DICTIONNAIRE FRANÇAIS ▸ ANGLAIS ANGLAIS ▸ FRANÇAIS FRENCH ▸ ENGLISH ENGLISH ▸ FRENCH DICTIONARY

COLLINS ROBERT FRENCH ▸ ENGLISH ENGLISH ▸ FRENCH DICTIONARY

Unabridged

by

Beryl T. Atkins
Alain Duval Rosemary C. Milne

and

Pierre-Henri Cousin
Hélène M. A. Lewis Lorna A. Sinclair
Renée O. Birks Marie-Noëlle Lamy

THIRD EDITION

HarperCollins*Publishers*

météorologie	*Mét, Met*	meteorology
métallurgie	*Métal, Metal*	metallurgy
masculin et féminin	*mf*	masculine and feminine
militaire	*Mil*	military
mines	*Min*	mining
minéralogie	*Minér, Miner*	mineralogy
masculin pluriel	*mpl*	masculine plural
musique	*Mus*	music
mythologie	*Myth*	mythology
nom	*n*	noun
nord de l'Angleterre	*N Angl*	North of England
nautique	*Naut*	nautical, naval
négatif	*nég, neg*	negative
nord de l'Angleterre	*N Engl*	North of England
nom féminin	*nf*	feminine noun
nom masculin	*nm*	masculine noun
nom masculin et féminin	*nmf*	masculine and feminine noun
nom masculin, féminin	*nm,f*	masculine, feminine noun
non comptable	*Non C*	uncountable
physique nucléaire	*Nucl Phys*	nuclear physics
numéral	*num*	numerical
objet	*obj*	object
opposé	*opp*	opposite
optique	*Opt*	optics
informatique	*Ordin*	computing
ornithologie	*Orn*	ornithology
emploi réfléchi	*o.s.*	oneself
parlement	*Parl*	parliament
passif	*pass*	passive
péjoratif	*péj, pej*	pejorative
personnel	*pers*	personal
pharmacie	*Pharm*	pharmacy
philatélie	*Philat*	philately
philosophie	*Philos*	philosophy
phonétique	*Phon*	phonetics
photographie	*Phot*	photography
verbe à particule	*phr vb elem*	phrasal verb element
physique	*Phys*	physics
physiologie	*Physiol*	physiology
pluriel	*pl*	plural
politique	*Pol*	politics
possessif	*poss*	possessive
préfixe	*préf, pref*	prefix
préposition	*prép, prep*	preposition
prétérit	*prét, pret*	preterite
pronom	*pron*	pronoun
proverbe	*Prov*	proverb
participe présent	*prp*	present participle
psychiatrie, psychologie	*Psych*	psychology, psychiatry
participe passé	*ptp*	past participle
quelque chose	*qch*	something
quelqu'un	*qn*	somebody, someone
marque déposée	®	registered trademark
radio	*Rad*	radio
chemin de fer	*Rail*	rail(ways)
relatif	*rel*	relative
religion	*Rel*	religion
quelqu'un	*sb*	somebody, someone
sciences	*Sci*	science
école	*Scol*	school
écossais, Écosse	*Scot*	Scottish, Scotland
sculpture	*Sculp*	sculpture
séparable	*sep*	separable
singulier	*sg*	singular
ski	*Ski*	skiing
argot	*sl*	slang
sociologie	*Sociol, Soc*	sociology, social work
terme de spécialiste	*SPÉC, SPEC*	specialist's term
Bourse	*St Ex*	Stock Exchange
quelque chose	*sth*	something
subjonctif	*subj*	subjunctive
suffixe	*suf*	suffix
superlatif	*superl*	superlative
chirurgie	*Surg*	surgery
arpentage	*Surv*	surveying
technique	*Tech*	technical
télécommunication	*Télec, Telec*	telecommunications
industrie textile	*Tex*	textiles
théâtre	*Théât, Theat*	theatre
télévision	*TV*	television
typographie	*Typ*	typography
université	*Univ*	university
américain, États-Unis	*US*	American, United States
verbe	*vb*	verb
médecine vétérinaire	*Vét, Vet*	veterinary medicine
verbe intransitif	*vi*	intransitive verb
verbe pronominal	*vpr*	pronominal verb
verbe transitif	*vt*	transitive verb
verbe transitif et intransitif	*vti*	transitive and intransitive verb
verbe transitif indirect	*vt indir*	indirect transitive verb
zoologie	*Zool*	zoology
langage familier, voir page xxvii	*	informal language, see page xxvii
langage très familier, voir page xxviii	**	very informal language, see page xxviii
langage vulgaire, voir page xxviii	***	offensive language, see page xxviii
emploi vielli, voir page xxviii	†	old-fashioned term or expression, see page xxviii
emploi archaïque, voir page xxviii	††	archaic term or expression, see page xxviii

LE ROBERT & COLLINS DICTIONNAIRE FRANÇAIS ▸ ANGLAIS ANGLAIS ▸ FRANÇAIS

Senior

par

Beryl T. Atkins
Alain Duval Rosemary C. Milne

et

Pierre-Henri Cousin
Hélène M. A. Lewis Lorna A. Sinclair
Renée O. Birks Marie-Noëlle Lamy

TROISIÈME ÉDITION

Dictionnaires Le Robert - Paris

third edition / troisième édition 1993

second edition reprinted / deuxième édition: réimpressions
1987 (twice) 1989 1991
1988 (twice) 1990 (twice)

Dictionnaires Le Robert
12, avenue d'Italie - 75013 Paris
ISBN 2-85036227-1

HarperCollins Publishers

P.O. Box, Glasgow G4 ONB, Great Britain
ISBN 0-00-433551-1
with thumb index 0-00-433552-X

1995 Markham Road, Scarborough, Canada, AM1B 5M8
ISBN 0-00-470277-8
with thumb index 0-06-275509-9

---

10 East 53rd Street, New York
New York 10022
ISBN 0-06-275509-9

First HarperCollins edition published 1993

The Library of Congress has catalogued the previous edition of this book as follows:

Collins-Robert French-English, English-French dictionary / by
Beryl T. Atkins ... [et al.]. – 2nd ed.
p. cm.
Title on added t.p.: Robert-Collins dictionnaire français-anglais, anglais-français.
Reprint. Originally published: London: Collins; Paris : Dictionnaires Le Robert, 1987.
ISBN 0-06-275503-X
1. French language–Dictionaries–English. 2. English language–Dictionaries–French I. Atkins, Beryl T. II. Title: Robert-Collins dictionnaire français-anglais, anglais-français.
PC2640.C69 1987
443'.21–dc20 90-4097

---

93 94 95 96 97 MI 10 9 8 7 6 5 4 3 2 1

Dépôt légal juin 1993

Typeset by Morton Word Processing Ltd, Scarborough
Printed in France by Maury-Imprimeur S. A. – Malesherbes

TROISIÈME ÉDITION/THIRD EDITION

direction rédactionnelle/general editors

Alain Duval Lorna Sinclair Knight

rédacteurs/editors

Diana Feri Stephen Clarke Dominique Le Fur
Laurence Hautekeur Françoise Morcellet Jill Campbell

chef de projet/editorial management

Vivian Marr

autres collaborateurs/other contributors

Christine Penman Jean-Benoît Ormal-Grenon Cécile Aubinière-Robb

administration, secrétariat et correction/editorial staff

Elspeth Anderson Luc Audrain Anne Baudrillard
Linda Chestnutt Chantal Combes Elizabeth Cunningham
Annick Dehais Anne Dickinson Susan Dunsmore
Sylvie Fontaine Élisabeth Huault Lesley Johnston Irene Lakhani
Joyce Littlejohn Dominique Lopin Kamal Loudiyi
Fiona MacGregor Maimie McGadie Janice McNeillie
Val McNulty Hellen Ranson Gonzague Raynaud
Diane Robinson Megan Thomson Lydia Vigné Silke Zimmermann

DEUXIÈME ÉDITION/SECOND EDITION

dirigée par/by

Beryl T. Atkins
Alain Duval Rosemary C. Milne Hélène M. A. Lewis
Lorna Sinclair Renée Birks

autres collaborateurs/other contributors

Guy Jean Forgue (*Américanismes/American language*)
Charles Lynn Clark Susan Lochrie Geneviève Lebaut
Joëlle Sampy Ann Goodman Renée Gillot-Gautier Florence Millar

administration, secrétariat et correction/administrative staff

William T. McLeod Richard Thomas Barbara Christie Carol Purdon
Elspeth Anderson Catherine E. Love Anne Marie Banks

PREMIÈRE ÉDITION/FIRST EDITION

par/by

Beryl T. Atkins
Alain Duval Rosemary C. Milne

et/and

Pierre-Henri Cousin
Hélène M. A. Lewis Lorna A. Sinclair
Renée O. Birks Marie-Noëlle Lamy

autres collaborateurs/other contributors

John Scullard Edwin Carpenter Margaret Curtin Kenneth Gibson
Gerry Kilroy Michael Janes Anthony Linforth Trevor Peach
Elise Thomson

avec/with
comité de lecture/readers' panel

Paul Robert
Martine Bercot Gilberte Gagnon Maryline Hira Lucette Jourdan
Denis Keen Jean Mambrino Jacques Mengin Robert Mengin
Marie Christine de Montoussé Alain Rey Josette Rey-Debove
Colette Thompson Elaine Williamson

Remerciements: première édition

Les auteurs tiennent à exprimer leurs remerciements à tous ceux qui ont apporté leur collaboration tout au long de la rédaction de cet ouvrage, et en particulier à Tom McArthur, dont les travaux sur les verbes anglais à particule ont été d'une aide précieuse; à Richard Wakely, qui a bien voulu les faire bénéficier de son concours pour le traitement des auxiliaires de mode anglais; à Colin Smith, qui leur a montré la voie; à Duncan McMillan pour ses conseils et sa collaboration à un stade avancé de la rédaction; à Guy Rondeau pour son concours lors de la compilation des emplois du français du Canada; enfin à tous ceux dont l'aide a concouru au parachèvement du texte.

Il faut aussi signaler et remercier les nombreux auxiliaires de rédaction, les correcteurs et les dactylographes qui ont permis de transformer en ouvrage imprimé un manuscrit volumineux – tout particulièrement Michèle Rodger, qui a dactylographié la majeure partie du dictionnaire.

Les auteurs tiennent enfin à exprimer leur gratitude à Geneviève McMillan pour sa longue et précieuse collaboration.

Acknowledgements: first edition

The editors are indebted to the following:

Tom McArthur for his original approach to English phrasal verbs; Richard Wakely for help with modal verbs in English; Colin Smith, editor of Collins Spanish Dictionary, for his inspiring example; Duncan McMillan for advice and help in the later stages of the book; Guy Rondeau for help with French Canadian usage; the many other individuals and organizations who helped on specific translation points.

Our thanks go also to the numerous copy editors and proofreaders who assisted in the conversion of our handwritten manuscript to the printed page, and especially to Michèle Rodger who typed most of the dictionary.

Finally we would like to express our gratitude to Geneviève McMillan for all that she contributed to this dictionary over a period of many years.

Remerciements: deuxième édition

Nous tenons à exprimer ici nos remerciements, une fois encore, à ceux et celles qui nous ont apporté leur concours lors du travail de révision de notre dictionnaire. Nous aimerions mentionner tout particulièrement:

Acknowledgements: second edition

We are again indebted to a number of people for their valuable contributions to this second edition:

J.-P. de Chezet J. Clear C. Cornilleau
T.H. & D. Elkins J. de Goiffon E. Hérault
P. Peronne J.S. Tassie

Il convient aussi de signaler et de remercier les traducteurs, en particulier Jean-François Allain, à qui nous avons soumis, à intervalles réguliers – et fréquents! – les problèmes les plus épineux, dans de nombreux domaines spécialisés:

And our thanks also go to our panel of professional translators, in particular Jean-François Allain, for solving some of our knottiest problems:

J.-F. Allain P. Collet D. Denby
C. Gordon G. Kilroy J.F. Lee
D.Marx J.B. Newsham A.-M. Noël
P. Reynes R. Schwartz B. Tulett

Remerciements: troisième édition

Nous tenons à remercier les nombreux correcteurs qui des deux côtés de la Manche ont vérifié et revérifié le texte. Nous tenons également à remercier les membres des services administratifs et du service de production à la fois chez Robert et chez Collins, et tout particulièrement dans ce domaine Gillian Hinton.

Nous présentons également nos remerciements aux personnes suivantes pour leur aide inestimable au cours de l'élaboration du texte:

Acknowledgements: third edition

We are indebted to the numerous proofreaders in France and the UK who checked and rechecked this text. Along with them, we must also thank the administrative and production staff at both Collins and Robert for all their hard work. Particular thanks, in this respect, are due to Gillian Hinton.

Our thanks also go to the following people for their invaluable help in preparing this edition:

Keith Foley (*business language consultant*) Anna-Louise Milne Elizabeth Mooney

Les auteurs

The editors

TABLE DES MATIÈRES

CONTENTS

PRÉFACE

Préface de la troisième édition

Une nouvelle édition constitue une étape capitale dans la vie d'un dictionnaire. Au delà des révisions ponctuelles permises par chaque réimpression, c'est une remise à plat de la totalité du texte, la relecture ligne à ligne de chaque article au travers du regard changeant de la langue.

Les événements politiques, les progrès de la science et de la technique, les nouvelles tendances de la musique et dans les loisirs, les changements dans les habitudes alimentaires entraînent tous la création d'un grand nombre de néologismes. Tout comme les phénomènes dont ils sont le reflet, beaucoup sont éphémères. Les autres entreront dans le vocabulaire courant.

Notre équipe est comme par le passé restée constamment à l'affût de ces nouveautés. Nous avions pour nous aider un précieux instrument de travail: notre banque de données qui contient des centaines de textes contemporains, allant des articles de journaux aux œuvres littéraires, ainsi que des enregistrements de conversations prises sur le vif.

Nous avons ainsi ajouté plus de 40.000 unités de traduction nouvelles, notamment un grand nombre de mots et de locutions tirés du monde des affaires, du monde géo-politique, ainsi que de nombreux exemples d'expressions courantes, sans oublier les derniers-nés de ces domaines en pleine évolution que sont, par exemple, l'écologie, l'informatique, la médecine et la Communauté européenne.

Il est bien sûr primordial de trouver facilement et rapidement tous ces renseignements. Nous avons donc entièrement changé la présentation du texte, pour la rendre encore plus claire et conviviale.

En présentant cette nouvelle édition du Robert & Collins, nous avons voulu nous mettre à l'écoute de la langue, repérer, choisir, doser les éléments nouveaux dans le respect du texte existant pour présenter une image fidèle du français, de l'anglais et de l'américain tels qu'ils sont parlés dans le monde à l'aube du vingt-et-unième siècle.

Les auteurs

Extrait de la préface de la première édition

Voici une œuvre faite en commun dans les deux vieux pays pour aider à la communication entre les anglophones et les francophones de l'ancien et du nouveau monde. . . .

Cependant il faudra la poursuivre, dans les années qui viennent. Car nos deux langues vivent et il faut vivre avec elles.

Paul Robert

PREFACE

Preface to the third edition

A new edition is a major step in the life of a dictionary. Minor alterations are made at every reprint, but a new edition is the result of a line-by-line examination of the text in the light of changes in the language.

Historical events, breakthroughs in science and technology, new fashions in music, in eating habits and leisure activities all produce their own new vocabulary at a startling rate. Some of these new words, like the phenomena themselves, will fade and be forgotten. Others will last and become established.

A good dictionary reflects such linguistic developments and our team of British and French lexicographers has been monitoring developments as closely as ever, aided by Collins' growing databank of real written and spoken language.

We have added over 40,000 new items, including an extensive new business list, a revised geographical list which takes into account the dramatic upheavals of the past few years, new examples taken from our massive collection of contemporary usage and vocabulary, and the latest terms used in such ever-changing fields as ecology, computing, medicine and the European Community.

Naturally, all this information must be easy to find in the dictionary, so we have redesigned the text using new typefaces, symbols and shading to allow the user to home in on the item he or she wishes to translate.

This new edition of the Collins-Robert is the result of meticulous observation of the way language has been evolving. We have monitored the changes, selected new elements and integrated them into the pattern of the existing text to give an accurate picture of the way English and French are being spoken and written as we approach the new millennium.

The editors

Extract from the first edition preface

This book embodies a fresh approach to bilingual lexicography, with its emphasis on the current, living language of everyday communication. . . .

We offer this new dictionary in the confident hope that the basic strength, and the many other features described in the pages that follow, will establish it in the appreciation of all who use it.

Jan Collins

INTRODUCTION

LE DICTIONNAIRE ROBERT & COLLINS est avant tout un outil qui cherche à répondre à un besoin pratique: permettre la communication entre le français et l'anglais de façon simple, rapide et sûre. Ses caractéristiques principales, notamment l'étendue et la nature du vocabulaire traité et l'agencement des indications servant à guider le lecteur, découlent directement de cette conception fonctionnelle d'un dictionnaire bilingue.

Étendue et nature du vocabulaire

L'accent est mis résolument sur la langue contemporaine. Le corpus très étendu s'attache à présenter au lecteur une image fidèle de la langue telle qu'elle est pratiquée quotidiennement, lue dans les journaux et les revues, parlée en société, entendue dans la rue.

Une attention toute particulière a été accordée aux emplois nouveaux et à de nombreux néologismes absents des dictionnaires bilingues et parfois monolingues existants, mais qui sont indispensables si l'on veut rendre compte de la pratique courante de la langue actuelle.

Une place non négligeable a été également réservée à la langue littéraire, au vocabulaire scientifique et aux domaines marquants de notre époque, tels que l'économie, l'informatique, l'éducation, l'environnement, la médecine et la politique.

Une autre préoccupation fondamentale a été de faire un dictionnaire qui s'adresse aussi bien au lecteur de langue française qu'à celui de langue anglaise. Suivant une politique rigoureuse, chaque mot français a été écrit et vérifié par des rédacteurs de langue française et chaque mot anglais par des rédacteurs de langue anglaise, travaillant en étroite collaboration pour s'assurer de la justesse de leurs traductions. Les utilisateurs de l'une ou l'autre langue peuvent donc se servir de ce dictionnaire avec une confiance égale: les auteurs ont veillé à ce que chacune des deux parties soit également valable dans le sens thème et dans le sens version.

La langue décrite ne se limite pas au français de France, à l'anglais de Grande-Bretagne. L'anglais nord-américain y est décrit avec un soin minutieux et ses emplois spécifiques précisés dans les deux parties de l'ouvrage. Les termes les plus répandus du français du Canada, mais aussi de Belgique et de Suisse sont également traités.

Indications servant à guider le lecteur

Un dictionnaire, si riche soit-il, perd une grande partie de sa valeur lorsque l'utilisateur ne peut pas trouver rapidement et sans incertitude ce qu'il cherche. Aussi une place importante a-t-elle été consacrée à l'établissement d'un système très complet d'indications qui guident le lecteur.

Tout article complexe est clairement divisé en catégories sémantiques introduites par une indication qui en fait ressortir le sens général. De plus, les variations de sens à l'intérieur de ces catégories sont soigneusement mises en évidence à l'aide de renseignements supplémentaires précisant chaque nuance. L'utilisation cohérente de ce système d'indications, sous forme de synonymes, de définitions partielles ou de compléments à valeur typique, est l'une des caractéristiques essentielles de ce dictionnaire. Les auteurs espèrent combler ainsi une lacune majeure de beaucoup d'ouvrages de ce type.

Les complexités et les subtilités de registre tendent à celui qui étudie une langue étrangère des pièges sournois. Les expressions qu'il utilise peuvent se trouver tout à fait déplacées – et parfois de façon grotesque – dans la situation du moment. Il est difficile d'acquérir une maîtrise parfaite des niveaux de langue à partir d'une page de dictionnaire, mais les auteurs ont tenté de créer un code très précis qui renseigne le lecteur, et indique pour chaque mot et expression, tant dans la langue de départ que dans la langue d'arrivée, les restrictions stylistiques qui s'imposent.

Les mots et expressions dont le niveau de style n'est pas précisé seront considérés comme neutres et pourront s'utiliser normalement dans les situations courantes. Chaque fois qu'il n'en est pas ainsi, une précision est apportée sur la nature de la restriction: par exemple langue soutenue ou littéraire, argot scolaire, connotation humoristique ou péjorative.

Les auteurs se sont en particulier attachés à élaborer un système aussi efficace que possible qui indique les différents degrés dans la familiarité, depuis les expressions légèrement familières jusqu'à celles qui sont ressenties comme très vulgaires. Un, deux ou trois astérisques avertissent le lecteur étranger. De même une croix ou une double croix indique que le mot est vieilli ou archaïque.

Un autre écueil des ouvrages traditionnels est constitué par le manque de renseignements d'ordre grammatical, ce qui ne permet généralement pas au lecteur étranger d'insérer correctement la traduction dans une structure plus complexe. Les auteurs ont donc tenu ici à indiquer soigneusement les exigences syntaxiques des deux langues en apportant toujours les précisions nécessaires (telles que la notation des constructions verbales ou des prépositions liées aux noms ou aux adjectifs). De nombreux exemples viennent en outre enrichir le contenu des articles, et montrent que le mot n'a pas d'existence en dehors de la phrase, et que les traductions ne sont pas fixes, mais peuvent changer suivant le contexte. Mettre le mot en situation permet de plus d'introduire les expressions idiomatiques nécessaires pour s'exprimer dans une langue authentique et éviter les erreurs d'usage.

Les pages qui suivent décrivent avec plus de détails les caractéristiques principales du dictionnaire.

INTRODUCTION

The Collins–Robert French Dictionary is first and foremost a practical tool designed for a specific function: to facilitate easy, rapid and reliable communication between French and English. Its major characteristics spring directly from this concept of the function of a bilingual dictionary. In particular, this concept has shaped two fundamental aspects: the scope and nature of the language treated; and the layout of the information presented and help provided.

The scope and nature of the language treated

The emphasis is firmly placed on contemporary language. The range is wide: the headwords and compounds, phrases and idioms have been selected and arranged to present the user with the authentic language he or she will meet daily in newspapers, journals, books and in the street.

Particular attention has been paid to recent coinages and new meanings, not found in existing bilingual dictionaries and even absent from some monolingual volumes, but essential if the dictionary is truly to reflect current, living language as it is spoken and written today.

Space has been found, too, for a considerable representation of the vocabulary of literature and science, and especially of those areas which have contributed notably to the modern consciousness – business, computing, education, the environment, medicine, politics, and so on.

One of our primary concerns has been to make the dictionary equally valid for French-speaking and English-speaking users. Our rigorous policy that every French word in the dictionary has been created and vetted by *French* lexicographers and every English word by *English* lexicographers, with constant discussion between them, means that French-speaking and English-speaking users can approach this dictionary with equal confidence. In addition, we have taken care that each side of the dictionary is equally helpful for translation from and into the foreign language.

The spread of language treated is not confined to British English or metropolitan French. North American English is described in great detail and its specific usages are pinpointed on both sides of the dictionary. The most common Canadian, Belgian and Swiss French terms are also covered.

Layout and help

However well-chosen the content of a dictionary may be, much of its value is instantly lost if the user cannot easily and quickly find his or her way to the meaning that meets his needs. So we have put considerable effort into devising and implementing a comprehensive system of indicating material.

Not only are all complex entries clearly divided into separate areas of meaning, but the sense of each area is signposted by 'indicators' which immediately highlight the group of meanings in that category. In addition, variations of meaning within each category are precisely pinpointed by further indicating material. The *systematic* and consistent use throughout the dictionary of indicating material, which may take the form of field labels, synonyms, typical subjects or objects of verbs, and so on, is a feature of the dictionary to which we attach the greatest importance. This indicating material is a very effective way of helping the user to pinpoint the exact translation he or she is looking for.

One of the most insidious linguistic traps that besets the student of any foreign language is to use words or expressions inappropriate – occasionally grotesquely so – to the context of the moment. The complexities and subtleties of register, especially of social overtones, are hardly to be acquired from the printed page, but we have created for this dictionary a range of 'style labels' that accurately characterize the stylistic restrictions that should be placed on any word or expression in the text – both in source language and in target language.

Words and expressions that are unmarked for style or register in source or target language are to be taken as standard language appropriate to any normal context or situation. Wherever this is not the case the nature of the restriction is indicated: formal, literary, school slang, humorous, pejorative, and so on.

In particular we gave much thought to how best to indicate the degrees of colloquialism ranging from expressions that are slightly informal through slang to those that are widely regarded as taboo. The foreign user of each language is warned by a label of one, two, or three asterisks of the degrees of care he or she must exercise in the use of expressions so marked. Similarly, a dagger and double dagger indicate words that are old-fashioned and obsolete, respectively.

Another feature of this dictionary is the wealth of phrases provided within many entries. Examples greatly expand the validity of the information provided by showing how translation and sometimes structure change in different contexts and by giving examples of the idioms and set expressions relating to the headword.

The pages that follow describe these and other features of the dictionary in greater detail.

COMMENT UTILISER LE DICTIONNAIRE

HOW TO USE THE DICTIONARY

Les principales caractéristiques de ce dictionnaire sont mentionnées dans les éclatés des pages xviii à xxi. Pour une explication détaillée de chacune de ces caractéristiques et pour tirer le meilleur parti de votre dictionnaire, reportez-vous aux pages xxii à xxxi.

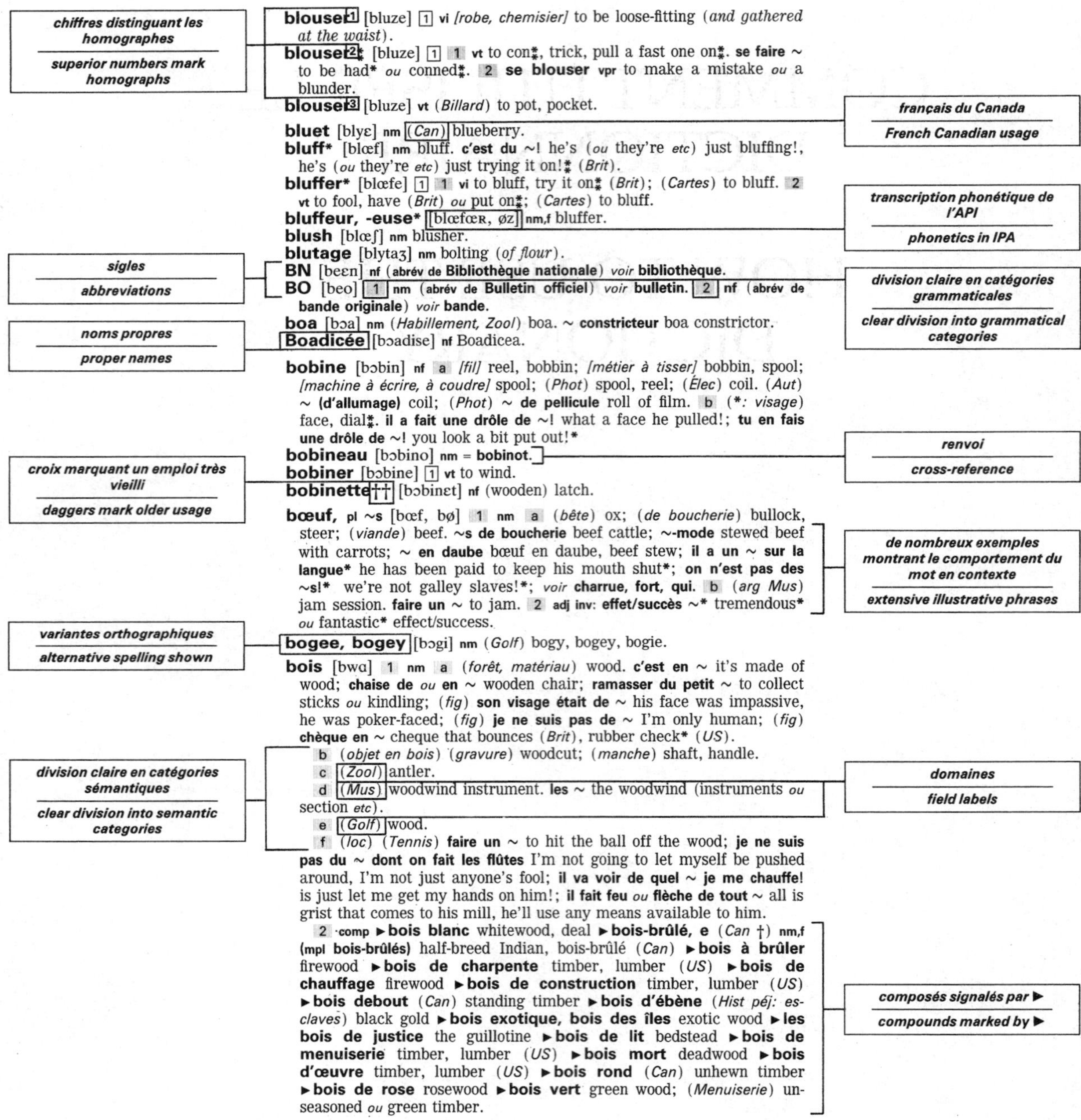

blouse[1] [bluze] 1 **vi** *[robe, chemisier]* to be loose-fitting (*and gathered at the waist*).
blouse[2]* [bluze] 1 1 **vt** to con*, trick, pull a fast one on*. **se faire ~** to be had* *ou* conned*. 2 **se blouser vpr** to make a mistake *ou* a blunder.
blouse[3] [bluze] **vt** (*Billard*) to pot, pocket.
bluet [blyɛ] **nm** (*Can*) blueberry.
bluff* [blœf] **nm** bluff. **c'est du ~!** he's (*ou* they're *etc*) just bluffing!, he's (*ou* they're *etc*) just trying it on!* (*Brit*).
bluffer* [blœfe] 1 1 **vi** to bluff, try it on* (*Brit*); (*Cartes*) to bluff. 2 **vt** to fool, have (*Brit*) *ou* put on*; (*Cartes*) to bluff.
bluffeur, -euse* [blœfœʀ, øz] **nm,f** bluffer.
blush [blœʃ] **nm** blusher.
blutage [blytaʒ] **nm** bolting (*of flour*).
BN [beɛn] **nf** (**abrév de Bibliothèque nationale**) *voir* **bibliothèque**.
BO [beo] 1 **nm** (**abrév de Bulletin officiel**) *voir* **bulletin**. 2 **nf** (**abrév de bande originale**) *voir* **bande**.
boa [bɔa] **nm** (*Habillement, Zool*) boa. **~ constricteur** boa constrictor.
Boadicée [bɔadise] **nf** Boadicea.
bobine [bɔbin] **nf** a *[fil]* reel, bobbin; *[métier à tisser]* bobbin, spool; *[machine à écrire, à coudre]* spool; (*Phot*) spool, reel; (*Élec*) coil. (*Aut*) **~ (d'allumage)** coil; (*Phot*) **~ de pellicule** roll of film. b (*: *visage*) face, dial*. **il a fait une drôle de ~!** what a face he pulled!; **tu en fais une drôle de ~!** you look a bit put out!*
bobineau [bɔbino] **nm** = **bobinot.**
bobiner [bɔbine] 1 **vt** to wind.
bobinette†† [bɔbinɛt] **nf** (wooden) latch.
bœuf, **pl ~s** [bœf, bø] 1 **nm** a (*bête*) ox; (*de boucherie*) bullock, steer; (*viande*) beef. **~s de boucherie** beef cattle; **~-mode** stewed beef with carrots; **~ en daube** bœuf en daube, beef stew; **il a un ~ sur la langue*** he has been paid to keep his mouth shut*; **on n'est pas des ~s!*** we're not galley slaves!*; *voir* **charrue, fort, qui.** b (*arg Mus*) jam session. **faire un ~** to jam. 2 **adj inv: effet/succès ~*** tremendous* *ou* fantastic* effect/success.
bogee, bogey [bɔgi] **nm** (*Golf*) bogy, bogey, bogie.
bois [bwɑ] 1 **nm** a (*forêt, matériau*) wood. **c'est en ~** it's made of wood; **chaise de** *ou* **en ~** wooden chair; **ramasser du petit ~** to collect sticks *ou* kindling; (*fig*) **son visage était de ~** his face was impassive, he was poker-faced; (*fig*) **je ne suis pas de ~** I'm only human; (*fig*) **chèque en ~** cheque that bounces (*Brit*), rubber check* (*US*).
b (*objet en bois*) (*gravure*) woodcut; (*manche*) shaft, handle.
c (*Zool*) antler.
d (*Mus*) woodwind instrument. **les ~** the woodwind (instruments *ou* section *etc*).
e (*Golf*) wood.
f (*loc*) (*Tennis*) **faire un ~** to hit the ball off the wood; **je ne suis pas du ~ dont on fait les flûtes** I'm not going to let myself be pushed around, I'm not just anyone's fool; **il va voir de quel ~ je me chauffe!** is just let me get my hands on him!; **il fait feu** *ou* **flèche de tout ~** all is grist that comes to his mill, he'll use any means available to him.
2 **comp ▸ bois blanc** whitewood, deal **▸ bois-brûlé, e** (*Can* †) **nm,f** (**mpl bois-brûlés**) half-breed Indian, bois-brûlé (*Can*) **▸ bois à brûler** firewood **▸ bois de charpente** timber, lumber (*US*) **▸ bois de chauffage** firewood **▸ bois de construction** timber, lumber (*US*) **▸ bois debout** (*Can*) standing timber **▸ bois d'ébène** (*Hist péj: esclaves*) black gold **▸ bois exotique, bois des îles** exotic wood **▸ les bois de justice** the guillotine **▸ bois de lit** bedstead **▸ bois de menuiserie** timber, lumber (*US*) **▸ bois mort** deadwood **▸ bois d'œuvre** timber, lumber (*US*) **▸ bois rond** (*Can*) unhewn timber **▸ bois de rose** rosewood **▸ bois vert** green wood; (*Menuiserie*) unseasoned *ou* green timber.

The main features of the dictionary are highlighted in the text extracts on pages xviii-xxi. For a detailed explanation of each of these features and information on how to get the most out of your dictionary, see pages xxii-xxxi.

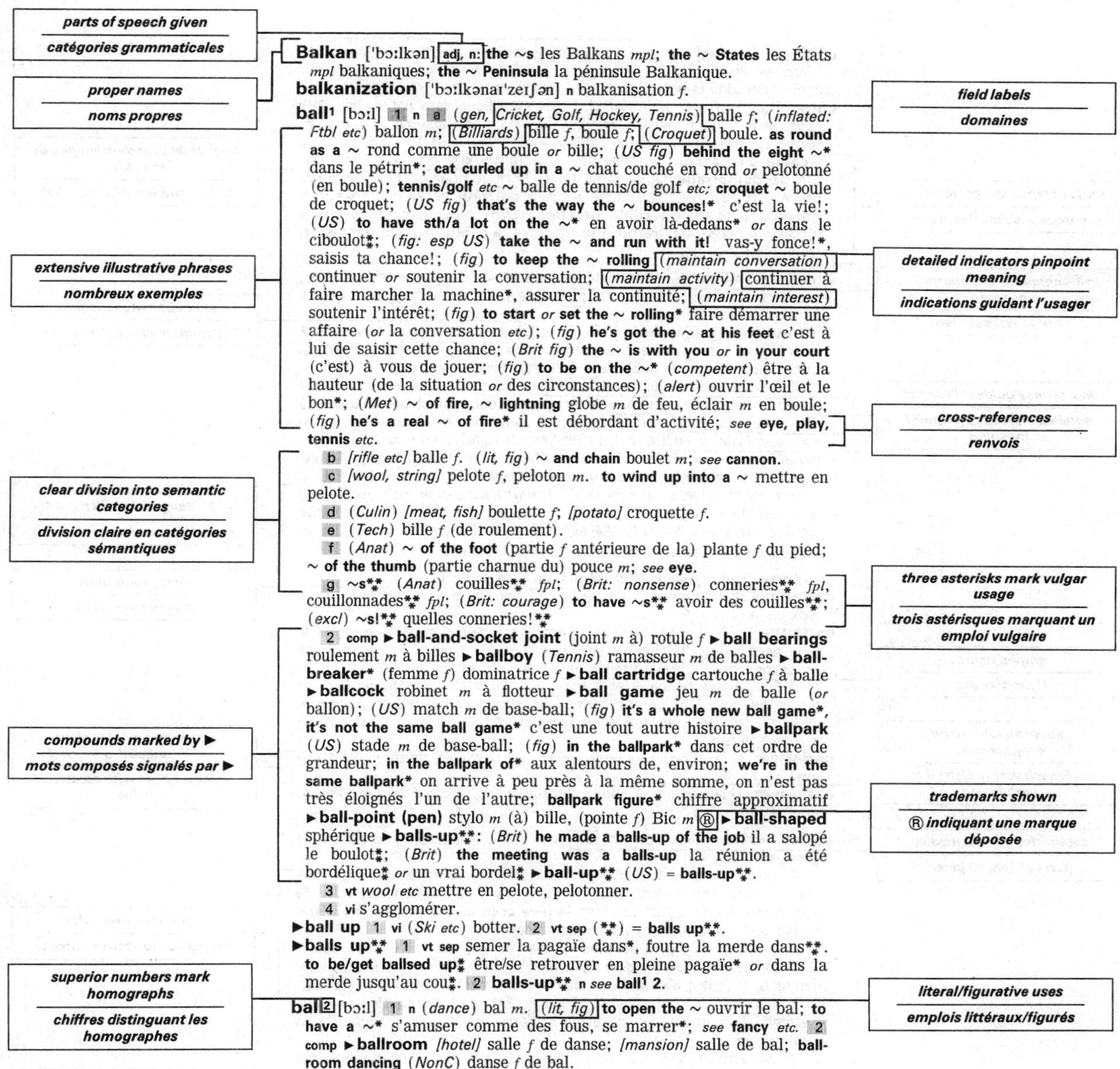

Balkan ['bɔːlkən] **adj, n**: **the ~s** les Balkans *mpl*; **the ~ States** les États *mpl* balkaniques; **the ~ Peninsula** la péninsule Balkanique.

balkanization [ˌbɔːlkənaɪ'zeɪʃən] **n** balkanisation *f*.

ball[1] [bɔːl] **1 n a** (*gen, Cricket, Golf, Hockey, Tennis*) balle *f*; (*inflated: Ftbl etc*) ballon *m*; (*Billiards*) bille *f*, boule *f*; (*Croquet*) boule. **as round as a ~** rond comme une boule *or* bille; (*US fig*) **behind the eight ~*** dans le pétrin*; **cat curled up in a ~** chat couché en rond *or* pelotonné (en boule); **tennis/golf** *etc* **~** balle de tennis/de golf *etc*; **croquet ~** boule de croquet; (*US fig*) **that's the way the ~ bounces!*** c'est la vie!; (*US*) **to have sth/a lot on the ~*** en avoir là-dedans* *or* dans le ciboulot**; (*fig: esp US*) **take the ~ and run with it!** vas-y fonce!*, saisis ta chance!; (*fig*) **to keep the ~ rolling** (*maintain conversation*) continuer *or* soutenir la conversation; (*maintain activity*) continuer à faire marcher la machine*, assurer la continuité; (*maintain interest*) soutenir l'intérêt; (*fig*) **to start** *or* **set the ~ rolling*** faire démarrer une affaire (*or* la conversation *etc*); (*fig*) **he's got the ~ at his feet** c'est à lui de saisir cette chance; (*Brit fig*) **the ~ is with you** *or* **in your court** (c'est) à vous de jouer; (*fig*) **to be on the ~*** (*competent*) être à la hauteur (de la situation *or* des circonstances); (*alert*) ouvrir l'œil et le bon*; (*Met*) **~ of fire, ~ lightning** globe *m* de feu, éclair *m* en boule; (*fig*) **he's a real ~ of fire*** il est débordant d'activité; *see* **eye, play, tennis** *etc*.

b [*rifle etc*] balle *f*. (*lit, fig*) **~ and chain** boulet *m*; *see* **cannon**.

c [*wool, string*] pelote *f*, peloton *m*. **to wind up into a ~** mettre en pelote.

d (*Culin*) [*meat, fish*] boulette *f*; [*potato*] croquette *f*.

e (*Tech*) bille *f* (de roulement).

f (*Anat*) **~ of the foot** (partie *f* antérieure de la) plante *f* du pied; **~ of the thumb** (partie charnue du) pouce *m*; *see* **eye**.

g ~s*** (*Anat*) couilles*** *fpl*; (*Brit: nonsense*) conneries*** *fpl*, couillonnades*** *fpl*; (*Brit: courage*) **to have ~s***** avoir des couilles***; (*excl*) **~s!***** quelles conneries!***

2 comp ▸**ball-and-socket joint** (joint *m* à) rotule *f* ▸**ball bearings** roulement *m* à billes ▸**ballboy** (*Tennis*) ramasseur *m* de balles ▸**ball-breaker*** (femme *f*) dominatrice *f* ▸**ball cartridge** cartouche *f* à balle ▸**ballcock** robinet *m* à flotteur ▸**ball game** jeu *m* de balle (*or* ballon); (*US*) match *m* de base-ball; (*fig*) **it's a whole new ball game***, **it's not the same ball game*** c'est une tout autre histoire ▸**ballpark** (*US*) stade *m* de base-ball; (*fig*) **in the ballpark*** dans cet ordre de grandeur; **in the ballpark of*** aux alentours de, environ; **we're in the same ballpark*** on arrive à peu près à la même somme, on n'est pas très éloignés l'un de l'autre; **ballpark figure*** chiffre approximatif ▸**ball-point (pen)** stylo *m* (à) bille, (pointe *f*) Bic *m* ® ▸**ball-shaped** sphérique ▸**balls-up*****: (*Brit*) **he made a balls-up of the job** il a salopé le boulot**; (*Brit*) **the meeting was a balls-up** la réunion a été bordélique** *or* un vrai bordel** ▸**ball-up***** (*US*) = **balls-up*****.

3 vt *wool etc* mettre en pelote, pelotonner.

4 vi s'agglomérer.

▸**ball up 1 vi** (*Ski etc*) botter. **2 vt sep** (***) = **balls up*****.

▸**balls up*** 1 vt sep** semer la pagaïe dans*, foutre la merde dans***. **to be/get ballsed up**** être/se retrouver en pleine pagaïe* *or* dans la merde jusqu'au cou**. **2 balls-up*** n** *see* **ball**[1] **2**.

ball[2] [bɔːl] **1 n** (*dance*) bal *m*. (*lit, fig*) **to open the ~** ouvrir le bal; **to have a ~*** s'amuser comme des fous, se marrer*; *see* **fancy** *etc*. **2 comp** ▸**ballroom** [*hotel*] salle *f* de danse; [*mansion*] salle de bal; **ballroom dancing** (*NonC*) danse *f* de bal.

câblage [kablaʒ] nm a (*voir* **câbler**) cabling; twisting together. b (*Élec: ensemble de fils*) wiring. c (*TV*) **le ~ du pays a commencé** cable television is being introduced into the country.
câble [kabl] 1 nm a (*filin*) cable. **~ métallique** wire cable. b (*TV*) cable. **le ~** cable television, cablevision (*US*); **être abonné au ~** to subscribe to cable television *ou* cablevision (*US*); *voir* **télévision.** 2 comp ▸**câble d'amarrage** mooring line ▸**câble coaxial** coaxial cable ▸**câble de démarrage** (*Aut*) jump lead (*Brit*), jumper cable (*US*) ▸**câble électrique** (electric) cable ▸**câble de frein** brake cable ▸**câble de halage** towrope ▸**câble hertzien** (*Élec*) radio link (*by hertzian waves*) ▸**câble de remorque** towrope ▸**câble de transmission** transmission cable.
caddie [kadi] nm a (*Golf*) caddie. **être le ~ de qn** to be sb's caddie, caddie for sb. b (*chariot*) **C~**® (supermarket *ou* shopping) trolley (*Brit*), caddy (*US*).
cadeau, pl **~x** [kado] nm a present, gift (*de qn* from sb). **faire un ~ à qn** to give sb a present *ou* gift; **~ de mariage/de Noël** wedding/Christmas present; **~ publicitaire** free gift, giveaway* (*US*).
b (*loc*) **faire ~ de qch à qn** (*offrir*) to make sb a present of sth, give sb sth as a present; (*laisser*) to let sb keep sth, give sb sth; **il a décidé d'en faire ~ (à qn)** he decided to give it away (to sb); **ils ne font pas de ~x** *[examinateurs etc]* they don't let you off lightly; **en ~** as a present; **garde la monnaie, je t'en fais ~** keep the change, I'm giving it to you; (*hum, iro*) **les petits ~x entretiennent l'amitié** there's nothing like a little present between friends (*iro*); (*hum*) **c'est pas un ~!*** *[personne]* he's (*ou* she's *etc*) a real pain!*; *[objet]* it's a real pain!*, it's more trouble than it's worth!; *[tâche]* it's a real pain!*; **c'était un ~ empoisonné** it was more of a curse than a blessing.

cadenas [kadna] nm padlock. **fermer au ~** to padlock.
cadenasser [kadnase] [1] 1 vt to padlock. 2 **se cadenasser** vpr to lock o.s. in.
cadence [kadɑ̃s] nf a (*rythme*) *[vers, chant, danse]* rhythm. **marquer la ~** to accentuate the rhythm. b (*vitesse, taux*) rate, pace. **~ de tir/de production** rate of fire/of production; **à la ~ de 10 par jour** at the rate of 10 a day; **à une bonne ~** at a good pace *ou* rate; (*fig*) **forcer la ~** to force the pace. c (*Mus*) *[succession d'accords]* cadence; *[concerto]* cadenza. d (*loc*) **en ~** (*régulièrement*) rhythmically; (*ensemble, en mesure*) in time.
cadencé, e [kadɑ̃se] (ptp **de cadencer**) adj (*rythmé*) rhythmic(al); *voir* **pas**[1].
cadencer [kadɑ̃se] [3] vt *débit, phrases, allure, marche* to put rhythm into, give rhythm to.
cadet, -ette [kadɛ, ɛt] 1 adj (*de deux*) younger; (*de plusieurs*) youngest.
2 nm a *[famille]* **le ~** the youngest child *ou* one; **le ~ des garçons** the youngest boy *ou* son; **mon (frère) ~** my younger brother; **le ~ de mes frères** my youngest brother; **le père avait un faible pour son ~** the father had a soft spot for his youngest boy.
b (*relation d'âges*) **il est mon ~** he's younger than me; **il est mon ~ de 2 ans** he's 2 years younger than me, he's 2 years my junior, he's my junior by 2 years; **c'est le ~ de mes soucis** it's the least of my worries.
c (*Sport*) *15-17 year-old player;* (*Hist*) cadet (*gentleman who entered the army to acquire military skill and eventually a commission*).
3 **cadette** nf a **la ~te** the youngest child *ou* girl *ou* one; **la ~te des filles** the youngest girl *ou* daughter; **ma (sœur) ~te** my younger sister.
b **elle est ma ~te** she's younger than me.
c (*Sport*) *15-17 year-old player.*

renvoi* / *cross-reference

anglais de Grande-Bretagne et des USA* / *British and American English

***mots composés signalés par* ▸ / *compounds marked by* ▸**

® indiquant une marque déposée* / *trademarks shown

indications syntaxiques* / *grammatical constructions

indications guidant l'usager* / *detailed indicators pinpoint meaning

astérisques marquant un emploi familier* / *asterisks mark informal usage

verbes pronominaux* / *pronominal verbs

emploi figuré* / *figurative use

renvoi au tableau de conjugaisons* / *all Franch verbs referred to verb tables

participe passé à valeur adjective* / *past participle with adjectival value

catégories grammaticales* / *parts of speech given

nombreux exemples* / *extensive illustrative phrases

glose, lorsqu'il n'est pas possible de traduire* / *explanation given when there is no equivalent

kiss [kɪs] **1** **n** baiser *m*. **to give sb a** ~ donner un baiser à qn, embrasser qn; **give me a** ~ embrasse-moi; (*to child*) fais-moi une bise*; (*Brit Med*) ~ **of life** bouche à bouche *m*; (*liter*) **the wind's** ~ **on her hair** le baiser du vent sur ses cheveux; (*in letter*) **love and** ~**es** bons baisers, grosses bises*; (*fig*) **to give the** ~ **of death to** porter le coup fatal à; *see* **blow**[1].

2 **comp** ▸**kiss curl** (*Brit*) accroche-cœur *m inv* ▸**kiss-off**‡: (*US*) **to give sb the kiss-off** (*employee*) virer qn; (*girlfriend etc*) plaquer‡ qn.

3 **vt** embrasser, donner un baiser à. **to** ~ **sb's cheek** embrasser qn sur la joue; **to** ~ **sb's hand** baiser la main de qn; (*Diplomacy etc*) **to** ~ **hands** être admis au baisemain (du roi *or* de la reine); **they** ~**ed each other** ils se sont embrassés; (*to hurt child*) **I'll** ~ **it better** un petit bisou* et ça ira mieux; **to** ~ **sb good night/goodbye** embrasser qn en lui souhaitant bonne nuit/en lui disant au revoir, souhaiter bonne nuit/dire au revoir à qn en l'embrassant; (*fig*) **you can** ~ **it goodbye!*** tu peux en faire ton deuil!; (*fig*) **to** ~ **the dust** *or* **ground** mordre la poussière.

4 **vi** s'embrasser. **to** ~ **and make up** faire la paix.

▸**kiss away** **vt sep**: **she kissed away the child's tears** elle a essuyé de ses baisers les larmes de l'enfant.

▸**kiss back** **vt sep** *person* rendre un baiser à.

kissagram [ˈkɪsəˌɡræm] **n** *baiser envoyé à l'occasion d'une célébration par l'intermédiaire d'une personne employée à cet effet.*

kisser‡ [ˈkɪsəʳ] **n** gueule‡ *f*.

kit [kɪt] **1** **n** **a** (*NonC*) (*equipment, gear*) [*camping, skiing, climbing, photography etc*] matériel *m*, équipement *m*; (*Mil*) fourniment *m*, barda‡ *m*, fourbi* *m*; (*tools*) outils *mpl*; (*luggage*) bagages *mpl*. **fishing** *etc* ~ matériel *or* attirail *m or* équipement de pêche *etc*; (*US*) **the whole** ~ **and caboodle*** tout le bataclan*, tout le fourbi*.

b (*NonC: belongings, gear*) effets *mpl* (personnels), affaires *fpl*.

c (*NonC: gen Sport: Brit: clothes*) équipement *m*, affaires *fpl*. **have you got your gym/football** ~? tu as tes affaires de gym/de football?

d (*set of items*) trousse *f*. **tool**~ trousse *f* à outils; **puncture-repair** ~ trousse de réparations; **first-aid** ~ trousse d'urgence *or* de premiers secours; *see* **survival** *etc*.

e (*parts for assembly*) kit *m*. **sold in** ~ **form** vendu en kit; **he built it from a** ~ il l'a assemblé à partir d'un kit; **model aeroplane** ~ maquette *f* d'avion (à assembler).

2 **comp** ▸**kitbag** sac *m* (*de voyage, de sportif, de soldat, de marin etc*) ▸**kit inspection** (*Mil*) revue *f* de détail.

▸**kit out, kit up** **vt sep** **a** (*Mil*) équiper (*with* de). **b** **to kit sb out with sth** équiper qn de qch; **he arrived kitted out in oilskins** il est arrivé équipé d'un ciré; **he had kitted himself out in a bright blue suit** il avait mis *or* il s'était acheté un costume bleu vif.

kitchen [ˈkɪtʃɪn] **1** **n** cuisine *f* (*pièce*); *see* **thief**.

2 **comp** *table, cutlery, scissors etc* de cuisine ▸**kitchen cabinet** buffet *m* de cuisine; (*fig Pol*) conseillers personnels *or* privés du Premier Ministre *or* (*US*) du Président ▸**kitchen-dinette** cuisine *f* avec coin-repas ▸**kitchen foil** papier *m* d'aluminium *or* d'alu* ▸**kitchen garden** (jardin *m*) potager *m* ▸**kitchenmaid** fille *f* de cuisine ▸**kitchen paper, kitchen roll** essuie-tout *m inv* ▸**kitchen police** (*US Mil*) corvée *f* de cuisine ▸**kitchen range** fourneau *m* (de cuisine), cuisinière *f* ▸**kitchen salt** sel *m* de cuisine, gros sel ▸**kitchen scales** balance *f* (de cuisine) ▸**kitchen sink** évier *m*; **I've packed everything but the kitchen sink*** j'ai tout empaqueté sauf les murs ▸**kitchen-sink* drama** (*Theat*) théâtre *m* naturaliste ▸**kitchen soap** savon *m* de Marseille ▸**kitchen unit** élément *m* de cuisine ▸**kitchen utensil** ustensile *m* de cuisine ▸**kitchenware** (*NonC*) (*dishes*) vaisselle *f or* faïence *f* (de cuisine); (*equipment*) ustensiles *mpl* de cuisine ▸**kitchen waste** *or* (*US*) **wastes** déchets *mpl* domestiques.

style indicated — ***indications de niveaux de langue***

clear division into grammatical categories — ***division claire en catégories grammaticales***

British and American English — ***anglais de Grande-Bretagne et des USA***

headword replaced by ~ — ***mot remplacé par ~***

phrasal verbs — ***verbes à particule***

explanation given when there is no equivalent — ***glose, lorsqu'il n'est pas possible de traduire***

phonetics in IPA — ***transcription phonétique de l'API***

asterisks mark informal or very informal usage — ***astérisques marquant un emploi familier ou très familier***

translation amplified — ***informations supplémentaires sur la traduction***

grammatical constructions — ***indication syntaxique***

translation disambiguated — ***explication de la traduction***

French genders given — ***indications de genres***

uncountable uses marked — ***emploi "non comptable"***

Ordre des mots

Le principe général est l'ordre alphabétique. Les variantes orthographiques qui ne se suivent pas immédiatement dans l'ordre alphabétique figurent à leur place dans la nomenclature avec un renvoi à la forme qui est traitée. Pour l'ordre d'apparition des composés, voir ***Les composés***.

Word order

Alphabetical order is followed throughout. If two variant spellings are not alphabetically adjacent each is treated as a separate headword and there is a cross-reference to the form treated in depth. For the alphabetical order of compounds, see ***Compounds***.

clé nm . . . = **clef**
caldron . . . n = **cauldron**

Les variantes orthographiques américaines sont traitées de la même manière.

American variations in spelling are treated in the same fashion.

honor . . . n (*US*) = **honour**

Les noms propres, ainsi que les sigles et acronymes, figurent à leur place dans l'ordre alphabétique général.

Proper names, as well as abbreviations and acronyms, will be found in their alphabetical place in the word list.

Les homographes sont suivis d'un chiffre qui permet de les distinguer, ex.: **raie**[1], **raie**[2]; **blow**[1], **blow**[2].

Superior numbers are used to separate words of like spelling, **raie**[1], **raie**[2]; **blow**[1], **blow**[2].

Les composés

Pour les besoins de ce dictionnaire, le terme 'composé' regroupe non seulement les mots formés de termes reliés par un trait d'union (ex.: **camion-citerne, arrière-pensée, body-building**), mais également les expressions anglaises formées à l'aide de noms adjectivés (ex.: **boat train, freedom fighter**) ou d'autres collocations similaires figées par la langue (ex.: **grand ensemble, modèle déposé, air traffic control, ear, nose and throat specialist**). Ils sont rassemblés et traités dans une catégorie à part suivant un ordre strictement alphabétique.

La catégorie des composés commence par l'étiquette **comp**. Chaque composé est précédé d'un triangle noir ► qui permet de la repérer rapidement et facilement.

Les composés français formés de termes soudés sont considérés comme mots à part entière et traités selon l'ordre alphabétique général (ex.: **portemanteau, portefeuille**). Les composés anglais formés de termes soudés figurent dans la catégorie des composés et ne font pas l'objet d'articles séparés (ex.: **bodyguard**); toutefois les vocables formés avec un suffixe (ex.: **childhood, friendship**) sont généralement traités dans la nomenclature à leur place alphabétique normale.

Les composés français formés à l'aide de préfixes d'origine verbale sont en général regroupés sous le verbe

Compounds

For the purposes of this dictionary the term 'compound' is taken to cover not only solid and hyphenated compounds (eg **camion-citerne, arrière-pensée, body-building**), but also attributive uses of English nouns (eg **boat train, freedom fighter**) and other collocations which function in a similar way (eg **grand ensemble, modèle déposé, air traffic control, ear, nose and throat specialist**). All of the above are normally treated in the compound section of the entry in alphabetical order.

All compound sections begin with the label **comp**. Each compound is directly preceded by a black triangle ► to make finding them quick and simple.

Solid compounds in French (eg **portefeuille, portemanteau**) are treated as headwords. Solid compounds in English (eg **bodyguard**) are normally treated in the compound section. However English words of the pattern *full word + suffix* (eg **childhood, friendship**) are not normally considered to be compounds and are usually treated as headwords.

French compounds of the pattern *verb root + noun* are generally given under the verb.

lave- . . . **préf** *voir* **laver**

et à l'article **laver**

and in the entry for **laver**

laver . . . 3 **comp** ► **lave-glace**

Dans la nomenclature anglaise, la catégorie grammaticale des composés est donnée lors-qu'elle n'est

In English, parts of speech are indicated for compounds in cases where the user might otherwise be

pas évidente ou que la forme composée appartient à plusieurs catégories grammaticales. Lorsque le composé appartient à plusieurs catégories grammaticales, le changement de catégorie est indiqué par un losange (◇).

confused. Where a compound has more than one part of speech, the change of part of speech is shown by a lozenge (◇).

► **cablecast** *(TV)* **n** émission *f* de télévision par câble ◇ **vt** transmettre par câble

Pour le français, la catégorie grammaticale et s'il y a lieu le genre des composés avec trait d'union sont donnés; ils sont aussi indiqués lorsqu'il y a risque d'erreur ou lorsque le terme traité appartient à plusieurs catégories grammaticales.

In French the part of speech, and if appropriate the gender, is given for all hyphenated compounds. It will also be given of course when the compound has several grammatical categories or if there is any risk of confusion.

Lorsque, pour des raisons pratiques, un composé anglais a été traité comme mot à part entière et doit être cherché à sa place dans la liste alphabétique générale, un renvoi prévient le lecteur.

When for practical reasons an English compound is treated as a headword in its alphabetical place, a cross-reference always makes this plain.

care . . . 2 **comp** . . . ► **careless** *etc see* **careless** *etc*

Les composés sont placés sous le premier élément, **grand ensemble** sous **grand**, **pont d'envol** sous **pont**, **freedom fighter** sous **freedom**, **general post office** sous **general**. Lorsque pour des raisons pratiques ce principe n'a pas été appliqué, un renvoi prévient le lecteur.

Compounds are placed under the first element, **grand ensemble** under **grand**, **pont d'envol** under **pont**, **freedom fighter** under **freedom**, **general post office** under **general**. Where for practical reasons an exception has been made to this rule a cross-reference alerts the user.

Les locutions et exemples

Les formules figées et les expressions idiomatiques figurent sous le premier terme qui reste inchangé, quelles que soient les modifications que l'on apporte à l'expression en question.

Monter sur ses grands chevaux et **monter un bateau à quelqu'un** sont traités sous **monter**. **Savoir quelque chose sur le bout du doigt** est placé sous **bout** parce que l'on peut dire également **connaître quelque chose sur le bout du doigt**.

Lorsque ce principe a été abandonné, un renvoi prévient l'utilisateur.

Un certain nombre de verbes français et anglais servent à former un très grand nombre de locutions verbales.

Set phrases and idioms

Set phrases and idiomatic expressions are also placed under the first element or the first word in the phrase which remains constant despite minor variations in the phrase itself.

To break somebody's heart and **to break a record** are both included under **break**. **To lend somebody a hand** is however under **hand** because it is equally possible to say **to give somebody a hand**.

Where this 'first element' principle has been abandoned a cross-reference alerts the user.

Certain very common French and English verbs form the basis of a very large number of phrases.

faire honneur à, faire du ski, faire la tête *etc*
to make sense of something, to make an appointment, to make a mistake *etc*

En pareil cas l'expression figurera sous le second élément: **faire la tête** sous **tête**, **to make sense of something** sous **sense**.

La liste qui suit indique les verbes que nous avons considérés comme 'vides' à cet égard:

en français: **avoir, être, faire, donner, mettre, passer, porter, prendre, remettre, reprendre, tenir, tirer.**

en anglais: **be, become, come, do, get, give, go, have, lay, make, put, set, take.**

We have considered such verbs to have a diminished meaning and in such cases the set phrases will be found under the second element, eg **faire la tête** under **tête**, **to make sense of something** under **sense**.

The following is a list of verbs which we consider to have a diminished meaning:

French: **avoir, être, faire, donner, mettre, passer, porter, prendre, remettre, reprendre, tenir, tirer.**

English: **be, become, come, do, get, give, go, have, lay, make, put, set, take.**

Répétition du mot dans l'article

Par souci d'économie de place, le mot est remplacé par le signe ~ lorsqu'il est répété dans le corps de l'article sans subir de modification orthographique.

Repetition of the headword within the entry

To save space, where the headword occurs in its full form within the entry it is replaced by ~.

age . . . **she stayed for ~s**
carry . . . **to ~ the can** . . . *but* **he carried his audience with him**

Les formes conjuguées des verbes français sont reprises en toutes lettres (ex.: **porter** . . . **il porte** . . . **ils porteront**), ainsi que les composés dans les deux langues et que les verbes anglais à particule.

Inflected forms of French verbs are shown in full (eg **porter** . . . **il porte** . . . **ils porteront**), as are compounds in both languages and phrasal verbs in English.

Pluriel

Les formes plurielles qui présentent des difficultés sont données dans la langue de départ.

En français, les pluriels autres que ceux qui se forment par le simple ajout du *-s* sont indiqués ex.: **cheval, -aux;** celui des composés avec trait d'union est également donné.

En anglais, les pluriels formés régulièrement ne sont pas donnés.

1 La plupart des noms prennent *-s* au pluriel: **bed-s, site-s.**

2 Les noms se terminant par *-s, -x, -z, -sh* et *-ch* [tʃ] prennent *-es* au pluriel: **boss-es, box-es, dish-es, patch-es.**

3 Les noms se terminant par *-y* non précédé d'une voyelle changent au pluriel le *-y* en *-ies*: **lady-ladies, berry-berries** (mais **tray-s, key-s**).

Quand le pluriel d'un mot est très différent du singulier, il figure à sa place dans la nomenclature générale avec un renvoi; il est répété sous le singulier.

Plurals

Irregular plural forms of English words are given in the English-French side, those of French words and compounds in the French-English side.

In French, all plurals which do not consist of *headword + s* are shown, eg **cheval, -aux.** The plural form of hyphenated compounds is also shown.

In English a knowledge of the basic rules is assumed.

1 Most English nouns take *-s* in the plural: **bed-s, site-s.**

2 Nouns that end in *-s, -x, -z, -sh* and some in *-ch* [tʃ] take *-es* in the plural: **boss-es, box-es, dish-es, patch-es.**

3 Nouns that end in *-y* not preceded by a vowel change the *-y* to *-ies* in the plural: **lady-ladies, berry-berries** (but **tray-s, key-s**).

Plural forms of the headword which differ substantially from the singular form are listed in their alphabetical place in the word list with a cross-reference, and repeated under the singular form.

yeux . . . **nmpl de œil**
œil, pl yeux . . . **nm**
children . . . **npl of child**
child, pl children . . . **n**

Dans la partie anglais-français, les mots français invariables au pluriel sont suivis de l'indication (*inv*).

French invariable plurals are marked (*inv*) on the English-French side for ease of reference.

Genre

Les formes féminines des mots français qui ne suivent pas directement le masculin dans l'ordre alphabétique sont données à leur place normale dans la nomenclature, avec un renvoi au masculin; elles sont répétées sous celui-ci.

Genders

Feminine forms in French which are separated alphabetically from the masculine form in the word list are shown as separate headwords with a cross reference to the masculine form.

belle . . . *voir* **beau**

Un mot féminin exigeant une traduction différente du masculin fait l'objet soit d'un article séparé soit d'une catégorie bien individualisée dans le cas d'articles complexes.

A feminine headword requiring a different translation from its masculine form is given either a separate entry or a separate category in the case of complex entries.

blanchisseur . . . **nm** launderer
blanchisseuse . . . **nf** laundress
coiffeur . . . **nm** *[dames]* hairdresser; *[hommes]* hairdresser, barber
coiffeuse . . . **nf** (*personne*) hairdresser; (*meuble*) . . .
baladeur, -euse . . . 1 **adj** . . . 2 **nm** . . . 3 **baladeuse nf**

Dans la partie anglais-français, le féminin des adjectifs français se construisant régulièrement n'est pas indiqué. Sont considérées comme régulières les formes suivantes:

In the English-French side the feminine forms of French adjectives are given only where these are not regular. The following are considered regular adjective inflections:

-, e ◇ -ef, -ève ◇ -eil, -eille ◇ -er, -ère ◇ -et, -ette ◇ -eur, -euse ◇ -eux, -euse ◇ -ien, -ienne ◇ -ier, -ière ◇ -if, -ive ◇ -il, -ille ◇ -on, -onne ◇ -ot, -otte

Par contre quand un nom anglais peut recevoir une traduction au masculin ou au féminin, selon le sexe, la forme du féminin est toujours mentionnée.

When the translation of an English noun could be either masculine or feminine, according to sex, the feminine form of the French noun translation is always given.

► **car-worker** (*Ind*) ouvrier *m*, -ière *f* de l'industrie automobile
► **computer scientist** informaticien(ne) *m(f)*

Indications d'emploi

Les indications guidant le lecteur prennent les formes suivantes.

Indicating material

General indicating material takes the following forms.

Entre parenthèses ( )

In parentheses ( )

1 Les synonymes et définitions partielles.

1 Synonyms and partial definitions.

décent, e . . . **adj** (*bienséant*) decent, proper; (*discret, digne*) proper; (*acceptable*) reasonable, decent
contender . . . **n** . . . (*in contest, competition, race*) concurrent(e) *m(f)*; (*in election, for a job*) candidat *m*

2 Les autres précisions et explications susceptibles de guider l'usager.

2 Other information and hints which guide the user.

décaper . . . **vt** (*gén*) to clean, cleanse; (*à l'abrasif*) to scour; . . . (*à la brosse*) to scrub
employment . . . **n** . . . (*a job*) emploi *m*, travail *m*; (*modest*) place *f*, (*important*) situation *f*

3 Les indications d'ordre grammatical permettant au lecteur étranger d'utiliser le mot correctement. Elles sont données après la traduction.

3 Syntactical information to allow the non-native speaker to use the word correctly. This is given after the translation.

différer . . . **vi** . . . to differ, be different (*de* from, *en, par* in)
dissimuler . . . **vt** . . . to conceal, hide (*à qn* from sb)
order . . . **vt** . . . ordonner (*sb to do* à qn de faire, *that* que + *subj*)
commit . . . **vt** . . . **to ~ o.s.** s'engager (*to sth* à qch; *to doing* à faire)

Entre crochets [ ]

In square brackets [ ]

1 Les noms sujets précisant le sens d'une entrée verbe.

1 Within verb entries, typical noun subjects of the headword.

décroître . . . **vi** *[nombre, population]* to decrease, diminish, decline; . . . *[eaux, fièvre]* to subside, go down; *[popularité]* to decline, drop
fade . . . **vi** *[flower]* se faner, se flétrir; *[light]* baisser, diminuer, s'affaiblir; *[colour]* passer, perdre son éclat; *[material]* passer, se décolorer

2 Les noms compléments d'une entrée nom.

2 Within noun entries, typical noun complements of the headword.

défiguration . . . **nf** *[vérité]* distortion; *[texte, tableau]* mutilation; *[visage]* disfigurement

branch . . . **n** . . . *[tree, candelabra]* branche *f*, . . . *[mountain chain]* ramification *f*, . . . *[subject, science etc]* branche

[vérité] doit se lire 'de la vérité'.

In such instances *[tree]* should be read as 'of tree'.

Sans parenthèses

Unbracketed indicating material

1 Les compléments d'objet d'une entrée verbe.

1 Typical objects of verbs.

défaire . . . **vt** . . . *couture, tricot* to undo, unpick (*Brit*); *écheveau* to undo, unravel, unwind; *corde, nœud, ruban* to undo, untie; . . . *valise* to unpack
impair . . . **vt** *abilities, faculties* détériorer, diminuer; *negotiations, relations* porter atteinte à; *health* abîmer, détériorer; *sight, hearing* abîmer, affaiblir

2 Les noms que peut qualifier une entrée adjectif.

2 Typical noun complements of adjectives.

élancé, e . . . **adj** *clocher, colonne, taille* slender
distinct . . . **adj** *landmark, voice, memory* distinct, clair, net; *promise, offer* précis, formel; *preference, likeness* marqué, net

3 Les verbes ou adjectifs modifiés par une entrée adverbe.

3 Typical verb or adjective complements of adverbs.

bien . . . **adv** . . . (*de façon satisfaisante*) *jouer, dormir, travailler* well; *conseiller, choisir* well, wisely; *fonctionner* properly, well
briskly . . . **adv** *move* vivement; *walk* d'un bon pas; *speak* brusquement; *act* sans tarder

NonC signifie 'non comptable'. Il est utilisé pour indiquer qu'un nom ne s'emploie pas normalement au pluriel et ne se construit pas, en règle générale, avec l'article indéfini ou un numéral. *NonC* a pour but d'avertir de lecteur étranger dans les cas où celui-ci risquerait d'employer le mot de manière incorrecte; mais notre propos n'est nullement de donner une liste exhaustive de ces mots en anglais. *NonC* est parfois utilisé comme indication dans la langue de départ, lorsque c'est le seul moyen de distinguer emplois 'non comptables' et 'comptables'.

NonC stands for 'uncountable' and serves to mark nouns which are not normally used in the plural or with the indefinite article or with numerals. *NonC* occurs only as a warning device in cases where a non-native speaker might otherwise use the word wrongly. There has been no attempt to give an exhaustive account of 'uncountability' in English. *NonC* has also been used as an indicator to distinguish meanings in the source language.

astuce . . . **nf** a (*NonC*) shrewdness, astuteness . . . b (*moyen, truc*) (clever) way, trick
clignement . . . **nm** . . . blinking (*NonC*)
Callanetics . . . **n** ® (*NonC*) *gymnastique douce* (*caractérisée par la répétition fréquente de légers exercises musculaires*)
implement . . . **n** . . . **~s** équipement *m* (*NonC*) matériel *m*

SPÉC signifie 'terme de spécialiste'.

SPEC stands for 'technical term'.

tympan . . . **nm** eardrum, tympanum (*SPEC*)

Cela veut dire que le mot anglais d'usage courant est 'eardrum' et que 'tympanum' ne se rencontre que dans le vocabulaire des spécialistes.

This indicates that the common English word is 'eardrum' and that 'tympanum' is restricted to the vocabulary of specialists.

≃ introduit une équivalence culturelle, lorsque ce que représente le terme de la langue de départ n'existe pas ou n'a pas d'équivalent exact dans la langue d'arrivée, et n'est donc pas à proprement parler traduisible.

≃ is used when the source language headword or phrase has no equivalent in the target language and is therefore untranslatable. In such cases the nearest cultural equivalent is given.

bêtise . . . **nf** . . . **~ de Cambrai** ≃ mint humbug (*Brit*), hard mint candy (*US*)
the Health Service ≃ la Sécurité sociale

Une glose explicative accompagne parfois l'équivalent culturel choisi; elle peut être donnée seule lorsqu'il n'existe pas d'équivalent culturel assez proche dans la langue d'arrivée.

Sometimes it is accompanied by an explanatory gloss (in italics). Such a gloss may be given alone in cases where there is no cultural equivalent in the target language.

baccalauréat ... **nm** ≃ A-levels (*Brit*), ≃ high school diploma (*US*), *Secondary School examination giving university entrance qualification*
Yorkshire pudding *pâte à crêpe cuite qui accompagne un rôti de bœuf*

On a eu recours aux petites capitales pour indiquer, dans certaines expressions anglaises, l'accent d'insistance qui rend, ou requiert, une nuance particulière du français.

Small capitals are used to indicate the spoken stress in certain English expressions.

mais enfin! je viens de te le dire! but I've just TOLD you!
I know HER but I've never seen HIM je la connais, elle, mais lui je ne l'ai jamais vu

Domaines

Les indications de domaine figurent dans les cas suivants:

1 Pour indiquer les différents sens d'un mot et introduire les traductions appropriées.

Field labels

Labels indicating subject fields occur in the following cases:

1 To differentiate various meanings of the headword.

cuirasse ... **nf** (*Hist*) *[chevalier]* breastplate; (*Naut*) armour(-plate *ou* -plating); (*Zool*) cuirass
grade ... **n** (*in hierarchy*) catégorie *f*, progression *f*, échelonnement *m*, grade *m*; (*Mil: rank*) rang *m*; (*Comm*) *[steel, butter, goods etc]* qualité *f*; (*Comm: size*) *[eggs, apples, anthracite, nuts etc]* calibre *m*; (*US: level*) niveau *m*; (*Climbing*) degré *m* (de difficulté)

2 Quand la langue de départ n'est pas ambiguë, mais que la traduction peut l'être.

2 When the meaning in the source language is clear but may be ambiguous in the target language.

comprimé ... **nm** (*Pharm*) tablet
parabola ... **n** parabole *f* (*Math*)

La liste des indications de domaine apparaissant sous forme abrégée figure sur les pages de garde.

A full list of the abbreviated field labels is given on the inside covers of the dictionary.

Niveaux de langue

Une quinzaine d'indications de registre accompagnent les mots et expressions qui présentent un écart par rapport à la langue courante. Ces indications sont données aussi bien dans la langue de départ que dans la langue d'arrivée et constituent avant tout un avertissement au lecteur utilisant la langue étrangère. Les paragraphes suivants précisent le sens des principaux niveaux de langue, dont la liste complète figure sous forme abrégée sur les pages de garde.

frm indique le style administratif, les formules officielles, la langue soignée.

Style labels

A dozen or so indicators of register are used to mark non-neutral words and expressions. These indicators are given for both source and target languages and serve mainly as a warning to the reader using the foreign language. The following paragraphs explain the meaning of the most common style labels, of which a complete list is given, with explanations, on the inside covers of the dictionary.

frm denotes formal language such as that used on official forms, in pronouncements and other formal communications.

agréer ... (*frm*) 1 **vt** (*accepter*) *demande, excuses* to accept
▶ **heretofore** (*frm*) jusque-là, jusqu'ici, ci-devant

* marque la majeure partie des expressions familières et les incorrections de langage employées dans la langue de tous les jours. Ce signe conseille au lecteur d'être prudent.

* indicates that the expression, while not forming part of standard language, is used by all educated speakers in a relaxed situation but would not be used in a formal essay or letter, or on an occasion when the speaker wishes to impress.

écraseur, -euse* ... **nm,f** roadhog*
discuter du sexe des anges* to discuss futilities
kidology* ... **n** (*Brit*) bluff *m*
he laughed himself silly* il a ri comme un bossu* *or* comme une baleine*

* marque les expressions très familières qui sont à employer avec la plus grande prudence par le lecteur étranger, qui devra posséder une grande maîtrise de la langue et savoir dans quel contexte elles peuvent être utilisées.

* indicates that the expression is used by some but not all educated speakers in a very relaxed situation. Such words should be handled with extreme care by the non-native speaker unless he is very fluent in the language and is very sure of his company.

doucement les basses!* take it easy!*, go easy!*
kisser* ... **n** gueule* *f*

** marque le petit nombre d'expressions courantes que le lecteur étranger doit pouvoir reconnaître, mais dont l'emploi risque d'être ressenti comme fortement indécent ou injurieux.

** means 'Danger!' Such words are liable to offend in any situation, and therefore are to be avoided by the non-native speaker.

baiser ... **vt** ... b (**) to screw**, lay**, fuck**
fart** ... **vi** péter**

† marque les termes ou expressions démodés, qui ont quitté l'usage courant mais que l'étranger peut encore rencontrer au cours de ses lectures.

† denotes old-fashioned terms which are no longer in wide current use but which the foreign user will certainly find in reading.

indéfrisable† ... **nf** perm, permanent (*US*)
botheration† ... **excl** zut!*, flûte!*, la barbe!*

†† marque les termes ou expressions archaïques, que le lecteur ne rencontrera en principe que dans les œuvres classiques.

†† denotes obsolete words which the user will normally find only in classical literature.

gageure ... **nf** b (††: *pari*) wager
burthen†† ... **= burden**

On évitera de confondre ces signes avec l'indication *Hist*, qui ne marque pas le niveau de langue du mot lui-même mais souligne que l'objet désigné ne se rencontre que dans un contexte historiquement daté.

The use of † and †† should not be confused with the label *Hist*. *Hist* does not apply to the expression itself but denotes the historical context of the object so named.

ordalie ... **nf** (*Hist*) ordeal

littér, liter marquent les expressions de style poétique ou littéraire.

liter, littér denote an expression which belongs to literary or poetic language.

ostentatoire ... **adj** (*littér*) ostentatious
beseech ... **vt** (*liter*) a (*ask for*) ... b (*entreat*) ...

Le lecteur veillera à ne pas confondre ces indications avec *lit* d'une part (sens propre, emploi littéral) et *Littérat, Literat* de l'autre (domaine de la littérature).

The user should not confuse these style labels with the field labels *Literat, Littérat* which indicate that the expression belongs to the field of literature. Similarly the user should note that the abbreviation *lit* indicates the literal, as opposed to the figurative *fig*, meaning of a word.

Les indications *arg* (argot) et *sl* (slang) désignent les termes appartenant au vocabulaire de groupes restreints (tels que les écoliers, les militaires) et l'indication du domaine approprié leur est adjoint dans la langue de départ.

For the purpose of this dictionary the indicators *sl* (slang) and *arg* (argot) mark specific areas of vocabulary restricted to clearly defined groups of speakers (eg schoolchildren, soldiers, etc) and for this reason a field label is added to the label *sl* or *arg* marking the departure language expression.

camer (se) ... (*arg Drogue*) to be on drugs
cooler ... (*Prison sl*) taule* *f*

Les indications de niveau de langue peuvent soit s'attacher à un mot ou à une expression isolés, soit marquer une catégorie entière ou même un article complet. Lorsqu'un mot est suivi d'astérisques, les locutions et exemples de l'article ne prendront à leur tour l'astérisque que si elles appartiennent à un niveau de langue différent. Tous les composés stylistiquement marqués prennent l'astérisque même s'ils sont du même niveau de langue que l'entrée.

The labels and symbols above are used to mark either an individual word or phrase, or a whole category, or even a complete entry. Where a headword is marked with asterisks any phrases in the entry will only have asterisks if they are of a different register from the headword. All compounds are marked even if their register matches that of the headword.

Ponctuation

Une virgule sépare les traductions considérées comme équivalentes ou pratiquement équivalentes des mots ou des expressions de la langue de départ.

Punctuation

A comma is used to separate translations which have the same or very similar meanings.

légitime ... 1 **adj** a (*légal*) *droits* legitimate, lawful
I haven't seen him for ages il y a un siècle que je ne le vois plus, il y a une éternité que je ne l'ai vu

Un point-virgule sépare les traductions qui ne sont pas interchangeables. En règle générale, le point-virgule est accompagné d'une indication qui précise la différence de sens.

A semi-colon separates translations which are not interchangeable. As a general rule, indicators are given to differentiate between non-interchangeable translations.

mettre en danger *personne* to put in danger; *vie, espèce* to endanger; *chances, réputation, carrière* to jeopardize
melting ... 1 **adj** *snow* fondant; (*fig*) *voice, look* attendri; *words* attendrissant

Les traductions offrant plusieurs variantes interchangeables à partir d'un tronc commun sont séparées par *ou* ou par *or*

In the translation of phrases, an alternative translation of only part of the phrase is preceded by either *or* or *ou*.

je serai ravi de vous retrouver I'll be delighted to see *ou* meet you again
to be eager to help être empressé à *or* très désireux d'aider

Le trait oblique / permet de regrouper des expressions de sens différent ayant un élément en commun, lorsque cette structure est reflétée dans la langue d'arrivée.

An oblique / indicates alternatives in the source language which are reflected exactly in the target language.

I'd give my eyeteeth* for a car like that/to go to China qu'est-ce que je ne donnerais pas pour avoir une voiture comme ça/pour aller en Chine
une voiture/maison haut/bas de gamme a car/house at the top/lower end of the range, an up-/down-market car/house

Les parenthèses figurant à l'intérieur des expressions ou de leur traduction indiquent que les mots qu'elles contiennent sont facultatifs.

Parentheses within illustrative phrases or their translations indicate that the material so contained is optional.

bas les mains* *ou* **les pattes!**** hands off!*, (keep your) paws off!**
(I've) got it! j'y suis!, ça y est!

Ces parenthèses peuvent figurer en corrélation.

Such parentheses may be given for phrases in both source and target language.

our (highly) esteemed colleague notre (très) estimé collègue *or* confrère

Renvois

Pour éviter d'avoir à répéter un ensemble d'indications, lorsqu'un mot a été traité en profondeur et que

Cross-references

To avoid repeating indicating material where one word has been treated in depth and derivatives of that

ses dérivés ont des divisions de sens correspondantes. Ceci se produit notamment pour les adverbes dérivés d'adjectifs et les nominalisations (voir aussi ***Verbes*** ci-dessous).

word have corresponding semantic divisions, eg adverbs which are cross-referred to adjectives, nouns which are cross-referred to verbs (see also ***Verbs*** below).

diffuser ... **vt** *lumière, chaleur* to diffuse; *bruit, idée* to spread (abroad), circulate, diffuse; *livres* to distribute; (*Jur*) *document* to circulate; *émission* to broadcast
diffusion ... **nf** (*voir* **diffuser**) diffusion; spreading; circulation; distribution; broadcasting

Pour renvoyer le lecteur à l'article dans lequel est traitée une certaine expression, où figure un certain composé (voir ***Les composés*** ci-dessus).

To refer the user to the headword under which a certain compound or idiom has been treated (see ***Compounds*** above).

Pour attirer l'attention de l'usager sur certains mots-clés qui ont été traités en profondeur: pour les numéraux, **six**, **sixième** et **soixante**; pour les jours de la semaine, **samedi**; pour les mois de l'année, **septembre**. Dans la nomenclature anglaise, ce seront les mots **six**, **sixth**, **sixty**, **Saturday**, **September**.

To draw the user's attention to the full treatment of such words as numerals, days of the week, and months of the year under certain key words. The key words which have been treated in depth are: French - **six**, **sixième**, **soixante**, **samedi**, **septembre**. English - **six**, **sixth**, **sixty**, **Saturday**, **September**.

Friday ... *for other phrases see* **Saturday** ...
vendredi ... *pour autres loc voir* **samedi**

Verbes

Les tables de conjugaison des verbes français et anglais sont données en annexe à la fin de l'ouvrage. Dans la nomenclature française, chaque verbe est suivi d'un numéro à l'intérieur d'un carré qui renvoie le lecteur à ces tables. Le prétérit et le participe passé des verbes forts anglais sont donnés après le verbe dans le corps de l'article. Une liste des principaux verbes forts figure également en annexe.

Dans la partie français-anglais, les emplois véritablement pronominaux des verbes sont traités dans une catégorie à part.

Verbs

Tables of French and English verbs are included in the supplements at the end of the book. At each verb headword in the French-English side of the dictionary, a number inside a box refers the user to these tables. The preterite and past participle of English strong verbs are given at the main verb entry.

In the French-English part of the dictionary verbs which are true pronominals are treated in a separate grammatical category.

baisser ... 3 **se baisser vpr** (*pour ramasser qch*) to bend down, stoop; (*pour éviter qch*) to duck

Les emplois pronominaux à valeur réciproque, réfléchie ou passive, ne figurent que lorsque la traduction l'exige. En pareil cas, ils peuvent être simplement donnés dans la catégorie appropriée du verbe transitif, à titre d'exemple.

Pronominal uses which indicate a reciprocal, reflexive or passive sense are shown only if the translation requires it. In such cases they may be given within the transitive category of the verb as an illustrative phrase.

grandir ... **vt** ... (*faire paraître grand*) ... **ces chaussures te grandissent** those shoes make you (look) taller; **il se grandit en se mettant sur la pointe des pieds** he made himself taller by standing on tiptoe

Les nominalisations des verbes français (mots en *-age*, *-ation*, *-ement* etc) reçoivent souvent des traductions qui ne sont données qu'à titre indicatif; ces traductions doivent être utilisées avec prudence, l'usager étant supposé savoir que dans de nombreux cas une construction verbale est plus courante en anglais.

French nouns formed from the *verb root* + *-ation* or *-age* or *-ement* etc are sometimes given only token translations. These translations must be treated with care by the user, who is assumed to know that in many cases a verbal construction is more common in English.

balbutiement ... **nm** (*paroles confuses*) stammering, mumbling; *[bébé]* babbling

Si la traduction d'un participe passé ne peut se déduire directement à partir du verbe, ou si le participe a pris une valeur adjective, il est traité comme

If the translation of a past participle cannot be reached directly from the verb entry or if the past participle has adjectival value then the past participle is

mot à part entière et figure à sa place alphabétique dans la nomenclature.

treated as a headword.

étendu, e ... **(ptp de étendre)** 1 **adj** a (*vaste*) ... b (*allongé*) ...
broken ... 1 **ptp of break.** 2 **adj** a (*lit*) cassé, brisé; ... b (*uneven*) ...; c (*interrupted*) ...; d (*spoilt, ruined*) ...

PRONONCIATION

PRONUNCIATION

PRONUNCIATION OF FRENCH

Transcription

The symbols used to record the pronunciation of French are those of the International Phonetic Association. The variety of French transcribed is that shown in *Le Nouveau Petit Robert*, i.e. standard Parisian speech. Within this variety of French, variant pronunciations are to be observed. In particular, there is a marked tendency among speakers today to make no appreciable distinction between: [a] and [ɑ], **patte** [pat] and **pâte** [pɑt] both tending towards the pronunciation [pat]; [ɛ̃] and [œ̃], **brin** [bʀɛ̃] and **brun** [bʀœ̃] both tending towards the pronunciation [bʀɛ̃]. The distinction between these sounds is maintained in the transcription.

Headwords

Each headword has its pronunciation transcribed between square brackets. In the case of words having a variant pronunciation (e.g. **tandis** [tɑ̃di], [tɑ̃dis]), the one pronunciation given is that regarded by the editorial team as preferable, often on grounds of frequency.

Morphological variations

Morphological variations of headwords are shown phonetically where necessary, without repetition of the root (e.g. **journal, pl -aux** [ʒuʀnal, o]).

Compound words

Compound words derived from headwords and shown within an entry are given without phonetic transcription (e.g. **passer** [pɑse], but **passe-lacet, passe-montagne**). The pronunciation of compounds is usually predictable, being that of the citation form of each element, associated with the final syllable stress characteristic of the language (see following paragraph).

Syllable stress

In normal, unemphatic speech, the final syllable of a word, or the final syllable of a sense group, carries a moderate degree of stress. The syllable stressed is given extra prominence by greater length and intensity. The exception to this rule is a final syllable containing a mute *e*, which is never stressed. In view of this simple rule, it has not been considered necessary to indicate the position of a stressed syllable of a word by a stress mark in the phonetic transcription.

Closing of [ɛ]

Under the influence of stressed [y], [i], or [e] vowels, an [ɛ] in an open syllable tends towards a closer [e] sound, even in careful speech. In such cases, the change has been indicated: **aimant** [ɛmɑ̃], but **aimer** [eme]; **bête** [bɛt], but **bêtise** [betiz].

Mute e [ə]

Within isolated words, a mute *e* [ə] preceded by a single pronounced consonant is regularly dropped (e.g. **follement** [fɔlmɑ̃]; **samedi** [samdi]).

Opening of [e]

As the result of the dropping of an [ə] within a word, an [e] occurring in a closed syllable tends towards [ɛ], as the transcription shows (e.g. **événement** [evɛnmɑ̃]; **élevage** [ɛlvaʒ]).

Aspirate h

Initial *h* in the spelling of a French word does not imply strong expulsion of breath, except in the case of certain interjections. Initial *h* is called 'aspirate' when it is incompatible with liaison (**des haricots** [de'aʀiko]) or elision (**le haricot** [lə'aʀiko]). Aspirate *h* is shown in transcriptions by an apostrophe placed at the beginning of the word (e.g. **hibou** ['ibu]).

Consonants and assimilation

Within a word and in normal speech, a voiceless consonant may be voiced when followed by a voiced consonant (e.g. **exemple** [ɛgzɑ̃pl]), and a voiced consonant may be devoiced when followed by a voiceless consonant (e.g. **absolument** [apsɔlymɑ̃]). When this phenomenon is regular in a word, it is shown in transcription (e.g. **abside** [apsid]). In speech, its frequency varies from speaker to speaker. Thus, while the citation form of **tasse** is [tɑs], the group **une tasse de thé** may be heard pronounced [yntɑsdəte] or [yntɑzdəte].

Sentence stress

Unlike the stress pattern of English associated with meaning, sentence stress in French is associated with rhythm. The stress falls on the final syllable of the sense groups of which the sentence is formed (see ***Syllable stress***). In the following example: *quand il m'a vu, il a traversé la rue en courant pour me dire un mot*, composed of three sense groups, the syllables **vu**, **-rant** and **mot** carry the stress, being slightly lengthened.

Intonation

French intonation is less mobile than English and is closely associated with sentence stress. It occurs normally on the final syllable of sense groups. Thus, in the sentence given above, the syllables **vu** and **-rant** are spoken with a slight rise (indicating continuity), while the syllable **mot** is accompanied by a fall in the voice (indicating finality). In the case of a question, the final syllable will normally also be spoken with rising voice.

PHONETIC TRANSCRIPTION OF FRENCH

Phonetic alphabet used

Vowels

[i] ***i**l, v**ie**, l**y**re*
[e] *bl**é**, jou**er***
[ɛ] *l**ait**, jou**et**, m**e**rci*
[a] *pl**a**t, p**a**tte*
[ɑ] *b**as**, p**â**te*
[ɔ] *m**o**rt, d**o**nner*
[o] *m**o**t, d**ô**me, **eau**, g**au**che*
[u] *gen**ou**, r**ou**e*
[y] *r**u**e, vêt**u***
[ø] *p**eu**, d**eu**x*
[œ] *p**eu**r, m**eu**ble*
[ə] *l**e**, pr**e**mier*
[ɛ̃] *mat**in**, pl**ein***
[ɑ̃] *s**an**s, v**en**t*
[ɔ̃] *b**on**, **om**bre*
[œ̃] *l**un**di, br**un***

Semi-consonants

[j] ***y**eux, pa**ill**e, p**i**ed*
[w] ***ou**i, n**ou**er*
[ɥ] *h**u**ile, l**u**i*

Consonants

[p] ***p**ère, sou**p**e*
[t] ***t**erre, vi**t**e*
[k] ***c**ou, **qu**i, sa**c**, **k**épi*
[b] ***b**on, ro**b**e*
[d] ***d**ans, ai**d**e*
[g] ***g**are, ba**gu**e*
[f] ***f**eu, neu**f**, **ph**oto*
[s] ***s**ale, **c**elui, **ç**a, de**ss**ous, ta**ss**e, na**t**ion*
[ʃ] ***ch**at, ta**ch**e*
[v] ***v**ous, rê**v**e*
[z] ***z**éro, mai**s**on, ro**s**e*
[ʒ] ***j**e, **g**ilet, **g**eôle*
[l] ***l**ent, so**l***
[ʀ] ***r**ue, veni**r***
[m] ***m**ain, fe**mm**e*
[n] ***n**ous, to**nn**e, a**n**imal*
[ɲ] *a**gn**eau, vi**gn**e*
[h] ***h**op! (exclamative)*
['] ***h**aricot (no liaison)*
[ŋ] *words borrowed from English: campi**ng***
[x] *words borrowed from Spanish or Arabic: **j**ota*

PRONONCIATION DE L'ANGLAIS

La notation adoptée est celle de l'Association phonétique internationale. L'ouvrage de base qui nous a servi constamment d'outil de référence est l'*English Pronouncing Dictionary* de Daniel Jones, qui, mis à jour par le Professeur A. C. Gimson, continue de faire autorité en France et partout ailleurs où l'on apprend l'anglais britannique.

La transcription correspond à la *received pronunciation* (*RP*), variété de l'anglais britannique la plus généralement étudiée dans le monde d'aujourd'hui. Elle correspond également, à quelques exceptions près, à celle de la 14e édition de l'*English Pronouncing Dictionary* (*EPD*) (Cambridge University Press). Ce système de transcription présente l'avantage d'utiliser des signes qui indiquent clairement la distinction à la fois quantitative et qualitative qui existe entre les voyelles tendues et relâchées (par exemple: 14e édition: [iː], [ɪ]; [ɜː], [ə].

Pour des raisons d'économie de place, une seule prononciation est donnée pour chaque mot, à l'exclusion des variantes éventuelles et connues. La prononciation ainsi transcrite est celle la plus fréquemment entendue selon l'*EPD*, ou, dans le cas de néologismes et de mots nouveaux, selon les membres de l'équipe Collins-Le Robert.

Il a été jugé inutile de compliquer la tâche de l'utilisateur en indiquant au moyen de symboles appropriés la prononciation de mots sortant du cadre du vocabulaire britannique. Ainsi, **aluminium**, **aluminum** sont transcrits: [ˌæljʊˈmɪnɪəm], [əˈluːmɪnəm], bien que la seconde forme, exclusivement américaine, ne s'entende normalement qu'avec un accent américain. Il s'agit, dans de tels cas, d'une approximation qui ne met pas en cause la compréhension du mot employé.

Les formes réduites

Certains mots monosyllabiques, en nombre limité, ayant une fonction plus structurale que lexicale, sont sujets, surtout à l'intérieur d'un énoncé, à une réduction vocalique plus ou moins importante. Le mot **and**, isolé, se prononce [ænd]; mais, dans la chaîne parlée, il se prononcera, à moins d'être accentué, [ənd, ən, n] selon le débit du locuteur et selon le contexte. Les mots qui sont le plus souvent touchés par cette réduction vocalique sont les suivants: *a, an, and, as, at, but, for, from, of, some, than, that, the, them, to, us, am, is, are, was, were, must, will, would, shall, should, have, has, had, do, does, can, could.*

L'accent tonique

Tout mot anglais, isolé, de deux syllabes ou plus, porte un accent tonique. Cet accent est noté au moyen du signe (ˈ) placé devant la syllabe intéressée; par exemple: **composer** [kəmˈpəʊzəʳ]. Le Français doit veiller à bien placer l'accent tonique sous peine de poser de sérieux problèmes de compréhension à ses interlocuteurs. Le tableau suivant indique un certain nombre de suffixes qui permettent de prévoir la place de l'accent tonique sur de nombreux mots. Ce tableau est donné à titre indicatif et ne cherche pas à être exhaustif.

Tableau des suffixes déterminant la position de l'accent tonique

SUFFIXE	*EXEMPLE*	*EXCEPTIONS*	*REMARQUES*
Accent sur syllabe finale			
-ee	refu'gee	'coffee, 'toffee, com'mittee, 'pedigree	
-eer	engi'neer		
-ese	Japa'nese		
-esque	pictu'resque		
-ette	quar'tette	'etiquette, 'omelette	
-ate	cre'ate		*verbes de 2 syllabes*
-fy	de'fy		*verbes de 2 syllabes*
-ise, -ize	ad'vise		*verbes de 2 syllabes*

SUFFIXE	EXEMPLE	EXCEPTIONS	REMARQUES
Accent sur pénultième			
-ial	com'mercial		
-ian	I'talian		
-ic, -ics	eco'nomics	'Arabic, a'rithmetic, 'Catholic, 'heretic, 'lunatic, 'politics	*les suffixes* -ical, -ically *ne modifient pas la place de l'accent tonique, et n'admettent pas d'exceptions. Par exemple*: po'litical, po'litically, arith'metical.
-ion	infor'mation	'dandelion, ('television)	
-ish	di'minish	im'poverish	*verbes en* -ish
-itis	appendi'citis		
-osis	diag'nosis	(meta'morphosis)	
Accent sur antépénultième			
-ety	so'ciety		
-ity	sin'cerity		
-itive	com'petitive		
-itude	'attitude		
-grapher	pho'tographer		
-graphy	pho'tography		
-logy	bi'ology		
-ate	ap'preciate		
-fy	'pacify		*pour les verbes de 2 syllabes, voir plus haut*
-ise, -ize	'advertise	'characterize, 'regularize, 'liberalize, 'nationalize	*pour les verbes de 2 syllabes, voir plus haut*

NB *Les mots placés entre parenthèses ont aussi une accentuation conforme au modèle.*

L'accent secondaire

Dans un mot, toute syllabe accentuée en plus de celle qui porte l'accent tonique porte un accent secondaire, c'est-à-dire un accent ayant moins d'intensité que l'accent tonique. L'accent secondaire est noté au moyen du signe (ˌ) devant la syllabe intéressée: Par exemple: **composition** [ˌkɒmpəˈzɪʃən] (accent secondaire sur [ˌkɒm]; accent tonique sur [ˈzɪʃ]).

Les composés

La prononciation des mots ou groupes de mots rassemblés dans la catégorie **comp** d'un article n'est pas indiquée, car elle correspond à celle du mot-souche suivie de celle du mot ou des mots formant le reste du composé mais avec une restriction importante: pour des raisons pratiques, on considérera que la grande majorité des composés à deux éléments ne sont accentués que sur le premier élément, cette accentuation s'accompagnant d'une chute de la voix. Exemple: '**foodstuffs**, '**food prices**.

L'accent de phrase

À la différence du français dont l'accent de phrase (syllabe allongée) tombe normalement sur la dernière syllabe des groupes de souffle, l'anglais met en relief la syllabe accentuée de chaque mot apportant un nouvel élément d'information. Dans la pratique cela veut dire que les mots lexicaux reçoivent un accent de phrase, tandis que les mots grammaticaux n'en reçoivent pas (voir ***Les formes réduites***). Il est logique, dans un tel système, que même les mots lexicaux ne soient pas accentués s'ils n'apportent pas de nouveaux éléments d'information; c'est le cas, notamment, de mots ou de concepts répétés dans une même séquence; ils sont accentués une première fois, mais ils perdent leur accent par la suite. De même, lorsqu'une idée est répétée dans une même séquence, les mots qui l'expriment ne sont plus mis en relief lors de sa réapparition. Par contre, les éléments contrastifs de la phrase anglaise sont toujours fortement accentués.

Exemple: *John's recently bought himself a car, and Peter's got a new one too.*

Accents sur: **John**, **recently**, **bought**, **car**, **Peter**, **too.**

Accents contrastifs sur: **John** (facultatif) et **Peter**. Absence d'accent sur: **'s got a new one**, qui n'apporte aucun nouvel élément d'information et pourrait être supprimé: (**and Peter, too.**)

L'intonation

L'intonation en anglais, beaucoup plus qu'en français, révèle le sentiment du locuteur vis-à-vis des propos qu'il tient. Dans les deux langues, l'intonation est liée à l'accent de phrase. L'intonation française, tout comme l'accent de phrase, se manifeste sur la dernière syllabe des groupes de souffle: légère montée de la voix à l'intérieur de la phrase, avec une chute ou une montée sur la syllabe finale, selon qu'il s'agit d'une déclarative ou d'une interrogative. En anglais, l'intonation est liée au sens, et se manifeste sur toutes les syllabes accentuées de la phrase (voir ***L'accent de phrase***). La phrase anglaise type présente une intonation commençant relativement haut, et descendant vers le grave progressivement sur les syllabes accentuées. Sur la dernière syllabe accentuée de la phrase, la voix marque soit une chute, soit une montée, plus importante qu'en français, selon le type de phrase: une chute, s'il s'agit d'une indication de finalité (déclaratives, impératives etc); une montée s'il s'agit d'une invitation au dialogue (interrogatives, requêtes polies etc). Plus le discours est animé et plus l'écart entre l'aigu et le grave se creuse. Des mots ayant un sens affectif intense tendent à faire monter la voix beaucoup plus haut que n'exigent les habitudes du discours français.

TRANSCRIPTION PHONÉTIQUE DE L'ANGLAIS

Alphabet phonétique et valeur des signes

Voyelles et diphtongues

[iː]	b***ea***d, s***ee***
[ɑː]	b***ar***d, c***al***m
[ɔː]	b***or***n, c***or***k
[uː]	b***oo***n, f***oo***l
[ɜː]	b***ur***n, f***er***n, w***or***k
[ɪ]	s***i***t, p***i***ty
[e]	s***e***t, l***e***ss
[æ]	s***a***t, ***a***pple
[ʌ]	f***u***n, c***o***me
[ɒ]	f***o***nd, w***a***sh
[ʊ]	f***u***ll, s***oo***t
[ə]	compos***er***, ***a***bove
[eɪ]	b***ay***, f***a***te
[aɪ]	b***uy***, l***ie***
[ɔɪ]	b***oy***, v***oi***ce
[əʊ]	n***o***, ag***o***
[aʊ]	n***ow***, pl***ou***gh
[ɪə]	***tier***, ***beer***
[ɛə]	t***are***, f***air***
[ʊə]	t***our***

Consonnes

[p]	***p***at, ***p***o***p***e
[b]	***b***at, ***b***a***b***y
[t]	***t***ab, s***t***ru***t***
[d]	***d***ab, men***ded***
[k]	***c***ot, ***k***iss, ***ch***ord
[g]	***g***ot, a***g***o***g***
[f]	***f***ine, ra***ff***le
[v]	***v***ine, ri***v***er
[s]	pot***s***, ***s***it, ri***ce***
[z]	pod***s***, bu***zz***
[θ]	***th***in, ma***th***s
[ð]	***th***is, o***th***er
[ʃ]	***sh***ip, ***s***ugar
[ʒ]	mea***s***ure
[tʃ]	***ch***ance
[dʒ]	***j***ust, e***dg***e
[l]	***l***ittle, p***l***ace
[r]	***r***an, sti***rr***ing
[m]	ra***m***, ***mumm***y
[n]	ra***n***, ***n***ut
[ŋ]	ra***ng***, ba***n***k
[h]	***h***at, re***h***eat
[j]	***y***et, mill***i***on
[w]	***w***et, be***w***ail
[x]	lo***ch***

Divers

	Un caractère en italique représente un son qui peut ne pas être prononcé
[ʳ]	représente un [r] entendu s'il forme une liaison avec le voyelle du mot suivant
[ˈ]	accent tonique
[ˌ]	accent secondaire

DICTIONNAIRE FRANÇAIS-ANGLAIS

FRENCH-ENGLISH DICTIONARY

A[1], a[1] [ɑ] **nm** (*lettre*) A, a. **de A (jusqu')à Z** from A to Z; **feuille A3/A4** sheet of A3/A4 paper; **c'est du format A4** it's A4 (paper); **prouver qch par a plus b** to prove sth conclusively.

A[2] (**abrév de ampère**) amp.

A[3] [a] **nf** (**abrév de autoroute**) ≃ M (*Brit*). **l'~ 10** the A10 motorway (*Brit*) *ou* highway (*US*).

a[2] (**abrév de are**) a.

Å (**abrév de angström**) Å.

A2† [adø] (**abrév de Antenne 2**) *former name for 2nd channel on French television.*

à [a] **prép** (*contraction avec le, les:* **au, aux**) a (*copule introduisant compléments après vb, loc verbale, adj, n*) **obéir/pardonner ~ qn** to obey/forgive sb; **rêver ~ qch** to dream of *ou* about sth; **se mettre ~ faire** to begin to do, set about *ou* start doing; **se décider ~ faire** to make up one's mind to do, decide (up)on doing; **s'habituer ~ faire** to get *ou* become *ou* grow used to doing; **prendre plaisir ~ faire** to take pleasure in doing, derive pleasure from doing; **c'est facile/difficile ~ faire** it's easy/difficult to do; **il est lent ~ s'habiller** he takes a long time dressing, he's slow at dressing (himself); **son aptitude ~ faire/au travail** his aptitude for doing/for work; **son empressement ~ aider** his eagerness *ou* willingness to help; **depuis son accession au trône/admission au club** since his accession to the throne/admission to the club; **je consens ~ ce que vous partiez** I consent *ou* agree to your leaving *ou* to your departure; *voir vb, n, adj appropriés.*

b (*déplacement, direction*) (*vers*) to; (*dans*) into. **aller** *ou* **se rendre ~ Paris/~ Bornéo/au Canada/aux Açores** to go to Paris/Borneo/Canada/the Azores; **le train de Paris ~ Reims** the train from Paris to Rheims; **aller ~ l'école/~ l'église/au marché/au théâtre** to go to school/church/(the) market/the theatre; **aller ~ la chasse/pêche** to go hunting/fishing; **aller** *ou* **partir ~ la recherche de qch** to go looking *ou* go and look for sth; **raconte ton voyage ~ Londres** tell us about your trip to London; **entrez donc au salon** (do) come into the lounge; **mets-toi ~ l'ombre** get into *ou* in the shade; **au lit/travail les enfants!** time for bed/work children!, off to bed/work children!

c (*position, localisation*) at; (*à l'intérieur de*) in; (*à la surface de*) on. **habiter ~ Carpentras/~ Paris/au Canada/aux Açores** to live at *ou* in Carpentras/in Paris/in Canada/in the Azores; **elle habite au 4e (étage)** she lives on the 4th floor; **être ~ l'école/~ la maison/au bureau/au théâtre** to be at school/home/the office/the theatre; **travailler ~ l'étranger/~ domicile** to work abroad/at home; **il faisait très chaud ~ l'église/au théâtre** it was very hot in church/the theatre; **Paris est ~ 400 km de Londres** Paris is 400 km from London; **il est seul au monde** he is (all) alone in the world; **c'est ~ 3 km/5 minutes (d'ici)** it's 3 km/5 minutes away (from here); **2e rue ~ droite/gauche** 2nd street on the right/left; **elle était assise ~ la fenêtre** she was sitting at *ou* by the window; **le magasin au coin de la rue** the shop *ou* store (*US*) on *ou* at the corner, the corner shop (*Brit*); **debout le dos au feu** standing with one's back to the fire; **j'ai froid aux jambes/aux mains** my legs/hands are cold, I've got cold legs/hands; **prendre qn au cou/~ la gorge** to take sb by the neck/throat; **il a été blessé ~ l'épaule/au genou** he was injured in the shoulder/knee; **il entra le sourire aux lèvres** he came in with a smile on his face; **il a de l'eau (jusqu')aux genoux** the water comes up to his knees, he's knee-deep in water; **regardez ~ la page 4** look at *ou* up page 4; **~ la télévision/radio** on television/the radio; *voir* **à-côté, bord, bout** *etc.*

d (*temps*) (*moment précis*) at; (*jour, date*) on; (*époque*) at, during; (*jusqu'à*) to, till, until. **~ quelle heure vient-il? — ~ 6 heures** what time is he coming? — at 6 *ou* (at) 6 o'clock; **je n'étais pas là ~ leur arrivée** I wasn't there when they arrived; **ils partirent au matin/le 3 au soir** they left in the morning/on the evening of the 3rd; **au printemps** in spring; **~ l'automne** in autumn; **la poésie au 19e siècle** poetry in the 19th century, 19th-century poetry; **aux grandes vacances** in *ou* during the summer holidays; **je vous verrai aux vacances/~ Noël/au retour** I'll see you in the holidays/at Christmas/when we come back; **~ demain/l'an prochain/dans un mois/samedi** see you tomorrow/next year/in a month's time/on Saturday; **le docteur reçoit de 2 ~ 4** the doctor has his surgery (*Brit*) *ou* sees patients from 2 to *ou* till 4; **remettre ~ huitaine** to postpone *ou* defer for a week *ou* until the next *ou* following week.

e (*condition, situation*) in, on, at. **être/rester au chaud/au froid/au vent/~ l'humidité** to be/stay in the warm/cold/wind/damp; **être ~ genoux/quatre pattes** to be on one's knees/on all fours; **il est ~ ménager/plaindre** he is to be handled carefully/pitied; **ils en sont ~ leurs derniers sous** they're down to their last few pence (*Brit*) *ou* cents (*US*); **elle n'est pas femme ~ faire cela** she is not the sort (of woman) to do that; **ce n'est pas le genre de docteur ~ oublier** he's not the sort of doctor to forget *ou* who would forget; **être/rester ~ travailler** to be/stay working *ou* at one's work; **il est toujours (là) ~ se plaindre** he's forever complaining; **il a été le premier ~ le dire, mais ils sont plusieurs ~ le penser** he was the first to say so, but there are quite a few who think like him *ou* the same; **ils sont 2 ~ l'avoir fait** there were 2 of them that did it; *voir* **à-coup, bout, cran.**

f (*rapport, évaluation, distribution etc*) by, per; (*approximation*) to. **faire du 50 ~ l'heure** to do 50 km an *ou* per hour; **consommer 9 litres aux 100 km** to use 9 litres to the *ou* per 100 km, do 100 km to 9 litres; **être payé ~ la semaine/l'heure** to be paid by the week/the hour; **vendre au détail/poids/mètre/kilo** to sell retail/by weight/by the metre/by the kilo; **il leur faut 4 ~ 5 heures/kilos** they need 4 to 5 hours/kilos; **entrer un ~ un/deux ~ deux** to come in one by one/two by two, come in one/two at a time; **gagner par 2 ~ zéro** to win by 2 goals to nil, win 2 nil; **~ chaque coup** every *ou* each time; **~ chaque pas** at each *ou* every step; **~ chaque page** on each *ou* every page; *voir* **bout, heure.**

g (*appartenance*) to, of. **être** *ou* **appartenir ~ qn/qch** to belong to sb/sth; **ce livre est ~ Pierre** this book belongs to Peter *ou* is Peter's; **le sac est ~ moi/~ elle** the bag is mine/hers; **c'est une amie ~ lui/eux** she is a friend of his/theirs; **ils n'ont pas de maison ~ eux** they haven't a house of their own; **le couteau ~ Jean*** John's knife; **c'est ~ lui de protester** (*sa responsabilité*) it's up to him *ou* it's his job to protest; (*son tour*) it's his turn to protest; **l'ananas a un goût bien ~ lui** pineapple has a flavour all (of) its own *ou* a distinctive flavour; **ce n'est pas ~ moi de le dire** it's not for me to say, it's not up to me to say; **c'est très gentil** *ou* **aimable ~ vous** that's very kind of you.

h (*avec vt à double complément*) (*attribution etc*) to (*souvent omis*); (*provenance*) from, out of; (*comparaison, préférence*) to. **donner/prêter/enseigner qch ~ qn** to give/lend/teach sb sth, give/lend/teach sth to sb; **prendre de l'eau au puits/~ la rivière/au seau** to take water from the well/from the river/out of *ou* from the bucket; **il préfère le vin ~ la bière** he prefers wine to beer; *voir* **aider, conseiller[1], emprunter, offrir.**

i (*moyen*) on, by, with. **faire qch ~ la machine/~ la main** to do sth by machine/hand; **fait ~ la machine/main** machine-/hand-made; **la cuisinière marche au gaz/au charbon/~ l'électricité** the cooker runs on *ou* uses gas/coal/electricity; **aller ~ bicyclette/~ pied/~ cheval** to cycle/walk/ride, go by bicycle/on foot/on horseback; **examiner qch au microscope/~ la loupe/~ l'œil nu** to examine sth under *ou* with a microscope/with a magnifying glass/with the naked eye; **il nous a joué l'air au piano/violon** he played us the tune on the piano/violin.

j (*manière: souvent traduit par adv*) at, in. **il est parti ~ toute allure/au galop** he rushed/galloped off, he left at full tilt*/at a gallop; **vivre ~ l'américaine** to live like an American *ou* in the American style; **une histoire ~ la (manière de) Tolstoï** a story in the style of Tolstoy *ou* à la Tolstoy; **elle fait la cuisine ~ l'huile/au beurre** she cooks with oil/butter; (*Culin*) **canard aux petits pois/aux pruneaux** duck with peas/prunes; **il l'a fait ~ sa manière** he did it in his own way; **il l'a fait ~ lui tout seul** he did it (all) on his own *ou* (all) by himself *ou* single-handed; **ils couchent ~ 3 dans la même chambre** they sleep 3 to a room; **ils ont fait le travail ~ 3/~ eux tous** they did the work between the 3 of them/between them (all).

k (*caractérisation: avec n*) with (*souvent omis*). **pompe ~ eau/essence** water/petrol (*Brit*) *ou* gasoline (*US*) pump; **bête ~ plumes/~ fourrure** feathered/furry creature; **enfant aux yeux bleus/aux cheveux**

longs blue-eyed/long-haired child, child with blue eyes/long hair; **robe ~ manches** dress with sleeves; **robe ~ manches courtes** short-sleeved dress; **canne ~ bout ferré** metal-tipped stick, stick with a metal tip; **bons ~ 10 ans** 10-year bonds; **la dame au chapeau vert** the lady in *ou* with the green hat; **le client au budget modeste** the customer on a tight *ou* small budget.

l (*destination*) (*avec n*) for (*souvent omis*); (*avec vb*) to; (*dédicace*) to, for. **tasse ~ thé** teacup; **pot ~ lait** milk jug; **~ mon épouse regrettée** in memory of my dear departed wife; **j'ai une maison ~ vendre/louer** I have a house to sell *ou* for sale/to let *ou* for letting; **donner une robe ~ nettoyer** to take a dress to be cleaned, take a dress in for cleaning; **il a un bouton ~ recoudre** he's got a button to sew on *ou* that needs sewing on; **je n'ai rien ~ lire/faire** I have nothing to read/do; **avez-vous ~ manger/boire?** have you anything to eat/drink?; **je peux vous donner ~ déjeuner/dîner** I can give you (some) lunch/dinner.

m (+ *infin: au point de*) **s'ennuyer ~ mourir** to be bored to death; **laid ~ faire peur** as ugly as sin; **ce bruit est ~ vous rendre fou** this noise is enough to drive you mad; **c'est ~ se demander si** it makes you wonder if.

n (+ *infin: valeur de gérondif: cause, hypothèse etc*) **~ le voir si maigre, j'ai eu pitié** (on) seeing him *ou* when I saw him so thin I took pity on him; **vous le buterez ~ le punir ainsi** you'll antagonize him if you punish him like that; **je me fatigue ~ répéter** I'm wearing myself out repeating; **il nous fait peur ~ conduire si vite** he frightens us (by) driving *ou* when he drives so fast; **~ bien considérer la chose, ~ bien réfléchir** if you think about it; **s'ennuyer ~ ne rien faire** to get bored doing nothing; *voir* **force**.

o (*conséquence, résultat*) to; (*cause*) at; (*d'après*) according to, from. **~ sa consternation** to his dismay; **~ leur grande surprise** much to their surprise, to their great surprise; **~ la demande de certains** at the request of certain people; **~ sa pâleur, on devinait son trouble** one could see *ou* tell by his paleness that he was distressed; **~ la nouvelle, il y eut des protestations** the news was greeted with protests; **~ ce qu'il prétend** according to what he says; **~ ce que j'ai compris** from what I understood; **c'est aux résultats qu'on le jugera** he will be judged on his results, it'll be on his results that he's judged.

p (*loc*) **~ ta** *ou* **votre santé!, ~ la tienne!** *ou* **la vôtre!** cheers!, your (good) health!; **aux absents!** to absent friends!; **~ la porte!** (get) out!; **~ la poubelle!** (it's) rubbish!, (let's) throw it out!; **au voleur!** stop thief!; **au feu!** fire!; *voir* **abordage, boire, souhait**.

q (*Prov*) **~ bon chat bon rat** tit for tat (*Prov*); **~ bon entendeur, salut** a word to the wise is enough; **~ chacun sa chacune*** every Jack has his Jill; **~ chacun selon son mérite** to each according to his merits; **~ chacun son métier** every man to his own trade; **~ chaque jour suffit sa peine** sufficient unto the day is the evil thereof (*Prov*); **~ cœur vaillant rien d'impossible** nothing is impossible to a willing heart (*Prov*); **aux grands maux les grands remèdes** desperate ills demand desperate measures; **~ l'impossible nul n'est tenu** no one is bound to do the impossible; **~ père avare, enfant prodigue** a miser will father a spendthrift son; **~ quelque chose malheur est bon** every cloud has a silver lining (*Prov*); **au royaume des aveugles les borgnes sont rois** in the kingdom of the blind the one-eyed man is king (*Prov*); **~ la Sainte Luce, les jours croissent du saut d'une puce** Lucy light, the shortest day and the longest night (*Prov*); **~ tout seigneur tout honneur** honour to whom honour is due.

Aaron [aʀɔ̃] **nm** Aaron.

AB (**abrév de assez bien**) quite good.

Abadan [abadɑ̃] **n** Abadan.

abaissable [abɛsabl] **adj** *siège* reclining (*épith*).

abaissant, e [abɛsɑ̃, ɑ̃t] **adj** degrading.

abaisse [abɛs] **nf** rolled-out pastry. **faites une ~ de 3 cm** roll out the pastry to a thickness of 3 cm.

abaisse-langue [abɛslɑ̃g] **nm inv** spatula (*Brit*), tongue depressor.

abaissement [abɛsmɑ̃] **nm** a (*action d'abaisser*) pulling down; pushing down; lowering; bringing down; reduction (*de* in); carrying; dropping; humiliation; debasing; humbling. b (*fait de s'abaisser*) *[température, valeur, taux]* fall, drop (*de* in); *[terrain]* downward slope. **l'~ de la moralité** the decline in morals. c (*conduite obséquieuse*) subservience, self-abasement; (*conduite choquante*) degradation.

abaisser [abese] 1 1 **vt** a *levier* (*tirer*) to pull down; (*pousser*) to push down; *store* to lower, pull down; *siège* to recline. (*littér*) **~ les yeux sur qn** to deign to look upon sb; **cette vitre s'abaisse-t-elle?** does this window go down?

b *température, valeur, taux* to lower, reduce, bring down; *niveau, mur* to lower.

c *chiffre* to bring down, carry; *perpendiculaire* to drop.

d (*rabaisser*) *[personne]* to humiliate; *[vice]* to debase; (*Rel*) to humble. **~ la puissance des nobles** to reduce the power of the nobles.

e (*Culin*) *pâte* to roll out.

2 **s'abaisser vpr** a (*diminuer*) *[température, valeur, taux]* to fall, drop, go down; *[terrain]* to slope down; (*Théât*) *[rideau]* to fall (*sur* on).

b (*s'humilier*) to humble o.s. **s'~ à** to stoop *ou* descend to.

abaisseur [abɛsœʀ] **adj m, nm: (muscle) ~** depressor.

abandon [abɑ̃dɔ̃] **nm** a (*délaissement*) *[personne, lieu]* desertion, abandonment. **~ de poste** desertion of one's post; (*Jur*) **~ du domicile conjugal** desertion.

b *[idée, privilège, fonction]* giving up; *[droit]* giving up, relinquishment, renunciation; *[course, championnat]* withdrawal (*de* from). (*Sport*) **après l'~ de notre équipe** after our team was forced to retire *ou* withdraw; **faire ~ de ses biens à qn** to make over one's property to sb; **faire ~ de ses droits sur** to relinquish *ou* renounce one's right(s) to; (*fig*) **~ de soi-même** self-abnegation.

c (*manque de soin*) neglected state, neglect. **l'(état d')~ où se trouvait la ferme** the neglected state (that) the farm was in; **jardin à l'~** neglected garden, garden run wild *ou* in a state of neglect; **laisser qch à l'~** to neglect sth.

d (*confiance*) lack of constraint. **parler avec ~** to talk freely *ou* without constraint; **dans ses moments d'~** in his moments of abandon, in his more expansive moments.

e (*nonchalance*) *[style]* easy flow. **étendu sur le sofa avec ~** stretched out luxuriously on the sofa; **l'~ de son attitude/ses manières** his relaxed *ou* easy-going attitude/manners.

f (*Ordin*) abort.

abandonné, e [abɑ̃dɔne] (**ptp de abandonner**) **adj** a *attitude, position* relaxed; (*avec volupté*) abandoned. b *route, usine, jardin* disused. **vieille maison ~e** deserted old house.

abandonner [abɑ̃dɔne] 1 1 **vt** a (*délaisser*) *lieu* to desert, abandon; *personne* (*gén*) to leave, abandon; (*intentionnellement*) to desert, abandon, forsake (*littér*); *voiture, animal* to abandon; *technique, appareil* to abandon, give up. **son courage l'abandonna** his courage failed *ou* deserted *ou* forsook (*littér*) him; **ses forces l'abandonnèrent** his strength failed *ou* deserted him; **l'ennemi a abandonné ses positions** the enemy abandoned their positions; (*Mil*) **~ son poste** to desert one's post; **~ le terrain** (*lit, Mil*) to take flight; (*fig*) to give up; (*Jur*) **~ le domicile conjugal** to desert *ou* abandon the family home.

b (*se retirer de*) *fonction* to give up, relinquish; *études, recherches* to give up, abandon; *matière d'examen* to drop, give up; *droit, privilèges* to give up, relinquish, renounce; *course* to withdraw *ou* retire from; *projet, hypothèse, espoir* to give up, abandon. **le joueur a dû ~** the player had to retire *ou* withdraw; **~ le pouvoir** to retire from *ou* give up *ou* leave office; (*lit, fig*) **~ la lutte** *ou* **la partie** to give up the fight *ou* struggle; (*Jur*) **~ les poursuites** to drop the charges; **j'abandonne!** I give up!

c (*donner, laisser*) **~ à** (*gén*) to give *ou* leave to; **~ ses biens à une bonne œuvre** to leave *ou* donate *ou* give one's wealth to a good cause; **elle lui abandonna sa main** she let him take her hand; **~ à qn le soin de faire qch** to leave it up to sb to do sth; **~ qn à son (triste) sort** to leave *ou* abandon (*littér*) sb to his fate; **~ au pillage/à la destruction/à la mort** to leave to be pillaged/to be destroyed/to die; **~ son corps au bien-être** to give o.s. up *ou* abandon o.s. to a sense of well-being.

2 **s'abandonner vpr** a (*se relâcher, se confier*) to let o.s. go. **il s'abandonna, me confia ses problèmes** he let himself go *ou* opened up and told me his problems; **elle s'abandonna dans mes bras** she sank into my arms.

b (*se laisser aller*) **s'~ à** *passion, joie, débauche* to give o.s. up to; *paresse, désespoir* to give way to; **s'~ à la rêverie/au bien-être** to indulge in *ou* give o.s. up to daydreaming/a sense of well-being; **il s'abandonna au sommeil** he let sleep overcome him, he let himself sink into sleep.

c (*s'en remettre à*) **s'~ à** to commit o.s. to, put o.s. in the hands of.

d (†: *se donner sexuellement*) to give o.s. (*à* to)

abaque [abak] **nm** abacus.

abasourdir [abazuʀdiʀ] 2 **vt** a (*étonner*) to stun, bewilder, dumbfound. **être abasourdi** to be stunned *ou* dumbfounded *ou* staggered*. b (*étourdir*) *[bruit]* to stun, daze.

abasourdissement [abazuʀdismɑ̃] **nm** bewilderment, stupefaction.

abat- [aba] **préf** *voir* **abattre**.

abâtardir [abɑtaʀdiʀ] 2 1 **vt** *race, vertu* to cause to degenerate; *qualité* to debase. 2 **s'abâtardir vpr** *[race, vertu]* to degenerate; *[qualité]* to become debased.

abâtardissement [abɑtaʀdismɑ̃] **nm** (*voir* **abâtardir**) degeneration; debasement.

abats [aba] **nmpl** *[volaille]* giblets; *[bœuf, porc]* offal.

abattage [abataʒ] **nm** a *[animal]* slaughter, slaughtering; *[arbre]* felling, cutting (down); (*Min*) extracting. b (*Comm*) **(vente à l')~** selling in bulk at knock-down prices. c (*) **avoir de l'~** (*entrain*) to be dynamic, have plenty of go*; (*force*) **il a de l'~** he's a strapping fellow. d *[prostituée]* **faire de l'~**‡ to turn dozens of tricks a day (*ou* night)‡ (*US*), get through dozens of punters (*Brit*) *ou* johns (*US*) a day (*ou* night)‡.

abattant [abatɑ̃] **nm** flap, leaf (*of table, desk*).

abattement [abatmɑ̃] **nm** a (*dépression*) dejection, despondency. **être dans un extrême ~** to be in very low spirits. b (*fatigue*) exhaustion; (*faiblesse*) enfeeblement. c (*Fin*) (*rabais*) reduction; (*fiscal*) (tax) allowance. **~ sur le prélèvement** abatement of the levy; **~ forfaitaire** standard deduction *ou* allowance.

abattis [abati] 1 **nmpl** *[volaille]* giblets; (*: *bras et jambes*) limbs; *voir* **numéroter**. 2 **nm** (*Can: terrain déboisé*) brushwood. **faire un ~** to clear fell (*Brit*) *ou* clear cut (*US*) land.

abattoir [abatwaʀ] **nm** slaughterhouse, abattoir. (*fig*) **envoyer des hommes à l'~*** to send men to be slaughtered *ou* massacred.

abattre [abatʀ] 41 1 **vt** a (*faire tomber*) *maison, mur* to pull *ou* knock down; *arbre* to cut down, fell; *adversaire* to fell, floor, knock down; *roche, minerai* to break away, hew; *quilles* to knock down; *avion* to bring *ou* shoot down. **le vent a abattu la cheminée** the wind blew the chimney down; **la pluie abat la poussière** the rain settles the dust; **il abattit son bâton sur ma tête** he brought his stick down on my head.
b (*tuer*) *personne, oiseau* to shoot down; *fauve* to shoot, kill; *animal domestique* to destroy, put down; *animal de boucherie* to slaughter. (*fig*) **c'est l'homme à ~** he's the one you've (*ou* we've *etc*) got to get rid of.
c (*fig: ébranler*) *[fièvre, maladie]* to weaken, drain (of energy); *[mauvaise nouvelle, échec]* to demoralize, shatter*; *[efforts]* to tire out, wear out. **la maladie l'a abattu** (the) illness left him prostrate *ou* very weak, (the) illness drained him of energy; **être abattu par la fatigue/la chaleur** to be overcome by tiredness/the heat; **se laisser ~ par des échecs** to be demoralized by failures, let failures get one down; **ne te laisse pas ~** keep your spirits up, don't let things get you down.
d (*fig: affaiblir*) *courage* to weaken; *forces* to drain, sap; *fierté* to humble.
e *carte* to lay down. (*lit, fig*) **~ son jeu *ou* ses cartes** to lay *ou* put one's cards on the table, show one's hand *ou* cards.
f **~ du travail** to get through a lot of work.
2 **s'abattre vpr** a (*tomber*) *[personne]* to fall (down), collapse; *[cheminée]* to fall *ou* crash down. **le mât s'abattit** the mast came *ou* went crashing down.
b **s'~ sur** *[pluie]* to beat down on(to); *[ennemi]* to swoop down on, fall on; *[oiseau de proie]* to swoop down on; *[moineaux]* to sweep down on(to); (*fig*) *[coups, injures]* to rain on.
3 **comp** ▸**abat-jour nm inv** *[lampe]* lampshade; (*Archit*) splay ▸**abat-son nm inv** louver *ou* luffer-boarding (*to deflect sound downwards*) ▸**abat-vent nm inv** *[cheminée]* chimney cowl; *[fenêtre, ouverture]* louver boarding; (*Agr*) wind screen.

abattu, e [abaty] (**ptp de abattre**) **adj** (*fatigué*) worn out, exhausted; (*faible*) *malade* very weak, feeble, prostrate; (*déprimé*) downcast, demoralized, despondent; *voir* **bride**.

abbatial, e, mpl -iaux [abasjal, jo] 1 **adj** abbey (*épith*). 2 **abbatiale nf** abbey-church.

abbaye [abei] **nf** abbey.

abbé [abe] **nm** *[abbaye]* abbot; (*prêtre*) priest. **~ mitré** mitred abbot; *voir* **monsieur**.

abbesse [abɛs] **nf** abbess.

abc [ɑbese] **nm** (*livre*) ABC *ou* alphabet book; (*rudiments*) ABC, fundamentals (*pl*), rudiments (*pl*). **c'est l'~ du métier** it's the most elementary *ou* the first requirement of the job.

abcès [apsɛ] **nm** (*Méd*) abscess; *[gencive]* gumboil, abscess. (*fig*) **il faut vider *ou* crever l'~!** we must root out the evil!; (*fig*) **~ de fixation** focal point for grievances.

Abdias [abdjas] **nm** Obadiah.

abdication [abdikasjɔ̃] **nf** (*lit, fig*) abdication. (*fig*) **l'~ des parents devant leurs enfants** parents' abdication of authority over their children.

abdiquer [abdike] 1 1 **vi** *[roi]* to abdicate. **la justice abdique devant le terrorisme** justice gives way in the face of *ou* before terrorism; **dans ces conditions j'abdique*** in that case I give up. 2 **vt: ~ la couronne** to abdicate the throne; **~ ses croyances/son autorité** to give up *ou* renounce one's beliefs/one's authority.

abdomen [abdɔmɛn] **nm** abdomen.

abdominal, e, mpl -aux [abdɔminal, o] 1 **adj** abdominal. 2 **nmpl: ~aux** stomach *ou* abdominal muscles; (*Sport*) **faire des ~aux** to do exercises for the stomach muscles, exercise the stomach muscles.

abdos* [abdo] **nmpl** (**abrév de abdominaux**) *voir* **abdominal**.

abducteur [abdyktœʀ] **nm** (*Anat*) abductor.

abduction [abdyksjɔ̃] **nf** (*Anat*) abduction.

abécédaire [ɑbesedɛʀ] **nm** alphabet primer.

abeille [abɛj] **nf** bee. **~ maçonne** mason bee; *voir* **nid, reine**.

Abel [abɛl] **nm** Abel.

aber [abɛʀ] **nm** (*Géog*) aber.

aberrant, e [abeʀɑ̃, ɑ̃t] **adj** a (*insensé*) *conduite* aberrant; *histoire* absurd, nonsensical. **il est ~ qu'il parte** it is absolutely absurd *ou* it is sheer nonsense for him to go *ou* that he should go. b (*Bio*) aberrant, abnormal, deviant; (*Ling*) irregular.

aberration [abeʀasjɔ̃] **nf** (*gén*) (mental) aberration; (*Astron, Phys*) aberration. **dans un moment *ou* instant d'~** in a moment of aberration; **par quelle ~ a-t-il accepté?** whatever possessed him to accept?; **~ chromosomique** chromosomal abnormality.

abêtir vt, s'abêtir vpr [abetiʀ] 2 to turn into a moron *ou* half-wit.

abêtissant, e [abetisɑ̃, ɑ̃t] **adj** *travail* stupefying.

abêtissement [abetismɑ̃] **nm** (*état*) stupidity, mindlessness. (*action*) **l'~ des masses par la télévision** the stupefying effect of television on the masses.

abhorrer [abɔʀe] 1 **vt** (*littér*) to abhor, loathe.

abîme [abim] **nm** a abyss, gulf, chasm. (*fig*) **l'~ qui nous sépare** the gulf *ou* chasm between us. b (*loc*) **au bord de l'~** *pays, banquier* on the brink *ou* verge of ruin; *personne* on the brink *ou* verge of despair; **être au fond de l'~** *[personne]* to be in the depths of despair *ou* at one's lowest ebb; *[pays]* to have reached rock-bottom; (*littér*) **les ~s de l'enfer/de la nuit/du temps** the depths of hell/night/time; **être plongé dans un ~ de perplexité** to be utterly *ou* deeply perplexed; **c'est un ~ de bêtise** he's abysmally *ou* incredibly stupid.

abîmer [abime] 1 1 **vt** a (*endommager*) to damage, spoil. **la pluie a complètement abîmé mon chapeau** the rain has ruined my hat. b (*‡: frapper*) **~ qn** to beat sb up; **~ le portrait à qn** to smash* *ou* bash* sb's face in. 2 **s'abîmer vpr** a *[objet]* to get spoilt *ou* damaged; *[fruits]* to go bad, spoil. **s'~ les yeux** to ruin *ou* strain one's eyes, spoil one's eyesight. b (*littér*) *[navire]* to sink, founder. *[personne]* **s'~ dans** *réflexion* to be deep *ou* sunk *ou* plunged in; *douleur* to lose o.s. in.

abject, e [abʒɛkt] **adj** despicable, contemptible, abject. **être ~ envers qn** to treat sb in a despicable manner, behave despicably towards sb.

abjectement [abʒɛktəmɑ̃] **adv** abjectly.

abjection [abʒɛksjɔ̃] **nf** abjection, abjectness.

abjuration [abʒyʀasjɔ̃] **nf** abjuration, renunciation, recantation (*de* of). **faire ~ de** to abjure.

abjurer [abʒyʀe] 1 **vt** to abjure, renounce, recant.

ablatif [ablatif] **nm** ablative. **à l'~** in the ablative; **~ absolu** ablative absolute.

ablation [ablasjɔ̃] **nf** (*Méd*) removal, ablation (*SPÉC*); (*Géol*) ablation.

ablette [ablɛt] **nf** bleak.

ablutions [ablysjɔ̃] **nfpl** (*gén*) ablutions. **faire ses ~** to perform one's ablutions.

abnégation [abnegasjɔ̃] **nf** (self-)abnegation, self-denial, self-sacrifice. **avec ~** selflessly.

aboiement [abwamɑ̃] **nm** a *[chien]* bark. **~s** barking (*NonC*). b (*péj*) (*cri*) cry. (*critiques, exhortations*) **~s** rantings, snarlings.

abois [abwa] **nmpl** baying. (*lit, fig*) **aux ~** at bay.

abolir [abɔliʀ] 2 **vt** *coutume, loi* to abolish, do away with.

abolition [abɔlisjɔ̃] **nf** abolition. **l'~ de l'esclavage** the Abolition of Slavery.

abolitionnisme [abɔlisjɔnism] **nm** abolitionism.

abolitionniste [abɔlisjɔnist] **adj, nmf** abolitionist.

abominable [abɔminabl] **adj** abominable, horrible; (*sens affaibli*) awful, frightful, terrible. **l'~ homme des neiges** the abominable snowman.

abominablement [abɔminabləmɑ̃] **adv** *se conduire, s'habiller* abominably. **~ cher** frightfully (*Brit*) *ou* terribly expensive; **~ laid** frightfully (*Brit*) *ou* horribly ugly.

abomination [abɔminasjɔ̃] **nf** a (*horreur, crime*) abomination. b (*loc*) **avoir qn/qch en ~** to loathe *ou* abominate sb/sth; **c'est une ~!** it's abominable!; **l'~ de la désolation** the abomination of desolation; **dire des ~s** to say abominable things.

abominer [abɔmine] 1 **vt** (*littér: exécrer*) to loathe, abominate.

abondamment [abɔ̃damɑ̃] **adv** abundantly, plentifully; *écrire* prolifically; *manger, boire* copiously; *rincer* thoroughly. **prouver ~ qch** to provide ample proof *ou* evidence of sth.

abondance [abɔ̃dɑ̃s] **nf** a (*profusion*) abundance. **des fruits en ~** plenty of *ou* an abundance of fruit, fruit in abundance *ou* in plenty; **larmes qui coulent en ~** tears falling in profusion *ou* profusely; **il y a (une) ~ de** there are plenty of, there is an abundance of; **année d'~** year of plenty; (*Prov*) **~ de biens ne nuit pas** an abundance of goods does no harm; *voir* **corne**. b (*richesses*) wealth, prosperity, affluence. **vivre dans l'~** to live in affluence; **~ d'idées** wealth of ideas. c **parler d'~** (*improviser*) to improvise, extemporize; (*parler beaucoup*) to speak at length.

abondant, e [abɔ̃dɑ̃, ɑ̃t] **adj** *récolte* good; *réserves* plentiful; *végétation* lush, luxuriant; *chevelure* thick, abundant (*frm*); *larmes* profuse, copious; *repas* copious, hearty (*épith*); *style* rich. **il me fit d'~es recommandations** he gave me copious advice, he lavished advice on me; **illustré d'~es photographies** illustrated with numerous photographs, richly *ou* lavishly illustrated with photographs; **la récolte est ~e cette année** there is a rich *ou* good *ou* fine harvest this year; **les pêches sont ~es sur le marché** peaches are in plentiful *ou* good *ou* generous supply (on the market); **il lui faut une nourriture ~e** he must have plenty to eat *ou* plenty of food.

abonder [abɔ̃de] 1 **vi** a to abound, be plentiful. **les légumes abondent cette année** there are plenty of vegetables this year, vegetables are plentiful *ou* in good supply this year. b **~ en** to be full of, abound in; **les forêts/rivières abondent en gibier/poissons** the forests/rivers are full of *ou* teeming with game/fish; **son œuvre abonde en images** his work is rich in *ou* is full of images. c **il abonda dans notre sens** he was in complete *ou* thorough *ou* full agreement with us.

abonné, e [abɔne] (**ptp de abonner**) 1 **adj: être ~ à un journal** to subscribe to a paper; **être ~ au téléphone** to be on the phone (*Brit*), have a phone; **être ~ au gaz** to have gas, be a gas consumer; (*fig*) **il y est ~!*** he's making (quite) a habit of it!; **il est ~ à la dernière place** he always comes last. 2 **nm,f** (*Presse, Téléc*) subscriber; (*Élec, Gaz*) consumer; (*Rail, Sport, Théât*) season-ticket holder. (*hum*) **c'est un ~ du bistrot**

he's always propping up the bar*; (*Téléc*) **se mettre aux ~s absents** to put one's phone on to the holiday answering service.

abonnement [abɔnmɑ̃] **nm** (*Presse*) subscription; (*Téléc*) rental; (*Rail, Sport, Théât*) season ticket. **prendre** *ou* **souscrire un ~ à un journal** to subscribe to *ou* take out a subscription to a paper.

abonner [abɔne] [1] **1 vt: ~ qn (à qch)** (*Presse*) to take out a subscription (to sth) for sb; (*Sport, Théât*) to buy sb a season ticket (for sth). **2 s'abonner vpr** (*Presse*) to subscribe, take out a subscription (*à* to); (*Sport, Théât*) to buy a season ticket (*à* for).

abord [abɔʀ] **nm a** (*environs*) **~s** (*gén*) surroundings; *[ville, village]* outskirts, surroundings; **aux ~s de** in the area around *ou* surrounding; **dans ce quartier et aux ~s** in this area and round about (*Brit*) *ou* and the area around it.

b (*manière d'accueillir*) manner. **être d'un ~** *ou* **avoir l'~ rude/rébarbatif** to have a rough/an off-putting manner; **être d'un ~ facile/difficile** to be approachable/not very approachable.

c (*accès*) access, approach. **lieu d'un ~ difficile** place with difficult means of access, place that is difficult to get to; **lecture d'un ~ difficile** reading matter which is difficult to get into *ou* difficult to get to grips with.

d (*loc*) **d'~** : (*en premier lieu*) **allons d'~ chez le boucher** let's go to the butcher's first; (*au commencement*) **il fut (tout) d'~ poli, puis il devint grossier** he was polite at first *ou* initially, and then became rude; (*introduisant une restriction*) **d'~, il n'a même pas 18 ans** for a start *ou* in the first place, he's not even 18; **dès l'~** from the outset, from the very beginning; **au premier ~** at first sight, initially; *voir* **prime, tout.**

abordable [abɔʀdabl] **adj** *prix* reasonable; *marchandise* affordable, reasonably priced; *personne* approachable; *lieu* accessible.

abordage [abɔʀdaʒ] **nm a** (*assaut*) attacking. **à l'~!** up lads and at 'em!, away boarders!; *voir* **sabre. b** (*accident*) collision.

aborder [abɔʀde] [1] **1 vt a** (*arriver à*) *rivage* to reach; *contrée* to arrive in *ou* at, reach; *tournant, montée* to reach. **les coureurs abordent la ligne droite** the runners are entering the home straight; (*fig*) **~ la vieillesse avec inquiétude** to approach old age with misgivings.

b (*approcher*) *personne* to approach, go *ou* come up to, accost. **il m'a abordé avec un sourire** he came up to me *ou* approached me with a smile.

c (*entreprendre*) *sujet* to start on, take up, tackle; *problème* to tackle. **il n'a abordé le roman que vers la quarantaine** he didn't take up writing *ou* move on to writing novels until he was nearly forty; **c'est le genre de question qu'il ne faut jamais ~ avec lui** that's the sort of question you should never get on to *ou* touch on with him; **j'aborde maintenant le second point** I'll now move on to the second point.

d (*Naut*) (*attaquer*) to board; (*heurter*) to collide with.

2 vi (*Naut*) to land, touch *ou* reach land. **~ dans** *ou* **sur une île** to land on an island.

aborigène [abɔʀiʒɛn] (*indigène*) **1 adj** (*gén*) aboriginal; (*relatif aux peuplades australiennes*) Aboriginal. **2 nmf** aborigine. **~ d'Australie** Aboriginal, Australian Aborigine.

abortif, -ive [abɔʀtif, iv] (*Méd*) **1 adj** abortive. **2 nm** abortifacient (*SPÉC*).

abouchement [abuʃmɑ̃] **nm** (*Tech*) joining up end to end.

aboucher [abuʃe] [1] **1 vt** (*Tech*) to join up (end to end). (*fig*) **~ qn avec** to put sb in contact *ou* in touch with. **2 s'aboucher vpr** (*péj*) **s'~ avec qn** to get in touch with sb, make contact with sb.

Abou Dhabî [abudabi] **n** Abu Dhabi.

abouler‡ [abule] [1] **1 vt** (*donner*) to hand over. **aboule!** hand it over!*, give it here!*, let's have it!* **2 s'abouler vpr** (*venir*) to come. **aboule-toi!** come (over) here!

aboulie [abuli] **nf** ab(o)ulia.

aboulique [abulik] **1 adj** ab(o)ulic (*SPÉC*). **2 nmf** (*Méd*) person suffering from ab(o)ulia. (*fig*) **son mari est un ~** her husband is utterly apathetic *ou* (totally) lacking in will power.

Abou Simbel [abusimbɛl] **n** Abu Simbel.

about [abu] **nm** (*Tech*) butt.

aboutement [abutmɑ̃] **nm** (*action*) joining (end to end); (*état*) join.

abouter [abute] [1] **vt** to join (up) (end to end).

abouti, e [abuti] **adj** *projet* successfully completed; *œuvre* accomplished.

aboutir [abutiʀ] [2] **vi a** (*réussir*) *[démarche]* to succeed, come off*; *[personne]* to succeed. **ses efforts/tentatives n'ont pas abouti** his efforts/attempts have had no effect *ou* have failed *ou* didn't come off*; **faire ~ des négociations/un projet** to bring negotiations/a project to a successful conclusion.

b (*arriver à, déboucher sur*) **~ à** *ou* **dans** to end (up) in *ou* at; **la route aboutit à un cul-de-sac** the road ends in a cul-de-sac; **une telle philosophie aboutit au désespoir** such a philosophy results in *ou* leads to despair; **~ en prison** to end up in prison; **les négociations n'ont abouti à rien** the negotiations have come to nothing, nothing has come of the negotiations; **en additionnant le tout, j'aboutis à 12 F** adding it all up I get 12 francs *ou* I get it to come to 12 francs; **il n'aboutira jamais à rien dans la vie** he'll never get anywhere in life.

aboutissants [abutisɑ̃] **nmpl** *voir* **tenant.**

aboutissement [abutismɑ̃] **nm** (*résultat*) *[efforts, opération]* outcome, result; (*succès*) *[plan]* success.

aboyer [abwaje] [8] **vi** to bark; (*péj: crier*) to shout, yell. **~ après** *ou* **contre qn** to bark *ou* yell at sb; *voir* **chien.**

aboyeur† [abwajœʀ] **nm** (*Théât*) barker†.

abracadabra [abʀakadabʀa] **excl** abracadabra.

abracadabrant, e [abʀakadabʀɑ̃, ɑ̃t] **adj** incredible, fantastic, preposterous.

Abraham [abʀaam] **nm** Abraham.

abraser [abʀɑze] [1] **vt** to abrade.

abrasif, -ive [abʀɑzif, iv] **adj, nm** abrasive.

abrasion [abʀɑzjɔ̃] **nf** (*gén, Géog*) abrasion.

abréaction [abʀeaksjɔ̃] **nf** abreaction.

abrégé [abʀeʒe] **nm** *[livre, discours]* summary, synopsis; *[texte]* summary, précis; (*manuel, guide*) short guide. **faire un ~ de** to summarize, précis; **~ d'Histoire** short guide to History; **en ~** (*en miniature*) in miniature; (*en bref*) in brief, in a nutshell; **répéter qch en ~** to repeat sth in a few words; **mot/phrase en ~** word/sentence in a shortened *ou* an abbreviated form; **voilà, en ~, de quoi il s'agissait** briefly *ou* to cut (*Brit*) *ou* make (*US*) a long story short, this is what it was all about.

abrégement [abʀɛʒmɑ̃] **nm** *[durée]* cutting short, shortening; *[texte]* abridgement.

abréger [abʀeʒe] [3] **et** [6] **vt** *vie* to shorten; *souffrances* to cut short; *durée, visite* to cut short, shorten; *texte* to shorten, abridge; *mot* to abbreviate, shorten. **pour ~ les longues soirées d'hiver** to while away the long winter evenings, to make the long winter evenings pass more quickly; **abrège!*** come *ou* get to the point!

abreuver [abʀœve] [1] **1 vt a** *animal* to water. **b** (*fig*) **~ qn de** to overwhelm *ou* shower sb with; **~ qn d'injures** to heap *ou* shower insults on sb; **le public est abreuvé de films d'horreur** (*inondé*) the public is swamped with horror films; (*saturé*) the public has had its fill of *ou* has had enough of horror films. **c** (*imbiber*) (*gén*) to soak, drench (*de* with); (*Tech*) to prime. **terre abreuvée d'eau** sodden *ou* waterlogged ground. **2 s'abreuver vpr** *[animal]* to drink; (*) *[personne]* to quench one's thirst, wet one's whistle*.

abreuvoir [abʀœvwaʀ] **nm** (*mare*) watering place; (*récipient*) drinking trough.

abréviation [abʀevjasjɔ̃] **nf** abbreviation.

abri [abʀi] **nm a** (*refuge, cabane*) shelter. **~ à vélos** bicycle shed; (*Mil*) **~ souterrain/antiatomique** air-raid/(atomic) fallout shelter; (*hum*) **tous aux ~s!** take cover!, run for cover!; **construire un ~ pour sa voiture** to build a carport.

b (*fig: protection*) refuge (*contre* from), protection (*contre* against). **~ fiscal** tax shelter.

c (*loc*) **à l'~: être/mettre à l'~** (*des intempéries*) to be/put under cover; (*du vol, de la curiosité*) to be/put in a safe place; **se mettre à l'~** to shelter, take cover; **être à l'~ de** (*protégé de*) *pluie, vent, soleil* to be sheltered from; *danger, soupçons* to be safe *ou* shielded from; *regards* to be hidden from; (*protégé par*) *mur, feuillage* to be sheltered *ou* shielded by; **je ne suis pas à l'~ d'une erreur** I'm not beyond making a mistake; **elle est à l'~ du besoin** she is free from financial worries; **se mettre à l'~ de** *pluie, vent, soleil* to take shelter from; *regards* to hide from; *soupçons* to shield o.s. from; **se mettre à l'~ du mur/du feuillage** to take cover *ou* shelter by the wall/under the trees; **mettre qch à l'~ de** *intempéries* to shelter sth from; *regards* to hide sth from; **mettre qch à l'~ d'un mur** to put sth in the shelter of a wall.

Abribus [abʀibys] **nm** ® bus shelter.

abricot [abʀiko] **1 nm** (*Bot*) apricot; *voir* **pêche**[1]. **2 adj inv** apricot (-coloured).

abricoté, e [abʀikɔte] **adj** *gâteau* apricot (*épith*); *voir* **pêche**[1].

abricotier [abʀikɔtje] **nm** apricot tree.

abriter [abʀite] [1] **1 vt** (*de la pluie, du vent*) to shelter (*de* from); (*du soleil*) to shelter, shade (*de* from); (*de radiations*) to screen (*de* from). **le bâtiment peut ~ 20 personnes** the building can accommodate 20 people; **abritant ses yeux de sa main** shading his eyes with his hand; **le côté abrité** (*de la pluie*) the sheltered side; (*du soleil*) the shady side; **maison abritée** house in a sheltered spot, sheltered house.

2 s'abriter vpr to (take) shelter (*de* from), take cover. (*fig*) **s'~ derrière la tradition** to shield o.s. *ou* hide behind tradition, use tradition as a shield; (*fig*) **s'~ derrière son chef/le règlement** to take cover behind one's boss/the rules.

abrogation [abʀɔgasjɔ̃] **nf** repeal, abrogation.

abrogeable [abʀɔʒabl] **adj** repealable.

abroger [abʀɔʒe] [3] **vt** to repeal, abrogate.

abrupt, e [abʀypt] **1 adj** *pente* abrupt, steep; *falaise* sheer; *personne* abrupt; *manières* abrupt, brusque. **2 nm** steep slope.

abruptement [abʀyptəmɑ̃] **adv** *descendre* steeply, abruptly; *annoncer* abruptly.

abruti, e [abʀyti] (**ptp de abrutir**) **1 adj a** (*hébété*) stunned, dazed (*de* with). **~ par l'alcool** besotted *ou* stupefied with drink. **b** (*: *bête*) idiotic*, moronic‡. **2 nm,f** (‡) idiot*, moron‡.

abrutir [abʀytiʀ] [2] **vt a** (*fatiguer*) to exhaust. **la chaleur m'abrutit** the heat makes me feel quite stupid; **~ qn de travail** to work sb silly *ou* stupid; **ces discussions m'ont abruti** these discussions have left me quite dazed; **s'~ à travailler** to work o.s. silly; **leur professeur les abrutit de travail** their teacher drives them stupid with work; **tu vas t'~ à force de lire** you'll overtax *ou* exhaust yourself reading so much. b (*abêtir*) ~ **qn** to deaden sb's mind; **l'alcool l'avait abruti** he was stupefied with drink; **s'~ à regarder la télévision** to become quite moronic *ou* mindless through watching (too much) television.

abrutissant, e [abʀytisɑ̃, ɑ̃t] **adj** *bruit* stunning, thought-destroying; *travail* mind-destroying. **ce bruit est ~** this noise drives you silly *ou* stupid *ou* wears you down.

abrutissement [abʀytismɑ̃] **nm** (*fatigue extrême*) (mental) exhaustion; (*abêtissement*) mindless *ou* moronic state. **l'~ des masses par la télévision** the stupefying effect of television on the masses.

ABS [abeɛs] **nm** (**abrév de Antiblockiersystem**) ABS.

abscisse [apsis] **nf** abscissa. **en ~** on the abscissa.

abscons, e [apskɔ̃, ɔ̃s] **adj** abstruse, recondite.

absence [apsɑ̃s] **nf** a (*gén, Jur*) *[personne]* absence. **son ~ à la réunion** his absence *ou* non-attendance at the meeting; (*Admin, Scol*) **3 ~s successives** 3 absences in succession; **cet élève/employé accumule les ~s** this pupil/employee is persistently absent; *voir* **briller**.
b (*manque*) absence, lack (*de* of). **~ de goût** lack of taste; **l'~ de rideaux** the absence of curtains; **il constata l'~ de sa valise** he noticed that his case was missing.
c (*défaillance*) **~ (de mémoire)** mental blank; **il a des ~s** at times his mind goes blank.
d **en l'~ de** in the absence of; **en l'~ de sa mère, c'est Anne qui fait la cuisine** in her mother's absence *ou* while her mother's away, Anne is *ou* it's Anne who is doing the cooking; **en l'~ de preuves** in the absence of proof.

absent, e [apsɑ̃, ɑ̃t] 1 **adj** a *personne* (*gén*) away (*de* from); (*pour maladie*) absent (*de* from), off*. **être ~ de son travail** to be absent from work, be off work*; **il est ~ de Paris/de son bureau en ce moment** he's out of *ou* away from Paris/his office at the moment; **conférence internationale dont la France était ~e** international conference from which France was absent.
b *sentiment* lacking, absent; *objet* missing. **discours d'où toute émotion était ~e** speech in which there was no trace of emotion; **il constata que sa valise était ~e** he noticed that his case was missing.
c (*distrait*) *air* vacant.
d (*Jur*) missing.
2 **nm,f** (*Scol Admin*) absentee; (*littér: mort, en voyage*) absent one (*littér*); (*disparu*) missing person. **le ministre/le champion a été le grand ~ de la réunion** the minister/the champion was the most notable absentee at the meeting; (*Prov*) **les ~s ont toujours tort** the absent are always in the wrong.

absentéisme [apsɑ̃teism] **nm** (*Agr, Écon, Ind*) absenteeism; (*Scol*) truancy.

absentéiste [apsɑ̃teist] **nmf** (*Agr*) absentee. (*gén*) **c'est un ~, il est du genre ~** he is always *ou* regularly absent *ou* off*; **propriétaire ~** absentee landlord; **élève ~** truant.

absenter (s') [apsɑ̃te] 1 **vpr** (*gén*) to go out, leave; (*Mil*) to go absent. **s'~ de** *pièce* to go out of, leave; *ville* to leave; **s'~ quelques instants** to go out for a few moments; **je m'étais absenté de Paris** I was away from *ou* out of Paris; **elle s'absente souvent de son travail** she is frequently off work* *ou* away from work; **élève qui s'absente trop souvent** pupil who is too often absent *ou* away (from school) *ou* off school.

abside [apsid] **nf** apse.

absidial, e, mpl -iaux [apsidjal, jo] **adj** apsidal.

absidiole [apsidjɔl] **nf** apsidiole.

absinthe [apsɛ̃t] **nf** (*liqueur*) absinth(e); (*Bot*) wormwood, absinth(e).

absolu, e [apsɔly] 1 **adj** a (*total*) absolute. **en cas d'~e nécessité** if absolutely essential; **être dans l'impossibilité ~e de faire qch** to find it absolutely impossible to do sth; **c'est une règle ~e** it's an absolutely unbreakable rule, it's a hard-and-fast rule; **j'ai la preuve ~e de sa trahison** I have absolute *ou* positive proof of his betrayal; *voir* **alcool**.
b (*entier*) *ton* peremptory; *jugement, caractère* rigid, uncompromising.
c (*opposé à relatif*) *valeur, température* absolute. **considérer qch de manière ~e** to consider sth absolutely *ou* in absolute terms.
d (*Hist, Pol*) *majorité, roi, pouvoir* absolute.
e (*Ling*) *construction* absolute. **verbe employé de manière ~e** verb used absolutely *ou* in the absolute; **génitif/ablatif ~** genitive/ablative absolute; *voir* **superlatif**.
2 **nm: l'~** the absolute; **juger dans l'~** to judge out of context *ou* in the absolute.

absolument [apsɔlymɑ̃] **adv** a (*entièrement*) absolutely. **avoir ~ tort** to be quite *ou* absolutely *ou* entirely wrong; **s'opposer ~ à qch** to be entirely *ou* absolutely opposed to sth, be completely *ou* dead* against sth; **il a tort! — ~!** he's wrong! — absolutely!; **vous êtes sûr? — ~!** are you sure? — positive! *ou* absolutely!; **~ pas!** certainly not!; **~ rien!** absolutely nothing!, nothing whatever. b (*à tout prix*) absolutely, positively. **vous devez ~** you absolutely *ou* positively *ou* simply must; **il veut ~ revenir** he (absolutely) insists upon returning. c (*Ling*) absolutely.

absolution [apsɔlysjɔ̃] **nf** a (*Rel*) absolution (*de* from). **donner l'~ à qn** to give sb absolution. b (*Jur*) dismissal (*of case, when defendant is considered to have no case to answer*).

absolutisme [apsɔlytism] **nm** absolutism.

absolutiste [apsɔlytist] 1 **adj** absolutistic. 2 **nmf** absolutist.

absorbable [apsɔʀbabl] **adj** absorbable.

absorbant, e [apsɔʀbɑ̃, ɑ̃t] 1 **adj** *matière* absorbent; *tâche* absorbing, engrossing; (*Bot, Zool*) *fonction, racines* absorptive. **société ~e** surviving company. 2 **nm** absorbent.

absorbé, e [apsɔʀbe] (**ptp de absorber**) **adj: avoir un air ~** to look engrossed *ou* absorbed (in one's thoughts *etc*).

absorber [apsɔʀbe] 1 1 **vt** a (*avaler*) *médicament, aliment* to take; (*fig*) *parti* to absorb; *firme* to take over, absorb.
b (*résorber*) (*gén*) to absorb; *liquide* to absorb, soak up; *tache* to remove, lift; (*Fin*) *dette* to absorb; *bruit* to deaden, absorb. **le noir absorbe la lumière** black absorbs light; **cet achat a absorbé presque toutes mes économies** I used up *ou* spent nearly all my savings on that purchase.
c (*accaparer*) *attention, temps* to occupy, take up. **mon travail m'absorbe beaucoup, je suis très absorbé par mon travail** my work takes up *ou* claims a lot of my time; **absorbé par son travail il ne m'entendit pas** he was engrossed in *ou* absorbed in his work and he didn't hear me; **cette pensée absorbait mon esprit, j'avais l'esprit absorbé par cette pensée** my mind was completely taken up with this thought.
2 **s'absorber vpr** (*se plonger*) **s'~/être absorbé dans une lecture** to become/be absorbed *ou* engrossed in reading; **s'~/être absorbé dans une profonde méditation** to become lost in/be plunged deep in thought.

absorption [apsɔʀpsjɔ̃] **nf** a (*voir* **absorber**) taking; absorption; takeover; removal. b (*méditation*) absorption.

absoudre [apsudʀ] 51 **vt** (*Rel*) to absolve (*de* from); (*littér*) to absolve (*de* from), pardon (*de* for); (*Jur*) to dismiss.

absoute [apsut] **nf** *[office des morts]* absolution; *[jeudi saint]* general absolution.

abstenir (s') [apstəniʀ] 22 **vpr** a **s'~ de qch** to refrain *ou* abstain from sth; **s'~ de faire** to refrain from doing; **s'~ de vin, s'~ de boire du vin** to abstain from wine, refrain from drinking wine; **s'~ de tout commentaire, s'~ de faire des commentaires** to refrain from (making) any comment, refrain from commenting; **dans ces conditions je préfère m'~** in that case I'd rather not; *voir* **doute**. b (*Pol*) to abstain (*de voter* from voting).

abstention [apstɑ̃sjɔ̃] **nf** abstention; (*non-intervention*) non-participation.

abstentionnisme [apstɑ̃sjɔnism] **nm** abstaining, non-voting.

abstentionniste [apstɑ̃sjɔnist] **adj, nmf** non-voter, abstainer.

abstinence [apstinɑ̃s] **nf** abstinence. (*Rel*) **faire ~** to refrain from eating meat.

abstinent, e [apstinɑ̃, ɑ̃t] **adj** abstemious, abstinent.

abstract [abstʀakt] **nm** abstract.

abstraction [apstʀaksjɔ̃] **nf** (*fait d'abstraire*) abstraction; (*idée abstraite*) abstraction, abstract idea. **faire ~ de** to set *ou* leave aside, disregard; **en faisant ~** *ou* **faite ~ des difficultés** setting aside *ou* leaving aside *ou* disregarding the difficulties.

abstraire [apstʀɛʀ] 50 1 **vt** (*isoler*) to abstract (*de* from), isolate (*de* from); (*conceptualiser*) to abstract. 2 **s'abstraire vpr** to cut o.s. off (*de* from).

abstrait, e [apstʀɛ, ɛt] 1 **adj** abstract. 2 **nm** a (*artiste*) abstract painter. (*genre*) **l'~** abstract art. b (*Philos*) **l'~** the abstract; **dans l'~** in the abstract.

abstraitement [apstʀɛtmɑ̃] **adv** abstractly, in the abstract.

abstrus, e [apstʀy, yz] **adj** abstruse, recondite.

absurde [apsyʀd] 1 **adj** (*Philos*) absurd; (*illogique*) absurd, preposterous; (*ridicule*) absurd, ridiculous, ludicrous. **ne sois pas ~!** don't talk such nonsense!, don't be ridiculous! *ou* absurd! 2 **nm** (*Littérat, Philos*) **l'~** the absurd; **l'~ de la situation** the absurdity of the situation; *voir* **prouver**.

absurdement [apsyʀdəmɑ̃] **adv** (*voir* **absurde**) absurdly; preposterously; ridiculously; ludicrously.

absurdité [apsyʀdite] **nf** a (*voir* **absurde**) absurdity; preposterousness; ridiculousness; ludicrousness. b (*parole, acte*) absurdity. **il vient de dire une ~** he has just said something (quite) absurd *ou* ridiculous; **dire des ~s** to talk nonsense.

Abû Dhabî [abudabi] **n = Abou Dhabî**.

Abuja [abuʒa] **n** Abuja.

abus [aby] 1 **nm** a (*excès*) *[médicaments, alcool]* abuse; *[force, autorité]* abuse, misuse. **faire ~ de** *sa force, son pouvoir* to abuse; **faire ~ de cigarettes** to smoke excessively; **l'~ (qu'il fait) d'aspirine** (his) excessive use *ou* (his) overuse of aspirin; **~ de boisson** excessive drinking, drinking to excess; **nous avons fait des** *ou* **quelques ~ hier soir** we overdid it *ou* things *ou* we overindulged last night; **il y a de l'~!*** that's going a bit too far!*, that's a bit steep!* (*Brit*) *ou* pushing a bit!* (*US*).
b (*injustice*) abuse, social injustice.
2 **comp** ▸ **abus d'autorité** abuse *ou* misuse of authority ▸ **abus de biens sociaux** misuse of company property ▸ **abus de confiance**

breach of trust; (*escroquerie*) confidence trick ▸**abus de langage** misnomer ▸**abus de pouvoir** abuse *ou* misuse of power.

abuser [abyze] 1 **1 abuser de vt indir a** (*exploiter*) *situation, crédulité* to exploit, take advantage of; *autorité, puissance* to abuse, misuse; *hospitalité, amabilité, confiance* to abuse; *ami, victime* to take advantage of. ~ **de sa force** to misuse one's strength; **je ne veux pas ~ de votre temps** I don't want to encroach on *ou* take up *ou* waste your time; **je ne voudrais pas ~ (de votre gentillesse)** I don't want to impose (upon your kindness); (*euph*) ~ **d'une femme** to take advantage of a woman (*euph*); **alors là, tu abuses!** now you're going too far! *ou* overstepping the mark!; **je suis compréhensif, mais il ne faudrait pas ~** I'm an understanding sort of person but don't try taking advantage *ou* don't push me too far; **elle abuse de la situation** she's trying it on a bit*.
b (*user avec excès*) *médicaments, citations* to overuse. ~ **de l'alcool** to drink too much *ou* excessively, drink to excess; ~ **de ses forces** to overexert o.s., overtax one's strength; **il ne faut pas ~ des bonnes choses** one mustn't overindulge in good things, enough is as good as a feast (*Prov*); **il use et (il) abuse de métaphores** he's too fond *ou* overfond of metaphors.
2 vt *[escroc]* to deceive; *[ressemblance]* to mislead. **se laisser ~ par de belles paroles** to be taken in *ou* misled by fine *ou* fair words.
3 s'abuser vpr (*frm*) (*se tromper*) to be mistaken, make a mistake; (*se faire des illusions*) to delude o.s. **si je ne m'abuse** if I'm not mistaken.

abusif, -ive [abyzif, iv] **adj** *pratique* improper; *mère, père* overpossessive; *prix* exorbitant, excessive; *punition* excessive. **usage ~ de son autorité** improper use *ou* misuse of one's authority; **usage ~ d'un mot** misuse *ou* improper use *ou* wrong use of a word; **c'est peut-être ~ de dire cela** it's perhaps putting it a bit strongly to say that.

Abû Simbel [abusimbɛl] **n** = **Abou Simbel**.

abusivement [abyzivmɑ̃] **adv** (*Ling: improprement*) wrongly, improperly; (*excessivement*) excessively, to excess. **il s'est servi ~ de lui** he took unfair advantage of him.

abyssal, e, mpl -aux [abisal, o] **adj** (*Géog*) abyssal; (*fig*) unfathomable.

abysse [abis] **nm** (*Géog*) abyssal zone.

abyssin, e [abisɛ̃, in] = **abyssinien**.

Abyssinie [abisini] **nf** Abyssinia.

abyssinien, -ienne [abisinjɛ̃, jɛn] **1 adj** Abyssinian. **2 nm,f: A~(ne)** Abyssinian.

AC [ɑse] **n** (**abrév de appellation contrôlée**) appellation contrôlée, *label guaranteeing district of origin of a wine*.

acabit [akabi] **nm** (*péj*) **être du même ~** to be cast in the same mould; **ils sont tous du même ~** they're all much of a muchness; **fréquenter des gens de cet ~** to mix with people of that type *ou* like that.

acacia [akasja] **nm** (*gén: faux acacia*) locust tree, false acacia; (*Bot: mimosacée*) acacia.

académicien, -ienne [akademisjɛ̃, jɛn] **nm,f** (*gén*) academician; *[Académie française] member of the French Academy*, Academician; (*Antiq*) academic.

académie [akademi] **nf a** (*société savante*) learned society; (*Antiq*) academy. **l'A~ royale de** the Royal Academy of; **l'A~ des Sciences** the Academy of Science; **l'A~ (française)** the (French) Academy. **b** (*école*) academy. ~ **de dessin/danse** art/dancing school, academy of art/dancing. **c** (*Univ*) ≃ regional (education) authority (*Brit*), school district (*US*). **d** (*Art: nu*) nude; (*: *anatomie*) anatomy (*hum*).

académique [akademik] **adj** (*péj, Art, littér*) academic; *[Académie française]* of the French Academy; (*Scol*) of the académie. (*Belgique, Can, Suisse*) **année ~** academic year; *voir* **inspection, palme**.

académisme [akademism] **nm** (*péj*) academicism.

Acadie [akadi] **nf** (*Hist*) Acadia. (*Géog*) **l'~** the Maritime Provinces.

acadien, -ienne [akadjɛ̃, jɛn] **1 adj** Acadian; (*de Louisiane*) Cajun. **2 nm** (*Ling*) Acadian. **3 nm,f: A~(ne)** Acadian; (*de Louisiane*) Cajun.

acajou [akaʒu] **1 nm** (*à bois rouge*) mahogany; (*anacardier*) cashew. **2 adj inv** mahogany (*épith*).

acalorique [akalɔʀik] **adj** calorie-free.

acanthe [akɑ̃t] **nf** (*Bot*) acanthus. (*Archit*) **(feuille d')~** acanthus.

a cap(p)ella [akapela] **adv, adj** a capella. **chanter ~** to sing a capella.

acariâtre [akaʀjɑtʀ] **adj** *caractère* sour, cantankerous; *femme* shrewish. **d'humeur ~** sour-tempered.

acarien [akaʀjɛ̃] **nm** acarid, acaridan.

accablant, e [akɑblɑ̃, ɑ̃t] **adj** *chaleur* exhausting, oppressive; *témoignage* overwhelming, damning; *responsabilité* overwhelming; *douleur* excruciating; *travail* exhausting.

accablement [akɑbləmɑ̃] **nm** (*abattement*) despondency, depression; (*oppression*) exhaustion.

accabler [akɑble] 1 **vt a** *[chaleur, fatigue]* to overwhelm, overcome; (*littér*) *[fardeau]* to weigh down. **accablé de chagrin** prostrate *ou* overwhelmed with grief; **les troupes, accablées sous le nombre** the troops, overwhelmed *ou* overpowered by numbers.
b *[témoignage]* to condemn, damn. **sa déposition m'accable** his evidence is overwhelmingly against me.
c (*faire subir*) ~ **qn d'injures** to heap *ou* shower abuse on sb; ~ **qn de reproches/critiques** to heap reproaches/criticism on sb; **il m'accabla de son mépris** he poured contempt upon me; ~ **qn d'impôts** to overburden sb with taxes; ~ **qn de travail** to overburden sb with work, pile work on sb; ~ **qn de questions** to overwhelm *ou* shower sb with questions; (*iro*) **il nous accablait de conseils** he overwhelmed us with advice.

accalmie [akalmi] **nf** (*gén*) lull; *[vent, tempête]* lull (*de* in); *[fièvre]* respite (*dans* in), remission (*dans* of); (*Comm*) *[affaires, transactions]* slack period; *[combat]* lull, break; *[crise politique ou morale]* period of calm, lull, calm spell (*de* in). **profiter d'une ~ pour sortir** to take advantage of a calm spell *ou* of a lull (in the wind) to go out; **nous n'avons pas eu un seul moment d'~ pendant la journée** we didn't have a single quiet moment during the whole day, there was no lull (in the activity) throughout the entire day.

accaparant, e [akapaʀɑ̃, ɑ̃t] **adj** *métier* demanding, all-absorbing, exacting; *enfant* demanding.

accaparement [akapaʀmɑ̃] **nm** (*voir* **accaparer**) *[pouvoir, production]* monopolizing; *[marché]* cornering, capturing; *[médecin etc]* involvement (*par* in).

accaparer [akapaʀe] 1 **vt a** (*monopoliser*) *production, pouvoir, conversation, hôte* to monopolize; *marché, vente* to corner, capture. **les enfants l'ont tout de suite accaparée** the children claimed all her attention straight away; **ces élèves brillants qui accaparent les prix** those bright pupils who carry off all the prizes. **b** (*absorber*) *[soucis, travail]* to take up the time and energy of. **accaparé par sa profession/les soucis** completely absorbed in *ou* wrapped up in his job/worries; **les enfants l'accaparent** the children take up all her time (and energy).

accapareur, -euse [akapaʀœʀ, øz] **1 adj** monopolistic, grabbing* (*épith*). **2 nm,f** (*péj*) monopolizer, grabber*.

accéder [aksede] 6 **accéder à vt indir a** (*atteindre*) *lieu, sommet* to reach, get to; *honneur, indépendance* to attain; *grade* to rise to; *responsabilité* to accede to. ~ **directement à** to have direct access to; **on accède au château par le jardin** you (can) get to the castle through the garden, (the) access to the castle is through the garden; ~ **au trône** to accede to the throne. **b** (*Ordin*) to access. **c** (*frm: exaucer*) *requête, prière* to grant, accede to (*frm*); *vœux* to meet, comply with; *demande* to accommodate, comply with.

accélérateur, -trice [akseleʀatœʀ, tʀis] **1 adj** accelerating. **2 nm** (*Aut, Phot, Phys*) accelerator. ~ **de particules** particle accelerator; **donner un coup d'~** (*lit*) to accelerate, step on it*; (*se dépêcher*) to step on it*, get a move on*; **donner un coup d'~ à l'économie** to give the economy a boost; **donner un coup d'~ aux réformes** to speed up the reforms.

accélération [akseleʀasjɔ̃] **nf** (*Aut, Tech*) acceleration; *[travail]* speeding up; *[pouls]* quickening. **l'~ de l'histoire** the speeding-up of the historical process.

accéléré [akseleʀe] **nm** (*Ciné*) speeded-up motion. **film en ~** speeded-up film; (*Univ*) **cours ~** crash course.

accélérer [akseleʀe] 6 **1 vt** *rythme* to speed up, accelerate; *travail* to speed up. ~ **le pas** to quicken *ou* speed up one's pace; (*fig*) ~ **le mouvement** to get things moving, hurry *ou* speed things up; **son pouls s'accéléra** his pulse quickened. **2 vi** (*Aut, fig*) to accelerate, speed up. **accélère!*** hurry up!, get a move on!*

accéléromètre [akseleʀɔmɛtʀ] **nm** accelerometer.

accent [aksɑ̃] **1 nm a** (*prononciation*) accent. **avoir l'~ paysan/du Midi** to have a country/southern (French) accent; **parler sans ~** to speak without an accent.
b (*Orthographe*) accent. **e ~ grave/aigu** e grave/acute; ~ **circonflexe** circumflex (accent).
c (*Phonétique*) accent, stress; (*fig*) stress. **mettre l'~ sur** (*lit*) to stress, put the stress *ou* accent on; (*fig*) to stress, emphasize; **l'~ est mis sur la production** (the) emphasis *ou* accent is (placed *ou* put) on production.
d (*inflexion*) tone (of voice). ~ **suppliant/plaintif** beseeching/plaintive tone; ~ **de sincérité/de détresse** note of sincerity/of distress; **récit qui a l'~ de la sincérité** story which has a ring of sincerity; **avec des ~s de rage** in accents of rage; **les ~s de cette musique** the strains of this music; **les ~s de l'espoir/de l'amour** the accents of hope/love; **les ~s déchirants de ce poète** the heartrending accents of this poet.
2 comp ▸**accent de hauteur** pitch ▸**accent d'intensité** tonic *ou* main stress ▸**accent de mot** word stress ▸**accent nasillard** nasal twang ▸**accent de phrase** sentence stress ▸**accent tonique** = **accent d'intensité** ▸**accent traînant** drawl.

accenteur [aksɑ̃tœʀ] **nm: ~ mouchet** dunnock, hedge sparrow.

accentuable [aksɑ̃tɥabl] **adj** *lettre* that can take an accent; *syllabe* that can be stressed *ou* accented.

accentuation [aksɑ̃tɥasjɔ̃] **nf** (*voir* **accentuer**) accentuation; stressing, emphasizing; intensification; marked increase. (*Phonétique*) **les règles de l'~** the rules of stress.

accentué, e [aksɑ̃tɥe] (**ptp de accentuer**) **adj** (*marqué*) marked, pronounced; (*croissant*) increased.

accentuel, -elle [aksɑ̃tɥɛl] **adj** (*Ling*) stressed, accented. **système ~ d'une langue** stress *ou* accentual system of a language.

accentuer [aksɑ̃tɥe] 1 **1 vt a** *lettre* to accent; *syllabe* to stress, accent. **syllabe (non) accentuée** (un)stressed *ou* (un)accented syllable. **b** *silhouette, contraste* to emphasize, accentuate; *goût* to bring out; *effort, poussée* to increase, intensify. **2 s'accentuer vpr** *[tendance,* *hausse]* to become more marked *ou* pronounced, increase; *[contraste, traits]* to become more marked *ou* pronounced. **l'inflation s'accentue** inflation is becoming more pronounced *ou* acute; **le froid s'accentue** it's becoming noticeably colder.

acceptabilité [akseptabilite] **nf** (*Ling*) acceptability.

acceptable [akseptabl] **adj** a (*passable*) *résultats, travail* satisfactory, fair. **ce café/vin est ~** this coffee/wine is reasonable *ou* quite decent* *ou* quite acceptable. b (*recevable*) *condition* acceptable. c (*Ling*) acceptable.

acceptation [akseptasjɔ̃] **nf** (*gén*) acceptance. **~ bancaire** bank acceptance.

accepter [aksepte] 1 **vt** a (*gén, Comm*) to accept; *proposition, condition* to agree to, accept; *pari* to take on, accept. **acceptez-vous les chèques?** do you take cheques?; **acceptez-vous X pour époux?** do you take X to be your husband?; **elle accepte tout de sa fille** she puts up with *ou* takes anything from her daughter; (*littér, hum*) **j'en accepte l'augure** I'd like to believe it; **~ le combat** *ou* **le défi** to take up *ou* accept the challenge; **elle a été bien acceptée dans le club** she's been well received at the club; **il n'accepte pas que la vie soit une routine** he won't accept that life should be a routine; **~ la compétence des tribunaux californiens** to defer to California jurisdiction.
b (*être d'accord*) to agree (*de faire* to do). **je n'accepterai pas que tu partes** I shall not agree to your leaving, I won't let you leave; **je n'accepte pas de partir** I refuse to leave, I will not leave.

acception [aksepsjɔ̃] **nf** (*Ling*) meaning, sense, acceptation. **dans toute l'~ du mot** *ou* **terme** in every sense *ou* in the full meaning of the word, using the word in its fullest sense; **sans ~ de** without distinction of.

accès [aksɛ] **nm** a (*possibilité d'approche*) access (*NonC*). **une grande porte interdisait l'~ du jardin** a big gate barred entry *ou* prevented access to the garden; **~ interdit à toute personne étrangère aux travaux** no entry *ou* no admittance to unauthorized persons; **d'~ facile** *lieu, port* (easily) accessible; *personne* approachable; *traité, manuel* easily understood; *style* accessible; **d'~ difficile** *lieu* hard to get to, not very accessible; *personne* not very approachable; *manuel* not easily understood.
b (*voie*) **les ~ de la ville** the approaches to *ou* means of access to the town; **les ~ de l'immeuble** the entrances to the building; **"~ aux quais"** "to the trains".
c (*loc*) **avoir ~ à qch** to have access to sth; **avoir ~ auprès de qn** to be able *ou* in a position to approach sb, have access to sb; **donner ~ à** *lieu* to give access to, (*en montant*) to lead up to; *carrière* to open the door *ou* way to.
d (*crise*) *[colère, folie]* fit; *[fièvre]* attack, bout; *[enthousiasme]* burst. **~ de toux** fit *ou* bout of coughing; **être pris d'un ~ de mélancolie/de tristesse** to be overcome by melancholy/sadness; **par ~** on and off.
e (*Ordin*) access. **port/temps d'~** access port/time; **~ protégé** restricted access; **~ aux données** access to data.

accessibilité [aksesibilite] **nf** accessibility (*à* to).

accessible [aksesibl] **adj** *lieu* accessible (*à* to), get-at-able*; *personne* approachable; *but* attainable; (*Ordin*) accessible (*par* by). **parc ~ au public** gardens open to the public; **elle n'est ~ qu'à ses amies** only her friends are able *ou* allowed to see her; **ces études sont ~s à tous** (*sans distinction*) this course is open to everyone; (*financièrement*) this course is within everyone's pocket; (*intellectuellement*) this course is within the reach of everyone; **être ~ à la pitié** to be capable of pity.

accession [aksesjɔ̃] **nf: ~ à** *pouvoir, fonction* accession to; *indépendance* attainment of; *rang* rise to; (*frm*) *requête, désir* granting of, compliance with; **pour faciliter l'~ à la propriété** to facilitate home ownership.

accessit [aksesit] **nm** (*Scol*) ≃ certificate of merit.

accessoire [akseswaʀ] 1 **adj** *idée* of secondary importance; *clause* secondary. **l'un des avantages ~s de ce projet** one of the added *ou* incidental advantages of this plan; **c'est d'un intérêt tout ~** this is only of minor *ou* incidental interest; **frais ~s** (*gén*) incidental expenses; (*Fin, Comm*) ancillary costs; (*Jur*) **dommages-intérêts ~s** incidental damages. 2 **nm** a (*Théât*) prop; (*Aut, Habillement*) accessory. **~s de toilette** toilet requisites; *voir* **magasin**. b (*Philos*) **l'~** the unessential, unessentials.

accessoirement [akseswaʀmɑ̃] **adv** (*secondairement*) secondarily, incidentally; (*si besoin est*) if need be, if necessary.

accessoiriser [akseswaʀize] 1 **vt** *tailleur, costume* to accessorize.

accessoiriste [akseswaʀist] 1 **nm** property man *ou* master. 2 **nf** property girl *ou* mistress.

accident [aksidɑ̃] 1 **nm** a (*gén*) accident; (*Aut, Rail*) accident, crash; (*Aviat*) crash. (*Admin*) **il n'y a pas eu d'~ de personnes** there were no casualties, no one was injured; **il y a eu plusieurs ~s mortels sur la route** there have been several road deaths *ou* several fatalities on the roads; **avoir un ~** to have an accident, meet with an accident.
b (*mésaventure*) **les ~s de sa carrière** the setbacks in his career; **les ~s de la vie** life's ups and downs, life's trials; **les ~s qui ont entravé la réalisation du projet** the setbacks *ou* hitches which held up the realization of the plan; **c'est un simple ~, il ne l'a pas fait exprès** it was just an accident, he didn't do it on purpose.
c (*Méd*) illness, trouble. **elle a eu un petit ~ de santé** she's had a little trouble with her health; **~ cardiaque** heart attack; **~ secondaire** minor complication.
d (*Philos*) accident.
e (*littér*) (*hasard*) (pure) accident; (*fait mineur*) minor event. **par ~** by chance, by accident; **si par ~ tu ...** if by chance you ..., if you happen to ... .
f (*Mus*) accidental.
2 **comp** ▸**accident d'avion** air *ou* plane crash ▸**accident de la circulation** road accident ▸**accidents domestiques** accidents in the home ▸**accident de montagne** mountaineering *ou* climbing accident ▸**accident de parcours** chance mishap ▸**accident de la route** = **accident de la circulation** ▸**accident de terrain** accident (*SPÉC*), undulation; **les accidents de terrain** the unevenness of the ground ▸**accident du travail** industrial injury ▸**accident de voiture** car accident *ou* crash.

accidenté, e [aksidɑ̃te] (**ptp de accidenter**) 1 **adj** a *région* undulating, hilly; *terrain* uneven, bumpy; *vie, carrière* chequered, eventful. b *véhicule* damaged; *avion* crippled. 2 **nm,f** casualty, injured person. **~ de la route** road accident victim; **~ du travail** victim of an accident at work *ou* of an industrial injury.

accidentel, -elle [aksidɑ̃tɛl] **adj** (*fortuit*) *événement* accidental, fortuitous; (*par accident*) *mort* accidental.

accidentellement [aksidɑ̃tɛlmɑ̃] **adv** a (*par hasard*) accidentally, by accident *ou* chance. **il était là ~** he just happened to be there. b *mourir* in an accident.

accidenter [aksidɑ̃te] 1 **vt** *personne* to injure, hurt; *véhicule* to damage.

accise [aksiz] **nf** (*Belgique, Can*) excise. **droits d'~** excise duties.

acclamation [aklamasjɔ̃] **nf: ~s** cheers, cheering; **il est sorti sous les ~s du public** he left to great cheering from the audience; **élire qn par ~** to elect sb by acclamation.

acclamer [aklame] 1 **vt** to cheer, acclaim. **on l'acclama roi** they acclaimed him king.

acclimatable [aklimatabl] **adj** acclimatizable, acclimatable (*US*).

acclimatation [aklimatasjɔ̃] **nf** acclimatization, acclimation (*US*); *voir* **jardin**.

acclimatement [aklimatmɑ̃] **nm** acclimatization, acclimation (*US*).

acclimater [aklimate] 1 1 **vt** (*Bot, Zool*) to acclimatize, acclimate (*US*); (*fig*) *idée, usage* to introduce. 2 **s'acclimater vpr** *[personne, animal, plante]* to become acclimatized, adapt (o.s. *ou* itself) (*à* to); (*fig*) *[usage, idée]* to become established *ou* accepted.

accointances [akwɛ̃tɑ̃s] **nfpl** (*péj*) contacts, links. **avoir des ~** to have contacts (*avec* with, *dans* in, among).

accolade [akɔlad] **nf** a (*embrassade*) embrace (*on formal occasion*); (*Hist: coup d'épée*) accolade. **donner/recevoir l'~** to embrace/be embraced. b (*Typ*) brace. **mots (mis) en ~** words bracketed together. c (*Archit, Mus*) accolade.

accoler [akɔle] 1 **vt** (*gén*) to place side by side; (*Typ*) to bracket together. **~ une chose à une autre** to place a thing beside *ou* next to another; **il avait accolé à son nom celui de sa mère** he had joined *ou* added his mother's maiden name to his surname.

accommodant, e [akɔmɔdɑ̃, ɑ̃t] **adj** accommodating.

accommodation [akɔmɔdasjɔ̃] **nf** (*Opt*) accommodation; (*adaptation*) adaptation.

accommodement [akɔmɔdmɑ̃] **nm** (*littér: arrangement*) compromise, accommodation (*littér*). (*hum*) **trouver des ~s avec le ciel/avec sa conscience** to come to an arrangement with the powers on high/with one's conscience.

accommoder [akɔmɔde] 1 1 **vt** a (*Culin*) *plat* to prepare (*à* in, with). **savoir ~ les restes** to be good at making the most of *ou* using up the left-overs.
b (*concilier*) **~ le travail avec le plaisir** to combine business with pleasure; **~ ses principes aux circonstances** to adapt *ou* alter one's principles to suit the circumstances.
c (††) (*arranger*) *affaire* to arrange; *querelle* to put right; (*réconcilier*) *ennemis* to reconcile, bring together; (*malmener*) to give harsh treatment to. (*installer confortablement*) **~ qn** to make sb comfortable.
2 **vi** (*Opt*) to focus (*sur* on).
3 **s'accommoder vpr** a (†: *s'adapter à*) **s'~ à** to adapt to.
b (*supporter*) **s'~ de** to put up with; **il lui a bien fallu s'en ~** he just had to put up with it *ou* accept it, he just had to make the best of a bad job; **je m'accommode de peu** I'm content *ou* I can make do with little; **elle s'accommode de tout** she can make do with anything.
c (††: *s'arranger avec*) **s'~ avec qn** to come to an agreement *ou* arrangement with sb (*sur* about).

accompagnateur, -trice [akɔ̃paɲatœʀ, tʀis] **nm,f** (*Mus*) accompanist; (*guide*) guide; (*Scol*) accompanying adult; *[voyage organisé]* courier.

accompagnement [akɔ̃paɲmɑ̃] **nm** a (*Mus*) accompaniment. **sans ~** unaccompanied. b (*Culin*) accompanying vegetables, trimmings*. c (*escorte*) escort; (*fig*) accompaniment; (*conséquence*) result, consequence. **l'~ d'un malade** being with a patient; *voir* **tir**.

accompagner [akɔ̃paɲe] 1 **vt** a (*escorter*) to accompany, go with, come with; (*fig*) *mourant* to be with, stay with. **~ un enfant à l'école** to take a child to school; ~ **qn chez lui/à la gare** to go home/to the station with sb, see sb home/to the station; **il s'était fait ~ de sa mère** he had got his mother to go with him *ou* to accompany him; **être accompagné de** *ou* **par qn** to be with sb, be accompanied by sb; **est-ce que vous êtes accompagné?** is there anybody with you?; **tous nos vœux vous accompagnent** all our good wishes go with you; **mes pensées t'accompagnent** I am with you in my thoughts; ~ **qn de ses huées** to catcall *ou* boo sb; ~ **qn du regard** to follow sb with one's eyes.

b (*assortir*) to accompany, go (together) with. **il accompagna ce mot d'une mimique expressive** he gestured expressively as he said the word; **une lettre accompagnait les fleurs** a letter came with the flowers; **crise de nerfs accompagnée de sanglots** hysteria accompanied by sobbing; **l'agitation qui accompagna son arrivée** the stir *ou* fuss that accompanied his arrival; **la guerre s'accompagne toujours de privations** war is always accompanied by *ou* always brings hardship.

c (*Mus*) to accompany (*à* on). **il s'accompagna (lui-même) à la guitare** he accompanied himself on the guitar.

d (*Culin*) **du chou accompagnait le rôti** cabbage was served with the roast; **le poisson s'accompagne d'un vin blanc sec** fish is served with a dry white wine; **le beaujolais est ce qui accompagne le mieux cette viande** a Beaujolais goes best with this meat, Beaujolais is the best wine to serve with this meat.

accompli, e [akɔ̃pli] (**ptp de accomplir**) **adj** a (*parfait, expérimenté*) accomplished; (*Ling*) accomplished. b (*révolu*) **avoir 60 ans ~s** to be over *ou* turned 60; *voir* **fait.**

accomplir [akɔ̃pliʀ] 2 **vt** a (*réaliser*) *devoir, promesse* to fulfil, carry out; *mauvaise action* to commit; *tâche, mission* to perform, carry out, accomplish; *exploit* to perform, achieve. ~ **des merveilles** to work wonders, perform miracles; **il a enfin pu ~ ce qu'il avait décidé de faire** at last he managed to achieve *ou* accomplish what he had decided to do; **la volonté de Dieu s'est accomplie** God's will was done. b *apprentissage, service militaire* (*faire*) to do; (*terminer*) to complete, finish.

accomplissement [akɔ̃plismɑ̃] **nm** (*voir* **accomplir**) fulfilment; accomplishment; committing; completion.

accord [akɔʀ] **nm** a (*entente*) agreement; (*concorde*) harmony. **l'~ fut général sur ce point** there was general agreement on this point; **le bon ~ régna pendant 10 ans** harmony reigned for 10 years; *voir* **commun.**

b (*traité*) agreement. **passer un ~ avec qn** to make an agreement with sb; **~ à l'amiable** informal *ou* amicable agreement; **~ de modération** restraint of trade clause; **~s bilatéraux** bilateral agreement; **~ général sur les tarifs douaniers et le commerce** General Agreement on Tariffs and Trade; **~-cadre** outline *ou* framework agreement; **~ de principe** agreement in principle; **les ~s d'Helsinki/de Camp David** *etc* the Helsinki/Camp David *etc* agreement; **~ monétaire européen** European Monetary Agreement; (*Jur*) **~ complémentaire** additional agreement; **~s de crédit** credit arrangements; **~ salarial** wage settlement; **~ de sûreté** security agreement.

c (*permission*) consent, agreement.

d (*harmonie*) *[couleurs]* harmony.

e (*Gram*) *[adjectif, participe]* agreement; (*Ling*) concord. **~ en genre/nombre** agreement in gender/number.

f (*Mus*) (*notes*) chord, concord; (*réglage*) tuning. **~ parfait** triad; **~ de tierce** third; **~ de quarte** fourth.

g (*loc*) **en ~ avec le paysage** in harmony *ou* in keeping with the landscape; **en ~ avec vos instructions** in accordance *ou* in line with your instructions; **en ~ avec le directeur** in agreement with the director; **être d'~** to agree, be in agreement (*frm*); **se mettre** *ou* **tomber d'~ avec qn** to agree *ou* come to an agreement with sb; **être d'~ pour faire** to agree to do; **il est d'~ pour nous aider** he will help us; **je ne suis pas d'~ pour le laisser en liberté** I don't agree that he should be left at large; **essayer de mettre 2 personnes d'~** to try to make 2 people come to *ou* reach an agreement *ou* agree with each other, try to make 2 people see eye to eye; **je les ai mis d'~ en leur donnant tort à tous les deux** I ended their disagreement by pointing out that they were both wrong; **c'est d'~** (we're) agreed, all right; **c'est d'~ pour demain** it's agreed for tomorrow, O.K. for tomorrow*; **d'~!** O.K.!*, (all) right!, right ho!* (*Brit*); **alors là, (je ne suis) pas d'~!*** I don't agree!, no way!*

accordable [akɔʀdabl] **adj** (*Mus*) tunable; *faveur* which can be granted.

accordage [akɔʀdaʒ] **nm, accordement** [akɔʀdəmɑ̃] **nm** tuning.

accordéon [akɔʀdeɔ̃] **nm** accordion. **~ à clavier** piano-accordion; **en ~*** *voiture* crumpled up; *pantalon, chaussette* wrinkled (up); **coup d'~*** sudden turnround (*Brit*) *ou* turnaround (*US*).

accordéoniste [akɔʀdeɔnist] **nmf** accordionist.

accorder [akɔʀde] 1 **1 vt** a (*donner*) *faveur, permission, demande* to grant; *allocation, pension* to give, award (*à* to). **on lui a accordé un congé exceptionnel** he's been given *ou* granted special leave; **il ne s'accorde jamais de répit** he never gives himself a rest, he never lets up*; **elle accorde à ses enfants tout ce qu'ils demandent** she lets her children have *ou* she gives her children anything they ask for; **pouvez-vous m'~ quelques minutes?** can you spare me a few minutes?; **je m'accorde 2 jours pour finir** I'm giving myself 2 days to finish; *voir* **main.**

b (*admettre*) **~ à qn que** to admit (to sb) that; **vous m'accorderez que j'avais raison** you'll admit *ou* concede I was right; **je vous l'accorde, j'avais tort** I admit *ou* accept *ou* concede that I was wrong, I was wrong I'll grant you that.

c (*attribuer*) **~ de l'importance à qch** to attach importance to sth; **~ de la valeur à qch** to attach value to sth, value sth.

d (*Mus*) *instrument* to tune. (*fig*) **ils devraient ~ leurs violons*** (*sur un récit, un témoignage*) they ought to get their story straight*; (*sur un projet*) they ought to come to an agreement.

e (*Gram*) **(faire) ~ un verbe/un adjectif** to make a verb/an adjective agree (*avec* with).

f (*mettre en harmonie*) *personnes* to bring together. **~ ses actions avec ses opinions** to match one's actions to one's opinions, act in accordance with one's opinions; **~ la couleur du tapis avec celle des rideaux** to match the colour of the carpet with (that of) the curtains, make the carpet match the curtains in colour.

2 **s'accorder vpr** a (*être d'accord*) to agree, be agreed; (*se mettre d'accord*) to agree. **ils s'accordent pour** *ou* **à dire que le film est mauvais** they agree that it's a poor film; **ils se sont accordés pour le faire élire** they agreed to get him elected.

b (*s'entendre*) *[personnes]* to get on together. **(bien/mal) s'~ avec qn** to get on (well/badly) with sb.

c (*être en harmonie*) *[couleurs]* to match, go together; *[opinions]* to agree; *[sentiments, caractères]* to be in harmony. **s'~ avec** *[opinion]* to agree with; *[sentiments]* to be in harmony *ou* in keeping with; *[couleur]* to match, go with; **il faut que nos actions s'accordent avec nos opinions** one's actions must be in keeping with one's opinions, one must act in accordance with one's opinions.

d (*Ling*) to agree (*avec* with). **s'~ en nombre/genre** to agree in number/gender.

accordeur [akɔʀdœʀ] **nm** (*Mus*) tuner.

accordoir [akɔʀdwaʀ] **nm** tuning hammer *ou* wrench.

accorte [akɔʀt] **adj f** (*hum*) winsome, comely.

accostable [akɔstabl] **adj**: **le rivage n'est pas ~** you can't get near the shore.

accostage [akɔstaʒ] **nm** (*Naut*) coming alongside; *[personne]* accosting.

accoster [akɔste] 1 **vt** a (*gén, péj*) *personne* to accost. b (*Naut*) *quai, navire* to come *ou* draw alongside; (*emploi absolu*) to berth.

accotement [akɔtmɑ̃] **nm** (*Aut*) shoulder, verge (*Brit*), berm (*US*); (*Rail*) shoulder. **~ non stabilisé, ~ meuble** soft verge (*Brit*) *ou* shoulder (*US*); **~ stabilisé** hard shoulder.

accoter [akɔte] 1 **1 vt** to lean, rest (*contre* against, *sur* on). **2 s'accoter vpr**: **s'~ à** *ou* **contre** to lean against.

accotoir [akɔtwaʀ] **nm** *[bras]* armrest; *[tête]* headrest.

accouchée [akuʃe] **nf** (new) mother.

accouchement [akuʃmɑ̃] **nm** (child)birth, delivery; (*travail*) labour, confinement. **~ provoqué** induced delivery; **~ à terme** delivery at full term, full-term delivery; **~ avant terme** early delivery, delivery before full term; **~ naturel** natural childbirth; **~ prématuré** premature birth; **~ sans douleur** painless childbirth; **pendant l'~** during the delivery.

accoucher [akuʃe] 1 **1 vt**: **~ qn** to deliver sb's baby, deliver sb. **2 vi** a (*être en travail*) to be in labour; (*donner naissance*) to have a baby, give birth. **où avez-vous accouché?** where did you have your baby?; **elle accouchera en octobre** her baby is due in October; **~ avant terme** to have one's baby prematurely *ou* early *ou* before it is due; **~ d'un garçon** to give birth to a boy, have a (baby) boy. b (*fig hum*) **~ de** *roman* to bring forth (*hum*), produce (*with difficulty*); **accouche!*** spit it out!*, out with it!*; *voir* **montagne.**

accoucheur, -euse [akuʃœʀ, øz] **1 nm,f**: **(médecin) ~** obstetrician. **2 accoucheuse nf** (*sage-femme*) midwife.

accouder (s') [akude] 1 **vpr** to lean (on one's elbows). **s'~ sur** *ou* **à** to lean (one's elbows) on, rest one's elbows on; **accoudé à la fenêtre** leaning (on one's elbows) at the window.

accoudoir [akudwaʀ] **nm** armrest.

accouplement [akupləmɑ̃] **nm** (*voir* **accoupler**) yoking; coupling (up); hitching (up); joining (up); connecting (up); bringing together; mating; coupling.

accoupler [akuple] 1 **1 vt** a (*ensemble*) *animaux de trait* to yoke; *roues* to couple (up); *wagons* to couple (up), hitch (up); *générateurs* to connect (up); *tuyaux* to join (up), connect (up); *moteurs* to couple, connect (up); (*fig*) *mots, images* to bring together, link. **ils sont bizarrement accouplés*** they make a strange couple, they're an odd match. b **~ une remorque/un cheval à** to hitch a trailer/horse (up) to; **~ un moteur/un tuyau à** to connect an engine/a pipe to. c (*faire copuler*) to mate (*à, avec, et* with). **2 s'accoupler vpr** *[animaux]* to mate, couple; (*hum péj*) *[humains]* to mate.

accourir [akuʀiʀ] 11 **vi** (*lit*) to rush up, run up (*à, vers* to); (*fig*) to hurry, hasten, rush (*à, vers* to). **à mon appel il accourut immédiatement** (*du salon*) at my call he ran up *ou* rushed up immediately; (*de province*) when I called on him he rushed *ou* hastened to see me immediately; **ils sont accourus (pour) le féliciter** they rushed up *ou* hurried to congratulate him.

accoutrement [akutʀəmɑ̃] nm (*péj*) getup*, rig-out* (*Brit*).
accoutrer [akutʀe] [1] (*péj*) 1 vt (*habiller*) to get up*, rig out* (*Brit*) (*de* in). 2 **s'accoutrer** vpr to get o.s. up*, rig o.s. out* (*Brit*) (*de* in). **il était bizarrement accoutré** he was strangely rigged out* (*Brit*) *ou* got up*, he was wearing the oddest rig-out* (*Brit*).
accoutumance [akutymɑ̃s] nf (*habitude*) habituation (*à* to); (*besoin*) addiction (*à* to).
accoutumé, e [akutyme] (ptp de **accoutumer**) adj usual. **comme à l'~e** as usual.
accoutumer [akutyme] [1] 1 vt: **~ qn à qch/à faire qch** to accustom sb *ou* get sb used to sth/to doing sth; **on l'a accoutumé à** *ou* **il a été accoutumé à se lever tôt** he has been used *ou* accustomed to getting up early. 2 **s'accoutumer** vpr: **s'~ à qch/à faire qch** to get used *ou* accustomed to sth/to doing sth; **il s'est lentement accoutumé** he gradually got used *ou* accustomed to it.
Accra [akʀa] n Accra.
accréditer [akʀedite] [1] 1 vt *rumeur* to substantiate, give substance to; *personne* to accredit (*auprès de* to). **banque accréditée** accredited bank. 2 **s'accréditer** vpr *[rumeur]* to gain ground.
accréditif, -ive [akʀeditif, iv] adj accreditive. **carte ~ive** credit card; **lettre ~ive** letter of credit.
accro [akʀo] 1 adj a (*arg Drogue*) **être ~** to have a habit (*arg*), be hooked (*arg*), have a monkey on one's back (*arg US*); **être ~ à l'héroïne** to be hooked on heroin (*arg*). b (*: *fanatique*) **être ~** to be hooked*. 2 nmf addict. **les ~s du deltaplane** hang-gliding addicts.
accroc [akʀo] nm a (*déchirure*) tear. **faire un ~ à** to make a tear in, tear. b (*fig*) *[réputation]* blot (*à* on); *[règle]* breach, infringement (*à* of). **faire un ~ à** *règle* to twist, bend; *réputation* to blot. c (*anicroche*) hitch, snag. **sans ~s** without a hitch, smoothly.
accrochage [akʀɔʃaʒ] nm a (*Aut: collision*) collision, bump*, fender-bender* (*US*); (*Mil: combat*) encounter, engagement; (*Boxe*) clinch; (*fig: dispute*) clash, brush. b (*action*) *[tableau]* hanging; *[wagons]* coupling, hitching (up) (*à* to).
accroche [akʀɔʃ] nf (*Publicité*) lead-in, catcher, catch line *ou* phrase.
accroché, e [akʀɔʃe] (ptp de **accrocher**) adj a (*: *amoureux*) **être ~** to be hooked*. b (*arg Drogue*) **être ~** to have a habit (*arg*), be hooked (*arg*), have a monkey on one's back (*arg US*); **être ~ à l'héroïne** to be hooked on heroin (*arg*).
accroche-cœur, pl **accroche-cœurs** [akʀɔʃkœʀ] nm kiss curl.
accrocher [akʀɔʃe] [1] 1 vt a (*suspendre*) *chapeau, tableau* to hang (up) (*à* on); (*attacher*) *wagons* to couple, hitch together. **~ un wagon/une remorque à** to hitch *ou* couple a carriage/a trailer (up) to; **~ un ver à l'hameçon** to fasten *ou* put a worm on the hook; **maison accrochée à la montagne** house perched on the mountainside; *voir* **cœur**.
b (*accidentellement*) *jupe, collant* to catch (*à* on); *aile de voiture* to catch (*à* on), bump (*à* against); *voiture* to bump into; *piéton* to hit; *pile de livres, meuble* to catch (on). **rester accroché aux barbelés** to be caught on (the) barbed wire.
c (*attirer*) **~ le regard** to catch the eye; **vitrine qui accroche les clients** window which attracts customers; **film qui accroche le public** picture that draws (in) *ou* pulls in the public.
d (*: *saisir*) *occasion* to get; *personne* to get hold of; *mots, fragments de conversation* to catch.
e (*Mil*) to engage; (*Boxe*) to clinch.
2 vi a *[fermeture éclair]* to stick, jam; (*fig*) *[pourparlers]* to come up against a hitch *ou* snag. (*fig*) **cette traduction accroche par endroits** this translation is a bit rough in places, there are one or two places where this translation does not run smoothly; **cette planche accroche quand on l'essuie** this board catches on the cloth when you wipe it.
b (*plaire*) *disque, slogan* to catch on. **ça accroche entre eux** they hit it off together*.
c (*: *s'intéresser*) **elle n'accroche pas en anglais** she's not really interested in English; **l'art abstrait, j'ai du mal à ~** I can't get into abstract art*.
3 **s'accrocher** vpr a (*se cramponner*) to hang on. **s'~ à** (*lit*) *branche* to cling to, hang on to; (*fig*) *espoir, personne* to cling to; **accroche-toi bien!** hold on tight!; **les vignes s'accrochent au flanc du coteau** the vineyards cling to the hillside.
b (*: *être tenace*) *[malade]* to cling on, hang on; *[étudiant]* to stick at it, stick in*; *[importun]* to cling. **pour enlever la tache, tiens, accroche-toi!** you'll have (a) hell of a job getting the stain out!*
c (*entrer en collision*) *[voitures]* to bump (each other), touch *ou* clip each other, have a bump; (*Boxe*) to go *ou* get into a clinch; (*Mil*) to engage; (*fig: se disputer*) to have a clash *ou* a brush (*avec* with). **ils s'accrochent tout le temps** they are always at loggerheads *ou* always quarrelling *ou* always getting across one another.
d (**: *en faire son deuil*) **se l'~: tu peux te l'~** you can kiss it goodbye*, you've got a hope* (*Brit*) (*iro*).
accrocheur, -euse [akʀɔʃœʀ, øz] adj a *joueur, concurrent* tenacious; *vendeur, représentant* persistent, aggressive. **c'est un ~** he's a sticker* *ou* fighter. b *affiche, titre* eye-catching; *méthode* calculated to appeal; *air de musique, slogan* catchy; *prix* very attractive; *film* which (really) pulls the crowds *ou* pulls them in*.
accroire [akʀwaʀ] vt (*frm, hum*) **faire** *ou* **laisser ~ à qn qch/que** to delude sb into believing sth/that; **et tu veux me faire ~ que ...** and you want me to believe that ...; **il veut nous en faire ~** he's trying to deceive us *ou* take us in, he's having us on* (*Brit*); **il ne s'en est pas laissé ~** he didn't let himself be taken in.
accroissement [akʀwasmɑ̃] nm (*gén*) increase (*de* in); *[nombre, production]* growth (*de* in), increase (*de* in). **~ démographique nul** zero population growth.
accroître [akʀwatʀ] [55] 1 vt *somme, plaisir, confusion etc* to increase, add to; *réputation* to enhance, add to; *gloire* to increase, heighten. **~ son avance sur qn** to widen *ou* increase one's lead over sb. 2 **s'accroître** vpr to increase, grow. **sa part s'accrut de celle de son frère** his share was increased by the addition of (what had been) his brother's.
accroupi, e [akʀupi] (ptp de **s'accroupir**) adj squatting *ou* crouching (down). **en position ~e** in a squatting *ou* crouching position.
accroupir (s') [akʀupiʀ] [2] vpr to squat *ou* crouch (down).
accroupissement [akʀupismɑ̃] nm squatting, crouching.
accu* [aky] nm (*Aut etc*) (abrév de **accumulateur**) battery. (*fig*) **recharger ses ~s** to recharge one's batteries.
accueil [akœj] nm (*gén: réception*) welcome, reception; *[sinistrés, film, idée]* reception. (*bureau*) **adressez-vous à l'~** ask at reception; **rien n'a été prévu pour l'~ des touristes** no plans have *ou* no provision has been made for accommodating the tourists *ou* putting up the tourists; **quel ~ a-t-on fait à ses idées?** what sort of reception did his ideas get?, how were his ideas received?; **faire bon ~ à** *idée, proposition* to welcome; **faire bon ~ à qn** to welcome sb, make sb welcome; **faire mauvais ~ à** *idée, suggestion* to receive badly; **faire mauvais ~ à qn** to make sb feel unwelcome, give sb a bad reception; **faire bon/mauvais ~ à un film** to give a film a good/bad reception; **d'~** *centre, organisation* reception (*épith*); *paroles, cérémonie* welcoming, of welcome; *voir* **terre**.
accueillant, e [akœjɑ̃, ɑ̃t] adj welcoming, friendly.
accueillir [akœjiʀ] [12] vt a (*aller chercher*) to meet, collect; (*recevoir*) to welcome, greet; (*donner l'hospitalité à*) to welcome, take in; (*pouvoir héberger*) to accommodate. **j'ai été l'~ à la gare** I went to meet *ou* collect him *ou* pick him up at the station; **il m'a bien accueilli** he made me very welcome, he gave me a warm welcome *ou* reception; **il m'a mal accueilli** he gave me a bad reception *ou* a poor welcome; **pendant la guerre il m'a accueilli sous son toit/dans sa famille** during the war he welcomed me into his house/his family; **cet hôtel peut ~ 80 touristes** this hotel can accommodate 80 tourists; **ils se sont fait ~ par des coups de feu/des huées, des coups de feu/des huées les ont accueillis** they were greeted with shots/jeers *ou* cat calls.
b *idée, demande, film, nouvelle* to receive. **être bien/mal accueilli** to be well/badly received; **il accueillit ma suggestion avec un sourire** he greeted *ou* received my suggestion with a smile.
acculer [akyle] [1] vt: **~ qn à** *mur* to drive sb back against; (*fig*) *ruine, désespoir* to drive sb to the brink of; (*fig*) *choix, aveu* to force sb into; **acculé à la mer** driven back to the edge of the sea; **~ qn contre** to drive sb back to *ou* against; **~ qn dans** *impasse, pièce* to corner sb in; (*lit, fig*) **nous sommes acculés, nous devons céder** we're cornered, we must give in.
acculturation [akyltyʀasjɔ̃] nf cultural integration.
accumulateur [akymylatœʀ] nm accumulator, (storage) battery. **~ de chaleur** storage heater.
accumulation [akymylasjɔ̃] nf a (*action, processus: voir* **accumuler**) accumulation; amassing; building up; piling up; stockpiling; accruing; (*tas*) heap, accumulation. (*résultat*) **une ~ de stocks** a build-up in stock. b (*Élec*) storage. **à ~ (nocturne)** (night-)storage (*épith*); *voir* **radiateur**.
accumuler [akymyle] [1] 1 vt *documents, richesses, preuves, erreurs* to accumulate, amass; *marchandises* to accumulate, build up (a stock of), stockpile; *énergie* to store. (*Fin*) **les intérêts accumulés pendant un an** the interest accrued over a year. 2 **s'accumuler** vpr to accumulate, pile up; (*Fin*) to accrue.
accusateur, -trice [akyzatœʀ, tʀis] 1 adj *doigt, regard* accusing; *documents, preuves* accusatory, incriminating. 2 nm,f accuser. (*Hist*) **~ public** public prosecutor (*during the French Revolution*).
accusatif, -ive [akyzatif, iv] 1 nm accusative case. **à l'~** in the accusative. 2 adj accusative.
accusation [akyzasjɔ̃] nf (*gén*) accusation; (*Jur*) charge, indictment. (*le procureur etc*) **l'~** the prosecution; **porter** *ou* **lancer une ~ contre** to make an accusation against; **mettre en ~** to indict; **mise en ~** indictment; **une terrible ~ contre notre société** a terrible indictment of our society; (*Jur*) **abandonner l'~** to drop the charge; *voir* **acte, chambre**.
accusatoire [akyzatwaʀ] adj (*Jur*) accusatory.
accusé, e [akyze] (ptp de **accuser**) 1 adj (*marqué*) marked, pronounced. 2 nm,f accused; *[procès]* defendant. **~ levez-vous!** ≃ the defendant will rise; *voir* **banc**. 3 comp ▸**accusé de réception** acknowledgement of receipt.
accuser [akyze] [1] 1 vt a *personne* (*gén*) to accuse (*de* of). (*Jur*) **~ de** to accuse of, charge with, indict for; **~ qn d'ingratitude** to tax sb with *ou* accuse sb of ingratitude; **~ qn d'avoir volé de l'argent** to accuse sb of stealing *ou* having stolen money; **tout l'accuse** everything points to his guilt *ou* his being guilty.
b (*rendre responsable*) *pratique, malchance, personne* to blame (*de*

for). **accusant son mari de ne pas s'être réveillé à temps** blaming her husband for not waking up in time; **accusant le médecin d'incompétence pour avoir causé la mort de l'enfant** blaming the doctor's incompetence for having caused the child's death, blaming the child's death on the doctor's incompetence.

c (*souligner*) *effet, contraste* to emphasize, accentuate, bring out. **robe qui accuse la sveltesse du corps** dress which accentuates *ou* emphasizes the slimness of the body.

d (*montrer*) to show. **la balance accusait 80 kg** the scales registered *ou* read 80 kg; ~ **la quarantaine** to show (all of) one's forty years; (*lit, fig*) ~ **le coup** to stagger under the blow, show that the blow has struck home; **elle accuse la fatigue de ces derniers mois** she's showing the strain of these last few months; **la Bourse accuse une baisse de 3 points/un léger mieux** the stock exchange is showing a 3-point fall/a slight improvement; ~ **réception de** to acknowledge receipt of.

2 **s'accuser** vpr a **s'~ de qch/d'avoir fait** (*se déclarer coupable*) to admit to sth/to having done; (*se rendre responsable de*) to blame o.s. for sth/for having done; (*Rel*) **mon père, je m'accuse (d'avoir péché)** Father, I have sinned; **en protestant, il s'accuse** by objecting, he is pointing to *ou* admitting his guilt.

b (*s'accentuer*) *[tendance]* to become more marked *ou* pronounced.

ace [ɛs] nm (*Tennis*) ace. **faire un ~** to serve an ace.

acerbe [asɛʀb] adj caustic, acid. **d'une manière ~** caustically, acidly.

acéré, e [aseʀe] adj *griffe, pointe* sharp; *lame* sharp, keen; *raillerie, réplique* scathing, biting, cutting. (*fig*) **critique à la plume ~e** critic with a scathing pen.

acétate [asetat] nm acetate.

acétique [asetik] adj acetic.

acétone [asetɔn] nf acetone.

acétylène [asetilɛn] nm acetylene; *voir* **lampe**.

acétylsalicylique [asetilsalisilik] adj: **acide ~** acetylsalicylic acid.

achalandé, e [aʃalɑ̃de] adj: **bien ~** (*bien fourni*) well-stocked; (†: *très fréquenté*) well-patronized.

achards [aʃaʀ] nmpl *spicy relish made with finely chopped fruit and vegetables*.

acharné, e [aʃaʀne] (ptp de **s'acharner**) adj *combat, concurrence, adversaire* fierce, bitter; *travail, efforts* relentless, unremitting, strenuous; *poursuivant, poursuite* relentless; *joueur, travailleur* relentless, determined. ~ **à faire** set *ou* bent *ou* intent on doing, determined to do; ~ **contre** set against; ~ **à sa destruction** set *ou* bent on destroying him, set *ou* bent on his destruction.

acharnement [aʃaʀnəmɑ̃] nm *[combattant, résistant]* fierceness, fury; *[poursuivant]* relentlessness; *[travailleur]* determination, unremitting effort. **son ~ au travail** the determination with which he tackles his work; **avec ~** *poursuivre* relentlessly; *travailler* relentlessly, furiously; *combattre* bitterly, fiercely; *résister* fiercely; **se battant avec ~** fighting tooth and nail; ~ **thérapeutique** prolongation of life by medical means (*when a patient would otherwise die*).

acharner (s') [aʃaʀne] 1 vpr: **s'~ sur** *victime, proie* to go at fiercely and unrelentingly; **s'~ contre qn** *[malchance]* to dog sb; *[adversaire]* to set o.s. against sb, have got one's knife into sb; **elle s'acharne après cet enfant** she's always hounding this child; **il s'acharne à prouver que c'est vrai** he is trying desperately to prove that it is true; **il s'acharne à son tableau** he is working furiously away at *ou* on his painting; **je m'acharne à le leur faire comprendre** I'm desperately trying to explain it to them, I'm straining every nerve to get them to understand; **il s'acharne inutilement, il n'y arrivera jamais** he's wasting his efforts, he'll never make it.

achat [aʃa] nm a (*action*) purchase, purchasing, buying; (*chose achetée*) purchase. **faire l'~ de qch** to purchase *ou* buy sth; **faire un ~** to make a purchase; ~ **d'impulsion** impulse buy *ou* purchase; ~ **groupé** package; (*Publicité*) ~ **d'espace** space buying; **il est allé faire quelques ~s** he has gone out to buy a few things *ou* to do some shopping; **faire des ~s** to shop, go shopping; **faire ses ~s (de Noël)** to do one's (Christmas) shopping; **c'est cher à l'~ mais c'est de bonne qualité** it's expensive (to buy) but it's good quality; **il a fait un ~ judicieux** he made a wise buy *ou* purchase.

b (*Bourse, Comm*) buying. **la livre vaut 11 F à l'~** the buying rate for sterling is 11 francs.

acheminement [aʃ(ə)minmɑ̃] nm (*voir* **acheminer**) forwarding, dispatch; conveying, transporting; routing; sending. (*Comm*) ~ **de marchandises** carriage of goods; **l'~ du courrier est rendu difficile par les récentes chutes de neige** the distribution *ou* transport of mail has been made difficult by the recent snowfalls.

acheminer [aʃ(ə)mine] 1 1 vt *courrier, colis* to forward, dispatch (*vers* to); *troupes* to convey, transport (*vers* to). ~ **des trains sur** *ou* **vers** to route trains to; ~ **un train supplémentaire sur Dijon** to put on *ou* send an extra train to Dijon; (*fig*) ~ **le pays vers la ruine** to lead the country to ruin. 2 **s'acheminer** vpr: **s'~ vers** *endroit* to make one's way towards, head for; *conclusion, solution* to move towards; *destruction, ruine* to head for.

acheter [aʃ(ə)te] 5 vt a to buy, purchase. ~ **qch à qn** (*à un vendeur*) to buy *ou* purchase sth from sb; (*pour un ami*) to buy sth for sb, buy sb sth; **je lui ai acheté une robe pour son anniversaire** I bought her a dress for her birthday; ~ **qch d'occasion** to buy sth secondhand; ~ **en grosses quantités** to bulk-buy (*Brit*); (*Bourse*) ~ **à la hausse/à la baisse** to buy for a rise/for a fall; **(s')~ une conduite** to turn over a new leaf, mend one's ways; *voir* **comptant, crédit, détail** *etc.* b (*péj*) *vote, appui* to buy; *électeur, juge* to bribe, buy. **se laisser ~** to let o.s. be bribed *ou* bought.

acheteur, -euse [aʃ(ə)tœʀ, øz] nm,f buyer, purchaser; (*Jur*) vendee; (*Comm: professionnel*) buyer. **il est ~** he wants to buy it; **il n'a pas encore trouvé d'~ pour sa voiture** he hasn't yet found anyone to buy his car *ou* a buyer for his car; **article qui ne trouve pas d'~** item which does not sell *ou* which finds no takers; **la foule des ~s** the crowd of shoppers.

achevé, e [aʃ(ə)ve] (ptp de **achever**) adj *canaille* downright, out-and-out, thorough; *artiste* accomplished; *art, grâce* perfect. **d'un ridicule ~** perfectly ridiculous; **tableau d'un mauvais goût ~** picture in thorough(ly) bad taste.

achèvement [aʃɛvmɑ̃] nm *[travaux]* completion; (*littér: perfection*) culmination; *voir* **voie**.

achever [aʃ(ə)ve] 5 1 vt a (*terminer*) *discours, repas* to finish, end; *livre* to finish, reach the end of; (*parachever*) *tâche, tableau* to complete, finish. ~ **ses jours à la campagne** to end one's days in the country; (*littér*) **le soleil achève sa course** the sun completes its course; ~ **(de parler)** to finish (speaking); **il partit sans ~ (sa phrase)** he left in mid sentence *ou* without finishing his sentence; ~ **de se raser/de se préparer** to finish shaving/getting ready; **le pays achevait de se reconstruire** the country was just finishing its *ou* coming to the end of its rebuilding.

b (*porter à son comble*) ~ **de: cette remarque acheva de l'exaspérer** this remark really brought his irritation to a head, this last remark really did make him cross; **cette révélation acheva de nous plonger dans la confusion** this revelation was all we needed to complete our confusion.

c (*tuer*) *blessé* to finish off; *cheval* to destroy; (*fatiguer, décourager*) to finish (off); (*: *vaincre*) to finish off. **cette mauvaise nouvelle acheva son père malade** this bad news finished his sick father *ou* dealt the final blow to his sick father; **cette longue promenade m'a achevé!** that long walk was the end of me! *ou* finished me!

2 **s'achever** vpr (*se terminer*) to end (*par, sur* with); (*littér*) *[jour, vie]* to come to an end, draw to a close. (*TV*) **ainsi s'achèvent nos émissions de la journée** that brings to an end our programmes for the day.

achigan [aʃigɑ̃] nm (*Can*) (black) bass. ~ **à grande bouche** large-mouth bass; ~ **à petite bouche** small-mouth bass; ~ **de roche** rock bass.

Achille [aʃil] nm Achilles; *voir* **talon**.

Achkhabad [akabad] n Achkhabad.

achoppement [aʃɔpmɑ̃] nm *voir* **pierre**.

achopper [aʃɔpe] 1 vi: ~ **sur** *difficulté* to stumble over; (*littér*) *pierre* to stumble against *ou* over.

achromatique [akʀɔmatik] adj achromatic.

acide [asid] 1 adj (*lit, fig*) acid, sharp, tart; (*Chim*) acid; *voir* **pluie**. 2 nm acid; (*arg Drogue*) acid. ~ **aminé** amino-acid; ~ **gras saturé/insaturé** saturated/unsaturated fatty acid.

acidificateur [asidifikatœʀ] nm acidifying agent, acidifier.

acidification [asidifikasjɔ̃] nf acidification.

acidifier vt, **s'acidifier** vpr [asidifje] 7 to acidify.

acidité [asidite] nf (*lit, fig*) acidity, sharpness, tartness; (*Chim*) acidity.

acidose [asidoz] nf acidosis.

acidulé, e [asidyle] adj *goût* slightly acid; *voir* **bonbon**.

acier [asje] nm steel. ~ **inoxydable/trempé** stainless/tempered steel; ~ **rapide** high-speed steel; **d'~** *poutre, colonne* steel (*épith*), of steel; (*fig*) *regard* steely; (*fig*) **muscles d'~** muscles of steel; **avoir un moral d'~** to have a fighting spirit; *voir* **gris**.

aciérie [asjeʀi] nf steelworks.

aciériste [asjeʀist] nm steelmaker.

acmé [akme] nf (*littér: apogée*) acme, summit; (*Méd*) crisis.

acné [akne] nf acne. ~ **juvénile** teenage acne.

acnéique [akneik] adj prone to acne (*attrib*).

acolyte [akɔlit] nm (*péj: associé*) confederate, associate; (*Rel*) acolyte, server.

acompte [akɔ̃t] nm (*arrhes*) deposit; (*sur somme due*) down payment; (*versement régulier*) instalment; (*sur salaire*) advance; (*à entrepreneur*) progress payment. (*sur somme due*) **un ~ de 10 F** 10 francs on account, a down payment of 10 francs; (*sur somme due*) **recevoir un ~** to receive something on account, receive a down payment; (*fig*) **ce week-end à la mer, c'était un petit ~ sur nos vacances** this weekend at the seaside was like snatching a bit of our holidays in advance *ou* was like a little foretaste of our holidays; *voir* **provisionnel**.

a contrario [akɔ̃tʀaʀjo] adv, adj a contrario.

acoquiner (s') [akɔkine] 1 vpr (*péj*) to get together, team up (*avec* with).

Açores [asɔʀ] nfpl: **les ~** the Azores.

à-côté, pl **à-côtés** [akote] nm *[problème]* side issue; *[situation]* side aspect; (*gain, dépense secondaire*) extra. **avec ce boulot, il se fait des petits ~s*** with this job, he makes a bit extra *ou* on the side*.

à-coup, pl **à-coups** [aku] nm *[moteur]* hiccough; *[machine]* jolt, jerk;

[économie, organisation] jolt. **travailler par ~s** to work by *ou* in fits and starts; **avancer par ~s** to move forward in *ou* by fits and starts, jerk *ou* jolt forward *ou* along; **sans ~s** smoothly; **le moteur eut quelques ~s** the engine gave a few (hic)coughs *ou* hiccoughed a bit.

acousticien, -ienne [akustisjɛ̃, jɛn] nm,f acoustician.

acoustique [akustik] 1 adj acoustic. (*Phon*) **trait distinctif ~** acoustic feature; *voir* **cornet.** 2 nf (*science*) acoustics (*sg*); (*sonorité*) acoustics (*pl*). **il y a une mauvaise ~** the acoustics are bad.

acquéreur [akeʀœʀ] nm buyer, purchaser. **j'ai trouvé/je n'ai pas trouvé ~ pour mon appartement** I have/I haven't found a purchaser *ou* buyer for my flat, I've found someone/I haven't found anyone to buy my flat; **cet objet n'a pas encore trouvé ~** this object has not yet found a purchaser *ou* buyer *ou* taker; **se porter ~ (de qch)** to announce one's intention of buying *ou* purchasing (sth); **se rendre ~ de qch** to purchase *ou* buy sth.

acquérir [akeʀiʀ] [21] vt a *propriété, meuble* to acquire, purchase, buy. **~ qch par succession** to come into sth, inherit sth; *voir* **bien.**

b (*obtenir*) *faveur, célébrité* to win, gain; *habileté, autorité, habitude* to acquire; *importance, valeur, expérience* to acquire, gain. **~ la certitude de** to become certain of; **c'est une chose qui s'acquiert facilement** it's something that's easy to pick up; **~ la preuve de** to gain *ou* obtain (the) proof of; **les certitudes que nous avions acquises** the facts we had clearly established.

c (*valoir, procurer*) to win, gain. **ceci lui acquit une excellente réputation** this won *ou* gained him an excellent reputation; **il s'est acquis l'estime/l'appui de ses chefs** he won *ou* gained his superiors' esteem/support.

acquêt [akɛ] nm acquest; *voir* **communauté.**

acquiescement [akjɛsmɑ̃] nm a (*approbation*) approval, agreement. **il leva la main en signe d'~** he raised his hand in (a sign of) approval *ou* agreement. b (*consentement*) acquiescence, assent. **donner son ~ à qch** to give one's assent to sth.

acquiescer [akjese] [3] vi a (*approuver*) to approve, agree. **il acquiesça d'un signe de tête** he nodded his approval *ou* agreement. b (*consentir*) to acquiesce, assent. **~ à une demande** to acquiesce to *ou* in a request, assent to a request.

acquis, e [aki, iz] (ptp de **acquérir**) 1 adj a *fortune, qualité, droit* acquired. (*Bio*) **caractères ~** acquired characteristics; *voir* **vitesse.**

b *fait* established, accepted. **tenir qch pour ~** (*comme allant de soi*) to take sth for granted; (*comme décidé*) to take sth as settled *ou* agreed; **il est maintenant ~ que** it has now been established that, it is now accepted that.

c **être ~ à qn: ce droit nous est ~** we have now established this right as ours; **ses faveurs nous sont ~es** we can count on *ou* be sure of his favour; **être ~ à un projet/qn** to be in complete support of *ou* completely behind a plan/sb.

2 nm (*savoir*) experience; (*droit*) legal right. **avoir de l'~** to have experience; **grâce à l'~ qu'il a obtenu en travaillant chez un patron** thanks to the experience he got *ou* the knowledge he acquired working for an employer; **la connaissance qu'il a de l'anglais représente pour lui un ~ précieux** his knowledge of English is a valuable aquisition; **~ sociaux** entitlements (*to social welfare, maternity leave, paid holidays etc*).

acquisition [akizisjɔ̃] nf (*action, processus*) acquisition, acquiring; (*objet*) acquisition; (*par achat*) purchase. **faire l'~ de qch** to acquire sth; (*par achat*) to purchase sth; **l'~ du langage** language acquisition; (*bibliothèque*) **nouvelle ~** accession.

acquit [aki] nm a (*Comm: décharge*) receipt. **"pour ~"** "received". b **par ~ de conscience** to set one's mind at rest, to be quite sure. c **~-à-caution** bond note.

acquittement [akitmɑ̃] nm (*voir* **acquitter**) acquittal; payment; discharge; settlement; fulfilment. (*Jur*) **verdict d'~** verdict of not guilty.

acquitter [akite] [1] 1 vt a *accusé* to acquit. b *droit, impôt* to pay; *dette* to pay (off), settle, discharge; *facture* (*gén*) to pay, settle; (*Comm*) to receipt. c **~ qn de** *dette, obligation* to release sb from. 2 **s'acquitter** vpr: **s'~ de** *dette* to pay (off), discharge, settle; *dette morale, devoir* to discharge; *promesse* to fulfil, carry out; *obligation* to fulfil, discharge; *fonction, tâche* to fulfil, carry out, perform; **comment m'~ (envers vous)?** how can I ever repay you? (*de* for).

acre [akʀ] 1 nf (*Hist*) ≃ acre. 2 nm (*Can*) acre (*4 046,86 m²*).

âcre [ɑkʀ] adj *odeur, saveur* acrid, pungent; (*fig littér*) acrid.

âcreté [ɑkʀəte] nf *[odeur, saveur]* acridness, acridity, pungency; (*fig littér*) acridness, acridity.

acrimonie [akʀimɔni] nf acrimony, acrimoniousness.

acrimonieux, -ieuse [akʀimɔnjø, jøz] adj acrimonious.

acrobate [akʀɔbat] nmf (*lit, fig*) acrobat.

acrobatie [akʀɔbasi] nf (*tour*) acrobatic feat; (*art, fig*) acrobatics (*sg*). **~ aérienne** aerobatics (*pl*); (*lit, fig*) **faire des ~s** to perform acrobatics; (*fig*) **mon emploi du temps tient de l'~*** I have to tie myself in knots* to cope with my timetable.

acrobatique [akʀɔbatik] adj (*lit, fig*) acrobatic.

acronyme [akʀɔnim] nm acronym.

Acropole [akʀɔpɔl] nf: **l'~** the Acropolis.

acrostiche [akʀɔstiʃ] nm acrostic.

acrylique [akʀilik] adj, nm acrylic.

actant [aktɑ̃] nm (*Ling*) agent.

acte [akt] 1 nm a (*action*) action, act. **~ instinctif/réflexe** instinctive/reflex action; **moins de paroles — des ~s** (let's have) less talk and more action; **plusieurs ~s de terrorisme ont été commis** several acts of terrorism have been committed; **~ de bravoure/de lâcheté/de cruauté** act of bravery/cowardice/cruelty, brave/cowardly/cruel act *ou* action *ou* deed; **ce crime est un ~ de folie/l'~ d'un fou** this crime is an act of madness/the act *ou* deed of a madman; (*Psych*) **passer à l'~** to act out one's desires *ou* fantasies; **après avoir menacé en paroles il passa aux ~s** having uttered verbal threats he proceeded to carry them out *ou* to put them into action; (*Philos*) **en ~** in actuality.

b (*Jur*) *[notaire]* deed; *[état civil]* certificate. (*Jur*) **dont ~** duly noted *ou* acknowledged.

c (*Théât, fig*) act. **comédie/pièce en un ~** one-act comedy/play; **le dernier ~ du conflit se joua en Orient** the final act of the struggle was played out in the East.

d *[congrès etc]* **~s** proceedings.

e (*loc*) **demander ~ que/de qch** to ask for formal acknowledgement that/of sth; **prendre ~ de** to note; **donner ~ que/de qch** to acknowledge formally that/sth; **faire ~ de citoyen/d'honnête homme** to act *ou* behave as a citizen/an honest man; **faire ~ d'autorité/d'énergie** to make a show of authority/energy; **faire ~ de candidature** to apply, submit an application; **faire ~ de présence** to put in a token appearance; **il a au moins fait ~ de bonne volonté** he has at least shown *ou* made a gesture of goodwill *ou* willingness; **prendre ~ que** to record formally that; **nous prenons ~ de votre promesse/proposition** we have noted *ou* taken note of your promise/proposal.

2 comp ▸**acte d'accusation** charge (*Brit*), bill of indictment ▸**acte d'amnistie** amnesty (*act*) ▸**les Actes des Apôtres** the Acts of the Apostles ▸**acte d'association** partnership agreement *ou* deed, articles of partnership ▸**acte authentique** = **acte notarié** ▸**acte de banditisme** criminal act ▸**acte de baptême** baptismal certificate ▸**acte de charité** act of charity ▸**acte de commerce** commercial act *ou* deed ▸**acte constitutif** (*société*) charter ▸**acte de contrition** act of contrition ▸**acte de décès** death certificate ▸**acte d'espérance** act of hope ▸**acte de l'état civil** *birth, marriage or death certificate* ▸**acte de foi** act of faith ▸**acte gratuit** acte gratuit, gratuitous act ▸**acte de guerre** act of war ▸**acte judiciaire** (*Jur*) judicial document; **signifier** *ou* **notifier un acte judiciaire** to serve legal process (*à* on) ▸**acte manqué** (*Psych*) subconsciously deliberate mistake ▸**acte de mariage** marriage certificate ▸**acte médical** (medical) consultation, medical treatment (*NonC*) ▸**acte de naissance** birth certificate ▸**acte notarié** notarial deed, deed executed by notary ▸**acte de notoriété** affidavit ▸**acte officiel** (*Jur*) instrument ▸**acte sexuel** sex act ▸**acte sous seing privé** private agreement, *document not legally certified* ▸**acte de succession** attestation of inheritance ▸**acte de vente** bill of sale.

acteur [aktœʀ] nm (*Théât, fig*) actor; *voir* **actrice.**

actif, -ive [aktif, iv] 1 adj *personne, participation* active; *poison, médicament* active, potent; (*au travail*) *population* working; (*Bourse*) *marché* buoyant; (*Phys*) *substance* activated, active; (*Ling*) active. **prendre une part ~ive à qch** to take an active part in sth; **dans la vie ~ive** in his (*ou* one's *etc*) working life; **entrer dans la vie ~ive** to begin one's working life; *voir* **armée², charbon** *etc.*

2 nm a (*Ling*) active (voice). **à l'~** in the active voice.

b (*Fin*) assets; *[succession]* credits. **~ circulant** current *ou* floating assets; **~ réalisable et disponible** current assets; **porter une somme à l'~** to put a sum on the assets side; (*fig*) **sa gentillesse est à mettre à son ~** his kindness is a point in his favour, on the credit *ou* positive *ou* plus* side there is his kindness (to consider); (*fig*) **il a plusieurs crimes à son ~** he has several crimes to his name; **il a plusieurs records à son ~** he has several records to his credit *ou* name.

c (*qui travaille*) person in active *ou* working life. **les ~s** people who work, the working population.

3 **active** nf (*Mil*) **l'~ive** the regular army.

actinium [aktinjɔm] nm actinium.

action [aksjɔ̃] 1 nf a (*acte*) action, act. **faire une bonne ~** to do a good deed; **~ audacieuse** act *ou* deed of daring, bold deed *ou* action; **vous avez commis là une mauvaise ~** you've done something (very) wrong, you've behaved badly.

b (*activité*) action. **être en ~** to be at work; **passer à l'~** to take action; **le moment est venu de passer à l'~** the time has come for action; (*Mil*) **passer à l'~, engager l'~** to go into battle *ou* action; **entrer en ~** *[troupes, canon]* to go into action; **mettre un plan en ~** to put a plan into action; **le dispositif de sécurité se mit en ~** the security device went off *ou* was set in action; *voir* **champ, feu¹, homme.**

c (*effet*) *[éléments naturels, loi, machine]* action; *[médicament]* action, effect. **ce médicament est sans ~** this medicine is ineffective *ou* has no effect; **sous l'~ du gel** under the action of frost, through the agency of frost; **machine à double ~** double-acting machine *ou* engine.

d (*initiative*) action. **engager une ~ commune** to take concerted action; **recourir à l'~ directe** to resort to *ou* have recourse to direct action; **politique d'~ régionale** regional development policy; **service d'~**

sanitaire et sociale health and social services departments.
e *[pièce, film]* (*mouvement, péripéties*) action; (*intrigue*) plot. ~! action!; **l'~ se passe en Grèce** the action takes place in Greece; **film d'~** action film; **roman d'~** action-packed novel.
f (*Jur*) action (at law), lawsuit. **~ juridique/civile** legal/civil action; *voir* **intenter**.
g (*Fin*) share. **~s** shares, stock(s); **~ ordinaire** ordinary share; **~s nominatives/au porteur** registered/bearer shares; **~ cotée** listed *ou* quoted share; **~ à dividende prioritaire** preference share (*Brit*), preferred share (*US*); **~ de chasse** hunting rights (*pl*); (*fig*) **ses ~s sont en hausse/baisse** things are looking up/are not looking so good for him; *voir* **société**.
h (*Mus*) *[piano]* action.
i (*Sport*) move.
2 comp ►**action en diffamation** (*Jur*) libel action ►**action d'éclat** dazzling *ou* brilliant feat *ou* deed ►**action de grâce(s)** thanksgiving ►**action revendicative** *[ouvriers]* industrial action (*NonC*); *[ménagères, étudiants]* protest (*NonC*) ►**l'action sociale** social welfare.

actionnaire [aksjɔnɛʀ] nmf shareholder.

actionnariat [aksjɔnaʀja] nm (*détention d'actions*) shareholding; (*personnes*) shareholders.

actionnement [aksjɔnmɑ̃] nm activating, activation.

actionner [aksjɔne] [1] vt a *mécanisme* to activate; *machine* to drive, work. **moteur actionné par la vapeur** steam-powered *ou* -driven engine; **~ la sonnette** to ring the bell. b (*Jur*) to sue, bring an action against. **~ qn en dommages et intérêts** to sue sb for damages.

activateur, -trice [aktivatœʀ, tʀis] 1 adj activating (*épith*). 2 nm activator.

activation [aktivasjɔ̃] nf (*Chim, Phys*) activation; (*Bio*) initiation of development.

activement [aktivmɑ̃] adv actively. **participer ~ à qch** to take an active part *ou* be actively involved in sth.

activer [aktive] [1] 1 vt a (*accélérer*) *processus, travaux* to speed up; (*aviver*) *feu* to stoke, pep up*. b (*Chim*) to activate. c (*Ordin*) to activate. 2 vi (*: *se dépêcher*) to get a move on*, get moving*. 3 **s'activer** vpr (*s'affairer*) to bustle about. **s'~ à faire** to be busy doing; **active-toi!*** get a move on!*

activisme [aktivism] nm activism.

activiste [aktivist] adj, nmf activist.

activité [aktivite] nf (*gén*) activity; (*emploi*) occupation. (*Scol*) **~s d'éveil** discovery; (*Scol*) **~s dirigées** class project work; **les rues sont pleines d'~** the streets are bustling with activity *ou* are very busy; **l'~ de la rue** the bustle of the street; **le passage de l'~ à la retraite** passing from active *ou* working life into retirement; (*Mil*) transfer from the active to the retired list; **avoir une ~ salariée** to be in paid employment; **ils ont étendu leurs ~s à la distribution** they have branched out into distribution; **être en ~** *[usine]* to function, be in operation; *[volcan]* to be active; *[fonctionnaire]* to be in active life; **être en pleine ~** *[usine, bureau]* to be operating at full strength, be in full operation; *[club]* to be running full-time; *[personne]* to be fully active; (*hum*) to be hard at it*.

actrice [aktʀis] nf (*Théât, fig*) actress.

actuaire [aktɥɛʀ] nmf actuary.

actualisation [aktɥalizasjɔ̃] nf (*voir* **actualiser**) actualization; updating; updated forecast; discounting.

actualiser [aktɥalize] [1] vt (*Ling, Philos*) to actualize; (*mettre à jour*) *ouvrage, règlement* to update, bring up to date; *coûts* to give an updated forecast of; *somme due* to discount. **cash-flow actualisé** discounted cash flow.

actualité [aktɥalite] nf a *[livre, sujet]* topicality. **livre d'~** topical book. b (*événements*) **l'~** current events; **l'~ sportive** the sporting *ou* sports news. c (*Ciné, Presse*) **les ~s** the news; **les ~s télévisées** (the) television news; **il est passé aux ~s*** he was on the news. d (*Philos*) actuality.

actuariel, -elle [aktɥaʀjɛl] adj actuarial.

actuel, -elle [aktɥɛl] adj a (*présent*) present, current. **à l'heure ~le** at the present time; **à l'époque ~le** nowadays, in this day and age; **le monde ~** the world today, the presentday world. b (*d'actualité*) *livre, problème* topical. c (*Philos, Rel*) actual.

actuellement [aktɥɛlmɑ̃] adv at the moment, at present.

acuité [akɥite] nf *[son]* shrillness; *[douleur]* acuteness, intensity; *[sens]* sharpness, acuteness; *[crise politique]* acuteness.

acuponcteur, acupuncteur [akypɔ̃ktœʀ] nm acupuncturist.

acuponcture, acupuncture [akypɔ̃ktyʀ] nf acupuncture.

acyclique [asiklik] adj (*gén*) non-cyclical; (*Chim*) acyclic.

a/d (abrév de **à dater, à la date de**) as from.

ADAC [adak] nm (abrév de **avion à décollage et atterrissage courts**) STOL.

adage [adaʒ] nm adage, saying.

adagio [ada(d)ʒjo] nm adagio.

Adam [adɑ̃] nm Adam. (*hum*) **en costume** *ou* **tenue d'~** in one's birthday suit; *voir* **pomme**.

adamantin, e [adamɑ̃tɛ̃, in] adj (*littér*) adamantine.

adaptabilité [adaptabilite] nf adaptability.

adaptable [adaptabl] adj adaptable.

adaptateur, -trice [adaptatœʀ, tʀis] 1 nm,f (*Ciné, Théât*) adapter. 2 nm (*Tech*) adapter.

adaptation [adaptasjɔ̃] nf (*gén, Ciné, Théât*) adaptation. **faire un effort d'~** to try to adapt; **faculté d'~** adaptability.

adapter [adapte] [1] 1 vt a (*appliquer*) **~ une prise/un mécanisme à** to fit a plug/a mechanism to; **ces mesures sont-elles bien adaptées à la situation?** are these measures really suited to the situation?; **~ la musique aux paroles** to fit the music to the words. b (*modifier*) *conduite, méthode, organisation* to adapt (*à* to); *roman, pièce* to adapt (*pour* for). 2 **s'adapter** vpr a (*s'habituer*) to adapt (o.s.) (*à* to). b (*s'appliquer*) *[objet, prise]* **s'~ à** to fit.

ADAV [adav] nm (abrév de **avion à décollage et atterrissage verticaux**) VTOL.

addenda [adɛ̃da] nm inv addenda.

Addis-Ababa [adisababa], **Addis Abeba** [adisabəba] n Addis Ababa.

additif, -ive [aditif, iv] 1 adj (*Math*) additive. 2 nm (*note, clause*) additional clause, rider; (*substance*) additive. **~ budgétaire** supplemental budget.

addition [adisjɔ̃] nf (*gén*) addition; (*problème*) addition, sum; (*facture*) bill, check (*US*). **par ~ de** by adding, by the addition of.

additionnel, -elle [adisjɔnɛl] adj additional; *voir* **centime**.

additionner [adisjɔne] [1] 1 vt (*lit, fig*) to add up. **~ qch à** to add sth to; **~ le vin de sucre** to add sugar to the wine, mix sugar with the wine; (*sur étiquette*) **additionné d'alcool** with alcohol added. 2 **s'additionner** vpr to add up.

additionneur [adisjɔnœʀ] nm adder (*machine*).

adducteur [adyktœʀ] adj m, nm: **(canal) ~** feeder (canal); **(muscle) ~** adductor.

adduction [adyksjɔ̃] nf (*Anat*) adduction. (*Tech*) **~ d'eau** water conveyance; **travaux d'~ d'eau** laying on water.

Adelaïde [adəlaid] nf Adelaide.

Aden [adɛn] n Aden.

adepte [adɛpt] nmf *[doctrine, mouvement]* follower; *[activité]* enthusiast. **faire des ~s** to win over *ou* gain followers; **les ~s du deltaplane** hang-gliding enthusiasts.

adéquat, e [adekwa(t), at] adj (*gén*) appropriate, suitable, fitting; (*Gram*) adequate. **utiliser le vocabulaire ~** to use the appropriate vocabulary; **ces installations ne sont pas ~es** these facilities are not suitable.

adéquation [adekwasjɔ̃] nf appropriateness; *[grammaire]* adequacy.

adhérence [adeʀɑ̃s] nf (*gén*) adhesion (*à* to); *[pneus, semelles]* grip (*à* on), adhesion (*à* to). *[voiture]* **~ (à la route)** roadholding.

adhérent, e [adeʀɑ̃, ɑ̃t] 1 adj: **~ à** which sticks *ou* adheres to. 2 nm,f member, adherent.

adhérer [adeʀe] [6] adhérer à vt indir a (*coller*) to stick to, adhere to. **~ à la route** *[pneu]* to grip the road; *[voiture]* to hold *ou* grip the road; **ça adhère bien** it sticks *ou* adheres well; it grips the road well. b (*se rallier à*) *point de vue* to support, adhere to (*frm*); *idéal* to adhere to. c (*devenir membre de*) to join; (*être membre de*) to be a member of, belong to.

adhésif, -ive [adezif, iv] 1 adj adhesive, sticky. **pansement ~** sticking plaster (*Brit*), Band-Aid ® (*US*); **papier ~** sticky(-backed) paper. 2 nm adhesive.

adhésion [adezjɔ̃] nf a (*accord*) support (*à* for), adherence (*frm*) (*à* to). b (*inscription*) joining; (*fait d'être membre*) membership (*à* of). **son ~ au club** his joining the club; **bulletin/campagne d'~** membership form/drive; **il y a 3 nouvelles ~s cette semaine** 3 new members joined this week, there have been 3 new memberships this week.

ad hoc [adɔk] adj inv appropriate, tailor-made.

adieu, pl ~x [adjø] 1 nm a (*salut*) farewell, goodbye. (*lit, fig*) **dire ~ à** to say goodbye *ou* farewell to; **baiser d'~** farewell kiss. b (*séparation*) **~x** farewells; **faire ses ~x (à qn)** to say one's farewells (to sb). 2 excl (*au revoir*) goodbye, cheerio* (*Brit*), farewell (††), adieu (††); (*dial: bonjour*) hullo, hi*. (*fig*) **~ la tranquillité/les vacances** goodbye to (our) peace and quiet/our holidays.

à-Dieu-va(t) [adjøva(t)] excl it's all in God's hands!

adipeux, -euse [adipø, øz] adj (*Anat*) adipose; *visage* fleshy.

adiposité [adipozite] nf adiposity.

adjacent, e [adʒasɑ̃, ɑ̃t] adj adjacent, adjoining. **~ à** adjacent to, adjoining; *voir* **angle**.

adjectif, -ive [adʒɛktif, iv] 1 adj adjectival, adjective (*épith*). 2 nm adjective. **~ substantivé/qualificatif** nominalized/qualifying adjective; **~ attribut/épithète** predicative/attributive adjective.

adjectival, e, mpl -aux [adʒɛktival, o] adj adjectival.

adjectivé, e [adʒɛktive] adj used as an adjective.

adjectivement [adʒɛktivmɑ̃] adv adjectivally, as an adjective.

adjoindre [adʒwɛ̃dʀ] [49] vt a (*associer*) **~ un collaborateur à qn** to appoint sb as an assistant to sb; **~ qn à un comité** to appoint sb to a committee; **s'~ un collaborateur** to take on *ou* appoint an assistant. b (*ajouter*) **~ une pièce/un dispositif à qch** to attach *ou* affix a part/device to sth; **~ un chapitre à un ouvrage** to add a chapter to a book; (*à la fin*) to append a chapter to a book.

adjoint, e [adʒwɛ̃, wɛ̃t] (**ptp de adjoindre**) 1 **adj: commissaire** *etc* ~ assistant commissioner *etc; voir* **professeur.** 2 **nm,f** assistant. ~ **au maire** deputy mayor; ~ **d'enseignement** non-certificated teacher. 3 **nm** (*Ling*) adjunct.

adjonction [adʒɔ̃ksjɔ̃] **nf** a (*action*) *[collaborateur]* addition; *[article, chapitre]* addition, (*à la fin*) appending (*à* to); *[dispositif]* attaching, affixing (*à* to). **l'~ de 2 secrétaires à l'équipe** the addition of 2 secretaries to the team, the appointment of 2 extra *ou* additional secretaries to the team. b (*chose ajoutée*) addition.

adjudant [adʒydɑ̃] **nm** (*gén*) warrant officer; (*Aviat US*) senior master sergeant. ~ **chef** warrant officer 1st class (*Brit*), chief warrant officer (*US*).

adjudicataire [adʒydikatɛʀ] **nmf** (*aux enchères*) purchaser; (*soumissionnaire*) successful bidder.

adjudicateur, -trice [adʒydikatœʀ, tʀis] **nm,f** *[enchères]* seller; *[contrat]* awarder.

adjudication [adʒydikasjɔ̃] **nf** a (*vente aux enchères*) sale by auction; (*marché administratif*) invitation to tender, putting up for tender; (*contrat*) contract. **par (voie d')~** by auction; by tender; **mettre en vente par** ~ to put up for sale by auction; **offrir par** ~ to put up for tender; ~ **forcée** compulsory sale. b (*attribution*) *[contrat]* awarding (*à* to); *[meuble, tableau]* auctioning (*à* to).

adjuger [adʒyʒe] [3] 1 **vt** a (*aux enchères*) to knock down, auction (*à* to). **une fois, deux fois, trois fois, adjugé(, vendu)!** going, going, gone!; **ceci fut adjugé pour 30 F** this went for *ou* was sold for 30 francs. b (*attribuer*) *contrat, avantage, récompense* to award; (**: donner*) *place, objet* to give. 2 **s'adjuger vpr** (*obtenir*) *contrat, récompense* to win; (*s'approprier*) to take for o.s. **il s'est adjugé la meilleure place** he has taken the best seat for himself, he has given himself the best seat.

adjuration [adʒyʀasjɔ̃] **nf** entreaty, plea.

adjurer [adʒyʀe] [1] **vt:** ~ **qn de faire** to implore *ou* beg sb to do.

adjuvant [adʒyvɑ̃] **nm** (*médicament*) adjuvant; (*additif*) additive; (*stimulant*) stimulant; (*Ling*) adjunct.

ad lib(itum) [adlib(itɔm)] **adv** ad lib.

admettre [admɛtʀ] [56] **vt** a (*laisser entrer*) *visiteur, démarcheur* to admit, let in. **la salle ne pouvait** ~ **que 50 personnes** the room could only accommodate *ou* seat *ou* admit 50 people; **les chiens ne sont pas admis dans le magasin** dogs are not allowed in the shop; (*sur écriteau*) no dogs (allowed); **il fut admis dans une grande pièce** he was ushered *ou* shown *ou* admitted into a large room; (*Tech*) **l'air/le liquide est admis dans le cylindre** the air/the liquid is allowed to pass into the cylinder.

b (*recevoir*) *hôte* to receive; *nouveau membre* to admit. ~ **qn à sa table** to receive sb at one's table; **il a été admis chez le ministre** he was received by the minister, he was admitted to see the minister; **se faire** ~ **dans un club** to gain admittance to *ou* be admitted to a club.

c (*Scol, Univ*) (*à un examen*) to pass; (*dans une classe*) to admit, accept. **ils ont admis 30 candidats** they passed 30 of the candidates; **il a été admis au concours** he passed *ou* got through the exam; **il a été admis dans un bon rang au concours** he came out well in *ou* got a good place in the exam; **il a/il n'a pas été admis en classe supérieure** he will move up into *ou* he will be admitted to/he didn't get into *ou* won't be admitted to the next class; **lire la liste des admis au concours** to read the list of successful candidates in *ou* of those who passed the (competitive) exam.

d (*convenir de*) *défaite, erreur* to admit, acknowledge. **il n'admet jamais ses torts** he never accepts *ou* admits he's in the wrong; **je suis prêt à** ~ **que vous aviez raison** I'm ready to accept *ou* admit *ou* concede *ou* acknowledge that you were right; **il est admis que, c'est chose admise que** it's an accepted *ou* acknowledged fact that, it's generally admitted that.

e (*accepter*) *excuses, raisons* to accept; (*Jur*) *pourvoi* to accept.

f (*supposer*) to suppose, assume. **en admettant que** supposing *ou* assuming that.

g (*tolérer*) *ton, attitude, indiscipline* to allow, accept. **je n'admets pas qu'il se conduise ainsi** I won't allow *ou* permit him to behave like that, I won't stand for *ou* accept such behaviour (from him); (*Admin*) ~ **qn à siéger** to admit sb (*as a new member*); (*Admin*) **admis à faire valoir ses droits à la retraite** entitled to retire.

h (*laisser place à*) to admit of. **ton qui n'admet pas de réplique** a tone which brooks no reply; **règle qui n'admet aucune exception** rule which allows of *ou* admits of no exception; **règle qui admet plusieurs exceptions** rule which allows for several exceptions.

administrateur, -trice [administʀatœʀ, tʀis] **nm,f** (*gén*) administrator; *[banque, entreprise]* director; *[fondation]* trustee. ~ **de biens** property manager; ~ **judiciaire** receiver; ~ **civil** *high-ranking civil servant acting as aide to a minister*.

administratif, -ive [administʀatif, iv] **adj** administrative.

administration [administʀasjɔ̃] **nf** a (*gérance: voir* **administrer**) management; running; administration; government. **je laisse l'~ de mes affaires à mon notaire** I leave my lawyer to deal with my affairs, I leave my affairs in the hands of my lawyer, I leave the handling of my affairs to my lawyer; ~ **légale** guardianship (*parental*); *[société]* **être placé sous** ~ **judiciaire** to go into receivership; *voir* **conseil.**

b *[médicament, sacrement]* administering, administration.

c (*service public*) (sector of the) public services. **l'A~** ≃ the Civil Service (*Brit*); **l'~ locale** local government; **être** *ou* **travailler dans l'~** to work in the public services; **l'~ des Douanes** ≃ the Customs and Excise (*Brit*); **l'~ des Eaux et Forêts** ≃ the Forestry Commission (*Brit*); **l'~ des Impôts** the tax department, ≃ the Inland Revenue (*Brit*), the Internal Revenue (*US*); (*Police*) **l'~ centrale** (the) police headquarters; **l'~ pénitentiaire** the prison authorities.

administrativement [administʀativmɑ̃] **adv** administratively. **interné** ~ formally committed (to mental hospital).

administré, e [administʀe] **nm,f** *[maire]* citizen. **informer ses ~s** to notify *ou* inform one's town (*ou* city).

administrer [administʀe] [1] **vt** a (*gérer*) *affaires, entreprise* to manage, run; *fondation* to administer; *pays* to run, govern; *commune* to run. b (*dispenser*) *justice, remède, sacrement* to administer; *coup, gifle* to deal, administer; (*Jur*) *preuve* to produce.

admirable [admiʀabl] **adj** admirable, wonderful. **être ~ de courage** to show admirable *ou* wonderful courage; **portrait ~ de vérité** portrait showing a wonderful likeness.

admirablement [admiʀabləmɑ̃] **adv** admirably, wonderfully.

admirateur, -trice [admiʀatœʀ, tʀis] **nm,f** admirer.

admiratif, -ive [admiʀatif, iv] **adj** admiring. **d'un air** ~ admiringly.

admiration [admiʀasjɔ̃] **nf** admiration. **faire l'~ de qn, remplir qn d'~** to fill sb with admiration; **tomber/être en ~ devant qch/qn** to be filled with/lost in admiration for sth/sb.

admirativement [admiʀativmɑ̃] **adv** admiringly, in admiration.

admirer [admiʀe] [1] **vt** to admire; (*iro*) to admire, marvel at.

admissibilité [admisibilite] **nf** *[postulant]* eligibility (*à* for); (*Scol, Univ*) *eligibility to sit the oral part of an exam.*

admissible [admisibl] 1 **adj** a *procédé* admissible, acceptable; *excuse* acceptable. **ce comportement n'est pas** ~ this behaviour is quite inadmissible *ou* unacceptable. b *postulant* eligible (*à* for); (*Scol, Univ*) *having passed the written part of an exam.* 2 **nmf** eligible candidate.

admission [admisjɔ̃] **nf** a (*dans un lieu, club*) admission, admittance, entry (*à* to). (*Univ*) ~ **à un concours** gaining a place in an exam, passing an exam; (*Scol, Univ*) ~ **à une école** (gaining) acceptance *ou* entrance to a school; **son ~ (au club) a été obtenue non sans mal** he had some difficulty in gaining admission *ou* entry (to the club); **faire une demande d'~ à un club** to apply to join *ou* make application to join a club, apply for membership of a club; (*Douane*) ~ **temporaire d'un véhicule** temporary importation of a vehicle; (*Univ*) **le nombre des ~s au concours a augmenté** the number of successful candidates in this exam has gone up.

b (*Tech: introduction*) intake; (*Aut*) induction; *voir* **soupape.**

admonestation [admɔnɛstasjɔ̃] **nf** (*littér*) admonition, admonishment.

admonester [admɔnɛste] [1] **vt** (*gén, Jur*) to admonish.

admonition [admɔnisjɔ̃] **nf** (*littér, Jur*) admonition, admonishment.

ADN [ɑdeɛn] **nm** (**abrév de acide désoxyribonucléique**) DNA.

adnominal, e, mpl -aux [adnɔminal, o] **adj** (*Ling*) adnominal.

ado* [ado] **nmf abrév de adolescent, e.**

adolescence [adɔlesɑ̃s] **nf** adolescence. **ses années d'~** his adolescent *ou* teenage years.

adolescent, e [adɔlesɑ̃, ɑ̃t] 1 **adj** (*littér*) adolescent (*épith*). 2 **nm,f** adolescent, teenager; (*Méd, Psych*) adolescent.

Adonis [adɔnis] **nm** (*Myth, fig*) Adonis.

adonner (s') [adɔne] [1] **vpr: s'~ à** *art, études* to devote o.s. to; *sport, hobby* to devote o.s. to, go in for; *boisson, vice* to give o.s. over to, take to; **adonné au jeu** addicted to gambling.

adoptant, e [adɔptɑ̃, ɑ̃t] **nm, f** person wishing to adopt.

adopter [adɔpte] [1] **vt** a *enfant* to adopt; (*fig: accueillir*) to adopt. b *attitude, religion, nom, mesure* to adopt; *cause* to take up, adopt. c *loi* to pass; *motion* to pass, adopt. **cette proposition a été adoptée à l'unanimité** this proposal was carried unanimously.

adoptif, -ive [adɔptif, iv] **adj** *enfant, patrie* adopted; *parent* adoptive.

adoption [adɔpsjɔ̃] **nf** (*voir* **adopter**) adoption; passing. **pays d'~** country of adoption; **un Londonien d'~** a Londoner by adoption.

adorable [adɔʀabl] **adj** *personne* adorable, delightful; *robe, village* lovely, delightful.

adorablement [adɔʀabləmɑ̃] **adv** delightfully, adorably.

adorateur, -trice [adɔʀatœʀ, tʀis] **nm,f** (*Rel, fig*) worshipper.

adoration [adɔʀasjɔ̃] **nf** adoration, worship. **être en ~ devant** to dote on, worship, idolize.

adorer [adɔʀe] [1] **vt** *personne, dieu etc* to adore, worship; *chose* to adore; *voir* **brûler.**

adosser [adose] [1] 1 **vt:** ~ **à** *ou* **contre qch** *meuble* to stand against sth; *échelle* to stand *ou* lean against sth; *bâtiment* to build against *ou* onto sth; **il était adossé au pilier** he was leaning with his back against the pillar. 2 **s'adosser vpr: s'~ à** *ou* **contre qch** *[personne]* to lean with one's back against sth; *[bâtiment]* to be built against *ou* onto sth, back onto sth.

adoubement [adubmɑ̃] **nm** (*Hist*) dubbing.

adouber [adube] [1] **vt** (*Hist*) to dub; (*Dames, Échecs*) to adjust.

adoucir [adusiʀ] [2] 1 **vt** a *saveur, acidité* to make milder *ou*

smoother; (*avec sucre*) to sweeten; *rudesse, voix, peau* to soften; *couleur, contraste* to soften, tone down; *caractère, personne* to mellow; *chagrin* to soothe, allay, ease; *conditions pénibles, épreuve* to ease; *dureté, remarque* to mitigate, soften. **pour ~ ses vieux jours** to comfort (him in) his old age; **pour ~ sa solitude** to ease his loneliness; **le vent du Midi a adouci la température** the south wind has made the weather warmer *ou* milder *ou* raised the temperature; **~ la condamnation de qn** to reduce sb's sentence; *voir* **musique**.
b (*Tech*) *eau* to soften.
2 **s'adoucir** vpr *[saveur, acidité]* to become milder *ou* smoother; (*avec sucre*) to become sweeter; *[voix, couleur, peau]* to soften; *[caractère, personne]* to mellow. **la température s'est adoucie** the weather has got milder; **vers le haut la pente s'adoucit** towards the top the slope became gentler *ou* less steep.

adoucissant, e [adusisɑ̃, ɑ̃t] 1 adj *crème, lotion* for smoother skin; *sirop* soothing. 2 nm fabric softener, fabric conditioner.

adoucissement [adusismɑ̃] nm (*voir* **adoucir**) sweetening; softening; toning-down; smoothing-out; mellowing; soothing; allaying; alleviation. **on espère un ~ de la température** we are hoping for milder weather *ou* a slight rise in the temperature; **apporter des ~s aux conditions de vie des prisonniers** to make the living conditions of the prisoners easier *ou* less harsh.

adoucisseur [adusisœʀ] nm: **~ (d'eau)** water softener.

ad patres* [adpatʀɛs] adv (*hum*) **expédier** *ou* **envoyer qn ~** to send sb to kingdom come*.

adrénaline [adʀenalin] nf adrenalin.

adressage [adʀesaʒ] nm mailing; (*Ordin*) addressing.

adresse[1] [adʀɛs] nf a (*domicile*) address. **partir sans laisser d'~** to leave without giving a forwarding address; **à Paris je connais quelques bonnes ~s de restaurants** in Paris I know (the names *ou* addresses of) some good restaurants; *voir* **carnet**. b (*frm: message*) address. **à l'~ de** for the benefit of. c (*Lexicographie*) headword; (*Ordin, Ling*) address.

adresse[2] [adʀɛs] nf (*habileté*) deftness, dexterity, skill; (*subtilité, finesse*) shrewdness, skill, cleverness; (*tact*) adroitness. **jeu/exercice d'~** game/exercise of skill; **il eut l'~ de ne rien révéler** he was adroit enough *ou* shrewd enough not to say anything; *voir* **tour**.

adresser [adʀese] [1] 1 vt a **~ une lettre/un colis à** (*envoyer*) to send a letter/parcel to; (*écrire l'adresse*) to address a letter/parcel to; **la lettre m'était personnellement adressée** the letter was addressed to me personally; **mon médecin m'a adressé à un spécialiste** my doctor sent *ou* referred me to a specialist.
b **~ une remarque/une requête à** to address a remark/a request to; **~ une accusation/un reproche à** to level an accusation/a reproach at *ou* against, aim an accusation/a reproach at; **~ une allusion/un coup à** to aim a remark/a blow at; **~ un compliment/ses respects à** to pay a compliment/one's respects to; **~ une prière à** to address a prayer to; (*à Dieu*) to offer (up) a prayer to; **~ un regard furieux à qn** to direct an angry look at sb; **il m'adressa un signe de tête/un geste de la main** he nodded/waved at me; **~ un sourire à qn** to give sb a smile, smile at sb; **~ la parole à qn** to speak to *ou* address sb; **il m'adressa une critique acerbe** he criticized me harshly; (*sur lettre*) **je vous adresse mes meilleurs vœux** please accept my best wishes.
c (*Ordin*) to address.
2 **s'adresser** vpr a (*adresser la parole à*) **s'~ à qn** to speak to sb, address sb; (*fig*) **il s'adresse à un public féminin** *[discours, magazine]* it is intended for *ou* aimed at a female audience; *[auteur]* he writes for *ou* is addressing a female audience; (*fig*) **ce livre s'adresse à notre générosité** this book is directed at *ou* appeals to our generosity; **cette remarque s'adresse à tout le monde** this remark is addressed to everyone.
b (*aller trouver*) **s'~ à** *personne* to go and see; (*Admin*) *personne, bureau* to apply to; **adressez-vous au concierge** go and see (*ou* ask, tell *etc*) the concierge; **adressez-vous au secrétariat** enquire at the office, go and ask at the office; (*hum*) **il vaut mieux s'~ à Dieu qu'à ses saints** it's best to go straight to the (man *ou* woman at the) top.

adret [adʀɛ] nm (*Géog*) south-facing slope.

Adriatique [adʀijatik] adj f, nf: **(mer) ~** Adriatic (Sea).

Adrien [adʀijɛ̃] nm Adrian.

adroit, e [adʀwa, wat] adj (*habile*) skilful, dext(e)rous, deft; (*subtil*) shrewd, skilled, clever; (*plein de tact*) adroit. **~ de ses mains** clever with one's hands, dext(e)rous.

adroitement [adʀwatmɑ̃] adv (*voir* **adroit**) skilfully; deftly; dext(e)rously; shrewdly; cleverly; adroitly.

adsorber [atsɔʀbe] [1] vt to adsorb.

adsorption [atsɔʀpsjɔ̃] nf adsorption.

adulateur, -trice [adylatœʀ, tʀis] nm,f (*littér*) (*admirateur*) adulator; (*flatteur*) sycophant.

adulation [adylasjɔ̃] nf (*littér*) (*admiration*) adulation; (*flatterie*) sycophancy.

aduler [adyle] [1] vt (*littér*) (*admirer*) to adulate; (*flatter*) to flatter.

adulte [adylt] 1 adj *personne* adult (*épith*); *animal, plante* fully-grown, mature; (*fig: mûr*) *attitude, comportement* adult, mature; *voir* **âge**. 2 nmf adult, grown-up.

adultère [adyltɛʀ] 1 adj *relations, désir* adulterous. **femme ~** adulteress; **homme ~** adulterer. 2 nm (*acte*) adultery; *voir* **constat**.

adultérin, e [adylteʀɛ̃, in] adj (*Jur*) *enfant* born of adultery.

ad valorem [advalɔʀɛm] loc adj ad valorem.

advenir [advəniʀ] [22] 1 vb impers a (*survenir*) **~ que** to happen that, come to pass that (*littér*); **~ à** to happen to, befall (*littér*); **qu'est-il advenu au prisonnier?** what has happened to the prisoner?; **il m'advient de faire** I sometimes happen to do; **advienne que pourra** come what may; **quoi qu'il advienne** whatever happens *ou* may happen. b (*devenir, résulter de*) **~ de** to become of; **qu'est-il advenu du prisonnier/du projet?** what has become of the prisoner/the project?; **on ne sait pas ce qu'il en adviendra** nobody knows what will come of it *ou* how it will turn out. 2 vi (*arriver*) to happen.

adventice [advɑ̃tis] adj (*Bot*) self-propagating; (*Philos, littér: accessoire*) adventitious.

adventif, -ive [advɑ̃tif, iv] adj (*Bot*) *bourgeon, racine* adventitious.

adventiste [advɑ̃tist] nmf Adventist.

adverbe [advɛʀb] nm adverb.

adverbial, e, mpl **-iaux** [advɛʀbjal, jo] adj adverbial.

adverbialement [advɛʀbjalmɑ̃] adv adverbially.

adversaire [advɛʀsɛʀ] nmf (*gén*) opponent, adversary; (*Mil*) adversary, enemy; *[théorie]* opponent.

adversatif, -ive [advɛʀsatif, iv] adj adversative.

adverse [advɛʀs] adj *partie, forces, bloc* opposing. (*littér*) **la fortune ~** adverse fortune; (*Jur*) **la partie ~** the other side.

adversité [advɛʀsite] nf adversity.

ad vitam æternam* [advitamεtɛʀnam] loc adv till kingdom come.

AE [aə] 1 nm (abrév de **adjoint d'enseignement**) *voir* **adjoint**. 2 nfpl (abrév de **affaires étrangères**) *voir* **affaire**.

aède [aɛd] nm (Greek) bard.

AEE [aəə] nf (abrév de **Agence pour les économies d'énergie**) *voir* **agence**.

AELE [aəɛlə] nf (abrév de **Association européenne de libre-échange**) EFTA.

AEN [aəɛn] nf (abrév de **Agence pour l'énergie nucléaire**) ≃ AEA.

aérage [aeʀaʒ] nm ventilation.

aérateur [aeʀatœʀ] nm ventilator.

aération [aeʀasjɔ̃] nf *[pièce, literie]* airing; *[terre, racine]* aeration; (*circulation d'air*) ventilation; *voir* **conduit**.

aéré, e [aeʀe] (ptp de **aérer**) adj *pièce* airy, well-ventilated; *page* well spaced out; *voir* **centre**.

aérer [aeʀe] [6] 1 vt *pièce, literie* to air; *terre, racine* to aerate; (*fig: alléger*) *exposé, présentation* to lighten. 2 **s'aérer** vpr *[personne]* to get some fresh air. **s'~ les idées** to clear one's mind.

aérien, -ienne [aeʀjɛ̃, jɛn] 1 adj a (*Aviat*) *espace, droit* air (*épith*); *navigation, photographie* aerial (*épith*); *attaque* aerial (*épith*), air (*épith*). **base ~ne** air base; *voir* **compagnie, ligne, métro**. b (*léger*) *silhouette* sylphlike; *démarche* light, floating; *musique, poésie* ethereal. c (*Bot*) *racine* aerial; (*Téléc*) *circuit, câble* overhead (*épith*); (*Géog*) *courant, mouvement* air (*épith*). 2 nm (*Rad: antenne*) aerial.

aérium [aeʀjɔm] nm sanatorium, sanitarium (*US*).

aérobic [aeʀɔbik] nf aerobics (*sg*).

aérobie [aeʀɔbi] adj aerobic.

aéro-club, pl **aéro-clubs** [aeʀoklœb] nm flying club.

aérodrome [aeʀodʀom] nm aerodrome (*Brit*), airfield.

aérodynamique [aeʀodinamik] 1 adj *soufflerie, expérience* aerodynamics (*épith*); *ligne, véhicule* streamlined, aerodynamic. 2 nf aerodynamics (*sg*).

aérodynamisme [aeʀodinamism] nm aerodynamic shape.

aérofrein [aeʀofʀɛ̃] nm air brake.

aérogare [aeʀogaʀ] nf (air) terminal.

aéroglisseur [aeʀoglisœʀ] nm hovercraft.

aérogramme [aeʀɔgʀam] nm airmail letter.

aérographe [aeʀɔgʀaf] nm airbrush.

aérolit(h)e [aeʀɔlit] nm aerolite, aerolith.

aéromodélisme [aeʀomɔdelism] nm model aircraft making.

aéronaute [aeʀonot] nmf aeronaut.

aéronautique [aeʀonotik] 1 adj aeronautical. 2 nf aeronautics (*sg*).

aéronaval, e, pl **~s** [aeʀonaval] adj *forces* air and sea (*épith*). **l'A~e** ≃ the Fleet Air Arm (*Brit*).

aéronef [aeʀɔnɛf] nm (*Admin*) aircraft.

aérophagie [aeʀɔfaʒi] nf: **il a** *ou* **fait de l'~** he suffers from abdominal wind.

aéroplane† [aeʀɔplan] nm aeroplane (*Brit*), airplane (*US*).

aéroport [aeʀɔpɔʀ] nm airport.

aéroporté, e [aeʀɔpɔʀte] adj *troupes* airborne (*Brit*), airmobile (*US*); *matériel* airlifted, brought *ou* ferried by air (*attrib*).

aéroportuaire [aeʀɔpɔʀtɥɛʀ] adj airport (*épith*).

aéropostal, e, mpl **-aux** [aeʀopɔstal, o] adj airmail (*épith*). (*Hist*) **l'A~e** the (French) airmail service.

aérosol [aeʀɔsɔl] nm aerosol. **déodorant en ~** deodorant spray, spray-on *ou* aerosol deodorant.

aérospatial, e, mpl **-iaux** [aeʀospasjal, jo] 1 adj aerospace (*épith*). 2 **aérospatiale** nf aerospace science.

aérostat [aeʀɔsta] nm aerostat.

aérostatique [aeʀɔstatik] 1 adj aerostatic. 2 nf aerostatics *(sg)*.
aérotrain [aeʀotʀɛ̃] nm ® hovertrain.
AF[1] [aɛf] nmpl (abrév de anciens francs) old francs.
AF[2] [aɛf] nf (abrév de allocations familiales) *voir* allocation.
AFAT [afat] nf (abrév de auxiliaire féminin de l'armée de terre) *member of the women's army*.
affabilité [afabilite] nf affability.
affable [afabl] adj affable.
affablement [afabləmɑ̃] adv affably.
affabulateur, -trice [afabylatœʀ, tʀis] nm,f inveterate liar, story-teller, romancer.
affabulation [afabylasjɔ̃] nf a (*mensonges*) **c'est de l'~, ce sont des ~s** it's all made up, it's pure fabrication. b *[roman]* (construction of the) plot.
affabuler [afabyle] 1 vi to invent *ou* make up stories.
affacturage [afaktyʀaʒ] nm (*Jur*) factoring.
affactureur [afaktyʀœʀ] nm (*Jur*) factor.
affadir [afadiʀ] 2 1 vt *aliment* to make tasteless *ou* insipid; *couleur, style* to make dull *ou* uninteresting *ou* colourless. 2 **s'affadir** vpr *[couleur, style]* to become dull, pall; *[aliment]* to lose (its) flavour, become tasteless *ou* insipid.
affadissement [afadismɑ̃] nm *[aliment]* loss of flavour (*de* in, from); *[saveur, style]* weakening (*de* of); *[couleurs, sensations]* dulling (*de* of).
affaiblir [afebliʀ] 2 1 vt (*gén*) to weaken.
2 **s'affaiblir** vpr *[personne, autorité, résolution, facultés]* to weaken, grow *ou* become weaker; *[vue]* to grow *ou* get dim *ou* weaker; *[son]* to fade (away), grow fainter; *[intérêt]* to wane; *[vent, tempête]* to abate, die down. **le sens de ce mot s'est affaibli** the meaning of this word has got weaker.
affaiblissement [afeblismɑ̃] nm (*gén*) weakening; *[bruit]* fading (away).
affaire [afɛʀ] 1 nf a (*problème*) matter, business. **j'ai à régler deux ou trois ~s urgentes** I've got two or three urgent matters to settle; **ce n'est pas une petite** *ou* **une mince ~** it's no small matter; **il faut tirer cette ~ au clair** we must get to the bottom of this business, we must sort out this business; **tirer** *ou* **sortir qn d'~** to help sb out, get sb out of a tight spot*; **il est assez grand pour se tirer d'~ tout seul** he's big enough to manage on his own *ou* to sort it out by himself; **c'est une ~ d'hommes** it's men's business; **c'est mon ~, non la tienne** it's my business *ou* affair, not yours; **ce n'est pas ton ~** it's none of your business; **j'en fais mon ~** I'll deal with that; **c'était une ~ bâclée en cinq minutes** it was a botched and hurried job; **comment je fais? — c'est TON ~!** what do I do? — that's YOUR problem!
b (*ce qui convient*) **j'ai là votre ~** I've got (just) what you want; **cet employé fera/ne fait pas l'~** this employee will do nicely/won't do (for the job); **ça fait mon ~** that's (just) what I want *ou* need; **cela fera bien l'~ de quelqu'un** that will (certainly) come in handy *ou* do nicely for somebody.
c (*scandale*) business, affair, matter. **on a voulu étouffer l'~** they wanted to hush the business *ou* matter up; **il a essayé d'arranger l'~** he tried to straighten out *ou* settle the matter; **c'est une sale ~** it's a nasty business; **l'~ Dreyfus** the Dreyfus affair; **l'~ de Suez** the Suez crisis; **une grave ~ de corruption/d'espionnage** a serious affair of corruption/espionage, a serious corruption/spy case; **c'est une ~ de gros sous** there's big money involved; **c'est une ~ à suivre** it's something *ou* a matter worth watching *ou* keeping an eye on.
d (*Jur, Police*) case. **l'~ X** the X case; **être sur une ~** to be on a case; **une ~ de vol** a case of theft; **son ~ est claire** it's an open and shut case.
e (*transaction*) deal, bargain, transaction. **une (bonne) ~** a good deal, a (good) bargain; **une mauvaise ~** a bad deal *ou* bargain; **faire ~ avec qn** to make a bargain with sb, conclude *ou* clinch a deal with sb; **ils font des ~s (d'or)** they're making money hand over fist, they're raking it in*; **ils font beaucoup d'~s** they do a lot of business; **l'~ est faite!** *ou* **conclue!** that's the deal settled!; **l'~ est dans le sac*** it's in the bag*.
f (*firme*) business, concern. **c'est une ~ qui marche/en or** it's a going concern/a gold mine; **il a repris l'~ de son père** he has taken on *ou* over his father's business.
g (*intérêts publics et privés*) **~s** affairs; **les ~s culturelles/de la municipalité/étrangères/publiques** cultural/municipal/foreign/public affairs; (*Can*) **A~s extérieures** External Affairs (*Can*); (*au Québec*) **A~s intergouvernementales** Intergovernmental Affairs (*Can*), Foreign Affairs; **mettre de l'ordre dans ses ~s** to put one's affairs in order; **occupe-toi de tes ~s** mind your own business; **se mêler des ~s des autres** to interfere in other people's business *ou* affairs; **il raconte ses ~s à tout le monde** he tells everyone about his affairs.
h (*activités commerciales*) **les ~s** business; **être dans les ~s** to be in business; **parler (d')~s** to talk *ou* discuss business; **il est venu pour ~s** he came on business; **il est dur en ~s** he's a tough businessman; **les ~s sont les ~s** business is business; **d'~s** *déjeuner, rendez-vous etc* business (*épith*); *voir* **cabinet, carré, chiffre.**
i **~s** (*habits*) clothes, things; (*objets personnels*) things, belongings; **range tes ~s!** put away *ou* tidy up your things!
j (*loc*) **avoir ~ à** *cas, problème* to be faced with, have to deal with; *personne* (*s'occuper de*) to be dealing with; (*être servi ou examiné par*) to be dealt with by; (*ton menaçant*) **tu auras ~ à moi/lui** you'll be hearing from me/him; **nous avons ~ à un dangereux criminel** we are dealing with a dangerous criminal; **être à son ~** to be in one's element; **il n'est pas à son ~** he doesn't feel at ease, he is self-conscious; **faire son ~ à qn*** to do sb in*; **cela ne fait rien à l'~** that's got nothing to do with it; **en voilà une ~!** what a (complicated) business!; **ce n'est pas une ~!** it's nothing to get worked up about!; **quelle ~!** what a carry-on!*; **c'est toute une ~ (que d'aller à Glasgow)** it's quite a business (getting to Glasgow); **il en a fait toute une ~** he made a dreadful fuss about it, he made a great song and dance about it; **c'est une tout autre ~** that's quite another matter *ou* quite another kettle of fish; **c'est une ~ classée** the matter is closed; **c'est une ~ entendue** it's a deal*; **toutes ~s cessantes** forthwith; **c'est (une) ~ de goût/de mode** it's a matter of taste/fashion; **c'est l'~ de quelques minutes/quelques clous** it's a matter of a few minutes/a few nails; **être sorti d'~** to be over the worst; *voir* **beau, connaître.**
2 comp ► **affaire de cœur** love affair ► **affaire d'État** (*Pol*) affair of state; **il en a fait une affaire d'état*** he made a song and dance about it *ou* a great issue of it ► **affaire d'honneur** affair of honour ► **affaire de mœurs** (*gén*) sex scandal; (*Jur*) sex case.
affairé, e [afeʀe] (ptp de s'affairer) adj busy.
affairement [afɛʀmɑ̃] nm bustling activity.
affairer (s') [afeʀe] 1 vpr to busy o.s., bustle about. **s'~ auprès** *ou* **autour de qn** to fuss around sb; **s'~ à faire** to busy o.s. doing, bustle about doing.
affairisme [afeʀism] nm (political) racketeering.
affairiste [afeʀist] nm (*péj*) huckster, wheeler-dealer*. **sous ce régime il n'y a pas de place pour l'~** there is no place under this government for political racketeering *ou* for those who want to use politics to line their purse.
affaissement [afɛsmɑ̃] nm (*voir* **affaisser**) subsidence; sagging; sinking. **~ de terrain** subsidence (*NonC*).
affaisser [afese] 1 1 **s'affaisser** vpr a (*fléchir*) *[route, sol]* to subside, sink; *[corps, poutre]* to sag; *[plancher]* to cave in, give way; (*fig*) *[forces, volonté]* to sink. **le sol était affaissé par endroits** the ground had subsided *ou* sunk in places. b (*s'écrouler*) *[personne]* to collapse. **il s'était affaissé sur le sol** he had collapsed *ou* crumpled in a heap on the ground; **il était affaissé dans un fauteuil/sur le sol** he was slumped in an armchair/on the ground. 2 vt *route, sol* to cause to subside.
affaler (s') [afale] 1 vpr (*tomber*) to collapse, fall; (*se laisser tomber*) to collapse, flop, slump. **affalé dans un fauteuil** slumped in an armchair; (*Naut*) **s'~ le long d'un cordage** to slide down a rope.
affamé, e [afame] (ptp de **affamer**) adj starving, famished, ravenous. (*fig*) **~ de gloire** hungry *ou* greedy for fame; *voir* **ventre.**
affamer [afame] 1 vt *personne, ville* to starve.
affameur, -euse [afamœʀ, øz] nm,f (*péj*) tight-fisted employer (*who pays starvation wages*).
affect [afɛkt] nm affect.
affectation [afɛktasjɔ̃] nf a *[immeuble, somme]* allocation, allotment, assignment (*à* to, for). **l'~ du signe + à un nombre** the addition of the plus sign to a number, the modification of a number by the plus sign. b (*nomination*) (*à un poste*) appointment; (*à une région, un pays*) posting. **rejoindre son ~** to take up one's appointment; to take up one's posting.
c (*manque de naturel*) affectation, affectedness. **avec ~** affectedly, with affectation *ou* affectedness.
d (*simulation*) affectation, show. **avec une ~ de** with an affectation *ou* show of.
affecté, e [afɛkte] (ptp de **affecter**) adj (*feint*) affected, feigned, assumed; (*maniéré*) affected.
affecter [afɛkte] 1 vt a (*feindre*) to affect, feign. **~ de faire qch** to pretend to do sth; **~ le bonheur/un grand chagrin** to affect *ou* feign happiness/great sorrow, put on a show of happiness/great sorrow; (*littér*) **~ un langage poétique** to affect *ou* favour a poetic style of language; **il affecta de ne pas s'y intéresser** he affected *ou* pretended not to be interested in it; **~ une forme** to take on *ou* assume a shape.
b (*destiner*) to allocate, allot, assign (*à* to, for). **~ des crédits à la recherche** to earmark funds for research, allocate *ou* allot *ou* assign funds to *ou* for research.
c (*nommer*) (*à une fonction, un bureau*) to appoint; (*à une région, un pays*) to post (*à* to).
d (*émouvoir*) to affect, move, touch; (*concerner*) to affect. **il a été très affecté par leur mort** he was deeply affected *ou* moved by their deaths.
e (*Math*) to modify. **nombre affecté du coefficient 2/du signe +** number modified by *ou* bearing the coefficient 2/a plus sign.
f (*Méd*) to affect. **les oreillons affectent surtout les jeunes enfants** mumps mostly affects young children.
affectif, -ive [afɛktif, iv] adj (*gén*) *vie* emotional; *terme, nuance* affective, emotional; (*Psych*) affective.
affection [afɛksjɔ̃] nf a (*tendresse*) affection. **avoir de l'~ pour** to feel affection for, be fond of; **prendre en ~, se prendre d'~ pour** to become fond of *ou* attached to.
b (*Méd*) ailment, affection.
c (*Psych*) affection.

affectionné, e [afɛksjɔne] (ptp de **affectionner**) adj (*frm*) **votre fils ~/fille ~e** your loving *ou* devoted son/daughter; **votre ~** yours affectionately.

affectionner [afɛksjɔne] 1 vt *chose* to have a liking for, be fond of; *personne* to have affection *ou* an attachment for.

affectivité [afɛktivite] nf affectivity.

affectueusement [afɛktɥøzmɑ̃] adv affectionately, fondly.

affectueux, -euse [afɛktɥø, øz] adj *personne* affectionate; *pensée, regard* affectionate, fond.

afférent, e [afeʀɑ̃, ɑ̃t] adj a (*Admin*) ~ **à** *fonction* pertaining to, relating to; **questions ~es** related questions; (*Jur*) **part ~e à** portion accruing to. b (*Méd*) afferent.

affermage [afɛʀmaʒ] nm (*voir* **affermer**) leasing; renting.

affermer [afɛʀme] 1 vt *[propriétaire]* to lease, let out on lease; *[fermier]* to rent, take on lease.

affermir [afɛʀmiʀ] 2 vt *pouvoir, position* to consolidate, strengthen; *muscles, chairs* to tone up; *prise, charge, coiffure* to make firm *ou* firmer; *arrimage* to tighten, make firm *ou* firmer. ~ **sa voix** to steady one's voice; **cela l'affermit dans sa résolution** that strengthened him in his resolution; **après cet événement son autorité s'est affermie** his authority was strengthened after that event.

affermissement [afɛʀmismɑ̃] nm strengthening.

affété, e [afete] adj (*littér*) precious, affected, mannered.

afféterie [afɛtʀi] nf (*littér*) preciosity, affectation (*NonC*).

affichage [afiʃaʒ] nm a (*voir* **afficher**) putting *ou* posting *ou* sticking up; billing. **l'~** billsticking, billposting; **"~ interdit"** "stick no bills", "post no bills"; **interdit à l'~** *magazine* not for public display; *voir* **panneau, tableau.** b (*Ordin*) display. ~ **à cristaux liquides** liquid-crystal display; **montre à ~ numérique** digital watch.

affiche [afiʃ] nf a (*officielle*) public notice; (*Admin, Théât*) bill; (*publicité, Art*) poster; (*électorale etc*) poster. **la vente a été annoncée par voie d'~** the sale was advertised on the public noticeboards; ~ **de théâtre** (play)bill; **par voie d'~** by (means of) public notices. b (*Théât*) **mettre à l'~** to bill; **quitter l'~** to come off, close; **tenir longtemps l'~** to have a long run; **la pièce a tenu l'~ pendant 6 mois** the play ran for 6 months *ou* had a 6-month run; **il y a une belle ~ pour cette pièce** this play has an excellent cast; *voir* **tête.**

afficher [afiʃe] 1 1 vt a *affiche, résultat* to put *ou* post *ou* stick up; (*Théât*) to bill; (*Ordin*) to display. **"défense d'~"** "stick no bills", "post no bills". b (*péj*) *émotion, mépris* to exhibit, display; *qualité, vice* to flaunt, parade, display. 2 **s'afficher** vpr *[personne]* to flaunt o.s. **s'~ avec sa secrétaire** to carry on openly in public with one's secretary; **l'hypocrisie qui s'affiche sur tous les visages** the hypocrisy which is plain to see *ou* flaunted *ou* displayed on everybody's face.

affichette [afiʃɛt] nf (*voir* **affiche**) small public notice; small bill; small poster.

afficheur, -euse [afiʃœʀ, øz] 1 nm,f billsticker, billposter. 2 nm (*Tech*) display.

affichiste [afiʃist] nmf poster designer *ou* artist.

affidé, e [afide] nm,f (*péj*) confederate, accomplice, henchman.

affilage [afilaʒ] nm (*voir* **affiler**) sharpening; whetting; honing.

affilé, e[1] [afile] (ptp de **affiler**) adj *outil, couteau* sharp; *intelligence* keen; *voir* **langue.**

affilée[2] [afile] nf: **d'~** at a stretch, running. **huit heures d'~** 8 hours at a stretch *ou* on end *ou* solid *ou* running; **boire plusieurs verres d'~** to drink several glasses in a row *ou* in succession *ou* one after the other.

affiler [afile] 1 vt *couteau, outil* to sharpen, whet; *rasoir* to sharpen, hone.

affiliation [afiljasjɔ̃] nf affiliation.

affilié, e [afilje] (ptp de **affilier**) nm,f affiliated member.

affilier [afilje] 7 1 vt to affiliate (*à* to). 2 **s'affilier** vpr to become affiliated, affiliate o.s. (*ou* itself) (*à* to).

affiloir [afilwaʀ] nm (*outil*) sharpener; (*pierre*) whetstone; (*pour couteau*) steel.

affinage [afinaʒ] nm *[métal]* refining; *[verre]* fining; *[fromage]* maturing.

affinement [afinmɑ̃] nm *[goût, manières, style]* refinement.

affiner [afine] 1 vt a *métal* to refine; *verre* to fine; *fromage* to complete the maturing (process) of. b *esprit, mœurs* to refine; *style* to polish, refine; *sens* to make keener, sharpen. **son goût s'est affiné** his taste has become more refined. c *taille, hanches* to slim (down); *[robe]* to slim (*fig*). **ce maquillage vous affinera le visage** this make-up will make your face look slimmer.

affineur, -euse [afinœʀ, øz] nm,f *[métal]* refiner; *[verre]* finer; *[fromage]* person in charge of the last stages of the maturing process.

affinité [afinite] nf (*gén*) affinity.

affirmatif, -ive [afiʀmatif, iv] 1 adj *réponse, proposition* affirmative; *personne, ton* assertive, affirmative; (*Ling*) affirmative, positive. **il a été ~ à ce sujet** he was quite positive on that score *ou* about that; (*Mil, hum*) ~! affirmative!; *voir* **signe.** 2 nm (*Ling*) affirmative, positive. **à l'~** in the affirmative, in the positive. 3 **affirmative** nf affirmative. **répondre par l'~ive** to answer yes *ou* in the affirmative; **dans l'~ive** in the event of the answer being yes *ou* of an affirmative reply (*frm*); **nous espérons que vous viendrez: dans l'~ive, faites-le-nous savoir** we hope you'll come and if you can (come) please let us know.

affirmation [afiʀmasjɔ̃] nf a (*allégation*) assertion. b (*Gram*) assertion. c (*manifestation*) *[talent, autorité]* assertion, affirmation.

affirmativement [afiʀmativmɑ̃] adv in the affirmative, affirmatively.

affirmer [afiʀme] 1 vt a (*soutenir*) to maintain, assert. **tu affirmes toujours tout sans savoir** you always assert everything *ou* you are always positive about everything without really knowing; **il affirme l'avoir vu s'enfuir** he maintains *ou* asserts that *ou* claims that he saw him run off; **il affirme que c'est de votre faute** he contends *ou* maintains *ou* asserts that it is your fault; **pouvez-vous l'~?** can you swear to it?, can you be positive about it?; **on ne peut rien ~ encore** we can't say anything positive *ou* for sure yet, we can't affirm anything yet; **c'est lui, affirma-t-elle** it's him, she affirmed; ~ **qch sur l'honneur** to maintain *ou* affirm sth on one's word of honour; ~ **sur l'honneur que** to give one's word of honour that, maintain *ou* affirm on one's word of honour that.

b (*manifester*) *originalité, autorité, position* to assert. **talent/personnalité qui s'affirme** talent/personality which is asserting itself; **il s'affirme comme l'un de nos meilleurs romanciers** he is asserting himself *ou* establishing himself as one of our best novelists.

c (*frm: proclamer*) to affirm, assert. **le président a affirmé sa volonté de régler cette affaire** the president affirmed *ou* asserted his wish to settle this matter.

affixe [afiks] nm affix.

affleurement [aflœʀmɑ̃] nm (*Géol*) outcrop; (*fig*) emergence; (*Tech*) flushing.

affleurer [aflœʀe] 1 1 vi *[rocs, récifs]* to show on the surface; *[filon, couche]* to show on *ou* through the surface, outcrop (SPÉC); (*fig*) *[sentiment, sensualité]* to show through the surface, come *ou* rise to the surface. **quelques récifs affleuraient (à la surface de l'eau)** a few reefs showed on the surface (of the water). 2 vt (*Tech*) to make flush, flush.

afflictif, -ive [afliktif, iv] adj (*Jur*) corporal.

affliction [afliksjɔ̃] nf (*littér*) affliction. **être dans l'~** to be in (a state of) affliction.

affligé, e [afliʒe] (ptp de **affliger**) adj: **être ~ de** *maladie* to be afflicted with; (*fig*) **il était ~ d'une femme acariâtre** he was afflicted *ou* cursed with a cantankerous wife; (*littér*) **les ~s** the afflicted.

affligeant, e [afliʒɑ̃, ɑ̃t] adj distressing; (*iro*) pathetic (*iro*).

affliger [afliʒe] 3 vt (*attrister*) to distress, grieve; (*littér: accabler*) to smite (*littér*) (*de* with). **s'~ de qch** to be grieved *ou* distressed about sth; (*hum*) **la nature l'avait affligé d'un nez crochu** nature had afflicted *ou* cursed him with a hooked nose.

affluence [aflyɑ̃s] nf *[gens]* crowds (*pl*), throng (*littér*); *voir* **heure.**

affluent [aflyɑ̃] nm tributary, affluent (SPÉC).

affluer [aflye] 1 vi *[fluide, sang]* to rush, flow (*à, vers* to); *[foule]* to flock. **les dons affluaient de partout** the donations were flooding in *ou* rolling in from all parts; **les télégrammes affluaient sur sa table** telegrams were pouring onto his table; **l'argent afflue dans les caisses de la banque** money is flowing *ou* flooding into the coffers of the bank.

afflux [afly] nm *[fluide]* inrush, inflow; *[argent, foule]* inrush, influx, flood; (*Élec*) flow. ~ **de capitaux** capital inflow; ~ **de main-d'œuvre** labour influx.

affolant, e [afɔlɑ̃, ɑ̃t] adj (*effrayant*) frightening; (*littér: troublant*) *situation, nouvelle* distressing, disturbing. **c'est ~!*** it's alarming!*; **à une vitesse ~e** at an alarming speed.

affolé, e [afɔle] (ptp de **affoler**) adj a (*effrayé*) panic- *ou* terror-stricken; (*littér: troublé*) driven wild *ou* crazy. **je suis ~ de voir ça*** I'm appalled *ou* horrified at that; **air ~** look of panic, panic-stricken look. b *boussole* wildly fluctuating.

affolement [afɔlmɑ̃] nm a (*effroi*) panic; (*littér: trouble*) (wild) turmoil. **pas d~!*** no panic!, dont panic! b *[boussole]* wild fluctuations.

affoler [afɔle] 1 1 vt (*effrayer*) to throw into a panic, terrify; (*littér: troubler*) to drive wild, throw into a turmoil. 2 **s'affoler** vpr to lose one's head. **ne nous affolons pas*** don't let's panic *ou* get in a panic*, let's keep our heads.

affouillement [afujmɑ̃] nm undermining (*by water*).

affouiller [afuje] 1 vt to undermine (SPÉC).

affranchi, e [afʀɑ̃ʃi] (ptp de **affranchir**) nm,f (*esclave*) emancipated *ou* freed slave; (*libertin*) emancipated man (*ou* woman).

affranchir [afʀɑ̃ʃiʀ] 2 vt a (*avec des timbres*) to put a stamp *ou* stamps on, stamp; (*à la machine*) to frank. **lettre affranchie/non affranchie** stamped/unstamped letter; franked/unfranked letter; **j'ai reçu une lettre insuffisamment affranchie** I received a letter with insufficient postage on it.

b *esclave* to enfranchise, emancipate, (set) free; *peuple, pays* to free; (*fig*) *esprit, personne* to free, emancipate. (*fig*) ~ **qn de** *contrainte* to free sb from, set sb free from; **s'~ d'une domination étrangère/des convenances** to free o.s. from foreign domination/from convention.

c (*arg Crime: mettre au courant*) ~ **qn** to give sb the low-down‡, put sb in the picture*.

d (*Cartes*) to clear.

affranchissement [afʀɑ̃ʃismɑ̃] nm a (*NonC: voir* **affranchir**) stamping; franking; emancipation; enfranchisement; freeing. b (*Poste: prix*

payé) postage.
affres [ɑfʀ] **nfpl** (*littér*) **les ~ de** the pangs *ou* the torments of; **être dans les ~ de la mort** to be in the throes of death.
affrètement [afʀɛtmɑ̃] **nm** (*voir* **affréter**) chartering; hiring.
affréter [afʀete] 6 **vt** (*Aviat, Naut*) to charter; (*Aut*) to hire, charter.
affréteur [afʀetœʀ] **nm** (*Aviat, Naut*) charterer; (*Aut*) hirer.
affreusement [afʀøzmɑ̃] **adv** *souffrir, blesser* horribly. **~ laid** hideously ugly; **pâlir ~** to turn ghastly pale; **ce plat est ~ mauvais** this dish is really horrible *ou* horrid; **on est ~ mal assis/en retard** we're dreadfully *ou* awfully badly seated/late.
affreux, -euse [afʀø, øz] 1 **adj** (*très laid*) hideous, horrible, horrid, ghastly; (*effroyable, abominable*) dreadful, awful, horrible. **quel temps ~!** what ghastly *ou* dreadful *ou* horrible weather!; **j'ai un mal de tête ~** I've got a splitting *ou* a dreadful *ou* an awful *ou* a horrible headache; **c'est un ~ Jojo*** (*drôle d'individu*) he's a strange character *ou* a bit of an oddball‡ *ou* oddbod‡ (*Brit*); (*enfant insupportable*) he's a little horror*. 2 **nm** (*arg Mil*) (white) mercenary (*gen serving in Africa*).
affriander [afʀijɑ̃de] 1 **vt** (*littér*) to attract, allure, entice.
affriolant, e [afʀijɔlɑ̃, ɑ̃t] **adj** *perspective, programme* enticing, appealing, tempting, exciting; *femme* enticing, inviting; *habit féminin* titillating, alluring.
affrioler [afʀijɔle] 1 **vt** to tempt, excite, arouse.
affriqué, e [afʀike] 1 **adj** affricative. 2 **affriquée nf** affricate.
affront [afʀɔ̃] **nm** (*frm: insulte*) affront. **faire (un) ~ à** to affront.
affrontement [afʀɔ̃tmɑ̃] **nm** (*Mil, Pol*) confrontation.
affronter [afʀɔ̃te] 1 1 **vt** *adversaire, danger* to confront, face, meet. **~ la mort** to face *ou* brave death; **~ le mauvais temps** to brave the bad weather. 2 **s'affronter vpr** *[adversaires]* to confront each other, be in confrontation. **ces deux théories s'affrontent** these two theories clash *ou* are in direct opposition.
affublement [afybləmɑ̃] **nm** (*péj*) attire, rig-out* (*Brit*).
affubler [afyble] 1 **vt: ~ qn de** *vêtement* to rig* (*Brit*) *ou* deck sb out in; **~ qn d'un sobriquet** to attach a nickname to sb; **il s'affubla d'un vieux manteau** he rigged* himself out (*Brit*) *ou* got* himself up in an old coat; **affublé d'un vieux chapeau** wearing an old hat.
affût [afy] **nm** a **~ (de canon)** (gun) carriage. b (*Chasse*) hide. **chasser à l'~** to lie in wait for game, hunt game from a hide; **être à l'~** to be (lying) in wait; **se mettre à l'~** to be in wait, hide out; (*fig*) **être à l'~ de qch** to be on the look-out for sth.
affûtage [afytaʒ] **nm** sharpening, grinding.
affûter [afyte] 1 **vt** to sharpen, grind.
affûteur [afytœʀ] **nm** (*personne*) grinder.
affûteuse [afytøz] **nf** (*machine*) grinder, sharpener.
afghan, e [afgɑ̃, an] 1 **adj** Afghan; *voir* **lévrier**. 2 **nm** (*Ling*) Afghan. 3 **nm,f: A~(e)** Afghan.
Afghanistan [afganistɑ̃] **nm** Afghanistan.
afin [afɛ̃] **prép: ~ de** to, in order to, so as to; **~ que** + *subj* so that, in order that.
AFME [afmə] **nf** (**abrév de Agence française pour la maîtrise de l'énergie**) *voir* **agence**.
AFNOR [ɑfnɔʀ] **nf** (**abrév de Association française de normalisation**) *French Industrial Standards Authority*, ≃ BSI (*Brit*), ≃ ANSI (*US*).
afocal, e, mpl -aux [afɔkal, o] **adj** afocal.
a fortiori [afɔʀsjɔʀi] **loc adv** a fortiori, all the more.
AFP [aɛfpe] **nf** (**abrév de Agence France-Presse**) French Press Agency.
AFPA [afpa] **nf** (**abrév de Association pour la formation professionnelle des adultes**) *adult professional education association*.
africain, e [afʀikɛ̃, ɛn] 1 **adj** African. 2 **nm,f: A~(e)** African.
africanisation [afʀikanizasjɔ̃] **nf** Africanization.
africanisme [afʀikanism] **nm** Africanism.
africaniste [afʀikanist] **nmf** Africanist.
afrikaans [afʀikɑ̃s] **nm, adj inv** Afrikaans.
afrikaner [afʀikanɛʀ] **nm** Afrikaner.
Afrique [afʀik] **nf** Africa. **l'~ australe/du Nord/du Sud-Ouest** Southern/North/South-West Africa; **la République d'~ du Sud** the Republic of South Africa; **l'~-Équatoriale/-Occidentale** French Equatorial/West Africa.
afro* [afʀo] **adj inv** afro. **coiffure ~** afro hairdo*.
afro- [afʀo] **préf** afro.
afro-asiatique, pl afro-asiatiques [afʀoazjatik] 1 **adj** Afro-Asian. 2 **nmf: A~** Afro-Asian.
AG* [aʒe] **nf** (**abrév de assemblée générale**) (*Écon*) AGM; *[étudiants]* EGM.
agaçant, e [agasɑ̃, ɑ̃t] **adj** irritating, aggravating*, annoying.
agacement [agasmɑ̃] **nm** irritation, annoyance.
agacer [agase] 3 **vt** a **~ qn** (*énerver*) to get on sb's nerves, irritate *ou* aggravate* sb; (*taquiner*) to pester *ou* tease sb; **~ les dents de qn** to set sb's teeth on edge; **~ les nerfs de qn** to get on sb's nerves; **ça m'agace!** it's getting on my nerves!; **agacé par le bruit** irritated *ou* annoyed by the noise; **agacé de l'entendre** irritated at hearing him. b (*littér: aguicher*) to excite, lead on.
agaceries [agasʀi] **nfpl** coquetries, provocative gestures.
Agamemnon [agamɛmnɔ̃] **nm** Agamemnon.
Agana [agana] **n** Agana.
agapes [agap] **nfpl** (*hum*) banquet, feast.
agar-agar [agaʀagaʀ] **nm** agar(-agar).
agate [agat] **nf** agate.
agave [agav] **nm** agave.
AGE [aʒeə] **nf** (**abrév de assemblée générale extraordinaire**) EGM.
âge [ɑʒ] 1 **nm** a (*gén*) age. **quel ~ avez-vous?** how old are you?, what age are you?; **à l'~ de 8 ans** at the age of 8; **j'ai votre ~** I'm your age, I'm the same age as you; **ils sont du même ~** they're the same age; (*hum*) **il est d'un ~ canonique** he's a venerable age (*hum*); **elle est d'un ~ avancé** she is getting on in age *ou* years, she is quite elderly; **d'~ moyen** middle-aged; **il ne paraît pas son ~** he doesn't look his age; **elle porte bien son ~** she looks well for her age, she carries her years well; **il fait plus vieux que son ~** he looks older than he is *ou* than his years; **sans ~, qui n'a pas d'~** ageless; **on a l'~ de ses artères** you're as old as you feel; **il a vieilli avant l'~** he has got *ou* is old before his time; **il a pris de l'~** he has aged; **amusez-vous, c'est de votre ~** enjoy yourself — you should (do) at your age; **j'ai passé l'~ de le faire** I've passed the age for doing it, I'm too old to do it; **avec l'~ il se calmera** as he grows *ou* gets older he'll settle down; **des gens de tout ~** people of all ages; **être en ~ de se marier** to be of marriageable age, be old enough to get married; **être en ~ de combattre** to be old enough to fight; *voir* **bas, moyen**.
b (*ère*) age. **l'~ de (la) pierre/du bronze/du fer** the Stone/Bronze/Iron Age.
2 **comp** ►**l'âge adulte** (*gén*) adulthood; (*pour un homme*) manhood; (*pour une femme*) womanhood; **à l'âge adulte** when one becomes an adult, on reaching adulthood (*frm*) ►**l'âge critique** the change of life ►**l'âge d'homme** manhood ►**l'âge ingrat** the awkward *ou* difficult age ►**l'âge légal** the legal age; **avoir l'âge légal** to be of age; **il n'a pas encore l'âge légal** he's under age ►**âge mental** mental age ►**l'âge mûr** maturity, middle age ►**l'âge d'or** the golden age ►**l'âge de la pierre polie** the neolithic age ►**l'âge de la pierre taillée** the palaeolithic age ►**l'âge de raison** the age of reason ►**l'âge de la retraite** retiring age ►**l'âge tendre** the tender years *ou* age ►**l'âge viril** = **l'âge d'homme**.
âgé, e [ɑʒe] **adj: être ~** to be old, be elderly (*euph*); **être ~ de 9 ans** to be 9 (years old), be 9 years of age; **enfant ~ de 4 ans** 4-year-old child; **dame ~e** elderly lady; **les personnes ~es** the elderly, old people.
agence [aʒɑ̃s] **nf** (*succursale*) branch (office); (*bureaux*) offices (*pl*); (*organisme*) agency, bureau, office. **~ commerciale** sales office *ou* agency; **A~ pour les économies d'énergie, A~ française pour la maîtrise de l'énergie** *French energy conservation agency*, ≃ Energy Efficiency Office (*Brit*); **A~ pour l'énergie nucléaire** Atomic Energy Authority; **A~ internationale de l'énergie atomique** International Atomic Energy Agency; **~ immobilière** estate agency (*Brit*), estate agent's (office) (*Brit*), real estate agency (*US*); **~ matrimoniale** marriage bureau; **A~ nationale pour l'emploi** *French national employment office*, ≃ job centre (*Brit*); **~ de placement** employment agency *ou* bureau; **~ de presse** news *ou* press agency, news service (*US*); **~ de publicité** advertising *ou* publicity agency; **~ de renseignements** information bureau *ou* office; **A~ spatiale européenne** European Space Agency; **~ de voyages** travel agency.
agencé, e [aʒɑ̃se] (**ptp de agencer**) **adj: local bien/mal ~** (*conçu*) well-/badly-laid-out *ou* -arranged premises; (*meublé*) well-/badly-equipped premises; **phrase bien ~e** well-put-together *ou* well-constructed sentence; **éléments bien ~s** well-organized elements.
agencement [aʒɑ̃smɑ̃] **nm** *[éléments]* organization, ordering; *[phrase, roman]* construction, organization; *[couleurs]* harmonization; *[local]* (*disposition*) arrangement, lay-out; (*équipement*) equipment. **muni d'~s modernes** provided with modern fittings, fitted with modern equipment.
agencer [aʒɑ̃se] 3 **vt** *éléments* to put together, organize, order; *couleurs* to harmonize; *phrase, roman* to put together, construct; *local* (*disposer*) to lay out, arrange; (*équiper*) to equip.
agenda [aʒɛ̃da] **nm** diary. **~ de bureau** desk diary; **~ électronique** electronic calendar.
agenouillement [aʒ(ə)nujmɑ̃] **nm** (*littér*) kneeling.
agenouiller (s') [aʒ(ə)nuje] 1 **vpr** to kneel (down). **être agenouillé** to be kneeling; (*fig*) **s'~ devant l'autorité** to bow before authority.
agenouilloir [aʒ(ə)nujwaʀ] **nm** (*escabeau*) hassock, kneeling stool; (*planche*) kneeling plank.
agent [aʒɑ̃] 1 **nm** a **~ (de police)** policeman, (police) constable (*Brit*), patrolman (*US*). **~ de la circulation** ≃ policeman on traffic duty, traffic policeman; **pardon monsieur l'~** excuse me, officer *ou* constable (*Brit*).
b (*Chim, Gram, Sci*) agent; *voir* **complément**.
c (*Comm, Pol: représentant*) agent; (*Admin*) officer, official. **les ~s du lycée/de l'hôpital** the ancillary staff of the school/hospital; **arrêter un ~ ennemi** to arrest an enemy agent; **~ consulaire/de publicité** *etc* consular/publicity *ou* advertising *etc* agent; **~ en franchise** franchised dealer.
2 **comp** ►**agent d'assurances** insurance agent ►**agent de change** stockbroker ►**agent commercial** (sales) representative ►**agent comptable** accountant ►**agent double** double agent ►**agent**

électoral campaign organizer *ou* aide ▸**agent du fisc** tax official ▸**agent de la force publique** member of the police force ▸**agent du gouvernement** government official ▸**agent immobilier** estate agent (*Brit*), real estate agent (*US*) ▸**agent de liaison** (*Mil*) liaison officer ▸**agent de maîtrise** supervisor ▸**agent maritime** shipping agent ▸**agent provocateur** agent provocateur ▸**agent de publicité** advertising agent ▸**agent de renseignements** intelligence agent ▸**agent secret** secret agent ▸**agent technique** technician ▸**agent de transmission** (*Mil*) despatch rider, messenger ▸**agent voyer** ≃ borough surveyor.

agentif [aʒɑ̃tif] **nm** (*Ling*) agentive.

agglo* [aglo] **nm abrév de aggloméré.**

agglomérat [aglɔmeʀa] **nm** (*Géol: volcanique*) agglomerate; (*Ling*) cluster.

agglomération [aglɔmeʀasjɔ̃] **nf** a (*Admin*) (*ville*) town; (*Aut*) built-up area. **l'~ parisienne** Paris and its suburbs, the urban area of Paris. b *[nations, idées]* conglomeration; *[matériaux]* conglomeration, agglomeration.

aggloméré [aglɔmeʀe] **nm** (*charbon*) briquette; (*bois*) chipboard, Masonite ® (*US*); (*pierre*) conglomerate.

agglomérer [aglɔmeʀe] 6 1 **vt** (*amonceler*) to pile up; (*Tech*) *charbon* to briquette; *bois, pierre* to compress. 2 **s'agglomérer vpr** (*Tech*) to agglomerate; (*s'amonceler*) to pile up; (*se rassembler*) to conglomerate, gather. (*Admin*) **population agglomérée** dense population.

agglutinant, e [aglytinɑ̃, ɑ̃t] 1 **adj** (*gén*) agglutinating; (*Ling*) agglutinative. 2 **nm** agglutinant.

agglutination [aglytinasjɔ̃] **nf** (*Bio, Ling*) agglutination.

agglutiner [aglytine] 1 **vt** to stick together; (*Bio*) to agglutinate. (*fig*) **les passants s'agglutinent devant la vitrine** the passers-by congregate in front of the window.

agglutinogène [aglytinɔʒɛn] **nm** agglutinogen.

aggravant, e [agʀavɑ̃, ɑ̃t] **adj** *facteur* aggravating; *voir* **circonstance.**

aggravation [agʀavasjɔ̃] **nf** *[mal, situation]* worsening, aggravation; *[impôt, chômage]* increase.

aggraver [agʀave] 1 1 **vt** (*faire empirer*) to make worse, worsen, aggravate; (*renforcer*) to increase. (*Sport*) **~ la marque** *ou* **le score** to increase one's lead. 2 **s'aggraver vpr** (*empirer*) to get worse; (*se renforcer*) to increase.

agile [aʒil] **adj** (*physiquement, mentalement*) agile, nimble. **être ~ de ses mains** to be nimble with one's hands; **d'un geste ~** with an agile *ou* a nimble *ou* quick gesture; **~ comme un singe** as nimble as a goat.

agilement [aʒilmɑ̃] **adv** nimbly, agilely.

agilité [aʒilite] **nf** agility, nimbleness.

agio [aʒjo] **nm** a (*différence de cours*) Exchange premium. b (*frais*) **~s** (bank) charges.

agiotage [aʒjɔtaʒ] **nm** (*Hist*) speculation on exchange business.

agioter [aʒjɔte] 1 **vi** (*gén*) to speculate; (*Bourse*) to gamble on the stock exchange.

agioteur [aʒjɔtœʀ] **nm** (*Hist*) speculator on exchange business.

agir [aʒiʀ] 2 1 **vi** a (*gén*) to act; (*se comporter*) to behave, act. **il faut ~ tout de suite** we must act *ou* do something at once, we must take action at once; **il a agi de son plein gré/en toute liberté** he acted quite willingly/freely; **il agit comme un enfant** he acts *ou* behaves like a child; **il a bien/mal agi envers sa mère** he behaved well/badly towards his mother; **il a sagement agi** he did the right thing, he acted wisely; **le syndicat a décidé d'~** the union has decided to take action *ou* to act; **~ en ami** to behave *ou* act like a friend; **~ au nom de** to act on behalf of; *voir* **façon, manière.**

b (*exercer une influence*) **~ sur qch** to act on sth; **~ sur qn** to bring pressure to bear on sb; (*Bourse*) **~ sur le marché** to influence the market; **~ auprès de qn** to use one's influence with sb.

c **faire ~: faire ~ la loi** to put *ou* set the law in motion; **il a fait ~ son syndicat/ses amis** he got his union/friends to act *ou* take action; **je ne sais pas ce qui le fait ~ ainsi** I don't know what prompts him to *ou* makes him act like that.

d (*opérer*) *[médicament]* to act, work; *[influence]* to have an effect (*sur* on). **le remède agit lentement** the medicine is slow to take effect, the medicine acts *ou* works slowly; **laisser ~ la nature** to let nature take its course; **la lumière agit sur les plantes** light acts on *ou* has an effect on plants.

2 **s'agir vb impers** a (*il est question de*) **il s'agit de** it is a matter *ou* question of; **dans ce film il s'agit de 3 bandits** this film is about 3 gangsters; **décide-toi, il s'agit de ton avenir** make up your mind, it's your future that's at stake; **les livres dont il s'agit** the books in question; **quand il s'agit de manger, il est toujours là** when it's a matter of eating, he's always there; **quand il s'agit de travailler, il n'est jamais là** when there's any work to be done, he's never there *ou* around; **on a trouvé des colonnes: il s'agirait/il s'agit d'un temple grec** some columns have been found: it would appear to be/it is a Greek temple; **de quoi s'agit-il?** what is it?, what's it (all) about?, what's the matter?; **voilà ce dont il s'agit** that's what it's (all) about; **il ne s'agit pas d'argent** it's not a question *ou* matter of money; **il ne s'agit pas de ça!** that's not it! *ou* the point!; (*iro*) **il s'agit bien de ça!** that's hardly the problem!; **il s'agissait bien de son frère** it WAS (about) his brother after all.

b (*il est nécessaire de faire*) **il s'agit de faire: il s'agit de faire vite** we must act quickly, the thing (to do) is to act quickly; **il s'agit pour lui de réussir** what he has to do is succeed; **maintenant, il ne s'agit pas de plaisanter** this is no time for joking; **avec ça, il ne s'agit pas de plaisanter** that's no joking matter; **maintenant il s'agit de garder notre avance** now it's a matter *ou* question of maintaining our lead, now what we have to do *ou* must do is maintain our lead; **il s'agit** *ou* **s'agirait de s'entendre: tu viens ou tu ne viens pas?** let's get one thing clear *ou* straight – are you coming or aren't you?; **il s'agit de savoir ce qu'il va faire** it's a question of knowing what he's going to do, what we have to establish is what he's going to do.

c (*† loc*) **s'agissant de qn/qch** as regards sb/sth; **s'agissant de sommes aussi importantes, il faut être prudent** when such large amounts are involved, one must be careful.

AGIRC [aʒiʀk] **nf** (**abrév de Association générale des institutions de retraite des cadres**) *confederation of executive pension funds.*

âgisme [ɑʒism] **nm** ageism.

agissant, e [aʒisɑ̃, ɑ̃t] **adj** (*actif*) active; (*efficace*) efficacious, effective. **minorité ~e** active *ou* influential minority.

agissements [aʒismɑ̃] **nmpl** (*péj*) schemes, intrigues. **surveiller les ~ de qn** to keep an eye on what sb is up to*.

agitateur, -trice [aʒitatœʀ, tʀis] 1 **nm,f** (*Pol*) agitator. 2 **nm** (*Chim*) stirring rod.

agitation [aʒitasjɔ̃] **nf** a *[mer]* roughness, choppiness; *[air]* turbulence; *[personne]* (*ayant la bougeotte*) restlessness, fidgetiness; (*affairé*) bustle; (*troublé*) agitation, nervousness; *[lieu, rue etc]* bustle, stir. b (*Pol*) unrest, agitation.

agité, e [aʒite] (**ptp de agiter**) **adj** a *personne* (*ayant la bougeotte*) restless, fidgety; (*affairé*) bustling (*épith*); (*troublé*) agitated, troubled, perturbed. (*Psych*) **les ~s** manic persons. b *mer* rough, choppy; *vie* hectic; *époque* troubled; *nuit* restless. **avoir le sommeil ~** to toss about in one's sleep, have broken sleep.

agiter [aʒite] 1 1 **vt** a (*secouer*) *bras, mouchoir* to wave; *ailes* to flap, flutter; *queue* to wag; *bouteille, liquide* to shake; (*fig*) *menace* to brandish. **~ avant l'emploi** shake (well) before use *ou* using; **~ l'air de ses bras** to fan the air with one's arms; **le vent agite doucement les branches** the wind stirs *ou* sways the branches (gently); **le vent agite violemment les branches** the wind shakes the branches; **les feuilles, agitées par le vent** the leaves, quivering *ou* fluttering in the wind; **bateau agité par les vagues** boat tossed *ou* rocked by the waves; **~ le spectre** *ou* **l'épouvantail de** to raise the spectre of.

b (*inquiéter*) to trouble, perturb, agitate.

c (*débattre*) *question, problème* to discuss, debate, air.

2 **s'agiter vpr** a *[employé, serveur]* to bustle about; *[malade]* to move about *ou* toss restlessly; *[enfant, élève]* to fidget; *[foule, mer]* to stir. **s'~ dans son sommeil** to toss and turn in one's sleep; **les pensées qui s'agitent dans ma tête** the thoughts that are stirring *ou* dancing about in my head; **le peuple s'agite** the masses are stirring *ou* getting restless; **s'~ sur sa chaise** to wriggle about on one's chair.

b (**: se dépêcher*) to get a move on*.

agit-prop [aʒitpʀɔp] **nf inv** agitprop.

agneau, **pl ~x** [aɲo] **nm** lamb; (*fourrure*) lambskin. (*fig*) **son mari est un véritable ~** her husband is as meek as a lamb; (*iro*) **mes ~x** my dears (*iro*); (*Rel*) **l'A~ de Dieu** the Lamb of God; (*Rel*) **A~ pascal** Paschal Lamb; (*Rel*) **l'~ sans tache** the lamb without stain; **l'~ du sacrifice** the sacrificial lamb; *voir* **doux, innocent.**

agnelage [aɲ(ə)laʒ] **nm** (*mise bas*) lambing; (*époque*) lambing season.

agneler [aɲ(ə)le] 5 **vt** to lamb.

agnelet [aɲ(ə)lɛ] **nm** small lamb, lambkin†.

agneline [aɲ(ə)lin] **nf** lamb's wool.

agnelle [aɲɛl] **nf** (she) lamb.

Agnès [aɲɛs] **nf** Agnes.

agnosticisme [agnɔstisism] **nm** agnosticism.

agnostique [agnɔstik] **adj, nmf** agnostic.

agonie [agɔni] **nf** (*Méd*) death pangs (*pl*). **entrer en ~** to begin to suffer the agony *ou* pangs of death, begin one's mortal agony (*frm*); **être à l'~** to be at death's door *ou* at the point of death; **longue ~** slow death; **son ~ fut longue** he died a slow death, he suffered the long agony of death (*frm*); (*fig*) **l'~ d'un régime** the death throes of a régime.

agonir [agɔniʀ] 2 **vt** to revile. **~ qn d'injures** to hurl insults *ou* abuse at sb, heap insults *ou* abuse on sb.

agonisant, e [agɔnizɑ̃, ɑ̃t] **adj** (*littér, fig*) dying. **la prière des ~s** prayers for the dying, last rites (*pl*).

agoniser [agɔnize] 1 **vi** (*littér, fig*) to be dying. **un blessé agonisait dans un fossé** a wounded man lay dying in a ditch.

agoraphobe [agɔʀafɔb] **adj, nmf** agoraphobic.

agoraphobie [agɔʀafɔbi] **nf** agoraphobia.

agrafage [agʀafaʒ] **nm** *[vêtement]* hooking (up), fastening (up); *[papiers]* stapling; (*Méd*) putting in of clips.

agrafe [agʀaf] **nf** *[vêtement]* hook, fastener; *[papiers]* staple; (*Méd*) clip.

agrafer [agʀafe] 1 **vt** *vêtement* to hook (up), fasten (up); *papiers* to staple; (*: *arrêter*) to nab*, grab*, bust* (*US*).

agrafeuse [agʀaføz] nf stapler.

agraire [agʀɛʀ] adj *politique, lois* agrarian; *mesure, surface* land (*épith*); *voir* **réforme**.

agrammatical, e, mpl **-aux** [agʀamatikal, o] adj agrammatical.

agrandir [agʀɑ̃diʀ] 2 1 vt a (*rendre plus grand*) *passage* to widen; *trou* to make bigger, enlarge; *usine, domaine* to enlarge, extend; *écart* to increase; *photographie, dessin* to enlarge, blow up*; (*à la loupe*) to magnify. **ce miroir agrandit la pièce** this mirror makes the room look bigger *ou* larger; **(faire) ~ sa maison** to extend one's house.
b (*développer*) to extend, expand. **pour ~ le cercle de ses activités** to widen *ou* extend *ou* expand the scope of one's activities.
c (*ennoblir*) *âme* to uplift, elevate, ennoble.
2 **s'agrandir** vpr *[ville, famille]* to grow, expand; *[écart]* to widen, grow, get bigger; *[passage]* to get wider; *[trou]* to get bigger. **il nous a fallu nous ~** we had to expand, we had to find a bigger place; **ses yeux s'agrandirent sous le coup de la surprise** his eyes widened *ou* grew wide with surprise.

agrandissement [agʀɑ̃dismɑ̃] nm *[local]* extension; *[puissance, ville]* expansion; (*Phot*) (*action*) enlargement; (*photo*) enlargement, blow-up*.

agrandisseur [agʀɑ̃disœʀ] nm enlarger.

agraphie [agʀafi] nf agraphia.

agrarien, -ienne [agʀaʀjɛ̃, jɛn] adj, nm (*Hist, Pol*) agrarian.

agréable [agʀeabl] adj pleasant, agreeable. **~ à voir** nice to see; **~ à l'œil** pleasing to the eye; **~ à vivre** *personne* easy *ou* pleasant to live with; *lieu* pleasant to live in; **il est toujours ~ de** it is always pleasant *ou* nice *ou* agreeable to; **ce que j'ai à dire n'est pas ~** what I have to say isn't (very) pleasant; **si ça peut lui être ~** if that will please him; **il me serait ~ de** it would be a pleasure for me to, I should be pleased to; **être ~ de sa personne**† to be pleasant-looking *ou* personable†; **l'~ de la chose** the pleasant *ou* nice thing about it; *voir* **joindre**.

agréablement [agʀeabləmɑ̃] adv pleasantly, agreeably. **nous avons ~ passé la soirée** we spent a pleasant *ou* an agreeable *ou* a nice evening, we spent the evening pleasantly *ou* agreeably; **~ surpris** pleasantly surprised.

agréé, e [agʀee] (ptp de **agréer**) 1 adj *bureau, infirmière* registered. **fournisseur ~** authorized *ou* registered dealer; (*Can*) **comptable ~** certified accountant (*Brit*), certified public accountant (*US*). 2 nm attorney, solicitor (*appearing for parties before a "tribunal de commerce"*).

agréer [agʀee] 1 (*frm*) 1 vt (*accepter*) *demande, excuses* to accept. **veuillez ~, Monsieur (ou Madame), l'expression de mes sentiments distingués** yours faithfully (*Brit*) *ou* sincerely (*US*); **veuillez ~ mes meilleures** *ou* **sincères salutations** yours sincerely. 2 **agréer à** vt indir *personne* to please, suit. **si cela vous agrée** if it suits *ou* pleases you, if you are agreeable.

agrèg [agʀɛg] nf (*arg Univ*) abrév de **agrégation**.

agrégat [agʀega] nm (*Constr, Écon, Géol*) aggregate; (*péj*) *[idées]* medley.

agrégatif, -ive [agʀegatif, iv] nm,f *candidate for the agrégation*.

agrégation [agʀegasjɔ̃] nf a (*Univ*) agrégation, *highest competitive examination for teachers in France*. b *[particules]* aggregation.

agrégé, e [agʀeʒe] (ptp de **agréger**) nm,f agrégé, *qualified secondary or high school teacher (holder of the agrégation)*; *voir* **professeur**.

agréger [agʀeʒe] 3 et 6 vt *particules* to aggregate. (*fig*) **~ qn à un groupe** to incorporate sb into a group; **s'~ à un groupe** to incorporate o.s. into a group.

agrément [agʀemɑ̃] nm a (*littér: charme*) *[personne]* charm; *[visage]* attractiveness, charm; *[conversation]* charm, pleasantness, agreeableness; *[lieu, climat]* pleasantness, agreeableness, amenity (*littér*). **sa compagnie est pleine d'~** his company is very enjoyable *ou* pleasant *ou* agreeable; **ville/maison sans ~** unattractive town/house, town/house with no agreeable *ou* attractive features; **les ~s de la vie** the pleasures of life, the pleasant things in life; **faire un voyage d'~** to go on *ou* make a pleasure trip; *voir* **art, jardin, plante**. b (*frm: consentement*) consent, approval; (*Jur*) assent. c (*Mus*) **(note d')~** grace note.

agrémenter [agʀemɑ̃te] 1 vt: **~ qch de** (*décorer*) to embellish *ou* adorn sth with; (*varier, relever*) to accompany sth with; **agrémenté de broderies** trimmed *ou* embellished *ou* adorned with embroidery; **conférence agrémentée de projections** lecture supplemented with *ou* accompanied by slides; **il agrémentait son récit d'anecdotes** he peppered *ou* accompanied *ou* enlivened his story with anecdotes; (*iro*) **dispute agrémentée de coups** argument enlivened with blows.

agrès [agʀɛ] nmpl (*Aviat, Naut*) tackle; (*Sport*) (gymnastics) apparatus. **exercices aux ~** exercises on the apparatus, apparatus work.

agresser [agʀese] 1 vt to attack. **il s'est senti agressé** (*physiquement*) he felt they (*ou* you *etc*) were being aggressive towards him; (*psychologiquement*) he felt they (*ou* you *etc*) were hostile towards him; **agressé par la vie moderne** feeling the strains *ou* stresses of modern life.

agresseur [agʀesœʀ] nm attacker, assailant, aggressor. **(pays) ~** aggressor.

agressif, -ive [agʀesif, iv] adj (*gén*) aggressive.

agression [agʀesjɔ̃] nf (*contre une personne*) attack; (*contre un pays*) aggression; (*dans la rue*) mugging; (*Psych*) aggression. **~ nocturne** attack *ou* assault at night; **être victime d'une ~** to be mugged; **les agressions de la vie moderne** the brutal stresses *ou* strains of modern living *ou* life.

agressivement [agʀesivmɑ̃] adv aggressively.

agressivité [agʀesivite] nf aggressiveness.

agreste [agʀɛst] adj (*littér*) rustic.

agricole [agʀikɔl] adj *ressources, enseignement* agricultural; *produits, travaux* farm (*épith*), agricultural; *population, peuple* farming (*épith*), agricultural. **ouvrier ~** farm *ou* field hand; *voir* **comice, exploitation**.

agriculteur, -trice [agʀikyltœʀ, tʀis] nm,f farmer.

agriculture [agʀikyltyʀ] nf agriculture, farming.

agripper [agʀipe] 1 1 vt (*se retenir à*) to grab *ou* clutch hold of; (*arracher*) to snatch, grab. 2 **s'agripper** vpr: **s'~ à qch** to cling on to sth, clutch *ou* grip sth; **ne t'agrippe pas à moi** don't cling on to *ou* hang on to me.

agro-alimentaire [agʀoalimɑ̃tɛʀ] 1 adj *industrie* farm-produce. 2 nm: **l'~** the farm-produce industry, agribusiness.

agronome [agʀɔnɔm] nm agronomist. **ingénieur ~** agricultural engineer.

agronomie [agʀɔnɔmi] nf agronomy, agronomics (*sg*).

agronomique [agʀɔnɔmik] adj agronomic(al).

agrume [agʀym] nm citrus fruit.

aguerrir [ageʀiʀ] 2 vt to harden. **~ qn contre** to harden sb to *ou* against, inure sb to; **des troupes aguerries** (*au combat*) seasoned troops; (*à l'effort*) trained troops; **s'~** to become hardened; **s'~ contre** to become hardened to *ou* against, inure o.s. to.

aguets [agɛ] nmpl: **aux ~** on the look-out, on the watch.

aguichant, e [agiʃɑ̃, ɑ̃t] adj enticing, tantalizing.

aguiche [agiʃ] nf teaser.

aguicher [agiʃe] 1 vt to entice, lead on, tantalize.

aguicheur, -euse [agiʃœʀ, øz] 1 adj enticing, tantalizing. 2 nm (*rare: enjôleur*) seducer. 3 **aguicheuse** nf (*allumeuse*) teaser, vamp.

ah ['ɑ] 1 excl a (*réponse, réaction exclamative*) ah!, oh!, ooh! (*question*) **~?, ~ bon?, ~ oui?** really?, is that so?; (*résignation*) **~ bon** oh *ou* ah well; (*insistance*) **~ oui** oh yes, yes indeed; (*insistance*) **~ non** oh no, certainly *ou* definitely not. b (*intensif*) **~ j'allais oublier** oh! *ou* ah! I nearly forgot; **~, ~! je t'y prends** aha! *ou* oho! I've caught you at it; **~, qu'il est lent!** oh how slow he is! 2 nm: **pousser un ~ de soulagement** to sigh with relief, give a sigh of relief; **des ~s d'allégresse** oohs and ahs of joy.

ahan†† [aɑ̃] nm *voir* **grand**.

ahaner [aane] 1 vi (††, *littér*) to labour, make great efforts. **ahanant sous le fardeau** labouring under the burden.

ahuri, e [ayʀi] (ptp de **ahurir**) 1 adj (*stupéfait*) stunned, flabbergasted; (*hébété, stupide*) stupefied, vacant. **avoir l'air ~** to have a stupefied look; **ne prends pas cet air ~** don't look so flabbergasted. 2 nm,f (*péj*) blockhead*, nitwit*.

ahurir [ayʀiʀ] 2 vt to dumbfound, astound, stun.

ahurissant, e [ayʀisɑ̃, ɑ̃t] adj stupefying, astounding; (*sens affaibli*) staggering.

ahurissement [ayʀismɑ̃] nm stupefaction.

aï [ai] nm (*Zool*) ai.

aiche [ɛʃ] nf = **èche**.

aide [ɛd] 1 nf a (*assistance*) help, assistance. **apporter son ~ à qn** to bring help *ou* assistance to sb; **son ~ nous a été précieuse** he was a great help *ou* of great help *ou* assistance to us, his help was invaluable to us; **appeler/crier à l'~** to call/shout for help; **appeler qn à son ~** to call for help from sb, call to sb for help; **venir/aller à l'~ de qn** to come/go to sb's aid *ou* assistance, come/go to help sb; **venir en ~ à qn** to help sb, come to sb's assistance *ou* aid; **à l'~!** help!; **sans l'~ de personne** without (any) help *ou* assistance, (completely) unassisted *ou* unaided, single-handed.
b (*secours financier*) aid.
c **à l'~ de** with the help *ou* aid of.
d (*Équitation*) **~s** aids.
2 nm,f assistant. **~-chimiste/-chirurgien** assistant chemist/surgeon.
3 comp ▸**aide de camp** nm aide-de-camp ▸**aide-comptable** nmf (pl **aides-comptables**) accountant's assistant ▸**aide de cuisine** nmf kitchen hand ▸**aide au développement** nf development aid ▸**aide-électricien** nm (pl **aides-électriciens**) electrician's mate (*Brit*) *ou* helper (*US*) ▸**aide familiale** mother's help, home help ▸**aide-jardinier** nm (pl **aides-jardiniers**) gardener's help *ou* mate (*Brit*), under-gardener ▸**aide judiciaire** nf legal aid ▸**aide de laboratoire** nmf laboratory assistant ▸**aide libérale** (*Écon*) concessionary aid ▸**aide-maçon** nm (pl **aides-maçons**) builder's mate (*Brit*) *ou* labourer ▸**aide maternelle** = **aide familiale** ▸**aide médicale (gratuite)** (free) medical aid ▸**aide ménagère** home help (*Brit*) ▸**aide-opérateur** nm (pl **aides-opérateurs**) (*Ciné*) assistant cameraman ▸**aide personnalisée au logement** ≃ housing benefit (*Brit*) *ou* subsidy (*US*) ▸**aide au retour** nf repatriation grant (*for immigrants returning to their country of origin*) ▸**aide sociale** ≃ social security, welfare; **recevoir l'aide sociale** ≃ to be on state aid *ou* social security (*Brit*) ▸**aide soignante** state enrolled

nurse (*Brit*), nursing auxiliary (*Brit*), nurse's aide (*US*).
aide-mémoire [ɛdmemwaʀ] nm inv (*gén*) aide-mémoire; (*Scol*) crib.
aider [ede] [1] 1 vt to help. **~ qn (à faire qch)** to help sb (to do sth); **~ qn à monter/à descendre/à traverser** to help sb up/down/across *ou* over; **il l'a aidé à sortir de la voiture** he helped him out of the car; **~ qn de ses conseils** to help *ou* assist sb with one's advice; **~ qn financièrement** to help sb (out) *ou* assist sb financially, give sb financial help *ou* aid; **il m'aide beaucoup** he helps me a lot, he's a great help to me; **je me suis fait ~ par *ou* de mon frère** I got my brother to help *ou* assist me *ou* to give me a hand*; **elle ne se déplace qu'aidée de sa canne** she can only get about with the help *ou* aid of her walking stick; (*hum*) **il n'est pas aidé!** nature hasn't been kind to him!
2 vi to help. **elle est venue pour ~** she came to help (out) *ou* to give *ou* lend a hand; **~ à la cuisine** to help (out) in *ou* give a hand in the kitchen; **le débat aiderait à la compréhension du problème** discussion would help (towards) *ou* contribute towards an understanding of the problem, discussion would help (one) to understand the problem; **ça aide à passer le temps** it helps to pass (the) time; **l'alcool aidant, il se mit à parler** helped on by the alcohol *ou* with the help of alcohol, he began to speak; *voir* **dieu**.
3 **s'aider** vpr a **s'~ de** to use, make use of. **atteindre le placard en s'aidant d'un escabeau** to reach the cupboard by using a stool *ou* with the aid of a stool; **en s'aidant de ses bras** using his arms to help him.
b (*loc*) **entre voisins il faut s'~** we neighbours should help each other (out); (*Prov*) **aide-toi, le Ciel t'aidera** God helps those who help themselves (*Prov*).
aïe [aj] excl (*douleur*) ouch!, ow! **~ ~ ~!, ça se présente mal** dear oh dear, things don't look too good!
AIEA [aiəa] nf (abrév de **Agence internationale de l'énergie atomique**) IAEA.
aïeul [ajœl] nm (*littér*) grandfather. **les ~s** the grandparents.
aïeule [ajœl] nf (*littér*) grandmother.
aïeux [ajø] nmpl (*littér*) forefathers, forebears, ancestors. **mes ~!*** my godfathers!* (†, *hum*), by jingo!*
aigle [ɛgl] 1 nm (*Zool, lutrin*) eagle. **~ royal** golden eagle; **~ d'Amérique** American eagle; **~ de mer** (*oiseau*) sea eagle; (*poisson*) eagle ray; (*fig*) **regard d'~** eagle look; **ce n'est pas un ~*** he's no genius. 2 nf (*Mil, Zool*) eagle.
aiglefin [ɛgləfɛ̃] nm haddock.
aiglon, -onne [ɛglɔ̃, ɔn] nm,f eaglet. (*Hist*) **l'A~** Napoleon II.
aigre [ɛgʀ] 1 adj a *fruit* sour, sharp; *vin* vinegary, sour, acid; *goût, odeur, lait* sour. b *son* shrill, piercing, sharp; *voix* sharp, cutting (*épith*). c *froid, vent* bitter, keen, cutting (*épith*). d *propos, critique* cutting (*épith*), harsh, acrid; *voir* **tourner**. 2 comp ▶**aigre-doux, aigre-douce** (mpl **aigres-doux**) adj *sauce* sweet and sour; *fruit* bitter-sweet; (*fig*) *propos* bitter-sweet.
aigrefin [ɛgʀəfɛ̃] nm swindler, crook.
aigrelet, -ette [ɛgʀəlɛ, ɛt] adj *petit-lait, pomme* sourish; *vin* vinegarish; *voix, son* shrillish.
aigrement [ɛgʀəmɑ̃] adv *répondre, dire* sourly.
aigrette [ɛgʀɛt] nf (*plume*) feather; (*oiseau*) egret; (*bijou*) aigret(te).
aigreur [ɛgʀœʀ] nf a (*acidité*) *[petit-lait]* sourness; *[vin]* sourness, acidity; *[pomme]* sourness, sharpness. b **~s: avoir des ~s (d'estomac)** to have heartburn. c (*acrimonie*) sharpness, harshness.
aigri, e [egʀi] (ptp de **aigrir**) adj embittered, bitter.
aigrir [egʀiʀ] [2] 1 vt *personne* to embitter; *caractère* to sour. 2 **s'aigrir** vpr *[aliment]* to turn sour; *[caractère]* to sour. **il s'est aigri** he has become embittered.
aigu, -uë [egy] 1 adj a *son, voix* high-pitched, shrill; *note* high-pitched, high. b *crise, phase* acute; *douleur* acute, sharp; *intelligence* keen, acute, sharp. c (*pointu*) sharp, pointed; *voir* **accent, angle**. 2 nm (*Mus*) (*sur bouton de réglage*) treble. **les ~s** the high notes; **passer du grave à l'~** to go from low to high pitch.
aigue-marine, pl **aigues-marines** [ɛgmaʀin] nf aquamarine.
aiguière [ɛgjɛʀ] nf ewer.
aiguillage [egɥijaʒ] nm (*Rail*) (*action*) shunting (*Brit*), switching (*US*); (*instrument*) points (*pl*) (*Brit*), switch (*US*). **le déraillement est dû à une erreur d'~** the derailment was due to faulty shunting (*Brit*) *ou* switching (*US*); (*fig*) **il y a eu une erreur d'~** there was a mix-up (in communication *etc*); *voir* **cabine**.
aiguille [egɥij] 1 nf a (*Bot, Couture, Méd*) needle. **~ à coudre/à tricoter/à repriser** sewing/knitting/darning needle; **travail à l'~** needlework; *voir* **chercher, fil, tirer**. b *[compteur, boussole, gramophone]* needle; *[horloge]* hand; *[balance]* pointer, needle; *[cadran solaire]* pointer, index; *[clocher]* spire; (*Rail*) point (*Brit*), switch (*US*); (*Géog*) (*pointe*) needle; (*cime*) peak. **en forme d'~** needle-shaped; **la petite/grande ~** the hour/minute hand, the little/big hand. 2 comp ▶**aiguille de glace** icicle ▶**aiguille de pin** pine needle.
aiguillée [egɥije] nf length of thread (*for use with needle at any one time*).
aiguiller [egɥije] [1] vt a (*orienter*) to direct. **~ un enfant vers le technique** to direct *ou* orientate *ou* steer a child towards technical studies; (*Scol*) **on l'a mal aiguillé** he was orientated *ou* steered in the wrong direction, he was misdirected; **~ la conversation sur un autre sujet** to direct *ou* steer the conversation onto another subject; **~ la police sur une mauvaise piste** to direct *ou* put the police onto the wrong track. b (*Rail*) to shunt (*Brit*), switch (*US*).
aiguillette [egɥijɛt] nf *[pourpoint]* aglet; (*Culin, Mil*) aiguillette.
aiguilleur [egɥijœʀ] nm (*Rail*) pointsman (*Brit*), switchman (*US*). (*Aviat*) **~ du ciel** air-traffic controller.
aiguillon [egɥijɔ̃] nm *[insecte]* sting; *[bouvier]* goad; (*Bot*) thorn; (*fig*) spur, stimulus.
aiguillonner [egɥijɔne] [1] vt *bœuf* to goad; (*fig*) to spur *ou* goad on.
aiguisage [egizaʒ] nm (*voir* **aiguiser**) sharpening; grinding.
aiguiser [egize] [1] vt a *couteau, outil* to sharpen, grind; *rasoir* to sharpen. b (*fig*) *appétit* to whet, stimulate; *sens* to excite, stimulate; *esprit* to sharpen; *style* to polish.
aiguiseur [egizœʀ] nm (*ouvrier*) sharpener, grinder.
aiguisoir [egizwaʀ] nm sharpener, sharpening tool.
aïkido [aikido] nm aikido.
ail, pl **~s, aulx** [aj, o] nm garlic; *voir* **gousse, saucisson, tête**.
aile [ɛl] nf a *[oiseau, château]* wing; *[moulin]* sail; *[hélice, ventilateur]* blade, vane; *[nez]* wing; *[voiture]* wing (*Brit*), fender (*US*). **~ marchante** (*Mil*) wheeling flank; (*fig*) *[groupe]* active element; **~ volante** hang-glider.
b (*loc*) **l'oiseau disparut d'un coup d'~** the bird disappeared with a flap of its wings; **d'un coup d'~ nous avons gagné Orly** we reached Orly in the twinkling of an eye *ou* in a trice; (*fig*) **avoir des ~s** to be quick as a flash; **l'espoir lui donnait des ~s** hope lent *ou* gave him wings; **prendre sous son ~ (protectrice)** to take under one's wing; **sous l'~ maternelle** under one's mother's *ou* the maternal wing; *voir* **peur, plomb, tire-d'aile(s)** *etc*.
ailé, e [ele] adj (*fig littér*) winged.
aileron [ɛlʀɔ̃] nm *[poisson]* fin; *[oiseau]* pinion; (*avion*) aileron; (*Aut: de stabilisation*) aerofoil; (*Archit*) console.
ailette [ɛlɛt] nf *[missile, radiateur]* fin; *[turbine, ventilateur]* blade. (*Aut*) **~ de refroidissement** cooling fan.
ailier [elje] nm (*gén*) winger; (*Rugby*) flanker, wing-forward.
aillade [ajad] nf garlic dressing *ou* sauce.
ailler [aje] [1] vt to flavour with garlic.
ailleurs [ajœʀ] adv a somewhere else, elsewhere. **nulle part ~** nowhere else; **partout ~** everywhere else; **il est ~, il a l'esprit ~** his thoughts are *ou* his mind is elsewhere, he's miles away (*fig*); **ils viennent d'~** they come from somewhere else; **j'ai gagné là ce que j'ai perdu (par) ~** I gained on this what I lost elsewhere; **nous sommes passés (par) ~** we went another way; **je l'ai su par ~** I heard of it from another source.
b **par ~** (*autrement*) otherwise, in other respects; (*en outre*) moreover, furthermore; **d'~** besides, moreover; **d'~ il faut avouer que ...** anyway *ou* besides *ou* moreover we have to confess that ...; **ce vin, d'~ très bon, n'est ...** this wine, which I may add is very good *ou* which is very good by the way, is not ...; **lui non plus d'~** neither does (*ou* is, has *etc*) he, for that matter.
ailloli [ajɔli] nm garlic mayonnaise.
aimable [ɛmabl] adj a (*gentil*) *parole* kind, nice; *personne* kind, nice, amiable (*frm*). **c'est un homme ~** he's a (very) nice man; **tu es bien ~ de m'avoir attendu** it was very nice *ou* kind of you to wait for me; **c'est très ~ à vous *ou* de votre part** it's most kind of you; (*frm*) **soyez assez ~ pour** be so kind *ou* good as to (*frm*); **~ comme une porte de prison** like a bear with a sore head. b (†: *agréable*) *endroit, moment* pleasant. c (††: *digne d'amour*) lovable, amiable††.
aimablement [ɛmabləmɑ̃] adv *agir* kindly, nicely; *répondre, recevoir* amiably, nicely; *refuser* politely. **il m'a offert ~ à boire** he kindly offered me a drink.
aimant[1] [ɛmɑ̃] nm magnet. **~ (naturel)** magnetite (*NonC*), lodestone.
aimant[2]**, e** [ɛmɑ̃, ɑ̃t] adj loving, affectionate.
aimantation [ɛmɑ̃tasjɔ̃] nf magnetization.
aimanté, e [ɛmɑ̃te] (ptp de **aimanter**) adj *aiguille, champs* magnetic.
aimanter [ɛmɑ̃te] [1] vt to magnetize.
aimer [eme] [1] 1 vt a (*d'amour*) to love, be in love with; (*d'amitié, attachement, goût*) to like, be fond of. **~ beaucoup** *personne* to like very much *ou* a lot, be very fond of; *animaux, choses* to like very much *ou* a lot, be very keen on *ou* fond of, love; **~ bien** to like, be fond of; **il l'aime d'amour** he loves her; **il l'aime à la folie** he adores her, he's crazy about her*; **j'aime une bonne tasse de café après déjeuner** I like *ou* enjoy *ou* love a good cup of coffee after lunch; **les hortensias aiment l'ombre** hydrangeas like shade; **tous ces trucs-là, tu aimes, toi?*** do you go in for all that kind of stuff?*; **je n'aime pas beaucoup cet acteur** I don't care for *ou* I don't like that actor very much, I'm not very keen on (*Brit*) that actor, I don't go much for that actor*; **elle n'aime pas le tennis** she doesn't like tennis *ou* care for tennis, she's not keen on (*Brit*) tennis; **les enfants aiment qu'on s'occupe d'eux** children like *ou* love attention; **elle n'aime pas qu'il sorte le soir** she doesn't like him going out *ou* him to go out at night; **~ faire,** (*littér*) **~ à faire** to like doing *ou* to do; (*frm, hum*) **j'aime à penser *ou* à croire que ...** I like to think that ...; *voir* **qui**.
b (*avec assez, autant, mieux*) **~ autant: j'aime autant vous dire que je n'irai pas!** I may as well tell you that I won't go!; **il aime *ou* aimerait autant ne pas sortir aujourd'hui** he'd just as soon not go out today, he'd

be just as happy not going out today; j'aimerais autant que ce soit elle qui m'écrive I'd rather it was she who wrote to me; j'aime autant qu'elle ne soit pas venue I'm just as happy *ou* it's (probably) just as well she didn't come; j'aime autant ça!* (*menace*) I'm pleased to hear it!; that sounds more like it!*; (*soulagement*) what a relief!; ~ mieux: on lui apporte des fleurs, elle aimerait mieux des livres they bring her flowers and she would rather *ou* sooner have *ou* she would prefer books; il aurait mieux aimé se reposer que d'aller au cinéma he would rather have rested *ou* he would have preferred to rest than go to the cinema; j'aime mieux te dire qu'il va m'entendre!* I'm going to give him a piece of my mind, and that's for sure; ~ assez: elle aime assez *ou* bien bavarder avec les commerçants she quite *ou* rather likes chatting with the tradesmen.

c (*au conditionnel = vouloir*) aimeriez-vous une tasse de thé? would you like a cup of tea?, would you care for a cup of tea?; elle aimerait bien aller se promener she would like to go for a walk; j'aimerais vraiment venir I'd really like to come, I'd love to come; je n'aimerais pas être dehors par ce temps I wouldn't want *ou* like to be out in this (sort of) weather; j'aimerais assez/je n'aimerais pas ce genre de manteau I would rather like/wouldn't like a coat like that.

2 **s'aimer** vpr a ils s'aiment they are in love, they love each other; aimez-vous les uns les autres love one another; ces deux collègues ne s'aiment guère there's no love lost between those two colleagues; se faire ~ de quelqu'un de riche *etc* to get somebody rich *etc* to fall in love with one; essayer de se faire ~ de qn to try to win the love *ou* affection of sb; je ne m'aime pas avec ce chapeau I don't like myself in that hat.

b (*faire l'amour*) to make love.

aine [ɛn] nf groin (*Anat*).

aîné, e [ɛne] 1 adj (*plus âgé*) older (*que* than), elder; (*le plus âgé*) eldest, oldest.

2 nm a *[famille]* l'~ (des garçons) the eldest boy; mon (frère) ~ (*plus âgé*) my older *ou* elder brother; (*le plus âgé*) my oldest *ou* eldest brother; le père était fier de son ~ the father was proud of his oldest *ou* eldest boy *ou* son.

b (*relation d'âges*) il est mon ~ he's older than me; il est mon ~ de 2 ans he's 2 years older than me, he's 2 years my senior; (*littér*) respectez vos ~s respect your elders.

3 **aînée** nf a l'~e (des filles) the oldest *ou* eldest girl *ou* daughter; ma sœur ~e, mon ~e (*plus âgée*) my older *ou* elder sister; (*la plus âgée*) my oldest *ou* eldest sister.

b elle est mon ~e she's older than me; elle est mon ~e de 2 ans she's 2 years older than me, she's 2 years my senior.

aînesse [ɛnɛs] nf *voir* droit.

ainsi [ɛ̃si] adv a (*de cette façon*) in this way *ou* manner. je préfère agir ~ I prefer to act in this way *ou* manner *ou* to act thus; il faut procéder ~ you have to proceed as follows *ou* thus *ou* in this manner; c'est ~ que ça s'est passé that's the way *ou* how it happened; est-ce ~ que tu me traites? is this the way *ou* is this how you treat me?; pourquoi me traites-tu ~? why do you treat me thus?†, why do you treat me like this? *ou* in this way?; ~ finit son grand amour thus ended his great love; il n'en est pas ~ pour tout le monde it's not so *ou* the case for everyone; s'il en est ~ *ou* puisque c'est ~, je m'en vais if *ou* since this is the way things are *ou* how things are, I am leaving, if *ou* since this is the case, I am leaving; s'il en était ~ if this were the case; il en sera ~ et pas autrement this is how *ou* the way it *ou* things will be and no other way.

b (*littér: en conséquence*) thus; (*donc*) so. ils ont perdu le procès, ~ ils sont ruinés they lost the case and so they are ruined; ~ tu vas partir! so, you're going to leave!

c (*littér: de même*) so, in the same way. comme le berger mène ses moutons, ~ le pasteur guide ses ouailles just as the shepherd leads his sheep, so *ou* in the same way does the minister guide his flock (*littér*).

d ~ que (just) as; (*littér*) ~ qu'il vous plaira (just) as it pleases you; ~ que nous avons dit hier just as we said yesterday; la jalousie, ~ qu'un poison subtil, s'insinuait en lui jealousy, (just) like a subtle poison, was slowly worming its way into him; sa beauté ~ que sa candeur me frappèrent I was struck by her beauty as well as her innocence.

e (*loc*) pour ~ dire so to speak, as it were; ils sont pour ~ dire ruinés they are ruined, so to speak *ou* as it were, you might say they are ruined; ~ soit-il (*gén*) so be it; (*Rel*) amen; et ~ de suite and so on (and so forth); ~ va le monde that's the way of the world.

air[1] [ɛʀ] 1 nm a (*gaz*) air; (*brise*) air, (light) breeze; (*courant d'air*) draught (*Brit*), draft (*US*). l'~ de la campagne/de la mer the country/sea air; l'~ de la ville ne lui convient pas town air *ou* the air of the town doesn't suit him; une pièce sans ~ a stuffy room; on manque d'~ ici there's no air (in) here, it's stuffy (in) here; donnez-nous un peu d'~ give us some (fresh) air; sortir à l'~ libre to come out into the open air; jouer à l'~ to play in the open air *ou* outdoors; mettre la literie à l'~ to put the bedclothes (out) to air *ou* out for an airing, air the bedclothes; sortir prendre l'~ to go out for some *ou* a breath of (fresh) air; (*Naut*) il y a des ~s there is a wind (up); il y a un peu d'~ aujourd'hui there's a light *ou* slight breeze today; on sent de l'~ qui vient de la porte you can feel a draught (*Brit*) *ou* draft (*US*) from the door; *voir* bol, chambre, courant *etc*.

b (*espace*) air. s'élever dans l'~ *ou* dans les ~s to rise (up) into the skies *ou* the air; regarder en l'~ to look up; avoir le nez en l'~ to gaze vacantly about one; jeter qch en l'~ to throw sth (up) into the air; transports par ~ air transport, transport by air; l'avion a pris l'~ the plane has taken off; de l'~ *hôtesse, ministère* air (*épith*); *voir* armée, école, mal.

c (*fig: atmosphère, ambiance*) atmosphere. dans l'~: ces idées étaient dans l'~ à cette époque those ideas were in the air at that time; il y a de la bagarre dans l'~ there's a quarrel in the wind *ou* brewing; il y a de l'orage dans l'~ there's a storm brewing; la grippe est dans l'~ there's flu about (*Brit*) *ou* going around; il est allé prendre l'~ du bureau he has gone to see how things look *ou* what things look like at the office; tout le monde se dispute, l'~ de la maison est irrespirable everyone's quarrelling and the atmosphere in the house is unbearable; il a besoin de l'~ de la ville he needs the atmosphere of the town.

d (*loc*) en l'~ *paroles, promesses* idle, empty; *agir* rashly; ce ne sont encore que des projets en l'~ these plans are still very much in the air; (*désordre*) tout était en l'~ dans la pièce the room was in a total mess; flanquer* *ou* ficher* *ou* foutre‡ tout en l'~ (*jeter*) to chuck‡ *ou* sling* (*Brit*) it all away *ou* out; (*abandonner*) to chuck it all up‡ (*Brit*) *ou* in‡; ce contretemps a fichu en l'~ mes vacances* this hitch has (completely) messed up my holidays*; en courant, il a flanqué le vase en l'~* as he was running he knocked over the vase; se ficher* *ou* se foutre‡ en l'~ to smash o.s. up*; vivre *ou* se nourrir de l'air du temps to live on air *ou* on nothing at all; *voir* parler.

2 comp ►**air-air** adj inv (*Mil*) air-to-air ►**air comprimé** compressed air ►**air conditionné** air conditioning ►**air liquide** liquid air ►**air-sol** adj inv (*Mil*) air-to-ground ►**air-terre** adj inv (*Mil*) air-to-ground.

air[2] [ɛʀ] nm a (*apparence, manière*) air. d'un ~ décidé in a resolute manner; sous son ~ calme c'est un homme énergique beneath his calm appearance he is a forceful man; un garçon à l'~ éveillé a lively-looking boy; ils ont un ~ de famille there's a family likeness between them; ça lui donne l'~ d'un clochard it makes him look like a tramp; *voir* faux, grand.

b (*expression*) look, air. d'un ~ perplexe with a look *ou* an air of perplexity, with a perplexed air *ou* look; je lui trouve un drôle d'~ I think he looks funny *ou* very odd; prendre un ~ éploré to put on *ou* adopt a tearful expression; elle a pris son petit ~ futé pour me dire she told me in her sly little manner, she put on that rather sly look she has *ou* of hers to tell me; prendre un ~ entendu to put on a knowing air; prendre un ~ pincé to put on a prim expression.

c (*loc*) avoir l'~: elle a l'~ d'une enfant she looks like a child; ça m'a l'~ d'un mensonge it looks to me *ou* sounds to me like a lie; ça m'a l'~ d'être assez facile it strikes me as being fairly easy, it looks fairly easy to me; elle a l'~ intelligent(e) she looks *ou* seems intelligent, she has an intelligent look; il a l'~ stupide – il en a l'~ et la chanson* he looks idiotic – he doesn't just look it either!*; il a eu l'~ de ne pas comprendre he looked as if *ou* as though he didn't understand, he didn't seem to understand; (*faire semblant*) he pretended not to understand; elle n'avait pas l'~ de vouloir travailler she didn't look as if *ou* as though she wanted to work; il est très ambitieux sans en avoir l'~ he might not look it but he's very ambitious, he's very ambitious although he might not *ou* doesn't really look it; ça (m')a tout l'~ d'être une fausse alerte it looks (to me) as if it's a false alarm; il a l'~ de vouloir neiger it looks like snow; de quoi j'ai l'~ maintenant!*, j'ai l'~ fin maintenant!* I really look like (a bit of) a fool (*Brit*) *ou* like a fine one (*Brit*) *ou* like an idiot now*; il n'a l'~ de rien, mais il sait ce qu'il fait you wouldn't think it to look at him but he knows what he's doing; cette plante n'a l'~ de rien, pourtant elle donne de très jolies fleurs this plant doesn't look much but it has very pretty flowers; sans avoir l'~ de rien, filons discrètement let's just behave naturally and slip away unnoticed; ça m'a tout de même coûté 5 000 F, l'~ de rien even so, it still cost me 5,000 francs; il a dit ça avec son ~ de ne pas y toucher he said it with the most innocent expression on his face.

air[3] [ɛʀ] nm *[opéra]* aria; (*mélodie*) tune, air. l'~ d'une chanson the tune of a song; ~ d'opéra operatic aria; ~ de danse dance tune; (*lit, fig*) ~ connu familiar tune; chanter des slogans sur l'~ des lampions to chant slogans.

airain [ɛʀɛ̃] nm (*littér*) bronze.

Airbus [ɛʀbys] nm ® Airbus ®.

aire [ɛʀ] nf (*zone*) area, zone; (*Math*) area; *[aigle]* eyrie. ~ d'atterrissage landing strip; (*pour hélicoptère*) landing pad; (*Agr*) ~ de battage threshing floor; (*Géol*) ~s continentales continental shields; ~ d'embarquement boarding area; (*Bio*) ~ embryonnaire germinal area; ~ de jeu adventure playground; ~ de lancement launching site; (*sur autoroute*) ~ de repos rest area (*on motorway etc*); ~ de service motorway services, service station; ~ de stationnement parking area; (*Naut*) ~ de vent rhumb; suivant l'~ de vent following the rhumb-line route, taking a rhumb-line course.

airelle [ɛʀɛl] nf (*myrtille*) bilberry, whortleberry, blueberry. ~ (rouge) (type of) cranberry.

aisance [ɛzɑ̃s] nf a (*facilité*) ease. s'exprimer avec une rare *ou* parfaite ~ to have great facility *ou* ease of expression, express o.s. with great ease *ou* facility; **il patinait avec une rare *ou* parfaite ~** he skated with the greatest of ease *ou* with great ease; **il y a beaucoup d'~ dans son style** he has an easy *ou* a flowing style *ou* a very fluent style. b (*richesse*) affluence. **vivre dans l'~** to be comfortably off *ou* well-off, live comfortably. c (*Couture*) **redonner de l'~ sous les bras** to give more freedom of movement *ou* more fullness under the arms; *voir* **pli.** d *voir* **fosse, lieu.**

aise [ɛz] 1 **nf** a (*littér*) joy, pleasure, satisfaction. **j'ai tant d'~ à vous voir** I'm overjoyed to see you, it gives me such joy *ou* pleasure *ou* satisfaction to see you; **sourire d'~** to smile with pleasure; **tous ces compliments la comblaient d'~** all these compliments made her overjoyed *ou* filled her with great joy *ou* satisfaction.

b (*loc*) **être à l'~, être à son ~** (*dans une situation*) to be *ou* feel at ease; (*dans un vêtement, fauteuil*) to feel *ou* be comfortable; (*être riche*) to be comfortably off *ou* comfortable; **être mal à l'~, être mal à son ~** (*dans une situation*) to be *ou* feel ill at ease; (*dans un vêtement, fauteuil*) to feel *ou* be uncomfortable; **mettez-vous à l'~ *ou* à votre ~** make yourself comfortable, make yourself at home; **leur hôtesse les mit tout de suite à l'~** their hostess immediately put them at (their) ease *ou* made them feel immediately at home; **faire qch à l'~*** to do sth easily; **tu comptes faire ça en deux heures? — à l'~!*** do you think you can do that in 2 hours? — easily! *ou* no problem!*; **en prendre à son ~ avec qch** to make free with sth, do exactly as one likes with sth; **vous en prenez à votre ~!** you're taking things nice and easy!; **tu en parles à ton ~!** it's easy (enough) *ou* it's all right for you to talk!; **à votre ~!** please yourself!, just as you like!; **on tient à 4 à l'~ dans cette voiture** this car holds 4 (quite) comfortably, 4 can get in this car (quite) comfortably.

c **~s: aimer ses ~s** to like *ou* be fond of one's creature comforts *ou* one's comforts; (*iro*) **tu prends tes ~s!** you're making yourself comfortable all right! (*iro*).

2 **adj** (*littér*) **être bien ~ d'avoir fini son travail** to be delighted *ou* most pleased to have finished one's work; **j'ai terminé — j'en suis fort ~** I've finished — I'm so glad.

aisé, e [eze] **adj** a (*facile*) easy. **~ à découvrir/faire** easy to find out/to do. b (*dégagé*) *démarche* easy, graceful; *style* flowing, fluent. c (*riche*) well-to-do, comfortably off (*attrib*), well-off.

aisément [ezemɑ̃] **adv** (*sans peine*) easily; (*sans réserves*) readily; (*dans la richesse*) comfortably.

aisselle [ɛsɛl] **nf** (*Anat*) armpit, axilla (*SPÉC*); (*Bot*) axil.

AIT [aite] **nf** (**abrév de Association internationale du tourisme**) *voir* **association.**

Aix-la-Chapelle [ɛkslaʃapɛl] **n** Aachen.

Ajax [aʒaks] **nm** Ajax.

ajonc [aʒɔ̃] **nm** gorse (*NonC*), furze (*NonC*).

ajour [aʒuʀ] **nm** (*gén pl*) *[broderie, sculpture]* openwork (*NonC*).

ajouré, e [aʒuʀe] (**ptp de ajourer**) **adj** *mouchoir* openwork (*épith*), hemstitched; *bijou, sculpture* which has an openwork design.

ajourer [aʒuʀe] 1 **vt** *sculpture* to ornament with openwork; *mouchoir* to hemstitch.

ajournement [aʒuʀnəmɑ̃] **nm** (*voir* **ajourner**) adjournment; deferment; postponement; referring; summons.

ajourner [aʒuʀne] 1 1 **vt** *assemblée* to adjourn; *réunion, élection, décision* to defer, postpone, adjourn; *rendez-vous* to postpone, put off; *candidat* to refer; *conscrit* to defer; (*Jur: convoquer*) to summon. **réunion ajournée d'une semaine/au lundi suivant** meeting adjourned *ou* delayed for a week/until the following Monday. 2 **s'ajourner vpr** (*Pol*) to adjourn.

ajout [aʒu] **nm** *[texte]* addition.

ajouter [aʒute] 1 1 **vt** a to add. **ajoute un peu de sel** put in *ou* add a bit more salt; **je dois ~ que** I should add that; **sans ~ un mot** without (saying *ou* adding) another word; **ajoutez à cela qu'il pleuvait** on top of that *ou* in addition to that *ou* what's more, it was raining; **ajoutez à cela sa maladresse naturelle** add to that his natural clumsiness.

b **~ foi aux dires de qn** to lend *ou* give credence to sb's statements, believe sb's statements.

2 **ajouter à vt indir** (*littér*) to add to, increase. **ton arrivée ajoute à mon bonheur** your arrival adds to *ou* increases my happiness.

3 **s'ajouter vpr: s'~ à** to add to; **ces malheurs venant s'~ à leur pauvreté** these misfortunes adding further to their poverty; **ceci, venant s'~ à ses difficultés** this coming on top of *ou* to add further to his difficulties; **à ces dépenses viennent s'~ les impôts** on top of *ou* in addition to these expenses there are taxes.

ajustage [aʒystaʒ] **nm** (*Tech*) fitting.

ajustement [aʒystəmɑ̃] **nm** *[statistique, prix]* adjustment; (*Tech*) fit. **~ monétaire** currency adjustment *ou* realignment.

ajuster [aʒyste] 1 1 **vt** a (*régler*) *ceinture, salaires* to adjust; *vêtement* to alter; *pièce réglable* to adjust, regulate. **robe ajustée** close-fitting dress; **il leur est difficile d'~ leurs vues** it is difficult for them to make their views agree *ou* to reconcile their views.

b (*adapter*) **~ qch à** to fit sth to; **~ un tuyau à qch** to fit a hose onto sth; **~ son style à un sujet** to fit *ou* adapt one's style to a subject.

c *tir* to aim. **~ son coup** to aim one's shot; **~ qn** to aim at sb.

d (†) *coiffure* to tidy, arrange; *tenue* to arrange; *cravate* to straighten.

2 **s'ajuster vpr** a (*Tech*) (*s'emboîter*) to fit (together); (*s'adapter*) to be adjustable. **s'~ à** to fit.

b (†: *se rajuster*) to adjust *ou* tidy one's dress†.

ajusteur [aʒystœʀ] **nm** metal worker.

Alabama [alabama] **nm** Alabama.

alacrité [alakʀite] **nf** (*littér*) alacrity.

Aladin [aladɛ̃] **nm** Aladdin.

Alain [alɛ̃] **nm** Alan.

alaise [alɛz] **nf** undersheet, drawsheet.

alambic [alɑ̃bik] **nm** (*Chim*) still.

alambiqué, e [alɑ̃bike] **adj** (*péj*) *style, discours* convoluted (*péj*), involved; *personne, esprit* over-subtle (*péj*).

alangui, e [alɑ̃gi] (**ptp de alanguir**) **adj** *attitude, geste* languid; *rythme, style* languid, lifeless.

alanguir [alɑ̃giʀ] 2 1 **vt** a *[fièvre]* to make feeble *ou* languid, enfeeble; *[chaleur]* to make listless *ou* languid; *[plaisirs, vie paresseuse]* to make indolent *ou* languid. **être tout alangui par la chaleur** to feel listless *ou* languid with the heat. b *récit* to make nerveless *ou* lifeless. 2 **s'alanguir vpr** to grow languid *ou* weak, languish.

alanguissement [alɑ̃gismɑ̃] **nm** languidness, languor.

alarmant, e [alaʀmɑ̃, ɑ̃t] **adj** alarming.

alarme [alaʀm] **nf** a (*signal de danger*) alarm, alert. **donner *ou* sonner l'~** to give *ou* sound *ou* raise the alarm, give the alert; *voir* **signal, sirène, sonnette.** b (*inquiétude*) alarm. **jeter l'~** to cause alarm; **à la première ~** at the first sign of danger.

alarmer [alaʀme] 1 1 **vt** to alarm. 2 **s'alarmer vpr** to become alarmed (*de, pour* about, at). **il n'a aucune raison de s'~** he has *ou* there is no cause for alarm.

alarmiste [alaʀmist] **adj, nmf** alarmist.

Alaska [alaska] **nm** Alaska. **la route de l'~** the Alaska Highway; **la chaîne de l'~** the Alaska Range.

albanais, e [albanɛ, ɛz] 1 **adj** Albanian. 2 **nm** (*Ling*) Albanian. 3 **nm,f: A~(e)** Albanian.

Albanie [albani] **nf** Albania.

albâtre [albɑtʀ] **nm** alabaster.

albatros [albatʀos] **nm** (*oiseau*) albatross; (*Golf*) albatross (*Brit*), double eagle (*US*).

Albert [albɛʀ] **nm** Albert.

Alberta [albɛʀta] **nm** Alberta.

albigeois, e [albiʒwa, waz] 1 **adj** a (*Géog*) of *ou* from Albi. b (*Hist*) Albigensian. 2 **nm,f: A~(e)** inhabitant *ou* native of Albi. 3 **nmpl** (*Hist*) **les ~** the Albigenses, the Albigensians; *voir* **croisade.**

albinisme [albinism] **nm** albinism.

albinos [albinos] **nmf, adj inv** albino.

Albion [albjɔ̃] **nf: (la perfide) ~** (perfidious) Albion.

album [albɔm] **nm** album. **~ (de) photos/de timbres** photo/stamp album; **~ à colorier** colouring *ou* painting book.

albumen [albymɛn] **nm** albumen.

albumine [albymin] **nf** albumin.

albumineux, -euse [albyminø, øz] **adj** albuminous.

albuminurie [albyminyʀi] **nf** albuminuria.

albuminurique [albyminyʀik] **adj** albuminuric.

alcade [alkad] **nm** alcalde.

alcaïque [alkaik] **adj** Alcaic. **vers ~s** Alcaics.

alcali [alkali] **nm** alkali. **~ volatil** ammonia.

alcalin, e [alkalɛ̃, in] **adj** alkaline.

alcalinité [alkalinite] **nf** alkalinity.

alcaloïde [alkalɔid] **nm** alkaloid.

alcalose [alkaloz] **nf** alkalosis.

Alceste [alsɛst] **nm** Alcestis.

alchimie [alʃimi] **nf** alchemy.

alchimique [alʃimik] **adj** alchemical, of alchemy.

alchimiste [alʃimist] **nm** alchemist.

alcool [alkɔl] **nm** a (*Chim*) alcohol. **~ absolu** pure alcohol; **~ à brûler** methylated spirit(s); **~ camphré** camphorated alcohol; **~ rectifié** rectified spirit; **~ à 90°** surgical spirit; **lampe à ~** spirit lamp.

b (*boisson*) alcohol (*NonC*). **l'~ au volant** drink-driving, drinking and driving; **boire de l'~** (*gén*) to drink alcohol; (*eau-de-vie*) to drink spirits; **il ne prend jamais d'~** he never drinks *ou* he never touches alcohol; **le cognac est un ~** cognac is a brandy *ou* spirit; **vous prendrez bien un petit ~** you won't say no to a little brandy *ou* liqueur; **~ de prune/poire** plum/pear brandy; **~ de menthe** medicinal mint spirit; **~ blanc** colourless spirit; **~ de grain** grain alcohol; **bière sans ~** non-alcoholic beer.

alcoolémie [alkɔlemi] **nf: taux d'~** alcohol level (in the blood).

alcoolique [alkɔlik] **adj, nmf** alcoholic.

alcooliser [alkɔlize] 1 1 **vt** to alcoholize. **boissons alcoolisées/non alcoolisées** alcoholic/soft drinks; **boisson légèrement alcoolisée** low-alcohol drink. 2 **s'alcooliser vpr** to become an alcoholic; (*hum: s'enivrer*) to get drunk.

alcoolisme [alkɔlism] **nm** alcoholism.

alcoolo‡ [alkɔlo] 1 **adj = alcoolique.** 2 **nmf** wino‡.

alcoomètre [alkɔmɛtʀ] **nm** alcoholometer.

Alcootest [alkɔtɛst] **nm** ® (*objet*) Breathalyser ® (*Brit*), Breathalyzer ® (*US*); (*épreuve*) breath test. **faire subir un ~ à qn** to breathalyse (*Brit*) *ou* breathalyze (*US*) sb, give sb a breath test, breath-test sb.
alcôve [alkov] **nf** alcove, recess (*in a bedroom*). (*fig*) **d'~** bedroom (*épith*), intimate; *voir* **secret.**
alcyon [alsjɔ̃] **nm** (*Myth*) Halcyon.
al dente [aldɛnte] **loc adv** al dente.
ALE [aɛlə] **nf** (**abrév de Association de libre-échange**) FTA.
aléa [alea] **nm** hazard. **en comptant avec tous les ~s** taking all the risks *ou* the unknown factors into account; **les ~s de l'examen** the hazards of the exam; **après bien des ~s** after many ups and downs *ou* many hazards.
aléatoire [aleatwaʀ] **adj** *gains, succès* uncertain; *marché* chancy, risky, uncertain; (*Ordin*) *nombre, accès* random; (*Mus*) aleatoric; *voir* **contrat.**
aléatoirement [aleatwaʀmɑ̃] **adv** randomly, haphazardly.
alémanique [alemanik] **adj, nm** (*Ling*) Alemannic; *voir* **suisse.**
alêne [alɛn] **nf** awl.
alentour [alɑ̃tuʀ] **adv** around, round about. **tout ~** *ou* **à l'entour††** all around; **~ de qch** (a)round sth; **les villages d'~** the villages around *ou* round about, the neighbouring *ou* surrounding villages.
alentours [alɑ̃tuʀ] **nmpl** a (*environs*) *[ville]* surroundings, neighbourhood. **les ~ sont très pittoresques** the surroundings *ou* environs are very picturesque; **dans les ~** in the vicinity *ou* neighbourhood; **aux ~ de Dijon** in the vicinity *ou* neighbourhood of Dijon; (*fig*) **étudier les ~ d'un problème** to study the side issues of a problem; **il gagne aux ~ de 1 000 F** he earns (something) in the region *ou* neighbourhood of 1,000 francs, he earns round about (*Brit*) 1,000 francs; **aux ~ de 8 heures** round about 8 (o'clock), some time around 8 (o'clock). b (*Art*) *[tapisserie]* border.
Aléoutiennes [aleusjɛn] **adj fpl, nfpl: les (îles) ~** the Aleutian Islands, the Aleutians.
Alep [alɛp] **nm** Aleppo.
alerte [alɛʀt] 1 **adj** *personne, geste* agile, nimble; *esprit* alert, agile, nimble; *vieillard* spry, agile; *style* brisk, lively. 2 **nf** a (*signal de danger, durée du danger*) alert, alarm. **donner l'~** to give the alert *ou* alarm; **donner l'~ à qn** to alert sb; **~ aérienne** air raid warning; **~ à la bombe** bomb scare; **système d'~** alarm system; (*guerre atomique*) early warning system; **les nuits d'~** nights on alert *ou* with an alert; *voir* **état, faux.** b (*fig*) (*avertissement*) warning sign; (*inquiétude*) alarm. **à la première ~** at the first warning sign; **l'~ a été chaude** *ou* **vive** there was intense *ou* considerable alarm. 3 **excl: ~!** watch out!
alertement [alɛʀt(ə)mɑ̃] **adv** (*voir* **alerte**) agilely; nimbly; alertly; spryly; briskly.
alerter [alɛʀte] 1 **vt** (*donner l'alarme*) to alert; (*informer*) to inform, notify; (*prévenir*) to warn. **~ l'opinion publique** to alert public opinion; **les pouvoirs publics ont été alertés** the authorities have been informed *ou* notified, it has been brought to the attention of the authorities.
alésage [alezaʒ] **nm** (*action*) reaming; (*diamètre*) bore.
alèse [alɛz] **nf = alaise.**
aléser [aleze] 6 **vt** to ream.
alevin [alvɛ̃] **nm** alevin, young fish (*bred artificially*).
alevinage [alvinaʒ] **nm** (*action*) stocking with alevins *ou* young fish; (*pisciculture*) fish farming.
aleviner [alvine] 1 1 **vt** (*empoissonner*) to stock with alevins *ou* young fish. 2 **vi** (*pondre*) to spawn.
Alexandre [alɛksɑ̃dʀ] **nm** Alexander.
Alexandrie [alɛksɑ̃dʀi] **n** Alexandria.
alexandrin, e [alɛksɑ̃dʀɛ̃, in] 1 **adj** *art, poésie,* (*Hist*) Alexandrian; *prosodie* alexandrine. 2 **nm** alexandrine.
alezan, e [alzɑ̃, an] **adj, nm,f** (*cheval*) chestnut. **~ clair** sorrel.
alfa [alfa] **nm** (*herbe*) Esparto (grass); (*papier*) Esparto paper.
Alfred [alfʀɛd] **nm** Alfred.
algarade [algaʀad] **nf** (*gronderie*) angry outburst; (*dispute*) row (*Brit*), spat*, run-in; (*Hist: attaque*) incursion.
algèbre [alʒɛbʀ] **nf** (*Math*) algebra. **par l'~** algebraically; **c'est de l'~ pour moi*** it's (all) Greek to me*.
algébrique [alʒebʀik] **adj** algebraic.
algébriquement [alʒebʀikmɑ̃] **adv** algebraically.
algébriste [alʒebʀist] **nmf** algebraist.
Alger [alʒe] **n** Algiers.
Algérie [alʒeʀi] **nf** Algeria.
algérien, -ienne [alʒeʀjɛ̃, jɛn] 1 **adj** Algerian. 2 **nm,f: A~(ne)** Algerian.
algérois, e [alʒeʀwa, waz] 1 **adj** of *ou* from Algiers. 2 **nm,f: A~(e)** inhabitant *ou* native of Algiers. 3 **nm** (*région*) **l'A~** the Algiers region.
algie [alʒi] **nf** algia.
ALGOL [algɔl] **nm** ALGOL.
algonkin, algonquin [algɔ̃kɛ̃] 1 **nm, adj m** (*Ling*) Algonquian. 2 **nmpl: A~s** Algonquians.
algorithme [algɔʀitm] **nm** algorithm.
algorithmique [algɔʀitmik] **adj** algorithmic.
algothérapie [algoteʀapi] **nf** seaweed bath(s).
algue [alg] **nf** (*gén*) seaweed (*NonC*); (*Bot*) alga. **~s** (*gén*) seaweed; (*Bot*) algae.
Alhambra [alɑ̃bʀa] **nm: l'~** the Alhambra.
alias [aljas] **adv** alias.
Ali Baba [alibaba] **nm: ~ et les quarante voleurs** Ali Baba and the Forty Thieves.
alibi [alibi] **nm** alibi.
Alice [alis] **nf** Alice. **~ au pays des merveilles** Alice in Wonderland.
aliénabilité [aljenabilite] **nf** alienability.
aliénable [aljenabl] **adj** alienable.
aliénant, e [aljenɑ̃, ɑ̃t] **adj** alienating.
aliénataire [aljenatɛʀ] **nmf** alienee.
aliénateur, -trice [aljenatœʀ, tʀis] **nm,f** (*Jur*) alienator.
aliénation [aljenasjɔ̃] **nf** (*gén*) alienation. (*Méd*) **~ (mentale)** (mental) derangement, insanity.
aliéné, e [aljene] (**ptp de aliéner**) **nm,f** insane person, lunatic (*péj*); *voir* **asile.**
aliéner [aljene] 6 **vt** a (*Jur: céder*) to alienate; *droits, liberté* to give up. (*Jur*) **~ un bien** to dispose of property; **~ sa liberté entre les mains de qn** to give (up) one's freedom into the hands of sb; **un traité qui aliène leur liberté** a treaty which alienates their freedom.
b (*rendre hostile*) *partisans, opinion publique* to alienate (*à qn* from sb). **cette mesure (lui) a aliéné les esprits** this measure alienated people (from him); **s'~ ses partisans/l'opinion publique** to alienate one's supporters/public opinion; **s'~ un ami** to alienate *ou* estrange a friend; **s'~ l'affection de qn** to alienate sb's affections, estrange sb.
c (*Philos, Sociol*) **~ qn** to alienate sb.
aliéniste† [aljenist] **nmf** psychiatrist.
alignement [aliɲ(ə)mɑ̃] **nm** a (*action*) aligning, lining up, bringing into alignment; (*rangée*) alignment, line. **les ~s de Carnac** the Carnac menhirs *ou* alignments (*SPÉC*). b (*Mil*) **être à l'~** to be in line; **se mettre à l'~** to fall into line, line up; **sortir de l'~** to step out of line (*lit*); **à droite/gauche, ~!** right/left, dress! c *[rue]* building line; (*Pol, Fin*) alignment. **~ monétaire** monetary alignment *ou* adjustment; **maison frappée d'~** house hit by the road widening scheme; *voir* **non.**
aligner [aliɲe] 1 1 **vt** a *objets* to align, line up, bring into alignment (*sur* with); (*fig*) *chiffres* to string together, string up a line of; (*fig*) *arguments* to reel off; (*Mil*) to form into lines, draw up in lines. **il alignait des cubes/allumettes sur la table** he was lining up *ou* making lines of building blocks/matches on the table; **des peupliers étaient alignés le long de la route** poplars stood in a straight line along the roadside; (*payer*) **pour acheter cette voiture, il va falloir les ~*** you'll have to lay out* *ou* cough up* a lot to buy this car.
b *rue* to modify the (statutory) building line of; (*Fin, Pol*) to bring into alignment (*sur* with). (*fig*) **~ sa conduite sur** to bring one's behaviour into line with, modify one's behaviour to conform with.
c (*: *punir*) **~ qn** to do sb*; **il s'est fait ~** he got done* (*pour* for).
2 **s'aligner vpr** *[soldats]* to fall into line, line up. (*Pol*) **s'~ sur** *politique* to conform to the line of; *pays, parti* to align o.s. with; **tu peux toujours t'~!*** just try and match *ou* beat that!*
aligoté [aligɔte] **adj m, nm** aligoté.
aliment [alimɑ̃] **nm** a (*nourriture*) food. **c'est un ~ riche** it's a rich food; **un ~ pauvre** a food with low nutritional value; **bien mâcher les ~s** to chew one's food well; **le pain est un ~** bread is (a) food *ou* a type of food; **le pain et le lait sont des ~s** bread and milk are foods *ou* (kinds of) food; **comment conserver vos ~s** how to keep (your) food *ou* foodstuffs fresh; **~ complet/liquide** whole/liquid food; (*Agr*) **~s industriels** factory feedstuffs; **~s organiques** wholefoods (*Brit*); (*fig*) **fournir un ~ à la curiosité de qn** to feed sb's curiosity, give sb's curiosity something to feed on; **ça a fourni un ~ à la conversation** it gave us something to talk about.
b (*Jur*) **~s** maintenance.
alimentaire [alimɑ̃tɛʀ] **adj** a *besoins* food (*épith*). **produits** *ou* **denrées ~s** foodstuffs; *voir* **bol, pâte, pension.** b (*péj*) *besogne, littérature* done to earn a living *ou* some cash. **c'est de la littérature ~** this sort of book is written as a potboiler *ou* as a money-spinner *ou* is written to earn a living.
alimentation [alimɑ̃tasjɔ̃] **nf** a (*action*) *[personne, chaudière]* feeding; *[moteur, circuit]* supplying, feeding. **l'~ en eau du moteur/des grandes villes** supplying water to *ou* the supply of water to the engine/large towns; *voir* **tuyau.** b (*régime*) diet. **~ de base** staple diet; **avoir une ~ équilibrée/mal équilibrée** to eat *ou* have a balanced/an unbalanced diet; **il lui faut une ~ lactée** he must have milky food(s) *ou* a milk diet. c (*Comm*) food trade; (*enseigne*) *[magasin]* grocery (store), groceries; *[rayon]* groceries.
alimenter [alimɑ̃te] 1 **vt** *personne, animal, chaudière* to feed; *conversation* to sustain, keep going, nourish; *curiosité* to feed, sustain; *moteur, circuit* to supply, feed. **le réservoir alimente le moteur en essence** the tank supplies the engine with petrol (*Brit*) *ou* gasoline (*US*) *ou* feeds *ou* supplies petrol *etc* to the engine; **~ une ville en gaz/électricité** to supply a town with gas/electricity; **le malade recommence à s'~** the patient is starting to eat again *ou* to take food again; **~ un compte** to provision an account.
alinéa [alinea] **nm** (*passage*) paragraph; (*ligne*) indented line (*at the beginning of a paragraph*). **nouvel ~** new line.

alitement [alitmɑ̃] nm confinement to (one's) bed.

aliter [alite] [1] 1 vt to confine to (one's) bed. **rester alité** to remain confined to (one's) bed, remain bedridden; **infirme alité** bedridden invalid. 2 **s'aliter** vpr to take to one's bed.

alizé [alize] adj m, nm: **(vent)** ~ trade wind.

Allah [ala] nm Allah.

allaitement [alɛtmɑ̃] nm a (*action: voir* **allaiter**) feeding; suckling; nursing. ~ **maternel** breast-feeding; ~ **mixte** mixed feeding; ~ **au biberon** bottle-feeding. b (*période*) breast-feeding.

allaiter [alete] [1] vt *[femme]* to (breast-)feed, give the breast to, suckle†, nurse; *[animal]* to suckle. ~ **au biberon** to bottle-feed; **elle allaite encore** she's still (breast-)feeding (the baby).

allant, e [alɑ̃, ɑ̃t] 1 adj (*littér: alerte*) sprightly, active. **musique ~e** lively music. 2 nm (*dynamisme*) drive, energy. **avoir de l'~** to have plenty of drive *ou* energy; **avec ~** energetically.

alléchant, e [aleʃɑ̃, ɑ̃t] adj (*voir* **allécher**) mouth-watering; enticing; tempting; alluring.

allécher [aleʃe] [6] vt *[odeur]* to make one's mouth water, tempt; (*fig*) *[proposition]* to entice, tempt, lure. **alléché par l'odeur** his (*ou* its) mouth watering at the smell, tempted by the smell.

allée [ale] nf a *[forêt]* lane, path; *[ville]* avenue; *[jardin]* path; *[parc]* path, walk, (*plus large*) avenue; (*menant à une maison*) drive, driveway; *[cinéma, autobus]* aisle. ~ **cavalière** bridle path; (*fig*) **les ~s du pouvoir** the corridors of power.

b **~s et venues** comings and goings; **que signifient ces ~s et venues dans le couloir?** what is the meaning of these comings and goings in the corridor?; **ceci l'oblige à de constantes ~s et venues (entre Paris et la province)** this forces him to go constantly back and forth *ou* backwards and forwards *ou* he is forced to be constantly coming and going (between Paris and the provinces); **j'ai perdu mon temps en ~s et venues pour avoir ce renseignement** I've wasted my time going back and forth *ou* to-ing and fro-ing to get this information; **le malade l'obligeait à de constantes ~s et venues** the patient kept her constantly on the run *ou* running about (for him).

allégation [a(l)legasjɔ̃] nf (*affirmation*) allegation; (*citation*) citation.

allégé, e [aleʒe] adj low-fat. **(produits) ~s** low-fat products.

allégeance [aleʒɑ̃s] nf allegiance. **faire ~ à qn** to swear allegiance to sb.

allégement [alɛʒmɑ̃] nm (*voir* **alléger**) lightening; unweighting; alleviation; reduction; mitigation; trimming. ~ **fiscal** tax relief.

alléger [aleʒe] [6] *et* [3] vt *poids, impôts* to lighten; *bagages, véhicule* to make lighter; *skis* to unweight; *douleur* to alleviate, relieve, soothe. ~ **les programmes scolaires** to lighten *ou* trim the school syllabus.

allégorie [a(l)legɔʀi] nf allegory.

allégorique [a(l)legɔʀik] adj allegorical.

allégoriquement [a(l)legɔʀikmɑ̃] adv allegorically.

allègre [a(l)lɛgʀ] adj *personne, humeur* gay, cheerful, light-hearted; *démarche* lively, jaunty; *musique* lively, merry. **il descendait la rue d'un pas ~** he was walking gaily *ou* cheerfully *ou* briskly down the street.

allégrement, allègrement [a(l)lɛgʀəmɑ̃] adv (*voir* **allègre**) gaily, cheerfully; light-heartedly; jauntily; merrily; (* *hum*) blithely, cheerfully.

allégresse [a(l)legʀɛs] nf elation, exhilaration. **ce fut l'~ générale** there was general rejoicing *ou* jubilation.

alléguer [a(l)lege] [6] vt a *fait* to put forward (as proof *ou* as an excuse *ou* as a pretext); *excuse, prétexte, raison, preuve* to put forward. **il allégua comme prétexte que ...** he put forward as a pretext that ...; **ils refusèrent de m'écouter, alléguant (comme raison) que ...** they refused to listen to me, arguing that ... *ou* alleging that ... . b (*littér: citer*) to cite, quote.

allèle [alɛl] nm allele.

alléluia [a(l)leluja] nm, excl (*Rel*) alleluia, hallelujah.

Allemagne [almaɲ] nf Germany. **l'~ fédérale** the Federal German Republic; ~ **de l'Ouest/de l'Est†** West/East Germany†; *voir* **république**.

allemand, e [almɑ̃, ɑ̃d] 1 adj German; *voir* **république**. 2 nm (*Ling*) German; *voir* **bas, haut**. 3 nm,f: **A~(e)** German. 4 **allemande** nf (*Danse, Mus*) allemande.

aller [ale] [9] 1 vi a (*se déplacer*) to go. ~ **à grands pas** to stride along; ~ **deux par deux** to go *ou* walk in twos *ou* pairs; **il va sans but par les rues** he wanders (aimlessly) through the streets; **il allait trop vite quand il a eu son accident (d'auto)** he was driving *ou* going too fast when he had his (car) accident; **en ville, on va plus vite à pied qu'en voiture** in town it is quicker to walk than to go by car, in town it is quicker to get around on foot than in a car; ~ **et venir** to come and go.

b (*se rendre à*) ~ **à/vers** to go to/towards; ~ **loin** to go a long way, go far (afield); ~ **à Paris/en Allemagne/à la campagne/chez le boucher** to go to Paris/to Germany/to the country/to the butcher's; **penses-tu y ~?** do you think you'll be going (there)?; ~ **au lit/à l'église/à l'école** to go to bed/to church/to school; ~ **à la chasse/à la pêche** to go hunting/fishing; ~ **aux champignons** to go mushroom-picking, go collecting mushrooms; ~ **à Paris en voiture/à** *ou* **en bicyclette/en avion** to drive/cycle/fly to Paris; **vas-tu à pied?** will you walk? *ou* go on foot?; ~ **sur Paris** to go in the direction of Paris, go towards Paris; ~ **aux renseignements/aux nouvelles** to go and inquire/and find out the news; (*fig*) **j'irai jusqu'au ministre** I'll take it to the minister; **il ira loin** he'll go far; **il est allé trop loin** he went too far; **on va à la catastrophe** we're heading for disaster; **il est allé jusqu'à dire** he went as *ou* so far as to say; ~ **sur ses 30 ans** to be getting on for (*Brit*) *ou* going on (*US*) 30; **où allons-nous?** what are things coming to?; **on ne va pas loin avec 100 F** you won't get far on 100 francs; **ce travail lui déplaît mais il ira jusqu'au bout** he doesn't like this job but he'll see it through.

c (*mener, s'étendre*) to go (*à* to). **cette route doit ~ quelque part** this road must go somewhere; **son champ va jusqu'à la forêt** his field goes *ou* stretches as far as the forest; **l'affaire pourrait ~ loin** this matter could turn out to be very serious.

d (*état de santé*) **comment allez-vous?** how are you?; **(comment) ça va?*** *ou* **comment va la santé?*** — **ça va*** how's things?* *ou* how are you keeping?* — fine *ou* not so bad*; **ça va mieux maintenant** I'm feeling better now; **comment va ton frère?** — **il va bien/mal** how's your brother? — he's well *ou* fine*/he isn't well *ou* he's unwell *ou* he's ill; **ça va?*** — **faudra bien que ça aille*** you all right?* — I'll have to be*; **ça va?** — **on fait ~*** you all right?* — so-so*.

e (*situation*) **(comment) ça va?*** — **ça va*** how's life?* *ou* how are you getting on?* — fine* *ou* not so bad*; **ça va à l'école?** — **ça va, ça vient*** how are you getting on at school? — it varies; **ça va, la réparation?*** — **faudra bien que ça aille*** is the repair all right? — it'll have to be*; **comment vont les affaires?** — **elles vont bien/mal** how's business? — (it's) fine/not too good; **ça va mal en Asie/à la maison** things aren't going too well *ou* things aren't looking so good in Asia/at home; **ça va mieux pour lui maintenant** things are looking better for him now, things are looking more hopeful for him now; **ça ne va pas mieux! il refuse d'obéir** whatever next! he's refusing to obey; **ça va mal ~ si tu continues** if you carry on, there's going to be trouble; **est-ce que ta pendule va bien?** *ou* **juste?** is your clock right?; **ça ne va pas sans difficulté** it's no easy job, there are problems; **non mais ça va pas (la tête)!*** you're crazy!*, you must be crazy!*; (*facile*) **ça va tout seul*** it's a cinch‡, it's a doddle‡ (*Brit*); **ça ne va pas tout seul*** it's no cinch‡, it's no doddle‡ (*Brit*); *voir* **chemin, cœur, main**.

f (*convenir*) ~ **à qn** *[forme, mesure]* to fit sb; *[style, genre]* to suit sb; ~ **(bien) avec** to go (well) with; ~ **bien ensemble** to go well together; **ce tableau va bien/mal sur ce mur** this picture goes well/doesn't go well on this wall; **la clef ne va pas dans la serrure** the key won't go in *ou* doesn't fit the lock; **cette robe lui va bien** (*couleur, style*) this dress suits her; (*pour la taille*) this dress fits her; **vos projets me vont parfaitement** your plans suit me fine; **rendez-vous demain 4 heures?** — **ça me va*** see you tomorrow at 4? — (it) suits me* *ou* it's all right by me; **ce climat ne leur va pas** this climate doesn't suit them *ou* agree with them; **les ciseaux ne vont pas pour couper du carton** scissors won't do *ou* are no good for cutting cardboard; **votre plan ne va pas** your plan won't do *ou* work; **ça lui va mal** *ou* (*hum*) **bien de critiquer les autres*** he's got a nerve* criticizing other people, he's a fine one* to criticize other people; **il a fait ce travail à la va-comme-je-te-pousse*** he did the work any old how*.

g ~ **aux cabinets** to go to the toilet; ~ **(à la selle)** to have a bowel movement; **le malade est-il allé à la selle?** have the patient's bowels moved?; **cela fait ~*** it keeps the bowels open, it clears you out* (*hum*).

h (*avec participe présent: pour exprimer la progression*) ~ **en augmentant** to keep increasing, increase more and more; ~ **en empirant** to get worse and worse; **le bruit va croissant** the noise is getting louder and louder.

i (*excl*) (*stimulation*) **allons!, allez!** go on!, come on!; (*incrédulité*) **allons donc!** really?, come on now!, come off it!*; (*agacement*) **allons bon! qu'est-ce qui t'est encore arrivé?** NOW what's happened!; (*impatience*) **allons, cesse de m'ennuyer!** will you just stop bothering me!; (*encouragement*) **allons, allons, il ne faut pas pleurer** come on now *ou* come, come, you mustn't cry; **ça va, ça va!*** all right, that's enough!, OK, OK*, don't go on!*; **allez, au revoir!** cheerio then! (*Brit*), 'bye then!, so long!*; ~ **de soi** to be self-evident, be obvious; **cela va de soi** it's obvious *ou* self-evident, it stands to reason, it goes without saying; **cela va sans dire** it goes without saying; **il va sans dire qu'il accepta** needless to say *ou* it goes without saying, he accepted; **il répète à tout va ce que tu lui as raconté** he's going round telling everyone what you told him; **va pour une nouvelle voiture!*** all right we'll HAVE a new car!; (*dans un marchandage*) **va pour 30 F!** OK, 30 francs then!; **va donc, eh imbécile!‡** get lost, you twit‡; **allez, allez, circulez** come on now, move along; **tu t'en remettras, va** don't worry, you'll get over it.

j (*avec en*) **il en va de: il en va de même pour tous les autres** the same applies to all the others; **il en va de cette affaire comme de la précédente** the same goes for this matter as for the previous one.

k (*avec y*) **on y va?*** shall we go?, are we off then?*; **allons-y!** let's go!; **allez-y, c'est votre tour** go on *ou* on you go, it's your turn; **allez-y, vous ne risquez rien** go ahead *ou* go on *ou* on you go, you've nothing to lose; **comme vous y allez!** you're going a bit far!*; **tu y vas mal!*** *ou* **un peu fort!*** you're going a bit far*; **vas-y doucement*** *ou* **mollo‡** gently does it, go gently; (*impers*) **il y ~ de: il y va de votre vie/de votre santé** your life/your health is at stake *ou* depends on it; **il y est allé de sa petite chanson*** he gave us his little song; **elle y va**

toujours de son porte-monnaie she's always the one who forks out‡; **il y est allé de sa petite larme*** he had a little cry.

2 **vb aux** (+ *infin*) a (*futur immédiat*) to be going to. **tu vas être en retard** you are going to be late, you'll be late; **il va descendre dans une minute** he'll be (coming) down in a minute; **ils allaient commencer** they were going to start, they were on the point of starting, they were about to start; **ça va prendre un quart d'heure** that'll take *ou* it's going to take a quarter of an hour.

b (*lit*) ~ **faire qch** to go and do sth; **il est allé me chercher mes lunettes** he went *ou* has gone to fetch (*Brit*) *ou* get my glasses; ~ **voir qn à l'hôpital** to go and visit sb in hospital; **je suis allé en courant chercher le docteur** I ran to fetch (*Brit*) *ou* get the doctor; ~ **faire le** *ou* **son marché** to go to the market.

c (*intensif*) ~ **se faire du souci inutilement** to go and worry for no reason at all; **allez donc voir si c'est vrai!** (well) you can believe it if you like!, you'll never know if it's true!; **n'allez pas vous imaginer que** don't you go imagining that; **pourvu qu'il n'aille pas penser que** as long as he doesn't go and think that; (*qui sait?*) **va savoir*!** who knows?, you never know.

3 **s'en aller vpr** a (*partir*) to go (away); (*déménager*) to move, leave. **s'en ~ subrepticement** to steal *ou* sneak away; **elle s'en va en vacances demain** she goes *ou* is going away on holiday tomorrow; **ils s'en vont à Paris** they are going *ou* off to Paris; **il s'en est allé furieux, il s'est en allé furieux*** he went away *ou* off in a huff, he left in a huff; **bon, je m'en vais** right, I'm off *ou* I'll be going; **ils s'en vont du quartier** they are leaving the district, they are moving away from the district.

b (*mourir*) to die. **il s'en va** he's sinking *ou* going; **il s'en est allé paisiblement** he passed away peacefully.

c (*prendre sa retraite*) to retire. **il s'en va cette année** he's retiring *ou* leaving this year.

d (*disparaître*) *[tache]* to come off; *[temps, années]* to pass, go by. **ça s'en ira au lavage** it'll wash off, it'll come off in the wash; **tous nos projets s'en vont en fumée** all our plans are going up in smoke; **tout son argent s'en va en disques** all his money goes on records.

e (*loc*) **je m'en vais leur montrer de quoi je suis capable** I'll show them what I'm made of!; **va-t'en voir si c'est vrai!*** you can believe it if you like!, you'll never know if it's true!

4 **nm** (*trajet*) outward journey; (*billet*) single (ticket) (*Brit*), one-way ticket (*US*). **l'~ s'est bien passé** the (outward) journey *ou* the journey there went off well; **j'irai vous voir à l'~** I'll come and see you on the *ou* my way there; **je ne fais que l'~-retour** I'm just going there and back; **3 ~s (simples) pour Tours** 3 singles (*Brit*) *ou* one-way tickets (*US*) to Tours; **prendre un ~-retour** to buy a return (ticket) (*Brit*) *ou* round-trip ticket (*US*); (*fig*) **donner/recevoir un ~-retour*** to give/get a box round the ears.

allergène [alɛʀʒɛn] **nm** allergen.

allergie [alɛʀʒi] **nf** allergy. (*lit, fig*) **faire une ~** to be allergic (*à* to).

allergique [alɛʀʒik] **adj** (*lit, fig*) allergic (*à* to).

allergisant, e [alɛʀʒizɑ̃, ɑ̃t] 1 **adj** *substance* allergenic. 2 **nm** allergen.

allergologie [alɛʀgɔlɔʒi] **nf** study of allergies.

allergologiste [alɛʀgɔlɔʒist] **nmf**, **allergologue** [alɛʀgɔlɔg] **nmf** allergist.

alliacé, e [aljase] **adj** alliaceous.

alliage [aljaʒ] **nm** alloy. (*fig péj*) **un ~ disparate de doctrines** a hotchpotch of doctrines; **roues en ~ léger** alloy wheels.

alliance [aljɑ̃s] 1 **nf** a (*pacte*) (*Pol*) alliance; (*entente*) union; (*Bible*) covenant. **faire** *ou* **conclure une ~ avec un pays** to enter into an alliance with a country; **il a fait ~ avec nos ennemis** he has allied himself with our enemies; **une étroite ~ s'était établie entre le vieillard et les enfants** a close bond had established itself between the old man and the children; *voir* **saint, triple.**

b (*frm: mariage*) union, marriage. **neveu/oncle par ~** nephew/uncle by marriage; **entrer par ~ dans une famille, faire ~ avec une famille** to marry into a family, become united by marriage with a family.

c (*bague*) (wedding) ring.

d (*fig: mélange*) combination. **l'~ de la musique et de la poésie dans cet opéra** the union of music and poetry in this opera.

2 **comp ▸alliance de mots** (*Littérat*) bold juxtaposition (of words), oxymoron.

allié, e [alje] (**ptp de allier**) 1 **adj** *pays, forces* allied. **famille ~e** family *ou* relations by marriage. 2 **nm,f** (*pays*) ally; (*fig: ami, soutien*) ally; (*parent*) relative by marriage. (*Pol*) **les A~s** the Allies.

allier [alje] 7 1 **vt** *efforts* to combine, unite; *couleurs* to match; *familles* to ally, unite by marriage; (*Pol*) to ally; (*Tech*) to alloy. **elle allie l'élégance à la simplicité** she combines elegance with simplicity; **ils sont alliés à une puissante famille** they are allied to *ou* related by marriage to a powerful family.

2 **s'allier vpr** *[efforts]* to combine, unite; *[couleurs]* to match; *[familles]* to become united by marriage, become allied; (*Pol*) to become allies *ou* allied; (*Tech*) to alloy. **s'~ à une famille riche** to become allied to *ou* with a wealthy family, marry into a wealthy family; **la France s'allia à l'Angleterre** France became allied to *ou* with England *ou* allied itself to *ou* with England.

alligator [aligatɔʀ] **nm** alligator.

allitération [a(l)liteʀasjɔ̃] **nf** alliteration.

allô [alo] **excl** (*Téléc*) hello!, hullo! (*Brit*).

allocataire [alɔkatɛʀ] **nmf** beneficiary.

allocation [alɔkasjɔ̃] 1 **nf** a (*voir* **allouer**) allocation; granting; allotment.

b (*somme*) allowance. **toucher les ~s*** to draw *ou* get family allowance(s).

2 **comp ▸allocation de chômage** unemployment benefit (*NonC*); **toucher l'allocation (de) chômage** to receive unemployment benefit (*Brit*) *ou* unemployment insurance (*US*) **▸allocations familiales** (*argent*) *state allowance paid to families with dependent children*, ≃ family allowance (*Brit*), ≃ child benefit (*Brit*), ≃ welfare (*US*); (*bureau*) ≃ family allowance department (*Brit*), child benefit office (*Brit*), ≃ welfare center (*US*), ≃ DSS (*Brit*) **▸allocation (de) logement** rent allowance *ou* subsidy **▸allocation de maternité** maternity allowance *ou* benefit **▸allocation (de) vieillesse** old-age pension.

allocs* [alɔk] **nfpl** (**abrév de allocations familiales**) *voir* **allocation.**

allocutaire [a(l)lɔkytɛʀ] **nmf** addressee.

allocution [a(l)lɔkysjɔ̃] **nf** short speech. **~ télévisée** short televised speech.

allogène [alɔʒɛn] **adj** *population* non-native; (*fig*) *éléments* foreign. **ces gens forment un groupe ~ en Grande-Bretagne** these people form a non-native racial group in Britain.

allonge [alɔ̃ʒ] **nf** (*Tech*) extension; *[table]* leaf; *[boucherie]* hook; (*Boxe*) reach. **avoir une bonne ~** to have a long reach.

allongé, e [alɔ̃ʒe] (**ptp de allonger**) **adj** a (*étendu*) **être ~** to be stretched out, be lying; **rester ~** *[blessé, malade]* to stay lying down, be lying down *ou* flat; (*se reposer*) to be lying down, have one's feet up, be resting; **~ sur son lit** lying on one's bed; **~ sur le dos** stretched out on *ou* lying on one's back, supine (*littér*); **les (malades) ~s** the recumbent patients; (*Art*) **figure ~e** recumbent figure. b (*long*) long; (*étiré*) elongated; (*oblong*) oblong. **faire une mine ~e** to pull *ou* make a long face.

allongement [alɔ̃ʒmɑ̃] **nm** a (*Métal*) elongation; (*Ling*) lengthening; (*Aviat*) aspect ratio. b (*voir* **allonger**) *[distance, vêtement]* lengthening; *[route, voie ferrée, congés, vie]* lengthening, extension. **l'~ des jours** the lengthening of the days, the longer days.

allonger [alɔ̃ʒe] 3 1 **vt** a (*rendre plus long*) to lengthen, make longer, extend (*de* by). **~ le pas** to hasten one's step(s); (*fig*) **cette coiffure lui allonge le visage** this hair style makes her face look longer *ou* long.

b (*étendre*) *bras, jambe* to stretch (out); *malade* to lay *ou* stretch out. **~ le cou (pour apercevoir qch)** to crane *ou* stretch one's neck (to see sth); **la jambe allongée sur une chaise** with one leg up on *ou* stretched out on a chair.

c (‡: *donner*) *somme* to dish out*, hand out; *coup, gifle* to deal, land*. **~ qn** to knock sb flat; **il va falloir les ~** we'll (*ou* you'll *etc*) have to lay out a lot.

d *sauce* to thin (down). (*fig*) **~ la sauce*** to spin it out.

2 **vi: les jours allongent** the days are growing longer *ou* drawing out.

3 **s'allonger vpr** a (*devenir ou paraître plus long*) *[ombres, jours]* to get longer, lengthen; *[enfant]* to grow taller; *[discours, visite]* to drag on. (*fig*) **son visage s'allongea à ces mots** at these words he pulled *ou* made a long face *ou* his face fell; **la route s'allongeait devant eux** the road stretched away before them.

b (*s'étendre*) to lie down (*full length*), stretch (o.s.) out. **s'~ dans l'herbe** to lie down on the grass, stretch (o.s.) out on the grass; (*pour dormir*) **je vais m'~ quelques minutes** I'm going to lie down for a few minutes; (*péj*) **elle s'allonge facilement‡** she's an easy lay‡.

allopathe [alɔpat] 1 **adj** allopathic. 2 **nmf** allopath, allopathist.

allopathie [alɔpati] **nf** allopathy.

allopathique [alɔpatik] **adj** allopathic.

allophone [alɔfɔn] **nm** allophone.

allotropie [alɔtʀɔpi] **nf** allotropy.

allotropique [alɔtʀɔpik] **adj** allotropic.

allouer [alwe] 1 **vt** *argent* to allocate; *indemnité* to grant; (*Fin*) *actions* to allot; *temps* to allot, allow, allocate. **pendant le temps alloué** during the allotted *ou* allowed time, during the time allowed *ou* allotted *ou* allocated.

allumage [alymaʒ] **nm** a (*action*) *[feu]* lighting, kindling; *[poêle]* lighting; *[électricité]* putting *ou* switching *ou* turning on; *[gaz]* lighting, putting *ou* turning on. b (*Aut*) ignition. **avance/retard à l'~** ignition advance/retard; **régler l'~** to adjust the timing; *voir* **auto-allumage.**

allumé, e‡ [alyme] **adj** (*fou*) crazy*, nuts*; (*ivre*) smashed‡, pissed‡ (*Brit*), lit up* (*US*).

allume-cigares [alymsigaʀ] **nm inv** cigar lighter.

allume-feu [alymfø] **nm inv** firelighter.

allume-gaz [alymgɑz] **nm inv** gas lighter (*for cooker*).

allumer [alyme] 1 1 **vt** a *feu* to light, kindle; *bougie, poêle* to light; *cigare, pipe* to light (up); *incendie* to start, light. **il alluma sa cigarette à celle de son voisin** he lit (up) his cigarette from his neighbour's, he got a light from his neighbour's cigarette; **le feu était allumé** the fire was lit *ou* alight, the fire was going; **laisse le poêle allumé** leave the stove on *ou* lit.

b *électricité, lampe, radio* to put *ou* switch *ou* turn on; *gaz* to light, put *ou* turn on. **laisse la lumière allumée** leave the light on; **allume dans la cuisine** put *ou* switch *ou* turn the kitchen light(s) on, put *ou* switch *ou* turn the lights on in the kitchen; **le bouton n'allume pas, ça n'allume pas** the light doesn't come on *ou* work; **où est-ce qu'on allume?** where is the switch?

c ~ **une pièce** to put *ou* switch *ou* turn the light(s) on in a room; **sa fenêtre était allumée** there was a light (on) at his window, his window was lit (up); **laisse le salon allumé** leave the light(s) on in the sitting-room, leave the sitting room light(s) on.

d *colère, envie, haine* to arouse, stir up, kindle; *amour* to kindle.

e (**: aguicher*) to turn on*.

f (*‡: tuer avec une arme à feu*) to burn‡.

2 **s'allumer** vpr *[incendie]* to blaze, flare up; *[lumière]* to come *ou* go on; *[radiateur]* to switch (itself) on; *[sentiment]* to be aroused. **ça s'allume comment?** how do you switch it on?; **le désir s'alluma dans ses yeux** his eyes lit up with desire; **ses yeux s'allumèrent/son regard s'alluma** his eyes/face lit up; **ce bois s'allume bien** this wood catches fire *ou* burns easily; **la pièce s'alluma** the light(s) came *ou* went on in the room; **sa fenêtre s'alluma** a light came *ou* went on at his window.

allumette [alymɛt] nf a match; (*morceau de bois*) match(stick). ~ **de sûreté** *ou* **suédoise** safety match; ~ **tison** fuse; **il a les jambes comme des ~s** he's got legs like matchsticks. b (*Culin*) flaky pastry finger. ~ **au fromage** cheese straw; *voir* **pomme**.

allumeur [alymœʀ] nm (*Aut*) distributor; (*Tech*) igniter. (*Hist*) ~ **de réverbères** lamplighter.

allumeuse [alymøz] nf (*péj*) teaser, tease, vamp.

allure [alyʀ] nf a (*vitesse*) *[véhicule]* speed; *[piéton]* pace. **rouler** *ou* **aller à grande/faible** ~ to drive *ou* go at (a) great/slow speed; **à toute** ~ *rouler* at top *ou* full speed, at full tilt; *réciter, dîner* as fast as one can; **manger à toute** ~ to gobble one's food; **à cette ~, nous n'aurons jamais fini à temps** at this rate we'll never be finished in time.

b (*démarche*) walk, gait (*littér*); (*prestance*) bearing; (*attitude*) air, look; (**: aspect*) *[objet, individu]* look, appearance. **avoir de l'~, ne pas manquer d'~** to have style, have a certain elegance; **avoir fière** *ou* **grande/piètre** ~ to cut a fine/shabby figure; **avoir une drôle d'~/bonne** ~ to look odd *ou* funny/fine; **d'~ louche/bizarre** fishy-/odd-looking; **les choses prennent une drôle d'~** things are taking a funny *ou* an odd turn.

c (*comportement*) **~s** ways; **choquer par sa liberté d'~s** to shock people with *ou* by one's free *ou* unconventional behaviour; **il a des ~s de voyou** he behaves *ou* carries on* like a hooligan.

d (*Équitation*) gait; (*Naut*) trim.

allusif, -ive [a(l)lyzif, iv] adj allusive.

allusion [a(l)lyzjɔ̃] nf (*référence*) allusion (*à* to); (*avec sous-entendu*) hint (*à* at). ~ **malveillante** innuendo; **faire ~ à** to allude *ou* refer to, hint at, make allusions to; **par** ~ allusively.

alluvial, e, mpl **-iaux** [a(l)lyvjal, jo] adj alluvial.

alluvionnement [a(l)lyvjɔnmɑ̃] nm alluviation.

alluvions [a(l)lyvjɔ̃] nfpl alluvial deposits, alluvium (*sg*).

Alma-Ata [almaata] n Alma Ata.

almanach [almana] nm almanac.

almée [alme] nf Egyptian dancing girl, almah.

aloès [alɔɛs] nm aloe.

aloi [alwa] nm: **de bon** ~ *plaisanterie, gaieté* honest, respectable; *individu* worthy, of sterling *ou* genuine worth; *produit* sound, worthy, of sterling *ou* genuine quality *ou* worth; **de mauvais** ~ *plaisanterie, gaieté* unsavoury, unwholesome; *individu* of little worth, of doubtful reputation; *produit* of doubtful quality.

alopécie [alɔpesi] nf alopecia.

alors [alɔʀ] adv a (*à cette époque*) then, in those days, at that time. **il était ~ étudiant** he was a student then *ou* at that time *ou* in those days; **les femmes d'~ portaient la crinoline** the women in *ou* of those days *ou* at *ou* of that time wore crinolines; **le ministre d'~ M. Dupont** the then minister Mr Dupont, the minister at that time, Mr Dupont; *voir* **jusque**.

b (*en conséquence*) then, in that case, so. **vous ne voulez pas de mon aide? ~ je vous laisse** you don't want my help? then *ou* in that case *ou* so I'll leave you *ou* I'll leave you then; **il ne connaissait pas l'affaire, ~ on l'a mis au courant** he wasn't familiar with the matter so they put him in the picture; ~ **qu'est-ce qu'on va faire?** what are we going to do then?, so what are we going to do?

c ~ **que** (*simultanéité*) while, when; (*opposition*) whereas; ~ **même que** (*même si*) even if, even though; (*au moment où*) while, just when; **on a sonné ~ que j'étais dans mon bain** the bell rang while *ou* when I was in my bath; **elle est sortie ~ que le médecin le lui avait interdit** she went out although *ou* even though the doctor had told her not to; **il est parti travailler à Paris ~ que son frère est resté au village** he went to work in Paris whereas *ou* while his brother stayed behind in the village; ~ **même qu'il me supplierait** even if he begged me, even if *ou* though he were to beg me.

d (*) ~ **tu viens (oui ou non)?** well (then), are you coming (or not)?, are you coming then (or not)?; ~ **ça, ça m'étonne** now that really does surprise me; ~ **là je ne peux pas vous répondre** well that I really can't tell you; ~ **là je vous arrête** well I must stop you there; **et (puis)** ~? and then what (happened)?; **il pleut — et** ~? it's raining — so (what)?; ~ ~!, ~ **quoi!** come on!; *voir* **non**.

alose [aloz] nf shad.

alouette [alwɛt] nf lark. ~ **(des champs)** skylark; **attendre que les ~s vous tombent toutes rôties dans la bouche** to wait for things to fall into one's lap; *voir* **miroir**.

alourdir [aluʀdiʀ] 2 1 vt *véhicule* to weigh *ou* load down, make heavy; *phrase* to make heavy *ou* cumbersome; *démarche, traits* to make heavy; *impôts* to increase; *esprit* to dull. **avoir la tête alourdie par le sommeil** to be heavy with sleep *ou* heavy-eyed; **vêtements alourdis par la pluie** clothes heavy with rain; **les odeurs d'essence alourdissaient l'air** petrol fumes hung heavy on the air, the air was heavy with petrol fumes. 2 **s'alourdir** vpr to become *ou* grow heavy. **sa taille/elle s'est alourdie** her waist/she has thickened out; **ses paupières s'alourdissaient** his eyes were growing *ou* becoming heavy.

alourdissement [aluʀdismɑ̃] nm *[véhicule, objet]* increased weight, heaviness; *[phrase, style, pas]* heaviness; *[impôts]* increase (*de* in); *[esprit]* dullness, dulling; *[taille]* thickening.

aloyau [alwajo] nm sirloin.

alpaga [alpaga] nm (*Tex, Zool*) alpaca.

alpage [alpaʒ] nm (*pré*) high mountain pasture; (*époque*) *season spent by sheep etc in mountain pasture*.

alpaguer‡ [alpage] 1 vt to nab*. **se faire** ~ to get nabbed*.

alpe [alp] nf a **les A~s** the Alps. b (*pré*) alpine pasture.

alpestre [alpɛstʀ] adj alpine.

alpha [alfa] nm alpha. (*Rel, fig*) **l'~ et l'oméga** the alpha and omega.

alphabet [alfabɛ] nm (*système*) alphabet; (*livre*) alphabet *ou* ABC book. ~ **morse** Morse code; ~ **phonétique international** International Phonetic Alphabet.

alphabétique [alfabetik] adj alphabetic(al). **par ordre** ~ in alphabetical order, alphabetically.

alphabétiquement [alfabetikmɑ̃] adv alphabetically.

alphabétisation [alfabetizasjɔ̃] nf elimination of illiteracy (*de* in). **l'~ d'une population** teaching a population to read and write; **campagne d'~** literacy campaign.

alphabétiser [alfabetize] 1 vt *pays* to eliminate illiteracy in; *population* to teach how to read and write.

alphanumérique [alfanymeʀik] adj alphanumeric.

Alphonse [alfɔ̃s] nm Alphonse, Alphonso.

alpin, e [alpɛ̃, in] adj alpine; *voir* **chasseur, ski**.

alpinisme [alpinism] nm mountaineering, climbing.

alpiniste [alpinist] nmf mountaineer, climber.

Alsace [alzas] nf Alsace.

alsacien, -ienne [alzasjɛ̃, jɛn] 1 adj Alsatian. 2 nm (*Ling*) Alsatian. 3 nm,f: **A~(ne)** Alsatian.

altérabilité [alteʀabilite] nf alterability.

altérable [alteʀabl] adj alterable. ~ **à l'air** liable to oxidization.

altérant, e [alteʀɑ̃, ɑ̃t] adj thirst-making.

altération [alteʀasjɔ̃] nf a (*action: voir* **altérer**) distortion, falsification; alteration; adulteration; debasement; change; modification. b (*voir* **s'altérer**) debasement; alteration; distortion; impairment. **l'~ de sa santé** the change for the worse in *ou* the deterioration of *ou* in his health. **l'~ de son visage/de sa voix** his distorted features/broken voice. c (*Mus*) accidental; (*Géol*) weathering.

altercation [altɛʀkasjɔ̃] nf altercation, dispute.

alter ego [altɛʀego] nm inv alter ego. **il est mon ~** he is my alter ego.

altérer [alteʀe] 6 1 vt a (*assoiffer*) to make thirsty. (*littér*) **altéré d'honneurs** thirsty *ou* thirsting for honours; **fauve altéré de sang** wild animal thirsting for blood; **il était altéré** his thirst was great, his throat was parched.

b (*fausser*) *texte, faits, vérité* to distort, falsify, alter, tamper with; *monnaie* to falsify; (*Comm*) *vin, aliments, qualité* to adulterate.

c (*abîmer*) *vin, aliments, qualité* to spoil, debase; *matière* to alter, debase; *sentiments* to alter, spoil; *couleur* to alter; *visage, voix* to distort; *santé, relations* to impair, affect. **la chaleur altère la viande** heat makes meat go off (*Brit*) *ou* spoils meat.

d (*modifier*) to alter, change, modify. **ceci n'a pas altéré mon amour pour elle** this has not altered my love for her.

2 **s'altérer** vpr *[vin]* to become spoiled; *[viande]* to go off (*Brit*), spoil (*US*); *[matière]* to become altered *ou* debased; *[couleur]* to become altered; *[visage]* to change, become distorted; *[sentiments]* to alter, be spoilt; *[santé, relations]* to deteriorate. **sa santé s'altère de plus en plus** his health is deteriorating further *ou* is getting progressively worse; **sa voix s'altéra sous le coup de la douleur** grief made his voice break, grief distorted his voice.

altérité [alteʀite] nf otherness.

alternance [altɛʀnɑ̃s] nf (*gén*) alternation; (*Pol*) changeover of political power between parties. **en ~: cette émission reprendra en ~ avec d'autres programmes** this broadcast will alternate with other programmes; **ils présentèrent le spectacle en ~** they took turns to present the show, they presented the show alternately; **il n'y avait pas eu d'~ (politique) en France depuis 23 ans** (political) power had not changed hands *ou* there had been no change in the (political) party in power in France for 23 years.

alternant, e [altɛʀnɑ̃, ɑ̃t] **adj** alternating.
alternateur [altɛʀnatœʀ] **nm** alternator.
alternatif, -ive[1] [altɛʀnatif, iv] **adj** (*périodique*) alternate; (*Philos*) alternative; (*Élec*) alternating.
alternative[2] [altɛʀnativ] **nf** (*dilemme*) alternative; (**: possibilité*) alternative, option; (*Philos*) alternative. **être dans une ~** to have to choose between two alternatives; **passer par des ~s de douleur et de joie** to alternate between pleasure and pain.
alternativement [altɛʀnativmɑ̃] **adv** alternately, in turn.
alterne [altɛʀn] **adj** (*Bot, Math*) alternate.
alterné, e [altɛʀne] (**ptp de alterner**) **adj** *rimes* alternate.
alterner [altɛʀne] [1] 1 **vt** *choses* to alternate; *cultures* to rotate, alternate. 2 **vi** to alternate (*avec* with). **ils alternèrent à la présidence** they took (it in) turns to be chairman *ou* to chair.
altesse [altɛs] **nf** (*prince*) prince; (*princesse*) princess. (*titre*) **votre A~** your Highness; **Son A~ sérénissime** (*prince*) His Serene Highness; (*princesse*) Her Serene Highness; **son A~ royale** His (*ou* Her) Royal Highness; **j'en ai vu entrer des ~s!** I saw lots of princes and princesses go in.
altier, -ière [altje, jɛʀ] **adj** *caractère* haughty. (*littér*) **cimes ~ières** lofty peaks (*littér*).
altimètre [altimɛtʀ] **nm** altimeter.
altimétrie [altimetʀi] **nf** altimetry.
altiport [altipɔʀ] **nm** altiport (*SPÉC*), mountain airfield.
altiste [altist] **nmf** viola player, violist.
altitude [altityd] **nf** a (*par rapport à la mer*) altitude, height above sea level; (*par rapport au sol*) height. (*fig*) **~s** heights; **être à 500 mètres d'~** to be at a height *ou* an altitude of 500 metres, be 500 metres above sea level; **en ~** at high altitude, high up; **l'air des ~s** the mountain air. b (*Aviat*) **perdre de l'~** to lose altitude *ou* height; **prendre de l'~** to gain altitude; **il volait à basse/haute ~** he was flying at low/high altitude.
alto [alto] 1 **nm** (*instrument*) viola. 2 **nf** = **contralto**. 3 **adj**: **saxo(phone)/flûte ~** alto sax(ophone)/flute.
altruisme [altʀɥism] **nm** altruism.
altruiste [altʀɥist] 1 **adj** altruistic. 2 **nmf** altruist.
Altuglas [altyglas] **nm** ® *thick form of Perspex* ®.
alu [aly] **nm abrév de aluminium.**
aluminate [alyminat] **nm** aluminate.
alumine [alymin] **nf** alumina.
aluminium [alyminjɔm] **nm** aluminium (*Brit*), aluminum (*US*).
alun [alœ̃] **nm** alum.
alunir [alyniʀ] [2] **vi** to land on the moon.
alunissage [alynisaʒ] **nm** (moon) landing.
alvéolaire [alveɔlɛʀ] **adj** alveolar.
alvéole [alveɔl] **nf** *ou* (*rare*) **nm** *[ruche]* alveolus, cell; (*Géol*) cavity. (*Méd*) **~ dentaire** tooth socket, alveolus (*SPÉC*); **~s dentaires** alveolar ridge, teeth ridge, alveoli (*SPÉC*); **~ pulmonaire** air cell, alveolus (*SPÉC*).
alvéolé, e [alveɔle] **adj** honeycombed, alveolate (*SPÉC*).
AM [aɛm] (**abrév de assurance maladie**) *health insurance*.
amabilité [amabilite] **nf** kindness. **ayez l'~ de** be so kind *ou* good as to; **plein d'~ envers moi** extremely kind *ou* polite to me; **faire des ~s à qn** to show politeness *ou* courtesy to sb.
amadou [amadu] **nm** touchwood, tinder.
amadouer [amadwe] [1] **vt** (*enjôler*) to coax, cajole; (*adoucir*) to mollify, soothe. **~ qn pour qu'il fasse qch** to coax *ou* wheedle *ou* cajole sb into doing sth.
amaigrir [amegʀiʀ] [2] 1 **vt** a to make thin *ou* thinner. **joues amaigries par l'âge** cheeks wasted with age; **je l'ai trouvé très amaigri** I found him much thinner, I thought he looked much thinner; **10 années de prison l'ont beaucoup amaigri** 10 years in prison have left him very much thinner. b (*Tech*) to thin down, reduce. 2 **s'amaigrir vpr** to get *ou* become thin *ou* thinner.
amaigrissant, e [amegʀisɑ̃, ɑ̃t] **adj** *régime* slimming (*Brit*), reducing (*US*).
amaigrissement [amegʀismɑ̃] **nm** (*pathologique*) *[corps]* loss of weight; *[visage, membres]* thinness. b (*volontaire*) slimming. **un ~ de 3 kg** a loss (in weight) of 3 kg; *voir* **cure**.
amalgamation [amalgamasjɔ̃] **nf** (*Métal*) amalgamation.
amalgame [amalgam] **nm** (*péj: mélange*) (strange) mixture *ou* blend; (*Métal, Dentisterie*) amalgam. **un ~ d'idées** a hotchpotch *ou* (strange) mixture of ideas; **faire l'~ entre deux idées** to confuse two ideas; (*fig Pol*) **il ne faut pas faire l'~** you shouldn't make generalizations.
amalgamer [amalgame] [1] 1 **vt** (*fig: mélanger*) to combine; (*Métal*) to amalgamate; (*fig: confondre*) to confuse. 2 **s'amalgamer vpr** (*fig: s'unir*) to combine; (*Métal*) to be amalgamated.
amande [amɑ̃d] **nf** a (*fruit*) almond. **~s amères/douces** bitter/sweet almonds; **~s pilées** ground almonds; **en ~** almond-shaped, almond (*épith*); *voir* **pâte**. b *[noyau]* kernel.
amandier [amɑ̃dje] **nm** almond (tree).
amandine [amɑ̃din] **nf** (*gâteau*) almond tart.
amanite [amanit] **nf** *any mushroom of the genus Amanita*. **~ phalloïde** death cap; **~ tue-mouches** fly agaric.
amant [amɑ̃] **nm** lover. **~ de passage** casual lover; **les deux ~s** the two lovers; **prendre un ~** to take a lover.
amante†† [amɑ̃t] **nf** (*fiancée*) betrothed††, mistress††.
amarante [amaʀɑ̃t] 1 **nf** amaranth. 2 **adj inv** amaranthine.
amariner [amaʀine] [1] **vt** a *navire ennemi* to take over and man. b *matelot* to accustom to life at sea. **elle n'est pas** *ou* **ne s'est pas encore amarinée** she has not got used to the sea *ou* not found her sea legs yet.
amarrage [amaʀaʒ] **nm** (*Naut*) mooring. **être à l'~** to be moored.
amarre [amaʀ] **nf** (*Naut: cordage*) rope *ou* line *ou* cable (for mooring). **les ~s** the moorings; *voir* **larguer, rompre**.
amarrer [amaʀe] [1] **vt** *navire* to moor, make fast; *cordage* to make fast, belay; (*fig*) *paquet, valise* to tie down, make fast.
amaryllis [amaʀilis] **nf** amaryllis.
amas [amɑ] **nm** a (*lit: tas*) heap, pile, mass; (*fig*) *[souvenirs, idées]* mass. **tout un ~ de** a whole heap *ou* pile *ou* mass of. b (*Astron*) star cluster. c (*Min*) mass.
amasser [amɑse] [1] 1 **vt** a (*amonceler*) *choses* to pile *ou* store up, amass, accumulate; *fortune* to amass, accumulate. **il ne pense qu'à ~ (de l'argent)** all he thinks of is amassing *ou* accumulating wealth. b (*rassembler*) *preuves, données* to amass, gather (together); *voir* **pierre**. 2 **s'amasser vpr** *[choses, preuves]* to pile up, accumulate; *[foule]* to gather, mass, muster. **les preuves s'amassent contre lui** the evidence is building up *ou* piling up against him.
amateur [amatœʀ] **nm** a (*non-professionnel*) amateur. **équipe ~** amateur team; **talent d'~** amateur talent; **c'est un peintre/musicien ~** he's an amateur painter/musician; **faire de la peinture en ~** to do a bit of painting (as a hobby); **photographe ~** amateur photographer, photo hobbyist (*US*).
b (*connaisseur*) **~ de** lover of; **~ d'art/de musique** art/music lover; **être ~ de films/de concerts** to be a keen (*Brit*) *ou* avid film-/concert-goer, be keen on (*Brit*) films/concerts; **elle est très ~ de framboises** she is very fond of *ou* she loves raspberries; **le jazz, je ne suis pas ~** I'm not a jazz fan, I'm not all that keen on jazz (*Brit*).
c (**: acheteur*) taker; (*volontaire*) volunteer. **il reste des carottes, il y a des ~s?** there are some carrots left – any takers?*; *voir* **trouver**.
d (*péj*) dilettante, mere amateur. **travail/talent d'~** amateurish work/talent; **faire qch en ~** to do sth amateurishly *ou* as a mere amateur.
amateurisme [amatœʀism] **nm** (*Sport*) amateurism; (*péj*) amateurishness. **c'est de l'~!** it's amateurish!
Amazone [amazon] **nf** (*Géog*) Amazon; (*Myth*) Amazon; (*fig*) amazon.
amazone [amazon] **nf** a (*écuyère*) horsewoman. **tenue d'~** woman's riding habit; **monter en ~** to ride sidesaddle. b (*jupe*) long riding skirt.
Amazonie [amazɔni] **nf** Amazonia.
amazonien, -ienne [amazɔnjɛ̃, jɛn] **adj** Amazonian.
ambages [ɑ̃baʒ] **nfpl**: **sans ~** without beating about the bush, in plain language.
ambassade [ɑ̃basad] **nf** a (*institution, bâtiment*) embassy; (*charge*) ambassadorship, embassy; (*personnel*) embassy staff (*pl*) *ou* officials (*pl*), embassy. **l'~ de France** the French Embassy. b (*fig: mission*) mission. **être envoyé en ~ auprès de qn** to be sent on a mission to sb.
ambassadeur [ɑ̃basadœʀ] **nm** (*Pol, fig*) ambassador. **~ extraordinaire** ambassador extraordinary (*auprès de* to); **l'~ de la pensée française** the representative *ou* ambassador of French thought.
ambassadrice [ɑ̃basadʀis] **nf** (*diplomate*) ambassador (*auprès de* to); (*femme de diplomate*) ambassador's wife, ambassadress; (*fig*) ambassador, ambassadress.
ambiance [ɑ̃bjɑ̃s] **nf** (*climat, atmosphère*) atmosphere; (*environnement*) surroundings (*pl*); *[famille, équipe]* atmosphere. **l'~ de la salle** the atmosphere in the house, the mood of the audience; **il vit dans une ~ calme** he lives in calm *ou* peaceful surroundings; **il y a de l'~!*** there's a great atmosphere here!*; **mettre de l'~** to liven things up*; *voir* **éclairage, musique**.
ambiant, e [ɑ̃bjɑ̃, jɑ̃t] **adj** *air* surrounding, ambient; *température* ambient. (*fig*) **déprimé par l'atmosphère ~e** depressed by the atmosphere around him *ou* the pervading atmosphere.
ambidextre [ɑ̃bidɛkstʀ] **adj** ambidextrous.
ambigu, -uë [ɑ̃bigy] **adj** ambiguous.
ambiguïté [ɑ̃bigɥite] **nf** a (*NonC*) ambiguousness, ambiguity. **une réponse sans ~** an unequivocal *ou* unambiguous reply; **parler/répondre sans ~** to speak/reply unambiguously *ou* without ambiguity. b (*Ling*) ambiguity. c (*terme*) ambiguity.
ambitieusement [ɑ̃bisjøzmɑ̃] **adv** ambitiously.
ambitieux, -ieuse [ɑ̃bisjø, jøz] **adj** ambitious. **c'est un ~** he's an ambitious man; (*littér*) **~ de plaire** anxious to please, desirous of pleasing (*littér*).
ambition [ɑ̃bisjɔ̃] **nf** ambition. **il met toute son ~ à faire** he makes it his sole aim to do; **il a l'~ de réussir** his ambition is to succeed.
ambitionner [ɑ̃bisjɔne] [1] **vt** to seek *ou* strive after. **il ambitionne d'escalader l'Everest** it's his ambition to *ou* his ambition is to climb Everest.
ambivalence [ɑ̃bivalɑ̃s] **nf** ambivalence.

ambivalent, e [ɑ̃bivalɑ̃, ɑ̃t] **adj** ambivalent.
amble [ɑ̃bl] **nm** *[cheval]* amble. **aller l'~** to amble.
ambler [ɑ̃ble] [1] **vi** *[cheval]* to amble.
amblyope [ɑ̃blijɔp] 1 **adj: il est ~** he has a lazy eye, he is amblyopic (*SPÉC*). 2 **nmf** person with a lazy eye *ou* amblyopia (*SPÉC*).
amblyopie [ɑ̃blijɔpi] **nf** lazy eye, amblyopia (*SPÉC*).
ambre [ɑ̃bʀ] **nm: ~ (jaune)** amber; **~ gris** ambergris; **couleur d'~** amber(-coloured).
ambré, e [ɑ̃bʀe] **adj** *couleur* amber; *parfum* perfumed with ambergris.
Ambroise [ɑ̃bʀwaz] **nm** Ambrose.
ambroisie [ɑ̃bʀwazi] **nf** (*Myth*) ambrosia; (*Bot*) ambrosia, ragweed. (*fig*) **c'est de l'~!** this is food fit for the gods!
ambrosiaque [ɑ̃bʀozjak] **adj** ambrosial.
ambulance [ɑ̃bylɑ̃s] **nf** ambulance.
ambulancier, -ière [ɑ̃bylɑ̃sje, jɛʀ] **nm** (*conducteur*) ambulance driver; (*infirmier*) ambulance man (*ou* woman).
ambulant, e [ɑ̃bylɑ̃, ɑ̃t] **adj** *comédien, musicien* itinerant, strolling, travelling. (*fig*) **c'est un squelette/dictionnaire ~*** he's a walking skeleton/dictionary; *voir* **marchand**.
ambulatoire [ɑ̃bylatwaʀ] **adj** (*Méd*) ambulatory.
AME [aɛmə] **nm** (**abrév de accord monétaire européen**) EMA.
âme [ɑm] **nf** a (*gén, Philos, Rel*) soul. **(que) Dieu ait son ~** (may) God rest his soul; (*fig*) **avoir l'~ chevillée au corps** to hang on to life, have nine lives (*fig*); **sur mon ~††** upon my soul†; *voir* **recommander, rendre**.
b (*centre de qualités intellectuelles et morales*) heart, soul, mind. **avoir** *ou* **être une ~ généreuse** to have great generosity of spirit; **avoir** *ou* **être une ~ basse** *ou* **vile** to have an evil heart *ou* mind, be evil-hearted *ou* evil-minded; **avoir** *ou* **être une ~ sensible** to be a sensitive soul, be very sensitive; **grandeur** *ou* (*frm*) **noblesse d'~** high- *ou* noble-mindedness; **en mon ~ et conscience** in all conscience *ou* honesty; (*littér*) **de toute mon ~** with all my soul; **il y a mis toute son ~** he put his heart and soul into it.
c (*centre psychique et émotif*) soul. **faire qch avec ~** to do sth with feeling; **ému jusqu'au fond de l'~** profoundly moved; **c'est un corps sans ~** he has no soul; **il est musicien dans l'~** he's a musician to the core; **il a la technique mais son jeu est sans ~** his technique is good but he plays without feeling *ou* his playing is soulless.
d (*personne*) soul. (*frm*) **un village de 600 ~s** a village of 600 souls; **on ne voyait ~ qui vive** you couldn't see a (living *ou* mortal) soul, there wasn't a (living *ou* mortal) soul to be seen; **bonne ~*** kind soul; **est-ce qu'il n'y aura pas une bonne ~ pour m'aider?** won't some kind soul give me a hand?; (*iro*) **il y a toujours de bonnes ~s pour critiquer** there's always some kind soul ready to criticize (*iro*); (*gén péj*) **~ charitable** kind(ly) *ou* well-meaning soul (*iro*); **il est là/il erre comme une ~ en peine** he looks like/he is wandering about like a lost soul; **être l'~ damnée de qn** to be sb's henchman *ou* tool; **il a trouvé l'~ sœur** he has found a soul mate.
e (*principe qui anime*) soul, spirit. **l'~ d'un peuple** the soul *ou* spirit of a nation; **l'~ d'un complot** the moving spirit in a plot; **être l'~ d'un parti** to be the soul *ou* leading light of a party; **elle a une ~ de sœur de charité** she is the very soul *ou* spirit of charity; **elle a une ~ de chef** she has the soul of a leader.
f (*Tech*) *[canon]* bore; *[aimant]* core; *[violon]* soundpost; *voir* **charge, état, fendre** *etc.*
Amélie [ameli] **nf** Amelia.
améliorable [ameljɔʀabl] **adj** improvable.
améliorant, e [ameljɔʀɑ̃, ɑ̃t] **adj** (*Agr*) soil-improving.
amélioration [ameljɔʀasjɔ̃] **nf** a (*NonC: voir* **améliorer**) improvement; betterment; amelioration. **l'~ de son état de santé** the improvement of *ou* in *ou* the change for the better in his health. b improvement. **faire des ~s dans, apporter des ~s à** to make *ou* carry out improvements in *ou* to; (*Écon*) **une ~ de la conjoncture** an economic upturn, an improvement in the state of the economy.
améliorer [ameljɔʀe] [1] 1 **vt** (*gén*) to improve; *situation, sort, statut* to improve, better, ameliorate (*frm*); *domaine, immeuble* to improve. **~ sa situation** to better *ou* improve o.s. *ou* one's situation; **pour ~ l'ordinaire** (*argent*) to top up one's basic income; (*repas*) to make things a bit more interesting. 2 **s'améliorer vpr** to improve.
amen [amɛn] **adv** (*Rel*) amen. **dire ~ à qch/à tout** to say amen to sth/everything, agree religiously to sth/everything.
aménageable [amenaʒabl] **adj** *horaire* flexible; *grenier* which can be converted (*en* into).
aménagement [amenaʒmɑ̃] **nm** (*voir* **aménager**) fitting-out; laying-out; converting, conversion; fixing-up; developing; planning; working out; adjusting; making, building; fitting up (*Brit*), putting in. **l'~ du territoire** national and regional development, ≃ town and country planning (*Brit*); **les nouveaux ~s d'un quartier/d'un centre hospitalier** the new developments in *ou* improvements to *ou* in a neighbourhood/hospital; **~ du temps de travail** (*réforme*) reform of working hours; (*gestion*) flexible time management; **demander des ~s financiers/d'horaire** to request certain financial adjustments/adjustments to one's timetable.
aménager [amenaʒe] [3] **vt** a (*équiper*) *local* to fit out; *parc* to lay out; *mansarde* to convert; *territoire* to develop; *horaire* (*gén*) to plan, work out; (*modifier*) to adjust. **~ une chambre en bureau** to convert a bedroom into a study, fit out a bedroom as a study. b (*créer*) *route* to make, build; *gradins, placard* to fit up (*Brit*), put in. **~ un bureau dans une chambre** to fit up (*Brit*) *ou* fix up a study in a bedroom.
amendable [amɑ̃dabl] **adj** (*Pol*) amendable; (*Agr*) which can be enriched.
amende [amɑ̃d] **nf** fine. **mettre à l'~** to penalize; **il a eu 500 F d'~** he got a 500-franc fine, he was fined 500 francs; **défense d'entrer sous peine d'~** trespassers will be prosecuted *ou* fined; **faire ~ honorable** to make amends.
amendement [amɑ̃dmɑ̃] **nm** (*Pol*) amendment; (*Agr*) (*opération*) enrichment; (*substance*) enriching agent.
amender [amɑ̃de] [1] 1 **vt** (*Pol*) to amend; (*Agr*) to enrich; *conduite* to improve, amend. 2 **s'amender vpr** to mend one's ways, amend.
amène [amɛn] **adj** (*littér: aimable*) *propos, visage* affable; *personne, caractère* amiable, affable. **des propos peu ~s** unkind words.
amener [am(ə)ne] [5] 1 **vt** a (*faire venir*) *personne, objet* to bring (along); (*acheminer*) *cargaison* to bring, convey. **on nous amène les enfants tous les matins** they bring the children (along) to us every morning, the children are brought (along) to us every morning; **amène-la à la maison** bring her round (*Brit*) *ou* around (*US*) *ou* along (to the house), bring her home; **le sable est amené à Paris par péniche** sand is brought *ou* conveyed to Paris by barges; **qu'est-ce qui vous amène ici?** what brings you here?; *voir* **bon[1], mandat**.
b (*provoquer*) to bring about, cause. **~ la disette** to bring about *ou* cause a shortage; **~ le typhus** to cause typhus.
c (*inciter*) **~ qn à faire qch** *[circonstances]* to induce *ou* lead *ou* bring sb to do sth; *[personne]* to bring sb round to doing sth, get sb to do sth; (*par un discours persuasif*) to talk sb into doing sth; **la crise pourrait ~ le gouvernement à agir** the crisis might induce *ou* lead *ou* bring the government to take action; **elle a été finalement amenée à renoncer à son voyage** she was finally induced *ou* driven to give up her trip; **je suis amené à croire que** I am led to believe *ou* think that; **c'est ce qui m'a amené à cette conclusion** that is what led *ou* brought me to that conclusion.
d (*diriger*) to bring. **~ qn à ses propres idées/à une autre opinion** to bring sb round to one's own ideas/another way of thinking; **~ la conversation sur un sujet** to bring the conversation round to a subject, lead the conversation on to a subject; **système amené à un haut degré de complexité** system brought to a high degree of complexity.
e *transition, conclusion, dénouement* to present, introduce. **exemple bien amené** well-introduced example.
f (*Pêche*) *poisson* to draw in; (*Naut*) *voile, pavillon* to strike. (*Mil*) **~ les couleurs** to strike colours.
g (*Dés*) *paire, brelan* to throw.
2 **s'amener* vpr** (*venir*) to come along. **tu t'amènes?** are you going to get a move on?*, come on!*; **il s'est amené avec toute sa bande** he came along *ou* turned up *ou* showed up* with the whole gang.
aménité [amenite] **nf** (*amabilité*) *[propos]* affability; *[personne, caractère]* amiability, affability. **sans ~** unkindly; (*iro*) **se dire des ~s** to exchange uncomplimentary remarks.
aménorrhée [amenɔʀe] **nf** amenorrhoea.
amenuisement [amənɥizmɑ̃] **nm** *[valeur, avance, espoir]* dwindling; *[chances]* lessening; *[ressources]* diminishing, dwindling.
amenuiser [amənɥize] [1] 1 **s'amenuiser vpr** *[valeur, avance, espoir]* to dwindle; *[chances]* to grow slimmer, lessen; *[provisions, ressources]* to run low, diminish, dwindle; *[temps]* to run out. 2 **vt** *objet* to thin down; (*fig*) to reduce.
amer[1] [amɛʀ] **nm** (*Naut*) seamark.
amer[2], -ère [amɛʀ] **adj** (*lit, fig*) bitter. **~ comme chicotin*** as bitter as wormwood; **avoir la bouche ~ère** to have a bitter taste in one's mouth.
amérasien, -ienne [ameʀazjɛ̃, jɛn] 1 **adj** Amerasian. 2 **nm,f: A~(ne)** Amerasian.
amèrement [amɛʀmɑ̃] **adv** bitterly.
américain, e [ameʀikɛ̃, ɛn] 1 **adj** American. **à l'~e** (*gén*) in the American style; (*Culin*) à l'Américaine; *voir* **œil**. 2 **nm** (*Ling*) American (English). 3 **nm,f: A~(e)** American. 4 **américaine nf** (*automobile*) American car.
américanisation [ameʀikanizasjɔ̃] **nf** americanization.
américaniser [ameʀikanize] [1] 1 **vt** to americanize. 2 **s'américaniser vpr** to become americanized.
américanisme [ameʀikanism] **nm** americanism.
américaniste [ameʀikanist] **nmf** Americanist, American specialist.
américium [ameʀisjɔm] **nm** americium.
amérindien, -ienne [ameʀɛ̃djɛ̃, jɛn] **adj, nm,f** Amerindian, American Indian.
Amérique [ameʀik] **nf** America. **~ centrale/latine/du Nord/du Sud** Central/Latin/North/South America.
Amerloque‡ [amɛʀlɔk] **nmf, Amerlo(t)** [amɛʀlo] **nm** Yankee*, Yank*.
amerrir [ameʀiʀ] [2] **vi** (*Aviat*) to land (on the sea), make a sea-landing; (*Espace*) to splash down.
amerrissage [ameʀisaʒ] **nm** (*Aviat*) (sea) landing; (*Espace*) splash-down.

amertume [amɛʀtym] **nf** (*lit, fig*) bitterness. **plein d'~** full of bitterness, very bitter.

améthyste [ametist] **nf, adj inv** amethyst.

ameublement [amœbləmɑ̃] **nm** (*meubles*) furniture; (*action*) furnishing. **articles d'~** furnishings; **commerce d'~** furniture trade.

ameublir [amœbliʀ] [2] **vt** (*Agr*) to loosen, break down.

ameuter [amøte] [1] 1 **vt** a (*attrouper*) *curieux, passants* to bring *ou* draw a crowd of; *voisins* to bring out; (*soulever*) *foule* to rouse, stir up, incite (*contre* against). **ses cris ameutèrent les passants** his shouts brought *ou* drew a crowd of passers-by; **tais-toi, tu vas ~ toute la rue!*** be quiet, you'll have the whole street out!; **tu n'as pas besoin d'~ tout le quartier!*** you don't have to tell the whole neighbourhood!, you don't have to shout it from the rooftops!
b *chiens* to form into a pack.
2 **s'ameuter vpr** (*s'attrouper*) *[passants]* to gather, mass; *[voisins]* to come out; (*se soulever*) to band together, gather into a mob. **des passants s'ameutèrent** a crowd of passers-by gathered (angrily).

ami, e [ami] 1 **nm,f** a friend. **c'est un vieil ~ de la famille** *ou* **de la maison** he's an old friend of the family; **c'est un/mon ~ d'enfance** he's a/my childhood friend; **~ intime** (very) close *ou* intimate friend, bosom friend; **il m'a présenté son ~e** he introduced his girlfriend to me; **elle est sortie avec ses ~es** she's out with her (girl)friends; **se faire un ~ de qn** to make *ou* become friends with sb, become a friend of sb; **faire ~-~ avec qn*** to make friends with sb; **nous sommes entre ~s** (*2 personnes*) we're friends; (*plus de 2*) we're all friends; **je vous dis ça en ~** I'm telling you this as a friend; **~s des bêtes/de la nature** animal/nature lovers; **société** *ou* **club des ~s de Balzac** Balzac club *ou* society; **un célibataire/professeur de mes ~s** a bachelor/teacher friend of mine; **être sans ~s** to be friendless, have no friends; **parents et ~s** friends and relations *ou* relatives; **~ des arts** patron of the arts; **l'~ de l'homme** man's best friend; **nos ~s à quatre pattes** our four-legged friends.
b (*euph*) (*amant*) boyfriend (*euph*); (*maîtresse*) girlfriend (*euph*). **l'~e de l'assassin** the murderer's lady-friend (*euph*); *voir* **bon[1], petit.**
c (*interpellation*) **mes chers ~s** gentlemen; (*auditoire mixte*) ladies and gentlemen; **mon cher ~** my dear fellow *ou* chap (*Brit*); **ça, mon (petit) ~** now look here; **ben mon ~!*** **si j'avais su** gosh!* *ou* blimey!* (*Brit*) *ou* crikey!* (*Brit*) if I had known that; (*entre époux*) **oui mon ~!** yes my dear.
2 **adj** *visage, pays* friendly; *regard* kindly, friendly. **tendre à qn une main ~e** to lend *ou* give sb a friendly *ou* helping hand; **être très ~ avec qn** to be very friendly *ou* (very) great *ou* good friends with sb; **nous sommes très ~s** we're very close *ou* good friends, we're very friendly; **être ~ de l'ordre** to be a lover of order.

amiable [amjabl] **adj** (*Jur*) amicable. **~ compositeur** conciliator; **à l'~: vente à l'~** private sale, sale by private agreement; **partage à l'~** private *ou* amicable partition; **accord** *ou* **règlement à l'~** friendly *ou* amicable agreement *ou* arrangement; **régler** *ou* **liquider une affaire à l'~** to settle a difference out of court.

amiante [amjɑ̃t] **nm** asbestos. **plaque/fils d'~** asbestos sheet *ou* plate/thread.

amibe [amib] **nf** amoeba.

amibiase [amibjɑz] **nf** amoebiasis.

amibien, -ienne [amibjɛ̃, jɛn] 1 **adj** *maladie* amoebic. 2 **nmpl: ~s** Amoebae.

amical, e, **mpl -aux** [amikal, o] 1 **adj** friendly. **match ~, rencontre ~e** friendly (match); **peu ~** unfriendly. 2 **amicale nf** association, club (*of people having the same interest*). **~e des anciens élèves** old boys' association (*Brit*), alumni association (*US*).

amicalement [amikalmɑ̃] **adv** in a friendly way. **il m'a salué ~** he gave me a friendly wave; (*formule épistolaire*) **(bien) ~** kind regards, best wishes, yours (ever).

amidon [amidɔ̃] **nm** starch.

amidonner [amidɔne] [1] **vt** to starch.

amincir [amɛ̃siʀ] [2] 1 **vt** to thin (down). **cette robe l'amincit** this dress makes her look slim(mer) *ou* thin(ner); **visage aminci par la tension** face drawn with tension *ou* hollow with anxiety. 2 **s'amincir vpr** *[couche de glace, épaisseur de tissu]* to get thinner.

amincissant, e [amɛ̃sisɑ̃, ɑ̃t] **adj: régime ~** slimming diet; **crème ~e** slimming cream.

amincissement [amɛ̃sismɑ̃] **nm** thinning (down). **l'~ de la couche de glace a causé l'accident** the ice had got thinner and it was this which caused the accident; *voir* **cure.**

aminé, e [amine] **adj** *voir* **acide.**

amiral, e, **mpl -aux** [amiʀal, o] 1 **adj: vaisseau** *ou* **bateau ~** flagship. 2 **nm** admiral; *voir* **contre, vice-.** 3 **amirale nf** admiral's wife.

amirauté [amiʀote] **nf** admiralty.

amitié [amitje] **nf** a (*sentiment*) friendship. **prendre qn en ~, se prendre d'~ pour qn** to take a liking to sb, befriend sb; **se lier d'~ avec qn** to make friends with sb; (*littér*) **nouer une ~ avec qn** to strike up a friendship with sb; **avoir de l'~ pour qn** to be fond of sb, have a liking for sb; **faites-moi l'~ de venir** do me the kindness *ou* favour of coming; **l'~ franco-britannique** Anglo-French *ou* Franco-British friendship; (*euph*) **~ particulière** (*entre hommes*) homosexual relationship; (*entre femmes*) lesbian relationship.
b (*formule épistolaire*) **~s** all the very best, very best wishes *ou* regards; **~s, Paul** kind regards, Paul, yours, Paul; **elle vous fait** *ou* **transmet toutes ses ~s** she sends her best wishes *ou* regards.
c (†: *civilités*) **faire mille ~s à qn** to give sb a warm and friendly welcome.

Amman [aman] **n** Amman.

ammoniac, -aque [amɔnjak] 1 **adj** ammoniac. **sel ~** sal ammoniac; *voir* **gomme.** 2 **nm** (*gaz*) ammonia. 3 **ammoniaque nf** ammonia (water).

ammoniacal, e, **mpl -aux** [amɔnjakal, o] **adj** ammoniacal.

ammoniaqué, e [amɔnjake] **adj** ammoniated.

ammonite [amɔnit] **nf** (*Zool*) ammonite.

ammonium [amɔnjɔm] **nm** ammonium.

amnésie [amnezi] **nf** amnesia.

amnésique [amnezik] 1 **adj** amnesic. 2 **nmf** amnesiac, amnesic.

amniocentèse [amnjosɛtɛz] **nf** amniocentesis.

amnios [amnjos] **nm** amnion.

amnioscopie [amnjɔskɔpi] **nf** fetoscopy.

amniotique [amnjɔtik] **adj** amniotic. **cavité/liquide ~** amniotic cavity/liquid.

amnistiable [amnistjabl] **adj** who may be amnestied.

amnistie [amnisti] **nf** amnesty. **loi d'~** law of amnesty.

amnistier [amnistje] [7] **vt** to amnesty, grant an amnesty to. **les amnistiés** the amnestied prisoners.

amocher‡ [amɔʃe] [1] **vt** *objet, personne* to mess up*, make a mess of*; *véhicule* to bash up*. **tu l'as drôlement amoché** you've made a terrible mess of him*, you've messed him up something terrible*; **se faire ~ dans un accident/une bagarre** to get messed up* in an accident/a fight; **il/la voiture était drôlement amoché(e)** he/the car was a terrible mess*; **il s'est drôlement amoché en tombant** he gave himself a terrible bash* (*Brit*) *ou* he pretty well smashed himself up (*US*) when he fell.

amoindrir [amwɛ̃dʀiʀ] [2] 1 **vt** *autorité* to lessen, weaken, diminish; *forces* to weaken; *fortune, quantité* to diminish, reduce; *personne* (*physiquement*) to make weaker, weaken; (*moralement, mentalement*) to diminish. **~ qn (aux yeux des autres)** to diminish *ou* belittle sb (in the eyes of others). 2 **s'amoindrir vpr** *[autorité, facultés]* to grow weaker, weaken, diminish; *[forces]* to weaken, grow weaker; *[quantité, fortune]* to diminish, grow less.

amoindrissement [amwɛ̃dʀismɑ̃] **nm** (*voir* **amoindrir**) lessening; weakening; diminishing; reduction.

amollir [amɔliʀ] [2] 1 **vt** *chose* to soften, make soft; *personne* (*moralement*) to soften; (*physiquement*) to weaken, make weak; *volonté, forces, résolution* to weaken. **cette chaleur vous amollit** this heat makes one feel (quite) limp *ou* weak. 2 **s'amollir vpr** *[chose]* to go soft; (*s'affaiblir*) *[courage, énergie]* to weaken; *[jambes]* to go weak; *[personne]* (*perdre courage, énergie*) to grow soft, weaken; (*s'attendrir*) to soften, relent.

amollissant, e [amɔlisɑ̃, ɑ̃t] **adj** *climat, plaisirs* enervating.

amollissement [amɔlismɑ̃] **nm** (*voir* **amollir**) softening; weakening. **l'~ général est dû à ...** the general weakening of purpose is due to ... .

amonceler [amɔ̃s(ə)le] [4] 1 **vt** *choses* to pile *ou* heap up; *richesses* to amass, accumulate; *difficultés* to accumulate; *documents, preuves* to pile up, accumulate, amass. 2 **s'amonceler vpr** *[choses]* to pile *ou* heap up; *[courrier, demandes]* to pile up, accumulate; *[nuages]* to bank up; *[neige]* to drift into banks, bank up. **les preuves s'amoncellent contre lui** the evidence is building up *ou* piling up against him.

amoncellement [amɔ̃sɛlmɑ̃] **nm** a (*voir* **amonceler**) piling up; heaping up; banking up; amassing; accumulating. b *[choses]* pile, heap, mass; *[idées]* accumulation.

amont [amɔ̃] **nm** *[cours d'eau]* upstream water; *[pente]* uphill slope. **en ~** (*rivière*) upstream, upriver; (*pente*) uphill; (*Écon*) upstream; **en ~ de** upstream *ou* upriver from; uphill from, above; (*fig*) before; **les rapides/l'écluse d'~** the upstream rapids/lock; **l'~ était coupé de rapides** the river upstream was a succession of rapids; **skieur/ski ~** uphill skier/ski.

amoral, e, **mpl -aux** [amɔʀal, o] **adj** amoral.

amoralisme [amɔʀalism] **nm** amorality.

amoralité [amɔʀalite] **nf** amorality.

amorçage [amɔʀsaʒ] **nm** a (*action: voir* **amorcer**) baiting; ground baiting; priming; energizing. b (*dispositif*) priming cap, primer.

amorce [amɔʀs] **nf** a (*Pêche*) *[hameçon]* bait; *[emplacement]* ground bait. b (*explosif*) *[cartouche]* cap, primer, priming; *[obus]* percussion cap; *[mine]* priming; *[pistolet d'enfant]* cap. c (*début*) *[route]* initial section; *[trou]* start; *[pellicule, film]* trailer; *[conversations, négociations]* beginning; *[idée, projet]* beginning, germ. **l'~ d'une réforme/d'un changement** the beginnings (*pl*) of a reform/change. d (*Ordin*) **(programme) ~** bootstrap.

amorcer [amɔʀse] [3] **vt** a *hameçon, ligne* to bait. **il amorce au ver de vase** (*ligne*) he baits his line with worms; (*emplacement*) he uses worms as ground bait.
b *dynamo* to energize; *syphon, obus, pompe* to prime.
c *route, tunnel* to start *ou* begin building, make a start on; *travaux* to begin, make a start on; *trou* to begin *ou* start to bore. **la construction**

est amorcée depuis 2 mois work has been in progress *ou* been under way for 2 months.

d (*commencer*) *réformes, évolution* to initiate, begin; *virage* to begin. **il amorça un geste pour prendre la tasse** he made as if to take the cup; ~ **la rentrée dans l'atmosphère** to initiate re-entry into the earth's atmosphere; **une descente s'amorce après le virage** after the bend the road starts to go down.

e (*Pol: entamer*) *conversations* to start (up); *négociations* to start, begin. **une détente est amorcée** *ou* **s'amorce** there are signs of (the beginnings of) a détente.

f (†: *attirer*) *client* to allure, entice.

amorphe [amɔRf] **adj** a (*apathique*) *personne* passive, lifeless, spiritless; *esprit, caractère, attitude* passive. b (*Minér*) amorphous.

amorti [amɔRti] (**ptp de amortir**) **nm** (*Tennis*) drop shot. (*Ftbl*) **faire un** ~ to trap the ball; **faire un ~ de la poitrine** to chest the ball down.

amortir [amɔRtiR] 2 **vt** a (*diminuer*) *choc* to absorb, cushion; *coup, chute* to cushion, soften; *bruit* to deaden, muffle; *passions, douleur* to deaden, dull. b (*Fin*) *dette* to pay off, amortize (SPÉC); *titre* to redeem; *matériel* to write off, depreciate (SPÉC). (*gén*) **il utilise sa voiture le plus souvent possible pour l'~** he uses his car as often as possible to make it pay *ou* to recoup the cost to himself; **maintenant, notre équipement est amorti** now we have written off the (capital) cost of the equipment. c (*Archit*) to put an amortizement *ou* amortization on.

amortissable [amɔRtisabl] **adj** (*Fin*) redeemable.

amortissement [amɔRtismɑ̃] **nm** a (*Fin*) *[dette]* paying off; *[titre]* redemption; (*provision comptable*) reserve *ou* provision for depreciation. **l'~ de ce matériel se fait en 3 ans** it takes 3 years to recoup *ou* to write off the cost of this equipment; (*Fin*) **~s admis par le fisc** capital allowances. b (*diminution: voir* **amortir**) absorption; cushioning; softening; deadening; muffling; dulling; (*Phys*) damping. c (*Archit*) amortizement, amortization.

amortisseur [amɔRtisœR] **nm** shock absorber.

amour [amuR] 1 **nm** a (*sentiment*) love. **parler d'~** to speak of love; **se nourrir** *ou* **vivre d'~ et d'eau fraîche*** to live on love alone; ~ **platonique** platonic love; **lettre/mariage/roman d'~** love letter/match/story; **fou d'~** madly *ou* wildly in love; ~ **fou** wild love *ou* passion, mad love; **ce n'est plus de l'~, c'est de la rage*** it's not love, it's raving madness!*; *voir* **filer, saison.**

b (*acte*) love-making (*NonC*). **pendant l'~, elle murmurait des mots tendres** while they were making love *ou* during their love-making, she murmured tender words; **l'~ libre** free love; **l'~ physique** physical love; **faire l'~** to make love (*avec* to, with).

c (*personne*) love; (*aventure*) love affair. **premier ~** (*personne*) first love; (*aventure*) first love (affair); **ses ~s de jeunesse** (*aventures*) the love affairs *ou* loves of his youth; (*personnes*) the loves *ou* lovers of his youth; **c'est un ~ de jeunesse** she's one of his old loves *ou* flames*†; **des ~s de rencontre** casual love affairs; (*hum*) **à tes ~s!*** (*quand on trinque*) here's to you!; (*quand on éternue*) bless you!; (*hum*) **comment vont tes ~s?*** how's your love life?* (*hum*).

d (*terme d'affection*) **mon ~** my love, my sweet; **cet enfant est un ~** that child's a real darling; **passe-moi l'eau, tu seras un ~** be a darling *ou* dear (*Brit*) and pass me the water, pass me the water, there's a darling *ou* a dear (*Brit*); **un ~ de bébé/de petite robe** a lovely *ou* sweet little baby/dress.

e (*Art*) cupid. (*Myth*) **(le dieu) A~** Eros, Cupid.

f (*loc*) **pour l'~ de Dieu** for God's sake, for the love of God; **pour l'~ de votre mère** for your mother's sake; **faire qch pour l'~ de l'art*** to do sth for the love of it *ou* for love*; **avoir l'~ du travail bien fait** to have a great love for work well done, love to see work well done; **faire qch avec ~** to do sth with loving care.

2 **nfpl** (*littér*) **~s** (*personnes*) loves; (*aventures*) love affairs; (*hum*) **~s ancillaires** amorous adventures with the servants.

3 **comp ▸amour-propre nm** self-esteem, pride; **blessure d'amour-propre** wound to one's self-esteem *ou* pride.

amouracher (s') [amuRaʃe] 1 **vpr** (*péj*) **s'~ de** to become infatuated with (*péj*).

amourette [amuRɛt] **nf** passing fancy, passing love affair.

amoureusement [amuRøzmɑ̃] **adv** lovingly, amorously.

amoureux, -euse [amuRø, øz] 1 **adj** a (*épris*) *personne* in love (*de* with). **être ~ de la musique/la nature** to be a music-/nature-lover, be passionately fond of music/nature; (*fig hum*) **il est ~ de sa voiture** he's in love with his car (*hum*); *voir* **tomber.** b (*d'amour*) *aventures* amorous, love (*épith*). **déboires ~** disappointments in love; **vie ~euse** love life. c (*ardent*) *tempérament, personne* amorous; *regard* (*tendre*) loving; (*voluptueux*) amorous. 2 **nm, f** (*gén*) lover; (†: *soupirant*) love, sweetheart. (*fig*) **~ de** lover of; **un ~ de la nature** a nature lover, a lover of nature; **~ transi** bashful lover; **partir en vacances en ~** to go off on holiday like a pair of lovers.

amovibilité [amɔvibilite] **nf** (*Jur*) removability.

amovible [amɔvibl] **adj** *doublure, housse, panneau* removable, detachable; (*Jur*) removable.

ampérage [ɑ̃peRaʒ] **nm** amperage.

ampère [ɑ̃pɛR] **nm** ampere, amp.

ampèremètre [ɑ̃pɛRmɛtR] **nm** ammeter.

amphétamine [ɑ̃fetamin] **nf** amphetamine.

amphi [ɑ̃fi] **nm** (*arg Univ*) **abrév de amphithéâtre.**

amphibie [ɑ̃fibi] 1 **adj** amphibious. 2 **nm** amphibian.

amphibiens [ɑ̃fibjɛ̃] **nmpl** amphibia, amphibians.

amphigouri [ɑ̃figuRi] **nm** amphigory.

amphigourique [ɑ̃figuRik] **adj** amphigoric.

amphithéâtre [ɑ̃fiteɑtR] **nm** (*Archit*) amphitheatre; (*Univ*) lecture hall *ou* theatre; (*Théât*) (upper) gallery. (*Géol*) **~ morainique** morainic cirque *ou* amphitheatre.

amphitryon [ɑ̃fitRijɔ̃] **nm** (*hum, littér: hôte*) host.

amphore [ɑ̃fɔR] **nf** amphora.

ample [ɑ̃pl] **adj** *manteau* roomy; *jupe, manche* full; *geste* wide, sweeping; *voix* sonorous; *style* rich, grand; *projet* vast; *vues, sujet* wide-ranging, extensive. **faire ~(s) provision(s) de** to gather a bountiful *ou* liberal *ou* plentiful supply of; **donner ~ matériel à discussion** to give ample material for discussion; (*frm*) **jusqu'à plus ~ informé** until fuller *ou* further information is available; **pour plus ~ informé je tenais à vous dire ...** for your further information I should tell you ...; **veuillez m'envoyer de plus ~s renseignements sur ...** please send me further details of ... *ou* further information about ... .

amplement [ɑ̃pləmɑ̃] **adv** *expliquer, mériter* fully, amply. **il a fait ~ ce qu'on lui demandait** he has more than done what was asked of him; **gagner ~ sa vie** to earn a very good *ou* ample living; **ça suffit ~, c'est ~ suffisant** that's more than enough, that's ample.

ampleur [ɑ̃plœR] **nf** a *[vêtement]* fullness, roominess; *[voix]* sonorousness; *[geste]* liberalness; *[style, récit]* opulence; *[vues, sujet, problème]* extent, scope, range; *[projet]* vastness, scope. **donner de l'~ à une robe** to give fullness to a dress.

b (*importance*) *[crise]* scale, extent; *[dégâts]* extent. **devant l'~ de la catastrophe** in the face of the sheer scale *ou* extent of the catastrophe; **vu l'~ des dégâts ...** in view of the scale *ou* the extent of the damage ...; **l'~ des moyens mis en œuvre** the sheer size *ou* the massive scale of the measures implemented; **sans grande ~** of limited scope, small-scale (*épith*); **ces manifestations prennent de l'~** these demonstrations are growing *ou* increasing in scale *ou* extent *ou* are becoming more extensive.

ampli* [ɑ̃pli] **nm** (**abrév de amplificateur**) amp*. **~-tuner** tuner amplifier.

ampliation [ɑ̃plijasjɔ̃] **nf** (*duplicata*) certified copy; (*développement*) amplification. **~ des offres de preuves** amplification of previous evidence.

amplificateur [ɑ̃plifikatœR] **nm** (*Phys, Rad*) amplifier; (*Phot*) enlarger (*permitting only fixed enlarging*).

amplification [ɑ̃plifikasjɔ̃] **nf** (*voir* **amplifier**) development; accentuation; expansion; increase; amplification; magnification; exaggeration; (*Phot*) enlarging; (*Opt*) magnifying.

amplifier [ɑ̃plifje] 7 1 **vt** a (*accentuer, développer*) *tendance* to develop, accentuate; *mouvement, échanges, coopération* to expand, increase, develop; *pensée* to expand, develop, amplify; (*péj*) *incident* to magnify, exaggerate. b (*Tech*) *son, courant* to amplify; *image* to magnify. 2 **s'amplifier vpr** *[mouvement, tendance, échange]* to grow, increase; *[pensée]* to expand, develop.

amplitude [ɑ̃plityd] **nf** a (*Astron, Phys*) amplitude. (*Géom*) **l'~ d'un arc** the length of the chord subtending an arc. b *[températures]* range. c (*fig: importance*) **l'~ de la catastrophe** the magnitude of the catastrophe.

ampoule [ɑ̃pul] **nf** (*Élec*) bulb; (*Pharm*) phial, vial; (*Méd*) *[main, pied]* blister, ampulla (SPÉC).

ampoulé, e [ɑ̃pule] **adj** *style* turgid, pompous, bombastic.

amputation [ɑ̃pytasjɔ̃] **nf** (*Anat*) amputation; (*fig*) *[texte, roman, fortune]* drastic cut *ou* reduction (*de* in); *[budget]* drastic cutback *ou* reduction (*de* in).

amputer [ɑ̃pyte] 1 **vt** a (*Anat*) to amputate. **il est amputé d'une jambe** he has had a leg amputated; **c'est un amputé** he has lost an arm (*ou* a leg), he has had an arm (*ou* a leg) off* (*Brit*). b (*fig*) *texte, roman, fortune* to cut *ou* reduce drastically; *budget* to cut back *ou* reduce drastically (*de* by). **~ un pays d'une partie de son territoire** to sever a country of a part of its territory.

Amsterdam [amstɛRdam] **n** Amsterdam.

amuïr (s') [amɥiR] 2 **vpr** (*Phonétique*) to become mute, be dropped (*in pronunciation*).

amuïssement [amɥismɑ̃] **nm** (*Phonétique*) *dropping of a phoneme in pronunciation.*

amulette [amylɛt] **nf** amulet.

amure [amyR] **nf** (*Naut*) tack. **aller bâbord/tribord ~s** to go on the port/starboard tack.

amurer [amyRe] 1 **vt** *voile* to haul aboard the tack of, tack.

amusant, e [amyzɑ̃, ɑ̃t] **adj** (*distrayant*) *jeu* amusing, entertaining; (*drôle*) *film, remarque, convive* amusing, funny. **c'est (très) ~** (*distrayant*) it's (great) fun *ou* (very) entertaining; (*surprenant*) it's (very) amusing *ou* funny; **l'~ de l'histoire c'est que** the funny part of the story is that, the amusing part about it all is that.

amuse-gueule [amyzgœl] **nm inv** appetizer, snack.

amusement [amyzmɑ̃] **nm** a (*divertissement*) amusement (*NonC*).

pour l'~ des enfants for the children's amusement *ou* entertainment, to amuse *ou* entertain the children. b (*jeu*) game; (*activité*) diversion, pastime. c (*hilarité*) amusement (*NonC*).

amuser [amyze] 1 1 **vt** a (*divertir*) to amuse, entertain; (*non intentionnellement*) to amuse.

b (*faire rire*) *histoire drôle* to amuse. **ces remarques ne m'amusent pas du tout** I don't find these remarks in the least bit funny *ou* amusing, I'm not in the least amused by such remarks; **tu m'amuses avec tes grandes théories** you make me laugh *ou* you amuse me with your great theories; **faire le pitre pour ~ la galerie** to clown about and play to the crowd, clown about to amuse the crowd.

c (*plaire*) **ça ne m'amuse pas de devoir aller leur rendre visite** I don't enjoy having to go and visit them; **si vous croyez que ces réunions m'amusent** if you think I enjoy these meetings.

d (*détourner l'attention de*) *ennemi, caissier* to distract (the attention of), divert the attention of. **pendant que tu l'amuses, je prends l'argent** while you keep him busy *ou* distract his attention, I'll take the money.

e (*tromper: par promesses etc*) to delude, beguile.

2 **s'amuser vpr** a (*jouer*) *[enfants]* to play. **s'~ avec** *jouet, personne, chien* to play with; *stylo, ficelle* to play *ou* fiddle *ou* toy with; **s'~ à un jeu** to play a game; **s'~ à faire** to amuse o.s. doing, play at doing; **pour s'~ ils allumèrent un grand feu de joie** they lit a big bonfire for a lark*; (*fig*) **ne t'amuse pas à recommencer, sinon!** don't you do *ou* start that again, or else!

b (*se divertir*) to have fun *ou* a good time, enjoy o.s.; (*rire*) to have a good laugh. **s'~ à faire** to have fun doing, enjoy o.s. doing; **nous nous sommes amusés comme des fous à écouter ses histoires** we laughed ourselves silly listening to his jokes; **nous nous sommes bien amusés** we had great fun *ou* a great time*; **qu'est-ce qu'on s'amuse!** this is great fun!; **j'aime autant te dire qu'on ne s'est pas amusés** it wasn't much fun, I can tell you; **on ne va pas s'~ à cette réunion** we're not going to have much fun *ou* enjoy it much at this meeting; **on ne faisait rien de mal, c'était juste pour s'~** we weren't doing any harm, it was just for fun *ou* for a laugh.

c (*batifoler*) to mess about* *ou* around*. **il ne faut pas que l'on s'amuse** (*il faut se dépêcher*) we mustn't dawdle; (*il faut travailler dur*) we mustn't idle.

d (*littér: se jouer de*) **s'~ de qn** to make a fool of sb.

amusette [amyzɛt] **nf** diversion. **elle n'a été pour lui qu'une ~** she was mere sport to him, she was just a passing fancy for him; **au lieu de perdre ton temps à des ~s tu ferais mieux de travailler** instead of frittering your time away on idle pleasures you'd do better to work.

amuseur, -euse [amyzœʀ, øz] **nm,f** entertainer. (*péj*) **ce n'est qu'un ~** he's just a clown.

amygdale [amidal] **nf** tonsil. **se faire opérer des ~s** to have one's tonsils removed *ou* out.

amygdalite [amidalit] **nf** tonsillitis.

amylacé, e [amilase] **adj** starchy.

amylase [amilɑz] **nf** amylase.

amyle [amil] **nm** amyl. **nitrite d'~** amyl nitrite.

amylique [amilik] **adj: alcool ~** amyl alcohol.

AN [aɛn] **nf** (**abrév de Assemblée nationale**) *voir* **assemblée.**

an [ɑ̃] **nm** a (*durée*) year. **après 5 ~s de prison** after 5 years in prison; **dans 3 ~s** in 3 years, in 3 years' time; **une amitié de 20 ~s** a friendship of 20 years' standing.

b (*âge*) year. **un enfant de six ~s** a six-year-old child, a six-year-old; **il a 22 ~s** he is 22 (years old); **il n'a pas encore 10 ~s** he's not yet 10.

c (*point dans le temps*) year. **4 fois par ~** 4 times a year; **il reçoit tant par ~** he gets so much a year *ou* annually *ou* per annum; **le jour *ou* le premier de l'~, le nouvel ~** New Year's Day; **en l'~ 300 de Rome** in the Roman year 300; **en l'~ 300 de notre ère/avant Jésus-Christ** in (the year) 300 A.D./B.C.; (*frm, hum*) **en l'~ de grâce ...** in the year of grace ...; **je m'en moque *ou* je m'en soucie comme de l'~ quarante** I couldn't care less (about it); *voir* **bon[1]**.

d (*littér*) **~s: les ~s l'ont courbé** he has become bowed *ou* hunched with age; **l'outrage des ~s** the ravages of time; **courbé sous le poids des ~s** bent under the weight of years *ou* age.

ana [ana] **nm** ana.

anabaptisme [anabatism] **nm** anabaptism.

anabaptiste [anabatist] **adj, nmf** anabaptist.

anabolisant, e [anabɔlizɑ̃, ɑ̃t] 1 **adj** anabolic. 2 **nm** anabolic steroid.

anabolisme [anabɔlism] **nm** anabolism.

anacarde [anakaʀd] **nm** cashew (nut).

anacardier [anakaʀdje] **nm** cashew (tree).

anachorète [anakɔʀɛt] **nm** anchorite.

anachronique [anakʀɔnik] **adj** anachronistic, anachronous.

anachronisme [anakʀɔnism] **nm** anachronism.

anacoluthe [anakɔlyt] **nf** anacoluthon.

anaconda [anakɔ̃da] **nm** anaconda.

Anacréon [anakʀeɔ̃] **nm** Anacreon.

anacréontique [anakʀeɔ̃tik] **adj** anacreontic.

anaérobie [anaeʀɔbi] 1 **adj** anaerobic. 2 **nm** anaerobe.

anaglyphe [anaglif] **nm** anaglyph.

anagrammatique [anagʀamatik] **adj** anagrammatical.

anagramme [anagʀam] **nf** anagram.

anal, e, mpl -aux [anal, o] **adj** anal.

analgésie [analʒezi] **nf** analgesia.

analgésique [analʒezik] **adj, nm** analgesic.

anallergique [analɛʀʒik] **adj** hypoallergenic.

analogie [analɔʒi] **nf** analogy. **par ~ avec** by analogy with.

analogique [analɔʒik] **adj** analogical.

analogiquement [analɔʒikmɑ̃] **adv** analogically.

analogue [analɔg] 1 **adj** analogous, similar (*à* to). 2 **nm** analogue.

analphabète [analfabɛt] **adj, nmf** illiterate.

analphabétisme [analfabetism] **nm** illiteracy.

analysable [analizabl] **adj** analysable (*Brit*), analyzable (*US*).

analyse [analiz] 1 **nf** a (*gén: examen*) analysis. **faire l'~ de** to analyse (*Brit*), analyze (*US*); **ce qu'il soutient ne résiste pas à l'~** what he maintains doesn't stand up to analysis; **avoir l'esprit d'~** to have an analytic(al) mind.

b (*Méd*) test. **~ de sang/d'urine** blood/urine test; **se faire faire des ~s** to have some tests (done); *voir* **laboratoire.**

c (*Psych*) psychoanalysis, analysis. **il poursuit une ~** he's undergoing *ou* having psychoanalysis *ou* analysis.

d (*Math*) (*discipline*) calculus; (*exercice*) analysis.

2 **comp ▸analyse combinatoire** combinatorial analysis **▸analyse en constituants immédiats** constituent analysis **▸analyse factorielle** factor *ou* factorial analysis **▸analyse financière** financial analysis **▸analyse fonctionnelle** functional job analysis **▸analyse grammaticale** parsing; **faire l'analyse grammaticale de** to parse **▸analyse logique** sentence analysis (*Brit*), diagramming (*US*) **▸analyse de marché** market analysis *ou* survey **▸analyse sectorielle** cross-section analysis **▸analyse spectrale** spectrum analysis **▸analyse de système** systems analysis **▸analyse transactionnelle** transactional analysis **▸analyse du travail** job analysis.

analyser [analize] 1 **vt** (*gén*) to analyse (*Brit*), analyze (*US*); (*Méd*) *sang, urine* to test; (*analyse grammaticale*) to parse.

analyste [analist] **nmf** (*gén, Math*) analyst; (*psychanalyste*) psychoanalyst, analyst. **~-programmeur** programme analyst; **~ financier/de marché** financial/market analyst; **~ de systèmes** systems analyst.

analytique [analitik] 1 **adj** analytic(al). 2 **nf** analytics (*sg*).

analytiquement [analitikmɑ̃] **adv** analytically.

anamorphose [anamɔʀfoz] **nf** anamorphosis.

ananas [anana(s)] **nm** (*fruit, plante*) pineapple.

anapeste [anapɛst] **nm** anapaest.

anaphore [anafɔʀ] **nf** anaphora.

anaphorique [anafɔʀik] **adj** anaphoric.

anar* [anaʀ] **nmf abrév de anarchiste.**

anarchie [anaʀʃi] **nf** (*Pol, fig*) anarchy.

anarchique [anaʀʃik] **adj** anarchic(al).

anarchiquement [anaʀʃikmɑ̃] **adv** anarchically.

anarchisant, e [anaʀʃizɑ̃, ɑ̃t] **adj** anarchistic.

anarchisme [anaʀʃism] **nm** anarchism.

anarchiste [anaʀʃist] 1 **adj** anarchistic. 2 **nmf** anarchist.

anarcho-syndicalisme [anaʀkosɛ̃dikalism] **nm** anarcho-syndicalism.

anarcho-syndicaliste, pl anarcho-syndicalistes [anaʀkosɛ̃dikalist] **nmf** anarcho-syndicalist.

anastigmat(e) [anastigma(t)] **adj m, nm: (objectif) ~** anastigmat, anastigmatic lens.

anastigmatique [anastigmatik] **adj** anastigmatic.

anastrophe [anastʀɔf] **nf** anastrophe.

anathématiser [anatematize] 1 **vt** (*lit, fig*) to anathematize.

anathème [anatɛm] **nm** (*excommunication, excommunié*) anathema. (*fig*) **jeter l'~ sur** to anathematize, curse; (*Rel*) **prononcer un ~ contre qn, frapper qn d'un ~** to excommunicate sb, anathematize sb.

Anatolie [anatɔli] **nf** Anatolia.

anatolien, -ienne [anatɔljɛ̃, jɛn] **adj** Anatolian.

anatomie [anatɔmi] **nf** a (*science*) anatomy. b (*corps*) anatomy. **elle a une belle ~*** she has a smashing figure*. c (*††: dissection*) (*Méd*) anatomy; (*fig*) analysis. **faire l'~ de** to dissect (*fig*), analyse; **pièce d'~** anatomical subject.

anatomique [anatɔmik] **adj** anatomical, anatomic.

anatomiquement [anatɔmikmɑ̃] **adv** anatomically.

anatomiste [anatɔmist] **nmf** anatomist.

ANC [aɛnse] **nm** (**abrév de African National Congress**) ANC.

ancestral, e, mpl -aux [ɑ̃sɛstʀal, o] **adj** ancestral.

ancêtre [ɑ̃sɛtʀ] **nmf** a (*aïeul*) ancestor; (**: vieillard*) old man (*ou* woman). **nos ~s du moyen âge** our ancestors *ou* forefathers *ou* forebears of the Middle Ages. b (*fig: précurseur*) *[personne, objet]* ancestor, forerunner, precursor. **c'est l'~ de la littérature moderne** he's the father of modern literature.

anche [ɑ̃ʃ] **nf** (*Mus*) reed.

anchoïade [ɑ̃ʃɔjad] **nf** ≃ anchovy paste.

anchois [ɑ̃ʃwa] **nm** anchovy.

anchoyade [ɑ̃ʃɔjad] **nf** = **anchoïade.**

ancien, -ienne [ɑ̃sjɛ̃, jɛn] 1 **adj** a (*vieux*) (*gén*) old; *coutume,* *château, loi* ancient; *objet d'art* antique. **dans l'~ temps** in olden days, in times gone by; **il est plus ~ que moi dans la maison** he has been with *ou* in the firm longer than me; **une ~ne amitié** an old friendship, a friendship of long standing; **compter en ~s francs** to count in old francs; **cela lui a coûté 10 millions ~s** it cost him 10 million old francs; *voir* **testament**.

b (*avant n: précédent*) former, old. **son ~ne femme** his ex-wife, his former *ou* previous wife; **c'est mon ~ quartier/~ne école** it's my old neighbourhood/school, that's where I used to live/go to school.

c (*antique*) *langue, civilisation* ancient. **dans les temps ~s** in ancient times; **la Grèce/l'Égypte ~ne** ancient Greece/Egypt.

2 nm (*mobilier ancien*) **l'~** antiques (*pl*).

3 nm,f (*personne*) a (*, †: *par l'âge*) elder, old man (*ou* woman). (*hum*) **et le respect pour les ~s?** and where's your respect for your elders?; **les ~s du village** the village elders.

b (*par l'expérience*) senior *ou* experienced person; (*Mil*) old soldier. **c'est un ~ dans la maison** he has been with *ou* in the firm a long time.

c (*Hist*) **les ~s** the Ancients; (*Littérat*) **les ~s et les modernes** the Ancients and the Moderns.

4 comp ▸**ancien combattant** war veteran, ex-serviceman ▸**ancien (élève)** old boy (*Brit*), alumnus (*US*), former pupil ▸**ancienne (élève)** old girl (*Brit*), alumna (*US*), former pupil ▸**l'Ancien Régime** the Ancien Régime.

anciennement [ɑ̃sjɛnmɑ̃] adv (*autrefois*) formerly.

ancienneté [ɑ̃sjɛnte] nf a (*durée de service*) (length of) service; (*privilèges obtenus*) seniority. **à l'~** by seniority; **il a 10 ans d'~ dans la maison** he has been with *ou* in the firm (for) 10 years. b *[maison]* oldness, (great) age, ancientness; *[statue, famille, objet d'art]* age, antiquity; *[loi, tradition]* ancientness. **de toute ~** from time immemorial.

ancillaire [ɑ̃silɛʀ] adj *voir* **amour**.

ancolie [ɑ̃kɔli] nf columbine.

ancrage [ɑ̃kʀaʒ] nm a (*Naut*) *[grand bateau]* anchorage; *[petit bateau]* moorage, moorings (*pl*). b (*attache*) *[poteau, câble]* anchoring; *[mur]* cramping.

ancre [ɑ̃kʀ] nf a (*Naut*) **~ (de marine)** anchor; **~ de miséricorde** *ou* **de salut** sheet anchor; **être à l'~** to be *ou* lie *ou* ride at anchor; **jeter l'~** to cast *ou* drop anchor; **lever l'~** (*lit*) to weigh anchor; (*: *fig*) to get going*, be on one's way*. b (*Constr*) cramp(-iron), anchor; (*Horlogerie*) anchor escapement, recoil escapement.

ancrer [ɑ̃kʀe] 1 1 vt a (*Naut*) to anchor.

b (*Tech*) *poteau, câble* to anchor; *mur* to cramp.

c (*fig*) to root. **~ qch dans la tête de qn** to fix sth firmly in sb's mind, get sth (to sink) into sb's head; **il a cette idée ancrée dans la tête** he's got this idea firmly fixed *ou* rooted in his head.

2 **s'ancrer** vpr a (*Naut*) to anchor, cast *ou* drop anchor.

b (*fig: s'incruster*) **il a l'habitude de s'~ chez les gens** when he visits people he usually stays for ages *ou* settles in for a good long while; **quand une idée s'ancre dans l'esprit des gens** when an idea takes root *ou* becomes fixed in people's minds; **il s'est ancré dans la tête que** ... he got it into *ou* fixed in his head that ... .

andain [ɑ̃dɛ̃] nm swath.

andalou, -ouse [ɑ̃dalu, uz] 1 adj Andalusian. 2 nm,f: **A~(se)** Andalusian.

Andalousie [ɑ̃daluzi] nf Andalusia, Andalucia.

Andes [ɑ̃d] nfpl: **les ~** the Andes.

andin, e [ɑ̃dɛ̃, in] adj Andean.

andorran, e [ɑ̃dɔʀɑ̃, an] 1 adj Andorran. 2 nm,f: **A~(e)** Andorran.

Andorre [ɑ̃dɔʀ] nf Andorra. **~-la-Vieille** Andorra la Vella.

andouille [ɑ̃duj] nf a (*Culin*) andouille (*sausage made of chitterlings*). b (‡: *imbécile*) prat‡ (*Brit*), clot* (*Brit*), dummy*, fool. **faire l'~** to act the fool; **espèce d'~!, triple ~!** you (stupid) prat!‡ (*Brit*), you (stupid) clot!* (*Brit*), you dummy!*

andouiller [ɑ̃duje] nm tine, (branch of) antler.

andouillette [ɑ̃dujɛt] nf andouillette (*small sausage made of chitterlings*).

André [ɑ̃dʀe] nm Andrew.

androcéphale [ɑ̃dʀosefal] adj with a human head.

androgène [ɑ̃dʀɔʒɛn] nm androgen.

androgyne [ɑ̃dʀɔʒin] 1 adj androgynous. 2 nm androgyne.

androïde [ɑ̃dʀɔid] nm android.

andrologie [ɑ̃dʀɔlɔʒi] nf andrology.

Andromaque [ɑ̃dʀɔmak] nf Andromache.

andropause [ɑ̃dʀopoz] nf male menopause.

androstérone [ɑ̃dʀosteʀɔn] nf androsterone.

âne [ɑn] nm a (*Zool*) donkey, ass. **être comme l'~ de Buridan** to be unable to decide between two alternatives; (*hum*) **il y a plus d'un ~ qui s'appelle Martin** a lot of people are called that, that's a very common name; *voir* **bonnet, dos, pont**. b (*fig*) ass, fool. **faire l'~ pour avoir du son** to act *ou* play dumb to find out what one wants to know, act the daft laddie (*ou* lassie)*; **~ bâté†** stupid ass; *voir* **bonnet, pont**.

anéantir [aneɑ̃tiʀ] 2 1 vt a (*détruire*) *ville, armée* to annihilate, wipe out; *efforts* to wreck, ruin, destroy; *espoirs* to dash, ruin, destroy; *sentiment* to obliterate, destroy. b (*déprimer, gén pass*) *[chaleur]* to overwhelm, overcome; *[fatigue]* to exhaust, wear out; *[chagrin]* to crush, prostrate; *[mauvaise nouvelle]* to overwhelm, crush. 2 **s'anéantir** vpr to vanish utterly; *[espoir]* to be dashed.

anéantissement [aneɑ̃tismɑ̃] nm a (*destruction: voir* **anéantir**) annihilation, wiping out; wrecking; ruin; destruction; dashing; obliteration. **c'est l'~ de tous mes espoirs** that's the end of *ou* that has wrecked all my hopes; **ce régime vise à l'~ de l'individu** this régime aims at the complete suppression *ou* annihilation of the individual('s rights). b (*fatigue*) state of exhaustion, exhaustion; (*abattement*) state of dejection, dejection.

anecdote [anɛkdɔt] nf (*gén, littér*) anecdote. **l'~** trivial detail *ou* details; (*péj*) **cet historien ne s'élève pas au-dessus de l'~** this historian doesn't rise above the anecdotal.

anecdotique [anɛkdɔtik] adj *histoire, description* anecdotal; *peinture* exclusively concerned with detail (*attrib*).

anémie [anemi] nf (*Méd*) anaemia; (*fig*) deficiency. **~ pernicieuse** pernicious anaemia.

anémié, e [anemje] (ptp de **anémier**) adj (*Méd*) anaemic; (*fig*) weakened, enfeebled.

anémier [anemje] 7 1 vt (*Méd*) to make anaemic; (*fig*) to weaken. 2 **s'anémier** vpr (*Méd*) to become anaemic.

anémique [anemik] adj (*Méd, fig*) anaemic.

anémomètre [anemɔmɛtʀ] nm *[fluide]* anemometer; *[vent]* anemometer, wind gauge.

anémone [anemɔn] nf anemone. **~ sylvie** wood anemone; **~ de mer** sea anemone.

ânerie [ɑnʀi] nf a (*NonC*) stupidity. **il est d'une ~!** he's a real ass!* b (*parole*) stupid *ou* idiotic remark; (*action*) stupid mistake, blunder. **arrête de dire des ~s!** stop talking rubbish! (*Brit*) *ou* nonsense!; **faire une ~** to make a blunder, do something silly.

anéroïde [aneʀɔid] adj *voir* **baromètre**.

ânesse [ɑnɛs] nf she-ass.

anesthésie [anɛstezi] nf (*état d'insensibilité, technique*) anaesthesia (*Brit*), anesthesia (*US*); (*opération*) anaesthetic (*Brit*), anesthetic (*US*). **sous ~** under anaesthetic (*Brit*) *ou* anesthetic (*US*), under anaesthesia (*Brit*) *ou* anesthesia (*US*); **~ générale/locale** general/local anaesthetic (*Brit*) *ou* anesthetic (*US*); **je vais vous faire une ~** I'm going to give you an anaesthetic (*Brit*) *ou* anesthetic (*US*).

anesthésier [anɛstezje] 7 vt (*Méd*) *organe* to anaesthetize (*Brit*), anesthetize (*US*); *personne* to give an anaesthetic (*Brit*) *ou* anesthetic (*US*) to, anaesthetize (*Brit*), anesthetize (*US*); (*fig*) to deaden, benumb, anaesthetize (*Brit*), anesthetize (*US*).

anesthésique [anɛstezik] adj, nm anaesthetic (*Brit*), anesthetic (*US*).

anesthésiste [anɛstezist] nmf anaesthetist (*Brit*), anesthesiologist (*US*).

aneth [anɛt] nm dill.

anévrisme [anevʀism] nm aneurism; *voir* **rupture**.

anfractuosité [ɑ̃fʀaktɥozite] nf *[falaise, mur, sol]* crevice.

ange [ɑ̃ʒ] 1 nm a (*Rel*) angel. **bon/mauvais ~** good/bad angel; (*fig*) **être le bon ~ de qn** to be sb's good *ou* guardian angel; (*fig*) **être le mauvais ~ de qn** to be an evil influence over *ou* on sb.

b (*personne*) angel. **oui mon ~** yes, darling; **va me chercher mes lunettes tu seras un ~** be an angel *ou* a darling and get me my glasses, go and look for my glasses, there's an angel *ou* a dear (*Brit*); **il est sage comme un ~** he's an absolute angel, he's as good as gold; **il est beau comme un ~** he's as pretty as a picture *ou* an angel, he looks quite angelic; **avoir une patience d'~** to have the patience of a saint; **c'est un ~ de douceur/de bonté** he's the soul of meekness/goodness.

c (*Zool*) angel fish.

d (*loc*) **un ~ passa** there was an awkward pause *ou* silence (in the conversation); **être aux ~s** to be in (the) seventh heaven.

2 comp ▸**ange déchu** (*Rel*) fallen angel ▸**l'ange exterminateur** (*Rel*) the exterminating angel ▸**ange gardien** (*Rel, fig*) guardian angel; (*fig: garde du corps*) bodyguard; *voir* **cheveux, faiseur, rire**.

angélique[1] [ɑ̃ʒelik] adj (*Rel, fig*) angelic(al).

angélique[2] [ɑ̃ʒelik] nf (*Bot, Culin*) angelica.

angéliquement [ɑ̃ʒelikmɑ̃] adv angelically, like an angel.

angélisme [ɑ̃ʒelism] nm (*Rel*) angelism; (*fig péj*) otherworldliness.

angelot [ɑ̃ʒ(ə)lo] nm (*Art*) cherub.

angélus [ɑ̃ʒelys] nm angelus.

angevin, e [ɑ̃ʒ(ə)vɛ̃, in] 1 adj (*d'Anjou*) Angevin (*épith*), of *ou* from Anjou; (*d'Angers*) of *ou* from Angers. 2 nm,f: **A~(e)** *[Anjou]* inhabitant *ou* native of Anjou; *[Angers]* inhabitant *ou* native of Angers.

angine [ɑ̃ʒin] nf (*amygdalite*) tonsillitis; (*pharyngite*) pharyngitis. **avoir une ~** to have a sore throat; **~ de poitrine** angina (pectoris); **~ couenneuse, ~ diphtérique** diphtheria.

angineux, -euse [ɑ̃ʒinø, øz] adj anginal.

angiome [ɑ̃ʒjom] nm angioma.

angioplastie [ɑ̃ʒjoplasti] nf angioplasty.

anglais, e [ɑ̃glɛ, ɛz] 1 adj English; *voir* **assiette, broderie, crème**. 2 nm a **A~** Englishman; **les A~** (*en général*) English people, the English; (*Britanniques*) British people, the British; (*hommes*) Englishmen; (*: *euph*) **les A~ ont débarqué** I've got the curse*, I've got my period. b (*Ling*) English. **~ canadien** Canadian English. 3 **anglaise**

nf a A~e Englishwoman. b (*Coiffure*) ~es ringlets. c (*Écriture*) ≃ modern English handwriting. d **à l'~e** *légumes* boiled; *voir* **filer, jardin.** 4 **adv: parler** ~ to speak English.

angle [ɑ̃gl] 1 nm a *[meuble, rue]* corner. **à l'~ de ces deux rues** at *ou* on the corner of these two streets; **le magasin qui fait l'~** the shop on the corner; **la maison est en ~** the house forms the corner *ou* stands directly on the corner.

b (*Math*) angle. ~ **saillant/rentrant** salient/re-entrant angle; ~ **aigu/obtus** acute/obtuse angle; ~**s alternes externes/internes** exterior/interior alternate angles.

c (*aspect*) angle, point of view. **vu sous cet** ~ seen from *ou* looked at from that angle *ou* point of view.

d (*fig*) *[caractère, personne]* rough edge; *voir* **arrondir.**

2 comp ►**angles adjacents** adjacent angles ►**angle de braquage** lock ►**angle de chasse** (*Aut*) castor angle ►**angle de couverture** (*Phot*) lens field ►**angle dièdre** dihedral angle ►**angle droit** right angle; **faire un angle droit** to be at right angles (*avec* to) ►**angle facial** facial angle ►**angle d'incidence** angle of incidence ►**angle d'inclinaison** angle of inclination ►**angle inscrit (à un cercle)** inscribed angle (of a circle) ►**angle de marche** = **angle de route** ►**angle mort** dead angle, blind spot ►**angle optique** optic angle ►**angle de réfraction** angle of refraction ►**angle de route** (*Mil*) bearing, direction of march ►**angle de tir** firing angle ►**angle visuel** visual angle; *voir* **grand.**

Angleterre [ɑ̃glətɛʀ] nf England; (*Grande Bretagne*) Britain.

anglican, e [ɑ̃glikɑ̃, an] adj, nm,f Anglican.

anglicanisme [ɑ̃glikanism] nm Anglicanism.

anglicisant, e [ɑ̃glisizɑ̃, ɑ̃t] nm,f (*étudiant*) student of English (*language and civilization*); (*spécialiste*) anglicist, English specialist.

angliciser [ɑ̃glisize] 1 1 vt to anglicize. 2 **s'angliciser** vpr to become anglicized.

anglicisme [ɑ̃glisism] nm anglicism.

angliciste [ɑ̃glisist] nmf (*étudiant*) student of English (*language and civilization*); (*spécialiste*) anglicist, English specialist.

anglo- [ɑ̃glɔ] préf anglo-.

anglo-américain, pl **anglo-américains** [ɑ̃gloameʀikɛ̃] 1 nm (*Ling*) American English. 2 adj Anglo-American.

anglo-arabe, pl **anglo-arabes** [ɑ̃gloaʀab] adj, nm (*cheval*) Anglo-Arab.

anglo-canadien, -ienne, mpl **anglo-canadiens** [ɑ̃glokanadjɛ̃, jɛn] 1 adj Anglo-Canadian. 2 nm (*Ling*) Canadian English. 3 nm,f: **A~(ne)** English Canadian.

anglomane [ɑ̃glɔman] nmf anglomaniac.

anglomanie [ɑ̃glɔmani] nf anglomania.

anglo-normand, e, mpl **anglo-normands** [ɑ̃glonɔʀmɑ̃, ɑ̃d] 1 adj Anglo-Norman; *voir* **île.** 2 nm a (*Ling*) Anglo-Norman, Norman French. b (*cheval*) Anglo-Norman (horse).

anglophile [ɑ̃glɔfil] 1 adj anglophilic. 2 nmf anglophile.

anglophilie [ɑ̃glɔfili] nf anglophilia.

anglophobe [ɑ̃glɔfɔb] 1 adj anglophobic. 2 nmf anglophobe.

anglophobie [ɑ̃glɔfɔbi] nf anglophobia.

anglophone [ɑ̃glɔfɔn] 1 adj *personne* English-speaking, Anglophone (*Can*); *littérature etc* English-Language (*épith*), in English (*attrib*). 2 nmf English-speaker, Anglophone (*Can*).

anglo-saxon, -onne, mpl **anglo-saxons** [ɑ̃glosaksɔ̃, ɔn] 1 adj Anglo-Saxon. **les pays ~s** Anglo-Saxon countries. 2 nm (*Ling*) Anglo-Saxon. 3 nm,f: **A~(ne)** Anglo-Saxon.

angoissant, e [ɑ̃gwasɑ̃, ɑ̃t] adj *situation, silence* harrowing, agonizing. **nous avons vécu des jours ~s** we went through *ou* suffered days of anguish *ou* agony.

angoisse [ɑ̃gwas] nf a (*NonC*) (*gén, Psych*) anguish, distress. (*Philos*) **l'~ métaphysique** metaphysical anguish, Angst; **une étrange ~ le saisit** a strange feeling of anguish gripped him; **l'~ de la mort** the anguish of death; **il vivait dans l'~/dans l'~ d'un accident** he lived in anguish/in fear and dread of an accident; **ils ont vécu des jours d'~** they went through *ou* suffered days of anguish *ou* agony; **c'est l'~*** it's panic stations*. b (*peur*) dread (*NonC*), fear. (*rare: sensation d'étouffement*) **avoir des ~s** to have feelings of suffocation.

angoissé, e [ɑ̃gwase] (ptp de **angoisser**) adj *geste, visage, voix* anguished; *question, silence* agonized. **regard/cri ~** look/cry of anguish; **être ~** (*inquiet*) to be distressed *ou* in anguish; (*oppressé*) to feel suffocated.

angoisser [ɑ̃gwase] 1 1 vt (*inquiéter*) to harrow, cause anguish *ou* distress to; (*oppresser*) to choke. 2 vi (**: être angoissé*) to be worried sick*.

Angola [ɑ̃gɔla] nm Angola.

angolais, e [ɑ̃gɔlɛ, ɛz] 1 adj Angolan. 2 nm,f: **A~(e)** Angolan.

angora [ɑ̃gɔʀa] adj, nm angora.

angstrœm, angström [aŋstʀœm] nm angstrom (unit).

anguille [ɑ̃gij] nf (*Culin, Zool*) eel. ~ **de mer** sea eel; ~ **de sable** sand eel; ~ **de roche** conger eel; **il m'a filé entre les doigts comme une ~** he slipped right through my fingers, he wriggled out of my clutches; (*fig*) **il y a ~ sous roche** there's something in the wind.

angulaire [ɑ̃gylɛʀ] adj angular; *voir* **grand, pierre.**

anguleux, -euse [ɑ̃gylø, øz] adj *menton, visage* angular, bony; *coude* bony.

anharmonique [anaʀmɔnik] adj anharmonic.

anhydre [anidʀ] adj anhydrous.

anhydride [anidʀid] nm anhydride.

anicroche* [anikʀɔʃ] nf hitch, snag. **sans ~s** smoothly, without a hitch.

ânier, -ière [ɑnje, jɛʀ] nm,f donkey-driver.

aniline [anilin] nf aniline.

animal, e, mpl **-aux** [animal, o] 1 adj (*Bio, fig*) animal (*épith*). (*péj: bestial*) **ses instincts ~aux** his animal instincts; **sa confiance était aveugle, ~e** his confidence was blind, instinctive; *voir* **esprit.** 2 nm (*Bio, fig*) animal. ~ **familier** *ou* **de compagnie** pet; ~ **de laboratoire** laboratory animal; **quel ~!*** (*personne grossière*) what a lout!; (*imbécile*) what a moron!*

animalcule [animalkyl] nm animalcule.

animalerie [animalʀi] nf *[laboratoire]* animal house; (*magasin*) pet shop.

animalier [animalje] 1 adj m *peintre, sculpteur* animal (*épith*). **cinéaste ~** maker of wildlife films; *voir* **parc.** 2 nm painter (*ou* sculptor) of animals, animal painter (*ou* sculptor).

animalité [animalite] nf animality.

animateur, -trice [animatœʀ, tʀis] nm,f a (*personne dynamique*) **c'est un ~ né** he's a born organizer; **l'~ de cette entreprise** the driving force behind *ou* the prime mover in this undertaking. b (*professionnel*) (*TV*) host; (*Music Hall*) compère; *[club]* leader, sponsor (*US*); *[camp de vacances]* activity leader, camp counselor (*US*); *[discothèque]* disc jockey, D.J.* c (*Ciné: technicien*) animator.

animation [animasjɔ̃] nf a (*vie*) *[quartier, regard, personne]* life, liveliness; *[discussion]* animation, liveliness; (*affairement*) *[rue, quartier, bureau]* (hustle and) bustle. **son arrivée provoqua une grande ~** his arrival caused a great deal of excitement *ou* a great commotion; **parler avec ~** to speak with great animation; **mettre de l'~ dans** *ou* **donner de l'~ à une réunion** to put some life into a meeting, liven a meeting up; **chargé de l'~ culturelle** in charge of cultural activities. b (*Ciné*) animation; *voir* **cinéma.**

animé, e [anime] (ptp de **animer**) adj a *rue, quartier* (*affairé*) busy; (*plein de vie*) lively; *regard, visage* lively; *discussion* animated, lively, spirited; (*Comm*) *enchères, marché* brisk. b (*Ling, Philos*) animate. c *voir* **dessin.**

animer [anime] 1 1 vt a (*être l'élément dynamique de, mener*) *débat, discussion, groupe* to lead; *réunion* to conduct; *entreprise* to lead, be prime mover in, mastermind; (*Rad, TV*) *spectacle* to compère. ~ **une course** to set the pace in a race.

b (*pousser*) *[haine]* to drive, impel; *[foi]* to impel; *[espoir]* to nourish, sustain. **animé seulement par le** *ou* **du désir de vous être utile** prompted only by the desire to be of service to you.

c (*stimuler*) *soldat* to rouse; *coureur* to urge on, drive on; *courage* to arouse. **la foi qui animait son regard** the faith which shone in his eyes.

d (*mouvoir*) to drive. **la fusée animée d'un mouvement ascendant** the rocket propelled *ou* driven by an upward thrust; **le balancier était animé d'un mouvement régulier** the pendulum was moving in a steady rhythm *ou* swinging steadily.

e (*donner de la vie à*) *ville, soirée, conversation* to liven up; *yeux* to put a sparkle into; *regard, visage* to put life into, light up; (*Art*) *peinture, statue* to bring to life; (*Philos*) *nature, matière* to animate.

2 **s'animer** vpr *[personne, rue]* to come to life, liven up; *[conversation]* to become animated, liven up; *[foule, objet inanimé]* to come to life; *[yeux, traits]* to light up.

animisme [animism] nm animism.

animiste [animist] 1 adj *théorie* animist(ic); *philosophe* animist. 2 nmf animist.

animosité [animozite] nf (*hostilité*) animosity (*contre* towards, against).

anion [anjɔ̃] nm anion.

anis [ani(s)] nm (*plante*) anise; (*Culin*) aniseed; (*bonbon*) aniseed ball. **à l'~** aniseed (*épith*).

aniser [anize] 1 vt to flavour with aniseed. **goût anisé** taste of aniseed.

anisette [anizɛt] nf anisette.

Ankara [ɑ̃kaʀa] n Ankara.

ankylose [ɑ̃kiloz] nf ankylosis.

ankyloser [ɑ̃kiloze] 1 1 vt to stiffen, ankylose (*SPÉC*); (*fig*) to benumb. **être tout ankylosé** to be stiff all over; **mon bras ankylosé** my stiff arm. 2 **s'ankyloser** vpr to stiffen up, ankylose (*SPÉC*); (*fig*) to become numb.

annales [anal] nfpl annals. **ça restera dans les ~*** that'll go down in history (*hum*).

annamite† [anamit] 1 adj Annamese, Annamite. 2 nmf: **A~** Annamese, Annamite.

Annapûrnâ [anapœʀna] nm Annapurna.

Anne [an] nf Ann, Anne.

anneau, pl **~x** [ano] 1 nm a (*gén: cercle*) ring; (*bague*) ring; *[serpent]* coil; *[chaîne]* link. ~ **de rideau** curtain ring. b (*Algèbre*) ring; (*Géom*) ring, annulus; *[colonne]* annulet; *[champignon]* annulus; *[ver]* segment, metamere. c (*Sport*) **les ~x** the rings; **exercices aux ~x**

ring exercises. 2 comp ▸**anneaux colorés** (*Opt*) Newton's rings ▸**anneau de croissance** *[arbre]* annual *ou* growth ring ▸**anneau épiscopal** bishop's ring ▸**anneau nuptial** wedding ring ▸**anneau oculaire** (*Opt*) eye ring ▸**anneau de Saturne** Saturn's ring ▸**anneau sphérique** (*Géom*) (spherical) annulus *ou* ring ▸**anneau de vitesse** (*Aut*) race track.

année [ane] 1 nf a (*durée*) year. **il y a bien des ~s qu'il est parti** he has been gone for many years, it's many years since he left; **la récolte d'une ~** a *ou* one year's harvest; **tout au long de l'~** the whole year (round), throughout the whole year; **payé à l'~** paid annually; **l'~ universitaire/scolaire** the academic/school year; **~ sabbatique** sabbatical year.
b (*âge, grade*) year. **il est dans sa vingtième ~** he is in his twentieth year; (*Scol*) **de première/deuxième ~** first-/second-year (*épith*).
c (*point dans le temps*) year. **les ~s de guerre** the war years; **~ de naissance** year of birth; (*Fin*) **~ budgétaire** financial year; (*Fin, Jur*) **~ de référence** relevant year; (*Statistiques*) **l'~ de référence 1984** the 1984 benchmark; **les ~s 20/30** the 20s/30s; **d'une ~ à l'autre** from one year to the next; **d'~ en ~** from year to year; (*littér*) **en l'~ 700 de notre ère/avant Jésus-Christ** in (the year) 700 A.D./B.C.; *voir* **bon**[1], **souhaiter**.
2 comp ▸**année bissextile** leap year ▸**année civile** calendar year ▸**année-lumière** nf (pl **années-lumières**) light year; **c'est à des années-lumières de mes préoccupations** it's the last thing on my mind ▸**année sainte** Holy Year ▸**année (de stage) de CPR** (*Scol*) induction year.

annelé, e [an(ə)le] adj ringed; (*Bot, Zool*) annulate; (*Archit*) annulated.

annexe [anɛks] 1 adj a (*secondaire*) *dépenses, tâches* subsidiary; *faits, considérations* related. **effets ~s** side effects; **revenus ~s** supplementary income. b (*attaché*) *document* annexed, appended. **les bâtiments ~s** the annexes. 2 nf (*Constr*) annex(e); *[document]* annex; *[contrat]* schedule (*de, à* to).

annexer [anɛkse] 1 1 vt *territoire* to annex; *document* to append, annex (*à* to). 2 **s'annexer*** vpr *personne, privilège* to hog*, monopolize.

annexion [anɛksjɔ̃] nf (*Pol*) annexation.

annexionnisme [anɛksjɔnism] nm annexationism.

annexionniste [anɛksjɔnist] adj, nmf annexationist.

Annibal [anibal] nm Hannibal.

annihilation [aniilasjɔ̃] nf a (*voir* **annihiler**) annihilation; wrecking; ruin; destruction; dashing; crushing. b (*Phys*) annihilation.

annihiler [aniile] 1 vt *efforts* to wreck, ruin, destroy; *espoirs* to dash, ruin, destroy, wreck; *résistance* to wipe out, destroy, annihilate; *personne, esprit* to crush. **le chef, par sa forte personnalité, annihile complètement ses collaborateurs** because of his strong personality, the boss completely overwhelms *ou* overshadows his colleagues.

anniversaire [anivɛʀsɛʀ] 1 adj anniversary (*épith*). **le jour ~ de leur mariage** (on) the anniversary of their marriage. 2 nm *[naissance]* birthday; *[événement, mariage, mort]* anniversary. **cadeau/carte d'~** birthday present/card.

annonce [anɔ̃s] nf a announcement; (*publicité*) (newspaper) advertisement; (*Cartes*) declaration. **petites ~s, ~s classées** classified advertisements *ou* ads*, small ads* (*Brit*), want ads* (*US*); **~ personnelle** personal message; **~ judiciaire** *ou* **légale** legal notice. b (*fig: indice*) sign, indication. **ce chômage grandissant est l'~ d'une crise économique** this growing unemployment heralds *ou* foreshadows an economic crisis.

annoncer [anɔ̃se] 3 1 vt a (*informer de*) *fait, décision, nouvelle* to announce (*à* to). **~ à qn que** to announce to sb that, tell sb that; **on m'a annoncé par lettre que** I was informed *ou* advised by letter that; **je lui ai annoncé la nouvelle** (*gén*) I announced the news to her, I told her the news; (*mauvaise nouvelle*) I broke the news to her; **on annonce l'ouverture d'un nouveau magasin** they're advertising the opening of a new shop; **on annonce la sortie prochaine de ce film** the forthcoming release of this film has been announced; **les journaux ont annoncé leur mariage** their marriage has been announced in the papers; **on annonce un grave incendie** a serious fire is reported to have broken out.
b (*prédire*) *pluie, détérioration* to forecast. **on annonce un ralentissement économique dans les mois à venir** a slowing-down in the economy is forecast *ou* predicted for the coming months.
c (*signaler*) *[présage]* to foreshadow, foretell; *[signe avant-coureur]* to herald; *[sonnerie, pas]* to announce, herald. **les nuages qui annoncent une tempête** the clouds that herald a storm; **ça n'annonce rien de bon** it bodes no good; **ce radoucissement annonce la pluie/le printemps** this warmer weather means that *ou* is a sign that rain/spring is on the way, this warmer weather is a sign of rain/spring; **la cloche qui annonce la fin des cours** the bell announcing *ou* signalling the end of classes; **il s'annonçait toujours en frappant 3 fois** he always announced himself by knocking 3 times.
d (*dénoter*) to bespeak, indicate, point to.
e (*introduire*) *personne* to announce. **il entra sans se faire ~** he went in without being announced *ou* without announcing himself; **annoncez-vous au concierge en arrivant** make yourself known *ou* say who you are to the concierge when you arrive; **qui dois-je ~?** what name shall I say?, whom shall I announce?
f (*Cartes*) to declare. (*fig*) **~ la couleur** to lay one's cards on the table, say where one stands.
2 **s'annoncer** vpr a (*se présenter*) *[situation]* to shape up. **comment est-ce que ça s'annonce?** how is it shaping up? *ou* looking?; **le temps s'annonce orageux** the weather looks (like being) stormy; **le retour s'annonce difficile** getting back promises to be difficult; **ça s'annonce bien** that looks promising, that looks like a promising *ou* good start.
b (*arriver*) to approach. **la révolution qui s'annonçait** the signs of the coming revolution; **l'hiver s'annonçait** winter was on its way.

annonceur [anɔ̃sœʀ] nm (*publicité*) advertiser; (*Rad, TV: speaker*) announcer.

annonciateur, -trice [anɔ̃sjatœʀ, tʀis] 1 adj: **~ de** *événement favorable* heralding; *événement défavorable* foreboding, forewarning; **signe ~ de** portent of. 2 nm,f herald, harbinger (*littér*).

Annonciation [anɔ̃sjasjɔ̃] nf: **l'~** (*événement*) the Annunciation; (*jour*) Annunciation Day, Lady Day.

annotateur, -trice [anɔtatœʀ, tʀis] nm,f annotator.

annotation [anɔtasjɔ̃] nf annotation.

annoter [anɔte] 1 vt to annotate.

annuaire [anɥɛʀ] nm yearbook, annual; *[téléphone]* (telephone) directory, phone book*.

annualisation [anɥalizasjɔ̃] nf (*Écon*) annualization. **l'~ de l'exposition** making the exhibition an annual event.

annualiser [anɥalize] 1 vt (*gén*) to make annual; (*Écon*) to annualize.

annualité [anɥalite] nf (*gén*) yearly recurrence. **l'~ du budget/de l'impôt** yearly budgeting/taxation.

annuel, -elle [anɥɛl] adj annual, yearly; *voir* **plante**[1].

annuellement [anɥɛlmɑ̃] adv annually, once a year, yearly.

annuité [anɥite] nf (*gén*) annual instalment (*Brit*) *ou* installment (*US*), annual payment; *[dette]* annual repayment. *[pension]* **avoir toutes ses ~s** to have (made) all one's years' contributions.

annulable [anylabl] adj annullable, liable to annulment (*attrib*).

annulaire [anylɛʀ] 1 adj annular, ring-shaped. 2 nm ring finger, third finger.

annulation [anylasjɔ̃] nf (*voir* **annuler**) invalidation; nullification; quashing; cancellation; annulment.

annuler [anyle] 1 1 vt *contrat* to invalidate, void, nullify; *jugement, décision* to quash; *engagement* to cancel, call off; *élection, acte, examen* to nullify, declare void; *mariage* to annul; *réservation* to cancel; *commande* to cancel, withdraw. 2 **s'annuler** vpr *[poussées, efforts]* to cancel each other out, nullify each other.

anoblir [anɔbliʀ] 2 vt to ennoble, confer a title of nobility on.

anoblissement [anɔblismɑ̃] nm ennoblement.

anode [anɔd] nf anode.

anodin, e [anɔdɛ̃, in] adj *personne* insignificant; *détail* trivial, trifling, insignificant; *critique* unimportant; *blessure* harmless; *propos* harmless, innocuous.

anodique [anɔdik] adj anodic.

anodiser [anɔdize] vt to anodize.

anomal, e, mpl **-aux** [anɔmal, o] adj (*Gram*) anomalous.

anomalie [anɔmali] nf (*gén, Astron, Gram*) anomaly; (*Bio*) abnormality; (*Tech*) (technical) fault.

anomie [anɔmi] nf anomie.

ânon [ɑnɔ̃] nm (*petit de l'âne*) ass's foal; (*petit âne*) little ass *ou* donkey.

anone [anɔn] nf annona.

ânonnement [anɔnmɑ̃] nm (*voir* **ânonner**) drone; faltering *ou* mumbling (speech).

ânonner [anɔne] 1 vti (*de manière inexpressive*) to read *ou* recite in a drone; (*en hésitant*) to read *ou* recite in a fumbling manner. **~ sa leçon** to mumble (one's way) through one's lesson.

anonymat [anɔnima] nm anonymity. **sous le couvert de l'~** anonymously; **garder l'~** to remain anonymous, preserve one's anonymity.

anonyme [anɔnim] adj (*sans nom*) anonymous; (*impersonnel*) *décor, meubles* impersonal.

anonymement [anɔnimmɑ̃] adv anonymously.

anophèle [anɔfɛl] nm anopheles.

anorak [anɔʀak] nm anorak.

anorexie [anɔʀɛksi] nf anorexia. **~ mentale** anorexia nervosa.

anorexique [anɔʀɛksik] adj, nmf anorexic.

anormal, e, mpl **-aux** [anɔʀmal, o] 1 adj (*gén, Sci*) abnormal; (*insolite*) unusual, abnormal; (*injuste*) abnormal. **il est ~ qu'il n'ait pas les mêmes droits** it isn't normal *ou* it's abnormal for him not to have the same rights. 2 nm,f (*Méd*) abnormal person.

anormalement [anɔʀmalmɑ̃] adv *se développer* abnormally; *se conduire, agir* unusually, abnormally. **~ chaud/grand** unusually *ou* abnormally hot/tall.

anormalité [anɔʀmalite] nf abnormality.

anoxie [anɔksi] nf anoxia.

anoxique [anɔksik] adj anoxic.

ANPE [aɛnpe] nf (abrév de **Agence nationale pour l'emploi**) *national employment agency.*

anse [ɑ̃s] nf *[panier, tasse]* handle; (*Géog*) cove; (*Anat*) loop, flexura (SPÉC). (*Archit*) ~ **(de panier)** basket-handle arch; (*hum*) **faire danser** *ou* **valser l'~ du panier** to make a bit out of the shopping money*.

antagonique [ɑ̃tagɔnik] adj antagonistic.

antagonisme [ɑ̃tagɔnism] nm antagonism.

antagoniste [ɑ̃tagɔnist] 1 adj *forces, propositions* antagonistic; (*Anat*) *muscles* antagonist. 2 nmf antagonist.

antalgique [ɑ̃talʒik] adj, nm analgesic.

antan [ɑ̃tɑ̃] nm (*littér*) **d'~** of yesteryear, of long ago; **ma jeunesse d'~** my long-lost youth, my youth of long ago; **ma force d'~** my strength of former days *ou* of days gone by *ou* of yesteryear; **mes plaisirs d'~** my erstwhile pleasures.

Antananarivo [ɑ̃tananaʀivo] n Antananarivo.

Antarctide [ɑ̃taʀktid] nf: **l'~** Antarctica.

antarctique [ɑ̃taʀktik] 1 adj antarctic. 2 nm: **l'A~** the Antarctic, Antarctica.

antécédence [ɑ̃tesedɑ̃s] nf antecedence.

antécédent, e [ɑ̃tesedɑ̃, ɑ̃t] 1 adj antecedent. 2 nm a (*Gram, Math, Philos*) antecedent; (*Méd*) past *ou* previous history. b **~s** *[personne]* past *ou* previous history, antecedents; *[affaire]* past *ou* previous history; **avoir de bons/mauvais ~s** to have a good/bad previous history.

antéchrist [ɑ̃tekʀist] nm Antichrist.

antécime [ɑ̃tesim] nf *[montagne]* foresummit, subsidiary summit.

antédiluvien, -ienne [ɑ̃tedilyvjɛ̃, jɛn] adj (*lit, fig*) antediluvian.

antenne [ɑ̃tɛn] nf a (*Zool*) antenna, feeler. (*fig*) **avoir des ~s** to have a sixth sense; (*fig*) **avoir des ~s dans un ministère** to have contacts in a ministry.

b (*pour capter*) (*Rad*) aerial, antenna; (*TV*) aerial; *[radar]* antenna. **~ parabolique** satellite dish.

c (*Rad, TV: écoute*) **être sur l'~** to be on the air; **passer à l'~** to go *ou* be on the air; **gardez l'~** stay tuned in; **je donne l'~ à Paris** we'll go over to Paris now; **je rends l'~ au studio** and now back to the studio; **temps d'~** airtime; **vous avez droit à 2 heures d'~** you are entitled to 2 hours' broadcasting time *ou* airtime *ou* to 2 hours on the air; **hors ~, le ministre a déclaré que** off the air, the minister declared that; **sur notre ~** on our station; **A~ 2**† *voir* **A2**.

d (*Naut: vergue*) lateen yard.

e (*petite succursale*) sub-branch, agency; (*de renseignements*) information service; (*Mil: poste avancé*) outpost. **~ chirurgicale** (*Mil*) advanced surgical unit; (*Aut*) emergency unit.

antépénultième [ɑ̃tepenyltjɛm] 1 adj antepenultimate. 2 nf antepenultimate syllable, antepenult.

antéposer [ɑ̃tepoze] [1] vt to place *ou* put in front of the word. **sujet antéposé** subject placed *ou* put in front of the verb.

antérieur, e [ɑ̃teʀjœʀ] adj a (*dans le temps*) *époque, situation* previous, earlier. **c'est ~ à la guerre** it was prior to the war; **cette décision était ~e à son départ** that decision was prior *ou* previous to his departure, that decision preceded his departure; **nous ne voulons pas revenir à la situation ~e** we don't want to return to the former *ou* previous situation; **dans une vie ~e** in a former life. b (*dans l'espace*) *partie* front (*épith*). **membre ~** forelimb; **patte ~e** forefoot. c (*Ling*) *voyelle* front (*épith*); *voir* **futur, passé**.

antérieurement [ɑ̃teʀjœʀmɑ̃] adv earlier. **~ à** prior *ou* previous to.

antériorité [ɑ̃teʀjɔʀite] nf *[événement, phénomène]* precedence; (*Gram*) anteriority.

anthologie [ɑ̃tɔlɔʒi] nf anthology; *voir* **morceau**.

anthozoaires [ɑ̃tozɔɛʀ] nmpl: **les ~** the Anthozoa.

anthracite [ɑ̃tʀasit] 1 nm anthracite. 2 adj inv dark grey (*Brit*) *ou* gray (*US*), charcoal grey.

anthrax [ɑ̃tʀaks] nm inv (*tumeur*) carbuncle.

anthropocentrique [ɑ̃tʀɔpɔsɑ̃tʀik] adj anthropocentric.

anthropocentrisme [ɑ̃tʀɔpɔsɑ̃tʀism] nm anthropocentrism.

anthropoïde [ɑ̃tʀɔpɔid] 1 adj anthropoid. 2 nm anthropoid (ape).

anthropologie [ɑ̃tʀɔpɔlɔʒi] nf anthropology.

anthropologique [ɑ̃tʀɔpɔlɔʒik] adj anthropological.

anthropologiste [ɑ̃tʀɔpɔlɔʒist] nmf, **anthropologue** [ɑ̃tʀɔpɔlɔg] nmf anthropologist.

anthropométrie [ɑ̃tʀɔpɔmetʀi] nf anthropometry.

anthropométrique [ɑ̃tʀɔpɔmetʀik] adj anthropometric(al).

anthropomorphique [ɑ̃tʀɔpɔmɔʀfik] adj anthropomorphic.

anthropomorphisme [ɑ̃tʀɔpɔmɔʀfism] nm anthropomorphism.

anthropomorphiste [ɑ̃tʀɔpɔmɔʀfist] 1 adj anthropomorphist, anthropomorphic. 2 nmf anthropomorphist.

anthroponymie [ɑ̃tʀɔpɔnimi] nf (*Ling*) anthroponomy.

anthropophage [ɑ̃tʀɔpɔfaʒ] 1 adj cannibalistic, cannibal (*épith*), anthropophagous (SPÉC). 2 nm cannibal, anthropophagite (SPÉC).

anthropophagie [ɑ̃tʀɔpɔfaʒi] nf cannibalism, anthropophagy (SPÉC).

anthropopithèque [ɑ̃tʀɔpɔpitɛk] nm anthropopithecus.

anti [ɑ̃ti] 1 préf **anti(-)** a (*rapport d'hostilité, d'opposition*) anti-; (*contraire à l'esprit de*) un-. **partis ~démocratiques** antidemocratic parties; **mesures ~grève** anti-strike laws; **ambiance/mesure ~démocratique** undemocratic atmosphere/measure; **campagne ~voitures/pollution** anti-car/antipollution campaign; **campagne ~bruit** noise abatement *ou* anti-noise campaign; **propagande ~tabac** anti-smoking propaganda.

b (*négation, contraire, inversion*) **style ~scientifique/poétique/érotique** unscientific/unpoetic/unerotic style; **démarche ~rationnelle** counter-rational approach; **l'~-art/-théâtre** anti-art/-theatre.

c (*protection*) anti-. (*Aut*) **dispositif ~-blocage** anti-lock device; (*Aut*) **traitement ~corrosion** rustproofing; (*Aut*) **bombe ~crevaison** (instant) puncture sealant; **mesures ~inflationnistes** anti- *ou* counter-inflationary measures; **mesures ~natalistes** birth-rate control measures; **dispositif ~friction/halo** anti-friction/-halo device; **dispositif ~radiations** radiation protection device; **crème ~(-)moustiques** anti-mosquito cream; **(médicament) ~dépresseur** antidepressant (drug); **~éblouissant/transpirant** anti-dazzle/antiperspirant; **produits/traitement ~cellulite** fat-reducing products/treatment.

2 nm (*hum*) **le parti des ~s** those who are anti *ou* against, the anti crowd*.

antiadhésif, -ive [ɑ̃tiadezif, iv] adj non-stick.

antiaérien, -ienne [ɑ̃tiaeʀjɛ̃, jɛn] adj *batterie, canon, missile* anti-aircraft; *abri* air-raid (*épith*).

anti-âge [ɑ̃tiɑʒ] adj inv anti-ageing.

antialcoolique [ɑ̃tialkɔlik] adj: **campagne ~** campaign against alcohol; **ligue ~** temperance league.

antiatomique [ɑ̃tiatɔmik] adj anti-radiation. **abri ~** fallout shelter.

anti-aveuglant, e [ɑ̃tiavœglɑ̃, ɑ̃t] adj (*Aut*) anti-dazzle.

antibalistique [ɑ̃tibalistik] adj *missile* antiballistic.

antibiothérapie [ɑ̃tibjoteʀapi] nf antibiotic therapy.

antibiotique [ɑ̃tibjɔtik] adj, nm antibiotic. **être/mettre sous ~s** to be/put on antibiotics.

antibois [ɑ̃tibwɑ] nm chair-rail.

antibrouillard [ɑ̃tibʀujaʀ] adj, nm (*Aut*) **(phare) ~** fog lamp (*Brit*), fog light (*US*).

antibruit [ɑ̃tibʀɥi] adj inv: **mur ~** (*qui empêche le bruit*) soundproof wall; (*qui diminue le bruit*) noise-reducing wall; **campagne ~** campaign against noise pollution.

antibuée [ɑ̃tibɥe] adj inv: **dispositif ~** demister; **bombe/liquide ~** anti-mist spray/liquid.

anticalcaire [ɑ̃tikalkɛʀ] 1 adj: **poudre ~** water softener. 2 nm water softener.

anticancéreux, -euse [ɑ̃tikɑ̃seʀø, øz] adj cancer (*épith*). **centre ~** (*laboratoire*) cancer research centre; (*hôpital*) cancer hospital.

anticasseur [ɑ̃tikasœʀ] adj: **loi ~(s)** anti-riot law.

anticerne [ɑ̃tisɛʀn] nm concealer (*to cover shadows under the eyes*).

antichambre [ɑ̃tiʃɑ̃bʀ] nf antechamber, anteroom. **faire ~**† to wait humbly *ou* patiently (for an audience with sb).

antichar [ɑ̃tiʃaʀ] adj anti-tank.

antichoc [ɑ̃tiʃɔk] adj *montre etc* shockproof.

antichute [ɑ̃tiʃyt] adj inv: **lotion ~** lotion preventing hair-loss.

anticipation [ɑ̃tisipasjɔ̃] nf a (*Fin*) **~ de paiement, paiement par ~** payment in advance *ou* anticipation, advance payment. b (*Littérat*) **littérature d'~** science fiction; **roman/film d'~** science fiction novel/film.

anticipé, e [ɑ̃tisipe] (ptp de **anticiper**) adj *retour* early (*épith*). **remboursement ~** repayment before due date; **retraite ~e** early retirement; **recevez mes remerciements ~s** thanking you in advance *ou* anticipation.

anticiper [ɑ̃tisipe] [1] 1 vi a (*prévoir, calculer*) to anticipate; (*en imaginant*) to look *ou* think ahead, anticipate what will happen; (*en racontant*) to jump ahead. **n'anticipons pas!** don't let's look *ou* think too far ahead, don't let's anticipate. b **~ sur** *récit, rapport* to anticipate; **~ sur l'avenir** to anticipate the *ou* look into the future; **sans vouloir ~ sur ce que je dirai tout à l'heure** without wishing to go into *ou* launch into what I shall say later; (*Sport*) **il anticipe bien (sur les balles)** he's got good anticipation. 2 vt (*Comm*) *paiement* to anticipate, pay before due; (*littér*) *avenir, événement* to anticipate, foresee.

anticlérical, e, mpl **-aux** [ɑ̃tikleʀikal, o] 1 adj anticlerical. 2 nm,f anticleric(al).

anticléricalisme [ɑ̃tikleʀikalism] nm anticlericalism.

anticlinal, e, mpl **-aux** [ɑ̃tiklinal, o] adj, nm anticlinal.

anticoagulant, e [ɑ̃tikɔagylɑ̃, ɑ̃t] adj, nm anticoagulant.

anticolonialisme [ɑ̃tikɔlɔnjalism] nm anticolonialism.

anticolonialiste [ɑ̃tikɔlɔnjalist] adj, nmf anticolonialist.

anticommunisme [ɑ̃tikɔmynism] nm anticommunism.

anticommuniste [ɑ̃tikɔmynist] adj, nmf anticommunist.

anticonceptionnel, -elle [ɑ̃tikɔ̃sɛpsjɔnɛl] adj contraceptive. **propagande ~le** birth-control propaganda; **moyens ~s** contraceptive methods, methods of birth control.

anticonformisme [ɑ̃tikɔ̃fɔʀmism] nm nonconformism.

anticonformiste [ɑ̃tikɔ̃fɔʀmist] adj, nmf nonconformist.

anticonstitutionnel, -elle [ɑ̃tikɔ̃stitysjɔnɛl] adj unconstitutional.

anticonstitutionnellement [ɑ̃tikɔ̃stitysjɔnɛlmɑ̃] adv unconstitutionally.

anticorps [ɑ̃tikɔʀ] nm antibody.

anticyclone [ɑ̃tisiklon] nm anticyclone.

anticyclonique [ɑ̃tisiklonik] adj anticyclonic.

antidater [ɑ̃tidate] [1] vt to backdate, predate, antedate.

antidémocratique [ɑ̃tidemɔkʀatik] **adj** (*opposé à la démocratie*) antidemocratic; (*peu démocratique*) undemocratic.
antidépresseur [ɑ̃tidepʀesœʀ] **adj m, nm** antidepressant.
antidérapant, e [ɑ̃tideʀapɑ̃, ɑ̃t] **adj** (*Aut*) non-skid; (*Ski*) non-slip.
antidétonant, e [ɑ̃tidetɔnɑ̃, ɑ̃t] **adj, nm** anti-knock.
antidiphtérique [ɑ̃tidifteʀik] **adj** *sérum* diphtheria (*épith*).
antidoping [ɑ̃tidɔpiŋ] **adj, antidopage** [ɑ̃tidɔpaʒ] **adj** *loi, test* anti-doping (*épith*); *contrôle* dope (*épith*).
antidote [ɑ̃tidɔt] **nm** (*lit, fig*) antidote (*contre, de* for, against).
antidrogue [ɑ̃tidʀɔg] **adj** *lutte, campagne* against drug abuse. **brigade ~** drug squad.
antiéconomique [ɑ̃tiekɔnɔmik] **adj** uneconomical.
antieffraction [ɑ̃tiefʀaksjɔ̃] **adj** *vitres* burglar-proof.
antiengin [ɑ̃tiɑ̃ʒɛ̃] **adj** antimissile.
antienne [ɑ̃tjɛn] **nf** (*Rel*) antiphony; (*fig littér*) chant, refrain.
antiesclavagisme [ɑ̃tiɛsklavaʒism] **nm** abolition (of slavery); (*US Hist*) abolitionism.
antiesclavagiste [ɑ̃tiɛsklavaʒist] 1 **adj** antislavery, opposed to slavery (*attrib*); (*US Hist*) abolitionist. 2 **nmf** opponent of slavery; abolitionist.
antifasciste [ɑ̃tifaʃist] **adj, nmf** antifascist.
anti-g [ɑ̃tiʒe] **adj inv: combinaison ~** G-suit.
antigang [ɑ̃tigɑ̃g] **adj inv: brigade ~** (police) commando squad.
antigel [ɑ̃tiʒɛl] **adj, nm** antifreeze.
antigène [ɑ̃tiʒɛn] **nm** antigen.
antigivrant, e [ɑ̃tiʒivʀɑ̃, ɑ̃t] 1 **adj** anti-icing (*épith*). 2 **nm** anti-icer.
Antigone [ɑ̃tigɔn] **nf** Antigone.
antigouvernemental, e, mpl -aux [ɑ̃tiguvɛʀnəmɑ̃tal, o] **adj** anti-government(al).
antigrippe [ɑ̃tigʀip] **adj inv: vaccin ~** flu vaccine; **vaccination ~** flu vaccination.
Antigua et Barbuda [ɑ̃tigwaebaʀbyda] **npl** Antigua and Barbuda.
antiguais, e [ɑ̃tigwɛ, ɛz] 1 **adj** Antiguan. 2 **nm,f: A~(e)** Antiguan.
antihausse [ɑ̃tios] **adj** *mesures* aimed at curbing price rises, anti-inflation (*épith*).
antihéros [ɑ̃tieʀo] **nm** anti-hero.
antihistaminique [ɑ̃tiistaminik] **adj, nm** antihistamine.
antihygiénique [ɑ̃tiiʒjenik] **adj** unhygienic.
anti-inflammatoire [ɑ̃tiɛ̃flamatwaʀ] **adj, nm** anti-inflammatory.
antijeu [ɑ̃tiʒø] **nm: faire de l'~** to be unsporting *ou* unsportsmanlike.
antillais, e [ɑ̃tijɛ, ɛz] 1 **adj** West Indian. 2 **nm,f: A~(e)** West Indian.
Antilles [ɑ̃tij] **nfpl: les ~** the West Indies; **les Grandes/Petites ~** the Greater/Lesser Antilles.
antilope [ɑ̃tilɔp] **nf** antelope.
antimatière [ɑ̃timatjɛʀ] **nf** antimatter.
antimilitarisme [ɑ̃timilitaʀism] **nm** antimilitarism.
antimilitariste [ɑ̃timilitaʀist] **adj, nmf** antimilitarist.
antimissile [ɑ̃timisil] **adj** antimissile.
antimite [ɑ̃timit] 1 **adj** (anti-)moth (*épith*). 2 **nm** mothproofing agent, moth repellent; (*boules de naphtaline*) mothballs.
antimoine [ɑ̃timwan] **nm** antimony.
antimonarchique [ɑ̃timɔnaʀʃik] **adj** antimonarchist, antimonarchic(al).
antimonarchiste [ɑ̃timɔnaʀʃist] **nmf** antimonarchist.
antinational, e, mpl -aux [ɑ̃tinasjɔnal, o] **adj** antinational.
antinomie [ɑ̃tinɔmi] **nf** antinomy.
antinomique [ɑ̃tinɔmik] **adj** antinomic(al).
antinucléaire [ɑ̃tinykleɛʀ] **adj** antinuclear.
Antioche [ɑ̃tjɔʃ] **n** Antioch.
ANTIOPE [ɑ̃tjɔp] **nf** (**abrév de acquisition numérique et télévisualisation d'images organisées en pages d'écriture**) *television sub-titles for the deaf*, ≃ Viewdata ®, ≃ Teletext ®, ≃ Videotex ®.
antipape [ɑ̃tipap] **nm** antipope.
antiparasitage [ɑ̃tipaʀazitaʒ] **nm** fitting of a suppressor to.
antiparasite [ɑ̃tipaʀazit] **adj** anti-interference. **dispositif ~** suppressor.
antiparasiter [ɑ̃tipaʀazite] [1] **vt** to fit a suppressor to.
antiparlementaire [ɑ̃tipaʀləmɑ̃tɛʀ] **adj** antiparliamentary.
antiparlementarisme [ɑ̃tipaʀləmɑ̃taʀism] **nm** antiparliamentarianism.
antipathie [ɑ̃tipati] **nf** antipathy. **l'~ entre ces deux communautés** the hostility *ou* antipathy between these two communities; **avoir de l'~ pour qn** to dislike sb.
antipathique [ɑ̃tipatik] **adj** *personne* disagreeable, unpleasant; *endroit* unpleasant. **il m'est ~** I don't like him, I find him disagreeable.
antipatriotique [ɑ̃tipatʀijɔtik] **adj** antipatriotic; (*peu patriote*) unpatriotic.
antipatriotisme [ɑ̃tipatʀijɔtism] **nm** antipatriotism.
antipelliculaire [ɑ̃tipelikylɛʀ] **adj** anti-dandruff.
antipersonnel [ɑ̃tipɛʀsɔnɛl] **adj inv** antipersonnel.
antiphrase [ɑ̃tifʀɑz] **nf** antiphrasis. **par ~** ironically.
antipode [ɑ̃tipɔd] **nm** (*Géog*) **les ~s** the antipodes; (*Géog*) **être à l'~** *ou* **aux ~s** to be on the other side of the world (*de* from, to); (*fig*) **votre théorie est aux ~s de la mienne** our theories are poles apart, your theory is the opposite extreme of mine.
antipoétique [ɑ̃tipɔetik] **adj** unpoetic.
antipoison [ɑ̃tipwazɔ̃] **adj inv: centre ~** treatment centre for poisoning cases.
antipoliomyélitique [ɑ̃tipɔljɔmjelitik] **adj** polio (*épith*).
antipollution [ɑ̃tipɔlysjɔ̃] **adj inv** antipollution (*épith*).
antiprotectionniste [ɑ̃tipʀɔtɛksjɔnist] 1 **adj** free-trade (*épith*). 2 **nmf** free trader.
antiprurigineux, -euse [ɑ̃tipʀyʀiʒinø, øz] **adj, nm** antipruritic.
antipsychiatrie [ɑ̃tipsikjatʀi] **nf** anti-psychiatry.
antipyrétique [ɑ̃tipiʀetik] **adj** antipyretic.
antipyrine [ɑ̃tipiʀin] **nf** antipyrine.
antiquaille [ɑ̃tikaj] **nf** (*péj*) piece of old junk.
antiquaire [ɑ̃tikɛʀ] **nmf** antique dealer.
antique [ɑ̃tik] **adj** (*de l'antiquité*) *vase, objet* antique, ancient; *style* ancient; (*littér: très ancien*) *coutume, objet* ancient; (*péj*) *véhicule, chapeau* antiquated, ancient. **style imitant l'~** mock-antique style; **il aime l'~** he is a lover of the art and style of antiquity.
antiquité [ɑ̃tikite] **nf** a (*période*) **l'~** antiquity. b (*ancienneté*) antiquity, (great) age. **de toute ~** from the beginning of time, from time immemorial. c **~s** (*œuvres de l'antiquité*) antiquities; (*meubles anciens etc*) antiques; **marchand d'~s** antique dealer.
antirabique [ɑ̃tiʀabik] **adj: vaccin ~** rabies vaccine; **vaccination ~** rabies vaccination.
antirachitique [ɑ̃tiʀaʃitik] **adj** antirachitic.
antiraciste [ɑ̃tiʀasist] **adj** antiracist, antiracialist.
antireflet [ɑ̃tiʀəflɛ] **adj inv** *surface* non-reflecting; (*Phot*) antiflare.
antireligieux, -ieuse [ɑ̃tiʀ(ə)liʒjø, jøz] **adj** antireligious.
antirépublicain, e [ɑ̃tiʀepyblikɛ̃, ɛn] **adj** antirepublican.
antirévolutionnaire [ɑ̃tiʀevɔlysjɔnɛʀ] **adj** antirevolutionary.
antirides [ɑ̃tiʀid] **adj inv** anti-wrinkle.
antiroman [ɑ̃tiʀɔmɑ̃] **nm: l'~** the antinovel, the anti-roman.
antirouille [ɑ̃tiʀuj] **adj inv** anti-rust.
antiroulis [ɑ̃tiʀuli] **adj inv** anti-roll (*épith*).
antiscorbutique [ɑ̃tiskɔʀbytik] **adj** antiscorbutic.
antisèche [ɑ̃tisɛʃ] **nf** (*arg Scol*) crib.
antiségrégationniste [ɑ̃tisegʀegasjɔnist] **adj** antisegregationist.
antisémite [ɑ̃tisemit] 1 **adj** anti-semitic. 2 **nmf** anti-semite.
antisémitisme [ɑ̃tisemitism] **nm** anti-semitism.
antisepsie [ɑ̃tisɛpsi] **nf** antisepsis.
antiseptique [ɑ̃tisɛptik] **adj, nm** antiseptic.
antisida [ɑ̃tisida] **adj inv** *campagne, vaccin* against AIDS, AIDS (*épith*); *traitement* for AIDS, AIDS (*épith*).
antisismique [ɑ̃tisismik] **adj** earthquake resistant.
antisocial, e, mpl -iaux [ɑ̃tisɔsjal, jo] **adj** (*Pol*) antisocial.
anti-sous-marin, e [ɑ̃tisumaʀɛ̃, in] **adj** anti-submarine.
antispasmodique [ɑ̃tispasmɔdik] **adj, nm** antispasmodic.
antisportif, -ive [ɑ̃tispɔʀtif, iv] **adj** (*opposé au sport*) anti-sport; (*peu élégant*) unsporting, unsportsmanlike.
antistatique [ɑ̃tistatik] **adj, nm** antistatic.
antistrophe [ɑ̃tistʀɔf] **nf** antistrophe.
antisubversif, -ive [ɑ̃tisybvɛʀsif, iv] **adj** counter-subversive.
antitabac [ɑ̃titaba] **adj inv: campagne ~** anti-smoking campaign.
antiterroriste [ɑ̃titeʀɔʀist] **adj** antiterrorist.
antitétanique [ɑ̃titetanik] **adj** *sérum etc* (anti-)tetanus (*épith*).
antithèse [ɑ̃titɛz] **nf** (*gén*) antithesis. (*fig: le contraire*) **c'est l'~ de** it is the opposite of.
antithétique [ɑ̃titetik] **adj** antithetic(al).
antitoxine [ɑ̃titɔksin] **nf** antitoxin.
antitoxique [ɑ̃titɔksik] **adj** antitoxic.
antitrust [ɑ̃titʀœst] **adj inv** *loi, mesures* anti-monopoly (*Brit*), anti-trust (*US*).
antituberculeux, -euse [ɑ̃titybɛʀkylø, øz] **adj** *sérum* tuberculosis (*épith*).
antitussif [ɑ̃titysif] **adj, nm: (sirop) ~** cough mixture.
antivariolique [ɑ̃tivaʀjɔlik] **adj: vaccin ~** smallpox vaccine.
antivénéneux, -euse [ɑ̃tivenenø, øz] **adj** antidotal.
antivenimeux, -euse [ɑ̃tivənimø, øz] **adj: sérum ~, substance ~euse** antivenom, antivenin.
antiviral, e, mpl -aux [ɑ̃tiviʀal, o] **adj** antiviral.
antivol [ɑ̃tivɔl] **nm, adj inv: (dispositif) ~** anti-theft device; **mettre un ~ sur son vélo** to put a (pad)lock on one's bike.
Antoine [ɑ̃twan] **nm** Ant(h)ony, Tony.
antonomase [ɑ̃tɔnɔmɑz] **nf** antonomasia.
antonyme [ɑ̃tɔnim] **nm** antonym.
antonymie [ɑ̃tɔnimi] **nf** antonymy.
antre [ɑ̃tʀ] **nm** (*littér: caverne*) cave; *[animal]* den, lair; (*fig*) den; (*Anat*) antrum.
anurie [anyʀi] **nf** anuria.
anus [anys] **nm** anus. **~ artificiel** colostomy (*SPÉC*).
Anvers [ɑ̃vɛʀ] **n** Antwerp.
anxiété [ɑ̃ksjete] **nf** (*inquiétude, Méd*) anxiety. **avec ~** with anxiety *ou* great concern; **être dans l'~** to be very anxious *ou* worried.
anxieusement [ɑ̃ksjøzmɑ̃] **adv** anxiously.
anxieux, -ieuse [ɑ̃ksjø, jøz] 1 **adj** *personne, regard* anxious, worried;

attente anxious. (*Méd*) **crises ~euses** crises of anxiety; **~ de** anxious to. 2 **nm,f** worrier.

anxiogène [ɑ̃ksjɔʒɛn] **adj** which causes anxiety *ou* distress.

anxiolytique [ɑ̃ksjɔlitik] 1 **adj** tranquillizing. 2 **nm** tranquillizer.

AOC [aose] **nf** (**abrév de appellation d'origine controlée**) *voir* **appellation**.

aoriste [aɔʀist] **nm** aorist.

aorte [aɔʀt] **nf** aorta.

aortique [aɔʀtik] **adj** aortic.

Aoste [aɔst] **n** Aosta.

août [u(t)] **nm** August; *pour loc voir* **septembre** *et* **quinze**.

aoûtat [auta] **nm** harvest tick *ou* mite.

aoûtien, -ienne* [ausjɛ̃, jɛn] **nm,f** August holiday-maker (*Brit*) *ou* vacationer (*US*).

AP [ape] **nf** (**abrév de Assistance publique**) *voir* **assistance**.

apache [apaʃ] **nm** a (*indien*) **A~** Apache. b (†: *voyou*) ruffian, tough. **il a une allure ~** he has a tough *ou* vicious look about him.

apaisant, e [apɛzɑ̃, ɑ̃t] **adj** (*chassant la tristesse, les soucis*) soothing; (*calmant les esprits*) mollifying, pacifying.

apaisement [apɛzmɑ̃] **nm** (*voir* **s'apaiser**) calming *ou* quietening down; cooling *ou* calming down; subsiding; abating; going *ou* dying down; appeasement; allaying. **donner des ~s à qn** to give assurances to sb, reassure sb; **cela lui procura un certain ~** this brought him some relief.

apaiser [apeze] [1] 1 **vt** a *personne, foule* to calm (down), pacify, placate. b (*adoucir*) (*gén*) to assuage; *désir, faim* to appease; *soif* to slake; *passion, excitation* to calm, quell, soothe; *conscience* to salve, soothe; *scrupules* to allay; *douleur* to soothe. 2 **s'apaiser vpr** a *[personne, malade]* to calm *ou* quieten down; *[coléreux]* to cool *ou* calm down. b *[vacarme, excitation, tempête]* to die down, subside; *[vagues, douleur]* to die down; *[passion, désir, soif, faim]* to be assuaged *ou* appeased; *[scrupules]* to be allayed.

apalachien, -ienne [apalaʃjɛ̃, jɛn] **adj** Appalachian.

apanage [apanaʒ] **nm** (*privilège*) **être l'~ de qn/qch** to be the privilege *ou* prerogative of sb/sth; **le pessimisme est le triste ~ des savants** it's the scholar's sorry privilege to be pessimistic; **avoir l'~ de qch** to have the sole *ou* exclusive right to sth, possess sth exclusively; **il croit avoir l'~ du bon sens** he thinks he's the only one with any common sense.

aparté [apaʀte] **nm** (*entretien*) private conversation (*in a group*); (*Théât, gén: remarque*) aside. **en ~** in an aside, in a stage whisper; (*Théât*) in an aside.

apartheid [apaʀtɛd] **nm** apartheid.

apathie [apati] **nf** apathy.

apathique [apatik] **adj** apathetic.

apathiquement [apatikmɑ̃] **adv** apathetically.

apatride [apatʀid] **nmf** stateless person.

APE [apeə] **nf** (**abrév de Assemblée parlementaire européenne**) EP.

APEC [apɛk] **nf** (**abrév de Association pour l'emploi des cadres**) executive employment agency.

Apennins [apenɛ̃] **nmpl: les ~** the Apennines.

aperception [apɛʀsɛpsjɔ̃] **nf** apperception.

apercevoir [apɛʀsəvwaʀ] [28] 1 **vt** a (*voir*) to see; (*brièvement*) to catch sight of *ou* a glimpse of; (*remarquer*) to notice, see. **on apercevait au loin un clocher** a church tower could be seen in the distance; **ça s'aperçoit à peine, c'est très bien réparé** it's hardly noticeable *ou* you can hardly see it, it's very well repaired.

b (*se rendre compte de*) *danger, contradictions* to see, perceive; *difficultés* to see, foresee. **si on fait cela, j'aperçois des problèmes** if we do that, I (can) see problems ahead *ou* I (can) foresee problems.

2 **s'apercevoir vpr: s'~ de** *erreur, omission* to notice; *présence, méfiance* to notice, become aware of; *dessein, manège* to notice, see through, become aware of; **s'~ que** to notice *ou* realize that; **sans s'en ~** without realizing, inadvertently.

aperçu [apɛʀsy] **nm** a (*idée générale*) general survey. **~ sommaire** brief survey; **cela vous donnera un bon ~ de ce que vous allez visiter** that will give you a good idea *ou* a general idea *ou* picture of what you are about to visit. b (*point de vue personnel*) insight (*sur* into).

apéritif, -ive [apeʀitif, iv] 1 **adj** (*littér*) *boisson* that stimulates the appetite. **ils firent une promenade ~ive** they took a walk to get up an appetite. 2 **nm** aperitif, aperitive, (pre-dinner *etc*) drink. **prendre l'~** to have an aperitif *ou* aperitive; **venez prendre l'~** come for drinks.

apéro* [apeʀo] **nm** (**abrév de apéritif**) aperitif, aperitive.

aperture [apɛʀtyʀ] **nf** (*Ling*) aperture.

apesanteur [apəzɑ̃tœʀ] **nf** weightlessness. **être en ~** to be weightless.

à-peu-près [apøpʀɛ] **nm inv** vague approximation; *voir* **près**.

apeuré, e [apœʀe] **adj** frightened, scared.

apex [apɛks] **nm** (*Astron, Bot, Sci*) apex; (*Ling*) *[langue]* apex, tip; (*accent latin*) macron.

aphasie [afazi] **nf** aphasia.

aphasique [afazik] **adj, nmf** aphasic.

aphérèse [afeʀɛz] **nf** aphaeresis.

aphone [afɔn] **adj** voiceless, aphonic (*SPÉC*). **je suis presque ~ d'avoir trop crié** I've nearly lost my voice *ou* I'm hoarse from so much shouting.

aphonie [afɔni] **nf** aphonia.

aphorisme [afɔʀism] **nm** aphorism.

aphrodisiaque [afʀɔdizjak] **adj, nm** aphrodisiac.

Aphrodite [afʀɔdit] **nf** Aphrodite.

aphte [aft] **nm** ulcer, aphtha (*SPÉC*). **~ buccal** mouth ulcer.

aphteux, -euse [aftø, øz] **adj** aphthous; *voir* **fièvre**.

api [api] *voir* **pomme**.

Apia [apja] **n** Apia.

à-pic [apik] **nm** cliff.

apical, e, mpl -aux [apikal, o] **adj** apical. **r ~** trilled r.

apico-alvéolaire [apikoalveɔlɛʀ] **adj, nf** apico-alveolar.

apico-dental, e, mpl -aux [apikodɑ̃tal, o] 1 **adj** apico-dental. 2 **apico-dentale nf** apico-dental.

apicole [apikɔl] **adj** beekeeping (*épith*), apiarian (*SPÉC*).

apiculteur, -trice [apikyltœʀ, tʀis] **nm,f** beekeeper, apiarist (*SPÉC*).

apiculture [apikyltyʀ] **nf** beekeeping, apiculture (*SPÉC*).

apitoiement [apitwamɑ̃] **nm** (*pitié*) pity, compassion.

apitoyer [apitwaje] [8] 1 **vt** to move to pity. **~ qn sur le sort de qn** to move sb to pity for *ou* make sb feel sorry for sb's lot; **n'essaie pas de m'~** don't try and make me feel sorry for you, don't try to get round me (*Brit*). 2 **s'apitoyer vpr: s'~ sur (qn/le sort de qn)** to feel pity *ou* compassion for (sb/sb's lot); **s'~ sur son propre sort** to feel sorry for o.s.

ap. J.-C. (**abrév de après Jésus-Christ**) AD.

aplanir [aplaniʀ] [2] 1 **vt** *terrain* to level; *difficultés* to smooth away *ou* out, iron out; *obstacles* to smooth away. **~ le chemin devant qn** to smooth sb's path *ou* way. 2 **s'aplanir vpr** *[terrain]* to become level. **les difficultés se sont aplanies** the difficulties smoothed themselves out *ou* were ironed out.

aplanissement [aplanismɑ̃] **nm** (*voir* **aplanir**) levelling; smoothing away; ironing out.

aplati, e [aplati] (**ptp de aplatir**) **adj** *forme, objet, nez* flat. **c'est ~ sur le dessus/à son extrémité** it's flat on top/at one end.

aplatir [aplatiʀ] [2] 1 **vt** *objet* to flatten; *couture* to press flat; *cheveux* to smooth down, flatten; *pli* to smooth (out); *surface* to flatten (out). **~ qch à coups de marteau** to hammer sth flat; **~ qn**‡ to flatten sb*; (*Rugby*) **~ le ballon** *ou* **un essai** to score a try. 2 **s'aplatir vpr** a *[personne]* **s'~ contre un mur** to flatten o.s. against a wall; **s'~ par terre** (*s'étendre*) to lie flat on the ground; (*: *tomber*) to fall flat on one's face; (*fig: s'humilier*) **s'~ devant qn** to crawl to sb, grovel before sb. b *[choses]* (*devenir plus plat*) to become flatter; (*être écrasé*) to be flattened *ou* squashed. (*s'écraser*) **s'~ contre*** to smash against.

aplatissement [aplatismɑ̃] **nm** (*gén*) flattening; (*fig: humiliation*) grovelling. **l'~ de la terre aux pôles** the flattening-out *ou* -off of the earth at the poles.

aplomb [aplɔ̃] **nm** a (*assurance*) composure, (self-)assurance; (*péj: insolence*) nerve, audacity, cheek*. **garder son ~** to keep one's composure, remain composed; **perdre son ~** to lose one's composure, get flustered.

b (*équilibre*) balance, equilibrium; (*verticalité*) perpendicular, plumb. *[personne]* **perdre l'~** *ou* **son ~** to lose one's balance; **à l'~ du mur** at the base of the wall.

c (*Équitation*) **~s** stand.

d **d'~** *corps* steady, balanced; *bâtiment, mur* plumb; **se tenir d'~ (sur ses jambes)** to be steady on one's feet; **être (posé) d'~** to be balanced *ou* level; **tu n'as pas l'air d'~*** you look off-colour* (*Brit*) *ou* out of sorts; **se remettre d'~ après une maladie*** to pick up *ou* get back on one's feet again after an illness; **ça va te remettre d'~*** that'll put you right *ou* on your feet again; **le soleil tombait d'~** the sun was beating straight down.

apnée [apne] **nf** apnoea (*Brit*), apnea (*US*). **plonger en ~** to dive without an aqualung *ou* while holding one's breath.

apocalypse [apɔkalips] **nf** (*Rel*) apocalypse. (*livre*) **l'A~** (the Book of) Revelation, the Apocalypse; **atmosphère d'~** doom-laden *ou* end-of-the-world atmosphere; **paysage/vision d'~** landscape/vision of doom.

apocalyptique [apɔkaliptik] **adj** (*Rel*) apocalyptic; (*fig*) *paysage* of doom; *vision* apocalyptic, of doom.

apocope [apɔkɔp] **nf** apocope.

apocryphe [apɔkʀif] 1 **adj** apocryphal, of doubtful authenticity; (*Rel*) Apocryphal. 2 **nm** apocryphal book. **les ~s** the Apocrypha.

apodictique [apɔdiktik] **adj** apodictic.

apogée [apɔʒe] **nm** (*Astron*) apogee; (*fig*) peak, apogee. **artiste à son ~** artist at her (*ou* his) peak; **elle était à l'~ de sa gloire** she was at the height of her fame.

apolitique [apɔlitik] **adj** (*indifférent*) apolitical, unpolitical; (*indépendant*) non-political.

apolitisme [apɔlitism] **nm** (*voir* **apolitique**) *[personne]* apolitical *ou* unpolitical attitude; non-political stand; *[organisme]* non-political character.

Apollon [apɔlɔ̃] **nm** (*Myth*) Apollo; (*fig*) Apollo, Greek god.

apologétique [apɔlɔʒetik] 1 **adj** (*Philos, Rel*) apologetic. 2 **nf** apologetics (*sg*).

apologie [apɔlɔʒi] **nf** apology. **faire l'~ de** (*gén*) to praise; (*Jur*) to vindicate.

apologiste [apɔlɔʒist] **nmf** apologist.

apologue [apɔlɔg] **nm** apologue.

apophyse [apɔfiz] nf apophysis.
apoplectique [apɔplɛktik] adj apoplectic.
apoplexie [apɔplɛksi] nf apoplexy. **attaque d'~** stroke, apoplectic fit.
apostasie [apɔstazi] nf apostasy.
apostasier [apɔstazje] 7 vi to apostatize, renounce the faith.
apostat, e [apɔsta, at] adj, nm,f apostate, renegade.
a posteriori [apɔsteʀjɔʀi] loc adv, adj (*Philos*) a posteriori; (*gén*) after the event. **il est facile, ~, de dire que ...** it is easy enough, after the event *ou* with hindsight, to say that ... .
apostille [apɔstij] nf apostil.
apostiller [apɔstije] 1 vt to add an apostil to.
apostolat [apɔstɔla] nm (*Bible*) apostolate, discipleship; (*prosélytisme*) proselytism, preaching, evangelism. (*fig*) **ce métier est un ~** this job requires total devotion *ou* has to be a vocation.
apostolique [apɔstɔlik] adj apostolic; *voir* **nonce**.
apostrophe [apɔstʀɔf] nf (*Gram, Rhétorique*) apostrophe; (*interpellation*) rude remark (*shouted at sb*). **mot mis en ~** word used in apostrophe; **lancer des ~s à qn** to shout rude remarks at sb.
apostropher [apɔstʀɔfe] 1 **1** vt (*interpeller*) to shout at, address sharply. **2 s'apostropher** vpr to shout at each other. **les deux automobilistes s'apostrophèrent violemment** the two motorists hurled violent abuse at each other.
apothème [apɔtɛm] nm apothem.
apothéose [apɔteoz] nf **a** (*consécration*) apotheosis. **cette nomination est pour lui une ~** this appointment is a supreme honour for him; **les tragédies de Racine sont l'~ de l'art classique** Racine's tragedies are the apotheosis *ou* pinnacle of classical art. **b** (*Théât, gén: bouquet*) grand finale. **finir dans une ~** to end in a blaze of glory. **c** (*Antiq: déification*) apotheosis.
apothicaire†† [apɔtikɛʀ] nm apothecary††; *voir* **compte**.
apôtre [apotʀ] nm (*Hist, Rel, fig*) apostle, disciple. **faire le bon ~** to play the saint; **se faire l'~ de** to make o.s. the spokesman *ou* advocate for.
Appalaches [apalaʃ] nmpl: **les (monts) ~** the Appalachian Mountains, the Appalachians.
appalachien, -ienne [apalaʃjɛ̃, jɛn] adj Appalachian.
apparaître [apaʀɛtʀ] 57 vi **a** (*se montrer*) *[jour, personne, fantôme]* to appear (*à* to); *[difficulté, vérité]* to appear, come to light; *[signes, obstacles]* to appear; *[fièvre, boutons]* to break out. **la vérité lui apparut soudain** the truth suddenly dawned on him; **la silhouette qui apparaît/les problèmes qui apparaissent à l'horizon** the figure/the problems looming up on the horizon.
b (*sembler*) to seem, appear (*à* to). **ces remarques m'apparaissent fort judicieuses** these seem *ou* sound very judicious remarks to me; **je dois t'~ comme un monstre** I must seem like *ou* appear a monster to you; **ça m'apparaît comme suspect** it seems slightly suspicious *ou* odd to me; **il apparaît que** it appears *ou* turns out that.
apparat [apaʀa] nm **a** (*pompe*) pomp. **d'~** *dîner, habit, discours* ceremonial; *voir* **grand**. **b** (*Littérat*) **~ critique** critical apparatus.
apparatchik [apaʀatʃik] nm apparatchik.
appareil [apaʀɛj] **1** nm **a** (*machine, instrument*) (*gén*) piece of apparatus, device; (*électrique, ménager*) appliance; (*Rad, TV: poste*) set; (*Phot*) camera; (*téléphone*) (tele)phone. **qui est à l'~?** who's speaking?; **Paul à l'~** Paul speaking.
b (*Aviat*) (aero)plane, aircraft (*inv*), craft (*inv*) (*US*).
c (*Méd*) appliance; (*contention dentaire*) brace; (*pour fracture*) splint; (*auditif*) hearing aid; (*: *dentier*) dentures, plate.
d (*Anat*) apparatus, system. **~ digestif/urogénital** digestive/urogenital system *ou* apparatus; **~ phonateur** vocal apparatus *ou* organs (*pl*).
e (*structure administrative*) machinery. **l'~ policier** the police machinery; **l'~ du parti** the party apparatus *ou* machinery; **l'~ des lois** the machinery of the law.
f (*littér*) (*dehors fastueux*) air of pomp; (*cérémonie fastueuse*) ceremony. **l'~ magnifique de la royauté** the trappings *ou* splendour of royalty; *voir* **simple**.
g (*Archit: agencement des pierres*) bond.
2 comp ►**appareil critique** critical apparatus ►**appareil de levage** lifting appliance, hoist ►**appareil de mesure** measuring device ►**appareil orthopédique** orthopaedic appliance ►**appareil-photo** nm (pl **appareils-photos**), **appareil photographique** camera ►**appareil à sous** (*distributeur*) slot machine; (*jeu*) fruit machine, one-armed bandit.
appareillage [apaʀɛjaʒ] nm **a** (*Naut*) (*départ*) casting off, getting under way; (*manœuvres*) preparations for casting off *ou* getting under way. **b** (*équipement*) equipment.
appareiller [apaʀeje] 1 **1** vi (*Naut*) to cast off, get under way. **2** vt **a** (*Naut*) *navire* to rig, fit out. **b** (*Archit: tailler*) *pierre* to dress. **c** (*Méd*) to fit with a prosthesis (*SPÉC*) *ou* an artificial limb (*ou* hand *ou* arm *etc*). **d** (*coupler*) to pair; (*assortir*) to match up; (*accoupler*) to mate (*avec* with).
apparemment [apaʀamɑ̃] adv apparently.
apparence [apaʀɑ̃s] nf **a** (*aspect*) *[maison, personne]* appearance, aspect. **ce bâtiment a (une) belle ~** it's a fine-looking building; **il a une ~ négligée** he is shabby-looking, he has a shabby *ou* uncared-for look about him.
b (*fig: extérieur*) appearance. **sous cette ~ souriante** under that smiling exterior; **sous l'~ de la générosité** under this (outward) show *ou* apparent display of generosity; **ce n'est qu'une (fausse) ~** it's a mere façade; **il ne faut pas prendre les ~s pour la réalité** one mustn't mistake appearance(s) for reality; **se fier aux/sauver les ~s** to trust/keep up appearances.
c (*semblant, vestige*) semblance.
d (*Philos*) appearance.
e (*loc*) **malgré l'~** *ou* **les ~s** in spite of appearances; **contre toute ~** against all expectations; **selon toute ~** in all probability; **en ~** apparently, seemingly, on the face of it; **des propos en ~ si contradictoires/si anodins** words apparently so contradictory/harmless; **ce n'est en ~ qu'il est heureux** it's only on the surface *ou* outwardly that he's happy.
apparent, e [apaʀɑ̃, ɑ̃t] adj **a** (*visible*) *appréhension, gêne* obvious, noticeable; *ruse* obvious. **de façon ~e** visibly, conspicuously; **sans raison/cause ~e** without apparent *ou* obvious reason/cause; **plafond avec poutres ~es** ceiling with visible *ou* exposed beams *ou* with beams showing; **coutures ~es** topstitched seams. **b** (*superficiel*) *solidité, causes* apparent (*épith*). **ces contradictions ne sont qu'~es** these are only outward *ou* surface discrepancies.
apparenté, e [apaʀɑ̃te] (ptp de **apparenter**) adj (*de la même famille*) related; (*qui ressemble à*) similar (*à* to). (*Pol*) **~ (au parti) socialiste** in alliance with the Socialists; **les libéraux et ~s** the Liberals and their electoral allies.
apparentement [apaʀɑ̃tmɑ̃] nm (*Pol*) grouping of electoral lists (*in proportional representation system*).
apparenter (s') [apaʀɑ̃te] 1 vpr: **s'~ à** (*Pol*) to ally o.s. with (*in elections*); (*par mariage*) to marry into; (*ressembler à*) to be similar to, have certain similarities to.
appariement [apaʀimɑ̃] nm (*voir* **apparier**) matching; pairing; mating.
apparier [apaʀje] 7 vt (*littér*) (*assortir*) to match; (*coupler*) to pair; (*accoupler*) to mate.
appariteur [apaʀitœʀ] nm (*Univ*) ≃ porter (*Brit*), ≃ campus policeman (*US*). (*hum*) **~ musclé** strong-arm attendant (*hired at times of student unrest*).
apparition [apaʀisjɔ̃] nf **a** (*manifestation*) *[étoile, symptôme, signe]* appearance; *[personne]* appearance, arrival; *[boutons, fièvre]* outbreak. **faire son ~** *[personne]* to make one's appearance, turn up, appear; *[symptômes]* to appear; *[fièvre]* to break out; **il n'a fait qu'une (courte** *ou* **brève) ~** (*à une réunion*) he only put in a brief appearance; (*dans un film*) he only made a brief appearance, he only appeared briefly. **b** (*vision*) apparition; (*fantôme*) apparition, spectre. **avoir des ~s** to see *ou* have visions.
apparoir [apaʀwaʀ] vb impers (*frm, hum*) **il appert (de ces résultats) que** it appears *ou* is evident (from these results) that.
appartement [apaʀtəmɑ̃] nm **a** flat (*Brit*), apartment (*US*); *[hôtel]* suite. **vivre dans un** *ou* **en ~** to live in a flat (*Brit*) *ou* apartment (*US*); *voir* **chien, plante**. **b** (*Can*) room.
appartenance [apaʀtənɑ̃s] nf *[race, famille]* belonging (*à* to), membership (*à* of); *[parti]* adherence (*à* to), membership (*à* of). (*Math*) **~ à un ensemble** membership of a set.
appartenir [apaʀtəniʀ] 22 **1 appartenir à** vt indir **a** (*être la possession de*) to belong to. **ceci m'appartient** this is mine, this belongs to me; **la maison m'appartient en propre** I'm the sole owner of the house; (*fig*) **pour des raisons qui m'appartiennent** for reasons of my own *ou* which concern me (alone); **un médecin ne s'appartient pas** a doctor's time *ou* life is not his own.
b (*faire partie de*) *famille, race, parti* to belong to, be a member of.
2 vb impers: **il appartient/n'appartient pas au comité de décider si ...** it is for *ou* up to/not for *ou* not up to the committee to decide if ..., it is/is not the committee's business to decide if ... .
appas [apɑ] nmpl (*littér*) charms.
appât [apɑ] nm (*Pêche*) bait; (*fig*) lure, bait. **mettre un ~ à l'hameçon** to bait one's hook; **l'~ du gain/d'une récompense** the lure of gain/a reward; *voir* **mordre**.
appâter [apɑte] 1 vt **a** (*pour attraper*) *poissons, gibier* to lure, entice; *piège, hameçon* to bait; (*fig*) *personne* to lure, entice. **b** (*engraisser*) *petits oiseaux* to feed (up); *volailles* to fatten (up).
appauvrir [apovʀiʀ] 2 **1** vt *personne, sol, langue* to impoverish; *sang* to make thin, weaken. **2 s'appauvrir** vpr *[personne, sol, langue]* to grow poorer, become (more) impoverished; *[sang]* to become thin *ou* weak; *[race]* to degenerate.
appauvrissement [apovʀismɑ̃] nm (*voir* **appauvrir, s'appauvrir**) impoverishment; thinning; degeneration.
appeau, pl **~x** [apo] nm (*instrument*) bird call; (*oiseau, fig*) decoy. **servir d'~ à qn** to act as a decoy *ou* a stool pigeon for sb.
appel [apɛl] **1** nm **a** (*cri*) call; (*demande pressante*) appeal. **accourir à l'~ de qn** to run in answer to sb's call; **~ à l'aide** *ou* **au secours** call for help; **elle a entendu des ~s** *ou* **des cris d'~** she heard someone calling out, she heard cries; **à son ~, elle se retourna** she turned round when he called; **~ à l'insurrection/aux armes/aux urnes** call to insurrection/to arms/to vote; **~ au calme** appeal *ou* call for calm; **à l'~**

des syndicats ... in response to the call of the trade unions ...; **manifestation à l'~ d'une organisation** demonstration called by an organization; **il me fit un ~ du regard** he gave me a meaningful glance; **il a fait un ~ du pied au chef de l'autre parti** he made covert advances to the leader of the other party; **faire l'~ nominal des candidats** to call out the candidates' names; **faire un ~ de phares** to flash one's headlights (*Brit*), flash the high beams (*US*); **offre/prix d'~** introductory offer/price; **produit d'~** loss leader; (*Hist*) **l'A~ du 18 juin** *General de Gaulle's radio appeal to the French people to resist the Nazi occupation.*

b **faire ~ à** (*invoquer*) to appeal to; (*avoir recours à*) to call on, resort to; (*fig: nécessiter*) to require; **faire ~ au bon sens/à la générosité de qn** to appeal to sb's common sense/generosity; **faire ~ à ses souvenirs** to call up one's memories; **il a dû faire ~ à tout son courage** he had to summon up *ou* muster all his courage; **faire ~ à l'armée** to call out the army; **on a dû faire ~ aux pompiers** they had to call on (the help of) the firemen; **ils ont fait ~ au président pour que** ... they appealed to *ou* called on the president to ...; **ce problème fait ~ à des connaissances qu'il n'a pas** this problem calls for *ou* requires knowledge he hasn't got.

c (*fig: voix*) call. **l'~ du devoir/de la religion** the call of duty/of religion; **l'~ de la raison/de sa conscience** the voice of reason/of one's conscience.

d (*vérification de présence*) (*Scol*) register, registration; (*Mil*) roll call. **faire l'~** (*Scol*) to call the register; (*Mil*) to call the roll; **absent/présent à l'~** (*Scol*) absent/present (for the register *ou* at registration); (*Mil*) absent/present at roll call; (*Jur*) **l'~ des causes** reading of the roll of cases (*to be heard*); *voir* **manquer, numéro.**

e (*Jur: recours*) appeal (*contre* against, from). **faire ~ d'un jugement** to appeal against a judgment; **faire ~** to appeal, lodge an appeal; **juger en ~/sans ~** to judge on appeal/without appeal; (*fig*) **sans ~** (**adj**) final; (**adv**) irrevocably; *voir* **cour.**

f (*Mil: mobilisation*) call-up. **~ de la classe 1985** 1985 call-up, call-up of the class of 1985; *voir* **devancer.**

g (*Téléc*) **~ (téléphonique)** (phone) call; *voir* **numéro.**

h (*Cartes*) signal (*à* for). **faire un ~ à pique** to signal for a spade.

i (*Athlétisme: élan*) take-off. **pied d'~** take-off foot.

j (*Ordin*) call.

2 **comp ▸appel d'air** in-draught (*Brit*), in-draft (*US*), intake of air **▸appel en couverture** (*Bourse*) request for cover **▸appel de fonds** call for capital; **faire un appel de fonds** to call up capital **▸appel à maxima** *appeal by prosecution against the harshness of a sentence* **▸appel à minima** *appeal by prosecution against the leniency of a sentence* **▸appel de note** (*Typ*) footnote reference, reference mark **▸appel d'offres** (*Comm*) invitation to tender *ou* bid (*US*) **▸appel au peuple** appeal *ou* call to the people.

appelant, e [ap(ə)lɑ̃, ɑ̃t] **nm,f** appellant.

appelé [ap(ə)le] **nm** (*Mil*) conscript, draftee (*US*), selectee (*US*). (*Rel, fig*) **il y a beaucoup d'~s et peu d'élus** many are called but few are chosen.

appeler [ap(ə)le] 4 1 **vt** a (*interpeller*) *personne, chien* to call; (*téléphoner à*) *personne* to ring (up), phone (up), call (up); *numéro* to dial, call, phone. **~ le nom de qn** to call out sb's name; (*Jur*) **~ une cause** to call (out) a case; **en attendant que notre cause soit appelée** waiting for our case to come up *ou* be called; **~ qn à l'aide** *ou* **au secours** to call to sb for help; **~ qn (d'un geste) de la main** to beckon (to) sb.

b (*faire venir: gén*) to summon; *médecin, taxi, police* to call, send for; *ascenseur* to call. **~ les fidèles à la prière** to summon *ou* call the faithful to prayer; **~ le peuple aux armes** to call *ou* summon the people to arms; (*Jur*) **~ qn en justice** to summon sb before the court; (*Jur*) **~ qn à comparaître comme témoin** to summon sb as a witness; (*Mil*) **~ une classe (sous les drapeaux)** to call up a class (of recruits); (*frm, hum*) **Dieu/la République vous appelle** God/the Republic is calling you; (*hum*) **le devoir m'appelle** duty calls; **les pompiers ont été appelés plusieurs fois dans la nuit** the firemen were called out several times during the night; **le patron l'a fait ~** the boss sent for him; **il a été appelé auprès de sa mère malade** he was called *ou* summoned to his sick mother's side; **~ la colère du ciel sur qn** to call down the wrath of heaven upon sb; **~ la bénédiction de Dieu sur qn** to confer God's blessing upon sb.

c (*nommer*) to call. **~ qn un imbécile** to call sb an imbecile; **j'appelle ceci une table/du bon travail** I call this a table/good work; **~ qn par son prénom** to call *ou* address sb by his first name; **nous nous appelons par nos prénoms** we are on first-name terms, we call each other by our first names; **~ qn Monsieur/Madame** to call sb Sir/Madam; **~ les choses par leur nom** to call things by their rightful name; **~ un chat un chat** to call a spade a spade; **voilà ce que j'appelle écrire!** that's what I call writing!; **il va se faire ~ Arthur!*** he's going to be in trouble!

d (*désigner*) **~ qn à** *poste* to appoint *ou* assign sb to; **être appelé à de hautes/nouvelles fonctions** to be assigned important/new duties; **sa nouvelle fonction l'appelle à jouer un rôle important** his new function will require him to play an important part; **être appelé à un brillant avenir** to be destined for a brilliant future; **la méthode est appelée à se généraliser** the method looks likely *ou* set to become general.

e (*réclamer*) *[situation, conduite]* to call for, demand. **j'appelle votre attention sur ce problème** I call your attention to this problem; **les affaires l'appellent à Lyon** business calls him to Lyons.

f (*entraîner*) **une lâcheté en appelle une autre** one act of cowardice leads to *ou* begets another; **ceci appelle une réflexion** *ou* **une remarque** this calls for comment.

g (*Cartes*) **~ le roi de cœur** to call for the king of hearts.

2 **vi** a (*crier*) **~ à l'aide** *ou* **au secours** to call for help; **elle appelait, personne ne venait** she called (out) but nobody came.

b **en ~ à** to appeal to; **en ~ de** to appeal against; **j'en appelle à votre bon sens** I appeal to your common sense.

3 **s'appeler vpr** (*être nommé*) to be called. **il s'appelle Paul** his name is Paul, he is called Paul; **comment s'appelle cet oiseau?** what's the name of this bird?, what's this bird called?; **comment cela s'appelle-t-il en français?** what's that (called) in French?, what do you call that in French?; **voilà ce qui s'appelle une gaffe/être à l'heure!** that's what's called a blunder/being on time!; **je te prête ce livre, mais il s'appelle Reviens!*** I'll lend you this book but you'd better give it back!*

appellatif [apelatif] **adj m, nm** (*Ling*) **(nom) ~** appellative.

appellation [apelasjɔ̃] **nf** designation, appellation; (*littér: mot*) term, name. (*Jur*) **~ d'origine** label of origin; **~ (d'origine) contrôlée** appellation contrôlée (*label guaranteeing the quality of wine*).

appendice [apɛ̃dis] **nm** *[livre]* appendix; (*Anat*) (*gén*) appendage, appendix. *[intestin]* **l'~** the appendix; (*hum: nez*) **~ nasal** proboscis (*hum*).

appendicectomie [apɛ̃disɛktɔmi] **nf** appendectomy.

appendicite [apɛ̃disit] **nf** appendicitis. **faire de l'~ chronique** to have a grumbling appendix; **avoir une crise d'~** to have appendicitis; **se faire opérer de l'~** to have one's appendix removed.

appentis [apɑ̃ti] **nm** (*petit bâtiment*) lean-to; (*toit en auvent*) penthouse (roof), sloping roof.

appert [apɛʀ] *voir* **apparoir.**

appesantir [apəzɑ̃tiʀ] 2 1 **vt** *tête, paupières* to weigh down; *objet* to make heavier; *gestes, pas* to slow (down); *esprit* to dull. (*littér*) **~ son bras** *ou* **autorité sur** to strengthen one's authority over. 2 **s'appesantir vpr** *[tête]* to grow heavier; *[gestes, pas]* to become slower; *[esprit]* to grow duller; *[autorité]* to grow stronger. **s'~ sur un sujet/des détails** to dwell at length on a subject/on details; **inutile de s'~** no need to dwell on that; **leur autorité s'est appesantie sur le peuple opprimé** their control over the oppressed nation has been strengthened.

appesantissement [apəzɑ̃tismɑ̃] **nm** *[démarche]* heaviness; *[esprit]* dullness; *[autorité]* strengthening.

appétence [apetɑ̃s] **nf** appetence. **avoir de l'~ pour** to have a partiality for, be partial to.

appétissant, e [apetisɑ̃, ɑ̃t] **adj** *nourriture* appetizing, mouth-watering; *femme* delectable. **peu ~** unappetizing.

appétit [apeti] **nm** a (*pour la nourriture*) appetite. **avoir de l'~, avoir bon ~, avoir un solide ~** to have a good *ou* hearty appetite; **perdre l'~** to lose one's appetite, go off one's food* (*Brit*); **il n'a pas d'~** he's got no appetite; **ouvrir l'~ de qn, donner de l'~ à qn** to give sb an appetite; (*lit*) **mettre qn en ~** to give sb an appetite; (*fig*) **ce premier essai m'a mis en ~** this first attempt gave me an appetite *ou* a taste for it; **avoir un ~ d'oiseau** to eat like a bird; **manger avec ~** to eat heartily *ou* with appetite; **manger sans ~** to eat without appetite; **avoir un ~ de loup** *ou* **d'ogre** to eat like a horse; **l'~ vient en mangeant** (*lit*) eating whets the appetite; (*fig*) the more you have the more you want; *voir* **bon**[1].

b (*désir naturel*) appetite; *[bonheur, connaissances]* appetite, thirst (*de* for). **~ sexuel** sexual appetite.

applaudimètre [aplodimɛtʀ] **nm** clapometer (*Brit*), applause meter.

applaudir [aplodiʀ] 2 1 **vt** to applaud, clap; (*fig littér: approuver*) to applaud, commend. **applaudissons notre sympathique gagnant** let's give the winner a big hand. 2 **vi** to applaud, clap. **~ à tout rompre** to bring the house down. 3 **applaudir à vt indir** (*littér: approuver*) *initiative* to applaud, commend. **~ des deux mains à qch** to approve heartily of sth, commend sth warmly. 4 **s'applaudir vpr** (*se réjouir de*) **je m'applaudis de n'y être pas allé!** I'm congratulating myself *ou* patting myself on the back for not having gone!

applaudissement [aplodismɑ̃] **nm** a (*acclamations*) **~s** applause (*NonC*), clapping (*NonC*); **des ~s nourris éclatèrent** loud applause *ou* clapping broke out; **sortir sous les ~s** to go off to great applause; **un tonnerre d'~s** thunderous applause. b (*littér: approbation*) approbation, commendation.

applicabilité [aplikabilite] **nf** applicability.

applicable [aplikabl] **adj** applicable. *[loi etc]* **être ~ à** to apply to, be applicable to.

applicateur [aplikatœʀ] 1 **adj m** applicator (*épith*). 2 **nm** (*dispositif*) applicator.

application [aplikasjɔ̃] **nf** a (*voir* **appliquer**) application; use; enforcement; implementation; administration. **mettre en ~** *décision* to put into practice, implement; *loi* to enforce, apply; *théorie* to put into practice, apply; **mise en ~** *[décision]* implementation; *[loi]* enforcement, application; *[théorie]* application; **mesures prises en ~ de la loi** measures taken to enforce *ou* apply the law.

b **~s** *[théorie, méthode]* applications; **les ~s de cette théorie sont très nombreuses** the (possible) applications of this theory are numerous.

c (*attention*) application, industry. **~ à qch** application to sth; **travailler avec ~** to work diligently, apply o.s. well; **son ~ à faire qch** the application *ou* zeal with which he does sth.

d (*Couture*) appliqué (work). **~ de dentelles** appliqué lace; **~ de velours** velvet appliqué.

e (*Math*) mapping.

applique [aplik] **nf** (*lampe*) wall lamp; (*Couture*) appliqué.

appliqué, e [aplike] (**ptp de appliquer**) **adj** *personne* industrious, assiduous; *écriture* careful. **bien ~** *baiser* firm; *coup* well-aimed; **linguistique** *etc* **~e** applied linguistics *etc*.

appliquer [aplike] 1 **1 vt a** (*poser*) *peinture, revêtement, cataplasme* to apply (*sur* to). (*Géom*) **~ une figure sur une autre** to apply one figure on another; **~ une échelle sur** *ou* **contre un mur** to put *ou* lean a ladder against a wall; **~ son oreille sur** *ou* **à une porte** to put one's ear to a door.

b (*mettre en pratique*) (*gén*) to apply; *peine* to enforce; *règlement, décision* to implement, put into practice; *loi* to enforce, apply; *remède* to administer; *recette* to use. **~ un traitement à une maladie** to apply a treatment to an illness.

c (*consacrer*) **~ son esprit à l'étude** to apply one's mind to study; **~ toutes ses forces à faire qch** to put all one's strength into doing sth.

d (*donner*) *gifle, châtiment* to give; *épithète, qualificatif* to apply. **~ un baiser/sobriquet à qn** to give sb a kiss/nickname; **je lui ai appliqué ma main sur la figure** I struck *ou* slapped him across the face, I struck *ou* slapped his face; **il s'est toujours appliqué cette maxime** he has always applied this maxim to himself.

2 s'appliquer vpr a (*coïncider avec*) **s'~ sur** to fit over; **le calque s'applique exactement sur son modèle** the tracing fits exactly on top of *ou* over its model.

b (*correspondre à*) **s'~ à** to apply to; **cette remarque ne s'applique pas à vous** this remark doesn't apply to you.

c (*se consacrer à*) **s'~ à** to apply o.s. to; **s'~ à cultiver son esprit** to apply o.s. to improving one's mind; **s'~ à l'étude de** to apply o.s. to the study of; **s'~ à paraître à la mode** to take pains to appear fashionable; **élève qui s'applique** pupil who applies himself.

appoggiature [apɔ(d)ʒjatyʀ] **nf** appoggiatura.

appoint [apwɛ̃] **nm a** (*monnaie*) **l'~** the right *ou* exact money *ou* change; **faire l'~** to give the right *ou* exact money *ou* change. **b** (*ressource, aide complémentaire*) (extra) contribution, (extra) help. **salaire d'~** secondary *ou* extra income; **travail d'~** second job; **radiateur d'~** back-up *ou* extra heater.

appointements [apwɛ̃tmɑ̃] **nmpl** salary.

appointer [apwɛ̃te] 1 **vt** to pay a salary to. **être appointé à l'année/au mois** to be paid yearly/monthly.

appontage [apɔ̃taʒ] **nm** landing (*on an aircraft carrier*).

appontement [apɔ̃tmɑ̃] **nm** landing stage, wharf.

apponter [apɔ̃te] 1 **vi** to land (*on an aircraft carrier*).

apport [apɔʀ] **nm a** (*approvisionnement*) *[capitaux]* contribution, supply; (*Tech*) *[chaleur, air frais, eau potable]* supply. **le tourisme grâce à son ~ de devises** tourism, thanks to the currency it brings in; **leur ~ financier/intellectuel** their financial/intellectual contribution; (*Fin*) **~ personnel** personal capital contribution; **terrain rendu plus fertile par l'~ d'alluvions d'une rivière** land made more fertile by the alluvia brought *ou* carried down by a river; **l'~ de** *ou* **en vitamines d'un aliment** the vitamins provided by *ou* the vitamin content of a food.

b (*contribution*) contribution. **l'~ de notre civilisation à l'humanité** our civilization's contribution to humanity.

c (*Jur*) **~s** property; **~s en communauté** *goods contributed by man and wife to the joint estate*; (*Fin*) **~s en société** capital invested.

apporter [apɔʀte] 1 **vt a** *objet* to bring. **apporte-le-moi** bring it to me, bring me it; **apporte-le-lui** take it to him; **apporte-le en montant** bring it up with you, bring it up when you come; **apporte-le en venant** bring it with you (when you come), bring it along; **qui a apporté toute cette boue?** who brought in all this mud?; **le vent d'ouest nous apporte toutes les fumées d'usine** the west wind blows *ou* sends *ou* carries all the factory fumes our way; **vent qui apporte la pluie** wind that brings rain.

b *satisfaction, repos, soulagement* to bring, give; *ennuis, argent, nouvelles* to bring; *modification* to bring about; *preuve, solution* to supply, provide, give. **~ sa contribution à qch** to make one's contribution to sth; **~ des modifications à qch** *[ingénieur]* to make *ou* introduce changes in sth, bring changes to sth; *[progrès]* to bring about changes in sth; **~ du soin à qch/à faire qch** to exercise care in sth/in doing sth; **~ de l'attention à qch/à faire qch** to bring one's attention to bear on sth/on doing sth; **elle y a apporté toute son énergie** she put all her energy into it; **son livre n'apporte rien de nouveau** his book contributes *ou* says nothing new, his book has nothing new to contribute *ou* say.

apposer [apoze] 1 **vt** (*frm*) *sceau, timbre, plaque* to affix; *signature* to append (*frm*); (*Jur*) *clause* to insert. (*Jur*) **~ les scellés** to affix the seals (*to prevent unlawful entry*).

apposition [apozisjɔ̃] **nf a** (*Gram*) apposition. **en ~** in apposition. **b** (*voir* **apposer**) affixing; appending; insertion.

appréciable [apʀesjabl] **adj** (*évaluable*) appreciable, noticeable; (*assez important*) appreciable. **un nombre ~ de gens** a good many *ou* a good few people, an appreciable number of people.

appréciateur, -trice [apʀesjatœʀ, tʀis] **nm,f** judge, appreciator.

appréciatif, -ive [apʀesjatif, iv] **adj** (*estimatif*) appraising, evaluative; (*admiratif*) appreciative; *voir* **état**.

appréciation [apʀesjasjɔ̃] **nf** (*voir* **apprécier**) estimation; assessment; appraisal; valuation. **je le laisse à votre ~** I leave you to judge for yourself, I leave it to your judgment *ou* assessment; **les ~s du professeur sur un élève** the teacher's assessment of a pupil; (*sur livret*) **"~ du professeur"** "teacher's comments *ou* remarks"; (*Assurances*) **~ des risques** estimation of risks, risk assessment.

apprécier [apʀesje] 7 **vt a** (*évaluer*) *distance, importance* to estimate, assess, appraise; (*expertiser*) *objet* to value, assess the value of. **b** (*discerner*) *nuance* to perceive, appreciate. **c** (*goûter*) *qualité, repas* to appreciate. **~ qn** (*le trouver sympathique*) to have a liking for sb; (*reconnaître ses qualités*) to appreciate sb; **un mets très apprécié** a much appreciated dish, a highly-rated dish; **son discours n'a pas été apprécié par la droite** his speech was not appreciated by the right wing; **il n'a pas apprécié!*** he didn't appreciate that!, he didn't much care for that!

appréhender [apʀeɑ̃de] 1 **vt a** (*arrêter*) to apprehend. **b** (*redouter*) to dread. **~ (de faire) qch** to dread (doing) sth; **~ que** to fear that. **c** (*Philos*) to apprehend.

appréhensif, -ive [apʀeɑ̃sif, iv] **adj** apprehensive, fearful (*de* of).

appréhension [apʀeɑ̃sjɔ̃] **nf a** (*crainte*) apprehension, anxiety. **envisager qch avec ~** to be apprehensive *ou* anxious about sth, dread sth; **avoir de l'~/un peu d'~** to be apprehensive/a little apprehensive; **son ~ de l'examen/d'un malheur** his apprehension about the exam/of a disaster. **b** (*littér, Philos*) apprehension.

apprenant, e [apʀənɑ̃, ɑ̃t] **nm,f** learner.

apprendre [apʀɑ̃dʀ] 58 **vt a** *leçon, métier* to learn. **~ que/à lire/à nager** to learn that/to read/to swim *ou* how to swim; **~ à se servir de** to learn (how) to use; **~ à connaître** to get to know; **l'espagnol s'apprend facilement** Spanish is easy to learn; **ce jeu s'apprend vite** this game is quickly learnt; **il apprend vite** he's a fast learner, he learns quickly; *voir* **cœur**.

b *nouvelle* to hear, learn; *événement, fait* to hear of, learn of; *secret* to learn (of) (*de qn* from sb). **j'ai appris hier que ...** I heard *ou* learnt *ou* it came to my knowledge (*frm*) yesterday that ...; **j'ai appris son arrivée par des amis/par la radio** I heard of *ou* learnt of his arrival through friends/on the radio; **apprenez que je ne me laisserai pas faire!** be warned that *ou* let me make it quite clear that I won't be trifled with!

c (*annoncer*) **~ qch à qn** to tell sb (of) sth; **il m'a appris la nouvelle** he told me the news; **il m'apprend à l'instant son départ/qu'il va partir** he has just told me of his departure/that he's going to leave; **vous ne m'apprenez rien!** you're not telling me anything new! *ou* anything I don't know already!, that's no news to me!

d (*enseigner*) **~ qch à qn** to teach sb sth, teach sth to sb; **~ à qn à faire** to teach sb (how) to do; **il a appris à son chien à obéir/qu'il doit obéir** he taught his dog to obey/that he must obey; (*iro*) **je vais lui ~ à répondre de cette façon** I'll teach him to answer back like that; (*iro*) **je vais lui ~ à vivre** I'll teach him a thing or two, I'll sort (*Brit*) *ou* straighten him out; (*iro*) **ça lui apprendra (à vivre)!** that'll teach him (a lesson)!; **on n'apprend pas à un vieux singe à faire des grimaces** you can't teach an old dog new tricks.

apprenti, e [apʀɑ̃ti] **nm,f** *[métier]* apprentice; (*débutant*) novice, beginner. **~ mécanicien** apprentice *ou* trainee mechanic, mechanic's apprentice; (*péj*) **~ philosophe** novice philosopher; **~ sorcier** sorcerer's apprentice.

apprentissage [apʀɑ̃tisaʒ] **nm** (*lit*) apprenticeship. **l'~ de la langue** language learning; **l'~ de l'anglais** learning English; **l'~ de l'amour** learning about love; **l'~ de la patience** learning to be patient, learning patience; **mettre qn en ~** to apprentice sb (*chez* to); **être en ~** to be apprenticed *ou* an apprentice (*chez* to); **faire son ~** to serve one's apprenticeship, do one's training (*chez* with); **faire son ~ de mécanicien** to train as a mechanic; **école** *ou* **centre d'~** training school; **faire l'~ de** (*lit*) *métier* to serve one's apprenticeship to; (*fig*) *douleur, vie active* to have one's first experience of, be initiated into; *voir* **contrat, taxe**.

apprêt [apʀɛ] **nm a** (*Tech: opération*) *[cuir, tissu]* dressing; *[papier]* finishing; (*Peinture*) sizing, priming. (*fig*) **sans ~** unaffectedly. **b** (*Tech: substance*) *[cuir, tissu]* dressing; (*Peinture*) size, primer. **couche d'~** coat of primer. **c** (*préparatifs*) **~s** *[voyage etc]* preparations (*de* for).

apprêtage [apʀɛtaʒ] **nm** (*voir* **apprêt**) dressing; finishing; sizing, priming.

apprêté, e [apʀete] (**ptp de apprêter**) **adj** (*affecté*) *manière, style* affected.

apprêter [apʀete] 1 **1 vt a** *nourriture* to prepare, get ready. (*habiller*) **~ un enfant/une mariée** to get a child/bride ready, dress a child/bride. **b** (*Tech*) *peau, papier, tissu* to dress, finish; (*Peinture*) to size, prime. 2 **s'apprêter** vpr a **s'~ à qch/à faire qch** to get ready for sth/to do sth, prepare (o.s.) for sth/to do sth; **nous nous apprêtions à partir** we were getting ready *ou* preparing to leave. b (*faire sa toilette*) to dress o.s., prepare o.s.

apprivoisable [apʀivwazabl] adj tameable.

apprivoisé, e [apʀivwaze] (ptp de **apprivoiser**) adj tame, tamed.

apprivoisement [apʀivwazmɑ̃] nm (*action*) taming; (*état*) tameness.

apprivoiser [apʀivwaze] 1 1 vt *animal* to tame, domesticate; *personne* to make more sociable. 2 **s'apprivoiser** vpr *[animal]* to become tame; *[personne]* to become more sociable. **le renard finit par s'~** the fox was finally tamed *ou* finally became tame.

approbateur, -trice [apʀɔbatœʀ, tʀis] 1 adj approving. **signe de tête ~** nod of approval, approving nod. 2 nm,f (*littér*) approver.

approbatif, -ive [apʀɔbatif, iv] adj = **approbateur.**

approbation [apʀɔbasjɔ̃] nf (*jugement favorable*) approval, approbation; (*acceptation*) approval. **donner son ~ à un projet** to give one's approval to a project; **ce livre a rencontré l'~ du grand public** this book has been well received by the public; **conduite/travail digne d'~** commendable behaviour/work; (*Fin*) **~ des comptes** approval of the accounts.

approchable [apʀɔʃabl] adj *chose* accessible; *personne* approachable. **il n'est pas ~ aujourd'hui, il est de mauvaise humeur** don't go near him today, he's in a bad mood; **le ministre est difficilement ~** the minister is rather inaccessible *ou* is not very accessible.

approchant, e [apʀɔʃɑ̃, ɑ̃t] adj *style, genre* similar (*de* to); *résultat* close (*de* to). **quelque chose d'~** something like that, something similar; **rien d'~** nothing like that.

approche [apʀɔʃ] nf a (*arrivée*) *[personne, véhicule, événement]* approach. **à mon ~ il sourit** he smiled as I drew nearer *ou* approached; **à l'~ de l'hiver/de la date prévue** at the approach of winter/the arranged date, as winter/the arranged date drew near *ou* approached; **pour empêcher l'~ de l'ennemi** to prevent the enemy's approaching *ou* the enemy from approaching; **s'enfuir à l'~ du danger** to flee at the approach of danger; **à l'~ *ou* aux ~s de la cinquantaine** as he neared *ou* approached fifty, as fifty drew nearer; *voir* **lunette.**

b (*abord*) **être d'~ difficile/aisée** *[personne]* to be unapproachable/approachable, be difficult/easy to approach; *[lieu]* to be inaccessible/(easily) accessible, be difficult/easy of access; *[musique, auteur]* to be difficult/easy to understand; **manœuvres *ou* travaux d'~** (*Mil*) approaches, saps; (*fig*) manoeuvres, manoeuvrings.

c (*parages*) **les ~s de** *ville, côte, région* the surrounding area of, the area (immediately) surrounding; **aux ~s de la ville elle pensa ...** as she neared *ou* approached the town she thought ... .

d (*façon d'aborder*) approach. **l'~ de ce problème** the approach to this problem; **ce n'est qu'une ~ sommaire de la question** this is only a brief introduction to *ou* a cursory glance at the question.

e (*Typ*) (*espace*) spacing; (*faute*) spacing error; (*signe*) close-up mark.

f (*Aviat*) **nous sommes maintenant en ~ finale et nous allons atterrir dans quelques minutes** we are now on our final aproach and shall be landing in a few minutes.

approché, e [apʀɔʃe] (ptp de **approcher**) adj *résultat, idée* approximate.

approcher [apʀɔʃe] 1 1 vt a *objet* to put near, move near. **~ un fauteuil/une table de la fenêtre** to move an armchair/a table near to the window; **approche ta chaise** draw *ou* bring up your chair, bring your chair nearer *ou* closer; **il approcha les deux chaises l'une de l'autre** he moved the two chairs close together; **il approcha le verre de ses lèvres** he lifted *ou* raised the glass to his lips; **elle approcha son visage du sien** she moved her face near to his.

b *personne* (*lit*) to go near, come near, approach; (*fig*) to approach. **ne l'approchez pas!** don't go near him!, keep away from him!, give him a wide berth!; (*fig*) **il approche tous les jours les plus hautes personnalités** he is in contact *ou* he has dealings every day with the top people.

2 vi a *[date, saison]* to approach, draw near; *[personne, orage]* to approach, come nearer; *[nuit, jour]* to approach, draw on. **le jour approche où** the day is near when; **approche que je t'examine** come here and let me look at you.

b **~ de qch: ~ d'un lieu** to near a place, get *ou* draw near to a place; **~ du but/du résultat** to draw near to *ou* to near the goal/result; **~ de la perfection** to come close to perfection, approach perfection; **il approche de la cinquantaine** he's getting on for (*Brit*) *ou* going on (*US*) *ou* approaching fifty; **devoir qui approche de la moyenne** exercise that is just below a pass mark; **l'aiguille du compteur approchait du 80** the needle on the speedometer was approaching *ou* nearing 80.

3 **s'approcher** vpr (*venir*) to come near, approach; (*aller*) to go near, approach. **un homme s'est approché pour me parler** a man came up to speak to me; **l'enfant s'approcha de moi** the child came up to me *ou* came close to *ou* near me; **ne t'approche pas de moi** don't come near me; **s'~ du micro** (*venir*) to come up to the mike; (*se rapprocher*) to get closer *ou* nearer to the mike; **approche-toi!** come here!; **approchez-vous du feu** come near (to) the fire; **à aucun moment ce roman ne s'approche de la réalité** at no time does this novel come anywhere near to *ou* approach reality; **il s'approcha du lit à pas de loup** he crept up to the bed.

approfondi, e [apʀɔfɔ̃di] (ptp de **approfondir**) adj *connaissances, étude* thorough, detailed; *débat* in-depth.

approfondir [apʀɔfɔ̃diʀ] 2 vt *canal, puits* to deepen, make deeper; (*fig*) *question, étude* to go (deeper) into; *connaissances* to deepen, increase. **la rivière s'est approfondie** the river has become deeper *ou* has deepened; **il vaut mieux ne pas ~ le sujet** it's better not to go into the matter too closely; **sans ~** superficially.

approfondissement [apʀɔfɔ̃dismɑ̃] nm *[canal, puits]* deepening (*NonC*); *[connaissances]* deepening (*NonC*), increasing (*NonC*). **l'~ de la question/de cette étude serait souhaitable** it would be a good idea to go deeper into the question/this study.

appropriation [apʀɔpʀijasjɔ̃] nf a (*Jur*) appropriation. **l'~ des terres par les conquérants** the appropriation of territory by the conquerors. b (*adaptation*) suitability, appropriateness.

approprié, e [apʀɔpʀije] (ptp de **approprier**) adj *réponse, méthode, remède* appropriate, suitable; *place* proper, right, appropriate. **il faut des remèdes ~s au mal** we need remedies that are suited *ou* appropriate to the evil; **fournir une réponse ~e à la question** to provide an apt *ou* a suitable *ou* an appropriate reply to the question.

approprier [apʀɔpʀije] 7 1 vt (*adapter*) to suit, fit, adapt (*à* to). **~ son style à l'auditoire** to suit one's style to the audience, adapt one's style to (suit) the audience. 2 **s'approprier** vpr a (*s'adjuger*) *bien* to appropriate; *pouvoir, droit, propriété* to take over, appropriate. **s'~ l'idée/la découverte de quelqu'un d'autre** to appropriate *ou* take over somebody else's idea/discovery. b (*s'adapter à*) **s'~ à** to be appropriate to, fit, suit.

approuver [apʀuve] 1 vt a (*être d'accord avec*) to approve of. **il a démissionné et je l'approuve** he resigned, and I agree with him *ou* approve (of his doing so); **on a besoin de se sentir approuvé** one needs to feel the approval of others; **nous n'approuvons pas ce genre d'attitude** we do not approve of that kind of behaviour; **je n'approuve pas qu'il parte maintenant** I don't approve of his leaving now. b (*formellement*) (*en votant*) *projet de loi* to approve, pass; (*par décret*) *méthode, médicament* to approve; (*en signant*) *contrat* to ratify; *procès-verbal, nomination* to approve; *voir* **lire**[1].

approvisionnement [apʀɔvizjɔnmɑ̃] nm (*action*) supplying (*en, de* of). (*réserves*) **~s** supplies, provisions, stock; **l'~ en légumes de la ville** supplying the town with vegetables, (the) supplying (of) vegetables to the town; **il avait tout un ~ d'alcool** he was well stocked with spirits, he had a large stock of spirits; (*Écon*) **~s sauvages** panic buying.

approvisionner [apʀɔvizjɔne] 1 1 vt *magasin, commerçant* to supply (*en, de* with); (*Fin*) *compte* to pay funds into; *fusil* to load. **commerçant bien approvisionné en fruits** tradesman well supplied *ou* stocked with fruit. 2 **s'approvisionner** vpr to stock up (*en* with), lay in supplies (*en* of). **s'~ en bois chez le grossiste** to stock up with wood *ou* get supplies of wood at the wholesaler's; **s'~ au supermarché le plus proche** to shop at the nearest supermarket.

approvisionneur, -euse [apʀɔvizjɔnœʀ, øz] nm,f supplier.

approximatif, -ive [apʀɔksimatif, iv] adj *calcul, évaluation* rough; *nombre* approximate; *termes* vague.

approximation [apʀɔksimasjɔ̃] nf (*gén*) approximation, (rough) estimate; (*Math*) approximation. **par ~s successives** by trial and error.

approximativement [apʀɔksimativmɑ̃] adv (*voir* **approximatif**) roughly; approximately; vaguely.

appt (abrév de **appartement**) apt.

appui [apɥi] 1 nm a (*lit, fig*) support; (*Alpinisme*) press hold. **prendre ~ sur** *[personne]* to lean on; (*du pied*) to stand on; *[objet]* to rest on; **son pied trouva un ~** he found a foothold; **avoir besoin d'~** to need (some) support; **trouver un ~** to find (some) support; **trouver un ~ chez qn** to receive support from sb; **j'ai cherché un ~ auprès de lui** I turned to him for support; **avoir l'~ de qn** to have sb's support *ou* backing; **donner son ~ à qn/à un projet** to give sb/a project one's support; **il a des ~s au ministère** he has connections in the ministry; **~ financier** financial support *ou* backing; **~ logistique** logistic backup *ou* support; *voir* **barre, point**[1].

b (*Mus*) *[voix]* placing. (*Poésie*) **consonne d'~** supporting consonant; **voyelle d'~** support vowel.

c **à l'~** in support of this, to back this up; **il me dit comment tapisser une pièce avec démonstration à l'~** he told me how to wallpaper a room and backed this up with a demonstration; **à l'~ de son témoignage il présenta cet écrit** he presented this document in support of his evidence *ou* to back up his evidence.

2 comp ►**appui aérien** (*Mil*) air support ►**appui-bras** nm (pl **appuis-bras**), **appuie-bras** nm inv armrest ►**appui de fenêtre** windowsill, window ledge ►**appui-main** nm (pl **appuis-main**), **appuie-main** nm inv maulstick ►**appui tactique** (*Mil*) tactical support ►**appui-tête** nm (pl **appuis-tête**), **appuie-tête** nm inv *[voiture, fauteuil de dentiste]* headrest, head restraint; *[fauteuil]* antimacassar.

appuie- [apɥi] préf *voir* **appui.**

appuyé, e [apɥije] (ptp de **appuyer**) adj (*insistant*) *regard* fixed, intent; *geste* emphatic; (*excessif*) *politesse* overdone; *compliment* laboured, overdone.

appuyer [apɥije] 8 1 vt a (*poser*) ~ **qch contre qch** to lean *ou* rest sth against sth; ~ **une échelle contre un mur** to lean *ou* rest *ou* stand a ladder against a wall, prop a ladder up against a wall; ~ **les coudes sur la table/son front contre la vitre** to rest *ou* lean one's elbows on the table/one's forehead against the window; ~ **sa main sur l'épaule/la tête de qn** to rest one's hand on sb's shoulder/head.

b (*presser*) to press. ~ **le pied sur l'accélérateur** to press *ou* put one's foot down on the accelerator; **il dut ~ son genou sur la valise pour la fermer** he had to press *ou* push the case down with his knee *ou* he had to kneel hard on the case to close it; **appuie ton doigt sur le pansement** put *ou* press your finger on the dressing; (*fig*) ~ **son regard sur qn** to stare intently at sb.

c (*étayer*) ~ **un mur par qch** to support *ou* prop up a wall with sth.

d (*fig: soutenir*) *personne, candidature, politique* to support, back (up). **il a appuyé sa thèse de documents convaincants** he backed up *ou* supported his thesis with convincing documents; ~ **la demande de qn** to support sb's request.

e (*Mil*) *attaque* to back up. **l'offensive sera appuyée par l'aviation** the offensive will be backed up from the air *ou* given air support.

2 vi a (*presser sur*) ~ **sur** *sonnette, bouton* to press, push; *frein* to press on, press down; *levier* to press (down *etc*); (*Aut*) ~ **sur le champignon*** to step on it*, put one's foot down (*Brit*).

b (*reposer sur*) ~ **sur** to rest on; **la voûte appuie sur des colonnes** the vault rests on columns *ou* is supported by columns.

c ~ **sur** (*insister sur*) *mot, argument* to stress, emphasize; (*accentuer*) *syllabe* to stress, emphasize, accentuate; (*Mus*) *note* to accentuate, accent; **n'appuyez pas trop** don't press the point; ~ **sur la chanterelle** to harp on.

d (*se diriger*) ~ **sur la droite** *ou* **à droite** to bear (to the) right.

3 **s'appuyer** vpr a (*s'accoter sur*) **s'~ sur/contre** to lean on/against; **appuie-toi sur mon épaule/à mon bras** lean on my shoulder/arm.

b (*fig: compter sur*) **s'~ sur qn/l'amitié de qn** to lean on sb/on sb's friendship; (*Pol*) **il s'appuie sur les groupements de gauche** he relies on the support of the groups of the left; **s'~ sur l'autorité de qn** to lean on sb's authority; **s'~ sur des découvertes récentes pour démontrer ...** to use recent discoveries to demonstrate ..., rely on recent discoveries in order to demonstrate ...; **sur quoi vous appuyez-vous pour avancer cela?** what evidence have you got to support what you're saying?

c (*‡: faire, subir*) *importun, discours ennuyeux* to put up with*; *corvée* to take on. **qui va s'~ le ménage?** who'll take on the housework?; **chaque fois c'est nous qui nous appuyons toutes les corvées** it's always us who get stuck* *ou* landed* with all the chores; **il s'est appuyé le voyage de nuit** he had to put up with travelling at night, he jolly well (*Brit*) had to travel by night*.

âpre [ɑpʀ] adj a *goût, vin* pungent, acrid; *hiver, vent* bitter, harsh; *temps* raw; *son, voix, ton* harsh. b (*dur*) *vie* harsh; *combat, discussion* bitter, grim; *détermination, résolution* grim; *concurrence, critique* fierce. c ~ **au gain** grasping, greedy.

âprement [ɑpʀəmɑ̃] adv *lutter* bitterly, grimly; *critiquer* fiercely.

après [apʀɛ] 1 prép a (*temps*) after. **il est entré ~ le début/~ elle** he came in after it started *ou* after the start/after her; **ne venez pas ~ 8 heures** don't come after 8; **cela s'est passé bien/peu ~ la guerre** this took place long *ou* a good while/shortly *ou* soon *ou* a short time after the war; ~ **beaucoup d'hésitations il a accepté** after much hesitation he accepted; **on l'a servie ~ moi** she was served after me; **l'un ~ l'autre** one after the other; ~ **cela il ne peut plus refuser** after that he can no longer refuse; ~ **tout ce que j'ai fait pour lui** after everything I did for him; (*hum*) ~ **nous le déluge!** *ou* **la fin du monde!** after us the heavens can fall!; ~ **coup** after the event, afterwards; **il n'a compris qu'~ coup** he did not understand until after the event *ou* afterwards; **elle l'a grondé, ~ quoi il a été sage** she gave him a scolding after which *ou* and afterwards he behaved himself; **nuit ~ nuit les bombes tombaient** bombs fell night after night; **page ~ page** page after page, page upon page; ~ **tout** after all; ~ **tout, il peut bien attendre** after all, he can wait; ~ **tout, ce n'est qu'un enfant** after all *ou* when all is said and done he is only a child; ~ **la pluie le beau temps** (*lit*) the sun is shining after the rain; (*fig*) everything's fine again; *voir* **Jésus**.

b (*espace*) (*plus loin que*) after, past; (*derrière*) behind, after. **j'étais ~ elle dans la queue** I was behind *ou* after her in the queue; **sa maison est (juste) ~ la mairie** his house is (just) past *ou* beyond the town hall; **elle traîne toujours ~ elle 2 petits chiens** she always trails 2 little dogs along behind her.

c (*espace: sur*) on. **c'est resté collé ~ le mur** it has stayed stuck on the wall; **grimper ~ un arbre** to climb (up) a tree; **sa jupe s'accrochait ~ les ronces** her skirt kept catching on *ou* in the brambles; **son chapeau est ~ le porte-manteau** his hat is on the peg.

d (*ordre d'importance*) after. **sa famille passe ~ ses malades** he puts his family after his patients; ~ **le capitaine vient le lieutenant** after captain comes lieutenant; ~ **vous, je vous prie** after you.

e (*poursuite*) after; (*aggressivité*) at. **courir ~ un ballon** to run after a ball; **aboyer/crier ~ qn** to bark/shout at sb; **il est furieux ~ ses enfants** he is furious with *ou* at* his children; ~ **qui en a-t-il?** who is he after?, who has he got it in for?*; **elle est toujours ~ lui** she's always (going) on at* (*Brit*) *ou* nagging (at) him, she keeps on at him all the time*; *voir* **courir, demander**.

f ~ + *infin* after; ~ **que** + *indic* after; ~ **manger** after meals *ou* food; **ce sont des propos d'~ boire** it's the drink talking; ~ **s'être reposé il reprit la route** after resting *ou* after he had rested *ou* (after) having rested he went on his way; **une heure ~ que je l'eus quittée elle me téléphona** an hour after I had left her she phoned me; **venez me voir ~ que vous lui aurez parlé** come and see me after *ou* when you have spoken to him.

g **d'~ lui/elle** according to him/her, in his/her opinion; **d'~ moi** in my opinion; **(à en juger) d'~ son regard/ce qu'il a dit** (to judge) from the look he gave/what he said; **ne jugez pas d'~ les apparences/ce qu'il dit** don't go by *ou* on appearances/what he says, don't judge by appearances/what he says; **d'~ le baromètre/les journaux** according to the barometer/the papers; **d'~ ma montre** by my watch, according to my watch; **portrait peint d'~ nature** portrait painted from life; **dessin d'~ Ingres** drawing after Ingres, drawing in the style *ou* manner of Ingres; **d'~ Balzac** adapted from Balzac.

2 adv a (*temps*) (*ensuite*) afterwards, after, next; (*plus tard*) later. **venez me voir ~** come and see me afterwards; **aussitôt/longtemps ~** immediately *ou* straight/long *ou* a long time after(wards); **2 jours/semaines ~** 2 days/weeks later.

b (*ordre d'importance, poursuite, espace*) **il pense surtout à ses malades, sa famille passe ~** he thinks of his patients first, his family comes second *ou* afterwards; ~ **nous avons des articles moins chers** otherwise we have cheaper things; **l'autobus démarra et il courut ~** as the bus started he ran after it; **va chercher le cintre, ton manteau est ~** fetch the coat hanger, your coat is on it; **laisse ta sœur tranquille, tu cries tout le temps ~** leave your sister alone, you're always (going) on at her* (*Brit*) *ou* nagging (at) her; **qu'est-ce qui vient ~?** what comes next?, what's to follow?; **et (puis) ~?** (*lit*) and then what?; (*fig*) so what?*, what of it?; ~ **tu iras dire que ...** next you'll be saying that ...; **la semaine/le mois d'~** the following *ou* next week/month, the week/month after; **qu'allons-nous faire ~?** what are we going to do next? *ou* afterwards?; **la page d'~** the next *ou* following page; **le train d'~ est plus rapide** the next train is faster.

3 comp ▸**après-demain** adv the day after tomorrow ▸**après-dîner** nm after dinner ▸**après-gaullisme** nm post-Gaullism ▸**après-guerre** nm (pl **après-guerres**) post-war years; **d'après-guerre** adj post-war ▸**après-midi** nm ou nf inv afternoon ▸**après-rasage** nm inv after-shave; **lotion d'après-rasage** after-shave lotion ▸**après-shampoing** nm inv conditioner ▸**après-ski** nm inv (*soulier*) snow boot; (*loisirs*) **l'après-ski** the après-ski ▸**après-soleil** nm inv after-sun cream *ou* milk ◊ adj after-sun ▸**après-vente** adj *voir* **service**.

âpreté [ɑpʀəte] nf (*voir* **âpre**) pungency; bitterness; rawness; harshness, grimness; fierceness.

a priori [apʀijɔʀi] 1 loc adv, adj a priori. 2 nm inv apriorism. **avoir des ~** to have prejudices (*sur* against, about).

apriorisme [apʀiɔʀism] nm apriorism.

aprioriste [apʀijɔʀist] 1 adj aprioristic, apriorist (*épith*). 2 nmf a priori reasoner, apriorist.

à-propos [apʀɔpo] nm *[remarque, acte]* aptness. **avec beaucoup d'~ le gouvernement a annoncé ...** with consummate timing the government has announced ...; **répondre avec ~** to make an apt *ou* a suitable reply; **avoir beaucoup d'~** (*dans ses réponses*) to have the knack of saying the right thing *ou* of making an apt reply; (*dans ses actes*) to have the knack of doing the right thing; **en cette circonstance imprévue, il a fait preuve d'~** in this unforeseen situation he showed great presence of mind; **il a manqué d'~ devant cette question** he seemed at (a bit of) a loss when faced with this question; **il n'a pas su répondre avec ~ devant cette question** he was unable to make an apt *ou* a suitable reply to this question; **son manque d'~ lui nuit** his inability to say *ou* do the right thing is doing him harm; *voir* **esprit**.

apte [apt] adj a ~ **à qch** capable of sth; ~ **à faire** capable of doing, able to do; ~ **à exercer une profession** (*intellectuellement*) (suitably) qualified for a job; (*physiquement*) capable of doing a job; **je ne suis pas ~ à juger** I'm not able to judge *ou* capable of judging, I'm no fit judge; (*Mil*) ~ **(au service)** fit for service. b (*Jur*) ~ **à** fit to *ou* for.

aptéryx [apteʀiks] nm apteryx, kiwi (*bird*).

aptitude [aptityd] nf a (*disposition, faculté*) aptitude, ability. **test d'~** aptitude test; **son ~ à étudier** *ou* **à** *ou* **pour l'étude** his aptitude for study *ou* studying, his ability to study; **avoir des ~s variées** to have varied gifts *ou* talents; **avoir de grandes ~s** to be very gifted *ou* talented. b (*Jur*) fitness.

apurement [apyʀmɑ̃] nm balancing.

apurer [apyʀe] 1 vt to balance.

aquaculteur, -trice [akwakyltœʀ, tʀis] nm,f (*gén*) aquiculturalist; *[poissons]* fish farmer.

aquaculture [akwakyltyʀ] nf (*gén*) aquiculture, aquaculture; *[poissons]* fish farming.

aquaplanage [akwaplanaʒ] nm aquaplaning.

aquaplane [akwaplan] nm aquaplane.

aquaplaning [akwaplaniŋ] nm = **aquaplanage**.

aquarelle [akwaʀɛl] nf (*technique*) watercolours; (*tableau*)

watercolour.
aquarelliste [akwaʀelist] nmf painter in watercolours.
aquarium [akwaʀjɔm] nm aquarium, fish tank.
aquatique [akwatik] adj *plante, animal* aquatic. **oiseau** ~ water bird, aquatic bird; **paysage** ~ (*sous l'eau*) underwater landscape; (*marécageux*) watery landscape.
aquavit [akwavit] nm aquavit.
aqueduc [ak(ə)dyk] nm aqueduct; (*Anat*) duct.
aqueux, -euse [akø, øz] adj aqueous; *voir* **humeur**.
à quia [akɥija] loc adv (*littér*) **mettre qn** ~ to nonplus sb; **être** ~ to be at a loss for a reply.
aquiculture [akɥikyltyʀ] nf = **aquaculture**.
aquifère [akɥifɛʀ] adj aquiferous.
aquilin, e [akilɛ̃, in] adj aquiline.
aquilon [akilɔ̃] nm (*Poésie*) north wind.
Aquitaine [akitɛn] nf: **l'**~ the Aquitaine.
AR [aɛʀ] nm (abrév de **accusé** *ou* **avis de réception**) *voir* **accusé, avis.**
A.R. a (abrév de **Altesse royale**) *voir* **altesse.** b abrév de **aller (et) retour.**
ara [aʀa] nm macaw.
arabe [aʀab] 1 adj *désert* Arabian; *nation, peuple* Arab; *art, langue, littérature* Arabic, Arab. **(cheval)** ~ Arab (horse); *voir* **république.** 2 nm (*Ling*) Arabic. **l'**~ **littéral** written Arabic. 3 nm: **A**~ Arab; **un jeune A**~ an Arab boy. 4 nf: **A**~ Arab woman (*ou* girl).
arabesque [aʀabɛsk] nf arabesque. ~ **de style** stylistic ornament, ornament of style.
arabica [aʀabika] nm arabica.
Arabie [aʀabi] nf Arabia. ~ **Saoudite,** ~ **Séoudite** Saudi Arabia; **le désert d'**~ the Arabian desert.
arabique [aʀabik] adj *voir* **gomme.**
arabisant, e [aʀabizɑ̃, ɑ̃t] nm,f Arabist, Arabic scholar.
arabisation [aʀabizasjɔ̃] nf arabization.
arabiser [aʀabize] 1 vt to arabize.
arabisme [aʀabism] nm Arabism.
arable [aʀabl] adj arable.
arabophone [aʀabɔfɔn] 1 adj Arabic-speaking. 2 nmf Arabic-speaker.
arac [aʀak] nm = **arack.**
arachide [aʀaʃid] nf (*plante*) groundnut (plant); (*graine*) peanut, monkey nut (*Brit*), groundnut. **huile d'**~ groundnut *ou* peanut oil.
arachnéen, -enne [aʀakneɛ̃, ɛn] adj (*littér: léger*) gossamer (*épith*), of gossamer, gossamery; (*Zool*) arachnidan.
arachnoïde [aʀaknɔid] nf arachnoid (membrane).
arachnoïdien, -ienne [aʀaknɔidjɛ̃, jɛn] adj arachnoid.
arack [aʀak] nm arrack.
araignée [aʀeɲe] nf a (*animal*) spider. ~ **de mer** spider crab; **il a une** ~ **dans le plafond*** *ou* **au plafond*** he's got a screw loose*, he's got bats in the belfry* (*Brit*); *voir* **toile.** b (*crochet*) grapnel.
araire [aʀɛʀ] nm swing plough (*Brit*) *ou* plow (*US*).
araméen, -enne [aʀameɛ̃, ɛn] 1 adj Aram(a)ean, Aramaic. 2 nm (*Ling*) Aramaic, Aram(a)ean. 3 nm,f: **A**~**(ne)** Aram(a)ean.
arasement [aʀɑzmɑ̃] nm (*voir* **araser**) levelling; planing(-down); sawing; erosion.
araser [aʀɑze] 1 vt *mur* to level; (*en rabotant*) to plane (down); (*en sciant*) to saw; (*Géol*) *relief* to erode (away).
aratoire [aʀatwaʀ] adj ploughing (*Brit*) (*épith*), plowing (*US*) (*épith*). **travaux** ~**s** ploughing; **instrument** ~ ploughing implement.
araucaria [aʀokaʀja] nm monkey puzzle (tree), araucaria.
arbalète [aʀbalɛt] nf crossbow.
arbalétrier [aʀbaletʀije] nm crossbowman.
arbitrage [aʀbitʀaʒ] nm a (*Comm, Pol: action*) arbitration; (*Bourse*) arbitrage; (*sentence*) arbitrament. ~ **obligatoire** compulsory arbitration; **recourir à l'**~ to go to arbitration. b (*Sport: voir* **arbitre**) refereeing; umpiring. **erreur d'**~ refereeing *ou* referee's error; umpiring *ou* umpire's error.
arbitragiste [aʀbitʀaʒist] nmf (*Bourse*) arbitrager, arbitragist.
arbitraire [aʀbitʀɛʀ] 1 adj (*despotique, contingent*) arbitrary. 2 nm: **l'**~: **le règne de l'**~ the reign of the arbitrary; **l'**~ **du signe linguistique/d'une décision** the arbitrary nature *ou* the arbitrariness of the linguistic sign/of a decision.
arbitrairement [aʀbitʀɛʀmɑ̃] adv arbitrarily.
arbitral, e, mpl **-aux** [aʀbitʀal, o] adj a (*Jur*) arbitral. b (*Sport: voir* **arbitre**) referee's (*épith*); umpire's (*épith*). **décision** ~**e** referee's *ou* umpire's decision *ou* ruling.
arbitralement [aʀbitʀalmɑ̃] adv (*Jur*) by arbitrators; (*Sport: voir* **arbitre**) by the referee; by the umpire.
arbitre [aʀbitʀ] nm a (*Boxe, Ftbl, Rugby*) referee, ref*; (*Cricket, Hockey, Tennis*) umpire. **faire l'**~ to (be the) referee *ou* umpire; (*Tennis*) ~ **de chaise** umpire; *voir* **libre.** b (*conciliateur*) arbiter; (*Jur*) arbitrator. **servir d'**~ **dans un conflit social** to act as an arbiter in an industrial dispute; (*fig*) ~ **du bon goût** arbiter of good taste.
arbitrer [aʀbitʀe] 1 vt a *conflit, litige* to arbitrate; *personnes* to arbitrate between. b (*Boxe, Ftbl, Rugby*) to referee, ref*; (*Cricket, Hockey, Tennis*) to umpire.
arboré, e [aʀbɔʀe] adj *région* wooded; *jardin* planted with trees.
arborer [aʀbɔʀe] 1 vt *vêtement* to sport; *sourire* to wear; *air* to display; *décoration, médaille* to sport, display; *drapeau* to bear, display; *bannière* to bear. **le journal arbore un gros titre** the paper is carrying a big headline; (*fig*) ~ **l'étendard de la révolte** to bear the standard of revolt.
arborescence [aʀbɔʀesɑ̃s] nf (*Agr*) arborescence; (*Ling*) branching.
arborescent, e [aʀbɔʀesɑ̃, ɑ̃t] adj arborescent, treelike. **fougère** ~**e** tree fern.
arborétum [aʀbɔʀetɔm] nm arboretum.
arboricole [aʀbɔʀikɔl] adj *technique etc* arboricultural; *animal* arboreal.
arboriculteur, -trice [aʀbɔʀikyltœʀ, tʀis] nm,f tree grower, arboriculturist (SPÉC).
arboriculture [aʀbɔʀikyltyʀ] nf tree cultivation, arboriculture (SPÉC).
arborisé, e [aʀbɔʀize] adj arborized.
arbouse [aʀbuz] nf arbutus berry.
arbousier [aʀbuzje] nm arbutus, strawberry tree.
arbre [aʀbʀ] 1 nm a (*Bot, Ling*) tree. ~ **fruitier/d'agrément** fruit/ornamental tree; **faire l'**~ **fourchu/droit** to do a handstand (with one's legs apart/together); (*fig*) **les** ~**s vous cachent la forêt** you can't see the wood (*Brit*) *ou* forest (*US*) for the trees; (*Prov*) **entre l'**~ **et l'écorce il ne faut pas mettre le doigt** do not meddle in other people's family affairs; **abattre** *ou* **couper l'**~ **pour avoir le fruit** to use a sledgehammer to crack a nut; **faire grimper** *ou* **faire monter qn à l'**~* to have sb on*, pull sb's leg*.
b (*Tech*) shaft.
2 comp ▸ **arbre à cames** camshaft; **avec arbre à cames en tête** with overhead camshaft ▸ **arbre de couche** driving shaft ▸ **arbre d'entraînement** drive shaft ▸ **arbre généalogique** family tree ▸ **arbre d'hélice** propeller shaft ▸ **arbre de Judée** Judas tree ▸ **arbre de mai** may tree ▸ **arbre-manivelle** nm (pl **arbres-manivelles**) crankshaft ▸ **arbre moteur** driving shaft ▸ **arbre de Noël** (*décoration, aussi Tech*) Christmas tree ▸ **arbre à pain** breadfruit tree ▸ **arbre de transmission** propeller shaft ▸ **arbre de vie** (*Anat*) arbor vitae, tree of life; (*Bible*) tree of life.
arbrisseau, pl ~**x** [aʀbʀiso] nm shrub.
arbuste [aʀbyst] nm small shrub, bush.
ARC [aʀk] nm (abrév de **AIDS-related complex**) ARC.
arc [aʀk] 1 nm (*arme*) bow; (*Géom*) arc; (*Anat, Archit*) arch. **l'**~ **de ses sourcils** the arch *ou* curve of her eyebrows; **la côte formait un** ~ the coastline formed an arc; *voir* **corde, lampe, soudure, tir.** 2 comp ▸ **arc brisé** gothic arch ▸ **arc de cercle** (*Géom*) arc of a circle; (*gén*) **ça forme un arc de cercle** it forms an arc; **en arc de cercle** in a circular arc ▸ **arc-en-ciel** nm (pl **arcs-en-ciel**) rainbow ▸ **arc électrique** electric arc ▸ **arc outrepassé** Moorish arch ▸ **arc en plein cintre** Roman arch ▸ **arc-rampant** nm (pl **arcs-rampants**) rampant arch ▸ **arc réflexe** reflex arc ▸ **arc de triomphe** triumphal arch ▸ **arc voltaïque** = **arc électrique.**
arcade [aʀkad] nf (*Archit*) arch, archway. ~**s** arcade, arches; **les** ~**s d'un cloître/d'un pont** the arches *ou* arcade of a cloister/of a bridge; **se promener sous les** ~**s** to walk through the arcade *ou* underneath the arches; ~ **dentaire** dental arch; ~ **sourcilière** (*gén*) arch of the eyebrows; (*Boxe*) **touché à l'**~ **sourcilière** cut above the eye; *voir* **jeu.**
Arcadie [aʀkadi] nf Arcadia.
arcadien, -ienne [aʀkadjɛ̃, jɛn] adj Arcadian.
arcane [aʀkan] nm a (*fig gén pl: mystère*) mystery. b (*Alchimie*) arcanum.
arcature [aʀkatyʀ] nf arcature.
arc-boutant, pl **arcs-boutants** [aʀkbutɑ̃] nm (*Archit*) flying buttress.
arc-bouter [aʀkbute] 1 1 vt (*Archit*) to buttress. 2 **s'arc-bouter** vpr to lean, press (*à, contre* (up) against, *sur* on). **arc-bouté contre le mur, il essayait de pousser la table** pressing (up) *ou* bracing himself against the wall, he tried to push the table.
arceau, pl ~**x** [aʀso] nm (*Archit*) arch; (*Croquet*) hoop; (*Méd*) cradle. (*Aut*) ~ **de sécurité** roll-over bar; ~ **de protection** roll bar.
archaïque [aʀkaik] adj archaic.
archaïsant, e [aʀkaizɑ̃, ɑ̃t] 1 adj archaistic. 2 nm,f archaist.
archaïsme [aʀkaism] nm archaism.
archange [aʀkɑ̃ʒ] nm archangel.
arche [aʀʃ] nf a (*Archit*) arch. b (*Rel*) ark. **l'**~ **de Noé** Noah's Ark; **l'**~ **d'alliance** the Ark of the Covenant.
archéologie [aʀkeɔlɔʒi] nf archaeology.
archéologique [aʀkeɔlɔʒik] adj archaeological.
archéologue [aʀkeɔlɔg] nmf archaeologist.
archer [aʀʃe] nm archer, bowman.
archet [aʀʃɛ] nm (*Mus, gén*) bow.
archétypal, e, mpl **-aux** [aʀketipal, o] adj archetypal.
archétype [aʀketip] 1 nm (*gén*) archetype; (*Bio*) prototype. 2 adj (*gén*) archetypal; (*Bio*) prototypal, prototypic.
archétypique [aʀketipik] adj archetypical.
archevêché [aʀʃəveʃe] nm (*territoire*) archdiocese, archbishopric; (*charge*) archbishopric; (*palais*) archbishop's palace.
archevêque [aʀʃəvɛk] nm archbishop.
archi... [aʀʃi] préf a (*: *extrêmement*) tremendously, enormously. ~**bondé,** ~**comble,** ~**plein** chock-a-block*, full to the gunwales; ~**connu**

tremendously *ou* enormously well-known; **~difficile** tremendously *ou* enormously difficult; **~millionnaire** millionaire several times over. b (*dans un titre*) arch... . **~diacre** archdeacon; **~duc** archduke.
archidiaconat [aʀʃidjakɔna] nm archdeaconry.
archidiaconé [aʀʃidjakɔne] nm archdeaconry.
archidiacre [aʀʃidjakʀ] nm archdeacon.
archidiocèse [aʀʃidjɔsɛz] nm archdiocese.
archiduc [aʀʃidyk] nm archduke.
archiduchesse [aʀʃidyʃɛs] nf archduchess.
archiépiscopal, e, mpl **-aux** [aʀʃiepiskɔpal, o] adj archiepiscopal.
archiépiscopat [aʀʃiepiskɔpa] nm archbishopric (*office*), archiepiscopate.
archimandrite [aʀʃimɑ̃dʀit] nm archimandrite.
Archimède [aʀʃimɛd] nm Archimedes; *voir* **principe, vis**[1].
archipel [aʀʃipɛl] nm archipelago. **L'~ malais** the Malay Archipelago.
archiphonème [aʀʃifɔnɛm] nm archiphoneme.
archiprêtre [aʀʃipʀɛtʀ] nm archpriest.
architecte [aʀʃitɛkt] nm (*lit, fig*) architect. **~ d'intérieur** interior designer; (*Ordin*) **~ de réseaux** network architect.
architectonique [aʀʃitɛktɔnik] 1 adj architectonic. 2 nf architectonics (*sg*).
architectural, e, mpl **-aux** [aʀʃitɛktyʀal, o] adj architectural.
architecture [aʀʃitɛktyʀ] nf (*lit, Ordin*) architecture; (*fig*) structure.
architrave [aʀʃitʀav] nf architrave.
archivage [aʀʃivaʒ] nm (*gén*) filing; (*Ordin*) filing, archival storage. **~ électronique** electronic filing *ou* storage.
archiver [aʀʃive] 1 vt to archive, file.
archives [aʀʃiv] nfpl archives, records. **les A~ Nationales** the National Archives, ≃ the Public Record Office (*Brit*); **ça restera dans les ~!*** that will go down in history!; **je vais chercher dans mes ~** I'll look through my files *ou* records.
archiviste [aʀʃivist] nmf archivist.
archivolte [aʀʃivɔlt] nf archivolt.
arçon [aʀsɔ̃] nm (*Équitation*) tree; *voir* **cheval, pistolet, vider.**
arctique [aʀktik] 1 adj (*Géog*) arctic. 2 nm: **l'A~** the Arctic.
ardemment [aʀdamɑ̃] adv ardently, fervently.
ardent, e [aʀdɑ̃, ɑ̃t] adj a (*brûlant*) (*gén*) burning; *tison* glowing; *flambeau, feu* blazing; *yeux* fiery (*de* with); *couleur* flaming, fiery; *chaleur, soleil* scorching, blazing; *fièvre* raging; *soif* raging; *voir* **buisson, chapelle, charbon.** b (*vif*) *conviction, foi* burning, fervent, passionate; *colère* burning, raging; *passion, désir* burning, ardent; *piété, haine, prière* fervent, ardent; *lutte* ardent, passionate; *discours* impassioned, inflamed. c (*bouillant*) *amant* ardent, hot-blooded; *jeunesse, caractère* fiery, passionate; *joueur* keen; *partisan* ardent, keen; *cheval* mettlesome, fiery. **être ~ au travail/au combat** to be a zealous worker/an ardent fighter.
ardeur [aʀdœʀ] nf (*voir* **ardent**) (*gén*) ardour; *[partisan, joueur]* keenness; *[caractère]* fieriness; *[foi, prière]* fervour. (*littér*) **les ~s de l'amour/de la haine** the ardour of love/hatred; (*littér, hum*) **modérez vos ~s!** control yourself!; **défendre une cause avec ~** to defend a cause ardently *ou* fervently; **son ~ au travail** *ou* **à travailler** his zeal *ou* enthusiasm for work; **l'~ du soleil** the heat of the sun; (*littér*) **les ~s de l'été** the heat of summer.
ardillon [aʀdijɔ̃] nm *[boucle]* tongue.
ardoise [aʀdwaz] 1 nf (*roche, plaque, tablette*) slate; (*: *dette*) unpaid bill. **toit d'~s** slate roof; **couvrir un toit d'~(s)** to slate a roof; (*fig*) **avoir une ~ de 300 F chez l'épicier** to owe a bill of 300 francs at the grocer's. 2 adj inv (*couleur*) slate-grey.
ardoisé, e [aʀdwaze] adj slate-grey.
ardoisier, -ière[1] [aʀdwazje, jɛʀ] 1 adj *gisement* slaty; *industrie* slate (*épith*). 2 nm (*ouvrier*) slate-quarry worker; (*propriétaire*) slate-quarry owner.
ardoisière[2] [aʀdwazjɛʀ] nf slate quarry.
ardu, e [aʀdy] adj *travail* arduous, laborious; *problème* difficult; *pente* steep.
are [aʀ] nm are, one hundred square metres.
areligieux, -ieuse [aʀ(ə)liʒjø, jøz] adj areligious.
aréna [aʀena] nf (*Can Sport*) arena, (skating) rink.
arène [aʀɛn] nf (*piste*) arena; (*Géol*) sand, arenite (*SPÉC*). (*Archit*) **~s** amphitheatre; (*fig*) **l'~ politique** the political arena; (*Géol*) **~ granitique** granitic sand; *voir* **descendre.**
arénicole [aʀenikɔl] nm sandworm.
aréole [aʀeɔl] nf areola.
aréomètre [aʀeɔmɛtʀ] nm hydrometer.
aréométrie [aʀeɔmetʀi] nf hydrometry.
aréopage [aʀeɔpaʒ] nm (*fig*) learned assembly. (*Hist*) **l'A~** the Areopagus.
arête [aʀɛt] nf a (*Zool*) (fish)bone. **~ centrale** backbone, spine; **c'est plein d'~s** it's full of bones, it's very bony; **enlever les ~s d'un poisson** to bone a fish. b (*bord*) *[cube, pierre, ski etc]* edge; *[toit]* arris; *[voûte]* groin; *[montagne]* ridge, crest; *[nez]* bridge. c (*Bot*) *[seigle, orge]* beard. **~s** beard.
argent [aʀʒɑ̃] nm a (*métal*) silver. **en ~, d'~** silver; *voir* **noce, parole, vif**[1].
b (*couleur*) silver. **cheveux/reflets (d')~** silvery hair/glints; **des souliers ~** silver *ou* silvery shoes.
c (*Fin*) money (*NonC*). **il a de l'~** he's got money, he's well off; **~ liquide** ready money, (ready) cash, spot cash; **~ bon marché** cheap money; **~ de poche** pocket money; **il l'a fait pour de l'~** he did it for money; **il se fait un ~ fou*** he makes lots *ou* loads* of money; **les puissances d'~** the controllers of wealth *ou* capital; **payer ~ comptant** to pay cash; *voir* **couleur, manger.**
d (*loc*) **l'~ leur fond dans les mains** they spend money like water; **j'en ai/j'en veux pour mon ~** I've got/I want (to get) my money's worth; **on en a pour son ~** we get good value (for money), it's worth every penny; **faire ~ de tout** to turn everything into cash, make money out of anything; **jeter** *ou* **flanquer* l'~ par la fenêtre** to throw *ou* chuck* money away, throw money down the drain; **prendre qch/les paroles de qn pour ~ comptant** to take sth/what sb says at (its) face value; (*Prov*) **l'~ n'a pas d'odeur** money has no smell; (*Prov*) **l'~ ne fait pas le bonheur** money can't buy happiness; (*Prov*) **l'~ va à l'~** money attracts money; (*Prov*) **point** *ou* **pas d'~, point** *ou* **pas de Suisse** nothing for nothing.
e (*Hér*) argent.
argenté, e [aʀʒɑ̃te] (ptp de **argenter**) adj *couleur, reflets, cheveux* silver, silvery. *couverts* **en métal ~** silver-plated; **je ne suis pas très ~ en ce moment*** I'm (rather) broke at the moment*, I'm not too well-off just now; **ils ne sont pas très ~s*** they're not very well-off; *voir* **renard.**
argenter [aʀʒɑ̃te] 1 vt *miroir* to silver; *couverts* to silver(-plate); (*fig littér*) to give a silvery sheen to, silver (*littér*).
argenterie [aʀʒɑ̃tʀi] nf silverware; (*de métal argenté*) silver plate.
argenteur [aʀʒɑ̃tœʀ] nm silverer.
argentier [aʀʒɑ̃tje] nm (*hum: ministre*) Minister of Finance; (*Hist*) Superintendent of Finance; (*meuble*) silver cabinet.
argentifère [aʀʒɑ̃tifɛʀ] adj silver-bearing, argentiferous (*SPÉC*).
argentin, e[1] [aʀʒɑ̃tɛ̃, in] adj silvery.
argentin, e[2] [aʀʒɑ̃tɛ̃, in] 1 adj Argentinian (*Brit*), Argentinean (*US*), Argentine (*épith*). 2 nm,f: **A~(e)** Argentinian (*Brit*), Argentinean (*US*), Argentine.
Argentine [aʀʒɑ̃tin] nf: **l'~** Argentina, the Argentine.
argenture [aʀʒɑ̃tyʀ] nf *[miroir]* silvering; *[couverts]* silver-plating, silvering.
argien, -ienne [aʀʒjɛ̃, jɛn] 1 adj Argos (*épith*), of Argos. 2 nm,f: **A~(ne)** inhabitant *ou* native of Argos.
argile [aʀʒil] nf clay. **~ à silex** clay-with-flints; *voir* **colosse.**
argileux, -euse [aʀʒilø, øz] adj clayey.
argon [aʀgɔ̃] nm argon.
argonaute [aʀgonot] nm (*Myth*) Argonaut; (*Zool*) argonaut, paper nautilus.
Argos [aʀgɔs] nm Argos.
argot [aʀgo] nm slang. **~ de métier** trade slang.
argotique [aʀgɔtik] adj (*de l'argot*) slang; (*très familier*) slangy.
argotisme [aʀgɔtism] nm slang term.
argousin†† [aʀguzɛ̃] nm (*péj hum: agent de police*) rozzer† (*péj*), bluebottle† (*péj*).
arguer [aʀgɥe] 1 (*littér*) 1 vt a (*déduire*) to deduce. **il ne peut rien ~ de ces faits** he can draw no conclusion from these facts. b (*prétexter*) **~ que** to put forward the reason that; **il argua qu'il n'avait rien entendu** he protested that he had heard nothing. 2 **arguer de** vt indir: **il refusa, arguant de leur manque de ressources** he refused, putting forward their lack of resources as an excuse *ou* as a reason.
argument [aʀgymɑ̃] nm (*raison, preuve, Littérat, Math*) argument. **tirer ~ de** to use as an argument *ou* excuse; **~ frappant** strong *ou* convincing argument; (*hum: coup*) blow; **~ massue** sledgehammer argument; **~ publicitaire** advertising claim; **~ de vente** selling proposition *ou* point.
argumentaire [aʀgymɑ̃tɛʀ] nm sales leaflet *ou* blurb.
argumentateur, -trice [aʀgymɑ̃tatœʀ, tʀis] adj argumentative.
argumentation [aʀgymɑ̃tasjɔ̃] nf argumentation.
argumenter [aʀgymɑ̃te] 1 vi to argue (*sur* about). **discours bien argumenté** well-argued speech.
argus [aʀgys] nm: **l'~ de l'automobile** ≃ Glass's directory (*Brit*), *guide to secondhand car prices*; **~ de la photo** *guide to secondhand photographic equipment prices*; *voir* **coté.**
argutie [aʀgysi] nf (*littér: gén péj*) quibble. **~s** pettifoggery, quibbles, quibbling.
aria[1] [aʀja] nm (†, *dial*) bother (*NonC*), nuisance (*NonC*).
aria[2] [aʀja] nf (*Mus*) aria.
Ariane [aʀjan] nf Ariadne; *voir* **fil.**
arianisme [aʀjanism] nm Arianism.
aride [aʀid] adj (*lit, fig*) arid; *vent* dry. **un travail ~** a thankless task; **cœur ~** heart of stone.
aridité [aʀidite] nf (*voir* **aride**) aridity; dryness; thanklessness. **~ du cœur** stony-heartedness.
ariette [aʀjɛt] nf arietta, ariette.
Arioste [aʀjɔst] nm: **l'~** Ariosto.
aristo‡ [aʀisto] nmf (*péj*) (abrév de **aristocrate**) toff*† (*Brit*), nob*†.
aristocrate [aʀistɔkʀat] nmf aristocrat.
aristocratie [aʀistɔkʀasi] nf aristocracy.

aristocratique [aʀistɔkʀatik] adj aristocratic.
aristocratiquement [aʀistɔkʀatikmɑ̃] adv aristocratically.
Aristophane [aʀistɔfan] nm Aristophanes.
Aristote [aʀistɔt] nm Aristotle.
aristotélicien, -ienne [aʀistɔtelisjɛ̃, jɛn] adj, nm,f Aristotelian.
aristotélisme [aʀistɔtelism] nm Aristotelianism.
arithméticien, -ienne [aʀitmetisjɛ̃, jɛn] nm,f arithmetician.
arithmétique [aʀitmetik] 1 nf (*science*) arithmetic; (*livre*) arithmetic book. 2 adj arithmetical.
arithmétiquement [aʀitmetikmɑ̃] adv arithmetically.
Arizona [aʀizɔna] nm: **l'~** Arizona.
Arkansas [aʀkɑ̃sas] nm: **l'~** Arkansas.
arlequin [aʀləkɛ̃] nm (*Théât*) Harlequin. **bas (d')~** harlequin stockings; *voir* **habit**.
arlequinade [aʀləkinad] nf (*fig*) buffoonery; (*Théât*) harlequinade.
armagnac [aʀmaɲak] nm armagnac.
armateur [aʀmatœʀ] nm (*propriétaire*) shipowner; (*exploitant*) ship's manager. **~-affréteur** owner-charterer.
armature [aʀmatyʀ] nf a (*gén: carcasse*) *[tente, montage, parapluie]* frame; (*Constr*) framework, armature (*SPÉC*); (*fig: infrastructure*) framework. **~ de corset** corset bones *ou* stays; **soutien-gorge à/sans ~** underwired/unwired bra. b (*Mus*) key signature. c (*Phys*) *[condensateur]* electrode; *[aimant]* armature.
arme [aʀm] nf a (*instrument*) (*gén*) weapon, arm; (*fusil, revolver*) gun. **fabrique d'~s** arms factory; **on a retrouvé l'~ du crime** the weapon used in the crime has been found; **il braqua** *ou* **dirigea son ~ vers** *ou* **contre moi** he aimed *ou* pointed his gun at me; **des policiers sans ~(s)** unarmed police; **se battre à l'~ blanche** to fight with knives; **~ atomique/biologique/chimique** atomic/biological/chemical weapon; **~ de poing** (*revolver*) handgun; (*couteau*) knife; **~ à feu** firearm; **~s de jet** projectiles; **l'~ absolue** the ultimate weapon; *voir* **bretelle, maniement, port[2]**.
b (*élément d'une armée*) arm. **l'~ de l'infanterie** the infantry arm; **dans quelle ~ sert-il?** which section is he in?; **les 3 ~s** the 3 services.
c (*Mil*) **la carrière** *ou* **le métier des ~s** soldiering; (*littér*) **le succès de nos ~s** the success of our armies; **être sous les ~s** to be a soldier; **appeler un régiment sous les ~s** to call up a regiment; **soldats en ~s** soldiers at arms; **un peuple en ~s** a nation at arms; **aux ~s!** to arms!; **compagnon** *ou* **frère d'~s** comrade-in-arms; *voir* **homme, place, prise**.
d (*fig: moyen d'action*) weapon. **donner** *ou* **fournir des ~s à qn** to give sb weapons (*contre* against); **le silence peut être une ~ puissante** silence can be a powerful weapon; **une ~ à double tranchant** a double-edged blade *ou* weapon; **il est sans ~ contre ce genre d'accusation** he's defenceless (*Brit*) *ou* defenseless (*US*) against that sort of accusation.
e (*Escrime*) **les ~s** fencing; **faire des ~s** to fence, do fencing; *voir* **maître, passe[1], salle**.
f (*Hér*) **~s** arms, coat of arms; **aux ~s de** bearing the arms of; *voir* **héraut**.
g (*loc*) **à ~s égales** on equal terms; **déposer** *ou* **mettre bas les ~s** to lay down (one's) arms; **rendre les ~s** to lay down one's arms, surrender; **faire ses premières ~s** to make one's début (*dans* in); **passer qn par les ~s** to shoot sb by firing squad; **partir avec ~s et bagages** to pack up and go; **passer l'~ à gauche**⁑ to kick the bucket⁑; **prendre le pouvoir/régler un différend par les ~s** to take power/settle a dispute by force; **porter les ~s** to be a soldier; **prendre les ~s** (*se soulever*) to rise up in arms; (*pour défendre son pays etc*) to take up arms; **avoir l'~ au bras** to be in arms; **~ à la bretelle!** ≃ slope arms!; **~ sur l'épaule!** shoulder arms!; **~ au pied!** attention! (*with rifle on ground*); **portez ~!** shoulder arms!; **présentez ~!** present arms!; **reposez ~!** order arms!; *voir* **appel, fait[1], gens[1], pris, suspension**.
armé, e[1] [aʀme] (ptp de **armer**) 1 adj *personne, forces, conflit* armed. **~ jusqu'aux dents, ~ de pied en cap** armed to the teeth; **bien ~ contre le froid** well-armed *ou* -equipped against the cold; **attention, il est ~!** careful, he's armed!; **~ d'un bâton/d'un dictionnaire** armed with a stick/a dictionary; **être bien ~ pour passer un examen** to be well-equipped to take an examination; (*fig*) **il est bien ~ pour se défendre** he is well-equipped for life; **il est bien ~ contre leurs arguments** he's well-armed against their arguments; **cactus ~ de piquants** cactus armed with spikes; **canne ~e d'un bout ferré** stick fitted with an iron tip, stick tipped with iron; *voir* **béton, ciment, force, main**.
2 nm (*position*) cock.
armée[2] [aʀme] 1 nf army. **~ de mercenaires/d'occupation/régulière** mercenary/occupying/regular army; **être dans l'~** to be in the army; **les ~s alliées** the allied armies; (*fig*) **une ~ de domestiques/rats** an army of servants/rats; (*péj*) **regardez-moi cette ~ (d'incapables)** just look at this (hopeless) bunch* *ou* crew*; *voir* **corps, grand, zone**. 2 comp ► **armée active** regular army ► **l'armée de l'air** the Air Force ► **l'armée de mer** the Navy ► **armée de réserve** reserve ► **l'Armée rouge** the Red Army ► **l'armée du Salut** the Salvation Army ► **l'armée de terre** the Army.
armement [aʀməmɑ̃] nm a (*action*) *[pays, armée]* armament; *[personne]* arming; *[fusil]* cocking; *[appareil-photo]* winding-on; *[navire]* fitting-out, equipping. b (*armes*) *[soldat]* arms, weapons; *[pays, troupe, avion, navire]* arms, armament(s). **usine d'~** arms factory; **la limitation des ~s** arms limitation; **dépenses d'~s de la France** France's expenditure on arms *ou* weapons, France's arms *ou* weapons expenditure; **vendre des ~s aux rebelles** to sell weapons *ou* arms to the rebels; *voir* **course**.
Arménie [aʀmeni] nf Armenia; *voir* **papier**.
arménien, -ienne [aʀmenjɛ̃, jɛn] 1 adj Armenian. 2 nm (*Ling*) Armenian. 3 nm,f: **A~(ne)** Armenian.
armer [aʀme] 1 1 vt a *pays, forteresse, personne* to arm (*de* with). **~ des rebelles contre un gouvernement** to arm rebels against a government; (*fig*) **~ le gouvernement de pouvoirs exceptionnels** to arm *ou* equip the government with exceptional powers; (*fig*) **~ qn contre les difficultés de la vie** to arm sb against life's difficulties, arm *ou* equip sb to deal with the difficulties of life.
b (*Hist*) **~ qn chevalier** to dub sb knight.
c (*Naut*) *navire* to fit out, equip.
d *fusil* to cock; *appareil-photo* to wind on.
e (*renforcer*) *béton, poutre* to reinforce (*de* with). **~ qch de** to fit sth with; **~ un bâton d'une pointe d'acier** to fit a stick with a steel tip, fit a steel tip on(to) a stick.
2 **s'armer** vpr (*s'équiper*) to arm o.s. (*de* with, *contre* against). **s'~ d'un fusil/d'un dictionnaire** to arm o.s. with a gun/a dictionary; (*fig*) **s'~ de courage/de patience** to arm o.s. with courage/patience.
armistice [aʀmistis] nm armistice.
armoire [aʀmwaʀ] nf (*gén*) (tall) cupboard; (*penderie*) wardrobe. **~ à pharmacie** medicine chest *ou* cabinet; **~ de toilette** bathroom cabinet (with a mirror); **~ frigorifique** cold room *ou* store; **~ à linge** linen cupboard (*Brit*) *ou* closet (*US*); **~ normande** large wardrobe; **~ à glace** (*lit*) wardrobe with a mirror; (* *fig: costaud*) great hulking brute*.
armoiries [aʀmwaʀi] nfpl coat of arms, armorial bearings.
armorial, e, mpl **-iaux** [aʀmɔʀjal, jo] adj, nm armorial.
armoricain, e [aʀmɔʀikɛ̃, ɛn] 1 adj Armorican. 2 nm,f (*Hist*) **A~(e)** Armorican.
armorier [aʀmɔʀje] 7 vt to emblazon.
armure [aʀmyʀ] nf (*Mil, Zool*) armour; (*fig*) defence; (*Phys*) armature; (*Tex*) weave.
armurerie [aʀmyʀʀi] nf (*voir* **armurier**) (*fabrique*) arms factory; (*magasin*) gunsmith's; armourer's; (*profession*) arms trade.
armurier [aʀmyʀje] nm (*fabricant, marchand*) *[armes à feu]* gunsmith; *[armes blanches]* armourer; (*Mil*) armourer.
ARN [aɛʀɛn] nm (abrév de **acide ribonucléique**) RNA.
arnaque⁑ [aʀnak] nm swindling. **c'est de l'~** it's a rip-off*, it's daylight robbery.
arnaquer⁑ [aʀnake] 1 vt (*escroquer*) to do⁑ (*Brit*), diddle* (*Brit*), swindle; (*arrêter*) to nab*. **on s'est fait ~ dans ce restaurant** we were done⁑ *ou* diddled* in that restaurant; **il leur a arnaqué des millions** he swindled *ou* did⁑ them out of millions.
arnaqueur, -euse⁑ [aʀnakœʀ, øz] nm,f swindler, cheat.
arnica [aʀnika] nf arnica.
Arno [aʀno] nm: **l'~** the Arno.
aromate [aʀɔmat] nm (*thym etc*) herb; (*poivre etc*) spice. **~s** seasoning (*NonC*); **ajoutez quelques ~s** add (some) seasoning *ou* a few herbs (*ou* spices).
aromathérapie [aʀɔmateʀapi] nf aromatherapy.
aromatique [aʀɔmatik] adj (*gén, Chim*) aromatic.
aromatiser [aʀɔmatize] 1 vt to flavour.
arôme, arome [aʀom] nm *[plat]* aroma; *[café, vin]* aroma, fragrance; *[fleur]* fragrance; (*goût*) flavour; (*ajouté à un aliment*) flavouring. **crème ~ chocolat** chocolate-flavoured cream dessert.
aronde†† [aʀɔ̃d] nf swallow; *voir* **queue**.
arpège [aʀpɛʒ] nm arpeggio. **faire des ~s** to play arpeggios.
arpéger [aʀpeʒe] 6 *et* 3 vt *passage* to play in arpeggios; *accord* to play as an arpeggio, spread.
arpent [aʀpɑ̃] nm (*Hist*) arpent (*about an acre*). (*fig*) **il a quelques ~s de terre en province** he's got a few acres in the country.
arpentage [aʀpɑ̃taʒ] nm (*technique*) (land) surveying; (*mesure*) measuring, surveying.
arpenter [aʀpɑ̃te] 1 vt to pace (up and down); (*Tech*) *terrain* to measure, survey.
arpenteur [aʀpɑ̃tœʀ] nm (land) surveyor; *voir* **chaîne**.
arpète* [aʀpɛt] nmf apprentice.
arpion⁑ [aʀpjɔ̃] nm hoof⁑, foot.
arqué, e [aʀke] (ptp de **arquer**) adj *forme, objet* curved, arched; *sourcils* arched, curved; *jambes* bow (*épith*), bandy. **avoir le dos ~** to be humpbacked *ou* hunchbacked; **le dos ~ sous l'effort** his back arched under the strain; **il a les jambes ~es** he's bandy(-legged) *ou* bow-legged; **nez ~** hooknose, hooked nose.
arquebuse [aʀkəbyz] nf (h)arquebus.
arquebusier [aʀkəbyzje] nm (*soldat*) (h)arquebusier.
arquer [aʀke] 1 1 vt *objet, tige* to curve; *dos* to arch. 2 vi *[objet]* to bend, curve; *[poutre]* to sag. **il ne peut plus ~**⁑ he can't walk any more. 3 **s'arquer** vpr to curve.
arrache- [aʀaʃ] préf *voir* **arracher**.
arraché [aʀaʃe] nm (*Sport*) snatch. **il soulève 130 kg à l'~** he can do a snatch using 130 kg; (*fig*) **obtenir la victoire à l'~** to snatch victory; **ils**

ont eu le contrat à l'~ they just managed to snatch the contract.

arrachement [aʀaʃmɑ̃] nm a (*chagrin*) wrench. quel ~ de le voir partir! it was a terrible wrench to see him leave! b (*voir* arracher) pulling out; tearing off.

arracher [aʀaʃe] 1 1 vt a (*extraire*) *légume* to lift; *souche, plante* to pull up, uproot; *mauvaises herbes* to pull up; *dent* to take out, extract, pull (*US*); *poil, clou* to pull out. il est parti ~ les mauvaises herbes he's out weeding; je vais me faire ~ une dent I'm going to have a tooth out *ou* extracted *ou* pulled (*US*).

b (*déchirer*) *chemise, affiche, membre* to tear off; *cheveux* to tear *ou* pull out; *feuille, page* to tear *ou* pull out (*de* of). (*fig*) je vais lui ~ les yeux I'll scratch *ou* claw his eyes out; (*fig*) j'ai arraché son voile *ou* masque I have torn down his mask, I've unmasked him; (*fig*) ce spectacle lui arracha le cœur the sight of it broke his heart, it was a heartrending sight for him; *[boisson, plat]* ça arrache (la gorge)‡ it will blow your head off*.

c (*enlever*) ~ à qn *portefeuille, arme* to snatch *ou* grab from sb; (*fig*) *argent* to extract from sb, get out of sb; *applaudissements, larmes* to wring from sb; *victoire* to wrest from sb; il lui arracha son sac à main he snatched *ou* grabbed her handbag from her; je lui ai arraché cette promesse/ces aveux/la vérité I dragged this promise/confession/the truth out of him, I wrung *ou* wrested this promise/this confession/the truth out of *ou* from him.

d (*soustraire*) ~ qn à *famille, pays* to tear *ou* drag sb away from; *passion, vice, soucis* to rescue sb from; *sommeil, rêve* to drag *ou* snatch sb out of *ou* from; *sort, mort* to snatch sb from; *habitudes, méditation* to force sb out of; ~ qn des mains d'un ennemi to snatch sb from (out of) the hands of an enemy; la mort nous l'a arraché death has snatched *ou* torn him from us; il m'a arraché du lit à 6 heures he got *ou* dragged me out of bed at 6 o'clock.

2 s'arracher vpr a (*se déchirer*) tu t'es encore arraché (les vêtements) après le grillage you've torn your clothes on the fence again; s'~ les cheveux (*lit*) to tear *ou* pull out one's hair; (*fig*) to tear one's hair; (*fig*) s'~ les yeux to scratch each other's eyes out.

b s'~ qn/qch to fight over sb/sth; (*hum*) on se m'arrache‡ they're all fighting over me* (*hum*).

c s'~ de *ou* à *pays, famille* to tear o.s. away from; *habitude, méditation, passion* to force o.s. out of; *lit* to drag o.s. from, force o.s. out of; on s'arrache?‡ let's split!‡

3 comp ▸arrache-clou nm (pl arrache-clous) nail wrench ▸arrache-pied: d'arrache-pied adv relentlessly.

arracheur [aʀaʃœʀ] nm *voir* mentir.

arracheuse [aʀaʃøz] nf (*Agr*) lifter, grubber.

arraisonnement [aʀɛzɔnmɑ̃] nm (*Naut*) inspection.

arraisonner [aʀɛzɔne] 1 vt (*Naut*) to inspect.

arrangeant, e [aʀɑ̃ʒɑ̃, ɑ̃t] adj accommodating, obliging.

arrangement [aʀɑ̃ʒmɑ̃] nm a (*action*) *[fleurs, coiffure, voyage]* arrangement. b (*agencement*) *[mobilier, maison]* layout, arrangement; *[fiches]* order, arrangement; *[mots]* order. l'~ de sa coiffure the way her hair is done *ou* arranged; l'~ de sa toilette the way she is dressed. c (*accord*) agreement, settlement, arrangement. arriver *ou* parvenir à un ~ to reach an agreement *ou* a settlement, come to an arrangement; sauf ~ contraire unless otherwise stated; (*Jur*) ~ de famille family settlement (*in financial matters*). d (*Mus*) arrangement. ~ pour guitare arrangement for guitar. e (*Math*) arrangement. f (*préparatifs*) ~s arrangements.

arranger [aʀɑ̃ʒe] 3 1 vt a (*disposer*) (*gén*) to arrange; *coiffure* to tidy up. ~ sa cravate/sa jupe to straighten (up) one's tie/skirt, set one's tie/skirt straight.

b (*organiser*) *voyage, réunion* to arrange, organize; *rencontre, entrevue* to arrange, fix (up). ~ sa vie/ses affaires to organize one's life/one's affairs; il a tout arrangé pour ce soir he has seen to *ou* he has arranged everything for tonight; ce combat de catch était arrangé à l'avance this wrestling match was fixed (in advance) *ou* was a put-up job*.

c (*régler*) *différend* to settle. je vais essayer d'~ les choses I'll try to sort things out; tout est arrangé, le malentendu est dissipé everything is settled *ou* sorted out, the disagreement is over; et ce qui n'arrange rien, il est en retard! and he's late, which doesn't help matters!; ce contretemps n'arrange pas nos affaires this setback doesn't help our affairs.

d (*contenter*) to suit, be convenient for. ça ne m'arrange pas tellement that doesn't really suit me; cela m'arrange bien that suits me nicely *ou* fine; à 6 heures si ça vous arrange at 6 o'clock if that suits you *ou* if that's convenient (for you); tu le crois parce que ça t'arrange you believe him because it suits you (to do so).

e (*réparer*) *voiture, montre* to fix, put right; *robe* (*recoudre*) to fix, mend; (*modifier*) to alter. il faudrait ~ votre devoir, il est confus you'll have to sort out your exercise as it's rather muddled.

f (**: malmener*) to sort out‡ (*Brit*). il s'est drôlement fait ~ he got a real working over*, they really sorted him out‡ (*Brit*); te voilà bien arrangé! what a state *ou* mess you've got yourself in!*

g (*Littérat, Mus*) to arrange.

2 s'arranger vpr a (*se mettre d'accord*) to come to an agreement *ou* arrangement. arrangez-vous avec le patron you'll have to come to an agreement *ou* arrangement with the boss *ou* sort it out with the boss; s'~ à l'amiable to come to a friendly *ou* an amicable agreement.

b (*s'améliorer*) *[querelle]* to be settled; *[situation]* to work out, sort itself out (*Brit*); *[santé]* to get better. le temps n'a pas l'air de s'~ it doesn't look as though the weather is improving *ou* getting any better; tout va s'~ everything will work out (all right) *ou* sort itself out (*Brit*), it'll all work out (all right) *ou* sort itself out (*Brit*); les choses s'arrangèrent d'elles-mêmes things sorted (*Brit*) *ou* worked themselves out unaided; ça ne s'arrange pas*, il est plus brouillon que jamais things are no better, he's more muddled than ever; il ne fait rien pour s'~ he doesn't do himself any favours; alors, ça s'arrange entre eux? are things getting (any) better between them?

c (*se débrouiller*) arrangez-vous comme vous voudrez mais je les veux demain I don't mind how you do it but I want them for tomorrow; (*iro*) tu t'arranges toujours pour avoir des taches! you always manage to get grubby! (*iro*); je ne sais pas comment tu t'arranges, mais tu as toujours des taches I don't know how you manage (it), but you're always grubby; il va s'~ pour finir le travail avant demain he'll see to it that *ou* he'll make sure (that) he finishes the job before tomorrow; il s'est arrangé pour avoir des places gratuites he has seen to it that he has got *ou* he has managed to get some free seats; arrangez-vous pour venir me chercher à la gare arrange it so that you can come and meet me at the station; c'est ton problème, arrange-toi! you work it out, it's your problem!

d s'~ de to make do with, put up with; il s'est arrangé du fauteuil pour dormir he made do with the armchair to sleep in; il faudra bien s'en ~ we'll just have to put up with it.

e (*se classer*) to be arranged. ses arguments s'arrangent logiquement his arguments are logically arranged.

f (*se rajuster*) to tidy o.s. up. elle s'arrange les cheveux she's tidying her hair.

g (**: se faire mal*) tu t'es bien arrangé! you've got yourself in a fine state!, you DO look a mess!*

arrangeur, -euse [aʀɑ̃ʒœʀ, øz] nm,f (*Mus*) arranger.

arrérages [aʀeʀaʒ] nmpl arrears.

arrestation [aʀɛstasjɔ̃] 1 nf arrest. procéder à l'~ de qn to arrest sb, take sb into custody; être en état d'~ to be under arrest; mettre en état d'~ to place *ou* put under arrest, take into custody; mise en ~ arrest; ils ont procédé à une douzaine d'~s they made a dozen arrests. 2 comp ▸arrestation préventive ≃ arrest ▸arrestation provisoire taking into preventive custody.

arrêt [aʀɛ] 1 nm a *[machine, véhicule]* stopping; *[développement, croissance]* stopping, checking, arrest; *[hémorragie]* stopping, arrest. attendez l'~ complet (du train/de l'avion) wait until the train/aircraft has come to a complete stop *ou* standstill; cinq minutes d'~ *[trajet]* a 5-minute stop; *[cours]* a 5-minute break; (*sur véhicule*) "~s fréquents" "frequent stops"; véhicule à l'~ stationary vehicle; *[véhicule]* être à l'~ to be stationary; faire un ~ *[train]* to stop, make a stop; *[gardien de but]* to make a save; le train fit un ~ brusque the train came to a sudden stop *ou* standstill; nous avons fait plusieurs ~s we made several stops *ou* halts; donner un coup d'~ à to check, put a brake on; *voir* chien.

b (*lieu*) stop. ~ d'autobus bus stop; ~ fixe/facultatif compulsory/request stop.

c (*Mil*) ~s arrest; ~s simples/de rigueur open/close arrest; ~s de forteresse confinement (*in military prison*); mettre qn aux ~s to put sb under arrest; *voir* maison, mandat.

d (*Jur: décision, jugement*) judgment, decision, ruling. (†, *littér*) les ~s du destin the decrees of destiny (*littér*).

e (*Couture*) faire un ~ to fasten off the thread; *voir* point².

f (*Tech*) *[machine]* stop mechanism; *[serrure]* ward; *[fusil]* safety catch. appuyez sur l'~ press the stop button.

g (*Ski*) stop.

h (*loc*) (*Jur*) faire ~ sur les appointements to issue a writ of attachment (on debtor's salary); rester *ou* tomber en ~ (*Chasse*) to point; (*fig*) to stop short; être en ~ (*Chasse*) to be pointing (*devant* at); (*fig*) to stand transfixed (*devant* before); marquer un ~ avant de continuer à parler to pause *ou* make a pause before speaking again; sans ~ (*sans interruption*) *travailler, pleuvoir* without stopping, non-stop; (*très fréquemment*) *se produire, se détraquer* continually, constantly; (*Rail*) "sans ~ jusqu'à Perpignan" "non-stop to Perpignan"; ce train est sans ~ jusqu'à Lyon this train is non-stop to Lyons.

2 comp ▸arrêt du cœur cardiac arrest, heart failure ▸l'arrêt des hostilités the cessation of hostilities ▸arrêt de jeu (*Sport*) stoppage; jouer les arrêts de jeu to play injury time *ou* stoppage time ▸arrêt (de) maladie sick leave; être en arrêt (de) maladie to be on sick leave ▸arrêt de mort sentence of death, death sentence ▸arrêt de travail (*grève*) stoppage (of work); (*congé de maladie*) sick leave; (*certificat*) doctor's *ou* medical certificate ▸arrêt de volée: faire un arrêt de volée (*Rugby*) to make a mark.

arrêté, e [aʀete] (ptp de arrêter) 1 adj *décision, volonté* firm, immutable; *idée, opinion* fixed, firm. c'est une chose ~e the matter *ou* it is settled. 2 nm (*décision administrative*) order, decree (*frm*). ~ ministériel departmental *ou* ministerial order; ~ municipal ≃ by(e)-law;

~ **préfectoral** order of the prefect; ~ **de compte** (*fermeture*) settlement of account; (*relevé*) statement of account (*to date*).

arrêter [aʀete] 1 1 vt a (*immobiliser*) *personne, machine, montre* to stop; *cheval* to stop, pull up; *moteur* to switch off, stop. **arrêtez-moi près de la poste** drop me by the post office; **il m'a arrêté dans le couloir pour me parler** he stopped me in the corridor to speak to me; (*dans la conversation*) **ici, je vous arrête!** I must stop *ou* interrupt you there!; **arrête ton char**‡ (*parler*) shut up!*, belt up!‡ (*Brit*); (*se vanter*) stop swanking!* (*Brit*) *ou* showing off!

b (*entraver*) *développement, croissance* to stop, check, arrest; *foule, ennemi* to stop, halt; *hémorragie* to stop, arrest. **le trafic ferroviaire est arrêté à cause de la grève** rail traffic is at a standstill *ou* all the trains have been cancelled *ou* halted because of the strike; **rien n'arrête la marche de l'histoire** nothing can stop *ou* check *ou* halt the march of history; (*hum*) **on n'arrête pas le progrès** there's no stopping progress; **nous avons été arrêtés par un embouteillage** we were held up *ou* stopped by a traffic jam; **seul le prix l'arrête** it's only the price that stops him; **rien ne l'arrête** there's nothing to stop him; **arrête les frais!*** drop it!*

c (*abandonner*) *études* to give up; (*Sport*) *compétition* to give up; (*Théât*) *représentations* to cancel. ~ **ses études/le tennis** to give up one's studies/tennis, stop studying/playing tennis; ~ **la fabrication d'un produit** to discontinue (the manufacture of) a product; **on a dû ~ les travaux à cause de la neige** we had to stop work *ou* call a halt to the work because of the snow.

d (*faire prisonnier*) to arrest. **il s'est fait ~ hier** he got himself arrested yesterday; **je vous arrête!** you're under arrest!

e (*Fin*) *compte* (*fermer*) to settle; (*relever*) to make up. **les comptes sont arrêtés chaque fin de mois** statements (of account) are made up at the end of every month.

f (*Couture*) *point* to fasten off.

g (*fixer*) *jour, lieu* to appoint, decide on; *plan* to decide on; *derniers détails* to finalize. ~ **son attention/ses regards sur** to fix one's attention/gaze on; ~ **un marché** to make a deal; **il a arrêté son choix** he has made his choice; **ma décision est arrêtée** my mind is made up; (*Admin*) ~ **que** to rule that; (*Jur*) ~ **les dispositions d'application** to adopt provisions to implement.

h (*Méd*) ~ **qn** to give sb sick leave; **elle est arrêtée depuis 3 semaines** she's been on sick leave for 3 weeks.

2 vi to stop. **il n'arrête pas** he's never still, he's always on the go; **il n'arrête pas de critiquer tout le monde** he never stops criticizing everyone, he's always criticizing everyone; **arrête de parler!** stop talking!; **il a arrêté de fumer après sa maladie** he gave up *ou* stopped smoking after his illness; **arrête!** stop it!, stop that!; **ça n'arrête pas!*** it never stops!

3 **s'arrêter** vpr a (*s'immobiliser*) [*personne, machine, montre*] to stop; [*train, voiture*] to stop, come to a stop *ou* a halt *ou* a standstill. **nous nous arrêtâmes sur le bas-côté/dans un village** we pulled up *ou* stopped by the roadside/at a village; **s'~ court** *ou* **net** [*personne*] to stop dead *ou* short; [*cheval*] to pull up; [*bruit*] to stop suddenly; **nous nous sommes arrêtés 10 jours à Lyon** we stayed *ou* stopped* 10 days in Lyons.

b (*s'interrompre*) to stop, break off. **s'~ de travailler/de parler** to stop working/speaking; **s'~ pour se reposer/pour manger** to break off *ou* stop for a rest/to eat; **arrête-toi un peu, tu vas t'épuiser** stop for a while *ou* take a break or you'll wear yourself out; **les ouvriers se sont arrêtés à 17 heures** (*grève*) the workmen downed tools (*Brit*) *ou* stopped work at 5 o'clock; (*heure de fermeture*) the workmen finished (work) *ou* stopped work at 5 o'clock; **sans s'~** without stopping, without a break; **ce serait dommage de s'~ en si bon chemin** it would be a shame to stop *ou* give up while one is doing so well.

c (*cesser*) [*développement, croissance*] to stop, come to a halt, come to a standstill; [*hémorragie*] to stop. **le travail s'est arrêté dans l'usine en grève** work has stopped in the striking factory, the striking factory is at a standstill; **s'~ de manger/marcher** to stop eating/walking; **s'~ de fumer/boire** to give up *ou* stop smoking/drinking; **l'affaire ne s'arrêtera pas là!** you (*ou* they *etc*) haven't heard the last of this!

d **s'~ sur** [*choix, regard*] to fall on; **il ne faut pas s'~ aux apparences** one must always look beneath appearances; **s'~ à des détails** to pay too much attention to details; **s'~ à un projet** to settle on *ou* fix on a plan; **arrêtons-nous un instant sur ce tableau** let us turn our attention to this picture for a moment.

arrhes [aʀ] nfpl deposit.

arrière [aʀjɛʀ] 1 nm a [*voiture*] back; [*bateau*] stern; [*train*] rear. (*Naut*) **à l'~** aft, at the stern; **à l'~ de** at the stern of, abaft; **se balancer d'avant en ~** to rock backwards and forwards; **avec le moteur à l'~** with the engine at the back; (*en temps de guerre*) **l'~ (du pays)** the home front, the civilian zone; **l'~ tient bon** morale on the home front *ou* behind the lines is high.

b (*Sport: joueur*) (*gén*) fullback; (*Volleyball*) back-line player. ~ **gauche/droit** (*Ftbl*) left/right back; (*Basketball*) left/right guard; (*Ftbl*) ~ **central** centre back; ~ **volant** sweeper.

c (*Mil*) **les ~s** the rear; **attaquer les ~s de l'ennemi** to attack the enemy in the rear; **assurer** *ou* **protéger ses ~s** (*lit*) to protect the rear; (*fig*) to leave o.s. a way out.

d **en ~** (*derrière*) behind; (*vers l'arrière*) backwards; **être/rester en ~** to be/lag *ou* drop behind; **regarder en ~** to look back *ou* behind; **faire un pas en ~** to step back(wards), take a step back; **aller/marcher en ~** to go/walk backwards; **se pencher en ~** to lean back(wards); (*Naut*) **en ~ toute!** full astern!; **100 ans en ~** 100 years ago *ou* back; **il faut remonter loin en ~ pour trouver une telle sécheresse** we have to go a long way back (in time) to find a similar drought; **revenir en ~** [*marcheur*] to go back, retrace one's steps; [*orateur*] to go back over what has been said; [*civilisation*] to regress; (*avec magnétophone*) to rewind; (*avec ses souvenirs, dans ses pensées*) to go back in time (*fig*), look back; **renverser la tête en ~** to tilt one's head back(wards); **le chapeau en ~** his hat tilted back(wards); **être peigné** *ou* **avoir les cheveux en ~** to have *ou* wear one's hair brushed *ou* combed back(wards).

e (*lit, fig*) **en ~ de** behind; **rester** *ou* **se tenir en ~ de qch** to stay behind sth; **il est très en ~ des autres élèves** he's a long way behind the other pupils.

2 adj inv: **roue/feu ~** rear wheel/light; **siège ~** back seat; [*moto*] pillion; *voir* **machine**[3], **marche**[1], **vent**.

3 excl: **en ~!** **vous gênez** stand *ou* get back! you're in the way; **~, misérable!**† behind me, wretch!†

4 comp ▸**arrière-ban** nm (pl **arrière-bans**) *voir* **ban** ▸**arrière-bouche** nf (pl **arrière-bouches**) back of the mouth ▸**arrière-boutique** nf (pl **arrière-boutiques**) back shop ▸**arrière-cour** nf (pl **arrière-cours**) backyard ▸**arrière-cuisine** nf (pl **arrière-cuisines**) scullery ▸**arrière-garde** nf (pl **arrière-gardes**) rearguard ▸**arrière-gorge** nf (pl **arrière-gorges**) back of the throat ▸**arrière-goût** nm (pl **arrière-goûts**) (*lit, fig*) aftertaste; **ses propos ont un arrière-goût de racisme** his comments smack of racism ▸**arrière-grand-mère** nf (pl **arrière-grand-mères**) great-grandmother ▸**arrière-grand-oncle** nm (pl **arrière-grands-oncles**) great-great-uncle ▸**arrière-grand-père** nm (pl **arrière-grands-pères**) great-grandfather ▸**arrière-grands-parents** nmpl great-grandparents ▸**arrière-grand-tante** nf (pl **arrière-grand-tantes**) great-great-aunt ▸**arrière-pays** nm inv hinterland ▸**arrière-pensée** nf (pl **arrière-pensées**) (*raison intéressée*) ulterior motive; (*réserves, doute*) mental reservation ▸**arrière-petit-cousin** nm (pl **arrière-petits-cousins**) cousin three times removed, distant cousin ▸**arrière-petite-fille** nf (pl **arrière-petites-filles**) great-granddaughter ▸**arrière-petit-fils** nm (pl **arrière-petits-fils**) great-grandson ▸**arrière-petits-enfants** nmpl great-grandchildren ▸**arrière-plan** nm (pl **arrière-plans**) background; (*lit, fig*) **à l'arrière-plan** in the background ▸**arrière-saison** nf (pl **arrière-saisons**) end of autumn, late autumn ▸**arrière-salle** nf (pl **arrière-salles**) back room, inner room (*esp of restaurant*) ▸**arrière-train** nm (pl **arrière-trains**) [*animal*], (*hum*) [*personne*] hindquarters.

arriéré, e [aʀjeʀe] 1 adj a (*Comm*) *paiement* overdue, in arrears (*attrib*); *dette* outstanding. b (*Psych*) *enfant, personne* backward, retarded; (*Scol*) educationally subnormal; *région, pays* backward, behind the times (*attrib*); *croyances, méthodes, personne* out-of-date, behind the times (*attrib*). 2 nm (*choses à faire, travail*) backlog; (*paiement*) arrears (*pl*). **il voulait régler l'~ de sa dette** he wanted to settle the arrears on his debt.

arriérer [aʀjeʀe] 6 (*Fin*) 1 vt *paiement* to defer. 2 **s'arriérer** vpr to fall into arrears, fall behind with payments.

arrimage [aʀimaʒ] nm (*Naut*) stowage, stowing.

arrimer [aʀime] 1 vt (*Naut*) *cargaison* to stow; (*gén*) *colis* to lash down, secure.

arrimeur [aʀimœʀ] nm stevedore.

arrivage [aʀivaʒ] nm [*marchandises*] consignment, delivery, load; (*fig hum*) [*touristes*] fresh load (*hum*) *ou* influx.

arrivant, e [aʀivɑ̃, ɑ̃t] nm,f newcomer. **nouvel ~** newcomer, new arrival; **combien d'~s y avait-il hier?** how many new arrivals were there yesterday?, how many newcomers *ou* people arrived yesterday?; **les premiers ~s de la saison** the first arrivals of the season.

arrivée [aʀive] nf a [*personne, train, courrier*] arrival; [*printemps, neige, hirondelles*] arrival, coming; [*course, skieur*] finish. **à mon ~, je ...** when I arrived *ou* upon my arrival, I ...; **à son ~ chez lui** on (his) arrival *ou* arriving home, when he arrived home; **attendant l'~ du courrier** waiting for the post *ou* mail to come *ou* arrive, waiting for the arrival of the post *ou* mail; **c'est l'~ des abricots sur le marché** apricots are beginning to arrive in *ou* are coming into the shops; *voir* **gare**[1], **juge, ligne**[1]. b (*Tech*) ~ **d'air/d'eau/de gaz** (*robinet*) air/water/gas inlet; (*processus*) inflow of air/water/gas.

arriver [aʀive] 1 vi a (*au terme d'un voyage*) [*train, personne*] to arrive. ~ **à** *ville* to arrive at, get to, reach; ~ **de** *ville, pays* to arrive from; ~ **en France** to arrive in *ou* reach France; ~ **chez des amis** to arrive at friends'; ~ **chez soi** to arrive *ou* get *ou* reach home; ~ **à destination** to arrive at one's *ou* its destination; ~ **à bon port** to arrive safe and sound; **nous sommes arrivés** we've arrived; **le train doit ~ à 6 heures** the train is due (to arrive) *ou* scheduled to arrive *ou* is due in at 6 o'clock; **il est arrivé par le train/en voiture** he arrived by train/by car *ou* in a car; **nous sommes presque arrivés, nous arrivons** we're almost there, we've almost arrived; **cette lettre m'est arrivée hier** this letter reached me yesterday; ~ **le premier** (*course*) to come in first; (*soirée, réception*) to be the first to arrive, arrive first; **les premiers arrivés** the first to arrive, the first arrivals; (*fig*) ~ **comme mars en carême** to come as sure as night follows day.

b (*approcher*) *[saison, nuit, personne, véhicule]* to come. ~ **à grands pas/en courant** to stride up/run up; **j'arrive!** (I'm) coming!, just coming!; **le train arrive en gare** the train is pulling *ou* coming into the station; **la voici qui arrive** here she comes (now); **allez, arrive, je suis pressé!** hurry up *ou* come on, I'm in a hurry!; **ton tour arrivera bientôt** it'll soon be your turn, your turn won't be long (in) coming; **on va commencer à manger, ça va peut-être faire ~ ton père** we'll start eating, perhaps that will make your father come; **pour faire ~ l'eau jusqu'à la maison** ... to lay the water on for (*Brit*) *ou* to bring the water (up) to the house ...; **l'air/l'eau arrive par ce trou** the air/water comes in through this hole; **pour qu'arrive plus vite le moment où il la reverrait** to hasten *ou* to bring nearer the moment when *ou* to bring the moment closer when he would see her again; *voir* **chien**.

c (*atteindre*) ~ **à** *niveau, lieu* to reach, get to, arrive at; *personne, âge* to reach, get to; *poste, rang* to attain, reach; *résultat, but, conclusion* to reach, arrive at; **la nouvelle est arrivée jusqu'à nous** the news has reached us *ou* got to us; **le bruit arrivait jusqu'à nous** the noise reached us; **je n'ai pas pu ~ jusqu'au chef** I wasn't able to get right to the boss; **comment arrive-t-on chez eux?** how do you get to their house?; **le lierre arrive jusqu'au 1er étage** the ivy goes up to *ou* goes up as far as the 1st floor; **l'eau lui arrivait (jusqu')aux genoux** the water came up to his knees, he was knee-deep in water; **et le problème des salaires? — j'y arrive** and what about the wages problem? — I'm just coming to that; (*fig*) **il ne t'arrive pas à la cheville** he's not a patch on you (*Brit*), he can't hold a candle to you; ~ **au pouvoir** to come to power.

d (*réussir à*) ~ **à faire qch** to succeed in doing sth, manage to do sth; **pour ~ à lui faire comprendre qu'il a tort** to get him to *ou* to succeed in making him understand he's wrong; **il n'arrive pas à le comprendre** he just doesn't understand it; **je n'arrive pas à comprendre son attitude** I just don't *ou* can't understand *ou* I fail to understand his attitude; **je n'arrive pas à faire ce devoir** I (just) can't manage (to do) this exercise; **tu y arrives? — je n'y arrive pas** can you do it? *ou* can you manage (to do) it? — I can't (manage it); ~ **à ses fins** to get one's way, achieve one's ends; **il n'arrivera jamais à rien** he'll never get anywhere, he'll never achieve anything; **on n'arrivera jamais à rien avec lui** it's impossible to get anywhere with him.

e (*réussir socialement*) to succeed (in life), get on (in life). **il veut ~** he wants to get on *ou* succeed (in life); **il se croit arrivé** he thinks he has made it* *ou* he has arrived.

f (*se produire*) to happen. **c'est arrivé hier** it happened *ou* occurred yesterday; **ce genre d'accident n'arrive qu'à lui!** that sort of accident only (ever) happens to him!; **ce sont des choses qui arrivent** these things (will) happen; **cela peut ~ à n'importe qui** it could *ou* can happen to anyone; **cela ne m'arrivera plus!** I won't let it happen again!; **il croit que c'est arrivé*** he thinks he has made it*; **cela devait lui ~** he had it coming to him*; **tu vas nous faire ~ des ennuis*** you'll get us into trouble *ou* bring trouble upon our heads.

g (*finir par*) **en ~ à** to come to; **on n'en est pas encore arrivé là!** (*résultat négatif*) we've not come to *ou* reached that (stage) yet!; (*résultat positif*) we've not got that far yet!; **on en arrive à se demander si** ... we're beginning to wonder whether ...; **il faudra bien en ~ là!** it'll have to come to that (eventually); **c'est triste d'en ~ là** it's sad to be reduced to that.

2 **vb impers** a **il est arrivé un accident** there has been an accident; **il (lui) est arrivé un malheur** something dreadful has happened (to him); **il lui est arrivé un accident/un malheur** he has had an accident/a misfortune, he has met with an accident/a misfortune; **il est arrivé un télégramme** a telegram has come *ou* arrived; **il lui arrivera des ennuis** he'll get (himself) into trouble; **il m'arrive toujours des aventures incroyables** incredible things are always happening to me, I'm always getting involved in incredible adventures; **quoiqu'il arrive** whatever happens; **elle est parfois arrogante comme il arrive souvent aux timides** she is sometimes arrogant as often happens *ou* as is often the case with shy people.

b **il arrive que** + *subj*, **il arrive de: il m'arrive d'oublier, il arrive que j'oublie** I sometimes forget; **il peut ~ qu'elle se trompe, il peut lui ~ de se tromper** she does occasionally make a mistake, it occasionally happens that she makes a mistake; **il peut ~ qu'elle se trompe mais ce n'est pas une raison pour la critiquer** she may (indeed) make mistakes but that's not a reason for criticizing her; **il pourrait ~ qu'ils soient sortis** it could be that they've gone out, they might have gone out; **s'il lui arrive** *ou* **arrivait de faire une erreur, prévenez-moi** if she should happen *ou* if she happens to make a mistake, let me know; **il m'est arrivé plusieurs fois de le voir/faire** I have seen him/done it several times; **il ne lui arrive pas souvent de mentir** it is not often that he lies, he does not often lie.

arrivisme [aʀivism] **nm** (*péj*) (ruthless) ambition, pushiness; (*social*) social climbing.

arriviste [aʀivist] **nmf** (*péj*) (ruthless) go-getter*, careerist; (*social*) social climber.

arrogamment [aʀɔgamɑ̃] **adv** arrogantly.

arrogance [aʀɔgɑ̃s] **nf** arrogance.

arrogant, e [aʀɔgɑ̃, ɑ̃t] **adj** arrogant.

arroger (s') [aʀɔʒe] 3 **vpr** *pouvoirs, privilèges* to assume (without right); *titre* to claim (falsely), claim (without right), assume. **s'~ le droit de** ... to assume the right to ..., take it upon o.s. to ... .

arroi [aʀwa] **nm** (*littér*) array. (*fig*) **être en mauvais ~** to be in a sorry state.

arrondi, e [aʀɔ̃di] (**ptp de arrondir**) 1 **adj** *objet, forme, relief* round, rounded; *visage* round; *voyelle* rounded. 2 **nm** (*gén: contour*) roundness; (*Aviat*) flare-out, flared landing; (*Couture*) hemline (*of skirt*).

arrondir [aʀɔ̃diʀ] 2 1 **vt** a *objet, contour* to round, make round; *rebord, angle* to round off; *phrases* to polish, round out; *gestes* to make smoother; *caractère* to make more agreeable, smooth the rough edges off; *voyelle* to round, make rounded; *jupe* to level; *visage, taille, ventre* to fill out, round out. (*fig*) **essayer d'~ les angles** to try to smooth things over.

b (*accroître*) *fortune* to swell; *domaine* to increase, enlarge. ~ **ses fins de mois** to supplement one's income.

c (*simplifier*) *somme, nombre* to round off. ~ **au franc supérieur** to round up to the nearest franc; ~ **au franc inférieur** to round down to the nearest franc.

2 **s'arrondir vpr** *[relief]* to become round(ed); *[taille, joues, ventre, personne]* to fill out; *[fortune]* to swell.

arrondissement [aʀɔ̃dismɑ̃] **nm** a (*Admin*) district.

b *[voyelle]* rounding; *[fortune]* swelling; *[taille, ventre]* rounding, filling out.

arrosage [aʀozaʒ] **nm** *[pelouse]* watering; *[voie publique]* spraying; *voir* **lance, tuyau**.

arroser [aʀoze] 1 **vt** a *[personne] plante, terre* (*gén*) to water; (*avec un tuyau*) to hose, water, spray; (*légèrement*) to sprinkle; *rôti* to baste. ~ **qch d'essence** to pour petrol over sth.

b *[pluie] terre* to water; *personne* (*légèrement*) to make wet; (*fortement*) to drench, soak. **Rouen est la ville la plus arrosée de France** Rouen is the wettest city *ou* the city with the highest rainfall in France; **se faire ~** to get drenched *ou* soaked.

c (*Géog*) *[fleuve]* to water.

d (*Mil*) (*avec fusil, balles*) to spray (*de* with); (*avec canon*) to bombard (*de* with). **leurs mitrailleuses/projectiles arrosèrent notre patrouille** they sprayed *ou* peppered our patrol with machine-gun fire/bullets.

e (*) *événement, succès* to drink to; *repas* to wash down (with wine)*; *café* to lace (with a spirit). **après un repas bien arrosé** after a meal washed down with plenty of wine; **tu as gagné, ça s'arrose!** you've won — that deserves a drink! *ou* we must drink to that!

f (**: soudoyer*) to grease *ou* oil the palm of.

g (*littér*) *[sang]* to soak. **visage arrosé de larmes** face bathed in *ou* awash with (*littér*) tears; ~ **de ses larmes une photographie** to bathe a photograph in tears, let one's tears fall upon a photograph; **terre arrosée de sang** blood-soaked earth.

arroseur [aʀozœʀ] **nm** a *[jardin]* waterer; *[rue]* water cartman. **c'est l'~ arrosé** his trick has backfired on him. b (*tourniquet*) sprinkler.

arroseuse [aʀozøz] **nf** *[rue]* water cart.

arrosoir [aʀozwaʀ] **nm** watering can.

arrt abrév de arrondissement.

arsenal, pl -aux [aʀsənal, o] **nm** (*stock, manufacture d'armes*) arsenal; *[mesures, lois]* arsenal; (**: attirail*) gear* (*NonC*), paraphernalia (*NonC*). **l'~ du pêcheur/du photographe** the gear *ou* paraphernalia of the fisherman/photographer; **tout un ~ de vieux outils** a huge collection *ou* assortment of old tools; (*Naut*) ~ **(de la marine** *ou* **maritime)** naval dockyard.

arsenic [aʀsənik] **nm** arsenic. **empoisonnement à l'~** arsenic poisoning.

arsenical, e, mpl -aux [aʀsənikal, o] **adj** *substance* arsenical.

arsénieux [aʀsenjø] **adj m** arsenic (*épith*). **oxyde** *ou* **anhydride ~** arsenic trioxide, arsenic.

arsouille† [aʀsuj] **nm ou nf** (*voyou*) ruffian. **il a un air ~** (*voyou*) he looks like a ruffian; (*malin*) he looks crafty.

art[1] [aʀ] 1 **nm** a (*esthétique*) art. **l'~ espagnol/populaire/nègre** Spanish/popular/black art; **les ~s plastiques** the visual arts, the fine arts; **l'~ pour l'~** art for art's sake; **livre/critique d'~** art book/critic; **aimer/protéger les ~s** to love/protect the arts; **c'est du grand ~!** (*activité*) it's poetry in motion!; (*tableau exécrable*) it's a work of art! (*iro*); (*travail excellent*) it's an excellent piece of work!; *voir* **amateur, beau, huitième** *etc*.

b (*technique*) art. ~ **culinaire/militaire/oratoire** the art of cooking/of warfare/of public speaking; **il est passé maître dans l'~ de faire rire** he's a past master in the art of making people laugh; **un homme/les gens de l'~** a man/the people in the profession; **demandons à un homme de l'~!** let's ask a professional!; *voir* **règle**.

c (*adresse*) *[artisan]* skill, artistry; *[poète]* skill, art, artistry. **faire qch avec un ~ consommé** to do sth with consummate skill; **il faut tout un ~ pour faire cela** doing that is quite an art, there's quite an art (involved) in doing that; **il a l'~ et la manière** he's got the know-how and he does it in style, he has both (great) skill and (great) style in what he does.

d **l'~ de faire qch** the art of doing sth, a talent *ou* flair for doing sth, the knack of doing sth*; **il a l'~ de me mettre en colère** he has a flair *ou* a talent for *ou* a knack of making me angry; **ce style a l'~ de me plaire** this style appeals to me; (*iro*) **ça a l'~ de m'endormir** it has the knack of sending me to sleep; **il y a un ~ de faire ceci** there's quite an art in doing this; **réapprendre l'~ de marcher** to re-learn the art of walking.

2 comp ▸**arts d'agrément** accomplishments ▸**arts appliqués** = **arts décoratifs** ▸**art déco** art deco ▸**arts décoratifs** decorative arts ▸**l'art dramatique** dramatic art, drama ▸**les arts du feu** ceramics ▸**les arts libéraux** the (seven) liberal arts ▸**arts martiaux** martial arts ▸**arts mécaniques** mechanical arts ▸**arts ménagers** (*technique*) home economics, homecraft (*NonC*), domestic science; **les Arts Ménagers** (*salon*) ≃ the Ideal Home Exhibition ▸**arts et métiers** applied *ou* industrial arts and crafts ▸**art nouveau** art nouveau ▸**art poétique** (*technique*) poetic art; (*doctrine*) ars poetica, poetics (*sg*) ▸**les arts de la scène** the performing arts ▸**art de vivre** art of living.

art[2] (**abrév de article**) art.

artefact [aʀtefakt] **nm** artefact.

Artémis [aʀtemis] **nf** Artemis.

artère [aʀtɛʀ] **nf** (*Anat*) artery. (*Aut*) **(grande) ~** (*en ville*) main road, thoroughfare; (*entre villes*) main (trunk) road.

artériel, -ielle [aʀteʀjɛl] **adj** (*Anat*) arterial; *voir* **tension**.

artériole [aʀteʀjɔl] **nf** arteriole.

artériosclérose [aʀteʀjoskleʀoz] **nf** arteriosclerosis.

artérite [aʀteʀit] **nf** arteritis.

artésien, -ienne [aʀtezjɛ̃, jɛn] **adj** Artois (*épith*), of *ou* from Artois; *voir* **puits**.

arthrite [aʀtʀit] **nf** arthritis. **avoir de l'~** to have arthritis.

arthritique [aʀtʀitik] **adj, nmf** arthritic.

arthritisme [aʀtʀitism] **nm** arthritism.

arthrodie [aʀtʀɔdi] **nf** gliding joint.

arthropode [aʀtʀɔpɔd] **nm** arthropod.

arthrose [aʀtʀoz] **nf** (degenerative) osteoarthritis.

Arthur [aʀtyʀ] **nm** Arthur; *voir* **appeler**.

artichaut [aʀtiʃo] **nm** artichoke; *voir* **cœur**.

article [aʀtikl] 1 **nm** a (*Comm*) item, article. **baisse sur tous nos ~s** all (our) stock *ou* all items reduced, reduction on all items; **~ d'importation** imported product; **nous ne faisons plus cet ~** we don't stock that item *ou* product any more; **faire l'~** (*pour vendre qch*) to give the sales pitch; (*fig*) to sing sth's *ou* sb's praises.

b (*Presse*) *[revue, journal]* article; *[dictionnaire]* entry.

c (*chapitre*) point; *[loi, traité]* article. **les 2 derniers ~s de cette lettre** the last 2 points in this letter; **pour** *ou* **sur cet ~** on this point; **sur l'~ de** in the matter of, in matters of.

d (*Gram*) article. **~ contracté/défini/élidé/indéfini/partitif** contracted/definite/elided/indefinite/partitive article.

e (*Ordin*) record, item.

f **à l'~ de la mort** at the point of death.

2 comp ▸**article d'appel** loss leader ▸**articles de bureau** office accessories ▸**articles de consommation courante** convenience goods ▸**article de foi** article of faith; **il prend ces recommandations pour articles de foi** for him these recommendations are articles of faith ▸**article de fond** (*Presse*) feature article ▸**articles de luxe** luxury goods ▸**articles de mode** fashion accessories ▸**articles de Paris** fancy goods ▸**article réclame** special offer ▸**articles de toilette** toiletries, toilet requisites *ou* articles ▸**articles de voyage** travel goods *ou* requisites; *voir* **pilote**.

articulaire [aʀtikylɛʀ] **adj** articular; *voir* **rhumatisme**.

articulation [aʀtikylasjɔ̃] **nf** a (*Anat*) joint; (*Tech*) articulation. **~s des doigts** knuckles, joints of the fingers; **~ du genou/de la hanche/de l'épaule** *etc* knee/hip/shoulder *etc* joint; **~ en selle** saddle joint. b (*fig*) *[discours, raisonnement]* linking sentence. **la bonne ~ des parties de son discours** the sound structuring of his speech. c (*Ling*) articulation. **point d'~** point of articulation. d (*Jur*) enumeration, setting forth.

articulatoire [aʀtikylatwaʀ] **adj** articulatory.

articulé, e [aʀtikyle] (**ptp de articuler**) 1 **adj** *langage* articulate(d); *membre* jointed, articulated; *objet* jointed; *poupée* with movable joints (*épith*). **autobus ~** articulated bus. 2 **nmpl** (*Zool*) **les ~s** the Arthropoda.

articuler [aʀtikyle] [1] **vt** a *mot* (*prononcer clairement*) to articulate, pronounce clearly; (*dire*) to pronounce, utter. **il articule bien/mal ses phrases** he articulates *ou* speaks/doesn't articulate *ou* speak clearly; **il articule mal** he doesn't articulate (his words) *ou* speak clearly; **articule!** speak clearly!

b (*joindre*) *mécanismes, os* to articulate, joint; *idées* to link (up *ou* together). **élément/os qui s'articule sur un autre** element/bone that is articulated with *ou* is jointed to another; **~ un discours sur deux thèmes principaux** to structure a speech round *ou* on two main themes; **toute sa défense s'articule autour de cet élément** his entire defence hinges *ou* turns on this factor; **les parties de son discours s'articulent bien** the different sections of his speech are well linked *ou* hang together well; **une grande salle autour de laquelle s'articulent une multitude de locaux** a large room surrounded by a multitude of offices.

c (*Jur*) *faits, griefs* to enumerate, set out.

artifice [aʀtifis] **nm** (artful *ou* clever *ou* ingenious) device, trick; (*péj*) trick, artifice. **~ de calcul** (clever) trick of arithmetic; **~ de style** stylistic device *ou* trick; **les femmes usent d'~s pour paraître belles** women use artful *ou* ingenious devices *ou* tricks to make themselves look beautiful; **l'~ est une nécessité de l'art** art cannot exist without (some) artifice; *voir* **feu**[1].

artificiel, -ielle [aʀtifisjɛl] **adj** (*gén*) artificial; *fibre* man-made; *soie* artificial; *colorant* artificial, synthetic; *dent* false; *bijou, fleur* artificial, imitation; *raisonnement, style* artificial, contrived; *vie, besoins* artificial; *gaieté* forced, unnatural.

artificiellement [aʀtifisjɛlmɑ̃] **adv** artificially. **fabriqué ~** man-made, synthetically made.

artificier [aʀtifisje] **nm** (*fabricant*) pyrotechnist; (*désamorçage*) bomb disposal expert.

artificieusement [aʀtifisjøzmɑ̃] **adv** (*littér*) guilefully, deceitfully.

artificieux, -ieuse [aʀtifisjø, jøz] **adj** (*littér*) guileful, deceitful.

artillerie [aʀtijʀi] **nf** artillery, ordnance. **~ de campagne** field artillery; **~ de marine** naval guns; (*lit, fig*) **grosse ~, ~ lourde** heavy artillery; **pièce d'~** piece of artillery, ordnance (*NonC*); **tir d'~** artillery fire.

artilleur [aʀtijœʀ] **nm** artilleryman, gunner.

artimon [aʀtimɔ̃] **nm** (*voile*) mizzen; (*mât*) mizzen(mast); *voir* **mât**.

artisan [aʀtizɑ̃] **nm** (self-employed) craftsman, artisan. **~ de la paix** peacemaker; **être l'~ de la victoire** to be the architect of victory; **il est l'~ de sa propre ruine** he has brought about *ou* he is the author of his own ruin.

artisanal, e, **mpl -aux** [aʀtizanal, o] **adj**: **activité ~e** craft work; **profession ~e** craft, craft industry; **retraite ~e** pension for self-employed craftsmen; **la fabrication se fait encore de manière très ~e** the style of production is still very much that of a cottage industry; **bombe de fabrication ~e** home-made bomb; **produits artisanaux** crafts, handicrafts.

artisanalement [aʀtizanalmɑ̃] **adv** by craftsmen.

artisanat [aʀtizana] **nm** (*métier*) craft industry; (*classe sociale*) artisans, artisan class. **l'~ local** (*industrie*) local crafts *ou* handicrafts.

artiste [aʀtist] 1 **nmf** a (*gén: musicien, cantatrice, sculpteur etc*) artist. **~ peintre** artist, painter; (*hum*) **~ capillaire** hair artiste; **les ~s quittèrent la salle de concert** the performers *ou* artists left the concert hall; *voir* **travail**.

b (*Ciné, Théât*) (*acteur*) actor (*ou* actress); (*chanteur*) singer; (*fantaisiste*) entertainer; *[music-hall, cirque]* artiste, entertainer. **~ dramatique/de cinéma** stage/film actor; **~-interprète** *[musique]* composer and performer; *[chanson, pièce]* writer and performer; **~ invité** *ou* **en représentation** guest soloist; **les ~s saluèrent** the performers took a bow; *voir* **entrée**.

c (*péj*) (*bohème*) bohemian; (*fantaisiste*) eccentric.

2 **adj** *personne, style* artistic. (*péj*) **il est du genre ~** he's the artistic *ou* bohemian type.

artistement [aʀtistəmɑ̃] **adv** artistically.

artistique [aʀtistik] **adj** artistic.

artistiquement [aʀtistikmɑ̃] **adv** artistically.

arum [aʀɔm] **nm** arum lily.

aryen, -yenne [aʀjɛ̃, jɛn] 1 **adj** Aryan. 2 **nm,f**: **A~(ne)** Aryan.

arythmie [aʀitmi] **nf** arrhythmia.

AS [aɛs] 1 **nfpl** (**abrév de assurances sociales**) *voir* **assurance**. 2 **nf** (**abrév de association sportive**) *voir* **association**.

as [ɑs] **nm** a (*carte, dé*) ace. (*Hippisme, loto*) **l'~** number one.

b (*fig: champion*) ace*. **un ~ de la route/du ciel** a crack driver/pilot; **l'~ de l'école** the school's star pupil.

c (*Tennis*) ace. **réussir** *ou* **servir un ~** to serve an ace.

d (*loc*) **être ficelé** *ou* **fagoté comme l'~ de pique*** to be dressed (all) anyhow*; **être (plein) aux ~‡** to be loaded*, be rolling in it*; **passer à l'~‡**: (*au restaurant*) **les apéritifs sont passés à l'~** we got away without paying for the drinks, we got the drinks for free*; **avec toutes les dépenses que l'on a faites, les vacances sont passées à l'~** with all the expense we'd had the holidays had to go by the board *ou* the holidays were completely written off*; **cet appareil ne marche pas, voilà 2 000 F passés à l'~** this camera doesn't work so that's 2,000 francs written off* *ou* 2,000 francs down the drain*.

ASA [aza] **nm** (*Phot*) ASA.

asbeste [asbɛst] **nm** asbestos.

asbestose [asbɛstoz] **nf** asbestosis.

ASBL [aɛsbeɛl] **nf** (**abrév de association sans but lucratif**) *voir* **association**.

ascendance [asɑ̃dɑ̃s] **nf** a (*généalogique*) ancestry. **son ~ paternelle** his paternal ancestry; **être d'~ bourgeoise** to be of middle-class descent. b (*Astron*) rising, ascent. (*Phys*) **~ thermique** thermal.

ascendant, e [asɑ̃dɑ̃, ɑ̃t] 1 **adj** *astre* rising, ascending; *mouvement, direction* upward; *progression* ascending; *trait* rising, mounting; (*Généalogie*) *ligne* ancestral. **mouvement ~ du piston** upstroke of the piston. 2 **nm** a (*influence*) (powerful) influence, ascendancy (*sur* over). **subir l'~ de qn** to be under sb's influence. b (*Admin*) **~s** ascendants. c (*Astron*) rising star; (*Astrol*) ascendant.

ascenseur [asɑ̃sœʀ] **nm** lift (*Brit*), elevator (*US*); *voir* **renvoyer**.

ascension [asɑ̃sjɔ̃] **nf** a *[ballon]* ascent, rising; *[fusée]* ascent; *[homme politique]* rise; (*sociale*) rise. (*Rel*) **l'A~** the Ascension; (*jour férié*) Ascension (Day); **l'île de l'A~** Ascension Island; (*Astron*) **~ droite** right ascension; ~ **professionnelle** professional advancement. b *[montagne]* ascent. **faire l'~ d'une montagne** to climb a mountain, make the ascent of a mountain; **la première ~ de l'Everest** the first ascent of Everest; **c'est une ~ difficile** it's a difficult climb; **faire des ~s** to go (mountain) climbing.

ascensionnel, -elle [asɑ̃sjɔnɛl] **adj** *mouvement* upward; *force* upward, elevatory. **vitesse ~le** climbing speed.

ascensionniste [asɑ̃sjɔnist] **nmf** ascensionist.

ascèse [asɛz] **nf** asceticism.

ascète [asɛt] **nmf** ascetic.

ascétique [asetik] **adj** ascetic.

ascétisme [asetism] **nm** asceticism.

ASCII [aski] **nm** ASCII. **code ~** ASCII code.

ascorbique [askɔʀbik] **adj** *acide* ascorbic.

ASE [aɛsə] **nf** (**abrév de Agence spatiale européenne**) ESA.

asémantique [asemɑ̃tik] **adj** asemantic.

asepsie [asɛpsi] **nf** asepsis.

aseptique [asɛptik] **adj** aseptic.

aseptisation [asɛptizasjɔ̃] **nf** (*voir* **aseptiser**) fumigation; sterilization; disinfection.

aseptiser [asɛptize] 1 **vt** *pièce* to fumigate; *pansement, ustensile* to sterilize; *plaie* to disinfect. **aseptisé** *roman* lifeless, sterile; *décor* cold.

asexué, e [asɛksɥe] **adj** (*Bio*) asexual; *personne* sexless, asexual.

ashkénaze [aʃkenɑz] **adj, nmf** Ashkenazi.

Asiate [azjat] **nmf** Asian.

asiatique [azjatik] 1 **adj** Asian. **la grippe ~** Asian flu. 2 **nmf: A~** Asian.

Asie [azi] **nf** Asia. ~ **Mineure** Asia Minor; ~ **centrale** Central Asia; ~ **du Sud-Est** Southeast Asia.

asile [azil] **nm** a (*institution*) ~ **(de vieillards)** old people's home, retirement home; ~ **(d'aliénés)** (lunatic) asylum; ~ **de nuit** night shelter, hostel, doss house* (*Brit*). b (*lit, fig: refuge*) refuge, sanctuary; (*Pol*) asylum. **sans ~** homeless; **droit d'~** (*Hist*) right of sanctuary; (*Pol*) right of asylum; ~ **de paix** haven of peace, peaceful retreat; **demander/donner ~** to seek/provide sanctuary (*Hist*) *ou* asylum (*Pol*) *ou* refuge (*gén*).

asocial, e, **mpl -iaux** [asɔsjal, jo] 1 **adj** *comportement* antisocial. 2 **nm,f** social misfit, socially maladjusted person.

asparagus [aspaʀagys] **nm** asparagus fern.

aspartam(e) [aspaʀtam] **nm** aspartame.

aspect [aspɛ] **nm** a (*allure*) *[personne]* look, appearance; *[objet, paysage]* appearance, look. **homme d'~ sinistre** sinister-looking man, man of sinister appearance; **l'intérieur de cette grotte a l'~ d'une église** the inside of this cave resembles *ou* looks like a church; **les nuages prenaient l'~ de montagnes** the clouds took on the appearance of mountains; **ce château a un ~ mystérieux** this castle has a look *ou* an air of mystery (about it).

b (*angle*) *[question]* aspect, side. **vu sous cet ~** seen from that angle *ou* side, seen in that light; **sous tous ses ~s** in all its aspects, from all its sides.

c (*Astrol, Ling*) aspect.

d (*littér: vue*) sight. **à l'~ de** at the sight of.

asperge [aspɛʀʒ] **nf** a (*Bot*) asparagus; *voir* **pointe**. b (*: *personne*) **(grande)** ~ beanpole*, string bean* (*US*).

asperger [aspɛʀʒe] 3 **vt** *surface* to spray, (*légèrement*) to sprinkle; *personne* to splash (*de* with). **s'~ le visage** to splash one's face with water; **le bus nous a aspergés au passage*** the bus splashed us *ou* sprayed water over us as it went past; **se faire ~*** (*par une voiture*) to get splashed.

aspérité [aspeʀite] **nf** a (*partie saillante*) bump. **les ~s de la table** the bumps on the table, the rough patches on the surface of the table. b (*littér*) *[caractère, remarques, voix]* harshness.

aspersion [aspɛʀsjɔ̃] **nf** spraying, sprinkling; (*Rel*) sprinkling of holy water, aspersion.

asphalte [asfalt] **nm** asphalt.

asphalter [asfalte] 1 **vt** to asphalt.

asphodèle [asfɔdɛl] **nm** asphodel.

asphyxiant, e [asfiksjɑ̃, jɑ̃t] **adj** *fumée* suffocating, asphyxiating; *atmosphère* stifling, suffocating; *voir* **gaz**.

asphyxie [asfiksi] **nf** (*gén*) suffocation, asphyxiation; (*Méd*) asphyxia; *[plante]* asphyxiation; (*fig*) *[personne]* suffocation; *[industrie]* stifling.

asphyxier [asfiksje] 7 1 **vt** (*lit*) to suffocate, asphyxiate; (*fig*) *industrie, esprit* to stifle. **mourir asphyxié** to die of suffocation *ou* asphyxiation. 2 **s'asphyxier vpr** (*accident*) to suffocate, asphyxiate, be asphyxiated; (*suicide*) to suffocate o.s.; (*fig*) to suffocate. **il s'est asphyxié au gaz** he gassed himself.

aspic [aspik] **nm** (*Zool*) asp; (*Bot*) aspic; (*Culin*) meat (*ou* fish *etc*) in aspic. ~ **de volaille** chicken in aspic.

aspirant, e [aspiʀɑ̃, ɑ̃t] 1 **adj** suction (*épith*), vacuum (*épith*); *voir* **pompe**[1]. 2 **nm,f** (*candidat*) candidate (*à* for). 3 **nm** (*Mil*) officer cadet; (*Naut*) midshipman, middie* (*US*).

aspirateur, -trice [aspiʀatœʀ, tʀis] 1 **adj** aspiratory. 2 **nm** (*domestique*) vacuum cleaner, Hoover ® (*Brit*); (*Constr, Méd etc*) aspirator. **passer les tapis à l'~** to vacuum *ou* hoover the carpets, run the vacuum cleaner *ou* Hoover over the carpets; **passer l'~** to vacuum, hoover; **passer un coup d'~ dans la voiture** to give the car a quick going-over with the vacuum cleaner *ou* Hoover.

aspiration [aspiʀasjɔ̃] **nf** a (*en inspirant*) inhaling (*NonC*), inhalation, breathing in (*NonC*); (*Ling*) aspiration. **de longues ~s** long deep breaths. b *[liquide]* (*avec une paille*) sucking (up); (*gén, Tech: avec une pompe etc*) sucking up, drawing up, suction; (*technique d'avortement*) vacuum extraction. c (*ambition*) aspiration (*vers, à* for, after); (*souhait*) desire, longing (*vers, à* for).

aspiré, e [aspiʀe] (**ptp de aspirer**) 1 **adj** (*Ling*) aspirated. **h ~** aspirate h. 2 **aspirée nf** aspirate.

aspirer [aspiʀe] 1 1 **vt** a *air, odeur* to inhale, breathe in; *liquide* (*avec une paille*) to suck (up); (*Tech: avec une pompe etc*) to suck *ou* draw up. ~ **et refouler** to pump in and out. b (*Ling*) to aspirate. 2 **aspirer à vt indir** *honneur, titre* to aspire to; *genre de vie, tranquillité* to desire, long for. **aspirant à quitter cette vie surexcitée** longing to leave this hectic life; ~ **à la main de qn**† to be sb's suitor†, aspire to sb's hand†.

aspirine [aspiʀin] **nf** aspirin. **(comprimé *ou* cachet d')~** aspirin; **prenez 2 ~s** take 2 aspirins; *voir* **blanc**.

aspiro-batteur, **pl aspiro-batteurs** [aspiʀobatœʀ] **nm** vacuum cleaner (*which beats as it sucks*).

assagir [asaʒiʀ] 2 1 **vt** a (*calmer*) *personne* to quieten (*Brit*) *ou* quiet (*US*) down, settle down; *passion* to subdue, temper, quieten (*Brit*), quiet (*US*). **n'arrivant pas à ~ ses cheveux rebelles** not managing to tame her rebellious hair. b (*littér: rendre plus sage*) to make wiser. 2 **s'assagir vpr** *[personne]* to quieten (*Brit*) *ou* quiet (*US*) down, settle down; *[style, passions]* to become subdued.

assagissement [asaʒismɑ̃] **nm** *[personne]* quietening (*Brit*) *ou* quieting (*US*) down, settling down; *[passions]* subduing.

assaillant, e [asajɑ̃, ɑ̃t] **nm,f** assailant, attacker.

assaillir [asajiʀ] 13 **vt** (*lit*) to assail, attack; (*fig*) to assail (*de* with). **il fut assailli de questions** he was assailed *ou* bombarded with questions.

assainir [aseniʀ] 2 **vt** *quartier, logement* to clean up, improve the living conditions in; *marécage* to drain; *air, eau* to purify, decontaminate; *finances, marché* to stabilize; *monnaie* to rehabilitate, re-establish. **la situation s'est assainie** the situation has become healthier; (*fig*) ~ **l'atmosphère** to clear the air.

assainissement [asenismɑ̃] **nm** (*voir* **assainir**) cleaning up; draining; purification; decontamination; stabilization. ~ **monétaire** rehabilitation *ou* re-establishment of the currency.

assaisonnement [asɛzɔnmɑ̃] **nm** (*méthode*) *[salade]* dressing, seasoning; *[plat]* seasoning; (*ingrédient*) seasoning.

assaisonner [asɛzɔne] 1 **vt** (*Culin*) to season, add seasoning to; *salade* to dress, season; (*fig*) *conversation etc* to spice, give zest to. **le citron assaisonne bien la salade** lemon is a good dressing for *ou* on a salad; ~ **qn**‡ (*physiquement*) to knock sb about*, give sb a thumping‡; (*verbalement*) to give sb a telling off*, tell sb off*, bawl sb out*; (*financièrement*) to clobber sb‡, sting sb‡.

assassin, e [asasɛ̃, in] 1 **adj** *œillade* provocative. 2 **nm** (*gén*) murderer; (*Pol*) assassin; (*Presse etc*) killer*, murderer. **l'~ court toujours** the killer* *ou* murderer is still at large; **à l'~!** murder!

assassinat [asasina] **nm** murder; (*Pol*) assassination.

assassiner [asasine] 1 **vt** to murder; (*Pol*) to assassinate. **mes créanciers m'assassinent!*** my creditors are bleeding me white!*

assaut [aso] **nm** (*Mil*) assault, attack (*de* on); (*Boxe, Escrime*) bout; (*Alpinisme*) assault. **donner l'~ à** to storm, attack, launch an attack on; **ils donnent l'~** they're attacking; **résister aux ~s de l'ennemi** to resist the enemy's attacks *ou* onslaughts; **partir à l'~ de** (*lit*) to attack, charge; (*fig*) **de petites firmes qui sont parties à l'~ d'un marché international** small firms who have set out to take the international market by storm *ou* to capture the international market; **prendre d'~** to take by storm, assault; (*fig*) **prendre une place d'~** to grab a seat; **les librairies étaient prises d'~** the bookshops were stormed by the public; **ils faisaient ~ de politesse** they were vying with each other *ou* rivalling each other in politeness; *voir* **char**.

assèchement [asɛʃmɑ̃] **nm** (*voir* **assécher**) draining; drainage, emptying; drying (out); drying (up); drying.

assécher [aseʃe] 6 **vt** *terrain* to drain; *réservoir* to drain, empty; *[vent, évaporation] terrain* to dry (out); *réservoir* to dry (up); *peau* to dry.

ASSEDIC [asedik] **nfpl** (**abrév de Associations pour l'emploi dans l'industrie et le commerce**) *organization managing unemployment insurance payments*.

assemblage [asɑ̃blaʒ] **nm** a (*action*) *[éléments, parties]* assembling, putting together; (*Menuiserie*) assembling, jointing; *[meuble, maquette, machine]* assembling, assembly; (*Ordin*) assembly; (*Typ*) *[feuilles]* gathering; (*Couture*) *[pièces]* sewing together; *[robe, pull-over]* sewing together *ou* up, making up. ~ **de pièces par soudure/collage** soldering/glueing together of parts.

b (*Menuiserie: jointure*) joint. ~ **à vis/par rivets/à onglet** screwed/rivet(ed)/mitre joint.

c (*structure*) **une charpente est un ~ de poutres** the framework of a roof is an assembly of beams; **toit fait d'~s métalliques** roof made of metal structures.

d (*réunion*) *[couleurs, choses, personnes]* collection.
e (*Art: tableau etc*) assemblage.

assemblé [asɑ̃ble] **nm** (*Danse*) assemblé.

assemblée [asɑ̃ble] **nf** (*gén: réunion, foule*) gathering; (*réunion convoquée*) meeting; (*Pol*) assembly. (*Rel*) **l'~ des fidèles** the congregation; **~ mensuelle/extraordinaire/plénière** monthly/extraordinary/plenary meeting; **~ générale** (*Écon*) annual general meeting; *[étudiants]* (extraordinary) general meeting; **~ générale extraordinaire** extraordinary general meeting; **réunis en ~** gathered *ou* assembled for a meeting; **à la grande joie de l'~** to the great joy of the assembled company *ou* of those present; **l'A~ nationale** the French National Assembly; **A~ parlementaire européenne** European Parliament; (*Pol*) **~ délibérante** deliberating assembly.

assembler [asɑ̃ble] 1 **1 vt a** (*réunir*) *données, matériaux* to gather (together), collect (together); (*Pol*) *comité* to convene, assemble; (†) *personnes* to assemble, gather (together); (*Typ*) *feuilles* to gather. (*Pol*) **les chambres assemblées ont voté la loi** the assembled chambers passed the law; (*Danse*) **~ les pieds** to take up third position; **l'amour les assemble†** love unites them (together) *ou* binds them together.
b (*joindre*) *idées, meuble, machine, puzzle* to assemble, put together; *pull, robe* to sew together *ou* up, make up; (*Menuiserie*) to assemble, joint; *couleurs, sons* to put together. **~ par soudure/collage** to solder/glue together.
2 s'assembler vpr *[foule]* to gather, collect; *[participants, conseil, groupe]* to assemble, gather; (*fig*) *[nuages]* to gather; *voir* **qui**.

assembleur, -euse [asɑ̃blœʀ, øz] **1 nm,f** (*ouvrier*) (*gén*) assembler, fitter; (*Typ*) gatherer. **2 nm** (*Ordin*) assembler. **3 assembleuse nf** (*Typ: machine*) gathering machine.

assener, asséner [asene] 5 **vt** *coup* to strike; (*fig*) *argument* to thrust forward; *propagande* to deal out; *réplique* to thrust *ou* fling back. **~ un coup à qn** to deal sb a blow.

assentiment [asɑ̃timɑ̃] **nm** (*consentement*) assent, consent; (*approbation*) approval. **donner son ~ à** to give one's assent *ou* consent *ou* approval to.

asseoir [aswaʀ] 26 **1 vt a ~ qn** (*personne debout*) to sit sb down; (*personne couchée*) to sit sb up; **~ qn sur une chaise/dans un fauteuil** to sit *ou* put sb on a chair/in an armchair, seat sb on a chair/in an armchair; **~ un enfant sur ses genoux** to sit *ou* take a child on one's knee; (*fig*) **~ un prince sur le trône** to put *ou* set a prince on the throne.
b faire ~ qn to ask sb to sit down; **faire ~ ses invités** to ask one's guests to sit down *ou* to take a seat; **je leur ai parlé après les avoir fait ~** I talked to them after asking them to sit down; **fais-la ~, elle est fatiguée** get her to sit down, she is tired.
c être assis to be sitting *ou* seated; **reste assis!** (*ne bouge pas*) sit still!; (*ne te lève pas*) don't get up!; **nous sommes restés assis pendant des heures** we sat *ou* remained seated for hours; **ils restèrent assis pendant l'hymne national** they remained seated during the national anthem; **nous étions très bien/mal assis** (*sur des chaises*) we had very comfortable/uncomfortable seats; (*par terre*) we were very comfortably/uncomfortably seated, we were sitting very comfortably/uncomfortably; **assis en tailleur** sitting cross-legged; **assis à califourchon sur** sitting astride, straddling; *voir* **entre**.
d (*frm*) (*affermir*) *réputation* to establish, assure; *autorité, théorie* to establish. **~ une maison sur du granit** to build a house on granite; **~ les fondations sur** to lay *ou* build the foundations on; **~ sa réputation sur qch** to build one's reputation on sth; **~ une théorie sur des faits** to base a theory on facts; **~ son jugement sur des témoignages dignes de foi** to base one's judgment on reliable evidence.
e (**: stupéfier*) to stagger, stun. **son inconscience m'assoit** his foolishness staggers me, I'm stunned by his foolishness; **j'en suis *ou* reste assis de voir que** I'm staggered *ou* stunned *ou* flabbergasted* to see that.
f (*Fin*) **~ un impôt** to base a tax, fix a tax.
2 s'asseoir vpr to sit (o.s.) down; *[personne couchée]* to sit up. **asseyez-vous donc** do sit down, do have *ou* take a seat; **asseyez-vous par terre** sit (down) on the floor; **il n'y a rien pour s'~** there is nothing to sit on; **le règlement, je m'assieds dessus!*** you know what you can do with the rule!‡; **s'~ à califourchon (sur qch)** to sit (down) astride (sth); **s'~ en tailleur** to sit (down) cross-legged.

assermenté, e [asɛʀmɑ̃te] **adj** *témoin, expert* on oath (*attrib*).

assertif, -ive [asɛʀtif, iv] **adj** *phrase etc* declarative.

assertion [asɛʀsjɔ̃] **nf** assertion.

asservi, e [asɛʀvi] (**ptp de asservir**) **adj** *peuple* enslaved; *presse* subservient. **moteur ~** servomotor.

asservir [asɛʀviʀ] 2 **vt** (*assujettir*) *personne* to enslave; *pays* to reduce to slavery, subjugate; (*littér: maîtriser*) *passions, nature* to overcome, master. **être asservi à** to be a slave to.

asservissement [asɛʀvismɑ̃] **nm** (*action*) enslavement; (*lit, fig: état*) slavery, subservience (*à* to); (*Élec*) servo-control (*NonC*) (*à* by).

assesseur [asesœʀ] **nm** assessor.

assez [ase] **adv a** (*suffisamment, avec vb*) enough; (*devant adj, adv*) enough, sufficiently. **bien ~** quite enough, plenty; **tu as (bien) ~ mangé** you've had *ou* eaten (quite) enough, you've had (quite) enough *ou* plenty to eat; **c'est bien ~ grand** it's quite big enough; **plus qu'~** more than enough; **je n'ai pas ~ travaillé** I haven't worked (hard) enough, I haven't worked sufficiently (hard); **la maison est grande mais elle ne l'est pas ~ pour nous** the house is big but it is not big enough for us; **il ne vérifie pas ~ souvent** he does not check often enough; **tu travailles depuis ~ longtemps** you've been working (for) long enough; **ça a ~ duré!** it has gone on long enough!; **combien voulez-vous? est-ce que 5 F c'est ~? — c'est bien ~** how much do you want? is 5 francs enough? *ou* will 5 francs do? — that will be plenty *ou* ample *ou* that will be quite *ou* easily enough; **il a juste ~ pour s'acheter ce livre** he has just enough to buy himself that book; *voir* **peu**.
b ~ de (*quantité, nombre*) enough; **avez-vous acheté ~ de pain/d'oranges?** have you bought enough *ou* sufficient bread/enough oranges?; **il n'y a pas ~ de viande pour tout le monde** there is not enough meat to go round *ou* for everyone; **c'est ~ de lui à me critiquer sans que tu t'en mêles** it's quite enough his criticizing me without your joining in (too); **ils sont ~ de deux pour ce travail** the two of them are enough *ou* will do* for this job; **j'en ai ~ de 3** 3 will be enough for me *ou* will do (for) me*; **n'apportez pas de pain/verres, il y en a ~** don't bring any bread/glasses, there is/are enough *ou* we have enough.
c (*en corrélation avec pour*) enough. **as-tu trouvé une boîte ~ grande pour tout mettre?** have you found a big enough box *ou* a box big enough to put it all in?; **le village est ~ près pour qu'elle puisse y aller à pied** the village is near enough for her to walk there; **je n'ai pas ~ d'argent pour m'offrir cette voiture** I can't afford (to buy myself) this car, I haven't enough money to buy myself this car; **il est ~ idiot pour refuser!** he's stupid enough to refuse!; **il n'est pas ~ sot pour le croire** he is not so stupid as to believe him.
d (*intensif*) rather, quite, fairly, pretty*. **la situation est ~ inquiétante** the situation is rather *ou* somewhat *ou* pretty* disturbing; **ce serait ~ agréable d'avoir un jour de congé** it would be rather *ou* quite nice to have a day off; **il était ~ tard quand ils sont partis** it was quite *ou* fairly *ou* pretty* late when they left; **j'ai oublié son adresse, est-ce ~ bête!** how stupid (of me), I've forgotten his address!; **je l'ai ~ vu!** I have seen (more than) enough of him!; **elle était déjà ~ malade il y a 2 ans** she was already quite ill 2 years ago; **je suis ~ de ton avis** I think I agree with you.
e (*loc*) **en voilà ~!, c'est ~!, c'en est ~!** I've had enough!, enough is enough!; **~!** that will do!, that's (quite) enough!; **~ parlé *ou* de discours, des actes!** enough talk *ou* enough said, let's have some action!; **(en) avoir ~ de qch/qn** to have (had) enough *ou* be sick* of sth/sb, be fed up with sth/sb*; **j'en ai ~ de toi et de tes jérémiades*** I've had enough of *ou* I'm sick (and tired) of* *ou* I'm fed up with* you and your moaning.

assidu, e [asidy] **adj a** (*ponctuel*) *présence* regular. **c'est un élève ~** he's a regular (and attentive) pupil; **ouvrier ~** workman who is regular in his work. **b** (*appliqué*) *soin, effort* assiduous, unremitting; *travail* assiduous, constant, painstaking; *personne* assiduous, painstaking. **c** (*empressé*) *personne* assiduous *ou* unremitting in one's attention (*auprès de* to). **faire une cour ~e à qn** to be assiduous in one's attentions to sb, woo sb assiduously.

assiduité [asidɥite] **nf** (*ponctualité*) regularity; (*empressement*) attentiveness, assiduity (*à* to). **son ~ aux cours** his regular attendance at classes; **fréquenter le bistrot avec ~** to be a regular at the pub (*Brit*) *ou* bar (*US*); (*frm, hum*) **poursuivre une femme de ses ~s** to pester a woman with one's assiduous attentions (*hum*).

assidûment [asidymɑ̃] **adv** *fréquenter* faithfully, assiduously; *travailler* assiduously.

assiégeant, e [asjeʒɑ̃, ɑ̃t] **1 nm,f** besieger. **2 adj: les troupes ~es** the besieging troops.

assiégé, e [asjeʒe] (**ptp de assiéger**) **1 nm,f: les ~s** the besieged. **2 adj** *garnison, ville* besieged, under siege (*attrib*).

assiéger [asjeʒe] 3 *et* 6 **vt** (*Mil*) *ville* to besiege, lay siege to; *armée* to besiege; (*fig*) (*entourer*) *guichet, porte, personne* to mob, besiege; (*harceler*) to beset. **assiégé par l'eau/les flammes** hemmed in by water/flames; **à Noël les magasins étaient assiégés** the shops (*Brit*) *ou* stores (*US*) were mobbed at Christmas; **ces pensées/tentations qui m'assiègent** these thoughts/temptations that beset *ou* assail me.

assiette [asjɛt] **1 nf a** (*vaisselle, quantité*) plate. **le nez dans son ~** with his head bowed over his plate.
b (*équilibre*) *[cavalier]* seat; *[navire]* trim; *[colonne]* seating. (*Équitation*) **perdre son ~** to lose one's seat, be unseated; (*Équitation*) **avoir une bonne ~** to have a good seat, sit one's horse well; (*fig*) **il n'est pas dans son ~ aujourd'hui** he's not feeling (quite) himself today, he's (feeling) a bit off-colour (*Brit*) today.
c *[hypothèque]* property *ou* estate on which a mortgage is secured. **~ de l'impôt** tax base; **~ de la TVA** basis upon which VAT is assessed.
2 comp ▸assiette anglaise assorted cold meats **▸assiette au beurre** (*manège*) rotor; (*fig*) **c'est l'assiette au beurre** it's a cushy job* **▸assiette de charcuterie** assorted cold meats **▸assiette composée** mixed salad (*of cold meats and vegetables*) **▸assiette creuse** (soup) dish, soup plate **▸assiette à dessert** side plate **▸assiette garnie** assorted cold meats **▸assiette plate** (dinner) plate **▸assiette à soupe = assiette creuse**.

assiettée [asjete] **nf** (*gén*) plate(ful); *[soupe]* plate(ful), dish.

assignable [asiɲabl] **adj** (*attribuable*) *cause, origine* ascribable, attributable (*à* to).

assignat [asiɲa] **nm** *banknote used during the French Revolution.*

assignation [asiɲasjɔ̃] **nf** (*Jur*) *[parts]* assignation, allocation. ~ **(à comparaître)** *[prévenu]* summons; *[témoin]* subpoena; ~ **en justice** ≃ writ of summons; subpoena; ~ **à résidence** house arrest.

assigner [asiɲe] 1 **vt** a (*attribuer*) *part, place, rôle* to assign, allocate, allot; *valeur, importance* to attach, ascribe, allot; *cause, origine* to ascribe, attribute (*à* to). b (*affecter*) *somme, crédit* to allot, allocate (*à* to), earmark (*à* for). c (*fixer*) *limite, terme* to set, fix (*à* to). ~ **un objectif à qn** to set sb a goal. d (*Jur*) ~ **(à comparaître)** *prévenu* to summons; *témoin* to subpoena, summon; ~ **qn en justice** to issue a writ against sb, serve a writ on sb; ~ **qn à résidence** to put sb under house arrest.

assimilable [asimilabl] **adj** a *immigrant* easily assimilated; *connaissances* easily assimilated *ou* absorbed; *nourriture* assimilable, easily assimilated. **ces connaissances ne sont pas ~s par un enfant** this knowledge could not be assimilated by a child, a child could not assimilate *ou* take in this knowledge. b (*comparable à*) ~ **à** comparable to; **ce poste est ~ à celui de contremaître** this job is comparable to *ou* may be considered like that of a foreman.

assimilateur, -trice [asimilatœʀ, tʀis] **adj** assimilative, assimilating. **c'est un admirable ~** he has fine powers of assimilation.

assimilation [asimilasjɔ̃] **nf** a (*absorption: gén, fig*) assimilation. ~ **chlorophyllienne** photosynthesis. b (*comparaison*) **l'~ de ce bandit à un héros/à Napoléon est un scandale** it's a scandal making this criminal out to be a hero/to liken *ou* compare this criminal to Napoleon; **l'~ des techniciens supérieurs aux ingénieurs** the classification of top-ranking technicians as engineers, the inclusion of top-ranking technicians in the same category as engineers.

assimilé, e [asimile] (**ptp de assimiler**) 1 **adj** (*similaire*) comparable, similar. **ce procédé et les autres méthodes ~es** this process and the other comparable methods; (*Écon*) **produits ~s** allied products. 2 **nm** (*Mil*) *non-combatant ranking with the combatants.* **les fonctionnaires et ~s** civil servants and comparable categories.

assimiler [asimile] 1 1 **vt** a (*absorber*) (*gén*) to assimilate; *connaissances* to take in. **un élève qui assimile bien** a pupil who assimilates *ou* takes things in easily; **ses idées sont du Nietzsche mal assimilé** his ideas are just a few ill-digested notions (taken) from Nietzsche.

b ~ **qn/qch à** (*comparer à*) to liken *ou* compare sb/sth to; (*classer comme*) to class sb/sth as, put sb/sth into the category of; (*faire ressembler à*) to make sb/sth similar to; **il s'assimila, dans son discours, aux plus grands savants** in his speech, he likened himself to *ou* classed himself alongside the greatest scientists; **les jardinières d'enfants demandent à être assimilées à des institutrices** kindergarten teachers are asking to be classed as *ou* given the same status as primary school teachers.

2 **s'assimiler vpr** (*être absorbé, s'intégrer*) to assimilate, be assimilated (*à* into, by).

assis, e¹ [asi, iz] (**ptp de asseoir**) **adj** a *personne* sitting (down), seated. **position** *ou* **station ~e** sitting position; **demeurer** *ou* **rester ~** to remain seated; **restez ~** (please) don't get up; **être ~** *voir* **asseoir;** *voir* **magistrature, place.** b (*fig*) *situation* stable, firm; *personne* stable; *autorité* (well-)established.

Assise [asiz] **n** Assisi.

assise² [asiz] **nf** (*Constr*) course; (*Bio, Géol*) stratum; (*fig*) basis, foundation.

assises [asiz] **nfpl** (*Jur*) assizes; (*fig*) meeting; *[parti politique]* conference. **tenir ses ~** to hold one's meeting; **ce parti tient ses ~ à Nancy** this party holds its annual meeting *ou* conference at Nancy; *voir* **cour.**

assistanat [asistana] **nm** (*Scol*) assistantship; (*Sociol*) (*aide financière*) aid; (*prestations sociales*) benefit (*Brit*), welfare (*US*), (*péj*) handouts, charity.

assistance [asistɑ̃s] 1 **nf** a (*assemblée*) *[conférence]* audience; *[débat]* audience, house; *[meeting]* house; *[cérémonie]* gathering, audience; *[messe]* congregation.

b (*aide*) assistance. **donner/prêter ~ à qn** to give/lend sb assistance; ~ **aux anciens détenus** prisoner after-care.

c (*présence*) attendance.

2 **comp** ▸**assistance judiciaire** legal aid ▸**assistance médicale (gratuite)** (free) medical care ▸**Assistance publique: les services de l'Assistance publique** ≃ the health and social security services; **être à l'Assistance publique** to be in (state *ou* public) care; **enfant de l'Assistance (publique)** child in care; **les hôpitaux de l'Assistance publique** state- *ou* publicly-owned hospitals ▸**assistance respiratoire** artificial respiration ▸**assistance sociale** (*aide*) social aid; (*métier*) social work ▸**assistance technique** technical aid.

assistant, e [asistɑ̃, ɑ̃t] 1 **nm,f** (*gén, Scol*) assistant; (*Univ*) ≃ assistant lecturer (*Brit*), teaching assistant (*US*). **~e sociale** social worker; (*Scol*) school counsellor, school social worker; **~e maternelle** child minder; **l'~ du professeur** the teacher's aide; **~e de direction** management secretary; **le directeur et son ~e** the manager and his personal assistant *ou* his PA; *voir* **maître.** 2 **nmpl: les ~s** those present.

assisté, e [asiste] (**ptp de assister**) 1 **adj** (*Jur, Méd, Sociol*) receiving (State) aid; *freins* servo-assisted. **enfant ~** child in care; *fabrication, traduction etc* **~ par ordinateur** computer-aided, computer-assisted; *voir* **direction.** 2 **nm,f les ~s** (*recevant une aide financière*) people receiving aid; (*recevant des prestations sociales*) people receiving benefit (*Brit*) *ou* welfare (*US*); (*péj*) people receiving handouts *ou* charity.

assister [asiste] 1 1 **assister à vt indir** (*être présent à*) *cérémonie, conférence, messe* to be (present) at, attend; *match, spectacle* to be at; *événement* to be present at, witness. **on assiste à une montée du chômage** we are witnessing a rise in unemployment. 2 **vt** (*aider*) to assist; (*financièrement*) *démunis* to give aid to. (*frm*) ~ **qn dans ses derniers moments** to succour (*frm*) *ou* comfort sb in his last hour; ~ **les pauvres**† to minister to† *ou* assist the poor.

associatif, -ive [asɔsjatif, iv] **adj** associative. (*Math*) **opération ~ive** associative operation; **la vie ~ive** community life.

association [asɔsjasjɔ̃] **nf** a (*gén: société*) association, society; (*Comm, Écon*) partnership. (*Jur*) ~ **de malfaiteurs** criminal conspiracy; ~ **sportive** sports association; ~ **syndicale** property owners' syndicate; **A~ internationale du tourisme** International Tourism Association; ~ **à but lucratif** profit-making association; ~ **sans but lucratif** *ou* **à but non lucratif** non-profit-making (*Brit*) *ou* not-for-profit (*US*) association; **A~ (européenne) de libre-échange** (European) Free Trade Association.

b *[idées, images]* association; *[couleurs, intérêts]* combination.

c (*participation*) association, partnership. **l'~ de ces deux écrivains a été fructueuse** these two writers have had a very fruitful partnership; **son ~ à nos travaux dépendra de ...** his joining us in our undertaking will depend on ...; **travailler en ~** to work in partnership (*avec* with).

associationnisme [asɔsjasjɔnism] **nm** (*Philos*) associationism.

associationniste [asɔsjasjɔnist] **adj, nmf** associationist.

associé, e [asɔsje] (**ptp de associer**) **nm,f** (*gén*) associate; (*Comm, Fin*) partner, associate. ~ **principal** senior partner; *voir* **membre.**

associer [asɔsje] 7 1 **vt** a (*faire participer à*) ~ **qn à** *profits* to give sb a share of; *affaire* to make sb a partner in; ~ **qn à son triomphe** to let sb share in one's triumph.

b ~ **qch à** (*rendre solidaire de*) to associate *ou* link sth with; (*allier à*) to combine sth with; **il associe la paresse à la malhonnêteté** he combines laziness with dishonesty.

c (*grouper*) *idées, images, mots* to associate; *couleurs, intérêts* to combine (*à* with).

2 **s'associer vpr** a (*s'unir*) *[firmes]* to join together, form an association; *[personnes]* (*gén*) to join forces, join together; (*Comm*) to form a partnership; *[pays]* to form an alliance. **s'~ à** *ou* **avec** *firme* to join with, form an association with; *personne* (*gén*) to join (forces) with; (*Comm*) to go into partnership with; *pays* to form an alliance with; *bandits* to fall in with.

b (*participer à*) **il s'est associé à nos projets** he joined us in our projects; **il finit par s'~ à notre point de vue** he finally came round to *ou* came to share our point of view; **s'~ à la douleur/aux difficultés de qn** to share in sb's grief/difficulties, feel for sb in his grief/difficulties; **je m'associe aux compliments que l'on vous fait** I should like to join with those who have complimented you.

c (*s'allier*) *[couleurs, qualités]* to be combined (*à* with). **ces 2 couleurs s'associent à merveille** these 2 colours go together beautifully.

d (*s'adjoindre*) **s'~ qn** to take sb on as a partner.

assoiffant, e [aswafɑ̃, ɑ̃t] **adj** *chaleur, travail* thirsty (*épith*), thirst-giving.

assoiffé, e [aswafe] **adj** (*lit*) thirsty. (*fig*) ~ **de** thirsting for *ou* after (*littér*); (*littér, hum*) **monstre ~ de sang** bloodthirsty monster.

assoiffer [aswafe] 1 **vt** *[temps, course]* to make thirsty.

assolement [asɔlmɑ̃] **nm** (systematic) rotation (of crops).

assoler [asɔle] 1 **vt** *champ* to rotate crops on.

assombri, e [asɔ̃bʀi] (**ptp de assombrir**) **adj** *ciel* darkened, sombre; *visage, regard* gloomy, sombre. **les couleurs ~es du crépuscule** the sombre shades of dusk.

assombrir [asɔ̃bʀiʀ] 2 1 **vt** a (*obscurcir*) (*gén*) to darken; *pièce* to make dark *ou* dull *ou* gloomy; *couleur* to make dark *ou* sombre. b (*attrister*) *personne* to fill with gloom; *assistance* to cast a gloom over; *visage, vie, voyage* to cast a shadow over. **les malheurs ont assombri son caractère** misfortune has given him a gloomy *ou* sombre outlook on life *ou* has made him a gloomier person. 2 **s'assombrir vpr** a *[ciel, pièce]* to darken, grow dark; *[couleur]* to grow sombre, darken. b *[personne, caractère]* to become gloomy *ou* morose; *[visage, regard]* to cloud over. **la situation politique s'est assombrie** the political situation has become gloomier.

assombrissement [asɔ̃bʀismɑ̃] **nm** *[ciel, pièce]* darkening. **ses amis s'inquiètent de l'~ progressif de son caractère** his friends are worried at the increasing gloominess of his attitude to life.

assommant, e* [asɔmɑ̃, ɑ̃t] **adj** (*ennuyeux*) deadly (boring)*, deadly (dull)*. **il est ~** he's a deadly* *ou* an excruciating bore, he's deadly (dull *ou* boring)*.

assommer [asɔme] 1 **vt** (*lit*) (*tuer*) to batter to death; (*étourdir*) *animal* to knock out, stun; *personne* to knock out, knock senseless, stun; (*fig: moralement*) to crush; (* *fig: ennuyer*) to bore stiff*, bore to tears* *ou* to death*. **être assommé par le bruit/la chaleur** to be overwhelmed by the noise/overcome by the heat; **si je lui mets la main dessus je l'assomme*** if I can lay my hands on him I'll beat his brains out.

assommoir†† [asɔmwaʀ] **nm** (*massue*) club; (*café*) grogshop† (*Brit*), bar.

Assomption [asɔ̃psjɔ̃] **nf: (*Rel*) (la fête de) l'~** (the feast of) the Assumption.

assonance [asɔnɑ̃s] **nf** assonance.

assonant, e [asɔnɑ̃, ɑ̃t] **adj** assonant, assonantal.

assorti, e [asɔʀti] (**ptp de assortir**) **adj** a (*en harmonie*) **des époux bien/mal ~s** a well/badly-matched *ou* suited couple, a good/bad match; **nos amis sont mal ~s** our friends are a mixed bunch; **être ~ à** *couleur* to match. b *bonbons* assorted. **"hors-d'œuvre/fromages ~s"** "assortment of hors d'œuvres/cheeses"; **magasin bien/mal ~** well/poorly-stocked shop. c **être ~ de** *conditions, conseils* to be accompanied with.

assortiment [asɔʀtimɑ̃] **nm** a (*gamme, série*) *[bonbons, hors-d'œuvre]* assortment; *[livres]* collection; *[vaisselle]* set. **je vous fais un ~?** shall I give you an assortment?; **il y avait tout un ~ d'outils** there was a whole set *ou* collection of tools. b (*association, harmonie*) *[couleurs, formes]* arrangement, ensemble. c (*Comm: lot, stock*) stock, selection.

assortir [asɔʀtiʀ] [2] 1 **vt** a (*accorder*) *couleurs, motifs* to match (*à, avec* to, with). **elle assortit la couleur de son écharpe à celle de ses yeux** she chose the colour of her scarf to match her eyes, she matched the colour of her scarf to her eyes; **elle avait su ~ ses invités** she had mixed *ou* matched her guests cleverly.

b (*accompagner de*) **~ qch de** *conseils, commentaires* to accompany sth with; **ce livre s'assortit de notes** this book has accompanying notes *ou* has notes with it.

c (*Comm: approvisionner*) *commerçant* to supply; *magasin* to stock (*de* with).

2 **s'assortir vpr** *[couleurs, motifs]* to match, go (well) together; *[caractères]* to go together, be well matched. **le papier s'assortit aux rideaux** the wallpaper matches *ou* goes (well) with the curtains.

assoupi, e [asupi] (**ptp de assoupir**) **adj** *personne* dozing; *sens, intérêt, douleur* dulled; *haine* lulled.

assoupir [asupiʀ] [2] 1 **vt** *personne* to make drowsy; *sens, intérêt, douleur* to dull; *passion* to lull. 2 **s'assoupir vpr** *[personne]* to doze off; (*fig*) to be dulled; to be lulled. **il est assoupi** he is dozing.

assoupissement [asupismɑ̃] **nm** a (*sommeil*) doze; (*fig: somnolence*) drowsiness. **être au bord de l'~** to be about to doze off. b (*action*) *[sens]* numbing; *[facultés, intérêt]* dulling; *[douleur]* deadening; *[chagrin]* lulling.

assouplir [asupliʀ] [2] 1 **vt** *cuir* to soften, make supple, make pliable; *membres, corps* to make supple; *règlements, mesures* to relax; *principes* to make more flexible, relax. **~ le caractère de qn** to make sb more manageable. 2 **s'assouplir vpr** to soften; to become supple; to become pliable; to relax; to become more flexible. **son caractère s'est assoupli** he has become more manageable.

assouplissant, e [asuplisɑ̃, ɑ̃t] 1 **adj** *produit, formule* softening. 2 **nm: ~ (textile)** (fabric) softener.

assouplissement [asuplismɑ̃] **nm** (*voir* **assouplir**) softening; suppling up; relaxing. **faire des exercices d'~** to limber up, do (some) limbering up exercises; (*Écon*) **mesures d'~ du crédit** easing of credit restrictions; **mesures d'~ des formalités administratives** measures to relax administrative regulations.

assouplisseur [asuplisœʀ] **nm** (fabric) softener.

assourdir [asuʀdiʀ] [2] 1 **vt** a (*rendre sourd*) *personne* to deafen. b (*amortir*) *bruit* to deaden, muffle. 2 **s'assourdir vpr** (*Ling*) to become voiceless, become unvoiced.

assourdissant, e [asuʀdisɑ̃, ɑ̃t] **adj** deafening.

assourdissement [asuʀdismɑ̃] **nm** a *[personne]* (*état*) (temporary) deafness; (*action*) deafening. b *[bruit]* deadening, muffling. c (*Ling*) devoicing.

assouvir [asuviʀ] [2] **vt** *faim, passion* to assuage, satisfy, appease.

assouvissement [asuvismɑ̃] **nm** assuaging, satisfaction, satisfying, appeasement.

ASSU [asy] **nf** (**abrév de Association du sport scolaire et universitaire**) *university and school sports association.*

assujetti, e [asyʒeti] (**ptp de assujettir**) **adj** *peuple* subject, subjugated. **~ à** *règle* subject to; *taxe* liable *ou* subject to; (*Admin*) **les personnes ~es à l'impôt** persons liable to tax *ou* affected by tax.

assujettir [asyʒetiʀ] [2] 1 **vt** (*contraindre*) *peuple* to subjugate, bring into subjection; (*fixer*) *planches, tableau* to secure, make fast. **~ qn à une règle** to subject sb to a rule. 2 **s'assujettir vpr** (*à une règle*) to submit (*à* to).

assujettissant, e [asyʒetisɑ̃, ɑ̃t] **adj** *travail, emploi* demanding, exacting.

assujettissement [asyʒetismɑ̃] **nm** (*contrainte*) constraint; (*dépendance*) subjection. **~ à l'impôt** tax liability.

assumer [asyme] [1] 1 **vt** a (*prendre*) (*gén*) to assume; *responsabilité, tâche, rôle* to take on; *commandement* to take over; *poste* to take up. **j'assume la responsabilité de faire ...** I'll take it upon myself to do ...; **~ les frais de qch** to meet the cost *ou* expense of sth; **tu as voulu te marier, alors assume!** you wanted to get married, so you'll just have to take the consequences! b (*remplir*) *poste* to hold; *rôle* to fulfil. **après avoir assumé ce poste pendant 2 ans** having held this post for 2 years. c (*accepter*) *conséquence, situation,* (*Philos*) *condition* to accept; *douleur* to accept. 2 **s'assumer vpr** to come to terms with o.s.

assurable [asyʀabl] **adj** insurable.

assurage [asyʀaʒ] **nm** (*Alpinisme*) belaying.

assurance [asyʀɑ̃s] 1 **nf** a (*confiance en soi*) self-confidence, (self-)assurance. **avoir de l'~** to be self-confident *ou* (self-)assured; **prendre de l'~** to gain (self-)confidence *ou* (self-)assurance; **parler avec ~** to speak with assurance *ou* confidence.

b (*garantie*) assurance, undertaking (*Brit*). **donner à qn l'~ formelle que** to give sb a formal assurance *ou* undertaking that; (*formule épistolaire*) **veuillez agréer l'~ de ma considération distinguée *ou* de mes sentiments dévoués** ≃ yours faithfully *ou* truly.

c (*contrat*) insurance (policy); (*firme*) insurance company. **contracter *ou* prendre une ~ contre** to take out insurance *ou* an insurance policy against; **il est dans les ~s** he's in insurance, he's in the insurance business; *voir* **police²**, **prime¹**.

d (*Alpinisme*) belaying. **longueur bénéficiant d'une bonne ~** well-protected pitch.

2 **comp ►assurance-automobile nf (pl assurances-automobile)** car *ou* motor (*Brit*) *ou* automobile (*US*) insurance **►assurance-bagages** luggage insurance **►assurance-chômage nf (pl assurances-chômage)** (*Can*) unemployment insurance **►assurance crédit** credit insurance **►assurance décès** whole-life insurance **►assurance-incendie nf (pl assurances-incendie)** fire insurance **►assurance invalidité-vieillesse** disablement insurance **►assurance maladie** health insurance **►assurance maritime** marine insurance **►assurance multirisque** comprehensive insurance **►assurance personnelle** personal insurance **►assurance responsabilité-civile = assurance au tiers ►assurances sociales** ≃ social security, ≃ welfare (*US*); **il est (inscrit) aux assurances sociales** he's in the state health scheme, he pays National Insurance (*Brit*) **►assurance au tiers** third-party insurance **►assurance tous risques** (*Aut*) comprehensive insurance **►assurance-vie nf (pl assurances-vie), assurance sur la vie** life assurance *ou* insurance **►assurance-vieillesse nf (pl assurances-vieillesse)** state pension scheme **►assurance contre le vol** insurance against theft **►assurance-voyage** travel insurance.

assuré, e [asyʀe] (**ptp de assurer**) 1 **adj** a *réussite, échec* certain, sure; *situation, fortune* assured. **son avenir est ~ maintenant** his future is certain *ou* assured now; **entreprise ~e du succès** undertaking which is sure *ou* assured of success.

b *air, démarche* assured, (self-)confident; *voix* assured, steady; *main, pas* steady. **mal ~** *voix, pas* uncertain, unsteady; **il est mal ~ sur ses jambes** he's unsteady on his legs.

c (*loc*) **tenir pour ~ que** to be confident that, take it as certain that; **il se dit ~ de** he says he is confident of; **tenez pour ~ que** rest assured that.

2 **nm,f** (*Assurance*) *[assurance-vie]* assured person; *[autres assurances]* insured person, policyholder. **l'~** the assured, the policyholder; **~ social** ≃ contributor to the National Insurance scheme (*Brit*) *ou* Social Security (*US*), person on Welfare (*US*).

assurément [asyʀemɑ̃] **adv** (*frm*) assuredly, most certainly. **~, ceci présente des difficultés** this does indeed present difficulties; **(oui) ~** yes indeed, (yes) most certainly; **~ il viendra** assuredly he'll come, he will most certainly come.

assurer [asyʀe] [1] 1 **vt** a (*certifier*) **~ à qn que** to assure sb that; **~ que** to affirm *ou* contend *ou* assert that; **cela vaut la peine, je vous assure** it's worth it, I assure you.

b (*confirmer*) **~ qn de** *amitié, bonne foi* to assure sb of; **sa participation nous est assurée** we have been assured of his participation, we're guaranteed that he'll take part.

c (*Fin: par contrat*) *maison, bijoux, véhicule* to insure (*contre* against); *personne* to assure. **~ qn sur la vie** to give sb (a) life assurance *ou* insurance, assure sb's life; **faire ~ qch** to insure sth, have *ou* get sth insured; **être assuré** to be insured.

d (*fournir*) *fonctionnement, permanence etc* to maintain; *surveillance* to ensure, provide, maintain; *service* to operate, provide. **pendant la grève, les mineurs n'assureront que les travaux d'entretien** during the strike the miners will carry out *ou* undertake maintenance work only; **on utilise des appareils électroniques pour ~ la surveillance des locaux** electronic apparatus is used to guard the premises *ou* to ensure that the premises are guarded; **l'avion qui assure la liaison entre Genève et Aberdeen** the plane that operates between Geneva and Aberdeen; **l'armée a dû ~ le ravitaillement des sinistrés** the army has had (to be moved in) to ensure *ou* provide supplies for the victims; (*Jur*) **~ sa propre défense** to conduct one's own defence; **~ la direction d'un service** to head up a department, be in charge of a department; **~ le remplacement de pièces défectueuses** to guarantee the replacement of faulty parts *ou* to replace faulty parts; **~ le suivi d'une commande** to follow up an order.

e (*procurer, garantir*) **~ une situation à son fils** to secure a position for one's son; **cela devrait leur ~ une vie aisée** that should ensure that they lead a comfortable life *ou* ensure a comfortable life for them; **ça lui a assuré la victoire** that ensured his victory *ou* made his victory certain.

f (*rendre sûr*) *bonheur, succès, paix* to ensure; *fortune* to secure; *avenir* to make certain. (*Mil*) ~ **les frontières contre** to make the frontiers secure from; (*fig*) ~ **ses arrières** to ensure one has something to fall back on; **cela m'assure un toit pour les vacances** that makes sure I'll have a roof over my head *ou* that ensures me a roof over my head for the holidays.

g (*affermir*) *pas, prise, échelle* to steady; (*fixer*) *échelle, volet* to secure; (*Alpinisme*) to belay. **il assura ses lunettes sur son nez** he fixed his glasses firmly on his nose.

2 **vi** (**: être à la hauteur*) to be very good. **il assure avec les femmes** he's very good with women; **ne pas** ~ to be useless* *ou* no good*; **je n'assure pas du tout en allemand** I'm useless* at German *ou* no good* at German at all.

3 **s'assurer vpr** a (*vérifier*) **s'~ que/de qch** to make sure that/of sth, check that/sth, ascertain that/sth; **assure-toi qu'on n'a rien volé** make sure *ou* check *ou* ascertain that nothing has been stolen; **assure-toi si le robinet est fermé** check if *ou* make sure the tap (*Brit*) *ou* faucet (*US*) is off; **je vais m'en** ~ I'll make sure *ou* check.

b (*contracter une assurance*) to insure o.s. (*contre* against). (*se prémunir*) **s'~ contre** *attaque, éventualité* to insure (o.s.) against; **s'~ sur la vie** to insure one's life, take out (a) life assurance *ou* insurance.

c (*se procurer*) ~ **l'aide de qn/la victoire** to secure *ou* ensure sb's help/victory; **il s'est ainsi assuré un revenu** in this way he made sure of an income for himself, he thus ensured *ou* secured himself an income; **s'~ l'accès de** to secure access to.

d (*s'affermir*) to steady o.s. (*sur* on); (*Alpinisme*) to belay o.s. **s'~ sur sa selle/ses jambes** to steady o.s. in one's saddle/on one's legs.

e (*littér: arrêter*) **s'~ d'un voleur** to apprehend a thief.

assureur [asyRœR] **nm** (*agent*) insurance agent; (*société*) insurance company; (*Jur: partie*) insurers (*pl*); [*entreprise*] underwriters. **~-conseil** insurance consultant.

Assyrie [asiRi] **nf** Assyria.

assyrien, -ienne [asiRjɛ̃, jɛn] 1 **adj** Assyrian. 2 **nm,f: A~(ne)** Assyrian.

aster [astɛR] **nm** aster.

astérisque [asteRisk] **nm** asterisk. **marqué d'un** ~ asterisked.

astéroïde [asteRɔid] **nm** asteroid.

asthénie [asteni] **nf** asthenia.

asthénique [astenik] **adj, nmf** asthenic.

asthmatique [asmatik] **adj, nmf** asthmatic.

asthme [asm] **nm** asthma.

asticot [astiko] **nm** (*gén*) maggot; (*pour la pêche*) gentle; (**: type*) bloke* (*Brit*), guy (*US*).

asticoter* [astikɔte] [1] **vt** to needle, get at*. **cesse donc d'~ ta sœur!** stop getting at* (*Brit*) *ou* plaguing (*Brit*) *ou* needling your sister!

astigmate [astigmat] 1 **adj** astigmatic. 2 **nmf** astigmat(ic).

astigmatisme [astigmatism] **nm** astigmatism.

astiquer [astike] [1] **vt** *arme, meuble, parquet* to polish; *bottes, métal* to polish, shine, rub up (*Brit*).

astragale [astRagal] **nm** (*Anat*) talus, astragalus; (*Bot*) astragalus; (*Archit*) astragal.

astrakan [astRakɑ̃] **nm** astrakhan.

astral, e, **mpl -aux** [astRal, o] **adj** astral.

astre [astR] **nm** star. (*littér*) **l'~ du jour/de la nuit** the day/night star (*littér*).

astreignant, e [astRɛɲɑ̃, ɑ̃t] **adj** *travail* exacting, demanding.

astreindre [astRɛ̃dR] [49] 1 **vt:** ~ **qn à faire** to compel *ou* oblige *ou* force sb to do; ~ **qn à un travail pénible/une discipline sévère** to force a trying task/a strict code of discipline upon sb. 2 **s'astreindre vpr: s'~ à faire** to force *ou* compel o.s. to do; **elle s'astreignait à un régime sévère** she forced herself to keep to a strict diet; **astreignez-vous à une vérification rigoureuse** apply yourself to a thorough check (*frm*), make yourself carry out a thorough check.

astreinte [astRɛ̃t] **nf** (*littér: obligation*) constraint, obligation; (*Jur*) penalty (*imposed on daily basis for non-completion of contract*).

astringence [astRɛ̃ʒɑ̃s] **nf** astringency.

astringent, e [astRɛ̃ʒɑ̃, ɑ̃t] **adj, nm** astringent.

astrolabe [astRɔlab] **nm** astrolabe.

astrologie [astRɔlɔʒi] **nf** astrology.

astrologique [astRɔlɔʒik] **adj** astrologic(al).

astrologue [astRɔlɔg] **nmf** astrologer.

astronaute [astRonot] **nmf** astronaut.

astronautique [astRonotik] **nf** astronautics (*sg*).

astronef† [astRɔnɛf] **nm** spaceship, spacecraft.

astronome [astRɔnɔm] **nmf** astronomer.

astronomie [astRɔnɔmi] **nf** astronomy.

astronomique [astRɔnɔmik] **adj** (*lit, fig*) astronomical, astronomic.

astronomiquement [astRɔnɔmikmɑ̃] **adv** astronomically.

astrophysicien, -ienne [astRofizisjɛ̃, jɛn] **nm,f** astrophysicist.

astrophysique [astRofizik] 1 **adj** astrophysical. 2 **nf** astrophysics (*sg*).

astuce [astys] **nf** a (*NonC*) shrewdness, astuteness. **il a beaucoup d'~** he is very shrewd *ou* astute. b (*moyen, truc*) (clever) way, trick. **là, l'~ c'est d'utiliser de l'eau au lieu de pétrole** now the trick *ou* the clever bit (*Brit*) here is to use water instead of oil; **les ~s du métier** the tricks of the trade; **c'est ça l'~!** that's the trick! *ou* the clever bit! (*Brit*). c (*) (*jeu de mots*) pun; (*plaisanterie*) wisecrack*. **faire des ~s** to make wisecracks*; ~ **vaseuse** lousy* pun.

astucieusement [astysjøzmɑ̃] **adv** shrewdly, cleverly, astutely.

astucieux, -ieuse [astysjø, jøz] **adj** *personne, réponse, raisonnement* shrewd, astute; *visage* shrewd, astute-looking; *moyen, solution* shrewd, clever.

Asturies [astyRi] **nfpl: les** ~ the Asturias.

asymétrie [asimetRi] **nf** asymmetry.

asymétrique [asimetRik] **adj** asymmetric(al).

asymptomatique [asɛ̃ptɔmatik] **adj** asymptomatic.

asymptote [asɛ̃ptɔt] 1 **adj** asymptotic. 2 **nf** asymptote.

asymptotique [asɛ̃ptɔtik] **adj** asymptotic.

asynchrone [asɛ̃kRon] **adj** asynchronous.

asyndète [asɛ̃dɛt] **nf** asyndeton.

asyntaxique [asɛ̃taksik] **adj** asyntactic(al).

atavique [atavik] **adj** atavistic.

atavisme [atavism] **nm** atavism. **c'est de l'~!** it's heredity coming out!, it's an atavistic trait!

atchoum [atʃum] **excl** atishoo.

atèle [atɛl] **nm** spider monkey.

atelier [atəlje] **nm** a (*local*) [*artisan*] workshop; [*artiste*] studio; [*couturières*] workroom; [*haute couture*] atelier. ~ **de fabrication** workshop. b (*groupe*) (*Art*) studio; (*Scol*) work-group; (*dans un colloque*) discussion group, workshop. (*Scol*) **les enfants travaillent en ~s** the children work in small groups; (*TV*) ~ **de production** production unit. c (*Ind*) [*usine*] shop, workshop; *voir* **chef¹**.

atemporel, -elle [atɑ̃pɔRɛl] **adj** *vérité* timeless.

atermoiement [atɛRmwamɑ̃] **nm** prevarication, procrastination (*NonC*).

atermoyer [atɛRmwaje] [8] **vi** (*tergiverser*) to procrastinate, temporize.

Athalie [atali] **nf** Athalia.

athée [ate] 1 **adj** atheistic. 2 **nmf** atheist.

athéisme [ateism] **nm** atheism.

Athéna [atena] **nf** Athena, (Pallas) Athene.

athénée [atene] **nm** (*Belgique: lycée*) ≈ secondary school (*Brit*), high school (*US*).

Athènes [atɛn] **n** Athens.

athénien, -ienne [atenjɛ̃, jɛn] 1 **adj** Athenian. 2 **nm,f: A~(ne)** Athenian; (*hum*) **c'est là que les A~s s'atteignirent** that's when all hell was let loose*.

athérome [ateRɔm] **nm** atheroma.

athérosclérose [ateRoskleRoz] **nf** atherosclerosis.

athlète [atlɛt] **nmf** athlete. **corps d'~** athletic body; (*hum*) **regarde l'~!, quel ~!** just look at muscleman! (*hum*).

athlétique [atletik] **adj** athletic.

athlétisme [atletism] **nm** athletics (*NonC*). ~ **sur piste** track athletics.

Atlantide [atlɑ̃tid] **nf: l'~** Atlantis.

atlantique [atlɑ̃tik] 1 **adj** Atlantic. (*Can*) **les Provinces** ~ the Atlantic Provinces; *voir* **heure.** 2 **nm: l'A~** the Atlantic (Ocean).

atlantisme [atlɑ̃tism] **nm** Atlanticism.

atlantiste [atlɑ̃tist] 1 **adj** *politique etc* Atlanticist, which promotes the Atlantic Alliance. 2 **nmf** Atlanticist.

atlas [atlɑs] **nm** (*livre, Anat*) atlas. (*Myth*) **A~** Atlas; (*Géog*) **l'A~** the Atlas Mountains.

atmosphère [atmɔsfɛR] **nf** (*lit, fig*) atmosphere.

atmosphérique [atmɔsfeRik] **adj** atmospheric; *voir* **courant, perturbation.**

atoca* [atɔka] **nm** (*Can: canneberge*) cranberry.

atoll [atɔl] **nm** atoll.

atome [atom] **nm** atom. **~-gramme** gram atom; **il n'a pas un ~ de bon sens** he hasn't an iota *ou* atom of common sense; **avoir des ~s crochus avec qn** to have a lot in common with sb, hit it off with sb*.

atomique [atɔmik] **adj** (*Chim, Phys*) atomic; (*Mil, Pol*) atomic, nuclear; *voir* **bombe.**

atomisation [atɔmizasjɔ̃] **nf** atomization.

atomiser [atɔmize] [1] **vt** (*gén*) to atomize; (*Mil*) to destroy by atomic *ou* nuclear weapons; (*fig*) to atomize, break up. **les atomisés d'Hiroshima** the victims of the Hiroshima atom bomb; (*fig*) **parti politique atomisé** atomized *ou* fragmented political party.

atomiseur [atɔmizœR] **nm** (*gén*) spray; [*parfum*] atomizer.

atomiste [atɔmist] **nmf** (*aussi* **savant, ingénieur** *etc* ~) atomic scientist.

atomistique [atɔmistik] **adj, nf: (théorie)** ~ atomic theory.

atonal, e, **mpl ~s** [atɔnal] **adj** atonal.

atonalité [atɔnalite] **nf** atonality.

atone [atɔn] **adj** a (*sans vitalité*) *être* lifeless; (*sans expression*) *regard* expressionless; (*Méd*) atonic. b (*Ling*) unstressed, unaccented, atonic.

atonie [atɔni] **nf** (*Ling, Méd*) atony; (*manque de vitalité*) lifelessness.

atours [atuR] **nmpl** (†, *hum*) attire, finery. **dans ses plus beaux** ~ in her loveliest attire (†, *hum*), in all her finery (*hum*).

atout [atu] **nm** a (*Cartes*) trump. **jouer** ~ to play a trump; (*en *commençant*) to lead trumps; **on jouait ~ cœur** hearts were trumps; **~ maître** master trump; **3 sans ~** 3 no trumps. **b** (*fig*) (*avantage*) asset; (*carte maîtresse*) trump card. **l'avoir dans l'équipe est un ~** it's a great advantage having him in the team, he is an asset to our team; **avoir tous les ~s (dans son jeu)** to hold all the trumps *ou* winning cards; **avoir plus d'un ~ dans sa manche** to have more than one ace up one's sleeve.

atoxique [atɔksik] **adj** non-poisonous.

ATP [atepe] **nf** (**abrév de Association des tennismen professionnels**) ATP.

atrabilaire [atʀabilɛʀ] **adj** (††, *hum*) bilious, atrabilious.

âtre [ɑtʀ] **nm** (*littér*) hearth.

Atrée [atʀe] **nm** Atreus.

Atrides [atʀid] **nmpl: les ~** the Atridae.

atroce [atʀɔs] **adj** **a** *crime* atrocious, heinous, foul; *douleur* excruciating; *spectacle* atrocious, ghastly, horrifying; *mort, sort, vengeance* dreadful, terrible. **b** (*sens affaibli*) *goût, odeur, temps* ghastly, atrocious, foul; *livre, acteur* atrocious, dreadful; *laideur, bêtise* dreadful.

atrocement [atʀɔsmɑ̃] **adv** **a** *souffrir* atrociously, horribly; *défigurer* horribly. **il s'est vengé ~** he wreaked a terrible *ou* dreadful revenge; **elle avait ~ peur** she was terror-stricken. **b** (*sens affaibli*) *laid* atrociously, dreadfully; *bête* dreadfully; *mauvais, ennuyeux* excruciatingly, dreadfully. **loucher ~** to have a dreadful squint.

atrocité [atʀɔsite] **nf** **a** (*qualité*) *[crime, action]* atrocity, atrociousness; *[spectacle]* ghastliness. **b** (*acte*) atrocity, outrage. **dire des ~s sur qn** to say wicked *ou* atrocious things about sb; **cette nouvelle tour est une ~** this new tower is an atrocity *ou* an eyesore.

atrophie [atʀɔfi] **nf** (*Méd*) atrophy; (*fig*) degeneration, atrophy.

atrophier [atʀɔfje] [7] **1 vt** (*Méd*) to atrophy; (*fig*) to atrophy, cause the degeneration of. **2 s'atrophier vpr** *[membres, muscle]* to waste away, atrophy; (*fig*) to atrophy, degenerate.

atropine [atʀɔpin] **nf** atropine, atropin.

attabler (s') [atable] [1] **vpr** (*pour manger*) to sit down at (the) table. **s'~ autour d'une bonne bouteille (avec des amis)** to sit (down) at the table *ou* settle down round (*Brit*) *ou* around (*US*) the table for a drink (with friends); **il retourna s'~ à la terrasse du café** he went back to sit at a table outside the café; **il traversa la salle et vint s'~ avec eux** he crossed the room and came to sit at their table; **les clients attablés** the seated customers.

attachant, e [ataʃɑ̃, ɑ̃t] **adj** *film, roman* captivating; *enfant* endearing.

attache [ataʃ] **nf** **a** (*en ficelle*) (piece of) string; (*en métal*) clip, fastener; (*courroie*) strap. **b** (*Anat*) **~s** (*épaules*) shoulders; (*aines*) groins; (*poignets et chevilles*) wrists and ankles. **c** (*fig*) (*lien*) tie. (*connaissances*) **~s** ties, connections; **avoir des ~s dans une région** to have family ties *ou* connections in a region. **d** (*Bot*) tendril. **e** (*loc*) **être à l'~** *[animal]* to be tied up; *[bateau]* to be moored; (*fig*) *[personne]* to be tied; *voir* **point[1]**, **port[1]**.

attaché, e [ataʃe] (**ptp de attacher**) **1 adj** **a** (*tenir à*) **être ~ à** (*gén*) to be attached to; *habitude* to be tied to; **~ à la vie** attached to life.

b (*frm: être affecté à*) **être ~ au service de qn** to be in sb's personal service; **les avantages ~s à ce poste** the benefits connected with *ou* attached to this position; **son nom restera ~ à cette découverte** his name will always be linked *ou* connected with this discovery.

2 nm attaché. **~ d'ambassade/de presse/militaire** embassy/press/military attaché; **~ d'administration** administrative assistant; **~ commercial/culturel** commercial/cultural attaché; (*Banque*) **~ de clientèle** account supervisor.

3 comp ▸ attaché-case [...kɛz] **nm inv** attaché case.

attachement [ataʃmɑ̃] **nm** **a** (*à une personne*) affection (*à* for), attachment (*à* to); (*à un lieu, à une doctrine, à la vie*) attachment (*à* to). **b** (*Constr*) daily statement (*of work done and expenses incurred*).

attacher [ataʃe] [1] **1 vt** **a** *animal, plante* to tie up; (*avec une chaîne*) to chain up; *volets* to fasten, secure. **~ une étiquette à un arbre/à une valise** to tie a label to a tree/on(to) a case; **attachez donc votre chien** please tie up your dog *ou* get your dog tied up; **il attacha sa victime sur une chaise** he tied his victim to a chair; **il a attaché son nom à cette découverte** he has linked *ou* put his name to this discovery; **s'~ à une corde** to tie o.s. with a rope; **s'~ à son siège** to fasten o.s. to one's seat.

b *paquet, colis* to tie up; *prisonnier* to tie up, bind; *plusieurs choses ensemble* to tie together, bind together. **~ les mains d'un prisonnier** to tie a prisoner's hands together, bind a prisoner's hands (together); **la ficelle qui attachait le paquet** the string that was round the parcel; **est-ce bien attaché?** is it well *ou* securely tied (up)?; **il ne les attache pas avec des saucisses*** he's a bit tight-fisted.

c *ceinture* to do up, fasten; *robe* (*à boutons*) to do up, button up, fasten; (*à fermeture éclair*) to do up, zip up; *lacets* to do up, tie up; *fermeture, bouton* to do up. **attache tes chaussures** do up *ou* tie up your shoes; (*Aviat*) **veuillez ~ votre ceinture** (please) fasten your seatbelts; (*hum*) **attachez vos ceintures!*** hold on to your hats!*

d *papiers* (*épingler*) to pin together, attach; (*agrafer*) to staple together, attach. **~ à** to pin to; to staple onto; **~ une affiche au mur avec du scotch** to stick a notice up on the wall with sellotape (*Brit*) *ou* Scotch tape, sellotape (*Brit*) *ou* Scotch-tape a notice to the wall.

e (*fig: lier à*) **des souvenirs l'attachent à ce village** (*qu'il a quitté*) he still feels attached to the village because of his memories; (*qu'il habite*) his memories keep him here in this village; **il a su s'~ ses étudiants** he has won the loyalty of his students; **plus rien ne l'attachait à la vie** nothing held her to life any more.

f (*attribuer*) **~ de l'importance à qch** to attach importance to sth; **~ de la valeur** *ou* **du prix à qch** to attach great value to sth, set great store by sth; **~ un certain sens à** to attach *ou* attribute a certain meaning to.

g (*frm: adjoindre*) **~ des gardes à qn** to give sb a personal guard; **~ qn à son service** to engage sb, take sb into one's service.

h (*fixer*) **~ son regard** *ou* **ses yeux sur** to fix one's eyes upon.

2 vi (*Culin*) to stick. **les pommes de terre ont attaché** the potatoes have stuck; **une poêle qui n'attache pas** a non-stick frying pan.

3 s'attacher vpr **a** (*gén*) to do up, fasten (up) (*avec, par* with); *[robe]* (*à boutons*) to button up, do up; (*à fermeture éclair*) to zip up, do up; *[fermeture, bouton]* to do up. **ça s'attache derrière** it does up (at) the back, it fastens (up) at the back.

b (*se prendre d'affection pour*) **s'~ à** to become attached to; **cet enfant s'attache vite** this child soon becomes attached to people.

c (*accompagner*) **s'~ aux pas de qn** to follow sb closely, dog sb's footsteps; **les souvenirs qui s'attachent à cette maison** the memories attached to *ou* associated with that house.

d (*prendre à cœur*) **s'~ à faire qch** to endeavour (*Brit frm*) *ou* endeavor (*US frm*) *ou* attempt to do sth.

attaquable [atakabl] **adj** (*Mil*) open to attack; *testament* contestable.

attaquant, e [atakɑ̃, ɑ̃t] **nm,f** (*Mil, Sport*) attacker; (*Ftbl*) striker, forward. **l'avantage est à l'~** the advantage is on the attacking side.

attaque [atak] **1 nf** **a** (*Mil, Police, Sport, fig*) attack; (*Alpinisme*) start. **aller à l'~** to go into the attack; **commettre des ~s nocturnes** to carry out night-time attacks *ou* assaults; **passer à l'~** to move into the attack; **une ~ virulente contre le gouvernement** a virulent attack *ou* onslaught on the Government; **~ d'artillerie** *etc* artillery *etc* attack; **~ à la bombe** bomb attack, bombing.

b (*Méd*) (*gén*) attack; *[épilepsie]* fit, attack (*de* of). **avoir une ~** (*cardiaque*) to have a heart attack; (*apoplexie*) to have a stroke, have a seizure.

c (*Mus*) striking up.

d (** loc*) **d'~** on form, in top form; **il est particulièrement d'~ ce soir** he is in particularly fine form tonight; **il n'est pas d'~ ce matin** he's a bit off form this morning; **se sentir** *ou* **être assez d'~ pour faire** to feel up to doing.

2 comp ▸ attaque aérienne air raid, air attack **▸ attaque d'apoplexie** apoplectic attack *ou* seizure **▸ attaque cardiaque** heart attack **▸ attaque à main armée** hold-up, armed attack **▸ attaque de nerfs** fit of hysterics, attack of nerves.

attaquer [atake] [1] **1 vt** **a** (*assaillir*) *pays* to attack, make *ou* launch an attack upon; *passant, jeune fille* to attack, assault, set upon; (*fig*) *abus, réputation, personne* to attack. **l'armée prussienne/l'équipe adverse attaqua** the Prussian army/the opposing team attacked *ou* went into the attack; **~ de front/par derrière** to attack from the front/from behind *ou* from the rear; **~ (qn) par surprise** to make a surprise attack ((up)on sb); **~ violemment qn pour avoir dit ...** to attack sb violently *ou* give sb a blasting* for saying ...; (*à un chien*) **allez, Rex attaque!** kill, Rex, kill!

b (*endommager*) *[rouille, acide]* to attack; (*Méd*) *[infection]* to affect, attack. **l'humidité a attaqué les peintures** damp has attacked *ou* damaged the paintings; **la pollution attaque notre environnement** pollution is having a damaging effect on *ou* is damaging our environment; **l'acide attaque le fer** acid attacks *ou* eats into iron.

c (*aborder*) *difficulté, obstacle* to tackle, attack; *chapitre* to tackle; *discours* to launch upon; *travail* to set about, buckle down to, get down to; (*Mus*) *morceau* to strike up, launch into; *note* to attack; (*Alpinisme*) to start. **il attaqua les hors-d'œuvre*** he tucked into* *ou* got going on* the hors d'œuvres.

d (*Jur*) *jugement, testament* to contest; *mesure* to challenge. **~ qn en justice** to bring an action against sb.

e (*Cartes*) **~ trêfle/de la reine** to lead with a club/the queen.

2 s'attaquer vpr: s'~ à *personne, abus, mal* to attack; *problème* to tackle, attack, take on; **s'~ à plus fort que soi** to take on more than one's match.

attardé, e [ataʀde] **1 adj** **a** (*Psych*) *enfant* backward. **b** (*en retard*) *promeneur* late, belated (*littér*). **c** (*démodé*) *personne, goût* old-fashioned, behind the times (*attrib*). **2 nm,f: ~ (mental)** backward *ou* mentally retarded child, (*mentally handicapped*) exceptional child (*US Scol*).

attarder [ataʀde] [1] **1 vt** to make late.

2 s'attarder vpr **a** (*se mettre en retard*) to linger (behind). **s'~ chez des amis** to stay on at friends'; **s'~ à boire** to linger over drinks *ou* a drink; **il s'est attardé au bureau pour finir un rapport** he has stayed late *ou* on at the office to finish a report; **s'~ au café** to linger at the café; **s'~ pour cueillir des fleurs** to stay behind to pick flowers; **elle s'est attardée en route** she dawdled *ou* lingered *ou* tarried (*littér*) on the way; **s'~ derrière les autres** to lag behind the others; **ne nous attardons pas ici** let's not linger *ou* hang about* here.

b (*fig*) **s'~ sur une description** to linger over a description; **s'~ à**

des détails to linger over *ou* dwell (up)on details.

atteindre [atɛ̃dʀ] 49 1 vt a (*parvenir à*) *lieu, limite* to reach; *objet haut placé* to reach, get at; *objectif* to reach, arrive at, attain. ~ **son but** *[personne]* to reach one's goal, achieve one's aim; *[mesure]* to be effective; *[missile]* to hit its target, reach its objective; **il ne m'atteint pas l'épaule** he doesn't come up to *ou* reach my shoulder; **la Seine a atteint la cote d'alerte** the Seine has risen to *ou* reached danger level; **il a atteint (l'âge de) 90 ans** he has reached his 90th birthday; **cette tour atteint 30 mètres** this tower is 30 metres high; **les peupliers peuvent ~ une très grande hauteur** poplars can grow to *ou* reach a very great height; **la corruption y atteint des proportions incroyables** corruption there has reached incredible proportions; *voir* **bave**.

b (*contacter*) *personne* to get in touch with, contact, reach.

c (*toucher*) *[pierre, balle, tireur]* to hit (*à* in); *[événement, maladie, reproches]* to affect. **il a eu l'œil atteint par un éclat d'obus** he was hit in the eye by a bit of shrapnel; **la maladie a atteint ses facultés mentales** the illness has affected *ou* impaired his mental faculties; **les reproches ne l'atteignent pas** reproaches don't affect him, he is unaffected by reproaches; **le malheur qui vient de l'~** the misfortune which has just struck him; **il a été atteint dans son amour-propre/ses sentiments** his pride has/his feelings have been hurt *ou* wounded.

2 **atteindre à** vt indir (*littér: parvenir à*) *but* to reach, achieve. ~ **à la perfection** to attain (to) *ou* achieve perfection.

atteint, e[1] [atɛ̃, ɛ̃t] adj a (*malade*) **être ~ de** (*maladie*) to be suffering from; **il a été atteint de surdité** he became *ou* went deaf; **le poumon** *etc* **est gravement/légèrement ~** the lung *etc* is badly/slightly affected; **il est gravement/légèrement ~** he is seriously/only slightly ill, he is a serious/mild case; **les malades les plus ~s** the worst cases, the worst affected. b (**: fou*) touched*, cracked*. c (*Admin*) **être ~ par la limite d'âge** to have to retire (*because one has reached the official retirement age*).

atteinte[2] [atɛ̃t] nf a (*préjudice*) attack (*à* on). (*Jur*) **~ à l'ordre public** breach of the peace; **~ à la sûreté de l'État** betrayal of national security; **~ à la vie privée** invasion of privacy; **porter ~ à** to strike a blow at, undermine. b (*Méd: crise*) attack (*de* of). **les premières ~s du mal** the first effects of the illness; *voir* **hors**.

attelage [at(ə)laʒ] nm a (*voir* **atteler**) harnessing; hitching up; yoking; coupling. b (*harnachement, chaînes*) *[chevaux]* harness; *[bœuf]* yoke; *[remorque]* coupling, attachment; (*Rail*) coupling. c (*équipage*) *[chevaux]* team; *[bœufs]* team, *[deux bœufs]* yoke.

atteler [at(ə)le] 4 1 vt *cheval* to harness, hitch up; *bœuf* to yoke, hitch up; *charrette, remorque* to hitch up; (*Rail*) *wagon* to couple on; *wagons* to couple. **le cocher était en train d'~** the coachman was in the process of getting the horses harnessed *ou* of harnessing up; (*fig*) **~ qn à un travail** to put sb on a job. 2 **s'atteler** vpr: **s'~ à** *travail, tâche* to get *ou* buckle down to; *problème* to get down to; **il est attelé à ce travail depuis ce matin** he has been working away at this job since this morning.

attelle [atɛl] nf *[cheval]* hame; (*Méd*) splint.

attenant, e [at(ə)nɑ̃, ɑ̃t] adj (*contigu*) adjoining. **jardin ~ à la maison** garden adjoining the house; **la maison ~e à la mienne (*ou* la sienne *etc*)** the house next door.

attendre [atɑ̃dʀ] 41 1 vt a *[personne] personne, événement* to wait for, await (*littér*). **maintenant, nous attendons qu'il vienne/de savoir** we are now waiting for him to come/waiting to find out; **attendez qu'il vienne/de savoir pour partir** wait until he comes/you know before you leave, wait for him to come/wait and find out before you leave; **~ la fin du film** to wait until the film is over *ou* until the end of the film; **(aller/venir) ~ un train/qn au train** to meet a train/sb off the train; **j'attends le *ou* mon train** I'm waiting for the *ou* my train; **~ le moment favorable** to bide one's time, wait for the right moment; **~ les vacances avec impatience** to look forward eagerly to the holidays, long for the holidays; **~ qn comme le Messie** to wait eagerly for sb; **nous n'attendons plus que lui pour commencer** we're only waiting for him to start, there's only him to come and then we can start; **il faut ~ un autre jour/moment pour lui parler** we'll have to wait till another day/time to speak to him; **je n'attends qu'une chose, c'est qu'elle s'en aille** I (just) can't wait for her to go; **il n'attendait que ça!** that's just what he was waiting for!; **qu'attendez-vous pour réclamer?** what are you waiting for? why don't you (go ahead and) complain?; **en attendant l'heure de partir, il jouait aux cartes** he played cards (while he waited) until it was time to go; **on ne peut rien faire en attendant de recevoir sa lettre** we can't do anything until we get his letter; **en attendant qu'il vienne, je vais vite faire une course** while I'm waiting for him to come I'm going to pop down* to the shop.

b *[voiture]* to be waiting for; *[maison]* to be ready for; *[mauvaise surprise]* to be in store for, await, wait for; *[gloire]* to be in store for, await. **il ne sait pas encore le sort qui l'attend!** he doesn't know yet what's in store for him! *ou* awaiting him!, he does not yet know what fate awaits him!; **une brillante carrière l'attend** he has a brilliant career in store (for him) *ou* ahead of him; **le dîner vous attend** dinner's ready (when you are).

c (*sans objet*) *[personne, chose]* to wait; *[chose]* (*se conserver*) to keep. **attendez un instant** wait a moment, hang on a minute*; **j'ai attendu deux heures** I waited (for) 2 hours; **attendez voir*** let me *ou* let's see *ou* think*; **attendez un peu** let's see, wait a second; (*menace*) just (you) wait!; (*Téléc*) **vous attendez ou vous voulez rappeler plus tard?** will you hold on or do you want to call back later?; (*iro*) **tu peux toujours ~!** you've got a hope! (*Brit*), you haven't a prayer! (*US*), you'll be lucky!; **ce travail attendra/peut ~** this work will wait/can wait; **ces fruits ne peuvent pas ~ (à demain)** this fruit won't keep (until tomorrow).

d **faire ~ qn** to keep sb waiting; **se faire ~** to keep people waiting, be a long time coming; **le conférencier se fait ~** the speaker is late *ou* is a long time coming; **il aime se faire ~** he likes to keep you *ou* people waiting; **excusez-moi de m'être fait ~** sorry to have kept you (waiting); **la paix se fait ~** peace is a long time coming; **la riposte ne se fit pas ~** the retort was not long in coming *ou* was quick to follow.

e (*escompter, prévoir*) *personne, chose* to expect. **~ qch de qn/qch** to expect sth from sb/sth; **il n'attendait pas un tel accueil** he wasn't expecting such a welcome; **elle est arrivée alors qu'on ne l'attendait plus** she came when she was no longer expected *ou* when they had given her up; **on attendait beaucoup de ces pourparlers** they had great hopes *ou* they expected great things* of these negotiations; **j'attendais mieux de cet élève** I expected better of this child, I expected this child to do better.

f (*loc*) **~ de pied ferme** to wait resolutely; **~ son tour** to wait one's turn; **~ un enfant** to be expecting a baby, be expecting*; **il attend son heure!** he's biding his time; **il m'attendait au tournant*** he waited for the chance to catch me out; **attendez-moi sous l'orme!†** you can wait for me till the cows come home!; **en attendant** (*pendant ce temps*) meanwhile, in the meantime; (*en dépit de cela*) all the same, be that as it may; **en attendant, j'ai le temps de finir le ménage** meanwhile *ou* in the meantime I've time to finish the housework; **en attendant, il est (quand même) très courageux** all the same *ou* be that as it may, he's (nonetheless) very brave.

2 **attendre après*** vt indir *chose* to be in a hurry for, be anxious for; *personne* to be waiting for, hang about waiting for*. **ne vous pressez pas de me rendre cet argent, je n'attends pas après** there's no rush to pay me back the money, I'm in no hurry for it; **je n'attends pas après lui/son aide!** I can get along without him/his help!

3 **s'attendre** vpr (*escompter, prévoir*) **s'~ à qch** to expect sth (*de* from); **il ne s'attendait pas à gagner** he wasn't expecting to win; **est-ce que tu t'attends vraiment à ce qu'il écrive?** do you really expect him to write?; **on ne s'attendait pas à cela de lui** we didn't expect that of him; **avec lui on peut s'~ à tout** you never know what to expect with him; **Marcel! si je m'attendais (à vous voir ici)!*** Marcel, fancy meeting you here!; **comme il fallait s'y ~ ...** as one would expect ..., predictably enough ... .

attendri, e [atɑ̃dʀi] (ptp de **attendrir**) adj *air, regard* melting (*épith*), tender.

attendrir [atɑ̃dʀiʀ] 2 1 vt *viande* to tenderize; (*fig*) *personne* to move (to pity); *cœur* to soften, melt. **il se laissa ~ par ses prières** her pleadings made him relent *ou* yield. 2 **s'attendrir** vpr to be moved *ou* touched (*sur* by), get emotional (*sur* over). **s'~ sur (le sort de) qn** to feel (sorry *ou* pity *ou* sympathy) for sb; **s'~ sur soi-même** to feel sorry for o.s.

attendrissant, e [atɑ̃dʀisɑ̃, ɑ̃t] adj moving, touching.

attendrissement [atɑ̃dʀismɑ̃] nm (*tendre*) emotion, tender feelings; (*apitoyé*) pity. **ce fut l'~ général** everybody got emotional; **pas d'~!** no soft-heartedness!, no displays of emotion!

attendrisseur [atɑ̃dʀisœʀ] nm (*Boucherie*) tenderizer. **viande passée à l'~** tenderized meat.

attendu, e [atɑ̃dy] (ptp de **attendre**) 1 adj *personne, événement, jour* long-awaited; (*prévu*) expected. 2 prép (*étant donné*) given, considering. **~ que** seeing that, since, given *ou* considering that; (*Jur*) whereas. 3 nm (*Jur*) **~s d'un jugement** reasons adduced for a judgment.

attentat [atɑ̃ta] nm (*gén: contre une personne*) murder attempt; (*Pol*) assassination attempt; (*contre un bâtiment*) attack (*contre* on). **~ à la bombe** bomb attack, (terrorist) bombing; **un ~ a été perpétré contre M. Dupont** an attempt has been made on the life of Mr Dupont, there has been an assassination attempt on Mr Dupont; **~ aux droits/à la liberté** violation of rights/of liberty; **~ contre la sûreté de l'État** conspiracy against the security of the State; (*Jur*) **~ aux mœurs** offence against public decency; (*Jur*) **~ à la pudeur** indecent assault.

attentatoire [atɑ̃tatwaʀ] adj prejudicial (*à* to), detrimental (*à* to).

attente [atɑ̃t] nf a wait, waiting (*NonC*). **cette ~ fut très pénible** it was a trying wait; **l'~ est ce qu'il y a de plus pénible** it's the waiting which is hardest to bear; **l'~ des résultats devenait insupportable** waiting for the results was becoming unbearable; **il y a dix minutes d'~ entre les deux trains** there is a 10-minute wait between the two trains; **l'~ se prolongeait** the wait was growing longer and longer; **vivre dans l'~ d'une nouvelle** to spend one's time waiting for (a piece of) news; **dans l'~ de vos nouvelles** looking forward to hearing *ou* hoping to hear from you; **le projet est en ~** the plan is in abeyance *ou* is hanging fire; **laisser un dossier en ~** to leave a file pending; *voir* **salle**.

b (*espoir*) expectation. **répondre à l'~ de qn** to come up to sb's expectations; **contre toute ~** contrary to (all) expectation(s).

attenter [atɑ̃te] 1 vi a ~ **à la vie de qn** to make an attempt on sb's life; ~ **à ses jours** to attempt suicide, make an attempt on one's life; ~ **à la sûreté de l'État** to conspire against the security of the State. b (*fig: violer*) ~ **à** *liberté, droits* to violate.

attentif, -ive [atɑ̃tif, iv] adj a (*vigilant*) *personne, air* attentive. **regarder qn d'un œil** ~ to look at sb attentively; **écouter d'une oreille ~ive** to listen attentively; **être ~ à tout ce qui se passe** to pay attention to all that goes on, heed all that goes on; **sois donc** ~ pay attention!
b (*scrupuleux*) *examen* careful, close, searching; *travail* careful; *soin* scrupulous. ~ **à son travail** careful *ou* painstaking in one's work; ~ **à ses devoirs** heedful *ou* mindful of one's duties; ~ **à ne blesser personne** careful *ou* cautious not to hurt anyone.
c (*prévenant*) *soins* thoughtful; *prévenance* watchful. ~ **à plaire** anxious to please; ~ **à ce que tout se passe bien** keeping a close watch to see that all goes (off) well.

attention [atɑ̃sjɔ̃] nf a (*concentration*) attention; (*soin*) care. **avec** ~ *écouter* carefully, attentively; *examiner* carefully, closely; **attirer/détourner l'~ de qn** to attract/divert *ou* distract sb's attention; **fixer son ~ sur** to focus one's attention on; **faire un effort d'~** to make an effort to concentrate; **demander un effort d'~** to require careful attention; **ce cas/projet mérite toute notre** ~ this case/project deserves our undivided attention; **"à l'~ de M. Dupont"** "for the attention of Mr Dupont"; **votre candidature a retenu notre** ~ we considered your application carefully; **je demande toute votre** ~ can I have your full attention?; *voir* **signaler.**
b **faire** *ou* **prêter ~ à** to pay attention *ou* heed to; **faire bien** *ou* **très** ~ to pay careful attention; **as-tu fait ~ à ce qu'il a dit?** did you pay attention to *ou* attend *ou* listen carefully to what he said?; **il n'a même pas fait ~ à moi/à ce changement** he didn't (even) take any notice of me/the change; **tu vas faire ~ quand il entrera et tu verras** look carefully *ou* have a good look when he comes in and you'll see what I mean; **ne faites pas ~ à lui** pay no attention to him, take no notice of him, never mind him.
c **faire** ~ (*prendre garde*) to be careful, take care; **(fais) ~ à ta ligne** watch *ou* mind (*Brit*) your waistline; **fais ~ à ne pas trop manger** mind *ou* be careful you don't eat too much; **fais ~ (à ce) que la porte soit fermée** be *ou* make sure *ou* mind the door's shut.
d (*loc*) **~! tu vas tomber** watch! *ou* mind (out)! *ou* careful! *ou* watch your step! you're going to fall! *ou* you'll fall!; ~ **chien méchant** beware of the dog; ~ **travaux** caution, work in progress; ~ **à la marche** mind the step; **~! je n'ai pas dit cela** careful! *ou* watch it!*, I didn't say that; ~ **au départ!** the train is now leaving!, all aboard!; ~ **à la peinture** (caution) wet paint; (*sur colis*) **"~, fragile"** "attention, handle with care", "caution, handle with care".
e (*prévenance*) attention, thoughtfulness (*NonC*). **être plein d'~s pour qn** to be very thoughtful *ou* attentive towards sb; **ses ~s me touchaient** I was touched by his attentions *ou* thoughtfulness; **quelle charmante ~!** how very thoughtful!, what a lovely thought!

attentionné, e [atɑ̃sjɔne] adj (*prévenant*) thoughtful, considerate (*pour, auprès de* towards).

attentisme [atɑ̃tism] nm wait-and-see policy, waiting-game.

attentiste [atɑ̃tist] 1 nmf partisan of a wait-and-see policy. 2 adj *politique* wait-and-see (*épith*).

attentivement [atɑ̃tivmɑ̃] adv *lire, écouter* attentively, carefully; *examiner* carefully, closely.

atténuantes [atenɥɑ̃t] adj fpl *voir* **circonstance.**

atténuation [atenɥasjɔ̃] nf a (*voir* **atténuer**) alleviation, easing; mollifying, appeasement; toning down; lightening; watering down; subduing; dimming; softening; toning down; (*Jur*) *[peine]* mitigation. b (*voir* **s'atténuer**) dying down; easing; subsiding, abatement; softening.

atténuer [atenɥe] 1 1 vt a *douleur* to alleviate, ease; *rancœur* to mollify, appease; *propos, reproches* to tone down; *faute* to mitigate; *responsabilité* to lighten; *punition* to lighten, mitigate; *coup, effets* to soften; *faits* to water down; (*Fin*) *pertes* to cushion. b *lumière* to subdue, dim; *couleur, son* to soften, tone down. 2 **s'atténuer** vpr a *[douleur]* to ease, die down; *[sensation]* to die down; *[violence, crise]* to subside, abate. b *[bruit]* to die down; *[couleur]* to soften. **leurs cris s'atténuèrent** their cries grew quieter *ou* died down.

atterrant, e [ateʀɑ̃, ɑ̃t] adj appalling.

atterrer [ateʀe] 1 vt to dismay, appal (*Brit*), appall (*US*), shatter. **il était atterré par cette nouvelle** he was aghast *ou* shattered at this piece of news; **sa bêtise m'atterre** his stupidity appals me, I am appalled by *ou* aghast at his stupidity; **on devinait à son air atterré que ...** we could tell by his look of utter dismay that ... .

atterrir [ateʀiʀ] 2 vi (*Aviat*) to land, touch down. ~ **sur le ventre** *[personne]* to land (up) flat on one's face; *[avion]* to make a belly landing; (*fig*) ~ **en prison/dans un village perdu*** to land up* (*Brit*) *ou* land* (*US*) in prison/in a village in the middle of nowhere; **le travail a finalement atterri sur mon bureau*** the job finally landed on my desk; **atterris!*** come back down to earth!

atterrissage [ateʀisaʒ] nm (*Aviat*) landing. **au moment de l'~** at the moment of landing, at touchdown; ~ **en catastrophe/sur le ventre/sans visibilité** crash/belly/blind landing; ~ **forcé** emergency *ou* forced landing; *voir* **piste, terrain, train.**

attestation [atɛstasjɔ̃] nf a *[fait]* attestation. b (*document*) certificate; *[diplôme]* certificate of accreditation *ou* of attestation. ~ **médicale** doctor's certificate; ~ **sur l'honneur** affidavit.

attester [atɛste] 1 vt a (*certifier*) *fait* to testify to, vouch for. ~ **que** to testify that, vouch for the fact that, attest that; *[témoin]* to attest that; ~ **(de) l'innocence de qn** to testify to *ou* vouch for sb's innocence; **ce fait est attesté par tous les témoins** this fact is borne out *ou* is attested by all the witnesses.
b (*démontrer*) *[preuve, chose]* to attest, testify to. **cette attitude atteste son intelligence** *ou* **atteste qu'il est intelligent** his intelligence is evidenced by this attitude, this attitude testifies to his intelligence; (*Ling*) **forme attestée** attested form; **mot non attesté dans** *ou* **par les dictionnaires** word not attested by the dictionaries.
c (*littér: prendre à témoin*) **j'atteste les dieux que ...** I call the gods to witness that ... .

attiédir [atjediʀ] 2 1 vt (*littér*) *eau* to make lukewarm; *climat* to make more temperate, temper; *désir, ardeur* to temper, cool. 2 **s'attiédir** vpr *[eau]* to become lukewarm; *[climat]* to become more temperate; (*littér*) *[désir, ardeur]* to cool down, wane. **l'eau s'est attiédie** (*plus chaude*) the water has got warmer *ou* has warmed up; (*moins chaude*) the water has got cooler *ou* has cooled down.

attiédissement [atjedismɑ̃] nm *[climat]* tempering; (*littér*) *[désir]* cooling, waning.

attifer* [atife] 1 1 vt (*habiller*) *femme* to get up*, doll up*; *homme* to get up* (*de* in). **regardez comme elle est attifée!** look at her get-up!* 2 **s'attifer** vpr *[femme]* to get *ou* doll o.s. up*; *[homme]* to get o.s. up* (*de* in).

attiger‡ [atiʒe] 3 vi to go a bit far*, overstep the mark.

Attila [atila] nm Attila.

attique¹ [atik] 1 adj (*Antiq*) Attic. **finesse/sel ~** Attic wit/salt. 2 nf: **l'A~** Attica.

attique² [atik] nm (*Constr*) attic (storey).

attirail* [atiʀaj] nm gear*, paraphernalia. ~ **de pêche** fishing tackle; ~ **de bricoleur/cambrioleur** handyman's/burglar's tools *ou* tool kit.

attirance [atiʀɑ̃s] nf attraction (*pour, envers* for). **éprouver de l'~ pour qch/qn** to be *ou* feel drawn towards sth/sb, be attracted to sth/sb; **l'~ du vide** the lure *ou* tug of the abyss.

attirant, e [atiʀɑ̃, ɑ̃t] adj attractive, appealing. **une femme très ~e** an alluring *ou* a very attractive woman.

attirer [atiʀe] 1 vt a (*gén, Phys*) to attract; (*en appâtant*) to lure, entice. **il m'attrapa et m'attira dans un coin** he caught hold of me and drew me into a corner; ~ **qn dans un piège/par des promesses** to lure *ou* entice sb into a trap/with promises; **spectacle fait pour ~ la foule** show guaranteed to bring in *ou* draw *ou* attract the crowds; **être attiré par une doctrine/qn** to be attracted *ou* drawn to a doctrine/sb; ~ **l'attention de qn sur qch** to draw sb's attention to sth; **il essaya d'~ son attention** he tried to attract *ou* catch his attention; **affiche/robe qui attire les regards** eye-catching poster/dress; **elle/son charme attire les hommes** she/her charm appeals to *ou* attracts men.
b (*causer*) ~ **des ennuis à qn** to cause *ou* bring sb difficulties; **cela va lui ~ des ennuis** that's going to cause *ou* give him problems; **tu vas t'~ des ennuis** you're going to cause trouble for yourself *ou* bring trouble upon yourself; **cela a attiré sur lui toute la colère de la ville** this brought the anger of the entire town down on him; **ses discours lui ont attiré des sympathies** his speeches won *ou* gained *ou* earned him sympathy; **s'~ des critiques/la colère de qn** to incur criticism/sb's anger, bring criticism on/sb's anger down on o.s.; **s'~ des ennemis** to make enemies for o.s.; **je me suis attiré sa gratitude** I won *ou* earned his gratitude.

attiser [atize] 1 vt *feu* to poke (up), stir up; *désir, querelle* to stir up, fan the flame of. **pour ~ la flamme** to make the fire burn up.

attitré, e [atitʀe] adj (*habituel*) *marchand, place* regular, usual; (*agréé*) *marchand* accredited, appointed, registered; *journaliste* accredited. **fournisseur ~ d'un chef d'état** purveyors by appointment to a head of state.

attitude [atityd] nf (*maintien*) bearing; (*comportement*) attitude; (*point de vue*) standpoint; (*affectation*) attitude, façade. **prendre des ~s gracieuses** to adopt graceful poses; **avoir une ~ décidée** to have an air of firmness; **prendre une ~ ferme** to adopt a firm standpoint *ou* attitude; **le socialisme chez lui ce n'est qu'une ~** his socialism is only a façade.

attouchement [atuʃmɑ̃] nm touch, touching (*NonC*); (*Méd*) palpation. **se livrer à des ~s sur qn** (*gén*) to fondle *ou* stroke sb; (*Jur*) to interfere with sb.

attractif, -ive [atʀaktif, iv] adj (*Phys*) *phénomène* attractive; (*attrayant*) *offre, prix* attractive.

attraction [atʀaksjɔ̃] nf a (*gén: attirance, Ling, Phys*) attraction. ~ **universelle** gravitation; ~ **moléculaire** molecular attraction. b (*centre d'intérêt*) attraction; (*partie d'un spectacle*) attraction; (*numéro d'un artiste*) number. **il est l'~ numéro un au programme** he is the star attraction on the programme; (*boîte de nuit*) **quand passent les ~s?** when is the cabaret (*Brit*) *ou* floorshow on?; (*cirque etc*) **ils ont renouvelé leurs ~s** they have changed their programme (of attractions *ou* entertainments), they have taken on some new acts; *voir* **parc**.

attrait [atʀɛ] **nm** a (*séduction*) *[femme, paysage, doctrine, plaisirs]* appeal, attraction; *[danger, aventure]* appeal. **ses romans ont pour moi beaucoup d'~** I find his novels very appealing *ou* attractive, his novels appeal to me very much; **éprouver un ~** *ou* **de l'~ pour qch** to be attracted to sth, find sth attractive *ou* appealing. b (*charmes*) **~s** attractions.

attrapade* [atʀapad] **nf** row*, telling off*.

attrape [atʀap] **nf** (*farce*) trick; *voir* **farce**[1].

attrape- [atʀap] **préf** *voir* **attraper**.

attraper [atʀape] 1 1 **vt** a *ballon* to catch; (* *fig*) *train* to catch, get, hop* (*US*); *contravention, gifle* to get; *journal, crayon* to pick up.
b *personne, voleur* to catch. **si je t'attrape!** if I catch you!; **~ qn à faire qch** to catch sb doing sth; **que je t'y attrape!*** don't let me catch you doing that!, if I catch you doing that!
c *maladie* to catch, get. **tu vas ~ froid** *ou* **du mal** you'll catch cold; **j'ai attrapé un rhume/son rhume** I've caught a cold/a cold from him *ou* his cold; **j'ai attrapé mal à la gorge** I've got a sore throat; **tu vas ~ la mort** you'll catch your death (of cold); **il a attrapé un coup de soleil** he got sunburnt; **la grippe s'attrape facilement** flu is very catching.
d (*intercepter*) *mots* to pick up.
e (*acquérir*) *style, accent* to pick up. **il faut ~ le coup** *ou* **le tour de main** you have to get *ou* learn the knack.
f (*gronder*) to tell off*. **se faire ~ (par qn)** to be told off (by sb)*, get a telling off (from sb)*; **mes parents vont m'~** I'll get it‡ from my parents, my parents will give me a telling off*; **ils se sont attrapés pendant une heure** they went at each other for a whole hour*.
g (*tromper*) to take in. **se laisser ~** to be had* *ou* taken in; **tu as été bien attrapé** (*trompé*) you were had all right*; (*surpris*) you were caught out there all right!
2 **comp ▸attrape-couillon‡ nm (pl attrape-couillon(s)) = attrape-nigaud* ▸attrape-mouche nm (pl attrape-mouche(s))** (*Bot*) fly trap; (*Orn*) flycatcher; (*piège*) flypaper **▸attrape-nigaud* nm (pl attrape-nigaud(s))** con*, con game* (*US*) **▸attrape-touristes nm inv** tourist trap.

attrayant, e [atʀɛjɑ̃, ɑ̃t] **adj** (*agréable, beau*) attractive; (*séduisant*) *idée* appealing, attractive. **c'est une lecture ~e** it makes *ou* it is pleasant reading; **peu ~** *travail* unappealing; *paysage* unattractive; *proposition* unattractive, unappealing.

attribuable [atʀibɥabl] **adj** attributable (*à* to).

attribuer [atʀibɥe] 1 **vt** a (*allouer*) *prix* to award; *avantages, privilèges* to grant, accord; *place, rôle* to allocate, assign; *biens, part* to allocate (*à* to). **s'~ le meilleur rôle/la meilleure part** to give o.s. the best role/the biggest share, claim the best role/the biggest share for o.s.
b (*imputer*) *faute* to attribute, impute; *pensée, intention* to attribute, ascribe (*à* to). **à quoi attribuez-vous cet échec/accident?** what do you put this failure/accident down to?, what do you attribute *ou* ascribe this failure/accident to?
c (*accorder*) *invention, mérite* to attribute (*à* to). **on lui attribue l'invention de l'imprimerie** the invention of printing has been attributed to him, he has been credited with the invention of printing; **la critique n'attribue que peu d'intérêt à son livre** the critics find little of interest in his book *ou* consider his book of little interest; **~ de l'importance à qch** to attach importance to sth; **s'~ tout le mérite** to claim all the merit for o.s.

attribut [atʀiby] **nm** (*caractéristique, symbole*) attribute; (*Gram*) complement. **adjectif ~** predicative adjective; **nom ~** noun complement.

attribution [atʀibysjɔ̃] **nf** a *[prix]* awarding; *[place, rôle, part]* allocation; *[œuvre, invention]* attribution. b (*prérogatives, pouvoirs*) **~s** attributions; **cela n'entre pas dans mes ~s** I'm not empowered to do that, that's not part of my job.

attristant, e [atʀistɑ̃, ɑ̃t] **adj** *nouvelle, spectacle* saddening.

attrister [atʀiste] 1 1 **vt** to sadden. **cette nouvelle nous a profondément attristés** we were greatly saddened by *ou* grieved at this news. 2 **s'attrister vpr** to be saddened (*de* by), become sad (*de qch* at sth, *de voir que* at seeing that).

attroupement [atʀupmɑ̃] **nm** *[foule]* gathering; (*groupe*) crowd, mob (*péj*).

attrouper (s') [atʀupe] 1 **vpr** to gather (together), flock together, form a crowd.

atypique [atipik] **adj** atypical.

au [o] *voir* **à**.

aubade [obad] **nf** dawn serenade. **donner une ~ à qn** to serenade sb at dawn.

aubaine [obɛn] **nf** godsend; (*financière*) windfall. **profiter de l'~** to make the most of one's good fortune *ou* of the opportunity; **quelle (bonne) ~!** what a godsend! *ou* stroke of luck!

aube[1] [ob] **nf** a dawn, daybreak, first light. **à l'~** at dawn *ou* daybreak *ou* first light; **avant l'~** before dawn *ou* daybreak. b (*fig*) dawn, beginning. **à l'~ de** at the dawn of.

aube[2] [ob] **nf** (*Rel*) alb.

aube[3] [ob] **nf** (*Tech*) *[bateau]* paddle, blade; *[moulin]* vane; *[ventilateur]* blade, vane. **roue à ~s** paddle wheel.

aubépine [obepin] **nf** hawthorn. **fleurs d'~** may (blossom), hawthorn blossom.

auberge [obɛʀʒ] **nf** inn. **il prend la maison pour une ~!*, il se croit à l'~!*** he uses this place as a hotel!; **~ de (la) jeunesse** youth hostel; **c'est l'~ espagnole** (*repas*) everyone's bringing some food along, it's a potluck party (*US*); (*situation chaotique*) it's a madhouse*; *voir* **sortir**.

aubergine [obɛʀʒin] 1 **nf** a (*légume*) aubergine (*Brit*), eggplant. b (†*: *contractuelle*) traffic warden (*Brit*), meter maid* (*US*). 2 **adj inv** aubergine(-coloured).

aubergiste [obɛʀʒist] **nmf** *[hôtel]* hotel-keeper; *[auberge]* innkeeper, landlord. *[auberge de jeunesse]* **père ~, mère ~** (youth-hostel) warden.

aubette [obɛt] **nf** (*Belgique*) bus shelter.

aubier [obje] **nm** sapwood.

auburn [obœʀn] **adj inv** auburn.

aucun, e [okœ̃, yn] 1 **adj** a (*nég*) no, not any. **~ commerçant ne le connaît** no tradesman (*Brit*) *ou* merchant knows him; **il n'a ~e preuve** he has no proof, he hasn't any proof; **sans faire ~ bruit** without making a noise *ou* any noise; **sans ~ doute** without (any) doubt, undoubtedly; **en ~e façon** in no way; **ils ne prennent ~ soin de leurs vêtements** they don't take care of their clothes (at all); **ils n'ont eu ~ mal à trouver le chemin** they had no trouble finding the way, they found the way without any trouble.
b (*positif*) any. **il lit plus qu'~ autre enfant** he reads more than any other child; **croyez-vous qu'~ auditeur aurait osé le contredire?** do you think that any listener would have dared to contradict him?
2 **pron** a (*nég*) **il n'aime ~ de ces films** he doesn't like any of these films; **~ de ses enfants ne lui ressemble** none of his children are like him; **je ne pense pas qu'~ d'entre nous puisse y aller** I don't think any of us can go; **combien de réponses avez-vous eues? — ~e** how many answers did you get? — not one *ou* none.
b (*positif*) any, any one. **il aime ses chiens plus qu'~ de ses enfants** he is fonder of his dogs than of any (one) of his children; **pensez-vous qu'~ ait compris?** do you think anyone *ou* anybody understood?
c (*littér*) **d'~s** some; **d'~s aiment raconter que ...** there are some who like to say that ... .

aucunement [okynmɑ̃] **adv** in no way, not in the least, not in the slightest. **il n'est ~ à blâmer** he's not in the slightest *ou* least to blame, he's in no way *ou* not in any way to blame; **accepterez-vous? — ~** are you going to accept? — indeed no *ou* (most) certainly not.

audace [odas] **nf** a (*NonC*) (*témérité*) daring, boldness, audacity; (*Art: originalité*) daring; (*effronterie*) audacity, effrontery. **avoir l'~ de** to have the audacity to, dare to. b (*geste osé*) daring gesture; (*innovation*) daring idea *ou* touch. **elle lui en voulait de ses ~s** she held his boldness *ou* his bold behaviour against him; **une ~ de génie** a daring touch of genius; **~s de style** daring innovations of style; **les ~s de la mode** the daring inventions *ou* creations of high fashion.

audacieusement [odasjøzmɑ̃] **adv** (*voir* **audacieux**) daringly; boldly; audaciously.

audacieux, -ieuse [odasjø, jøz] **adj** *soldat, action* daring, bold; *artiste, projet* daring; *geste* audacious, bold; *voir* **fortune**.

au-deçà, au-dedans, au-dehors *voir* **deçà, dedans, dehors**.

au-delà [od(ə)la] 1 **loc adv** *voir* **delà**. 2 **nm: l'~** the beyond.

au-dessous, au-dessus *voir* **dessous, dessus**.

au-devant [od(ə)vɑ̃] 1 **loc prép: ~ de** ahead of; **aller ~ de qn** to go and meet sb; **aller ~ des désirs de qn** to anticipate sb's wishes. 2 **loc adv** ahead.

audibilité [odibilite] **nf** audibility.

audible [odibl] **adj** audible.

audience [odjɑ̃s] **nf** a (*frm: entretien*) interview, audience. **donner ~ à qn** to give audience to sb. b (*Jur: séance*) hearing. c (*attention*) (interested) attention. **ce projet eut beaucoup d'~** this project aroused much interest; **cet écrivain a trouvé ~ auprès des étudiants** this author has had a favourable reception from students. d (*spectateurs, auditeurs*) audience. (*Rad, TV*) **faire de l'~** to attract a large audience; **gagner des points d'~** to go up in the ratings.

audimat [odimat] **nm inv** ® (*appareil*) audiometer; (*taux d'écoute*) ratings. **avoir un bon ~** to have good ratings.

audimètre [odimɛtʀ] **nm** audiometer.

audio- [odjo] **préf** audio.

audioconférence [odjokɔ̃feʀɑ̃s] **nf** conference call.

audio-électronique, pl audio-électroniques [odjoelɛktʀɔnik] **adj** audiotronic.

audiofréquence [odjofʀekɑ̃s] **nf** audio frequency.

audiogramme [odjogʀam] **nm** audiogram.

audiomètre [odjomɛtʀ] **nm** audiometer.

audiométrie [odjometʀi] **nf** audiometry.

audionumérique [odjonymeʀik] **adj** digital.

audio-oral, e, mpl audio-oraux [odjooʀal, o] **adj** *exercices, méthode* audio (*épith*).

audiophone [odjofɔn] **nm** hearing aid.

audioprothésiste [odjopʀɔtezist] **nmf** hearing aid specialist.

audiotypie [odjotipi] **nf** audiotyping.

audiotypiste [odjotipist] **nmf** audiotypist.

audiovisuel, -elle [odjovizɥɛl] 1 adj audiovisual. 2 nm (*équipement*) audiovisual aids; (*méthodes*) audiovisual techniques *ou* methods; (*radio et télévision*) radio and television.
audit [odit] nm a (*contrôle*) audit. **faire l'~ de** to audit. b (*personne*) auditor.
auditer [odite] 1 vt to audit.
auditeur, -trice [oditœʀ, tʀis] nm,f (*gén, Rad*) listener; (*Ling*) hearer; (*Fin*) auditor. **le conférencier avait charmé ses ~s** the lecturer had captivated his audience; (*Univ*) ~ **libre** unregistered student (*who is allowed to attend lectures*) (*Brit*), auditor (*US*); (*Admin*) ~ **à la Cour des comptes** junior official (*at the Cour des Comptes*).
auditif, -ive [oditif, iv] adj auditory. **troubles ~s** hearing problems *ou* difficulties; **aide** *ou* **prothèse ~ive** hearing aid.
audition [odisjɔ̃] nf a (*Mus, Théât*) (*essai*) audition; (*récital*) recital; (*concert d'élèves*) concert (*de* by). (*Mus, Théât*) **passer une ~** to audition, have an audition. b (*Jur*) **procéder à l'~ d'un témoin** to examine a witness. c (*écoute*) *[musique, disque]* hearing. **salle conçue pour l'~ de la musique** room designed for listening to music; **avec l'orage l'~ est très mauvaise** with the storm the sound is very bad. d (*ouïe*) hearing.
auditionner [odisjɔne] 1 1 vt to audition, give an audition to. 2 vi to be auditioned, audition.
auditoire [oditwaʀ] 1 nm audience. 2 adj (*Ling*) auditory.
auditorium [oditɔʀjɔm] nm (*Rad*) public studio.
auge [oʒ] nf (*Agr, Constr*) trough. (*Géog*) **vallée en ~** U-shaped valley, trough; (*hum*) **passe ton ~!*** give us your plate!*
augmentatif, -ive [ɔgmɑ̃tatif, iv] adj (*Gram*) augmentative.
augmentation [ɔgmɑ̃tasjɔ̃] nf (*accroissement*) (*gén*) increase; *[prix, population, production]* increase, rise, growth (*de* in). ~ **de salaire/prix** pay/price rise, salary/price increase, increase in salary/price; (*Fin*) ~ **de capital** increase in capital; **l'~ des salaires par la direction** the management's raising of salaries; **réclamer une ~ (de salaire)** (*collectivement*) to make a wage claim; (*individuellement*) to put in for a rise (*Brit*) *ou* raise (*US*); **l'~ des prix par les commerçants** the raising *ou* putting up of prices by shopkeepers (*Brit*) *ou* storekeepers (*US*).
augmenter [ɔgmɑ̃te] 1 1 vt a *salaire, prix, impôts* to increase, raise, put up; *nombre* to increase, raise, augment; *production, quantité, dose* to increase, step up, raise; *durée* to increase; *difficulté, inquiétude* to add to, increase; *intérêt* to heighten. ~ **les prix de 10 %** to increase *ou* raise *ou* put up prices by 10%; **il augmente ses revenus en faisant des heures supplémentaires** he augments *ou* supplements his income by working overtime; **sa collection s'est augmentée d'un nouveau tableau** he has extended *ou* enlarged his collection with a new painting, he has added a new painting to his collection; (*Tricot*) ~ **(de 5 mailles)** to increase (5 stitches); (*Mus*) **tierce augmentée** augmented third; **ceci ne fit qu'~ sa colère** this only added to his anger; *voir* **édition**.
b ~ **qn (de 500 F)** to increase sb's salary (by 500 francs), give sb a (500-franc) rise (*Brit*) *ou* raise (*US*); **il n'a pas été augmenté depuis 2 ans** he has not had *ou* has not been given a rise (*Brit*) *ou* raise (*US*) *ou* a salary increase for 2 years.
2 vi (*grandir*) *[salaire, prix, impôts]* to increase, rise, go up; *[marchandises]* to go up; *[poids, quantité]* to increase; *[population, production]* to grow, increase, rise; *[douleur]* to grow *ou* get worse, increase; *[difficulté, inquiétude]* to grow, increase. ~ **de poids/volume** to increase in weight/volume; *voir* **vie**.
augure [ogyʀ] nm a (*devin*) (*Hist*) augur; (*fig hum*) soothsayer, oracle. **consulter les ~s** to consult the oracle. b (*présage*) omen; (*Hist*) augury. **être de bon ~** to be of good omen, augur well; **résultat de bon ~** promising *ou* encouraging result; **être de mauvais ~** to be ominous *ou* of ill omen, augur ill; **cela me paraît de bon/mauvais ~** that's a good/bad sign, that augurs well/badly; *voir* **accepter, oiseau**.
augurer [ogyʀe] 1 vt: **que faut-il ~ de son silence?** what must we gather *ou* understand from his silence?; **je n'augure rien de bon de cela** I don't foresee *ou* see any good coming from *ou* out of it; **cela augure bien/mal de la suite** that augurs well/ill (for what is to follow).
Auguste [ogyst] nm Augustus. (*Antiq*) **le siècle d'~** the Augustan age.
auguste [ogyst] 1 adj *personnage, assemblée* august; *geste* noble, majestic. 2 nm: **A~** ≃ Coco the clown.
augustin, e [ogystɛ̃, in] 1 nm: **A~** Augustine. 2 nm,f (*Rel*) Augustinian.
augustinien, -ienne [ogystinjɛ̃, jɛn] adj Augustinian.
aujourd'hui [oʒuʀdɥi] adv a (*ce jour-ci*) today. ~ **en huit** a week today (*Brit*), today week (*Brit*), a week from today; **il y a ~ 10 jours que** it's 10 days ago today that; **c'est tout pour ~** that's all *ou* that's it for today; **à dater** *ou* **à partir d'~** (as) from today, from today onwards; ~ **après-midi** this afternoon; **je le ferai dès ~** I'll do it this very day; *voir* **jour**. b (*de nos jours*) today, nowadays, these days. **ça ne date pas d'~** *[objet]* it's not exactly new; *[situation, attitude]* it's nothing new; **les jeunes d'~** young people nowadays, (the) young people of today.
aulne [o(l)n] nm alder.
aulx [o] nmpl *voir* **ail**.
aumône [omon] nf (*don*) charity (*NonC*), alms; (*action de donner*) almsgiving. **vivre d'~(s)** to live on charity; **demander l'~** (*lit*) to ask *ou* beg for charity *ou* alms; (*fig*) to beg (for money *etc*); **faire l'~** to give alms (*à* to); **cinquante francs! c'est une ~** fifty francs, that's a beggarly sum (from him)!; (*fig*) **faire** *ou* **accorder l'~ d'un sourire à qn** to favour sb with a smile, spare sb a smile.
aumônerie [omonʀi] nf chaplaincy.
aumônier [omonje] nm chaplain.
aumônière [omonjɛʀ] nf (*Hist, Rel*) purse.
aune[1] [on] nm = **aulne**.
aune[2] [on] nf ≃ ell. (*fig*) **il fit un nez long d'une ~, son visage s'allongea d'une ~** he pulled a long face *ou* a face as long as a fiddle (*Brit*).
auparavant [opaʀavɑ̃] adv (*d'abord*) before(hand), first; (*avant*) before(hand), previously.
auprès [opʀɛ] 1 prép: ~ **de** a (*près de, à côté de*) next to, close to, by; (*au chevet de, aux côtés de*) with. **rester ~ d'un malade** to stay with an invalid; **s'asseoir ~ de la fenêtre/de qn** to sit down by *ou* close to the window/by *ou* next to *ou* close to sb.
b (*comparé à*) compared with, in comparison with, next to. **notre revenu est élevé ~ du leur** our income is high compared with *ou* in comparison with *ou* next to theirs.
c (*s'adressant à*) with, to. **faire une demande ~ des autorités** to apply to the authorities, lodge a request with the authorities; **faire une démarche ~ du ministre** to approach the minister, apply to the minister; **déposer une plainte ~ des tribunaux** to instigate legal proceedings; **avoir accès ~ de qn** to have access to sb; **ambassadeur ~ du Vatican** ambassador to the Vatican.
d (*dans l'opinion de*) in the view of, in the opinion of. **il passe pour un incompétent ~ de ses collègues** he is incompetent in the view *ou* opinion of his colleagues; **jouir ~ de qn de beaucoup d'influence** to have *ou* carry a lot of influence with sb.
2 adv (*littér*) nearby.
auquel [okɛl] *voir* **lequel**.
aura [ɔʀa] nf aura.
auréole [ɔʀeɔl] nf a (*Art, Astron*) halo, aureole. (*fig*) **entouré de l'~ du succès** surrounded by a glow of success; (*fig*) **paré de l'~ du martyre** wearing a martyr's crown *ou* the crown of martyrdom; **parer qn d'une ~** to glorify sb. b (*tache*) ring.
auréoler [ɔʀeɔle] 1 1 vt (*gén ptp*) (*glorifier*) to glorify; (*Art*) to encircle with a halo. **tête auréolée de cheveux blancs** head with a halo of white hair; **auréolé de gloire** wreathed in *ou* crowned with glory; **être auréolé de prestige** to have an aura of prestige. 2 **s'auréoler** vpr: **s'~ de** to take on an aura of.
auréomycine [ɔʀeomisin] nf aureomycin (*Brit*), Aureomycin ® (*US*).
auriculaire [ɔʀikylɛʀ] 1 nm little finger. 2 adj auricular; *voir* **témoin**.
auriculothérapie [ɔʀikyloteʀapi] nf aural acupuncture.
aurifère [ɔʀifɛʀ] adj gold-bearing.
aurification [ɔʀifikasjɔ̃] nf *[dent]* filling with gold.
aurifier [ɔʀifje] 7 vt *dent* to fill with gold.
Aurigny [ɔʀiɲi] nf Alderney.
aurochs [ɔʀɔk] nm aurochs.
aurore [ɔʀɔʀ] nf a dawn, daybreak, first light. **à l'~** at dawn *ou* first light *ou* daybreak; **avant l'~** before dawn *ou* daybreak; **se lever/partir aux ~s** to get up/leave at the crack of dawn; ~ **australe** aurora australis; ~ **boréale** northern lights, aurora borealis; ~ **polaire** polar lights. b (*fig*) dawn, beginning. **à l'~ de** at the dawn of.
auscultation [ɔskyltasjɔ̃] nf auscultation.
ausculter [ɔskylte] 1 vt to sound (the chest of), auscultate (*SPÉC*).
auspices [ɔspis] nmpl a (*Antiq*) auspices. b **sous de bons/mauvais ~s** under favourable/unfavourable auspices; **sous les ~s de qn** under the patronage *ou* auspices of sb.
aussi [osi] 1 adv a (*également*) too, also. **je suis fatigué et lui/eux ~** I'm tired and so is he/are they, I'm tired and he is/they are too; **il travaille bien et moi ~** he works well and so do I; **il parle ~ l'anglais** he also speaks ENGLISH, he speaks ENGLISH as well, he speaks ENGLISH too; **lui ~ parle l'anglais** HE speaks English too *ou* as well, he too speaks English; **il parle l'italien et ~ l'anglais** he speaks Italian and English too *ou* as well, he speaks Italian and also English; **il a la grippe — lui ~?** he's got flu — him too?* *ou* him as well?, he has flu — he too? (*frm*); **c'est ~ mon avis** I think so too *ou* as well, that's my view too *ou* as well; **faites bon voyage — vous ~** have a good journey — you too *ou* (the) same to you; **il ne suffit pas d'être doué, il faut ~ travailler** it's not enough to be talented, you also have to work; **toi ~, tu as peur?** so you too are afraid?, so you are afraid too? *ou* as well?
b (*comparaison*) ~ **grand** *etc* **que** as tall *etc* as; **il est ~ bête que méchant** *ou* **qu'il est méchant** he's as stupid as he is ill-natured; **viens ~ souvent que tu voudras** come as often as you like; **s'il pleut ~ peu que l'an dernier** if it rains as little as last year; **il devint ~ riche qu'il l'avait rêvé** he became as rich as he had dreamt he would; **pas ~ riche qu'on le dit** not as rich as he is said to be; **la piqûre m'a fait tout ~ mal que la blessure** the injection hurt me just as much as the injury (did); ~ **vite que possible** as quickly as possible; **d'~ loin qu'il nous vit il cria** far away though he was he shouted as soon as he saw us.
c (*si, tellement*) so. **je ne te savais pas ~ bête** I didn't think you were so *ou* that* stupid; **comment peut-on laisser passer une ~ bonne occasion?** how can one let slip such a good opportunity? *ou* so good an

opportunity?; **je ne savais pas que cela se faisait ~ facilement (que ça)** I didn't know that could be done as easily (as that) *ou* so easily *ou* that easily*; **~ léger qu'il fût** light though he was; **~ idiot que ça puisse paraître** silly though *ou* as it may seem.

d (*tout autant*) **~ bien** just as well, just as easily; **tu peux ~ bien dire non** you can just as easily *ou* well say no; (*littér*) **puisqu'~ bien tout est fini** since, moreover, everything is finished; **mon tableau peut ~ bien représenter une montagne qu'un animal** my picture could just as well *ou* easily represent a mountain as an animal; **~ sec*** on the spot*, quick as a flash.

2 **conj** (*en conséquence*) therefore, consequently; (*d'ailleurs*) well, moreover. **je suis faible, ~ ai-je besoin d'aide** I'm weak, therefore *ou* consequently I need help; **tu n'as pas compris, ~ c'est ta faute: tu n'écoutais pas** you haven't understood, well, it's your own fault – you weren't listening.

aussitôt [osito] 1 **adv** straight away, immediately. **~ arrivé/descendu il s'attabla** as soon as he arrived/came down he sat down at table; **~ le train arrêté, elle descendit** as soon as *ou* immediately (*Brit*) the train stopped she got out; **~ dit, ~ fait** no sooner said than done; **~ après son retour** straight *ou* directly *ou* immediately after his return; **il est parti ~ après** he left straight *ou* directly *ou* immediately after; **~ que** as soon as; **~ que je le vis** as soon as *ou* the moment I saw him. 2 **prép**: **~ arrivée, je lui ai téléphoné** immediately (up)on my arrival I phoned him, immediately (*Brit*) I arrived I phoned him.

austère [ostɛʀ] **adj** *personne, vie, style, monument* austere; *livre, lecture* dry. **coupe ~ d'un manteau** severe cut of a coat.

austèrement [ostɛʀmɑ̃] **adv** austerely.

austérité [osteʀite] **nf** (*voir* **austère**) austerity; dryness. (*Rel*) **~s** austerities; (*Pol*) **mesures/politiques d'~** austerity measures/policies.

austral, e, **mpl ~s** [ɔstʀal] **adj** southern, austral (*SPÉC*). **pôle ~** south pole; *voir* **aurore**.

Australasie [ɔstʀalazi] **nf** Australasia. *produit, habitant* **d'~** Australasian.

Australie [ostʀali] **nf** Australia. (*Pol*) **l'~** the commonwealth of Australia; **~-Méridionale/-Occidentale** South/Western Australia.

australien, -ienne [ostʀaljɛ̃, jɛn] 1 **adj** Australian. 2 **nm,f**: **A~(ne)** Australian.

australopithèque [ɔstʀalɔpitɛk] **nm** Australopithecus.

autant [otɑ̃] **adv** a **~ de** (*quantité*) as much (*que* as); (*nombre*) as many (*que* as); **il y a (tout) ~ de place ici (que là-bas)** there's (just) as much room here (as over there); **il n'y a pas ~ de neige que l'année dernière** there isn't as much *ou* there's not so much snow as last year; **nous employons ~ d'hommes qu'eux** we employ as many men as they do *ou* as them; **nous sommes ~ qu'eux** we are as many as they are *ou* as them, there are as many of us as of them; **il nous prêtera ~ de livres qu'il pourra** he'll lend us as many books as he can; **ils sont ~ à plaindre l'un que l'autre** you have to feel just as sorry for both of them; **ils ont ~ de mérite l'un que l'autre** they have equal merit; **ils ont ~ de talents l'un que l'autre** they are both equally talented; **elle mange deux fois ~ que lui** she eats twice as much as him *ou* as he does; **j'en voudrais encore ~** I'd like as much again; **tous ces enfants sont ~ de petits menteurs** all these children are so many little liars; **tous ~ que vous êtes** the whole lot of you.

b (*intensité*) as much (*que* as). **il travaille toujours ~** he works as hard as ever, he's still working as hard; **pourquoi travaille-t-il ~?** why does he work so much? *ou* so hard?; **rien ne lui plaît ~ que de regarder les autres travailler** there is nothing he likes so much as *ou* likes better than watching others work; **intelligent, il l'est ~ que vous** he's quite as clever as you are; **il peut crier ~ qu'il veut** he can scream as much as he likes; **cet avertissement vaut pour vous ~ que pour lui** this warning applies to you as much as to him; **courageux ~ que compétent** courageous as well as competent, as courageous as he is competent; **~ prévenir la police** it would be as well to tell the police; *voir* **aimer**.

c (*tant*) (*quantité*) so much, such; (*nombre*) so many, such a lot of. **elle ne pensait pas qu'il aurait ~ de succès/qu'il mangerait ~** she never thought that he would have so much *ou* such success/that he would eat so much *ou* such a lot; **vous invitez toujours ~ de gens?** do you always invite so many people? *ou* such a lot of people?; **j'ai rarement vu ~ de monde** I've seldom seen such a crowd *ou* so many people.

d (*avec en: la même chose*) the same. **je ne peux pas en dire ~** I can't say the same (for myself); **je ne peux pas en faire ~** I can't do as much *ou* the same.

e (*avec de: exprimant une proportion*) **d'~: ce sera augmenté d'~** it will be increased accordingly *ou* in proportion; **d'~ que, d'~ plus que** all the more so since *ou* because; **c'est d'~ plus dangereux qu'il n'y a pas de parapet** it's all the more dangerous since *ou* because there is no parapet; **écrivez-lui, d'~ que** *ou* **d'~ plus que je ne suis pas sûr qu'il vienne demain** you'd better write to him especially since I'm not sure if he's coming tomorrow; **d'~ plus!** all the more reason!; **cela se gardera d'~ mieux (que ...)** it will keep even better *ou* all the better (since ...); **nous le voyons d'~ moins qu'il habite très loin maintenant** we see him even less *ou* all the less now that he lives a long way away.

f (*loc*) **~ il est généreux, ~ elle est avare** he is as generous as she is miserly; **~ il aime les chiens, ~ il déteste les chats** he likes dogs as much as he hates cats; **~ que possible** as much *ou* as far as possible; **il voudrait, ~ que possible, éviter les grandes routes** he would like to avoid the major roads as much *ou* as far as possible; (*Prov*) **~ d'hommes, ~ d'avis** every man to his own opinion; **"A~ en emporte le vent"** "Gone with the Wind"; **(pour) ~ que je** (*ou* **qu'il** *etc*) **sache** as far as I know (*ou* he *etc* knows), to the best of my (*ou* his *etc*) knowledge; **c'est ~ de gagné** *ou* **de pris** at least that's something; **c'est ~ de fait** that's that done at least; **~ dire qu'il ne sait rien/qu'il est fou** you *ou* one might as well say that he doesn't know anything/that he's mad; **pour ~** for all that; **vous l'avez aidé mais il ne vous remerciera pas pour ~** you helped him but for all that you won't get any thanks from him; **il ne le fera qu'~ qu'il saura que vous êtes d'accord** he'll only do it in so far as he knows you agree.

autarcie [otaʀsi] **nf** autarky.

autarcique [otaʀsik] **adj** autarkical.

autel [otɛl] **nm** a (*Rel*) altar. (*fig: épouser*) **conduire qn à l'~** to lead sb to the altar; **conduire** *ou* **mener sa fille à l'~** to give one's daughter away (in marriage); *voir* **trône**. b (*fig littér*) altar. **dresser un ~** *ou* **des ~s à qn** to worship sb, put sb on a pedestal; **sacrifier qch sur l'~ de** to sacrifice sth on the altar of.

auteur [otœʀ] **nm** a *[invention, plan, crime]* author; *[texte, roman]* author, writer; *[opéra, concerto]* composer; *[procédé]* originator, author. **il/elle en est l'~** (*invention*) he/she invented it; (*texte*) he/she wrote it, he's/she's the author (of it); **l'~ de cette plaisanterie** the author of this prank, the person who played this prank; **l'~ de l'accident s'est enfui** the person who caused the accident ran off; **l'~ de ce tableau** the painter of this picture, the artist who painted this picture; **qui est l'~ de cette affiche?** who designed this poster?; (*musée*) **"~ inconnu"** "anonymous", "artist unknown"; **il fut l'~ de sa propre ruine** he was the author of his own ruin; **Prévert est l'~ des paroles, Kosma de la musique** Prévert wrote the words *ou* lyrics and Kosma composed the music; (†, *hum*) **l'~ de mes jours** my noble progenitor (†, *hum*); (*Mus*) **~-compositeur** composer-songwriter; *voir* **droit**[3].

b (*écrivain*) author. **lire tout un ~** to read all of an author's works; (*femme*) **c'est un ~ connu** she is a well-known author *ou* authoress; *voir* **femme**.

authenticité [otɑ̃tisite] **nf** (*voir* **authentique**) authenticity; genuineness.

authentification [otɑ̃tifikasjɔ̃] **nf** authentication.

authentifier [otɑ̃tifje] 7 **vt** to authenticate.

authentique [otɑ̃tik] **adj** *œuvre d'art, récit* authentic, genuine; *signature, document* authentic; *sentiment* genuine; *voir* **acte**.

authentiquement [otɑ̃tikmɑ̃] **adv** genuinely, authentically; *rapporter* faithfully.

autisme [otism] **nm** autism.

autiste [otist] **adj, nmf** autistic.

autistique [otistik] **adj** autistic.

auto [oto] 1 **nf** (*voiture*) car, automobile (*US*). **~s tamponneuses** dodgems (*Brit*), bumper cars; *voir* **salon, train.** 2 **adj inv**: **assurance ~** car *ou* motor (*Brit*) *ou* automobile (*US*) insurance; **frais ~** running costs (*of a car*).

auto... [oto] **préf** a (*fait sur soi*) self-. (*Alpinisme*) **~-assurance** self-belay, self-belaying system; **~discipline** self-discipline; **s'~gérer/financer** to be self-managing *ou* -running/self-financing; **organisme ~géré** self-managed *ou* -run body; **tendances ~destructrices** self-destructive tendencies. b (*qui se fait tout seul*) self-. **~(-)contrôle** automatic control; **~(-)régulation** self-regulating system; **~(-)adhésif** self-adhesive. c (*se rapportant à l'automobile*) **train ~-couchettes** car sleeper train.

auto-allumage [otoalymaʒ] **nm** pre-ignition.

autoberge [otobɛʀʒ] **nm** riverside *ou* embankment expressway.

autobiographie [otobjɔgʀafi] **nf** autobiography.

autobiographique [otobjɔgʀafik] **adj** autobiographic(al).

autobronzant, e [otobʀɔ̃zɑ̃, ɑ̃t] **adj** instant tanning (*épith*).

autobus [ɔtɔbys] **nm** bus. (*Hist*) **~ à impériale** double decker (bus).

autocar [ɔtɔkaʀ] **nm** coach (*Brit*), bus (*US*); (*de campagne*) country bus.

autocaravane [otokaʀavan] **nf** motor caravan (*Brit*), motorhome (*US*), camper (*US*).

autocassable [otokɑsabl] **adj**: **ampoule ~** ampoule, ampule (*surtout US*) (*with a snap-off top*).

autocensure [otosɑ̃syʀ] **nf** self-censorship.

autocensurer (s') [otosɑ̃syʀe] 1 **vpr** to practise self-censorship, censor o.s.

autochenille [otoʃ(ə)nij] **nf** half-track.

autochtone [ɔtɔktɔn] 1 **adj** native, autochthonous (*SPÉC*); (*Géol*) autochthonous. 2 **nmf** native, autochton (*SPÉC*).

autoclave [otoklav] **adj, nm** (*Méd, Tech*) **(appareil** *m ou* **marmite** *f*) **~** autoclave.

autocoat [otokot] **nm** car coat.

autocollant, e [otokɔlɑ̃, ɑ̃t] 1 **adj** *étiquette* self-adhesive, self-sticking; *papier* self-adhesive; *enveloppe* self-seal, self-adhesive. 2 **nm** sticker.

autocopiant, e [otokɔpjɑ̃, ɑ̃t] **adj**: **papier ~** carbon paper.

autocorrection [otokɔʀɛksjɔ̃] **nf** autocorrection.

autocrate [otokʀat] nm autocrat.
autocratie [otokʀasi] nf autocracy.
autocratique [otokʀatik] adj autocratic.
autocratiquement [otokʀatikmɑ̃] adv autocratically.
autocritique [otokʀitik] nf self-criticism. **faire son ~** to criticize o.s.
autocuiseur [otokɥizœʀ] nm pressure cooker.
autodafé [otodafe] nm auto-da-fé.
autodéfense [otodefɑ̃s] nf self-defence. **groupe d'~** vigilante group *ou* committee.
autodestruction [otodɛstʀyksjɔ̃] nf self-destruction.
autodétermination [otodetɛʀminasjɔ̃] nf self-determination.
autodidacte [otodidakt] adj self-taught. **c'est un ~** he is self-taught, he is a self-taught man.
autodrome [otodʀom] nm motor-racing track, autodrome.
auto-école, pl **auto-écoles** [otoekɔl] nf driving school. **moniteur d'~** driving instructor.
auto-érotique [otoeʀɔtik] adj auto-erotic.
auto-érotisme [otoeʀɔtism] nm auto-eroticism, auto-erotism.
autofécondation [otofekɔ̃dasjɔ̃] nf (*Bio*) self-fertilization.
autofinancement [otofinɑ̃smɑ̃] nm self-financing.
autofinancer (s') [otofinɑ̃se] 1 vpr *[entreprise]* to be *ou* become self-financing. **programme de recherches autofinancé** self-supporting *ou* self-financed research programme.
autofocus [otofɔkys] adj, nm autofocus.
autogène [otoʒɛn] adj *voir* **soudure**.
autogérer (s') [otoʒeʀe] 1 vpr to be self-managing.
autogestion [otoʒɛstjɔ̃] nf (*gén*) self-management; (*avec les ouvriers*) joint worker-management control.
autogestionnaire [otoʒɛstjɔnɛʀ] adj self-managing (*épith*).
autogire [otoʒiʀ] nm autogiro, autogyro.
autographe [ɔtɔgʀaf] adj, nm autograph.
autogreffe [otogʀɛf] nf autograft.
autoguidage [otogidaʒ] nm self-steering.
autoguidé, e [otogide] adj self-guided.
auto-immun, e [otoi(m)mœ̃, yn] adj autoimmune.
auto-immunisation [otoimynizasjɔ̃] nf autoimmunization.
auto-induction [otoɛ̃dyksjɔ̃] nf (*Phys*) self-induction.
auto-intoxication [otoɛ̃tɔksikasjɔ̃] nf auto-intoxication.
autolyse [otoliz] nf autolysis.
automate [ɔtɔmat] nm (*lit, fig*) automaton. **marcher comme un ~** to walk like a robot.
automation [ɔtɔmɑsjɔ̃] nf automation.
automatique [ɔtɔmatik] 1 adj automatic. 2 nm (*Téléc*) ≃ subscriber trunk dialling (*Brit*), STD (*Brit*), direct distance dialing (*US*); (*revolver*) automatic; *voir* **distributeur**.
automatiquement [ɔtɔmatikmɑ̃] adv automatically.
automatisation [ɔtɔmatizasjɔ̃] nf automation.
automatiser [ɔtɔmatize] 1 vt to automate.
automatisme [ɔtɔmatism] nm automatism; *[machine]* automatic functioning, automatism.
automédication [otomedikasjɔ̃] nf self-medication. **faire de l'~** to medicate o.s.
automédon [ɔtɔmedɔ̃] nm (†, *hum*) coachman.
automitrailleuse [otomitʀɑjøz] nf armoured car.
automnal, e, mpl **-aux** [ɔtɔnal, o] adj autumnal.
automne [ɔtɔn] nm autumn, fall (*US*). **en ~** in (the) autumn, in the fall; (*fig*) **c'est l'~ de ses jours** he's in the autumn (*Brit*) *ou* fall (*US*) of his life.
automobile [ɔtɔmɔbil] 1 adj *véhicule* self-propelled, motor (*épith*), automotive; *course, sport* motor (*épith*); *assurance, industrie* motor, car, automobile (*US*); *voir* **canot**. 2 nf (*voiture*) motor car (*Brit*), automobile (*US*). (*industrie*) **l'~** the car *ou* motor industry, the automobile industry (*US*); (*Sport, conduite*) **l'~** motoring; **termes d'~** motoring terms; **être passionné d'~** to be a car fanatic; **aimer les courses d'~s** to like motor racing.
automobilisme [ɔtɔmɔbilism] nm motoring.
automobiliste [ɔtɔmɔbilist] nmf motorist.
automoteur, -trice [otomɔtœʀ, tʀis] 1 adj self-propelled, motorized, motor (*épith*), automotive. 2 **automotrice** nf electric railcar.
automutilation [otomytilasjɔ̃] nf self-mutilation.
autoneige [otonɛʒ] nf (*Can*) snowmobile (*US, Can*), snowcat.
autonettoyant, e [otonetwajɑ̃, ɑ̃t] adj self-cleaning (*épith*).
autonome [ɔtɔnɔm] adj a *port* independent, autonomous; *territoire* autonomous, self-governing. **groupuscule ~** group of political extremists. b *personne* self-sufficient; (*Philos*) *volonté* autonomous; (*Ordin*) off-line; *voir* **scaphandre**.
autonomie [ɔtɔnɔmi] nf (*Admin, Fin, Philos, Pol*) autonomy; (*Aut, Aviat*) range. **certains Corses/Bretons veulent l'~** some Corsicans/Bretons want home rule *ou* autonomy *ou* self-government.
autonomiste [ɔtɔnɔmist] nmf, adj (*Pol*) separatist.
autonyme [otonim] adj autonymous.
autopont [otopɔ̃] nm flyover (*Brit*), overpass (*US*).
autoportrait [otopɔʀtʀɛ] nm self-portrait.
autopropulsé, e [otopʀɔpylse] adj self-propelled.
autopropulsion [otopʀɔpylsjɔ̃] nf self-propulsion.
autopsie [ɔtɔpsi] nf autopsy, post-mortem (examination); (*fig*) dissection.
autopsier [ɔtɔpsje] 7 vt to carry out an autopsy *ou* a post-mortem (examination) on.
autopunition [otopynisjɔ̃] nf self-punishment.
autoradio [otoʀadjo] nm car radio.
autoradiographie [otoʀadjɔgʀafi] nf autoradiograph.
autorail [otoʀaj] nm railcar.
autorisation [ɔtɔʀizasjɔ̃] nf (*permission*) permission, authorization (*de qch* for sth, *de faire* to do); (*permis*) permit. **nous avions l'~ du professeur** we had the teacher's permission; **avoir l'~ de faire qch** to have permission *ou* be allowed to do sth; (*Admin*) to be authorized to do sth; **le projet doit recevoir l'~ du comité** the project must be authorized *ou* passed by the committee; **~ d'absence** leave of absence; (*Ordin*) **~ d'accès** access permission; (*Fin*) **~ de crédit** credit line, line of credit; (*Écon*) **~ de mise sur le marché** *permit to market a product;* (*Aviat*) **~ de vol** flight clearance; **~ parentale** parental consent.
autorisé, e [ɔtɔʀize] (ptp de **autoriser**) adj *agent, version* authorized; *opinion* authoritative. **dans les milieux ~s** in official circles; **nous apprenons de source ~e que ...** we have learnt from official sources that ... .
autoriser [ɔtɔʀize] 1 1 vt a **~ qn à faire** (*donner la permission de*) to give *ou* grant sb permission to do, authorize sb to do; (*habiliter à*) *[personne, décret]* to give sb authority to do, authorize sb to do; **il nous a autorisés à sortir** he has given *ou* granted us permission to go out, we have his permission to go out; **sa faute ne t'autorise pas à le condamner** his mistake does not entitle you *ou* give you the right to pass judgment on him; **tout nous autorise à croire que ...** everything leads us to believe that ...; **se croire autorisé à dire que ...** to feel one is entitled *ou* think one has the right to say that ... .
b (*permettre*) *[personne] manifestation, sortie* to authorize, give permission for; *projet* to pass, authorize. **le sel ne m'est pas autorisé** I'm not allowed to eat salt.
c (*rendre possible*) *[chose]* to admit of, allow (of), sanction. **l'imprécision de cette loi autorise les abus** the imprecisions in this law admit of *ou* allow of *ou* appear to sanction abuses; **expression autorisée par l'usage** expression sanctioned *ou* made acceptable by use.
d (*littér: justifier*) to justify.
2 **s'autoriser** vpr: **s'~ de qch pour faire** (*idée de prétexte*) to use sth as an excuse to do; (*invoquer*) **je m'autorise de notre amitié pour** in view of our friendship I permit myself to; **on s'autorise à penser que ...** one is justified in thinking that ... .
autoritaire [ɔtɔʀitɛʀ] adj, nmf authoritarian.
autoritairement [ɔtɔʀitɛʀmɑ̃] adv in an authoritarian way.
autoritarisme [ɔtɔʀitaʀism] nm authoritarianism.
autorité [ɔtɔʀite] nf a (*pouvoir*) authority (*sur* over). **l'~ que lui confère son expérience/âge** the authority conferred upon him by experience/age; **avoir de l'~ sur qn** to have authority over sb; **être sous l'~ de qn** to be under sb's authority; **avoir ~ pour faire** to have authority to do; **ton/air d'~** authoritative tone/air, tone/air of authority.
b (*expert, ouvrage*) authority. **c'est l'une des grandes ~s en la matière** it *ou* he is one of the great authorities on the subject.
c (*Admin*) **l'~** those in authority, the powers that be (*gén iro*); **les ~s** the authorities; **l'~ militaire/législative** *etc* the military/legislative *etc* authorities; **les ~s civiles et religieuses/locales** the civil and religious/local authorities; **agent** *ou* **représentant de l'~** representative of authority; **adressez-vous à l'~** *ou* **aux ~s compétente(s)** apply to the proper authorities.
d (*Jur*) **l'~ de la loi** the authority *ou* power of the law; **l'~ de la chose jugée** res judicata; **être déchu de son ~ paternelle** to lose one's parental rights; **fermé/vendu par ~ de justice** closed/sold by order of the court.
e (*loc*) **d'~** (*de façon impérative*) on one's own authority; (*sans réflexion*) out of hand, straight off, unhesitatingly; **de sa propre ~** on one's own authority; **faire ~** *[livre, expert]* to be accepted as an authority, be authoritative.
autoroute [otoʀut] nf motorway (*Brit*), highway (*US*), freeway (*US*). **~ de dégagement** *toll-free stretch of motorway leading out of a big city;* **~ de liaison** intercity motorway (*Brit*), highway (*US*), freeway (*US*); **~ urbaine** urban *ou* inner-city motorway (*Brit*), throughway (*US*), expressway (*US*); **~ à péage** toll motorway (*Brit*), turnpike (*US*).
autoroutier, -ière [otoʀutje, jɛʀ] adj motorway (*Brit*) (*épith*), freeway (*US*) (*épith*).
autosatisfaction [otosatisfaksjɔ̃] nf self-satisfaction.
auto-stop [otostɔp] nm hitch-hiking, hitching*. **pour rentrer, il a fait de l'~** (*long voyage*) he hitched* *ou* hitch-hiked home; (*courte distance*) he thumbed *ou* hitched* a lift home; **il a fait le tour du monde en ~** he hitch-hiked round the world, he hitched* his way round the world; **j'ai pris quelqu'un en ~** I picked up a *ou* gave a lift to a hitch-hiker *ou* hitcher*; **il nous a pris en ~** he picked us up, he gave us a lift.
auto-stoppeur, -euse, mpl **auto-stoppeurs** [otostɔpœʀ, øz] nm,f hitch-hiker, hitcher*. **prendre un ~** to pick up a hitch-hiker *ou* hitcher*.

autostrade† [otostʀad] **nf** motorway (*Brit*), freeway (*US*), highway (*US*).

autosuffisance [otosyfizɑ̃s] **nf** self-sufficiency.

autosuffisant, e [otosyfizɑ̃, ɑ̃t] **adj** self-sufficient.

autosuggestion [otosygʒɛstjɔ̃] **nf** autosuggestion.

autotracté, e [ototʀakte] **adj** self-propelled.

autotransfusion [ototʀɑ̃sfyzjɔ̃] **nf** autologous transfusion.

autour[1] [otuʀ] 1 **adv** around. **tout ~** all around; **une maison avec un jardin ~** a house surrounded by a garden, a house with a garden around *ou* round (*Brit*) it. 2 **prép: ~ de** *lieu* around, round (*Brit*); *temps, somme* about, around, round about (*Brit*); **il regarda ~ de lui** he looked around him *ou* about him, he looked around; **discussion ~ d'un projet** discussion on *ou* about a project; **~ d'un bon café** over a nice cup of coffee; *voir* **tourner.**

autour[2] [otuʀ] **nm** (*Orn*) goshawk.

autovaccin [otovaksɛ̃] **nm** autogenous vaccine, autovaccine.

autre [otʀ] 1 **adj indéf** a (*différent*) other, different. **ils ont un (tout) ~ mode de vie/point de vue** they have a (completely) different way of life/point of view; **chercher un ~ mode de vie** to try to find an alternative lifestyle *ou* a different way of living; **c'est une ~ question/un ~ problème** that's another *ou* a different question/problem; **c'est (tout) ~ chose** that's a different *ou* another matter (altogether); **parlons d'~ chose** let's talk about something else *ou* different; **revenez une ~ fois/un ~ jour** come back some other *ou* another time/another *ou* some other day; **je fais cela d'une ~ façon** I do it a different way *ou* another way *ou* differently; **il n'y a pas d'~ moyen d'entrer que de forcer la porte** there's no other way *ou* there isn't any other way of getting in but to force open the door; **vous ne le reconnaîtrez pas, il est (devenu) tout ~** you won't know him, he's completely different *ou* he is a changed man; **après ce bain je me sens un ~ homme** after that swim, I feel a new man; (*Prov*) **~s temps ~s mœurs** customs change with the times, autres temps autres mœurs; *voir* **part.**

b (*supplémentaire*) other. **elle a 2 ~s enfants** she has 2 other *ou* 2 more children; **donnez-moi un ~ kilo/une ~ tasse de thé** give me another kilo/cup of tea; **il y a beaucoup d'~s solutions** there are many other *ou* many more solutions; **bien *ou* beaucoup d'~s choses encore** plenty more besides; **c'est un ~ Versailles** it's another Versailles; **c'est un ~ moi-même** he's my alter ego; **des couteaux, des verres et ~s objets indispensables** knives, glasses and other necessary items.

c (*de deux: marque une opposition*) other. **il habite de l'~ côté de la rue/dans l'~ sens** he lives on the other *ou* opposite side of the street/in the other *ou* opposite direction; **mets l'~ manteau** put on the other coat; **mets ton ~ manteau** put on your other coat; (*Rel*) **l'~ monde** the next world; **expédier *ou* envoyer qn dans l'~ monde** to send sb to meet his (*ou* her) maker.

d (*loc*) **l'~ jour, l'~ fois** the other day; **l'~ lundi** one Monday recently; **l'~ semaine** the other week; **nous/vous ~s*: faut pas nous raconter des histoires, à nous ~s!*** there's no point telling fibs to US!; **nous ~s*, on est prudents** WE are *ou* WE'RE cautious; **taisez-vous, vous ~s*** be quiet, you lot* (*Brit*) *ou* you people *ou* the rest of you; **et vous ~s qu'en pensez-vous?** what do you people *ou* you lot* (*Brit*) think?; **nous ~ Français, nous aimons la bonne cuisine** we Frenchmen like good cooking; **j'aimerais bien entendre un ~ son de cloche** I'd like to have a second opinion; **c'est un ~ son de cloche** that's quite another story; **j'ai d'~s chats à fouetter** I've other fish to fry; **vous êtes de l'~ côté de la barrière** you see it from the other side; **voilà ~ chose!*** (*incident*) that's all I need!; (*impertinence*) what a cheek!, the cheek of it!; **c'est quand même ~ chose!** it's altogether something else!; **c'est cela et pas ~ chose** it's that or nothing; **~ chose, Madame?** anything *ou* something else, madam?; **ce n'est pas ~ chose que de la jalousie** that's just jealousy, that's nothing but jealousy; **ah ~ chose! j'ai oublié de vous dire que** oh, one more thing! I forgot to tell you that; **une chose est de rédiger un rapport, ~ chose est d'écrire un livre** it's one thing to draw up a report, but quite another thing *ou* but another thing altogether to write a book; **~ part** somewhere else; **d'~ part** on the other hand; (*de plus*) moreover; **d'un ~ côté** on the other hand; **c'est une ~ paire de manches*** that's another kettle of fish, that's another story.

2 **pron indéf** a (*qui est différent*) another (one). **d'~s** others; **aucun ~, nul ~, personne d'~** no one else, nobody else; **prendre qn pour un ~/une chose pour une ~** to take sb for sb else/sth for sth else; **envoyez-moi bien ce livre je n'en veux pas d'~** make sure you send me this book, I don't want any other (one) *ou* I want no other; **à d'~s!*** (go and) tell that to the marines!*, (that's) a likely story!; **il n'en fait jamais d'~s!** that's just typical of him!, that's just what he always does!; **un ~ que moi/lui aurait refusé** anyone else (but me/him) would have refused; **elle n'est pas plus bête qu'une ~** she's no more stupid than anyone else; **il en a vu d'~s!** he's seen worse!; **les deux ~s** the other two, the two others; **et l'~ (là)*, il vient avec nous?** what about him, is he coming with us?; **vous en êtes un ~!***† you're a fool!; **X, Y, Z, et ~s** X, Y, Z and others *ou* etc; **d'~s diraient que ...** others would say that ...; *voir* **entre, rien.**

b (*qui vient en plus*) **deux enfants, c'est assez, je n'en veux pas d'~/d'~s** two children are enough, I don't want another (one)/(any) more; **donnez m'en un ~** give me another (one) *ou* one more; **qui/quoi d'~?** who/what else?; **rien/personne d'~** nothing/nobody else.

c (*marque une opposition*) **l'~** the other (one); **les ~s** (*choses*) the others, the other ones; (*personnes*) the others; **les ~s ne veulent pas venir** the others don't want to come; **penser du mal des ~s** to think ill of others *ou* of other people; **avec toi, c'est toujours les ~s qui ont tort** with you, it's always the others who are *ou* the other person who is in the wrong; **d'une minute/semaine à l'~** (*bientôt*) any minute/week (now); **d'une minute à l'~** (*n'importe quand*) any moment *ou* minute *ou* time; (*soudain*) from one minute *ou* moment to the next; *voir* **côté, ni.**

3 **nm** (*Philos*) **l'~** the other.

autrefois [otʀəfwa] **adv** in the past, in bygone days (*littér*). **d'~** of the past, of old, past; **~ ils s'éclairaient à la bougie** in the past *ou* in bygone days they used candles for lighting; **~ je préférais le vin** (in the past) I used to prefer wine.

autrement [otʀəmɑ̃] **adv** a (*d'une manière différente*) differently. **il faut s'y prendre (tout) ~** we'll have to go about it in (quite) another way *ou* (quite) differently; **avec ce climat il ne peut en être ~** with this climate it can't be any other way *ou* how else could it be!; **cela ne peut s'être passé ~** it can't have happened any other way; **agir ~ que d'habitude *ou* qu'on ne fait d'habitude** to act differently from usual; **comment aller à Londres ~ que par le train?** how can we get to London other than by train?; **~ appelé** otherwise known as.

b **faire ~: il n'y a pas moyen de faire ~, on ne peut pas faire ~** it's impossible to do otherwise *ou* to do anything else; **il n'a pas pu faire ~ que de me voir** he couldn't help seeing me *ou* help but see me; **quand il voit une pâtisserie il ne peut pas faire ~ que d'y entrer** whenever he sees a cake shop he can't help going in *ou* he just HAS to go in; **elle a fait ~ que je lui avais dit** she did something different from *ou* other than what I told her.

c (*sinon*) otherwise; (*idée de menace*) otherwise, or else. **travaille bien, ~ tu auras de mes nouvelles!** work hard, otherwise *ou* or else you'll be hearing a few things from me!

d (**: à part cela*) otherwise, apart *ou* aside from that. **la viande était bonne, ~ le repas était quelconque** the meat was good but apart *ou* aside from that *ou* but otherwise the meal was pretty nondescript.

e (**: comparatif*) far (more). **il est ~ intelligent** he is far more intelligent, he is more intelligent by far; **c'est ~ meilleur** it's far better, it's better by far (*que* than).

f **pas ~** (**: pas spécialement*) not particularly *ou* especially; **cela ne m'a pas ~ surpris** that didn't particularly surprise me.

g **~ dit** (*en d'autres mots*) in other words; (*c'est-à-dire*) that is.

Autriche [otʀiʃ] **nf** Austria.

autrichien, -ienne [otʀiʃjɛ̃, jɛn] 1 **adj** Austrian. 2 **nm,f: A~(ne)** Austrian.

autruche [otʀyʃ] **nf** ostrich. (*fig*) **faire l'~** to bury one's head in the sand; *voir* **estomac, politique.**

autrui [otʀɥi] **pron** (*littér*) others. **respecter le bien d'~** to respect the property of others *ou* other people's property.

auvent [ovɑ̃] **nm** *[maison]* canopy; *[tente]* awning, canopy.

auvergnat, e [ovɛʀɲa, at] 1 **adj** of *ou* from (the) Auvergne. 2 **nm** (*Ling*) Auvergne dialect. 3 **nm,f: A~(e)** inhabitant *ou* native of (the) Auvergne.

Auvergne [ovɛʀɲ] **nf: l'~** (the) Auvergne.

aux [o] *voir* **à.**

auxiliaire [ɔksiljɛʀ] 1 **adj** (*Ling, Mil, gén*) auxiliary (*épith*); *cause, raison* secondary, subsidiary; (*Scol*) assistant (*épith*). **bureau ~** sub-office; (*Ordin*) **mémoire ~** additional *ou* extra memory; (*Ordin*) **programme ~** auxiliary routine. 2 **nmf** (*assistant*) assistant, helper. (*Jur*) **~ de (la) justice** representative of the law; **~ médical** medical auxiliary. 3 **nm** (*Gram, Mil*) auxiliary.

auxiliairement [ɔksiljɛʀmɑ̃] **adv** (*Ling*) as an auxiliary; (*fig: secondairement*) secondarily, less importantly.

auxiliariat [ɔksiljaʀja] **nm** (*Scol*) **pendant mon ~** during my time as a supply teacher (*Brit*) *ou* substitute teacher (*US*).

AV [ave] (**abrév de avis de virement**) *voir* **avis.**

av **abrév de avenue.**

avachi, e [avaʃi] (**ptp de avachir**) **adj** a *cuir, feutre* limp; *chaussure, vêtement* misshapen, out of shape. **pantalon ~** baggy trousers. b *personne* (*par la chaleur*) limp; (*moralement*) flabby, sloppy. **~ sur son pupitre** slumped on his desk.

avachir [avaʃiʀ] [2] 1 **vt** a *cuir, feutre* to make limp; *chaussure, vêtement* to make shapeless, put out of shape. b (*état*) *personne* (*physiquement*) to make limp; (*moralement*) to make sloppy. 2 **s'avachir vpr** a *[cuir]* to become limp; *[vêtement]* to go out of shape, become shapeless. b *[personne]* (*physiquement*) to become limp; (*moralement*) to become sloppy.

avachissement [avaʃismɑ̃] **nm** a *[vêtement, cuir]* loss of shape. b (*état*) *[personne]* (*physiquement*) limpness; (*moralement*) sloppiness, flabbiness. **leur ~ faisait peine à voir** it was a shame to see them becoming so sloppy *ou* to see them letting themselves go like this.

aval[1] [aval] **nm** *[cours d'eau]* downstream water; *[pente]* downhill slope. **en ~** (*lit*) below, downstream, down-river; downhill; (*Écon*) downstream; (*dans une hiérarchie*) lower down; **en ~ de** (*lit*) below, downstream *ou* down-river from; downhill from; (*fig: après*) after; **les**

rapides/l'écluse d'~ the downstream rapids/lock; **l'~ était coupé de rapides** the river downstream was a succession of rapids; **skieur/ski ~** downhill skier/ski.

aval², pl **~s** [aval] **nm** (*fig: soutien*) backing, support; (*Comm, Jur*) guarantee (*de* for). **donner son ~ à qn** to give sb one's support, back sb; **donner son ~ à une traite** to guarantee *ou* endorse a draft.

avalanche [avalɑ̃ʃ] **nf** (*Géog*) avalanche; *[coups]* hail, shower; *[compliments]* flood, torrent; *[réclamations, prospectus]* avalanche; *voir* **couloir.**

avalancheux, -euse [avalɑ̃ʃø, øz] **adj** *zone, pente* avalanche-prone.

avaler [avale] 1 **vt** a *nourriture* to swallow (down); *repas* to swallow; *boisson* to swallow (down), drink (down); (*fig*) *roman* to devour; (*Alpinisme*) *mou, corde* to take in. *[fumeur]* **~ la fumée** to inhale (the smoke); **~ qch d'un trait** *ou* **d'un seul coup** to swallow sth in one gulp, down sth in one*; **~ son café à petites gorgées** to sip one's coffee; **~ sa salive** to swallow; (*fig*) **j'ai eu du mal à ~ ma salive** I gulped; **il a avalé de travers** it went down the wrong way; **il n'a rien avalé depuis 2 jours** he hasn't eaten a thing *ou* had a thing to eat for 2 days.

b (*) *mensonge, histoire* to swallow; *affront* to swallow, take; *mauvaise nouvelle* to accept. **on lui ferait ~ n'importe quoi** he would swallow anything; (*fig*) **~ la pilule** *ou* **le morceau** to take one's medicine, bite the bullet; **c'est dur** *ou* **difficile à ~** it's hard *ou* difficult to swallow; **~ des couleuvres** (*affront*) to swallow an affront; (*mensonge*) to swallow a lie, be taken in; **j'ai cru qu'il allait m'~ tout cru** I thought he was going to eat me alive; **c'est un ambitieux qui veut tout ~** he's an ambitious man who thinks he can take on anything; **~ ses mots** to mumble; **~ les kilomètres** ≈ to eat up the miles; (*Sport*) **~ l'obstacle** to make short work of the obstacle, take the obstacle in one's stride.

c (*loc fig*) **tu as avalé ta langue?** have you lost your tongue?; **on dirait qu'il a avalé son parapluie** he's so (stiff and) starchy; (*hum*) **~ son bulletin de naissance** to kick the bucket*, snuff it*.

avaleur, -euse [avalœʀ, øz] **nm,f: ~ de sabres** sword swallower.

avaliser [avalize] 1 **vt** *plan, entreprise* to back, support; (*Comm, Jur*) to endorse, guarantee.

à-valoir [avalwaʀ] **nm inv** advance.

avance [avɑ̃s] **nf** a (*marche, progression*) advance. **accélérer/ralentir son ~** to speed up/slow down one's advance.

b (*sur un concurrent etc*) lead. **avoir/prendre de l'~ sur qn** to have/take the lead over sb; **dix minutes/km d'~** a 10-minute/km lead; **avoir une longueur d'~** to be a length ahead; (*Scol*) **il a un an d'~** he's a year ahead; **l'~ des Russes dans le domaine scientifique** the Russians' lead in the world of science; **perdre son ~** to lose one's *ou* the lead; **cet élève est tombé malade et a perdu son ~** this pupil fell ill and lost the lead he had (on the rest of the class).

c (*sur un horaire*) **avoir/prendre de l'~** to be/get ahead of schedule; **avoir beaucoup d'~/une ~ de 2 ans** to be well/2 years ahead of schedule; **avoir/prendre de l'~ dans son travail** to be/get ahead in *ou* with one's work; **le train a dix minutes d'~** the train is 10 minutes early; **le train a pris de l'~/dix minutes d'~** the train has got ahead/has got 10 minutes ahead of schedule; **arriver avec cinq minutes d'~** to arrive 5 minutes early *ou* 5 minutes ahead of time; **avec cinq minutes d'~ sur les autres** 5 minutes earlier than the others; **le train a perdu son ~** the train has lost the time it had gained; (*Aut, Tech*) **~ à l'allumage** ignition advance; **ma montre a dix minutes d'~** my watch is 10 minutes fast; **ma montre prend de l'~** my watch is gaining *ou* gains; **ma montre prend beaucoup d'~** my watch gains a lot.

d (*Comm, Fin: acompte*) advance. **~ de fonds** advance; **faire une ~ de 100 F à qn** to advance sb 100 francs, make sb an advance of 100 francs; **donner à qn une ~ sur son salaire** to give sb an advance on his salary; (*Ciné*) **~ sur recettes** advance against takings (*grant given to film makers by the Government*).

e (*ouvertures*) **~s** overtures, (*galantes*) advances; **faire des ~s à qn** to make overtures *ou* advances to sb.

f **en ~** (*sur l'heure fixée*) early; (*sur l'horaire etc*) ahead of schedule; **être en ~ sur qn** to be ahead of sb; **être en ~ d'une heure** (*sur l'heure fixée*) to be an hour early; (*sur l'horaire*) to be an hour ahead of schedule; **dépêche-toi, tu n'es pas en ~!** hurry up, you've not got much time! *ou* you're running out of time!; **tous ces problèmes ne m'ont pas mis en ~** all these problems haven't helped; **les crocus sont en ~ cette année** the crocuses are early this year; **leur fils est très en ~ dans ses études/sur les autres enfants** their son is well ahead in his studies/of the other children; **il est en ~ pour son âge** he is advanced for his age, he is ahead of his age group; **leur pays est en ~ dans le domaine scientifique** their country leads *ou* is ahead in the field of science; **ses idées étaient/il était très en ~ sur son temps** *ou* **son époque** his ideas were/he was well ahead of *ou* in advance of his time; **nous sommes en ~ sur le programme** we're ahead of schedule.

g (*loc*) **à l'~** in advance, beforehand; **réserver une place un mois à l'~** to book a seat one month ahead *ou* in advance; **prévenir qn deux heures à l'~** to give sb 2 hours' notice, notify *ou* warn sb 2 hours beforehand *ou* in advance; **payable à l'~** payable in advance; **je vous remercie à l'~** *ou* **d'~** thanking you in advance *ou* in anticipation; **merci d'~** thanks (in advance); **d'~** in advance; **d'~ je peux vous dire que ...** I can tell you in advance *ou* right now that ...; **d'~ il pouvait deviner** already *ou* even then he could guess; **je m'en réjouis d'~** I look forward to it with pleasure; **il faut payer d'~** one must pay in advance; **ça a été arrangé d'~** it was prearranged, it was arranged beforehand *ou* in advance; **par ~** in advance.

avancé, e¹ [avɑ̃se] (**ptp de avancer**) **adj** a *élève, civilisation, technique* advanced. **la saison/journée était ~e** it was late in the season/day; **la nuit était ~e** it was well into the night; **il est très ~ dans son travail** he is well on with his work; **à une heure ~e de la nuit** well on into the night; **son roman est déjà assez ~** he's already quite a long way on *ou* quite far ahead with his novel; **je suis peu/très ~ dans la lecture de mon roman** I haven't got very far into/I'm well into my novel; **les pays les moins ~s** the least developed countries; **cet enfant n'est vraiment pas ~ pour son âge** this child is rather backward *ou* is not at all advanced for his age; **être d'un âge ~** to be advanced in years *ou* well on in years; **dans un état ~ de ...** in an advanced state of ...; **après toutes ses démarches, il n'en est pas plus ~** after all the steps he has taken, he's no further on than he was; (*iro*) **nous voilà bien ~s!*** a long way that's got us! (*iro*), a (fat) lot of good that's done us!* (*iro*); *voir* **heure.**

b (*d'avant-garde*) *opinion, idée* progressive, advanced.

c (*qui se gâte*) *fruit, fromage* overripe. **ce poisson est ~** this fish is going off (*Brit*) *ou* is bad.

d (*Mil*) *poste* advanced.

avancée² [avɑ̃se] **nf** overhang.

avancement [avɑ̃smɑ̃] **nm** a (*promotion*) promotion. **avoir** *ou* **prendre de l'~** to be promoted, get promotion; **~ à l'ancienneté** promotion according to length of service; **possibilités d'~** career prospects, prospects *ou* chances of promotion. b (*progrès*) *[travaux]* progress; *[sciences, techniques]* advancement. c (*mouvement*) forward movement. d (*Jur*) **~ d'hoirie** advancement.

avancer [avɑ̃se] 3 1 **vt** a (*porter en avant*) *objet* to move *ou* bring forward; *tête* to move forward; *main* to hold out, put out (*vers* to); *pion* to move forward. **~ le cou** to crane one's neck; **~ un siège à qn** to draw up *ou* bring forward a seat for sb; **le blessé avança les lèvres pour boire** the injured man put his lips forward to drink; (†, *hum*) **la voiture de Madame est avancée** Madam's carriage awaits (†, *hum*); **~ (les aiguilles d')une pendule** to put (the hands of) a clock forward *ou* on (*Brit*).

b (*fig*) *opinion, hypothèse* to put forward, advance. **ce qu'il avance paraît vraisemblable** what he is putting forward *ou* suggesting seems quite plausible.

c *date, départ* to bring forward. **il a dû ~ son retour** he had to bring forward the date of his return.

d (*faire progresser*) *travail* to speed up. **est-ce que cela vous avancera si je vous aide?** will it speed things up (for you) *ou* will you get on more quickly if I lend you a hand?; **ça n'avance pas nos affaires** that doesn't improve matters for us; **cela t'avancera à quoi de courir?** what good will it do you to run?; **cela ne t'avancera à rien de crier*** shouting won't get you anywhere, you won't get anywhere by shouting.

e *somme d'argent, fonds* to advance; (*: *prêter*) to lend.

2 **vi** a (*progresser*) to advance, move forward; *[bateau]* to make headway. **l'armée avance sur Paris** the army is advancing on Paris; **il avança d'un pas** he took *ou* moved a step forward; **il avança d'un mètre** he moved three feet forward, he came three feet nearer; **mais avance donc!** move on *ou* forward *ou* up, will you!; **le paysan essayait de faire ~ son âne** the peasant tried to get his donkey to move (on) *ou* to make his donkey move (on); **ça n'avançait pas sur l'autoroute** traffic on the motorway was almost at a standstill *ou* was crawling along.

b (*fig*) to make progress. **la nuit avance** night is wearing on; **faire ~** *travail* to speed up; *élève* to bring on, help to make progress; *science* to further; **~ vite/lentement dans son travail** to make good/slow progress in one's work; **~ péniblement dans son travail** to plod on slowly with *ou* make halting progress in one's work; **~ en âge** to be getting on (in years); **~ en grade** to be promoted, get promotion; **et les travaux, ça avance?*** how's the work coming on?*; **son livre n'avance guère** he's not making much headway *ou* progress with his book; **tout cela n'avance à rien** that doesn't get us any further *ou* anywhere; **je travaille mais il me semble que je n'avance pas** I'm working but I don't seem to be getting anywhere.

c *[montre, horloge]* to gain. **~ de dix minutes par jour** to gain 10 minutes a day; **ma montre avance** *ou* **j'avance (de dix minutes)** my watch is *ou* I'm (10 minutes) fast.

d *[cap, promontoire]* to project, jut out (*dans* into); *[lèvre, menton]* to protrude. **un balcon qui avance (de 3 mètres) sur la rue** a balcony that juts out *ou* projects (3 metres) over the street.

3 **s'avancer vpr** a (*aller en avant*) to move forward; (*progresser*) to advance. **il s'avança vers nous** he came towards us; **la procession s'avançait lentement** the procession advanced slowly *ou* moved slowly forward; **il s'est avancé dans son travail** he made some progress with his work.

b (*fig: s'engager*) to commit o.s. **il n'aime pas beaucoup s'~** he does not like to commit himself *ou* stick his neck out*; **je ne peux pas m'~ sans connaître la question** I don't know enough about it to venture *ou* hazard an opinion, I can't commit myself without knowing more about it; **ne t'avance pas trop si tu ne veux pas le regretter** don't do (*ou* say) anything you might regret.

avanie [avani] nf: **subir une ~** to be snubbed; **faire** *ou* **infliger des ~s à qn** to snub sb; **les ~s qu'il avait subies** the snubs he had received.

avant [avɑ̃] 1 prép a (*temps, lieu*) before; (*avec limite de temps*) by, before. **il est parti ~ la pluie/la fin** he left before the rain started/the end; **il est parti ~ nous** he left before us; **cela s'est passé bien/peu ~ son mariage** this took place long *ou* a good while/shortly *ou* a short time before he was *ou* got married *ou* before his marriage; **ne venez pas ~ 10 heures** don't come until *ou* before 10; **il n'arrivera pas ~ une demi-heure** he won't be here for another half hour (yet) *ou* for half an hour (yet); **~ cela il était très gai** before that *ou* (up) until then he had been very cheerful; **j'étais ~ lui dans la queue mais on l'a servi ~ moi** I was in front of him *ou* before him in the queue (*Brit*) *ou* line (*US*) but he was served before me *ou* before I was; **il me le faut ~ demain/minuit** I must have it by *ou* before tomorrow/midnight; **il me le faut ~ une semaine/un mois** I must have it within a week/a month; **~ peu** shortly; **sa maison est (juste) ~ la mairie** his house is (just) before *ou* this side of the town hall; **X, ce féministe (bien) ~ la lettre** X, a feminist (long) before the term existed *ou* had been coined; *voir* **Jésus**.

b (*priorité*) before, in front of, above. **~ tout, ~ toute chose** above all, first and foremost; **le travail passe ~ tout** work comes before everything; **~ tout, il faut éviter la guerre** above all (things) war must be avoided; **il faut ~ tout vérifier l'état du toit** first and foremost *ou* above all else we must see what state the roof is in; **en classe, elle est ~ sa sœur** at school she is ahead of her sister; **il met sa santé ~ sa carrière** he puts his health before *ou* above his career, he values his health above his career; **le capitaine est ~ le lieutenant** captain comes before lieutenant.

c **~ de** + *infin* before; **~ que** + *subj* before; **à prendre ~ (de) manger** to be taken before food *ou* meals; **dînez donc ~ de partir** do have a meal before you go; **consultez-moi ~ de prendre une décision** consult me before making your decision *ou* before you decide; **je veux lire sa lettre ~ qu'elle (ne) l'envoie** I want to read her letter before she sends it (off); **n'envoyez pas cette lettre ~ que je (ne) l'aie lue** don't send this letter before *ou* until I have read it; **la poste est juste ~ d'arriver à la gare** the post office is just before you come to the station.

2 adv a (*temps*) before, beforehand. **le voyage sera long, mangez ~** it's going to be a long journey so have something to eat beforehand *ou* before you go; **quelques semaines/mois ~** a few *ou* some weeks/months before(hand) *ou* previously *ou* earlier; **peu de temps/longtemps ~** shortly/well *ou* long before(hand); **la semaine/le mois d'~** the week/month before, the previous week/month; **fort ~ dans la nuit** far *ou* well into the night; **les gens d'~ étaient plus aimables** the previous people were nicer, the people (who were there) before were nicer; **réfléchis ~, tu parleras après** think before you speak, think first then (you can) speak; **le train d'~ était plein** the earlier *ou* previous train was full; **~ je préférais le bateau au train** (before) I used to prefer the boat to the train; **venez me parler ~** come and talk to me first *ou* beforehand.

b (*lieu: fig*) before; (*avec mouvement*) forward, ahead. **tu vois la gare? il habite juste ~** (you) see the station? he lives just this side (of it) *ou* before it; **n'avancez pas trop** *ou* **plus ~, c'est dangereux** don't go any further (forward), it's dangerous; **il s'était engagé trop ~ dans le bois** he had gone too far *ou* too deep into the wood; (*fig*) **il s'est engagé trop ~** he has got* *ou* become too involved, he has committed himself too deeply; **n'hésitez pas à aller plus ~** don't hesitate to go further *ou* on; **ils sont assez ~ dans leurs recherches** they are well into *ou* well advanced in *ou* far ahead in their research.

c **en ~** (*mouvement*) forward; (*temps, position*) in front, ahead (*de* of); **en ~, marche!** forward march!; (*Naut*) **en ~ toute!** full steam ahead!; **la voiture fit un bond en ~** the car lurched forward; **être en ~** (*d'un groupe de personnes*) to be (out) in front; **marcher en ~ de la procession** to walk in front of the procession; **les enfants sont partis en ~** the children have gone on ahead *ou* in front; **partez en ~, on vous rejoindra** you go on (ahead *ou* in front), we'll catch up with you; (*fig*) **regarder en ~** to look ahead; (*fig*) **mettre qch en ~** to put sth forward, advance sth; (*fig*) **mettre qn en ~** (*pour se couvrir*) to use sb as a front; (*pour aider qn*) to push sb forward *ou* to the front; (*fig*) **il aime se mettre en ~** he likes to push himself forward, he likes to be in the forefront.

3 nm a [*voiture, train*] front; [*navire*] bow(s), stem. **voyager à l'~ du train** to travel in the front of the train; **dans cette voiture on est mieux à l'~** it's more comfortable in the front of this car; (*fig*) **aller de l'~** to forge ahead.

b (*Sport: joueur*) (*gén*) forward; (*Volleyball*) frontline player. **la ligne des ~s** the forward line.

c (*Mil*) front.

4 adj inv *roue, siège* front; *marche* forward. **traction ~** front-wheel drive; **la partie ~** the front part.

5 comp ►**avant-bras** nm inv forearm ►**avant-centre** nm (pl **avant-centres**) centre-forward ►**avant-coureur** adj inv precursory, premonitory; **signe avant-coureur** forerunner, harbinger (*littér*) ►**avant-dernier, -ière** nm,f, adj (mpl **avant-derniers**) next to last, last but one (*Brit*), (*sg seulement*) penultimate ►**avant-garde** nf (pl **avant-gardes**) (*Mil*) vanguard; (*Art, Pol*) avant-garde; **art/poésie/idées d'avant-garde** avant-garde art/poetry/ideas ►**avant-gardisme** nm avant-gardism ►**avant-gardiste** adj, nmf (pl **avant-gardistes**) avant-gardist ►**avant-goût** nm foretaste ►**avant-guerre** nm pre-war years; **d'avant-guerre** adj pre-war ►**avant-hier** adv the day before yesterday ►**avant-midi*** nm ou nf inv (*Belgique, Can*) morning ►**avant-port** nm (pl **avant-ports**) outer harbour ►**avant-poste** nm (pl **avant-postes**) outpost ►**avant-première** nf (pl **avant-premières**) preview ►**avant-projet** nm (pl **avant-projets**) pilot study ►**avant-propos** nm inv foreword ►**avant-scène** nf (pl **avant-scènes**) (*Théât*) (*scène*) apron, proscenium; (*loge*) box (*at the front of the house*) ►**avant-train** nm (pl **avant-trains**) [*animal*] foreparts, forequarters; [*véhicule*] front axle assembly *ou* unit ►**avant-veille** nf: **l'avant-veille** two days before *ou* previously; **c'était l'avant-veille de Noël** it was the day before Christmas Eve *ou* two days before Christmas.

avantage [avɑ̃taʒ] nm a (*intérêt*) advantage. **cette solution a l'~ de ne léser personne** this solution has the advantage of not hurting anyone; **il a ~ à y aller** it will be to his advantage to go, it will be worth his while to go; **j'ai ~ à acheter en gros** it's worth my while to *ou* it's worth it for me to buy in bulk; **tirer ~ de la situation** to take advantage of the situation, turn the situation to one's advantage; **tu aurais ~ à te tenir tranquille*** you'd be *ou* do better to keep quiet*, you'd do well to keep quiet.

b (*supériorité*) advantage. **avoir un ~ sur qn** to have an advantage over sb; **j'ai sur vous l'~ de l'expérience** I have the advantage of experience over you; **ils ont l'~ du nombre sur leurs adversaires** they have the advantage of numbers over their enemies.

c (*Fin: gain*) benefit. **~s accessoires** additional benefits; **~s en nature** fringe benefits, payment in kind; **gros ~s matériels d'un métier** overall material benefits of a job; **~ pécuniaire** financial benefit; **~s sociaux** welfare benefits.

d (*Mil, Sport, fig*) advantage; (*Tennis*) vantage (*Brit*), advantage. **avoir l'~** to have the advantage, have the upper hand, be one up*; (*Tennis*) **~ service/dehors** van(tage) in/out (*Brit*), ad in/out* (*US*), advantage in/out.

e (*frm: plaisir*) **j'ai (l'honneur et) l'~ de vous présenter M. X** I have the (honour and) privilege of introducing Mr X to you (*frm*); **que me vaut l'~ de votre visite?** to what do I owe the pleasure *ou* honour of your visit? (*frm*).

f (*loc*) **être à son ~** (*sur une photo*) to look one's best; (*dans une conversation*) to be at one's best; **elle est à son ~ avec cette coiffure** she looks her best with that hair style, that hair style flatters her; **il s'est montré à son ~** he was seen in a favourable light *ou* to advantage; **c'est (tout) à ton ~** it's (entirely) to your advantage; **changer à son ~** to change for the better; **tourner qch à son ~** to turn sth to one's advantage.

avantager [avɑ̃taʒe] 3 vt a (*donner un avantage à*) to favour, give an advantage to. **elle a été avantagée par la nature** she was favoured by nature; **il a été avantagé par rapport à ses frères** he has been given an advantage over his brothers; (*dans la vie*) **être avantagé dès le départ** to have a head start (*par rapport à* on). b (*mettre en valeur*) to flatter. **ce chapeau l'avantage** that hat flatters her, she looks good in that hat.

avantageusement [avɑ̃taʒøzmɑ̃] adv *vendre* at a good price; *décrire* favourably, flatteringly. **la situation se présente ~** the situation looks favourable; **une robe qui découvrait ~ ses épaules magnifiques** a dress which showed off her lovely shoulders to great advantage.

avantageux, -euse [avɑ̃taʒø, øz] adj a (*profitable*) *affaire* worthwhile, profitable; *prix* attractive. **ce serait plus ~ de faire comme cela** it would be more profitable *ou* worthwhile to do it this way; **c'est une occasion ~euse** it's an attractive *ou* a good bargain. b (*présomptueux*) *air, personne* conceited. c (*qui flatte*) *portrait, chapeau* flattering.

avare [avaʀ] 1 adj a *personne* miserly, avaricious, tight-fisted*. **il est ~ de paroles** he's sparing of words; **il est ~ de compliments** he's sparing with his compliments *ou* sparing of compliments; *voir* **à**. b (*littér: peu abondant*) *terre* meagre. **une lumière ~ pénétrait dans la pièce** a dim *ou* weak light filtered into the room. 2 nmf miser.

avarice [avaʀis] nf miserliness, avarice.

avaricieux, -ieuse [avaʀisjø, jøz] (*littér*) 1 adj miserly, niggardly, stingy. 2 nm miser, niggard, skinflint.

avarie [avaʀi] nf [*navire, véhicule*] damage (*NonC*); (*Tech*) [*cargaison, chargement*] damage (*NonC*) (in transit), average (*SPÉC*).

avarié, e [avaʀje] (ptp de **avarier**) adj *aliment* rotting; *navire* damaged. **une cargaison de viande ~e** a cargo of rotting meat; **cette viande est ~e** this meat has gone off (*Brit*) *ou* gone bad.

avarier [avaʀje] 7 1 vt to spoil, damage. 2 **s'avarier** vpr [*fruits, viande*] to go bad, rot.

avatar [avataʀ] nm (*Rel*) avatar; (*fig*) metamorphosis. (*péripéties*) **~s*** misadventures.

à vau-l'eau [avolo] adv *voir* **vau-l'eau**.

Avé [ave] nm inv (*prière: aussi* **~ Maria**) Hail Mary, Ave Maria.

avec [avɛk] 1 prép a (*accompagnement, accord*) with. **elle est sortie ~ les enfants** she is out *ou* has gone out with the children; **son mariage ~ X a duré 8 ans** her marriage to X lasted (for) 8 years; **ils ont les**

syndicats ~ eux they've got the unions on their side *ou* behind them; je pense ~ cet auteur que ... I agree with this writer that ...; elle est ~ Robert (*elle le fréquente*) she's going out with Robert; (*ils vivent ensemble*) she's living with Robert.

b (*comportement: envers*) to, towards, with. comment se comportent-ils ~ vous? how do they behave towards *ou* with you?; il est très doux ~ les animaux he is very gentle with animals; il a été très gentil ~ nous he was very kind to us.

c (*moyen, manière*) with; (*ingrédient*) with, from, out of. vous prenez votre thé ~ du lait ou du citron? do you have *ou* take your tea with milk or (with) lemon?, do you have *ou* take milk or lemon in your tea?; boire ~ une paille to drink with a straw; une maison ~ jardin a house with a garden; faire qch ~ (grande) facilité to do sth with (great) ease *ou* (very) easily; (il) faudra bien faire ~ he (*ou* we *etc*) will have to make do; parler ~ colère/bonté/lenteur to speak angrily *ou* with anger/kindly/slowly; chambre ~ salle de bain room with a bathroom *ou* its own bathroom; couteau ~ (un) manche en bois knife with a wooden handle, wooden-handled knife; gâteau fait ~ du beurre cake made with butter; ragoût fait ~ des restes stew made out of *ou* from (the) left-overs; c'est fait (entièrement) ~ du plomb it's made (entirely) of lead; voyageant ~ un passeport qui ... travelling on a passport which ... .

d (*cause, simultanéité, contraste etc*) with. on oublie tout ~ le temps one forgets everything in time *ou* in the course of time *ou* with the passing of time; ~ les élections, on ne parle plus que politique with the elections (on) no one talks anything but politics; ~ l'inflation et le prix de l'essence, les voitures se vendent mal what with inflation and the price of petrol, cars aren't selling very well; il est difficile de marcher ~ ce vent it is difficult to walk in *ou* with this wind; ~ un peu de travail, il aurait gagné le prix with a little work *ou* if (only) he had done a little work he would have won the prize; ~ toute ma bonne volonté, je ne suis pas parvenu à l'aider with the best will in the world *ou* for all my goodwill I did not manage to help him; se lever ~ le jour to get up *ou* rise with the sun *ou* dawn, get up at daybreak; ils sont partis ~ la pluie they left in the rain.

e (*opposition*) with. rivaliser/combattre ~ qn to vie/fight with sb; elle s'est fâchée ~ tous leurs amis she has fallen out with all their friends.

f d'~: séparer/distinguer qch d'~ qch d'autre to separate/distinguish sth from sth else; divorcer d'~ qn to divorce sb; se séparer d'~ qn to leave sb, part from sb (*littér*); elle s'est séparée d'~ X she has separated from X.

g ~ cela*: (*dans un magasin*) et ~ ça, madame? anything else?; il conduit mal et ~ ça il conduit trop vite he drives badly and what's more *ou* on top of that he drives too fast; ~ cela que tu ne le savais pas! what do you mean you didn't know!, as if you didn't know!; (*iro*) et ~ ça qu'il est complaisant! and it's not as if he were helpful (either *ou* at that)!, and he's not exactly *ou* even helpful either! *ou* at that!; ~ tout ça j'ai oublié le pain in the midst of all this I forgot about the bread.

2 adv (*) tiens mes gants, je ne peux pas conduire ~ hold my gloves, I can't drive with them on; rends-moi mon stylo, tu allais partir ~! give me back my pen, you were going to walk off with it!

aveline [av(ə)lin] nf (*noix*) filbert.

avelinier [av(ə)linje] nm (*arbre*) filbert.

aven [avɛn] nm swallow hole (*Brit*), sinkhole, pothole.

avenant, e [av(ə)nɑ̃, ɑ̃t] 1 adj *personne* pleasant, welcoming; *manières* pleasant, pleasing; *maison* of pleasing appearance. 2 nm a à l'~ in keeping (*de* with); la maison était luxueuse, et le mobilier était à l'~ the house was luxurious, and the furniture was in keeping (with it); la table coûtait 8 000 F, et tout était à l'~ the table cost 8,000 francs and everything else was just as expensive. b (*Jur*) *[police d'assurance]* endorsement; *[contrat]* amendment (*à* to). faire un ~ à to endorse; to amend.

avènement [avɛnmɑ̃] nm *[roi]* accession, succession (*à* to); *[régime, politique, idée]* advent; *[Messie]* Advent, Coming.

avenir[1] [av(ə)niʀ] nm a (*futur*) future; (*postérité*) future generations. avoir des projets d'~ to have plans for the future, have future plans; dans un proche ~ in the near future; elle m'a prédit mon ~ she told my fortune.

b (*bien-être*) future (well-being). assurer l'~ de ses enfants to take care of *ou* ensure one's children's future.

c (*carrière*) future, prospects. il a de l'~, c'est un homme d'~ *ou* plein d'~ he's a man with a future *ou* with good prospects, he's an up-and-coming man; métier d'~ job with a future *ou* with prospects; il n'y a aucun ~ dans ce métier there's no future in this job, this is a dead-end job; projet sans ~ project without prospects of success *ou* without a future.

d (*dorénavant*) à l'~ from now on, in future.

avenir[2] [av(ə)niʀ] nm (*Jur*) writ of summons (*from one counsel to another*).

Avent [avɑ̃] nm: l'~ Advent.

aventure [avɑ̃tyʀ] nf a (*péripétie, incident*) adventure; (*entreprise*) venture; (*liaison amoureuse*) affair. fâcheuse ~ unfortunate experience; une ~ effrayante a terrifying experience; film/roman d'~s adventure film/story; une ~ sentimentale a love affair; avoir une ~ (galante) avec qn to have an affair with sb. b l'~ adventure; esprit d'~ spirit of adventure; *voir* dire, diseuse. c (*loc*) marcher à l'~ to walk aimlessly; (*littér*) si, par ~ *ou* d'~ if by any chance; quand, par ~ *ou* d'~ when by chance.

aventuré, e [avɑ̃tyʀe] (ptp de aventurer) adj *entreprise* risky, chancy; *hypothèse* risky, venturesome.

aventurer [avɑ̃tyʀe] 1 1 vt *somme, réputation, vie* to risk, put at stake, chance; *remarque, opinion* to venture. 2 s'aventurer vpr to venture (*dans* into, *sur* onto). s'~ à faire qch to venture to do sth; (*fig*) s'~ en terrain *ou* sur un chemin glissant to tread on dangerous ground, skate on thin ice.

aventureusement [avɑ̃tyʀøzmɑ̃] adv (*gén*) adventurously; (*dangereusement*) riskily.

aventureux, -euse [avɑ̃tyʀø, øz] adj *personne, esprit* adventurous, enterprising, venturesome; *imagination* bold; *projet, entreprise* risky, rash, chancy; *vie* adventurous.

aventurier [avɑ̃tyʀje] nm adventurer.

aventurière [avɑ̃tyʀjɛʀ] nf adventuress.

aventurisme [avɑ̃tyʀism] nm (*Pol*) adventurism.

aventuriste [avɑ̃tyʀist] adj (*Pol*) adventurist.

avenu, e[1] [av(ə)ny] adj *voir* nul.

avenue[2] [av(ə)ny] nf *[ville]* (*boulevard*) avenue; *[parc]* (*allée*) drive, avenue. (*littér*) les ~s du pouvoir the avenues of *ou* to power.

avéré, e [aveʀe] (ptp de s'avérer) adj *fait* known, recognized. il est ~ que it is a known *ou* recognized fact that.

avérer (s') [aveʀe] 6 vpr: il s'avère que it turns out that; ce remède s'avéra inefficace this remedy proved (to be) *ou* turned out to be ineffective; il s'est avéré un employé consciencieux he proved (to be) *ou* turned out to be *ou* showed himself to be a conscientious employee.

avers [avɛʀ] nm obverse (*of coin, medal*).

averse [avɛʀs] nf (*pluie*) shower (of rain); (*fig*) *[insultes, pierres]* shower. forte ~ heavy shower, downpour; ~ orageuse thundery shower; être pris par *ou* recevoir une ~ to be caught in a shower.

aversion [avɛʀsjɔ̃] nf aversion (*pour* to), loathing (*pour* for). avoir en ~, avoir de l'~ pour to have an aversion to, have a loathing for *ou* a strong dislike of, loathe; prendre en ~ to take a (violent) dislike to.

averti, e [avɛʀti] (ptp de avertir) adj *public* informed, mature; *connaisseur, expert* well-informed. c'est un film réservé à des spectateurs ~s it's a film suitable for a mature *ou* an informed audience; ~ de *problèmes etc* aware of; être très ~ des travaux cinématographiques contemporains to be very well up on *ou* well informed about the contemporary film scene; *voir* homme.

avertir [avɛʀtiʀ] 2 vt (*mettre en garde*) to warn (*de qch* of sth); (*renseigner*) to inform (*de qch* of sth). avertissez-le de ne pas recommencer warn him not to do it again; tenez-vous pour averti be warned, don't say you haven't been warned; avertissez-moi dès que possible let me know as soon as possible.

avertissement [avɛʀtismɑ̃] nm (*avis*) warning; (*présage*) warning, warning sign; (*réprimande*) (*Sport*) warning, caution; (*Scol*) warning. recevoir un ~ to receive a warning, be admonished; (*préface*) ~ (au lecteur) foreword; ~ sans frais (*Jur*) notice of assessment; (*fig*) clear warning (*à* to).

avertisseur, -euse [avɛʀtisœʀ, øz] 1 adj warning. 2 nm (*Aut*) horn, hooter (*Brit*). ~ (d'incendie) (fire) alarm.

aveu, pl ~x [avø] nm a *[crime, amour]* confession, avowal (*littér*); *[fait, faiblesse]* acknowledgement, admission, confession. c'est l'~ (déguisé) d'un échec de la part du gouvernement it's a (tacit) admission of defeat on the part of the government; c'est un ~ d'impuissance it's a confession *ou* an admission of helplessness *ou* powerlessness; faire l'~ d'un crime to confess to a crime; faire des ~x complets to make a full confession; passer aux ~x to make a confession; revenir sur ses ~x to retract one's confession.

b (*frm: selon*) de l'~ de qn according to sb; de l'~ même du témoin on the witness's own testimony.

c (*frm*) sans ~ *homme, politicien* disreputable.

d (*littér: assentiment*) consent. sans l'~ de qn without sb's authorization *ou* consent.

aveuglant, e [avœglɑ̃, ɑ̃t] adj *lumière* blinding, dazzling; *vérité* blinding (*épith*), glaring (*épith*), overwhelming.

aveugle [avœgl] 1 adj *personne* blind, sightless (*épith*); (*fig*) *passion, dévouement, obéissance* blind; *attentat* indiscriminate, random; *fenêtre, façade, mur, couloir* blind. devenir ~ to go blind; ~ d'un œil blind in one eye; il est ~ de naissance he was born blind, he has been blind from birth; son amour le rend ~ love is blinding him, he is blinded by love; avoir une confiance ~ en qn to trust sb blindly *ou* implicitly; une confiance ~ dans la parole de qn (an) implicit trust *ou* faith in sb's word; être ~ aux défauts de qn to be blind to sb's faults; l'~ instrument du destin the blind *ou* unwitting instrument of fate.

2 nmf blind man (*ou* woman). les ~s the blind; faire qch en ~ to do sth blindly; ~-né person blind from birth; c'est un ~-né he was born blind; *voir* à, double.

aveuglement [avœgləmɑ̃] nm (*littér: égarement*) blindness.

aveuglément [avœglemɑ̃] adv (*fidèlement*) blindly; (*inconsidérément*) blindly, blindfold.

aveugler [avœgle] 1 **1 vt a** (*lit, fig*) (*rendre aveugle*) to blind; (*éblouir*) to dazzle, blind. **b** *fenêtre* to block *ou* brick up; *voie d'eau* to stop up. **2 s'aveugler vpr: s'~ sur qn** to be blind to *ou* shut one's eyes to sb's defects.

aveuglette [avœglɛt] **nf: avancer à l'~** to grope (one's way) along, feel one's way along; **descendre à l'~** to grope one's way down; **prendre des décisions à l'~** to take decisions in the dark *ou* blindly.

aveulir [avølir] 2 **1 vt** to enfeeble, enervate. **2 s'aveulir vpr** to lose one's will (power), degenerate.

aveulissement [avølismɑ̃] **nm** enfeeblement, enervation; loss of will (power).

aviateur [avjatœr] **nm** airman, aviator, pilot.

aviation [avjasjɔ̃] **1 nf** (*Mil*) (*corps d'armée*) air force; (*avions*) aircraft, air force. **l'~** (*sport, métier de pilote*) flying; (*secteur commercial*) aviation; (*moyen de tranport*) air travel; **coupe/meeting d'~** flying cup/meeting; **usine d'~** aircraft factory; **services/base d'~** air services/base; *voir* **champ, ligne[1], terrain. 2 comp ▸aviation de chasse** fighter force **▸aviation navale** fleet air arm (*Brit*), naval air force (*US*).

aviatrice [avjatris] **nf** woman pilot, aviator.

avicole [avikɔl] **adj** (*voir* **aviculture**) *élevage* poultry (*épith*); bird (*épith*); *établissement* bird-breeding; poultry farming *ou* breeding; *ferme* poultry.

aviculteur, -trice [avikyltœr, tris] **nm,f** (*voir* **aviculture**) poultry farmer *ou* breeder; aviculturist (*SPÉC*), bird breeder, bird fancier.

aviculture [avikyltyr] **nf** (*volailles*) poultry farming *ou* breeding; (*oiseaux*) aviculture (*SPÉC*), bird breeding, bird fancying.

avide [avid] **adj** (*par intensité*) eager; (*par cupidité*) greedy, grasping; *lecteur* avid, eager. **~ de** *plaisir, sensation* eager *ou* avid for; *argent, nourriture* greedy for; *pouvoir, honneurs* greedy *ou* avid for; **~ de faire qch** eager to do sth; **~ de sang** *ou* **de carnage** bloodthirsty (*épith*), thirsting for blood (*attrib*).

avidement [avidmɑ̃] **adv** (*voir* **avide**) eagerly; greedily; avidly.

avidité [avidite] **nf** (*voir* **avide**) eagerness; greed; avidity (*de* for). **manger avec ~** to eat greedily.

avilir [avilir] 2 **1 vt** *personne* to degrade, debase, demean; *monnaie* to debase; *marchandise* to depreciate. **2 s'avilir vpr** *[personne]* to degrade o.s., debase o.s., demean o.s.; *[monnaie, marchandise]* to depreciate.

avilissant, e [avilisɑ̃, ɑ̃t] **adj** *spectacle* degrading, shameful, shaming (*épith*); *conduite, situation, travail* degrading, demeaning.

avilissement [avilismɑ̃] **nm** (*voir* **avilir**) degradation; debasement; depreciation.

aviné, e [avine] **adj** (*littér*) *personne* inebriated, intoxicated; *voix* drunken. **il a l'haleine ~e** his breath smells of alcohol.

avion [avjɔ̃] **1 nm** (*appareil*) aeroplane (*Brit*), plane, airplane (*US*), aircraft (*pl inv*). (*sport*) **l'~** flying; **défense/batterie contre ~s** anti-aircraft defence/battery; **il est allé à Paris en ~** he went to Paris by air *ou* by plane, he flew to Paris; **par ~** by air(mail).

2 comp ▸avion de bombardement bomber **▸avion-cargo nm (pl avions-cargos)** (air) freighter, cargo aircraft **▸avion de chasse** interceptor, fighter **▸avion-cible nm (pl avions-cibles)** target aircraft **▸avion-citerne nm (pl avions-citernes)** air tanker **▸avion commercial** commercial aircraft **▸avion-école nm (pl avions-écoles)** training plane **▸avion furtif** Stealth plane **▸avion-fusée nm (pl avions-fusées)** rocket-propelled plane **▸avion de ligne** airliner **▸avion en papier** paper aeroplane **▸avion postal** mail plane **▸avion à réaction** jet (plane) **▸avion de reconnaissance** reconnaissance aircraft **▸avion-suicide nm (pl avions-suicide)** suicide plane **▸avion-taxi nm (pl avions-taxis)** taxiplane (*US*) **▸avion de tourisme** private aeroplane **▸avion de transport** transport aircraft.

avionique [avjɔnik] **nf** avionics (*sg*).

avionneur [avjɔnœr] **nm** aircraft manufacturer.

aviron [avirɔ̃] **nm a** (*rame*) oar; (*sport*) rowing. **faire de l'~** to row. **b** (*Can*) paddle.

avironner [avirɔne] 1 **vt** (*Can*) to paddle.

avis [avi] **1 nm a** (*opinion*) opinion. **donner son ~** to give one's opinion *ou* views (*sur* on, about); **les ~ sont partagés** opinion is divided; **être du même ~ que qn, être de l'~ de qn** to be of the same opinion *ou* of the same mind as sb, share the view of sb; **on ne te demande pas ton ~!** who asked you?; **je ne suis pas de votre ~** I'm not of your opinion *ou* view; **à mon ~ c'est ...** in my opinion *ou* to my mind it is ...; **si tu veux mon ~, il est ...** if you ask me *ou* if you want my opinion he is ...; **c'est bien mon ~** I quite agree; (*iro*) **à mon humble ~** in my humble opinion; **de l'~ de tous, il ne sera pas élu** the unanimous view *ou* the general opinion is that he won't be elected; *voir* **changer, deux.**

b (*conseil*) advice (*NonC*). **un ~ amical** a friendly piece of advice, a piece of friendly advice, some friendly advice; **suivre l'~** *ou* **les ~ de qn** to take *ou* follow sb's advice; **sur l'~ de qn** on sb's advice; **suivant l'~ donné** following the advice given.

c (*notification*) notice; (*Fin*) advice. **lettre d'~** letter of advice; **~ de crédit/de débit** credit/debit advice; **(~ d')appel d'offres** invitation to tender *ou* to bid; **sans ~ préalable** without prior notice; **jusqu'à nouvel ~** until further notice; **sauf ~ contraire** unless otherwise informed, unless one hears to the contrary; (*sur étiquette, dans préface etc*) unless otherwise indicated; (*Naut*) **~ de coup de vent** gale warning; **~ de tempête** storm warning; **~ aux amateurs!*** any takers?*; **donner ~ de/que†** to give notice of/that.

d (*Admin: consultation officielle*) opinion. **les membres ont émis un ~** the members put forward an opinion; **on a pris l'~ du conseil** they took the opinion of the council; **~ favorable/défavorable** (*Scol*) passed/failed; (*Admin*) accepted/rejected.

e (*loc*) **être d'~ que/de: il était d'~ de partir** *ou* **qu'on parte immédiatement** he thought we should leave immediately, he was of the opinion that we should leave at once, he was for leaving at once*; **je suis d'~ qu'il vaut mieux attendre** I think *ou* I am of the opinion that it is better to wait; (†, *hum*) **m'est ~ que** methinks (†, *hum*).

2 comp ▸avis de décès announcement of death, death notice* **▸avis d'expédition** (*Comm*) advice of dispatch **▸avis d'imposition** tax notice **▸avis au lecteur** foreword **▸avis de mise en recouvrement** (*Fin*) notice of assessment **▸avis de mobilisation** mobilization notice **▸avis au public** public notice; (*en-tête*) notice to the public **▸avis de réception** acknowledgement of receipt **▸avis de recherche** *[criminel]* wanted notice; *[disparu]* missing person notice; **lancer un avis de recherche** (*pour criminel*) to issue a wanted notice, declare sb wanted; (*pour disparu*) to issue a missing person notice, declare sb a missing person **▸avis de virement** advice of bank transfer.

avisé, e [avize] (**ptp de aviser**) **adj** sensible, wise. **bien ~** well-advised; **mal ~** rash, ill-advised.

aviser [avize] 1 **1 vt a** (*frm, littér: avertir*) to advise, inform (*de* of), notify (*de* of, about). **il ne m'en a pas avisé** he didn't notify me of *ou* about it.

b (*littér: apercevoir*) to catch sight of, notice.

2 vi: cela fait, nous aviserons once that's done, we'll see where we stand *ou* we'll take stock *ou* we'll review the situation; **sur place, nous aviserons** once (we're) there, we'll try and sort (*Brit*) *ou* work something out *ou* we'll assess the situation; **il va falloir ~** well, we'll have to think about it *ou* give it some thought; **~ à qch** to see to sth; **nous aviserons au nécessaire** we shall see to the necessary *ou* do what is necessary.

3 s'aviser vpr a (*remarquer*) **s'~ de qch** to become suddenly aware of sth, realize sth suddenly; **il s'avisa que ...** he suddenly realized that ... .

b (*s'aventurer à*) **s'~ de faire qch** to dare to do sth, take it into one's head to do sth; **et ne t'avise pas d'aller lui dire** and don't you dare go and tell him, and don't you take it into your head to go and tell him.

avitaminose [avitaminoz] **nf** vitamin deficiency, avitaminosis (*SPÉC*).

aviver [avive] 1 **1 vt a** *douleur physique, appétit* to sharpen; *regrets, chagrin* to deepen; *intérêt, désir* to kindle, arouse; *colère* to stir up; *souvenirs* to stir up, revive; *querelle* to stir up, add fuel to; *passion* to arouse, excite, stir up; *regard* to brighten; *couleur* to revive, brighten (up); *feu* to revive, stir up. **l'air frais leur avait avivé le teint** the fresh air had given them some colour *ou* put colour into their cheeks.

b (*Méd*) *plaie* to open up; (*Tech*) *bronze* to burnish; *poutre* to square off.

2 s'aviver vpr (*voir* **aviver**) to sharpen; to deepen; to be kindled; to be aroused; to be stirred up; to be excited; to brighten; to revive, be revived; to brighten up.

av. J.-C. (**abrév de avant Jésus-Christ**) BC.

avocaillon [avɔkajɔ̃] **nm** (*péj*) pettifogging lawyer, small-town lawyer.

avocasserie [avɔkasri] **nf** (*péj*) pettifoggery, chicanery.

avocassier, -ière [avɔkasje, jɛr] **adj** (*péj*) pettifogging, chicaning.

avocat[1], e [avɔka, at] **1 nm,f a** (*Jur: personne inscrite au barreau*) barrister, advocate (*Écos*), attorney(-at-law) (*US*). **consulter son ~** to consult one's lawyer; **l'accusé et son ~** the accused and his counsel.

b (*fig: défenseur*) advocate, champion. **se faire l'~ d'une cause** to advocate *ou* champion *ou* plead a cause; **fais-toi mon ~ auprès de lui** plead with him on my behalf.

2 comp ▸avocat d'affaires business lawyer **▸avocat-conseil nm (pl avocats-conseils)** ≃ consulting barrister (*Brit*), ≃ counsel-in-chambers (*Brit*), ≃ attorney (*US*) **▸l'avocat de la défense** the counsel for the defence *ou* defendant, the defending counsel (*Brit*), the defense counsel (*US*) **▸l'avocat du diable** (*Rel, fig*) the devil's advocate; (*fig*) **se faire l'avocat du diable** to be *ou* play devil's advocate **▸avocat d'entreprise** company lawyer (*Brit*), corporation lawyer (*US*) **▸avocat général** counsel for the prosecution, assistant procurator fiscal (*Écos*), prosecuting attorney (*US*) **▸l'avocat de la partie civile** the counsel for the plaintiff **▸avocat plaidant** court lawyer (*Brit*), trial attorney (*US*) **▸avocat sans cause** briefless barrister (*Brit*) *ou* attorney (*US*).

avocat[2] [avɔka] **nm** avocado (pear).

avocatier [avɔkatje] **nm** avocado (tree), avocado pear tree.

avocette [avɔsɛt] **nf** avocet.

avoine [avwan] **nf** oats; *voir* **farine, flocon, fou.**

avoir [avwar] 34 **1 vt a** (*posséder, disposer de*) *maison, patron, frère* to have. **il n'a pas d'argent** he has no money, he hasn't got any money; **on ne peut pas tout ~** you can't have everything; **avez-vous du feu?**

have you got a light?; **j'ai (tout) le temps de le faire** I have *ou* have got (plenty of) time to do it; ~ **qn pour ami** to have sb as a friend; **pour tout mobilier ils ont deux chaises et une table** the only furniture they have is two chairs and a table.

b (*obtenir, attraper*) *renseignement, prix, train* to get. **j'ai eu un coup de téléphone de Richard** I had *ou* got a phone call from Richard; **il a eu sa licence en 1939** he graduated in 1939, he got his degree in 1939; **nous avons très bien la BBC** we (can) get the BBC very clearly; **pouvez-vous nous ~ ce livre?** can you get this book for us?, can you get us this book?; **elle a eu 3 pommes pour un franc** she got 3 apples for one franc; **j'avais Jean au téléphone quand on nous a coupés** I was on the phone to John when we were cut off; **essayez de m'~ Paris (au téléphone)** could you put me through to Paris *ou* get me Paris; **je n'arrive pas à ~ Paris** I can't get through to Paris; (*Sport*) **j'ai!** mine!

c (*souffrir de*) *rhume, maladie* to have. ~ **de la fièvre** to have *ou* run a high temperature; **il a la rougeole** he's got measles; **il a eu la rougeole à 10 ans** he had *ou* got measles at the age of 10.

d (*porter*) *vêtements* to have on, wear. **la femme qui a le chapeau bleu et une canne** the woman with the blue hat and a stick.

e *caractéristiques physiques ou morales* to have. **il a les yeux bleus** he has *ou* has got blue eyes; **il a du courage/de l'ambition/du toupet** he has (got) courage/ambition/cheek, he is courageous/ambitious/cheeky; **son regard a quelque chose de méchant, il a quelque chose de méchant dans le regard** he's got a nasty look in his eye; ~ **la tête qui tourne** to feel giddy; **j'ai le cœur qui bat** my heart is thumping; **regardez, il a les mains qui tremblent** look, his hands are shaking; **en ~**‡ to have guts* *ou* balls**.

f *âge* to be. **quel âge avez-vous?** how old are you?; **il a dix ans** he is ten (years old); **ils ont le même âge** they are the same age.

g *formes, dimensions, couleur* to be. ~ **3 mètres de haut/4 mètres de long** to be 3 metres high/4 metres long; **cette armoire a une jolie ligne** this cupboard is a nice shape; **qu'est-ce qu'elle a comme tour de taille?** what's her waist measurement?, what waist is she? (*Brit*); **la maison a 5 étages** the house has 5 floors; **la voiture qui a cette couleur** the car which is that colour.

h (*éprouver*) *joie, chagrin* to feel; *intérêt* to show. ~ **faim/froid/honte** to be *ou* feel hungry/cold/ashamed; ~ **le sentiment/l'impression que** to have the feeling/the impression that; **qu'est-ce qu'il a?** what's the matter with him?, what's wrong with him?; **il a sûrement quelque chose** there's certainly something the matter with him, there's certainly something wrong with him; **il a qu'il est furieux** he's furious, that's what's wrong *ou* the matter with him; **qu'est-ce qu'il a à pleurer?** what's he crying for?; *voir* **besoin, envie, mal** *etc.*

i *idées, raisons* to have; *opinion* to hold, have. **cela n'a aucun intérêt pour eux** it is of no interest to them; **la danse n'a aucun charme pour moi** dancing doesn't appeal to me at all; *voir* **raison, tort.**

j *geste* to make; *rire* to give; *cri* to utter. **elle eut un sourire malin** she gave a knowing smile, she smiled knowingly; **il eut une grimace de douleur** he winced; **ils ont eu des remarques malheureuses** they made *ou* passed (*Brit*) some unfortunate remarks; *voir* **mot.**

k (*recevoir*) *visites, amis* to have. **il aime ~ des amis** he likes to have friends round (*Brit*) *ou* over (*US*), he likes to entertain friends; ~ **des amis à dîner** to have friends to dinner.

l *obligation, activité, conversation* to have. **ils ont des soirées 2 ou 3 fois par semaine** they have parties 2 or 3 times a week; **je n'ai rien ce soir** I've nothing on this evening, I'm not doing anything this evening; (*Scol*) **j'ai français à 10 heures** I've got French at 10.

m (*: *vaincre*) **on les aura!** we'll have *ou* get them!*; **ils ont fini par ~ le coupable** they got the culprit in the end; **je t'aurai!** I'll get you!*; **dans la fusillade, ils ont eu le chef de la bande** in the shoot-out they got the gang leader*; **elle m'a eu au sentiment** she took advantage of my better nature.

n (*: *duper*) *personne* to take in, con‡. **je les ai eus** I took them in, I conned them‡; **ils m'ont eu** I've been had*; **se faire ~** to be had*, be taken in; **je me suis fait ~ de 30 F** I was conned out of 30 francs‡.

o (*loc*) **en ~ après* qn** to be mad at sb*; **elle en a toujours après moi** she's always on at me; **après qui en as-tu?*** who have you got a grudge against?; **qu'est-ce que tu as contre lui?** what have you got against him?; **en ~ pour son argent** to have *ou* get one's money's worth; **j'en ai pour 100 F** it will cost me *ou* set me back* 100 francs; **il en a pour deux heures** it will take him 2 hours; **il en a pour deux secondes** it'll take him 2 seconds; **tu en as pour combien de temps?** how long are you going to be?, how long will it take you?; **en ~ assez*** *ou* **par-dessus la tête*** *ou* **plein le dos*** to be fed up*, be cheesed off* *ou* browned off* (*Brit*) (*de qch* with sth); **on en a encore pour 20 km de cette mauvaise route** there's another 20 km of this awful road; **quand il se met à pleuvoir, on en a pour 3 jours** once it starts raining, it goes on *ou* sets in for 3 days; *voir* **estime, horreur.**

2 **vb aux** a (*avec ptp*) **j'étais pressé, j'ai couru** I was in a hurry so I ran; **j'ai déjà couru 10 km** I've already run 10 km; **quand il eut** *ou* **a eu parlé** when he had spoken; **il n'est pas bien, il a dû trop manger** he is not well, he must have eaten too much; **nous aurons terminé demain** we shall have finished tomorrow; **si je l'avais vu** if I had seen him; **il a été tué hier** he was killed yesterday; **il a été renvoyé deux fois** he has been dismissed twice; **il aura été retardé par la pluie** he must *ou* will have been held up by the rain; *voir* **vouloir.**

b (+ *infin: devoir*) ~ **qch à faire** to have sth to do; **j'ai des lettres à écrire** I've (got) some letters to write; **j'ai à travailler** I have to work, I must work; **il n'a pas à se plaindre** he can't complain; **vous aurez à parler** you will have to speak; **vous n'avez pas à vous en soucier** you mustn't *ou* needn't worry about it; *voir* **maille, rien, voir.**

c **n'~ qu'à: tu n'as qu'à me téléphoner demain** just give me a ring tomorrow, why don't you ring me up tomorrow?; **tu n'as qu'à appuyer sur le bouton, et ça se met en marche** (you) just press the knob, and it starts working; **il n'a qu'un mot à dire pour nous sauver** he need only say the word, and we're saved; **c'est simple, vous n'avez qu'à lui écrire** it's simple, just write to him *ou* you need only write to him *ou* you've only (got) to write to him; **tu n'avais qu'à ne pas y aller** you shouldn't have gone (in the first place); **tu n'as qu'à faire attention/te débrouiller** you'll just have to take care/sort (*Brit*) *ou* work it out for yourself; **s'il n'est pas content, il n'a qu'à partir** if he doesn't like it, he can just go.

d **ils ont eu leurs carreaux cassés par la grêle** they had their windows broken by the hail; **vous aurez votre robe nettoyée gratuitement** your dress will be cleaned free of charge.

3 **vb impers** a **il y a** (*avec sg*) there is; (*avec pl*) there are; **il y a eu 3 blessés** 3 people were injured, there were 3 injured; **il n'y avait que moi** I was the only one; **il y avait une fois** ... once upon a time, there was ...; **il y en a pour dire** *ou* **qui disent** there are some *ou* those who say, some say; **il y a enfant et enfant** there are children and children!; **il y en a, je vous jure*** some people, honestly!*, really, some people!*; **il n'y a pas de quoi** don't mention it; **qu'y a-t-il?, qu'est-ce qu'il y a?** what is it?, what's the matter?, what's up?*; **il y a que nous sommes mécontents*** we're annoyed, that's what*; **il n'y a que lui pour faire cela!** only he would do that!, trust him to do that!, it takes him to do that!; **il n'y a pas que nous à le dire** we're not the only ones who say *ou* to say that; **il n'y a pas à dire*, il est très intelligent** there's no denying he's very intelligent; **(il n')y a pas, (il) faut que je parte*** there's nothing else for it, I've got to go; **il doit/peut y ~ une raison** there must/may be a reason; **il n'y a qu'à les laisser partir** just let them go; **il n'y a qu'à protester** we shall just have to protest, why don't we protest; **quand il n'y en a plus, il y en a encore!** there's plenty more where that came from!*; **quand (il) y en a pour deux, (il) y en a pour trois** *nourriture* there's plenty for everyone; *place* there's plenty of room for everyone; **il n'y a pas que toi** you're not the only one!; **il n'y en a que pour mon petit frère, à la maison** my little brother gets all the attention at home.

b (*pour exprimer le temps écoulé*) **il y a 10 ans que je le connais** I have known him (for) 10 years; **il y aura 10 ans demain que je ne l'ai vu** it will be 10 years tomorrow since I last saw him; **il y avait longtemps qu'elle désirait ce livre** she had wanted this book for a long time; **il y a 10 ans, nous étions à Paris** 10 years ago we were in Paris; **il y a 10 jours que nous sommes rentrés, nous sommes rentrés il y a 10 jours** we got back 10 days ago, we have been back 10 days.

c (*pour exprimer la distance*) **il y a 10 km d'ici à Paris** it is 10 km from here to Paris; **combien y a-t-il d'ici à Paris?** how far is it from here to Paris?

4 **nm** a (*bien*) assets, resources. **son ~ était bien peu de chose** what he had wasn't much.

b (*Comm*) (*actif*) credit (side); (*billet de crédit*) credit note. (*Fin*) ~ **fiscal** tax credit; *voir* **doit.**

c **~s** holdings, assets; **~s à l'étranger** foreign assets *ou* holdings; **~s en caisse** *ou* **en numéraire** cash holdings.

avoirdupoids [avwaʀdypwɑ] **nm** avoirdupoids.

avoisinant, e [avwazinɑ̃, ɑ̃t] **adj** *région, pays* neighbouring; *rue, ferme* nearby, neighbouring. **dans les rues ~es** in the nearby streets, in the streets close by *ou* nearby.

avoisiner [avwazine] 1 **vt** *lieu* to be near *ou* close to, border on; (*fig*) to border *ou* verge on *ou* upon.

avortement [avɔʀtəmɑ̃] **nm** (*Méd*) abortion. (*fig*) ~ **de** failure of; **campagne contre l'~** anti-abortion campaign; ~ **thérapeutique** termination (of pregnancy) (*for medical reasons*).

avorter [avɔʀte] 1 **vi** a (*Méd*) to have an abortion, abort. **faire ~ qn** *[personne]* to give sb an abortion, abort sb; *[remède etc]* to make sb abort; **se faire ~** to have an abortion. b (*fig*) to fail, come to nothing. **faire ~ un projet** to frustrate *ou* wreck a plan; **projet avorté** abortive plan.

avorteur, -euse [avɔʀtœʀ, øz] **nm,f** abortionist.

avorton [avɔʀtɔ̃] **nm** (*péj: personne*) little runt (*péj*); (*arbre, plante*) puny *ou* stunted specimen; (*animal*) puny specimen.

avouable [avwabl] **adj** blameless, worthy (*épith*), respectable. **il a utilisé des procédés peu ~s** he used fairly disreputable methods *ou* methods which don't bear mentioning.

avoué, e [avwe] (**ptp de avouer**) 1 **adj** *ennemi, revenu, but* avowed. 2 **nm** ≃ solicitor, attorney-at-law (*US*).

avouer [avwe] 1 1 **vt** *amour* to confess, avow (*littér*); *crime* to confess (to), own up to; *fait* to acknowledge, admit; *faiblesse, vice* to admit to, confess to. ~ **avoir menti** to admit *ou* confess that one has lied, admit *ou* own up to lying; ~ **que** to admit *ou* confess that; **elle est douée, je**

l'avoue she is gifted, I must admit; *voir* **faute**.

2 **vi** a (*se confesser*) *[coupable]* to confess, own up. b (*admettre*) to admit, confess. **tu avoueras, c'est un peu fort!** you must admit *ou* confess, it is a bit much!

3 **s'avouer vpr: s'~ coupable** to admit *ou* confess one's guilt; **s'~ vaincu** to admit *ou* acknowledge defeat; **s'~ déçu** to admit to being disappointed, confess o.s. disappointed.

avril [avʀil] **nm** April. (*Prov*) **en ~ ne te découvre pas d'un fil** ≃ never cast a clout till May is out (*Prov*); *pour autres loc voir* **septembre** *et* **poisson, premier.**

avunculaire [avɔ̃kylɛʀ] **adj** avuncular.

axe [aks] **nm** a (*Tech*) axle; (*Anat, Astron, Bot, Math*) axis. b (*route*) trunk road (*Brit*), main highway (*US*). **les grands ~s (routiers)** the major trunk roads (*Brit*), the main roads; **l'~ Paris-Marseille** the main Paris-Marseilles road, the main road between Paris and Marseilles; (*à Paris*) **~ rouge** clearway (*Brit*), no stopping zone. c (*fig*) *[débat, théorie, politique]* main line. d (*Hist*) **l'A~** the Axis. e (*dans le prolongement*) **dans l'~: cette rue est dans l'~ de l'église** this street is directly in line with the church; **mets-toi bien dans l'~ (de la cible)** line up on the target, get directly in line with the target.

axel [aksɛl] **nm** axel.

axer [akse] [1] **vt: ~ qch sur/autour de** to centre sth on/round.

axial, e, mpl -iaux [aksjal, jo] **adj** axial. **éclairage ~** central overhead lighting.

axillaire [aksilɛʀ] **adj** axillary.

axiomatique [aksjɔmatik] 1 **adj** axiomatic. 2 **nf** axiomatics (*sg*).

axiome [aksjom] **nm** axiom.

axis [aksis] **nm** axis (vertebra).

ayant cause, pl ayants cause [ɛjɑ̃koz] **nm** (*Jur*) legal successor, successor in title. **les ayants cause du défunt** the beneficiaries of the deceased.

ayant droit, pl ayants droit [ɛjɑ̃dʀwa] **nm** a (*Jur*) = **ayant cause.** b *[prestation, pension]* eligible party. **~ à** party entitled to *ou* eligible for.

ayatollah [ajatɔla] **nm** ayatollah.

azalée [azale] **nf** azalea.

Azerbaïdjan [azɛʀbaidʒɑ̃] **nm** Azerbaijan.

azerbaïdjanais, e [azɛʀbaidʒanɛ, ɛz] 1 **adj** Azerbaijani. 2 **nm** (*Ling*) Azerbaijani. 3 **nm,f: A~(e)** Azerbaijani.

azimut [azimyt] **nm** azimuth. *téléphoner* **tous ~s*** (*partout*) everywhere, all over the place*; (*frénétiquement*) frantically; **chercher qn dans tous les ~s*** to look all over the place for sb*; (*fig*) **offensive tous ~s contre les fraudeurs du fisc** all-out attack on tax-evaders.

azimutal, e, mpl -aux [azimytal, o] **adj** azimuthal.

azimuté, e* [azimyte] **adj** crazy*, nuts*, mad.

Azincourt [azɛ̃kuʀ] **n** Agincourt.

azote [azɔt] **nm** nitrogen.

azoté, e [azɔte] **adj** nitrogenous; *voir* **engrais.**

AZT [azɛdte] **nm** (**abrév de azidothymidine**) AZT.

aztèque [astɛk] 1 **adj** Aztec. 2 **nmf: A~** Aztec.

azur [azyʀ] **nm** (*littér*) (*couleur*) azure, sky blue; (*ciel*) skies, sky; *voir* **côte.**

azuré, e [azyʀe] (**ptp de azurer**) **adj** azure.

azurer [azyʀe] [1] **vt** *linge* to blue; (*littér*) to azure, tinge with blue.

azyme [azim] **adj** unleavened; *voir* **pain.**

B

B, b [be] nm (*lettre*) B, b. **B comme Berthe** ≃ B for Baker.

b (**abrév de bien**) g, good.

B. A. [bea] nf (**abrév de bonne action**) good deed. **faire sa ~ (quotidienne)** to do one's good deed for the day.

baba[1] [baba] nm (*Culin*) baba. **~ au rhum** rum baba.

baba[2] [baba] 1 nm: **il l'a eu dans le ~**‡ it was one in the eye for him*. 2 adj inv (*) **en être** *ou* **en rester ~** to be flabbergasted* *ou* dumbfounded; **j'en suis resté ~** you could have knocked me down with a feather*.

baba[3] [baba] nmf (*personne*) ≃ hippy.

B.A.-BA [beaba] nm sg A.B.C.-stage.

baba cool, pl **baba cools** [babakul] nmf = **baba**[3].

Babel [babɛl] n *voir* **tour**[1].

Babette [babɛt] nf Betty, Bess.

babeurre [babœʀ] nm buttermilk.

babil [babil] nm (*littér*) (*voir* **babillard**) babble; prattle; twitter; chatter.

babillage [babijaʒ] nm (*voir* **babillard**) babble, babbling; prattling; twitter(ing); chatter(ing).

babillard, e [babijaʀ, aʀd] 1 adj (*littér*) *personne* prattling, chattering; *bébé* babbling; *oiseau* twittering; *ruisseau* babbling, chattering. 2 nm,f chatterbox. 3 **babillarde*** nf (*lettre*) letter, note.

babiller [babije] 1 vi (*voir* **babillard**) to prattle; to chatter; to babble; to twitter.

babines [babin] nfpl (*lit, fig*) chops; *voir* **lécher**.

babiole [babjɔl] nf (*bibelot*) trinket, knick-knack; (*fig: vétille*) trifle, triviality. (*cadeau sans importance*) **offrir une ~** to give a small token *ou* a little something.

bâbord [bɑbɔʀ] nm (*Naut*) port (side). **par** *ou* **à ~** on the port side, to port.

babouche [babuʃ] nf babouche, Turkish *ou* oriental slipper.

babouin [babwɛ̃] nm baboon.

baby-boom, pl **baby-booms** [babibum] nm baby boom.

baby-foot, pl **baby-foots** [babifut] nm table football.

Babylone [babilɔn] n Babylon.

babylonien, -ienne [babilɔnjɛ̃, jɛn] 1 adj Babylonian. 2 nm,f: **B~(ne)** inhabitant *ou* native of Babylon.

baby-sitter, pl **baby-sitters** [babisitœʀ] nmf baby-sitter.

baby-sitting, pl **baby-sittings** [babisitiŋ] nm baby-sitting. **faire du ~** to baby-sit.

bac[1]* [bak] nm (**abrév de baccalauréat**) **un ~ + 2/+ 5** someone with 2/5 years' higher education; **(une formation) ~ + 2** 2 years' higher education.

bac[2] [bak] nm a (*bateau*) ferry, ferryboat. **~ à voitures** car-ferry. b (*récipient*) tub; (*abreuvoir*) trough; (*Ind*) tank, vat; (*Peinture, Phot*) tray; *[évier]* sink. **évier avec deux ~s** double sink unit; **~ à glace** ice-tray; **~ à laver** washtub, (deep) sink; **~ à légumes** vegetable compartment *ou* tray; **~ à sable** sandpit.

bacantes* [bakɑ̃t] nfpl = **bacchantes;** *voir* **bacchante b.**

baccalauréat [bakalɔʀea] nm ≃ A-levels (*Brit*); ≃ high school diploma (*US*), *Secondary School examination giving university entrance qualification.* (*Jur*) **~ en droit** diploma in law.

baccara [bakaʀa] nm baccara(t).

baccarat [bakaʀa] nm: **(cristal de) ~** Baccarat crystal.

bacchanale [bakanal] nf a (*danse*) bacchanalian *ou* drunken dance; (†: *orgie*) orgy, drunken revel. b (*Antiq*) **~s** Bacchanalia.

bacchante [bakɑ̃t] nf a (*Antiq*) bacchante. b **~s*** moustache, whiskers (*hum*).

Bacchus [bakys] nm Bacchus.

Bach [bak] nm Bach.

bâchage [bɑʃaʒ] nm covering, sheeting over.

bâche [bɑʃ] nf canvas cover *ou* sheet. **~ goudronnée** tarpaulin.

bachelier, -ière [baʃəlje, jɛʀ] nm,f *person who has passed the baccalauréat.* (*Jur*) **~ en droit** holder of a diploma in law.

bâcher [bɑʃe] 1 vt to cover (with a canvas sheet *ou* a tarpaulin), put a canvas sheet *ou* a tarpaulin over. **camion bâché** covered lorry (*Brit*) *ou* truck.

bachique [baʃik] adj (*Antiq, fig*) Bacchic. **chanson ~** drinking song.

bachot[1]* [baʃo] nm (*Scol*) = **baccalauréat;** *voir* **boîte.**

bachot[2] [baʃo] nm (small) boat, skiff.

bachotage [baʃɔtaʒ] nm (*Scol*) cramming. **faire du ~** to cram (for an exam).

bachoter [baʃɔte] 1 vi (*Scol*) to cram (for an exam).

bacillaire [basi(l)lɛʀ] adj *maladie* bacillary; *malade* tubercular. **les ~s** tubercular cases *ou* patients.

bacille [basil] nm (*gén*) germ, bacillus (*SPÉC*).

bacillose [basi(l)loz] nf (*gén*) bacillus infection; (*tuberculose*) tuberculosis.

bâclage [bɑklaʒ] nm botching, scamping.

bâcler [bɑkle] 1 vt *travail, devoir* to botch (up), scamp (*Brit*); *ouvrage* to throw together; *cérémonie* to skip through, hurry over. **~ sa toilette** to have a quick wash, give o.s. a lick and a promise; **c'est du travail bâclé** it's slapdash work.

bacon [bekɔn] nm (*lard*) bacon; (*jambon fumé*) smoked loin of pork.

baconien, -ienne [bakɔnjɛ̃, jɛn] adj Baconian.

bactéricide [baktеʀisid] adj bactericidal.

bactérie [bakteʀi] nf bacterium.

bactérien, -ienne [bakteʀjɛ̃, jɛn] adj bacterial.

bactériologie [bakteʀjɔlɔʒi] nf bacteriology.

bactériologique [bakteʀjɔlɔʒik] adj bacteriological.

bactériologiste [bakteʀjɔlɔʒist] nmf bacteriologist.

bactériophage [bakteʀjɔfaʒ] nm bacteriophage.

badaboum [badabum] excl crash, bang, wallop!

badaud, e [bado, od] 1 adj: **les Parisiens sont très ~s** Parisians love to stop and stare *ou* are full of idle curiosity. 2 nm,f (*qui regarde*) curious *ou* gaping (*péj*) *ou* gawking (*péj*) onlooker; (*qui se promène*) stroller.

badauder [badode] 1 vi (*se promener*) to stroll (*dans* about); (*regarder*) to gawk (*devant* at).

badauderie [badodʀi] nf (idle) curiosity.

baderne [badɛʀn] nf (*péj*) **(vieille) ~** old fogey*.

badge [badʒ] nm badge.

badigeon [badiʒɔ̃] nm (*voir* **badigeonner**) distemper; whitewash; colourwash (*Brit*). **donner un coup de ~** to give a coat of distemper *ou* whitewash.

badigeonnage [badiʒɔnaʒ] nm (*voir* **badigeonner**) distempering; whitewashing; colourwashing; painting.

badigeonner [badiʒɔne] 1 vt a *mur intérieur* to distemper; *mur extérieur* to whitewash (*Brit*); (*en couleur*) to colourwash (*Brit*), give a colourwash (*Brit*) to; (*barbouiller*) *visage, surface* to smear, daub, cover (*de* with). b (*Méd*) *plaie* to paint (*à, avec* with). **se ~ la gorge** to paint one's throat (*à* with). c (*Culin*) to brush (*de* with).

badigeonneur [badiʒɔnœʀ] nm (*péj*) dauber (*péj*); (*Tech*) painter.

badin[1]**, e**[1]† [badɛ̃, in] adj (*gai*) light-hearted, jocular; (*taquin*) playful. **sur un** *ou* **d'un ton ~** light-heartedly, jocularly; playfully.

badin[2] [badɛ̃] nm (*Aviat*) airspeed indicator.

badinage [badinaʒ] nm (*propos légers*) banter (*NonC*), jesting talk (*NonC*). **sur un ton de ~** in a jesting *ou* bantering *ou* light-hearted tone.

badine[2] [badin] nf switch.

badiner [badine] 1 vi a (†: *plaisanter*) to exchange banter, jest†. **pour ~** for a jest†, in jest. b **c'est quelqu'un qui ne badine pas** he's a man who really means what he says; **il ne badine pas sur la discipline** he's a stickler for discipline, he has strict ideas about discipline; **il ne faut pas ~ avec ce genre de maladie** this sort of illness is not to be treated lightly, an illness of this sort should be taken seriously; **et je ne badine pas!** I'm in no mood for joking!, I'm not joking!

badinerie† [badinʀi] nf jest†.

badminton [badmintɔn] nm badminton.

baffe* [bɑf] nf slap, clout*. **tu veux une ~?** do you want your face slapped? *ou* want a clip on the ear?*

Baffin [bafin] nm: **mer** *ou* **baie de ~** Baffin Bay; **terre de ~** Baffin Island.

baffle [bafl] nm baffle.

bafouer [bafwe] 1 vt *autorité* to flout, scorn. **mari bafoué** cuckold†.

bafouillage [bafujaʒ] nm (*bredouillage*) spluttering, stammering; (*propos stupides*) gibberish (*NonC*), babble (*NonC*).

bafouille* [bafuj] nf (*lettre*) letter, note.

bafouiller [bafuje] 1 1 vi *[personne]* (*bredouiller*) to splutter, stammer; (*tenir des propos stupides*) to talk gibberish, babble; *[moteur]* to splutter, misfire. 2 vt to splutter (out), stammer (out). **qu'est-ce qu'il bafouille?** what's he babbling *ou* jabbering on about?*

bafouilleur, -euse [bafujœʀ, øz] nm,f splutterer, stammerer.

bâfrer‡ [bɑfʀe] 1 1 vi to guzzle*, gobble, wolf*. 2 vt to guzzle (down)*, gobble (down), bolt (down), wolf (down)*.

bâfreur, -euse‡ [bɑfʀœʀ, øz] nm,f greedy guts* (*Brit*), guzzler*.

bagage [bagaʒ] nm a (*gén pl: valises*) luggage (*NonC*), baggage (*NonC*). **faire/défaire ses ~s** to pack/unpack (one's luggage), do one's packing/unpacking; **envoyer qch en ~s accompagnés** to send sth as registered luggage; **~s à main** hand luggage, carry-on bags. b (*valise*) bag, piece of luggage; (*Mil*) kit. **il avait pour tout ~ une serviette** his only luggage was a briefcase. c (*fig*) (*connaissances*) stock of knowledge; (*diplômes*) qualifications. **son ~ intellectuel/littéraire** his stock *ou* store of general/literary knowledge.

bagagerie [bagagʀi] nf bag shop.

bagagiste [bagaʒist] nm porter, luggage *ou* baggage handler.

bagarre [bagaʀ] nf a **la ~** fighting; **il veut** *ou* **cherche la ~** he wants *ou* is looking for a fight; **il aime la ~** he loves fighting *ou* a fight. b (*rixe*) fight, scuffle, brawl; (*fig: entre deux orateurs*) set-to, clash, barney* (*Brit*). **~ générale** free-for-all; **violentes ~s** rioting.

bagarrer* [bagaʀe] 1 1 vi (*se disputer*) to argue, wrangle; (*lutter*) to fight. 2 **se bagarrer** vpr (*se battre*) to fight, scuffle, scrap*; (*se disputer*) to have a set-to *ou* a barney* (*Brit*). **ça s'est bagarré (dur) dans les rues** there was (heavy *ou* violent) rioting in the streets.

bagarreur, -euse* [bagaʀœʀ, øz] 1 adj *caractère* aggressive, fighting (*épith*). **il est ~** he loves a fight. 2 nm,f (*pour arriver dans la vie*) fighter; (*Sport*) battler.

bagatelle [bagatɛl] nf a (*chose de peu de prix*) small thing, trinket; (*†: bibelot*) knick-knack, trinket. b (*petite somme*) small *ou* paltry sum, trifle. **je l'ai eu pour une ~** I got it for next to nothing; (*iro*) **un accident qui m'a coûté la ~ de 3 000 F** an accident which cost me the paltry sum of 3,000 francs *ou* a mere 3,000 francs (*iro*). c (*fig: vétille*) trifle. **s'amuser à** *ou* **perdre son temps à des ~s** to fritter away one's time. d († *ou hum: amour*) philandering. **être porté sur la ~** *[homme]* to be a bit of a philanderer *ou* womanizer; *[femme]* to be a bit of a lass. e (††) **~s!** fiddlesticks!†

Bagdad [bagdad] n Baghdad.

bagnard [baɲaʀ] nm convict.

bagne [baɲ] nm (*Hist*) (*prison*) penal colony; (*peine*) penal servitude, hard labour. **être condamné au ~** to be sentenced to hard labour; (*fig*) **quel ~!*, c'est un vrai ~!*** it's a hard grind!, it's sheer slavery!

bagnole* [baɲɔl] nf motorcar (*Brit*), automobile (*US*), buggy‡. **vieille ~** old banger* (*Brit*), jalopy*.

bagou(t)* [bagu] nm volubility, glibness (*péj*). **avoir du ~** to have the gift of the gab, have a glib tongue (*péj*).

bagouse‡ [baguz] nf ring.

baguage [bagaʒ] nm *[oiseau, arbre]* ringing.

bague [bag] nf (*bijou*) ring; *[cigare]* band; *[oiseau]* ring; *[boîte de bière]* pull-tab, ring-pull; (*Tech*) collar. **elle lui a mis la ~ au doigt*** she has hooked him*; **~ de fiançailles** engagement ring; **~ de serrage** jubilee clip; (*Phot*) **~ intermédiaire/de réglage** adapter/setting ring; **~ allonge** extension tube.

baguenaude* [bagnod] nf: **être en ~** to be gallivanting about.

baguenauder (se)* [bagnode] 1 vpr (*faire un tour*) to go for a stroll, go for a jaunt; (*traîner*) to mooch about* (*Brit*), trail around.

baguer [bage] 1 vt a *oiseau, arbre* to ring; (*Tech*) to collar. **elle avait les mains baguées** she had rings on her fingers; **cigare bagué** cigar with a band round it. b (*Couture*) to baste, tack.

baguette [bagɛt] 1 nf a (*bâton*) switch, stick. (*pour manger*) **~s** chopsticks; **~ de chef d'orchestre** (conductor's) baton; **sous la ~ de X** conducted by X, with X conducting; (*fig*) **mener** *ou* **faire marcher qn à la ~** to rule sb with an iron hand, keep a strong hand on sb.

b (*pain*) loaf *ou* stick of French bread.

c (*Constr*) beading, strip of wood; (*Élec: cache-fils*) wood casing *ou* strip.

d (*dessin de chaussette*) clock.

2 comp ▸**baguette de coudrier** hazel stick *ou* switch, divining rod ▸**baguette de fée** = **baguette magique** ▸**baguette de fusil** ramrod ▸**baguette magique** magic wand; **il ne va pas résoudre tous les problèmes d'un coup de baguette magique** he can't wave a magic wand and solve all the problems ▸**baguette de protection** (*Aut*) side trim ▸**baguette de sourcier** divining rod ▸**baguette de tambour** drumstick; **cheveux en baguettes de tambour** dead (*Brit*) *ou* perfectly straight hair.

bah [bɑ] excl (*indifférence*) pooh!; (*doute*) well ...!, really!

Bahamas [baamas] nfpl: **les (îles) ~** the Bahamas.

bahamien, ienne [baamjɛ̃, ɛn] 1 adj Bahamian. 2 nm,f: **B~(ne)** Bahamian.

Bahrein [baʀɛn] nm Bahrain. **à ~** in Bahrain.

bahreinite [baʀɛnit] 1 adj Bahraini. 2 nmf: **B~** Bahraini.

bahut [bay] nm a (*coffre*) chest; (*buffet*) sideboard. b (*arg Scol*) school.

bai, e¹ [bɛ] adj *cheval* bay.

baie² [bɛ] nf a (*Géog*) bay. **la ~ d'Hudson/de la Table** Hudson/Table Bay. b (*Archit*) opening. (*fenêtre*) **~ (vitrée)** picture window.

baie³ [bɛ] nf (*Bot*) berry.

baignade [bɛɲad] nf (*action*) bathing (*Brit*), swimming; (*bain*) bathe, swim; (*lieu*) bathing (*Brit*) *ou* swimming place. **~ interdite** no bathing *ou* swimming; **c'est l'heure de la ~** it's time for a bathe *ou* a swim.

baigner [beɲe] 1 1 vt a *bébé, chien* to bath; *pieds, visage, yeux* to bathe. **des larmes baignaient ses joues** his face was bathed in tears.

b **baigné de** bathed in; (*trempé de*) soaked with; **visage baigné de larmes/sueur** face bathed in tears/sweat; **chemise baignée de sang/sueur** shirt soaked with blood/sweat, blood-/sweat-soaked shirt; **forêt baignée de lumière** forest bathed in *ou* flooded with light.

c *[mer, rivière]* to wash, bathe; *[lumière]* to bathe, flood.

2 vi a (*tremper dans l'eau*) *[linge]* to soak, lie soaking (*dans* in); (*tremper dans l'alcool*) *[fruits]* to steep, soak (*dans* in). **la viande baignait dans la graisse** the meat was swimming in fat *ou* lay in a pool of fat; **la victime baignant dans son sang** the victim lying in a pool of blood; (*fig*) **la ville baigne dans la brume** the town is shrouded *ou* wrapped in mist; (*fig*) **tout baigne dans l'huile*** everything's hunky-dory*, everything's looking great*; **ça baigne!*** great!*, couldn't be better!*

b (*fig: être plongé dans*) **il baigne dans la joie** his joy knows no bounds, he is bursting with joy; **~ dans le mystère** *[affaire]* to be shrouded *ou* wrapped *ou* steeped in mystery; *[personne]* to be completely mystified *ou* baffled.

3 **se baigner** vpr (*dans la mer, une rivière*) to go bathing (*Brit*) *ou* swimming, have a bathe *ou* a swim; (*dans une piscine*) to go swimming, have a swim; (*dans une baignoire*) to have a bath.

baigneur, -euse [bɛɲœʀ, øz] 1 nm,f bather (*Brit*), swimmer. 2 nm (*jouet*) dolly, baby doll.

baignoire [bɛɲwaʀ] nf a bath(tub). **~ sabot** ≃ hip-bath. b (*Théât*) ground floor box, baignoire. c *[sous-marin]* conning tower.

Baïkal [bajkal] nm *voir* **lac**.

bail, pl **baux** [baj, bo] 1 nm a (*Jur*) lease. **prendre à ~** to lease, take out a lease on; **donner à ~** to lease (out); **faire/passer un ~** to draw up/enter into a lease. b (*fig*) **ça fait un ~ que je ne l'ai pas vu!*** it's ages* since I (last) saw him! 2 comp ▸**bail commercial** commercial lease ▸**bail à ferme** farming lease ▸**bail à loyer** (house-)letting lease (*Brit*), rental lease (*US*).

baille [bɑj] nf (*Naut*) (wooden) bucket. **à la ~!*** into the drink (with him)!*

bâillement [bɑjmɑ̃] nm a *[personne]* yawn. b *[col]* gaping *ou* loose fit.

bailler [baje] 1 vt (†† *ou hum*) to give (*fig*). **vous me la baillez belle!** *ou* **bonne!** that's a tall tale!

bâiller [bɑje] 1 vi a *[personne]* to yawn. **~ de sommeil** *ou* **de fatigue** to yawn with tiredness; **~ d'ennui** to yawn with *ou* from boredom; **~ à s'en décrocher la mâchoire** *ou* **comme une carpe** to yawn one's head off. b (*être trop large*) *[col, décolleté]* to hang *ou* sit loose, gape; *[soulier]* to gape. c (*être entrouvert*) *[couture, boutonnage]* to gape; *[porte]* to be ajar *ou* half-open; *[soulier]* to gape, be split open.

bailleur, bailleresse [bajœʀ, bajʀɛs] nm,f lessor. **~ de fonds** backer, sponsor; **~ de licence** licensor, licenser.

bailli [baji] nm bailiff.

bailliage [bajaʒ] nm bailiwick.

bâillon [bɑjɔ̃] nm (*lit, fig*) gag. **mettre un ~ à qn** to gag sb.

bâillonnement [bɑjɔnmɑ̃] nm (*voir* **bâillonner**) gagging; stifling.

bâillonner [bɑjɔne] 1 vt *personne* to gag; (*fig*) *presse, opposition, opinion* to gag, stifle.

bain [bɛ̃] 1 nm a (*dans une baignoire*) bath; (*dans une piscine*) swim; (*dans la mer*) bathe (*Brit*), swim. **~ de boue/sang** mud/blood bath; (*fig*) **ce séjour à la campagne fut pour elle un ~ de fraîcheur** that stay in the country put new life into her *ou* revitalized her; **prendre un ~** (*dans une baignoire*) to have a bath; (*dans la mer, une rivière*) to have a swim *ou* bathe; (*dans une piscine*) to have a swim.

b (*liquide*) bath(water); (*Chim, Phot*) bath. **fais chauffer mon ~** heat my bath *ou* bathwater; **fais couler mon ~** run my bath (for me); (*Phot*) **~ de fixateur/de révélateur** fixing/developing bath.

c (*récipient*) (*baignoire*) bath(tub); *[teinturier]* vat.

d (*piscine*) **petit/grand ~** shallow/deep end; (*lieu*) **~s** baths; **~s publics/romains** public/Roman baths.

e (* *loc*) **mettre qn dans le ~** (*informer*) to put sb in the picture; (*compromettre*) to incriminate sb, implicate sb; **en avouant, il nous a tous mis dans le ~** by owning up, he has involved us all (in it); **nous sommes tous dans le même ~** we're all in the same boat, we're in this together; **tu seras vite dans le** ~ you'll soon pick it up *ou* get the hang of it* *ou* find your feet (*Brit*).

2 comp ►**bain de foule** walkabout; **prendre un bain de foule** to mingle with the crowd, go on a walkabout ►**j'ai pris un bain de jouvence** it was a rejuvenating experience, it made me feel years younger ►**bain linguistique** *ou* **de langue: il n'y a rien de tel que le bain linguistique** *ou* **de langue pour apprendre l'anglais** there is nothing like being steeped in the language to learn English ►**bain-marie** nm (pl **bains-marie**) (hot water in) double boiler, bain-marie; **faire chauffer au bain-marie** *sauce* to heat in a bain-marie *ou* a double boiler; *boîte de conserve* to immerse in boiling water ►**bains de mer** sea bathing (*Brit*) *ou* swimming ►**bain moussant** *ou* **de mousse** bubble *ou* foam bath ►**bain de pieds** (*récipient*) foot-bath; (*baignade*) paddle ►**bains douches municipaux** public baths (with showers) ►**bain de siège** sitzbath; **prendre un bain de siège** to have a sitzbath, have a hip-bath; (*hum*) to sit at the edge of the water ►**bain de soleil: prendre un bain de soleil** to sunbathe; **les bains de soleil lui sont déconseillés** he has been advised against sunbathing ►**bain turc** Turkish bath ►**bain de vapeur** steam bath.

baïonnette [bajɔnɛt] nf (*Élec, Mil*) bayonet. **charge à la** ~ bayonet charge; **charger** ~ **au canon** to charge with fixed bayonets.

baise** [bɛz] nf screwing**. **il ne pense qu'à la** ~ he only ever thinks about getting his end away**; **une bonne** ~ a good screw** *ou* fuck**.

baise-en-ville* [bɛzɑ̃vil] nm inv overnight bag.

baisemain [bɛzmɛ̃] nm: **il lui fit le** ~ he kissed her hand; **le** ~ **ne se pratique plus** it is no longer the custom to kiss a woman's hand.

baisement [bɛzmɑ̃] nm: ~ **de main** kissing of hands.

baiser [beze] 1 nm kiss. **gros** ~ smacking kiss*, smacker*; ~ **rapide** quick kiss, peck; (*fin de lettre*) **bons** ~**s** love (and kisses); ~ **de paix** kiss of peace; **le** ~ **de Judas** the kiss of Judas. 2 [1] vt a (*frm*) *main, visage* to kiss. b (**) to screw**, lay**, fuck**. c (‡: *avoir, l'emporter sur*) to outdo, have‡. **il a été baisé, il s'est fait** ~ he was really had‡. 3 vi (**) to screw**, fuck**. **elle baise bien** she's a good fuck**.

baiseur, -euse** [bɛzœʀ, øz] nm,f: **c'est un sacré** ~ he's always at it‡.

baisse [bɛs] nf *[température, prix, provisions]* fall, drop; *[baromètre]* fall; (*Bourse*) fall; *[pression, régime d'un moteur]* drop; *[niveau]* fall, drop, lowering; *[eaux]* drop, fall; *[popularité]* decline, drop, lessening (*de* in). **être en** ~ to be falling; to be dropping; to be sinking; to be declining *ou* lessening; ~ **de l'activité économique** downturn *ou* downswing in the economy; ~ **sur les légumes** (*par surproduction*) vegetables down in price; (*en réclame*) special offer on vegetables.

baisser [bese] [1] 1 vt a *objet* to lower; *store* to lower, pull down; *vitre* to lower, let down; (*à l'aide d'une manivelle*) to wind down; *col* to turn down; (*Théât*) *rideau* to lower, ring down. **baisse la branche pour que je puisse l'attraper** pull the branch down so (that) I can reach it; ~ **pavillon** (*Naut*) to lower *ou* strike the flag; (*fig*) to show the white flag, give in; (*Théât*) **une fois le rideau baissé** once the curtain was down.

b *main, bras* to lower. ~ **la tête** to lower *ou* bend one's head; (*de chagrin, honte*) to hang *ou* bow one's head (*de* in); (*) *[plantes]* to wilt, droop; ~ **les yeux** to look down, lower one's eyes; **elle entra, les yeux baissés** she came in with downcast eyes; **faire** ~ **les yeux à qn** to outstare sb, stare sb out of countenance; ~ **le nez*** (*de honte*) to hang one's head; ~ **le nez dans son livre*** to bury one's nose in one's book; ~ **le nez dans son assiette*** to bend over one's plate; (*fig*) ~ **les bras** to give up, throw in the sponge*.

c *chauffage, lampe, radio* to turn down, turn low; *voix, ton* to lower. (*Aut*) ~ **ses phares** to dip (*Brit*) *ou* dim one's headlights; ~ **le ton** (*lit*) to modify one's tone; (*fig*) to climb down; **baisse un peu le ton!*** pipe down!*

d *prix* to lower, bring down, reduce.

e *mur* to lower.

2 vi a *[température]* to fall, drop, go down; *[baromètre]* to fall; *[pression]* to drop, fall; *[marée]* to go out, ebb; *[eaux]* to subside, go down, sink; *[réserves, provisions]* to run *ou* get low; *[prix]* to come down, go down, drop, fall; (*Bourse*) to fall, drop; *[popularité]* to decline, lessen, drop; *[soleil]* to go down, sink. **il a baissé dans mon estime** he has sunk *ou* gone down *ou* dropped in my estimation.

b *[vue, mémoire, forces, santé]* to fail, dwindle; *[talent]* to decline, drop, fall off. **le jour baisse** the light is failing *ou* dwindling, it is getting dark; **il a beaucoup baissé ces derniers temps** (*physiquement*) he has got a lot weaker recently; (*mentalement*) his mind has got a lot weaker recently.

3 **se baisser** vpr (*pour ramasser qch*) to bend down, stoop; (*pour éviter qch*) to duck. **il n'y a qu'à se** ~ **pour les ramasser*** there are loads* of them, they are lying thick on the ground.

baissier [besje] nm (*Bourse*) bear.

bajoues [baʒu] nfpl *[animal]* chops; *[personne]* jowls, heavy cheeks.

bakchich [bakʃiʃ] nm baksheesh.

Bakélite [bakelit] nf ® Bakelite ®.

Bakou [baku] n Baku.

bal, pl ~**s** [bal] 1 nm (*réunion*) dance; (*habillé*) ball; (*lieu*) dance hall. **aller au** ~ to go dancing. 2 comp ►**bal champêtre** open-air dance ►**bal costumé** fancy dress ball ►**bal des débutantes** coming-out ball ►**bal masqué** = **bal costumé** ►**bal musette** popular dance (*to the accordion*) ►**bal populaire** ≃ local hop* (*US*), ≃ barn dance, ≃ village dance (*Brit*) ►**bal public** = **bal populaire** ►**bal du 14 juillet** Bastille Day dance (*free and open to all*) ►**bal travesti** costume ball.

balade* [balad] nf (*à pied*) walk, stroll; (*en auto*) drive run; (*à vélo*) ride, run. **être en** ~ to be out for a walk (*ou* a drive); **faire une** ~, **aller en** ~ to go for a walk (*ou* a drive).

balader* [balade] [1] 1 vt a (*traîner*) *chose* to trail round, carry about; *personne* to trail round. b (*promener*) *personne, animal* to take for a walk. (*fig*) **leur équipe a baladé la nôtre** their team was all over ours*. 2 **se balader** vpr (*à pied*) to go for a walk *ou* a stroll *ou* a saunter; (*en auto*) to go for a drive *ou* run; (*à vélo*) to go for a ride *ou* run; (*traîner*) to traipse round. **pendant qu'ils se baladaient** while they were out on a walk (*ou* drive *etc*); **aller se** ~ **en Afrique** to go touring *ou* gallivanting round Africa; **la lettre s'est baladée de bureau en bureau** the letter has been pushed round *ou* sent around from one office to another.

baladeur, -euse [baladœʀ, øz] 1 adj wandering, roving. **avoir la main** ~**euse** *ou* **les mains** ~**euses** to have wandering *ou* roving hands. 2 nm (*magnétophone*) walkman, personal stereo. 3 **baladeuse** nf (*lampe*) inspection lamp.

baladin† [baladɛ̃] nm wandering entertainer *ou* actor, strolling player.

balafre [balɑfʀ] nf (*blessure*) gash; (*intentionnelle*) slash; (*cicatrice*) scar.

balafrer [balɑfʀe] [1] vt (*voir* **balafre**) to gash; to slash; to scar. **il s'est balafré** he gashed his face.

balai [balɛ] 1 nm a (*gén*) broom, brush; *[bruyère, genêt]* besom, broom; (*Élec*) brush; (*Aut*) *[essuie-glace]* blade. **passer le** ~ to sweep the floor, give the floor a sweep; **donner un coup de** ~ (*lit*) to give the floor a (quick) sweep; (*fig*) to make a clean sweep. b (‡: *an*) **il a 80** ~**s** he's 80. 2 comp ►**balai-brosse** nm (pl **balai-brosses**) (long-handled) scrubbing brush ►**balai de crin** horsehair brush ►**balai éponge** squeezy (*Brit*) *ou* sponge (*US*) mop ►**balai mécanique** carpet sweeper.

balaise‡ [balɛz] adj = **balèze‡**.

balalaïka [balalaika] nf balalaika.

balance [balɑ̃s] 1 nf a (*instrument*) pair of scales; (*à bascule*) weighing machine; (*pour salle de bains*) (bathroom) scales (*pl*); (*pour cuisine*) (kitchen) scales (*pl*); (*Chim, Phys*) balance.

b (*loc*) **(main)tenir la** ~ **égale entre 2 rivaux** to hold the scales even between 2 rivals; **être en** ~ *[proposition]* to hang in the balance; *[candidat]* to be under consideration; **être en** ~ **entre 2 idées** to be wavering between 2 ideas; **mettre dans la** *ou* **en** ~ **le pour et le contre** to weigh up the pros and cons; **il a mis** *ou* **jeté toute son autorité dans la** ~ he used his authority to tip the scales; **si on met dans la** ~ **son ancienneté** if you take his seniority into account, if you include his seniority in his favour.

c (*Comm, Écon, Élec, Pol*) balance. ~ **de l'actif et du passif** balance of assets and liabilities.

d (*Astron*) **la B**~ Libra, the Balance. **être (de la) B**~ to be (a) Libra *ou* a Libran.

e (*Pêche*) drop-net.

2 comp ►**balance automatique** shop scales (*pl*) ►**balance à bascule** (*à marchandises*) weighbridge; (*à personnes*) weighing machine ►**balance commerciale** *ou* **du commerce** balance of trade ►**balance des comptes** balance of payments ►**balance des forces** balance of power ►**balance de ménage** kitchen scales (*pl*) ►**balance des paiements** = **balance des comptes** ►**balance des pouvoirs** balance of power ►**balance de précision** precision balance ►**balance de Roberval** (Roberval's) balance ►**balance romaine** steelyard.

balancé, e [balɑ̃se] (ptp de **balancer**) adj: **phrase bien/harmonieusement** ~**e** well-turned/nicely balanced phrase; *[personne]* **être bien** ~* to be well-built; **elle est bien** ~**e*** she's got a smashing (*Brit*) *ou* stunning figure*, she's got what it takes*.

balancelle [balɑ̃sɛl] nf (*dans un jardin*) couch hammock (*Brit*), glider (*US*).

balancement [balɑ̃smɑ̃] nm a (*mouvement*) *[corps]* sway; *[bras]* swing(ing); *[bateau]* rocking, motion; *[hanches, branches]* swaying. b (*Littérat, Mus*) balance.

balancer [balɑ̃se] [3] 1 vt a *chose, bras, jambe* to swing; *bateau, bébé* to rock; (*sur une balançoire*) to swing, push, give a push to. **veux-tu que je te balance?** do you want me to push you? *ou* give you a push?; **le vent balance les branches** the wind rocks the branches *ou* sets the branches swaying.

b (‡: *lancer*) to fling, chuck*. **balance-moi mon crayon** fling *ou* chuck* me over my pencil (*Brit*), toss me my pencil; ~ **qch à la tête de qn** to fling *ou* chuck* sth at sb's head; (*fig*) **qu'est-ce qu'il leur a balancé!** he didn't half give them a telling-off!*, he didn't half bawl them out!‡

c (‡: *se débarrasser de*) *vieux meubles* to chuck out* *ou* away*, toss out. ~ **qn** to give sb the push‡ (*Brit*), give sb the boot‡, chuck sb out*; **balance-ça à la poubelle** chuck it in the dustbin*; **il s'est fait** ~ **du lycée** he got kicked out* *ou* chucked out* of school; **j'ai envie de tout** ~

(*métier, travail*) I feel like chucking it all up‡; (*vieux objets*) I feel like chucking the whole lot out* *ou* away*.
d (*équilibrer*) *compte, phrases, paquets* to balance. ~ **le pour et le contre**† to weigh (up) the pros and cons; **tout bien balancé** everything considered.
e (*arg crime: dénoncer*) to finger (*arg*).
2 **vi** a (†: *hésiter*) to waver, hesitate, dither. (*hum*) **entre les deux mon cœur balance** I can't bring myself to choose (between them).
b (*osciller*) *[objet]* to swing.
3 **se balancer vpr** a (*osciller*) *[bras, jambes]* to swing; *[bateau]* to rock; *[branches]* to sway; *[personne]* (*sur une balançoire*) to swing, have a swing; (*sur une bascule*) to seesaw, play on a seesaw. **se ~ sur ses jambes** *ou* **sur un pied** to sway about, sway from side to side; **ne te balance pas sur ta chaise!** don't tip back on your chair!; (*Naut*) **se ~ sur ses ancres** to ride at anchor.
b (*: *se ficher de*) **se ~ de** not to give a darn about*; **je m'en balance** I don't give a darn* (about it), I couldn't care a hoot* *ou* less (about it).

balancier [balɑ̃sje] **nm** *[pendule]* pendulum; *[montre]* balance wheel; *[équilibriste]* (balancing) pole.

balançoire [balɑ̃swaʀ] **nf** (*suspendue*) swing; (*sur pivot*) seesaw. **faire de la ~** to have (a go on) a swing *ou* a seesaw.

balayage [balɛjaʒ] **nm** sweeping; (*Élec, Rad*) scanning.

balayer [baleje] 8 **vt** a (*ramasser*) *poussière, feuilles mortes* to sweep up, brush up.
b (*nettoyer*) *pièce* to sweep (out); *trottoir* to sweep. (*fig*) **le vent balaie la plaine** the wind sweeps across *ou* scours the plain.
c (*chasser*) *feuilles* to sweep away; *soucis, obstacles* to brush aside, sweep away, get rid of; *personnel* to sack* (*Brit*), fire*; *objections* to brush aside. **l'armée balayant tout sur son passage** the army sweeping aside all that lies (*ou* lay) in its path; **le gouvernement a été balayé par ce nouveau scandale** the government was swept out of office by this new scandal.
d (*Tech*) *[phares]* to sweep (across); *[vague]* to sweep over; (*Élec, Rad*) *[radar]* to scan; *[tir]* to sweep (across).

balayette [balɛjɛt] **nf** small (hand)brush.

balayeur, -euse [balɛjœʀ, øz] 1 **nm,f** roadsweeper (*Brit*), streetsweeper (*US*). 2 **balayeuse nf** roadsweeping (*Brit*) *ou* streetsweeping (*US*) machine, roadsweeper (*Brit*), streetsweeper (*US*).

balayures [balejyʀ] **nfpl** sweepings.

balbutiant, e [balbysjɑ̃, ɑ̃t] **adj** *science* in its infancy (*attrib*).

balbutiement [balbysimɑ̃] **nm** (*paroles confuses*) stammering, mumbling; *[bébé]* babbling. **les premiers ~s de l'enfant** the child's first faltering attempts at speech; (*fig: débuts*) **~s** beginnings; **cette science en est à ses premiers ~s** this science is still in its infancy.

balbutier [balbysje] 7 1 **vi** (*bredouiller*) to stammer, mumble. 2 **vt** to stammer (out), falter out, mumble.

balbuzard [balbyzaʀ] **nm: ~ (pêcheur)** osprey.

balcon [balkɔ̃] **nm** (*Constr*) balcony. (*Théât*) **(premier) ~** dress circle; **deuxième ~** upper circle; **loge/fauteuil de ~** box/seat in the dress circle.

balconnet [balkɔnɛ] **nm** half-cup bra.

baldaquin [baldakɛ̃] **nm** (*dais*) baldaquin, canopy; *[lit]* tester, canopy.

Bâle [bɑl] **n** Basle, Basel.

Baléares [baleaʀ] **nfpl: les (îles) ~** the Balearic Islands, the Baleares; **en vacances aux ~** ≃ on holiday in Majorca.

baleine [balɛn] **nf** a whale. **~ blanche/bleue/franche** white/blue/right whale; **~ à bosse** humpback whale; **rire** *ou* **se marrer comme une ~*** to laugh like a drain*. b (*fanon*) (piece of) whalebone, baleen; (*pour renforcer*) stiffener. **~ de corset** (corset-)stay; **~ de parapluie** umbrella rib.

baleiné, e [balene] **adj** *col* stiffened; *gaine, soutien-gorge* boned.

baleineau, pl **~x** [balɛno] **nm** whale calf.

baleinier, -ière [balenje, jɛʀ] 1 **adj** whaling. 2 **nm** (*pêcheur, bateau*) whaler. 3 **baleinière nf** whale *ou* whaling boat.

balèze‡ [balɛz] **adj** (*musclé*) brawny, hefty*; (*doué*) terrific*, great* (*en* at).

balisage [balizaʒ] **nm** (*voir* **balise**) a (*action*) beaconing; marking-out. b (*signaux*) beacons, buoys; runway lights; (road) signs; markers.

balise [baliz] **nf** (*Naut*) beacon, (marker) buoy; (*Aviat*) beacon, runway light; (*Aut*) (road) sign; *[piste de ski]* marker.

baliser [balize] 1 1 **vt** (*voir* **balise**) to mark out with beacons *ou* buoys *ou* lights; to signpost, put signs (up) on; to mark out. 2 **vi** (*: *avoir peur*) to be worked up. **il balise pour son examen** he's worked up about his exam.

baliseur [balizœʀ] **nm** (*personne*) ≃ (Trinity House) buoy-keeper; (*bateau*) ≃ Trinity House boat.

balistique [balistik] 1 **adj** ballistic. 2 **nf** ballistics (*sg*).

baliverne [balivɛʀn] **nf: ~s** twaddle, nonsense; **dire des ~s** to talk nonsense *ou* twaddle; **s'amuser à des ~s** to fool around; **~s!**† nonsense!, balderdash!†, fiddlesticks!†

balkanique [balkanik] **adj** Balkan. **les États ~s** the Balkan States.

balkanisation [balkanizasjɔ̃] **nf** balkanization.

balkaniser [balkanize] 1 **vt** to balkanize.

Balkans [balkɑ̃] **nmpl: les ~** the Balkans.

ballade [balad] **nf** (*poème court, Mus*) ballade; (*poème long*) ballad.

ballant, e [balɑ̃, ɑ̃t] 1 **adj: les bras ~s** with arms dangling, with swinging arms; **les jambes ~es** with dangling legs; **ne reste pas là, les bras ~s*** don't stand there looking helpless *ou* with your arms dangling at your sides. 2 **nm** (*mou*) *[câble]* slack, play; *[chargement]* sway, roll. **avoir du ~** *[câble]* to be slack; *[chargement]* to be slack *ou* loose; **donner du ~ (à une corde)** to give some slack *ou* play (to a rope).

ballast [balast] **nm** (*Rail*) ballast, roadbed (*US*); (*Naut*) ballast tank.

balle[1] [bal] **nf** a (*projectile*) bullet. **~ dum-dum/explosive/traçante** dum-dum/explosive/tracer bullet; **~ en caoutchouc/de plastique** rubber/plastic bullet; **~ perdue** stray bullet; **percé** *ou* **criblé de ~s** *chose* full of *ou* riddled with bullet holes; *personne* riddled with bullet holes *ou* bullets; **prendre une ~ dans la peau*** to get shot *ou* plugged‡; **finir avec douze ~s dans la peau*** to end up in front of a firing squad.
b (*Sport*) ball. **~ de golf/de ping-pong** golf/table tennis ball; **jouer à la ~** to play (with a) ball; **à toi la ~!** catch!; (*fig*) **saisir la ~ au bond** to jump at the opportunity.
c (*Sport: coup*) shot, ball. **c'est une ~ bien placée** *ou* **une belle ~** that's a nice ball, that's a well placed *ou* good shot; **faire des** *ou* **quelques ~s** to have a knock-up (*Brit*), knock the ball around a bit; (*Tennis*) **~ de jeu/match/set** game/match/set point; **~ let** let ball; **jouer une ~ let** to play a let.
d **~s*** francs.

balle[2] [bal] **nf** (*Agr, Bot*) husk, chaff.

balle[3] [bal] **nf** *[coton, laine]* bale.

balle[4]* [bal] **nf** chubby face. **il a une bonne ~** he has a jolly face.

baller [bale] 1 **vi** *[bras, jambes]* to dangle, hang loosely; *[tête]* to hang; *[chargement]* to be slack *ou* loose.

ballerine [bal(ə)ʀin] **nf** (*danseuse*) ballerina, ballet dancer; (*soulier*) ballet shoe.

ballet [balɛ] **nm** (*danse, spectacle*) ballet; (*musique*) ballet music. (*fig*) **~ diplomatique** flurry of diplomatic activity; (*compagnie*) **les B~s russes** the Russian Ballet.

ballon [balɔ̃] 1 **nm** a (*Sport*) ball. **~ de football** football (*Brit*), soccer ball (*US*); **~ de rugby** rugby ball; (*fig*) **le ~ rond** soccer; **le ~ ovale** rugger (*Brit*), football (*US*).
b **~ (en** *ou* **de baudruche)** (child's toy) balloon.
c (*Aviat*) balloon. **monter en ~** to go up in a balloon; **voyager en ~** to travel by balloon.
d (*Géog*) round-topped mountain.
e (*verre*) wineglass, brandy glass; (*contenu*) glass (of wine).
f (*Alcootest*) **souffler dans le ~** to take a breath test *ou* Breathalyzer test ® (*Brit*); **soufflez dans le ~, s'il vous plaît** blow in(to) the bag, please.
g **avoir le ~‡** to be expecting*, be in the family way*.
2 **comp ▸ ballon de barrage** barrage balloon **▸ ballon captif** captive balloon **▸ ballon dirigeable** airship **▸ ballon d'eau chaude** hot-water tank **▸ ballon d'essai** (*Mét*) pilot balloon; (*fig*) test of public opinion, feeler, trial balloon (*US*); (*fig*) **lancer un ballon d'essai** to fly a kite **▸ ballon d'oxygène** oxygen bottle **▸ ballon-sonde nm (pl ballons-sondes)** sounding balloon.

ballonnement [balɔnmɑ̃] **nm** feeling of distension, flatulence; (*Vét*) bloat.

ballonner [balɔne] 1 **vt** *ventre* to distend; *personne* to blow out; (*Vét*) *animal* to cause bloat in. **j'ai le ventre ballonné, je me sens ballonné, je suis ballonné** I feel bloated, my stomach feels distended.

ballonnet [balɔnɛ] **nm** (*gén, Aviat, Mét*) (small) balloon.

ballot [balo] **nm** a (*paquet*) bundle, package. b (*: *nigaud*) nitwit‡, silly ass‡. **tu es/c'est ~ de l'avoir oublié** you're/it's a bit daft (*Brit*) *ou* crazy (*US*) to have forgotten it*.

ballotin [balɔtɛ̃] **nm: ~ de chocolats** (*small, punnet-shaped*) box of chocolates.

ballottage [balɔtaʒ] **nm** (*Pol*) **il y a ~** there will have to be a second ballot, people will have to vote again; **M. Dupont est en ~** Mr Dupont has to stand again at (*Brit*) *ou* run again on (*US*) the second ballot.

ballottement [balɔtmɑ̃] **nm** (*voir* **ballotter**) banging about; rolling; lolling; bouncing; tossing, bobbing; shaking.

ballotter [balɔte] 1 1 **vi** *[objet]* to roll around, bang about; *[tête, membres]* to loll; *[poitrine]* to bounce; *[bateau]* to toss, bob about. 2 **vt** (*gén pass*) *personne* to shake about, jolt; *bateau* to toss (about). **on est ballotté dans ce train** you get shaken about *ou* thrown about in this train; (*fig*) **être ballotté entre 2 sentiments contraires** to be torn between 2 conflicting feelings; **cet enfant a été ballotté entre plusieurs écoles** this child has been shifted around *ou* shunted around* from school to school.

ballottine [balɔtin] **nf** (*Culin*) ≃ meat loaf (*made with poultry*).

ball-trap, pl **ball-traps** [baltʀap] **nm** (*lieu*) shooting ground; (*Sport*) clay-pigeon shooting, trap-shooting, skeet-shooting; (*machine*) trap.

balluchon [balyʃɔ̃] **nm** (†) bundle (*of clothes*); (*) belongings. **faire son ~*** to pack up one's traps.

balnéaire [balneɛʀ] **adj** bathing (*Brit*), swimming; *voir* **station**.

balnéothérapie [balneoteʀapi] **nf** balneotherapy.

balourd, e [baluʀ, uʀd] 1 nm,f (*: *lourdaud*) dolt, fathead*, clumsy oaf*. **qu'il est ~!** what a dolt he is! 2 nm (*Tech*) unbalance.
balourdise [baluʀdiz] nf a (*maladresse manuelle*) clumsiness; (*manque de finesse*) fatheadedness*, doltishness. b (*gaffe*) blunder, boob*.
balsa [balza] nm balsa (wood).
balsamier [balzamje] nm balsam tree.
balsamine [balzamin] nf balsam.
balsamique [balzamik] adj balsamic.
balte [balt] adj *pays, peuple* Baltic. **les pays ~s** the Baltic States.
balthazar [baltazaʀ] nm a (*Antiq, Rel*) **B~** Belshazzar. b (†: *banquet*) feast, banquet. c (*bouteille*) balthazar.
baltique [baltik] 1 adj *mer, région* Baltic. 2 nf: **la (mer) B~** the Baltic (Sea).
baluchon [balyʃɔ̃] nm = **balluchon**.
balustrade [balystʀad] nf (*Archit*) balustrade; (*garde-fou*) railing, handrail.
balustre [balystʀ] nm (*Archit*) baluster; *[siège]* spoke.
balzacien, -ienne [balzasjɛ̃, jɛn] adj of Balzac, typical of Balzac.
balzan, e [balzɑ̃, an] 1 adj *cheval* with white stockings. 2 **balzane** nf white stocking.
Bamako [bamako] n Bamako.
bambin [bɑ̃bɛ̃] nm small child, little lad* (*Brit*) *ou* guy* (*US*).
bambochard, e [bɑ̃bɔʃaʀ, aʀd] = **bambocheur**.
bambocher* [bɑ̃bɔʃe] 1 vi (*faire la noce*) to live it up*, have a wild time.
bambocheur, -euse [bɑ̃bɔʃœʀ, øz] 1 adj *tempérament* revelling. 2 nm,f (*: *noceur*) reveller, fast liver.
bambou [bɑ̃bu] nm a (*plante*) bamboo; (*canne*) bamboo (walking) stick; *voir* **pousse**. b **coup de ~*** (*insolation*) **attraper un coup de ~**† to get a touch of the sun* *ou* a touch of sunstroke; **avoir le coup de ~** (*folie*) to be round the bend* (*Brit*) *ou* a bit touched*; (*fatigue*) to be shattered* *ou* bushed*; (*prix exorbitant*) **c'est le coup de ~** the prices are sky-high.
bamboula* [bɑ̃bula] nf: **faire la ~** to live it up*, have a wild time.
ban [bɑ̃] nm a *[mariage]* **~s** banns. b *[applaudissements]* round of applause, cheer; *[tambour]* drum roll; *[clairon]* bugle call, fanfare. **faire un ~ à qn** to applaud *ou* cheer sb; **un ~ pour X!, ouvrez le ~!** (let's have) a big hand for* *ou* a round of applause for X!, ≃ three cheers for X! c (*Hist*) proclamation. d (*loc*) (*Hist*) **être/mettre au ~ de l'Empire** to be banished/banish from the Empire; (*fig*) **être/mettre au ~ de la société** to be outlawed/outlaw from society; (*Hist*) **le ~ et l'arrière-~** the barons and vassals; **le ~ et l'arrière-~ de sa famille/de ses amis** every last one of *ou* the entire collection of his relatives/his friends.
banal, e[1], mpl **~s** [banal] adj (*ordinaire*) *roman, conversation* banal, trite; *idée* banal, trite, well-worn; *vie* humdrum, banal; *personne* run-of-the-mill, ordinary; *nouvelle, incident* (*courant*) commonplace, everyday (*épith*); (*insignifiant*) trivial. **il n'y a rien là que de très ~** there is nothing at all unusual *ou* out of the ordinary about that; **une grippe ~e** a common or garden case of flu; **un personnage peu ~** an unusual character; **haïr le ~** to hate what is banal *ou* what is trite.
banal, e[2], mpl **-aux** [banal, o] adj (*Hist*) **four/moulin ~** communal *ou* village oven/mill.
banalement [banalmɑ̃] adv (*voir* **banal**[1]) tritely; in a humdrum way. **tout ~** quite simply; **c'est arrivé très ~** it happened in the most ordinary way.
banalisation [banalizasjɔ̃] nf *[campus]* opening to the police. **la ~ de la violence** the way in which violence has become an everyday fact *ou* feature of life.
banaliser [banalize] 1 vt a *expression* to make commonplace *ou* trite; *vie* to rob of its originality. **ce qui banalise la vie quotidienne** what makes life humdrum *ou* robs life of its excitement. b *voiture de police* to disguise; *campus* to open to the police. (*Police*) **voiture banalisée** unmarked police car.
banalité [banalite] nf (*voir* **banal**[1]) a (*caractère*) banality; triteness; ordinariness; triviality. b (*propos*) truism, platitude, trite remark.
banane [banan] nf a (*fruit*) banana. b (*Aut*) overrider. c (*Coiffure*) quiff (*Brit*), pompadour (*US*). d (*arg Mil*) medal, decoration, gong*. e (*arg Aviat*) twin-rotor helicopter, chopper‡. f (*sac*) waist-bag, bum-bag.
bananeraie [bananʀɛ] nf banana plantation.
bananier [bananje] nm (*arbre*) banana tree; (*bateau*) banana boat.
banc [bɑ̃] 1 nm a (*siège*) seat, bench. **~ (d'école)** (desk) seat; **nous nous sommes connus sur les ~s de l'école** we've known each other since we were at school together.
b (*Géol*) (*couche*) layer, bed; *[coraux]* reef. **~ de sable/vase** sand/mudbank; (*Can*) **~ de neige** snowdrift, snowbank.
c *[poissons]* shoal (*Brit*), school (*US*).
d (*Tech*) (work) bench.
e (*Mét*) bank, patch.
2 comp ►**banc des accusés** (*Jur*) dock, bar ►**banc des avocats** (*Jur*) bar ►**banc d'église** pew ►**banc d'essai** (*Tech*) test bed; (*fig*) testing ground; **émission qui sert de banc d'essai pour jeunes chanteurs** programme that gives young singers a chance to show their talents ►**banc des ministres** (*Parl*) ≃ government front bench (*Brit*) ►**banc d'œuvre** (*Rel*) ≃ churchwardens' pew ►**banc des témoins** (*Jur*) witness box (*Brit*), witness stand (*US*).
bancable [bɑ̃kabl] adj bankable.
bancaire [bɑ̃kɛʀ] adj *système etc* banking. **chèque ~** (bank) cheque (*Brit*) *ou* check (*US*).
bancal, e, mpl **~s** [bɑ̃kal] adj a *personne* (*boiteux*) lame; (*aux jambes arquées*) bandy-legged. b *table, chaise* wobbly, rickety. c *idée, raisonnement* shaky, unsound.
banco [bɑ̃ko] nm banco. **faire ~** to go banco.
bandage [bɑ̃daʒ] nm a (*objet*) *[blessé]* bandage; *[roue]* (*en métal*) band, hoop; (*en caoutchouc*) tyre. **~ herniaire** surgical appliance, truss. b (*action*) *[blessé]* bandaging; *[ressort]* stretching; *[arc]* bending.
bandana [bɑ̃dana] nm banda(n)na.
bandant, e‡ [bɑ̃dɑ̃, ɑ̃t] adj *film, livre* sexy‡. **elle est vachement ~e** she's a real turn-on‡.
Bandar Seri Begawan [bɑ̃daʀseʀibegawan] n Bandar Seri Begawan.
bande[1] [bɑ̃d] 1 nf a (*ruban*) (*en tissu, métal*) band, strip; (*en papier*) strip; (*de sable*) strip, tongue; (*Ciné*) film; *[magnétophone]* tape; (*Presse*) wrapper; (*Méd*) bandage. (*Mil*) **~ (de mitrailleuse)** (ammunition) belt; **journal sous ~** mailed newspaper.
b (*dessin, motif*) stripe; *[chaussée]* line; *[assiette]* band; (*Hér*) bend.
c (*Billard*) cushion. **jouer la ~** to play (the ball) off the cushion; (*fig*) **faire/obtenir qch par la ~** to do/get sth by devious means *ou* in a roundabout way; **apprendre qch par la ~** to hear of sth indirectly *ou* through the grapevine*.
d (*Naut*) list. **donner de la ~** to list.
2 comp ►**bande d'absorption** (*Phys*) absorption band ►**bande-annonce** (*Ciné*) (pl **bandes-annonces**) trailer ►**bande d'arrêt d'urgence** hard shoulder (*Brit*), berm (*US*) ►**bande dessinée** comic strip, strip cartoon (*Brit*) ►**bande d'essai** (*Phot*) test strip ►**bande étalon** (*Phot*) reference strip, test gauge ►**bande de fréquence** (*Rad*) waveband, frequency band ►**bande gaufrée** (*Phot*) apron ►**bande illustrée** = **bande dessinée** ►**bande magnétique** magnetic tape ►**bande de manœuvre** (*Ordin*) scratch tape ►**bande molletière** puttee ►**bande originale** (original) soundtrack ►**bande perforée** punched *ou* perforated *ou* paper tape ►**bande protectrice** (*Phot*) duplex paper ►**bande de roulement** *[pneu]* tread ►**bande-son** (pl **bandes-son**), **bande sonore** (*Ciné*) soundtrack ►**bande de terre** strip *ou* tongue of land ►**bande Velpeau** ® (*Méd*) crêpe bandage (*Brit*), Ace ® bandage (*US*).
bande[2] [bɑ̃d] nf a (*groupe*) *[gens]* band, group, gang*; *[oiseaux]* flock. **~ de loups/chiens** pack of wolves/dogs; **~ de lions** troop *ou* pride (*littér*) of lions; **~ de singes** troop of monkeys; **ils sont partis en ~** they set off in a group, they all went off together.
b (*groupe constitué*) set, gang; *[pirates]* band; *[voleurs]* gang, band. **~ armée** armed band *ou* gang; **il ne fait pas partie de leur ~** he's not in their crowd *ou* set *ou* gang; **ils sont toute une ~ d'amis** they make up a whole crowd *ou* group of friends; (*Pol*) **la ~ des Quatre** the Gang of Four; **faire ~ à part** *[groupe]* to make a separate group; *[personne]* to keep to o.s.; (*fig: faire exception*) to be an exception; **venez avec nous, ne faites pas ~ à part** come with us, don't stay on your own.
c (*: *groupe de*) **~ de** bunch of*, pack of*; **~ d'imbéciles!** pack of idiots!*, bunch of fools!*; **c'est une ~ de paresseux** they're a lazy lot (*Brit*) *ou* bunch* *ou* crowd*.
bandeau, pl **~x** [bɑ̃do] nm a (*ruban*) headband, bandeau; (*pansement*) head bandage; (*pour les yeux*) blindfold. **mettre un ~ à qn** to blindfold sb; **avoir un ~ sur l'œil** to wear an eye patch; (*fig*) **avoir un ~ sur les yeux** to be blind. b (*Coiffure*) **porter les cheveux en ~** to wear one's hair coiled round one's head.
bandelette [bɑ̃dlɛt] nf strip of cloth, (narrow) bandage; *[momie]* wrapping, bandage.
bander [bɑ̃de] 1 1 vt a (*entourer*) *genou, plaie* to bandage. **~ les yeux à qn** to blindfold sb; **les yeux bandés** blindfold(ed). b (*tendre*) *corde* to strain, tauten; *arc* to bend; *ressort* to stretch, tauten; *muscles* to tense. 2 vi (**‡**) to have an erection, have a hard-on**‡**.
banderille [bɑ̃dʀij] nf banderilla.
banderole [bɑ̃dʀɔl] nf (*drapeau*) banderole. **~ publicitaire** advertizing streamer.
bandit [bɑ̃di] nm (*voleur*) gangster, thief; (*assassin*) gangster; (*brigand*) bandit; (*fig: escroc*) crook, shark*; (*: *enfant*) rascal. **~ armé** gunman, armed gangster; **~ de grand chemin** highwayman.
banditisme [bɑ̃ditism] nm (*actions criminelles*) crime. **le grand ~** organized crime; (*fig*) **300 F pour cette réparation, c'est du ~!** 300 francs for this repair job — it's daylight robbery!
bandoulière [bɑ̃duljɛʀ] nf (*gén*) shoulder strap; (*Mil*) bandoleer, bandolier. **en ~** slung across the shoulder.
bang [bɑ̃g] 1 nm inv: **~ (supersonique)** supersonic bang, sonic boom. 2 excl bang!, crash!
Bangkok [bɑ̃ŋkɔk] n Bangkok.
bangladais, e [bɑ̃gladɛ, ɛz] 1 adj Bangladeshi. 2 nm,f: **B~(e)** Bangladeshi.

Bangladesh [bɑ̃gladɛʃ] nm Bangladesh. *économie, population* **du ~** Bangladeshi; **un habitant du ~** a Bangladeshi.
Bangui [bɑ̃gi] n Bangui.
banjo [bɑ̃(d)ʒo] nm banjo.
Banjul [bɑ̃ʒul] n Banjul.
banlieue [bɑ̃ljø] nf suburbs, outskirts. **proche/moyenne/grande ~** inner *ou* immediate/inner *ou* near/outer suburbs; **Paris et sa (grande) ~** greater Paris; **la grande ~ de Paris** the outer suburbs of Paris, the commuter belt of Paris; **la ~ rouge** the Communist-controlled suburbs of Paris; **habiter en ~** to live in the suburbs; **de ~** *maison, ligne de chemin de fer* suburban (*épith*); *train* commuter (*épith*).
banlieusard, e [bɑ̃ljøzaʀ, aʀd] nm,f suburbanite, (suburban) commuter.
banne [ban] nf a (*toile*) canopy. b (*panier*) wicker basket.
banni, e [bani] (ptp de **bannir**) nm,f exile.
bannière [banjɛʀ] nf a banner. **la ~ étoilée** the Star-Spangled Banner; (*fig*) **se battre** *ou* **se ranger sous la ~ de qn** to fight on sb's side *ou* under sb's banner. b (*: *pan de chemise*) shirttail. **il se promène toujours en ~** he's always walking round with his shirt-tail hanging out.
bannir [baniʀ] [2] vt *citoyen* to banish; *pensée* to banish, dismiss; *mot, sujet, aliment* to banish, exclude (*de* from); *usage* to prohibit, put a ban on. (*frm*) **je l'ai banni de ma maison** I forbade him to darken my door (*frm*), I told him never to set foot in my house again.
bannissement [banismɑ̃] nm banishment.
banque [bɑ̃k] 1 nf a (*établissement*) bank; (*ensemble*) banks. **il a 3 millions en** *ou* **à la ~** he's got 3 million in the bank; **mettre** *ou* **porter des chèques à la ~** to bank cheques; **la grande ~ appuie sa candidature** the big banks are backing his candidature.
b (*activité, métier*) banking.
c (*Jeux*) bank. **tenir la ~** to be (the) banker.
d (*Méd*) **~ des yeux/du sang/du sperme** eye/blood/sperm bank; **~ d'organes** organ bank.
2 comp ►**banque d'affaires** commercial *ou* mercantile bank ►**banque centrale** central bank ►**Banque centrale européenne** European Central Bank ►**banque de dépôt** deposit bank ►**banque de données** data bank ►**banque d'émission** bank of issue ►**banque d'escompte** discount bank ►**Banque européenne d'investissement** European Investment Bank ►**Banque internationale pour la reconstruction et le développement** International Bank for Reconstruction and Development ►**Banque mondiale** World Bank ►**Banque des règlements internationaux** Bank for International Settlements.
banquer* [bɑ̃ke] [1] vi to cough up*, stump up* (*Brit*).
banqueroute [bɑ̃kʀut] nf (*Fin*) (fraudulent) bankruptcy; (*Pol*) bankruptcy; (*fig littér*) failure. **faire ~** to go bankrupt.
banqueroutier, -ière [bɑ̃kʀutje, jɛʀ] nm,f (fraudulent) bankrupt.
banquet [bɑ̃kɛ] nm dinner; (*d'apparat*) banquet.
banqueter [bɑ̃k(ə)te] [4] vi (*lit*) to banquet; (*festoyer*) to feast.
banquette [bɑ̃kɛt] nf a *[train]* seat; *[auto]* (bench) seat; *[restaurant]* (wall) seat; *[piano]* (duet) stool. b (*Archit*) window seat. c (*Mil*) **~ de tir** banquette, fire-step.
banquier [bɑ̃kje] nm (*Fin, Jeux*) banker.
banquise [bɑ̃kiz] nf ice field; (*flottante*) ice floe.
bantou, e [bɑ̃tu] 1 adj Bantu. 2 nm (*Ling*) Bantu. 3 nm,f: **B~(e)** Bantu.
Bantoustan [bɑ̃tustɑ̃] nm Bantustan.
baobab [baɔbab] nm baobab.
baptême [batɛm] 1 nm a (*sacrement*) baptism; (*cérémonie*) christening, baptism. **donner le ~ à** to baptize, christen; **recevoir le ~** to be baptized *ou* christened. b *[cloche]* blessing, dedication; *[navire]* naming, christening. 2 comp ►**baptême de l'air** first flight ►**baptême du feu** baptism of fire ►**baptême de la ligne** (*Naut*) (first) crossing of the line.
baptiser [batize] [1] vt a (*Rel*) to baptize, christen. b *cloche* to bless, dedicate; *navire* to name, christen. c (*appeler*) to call, christen, name. **on le baptisa Paul** he was christened Paul; **on baptisa la rue du nom du maire** the street was named *ou* called after the mayor. d (*: *surnommer*) to christen, dub. (*hum*) **la pièce qu'il baptisait pompeusement salon** the room which he pompously dubbed the drawing room, the room to which he gave the pompous title of drawing room. e (* *fig*) *vin, lait* to water down.
baptismal, e, mpl **-aux** [batismal, o] adj baptismal.
baptisme [batism] nm baptism.
baptiste [batist] adj, nmf Baptist.
baptistère [batistɛʀ] nm baptistry.
baquet [bakɛ] nm tub; *voir* **siège**[1].
bar[1] [baʀ] nm (*établissement, comptoir*) bar. **~ américain** bar; **~-tabac** bar (*which sells tobacco and stamps*).
bar[2] [baʀ] nm (*poisson*) bass.
bar[3] [baʀ] nm (*Phys*) bar.
Barabbas [baʀabas] nm Barabbas.
barachois [baʀaʃwa] nm (*Can*) lagoon.
baragouin* [baʀagwɛ̃] nm gibberish, double Dutch.
baragouinage* [baʀagwinaʒ] nm (*façon de parler*) gibbering; (*propos*) gibberish, double Dutch.
baragouiner* [baʀagwine] [1] 1 vi to gibber, talk gibberish *ou* double Dutch. 2 vt *langue* to speak badly; *discours, paroles* to jabber out, gabble. **il baragouine un peu l'espagnol** he can speak a bit of Spanish *ou* say a few words of Spanish; (*péj*) **qu'est-ce qu'il baragouine?** what's he jabbering on about?*
baragouineur, -euse* [baʀagwinœʀ, øz] nm,f jabberer.
baraka‡ [baʀaka] nf luck. **avoir la ~** to be lucky.
baraque [baʀak] nf a (*abri en planches*) shed, hut; (*servant de boutique*) stand, stall. **~ foraine** fairground stall. b (*: *maison*) place*, shack*; (*appartement*) pad‡, place*; (*péj: maison, entreprise etc*) dump*, hole‡. **une belle ~** a smart place*; **quand je suis rentré à la ~** when I got back to my place* *ou* shack‡ *ou* pad‡; **quelle (sale) ~!** what a lousy dump!‡, what a hole!‡; *voir* **casser.**
baraqué, e* [baʀake] adj: **bien ~** *homme* hefty, well-built; *femme* well-built.
baraquement [baʀakmɑ̃] nm: **~(s)** group of huts; (*Mil*) camp.
baratin* [baʀatɛ̃] nm (*boniment*) sweet talk*, smooth talk*; (*verbiage*) chatter, hot air‡; (*Comm*) patter*, sales talk, pitch (*US*). **assez de ~!** cut the chat!* (*Brit*) *ou* the chatter *ou* the cackle!* (*Brit*); (*gén*) **faire son** *ou* **du ~ à qn** to sweet-talk sb‡, chat sb up* (*Brit*), hand sb a line* (*US*); (*Comm*) **faire son** *ou* **le ~ à un client** to give a customer the sales talk *ou* patter*; **avoir du ~** to have all the patter*, be a smooth talker.
baratiner* [baʀatine] [1] 1 vt: **~ qn** (*amadouer par un boniment*) to chat sb up* (*Brit*), sweet-talk* sb; (*draguer*) to chat sb up* (*Brit*), hand sb a line* (*US*); (*Comm*) **~ (le client)** to give a customer the sales talk *ou* spiel* *ou* patter*. 2 vi (*bavarder*) to natter* (*Brit*), chatter.
baratineur, -euse* [baʀatinœʀ, øz] 1 nm,f (*beau parleur, menteur*) smooth talker; (*bavard*) gasbag‡, windbag‡. 2 nm (*dragueur*) smooth talker.
baratte [baʀat] nf *[beurre]* churn.
baratter [baʀate] [1] vt to churn.
Barbade [baʀbad] nf: **la ~** Barbados.
barbadien, -ienne [baʀbadjɛ̃, ɛn] 1 adj Barbadian. 2 nm,f: **B~(ne)** Barbadian.
barbant, e* [baʀbɑ̃, ɑ̃t] adj (*ennuyeux*) boring, deadly dull. **qu'il est/que c'est ~!** what a bore he/it is!, he's/it's deadly boring!*
barbaque‡ [baʀbak] nf (*péj*) meat.
barbare [baʀbaʀ] 1 adj *invasion, peuple* barbarian, barbaric; *mœurs, musique, crime* barbarous, barbaric. 2 nm (*Hist, fig*) barbarian.
barbarement [baʀbaʀmɑ̃] adv barbarously, barbarically.
barbaresque [baʀbaʀɛsk] adj (*Hist: d'Afrique du Nord*) *régions, peuples, pirate* Barbary Coast (*épith*). **les États ~s** the Barbary Coast.
Barbarie [baʀbaʀi] nf: **la ~** the Barbary Coast.
barbarie [baʀbaʀi] nf (*manque de civilisation*) barbarism; (*cruauté*) barbarity, barbarousness.
barbarisme [baʀbaʀism] nm (*Gram*) barbarism.
barbe[1] [baʀb] 1 nf a (*Anat*) beard. **une ~ de 3 mois** 3 months' (growth of) beard; **il a une ~ de 3 jours** he has got 3 days' stubble on his chin; **sans ~** *adulte* clean-shaven, beardless; *adolescent* (*imberbe*) beardless; **il a de la ~ (au menton)** *[adulte]* he needs a shave; *[adolescent]* he has already a few hairs on his chin; **avoir une ~, porter la** *ou* **une ~** to have a beard, be bearded; **faire la ~ à qn** to trim sb's beard; (*fig hum*) **il n'a pas encore de ~ au menton et il croit tout savoir** he's still in short pants *ou* he's still wet behind the ears* and he thinks he knows it all.
b *[chèvre, singe, oiseau]* beard.
c *[plume]* barb; *[poisson]* barbel, wattle; *[orge]* beard (*NonC*). **~s** whiskers.
d (*aspérités*) **~s** *[papier]* ragged edge; *[métal]* jagged edge.
e (*loc*) **à la ~ de qn** under sb's nose; **dérober qch à la ~ de qn** to swipe* sth from under sb's nose; **vieille ~*** old stick-in-the-mud*, old fogey*; **marmonner dans sa ~** to mumble *ou* mutter into one's beard; **rire dans sa ~** to laugh up one's sleeve; **la ~!*** damn (it)!‡, blast!*; **il faut que j'y retourne, quelle ~!*** I've got to go back — what a drag!*; **oh toi, la ~!*** oh shut up, you!*, shut your mouth, you!‡
2 comp ►**Barbe-Bleue** nm Bluebeard ►**barbe de capucin** wild chicory ►**barbe à papa** candy-floss (*Brit*), cotton candy (*US*).
barbe[2] [baʀb] nm (*Zool*) **(cheval) ~** barb.
barbeau, pl **~x** [baʀbo] nm (*Zool*) barbel; (*Bot*) cornflower; (‡: *souteneur*) pimp, ponce.
barbecue [baʀbəkju] nm (*repas, cuisine*) barbecue; (*matériel*) barbecue set.
barbelé, e [baʀbəle] adj, nm: **(fil de fer) ~** barbed wire (*NonC*); **les ~s** the barbed wire fence *ou* fencing; **s'égratigner après les ~s** to get scratched on the barbed wire; **derrière les ~s** in a P.O.W. camp.
barber* [baʀbe] [1] 1 vt to bore stiff*, bore to tears*. 2 **se barber** vpr to be bored stiff*, be bored to tears* (*à faire qch* doing sth).
Barberousse [baʀbəʀus] nm Barbarossa.
barbet [baʀbɛ] nm: **(chien) ~** water spaniel.
barbiche [baʀbiʃ] nf goatee (beard).
barbichette* [baʀbiʃɛt] nf (small) goatee (beard).

barbier [barbje] nm (††) barber; (Can) (men's) hairdresser.

barbillon [barbijɔ̃] nm a [plume, hameçon] barb; [poisson] barbel. [bœuf, cheval] ~s barbs. b (Zool: petit barbeau) (small) barbel.

barbiturique [barbityrik] 1 adj barbituric. 2 nm barbiturate.

barbon [barbɔ̃] nm (†† ou péj) (vieux) ~ greybeard, old fogey*.

barbotage [barbɔtaʒ] nm (voir **barboter**) pinching* (Brit); filching*; paddling, splashing about, squelching around (Brit); bubbling.

barboter [barbɔte] 1 1 vt (*: voler) to pinch* (Brit), filch* (à from, off*). **elle lui a barboté son briquet** she has filched* his lighter. 2 vi a (patauger) [canard] to dabble; [enfant] to paddle; (en éclaboussant) to splash about. ~ **dans la boue** to squelch around in (Brit) ou paddle through the mud. b [gaz] to bubble.

barboteur, -euse¹ [barbɔtœr, øz] 1 adj (*) **il est (du genre) ~, c'est un ~** he's a bit light-fingered (Brit) ou sticky-fingered (US). 2 nm (Chim) bubble chamber.

barboteuse² [barbɔtøz] nf (vêtement) rompers.

barbouillage [barbujaʒ] nm a (peinture) daub; (écriture) scribble, scrawl. b (action) daubing; scribbling, scrawling.

barbouille* [barbuj] nf (péj) painting. (hum) **il fait de la ~** he does a bit of painting.

barbouiller [barbuje] 1 vt a (couvrir, salir) to smear, daub (de with), cover (de with, in). **il a le visage tout barbouillé de chocolat** he's got chocolate (smeared) all over his face, he's got his face covered in chocolate.

b (péj: peindre) mur to daub ou slap paint on. **il barbouille (des toiles) de temps en temps** he does an odd bit of painting from time to time; **il barbouille des toiles en amateur** he messes about with paints and canvas, he does a bit of painting on the side.

c (péj: écrire, dessiner) to scribble (sur on). ~ **une feuille de dessins** to scribble ou scrawl drawings on a piece of paper; ~ **du papier** to cover a piece of paper with scrawls, scrawl all over a piece of paper; ~ **un slogan sur un mur** to daub a slogan on a wall.

d (*) ~ **l'estomac** to upset the stomach; **être barbouillé, avoir l'estomac** ou **le cœur barbouillé** to feel queasy ou sick.

barbouilleur, -euse [barbujœr, øz] nm,f a (péj: artiste) dauber; (péj: peintre en bâtiment) bad ou slapdash painter. b ~ **de papier** hack (writer).

barbouillis [barbuji] nm (écriture) scribble, scrawl; (peinture) daub.

barbouze* [barbuz] nf a beard. b (policier) secret (government) police agent; (garde du corps) bodyguard.

barbu, e [barby] 1 adj bearded. **un ~** a bearded man, a man with a beard. 2 **barbue** nf (Zool) brill.

barcarolle [barkarɔl] nf barcarolle.

barcasse [barkas] nf boat.

Barcelone [barsəlɔn] n Barcelona.

barda* [barda] nm gear*; (Mil) kit. **il a tout un ~ dans la voiture** he's got a whole load* of stuff in the car.

barde¹ [bard] nm (poète) bard.

barde² [bard] nf (Culin, Mil) bard.

bardeau¹, pl ~x [bardo] nm [toit] shingle.

bardeau², pl ~x [bardo] nm = **bardot**.

barder [barde] 1 1 vt a (Culin) to bard. b (Mil) cheval to bard. **bardé de fer** cheval barded; soldat armour-clad; porte with iron bars; **discours bardé de citations** speech packed ou larded with quotations; **poitrine bardée de décorations** chest covered with medals. c (fig) **être bardé (contre)** to be immune (to). 2 vb impers (*) **ça va ~** things are going to get hot, all hell is going to break loose; **ça a bardé!** (dans une réunion) the sparks really flew!; (dans les rues) things got hot!

bardot [bardo] nm hinny.

barème [barɛm] nm (table de référence) table, list; (tarif) (Comm) scale of charges, price list; (Rail) fare schedule. ~ **des salaires** salary scale; ~ **des impôts** tax scale; (Scol) ~ **de correction** scale of marking (Brit) ou grading (US).

barge [barʒ] nf (Naut) barge.

barguigner [bargiɲe] 1 vi (littér, hum) **sans ~** without humming and hawing (Brit) ou hemming and hawing (US), without shilly-shallying.

baril [bari(l)] nm [pétrole] barrel; [vin] barrel, cask; [poudre] keg, cask; [harengs] barrel. ~ **de lessive** drum of detergent.

barillet [barijɛ] nm a (petit baril) small barrel ou cask. b (Tech) [serrure, revolver] cylinder; [pendule] barrel. **serrure à ~** Yale ® lock.

bariolage [barjɔlaʒ] nm (résultat) riot ou medley of colours; (action) daubing.

bariolé, e [barjɔle] (ptp de **barioler**) adj vêtement many-coloured, rainbow-coloured, gaudy (péj); groupe colourfully dressed, gaily-coloured.

barioler [barjɔle] 1 vt to splash ou daub bright colours on, streak with bright colours.

bariolure [barjɔlyr] nf gay ou gaudy (péj) colours.

barjo(t)⁑ [barʒo] adj nuts*, crazy*, barmy*.

barmaid [barmɛd] nf barmaid.

barman [barman], pl **barmans** ou **barmen** [barmɛn] nm barman, bartender.

barnache [barnaʃ], **barnacle** [barnakl] nf = **bernache**.

baromètre [barɔmɛtr] nm (lit, fig) barometer; (lit) glass. **le ~ baisse** the glass ou barometer is falling; **le ~ est au beau fixe/à la pluie** the barometer is set at fair/is pointing to rain; (fig) **le ~ est au beau (fixe)*** things are looking good*; ~ **enregistreur/anéroïde** recording/aneroid barometer.

barométrique [barɔmetrik] adj barometric(al).

baron [barɔ̃] nm a (titre) baron; voir **monsieur**. b (fig: magnat) baron, lord. **les ~s de la presse** the press lords ou barons.

baronnage [barɔnaʒ] nm (titre) barony; (corps des barons) baronage.

baronne [barɔn] nf baroness; voir **madame**.

baronnet [barɔnɛ] nm baronet.

baronnie [barɔni] nf barony.

baroque [barɔk] 1 adj idée weird, strange, wild; (Archit, Art) baroque. 2 nm baroque.

baroud [barud] nm (arg Mil) fighting. ~ **d'honneur** last-ditch struggle, gallant last stand.

baroudeur [barudœr] nm (arg Mil) firebrand, fighter.

barouf(le)⁑ [baruf(lə)] nm (vacarme) row*, din*, racket*. **faire du ~** to kick up a din*, make a row*; (protester) to kick up a fuss* ou stink⁑.

barque [bark] nf small boat, small craft. ~ **à moteur** (small) motor-boat; ~ **de pêche** small fishing boat.

barquette [barkɛt] nf (Culin) pastry boat, small tart.

barracuda [barakyda] nm barracuda.

barrage [baraʒ] nm a [rivière, lac] dam, barrage; (à fleur d'eau) weir. b (barrière) barrier; (d'artillerie, de questions) barrage. ~ **de police** (gén) (police) roadblock; (cordon d'agents) police cordon; (chevaux de frise) (police) barricade; **faire ~ à** to hinder, stand in the way of; **le ~ de la rue** the blocking of the street; (avec barricades) the barricading of the street. c (Cartes) pre-emptive bid, pre-empt.

barre [bar] 1 nf a (gén, Hér: tige, morceau) bar; (de fer) rod, bar; (de bois) piece, rod. (Ftbl, Rugby) ~ **(transversale)** crossbar; ~ **de chocolat** bar of chocolate; ~ **de savon** cake ou bar of soap.

b (Danse) barre. **exercices à la ~** exercises at the barre, barre exercises.

c (Naut) helm; [petit bateau] tiller. (lit, fig) **être à la** ou **tenir la ~** to be at the helm; (lit, fig) **prendre la ~** to take the helm.

d (Jur) ~ **du tribunal** bar; ~ **(des témoins)** witness box (Brit), witness stand (US); **être appelé à la ~** to be called as a witness; **comparaître à la ~** to appear as a witness.

e (Géog: houle) (gén) race; (à l'estuaire) bore; (banc de sable) (sand) bar; (crête de montagne) ridge.

f (trait) line, dash, stroke; (du t, f) stroke. **faire** ou **tirer des ~s** to draw lines (on a page); **mets une ~ à ton t** cross your t; (Math) ~ **de fraction/d'addition** etc fraction/addition etc line.

g (niveau) mark. **dépasser la ~ des 10 %** to pass the 10 % mark; (Scol) **placer la ~ à 10** to set the pass mark at 10.

h (†: jeu) ~s ≈ prisoners' base; (frm) **avoir ~(s) sur qn** (avantage) to have an advantage over sb; (pouvoir) to have power over ou a hold on sb.

i (Zool) [cheval] bar.

2 comp ▸**barre d'accouplement** (Aut) tie-rod ▸**barre anti-roulis** (Aut) anti-roll bar ▸**barre d'appui** (window) rail ▸**barre à disques** (Sport) barbell ▸**barre fixe** (Sport) horizontal ou chinning bar ▸**barre de mesure** (Mus) bar line ▸**barre à mine** (Tech) crowbar ▸**barre de remorquage** (Aut) tow bar ▸**barre de reprise** (Mus) repeat mark(s) ou sign ▸**barres asymétriques** (Sport) asymetric bars ▸**barres parallèles** (Sport) parallel bars ▸**barre de torsion** (Aut) torsion bar.

barreau, pl ~x [baro] nm a [échelle] rung; [cage, fenêtre] bar. **être derrière les ~x** [prisonnier] to be behind bars; ~ **de chaise** (lit) (chair) rung ou crossbar; (*: cigare) fat cigar. b (Jur) bar. **entrer** ou **être admis** ou **reçu au ~** to be called to the bar.

barrement [barmɑ̃] nm [chèque] crossing.

barrer [bare] 1 1 vt a (obstruer) porte to bar; fenêtre to bar up; chemin, route (par accident) to block; (pour travaux, par la police) to close (off), shut off; (par barricades) to barricade. ~ **le passage** ou **la route à qn** (lit) to stand in sb's way, block ou bar sb's way, stop sb getting past; (fig) to stand in sb's way; **des rochers nous barraient la route** rocks blocked ou barred our way.

b (rayer) mot, phrase to cross out, score out; surface, feuille to cross. ~ **un chèque** to cross a cheque; **chèque barré/non barré** crossed/open ou uncrossed cheque; **les rides qui barraient son front** the wrinkles which lined his forehead.

c (Naut) to steer. (Sport) **quatre barré** coxed four.

2 vi (Naut) to steer, take the helm.

3 **se barrer⁑** vpr (s'enfuir) to clear off*, clear out*. **barre-toi!** clear off!*, beat it!*, scram!⁑, hop it!* (Brit).

barrette [barɛt] nf a (pour cheveux) (hair) slide (Brit), barrette (US); (bijou) brooch; [médaille] bar. b (Rel) biretta. **recevoir la ~** to receive the red hat, become a cardinal.

barreur, -euse [barœr, øz] nm,f (gén) helmsman, coxswain; (Aviron) cox(swain). **quatre avec/sans ~** coxed/coxless four.

barricade [barikad] nf barricade; voir **côté**.

barricader [barikade] 1 1 vt porte, fenêtre, rue to barricade. 2 **se barricader** vpr: **se ~ dans/derrière** to barricade o.s. in/behind; (fig) **se**

~ **chez soi** to lock *ou* shut o.s. in.

barrière [baʀjɛʀ] 1 nf (*clôture*) fence; (*porte*) gate; (*lit, fig: obstacle*) barrier; (*Hist: octroi*) tollgate. 2 comp ▸**barrière de dégel** *roadsign warning of dangerous road conditions for heavy vehicles during a thaw* ▸**barrière douanière** trade *ou* tariff barrier ▸**barrière naturelle** natural barrier ▸**barrière (de passage à niveau)** level (*Brit*) *ou* grade (*US*) crossing gate.

barrique [baʀik] nf barrel, cask; *voir* **plein.**

barrir [baʀiʀ] 2 vi to trumpet.

barrissement [baʀismɑ̃] nm trumpeting.

bartavelle [baʀtavɛl] nf rock partridge.

Barthélemy [baʀtelemi] nm Bartholomew.

baryton [baʀitɔ̃] adj, nm baritone. ~**-basse** base-baritone.

baryum [baʀjɔm] nm barium.

bas¹, basse [bɑ, bɑs] 1 adj a *siège, colline, voix,* (*Mus*) *note* low; *maison* low-roofed; *terrain* low(-lying). **le soleil est ~ sur l'horizon** the sun is low on the horizon; **pièce basse de plafond** room with a low ceiling; **le feu est ~** the fire is low; **les basses branches** *ou* **les branches basses d'un arbre** the lower *ou* bottom branches of a tree; **les branches de cet arbre sont basses** the branches of this tree hang low; **~ sur pattes** short-legged, stumpy-legged; **il parle sur un ton trop ~** he speaks too softly; *voir* **main, messe, oreille** *etc.*

b *prix, baromètre, altitude, chiffre* low; (*Élec*) *fréquence* low. **je l'ai eu à ~ prix** I got it cheap *ou* for a small sum.

c *marée, fleuve* low. **c'est la basse mer, c'est (la) marée basse** the tide is low *ou* out, it's low tide; **à marée basse** at low tide *ou* water; **pendant les basses eaux** when the waters are low, when the water level is low.

d (*humble*) *condition, naissance* low, lowly; (*subalterne*) menial; (*mesquin*) *jalousie, vengeance* base, petty; (*abject*) *action* base, mean, low. **basses besognes** (*humbles*) menial tasks; (*désagréables*) dirty work.

e (*Hist, Ling*) **le B~-Empire** the late Empire; **le ~ latin** low Latin; **le ~ allemand** Low German, plattdeutsch (*SPÉC*).

f (*Géog*) **la Basse Seine** the Lower Seine; **le B~ Languedoc** Lower Languedoc; **les B~ Bretons** the inhabitants of Lower Britanny; (*Hist Can*) **le B~ Canada** Lower Canada.

g (*loc*) **être au plus ~** *[personne]* to be very low, be at a very low ebb; *[prix]* to have reached rock bottom, be at their lowest; **au ~ mot** at the very least, at the lowest estimate; **en ce ~ monde** here below; **de ~ étage** (*humble*) lowborn; (*médiocre*) poor, second-rate; **un enfant en ~ âge** a young *ou* small child.

2 adv a **très/trop** *etc* **~** very/too *etc* low; **mettez vos livres plus ~** put your books lower down; **comme l'auteur le dit plus ~** as the author says further on *ou* says below; **voir plus ~** see below.

b *parler, dire* softly, in a low voice. **mettez la radio/le chauffage plus ~** turn the radio/heating down; **mets la radio tout ~** put the radio on very low; **parler tout ~** to speak in a whisper *ou* in a very low voice.

c (*fig*) **mettre** *ou* **traiter qn plus ~ que terre** to treat sb like dirt; **son moral est (tombé) très ~** his morale is very low *ou* is at a low ebb, he's in very low spirits; (*dans l'abjection*) **tomber bien ~** to sink really low; **le malade est bien ~** the patient is very weak *ou* low; **les prix n'ont jamais été** *ou* **ne sont jamais tombés aussi ~** prices have reached a new low *ou* an all-time low, prices have never fallen so low.

d (*loc*) (*Vét*) **mettre ~** to give birth, drop; **mettre ~ les armes** (*Mil*) to lay down one's arms; (*fig*) to throw in the sponge; **mettre ~ qch†** to lay sth down; **~ les mains*** *ou* **les pattes!⁑** hands off!*, (keep your) paws off!⁑; (*à un chien*) **~ les pattes!** down!; **à ~ le fascisme!** down with fascism!; *voir* **chapeau, jeter.**

3 nm a *[page, escalier, colline]* foot, bottom; *[visage]* lower part; *[mur]* foot; *[pantalon]* bottom; *[jupe]* hem, bottom. **dans le ~** at the bottom; **au ~ de la page** at the foot *ou* bottom of the page; **l'étagère/le tiroir du ~** the bottom shelf/drawer; **les appartements du ~** the downstairs flats, the flats downstairs *ou* down below; **au ~ de l'échelle sociale** at the bottom of the social ladder; **compter/lire de ~ en haut** to count/read starting at the bottom *ou* from the bottom up.

b **en ~: il habite en ~** he lives downstairs *ou* down below; **marcher la tête en ~** to walk on one's hands; **le bruit vient d'en ~** the noise is coming from downstairs *ou* from down below; **les voleurs sont passés par en ~** the thieves got in downstairs; **en ~ de la côte** at the bottom *ou* foot of the hill; *voir* **haut.**

4 **basse** nf (*Mus*) (*chanteur*) bass; (*voix*) bass (voice); (*instrument*) (double) bass. **basse continue** (basso) continuo, thorough bass; **basse contrainte** ground bass; **flûte/trombone basse** bass flute/trombone.

5 comp ▸**bas de casse** (*Typ*) nm lower case ▸**le bas clergé** (*Rel*) the lower clergy ▸**bas-côté** nm (pl **bas-côtés**) *[route]* verge; *[église]* (side) aisle; (*Can*) penthouse, lean-to extension ▸**basse-cour** nf (pl **basses-cours**) (*lieu*) farmyard; (*volaille*) poultry (*NonC*) ▸**bas-fond** nm (pl **bas-fonds**) (*Naut*) shallow, shoal; **les bas-fonds de la société** the lowest depths *ou* the dregs of society; **les bas-fonds de la ville** the seediest *ou* slummiest parts of the town ▸**basse-fosse** nf (pl **basses-fosses**) *voir* **cul** ▸**les bas morceaux** (*Boucherie*) the cheap cuts ▸**le bas peuple** the lower classes ▸**les bas quartiers de la ville** the seedy *ou* poor parts of the town ▸**bas-relief** nm (pl **bas-reliefs**) bas relief, low relief ▸**basse saison** (*Tourisme*) low season, off season ▸**basse-taille** nf (pl **basses-tailles**) (*Mus*) bass baritone ▸**Basse-Terre** n Basse-Terre ▸**bas-ventre** nm (pl **bas-ventres**) stomach, guts.

bas² [bɑ] nm stocking; (*de footballeur*) sock; (*de bandit masqué*) stocking mask. **~ fins** sheer stockings; **~ de nylon** nylon stockings, nylons; **~ sans couture** seamless stockings; **~ à varices** support stockings (*Brit*) *ou* hose; **~ de laine** (*lit*) woollen stockings; (*fig*) savings, nest egg (*fig*); (*péj*) **~-bleu** bluestocking.

basal, e, mpl **-aux** [bɑzal, o] adj basal.

basalte [bazalt] nm basalt.

basaltique [bazaltik] adj basalt(ic).

basané, e [bazane] adj *teint, visage [vacancier]* (sun) tanned, sunburnt (*Brit*); *[marin]* tanned, weather-beaten; *[indigène]* swarthy.

basculant, e [baskylɑ̃, ɑ̃t] adj *voir* **benne.**

bascule [baskyl] nf a (*balance*) *[marchandises]* weighing machine. *[personne]* **~ (automatique)** scales (*pl*); *voir* **pont.** b (*balançoire*) **(jeu de) ~** seesaw; **cheval/fauteuil à ~** rocking horse/chair; **faire tomber qn/qch par un mouvement de ~** to topple sb/sth over; **pratiquer une politique de ~** to have a policy of maintaining the balance of power. c (*mécanisme*) bascule. (*Ordin*) **~ (bistable)** flip-flop. d (*Lutte*) lift-over.

basculer [baskyle] 1 1 vi *[personne]* to topple *ou* fall over, overbalance; *[objet]* to fall *ou* tip over; *[benne, planche, wagon]* to tip up; *[tas]* to topple (over). **il bascula dans le vide** he toppled over the edge; (*fig, Pol*) **~ dans l'opposition** to swing *ou* go over to the opposition. 2 vt (*plus gén* **faire ~**) *benne* to tip up; *contenu* to tip out; *personne* to knock off balance, topple over.

basculeur [baskylœʀ] nm a (*Élec*) rocker switch. b (*benne*) tipper.

base [bɑz] 1 nf a *[bâtiment, colonne, triangle]* base; *[montagne]* base, foot; (*Anat, Chim, Math*) base; (*Ling: racine*) root. (*Ordin*) **~ 2/10** base 2/10.

b (*Mil etc: lieu*) base. **~ navale/aérienne** naval/air base; **rentrer à sa** *ou* **la ~** to return to base.

c (*Pol*) **la ~** the rank and file, the grass roots.

d (*principe fondamental*) basis. **~s** basis, foundations; **~s d'un traité/accord** basis of a treaty/an agreement; **raisonnement fondé sur des ~s solides** solidly-based argument; **il a des ~s solides en anglais** he has a good grounding in English *ou* a sound basic knowledge of English; **saper/renverser les ~s de ...** to undermine/destroy the foundations of ...; **établir** *ou* **jeter** *ou* **poser les ~s de ...** to lay the foundations of ... .

e (*loc*) **à ~ de: un produit à ~ de soude** a soda-based product; **être à la ~ de** to be at the root of; **sur la ~ de ces renseignements** on the basis of this information; **de ~** *prix, modèle, règles* basic; **le français de ~** basic French; (*Ling*) **forme de ~** base form; **camp de ~** base camp.

2 comp ▸**base de départ** (*fig*) starting point (*fig*) ▸**base de données** database ▸**base d'imposition** taxable amount ▸**base de lancement** launching site ▸**base de maquillage** make-up base ▸**base d'opération** base of operations, operations base ▸**base de ravitaillement** supply base ▸**base de temps** (*Ordin*) clock.

base-ball, pl **base-balls** [bɛzbol] nm baseball.

baser [bɑze] 1 vt *opinion, théorie* to base (*sur* on). (*Mil*) **être basé à/dans/sur** to be based at/in/on; **sur quoi vous basez-vous pour le dire?** (*preuves*) what basis *ou* grounds have you for saying that?; (*données*) what are you basing your argument on?, what is the basis of your argument?; **économie basée sur le pétrole** oil-based economy.

BASIC [bazik] nm BASIC.

basilic [bazilik] nm (*Bot*) basil; (*Zool*) basilisk.

basilique [bazilik] nf basilica.

basique [bɑzik] adj (*gén, Chim*) basic.

basket [baskɛt] nm basketball. **~s** basketball boots (*Brit*), trainers (*Brit*), sneakers, tennis shoes (*US*).

basket-ball, pl **basket-balls** [baskɛtbol] nm basketball.

basketteur, -euse [basketœʀ, øz] nm,f basketball player.

basquaise [baskɛz] 1 adj f (*Culin*) **poulet/sauce ~** basquaise chicken/sauce. 2 nf: **B~** Basque (woman).

basque¹ [bask] 1 adj Basque. **le Pays ~** the Basque Country. 2 nm (*Ling*) Basque. 3 nmf: **B~** Basque.

basque² [bask] nf *[habit]* skirt(s); *[robe]* basque; *voir* **pendu.**

basse [bɑs] *voir* **bas¹.**

bassement [bɑsmɑ̃] adv basely, meanly, despicably.

bassesse [bɑsɛs] nf a (*NonC*) (*servilité*) servility; (*mesquinerie*) meanness, baseness, lowness; (*vulgarité*) vulgarity, vileness. b (*acte servile*) servile act; (*acte mesquin*) low *ou* mean *ou* base *ou* despicable act. **faire des ~s à qn pour obtenir** to kowtow *ou* grovel to sb in order to get; **faire des ~s à un ennemi** to play underhand tricks on an enemy.

basset [bɑsɛ] nm (*Zool*) basset (hound).

bassin [basɛ̃] nm a (*pièce d'eau*) ornamental lake, pond; *[piscine]* pool; *[fontaine]* basin. b (*cuvette*) bowl; (*Méd*) bedpan. c (*Géog*) basin. **~ houiller/minier** coal/mineral field *ou* basin. d (*Anat*) pelvis. e (*Naut*) dock. **~ de radoub/de marée** dry/tidal dock.

bassine [basin] nf a (*cuvette*) bowl, basin. **~ à confiture** preserving pan. b (*contenu*) bowl(ful).

bassiner [basine] 1 vt a *plaie* to bathe; (*Agr*) to sprinkle *ou* spray (water on). b *lit* to warm (with a warming pan). c (*: *ennuyer*) to bore. **elle nous bassine** she's a pain in the neck*.

bassinet [basinɛ] **nm** *voir* **cracher**.

bassinoire [basinwaʀ] **nf** (*Hist*) warming pan; (*) bore, pain in the neck*.

bassiste [bɑsist] **nmf** (double) bass player.

basson [bɑsɔ̃] **nm** (*instrument*) bassoon; (*musicien*) bassoonist.

bassoniste [bɑsɔnist] **nmf** bassoonist.

basta* [basta] **excl** that's enough!

baste†† [bast] **excl** (*indifférence*) never mind!, who cares?; (*dédain*) pooh!

bastide [bastid] **nf** a (country) house (*in Provence*). b (*Hist*) walled town (*in S.W. France*).

bastille [bastij] **nf** fortress, castle. (*Hist*) **la B~** the Bastille.

bastingage [bastɛ̃gaʒ] **nm** (*Naut*) (ship's) rail; (*Hist*) bulwark.

bastion [bastjɔ̃] **nm** bastion; (*fig*) bastion, stronghold.

baston‡ [bastɔ̃] **nm ou f** punch-up* (*Brit*), fight. **il va y avoir du ~** there's going to be a bit of a punch-up* (*Brit*) *ou* fight.

bastonnade†† [bastɔnad] **nf** drubbing, beating.

bastonner (se)‡ [bastɔne] [1] **vpr** to fight.

bastos [bastos] **nf** (*arg Crime: balle*) slug*.

bastringue* [bastʀɛ̃g] **nm** a (*objets*) junk*, clobber‡ (*Brit*). **et tout le ~** the whole caboodle (*Brit*) *ou* kit and caboodle (*US*). b (*bruit*) racket*, din*. c (*bal*) (local) dance hall; (*orchestre*) band.

Basutoland [basytɔlɑ̃d] **nm** Basutoland.

bat **abrév de bâtiment**.

bât [bɑ] **nm** packsaddle. (*fig*) **c'est là où le ~ blesse** that's where the shoe pinches.

bataclan* [bataklɑ̃] **nm** junk*, clobber‡ (*Brit*). **... et tout le ~** ... and everything else, ... the whole kit and caboodle (*US*), ... and what have you*.

bataille [bataj] 1 **nf** a (*Mil*) battle; (*rixe*) fight; (*fig*) fight, struggle; (*controverse*) fight, dispute. **~ de rue** street fight *ou* battle; **la vie est une dure ~** life is a hard fight *ou* struggle. b (*Cartes*) beggar-my-neighbour. c (*loc*) **en ~** (*Mil, Naut*) in battle order *ou* formation; **il a les cheveux en ~** his hair's all dishevelled *ou* tousled; **le chapeau en ~** with his hat on askew; **être garé en ~** to be parked at an angle to the kerb. 2 **comp ▸ bataille aérienne** air battle **▸ bataille de boules de neige** snowball fight **▸ bataille électorale** election **▸ bataille navale** naval battle **▸ bataille rangée** pitched battle.

batailler [bataje] [1] **vi** (*fig: lutter*) to fight, battle.

batailleur, -euse [batajœʀ, øz] 1 **adj** pugnacious, aggressive. **il est ~** he loves a fight. 2 **nm,f** fighter (*fig*).

bataillon [batajɔ̃] **nm** (*Mil*) battalion; (*fig*) crowd, herd.

bâtard, e [bɑtaʀ, aʀd] 1 **adj** *enfant* illegitimate, bastard† (*péj, épith*); (*fig*) *œuvre, solution* hybrid (*épith*). **chien ~** mongrel. 2 **nm,f** (*personne*) illegitimate child, bastard† (*péj*); (*chien*) mongrel. 3 **nm** (*Boulangerie*) ≈ Vienna roll. 4 **bâtarde nf** (*Typ: aussi* **écriture ~e**) slanting round-hand.

bâtardise [bɑtaʀdiz] **nf** bastardy† (*péj*), illegitimacy.

batavia [batavja] **nf** Webb lettuce.

bateau, pl ~x [bato] 1 **nm** a (*gén*) boat; (*grand*) ship. **~ à moteur/à rames/à voiles** motor/rowing/sailing boat; **prendre le ~** (*embarquer*) to embark, take the boat (*à* at); (*voyager*) to go by boat, sail; **aller en ~** to go by boat, sail; **faire du ~** (*à voiles*) to go sailing; (*à rames etc*) to go boating.
b *[trottoir]* driveway entrance (*depression in kerb*).
c **encolure** *ou* **décolleté ~** boat neck.
2 **adj inv** (‡: *banal*) hackneyed. **c'est (un sujet** *ou* **thème) ~** it's the same old theme* *ou* the favourite topic (that crops up every time).
3 **comp ▸ bateau amiral** flagship **▸ bateau-citerne nm (pl bateaux-citernes)** tanker **▸ bateau de commerce** merchant ship *ou* vessel **▸ bateau-école nm (pl bateaux-écoles)** training ship **▸ bateau-feu nm (pl bateaux-feux)** lightship **▸ bateau de guerre** warship, battleship **▸ bateau-lavoir nm (pl bateaux-lavoirs)** wash-shed (on river); (*péj*) **capitaine** *ou* **amiral de bateau-lavoir** freshwater sailor **▸ bateau-mouche nm (pl bateaux-mouches)** pleasure steamer, river boat (*on the Seine*) **▸ bateau de pêche** fishing boat **▸ bateau-phare nm (pl bateaux-phares)** lightship **▸ bateau-pilote nm (pl bateaux-pilotes)** pilot boat **▸ bateau de plaisance** yacht **▸ bateau-pompe nm (pl bateaux-pompes)** fireboat **▸ bateau de sauvetage** lifeboat **▸ bateau à vapeur** steamer, steamship.

bateleur, -euse [batlœʀ, øz] **nm,f** (†) tumbler; (*péj*) buffoon.

batelier [batəlje] **nm** boatman, waterman; *[bac]* ferryman.

batelière [batəljɛʀ] **nf** boatwoman; *[bac]* ferrywoman.

batellerie [batɛlʀi] **nf** a (*transport*) inland water transport *ou* navigation, canal transport. b (*bateaux*) river and canal craft.

bâter [bɑte] [1] **vt** to put a packsaddle on.

bat-flanc [baflɑ̃] **nm inv** (*lit de cellule etc*) boards.

bath* [bat] **adj inv** *personne, chose* super*, great*, smashing*.

bathymètre [batimɛtʀ] **nm** bathometer, bathymeter.

bathymétrie [batimetʀi] **nf** bathometry, bathymetry.

bathymétrique [batimetʀik] **adj** bathymetric.

bathyscaphe [batiskaf] **nm** bathyscaphe.

bathysphère [batisfɛʀ] **nf** bathysphere.

bâti, e [bɑti] (**ptp de bâtir**) 1 **adj** a **être bien/mal ~** *[personne]* to be well-built/of clumsy build; *[dissertation]* to be well/badly constructed. b **terrain ~/non ~** developed/undeveloped site. 2 **nm** a (*Couture*) tacking (*NonC*). **point de ~** tacking stitch. b (*Constr*) *[porte]* frame; *[machine]* stand, support, frame.

batifolage [batifɔlaʒ] **nm** (*voir* **batifoler**) frolicking about; larking about (*Brit*); dallying; flirting.

batifoler [batifɔle] [1] **vi** (†, *hum*) a (*folâtrer*) to lark (*Brit*) *ou* frolic about; (*péj: perdre son temps*) to dally†, lark about. b (*flirter*) to dally, flirt (*avec* with).

batik [batik] **nm** batik.

bâtiment [bɑtimɑ̃] **nm** a (*édifice*) building. (*Agr*) **~s d'élevage** livestock buildings; **~s d'habitation** living quarters; **~s d'exploitation** farm buildings *ou* sheds. b (*industrie*) **le ~** the building industry *ou* trade; **être dans le ~** to be in the building trade, be a builder. c (*Naut*) ship, vessel.

bâtir [bɑtiʀ] [2] **vt** a (*Constr*) to build. **(se) faire ~ une maison** to have a house built; **se ~ une maison** to build o.s. a house; **la maison s'est bâtie en 3 jours** the house was built *ou* put up in 3 days; **~ sur le roc/sable** to build on rock/sand; **terrain/pierre à ~** building land/stone. b (*fig*) *hypothèse* to build (up); *phrase* to construct, build; *fortune* to amass, build up; *réputation* to build (up), make (*sur* on); *plan* to draw up. c (*Couture*) to tack (*Brit*), baste. **fil/coton à ~** tacking *ou* basting thread/cotton.

bâtisse [bɑtis] **nf** a (*maison*) building; (*péj*) great pile *ou* edifice. b (*Tech*) masonry.

bâtisseur, -euse [bɑtisœʀ, øz] **nm,f** builder. **~ d'empire** empire builder.

batiste [batist] **nf** batiste, cambric, lawn.

bâton [bɑtɔ̃] 1 **nm** a (*canne*) stick, staff (*littér*); (*Rel: insigne*) staff; (*trique*) club, cudgel; (*à deux mains*) staff.
b *[craie, encens, réglisse]* stick. **~ de rouge (à lèvres)** lipstick.
c (*trait*) vertical line *ou* stroke. (*Scol*) **faire des ~s** to draw vertical lines (*when learning to write*).
d (*: *million de centimes*) ten thousand francs.
e (*loc*) **il m'a mis des ~s dans les roues** he put a spoke in my wheel, he put a spanner (*Brit*) *ou* wrench (*US*) in the works (for me); **parler à ~s rompus** to talk about this and that; (*fig hum*) **il est mon ~ de vieillesse** he is the prop *ou* staff of my old age (*hum*).
2 **comp ▸ bâton de berger** shepherd's crook **▸ bâton blanc†** (*d'agent de police*) policeman's baton **▸ bâton de chaise** chair rung **▸ bâton de chef d'orchestre** conductor's baton **▸ bâton de maréchal** (*lit*) marshal's baton; (*fig*) **ce poste, c'est son bâton de maréchal** that's the highest post he'll ever hold **▸ bâton de pèlerin** (*Rel*) pilgrim's staff; (*fig*) **prendre son bâton de pèlerin** to set out on a peace mission **▸ bâton de ski** ski stick *ou* pole.

bâtonner†† [bɑtɔne] [1] **vt** to beat with a stick, cudgel.

bâtonnet [bɑtɔnɛ] **nm** short stick *ou* rod; (*Opt*) rod.

bâtonnier [bɑtɔnje] **nm** ≈ president of the Bar.

batracien [batʀasjɛ̃] **nm** batrachian.

battage [bataʒ] **nm** a *[tapis, or]* beating; *[céréales]* threshing. b (*: *publicité*) publicity campaign. **faire du ~ autour de qch/qn** to give sth/sb a plug*, sell sth/sb hard*, give sth/sb the hype*.

battant, e [batɑ̃, ɑ̃t] 1 **adj** *voir* **battre, pluie, tambour.** 2 **nm** a *[cloche]* clapper, tongue. **~ (de porte)** left-hand *ou* right-hand flap *ou* door (*of a double door*); **~ (de fenêtre)** (left-hand *ou* right-hand) window; *[volet]* shutter, flap; **porte à double ~** double door; **ouvrir une porte à deux ~s** to open both sides *ou* doors (*of a double door*). b (*personne*) fighter (*fig*).

batte [bat] **nf** a (*outil*) (*à beurre*) dasher; *[blanchisseuse]* washboard; (*Sport*) bat; (*sabre de bois*) wooden sword. b (*battage*) beating.

battement [batmɑ̃] **nm** a (*claquement*) *[porte, volet]* banging (*NonC*); *[marteau]* banging (*NonC*), thud; *[pluie]* beating (*NonC*), (pitter-)patter (*NonC*); *[tambour]* beating (*NonC*), rattle (*NonC*); *[voile, toile]* flapping (*NonC*).
b (*mouvement*) *[ailes]* flapping (*NonC*), flutter (*NonC*), beating (*NonC*); *[cils]* fluttering (*NonC*); *[rames]* plash (*NonC*), splash (*NonC*). **~ de paupières** blinking of eyelids (*NonC*); **~s de jambes** leg movement; **accueillir qn avec des ~s de mains** to greet sb with clapping *ou* applause.
c (*Méd*) *[cœur]* beat, beating (*NonC*); *[pouls]* beat, throbbing (*NonC*), beating (*NonC*); (*irrégulier*) fluttering (*NonC*); *[tempes]* throbbing (*NonC*). **avoir des ~s de cœur** to get *ou* have palpitations; **cela m'a donné des ~s de cœur** it set my heart beating, it gave me palpitations, it set me all of a flutter*.
d (*intervalle*) interval. **2 minutes de ~** (*pause*) a 2-minute break; (*attente*) 2 minutes' wait; (*temps libre*) 2 minutes to spare; **j'ai une heure de ~ de 10 à 11** I'm free for an hour *ou* I've got an hour to spare between 10 and 11.
e (*Rad*) beat; (*Phon*) flap.

batterie [batʀi] **nf** a (*Mil*) battery. **mettre des canons en ~** to unlimber guns; **~ de canons** battery of artillery; **~ antichars/de D.C.A** anti-tank/anti-aircraft battery; **~ côtière** coastal battery; (*fig*)

changer/dresser ses ~s to change/lay *ou* make one's plans; (*fig*) **démasquer** *ou* **dévoiler ses ~s** to unmask one's guns.
b (*Mus: percussion*) percussion (instruments); (*Jazz: instruments*) drum kit. **X à la ~** X on drums *ou* percussion; **on entend mal la ~** you can hardly hear the drums.
c (*Aut, Élec*) battery.
d (*groupe*) *[tests, chaudières]* battery. **~ de projecteurs** bank of spotlights; **~ de satellites** array of satellites.
e **~ de cuisine** (*Culin*) pots and pans, kitchen utensils; (**: décorations*) gongs*, ironmongery*; **toute la ~ de cuisine*** everything but the kitchen sink, the whole caboodle*.

batteur [batœʀ] **nm** a (*Culin*) whisk, beater. b (*Mus*) drummer, percussionist. c (*métier*) (*Agr*) thresher; (*Métal*) beater; (*Cricket*) batsman; (*Base-ball*) batter.

batteuse [batøz] **nf** a (*Agr*) threshing machine; *voir* **moissonneuse**. b (*Métal*) beater.

battle-dress [batœldʀɛs] **nm inv** battle-dress.

battoir [batwaʀ] **nm** a *[laveuse]* beetle, battledore; (*à tapis*) (carpet) beater. b (*grandes mains*) **~s*** (great) mitts‡ *ou* paws‡.

battre [batʀ] [41] 1 **vt** a *personne* to beat, strike, hit. **elle ne bat jamais ses enfants** she never hits *ou* smacks her children; **~ qn comme plâtre*** to beat the living daylights out of sb*, thrash *ou* beat sb soundly; **~ qn à mort** to batter *ou* beat sb to death; **regard de chien battu** cowering look.
b (*vaincre*) *adversaire, équipe* to beat, defeat; *record* to beat. **se faire ~** to be beaten *ou* defeated; **il ne se tient pas pour battu** he doesn't consider himself beaten *ou* defeated; (*Sport*) **~ qn (par) 6 à 3** to beat sb 6-3; **~ qn à plate(s) couture(s)** to beat sb hollow (*Brit*), beat the pants off sb*, beat sb hands down.
c (*frapper*) *tapis, linge, fer, or* to beat; *blé* to thresh. (*Prov*) **~ le fer pendant qu'il est chaud** to strike while the iron is hot (*Prov*); **il battit l'air/l'eau des bras** his arms thrashed the air/water; **~ le fer à froid** to cold hammer iron; **son manteau lui bat les talons** his coat is flapping round his ankles; **~ le briquet†** to strike a light.
d (*agiter*) *beurre* to churn; *blanc d'œuf* to beat (up), whip, whisk; *crème* to whip; *cartes* to shuffle. **œufs battus en neige** stiff egg whites, stiffly-beaten egg whites.
e (*parcourir*) *région* to scour, comb. **~ le pays** to scour the countryside; (*Chasse*) **~ les buissons/les taillis** to beat the bushes/undergrowth (for game); **hors des sentiers battus** off the beaten track; (*fig*) **~ la campagne** to wander in one's mind; **~ le pavé** to wander aimlessly about *ou* around.
f (*heurter*) *[pluie]* to beat *ou* lash against; *[mer]* to beat *ou* dash against; (*Mil*) *positions, ennemis* to batter. **littoral battu par les tempêtes** storm-lashed coast.
g (*Mus*) **~ la mesure** to beat time; (*Mil*) **~ le tambour** (*lit*) to beat the drum; (*fig*) to shout from the housetops; **~ le rappel** to call to arms; (*fig*) **~ le rappel de ses souvenirs** to summon up one's old memories; **~ le rappel de ses amis** to rally one's friends; (*Mil*) **~ la retraite** to sound the retreat.
h (*loc*) **~ la breloque†** *[appareil]* to be on the blink*, be erratic; *[cœur]* to be giving out; **son cœur battait la chamade** his heart was pounding *ou* beating wildly; **~ en brèche une théorie** to demolish a theory; **~ froid à qn** to cold-shoulder sb, give sb the cold shoulder; **~ son plein** *[saison touristique]* to be at its height; *[fête]* to be going full swing; **~ la semelle** to stamp one's feet (to keep warm); (*Naut*) **~ pavillon britannique** to fly the British flag, sail under the British flag; (*Fin*) **~ monnaie** to strike *ou* mint coins; (*Rel*) **~ sa coulpe** to beat one's breast (*fig*).
2 **vi** a *[cœur, pouls]* to beat; *[montre, métronome]* to tick; *[pluie]* to beat, lash (*contre* against); *[porte, volets]* to bang, rattle; *[voile, drapeau]* to flap; *[tambour]* to beat. (*fig hum*) **son cœur bat pour lui** he is her heart-throb; **son cœur battait d'émotion** his heart was beating wildly *ou* pounding *ou* thudding with emotion; **le cœur battant** with beating heart.
b **~ en retraite** to beat a retreat, fall back.
3 **battre de vt indir: ~ des mains** to clap one's hands; (*fig*) to dance for joy, exult; **~ du tambour** to beat the drum; **l'oiseau bat des ailes** the bird is beating *ou* flapping its wings; (*fig*) **~ de l'aile** to be in a bad *ou* in a dicky* (*Brit*) *ou* shaky state.
4 **se battre vpr** a (*dans une guerre, un combat*) to fight (*avec* with, *contre* against); (*se disputer*) to fall out; (*fig*) to fight, battle, struggle (*contre* against). **se ~ comme des chiffonniers** to fight like cat and dog; **se ~ au couteau/à la baïonnette** to fight with knives/bayonets; **nos troupes se sont bien battues** our troops fought well *ou* put up a good fight; **se ~ en duel** to fight a duel; (*fig*) **se ~ contre les préjugés** to battle *ou* fight *ou* struggle against prejudice; **se ~ contre des moulins à vent** to tilt at windmills; **il faut se ~ pour arriver à obtenir quelque chose** you have to fight to get what you want; **voilà une heure qu'il se bat avec ce problème** he's been struggling *ou* battling with that problem for an hour now.
b **se ~ la poitrine** to beat one's breast; (*fig*) **se ~ les flancs** to rack one's brains.
c **je m'en bats l'œil‡** I don't care a fig* *ou* a damn‡.

battu, e[1] [baty] (**ptp de battre**) **adj** *voir* **battre, jeté, œil, pas**[1], **terre**.

battue[2] [baty] **nf** (*Chasse*) battue, beat.

batture [batyʀ] **nf** (*Can*) sand bar, strand.

bau, pl ~x [bo] **nm** (*Naut*) beam.

baud [bo] **nm** (*Ordin*) baud.

baudelairien, -ienne [bodlɛʀjɛ̃, jɛn] **adj** of Baudelaire, Baudelairean.

baudet [bodɛ] **nm** a (*Zool*) donkey, ass. b (*Menuiserie*) trestle, sawhorse.

baudrier [bodʀije] **nm** *[épée]* baldric; *[drapeau]* shoulder-belt; (*Alpinisme*) harness; (*pour matériel*) gear sling.

baudroie [bodʀwa] **nf** angler (fish).

baudruche [bodʀyʃ] **nf** (*personne*) windbag*; (*théorie*) empty theory, humbug*; *voir* **ballon**.

bauge [boʒ] **nf** *[sanglier, porc]* wallow.

baume [bom] **nm** (*lit*) balm, balsam; (*fig*) balm. **ça lui a mis du ~ au cœur** *ou* **dans le cœur** it heartened him.

Baumé [bome] **nm** *voir* **degré**.

baux [bo] **pl de bail, bau**.

bauxite [boksit] **nf** bauxite.

bavard, e [bavaʀ, aʀd] 1 **adj** *personne* talkative, garrulous; *discours, récit* long-winded, wordy. 2 **nm,f** chatterbox*, talkative person, prattler; (*péj*) gossip, blabbermouth*.

bavardage [bavaʀdaʒ] **nm** (*voir* **bavarder**) chatting, talking; chattering, prattling; gossiping. **j'entendais leur ~** *ou* **leurs ~s** I could hear their talking *ou* chattering.

bavarder [bavaʀde] [1] **vi** (*gen: parler*) to chat, talk; (*jacasser*) to chatter, prattle; (*commérer*) to gossip; (*divulguer un secret*) to blab*, give the game away, talk. (*Scol*) **arrêtez de ~** stop talking *ou* chattering.

bavarois, e [bavaʀwa, waz] 1 **adj** Bavarian. 2 **nm,f** a (*personne*) **B~(e)** Bavarian. b (*Culin*) bavarois. **~e aux fraises** strawberry bavarois.

bavasser* [bavase] [1] **vi** (*bavarder*) to natter* (*Brit*), gas‡.

bave [bav] **nf** *[personne]* dribble; *[animal]* slaver, slobber; *[chien enragé]* foam, froth; *[escargot]* slime; *[crapaud]* spittle; (*fig*) venom, malicious words. **la ~ du crapaud n'atteint pas la blanche colombe!** your spiteful words can't touch me!

baver [bave] [1] 1 **vi** a *[personne]* to dribble; (*beaucoup*) to slobber, drool; *[animal]* to slaver, slobber; *[chien enragé]* to foam *ou* froth at the mouth; *[stylo]* to leak; *[pinceau]* to drip; *[liquide]* to run. b (*loc*) **en ~ d'admiration*** to gasp in admiration; **en ~‡** to have a rough *ou* hard time of it*; **il m'en a fait ~‡** he really made me sweat*, he really gave me a rough *ou* hard time*. c (*littér*) **~ sur la réputation de qn** to besmear *ou* besmirch sb's reputation. 2 **vt: il en a bavé des ronds de chapeau‡** his eyes nearly popped out of his head*.

bavette [bavɛt] **nf** a *[tablier, enfant]* bib; (*Aut: garde-boue*) mudguard, mud flap. b (*Culin*) undercut; *voir* **tailler**.

baveux, -euse [bavø, øz] **adj** *bouche* dribbling, slobbery; *enfant* dribbling. **omelette ~euse** runny omelette; (*Typ*) **lettre ~euse** blurred *ou* smeared letter.

Bavière [bavjɛʀ] **nf** Bavaria.

bavoir [bavwaʀ] **nm** bib.

bavure [bavyʀ] **nf** (*tache*) smudge, smear; (*Tech*) burr; (*fig*) hitch, flaw; (*Admin euph*) unfortunate mistake (*euph*). (*fig*) **sans ~** (**adj**) flawless, faultless; (**adv**) flawlessly, faultlessly.

bayadère [bajadɛʀ] 1 **nf** bayadère. 2 **adj** *tissu* colourfully striped.

bayer [baje] [1] **vi: ~ aux corneilles** to stand gaping, stand and gape.

bazar [bazaʀ] **nm** a (*magasin*) general store; (*oriental*) bazaar. b (**: effets personnels*) junk* (*NonC*), gear‡ (*NonC*), things*. c (**: désordre*) clutter, jumble, shambles (*NonC*). **quel ~!** what a shambles!*; **et tout le ~** and all the rest, and what have you*, the whole caboodle*, the whole kit and caboodle (*US*).

bazarder* [bazaʀde] [1] **vt** (*jeter*) to get rid of, chuck out*, ditch*; (*vendre*) to flog‡, get rid of, sell off.

bazooka [bazuka] **nm** bazooka.

BCBG [besebeʒe] **adj** (**abrév de bon chic bon genre**) *voir* **bon**.

BCE [beseə] **nf** (**abrév de Banque centrale européenne**) ECB.

BCG [beseʒe] **nm** (**abrév de vaccin Bilié Calmette et Guérin**) BCG.

bd abrév de boulevard.

BD [bede] **nf** a (**abrév de bande dessinée**) **la ~** strip cartoons; **une ~** a strip cartoon; **auteur de ~** strip cartoonist. b (**abrév de base de données**) DB.

bê [bɛ] **excl** baa!

beagle [bigl] **nm** beagle.

béant, e [beɑ̃, ɑ̃t] **adj** *blessure* gaping, open; *bouche* gaping, wide open; *yeux* wide open; *gouffre* gaping, yawning; *personne* wide-eyed, open-mouthed (*de* with, in), gaping (*de* in).

béarnais, e [bearnɛ, ɛz] 1 **adj** *personne* from the Béarn. (*Culin*) (**sauce** *f*) **~e** Béarnaise sauce. 2 **nm,f: B~(e)** inhabitant *ou* native of the Béarn.

béat, e [bea, at] **adj** (*hum*) *personne* blissfully happy; (*content de soi*) smug, self-satisfied, complacent; *sourire, air* (*niaisement heureux*) beatific, blissful. **optimisme ~** smug optimism; **admiration ~e** blind *ou* dumb admiration; **être ~ d'admiration** to be struck dumb with admiration; **regarder qn d'un air ~** to look at sb in open-eyed wonder *ou* with dumb admiration.

béatement [beatmɑ̃] **adv** (*voir* **béat**) smugly; complacently; beatifically, blissfully.

béatification [beatifikasjɔ̃] **nf** beatification.

béatifier [beatifje] 7 **vt** to beatify.

béatitude [beatityd] **nf** (*Rel*) beatitude; (*bonheur*) bliss. **les B~s** the Beatitudes.

beatnik [bitnik] **nmf** beatnik. **la génération ~** *ou* **des ~s** the beat generation.

Béatrice [beatʀis] **nf** Beatrice.

beau [bo] , **bel** *devant n commençant par voyelle ou h muet*, **belle** [bɛl] *f*, **mpl beaux** [bo] **1** **adj** **a** (*qui plaît au regard, à l'oreille*) *objet, paysage* beautiful, lovely; *femme* beautiful, fine-looking, lovely; *homme* handsome, good-looking. **les belles dames et les beaux messieurs** the smart ladies and gentlemen; **les beaux quartiers** the smart *ou* posh* districts; **il est ~ comme le jour** *ou* **comme un dieu** he's like a Greek god; **mettre ses beaux habits** to put on one's best clothes; **il est ~ garçon** he's good-looking, he's a good-looking lad* (*Brit*) *ou* guy* (*US*); **il est ~ gosse*** he's a good looker*.

b (*qui plaît à l'esprit, digne d'admiration*) *discours, match* fine; *poème, roman* fine, beautiful. **il a un ~ talent** he has a fine gift, he's very talented *ou* gifted; **une belle mort** a fine death; **une belle âme** a fine *ou* noble nature; **un ~ geste** a noble act, a fine gesture; **toutes ces belles paroles/tous ces beaux discours n'ont convaincu personne** all these fine(-sounding) words/all these grand speeches failed to convince anybody.

c (*agréable*) *temps* fine, beautiful; *voyage* lovely. **aux beaux jours, à la belle saison** in (the) summertime; (*fig*) **il y a encore de beaux jours pour les escrocs** there are good times ahead *ou* there's a bright future for crooks; **par une belle soirée d'été** on a beautiful *ou* fine summer's evening; **il fait (très) ~ (temps)** the weather's very good, it's beautiful weather, it's very fine; **la mer était belle** the sea was calm; **c'est le bel âge** those are the best years of life; **c'est la belle vie!** this is the (good) life!; (*Hist*) **la Belle Époque** the Belle Époque, the Edwardian era.

d (**: intensif*) *revenu, profit* handsome, tidy*; *résultat, occasion* excellent, fine. **il a une belle situation** he has an excellent position; **cela fait une belle somme!** that's a tidy* sum of money!; **il en reste un ~ morceau** there's still a good bit (of it) left; **95 ans, c'est un bel âge** it's a good age, 95; **un ~ jour** (*passé*) one (fine) day; (*futur*) one of these (fine) days, one (fine) day; **il est arrivé un ~ matin/jour** he came one morning/day.

e (*iro: déplaisant*) **il a attrapé une belle bronchite** he's got a nasty attack *ou* a bad bout of bronchitis; **une belle gifle** a good slap; **une belle brûlure/peur** a nasty burn/fright; **ton frère est un ~ menteur** your brother is a terrible *ou* the most awful liar; **c'est un beau salaud**‡ he's a real bastard**; **un ~ désordre** *ou* **gâchis** a fine mess; **un ~ vacarme** a terrible din; **la belle affaire!** big deal!*, so what?*; **en faire de belles** to get up to mischief; **embarquez tout ce ~ monde!** cart this fine crew* *ou* bunch* away!; (*iro*) **en apprendre/dire de belles sur qn*** to hear/say some nice things about sb (*iro*); **être dans un ~ pétrin** *ou* **dans de beaux draps** to be in a fine old mess*.

f (*loc*) **ce n'est pas ~ de mentir** it isn't nice to tell lies; **ça me fait une belle jambe!*** a fat lot of good it does me!*; (*iro*) **c'est du ~ travail!** well done! (*iro*); **de plus belle** all the more, more than ever, even more; **crier de plus belle** to shout louder than ever *ou* all the louder *ou* even louder; **recommencer de plus belle** to start off *ou* up again, start up even worse than before *ou* ever; **dormir** *ou* **coucher à la belle étoile** to sleep out in the open; **il y a belle lurette de cela** that was ages ago *ou* donkey's years* (*Brit*) ago; **il y a belle lurette que** it is ages *ou* donkey's years* (*Brit*) since; **il l'a eu(e) belle de s'échapper** they made it easy *ou* child's play for him to escape; **faire qch pour les beaux yeux de qn** to do sth just for sb *ou* just to please sb; **tout ~, tout ~!**† steady on!, easy does it!; **le plus ~ de l'histoire, c'est que ...** the best bit of it *ou* part about it is that ...; **c'est trop ~ pour être vrai** it's too good to be true; **ce serait trop ~!** that would be too much to hope for!; **avoir ~ jeu de** to have every opportunity to; **avoir le ~ rôle** to show o.s. in a good light, come off best (in a situation); **se faire ~** to get spruced up *ou* dressed up; **se faire** *ou* **se mettre ~** to beautify o.s.; **avec lui, c'est soit belle et tais-toi** he expects you just to sit and look pretty; (*littér*) **porter ~** to look dapper; **avoir ~: on a ~ faire/dire ils n'apprennent rien** whatever you do/say they don't learn anything, try as you may they don't learn anything; **on a ~ protester, personne n'écoute** however much you protest no one listens; **on a ~ dire, il n'est pas bête** say what you like, he is not stupid; **il eut ~ essayer** however much *ou* whatever he tried, try as he might; **il ferait ~ voir qu'il mente!** he'd better not be lying!; **bel et bien** well and truly; **ils sont bel et bien entrés par la fenêtre** they really did get in through the window, they got in through the window all right *ou* no doubt about it *ou* no doubt about that; **il s'est bel et bien trompé** he got it well and truly wrong; *voir* **bailler, échapper.**

2 **nm** **a** **le ~** the beautiful; **le culte du ~** the cult of beauty; **elle n'aime que le ~** she only likes what is beautiful; **elle n'achète que le ~** she only buys the best quality.

b (*loc*) **faire le ~** *[chien]* to sit up and beg; (*péj*) *[personne]* to curry favour (*devant* with); *[temps]* **être au ~** to be fine, be set fair; *[baromètre]* **être au ~ (fixe)** to be set fair, be settled; (*fig*) *[relations, atmosphère]* to be looking rosy; **c'est du ~!** (*reproche*) that was a fine thing to do! (*iro*); (*consternation*) this is a fine business! (*iro*) *ou* a fine mess! (*iro*).

3 **belle** **nf** **a** beauty, belle; (*compagne*) lady friend. **ma belle!*** my girl!; **la Belle au bois dormant** Sleeping Beauty; **la Belle et la Bête** Beauty and the Beast; *[prisonnier]* **se faire la belle** to do a runner.

b (*Jeux, Sport*) decider, deciding match.

4 **comp** ►**les beaux-arts** **nmpl** (*Art*) fine art; (*école*) the Art School ►**bel esprit** wit; **faire le bel esprit** to show off one's wit ►**belle-famille** **nf (pl belles-familles)** *[homme]* wife's family, in-laws*; *[femme]* husband's family, in-laws* ►**belle-fille** **nf (pl belles-filles)** (*bru*) daughter-in-law; (*remariage*) stepdaughter ►**beau-fils** **nm (pl beaux-fils)** (*gendre*) son-in-law; (*remariage*) stepson ►**beau-frère** **nm (pl beaux-frères)** brother-in-law ►**belle-de-jour** **nf (pl belles-de-jour)** (*Bot*) convolvulus, morning glory; (**: prostituée*) prostitute ►**belles-lettres** **nfpl** great literature ►**belle-maman*** **nf (pl belles-mamans)** mother-in-law, mum-in-law* (*Brit*) ►**belle-mère** **nf (pl belles-mères)** mother-in-law; (*nouvelle épouse du père*) stepmother ►**le beau monde** high society; **fréquenter du beau monde** to move in high society ►**belle-de-nuit** **nf (pl belles-de-nuit)** (*Bot*) marvel of Peru; (**: prostituée*) prostitute ►**beau-papa*** **nm (pl beaux-papas)** father-in-law, dad-in-law* (*Brit*) ►**beaux-parents** **nmpl** *[homme]* wife's parents, in-laws*; *[femme]* husband's parents, in-laws* ►**beau parleur** smooth *ou* glib talker ►**beau-père** **nm (pl beaux-pères)** father-in-law; (*nouveau mari de la mère*) stepfather ►**le beau sexe** the fair sex ►**belle-sœur** **nf (pl belles-sœurs)** sister-in-law ►**beau ténébreux** (*hum*) dashing young man with a sombre air.

beauceron, -onne [bosʀɔ̃, ɔn] **1** **adj** of *ou* from the Beauce. **2** **nm,f: B~(ne)** inhabitant *ou* native of the Beauce.

beaucoup [boku] **adv** **a** a lot, (very) much, a great deal. **il mange ~** he eats a lot; **elle lit ~** she reads a great deal *ou* a lot; **elle ne lit pas ~** she doesn't read much *ou* a great deal *ou* a lot; **la pièce ne m'a pas ~ plu** I didn't like the play very much, I didn't greatly like the play; **il s'intéresse ~ à la peinture** he is very *ou* greatly interested in painting, he takes a lot *ou* a great deal of interest in painting; **il y a ~ à faire/voir** there's a lot to do/see; **il a ~ voyagé/lu** he has travelled/read a lot *ou* extensively *ou* a great deal.

b **~ de** (*quantité*) a great deal of, a lot of, much; (*nombre*) many, a lot of, a good many; **~ de monde** a lot of people, a great *ou* good many people; **avec ~ de soin/plaisir** with great care/pleasure; **il ne reste pas ~ de pain** there isn't a lot of *ou* isn't (very) much bread left; **j'ai ~ (de choses) à faire** I have a lot (of things) to do; **pour ce qui est de l'argent/du lait, il en reste ~/il n'en reste pas ~** as for money/milk, there is a lot left/there isn't a lot *ou* much left; **vous attendiez des touristes, y en a-t-il eu ~? — oui (il y en a eu) ~** you were expecting tourists and were there many *ou* a lot (of them)? — yes there were (a good many *ou* a lot of them); **j'en connais ~ qui pensent que** I know a great many (people) *ou* a lot of people who think that; **il a ~ d'influence** he has a great deal *ou* a lot of influence, he is very influential; **il a eu ~ de chance** he's been very lucky.

c (*employé seul: personnes*) many. **ils sont ~ à croire que ..., ~ croient que ...** many *ou* a lot of people think that ...; **~ d'entre eux sont partis** a lot *ou* many of them have left.

d (*modifiant adv trop, plus, moins, mieux et adj*) much, far, a good deal; (*nombre*) a lot. **~ plus rapide** much *ou* a good deal *ou* a lot quicker; **elle travaille ~ trop** she works far too much; **elle travaille ~ trop lentement** she works much *ou* far too slowly; **se sentir ~ mieux** to feel much *ou* miles* better; **~ plus d'eau** much *ou* a lot *ou* far more water; **~ moins de gens** many *ou* a lot *ou* far fewer people; **il est susceptible, il l'est même ~** he's touchy, in fact very much so.

e **de ~** by far, by a long way, by a long chalk* (*Brit*); **elle est de ~ la meilleure élève** she is by far *ou* is far and away the best pupil, she's the best pupil by far *ou* by a long chalk* (*Brit*); **il l'a battu de ~** he beat him by miles* *ou* by a long way; **il est de ~ ton aîné** he is very much *ou* is a great deal older than you; **il est de ~ supérieur** he is greatly *ou* far superior; **il préférerait de ~ s'en aller** he'd much *ou* far rather go; **il s'en faut de ~ qu'il soit au niveau** he is far from being up to standard, he's nowhere near the standard, he isn't anything like up to standard.

f (*loc*) **c'est déjà ~ de l'avoir fait** *ou* **qu'il l'ait fait** it was quite something *ou* quite an achievement to have done it at all; **à ~ près** far from it; **c'est ~ dire** that's an exaggeration *ou* an overstatement, that's saying a lot; **être pour ~ dans une décision/une nomination** to be largely responsible for a decision/an appointment, have a big hand in making a decision/an appointment; **il y est pour ~** he's largely responsible for it, he's had a lot to do with it, he had a big hand in it.

beauf‡ [bof] **nm** **a** (*beau-frère*) brother-in-law. **b** (*péj*) (small-minded) petty bourgeois.

beaujolais [boʒɔlɛ] **nm** **a** (*région*) **le B~** the Beaujolais region. **b** (*vin*) beaujolais, Beaujolais. **le ~ nouveau** (the) beaujolais *ou* Beaujolais nouveau, (the) new beaujolais *ou* Beaujolais.

beaupré [bopʀe] **nm** bowsprit.

beauté [bote] **nf** a (*gén*) beauty; *[femme]* beauty, loveliness; *[homme]* handsomeness. **de toute ~** very beautiful, magnificent; **se (re)faire une ~** to powder one's nose, do one's face*; **vous êtes en ~ ce soir** you look radiant this evening; **finir** *ou* **terminer qch en ~** to complete sth brilliantly, finish sth with a flourish; **finir en ~** to end with a flourish, finish brilliantly; **faire qch pour la ~ du geste** to do sth for the sake of it; **la ~ du diable** youthful beauty *ou* bloom. b (*belle femme*) beauty. c **~s** beauties; **les ~s de Rome** the beauties *ou* sights of Rome.

bébé [bebe] **nm** (*enfant, animal*) baby; (*poupée*) dolly. **faire le ~** to behave *ou* act like a baby; **c'est un vrai ~** he's a real baby; **il est resté très ~** he has stayed very babyish; **~ éléphant/girafe** baby elephant/giraffe; **~-éprouvette** test-tube baby.

bébête* [bebɛt] 1 **adj** silly. 2 **nf: une petite ~** a little insect, a creepy crawly* (*Brit*).

bec [bɛk] 1 **nm** a (*Orn*) beak, bill. **oiseau qui se fait le ~ (contre)** bird that sharpens its beak (on); **(nez en) ~ d'aigle** aquiline *ou* hook nose.
b (*pointe*) *[plume]* nib; *[carafe, casserole]* lip; *[théière]* spout; *[flûte, trompette]* mouthpiece; (*Géog*) bill, headland.
c (*: *bouche*) mouth. **ouvre ton ~!** open your mouth!, mouth open!*; **ferme ton ~!** just shut up!*; **il n'a pas ouvert le ~** he never opened his mouth, he didn't say a word; **la pipe au ~** with his pipe stuck* in his mouth; **clore** *ou* **clouer le ~ à qn** to reduce sb to silence, shut sb up*; *voir* **prise**.
d (*loc*) **tomber sur un ~*** to be stymied*, come unstuck*; **être** *ou* **rester le ~ dans l'eau*** to be left in the lurch, be left high and dry.
2 **comp** ▸**bec Auer** Welsbach burner ▸**bec Bunsen** Bunsen burner ▸**bec-de-cane nm (pl becs-de-cane)** (*poignée*) doorhandle; (*serrure*) catch ▸**bec-croisé nm (pl becs-croisés)** crosshill ▸**bec fin*** gourmet ▸**bec de gaz** lamppost, gaslamp ▸**bec-de-lièvre nm (pl becs-de-lièvre)** (*Méd*) harelip ▸**bec verseur** pourer, pouring lip.

bécane* [bekan] **nf** (*vélo*) bike*; (*machine*) machine.

bécarre [bekaʀ] **nm** (*Mus*) natural. **sol ~** G natural.

bécasse [bekas] **nf** (*Zool*) woodcock; (*: *sotte*) (silly) goose*.

bécasseau, pl ~x [bekaso] **nm** sandpiper; (*petit de la bécasse*) young woodcock.

bécassine [bekasin] **nf** snipe.

bêchage [bɛʃaʒ] **nm** digging, turning over.

béchamel [beʃamɛl] **nf: (sauce) ~** béchamel (sauce), white sauce.

bêche [bɛʃ] **nf** spade.

bêcher [beʃe] [1] 1 **vt** (*Agr*) to dig, turn over. 2 **vi** (*: *crâner*) to be stuck-up *ou* toffee-nosed* (*Brit*).

bêcheur, -euse* [bɛʃœʀ, øz] 1 **adj** stuck-up*, toffee-nosed* (*Brit*). 2 **nm,f** stuck-up person*, toffee-nosed person* (*Brit*).

bécot* [beko] **nm** kiss, peck. **gros ~** smacker*.

bécoter* [bekɔte] [1] 1 **vt** to kiss. 2 **se bécoter* vpr** to smooch.

becquée [beke] **nf** beakful. **donner la ~ à** to feed.

becquet [bekɛ] **nm** (*Alpinisme*) (rocky) spike. (*Aut*) **~ (arrière)** spoiler.

becquetance‡ [bɛktɑ̃s] **nf** grub‡.

becqueter [bɛkte] [4] **vt** (*Orn*) to peck (at); (‡) to eat. **qu'y a-t-il à ~ ce soir?** what's for grub tonight?‡, what's tonight's nosh?‡ (*Brit*) *ou* grub?‡

bectance nf = becquetance.

becter vt = becqueter.

bedaine* [bədɛn] **nf** paunch, potbelly‡.

bedeau, pl ~x [bədo] **nm** verger, beadle†.

bedon* [bədɔ̃] **nm** paunch, corporation (*Brit*), potbelly‡.

bedonnant, e* [bədɔnɑ̃, ɑ̃t] **adj** potbellied‡, paunchy, portly.

bedonner* [bədɔne] [1] **vi** to get a paunch, get potbellied‡.

bédouin, -ouine [bedwɛ̃, win] 1 **adj** Bedouin. 2 **nm,f: B~(e)** Bedouin.

BEE [beøø] **nm** (**abrév de Bureau européen de l'environnement**) *voir* **bureau 2.**

bée [be] **adj: être** *ou* **rester bouche ~** (*lit*) to stand open-mouthed *ou* gaping; (*d'admiration*) to be lost in wonder; (*de surprise*) to be flabbergasted* (*devant* at); **il en est resté bouche ~** his jaw dropped, he was flabbergasted*.

béer [bee] [1] **vi** a to be (wide) open. b **~ d'admiration/d'étonnement** to gape in admiration/amazement, stand gaping in admiration/amazement.

beethovénien, -ienne [betɔvenjɛ̃, jɛn] **adj** Beethovenian, of Beethoven.

beffroi [befʀwa] **nm** belfry.

bégaiement, bégayement [begɛmɑ̃] **nm** (*lit*) stammering, stuttering. (*fig: débuts*) **~s** faltering *ou* hesitant beginnings.

bégayer [begeje] [8] 1 **vi** to stammer, stutter, have a stammer. 2 **vt** to stammer (out), falter (out).

bégonia [begɔnja] **nm** begonia.

bègue [bɛg] 1 **nmf** stammerer, stutterer. 2 **adj: être ~** to stammer, have a stammer.

bégueule [begœl] 1 **nf** prude. 2 **adj** prudish.

bégueulerie [begœlʀi] **nf** prudishness, prudery.

béguin [begɛ̃] **nm** a (*: *toquade*) **avoir le ~ pour qn** to have a crush on sb*, be sweet on sb*; **elle a eu le ~ pour cette petite ferme** she took a great fancy to that little farmhouse. b (*bonnet*) bonnet.

béguinage [beginaʒ] **nm** (*Rel*) Beguine convent.

béguine [begin] **nf** (*Rel*) Beguine.

bégum [begɔm] **nf** begum.

behaviorisme [bievjɔʀism] **nm** behaviourism.

behavioriste [bievjɔʀist] **adj, nmf** behavio(u)rist.

Behring nm = Béring.

BEI [beəi] **nf** (**abrév de Banque européenne d'investissement**) EIB.

beige [bɛʒ] **adj, nm** beige.

beigne[1]‡ [bɛɲ] **nf** slap, clout*. **donner une ~ à qn** to clout sb *, give sb a clout*.

beigne[2] [bɛɲ] **nm** (*Can*) doughnut.

beignet [bɛɲɛ] **nm** *[fruits, légumes]* fritter; (*pâte frite*) doughnut. **~ aux pommes** apple doughnut *ou* fritter.

Beijing [beidʒin] **n** Beijing.

bel [bɛl] **adj** *voir* **beau.**

bel canto [bɛlkɑ̃to] **nm** bel canto.

bêlement [bɛlmɑ̃] **nm** (*Zool, fig*) bleat(ing).

bêler [bele] [1] **vi** (*Zool, fig*) to bleat.

belette [bəlɛt] **nf** weasel.

Belfast [bɛlfast] **n** Belfast.

belge [bɛlʒ] 1 **adj** Belgian. 2 **nmf: B~** Belgian.

belgicisme [bɛlʒisism] **nm** Belgian-French word (*ou* phrase).

Belgique [bɛlʒik] **nf** Belgium.

Belgrade [bɛlgʀad] **n** Belgrade.

bélier [belje] **nm** (*Zool*) ram; (*Tech*) ram, pile driver; (*Mil*) (battering) ram. **coup de ~** waterhammer; **~ hydraulique** hydraulic ram; (*Astron*) **le B~** Aries, the Ram; **être (du) B~** to be (an) Aries *ou* an Arian.

bélître†† [belitʀ] **nm** rascal, knave†.

Bélize [beliz] **nm** Belize.

bélizien,-ienne [belizjɛ̃, jɛn] 1 **adj** Belizean. 2 **nm,f: B~(ne)** Belizean.

belladone [beladɔn] **nf** (*Bot*) deadly nightshade, belladonna; (*Méd*) belladonna.

bellâtre [bɛlɑtʀ] **nm** buck, swell*.

belle [bɛl] *voir* **beau.**

belle-doche‡, pl belles-doches [bɛldɔʃ] **nf** (*péj*) mother-in-law.

bellement [bɛlmɑ̃] **adv** (*bel et bien*) well and truly; (†: *avec art*) nicely, gently.

bellicisme [belisism] **nm** bellicosity, warmongering.

belliciste [belisist] 1 **adj** warmongering, bellicose. 2 **nmf** warmonger.

belligérance [beliʒeʀɑ̃s] **nf** belligerence, belligerency.

belligérant, e [beliʒeʀɑ̃, ɑ̃t] **adj, nm,f** belligerent.

belliqueux, -euse [belikø, øz] **adj** *humeur, personne* quarrelsome, aggressive; *politique, peuple* warlike, bellicose, aggressive.

bellot, -otte*† [bɛlo, ɔt] **adj** *enfant* pretty, bonny (*Brit*).

Belmopan [bɛlmɔpan] **n** Belmopan.

belon [bəlɔ̃] **nm ou f** Belon oyster.

belote [bəlɔt] **nf** *card game.*

bélouga, béluga [beluga] **nm** beluga.

belvédère [bɛlvedɛʀ] **nm** (*terrasse*) panoramic viewpoint, belvedere; (*édifice*) belvedere.

bémol [bemɔl] **nm** (*Mus*) flat. **en si ~** in B flat; (*: *fig*) **mettre un ~** to tone it *ou* things down a bit*; (*: *fig*) **mettre un ~ à qch** to tone sth down a bit*.

ben* [bɛ̃] **adv** well, er*. **~, je n'en sais rien du tout** well, I really don't know; **~ oui/non** well yes/no; **~ quoi?** so (what)?; **eh ~** well, er*; **c'est ~ vrai** it's true enough, it's true you know.

bénédicité [benedisite] **nm** grace, blessing. **dire le ~** to say grace *ou* the blessing.

bénédictin, e [benediktɛ̃, in] 1 **adj** Benedictine. 2 **nm,f** Benedictine; *voir* **travail[1]**. 3 **nf: Bénédictine** (*liqueur*) Benedictine.

bénédiction [benediksjɔ̃] **nf** a (*Rel: consécration*) benediction, blessing; *[église]* consecration; *[drapeau, bateau]* blessing. **recevoir la ~** to be given a blessing; **donner la ~ à** to bless; **~ nuptiale** marriage blessing; **la ~ nuptiale leur sera donnée ...** the marriage ceremony will take place ... . b (*assentiment, faveur*) blessing. **donner sa ~ à** to give one's blessing to. c (*: *aubaine*) blessing, godsend. **c'est une ~ (du ciel)!** it's a blessing! *ou* a godsend!

bénef* [benɛf] **nm** (**abrév de bénéfice**) profit.

bénéfice [benefis] 1 **nm** a (*Comm*) profit. **vendre à ~** to sell at a profit; **réaliser de gros ~s** to make a big profit *ou* big profits; **faire du ~** to make *ou* turn a profit; **c'est tout ~** it's to your advantage.
b (*avantage*) advantage, benefit. (*Jur*) **il a obtenu un divorce à son ~** he obtained a divorce in his favour; **il perd tout le ~ de sa bonne conduite** he loses all the benefits he has gained from his good behaviour; **concert donné au ~ des aveugles** concert given to raise funds for *ou* in aid of the blind; **conclure une affaire à son ~** to complete a deal to one's advantage; **il a tiré un ~ certain de ses efforts** his efforts certainly paid off; **quel ~ as-tu à le nier?** what's the point of (your) denying it?, what good is there in (your) denying it?; **laissons-lui le ~ du doute** let us give him the benefit of the doubt; (*Jur*) **au ~ de l'âge** by prerogative of age.
c (*Rel*) benefice, living.
2 **comp** ▸**bénéfice des circonstances atténuantes** (*Jur*) benefit

of mitigating circumstances ▸**bénéfice d'exploitation** (*Fin*) operating profit ▸**sous bénéfice d'inventaire** (*Fin*) without liability to debts beyond assets descended ▸**bénéfice net par action** (*Fin*) price earning ratio; (*fig: jusqu'à preuve du contraire*) until there is evidence to the contrary ▸**bénéfices non distribués** (*Fin*) (accumulated) retained earnings.

bénéficiaire [benefisjɛʀ] 1 **adj** *opération* profit-making, profitable; *voir* **marge.** 2 **nmf** (*gén*) beneficiary; *[testament]* beneficiary; *[chèque]* payee. **être le ~ d'une nouvelle mesure** to benefit by a new measure.

bénéficier [benefisje] 7 bénéficier de **vt indir** (*jouir de*) to have, enjoy; (*obtenir*) to get, have; (*tirer profit de*) to benefit by *ou* from, gain by. **~ de certains avantages** to have *ou* enjoy certain advantages; **~ d'une remise** to get a reduction *ou* discount; **~ d'un préjugé favorable** to be favourably considered; **~ d'une mesure/d'une situation** to benefit by *ou* gain by a measure/situation; (*Jur*) **~ d'un non-lieu** to be (unconditionally) discharged; (*Jur*) **~ de circonstances atténuantes** to be granted mitigating circumstances; **faire ~ qn de certains avantages** to enable sb to enjoy certain advantages; **faire ~ qn d'une remise** to give *ou* allow sb a discount.

bénéfique [benefik] **adj** beneficial.

Bénélux [benelyks] **nm: le ~** the Benelux countries.

benêt [bənɛ] 1 **nm** simpleton, silly. **grand ~** big ninny*, stupid lump‡; **faire le ~** to act stupid *ou* daft‡ (*Brit*). 2 **adj m** simple, simple(-minded), silly.

bénévolat [benevɔla] **nm** voluntary help.

bénévole [benevɔl] 1 **adj** *aide, travail, personne* voluntary, unpaid. 2 **nmf** volunteer, voluntary helper *ou* worker.

bénévolement [benevɔlmɑ̃] **adv** *travailler* voluntarily, for nothing.

Bengale [bɛ̃gal] **nm** Bengal; *voir* **feu**[1].

bengali [bɛ̃gali] 1 **adj** Bengali, Bengalese. 2 **nm** (*Ling*) Bengali; (*oiseau*) waxbill. 3 **nmf: B~** Bengali, Bengalese.

bénigne [beniɲ] **adj f** *voir* **bénin.**

bénignement [beniɲmɑ̃] **adv** (*littér*) benignly, in a kindly way.

bénignité [beniɲite] **nf** *[maladie]* mildness; (*littér*) *[personne]* benignancy, kindness.

Bénin [benɛ̃] **nm** Benin. **République populaire du ~** People's Republic of Benin.

bénin, -igne [benɛ̃, iɲ] **adj** a *accident* slight, minor; *punition* mild; *maladie, remède* mild, harmless; *tumeur* benign. b (*littér*) *humeur, critique* benign, kindly.

béninois, e [beninwa,waz] 1 **adj** Beninese. 2 **nm,f: B~(e)** Beninese.

béni-oui-oui* [beniwiwi] **nmf inv** (*péj*) yes man* (*péj*).

bénir [beniʀ] 2 **vt** a (*Rel*) *fidèle, objet* to bless; *mariage* to bless, solemnize; *voir* **dieu.** b (*remercier*) to be eternally grateful to, thank God for. **il bénissait l'arrivée providentielle de ses amis** he thanked God for *ou* was eternally grateful for the providential arrival of his friends; **soyez béni!** bless you!; (*iro*) **ah, toi, je te bénis!** oh curse you! *ou* damn you!‡; **~ le ciel de qch** to thank God for sth; **béni soit le jour où ...** thank God for the day (when) ...; **je bénis cette coïncidence** (I) thank God for this coincidence.

bénit, e [beni, it] **adj** *pain, cierge* consecrated; *eau* holy.

bénitier [benitje] **nm** (*Rel*) stoup, font; *voir* **diable, grenouille.**

Benjamin [bɛ̃ʒamɛ̃] **nm** Benjamin.

benjamin [bɛ̃ʒamɛ̃] **nm** youngest son, youngest child.

benjamine [bɛ̃ʒamin] **nf** youngest daughter, youngest child.

benjoin [bɛ̃ʒwɛ̃] **nm** benzoin.

benne [bɛn] **nf** a (*Min*) skip (*Brit*), truck, tub. b *[camion]* (*basculante*) tipper (lorry) (*Brit*), dump truck; (*amovible*) skip; *[grue]* scoop, bucket; *[téléphérique]* (cable-)car.

Benoît [bənwa] **nm** Benedict.

benoît, e [bənwa, wat] **adj** (*littér*) bland, ingratiating.

benoîtement [bənwatmɑ̃] **adv** (*littér*) blandly, ingratiatingly.

benzène [bɛ̃zɛn] **nm** benzene.

benzine [bɛ̃zin] **nf** benzine.

benzol [bɛ̃zɔl] **nm** benzol.

Béotie [beɔsi] **nf** Boeotia.

béotien, -ienne [beɔsjɛ̃, jɛn] 1 **adj** Boeotian. 2 **nm** (*péj*) philistine. 3 **nm,f: B~(ne)** Boeotian.

BEP [beøpe] **nm** (**abrév de brevet d'études professionnelles**) *voir* **brevet.**

BEPA [beøpea] **nm** (**abrév de brevet d'études professionnelles agricoles**) *voir* **brevet.**

BEPC [beəpese] **nm** (**abrév de brevet d'études du premier cycle**) *voir* **brevet.**

béquée **nf** = **becquée.**

béquet **nm** = **becquet.**

béqueter **vt** = **becqueter.**

béquille [bekij] **nf** a *[infirme]* crutch. **marcher avec des ~s** to walk *ou* be on crutches. b *[motocyclette, mitrailleuse]* stand; (*Aviat*) tail skid; (*Naut*) shore, prop. **mettre une ~ sous qch** to prop *ou* shore sth up. c *[serrure]* handle.

béquiller [bekije] 1 1 **vt** (*Naut*) to shore up. 2 **vi** (*) to walk with *ou* on crutches.

ber [bɛʀ] **nm** (*Can: berceau*) cradle.

berbère [bɛʀbɛʀ] 1 **adj** Berber. 2 **nm** (*Ling*) Berber. 3 **nmf: B~** Berber.

bercail [bɛʀkaj] **nm** (*Rel, fig*) fold. **rentrer au ~*** to return to the fold.

berçante [bɛʀsɑ̃t] **nf** (*Can *: aussi* **chaise ~**) rocking chair.

berceau, **pl ~x** [bɛʀso] **nm** a (*lit*) cradle, crib; (*lieu d'origine*) birthplace. **dès le ~** from birth, from the cradle; **il les prend au ~!*** he snatches them straight from the cradle!, he's a baby *ou* cradle snatcher! b (*Archit*) barrel vault; (*charmille*) bower, arbour; (*Naut*) cradle.

bercelonnette [bɛʀsəlɔnɛt] **nf** rocking cradle, cradle on rockers.

bercement [bɛʀsəmɑ̃] **nm** rocking (movement).

bercer [bɛʀse] 3 1 **vt** a *bébé* to rock; (*dans ses bras*) to rock, cradle; *navire* to rock. **il a été bercé au son du canon** he was reared with the sound of battle in his ears. b (*apaiser*) *douleur* to lull, soothe. c (*tromper*) **~ de** to delude with. 2 **se bercer** **vpr: se ~ de** to delude o.s. with; **se ~ d'illusions** to harbour illusions, delude o.s.

berceur, -euse [bɛʀsœʀ, øz] 1 **adj** *rythme* lulling, soothing. 2 **berceuse** **nf** a (*chanson*) lullaby, cradlesong; (*Mus*) berceuse. b (*fauteuil*) rocking chair.

Bérénice [beʀenis] **nf** Ber(e)nice.

béret [beʀɛ] **nm** beret.

bergamasque [bɛʀgamask] **nf** bergamask.

bergamote [bɛʀgamɔt] **nf** bergamot orange.

bergamotier [bɛʀgamɔtje] **nm** bergamot.

berge [bɛʀʒ] **nf** *[rivière]* bank. (‡: *année*) **il a 50 ~s** he's 50 (years old).

berger [bɛʀʒe] **nm** (*lit, Rel*) shepherd. **(chien de) ~** sheepdog; **~ allemand** alsatian (*Brit*), German sheepdog *ou* shepherd; *voir* **étoile.**

bergère [bɛʀʒɛʀ] **nf** a (*personne*) shepherdess. b (*fauteuil*) wing chair.

bergerie [bɛʀʒəʀi] **nf** a sheepfold; *voir* **loup.** b (*Littérat*) **~s** pastorals.

bergeronnette [bɛʀʒəʀɔnɛt] **nf** wagtail. **~ flavéole/des ruisseaux** yellow/grey wagtail.

béribéri [beʀibeʀi] **nm** beriberi.

Béring [beʀiŋ] **nm: le détroit de ~** the Bering Strait; **mer de ~** Bering Sea.

berk* [bɛʀk] **excl** yuk‡.

berkélium [bɛʀkeljɔm] **nm** berkelium.

berlander* [bɛʀlɑ̃de] 1 **vi** (*Can*) to prevaricate, equivocate.

Berlin [bɛʀlɛ̃] **n** Berlin. **~-Est/-Ouest** East/West Berlin.

berline [bɛʀlin] **nf** a (*Aut*) saloon (car) (*Brit*), sedan (*US*); (††: *à chevaux*) berlin. b (*Min*) truck.

berlingot [bɛʀlɛ̃go] **nm** a (*bonbon*) boiled sweet, humbug (*Brit*). b (*emballage*) (pyramid-shaped) carton; (*pour shampooing*) sachet.

berlinois, e [bɛʀlinwa, waz] 1 **adj** of *ou* from Berlin. 2 **nm,f: B~(e)** Berliner.

berlot [bɛʀlo] **nm** (*Can*) sleigh.

berlue [bɛʀly] **nf: j'ai la ~** I must be seeing things.

berme [bɛʀm] **nf** *[canal]* path; *[fossé]* verge.

bermuda(s) [bɛʀmyda] **nm** bermuda shorts, bermudas.

Bermudes [bɛʀmyd] **nfpl** Bermuda; *voir* **triangle.**

bermudien, -ienne [bɛʀmydjɛ̃, jɛn] 1 **adj** Bermudan, Bermudian. 2 **nm,f: B~(ne)** Bermudan, Bermudian.

bernache [bɛʀnaʃ] **nf** (*crustacé*) barnacle. (*oie*) **~ (nonnette)** barnacle goose; **~ cravant** brent goose.

bernacle [bɛʀnakl] **nf** barnacle goose.

Bernard [bɛʀnaʀ] **nm** Bernard.

bernardin, e [bɛʀnaʀdɛ̃, in] **nm,f** Bernardine, Cistercian.

bernard-l'(h)ermite [bɛʀnaʀlɛʀmit] **nm inv** hermit crab.

Berne [bɛʀn] **n** Bern.

berne [bɛʀn] **nf: en ~** ≃ at half-mast; **mettre en ~** ≃ to half-mast.

berner [bɛʀne] 1 **vt** (*littér: tromper*) to fool, hoax; (*Hist*) *personne* to toss in a blanket.

bernicle [bɛʀnikl] **nf** = **bernique.**

Bernin [bɛʀnɛ̃] **nm: le ~** Bernini.

bernique[1] [bɛʀnik] **nf** limpet.

bernique[2]* [bɛʀnik] **excl** (*rien à faire*) nothing doing!*, not a chance! *ou* hope!

bernois, e [bɛʀnwa, waz] 1 **adj** Bernese. 2 **nm,f: B~(e)** Bernese.

berrichon, -onne [bɛʀiʃɔ̃, ɔn] 1 **adj** of *ou* from the Berry. 2 **nm,f: B~(ne)** inhabitant *ou* native of the Berry.

Berthe [bɛʀt] **nf** Bertha.

Bertrand [bɛʀtʀɑ̃] **nm** Bertrand, Bertram.

béryl [beʀil] **nm** beryl.

berzingue‡ [bɛʀzɛ̃g] **adv: à tout(e) ~** flat out*.

besace [bəzas] **nf** beggar's bag *ou* pouch.

bésef‡ [bezɛf] **adv: il n'y en a pas ~** (*quantité*) there's not much (of it) *ou* a lot (of it); (*nombre*) there aren't many (of them) *ou* a lot (of them).

besicles [bezikl] **nfpl** (*Hist*) spectacles; (*hum*) glasses, specs*.

bésigue [bezig] **nm** bezique.

besogne [bəzɔɲ] **nf** (*travail*) work (*NonC*), job. **se mettre à la ~** to set to work; **c'est de la belle ~** (*lit*) it's nice work; (*iro*) it's a nice mess; **une sale ~** a nasty job; **il est allé vite en ~** he didn't hang about*.

besogner [bəzɔɲe] 1 **vi** to toil (away), drudge.

besogneux, -euse [bəzɔɲø, øz] adj (†: *miséreux*) needy, poor; (*travailleur*) industrious, hard-working.

besoin [bəzwɛ̃] nm a (*exigence*) need (*de* for). **~s essentiels** basic needs; **subvenir** *ou* **pourvoir aux ~s de qn** to provide for sb's needs; **il a de grands/petits ~s** his needs are great/small; **éprouver le ~ de faire qch** to feel the need to do sth; **mentir est devenu un ~ chez lui** lying has become compulsive *ou* a need with him.
b (*pauvreté*) **le ~** need, want; **être dans le ~** to be in need *ou* want; **cela les met à l'abri du ~** that will keep the wolf from their door; **une famille dans le ~** a needy family; **pour ceux qui sont dans le ~** for the needy, for those in straitened circumstances.
c (*euph*) **~s naturels** nature's needs; **faire ses ~s** *[personne]* to relieve o.s., spend a penny* (*Brit*), go to the john* (*US*); *[animal domestique]* to do its business; **satisfaire un ~ pressant** to relieve o.s.
d (*avec avoir*) **avoir ~ de qn** to need sb; **avoir ~ de qch** to need sth, be in need of sth, want sth; **avoir ~ de faire qch** to need to do sth; **il n'a pas ~ de venir** he doesn't need *ou* have to come, there's no need for him to come; **il a ~ que vous l'aidiez** he needs your help *ou* you to help him; **pas ~ de dire qu'il ne m'a pas cru** it goes without saying *ou* needless to say he didn't believe me; **je n'ai pas ~ de vous rappeler que ...** there's no need (for me) to remind you that ...; **ce tapis a ~ d'être nettoyé** this carpet needs *ou* wants (*Brit*) cleaning; **vous pouvez jouer mais il n'y a pas ~ de faire autant de bruit** you can play but you don't have *ou* need to be so noisy; **il a grand ~ d'aide** he needs help badly, he's badly in need of help; (*iro*) **il avait bien ~ de ça!** that's just what he needed! (*iro*); **est-ce que tu avais ~ d'y aller?***why on earth did you go?, did you really have to go?, what did you want to go for anyway!*
e (*avec être: littér*) **si ~ est, s'il en est ~** if need(s) be, if necessary; **il n'est pas ~ de mentionner que ...** there is no need to mention that ... .
f (*loc*) **au ~** if necessary, if need(s) be; **si le ~ s'en fait sentir** if the need arises, if it's felt to be necessary; **en cas de ~** if the need arises, in case of necessity; **pour les ~s de la cause** for the purpose in hand.

Bessarabie [besaʀabi] nf Bessarabia.

bestiaire [bɛstjɛʀ] nm a (*livre*) bestiary. b (*gladiateur*) gladiator.

bestial, e, mpl **-iaux** [bɛstjal, jo] adj bestial, brutish.

bestialement [bɛstjalmɑ̃] adv bestially, brutishly.

bestialité [bɛstjalite] nf (*sauvagerie*) bestiality, brutishness; (*perversion*) bestiality.

bestiaux [bɛstjo] nmpl (*gén*) livestock; (*bovins*) cattle.

bestiole [bɛstjɔl] nf (tiny) creature, creepy crawly* (*Brit*).

bêta¹, -asse* [bɛta, ɑs] 1 adj silly, stupid. 2 nm,f goose*, silly billy*. **gros ~!** big ninny!*, silly goose!*

bêta² [bɛta] nm (*Ling, Phys*) beta. (*Méd*) **~-bloquant** beta-blocking.

bétail [betaj] nm (*gén*) livestock; (*bovins, fig*) cattle. **gros ~** cattle; **petit ~** small livestock; **le ~ humain qu'on entasse dans les camps** the people who are crammed like cattle into the camps.

bétaillère [betajɛʀ] nf livestock truck.

bête [bɛt] 1 nf a (*animal*) animal; (*insecte*) insect, bug*, creature. **~ (sauvage)** (wild) beast; **nos amies les ~s** our friends the animals, our four-legged friends; **aller soigner les ~s** to go and see to the animals; **gladiateur livré aux ~s** gladiator flung to the beasts; **pauvre petite ~** poor little thing* *ou* creature; **ce chien est une belle ~** this dog is a fine animal *ou* beast; **tu as une petite ~ sur ta manche** there's an insect *ou* a creepy crawly* (*Brit*) on your sleeve; **ces sales ~s ont mangé mes salades** those wretched creatures have been eating my lettuces.
b (*personne*) (*bestial*) beast; (†: *stupide*) fool. **c'est une méchante ~** he is a wicked creature; **quelle sale ~!** (*enfant*) what a wretched pest!; (*adulte*) what a horrible creature!, what a beast!; (*hum*) **c'est une brave** *ou* **une bonne ~!** he is a good-natured sort *ou* soul; (*terme d'affection*) **grande** *ou* **grosse ~!*** you big silly!*; **faire la ~** to act stupid *ou* daft*, play the fool.
2 adj a (*stupide*) *personne, idée, sourire* stupid, silly, foolish, idiotic. **ce qu'il peut être ~!** what a fool he is!; **il est plus ~ que méchant** he may be stupid but he's not malicious, he's stupid rather than really nasty; **il est loin d'être ~** he's far from stupid, he's no fool, he's quite the reverse of stupid; **être ~ comme ses pieds*** *ou* **à manger du foin*** to be too stupid for words, be as thick as a brick*; **lui, pas si ~, est parti à temps** knowing better *ou* being no fool, he left in time; **ce film est ~ à pleurer** this film is too stupid for words; **c'est ~, on n'a pas ce qu'il faut pour faire des crêpes** it's a shame *ou* it's stupid we haven't got what we need for making pancakes; **que je suis ~!** how silly *ou* stupid of me!, what a fool I am!; **ce n'est pas ~** that's not a bad idea.
b (*: *très simple*) **c'est tout ~** it's quite *ou* dead* (*Brit*) simple; **~ comme chou** simplicity itself, as easy as pie* *ou* as winking*.
3 comp ▸**bête à bon dieu** ladybird ▸**bête à concours** swot* (*Brit*), grind* (*US*) ▸**bête à cornes** horned animal; (*hum*) snail ▸**bête curieuse** (*iro*) queer *ou* strange animal; **regarder qn comme une bête curieuse** to stand and stare at sb ▸**bête fauve** big cat, wild beast ▸**bête féroce** wild animal *ou* beast ▸**bête noire: c'est ma bête noire** *[chose]* that's my pet hate *ou* bête noire *ou* pet peeve* (*US*); *[personne]* I just can't stand him ▸**bête de race** pedigree animal ▸**bête sauvage** = **bête féroce** ▸**bête de somme** beast of burden ▸**bête de trait** draught animal.

bétel [betɛl] nm betel.

bêtement [bɛtmɑ̃] adv stupidly, foolishly, idiotically. **tout ~** quite simply.

Béthanie [betani] n Bethany.

Bethléem [bɛtleɛm] n Bethlehem.

Bethsabée [bɛtsabe] nf Bathsheba.

bêtifiant, e [betifjɑ̃, jɑ̃t] adj *livre, film* idiotic.

bêtifier [betifje] 7 vi to prattle stupidly, talk twaddle.

bêtise [betiz] nf a (*NonC: stupidité*) stupidity, foolishness, folly. **être d'une ~ crasse** to be incredibly stupid; **j'ai eu la ~ d'accepter** I was foolish enough to accept; **c'était de la ~ d'accepter** it was folly to accept.
b (*action stupide*) silly *ou* stupid thing; (*erreur*) blunder; (*frasque*) stupid prank. **ne dis pas de ~s** don't talk nonsense *ou* rubbish (*Brit*); **ne faites pas de ~s, les enfants** don't do anything silly children, don't get into *ou* up to mischief children; **faire une ~** (*action stupide, frasque*) to do something stupid; (*erreur*) to make a blunder, boob*.
c (*bagatelle*) trifle, triviality. **dépenser son argent en ~s** to spend *ou* squander one's money on rubbish (*Brit*) *ou* trash (*US*).
d **~ de Cambrai** ≈ mint humbug (*Brit*), hard mint candy (*US*).
e (*Can*) **~s*** insults, rude remarks.

bêtisier [betizje] nm collection of foolish quotations.

béton [betɔ̃] nm concrete. **~ armé** reinforced concrete; (*fig*) **accord en ~ armé** ironclad agreement; (*Ftbl*) **faire** *ou* **jouer le ~** to play defensively.

bétonnage [betɔnaʒ] nm (*voir* **bétonner**) concreting; defensive play.

bétonner [betɔne] 1 1 vt (*Constr*) to concrete. 2 vi (*Ftbl*) to play defensively.

bétonneuse [betɔnøz] nf, **bétonnière** [betɔnjɛʀ] nf cement mixer.

bette [bɛt] nf: **~s** Chinese cabbage *ou* leaves.

betterave [bɛtʀav] nf: **~ fourragère** mangel-wurzel, beet; **~ (rouge)** beetroot (*Brit*), beet (*US*); **~ sucrière** sugar beet.

betteravier, -ière [bɛtʀavje, jɛʀ] 1 adj beetroot (*épith*), of beetroots (*Brit*) *ou* beets (*US*). 2 nm beet grower.

beuglant* [bøglɑ̃] nm honky-tonk*.

beuglante‡ [bøglɑ̃t] nf (*cri*) yell, holler*; (*chanson*) song. **pousser une ~** to yell, give a yell *ou* holler*.

beuglement [bøgləmɑ̃] nm (*voir* **beugler**) lowing (*NonC*), mooing (*NonC*); bellowing (*NonC*); bawling (*NonC*), hollering* (*NonC*); blaring (*NonC*). **pousser des ~s** to bawl, bellow.

beugler [bøgle] 1 1 vi a *[vache]* to low, moo; *[taureau]* to bellow. b (*) *[personne]* to bawl, bellow, holler*; *[radio]* to blare. **faire ~ sa télé** to have one's TV on (at) full blast*. 2 vt (*péj*) *chanson* to bellow out, belt out*.

beur [bœʀ] 1 nmf *young North African born in France.* 2 adj *culture, musique of young North African born in France.*

beurk* excl = **berk***.

beurre [bœʀ] 1 nm a (*laitier*) butter. **~ salé/demi-sel** salted/slightly salted butter; **au ~** *plat* (cooked) in butter; *pâtisserie* made with butter; **faire la cuisine au ~** to cook with butter; **~ fondu** melted butter (*Brit*), drawn butter (*US*); *voir* **inventer, motte, œil.**
b (*Culin*) paste. **~ d'anchois/d'écrevisses** anchovy/shrimp paste; (*substance végétale*) **~ de cacao/de cacahuètes** cocoa/peanut butter.
c (* *loc*) **entrer comme dans du ~** to go *ou* get in with the greatest (of) ease; **le couteau entre dans cette viande comme dans du ~** this meat is like butter to cut; **cette viande, c'est du ~!** this is very tender meat; **ça va mettre du ~ dans les épinards** that will add a little to the kitty; **faire son ~** to make a packet* *ou* one's pile*, feather one's nest; **il n'y en a pas plus que de ~ en broche** there is (*ou* are) none at all; *voir* **compter.**
2 comp ▸**beurre d'escargot** = **beurre persillé** ▸**beurre-frais** adj inv (*couleur*) buttercup yellow ▸**beurre laitier** dairy butter ▸**beurre noir** (*Culin*) brown (butter) sauce ▸**beurre persillé** *ou* **d'escargots** garlic and parsley butter ▸**beurre roux** roux.

beurré, e [bœʀe] (ptp de **beurrer**) 1 adj (‡: *ivre*) canned‡, plastered‡. 2 nm butter-pear, beurré. 3 **beurrée** nf (*Can* †) slice of bread and butter.

beurrer [bœʀe] 1 1 vt a to butter. **tartine beurrée** slice of bread and butter. b (*Can* †) to smear. 2 **se beurrer‡** vpr to get canned‡ *ou* plastered‡.

beurrier, -ière [bœʀje, jɛʀ] 1 adj *industrie, production* butter (*épith*). **région ~ière** butter-producing region. 2 nm butter dish.

beuverie [bøvʀi] nf drinking bout *ou* session, binge*.

bévue [bevy] nf blunder.

bey [bɛ] nm bey.

Beyrouth [beʀut] n Beirut.

bézef‡ [bezɛf] adv = **bésef‡**.

bhotia [bɔtja] 1 adj Bhutanese. 2 nmf: **B~** Bhutanese.

Bhoutan, Bhutân [butɑ̃] nm Bhutan.

bi... [bi] préf bi... .

biacide [biasid] adj, nm diacid.

Biafra [bjafʀa] nm Biafra.

biafrais, e [bjafʀɛ, ɛz] 1 adj Biafran. 2 nm,f: **B~(e)** Biafran.

biais [bjɛ] nm a (*détour, artifice*) device, expedient, dodge*. **chercher un ~ pour obtenir qch** to find some means of getting sth *ou* expedient for getting sth; **il a trouvé le** *ou* **un ~ (pour se faire exempter)** he found a dodge* (to get himself exempted); **par quel ~ vais-je m'en tirer?** what means can I use to get out of it?, how on earth am I going to get out of it?; **par le ~ de** by means of, using the expedient of.

b (*aspect*) angle, way. **c'est par ce ~ qu'il faut aborder le problème** the problem should be approached from this angle *ou* in this way.

c (*Tex*) (*sens*) bias; (*bande*) piece of cloth cut on the bias *ou* the cross. **coupé** *ou* **taillé dans le ~** cut on the bias *ou* the cross.

d (*ligne oblique*) slant.

e (*loc*) **en ~, de ~** slantwise, at an angle; **une allée traverse le jardin en ~** a path cuts diagonally across the garden; **regarder qn de ~** to give sb a sidelong glance; **prendre une question de ~** to tackle a question indirectly *ou* in a roundabout way.

biaiser [bjeze] 1 **vi** a (*louvoyer*) to sidestep the issue, prevaricate. b (*obliquer*) to change direction.

biathlon [biatlɔ̃] **nm** biathlon.

bibelot [biblo] **nm** (*objet sans valeur*) trinket, knick-knack; (*de valeur*) bibelot, curio.

biberon [bibʀɔ̃] **nm** feeding bottle, baby's bottle. **élevé au ~** bottle-fed; **l'heure du ~** (baby's) feeding time; **élever** *ou* **nourrir au ~** to bottle-feed.

biberonner‡ [bibʀɔne] 1 **vi** to tipple*, booze‡.

bibi[1]* [bibi] **nm** woman's hat.

bibi[2]‡ [bibi] **pron** me, yours truly (*hum*).

bibine* [bibin] **nf** (weak) beer, dishwater (*hum*). **une infâme ~** a loathsome brew.

bibi(t)te [bibit] **nf** (*Can*) insect, bug*.

bible [bibl] **nf** (*livre, fig*) bible. **la B~** the Bible.

bibliobus [biblijobys] **nm** mobile library.

bibliographe [biblijɔgʀaf] **nmf** bibliographer.

bibliographie [biblijɔgʀafi] **nf** bibliography.

bibliographique [biblijɔgʀafik] **adj** bibliographic(al).

bibliomane [biblijɔman] **nmf** booklover.

bibliomanie [biblijɔmani] **nf** bibliomania.

bibliophile [biblijɔfil] **nmf** bibliophile, booklover.

bibliophilie [biblijɔfili] **nf** bibliophilism, love of books.

bibliothécaire [biblijɔtekɛʀ] **nmf** librarian.

bibliothéconomie [biblijtekɔnɔmi] **nf** library science.

bibliothèque [biblijɔtɛk] **nf** (*édifice, pièce*) library; (*meuble*) bookcase; (*collection*) library, collection (of books). **~ de gare** station bookstall (*Brit*) *ou* newsstand (*US*); **B~ nationale** *French national library;* **~ de prêt** lending library; **~ universitaire** university library.

biblique [biblik] **adj** biblical.

Bic [bik] **nm** ® **(pointe)** ≃ Biro ®, ball-point pen.

bicaméral, e, **mpl -aux** [bikameʀal, o] **adj** bicameral, two-chamber (*épith*).

bicaméralisme [bikameʀalism] **nm, bicamérisme** [bikameʀism] **nm** bicameral *ou* two-chamber system.

bicarbonate [bikaʀbɔnat] **nm** bicarbonate. **~ de soude** bicarbonate of soda, sodium bicarbonate, baking soda.

bicarré, e [bikɑʀe] **adj** (*Math*) biquadratic.

bicentenaire [bisɑ̃t(ə)nɛʀ] **nm** bicentenary, bicentennial.

bicéphale [bisefal] **adj** two-headed, bicephalous (*SPÉC*).

biceps [bisɛps] **nm** biceps. **avoir des** *ou* **du ~*** to have a strong *ou* good pair of arms.

biche [biʃ] **nf** hind, doe. **un regard** *ou* **des yeux de ~ aux abois** frightened doe-like eyes; (*fig*) **ma ~** darling, pet.

bicher* [biʃe] 1 **vi** a [*personne*] to be pleased with o.s. b **ça biche?** how's things?*, things O.K. with you?*

bichette [biʃɛt] **nf** (*terme d'affection*) **(ma) ~** darling, pet.

bichlorure [biklɔʀyʀ] **nm** bichloride.

bichon, -onne [biʃɔ̃, ɔn] **nm,f** (*chien*) toy dog. **mon ~*** pet, love.

bichonnage [biʃɔnaʒ] **nm** titivation.

bichonner [biʃɔne] 1 **vt** a (*pomponner*) to dress up, doll up*. (*péj*) **elle est en train de se ~ dans sa chambre** she's sprucing herself up *ou* she's titivating (herself) *ou* getting dolled up* in her room. b (*prendre soin de*) **~ qn** to wait on sb hand and foot, cosset sb.

bichromate [bikʀɔmat] **nm** bichromate.

bichromie [bikʀɔmi] **nf** two-colour process.

bicolore [bikɔlɔʀ] **adj** bicolour(ed), two-colour(ed), two-tone; (*Cartes*) two-suited.

biconcave [bikɔ̃kav] **adj** biconcave.

biconvexe [bikɔ̃vɛks] **adj** biconvex.

bicoque [bikɔk] **nf** (*péj*) shack*, dump*; (*: *maison*) shack*, place*.

bicorne [bikɔʀn] 1 **nm** cocked hat. 2 **adj** two-horned.

bicot** [biko] **nm** (*péj: Arabe*) wog**.

bicycle [bisikl] **nm** (*Can*) bicycle.

bicyclette [bisiklɛt] **nf** a bicycle, bike*. **aller à la ville à** *ou* **en ~** to go to town by bicycle, cycle to town; **faire de la ~** to go cycling, cycle; **sais-tu faire de la ~?** can you cycle?, can you ride a bike?* b (*Sport*) cycling.

bidasse* [bidas] **nm** (*conscrit*) soldier, swaddy (*arg Mil*).

bide [bid] **nm** a (‡: *ventre*) belly‡. **avoir du ~** to have a potbelly. b (*: *échec*) (*gén*) **ça a été le ~** it was a total flop*; **il a essayé de la draguer, mais ça a été le ~** he tried to chat her up but she wasn't having any of it*; (*Théât, Ciné*) **être** *ou* **faire un ~** to be a flop* *ou* a wash-out, bomb* (*US*).

bidet [bidɛ] **nm** a (*cuvette*) bidet. b (*cheval*) (old) nag.

bidirectionnel, -elle [bidiʀɛksjɔnɛl] **adj** bi-directional.

bidoche‡ [bidɔʃ] **nf** meat.

bidon [bidɔ̃] 1 **nm** a (*gén*) can, tin; (*à huile*) can; (*à peinture*) tin; [*campeur, soldat*] water bottle, flask. **~ à lait** milk-churn; **huile en ~** oil in a can. b (‡: *ventre*) belly‡. c (‡: *bluff*) **c'est du ~** that's a load of bull‡ *ou* codswallop‡ (*Brit*) *ou* hot air; **ce n'est pas du ~** I'm (*ou* he's *etc*) not kidding!‡, that's the God's honest truth*. 2 **adj inv** (‡: *simulé*) *attentat, attaque* mock (*épith*); *déclaration, prétexte* phoney*; *élection* rigged; *maladie, émotion* sham (*épith*). **société ~** ghost company.

bidonnant, e‡ [bidɔnɑ̃, ɑ̃t] **adj** hilarious. **c'était ~** it was a hell‡ of a laugh, it had us (*ou* them *etc*) doubled up (with laughter).

bidonner (se)‡ [bidɔne] 1 **vpr** to split one's sides laughing*, be doubled up (with laughter), crease up‡.

bidonville [bidɔ̃vil] **nm** shanty town.

bidouillage* [bidujaʒ] **nm: c'est du ~** (*gén*) it's a bit of a rush job; (*Ordin*) it's just something I've (*ou* we've *etc*) hacked up.

bidouiller* [biduje] 1 **vt** (*gén*) to (have a) tinker with; (*Ordin*) *programme* to hack up. **j'ai réussi à le ~** I've managed to fix it for the time being.

bidouilleur, -euse* [bidujœʀ, øz] **nm,f: c'est un ~** (*habile*) he's quite good with his hands; (*péj*) he's a bit of a botcher*.

bidous [bidu] **nmpl** (*Can*) money.

bidule* [bidyl] **nm** (*machin*) thingummy* (*Brit*), thingumabob*, contraption, whatsit; (*personne*) what's-his-name* (*ou* what's-her-name*), whatsit*. **eh ~!** hey (you) what's-your-name!*

bief [bjɛf] **nm** a [*canal*] reach. b [*moulin*] **~ d'amont** mill race; **~ d'aval** tail race *ou* water.

bielle [bjɛl] **nf** (*locomotive*) connecting rod; (*voiture*) track rod.

biellette [bjelɛt] **nf** (*Aut*) stub axle.

biélorusse [bjelɔʀys] 1 **adj** Bielorussian. 2 **nmf: B~** Bielorussian.

Biélorussie [bjelɔʀysi] **nf** Bielorussia.

bien [bjɛ̃] 1 **adv** a (*de façon satisfaisante*) *jouer, dormir, travailler* well; *conseiller, choisir* well, wisely; *fonctionner* properly, well. **aller** *ou* **se porter ~, être ~ portant** to be well, be in good health; **comment vas-tu? — ~/très ~ merci** how are you? — fine/very well, thanks; **il a ~ réussi** he's done well (for himself); **cette porte ferme ~** this door shuts properly *ou* well; **la télé* ne marche pas ~** the TV isn't working properly *ou* right; **il s'habille ~** he dresses well *ou* smartly; **il parle ~ l'anglais** he speaks good English, he speaks English well; **elle est ~ coiffée aujourd'hui** her hair looks nice today; **nous sommes ~ nourris à l'hôtel** we get good food *ou* we are well fed at the hotel; **il a ~ pris ce que je lui ai dit** he took what I had to say in good part *ou* quite well; **il s'y est ~ pris (pour le faire)** he went about it the right way; **si je me rappelle ~** if I remember right(ly) *ou* correctly; **ils vivent très ~ avec son salaire** they live very comfortably *ou* get along very well on his salary.

b (*selon les convenances, la morale, la raison*) *se conduire, agir* well, decently. **il pensait ~ faire** he thought he was doing the right thing; **vous avez ~ fait** you did the right thing, you did right; **se tenir ~ à table** to behave properly *ou* well at table; **il faut te tenir particulièrement ~ aujourd'hui** you must behave especially well *ou* be especially good today, you must be on your best behaviour today; **pour ~ faire, il faudrait ...** (in order) to do it *ou* to do things properly one should ...; **faire ~ les choses** to do things properly *ou* in style; **vous faites ~ de me le dire!** you've done well to tell me!, it's a good thing you've told me!; **vous feriez ~ de partir tôt** you'd do well *ou* you'd be well advised to leave early.

c (*sans difficulté*) *supporter* well; *se rappeler* well, clearly. **on comprend ~/très ~ pourquoi** one can quite/very easily understand *ou* see why; **il peut très ~ le faire** he can quite easily do it.

d (*exprimant le degré*) (*très*) very, really, awfully*; (*beaucoup*) very much, thoroughly; (*trop*) rather, jolly* (*Brit*), pretty*. **~ mieux** much better; **~ souvent** quite often; **nous sommes ~ contents de vous voir** we're very glad *ou* awfully* pleased to see you; **~ plus heureux/cher** far *ou* much happier/more expensive; **c'est un ~ beau pays** it's a really *ou* truly beautiful country; **nous avons ~ ri** we had a good laugh; **les enfants se sont ~ amusés** the children thoroughly enjoyed themselves *ou* had great fun; **vos œufs sont ~ frais?** are your eggs really fresh?; **question ~ délicate** highly sensitive question; **~ trop bête** far too stupid; **tout cela est ~ joli mais** that's all very well but; **elle est ~ jeune (pour se marier)** she is very *ou* rather young (to be getting married); **nous avons ~ travaillé aujourd'hui** we've done some good work today; **c'est ~ moderne pour mes goûts** it's rather too modern for my taste; **il me paraît ~ sûr de lui** he seems to me to be rather *ou* jolly* (*Brit*) *ou* pretty* sure of himself.

e (*effectivement*) indeed, definitely; (*interrog: réellement*) really. **nous savons ~ où il se cache** we know perfectly well *ou* quite well where he's hiding; **j'avais ~ dit que je ne viendrais pas** I DID say *ou* I certainly did say that I wouldn't come; **je trouve ~ que c'est un peu cher mais tant pis** I DO think it's rather expensive *ou* I agree it's rather expensive but too bad; **je sais ~ mais ...** I know (full well) but ..., I agree but ...; **c'est ~ une erreur** it's definitely *ou* certainly a mistake; **c'est ~ à ton frère que je pensais** it was indeed your brother I was thinking of; **ce n'est pas lui mais ~ son frère qui est docteur** it's not he but his brother who is a doctor, it's his brother not he who is a doctor; **dis-lui ~ que** be sure to *ou* and tell him that, make sure you tell him that; **je vous avais ~ averti** I gave you due *ou* ample warning; **est-ce ~ mon manteau?** is it really my coat?; **était-ce ~ une erreur?** was it really *ou* in fact a mistake?

f (*exclamatif: vraiment, justement*) **il s'agit ~ de cela!** as if that's the point!; **voilà ~ les femmes!** how like women!, that's just like women!, that's women all over!; **c'est ~ ma veine!*** (it's) just my luck!; **c'était ~ la peine!** after all that trouble!, it wasn't worth the trouble!; **c'est ~ cela, on t'invite et tu te décommandes!** that's right *ou* that's just like it! — you're invited and you call off!

g (*intensif*) **ferme ~ la porte** shut the door properly, make sure you shut the door; **tourne ~ ton volant à droite** turn your wheel hard to the right; **écoute-moi ~** listen to me carefully; **regardez ~ ce qu'il va faire** watch what he does carefully; **mets-toi ~ en face** stand right *ou* straight opposite; **percer un trou ~ au milieu** to knock a hole right *ou* bang* (*Brit*) in the centre; **tiens-toi ~ droit** stand quite straight; **ça m'est ~ égal** it's all one *ou* the same to me; **il est mort et ~ mort** he is dead and buried *ou* gone; **c'est ~ compris?** is that clearly *ou* quite understood?; **c'est ~ promis?** is that a firm promise?; **il arrivera ~ à se débrouiller** he'll manage to cope all right; **ça finira ~ par s'arranger** it's bound to work out all right in the end; **j'espère ~!** I should hope so (too)!; **on verra ~** we'll see, time will tell; **où peut-il ~ être?** where on earth can he be?, where CAN he be?; **il se pourrait ~ qu'il pleuve** it could well rain.

h (*malgré tout*) **il fallait ~ que ça se fasse** it had to be done; **il fallait ~ que ça arrive** it was bound to happen; **j'étais ~ obligé d'accepter** I was more or less *ou* pretty well* obliged *ou* bound to accept; **il faut ~ le supporter** one just has to put up with it; **il pourrait ~ venir nous voir de temps en temps!** he could at least come and see us now and then!

i (*volontiers*) **je mangerais ~ un morceau** I could do with a bite to eat, I wouldn't mind something to eat; **il partirait ~ en vacances mais il a trop de travail** he would gladly go *ou* he'd be only too glad to go on holiday but he has too much work to do; **j'irais ~ mais ...** I'd willingly *ou* happily *ou* gladly go but ...; **je voudrais ~ t'y voir!** I wouldn't half‡ like (*Brit*) *ou* I'd sure* like (*US*) to see you do it!; **je verrais très ~ un vase sur la cheminée** I think a vase on the mantelpiece might look very nice.

j (*au moins*) at least. **il y a ~ 3 jours que je ne l'ai vu** I haven't seen him for at least 3 days; **cela vaut ~ ce prix là** it's well worth the price *ou* that much, it's worth at least that price.

k **~ des ...** a good many ..., many a ...; **~ du, ~ de la** a great deal of; **je connais ~ des gens qui auraient protesté** I know a good many *ou* quite a few who would have protested; **ils ont eu ~ de la chance** they were really very lucky; **elle a eu ~ du mal** *ou* **de la peine à le trouver** she had a good *ou* great deal of difficulty in *ou* no end of trouble* in finding it; **ça fait ~ du monde** that makes an awful lot of people.

l **~ que** although, though; **~ que je ne puisse pas venir** although *ou* though I can't come.

m (*loc*) **ah ~ (ça) alors!** (*surprise*) well, well!, just fancy!; (*indignation*) well really!; **ah ~ oui** well of course; **~ entendu, ~ sûr, ~ évidemment** of course; (*dans une lettre*) **~ à vous** yours; **ni ~ ni mal** so-so*; **~ lui en a pris** it was just as well he did it; **c'est ~ fait (pour lui)** it serves him right.

2 **adj inv** **a** (*satisfaisant*) *personne* good; *film, tableau, livre* good, fine. **elle est très ~ comme secrétaire** she's a very good *ou* competent secretary; **donnez-lui quelque chose de ~** give him something really good; **ce serait ~ s'il venait** it would be good if he were to come; **~!** (*approbation*) good!, fine!; (*pour changer de sujet*) O.K., all right; (*exaspération*) **~! ~!, c'est ~!** all right! all right!, O.K.! O.K.!*

b (*Scol: sur copie*) good. **assez ~** quite good; **très ~** very good.

c (*en bonne forme*) well, in good form *ou* health *ou* shape. **il n'était pas très ~ ce matin** he was out of sorts *ou* off colour* (*Brit*) *ou* he wasn't in very good form this morning.

d (*beau*) *personne* good-looking, nice-looking; *chose* nice. **elle était très ~ quand elle était jeune** she was very attractive *ou* good-looking when she was young; **il est ~ de sa personne** he's a good-looking man *ou* a fine figure of a man; **ils ont une maison tout ce qu'il y a de ~*** they've got a smashing* (*Brit*) *ou* really lovely *ou* nice house; **ce bouquet fait ~ sur la cheminée** the flowers look nice on the mantelpiece.

e (*à l'aise*) **il est ~ partout** he is *ou* feels at home anywhere; **on est ~ à l'ombre** it's pleasant *ou* nice in the shade; **on est ~ ici** it's nice here, we like it here; **je suis ~ dans ce fauteuil** I'm very comfortable in this chair; **elle se trouve ~ dans son nouveau poste** she's very happy in her new job; **laisse-le, il est ~ où il est!** leave him alone — he's quite all right where he is *ou* he's fine where he is; (*iro*) **vous voilà ~!** now you've done it!, you're in a fine mess now!

f (*moralement, socialement acceptable*) nice. **c'est pas ~ de dire ça** it's not nice to say that; **ce n'est pas ~ de faire ça** it's not nice to do that, it's wrong to do that; **c'est ~ ce qu'il a fait là** it was very good *ou* decent *ou* nice of him to do that; **c'est ~ à vous de les aider** it's good *ou* nice of you to help them; **c'est un type ~*** he's a decent *ou* nice fellow; **trouves-tu ~ qu'il ait fait cela?** do you think it was very nice of him to do that?; **c'est une femme ~** she's a very nice woman; **des gens ~** very nice *ou* decent people.

g (*en bons termes*) **être ~ avec qn** to be on good terms *ou* get on well with sb; **ils sont ~ ensemble** they're on the best of terms; **se mettre ~ avec qn** to get on the good *ou* right side of sb, get into sb's good books*.

3 **nm** **a** (*ce qui est avantageux, agréable*) good. **le ~ public** the public good; **pour le ~ de l'humanité** for the good of humanity; **c'est pour ton ~!** it's for your own good!; **pour son (plus grand) ~** for his (greater) benefit; **finalement cet échec temporaire a été un ~** in the end this setback was a good thing; **je trouve qu'il a changé en ~** I find he has changed for the better *ou* he has improved; **faire du ~ à qch/qn** to do sth/sb good; **ses paroles m'ont fait du ~** his words did me good, I took comfort from his words; **dire du ~ de** to speak well of; **parler en ~ de qn** to speak favourably *ou* well of sb; **vouloir du ~ à qn** to wish sb well; (*iro*) **un ami qui vous veut du ~** a well-wisher (*iro*); **on a dit le plus grand ~ de ce livre/de cet acteur** this book/this actor has been highly praised, people spoke very highly *ou* favourably of this book/this actor; **on dit beaucoup de ~ de ce restaurant** this restaurant has got a very good name, people speak very highly of this restaurant; **grand ~ vous fasse!** much good may it do you!, you're welcome to it!; (*littér*) **être du dernier ~ avec qn** to be on the closest terms possible *ou* on intimate terms with sb.

b (*ce qui a une valeur morale*) **savoir discerner le ~ du mal** to be able to tell good from evil *ou* right from wrong; **faire le ~** to do good; **rendre le ~ pour le mal** to return good for evil.

c (*gén: possession*) possession, property (*NonC*); (*argent*) fortune; (*terres*) estate. **~s** goods, possessions, property; **cette bibliothèque est son ~ le plus cher** this bookcase is his most treasured possession; **la tranquillité est le seul ~ qu'il désire** peace of mind is all he asks for; **il considère tout comme son ~** he regards everything as being his property *ou* his own; **il est très attaché aux ~s de ce monde** he lays great store by worldly goods *ou* possessions; (*Prov*) **~ mal acquis ne profite jamais** ill gotten ill spent, ill-gotten goods *ou* gains seldom prosper; **il a dépensé tout son ~** he has gone through all his fortune; **avoir du ~ (au soleil)** to have property; **laisser tous ses ~s à ...** to leave all one's (worldly) goods *ou* possessions to ... .

4 **comp** ▸ **bien-aimé(e)** **adj, nmf** (**pl bien-aimé(e)s**) beloved ▸ **biens de consommation** consumer goods ▸ **biens durables** consumer durables ▸ **biens d'équipement** capital equipment *ou* goods; (*Ind*) plant ▸ **biens d'équipement ménager** household goods ▸ **bien-être** **nm inv** (*physique*) well-being; (*matériel*) comfort, material well-being ▸ **bien de famille** family estate ▸ **biens fonciers** = **biens immeubles** ▸ **bien-fondé** **nm** (**pl bien-fondés**) [*opinion, assertion*] validity; (*Jur*) [*plainte*] cogency ▸ **biens immeubles, biens immobiliers** real estate *ou* property (*Brit*), landed property ▸ **biens immédiatement disponibles** off-the-shelf goods ▸ **biens intermédiaires** (*Admin*) intermediate goods ▸ **bien marchand** commodity ▸ **biens meubles, biens mobiliers** personal property *ou* estate, movables ▸ **bien-pensant** **adj** (*Rel*) God-fearing; (*Pol, gén*) right-thinking; (*péj*) **les bien-pensants** right-thinking people ▸ **biens privés** private property ▸ **biens publics** public property.

bienfaisance [bjɛ̃fəzɑ̃s] **nf** charity. **association** *ou* **œuvre de ~** charitable organization; **l'argent sera donné à des œuvres de ~** the money will be given to charity.

bienfaisant, e [bjɛ̃fəzɑ̃, ɑ̃t] **adj** **a** *climat, cure, influence* salutary, beneficial; *pluie* refreshing, beneficial. **b** *personne* beneficent, kind, kindly.

bienfait [bjɛ̃fɛ] **nm** (*faveur*) kindness; (*avantage*) benefit. **c'est un ~ du ciel!** it's a godsend! *ou* a blessing!; (*Prov*) **un ~ n'est jamais perdu** a favour is never wasted; **les ~s de la science** the benefits of science; **les ~s d'un traitement** the beneficial action *ou* effects of a treatment; **il commence à ressentir les ~s de son séjour à la campagne** he is beginning to feel the beneficial effects *ou* the benefit of his stay in the country *ou* the good his stay in the country has done him.

bienfaiteur [bjɛ̃fɛtœʀ] **nm** benefactor.

bienfaitrice [bjɛ̃fɛtʀis] **nf** benefactress.

bienheureux, -euse [bjɛ̃nœʀø, øz] **adj** **a** (*Rel*) blessed, blest. **les ~** the blessed, the blest. **b** (*littér*) happy. **~ celui qui ...** lucky are those who ... .

biennal, e, **mpl -aux** [bjenal, o] **1** **adj** biennial. **2** **biennale** **nf** biennial event.

bien-pensant, e [bjɛ̃pɑ̃sɑ̃, ɑ̃t] **adj** *voir* **bien**.

bienséance [bjɛ̃seɑ̃s] **nf** propriety, decorum. **les ~s** the proprieties, the rules of etiquette.

bienséant, e [bjɛ̃seɑ̃, ɑ̃t] **adj** *action, conduite* proper, seemly, becoming. **il n'est pas ~ de bâiller** it is unbecoming *ou* unseemly to yawn, it isn't the done thing to yawn.

bientôt [bjɛ̃to] **adv** soon. **à ~!** see you soon!, bye for now!*; **c'est ~ dit** it's easier said than done, it's easy to say; **on est ~ arrivé** we'll soon be there, we'll be there shortly; **on ne pourra ~ plus circuler dans Paris** before long it will be impossible to drive in Paris; **c'est pour ~?** is it due soon?, any chance of its being ready soon?; (*naissance*) is the baby expected *ou* due soon?; **il est ~ minuit** it's nearly midnight; **il aura ~ 30 ans** he'll soon be 30, it will soon be his 30th birthday; **il eut ~ fait de finir son travail**† he finished his work in no time, he lost no time in finishing his work.

bienveillance [bjɛ̃vɛjɑ̃s] **nf** benevolence, kindness (*envers* to). **avec ~** *dire, regarder* benevolently, kindly; *parler* kindly; **examiner un cas avec ~** to give favourable consideration to a case; (*Admin*) **je sollicite de votre haute ~ ...** I beg (leave) to request ... .

bienveillant, e [bjɛ̃vɛjɑ̃, ɑ̃t] **adj** benevolent, kindly.

bienvenu, e [bjɛ̃v(ə)ny] 1 **adj: remarque ~e** apposite *ou* well-chosen remark. 2 **nm,f: vous êtes le ~, soyez le ~** you are very welcome, pleased to see you*; **une tasse de café serait la ~e** a cup of coffee would be (most) welcome. 3 **bienvenue nf** welcome. **souhaiter la ~e à qn** to welcome sb; **~e à vous!** welcome (to you)!, you are most welcome!; **allocution de ~e** welcoming speech; **~e à Paris/en Italie!** welcome to Paris/to Italy!; **~e parmi nous!** welcome (to the department *ou* company *ou* neighbourhood *etc*)!; (*Can: je vous en prie*) **~e!** you're welcome!

bière[1] [bjɛʀ] **nf** beer. **garçon, 2 ~s!** waiter, 2 beers!; **~ blonde** ≃ lager, ≃ light ale (*Brit*), ≃ light beer (*US*); **~ brune** ≃ brown ale, ≃ stout (*Brit*); **~ (à la) pression** draught (*Brit*) *ou* draft (*US*) beer, beer on draught (*Brit*) *ou* draft (*US*); *voir* **petit**.

bière[2] [bjɛʀ] **nf** coffin (*Brit*), casket (*US*). **mettre qn en ~** to put *ou* place sb in his coffin; **la mise en ~ a eu lieu ce matin** the body was placed in the coffin this morning.

biffage [bifaʒ] **nm** crossing out.

biffer [bife] [1] **vt** to cross out, strike out. **~ à l'encre/au crayon** to ink/pencil out.

biffure [bifyʀ] **nf** crossing out.

bifidus [bifidys] **nm** bifidus.

bifocal, e, mpl -aux [bifɔkal, o] **adj** bifocal. **lunettes ~es** bifocals.

bifteck [biftɛk] **nm** steak. **~ de cheval** horsemeat steak; **deux ~s** two steaks, two pieces of steak; *voir* **défendre, gagner**.

bifurcation [bifyʀkasjɔ̃] **nf** *[route]* fork, junction; (*Rail*) fork; *[artère, tige]* branching; (*fig: changement*) change.

bifurquer [bifyʀke] [1] **vi** a *[route, voie ferrée]* to fork, branch off. b *[véhicule]* to turn off (*vers, sur* for, towards); (*fig*) *[personne]* to branch off (*vers* into). **~ sur la droite** to bear *ou* turn right.

bigame [bigam] 1 **adj** bigamous. 2 **nmf** bigamist.

bigamie [bigami] **nf** bigamy.

bigarré, e [bigaʀe] (**ptp de bigarrer**) **adj** a (*bariolé*) *vêtement* many-coloured *ou* -hued, rainbow-coloured; *groupe* colourfully dressed, gaily coloured. b (*fig*) *foule* motley (*épith*); *société, peuple* heterogeneous, mixed.

bigarreau, pl ~x [bigaʀo] **nm** bigarreau, bigaroon (cherry).

bigarrer [bigaʀe] [1] **vt** to colour in many hues.

bigarrure [bigaʀyʀ] **nf** coloured pattern. **la ~** *ou* **les ~s d'un tissu** the medley of colours in a piece of cloth, the gaily-coloured pattern of a piece of cloth.

big-bang [bigbɑ̃g] **nm inv** big bang.

bigle† [bigl] **adj** (*hum*) squint(-eyed), cross-eyed.

bigler⁑ [bigle] [1] 1 **vt** *femme* to eye up* (*Brit*), eye (*US*); *objet* to take a squint at*. 2 **vi** (*loucher*) to squint, have a squint. **arrête de ~ sur** *ou* **dans mon jeu** stop squinting at my cards*, take your beady eyes off my cards*.

bigleux, -euse* [biglø, øz] **adj** (*myope*) short-sighted. **quel ~ tu fais!** you need glasses!

bigophone* [bigofɔn] **nm** phone, blower⁑ (*Brit*), horn* (*US*). **passer un coup de ~ à qn** to get sb on the blower⁑ (*Brit*) *ou* horn* (*US*), give sb a buzz* *ou* ring.

bigophoner* [bigɔfɔne] [1] **vi** to be on the blower⁑ (*Brit*) *ou* horn* (*US*). **~ à qn** to give sb a buzz* *ou* ring.

bigorneau, pl ~x [bigɔʀno] **nm** winkle.

bigorner⁑ [bigɔʀne] [1] 1 **vt** *voiture* to smash up. 2 **se bigorner vpr** (*se battre*) to come to blows, scrap* (*avec* with); (*se disputer*) to have a brush *ou* an argument *ou* a barney⁑ (*Brit*) (*avec* with).

bigot, e [bigo, ɔt] (*péj*) 1 **adj** over-pious, sanctimonious, holier-than-thou. 2 **nm,f** (religious) bigot.

bigoterie [bigɔtʀi] **nf** (*péj*) (religious) bigotry, pietism.

bigoudi [bigudi] **nm** (hair-)curler *ou* roller. **une femme en ~s** a woman (with her hair) in curlers *ou* rollers.

bigre [bigʀ] **excl** (*hum*) gosh!*, holy smoke!*

bigrement [bigʀəmɑ̃] **adv** *chaud, bon* dashed*, jolly* (*Brit*); *changer* a heck of a lot*. **on a ~ bien mangé** we had a jolly good meal*.

biguine [bigin] **nf** beguine.

Bihâr [biaʀ] **nm: le ~** Bihar.

bihebdomadaire [biɛbdɔmadɛʀ] **adj** twice-weekly.

bijection [biʒɛksjɔ̃] **nf** bijection.

bijou, pl ~x [biʒu] **nm** jewel; (*chef-d'œuvre*) gem. **les ~x d'une femme** a woman's jewels *ou* jewellery; **un ~ de précision** a marvel of precision; (*terme d'affection*) **mon ~** my love, pet; (*fig, hum*) **~x de famille**⁑ wedding tackle⁑ (*Brit*), family jewels⁑ (*US*).

bijouterie [biʒutʀi] **nf** (*boutique*) jeweller's (shop); (*commerce*) jewellery business *ou* trade; (*art*) jewellery-making; (*bijoux*) jewellery.

bijoutier, -ière [biʒutje, jɛʀ] **nm,f** jeweller.

bikini [bikini] **nm** ® bikini.

bilabial, e, mpl -iaux [bilabjal, jo] (*Ling*) 1 **adj** bilabial. 2 **bilabiale nf** bilabial.

bilame [bilam] **nm** (*Phys*) bimetallic strip.

bilan [bilɑ̃] **nm** a (*évaluation*) appraisal, assessment; (*résultats*) results; (*conséquences*) consequences. **le ~ d'une catastrophe** the final toll of a disaster; **faire le ~ d'une situation** to take stock of *ou* assess a situation; **quand on arrive à 50 ans on fait le ~** when you reach 50 you take stock (of your life); **"camion fou sur l'autoroute, ~: 3 morts"** "runaway lorry on motorway: 3 dead"; (*Méd*) **~ de santé** (medical) checkup; **se faire faire un ~ de santé** to go for *ou* have a checkup; (*fig*) **faire le ~ de santé de l'économie/d'une entreprise** to assess the current state of the economy/a company.

b (*Fin*) balance sheet, statement of accounts. **dresser** *ou* **établir son ~** to draw up the balance sheet; **~ de liquidation** statement of affairs (*in a bankruptcy petition*).

bilatéral, e, mpl -aux [bilateʀal, o] **adj** bilateral. **stationnement ~** parking on both sides (of the road).

bilboquet [bilbɔkɛ] **nm** ≃ cup-and-ball game.

bile [bil] **nf** (*Anat, fig: amertume*) bile. (*fig*) **se faire de la ~ (pour)** to get worried (about), worry o.s. sick (about)*; *voir* **échauffer**.

biler (se)* [bile] [1] **vpr** (*gén nég*) to worry o.s. sick* (*pour* about). **ne vous bilez pas!** don't get all worked up!* *ou* het up!*, don't get yourself all worried!; **il ne se bile pas** he takes it nice and easy*.

bileux, -euse* [bilø, øz] **adj** easily upset *ou* worried. **il n'est pas ~!, ce n'est pas un ~!** he's not one to worry *ou* to let things bother him, he doesn't let things bother him; **quel ~ tu fais!** what a fretter* *ou* worrier you are!

biliaire [biljɛʀ] **adj** biliary; *voir* **calcul, vésicule**.

bilieux, -euse [biljø, øz] **adj** *teint* bilious, yellowish; *personne, tempérament* irritable, testy, irascible.

bilingue [bilɛ̃g] **adj** bilingual.

bilinguisme [bilɛ̃gɥism] **nm** bilingualism.

billard [bijaʀ] 1 **nm** a (*jeu*) billiards (*sg*); (*table*) billiard table; (*salle*) billiard room. **boule de ~** billiard ball; **faire un ~** *ou* **une partie de ~** to play (a game of) billiards. b (* *loc*) **passer sur le ~** to be operated on, have an operation; **c'est du ~** it's quite *ou* dead* (*Brit*) easy, it's a piece of cake* (*Brit*) *ou* a cinch*; **cette route est un vrai ~** this road is like a billiard table. 2 **comp ▸billard américain** pool **▸billard électrique** pinball machine **▸billard français** French billiards **▸billard japonais** (*partie*) (game of) pinball; (*table*) pinball machine **▸billard russe** bar billiards.

bille [bij] **nf** a (*boule*) *[enfant]* marble; *[billard]* (billiard) ball. **jouer aux ~s** to play marbles, have a game of marbles; **déodorant à ~** roll-on deodorant; (*fig*) **il a attaqué** *ou* **foncé ~ en tête*** he didn't beat about the bush*; (*fig*) **reprendre** *ou* **récupérer** *ou* **retirer ses ~s** to pull out; (*fig*) **il a su placer ses ~s*** he made all the right moves; **toucher sa ~ au tennis/en maths*** to know a thing or two about tennis/maths. b **~ de bois** billet, block of wood. c (*: *visage*) mug⁑, face. **il a fait une drôle de ~!** you should have seen his face!; **~ de clown** funny face; **il a une bonne ~** he's got a jolly face.

billet [bijɛ] 1 **nm** a ticket. **~ de quai/train/loterie** platform/train/lottery ticket; **~ circulaire/collectif** round-trip/group ticket; **est-ce que tu as ton ~ de retour?** have you got your return (*Brit*) *ou* round-trip (*US*) ticket?; **prendre un ~ aller/aller-retour** to take a single (*Brit*) *ou* one-way (*US*)/return (*Brit*) *ou* round-trip (*US*) ticket.

b (*argent*) note, bill (*US*). **~ de 10 francs** 10-franc note; **ça coûte 500 ~s*** it costs 500 francs; *voir* **faux**[2].

c (*littér ou †: lettre*) note, short letter.

d (*loc*) **je te fiche** *ou* **flanque mon ~ qu'il ne viendra pas!**⁑ I bet you my bottom dollar* *ou* a pound to a penny* (*Brit*) *ou* a dollar to a doughnut* (*US*) he won't come.

2 **comp ▸billet de banque** banknote **▸billet de commerce** promissory note **▸billet doux** billet doux, love letter **▸billet de faveur** complimentary ticket **▸billet de logement** (*Mil*) billet **▸billet à ordre** promissory note, bill of exchange **▸billet de parterre***†: **prendre** *ou* **ramasser un billet de parterre** to come a cropper*, fall flat on one's face **▸billet au porteur** bearer order **▸billet de retard** (*Scol*) late slip (*Brit*), tardy slip (*US*); (*Admin*) *note from public transport authorities attesting late running of train etc* **▸le billet vert** the dollar.

billetterie [bijɛtʀi] **nf** (*Banque*) cash dispenser, automatic teller machine (*US*).

billevesées [bijvəze] **nfpl** (*littér: sornettes*) nonsense (*NonC*).

billion [biljɔ̃] **nm** (*million de millions*) billion (*Brit*), trillion (*US*); (†: *milliard*) thousand million, milliard (*Brit*), billion (*US*).

billot [bijo] **nm** *[boucher, bourreau, cordonnier]* block; (*Can*) log (of wood). (*fig*) **j'en mettrais ma tête sur le ~** I'd stake my life on it.

bilobé, e [bilɔbe] **adj** bilobed.

bimbeloterie [bɛ̃blɔtʀi] **nf** (*objets*) knick-knacks, fancy goods (*Brit*); (*commerce*) knick-knack *ou* fancy goods (*Brit*) business.

bimbelotier, -ière [bɛ̃blɔtje, jɛʀ] nm,f (*fabricant*) fancy goods manufacturer (*Brit*), gifts manufacturer (*US*); (*marchand*) fancy goods dealer (*Brit*), gift store owner (*US*).
bimensuel, -elle [bimɑ̃sɥɛl] 1 adj fortnightly (*Brit*), twice monthly, bimonthly. 2 nm (*revue*) fortnightly review (*Brit*), semimonthly (*US*).
bimensuellement [bimɑ̃sɥɛlmɑ̃] adv fortnightly (*Brit*), twice a month.
bimestriel, -elle [bimɛstʀijɛl] adj: **revue ~elle** bimonthly review, review which appears six times a year.
bimétallique [bimetalik] adj bimetallic.
bimétallisme [bimetalism] nm bimetallism.
bimoteur [bimɔtœʀ] 1 adj twin-engined. 2 nm twin-engined plane.
binage [binaʒ] nm hoeing, harrowing.
binaire [binɛʀ] adj binary.
biner [bine] 1 vt to hoe, harrow.
binette [binɛt] nf a (*Agr*) hoe. b (*: *visage*) face, dial‡.
bing [biŋ] excl smack!, thwack!
bingo [biŋgo] nm (*Can*) (*jeu*) ≃ bingo (*using letters as well as numbers*); (*partie*) ≃ game of bingo.
biniou [binju] nm (*Mus*) (Breton) bagpipes. (*: *téléphone*) **donner un coup de ~ à qn** to give sb a buzz* *ou* a ring.
binoclard, e* [binɔklaʀ, aʀd] adj, nm,f: **il est ~, c'est un ~** he wears specs*.
binocle [binɔkl] nm pince-nez.
binoculaire [binɔkylɛʀ] adj binocular.
binôme [binom] nm binomial.
biochimie [bjoʃimi] nf biochemistry.
biochimique [bjoʃimik] adj biochemical.
biochimiste [bjoʃimist] nmf biochemist.
biodégradable [bjodegʀadabl] adj biodegradable.
bioénergétique [bjoenɛʀʒetik] adj bioenergetic.
bioénergie [bjoenɛʀʒi] nf bioenergy.
bioéthique [bjoetik] nf bioethics (*sg*).
biographe [bjɔgʀaf] nmf biographer.
biographie [bjɔgʀafi] nf biography. **~ romancée** biographical novel.
biographique [bjɔgʀafik] adj biographical.
biologie [bjɔlɔʒi] nf biology.
biologique [bjɔlɔʒik] adj biological; *produits, aliments* natural, organic.
biologiste [bjɔlɔʒist] nmf biologist.
biomasse [bjomas] nf biomass.
bionique [bjɔnik] 1 nf bionics (*sg*). 2 adj bionic.
biophysique [bjofizik] nf biophysics (*sg*).
biopsie [bjɔpsi] nf biopsy.
biorythme [bjoʀitm] nm biorhythm.
biosphère [bjɔsfɛʀ] nf biosphere.
biosynthèse [bjosɛ̃tɛz] nf biosynthesis.
bioxyde [b(j)ɔksid] nm dioxide.
bip [bip] nm a (*son*) (*court*) b(l)eep; (*continu*) b(l)eeping. **faire ~** to b(l)eep; **parlez après le ~ sonore** speak after the tone *ou* beep. b (*appareil*) bleep(er), beeper.
bipale [bipal] adj twin-bladed.
biparti, e [bipaʀti] adj, **bipartite** [bipaʀtit] adj (*Bot*) bipartite; (*Pol*) two-party, bipartite, bipartisan.
bipartisme [bipaʀtism] nm (*Pol*) bipartisanship.
bipasse [bipas] nm = **by-pass.**
bip-bip, pl **bips-bips** [bipbip] nm = **bip b.**
bipède [bipɛd] adj, nm biped.
biper [bipe] 1 vt to page.
biphasé, e [bifɑze] adj diphase, two-phase.
biplace [biplas] adj, nm two-seater.
biplan [biplɑ̃] 1 adj: **avion ~** biplane. 2 nm biplane.
bipolaire [bipɔlɛʀ] adj bipolar.
bipolarité [bipɔlaʀite] nf bipolarity.
bique [bik] nf nanny-goat. (*péj*) **vieille ~** old hag, old trout* (*Brit*), old witch*.
biquet, -ette [bikɛ, ɛt] nm,f (*Zool*) kid. (*terme d'affection*) **mon ~** love, ducky* (*Brit*).
biquotidien, -ienne [bikɔtidjɛ̃, jɛn] adj twice-daily.
birbe [biʀb] nm (*péj*) **vieux ~** old fuddy-duddy‡, old fogey*.
BIRD [biʀd] nf (abrév de **Banque internationale pour la reconstruction et le développement**) IBRD.
biréacteur [biʀeaktœʀ] nm twin-engined jet.
biréfringence [biʀefʀɛ̃ʒɑ̃s] nf birefringence.
biréfringent, e [biʀefʀɛ̃ʒɑ̃, ɑ̃t] adj birefringent.
birème [biʀɛm] nf (*Antiq*) bireme.
birman, e [biʀmɑ̃, an] 1 adj Burmese. 2 nm (*Ling*) Burmese. 3 nm,f: **B~(e)** Burmese.
Birmanie [biʀmani] nf Burma.
biroute‡ [biʀut] nf willy‡ (*Brit*), wang‡ (*US*).
bis¹ [bis] 1 adv (*Mus: sur partition*) repeat, twice. **~!** (*Théât*) encore!; (*numéro*) **12 ~** 12a; *voir* **itinéraire.** 2 nm (*Théât*) encore.
bis², e¹ [bi, biz] adj greyish-brown, brownish-grey; *voir* **pain.**
bisaïeul [bizajœl] nm great-grandfather.
bisaïeule [bizajœl] nf great-grandmother.
bisannuel, -elle [bizanɥɛl] adj biennial.
bisbille* [bisbij] nf squabble, tiff. **être en ~ avec qn** to be at loggerheads *ou* at odds with sb.
biscornu, e [biskɔʀny] adj *forme* irregular, crooked; *maison* crooked, oddly shaped; *idée, esprit* cranky, peculiar; *raisonnement* tortuous, cranky. **un chapeau ~** a shapeless hat.
biscoteaux* [biskɔto] nmpl biceps. **avoir des ~** to have a good pair of biceps.
biscotte [biskɔt] nf rusk (*Brit*), melba toast (*US*).
biscuit [biskɥi] 1 nm a (*Culin*) sponge cake. **~ (sec)** biscuit (*Brit*), cookie (*US*); **~ salé** cheese biscuit (*Brit*), cracker (*US*). b (*céramique*) biscuit, bisque. 2 comp ▸**biscuit pour chien** dog biscuit ▸**biscuit à la cuiller** sponge finger (*Brit*), lady finger (*US*) ▸**biscuit de Savoie** sponge cake.
biscuiterie [biskɥitʀi] nf (*usine*) biscuit (*Brit*) *ou* cookie (*US*) factory; (*commerce*) biscuit (*Brit*) *ou* cookie (*US*) trade.
bise² [biz] nf North wind.
bise³ [biz] nf kiss. **faire une** *ou* **la ~ à qn** to kiss sb, give sb a kiss; **il lui a fait une petite ~** he gave her a quick peck* *ou* kiss; (*sur lettre*) **grosses ~s** love and kisses (*de* from).
biseau, pl **~x** [bizo] nm (*bord*) *[glace, vitre]* bevel, bevelled edge; (*Menuiserie*) chamfer, chamfered edge; (*outil*) bevel. **en ~** bevelled, with a bevelled edge; chamfered, with a chamfered edge.
biseautage [bizotaʒ] nm (*voir* **biseau**) bevelling; chamfering.
biseauter [bizote] 1 vt *glace, vitre* to bevel; (*Menuiserie*) to chamfer; *cartes* to mark.
bisexualité [bisɛksɥalite] nf bisexuality, bisexualism.
bisexué, e [bisɛksɥe] adj bisexual.
bisexuel, elle [bisɛksɥɛl] 1 adj bisexual. 2 nm,f bisexual.
bismuth [bismyt] nm bismuth.
bison [bizɔ̃] nm bison, American buffalo.
bisou* [bizu] nm kiss. **faire un ~ à qn** to give sb a kiss; **faire un petit ~ à qn** to give sb a peck* *ou* kiss; (*sur lettre*) **gros ~s** love and kisses (*de* from).
bisque [bisk] nf (*Culin*) bisk, bisque. **~ de homard** lobster soup, bisque of lobster.
bisquer* [biske] 1 vi to be riled* *ou* nettled. **faire ~ qn** to rile* *ou* nettle sb.
Bissau [bisao] n Bissau.
bissecteur, -trice [bisɛktœʀ, tʀis] 1 adj bisecting. 2 **bissectrice** nf bisector, bisecting line.
bisser [bise] 1 vt (*faire rejouer*) *acteur, chanson* to encore; (*rejouer*) *morceau* to play again, sing again.
bissextile [bisɛkstil] adj f *voir* **année.**
bissexué, e [bisɛksɥe] adj = **bisexué.**
bissexuel, elle [bisɛksɥɛl] adj, nm,f = **bisexuel, elle.**
bistable [bistabl] adj (*Ordin*) bistable.
bistouri [bistuʀi] nm bistoury (SPÉC), scalpel.
bistre [bistʀ] 1 adj *couleur* blackish-brown, bistre; *objet* bistre-coloured, blackish-brown; *peau, teint* swarthy. 2 nm bistre.
bistré, e [bistʀe] (ptp de **bistrer**) adj *teint* tanned, swarthy.
bistrer [bistʀe] 1 vt *objet* to colour with bistre; *peau* to tan.
bistro(t) [bistʀo] nm a (*: *café*) ≃ pub (*Brit*), bar (*US*), café. b (†: *cafetier*) ≃ publican (*Brit*), bartender (*US*), café owner.
bit [bit] nm (*Ordin*) bit.
B.I.T. [beite] nm (abrév de **Bureau international du travail**) ILO.
bite** [bit] nf = **bitte b.**
bitoniau* [bitɔnjo] nm whatsit*.
bitos* [bitos] nm hat, headgear* (*NonC*).
bitte [bit] nf a *[navire]* bitt. **~ (d'amarrage)** *[quai]* mooring post, bollard. b (**) prick**, cock**, dick**.
bitterois, e [bitɛʀwa, waz] 1 adj of *ou* from Béziers. 2 nm,f: **B~(e)** inhabitant *ou* native of Béziers.
bitture‡ [bityʀ] nf = **biture‡.**
bitumage [bitymaʒ] nm asphalting.
bitume [bitym] nm (*Chim, Min*) bitumen; (*revêtement*) asphalt, Tarmac ®.
bitumé, e [bityme] (ptp de **bitumer**) adj *route* asphalted, asphalt, tarmac (*épith*); *carton* bitumized.
bitum(in)er [bitym(in)e] 1 vt to asphalt, tarmac.
bitum(in)eux, -euse [bitym(in)ø, øz] adj bituminous.
biture‡ [bityʀ] nf: **prendre une ~** to get drunk *ou* canned‡ *ou* plastered‡; **il tient une de ces ~s** he's plastered‡, he's blind drunk*.
biturer (se)‡ [bityʀe] 1 vpr to get drunk *ou* canned‡ *ou* plastered‡.
biunivoque [biynivɔk] adj (*fig*) one-to-one; (*Math*) *voir* **correspondance.**
bivalent, e [bivalɑ̃, ɑ̃t] adj bivalent.
bivalve [bivalv] adj, nm bivalve.
bivouac [bivwak] nm bivouac.
bivouaquer [bivwake] 1 vi to bivouac.
bizarre [bizaʀ] 1 adj *personne, conduite* strange, odd, peculiar, freaky*; *idée, raisonnement, temps* odd, queer, strange, funny*; *vêtement* strange *ou* funny(-looking). **tiens, c'est ~** that's odd *ou* queer *ou* funny*. 2 nm: **le ~** the bizarre; **le ~ dans tout cela ...** what is strange *ou* odd *ou* queer *ou* peculiar about all that ..., the strange *ou*

odd part about it all ... .

bizarrement [bizaʀmɑ̃] adv strangely, oddly, peculiarly, queerly.

bizarrerie [bizaʀʀi] nf *[personne]* odd *ou* strange *ou* peculiar ways; *[idée]* strangeness, oddness, queerness; *[situation, humeur]* queer *ou* strange *ou* odd nature. ~s *[langue, règlement]* peculiarities, oddities, vagaries.

bizarroïde [bizaʀɔid] adj odd.

bizut [bizy] nm (*arg Scol*) fresher (*Brit*), freshman, first-year student *ou* scholar.

bizutage [bizytaʒ] nm (*arg Scol*) ragging (*Brit*), hazing (*US*) (*of new student etc*).

bizuter [bizyte] 1 vt (*arg Scol*) to rag (*Brit*), haze (*US*) (*new student etc*).

bizuth [bizy] nm = **bizut**.

BK [beka] nm (abrév de **bacille de Koch**) tubercle bacillus.

blablabla* [blablabla] nm blah*, claptrap*, waffle* (*Brit*).

blablater* [blablate] 1 vi to blabber on*, waffle on* (*Brit*).

blackboulage [blakbulaʒ] nm blackballing.

blackbouler [blakbule] 1 vt (*à une élection*) to blackball; (*: *à un examen*) to fail.

black-out [blakaut] nm (*Élec, Mil, fig*) blackout. (*fig*) **faire le ~ sur qch** to impose a (news) blackout on sth.

blafard, e [blafaʀ, aʀd] adj *teint* pale, pallid, wan; *couleur, lumière, soleil* wan, pale. **l'aube ~e** the pale light of dawn.

blague [blag] nf a (*) (*histoire, plaisanterie*) joke; (*farce*) practical joke, trick. **faire une ~ à qn** to play a trick *ou* a joke on sb; **sans ~?** really?, you're kidding!‡, you don't say!*; **sans ~, ~ à part** seriously, joking apart, kidding aside* (*US*); **il prend tout à la ~** he can never take anything seriously; **ne me raconte pas de ~s!** stop having (*Brit*) *ou* putting (*US*) me on!* *ou* kidding me!‡, pull the other one!‡; **c'est de la ~ tout ça!** it's all talk, it's all bull‡.
b (*: *erreur*) silly thing, blunder, stupid mistake. **faire une ~** to make a blunder *ou* a stupid mistake; **faire des ~s** to do silly *ou* stupid things; **attention, pas de ~s!** be careful, no messing about!*
c **~ (à tabac)** (tobacco) pouch.

blaguer* [blage] 1 1 vi to be joking *ou* kidding‡ (*sur* about). **j'ai dit cela pour ~** I said it for a lark* (*Brit*) *ou* joke (*US*); **on ne blague pas avec ça** you shouldn't joke about that, that's not something to joke about. 2 vt to tease, make fun of, kid‡, take the mickey out of‡ (*Brit*).

blagueur, -euse [blagœʀ, øz] 1 adj *sourire, air* ironical, teasing; *ton, manière* jokey*. **il est (très) ~** he is (really) good fun. 2 nm,f (*gén*) joker; (*farceur*) practical joker.

blair‡ [blɛʀ] nm nose, hooter‡ (*Brit*), beak‡.

blaireau, pl **~x** [blɛʀo] nm a (*Zool*) badger. b (*pour barbe*) shaving brush.

blairer‡ [bleʀe] 1 vt: **je ne peux pas le ~** he gives me the creeps‡, I can't stand *ou* bear him.

blâmable [blɑmabl] adj blameful.

blâme [blɑm] nm a (*désapprobation*) blame; (*réprimande*) reprimand, rebuke. b (*punition: Admin, Sport*) reprimand. **donner un ~ à qn** to reprimand sb; **recevoir un ~** to be reprimanded, incur a reprimand.

blâmer [blɑme] 1 vt (*désavouer*) to blame; (*réprimander*) to reprimand, rebuke. **je ne te blâme pas de** *ou* **pour l'avoir fait** I don't blame you for having done it.

blanc, blanche [blɑ̃, blɑ̃ʃ] 1 adj a (*de couleur blanche*) white. **il était ~ à 30 ans** he had white hair at 30; **ils sont rentrés de vacances ~s comme ils sont partis** they came back from holiday as pale as when they left; **elle avait honte de ses jambes blanches** she was ashamed of her lily-white (*hum*) *ou* pale legs; **~ de colère/de peur** white with anger/fear; **~ comme neige** (as) white as snow, snow-white; **~ comme un cachet d'aspirine** white as a sheet; **il devint ~ comme un linge** he went *ou* turned as white as a sheet; *voir* **arme, bois, bonnet**.
b *page, bulletin de vote* blank; *papier non quadrillé* unlined, plain. (*Scol*) **il a rendu copie blanche** *ou* **sa feuille blanche** he handed in a blank paper; **prenez une feuille blanche** take a clean *ou* blank piece of paper; *voir* **carte, examen**.
c (*innocent*) pure, innocent. **~ comme neige** *ou* **comme la blanche hermine** as pure as the driven snow.
d (*de la race blanche*) *domination, justice* white. **l'Afrique blanche** white Africa.
2 nm a (*couleur*) white. **peindre qch en ~** to paint sth white; **le ~ de sa robe tranchait sur sa peau brune** her white dress *ou* the white of her dress contrasted sharply with her dark skin; *voir* **but**.
b (*linge*) **laver séparément le ~ et la couleur** to wash whites and coloureds separately; **vente de ~** white sale, sale of household linen; **magasin de ~** linen shop; **la quinzaine du ~** (annual) sale of household linen, (annual) white sale.
c (*cosmétique*) **elle se met du ~** she wears white powder.
d (*espace non écrit*) blank, space; *[bande magnétique]* blank; *[domino]* blank. **laisser un ~** to leave a blank *ou* space; **il faut laisser le nom en ~** the name must be left blank *ou* must not be filled in; *voir* **chèque, signer**.
e (*vin*) white wine.
f (*Culin*) **~ (d'œuf)** (egg) white; **~ (de poulet)** white (meat), breast of chicken; **elle n'aime pas le ~** she doesn't like the white (meat) *ou* the breast.
g **le ~ (de l'œil)** the white (of the eye); *voir* **regarder, rougir**.
h (*homme blanc*) **un B~** a White, a white man; **les B~s** the Whites, white men.
i (*loc*) **à ~** *charger* with blanks; **tirer à ~** to fire blanks; **cartouche à ~** blank (cartridge); *voir* **chauffer, saigner**.
3 **blanche** nf a (*femme*) **une Blanche** a white woman.
b (*Mus*) minim (*Brit*), half-note (*US*).
c (*Billard*) white (ball).
d (*arg Drogue*) horse (*arg*), smack (*arg*).
4 comp ▸**blanc de baleine** spermaceti ▸**blanc bec*** greenhorn*, tenderfoot* ▸**blanc de blanc(s)** blanc de blanc(s) ▸**blanc cassé** off-white ▸**blanc-cassis** nm (pl **blancs-cassis**) (apéritif of) white wine and blackcurrant liqueur ▸**blanc de céruse** white lead ▸**blanc de chaux** whitewash ▸**blanc d'Espagne** whiting, whitening ▸**blanc-manger** (*Culin*) nm (pl **blancs-mangers**) blancmange ▸**Blanche-Neige (et les Sept Nains)** Snow White (and the Seven Dwarfs) ▸**blanc seing** (*lit*) signature to a blank document; (*fig*) **donner un blanc seing à qn** to give sb a free rein *ou* free hand ▸**blanc de zinc** zinc oxide.

blanchâtre [blɑ̃ʃɑtʀ] adj whitish, off-white.

blanche [blɑ̃ʃ] *voir* **blanc**.

blancheur [blɑ̃ʃœʀ] nf whiteness.

blanchiment [blɑ̃ʃimɑ̃] nm (*décoloration*) bleaching; (*badigeonnage*) whitewashing; *[argent]* laundering.

blanchir [blɑ̃ʃiʀ] 2 1 vt a (*gén*) to whiten, lighten; *mur* to whitewash; *cheveux* to turn grey *ou* white; *toile* to bleach. **le soleil blanchit l'horizon** the sun is lighting up the horizon; **la neige blanchit les collines** the snow is turning the hills white; **~ à la chaux** to whitewash.
b (*nettoyer*) *linge*, (*fig*) *argent* to launder. **il est logé, nourri et blanchi** he gets bed and board and his washing *ou* his laundry is done for him.
c (*disculper*) *personne* to exonerate, absolve, clear; *réputation* to clear. **il en est sorti blanchi** he cleared his name.
d **(faire) ~** (*Culin*) *légume* to blanch; (*Agr*) to blanch.
2 vi *[personne, cheveux]* to turn *ou* go grey *ou* white; *[couleur, horizon]* to become lighter. **son teint a blanchi** he is looking *ou* has got paler, he has lost colour; **~ de peur** to blanch *ou* blench *ou* go white with fear.
3 **se blanchir** vpr to exonerate o.s. (*de* from), clear one's name.

blanchissage [blɑ̃ʃisaʒ] nm *[linge]* laundering; *[sucre]* refining. **donner du linge au ~** to send linen to the laundry; **note de ~** laundry bill.

blanchissement [blɑ̃ʃismɑ̃] nm whitening. **ce shampooing retarde le ~ des cheveux** this shampoo stops your hair going grey *ou* white.

blanchisserie [blɑ̃ʃisʀi] nf laundry.

blanchisseur [blɑ̃ʃisœʀ] nm launderer.

blanchisseuse [blɑ̃ʃisøz] nf laundress.

blanquette [blɑ̃kɛt] nf a (*Culin*) **~ de veau/d'agneau** blanquette of veal/of lamb, veal/lamb in white sauce. b (*vin*) sparkling white wine.

blase‡ [blɑʒ] nm = **blaze**.

blasé, e [blɑze] (ptp de **blaser**) 1 adj blasé. 2 nm,f blasé person. **faire le ~** to affect a blasé indifference to everything.

blaser [blɑze] 1 1 vt to make blasé *ou* indifferent. **être blasé de** to be bored with *ou* tired of. 2 **se blaser** vpr to become bored (*de* with), become tired (*de* of), become blasé (*de* about).

blason [blɑzɔ̃] nm a (*armoiries*) coat of arms, blazon; *voir* **redorer**. b (*science*) heraldry. c (*Littérat: poème*) blazon.

blasphémateur, -trice [blasfematœʀ, tʀis] 1 adj *personne* blaspheming, blasphemous. 2 nm,f blasphemer.

blasphématoire [blasfematwaʀ] adj *parole* blasphemous.

blasphème [blasfɛm] nm blasphemy.

blasphémer [blasfeme] 6 vti to blaspheme.

blatte [blat] nf cockroach.

blaze‡ [blɑʒ] nm (*nez*) beak‡, hooter‡ (*Brit*), conk‡ (*Brit*); (*nom*) name.

blazer [blazɛʀ] nm blazer.

blé [ble] nm wheat, corn (*Brit*); (‡: *argent*) dough‡, lolly‡. **le ~ en herbe** (*Agr*) corn on the blade; (*fig*) young shoots, young bloods; **~ dur** hard wheat, durum wheat; **~ noir** buckwheat; (*Can*) **~ d'Inde*** maize, (Indian) corn (*US, Can*); *voir* **blond, fauché**.

bled [blɛd] nm a (*) village; (*péj*) hole*, godforsaken place*, dump‡. **c'est un ~ perdu** *ou* **paumé** it's a godforsaken place* *ou* hole* (in the middle of nowhere). b (*Afrique du Nord*) **le ~** the interior (of North Africa). (*fig*) **habiter dans le ~*** to live in the middle of nowhere *ou* at the back of beyond.

blême [blɛm] adj *teint* pallid, deathly pale, wan; *lumière* pale, wan. **~ de rage/de colère** livid *ou* white with rage/anger.

blêmir [blemiʀ] 2 vi *[personne]* to turn *ou* go pale, pale; *[lumière]* to grow pale. **~ de colère** to go livid *ou* white with anger.

blêmissement [blemismɑ̃] nm *[teint, lumière]* paling.

blende [blɛ̃d] nf blende.

blennie [bleni] nf (*Zool*) blenny.

blennorragie [blenɔʀaʒi] nf blennorrhoea, gonorrhoea.

blèsement [blɛzmɑ̃] nm lisping.

bléser [bleze] 6 vi to lisp.

blessant, e [blesɑ̃, ɑ̃t] adj (*offensant*) cutting, biting, hurtful.

blessé, e [blese] (ptp de **blesser**) 1 adj (*voir* **blesser**) hurt, injured; wounded; (*offensé*) hurt, upset. **être ~ à la tête/au bras** to have a head/an arm injury *ou* wound.
2 nm wounded *ou* injured man, casualty; (*Mil*) wounded soldier, casualty. **les ~s** (*gén*) the injured; (*Mil*) the wounded; **l'accident a fait 10 ~s** 10 people were injured *ou* hurt in the accident.
3 **blessée** nf wounded *ou* injured woman, casualty.
4 comp ▶**blessé grave** seriously *ou* severely injured *ou* wounded person ▶**blessé de guerre** person who was wounded in the war; **les blessés de guerre** the war wounded ▶**blessé léger** slightly injured person ▶**blessés de la route** road casualties, people *ou* persons injured in road accidents.

blesser [blese] 1 vt a (*gén, accidentellement*) to hurt, injure; (*Mil, dans une aggression*) to wound. **il a été blessé d'un coup de couteau** he received a knife wound, he was stabbed (with a knife); **être blessé dans un accident de voiture** to be injured in a car accident; **il s'est blessé en tombant** he fell and injured himself; **il s'est blessé (à) la jambe** he has injured *ou* hurt his leg.
b *[ceinture, soulier]* to hurt; (*fig*) to offend. **ses souliers lui blessent le talon** his shoes hurt his heel *ou* make his heel sore; **sons qui blessent l'oreille** sounds which offend the ear *ou* grate on the ear; **couleurs qui blessent la vue** colours which offend *ou* shock the eye.
c (*offenser*) to hurt (the feelings of), upset, wound. **~ qn au vif** to cut sb to the quick; **il s'est senti blessé dans son orgueil** his pride was hurt, he felt wounded in his pride; **des paroles qui blessent** cutting words, wounding *ou* cutting remarks; **il se blesse pour un rien** he's easily hurt *ou* offended, he's quick to take offence.
d (*littér: porter préjudice à*) *règles, convenances* to offend against; *intérêts* to go against, harm. **cela blesse son sens de la justice** that offends his sense of justice.

blessure [blesyʀ] nf (*accidentelle*) injury; (*intentionnelle, morale*) wound. **quelle ~ d'amour-propre pour lui!** what a blow to his pride!; *voir* **coup**.

blet, blette[1] [blɛ, blɛt] adj *fruit* overripe, soft.

blette[2] [blɛt] nf = **bette**.

blettir [bletiʀ] 2 vi to become overripe *ou* soft.

blettissement [bletismɑ̃] nm overripeness.

bleu, e [blø] 1 adj *couleur* blue; *steak* very rare, underdone. **~ de froid** blue with cold; **être ~ de colère** to be livid *ou* purple with rage; *voir* **enfant, fleur, peur**.
2 nm a (*couleur*) blue. (*fig*) **il n'y a vu que du ~** he didn't twig* (*Brit*), he didn't smell a rat*; **regarde le ~ de ce ciel** look at the blueness of that sky, look how blue the sky is.
b **~ (de lessive)** (dolly) blue; **passer le linge au ~** to blue the laundry.
c (*marque sur la peau*) bruise. **être couvert de ~s** to be covered in bruises, be black and blue*; **se faire un ~ au genou/bras**to bruise one's knee/arm.
d (*vêtement*) **~(s) (de travail)** dungarees, overalls; **~ (de chauffe)** boiler suit (*Brit*), overalls.
e (*arg Mil: recrue*) rookie (*arg*), new *ou* raw recruit; (*gén: débutant*) beginner, greenhorn*. **tu me prends pour un ~?** do you think I was born yesterday?*
f (*fromage*) blue(-veined) cheese.
g (*Culin*) **truite au ~** trout au bleu.
h (*Can*) **les B~s** the Conservatives.
3 comp ▶**bleu ardoise** slaty *ou* slate blue ▶**bleu canard** peacock blue ▶**bleu ciel** sky blue ▶**bleu de cobalt** cobalt blue ▶**bleu horizon** skyblue ▶**bleu lavande** lavender blue ▶**bleu marine** navy blue ▶**bleu de méthylène** (*Méd*) methylene blue ▶**bleu noir** blue-black ▶**bleu nuit** midnight blue ▶**bleu outremer** ultramarine ▶**bleu pétrole** dark greenish-blue ▶**bleu de Prusse** Prussian blue ▶**bleu roi** royal blue ▶**bleu turquoise** turquoise blue ▶**bleu vert** blue-green.

bleuâtre [bløɑtʀ] adj bluish.

bleuet [bløɛ] nm cornflower; (*Can*) blueberry.

bleuetière [bløɛtjɛʀ] nf (*Can*) blueberry grove.

bleuir [bløiʀ] 2 vti to turn blue.

bleuissement [bløismɑ̃] nm turning blue.

bleuté, e [bløte] adj *reflet* bluish; *verre* blue-tinted.

bleusaille [bløzaj] nf (*arg Mil*) (*recrue*) rookie (*arg*), new *ou* raw recruit; (*collectivement*) **la ~** the rookies (*arg*).

blindage [blɛ̃daʒ] nm (*voir* **blinder**) armour plating; screening; timbering, shoring up.

blindé, e [blɛ̃de] (ptp de **blinder**) 1 adj a (*Mil*) *division* armoured; *engin, train* armoured, armour-plated; *abri* bombproof; *porte* reinforced. b (*: *endurci*) immune, hardened (*contre* to). **il a essayé de me faire peur mais je suis ~** he tried to frighten me but I'm too thickskinned*. c (‡: *ivre*) stewed‡, canned‡, plastered‡. 2 nm (*Mil*) tank. **~ léger de campagne** combat car; **~ de transport de troupes** armoured personnel carrier; **les ~s** the armour.

blinder [blɛ̃de] 1 vt a (*Mil*) to armour, put armour plating on; (*Élec*) to screen; (*Constr*) to shore up, timber. b (*: *endurcir*) to harden, make immune (*contre* to). c (‡: *soûler*) to make *ou* get drunk *ou* plastered‡ *ou* canned‡.

blinis [blinis] nm blin.

blizzard [blizaʀ] nm blizzard.

bloc [blɔk] 1 nm a *[pierre, marbre, bois]* block. **table faite d'un seul ~** table made from one piece.
b (*papeterie*) pad. **~ de bureau** office notepad, desk pad; **~ de papier à lettres** writing pad.
c (*système d'éléments*) unit; (*Ordin*) block. **ces éléments forment (un) ~** these elements make up a unit.
d (*groupe, union*) group; (*Pol*) bloc. **ces entreprises forment un ~** these companies make up a group; (*Pol*) **le ~ communiste/des pays capitalistes** the communist/capitalist bloc; (*Pol*) **pays divisé en deux ~s adverses** country split into two opposing blocks *ou* factions; (*Fin*) **~ monétaire** monetary bloc.
e (*Bourse*) *[actions]* block. **achat/vente en ~** block purchase/sale; *voir aussi* **1g**.
f (‡: *prison*) **mettre qn au ~** to clap sb in clink‡ *ou* jug ‡; **j'ai eu 10 jours de ~** I got 10 days in clink‡ *ou* jug‡.
g (*loc*) **faire ~** to join forces, unite (*avec* with; *contre* against); **à ~: serrer *ou* visser qch à ~** to screw sth up as tight as possible *ou* as far as it will go; **fermer un robinet à ~** to turn a tap right *ou* hard off; **en ~: acheter/vendre qch en ~** to buy/sell sth as a whole; **il refuse en ~ tous mes arguments** he rejects all my arguments out of hand *ou* outright; **les pays du Marché commun ont condamné en ~ l'attitude des USA** the Common Market countries were united *ou* unanimous in their condemnation of the US attitude; **se retourner tout d'un ~** to swivel round; *voir* **freiner, gonflé**.
2 comp ▶**bloc-calendrier** nm (pl **blocs-calendriers**) tear-off calendar ▶**bloc-cuisine** nm (pl **blocs-cuisines**) kitchen unit ▶**bloc de culasse** breech-block ▶**bloc-cylindres** (*Aut*) nm (pl **blocs-cylindres**) cylinder block ▶**bloc de départ** (*Sport*) starting-block ▶**bloc-diagramme** (*Géog*) nm (pl **blocs-diagrammes**) block diagram ▶**bloc-évier** nm (pl **blocs-éviers**) sink unit ▶**bloc-moteur** (*Aut*) nm (pl **blocs-moteurs**) engine block ▶**bloc-notes** nm (pl **blocs-notes**) (*cahier*) desk pad, scratch pad; (*avec pince*) clipboard ▶**bloc opératoire** (*Méd*) operating theatre suite ▶**bloc optique** (*Aut*) headlamp assembly ▶**bloc sonore** (*Ciné*) sound unit ▶**bloc-système** (*Rail*) nm (pl **blocs-systèmes**) block system.

blocage [blɔkaʒ] nm a *[prix, salaires]* freeze, freezing; *[compte bancaire]* freezing. b (*Constr*) rubble. c (*Psych*) block. **avoir *ou* faire un ~** to have a mental block. d *[frein, roues]* locking; *[écrou]* overtightening. (*Ordin*) **~ de mémoire** memory block.

blockhaus [blɔkos] nm (*Mil*) blockhouse, pillbox.

blocus [blɔkys] nm blockade. (*Hist*) **le ~ continental** the Continental System; **lever/forcer le ~** to raise/run the blockade; **faire le ~ de** to blockade.

blond, blonde [blɔ̃, blɔ̃d] 1 adj *cheveux* fair, blond(e); *personne* fair, fair-haired, blond(e); *blé, sable* golden. **~ cendré** ash-blond; **~ roux** sandy, light auburn; **~ vénitien** strawberry blonde; **tabac ~** mild *ou* light *ou* Virginia tobacco; **bière ~e** ≃ lager, ≃ light ale (*Brit*), ≃ light beer (*US*); **il est ~ comme les blés** his hair is golden blond(e), he has golden blond(e) hair. 2 nm (*couleur*) blond, light gold; (*homme*) fair-haired man. 3 **blonde** nf (*bière*) ≃ lager, ≃ light ale (*Brit*), ≃ light beer (*US*); (*cigarette*) Virginia cigarette; (*femme*) blonde; (*Can* *) girl friend, sweetheart. **~e incendiaire** blonde bombshell (*hum*); **~e oxygénée** peroxide blonde.

blondasse [blɔ̃das] adj (*péj*) dull blond(e).

blondeur [blɔ̃dœʀ] nf (*littér*) *[cheveux]* fairness; *[blés]* gold.

blondin [blɔ̃dɛ̃] nm fair-haired child *ou* young man; (††: *élégant*) dandy.

blondine [blɔ̃din] nf fair-haired child *ou* young girl.

blondinet [blɔ̃dinɛ] nm light-haired boy.

blondinette [blɔ̃dinɛt] nf light-haired girl.

blondir [blɔ̃diʀ] 2 1 vi *[cheveux]* to go fairer; (*littér*) *[blés]* to turn golden; *[oignons]* to become transparent. **faire ~ des oignons** to fry onions lightly (until they are transparent). 2 vt *cheveux, poils* to bleach.

bloquer [blɔke] 1 1 vt a (*grouper*) to lump together, put *ou* group together, combine. **~ ses jours de congé** to lump one's days off together; **~ les notes en fin de volume** to put *ou* group all the notes together at the end of the book; (*Scol*) **des cours bloqués sur six semaines** a six-week modular course.
b (*immobiliser*) *machine* to jam; *écrou* to overtighten; *roue* (*accidentellement*) to lock; (*exprès*) to put a block under, chock; *porte* to jam, wedge. **~ les freins** to jam on the brakes; **~ qn contre un mur** to pin sb against a wall; **être bloqué par les glaces** to be stuck in the ice, be icebound; **être bloqué par un accident/la foule** to be held up by an accident/the crowd; **je suis bloqué chez moi** I'm stuck at home; **les négociations sont bloquées** the talks are blocked *ou* are at a standstill.
c (*obstruer*) to block (up); (*Mil*) to blockade. **route bloquée par la glace/la neige** icebound/snowbound road; **un camion bloque la route** a truck is blocking the road, the road is blocked by a truck; **des travaux bloquent la route** there are road works in *ou* blocking the way; **les enfants bloquent le passage** the children are standing in *ou* blocking the

way, the children are stopping me (*ou* us *etc*) getting past.
d (*Sport*) *ballon* to block; (*Billard*) *bille* to jam, wedge.
e *marchandises* to stop, hold up; *crédit, salaires* to freeze; *compte en banque* to stop, freeze.
f (*Psych*) **ça me bloque d'être devant un auditoire** I freeze if I have to speak in public; **quand on le critique, ça le bloque** when you criticize him, he just clams up*.
g (*: *Belgique*) *examen* to swot for* (*Brit*), cram for.
2 **se bloquer** vpr *[porte]* to jam, get stuck, stick; *[machine]* to jam; *[roue]* to lock; *[frein]* to jam, lock on; *[clé]* to get stuck; (*Psych*) to have a mental block. **devant un auditoire, il se bloque** in front of an audience he just freezes.

bloqueur [blɔkœʀ] nm (*Can Ftbl*) lineman.

blottir (se) [blɔtiʀ] [2] vpr to curl up, snuggle up, huddle up. **se ~ contre qn** to snuggle up to sb; **se ~ dans les bras de qn** to snuggle up in sb's arms; **blottis les uns contre les autres** curled up *ou* huddled up (close) against one another; **blotti parmi les arbres** nestling *ou* huddling among the trees.

blousant, e [bluzɑ̃, ɑ̃t] adj *robe, chemisier* loose-fitting (*and gathered at the waist*).

blouse [bluz] nf (*tablier*) overall; (*chemisier*) blouse, smock; *[médecin]* (white) coat; *[paysan]* smock; (*Billard*) pocket.

blouser¹ [bluze] [1] vi *[robe, chemisier]* to be loose-fitting (*and gathered at the waist*).

blouser²⁑ [bluze] [1] 1 vt to con⁑, trick, pull a fast one on⁑. **se faire ~** to be had* *ou* conned⁑. 2 **se blouser** vpr to make a mistake *ou* a blunder.

blouser³ [bluze] vt (*Billard*) to pot, pocket.

blouson [bluzɔ̃] nm windjammer, blouson-style jacket. **~ de laine** lumber jacket; **~ d'aviateur** bomber *ou* pilot jacket; **les ~s dorés†** rich delinquents; **~ noir†** ≃ teddy-boy, hell's angel (*US*).

blue-jean, pl **blue-jeans** [bludʒin] nm (pair of) jeans.

blues [bluz] nm inv (*Mus*) blues. **aimer le ~** to like (the) blues.

bluet [blyɛ] nm (*Can*) blueberry.

bluff* [blœf] nm bluff. **c'est du ~!** he's (*ou* they're *etc*) just bluffing!, he's (*ou* they're *etc*) just trying it on!⁑ (*Brit*).

bluffer* [blœfe] [1] 1 vi to bluff, try it on⁑ (*Brit*); (*Cartes*) to bluff. 2 vt to fool, have (*Brit*) *ou* put on⁑; (*Cartes*) to bluff.

bluffeur, -euse* [blœfœʀ, øz] nm,f bluffer.

blush [blœʃ] nm blusher.

blutage [blytaʒ] nm bolting (*of flour*).

BN [beɛn] nf (abrév de **Bibliothèque nationale**) *voir* **bibliothèque**.

BO [beo] 1 nm (abrév de **Bulletin officiel**) *voir* **bulletin**. 2 nf (abrév de **bande originale**) *voir* **bande**.

boa [bɔa] nm (*Habillement, Zool*) boa. **~ constricteur** boa constrictor.

Boadicée [bɔadise] nf Boadicea.

boat people [botpipœl] nmpl boat people.

bob¹ [bɔb] nm (*Sport*) bob(sleigh).

bob² [bɔb] nm (*chapeau*) cotton sunhat.

bobard* [bɔbaʀ] nm (*mensonge*) lie, fib*; (*histoire*) tall story, yarn.

bobèche [bɔbɛʃ] nf candle-ring.

bobinage [bɔbinaʒ] nm (*gén: action*) winding; (*Élec*) coil(s).

bobine [bɔbin] nf a *[fil]* reel, bobbin; *[métier à tisser]* bobbin, spool; *[machine à écrire, à coudre]* spool; (*Phot*) spool, reel; (*Élec*) coil. (*Aut*) **~ (d'allumage)** coil; (*Phot*) **~ de pellicule** roll of film. b (*: *visage*) face, dial⁑. **il a fait une drôle de ~!** what a face he pulled!; **tu en fais une drôle de ~!** you look a bit put out!*

bobineau [bɔbino] nm = **bobinot**.

bobiner [bɔbine] [1] vt to wind.

bobinette†† [bɔbinɛt] nf (wooden) latch.

bobineuse [bɔbinøz] nf winding machine.

bobinoir [bɔbinwaʀ] nm winding machine.

bobinot [bɔbino] nm (*Tex*) reel, bobbin.

bobsleigh [bɔbslɛg] nm bobsleigh.

bobo [bobo] nm (*langage enfantin*) (*plaie*) sore; (*coupure*) cut. **avoir ~** to be hurt, have a pain; **avoir ~ à la gorge** to have a sore throat; **ça (te) fait ~?** does it hurt?, is it sore?; **il n'y a pas eu de ~** there was no harm done.

bobonne*† [bɔbɔn] nf: **il est sorti avec (sa) ~** he's gone out with his old woman⁑ *ou* his missus* (*Brit*); (*hum*) **oui ~** yes love* *ou* dearie*.

bocage [bɔkaʒ] nm a (*Géog*) bocage, *farmland criss-crossed by hedges and trees*. b (*littér: bois*) grove, copse.

bocager, -ère [bɔkaʒe, ɛʀ] adj (*littér: boisé*) wooded. (*Géog*) **paysage ~** bocage landscape.

bocal, pl **-aux** [bɔkal, o] nm jar. **~ à poissons rouges** goldfish bowl; **mettre en ~aux** *fruits* to preserve, bottle.

Boccace [bɔkas] nm Boccaccio.

boche*⁑ [bɔʃ] (*péj*) 1 adj Boche. 2 nm: **B~** Jerry, Boche, Hun, Kraut⁑.

bock [bɔk] nm (*verre*) beer glass; (*bière*) glass of beer.

body [bɔdi] nm (*gén*) body(suit); (*Sport*) leotard.

Boers [buʀ] nmpl: **les ~** the Boers.

bœuf, pl **~s** [bœf, bø] 1 nm a (*bête*) ox; (*de boucherie*) bullock, steer; (*viande*) beef. **~s de boucherie** beef cattle; **~-mode** stewed beef with carrots; **~ en daube** bœuf en daube, beef stew; **il a un ~ sur la langue*** he has been paid to keep his mouth shut*; **on n'est pas des ~s!*** we're not galley slaves!*; *voir* **charrue, fort, qui**. b (*arg Mus*) jam session. **faire un ~** to jam. 2 adj inv: **effet/succès ~*** tremendous* *ou* fantastic* effect/success.

bof! [bɔf] excl: **il est beau!** – **~** he's handsome! – do you really think so? *ou* d'you reckon?*; **qu'en penses-tu?** – **~** what do you think of it? – not a lot; **ça t'a plu?** – **~** did you like it? – not really.

bogee, bogey [bɔgi] nm (*Golf*) bogy, bogey, bogie.

bog(g)ie [bɔgi] nm (*Rail*) bogie.

Bogota [bogota] n Bogota.

bogue¹ [bɔg] nf (*Bot*) husk.

bogue² [bɔg] nm (*Ordin*) bug.

Bohême, Bohème [bɔɛm] nf Bohemia.

bohème [bɔɛm] 1 adj bohemian. 2 nmf bohemian. **mener une vie de ~** to lead a bohemian life. 3 nf (*milieu*) **la B~** Bohemia.

bohémien, -ienne [bɔemjɛ̃, jɛn] 1 adj Bohemian. 2 nm (*Ling*) Bohemian. 3 nm,f (*gitan*) gipsy. (*de Bohême*) **B~(ne)** Bohemian.

boire [bwaʀ] [53] 1 vt a to drink. **~ un verre, ~ un coup*** to have a drink; **aller ~ un coup*** to go for a drink; **un coup à ~*** a drink; **~ qch à longs traits** to take great gulps of sth, gulp sth down; **offrir/donner à ~ à qn** to get sb/give sb something to drink *ou* a drink; **~ à la santé/au succès de qn** to drink sb's health/to sb's success; **on a bu une bouteille à nous deux** we drank a (whole) bottle between the two of us; **ce vin se boit bien** *ou* **se laisse ~** this wine goes down nicely*, this wine is very drinkable.
b **faire ~ un enfant** to give a child something to drink; **faire ~ un cheval** to water a horse.
c (*gén emploi absolu: boire trop*) to drink. **~ comme un trou*** to drink like a fish; **~ sans soif** to drink heavily; **c'est un homme qui boit (sec)** he's a (heavy) drinker; **il s'est mis à ~** he has taken to drink, he has started drinking; **il a bu, c'est évident** he has obviously been drinking.
d (*absorber*) to soak up, absorb. **ce papier boit l'encre** the ink soaks into this paper; **ce buvard boit bien l'encre** this blotter soaks up the ink well; **la plante a déjà tout bu** the plant has already soaked up all the water.
e (*loc*) **~ les paroles de qn** to drink in sb's words, lap up what sb says*; **~ le calice jusqu'à la lie** to drain one's cup to the (last) dregs *ou* last drop; **~ un bouillon*** (*revers de fortune*) to make a big loss, be ruined; (*en se baignant*) to swallow *ou* get a mouthful; **~ la tasse*** to swallow *ou* get a mouthful; **~ du petit lait** to lap it up*; **il y a à ~ et à manger là-dedans** (*dans une boisson*) there are bits floating about in it; (*fig*) (*qualités et défauts*) it's got its good points and its bad; (*vérités et mensonges*) you have to pick and choose what to believe.
2 nm: **le ~ et le manger** food and drink; (*fig*) **il en perd le ~ et le manger** he's losing sleep over it (*ou* her *etc*), he can't eat or sleep because of it (*ou* her *etc*).

bois [bwɑ] 1 nm a (*forêt, matériau*) wood. **c'est en ~** it's made of wood; **chaise de** *ou* **en ~** wooden chair; **ramasser du petit ~** to collect sticks *ou* kindling; (*fig*) **son visage était de ~** his face was impassive, he was poker-faced; (*fig*) **je ne suis pas de ~** I'm only human; (*fig*) **chèque en ~** cheque that bounces (*Brit*), rubber check* (*US*).
b (*objet en bois*) (*gravure*) woodcut; (*manche*) shaft, handle.
c (*Zool*) antler.
d (*Mus*) woodwind instrument. **les ~** the woodwind (instruments *ou* section *etc*).
e (*Golf*) wood.
f (*loc*) (*Tennis*) **faire un ~** to hit the ball off the wood; **je ne suis pas du ~ dont on fait les flûtes** I'm not going to let myself be pushed around, I'm not just anyone's fool; **il va voir de quel ~ je me chauffe!** is just let me get my hands on him!; **il fait feu** *ou* **flèche de tout ~** all is grist that comes to his mill, he'll use any means available to him.
2 comp ▸**bois blanc** whitewood, deal ▸**bois-brûlé, e** (*Can* †) nm,f (mpl **bois-brûlés**) half-breed Indian, bois-brûlé (*Can*) ▸**bois à brûler** firewood ▸**bois de charpente** timber, lumber (*US*) ▸**bois de chauffage** firewood ▸**bois de construction** timber, lumber (*US*) ▸**bois debout** (*Can*) standing timber ▸**bois d'ébène** (*Hist péj: esclaves*) black gold ▸**bois exotique, bois des îles** exotic wood ▸**les bois de justice** the guillotine ▸**bois de lit** bedstead ▸**bois de menuiserie** timber, lumber (*US*) ▸**bois mort** deadwood ▸**bois d'œuvre** timber, lumber (*US*) ▸**bois rond** (*Can*) unhewn timber ▸**bois de rose** rosewood ▸**bois vert** green wood; (*Menuiserie*) unseasoned *ou* green timber.

boisage [bwɑzaʒ] nm (*action*) timbering; (*matière*) timber work.

boisé, e [bwɑze] (ptp de **boiser**) adj wooded, woody. **pays ~** woodland(s), wooded *ou* woody countryside.

boisement [bwɑzmɑ̃] nm afforestation.

boiser [bwɑze] [1] vt *région* to afforest, plant with trees; *galerie* to timber.

boiserie [bwɑzʀi] nf: **~(s)** panelling, wainscot(t)ing, wood trim (*US*).

boisseau, pl **~x** [bwaso] nm (††) ≃ bushel; (*Can*) bushel (*36,36 litres*). **c'est un vrai ~ de puces!*** he's a menace!* *ou* a pest!*; **garder** *ou* **laisser** *ou* **mettre qch sous le ~** to keep sth dark *ou* in the dark.

boisson [bwasɔ̃] nf drink; (*Can* *) hard liquor, spirits. **ils apportent la** ~ they are bringing the drinks; **usé par la** ~ worn out with drinking; (*littér*) **être pris de** ~ to be drunk, be under the influence; ~ **alcoolisée** alcoholic beverage (*frm*) *ou* drink; ~ **non alcoolisée** soft drink.

boîte [bwat] 1 nf a (*récipient*) (*en carton, bois*) box; (*en métal*) box, tin; *[conserves]* tin (*Brit*), can (*US*). **mettre des haricots en** ~ to can beans; **des tomates en** ~ tinned (*Brit*) *ou* canned (*US*) tomatoes; (*fig*) **mettre qn en** ~* to pull sb's leg*, take the mickey out of sb‡ (*Brit*); **il a mangé toute la** ~ **de caramels** he ate the whole box of toffees.
b (*: *cabaret*) nightclub; (*: *lieu de travail*) (*firme*) firm, company; (*bureau*) office; (*école*) school. **aller** *ou* **sortir en** ~ to go (out) to a nightclub, to go (out) nightclubbing*; **quelle (sale)**~! what a joint!‡ *ou* dump!‡, what a crummy hole!‡; **je veux changer de** ~ (*usine*) I want to change my job; (*lycée*) I want to change schools; **il s'est fait renvoyer de la** ~ he got chucked out‡.
2 comp ▸**boîte d'allumettes** box of matches ▸**boîte à bachot** (*péj*) cramming school ▸**boîte à bijoux** jewel box ▸**boîte de conserve** tin (*Brit*) *ou* can (*US*) of food ▸**boîte de couleurs** box of paints, paintbox ▸**boîte à couture** = **boîte à ouvrage** ▸**boîte crânienne** (*Anat*) cranium, brainpan ▸**boîte expressive** (*Orgue*) swell (box) ▸**boîte à gants** (*Aut*) glove locker (*Brit*) *ou* compartment ▸**boîte à idées** suggestion box ▸**boîte à** *ou* **aux lettres** (*publique*) pillar box (*Brit*), mailbox (*US*), letterbox; (*privée*) letterbox; **je leur sers de boîte à lettres** I'm their go-between ▸**boîte à lettres électronique** electronic mailbox ▸**boîte à malice** bag of tricks ▸**boîte à musique** musical box ▸**boîte noire** (*Aviat*) flight recorder, black box ▸**boîte de nuit** nightclub ▸**boîte à ordures** dustbin (*Brit*), garbage *ou* trash can (*US*) ▸**boîte à outils** toolbox ▸**boîte à ouvrage** sewing box, workbox ▸**boîte de Pandore** Pandora's box ▸**boîte postale 150** P.O. Box 150 ▸**boîte de vitesses** (*Aut*) gearbox.

boitement [bwatmɑ̃] nm limping.

boiter [bwate] [1] vi *[personne]* to limp, walk with a limp *ou* gimp; *[meuble]* to wobble; *[raisonnement]* to be unsound *ou* shaky. ~ **bas** to limp badly; ~ **de la jambe gauche** to limp with one's left leg.

boiteux, -euse [bwatø, øz] 1 adj *personne* lame, who limps (*attrib*); *meuble* wobbly, rickety; *paix, projet* shaky; *union* ill-assorted; *raisonnement* unsound, shaky; *explication* lame, clumsy, weak; *vers* faulty; *phrase* (*incorrecte*) grammatically wrong, (*mal équilibrée*) unbalanced, clumsy. 2 nm,f lame person, gimp‡.

boîtier [bwatje] nm case; (*pour appareil-photo*) body. (*Aut*) ~ **de différentiel** differential housing; ~ **électrique** electric torch (*Brit*), flashlight (*US*); ~ **de montre** watchcase.

boitillement [bwatijmɑ̃] nm slight limp, hobble.

boitiller [bwatije] [1] vi to limp slightly, have a slight limp, hobble.

bol [bɔl] nm a (*récipient*) bowl; (*contenu*) bowl, bowlful. (*fig*) **prendre un (bon)** ~ **d'air** to get a good breath of fresh air. b (*Pharm*) bolus. (*Méd*) ~ **alimentaire** bolus. c (‡ *loc*) **avoir du** ~ to be lucky *ou* jammy‡ (*Brit*); **ne pas avoir de** ~ to be unlucky; **pas de** ~! hard luck!; **pas de** ~, **il est déjà parti** you're (*ou* we're *etc*) out of luck, he has already left. d (*Can* *) = **bolle***.

bolchevique [bɔlʃəvik] adj, nmf Bolshevik, Bolshevist.

bolchevisme [bɔlʃəvism] nm Bolchevism.

bolcheviste [bɔlʃəvist] = **bolchevique**.

bolduc [bɔldyk] nm curling ribbon, gift-wrap ribbon, bolduc (*SPÉC*).

bolée [bɔle] nf bowl(ful).

boléro [bɔleʀo] nm (*Habillement, Mus*) bolero.

bolet [bɔlɛ] nm ≃ wild mushroom, boletus (*SPÉC*).

bolide [bɔlid] nm (*Astron*) meteor, bolide (*SPÉC*); (*voiture*) (high-powered) racing car. **comme un** ~ *arriver, passer* at top speed; *s'éloigner* like a rocket.

bolivar [bɔlivaʀ] nm bolivar.

Bolivie [bɔlivi] nf Bolivia.

bolivien, -ienne [bɔlivjɛ̃, jɛn] 1 adj Bolivian. 2 nm,f: **B~(ne)** Bolivian.

bollard [bɔlaʀ] nm (*Naut*) bollard.

bolle* [bɔl] nf (*Can*) head. **j'ai mal à la** ~ I have a headache.

bolognais, e [bɔlɔɲɛ, ɛz] 1 adj Bolognese; (*Culin*) bolognese. 2 nm,f: **B~(e)** Bolognese.

Bologne [bɔlɔɲ] n Bologna.

bombance*† [bɔ̃bɑ̃s] nf feast, revel, beanfeast* (*Brit*). **faire** ~ to revel, have a beanfeast* (*Brit*).

bombarde [bɔ̃baʀd] nf (*Mil*) bombard.

bombardement [bɔ̃baʀdəmɑ̃] nm (*voir* **bombarder**) (*Mil*) bombardment; bombing; shelling; (*fig*) pelting; showering; bombarding; (*Phys*) bombardment. ~ **aérien** air raid, aerial bombing (*NonC*); ~ **atomique** (*Mil*) atom-bomb attack, atomic attack; (*Phys*) atomic bombardment.

bombarder [bɔ̃baʀde] [1] vt (*Mil*) to bombard; (*avec bombes*) to bomb; (*par obus*) to shell; (*Phys*) to bombard. (*fig*) ~ **de** *cailloux, tomates* to pelt with; *questions* to bombard with; **on l'a bombardé directeur*** he was suddenly thrust into *ou* pitchforked into the position of manager.

bombardier [bɔ̃baʀdje] nm (*avion*) bomber; (*aviateur*) bomb-aimer, bombardier.

Bombay [bɔ̃bɛ] n Bombay.

bombe [bɔ̃b] 1 nf a (*Mil*) bomb. **attentat à la** ~ bombing, bomb *ou* bombing attack; (*fig*) **comme une** ~ unexpectedly, (like a bolt) out of the blue; **la nouvelle a éclaté comme une** ~ *ou* **a fait l'effet d'une** ~ the news came as a bombshell *ou* was like a bolt out of the blue.
b (*atomiseur*) spray. (*gén*) **en** ~ in an aerosol (*attrib*); **peinture/Chantilly en** ~ aerosol paint/cream; **déodorant/insecticide en** ~ deodorant/insect spray.
c (*Équitation*) riding cap *ou* hat.
d (*loc*) **faire la** ~* to go on a spree *ou* a binge*.
2 comp ▸**bombe anti-crevaison** instant puncture sealant ▸**bombe antigel** (*Aut*) de-icing spray ▸**bombe atomique** atom(ic) bomb; **lancer** *ou* **lâcher une bombe atomique sur** to make an atomic *ou* nuclear attack on; **la bombe atomique** the Bomb ▸**bombe au cobalt** (*Méd*) cobalt therapy unit, telecobalt machine ▸**bombe déodorante** deodorant spray ▸**bombe à eau** water bomb ▸**bombe à fragmentation** cluster bomb ▸**bombe glacée** (*Culin*) bombe glacée, iced *ou* ice-cream pudding ▸**bombe H** H-bomb ▸**bombe à hydrogène** hydrogen bomb ▸**bombe incendiaire** incendiary *ou* fire bomb ▸**bombe insecticide** insect spray, fly spray ▸**bombe lacrymogène** teargas grenade ▸**bombe de laque** hair spray ▸**bombe de peinture** paint spray, can of aerosol paint ▸**bombe à retardement** time bomb ▸**bombe volcanique** (*Géol*) volcanic bomb.

bombé, e [bɔ̃be] (ptp de **bomber**) adj *forme* rounded, convex; *cuiller* rounded; *poitrine* thrown out; *front* domed; *mur* bulging; *dos* humped, hunched; *route* steeply cambered. **verre** ~ balloon-shaped glass.

bombement [bɔ̃bmɑ̃] nm *[forme]* convexity; *[route]* camber; *[front]* bulge.

bomber [bɔ̃be] [1] 1 vt a ~ **le torse** *ou* **la poitrine** (*lit*) to stick out *ou* throw out one's chest; (*fig*) to puff out one's chest, swagger about. b (*Peinture*) to spray(-paint). 2 vi *[route]* to camber; *[mur]* to bulge; (*Menuiserie*) to warp; (*: *rouler vite*) to belt along*.

bombonne [bɔ̃bɔn] nf = **bonbonne**.

bombyx [bɔ̃biks] nm bombyx.

bôme [bom] nf (*Voile*) boom.

bon¹, bonne¹ [bɔ̃, bɔn] 1 adj a (*de qualité*) (*gén*) good; *fauteuil, lit* good, comfortable. **il a une bonne vue** *ou* **de ~s yeux** he has good eyesight, his eyesight is good; **il a de bonnes jambes** he has a good *ou* strong pair of legs; **il a fait du** ~ **travail** he has done a good job of work; **marchandises/outils de bonne qualité** good quality goods/tools.
b (*compétent*) *docteur, élève, employé* good; (*efficace*) *instrument, système, remède* good, reliable; (*sage*) *conseil* good, sound; (*valable*) *excuse, raison* good, valid, sound; (*sain, sûr*) *placement, monnaie, entreprise* sound. **être** ~ **en anglais** to be good at English; **une personne de** ~ **conseil** a man of sound judgment; **pour le** ~ **fonctionnement du moteur** for the efficient working of the motor, for the motor to work efficiently *ou* properly; **quand on veut réussir tous les moyens sont ~s** anything goes when one wants to succeed; **tout lui est** ~ **pour me discréditer** he'll stop at nothing to discredit me.
c (*agréable*) *odeur, vacances, surprise, repas* good, pleasant, nice. **un** ~ **petit vin** a nice (little) wine; **elle aime les bonnes choses** she likes the good things in life; **nous avons passé une bonne soirée** we had a pleasant *ou* nice evening; **c'était vraiment** ~ (*à manger, à boire*) it was *ou* tasted really good *ou* nice; **l'eau est bonne** the water is warm *ou* fine *ou* nice; **il a la bonne vie** he's got it easy*, life is a bed of roses for him; **être en bonne compagnie** to be in good company *ou* with pleasant companions; (*littér*) **être de bonne compagnie** to be pleasant *ou* good company.
d (*moralement ou socialement irréprochable*) *lectures, fréquentations, pensées, famille* good. **il est** ~ **père et** ~ **fils** he's a good father and a good son; **libéré pour bonne conduite** released for good conduct; **de bonne renommée** of good repute; **d'un** ~ **milieu social** from a good social background; **dans la bonne société** in polite society.
e (*charitable*) *personne* good, kind(-hearted), kindly; *action* good, kind, kindly; *parole* kind, comforting, kindly. **la bonne action** *ou* **la B.A. quotidienne de l'éclaireur** the scout's good deed for the day; **il a eu un** ~ **mouvement** he made a nice gesture; **être** ~ **pour les animaux** to be kind to animals; **avoir** ~ **cœur** to have a good *ou* kind heart, be kind- *ou* good-hearted; **vous êtes bien** *ou* **trop** ~ you are really too kind, it's really too kind *ou* good of you; **il est** ~ **comme du** ~ **pain** he has a heart of gold; **elle est bonne fille** she's a nice *ou* good-hearted girl, she's a good sort*; **une bonne âme** a good soul; (*iro*) **vous êtes** ~ **vous (avec vos idées impossibles)!*** you're a great help (with your wild ideas)!; (*péj*) **c'est un** ~ **pigeon** *ou* **une bonne poire** he is a bit of a sucker‡ *ou* mug‡ (*Brit*) *ou* dope*.
f (*valable, utilisable*) *billet, passeport, timbre* valid. **médicament/yaourt** ~ **jusqu'au 5 mai** medicine/yoghurt to be consumed *ou* used before 5th May; **est-ce que la soupe va être encore bonne avec cette chaleur?** will the soup have kept *ou* will the soup still be all right in this heat?; **ce joint de caoutchouc n'est plus** ~ this rubber washer has perished (*Brit*) *ou* is no longer any good; **est-ce que ce pneu/ce vernis est encore ~?** is this tyre/varnish still fit to be used? *ou* still usable?; (*au tennis*) **la balle est/n'est pas bonne** the ball was in/was out.
g (*favorable*) *opinion, rapport* good, favourable; (*Scol*) *bulletin, note*

good. **dans le ~ sens du terme** in the favourable sense of the word.

h (*recommandé*) *alimentation* good. **~ pour la santé/pour le mal de tête** good for one's health/for headaches; **ces champignons ne sont pas ~s (à manger)** these mushrooms aren't safe (to eat); **est-ce que cette eau est bonne?** is this water fit *ou* all right to drink?, is this water drinkable?; **est-ce bien ~ de fumer tant?** is it a good thing *ou* very wise to smoke so much?; **ce serait une bonne chose s'il restait là-bas** it would be a good thing if he stayed there; **il serait ~ que vous les préveniez** you would do well *ou* it would be a good idea *ou* thing to let them know; **il est ~ de louer de bonne heure** it's as well *ou* it's advisable to book early; **croire** *ou* **juger** *ou* **trouver ~ de faire** to think *ou* see fit to do; **il semblerait ~ de** it would seem sensible *ou* a good idea to; **trouvez-vous ~ qu'il y aille?** do you think it's a good thing for him to go?; **quand/comme vous le jugerez ~** when/as you see fit; **quand/comme ~ vous semble** when/as you think best; **allez-y si ~ vous semble** go ahead if you think it best.

i (**: attrapé*) **je suis ~!*** I've had it!*; **le voilà ~ pour une contravention** he's in for a fine (now)*.

j **~ pour:** (*Mil*) **~ pour le service** fit for service; **le voilà ~ pour recommencer** now he'll have to start all over again; **la télévision, c'est ~ pour ceux qui n'ont rien à faire** television is all right *ou* fine for people who have nothing to do; **cette solution, c'est ~ pour toi, mais pas pour moi** that may be a solution for you but it won't do for me; (*sur imprimé*) **~ pour pouvoir** procuration given by; (*sur chèque*) **~ pour franco** pay bearer to the amount of; (*Comm: sur coupon*) **~ pour un lot de 6 bouteilles** this voucher *ou* coupon may be exchanged for a pack of 6 bottles; **~ pour une réduction de 2 F** 2 francs off next purchase.

k **~ à: cet enfant n'est ~ à rien** this child is no good *ou* use at anything; **cet appareil n'est ~ à rien/n'est pas ~ à grand-chose** this instrument is useless/isn't much good *ou* use for anything; **c'est ~ à jeter** it's fit for the dustbin, it might as well be thrown out; **c'est (tout juste) ~ à nous créer des ennuis** it will only create problems for us, all it will do is (to) create problems for us; **ce drap est (tout juste) ~ à faire des torchons** this sheet is (just) about good enough for *ou* is only fit for dusters (*Brit*) *ou* dustcloths (*US*); **c'est ~ à savoir** it's useful *ou* just as well to know that, that's worth knowing; **c'est toujours ~ à prendre** there's no reason to turn it down, it's better than nothing; **tout n'est pas ~ à dire** some things are better left unsaid; **puis-je vous être ~ à quelque chose?** can I be of any use *ou* help to you?, can I do anything for you?

l (*correct*) *solution, méthode, réponse, calcul* right, correct. **au ~ moment** at the right *ou* proper time; **le ~ numéro/cheval** the right number/horse; **sur le ~ côté de la route** on the right *ou* proper side of the road; **le ~ côté du couteau** the cutting *ou* sharp edge of the knife; **le ~ usage** correct usage (of language); (*en positionnant qch*) **je suis ~ là?*** is this O.K.?, how's that?; (*fig*) **ils sont sur la bonne route** they're on the right track; (*Prov*) **les ~s comptes font les ~s amis** bad debts make bad friends.

m (*intensif de quantité*) good. **un ~ kilomètre** a good kilometre; **une bonne livre/semaine/heure** a good pound/week/hour; **une bonne raclée*** a thorough *ou* sound hiding; **un ~ savon*** a thorough *ou* sound telling-off*; **il a reçu une bonne paire de claques** he got a smart clip on the ear* (*Brit*) *ou* a good slap in the face; **la voiture en a pris un ~ coup*** the car has got *ou* had a real bash*; **ça fait un ~ bout de chemin!** that's quite a good way! *ou* a step!, that's quite some way!; **il est tombé une bonne averse/couche de neige** there has been a heavy shower/fall of snow; **après un ~ moment** after quite some time *ou* a good while; **laissez une bonne marge** leave a good *ou* wide margin; **il faudrait une bonne gelée pour tuer la vermine** what is needed is a hard frost to kill off the vermin; **ça aurait besoin d'une bonne couche de peinture/d'un ~ coup de balai** it needs *ou* would need a good coat of paint/a good sweep-out; **ça fait un ~ poids à traîner!** that's quite a *ou* some load to drag round!; **d'un ~ pas** at a good pace *ou* speed; **faire ~ poids/bonne mesure** to give good weight/measure; **il faudrait qu'il pleuve une bonne fois** what's needed is a good downpour; **je te le dis une bonne fois (pour toutes)** I'm telling you once and for all, I'll tell you one last time; **(un) ~ nombre de** a good many; **une bonne moitié** at least half.

n (*intensif de qualité*) **une bonne paire de souliers** a good (strong) pair of shoes; **une bonne robe de laine** a nice warm woollen dress; **une bonne tasse de thé** a nice (hot) cup of tea; **un ~ bain chaud** a nice hot bath; **le ~ vieux temps** the good old days; **c'était le ~ temps!** those were the days!

o **mon ~ monsieur** my good man; **ma bonne dame** my good woman; **les bonnes gens** good *ou* honest people; **mon ~ ami** my dear *ou* good friend; **une bonne dame m'a fait entrer** some good woman let me in.

p (*souhaits*) **bonne (et heureuse) année!** happy New Year!; **~ anniversaire!** happy birthday!; **~ appétit!** have a nice meal!, enjoy your meal!; **bonne chance!** good luck!, all the best!; **~ courage!** good luck!; **~ dimanche!** have a good time on Sunday!, have a nice Sunday!; **bonne fin de semaine!** enjoy the rest of the week!, have a good weekend!; **bonne nuit!** good night!; **bonne rentrée!** I hope you get back all right! *ou* safely!, safe return!; (*Scol*) I hope the new term starts well!; **~ retour!** safe journey back!, safe return!; **bonne route!** safe journey!; **bonne santé!** (I) hope you keep well!; **bonnes vacances!** have a good holiday! (*Brit*) *ou* vacation! (*US*); **~ voyage!** safe journey!, have a good journey!; **au revoir et bonne continuation** goodbye and I hope all goes well (for you) *ou* and all the best!

q (*amical*) *ambiance* good, pleasant, nice; *regard, sourire* warm, pleasant. **relations de ~ voisinage** good neighbourly relations; **un ~ (gros) rire** a hearty *ou* cheery laugh; **c'est un ~ camarade** he's a good friend.

r (*loc*) **~!** right!, O.K.!*; **~! ~!** all right! all right!; **c'est ~! je le ferai moi-même** (all) right then I'll do it myself; **~ Dieu!*, ~ sang (de bonsoir)!** damn and blast it!‡, hells bells!‡; **à ~ droit** with good reason, legitimately; **~s baisers** much love, love and kisses; **~ débarras!** good riddance!; **~ vent!** good riddance!, go to blazes!*; **~ an mal an** taking one year with another, on average; **~ gré mal gré** whether you (*ou* they *etc*) like it or not, willy-nilly; **à bonne fin** to a successful conclusion; **être en bonnes mains** to be in good hands; **(à) ~ marché** *acheter* cheap; **de ~ cœur** *manger, rire* heartily; *faire, accepter* willingly, readily; **être de bonne composition** to be biddable, be easy to deal with; **à ~ compte** *obtenir* (on the) cheap, for very little, for a song; **s'en tirer à ~ compte** to get off lightly; **à la bonne franquette*** *recevoir, agir* informally; **on a dîné à la bonne franquette*** we took pot luck together; **de bonne heure** early; **à la bonne heure!** that's fine!; (*iro*) that's a fine idea! (*iro*); **manger de ~ appétit** to eat heartily; **de ~ matin** early; **une bonne pâte** an easy-going fellow, a good sort; **avoir ~ pied ~ œil** to be as fit as a fiddle, be hale and hearty; **c'est de bonne guerre** that's fair enough; (*iro*) **elle est bien bonne celle-là** that's a good one!; (*littér*) **faire bonne chère** to eat well, have a good meal; (*littér*) **faire ~ visage à qn** to put on a pleasant face for sb; **faire le ~ apôtre** to have a holier-than-thou attitude; **tenir le ~ bout*** to be getting near the end of one's work, be past the worst; (*hum*) **pour la bonne cause†** with honourable motives *ou* intentions; **voilà une bonne chose de faite** that's one good job got out of the way *ou* done; (*Prov*) **~ chien chasse de race** like father like son (*Prov*); (*Prov*) **bonne renommée vaut mieux que ceinture dorée** a good name is better than riches; (*Prov*) **~ sang ne saurait mentir** what's bred in the bone will (come) out in the flesh (*Prov*); **avoir** *ou* **se donner** *ou* **prendre du ~ temps** to enjoy o.s., have a good time; *voir* **allure, garder, vent.**

2 adv: **il fait ~ ici** it's nice *ou* pleasant here; **il fait ~ au soleil** it's nice and warm in the sun; **il fait ~ vivre à la campagne** it is a nice life in the country; **il fait ~ vivre** it's good to be alive; **il ne ferait pas ~ le contredire** we (*ou* you *etc*) would be ill-advised to contradict him.

3 nm a (*personne*) good *ou* upright person, welldoer. **les ~s et les méchants** good people and wicked people, welldoers and evildoers; (*westerns*) the goodies and the baddies (*Brit*), the good guys and the bad guys (*US*).

b (*morceau, partie*) **mange le ~ et laisse le mauvais** eat what's good *ou* the good part and leave what's bad *ou* the bad part.

c (*loc*) **avoir du ~: cette solution a du ~** this solution has its merits *ou* advantages *ou* its (good) points; **il y a du ~: il y a du ~ dans ce qu'il dit** there is some merit *ou* there are some good points in what he says; **il y a du ~ et du mauvais** it has its good and its bad points; **il y a du ~ et du moins ~** parts of it are good and parts of it are not so good, some bits are better than others.

4 **bonne** nf: **en voilà une bonne!** that's a good one!; (*iro*) **tu en as de bonnes, toi!*** you're kidding!‡, you must be joking!*; **avoir qn à la bonne*** to like sb, be in (solid) with sb (*US*); **il m'a à la bonne*** I'm in his good books*.

5 comp ►**bonne action** good deed; **faire sa bonne action quotidienne** to do one's good deed for the day ►**bonne amie†** (*hum*) girlfriend, sweetheart ►**bon chic bon genre*** *personne* smart but fogeyish*, preppy (*US*); *bar, soirée* smart but fogeyish*, Sloany (*Brit*) ►**le Bon Dieu** God, the good *ou* dear Lord ►**bon enfant** adj inv *personne, sourire* good-natured; *atmosphère* friendly ►**bonne étoile** lucky star ►**bonne femme** (*péj: femme*) woman; (*péj: épouse*) **sa bonne femme** his old woman‡, his missus* ►**bonne maman*** granny*, grandma ►**bon marché** adj inv cheap, inexpensive ►**bon mot** witty remark, witticism ►**bonnes œuvres** charity ►**bon papa*** grandpa, grandad* ►**la bonne parole** (*Rel*) (*lit*) the word of God; (*fig*) the gospel (*fig*) ►**bon point** (*Scol*) star; (*fig*) **un bon point pour vous!** that's a point in your favour! ►**bon à rien, bonne à rien** nm,f good-for-nothing, ne'er-do-well ►**bon Samaritain** (*Bible, fig*) good Samaritan ►**bon sens** common sense ►**bonne sœur*** nun ►**bon teint** *couleur* fast; (*fig*) *syndicaliste* staunch, dyed-in-the-wool (*fig*) ►**le bon ton** good form, good manners; **il est de bon ton de** it is good form *ou* good manners to ►**bon vivant** adj jovial ◊ nm jovial fellow; *voir aussi* **1e**.

bon² [bɔ̃] 1 nm (*formulaire*) slip, form; (*coupon d'échange*) coupon, voucher; (*Fin: titre*) bond. 2 comp ►**bon de caisse** cash voucher ►**bon de commande** order form ►**bon d'épargne** savings certificate ►**bon d'essence** petrol (*Brit*) *ou* gas (*US*) coupon ►**bon de garantie** guarantee (slip) ►**bon de livraison** delivery slip ►**bon de réduction** reduction coupon *ou* voucher ►**bon à tirer** (*Typ*) adj passed for press ◊ nm final corrected proof; **donner le bon à tirer** to pass for press ►**bon du Trésor** (Government) Treasury bill ►**bon à**

vue demand note.

Bonaparte [bɔnapaʀt] nm Bonaparte.

bonapartisme [bɔnapaʀtism] nm Bonapartism.

bonapartiste [bɔnapaʀtist] adj, nmf Bonapartist.

bonard, e* [bɔnaʀ, aʀd] adj a (*dupe*) gullible. **il est vachement ~** he'll swallow anything*, he's so gullible. b (*facile*) **c'est ~** it is no sweat‡, we (*ou* you *etc*) can take it easy.

bonasse [bɔnas] adj (*gén*) easy-going; (*péj*) meek. **accepter qch d'un air ~** (*gén*) to accept sth good-naturedly; (*péj*) to accept sth meekly.

bonbon [bɔ̃bɔ̃] 1 nm sweet (*Brit*), sweetie* (*Brit*), candy (*US*). 2 comp ▸**bonbon acidulé** acid drop ▸**bonbon anglais** fruit drop ▸**un bonbon au chocolat** a chocolate ▸**bonbon fourré** sweet (*Brit*) *ou* candy (*US*) with soft centre ▸**bonbon à la menthe** mint, humbug (*Brit*) ▸**bonbon au miel** honey drop.

bonbonne [bɔ̃bɔn] nf (*recouverte d'osier*) demijohn; (*à usage industriel*) carboy.

bonbonnière [bɔ̃bɔnjɛʀ] nf (*boîte*) sweet (*Brit*) *ou* candy (*US*) box, bonbonnière; (*fig: appartement*) bijou flat (*Brit*), exquisite apartment (*US*), bijou residence (*hum*).

bond [bɔ̃] nm *[personne, animal]* leap, bound, jump, spring; *[balle]* bounce. **faire des ~s** (*sauter*) to leap *ou* spring up *ou* into the air; (*gambader*) to leap *ou* jump about; **faire un ~ d'indignation** to leap *ou* jump up in indignation *ou* indignantly; **faire un ~ de surprise** to start with surprise; **franchir qch d'un ~** to clear sth at one jump *ou* bound; **se lever d'un ~** to leap *ou* jump *ou* spring up; **d'un ~ il fut près d'elle** in a single leap *ou* bound he was at her side; **il ne fit qu'un ~ jusqu'à l'hôpital** he rushed *ou* dashed off to the hospital, he was at the hospital in a trice; **progresser par ~s** to progress by leaps and bounds; (*Mil*) to advance by successive dashes; **l'économie nationale a fait un ~ (en avant)** the country's economy has leapt forward, there has been a boom *ou* surge in the country's economy; **un grand ~ en avant pour la science** a great leap forward for science; **les prix ont fait un ~** prices have shot up *ou* soared; *voir* **balle**[1], **faux**[2].

bonde [bɔ̃d] nf a (*bouchon*) *[tonneau]* bung, stopper; *[évier, baignoire]* plug; *[étang]* sluice gate. b (*trou*) *[tonneau]* bunghole; *[évier, baignoire]* plughole.

bondé, e [bɔ̃de] adj packed(-full), cram-full, jam-packed*.

bondieuserie [bɔ̃djøzʀi] nf (*péj*) (*piété*) religiosity, devoutness; (*bibelot*) religious trinket *ou* bric-à-brac (*NonC*).

bondir [bɔ̃diʀ] 2 vi a (*sauter*) *[homme, animal]* to jump *ou* leap *ou* spring up; *[balle]* to bounce (up). **~ de joie** to jump *ou* leap for joy; **~ de colère** to fume with anger; **il bondit d'indignation** he leapt up indignantly; (*fig*) **cela me fait ~*** it makes me hopping mad*, it makes my blood boil*. b (*gambader*) to jump *ou* leap about. c (*sursauter*) to start. **~ de surprise/de frayeur** to start with surprise/fright. d (*se précipiter*) **~ vers** *ou* **jusqu'à** to dash *ou* rush to; **~ sur sa proie** to pounce on one's prey.

bondissement [bɔ̃dismɑ̃] nm bound, leap. **regarder les ~s d'une chèvre** to watch a goat bounding *ou* leaping *ou* skipping about.

bongo [bɔ̃go] nm (*Mus*) bongo (drum).

bonheur [bɔnœʀ] 1 nm a (*NonC: félicité*) happiness, bliss.
b (*joie*) joy (*NonC*), source of happiness *ou* joy. **le ~ de vivre/d'aimer** the joy of living/of loving; **avoir le ~ de voir son fils réussir** to have the joy of seeing one's son succeed; **faire le ~ de qn** to make sb happy, bring happiness to sb; **si ce ruban peut faire ton ~, prends-le*** if this ribbon is what you're looking for *ou* can be any use to you take it; **des vacances! quel ~!** holidays! what bliss! *ou* what a delight!; **quel ~ de vous revoir!** what a pleasure it is to see you again!
c (*chance*) (good) luck, good fortune. **il ne connaît pas son ~!** he doesn't know *ou* realize (just) how lucky he is!, he doesn't know *ou* realize his luck!*; **avoir le ~ de faire** to be lucky enough *ou* have the good fortune to do; **il eut le rare ~ de gagner 3 fois** he had the unusual good fortune *ou* luck of winning *ou* to win 3 times; **porter ~ à qn** to bring sb luck; **ça porte ~ de ...** it's lucky to ...; **par ~** fortunately, luckily; **par un ~ inespéré** by an unhoped-for stroke of luck *ou* good fortune.
d (*loc*) (*littér*) **avec ~** felicitously; **mêler avec ~ le tragique et le comique** to make a happy *ou* skilful blend of the tragic and the comic; **au petit ~ (la chance)*** *répondre* off the top of one's head*; *faire* haphazardly, any old how*; **il n'y a pas de véritable sélection, c'est au petit ~ la chance** there is no real selection (process), it is just pot luck *ou* the luck of the draw.
2 comp ▸**bonheur-du-jour** nm (pl **bonheurs-du-jour**) escritoire, writing desk.

bonhomie [bɔnɔmi] nf good-naturedness, good-heartedness, bonhomie.

bonhomme [bɔnɔm], pl **bonshommes** [bɔ̃zɔm] 1 nm (*) (*homme*) chap* (*Brit*), fellow*, bloke* (*Brit*), guy*; (*mari*) old man‡; (‡ *Can: père*) old man‡, father. **dessiner des bonshommes** to draw little men; **un petit ~ de 4 ans** a little chap* *ou* lad* *ou* fellow* of 4; **dis-moi, mon ~** tell me, sonny* *ou* little fellow*; (*fig*) **aller** *ou* **suivre son petit ~ de chemin** to carry on *ou* go on in one's own sweet way. 2 adj inv: **air/regard ~** good-natured expression/look. 3 comp ▸**bonhomme de neige** snowman ▸**bonhomme de pain d'épice** gingerbread man.

boni† [bɔni] nm (*bénéfice*) profit. **100 F de ~** a 100-franc profit.

boniche [bɔniʃ] nf (*péj*) servant (maid), skivvy* (*Brit*). **faire la ~ (pour qn)** to skivvy for sb*.

bonification [bɔnifikasjɔ̃] nf a (*amélioration*) *[terre, vins]* improvement. b (*en compétition*) bonus (points); (*avantage*) advantage, start.

bonifier vt, **se bonifier** vpr [bɔnifje] 7 to improve.

boniment [bɔnimɑ̃] nm (*baratin*) sales talk (*NonC*), patter* (*NonC*); (*: *mensonge*) tall story, humbug (*NonC*). **faire le** *ou* **du ~ à qn** to give sb the sales talk *ou* patter*; **faire du ~ à une femme** to chat a woman up* (*Brit*), try and pick up a woman*; **raconter des ~s*** to spin yarns *ou* tall stories.

bonimenter [bɔnimɑ̃te] 1 vi to give the sales talk *ou* patter*.

bonimenteur [bɔnimɑ̃tœʀ] nm smooth talker; *[foire]* barker.

bonjour [bɔ̃ʒuʀ] nm (*gén*) hello, how d'you do?; (*matin*) (good) morning; (*après-midi*) (good) afternoon; (*Can: au revoir*) good day (*frm*), good morning, good afternoon. **donnez-lui le ~ de ma part** give him my regards, remember me to him; **dire ~ à qn** to say hello to sb; **le bus aux heures de pointe, ~ (les dégâts)!*** the bus in the rush hour is hell!*; **tu aurais vu sa moto après l'accident! ~ (les dégâts)!*** you should've seen his bike after the accident! what a mess!; **si son père l'apprend, ~ (les dégâts)!** if his father finds out about it, sparks will fly *ou* all hell will be let loose!*

Bonn [bɔn] n Bonn.

bonne[2] [bɔn] nf maid, domestic. **~ d'enfants** nanny (*Brit*), child's nurse (*US*); **~ à tout faire** general help, skivvy (*Brit*); (*hum*) maid of all work; *voir aussi* **bon**[1].

bonnement [bɔnmɑ̃] adv: **tout ~** just, (quite) simply; **dire tout ~ que** to say (quite) frankly *ou* openly *ou* plainly that.

bonnet [bɔnɛ] 1 nm a (*coiffure*) bonnet, hat; *[bébé]* bonnet. b *[soutien-gorge]* cup. c (*Zool*) reticulum. d (*loc*) **prendre qch sous son ~** to make sth one's concern *ou* responsibility, take it upon o.s. to do sth; **c'est ~ blanc et blanc ~** it's six of one and half a dozen of the other (*Brit*), it amounts to the same thing; *voir* **gros, jeter, tête**. 2 comp ▸**bonnet d'âne** dunce's cap ▸**bonnet de bain** bathing cap ▸**bonnet de nuit** (*Habillement*) nightcap; (* *fig*) wet blanket*, killjoy, spoilsport ▸**bonnet phrygien** Phrygian cap ▸**bonnet à poils** bearskin ▸**bonnet de police** forage cap, garrison *ou* overseas cap (*US*).

bonneteau [bɔnto] nm three card trick.

bonneterie [bɔnɛtʀi] nf (*objets*) hosiery; (*magasin*) hosier's shop, hosiery; (*commerce*) hosiery trade.

bonnetier, -ière [bɔntje, jɛʀ] nm,f hosier.

bonnette [bɔnɛt] nf (*Phot*) supplementary lens; (*Naut*) studding sail, stuns'l; (*Mil*) *[fortification]* bonnet.

bonniche [bɔniʃ] nf = **boniche**.

bonsaï [bɔ̃zaj] nm bonsai.

bonsoir [bɔ̃swaʀ] nm (*en arrivant*) hello, good evening; (*en partant*) good evening, good night; (*en se couchant*) good night. **souhaiter le ~ à qn** to say good night to sb; **~!*** (that's just) too bad!* (*Brit*), tough (luck)!*; (*rien à faire*) nothing doing!*, not a chance!*, not on your life!*; **pour s'en débarrasser/le convaincre, ~!** it's going to be sheer *ou* absolute hell* getting rid of it/convincing him!

bonté [bɔ̃te] nf a (*NonC*) kindness, goodness. **ayez la ~ de faire** would you be so kind *ou* good as to do?; **faire qch par pure ~ d'âme** to do sth out of the goodness of one's heart; **avec ~** kindly; **~ divine!** *ou* **du ciel!** good heavens!* b (act of) kindness. **merci de toutes vos ~s** thank you for all your kindnesses to me *ou* for all the kindness you've shown me.

bonus [bɔnys] nm (*Assurances*) no-claims bonus.

bonze [bɔ̃z] nm (*Rel*) bonze; (*: *personnage important*) bigwig*. **vieux ~‡** old fossil‡.

bonzerie [bɔ̃zʀi] nf Buddhist monastery.

bonzesse [bɔ̃zɛs] nf bonze.

boogie-woogie, pl **boogie-woogies** [bugiwugi] nm boogie-woogie.

bookmaker [bumɛkœʀ] nm bookmaker.

booléen, -enne [buleɛ̃, ɛn] adj (*Math, Ordin*) boolean.

boom [bum] nm (*expansion*) boom. **le baby ~** the baby boom.

boomerang [bumʀɑ̃g] nm (*lit, fig*) boomerang. (*fig*) **faire ~, avoir un effet ~** to backfire.

boots [buts] nmpl boots.

boqueteau, pl **~x** [bɔkto] nm copse.

borborygme [bɔʀbɔʀigm] nm rumble, rumbling noise (in one's stomach).

bord [bɔʀ] nm a *[route]* side, edge; *[rivière]* side, bank; *[lac]* edge, side, shore; *[cratère]* edge, rim, lip; *[forêt, table]* edge; *[précipice]* edge, brink; *[verre, tasse]* brim, rim; *[assiette]* edge, rim; *[plaie]* edge. **le ~ de la mer** the seashore; **~ du trottoir** edge of the pavement, kerb (*Brit*), curb (*US*); **une maison au ~ du lac** a house by the lake *ou* at the lakeside, a lakeside house; **se promener au ~ de la rivière** to go for a walk along the riverside *ou* the river bank *ou* by the river; **passer ses vacances au ~ de la mer** to spend one's holidays at the seaside *ou* by the sea, go to the seaside for one's holidays; **pique-niquer au ~** *ou* **sur le ~ de la route** to (have a) picnic at *ou* by the roadside; **au ~ de l'eau** at the water's edge; **se promener au ~ de l'eau** to go for a walk by the lake *ou* river *ou* sea; **en été les ~s du lac sont envahis de touristes** in summer the shores of the lake are overrun by tourists; **il a regagné le ~ à la nage** (*dans la mer*) he swam ashore *ou* to the shore; (*dans une rivière*) he swam to the bank; **verre rempli jusqu'au ~ *ou* à ras ~** glass full *ou* filled to the brim.

b *[vêtement, mouchoir]* edge, border; *[chapeau]* brim. **chapeau à large(s) ~(s)** wide- *ou* broad-brimmed hat; **le ~ ourlé *ou* roulotté d'un mouchoir** the rolled hem of a handkerchief; **veste ~ à ~** edge-to-edge jacket; **coller du papier ~ à ~** to hang wallpaper edge to edge.

c (*Naut*) side. **les hommes du ~** the crew; (*Aviat, Naut*) **à ~** on board, aboard; **monter à ~** to go on board *ou* aboard; **prendre qn à son ~** to take sb aboard *ou* on board; **monter à ~ d'un navire** to board a ship, go on board *ou* aboard ship; **la marchandise a été expédiée à ~ du SS Wallisdown** the goods were shipped on SS Wallisdown; (*Naut*) **passer/jeter par-dessus ~** to hand/throw overboard; **M. X, à ~ d'une voiture bleue** Mr X, driving *ou* in a blue car; **journal *ou* livre de ~** log(book), ship's log.

d (*Naut: bordée*) tack. **tirer des ~s** to tack, make tacks; **tirer un ~** to tack, make a tack.

e (*Can* *) side. **de mon ~** on my side; **prendre le ~** to make off.

f (*loc*) **être au ~ de la ruine/du désespoir** to be on the verge *ou* brink of ruin/despair; **au ~ de la tombe** on the brink of death, at death's door; **au ~ des larmes** on the verge of tears, almost in tears; **nous sommes du même ~** we are on the same side, we are of the same opinion; (*socialement*) we are all of a kind; **à pleins ~s** abundantly, freely; **il est un peu fantaisiste/sadique sur les ~s*** he is a bit of an eccentric/sadist.

bordage [bɔʀdaʒ] nm a (*Couture*), edging, bordering. b (*Naut*) **~s** (*en bois*) planks, planking; (*en fer*) plates, plating. c (*Can*) **~s** inshore ice.

bordé [bɔʀde] nm a (*Couture*) braid, trimming. b (*Naut*) (*en bois*) planking; (*en fer*) plating.

bordeaux [bɔʀdo] 1 nm a (*ville*) **B~** Bordeaux. b (*vin*) Bordeaux (wine). **~ rouge** claret. 2 adj inv maroon, burgundy.

bordée [bɔʀde] nf a (*salve*) broadside. (*fig*) **~ d'injures** torrent *ou* volley of abuse. b (*Naut: quart*) watch. c (*parcours*) tack. **tirer des ~s** to tack, make tacks; (*fig*) **tirer une ~** to go on a spree* *ou* binge*. d (*Can* *) **une bordée de neige** a heavy snowfall.

bordel‡ [bɔʀdɛl] nm (*hôtel*) brothel, whorehouse*; (*chaos*) mess, shambles (*sg*). **quel ~!** what a bloody*‡ (*Brit*) *ou* goddamned‡ shambles!; **si tout le monde a accès aux dossiers, ça va être le ~** if everyone has access to the files it'll be bloody*‡ (*Brit*) *ou* goddamned‡ chaos; **mettre *ou* foutre‡ le ~** to create havoc, cause bloody*‡ (*Brit*) *ou* goddamned‡ chaos; **mettre *ou* foutre‡ le ~ dans qch** to screw‡ *ou* bugger*‡ (*Brit*) sth up; **~!** bloody hell!‡ (*Brit*), hell!‡, shit!*‡; **arrête de gueuler, ~ (de merde)!** stop shouting for Christ's sake!*‡

bordelais, e [bɔʀdəlɛ, ɛz] 1 adj of *ou* from Bordeaux, Bordeaux (*épith*). 2 nm,f: **B~(e)** inhabitant *ou* native of Bordeaux. 3 nm (*région*) **le B~** the Bordeaux region.

bordélique‡ [bɔʀdelik] adj shambolic*.

border [bɔʀde] 1 vt a (*Couture*) (*entourer*) to edge, trim (*de* with); (*ourler*) to hem, put a hem on. b *rue, rivière [arbres, immeubles, maisons]* to line; *[sentier]* to run alongside. **allée bordée de fleurs** path edged *ou* bordered with flowers; **rue bordée de maisons** road lined with houses; **rue bordée d'arbres** tree-lined road. c *personne, couverture* to tuck in. **~ un lit** to tuck the blankets in. d (*Naut*) (*en bois*) to plank; (*en fer*) to plate. e (*Naut*) *voile* to haul on, pull on; *avirons* to ship.

bordereau, pl ~x [bɔʀdəʀo] 1 nm (*formulaire*) note, slip; (*relevé*) statement, summary; (*facture*) invoice. 2 comp ►**bordereau d'achat** purchase note ►**bordereau d'envoi** dispatch note ►**bordereau de livraison** delivery slip *ou* note ►**bordereau de salaire** salary advice ►**bordereau de versement** pay(ing)-in slip.

bordure [bɔʀdyʀ] nf (*bord*) edge; (*cadre*) surround, frame; (*de gazon, fleurs*) border; (*d'arbres*) line; (*Couture*) border, edging, edge. **~ de trottoir** kerb (*Brit*), curb (*US*), kerbstones (*Brit*), curbstones (*US*); **en ~ de** (*le long de*) running along, alongside, along the edge of; (*à côté de*) next to, by; (*près de*) near (to); **en ~ de route** *maison, champ* by the roadside (*attrib*); *restaurant, arbre* roadside (*épith*); **papier à ~ noire** black-edged paper, paper with a black edge.

bore [bɔʀ] nm boron.

boréal, e, mpl -aux [bɔʀeal, o] adj boreal; *voir* **aurore**.

Borgia [bɔʀʒja] n Borgia.

borgne [bɔʀɲ] adj a *personne* one-eyed, blind in one eye. **fenêtre ~** obstructed window. b (*fig: louche*) *hôtel, rue* shady.

borique [bɔʀik] adj boric.

bornage [bɔʀnaʒ] nm *[champ]* boundary marking, demarcation.

borne [bɔʀn] 1 nf a (*kilométrique*) kilometre-marker, ≃ milestone; *[terrain]* boundary stone *ou* marker; (*autour d'un monument etc*) stone post. **ne reste pas là planté comme une ~!*** don't just stand there like a statue! b (*fig*) **~s** limit(s), bounds; **il n'y a pas de ~s à la bêtise humaine** human folly knows no bounds; **franchir *ou* dépasser les ~s** to go too far; **sans ~s** limitless, unlimited, boundless; **mettre des ~s à** to limit. c (*) kilometre. d (*Élec*) terminal. 2 comp ►**borne-fontaine** (*Can*) nf (**pl borne-fontaines**) fire hydrant.

borné, e [bɔʀne] (**ptp de borner**) adj *personne* narrow-minded, short-sighted; *esprit, vie* narrow; *intelligence* limited.

Bornéo [bɔʀneo] n Borneo.

borner [bɔʀne] 1 1 vt a *ambitions, besoins, enquête* to limit, restrict (*à faire* to doing, *à qch* to sth).

b *terrain* to mark out *ou* off, mark the boundary of. **arbres qui bornent un champ** trees which border a field; **immeubles qui bornent la vue** buildings which limit *ou* restrict one's view.

2 **se borner** vpr (*se contenter de*) **se ~ à faire** to content o.s. with doing, be content to do; **se ~ à qch** to content o.s. with sth; (*se limiter à*) **se ~ à faire/à qch** *[personne]* to restrict *ou* confine *ou* limit o.s. to doing/to sth; *[visite, exposé]* to be limited *ou* restricted *ou* confined to doing/to sth; **je me borne à vous faire remarquer que ...** I would just *ou* merely like to point out to you that ...; **il s'est borné à resserrer les vis** he merely tightened up the screws, he contented himself with tightening up the screws.

bosco [bɔsko] nm (*Naut*) quartermaster.

bosniaque [bɔznjak] 1 adj Bosnian. 2 nmf: **B~** Bosnian.

Bosnie [bɔsni] nf Bosnia.

bosnien, -ienne [bɔznjɛ̃, jɛn] 1 adj Bosnian. 2 nm,f: **B~(ne)** Bosnian.

Bosnie-Herzégovine [bɔsniɛʀzegɔvin] nf Bosnia and Herzegovina.

Bosphore [bɔsfɔʀ] nm: **le ~** the Bosphorus.

bosquet [bɔskɛ] nm copse, grove.

bossage [bɔsaʒ] nm (*Archit*) boss. **~s** bosses, bossage.

bosse [bɔs] nf a *[chameau, bossu]* hump; (*en se cognant*) bump, lump; (*éminence*) bump; (*Ski*) mogul, bump. **se faire une ~ au front** to get a bump on one's forehead; **route pleine de ~s** (very) bumpy road; *voir* **rouler**. b (* *loc*) **avoir la ~ des maths** to have a good head for maths, be good at maths; **avoir la ~ du commerce** to be a born businessman (*ou* businesswoman).

bosselage [bɔslaʒ] nm embossment.

bosseler [bɔsle] 4 vt (*déformer*) to dent, bash about; (*marteler*) to emboss. **tout bosselé** *théière* battered, badly dented, all bashed* about *ou* in (*attrib*); *front* bruised, covered in bumps (*attrib*); *sol* bumpy.

bossellement [bɔsɛlmɑ̃] nm embossing.

bosselure [bɔslyʀ] nf (*défaut*) dent; (*relief*) embossment.

bosser* [bɔse] 1 1 vi (*travailler*) to work; (*travailler dur*) (*intellectuellement*) to swot (*Brit*), work hard, slog away*; (*physiquement*) to slave away, work one's guts out‡. 2 vt *examen* to swot for (*Brit*), slog away for*. **~ son anglais** to swot up *ou* slog away at* one's English.

bosseur, -euse [bɔsœʀ, øz] nm,f slogger*, hard worker.

bossoir [bɔswaʀ] nm *[bateau]* davit; *[ancre]* cathead.

bossu, e [bɔsy] 1 adj *personne* hunchbacked. **dos ~** hunch(ed) back; **redresse-toi, tu es tout ~** sit up, you're getting round-shouldered. 2 nm,f hunchback; *voir* **rire**.

Boston [bɔstɔn] n Boston.

boston [bɔstɔ̃] nm (*danse, jeu*) boston.

Bostonien, -ienne [bɔstɔnjɛ̃, jɛn] nm,f Bostonian.

bostonnais, e [bɔstɔnɛ, ɛz] nm,f (*Can Hist*) Bostonian, American.

bot, bote [bo, bɔt] adj: **main bote** club-hand; **pied ~** club-foot.

botanique [bɔtanik] 1 adj botanical. 2 nf botany.

botaniste [bɔtanist] nmf botanist.

Botnie [bɔtni] nf: **le golfe de ~** the Gulf of Bothnia.

Botswana [bɔtswana] nm Botswana.

botswanais, e [bɔtswanɛ, ɛz] 1 adj of *ou* from Botswana. 2 nm,f: **B~(e)** inhabitant *ou* native of Botswana.

botte[1] [bɔt] nf (high) boot. **~ de caoutchouc** wellington (boot), gumboot, welly‡; **~ de cheval, ~ de cavalier** riding boot; **~ d'égoutier** wader; **être à la ~ de qn** to be under sb's heel *ou* thumb, be sb's puppet; **avoir qn à sa ~** to have sb under one's heel *ou* thumb; (*fig*) **cirer *ou* lécher les ~s de qn*** to lick sb's boots; **être sous la ~ de l'ennemi** to be under the enemy's heel.

botte[2] [bɔt] nf *[fleurs, légumes]* bunch; *[foin]* (*en gerbe*) bundle, sheaf; (*au carré*) bale.

botte[3] [bɔt] nf (*Escrime*) thrust. **porter une ~ à** (*lit*) to make a thrust at; (*fig*) to hit out at; (*fig*) **~ secrète** secret weapon.

botte[4] [bɔt] nf (*arg Scol: École polytechnique*) **sortir dans la ~** to be among the top students in one's year.

botter [bɔte] 1 1 vt a (*mettre des bottes à*) to put boots on; (*vendre des bottes à*) to sell boots to. **se ~** to put one's boots on; **il se botte chez X** he buys his boots at X's; **botté de cuir** with leather boots on, wearing leather boots. b **~ les fesses *ou* le derrière de qn‡** to kick *ou* boot‡ sb in the behind*, give sb a kick up the backside‡ *ou* in the pants‡. c **ça me botte‡** I fancy* (*Brit*) *ou* like *ou* dig‡ that; **ce film m'a botté*** I really liked *ou* went for* that film. d (*Ftbl*) to kick. 2 vi (*Ftbl*) to kick the ball; (*Ski*) to ball up.

bottier [bɔtje] nm *[bottes]* bootmaker; *[chaussures]* shoemaker.

bottillon [bɔtijɔ̃] nm ankle boot; *[bébé]* bootee.

Bottin [bɔtɛ̃] nm ® directory, phonebook. **~ mondain** ≃ Who's Who.

bottine [bɔtin] nf (ankle) boot, bootee. **~ à boutons** button-boot.

botulisme [bɔtylism] nm botulism.

boubou [bubu] nm boubou, bubu.

bouc [buk] nm (*Zool*) (billy) goat; (*barbe*) goatee (beard). **sentir *ou* puer le ~‡** to stink*, pong‡ (*Brit*); (*fig*) **~ émissaire** scapegoat, fall guy.

boucan* [bukɑ̃] nm din*, racket*. faire du ~ (*bruit*) to kick up* a din* *ou* a racket*; (*protestation*) to kick up* a fuss *ou* a shindy*.

boucane‡ [bukan] nf (*Can*) smoke.

boucaner [bukane] [1] vt *viande* to smoke, cure; *peau* to tan.

boucanier [bukanje] nm (*pirate*) buccaneer.

bouchage [buʃaʒ] nm (*voir* boucher) corking; filling up *ou* in; plugging, stopping; blocking (up); choking up.

bouche [buʃ] 1 nf a (*Anat*) mouth; *[volcan, fleuve, four]* mouth. embrasser à pleine ~ to kiss full on the lips; parler la ~ pleine to talk with one's mouth full; avoir la ~ amère to have a bitter taste in one's mouth; j'ai la ~ sèche my mouth feels *ou* is dry; j'ai la ~ pâteuse my tongue feels thick *ou* coated; (*fig*) il a 5 ~s à nourrir he has 5 mouths to feed; (*dans une population*) les ~s inutiles the non-active *ou* unproductive population; dans leur tribu, une fille est une ~ inutile in their tribe a girl is just another mouth to feed; provisions de ~ provisions; dépenses de ~food bills.

b (*organe de la communication*) mouth. fermer la ~ à qn to shut sb up; garder la ~ close to keep one's mouth shut; dans sa ~, ce mot choque when he says *ou* uses it, that word sounds offensive; il a toujours l'injure à la ~ he's always ready with an insult; il n'a que ce mot-là à la ~ that is all he ever talks about; de ~ à oreille by word of mouth, confidentially; ta ~ (bébé)!‡ shut your mouth!‡ *ou* trap!‡; ~ cousue!* don't breathe a word!, mum's the word!*; l'histoire est dans toutes les ~s the story is on everyone's lips, everyone's talking about it; son nom est dans toutes les ~s his name is a household word *ou* is on everyone's lips; aller *ou* passer de ~ en ~ to be rumoured about; il a la ~ pleine de cet acteur he can talk of nothing but this actor; il en a plein la ~ he can talk of nothing else; nos sentiments s'expriment par sa ~ our feelings are expressed by him *ou* by what he says.

c (*loc*) s'embrasser à ~ que veux-tu to kiss eagerly; faire la fine *ou* petite ~ to turn one's nose up (*fig*); avoir la ~ en cœur to simper; avoir la ~ en cul-de-poule to purse one's lips; *voir* bée.

2 comp ▸ **bouche d'aération** air vent *ou* inlet ▸ **bouche-à-bouche** nm inv kiss of life (*Brit*), mouth-to-mouth resuscitation (*Brit*) *ou* respiration (*US*); faire du bouche-à-bouche à qn to give sb the kiss of life *ou* mouth to mouth resuscitation ▸ **bouche de chaleur** hot-air vent *ou* inlet ▸ **bouche d'égout** manhole ▸ **bouche à feu** (*Hist*) piece (of ordnance), gun ▸ **bouche d'incendie** fire hydrant ▸ **bouche de métro** metro entrance.

bouché, e[1] [buʃe] (ptp de boucher) adj *temps* cloudy, overcast; (‡ *fig*) *personne* stupid, thick‡ (*Brit*). ~ à l'émeri *flacon* with a ground glass stopper; (*) *personne* wood from the neck up*, thick as a brick‡ (*Brit*); les mathématiques sont ~es there is no future in maths; *voir* cidre.

bouchée[2] [buʃe] nf a mouthful. (*fig*) pour une ~ de pain for a song, for next to nothing; (*fig*) mettre les ~s doubles to get stuck in* (*Brit*), put on a spurt; ne faire qu'une ~ d'un plat to gobble up *ou* polish off a dish in next to no time; (*fig*) ne faire qu'une ~ d'un adversaire to make short work of an opponent. b (*Culin*) une ~ (au chocolat) a chocolate; ~ à la reine chicken vol-au-vent.

boucher[1] [buʃe] [1] 1 vt a *bouteille* to cork, put the *ou* a cork in; *trou, fente* to fill up *ou* in; *fuite* to plug, stop; *fenêtre* to block (up); *lavabo* to block (up), choke (up). sécrétions qui bouchent les pores secretions which block up *ou* clog up the pores; j'ai les oreilles bouchées my ears are blocked (up); j'ai le nez bouché my nose is blocked (up) *ou* stuffed up *ou* bunged up*; ~ le passage to be *ou* stand in the way; ~ le passage à qn to be *ou* stand in sb's way, block sb's way; ~ la vue to block the view; tu me bouches le jour you're in my *ou* the light; prends une pomme, ça te bouchera un trou* have an apple, that will keep you going (for now); on l'a employé pour ~ les trous we used him as a stopgap.

b ça/elle lui en a bouché un coin‡ he was staggered* *ou* flabbergasted* *ou* gobsmacked‡ (*Brit*).

2 **se boucher** vpr *[évier]* to get blocked *ou* choked *ou* clogged up; *[temps]* to get cloudy, become overcast. se ~ le nez to hold one's nose; se ~ les oreilles to put one's fingers in one's ears; se ~ les yeux to put one's hands over one's eyes, hide one's eyes.

boucher[2] [buʃe] nm (*lit, fig*) butcher.

bouchère [buʃɛʀ] nf (woman) butcher; (*épouse*) butcher's wife.

boucherie [buʃʀi] nf (*magasin*) butcher's (shop); (*métier*) butchery (trade); (*fig*) slaughter. ~ chevaline horse(meat) butcher's.

bouche-trou, pl bouche-trous [buʃtʀu] nm (*personne*) fill-in, stopgap, stand-in; (*chose*) stopgap, pinch-hitter* (*NonC*).

bouchon [buʃɔ̃] nm a (*en liège*) cork; (*en verre*) stopper; (*en plastique*) stopper, top; (*en chiffon, papier*) plug, bung; *[bidon, réservoir]* cap; *[tube]* top; *[évier]* plug. (*Phot*) ~ d'objectif lens cap; ~ anti-vol locking petrol cap (*Brit*), locking fuel filler cap; ~ de vidange drain plug; vin qui sent le ~ corked wine; *voir* pousser. b (*Pêche*) float. c ~ (de paille) wisp. d (*Aut: embouteillage*) holdup, traffic jam. un ~ de 12 km a 12-km tailback.

bouchonnage [buʃɔnaʒ] nm *[cheval]* rubbing-down, wisping-down (*Brit*).

bouchonner [buʃɔne] [1] 1 vt *cheval* to rub down, wisp down (*Brit*). 2 vi (*Aut*) ça bouchonne en ville there's heavy congestion in town.

bouchot [buʃo] nm mussel bed.

bouclage [buklaʒ] nm (*: *mise sous clefs*) locking up *ou* away, imprisonment; (*encerclement*) surrounding, sealing off.

boucle [bukl] nf *[ceinture, soulier]* buckle; *[cheveux]* curl, lock; *[ruban, voie ferrée, rivière]* loop; (*Sport*) lap; (*Aviat*) loop; (*Ordin*) loop. fais une ~ à ton j put a loop on your j; fais une ~ à ton lacet tie your shoelace in a bow; B~s d'or Goldilocks; ~ d'oreille earring; ~ d'oreille à vis (*ou* à crochets) pierced earring, earring for pierced ear.

bouclé, e [bukle] (ptp de boucler) adj *cheveux, fourrure* curly; *personne* curly-haired. il avait la tête ~e his hair was curly *ou* all curls.

boucler [bukle] [1] 1 vt a (*fermer*) *ceinture* to buckle, fasten (up); (*) *porte* to lock. ~ sa valise (*lit*) to fasten one's suitcase; (*fig*) to pack one's bags; tu vas la ~!‡ will you belt up!‡ (*Brit*), will you shut your trap!‡

b (*fig: terminer*) *affaire* to finish off, get through with, settle; *circuit* to complete, go round; *budget* to balance. arriver à ~ ses fins de mois to manage to stay in the black at the end of the month; (*Aviat*) ~ la boucle to loop the loop; (*fig*) on est revenu par l'Espagne pour ~ la boucle we came back through Spain to make (it) a round trip; (*fig*) nous revoilà dans ce village, on a bouclé la boucle we're back in the village, so we've come full circle; dans le cycle de production la boucle est bouclée the cycle of production is now completed.

c (*: *enfermer*) to shut up *ou* away, lock up, put inside*. ils ont bouclé le coupable they've locked up the criminal *ou* put the criminal under lock and key; être bouclé chez soi to be cooped up *ou* stuck* at home.

d (*Mil, Police: encercler*) to surround, seal off, cordon off. la police a bouclé le quartier the police surrounded the area *ou* sealed off the area.

2 vi to curl, be curly.

bouclette [buklɛt] nf small curl, ringlet.

bouclier [buklije] nm (*Mil, fig*) shield; (*Police*) riot shield. faire un ~ de son corps à qn to shield sb with one's body; (*Espace*) ~ thermique heat shield; ~ atomique *ou* nucléaire nuclear defences (*pl*); ~ humain human shield.

Bouddha [buda] nm Buddha. (*statuette*) b~ Buddha.

bouddhique [budik] adj Buddhist.

bouddhisme [budism] nm Buddhism. ~ zen zen Buddhism.

bouddhiste [budist] adj, nmf Buddhist. ~ zen zen Buddhist.

bouder [bude] [1] 1 vi to sulk, have a sulk *ou* the sulks*. 2 vt *personne* to refuse to talk to *ou* have anything to do with; *chose* to refuse to have anything to do with, keep away from; (*Comm*) *produit* to be reluctant to buy, stay away from. ~ la nourriture to have no appetite; ~ son plaisir to deny o.s.; spectacle boudé par le public show that is ignored by the public; les électeurs ont boudé ce scrutin a lot of voters stayed at home; le soleil va ~ le nord du pays the north of the country won't see much of the sun; ils se boudent they're not on speaking terms, they're not speaking.

bouderie [budʀi] nf (*état*) sulkiness (*NonC*); (*action*) sulk.

boudeur, -euse [budœʀ, øz] adj sulky, sullen.

boudin [budɛ̃] nm a (*Culin*) ~ (noir) ≃ black pudding (*Brit*), blood sausage (*US*); ~ blanc ≃ white pudding; (*: *bouder*) faire du ~ to sulk; *voir* eau. b (*gonflable*) ring, tube. c (*: *doigt*) podgy *ou* fat finger. d (*: *fille*) fat lump (of a girl)‡ (*péj*), fatty‡ (*péj*), fatso‡ (*péj*).

boudiné, e [budine] (ptp de boudiner) adj a *doigt* podgy. b (*serré*) ~ dans squeezed into, bursting out of; ~ dans un corset strapped into *ou* bulging out of a tight-fitting corset.

boudiner [budine] [1] 1 vt (*Tex*) to rove; *fil* to coil. sa robe la boudine her dress makes her look all bulges. 2 **se boudiner** vpr: se ~ dans ses vêtements to squeeze o.s. into one's clothes, wear too tight-fitting clothes.

boudoir [budwaʀ] nm (*salon*) boudoir; (*biscuit*) sponge (*Brit*) *ou* lady (*US*) finger.

boue [bu] nf (*gén*) mud; *[mer, canal]* sludge, silt; (*dépôt*) sediment. (*Méd*) ~s activées activated sludge; (*fig*) traîner qn dans la ~ to drag sb in the mud; (*fig*) couvrir qn de ~ to throw *ou* sling mud at sb.

bouée [bwe] nf (*de signalisation*) buoy; (*d'enfant*) rubber ring. ~ de sauvetage (*lit*) lifebelt; (*fig*) lifeline; ~ sonore radio buoy.

boueux, -euse [bwø, øz] 1 adj muddy; (*Typ*) blurred, smudged. 2 nm dustman (*Brit*), refuse collector (*Brit Admin*), garbage collector (*US*).

bouffant, e [bufɑ̃, ɑ̃t] 1 adj *manche* puff(ed) (*épith*), full; *cheveux* full; *pantalon* baggy. 2 nm *[jupe, manche]* fulness; *[cheveux]* fullness, volume; *[pantalon]* bagginess.

bouffarde* [bufaʀd] nf pipe.

bouffe[1] [buf] adj *voir* opéra.

bouffe[2]‡ [buf] nf grub‡. il ne pense qu'à la ~ he only thinks of his stomach *ou* of his grub‡ *ou* nosh‡ (*Brit*); faire la ~ to cook, do the cooking, make the grub‡.

bouffée [bufe] nf *[parfum]* whiff; *[pipe, cigarette]* puff, drag*; *[colère]* outburst; *[orgueil]* fit. ~ d'air *ou* de vent puff *ou* breath *ou* gust of wind; (*lit, fig*) une ~ d'air pur a breath of fresh air; ~ de chaleur (*Méd*) hot flush (*Brit*) *ou* flash (*US*); (*gén*) gust *ou* blast of hot air; par ~s in gusts.

bouffer[1] [bufe] [1] **vi** *[cheveux]* to be full, have volume. **faire ~ une jupe/une manche** to make a skirt fuller/a sleeve puff out; **faire ~ ses cheveux** to add volume *ou* fullness to one's hair.

bouffer[2]‡ [bufe] [1] **vt** a (*gén*) to eat; (*engloutir*) to gobble up*, wolf down. **cette voiture bouffe de l'essence** this car drinks petrol (*Brit*) *ou* guzzles gas (*US*); **se ~ le nez** to have a go at one another*, scratch each other's eyes out*; **~ du curé** to be violently anti-church *ou* anti-clerical; **je l'aurais bouffé!** I could have murdered him!; **j'ai cru qu'elle allait le ~** I thought she was going to eat him alive. b (*emploi absolu*) to eat. **on bouffe mal ici** the grub‡ here isn't up to much; **on a bien bouffé ici** the grub was great here‡.

bouffetance‡ [buftɑ̃s] **nf** = **bouffe**[2].

bouffeur, -euse‡ [bufœʀ, øz] **nm,f** greedy guts‡, (greedy) pig*.

bouffi, e [bufi] (**ptp de bouffir**) **adj** *visage* puffed up, bloated; *yeux* swollen, puffy; (*fig*) swollen, puffed up (*de* with). (**hareng**) **~** bloater.

bouffir [bufiʀ] [2] 1 **vt** to puff up. 2 **vi** to become bloated, puff up.

bouffissure [bufisyʀ] **nf** puffiness (*NonC*), bloatedness (*NonC*); puffy swelling.

bouffon, -onne [bufɔ̃, ɔn] 1 **adj** farcical, comical. 2 **nm** (*pitre*) buffoon, clown; (*Hist*) jester.

bouffonnerie [bufɔnʀi] **nf** a (*NonC*) *[personne]* clownishness; *[situation]* drollery. b **~s** (*comportement*) antics, foolery, buffoonery; (*paroles*) jesting; **faire des ~s** to clown about, play the fool.

bougainvillée [bugɛ̃vile] **nf**, **bougainvillier** [bugɛ̃vilje] **nm** bougainvillea.

bouge [buʒ] **nm** (*taudis*) hovel, dump*; (*bar louche*) low dive*.

bougeoir [buʒwaʀ] **nm** (*bas*) candle-holder; (*haut*) candlestick.

bougeotte* [buʒɔt] **nf: avoir la ~** (*voyager*) to be always on the move; (*remuer*) to fidget (about), have the fidgets*, have ants in one's pants‡.

bouger [buʒe] [3] 1 **vi** a (*remuer*) to move; (*se révolter*) to be restless. **ne bouge pas** keep still, don't move *ou* budge; **il n'a pas bougé (de chez lui)** he stayed in *ou* at home, he didn't stir out; (*tremblement de terre*) **la terre a bougé** the ground shook; **un métier où l'on bouge** an active job, a job where you are always on the move; (*fig*) **quand la police l'a arrêté, personne n'a bougé** when the police arrested him no-one lifted a finger (to help).
b (*changer*) **ça bouge toujours dans cette industrie/ce service** this is a fast-moving industry/lively department; **ça ne bouge pas beaucoup dans ce service** nothing much ever changes in this department; **ce tissu ne bouge pas** (*gén*) this cloth wears *ou* will wear well; (*dimension*) this cloth is shrink-resistant; (*couleur*) this cloth will not fade; **ses idées n'ont pas bougé** his ideas haven't altered, he hasn't changed his ideas; **les prix n'ont pas bougé** prices have stayed put* *ou* the same.
2 **vt** (*) *objet* to move, shift*. **il n'a pas bougé le petit doigt** he didn't lift a finger (to help).
3 **se bouger*** **vpr** to move. **bouge-toi de là!** shift over!‡, shift out of the way!‡, scoot over!* (*US*); **je m'ennuie — alors bouge-toi un peu!** I'm bored — then get up off your backside*! (*Brit*) *ou* butt‡! (*US*); **il faut se ~ pour obtenir satisfaction** you have to put yourself out to get satisfaction.

bougie [buʒi] **nf** a (*chandelle*) candle; (*Aut*) spark(ing) plug, plug. **ampoule de 40 ~s**† 40 candle-power bulb. b (‡: *visage*) face, dial‡. **faire une drôle de ~** to pull (*Brit*) *ou* make a (wry) face.

bougna(t)†* [buɲa] **nm** (*charbonnier*) coalman; (*marchand de charbon*) coal merchant (*who also runs a small café*).

bougnoul(e)** [buɲul] **nmf** (*péj*) (*Noir*) nigger**; (*Arabe*) wog**, fucking** *ou* bloody** (*Brit*) Arab.

bougon, -onne [bugɔ̃, ɔn] 1 **adj** grumpy, grouchy*. 2 **nm,f** grumbler, grouch*.

bougonnement [bugɔnmɑ̃] **nm** grumbling, grouching*.

bougonner [bugɔne] [1] **vi** to grouch* (away) (to o.s.), grumble.

bougre* [bugʀ] 1 **nm** (*type*) guy*, chap* (*Brit*), fellow*, blighter* (*Brit*); (*enfant*) (little) rascal. **bon ~** good sort* *ou* chap*; **pauvre ~** poor devil* *ou* blighter*; **ce ~ d'homme** that confounded man; **~ d'idiot! *ou* d'animal!** stupid *ou* confounded idiot!*, silly blighter!* (*Brit*); **il le savait, le ~!** the so-and-so knew it! 2 **excl** good Lord!*, strewth!* (*Brit*), I'll be darned!* (*US*).

bougrement* [bugʀəmɑ̃] **adv** (*hum*) damn*, damned*.

bougresse‡ [bugʀɛs] **nf** woman; (*péj*) hussy, bitch‡.

boui-boui, **pl bouis-bouis*** [bwibwi] **nm** (*gén*) unpretentious (little) restaurant; (*péj*) greasy spoon*.

bouif*† [bwif] **nm** cobbler.

bouillabaisse [bujabɛs] **nf** bouillabaisse, fish soup.

bouillant, e [bujɑ̃, ɑ̃t] **adj** (*brûlant*) *boisson* boiling (hot), scalding; (*qui bout*) *eau, huile* boiling; *tempérament* fiery; *personne* (*emporté*) fiery-natured, hotheaded; (*fiévreux*) boiling (hot)*. **~ de colère** seething *ou* boiling with anger.

bouillasse* [bujas] **nf** (*gadoue*) muck.

bouille* [buj] **nf** (*visage*) face, mug‡ (*péj*). **avoir une bonne ~** to have a cheerful friendly face.

bouilleur [bujœʀ] **nm** (*distillateur*) distiller. **~ de cru** home distiller; **~ de cru clandestin** moonshiner.

bouilli, e[1] [buji] 1 **adj** boiled. 2 **nm** boiled meat. **~ de bœuf** *beef stew*.

bouillie[2] [buji] **nf** *[bébé]* baby's cereal; *[vieillard]* gruel, porridge. **mettre en ~** *légumes, fruits* to pulp, mash *ou* reduce to a pulp; (*fig*) *adversaire* to beat to a pulp; (*fig*) **c'est de la ~ pour les chats** it's a (proper) dog's dinner*; **réduit en ~** (*lit*) *légumes* cooked to a pulp *ou* mush; (*fig*) *adversaire* to a pulp beaten; *voiture* crushed to pieces, flattened*.

bouillir [bujiʀ] [15] 1 **vi** a (*lit*) to boil, be boiling. **commencer à ~** to reach boiling point, be nearly boiling; **l'eau bout** the water is boiling; **l'eau ne bout plus** the water has stopped boiling, the water has gone *ou* is off the boil (*Brit*); **faire ~ de l'eau** to boil water, bring water to the boil; **faire ~ du linge/des poireaux** to boil clothes/leeks; **faire ~ un biberon** to sterilize a (baby's) bottle by boiling; **~ à gros bouillons** to boil fast; (*fig*) **avoir de quoi faire ~ la marmite** to have enough to keep the pot boiling; **c'est elle qui fait ~ la marmite**she's the breadwinner.
b (*fig*) to boil. **à voir ça, je bous!** seeing that makes my blood boil!, I boil at seeing that!; **faire ~ qn** to make sb's blood boil, make sb mad*; **~ d'impatience** to seethe with impatience; **~ de rage/de haine** to seethe *ou* boil with anger/hatred.
2 **vt** *eau, linge* to boil.

bouilloire [bujwaʀ] **nf** kettle. **~ électrique** (*gén*) electric kettle; (*haute*) jug kettle.

bouillon [bujɔ̃] 1 **nm** a (*soupe*) broth, stock, bouillon. **~ de légumes/poulet** vegetable/chicken stock; **prendre *ou* boire un ~*** (*en nageant*) to swallow *ou* get a mouthful; (*Fin*) to take a tumble*, come a cropper* (*Brit*). b (*bouillonnement*) bubble (in boiling liquid). **au premier ~** as soon as it boils *ou* comes to the boil; **couler à gros ~s** to gush out, come gushing out. c (*arg Presse*) **~s** unsold copies, returns. d (*Couture*) puff. 2 **comp** ▸**bouillon cube** stock *ou* bouillon cube ▸**bouillon de culture** (*Bio*) (culture) medium ▸**bouillon gras** meat stock ▸**bouillon d'onze heures*** poisoned drink, lethal potion.

bouillonnant, e [bujɔnɑ̃, ɑ̃t] **adj** (*voir* **bouillonner**) bubbling; seething; foaming, frothing.

bouillonnement [bujɔnmɑ̃] **nm** (*voir* **bouillonner**) bubbling; seething; foaming, frothing.

bouillonner [bujɔne] [1] **vi** *[liquide chaud]* to bubble, seethe; *[torrent]* to foam, froth; *[idées]* to bubble up; *[esprit]* to seethe. (*fig*) **~ de colère** to seethe *ou* boil with anger; **il bouillonne d'idées** his mind is teeming with ideas, he's bubbling with ideas.

bouillotte [bujɔt] **nf** hot-water bottle.

boulange* [bulɑ̃ʒ] **nf** bakery trade. **être dans la ~** to be a baker (by trade).

boulanger [bulɑ̃ʒe] **nm** baker.

boulangère [bulɑ̃ʒɛʀ] **nf** (woman) baker; (*épouse*) baker's wife.

boulangerie [bulɑ̃ʒʀi] **nf** (*magasin*) baker's (shop), bakery; (*commerce*) bakery trade. **~-pâtisserie** baker's and confectioner's (shop).

boule[1] [bul] 1 **nf** a (*Billard, Croquet*) ball; (*Boules*) bowl; (*Géol*) tor. **jouer aux ~s** to play bowls; (*Casino*) **jouer à la ~** to play (at) boule; **roulé en ~** *animal* curled up in a ball; *paquet* rolled up in a ball; (*fig*) **être en ~*** to be in a temper *ou* paddy* (*Brit*); **se mettre en ~** *[hérisson]* to roll up into a ball; (*) *[personne]* to fly off the handle*; **cela me met en ~*** that makes me mad* *ou* gets my goat‡ *ou* gets me‡.
b (*: *grosseur*) lump. (*fig*) **avoir une ~ dans la gorge** to have a lump in one's throat; **j'ai les ~s**‡ (*anxieux*) I've got butterflies*; (*mécontent*) I'm hopping mad*; **ça fait les ~s**‡ (*ça angoisse*) it's really scary*; (*ça énerve*) it's damn annoying‡.
c (*: *tête*) head, nut*. **perdre la ~** to go bonkers‡ (*Brit*) *ou* nuts*, go off one's rocker‡; **coup de ~** head-butt; **avoir la ~ à zéro** to have a shaven head.
2 **comp** ▸**boule de billard** billiard ball; (*fig*) **avoir une boule de billard** to be as bald as a coot* *ou* an egg* ▸**boule de cristal** crystal ball; (*fig*) **je ne lis pas dans les boules de cristal!** I haven't got a crystal ball!, I'm not a clairvoyant! ▸**boule de feu** fireball ▸**boule de gomme** (*Pharm*) throat pastille; (*bonbon*) fruit pastille *ou* gum, gumdrop ▸**boule de neige** snowball; (*fig*) **faire boule de neige** to snowball ▸**boule-de-neige nf (pl boules-de-neige)** (*fleur*) guelder-rose; (*arbre*) snowball tree ▸**boule puante** stink bomb ▸**boule Quiès** ® earplug, ear stopper.

boule[2] [bul] **nm** (*Menuiserie*) boule, buhl. **commode ~** boule *ou* buhl chest of drawers.

bouleau, **pl ~x** [bulo] **nm** (silver) birch.

bouledogue [buldɔg] **nm** bulldog.

bouler [bule] [1] **vi** to roll along. **elle a boulé dans l'escalier** she fell head over heels down the stairs; **envoyer ~ qn*** to send sb packing*, send sb away with a flea in his ear*.

boulet [bulɛ] **nm** a *[forçat]* ball and chain. **~ (de canon)** cannonball; (*fig*) **traîner un ~** to have a millstone round one's neck; **c'est un (véritable) ~ pour ses parents** he is a millstone round his parents' neck; **arriver comme un ~ de canon** to come bursting in *ou* crashing in; **tirer à ~s rouges sur qn** to lay into sb tooth and nail. b *[charbon]* (coal) nut. c (*Vét*) fetlock.

boulette [bulɛt] **nf** a *[papier]* pellet; (*Culin*) meat croquette, meatball; (*empoisonnée*) poison ball. b (* *fig*) blunder, bloomer*. **faire**

une ~ to make a blunder *ou* bloomer*, drop a brick* *ou* clanger* (*Brit*).

boulevard [bulvaʀ] nm boulevard. **les ~s extérieurs** the outer boulevards of Paris; **les grands ~s** the grand boulevards; **pièce** *ou* **comédie de ~** light comedy; *voir* **théâtre**.

bouleversant, e [bulvɛʀsɑ̃, ɑ̃t] adj *spectacle, récit* deeply moving; *nouvelle* shattering, overwhelming.

bouleversement [bulvɛʀsəmɑ̃] nm *[habitudes, vie politique etc]* upheaval, disruption. **le ~ de son visage** the utter distress on his face, his distraught face.

bouleverser [bulvɛʀse] [1] vt a (*émouvoir*) to distress deeply; (*causer un choc*) to overwhelm, bowl over, shatter. **bouleversé par l'angoisse/la peur** distraught with anxiety/fear; **la nouvelle les a bouleversés** they were shattered *ou* deeply distressed by the news. b (*modifier*) *plan, habitude* to disrupt, change completely *ou* drastically. c (*déranger*) to turn upside down.

boulier [bulje] nm (*calcul*) abacus; (*Billard*) scoring board.

boulimie [bulimi] nf bulimia (*SPÉC*). **il fait de la ~*** he is a compulsive eater; (*fig*) **être saisi d'une ~ de lecture/de cinéma** to be seized by a compulsive desire to read/to go the cinema.

boulimique [bulimik] 1 adj bulimic (*SPÉC*). 2 nmf bulimiac (*SPÉC*), compulsive eater.

boulingrin [bulɛ̃gʀɛ̃] nm lawn.

bouliste [bulist] nmf bowls player.

boulle [bul] nm = **boule[2]**.

boulodrome [bulodʀom] nm bowling pitch.

boulon [bulɔ̃] nm bolt; (*avec son écrou*) nut and bolt. (*fig*) **(res)serrer les ~s** to tighten a few screws.

boulonnage [bulɔnaʒ] nm (*voir* **boulonner**) bolting (on); bolting (down).

boulonner [bulɔne] [1] 1 vt (*serrer à force*) to bolt (down); (*assembler*) to bolt (on). 2 vi (*) to work. **~ (dur)** to slog* *ou* slave* away.

boulot[1], -otte [bulo, ɔt] adj plump, tubby*.

boulot[2]* [bulo] nm (*travail*) work (*NonC*); (*dur labeur*) grind* (*NonC*); (*emploi*) job, work (*NonC*); (*lieu de travail*) work (*NonC*), place of work. **elle a 4 enfants à élever, quel ~!** she has 4 children to bring up, what a job!; **être sans ~** to be out of work *ou* unemployed; **j'ai un ~ fou en ce moment** I'm up to my eyes in work *ou* I'm snowed under with work at the moment*; **ce n'est pas du ~** that's not work!, (do you) call that work!; **on a du ~** (*gén*) we've got work to do; (*tâche difficile*) that will take some doing*; **il a trouvé du ~** *ou* **un ~** he's found work *ou* a job; **allons, au ~!** let's get cracking!*, let's get the show on the road!*; **il est ~ ~** with him it is just work, work, work*; *voir* **métro**.

boulotter* [bulɔte] [1] 1 vi to eat, nosh‡ (*Brit*). **on a bien boulotté** we had a good meal‡. 2 vt to eat.

boum [bum] 1 excl (*chute*) bang!, wallop!; (*explosion*) boom!, bang! (*langage enfantin*) **faire ~** to go bang*; **~ par terre!** whoops a daisy! 2 nm (*explosion*) bang. **on entendit un grand ~** there was an enormous bang; (*loc*) **être en plein ~‡** to be in full swing, be going full blast*. 3 nf (*: *fête*) party, rave-up‡, knees-up‡ (*Brit*).

boumer‡ [bume] [1] vi: **ça boume** everything's going fine *ou* swell* (*US*); **ça boume?** how's things?* *ou* tricks?*

boumerang [bumʀɑ̃g] nm = **boomerang**.

bounioul [bunjul] nm = **bougnoul(e)**.

bouquet[1] [bukɛ] nm a (*Bot*) **~ (de fleurs)** bunch (of flowers); (*soigneusement composé*) (*grand*) bouquet, (*petit*) posy; **~ d'arbres** clump of trees; **faire un ~** to make up a bouquet; **le ~ de mariée** the bride's bouquet; **~ de persil/thym** bunch of parsley/thyme; (*Culin*) **~ garni** bouquet garni, *bunch of mixed herbs;* (*Can* ‡) **~s** (garden *ou* cut) flowers; (house) plants. b *[feu d'artifice]* finishing *ou* crowning piece (*in a firework display*). (*fig*) **c'est le ~!*** that takes the cake!* *ou* the biscuit!* (*Brit*), that's the last straw! c *[vin]* bouquet. **vin qui a du ~** wine which has a good bouquet *ou* nose. d (*Jur*) *[viager]* initial payment.

bouquet[2] [bukɛ] nm (*Zool: crevette*) prawn.

bouquetière [buk(ə)tjɛʀ] nf flower seller, flower girl.

bouquetin [buk(ə)tɛ̃] nm ibex.

bouquin* [bukɛ̃] nm book.

bouquiner* [bukine] [1] vti to read. **il passe son temps à ~** he always has his nose in a book.

bouquiniste [bukinist] nmf secondhand bookseller (*esp along the Seine in Paris*).

bourbe [buʀb] nf mire, mud.

bourbeux, -euse [buʀbø, øz] adj miry, muddy.

bourbier [buʀbje] nm (quag)mire; (*fig*) (*situation*) mess; (*entreprise*) unsavoury *ou* nasty business, quagmire.

Bourbon [buʀbɔ̃] 1 n Bourbon. 2 nm (*whisky*) **b~** bourbon.

bourde* [buʀd] nf (*gaffe*) blunder, bloomer*, boob*; (*faute*) slip, mistake, bloomer*; howler* (*surtout Scol*). **faire une ~** (*gaffe*) to boob* (*Brit*), blunder, drop a clanger* (*Brit*); (*faute*) to make a (silly) mistake, goof up* (*US*).

bourdon[1] [buʀdɔ̃] nm a (*Zool*) bumblebee, humble-bee. **avoir le ~*** to have the blues*; *voir* **faux[2]**. b (*Mus*) (*cloche*) great bell; *[cornemuse]* bourdon, drone; *[orgue]* bourdon; *voir* **faux[2]**.

bourdon[2] [buʀdɔ̃] nm (*Typ*) omission, out.

bourdon[3] [buʀdɔ̃] nm pilgrim's staff.

bourdonnement [buʀdɔnmɑ̃] nm *[insecte]* humming (*NonC*), buzzing (*NonC*); *[abeille]* drone (*NonC*); *[voix]* buzz (*NonC*), hum (*NonC*); *[moteur]* hum (*NonC*), humming (*NonC*), drone (*NonC*); *[avion]* drone (*NonC*). **avoir un ~ dans les oreilles** *ou* **des ~s d'oreilles** to have a singing *ou* buzzing noise in one's ears.

bourdonner [buʀdɔne] [1] vi *[insecte]* to buzz, hum; *[abeille]* to drone; *[moteur]* to hum, drone. **ça bourdonne dans mes oreilles** my ears are buzzing, there is a buzzing in my ears.

bourg [buʀ] nm market town; (*petit*) village. **au ~, dans le ~** in town, in the village.

bourgade [buʀgad] nf village, (small) town.

bourgeois, e [buʀʒwa, waz] 1 adj a middle-class; *appartement* comfortable, snug. **quartier ~** middle-class *ou* residential district.

b (*gén péj: conventionnel*) *culture, préjugé* bourgeois, middle-class; *valeurs, goûts* bourgeois, middle-class, conventional. **avoir l'esprit (petit-)~** to have a conventional *ou* narrow outlook; **mener une petite vie ~e** to live a boring middle-class existence; *voir* **petit**.

2 nm,f a bourgeois, middle-class person. **grand ~** upper middle-class person; (*péj*) **les ~** the wealthy (classes); **sortir en ~*†** to go out in mufti*† *ou* in civvies*; *voir* **épater**.

b (*Hist*) (*citoyen*) burgess; (*riche roturier*) bourgeois.

3 nm (*Can*) head of household, master.

4 **bourgeoise*** nf (*hum: épouse*) **la** *ou* **ma ~e** the wife*, the missus*.

bourgeoisement [buʀʒwazmɑ̃] adv *penser, réagir* conventionally; *vivre* comfortably.

bourgeoisie [buʀʒwazi] nf a middle class(es), bourgeoisie. **petite/moyenne/haute ~** lower middle/middle/upper middle class. b (*Hist: citoyenneté*) bourgeoisie, burgesses.

bourgeon [buʀʒɔ̃] nm (*Bot*) bud; († *fig*) spot, pimple.

bourgeonnement [buʀʒɔnmɑ̃] nm (*Bot*) budding; (*Méd*) granulation (*SPÉC*).

bourgeonner [buʀʒɔne] [1] vi (*Bot*) to (come into) bud; (*Méd*) *[plaie]* to granulate (*SPÉC*). (*fig*) **son visage bourgeonne** he's getting spots *ou* pimples on his face.

bourgmestre [buʀgmɛstʀ] nm burgomaster.

bourgogne [buʀgɔɲ] 1 nm (*vin*) burgundy. 2 nf (*région*) **la B~** Burgundy.

bourguignon, -onne [buʀgiɲɔ̃, ɔn] 1 adj Burgundian. (*Culin*) **un (bœuf) ~** bœuf bourguignon, beef stewed in red wine. 2 nm,f: **B~(ne)** Burgundian.

bourlinguer [buʀlɛ̃ge] [1] vi a (*naviguer*) to sail; (*: *voyager*) to get around a lot*, knock about a lot*. b (*Naut*) to labour.

bourrache [buʀaʃ] nf borage.

bourrade [buʀad] nf (*du poing*) thump; (*du coude*) dig, poke, prod.

bourrage [buʀaʒ] nm *[coussin]* stuffing; *[poêle, pipe]* filling; *[fusil]* wadding. **~ de crâne*** (*propagande*) brainwashing; (*récits exagérés*) eyewash*, hot air*; (*Scol*) cramming.

bourrasque [buʀask] nf gust of wind, squall. **~ de neige** flurry of snow; **le vent souffle en ~** the wind is blowing in gusts.

bourrasser* [buʀase] [1] vt (*Can*) to browbeat, bully.

bourratif, -ive [buʀatif, iv] adj (*gén*) filling; (*péj*) stodgy.

bourre[1] [buʀ] nf *[coussin]* stuffing; (*en poils*) hair; (*en laine, coton*) wadding, flock; *[bourgeon]* down; *[fusil]* wad. **de première ~*** great*, brilliant* (*Brit*); **à la ~‡** (*en retard*) late; (*pressé*) pushed for time*; **être à la ~ dans son travail‡** to be behind with one's work.

bourre[2]‡ [buʀ] nm (*policier*) cop*. **les ~s** the fuzz‡, the cops*.

bourré, e[1] [buʀe] (ptp de **bourrer**) adj a (*plein à craquer*) *salle, sac, compartiment* packed, jam-packed*, crammed (*de* with). **portefeuille ~ de billets** wallet cram-full of *ou* stuffed with notes; **devoir ~ de fautes** exercise packed *ou* crammed with mistakes; **il est ~ de tics** he is always twitching; **il est ~ de complexes** he has got loads of hang-ups*, he is really hung-up*; **~ de vitamines** *aliment* crammed *ou* packed with vitamins. b (‡: *ivre*) tight*, canned‡, plastered‡.

bourreau, pl **~x** [buʀo] 1 nm a (*tortionnaire*) torturer. b (*Hist*) *[guillotine]* executioner, headsman; *[pendaison]* executioner, hangman. 2 comp ▸**bourreau des cœurs** ladykiller ▸**bourreau d'enfants** child-batterer, baby-batterer ▸**bourreau de travail** glutton for work*, workaholic*.

bourrée[2] [buʀe] nf (*Mus*) bourrée.

bourreler [buʀle] [4] vt: **bourrelé de remords** racked by remorse.

bourrelet [buʀlɛ] nm a (*gén*) roll; *[porte, fenêtre]* draught excluder (*Brit*), weather strip (*US*). b **~ (de chair)** fold *ou* roll of flesh; **~ (de graisse)** roll of fat, spare tyre*.

bourrelier [buʀəlje] nm saddler.

bourrellerie [buʀɛlʀi] nf saddlery.

bourrer [buʀe] [1] 1 vt a (*remplir*) *coussin* to stuff; *pipe, poêle* to fill; *valise* to stuff *ou* cram full; (*Mil, Min*) to ram home. **~ une dissertation de citations** to cram an essay with quotations; **~ un sac de papiers** to stuff *ou* cram papers into a bag.

b **~ qn de nourriture** to stuff sb with food; **ne te bourre pas de gâteaux** don't stuff* yourself *ou* fill yourself up* with cakes; **les frites,**

ça bourre! chips are very filling!

c (*loc*) ~ **le crâne à qn*** (*endoctriner*) to stuff* sb's head full of ideas, brainwash sb; (*en faire accroire*) to feed sb a lot of eyewash*; (*Scol*) to cram sb; ~ **qn de coups** to pummel sb, beat sb up, hammer blows on sb; **se faire ~ la gueule*‡** to get one's head bashed in‡; **se ~ la gueule*‡** (*se battre*) to bash one another up‡; (*se soûler*) to get sloshed‡ *ou* pissed*‡ (*Brit*) *ou* plastered‡; ~ **le mou à qn‡** to have sb on* (*Brit*), kid sb (on)*.

2 **vi** (‡: *se dépêcher*) (*en voiture, en moto*) to go flat out*, tear along*, belt along‡ (*Brit*); (*au travail*) to go *ou* work flat out*.

bourriche [buʀiʃ] **nf** *[huîtres]* hamper, basket; (*Pêche*) keep-net.

bourrichon* [buʀiʃɔ̃] **nm**: **se monter le ~** to get a notion in one's head; **monter le ~ à qn** to put ideas into sb's head, stir sb up (*contre* against).

bourricot [buʀiko] **nm** (small) donkey.

bourrin* [buʀɛ̃] **nm** horse, nag*.

bourrique [buʀik] **nf** a (*Zool*) (*âne*) donkey, ass; (*ânesse*) she-ass. b (* *fig*) (*imbécile*) ass, blockhead*; (*têtu*) pigheaded* person. **faire tourner qn en ~** to drive sb to distraction *ou* up the wall*; *voir* **soûl, têtu.**

bourriquot [buʀiko] **nm** = **bourricot.**

bourru, e [buʀy] **adj** *personne, air* surly; *voix* gruff.

bourrure [buʀyʀ] **nf** (*Can*) stuffing (*in saddle etc*).

bourse [buʀs] 1 **nf** a (*porte-monnaie*) purse. **la ~ ou la vie!** your money or your life!, stand and deliver!; **sans ~ délier** without spending a penny; **avoir la ~ dégarnie/bien garnie** to have an empty/a well-lined purse; **ils font ~ commune** they share expenses, they pool their resources; **ils font ~ à part** they keep separate accounts, they keep their finances separate; **il nous a ouvert sa ~** he lent us some money, he helped us out with a loan; **devoir faire appel à la ~ de qn** to have to ask sb for a loan; **c'est trop cher pour ma ~** I can't afford it, it's more than I can afford; *voir* **cordon, portée.**

b (*Bourse*) **la B~** (*activité*) the Stock Exchange (*Brit*) *ou* Market; (*bâtiment*) *[Paris]* the Bourse; *[Londres]* the (London) Stock Exchange; *[New York]* Wall Street; **la B~ monte/descend** share (*Brit*) *ou* stock (*US*) prices are going up/down, the market is going up/down; **valoir tant en B~** to be worth so much on the Stock Exchange *ou* Market; **jouer à la B~** to speculate *ou* gamble on the Stock Exchange *ou* Market; *voir* **coté.**

c ~ **(d'études)** (*Scol*) school maintenance allowance (*NonC*); (*Univ*) grant; (*obtenue par concours*) scholarship.

d (*Anat*) ~ **séreuse** bursa; **~s** scrotum.

2 **comp ▸ Bourse du** *ou* **de commerce** *ou* **des marchandises** produce exchange, commodity market **▸ Bourse du travail** (*Ind*) (*lieu de réunion des syndicats*) ≃ trades union centre **▸ Bourse des valeurs** Stock Market, Stock *ou* Securities Exchange.

boursicotage [buʀsikɔtaʒ] **nm** (*Bourse*) speculation (on a small scale), dabbling on the Stock Exchange.

boursicoter [buʀsikɔte] 1 **vi** (*Bourse*) to speculate in a small way, dabble on the Stock Exchange.

boursicoteur, -euse [buʀsikɔtœʀ, øz] **nm,f**, **boursicotier, -ière** [buʀsikɔtje, jɛʀ] **nm,f** (*Bourse*) small-time speculator, small investor.

boursier, -ière [buʀsje, jɛʀ] 1 **adj** a **étudiant ~** grant holder; (*par concours*) scholarship holder. b (*Bourse*) *marché, valeurs* stock-exchange (*épith*). 2 **nm,f** (*étudiant*) grant holder; (*par concours*) scholarship holder.

boursouflage [buʀsuflaʒ] **nm** *[visage]* swelling, puffing-up; *[style]* turgidity.

boursouflé, e [buʀsufle] (**ptp de boursoufler**) **adj** *visage* puffy, swollen, bloated; *main* swollen; *surface peinte* blistered; (*fig*) *style, discours* bombastic, turgid.

boursouflement [buʀsufləmɑ̃] **nm** = **boursouflage.**

boursoufler [buʀsufle] 1 1 **vt** to puff up, bloat. 2 **se boursoufler vpr** *[peinture]* to blister; *[visage, main]* to swell (up).

boursouflure [buʀsuflyʀ] **nf** *[visage]* puffiness; *[style]* turgidity, pomposity; (*cloque*) blister; (*enflure*) swelling.

bouscaud, e [busko, od] **adj** (*Can*) thickset.

bouscueil [buskœj] **nm** (*Can*) break-up of ice (in rivers and lakes).

bousculade [buskylad] **nf** (*remous*) hustle, jostle, crush; (*hâte*) rush, scramble.

bousculer [buskyle] 1 1 **vt** a *personne* (*pousser*) to jostle, shove; (*heurter*) to bump into *ou* against, knock into *ou* against; (*presser*) to rush, hurry (up); (*Mil*) to drive from the field. (*fig*) **je n'aime pas qu'on me bouscule** I don't like to be pressured *ou* rushed; (*fig*) **être (très) bousculé** to be rushed off one's feet.

b *objet* (*heurter*) to knock *ou* bump into; (*faire tomber*) to knock over; (*déranger*) to knock about.

c (*fig*) *idées* to shake up, liven up; *habitudes* to upset; *emploi du temps* to upset, disrupt.

2 **se bousculer vpr** (*se heurter*) to jostle each other; (*: *se dépêcher*) to get a move on*. **les souvenirs/idées se bousculaient dans sa tête** his head was buzzing with memories/ideas; (*bégayer*) **ça se bouscule au portillon*** he can't get his words out fast enough; (*s'enthousiasmer*) **les gens ne se bousculent pas (au portillon)*** people aren't exactly queuing up*.

bouse [buz] **nf** (cow *ou* cattle) dung (*NonC*), cow pat.

bouseux‡ [buzø] **nm** (*péj*) bumpkin, yokel.

bousier [buzje] **nm** dung-beetle.

bousillage [buzijaʒ] **nm** (*: *voir* **bousiller**) botching; bungling; wrecking; busting-up‡; smashing-up*; pranging* (*Brit*).

bousiller* [buzije] 1 **vt** *travail* to botch, bungle, louse up‡; *appareil, moteur* to bust up‡, wreck; *voiture, avion* to smash up*, prang* (*Brit*), total* (*US*); *personne* to bump off‡, do in‡. **ça a bousillé sa vie/carrière** it wrecked his life/career; **se ~ la santé** to ruin one's health; **se faire ~** to get done in‡ *ou* bumped off‡.

bousilleur, -euse* [buzijœʀ, øz] **nm,f** bungler, botcher.

boussole [busɔl] **nf** compass. (*fig*) **perdre la ~*** to go off one's head.

boustifaille‡ [bustifɑj] **nf** grub‡, nosh‡ (*Brit*), chow‡.

bout [bu] 1 **nm** a (*extrémité*) *[ficelle, planche, perche]* end; *[nez, doigt, langue, oreille]* tip; *[table]* end; *[canne]* end, tip. ~ **du sein** nipple; **à ~ rond/carré** round-/square-ended; **à ~ ferré** *canne* with a steel *ou* metal tip, steel-tipped; *souliers* with a steel toecap; **cigarette à ~ de liège** cork-tipped cigarette; **il écarta les feuilles mortes du ~ du pied** he pushed aside the dead leaves with his toe; **à ~ de bras** at arm's length; (*fig*) **du ~ des lèvres** reluctantly, half-heartedly; (*fig*) **avoir qch sur le ~ de la langue** to have sth on the tip of one's tongue; **il est artiste jusqu'au ~ des ongles** he is an artist to his fingertips; **savoir** *ou* **connaître qch sur le ~ du doigt** to have sth at one's fingertips; **regarder** *ou* **voir les choses par le petit ~ de la lorgnette** to take a narrow view of things; **il a mis le ~ du nez à** *ou* **passé le ~ du nez par la porte et il a disparu** he popped his head round the door *ou* he just showed his face then disappeared; *voir* **manger, montrer, savoir.**

b *[espace, durée]* end. **au ~ de la rue** at the end of the street; **au ~ du jardin** at the bottom *ou* end of the garden; **au ~ d'un mois** at the end of a month, after a month, a month later; **au ~ d'un moment** after a while; **à l'autre ~ de** at the other *ou* far end of; **on n'en voit pas le ~** there doesn't seem to be any end to it; **d'un ~ à l'autre de la ville** from one end of the town to the other; **d'un ~ à l'autre de ses œuvres** throughout *ou* all through his works; **d'un ~ de l'année à l'autre** all the year round, from one year's end to the next; **d'un ~ à l'autre du voyage** from the beginning of the journey to the end, throughout *ou* right through the journey; (*fig*) **ce n'est pas le ~ du monde!** it's not impossible!; **si tu as 5 F à payer c'est (tout) le ~ du monde*** 5 francs is the very most it might cost you, at the (very) worst it might cost you 5 francs; **commençons par un ~ et nous verrons** let's get started *ou* make a start and then we'll see.

c (*morceau*) *[ficelle]* piece, bit; *[pain, papier]* piece, bit, scrap; (*Naut*) (length of) rope. **on a fait un ~ de chemin ensemble** (*lit*) we walked part of the way *ou* some of the way *ou* a bit of the way together; (*fig*) (*en couple*) we were together for a while; (*au travail*) we worked together for a while; **il m'a fait un ~ de conduite** he went part of the way with me; **jusqu'à Paris, cela fait un ~*** it's some distance *ou* quite a long way to Paris; **il est resté un (bon) ~ de temps** he stayed a while *ou* quite some time; **avoir un ~ de rôle dans une pièce** to have a small *ou* bit part in a play; **un ~ de terrain** a patch *ou* plot of land; **un ~ de pelouse** a patch of lawn; **un ~ de ciel bleu** a patch of blue sky; **un petit ~ d'homme*** a (mere) scrap of a man; **un petit ~ de femme** a slip of a woman; **un petit ~ de chou*** a little kid* *ou* nipper* (*Brit*); *voir* **connaître.**

d **à ~**: **être à ~** (*fatigué*) to be all in*, be at the end of one's tether; (*en colère*) to have had enough, be at the end of one's patience; **ma patience est à ~** my patience is exhausted; **être à ~ de force(s)/ressources** to have no strength/money left; **être à ~ d'arguments** to have run out of arguments; **être à ~ de nerfs** to be at the end of one's tether, be just about at breaking *ou* screaming* point; **à tout ~ de champ** all the time; **mettre** *ou* **pousser qn à ~** to push sb to the limit (of his patience); *voir* **souffle.**

e (*loc*) **au ~ du compte** in the last analysis, all things considered; **être au ~ de son** *ou* **du rouleau*** (*n'avoir plus rien à dire*) to have run out of ideas; (*être sans ressources*) to be running short (of money); (*être épuisé*) to be at the end of one's tether; (*être près de la mort*) to have come to the end of the road; **il n'est pas au ~ de ses peines** he's not out of the wood (*Brit*) *ou* woods (*US*) yet, his troubles still aren't over; **je suis** *ou* **j'arrive au ~ de mes peines** I am out of the wood (*Brit*) *ou* woods (*US*), the worst of my troubles are over; **jusqu'au ~**: **nous sommes restés jusqu'au ~** we stayed right to the end; **ils ont combattu jusqu'au ~** they fought to the bitter end; **rebelle jusqu'au ~** rebellious to the end *ou* the last; **il faut aller jusqu'au ~ de ce qu'on entreprend** if you take something on you must see it through (to the end); **aller jusqu'au ~ de ses idées** to follow one's ideas through to their logical conclusion; **~ à ~** end to end; **mettre des planches/cordes ~ à ~** to put planks/ropes end to end; **de ~ en ~**: **lire un livre de ~ en ~** to read a book from cover to cover *ou* right through *ou* from start to finish; **parcourir une rue de ~ en ~** to go from one end of a street to the other; **à ~ portant** point-blank, at point-blank range; **mettre les ~s‡** to hop it‡ (*Brit*), skedaddle*, scarper‡ (*Brit*); *voir* **bon[1], brûler, joindre, porter.**

2 **comp ▸ bout de l'an** (*Rel*) memorial service (*held on the first anniversary of a person's death*) **▸ bout-dehors** (*Naut*) **nm** (**pl bouts-**

dehors) boom ►**bout d'essai** (*Ciné*) screen test, test film; **tourner un bout d'essai** to do a screen test ►**bout filtre** nm filter tip; **cigarettes (à) bout filtre** filter tip cigarettes, tipped cigarettes ►**bout-rimé** (*Littérat*) nm (pl **bouts-rimés**) bouts rimés, poem in set rhymes.

boutade [butad] nf a (*plaisanterie*) jest, sally. b (*caprice*) whim. **par ~** as the whim takes him (*ou* her *etc*), by fits and starts.

boute-en-train [butɑ̃tʀɛ̃] nm inv live wire*. **c'était le ~ de la soirée** he was the life and soul of the party.

bouteille [butɛj] nf a (*récipient*) bottle; (*contenu*) bottle(ful). **~ d'air comprimé/de butane** cylinder of compressed air/of butane gas; ® **~ Thermos** Thermos ® flask (*Brit*) *ou* bottle (*US*); **~ de Leyde** Leyden jar; **~ d'un litre/de 2 litres** litre/2-litre bottle; **~ de vin** (*récipient*) wine bottle; (*contenu*) bottle of wine; **bière en ~** bottled beer; **mettre du vin en ~s** to bottle wine; **vin qui a 10 ans de ~** wine that has been in (the) bottle for 10 years.
b (*loc*) **prendre de la ~*** to be getting on in years, be getting long in the tooth* (*hum*); (*dans son métier*) **il a de la ~*** he's been around a long time; **boire une (bonne) ~** to drink *ou* have a bottle of (good) wine; (*gén hum*) **aimer la ~** to be fond of drink *ou* the bottle, like one's tipple*; **c'est la ~ à l'encre** the whole business is about as clear as mud, you can't make head nor tail of it.

bouter†† [bute] [1] vt to drive, push (*hors de* out of).

bouteur [butœʀ] nm bulldozer. **~ biais** angledozer.

boutique [butik] nf shop, store (*surtout US*); [*grand couturier*] boutique; (‡ *fig*) dump‡. **~ en plein vent** open-air stall; **~ de produits diététiques** health food shop; **~ de droit** law centre; **robe/tailleur ~** designer dress/suit; **quelle sale ~!** what a crummy‡ place! *ou* a dump!‡; *voir* **fermer, parler**.

boutiquier, -ière [butikje, jɛʀ] nm,f shopkeeper (*Brit*), storekeeper (*US*).

boutoir [butwaʀ] nm [*sanglier*] snout. **coup de ~** (*Mil, Sport, gén*) thrust; [*vent, vagues*] battering (*NonC*).

bouton [butɔ̃] 1 nm a (*Couture*) button. **~ de chemise** shirt button; **~ de culotte** trouser (*Brit*) *ou* pants (*US*) button; (*fig*) **il ne manque pas un ~ de guêtre** everything is perfect. b (*mécanisme*) (*Elec*) switch; [*porte, radio*] knob; [*sonnette*] (push-)button. c (*Bot*) bud. **en ~** in bud; **~ de rose** rosebud. d (*Méd*) spot, pimple, zit* (*US*). **~ d'acné** spot (*caused by acne*); **avoir des ~s** to have spots *ou* pimples, have a pimply face; (*: *fig*) **ça lui donne des ~s** that brings him out in a rash*. 2 comp ►**bouton de col** collar stud ►**bouton de manchette** cufflink ►**bouton-d'or** nm (pl **boutons-d'or**) buttercup ►**bouton-pression** nm (pl **boutons-pression**) press stud (*Brit*), snap fastener.

boutonnage [butɔnaʒ] nm buttoning(-up). **avec ~ à droite/à gauche** right/left buttoning (*épith*), which buttons on the right/left; **manteau à double ~** double-buttoning coat.

boutonner [butɔne] [1] 1 vt a *vêtement* to button *ou* fasten (up). b (*Escrime*) to button. 2 **se boutonner** vpr [*vêtement*] to button (up); [*personne*] to button (up) one's coat *ou* trousers *etc*.

boutonneux, -euse [butɔnø, øz] adj pimply, spotty.

boutonnière [butɔnjɛʀ] nf (*Couture*) buttonhole; (*bouquet*) buttonhole (*Brit*), boutonniere (*US*). **avoir une fleur à la ~** to wear a flower in one's buttonhole, wear a buttonhole (*Brit*) *ou* boutonniere (*US*); **porter une décoration à la ~** to wear a decoration on one's lapel; (*Chirurgie*) **faire une ~ (à qn)** to make a small incision (in sb's abdomen).

bouturage [butyʀaʒ] nm taking (of) cuttings, propagation (by cuttings).

bouture [butyʀ] nf cutting. **faire des ~s** to take cuttings.

bouturer [butyʀe] [1] 1 vt to take a cutting from, propagate (by cuttings). 2 vi to put out suckers.

bouvet [buvɛ] nm (*Menuiserie*) rabbet plane.

bouvier [buvje] nm (*personne*) herdsman, cattleman; (*chien*) sheep dog.

bouvillon [buvijɔ̃] nm bullock, steer (*US*).

bouvreuil [buvʀœj] nm bullfinch.

bouzouki [buzuki] nm bouzouki.

bovarysme [bɔvaʀism] nm bovarism, bovarysm.

bovidé [bɔvide] 1 adj m bovid. 2 nm bovid. **~s** bovids, bovidae (SPÉC).

bovin, e [bɔvɛ̃, in] 1 adj (*lit, fig*) bovine. 2 nm bovine. **~s** cattle, bovini (SPÉC).

bowling [buliŋ] nm (*jeu*) (tenpin) bowling; (*salle*) bowling alley.

box, pl **boxes** [bɔks] nm [*hôpital, dortoir*] cubicle; [*écurie*] loose-box; [*porcherie*] stall, pen; (*garage*) lock-up (garage). (*Jur*) **~ des accusés** dock.

box(-calf) [bɔks(kalf)] nm box calf. **sac en ~ noir** black calfskin bag.

boxe [bɔks] nf boxing. **match de ~** boxing match; **~ anglaise** boxing; **~ française** kick boxing.

boxer[1] [bɔkse] [1] 1 vi to box, be a boxer. **~ contre** to box against, fight. 2 vt (*Sport*) to box against, fight; (‡: *frapper*) to thump*, punch.

boxer[2] [bɔksɛʀ] nm boxer (dog).

boxeur [bɔksœʀ] nm boxer.

box-office, pl **box-offices** [bɔksɔfis] nm box office. **film en tête du ~** box-office success *ou* hit.

boxon‡ [bɔksɔ̃] nm brothel, whorehouse*†. **c'est le ~!** it's a shambolic mess!‡ (*Brit*), it's a shambles!

boy [bɔj] nm (*serviteur*) (native) servant boy, boy; (*Music-hall*) ≃ male dancer.

boyard [bɔjaʀ] nm (*Hist*) boyar(d).

boyau, pl **~x** [bwajo] nm a (*intestins*) **~x** [*animal*] guts, entrails; (*) [*homme*] insides*, guts*; **avoir le ~ de la rigolade*** to have the giggles; *voir* **tripe**. b (*corde*) **~ (de chat)** (cat)gut. c (*passage*) (narrow) passageway; (*tuyau*) narrow pipe; (*Mil*) communication trench, sap; (*Min*) (narrow) gallery. d [*bicyclette*] (racing) tyre, tubeless tyre. e (*pour saucisse*) casing.

boycott [bɔjkɔt] nm, **boycottage** [bɔjkɔtaʒ] nm boycotting (*NonC*), boycott.

boycotter [bɔjkɔte] [1] vt to boycott.

boy-scout, pl **boy(s)-scouts** [bɔjskut] nm (boy) scout. **avoir une mentalité de ~*** to have a (rather) naïve *ou* ingenuous outlook.

BP [bepe] (abrév de **boîte postale**) *voir* **boîte**.

BPF (abrév de **bon pour francs**) *amount payable on a cheque*.

brabançon, -onne [bʀabɑ̃sɔ̃, ɔn] 1 adj of *ou* from Brabant. 2 nm,f: **B~(ne)** inhabitant *ou* native of Brabant. 3 nf: **la B~ne** the Belgian national anthem.

brabant [bʀabɑ̃] nm a (*Agr: aussi* **double ~**) swivel plough, turnwrest plow (*US*). b (*Géog*) **le B~** Brabant.

bracelet [bʀaslɛ] 1 nm [*poignet*] bracelet; [*bras, cheville*] bangle; [*montre*] strap, bracelet. 2 comp ►**bracelet de force** (leather) wristband ►**bracelet-montre** nm (pl **bracelets-montres**) wristwatch.

brachial, e, mpl **-iaux** [bʀakjal, jo] adj brachial.

brachiopode [bʀakjɔpɔd] nm brachiopod.

brachycéphale [bʀakisefal] 1 adj brachycephalic. 2 nmf brachycephalic person.

brachycéphalie [bʀakisefali] nf brachycephaly.

braconnage [bʀakɔnaʒ] nm poaching.

braconner [bʀakɔne] [1] vi to poach.

braconnier [bʀakɔnje] nm poacher.

bradage [bʀadaʒ] nm selling off.

brader [bʀade] [1] vt (*vendre à prix réduit*) to sell cut-price (*Brit*) *ou* cut-rate (*US*); (*vendre en solde*) to have a clearance sale of; (*lit, fig: se débarrasser de*) to sell off.

braderie [bʀadʀi] nf (*magasin*) discount centre; (*sur un marché*) stall selling cut-price (*Brit*) *ou* cut-rate (*US*) goods.

bradycardie [bʀadikaʀdi] nf abnormally low rate of heartbeat, bradycardia (SPÉC).

braguette [bʀagɛt] nf fly, flies (*of trousers*); (*Hist*) codpiece.

brahmane [bʀɑman] nm Brahmin, Brahman.

brahmanique [bʀɑmanik] adj Brahminical.

brahmanisme [bʀɑmanism] nm Brahminism, Brahmanism.

Brahmapoutre [bʀamaputʀ] nm, **Brahmaputra** [bʀamaputʀa] nm Brahmaputra.

brahmine [bʀɑmin] nf Brahmani, Brahmanee.

brai [bʀɛ] nm pitch, tar.

braies [bʀɛ] nfpl (*Hist*) breeches (*worn by Gauls*).

braillard, e [bʀɑjaʀ, aʀd] (*voir* **brailler**) 1 adj bawling (*épith*); yelling (*épith*); howling (*épith*); squalling (*épith*). 2 nm,f bawler.

braille [bʀɑj] nm Braille.

braillement [bʀɑjmɑ̃] nm (*voir* **brailler**) bawling (*NonC*); yelling (*NonC*); howling (*NonC*); squalling (*NonC*). **les ~s de l'enfant** the bawling *ou* bawls of the child.

brailler [bʀɑje] [1] 1 vi (*crier*) to bawl, yell; (*pleurer*) to bawl, howl, squall. **il faisait ~ sa radio** his radio was blaring, he had his radio blaring. 2 vt *chanson, slogan* to bawl out.

brailleur, -euse [bʀɑjœʀ, øz] = **braillard**.

braiment [bʀɛmɑ̃] nm bray(ing).

brain-trust, pl **brain-trusts** [bʀɛntʀœst] nm brain trust, brains trust.

braire [bʀɛʀ] [50] vi (*lit, fig*) to bray. **faire ~ qn‡** to get on sb's wick‡.

braise [bʀɛz] nf a [*feu*] **la ~, les ~s** the (glowing) embers; (*charbon de bois*) live charcoal; (*fig*) **être sur la ~** to be on tenterhooks; **yeux de ~** fiery eyes, eyes like coals. b (‡: *argent*) cash*, dough‡, bread‡.

braiser [bʀeze] [1] vt to braise. **bœuf/chou braisé** braised beef/cabbage.

bramement [bʀɑmmɑ̃] nm (*voir* **bramer**) bell, troat; wailing.

bramer [bʀɑme] [1] vi [*cerf*] to bell, troat; (* *fig*) to wail.

bran [bʀɑ̃] nm bran. **~ de scie** sawdust.

brancard [bʀɑ̃kaʀ] nm a (*bras*) [*charrette*] shaft; [*civière*] shaft, pole; *voir* **ruer**. b (*civière*) stretcher.

brancardier, -ière [bʀɑ̃kaʀdje, jɛʀ] nm,f stretcher-bearer.

branchage [bʀɑ̃ʃaʒ] nm branches, boughs. **~s** fallen *ou* lopped-off branches, lops.

branche [bʀɑ̃ʃ] nf a (*Bot*) branch, bough. **~ mère** main branch; **sauter de ~ en ~** to leap from branch to branch; **asperges en ~s** whole asparagus, asparagus spears; **céleri en ~s** (sticks of) celery; *voir* **vieux**.
b (*ramification*) [*nerfs, veines*] branch, ramification; [*rivière, canalisation, bois de cerf*] branch; [*lunettes*] side-piece; [*compas*] leg; [*ciseaux*] blade; [*fer à cheval*] half; [*famille*] branch. **la ~ aînée** the elder *ou* eldest branch of the family; **la ~ maternelle** the maternal branch of the family, the mother's side of the family; **avoir de la ~*** to be of good stock; *voir* **chandelier**.

c (*secteur*) branch. **les ~s de la science moderne** the different branches of modern science; **notre fils s'orientera vers une ~ technique** our son will go in for the technical side.

branché,e* [bʀɑ̃ʃe] (**ptp de brancher**) **adj** (*dans le vent*) switched-on*. **il est ~** he's a swinger*, he is switched-on*.

branchement [bʀɑ̃ʃmɑ̃] **nm** (*action: voir* **brancher**) plugging-in; connecting(-up); linking-up; (*objet*) connection, installation; (*Rail*) branch line; (*Ordin*) branch; (*Gram*) branching.

brancher [bʀɑ̃ʃe] 1 **vt** a *appareil électrique* to plug in; (*installer*) to connect up; *appareil à gaz, tuyau* to connect up; *téléphone* to connect (up); *réseau* to link up (*sur* with). **~ qch sur qch** to plug sth into sth; to connect sth up with sth; **où est-ce que ça se branche?** where does that plug in?; **où est-ce que je peux me ~?** where can I plug it in?

b (*fig*) **~ qn sur un sujet** to start sb off on a subject; **~ la conversation sur un sujet** to start the conversation off on a subject; **ce qui me branche*** what grabs* me *ou* gives me a buzz*; **quand on l'a branché** *ou* **quand il est branché là-dessus il est intarissable** when he's launched on that *ou* when somebody gets him started on that he can go on forever.

branchette [bʀɑ̃ʃɛt] **nf** small branch, twig.

branchial, e, mpl -iaux [bʀɑ̃ʃjal, jo] **adj** branchial.

branchies [bʀɑ̃ʃi] **nfpl** (*Zool*) branchiae (*SPÉC*), gills.

branchiopode [bʀɑ̃ʃjɔpɔd] **nm** branchiopod.

branchu, e [bʀɑ̃ʃy] **adj** branchy.

brandade [bʀɑ̃dad] **nf: ~ (de morue)** brandade (*dish made with cod*).

brande [bʀɑ̃d] **nf** (*lande*) heath(land); (*plantes*) heath, heather, brush.

brandebourg [bʀɑ̃dbuʀ] **nm** (*Habillement*) frog. **à ~(s)** frogged.

brandebourgeois, e [bʀɑ̃dbuʀʒwa, waz] 1 **adj** Brandenburg (*épith*). 2 **nm,f: B~(e)** inhabitant *ou* native of Brandenburg.

brandir [bʀɑ̃diʀ] 2 **vt** *arme, document* to brandish, flourish, wave.

brandon [bʀɑ̃dɔ̃] **nm** firebrand (*lit*). **~ de discorde** bone of contention.

branlant, e [bʀɑ̃lɑ̃, ɑ̃t] **adj** *dent* loose; *mur* shaky; *escalier, meuble* rickety, shaky; *pas* unsteady, tottering, shaky; (*fig*) *régime* tottering, shaky; *raison* shaky.

branle [bʀɑ̃l] **nm** *[cloche]* swing. **mettre en ~** *cloche* to swing, set swinging; (*fig*) *forces* to set in motion, set off, get moving; **donner le ~ à** to set in motion, set rolling; **se mettre en ~** to get going *ou* moving.

branle-bas [bʀɑ̃lbɑ] **nm inv** bustle, commotion, pandemonium. **dans le ~ du départ** in the confusion *ou* bustle of departure; **être en ~** to be in a state of commotion; **mettre qch en ~** to turn sth upside down, cause commotion in sth; (*Naut*) **~ de combat** (*manœuvre*) preparations for action; (*ordre*) "action stations!"; **sonner le ~ de combat** to sound action stations; **mettre en ~ de combat** to clear the decks (for action).

branlée‡ [bʀɑ̃le] **nf** hammering*. **recevoir une ~** to get hammered*, get a hammering*.

branlement [bʀɑ̃lmɑ̃] **nm** *[tête]* wagging, shaking.

branler [bʀɑ̃le] 1 1 **vt** a **~ la tête** *ou* (*hum*) **du chef** to shake *ou* wag one's head. b (**‡**) **qu'est-ce qu'ils branlent?** what the hell are they up to?‡; **il n'en branle pas une** he does bugger** *ou* fuck** all; **j'en ai rien à ~** I don't give a fuck** 2 **vi** *[échafaudage]* to be shaky *ou* unsteady; *[meuble]* to be shaky *ou* rickety; *[dent]* to be loose. (*fig*) **~ dans le manche** to be shaky *ou* precarious. 3 **se branler**** **vpr** to wank** (*Brit*), jerk off** (*US*). (*fig*) **je m'en branle** I don't give a fuck**.

branleur, -euse‡ [bʀɑ̃lœʀ, øz] **nm,f** (*paresseux*) lazy bugger**.

branleux, -euse‡ [bʀɑ̃lø, øz] **adj** (*Can*) equivocating, slow, shilly-shallying*.

branque* [bʀɑ̃k], **branquignol*** [bʀɑ̃kiɲɔl] 1 **adj** barmy* (*Brit*), crazy*. 2 **nm** nutter‡ (*Brit*), crackpot*.

braquage [bʀakaʒ] **nm** (*Aut*) (steering) lock; (*arg Crime*) stickup (*arg*); *voir* **angle, rayon.**

braque [bʀak] 1 **adj** (*) barmy* (*Brit*), crazy*. 2 **nm** (*Zool*) pointer.

braquer [bʀake] 1 1 **vt** a **~ une arme** *etc* **sur** to point *ou* aim *ou* level a weapon *etc* at; **~ un télescope** *etc* **sur** to train a telescope *etc* on; **~ son regard/attention** *etc* **sur** to turn one's gaze/attention *etc* towards, fix one's gaze/attention *etc* on; **~ les yeux sur qch** to fix one's eyes on sth, stare hard at sth; **~ (son arme sur) qn** to pull one's gun on sb*.

b (*Aut*) *roue* to swing.

c (*‡: attaquer*) *banque* to hold up, stick up‡; *caissier, commerçant* to hold up.

d (*fig: buter*) **~ qn** to put sb's back up*, make sb dig in his heels; **~ qn contre qch** to turn sb against sth; **il est braqué** he is not to be budged, he has dug his heels in.

2 **vi** (*Aut*) to turn the (steering) wheel. *[voiture]* **~ bien/mal** to have a good/bad lock; **~ à fond** to put on the full lock; **braquez vers la gauche/la droite!** left hand/right hand hard down! (*Brit*), turn hard left/right.

3 **se braquer vpr** to dig one's heels in. **se ~ contre** to set one's face against.

braquet [bʀakɛ] **nm** *[bicyclette]* gear ratio.

braqueur‡ [bʀakœʀ] **nm** (*gangster*) hold-up man*.

bras [bʀɑ] 1 **nm** a (*Anat*) arm. **une serviette sous le ~** with a briefcase under one's arm; **un panier au ~** with a basket on one's arm; **donner le ~ à qn** to give sb one's arm; **prendre le ~ de qn** to take sb's arm; **être au ~ de qn** to be on sb's arm; **se donner le ~** to link arms; **~ dessus, ~ dessous** arm in arm; (*lit*) **les ~ croisés** with one's arms folded; (*fig*) **rester les ~ croisés** to sit idly by; **tendre** *ou* **allonger le ~ vers qch** to reach out for sth, stretch out one's hand *ou* arm for sth; *voir* **arme, force, plein** *etc.*

b (*travailleur*) hand, worker. **manquer de ~** to be short-handed, be short of manpower *ou* labour; **c'est lui la tête, moi je suis le ~** he does the thinking and I do the (actual) work, he supplies the brain and I supply the brawn.

c (*pouvoir*) **le ~ de la justice** the arm of the law; (*Rel*) **le ~ séculier** the secular arm.

d *[manivelle, outil, pompe]* handle; *[fauteuil]* arm(rest); *[grue]* jib; *[sémaphore, ancre, électrophone, moulin]* arm; *[croix]* limb; *[aviron, brancard]* shaft; (*Naut*) *[vergue]* brace.

e *[fleuve]* branch.

f *[cheval]* shoulder; *[mollusque]* tentacle.

g (*loc*) **en ~ de chemise** in (one's) shirt sleeves; **saisir qn à ~-le-corps** to seize sb round the waist, seize sb bodily; (*fig*) **avoir le ~ long** to have a long arm; (*lit, fig*) **à ~ ouverts, les ~ ouverts** with open arms (*lit, fig*); **à ~ tendus** with outstretched arms; **tomber sur qn à ~ raccourcis*** to set (up)on sb, pitch into sb*; **lever les ~ au ciel** to throw up one's arms; **les ~ m'en tombent** I'm flabbergasted* *ou* stunned; **avoir qch/qn** *ou* **se retrouver avec qch/qn sur les ~*** to have sth/sb on one's hands, be stuck* *ou* landed* with sth/sb; **il a une nombreuse famille sur les ~*** he's got a large family to look after; **avoir une sale histoire sur les ~*** to have a nasty business on one's hands; (*hum*) **(être) dans les ~ de Morphée** (to be) in the arms of Morpheus; **faire un ~ d'honneur à qn** ≃ put two fingers up at sb*, give sb the V-sign (*Brit*) *ou* the finger** (*US*); *voir* **bout, couper, gros** *etc.*

2 **comp ▸bras droit** (*fig*) right-hand man **▸bras d'essuie-glace** (*Aut*) wiper arm **▸bras de fer** (*Sport*) Indian wrestling (*NonC*), arm-wrestling (*NonC*); **faire une partie de bras de fer avec qn** to arm-wrestle with sb; (*fig*) **la partie de bras de fer entre patronat et syndicats** the wrestling match between the bosses and the unions **▸bras de levier** lever arm; **faire bras de levier** to act as a lever **▸bras de mer** arm of the sea, sound **▸bras mort** oxbow lake, cutoff.

brasage [bʀɑzaʒ] **nm** brazing.

braser [bʀɑze] 1 **vt** to braze.

brasero [bʀɑzeʀo] **nm** brazier.

brasier [bʀɑzje] **nm** (*incendie*) (blazing) inferno, furnace; (*fig: foyer de guerre*) inferno. **son cœur/esprit était un ~** his heart/mind was on fire *ou* ablaze.

Brasilia [bʀazilja] **n** Brasilia.

brasiller [bʀɑzije] 1 **vi** *[mer]* to glimmer; *[bougie]* to glow red.

brassage [bʀasaʒ] **nm** a *[bière]* brewing. b (*mélange*) mixing. **~ de races** intermixing of races; (*Aut*) **~ des gaz** mixing. c (*Naut*) bracing.

brassard [bʀasaʀ] **nm** armband. **~ de deuil** black armband.

brasse [bʀas] **nf** a (*sport*) breast-stroke; (*mouvement*) stroke. **~ coulée** breast-stroke; **~ papillon** butterfly(-stroke); **nager la ~** to swim breast-stroke; **faire quelques ~s** to do a few strokes. b (*††: mesure*) ≃ 6 feet; (*Naut*) fathom.

brassée [bʀase] **nf** armful; (*Can* ‡) *[machine à laver etc]* load. **par ~s** in armfuls;

brasser [bʀase] 1 **vt** a (*remuer*) to stir (up); (*mélanger*) to mix; *pâte* to knead; *salade* to toss; *cartes* to shuffle; *argent* to handle a lot of. **~ des affaires** to be in big business; (*fig*) **~ du vent** to blow hot air*. b *bière* to brew. c (*Naut*) to brace.

brasserie [bʀasʀi] **nf** a (*café*) ≃ pub (*Brit*), bar (*US*), brasserie. b (*fabrique de bière*) brewery; (*industrie*) brewing industry.

brasseur, -euse [bʀasœʀ, øz] **nm,f** a *[bière]* brewer. b (*Comm*) **~ d'affaires** big businessman. c (*Sport*) breast-stroke swimmer.

brassière [bʀasjɛʀ] **nf** a *[bébé]* (baby's) vest (*Brit*) *ou* undershirt (*US*). **~ (de sauvetage)** life jacket. b (*Can: soutien-gorge*) bra.

brasure [bʀɑzyʀ] **nf** (*procédé*) brazing; (*résultat*) brazed joint, braze; (*métal*) brazing metal.

bravache [bʀavaʃ] 1 **nm** braggart, blusterer. **faire le ~** to swagger about. 2 **adj** swaggering, blustering.

bravade [bʀavad] **nf** act of bravado. **par ~** out of bravado.

brave [bʀav] 1 **adj** a (*courageux*) *personne, action* brave, courageous, gallant (*littér*). **faire le ~** to act brave, put on a bold front. b (*avant n: bon*) good, nice, fine; (*honnête*) decent, honest. **c'est une ~ fille** she's a nice girl; **c'est un ~ garçon** he's a good *ou* nice lad (*Brit*) *ou* fellow; **ce sont de ~s gens** they're good *ou* decent people *ou* souls; **il est bien ~** he's not a bad chap* (*Brit*) *ou* guy* (*US*), he's a nice enough fellow; **mon ~ (homme)** my good man *ou* fellow; **ma ~ dame** my good woman. 2 **nm** (*gén*) brave man; (*indien*) brave.

bravement [bʀavmɑ̃] **adv** (*courageusement*) bravely, courageously, gallantly (*littér*); (*résolument*) boldly, unhesitatingly.

braver [bʀave] 1 **vt** (*défier*) *autorité, parents* to stand up to, hold out against, defy; *règle* to defy, disobey; *danger, mort* to brave. **~ l'opinion** to fly in the face of (public) opinion.

bravo [bʀavo] 1 **excl** (*félicitation*) well done!, bravo!, right on!*; (*approbation*) hear! hear! 2 **nm** cheer. **un grand ~ pour ...!** a big cheer for ...!, let's hear it for ...! (*US*).

bravoure [bʀavuʀ] nf bravery, braveness, gallantry; *voir* **morceau.**
Brazzaville [bʀazavil] n Brazzaville.
break [bʀɛk] nm **a** (*Aut*) estate (car) (*Brit*), shooting brake† (*Brit*), station wagon (*US*). **b** (*pause*) break. **faire un ~** to take a break. **c** (*Boxe, Tennis*) break. **balle de ~** break point; **faire le ~** to break.
brebis [bʀəbi] nf (*Zool*) ewe; (*Rel: pl*) flock. **~ égarée** stray *ou* lost sheep; **~ galeuse** black sheep; **à ~ tondue Dieu mesure le vent** the Lord tempers the wind to the shorn lamb.
brèche [bʀɛʃ] nf *[mur]* breach, opening, gap; (*Mil*) breach; *[lame]* notch, nick. (*Mil*) **faire** *ou* **ouvrir une ~ dans le front ennemi** to make a breach in *ou* breach the enemy line; (*fig*) **faire une ~ à sa fortune** to make a hole in one's fortune; (*fig*) **il est toujours sur la ~** he's still beavering away *ou* hard at it*; *voir* **battre.**
bréchet [bʀeʃɛ] nm wishbone.
brechtien, -ienne [bʀɛʃtjɛ̃, jɛn] adj Brechtian.
bredouillage [bʀədujaʒ] nm spluttering, mumbling.
bredouille [bʀəduj] adj (*gén*) empty-handed. (*Chasse, Pêche*) **rentrer ~** to go *ou* come home empty-handed *ou* with an empty bag.
bredouillement [bʀədujmɑ̃] nm = **bredouillage.**
bredouiller [bʀəduje] [1] **1** vi to stammer, mumble. **2** vt to mumble, stammer (out), falter out. **~ une excuse** to splutter out *ou* falter out *ou* stammer an excuse.
bredouilleur, -euse [bʀədujœʀ, øz] **1** adj mumbling, stammering. **2** nm,f mumbler, stammerer.
bref, brève [bʀɛf, ɛv] **1** adj *rencontre, discours, lettre* brief, short; *voyelle, syllabe* short. **d'un ton ~** sharply, curtly; **soyez ~ et précis** be brief and to the point; **à ~ délai** shortly. **2** adv: **(enfin) ~** (*pour résumer*) to cut a long story short, in short, in brief; (*passons*) let's not waste any more time; (*donc*) anyway; **en ~** in short, in brief. **3** nm (*Rel*) (papal) brief. **4 brève** nf (*syllabe*) short syllable; (*voyelle*) short vowel; (*Journalisme*) news (*sg*) in brief.
breffage [bʀɛfaʒ] nm briefing.
bréhaigne [bʀeɛɲ] adj (*Zool* †) barren, sterile.
brelan [bʀəlɑ̃] nm (*Cartes*) three of a kind. **~ d'as** three aces.
breloque [bʀəlɔk] nf (bracelet) charm; *voir* **battre.**
brème [bʀɛm] nf **a** (*Zool*) bream. **b** (*arg Cartes*) card.
Brésil [bʀezil] nm Brazil.
brésil [bʀezil] nm brazil (wood).
brésilien, -ienne [bʀeziljɛ̃, jɛn] **1** adj Brazilian. **maillot de bain/slip ~** high-cut swimsuit/panties. **2** nm,f: **B~(ne)** Brazilian.
bressan, e [bʀɛsɑ̃, an] **1** adj of *ou* from Bresse. **2** nm,f: **B~(e)** inhabitant *ou* native of Bresse.
Bretagne [bʀətaɲ] nf Brittany; *voir* **grand.**
bretèche [bʀətɛʃ] nf gatehouse, bartizan.
bretelle [bʀətɛl] nf **a** *[sac]* (shoulder) strap; *[lingerie]* strap; *[fusil]* sling. *[pantalon]* **~s** braces (*Brit*), suspenders (*US*); **porter l'arme** *ou* **le fusil à la ~** to carry one's weapon slung over one's shoulder; *voir* **remonter. b** (*Rail*) crossover; (*Aut*) slip road (*Brit*), entrance (*ou* exit) ramp (*US*). **~ de raccordement** access road; **~ de contournement** bypass.
breton, -onne [bʀətɔ̃, ɔn] **1** adj Breton. **2** nm (*Ling*) Breton. **3** nm,f: **B~(ne)** Breton.
bretonnant, e [bʀətɔnɑ̃, ɑ̃t] adj Breton-speaking. **la Bretagne ~e** Breton-speaking Brittany.
bretteur [bʀɛtœʀ] nm (††) swashbuckler; (*duelliste*) duellist.
bretteux, -euse‡ [bʀɛtø, øz] adj (*Can*) idling, dawdling. **un ~** an idler, a slowcoach (*Brit*), a slowpoke (*US*).
bretzel [bʀɛtzɛl] nm pretzel.
breuvage [bʀœvaʒ] nm drink, beverage; (*magique*) potion.
brève [bʀɛv] *voir* **bref.**
brevet [bʀəvɛ] **1** nm **a** (*diplôme*) diploma, certificate; (*Hist: note royale*) royal warrant; (*Scol*) ≃ G.C.S.E. (*Brit*), *exam taken at the age of 16.* (*Scol*) **avoir son ~** ≃ to have (passed) one's G.C.S.E.s (*Brit*).
b (*Naut*) certificate, ticket. **~ de capitaine** master's certificate *ou* ticket; (*Mil*) **~ de commandant** major's brevet.
c (*Jur*) **~ (d'invention)** letters patent, patent; **~ en cours d'homologation** patent pending.
d (*fig: garantie*) guarantee. **donner à qn un ~ d'honnêteté** to testify to *ou* guarantee sb's honesty; **on peut lui décerner un ~ de persévérance** you could give him a medal for perseverance.
2 comp ▸**brevet d'apprentissage** ≃ certificate of apprenticeship ▸**brevet d'études du premier cycle**† (*Scol*) *exam taken at the age of 16,* ≃ G.C.S.E. (*Brit*) ▸**brevet d'études professionnelles** *technical school certificate* ▸**brevet d'études professionnelles agricoles** *agricultural school certificate* ▸**brevet de pilote** pilot's licence ▸**brevet de technicien** *vocational training certificate taken at age 16* ▸**brevet de technicien agricole** *vocational training certificate in agriculture* ▸**brevet de technicien supérieur** *vocational training certificate taken after the age of 18.*
brevetable [bʀəv(ə)tabl] adj patentable.
breveté, e [bʀəv(ə)te] (ptp de **breveter**) **1** adj **a** *invention* patented. **~ sans garantie du gouvernement** patented (*without official government approval*). **b** (*diplômé*) *technicien* qualified, certificated; (*Mil*) *officier* commissioned. **2** nm,f (*Jur etc*) patentee.
breveter [bʀəv(ə)te] [4] vt *invention* to patent. **faire ~ qch** to take out a patent for sth.
bréviaire [bʀevjɛʀ] nm (*Rel*) breviary; (*fig*) bible.
BRI [beɛʀi] nf (abrév de **Banque des règlements internationaux**) BIS.
briard, e [bʀijaʀ, aʀd] **1** adj of *ou* from Brie. **2** nm,f: **B~(e)** inhabitant *ou* native of Brie. **3** nm (*chien*) Brie shepherd.
bribe [bʀib] nf (*fragment*) bit, scrap. **~s de conversation** snatches of conversation; **~s de nourriture** scraps of food; **les ~s de sa fortune** the remnants of his fortune; **par ~s** in snatches, piecemeal.
bric-à-brac [bʀikabʀak] nm inv **a** (*objets*) bric-a-brac, odds and ends; (*fig*) bric-a-brac, trimmings. **b** (*magasin*) junk shop.
bric et de broc [bʀikedbʀɔk] loc adv: **de ~** (*de manière disparate*) in any old way*, any old how*; **meublé de ~** furnished with bits and pieces *ou* with odds and ends.
brick [bʀik] nm **a** (*Naut*) brig. **b** (*Culin*) ≃ fritter (*with a filling*). **~ à l'œuf/au thon** egg/tuna fritter.
bricolage [bʀikɔlaʒ] nm **a** (*passe-temps*) tinkering about, do-it-yourself, D.I.Y.* (*Brit*); (*travaux*) odd jobs. **j'ai du ~ à faire** I've got a few (odd) jobs to do; **rayon ~** do-it-yourself department. **b** (*réparation*) makeshift repair *ou* job. (*péj*) **c'est du ~!** it's a rush job!*
bricole [bʀikɔl] nf **a** (*) (*babiole*) trifle; (*cadeau*) something small, token; (*menu travail*) easy job, small matter. **il ne reste que des ~s** there are only a few bits and pieces *ou* a few odds and ends left; **ça coûte 10 F et des ~s** it costs 10 francs odd*. **b** *[cheval]* breast harness. **c** (*Can*) **~s*** braces (*Brit*), suspenders (*US*).
bricoler [bʀikɔle] [1] **1** vi (*menus travaux*) to do odd jobs, potter about (*Brit*); (*réparations*) to do odd repairs, do odd jobs; (*passe-temps*) to tinker about *ou* around. **2** vt (*réparer*) to fix (up), mend; (*mal réparer*) to tinker *ou* mess (about) with; (*fabriquer*) to knock up* (*Brit*), cobble up *ou* together.
bricoleur [bʀikɔlœʀ] nm handyman, D.I.Y. man* (*Brit*), do-it-yourselfer*. **il est ~** he is good with his hands, he's very handy*; **je ne suis pas très ~** I'm not much of a handyman.
bricoleuse [bʀikɔløz] nf handywoman, D.I.Y. woman* (*Brit*), do-it-yourselfer*.
bride [bʀid] nf **a** (*Équitation*) bridle. **tenir un cheval en ~** to curb a horse; (*fig*) **tenir ses passions/une personne en ~** to keep one's passions/a person in check, keep a tight hand *ou* rein on one's passions/a person; **jeter** *ou* **laisser** *ou* **mettre la ~ sur le cou** *ou* **col à un cheval** to give a horse the reins, give a horse his head; (*fig*) **laisser la ~ sur le cou à qn** to give *ou* leave sb a free hand; **les jeunes ont maintenant la ~ sur le cou** young people have free rein to do as they like nowadays; **tenir la ~ haute à un cheval** to rein in a horse; (*fig*) **tenir la ~ haute à qn** to keep a tight rein on sb; **aller à ~ abattue** *ou* **à toute ~** to ride flat out*, ride hell for leather*; *voir* **lâcher, tourner.**
b *[bonnet]* string; (*en cuir*) strap.
c (*Couture*) *[boutonnière]* bar; *[bouton]* loop; *[dentelle]* bride.
d (*Tech*) *[bielle]* strap; *[tuyau]* flange.
bridé, e [bʀide] (ptp de **brider**) adj: **avoir les yeux ~s** to have slanting *ou* slit eyes.
brider [bʀide] [1] vt **a** *cheval* to bridle; *moteur* to restrain; (*fig*) *impulsion, colère* to bridle, restrain, keep in check, quell; *personne* to keep in check, hold back. **logiciel bridé** restricted-access software, crippleware*; (*fig*) **il est bridé dans son costume, son costume le bride** his suit is too tight for him. **b** (*Culin*) to truss. **c** *boutonnière* to bind; *tuyau* to clamp, flange; (*Naut*) to lash together.
bridge [bʀidʒ] nm (*Cartes*) bridge; (*prothèse dentaire*) bridge. **~ contrat** contract bridge; **~ aux enchères** auction bridge; **faire un ~** to play *ou* have a game of bridge.
bridger [bʀidʒe] [3] vi to play bridge.
Bridgetown [bʀidʒtaun] n Bridgetown.
bridgeur, -euse [bʀidʒœʀ, øz] nm,f bridge player.
bridon [bʀidɔ̃] nm snaffle.
brie [bʀi] nm Brie (cheese).
briefer [bʀife] [1] vt to brief.
briefing [bʀifiŋ] nm briefing. **faire un ~ à l'intention de l'équipe de vente** to brief the sales force.
brièvement [bʀijɛvmɑ̃] adv briefly, concisely.
brièveté [bʀijɛvte] nf brevity, briefness.
brigade [bʀigad] nf (*Mil*) brigade; (*Police*) squad; (*gén: équipe*) gang, team. **~ criminelle** crime *ou* murder squad; **B~s internationales** International Brigades; **~ des mineurs** juvenile liaison police, juvenile bureau; **~ des mœurs, ~ mondaine** vice squad; **~ de recherche dans l'intérêt des familles** ≃ missing persons bureau; **~ des stupéfiants** *ou* **des stups*** drug(s) squad; **~ volante** flying squad; **~ anti-gang** anti-terrorist squad; **~ anti-émeute** riot police (*NonC*) *ou* squad; **~ de gendarmerie** gendarmerie squad.
brigadier [bʀigadje] nm (*Police*) ≃ sergeant; (*Mil*) *[artillerie]* bombardier; *[blindés, cavalerie, train]* corporal. **~-chef** ≃ lance sergeant.
brigand [bʀigɑ̃] nm (†: *bandit*) brigand, bandit; (*péj: filou*) twister (*Brit*), sharpie* (*US*), crook; (*hum: enfant*) rascal, imp.
brigandage [bʀigɑ̃daʒ] nm (armed) robbery, banditry; (†) brigandage. **commettre des actes de ~** to engage in robbery with violence; (*fig*) **c'est du ~!** it's daylight robbery!

brigantin [bʀigɑ̃tɛ̃] nm (*Naut*) brig.

brigantine [bʀigɑ̃tin] nf (*Naut*) spanker.

Brigitte [bʀiʒit] nf Bridget.

brigue [bʀig] nf (*littér*) intrigue. **obtenir qch par ~** to get sth by intrigue.

briguer [bʀige] [1] vt *emploi* to covet, aspire to, bid for; *honneur, faveur* to aspire after, crave; *amitié* to court, solicit; *suffrages* to solicit, canvass (for).

brillamment [bʀijamɑ̃] adv brilliantly. **réussir ~ un examen** to pass an exam with flying colours.

brillance [bʀijɑ̃s] nf (*Astron*) brilliance.

brillant, e [bʀijɑ̃, ɑ̃t] 1 adj a (*luisant*) shiny, glossy; (*étincelant*) sparkling, bright; *chaussures* well-polished, shiny; *couleur* bright, brilliant. **elle avait les yeux ~s de fièvre/d'impatience** her eyes were bright with fever/impatience; **il avait les yeux ~s de convoitise/colère** his eyes glittered with envy/anger; *voir* **peinture, sou.**

b (*remarquable*) brilliant, outstanding; *situation* excellent, brilliant; *succès* brilliant, dazzling, outstanding; *avenir* brilliant, bright; *conversation* brilliant, sparkling. **avoir une intelligence ~e** to be outstandingly intelligent, be brilliant; **sa santé n'est pas ~e** his health isn't too good; **ce n'est pas ~** it's not up to much, it's not too good, it's not brilliant*.

2 nm a (*NonC: éclat*) (*étincelant*) sparkle, brightness; (*luisant*) shine, glossiness; *[couleur]* brightness, brilliance; *[étoffe]* sheen; (*par usure*) shine. (*fig*) **le ~ de son esprit/style** the brilliance of his mind/style; **il a du ~ mais peu de connaissances réelles** he has a certain brilliance but not much serious knowledge; **donner du ~ à un cuir** to polish up a piece of leather.

b (*diamant*) brilliant. **taillé/monté en ~** cut/mounted as a brilliant.

brillantine [bʀijɑ̃tin] nf brilliantine.

briller [bʀije] [1] vi a (*gén*) *[lumière, soleil]* to shine; *[diamant, eau]* to sparkle, glitter; *[étoile]* to twinkle, shine (brightly); *[métal]* to glint, shine; *[feu, braises]* to glow (brightly); *[flammes]* to blaze; *[éclair]* to flash; *[chaussures]* to shine; *[surface polie, humide]* to shine, glisten. **faire ~ les meubles/l'argenterie** to polish the furniture/the silver; **faire ~ ses chaussures** to shine *ou* polish one's shoes; *voir* **tout.**

b *[yeux]* to shine, sparkle; *[nez]* to be shiny; *[larmes]* to glisten. **ses yeux brillaient de joie** his eyes sparkled with joy; **ses yeux brillaient de convoitise** his eyes glinted greedily.

c *[personne]* to shine, stand out. **~ en société** to be a success in society; **~ à un examen** to come out (on) top in *ou* do brilliantly *ou* shine in an exam; **~ par son talent/éloquence** to be outstandingly talented/eloquent; **il ne brille pas par le courage/la modestie** courage/modesty is not his strong point; **~ par son absence** to be conspicuous by one's absence; **le désir de ~** the longing to stand out (from the crowd), the desire to be the centre of attention; **faire ~ les avantages de qch à qn** to paint a glowing picture of sth to sb.

brimade [bʀimad] nf (*vexation*) vexation; (*Mil, Scol: d'initiation*) ragging (*NonC*) (*Brit*), hazing (*NonC*) (*US*). **faire subir des ~s à qn** to harry sb, harass sb; (*Mil, Scol*) to rag sb (*Brit*), haze sb (*US*).

brimbalement* [bʀɛ̃balmɑ̃] nm = **bringuebalement***.

brimbaler* [bʀɛ̃bale] [1] = **bringuebaler***.

brimborion [bʀɛ̃bɔʀjɔ̃] nm (*colifichet*) bauble, trinket.

brimer [bʀime] [1] vt (*soumettre à des vexations*) to aggravate, bully; (*Mil, Scol*) *nouveaux* to rag (*Brit*), haze (*US*). **se sentir brimé** to feel one's being got at* *ou* being done down* (*Brit*); **je suis brimé*** I'm being got at* *ou* done down* (*Brit*).

brin [bʀɛ̃] nm a *[blé, herbe]* blade; *[bruyère, mimosa, muguet]* sprig; *[osier]* twig; *[paille]* wisp. (*fig*) **un beau ~ de fille** a fine-looking girl.

b *[chanvre, lin]* yarn, fibre; *[corde, fil, laine]* strand.

c (*un peu*) **un ~ de** a touch *ou* grain *ou* bit of; **il n'a pas un ~ de bon sens** he hasn't got an ounce *ou* a grain of common sense; **avec un ~ de nostalgie** with a touch *ou* hint of nostalgia; **il y a en lui un ~ de folie/méchanceté** there's a touch of madness/malice in him; **faire un ~ de causette** to have a bit of a chat* (*Brit*), have a little chat; **faire un ~ de toilette** to have a lick and a promise, have a quick wash; **il n'y a pas un ~ de vent** there isn't a breath of wind; **s'amuser un ~** to have a bit of fun; **un ~ +** *adj* a shade *ou* bit *ou* little + *adj*; **un ~ plus grand/haut** a bit *ou* a little *ou* a fraction *ou* a shade bigger/higher; **je suis un ~ embêté*** I'm a trifle *ou* a shade worried.

d (*Rad*) *[antenne]* wire.

brindezingue * [bʀɛ̃dzɛ̃g] adj nutty*, crazy*.

brindille [bʀɛ̃dij] nf twig.

bringue[1]* [bʀɛ̃g] nf: **grande ~** beanpole*.

bringue[2]* [bʀɛ̃g] nf (*beuverie*) binge*; (*débauche*) spree. **faire la ~** to go on a binge* *ou* a spree; **~ à tout casser** rave-up*.

bringuebalement* [bʀɛ̃g(ə)balmɑ̃] nm, **brinquebalement*** [bʀɛ̃kbalmɑ̃] nm (*mouvement*) shaking (about); (*bruit*) rattle.

bringuebaler* [bʀɛ̃g(ə)bale] [1], **brinquebaler*** [bʀɛ̃kbale] [1] 1 vi *[tête]* to shake about, joggle; *[voiture]* to shake *ou* rock about, joggle; (*avec bruit*) to rattle. **une vieille auto toute bringuebalante** a ramshackle *ou* broken-down old car; **il y a quelque chose qui bringuebale dans ce paquet** something is rattling in this packet. 2 vt to cart (about).

brio [bʀijo] nm (*virtuosité*) brilliance; (*Mus*) brio. **faire qch avec ~** to do sth brilliantly, carry sth off with great panache.

brioche [bʀijɔʃ] nf brioche (*sort of bun*). **jambon en ~** *ham in a pastry case;* (*fig*) **prendre de la ~*** to develop a paunch *ou* a corporation (*Brit*), get a bit of a tummy*.

brioché, e [bʀijɔʃe] adj (baked) like a brioche; *voir* **pain.**

brique [bʀik] 1 nf a (*Constr*) brick; *[savon]* bar, cake; *[tourbe]* block, slab; *[lait]* carton. **mur de** *ou* **en ~(s)** brick wall; **~ pleine/creuse** solid/hollow brick; (*fig*) **bouffer des ~s**‡ to have nothing to eat. b (*) a million (old) francs. c (*Naut*) **~ à pont** holystone. 2 adj inv brick red.

briquer [bʀike] [1] vt (*) to polish up; (*Naut*) to holystone, scrub down.

briquet[1] [bʀikɛ] nm (cigarette) lighter. **~-tempête** windproof lighter; *voir* **battre.**

briquet[2] [bʀikɛ] nm (*Zool*) beagle.

briquetage [bʀik(ə)taʒ] nm (*mur*) brickwork; (*enduit*) imitation brickwork.

briqueter [bʀik(ə)te] [4] vt a (*bâtir*) to brick, build with bricks. b (*peindre*) to face with imitation brickwork.

briqueterie [bʀik(ə)tʀi] nf brickyard, brickfield.

briqueteur [bʀik(ə)tœʀ] nm bricklayer.

briquetier [bʀik(ə)tje] nm (*ouvrier*) brickyard worker, brickmaker; (*entrepreneur*) brick merchant.

briquette [bʀikɛt] nf briquette. **c'est de la ~*** it's not up to much.

bris [bʀi] nm breaking. (*Jur*) **~ de clôture** trespass, breaking-in; (*Aut*) **~ de glaces** broken windows; (*Jur*) **~ de scellés** breaking of seals.

brisant, e [bʀizɑ̃, ɑ̃t] 1 adj high-explosive (*épith*). **obus ~** high-explosive shell. 2 nm a (*vague*) breaker. b (*écueil*) shoal, reef. c (*brise-lames*) groyne, breakwater.

Brisbane [bʀizban] n Brisbane.

briscard [bʀiskaʀ] nm (*Hist Mil*) veteran, old soldier.

brise [bʀiz] nf breeze.

brise- [bʀiz] préf *voir* **briser.**

brisé, e [bʀize] (**ptp de briser**) adj: **~ (de fatigue)** worn out, exhausted; **~ (de chagrin)** overcome by sorrow, brokenhearted; *voir* **arc, ligne**[1]**, pâte.**

brisées [bʀize] nfpl: **marcher sur les ~ de qn** to poach on sb's preserves (*fig*); **suivre les ~ de qn** to follow in sb's footsteps.

briser [bʀize] [1] 1 vt a (*casser*) *objet* to break, smash; *mottes de terre* to break up; *chaîne, fers* to break. **~ qch en mille morceaux** to smash sth to smithereens, break sth into little pieces *ou* bits, shatter sth (into little pieces); (*lit, fig*) **~ la glace** to break the ice.

b (*saper, détruire*) *carrière, vie* to ruin, wreck; *personne* (*épuiser*) to tire out, exhaust; (*abattre la volonté de*) to break, crush; *espérance* to smash, shatter, crush; *cœur, courage* to break; *traité, accord* to break; *amitié* to break up, bring to an end. **d'une voix brisée par l'émotion** in a voice choked with emotion; **ces épreuves l'ont brisé** these trials and tribulations have left him a broken man; **il en a eu le cœur brisé** it broke his heart, he was heartbroken about it.

c (*avoir raison de*) *volonté* to break, crush; *rebelle* to crush, subdue; *opposition, résistance* to crush, break down; *grève* to break (up); *révolte* to crush, quell. **il était décidé à ~ les menées de ces conspirateurs** he was determined to put paid to (*Brit*) *ou* put a stop to the schemings of these conspirators.

d (†: *mettre fin à*) *entretien* to break off.

2 vi (*littér*) a (*rompre*) **~ avec qn** to break with sb; **brisons là!**† enough said!

b (*déferler*) *[vagues]* to break.

3 **se briser** vpr a *[vitre, verre]* to break, shatter, smash; *[bâton, canne]* to break, snap.

b *[vagues]* to break (*contre* against).

c *[résistance]* to break down, snap; *[assaut]* to break up (*sur* on, *contre* against); *[espoir]* to be dashed. **nos efforts se sont brisés sur cette difficulté** our efforts were frustrated *ou* thwarted by this difficulty.

d *[cœur]* to break, be broken; *[voix]* to falter, break.

4 comp ▸ **brise-bise** nm inv half-curtain (*on window*) ▸ **brise-fer** nm inv (*enfant*) wrecker ▸ **brise-glace** nm inv (*navire*) icebreaker; *[pont]* icebreaker, ice apron ▸ **brise-jet** nm inv tap swirl (*Brit*), anti-splash faucet nozzle (*US*) ▸ **brise-lames** nm inv breakwater, mole ▸ **brise-mottes** nm inv harrow ▸ **brise-soleil** nm inv (slatted) canopy *ou* awning ▸ **brise-tout** nm inv = **brise-fer** ▸ **brise-vent** nm inv windbreak.

briseur, -euse [bʀizœʀ, øz] nm,f breaker, wrecker. **~ de grève** strikebreaker.

brisquard [bʀiskaʀ] nm = **briscard.**

bristol [bʀistɔl] nm (*papier*) Bristol board; (*carte de visite*) visiting card.

brisure [bʀizyʀ] nf (*cassure*) break, crack; *[charnière]* joint, break; (*Hér*) mark of cadency, brisure. (*Culin*) **~s de riz** *rice which has not been sorted and is of inconsistent quality.*

britannique [bʀitanik] 1 adj British. 2 nmf: **B~** Briton, British person, Britisher (*US*); **c'est un B~** he's British *ou* a Britisher (*US*), he's a Brit*; **les B~s** the British (people), the Brits*.

broc [bʀo] nm pitcher, ewer.

brocante [bʀɔkɑ̃t] nf (*commerce*) secondhand trade, secondhand market; (*objets*) secondhand goods. **il est dans la ~** he deals in secondhand goods; **acheter qch à la ~** to buy sth at the flea market.

brocanter [bʀɔkɑ̃te] 1 vi to deal in secondhand goods.
brocanteur, -euse [bʀɔkɑ̃tœʀ, øz] nm,f secondhand goods dealer.
brocard[1] [bʀɔkaʀ] nm (*Zool*) brocket.
brocard[2] [bʀɔkaʀ] nm (*littér*, †) gibe, taunt.
brocarder [bʀɔkaʀde] 1 vt (*littér*, †) to gibe at, taunt.
brocart [bʀɔkaʀ] nm brocade.
brochage [bʀɔʃaʒ] nm (*voir* **brocher**) binding (*with paper*); brocading.
broche [bʀɔʃ] nf a (*bijou*) brooch. b (*Culin*) spit; (*Tex*) spindle; (*Tech*) drift, pin; (*Élec*) pin; (*Méd*) pin. (*Alpinisme*) ~ **(à glace)** ice piton; (*Culin*) **faire cuire à la** ~ to spit-roast.
broché [bʀɔʃe] 1 nm (*Tex*) (*procédé*) brocading; (*tissu*) brocade. 2 adj m: **livre** ~ soft-cover book, book with paper binding.
brocher [bʀɔʃe] 1 vt a *livre* to bind (*with paper*), put a paper binding on. b (*Tex*) to brocade. **tissu broché d'or** gold brocade.
brochet [bʀɔʃɛ] nm (*Zool*) pike.
brochette [bʀɔʃɛt] nf (*Culin: ustensile*) skewer; (*plat*) kebab, brochette. (*fig*) ~ **de décorations** row of medals; (*fig*) ~ **de personnalités** bevy *ou* band of VIPs.
brocheur, -euse [bʀɔʃœʀ, øz] 1 nm,f (*voir* **brocher**) book binder; brocade weaver. 2 nm brocade loom. 3 **brocheuse** nf binder, binding machine.
brochure [bʀɔʃyʀ] nf a (*magazine*) brochure, booklet, pamphlet. ~ **touristique** tourist brochure. b *[livre]* (paper) binding. c (*Tex*) brocaded pattern *ou* figures.
brocoli [bʀɔkɔli] nm broccoli.
brodequin [bʀɔd(ə)kɛ̃] nm (laced) boot; (*Hist Théât*) buskin, sock. (*Hist: supplice*) **les** ~**s** the boot.
broder [bʀɔde] 1 1 vt *tissu* to embroider (*de* with); (*fig*) *récit* to embroider. 2 vi (*exagérer*) to embroider, embellish; (*trop développer*) to elaborate. ~ **sur un sujet** to elaborate on a subject.
broderie [bʀɔdʀi] nf (*art*) embroidery; (*objet*) piece of embroidery, embroidery (*NonC*); (*industrie*) embroidery trade. **faire de la** ~ to embroider, do embroidery; ~ **anglaise** broderie anglaise.
brodeur [bʀɔdœʀ] nm embroiderer.
brodeuse [bʀɔdøz] nf (*ouvrière*) embroideress; (*machine*) embroidery machine.
broiement [bʀwamɑ̃] nm = **broyage**.
bromate [bʀɔmat] nm bromate.
brome [bʀom] nm (*Chim*) bromine.
bromique [bʀɔmik] adj bromic.
bromure [bʀɔmyʀ] nm bromide. ~ **d'argent/de potassium** silver/potassium bromide.
bronche [bʀɔ̃ʃ] nf bronchus (*SPÉC*). **les** ~**s** the bronchial tubes; **il est faible des** ~**s** he has a weak chest.
broncher [bʀɔ̃ʃe] 1 vi *[cheval]* to stumble. **personne n'osait** ~* no one dared move a muscle *ou* say a word; **le premier qui bronche ...!*** the first person to budge ...!* *ou* make a move ...!; **sans** ~ (*sans peur*) without turning a hair, without flinching; (*: *sans protester*) uncomplainingly, meekly; (*sans se tromper*) faultlessly, without faltering.
bronchiole [bʀɔ̃ʃjɔl] nf (*Anat*) bronchiole.
bronchique [bʀɔ̃ʃik] adj bronchial.
bronchite [bʀɔ̃ʃit] nf bronchitis (*NonC*). **avoir une bonne** ~ to have (got) a bad bout *ou* attack of bronchitis.
bronchitique [bʀɔ̃ʃitik] adj bronchitic (*SPÉC*). **il est** ~ he suffers from bronchitis.
broncho-pneumonie, pl **broncho-pneumonies** [bʀɔ̃kopnømɔni] nf bronchopneumonia (*NonC*).
brontosaure [bʀɔ̃tozɔʀ] nm brontosaurus.
bronzage [bʀɔ̃zaʒ] nm (*voir* **bronzer**) (sun) tan; bronzing. ~ **intégral** allover tan.
bronzant, e [bʀɔ̃zɑ̃, ɑ̃t] adj *lait, lotion* tanning (*épith*), suntan (*épith*).
bronze [bʀɔ̃z] nm (*métal, objet*) bronze.
bronzé, e [bʀɔ̃ze] (ptp de **bronzer**) adj (sun)tanned, sunburnt (*Brit*).
bronzer [bʀɔ̃ze] 1 1 vt *peau* to tan; *métal* to bronze. 2 vi *[peau, personne]* to get a tan. **les gens qui (se) bronzent sur la plage** people who sunbathe on the beach.
bronzette* [bʀɔ̃zɛt] nf: **faire de la** ~ to do a bit of sunbathing.
bronzeur [bʀɔ̃zœʀ] nm (*fondeur*) bronze-smelter; (*fabricant*) bronze-smith.
broquette [bʀɔkɛt] nf (tin)tack.
brossage [bʀɔsaʒ] nm brushing.
brosse [bʀɔs] 1 nf a brush; *[peintre]* (paint)brush. (*fig hum*) **l'art de manier la** ~ **à reluire** the art of sucking up to people* *ou* buttering people up; **donne un coup de** ~ **à ta veste** give your jacket a brush; **passer le tapis à la** ~ to give the carpet a brush; **passer le carrelage à la** ~ to give the (stone) floor a scrub. b (*Coiffure*) crew cut. **avoir les cheveux en** ~ to have a crew-cut. c (*Can*) **prendre une** ~⁑ to get drunk *ou* smashed⁑. 2 comp ▸**brosse à chaussures** shoebrush ▸**brosse à cheveux** hairbrush ▸**brosse en chiendent** scrubbing brush ▸**brosse à dents** toothbrush ▸**brosse à habits** clothesbrush ▸**brosse métallique** wire brush ▸**brosse à ongles** nailbrush.
brosser [bʀɔse] 1 1 vt a (*nettoyer*) to brush; *cheval* to brush down; *plancher, carrelage* to scrub. ~ **qn** to brush sb's clothes. b (*Art, fig*) to paint. ~ **un vaste tableau de la situation** to paint a broad picture of the situation. c (*Sport*) to put spin on. 2 **se brosser** vpr a to brush one's clothes, give one's clothes a brush. **se** ~ **les dents** to brush *ou* clean one's teeth; **se** ~ **les cheveux** to brush one's hair. b (⁑) **se** ~ **le ventre** to go without food; **tu peux (toujours) te** ~! you'll have to do without!, nothing doing!⁑, you can whistle for it!⁑
brosserie [bʀɔsʀi] nf (*usine*) brush factory; (*commerce*) brush trade.
brossier [bʀɔsje] nm (*ouvrier*) brush maker; (*commerçant*) brush dealer.
brou [bʀu] nm (*écorce*) husk, shuck (*US*). ~ **de noix** (*Menuiserie*) walnut stain; (*liqueur*) walnut liqueur.
broue⁑ [bʀu] nf (*Can*) *[bière]* froth; *[mer]* foam.
brouet [bʀuɛ] nm (††: *potage*) gruel; (*péj, hum*) brew.
brouette [bʀuɛt] nf wheelbarrow.
brouettée [bʀuete] nf (wheel)barrowful.
brouetter [bʀuete] 1 vt to (carry in a) wheelbarrow.
brouhaha [bʀuaa] nm (*tintamarre*) hubbub.
brouillage [bʀujaʒ] nm (*Rad*) (*intentionnel*) jamming; (*accidentel*) interference.
brouillard [bʀujaʀ] nm a (*dense*) fog; (*léger*) mist; (*mêlé de fumée*) smog. ~ **de chaleur** heat haze; ~ **givrant** freezing fog; ~ **à couper au couteau** thick *ou* dense fog, peasouper*; **il fait** *ou* **il y a du** ~ it's foggy; (*fig*) **être dans le** ~ to be lost, be all at sea; *voir* **foncer**. b (*Comm*) daybook.
brouillasser [bʀujase] 1 vi to drizzle.
brouille [bʀuj] nf disagreement, breach, quarrel. ~ **légère** tiff; **être en** ~ **avec qn** to have fallen out with sb, be on bad terms with sb.
brouillé, e [bʀuje] (ptp de **brouiller**) adj a (*fâché*) **être** ~ **avec qn** to have fallen out with sb, be on bad terms with sb; **être** ~ **avec les dates/l'orthographe/les maths*** to be hopeless *ou* useless* at dates/spelling/maths. b **avoir le teint** ~ to have a muddy complexion; *voir* **œuf**.
brouiller [bʀuje] 1 1 vt a (*troubler*) *contour, vue, yeux* to blur; *papiers, idées* to mix *ou* muddle up; *message, combinaison de coffre* to scramble. **la buée brouille les verres de mes lunettes** my glasses are misting up; **la pluie a brouillé l'adresse** the rain has smudged *ou* blurred the address; **son accident lui a brouillé la cervelle*** since he had that accident his mind has been a bit muddled *ou* confused; (*fig*) ~ **les pistes** *ou* **cartes** to confuse *ou* cloud the issue, draw a red herring across the trail.
b (*fâcher*) to set at odds, put on bad terms. **cet incident l'a brouillé avec sa famille** this incident set him at odds with *ou* put him on bad terms with his family.
c (*Rad*) *émission* (*avec intention*) to jam; (*par accident*) to cause interference to.
2 **se brouiller** vpr a (*se troubler*) *[vue]* to become blurred; *[souvenirs, idées]* to get mixed *ou* muddled up, become confused. **tout se brouilla dans sa tête** everything became confused *ou* muddled in his mind.
b (*se fâcher*) **se** ~ **avec qn** to fall out *ou* quarrel with sb; **depuis qu'ils se sont brouillés** since they fell out (with each other).
c (*Mét*) *[ciel]* to cloud over. **le temps se brouille** it's going *ou* turning cloudy, the weather is breaking.
brouillerie [bʀujʀi] nf = **brouille**.
brouilleur [bʀujœʀ] nm jammer.
brouillon, -onne [bʀujɔ̃, ɔn] 1 adj (*qui manque de soin*) untidy; (*qui manque d'organisation*) unmethodical, unsystematic, muddle-headed. **élève** ~ careless pupil; **avoir l'esprit** ~ to be muddle-headed. 2 nm,f muddler, muddlehead. 3 nm *[lettre, devoir]* rough copy; (*ébauche*) (rough) draft; (*calculs, notes etc*) rough work. **(papier)** ~ rough paper; **prendre qch au** ~ to make a rough copy of sth; *voir* **cahier**.
broum! [bʀum] excl brum, brum!
broussaille [bʀusɑj] nf: ~**s** undergrowth, brushwood, scrub; **avoir les cheveux en** ~ to have unkempt *ou* untidy *ou* tousled hair; **sourcils en** ~ bushy eyebrows.
broussailleux, -euse [bʀusɑjø, øz] adj *terrain, sous-bois* bushy, scrubby; *ronces* brambly; *jardin* overgrown; *sourcils, barbe* bushy; *cheveux* bushy, tousled.
broussard* [bʀusaʀ] nm bushman.
brousse [bʀus] nf: **la** ~ the bush; (*fig*) **c'est en pleine** ~* it's at the back of beyond* (*Brit*), it's in the middle of nowhere.
broutage [bʀutaʒ] nm = **broutement**.
broutard [bʀutaʀ] nm grass-fed calf.
broutement [bʀutmɑ̃] nm (*voir* **brouter**) grazing; nibbling; browsing; chattering; grabbing; juddering.
brouter [bʀute] 1 1 vt *herbe* to graze (on); *[lapin]* to nibble. (*fig*) **il nous les broute!⁑** he's a pain in the neck!⁑, he's a bloody*⁑ (*Brit*) *ou* damned⁑ nuisance. 2 vi a *[mouton]* to graze; *[vache, cerf]* to browse; *[lapin]* to nibble. b (*Tech*) *[rabot]* to chatter; (*Aut*) *[freins]* to grab; *[embrayage]* to judder.
broutille [bʀutij] nf (*bagatelle*) trifle. **c'est de la** ~* (*de mauvaise qualité*) it's cheap rubbish; (*sans importance*) it's not worth mentioning, it's nothing of any consequence.
brownien, -ienne [bʀonjɛ̃, jɛn] adj Brownian. **mouvement** ~ Brownian movement; **particules** ~**nes** Brownian particles; (*fig*) **agité**

de mouvements ~s rushing about in all directions.

broyage [bʀwajaʒ] **nm** (*voir* **broyer**) grinding; crushing; braking.

broyer [bʀwaje] [8] **vt** *pierre, sucre, os* to grind (to powder), crush; *chanvre, lin* to brake; *poivre, blé* to grind; *aliments* to grind, break up; *couleurs* to grind; *doigt, main* to crush. (*fig*) ~ **du noir** to be in the doldrums *ou* down in the dumps*.

broyeur, -euse [bʀwajœʀ, øz] **1 adj** crushing, grinding. **2 nm** (*ouvrier*) grinder, crusher; (*machine*) grinder, crusher; *[chanvre, lin]* brake. ~ **(de cailloux)** pebble grinder.

brrr [bʀʀ] **excl** brr!

bru [bʀy] **nf** daughter-in-law.

bruant [bʀyɑ̃] **nm** bunting (*bird*). ~ **jaune** yellowhammer; ~ **des roseaux** reed bunting.

brucelles [bʀysɛl] **nfpl** tweezers.

brucellose [bʀyseloz] **nf** brucellosis.

Bruges [bʀyʒ] **n** Bruges.

brugnon [bʀyɲɔ̃] **nm** nectarine.

brugnonier [bʀyɲɔnje] **nm** nectarine tree.

bruine [bʀɥin] **nf** (fine) drizzle, Scotch mist.

bruiner [bʀɥine] [1] **vi** to drizzle.

bruineux, -euse [bʀɥinø, øz] **adj** drizzly.

bruire [bʀɥiʀ] [2] **vi** *[feuilles, tissu, vent]* to rustle; *[ruisseau]* to murmur; *[insecte]* to buzz, hum.

bruissement [bʀɥismɑ̃] **nm** (*voir* **bruire**) rustle, rustling; murmur; buzz(ing), humming.

bruit [bʀɥi] **nm a** (*gén*) sound, noise; (*avec idée d'intensité désagréable*) noise. **j'entendis un ~** I heard a noise; **un ~ de vaisselle** the clatter of dishes; **un ~ de moteur/voix** the sound of an engine/of voices; **un ~ de verre brisé** the tinkle *ou* sound of broken glass; **un ~ de pas** (the sound of) footsteps; **le ~ d'un plongeon** (the sound of) a splash; **le ~ de la pluie contre les vitres** the sound *ou* patter of the rain against the windows; **le ~ des radios** the noise *ou* blare of radios; **les ~s de la rue** street noises; **un ~ ou des ~s de marteau** (the sound of) hammering; **~ de fond** background noise; **le ~ familier des camions** the familiar rumble of the lorries; **un ~ parasite** interference (*NonC*); **~ sourd** thud; **~ strident** screech, shriek; **on n'entend aucun ~ d'ici** you can't hear a sound from here; **dans un ~ de tonnerre** with a thunderous roar.
b (*opposé à silence*) **le ~** noise; **on ne peut pas travailler dans le ~** one cannot work against noise; **le ~ est insupportable ici** the noise is unbearable here; **cette machine fait un ~ infernal** this machine makes a dreadful noise *ou* racket*; **sans ~** noiselessly, without a sound, silently.
c il y a trop de ~ there's too much noise, it's too noisy; **s'il y a du ~ je ne peux pas travailler** if there's (a) noise I can't work; **les enfants font du ~, c'est normal** it's natural that children are noisy; **arrêtez de faire du ~** stop making a noise *ou* being (so) noisy; **faites du ~ pour chasser les pigeons** make a *ou* some noise to scare the pigeons away; **j'entendis du ~** I heard a noise.
d (*fig*) **beaucoup de ~ pour rien** much ado about nothing, a lot of fuss about nothing; **faire grand ~ ou beaucoup de ~ autour de qch** to make a great fuss *ou* to-do about sth; **cette nouvelle a été annoncée à grand ~** they made a big splash with the news; **il fait plus de ~ que de mal** his bark is worse than his bite.
e (*nouvelle*) rumour. **le ~ de son départ ...** the rumour of his leaving ...; **le ~ court qu'il doit partir** there is a rumour going about *ou* rumour has it that he is to go; **c'est un ~ qui court** it's a rumour that's going round; **se faire l'écho d'un ~** to repeat a rumour; **répandre de faux ~s (sur)** to spread false rumours *ou* tales (about); **les ~s de couloir à l'Assemblée nationale** parliamentary rumours; **~s de guerre** rumours of war; **~ de bottes** sabre-rattling; (††) **il n'est ~ dans la ville que de son arrivée** his arrival is the talk of the town, his arrival has set the town agog.
f (*Téléc*) noise. (*Méd*) **~ de souffle** murmur.

bruitage [bʀɥitaʒ] **nm** sound effects.

bruiter [bʀɥite] [1] **vt** to add the sound effects to.

bruiteur [bʀɥitœʀ] **nm** sound-effects engineer.

brûlage [bʀylaʒ] **nm** *[cheveux]* singeing; *[café]* roasting; *[herbes]* burning. **faire un ~ à qn** to singe sb's hair.

brûlant, e [bʀylɑ̃, ɑ̃t] **adj a** (*chaud*) *objet* burning (hot), red-hot; *plat* piping hot; *liquide* boiling (hot), scalding; *soleil* scorching, blazing; *air* burning. **il a le front ~ (de fièvre)** his forehead is burning (with fever). **b** (*passionné*) *regard, pages* fiery, impassioned. **c** (*controversé*) *sujet* ticklish. **être sur un terrain ~** to touch on a hotly debated issue; **c'est d'une actualité ~e** it's the burning question of the hour.

brûle- [bʀyl] **préf** *voir* **brûler**.

brûlé, e [bʀyle] (**ptp de brûler**) **1 adj** (*) **il est ~** (*gén*) he's had* *ou* blown* it; *[espion]* his cover is blown*; *voir* **crème, terre, tête. 2 nm a ça sent le ~** (*lit*) there's a smell of burning; (*fig*) trouble's brewing; **cela a un goût de ~** it tastes burnt *ou* has a burnt taste. **b** (*personne*) **grand ~** victim of third-degree burns, badly burnt person.

brûler [bʀyle] [1] **1 vt a** (*détruire*) *objet, ordures, corps* to burn; *maison* to burn down. **être brûlé vif** (*accident*) to be burnt alive *ou* burnt to death; (*supplice*) to be burnt at the stake; (*fig*) **il a brûlé ses dernières cartouches** he has shot his bolt; (*fig*) **~ ses vaisseaux** to burn one's boats; **~ le pavé†** to ride *ou* run *etc* hell for leather*; (*Théât*) **~ les planches** to give a spirited performance; **~ ce que l'on a adoré** to burn one's old idols.
b (*endommager*) *[flamme]* (*gén*) to burn; *cheveux* to singe; *[eau bouillante]* to scald; *[fer à repasser]* to singe, scorch; *[soleil] herbe* to scorch; *peau* to burn; *[gel] bourgeon* to nip, damage; *[acide] peau* to burn, sear; *métal* to burn, attack, corrode. **il a la peau brûlée par le soleil** (*bronzage*) his skin is sunburnt (*Brit*) *ou* tanned; (*lésion*) his skin *ou* he has been burnt by the sun; **le soleil nous brûle** the sun is scorching *ou* burning.
c (*traiter*) *café* to roast; (*Méd*) to cauterize.
d (*consommer*) *électricité, charbon* to burn, use; *cierge, chandelle* to burn. **ils ont brûlé tout leur bois** they've burnt up *ou* used up all their wood; **~ la chandelle par les deux bouts** to burn the candle at both ends; **~ de l'encens** to burn incense.
e (*dépasser*) (*Aut*) **~ un stop** to ignore a stop sign; **~ un feu rouge** to go through a red light (without stopping), to run a red light (*US*); (*Rail*) **~ un signal/une station** to go through *ou* past a signal/a station (without stopping); **~ une étape** to cut out a stop; (*fig*) **~ les étapes** (*réussir rapidement*) to shoot ahead; (*trop se précipiter*) to cut corners, take short cuts; **~ la politesse à qn** to leave sb abruptly (without saying goodbye).
f (*donner une sensation de brûlure*) to burn. **le radiateur me brûlait le dos** the radiator was burning my back; **j'ai les yeux qui me brûlent, les yeux me brûlent** my eyes are smarting *ou* stinging; **j'ai la figure qui (me) brûle** my face is burning; **la gorge lui brûle** he's got a burning sensation in his throat; (*fig*) **l'argent lui brûle les doigts** money burns a hole in his pocket.
g (*fig: consumer*) **le désir de l'aventure le brûlait, il était brûlé du désir de l'aventure** he was burning *ou* longing for adventure.
2 vi a *[charbon, feu]* to burn; *[maison, forêt]* to be on fire; (*Culin*) to burn. **on a laissé ~ l'électricité ou l'électricité a brûlé toute la journée** the lights have been left on *ou* have been burning away all day; **ce bois brûle très vite** this wood burns (up) very quickly; *voir* **torchon**.
b (*être brûlant*) to be burning (hot) *ou* scalding. **son front brûle de fièvre** his forehead is burning; **ne touche pas, ça brûle** don't touch that, you'll burn yourself *ou* you'll get burnt; (*jeu, devinette*) **tu brûles!** you're getting hot!
c (*fig*) **~ de faire qch** to be burning *ou* be dying to do sth; **~ d'impatience** to seethe with impatience; († *ou hum*) **~ (d'amour) pour qn** to be infatuated *ou* madly in love with sb; **~ d'envie ou du désir de faire qch** to be dying *ou* longing to do sth.
3 se brûler vpr a to burn o.s.; (*se tuer*) to set o.s. on fire; (*s'ébouillanter*) to scald o.s. **se ~ les doigts** (*lit*) to burn one's fingers; (*fig*) to get one's fingers burnt (*fig*); **le papillon s'est brûlé les ailes à la flamme** the butterfly burnt its wings in the flame; (*se compromettre*) **se ~ les ailes†** to burn one's fingers; **se ~ la cervelle** to blow one's brains out.
b (* *Can*) to exhaust o.s., wear o.s. out.
4 comp ▸ brûle-gueule nm inv short (clay) pipe **▸ brûle-parfum nm inv** perfume burner **▸ brûle-pourpoint adv: à brûle-pourpoint** point-blank; (†: *à bout portant*) at point-blank range.

brûlerie [bʀylʀi] **nf** *[café]* coffee-roasting plant *ou* shop; *[alcool]* (brandy) distillery.

brûleur [bʀylœʀ] **nm** (*dispositif*) burner.

brûlis [bʀyli] **nm** (*technique*) ≃ stubble-burning; (*terrain*) field (*where stubble has been burnt*).

brûloir [bʀylwaʀ] **nm** coffee roaster (*machine*).

brûlot [bʀylo] **nm a** (*Hist Naut*) fire ship; (*personne*) firebrand. (*fig*) **lancer un ~ contre** to launch a scathing attack on. **b** (*Can*) midge, gnat.

brûlure [bʀylyʀ] **nf** (*lésion*) burn; (*sensation*) burning sensation. **~ (d'eau bouillante)** scald; **~ de cigarette** cigarette burn; **~ du premier degré** first-degree burn; **~s d'estomac** heartburn (*NonC*).

brumaire [bʀymɛʀ] **nm** Brumaire (*second month of French Republican calendar*).

brumasser [bʀymase] [1] **vb impers: il brumasse** it's a bit misty, there's a slight mist.

brume [bʀym] **nf** (*gén*) mist; (*dense*) fog; (*Mét*) mist; (*Naut*) fog. **~ légère** haze; **~ de chaleur ou de beau temps** heat haze; *voir* **corne**.

brumeux, -euse [bʀymø, øz] **adj** misty; foggy; (*fig*) obscure, hazy.

brumisateur [bʀymizatœʀ] **nm** spray, atomiser.

brun, brune [bʀœ̃, bʀyn] **1 adj** *yeux, couleur* brown; *cheveux* brown, dark; *peau* dusky, swarthy, dark; (*bronzé*) tanned, brown; *tabac* dark; *bière* brown. **il est ~** (*cheveux*) he's dark-haired; (*bronzé*) he's tanned; **il est ~ (de peau)** he's dark-skinned; **~ roux** (dark) auburn. **2 nm** (*couleur*) brown; (*homme*) dark-haired man. **3 brune nf a** (*bière*) brown ale, stout. **b** (*cigarette*) *cigarette made of dark tobacco.* **c** (*femme*) brunette. **d** (*littér*) **à la ~** at twilight, at dusk.

brunante [bʀynɑ̃t] **nf** (*Can*) **à la ~** at twilight, at dusk.

brunâtre [bʀynɑtʀ] **adj** brownish.

Brunéi [bʀynei] **nm** Brunei.

brunéien, -ienne [bʀynejɛ̃, jɛn] **1 adj** of *ou* from Brunei. **2 nm,f: B~(ne)** inhabitant *ou* native of Brunei.

brunette [bʀynɛt] **nf** brunette.

brunir [bʀyniʀ] 2 1 vi *[personne, peau]* to get sunburnt (*Brit*), get a tan; *[cheveux]* to go darker; *[caramel]* to brown. 2 vt a *peau* to tan; *cheveux* to darken. b *métal* to burnish, polish.

brunissage [bʀynisaʒ] nm burnishing.

brunissement [bʀynismɑ̃] nm *[peau]* tanning.

brunissoir [bʀyniswaʀ] nm burnisher.

brunissure [bʀynisyʀ] nf *[métal]* burnish; (*Agr*) potato rot; *[vigne]* brown rust.

brushing [bʀœʃiŋ] nm blow-dry. **faire un ~ à qn** to blow-dry sb's hair.

brusque [bʀysk] adj a (*rude, sec*) *personne, manières* brusque, abrupt, blunt; *geste* brusque, abrupt, rough; *ton* curt, abrupt, blunt. **être ~ avec qn** to be curt *ou* abrupt with sb. b (*soudain*) *départ, changement* abrupt, sudden; *virage* sharp; *envie* sudden.

brusquement [bʀyskəmɑ̃] adj (*voir* **brusque**) brusquely; abruptly; bluntly; roughly; curtly; suddenly; sharply.

brusquer [bʀyske] 1 vt a (*précipiter*) to rush, hasten. **attaque brusquée** surprise attack; **il ne faut rien ~** we mustn't rush things. b *personne* to rush, chivvy*.

brusquerie [bʀyskəʀi] nf brusqueness, abruptness.

brut, e[1] [bʀyt] 1 adj a *diamant* uncut, rough; *pétrole* crude; *minerai* crude, raw; *sucre* unrefined; *soie, métal* raw; *toile* unbleached; *laine* untreated; *champagne* brut, extra dry; (*fig*) *fait* crude; *idée* crude, raw; *art* primitive. **à l'état ~** (*lit*) *matière* untreated, in the rough; (*fig*) *idées* in the rough; **~ de béton** *ou* **de décoffrage** *mur* concrete; **~ de fonderie** *pièce* unpolished; (*fig*) **~ de béton** *ou* **de fonderie** rough and ready; *voir* **poids**.

b (*Comm*) *bénéfice, poids, traitement* gross. **produire ~ un million** to gross a million; **ça fait 100 F/100 kg ~, ça fait ~ 100 F/100 kg** that makes 100 francs/100 kg gross; *voir* **produit**.

2 nm a (*pétrole*) crude (oil). **~ lourd** heavy crude; **~ léger** light crude.

b (*salaire*) gross salary.

brutal, e, mpl **-aux** [bʀytal, o] adj a (*violent*) *personne, caractère* rough, brutal, violent; *instinct* savage; *jeu* rough. **être ~ avec qn** to be rough with sb; **force ~e** brute force. b (*choquant*) *langage, franchise* blunt; *vérité* plain, unvarnished; *réalité* stark. **il a été très ~ dans sa réponse** he was very outspoken in his answer, he gave a very blunt answer. c (*soudain*) *mort* sudden; *choc, coup* brutal.

brutalement [bʀytalmɑ̃] adv (*voir* **brutal**) roughly; brutally; violently; bluntly; plainly; suddenly.

brutaliser [bʀytalize] 1 vt *personne* to bully, knock about, handle roughly, manhandle; *machine* to ill-treat.

brutalité [bʀytalite] nf (*NonC: violence*) brutality, violence, roughness; (*acte brutal*) brutality; (*Sport*) rough play (*NonC*); (*soudaineté*) suddenness. **~s policières** police brutality.

brute[2] [bʀyt] nf (*homme brutal*) brute, animal; (*homme grossier*) boor, lout; (*littér: animal*) brute, beast. **taper sur qch comme une ~*** to bash* away at sth (savagely); **frapper qn comme une ~** to hit out at sb brutishly; **~ épaisse*** brutish lout; **c'est une sale ~!*** he's a real brute!*; **tu es une grosse ~!*** you're a big bully!

Brutus [bʀytys] n Brutus.

Bruxelles [bʀysɛl] n Brussels; *voir* **chou**[1].

bruyamment [bʀɥijamɑ̃] adv *rire, parler* noisily, loudly; *protester* loudly.

bruyant, e [bʀɥijɑ̃, ɑ̃t] adj *personne, réunion* noisy, boisterous; *rue* noisy; *rire* loud; *succès* resounding (*épith*). **ils ont accueilli la nouvelle avec une joie ~e** they greeted the news with whoops* *ou* with loud cries of joy.

bruyère [bʀyjɛʀ] nf (*plante*) heather; (*terrain*) heath(land). **pipe en (racine de) ~** briar pipe; *voir* **coq**[1], **terre**.

BT [bete] nm (**abrév de brevet de technicien**) *voir* **brevet**

BTA [betea] nm (**abrév de brevet de technicien agricole**) *voir* **brevet.**

BTP [betepe] nmpl (**abrév de bâtiments et travaux publics**) *public buildings and works sector.*

BTS [beteɛs] nm (**abrév de brevet de technicien supérieur**) *voir* **brevet.**

BU [bey] nf (**abrév de bibliothèque universitaire**) *voir* **bibliothèque.**

bu, e [by] ptp de **boire.**

buanderette [bɥɑ̃dʀɛt] nf (*Can*) launderette (*Brit*), Laundromat ® (*US*).

buanderie [bɥɑ̃dʀi] nf wash house, laundry; (*Can: blanchisserie*) laundry.

bubale [bybal] nm bubal.

bubon [bybɔ̃] nm bubo.

bubonique [bybɔnik] adj bubonic; *voir* **peste.**

Bucarest [bykaʀɛst] n Bucharest.

buccal, e, mpl **-aux** [bykal, o] adj oral; *voir* **cavité, voie.**

buccin [byksɛ̃] nm whelk.

bucco-dentaire, pl **bucco-dentaires** [bykodɑ̃tɛʀ] adj *hygiène* oral.

bûche [byʃ] nf a *[bois]* log. (*Culin*) **~ de Noël** Yule log. b (*: *lourdaud*) blockhead‡, clot‡ (*Brit*), clod‡ (*US*), lump*. **rester (là) comme une ~** to sit there like a (great) lump*. c (*: *chute*) fall, spill. **ramasser une ~** to come a cropper* (*Brit*), take a (headlong) spill (*US*).

bûcher[1] [byʃe] nm a (*remise*) woodshed. b (*funéraire*) (funeral) pyre; (*supplice*) stake. **être condamné au ~** to be condemned to (be burnt at) the stake.

bûcher[2]* [byʃe] 1 1 vt to swot up* (*Brit*), slog away at*, bone up on*. 2 vi to swot* (*Brit*), slog away*.

bûcher[3] [byʃe] 1 (*Can*) 1 vt *arbres* to fell, cut down, chop down. 2 vi to fell trees.

bûcheron [byʃʀɔ̃] nm woodcutter, lumberjack, lumberman (*US*).

bûchette [byʃɛt] nf (dry) twig, stick (of wood); (*pour compter*) rod, stick.

bûcheur, -euse* [byʃœʀ, øz] 1 adj hard-working. 2 nm,f slogger*, grind* (*US*).

bucolique [bykɔlik] 1 adj bucolic, pastoral. 2 nf bucolic, pastoral (poem).

Budapest [bydapɛst] n Budapest.

budget [bydʒɛ] nm budget. **~ d'exploitation** working *ou* operating *ou* trading budget; **~ de fonctionnement** operating budget; **~ publicitaire** *[annonceur]* advertising budget; *[agence de publicité]* advertising account; **~ prévisionnel** provisional budget; **le client au ~ modeste** the customer on a tight budget; **vacances pour petits ~s** *ou* **~s modestes** low-cost *ou* budget holidays; *voir* **boucler.**

budgétaire [bydʒetɛʀ] adj *dépenses, crise* budgetary. **prévisions ~s** budget forecasts; **collectif ~** minibudget, interim budget; **année ~** financial year.

budgéter [bydʒete] 1 vt = **budgétiser.**

budgétisation [bydʒetizasjɔ̃] nf inclusion in the budget.

budgétiser [bydʒetize] 1 vt (*Fin*) to include in the budget, budget for.

budgétivore [bydʒetivɔʀ] adj high-spending (*épith*).

buée [bɥe] nf *[haleine]* condensation, steam; *[eau chaude]* steam; (*sur vitre*) mist, steam, condensation; (*sur miroir*) mist, blur. **couvert de ~** misted up, steamed up; **faire de la ~** to make steam.

Buenos Aires [bwenɔzɛʀ] n Buenos Aires.

buffet [byfɛ] nm a (*meuble*) *[salle à manger]* sideboard. **~ de cuisine** kitchen dresser *ou* cabinet; *voir* **danser.** b *[réception]* (*table*) buffet; (*repas*) buffet (meal). **~ campagnard** ≈ cold table; **~ froid** cold buffet; **~ (de gare)** station buffet, refreshment room. c (‡ *fig: ventre*) stomach, belly‡. **il n'a rien dans le ~** he hasn't had anything to eat; (*manque de courage*) he has no guts*. d **~ (d'orgue)** (organ) case.

buffle [byfl] nm buffalo.

buggy [bygi] nm (*Aut*) buggy.

bugle[1] [bygl] nm (*Mus*) bugle.

bugle[2] [bygl] nf (*Bot*) bugle.

buire [bɥiʀ] nf ewer.

buis [bɥi] nm (*arbre*) box(wood) (*NonC*), box tree; (*bois*) box(wood).

buisson [bɥisɔ̃] nm (*Bot*) bush. (*Culin*) **~ de langoustines** scampi en buisson *ou* in a bush; (*Bible*) **~ ardent** burning bush.

buissonneux, -euse [bɥisɔnø, øz] adj *terrain* bushy, full of bushes; *végétation* scrubby.

buissonnière [bɥisɔnjɛʀ] adj f *voir* **école.**

Bujumbura [buʒumbuʀa] n Bujumbura.

bulbe [bylb] nm (*Bot*) bulb, corm; (*Archit*) onion-shaped dome. (*Anat*) **~ pileux** hair bulb; **~ rachidien** medulla.

bulbeux, -euse [bylbø, øz] adj (*Bot*) bulbous; *forme* bulbous, onion-shaped.

bulgare [bylgaʀ] 1 adj Bulgarian. 2 nm (*Ling*) Bulgarian. 3 nmf: **B~** Bulgarian, Bulgar.

Bulgarie [bylgaʀi] nf Bulgaria.

bulldozer [buldozɛʀ] nm bulldozer. (*fig*) **c'est un vrai ~** he steamrollers (his way) through everything.

bulle [byl] 1 nf a *[air, savon, verre]* bubble; (*Méd: cloque*) blister; (*Méd: enceinte stérile*) bubble; *[bande dessinée]* balloon. **faire des ~s** to blow bubbles; **bébé-/enfant-~** baby/child who has to live in a sterile environment (*because he or she lacks immunity to disease*). b (*Rel*) bull; *voir* **coincer.** 2 nm: **(papier) ~** Manilla paper.

bullé, e [byle] adj bubble (*épith*). **verre ~** bubble glass.

buller* [byle] 1 vi (*paresser*) to laze around.

bulletin [byltɛ̃] 1 nm (*reportage, communiqué*) bulletin, report; (*magazine*) bulletin; (*formulaire*) form; (*certificat*) certificate; (*billet*) ticket; (*Scol*) report; (*Pol*) ballot paper.

2 comp ▸**bulletin de bagage** luggage ticket, baggage check (*surtout US*) ▸**bulletin blanc** (*Pol*) blank vote ▸**bulletin de commande** order form ▸**bulletin de consigne** left-luggage (*Brit*) *ou* checkroom (*US*) ticket ▸**bulletin des cours** (*Bourse*) official list, stock-exchange list ▸**bulletin d'état civil** identity document (*issued by local authorities*) ▸**bulletin d'information** news bulletin ▸**bulletin météorologique** weather forecast *ou* report *ou* check ▸**bulletin de naissance** birth certificate ▸**bulletin de notes** = **bulletin scolaire** ▸**bulletin nul** (*Pol*) spoilt ballot paper ▸**Bulletin officiel** official bulletin ▸**bulletin-réponse** nm (pl **bulletins-réponses**) (*dans un concours*) entry form ▸**bulletin de salaire** salary advice, pay-slip ▸**bulletin de santé** medical bulletin ▸**bulletin scolaire** (*Scol*) (*school*) report ▸**bulletin trimestriel** end-of-term report ▸**bulletin de vote** (*Pol*) ballot paper; **bulletin de vote par correspondance** postal vote (*Brit*), absentee ballot (*US*).

bullpack [bylpak] nm ® bubble wrap.

bulot [bylo] nm whelk.

bungalow [bœ̃galo] nm (*en Inde*) bungalow; *[motel]* chalet.

bunker [bunkœʀ] nm (*Golf*) bunker (*Brit*), sand trap (*US*).

buraliste [byʀalist] nmf *[bureau de tabac]* tobacconist (*Brit*), tobacco dealer (*US*); *[poste]* clerk.

bure [byʀ] nf (*étoffe*) frieze, homespun; (*vêtement*) *[moine]* frock, cowl. **porter la ~** to be a monk.

bureau, pl **~x** [byʀo] 1 nm a (*meuble*) desk.

b (*cabinet de travail*) study.

c (*lieu de travail: pièce, édifice*) office. **le ~ du directeur** the manager's office; **pendant les heures de ~** during office hours; **nos ~x seront fermés** our premises *ou* the office will be closed; (*hum*) **le ~ des pleurs est fermé** moaning (about it) will get you nowhere; *voir* **chef**[1]**, deuxième, employé.**

d (*section*) department; (*Mil*) branch, department.

e (*comité*) committee; (*exécutif*) board. **aller à une réunion du ~** to go to a committee meeting; *[syndicats]* **élire le ~** to elect the officers (of the committee).

2 comp ▸**bureau d'accueil** reception ▸**bureau d'aide sociale** welfare office ▸**bureau de bienfaisance** welfare office ▸**bureau de change** bureau de change, foreign exchange office (*US*) ▸**bureau des contributions** tax office ▸**bureau à cylindre** roll-top desk ▸**bureau de douane** customs house ▸**bureau d'études** *[entreprise]* research department; *cabinet* research consultancy ▸**Bureau européen de l'environnement** European Environment Office ▸**Bureau international du travail** International Labour Office ▸**bureau de location** booking *ou* box office ▸**bureau ministre** pedestal desk ▸**bureau des objets trouvés** lost property (*Brit*) *ou* lost and found (*US*) office ▸**bureau de placement** employment agency ▸**bureau postal d'origine** dispatching (post) office ▸**bureau de poste** post office ▸**bureau de renseignements** information service ▸**bureau de tabac** tobacconist's (shop) (*Brit*), tobacco *ou* smoke shop (*US*) ▸**bureau de tri** sorting office ▸**Bureau de vérification de la publicité** ≃ Advertising Standards Authority (*Brit*), *independent body which regulates the advertising industry* ▸**bureau de vote** polling station.

bureaucrate [byʀokʀat] nmf bureaucrat.

bureaucratie [byʀokʀasi] nf (*péj*) (*gén*) bureaucracy; (*employés*) officials, officialdom (*NonC*). **toute cette ~ m'agace** all this red tape gets on my nerves.

bureaucratique [byʀokʀatik] adj bureaucratic.

bureaucratisation [byʀokʀatizasjɔ̃] nf bureaucratization.

bureaucratiser [byʀokʀatize] 1 vt to bureaucratize.

bureautique [byʀotik] nf office automation.

burette [byʀɛt] nf (*Chim*) burette; (*Culin, Rel*) cruet; *[mécanicien]* oilcan. (*‡: testicules*) **~s** balls*‡.

burgrave [byʀgʀav] nm burgrave.

burin [byʀɛ̃] nm (*Art*) (*outil*) burin, graver; (*gravure*) engraving, print; (*Tech*) (cold) chisel.

buriné, e [byʀine] (ptp de **buriner**) adj (*fig*) *visage* seamed, craggy.

buriner [byʀine] 1 vt (*Art*) to engrave; (*Tech*) to chisel, chip.

Burkina(-Faso) [byʀkina(faso)] nm Burkina-Faso.

burkinabé [byʀkinabe] 1 adj of *ou* from Burkina-Faso. 2 nmf: **B~** inhabitant *ou* native of Burkina-Faso.

burlat [byʀla] nf *type of cherry.*

burlesque [byʀlɛsk] adj (*Théât*) burlesque; (*comique*) comical, funny; (*ridicule*) ludicrous, ridiculous, absurd. **le ~** the burlesque.

burlingue‡ [byʀlɛ̃g] nm (*lieu de travail*) office.

burnous [byʀnu(s)] nm *[Arabe]* burnous(e); *[bébé]* baby's cape; *voir* **suer.**

burundais, e [buʀundɛ, ɛz] 1 adj of *ou* from Burundi. 2 nm,f: **B~(e)** inhabitant *ou* native of Burundi.

Burundi [buʀundi] nm Burundi.

bus [bys] nm (*Aut, Ordin*) bus.

busard [byzaʀ] nm (*Orn*) harrier. **~ Saint-Martin** hen harrier.

buse[1] [byz] nf (*Orn*) buzzard; (**: imbécile*) dolt*.

buse[2] [byz] nf (*tuyau*) (*gén*) pipe; (*Tech*) duct. **~ d'aération** ventilation duct; **~ de carburateur** carburettor choke tube; **~ de haut fourneau** blast nozzle; **~ d'injection** injector (nozzle).

business‡ [biznɛs] nm (*truc, machin*) thingummy* (*Brit*), thingumajig, whatnot*; (*affaire louche*) piece of funny business*. **qu'est-ce que c'est que ce ~?** what's all this business about?

busqué, e [byske] adj: **avoir le nez ~** to have a hooked *ou* a hook nose.

buste [byst] nm (*torse*) chest; (*seins*) bust; (*sculpture*) bust.

bustier [bystje] nm long-line (strapless) bra.

but [by(t)] nm a (*destination*) goal. **prenons comme ~ (de promenade) le château** let's go (for a walk) as far as the castle, let's aim to walk as far as the castle; **leur ~ de promenade favori** their favourite walk; **aller** *ou* **errer sans ~** to wander aimlessly about.

b (*objectif*) aim, goal, objective. **il n'a aucun ~ dans la vie** he has no aim in life; **il a pour ~** *ou* **il s'est donné pour ~ de faire** his aim is to do, he is aiming to do; **aller droit au ~** to come *ou* go straight to the point; **nous touchons au ~** the end *ou* our goal is in sight; **être encore loin du ~** to have a long way to go; **à ~ lucratif** profit-making, profit-seeking.

c (*intention*) aim, purpose, object; (*raison*) reason. **dans le ~ de faire** with the intention *ou* aim of doing, in order to do; **je lui écris dans le ~ de ...** my aim in writing to him is to ...; **je fais ceci dans le seul ~ de ...** my sole aim in doing this is to ...; **c'est dans ce ~ que nous partons** it's with this aim in view that we're leaving; **faire qch dans un ~ déterminé** to do sth for a definite reason *ou* aim, do sth with one aim *ou* object in view; **c'était le ~ de l'opération** that was the object *ou* point of the operation; **qui va à l'encontre du ~ recherché** self-defeating.

d [by(t)] (*Sport*) (*Ftbl etc*) goal; (*Tir*) target, mark; (*Pétanque: cochonnet*) jack. **gagner/perdre (par) 3 ~s à 2** to win/lose by 3 goals to 2.

e **de ~ en blanc** suddenly, point-blank, just like that*; **comment puis-je te répondre de ~ en blanc?** how can I possibly give you an answer on the spur of the moment? *ou* just like that?*; **il me demanda de ~ en blanc si ...** he asked me point-blank if ... .

butane [bytan] nm: **(gaz) ~** (*Camping, Ind*) butane; (*usage domestique*) calor gas ®.

butanier [bytanje] nm butane tanker.

buté, e[1] [byte] (ptp de **buter**) adj *personne, air* stubborn, obstinate, mulish.

butée[2] [byte] nf a (*Archit*) abutment. b (*Tech*) stop; *[piscine]* end wall; (*Ski*) toe-piece.

buter [byte] 1 1 vi a to stumble, trip. **~ contre qch** (*trébucher*) to stumble over sth, catch one's foot on sth; (*cogner*) to bump *ou* bang into *ou* against sth; (*s'appuyer*) to be supported by sth, rest against sth; (*fig*) **~ contre une difficulté** to come up against a difficulty, hit a snag*; **nous butons sur ce problème depuis le début** it is a problem which has balked *ou* stymied* us from the start.

b (*Ftbl*) to score a goal.

2 vt a *personne* to antagonize. **cela l'a buté** it made him dig his heels in.

b (*renforcer*) *mur, colonne* to prop up.

c (*‡: tuer*) to bump off‡, do in‡.

3 **se buter** vpr a (*s'entêter*) to dig one's heels in, get obstinate *ou* mulish.

b (*se heurter*) **se ~ à une personne** to bump into a person; **se ~ à une difficulté** to come up against a difficulty, hit a snag*.

buteur [bytœʀ] nm (*Ftbl*) striker.

butin [bytɛ̃] nm a *[armée]* spoils, booty, plunder; *[voleur]* loot; (*fig*) booty. **~ de guerre** spoils of war. b (** Can*) linen, calico; (*tissu*) material; (*vêtements*) clothes.

butiner [bytine] 1 1 vi *[abeilles]* to gather nectar. 2 vt *[abeilles]* *nectar* to gather; (*fig*) to gather, glean, pick up.

butoir [bytwaʀ] nm (*Rail*) buffer; (*Tech*) stop. **~ de porte** doorstop, door stopper; *voir* **date.**

butor [bytɔʀ] nm (*péj: malotru*) boor, lout, yob‡ (*Brit*); (*Orn*) bittern.

buttage [bytaʒ] nm earthing-up.

butte [byt] nf (*tertre*) mound, hillock. **~ de tir** butts; **~-témoin** outlier; (*fig*) **être en ~ à** to be exposed to.

butter [byte] 1 vt a (*Agr*) *plante* to earth up; *terre* to ridge. b (*‡: tuer*) to bump off‡, do in‡.

buvable [byvabl] adj drinkable, fit to drink. (*fig*) **c'est ~!*** it's not too bad!; (*Méd*) **ampoule ~** phial to be taken orally.

buvard [byvaʀ] nm (*papier*) blotting paper (*Brit*), fleece paper; (*sous-main*) blotter.

buvette [byvɛt] nf a (*café*) refreshment room; (*en plein air*) refreshment stall. b *[ville d'eaux]* pump room.

buveur, -euse [byvœʀ, øz] nm,f a (*ivrogne*) drinker. b (*consommateur*) drinker; *[café]* customer. **~ de bière** beer drinker.

BVP [bevepe] nm (abrév de **Bureau de vérification de la publicité**) ≃ ASA (*Brit*).

by-pass [bajpas] nm (*Élec, Tech*) by-pass; (*Méd*) by-pass operation.

byronien, -ienne [biʀɔnjɛ̃, jɛn] adj Byronic.

Byzance [bizɑ̃s] n Byzantium. (*fig*) **c'est ~!*** what luxury!

byzantin, e [bizɑ̃tɛ̃, in] adj (*Hist*) Byzantine; (*fig*) protracted and trivial, wrangling.

byzantinisme [bizɑ̃tinism] nm argumentativeness, logic-chopping, (love of) hair-splitting.

byzantiniste [bizɑ̃tinist] nmf Byzantinist, specialist in Byzantine art.

BZH (abrév de **Breizh**) Brittany.

C

C[1], **c**[1] [se] nm (*lettre*) C, c. (*Ordin*) (**langage**) **C** C.
C[2] (abrév de **Celsius, centigrade**) C.
c[2] abrév de **centime**.
c' [s] abrév de **ce**.
CA [sea] nm a (abrév de **chiffre d'affaires**) *voir* **chiffre**. b (abrév de **conseil d'administration**) *voir* **conseil**.
ça[1] [sa] nm (*Psych: inconscient*) id.
ça[2] [sa] pron dém (= **cela** *mais plus courant et plus familier*) a (*gén*) that, it; (**: pour désigner*) (*près*) this; (*plus loin*) that. **je veux ~, non pas ~, ~ là dans le coin** I want that, no, not this, that over there in the corner; **qu'est-ce que ~ veut dire?** what does that *ou* it *ou* this mean?; **on ne s'attendait pas à ~** that was (quite) unexpected, we weren't expecting that; **~ n'est pas très facile** that's not very easy; **~ m'agace de l'entendre se plaindre** it gets on my nerves hearing him complain; **~ vaut la peine qu'il essaie** it's worth his having a go; **~ donne bien du souci, les enfants** children are a lot of worry; **faire des études, ~ ne le tentait guère** studying didn't really appeal to him.
b (*péj: désignant qn*) he, she, they. **et ~ va à l'église!** and to think he (*ou* she *etc*) goes to church!
c (*renforçant qui, pourquoi, comment etc*) **il ne veut pas venir — pourquoi ~?** he won't come — why not? *ou* why's that? *ou* why won't he?; **j'ai vu X — qui ~?/quand ~?/où ~?** I've seen X — who (do you mean)? *ou* who's that?/when was that?/where was that?
d **~ fait 10 jours/longtemps qu'il est parti** it's 10 days/a long time since he left, he has been gone 10 days/a long time; **voilà, Madame, ~ (vous) fait 10 F** here you are, Madam, that will be 10 francs.
e (*loc*) **tu crois ~!** *ou* **cela!, on croit ~!** *ou* **cela!** that's what YOU think!; **~ ne fait rien** it doesn't matter; **on dit ~!** *ou* **cela!** that's what they (*ou* you *etc*) SAY!; **voyez-vous ~!** how do you like that!, did you ever hear of such a thing!; **~ va?** *ou* **marche?** *etc* how are things?*, how goes it?*; **oui ~ va, continuez comme ~** yes that's fine *ou* O.K.*, carry on like that; **(ah) ~ non!** most certainly not!; **(ah) ~ oui!** absolutely!, (yes) definitely!; (*iro*) **c'est ~, continue!** that's right, just you carry on!* (*iro*); **~ par exemple!** (*indignation*) well!, well really!; (*surprise*) well I never!; **~ alors!** (my) goodness!*; **me faire ~ à moi!** fancy doing that to me (of all people)!; **on dirait un Picasso/du champagne — il y a de ~*** it looks like a Picasso/tastes like champagne — yes (I suppose) it does a bit; **tu pars à cause du salaire? — il y a de ~*** are you leaving because of the salary? — it is partly that; **j'ai 5 jours de vacances, c'est déjà** *ou* **toujours ~ (de pris)** I've got 5 days holiday, that is something; *voir* **pas**[2].
çà [sa] adv a **~ et là** here and there. b (††: *ici*) hither (†† *ou hum*).
cabale [kabal] nf a (*complot, comploteurs*) cabal, conspiracy. **monter** *ou* **organiser une ~ contre qn** to mount a conspiracy against sb. b (*Hist*) cab(b)ala, kab(b)ala.
cabaliste [kabalist] nmf cab(b)alist.
cabalistique [kabalistik] adj (*mystérieux*) *signe* cabalistic, arcane; (*Hist*) cabalistic.
caban [kabɑ̃] nm (*veste longue*) car coat, three-quarter (length) coat; *[marin]* reefer jacket.
cabane [kaban] 1 nf a (*en bois*) hut, cabin; (*en terre*) hut; (*pour rangements, animaux*) shed. b (*péj: bicoque*) shack. c (**: prison*) **en ~** in (the) clink‡, in the nick‡ (*Brit*), in jug‡; **3 ans de ~** 3 years in (the) clink‡ *ou* in the nick‡ (*Brit*) *ou* inside‡. 2 comp ► **cabane à lapins** (*lit*) rabbit hutch; (*fig*) box ► **cabane à outils** toolshed ► **cabane de rondins** log cabin ► **cabane à sucre*** (*Can*) sap house (*Can*).
cabanon [kabanɔ̃] nm a (*en Provence: maisonnette*) *[campagne]* (country) cottage; *[littoral]* cabin, chalet. b (*remise*) shed, hut. c (*cellule*) *[aliénés]* padded cell. **il est bon pour le ~*†** he should be locked up, he's practically certifiable*.
cabaret [kabaʀɛ] nm (*boîte de nuit*) night club, cabaret; (†: *café*) tavern, inn; *voir* **danseuse**.
cabaretier, -ière† [kabaʀ(ə)tje, jɛʀ] nm,f innkeeper.
cabas [kabɑ] nm (*sac*) shopping bag.
cabestan [kabɛstɑ̃] nm capstan; *voir* **virer**.
cabillaud [kabijo] nm (fresh) cod (*pl inv*).
cabine [kabin] 1 nf *[navire, véhicule spatial]* cabin; *[avion]* cockpit; *[train, grue]* cab; *[piscine]* cubicle; *[laboratoire de langues]* booth; (*Can*) motel room, cabin (*US, Can*). (*Scol, Univ*) **entraînement en ~s** language lab training *ou* practice.
2 comp ► **cabine d'aiguillage** signal box ► **cabine (d'ascenseur)** lift (cage) (*Brit*), (elevator) car (*US*) ► **cabine de bain** (bathing *ou* beach) hut ► **cabine de douche** shower cubicle ► **cabine d'essayage** fitting room ► **cabine de pilotage** (*gén*) cockpit; (*dans avion de ligne*) flight deck ► **cabine de projection** projection room ► **cabine spatiale** cabin (*of a spaceship*) ► **cabine de téléphérique** cablecar ► **cabine téléphonique** call *ou* (tele)phone box, telephone booth *ou* kiosk, pay-phone.
cabinet [kabinɛ] 1 nm a (*toilettes*) **~s** toilet, loo* (*Brit*), john* (*US*). **il est aux ~s** he's in the toilet *ou* loo* (*Brit*) *ou* john* (*US*).
b (*local professionnel*) *[dentiste]* surgery (*Brit*), office (*US*); *[médecin]* surgery (*Brit*), office (*US*), consulting-room; *[notaire]* office; *[avocat]* chambers (*pl*); *[agent immobilier]* agency.
c (*clientèle*) *[avocat, médecin]* practice.
d (*Pol*) (*gouvernement*) cabinet; *[ministre]* advisers (*pl*); *voir* **chef**[1].
e *[exposition]* exhibition room.
f (*meuble*) cabinet.
g (†) (*bureau*) study; (*réduit*) closet †.
2 comp ► **cabinet d'affaires** business consultancy ► **cabinet d'aisances†** water closet† (*Brit*), lavatory ► **cabinet-conseil** consulting firm ► **cabinet de consultation** surgery (*Brit*), doctor's office (*US*), consulting-room ► **cabinet d'étude†** study ► **cabinet de lecture†** reading room ► **cabinet médical** = **cabinet de consultation** ► **cabinet particulier** private dining room ► **cabinet de recrutement** recruitment consultancy ► **cabinet de toilette** ≃ bathroom ► **cabinet de travail** study.
câblage [kɑblaʒ] nm a (*voir* **câbler**) cabling; twisting together. b (*Élec: ensemble de fils*) wiring. c (*TV*) **le ~ du pays a commencé** cable television is being introduced into the country.
câble [kɑbl] 1 nm a (*filin*) cable. **~ métallique** wire cable. b (*TV*) cable. **le ~** cable television, cablevision (*US*); **être abonné au ~** to subscribe to cable television *ou* cablevision (*US*); *voir* **télévision**. 2 comp ► **câble d'amarrage** mooring line ► **câble coaxial** coaxial cable ► **câble de démarrage** (*Aut*) jump lead (*Brit*), jumper cable (*US*) ► **câble électrique** (electric) cable ► **câble de frein** brake cable ► **câble de halage** towrope ► **câble hertzien** (*Élec*) radio link (*by hertzian waves*) ► **câble de remorque** towrope ► **câble de transmission** transmission cable.
câbler [kɑble] 1 vt a *dépêche, message* to cable. b (*Tech*) *torons* to twist together (into a cable). (*TV*) **~ un pays/un quartier** to put cable television into a country/an area; **quand l'Europe sera câblée** when Europe has cable television.
câblerie [kɑbləʀi] nf cable-manufacturing plant.
câblier [kɑblije] nm (*navire*) cable ship.
câblodistribution [kɑblodistʀibysjɔ̃] nf (*Québec*) cable television; cable vision (*US*), community antenna television (*US*).
cabochard, e* [kabɔʃaʀ, aʀd] adj (*têtu*) pigheaded*, mulish. **c'est un ~** he's pigheaded*.
caboche [kabɔʃ] nf a (**: tête*) noddle*, nut*, head. **mets-toi ça dans la ~** get that into your head *ou* noddle* *ou* thick skull*; **quand il a quelque chose dans la ~** when he has something in his head; **il a la ~ solide** he must have a thick skull; **quelle ~ il a!** he's so pigheaded!* b (*clou*) hobnail.
cabochon [kabɔʃɔ̃] nm a (*bouchon*) *[carafe]* stopper; (*brillant*) cabochon. b (*clou*) stud.
cabosser [kabɔse] 1 vt (*bosseler*) to dent. **une casserole toute cabossée** a battered *ou* badly dented saucepan.

cabot [kabo] 1 nm a (*péj: chien*) dog, cur (*péj*), mutt. b (*arg Mil: caporal*) ≃ corp (*arg Mil Brit*). 2 adj, nm = **cabotin**.

cabotage [kabɔtaʒ] nm (*Naut*) coastal navigation. **petit/grand ~** inshore/seagoing navigation.

caboter [kabɔte] [1] vi (*Naut*) to coast, ply (along the coast). **~ le long des côtes d'Afrique** to ply along the African coast.

caboteur [kabɔtœʀ] nm (*bateau*) tramp, coaster.

cabotin, e [kabɔtɛ̃, in] 1 adj (*péj*) theatrical. **il est très ~** he likes to show off *ou* hold the centre of the stage. 2 nm,f (*péj*) (*personne maniérée*) show-off, poseur; (*acteur*) ham (actor).

cabotinage [kabɔtinaʒ] nm *[personne, enfant]* showing off, playacting; *[acteur]* ham *ou* third-rate acting.

cabotiner [kabɔtine] [1] vi *[élève, m'as-tu-vu]* to playact.

caboulot [kabulo] nm (*péj: bistro*) sleazy* *ou* seedy* dive* (*péj*) *ou* pub.

cabrer [kɑbʀe] [1] 1 vt *cheval* to rear up; *avion* to nose up. **faire ~ son cheval** to make one's horse rear up; (*fig*) **~ qn** to put sb's back up; (*fig*) **~ qn contre qn** to turn *ou* set sb against sb. 2 **se cabrer** vpr *[cheval]* to rear up; *[avion]* to nose up; (*fig*) *[personne, orgueil]* to revolt, rebel. **se ~ contre qn** to turn *ou* rebel against sb; **se ~ à** *ou* **devant** to jib at.

cabri [kabʀi] nm (*Zool*) kid.

cabriole [kabʀijɔl] nf (*bond*) *[enfant, chevreau]* caper; (*culbute*) *[clown, gymnaste]* somersault; (*Danse*) cabriole; (*Équitation*) capriole, spring; (*fig*) *[politicien]* skilful manoeuvre, clever caper. **faire des ~s** *[chevreau, enfant]* to caper *ou* cavort (about); *[cheval]* to cavort.

cabrioler [kabʀijɔle] [1] vi (*gambader*) to caper *ou* cavort about.

cabriolet [kabʀijɔlɛ] nm (*Hist*) cabriolet; (*voiture décapotable*) convertible.

cabus [kaby] nm *voir* **chou**[1].

CAC [kak] nf (abrév de **compagnie des agents de change**) *institute of stockbrokers*. **l'indice ~ 40** the CAC index.

caca* [kaka] nm (*langage enfantin*) pooh* (*langage enfantin Brit*). **faire ~** to do a pooh* (*langage enfantin Brit*) *ou* a number two* (*langage enfantin US*) *ou* a big job* (*langage enfantin*); **il a marché dans du ~ de chien** he stepped in some dog's dirt; (*fig*) **son travail, c'est (du) ~** his work is (a load of) rubbish*; (*couleur*) **~ d'oie** greenish-yellow.

cacah(o)uète, cacahouette [kakawɛt] nf peanut, monkey nut (*Brit*); *voir* **beurre**.

cacao [kakao] nm (*Culin*) (*poudre*) cocoa (powder); (*boisson*) cocoa; (*Bot*) cocoa bean.

cacaoté, e [kakaɔte] adj *farine* cocoa- *ou* chocolate-flavoured.

cacaotier [kakaɔtje] nm, **cacaoyer** [kakaɔje] nm cacao (tree).

cacaoui [kakawi] nm (*Can*) old squaw (duck), cockawee (*Can*).

cacatoès [kakatɔɛs] nm (*oiseau*) cockatoo.

cacatois [kakatwa] nm (*Naut*) (*voile*) royal; (*aussi* **mât de ~**) royal mast. **grand/petit ~** main/fore royal.

cachalot [kaʃalo] nm sperm whale.

cache[1] [kaʃ] nm (*Ciné, Phot*) mask; (*gén*) card (*for covering one eye, masking out a section of text*).

cache[2] [kaʃ] nf (*†: cachette*) hiding place; (*pour butin*) cache.

cache- [kaʃ] préf *voir* **cacher**.

caché, e [kaʃe] (ptp de **cacher**) adj *trésor* hidden; *asile* secluded, hidden; *sentiments* inner(most), secret; *sens* hidden, secret; *charmes, vertus* hidden. **je n'ai rien de ~ pour eux** I have no secrets from them; **mener une vie ~e** (*secrète*) to have a secret *ou* hidden life; (*retirée*) to lead a secluded life.

Cachemire [kaʃmiʀ] nm Kashmir.

cachemire [kaʃmiʀ] nm (*laine*) cashmere. **motif** *ou* **impression** *ou* **dessin ~** paisley pattern; **écharpe en ~** cashmere scarf; **écharpe ~** paisley(-pattern) scarf.

Cachemirien, -ienne [kaʃmiʀjɛ̃, ɛn] nm,f Kashmiri.

cacher [kaʃe] [1] 1 vt a (*dissimuler volontairement*) *objet* to hide, conceal; *malfaiteur* to hide. **le chien est allé ~ son os** the dog has gone (away) to bury its bone; **~ ses cartes** *ou* **son jeu** (*lit*) to keep one's cards up, play a close game; (*fig*) to keep one's cards close to one's chest, hide one's game, hold out on sb.

b (*masquer*) *accident de terrain, trait de caractère* to hide, conceal. **les arbres nous cachent le fleuve** the trees hide *ou* conceal the river from our view *ou* from us; **tu me caches la lumière** you're in my light; **son silence cache quelque chose** he's hiding something by his silence; **les mauvaises herbes cachent les fleurs** you can't see the flowers for the weeds; **ces terrains cachent des trésors minéraux** mineral treasures lie hidden in this ground; *voir* **arbre**.

c (*garder secret*) *fait, sentiment* to hide, conceal (*à qn* from sb). **~ son âge** to keep one's age a secret; **on ne peut plus lui ~ la nouvelle** you can't keep *ou* hide *ou* conceal the news from her any longer; **il ne m'a pas caché qu'il désire partir** he hasn't hidden *ou* concealed it from me that he wants to leave, he hasn't kept it (a secret) from me that he wants to leave; **il n'a pas caché que** he made no secret (of the fact) that.

2 **se cacher** vpr a (*volontairement*) *[personne, soleil]* to hide. **va te ~!** get out of my sight!, be gone!*; **se ~ de qn** to hide from sb; **il se cache pour fumer** he goes and hides to have a smoke; **il se cache d'elle pour boire** he drinks behind her back; (*littér*) **se ~ de ses sentiments** to hide *ou* conceal one's feelings; **je ne m'en cache pas** I am quite open about it, I make no secret of it, I do not hide *ou* conceal it.

b (*être caché*) *[personne]* to be hiding; *[malfaiteur, évadé]* to be in hiding; *[chose]* to be hiding *ou* hidden. **il se cache de peur d'être puni** he is keeping out of sight *ou* he's hiding for fear of being punished.

c (*être masqué*) *[accident de terrain, trait de caractère]* to be concealed. **la maison se cache derrière le rideau d'arbres** the house is concealed *ou* hidden behind the line of trees.

d **sans se ~: faire qch sans se ~** *ou* **s'en ~** to do sth openly, do sth without hiding *ou* concealing the fact, do sth and make no secret of it; **il l'a fait sans se ~ de nous** he did it without hiding *ou* concealing it from us.

3 comp ►**cache-cache** nm inv (*lit, fig*) hide-and-seek ►**cache-cœur** nm inv crossover top (*ou* sweater *etc*) ►**cache-col** nm inv scarf, muffler ►**cache-misère*** nm inv *wrap or coat worn to hide old or dirty clothes* ►**cache-nez** nm inv = **cache-col** ►**cache-plaque** nm inv hob cover ►**cache-pot** nm inv flowerpot holder ►**cache-prise** nm inv socket cover ►**cache-radiateur** nm inv radiator cover ►**cache-sexe** nm inv G-string ►**cache-tampon** nm inv hunt-the-thimble, hide-the-thimble ►**cache-théière** nm inv tea cosy (*Brit*) *ou* cozy (*US*).

cachère [kaʃɛʀ] adj inv = **kasher**.

cachet [kaʃɛ] nm a (*Pharm*) (*gén: comprimé*) tablet; (*††: enveloppe*) cachet. **un ~ d'aspirine** an aspirin (tablet); *voir* **blanc**.

b (*timbre*) stamp; (*sceau*) seal. **~ (de la poste)** postmark; **sa lettre porte le ~ de Paris** his letter is postmarked from Paris *ou* has a Paris postmark; *voir* **lettre**.

c (*fig: style, caractère*) style, character. **cette petite église avait du ~** there was something very characterful about that little church, that little church had (great) character *ou* style; **une robe qui a du ~** a stylish *ou* chic dress, a dress with some style about it; **ça porte le ~ de l'originalité/du génie** it bears the stamp of originality/genius, it has the mark of originality/genius on it.

d (*rétribution*) fee; *voir* **courir**.

cachetage [kaʃtaʒ] nm sealing.

cacheter [kaʃte] [4] vt to seal; *voir* **cire**.

cachette [kaʃɛt] nf *[objet]* hiding-place; *[personne]* hideout, hiding-place. **en ~** *agir, fumer* on the sly *ou* quiet; *rire* to oneself, up one's sleeve; *économiser* secretly; **en ~ de qn** (*action répréhensible*) behind sb's back; (*action non répréhensible*) unknown to sb.

cachexie [kaʃɛksi] nf cachexia, cachexy.

cachot [kaʃo] nm (*cellule*) dungeon; (*punition*) solitary confinement.

cachotterie [kaʃɔtʀi] nf (*secret*) mystery. **c'est une nouvelle ~ de sa part** it's another of his (little) mysteries; **faire des ~s** to be secretive, act secretively, make mysteries about things; **faire des ~s à qn** to make a mystery of sth to sb, be secretive about sth to sb.

cachottier, -ière [kaʃɔtje, jɛʀ] adj secretive. **cet enfant est (un) ~** he's a secretive child.

cachou [kaʃu] nm (*bonbon*) cachou.

cacique [kasik] nm (*Ethnologie*) cacique. (*arg Scol*) **c'était le ~** he came first, he got first place.

cacochyme [kakɔʃim] adj († *ou hum*) **un vieillard ~** a doddery old man.

cacophonie [kakɔfɔni] nf cacophony.

cacophonique [kakɔfɔnik] adj cacophonous.

cactée [kakte] nf, **cactacée** [kaktase] nf cactacea.

cactus [kaktys] nm inv cactus.

c.-à.-d. (abrév de **c'est-à-dire**) i.e.

cadastral, e, mpl **-aux** [kadastʀal, o] adj cadastral.

cadastre [kadastʀ] nm (*registre*) cadastre; (*service*) cadastral survey.

cadastrer [kadastʀe] [1] vt to survey and register (*in the cadastre*).

cadavéreux, -euse [kadɑveʀø, øz] adj *teint* deathly (pale), deadly pale; *pâleur* deathly. **les blessés au teint ~** the deathly-looking *ou* deathly pale injured.

cadavérique [kadɑveʀik] adj *teint* deathly (pale), deadly pale; *pâleur* deathly; *voir* **rigidité**.

cadavre [kadɑvʀ] nm a (*humain*) corpse, (dead) body; (*animal*) carcass, body. (*fig*) **c'est un ~ ambulant** he's a living corpse. b (**: bouteille vide, de vin etc*) empty (bottle), dead man* (*Brit*), soldier*.

caddie [kadi] nm a (*Golf*) caddie. **être le ~ de qn** to be sb's caddie, caddie for sb. b (*chariot*) **C~** ® (supermarket *ou* shopping) trolley (*Brit*), caddy (*US*).

cadeau, pl **~x** [kado] nm a present, gift (*de qn* from sb). **faire un ~ à qn** to give sb a present *ou* gift; **~ de mariage/de Noël** wedding/Christmas present; **~ publicitaire** free gift, giveaway* (*US*).

b (*loc*) **faire ~ de qch à qn** (*offrir*) to make sb a present of sth, give sb sth as a present; (*laisser*) to let sb keep sth, give sb sth; **il a décidé d'en faire ~ (à qn)** he decided to give it away (to sb); **ils ne font pas de ~x** *[examinateurs etc]* they don't let you off lightly; **en ~** as a present; **garde la monnaie, je t'en fais ~** keep the change, I'm giving it to you; (*hum, iro*) **les petits ~x entretiennent l'amitié** there's nothing like a little present between friends (*iro*); (*hum*) **c'est pas un ~!*** *[personne]* he's (*ou* she's *etc*) a real pain!*; *[objet]* it's a real pain!*, it's more trouble than it's worth!; *[tâche]* it's a real pain!*; **c'était un ~**

empoisonné it was more of a curse than a blessing.

cadenas [kadnɑ] nm padlock. **fermer au ~** to padlock.

cadenasser [kadnɑse] ① 1 vt to padlock. 2 **se cadenasser** vpr to lock o.s. in.

cadence [kadɑ̃s] nf a (*rythme*) *[vers, chant, danse]* rhythm. **marquer la ~** to accentuate the rhythm. b (*vitesse, taux*) rate, pace. **~ de tir/de production** rate of fire/of production; **à la ~ de 10 par jour** at the rate of 10 a day; **à une bonne ~** at a good pace *ou* rate; (*fig*) **forcer la ~** to force the pace. c (*Mus*) *[succession d'accords]* cadence; *[concerto]* cadenza. d (*loc*) **en ~** (*régulièrement*) rhythmically; (*ensemble, en mesure*) in time.

cadencé, e [kadɑ̃se] (ptp de **cadencer**) adj (*rythmé*) rhythmic(al); *voir* **pas**[1].

cadencer [kadɑ̃se] ③ vt *débit, phrases, allure, marche* to put rhythm into, give rhythm to.

cadet, -ette [kadɛ, ɛt] 1 adj (*de deux*) younger; (*de plusieurs*) youngest.

2 nm a *[famille]* **le ~** the youngest child *ou* one; **le ~ des garçons** the youngest boy *ou* son; **mon (frère) ~** my younger brother; **le ~ de mes frères** my youngest brother; **le père avait un faible pour son ~** the father had a soft spot for his youngest boy.

b (*relation d'âges*) **il est mon ~** he's younger than me; **il est mon ~ de 2 ans** he's 2 years younger than me, he's 2 years my junior, he's my junior by 2 years; **c'est le ~ de mes soucis** it's the least of my worries.

c (*Sport*) *15-17 year-old player;* (*Hist*) cadet (*gentleman who entered the army to acquire military skill and eventually a commission*).

3 **cadette** nf a **la ~te** the youngest child *ou* girl *ou* one; **la ~te des filles** the youngest girl *ou* daughter; **ma (sœur) ~te** my younger sister.

b **elle est ma ~te** she's younger than me.

c (*Sport*) *15-17 year-old player*.

cadmium [kadmjɔm] nm cadmium.

cadogan [kadɔgɑ̃] nm = **catogan**.

cadrage [kɑdʀaʒ] nm (*Phot*) *[image]* centring (*Brit*), centering (*US*).

cadran [kadʀɑ̃] 1 nm *[téléphone, boussole, compteur]* dial; *[montre, horloge]* dial, face; *[baromètre]* face; *voir* **tour**[2]. 2 comp ▸**cadran solaire** sundial.

cadre [kɑdʀ] nm a *[tableau, porte, bicyclette]* frame. **mettre un ~ à un tableau** to put a picture in a frame, frame a picture; **il roulait à bicyclette avec son copain sur le ~** he was riding along with his pal on the crossbar.

b (*caisse*) **~ (d'emballage** *ou* **de déménagement)** crate, packing case; **~-conteneur** *ou* **-container** container.

c (*sur formulaire*) space, box. **ne rien écrire dans ce ~** do not write in this space, leave this space blank.

d (*décor*) setting; (*entourage*) surroundings. **vivre dans un ~ luxueux** to live in luxurious surroundings; **son enfance s'écoula dans un ~ austère** he spent his childhood in austere surroundings; **une maison située dans un ~ de verdure** a house in a leafy setting; **sortir du ~ étroit de la vie quotidienne** to get out of the straitjacket *ou* the narrow confines of everyday life; **quel ~ magnifique!** what a magnificent setting!; **~ de vie** (living) environment.

e (*limites*) scope. **rester/être dans le ~ de** to remain/be *ou* fall within the scope of; **cette décision sort du ~ de notre accord** this decision is outside *ou* beyond the scope of our agreement; **il est sorti du ~ de ses fonctions** he went beyond the scope of *ou* overstepped the limits of his responsibilities; **respecter le ~ de la légalité** to remain within (the bounds of) the law; *voir* **loi**.

f (*contexte*) **dans le ~ des réformes/des recherches** within the context of *ou* the framework of the reforms/research; **une manifestation qui aura lieu dans le ~ du festival** an event which will take place within the context *ou* framework of the festival *ou* as part of the festival.

g (*structure*) scope. **le ~** *ou* **les ~s de la mémoire/de l'inconscient** the structures of the memory/the unconscious.

h (*chef, responsable*) executive, manager; (*Mil*) officer. **les ~s** the managerial staff; **elle est passée ~** she has been upgraded to a managerial position *ou* to the rank of manager, she's been made an executive; **~ subalterne** junior manager *ou* executive; **~ supérieur** executive, senior manager; **~ moyen** middle executive, middle manager; **les ~s moyens** middle management, middle-grade managers (*US*); (*hum*) **jeune ~ dynamique** upwardly mobile young executive.

i (*Admin: liste du personnel*) **entrer dans/figurer sur les ~s (d'une compagnie)** to be (placed) on/be on the books (of a company); **être rayé des ~s** (*licencié*) to be dismissed; (*libéré*) to be discharged; *voir* **hors**.

j *[radio]* frame antenna.

k (*Phot*) **~ de développement** processing rack; **viseur à ~ lumineuse** collimator viewfinder.

cadrer [kɑdʀe] ① 1 vi (*coïncider*) to tally (*avec* with), conform (*avec* to, with). 2 vt a (*Ciné, Phot*) to centre. b (*définir*) *projet* to define the parameters of.

cadreur [kɑdʀœʀ] nm (*Ciné*) cameraman.

caduc, caduque [kadyk] adj a (*Bot*) deciduous. b (*Jur*) null and void. **devenir ~** to lapse; **rendre ~** to render null and void, invalidate. c (*périmé*) *théorie* outmoded, obsolete. d (*Ling*) **e ~** mute e. e **âge ~** declining years.

caducée [kadyse] nm caduceus.

cæcum [sekɔm] nm caecum.

cæsium [sezjɔm] nm caesium.

CAF[1] [kaf] (abrév de **coût, assurance, frêt**) CIF.

CAF[2] (abrév de **caisse d'allocations familiales**) *voir* **caisse**.

cafard[1] [kafaʀ] nm a (*insecte*) cockroach. b (*: *mélancolie*) **un accès** *ou* **coup de ~** a fit of depression *ou* of the blues*; **avoir le ~** to be down in the dumps*, be feeling gloomy *ou* low*; **ça lui donne le ~** that depresses him, that gets him down*.

cafard[2], **e** [kafaʀ, aʀd] nm,f (*péj*) (*rapporteur*) sneak, telltale, tattletale (*US*); (*rare: tartufe*) hypocrite.

cafardage* [kafaʀdaʒ] nm (*rapportage*) sneaking, taletelling.

cafarder* [kafaʀde] ① 1 vt (*dénoncer*) to tell tales on, sneak on* (*Brit*). 2 vi a (*rapporter*) to tell tales, sneak* (*Brit*). b (*être déprimé*) to be down in the dumps*, be feeling gloomy *ou* low*.

cafardeur, -euse[1] [kafaʀdœʀ, øz] nm,f (*péj*) sneak, telltale, tattletale (*US*).

cafardeux, -euse[2] [kafaʀdø, øz] adj (*déprimé*) *personne* down in the dumps* (*attrib*), gloomy, feeling gloomy *ou* low* (*attrib*); *tempérament* gloomy, melancholy; (*déprimant*) depressing.

café [kafe] 1 nm a (*plante, boisson, produit*) coffee.

b (*moment du repas*) coffee. **au ~, on parlait politique** we talked politics over coffee; **il est arrivé au ~** he came in when we were having coffee.

c (*lieu*) café, ≃ pub (*Brit*). **ce n'est qu'une discussion de** *ou* **ce ne sont que des propos de café du Commerce** (*gén*) it's just barroom philosophizing; (*politique*) it's just barroom politics.

2 comp ▸**café bar** café (*serving spirits, coffee, snacks*) ▸**café complet** ≃ continental breakfast ▸**café-concert** (*Hist*) nm (pl **cafés-concerts**), **caf'conc'** *café where singers entertain customers* ▸**café crème** white coffee (*Brit*), coffee with cream ▸**café décaféiné** decaffeinated coffee ▸**café express** espresso coffee ▸**café filtre** filter(ed) coffee ▸**café en grains** coffee beans ▸**café instantané** instant coffee ▸**café au lait** nm white coffee (*Brit*), coffee with milk ◊ adj inv coffee-coloured ▸**café liégeois** coffee ice cream (*with whipped cream*) ▸**café lyophilisé** (freeze-dried) instant coffee ▸**café noir** *ou* **nature** black coffee ▸**café en poudre** = **café instantané** ▸**café-restaurant** nm (pl **cafés-restaurants**) restaurant, *café serving meals* ▸**café soluble** = **café instantané** ▸**café tabac** *tobacconist's* (*Brit*) *or tobacco shop* (*US*) *also serving coffee and spirits* ▸**café-théâtre** theatre workshop ▸**café turc** Turkish coffee ▸**café vert** unroasted coffee.

caféier [kafeje] nm coffee tree.

caféière [kafejɛʀ] nf coffee plantation.

caféine [kafein] nf caffeine.

cafet* [kafɛt] nf abrév de **cafétéria**.

cafetan [kaftɑ̃] nm caftan.

cafeter* [kafte] vti = **cafter**.

cafétéria [kafeteʀja] nf cafeteria.

cafeteur, -euse* [kaftœʀ, øz] nm,f = **cafteur, euse**.

cafetier, -ière [kaftje, jɛʀ] 1 nm,f café-owner. 2 **cafetière** nf a (*pot*) coffeepot; (*percolateur*) coffee-maker. b (‡: *tête*) nut*, noddle* (*Brit*), noodle* (*US*).

cafouillage* [kafujaʒ] nm muddle, shambles (*sg*).

cafouiller* [kafuje] ① vi *[organisation, administration, gouvernement]* to be in *ou* get into a (state of) shambles *ou* a mess; *[discussion]* to turn into a shambles, fall apart; *[équipe]* to get into a shambles, go to pieces; *[candidat]* to flounder; *[moteur, appareil]* to work in fits and starts. **dans cette affaire le gouvernement cafouille** the government's in a real shambles over this business; (*Sport*) **~ (avec) le ballon** to fumble the ball.

cafouilleur, -euse* [kafujœʀ, øz], **cafouilleux, -euse*** [kafujø, øz] 1 adj *organisation, discussion* shambolic* (*Brit*), chaotic. **il est ~** he always gets (things) into a muddle, he's a bungler *ou* muddler. 2 nm,f muddler, bungler.

cafouillis [kafuji] nm = **cafouillage**.

cafre [kafʀ] 1 adj kaf(f)ir. 2 nmf: **C~** Kaf(f)ir.

cafter* [kafte] ① 1 vt (*dénoncer*) to tell tales on, sneak on* (*Brit*). 2 vi to tell tales, sneak* (*Brit*).

cafteur, -euse* [kaftœʀ, øz] nm,f sneak, telltale, tattletale (*US*).

cage [kaʒ] 1 nf a *[animaux]* cage. **mettre en ~** (*lit*) to put in a cage; (*fig*) *voleur* to lock up; **dans ce bureau, je me sens comme un animal en ~** in this office I feel caged up *ou* in. b (*Tech*) *[roulement à billes, pendule]* casing; *[maison]* shell; (*Sport*: *buts*) goal. 2 comp ▸**cage d'escalier** (stair)well ▸**cage d'ascenseur** lift (*Brit*) *ou* elevator (*US*) shaft ▸**cage d'extraction** (*Min*) cage ▸**cage de Faraday** (*Élec*) Faraday cage ▸**cage à lapins** (*lit*) (rabbit) hutch; (*fig péj: maison*) poky little hole*, box ▸**cage à poules** (*lit*) hen-coop; (*fig: pour enfants*) jungle-gym, climbing frame; (*fig péj: maison*) shack, poky little hole*, box ▸**cage thoracique** rib cage.

cageot [kaʒo] nm a *[légumes, fruits]* crate. b (‡: *femme laide*) dog‡.

cagette [kaʒɛt] nf *[légumes, fruits]* crate.

cagibi* [kaʒibi] nm (*débarras*) boxroom (*Brit*), storage room (*US*), glory hole* (*Brit*); (*remise*) shed.

cagne [kaɲ] nf (*arg Scol*) *Arts class preparing entrance exam for the École normale supérieure*.

cagneux, -euse[1] [kaɲø, øz] adj *cheval, personne* knock-kneed; *jambes* crooked. **genoux ~** knock knees.

cagneux, -euse[2] [kaɲø, øz] nm,f (*arg Scol*) *pupil in the "cagne"*; voir **cagne**.

cagnotte [kaɲɔt] nf (*caisse commune*) kitty; *[jeu]* pool, kitty; (*: *économies*) nest egg.

cagot, e [kago, ɔt] (†† *ou péj*) 1 adj *allure, air* sanctimonious. 2 nm,f sanctimonious *ou* canting hypocrite.

cagoule [kagul] nf *[moine]* cowl; *[pénitent]* hood, cowl; *[bandit]* hood, mask; (*passe-montagne*) balaclava.

cahier [kaje] 1 nm (*Scol*) notebook, exercise book; (*Typ*) gathering; (*revue littéraire*) journal. 2 comp ▸**cahier de brouillon** roughbook (*Brit*), notebook (for rough drafts) (*US*) ▸**cahier des charges** *[production]* specifications, requirements (*US*); *[contrat]* terms of reference, terms and conditions ▸**cahier de cours** notebook, exercise book ▸**cahier de devoirs** (home) exercise book, homework book ▸**cahier de doléances** (*Hist*) register of grievances ▸**cahier d'exercices** exercise book ▸**cahier de textes** homework notebook *ou* diary ▸**cahier de travaux pratiques** lab book.

cahin-caha* [kaɛ̃kaa] adv: **aller ~** *[troupe, marcheur]* to jog along; *[vie, affaires]* to struggle along; *[santé]* **alors ça va? — ~** how are you? — (I'm) so-so *ou* middling*, I'm struggling along.

cahot [kao] nm (*secousse*) jolt, bump. (*fig*) **~s** ups and downs.

cahotant, e [kaɔtɑ̃, ɑ̃t] adj *route* bumpy, rough; *véhicule* bumpy, jolting.

cahotement [kaɔtmɑ̃] nm bumping, jolting.

cahoter [kaɔte] [1] 1 vt *voyageurs* to jolt, bump about; *véhicule* to jolt; (*fig*) *[vicissitudes]* to buffet about. **une famille cahotée par la guerre** a family buffeted *ou* tossed about by the war. 2 vi *[véhicule]* to jog *ou* trundle along. **le petit train cahotait le long du canal** the little train jogged *ou* trundled along by the canal.

cahoteux, -euse [kaɔtø, øz] adj *route* bumpy, rough.

cahute [kayt] nf (*cabane*) shack, hut; (*péj*) shack.

caïd [kaid] nm a (*meneur*) *[pègre]* boss, big chief*, top man; (*) *[classe, bureau]* big shot*. (*as, crack*) **le ~ de l'équipe*** the star of the team, the team's top man; **en maths/en mécanique, c'est un ~*** he's an ace* at maths/at mechanics. b (*en Afrique du Nord: fonctionnaire*) kaid.

caillasse [kajas] nf (*pierraille*) loose stones. **pente couverte de ~** scree-covered slope, slope covered with loose stones; (*péj*) **ce n'est pas du sable ni de la terre, ce n'est que de la ~** it's neither sand nor soil, it's just like gravel *ou* it's just loose stones.

caille [kaj] nf (*oiseau*) quail. **chaud comme une ~** snug as a bug in a rug; **rond comme une ~** plump as a partridge; (*affectueusement*) **oui ma ~*** yes poppet* (*Brit*) *ou* honey* (*US*).

caillé [kaje] nm curds.

caillebotis [kajbɔti] nm (*treillis*) grating; (*plancher*) duckboard.

caillement [kajmɑ̃] nm (voir **cailler**) curdling; coagulating, clotting.

cailler [kaje] [1] 1 vt (*plus courant* **faire** *ou* **laisser ~**) *lait* to curdle. 2 vi, **se cailler** vpr a *[lait]* to curdle; *[sang]* to coagulate, clot; voir **lait**. b (‡) (*avoir froid*) to be cold. (*faire froid*) **ça caille** it's freezing; **qu'est-ce qu'on (se) caille*** it's freezing cold *ou* perishing* (cold) (*Brit*).

caillette [kajɛt] nf (*Zool*) rennet stomach, abomasum (SPÉC).

caillot [kajo] nm (blood) clot.

caillou, pl **~x** [kaju] nm (*gén*) stone; (*petit galet*) pebble; (*grosse pierre*) boulder; (*: *tête, crâne*) head, nut*; (*: *diamant etc*) stone. **des tas de ~x d'empierrement** heaps of road metal, heaps of chips for the road; **on ne peut rien faire pousser ici, c'est du ~** you can't get anything to grow here, it's nothing but stones; (*fig*) **il a un ~ à la place du cœur** he has a heart of stone; **il n'a pas un poil** *ou* **cheveu sur le ~*** he's as bald as a coot *ou* an egg; (*Géog*) **le C~*** New Caledonia.

cailloutage [kajutaʒ] nm (*action*) metalling; (*cailloux*) (road) metal, ballast.

caillouter [kajute] [1] vt (*empierrer*) to metal.

caillouteux, -euse [kajutø, øz] adj *route, terrain* stony; *plage* pebbly, shingly.

cailloutis [kajuti] nm (*gén*) gravel; *[route]* (road) metal, ballast.

caïman [kaimɑ̃] nm cayman, caiman.

Caïmans [kaimɑ̃] nfpl voir **île**.

Caïn [kaɛ̃] nm Cain.

Caire [kɛʀ] n: **le ~** Cairo.

cairn [kɛʀn] nm a (*Alpinisme*) cairn. b (*chien*) cairn (terrier).

caisse [kɛs] 1 nf a (*container*) box; *[fruits, légumes]* crate; *[plantes]* box. **mettre des arbres en ~** to plant trees in boxes *ou* tubs.

b (*Tech: boîte, carcasse*) *[horloge]* casing; *[orgue]* case; *[véhicule]* bodywork (voir aussi **1h**); *[tambour]* cylinder.

c (*contenant de l'argent*) (*tiroir*) till; (*machine*) cash register, till; (*portable*) cashbox. (*somme d'argent*) **petite ~** petty cash, float* (*US*); **avoir de l'argent en ~** to have ready cash; **ils n'ont plus un sou en ~** they haven't a penny *ou* a cent (*US*) left in the bank; **faire la ~** to count up the money in the till, do the till; **être à la ~** (*temporairement*) to be at *ou* on the cashdesk; (*être caissier*) to be the cashier; **tenir la ~** to be the cashier; (*fig hum*) to hold the purse strings; **les ~s (de l'état) sont vides** the coffers (of the state) are empty; **voler la ~, partir avec la ~** to steal *ou* make off with the contents of the till *ou* the takings; voir **bon**[2], **livre**[1].

d (*guichet*) *[boutique]* cashdesk; *[banque]* cashier's desk; *[supermarché]* check-out. **passer à la ~** (*lit*) to go to the cashdesk *ou* cashier; (*être payé*) to collect one's money; (*être licencié*) to get paid off, get one's books (*Brit*) *ou* cards* (*Brit*); **on l'a prié de passer à la ~** he was asked to take his cards (*Brit*) and go *ou* collect his (last) wages and go.

e (*établissement, bureau*) office; (*organisme*) fund. **~ de retraite/d'entraide** pension/mutual aid fund; **~ d'allocations familiales** family allowance office (*Brit*), ≃welfare center (*US*); **~ primaire d'assurance maladie** *state health insurance office*, ≃ Department of Health office (*Brit*), ≃ Medicaid office (*US*).

f (*Mus: tambour*) drum; voir **gros**.

g (‡: *poitrine*) chest. **il s'en va** *ou* **part de la ~** his lungs are giving out.

h (*: *voiture*) motor * (*Brit*), auto* (*US*). **vieille ~** old heap‡, old banger* (*Brit*).

2 comp ▸**caisse claire** (*Mus*) side *ou* snare drum ▸**caisse comptable** = **caisse enregistreuse** ▸**caisse des dépôts et consignations** deposit and consignment office ▸**caisse à eau** (*Naut, Rail*) water tank ▸**caisse d'emballage** packing case ▸**caisse enregistreuse** cash register ▸**caisse d'épargne** savings bank ▸**caisse noire** secret funds ▸**caisse à outils** toolbox ▸**caisse de résonance** resonance chamber ▸**caisse de retraite** superannuation *ou* pension fund ▸**caisse à savon** (*lit*) soapbox; (*péj: meuble*) old box ▸**caisse de solidarité** (*Scol*) school fund ▸**caisse du tympan** middle ear, tympanic cavity (SPÉC).

caissette [kɛsɛt] nf (small) box.

caissier, -ière [kesje, jɛʀ] nm,f *[banque]* cashier; *[magasin]* cashier, assistant at the cashdesk; *[supermarché]* check-out assistant (*Brit*) *ou* clerk (*US*); *[cinéma]* cashier, box-office assistant (*Brit*).

caisson [kɛsɔ̃] nm a (*caisse*) box, case; *[bouteilles]* crate; (*coffrage*) casing; (*Mil: chariot*) caisson. b (*Tech: immergé*) caisson. **le mal** *ou* **la maladie des ~s** caisson disease, the bends*. c *[plafond]* caisson, coffer; voir **plafond, sauter**.

cajoler [kaʒɔle] [1] vt (*câliner*) to pet, cuddle, make a fuss of; (†: *amadouer*) to wheedle, coax, cajole. **~ qn pour qu'il donne qch** to try to wheedle sb into giving sth; **~ qn pour obtenir qch** to try to wheedle sth out of sb, cajole sb to try and get sth from him.

cajolerie [kaʒɔlʀi] nf a (*caresses*) cuddle. **faire des ~s à qn** to make a fuss of sb, give sb a cuddle. b (†: *flatterie*) flattery, cajoling (*NonC*). **arracher une promesse à qn à force de ~s** to coax *ou* cajole a promise out of sb.

cajoleur, -euse [kaʒɔlœʀ, øz] 1 adj (*câlin*) *mère* loving, affectionate; (*flatteur*) *voix, personne* wheedling, coaxing. 2 nm,f (*flatteur*) wheedler, coaxer.

cajou [kaʒu] nm: **(noix de) ~** cashew nut.

cajun [kaʒœ̃] 1 adj inv Cajun. 2 nm (*Ling*) Cajun. 3 nmf: **C~** Cajun.

cake [kɛk] nm fruit cake.

cal[1] [kal] nm (*Bot, Méd*) callus.

cal[2] (abrév de **calorie**) cal.

Calabrais, e [kalabʀɛ, ɛz] 1 adj Calabrian. 2 nm,f: **C~(e)** Calabrian.

Calabre [kalabʀ] nf Calabria.

calage [kalaʒ] nm (voir **caler**) wedging; chocking; keying; locking.

calamar [kalamaʀ] nm = **calmar**.

calamine [kalamin] nf a (*Minér*) calamine. b (*Aut: résidu*) carbon deposits.

calaminer (se) [kalamine] [1] vpr *cylindre etc* to be caked with soot, coke up (*Brit*), get coked up (*Brit*).

calamistré, e [kalamistʀe] adj *cheveux* waved and brilliantined.

calamité [kalamite] nf (*malheur*) calamity. (*hum*) **ce type est une ~*** this bloke* (*Brit*) *ou* guy* is a (walking) disaster; **quelle ~!*** what a disaster!

calamiteux, -euse [kalamitø, øz] adj calamitous.

calandre [kalɑ̃dʀ] nf *[automobile]* radiator grill; (*machine*) calender.

calanque [kalɑ̃k] nf (*crique: en Méditerranée*) rocky inlet.

calao [kalao] nm hornbill.

calcaire [kalkɛʀ] 1 adj a (*qui contient de la chaux*) *sol, terrain* chalky, calcareous (SPÉC); *eau* hard. b (*Géol*) *roche, plateau, relief* limestone (*épith*). c (*Méd*) *dégénérescence* calcareous; (*Chim*) *sels* calcium (*épith*). 2 nm (*Géol*) limestone; *[bouilloire]* fur (*Brit*), sediment (*US*).

calcanéum [kalkaneɔm] nm calcaneum.

calcification [kalsifikasjɔ̃] nf (*Méd*) calcification.

calcination [kalsinasjɔ̃] nf calcination.

calciné, e [kalsine] (ptp de **calciner**) adj *débris, os* charred, burned to ashes (*attrib*); *rôti* charred, burned to a cinder (*attrib*).

calciner [kalsine] [1] 1 vt (*Tech: brûler*) *pierre, bois, métal* to calcine (SPÉC); *rôti* to burn to a cinder. (*littér*) **la plaine calcinée par le soleil** the plain scorched by the sun, the sun-scorched *ou* sun-baked plain. 2

se calciner vpr *[rôti]* to burn to a cinder; *[débris]* to burn to ashes.
calcium [kalsjɔm] nm calcium.
calcul [kalkyl] 1 nm a *(opération)* calculation; *(exercice scolaire)* sum. **se tromper dans ses ~s, faire une erreur de ~** to miscalculate, make a miscalculation, make a mistake in one's calculations; *voir* **règle.**
b *(discipline)* **le ~** arithmetic; **fort en ~** good at arithmetic *ou* sums; **le ~ différentiel/intégral** differential/integral calculus.
c *(estimation)* **~s** reckoning(s), calculations, computations; **tous ~s faits** with all factors reckoned up, having done all the reckonings *ou* calculations; **d'après mes ~s** by my reckoning, according to my calculations *ou* computations.
d *(plan)* calculation *(NonC)*. **par ~** with an ulterior motive, out of (calculated) self-interest; **sans (aucun) ~** without any ulterior motive *ou* (any) self-interest; **faire un bon ~** to calculate correctly *ou* right; **faire un mauvais ~** to miscalculate, make a miscalculation; **c'est le ~ d'un arriviste** it's the calculated move of an ambitious man; **~s intéressés** self-interested motives.
e *(Méd)* stone, calculus *(SPÉC)*.
2 comp ►**calcul algébrique** calculus ►**calcul biliaire** *(Méd)* gallstone ►**calcul mental** *(discipline)* mental arithmetic; *(opération)* mental calculation ►**calcul des probabilités** probability theory ►**calcul rénal** *(Méd)* stone in the kidney, renal calculus *(SPÉC)*.
calculable [kalkylabl] adj calculable, which can be calculated *ou* worked out.
calculateur, -trice [kalkylatœʀ, tʀis] 1 adj *(intéressé)* calculating. 2 nm *(machine)* computer. **~ numérique/analogique** digital/analog computer. 3 **calculatrice** nf *(machine)* calculator. **~ de poche** handheld *ou* pocket calculator, minicalculator. 4 nm,f *(personne)* calculator. **c'est un bon ~** he's good at counting *ou* at figures *ou* at calculations.
calculer [kalkyle] [1] 1 vt a *prix, quantité* to work out, calculate, reckon; *surface* to work out, calculate. **apprendre à ~** to learn to calculate; **il calcule vite** he calculates quickly, he's quick at figures *ou* at calculating; **~ (un prix) de tête *ou* mentalement** to work out *ou* reckon *ou* calculate (a price) in one's head; *voir* **machine**[3], **règle.**
b *(évaluer, estimer) chances, conséquences* to calculate, work out, weigh up. *(Sport)* **~ son élan** to judge one's run-up; **~ que** to work out *ou* calculate that; **tout bien calculé** everything *ou* all things considered; *voir* **risque.**
c *(combiner) geste, attitude, effets* to plan, calculate; *plan, action* to plan. **elle calcule continuellement** she's always calculating; **~ son coup** to plan one's move (carefully); **ils avaient calculé leur coup** they had it all figured out*; **avec une gentillesse calculée** with calculated kindness.
2 vi *(économiser, compter)* to budget carefully, count the pennies. *(péj)* **ces gens qui calculent** those (people) who are always counting their pennies *ou* who work out every penny *(péj)*.
calculette [kalkylɛt] nf hand-held *ou* pocket calculator, minicalculator.
caldoche [kaldɔʃ] 1 adj white New Caledonian *(épith)*. 2 nmf: **C~** white New Caledonian.
cale[1] [kal] nf a *(Naut: soute)* hold; *voir* **fond.** b *(chantier, plan incliné)* slipway. **~ de chargement** slipway; **~ de radoub** graving dock; **~ sèche** dry dock.
cale[2] [kal] nf *(coin) [meuble, caisse]* wedge; *(Golf)* wedge; *[roue]* chock, wedge. **mettre une voiture sur ~s** to put a car on blocks.
calé, e* [kale] (ptp de **caler**) adj a *(savant) personne* bright. **être ~ en maths** to be a wizard* at maths; **c'est drôlement ~ ce qu'il a fait** what he did was terribly clever. b *(ardu) problème* tough.
calebasse [kalbɑs] nf *(récipient)* calabash, gourde.
calèche [kalɛʃ] nf barouche.
calecif‡ [kalsif] nm pants *(Brit)*, shorts *(US)*.
caleçon [kalsɔ̃] nm a *[homme]* boxer shorts *(Brit)*, shorts *(US)*. **3 ~s** 3 pairs of boxer shorts *(Brit) ou* shorts *(US)*; **où est mon ~, où sont mes ~s?** where are my boxer shorts *(Brit) ou* shorts *(US)*?; **~(s) de bain** swimming *ou* bathing trunks; **~(s) long(s)** long johns*. b *[femme]* leggings.
calédonien, -ienne [kaledɔnjɛ̃, jɛn] adj Caledonian.
calembour [kalɑ̃buʀ] nm pun, play on words *(NonC)*.
calembredaine [kalɑ̃bʀədɛn] nf *(plaisanterie)* silly joke. *(balivernes)* **~s** balderdash *(NonC)*, nonsense.
calencher‡ [kalɑ̃ʃe] [1] vi to snuff it‡, croak‡ *(US)*.
calendes [kalɑ̃d] nfpl *(Antiq)* calends; *voir* **renvoyer.**
calendos‡ [kalɑ̃dos] nm Camembert (cheese).
calendrier [kalɑ̃dʀije] nm *(jours et mois)* calendar; *(programme)* timetable. **~ d'amortissement** repayment schedule; **~ à effeuiller/perpétuel** tear-off/everlasting calendar; **~ des examens** exam timetable; *(Ftbl)* **~ des rencontres** fixture(s) timetable *ou* list; **~ de travail** work schedule *ou* programme; *voir* **bloc.**
cale-pied [kalpje] nm inv *[vélo]* toe clip.
calepin [kalpɛ̃] nm notebook.
caler [kale] [1] 1 vt a *(avec une cale, un coin) meuble* to put a wedge under, wedge; *fenêtre, porte* to wedge; *roue* to chock, wedge.
b *(avec une vis, une goupille) poulie* to key; *cheville, objet pivotant* to wedge, lock.
c *(avec des coussins etc) malade* to prop up. **~ sa tête sur l'oreiller** to prop *ou* rest one's head on the pillow; **des coussins lui calaient la tête, il avait la tête (bien) calée par des coussins** his head was (well) propped up on *ou* supported by cushions.
d *(appuyer) pile de livres, de linge* to prop up. **~ dans un coin/contre** to prop up in a corner/against.
e *moteur, véhicule* to stall.
f *(Naut: baisser) mât* to house.
g (*: *bourrer*) **ça vous cale l'estomac** it fills you up; **je suis calé pour un bon moment** that's me full up for a while*.
2 vi a *[véhicule, moteur, conducteur]* to stall.
b (*) *(céder)* to give in; *(abandonner)* to give up. **il a calé avant le dessert** he gave up before the dessert; **il a calé sur le dessert** he couldn't finish his dessert.
c *(Naut)* **~ trop** to have too great a draught; **~ 8 mètres** to draw 8 metres of water.
3 **se caler** vpr: **se ~ dans un fauteuil** to plant o.s. firmly *ou* settle o.s. comfortably in an armchair; **se ~ les joues*** to have a good feed* *ou* tuck-in* *(Brit)*.
caleter‡ vi, **se caleter** vpr [kalte] [1] = **calter‡.**
calfatage [kalfataʒ] nm ca(u)lking.
calfater [kalfate] [1] vt *(Naut)* to ca(u)lk.
calfeutrage [kalføtʀaʒ] nm *(voir* **calfeutrer***)* draughtproofing; filling, stopping-up.
calfeutrer [kalføtʀe] [1] 1 vt *pièce, porte* to (make) draughtproof; *fissure* to fill, stop up. 2 **se calfeutrer** vpr *(s'enfermer)* to shut o.s. up *ou* away; *(pour être au chaud)* to hole (o.s.) up, make o.s. snug.
calibrage [kalibʀaʒ] nm *(voir* **calibrer***)* grading; calibration; gauging.
calibre [kalibʀ] nm a *(diamètre) [fusil, canon]* calibre, bore; *[conduite, tuyau]* bore, diameter; *[obus, balle]* calibre; *[cylindre, instrument de musique]* bore; *[câble]* diameter; *[œufs, fruits]* grade; *[boule]* size. **de gros ~** *pistolet* large-bore *(épith)*; *obus* large-calibre *(épith)*; **pistolet de ~ 7,35** 7.35 mm pistol. b *(arg Crime: pistolet)* rod *(arg)*, gat *(arg)*. c *(instrument) (gradué et ajustable)* gauge; *(réplique)* template. d *(fig: envergure)* calibre. **son frère est d'un autre ~** his brother is of another calibre altogether; **c'est rare un égoïsme de ce ~** you don't often see selfishness on such a scale.
calibrer [kalibʀe] [1] vt a *(mesurer) œufs, fruits, charbon* to grade; *conduit, cylindre, fusil* to calibrate. b *(finir) pièce travaillée* to gauge.
calice [kalis] nm *(Rel)* chalice; *(Bot, Physiol)* calyx; *voir* **boire.**
calicot [kaliko] nm a *(tissu)* calico; *(banderole)* banner. b (†: *vendeur)* draper's assistant *(Brit)*, fabric clerk *(US)*.
califat [kalifa] nm caliphate.
calife [kalif] nm caliph. **il veut être ~ à la place du ~** he likes to play God.
Californie [kalifɔʀni] nf California.
californien, -ienne [kalifɔʀnjɛ̃, jɛn] 1 adj Californian. 2 nm,f: **C~(ne)** Californian.
californium [kalifɔʀnjɔm] nm californium.
califourchon [kalifuʀʃɔ̃] nm: **à ~** astride; **s'asseoir à ~ sur qch** to straddle sth, sit astride sth; **être à ~ sur qch** to bestride sth, be astride sth; *(Équitation)* **monter à ~** to ride astride.
câlin, e [kɑlɛ̃, in] 1 adj *(qui aime les caresses) enfant, chat* cuddly, cuddlesome; *(qui câline) mère, ton, regard* tender, loving. 2 nm cuddle. **faire un (petit) ~ à qn** to give sb a cuddle.
câliner [kɑline] [1] vt *(cajoler)* to fondle, cuddle.
câlinerie [kɑlinʀi] nf *(tendresse)* tenderness. *(caresses, cajoleries)* **~s** caresses; **faire des ~s à qn** to fondle *ou* cuddle sb.
calisson [kalisɔ̃] nm calisson *(lozenge-shaped sweet made of ground almonds)*.
calleux, -euse [kalø, øz] adj *peau* horny, callous.
calligramme [kaligʀam] nm *(poème)* calligramme.
calligraphe [ka(l)ligʀaf] nmf calligrapher, calligraphist.
calligraphie [ka(l)ligʀafi] nf *(technique)* calligraphy, art of handwriting. **c'est de la ~** it's lovely handwriting, the (hand)writing is beautiful.
calligraphier [ka(l)ligʀafje] [7] vt *titre, phrase* to write artistically, calligraph *(SPÉC)*.
calligraphique [ka(l)ligʀafik] adj calligraphic.
callosité [kalozite] nf callosity.
calmant, e [kalmɑ̃, ɑ̃t] 1 adj a *(Pharm) (tranquillisant)* tranquillizing *(épith)*; *(contre la douleur)* painkilling *(épith)*. b *(apaisant) paroles* soothing. 2 nm *(Pharm)* tranquillizer, sedative; painkiller.
calmar [kalmaʀ] nm squid.
calme [kalm] 1 adj *(gén)* quiet, calm; *(paisible)* peaceful; *nuit, air* still. **malgré leurs provocations il restait très ~** he remained quite calm *ou* cool *ou* unruffled in spite of their taunts; **le malade a eu une nuit ~** the invalid has had a quiet *ou* peaceful night.
2 nm a *(sang-froid)* coolness. **garder son ~** to keep cool *ou* calm, keep one's cool* *ou* head; **perdre son ~** to lose one's composure *ou* cool*; **avec un ~ incroyable** with incredible sangfroid *ou* coolness; **recouvrant son ~** recovering his equanimity.
b *(tranquillité) (gén)* quietness, peace (and quiet); *[nuit]* stillness; *[endroit]* peacefulness, quietness. **chercher le ~** to look for (some) peace and quiet; **le ~ de la campagne** the peace (and quiet) of the country-

side; **il me faut du ~ pour travailler** I need quietness *ou* peace to work; **du ~!** (*restez tranquille*) let's have some quiet!, quieten down! (*Brit*), quiet down! (*US*); (*pas de panique*) keep cool! *ou* calm!; *[malade]* **rester au ~** to avoid excitement, take things quietly; **ramener le ~** (*arranger les choses*) to calm things down; (*rétablir l'ordre*) to restore order; **le ~ avant la tempête** the lull before the storm.

c (*Naut*) **~ plat** dead calm; (*fig*) **en août c'est le ~ plat dans les affaires** in August business is dead quiet *ou* at a standstill; (*fig*) **depuis que je lui ai envoyé cette lettre c'est le ~ plat** since I sent him that letter I haven't heard a thing *ou* a squeak; **~s équatoriaux** doldrums (*lit*).

calmement [kalmәmɑ̃] adv *agir* calmly. **la journée s'est passée ~** the day passed quietly.

calmer [kalme] [1] **1** vt **a** (*apaiser*) *personne* to calm (down), pacify; *querelle, discussion* to quieten down (*Brit*), quiet down (*US*); *sédition, révolte* to calm; (*littér*) *tempête, flots* to calm. **~ les esprits** to calm people down, pacify people; **attends un peu, je vais te ~!*** just you wait, I'll (soon) quieten (*Brit*) *ou* quiet (*US*) you down!; (*lit, fig*) **~ le jeu** to calm things down.

b (*réduire*) *douleur, inquiétude* to soothe, ease; *nerfs, agitation, crainte, colère* to calm, soothe; *fièvre* to bring down, reduce, soothe; *impatience* to curb; *faim* to appease; *soif* to quench; *désir, ardeur* to cool, subdue.

2 se calmer vpr **a** *[personne]* (*s'apaiser*) to calm down, cool down; (*faire moins de bruit*) to quieten down (*Brit*), quiet down (*US*); (*se tranquilliser*) to calm down; *[discussion, querelle]* to quieten down (*Brit*), quiet down (*US*); *[tempête]* to calm down, die down; *[mer]* to calm down. **on se calme!*** (*taisez-vous*) be quiet!; (*pas de panique*) don't panic!, calm down!

b (*diminuer*) *[douleur]* to ease, subside; *[faim, soif, inquiétude]* to ease; *[crainte, impatience, fièvre]* to subside; *[colère, désir, ardeur]* to cool, subside.

calomel [kalɔmɛl] nm calomel.

calomniateur, -trice [kalɔmnjatœʀ, tʀis] (*voir* **calomnier**) **1** adj slanderous; libellous. **2** nm,f slanderer; libeller.

calomnie [kalɔmni] nf slander, calumny; (*écrite*) libel; (*sens affaibli*) maligning (*NonC*). **cette ~ l'avait profondément blessé** he'd been deeply hurt by this slander *ou* calumny; **écrire une ~/des ~s** to write something libellous/libellous things; **dire une ~/des ~s** to say something slanderous/slanderous things.

calomnier [kalɔmnje] [7] vt (*diffamer*) to slander; (*par écrit*) to libel; (*sens affaibli: vilipender*) to malign.

calomnieux, -ieuse [kalɔmnjø, jøz] adj (*voir* **calomnier**) slanderous; libellous.

caloporteur [kalopɔʀtœʀ] adj, nm = **caloriporteur**.

calorie [kalɔʀi] nf calorie. **aliment riche/pauvre en ~s** food with a high/low calorie content, high-/low-calorie food; **ça donne des ~s*** it warms you up; **tu aurais besoin de ~s!*** you need building up!

calorifère [kalɔʀifɛʀ] **1** adj heat-giving. **2** nm (†) stove.

calorifique [kalɔʀifik] adj calorific.

calorifuge [kalɔʀifyʒ] **1** adj (heat-)insulating, heat-retaining. **2** nm insulating material.

calorifugeage [kalɔʀifyʒaʒ] nm lagging, insulation.

calorifuger [kalɔʀifyʒe] [3] vt to lag, insulate (against loss of heat).

calorimètre [kalɔʀimɛtʀ] nm calorimeter.

calorimétrie [kalɔʀimetʀi] nf calorimetry.

calorimétrique [kalɔʀimetʀik] adj calorimetric(al).

caloriporteur [kalɔʀipɔʀtœʀ] **1** adj (*gén*) heat-conducting; (*rafraîchissant*) coolant. **2** nm (*gén*) heat conductor; (*qui rafraîchit*) coolant.

calorique [kalɔʀik] adj (*diététique*) calorie (*épith*); (*chaleur*) calorific. **ration ~** calorie requirements (*pl*).

calot [kalo] nm **a** (*coiffure*) forage cap, overseas cap (*US*). **b** (*bille*) (large) marble.

calotin, e [kalɔtɛ̃, in] (*péj*) **1** adj sanctimonious, churchy*. **2** nm,f (*bigot*) sanctimonious churchgoer.

calotte [kalɔt] **1** nf **a** (*bonnet*) skullcap. **b** (*péj*) **la ~** (*le clergé*) the priests, the cloth; (*le parti dévot*) the church party. **c** (*partie supérieure*) *[chapeau]* crown; (*Archit*) *[voûte]* calotte. **d** (*: *gifle*) slap. **il m'a donné une ~** he gave me a slap in the face *ou* a box on the ears* (*Brit*). **2** comp ►**la calotte des cieux** the dome *ou* vault of heaven ►**calotte crânienne** (*Anat*) top of the skull ►**calotte glaciaire** (*Géog*) icecap ►**calotte sphérique** segment of a sphere.

calotter* [kalɔte] [1] vt (*gifler*) to cuff, box the ears of (*Brit*), clout*.

calquage [kalkaʒ] nm tracing.

calque [kalk] nm **a** (*dessin*) tracing. **prendre un ~ d'un plan** to trace a plan. **b** **(papier-)~** tracing paper. **c** (*fig: reproduction*) *[œuvre d'art]* exact copy; *[incident, événement]* carbon copy; *[personne]* spitting image. **d** (*Ling*) calque, loan translation.

calquer [kalke] [1] vt (*copier*) *plan, dessin* to trace; (*fig*) to copy exactly. (*Ling*) **calqué de l'anglais** translated literally from English; **~ son comportement sur celui de son voisin** to model one's behaviour on that of one's neighbour, copy one's neighbour's behaviour exactly.

calter‡ vi, **se calter‡** vpr [kalte] [1] (*décamper*) to scarper‡ (*Brit*), make o.s. scarce‡, buzz off‡ (*Brit*).

calumet [kalymɛ] nm peace pipe. **fumer le ~ de la paix** (*lit*) to smoke the pipe of peace; (*fig*) to bury the hatchet.

calva* [kalva] nm abrév de **calvados**.

calvados [kalvados] nm (*eau-de-vie*) calvados.

calvaire [kalvɛʀ] nm **a** (*croix*) (*au bord de la route*) roadside cross *ou* crucifix, calvary; (*peinture*) Calvary, road *ou* way to the Cross. **b** (*épreuve*) suffering, martyrdom. **le ~ du Christ** Christ's martyrdom *ou* suffering on the cross; **sa vie fut un long ~** his life was one long martyrdom *ou* agony *ou* tale of suffering; **un enfant comme ça, c'est un ~ pour la mère** a child like that must be a sore *ou* bitter trial *ou* sore burden to his mother. **c** (*Rel*) **Le C~** Calvary.

Calvin [kalvɛ̃] nm Calvin.

calvinisme [kalvinism] nm Calvinism.

calviniste [kalvinist] **1** adj Calvinist, Calvinistic. **2** nmf Calvinist.

calvitie [kalvisi] nf baldness (*NonC*). **~ précoce** premature baldness (*NonC*).

calypso [kalipso] nm calypso.

camaïeu [kamajø] nm (*peinture*) monochrome. **en ~** *paysage, motif* monochrome (*épith*); **en ~ bleu** in blue monochrome; **peint en ~** painted in monochrome.

camail [kamaj] nm (*Rel*) cappa magna.

camarade [kamaʀad] **1** nmf companion, friend, mate*, pal*. (*Pol*) **le ~ X** comrade X; **elle voyait en lui un bon ~** she saw him as a good friend. **2** comp ►**camarade d'atelier** workmate (*Brit*), shop buddy* (*US*) ►**camarade d'école** schoolmate, school friend ►**camarade d'étude** fellow student ►**camarade de jeu** playmate ►**camarade de régiment** mate from one's army days, old army mate *ou* buddy*.

camaraderie [kamaʀadʀi] nf good-companionship, good-fellowship, camaraderie. **la ~ mène à l'amitié** good-companionship *ou* a sense of companionship leads to friendship.

camard, e [kamaʀ, aʀd] adj *nez* pug (*épith*); *personne* pug-nosed.

camarguais, e [kamaʀgɛ, ɛz] **1** adj of *ou* from the Camargue. **2** nm,f: **C~(e)** inhabitant *ou* native of the Camargue.

Camargue [kamaʀg] nf: **la ~** the Camargue.

cambiste [kɑ̃bist] nm foreign exchange broker *ou* dealer; *[devises des touristes]* moneychanger.

Cambodge [kɑ̃bɔdʒ] nm Cambodia.

cambodgien, -ienne [kɑ̃bɔdʒjɛ̃, jɛn] **1** adj Cambodian. **2** nm,f: **C~(ne)** Cambodian.

cambouis [kɑ̃bwi] nm dirty oil *ou* grease.

cambré, e [kɑ̃bʀe] (ptp de **cambrer**) adj: **avoir les reins ~s** *ou* **le dos ~** to have an arched back; **être un peu/très ~** to have a slightly/very arched back; **avoir le pied très ~** to have very high insteps *ou* arches; **chaussures ~es** shoes with a high instep.

cambrer [kɑ̃bʀe] [1] **1** vt **a** *pied* to arch. **~ la taille** *ou* **le corps** *ou* **les reins** to throw back one's shoulders, arch one's back. **b** (*Tech*) *pièce de bois* to bend; *métal* to curve; *tige, semelle* to arch. **2 se cambrer** vpr (*se redresser*) to throw back one's shoulders, arch one's back.

cambrien, -ienne [kɑ̃bʀijɛ̃, ijɛn] adj, nm Cambrian.

cambriolage [kɑ̃bʀijɔlaʒ] nm (*activité, méthode*) burglary, housebreaking, breaking and entering (*Jur*); (*coup*) break-in, burglary.

cambrioler [kɑ̃bʀijɔle] [1] vt to break into, burgle (*Brit*), burglarize (*US*).

cambrioleur [kɑ̃bʀijɔlœʀ] nm burglar, housebreaker.

cambrouse‡ [kɑ̃bʀuz] nf, **cambrousse‡** [kɑ̃bʀus] nf (*campagne*) country. **en pleine ~** in the middle of nowhere, at the back of beyond (*Brit*); (*péj*) **frais arrivé de sa ~** fresh from the backwoods *ou* the sticks.

cambrure [kɑ̃bʀyʀ] nf **a** (*courbe, forme*) *[poutre, taille, reins]* curve; *[semelle, pied]* arch; *[route]* camber. **sa ~ de militaire** his military bearing. **b** (*partie*) **~ du pied** instep; **~ des reins** small *ou* hollow of the back; **pieds qui ont une forte ~** feet with high insteps; **reins qui ont une forte ~** back which is very hollow *ou* arched.

cambuse [kɑ̃byz] nf **a** (‡) (*pièce*) pad‡; (*maison*) shack*, place; (*taudis*) hovel. **b** (*Naut*) storeroom.

came¹ [kam] nf (*Tech*) cam; *voir* **arbre**.

came² [kam] nf (*arg Drogue*) (*gén*) junk (*arg*), stuff (*arg*); (*cocaïne*) snow (*arg*); (‡: *marchandise*) stuff*; (*péj: pacotille*) junk*, trash*.

camé, e¹ [kame] **1** adj (*arg Drogue*) stoned‡. **complètement ~** stoned out of one's mind‡. **2** nm,f (*arg Drogue*) junkie (*arg*), druggy‡.

camée² [kame] nm cameo.

caméléon [kameleɔ̃] nm (*Zool*) chameleon; (*fig*) chameleon; (*péj*) turncoat.

camélia [kamelja] nm camellia.

camelot [kamlo] nm street pedlar *ou* vendor. (*Hist*) **les C~s du roi** *militant royalist group in 1930s*.

camelote* [kamlɔt] nf **a** (*pacotille*) **c'est de la ~** it's junk* *ou* trash* *ou* rubbish* (*Brit*) *ou* schlock‡ (*US*). **b** (*marchandise*) stuff*. **il vend de la belle ~** he sells nice stuff.

camembert [kamɑ̃bɛʀ] nm (*fromage*) Camembert (cheese); (*: *Ordin*) pie chart.

camer (se) [kame] vpr (*arg Drogue*) to be on drugs.

caméra [kameʀa] nf (*Ciné, TV*) camera; *[amateur]* cine-camera, movie camera (*US*). **devant les ~s de la télévision** in front of the television cameras, on TV.

cameraman [kameʀaman], pl **cameramen** [kameʀamɛn] nm cameraman.

camériste [kameʀist] nf (*femme de chambre*) chambermaid; (*Hist*) lady-in-waiting.

Cameroun [kamʀun] nm Cameroon; (*Hist*) Cameroons. **République unie du ~** United Republic of Cameroon.

camerounais, e [kamʀunɛ, ɛz] 1 adj Cameroonian. 2 nm,f: **C~(e)** Cameroonian.

caméscope [kameskɔp] nm ® camcorder, video camera.

camion [kamjɔ̃] 1 nm a (*véhicule*) (*ouvert*) lorry (*Brit*), truck (*US*); (*fermé*) van, truck (*US*). b (*chariot*) wag(g)on, dray. c *[peintre]* (*seau*) (paint-)pail. 2 comp ▸**camion-citerne** nm (pl **camions-citernes**) tanker (lorry) (*Brit*), tank truck (*US*) ▸**camion de déménagement** removal (*Brit*) *ou* moving (*US*) van, pantechnicon (*Brit*) ▸**camion (à) remorque** lorry (*Brit*) *ou* truck (*US*) with a trailer, tractor-trailer (*US*) ▸**camion (à) semi-remorque** articulated lorry (*Brit*), trailer truck (*US*).

camionnage [kamjɔnaʒ] nm haulage, transport.

camionnette [kamjɔnɛt] nf (small) van; (*ouverte*) pick-up (truck).

camionneur [kamjɔnœʀ] nm (*chauffeur*) lorry (*Brit*) *ou* truck (*US*) driver, trucker (*US*); van driver; (*entrepreneur*) haulage contractor (*Brit*), road haulier (*Brit*), trucking contractor (*US*).

camisole [kamizɔl] 1 nf (††) (*blouse*) camisole†; (*chemise de nuit*) nightshirt. 2 comp ▸**camisole chimique** suppressants (*pl*) ▸**camisole de force** straitjacket.

camomille [kamɔmij] nf (*Bot*) camomile; (*tisane*) camomile tea.

camouflage [kamuflaʒ] nm a (*Mil*) (*action*) camouflaging; (*résultat*) camouflage. b (*gén*) *[argent]* concealing, hiding; *[erreur]* camouflaging, covering-up. **le ~ d'un crime en accident** disguising a crime as an accident.

camoufler [kamufle] 1 vt (*Mil*) to camouflage; (*fig*) (*cacher*) *argent* to conceal, hide; *erreur, embarras* to conceal, cover up; (*déguiser*) *défaite, intentions* to disguise. **~ un crime en accident** to disguise a crime as an accident, make a crime look like an accident.

camouflet [kamuflɛ] nm (*littér*) snub. **donner un ~ à qn** to snub sb.

camp [kɑ̃] 1 nm a (*Alpinisme, Mil, Sport, emplacement*) camp. **~ de prisonniers/de réfugiés** prison/refugee camp; **rentrer au ~** to come *ou* go back to camp; *voir* **aide, feu**[1] *etc.*

b (*séjour*) **faire un ~ d'une semaine dans les Pyrénées** to go camping for a week *ou* go for a week's camping holiday (*Brit*) *ou* vacation (*US*) in the Pyrenees; **le ~ vous fait découvrir beaucoup de choses** camping lets you discover lots of things.

c (*parti, faction*) (*Jeux, Sport*) side; (*Pol*) camp. **changer de ~** *[joueur]* to change sides; *[soldat]* to go over to the other side; (*fig*) **à cette nouvelle la consternation/l'espoir changea de ~** on hearing this, it was the other side which began to feel dismay/hopeful; **dans le ~ opposé/victorieux** in the opposite/winning camp; **passer au ~ adverse** to go over to the opposite *ou* enemy camp; *voir* **balle.**

2 comp ▸**camp de base** base camp ▸**camp de camping** campsite, camping site ▸**camp de concentration** concentration camp ▸**camp d'extermination** death camp ▸**camp fortifié** fortified camp ▸**camp de la mort** = **camp d'extermination** ▸**camp retranché** = **camp fortifié** ▸**camp de toile** campsite, camping site ▸**camp de travail** labour camp ▸**camp de vacances** ≃ summer camp (*US*), ≃ children's holiday camp (*Brit*) ▸**camp volant** camping tour *ou* trip; (*Mil*) temporary camp; (*fig*) **vivre** *ou* **être en camp volant** to live out of a suitcase.

campagnard, e [kɑ̃paɲaʀ, aʀd] 1 adj *vie, allure, manières* country (*épith*); (*péj*) rustic (*péj*); *voir* **gentilhomme.** 2 nm countryman, country fellow; (*péj*) rustic (*péj*), hick (*pej*). **~s** countryfolk; (*péj*) rustics (*péj*). 3 **campagnarde** nf countrywoman, country lass (*Brit*) *ou* girl.

campagne [kɑ̃paɲ] nf a (*gén: habitat*) country; (*paysage*) countryside; (*Agr: champs ouverts*) open country. **la ville et la ~** town and country; **la ~ anglaise** the English countryside; **dans la ~ environnante** in the surrounding countryside; **nous sommes tombés en panne en pleine ~** we broke down right in the middle of the country(side), we broke down away out in the country; **à la ~** in the country; **auberge/chemin de ~** country inn/lane; **les travaux de la ~** farm *ou* agricultural work; *voir* **battre, maison** *etc.*

b (*Mil*) campaign. **faire ~** to fight (a campaign); **les troupes en ~** the troops on campaign *ou* in the field; **entrer en ~** to embark on a campaign; **la ~ d'Italie/de Russie** the Italian/Russian campaign; **artillerie/canon de ~** field artillery/gun; *voir* **tenue.**

c (*Pol, Presse etc*) campaign (*pour* for, *contre* against). **~ électorale** election campaign; **~ commerciale** *ou* **publicitaire** marketing *ou* sales campaign, sales drive; **~ publicitaire, ~ de publicité** advertising *ou* publicity drive *ou* campaign; (*Pol*) **faire ~ pour un candidat** to campaign *ou* canvass for *ou* on behalf of a candidate; **partir en ~** to launch a campaign (*contre* against); **mener une ~ pour/contre** to campaign for/against, lead a campaign for/against; **tout le monde se mit en ~ pour lui trouver une maison** everybody set to work *ou* got busy to find him a house.

campagnol [kɑ̃paɲɔl] nm vole.

campanile [kɑ̃panil] nm *[église]* campanile; (*clocheton*) bell-tower.

campanule [kɑ̃panyl] nf bellflower, campanula.

campement [kɑ̃pmɑ̃] nm (*camp*) camp, encampment. **matériel de ~** camping equipment; **chercher un ~ pour la nuit** to look for somewhere to set up camp *ou* for a camping place for the night; **établir son ~ sur les bords d'un fleuve** to set up one's camp on the bank of a river; **~ de nomades/d'Indiens** camp *ou* encampment of nomads/of Indians; (*Mil*) **revenir à son ~** to return to camp.

camper [kɑ̃pe] 1 1 vi (*lit*) to camp. (*fig hum*) **on campait à l'hôtel/dans le salon** we were camping out at *ou* in a hotel/in the lounge; *voir* **position.**

2 vt a *troupes* to camp out. **campés pour 2 semaines près du village** camped (out) for 2 weeks by the village.

b (*fig: esquisser*) *caractère, personnage* to portray; *récit* to construct; *portrait* to fashion, shape. **personnage bien campé** vividly sketched *ou* portrayed character.

c (*fig: poser*) **~ sa casquette sur l'oreille** to pull *ou* clap one's cap on firmly over one ear; **se ~ des lunettes sur le nez** to plant* a pair of glasses on one's nose.

3 **se camper** vpr: **se ~ devant** to plant o.s. in front of; **se ~ sur ses jambes** to plant o.s. *ou* stand firmly on one's feet.

campeur, -euse [kɑ̃pœʀ, øz] nm,f camper.

camphre [kɑ̃fʀ] nm camphor.

camphré, e [kɑ̃fʀe] adj camphorated; *voir* **alcool.**

camphrier [kɑ̃fʀije] nm camphor tree.

camping [kɑ̃piŋ] nm a (*activité*) **le ~** camping; **faire du ~** to go camping; *voir* **sauvage.** b (*lieu*) campsite, camping site. c (*voiture*) **~-car** camper, motorhome (*US*); (*réchaud*) **~-gaz** camp(ing) stove.

campos*† [kɑ̃po] nm: **demain on a ~** tomorrow is a day off, we've got tomorrow off *ou* free; **on a eu** *ou* **on nous a donné ~ à 4 heures** we were free *ou* told to go at 4 o'clock, we were free from 4 o'clock.

campus [kɑ̃pys] nm campus.

camus, e [kamy, yz] adj *nez* pug (*épith*); *personne* pug-nosed.

Canaan [kanaɑ̃] nm Canaan.

Canada [kanada] nm Canada.

Canadair [kanadɛʀ] nm ® fire-fighting aircraft, tanker plane (*US*).

canadianisme [kanadjanism] nm Canadianism.

canadien, -ienne [kanadjɛ̃, jɛn] 1 adj Canadian. 2 nm,f: **C~(ne)** Canadian; **C~(ne) français(e)** French Canadian. 3 **canadienne** nf (*veste*) fur-lined jacket; (*canoë*) (Canadian) canoe; (*tente*) (ridge) tent.

canaille [kanɑj] 1 adj *air, manières* low, cheap, coarse. **sous ses airs ~s, il est sérieux** he might look a bit rough and ready, but he is reliable. 2 nf (*péj*) (*salaud*) bastard‡ (*péj*); (*escroc*) crook, shyster (*US*), chiseler (*US*); (*hum: enfant*) rascal, rogue, (little) devil. (*péj: la populace*) **la ~**† the rabble (*péj*), the riffraff (*péj*).

canaillerie [kanɑjʀi] nf a *[allure, ton, manières]* vulgarity, coarseness. b (*malhonnêteté*) *[procédés, personne]* crookedness. c (*action malhonnête*) dirty *ou* low trick.

canal, pl **-aux** [kanal, o] 1 nm a (*artificiel*) canal; (*détroit*) channel; (*tuyau, fossé*) conduit, duct; (*Anat*) canal, duct; (*TV, Ordin*) channel. **le C~ de Panama/Suez** the Panama/Suez Canal; **C~ Plus, C~** + *French pay TV channel.*

b (*intermédiaire*) **par le ~ d'un collègue** through *ou* via a colleague; **par le ~ de la presse** through the medium of the press; (*littér*) **par un ~ amical** through a friendly channel.

2 comp ▸**canal d'amenée** feeder canal ▸**canal biliaire** (*Anat*) biliary canal, bile duct ▸**canal déférent** vas deferens ▸**canal de dérivation** diversion canal ▸**canal de distribution** distribution channel ▸**canal de fuite** tail-race ▸**canal d'irrigation** irrigation canal ▸**canal maritime** ship canal ▸**canal médullaire** (*Anat, Bot*) medullary cavity *ou* canal ▸**canal de navigation** ship canal.

canalisation [kanalizasjɔ̃] nf a (*tuyau*) (main) pipe. **~s** (*réseau*) pipes, piping, pipework; (*Élec*) cables. b (*aménagement*) *[cours d'eau]* canalization. c *[demandes, foule]* channelling, funnelling.

canaliser [kanalize] 1 vt a *foule, demandes, pensées, énergie* to channel, funnel. b *fleuve* to canalize; *région, plaine* to provide with a network of canals.

cananéen, -enne [kananeɛ̃, ɛn] 1 adj Canaanite. 2 nm (*Ling*) Canaanite. 3 nm,f: **C~(ne)** Canaanite.

canapé [kanape] nm a (*meuble*) sofa, settee, couch. **~ transformable** *ou* **convertible, ~-lit** bed settee (*Brit*), sofa bed. b (*Culin*) open sandwich; (*pour apéritif*) canapé. **crevettes sur ~** shrimp canapé, canapé of shrimps.

canaque [kanak] 1 adj Kanak. 2 nmf: **C~** Kanak.

canard [kanaʀ] 1 nm a (*oiseau, Culin*) duck; (*mâle*) drake; *voir* **froid, mare.** b (*) (*journal*) rag*; (*fausse nouvelle*) false report, rumour, canard. c (*Mus: couac*) false note. **faire un ~** to hit a false note. d (*terme d'affection*) **mon (petit) ~** pet, poppet* (*Brit*). e (*: *sucre arrosé*) *sugar lump dipped in brandy or coffee.* **tu veux (prendre) un ~?** would you like a sugar lump dipped in brandy? 2 comp

►**canard de Barbarie** Muscovy *ou* musk duck ►**canard boiteux*** (*fig*) lame duck ►**canard laqué** Peking duck ►**canard mandarin** mandarin duck ►**canard à l'orange** (*Culin*) duck in orange sauce ►**canard sauvage** wild duck ►**canard siffleur** wigeon ►**canard souchet** shoveler.

canardeau, pl ~x [kanaʀdo] nm duckling.

canarder* [kanaʀde] 1 **1** vt (*au fusil*) to snipe at, take potshots at; (*avec des pierres etc*) to pelt (*avec* with). ~ **qn avec des boules de neige** to pelt sb with snowballs; **ça canardait de tous les côtés** there was firing *ou* firing was going on on all sides. **2** vi (*Mus*) to hit a false note.

canardière [kanaʀdjɛʀ] nf (*mare*) duck-pond; (*fusil*) punt gun.

canari [kanaʀi] nm canary. **(jaune)** ~ canary (yellow).

Canaries [kanaʀi] nfpl: **les (îles)** ~ the Canary Islands, the Canaries.

canasson [kanasɔ̃] nm (*péj: cheval*) nag (*péj*).

canasta [kanasta] nf canasta.

Canberra [kɑ̃beʀa] n Canberra.

cancan [kɑ̃kɑ̃] nm **a** (*racontar*) piece of gossip. ~s gossip; **faire courir des ~s (sur qn)** to spread gossip *ou* stories (about sb), tittle-tattle (about sb). **b** (*danse*) cancan.

cancaner [kɑ̃kane] 1 vi **a** (*bavarder*) to gossip; (*médire*) to spread scandal *ou* gossip, tittle-tattle. **b** [*canard*] to quack.

cancanier, -ière [kɑ̃kanje, jɛʀ] **1** adj gossipy, scandalmongering (*épith*), tittle-tattling (*épith*). **2** nm,f gossip, scandalmonger, tittle-tattle.

cancer [kɑ̃sɛʀ] nm **a** (*Méd, fig*) cancer. **avoir un ~ du sein/du poumon** to have breast/lung cancer, have cancer of the breast/lung; ~ **du sang** leukaemia. **b** (*Astron*) **le C~** Cancer; **être (du) C~** to be (a) Cancer *ou* a Cancerian; *voir* **tropique**.

cancéreux, -euse [kɑ̃seʀø, øz] **1** adj *tumeur* cancerous; *personne* with cancer. **2** nm,f person with cancer; (*à l'hôpital*) cancer patient.

cancériforme [kɑ̃seʀifɔʀm] adj cancer-like.

cancérigène [kɑ̃seʀiʒɛn] adj carcinogenic, cancer-producing.

cancérisation [kɑ̃seʀizasjɔ̃] nf: **on peut craindre la ~ de l'organe** there is a risk of the organ becoming cancerous.

cancériser (se) [kɑ̃seʀize] 1 vpr to become cancerous. **cellules cancérisées** cancerous cells.

cancérogène [kɑ̃seʀɔʒɛn] adj = **cancérigène**.

cancérologie [kɑ̃seʀɔlɔʒi] nf cancerology.

cancérologue [kɑ̃seʀɔlɔg] nmf cancerologist.

cancre [kɑ̃kʀ] nm (*péj: élève*) dunce.

cancrelat [kɑ̃kʀəla] nm cockroach.

candélabre [kɑ̃delɑbʀ] nm (*chandelier*) candelabra, candelabrum.

candeur [kɑ̃dœʀ] nf ingenuousness, guilelessness, naïvety.

candi [kɑ̃di] adj m *voir* **sucre**.

candidat, e [kɑ̃dida, at] nm,f [*examen, élection*] candidate (*à* at); [*poste*] applicant, candidate (*à* for). ~ **sortant** present *ou* outgoing incumbent; **les ~s à l'examen** the examination candidates; **être ~ à la députation** ≃ to stand for Parliament (*Brit*), ≃ run for congress (*US*); **être ~ à un poste** to be an applicant *ou* a candidate for a job, have applied for a job; **se porter ~ à un poste** to apply for a job, put o.s. forward for a job; (*Pol*) **être ~ à la présidence** to stand (*Brit*) *ou* run for president, run for the presidency; (*fig*) **les ~s à la retraite** candidates for retirement.

candidature [kɑ̃didatyʀ] nf (*Pol*) candidature, candidacy (*US*); [*poste*] application (*à* for). ~ **officielle** [*poste*] formal application; (*Pol*) official candidature *ou* candidacy (*US*); ~ **spontanée** [*poste*] (*action*) unsolicited application; (*lettre*) unsolicited letter of application; **poser sa ~ à un poste** to apply for a job, submit one's application for a job; **poser sa ~ à une élection** to stand in *ou* at (*Brit*) an election, put o.s. forward as a candidate in an election, run for election (*US*).

candide [kɑ̃did] adj ingenuous, guileless, naïve.

candidement [kɑ̃didmɑ̃] adv ingenuously, guilelessly, naïvely.

candir [kɑ̃diʀ] 2 vi: **faire ~** to candy.

cane [kan] nf (female) duck.

caner‡ [kane] 1 vi (*mourir*) to kick the bucket‡, snuff it‡; (*flancher*) to chicken out‡, funk it‡ (*devant* in the face of).

caneton [kantɔ̃] nm duckling.

canette[1] [kanɛt] nf duckling.

canette[2] [kanɛt] nf [*machine à coudre*] spool. ~ **(de bière)** small bottle of beer.

canevas [kanvɑ] nm **a** [*livre, discours*] framework, basic structure. **b** (*Couture*) (*toile*) canvas; (*ouvrage*) tapestry (work). **c** (*Cartographie*) network.

caniche [kaniʃ] nm poodle. ~ **nain** toy poodle.

caniculaire [kanikylɛʀ] adj *chaleur, jour* scorching. **une journée ~** a scorcher*, a scorching (hot) day.

canicule [kanikyl] nf (*forte chaleur*) scorching heat. **une ~ qui dure depuis 3 jours** a heatwave which has been going on for 3 days; (*spécialement juillet-août*) **la ~** the midsummer heat, the dog days; **cette ~ précoce** this early (summer) heatwave; **aujourd'hui c'est la ~** today is *ou* today it is a scorcher*.

canif [kanif] nm penknife, pocket knife. (*fig*) **donner un coup de ~ dans le contrat de mariage*** to have a bit on the side*.

canin, e [kanɛ̃, in] **1** adj *espèce* canine; *exposition* dog (*épith*). **2 canine** nf (*dent*) canine (tooth); (*supérieure*) eyetooth.

caninette [kaninɛt] nf pooper-scooper motor bike*; *motor bike used to clean streets of dogs' dirt.*

canisses [kanis] nfpl (type of) wattle fence.

caniveau, pl ~x [kanivo] nm gutter (*in roadway etc*).

canna [kana] nm (*fleur*) canna.

cannabis [kanabis] nm cannabis.

cannage [kanaʒ] nm (*partie cannée*) canework; (*opération*) caning.

canne [kan] **1** nf (*bâton*) (walking) stick, cane; [*souffleur de verre*] rod; (*:*jambe*) leg. ~s pins‡; **il ne tient pas sur ses ~s** he's not very steady on his pins‡; *voir* **sucre**. **2** comp ►**canne blanche** [*aveugle*] white stick ►**canne-épée** nf (pl **cannes-épées**) swordstick ►**canne à pêche** fishing rod ►**canne à sucre** sugar cane.

canné, e [kane] (*ptp de* **canner**) adj *siège* cane (*épith*).

cannelé, e [kanle] (*ptp de* **canneler**) adj *colonne* fluted.

canneler [kanle] 4 vt to flute.

cannelier [kanəlje] nm cinnamon tree.

cannelle [kanɛl] nf (*Culin*) cinnamon; (*robinet*) tap, spigot.

cannelure [kan(ə)lyʀ] nf [*meuble, colonne*] flute; [*plante*] striation. ~s [*colonne*] fluting; [*neige*] corrugation; (*Géol*) ~**s glaciaires** striae, striations.

canner [kane] 1 vt *chaise* to cane.

cannette [kanɛt] nf = **canette**[2].

canneur, -euse [kanœʀ, øz] nm,f cane worker, caner.

cannibale [kanibal] **1** adj *tribu, animal* cannibal (*épith*), canibalistic. **2** nmf cannibal, man-eater.

cannibalisation [kanibalizasjɔ̃] nf [*machine*] cannibalization; (*Comm*) [*produit*] cannibalization (*US*).

cannibaliser [kanibalize] 1 vt *machine* to cannibalize; (*Comm*) *produit* to eat into the market share of, cannibalize (*US*). **ce produit a été cannibalisé par ...** this product has lost (some of its) market share to ... .

cannibalisme [kanibalism] nm cannibalism.

cannisses [kanis] nfpl = **canisses**.

canoë [kanɔe] nm (*bateau*) canoe; (*sport*) canoeing. **faire du ~(-kayak)** to go canoeing, canoe.

canoéisme [kanɔeism] nm canoeing.

canoéiste [kanɔeist] nmf canoeist.

canon[1] [kanɔ̃] **1** nm **a** (*arme*) gun; (*Hist*) cannon. ~ **de 75/125** 75/125-mm gun; **coup de ~** (*moderne*) artillery shot; (*Hist*) cannon shot; **des coups de ~** (*moderne*) artillery fire; (*Hist*) cannon fire; (*Sport*) **service/tir ~*** bullet-like serve/shot; *voir* **chair**.

b (*tube*) [*fusil, revolver*] barrel. **fusil à ~ scié** sawn-off (*Brit*) *ou* sawed-off (*US*) shotgun; **à deux ~s** double-barrelled; *voir* **baïonnette**.

c (*Tech*) [*clef, seringue*] barrel; [*arrosoir*] spout.

d (*Vét*) [*bœuf, cheval*] cannonbone.

e (*Hist Habillement*) canion.

f (*: *verre*) glass (of wine).

2 comp ►**canon à eau** water cannon ►**canon anti-aérien** (*Mil*) anti-aircraft *ou* A.A. gun ►**canon anti-char** (*Mil*) anti-tank gun ►**canon anti-grêle** anti-hail gun ►**canon à électrons** (*Phys*) electron gun ►**canon lisse** smooth *ou* unrifled bore ►**canon de marine** naval gun ►**canon à neige** snow cannon ►**canon rayé** rifled bore.

canon[2] [kanɔ̃] nm **a** (*norme, modèle*) model, perfect example. (*normes, code*) ~s canons; **les ~s de la beauté** aesthetic values; **elle est ~*, c'est un ~*** *ou* **une fille ~*** she is a (real) peach (of a girl)‡. **b** (*Rel*) (*loi*) canon; [*messe, Nouveau Testament*] canon; *voir* **droit**[3].

canon[3] [kanɔ̃] nm (*Mus*) ~ **à 2 voix** canon for 2 voices; **chanter en ~** to sing in a round *ou* in canon.

cañon [kaɲɔ̃, kaɲɔn] nm canyon, cañon.

canonique [kanɔnik] adj canonical; *voir* **âge**.

canonisation [kanɔnizasjɔ̃] nf canonization.

canoniser [kanɔnize] 1 vt to canonize.

canonnade [kanɔnad] nf cannonade. **le bruit d'une ~** the noise of a cannonade *ou* of (heavy) gunfire.

canonner [kanɔne] 1 vt to bombard, shell.

canonnier [kanɔnje] nm gunner.

canonnière [kanɔnjɛʀ] nf gunboat.

canot [kano] nm (*barque*) (small *ou* open) boat, dinghy; (*Can*) Canadian canoe. ~ **automobile** motorboat; ~ **de pêche** (open) fishing boat; ~ **pneumatique** rubber *ou* inflatable ding(h)y; ~ **de sauvetage** lifeboat.

canotage [kanɔtaʒ] nm boating, rowing; (*Can*) canoeing. **faire du ~** to go boating *ou* rowing; (*Can*) to go canoeing.

canoter [kanɔte] 1 vi to go boating *ou* rowing *ou* (*Can*) canoeing.

canoteur [kanɔtœʀ] nm rower.

canotier [kanɔtje] nm (*chapeau*) boater.

cantabrique [kɑ̃tabʀik] adj: **les monts ~s** the Cantabrian Mountains, the Cantabrians.

cantaloup [kɑ̃talu] nm cantaloup, muskmelon.

cantate [kɑ̃tat] nf cantata.

cantatrice [kɑ̃tatʀis] nf [*opéra*] (opera) singer, prima donna; [*chants classiques*] (professional) singer.

cantilène [kɑ̃tilɛn] **nf** song, cantilena.
cantine [kɑ̃tin] **nf** a (*réfectoire*) *[usine]* canteen; *[école]* dining hall (*Brit*), cafeteria; (*service*) school meals *ou* dinners. **manger à la ~** to eat in the canteen; to have school meals. b (*malle*) tin trunk.
cantinière [kɑ̃tinjɛʀ] **nf** (*Hist Mil*) canteen woman.
cantique [kɑ̃tik] **nm** (*chant*) hymn; *[Bible]* canticle. **le ~ des ~s** the Song of Songs, the Song of Solomon.
canton [kɑ̃tɔ̃] **nm** a (*Pol*) (*en France*) canton, ≃ district; (*en Suisse*) canton. b (*section*) *[voie ferrée, route]* section. c (†: *région*) district; (*Can*) township.
cantonade [kɑ̃tɔnad] **nf**: **parler à la ~** (*gén*) to speak to no one in particular *ou* to everyone in general; (*Théât*) to speak (an aside) to the audience; **c'est à qui? dit-elle à la ~** whose is this? she asked the assembled company.
cantonais, e [kɑ̃tɔnɛ, ɛz] 1 **adj** Cantonese. 2 **nm** (*Ling*) Cantonese. 3 **nm,f**: **C~(e)** Cantonese.
cantonal, e, **mpl -aux** [kɑ̃tɔnal, o] **adj** (*en France*) cantonal, ≃ district (*épith*); (*en Suisse*) cantonal. **sur le plan ~** (*en France*) at (the) local level; (*en Suisse*) at the level of the cantons; **les (élections) ~es** cantonal elections.
cantonnement [kɑ̃tɔnmɑ̃] **nm** (*voir* **cantonner**) (*Mil*) (*action*) stationing; billeting, quartering; (*lieu*) quarters (*pl*), billet; (*camp*) camp. **établir un ~ en pleine nature** to set up (a) camp in the wilds.
cantonner [kɑ̃tɔne] [1] 1 **vt** (*Mil*) to station; (*chez l'habitant etc*) to quarter, billet (*chez, dans* on). (*fig*) **~ qn dans un travail** to confine sb to a job. 2 **vi** (*Mil*) *[troupe]* to be quartered *ou* billetted; be stationed (*à, dans* at). 3 **se cantonner vpr** (*se limiter*) **se ~ à** *ou* **dans** to confine o.s. to.
cantonnier [kɑ̃tɔnje] **nm** (*ouvrier*) roadmender, roadman.
cantonnière [kɑ̃tɔnjɛʀ] **nf** (*tenture*) pelmet.
canular [kanylaʀ] **nm** (*farce, mystification*) hoax. **monter un ~** to think up *ou* plan a hoax; **faire un ~ à qn** to hoax sb, play a hoax on sb.
canule [kanyl] **nf** cannula.
canuler‡ [kanyle] [1] **vt** (*ennuyer*) to bore; (*agacer*) to pester.
canut, -use [kany, yz] **nm,f** (*f rare*) silk worker (*at Lyons*).
Canut [kanyt] **nm** Canute, Knut.
CAO [seao] **nf** (**abrév de conception assistée par ordinateur**) **CAD**.
caoua* [kawa] **nm** = **kawa***.
caoutchouc [kautʃu] **nm** a (*matière*) rubber. **en ~** rubber (*épith*); ® **~ mousse** foam *ou* sponge rubber; **une balle en ~ mousse** a rubber *ou* sponge ball; *voir* **botte¹**. b (*élastique*) rubber *ou* elastic band. c (†) (*imperméable*) waterproof. (*chaussures*) **~s** overshoes, galoshes. d (*plante verte*) rubber plant.
caoutchouter [kautʃute] [1] **vt** to rubberize, coat with rubber.
caoutchouteux, -euse [kautʃutø, øz] **adj** rubbery.
CAP [seape] **nm** (**abrév de certificat d'aptitude professionnelle**) vocational training certificate, ≃ City and Guilds examination (*Brit*). **il a un ~ de menuisier/soudeur** he's a qualified joiner/welder, ≃ he's got a City and Guilds in joinery/welding (*Brit*).
cap [kap] 1 **nm** a (*Géog*) cape; (*promontoire*) point, headland. **le ~ Canaveral** Cape Canaveral; **le ~ Horn** Cape Horn; **le ~ de Bonne Espérance** the Cape of Good Hope; **les îles du C~ Vert** the Cape Verde Islands; (*Naut*) **passer** *ou* **doubler un ~** to round a cape; *[malade etc]* **il a passé le ~** he's over the hump *ou* the worst, he's turned the corner; **il a passé le ~ de l'examen** he has got over the hurdle of the exam; **dépasser** *ou* **franchir** *ou* **passer le ~ des 40 ans** to turn 40; **dépasser** *ou* **franchir le ~ des 50 millions** to pass the 50-million mark.
b (*direction*) (*lit, fig*) **changer de ~** to change course; (*Naut*) **mettre le ~ au vent** to head into the wind; **mettre le ~ au large** to stand out to sea; (*Aut, Naut*) **mettre le ~ sur** to head for, steer for; *voir* **pied**.
c (*ville*) **Le C~** Cape Town; **la province du C~** the Cape Province.
2 **comp ►cap-hornier nm** (**pl cap-horniers**) Cape Horner.
capable [kapabl] **adj** a (*compétent*) able, capable.
b (*apte à*) **~ de faire** capable of doing; **te sens-tu ~ de tout manger?** do you feel you can eat it all?, do you feel up to eating it all?; **tu n'en es pas ~** you're not up to it, you're not capable of it; **viens te battre si tu en es ~** come and fight if you've got it in you *ou* if you dare; **cette conférence est ~ d'intéresser beaucoup de gens** this lecture is liable to interest *ou* likely to interest a lot of people.
c (*qui peut faire preuve de*) **~ de** *dévouement, courage, éclat, incartade* capable of; **il est ~ du pire comme du meilleur** he's capable of (doing) the worst as well as the best; **il est ~ de tout** he'll stop at nothing, he's capable of anything.
d (*) **il est ~ de l'avoir perdu/de réussir** he's quite likely to have lost it/to succeed, he's quite capable of having lost it/of succeeding; **il est bien ~ d'en réchapper** he may well get over it.
e (*Jur*) competent.
capacité [kapasite] 1 **nf** a (*contenance, potentiel*) capacity; (*Élec*) *[accumulateur]* capacitance, capacity. (*Tourisme*) **la ~ d'accueil d'une ville** the total amount of tourist accommodation in a town.
b (*aptitude*) ability (*à* to). **d'une très grande ~** of very great ability; **~s intellectuelles** intellectual abilities *ou* capacities; **en-dehors de mes ~s** beyond my capabilities *ou* capacities; **sa ~ d'analyse/ d'analyser les faits** his capacity for analysis/analysing facts.
c (*Jur*) capacity. **avoir ~ pour** to be (legally) entitled to.
2 **comp ►capacité civile** (*Jur*) civil capacity **►capacité contributive** ability to pay tax **►capacité en droit** *basic legal qualification* **►capacité électrostatique** capacitance **►capacité légale** legal capacity **►capacité thoracique** (*Méd*) vital capacity.
caparaçon [kapaʀasɔ̃] **nm** (*Hist*) caparison.
caparaçonner [kapaʀasɔne] [1] **vt** (*Hist*) *cheval* to caparison. (*fig hum*) **caparaçonné de cuir** all clad in leather.
cape [kap] **nf** (*Habillement*) (*courte*) cape; (*longue*) cloak. **roman/film de ~ et d'épée** cloak and dagger novel/film; *voir* **rire**.
capeline [kaplin] **nf** wide-brimmed hat.
CAPES [kapɛs] **nm** (**abrév de certificat d'aptitude au professorat de l'enseignement de second degré**) *voir* **certificat**.
capésien, -ienne [kapesjɛ̃, jɛn] **nm,f** student preparing the CAPES; holder of the CAPES, ≃ qualified graduate teacher.
CAPET [kapɛt] **nm** (**abrév de certificat d'aptitude au professorat de l'enseignement technique**) *voir* **certificat**.
capétien, -ienne [kapesjɛ̃, jɛn] **adj, nm,f** Capetian.
Capharnaüm [kafaʀnaɔm] **n** Capernaum.
capharnaüm* [kafaʀnaɔm] **nm** (*bric-à-brac, désordre*) shambles* (*NonC*), pigsty. **quel ~ dans le grenier** what a pigsty the attic is, what a shambles in the attic.
capillaire [kapilɛʀ] 1 **adj** (*Anat, Bot, Phys*) capillary; *soins, lotion* hair (*épith*); *voir* **artiste, vaisseau**. 2 **nm** (*Anat*) capillary; (*Bot: fougère*) maidenhair fern.
capillarité [kapilaʀite] **nf** capillarity.
capilliculteur [kapilikyltœʀ] **nm** specialist in hair care.
capilotade [kapilɔtad] **nf**: **en ~** *gâteau* in crumbs; *fruits, visage* in a pulp; *objet cassable* in smithereens; **mettre en ~** (*écraser*) *gâteau* to squash to bits; *fruits* to squash to a pulp; *adversaire* to beat to a pulp; (*casser*) to smash to smithereens; **il avait les reins/les jambes en ~** his back was/his legs were aching like hell‡ *ou* giving him hell‡.
capitaine [kapitɛn] 1 **nm** (*Mil*) (*armée de terre*) captain; (*armée de l'air*) flight lieutenant (*Brit*), captain (*US*); (*Naut*) *[grand bateau]* captain, master; *[bateau de pêche etc]* captain, skipper; (*Sport*) captain, skipper*; (*littér: chef militaire*) (military) leader; *voir* **instructeur, mon**.
2 **comp ►capitaine de corvette** lieutenant commander **►capitaine de frégate** commander **►capitaine de gendarmerie** captain of the gendarmerie **►capitaine d'industrie** captain of industry **►capitaine au long cours** master mariner **►capitaine de la marine marchande** captain in the merchant navy (*Brit*) *ou* in the marine (*US*) **►capitaine des pompiers** fire chief, firemaster (*Brit*), marshall (*US*) **►capitaine de port** harbour master **►capitaine de vaisseau** captain.
capitainerie [kapitɛnʀi] **nf** harbour master's office.
capital, e, **mpl -aux** [kapital, o] 1 **adj** a (*fondamental*) *œuvre* major (*épith*), main (*épith*); *point, erreur, question* major (*épith*), chief (*épith*), fundamental; *rôle* cardinal, major (*épith*), fundamental; *importance* cardinal (*épith*), capital (*épith*). **d'une importance ~e** of cardinal *ou* capital importance; **lettre ~e** *voir* **3**; *voir* **péché, sept**.
b (*principal*) major, main. **c'est l'œuvre ~e de X** it is X's major work; **son erreur ~e est d'avoir ...** his major *ou* chief mistake was to have ... .
c (*essentiel*) **c'est ~** it's essential; **il est ~ d'y aller** *ou* **que nous y allions** it is of paramount *ou* the utmost importance *ou* it is absolutely essential that we go there.
d (*Jur*) capital; *voir* **peine**.
2 **nm** a (*Fin: avoirs*) capital. **50 millions de francs de ~** a 50-million-franc capital, a capital of 50 million francs; **au ~ de** with a capital of; *voir* **augmentation**.
b (*placements*) **~aux** money, capital; **investir des ~aux dans une affaire** to invest money *ou* capital in a business; **la circulation/fuite des ~aux** the circulation/flight of money *ou* capital.
c (*possédants*) **le ~** capital; **le ~ et le travail** capital and labour; *voir* **grand**.
d (*fig: fonds, richesse*) stock, fund. **le ~ de connaissances acquis à l'école** the stock *ou* fund of knowledge acquired at school; **la connaissance d'une langue constitue un ~ appréciable** knowing a language is a significant *ou* major asset; **le ~ artistique du pays** the artistic wealth *ou* resources of the country; **accroître son ~-santé** to build up one's reserves of health.
3 **capitale nf** a (*Typ*) **(lettre) ~e** capital (letter); **en grandes/ petites ~es** in large/small capitals; **en ~es d'imprimerie** in block letters *ou* block capitals.
b (*métropole*) capital (city). **Paris est la ~e de la France** Paris is the capital (city) of France; **le dimanche, les Parisiens quittent la ~e** on Sundays Parisians leave the capital; **grande/petite ~e régionale** large/ small regional capital; (*fig*) **la ~e du vin/de la soie** the capital of winegrowing/of the silk industry.
4 **comp ►capital circulant** working capital, circulating capital **►capital constant** constant capital **►capital d'exploitation** working capital **►capitaux fébriles** hot money **►capital fixe** fixed (capital) assets **►capitaux flottants** = **capitaux fébriles ►capital initial** *ou* **de**

lancement seed *ou* start-up money ►**capital-risque** venture capital ►**capital social** authorized capital, share capital ►**capitaux spéculatifs** = **capitaux fébriles** ►**capital variable** variable capital.

capitalisable [kapitalizabl] adj capitalizable.

capitalisation [kapitalizasjɔ̃] nf capitalization. ~ **boursière** market capitalization *ou* valuation.

capitaliser [kapitalize] 1 1 vt a (*amasser*) *somme* to amass; (*fig*) *expériences, connaissances* to build up, accumulate. **l'intérêt capitalisé pendant un an** interest accrued *ou* accumulated in a year. b (*Fin: ajouter au capital*) *intérêts* to capitalize. c (*calculer le capital de*) *rente* to capitalize. 2 vi to save, put money by.

capitalisme [kapitalism] nm capitalism.

capitaliste [kapitalist] adj, nmf capitalist.

capitation [kapitasjɔ̃] nf (*Hist*) poll tax, capitation.

capiteux, -euse [kapitø, øz] adj *vin, parfum* heady; *femme, beauté* intoxicating, alluring.

Capitole [kapitɔl] nm: **le** ~ the Capitole.

capiton [kapitɔ̃] nm (*bourre*) padding; *[cellulite]* node of fat (*SPÉC*). **les** ~**s** the orange peel effect.

capitonnage [kapitɔnaʒ] nm padding.

capitonner [kapitɔne] 1 vt *siège, porte* to pad (*de* with). (*fig*) **capitonné de** lined with; **nid capitonné de plumes** feather-lined nest.

capitulaire [kapitylɛʀ] adj (*Rel*) capitular. **salle** ~ chapter house.

capitulard, e [kapitylaʀ, aʀd] (*péj*) 1 adj (*Mil*) partisan of surrender; (*fig*) defeatist. 2 nm,f (*Mil*) advocate of surrender; (*fig*) defeatist.

capitulation [kapitylasjɔ̃] nf (*Mil*) (*reddition*) capitulation, surrender; (*traité*) capitulation (treaty); (*fig: défaite, abandon*) capitulation, surrender. ~ **sans conditions** unconditional surrender.

capituler [kapityle] 1 vi (*Mil: se rendre*) to capitulate, surrender; (*fig: céder*) to surrender, give in, capitulate.

capon, -onne†† [kapɔ̃, ɔn] 1 adj cowardly. 2 nm,f coward.

caporal, pl **-aux** [kapɔʀal, o] nm a (*Mil*) corporal. ~ **d'ordinaire** *ou* **de cuisine** mess corporal; ~**-chef** corporal. b (*tabac*) caporal.

caporalisme [kapɔʀalism] nm *[personne, régime]* petty officiousness.

capot [kapo] 1 nm a *[véhicule, moteur]* bonnet (*Brit*), hood (*US*). b (*Naut*) (*bâche de protection*) cover; (*trou d'homme*) companion hatch. 2 adj inv (*Cartes*) **être** ~ to have lost all the tricks; **il nous a mis** ~ he took all the tricks.

capotage [kapɔtaʒ] nm *[avion, véhicule]* overturning.

capote [kapɔt] nf a *[voiture]* hood (*Brit*), top. b (*gén Mil: manteau*) greatcoat. c (*‡*) ~ **(anglaise)** French letter‡ (*Brit*), rubber‡, safe‡ (*US*). d (*†: chapeau*) bonnet.

capoter [kapɔte] 1 1 vi *[véhicule]* to overturn; *[négociations]* to founder. **faire** ~ *véhicule* to overturn; *negociations, projet* to scupper*, put paid to. 2 vt (*Aut*) (*garnir d'une capote*) to fit with a hood (*Brit*) *ou* top.

cappuccino [kaputʃino] nm cappuccino.

câpre [kɑpʀ] nf (*Culin*) caper.

Capri [kapʀi] nf Capri.

caprice [kapʀis] nm a (*lubie*) whim, caprice; (*toquade amoureuse*) (passing) fancy. **agir par** ~ to act out of capriciousness; **ne lui cède pas, c'est seulement un** ~ don't give in to him, it's only a whim; **faire un** ~ to throw a tantrum; **cet enfant fait des** ~**s** this child is being awkward *ou* temperamental; **cet arbre est un vrai** ~ **de la nature** this tree is a real freak of nature; **une récolte exceptionnelle due à quelque** ~ **de la nature** an exceptional crop due to some quirk *ou* trick of nature.

b (*variations*) ~**s** (*littér*) *[nuages, vent]* caprices, fickle play; *[chemin]* wanderings, windings; **les** ~**s de la mode** the vagaries *ou* whims of fashion; **les** ~**s du sort** *ou* **du hasard** the quirks of fate.

capricieusement [kapʀisjøzmɑ̃] adv capriciously, whimsically.

capricieux, -ieuse [kapʀisjø, jøz] adj a (*fantasque*) (*gén*) capricious, whimsical; *appareil* temperamental; (*littér*) *brise* capricious; *chemin* winding. b (*coléreux*) wayward. **cet enfant est (un)** ~ this child is awkward *ou* temperamental, this child throws tantrums.

capricorne [kapʀikɔʀn] nm a (*Astron*) **le C**~ Capricorn; **être (du) C**~ to be (a) Capricorn; *voir* **tropique.** b (*Zool*) capricorn beetle.

câprier [kɑpʀije] nm caper bush *ou* shrub.

caprin, e [kapʀɛ̃, in] adj (*Zool*) *espèce* goat (*épith*), caprine (*SPÉC*); *allure* goat-like.

capsulage [kapsylaʒ] nm capsuling.

capsule [kapsyl] nf a (*Anat, Bot, Pharm*) capsule. ~ **spatiale** space capsule. b *[bouteille]* capsule, cap. c *[arme à feu]* (percussion) cap, primer; *[pistolet d'enfant]* cap; *voir* **pistolet.**

capsuler [kapsyle] 1 vt to put a capsule *ou* cap on.

captage [kaptaʒ] nm *[cours d'eau]* harnessing; *[message,émission]* picking up.

captateur, -trice [kaptatœʀ, tʀis] nm,f (*Jur*) ~ **de testament** *ou* **de succession** legacy hunter.

captation [kaptasjɔ̃] nf (*Jur*) improper sollicitation of a legacy.

capter [kapte] 1 vt a *suffrages, attention* to win, capture; *confiance, faveur, bienveillance* to win, gain. b (*Téléc*) *message, émission* to pick up. c *source, cours d'eau* to harness. d (*Élec*) *courant* to tap.

capteur [kaptœʀ] nm sensor. ~ **solaire** solar panel.

captieusement [kapsjøzmɑ̃] adv (*littér*) speciously.

captieux, -ieuse [kapsjø, jøz] adj specious.

captif, -ive [kaptif, iv] 1 adj *soldat, personne, marché, clientèle* captive; (*Géol*) *nappe d'eau* confined; *voir* **ballon.** 2 nm,f (*lit, fig*) captive, prisoner.

captivant, e [kaptivɑ̃, ɑ̃t] adj *film, lecture* gripping, enthralling, captivating; *personne* fascinating, captivating.

captiver [kaptive] 1 vt *personne* to fascinate, enthrall, captivate; *attention, esprit* to captivate.

captivité [kaptivite] nf captivity. **en** ~ in captivity.

capture [kaptyʀ] nf a (*action: voir* **capturer**) catching; capture. b (*animal*) catch; (*personne*) capture.

capturer [kaptyʀe] 1 vt *malfaiteur, animal* to catch, capture; *navire* to capture.

capuche [kapyʃ] nf hood.

capuchette [kapyʃɛt] nf rainhood.

capuchon [kapyʃɔ̃] nm a (*Couture*) hood; (*Rel*) cowl; (*pèlerine*) hooded raincoat. b *[stylo]* top, cap. c *[cheminée]* cowl.

capucin [kapysɛ̃] nm (*Rel*) Capuchin; (*Zool: singe*) capuchin; *voir* **barbe**[1].

capucine [kapysin] nf (*Bot*) nasturtium; (*Rel*) Capuchin nun.

cap-verdien, -ienne [kapvɛʀdjɛ̃, jɛn] 1 adj Cape Verdean. 2 nm,f: **C~(ne)** Cape Verdean.

caque [kak] nf herring barrel. (*Prov*) **la** ~ **sent toujours le hareng** what's bred in the bone will (come) out in the flesh (*Prov*).

caquelon [kaklɔ̃] nm earthenware *ou* cast-iron fondue-dish.

caquet [kakɛ] nm (*) *[personne]* blether* (*Brit*), gossip, prattle; *[poule]* cackle, cackling. **rabattre** *ou* **rabaisser le** ~ **de** *ou* **à qn*** to bring *ou* pull sb down a peg or two.

caquetage [kaktaʒ] nm (*voir* **caqueter**) cackle, cackling, blether* (*Brit*).

caqueter [kakte] 4 vi *[personne]* to gossip, prattle, blether* (*Brit*); *[poule]* to cackle.

car[1] [kaʀ] nm coach (*Brit*), bus (*US*). ~ **de police** police van; ~ **de (radio)reportage** outside-broadcasting van; ~ **(de ramassage) scolaire** school bus.

car[2] [kaʀ] conj because, for.

carabin [kaʀabɛ̃] nm (*arg Méd*) medical student, medic*.

carabine [kaʀabin] nf rifle, gun, carbine (*SPÉC*); *[stand de tir]* rifle. ~ **à air comprimé** air rifle *ou* gun.

carabiné, e* [kaʀabine] adj *fièvre, vent, orage* raging, violent; *cocktail, facture, punition* stiff. **amende** ~**e** heavy *ou* stiff fine; **rhume** ~ stinking‡ *ou* shocking* cold; **mal de tête** ~ splitting *ou* blinding headache; **mal de dents** ~ raging *ou* screaming* (*Brit*) toothache.

carabinier [kaʀabinje] nm (*en Espagne*) carabinero, customs officer; (*en Italie*) carabinieri, police officer; (*Hist Mil*) carabineer.

carabosse [kaʀabɔs] nf *voir* **fée.**

Caracas [kaʀakas] n Caracas.

caraco [kaʀako] nm (*†: chemisier*) (woman's) loose blouse; (*sous-vêtement*) camisole.

caracoler [kaʀakɔle] 1 vi *[cheval]* to caracole, prance; *[cavalier]* to caracole; (*fig: gambader*) to gambol *ou* caper about.

caractère [kaʀaktɛʀ] nm a (*tempérament*) character, nature. **être d'un** *ou* **avoir un** ~ **ouvert/fermé** to have an outgoing/withdrawn nature; **être d'un** *ou* **avoir un** ~ **froid/passionné** to be a cold(-natured)/passionate(-natured) person; **avoir bon/mauvais** ~ to be good-/ill-natured, be good-/bad-tempered; **il est très jeune de** ~ *[adolescent]* he's very immature; *[adulte]* he has a very youthful outlook; **son** ~ **a changé** his character has changed; **les chats ont un** ~ **sournois** cats have a sly nature; **il a** *ou* **c'est un heureux** ~ he has a happy nature; **ce n'est pas dans son** ~ **de faire, il n'a pas un** ~ **à faire** it is not in his nature to do, it is not like him to do; **le** ~ **méditerranéen/latin** the Mediterranean/Latin character; **il a un sale** ~* he is a difficult *ou* pig-headed* customer; **il a un** ~ **de cochon*** he is an awkward *ou* a cussed* so-and-so*; **il a un** ~ **en or** he's very good-natured, he has a delightful nature.

b (*nature, aspect*) nature. **sa présence confère à la réception un** ~ **officiel** his being here gives an official character *ou* flavour to the reception; **la situation n'a aucun** ~ **de gravité** the situation shows no sign *ou* evidence of seriousness; **le** ~ **difficile de cette mission est évident** the difficult nature of this mission is quite clear; **le récit a le** ~ **d'un plaidoyer** the story is (in the nature of) a passionate plea.

c (*fermeté*) character. **il a du** ~ he has *ou* he's got* character; **il n'a pas de** ~ he has no character *ou* spirit *ou* backbone; **un style sans** ~ a characterless style.

d (*cachet, individualité*) character. **la maison/cette vieille rue a du** ~ the house/this old street has (got) character.

e (*littér: personne*) character. **ces** ~**s ne sont pas faciles à vivre** these characters are not easy to live with; *voir* **comique.**

f (*gén pl: caractéristique*) characteristic, feature; *[personne]* trait. ~**s nationaux/d'une race** national/racial characteristics *ou* features *ou* traits; ~ **héréditaire/acquis** hereditary/acquired characteristic *ou* feature.

g (*Écriture, Typ*) character. ~ **gras/maigre** heavy-/light-faced letter;

(*Typ*) ~**s gras** bold type (*NonC*); **écrire en gros/petits ~s** to write in large/small characters; **écrivez en ~s d'imprimerie** write in block capitals; **les ~s de ce livre sont agréables à l'œil** the print of this book is easy on the eye.

caractériel, -elle [kaʀaktɛʀjɛl] 1 adj a *enfant* emotionally disturbed, maladjusted. b **traits ~s** traits of character; **troubles ~s** emotional disturbance *ou* problems. 2 nm,f problem *ou* maladjusted child.

caractérisation [kaʀakteʀizasjɔ̃] nf characterization.

caractérisé, e [kaʀakteʀize] (ptp de **caractériser**) adj *erreur* blatant. **une rubéole ~e** a clear *ou* straightforward case of German measles; **c'est de l'insubordination ~e** it's sheer *ou* downright insubordination.

caractériser [kaʀakteʀize] 1 vt (*être typique de*) to characterize, be characteristic of; (*décrire*) to characterize. **avec l'enthousiasme qui le caractérise** with his characteristic enthusiasm; **ça se caractérise par** it is characterized *ou* distinguished by; **l'art de ~ un paysage** the knack of picking out the main features of a landscape; **ce qui caractérise ce paysage** the main *ou* characteristic features of this landscape.

caractéristique [kaʀakteʀistik] 1 adj characteristic (*de* of). 2 nf characteristic, (typical) feature. (*Admin*) ~**s signalétiques** particulars, personal details; ~**s techniques** design features.

caractérologie [kaʀakteʀɔlɔʒi] nf characterology.

carafe [kaʀaf] nf decanter; *[eau, vin ordinaire]* carafe; (*: *tête*) head, nut*. **tomber en ~*** to break down; **rester en ~*** to be left stranded, be left high and dry.

carafon [kaʀafɔ̃] nm (*voir* **carafe**) small decanter; small carafe; (*: *tête*) head, nut*.

caraïbe [kaʀaib] adj Caribbean. **les C~s** the Caribbean.

carambolage [kaʀɑ̃bɔlaʒ] nm *[autos]* multiple crash, pile-up; (*Billard*) cannon.

carambole [kaʀɑ̃bɔl] nf a (*Billard*) red (ball). b (*fruit*) star fruit, carambola.

caramboler [kaʀɑ̃bɔle] 1 1 vt to collide with, go *ou* cannon into. **5 voitures se sont carambolées** there was a pile-up of 5 cars, 5 cars ran into each other *ou* collided. 2 vi (*Billard*) to cannon, get *ou* make a cannon.

carambouillage [kaʀɑ̃bujaʒ] nm, **carambouille** [kaʀɑ̃buj] nf (*Jur*) reselling of unlawfully owned goods.

caramel [kaʀamɛl] 1 nm (*sucre fondu*) caramel; (*bonbon*) (*mou*) caramel, fudge, chewy toffee; (*dur*) toffee. 2 adj inv caramel(-coloured).

caramélisation [kaʀamelizasjɔ̃] nf caramelization.

caraméliser [kaʀamelize] 1 1 vt *sucre* to caramelize; *moule, pâtisserie* to coat with caramel; *boisson, aliment* to flavour with caramel. 2 vi, **se caraméliser** vpr *[sucre]* to caramelize.

carapace [kaʀapas] nf *[crabe, tortue]* shell, carapace. **~ de boue** crust of mud; **sommet recouvert d'une ~ de glace** summit encased in a sheath of ice; **il est difficile de percer sa ~ d'égoïsme** it's difficult to penetrate the armour of his egoism *ou* his thickskinned self-centredness.

carapater (se)* [kaʀapate] 1 vpr to skedaddle*, hop it*, run off.

carat [kaʀa] nm carat. **or à 18 ~s** 18-carat gold; *voir* **dernier**.

Caravage [kaʀavaʒ] nm: **le ~** Caravaggio.

caravane [kaʀavan] nf (*convoi*) caravan; (*véhicule*) caravan, trailer (*US*). **une ~ de voitures** a procession *ou* stream of cars; **une ~ de touristes** a stream of tourists; **la ~ du Tour de France** the whole retinue of the Tour de France; *voir* **chien**.

caravanier, -ière [kaʀavanje, jɛʀ] 1 adj *itinéraire, chemin* caravan (*épith*). **tourisme ~** caravanning. 2 nm a (*conducteur de caravane*) caravaneer. b (*vacancier*) caravanner.

caravaning [kaʀavaniŋ] nm (*mode de déplacement*) caravanning; (*emplacement*) caravan site.

caravansérail [kaʀavɑ̃seʀaj] nm (*lit, fig*) caravanserai.

caravelle [kaʀavɛl] nf (*Hist Naut*) caravel. (*Aviat*) ® **C~** Caravelle.

carbochimie [kaʀbɔʃimi] nf organic chemistry.

carbonate [kaʀbɔnat] nm carbonate. **~ de soude** sodium carbonate, washing soda.

carbone [kaʀbɔn] nm (*matière, feuille*) carbon. **le ~ 14** carbon-14; **(papier) ~** carbon (paper); *voir* **datation**.

carbonifère [kaʀbɔnifɛʀ] 1 adj (*Minér*) carboniferous; (*Géol*) Carboniferous. 2 nm Carboniferous.

carbonique [kaʀbɔnik] adj carbonic; *voir* **gaz, neige** *etc.*

carbonisation [kaʀbɔnizasjɔ̃] nf carbonization.

carbonisé, e [kaʀbɔnize] (ptp de **carboniser**) adj *arbre, restes* charred. **il est mort ~** he was burned to death.

carboniser [kaʀbɔnize] 1 vt *bois, substance* to carbonize; *forêt, maison* to burn to the ground, reduce to ashes; *rôti* to burn to a cinder.

carbon(n)ade [kaʀbɔnad] nf (*méthode*) grilling (of meat) on charcoal; (*mets*) meat grilled on charcoal.

carburant [kaʀbyʀɑ̃] 1 adj m: **mélange ~** mixture (of petrol (*Brit*) *ou* gas (*US*) and air) (*in internal combustion engine*). 2 nm fuel. **les ~s** fuel oils.

carburateur [kaʀbyʀatœʀ] nm carburettor.

carburation [kaʀbyʀasjɔ̃] nf *[essence]* carburation; *[fer]* carburization.

carbure [kaʀbyʀ] nm carbide; *voir* **lampe**.

carburé, e [kaʀbyʀe] (ptp de **carburer**) adj *air, mélange* carburetted; *métal* carburized.

carburer [kaʀbyʀe] 1 1 vi a *[moteur]* **ça carbure bien/mal** it is well/badly tuned. b (*‡*) *[santé, travail]* **~ bien/mal** to be doing fine/badly; **alors, ça carbure?** well, are things going O.K.?; **il carbure au rouge** red wine is his tipple; **ça carbure sec ici!** (*boisson*) they're really knocking it back in here!; (*travail*) they're working flat out*! 2 vt *air* to carburet; *métal* to carburize.

carburol [kaʀbyʀɔl] nm gasohol.

carcajou [kaʀkaʒu] nm wolverine.

carcan [kaʀkɑ̃] nm (*Hist*) iron collar; (*fig: contrainte*) yoke, shackles (*pl*). **ce col est un vrai ~** this collar is like a vice.

carcasse [kaʀkas] nf a *[animal],* (*) *[personne]* carcass. **je vais réchauffer ma ~ au soleil*** I'm going to toast myself in the sun*. b (*armature*) *[abat-jour]* frame; *[bateau]* skeleton; *[immeuble]* shell, skeleton. **pneu à ~ radiale/diagonale** radial/cross-ply tyre.

carcéral, e, mpl **-aux** [kaʀseʀal, o] adj prison (*épith*). **régime ~** prison regime.

carcinogène [kaʀsinɔʒɛn] adj carcinogenic.

carcinome [kaʀsinom] nm carcinoma.

cardage [kaʀdaʒ] nm carding.

cardamome [kaʀdamɔm] nf cardamom.

cardan [kaʀdɑ̃] nm universal joint; *voir* **joint**.

carde [kaʀd] nf (*Tex*) card.

carder [kaʀde] 1 vt to card.

cardeur, -euse [kaʀdœʀ, øz] 1 nm,f carder. 2 **cardeuse** nf (*machine*) carding machine, carder.

cardiaque [kaʀdjak] 1 adj (*Anat*) cardiac. **malade ~** heart case *ou* patient; **être ~** to suffer from *ou* have a heart condition; *voir* **crise**. 2 nmf heart case *ou* patient.

Cardiff [kaʀdif] n Cardiff.

cardigan [kaʀdigɑ̃] nm cardigan.

cardinal, e, mpl **-aux** [kaʀdinal, o] 1 adj *nombre* cardinal; (*littér: capital*) cardinal; *voir* **point¹**. 2 nm a (*Rel*) cardinal. **~-évêque** cardinal bishop; **~-prêtre** cardinal priest. b (*nombre*) cardinal number. c (*Orn*) cardinal (bird).

cardinalat [kaʀdinala] nm cardinalship.

cardinalice [kaʀdinalis] adj of a cardinal. **conférer à qn la dignité ~** to make sb a cardinal, raise sb to the purple; *voir* **pourpre**.

cardiogramme [kaʀdjɔgʀam] nm cardiogram.

cardiographe [kaʀdjɔgʀaf] nm cardiograph.

cardiographie [kaʀdjɔgʀafi] nf cardiography.

cardiologie [kaʀdjɔlɔʒi] nf cardiology.

cardiologue [kaʀdjɔlɔg] nmf cardiologist, heart specialist.

cardio-vasculaire, pl **cardio-vasculaires** [kaʀdjovaskylɛʀ] adj cardiovascular.

cardite [kaʀdit] nf (*Méd*) carditis.

cardon [kaʀdɔ̃] nm (*Culin*) cardoon.

carême [kaʀɛm] 1 nm (*jeûne*) fast. (*Rel: période*) **le C~** Lent; **sermon de ~** Lent sermon; **faire ~** to observe *ou* keep Lent, fast during Lent; **rompre le ~** to break the Lent fast *ou* the fast of Lent; (*fig*) **le ~ qu'il s'est imposé** the fast he has undertaken; **face** *ou* **figure** *ou* **mine de ~*** long face (*fig*). 2 comp ▶ **carême-prenant††** nm (pl **carêmes-prenants**) Shrovetide††.

carénage [kaʀenaʒ] nm a (*Naut*) (*action*) careening; (*lieu*) careenage. b *[véhicule]* (*action*) streamlining; (*partie*) fairing.

carence [kaʀɑ̃s] nf a (*Méd: manque*) deficiency. **maladie de** *ou* **par ~** deficiency disease; **~ vitaminique** *ou* **en vitamines** vitamin deficiency; **~ affective** emotional deprivation; **~ alimentaire** nutritional deficiency; (*fig*) **une grave ~ en personnel qualifié** a grave deficiency *ou* shortage of qualified staff. b (*NonC: incompétence*) *[gouvernement]* shortcomings, incompetence; *[parents]* inadequacy. c (*défauts*) **les ~s de** the inadequacies *ou* shortcomings of. d (*Jur*) insolvency.

carène [kaʀɛn] nf a (*Naut*) (lower part of the) hull. **mettre en ~** to careen. b (*Bot*) carina, keel.

caréner [kaʀene] 6 vt a (*Naut*) to careen. b (*Tech*) *véhicule* to streamline.

caressant, e [kaʀesɑ̃, ɑ̃t] adj *enfant, animal* affectionate; *regard, voix* caressing, tender; *brise* caressing.

caresse [kaʀɛs] nf a caress; (*à un animal*) stroke, pet. **faire des ~s à** *personne* to caress; *animal* to stroke, pet; (*littér*) **la ~ de la brise/des vagues** the caress of the breeze/of the waves. b (*††: flatterie*) cajolery (*NonC*), flattery (*NonC*). **endormir la méfiance de qn par des ~s** to use cajolery to allay *ou* quieten sb's suspicions.

caresser [kaʀese] 1 vt a *personne* to caress; *animal* to stroke, pet; *objet* to stroke. **il lui caressait les jambes/les seins** he was stroking *ou* caressing her legs/fondling her breasts; **il caressait les touches du piano** he stroked *ou* caressed the keys of the piano; **~ qn du regard** to give sb a fond *ou* caressing look, look lovingly *ou* fondly at sb; (*hum*) **je vais lui ~ les côtes*** I'm going to give him a drubbing. b *projet, espoir* to entertain, toy with. **~ le projet de faire qch** to toy with the idea of doing sth. c (*††: flatter*) to flatter, fawn on.

cargaison [kaʀgɛzɔ̃] nf a (*Aviat, Naut*) cargo, freight. **une ~ de bananes** a cargo of bananas. b (*) load, stock. **des ~s de** *lettres,* *demandes* heaps *ou* piles of; **des ~s de touristes** busloads (*ou* shiploads *ou* planeloads) of tourists.

cargo [kaʀgo] **nm** cargo boat, freighter. **~ mixte** cargo and passenger vessel.

cargue [kaʀg] **nf** (*Naut*) brail.

carguer [kaʀge] 1 **vt** *voiles* to brail, furl.

cari [kaʀi] **nm** = **curry**.

cariatide [kaʀjatid] **nf** caryatid.

caribou [kaʀibu] **nm** caribou.

caricatural, e, mpl -aux [kaʀikatyʀal, o] **adj** (*ridicule*) *aspect, traits* ridiculous, grotesque; (*exagéré*) *description, interprétation* caricatured.

caricature [kaʀikatyʀ] **nf** a (*dessin, description, représentation*) caricature; (*dessin à intention politique*) (satirical) cartoon. **faire la ~ de** to make a caricature of, caricature; **ce n'est qu'une ~ de procès** it's a mere mockery of a trial; **ce n'est qu'une ~ de la vérité** it's a caricature *ou* gross distortion of the truth; **c'est une ~ de l'Anglais en vacances** he is a caricature of the Englishman on holiday. b (**: personne laide*) fright*.

caricaturer [kaʀikatyʀe] 1 **vt** to caricature.

caricaturiste [kaʀikatyʀist] **nmf** caricaturist; (*à intention politique*) (satirical) cartoonist.

carie [kaʀi] **nf** a (*Méd*) *[dents, os]* caries (*NonC*). **la ~ dentaire** tooth decay, (dental) caries; **j'ai une ~** I've got a bad tooth *ou* a hole in my tooth. b (*Bot*) *[arbre]* blight; *[blé]* smut, bunt.

carier [kaʀje] 7 1 **vt** to decay, cause to decay. **dent cariée** bad *ou* decayed tooth. 2 **se carier vpr** to decay.

carillon [kaʀijɔ̃] **nm** a *[église]* (*cloches*) (peal *ou* set of) bells; (*air*) chimes. **on entendait le ~ de St Pierre/des ~s joyeux** we could hear the chimes of St Pierre/hear joyful chimes. b *[horloge]* (*système de sonnerie*) chime; (*air*) chimes. **une horloge à ~, un ~** a chiming clock. c *[vestibule, entrée]* (door) chime.

carillonner [kaʀijɔne] 1 1 **vi** a *[cloches]* to ring, chime; (*à toute volée*) to peal out. b (*à la porte*) to ring very loudly. **ça ne sert à rien de ~, il n'y a personne** it's no use jangling *ou* ringing the doorbell like that – there's no one in. 2 **vt** *fête* to announce with a peal of bells; *heure* to chime, ring; (*fig*) *nouvelle* to broadcast.

carillonneur [kaʀijɔnœʀ] **nm** bell ringer.

cariste [kaʀist] **nm** fork-lift truck operator.

caritatif, -ive [kaʀitatif, iv] **adj** charitable. **association** *ou* **organisation ~ive** charity, charitable organization.

carlin [kaʀlɛ̃] **nm** pug(dog).

carlingue [kaʀlɛ̃g] **nf** (*Aviat*) cabin; (*Naut*) keelson.

carliste [kaʀlist] **adj, nmf** Carlist.

carmagnole [kaʀmaɲɔl] **nf** (*chanson, danse*) carmagnole; (*Hist: veste*) short jacket (*worn during the French revolution*).

carme [kaʀm] **nm** Carmelite, White Friar.

carmel [kaʀmɛl] **nm** (*monastère*) *[carmes]* Carmelite monastery; *[carmélites]* Carmelite convent. (*ordre*) **le C~** the Carmelite order.

carmélite [kaʀmelit] **nf** Carmelite nun.

carmin [kaʀmɛ̃] 1 **nm** (*colorant*) cochineal; (*couleur*) carmine, crimson. 2 **adj inv** carmine, crimson.

carminé, e [kaʀmine] **adj** carmine, crimson.

carnage [kaʀnaʒ] **nm** (*lit, fig*) carnage, slaughter. **quel ~!** what a slaughter! *ou* massacre!; (*fig*) **je vais faire un ~** I'm going to massacre someone.

carnassier, -ière [kaʀnasje, jɛʀ] 1 **adj** *animal* carnivorous, flesh-eating; *dent* carnassial. 2 **nm** carnivore. **~s** carnivores, carnivora (*SPÉC*). 3 **carnassière nf** (*dent*) carnassial; (*gibecière*) gamebag.

carnation [kaʀnasjɔ̃] **nf** (*teint*) complexion; (*Peinture*) **~s** flesh tints.

carnaval, pl ~s [kaʀnaval] **nm** (*fête*) carnival; (*période*) carnival (time). (*mannequin*) **(Sa Majesté) C~** King Carnival; (*fig: excentrique*) **une espèce de ~** a sort of gaudily-dressed person *ou* clown; **de ~** *tenue, ambiance* carnival (*épith*).

carnavalesque [kaʀnavalɛsk] **adj** (*grotesque*) carnivalesque; (*relatif au carnaval*) of the carnival.

carne [kaʀn] **nf** (*péj*) (**: viande*) tough *ou* leathery meat; (*†: cheval*) nag, hack. (*fig*) **quelle ~!⁑** (*homme*) what a swine!⁑ *ou* bastard!*⁑; (*femme*) what a bitch!⁑

carné, e [kaʀne] **adj** a *alimentation* meat (*épith*). b *fleur* flesh-coloured.

carnet [kaʀnɛ] 1 **nm** (*calepin*) notebook; (*liasse*) book. 2 **comp** ►**carnet d'adresses** address book ►**carnet de bal** dance card ►**carnet de billets** book of tickets ►**carnet de bord** (*Naut, Aviat*) log(book) ►**carnet de chèques** cheque book ►**carnet de commandes** order book; **nos carnets de commandes sont pleins** we have a full order book ►**carnet de notes** (*Scol*) school report (*Brit*), report card; **avoir un bon carnet (de notes)** to have a good report ►**carnet de route** travel diary ►**carnet de santé** health record ►**carnet à souches** counterfoil book ►**carnet de timbres** book of stamps ►**carnet de vol** (*Aviat*) log(book).

carnier [kaʀnje] **nm** gamebag.

carnivore [kaʀnivɔʀ] 1 **adj** *animal* carnivorous, flesh-eating; *insecte, plante* carnivorous. *[personne]* **il est ~** he's a meat-lover. 2 **nm** carnivore. **~s** carnivores, carnivora (*SPÉC*).

Caroline [kaʀɔlin] **nf: ~ du Nord** North Carolina; **~ du Sud** South Carolina.

carolingien, -ienne [kaʀɔlɛ̃ʒjɛ̃, jɛn] 1 **adj** Carolingian. 2 **nm,f: C~(ne)** Carolingian.

carotène [kaʀɔtɛn] **nm** carotene, carotin.

carotide [kaʀɔtid] **adj, nf** carotid.

carottage⁑ [kaʀɔtaʒ] **nm** (*vol*) swiping⁑, nicking⁑ (*Brit*), pinching*.

carotte [kaʀɔt] 1 **nf** a (*Bot, Culin*) carrot. (*fig*) **les ~s sont cuites!*** they've (*ou* we've *etc*) had it!*, it's all up with* (*Brit*) *ou* over for them (*ou* us *etc*); *voir* **poil**. b (**: promesse*) carrot. **on ne peut le faire travailler qu'à la ~ et au bâton** to get him to work you have to use the carrot and stick approach. c (*Tech*) core. d *[tabac]* plug; (*enseigne*) tobacconist's (*Brit*) *ou* tobacco shop (*US*) sign. 2 **adj inv** *cheveux* red, carroty* (*péj*); *couleur* carroty. **objet (couleur) ~** carrot-coloured object; **rouge ~** carrot red.

carotter⁑ [kaʀɔte] 1 1 **vt** (*voler*) *objet* to swipe⁑, nick⁑ (*Brit*), pinch*; *client* to cheat, do* (*Brit*). **~ qch à qn** to nick⁑ sth from sb; **il m'a carotté (de) 5 F, je me suis fait ~ (de) 5 F** he did* *ou* diddled* me out of 5 francs. 2 **vi: il essaie toujours de ~** he's always trying to fiddle a bit for himself; **~ sur: elle carotte sur l'argent des commissions** she fiddles the housekeeping money.

carotteur, -euse⁑ [kaʀɔtœʀ, øz] **nm,f** pincher*, diddler*.

caroube [kaʀub] **nf** (*fruit*) carob.

caroubier [kaʀubje] **nm** carob (tree).

carpaccio [kaʀpatʃ(j)o] **nm** carpaccio.

Carpates [kaʀpat] **nfpl: les ~** the Carpathians.

carpe¹ [kaʀp] **nf** (*Zool*) carp; *voir* **muet, saut.**

carpe² [kaʀp] **nm** (*Anat*) carpus.

carpeau, pl ~x [kaʀpo] **nm** young carp.

carpette [kaʀpɛt] **nf** (*tapis*) rug; (*péj: personne servile*) fawning *ou* servile person, doormat (*fig*). **s'aplatir comme une ~ devant qn** to fawn on sb.

carpien, -ienne [kaʀpjɛ̃, jɛn] **adj** carpal.

carquois [kaʀkwa] **nm** quiver.

carrare [kaʀaʀ] **nm** (*marbre*) Carrara (marble).

carre [kaʀ] **nf** *[ski]* edge. (*Ski*) **faire mordre les ~s** to dig in the edges of one's skis; *voir* **prise**.

carré, e [kaʀe] (**ptp de carrer**) 1 **adj** a *table, jardin, menton* square. **aux épaules ~es** square-shouldered; *voir* **partie²**.

b (*Math*) square. **mètre/kilomètre ~** square metre/kilometre; **il n'y avait pas un centimètre ~ de place** there wasn't a square inch of room, there wasn't room *ou* there was no room to swing a cat (*Brit*); *voir* **racine**.

c (*fig: franc*) *personne* forthright, straightforward; *réponse* straight, straightforward. **être ~ en affaires** to be aboveboard *ou* forthright in one's (business) dealings.

2 **nm** a (*gén*) square. **découper qch en petits ~s** to cut sth up into little squares; **un ~ de soie** a silk square; **un ~ de terre** a patch *ou* plot (of land); **un ~ de choux/de salades** a cabbage/lettuce patch; **avoir les cheveux coupés au ~, avoir une coupe au ~** to wear *ou* have one's hair in a bob.

b (*Mil: disposition*) square; *voir* **former.**

c (*Naut: mess, salon*) wardroom. **le ~ des officiers** the (officers') wardroom.

d (*Math*) square. **le ~ de 4** 4 squared, the square of 4; **3 au ~** 3 squared; **élever** *ou* **mettre** *ou* **porter un nombre au ~** to square a number.

e (*Cartes*) **un ~ d'as** four aces.

f (*Culin*) **~ de l'Est** *soft, mild, fermented cheese*; (*Boucherie*) **~ d'agneau** loin of lamb.

g (*groupe*) **le dernier ~** the last handful.

3 **carrée nf** (*⁑: chambre*) pad⁑; (*Hist Mus*) breve.

carreau, pl ~x [kaʀo] **nm** a (*par terre*) (floor) tile; (*au mur*) (wall) tile. **~ de plâtre** plaster block.

b (*carrelage, sol*) tiled floor. **le ~ des Halles** les Halles market.

c (*vitre*) (window) pane. **remplacer un ~** to replace a pane; **regarder au ~** to look out of the window; **des vandales ont cassé les ~x** vandals have smashed the windows; (**: lunettes*) **enlève tes ~x** take off your specs*.

d (*sur un tissu*) check; (*sur du papier*) square. **à ~x** *papier* squared; *mouchoir* check (*épith*), checked; **veste à grands/petits ~x** jacket with a large/small check; (*Scol*) **laisser 3 ~x de marge** leave 3 squares' margin, leave a margin of 3 squares; (*Tech*) **mettre un plan au ~** to square a plan.

e (*Cartes*) diamond.

f *[mine]* bank.

g (*Hist: flèche*) bolt.

h (** loc*) (*bagarre*) **laisser qn sur le ~** to lay sb out*; **il est resté sur le ~** (*bagarre*) he was laid out*; (*examen*) he didn't make the grade; **se tenir à ~** to keep one's nose clean⁑, watch one's step.

carrefour [kaʀfuʀ] **nm** a *[routes, rues]* crossroads. (*fig*) **la Belgique, ~ de l'Europe** Belgium, the crossroads of Europe; (*fig*) **Marseille, ~ de la drogue** Marseilles, the crossroads of the drug traffic; (*fig*) **discipline au ~ de plusieurs sciences** subject at the junction *ou* meeting point of many different sciences; (*fig*) **cette manifestation est un ~ d'idées** this event is a forum for ideas. b (*fig: tournant*) crossroads. **se trouver à un ~ (de sa vie/carrière)** to be at a crossroads (in one's life/career). c (*rencontre, forum*) forum, symposium. **~ des métiers** careers convention.

carrelage [kaʀlaʒ] **nm** (*action*) tiling; (*carreaux*) tiles, tiling. **poser un ~** to lay a tiled floor; **laver le ~** to wash the floor.

carreler [kaʀle] 4 **vt** *mur, sol* to tile; *papier* to draw squares on.

carrelet [kaʀlɛ] **nm** a (*poisson*) plaice. b (*filet*) *square fishing net.* c (*Tech*) *[bourrelier]* half-moon needle; *[dessinateur]* square ruler.

carreleur [kaʀlœʀ] **nm** tiler.

carrément [kaʀemɑ̃] **adv** a (*franchement*) bluntly, straight out. **je lui ai dit ~ ce que je pensais** I told him bluntly *ou* straight out what I thought. b (*sans hésiter*) straight. **il a ~ écrit au proviseur** he wrote straight to the headmaster; **vas-y ~** go right ahead; **j'ai pris ~ à travers champs** I struck straight across the fields. c (*intensif*) **il est ~ timbré*** he's definitely cracked*; **cela nous fait gagner ~ 10 km/2 heures** it saves us 10 whole km *ou* a full 10 km/a whole 2 hours *ou* 2 full hours. d (*rare: d'aplomb*) squarely, firmly.

carrer [kaʀe] 1 1 **vt** (*Math, Tech*) to square. 2 **se carrer vpr: se ~ dans** to settle (o.s.) comfortably *ou* ensconce o.s. in; **bien carré dans son fauteuil** comfortably settled *ou* ensconced in his armchair.

carrier [kaʀje] **nm** (*ouvrier*) quarryman, quarrier; (*propriétaire*) quarry owner. **maître ~** quarry master.

carrière[1] [kaʀjɛʀ] **nf** *[sable]* (sand)pit; *[roches etc]* quarry.

carrière[2] [kaʀjɛʀ] **nf** a (*profession*) career. **en début/fin de ~** at the beginning/end of one's career; (*Pol*) **la ~** the diplomatic service; **embrasser la ~ des armes†** to embark on a career of arms†; **faire ~ dans l'enseignement** to make one's career in teaching; **il est entré dans l'industrie et y a fait (rapidement) ~** he went into industry and (quickly) made a career for himself (in it); *voir* **militaire.** b (*littér: cours*) **le jour achève sa ~** the day is drawing to a close *ou* has run its course; **donner (libre) ~ à** to give free rein to.

carriérisme [kaʀjeʀism] **nm** (*péj*) careerism.

carriériste [kaʀjeʀist] **nmf** (*péj*) careerist.

carriole [kaʀjɔl] **nf** a (*péj*) (ramshackle) cart. b (*Can*) sleigh, ca(r)riole (*US, Can*), carryall (*US, Can*).

carrossable [kaʀɔsabl] **adj** *route etc* suitable for (motor) vehicles.

carrosse [kaʀɔs] **nm** coach (*horse-drawn*). **~ d'apparat** state coach; *voir* **cinquième, rouler.**

carrosser [kaʀɔse] 1 **vt** (*Aut*) (*mettre une carrosserie à*) to fit a body to; (*dessiner la carrosserie de*) to design a body for *ou* the body of. **voiture bien carrossée** car with a well-designed body; *[personne]* **elle est bien carrossée‡** she's got curves in all the right places.

carrosserie [kaʀɔsʀi] **nf** (*Aut*) (*coque*) body(work), coachwork; (*métier*) coachbuilding (*Brit*). **atelier de ~** body shop, coachbuilder's workshop (*Brit*).

carrossier [kaʀɔsje] **nm** (*constructeur*) coachbuilder (*Brit*); (*dessinateur*) car designer. **ma voiture est chez le ~** my car is at the coachbuilder's (*Brit*) *ou* in the body shop (*US*).

carrousel [kaʀuzɛl] **nm** a (*Équitation*) carousel; (*fig: tourbillon*) merry-go-round. **un ~ d'avions dans le ciel** planes weaving patterns *ou* circling in the sky. b *[diapositives]* Carousel ®.

carrure [kaʀyʀ] **nf** a (*largeur d'épaules*) *[personne]* build; *[vêtement]* breadth across the shoulders. **manteau un peu trop étroit de ~** coat which is a little tight across the shoulders; **une ~ d'athlète** an athlete's build; **homme de belle/forte ~** well-built/burly man. b *[mâchoire]* squareness; *[bâtiment]* square shape. c (*fig: envergure*) calibre, stature.

carry [kaʀi] **nm = curry.**

cartable [kaʀtabl] **nm** *[écolier]* (*à poignée*) (school)bag; (*à bretelles*) satchel.

carte [kaʀt] 1 **nf** a (*gén*) card. **~ (postale)** (post)card; **~ de visite** visiting card, calling card (*US*).

b (*Jeux*) **~ (à jouer)** (playing) card; **battre** *ou* **brasser** *ou* **mêler les ~s** to shuffle the cards; **donner les ~s** to deal (the cards); **faire** *ou* **tirer les ~s à qn** to read sb's cards; **avoir toutes les ~ en main** (*lit*) to have all the cards; (*fig*) to hold all the cards; **jouer la ~ du charme** to turn on the charm; **jouer la ~ de la solidarité/de la concurrence** to play the solidarity/competition card; **~ maîtresse** (*lit*) master (card); (*fig*) trump card; (*lit*) **~ forcée** forced card; (*fig*) **c'est la ~ forcée!** we've no choice!, it's Hobson's choice!; (*lit, fig*) **~s sur table** cards on the table; *voir* **brouiller, château.**

c (*Géog*) map; (*Astron, Mét, Naut*) chart. **~ du relief/géologique** relief/geological map; **~ routière** roadmap; **~ du ciel** sky chart; **~ de la lune** chart *ou* map of the moon; **~ météorologique** *ou* **du temps** weather chart; *voir* **rayer.**

d (*au restaurant*) menu. **on prend le menu ou la ~?** shall we have the set menu or shall we eat à la carte?; **repas à la ~** à la carte meal; **une très bonne/très petite ~** a very good/very small menu *ou* choice of dishes; (*fig*) **à la ~** *retraite, plan d'investissement, voyage* tailor-made; **faire du tourisme à la ~** to go on a tour (*which one has organized oneself*); (*Scol*) **programme à la ~** free-choice curriculum, curriculum allowing pupils a choice of subjects; **avoir un horaire à la ~** to have flexible working hours.

e (*Fin*) credit card. **payer par ~** to pay by credit card.

f (*Ordin*) board.

g (*loc*) **en ~: fille** *ou* **femme en ~** registered prostitute.

2 **comp** ►**carte d'abonnement** (*train*) season ticket, pass; (*Théâtre*) season ticket ►**carte d'alimentation** = **carte de rationnement** ►**carte d'anniversaire** birthday card ►**carte d'assuré social** *ou* **de Sécurité sociale** ≃ National insurance Card (*Brit*), social security card (*US*) ►**carte bancaire** banker's card ►**carte blanche: avoir carte blanche** to have carte blanche *ou* a free hand; **donner carte blanche à qn** to give sb carte blanche *ou* a free hand ►**Carte Bleue** ® (*Banque*) ≃ Visa Card ® ►**carte de chemin de fer** railway (*Brit*) *ou* train (*US*) season ticket ►**carte de correspondance** (plain) postcard ►**carte de crédit** credit card ►**carte d'électeur** elector's card, voter registration card (*US*) ►**carte d'état-major** Ordnance Survey map (*Brit*), Geological Survey map (*US*) ►**carte d'étudiant** student card ►**carte d'extension de mémoire** memory expansion board ►**carte de famille nombreuse** *card issued to members of large families, allowing reduced fares etc* ►**carte de fidélité** (regular customer's) discount card ►**carte graphique** graphics board ►**carte grise** ≃ (car) registration book (*Brit*) *ou* papers (*US*), logbook (*Brit*) ►**carte d'identité** identity *ou* I.D. card ►**carte d'identité scolaire** pupil's identity card, student I.D. (card) ►**carte d'interface** interface board ►**carte d'invitation** invitation card ►**carte jeune** young persons' discount card ►**carte journalière** (*Ski*) day-pass, day-ticket ►**carte de lecteur** reader's ticket (*Brit*), library ticket (*Brit*), library card ►**carte-lettre nf** (**pl cartes-lettres**) letter-card ►**carte mécanographique** = **carte perforée** ►**carte à mémoire** smart card, intelligent card; (*pour téléphone*) phone card ►**carte de Noël** Christmas card ►**carte orange** monthly (*or* weekly *ou* yearly) season ticket (*for all types of transport in Paris*) ►**carte de paiement** credit card ►**carte perforée** punch card ►**carte de presse** press card ►**carte privative** charge *ou* store card ►**carte à puce** smart card, intelligent card ►**carte de rationnement** ration card ►**carte-réponse nf** (**pl cartes-réponses**) (*gén*) reply card; *[concours]* entry form ►**carte scolaire** list of schools (*showing forecasts for regional requirements*) ►**carte de séjour** residence permit ►**carte syndicale** union card ►**carte téléphonique** phonecard ►**carte de travail** work permit ►**carte vermeille** ≃ senior citizen's rail pass ►**carte verte** (*Aut*) green card ►**carte des vins** wine list ►**carte de vœux** greetings card.

cartel [kaʀtɛl] **nm** a (*Pol*) cartel, coalition; (*Écon*) cartel, combine. b (*pendule*) wall clock. c (*Hist: défi*) cartel.

cartellisation [kaʀtelizasjɔ̃] **nf** (*Écon*) formation of combines.

carter [kaʀtɛʀ] **nm** *[bicyclette]* chain guard; (*Aut*) *[huile]* sump, oilpan (*US*); *[boîte de vitesses]* (gearbox) casing; *[différentiel]* cage; *[moteur]* crankcase.

carterie [kaʀt(ə)ʀi] **nf** postcard shop.

cartésianisme [kaʀtezjanism] **nm** Cartesianism.

cartésien, -ienne [kaʀtezjɛ̃, jɛn] **adj, nm,f** Cartesian.

Carthage [kaʀtaʒ] **n** Carthage.

carthaginois, e [kaʀtaʒinwa, waz] 1 **adj** Carthaginian. 2 **nm,f: C~(e)** Carthaginian.

cartilage [kaʀtilaʒ] **nm** (*Anat*) cartilage; *[viande]* gristle.

cartilagineux, -euse [kaʀtilaʒinø, øz] **adj** (*Anat*) cartilaginous; *viande* gristly.

cartographe [kaʀtɔgʀaf] **nmf** cartographer.

cartographie [kaʀtɔgʀafi] **nf** cartography, map-making.

cartographique [kaʀtɔgʀafik] **adj** cartographic(al).

cartomancie [kaʀtɔmɑ̃si] **nf** fortune-telling (*with cards*), cartomancy.

cartomancien, -ienne [kaʀtɔmɑ̃sjɛ̃, jɛn] **nm,f** fortune-teller (*who uses cards*).

carton [kaʀtɔ̃] 1 **nm** a (*matière*) cardboard. **écrit/collé sur un ~** written/pasted on (a piece of) cardboard; **masque de** *ou* **en ~** cardboard mask.

b (*boîte*) (cardboard) box, carton (*US*); (*contenu*) boxful; (*†: cartable*) (school)bag, satchel. **~ de lait** (*boîte*) carton of milk; (*plusieurs boîtes*) pack of milk; **~-repas** pre-packaged meal; (*fig*) **c'est quelque part dans mes ~s** it's somewhere in my files; *voir* **taper.**

c (*cible*) target. **faire un ~** (*à la fête*) to have a go at the rifle range; (**: sur l'ennemi*) to take a potshot* (*sur* at); **faire un bon ~** to make a good score, do a good shoot (*Brit*); (*fig*) **j'ai fait un ~ en anglais*** I did brilliantly at English*.

d (*Peinture*) sketch; (*Géog*) inset map; *[tapisserie, mosaïque]* cartoon.

e (*carte*) card. **~ d'invitation** invitation card.

2 **comp** ►**carton à chapeau** hatbox ►**carton à chaussures** shoebox ►**carton à dessin** portfolio ►**carton jaune** (*Ftbl*) yellow card; **il a reçu un carton jaune** he got a yellow card, he was booked ►**carton pâte** pasteboard; **de carton pâte** *décor,* (*fig*) *personnages* cardboard (*épith*) ►**carton rouge** (*Ftbl*) red card; **il a reçu un carton rouge** he got the red card, he was sent off.

cartonnage [kaʀtɔnaʒ] **nm** a (*industrie*) cardboard industry. b (*emballage*) cardboard (packing). c (*Reliure*) (*action*) boarding. (*couverture*) **~ pleine toile** cloth binding; **~ souple** limp cover.

cartonner [kaʀtɔne] [1] 1 vt a (*relier*) to bind in boards. **livre cartonné** hardback (book). b (**: heurter*) to smash into*. 2 vi* a (*réussir*) to do brilliantly* (*en* in). b (*échouer*) to do terribly *ou* really badly (*en* in). c (*en voiture*) to have a smash(-up)*. **ça cartonne souvent à ce carrefour** you get quite a few crashes at this crossroads*.

cartonnerie [kaʀtɔnʀi] nf (*industrie*) cardboard industry; (*usine*) cardboard factory.

cartonnier [kaʀtɔnje] nm a (*artiste*) tapestry *ou* mosaic designer. b (*meuble*) filing cabinet.

cartouche¹ [kaʀtuʃ] nf *[fusil, stylo, magnétophone, ordinateur]* cartridge; *[cigarettes]* carton; *voir* **brûler**.

cartouche² [kaʀtuʃ] nm (*Archéol, Archit*) cartouche.

cartoucherie [kaʀtuʃʀi] nf (*fabrique*) cartridge factory; (*dépôt*) cartridge depot.

cartouchière [kaʀtuʃjɛʀ] nf (*ceinture*) cartridge belt; (*sac*) cartridge pouch.

caryatide [kaʀjatid] nf = **cariatide**.

cas [kɑ] 1 nm a (*situation*) case, situation; (*événement*) occurrence. **~ tragique/spécial** tragic/special case; **un ~ imprévu** an unforeseen case *ou* situation; **~ urgent** urgent case, emergency; (*Écon*) **étude de ~** case study; **comme c'est son ~** as is the case with him; **il neige à Nice, et c'est un ~ très rare** it's snowing in Nice and that's a very rare occurrence *ou* which is very rare; **exposez-lui votre ~** state your case, explain your position; (*à un médecin*) describe your symptoms; **il s'est mis dans un mauvais ~** he's got himself into a tricky situation *ou* position; **dans le premier ~** in the first case *ou* instance.

b (*Jur*) case. **~ d'homicide/de divorce** murder/divorce case; **l'adultère est un ~ de divorce** adultery is grounds for divorce; **soumettre un ~ au juge** to submit a case to the judge; (*hum*) **c'est un ~ pendable** he deserves to be shot (*hum*).

c (*Méd, Sociol*) case. **il y a plusieurs ~ de variole dans le pays** there are several cases of smallpox in the country; **~ social** person with social problems, social misfit; (*fig*) **c'est vraiment un ~!** he's (*ou* she's) a real case!*

d (*Ling*) case.

e (*loc*) **faire (grand) ~ de/peu de ~ de** to attach great/little importance to, set great/little store by; **il ne fait jamais aucun ~ de nos observations** he never pays any attention to *ou* takes any notice of our comments; **c'est le ~ ou jamais** it's now or never; **c'est le ~ ou jamais de réclamer** if ever there was a case for complaint this is it; **... c'est (bien) le ~ de le dire!** ... you've said it!, ... and no mistake about that!; **au ~ *ou* dans le ~ *ou* pour le ~ où il pleuvrait, en ~ qu'il pleuve†** in case it rains, in case it should rain; **je prends un parapluie au ~ où* *ou* en ~*** I am taking an umbrella (just) in case; **dans ce ~-là *ou* en ce ~ *ou* auquel ~ téléphonez-nous** in that case give us a ring; **dans le ~ présent** in this particular case; **le ~ échéant** if the case arises, if need be; **en ~ de réclamation/d'absence** in case of *ou* in the event of complaint/absence; **en ~ de besoin nous pouvons vous loger** if need be we can put you up; **en ~ d'urgence** in an emergency, in emergencies; **en aucun ~ vous ne devez vous arrêter** on no account *ou* under no circumstances are you to stop; **en tout ~, en *ou* dans tous les ~** anyway, in any case, at any rate; **mettre qn dans le ~ d'avoir à faire** to put sb in the situation *ou* position of having to do; **il accepte ou il refuse selon les ~** he accepts or refuses as the case may be.

2 comp ▶**cas de conscience** matter *ou* case of conscience; **il a un cas de conscience** he's in a moral dilemma, he has a moral problem ▶**cas d'école** textbook case ▶**cas d'égalité des triangles** congruence of triangles ▶**cas d'espèce** individual case ▶**cas de figure** scenario; **dans ce cas de figure** in this case ▶**cas de force majeure** case of absolute necessity ▶**cas de légitime défense** case of legitimate self-defence; **c'était un cas de légitime défense** he acted in self-defence ▶**cas limite** borderline case.

casanier, -ière [kazanje, jɛʀ] 1 adj *personne, habitudes, vie* stay-at-home (*épith*). 2 nm,f stay-at-home, homebody (*US*).

casaque [kazak] nf *[jockey]* blouse; (†) *[femme]* overblouse; (*Hist*) *[mousquetaire]* tabard; *voir* **tourner**.

casbah [kazba] nf (*en Afrique*) kasbah; (*‡: maison*) house, place*. **rentrer à la ~** to go home.

cascade [kaskad] nf a *[eau]* waterfall, cascade; (*fig*) *[mots, événements, chiffres]* stream, torrent, spate; *[rires]* peal. (*fig*) **des démissions en ~** a chain *ou* spate of resignations; *voir* **montage**. b (*acrobatie*) stunt. **faire des ~s en voiture/moto** to do stunt driving/riding.

cascader [kaskade] [1] vi (*littér*) to cascade.

cascadeur [kaskadœʀ] nm *[film]* stuntman; *[cirque]* acrobat.

cascadeuse [kaskadøz] nf *[film]* stuntgirl; *[cirque]* acrobat.

case [kɑz] nf a (*sur papier*) square, space; (*sur formulaire*) box; *[échiquier]* square. (*Jeux*) **la ~ départ** the start; (*fig*) **nous voilà revenus à la ~ départ** we're back to square one. b *[pupitre]* compartment, shelf; *[courrier]* pigeonhole; *[boîte, tiroir]* compartment. **~ postale** post-office box; (*Ordin*) **~ de réception** card stacker; **il a une ~ vide* *ou* en moins*, il lui manque une ~*** he has a screw loose*. c (*hutte*) hut. **la C~ de l'Oncle Tom** Uncle Tom's Cabin.

caséeux, -euse [kazeø, øz] adj caseous.

caséine [kazein] nf casein.

casemate [kazmat] nf blockhouse, pillbox.

caser* [kɑze] [1] 1 vt a (*placer*) *objets* to shove*, stuff; (*loger*) *amis* to put up. **il a casé les chaussures dans une poche** he tucked *ou* stuffed the shoes into a pocket.

b (*marier*) *fille* to find a husband for; (*pourvoir d'une situation*) to find a job for. **il a casé son fils dans une grosse maison d'édition** he got his son a job *ou* got his son set up in a big publishing house; **ses enfants sont casés maintenant** (*emploi*) his children have got jobs now *ou* are fixed up now; (*mariage*) his children are (married and) off his hands now.

2 **se caser** vpr (*se marier, se mettre en couple*) to settle down; (*trouver un emploi*) to find a (steady) job; (*se loger*) to find a place (to live). (*personne seule*) **il va avoir du mal à se caser** he's going to have a job finding someone to settle down with.

caserne [kazɛʀn] nf (*Mil, fig*) barracks. **~ de pompiers** fire station (*Brit*), fire *ou* station house (*US*); **cet immeuble est une vraie ~** this building looks like a barracks.

casernement [kazɛʀnəmɑ̃] nm (*Mil*) (*action*) quartering in barracks; (*bâtiments*) barrack buildings.

caserner [kazɛʀne] [1] vt (*Mil*) to barrack, quarter in barracks.

casernier [kazɛʀnje] nm barrack quartermaster.

cash* [kaʃ] 1 adv (*comptant*) **payer ~** to pay cash down; **il m'a donné 40 000 F ~** he gave me 40,000 francs cash down *ou* on the nail* (*Brit*) *ou* on the barrel* (*US*). 2 nm cash (*NonC*).

cash-flow [kaʃflo] nm cash flow.

casier [kɑzje] 1 nm a (*compartiment*) compartment; (*tiroir*) drawer; (*fermant à clef*) locker; *[courrier]* pigeonhole (*Brit*), box (*US*). **~ de consigne automatique** luggage locker. b (*meuble*) set of compartments *ou* pigeonholes; (*à tiroirs*) filing cabinet. c (*Pêche*) (lobster *etc*) pot. **poser des ~s** to put out lobster pots. 2 comp ▶**casier à bouteilles** bottle rack ▶**casier fiscal** tax record ▶**casier à homards** lobster pot ▶**casier judiciaire** police *ou* criminal record; **avoir un casier judiciaire vierge** to have a clean (police) record; **avoir un casier judiciaire chargé** to have a long record ▶**casier à musique** music cabinet.

casino [kazino] nm casino.

casoar [kazɔaʀ] nm (*Orn*) cassowary; (*plumet*) plume.

casque [kask] 1 nm a (*qui protège*) *[soldat, alpiniste]* helmet; *[motocycliste]* crash helmet; *[ouvrier]* hard hat. **"le port du ~ est obligatoire"** "this is a hard hat area", "hard hats must be worn at all times". b (*pour sécher les cheveux*) (hair-)drier. c **~ (à écouteurs)** (*gen*) headphones, headset, earphones; *[hi-fi]* headphones. d (*Zool*) casque. e (*Bot*) helmet, galea. 2 comp ▶**Casque bleu** blue helmet *ou* beret; **les Casques bleus** the U.N. peacekeeping force, the blue helmets *ou* berets ▶**casque colonial** pith helmet, topee ▶**casque intégral** full-face helmet ▶**casque à pointe** spiked helmet.

casqué, e [kaske] 1 ptp de **casquer***. 2 adj *motocycliste, soldat* wearing a helmet, helmeted. **~ de cuir** wearing a leather helmet.

casquer* [kaske] [1] vti (*payer*) to cough up*, fork out*.

casquette [kaskɛt] nf cap. **~ d'officier** officer's (peaked) cap; (*fig*) **avoir plusieurs ~s/une double ~** to wear several hats/two hats.

cassable [kɑsabl] adj breakable.

cassandre [kasɑ̃dʀ] nf (*Myth*) **C~** Cassandra. (*fig*) **jouer les ~** to be a prophet of doom.

cassant, e [kɑsɑ̃, ɑ̃t] adj a *glace, substance* brittle; *métal* short; *bois* easily broken *ou* snapped. b (*fig*) *ton* curt, abrupt, brusque; *attitude, manières* brusque, abrupt. c (**: difficile*) **ce n'est pas ~** it's not exactly back-breaking *ou* tiring work.

cassate [kasat] nf cassata.

cassation [kɑsasjɔ̃] nf a (*Jur*) cassation; *voir* **cour, pourvoir**. b (*Mil*) reduction to the ranks.

casse [kɑs] 1 nf a (*action*) breaking, breakage; (*objets cassés*) damage, breakages. **il y a eu beaucoup de ~ pendant le déménagement** there were a lot of things broken *ou* a lot of breakages during the move; **payer la ~** to pay for the damage *ou* breakages; (*fig*) **il va y avoir de la ~*** there's going to be (some) rough stuff*; **pas de ~!** (*lit*) don't break anything!; (** fig*) no rough stuff!*

b (**: endroit*) scrap yard. (*récupération*) **mettre à la ~** to scrap; **vendre à la ~** to sell for scrap; **bon pour la ~** fit for scrap, ready for the scrap heap; **envoyer une voiture à la ~** to send a car to the breakers.

c (*Typ*) **lettres du haut de/du bas de ~** upper-case/lower-case letters.

d (*Bot*) cassia.

2 nm (*arg Crime: cambriolage*) break-in. **faire un ~ dans une bijouterie** to break into a jeweller's shop, do a break-in at a jeweller's shop.

casse- [kɑs] préf *voir* **casser**.

cassé, e [kɑse] (ptp de **casser**) adj *voix* broken, cracked; *vieillard* bent; *voir* **blanc, col**.

cassement [kɑsmɑ̃] nm a **~ de tête*** headache (*fig*), worry. b = **casse 2**.

casser [kɑse] [1] 1 vt a (*briser*) *objet, volonté, moral, rythme* to break; *noix* to crack; *latte, branche* to snap, break; *vin* to spoil the flavour of; (*) *appareil* to bust*. ~ **une dent/un bras à qn** to break sb's tooth/arm; ~ **qch en deux/en morceaux** to break sth in two/into pieces; ~ **un morceau de chocolat** to break off *ou* snap off a piece of chocolate; ~ **un carreau** (*volontairement*) to smash a pane; (*accidentellement*) to break a pane; **il s'est mis à tout** ~ **autour de lui** he started smashing *ou* breaking everything about him; **cette bonne casse tout** *ou* **beaucoup** this maid is always breaking things; **cette maladie lui a cassé la voix** this illness has ruined his voice.

b (*dégrader*) *personne* (*Mil*) to reduce to the ranks, break; (*Admin*) to demote.

c (*Admin, Jur: annuler*) *jugement* to quash; *arrêt* to nullify, annul. **faire** ~ **un jugement pour vice de forme** to have a sentence quashed on a technicality.

d (*Comm*) ~ **les prix** to slash prices.

e (‡: *tuer*) ~ **du Viet/du Boche** to go Viet-/Jerry-smashing.

f (*loc*) (*Aviat*) ~ **du bois** to smash up one's plane; (*fig: avoir du succès*) ~ **la baraque*** to bring the house down; (*fig: tout gâcher*) ~ **la baraque à qn*** to mess *ou* foul‡ everything up (for sb); ~ **la croûte*** *ou* **la graine*** to have a bite *ou* something to eat; ~ **la figure*** *ou* **la gueule‡ à qn** to smash sb's face in‡, knock sb's block off‡; ~ **le morceau‡** (*avouer*) to spill the beans, come clean; (*trahir*) to blow the gaff* (*Brit*), give the game away*; ~ **les pieds à qn*** (*fatiguer*) to bore sb stiff; (*irriter*) to get on sb's nerves; **il nous les casse!‡** he's a pain (in the neck)!‡; **tu me casses les bonbons!‡** you're a pain in the neck!‡, you're getting on my nerves *ou* wick (*Brit*)!‡; ~ **sa pipe*** to kick the bucket‡, snuff it* (*Brit*); **ça/il ne casse pas des briques*, ça/il ne casse rien, ça/il ne casse pas trois pattes à un canard** it's/he's nothing special, it's/he's nothing to shout about *ou* to get excited about; ~ **du sucre sur le dos de qn** to gossip *ou* talk about sb behind his back; **il nous casse la tête** *ou* **les oreilles* avec sa trompette** he deafens us with his trumpet; **il nous casse la tête avec ses histoires*** he bores us stiff with his stories; **à tout** ~* (*extraordinaire*) *film, repas* stupendous, fantastic; *succès* runaway (*épith*); (*tout au plus*) **tu en auras pour 100 F à tout** ~ that'll cost you at the outside *ou* at the most 100 francs; *voir* **omelette, rein.**

2 **vi** (*se briser*) *[objet]* to break; *[baguette, corde, plaque]* to break, snap. **ça casse facilement** it breaks easily; **ça casse comme du verre** it breaks like glass; **le pantalon doit** ~ **sur la chaussure** the trouser (leg) should rest on the shoe.

3 **se casser vpr** a (*se briser*) *[objet]* to break. **la tasse s'est cassée en tombant** the cup fell and broke; **l'anse s'est cassée** the handle came off *ou* broke (off); **se** ~ **net** to break clean off *ou* through.

b *[personne]* **se** ~ **la jambe/une jambe/une dent** to break one's leg/a leg/a tooth; (*fig*) **se** ~ **le cou** *ou* **la figure*** *ou* **la gueule‡** (*tomber*) to come a cropper*, fall flat on one's face; (*d'une certaine hauteur*) to crash down; (*faire faillite*) to come a cropper*, go bankrupt; (*se tuer*) to smash o.s. up*; **se** ~ **la figure contre** to crash into; (*fig*) **se** ~ **le nez** (*trouver porte close*) to find no one in; (*échouer*) to come a cropper*, fail; (*fig*) **il ne s'est pas cassé la tête*** *ou* **la nénette‡** *ou* **le tronc‡** *ou* **le cul**‡** he didn't overtax himself *ou* overdo it; (*fig*) **cela fait 2 jours que je me casse la tête sur ce problème** I've been racking my brains for 2 days over this problem; (*fig*) **se** ~ **les dents** to come a cropper*.

c (*: *se fatiguer*) **il ne s'est rien cassé** *ou* **il ne s'est pas cassé pour écrire cet article** he didn't strain himself writing this article.

d (‡: *partir*) to split‡. **casse-toi!** get the hell out of here!‡

4 **comp** ▶**casse-cou*** **nmf inv** (*sportif etc*) daredevil, reckless person; (*en affaires*) reckless person; **il/elle est casse-cou** he/she is reckless *ou* a daredevil ▶**crier casse-cou à qn** to warn sb ▶**casse-couilles**‡** **nmf inv** pain in the arse**‡ (*Brit*) *ou* ass**‡ (*US*) *ou* butt**‡ ▶**casse-croûte nm inv** snack, lunch (*US*); (*Can*) snack bar; **prendre/emporter un petit casse-croûte** to have/take along a bite to eat *ou* a snack ▶**casse-cul**‡** **adj inv** bloody (*Brit*) *ou* damn annoying‡!; he's a pain in the arse**‡ (*Brit*) *ou* ass**‡ (*US*) ▶**casse-dalle*** = **casse-croûte** ▶**casse-graine*** = **casse-croûte** ▶**casse-gueule‡ adj inv** *sentier* dangerous, treacherous; *opération, entreprise* dicey* (*Brit*), dangerous ◊ **nm inv** (*opération, entreprise*) dicey* (*Brit*) business; (*endroit*) dangerous *ou* nasty spot; **aller au casse-gueule***† to go to war (to be killed) ▶**casse-noisettes nm inv, casse-noix nm inv** nutcrackers (*Brit*), nutcracker (*US*); **as-tu un casse-noisettes?** have you got a pair of nutcrackers? (*Brit*) *ou* a nutcracker? (*US*); **le casse-noisettes est sur la table** the nutcrackers (*Brit*) are *ou* the nutcracker (*US*) is on the table ▶**Casse-Noisette** (*Mus*) the Nutcracker ▶**casse-pattes*: nm inv** *[escalier, côte]* **c'est un vrai casse-pattes*** it's a real slog* ▶**casse-pieds* nmf inv** (*importun*) nuisance, pain in the neck‡; (*ennuyeux*) bore; **ce qu'elle est casse-pieds*!** (*importune*) she's a pain in the neck!‡; (*ennuyeuse*) what a bore *ou* drag* she is! ▶**casse-pipes*: nm inv aller au casse-pipes** to go to the front ▶**casse-tête nm inv** (*Hist: massue*) club; **casse-tête (chinois)** (*problème difficile*) headache (*fig*); (*jeu*) puzzle, brain-teaser ▶**casse-vitesse** sleeping policeman (*Brit*), speed bump.

casserole [kasʀɔl] **nf** a (*Culin*) (*ustensile*) saucepan; (*contenu*) saucepan(ful). **du veau à la** *ou* **en** ~ braised veal. b (*péj*) **c'est une vraie** ~* *[piano]* it's a tinny piano; *[voiture]* it's a tinny car; *[chanteur]* he's a lousy singer*, he can't sing for toffee*; **chanter comme une** ~* to be a lousy singer*, squawk like a parrot*. c (*arg Ciné*) projector. d (*loc*) **passer à la** ~‡ *fille* to screw**‡, lay**‡; *prisonnier* (*tuer*) to bump off‡; **elle est passée à la** ~‡ she got screwed**‡ *ou* laid**‡.

cassette [kasɛt] **nf** a (*coffret*) casket; (*trésor*) *[roi]* privy purse. (*hum*) **il a pris l'argent sur sa** ~ **personnelle** he took the money *ou* paid out of his own pocket. b *[magnétophone, ordinateur]* cassette; *voir* **magnétophone.**

casseur [kasœʀ] **nm** (*: *bravache*) tough *ou* big guy*; (*Aut: ferrailleur*) scrap merchant (*Brit*) *ou* dealer; (*Pol: manifestant*) rioter, rioting demonstrator; (‡: *cambrioleur*) burglar. **jouer les** ~**s*** to come the rough stuff*; ~ **de pierres** stone breaker; (*Tech*) ~ **de vitesse** ramp, sleeping policeman (*Brit*), speed bump.

cassis [kasis] **nm** a (*fruit*) blackcurrant; (*arbuste*) blackcurrant bush; (*liqueur*) blackcurrant liqueur; *voir* **blanc.** b (‡: *tête*) nut*, block*. c *[route]* bump, ridge.

cassolette [kasɔlɛt] **nf** (*ustensile*) *earthenware dish;* (*mets*) cassolette.

cassonade [kasɔnad] **nf** brown sugar.

cassoulet [kasulɛ] **nm** cassoulet (*casserole dish of S.W. France*).

cassure [kɑsyʀ] **nf** a (*lit, fig*) break; *[col]* fold. **à la** ~ **du pantalon** where the trousers rest on the shoe. b (*Géol*) (*gén*) break; (*fissure*) crack; (*faille*) fault.

castagne‡ [kastaɲ] **nf** a (*action*) fighting. **il aime la** ~ he loves a good punch-up* (*Brit*) *ou* fight. b (*rixe*) fight, punch-up* (*Brit*).

castagner (se)‡ [kastaɲe] 1 **vpr** to fight, have a punch-up* (*Brit*). **ils se sont castagnés** they beat (the) hell out of each other‡, they had a punch-up* (*Brit*) *ou* fight.

castagnettes [kastaɲɛt] **nfpl** castanets. **il avait les dents/les genoux qui jouaient des** ~* he could feel his teeth chattering *ou* rattling/knees knocking, his teeth were chattering *ou* rattling/his knees were knocking.

caste [kast] **nf** (*lit, péj*) caste; *voir* **esprit.**

castel [kastɛl] **nm** mansion, small castle.

castillan, e [kastijɑ̃, an] 1 **adj** Castilian. 2 **nm** (*Ling*) Castilian. 3 **nm,f: C~(e)** Castilian.

Castille [kastij] **nf** Castile.

castor [kastɔʀ] **nm** (*Zool, fourrure*) beaver.

castrat [kastʀa] **nm** (*chanteur*) castrato.

castrateur, -trice [kastʀatœʀ, tʀis] **adj** (*Psych*) castrating.

castration [kastʀasjɔ̃] **nf** (*voir* **castrer**) castration; spaying; gelding; doctoring. **complexe de** ~ castration complex.

castrer [kastʀe] 1 **vt** (*gén*) *homme, animal mâle* to castrate; *animal femelle* to castrate, spay; *cheval* to geld; *chat, chien* to doctor, fix (*US*).

Castries [kastʀi] **n** Castries.

castrisme [kastʀism] **nm** Castroism.

castriste [kastʀist] 1 **adj** Castro (*épith*), Castroist. 2 **nmf** supporter *ou* follower of Castro.

casuel, -elle [kɑzɥɛl] 1 **adj** a (*Ling*) **désinences** ~**les** case endings; **système** ~ case system. b (*littér*) fortuitous. 2 **nm** (†) (*gain variable*) commission money; *[curé]* casual offerings (*pl*).

casuiste [kɑzɥist] **nm** (*Rel, péj*) casuist.

casuistique [kɑzɥistik] **nf** (*Rel, péj*) casuistry.

casus belli [kɑzysbɛlli] **nm inv** casus belli.

catabolisme [katabɔlism] **nm** catabolism.

catachrèse [katakʀɛz] **nf** catachresis.

cataclysme [kataklism] **nm** cataclysm.

cataclysmique [kataklismik] **adj** cataclysmic, cataclysmal.

catacombes [katakɔ̃b] **nfpl** catacombs.

catadioptre [katadjɔptʀ] **nm** (*sur voiture*) reflector; (*sur chaussée*) Catseye ® (*Brit*), cat's eye.

catafalque [katafalk] **nm** catafalque.

catalan, e [katalɑ̃, an] 1 **adj** Catalan, Catalonian. 2 **nm** (*Ling*) Catalan. 3 **nm,f: C~(e)** Catalan.

catalepsie [katalɛpsi] **nf** catalepsy. **tomber en** ~ to have a cataleptic fit.

cataleptique [katalɛptik] **adj, nmf** cataleptic.

Catalogne [katalɔɲ] **nf** Catalonia.

catalogne [katalɔɲ] **nf** (*Can Artisanat*) *piece of cloth woven into drapes, covers and rugs.*

catalogue [katalɔg] **nm** (*gén*) catalogue; (*Ordin*) directory. **prix de** ~ list price; **faire le** ~ **de** to catalogue, list; **acheter qch sur** ~ to buy sth from a catalogue.

cataloguer [katalɔge] 1 **vt** *articles, objets* to catalogue, list; *bibliothèque, musée* to catalogue; (*) *personne* to categorize, label (*comme* as).

catalyse [kataliz] **nf** catalysis.

catalyser [katalize] 1 **vt** (*Chim, fig*) to catalyse.

catalyseur [katalizœʀ] **nm** (*Chim, fig*) catalyst.

catalytique [katalitik] **adj** catalytic; *voir* **pot.**

catamaran [katamaʀɑ̃] **nm** (*voilier*) catamaran; *[hydravion]* floats.

cataphote [katafɔt] **nm** ® = **catadioptre.**

cataplasme [kataplasm] **nm** (*Méd*) poultice, cataplasm. ~ **sinapisé** mustard poultice *ou* plaster; (*fig*) **cet entremets est un véritable** ~ **sur l'estomac** the dessert lies like a lead weight *ou* lies heavily on the stomach.

catapultage [katapyltaʒ] **nm** (*lit, fig*) catapulting; (*Aviat*) catapult launch.

catapulte [katapylt] **nf** (*Aviat, Hist*) catapult.
catapulter [katapylte] [1] **vt** (*lit*) to catapult. **il a été catapulté à ce poste** he was pitchforked into this job.
cataracte [kataʀakt] **nf** a (*chute d'eau*) cataract. (*fig*) **des ~s de pluie** torrents of rain. b (*Méd: NonC*) cataract. **il a été opéré de la ~** he's had a cataract operation, he's been operated on for (a) cataract.
catarrhal, e, **mpl -aux** [kataʀal, o] **adj** catarrhal.
catarrhe [kataʀ] **nm** catarrh.
catarrheux, -euse [kataʀø, øz] **adj** *voix* catarrhal, thick. **vieillard ~** wheezing old man.
catastase [katastaz] **nf** (*Phon*) on-glide.
catastrophe [katastʀɔf] **nf** disaster, catastrophe. **~ aérienne** air crash *ou* disaster; **~ naturelle** natural disaster (*gén*); (*Assurances*) act of God; **~! le prof est arrivé!*** panic stations! the teacher's here!; **~! je l'ai perdu!** Hell's bells!* I've lost it!; **en ~: atterrir en ~** to make a forced *ou* an emergency landing; **ils sont partis en ~** they left in a terrible *ou* mad rush; **c'est la ~ cette voiture/ces chaussures!*** this car is/these shoes are a disaster!; **film ~** disaster movie *ou* film; (*fig*) **scénario ~** nightmare scenario.
catastrophé, e* [katastʀɔfe] **adj** *personne, air* stunned. **être ~** to be shattered* *ou* stunned.
catastropher* [katastʀɔfe] [1] **vt** to shatter*, stun.
catastrophique [katastʀɔfik] **adj** disastrous, catastrophic.
catastrophisme [katastʀɔfism] **nm** a (*Géol*) catastrophism. b (*pessimisme*) gloom-mongering. **faire du ~** to preach doom and gloom.
catastrophiste [katastʀɔfist] 1 **adj** *vision* gloomy, (utterly) pessimistic. 2 **nmf** a (*Géol*) catastrophist. b (*pessimiste*) gloom-monger, (utter) pessimist.
catch [katʃ] **nm** wrestling. **il fait du ~** he's an all-in wrestler, he's a wrestler.
catcher [katʃe] [1] **vi** to wrestle.
catcheur, -euse [katʃœʀ, øz] **nm,f** wrestler.
catéchèse [kateʃɛz] **nf** catechetics (*pl*), catechesis.
catéchisation [kateʃizasjɔ̃] **nf** catechization.
catéchiser [kateʃize] [1] **vt** (*Rel*) to catechize; (*endoctriner*) to indoctrinate, catechize; (*sermonner*) to lecture.
catéchisme [kateʃism] **nm** (*enseignement, livre, fig*) catechism. **aller au ~** to go to catechism (class), ≃ go to Sunday school.
catéchiste [kateʃist] **nmf** catechist; *voir* **dame**.
catéchumène [katekymɛn] **nmf** (*Rel*) catechumen; (*fig*) novice.
catégorie [kategɔʀi] **nf** (*gén, Philos*) category; (*Boxe, Hôtellerie*) class; (*Admin*) *[personnel]* grade. (*Boucherie*) **morceaux de première/deuxième ~** prime/second cuts; **ranger par ~** to categorize; **il est de la ~ de ceux qui ...** he comes in *ou* he belongs to the category of those who ...; (*Sociol*) **~ socio(-)professionnelle** socio-professional group.
catégoriel, -elle [kategɔʀjɛl] **adj** a (*Pol, Syndicats*) **revendications ~elles** sectional claims. b (*Gram*) **indice ~** category index.
catégorique [kategɔʀik] **adj** a (*net*) *ton, personne* categorical, dogmatic; *démenti, refus* flat (*épith*), categorical. b (*Philos*) categorical.
catégoriquement [kategɔʀikmɑ̃] **adv** (*voir* **catégorique**) categorically; dogmatically; flatly.
catégorisation [kategɔʀizasjɔ̃] **nf** categorization.
catégoriser [kategɔʀize] [1] **vt** to categorize. **le risque de ~ à outrance** the risk of over-categorizing.
caténaire [katenɛʀ] **adj, nf** (*Rail*) catenary.
catgut [katgyt] **nm** (*Méd*) catgut.
cathare [kataʀ] 1 **adj** Cathar. 2 **nmf: C~** Cathar.
catharsis [kataʀsis] **nf** (*Littérat, Psych*) catharsis.
Cathay [katɛ] **nm** Cathay.
cathédrale [katedʀal] **nf** cathedral; *voir* **verre**.
Catherine [katʀin] **nf** Catherine, Katherine. **~ la Grande** Catherine the Great.
catherinette [katʀinɛt] **nf** *girl of 25 still unmarried by the Feast of St Catherine.*
cathéter [katetɛʀ] **nm** catheter.
cathétérisme [kateteʀism] **nm** catheterization.
catho* [kato] **adj, nmf abrév de catholique.**
cathode [katɔd] **nf** cathode.
cathodique [katɔdik] **adj** (*Phys*) cathodic; *voir* **rayon**.
catholicisme [katɔlisism] **nm** (Roman) Catholicism.
catholicité [katɔlisite] **nf** a (*fidèles*) **la ~** the (Roman) Catholic Church. b (*orthodoxie*) catholicity.
catholique [katɔlik] 1 **adj** a (*Rel*) *foi, dogme* (Roman) Catholic. b (*) **pas (très) ~** fishy*, shady, a bit doubtful, not very kosher* (*US*). 2 **nmf** (Roman) Catholic.
catimini [katimini] **adv: en ~** on the sly *ou* quiet; **sortir en ~** to steal *ou* sneak out; **il me l'a dit en ~** he whispered it in my ear.
catin† [katɛ̃] **nf** (*prostituée*) trollop†, harlot††.
cation [katjɔ̃] **nm** cation.
catogan [katɔgɑ̃] **nm** *bow tying hair on the neck.*
Caton [katɔ̃] **nm** Cato.
Catulle [katyl] **nm** Catullus.
Caucase [kɔkɑz] **nm: le ~** the Caucasus.
caucasien, -ienne [kɔkɑzjɛ̃, jɛn] 1 **adj** Caucasian. 2 **nm,f: C~(ne)** Caucasian.
cauchemar [koʃmaʀ] **nm** nightmare. (*fig*) **l'analyse grammaticale était son ~** parsing was a nightmare to him; **vision de ~** nightmarish sight.
cauchemarder [koʃmaʀde] [1] **vi** to have a nightmare, have nightmares. **faire ~ qn** to give sb nightmares.
cauchemardesque [koʃmaʀdɛsk] **adj** *impression, expérience* nightmarish.
cauchemardeux, -euse [koʃmaʀdø, øz] **adj** a = **cauchemardesque.** b **sommeil ~** sleep full of nightmares.
caudal, e, **mpl -aux** [kodal, o] **adj** caudal.
cauri [kɔʀi] **nm** cowrie *ou* cowry (shell).
causal, e, **mpl -aux** [kozal, o] **adj** causal.
causalité [kozalite] **nf** causality.
causant, e* [kozɑ̃, ɑ̃t] **adj** talkative, chatty. **il n'est pas très ~** he doesn't say very much, he's not very forthcoming *ou* talkative.
causatif, -ive [kozatif, iv] **adj** (*Gram*) *conjonction* causal; *construction, verbe* causative.
cause [koz] **nf** a (*motif, raison*) cause. **quelle est la ~ de l'accident?** what caused the accident?, what was the cause of the accident?; **on ne connaît pas la ~ de son absence** the reason for *ou* the cause of his absence is not known; **être (la) ~ de qch** to be the cause of sth; **la chaleur en est la ~** it is caused by the heat; **la ~ en demeure inconnue** the cause remains unknown, the reason for it remains unknown; **les ~s qui l'ont poussé à agir** the reasons that caused him to act; **être ~ que†: cet accident est ~ que nous sommes en retard** this accident is the cause of our being late; **elle est ~ que nous sommes en retard** she is responsible for our being late; *voir* **relation.**

b (*Jur*) lawsuit, case; (*à plaider*) brief. **~ civile** civil action; **~ criminelle** criminal proceedings; **la ~ est entendue** (*lit*) the sides have been heard; (*fig*) there's no doubt in our minds; **~ célèbre** cause célèbre, famous trial *ou* case; **plaider sa ~** to plead one's case; **un avocat sans ~(s)** a briefless barrister; *voir* **connaissance.**

c (*ensemble d'intérêts*) cause. **une juste/grande/noble/bonne ~** a just/great/noble/good cause; **une ~ perdue** a lost cause; **faire ~ commune avec qn** to make common cause with sb, side *ou* take sides with sb; *voir* **fait.**

d (*Philos*) cause. **~ première/seconde/finale** primary/secondary/final cause.

e (*loc*) **à ~ de** (*en raison de*) because of, owing to; (*par égard pour*) because of, for the sake of; **à ~ de cet incident technique** owing to *ou* because of this technical failure; **c'est à ~ de lui que nous sommes perdus** it's because of him we got lost, he is responsible for our getting lost; **à ~ de son âge** on account of *ou* because of his age; **il est venu à ~ de vous** he came for your sake *ou* because of you; (*iro*) **ce n'est pas à ~ de lui que j'y suis arrivé!** it's no thanks to him I managed to do it!; **être en ~** *[personne]* to be involved *ou* concerned; *[intérêts etc]* to be at stake, be involved; **son honnêteté n'est pas en ~** there is no question about his honesty, his honesty is not in question; **mettre en ~** *innocence, nécessité, capacité* to (call into) question; *personne* to implicate; **remettre en ~** *principe, tradition* to question, challenge; **sa démission remet tout en ~** his resignation re-opens the whole question, we're back to square one* (*Brit*) *ou* where we started from because of his resignation; **mettre qn hors de ~** to clear *ou* exonerate sb; **c'est hors de ~** it is out of the question; **pour ~ de** on account of; **fermé pour ~ d'inventaire/de maladie** closed for stocktaking/on account of illness; **et pour ~!** and for (a very) good reason!; **non sans ~!** not without (good) cause *ou* reason!; **ils le regrettent — non sans ~!** they are sorry — as well they might be! *ou* not without reason!
causer¹ [koze] [1] **vt** (*provoquer*) to cause; (*entraîner*) to bring about. **~ des ennuis à qn** to get sb into trouble, bring trouble to sb; **~ de la peine à qn** to hurt sb; **~ du plaisir à qn** to give pleasure to sb.
causer² [koze] [1] **vti** a (*s'entretenir*) to chat, talk; (*: *discourir*) to speak, talk. **~ de qch** to talk about sth; (*propos futiles*) to chat about sth; **~ politique/travail** to talk politics/shop; **elles causaient chiffons** they were chatting about *ou* discussing clothes; **~ à qn*** to talk *ou* speak to sb; (*iro*) **cause toujours, tu m'intéresses!** keep going *ou* talking, I'm all ears *ou* I'm hanging on your every word (*iro*). b (*jaser*) to talk, gossip (*sur qn* about sb). **on en cause** people are talking; **on cause dans le village/le bureau** people are talking in the village/the office. c (‡: *avouer*) to talk. **pour le faire ~** to loosen his tongue, to make him talk.
causerie [kozʀi] **nf** (*conférence*) talk; (*conversation*) chat.
causette [kozɛt] **nf: faire la ~, faire un brin de ~** to have a chat* *ou* natter* (*Brit*) (*avec* with).
causeur, -euse [kozœʀ, øz] 1 **adj** (*rare*) talkative, chatty. 2 **nm,f** talker, conversationalist. 3 **causeuse nf** (*siège*) causeuse, love seat.
causse [kos] **nm** causse, *limestone plateau (in south-central France).*
causticité [kostisite] **nf** (*lit, fig*) causticity.
caustique [kostik] **adj, nmf** (*Sci, fig*) caustic.
caustiquement [kostikmɑ̃] **adv** caustically.
cautèle [kotɛl] **nf** (*littér*) cunning, guile.
cauteleusement [kotløzmɑ̃] **adv** (*littér*) in a cunning way.

cauteleux, -euse [kotlø, øz] adj (*littér*) cunning.
cautère [kɔtɛʀ] nm cautery. **c'est un ~ sur une jambe de bois** it's as much use as a poultice on a wooden leg.
cautérisation [kɔteʀizasjɔ̃] nf cauterization.
cautériser [kɔteʀize] 1 vt to cauterize.
caution [kosjɔ̃] nf a (*somme d'argent*) (*Fin*) guarantee, security; (*Jur*) bail (bond). **~ de soumission** bid bond; **~ solidaire** joint and several guarantee; **verser une ~ (de 1 000 F)** to put *ou* lay down a security *ou* a guarantee (of 1,000 francs); **mettre qn en liberté sous ~** to release *ou* free sb on bail; **libéré sous ~** freed *ou* released *ou* out on bail; **payer la ~ de qn** to stand (*Brit*) *ou* go (*US*) bail for sb, bail sb out.
b (*fig: garantie morale*) guarantee. **sa parole est ma ~** his word is my guarantee.
c (*appui*) backing, support. **avoir la ~ d'un parti/de son chef** to have the backing *ou* support of a party/one's boss.
d (*personne, garant*) **se porter ~ pour qn** to stand security (*Brit*) *ou* surety for sb; *voir* **sujet**.
cautionnement [kosjɔnmɑ̃] nm (*somme*) guaranty, guarantee, security (*Brit*), surety; (*contrat*) security *ou* surety bond; (*soutien*) support, backing.
cautionner [kosjɔne] 1 vt a (*répondre de*) (*moralement*) to answer for, guarantee; (*financièrement*) to guarantee, stand surety *ou* guarantor for. b *politique, gouvernement* to support, give one's support *ou* backing to.
cavaillon [kavajɔ̃] nm cavaillon melon.
cavalcade [kavalkad] nf a (*course tumultueuse*) stampede; (**: troupe désordonnée*) stampede, stream. b *[cavaliers]* cavalcade. c (*défilé, procession*) cavalcade, procession.
cavalcader [kavalkade] 1 vi (*gambader, courir*) to stream, swarm, stampede; (*†: chevaucher*) to cavalcade, ride in a cavalcade.
cavale [kaval] nf a (*littér*) mare. b (*arg Prison: évasion*) **être en ~** to be on the run.
cavaler‡ [kavale] 1 1 vi a (*courir*) to run. **j'ai dû ~ dans tout Londres pour le trouver** I had to rush all round London to find it. b (*draguer*) *[homme]* to chase anything in a skirt*; *[femme]* to chase anything in trousers*. 2 vt (*ennuyer*) to bore, annoy. **il commence à nous ~** we're beginning to get cheesed off* (*Brit*) *ou* browned off* (*Brit*) *ou* teed off* (*US*) with him, he's beginning to get on our wick‡ (*Brit*). 3 **se cavaler** vpr (*se sauver*) to clear off‡, get the hell out of it‡, scarper‡ (*Brit*), skedaddle*. **les animaux se sont cavalés** the animals legged it* *ou* scarpered‡ (*Brit*) *ou* skedaddled*; **il s'est cavalé à la maison** he cleared off home‡.
cavalerie [kavalʀi] nf (*Mil*) cavalry; *[cirque]* horses. (*Mil*) **~ légère** light cavalry *ou* horse; **c'est de la grosse ~** (*nourriture*) it is heavy stuff; (*objets*) it is uninspiring stuff.
cavaleur‡ [kavalœʀ] nm wolf, womanizer. **il est ~** he is a womanizer, he chases anything in a skirt*.
cavaleuse‡ [kavaløz] nf hot piece‡. **elle est ~** she chases anything in trousers*.
cavalier, -ière [kavalje, jɛʀ] 1 adj a (*impertinent*) casual, cavalier, offhand. **je trouve que c'est un peu ~ de sa part (de faire cela)** I think he's being a bit offhand (doing that). b **allée/piste ~ière** riding/bridle path. 2 nm,f a (*Équitation*) rider. (*fig*) **faire ~ seul** to go it alone, be a loner*. b (*partenaire: au bal etc*) partner. 3 nm a (*Mil*) trooper, cavalryman. **une troupe de 20 ~s** a troop of 20 horses. b (*accompagnateur*) escort; (*Can **) boyfriend, beau (*US*). **être le ~ d'une dame** to escort a lady. c (*Échecs*) knight. d (*clou*) staple; *[balance]* rider; *[dossier]* tab. e (*Hist Brit*) cavalier. f (*††: gentilhomme*) gentleman.
cavalièrement [kavaljɛʀmɑ̃] adv casually, in cavalier fashion, offhandedly.
cavatine [kavatin] nf (*Mus*) cavatina.
cave¹ [kav] nf a (*pièce*) cellar; (*voûtée*) vault; (*cabaret*) cellar nightclub. **chercher** *ou* **fouiller de la ~ au grenier** to search the house from top to bottom. b (*Vin*) cellar. **avoir une bonne ~** to have *ou* keep a fine cellar. c (*coffret à liqueurs*) liqueur cabinet; (*coffret à cigares*) cigar box. d (*Can*) *[maison]* basement.
cave² [kav] adj (*creux*) *yeux, joues* hollow, sunken; *voir* **veine**.
cave³‡ [kav] nm a straight (*arg*), *someone who does not belong to the underworld.* b (*imbécile*) sucker‡. **il est ~** he's a sucker‡.
caveau, pl **~x** [kavo] nm (*sépulture*) vault, tomb; (*cabaret*) nightclub; (*cave*) (small) cellar. **~ de famille** family vault.
caverne [kavɛʀn] nf a (*grotte*) cave, cavern; *voir* **homme**. b (*Anat*) cavity.
caverneux, -euse [kavɛʀnø, øz] adj a *voix* hollow, cavernous. b (*Anat, Méd*) *respiration* cavernous; *poumon* with cavitations, with a cavernous lesion; *voir* **corps**. c (*littér*) *montagne, tronc* cavernous.
caviar [kavjaʀ] nm a (*Culin*) caviar(e). **~ rouge** salmon roe. b (*Presse*) **passer au ~** to blue-pencil, censor.
caviarder [kavjaʀde] 1 vt (*Presse*) to blue-pencil, censor.
caviste [kavist] nm cellarman.
cavité [kavite] nf cavity. **~ articulaire** socket (*of bone*); **~ pulpaire** (tooth) pulp cavity; **~ buccale** oral cavity.
Cayenne [kajɛn] n Cayenne; *voir* **poivre**.
CB (abrév de **Carte Bleue**) *voir* **carte**.
C.B. [sibi] nf (abrév de **Citizens' Band**) **la ~** CB radio.
C.C. [sese] a nm (abrév de **compte courant**) C/A. b (abrév de **corps consulaire**) *voir* **corps**.
CCP [sesepe] nm a (abrév de **centre de chèques postaux**) *voir* **centre**. b (abrév de **compte chèque postal**) *voir* **compte**.
CD¹ [sede] nm (abrév de **compact disc**) CD.
CD² [sede] (abrév de **corps diplomatique**) CD.
CDD [sedede] nm (abrév de **contrat à durée déterminée**) *voir* **contrat**.
CDDP [sededepe] nm (abrév de **centre départemental de documentation pédagogique**) *voir* **centre**.
CDI [sedei] nm a (abrév de **centre de documentation et d'information**) *voir* **centre**. b (abrév de **centre des impôts**) *voir* **centre**. c (abrév de **contrat à durée indéterminée**) *voir* **contrat**. d (abrév de **compact disc interactif**) CDI.
CD-ROM [sedeʀɔm] nm (abrév de **compact disc read only memory**) CD-ROM.
CDS [sedeɛs] nm (abrév de **Centre des démocrates sociaux**) *French political party.*
CDV [sedeve] nm (abrév de **compact disc video**) CDV.
CE [seə] 1 nm a (abrév de **comité d'entreprise**) *voir* **comité**. b (abrév de **Conseil de l'Europe**) *voir* **conseil**. c (abrév de **cours élémentaire**) *voir* **cours**. 2 nf (abrév de **Communauté européenne**) EC.
ce [sə] , **cet** [sɛt] *devant voyelle ou h muet au masculin,* **cette** [sɛt] *f,* **ces** [se] *pl* 1 adj dém a (*proximité*) this; (*pl*) these; (*non-proximité*) that; (*pl*) those. **ce chapeau(-ci)/(-là)** this/that hat; **si seulement ce mal de tête s'en allait** if only this headache would go away; **un de ces films sans queue ni tête** one of those films without beginning or end; **ah ces promenades dans la campagne anglaise!** (*en se promenant*) ah these walks in the English countryside!; (*évocation*) ah those walks in the English countryside!; **je ne peux pas voir cet homme** I can't stand (the sight of) that man; **cet imbécile d'enfant a perdu ses lunettes** this *ou* that stupid child has lost his (*ou* her) glasses; **et ce rhume/cette jambe, comment ça va?*** and how's the cold/leg (doing)?*
b (*loc de temps*) **venez ce soir/cet après-midi** come tonight *ou* this evening/this afternoon; **cette nuit** (*qui vient*) tonight; (*passée*) last night; **ce mois(-ci)** this month; **ce mois-là** that month; **il faudra mieux travailler ce trimestre(-ci)** you'll have to work harder this term; **il a fait très beau ces jours(-ci)** the weather's been very fine lately *ou* these last few days; **en ces temps troublés** (*de nos jours*) in these troubled days; (*dans le passé*) in those troubled days; **j'irai la voir un de ces jours** I'll call on her one of these days.
c (*intensif*) **comment peut-il raconter ces mensonges!** how can he tell such lies!; **aurait-il vraiment ce courage?** would he really have that sort of *ou* that much courage?; **cette idée!** what an idea!; **ce toupet!*** what (a) nerve!*, such cheek!*; **cette générosité me semble suspecte** such *ou* this generosity looks suspicious to me; **elle a de ces initiatives!** she gets hold of *ou* has some *ou* these wild ideas!; *voir* **un**.
d (*frm*) **si ces dames veulent bien me suivre** if the ladies will be so kind as to follow me; **ces messieurs sont en réunion** the gentlemen are in a meeting.
e (*avec qui, que*) **cette amie chez qui elle habite est docteur** the friend she's living with is a doctor; **elle n'est pas de ces femmes qui se plaignent toujours** she's not one of those *ou* these women who are always complaining; **c'est un de ces livres que l'on lit en vacances** it's one of those books *ou* the sort of book you read on holiday; **il a cette manie qu'ont les jeunes de ...** he has this *ou* that habit common to young people of ... *ou* that young people have of ... .
2 pron dém a **c'est, ce sont: qui est-ce?** *ou* **c'est?* — c'est un médecin/l'instituteur** (*en désignant*) who's he? *ou* who's that? — he is a doctor/the schoolteacher; (*au téléphone, à la porte*) who is it? — it's a doctor/the schoolteacher; **c'est la camionnette du boucher** it's *ou* that's the butcher's van; **ce sont des hôtesses de l'air/de bons souvenirs** they are air hostesses/happy memories; **c'est la plus intelligente de la classe** she is the most intelligent in the class; **c'est une voiture rapide** it's a fast car; **c'était le bon temps!** those were the days!; **je vais acheter des pêches, ce n'est pas cher en ce moment** I am going to buy some peaches — they're quite cheap just now; **qui est-ce qui a crié? — c'est lui** who shouted? — HE did *ou* it was him; **à qui est ce livre? — c'est à elle/à ma sœur** whose book is this? — it's hers/my sister's; **c'est impossible à faire** it's impossible to do; **c'est impossible de le faire*** it's impossible to do it.
b (*tournure emphatique*) **c'est le vent qui a emporté la toiture** it was the wind that blew the roof off; **c'est eux*** *ou* **ce sont eux** *ou* **c'étaient eux qui mentaient** they are the ones who *ou* it's they who were lying; **c'est vous qui devez décider, c'est à vous de décider** it's up to you to decide, it's you who must decide; **c'est toi qui le dis!** that's what YOU say!; **c'est avec plaisir que nous acceptons** we accept with pleasure; **c'est une bonne voiture que vous avez là** that's a good car you've got there; **un hôtel pas cher, c'est difficile à trouver** a cheap hotel isn't easy to find; **c'est à se demander s'il n'est pas fou** you really wonder *ou* it makes you wonder if he isn't mad.
c **ce qui, ce que** what; (*reprenant une proposition*) which; **tout ce que je sais** all (that) I know; **ce qui est important c'est ...** what really

matters is ...; **elle fait ce qu'on lui dit** she does what she is told *ou* as she is told; **il ne sait pas ce que sont devenus ses amis** he doesn't know what has become of his friends; **il ne comprenait pas ce à quoi on faisait allusion/ce dont on l'accusait** he didn't understand what they were hinting at/what he was being accused of; **nous n'avons pas de jardin, ce qui est dommage** we haven't got a garden, which is a pity; **il faut être diplômé, ce qu'il n'est pas** you have to have qualifications, which he hasn't; **il a été reçu à son examen, ce à quoi il s'attendait fort peu** he passed his exam, which he wasn't expecting (to do); **voilà tout ce que je sais** that's all I know.

d **à ce que, de ce que: on ne s'attendait pas à ce qu'il parle** they were not expecting him *ou* he was not expected to speak; **il se plaint de ce qu'on ne l'ait pas prévenu** he is complaining that no one warned him.

e (**: intensif*) **ce que** *ou* **qu'est-ce que ce film est lent!** how slow this film is!, what a slow film this is!; **ce qu'on peut s'amuser!** what fun (we are having)!; **ce qu'il parle bien!** what a good speaker he is!, how well he speaks!; **ce que c'est que le destin!** that's fate for you!; **voilà ce que c'est que de conduire trop vite** that's what comes of driving too fast.

f (*explication*) **c'est que: quand il écrit, c'est qu'il a besoin d'argent** when he writes, it means (that) *ou* it's because he needs money; **c'est qu'elle n'entend rien, la pauvre!** but the poor woman can't hear a thing!, but she can't hear, poor woman!; **ce n'est pas qu'elle soit bête, mais elle ne travaille pas** it's not that she's stupid, but she just doesn't work.

g (*loc*) **c'est (vous) dire s'il a eu peur** that shows you how frightened he was; **c'est tout dire** that (just) shows; **à ce qu'on dit/que j'ai appris** from what they say/what I've heard; **qu'est-ce à dire?**† what does that mean?; **ce faisant** in so doing, in the process; **ce disant** so saying, saying this; **pour ce faire** to this end, with this end in view; (*frm*) **et ce: il a refusé, et ce, après toutes nos prières** he refused, (and this) after all our entreaties.

CEA [seəa] a **nm** (**abrév de compte d'épargne en actions**) *voir* **compte.** b **nf** (**abrév de Commissariat à l'énergie atomique**) AEC.

céans†† [seɑ̃] **adv** here, in this house; *voir* **maître.**

CECA [seka] **nf** (**abrév de Communauté européenne du charbon et de l'acier**) ECSC.

ceci [səsi] **pron dém** this. **ce cas a ~ de surprenant que ...** this case is surprising in that ..., there is one surprising thing about this case which is that ...; **à ~ près que** except that, with the *ou* this exception that; **~ compense cela** one thing makes up for another.

Cécile [sesil] **nf** Cecilia.

cécité [sesite] **nf** blindness. (*Ski*) **~ des neiges** snow-blindness; **~ verbale** word blindness; **il a été frappé de ~ à l'âge de 5 ans** he was struck blind *ou* he went blind at the age of 5.

cédant, e [sedɑ̃, ɑ̃t] (*Jur*) 1 **adj** assigning. 2 **nm,f** assignor.

céder [sede] 6 1 **vt** a (*donner*) *part, place, tour* to give up. **~ qch à qn** to let sb have sth, give sth up to sb; **~ la place (à qn)** to let sb take one's place; **je m'en vais, je vous cède ma place** *ou* **je cède la place** I'm going so you can have my place *ou* I'll let you have my place; (*Rad*) **et maintenant je cède l'antenne à notre correspondant à Paris** now (I'll hand you) over to our Paris correspondent; (*Jur*) **~ ses biens** to make over *ou* transfer one's property; *voir* **parole.**

b (*vendre*) *commerce* to sell, dispose of. **~ qch à qn** to let sb have sth, sell sth to sb; **le fermier m'a cédé un litre de lait** the farmer let me have a litre of milk; **~ à bail** to lease; **"bail à ~"** "lease for sale"; **il a bien voulu ~ un bout de terrain** he agreed to part with a plot of ground.

c (*loc*) **~ le pas à qn/qch** to give precedence to sb/sth; **son courage ne le cède en rien à son intelligence** he's as brave as he is intelligent; **il ne le cède à personne en égoïsme** as far as selfishness is concerned he's second to none; **il ne lui cède en rien** he is every bit his equal; *voir* **terrain.**

2 **vi** a (*capituler*) to give in. **~ par faiblesse/lassitude** to give in out of weakness/tiredness; **aucun ne veut ~** no one wants to give in *ou* give way.

b **~ à** (*succomber à*) to give way to, yield to; (*consentir*) to give in to; **~ à la force/tentation** to give way *ou* yield to force/temptation; **~ à qn** (*à ses raisons, ses avances*) to give in *ou* yield to sb; **~ aux caprices/prières de qn** to give in to sb's whims/entreaties; **il cède facilement à la colère** he gives way easily to anger.

c (*se rompre*) *[digue, chaise, branche]* to give way; (*fléchir, tomber*) *[fièvre, colère]* to subside. **la glace a cédé sous le poids** the ice gave (way) under the weight.

cédétiste [sedetist] 1 **adj** CFDT (*épith*). 2 **nmf** member of the CFDT.

CEDEX [sedɛks] **nm** (**abrév de courrier d'entreprise à distribution exceptionnelle**) express postal service (*for bulk users*).

cédille [sedij] **nf** cedilla.

cédrat [sedʀa] **nm** (*fruit*) citron; (*arbre*) citron (tree).

cèdre [sɛdʀ] **nm** (*arbre*) cedar (tree); (*Can: thuya*) cedar, arbor vitae; (*bois*) cedar (wood).

cédrière [sedʀijɛʀ] **nf** (*Can*) cedar grove.

cédulaire [sedylɛʀ] **adj** (*Jur*) **impôts ~s** scheduled taxes.

cédule [sedyl] **nf** (*Impôts*) schedule.

CEE [seəə] **nf** (**abrév de Communauté économique européenne**) EEC.

CEEA [seəəa] **nf** (**abrév de Communauté européenne de l'énergie atomique**) EAEC.

cégétiste [seʒetist] 1 **adj** CGT (*épith*). 2 **nmf** member of the CGT.

CEI [seəi] **nf** (**abrév de Communauté des États indépendants**) CIS.

ceindre [sɛ̃dʀ] 52 **vt** (*littér*) a (*entourer*) **~ sa tête d'un bandeau** to put a band round one's head; **la tête ceinte d'un diadème** wearing a diadem; **~ une ville de murailles** to encircle a town with walls; (*Bible*) **se ~ les reins** to gird one's loins. b (*mettre*) *armure, insigne d'autorité* to don, put on. **~ son épée** to buckle *ou* gird on one's sword; (*lit, fig*) **~ l'écharpe municipale** ≃ to put on *ou* don the mayoral chain; (*lit, fig*) **~ la couronne** to assume the crown.

ceint, e [sɛ̃, ɛ̃t] **ptp de ceindre.**

ceinture [sɛ̃tyʀ] 1 **nf** a *[manteau, pantalon]* belt; *[pyjama, robe de chambre]* cord; (*écharpe*) sash; (*gaine, corset*) girdle. **se mettre** *ou* **se serrer la ~*** to tighten *ou* pull in one's belt (*fig*); **elle a tout, et nous ~!*** she's got everything and we've got sweet FA‡ *ou* nix!‡ (*US*) *ou* zilch!* (*US*); **faire ~*** to have to go without.

b (*Couture: taille*) *[pantalon, jupe]* waistband.

c (*Anat*) waist. **nu jusqu'à la ~** stripped to the waist; **l'eau lui arrivait (jusqu')à la ~** the water came up to his waist, he was waist-deep in *ou* up to his waist in water.

d (*Sport*) (*prise*) waistlock. (*Judo*) **~ noire** *etc* black *etc* belt; (*Boxe, fig*) **coup au-dessous de la ~** blow below the belt.

e *[fortifications, murailles]* ring; *[arbres, montagnes]* belt.

f (*métro, bus*) circle line. **petite/grande ~** inner/outer circle.

2 **comp ►ceinture de chasteté** chastity belt **►ceinture de flanelle** flannel binder **►ceinture fléchée** (*Can*) arrow sash **►ceinture de grossesse** maternity girdle *ou* support **►ceinture herniaire** truss **►ceinture médicale** = **ceinture orthopédique ►ceinture de natation** swimmer's float belt **►ceinture orthopédique** surgical corset **►ceinture pelvienne** (*Anat*) pelvic girdle **►ceinture de sauvetage** lifebelt **►ceinture scapulaire** (*Anat*) pectoral girdle **►ceinture de sécurité (à enrouleur)** (inertia reel) seat *ou* safety belt **►ceinture verte** green belt.

ceinturer [sɛ̃tyʀe] 1 **vt** *personne* (*gén*) to grasp *ou* seize round the waist; (*Sport*) to tackle (round the waist); *ville* to surround, encircle.

ceinturon [sɛ̃tyʀɔ̃] **nm** *[uniforme]* belt.

cela [s(ə)la] **pron dém** a (*gén, en opposition à ceci*) that; (*en sujet apparent*) it. **qu'est-ce que ~ veut dire?** what does that *ou* this mean?; **on ne s'attendait pas à ~** that was (quite) unexpected, we weren't expecting that; **~ n'est pas très facile** that's not very easy; **~ m'agace de l'entendre se plaindre** it annoys me to hear him complain; **~ vaut la peine qu'il essaie** it's worth his trying; **~ me donne du souci** it *ou* that gives me a lot of worry; **faire des études, ~ ne le tentait guère** studying did not really appeal to him.

b (*renforce comment, où, pourquoi etc*) **il ne veut pas venir — pourquoi ~?** he won't come — why not? *ou* why won't he?; **j'ai vu X — qui ~?/quand ~?/où ~?** I've seen X — who (do you mean)? *ou* who is that?/when was that?/where was that?

c **~ fait 10 jours/longtemps qu'il est parti** it is 10 days/a long time since he left, he has been gone 10 days/a long time, he left 10 days/a long time ago.

d (*loc*) **voyez-vous ~!** did you ever hear of such a thing!; **~ ne fait rien** it *ou* that does not matter; **et en dehors de** *ou* **à part ~?** apart from that?; **à ~ près que** except that, with the exception that; **il y a 2 jours de ~, il y a de ~ 2 jours** 2 days ago; **avec eux, il y a ~ de bien qu'ils ...** there's one thing to their credit and that's that they ..., I'll say this *ou* that for them, they ... .

CEL [seəɛl] **nm** (**abrév de compte d'épargne logement**) *voir* **compte.**

céladon [seladɔ̃] **nm, adj inv: (vert) ~** celadon.

célébrant [selebʀɑ̃] (*Rel*) 1 **adj m** officiating. 2 **nm** celebrant.

célébration [selebʀasjɔ̃] **nf** celebration.

célèbre [selɛbʀ] **adj** famous, celebrated (*par* for). **cet escroc, tristement ~ par ses vols** this crook, notorious for his robberies *ou* whose robberies have won him notoriety; **se rendre ~ par** to achieve celebrity for *ou* on account of.

célébrer [selebʀe] 6 **vt** a *anniversaire, fête* to celebrate; *cérémonie* to hold; *mariage* to celebrate, solemnize. **~ la messe** to celebrate mass.

b (*glorifier*) to celebrate, extol. **~ les louanges de qn** to sing sb's praises.

célébrité [selebʀite] **nf** (*renommée*) fame, celebrity; (*personne*) celebrity. **parvenir à la ~** to rise to fame.

celer [səle] 5 **vt** († *ou littér*) to conceal (*à qn* from sb).

céleri [sɛlʀi] **nm: ~ en branche(s)** celery; **~(-rave)** celeriac; **~ rémoulade** celeriac in remoulade (dressing); *voir* **pied.**

célérité [seleʀite] **nf** promptness, speed, swiftness. **avec ~** promptly, swiftly.

célesta [selɛsta] **nm** celeste, celesta.

céleste [selɛst] **adj** a (*du ciel, divin*) celestial, heavenly. **colère/puissance ~** celestial anger/power, anger/power of heaven; **le C~ Empire** the Celestial Empire. b (*fig: merveilleux*) heavenly.

célibat [seliba] **nm** *[homme]* bachelorhood, celibacy; *[femme]* spinsterhood; (*par abstinence*) (period of) celibacy; *[prêtre]* celibacy. **vivre dans le ~** (*gén*) to live a single life, be unmarried; *[prêtre]* to be

celibate.
célibataire [selibatɛʀ] 1 adj (*gén*) single, unmarried; *prêtre* celibate; (*Admin*) single. **mère ~** unmarried mother; **père (*ou* mère) ~** single parent. 2 nm (*homme*) bachelor; (*Admin*) single man. **la vie de ~** the life of a single man, the bachelor's life, (the) single life; **club pour ~s** singles club. 3 nf (*femme jeune*) single girl, unmarried woman; (*moins jeune*) spinster; (*Admin*) single woman. **la vie de ~** (the) single life, the life of a single woman.
célioscopie [seljɔskɔpi] nf = **cœlioscopie**.
celle [sɛl] pron dém *voir* **celui**.
cellier [selje] nm storeroom (*for wine and food*).
Cellophane [selɔfan] nf ® Cellophane ®. *aliment* **sous C~** wrapped in Cellophane.
cellulaire [selylɛʀ] adj a (*Bio*) cellular. b **régime ~** confinement; **voiture *ou* fourgon ~** prison van; *voir* **téléphone**.
cellule [selyl] nf (*Bio, Bot, Jur, Mil, Phot, Pol*) cell; *[avion]* airframe; *[électrophone]* cartridge. (*Sociol*) **~ familiale** family unit; **réunir une ~ de crise** to convene an emergency committee; (*Mil*) **6 jours de ~** 6 days in the cells, 6 days' cells; **~ photo-électrique** electric eye.
cellulite [selylit] nf (*graisse*) cellulite; (*inflammation*) cellulitis. **avoir de la ~** to have cellulite (*SPÉC*).
celluloïd [selylɔid] nm celluloid.
cellulose [selyloz] nf cellulose. **~ végétale** dietary fibre.
cellulosique [selylozik] adj cellulose (*épith*).
celte [sɛlt] 1 adj Celtic. 2 nmf: **C~** Celt.
celtique [sɛltik] adj, nm Celtic.
celui [səlɥi], **celle** [sɛl], mpl **ceux** [sø], fpl **celles** [sɛl] pron dém a (*fonction démonstrative*) **celui-ci, celle-ci** this one; **ceux-ci, celles-ci** these (ones); **celui-là, celle-là** that one; **ceux-là, celles-là** those (ones); **j'hésite entre les deux chaises, celle-ci est plus élégante, mais on est mieux sur celle-là** I hesitate between the two chairs – this one's more elegant, but that one's more comfortable; **une autre citation, plus littéraire celle-là** another quotation, this time a more literary one *ou* this next one is more literary.
b (*référence à un antécédent*) **j'ai rendu visite à mon frère et à mon oncle, celui-ci était malade** I visited my brother and my uncle and the latter was ill; **elle écrivit à son frère: celui-ci ne répondit pas** she wrote to her brother, who did not answer *ou* but he did not answer; **ceux-là, ils auront de mes nouvelles** that lot* *ou* as for them, I'll give them a piece of my mind; **il a vraiment de la chance, celui-là!** that chap* (*Brit*) *ou* guy* certainly has a lot of luck!; **elle est forte *ou* bien bonne, celle-là!** that's a bit much! *ou* steep!* *ou* stiff!*
c (+ *de*) **celui de: je n'aime pas cette pièce, celle de X est meilleure** I don't like this play, X's is better; **c'est celui des 3 frères que je connais le mieux** of the 3 brothers he's the one I know (the) best, he's the one I know (the) best of the 3 brothers; **il n'a qu'un désir, celui de devenir ministre** he only wants one thing – (that's) to become a minister; **s'il cherche un local, celui d'en-dessous est libre** if he's looking for a place, the one below is free; **ce livre est pour celui d'entre vous que la peinture intéresse** this book is for whichever one of you who is interested in painting; **pour ceux d'entre vous qui ...** for those of *ou* among you who ... .
d **celui qui/que/dont: ses romans sont ceux qui se vendent le mieux** his novels are the ones *ou* those that sell best; **c'est celle que l'on accuse** she is the one who is being accused; **donnez-lui le ballon jaune, c'est celui qu'il préfère** give him the yellow ball – it's *ou* that's the one he likes best; **celui dont je t'ai parlé** the one I told you about.
e (*: *avec adj, participe*) **cette marque est celle recommandée par X** this brand is the one recommended by X, this is the brand recommended by X; **celui proche de la fontaine** the one near the fountain; **tous ceux ayant le même âge** all those of the same age.
cément [semɑ̃] nm (*Métal*) cement; *[dents]* cementum, cement.
cénacle [senakl] nm (*réunion, cercle*) (literary) coterie *ou* set; (*Rel*) cenacle.
cendre [sɑ̃dʀ] nf (*gén: substance*) ash, ashes. *[charbon]* ~, ~s ash, ashes, cinders; *[mort]* ~s ashes; **~ de bois** wood ash; **des ~s *ou* de la ~ (de cigarette)** (cigarette) ash; **réduire en ~s** to reduce to ashes; **couleur de ~** ashen, ash-coloured; **le jour des C~s, les C~s** Ash Wednesday; **cuire qch sous la ~** to cook sth in (the) embers; (*Géol*) **~s volcaniques** volcanic ash; *voir* **couver, renaître**.
cendré, e [sɑ̃dʀe] 1 adj (*couleur*) ashen. **gris/blond ~** ash grey/blond. 2 **cendrée** nf (*piste*) cinder track. (*Chasse*) **de la ~e** dust shot.
cendreux, -euse [sɑ̃dʀø, øz] adj *terrain, substance* ashy; *couleur* ash (*épith*), ashy; *teint* ashen.
cendrier [sɑ̃dʀije] nm *[fumeur]* ashtray; *[poêle]* ash pan. *[locomotive]* **~ de foyer** ash box.
cendrillon [sɑ̃dʀijɔ̃] nf (†: *humble servante*) Cinderella. **C~** Cinderella.
cène [sɛn] nf a (*Peinture, Bible*) **la C~** the Last Supper. b (*communion protestante*) (Holy) Communion, Lord's Supper, Lord's Table.
cénesthésie [senɛstezi] nf coen(a)esthesia.
cénesthésique [senɛstezik] adj cenesthesic, cenesthetic.
cénobite [senɔbit] nm coenobite.
cénotaphe [senɔtaf] nm cenotaph.
cens [sɑ̃s] nm (*Hist*) (*quotité imposable*) taxable quota *ou* rating (*as an electoral qualification*); (*redevance féodale*) rent (*paid by tenant of a piece of land to feudal superior*); (*recensement*) census. **~ électoral** ≃ poll tax.
censé, e [sɑ̃se] adj: **être ~ faire qch** to be supposed to do sth; **je suis ~ travailler** I'm supposed to be *ou* I should be working; **nul n'est ~ ignorer la loi** ignorance of the law is no excuse.
censément [sɑ̃semɑ̃] adv (*en principe*) supposedly; (*pratiquement*) virtually; (*pour ainsi dire*) to all intents and purposes.
censeur [sɑ̃sœʀ] nm a (*Ciné, Presse*) censor. b (*fig: critique*) critic. c (*Scol*) ≃ deputy *ou* assistant head (*Brit*), ≃ assistant *ou* vice-principal (*US*). **Madame le ~** the deputy headmistress (*Brit*), the assistant principal (*US*). d (*Hist*) censor.
censitaire [sɑ̃sitɛʀ] 1 adj: **suffrage *ou* système ~** voting system based on the poll tax. 2 nm: **(électeur) ~** eligible voter (*through payment of the poll tax*).
censurable [sɑ̃syʀabl] adj censurable.
censure [sɑ̃syʀ] nf a (*Ciné, Presse*) (*examen*) censorship; (*censeurs*) (board of) censors; (*Psych*) censor. b (†: *critique*) censure (*NonC*); (*Jur, Pol: réprimande*) censure. **les ~s de l'Église** the censure of the Church; *voir* **motion**.
censurer [sɑ̃syʀe] [1] vt a (*Ciné, Presse*) *spectacle, journal* to censor. b (*critiquer: Jur, Pol, Rel*) to censure.
cent[1] [sɑ̃] 1 adj a (*cardinal: gén*) a hundred; (*100 exactement*) one hundred, a hundred. (*multiplié par un nombre*) **quatre ~s** four hundred; **quatre ~ un/treize** four hundred and one/thirteen; **~/deux ~s chaises** a hundred/two hundred chairs.
b (*ordinal: inv*) **en l'an treize ~** in the year thirteen hundred.
c (*beaucoup de*) **il a eu ~ occasions de le faire** he has had hundreds of opportunities to do it; **je te l'ai dit ~ fois** I've told you a hundred times, if I've told you once I've told you a hundred times; **il a ~ fois raison** he's absolutely right; **~ fois mieux/pire** a hundred times better/worse; **je préférerais ~ fois faire votre travail** I'd far rather do your job, I'd rather do your job any day*; **c'est ~ fois trop grand** it's far too big; *voir* **mot**.
d (*loc*) **il est aux ~ coups** he is frantic, he doesn't know which way to turn; **faire les ~ pas** to pace up and down; (*Sport*) **(course de) quatre ~s mètres haies** 400 metres hurdles; **tu ne vas pas attendre ~ sept ans*** you can't wait for ever; (*Hist*) **les C~-Jours** the Hundred Days; **s'ennuyer *ou* s'emmerder‡ à ~ sous l'heure*** to be bored to tears*, be bored out of one's mind‡; *voir* **donner, quatre**.
2 nm a (*nombre*) a hundred. **il y a ~ contre un à parier que ...** it's a hundred to one that ...; *voir* **gagner**.
b **pour ~** per cent; **argent placé à 5 pour ~** money invested at 5 per cent; (*fig*) **être ~ pour ~ français, être français (à) ~ pour ~** to be a hundred per cent French, be French through and through; **je suis ~ pour ~ sûr** I'm a hundred per cent certain; **j'en suis à 90 pour ~ sûr** I'm ninety per cent certain of it.
c (*Comm: centaine*) **un ~** a *ou* one hundred; **un ~ de billes/d'œufs** a *ou* one hundred marbles/eggs; **c'est 12 F le ~** they're 12 francs a hundred; *pour autres loc voir* **six**.
cent[2] [sɛnt], (*Can*) [sɛn] nm (*US, Can: monnaie*) cent. (*Can* †) **quinze-~** cheap store, dime store (*US, Can*), five-and-ten (*US, Can*).
centaine [sɑ̃tɛn] nf a (*environ cent*) **une ~ de** about a hundred, a hundred or so; **la ~ de spectateurs qui ...** the hundred or so spectators who ...; **plusieurs ~s (de)** several hundred; **des ~s de personnes** hundreds of people; **ils vinrent par ~s** they came in (their) hundreds. b (*cent unités*) hundred. **10 F la ~** 10 francs a hundred; **atteindre la ~** (*âge*) to live to be a hundred; (*collection etc*) to reach the (one) hundred mark; **il les vend à la ~** he sells them by the hundred; (*Math*) **la colonne des ~s** the hundreds column.
centaure [sɑ̃tɔʀ] nm centaur.
centenaire [sɑ̃t(ə)nɛʀ] 1 adj hundred-year-old (*épith*). **cet arbre est ~** this tree is a hundred years old, this is a hundred-year-old tree. 2 nmf (*personne*) centenarian. 3 nm (*anniversaire*) centenary.
centenier [sɑ̃tənje] nm (*Hist*) centurion.
centésimal, e, mpl **-aux** [sɑ̃tezimal, o] adj centesimal.
centiare [sɑ̃tjaʀ] nm centiare.
centième [sɑ̃tjɛm] 1 adj, nmf hundredth; **je n'ai pas retenu le ~ de ce qu'il a dit** I can only remember a fraction of what he said; **je ne répéterai pas le ~ de ce qu'il a dit** almost everything he said was unrepeatable; *pour autres loc voir* **sixième**. 2 nf (*Théât*) hundredth performance.
centigrade [sɑ̃tigʀad] adj centigrade.
centigramme [sɑ̃tigʀam] nm centigramme.
centilitre [sɑ̃tilitʀ] nm centilitre.
centime [sɑ̃tim] nm centime. (*fig*) **je n'ai pas un ~** I haven't got a penny (*Brit*) *ou* a cent (*US*); **~ additionnel** ≃ additional tax.
centimètre [sɑ̃timɛtʀ] nm (*mesure*) centimetre; (*ruban*) tape measure, measuring tape.
centrafricain, e [sɑ̃tʀafʀikɛ̃, ɛn] adj of the Central African Republic. **République ~e** Central African Republic.
centrage [sɑ̃tʀaʒ] nm centring.
central, e, mpl **-aux** [sɑ̃tʀal, o] 1 adj a (*du centre*) *quartier* central;

partie, point centre (*épith*), central. **mon bureau occupe une position très ~e** my office is very central; **Amérique/Asie ~e** Central America/ Asia; *voir* **chauffage.**

b (*le plus important*) *problème, idée* central; *bureau* central (*épith*), head (*épith*), main (*épith*).

c (*Jur*) *pouvoir, administration* central.

2 nm (*Téléc*) ~ **(téléphonique)** (telephone) exchange, central (*US* †).

3 centrale nf a ~e (électrique) power station *ou* plant (*US*).

b ~e syndicale *ou* **ouvrière** *group of affiliated trade unions.*

c ~e d'achat(s) central buying office.

d (*prison*) prison, ≃ county jail (*US*), ≃ (state) penitentiary (*US*).

e *voyelle* centre.

f C~e = **École ~e des arts et manufactures.**

centralien, -ienne [sɑ̃tʀaljɛ̃, jɛn] **nm,f** student (*ou* former student) of the École centrale.

centralisateur, -trice [sɑ̃tʀalizatœʀ, tʀis] **adj** centralizing (*épith*).

centralisation [sɑ̃tʀalizasjɔ̃] **nf** centralization.

centraliser [sɑ̃tʀalize] 1 **vt** to centralize. **économie centralisée** centralized economy.

centralisme [sɑ̃tʀalism] **nm** centralism.

centre [sɑ̃tʀ] **1 nm a** (*gén, Géom*) centre; (*fig*) *[problème]* centre, heart. **le C~ (de la France)** central France, the central region *ou* area of France; **il habite en plein ~ (de la ville)** he lives right in the centre (of town); **~-ville** town centre, city centre; **il se croit le ~ du monde** he thinks the universe revolves around him; **au ~ du débat** at the centre of the debate; **mot ~** key word; **une idée ~** a central idea.

b (*lieu d'activités*) centre; (*bureau*) office, centre; (*bâtiment, services*) centre. **les grands ~s urbains/industriels/universitaires** the great urban/industrial/academic centres.

c (*Pol*) centre. **~ gauche/droit** centre left/right; **député du ~** deputy of the centre.

d (*Ftbl*) (†: *joueur*) centre (half *ou* forward)†; (*passe*) centre pass; *voir* **avant.**

2 comp ►centre d'accueil reception centre **►centre aéré** (school's) outdoor centre **►centre d'attraction** centre of attraction **►centre de chèques postaux** ≃ National Girobank (*Brit*) **►centre commercial** shopping centre *ou* arcade, shopping mall (*US*) **►centre de contrôle** (*Espace*) mission control **►centre culturel** arts centre **►centre départemental de documentation pédagogique** *local teachers' resource centre* **►centre de détention préventive** remand prison **►centre de documentation** resource centre, reference library **►centre de documentation et d'information** school library **►centre d'éducation surveillée** community home with education (*Brit*), reformatory (*US*) **►centre de formation professionnelle** professional training centre **►centre de gravité** (*Phys*) centre of gravity **►centre d'hébergement** lodging house, reception centre **►centre hospitalier** hospital complex **►centre des impôts** tax collection office **►centre d'influence** centre of influence **►centre d'information et de documentation de la jeunesse** careers advisory centre **►centre d'information et d'orientation** careers advisory centre **►centre d'intérêt** centre of interest **►centre médical** medical *ou* health centre **►Centre national de cinématographie** *French national film institute*, ≃ British Film Institute (*Brit*), ≃ Academy of Motion Picture Arts and Sciences (*US*) **►Centre national de documentation pédagogique** national teachers' resource centre **►Centre national d'enseignement à distance** national centre for distance learning, ≃ Open University (*Brit*) **►Centre national des industries et des techniques** *exhibition centre in Paris* **►Centre national du patronat français** *French national employers' federation*, ≃ Confederation of British Industry (*Brit*) **►Centre national de la recherche scientifique** ≃ Science and Engineering Research council (*Brit*), ≃ National Science Foundation (*US*) **►Centre national de télé-enseignement** national distance learning centre **►centres nerveux** (*Physiol, fig*) nerve centres **►Centre régional de documentation pédagogique** *regional teachers' resource centre* **►Centre régional des œuvres universitaires et scolaires** students' representative body **►centre de tri** (*Poste*) sorting office **►centre de villégiature** (holiday) resort **►centres vitaux** (*Physiol*) vital organs, vitals; (*fig*) *[entreprise]* vital organs (*fig*); *voir* **serveur.**

centrer [sɑ̃tʀe] 1 **vt** (*Sport, Tech*) to centre. (*fig*) **~ une pièce/une discussion sur** to focus a play/a discussion (up)on.

centrifugation [sɑ̃tʀifygasjɔ̃] **nf** centrifugation.

centrifuge [sɑ̃tʀifyʒ] **adj** centrifugal.

centrifuger [sɑ̃tʀifyʒe] 3 **vt** to centrifuge.

centrifugeur [sɑ̃tʀifyʒœʀ] **nm, centrifugeuse** [sɑ̃tʀifyʒøz] **nf** (*Tech*) centrifuge; (*Culin*) juice extractor.

centripète [sɑ̃tʀipɛt] **adj** centripetal.

centrisme [sɑ̃tʀism] **nm** (*Pol*) centrism, centrist policies.

centriste [sɑ̃tʀist] **adj, nmf** centrist.

centuple [sɑ̃typl] **1 adj** a hundred times as large (*de* as). **mille est un nombre ~ de dix** a thousand is a hundred times ten. **2 nm: le ~ de 10** a hundred times 10; **au ~** a hundredfold; **on lui a donné le ~ de ce qu'il mérite** he was given a hundred times more than he deserves.

centupler [sɑ̃typle] 1 **vti** to increase a hundred times *ou* a hundredfold. **~ un nombre** to multiply a number by a hundred.

centurie [sɑ̃tyʀi] **nf** (*Hist Mil*) century.

centurion [sɑ̃tyʀjɔ̃] **nm** centurion.

CEP [seəpe] **nm** (**abrév de certificat d'études primaires**) *voir* **certificat.**

cep [sɛp] **nm a ~ (de vigne)** (vine) stock. **b** *[charrue]* stock.

cépage [sepaʒ] **nm** (type of) vine.

cèpe [sɛp] **nm** (*Culin*) cep; (*Bot*) (edible) boletus.

cependant [s(ə)pɑ̃dɑ̃] **conj a** (*pourtant*) nevertheless, however, yet. **ce travail est dangereux, nous allons ~ essayer de le faire** this job is dangerous – however *ou* nevertheless *ou* still we shall try to do it; **c'est incroyable et ~ c'est vrai** it's incredible, yet *ou* but nevertheless it is true *ou* but it's true nevertheless. **b** (*littér*) (*pendant ce temps*) meanwhile, in the meantime. (*tandis que*) **~ que** while.

céphalée [sefale] **nf** cephalalgia (*SPÉC*), headache.

céphalique [sefalik] **adj** cephalic.

céphalopode [sefalɔpɔd] **nm** cephalopod. **~s** cephalopods, Cephalopoda (*SPÉC*).

céphalo-rachidien, -ienne [sefaloʀaʃidjɛ̃, jɛn] **adj** cephalo-rachidian (*SPÉC*), cerebrospinal.

céramique [seʀamik] **1 adj** ceramic. **2 nf** (*matière*) ceramic; (*objet*) ceramic (*ornament etc*). (*art*) **la ~** ceramics, pottery; **vase en ~** ceramic *ou* pottery vase; **~ dentaire** dental ceramics.

céramiste [seʀamist] **nmf** ceramist.

cerbère [sɛʀbɛʀ] **nm** (*fig péj*) fierce doorkeeper *ou* doorman; (*hum: concierge*) janitor. (*Myth*) **C~** Cerberus.

cerceau, pl ~x [sɛʀso] **nm** *[enfant, tonneau, crinoline]* hoop; *[capote, tonnelle]* half-hoop. **jouer au ~** to play with *ou* bowl a hoop; **avoir les jambes en ~** to be bandy-legged *ou* bow-legged, have bandy *ou* bow legs.

cerclage [sɛʀklaʒ] **nm** hooping.

cercle [sɛʀkl] **1 nm a** (*forme, figure*) circle, ring; (*Géog, Géom*) circle. **l'avion décrivait des ~s** the plane was circling (overhead); **itinéraire décrivant un ~** circular itinerary; **entourer d'un ~ le chiffre correct** to circle *ou* ring *ou* put a circle *ou* a ring round the correct number; **faire ~ (autour de qn/qch)** to gather round (sb/sth) in a circle *ou* ring, make a circle *ou* ring (round sb/sth); **~s imprimés sur la table par les (fonds de) verres** rings left on the table by the glasses; **un ~ de badauds/de chaises** a circle *ou* ring of onlookers/chairs; *voir* **arc, quadrature.**

b (*fig: étendue*) scope, circle, range. **le ~ des connaissances humaines** the scope *ou* range of human knowledge; **étendre le ~ de ses relations/de ses amis** to widen the circle of one's acquaintances/one's circle of friends.

c (*groupe*) circle. **le ~ de famille** the family circle; **un ~ d'amis** a circle of friends; **~ de qualité** quality circle.

d (*cerceau*) hoop, band. **~ de tonneau** barrel hoop *ou* band; **~ de roue** tyre (*made of metal*).

e (*club*) society, club. **~ littéraire** literary circle *ou* society; **~ d'études philologiques** philological society *ou* circle; **aller dîner au ~** to go and dine at the club.

f (*instrument*) protractor.

2 comp ►cercle horaire horary circle **►cercle polaire** polar circle; **cercle polaire arctique** Arctic Circle; **cercle polaire austral** Antarctic Circle **►cercle vicieux** (*fig*) vicious circle.

cercler [sɛʀkle] 1 **vt** (*gén*) to ring; *tonneau* to hoop; *roue* to tyre (*de* with). **lunettes cerclées d'écaille** horn-rimmed spectacles.

cercueil [sɛʀkœj] **nm** coffin, casket (*US*).

céréale [seʀeal] **nf** cereal (*Bot*). **~s vivrières** *ou* **alimentaires** food grains.

céréaliculture [seʀealikyltyʀ] **nf** cereal growing.

céréalier, -ière [seʀealje, jɛʀ] **1 adj** cereal (*épith*). **2 nm** (*producteur*) cereal grower. **(navire) ~** grain carrier *ou* ship.

cérébelleux, -euse [seʀebelø, øz] **adj** cerebellar.

cérébral, e, mpl -aux [seʀebʀal, o] **adj** (*Méd*) cerebral; (*intellectuel*) *travail* mental. **c'est un ~** he's a cerebral type.

cérébro-spinal, e, mpl -aux [seʀebʀospinal, o] **adj** cerebrospinal.

cérémonial, pl ~s [seʀemɔnjal] **nm** ceremonial.

cérémonie [seʀemɔni] **nf** ceremony. **sans ~** *manger* informally; *proposer* without ceremony, unceremoniously; *réception* informal; **avec ~** ceremoniously; **faire des ~s** to stand on ceremony, make a to-do* *ou* fuss; **tenue** *ou* **habit de ~** formal dress (*NonC*), ceremonial dress (*NonC*); (*Mil*) **tenue de ~** dress uniform; *voir* **maître.**

cérémonieusement [seʀemɔnjøzmɑ̃] **adv** ceremoniously, formally.

cérémonieux, -ieuse [seʀemɔnjø, jøz] **adj** *ton, accueil, personne* ceremonious, formal. **il est très ~** he's very formal *ou* ceremonious.

cerf [sɛʀ] **nm** stag, hart (*littér*).

cerfeuil [sɛʀfœj] **nm** chervil.

cerf-volant, pl cerfs-volants [sɛʀvɔlɑ̃] **nm a** (*jouet*) kite. **jouer au ~** to fly a kite. **b** (*Zool*) stag beetle.

cerisaie [s(ə)ʀizɛ] **nf** cherry orchard.

cerise [s(ə)ʀiz] **1 nf** cherry. (*fig*) **la ~ sur le gâteau** the icing on the cake. **2 adj inv** cherry(-red), cerise; *voir* **rouge.**

cerisier [s(ə)ʀizje] **nm** (*arbre*) cherry (tree); (*bois*) cherry (wood).

cérium [seʀjɔm] nm cerium.
CERN [sɛʀn] nm (abrév de **Conseil européen pour la recherche nucléaire**) CERN.
cerne [sɛʀn] nm *[yeux, lune]* ring; (*tache*) ring, mark. **les ~s de** *ou* **sous ses yeux** the (dark) rings *ou* shadows under his eyes.
cerné, e [sɛʀne] adj: **avoir les yeux ~s** to have (dark) shadows *ou* rings under one's eyes; **ses yeux ~s trahissaient sa fatigue** the dark shadows *ou* rings under his eyes revealed his tiredness.
cerneau, pl **~x** [sɛʀno] nm unripe walnut; (*Culin*) half-shelled walnut.
cerner [sɛʀne] 1 vt a (*entourer*) to encircle, surround; (*Peinture*) *visage, silhouette* to outline (*de* with, in). **ils étaient cernés de toute(s) part(s)** they were surrounded on all sides, they were completely surrounded *ou* encircled. b (*comprendre*) *problème* to delimit, define, zero in on; *personne* to work out, figure out. c *noix* to shell (*while unripe*); *arbre* to ring.
CERS [seəɛʀɛs] nm (abrév de **Centre européen de recherche spatiale**) ESRO.
certain, e [sɛʀtɛ̃, ɛn] 1 adj a (*après n: incontestable*) *fait, succès, événement* certain; *indice* sure; *preuve* positive, sure; *cause* undoubted, sure. **c'est la raison ~e de son départ** it's undoubtedly the reason for his going; **ils vont à une mort ~e** they're heading for certain death; **il a fait des progrès ~s** he has made definite *ou* undoubted progress; **la victoire est ~e** victory is assured *ou* certain; **c'est une chose ~e** it's absolutely certain; **c'est ~** there's no doubt about it *ou* that, that's quite certain, that's for sure*; **il est maintenant ~ qu'elle ne reviendra plus** it's now (quite) certain that she won't come back, she's sure *ou* certain not to come back now; **il est aujourd'hui ~ que la terre tourne autour du soleil** there is nowadays no doubt that *ou* these days we are certain that the earth revolves around the sun; **je le tiens pour ~!** I'm certain *ou* sure of it!; **il est ~ que ce film ne convient guère à des enfants** this film is undoubtedly not suitable *ou* is certainly unsuitable for children.
b (*convaincu, sûr*) *personne* sure, certain (*de qch* of sth, *de faire* of doing), convinced (*de qch* of sth, *que* that). **es-tu ~ de rentrer ce soir?** are you sure *ou* certain you'll be back this evening? *ou* of being back this evening?; **il est ~ de leur honnêteté** he's certain *ou* convinced *ou* sure of their honesty; **on n'est jamais ~ du lendemain** you can never be sure *ou* tell what tomorrow will bring; **elle est ~e qu'ils viendront** she's sure *ou* certain *ou* convinced (that) they'll come; *voir* **sûr**.
c (*Comm: déterminé*) *date, prix* definite.
2 adj indéf (*avant n*) a (*plus ou moins défini*) **un ~** a certain, some; **elle a un ~ charme** she's got a certain charm; **dans une ~e mesure** to some extent; **il y a un ~ village où** there is a certain *ou* some village where; **dans un ~ sens, je le comprends** in a way *ou* in a certain sense *ou* in some senses I can see his point; **jusqu'à un ~ point** up to a (certain) point; **il a manifesté un ~ intérêt** he showed a certain (amount of) *ou* some interest; **un ~ nombre d'éléments font penser que** ... a (certain) number of things lead one to think that ... .
b (*parfois péj: personne*) **un ~** a (certain), one; **un ~ M. X vous a demandé** a *ou* one Mr X asked for you; **il y a un ~ Robert dans la classe** there is a certain Robert in the class; **un ~ ministre disait même que** a certain minister even said that.
c (*intensif*) some. **il a un ~ âge** he is getting on; **une personne d'un ~ âge** an oldish person; **c'est à une ~e distance d'ici** it's quite a *ou* some distance from here; **cela demande une ~e patience** it takes a fair amount of patience; **ça demande un ~ courage!** it takes some courage!*; **au bout d'un ~ temps** after a while *ou* some time.
d (*pl: quelques*) **~s** some, certain; **dans ~s cas** in some *ou* certain cases; **~es personnes ne l'aiment pas** some people don't like him; **~es fois, à ~s moments** at (certain) times; **sans ~es notions de base** without some *ou* certain (of the) basic notions.
3 pron indéf pl: **~s** (*personnes*) some (people); (*choses*) some; **dans ~s de ces cas** in certain *ou* some of these cases; **parmi ses récits ~s sont amusants** some of his stories are amusing; **pour ~s** for some (people); **~s disent que** some say that; **~s d'entre vous** some of you; **il y en a ~s qui** there are some (people) *ou* there are those who.
4 nm (*Fin*) fixed *ou* direct rate of exchange.
certainement [sɛʀtɛnmɑ̃] adv (*très probablement*) most probably, most likely, surely; (*sans conteste*) certainly; (*bien sûr*) certainly, of course. **il va ~ venir ce soir** he'll certainly *ou* most probably *ou* most likely come tonight; **il est ~ le plus intelligent** he's certainly *ou* without doubt the most intelligent; **il y a ~ un moyen de s'en tirer** there must certainly *ou* surely be some way out; **puis-je emprunter votre stylo? — ~** can I borrow your pen? — certainly *ou* of course.
certes [sɛʀt] adv a (*de concession*) (*sans doute*) certainly, admittedly; (*bien sûr*) of course. **il est ~ le plus fort, mais ...** he is admittedly *ou* certainly the strongest, but ...; **~ je n'irai pas jusqu'à le renvoyer mais ...** of course I shan't *ou* I certainly shan't go as far as dismissing him but ... . b (*d'affirmation*) indeed, most certainly. **l'avez-vous apprécié? — ~** did you like it? — I did indeed *ou* I most certainly did.
certificat [sɛʀtifika] 1 nm (*attestation*) certificate, attestation; (*diplôme*) certificate, diploma; (*recommandation*) *[domestique]* testimonial; (*fig*) guarantee.
2 comp ►**certificat d'aptitude pédagogique** teaching diploma ►**certificat d'aptitude pédagogique à l'enseignement secondaire** *secondary school (Brit) or high school (US) teacher's diploma* ►**certificat d'aptitude professionnelle** vocational training certificate, ≃ City and Guilds examination (*Brit*) ►**certificat d'aptitude au professorat de l'enseignement du second degré** *secondary school (Brit) ou high school (US) teacher's diploma* ►**certificat d'aptitude au professorat de l'enseignement technique** *technical teaching diploma* ►**certificat de bonne vie et mœurs** character reference ►**certificat de concubinage** *document certifying that an unmarried couple are living together as man and wife* ►**certificat de dépôt** (*Fin*) certificate of deposit ►**certificat d'études primaires** *primary leaving certificate* ►**certificat d'investissement** non-voting preference share ►**certificat de licence** (*Univ* †) *part of first degree* ►**certificat médical** medical *ou* doctor's certificate ►**certificat de navigabilité** (*Naut*) certificate of seaworthiness; (*Aviat*) certificate of airworthiness ►**certificat d'origine** (*Comm*) certificate of origin ►**certificat de résidence** (*Admin*) certificate of residence *ou* domicile ►**certificat de scolarité** attestation of attendance at school *ou* university ►**certificat de travail** attestation of employment.
certification [sɛʀtifikasjɔ̃] nf (*Jur: assurance*) attestation, witnessing. **~ de signature** attestation of signature.
certifié, e [sɛʀtifje] (ptp de **certifier**) nm,f (qualified) secondary school *ou* high-school (*US*) teacher, *holder of the CAPES*.
certifier [sɛʀtifje] 7 vt a (*assurer*) **~ qch à qn** to assure sb of sth, guarantee sb sth *ou* sth to sb; **je te certifie qu'ils vont avoir affaire à moi!** I can assure you *ou* I'm telling you* they'll have ME to reckon with! b (*Jur: authentifier*) *document* to certify, guarantee; *signature* to attest, witness; *caution* to counter-secure. **copie certifiée conforme à l'original** certified copy of the original.
certitude [sɛʀtityd] nf certainty, certitude (*rare*). **c'est une ~/une ~ absolue** it's certain *ou* a certainty/absolutely certain *ou* an absolute certainty; **avoir la ~ de qch/de faire** to be certain *ou* (quite) sure *ou* confident of sth/of doing; **j'ai la ~ d'être le plus fort** I am certain of being *ou* that I am the stronger, I am convinced that I am the stronger.
cérumen [seʀymɛn] nm (ear) wax, cerumen (*SPÉC*).
cérumineux, -euse [seʀyminø, øz] adj ceruminous.
céruse [seʀyz] nf ceruse.
Cervantes [sɛʀvɑ̃tɛs] nm Cervantes.
cerveau, pl **~x** [sɛʀvo] 1 nm a (*Anat*) brain; (*fig: intelligence*) brain(s), mind; (*fig: centre de direction*) brain(s). **avoir un ~ étroit/puissant** to have limited mental powers/a powerful mind; **ce bureau est le ~ de l'entreprise** this department is the brain(s) of the company; **avoir le ~ dérangé** *ou* (*hum*) **fêlé** to be deranged *ou* (a bit) touched* *ou* cracked*; **fais travailler ton ~** use your brain; *voir* **rhume, transport.** b (*fig: personne*) brain, mind. **c'est un (grand) ~** he has a great brain *ou* mind, he is a mastermind; **c'était le ~ de l'affaire** he masterminded the job, he was the brain(s) *ou* mind behind the job; **c'est le ~ de la bande** he's the brain(s) of the gang; **la fuite** *ou* **l'exode des ~x** the brain drain.
2 comp ►**cerveau antérieur** forebrain ►**cerveau électronique** electronic brain ►**cerveau moyen** midbrain ►**cerveau postérieur** hindbrain.
cervelas [sɛʀvəla] nm saveloy.
cervelet [sɛʀvəlɛ] nm cerebellum.
cervelle [sɛʀvɛl] nf (*Anat*) brain; (*Culin*) brains. (*Culin*) **~ d'agneau** lamb's brains; **se brûler** *ou* **se faire sauter la ~** to blow one's brains out; **quand il a quelque chose dans la ~** when he gets something into his head; **sans ~** brainless; **il n'a rien dans la ~*** he's completely brainless, he's as thick as two short planks*; **avoir une ~ d'oiseau** to be feather-brained *ou* bird-brained; **toutes ces ~s folles** (all) these scatterbrains; *voir* **creuser, trotter.**
cervical, e, mpl **-aux** [sɛʀvikal, o] adj cervical.
cervidé [sɛʀvide] nm: **~s** cervidae (*SPÉC*); **le daim est un ~** the deer is a member of *ou* is one of the cervidae family *ou* species.
cervier [sɛʀvje] adj m *voir* **loup.**
Cervin [sɛʀvɛ̃] nm: **le ~** the Matterhorn.
cervoise [sɛʀvwaz] nf barley beer.
CES [seəɛs] nm (abrév de **collège d'enseignement secondaire**) *voir* **collège.**
ces [se] pron dém *voir* **ce.**
César [sezaʀ] nm a (*Hist*) Caesar. b (*Ciné*) ≃ Oscar, ≃ BAFTA award (*Brit*).
Césarée [sezaʀe] nf Caesarea.
césarien, -ienne [sezaʀjɛ̃, jɛn] 1 adj (*Hist*) Caesarean. 2 **césarienne** nf (*Méd*) Caesarean (section). **elle a eu** *ou* **on lui a fait une ~ne** she had a Caesarean.
césium [sezjɔm] nm = **cæsium.**
cessant, e [sesɑ̃, ɑ̃t] adj *voir* **affaire.**
cessation [sesasjɔ̃] nf (*frm*) *[activité, pourparlers]* cessation; *[hostilités]* cessation, suspension; *[paiements]* suspension. (*Ind*) **~ de travail** stoppage (*of work*).
cesse [sɛs] nf a **sans ~** (*tout le temps*) continually, constantly, incessantly; (*sans interruption*) continuously, without ceasing, incessantly; **elle est sans ~ après lui** she's continually *ou* constantly nagging (at) him, she keeps *ou* is forever nagging (at) him; **la pluie tombe sans ~ depuis hier** it has been raining continuously *ou* non-stop

since yesterday. b **il n'a de ~ que ...** he will not rest until ...; **il n'a eu de ~ qu'elle ne lui cède** he gave her no peace *ou* rest until she gave in to him.

cesser [sese] 1 1 vt a *bavardage, bruit, activité* to stop, cease (*frm ou* †); *relations* to (bring to an) end, break off. **nous avons cessé la fabrication de cet article** we have stopped making this item, this line has been discontinued; (*Admin*) ~ **ses fonctions** to relinquish *ou* give up (one's) office; (*Comm*) ~ **tout commerce** to cease trading; (*Fin*) ~ **ses paiements** to stop *ou* discontinue payment; (*Mil*) ~ **le combat** to stop (the) fighting; ~ **le travail** to stop work *ou* working.

b ~ **de faire qch** to stop doing sth, cease doing sth; **il a cessé de fumer** he's given up *ou* stopped smoking; **il a cessé de venir il y a un an** he ceased *ou* gave up *ou* left off* coming a year ago; **il n'a pas cessé de pleuvoir de toute la journée** it hasn't stopped raining all day; **la compagnie a cessé d'exister en 1943** the company ceased to exist *ou* ceased trading in 1943; **quand cesseras-tu** *ou* **tu vas bientôt ~ de faire le clown?** when are you going to give up *ou* leave off* *ou* stop acting the fool?; **son effet n'a pas cessé de se faire sentir** its effect is still making itself felt.

c (*frm: répétition fastidieuse*) **ne ~ de: il ne cesse de m'importuner** he's continually *ou* incessantly worrying me; **il ne cesse de dire que ...** he is constantly *ou* continually saying that ..., he keeps repeating (endlessly) that ... .

2 vi a *[bavardage, bruit, activités, combat]* to stop, cease; *[relations, fonctions]* to come to an end; *[douleur]* to stop; *[fièvre]* to pass, die down. **le vent a cessé** the wind has stopped (blowing); **tout travail a cessé** all work has stopped *ou* come to a halt *ou* a standstill.

b **faire ~** *bruit* to put a stop to, stop; *scandale* to put an end *ou* a stop to; (*Jur*) **pour faire ~ les poursuites** in order to have the action *ou* proceedings dropped.

cessez-le-feu [sesel(ə)fø] nm inv ceasefire.

cessible [sesibl] adj (*Jur*) transferable, assignable.

cession [sesjɔ̃] nf *[bail, biens, droit]* transfer. **faire ~ de** to transfer, assign; **~-bail** lease-back.

cessionnaire [sesjɔnɛʀ] nm (*Jur*) *[bien, droit]* transferee, assignee.

c'est-à-dire [sɛtadiʀ] conj a (*à savoir*) that is (to say), i.e. **un lexicographe, ~ quelqu'un qui fait un dictionnaire** a lexicographer, that is (to say), someone who compiles a dictionary.

b **~ que** (*en conséquence*): **l'usine a fermé, ~ que son frère est maintenant en chômage** the factory has shut down which means that his brother is unemployed now; (*manière d'excuse*) **viendras-tu dimanche? — ~ que j'ai arrangé un pique-nique avec mes amis** will you come on Sunday? – well actually *ou* well the thing is *ou* I'm afraid I've arranged a picnic with my friends; (*rectification*) **je suis fatigué — ~ que tu as trop bu hier** I'm tired – you mean *ou* what you mean is you had too much to drink yesterday.

césure [sezyʀ] nf caesura.

cet [sɛt] adj dém *voir* **ce**.

CET [seəte] nm (abrév de **collège d'enseignement technique**) *voir* **collège**.

cétacé [setase] nm cetacean.

ceux [sø] pron dém *voir* **celui**.

Cévennes [sevɛn] nfpl: **les C~** the Cévennes.

cévenol, e [sevnɔl] 1 adj of *ou* from the Cévennes (region). 2 nm,f: **C~(e)** inhabitant *ou* native of the Cévennes (region).

Ceylan [selɑ̃] nm Ceylon.

cf [seɛf] (abrév de **confer**) cf.

CFA [seɛfa] (abrév de **Communauté financière africaine**) *voir* **franc**[2].

CFAO [seɛfao] nf (abrév de **conception et fabrication assistées par ordinateur**) CADCAM.

CFC [seɛfse] nmpl (abrév de **chloro-fluoro-carbures**) CFCs.

CFDT [seɛfdete] nf (abrév de **Confédération française démocratique du travail**) *French trade union.*

CFP [seɛfpe] nm (abrév de **centre de formation professionnelle**) *voir* **centre**.

CFTC [seɛftese] nf (abrév de **Confédération française des travailleurs chrétiens**) *French trade union.*

cg (abrév de **centigramme**) cg.

CGC [segese] nf (abrév de **Confédération générale des cadres**) *French management union.*

CGT [seʒete] nf (abrév de **Confédération générale du travail**) *French trade union.*

chacal, pl **~s** [ʃakal] nm jackal.

chaconne [ʃakɔn] nf chaconne.

chacun, e [ʃakœ̃, yn] pron indéf a (*d'un ensemble bien défini*) each (one). **~ de** each (one) *ou* every one of; **~ d'entre eux** each (one) of them, every one of them; **~ des deux** each *ou* both of them, each of the two; **ils me donnèrent ~ 10 F/leur chapeau** they each (of them) gave me 10 francs/their hat, each (one) of them gave me 10 francs/their hat; **il leur donna (à) ~ 10 F, il leur donna 10 F (à) ~** he gave them 10 francs each, he gave them each 10 francs, he gave each (one) of them 10 francs; **il remit les livres ~ à sa** *ou* **leur place** he put back each of the books in its (own) place; **nous sommes entrés ~ à notre tour** we each went in in turn, we went in each in turn.

b (*d'un ensemble indéfini: tout le monde*) everyone, everybody. **comme ~ le sait** as everyone *ou* everybody *ou* each person knows; **~ son tour!** wait your turn!, everyone's got to have a turn!; **~ son goût** *ou* **ses goûts** every man to his (own) taste; **~ pour soi (et Dieu pour tous!)** every man for himself (and God for us all!); **~ voit midi à sa porte** people always act in their own interests; *voir* **à, tout**.

chafouin, e [ʃafwɛ̃, in] adj *visage* sly(-looking), foxy(-looking). **à la mine ~e** sly- *ou* foxy-looking, with a sly expression.

chagrin[1], e [ʃagʀɛ̃, in] 1 adj (*littér*) (*triste*) *air, humeur, personne* despondent, woeful, dejected; (*bougon*) *personne* ill-humoured, morose. **les esprits ~s disent que ...** disgruntled people say that ... .

2 nm a (*affliction*) grief, sorrow. **un ~ d'enfant** a child's disappointment *ou* distress *ou* sorrow; (*à un enfant*) **alors, on a un gros ~!** well, we do look sorry for ourselves! *ou* unhappy! *ou* woeful!; **avoir un ~ d'amour** to have an unhappy love affair, be disappointed in love; **plonger qn dans un profond ~** to plunge sb deep in grief; **faire du ~ à qn** to grieve *ou* distress sb, cause sb grief *ou* distress *ou* sorrow; **avoir du ~** to be grieved *ou* distressed; *voir* **noyer**[2].

b (††: *mélancolie*) ill-humour.

chagrin[2] [ʃagʀɛ̃] nm (*cuir*) shagreen; *voir* **peau**.

chagrinant, e [ʃagʀinɑ̃, ɑ̃t] adj distressing, grievous.

chagriner [ʃagʀine] 1 vt (*désoler*) to grieve, distress, upset; (*tracasser*) to worry, bother.

chah [ʃa] nm = **shah**.

chahut [ʃay] nm (*tapage*) uproar, rumpus*, hullabaloo*; (*Scol*) uproar. **faire du ~** to kick up* *ou* make *ou* create a rumpus* *ou* a hullabaloo*; (*Scol*) to make *ou* create an uproar.

chahuter [ʃayte] 1 1 vi (*Scol: faire du bruit*) to make *ou* create an uproar; (*faire les fous*) to kick up* *ou* create a rumpus*, make a commotion. 2 vt a *professeur* to play up, rag, bait; (†) *fille* to tease. **un professeur chahuté** a teacher who is baited *ou* ragged (by his pupils); (*Bourse*) *valeur* unstable. b (*: *cahoter*) *objet* to knock about.

chahuteur, -euse [ʃaytœʀ, øz] 1 adj rowdy, unruly. 2 nm,f rowdy.

chai [ʃɛ] nm wine and spirit store(house).

chaîne [ʃɛn] 1 nf a (*de métal, ornementale*) chain. **~ de bicyclette/de montre** bicycle/watch chain; **attacher un chien à une ~** to chain up a dog, put a dog on a chain; (*Aut*) **~s** (snow) chains.

b (*fig: esclavage*) **~s** chains, bonds, fetters, shackles; **les travailleurs ont brisé leurs ~s** the workers have cast off their chains *ou* bonds *ou* shackles.

c (*suite, succession*) (*gén, Anat, Chim, Méd*) chain; (*Géog*) *[montagnes]* chain, range. **la ~ des Alpes** the alpine range; (*fig*) **faire la ~** to form a (human) chain; *voir* **réaction**.

d (*Ind*) **~ (de fabrication)** production line; **produire qch à la ~** to mass-produce sth, make sth on an assembly line *ou* a production line; **travailler à la ~** to work on an assembly line *ou* a production line; (*fig*) **il produit des romans à la ~** he churns out one novel after another; *voir* **travail**[1].

e (*TV: longueur d'onde*) channel. **première/deuxième ~** first/second channel.

f (*Rad: appareil*) **~ (hi-fi/stéréophonique)** hi-fi/stereophonic system; **~ compacte** music centre.

g (*Comm*) *[journaux]* string; *[magasins]* chain, string.

h (*Tex*) warp.

i (*lettre*) chain letter.

2 comp ▸**chaîne alimentaire** (*Écologie*) food chain ▸**chaîne d'arpenteur** (*Tech*) (surveyor's) chain, chain measure ▸**chaîne de caractères** (*Ordin*) character string ▸**chaîne de fabrication** (*Ind*) production line ▸**chaîne du froid** (*Ind*) refrigeration procedure ▸**chaîne de montage** (*Ind*) assembly line ▸**chaîne à neige** (*Aut*) snow chain ▸**la chaîne parlée** (*Ling*) connected speech ▸**chaîne payante** *ou* **à péage** (*TV*) pay TV channel ▸**chaîne publique** (*TV*) publicly-owned channel, public service channel (*US*), ≃ PBS channel (*US*) ▸**chaîne sans fin** (*Tech*) endless chain ▸**chaîne de solidarité: former une chaîne de solidarité pour aider les réfugiés** to form a human chain to help the refugees ▸**chaîne de sûreté** (*gén*) safety chain; *[porte]* door *ou* safety chain.

chaîner [ʃene] 1 vt (*Ordin*) to chain.

chaînette [ʃɛnɛt] nf (small) chain. (*Math*) **courbe** *ou* **arc en ~** catenary curve; *voir* **point**[2].

chaînon [ʃɛnɔ̃] nm (*lit, fig*) *[chaîne]* link; *[filet]* loop; (*Géog*) secondary range (of mountains). **le ~ manquant** the missing link; (*Ordin*) **~ de données** data link.

chair [ʃɛʀ] nf a *[homme, animal, fruit]* flesh. **entrer dans les ~s** to penetrate the flesh; **en ~ et en os** in the flesh, as large as life (*hum*); **être ni ~ ni poisson** (*indécis*) to have an indecisive character; (*de caractère flou*) to be neither fish, fowl nor good red herring; **collant (couleur) ~** flesh-coloured tights; **l'ogre aime la ~ fraîche** the ogre likes a diet of warm young flesh; (*hum*) **il aime la ~ fraîche** (*des jeunes femmes*) he likes firm young flesh *ou* bodies; **avoir/donner la ~ de poule** (*froid*) to have/give goosepimples *ou* gooseflesh; *[chose effrayante]* **ça vous donne** *ou* **on en a la ~ de poule** it makes your flesh creep, it gives you gooseflesh; (*fig*) **~ à canon** cannon fodder; (*Culin*) **~ (à saucisse)** sausage meat; (*fig*) **je vais en faire de la ~ à pâté** *ou* **à saucisse** *ou* **le transformer en ~ à pâté** *ou* **à saucisse** I'm going to make mincemeat of him; **bien en ~** well-padded (*hum*), plump.

b (*littér, Rel: opposé à l'esprit*) flesh. **souffrir dans/mortifier sa ~** to suffer in/mortify the flesh; **fils/parents selon la ~** natural son/parents; **sa propre ~, la ~ de sa ~** his own flesh and blood; **la ~ est faible** the flesh is weak; *voir* **péché.**
c (*Peinture*) **~s** flesh tones *ou* tints.
chaire [ʃɛʀ] **nf** a (*estrade*) *[prédicateur]* pulpit; *[professeur]* rostrum. **monter en ~** to go up into the pulpit. b (*Univ: poste*) chair. **créer une ~ de français** to create a chair of French. c **la ~ pontificale** the papal throne.
chaise [ʃɛz] 1 **nf** chair. **faire la ~** (*pour porter un blessé*) to link arms to make a seat *ou* chair; *voir* **politique.** 2 **comp** ►**chaise de bébé** high-chair ►**chaise de cuisine** kitchen chair ►**chaise électrique** electric chair ►**chaise haute** highchair ►**chaise de jardin** garden chair ►**chaise longue** (*siège pliant*) deckchair; (*canapé*) chaise longue; **faire de la chaise longue** to lie back *ou* relax in a deckchair; (*se reposer*) to put one's feet up ►**chaises musicales** (*jeu*) musical chairs ►**chaise percée** commode ►**chaise (à porteurs)** sedan(-chair) ►**chaise de poste** poste chaise ►**chaise roulante** wheelchair, bathchair† (*Brit*).
chaisière [ʃɛzjɛʀ] **nf** (female) chair attendant.
chaland[1] [ʃalɑ̃] **nm** (*Naut*) barge.
chaland[2], **e**† [ʃalɑ̃, ɑ̃d] **nm,f** (*client*) customer.
chalazion [ʃalɑzjɔ̃] **nm** (*Méd*) sty.
Chaldée [kalde] **nf** Chaldea.
chaldéen, -enne [kaldeɛ̃, ɛn] 1 **adj** Chaldean, Chaldee. 2 **nm** (*Ling*) Chaldean. 3 **nm,f: C~(ne)** Chaldean, Chaldee.
châle [ʃɑl] **nm** shawl; *voir* **col.**
chalet [ʃalɛ] **nm** chalet; (*Can*) summer cottage. **~ de nécessité††** public convenience.
chaleur [ʃalœʀ] **nf** a (*gén, Phys*) heat; (*modérée, agréable*) warmth. **il fait une ~ accablante** the heat is oppressive, it is oppressively hot; **il faisait une ~ lourde** the air was sultry, it was very close; **les grandes ~s (de l'été)** the hot (summer) days *ou* weather; (*sur étiquette*) **"craint la ~"** "keep *ou* to be kept in a cool place"; **~ massique** *ou* **spécifique/latente** specific/latent heat; **~ animale** body heat.
b (*fig*) *[discussion, passion]* heat; *[accueil, voix, couleur]* warmth; *[convictions]* fervour. **manquer de ~ humaine** to lack the human touch; **je vais dans ce club pour trouver un peu de ~ humaine** I go to that club for a bit of company; **prêcher avec ~** to preach with fire *ou* fervour; **défendre une cause/un ami avec ~** to defend a cause/a friend hotly *ou* heatedly *ou* fervently.
c (*Zool: excitation sexuelle*) **la période des ~s** the heat; **en ~** on *ou* in heat.
d (†*: malaise*) flush. **éprouver des ~s** to have hot flushes (*Brit*) *ou* flashes (*US*); *voir* **bouffée.**
chaleureusement [ʃalœʀøzmɑ̃] **adv** warmly.
chaleureux, -euse [ʃalœʀø, øz] **adj** *accueil, applaudissements, remerciements* warm; *félicitations* hearty, warm. **il parla de lui en termes ~** he spoke of him most warmly.
châlit [ʃɑli] **nm** bedstead.
challenge [ʃalɑ̃ʒ] **nm** (*épreuve*) contest, tournament (*in which a trophy is at stake*); (*trophée*) trophy; (*gageure, défi*) challenge.
challengeur [ʃalɑ̃ʒœʀ], **challenger** [ʃalɑ̃ʒɛʀ] **nm** challenger.
chaloir [ʃalwaʀ] **vi** *voir* **chaut.**
chaloupe [ʃalup] **nf** launch; (*Can* *) rowing boat (*Brit*), rowboat (*US, Can*). **~ de sauvetage** lifeboat.
chaloupé, e [ʃalupe] **adj** *danse* swaying. **démarche ~e** rolling gait.
chalumeau, pl **~x** [ʃalymo] **nm** a (*Tech*) blowlamp (*Brit*), blowtorch (*US*). **~ oxyacétylénique** oxyacetylene torch; **ils ont découpé le coffre-fort au ~** they used a blowlamp (*Brit*) *ou* blowtorch (*US*) to cut through the safe. b (*Mus*) pipe. c (†*: paille*) (drinking) straw. d (*Can*) spout (fixed on the sugar maple tree) for collecting maple sap.
chalut [ʃaly] **nm** trawl (net). **pêcher au ~** to trawl.
chalutage [ʃalytaʒ] **nm** trawling.
chalutier [ʃalytje] **nm** (*bateau*) trawler; (*pêcheur*) trawlerman.
chamade [ʃamad] **nf** *voir* **battre.**
chamaille [ʃamɑj] **nf** squabble, (petty) quarrel.
chamailler (se) [ʃamɑje] 1 **vpr** to squabble, bicker.
chamaillerie [ʃamɑjʀi] **nf** (*gén pl*) squabble, (petty) quarrel. **~s** squabbling (*NonC*), bickering (*NonC*).
chamailleur, -euse [ʃamɑjœʀ, øz] **adj** quarrelsome. **c'est un ~** he's a quarrelsome one, he's a squabbler.
Chaman [ʃaman] **nm** Shaman.
Chamanisme [ʃamanism] **nm** shamanism.
chamarré, e [ʃamaʀe] (**ptp de chamarrer**) **adj** *étoffe, rideaux* richly coloured *ou* brocaded. **~ d'or/de pourpre** bedecked with gold/purple.
chamarrer [ʃamaʀe] 1 **vt** (*littér: orner*) to bedeck, adorn.
chamarrure [ʃamaʀyʀ] **nf** (*gén pl*) *[étoffe]* vivid *ou* loud (*péj*) combination of colours; *[habit, uniforme]* rich trimming.
chambard* [ʃɑ̃baʀ] **nm** (*vacarme*) racket*, row*, rumpus*; (*protestation*) rumpus*, row*, shindy*; (*bagarre*) scuffle, brawl; (*désordre*) shambles* (*sg*), mess; (*bouleversement*) upheaval. **faire du ~** (*protester*) to kick up a rumpus* *ou* a row* *ou* a shindy*; **ça va faire du ~!** there'll be a row* *ou* a rumpus* over that!
chambardement* [ʃɑ̃baʀdəmɑ̃] **nm** (*bouleversement*) upheaval; (*nettoyage*) clear-out.
chambarder* [ʃɑ̃baʀde] 1 **vt** (*bouleverser*) *objets, pièce* to turn upside down; *projets, habitudes* to turn upside down, upset; (*se débarrasser de*) to chuck out‡, throw out, get rid of. **il a tout chambardé** (*bouleversé*) he turned everything upside down; (*liquidé*) he chucked‡ *ou* threw the whole lot out, he got rid of the whole lot.
chambellan [ʃɑ̃belɑ̃] **nm** chamberlain.
chamboulement* [ʃɑ̃bulmɑ̃] **nm** (*désordre*) chaos, confusion; (*bouleversement*) upheaval.
chambouler* [ʃɑ̃bule] 1 **vt** (*bouleverser*) *objets, pièce* to turn upside down (*fig*); *projets* to mess up*, make a mess of*, cause chaos in. **cela a chamboulé nos projets** that caused chaos in *ou* messed up* our plans *ou* threw our plans right out*; **il a tout chamboulé dans la maison** he has turned the (whole) house upside down; **pour bien faire, il faudrait tout ~** to do things properly we should have to turn the whole thing *ou* everything upside down.
chambranle [ʃɑ̃bʀɑ̃l] **nm** *[porte]* (door) frame, casing; *[fenêtre]* (window) frame, casing; *[cheminée]* mantelpiece. **il s'appuya au ~** he leant against the doorpost.
chambre [ʃɑ̃bʀ] 1 **nf** a (*pour dormir*) bedroom; (*††: pièce*) chamber††, room. **~ à un lit/à deux lits** single-/twin-bedded room; **~ pour deux personnes** double room; **va dans ta ~!** go to your (bed)room!; **faire ~ à part** to sleep apart *ou* in separate rooms; *voir* **femme, robe, valet.**
b (*Pol*) House, Chamber. **à la C~** in the House; **système à deux ~s** two-house *ou* -chamber system; **C~ haute/basse** Upper/Lower House *ou* Chamber.
c (*Jur: section judiciaire*) division; (*Admin: assemblée, groupement*) chamber. **première/deuxième ~** upper/lower chamber.
d (*Tech*) *[fusil, mine, canon]* chamber.
e (*loc*) **en ~: travailler en ~** to work at home, do outwork; **couturière en ~** dressmaker working at home; (*iro*) **stratège/alpiniste en ~** armchair strategist/mountaineer; *voir* **musique, orchestre.**
2 **comp** ►**chambre d'accusation** (*Jur*) court of criminal appeal ►**chambre à air** (*Aut*) (inner) tube; **sans chambre à air** tubeless ►**chambre d'amis** spare *ou* guest room ►**chambre de bonne** maid's room ►**chambre des cartes** (*Naut*) chart-house ►**chambre à cartouches** (cartridge) chamber ►**chambre claire** (*Opt*) camera lucida ►**chambre de combustion** (*Aut*) combustion chamber ►**chambre de commerce (et d'industrie)** (*Comm*) Chamber of Commerce ►**la Chambre des communes** (*Brit Pol*) the House of Commons ►**chambre de compensation** (*Comm*) clearing house ►**chambre correctionnelle** (*Jur*) ≃ magistrates' *ou* district court ►**chambre à coucher** (*pièce*) bedroom; (*mobilier*) bedroom suite ►**chambre criminelle** (*Jur*) court of criminal appeal (*in the Cour de Cassation*) ►**la Chambre des députés** (*Pol*) the Chamber of Deputies ►**chambre d'enfant** child's (bed)room, nursery ►**chambre d'étudiant** student room ►**chambre d'explosion** = **chambre de combustion** ►**chambre forte** strongroom ►**chambre frigorifique, chambre froide** cold room; **mettre qch en chambre froide** *ou* **frigorifique** to put sth into cold storage *ou* in the cold room ►**chambre à gaz** gas chamber ►**la Chambre des lords** (*Brit Pol*) the House of Lords ►**chambre des machines** (*Naut*) engine room ►**chambre des métiers** guild chamber, chamber of trade ►**chambre meublée** furnished room, bed-sitter (*Brit*) ►**chambre noire** (*Phot*) darkroom ►**les chambres de l'œil** (*Anat*) the aqueous chambers of the eye ►**chambre des requêtes** (*Jur*) (preliminary) civil appeal court ►**chambre syndicale** employers' federation.
chambrée [ʃɑ̃bʀe] **nf** (*pièce, occupants*) room; *[soldats]* barrack-room.
chambrer [ʃɑ̃bʀe] 1 **vt** a *vin* to bring to room temperature, chambré; *personne* (*prendre à l'écart*) to corner, collar*; (*tenir enfermé*) to keep in, confine, keep cloistered. **les organisateurs ont chambré l'invité d'honneur** the organisers kept the V.I.P. guest out of circulation *ou* to themselves. b (**: taquiner*) to tease. (*canular*) **tu me chambres?** are you having me on?*, are you pulling my leg?*
chambrette [ʃɑ̃bʀɛt] **nf** small bedroom.
chambrière [ʃɑ̃bʀijɛʀ] **nf** (*béquille de charrette*) cart-prop; (†*: servante*) chambermaid.
chameau, pl **~x** [ʃamo] **nm** a (*Zool*) camel; *voir* **poil.** b (** péj*) beast*. **elle devient ~ avec l'âge** the older she gets the more beastly she becomes.
chamelier [ʃaməlje] **nm** camel driver.
chamelle [ʃamɛl] **nf** (*Zool*) she-camel.
chamois [ʃamwa] 1 **nm** (*Zool*) chamois; (*Ski*) skiing badge (*marking degree of ability*); *voir* **peau.** 2 **adj inv** fawn, buff(-coloured).
chamoisine [ʃamwazin] **nf** shammy leather.
champ [ʃɑ̃] 1 **nm** a (*Agr*) field. **~ de blé** wheatfield, field of corn (*Brit*) *ou* wheat; **~ d'avoine/de trèfle** field of oats/clover; **travailler aux ~s** to work in the fields; **on s'est retrouvé en plein(s) ~(s)** we found ourselves in the middle of *ou* surrounded by fields.
b (*campagne*) **~s** country(side); **la vie aux ~s** life in the country, country life; **fleurs des ~s** wild flowers, flowers of the countryside; *voir* **clef, travers**[2].

c (*fig: domaine*) field, area. **il a dû élargir le ~ de ses recherches/de ses investigations** he had to widen *ou* extend the field *ou* area of his research/his investigations.
d (*Élec, Ling, Ordin, Phys*) field.
e (*Ciné, Phot*) **dans le ~** in (the) shot *ou* the picture; **être dans le ~** to be in shot; **sortir du ~** to go out of shot; **pas assez de ~** not enough depth of focus; *voir* **profondeur.**
f (*Hér*) *[écu, médaille]* field.
g (*loc*) **avoir du ~** to have elbowroom *ou* room to move; **laisser du ~ à qn** to leave sb room to manoeuvre; **laisser le ~ libre** to leave the field open *ou* clear; **vous avez le ~ libre** I'll (*ou* we'll *etc*) leave you to it, it's all clear for you; **laisser le ~ libre à qn** to leave sb a clear field; **prendre du ~** (*lit*) to step back, draw back; (*fig*) to draw back; (*Mil*) **sonner aux ~s** to sound the general salute; *voir* **sur**[1], **tout.**
2 **comp ►champ d'action, champ d'activité** sphere of activity **►champ d'aviation** (*Aviat*) airfield **►champ de bataille** (*Mil, fig*) battlefield **►champ clos** combat area; (*fig*) **en champ clos** behind closed doors **►champ de courses** racecourse **►champ de foire** fairground **►champ d'honneur** (*Mil*) field of honour; **mourir** *ou* **tomber au champ d'honneur** to be killed in action **►champ magnétique** (*Phys*) magnetic field **►champ de manœuvre** (*Mil*) parade ground **►champ de Mars** ≃ military esplanade **►champ de mines** minefield **►champ de neige** snowfield **►champ opératoire** (*Méd*) operative field **►champ optique** (*Phys*) optical field **►champ ouvert** (*Agr*) open field **►champ sémantique** (*Ling*) semantic field **►champ de tir** (*terrain*) rifle *ou* shooting range, practice ground; (*angle de vue*) field of fire **►champ visuel** *ou* **de vision** field of vision *ou* view, visual field.

champagne [ʃɑ̃paɲ] 1 **nm** champagne. 2 **nf: la C~** Champagne, the Champagne region; *voir* **fine**[2].

champagnisation [ʃɑ̃paɲizasjɔ̃] **nf** *[vin]* champagnization.

champagniser [ʃɑ̃paɲize] [1] **vt** *vin* to champagnize.

champenois, e [ʃɑ̃pənwa, waz] 1 **adj** of *ou* from Champagne. (*Vin*) **méthode ~e** champagne method; **vin (mousseux) méthode ~e** champagne-type *ou* sparkling wine. 2 **nm,f: C~(e)** inhabitant *ou* native of Champagne.

champêtre [ʃɑ̃pɛtʀ] **adj** (*rural*) (*gén*) rural; *vie* country (*épith*), rural; *odeur* country (*épith*); *bal, fête* village (*épith*); *voir* **garde**[2].

champignon [ʃɑ̃piɲɔ̃] **nm** a (*gén*) mushroom; (*terme générique*) fungus; (*vénéneux*) toadstool, poisonous mushroom *ou* fungus; (*Méd*) fungus. **~ comestible** (edible) mushroom, edible fungus; **certains ~s sont comestibles** some fungi are edible; **~ de Paris** *ou* **de couche** cultivated mushroom; **~ hallucinogène** hallucinogenic mushroom, magic mushroom*; *voir* **pousser, ville.** b (*aussi* **~ atomique**) mushroom cloud. c (*: *Aut*) accelerator; *voir* **appuyer.**

champignonnière [ʃɑ̃piɲɔnjɛʀ] **nf** mushroom bed.

champion, -ionne [ʃɑ̃pjɔ̃, jɔn] 1 **adj** (*) A1, first-rate. **c'est ~!** that's great! *ou* first-rate! *ou* top-class! (*Brit*). 2 **nm,f** (*Sport, défenseur*) champion. **~ du monde de boxe** world boxing champion; **se faire le ~ d'une cause** to champion a cause; (*hum*) **c'est le ~ de la gaffe** there's no one to beat him for tactlessness.

championnat [ʃɑ̃pjɔna] **nm** championship. **~ du monde/d'Europe** world/European championship.

chançard, e* [ʃɑ̃saʀ, aʀd] 1 **adj** lucky. 2 **nm,f** lucky devil*, lucky dog*.

chance [ʃɑ̃s] **nf** a (*bonne fortune*) (good) luck. **tu as de la ~ d'y aller** you're lucky *ou* fortunate to be going; **il a la ~ d'y aller** he's lucky *ou* fortunate enough to be going, he has the good luck *ou* good fortune to be going; **avec un peu de ~** with a bit of luck; **quelle ~!** what a bit *ou* stroke of (good) luck!, how lucky!; **c'est une ~ que ...** it's lucky *ou* fortunate that ..., it's a bit of *ou* a stroke of luck that ...; **coup de ~** stroke of luck; **il était là, une ~!** *ou* **un coup de ~!** he was there, luckily; **c'est mon jour de ~!** it's my lucky day!; **ce n'est pas mon jour de ~!** it's not my day!; **la ~ a voulu qu'il y eût un médecin sur place** by a stroke of luck *ou* luckily there was a doctor on the spot; **par ~** luckily, fortunately; **pas de ~!** hard *ou* bad *ou* tough* luck!, hard lines!* (*Brit*); (*iro*) **c'est bien ma ~** (that's) just my luck!; *voir* **porter.**
b (*hasard, fortune*) luck, chance. **courir** *ou* **tenter sa ~** to try one's luck; **la ~ a tourné** his (*ou* her *etc*) luck has changed; **la ~ lui sourit** luck favours him, (good) fortune smiles on him; **mettre la ~** *ou* **toutes les ~s de son côté** to take no chances; **sa mauvaise ~ le poursuit** he is dogged by ill-luck, bad luck dogs his footsteps (*littér*); *voir* **bon**[1].
c (*possibilité de succès*) chance. **donner sa ~** *ou* **ses ~s à qn** to give sb his chance; **quelles sont ses ~s (de réussir** *ou* **de succès)?** what are his chances *ou* what chance has he got (of succeeding *ou* of success)?; **il a ses** *ou* **des ~s (de gagner)** he's got *ou* stands a *ou* some chance (of winning); **il/son tir n'a laissé aucune ~ au gardien de but** he/his shot didn't give the goalkeeper a chance; **les ~s d'un accord ...** the chances of a settlement ...; **il n'a aucune ~** he hasn't got *ou* doesn't stand a (dog's) chance; **il y a une ~ sur cent (pour) que ...** there's one chance in a hundred *ou* a one-in-a-hundred chance that ...; **il y a peu de ~s (pour) qu'il la voie** there's little chance (that) he'll see her, there's little chance of his seeing her, the chances of his seeing her are slim; **il y a toutes les ~s** *ou* **de grandes ~s que ...** there's every chance that ..., the chances *ou* odds are that ...; **il y a des ~s*** it's very likely, I wouldn't be surprised; **ils ont des ~s égales** they have equal chances *ou* an equal chance; **elle a une ~ sur deux de s'en sortir** she's got a fifty-fifty chance of pulling through.

chancelant, e [ʃɑ̃s(ə)lɑ̃, ɑ̃t] **adj** *démarche, pas* unsteady, faltering, tottering; *meuble, objet* wobbly, unsteady; *mémoire, santé* uncertain, shaky; *conviction, courage, résolution* wavering, faltering, shaky; *autorité* tottering, wavering, shaky. **dynasties ~es** tottering dynasties.

chanceler [ʃɑ̃s(ə)le] [4] **vi** *[personne]* to totter, stagger; *[ivrogne]* to reel; *[objet]* to wobble, totter; *[autorité]* to totter, falter; *[conviction, résolution, courage]* to waver, falter. **il s'avança en chancelant** he tottered *ou* staggered *ou* reeled forward; **une société qui chancelle sur ses bases** a society which is tottering upon its foundations; **il chancela dans sa résolution** he wavered in his resolve.

chancelier [ʃɑ̃səlje] **nm** *[Allemagne, Autriche]* chancellor; *[ambassade]* secretary; (*Hist*) chancellor. (*Brit*) **le ~ de l'Échiquier** the Chancellor of the Exchequer.

chancelière [ʃɑ̃səljɛʀ] **nf** foot-muff (*Brit*).

chancellerie [ʃɑ̃sɛlʀi] **nf** *[ambassade, consulat]* chancellery, chancery; (*Hist*) chancellery.

chanceux, -euse [ʃɑ̃sø, øz] **adj** lucky, fortunate; (††: *hasardeux*) hazardous.

chancre [ʃɑ̃kʀ] **nm** (*Bot, Méd, fig: abcès*) canker. **~ syphilitique** chancre; **~ mou** chancroid, soft chancre; **manger** *ou* **bouffer comme un ~**‡ to pig oneself‡ (*Brit*), stuff oneself like a pig*.

chandail [ʃɑ̃daj] **nm** (thick) jumper (*Brit*), (thick) sweater.

Chandeleur [ʃɑ̃dlœʀ] **nf: la ~** Candlemas.

chandelier [ʃɑ̃dəlje] **nm** (*à une branche*) candlestick; (*à plusieurs branches*) candelabra.

chandelle [ʃɑ̃dɛl] **nf** a (*bougie*) (tallow) candle. **dîner/souper aux ~s** dinner/supper by candlelight, candlelit dinner/supper. b (*fig*) (*Aviat*) chandelle; (*Rugby, Ftbl*) up-and-under; (*Tennis*) lob; (*Gym*) shoulder stand; (‡: *au nez*) trickle of snot*. (*fusée d'artifice*) **~ romaine** roman candle. c (*loc*) (*hum*) **tenir la ~** to play gooseberry (*Brit*), be a third wheel (*US*); (*Aviat*) **monter en ~** to climb vertically; (*Golf*) **lancer en ~** to loft; *voir* **brûler, économie, jeu.**

chanfrein [ʃɑ̃fʀɛ̃] **nm** a (*Tech*) chamfer, bevelled edge. b *[cheval]* nose.

change [ʃɑ̃ʒ] **nm** a (*Fin*) *[devises]* exchange. (*Banque*) **faire le ~** to exchange money; **opération de ~** (foreign) exchange transaction; *voir* **agent, bureau** *etc.* b (*Fin: taux d'échange*) exchange rate. **le ~ est avantageux** the exchange rate is favourable; **la cote des ~s** the (list of) exchange rates; **au cours actuel du ~** at the current rate of exchange.
c (*Can: petite monnaie*) change. d **~ (complet)** (disposable) nappy (*Brit*) *ou* diaper (*US*). e (*loc*) **gagner/perdre au ~** to gain/lose on the exchange *ou* deal; **donner le ~** to allay suspicion; **donner le ~ à qn** to put sb off the scent *ou* off the track.

changeable [ʃɑ̃ʒabl] **adj** (*transformable*) changeable, alterable.

changeant, e [ʃɑ̃ʒɑ̃, ɑ̃t] **adj** *personne, fortune, humeur* changeable, fickle, changing (*épith*); *couleur, paysage* changing (*épith*); *temps* changeable, unsettled. **son humeur est ~e** he's a man of many moods *ou* of uneven temper.

changement [ʃɑ̃ʒmɑ̃] **nm** a (*remplacement*) changing. **le ~ de la roue nous a coûté 100 F** the wheel change cost us 100 francs; **le ~ de la roue nous a pris une heure** changing the wheel *ou* the wheel change took us an hour, it took us an hour to change the wheel.
b (*fait de se transformer*) change (*de* in). **le ~ soudain de la température/de la direction du vent** the sudden change in temperature/(the) direction of the wind.
c (*transformation*) change, alteration. **il n'aime pas le(s) ~(s)** he doesn't like change(s); **elle a trouvé de grands ~s dans le village** she found great changes in the village, she found the village greatly changed *ou* altered; **il y a eu du ~** (*situation*) things have changed; (*objets*) things have been changed; **la situation reste sans ~** there has been no change in the situation, the situation remains unchanged *ou* unaltered; **~ en bien** *ou* **en mieux** change for the better.
d (*voir* **changer 2**) **~ de** change of; **~ d'adresse/d'air/de ministère** change of address/air/government; **~ de programme** (*projet*) change of plan *ou* in the plan(s); (*spectacle etc*) change of programme *ou* in the programme; **~ de direction** (*sens*) change of course *ou* direction; (*dirigeants*) change of management; (*sur un écriteau*) under new management; **il y a eu un ~ de propriétaire** it has changed hands, it has come under new ownership; (*Mus*) **~ de ton** change of key; **~ de décor** (*paysage*) change of scenery; (*Théât*) scene-change; (*Théât*) **~ à vue** transformation (scene).
e (*Admin: mutation*) transfer. **demander son ~** to apply for a transfer.
f (*Aut*) **~ de vitesse** (*dispositif*) gears, gear stick *ou* lever (*Brit*), gear change; (*action*) change of gears, gear changing (*NonC*), gear change; *[bicyclette]* gear(s).
g (*Transport*) change. **il y a 2 ~s pour aller de X à Y** you have to change twice *ou* make 2 changes to get from X to Y.

changer [ʃɑ̃ʒe] [3] 1 **vt** a (*modifier*) *projets, personne* to change, alter. **on ne le changera pas** nothing will change him *ou* make him change, you'll never change him; **ce chapeau la change** this hat makes her look different; **cela change tout!** that makes all the difference!, that changes everything!; **une promenade lui changera les idées** a walk will take his mind off things; **il n'a pas changé une virgule au rapport** he hasn't changed *ou* altered a comma in the report; **il ne veut rien ~ à ses habitudes** he doesn't want to change *ou* alter his habits in any way; **cela ne change rien à l'affaire** it doesn't make the slightest difference, it doesn't alter things a bit; **cela ne change rien au fait que** it doesn't change *ou* alter the fact that; **vous n'y changerez rien!** there's nothing you can do (about it)!

b (*remplacer, échanger*) to change; (*Théât*) *décor* to change, shift; (*Fin*) *argent, billet* to change; (*Can*) *chèque* to cash. **~ 100 F contre des livres** to change 100 francs into pounds, exchange 100 francs for pounds; **~ les draps/une ampoule** to change the sheets/a bulb; **il a changé sa voiture contre** *ou* **pour une nouvelle** he changed his car for a new one; **ce manteau était trop petit, j'ai dû le ~** that coat was too small – I had to change *ou* exchange it; **j'ai changé ma place contre la sienne** I changed *ou* swapped* places with him, I exchanged my place for his; **il a changé sa montre contre celle de son ami** he exchanged his watch for his friend's, he swapped* watches with his friend.

c (*déplacer*) **~ qn de poste** to move sb to a different job; **~ qn/qch de place** to move sb/sth to a different place, shift sb/sth; **ils ont changé tous les meubles de place** they've changed *ou* moved all the furniture round, they've shifted all the furniture (about); (*fig*) **~ son fusil d'épaule** to have a change of heart.

d (*transformer*) **~ qch/qn en** to change *ou* turn sth/sb into; **la citrouille fut changée en carrosse** the pumpkin was changed *ou* turned into a carriage.

e **~ un enfant/malade** to change a child/patient; **~ ses couches à un enfant** to change a child's nappies (*Brit*) *ou* diapers (*US*).

f (*procurer un changement à*) **cela nous a changés agréablement de ne plus entendre de bruit** it was a pleasant *ou* nice change for us not to hear any noise; **ils vont en Italie, cela les changera de leur pays pluvieux** they are going to Italy – it will be *ou* make a change from their rainy country.

2 **changer de** vt indir a (*remplacer*) to change; (*modifier*) to change, alter. **~ d'adresse/de nom/de voiture** to change one's address/name/car; **~ de domicile** *ou* **d'appartement** to move (house); **~ de peau** (*lit*) to shed one's skin; (*fig*) to become a different person; **~ de vêtements** *ou* **de toilette** to change (one's clothes); **elle a changé de coiffure** she has changed *ou* altered her hairstyle; **~ d'avis** *ou* **d'idée/de ton** to change one's mind/tune; **il change d'avis comme de chemise*** he's as changeable as the weather; **elle a changé de couleur quand elle m'a vu** she changed colour when she saw me; **la rivière a changé de cours** the river has altered *ou* shifted its course; **elle a changé de visage** her face has changed *ou* altered; (*d'émotion*) her expression changed *ou* altered; **change de disque!**‡ put another record on!‡, don't keep (harping) on *ou* don't go on about it!*

b (*passer dans une autre situation*) to change. **~ de train/compartiment/pays** to change trains/compartments/countries; **~ de camp** *[victoire, soldat]* to change camps *ou* sides; (*Aut*) **~ de vitesse** to change gear; **changeons de crémerie**‡ *ou* **d'auberge**‡ let's take our custom (*Brit*) *ou* business elsewhere; **~ de position** to alter *ou* shift *ou* change one's position; **j'ai besoin de ~ d'air** I need a change of air; **pour ~ d'air** for a change of air, to get a change of air; **~ de côté** (*gén*) to go over *ou* across to the other side, change sides; (*dans la rue*) to cross over (to the other side); **~ de propriétaire** *ou* **de mains** to change hands; **changeons de sujet** let's change the subject; **il a changé de route pour m'éviter** he went a different way *ou* changed his route to avoid me; (*Naut*) **~ de cap** to change *ou* alter course.

c (*échanger*) to exchange, change, swap* (*avec qn* with sb). **~ de place avec qn** to change *ou* exchange *ou* swap* places with sb; **j'aime bien ton sac, tu changes avec moi?*** I like your bag – will you swap* (with me)? *ou* will you exchange *ou* do a swap* (with me)?

3 vi a (*se transformer*) to change, alter. **~ en bien** *ou* **en mieux/en mal** *ou* **en pire** to change for the better/the worse; **il n'a pas du tout changé** he hasn't changed *ou* altered at all *ou* a bit; **les temps ont bien changé!** *ou* **sont bien changés!** (how) times have changed!; **le vent a changé** the wind has changed (direction) *ou* has veered round.

b (*Aviat, Rail etc*) to change. **j'ai dû ~ à Rome** I had to change at Rome.

c (*lit, iro*) **pour ~!** (just) for a change!, by way of a change!; **et pour (pas) ~ c'est nous qui faisons le travail*** and as per usual* *ou* and just by way of a change (*iro*) we'll be doing the work.

d (*procurer un changement*) **ça change des films à l'eau de rose** it makes a change from these sentimental films.

4 **se changer** vpr a (*mettre d'autres vêtements*) to change (one's clothes). **va te ~ avant de sortir** go and change (your clothes) before you go out.

b **se ~ en** to change *ou* turn into.

changeur [ʃɑ̃ʒœʀ] nm a (*personne*) moneychanger. b (*machine*) **~ (de disques)** record changer; **~ de monnaie** change machine.

chanoine [ʃanwan] nm (*Rel*) canon (*person*); *voir* **gras**.

chanoinesse [ʃanwanɛs] nf (*Rel*) canoness.

chanson [ʃɑ̃sɔ̃] 1 nf song. **~ d'amour/à boire/de marche/populaire** love/drinking/marching/popular song; **~ enfantine/d'étudiant** children's/student song; (*fig*) **c'est toujours la même ~** it's always the same old story; **~s que tout cela!**†† fiddle-de-dee!††, poppycock!††; **ça, c'est une autre ~** that's quite a different matter *ou* quite another story; *voir* **connaître**. 2 comp ▸**chanson folklorique** folksong ▸**chanson de geste** (*Littérat*) chanson de geste ▸**chanson de marins** (sea) shanty ▸**chanson de Noël** (Christmas) carol ▸**la Chanson de Roland** the Chanson de Roland, the Song of Roland ▸**chanson de toile** (*Littérat*) chanson de toile, weaving song.

chansonnette [ʃɑ̃sɔnɛt] nf ditty, light-hearted song.

chansonnier [ʃɑ̃sɔnje] nm (*artiste*) chansonnier, cabaret singer (*specializing in political satire*); (*livre*) song-book.

chant[1] [ʃɑ̃] nm a (*sons*) *[personne]* singing; *[oiseau]* singing, warbling; (*mélodie habituelle*) song; *[insecte]* chirp(ing); *[coq]* crow(ing); *[mer, vent, instrument]* song. **entendre des ~s mélodieux** to hear melodious singing; **au ~ du coq** at cockcrow; (*fig*) **le ~ du cygne d'un artiste** an artist's swan song; (*fig*) **écouter le ~ des sirènes** to let o.s. be led astray.

b (*chanson*) song. **~ patriotique/populaire** patriotic/popular song; **~ de Noël** (Christmas) carol; **~ religieux** *ou* **sacré** *ou* **d'Église** hymn; **~ de guerre** battle song.

c (*action de chanter, art*) singing. **nous allons continuer par le ~ d'un cantique** we shall continue by singing a hymn; **cours/professeur de ~** singing lessons/teacher; **apprendre le ~** to learn singing; **j'aime le ~ choral** I like choral *ou* choir singing; **~ grégorien** Gregorian chant; **~ à une/à plusieurs voix** song for one voice/several voices.

d (*mélodie*) melody.

e (*Poésie*) (*genre*) ode; (*division*) canto. **~ funèbre** funeral lament; **~ nuptial** nuptial song *ou* poem; **épopée en douze ~s** epic in twelve cantos; (*fig*) **le ~ désespéré de ce poète** the despairing song of this poet.

chant[2] [ʃɑ̃] nm edge. **de** *ou* **sur ~** on edge, edgewise.

chantage [ʃɑ̃taʒ] nm blackmail. **se livrer à un** *ou* **exercer un ~ sur qn** to blackmail sb; **faire du ~** to use *ou* apply blackmail; **on lui a extorqué des millions à coup de ~** they blackmailed him into parting with millions; **~ affectif** emotional blackmail; **il (nous) a fait le ~ au suicide** he threatened suicide to blackmail us, he blackmailed us with the threat of *ou* by threatening suicide.

chantant, e [ʃɑ̃tɑ̃, ɑ̃t] adj a (*mélodieux*) *accent, voix* singsong, lilting. b (*qui se chante aisément*) *air, musique* tuneful, catchy.

chanter [ʃɑ̃te] [1] 1 vt a *chanson, opéra, messe* to sing. **l'oiseau chante ses trilles** the bird sings *ou* warbles *ou* chirrups its song; **chante-nous quelque chose!** sing us a song!, sing something for us!

b (*célébrer*) to sing of, sing. **~ les exploits de qn** to sing (of) sb's exploits; **~ l'amour** to sing of love; (*fig*) **~ les louanges de qn** to sing sb's praises; *voir* **victoire**.

c (**: raconter*) **qu'est-ce qu'il nous chante là?** what's this he's telling us?, what's he on about now?*; **~ qch sur tous les tons** to harp on about sth, go on about sth*.

2 vi a *[personne]* to sing; (** fig: de douleur*) to yell (out), sing out*; *[oiseau]* to sing, warble; *[coq]* to crow; *[poule]* to cackle; *[insecte]* to chirp; *[ruisseau]* to babble; *[bouilloire]* to sing; *[eau qui bout]* to hiss, sing. **~ juste/faux** to sing in tune/out of tune *ou* flat; **~ pour endormir un enfant** to sing a child to sleep; **chantez donc plus fort!** sing up! (*Brit*) *ou* out! (*US*); **c'est comme si on chantait*** it's like talking to a deaf man, it's a waste of breath; **il chante en parlant** he's got a lilting *ou* singsong voice *ou* accent, he speaks with a lilt.

b (*par chantage*) **faire ~ qn** to blackmail sb.

c (**: plaire*) **vas-y si le programme te chante** (you) go if the programme appeals to you *ou* if you fancy (*Brit*) the programme; **cela ne me chante guère de sortir ce soir** I don't really feel like *ou* fancy (*Brit*) going out *ou* I am not very keen (*Brit*) on going out tonight; **il vient quand** *ou* **si** *ou* **comme ça lui chante** he comes when *ou* if *ou* as the fancy takes him.

chanterelle [ʃɑ̃tʀɛl] nf a (*Bot*) chanterelle. b (*Mus*) E-string; *voir* **appuyer**. c (*oiseau*) decoy (bird).

chanteur, -euse [ʃɑ̃tœʀ, øz] nm,f singer. **~ de charme** crooner; **~ de(s) rues** street singer, busker (*Brit*); *voir* **maître, oiseau**.

chantier [ʃɑ̃tje] 1 nm a (*Constr*) building site; (*lieu de travail d'un plombier, d'un peintre etc*) job; (*Can *†: exploitation forestière*) logging *ou* lumbering industry (*US, Can*); (*Can: pour bûcherons*) lumber camp (*US, Can*), shanty (*Can*). **le matin il est au ~** he's on the (building *etc*) site in the mornings; **j'ai laissé mes pinceaux sur le ~** I left my brushes at the job; (*sur une route*) **il y a un ~** there are roadworks; (*écriteau*) **"~ interdit au public"** "no entry *ou* admittance (to the public)"; (*écriteau*) **"fin de ~"** "road clear", "end of roadworks".

b (*entrepôt*) depot, yard.

c (** fig: désordre*) shambles*. **quel ~ dans ta chambre!** what a shambles* *ou* mess in your room!

d (*loc*) **en ~, sur le ~: il a 2 livres en ~** *ou* **sur le ~** he has 2 books in hand *ou* on the go, he's working on 2 books; **mettre un ouvrage en ~** *ou* **sur le ~** to put a piece of work in hand; **dans l'appartement, nous sommes en ~ depuis 2 mois** we've had work *ou* alterations going on in the flat for 2 months now.

2 comp ▸**chantier de construction** building site ▸**chantier de démolition** demolition site ▸**chantier d'exploitation** (*Min*) opencast working ▸**chantier d'exploitation forestière** tree-felling *ou* lumber (*US, Can*) site ▸**chantier naval** shipyard, shipbuilding yard ▸**chantier de réarmement** refit yard.

chantilly [ʃɑ̃tiji] **nf** = **crème chantilly**; *voir* **crème 4**.

chantonnement [ʃɑ̃tɔnmɑ̃] **nm** (soft) singing, humming, crooning.

chantonner [ʃɑ̃tɔne] 1 1 **vi** *[personne]* to sing to oneself, hum, croon; *[eau qui bout]* to hiss, sing. ~ **pour endormir un bébé** to croon *ou* sing a baby to sleep. 2 **vt** to sing, hum. ~ **une mélodie** to sing *ou* hum a tune (to oneself); ~ **une berceuse à** *ou* **pour un bébé** to croon *ou* sing a lullaby to a baby.

chantoung [ʃɑ̃tuŋ] **nm** Shantung (silk).

chantourner [ʃɑ̃tuʀne] 1 **vt** to jig-saw; *voir* **scie**.

chantre [ʃɑ̃tʀ] **nm** (*Rel*) cantor; (*fig littér*) (*poète*) bard, minstrel; (*laudateur*) exalter, eulogist. (*littér*) **les ~s des bois** the songsters; *voir* **grand**.

chanvre [ʃɑ̃vʀ] **nm** (*Bot, Tex*) hemp. **de ~** hemp (*épith*), hempen (*épith*); ~ **du Bengale** jute; ~ **indien** Indian hemp; ~ **de Manille** Manila hemp, abaca; *voir* **cravate**.

chanvrier, -ière [ʃɑ̃vʀije, ijɛʀ] 1 **adj** hemp (*épith*). 2 **nm,f** (*cultivateur*) hemp grower; (*ouvrier*) hemp dresser.

chaos [kao] **nm** (*lit, fig*) chaos. **dans le ~** in (a state of) chaos.

chaotique [kaɔtik] **adj** chaotic.

chap. (**abrév de chapitre**) chap.

chapardage* [ʃapaʀdaʒ] **nm** petty theft, pilfering (*NonC*).

chaparder* [ʃapaʀde] 1 **vti** to pinch, pilfer (*à* from).

chapardeur, -euse* [ʃapaʀdœʀ, øz] 1 **adj** light-fingered. 2 **nm,f** pilferer, petty thief.

chape [ʃap] **nf** a (*Rel*) cope. b (*Tech*) *[pneu]* tread; *[bielle]* strap; *[poulie]* shell; *[voûte]* coating; (*sur béton*) screed. (*fig*) **toute cette bureaucratie est une ~ de plomb** all this bureaucracy is like a millstone around our necks.

chapeau, pl ~x [ʃapo] 1 **nm** a (*coiffure*) hat. **saluer qn ~ bas** (*lit*) to doff one's hat to sb; (*fig*) to take one's hat off to sb; **saluer qn d'un coup de ~** to raise one's hat to sb; **ça mérite un coup de ~** you've got to take your hat off to it (*ou* him *etc*); **coup de ~ à Paul pour sa nouvelle chanson** hats off to Paul for his new song; **tirer son ~ à qn*** to take one's hat off to sb; **il a réussi? eh bien ~ !*** he managed it? hats off to him! *ou* you've got to hand it to him!; **~, mon vieux!*** well done *ou* jolly good, old man!* (*Brit*); *voir* **porter, travailler**.

b (*Tech*) *[palier]* cap. (*Aut*) ~ **de roue** hub cap; **démarrer sur les ~x de roues*** *[véhicule, personne]* to shoot off at top speed, take off like a shot; *[affaire, soirée]* to get off to a good start; **prendre un virage sur les ~x de roues** to screech round a corner.

c (*Presse*) *[article]* introductory paragraph.

d (*Bot*) *[champignon]* cap; (*Culin*) *[vol-au-vent]* lid, top.

2 comp ▸**chapeau de brousse** safari hat ▸**chapeau chinois** (*Mus*) crescent, jingling Johnny; (*Zool*) limpet ▸**chapeau cloche** cloche hat ▸**chapeau de gendarme** (*en papier*) (folded) paper hat ▸**chapeau haut-de-forme** top hat, topper* ▸**chapeau melon** bowler (hat) ▸**chapeau mou** trilby (hat) (*Brit*), fedora (*US*) ▸**chapeau de paille** straw hat ▸**chapeau de plage** *ou* **de soleil** sun hat ▸**chapeau tyrolien** Tyrolean hat.

chapeauté, e [ʃapote] 1 **ptp de chapeauter**. 2 **adj** with a hat on, wearing a hat.

chapeauter [ʃapote] 1 **vt** (*superviser*) to head (up), oversee.

chapelain [ʃaplɛ̃] **nm** chaplain.

chapelet [ʃaplɛ] **nm** a (*objet*) rosary, beads; (*prières*) rosary. **réciter** *ou* **dire son ~** to say the rosary, tell *ou* say one's beads†; **le ~ a lieu à 5 heures** the rosary is at 5 o'clock; (*fig*) **dévider** *ou* **défiler son ~*** to recite one's grievances. b (*fig: succession, chaîne*) ~ **d'oignons/d'injures/d'îles** string of onions/of insults/of islands; ~ **de bombes** stick of bombs.

chapelier, -ière [ʃapəlje, jɛʀ] 1 **adj** hat (*épith*). 2 **nm,f** hatter.

chapelle [ʃapɛl] **nf** a (*Rel*) (*lieu*) chapel; (*Mus: chœur*) chapel. ~ **absidiale/latérale** absidial/side chapel; ~ **de la Sainte Vierge** Lady Chapel; ~ **ardente** (*dans une église*) chapel of rest; **l'école a été transformé en ~ ardente** the school was turned into a temporary morgue; *voir* **maître**. b (*coterie*) coterie, clique.

chapellerie [ʃapɛlʀi] **nf** (*magasin*) hat shop, hatter('s); (*commerce*) hat trade, hat industry.

chapelure [ʃaplyʀ] **nf** (*Culin*) (dried) bread-crumbs.

chaperon [ʃapʀɔ̃] **nm** a (*personne*) chaperon. b (*Constr*) *[mur]* coping. c (†: *capuchon*) hood. *voir* **petit 5**.

chaperonner [ʃapʀɔne] 1 **vt** a *personne* to chaperon. b (*Constr*) *mur* to cope.

chapiteau, pl ~x [ʃapito] **nm** a *[colonne]* capital. b *[cirque]* big top, marquee. **sous le ~** under the big top. c *[alambic]* head.

chapitre [ʃapitʀ] **nm** a *[livre, traité]* chapter; *[budget, statuts]* section, item. **inscrire un nouveau ~ au budget** to make out a new budget head; (*fig*) **c'était un nouveau ~ de sa vie qui commençait** a new chapter of *ou* in his life was beginning.

b (*fig: sujet, rubrique*) subject, matter. **il est imbattable sur ce ~** he's unbeatable on that subject *ou* score; **il est très strict sur le ~ de la discipline** he's very strict in the matter of discipline *ou* about discipline; **au ~ des faits divers** under the heading of news in brief; **on pourrait dire sur ce ~ que ...** one might say on that score *ou* subject that ... .

c (*Rel: assemblée*) chapter; *voir* **salle, voix**.

chapitrer [ʃapitʀe] 1 **vt** a (*réprimande*) to admonish, reprimand; (*recommandation*) to lecture (*sur* on, about). b *texte* to divide into chapters; *budget* to divide into headings, itemize.

chapka [ʃapka] **nf** Russian fur hat.

chapon [ʃapɔ̃] **nm** capon.

chaptalisation [ʃaptalizasjɔ̃] **nf** *[vin]* chaptalization.

chaptaliser [ʃaptalize] 1 **vt** *vin* to chaptalize.

chaque [ʃak] **adj** a (*d'un ensemble bien défini*) every, each. ~ **élève (de la classe)** every *ou* each pupil (in the class); **ils coûtent 10 F ~*** they're 10 francs each *ou* apiece. b (*d'un ensemble indéfini*) every. ~ **homme naît libre** every man is born free; **il m'interrompt à ~ instant** he interrupts me every other second, he keeps interrupting me; ~ **10 minutes, il éternuait*** he sneezed every 10 minutes; ~ **chose à sa place** everything in its place; ~ **chose en son temps** everything in its own time; *voir* **à**.

char [ʃaʀ] 1 **nm** a (*Mil*) tank. **régiment de ~s** tank regiment. b *[carnaval]* (carnival) float. **le défilé des ~s fleuris** the procession of flower-decked floats. c (†: *charrette*) waggon, cart. **les ~s de foin rentraient** the hay waggons *ou* carts were returning. d (*Can* ‡) car, automobile (*US*). e (*Antiq*) chariot. (*littér*) **le ~ de l'Aurore** the chariot of the dawn (*littér*); (*fig*) **le ~ de l'État** the ship of state; *voir* **arrêter**. 2 **comp** ▸**char d'assaut** (*Mil*) tank ▸**char à banc** charabanc, char-à-banc ▸**char à bœufs** oxcart ▸**char de combat** (*Mil*) = **char d'assaut** ▸**char funèbre** hearse ▸**char à voile** sand yacht, land yacht; **faire du char à voile** to go sand-yachting.

charabia* [ʃaʀabja] **nm** gibberish, gobbledygook*.

charade [ʃaʀad] **nf** (*parlée*) riddle, word puzzle; (*mimée*) charade.

charançon [ʃaʀɑ̃sɔ̃] **nm** weevil.

charançonné, e [ʃaʀɑ̃sɔne] **adj** weevilly, weevilled.

charbon [ʃaʀbɔ̃] 1 **nm** a (*combustible*) coal (*NonC*); (*escarbille*) speck of coal dust, piece of grit. **faire cuire qch sur des ~s** to cook sth over a coal fire; (*fig*) **être sur des ~s ardents** to be like a cat on hot bricks (*Brit*) *ou* on a hot tin roof (*US*); (*fig*) **aller au ~*** to go to work; **c'est toujours moi qui vais au ~!‡** it's always me that gets lumbered!*

b (*maladie*) *[blé]* smut, black rust; *[bête, homme]* anthrax.

c (*Art*) (*instrument*) piece of charcoal; (*dessin*) charcoal drawing.

d (*Pharm*) charcoal. **pastilles au ~** charcoal tablets.

e (*Élec*) *[arc électrique]* carbon.

2 **comp** ▸**charbon actif** *ou* **activé** active *ou* activated carbon ▸**charbon animal** animal black ▸**charbon de bois** charcoal; **cuit au charbon de bois** charcoal-grilled, barbecued ▸**charbon de terre**†† coal.

charbonnage [ʃaʀbɔnaʒ] **nm** (*gén pl: houillère*) colliery, coalmine. **les C~s (de France)** the French Coal Board.

charbonner [ʃaʀbɔne] 1 1 **vt** (*noircir*) *inscription* to scrawl in charcoal. ~ **un mur de dessins** to scrawl (charcoal) drawings on a wall; **avoir les yeux charbonnés** to have eyes heavily rimmed with black; **se ~ le visage** to blacken *ou* black one's face. 2 **vi** *[lampe, poêle, rôti]* to char, go black; (*Naut*) to take on coal.

charbonneux, -euse [ʃaʀbɔnø, øz] **adj** a *apparence, texture* coal-like; (*littér: noirci, souillé*) sooty. b (*Méd*) **tumeur ~euse** anthracoid *ou* anthrasic tumour; **mouche ~euse** anthrax-carrying fly.

charbonnier, -ière [ʃaʀbɔnje, jɛʀ] 1 **adj** coal (*épith*). **navire ~** collier, coaler; *voir* **mésange**. 2 **nm** (*personne*) coalman; (††: *fabriquant de charbon de bois*) charcoal burner. (*Prov*) ~ **est maître dans sa maison** *ou* **chez soi** a man is master in his own home, an Englishman's home is his castle (*Brit*); *voir* **foi**.

charcutage [ʃaʀkytaʒ] **nm** (*péj*) ~ **électoral** gerrymandering.

charcuter* [ʃaʀkyte] 1 **vt** *personne* to hack about*; *rôti, volaille* to mangle, hack to bits. (*hum: en se rasant*) **se ~** to cut o.s. to ribbons; (*bagarre*) **ils se sont charcutés** they cut each other to ribbons, they hacked each other about*.

charcuterie [ʃaʀkytʀi] **nf** (*magasin*) pork butcher's shop and delicatessen; (*produits*) cooked pork meats; (*commerce*) pork meat trade; delicatessen trade.

charcutier, -ière [ʃaʀkytje, jɛʀ] **nm,f** pork butcher; (*traiteur*) delicatessen dealer; (* *fig: chirurgien*) butcher* (*fig*).

chardon [ʃaʀdɔ̃] **nm** (*Bot*) thistle. *[grille, mur]* **~s** spikes.

chardonneret [ʃaʀdɔnʀɛ] **nm** goldfinch.

charentais, e [ʃaʀɑ̃tɛ, ɛz] 1 **adj** of *ou* from Charente. 2 **nm,f**: **C~(e)** inhabitant *ou* native of Charente. 3 **charentaise nf** carpet slippers.

charge [ʃaʀʒ] 1 **nf** a (*lit, fig: fardeau*) burden; *[véhicule]* load; *[navire]* freight, cargo; (*Archit: poussée*) load. *[camion]* ~ **maximale** maximum load; **fléchir** *ou* **plier sous la ~** to bend under the load *ou* burden; (*fig*) **l'éducation des enfants est une lourde ~ pour eux** educating the children is a heavy burden for them; (*fig*) **leur mère infirme est une ~ pour eux** their invalid mother is a burden to *ou* upon them.

b (*rôle, fonction*) responsibility; (*Admin*) office; (*Jur*) practice. **~ publique/élective** public/elective office; **les hautes ~s qu'il occupe** the high office that he holds; **les devoirs de la ~** the duties of (the) office; **on lui a confié la ~ de (faire) l'enquête** he was given the responsibility of (carrying out) the inquiry; **être en ~ de** (*Jur*) to be in charge of, handle; (*Comm*) to deal with, handle; *voir* **femme**.

c (*obligations financières*) **~s** *[commerçant]* expenses, costs, outgoings; *[locataire]* maintenance *ou* service charges; **il a de grosses ~s familiales** his family expenses *ou* outgoings are high; **dans ce commerce, nous avons de lourdes ~s** we have heavy expenses *ou* costs *ou* our overheads are high in this trade; **avoir des ~s excessives** to be over-committed; **les ~s de l'État** government expenditure; *voir* **cahier**.

d (*Jur*) charge. **les ~s qui pèsent contre lui** the charges against him; *voir* **témoin**.

e (*Mil: attaque*) charge. (*Sport*) **~ irrégulière** illegal tackle; *voir* **pas[1], revenir, sonner**.

f (*Tech*) *[fusil]* (*action*) loading, charging; (*explosifs*) charge; (*Élec*) (*action*) charging; (*quantité*) charge. (*Élec*) **conducteur en ~** live conductor; (*Élec*) **mettre une batterie en ~** to charge a battery, put a battery on charge (*Brit*); **la batterie est en ~** the battery is being charged *ou* is on charge (*Brit*).

g (*caricature, satire*) caricature; *voir* **portrait**.

h (*Naut: chargement*) loading.

i (*loc*) **être à la ~ de qn** *[frais, réparations]* to be chargeable to sb, be payable by sb; *[personne, enfant]* to be dependent upon sb, be a charge on sb, be supported by sb; **les frais sont à la ~ de l'entreprise** the costs will be borne by the firm, the firm will pay the expenses; **il a sa mère à (sa) ~** he has a dependent mother, he has his mother to support; **enfants à ~** dependent children; **personnes à ~** dependents; **les enfants confiés à sa ~** the children in his care; (*littér*) **être à ~ à qn** to be a burden to *ou* upon sb; **avoir la ~ de qn** to be responsible for sb, have charge of sb; **à ~ pour lui de payer** on condition that he meets the costs; **il a la ~ de faire, il a pour ~ de faire** the onus is upon him to do, he is responsible for doing; **j'accepte ton aide, à ~ de revanche** I accept your help on condition *ou* provided that you'll let me do the same for you one day *ou* for you in return; **prendre en ~** *frais, remboursement* to take care of; *passager* to take on; **prendre un enfant en ~** (*gén*) to take charge of a child; *[Assistance publique]* to take a child into care; (*fig*) **l'adolescent doit se prendre en ~** the adolescent must take responsibility for himself; **prise en ~** *[taxi etc]* minimum (standard) charge; *[Sécurité sociale]* acceptance (of financial liability); **avoir ~ d'âmes** *[prêtre]* to be responsible for people's spiritual welfare, have the cure of souls; *[père, conducteur]* to be responsible for the welfare of children, passengers, have lives in one's care; *voir* **pris**.

2 comp ▸**charge affective** (*Psych*) emotive power ▸**charge d'appoint** (*Chauffage*) booster ▸**charge creuse** (*Mil*) hollow-charge ▸**charge d'explosifs** explosive charge ▸**charges de famille** dependents ▸**charge(s) fiscale(s)** tax burden ▸**charges locatives** maintenance *ou* service charges ▸**charges sociales** social security contributions ▸**charge utile** live load ▸**charge à vide** weight (when) empty, empty weight.

chargé, e [ʃaʀʒe] (ptp de **charger**) 1 adj a (*lit*) *personne, véhicule* loaded, laden (*de* with). **être ~ comme un mulet*** *ou* **une bourrique*** *ou* **un baudet*** to be loaded *ou* laden (down) like a mule.

b (*responsable de*) **être ~ de** *travail, enfants* to be in charge of.

c (*fig: rempli de*) **un homme ~ d'honneurs** a man laden with honours; (*littér*) **~ d'ans** *ou* **d'années** weighed down by (the) years (*littér*), ancient in years (*littér*); **passage/mot ~ de sens** passage/word full of *ou* pregnant with meaning; **un regard ~ de menaces** a look full of threats; **nuage ~ de neige** snow-laden cloud, cloud laden *ou* heavy with snow; **air ~ de parfums** air heavy with fragrance (*littér*), air heavy with sweet smells.

d (*occupé*) *emploi du temps, journée* full, heavy. **notre programme est très ~ en ce moment** we have a very busy schedule *ou* a very full programme *ou* we are very busy at the moment.

e (*fig: lourd*) *conscience* troubled; *ciel* overcast, heavy; *style* over-elaborate, intricate. **j'ai la conscience ~e de** my conscience is burdened *ou* troubled with; **c'est un homme qui a un passé ~** he is a man with a past; *voir* **hérédité**.

f (*Méd*) *estomac* overloaded. **avoir la langue ~e** to have a coated *ou* furred tongue; **il a l'haleine ~e** his breath smells.

g (*Tech*) *arme, appareil* loaded.

h (‡: *ivre*) plastered‡ (*attrib*), slashed‡ (*surtout Brit*) (*attrib*); (‡: *drogué*) stoned‡ (*attrib*), spaced (out)‡ (*attrib*).

2 comp ▸**chargé d'affaires** nm chargé d'affaires ▸**chargé de cours** nm junior lecturer *ou* fellow ▸**chargé de famille** adj with family responsibilities ▸**chargé de mission** nm (official) representative.

chargement [ʃaʀʒəmɑ̃] nm a (*action*) loading. **le ~ d'un camion** the loading(-up) of a lorry; **le ~ des bagages** the loading of the luggage. b (*gén: marchandises*) load; *[navire]* freight, cargo. **le ~ a basculé** the load toppled over. c (*Comm*) (*remise*) registering; (*paquet*) registered parcel. d *[arme, caméra]* loading; *[chaudière]* stoking.

charger [ʃaʀʒe] [3] 1 vt a (*lit, fig*) *animal, personne, véhicule, logiciel* to load; *table, étagère* to load. **~ qn de paquets** to load sb up *ou* weigh sb down with parcels; **je vais ~ la voiture** I'll go and load the car (up); **on a trop chargé cette voiture** this car has been overloaded; **table chargée de mets appétissants** table laden *ou* loaded with mouth-watering dishes; **~ le peuple d'impôts** to burden the people with *ou* weigh the people down with taxes; **~ sa mémoire (de faits)/un texte de citations** to overload one's memory (with facts)/a text with quotations; **un plat qui charge l'estomac** a dish that lies heavy on *ou* overloads the stomach; **ne lui chargez pas l'estomac** don't overload his stomach.

b (*placer, prendre*) *objet, bagages* to load (*dans* into). **il a chargé le sac/le cageot sur son épaule** he loaded the sack/the crate onto his shoulder, he heaved the sack over/the crate onto his shoulder; *[taxi]* **~ un client** to pick up a passenger *ou* a fare.

c *fusil, caméra* to load; (*Élec*) *batterie* to charge; *chaudière* to stoke, fire; (*Couture*) *bobine, canette* to load *ou* fill with thread.

d (*donner une responsabilité*) **~ qn de qch** to put sb in charge of sth; **~ qn de faire** to give sb the responsibility *ou* job of doing, ask sb to do; **être chargé de faire** to be put in charge of doing, be made responsible for doing; **il m'a chargé d'un petit travail** he gave me a little job to do; **on l'a chargé d'une mission importante** he was assigned an important mission; **on l'a chargé de la surveillance des enfants** *ou* **de surveiller les enfants** he was put in charge of the children, he was given the job of looking after the children; **il m'a chargé de mettre une lettre à la poste** he asked me to post a letter; **on m'a chargé d'appliquer le règlement** I've been instructed to apply the rule; **il m'a chargé de m'occuper de la correspondance** he gave me the responsibility *ou* job of seeing to the correspondence; **il m'a chargé de ses amitiés pour vous** *ou* **de vous transmettre ses amitiés** he sends you his regards, he asked me to give you his regards *ou* to convey his regards.

e (*accuser*) *personne* to bring all possible evidence against. (*littér*) **~ qn de** *crime* to charge sb with.

f (*attaquer*) (*Mil*) to charge (at); (*Sport*) to charge, tackle. **chargez!** charge!; **il a chargé dans le tas*** he charged into them.

g (*caricaturer*) *portrait* to make a caricature of; *description* to overdo, exaggerate; (*Théât*) *rôle* to overact, ham (up)*. **il a tendance à ~** he has a tendency to overdo it *ou* to exaggerate.

2 **se charger** vpr a **se ~ de** *tâche* to see to, take care *ou* charge of, take on; *enfant, prisonnier, élève,* (*iro*) *ennemi* to see to, attend to, take care of; **se ~ de faire** to undertake to do, take it upon o.s. to do; **il s'est chargé des enfants** he is seeing to *ou* taking care *ou* charge of the children; **d'accord je m'en charge** O.K., I'll see to it *ou* I'll take care of that; **je me charge de le faire venir** I'll make sure *ou* I'll see to it that he comes, I'll make it my business to see that he comes.

b ‡ (*se soûler*) to get plastered‡; (*se droguer*) to get stoned‡.

chargeur [ʃaʀʒœʀ] nm a (*personne*) (*gén, Mil*) loader; (*Naut: négociant*) shipper; (*affréteur*) charterer. b (*dispositif*) *[arme à feu]* magazine, cartridge clip; (*Phot*) cartridge. **il vida son ~ sur les gendarmes** he emptied his magazine at the police; (*Élec*) **~ de batterie** (battery) charger.

chariot [ʃaʀjo] nm (*charrette*) waggon (*Brit*), wagon, (*plus petit*) truck, cart; (*table, panier à roulettes*) trolley (*Brit*), cart (*US*); (*appareil de manutention*) truck, float (*Brit*); (*Tech*) *[machine à écrire, machine-outil]* carriage; *[hôpital]* trolley. *[gare, aéroport]* **~ (à bagages)** (baggage *ou* luggage) trolley; (*Ciné*) **~ (de caméra)** dolly; **~ élévateur (à fourche)** fork-lift truck; (*Astron*) **le petit/grand C~** the Little/Great Bear.

charismatique [kaʀismatik] adj charismatic.

charisme [kaʀism] nm charisma.

charitable [ʃaʀitabl] adj (*qui fait preuve de charité*) charitable (*envers* towards); (*gentil*) kind (*envers* to, towards). (*iro*) **... et c'est un conseil ~** ... that's just a friendly *ou* kindly bit of advice (*iro*); *voir* **âme**.

charitablement [ʃaʀitabləmɑ̃] adv (*voir* **charitable**) charitably; kindly. (*iro*) **je vous avertis ~ que la prochaine fois ...** let me give you a friendly *ou* kindly warning that the next time ... .

charité [ʃaʀite] nf a (*gén: bonté, amour*) charity; (*gentillesse*) kindness; (*Rel*) charity, love. **il a eu la ~ de faire** he was kind enough to do; **faites-moi la ~ de, ayez la ~ de** have the kindness to, be so kind as to, be kind enough to; **ce serait une ~ à lui faire que de** it would be doing him a kindness *ou* a good turn to; *voir* **dame, sœur**.

b (*aumône*) charity. **demander la ~** (*lit*) to ask *ou* beg for charity; (*fig*) to come begging; **faire la ~** to give to charity; **faire la ~ à** *mendiant, déshérités* to give (something) to; **je ne veux pas qu'on me fasse la ~** I don't want charity *ou* a handout; **la ~, ma bonne dame!** have you got a penny, kind lady?; **vivre de la ~ publique** to live on (public) charity; **vivre des ~s de ses voisins** to live on the charity of one's neighbours; (*Prov*) **~ bien ordonnée commence par soi-même** charity begins at home (*Prov*); **fête de ~** fête in aid of charity; *voir* **vente**.

Charites [ʃaʀit] nfpl (*Myth*) **les ~** the Charities.

charivari [ʃaʀivaʀi] nm hullabaloo.

charlatan [ʃaʀlatɑ̃] nm (*péj*) (*médecin*) quack, charlatan; (*pharmacien, vendeur*) mountebank; (*politicien*) charlatan, trickster; *voir* **remède**.

charlatanerie [ʃaʀlatanʀi] nf = **charlatanisme**.

charlatanesque [ʃaʀlatanɛsk] adj (*de guérisseur*) *remède, méthodes*

quack (*épith*); (*de démagogue, d'escroc*) *méthodes* phoney, bogus.
charlatanisme [ʃaʀlatanism] **nm** *[guérisseur]* quackery, charlatanism; *[politicien etc]* charlatanism, trickery.
Charlemagne [ʃaʀləmaɲ] **nm** Charlemagne.
Charles [ʃaʀl] **nm** Charles. ~ **le Téméraire** Charles the Bold; **~-Quint** Charles the Fifth (of Spain).
charleston [ʃaʀlɛstɔn] **nm** (*danse*) charleston.
charlot [ʃaʀlo] **nm** **a** (*Ciné*) **C~** Charlie Chaplin. **b** (*péj: fumiste*) (*peu sérieux*) phoney*; (*paresseux*) shirker, skiver‡.
charlotte [ʃaʀlɔt] **nf** (*Culin*) charlotte; (*coiffure*) mobcap.
charmant, e [ʃaʀmɑ̃, ɑ̃t] **adj** **a** (*aimable*) *hôte, jeune fille, employé* charming; *enfant* sweet, delightful; *sourire, manières* charming, engaging. **il s'est montré ~ et nous a aidé du mieux qu'il a pu** he was charming and helped us as much as he could; **c'est un collaborateur ~** he is a charming *ou* delightful man to work with; *voir* **prince**. **b** (*très agréable*) *séjour, soirée* delightful, lovely. (*iro*) **eh bien c'est ~** charming! (*iro*); (*iro*) **~e soirée** delightful time! (*iro*). **c** (*ravissant*) *robe, village, jeune fille, film, sourire* lovely, charming.
charme¹ [ʃaʀm] **nm** (*Bot*) hornbeam.
charme² [ʃaʀm] **nm** **a** (*attrait*) *[personne, musique, paysage]* charm. **le ~ de la nouveauté** the attraction(s) of novelty; **elle a beaucoup de ~** she has great charm; **ça lui donne un certain ~** that gives him a certain charm *ou* appeal; **cette vieille maison a son ~** this old house has its charm; **c'est ce qui en fait (tout) le ~** that's where its attraction lies, that's what is so delightful about it; **ça ne manque pas de ~** it's not without (a certain) charm; **ça a peut-être du ~ pour vous, mais ...** it may appeal to you but ...; (*hum, iro*) **je suis assez peu sensible aux ~s d'une promenade sous la pluie** a walk in the rain holds few attractions for me.
b (*hum: attraits d'une femme*) **~s** charms (*hum*); *voir* **commerce**.
c (*envoûtement*) spell. **subir le ~ de qn** to be under sb's spell, be captivated by sb; **exercer un ~ sur qn** to have sb under one's spell; **il est tombé sous son ~** he has fallen beneath her spell; **être sous le ~ de** to be held spellbound by, be under the spell of; **tenir qn sous le ~ (de)** to captivate sb (with), hold sb spellbound (with); **le ~ est rompu** the spell is broken; *voir* **chanteur**.
d (*loc*) **faire du ~** to turn on the charm; **faire du ~ à qn** to make eyes at sb; **aller** *ou* **se porter comme un ~** to be *ou* feel as fit as a fiddle.
charmé, e [ʃaʀme] (**ptp de charmer**) **adj: être ~ de faire** to be delighted to do.
charmer [ʃaʀme] [1] **vt** *public* to charm, enchant; *serpents* to charm; (†, *littér*) *peine, douleur* to charm away. **elle a des manières qui charment** she has charming *ou* delightful ways; **spectacle qui charme l'oreille et le regard** performance that charms *ou* enchants both the ear and the eye.
charmeur, -euse [ʃaʀmœʀ, øz] **1** **adj** *sourire, manières* winning, engaging. **2** **nm,f** (*séducteur*) charmer. **~ de serpent** snake charmer.
charmille [ʃaʀmij] **nf** arbour; (*allée d'arbres*) tree-covered walk.
charnel, -elle [ʃaʀnɛl] **adj** (*frm*) *passions, instincts* carnal; *désirs* carnal, fleshly. **l'acte ~, l'union ~le** the carnal act (*frm*); **un être ~** an earthly creature, a creature of blood *ou* flesh; **liens ~s** blood ties.
charnellement [ʃaʀnɛlmɑ̃] **adv** (*frm, littér*) **convoiter** *ou* **désirer qn ~** to desire sb sexually; **connaître ~** to have carnal knowledge of (*littér*); **pécher ~** to commit the sin of the flesh (*littér*).
charnier [ʃaʀnje] **nm** *[victimes]* mass grave; (††: *ossuaire*) charnel house.
charnière [ʃaʀnjɛʀ] **nf** **a** *[porte, fenêtre, coquille]* hinge; *[timbre de collection]* (stamp) hinge; *voir* **nom**. **b** (*fig*) turning point; (*Mil*) pivot. **à la ~ de deux époques** at the turning point between two eras; **une discipline-~** an interlinking field of study; **un roman-~** a novel marking a turning point *ou* a transition; **une époque-~** a transition period.
charnu, e [ʃaʀny] **adj** *lèvres* fleshy, thick; *fruit, bras* plump, fleshy. **les parties ~es du corps** the fleshy parts of the body; (*hum*) **sur la partie ~e de son individu** on the fleshy part of his person (*hum*).
charognard [ʃaʀɔɲaʀ] **nm** (*lit*) vulture, carrion crow; (*fig*) vulture.
charogne [ʃaʀɔɲ] **nf** (*cadavre*) carrion, decaying carcass; (‡: *salaud*) (*femme*) bitch‡; (*homme*) bastard‡, sod‡ (*Brit*).
charolais, e [ʃaʀɔlɛ, ɛz] **1** **adj** of *ou* from the Charolais. **2** **nm: le C~** the Charolais. **3** **nm,f** (*bétail*) Charolais.
charpente [ʃaʀpɑ̃t] **nf** **a** *[maison, bâtiment]* frame(work), skeleton; *voir* **bois**. **b** (*fig: structure*) *[feuille]* skeleton; *[roman, pièce de théâtre]* structure, framework. **le squelette est la ~ du corps** the skeleton is the framework of the body. **c** (*carrure*) build, frame. **quelle solide ~!** what a solid build (he is)!, what a strong frame he has!; **~ fragile/forte/épaisse** fragile/strong/stocky build.
charpenté, e [ʃaʀpɑ̃te] **adj: bien/solidement/puissamment ~** *personne* well/solidly/powerfully built; *texte* well/solidly/powerfully structured *ou* constructed.
charpentier [ʃaʀpɑ̃tje] **nm** (*Constr*) carpenter; (*Naut*) shipwright.
charpie [ʃaʀpi] **nf** **a** (*Hist: pansement*) shredded linen (*used to dress wounds*). **b** (*loc*) **cette viande est trop cuite, c'est de la ~** this meat has been cooked to shreds; **ces vêtements sont tombés en ~** these clothes are (all) in shreds *ou* ribbons, these clothes are falling to bits; **mettre** *ou* **réduire en ~** *papier, vêtements* (*déchirer*) to tear to shreds; *viande* (*hacher menu*) to mince; **je vais le mettre en ~!** I'll tear him to shreds!, I'll make mincemeat of him!; **il s'est fait mettre en ~ par le train** he was mashed up* *ou* hacked to pieces by the train.
charretée [ʃaʀte] **nf** (*lit*) cartload (*de* of). (* *fig: grande quantité de*) **une ~ de, des ~s de** loads* *ou* stacks* of.
charretier, -ière [ʃaʀtje, jɛʀ] **nm,f** carter. (*péj*) **de ~** *langage, manières* coarse; *voir* **chemin, jurer**.
charrette [ʃaʀɛt] **nf** cart. **~ à bras** handcart, barrow. **~ des condamnés** tumbrel; (*fig*) **il a fait partie de la dernière ~** he went in the last round of redundancies; (*Comm*) **faire une ~*** to work flat out*; (*Comm*) **être en (pleine) ~*** to be working against the clock.
charriage [ʃaʀjaʒ] **nm** **a** (*transport*) carriage, cartage. **b** (*Géol: déplacement*) overthrusting; *voir* **nappe**.
charrier [ʃaʀje] [7] **1** **vt** **a** (*transporter*) *[personne]* (*avec brouette etc*) to cart (along), trundle along, wheel (along); (*sur le dos*) to hump (*Brit*) *ou* lug along, heave (along), cart (along); *[camion etc]* to carry, cart. **on a passé des heures à ~ du charbon** we spent hours heaving *ou* carting coal.
b (*entraîner*) *[fleuve]* to carry (along), wash along, sweep (along); *[coulée, avalanche]* to carry (along), sweep (along). (*littér*) **le ciel** *ou* **le vent charriait de lourds nuages** the sky *ou* the wind carried past *ou* along heavy clouds.
c (*: *se moquer de*) **~ qn** to take sb for a ride, kid sb on* (*Brit*), have sb on* (*Brit*), put sb on* (*US*); **se faire ~ par ses amis** to be kidded on* *ou* had on* *ou* put on* by one's friends.
2 **vi** (‡) (*abuser*) to go too far, overstep the mark; (*plaisanter*) to be kidding* (*Brit*), be joking*. **vraiment il charrie** he's really going too far, he's really overstepping the mark; **tu charries, elle n'est pas si vieille!** come off it* (*Brit*) – she's not that old!, come on* – she's not that old!; **je ne suis pas ta bonne, faut pas ~** *ou* **faudrait pas ~!** come off it* (*Brit*) I'm not your servant!, come on* – I'm not your servant!; **je ne suis pas sa/leur bonne – faut pas ~** *ou* **faudrait pas ~!** he/they must be joking *ou* kidding* – I'm not their servant!
charrieur, -euse‡ [ʃaʀjœʀ, øz] **nm,f: c'est un ~** (*il abuse*) he's always going too far *ou* overstepping the mark; (*il plaisante*) he's always having (*Brit*) *ou* kidding (*Brit*) *ou* putting (*US*) people on‡; **il est un peu ~** he's a bit of a joker*.
charroi†† [ʃaʀwɑ] **nm** (*transport*) cartage.
charron [ʃaʀɔ̃] **nm** cartwright, wheelwright.
charroyer [ʃaʀwaje] [8] **vt** (*littér*) (*transporter par charrette*) to cart; (*transporter laborieusement*) to cart (along), heave (along).
charrue [ʃaʀy] **nf** plough (*Brit*), plow (*US*). (*fig*) **mettre la ~ devant** *ou* **avant les bœufs** to put the cart before the horse.
charte [ʃaʀt] **nf** (*Hist, Pol: convention*) charter; (*Hist: titre, contrat*) title, deed. (*Hist*) **accorder une ~ à** to grant a charter to, charter; (*Pol*) **la C~ des Nations Unies** the Charter of the United Nations.
charter [ʃaʀtɛʀ] **1** **nm** (*vol*) charter flight; (*avion*) chartered plane. **2** **adj inv** *vol, billet, prix* charter (*épith*). **avion ~** chartered plane.
chartisme [ʃaʀtism] **nm** (*Pol Brit*) Chartism.
chartiste [ʃaʀtist] **1** **adj, nmf** (*Hist*) Chartist. **2** **nmf** (*élève*) student of the École des Chartes (*in Paris*).
chartreuse [ʃaʀtʀøz] **nf** (*liqueur*) chartreuse; (*couvent*) Charterhouse, Carthusian monastery; (*religieuse*) Carthusian nun.
chartreux [ʃaʀtʀø] **nm** (*religieux*) Carthusian monk; (*chat*) Chartreux.
Charybde [kaʀibd] **nm** Charybdis; *voir* **tomber**.
chas [ʃɑ] **nm** eye (*of needle*).
chasse¹ [ʃas] **1** **nf** **a** (*gén*) hunting; (*au fusil*) shooting, hunting. **aller à la ~** to go hunting; **aller à la ~ aux papillons** to go butterfly hunting; **~ au faisan** pheasant shooting; **~ au lapin** rabbit shooting, rabbiting; **~ au renard/au chamois/au gros gibier** fox/chamois/big game hunting; **air/habits de ~** hunting tune/clothes; *voir* **chien, cor¹, fusil** *etc*.
b (*période*) hunting season, shooting season. **la ~ est ouverte/fermée** it is the open/close season (*Brit*), it is open/closed season (*US*).
c (*gibier tué*) **manger/partager la ~** to eat/share the game; **faire (une) bonne ~** to get a good bag.
d (*terrain, domaine*) shoot, hunting ground. **louer une ~** to rent a shoot *ou* land to shoot *ou* hunt on; **une ~ giboyeuse** well-stocked shoot; **~ gardée** (*lit*) private hunting (ground), private shoot(ing); (*fig*) private ground; **c'est ~ gardée!** no poaching on *ou* keep off our (*ou* their *etc*) preserve!, out of bounds!; *voir* **action**.
e (*chasseurs*) **la ~** the hunt.
f (*Aviat*) **la ~** the fighters (*pl*); *voir* **avion, pilote**.
g (*poursuite*) chase. **une ~ effrénée dans les rues de la ville** a frantic chase through the streets of the town.
h (*loc*) **faire la ~ aux souris/aux moustiques** to hunt down *ou* chase mice/mosquitoes; **faire la ~ aux abus/erreurs** to hunt down *ou* track down abuses/errors; **faire la ~ aux appartements/occasions** to be *ou* go flat- (*Brit*) *ou* apartment- (*US*)/bargain-hunting; **faire la ~ au mari** to be hunting for a husband, be on the hunt for a husband*; **prendre en ~, donner la ~ à** *fuyard, voiture* to give chase to, chase after; *avion, navire, ennemi* to give chase to; (*Aviat, Mil, Naut*) **donner la ~** to give chase; **se mettre en ~ pour trouver qch** to go hunting for sth; **être en ~** *[chienne]* to be in *ou* on heat; *[chien]* to be on the trail.

2 comp ▸**chasse à l'affût** hunting (from a hide) ▸**chasse au chevreuil** deer hunting, deer-stalking ▸**chasse à courre** hunting ▸**chasse au furet** ferreting ▸**chasse au fusil** shooting ▸**chasse à l'homme** manhunt ▸**chasse aux sorcières** (*Pol*) witch hunt ▸**chasse sous-marine** harpooning, harpoon fishing ▸**chasse au trésor** treasure hunt.

chasse[2] [ʃas] nf a ~ **(d'eau** *ou* **des cabinets)** (toilet) flush; **actionner** *ou* **tirer la** ~ to pull the chain (*Brit*), flush the toilet *ou* lavatory (*Brit*). b (*Typ*) body (width), set (width).

châsse [ʃɑs] nf (*reliquaire*) reliquary, shrine; (*‡: œil*) peeper*; (*monture*) *[bague, bijou]* setting; *[lancette]* handle.

chasse- [ʃas] préf *voir* **chasser.**

chassé [ʃase] 1 nm (*danse*) chassé. 2 comp ▸**chassé-croisé** nm **(pl chassés-croisés)** (*Danse*) chassé-croisé, set to partners; (*fig*) **avec tous ces chassés-croisés nous ne nous sommes pas vus depuis 6 mois** amid *ou* with all these to-ings and fro-ings we haven't seen each other for 6 months; (*fig*) **par suite d'un chassé-croisé nous nous sommes manqués** we missed each other because of a mix-up *ou* confusion about where to meet; (*fig*) **une période de chassés-croisés sur les routes** a period of heavy (two-way) traffic; (*fig*) **c'est un chassé-croisé à la sortie des bureaux** there's a mad scramble when the offices close.

chasselas [ʃasla] nm chasselas grape.

chassepot [ʃaspo] nm (*Hist*) chassepot (rifle).

chasser [ʃase] 1 1 vt a (*gén*) to hunt; (*au fusil*) to shoot, hunt. ~ **à l'affût/au filet** to hunt from a hide/with a net; ~ **le faisan/le cerf** to go pheasant-shooting/deer hunting; ~ **le lapin au furet** to go ferreting; **il chasse le lion en Afrique** he is shooting lions *ou* lion-shooting in Africa; (*fig*) **il est ministre, comme son père et son grand-père: il chasse de race** he's a minister like his father and grandfather before him – it runs in the family *ou* he is carrying on the family tradition; *voir* **bon**[1].

b (*faire partir*) *importun, animal, ennemi* to drive *ou* chase out *ou* away; *domestique, fils indigne, manifestant* to send packing, turn out; *immigrant* to drive out, expel; *touristes, clients* to drive away, chase away. **chassant de la main les insectes** brushing away *ou* driving off (the) insects with his hand; **il a chassé les gamins du jardin** he chased *ou* drove the lads out of the garden; **mon père m'a chassé de la maison** my father has turned me out of the house *ou* has sent me packing; **le brouillard nous a chassés de la plage** we were driven away from *ou* off the beach by the fog; **ces touristes, ils vont finir par nous** ~ **de chez nous** these tourists will end up driving us away from *ou* out of *ou* hounding us from our own homes; **il a été chassé de son pays par le nazisme** he was forced by Nazism to flee his country, Nazism drove him from his country; (*Prov*) **chassez le naturel, il revient au galop** what's bred in the bone comes out in the flesh (*Prov*); *voir* **faim.**

c (*dissiper*) *odeur* to dispel, drive away; *idée* to dismiss, chase away; *souci, doute* to dispel, drive away, chase away. **essayant de** ~ **ces images obsédantes** trying to chase away *ou* dismiss these haunting images; **il faut** ~ **cette idée de ta tête** you must get that idea out of your head *ou* dismiss that idea from your mind; **le vent a chassé le brouillard** the wind dispelled *ou* blew away the fog.

d (*pousser*) *troupeau, nuages, pluie* to drive; (*Tech*) *clou* to drive in.

e (*éjecter*) *douille, eau d'un tuyau* to drive out; *voir* **clou.**

2 vi a (*aller à la chasse*) (*gén*) to go hunting; (*au fusil*) to go shooting. (*fig*) ~ **sur les terres de qn** to poach on sb's territory.

b (*déraper*) *[véhicule, roues]* to skid; *[ancre]* to drag. (*Naut*) ~ **sur ses ancres** to drag its anchors.

3 comp ▸**chasse-clou** nm **(pl chasse-clous)** nail punch ▸**chasse-mouches** nm inv flyswatter, fly whisk (*Brit*) ▸**chasse-neige** nm inv (*instrument*) snowplough; (*position du skieur*) snowplough, wedge; **descendre une pente en chasse-neige** to snowplough down a slope ▸**chasse-neige à soufflerie** snow-blower ▸**chasse-pierres** nm inv cowcatcher.

chasseresse [ʃasʀɛs] nf (*littér*) huntress (*littér*); *voir* **Diane.**

chasseur [ʃasœʀ] 1 nm a (*gén*) hunter; (*à courre*) hunter, huntsman. **c'est un très bon** ~ (*gibier à poil*) he's a very good hunter; (*gibier à plume*) he's an excellent shot; **c'est un grand** ~ **de perdrix** he's a great one for partridge-shooting; **c'est un grand** ~ **de renards** he's a great one for foxhunting, he's a great foxhunter.

b (*Mil*) (*soldat*) chasseur. (*régiment*) **le 3e** ~ the 3rd (regiment of) chasseurs.

c (*Mil*) (*avion*) fighter.

d (*garçon d'hôtel*) page (boy), messenger (boy), bellboy (*US*).

2 comp ▸**chasseur alpin** (*Mil*) mountain infantryman; (*troupe*) **les chasseurs alpins** the mountain infantry, the alpine chasseurs ▸**chasseur d'autographes** autograph hunter ▸**chasseur-bombardier** (*Aviat, Mil*) nm **(pl chasseurs-bombardiers)** fighter-bomber ▸**chasseur à cheval** (*Hist Mil*) cavalryman; (*troupe*) **les chasseurs à cheval** the cavalry ▸**chasseur d'images** roving photography enthusiast ▸**chasseur à pied** (*Hist Mil*) infantryman; (*troupe*) **les chasseurs à pied** the infantry ▸**chasseur de prime** bounty hunter ▸**chasseur à réaction** (*Aviat*) jet fighter ▸**chasseur de sous-marins** submarine chaser ▸**chasseur de têtes** (*lit, fig*) headhunter.

chasseuse [ʃasøz] nf (*rare*) huntswoman, hunter, huntress (*littér*).

chassie [ʃasi] nf *[yeux]* sticky matter (*in eye*).

chassieux, -ieuse [ʃasjø, jøz] adj *yeux* sticky, gummy; *personne, animal* gummy- *ou* sticky-eyed.

châssis [ʃɑsi] nm a *[véhicule]* chassis; *[machine]* sub- *ou* under-frame. b (*encadrement*) *[fenêtre]* frame; *[toile, tableau]* stretcher; (*Typ*) chase; (*Phot*) (printing) frame. ~ **mobile/dormant** opening/fixed frame. c (*‡*) (*corps féminin*) body, figure, chassis‡ (*US*). **elle a un beau** ~! what a smashing figure she's got!*, she's a knockout!‡ d (*Agr*) cold frame.

chaste [ʃast] adj *personne, pensées, amour, baiser* chaste; *yeux, oreilles* innocent. **de ~s jeunes filles** chaste *ou* innocent young girls.

chastement [ʃastəmɑ̃] adv chastely, innocently.

chasteté [ʃastəte] nf chastity; *voir* **ceinture.**

chasuble [ʃazybl] nf chasuble; *voir* **robe.**

chat [ʃa] 1 nm a (*animal*) (*gén*) cat; (*mâle*) tomcat. ~ **persan/siamois** Persian/Siamese cat; **petit** ~ kitten; (*terme d'affection*) **mon petit** ~ (*à un enfant*) pet*, poppet* (*Brit*); (*à une femme*) sweetie*, lovie*.

b (*jeu*) tig (*Brit*), tag. **jouer à** ~ to play tig (*Brit*) *ou* tag, have a game of tig (*Brit*) *ou* tag; **(c'est toi le)** ~! you're it!

c (*loc*) **il n'y avait pas un** ~ **dehors** there wasn't a soul outside; **avoir un** ~ **dans la gorge** to have a frog in one's throat; **il a acheté cette voiture** ~ **en poche** he bought a pig in a poke when he got that car, he hardly even looked at the car before buying it; (*Prov*) ~ **échaudé craint l'eau froide** once bitten, twice shy (*Prov*); (*Prov*) **quand le** ~ **n'est pas là les souris dansent** when the cat's away the mice will play (*Prov*); *voir* **appeler, chien, fouetter** *etc.*

2 comp ▸**le Chat Botté** Puss in Boots ▸**chat de gouttière** ordinary cat, alley cat (*péj*) ▸**chat-huant** (*Zool*) nm **(pl chats-huants)** screech owl, barn owl ▸**chat à neuf queues** (*Hist Naut*) cat-o'-nine-tails ▸**chat perché** (*jeu*) "off-ground" tag *ou* tig (*Brit*) ▸**chat sauvage** wildcat ▸**chat-tigre** nm **(pl chats-tigres)** tiger cat.

châtaigne [ʃɑtɛɲ] nf a (*fruit*) (sweet) chestnut. ~ **d'eau** water chestnut. b (*‡: coup de poing*) clout*, biff*. **flanquer une** ~ **à qn** to clout* *ou* biff* sb, give sb a clout* *ou* biff*. c (**: décharge électrique*) (electric) shock.

châtaigneraie [ʃɑtɛɲʀɛ] nf chestnut grove.

châtaignier [ʃɑteɲe] nm (*arbre*) (sweet) chestnut tree; (*bois*) chestnut.

châtain [ʃɑtɛ̃] 1 nm chestnut brown. 2 adj *cheveux* chestnut (brown); *personne* brown-haired. **elle est** ~ **clair/roux** she has light brown hair/auburn hair.

château, pl ~x [ʃɑto] 1 nm (*forteresse*) castle; (*résidence royale*) palace, castle; (*manoir, gentilhommière*) mansion, stately home; (*en France*) château. **les ~x de la Loire** the Loire châteaux; (*vignobles*) **les ~x du Bordelais** the châteaux of the Bordeaux region; (*fig*) **bâtir** *ou* **faire des ~x en Espagne** to build castles in the air *ou* in Spain; **il est un peu** ~ **branlant** he's a bit wobbly on his pins; *voir* **vie.**

2 comp ▸**château d'arrière** (*Naut*) aftercastle ▸**château d'avant** (*Naut*) forecastle, fo'c'sle ▸**château de cartes** (*Cartes, fig*) house of cards ▸**château d'eau** water tower ▸**château fort** stronghold, fortified castle ▸**Château-la-Pompe**† nm inv Adam's ale† ▸**château de poupe** (*Naut*) = **château d'arrière** ▸**château de proue** (*Naut*) = **château d'avant.**

chateaubriand, châteaubriant [ʃatobʀijɑ̃] nm (*Culin*) chateaubriand, chateaubriant.

châtelain [ʃɑt(ə)lɛ̃] nm a (*Hist: seigneur*) (feudal) lord. **le** ~ the lord of the manor. b (*propriétaire d'un manoir*) (*d'ancienne date*) squire; (*nouveau riche*) owner of a manor. **le** ~ **vint nous ouvrir** the owner of the manor *ou* the squire came to the door.

châtelaine [ʃɑt(ə)lɛn] nf a (*propriétaire d'un manoir*) owner of a manor. **la** ~ **vint nous recevoir** the lady of the manor came to greet us. b (*épouse du châtelain*) lady (of the manor), chatelaine. c (*ceinture*) chatelaine, châtelaine.

châtié, e [ʃɑtje] (**ptp de châtier**) adj *style* polished, refined; *langage* refined.

châtier [ʃɑtje] 7 vt a (*littér: punir*) *coupable* to chastise (*littér*), castigate (*littér*), punish; *faute* to punish; (*Rel*) *corps* to chasten, mortify. ~ **l'insolence de qn** to chastise *ou* punish sb for his insolence; *voir* **qui.** b (*soigner, corriger*) *style* to polish, refine, perfect; *langage* to refine.

chatière [ʃatjɛʀ] nf (*porte*) cat-flap; (*trou d'aération*) (air-)vent, ventilation hole; (*piège*) cat-trap.

châtiment [ʃɑtimɑ̃] nm (*littér*) chastisement (*littér*), castigation (*littér*), punishment. ~ **corporel** corporal punishment; **subir un** ~ to receive *ou* undergo punishment.

chatoiement [ʃatwamɑ̃] nm (*voir* **chatoyant**) glistening; shimmer(ing); sparkle.

chaton[1] [ʃatɔ̃] nm a (*Zool*) kitten. b (*Bot*) catkin. **~s de saule** pussy willows; (*fig*) **~s de poussière** balls of fluff.

chaton[2] [ʃatɔ̃] nm (*monture*) bezel, setting; (*pierre*) stone.

chatouille* [ʃatuj] nf tickle. **faire des ~s à qn** to tickle sb; **craindre les ~s** *ou* **la** ~ to be ticklish.

chatouillement [ʃatujmɑ̃] nm (*gén*) tickling; (*dans le nez, la gorge*) tickle. **des ~s la faisaient se trémousser** a tickling sensation made her fidget.

chatouiller [ʃatuje] 1 **vt** a (*lit*) to tickle. **arrête, ça chatouille!** don't, that tickles! *ou* you're tickling! b (*fig*) *amour-propre, curiosité* to tickle, titillate; *palais, odorat* to titillate. c († *hum*) **~ les côtes à qn** to tan sb's hide.

chatouilleux, -euse [ʃatujø, øz] **adj** a (*lit*) ticklish. b (*fig: susceptible*) *personne, caractère* touchy, (over)sensitive. **individu à l'amour-propre ~** person who easily takes offence *ou* whose pride is sensitive; **être ~ sur l'honneur/l'étiquette** to be touchy *ou* sensitive on points of honour/etiquette.

chatouillis* [ʃatuji] **nm** (*sensation*) light tickling, gentle tickling. **faire des ~ à qn** to tickle sb lightly *ou* gently.

chatoyant, e [ʃatwajɑ̃, ɑ̃t] **adj** *vitraux* glistening; *reflet, étoffe* shimmering; *bijoux, plumage* glistening, shimmering; *couleurs, style* sparkling. **l'éclat ~ des pierreries** the glistening *ou* shimmering of the gems.

chatoyer [ʃatwaje] 8 **vi** (*voir* **chatoyant**) to glisten; to shimmer; to sparkle.

châtré⁑ [ʃɑtʀe] **nm** (*lit, fig*) eunuch. **voix de ~** squeaky little voice.

châtrer [ʃɑtʀe] 1 **vt** *taureau, cheval* to castrate, geld; *chat* to neuter, castrate, fix (*US*); *homme* to castrate, emasculate; (*littér*) *texte* to mutilate, bowdlerize.

chatte [ʃat] **nf** (*Zool*) (she-)cat; (⁑: *vagin*) pussy⁑⁑ **elle est très ~** she's very kittenish; (*terme d'affection*) **ma (petite) ~** (my) pet*, sweetie(-pie)*.

chattemite [ʃatmit] **nf: faire la ~** to be a bit of a coaxer.

chatterie [ʃatʀi] **nf** a (*caresses*) **~s** playful attentions *ou* caresses; (*minauderies*) kittenish ways; **faire des ~s à qn** to pet sb. b (*friandise*) titbit, dainty morsel. **aimer les ~s** to love a little delicacy *ou* a dainty morsel.

chatterton [ʃatɛʀtɔn] **nm** (*Élec*) (adhesive) insulating tape.

chaud, chaude [ʃo, ʃod] 1 **adj** a warm; (*très chaud*) hot. **les climats ~s** warm climates; (*très chaud*) hot climates; **l'eau du lac n'est pas assez ~e pour se baigner** the water in the lake is not warm enough for bathing; **bois ton thé pendant qu'il est ~** drink your tea while it's hot; **tous les plats étaient servis très ~s** all the dishes were served up piping hot; **cela sort tout ~ du four** it's (piping) hot from the oven; (*fig*) **il a des nouvelles toutes ~es** he's got some news hot from the press (*fig*) *ou* some hot news; *voir* **battre, main** *etc.*

b *couverture, vêtement* warm, cosy.

c (*vif, passionné*) *félicitations* warm, hearty; (*littér*) *amitié* warm; *partisan* keen, ardent; *admirateur* warm, ardent; *recommandation* wholehearted, enthusiastic; *discussion* heated. **la bataille a été ~e** it was a fierce battle, the battle was fast and furious; **être ~ (pour faire/pour qch)*** to be enthusiastic (about doing/about sth), be keen (on doing/on sth) (*Brit*); **il n'est pas très ~ pour conduire de nuit*** he doesn't much like driving at night, he is not very *ou* too keen (*Brit*) on driving at night.

d (*dangereux*) **l'alerte a été ~e** it was a near *ou* close thing; **les points ~s du globe** the world's hot spots; **les journaux prévoient un été "~"** newspapers forecast a long hot summer (of unrest).

e *voix, couleur* warm.

f (*: *sensuel*) *personne, tempérament* hot.

2 **nm** a (*chaleur*) **le ~** (the) heat, the warmth; **elle souffre autant du ~ que du froid** she suffers as much from the heat as from the cold; **restez donc au ~** stay in the warmth, stay where it's warm; **garder qch au ~** to keep sth warm *ou* hot; **garder un enfant enrhumé au ~** to keep a child with a cold (indoors) in the warmth; **être bien au ~** to be nice and warm.

b **à ~** *opération* emergency; (*Tech*) *travailler* under heat; **reportage à ~** on-the-spot report; **il a été opéré à ~** he had an emergency operation; *voir* **souder**.

3 **adv: avoir ~** to be warm, feel warm; (*très chaud*) to be hot, feel hot; **avez-vous assez ~?** are you warm enough?; **on a trop ~ ici** it's too hot *ou* too warm in here; (*fig*) **ma voiture a dérapé, j'ai eu ~!*** my car skidded, I got a real fright *ou* it gave me a nasty fright; **il fait ~** it is hot *ou* warm; (*iro*) **il fera ~ le jour où il voudra bien travailler*** that will be the day when he decides to work (*iro*); **ça ne me fait ni ~ ni froid** it makes no odds to me, I couldn't care less either way, it cuts no ice with me; **ça fait ~ au cœur** it's heart-warming; **manger ~** to have a hot meal, eat something hot; **boire ~** to have *ou* take hot drinks; **il a fallu tellement attendre qu'on n'a pas pu manger ~** we had to wait so long the food was no longer hot; **"servir ~"** "serve hot"; **~ devant!** mind your back (*ou* backs)!; **tenir ~ à qn** to keep sb warm; (*tenir trop chaud*) to make sb too hot; **donner ~ à qn** to warm sb up; *voir* **souffler**.

4 **chaude nf** (†: *flambée*) blaze.

5 **comp ►chaud et froid** (*Méd*) **nm, pl inv** chill **►chaud-froid** (*Culin*) **nm (pl chauds-froids)** chaudfroid **►chaud lapin**⁑ randy (*Brit*) *ou* horny devil⁑ **►chaude-pisse**⁑ **nf inv** clap⁑.

chaudement [ʃodmɑ̃] **adv** (*contre le froid*) *s'habiller* warmly; (*chaleureusement*) *féliciter, recommander* warmly, heartily; (*avec passion, acharnement*) heatedly, hotly. **~ disputé** hotly disputed; (*hum*) **comment ça va? — ~!** how are you? — (I'm) hot! (*hum*).

chaudière [ʃodjɛʀ] **nf** *[locomotive, chauffage central]* boiler.

chaudron [ʃodʀɔ̃] **nm** cauldron.

chaudronnerie [ʃodʀɔnʀi] **nf** a (*métier*) boilermaking, boilerwork; (*industrie*) boilermaking industry. b (*boutique*) coppersmith's workshop; (*usine*) boilerworks. c (*produits*) **grosse ~** industrial boilers; **petite ~** pots and pans, hollowware (*Brit*).

chaudronnier, -ière [ʃodʀɔnje, jɛʀ] **nm,f** (*artisan*) coppersmith; (*ouvrier*) boilermaker.

chauffage [ʃofaʒ] **nm** (*action*) heating; (*appareils*) heating (system). **il y a le ~?** is there any heating?, is it heated?; **avoir un bon ~** to have a good heating system; **~ au charbon/au gaz/à l'électricité** solid fuel/gas/electric heating; **~ central** central heating; **~ par le sol** underfloor heating; **~ urbain** urban *ou* district heating system; **mets le ~** (*maison*) put on the heating; (*voiture*) put on the heater; *voir* **bois**.

chauffagiste [ʃofaʒist] **nm** heating engineer *ou* specialist.

chauffant, e [ʃofɑ̃, ɑ̃t] **adj** *surface, élément* heating (*épith*); *voir* **couverture, plaque**.

chauffard* [ʃofaʀ] **nm** (*péj*) reckless driver. **(espèce de) ~!** roadhog!; **c'est un vrai ~** he's a real menace *ou* maniac on the roads; **il a été renversé/tué par un ~** he was run over/killed by a reckless driver; **on n'a pas retrouvé le ~ responsable de l'accident** the driver responsible for the accident has not yet been found; **il pourrait s'agir d'un ~** the police are looking for a hit-and-run driver.

chauffe [ʃof] **nf** (*lieu*) fire-chamber; (*processus*) stoking. **surface de ~** heating-surface, fire surface; (*Naut*) **chambre de ~** stokehold; *voir* **bleu**.

chauffe- [ʃof] **préf** *voir* **chauffer**.

chauffer [ʃofe] 1 1 **vt** a (*plus gén* **faire ~, mettre à ~**) *soupe* to warm up, heat up; *assiette* to warm, heat; *eau du bain* to heat (up); *eau du thé* to boil, heat up. **~ qch au four** to heat sth up in the oven, put sth in the oven to heat up; **mets l'eau/les assiettes à ~** put the water on/the plates in to heat up; (*hum: quand on casse qch*) **faites ~ la colle!** bring out the glue!; **je vais te ~ les oreilles!** I'll box your ears!, you'll get a clip round the ear!*

b *appartement* to heat. **on va ~ un peu la pièce** we'll heat (up) the room a bit.

c *[soleil]* to warm, make warm; *[soleil brûlant]* to heat, make hot.

d (*Tech*) *métal, verre, liquide* to heat; *chaudière, locomotive* to stoke (up), fire. (*lit, fig*) **~ qch à blanc** to make sth white-hot; (*fig*) **~ qn à blanc** to galvanize sb into action.

e (*: *préparer*) *candidat* to cram; *commando* to train up; *salle, public* to warm up.

f *muscle* to warm up.

g (†*: *voler*) to pinch*, whip* (*Brit*), swipe*.

2 **vi** a (*être sur le feu*) *[aliment, eau du bain]* to be heating up, be warming up; *[assiette]* to be heating (up), be warming (up); *[eau du thé]* to be heating up.

b (*devenir chaud*) *[moteur, télévision]* to warm up; *[four]* to heat up; *[chaudière, locomotive]* to get up steam.

c (*devenir trop chaud*) *[freins, appareil, moteur]* to overheat.

d (*donner de la chaleur*) *[soleil]* to be hot; *[poêle]* to give out a good heat. **ils chauffent au charbon** they use coal for heating, their house is heated by coal; **le mazout chauffe bien** oil gives out a good heat.

e (**loc*) **ça chauffe dans le coin!** things are getting heated over there!, sparks are about to fly over there!; **ça va ~!** sparks will fly!; (*Sport*) **le but/l'essai chauffe** there must be a goal/try now!, they're on the brink of a goal/try; (*cache-tampon*) **tu chauffes!** you're getting warm(er)!

3 **se chauffer vpr** a (*près du feu*) to warm o.s.; (*: *en faisant des exercices*) to warm o.s. up. **se ~ au soleil** to warm o.s. in the sun.

b **se ~ au bois/charbon** to burn wood/coal, use wood/coal for heating; **se ~ à l'électricité** to have electric heating, use electricity for heating; *voir* **bois**.

4 **comp ►chauffe-assiettes nm inv** plate-warmer **►chauffe-bain nm (pl chauffe-bains)** water-heater **►chauffe-biberon nm inv** bottle-warmer **►chauffe-eau nm inv** water-heater; (*à élément chauffant*) immersion heater, immerser **►chauffe-pieds nm inv** foot-warmer **►chauffe-plats nm inv** dish-warmer, chafing dish.

chaufferette [ʃofʀɛt] **nf** (*chauffe-pieds*) foot-warmer; (*réchaud*) plate warmer.

chaufferie [ʃofʀi] **nf** *[maison, usine]* boiler room; *[navire]* stokehold.

chauffeur [ʃofœʀ] 1 **nm** a (*conducteur*) (*gén*) driver; (*privé*) chauffeur. **~ d'autobus** bus driver; **voiture avec/sans ~** chauffeur-driven/self-drive car. b *[chaudière]* fireman, stoker. 2 **comp ►chauffeur de camion** lorry (*Brit*) *ou* truck (*US*) driver **►chauffeur du dimanche** (*hum*) Sunday driver, weekend motorist **►chauffeur de maître** chauffeur **►chauffeur de taxi** taxi driver, cab driver.

chauffeuse [ʃoføz] **nf** low armless chair, unit chair.

chaulage [ʃolaʒ] **nm** (*voir* **chauler**) liming; whitewashing.

chauler [ʃole] 1 **vt** *sol, arbre, raisins* to lime; *mur* to whitewash.

chaume [ʃom] **nm** a (*reste des tiges*) stubble. (*littér: champs*) **les ~s** the stubble fields. b (*couverture de toit*) thatch. **couvrir de ~** to thatch; *voir* **toit**. c (*rare: tige*) *[graminée, céréale]* culm.

chaumer [ʃome] 1 1 **vt** to clear stubble from. 2 **vi** to clear the stubble.

chaumière [ʃomjɛʀ] nf (*littér, hum: maison*) (little) cottage; (*maison à toit de chaume*) thatched cottage. **on en parlera encore longtemps dans les ~s** it will be talked of in the countryside *ou* in the villages for a long time to come; **un feuilleton qui fait pleurer dans les ~s** a serial which will bring tears to the eyes of all simple folk.

chaumine [ʃomin] nf (*littér ou* †) little cottage (*often thatched*), cot (*Poésie*).

chaussant, e [ʃosɑ̃, ɑ̃t] adj (*confortable*) well-fitting, snug-fitting. **articles ~s** footwear (*NonC*); **ces souliers sont très ~s** these shoes are a very good fit *ou* fit very well.

chausse [ʃos] nf *voir* **chausses**.

chausse- [ʃos] préf *voir* **chausser**.

chaussée [ʃose] nf a (*route, rue*) road, roadway. **s'élancer sur la ~** to rush out into the road *ou* onto the roadway; **traverser la ~** to cross the road; **ne reste pas sur la ~** don't stay in *ou* on the road *ou* on the roadway; **l'entretien de la ~** the maintenance of the roadway, road maintenance; **~ pavée** cobbled street; (*route*) cobbled *ou* flagged road; **~ bombée** cambered road; "**~ glissante**" "slippery road"; "**~ déformée**" "uneven road surface"; *voir* **pont**. b (*chemin surélevé*) causeway; (*digue*) embankment. **la ~ des Géants** the Giants' Causeway.

chausser [ʃose] [1] 1 vt a (*mettre des chaussures à*) *enfant* to put shoes on. **chausse les enfants pour sortir** put the children's shoes on (for them) *ou* help the children on with their shoes and we'll go out; **se ~** to put one's shoes on; **se faire ~ par** to have one's shoes put on by; **~ qn de bottes** to put boots on sb; **chaussé de bottes/sandales** wearing boots/sandals, with boots/sandals on; *voir* **cordonnier**.

b (*mettre*) *souliers, lunettes* to put on. **~ du 40** to take size 40 in shoes, take a (size) 40 shoe; **~ des bottes à un client** to put boots on a customer; (*Équitation*) **~ les étriers** to put one's feet into the stirrups.

c (*fournir en chaussures*) **ce marchand nous chausse depuis 10 ans** this shoemaker has been supplying us with shoes for 10 years; **se (faire) ~ chez ...** to buy *ou* get one's shoes at ...; **se (faire) ~ sur mesure** to have one's shoes made to measure.

d [*chaussure*] to fit. **ces chaussures chaussent large** these shoes come in a wide fitting (*Brit*) *ou* size (*US*), these are wide-fitting shoes; **ces chaussures vous chaussent bien** those shoes fit you well *ou* are a good fit; **ces souliers chaussent bien (le pied)** these are well-fitting shoes.

e (*Agr*) *arbre* to earth up.

f (*Aut*) *voiture* to fit tyres on. **voiture bien chaussée** car with good tyres.

2 comp ▸**chausse-pied** nm (pl **chausse-pieds**) shoehorn ▸**chausse-trappe** (*lit, fig*) nf (pl **chausse-trappes**) trap; **tomber dans/éviter une chausse-trappe** to fall into/avoid a trap.

chausses [ʃos] nfpl (*Hist Habillement*) chausses; *voir* **haut**.

chaussette [ʃosɛt] nf sock. **j'étais en ~s** I was in my socks; **~s à clous**‡ [*agent de police*] (policeman's) hobnailed boots; **~s russes** footbindings.

chausseur [ʃosœʀ] nm (*fabricant*) shoemaker; (*fournisseur*) footwear specialist, shoemaker. **mon ~ m'a déconseillé cette marque** my shoemaker has advised me against that make.

chausson [ʃosɔ̃] nm a (*pantoufle*) slipper; [*bébé*] bootee; [*danseur*] ballet shoe *ou* pump; **~ à pointe** blocked shoe; *voir* **point²**. b (*Culin*) turnover.

chaussure [ʃosyʀ] 1 nf a (*soulier*) shoe. **la ~ est une partie importante de l'habillement** footwear is *ou* shoes are an important part of one's dress; **ils ont de la belle ~** they do a beautiful line in footwear; **rayon (des) ~s** shoe *ou* footwear department; *voir* **trouver**. b **la ~** (*industrie*) shoe industry; (*commerce*) shoe trade (*Brit*) *ou* business.

2 comp ▸**chaussures basses** flat shoes ▸**chaussures cloutées** *ou* **à clous** hobnailed boots ▸**chaussures montantes** ankle boots ▸**chaussures de ski** ski boots ▸**chaussures à talon** high-heeled shoes, (high) heels*.

chaut [ʃo] vi (†† *ou hum*) **peu me ~** it matters little to me, it is of no import († *ou hum*) *ou* matter† to me.

chauve [ʃov] 1 adj *personne* bald(-headed); *crâne* bald; (*fig littér*) *colline, sommet* bare. **~ comme un œuf*** *ou* **une bille*** *ou* **mon genou*** as bald as a coot. 2 comp ▸**chauve-souris** (*Zool*) nf (pl **chauves-souris**) bat.

chauvin, e [ʃovɛ̃, in] 1 adj chauvinistic, jingoistic. 2 nm,f chauvinist, jingoist.

chauvinisme [ʃovinism] nm chauvinism, jingoism.

chauviniste [ʃovinist] 1 adj chauvinistic, jingoistic. 2 nmf chauvinist, jingoist.

chaux [ʃo] nf lime. **~ vive/éteinte** quick/slaked lime; **blanchi** *ou* **passé à la ~** whitewashed.

chavirer [ʃaviʀe] [1] 1 vi a [*bateau*] to capsize, keel over, overturn; (*fig*) [*gouvernement*] to founder, crumble, sink. **faire ~ un bateau** to keel a boat over, capsize *ou* overturn a boat.

b [*pile d'objets*] to keel over, overturn; [*charrette*] to overturn, tip over; (*fig*) [*yeux*] to roll; [*paysage, chambre*] to reel, spin; [*esprit*] to reel; [*cœur*] to turn over (*fig*).

2 vt a (*renverser*) *bateau* [*vagues*] to capsize, overturn; (*Tech: en cale sèche*) to keel over; *meubles* to overturn.

b (*bouleverser*) *personne* to bowl over. **j'en suis toute chavirée*** I'm completely shattered by it, it gave me a nasty fright *ou* turn*; **musique qui chavire l'âme** music that tugs at the heartstrings.

chéchia [ʃeʃja] nf tarboosh, fez.

check-list, pl **check-lists** [(t)ʃɛklist] nf check list.

check-up [(t)ʃɛkœp] nm inv check-up.

chef¹ [ʃɛf] 1 nmf a (*patron, dirigeant*) head, boss*, top man*; [*tribu*] chief(tain), headman. **il a l'estime de ses ~s** he is highly thought of by his superiors *ou* bosses*; **la ~*** the boss; (*péj*) **faire le** *ou* **jouer au petit ~** to throw one's weight around.

b [*expédition, révolte, syndicat*] leader. (*: *as*) **tu es un ~** you're the greatest*, you're the tops*; **avoir une âme** *ou* **un tempérament de ~** to be a born leader; **elle/il se débrouille comme un ~** she/he is doing a first-class job.

c (*Mil: au sergent*) **oui, ~!** yes, Sarge!

d chef. (*Culin*) **spécialité du ~** chef's speciality; **pâté du ~** chef's special pâté; **~ de cuisine** head chef.

e **en ~**: **commandant en ~** commander-in-chief; **général en ~** general-in-chief; **ingénieur/rédacteur en ~** chief engineer/editor; **le général commandait en ~ les troupes alliées** the general was the commander-in-chief of the allied troops.

2 adj inv: **gardien/médecin ~** chief warden/consultant.

3 comp ▸**chef d'atelier** (shop) foreman ▸**chef de bande** gang leader ▸**chef de bataillon** major ▸**chef de bureau** head clerk ▸**chef de cabinet** (*Admin*) principal private secretary ▸**chef de chantier** (works (*Brit*) *ou* site) foreman ▸**chef des chœurs** (*Mus*) choirmaster ▸**chef de classe** class prefect *ou* monitor (*Brit*), class president (*US*) ▸**chef de clinique** ≃ senior registrar ▸**chef comptable** chief accountant ▸**chef de dépôt** shed *ou* yard master ▸**chef d'école** (*Art, Littérat*) leader of a school ▸**chef d'entreprise** company manager *ou* head ▸**chef d'équipe** foreman ▸**chef d'escadron** major ▸**chef d'État** head of state ▸**le chef de l'État** the Head of State ▸**chef d'état-major** (*Mil*) chief of staff ▸**chefs d'État-Major** Joint Chiefs of Staff ▸**chef de famille** head of the family *ou* household; (*Admin*) householder ▸**chef de file** leader; (*Pol*) party leader; (*Naut*) leading ship ▸**chef de gare** (*Rail*) station master ▸**chef des jurés** (*Jur*) foreman of the jury ▸**chef-lieu** (*Admin, Géog*) nm (pl **chef-lieux**) ≃ county town ▸**chef mécanicien** chief mechanic; (*Rail*) head driver (*Brit*), chief engineer (*US*) ▸**chef de musique** bandmaster ▸**chef de nage** stroke (oar) ▸**chef-d'œuvre** nm (pl **chefs-d'œuvre** [ʃɛdœvʀ]) masterpiece, chef-d'œuvre; (*fig*) **c'est un chef-d'œuvre d'hypocrisie/d'ironie** it is the ultimate hypocrisy/irony ▸**chef d'orchestre** (*Mus*) conductor (*Brit*), leader (*US*) ▸**chef de patrouille** patrol leader ▸**chef de pièce** (*Mil*) captain of a gun ▸**chef de produit** product manager, brand manager ▸**chef de projet** (*Admin*) project manager ▸**chef de rayon** (*Comm*) department(al) supervisor, departmental manager ▸**chef de service** (*Admin*) section *ou* departmental head; (*Méd*) ≃ consultant ▸**chef de train** (*Rail*) guard (*Brit*), conductor (*US*).

chef² [ʃɛf] nm a (†† *ou hum: tête*) head. (*Jur*) **~ d'accusation** charge, count (of indictment). b (*loc*) (*Jur*) **du ~ de sa femme** in one's wife's right; (*frm*) **de son propre ~** on his own initiative, on his own authority; (*littér*) **au premier ~** greatly, exceedingly; (*littér*) **de ce ~** accordingly, hence.

cheftaine [ʃɛftɛn] nf [*louveteaux*] cubmistress (*Brit*), den mother (*US*); [*jeunes éclaireuses*] Brown Owl (*Brit*), den mother (*US*); [*éclaireuses*] (guide) captain.

cheik [ʃɛk] nm sheik.

chelem [ʃlɛm] nm (*Cartes*) slam. **petit/grand ~** small/grand slam. (*Sport*) **faire le grand ~** to do the grand slam.

chemin [ʃ(ə)mɛ̃] 1 nm a (*gén*) path; (*route*) lane; (*piste*) track; *voir* **croisée², voleur**.

b (*parcours, trajet, direction*) way (*de, pour* to). **demander/trouver le** *ou* **son ~** to ask/find the *ou* one's way; **montrer le ~ à qn** to show sb the way; **il y a bien une heure de ~** it takes a good hour to get there; **quel ~ a-t-elle pris?** which way did she go?; **de bon matin, ils prirent le ~ de X** they set out *ou* off for X early in the morning; **le ~ le plus court entre deux points** the shortest distance between two points; **ils ont fait tout le ~ à pied/en bicyclette** they walked/cycled all the way *ou* the whole way; **on a fait du ~ depuis une heure** we've come quite a (good) way in an hour; **se mettre en ~** to set out *ou* off; **poursuivre son ~** to carry on *ou* keep on one's way; (*littér*) **passez votre ~** go your way (*littér*), be on your way; **~ faisant, en ~** on the way; **pour venir, nous avons pris le ~ des écoliers** we came the long way round; (*fig*) **aller son ~** to go one's own sweet way; **être toujours sur les ~s** to be always on the road; *voir* **rebrousser**.

c (*fig*) path, way, road. **le ~ de l'honneur/de la gloire** the path *ou* way of honour/to glory; **le ~ de la ruine** the road to ruin; **nos ~s se sont croisés** our paths crossed; *voir* **droit², tout**.

d (*loc*) **il a encore du ~ à faire** he's still got a long way to go, he's not there yet; (*iro*) there's still room for improvement; **faire son ~ dans la vie** to make one's way in life; **se mettre dans** *ou* **sur le ~ de qn** to stand *ou* get in sb's way, stand in sb's path; (*fig*) **il est toujours sur mon ~** (*présent*) he turns up wherever I go; (*comme obstacle*) he always stands in my way; **il a fait du ~!** (*arriviste, jeune cadre*) he has come up in the world; (*savant, chercheur*) he has come a long way; **cette idée a fait du ~** this idea has gained ground; (*concession*) **faire la moitié du ~** to go half-way (to meet sb); **montrer le ~** to lead the way; **cela n'en prend pas le ~** it doesn't look likely; **il n'y arrivera pas par ce ~** he won't achieve anything this way, he won't get far if he goes about it this way; (*fig*) **être sur le** *ou* **en bon ~** to be on the right track; **elle est en bon ~ pour avoir son diplôme** she's going the right way about it if she wants to get her diploma; **ne t'arrête pas en si bon~!** don't stop now when you're doing so well *ou* after such a good start; **trouver des difficultés sur son ~** to meet difficulties on one's path; **est-ce qu'il va réussir? — il n'en prend pas le ~** will he succeed? — he's not going the right way about it; (*Rel*) **le ~ de Damas** the road to Damascus; (*fig*) **trouver son ~ de Damas** to see the light (*fig*).

2 **comp** ►**chemin d'accès** (*Ordin*) access path ►**chemin charretier** cart track ►**chemin creux** sunken lane ►**chemin critique** (*Ordin*) critical path ►**le chemin de (la) croix** (*Rel*) the Way of the Cross ►**chemin de fer** (*Rail*) railway (*Brit*), railroad (*US*); (*moyen de transport*) rail; **par chemin de fer** by rail; **employé des chemins de fer** railway (*Brit*) *ou* railroad (*US*) worker ►**chemin de halage** towpath ►**chemin de ronde** (*Archit*) covered way ►**chemin de table** table runner ►**chemin de terre** dirt track ►**chemin de traverse** path across *ou* through the fields ►**chemin vicinal** country road *ou* lane, minor road.

chemineau, pl **~x** [ʃ(ə)mino] **nm** (*littér ou ††: vagabond*) vagabond, tramp.

cheminée [ʃ(ə)mine] 1 **nf** a (*extérieure*) *[maison, usine]* chimney (stack); *[paquebot, locomotive]* funnel, smokestack. b (*intérieure*) fireplace; (*foyer*) fireplace, hearth; (*encadrement*) mantelpiece, chimney piece. **un feu crépitait dans la ~** a fire was crackling in the hearth *ou* fireplace *ou* grate; *voir* **feu**[1]. c (*Alpinisme*) chimney; *[lampe]* chimney.

2 **comp** ►**cheminée d'aération** ventilation shaft ►**cheminée prussienne** (closed) stove ►**cheminée d'usine** factory chimney.

cheminement [ʃ(ə)minmɑ̃] **nm** (*progression*) *[caravane, marcheurs]* progress, advance; (*Mil*) *[troupes]* advance (under cover); *[sentier, itinéraire, eau]* course, way; (*fig*) *[idées, pensée]* development, progression. **il est difficile de suivre son ~ intellectuel** it is difficult to follow his reasoning *ou* line of thought.

cheminer [ʃ(ə)mine] 1 **vi** (*littér*) a (*marcher, Mil: avancer à couvert*) to walk (along). **~ péniblement** to trudge (wearily) along; **après avoir longtemps cheminé** having plodded along for ages; **nous cheminions vers la ville** we wended (*littér*) *ou* made our way towards the town.

b (*progresser*) *[sentier]* to make its way (*dans* along); *[eau]* to make its way, follow its course (*dans* along); *[idées]* to follow their course. **l'idée cheminait lentement dans sa tête** the idea was slowly taking root in his mind, he was slowly coming round to the idea; **sa pensée cheminait de façon tortueuse** his thoughts followed a tortuous course; **les eaux de la Durance cheminent pendant des kilomètres entre des falaises** the waters of the Durance flow for miles between cliffs *ou* make their way between cliffs for miles (and miles).

cheminot [ʃ(ə)mino] **nm** railwayman (*Brit*), railroad man (*US*).

chemisage [ʃ(ə)mizaʒ] **nm** (*intérieur*) lining; (*extérieur*) jacketing.

chemise [ʃ(ə)miz] 1 **nf** a (*Habillement*) *[homme]* shirt; (††) *[femme]* chemise††, shift†; *[bébé]* vest. **~ de soirée/de sport** dress/sports shirt; **être en manches** *ou* **bras de ~** to be in one's shirt sleeves; **col/manchette de ~** shirt collar/cuff; *voir* **premier**.

b *[dossier]* folder; (*Tech*) (*revêtement intérieur*) lining; (*revêtement extérieur*) jacket. (*Aut*) **~ de cylindre** cylinder liner.

2 **comp** ►**chemise (américaine)** (woman's) vest (*Brit*) *ou* undershirt (*US*) ►**chemises brunes** (*Hist*) Brown Shirts ►**chemise d'homme** man's shirt ►**chemise de maçonnerie** facing ►**chemises noires** (*Hist*) Blackshirts ►**chemise de nuit** *[femme]* nightdress, nightgown, nightie*; *[homme]* nightshirt ►**chemises rouges** (*Hist*) Redshirts.

chemiser [ʃ(ə)mize] 1 **vt** *intérieur* to line; *extérieur* to jacket.

chemiserie [ʃ(ə)mizʀi] **nf** (*magasin*) (gentlemen's) outfitters' (*Brit*), man's shop; (*rayon*) shirt department; (*commerce*) shirt(-making) trade (*Brit*) *ou* business.

chemisette [ʃ(ə)mizɛt] **nf** *[homme]* short-sleeved shirt; *[femme]* short-sleeved blouse.

chemisier, -ière [ʃ(ə)mizje, jɛʀ] 1 **nm,f** (*marchand*) (gentlemen's) shirtmaker; (*fabricant*) shirtmaker. 2 **nm** (*vêtement*) blouse; *voir* **col, robe**.

chênaie [ʃɛnɛ] **nf** oak grove.

chenal, pl **-aux** [ʃənal, o] 1 **nm** (*canal*) channel, fairway; (*rigole*) channel; *[moulin]* millrace; *[forge, usine]* flume. 2 **comp** ►**chenal de coulée** (*Ind*) gate, runner ►**chenal pro-glaciaire** (*Géol*) glaciated valley.

chenapan [ʃ(ə)napɑ̃] **nm** (*hum: garnement*) scallywag (*hum*), rascal (*hum*); (*péj: vaurien*) scoundrel, rogue.

chêne [ʃɛn] 1 **nm** (*arbre*) oak (tree); (*bois*) oak. 2 **comp** ►**chêne-liège** **nm** (**pl chênes-lièges**) cork oak ►**chêne rouvre** durmast *ou* sessile oaktree ►**chêne vert** holm oak, ilex.

chéneau, pl **~x** [ʃeno] **nm** *[toit]* gutter.

chenet [ʃ(ə)nɛ] **nm** firedog, andiron.

chènevis [ʃɛnvi] **nm** hempseed.

chenil [ʃ(ə)nil] **nm** kennels. **mettre son chien dans un ~** to put one's dog in kennels.

chenille [ʃ(ə)nij] 1 **nf** a (*Aut, Zool*) caterpillar. **véhicule à ~s** tracked vehicle. b (*Tex*) chenille. 2 **comp** ►**chenille du mûrier** silkworm ►**chenille processionnaire** processionary caterpillar.

chenillé, e [ʃ(ə)nije] **adj** *véhicule* with caterpillar tracks, tracked.

chenillette [ʃ(ə)nijɛt] **nf** (*véhicule*) tracked vehicle.

chenu, e [ʃəny] **adj** (*littér*) *vieillard, tête* hoary; *arbre* leafless with age.

cheptel [ʃɛptɛl] 1 **nm** (*bétail*) livestock; (*Jur*) livestock (*leased*). **~ ovin/porcin d'une région** sheep/pig *ou* swine population of an area; *voir* **bail**. 2 **comp** ►**cheptel mort** (*Jur*) farm implements ►**cheptel vif** (*Jur*) livestock.

chèque [ʃɛk] 1 **nm** a (*Banque*) cheque (*Brit*), check (*US*). **faire/toucher un ~** to write/cash a cheque; **~ de 100 F** cheque for 100 francs (*Brit*) *ou* in the amount of 100 francs (*US*).

b (*bon*) voucher. **~-déjeuner** ® *ou* **-repas** *ou* **-restaurant** ® luncheon voucher (*Brit*), meal ticket (*US*); **~-cadeau** gift token; **~-essence** petrol (*Brit*) *ou* gasoline (*US*) coupon *ou* voucher.

2 **comp** ►**chèque bancaire** cheque ►**chèque barré** crossed cheque (*Brit*), check for deposit only (*US*) ►**chèque en blanc** (*lit, fig*) blank cheque ►**chèque en bois*** dud cheque*, rubber check* (*US*) ►**chèque certifié** certified cheque ►**chèque de dépannage** loose cheque (*supplied by bank when customer does not have his own chequebook*) ►**chèque non barré** uncrossed *ou* open cheque (*Brit*), check payable to bearer (*US*) ►**chèque à ordre** cheque to order, order cheque ►**chèque au porteur** bearer cheque ►**chèque postal** ≃ (Post Office) Girocheque (*Brit*) ►**chèque sans provision** bad *ou* dud* cheque, rubber check* (*US*) ►**chèque de voyage** traveller's cheque.

chéquier [ʃekje] **nm** cheque (*Brit*) *ou* check (*US*) book.

cher, chère[1] [ʃɛʀ] 1 **adj** a (*gén après n: aimé*) *personne, souvenir, vœu* dear (*à* to). **ceux qui nous sont ~s** our nearest and dearest, our dear ones; **des souvenirs ~s** fond memories; **des souvenirs ~s à mon cœur** memories dear to my heart; **les êtres ~s** the loved ones; **c'est mon vœu le plus ~** it's my fondest *ou* dearest wish; **mon désir le plus ~** *ou* **mon plus ~ désir est de** my greatest *ou* most cherished desire is to; **l'honneur est le bien le plus ~** honour is one's most precious possession, one's honour is to be treasured above all else.

b (*avant n*) dear. **(mes) ~s auditeurs** dear listeners; (*Rel*) **mes bien ~s frères** my dear(est) brethren; **Monsieur et ~ collègue** dear colleague; **ce ~ (vieux) Louis!*** dear old Louis!*; (*hum*) **le ~ homme n'y entendait pas malice** the dear man didn't mean any harm by it; **retrouver ses ~s parents/chères pantoufles** to find one's beloved parents/slippers again; **retrouver ses chères habitudes** to slip back into one's dear old habits; (*sur lettre*) **~s tous** dear all.

c (*coûteux: après n*) *marchandise* expensive, dear (*Brit*), costly; *boutique, commerçant* expensive, dear (*Brit*). **un petit restaurant pas ~** an inexpensive *ou* reasonably priced little restaurant; **la vie est chère à Paris** the cost of living is high in Paris, Paris is an expensive place to live; **c'est moins ~ qu'en face** it's cheaper than *ou* less expensive than in the shop opposite; **cet épicier est trop ~** this grocer is too expensive *ou* too dear (*Brit*) *ou* charges too much; **c'est trop ~ pour ce que c'est** it's overpriced; *voir* **vie**.

2 **nm,f** (*frm, hum*) **mon ~, ma chère** my dear; **oui, très ~** yes, dearest.

3 **adv** *valoir, coûter, payer* a lot (of money), a great deal (of money). **article qui vaut** *ou* **coûte ~** expensive item, item that costs a lot *ou* a great deal; **as-tu payé ~ ton costume?** did you pay much *ou* a lot for your suit?, was your suit (very) expensive? *ou* (very) dear (*Brit*)?; **il se fait payer ~, il prend ~** he charges high rates, his rates are high, he's expensive; **il vend ~** his prices are high, he charges high prices; **ça s'est vendu ~** it went for *ou* fetched a high price *ou* a lot (of money), it cost a mint*; **je ne l'ai pas acheté ~, je l'ai eu pour pas ~*** I bought it very cheaply *ou* bought it cheap*, I got it dirt cheap*, I didn't pay much for it; **je donnerais ~ pour savoir ce qu'il fait*** I'd give anything to know what he's doing; **je ne donne pas ~ de sa vie/de sa réussite** I wouldn't like to bet on his chances of surviving/succeeding; (*fig*) **garnement qui ne vaut pas ~** ne'er-do-well, good-for-nothing; (*fig*) **tu ne vaux pas plus ~ que lui** you're no better than him, you're just as bad as he is; (*fig*) **son imprudence lui a coûté ~** his rashness cost him dear (*Brit*) *ou* a great deal (*US*); (*fig*) **il a payé ~ son imprudence** he paid dearly (*Brit*) *ou* heavily for his rashness.

chercher [ʃɛʀʃe] 1 1 **vt** a (*essayer de trouver*) *personne, chose égarée, emploi* to look for, search for, try to find, hunt for; *solution, moyen* to look for, seek, try to find; *ombre, lumière, tranquillité* to seek; *citation, heure de train* to look up; *nom, mot* to try to find, try to think of; *raison, excuse* to cast about for, try to find, look for. **~ qn du regard** *ou* **des yeux** to look (around) for sb; **~ qch à tâtons** to grope *ou* fumble for sth; **attends, je cherche** wait a minute, I'm trying to think; **il n'a pas bien cherché** he didn't look *ou* search very hard; **~ partout qch/qn** to search *ou* hunt everywhere for sth/sb; **~ sa voie** to look for *ou* seek a path in life; **~ ses mots** to search for words; (*à un chien*) **cherche! cherche!** find it, boy!

b (*viser à*) *gloire, succès* to seek (after); (*rechercher*) *alliance, faveur* to seek. **il ne cherche que son intérêt** he is concerned only with his own interest.

c (*provoquer*) *danger, mort* to court. **~ la difficulté** to look for difficulties; **~ la bagarre** to be looking *ou* spoiling for a fight; **tu l'auras cherché!** you've been asking for it!; **si on me cherche, on me trouve*** if anyone asks for it, they'll get it*; **~ le contact avec l'ennemi** to try to engage the enemy in combat.

d (*prendre, acheter*) **aller ~ qch/qn** to go for sth/sb, go and fetch (*Brit*) *ou* get sth/sb; **il est venu ~ Paul** he called *ou* came for Paul, he came to fetch (*Brit*) *ou* to get Paul; **il est allé me ~ de la monnaie** he has gone to get some change for me; **va me ~ mon sac** go and fetch (*Brit*) *ou* get me my bag; **qu'est-ce que tu vas ~? je n'ai rien dit!** whatever do you mean? *ou* whatever are you trying to read into it? I didn't say a thing!; **où est-ce qu'il va ~ toutes ces idées idiotes!** where does he get all those stupid ideas from!; **monter/descendre ~ qch** to go up/down for sth *ou* to get sth; **aller ~ qch dans un tiroir** to go and get sth out of a drawer; **il est allé/venu le ~ à la gare** he went/came to meet *ou* collect him at the station; **aller ~ les enfants à l'école** to go to fetch (*Brit*) *ou* get *ou* collect the children from school; **envoyer (qn) ~ le médecin** to send (sb) for the doctor; **ça va ~ dans les 300 F** it'll add up to *ou* come to something like 300 francs; **ça va ~ dans les 5 ans de prison** it will mean something like 5 years in prison; (*amende*) **ça peut aller ~ loin** it could mean a heavy fine.

e **~ à faire** to try to do, attempt to do; **~ à comprendre** to try to understand; **faut pas ~ à comprendre*** don't (even) try and understand; **~ à faire plaisir à qn** to try *ou* endeavour to please sb; **~ à obtenir qch** to try to obtain sth; **~ à savoir qch** to try *ou* attempt to find out sth.

f (*loc*) **~ des crosses à qn*** to try and pick a fight with sb; **~ fortune** to seek one's fortune; **~ des histoires à qn** to try to make trouble for sb; **~ midi à quatorze heures** to complicate the issue, look for complications; **~ noise à qn** to pick a quarrel with sb; **~ la petite bête** to split hairs; **~ une aiguille dans une botte** *ou* **meule de foin** to look for a needle in a haystack; **~ des poux dans la tête de qn** to try and make trouble for sb; **~ querelle à qn** to pick a quarrel with sb; **~ son salut dans la fuite** to seek *ou* take refuge in flight; **cherchez la femme!** cherchez la femme!

2 **se chercher** vpr (*chercher sa voie*) to search for an identity.

chercheur, -euse [ʃɛʀʃœʀ, øz] 1 adj *esprit* inquiring; *voir* **tête**. 2 nm (*Tech*) *[télescope]* finder; *[détecteur à galène]* cat's whisker. **~ de fuites** gas-leak detector. 3 nm,f (*personne qui étudie, cherche*) researcher; (*Univ: chargé de recherches*) researcher, research worker. (*personne qui cherche qch*) **~ de** seeker of; **~ d'aventure(s)** adventure seeker, seeker after adventure; **~ d'or** gold digger; **~ de trésors** treasure hunter.

chère² [ʃɛʀ] nf (*†† ou hum*) food, fare, cheer†. **faire bonne ~** to eat well; **aimer la bonne ~** to love one's food.

chèrement [ʃɛʀmɑ̃] adv a (*avec affection*) *aimer* dearly, fondly. **conserver ~ des lettres** to keep letters lovingly, treasure letters; **conserver ~ le souvenir de qn/qch** to treasure *ou* cherish the memory of sb/sth. b (*non sans pertes, difficultés*) **~ acquis** *ou* **payé** *avantage, victoire, succès* dearly bought *ou* won; **vendre** *ou* **faire payer ~ sa vie** to sell one's life dearly. c (*†: au prix fort*) *vendre* at a high price, dearly†.

chéri, e [ʃeʀi] (ptp de **chérir**) 1 adj (*bien-aimé*) beloved, darling, dear(est). **quand il a revu son fils ~** when he saw his beloved son again; **dis-moi, maman ~e** tell me, mother dear *ou* mother darling; (*sur tombe*) **à notre père ~** to our dearly loved *ou* beloved father. 2 nm,f a (*terme d'affection*) darling. **mon (grand) ~** (my) darling, my (little) darling; (*hum*) **bonjour mes ~s** hullo (my) darlings (*hum*). b (*péj: chouchou*) **c'est le ~ à sa maman** he's mummy's little darling *ou* mummy's blue-eyed boy, his mother dotes on him; **c'est le ~ de ses parents** his parents dote on him, he's the apple of his parents' eye.

chérir [ʃeʀiʀ] [2] vt (*littér*) *personne* to cherish, love dearly; *liberté, idée* to cherish, hold dear; *souvenir* to cherish, treasure.

chérot* [ʃeʀo] adj m (*coûteux*) pricey* (*Brit*), dear.

cherry [ʃeʀi] nm, **cherry brandy** [ʃeʀibʀɑ̃di] nm cherry brandy.

cherté [ʃɛʀte] nf *[article]* high price, dearness (*Brit*); *[époque, région]* high prices (*de* in). **la ~ de la vie** the high cost of living, the cost of things*.

chérubin [ʃeʀybɛ̃] nm (*lit, fig*) cherub. **~s** (*Art*) cherubs; (*Rel*) cherubim.

chétif, -ive [ʃetif, iv] adj a (*malingre*) *enfant* puny, sickly; *adulte* puny; *arbuste, plante* puny, weedy, stunted. **enfant/végétaux à l'aspect ~** weedy-looking *ou* puny-looking child/plants. b (*minable*) *récolte* meagre, poor; *existence* meagre, mean; *repas* skimpy, scanty; *raisonnement* paltry, feeble.

chétivement [ʃetivmɑ̃] adv *pousser* punily.

chevaine [ʃ(ə)vɛn] nm = **chevesne**.

cheval, pl **-aux** [ʃ(ə)val, o] 1 nm a (*animal*) horse; (*viande*) horsemeat. **carosse à deux/à six ~aux** coach and pair/and six; **faire du ~** to go horse-riding; **tu sais faire du ~?** can you ride (a horse)?; (*péj*) **c'est un grand ~, cette fille** she's built like a carthorse (*Brit péj*), she's a great horse of a girl (*péj*); **au travail, c'est un vrai ~** he works like a carthorse (*Brit*), he works like a Trojan; (*fig*) **ce n'est pas le mauvais ~** he's not a bad sort *ou* soul; **tu as mangé** *ou* **bouffé du ~!*** you're lively!; *voir* **miser, monter, petit 5**.

b (*Aut*) horsepower (*NonC*). **elle fait combien de ~aux?** how many cc's is the engine?, what horsepower is it?; **c'est une 6 ~aux** it's a 6 horsepower car.

c (*arg Drogue*) horse, (big) H.

d (*loc*) **à ~** on horseback; **se tenir bien à ~** to have a good seat, sit well on horseback; **être à ~ sur une chaise** to be (sitting) astride a chair, be straddling a chair; **village à ~ sur deux départements** village straddling two departments; **à ~ sur deux mois** overlapping two (different) months, running from one month into the next; **être à ~ sur deux cultures** *[ville, pays]* to be at the crossroads of two cultures; *[personne]* to have roots in two cultures; *[œuvre]* to be rooted in *ou* to span two cultures; **être (très) à ~ sur le règlement/les principes** to be a (real) stickler for the rules/for principles; **de ~*** *remède* drastic; *fièvre* raging.

2 comp ►**cheval d'arçons** pommel horse ►**cheval d'attelage** plough horse ►**cheval à bascule** rocking horse ►**cheval de bataille** (*Mil*) battle horse, charger; (*fig*) **il a ressorti son cheval de bataille** he's back on his hobby-horse *ou* his favourite theme again ►**cheval de bois** wooden horse; **monter** *ou* **aller sur les chevaux de bois** to go on the roundabout (*Brit*) *ou* merry-go-round; (*† ou hum*) **déjeuner** *ou* **dîner** *ou* **manger avec les chevaux de bois** to miss a meal, go dinnerless ►**cheval de chasse** hunter ►**cheval de cirque** circus horse ►**cheval de course** racehorse ►**cheval de fiacre** carriage horse ►**cheval fiscal** horsepower (*for tax purposes*) ►**chevaux de frise** chevaux-de-frise ►**cheval de labour** carthorse, plough horse ►**cheval de manège** school horse ►**cheval marin** *ou* **de mer** sea horse ►**cheval de poste** *ou* **de relais** post horse ►**cheval de renfort** remount ►**(vieux) cheval de retour** recidivist, old lag* (*Brit*) ►**cheval de saut** vaulting horse ►**cheval de selle** saddle horse ►**cheval de trait** draught horse (*Brit*), draft horse (*US*) ►**le cheval de Troie** (*lit, fig*) the Trojan horse, the Wooden Horse of Troy ►**cheval vapeur** nm (pl **chevaux vapeur**) horsepower.

chevalement [ʃ(ə)valmɑ̃] nm *[mur]* shoring; *[galerie]* (pit)head frame.

chevaler [ʃ(ə)vale] [1] vt *mur* to shore up.

chevaleresque [ʃ(ə)valʀɛsk] adj *caractère, conduite* chivalrous, gentlemanly. **règles ~s** rules of chivalry; **l'honneur ~** the honour of a knight, knightly honour; *voir* **littérature**.

chevalerie [ʃ(ə)valʀi] nf (*Hist: institution*) chivalry; (*dignité, chevaliers*) knighthood; *voir* **roman¹**.

chevalet [ʃ(ə)valɛ] nm *[peintre]* easel; (*Menuiserie*) trestle, sawhorse (*Brit*), sawbuck (*US*); *[violon etc]* bridge; (*Hist: torture*) rack.

chevalier [ʃ(ə)valje] 1 nm a (*Hist*) knight. **faire qn ~** to knight sb, dub sb knight; **"je te fais ~"** "I dub you knight". b (*oiseau*) sandpiper. 2 comp ►**chevalier aboyeur** (*Orn*) greenshank ►**chevalier blanc** (*Fin*) white knight ►**chevalier errant** knight-errant ►**chevalier gambette** (*Orn*) redshank ►**chevalier gris** (*Fin*) grey knight ►**chevalier d'industrie** crook, swindler ►**chevalier de la Légion d'honneur** chevalier of the Legion of Honour ►**chevalier noir** (*Fin*) black knight ►**chevalier servant** (attentive) escort ►**chevalier de la Table ronde** Knight of the Round Table ►**le chevalier de la Triste Figure** the Knight of the Sorrowful Countenance.

chevalière [ʃ(ə)valjɛʀ] nf signet ring.

chevalin, e [ʃ(ə)valɛ̃, in] adj *race* of horses, equine; *visage, œil* horsy; *voir* **boucherie**.

chevauchant, e [ʃ(ə)voʃɑ̃, ɑ̃t] adj *pans, tuiles, dents* overlapping.

chevauchée [ʃ(ə)voʃe] nf (*course*) ride; (*cavaliers, cavalcade*) cavalcade.

chevauchement [ʃ(ə)voʃmɑ̃] nm (*gén*) overlapping; (*Géol*) thrust fault.

chevaucher [ʃ(ə)voʃe] [1] 1 vt a (*être à cheval sur*) *cheval, âne* to be astride; *chaise* to sit astride, straddle, bestride. (*fig*) **de grosses lunettes lui chevauchaient le nez** a large pair of glasses sat on his nose; (*fig*) **le pont chevauche l'abîme** the bridge spans the abyss. b (*recouvrir partiellement*) *ardoise, pan* to overlap, lap over. 2 **se chevaucher** vpr (*se recouvrir partiellement*) *[dents, tuiles, lettres]* to overlap (each other); (*Géol*) *[couches]* to overthrust, override. 3 vi a († *ou littér: aller à cheval*) to ride (on horseback). b = **se chevaucher**.

chevau-léger, pl **chevau-légers** [ʃ(ə)voleʒe] nm (*Hist*) (*soldat*) member of the Household Cavalry. (*troupe*) **~s** Household Cavalry.

chevêche [ʃ(ə)vɛʃ] nf little owl.

chevelu, e [ʃəv(ə)ly] adj *personne* (*gén*) with a good crop of *ou* long mane of hair, long-haired; (*péj*) hairy (*péj*), long-haired; *tête* hairy; (*fig*) *épi* tufted; *racine* bearded; *voir* **cuir**.

chevelure [ʃəv(ə)lyʀ] nf a (*cheveux*) hair (*NonC*). **une ~ malade/terne** unhealthy/dull hair; **elle avait une ~ abondante/une flamboyante ~ rousse** she had thick hair *ou* a thick head of hair/a shock of flaming red hair; **sa ~ était magnifique** her hair was magnificent. b *[comète]* tail.

chevesne [ʃ(ə)vɛn] nm chub.

chevet [ʃ(ə)vɛ] nm a *[lit]* bed(head). **au ~ de qn** at sb's bedside; *voir* **lampe, livre¹, table**. b (*Archit*) *[église]* chevet.

cheveu, pl ~x [ʃ(ə)vø] 1 nm a (gén pl) hair. (chevelure) ~x hair (NonC); (collectif) il a le ~ rare he is balding, his hair is going thin; une femme aux ~x blonds/frisés a fair-haired/curly-haired woman, a woman with fair/curly hair; avoir les ~x en désordre ou en bataille ou hirsutes to have untidy ou tousled hair, be dishevelled; (les) ~x au vent hair hanging loose; elle s'est trouvé 2 ~x blancs she has found 2 white hairs; épingle/brosse/filet à ~x hairpin/brush/net; en ~x† hatless†, bareheaded; il n'a pas un ~ sur la tête ou le caillou* he hasn't a (single) hair on his head; voir coupe².

b (loc) tenir à un ~: leur survie n'a tenu qu'à un ~ their survival hung by a thread, they survived but it was a very close thing; son accord n'a tenu qu'à un ~ it was touch and go whether he would agree; il s'en faut d'un ~ qu'il ne change d'avis it's touch and go whether he'll change his mind; il s'en est fallu d'un ~ qu'ils ne se tuent they escaped death by the skin of their teeth ou by a hair's breadth, they were within an ace of being killed; si vous osez toucher à un ~ de cet enfant if you dare touch a hair of this child's head; avoir mal aux ~x* to have a morning-after headache; avoir un ~* (sur la langue) to have a lisp; se faire des ~x* (blancs) to worry o.s. grey ou stiff*, worry o.s. to death; comme un ~ sur la soupe* arriver at the most awkward moment, just at the right time (iro); ça arrive ou ça vient comme un ~ sur la soupe, ce que tu dis that remark is completely irrelevant ou quite out of place; tiré par les ~x histoire far-fetched; il y a un ~* there's a hitch* ou snag*; il va y trouver un ~* he's not going to like it one bit; se prendre aux ~x to come to blows; voir arracher, couper, saisir.

2 comp ▸cheveux d'ange (vermicelle) fine vermicelli; (décoration) silver floss (Brit), icicles (US) (for Christmas tree) ▸cheveux de Vénus maidenhair (fern).

chevillard [ʃ(ə)vijaʀ] nm wholesale butcher.

cheville [ʃ(ə)vij] nf a (Anat) ankle. l'eau lui venait ou arrivait à la ~ ou aux ~s he was ankle-deep in water, the water came up to his ankles; (fig) aucun ne lui arrive à la ~ he is head and shoulders above the others, there's no one to touch him, no one else can hold a candle to him; (péj) avoir les ~s qui enflent* to be full of oneself, have a swollen ou swelled head* (US); (péj) t'as pas les ~s qui enflent?* you're very full of yourself, aren't you?; (péj) ça va les ~s?* bighead!*

b (fiche) (pour joindre) dowel, peg, pin; (pour y enfoncer un clou) plug; (Mus) [instrument à cordes] peg; (Boucherie: crochet) hook. vendre qch à la ~ to sell sth wholesale; vente à la ~ wholesaling; ~ ouvrière (Aut) kingpin; (fig) kingpin, mainspring.

c (Littérat) [poème] cheville; (péj: remplissage) padding (NonC).

d (loc) être en ~ avec qn pour faire qch to be in cahoots* with sb to do sth, to collude with sb in doing sth.

cheviller [ʃ(ə)vije] 1 vt (Menuiserie) to peg; voir âme.

chèvre [ʃɛvʀ] 1 nf a (Zool) (gén) goat; (femelle) she-goat, nanny-goat. (fig) devenir ~* to go crazy; (fig) je deviens ~ moi avec tous ces formulaires/enfants!* all these forms/these children are driving me up the wall!*; (fig) rendre ou faire devenir qn ~* to drive sb up the wall*; voir fromage. b (Tech) (treuil) hoist, gin; (chevalet) sawhorse (Brit), sawbuck (US), trestle. 2 nm (fromage) goat cheese, goat's-milk cheese.

chevreau, pl ~x [ʃəvʀo] nm (animal, peau) kid. bondir comme un ~ to frisk like a lamb.

chèvrefeuille [ʃɛvʀəfœj] nm honeysuckle.

chevrette [ʃəvʀɛt] nf a (jeune chèvre) kid, young she-goat. b (chevreuil femelle) roe, doe; (fourrure) goatskin. c (trépied) (metal) tripod.

chevreuil [ʃəvʀœj] nm (Zool) roe deer; (mâle) roebuck; (Can: cerf de Virginie) deer; (Culin) venison.

chevrier [ʃəvʀije] nm (berger) goatherd; (haricot) (type of) kidney bean.

chevrière [ʃəvʀijɛʀ] nf (rare) goat-girl.

chevron [ʃəvʀɔ̃] nm (poutre) rafter; (galon) stripe, chevron; (motif) chevron, V(-shape). ~s herringbone (pattern), chevron pattern; à ~s (petits) herringbone; (grands) chevron-patterned; (Aviat Mil) formation en ~; voir -formation, engrenage.

chevronné, e [ʃəvʀɔne] adj alpiniste practised, seasoned, experienced; (soldat) seasoned, veteran; (conducteur) experienced, practised. un parlementaire ~ a seasoned parliamentarian, an old parliamentary hand.

chevrotant, e [ʃəvʀɔtɑ̃, ɑ̃t] adj voix quavering, shaking; vieillard with a quavering voice.

chevrotement [ʃəvʀɔtmɑ̃] nm [voix] quavering, shaking; [vieillard] quavering (voice).

chevroter [ʃəvʀɔte] 1 vi [personne] to quaver; [voix] to quaver, shake.

chevrotine [ʃəvʀɔtin] nf buckshot (NonC).

chewing-gum, pl chewing-gums [ʃwiŋgɔm] nm chewing gum (NonC).

chez [ʃe] prép a (à la maison) ~ soi at home; être/rester ~ soi to be/stay at home, be/stay in; est-ce qu'elle sera ~ elle aujourd'hui? will she be at home ou in today?; nous rentrons ~ nous we are going home; j'ai des nouvelles de ~ moi I have news from home; faites comme ~ vous make yourself at home; on n'est plus ~ soi avec tous ces étrangers! it doesn't feel like home any more with all these foreigners about!; je l'ai accompagné ~ lui I saw ou walked him home; nous l'avons trouvée ~ elle we found her at home; avoir un ~ soi to have a home to call one's own ou a home of one's own.

b ~ qn (maison) at sb's house ou place; (appartement) at sb's place ou flat (Brit) ou apartment (US); (famille) in sb's family ou home; (sur une adresse) c/o sb; ~ moi nous sommes 6 there are 6 of us in my ou our family; près de/devant/de ~ qn near/in front of/from sb's place ou house; de/près de ~ nous from/near (our) home ou our place ou our house; ~ Robert/le voisin at Robert's (house)/the neighbour's (house); ~ moi/son frère, c'est tout petit my/his brother's place is tiny; je vais ~ lui/Robert I'm going to his place/to Robert's (place); il séjourne ~ moi he is staying at my place ou with me; la personne ~ qui je suis allé the person to whose house I went; passons par ~ eux/mon frère let's drop in on them/my brother, let's drop by their place/my brother's place; (enseigne de café) ~ Rosalie Rosalie's, chez Rosalie; ~ nous (pays) in our country, at home, back home*; (région) at home, back home*; (maison) in our house, at home; ~ nous au Canada/en Bretagne (là-bas) back (home)* in Canada/Brittany; (ici) here in Canada/Brittany; c'est une paysanne/coutume (bien) de ~ nous she/it is one of our typical local country girls/customs; ~ eux/vous, il n'y a pas de parlement in their/your country there's no parliament; il a été élevé ~ les Jésuites he was brought up in a Jesuit school ou by the Jesuits.

c ~ l'épicier/le coiffeur/le docteur at the grocer's/the hairdresser's/the doctor's; je vais ~ le boucher I'm going to the butcher's; il va ~ le dentiste/le docteur he's going to the dentist('s)/the doctor('s).

d (avec peuple, groupe humain ou animal) among. ~ les Français/les Sioux/les Romains among the French/the Sioux/the Romans; ~ l'ennemi, les pertes ont été élevées the enemy's losses were heavy; ~ les fourmis/le singe among (the) ants/(the) monkeys; on trouve cet instinct ~ les animaux you find this instinct in animals; ~ les politiciens among politicians.

e (avec personne, œuvre) ~ Balzac/Picasso on trouve de tout in Balzac/Picasso you find a bit of everything; c'est rare ~ un enfant de cet âge it's rare in a child of that age; ~ lui, c'est une habitude it's a habit with him; ~ lui c'est le foie qui ne va pas it's his liver that gives him trouble.

chiadé, e [ʃjade] (ptp de chiader) adj (arg Scol) (difficile) problème tough*, stiff*; (approfondi) exposé, leçon brainy*, powerful*; (perfectionné) appareil clever, nifty*.

chiader [ʃjade] 1 1 vt (arg Scol) leçon to swot up* (Brit); examen to swot for* (Brit), cram for*; exposé to swot up* for (Brit), work on. 2 vi (travailler) to swot* (Brit), slog away*.

chiadeur, -euse* [ʃjadœʀ, øz] nm,f swot* (Brit), slogger*.

chialer‡ [ʃjale] 1 vi (pleurer) to blubber*.

chialeur, -euse‡ [ʃjalœʀ, øz] nm,f crybaby*, blubberer*.

chiant, chiante** [ʃjɑ̃, ʃjɑ̃t] adj (ennuyeux) personne, problème, difficulté bloody** (Brit) ou damn** annoying. ce roman est ~ this novel's a bloody (Brit) ou damn‡ pain; c'est ~, je vais être en retard it's a bloody** (Brit) ou damn‡ nuisance ou it's bloody (Brit) ou damn annoying ou sickening‡, I'm going to be late; tu es ~ avec tes questions! you're a pain in the arse** (Brit) ou ass** (US) with all your questions!, your questions are a real pain in the arse!** (Brit) ou ass!** (US).

chiard‡ [ʃjaʀ] nm brat.

chiasme [kjasm] nm (Littérat) chiasmus; (Anat) chiasm, chiasma.

chiasse [ʃjas] 1 nf (**) a (colique) runs*, trots*, skitters‡ (Brit). avoir/attraper la ~ (lit) to have/get the runs* ou the trots*; (peur) to have/get the willies*, be/get scared shitless**, be/get in a funk‡; ça lui donne la ~ (lit) it gives him the runs*; (peur) it gets him scared witless‡. b (poisse) c'est la ~, quelle ~ what a bloody** (Brit) ou damn‡ pain, what a bloody** (Brit) ou damn‡ drag. 2 comp ▸chiasse(s) de mouche(s) fly speck(s).

chiatique** [ʃjatik] adj personne, problème, difficulté bloody** (Brit) ou damn‡ annoying, a pain in the arse** (Brit) ou ass** (US) (attrib).

chic [ʃik] 1 nm a (élégance) [toilette, chapeau] stylishness; [personne] style. avoir du ~ [toilette, chapeau] to have style, be stylish; [personne] to have (great) style; être habillé avec ~ to be stylishly dressed; voir bon.

b (loc) avoir le ~ pour faire qch to have the knack of doing sth; de ~ peindre, dessiner without a model, from memory; traduire/écrire qch de ~ to translate/write sth off the cuff.

2 adj inv a (élégant) chapeau, toilette, personne stylish, smart.

b (de la bonne société) dîner smart, posh*. 2 messieurs ~ 2 well-to-do ou smart(-looking) gentlemen; les gens ~ vont à l'opéra le vendredi the smart set ou posh people go to the opera on Fridays; elle travaille chez des gens ~ she's working for some posh* ou well-to-do people.

c (*: gentil, généreux) decent*, nice. c'est une ~ fille she's a decent sort* ou a nice girl; c'est un ~ type he's a decent sort* ou a nice bloke* (Brit) ou a nice guy*; elle a été très ~ avec moi she's been very nice ou decent to me; c'est très ~ de sa part that's very decent ou nice of him.

3 excl: ~ (alors)!* great!*

chicane [ʃikan] nf a (zigzag) [barrage routier] ins and outs, twists and turns; [circuit automobile] chicane; [gymkhana] in and out, zigzag. des

camions stationnés en ~ gênaient la circulation lorries parked at intervals on both sides of the street held up the traffic. b († *Jur*) (*objection*) quibble; (*querelle*) squabble, petty quarrel. **aimer la ~** (*disputes*) to enjoy picking quarrels with people, enjoy bickering; (*procès*) to enjoy pettifogging *ou* bickering over points of procedure; **faire des ~s à qn** to pick petty quarrels with sb; **gens de ~** pettifoggers.

chicaner [ʃikane] 1 1 vt a (†, *littér*) (*mesurer*) ~ **qch à qn** to quibble *ou* haggle with sb over sth; (*contester*) **nul ne lui chicane son courage** no one disputes *ou* denies his courage *ou* calls his courage into question. b (†, *littér: chercher querelle à*) ~ **qn (sur** *ou* **au sujet de qch)** to quibble *ou* squabble with sb (over sth); **ils se chicanent continuellement** they wrangle constantly (with each other), they are constantly bickering. 2 vi a (*ergoter sur*) ~ **sur** to quibble about, haggle over. b († *Jur*) to pettifog†.

chicanerie [ʃikanʀi] nf (†) (*disputes*) wrangling, petty quarrelling (*NonC*); (*tendance à ergoter*) (constant) quibbling. **toutes ces ~s** all this quibbling *ou* haggling.

chicaneur, -euse [ʃikanœʀ, øz] (*ergoteur*) 1 adj argumentative, pettifogging. 2 nm,f quibbler.

chicanier, -ière [ʃikanje, jɛʀ] 1 adj quibbling. 2 nm,f quibbler.

Chicano [ʃikano] nmf Chicano.

chiche[1] [ʃiʃ] adj *voir* **pois**.

chiche[2] [ʃiʃ] adj a (*mesquin*) *personne* niggardly, mean; *rétribution* niggardly, paltry, mean; *repas* scanty, meagre. **comme cadeau, c'est un peu ~** it's a rather mean *ou* paltry gift; **être ~ de paroles/compliments** to be sparing with one's words/compliments. b (*: *capable de*) **être ~ de faire qch** to be able to do sth *ou* capable of doing sth; **tu n'es pas ~ (de le faire)** you couldn't (do that); ~ **que je le fais!** I bet you I do it!*, (I) bet you I will!*; ~? — ~! am I on?* *ou* are you game?* — you're on!*

chichement [ʃiʃmɑ̃] adv *récompenser, nourrir* meanly, meagrely; *vivre, se nourrir* (*pauvrement*) poorly; (*mesquinement*) meanly.

chichi* [ʃiʃi] nm a ~**(s)** (*embarras*) fuss (*NonC*), carry-on* (*NonC*); (*manières*) fuss (*NonC*); **faire des ~s** *ou* **du ~** (*embarras*) to fuss, make a fuss; (*manières*) to make a fuss; **ce sont des gens à ~(s)** they're the sort of people who make a fuss; **on vous invite sans ~(s)** we're inviting you informally; **ce sera sans ~** it'll be quite informal. b (*beignet*) ≃ doughnut.

chichiteux, -euse* [ʃiʃitø, øz] adj (*péj*) (*faiseur d'embarras*) troublesome; (*maniéré*) affected, fussy.

chicon [ʃikɔ̃] nm (*romaine*) cos (lettuce) (*Brit*), romaine (*US*); (*Belgique: endive*) endive.

chicorée [ʃikɔʀe] nf (*salade*) endive; (*à café*) chicory. ~ **frisée** curly endive (lettuce).

chicot [ʃiko] nm (*dent*) stump; (*rare: souche*) (tree) stump. **elle souriait, découvrant des ~s jaunis par le tabac** she smiled, revealing the stumps of her nicotine-stained teeth.

chicotin [ʃikɔtɛ̃] nm *voir* **amer**[2].

chié, e[1]‡ [ʃje] adj a (*réussi, calé*) bloody (*Brit*) *ou* damned good‡. **elle est ~e leur maison** their house is something else!*; (*iro*) **c'est ~ comme bled!** it's a bloody dump!** (*Brit*) *ou* damned hole‡ (*US*); **il est ~ ce problème** it's a hell of a problem‡. b (*qui exagère*) **t'es (pas) ~ d'arriver toujours en retard!** it's a bit much you always turning up late!*

chiée[2]** [ʃje] nf: **une ~ de, des ~s de** a hell of a lot of‡.

chien [ʃjɛ̃] 1 nm a (*animal*) dog. **petit ~** (*jeune*) pup, puppy; (*de petite taille*) small dog; **"(attention) ~ méchant"** "beware of the dog"; **faire le ~ fou** to fool about.

b [*fusil*] hammer, cock.

c (††: *injure*) ~! (you) cur!††

d (*: *frange*) ~**s** fringe.

e (*loc*) **coiffée à la ~** wearing a fringe; **en ~ de fusil** curled up; **quel ~ de temps!** *ou* **temps de ~!** what filthy *ou* foul weather!; **vie de ~** dog's life; **ce métier de ~** this rotten job; **comme un ~** *mourir, traiter* like a dog; **elle a du ~*** she has a certain something*, she's very attractive; **entre ~ et loup** in the twilight *ou* dusk; **c'est pas fait pour les ~s!*** it's there to be used; **être** *ou* **vivre** *ou* **s'entendre comme ~ et chat** to fight like cat and dog, always be at one another's throats; **ils se sont regardés en ~s de faïence** they just stood staring at each other; **arriver comme un ~ dans un jeu de quilles** to turn up when least needed *ou* wanted; **recevoir qn comme un ~ dans un jeu de quilles** to give sb a cold reception; (*dans journal*) ~**s écrasés*** news (*sg*) in brief; **faire les** *ou* **tenir la rubrique des ~s écrasés*** to write nothing but fillers; **je ne suis pas ton ~!** I'm not your slave *ou* servant!; **je lui garde** *ou* **réserve un ~ de ma chienne*** I'll get even with him*; (*Prov*) **un ~ regarde bien un évêque** a cat may look at a king (*Prov*); (*Prov*) **les ~s aboient, la caravane passe** let the world say what it will; *voir* **regarder**.

f (*Naut*) **coup de ~** squall.

2 adj inv a (*avare*) mean, stingy*.

b (*méchant*) rotten. **elle n'a pas été ~ avec toi** she was quite decent to you.

3 comp ▸**chien d'appartement** house dog ▸**chien d'arrêt** pointer ▸**chien assis** (*Constr*) ≃ dormer window (*Brit*), dormer (*US*) ▸**chien d'aveugle** guide dog, blind dog ▸**chien de berger** sheepdog ▸**chien de chasse** retriever, gun dog ▸**chien couchant** setter; **faire le chien couchant** to kowtow, toady (*auprès de* to) ▸**chien courant** hound ▸**chien de garde** guard dog, watchdog ▸**chien-loup** nm (pl **chiens-loups**) wolfhound ▸**chien de manchon** lapdog ▸**chien de mer** dogfish ▸**chien polaire** = **chien de traîneau** ▸**chien policier** police dog, tracker dog ▸**chien de race** pedigree dog ▸**chien de salon** = **chien de manchon** ▸**chien savant** (*lit*) performing dog; (*fig*) know-all ▸**chien de traîneau** husky.

chien-chien, pl **chiens-chiens** [ʃjɛ̃ʃjɛ̃] nm (*langage enfantin*) doggy (*langage enfantin*). **oh le beau ~** nice doggy!, good doggy!

chiendent [ʃjɛ̃dɑ̃] nm a (*Bot*) (couch) grass, quitch (grass); (*mauvaise herbe*) couch (grass); *voir* **brosse**. b (†*: *l'ennui*) **le ~** the trouble *ou* rub (†, *hum*).

chienlit [ʃjɑ̃li] nf a (*pagaille*) havoc. b (†: *mascarade*) fancy-dress parade.

chienne [ʃjɛn] nf bitch. (*injure*) ~! (you) bitch!‡; **quelle ~ de vie!*** what a dog's life!

chier** [ʃje] 7 vi a to shit**, crap**~ **un coup** to have a crap** *ou* shit**.

b (*loc*) **faire ~ qn** *[personne]* (*ennuyer*) to give sb a pain in the butt‡ *ou* arse** (*Brit*) *ou* ass** (*US*), bore the pants off sb‡; (*tracasser, harceler*) to get up sb's nose‡ (*Brit*), bug sb‡; **ça me fait ~** it's a *ou* it gives me a pain in the arse** *ou* butt‡; **envoyer ~ qn** to tell sb to piss off** *ou* bugger off** (*Brit*) *ou* fuck off**; **se faire ~: je me suis fait ~ pendant 3 heures à réparer la voiture** I sweated my guts out‡ for 3 hours repairing the car; **qu'est-ce qu'on se fait ~ à ses conférences** what a bloody‡ (*Brit*) *ou* fucking bore his lectures are**, his lectures bore the pants off you‡; **ça va ~ (des bulles)** there'll be one hell of a (bloody**) (*Brit*) row!‡; **y a pas à ~, c'est lui le meilleur** say what you bloody (*Brit*) *ou* damn well like**, he's the best!; **il faut quand même pas ~ dans la colle!** you've got a bloody (*Brit*) *ou* fucking cheek!**; **(nul) à ~** (*mauvais*) *film, livre, service* crappy**, crap** (*attrib*); *personne incompétente, voiture inutilisable* bloody (*Brit*) *ou* fucking useless**; (*laid*) bloody (*Brit*) *ou* fucking hideous**.

chierie‡ [ʃiʀi] nf (real) pain in the butt‡ *ou* arse** (*Brit*) *ou* ass** (*US*).

chiffe [ʃif] nf a (*personne sans volonté*) spineless individual, wet*, drip*. **être une ~ (molle)** to be spineless *ou* wet*; **je suis comme une ~ (molle)** (*fatigué*) I feel like a wet rag; *voir* **mou**[1]. b (*chiffon*) rag.

chiffon [ʃifɔ̃] 1 nm a (*tissu usagé*) (piece of) rag. **jeter de vieux ~s** to throw out old rags; (*fig*) **ce devoir est un vrai ~** this exercise is extremely messy *ou* a dreadful mess; **mettre ses vêtements en ~** to throw down one's clothes in a crumpled heap; **parler ~s*** to talk (about) clothes*.

b (*Papeterie*) **le ~** rag; **fait avec du ~** made from rags (*linen, cotton*); *voir* **papier**.

2 comp ▸**chiffon à chaussures** shoe cloth *ou* duster (*Brit*) *ou* rag ▸**chiffon à meubles** = **chiffon à poussière** ▸**chiffon de papier: écrire qch sur un chiffon de papier** to write sth (down) on a (crumpled) scrap of paper; **ce traité n'est qu'un chiffon de papier** this treaty isn't worth the paper it's written on *ou* is no more than a useless scrap of paper ▸**chiffon à poussière** duster (*Brit*), dustcloth (*US*).

chiffonnade [ʃifɔnad] nf chiffonnade.

chiffonné, e [ʃifɔne] (ptp de **chiffonner**) adj a (*fatigué*) *visage* worn-looking. b (*sympathique*) **un petit nez ~** a funny little face.

chiffonner [ʃifɔne] 1 vt a (*lit*) *papier* to crumple; *habits* to crease, rumple, crumple; *étoffe* to crease, crumple. **ce tissu se chiffonne facilement** this material creases *ou* crumples easily *ou* is easily creased. b (*: *contrarier*) **ça me chiffonne** it bothers *ou* worries me; **qu'est-ce qui te chiffonne?** what's the matter (with you)?, what's bothering *ou* worrying you?

chiffonnier [ʃifɔnje] nm a (*personne*) ragman, rag-and-bone man (*Brit*). **se battre/se disputer comme des ~s** to fight/quarrel like fishwives. b (*meuble*) chiffonier.

chiffrable [ʃifʀabl] adj: **ce n'est pas ~** one can't put a figure to it.

chiffrage [ʃifʀaʒ] nm (*voir* **chiffrer**) (en)coding, ciphering; assessing; numbering; marking; figuring.

chiffre [ʃifʀ] nm a (*caractère*) figure, numeral, digit (*Math*). ~ **arabe/romain** Arab/Roman numeral; **nombre** *ou* **numéro de 7 ~s** 7-figure *ou* 7-digit number; **inflation à deux/trois ~s** two/three figure *ou* double/triple digit inflation; **écrire un nombre en ~s** to write out a number in figures; **science des ~s** science of numbers; **employé qui aligne des ~s toute la journée** clerk who spends all day adding up columns of figures; **il aime les ~s** he likes working with figures.

b (*montant*) *[dépenses]* total, sum. **en ~s ronds** in round figures; **ça atteint des ~s astronomiques** it reaches an astronomical figure *ou* sum; **le ~ des naissances** the total *ou* number of births *ou* the birth total; **le ~ des chômeurs** the unemployment figures *ou* total, the total *ou* figure of those unemployed, the number of unemployed *ou* of those out of work.

c (*Comm*) ~ **(d'affaires)** turnover; **il fait un ~ (d'affaires) de 3 millions** he has a turnover of 3 million francs; ~ **net/brut** net/gross figure *ou* sum; **faire du ~*** to rake it in*; *voir* **impôt**.

d (*code*) *[message]* code, cipher; *[coffre-fort]* combination. **écrire une lettre en ~s** to write a letter in code *ou* cipher; **on a trouvé leur ~** their code has been broken; **le (service du) ~** the cipher office.
e (*initiales*) (set of) initials, monogram. **mouchoir brodé à son ~** handkerchief embroidered with one's initials *ou* monogram.
f (*Mus: indice*) figure.

chiffrement [ʃifʀəmɑ̃] **nm** *[texte]* (en)coding, ciphering.

chiffrer [ʃifʀe] 1 **1 vt a** (*coder*) *message* to (en)code, cipher; (*Informatique*) *données, télégramme* to encode; *voir* **message**.
b (*évaluer*) *dépenses, dommages* to put a figure to, assess (the amount of).
c (*numéroter*) *pages* to number.
d (*marquer*) *effets personnels, linge* to mark (with one's *ou* sb's initials).
e (*Mus*) *accord* to figure. **basse chiffrée** figured bass.
2 **vi, se chiffrer vpr: (se) ~ à** to add up to, amount to, come to; **ça (se) chiffre à combien?** what *ou* how much does that add up to? *ou* amount to? *ou* come to?; **ça (se) chiffre par millions** that adds up to *ou* amounts to *ou* comes to millions; **ça commence à ~!** it's starting to mount up!; **ça finit par ~*** it adds up to *ou* amounts to *ou* comes to quite a lot in the end.

chiffreur, -euse [ʃifʀœʀ, øz] **nm,f** coder.

chignole [ʃiɲɔl] **nf** (*outil*) (*à main*) (hand) drill; (*électrique*) (electric) drill; (**: voiture*) jalopy* (*hum*).

chignon [ʃiɲɔ̃] **nm** bun, chignon. **se faire un ~** to put one's hair into a bun; *voir* **crêper**.

chihuahua [ʃiwawa] **nm** Chihuahua.

chi'ite [ʃiit] **adj, nmf** Shiite.

Chili [ʃili] **nm** Chile.

chilien, -ienne [ʃiljɛ̃, jɛn] **1 adj** Chilean. **2 nm,f: C~(ne)** Chilean.

chimère [ʃimɛʀ] **nf a** (*utopie*) (wild) dream, chimera; (*illusion, rêve*) pipe dream, (idle) fancy. **le bonheur est une ~** happiness is a figment of the imagination *ou* is just a (wild) dream *ou* is a chimera; **c'est une ~ que de croire ...** it is fanciful *ou* unrealistic to believe ...; **ce projet de voyage est une ~ de plus** these travel plans are just another pipe dream *ou* (idle) fancy; **se repaître de ~s** to live on dreams *ou* in a fool's paradise; **se forger des ~s** to fabricate wild *ou* impossible dreams; **tes grands projets, ~s (que tout cela)!** your grand plans are nothing but pipe dreams *ou* (idle) fancies; **un monde peuplé de vagues ~s** a world filled with vague imaginings.
b (*Myth*) chim(a)era, Chim(a)era.

chimérique [ʃimeʀik] **adj a** (*utopique*) *esprit, projet, idée* fanciful; *rêve* wild (*épith*), idle (*épith*). **c'est un esprit ~** he's very fanciful, he's a great dreamer. **b** (*imaginaire*) *personnage* imaginary, chimerical.

chimie [ʃimi] **nf** chemistry. **~ organique/minérale** organic/inorganic chemistry; **cours/expérience de ~** chemistry class/experiment; **la merveilleuse ~ de l'amour** love's marvellous chemistry.

chimiothérapie [ʃimjoteʀapi] **nf** chemotherapy.

chimique [ʃimik] **adj** chemical; *voir* **produit**.

chimiquement [ʃimikmɑ̃] **adv** chemically.

chimiste [ʃimist] **nmf** chemist (*scientist*); *voir* **ingénieur**.

chimpanzé [ʃɛ̃pɑ̃ze] **nm** chimpanzee, chimp*.

chinchilla [ʃɛ̃ʃila] **nm** (*Zool, fourrure*) chinchilla.

Chine [ʃin] **nf** China. **~ populaire/nationaliste** red *ou* communist/nationalist China; *voir* **crêpe**[2], **encre**.

chine[1] [ʃin] **nm a** (*papier*) Chinese *ou* rice paper. **b** (*vase*) china vase; (*NonC: porcelaine*) china.

chine[2]* [ʃin] **nf: j'aime bien (faire de) la ~** I love hunting (around) for antiques; **il est dans le milieu de la ~** he's in *ou* he deals in antiques; **vente à la ~** door-to-door selling.

chiner [ʃine] 1 **1 vt a** (*Tex*) *étoffe* to dye the warp of. **manteau/tissu chiné** chiné coat/fabric. **b** (**: taquiner*) to kid , have on* (*Brit*), rag*. **tu ne vois pas qu'il te chine** don't you see he's kidding you *ou* ragging* you *ou* having you on* (*Brit*); **je n'aime pas qu'on me chine** I don't like being ragged*. **2 vi** (*) to hunt (around) for antiques.

Chinetoque** [ʃintɔk] **nmf** (*péj: Chinois*) Chink* (*péj*).

chineur, -euse* [ʃinœʀ, øz] **nm,f** (*brocanteur*) antique dealer; (*amateur*) antique-hunter.

chinois, e [ʃinwa, waz] **1 adj a** (*de Chine*) Chinese; *voir* **ombre**[1]. **b** (*péj: pointilleux*) *personne* pernickety (*péj*), fussy (*péj*); *règlement* hair-splitting (*péj*). **2 nm a** (*Ling*) Chinese. (*péj*) **c'est du ~*** it's double Dutch* (*Brit*), it's all Greek to me*. **b C~** Chinese, Chinese man, Chinaman (*hum*); **les C~** the Chinese. **c** (* *péj: maniaque*) hair-splitter (*péj*). **d** (*Culin*) (*passoire*) (small conical) strainer. **3 nf: Chinoise** Chinese, Chinese woman.

chinoiser [ʃinwaze] 1 **vi** to split hairs. **~ sur** to quibble over.

chinoiserie [ʃinwazʀi] **nf a** (*subtilité excessive*) hair-splitting (*NonC*). **b** (*complications*) **~s** unnecessary complications *ou* fuss; **les ~s de l'administration** red tape; **tout ça, ce sont des ~s** that is all nothing but unnecessary complications. **c** (*Art*) (*décoration*) chinoiserie; (*objet*) Chinese ornament, Chinese curio.

chintz [ʃints] **nm** (*Tex*) chintz.

chiot [ʃjo] **nm** pup(py).

chiotte [ʃjɔt] **nf a** (*W.-C.*) **~s**** bog** (*Brit*), john** (*US*), can**; **aux ~s l'arbitre!**** what a shitty referee!**; *voir* **corvée**. **b** (**: *voiture*) jalopy*† (*hum*).

chiourme [ʃjuʀm] **nf** *voir* **garder**.

chiper* [ʃipe] 1 **vt** (*voler*) *portefeuille, idée* to pinch*, filch*, make off with; *rhume* to catch.

chipeur, -euse* [ʃipœʀ, øz] **adj** *gamin* thieving.

chipie* [ʃipi] **nf** vixen (*péj*). **petite ~!** you little devil!*

chipolata [ʃipɔlata] **nf** chipolata.

chipotage* [ʃipɔtaʒ] **nm** (*marchandage, ergotage*) quibbling; (*pour manger*) picking *ou* nibbling (at one's food).

chipoter* [ʃipɔte] 1 **vi** (*manger*) to be a fussy eater; (*ergoter*) to quibble (*sur* about, over); (*marchander*) to quibble (*sur* over). **~ sur la nourriture** to nibble *ou* pick at one's food; **tu chipotes là!** now you're quibbling!; **vous n'allez pas ~ pour 2 minutes de retard/pour 2 F!** you're not going to quibble about (my) being 2 minutes late/about 2 francs!

chipoteur, -euse* [ʃipɔtœʀ, øz] **1 adj** (*marchandeur*) haggling; (*ergoteur*) quibbling; (*en mangeant*) fussy. **2 nm,f** (*marchandeur*) haggler; (*ergoteur*) quibbler; (*en mangeant*) fussy eater.

chips [ʃips] **nmpl** (*Culin*) crisps (*Brit*), chips (*US*); *voir* **pomme**.

chique [ʃik] **nf** (*tabac*) quid, chew; (**: enflure*) (facial) swelling, lump (on the cheek); *voir* **couper**.

chiqué* [ʃike] **nm a** (*bluff*) pretence (*NonC*), bluffing (*NonC*). **il a fait ça au ~** he bluffed it out; **il prétend que cela le laisse froid mais c'est du ~** he pretends it leaves him cold but it's all put on* *ou* a great pretence. **b** (*factice*) sham (*NonC*). **ces combats de catch c'est du ~** these wrestling matches are all sham *ou* all put on* *ou* are faked; **combat sans ~** fight that's for real*; **~!, remboursez!** what a sham!, give us our money back! **c** (*manières*) putting on airs (*NonC*), airs and graces (*pl*). **faire du ~** to put on airs (and graces).

chiquement* [ʃikmɑ̃] **adv** *s'habiller* smartly, stylishly; *traiter, accueillir* kindly, decently.

chiquenaude [ʃiknod] **nf** (*pichenette*) flick, flip. **il l'écarta d'une ~** he flicked *ou* flipped it off; (*fig*) **une ~ suffirait à renverser le gouvernement** the government could be overturned by a flick *ou* snap of the fingers.

chiquer [ʃike] 1 **1 vt** *tabac* to chew; *voir* **tabac**. **2 vi** to chew tobacco.

chiqueur, -euse [ʃikœʀ, øz] **nm,f** tobacco-chewer.

chirographaire [kiʀɔgʀafɛʀ] **adj** unsecured.

chirographie [kiʀɔgʀafi] **nf** = **chiromancie**.

chiromancie [kiʀɔmɑ̃si] **nf** palmistry, chiromancy (*SPÉC*).

chiromancien, -ienne [kiʀɔmɑ̃sjɛ̃, jɛn] **nm,f** palmist, chiromancer (*SPÉC*).

chiropracteur [kiʀɔpʀaktœʀ] **nm** chiropractor.

chiropracticien, -ienne [kiʀɔpʀaktisjɛ̃, jɛn] **nm,f** chiropractor.

chiropractie [kiʀɔpʀakti] **nf** chiropractic.

chiropraxie [kiʀɔpʀaksi] **nf** chiropractic.

chirurgical, e, mpl -aux [ʃiʀyʀʒikal, o] **adj** surgical.

chirurgie [ʃiʀyʀʒi] **nf** surgery (*science*). **~ esthétique/dentaire** plastic/dental surgery.

chirurgien, -ienne [ʃiʀyʀʒjɛ̃, jɛn] **nm,f** surgeon. **~-dentiste** dental surgeon; (*Mil*) **~-major** army surgeon.

chiure [ʃjyʀ] **nf: ~(s) de mouche(s)** fly speck(s).

chlâsse** [ʃlas] **adj** zonked**.

chleuh** [ʃlø] (*péj*) **1 adj** Boche**. **2 nmf: C~** Boche**, Jerry**†.

chlinguer [ʃlɛ̃ge] = **schlinguer**.

chlorate [klɔʀat] **nm** chlorate.

chlore [klɔʀ] **nm** chlorine.

chloré, e [klɔʀe] (**ptp de chlorer**) **adj** chlorinated.

chlorer [klɔʀe] 1 **vt** to chlorinate.

chlorhydrique [klɔʀidʀik] **adj** hydrochloric.

chlorique [klɔʀik] **adj** chloric.

chloroforme [klɔʀɔfɔʀm] **nm** chloroform.

chloroformer [klɔʀɔfɔʀme] 1 **vt** to chloroform.

chlorophylle [klɔʀɔfil] **nf** chlorophyll.

chlorophyllien, -ienne [klɔʀɔfiljɛ̃, jɛn] **adj** chlorophyllous.

chlorure [klɔʀyʀ] **nm** chloride. **~ de sodium** sodium chloride; **~ de chaux** chloride of lime.

chlorurer [klɔʀyʀe] 1 **vt** = **chlorer**.

choc [ʃɔk] **1 nm a** (*heurt*) *[objets]* impact, shock; *[vagues]* crash, shock. **le ~ de billes d'acier qui se heurtent** the impact of steel balls as they collide; **cela se brise au moindre ~** it breaks at the slightest bump *ou* knock; **"résiste au(x) ~(s)"** "shock-resistant"; **la résistance au ~ d'un matériau** a material's resistance to shock; **la carosserie se déforma sous le ~** the coachwork twisted with *ou* under the impact; **la corde se rompit sous le ~** the sudden wrench made the rope snap *ou* snapped the rope.
b (*collision*) *[véhicules]* crash, smash; *[personnes]* blow; (*plus léger*) bump. **le ~ entre les véhicules fut très violent** the vehicles crashed together with a tremendous impact; **encore un ~ meurtrier sur la RN7** another fatal crash *ou* smash on the RN7; **il tituba sous le ~** the blow *ou* bump put *ou* sent him off balance.
c (*bruit d'impact*) (*violent*) crash, smash; (*sourd*) thud, thump; (*métallique*) clang, clash; (*cristallin*) clink, chink; *[gouttes, grêlons]* drumming (*NonC*). **le ~ sourd des obus** the thud of shellfire;

j'entendais au loin le ~ des pesants marteaux d'acier in the distance I could hear the clang *ou* clash of the heavy steel hammers.

d (*affrontement*) *[troupes, émeutiers]* clash; (*fig*) *[intérêts, cultures, passions]* clash, collision. il y a eu un ~ sanglant entre la police et les émeutiers there has been a violent clash between police and rioters; la petite armée ne put résister au ~ the little army could not stand up to the onslaught.

e (*émotion brutale*) shock. il ne s'est pas remis du ~ he hasn't got over the shock *ou* recovered from the shock; ça m'a fait un drôle de ~ de le voir dans cet état it gave me a nasty shock *ou* quite a turn* to see him in that state; il est encore sous le ~ (*à l'annonce d'une nouvelle*) he's still in a state of shock; (*après un accident*) he's still in shock; tenir le ~* *[machine]* to hold out; *[personne]* to cope; après la mort de sa femme il n'a pas tenu le ~ after the death of his wife he couldn't cope; *voir* état.

f de ~ *troupe, unité* shock; *traitement, thérapeutique, tactique* shock; *enseignement* avant-garde, futuristic; *évêque, patron* high-powered, supercharged*.

2 adj inv (*à sensation*) argument/discours/formule(-)~ shock argument/speech/formula; film/photo(-)~ shock film/photo; mesures(-)~ shock measures; "prix(-)~" "amazing *ou* drastic reductions"; "notre prix-~: 99 F" "our special price: 99 francs".

3 comp ▸**choc culturel** culture shock ▸**choc électrique** electric shock ▸**choc nerveux** (nervous) shock ▸**choc opératoire** post-operative shock ▸**choc pétrolier** (*Écon*) oil crisis ▸**choc en retour** (*Élec*) return shock; (*fig*) backlash ▸**choc thermique** thermal shock.

chochotte* [ʃɔʃɔt] **1** nf (*femme chichiteuse*) fusspot*; (*homme: mauviette*) sissy*; (*homme efféminé*) namby-pamby*. arrête de faire la *ou* ta ~! stop making such a fuss (about nothing)!* **2** adj inv: elle est très ~ she fusses too much; il est très ~ (*mauviette*) he's a real sissy*; (*efféminé*) he's a real namby-pamby*.

chocolat [ʃɔkɔla] **1** nm **a** (*substance*) chocolate; (*bonbon*) chocolate, choc* (*Brit*); (*boisson*) chocolate. "un ~ s'il vous plaît" "a (cup of) chocolate please"; mousse/crème au ~ chocolate mousse/cream; ~ au lait/aux noisettes milk/hazelnut chocolate; *voir* barre, plaque.

b (*couleur*) chocolate (brown), dark brown.

c être ~*† to be thwarted *ou* foiled.

2 adj inv chocolate(-coloured).

3 comp ▸**chocolat blanc** white chocolate ▸**chocolat chaud** hot chocolate ▸**chocolat à croquer** plain (eating) chocolate ▸**chocolat à cuire** cooking chocolate ▸**chocolat fondant** fondant chocolate ▸**chocolat liégeois** chocolate ice cream (*with whipped cream*) ▸**chocolat de ménage** = chocolat à cuire ▸**chocolat en poudre** drinking chocolate.

chocolaté, e [ʃɔkɔlate] adj (*additionné de chocolat*) chocolate-flavoured, chocolate (*épith*); (*au goût de chocolat*) chocolate-flavoured, chocolat(e)y*.

chocolaterie [ʃɔkɔlatʀi] nf (*fabrique*) chocolate factory; (*magasin*) (quality) chocolate shop.

chocolatier, -ière [ʃɔkɔlatje, jɛʀ] **1** adj: l'industrie ~ière the chocolate industry. **2** nm,f (*fabricant*) chocolate maker; (*commerçant*) chocolate seller.

chocottes‡ [ʃɔkɔt] nfpl: avoir les ~ to have the jitters* *ou* the heebie-jeebies* *ou* the willies*; ça m'a filé les ~ it gave me the jitters* *ou* the heebie-jeebies* *ou* the willies*.

chœur [kœʀ] nm **a** (*chanteurs*) (*gén, Rel*) choir; *[opéra, oratorio]* chorus. **b** (*Théât: récitants*) chorus. **c** (*fig*) (*concert*) un ~ de récriminations a chorus of recriminations; (*groupe*) le ~ des mécontents the band of malcontents. **d** (*Archit*) choir, chancel; *voir* enfant. **e** (*Mus: composition*) chorus; (*hymne*) chorale; (*Théât: texte*) chorus. ~ à 4 parties (*opéra*) 4-part chorus; (*Rel*) 4-part chorale. **f** (*loc*) en ~ (*Mus*) in chorus; (*fig: ensemble*) *chanter* in chorus; *répondre, crier* in chorus *ou* unison; (*fig hum*) on s'ennuyait en ~ we were all getting bored (together); tous en ~! all together now!

choir [ʃwaʀ] vi (*littér ou † ou hum*) to fall. faire ~ to cause to fall; laisser ~ un objet to drop an object; (*fig*) laisser ~ ses amis to let one's friends down; se laisser ~ dans un fauteuil to sink into an armchair.

choisi, e [ʃwazi] (ptp de choisir) adj **a** (*sélectionné*) *morceaux, passages* selected. **b** (*raffiné*) *langage, termes* carefully chosen; *clientèle, société* select.

choisir [ʃwaziʀ] ② vt **a** (*gén*) to choose. nous avons choisi ces articles pour nos clients we have selected these items for our customers; des 2 solutions, j'ai choisi la première I chose *ou* picked the first of the 2 solutions, I opted *ou* plumped (*Brit*) for the first of the 2 solutions; choisissez une carte/un chiffre pick a card/a number; il faut savoir ~ ses amis you must know how to pick *ou* choose your friends; dans les soldes, il faut savoir ~ in the sales, you've got to know what to choose *ou* you've got to know how to be selective; se ~ un mari to choose a husband; on l'a choisi parmi des douzaines de candidats he was picked (out) *ou* selected *ou* chosen from among dozens of applicants; (*iro*) tu as (bien) choisi ton moment! what a time to choose!; tu as mal choisi ton moment si tu veux une augmentation! you picked the wrong time to ask for a rise!

b ~ de faire qch to choose to do sth; à toi de ~ si et quand tu veux partir it's up to you to choose if and when you want to leave.

choix [ʃwa] nm **a** (*décision*) choice. il a fait un bon/mauvais ~ he has made a good/bad choice, he has chosen well/badly; je n'avais pas d'autre ~ I had no choice, I had no other option; un aménagement de son ~ alterations of one's (own) choosing; ce ~ de poèmes plaira aux plus exigeants this selection of poems will appeal to the most demanding reader; le ~ d'un cadeau est souvent difficile choosing a gift *ou* the choice of a gift is often difficult; faire un ~ de société to choose the kind of society one wants to live in; *voir* embarras.

b (*variété*) choice, selection, variety. ce magasin offre un grand ~ this shop has a wide *ou* large selection (of goods); il y a du ~ there is a choice; il y a tout le ~ qu'on veut there is plenty of choice, there are plenty to choose from; il n'y a pas beaucoup de ~ there isn't a great deal of *ou* much choice, there isn't a great selection (to choose from).

c (*échantillonnage de*) ~ de selection of; il avait apporté un ~ de livres he had brought a selection *ou* collection of books.

d (*qualité*) de ~ choice, selected; morceau de ~ (*viande*) prime cut; de premier ~ *fruits* class *ou* grade one; *viande* top grade, highest quality; de ~ courant standard quality; de second ~ *fruits, viande* class *ou* grade two (*Brit*), market grade (*US*); articles de second ~ seconds.

e (*loc*) au ~: vous pouvez prendre, au ~, fruits ou fromages you may have fruit or cheese, as you wish *ou* prefer, you have a choice between *ou* of fruit or cheese; "dessert au ~" "choice of desserts"; avancement au ~ promotion on merit *ou* by selection; au ~ du client as the customer chooses, according to (the customer's) preference; faire son ~ to take *ou* make one's choice, take one's pick; mon ~ est fait my choice is made; c'est un ~ à faire it's a choice you have (*ou* he has *etc*) to make; avoir le ~ to have a *ou* the choice; je n'avais pas le ~ I had no option *ou* choice; (*frm*) faire ~ de qch to select sth; laisser le ~ à qn (de faire) to leave sb (free) to choose (to do); donner le ~ à qn (de faire) to give sb the choice (of doing); arrêter *ou* fixer *ou* porter son ~ sur qch to fix one's choice (up)on sth, settle on sth; il lit sans (faire de) ~ he's an indiscriminate reader, he reads indiscriminately.

choléra [kɔleʀa] nm cholera.

cholérique [kɔleʀik] **1** adj choleraic. **2** nmf cholera patient *ou* case.

cholestérol [kɔlɛsteʀɔl] nm cholesterol.

cholestérolémie [kɔlɛsteʀɔlemi] nf cholestorolaemia (*Brit*), cholestorolemia (*US*).

chômage [ʃomaʒ] **1** nm *[travailleurs]* unemployment; *[usine, industrie]* inactivity. les chiffres/le taux de ~ the unemployment *ou* jobless figures/rate; ~ saisonnier/chronique seasonal/chronic unemployment; de ~ *allocation, indemnité* unemployment (*épith*); (être) en *ou* au ~ (to be) unemployed *ou* out of work; être/s'inscrire au ~ to be/sign on the dole* (*Brit*), receive/apply for unemployment benefit; mettre qn au *ou* en ~ to make sb redundant (*Brit*), put sb out of work *ou* a job, lay sb off; beaucoup ont été mis en ~ many have been made redundant *ou* have been put out of work *ou* a job, there have been many redundancies (*Brit*); toucher le ~* to get dole* (*Brit*) *ou* unemployment money.

2 comp ▸**chômage partiel** short-time working; mettre qn en *ou* au chômage partiel to put sb on short-time (working) ▸**chômage structurel** structural unemployment ▸**chômage technique** lay-offs (*pl*); mettre en chômage technique to lay off; le nombre de travailleurs en chômage technique the number of workers laid off, the number of lay-offs.

chômé, e [ʃome] (ptp de chômer) adj: jour ~, fête ~e public holiday, ≃ bank holiday (*Brit*).

chômedu‡ [ʃomdy] nm (*inactivité*) unemployment; (*indemnités*) dole* (*Brit*), welfare* (*US*). être au ~ to be on the dole* (*Brit*) *ou* on welfare* (*US*).

chômer [ʃome] ① **1** vi **a** (*fig: être inactif*) *[capital, équipements]* to be unemployed, be idle, lie idle; *[esprit, imagination]* to be idle, be inactive. son imagination ne chômait pas his imagination was not idle *ou* inactive; ses mains ne chômaient pas his hands were not idle *ou* inactive; j'aime autant te dire qu'on n'a pas chômé I don't need to tell you that we didn't just sit around idly *ou* we weren't idle.

b (*être sans travail*) *[travailleur]* to be unemployed, be out of work *ou* a job; *[usine, installation]* to be *ou* stand idle, be at a standstill; *[industrie]* to be at a standstill.

c (*††: être en congé*) to have a holiday, be on holiday.

2 vt (*††*) *jour férié* to keep.

chômeur, -euse [ʃomœʀ, øz] nm,f (*gén*) unemployed person *ou* worker; (*mis au chômage*) redundant worker (*Brit*). les ~s (de longue durée) the (long-term) unemployed; le nombre des ~s the number of unemployed, the number of people out of work; un million de/3 000 ~s a million/3,000 unemployed *ou* out of work; un ~ n'a pas droit à ces prestations an unemployed person is not entitled to these benefits.

chope [ʃɔp] nf (*récipient*) tankard, mug; (*contenu*) pint.

choper‡ [ʃɔpe] ① vt **a** (*voler*) to pinch*, nick* (*Brit*). **b** (*attraper*) *balle, personne, maladie* to catch. se faire ~ par la police to get nabbed* by the police.

chopine [ʃɔpin] nf (*: bouteille*) bottle (of wine); (*††: mesure*) half-litre, pint; (*Can: 1/2 pinte, 0,568 l*) pint. on a été boire une ~* we went for a drink.

choquant, e [ʃɔkɑ̃, ɑ̃t] adj (*qui heurte le goût*) shocking, appalling; (*qui heurte le sens de la justice*) outrageous, scandalous; (*qui heurte la pudeur*) shocking, offensive. **le spectacle ~ de ces blessés** the harrowing *ou* horrifying sight of those injured people; **c'est un film ~, même pour les adultes** it's a film that shocks even adults.

choquer [ʃɔke] 1 1 vt a (*scandaliser*) to shock, (*plus fort*) appal; (*heurter, blesser*) to offend, shock. **ça m'a choqué de le voir dans cet état** I was shocked *ou* appalled to see him in that state; **de tels films me choquent** I find such films shocking, I am shocked by films like that; **ce roman risque de ~** this novel may well be offensive *ou* shocking (to some people), people may find this novel offensive *ou* shocking; **j'ai été vraiment choqué par son indifférence** I was really shocked *ou* appalled by his indifference; **ne vous choquez pas de ma question** don't be shocked at *ou* by my question; **il a été très choqué de ne pas être invité** he was most offended *ou* very put out at not being invited *ou* not to be invited; **ce film/cette scène m'a beaucoup choqué** I was deeply shocked by that film/scene.

b (*aller à l'encontre de*) *délicatesse, pudeur, goût* to offend (against); *bon sens, raison* to offend against, go against; *vue* to offend; *oreilles [son, musique]* to jar on, offend; *[propos]* to shock, offend. **cette question a choqué sa susceptibilité** that question offended his sensibilities *ou* made him take umbrage.

c (*commotionner*) *[chute]* to shake (up); *[accident]* to shake (up), shock; *[deuil, maladie]* to shake. (*Méd*) **être choqué** to be in shock; **il sortit du véhicule, durement choqué** he climbed out of the vehicle badly shaken *ou* shocked; **la mort de sa mère l'a beaucoup choqué** the death of his mother has shaken him badly, he has been badly shaken by his mother's death.

d (*taper, heurter*) (*gén*) to knock (against); *verres* to clink. **il entendait les ancres se ~ dans le petit port** he could hear the anchors clanking against each other in the little harbour; **choquant son verre contre le mien** clinking his glass against mine.

e (*Naut*) *cordage, écoute* to slacken.

2 **se choquer** vpr (*s'offusquer*) to be shocked. **il se choque facilement** he's easily shocked.

choral, e, mpl **~s** [kɔʀal] 1 adj choral. 2 nm choral(e). 3 **chorale** nf choral society, choir.

chorégraphe [kɔʀegʀaf] nmf choreographer.

chorégraphie [kɔʀegʀafi] nf choreography.

chorégraphique [kɔʀegʀafik] adj choreographic.

choreute [kɔʀøt] nm chorist.

choriste [kɔʀist] nmf *[église]* choir member, chorister; *[opéra, théâtre antique]* member of the chorus. **les ~s** the choir; the chorus.

chorus [kɔʀys] nm: **faire ~** to chorus *ou* voice one's agreement *ou* approval; **faire ~ avec qn** to voice one's agreement with sb; **ils ont fait ~ avec lui pour condamner ces mesures** they joined with him in voicing their condemnation of the measures.

chose [ʃoz] 1 nf a thing. **on m'a raconté une ~ extraordinaire** I was told an extraordinary thing; **j'ai pensé (à) une ~** I thought of one thing; **il a un tas de ~s à faire à Paris** he has a lot of things *ou* lots to do in Paris; **il n'y a pas une seule ~ de vraie là-dedans** there isn't a (single) word of truth in it; **critiquer est une ~, faire le travail en est une autre** criticizing is one thing, doing the work is another (matter); **ce n'est pas ~ facile** *ou* **aisée de ...** it's not an easy thing *ou* easy to ...; **~ étrange** *ou* **curieuse, il a accepté** strangely *ou* curiously enough, he accepted, the strange *ou* curious thing is (that) he accepted; **c'est une ~ admise que ...** it's an accepted fact that ... .

b (*événements, activités*) **les ~s** things; **les ~s se sont passées ainsi** it (all) happened like this; **les ~s vont mal** things are going badly *ou* are in a bad way; **dans l'état actuel des ~s, au point où en sont les ~s** as things *ou* matters stand at present, the way things stand at present; **ce sont des ~s qui arrivent** it's one of those things, these things (just) happen; **regarder les ~s en face** to face up to things; **prendre les ~s à cœur/comme elles sont** to take things to heart/as they come; **mettons les ~s au point** let's get things clear *ou* straight; **en mettant les ~s au mieux/au pire** at best/worst; **parler/discuter de ~(s) et d'autre(s)** to talk about/discuss this and that *ou* one thing and another; **elle a fait de grandes ~s** she has done great things; *voir* **force, leçon, ordre[1]**.

c (*ce dont il s'agit*) **la ~: la ~ est d'importance** it's no trivial matter, it's a matter of some importance; **la ~ dont j'ai peur, c'est que** what *ou* the thing I'm afraid of is that; **il va vous expliquer la ~** he'll tell you all about it *ou* what it's all about; **la ~ en question** the matter in hand, the case in point, what we are discussing; **la ~ dont je parle** the thing I'm talking about; **il a très bien pris la ~** he took it all very well; **c'est la ~ à ne pas faire** that's the one thing *ou* the very thing not to do.

d (*réalités matérielles*) **les ~s** things; **les bonnes/belles ~s** good/beautiful things; **les ~s de ce monde** the things of this world; **chez eux, quand ils reçoivent, ils font bien les ~s** when they have guests they really go to town* *ou* do things in style; **elle ne fait pas les ~s à demi** *ou* **à moitié** she doesn't do things by halves.

e (*mot*) thing. **j'ai plusieurs ~s à vous dire** I've got several things to tell you; **vous lui direz bien des ~s de ma part** give him my regards.

f (*objet*) thing. **ils vendent/fabriquent de jolies ~s** they sell/make some nice things.

g (*personne, animal*) thing. **pauvre ~!** poor thing!; **c'est une petite ~ si fragile encore** he (*ou* she) is still such a delicate little thing; **être la ~ de qn** to be sb's plaything.

h (*Jur*) **la ~ jugée** the res judicata, the final decision; (*Pol*) **la ~ publique** the state *ou* nation; († *ou hum*) **la ~ imprimée** the printed word.

i (*loc*) **c'est ~ faite** it's done; **c'est bien peu de ~** it's nothing really; **(très) peu de ~** nothing much, very little; **avant toute ~** above all (else); **toutes ~s égales** all (other) things being equal; all things considered; **de deux ~s l'une** it's got to be one thing or the other; (*Prov*) **~ promise, ~ due** promises are made to be kept; *voir* **porté**.

2 nm (*) a (*truc, machin*) thing, contraption, thingumajig*. **qu'est-ce que c'est que ce ~?** what's this thing here?, what's this thingumajig?*

b (*personne*) what's-his-name*, thingumajig*. **j'ai vu le petit ~** I saw young what's-his-name* *ou* what do you call him; **Monsieur C~** Mr what's-his-name* *ou* thingumajig*; **eh! C~** hey, you.

3 adj inv (*) **être/se sentir tout ~** (*bizarre*) to be/feel not quite oneself, feel a bit peculiar; (*malade*) to be/feel out of sorts *ou* under the weather; **ça l'a rendu tout ~ d'apprendre cette nouvelle** hearing that piece of news made him go all funny.

chosifier [ʃozifje] 7 vt to reify.

Chostakovitch [ʃɔstakɔvitʃ] n Shostakovich.

chou[1], pl **~x** [ʃu] 1 nm a (*Bot*) cabbage.

b (*ruban*) rosette.

c (*gâteau*) puff; *voir* **pâte**.

d (**loc*) **être dans les ~x** *[projet]* to be up the spout* (*Brit*), be a write-off; (*Sport*) to be right out of the running; *[candidat]* to have had it; **faire ~ blanc** to draw a blank; **le gouvernement va faire ses ~x gras de la situation** the government will capitalize *ou* cash in on the situation; **ils vont faire leurs ~x gras de ces vieux vêtements** they'll be only too glad to make use of these old clothes, they'll be as pleased as Punch with these old clothes; *voir* **bout**.

2 comp ►**chou de Bruxelles** Brussels sprout ►**chou cabus** white cabbage ►**chou à la crème** (*Culin*) cream puff ►**chou-fleur** nm (pl **choux-fleurs**) cauliflower ►**chou frisé** kale ►**chou-navet** nm (pl **choux-navets**) swede (*Brit*), rutabaga (*US*) ►**chou palmiste** nm (pl **choux-palmistes**) cabbage tree ►**chou-rave** nm (pl **choux-raves**) kohlrabi ►**chou rouge** red cabbage.

chou[2], -te*, mpl **~x** [ʃu, ʃut, ʃu] 1 nm,f (*amour, trésor*) darling. **c'est un ~** he's a darling *ou* a dear; **oui ma ~te** yes darling *ou* honey (*US*) *ou* poppet* (*Brit*). 2 adj inv (*ravissant*) delightful, cute* (*surtout US*). **ce que c'est ~, cet appartement** what a delightful *ou* lovely little flat, what an absolute darling of a flat; **ce qu'elle est ~ dans ce manteau** doesn't she look just delightful *ou* adorable in this coat?

chouan [ʃwɑ̃] nm *18th century French counter-revolutionary*.

choucas [ʃuka] nm jackdaw.

chouchou, -te* [ʃuʃu, ut] nm,f pet, darling, blue-eyed boy (*ou* girl). **le ~ du prof** the teacher's pet.

chouchouter* [ʃuʃute] 1 vt to pamper, coddle, pet.

choucroute [ʃukʀut] nf sauerkraut. **~ garnie** *sauerkraut with meat*.

chouette[1]* [ʃwɛt] 1 adj a (*beau*) *objet, personne* smashing* (*Brit*), great*, cute* (*surtout US*). b (*gentil*) nice; (*sympathique*) smashing* (*Brit*), great*. **sois ~, prête-moi 100 F** be a dear *ou* sport* and lend me 100 francs. 2 excl: **~ (alors)!** smashing!* (*Brit*), great!*

chouette[2] [ʃwɛt] nf (*Zool*) owl. **~-effraie** barn owl, screech owl; **~ hulotte** tawny owl; (*fig péj*) **quelle vieille ~!** what an old harpy!

chouettement* [ʃwɛtmɑ̃] adv nicely.

chouïa* [ʃuja] nm *[sucre, bonne volonté, impatience, place etc]* smidgin. **c'est pas ~** that's not much; **un ~ trop grand/petit/étroit** (just) a shade too big/small/narrow; **il manque un ~ pour que tu puisses te garer** there's not quite enough room for you to park.

choupette [ʃupɛt] nf *[cheveux]* top-knot.

chouquette [ʃukɛt] nf *ball of choux pastry sprinkled with sugar*.

chouraver⁑ [ʃuʀave] , **chourer⁑** [ʃuʀe] 1 vt to pinch*, nick⁑ (*Brit*), swipe⁑.

chow-chow, pl **chows-chows** [ʃoʃo] nm chow (*dog*).

choyer [ʃwaje] 8 vt (*frm: dorloter*) to cherish; (*avec excès*) to pamper; (*fig*) *idée* to cherish.

chrême [kʀɛm] nm chrism, holy oil.

chrétien, -ienne [kʀetjɛ̃, jɛn] adj, nm,f Christian.

chrétiennement [kʀetjɛnmɑ̃] adv *agir* in a Christian way. **mourir ~** to die as a Christian, die like a good Christian; **être enseveli ~** to have a Christian burial.

chrétienté [kʀetjɛ̃te] nf Christendom.

christ [kʀist] nm a **le C~** Christ. b (*Art*) crucifix, Christ (*on the cross*). **un grand ~ en** *ou* **de bois** a large wooden crucifix *ou* figure of Christ on the cross; **peindre un ~** to paint a figure of Christ.

christiania [kʀistjanja] nm (*Ski*) (parallel) christie, christiania.

christianisation [kʀistjanizasjɔ̃] nf conversion to Christianity.

christianiser [kʀistjanize] 1 vt to convert to Christianity.

christianisme [kʀistjanism] nm Christianity.

christique [kʀistik] adj Christlike.

Christmas [kʀistmas] n: **île ~** Christmas Island.

Christophe [kʀistɔf] **nm** Christopher.
chromage [kʀomaʒ] **nm** chromium-plating.
chromate [kʀɔmat] **nm** chromate.
chromatique [kʀɔmatik] **adj** a (*Mus, Peinture*) chromatic. b (*Bio*) chromosomal.
chromatisme [kʀɔmatism] **nm** (*Mus*) chromaticism; (*Peinture: aberration chromatique*) chromatum, chromatic aberration; (*coloration*) colourings.
chromatographie [kʀɔmatɔgʀafi] **nf** chromatography.
chrome [kʀom] **nm** (*Chim*) chromium. (*Peinture*) **jaune/vert de** ~ chrome yellow/green; (*Aut*) **faire les ~s*** to polish the chrome.
chromer [kʀome] 1 **vt** to chromium-plate. **métal chromé** chromium-plated metal.
chromo [kʀomo] **nm** chromo.
chromosome [kʀomozom] **nm** chromosome.
chromosomique [kʀomozomik] **adj** chromosomal.
chronicité [kʀɔnisite] **nf** chronicity.
chronique [kʀɔnik] 1 **adj** chronic. 2 **nf** (*Littérat*) chronicle; (*Presse*) column, page. ~ **financière** financial column *ou* page *ou* news; ~ **locale** local news and gossip; (*Bible*) **le livre des C~s** the Book of Chronicles; *voir* **défrayer**.
chroniquement [kʀɔnikmɑ̃] **adv** chronically.
chroniqueur, -euse [kʀɔnikœʀ, øz] **nm,f** (*Littérat*) chronicler; (*Presse, gén*) columnist. ~ **parlementaire/sportif** parliamentary/sports editor; ~ **dramatique** drama critic.
chrono* [kʀono] **nm** (**abrév de chronomètre**) stopwatch. (*Aut*) **faire du 80 (km/h)** ~ *ou* **au** ~ to be timed *ou* clocked at 80; (*temps chronométré*) **faire un bon** ~ to do a good time.
chronologie [kʀɔnɔlɔʒi] **nf** chronology.
chronologique [kʀɔnɔlɔʒik] **adj** chronological.
chronologiquement [kʀɔnɔlɔʒikmɑ̃] **adv** chronologically.
chronométrage [kʀɔnɔmetʀaʒ] **nm** (*Sport*) timing.
chronomètre [kʀɔnɔmɛtʀ] **nm** (*montre de précision*) chronometer; (*Sport*) stopwatch. ~ **de marine** marine *ou* box chronometer.
chronométrer [kʀɔnɔmetʀe] 6 **vt** to time.
chronométreur, -euse [kʀɔnɔmetʀœʀ, øz] **nm,f** (*Sport*) timekeeper.
chronométrique [kʀɔnɔmetʀik] **adj** chronometric.
chrysalide [kʀizalid] **nf** chrysalis. (*fig*) **sortir de sa** ~ to blossom out, come out of one's shell.
chrysanthème [kʀizɑ̃tɛm] **nm** chrysanthemum.
chrysolithe [kʀizɔlit] **nf** chrysolite, olivine.
CHU [seaʃy] **nm** (**abrév de centre hospitalier universitaire**) *voir* **centre**.
chu [ʃy] **ptp de choir**.
chuchotement [ʃyʃɔtmɑ̃] **nm** (*voir* **chuchoter**) whisper, whispering (*NonC*); murmur.
chuchoter [ʃyʃɔte] 1 **vti** *[personne, vent, feuilles]* to whisper; *[ruisseau]* to murmur. ~ **qch à l'oreille de qn** to whisper *ou* murmur sth in sb's ear.
chuchoterie [ʃyʃɔtʀi] **nfpl:** ~**s** whispers; **faire des ~s** to whisper.
chuchoteur, -euse [ʃyʃɔtœʀ, øz] 1 **adj** whispering. 2 **nm,f** whisperer.
chuchotis [ʃyʃɔti] **nm** = **chuchotement**.
chuintant, e [ʃɥɛ̃tɑ̃, ɑ̃t] **adj, nf** (*Ling*) **(consonne)** ~**e** palato-alveolar fricative, hushing sound.
chuintement [ʃɥɛ̃tmɑ̃] **nm** (*Ling*) pronunciation of *s* sound as *sh*; (*bruit*) soft *ou* gentle hiss.
chuinter [ʃɥɛ̃te] 1 **vi** a (*Ling*) to pronounce *s* as *sh*. b *[chouette]* to hoot, screech. c (*siffler*) to hiss softly *ou* gently.
chut [ʃyt] **excl** sh!
chute [ʃyt] **nf** a *[pierre etc]* fall; (*Théât*) *[rideau]* fall. **faire une** ~ *[personne]* to (have a) fall; *[chose]* to fall; **faire une ~ de 3 mètres** to fall 3 metres; **faire une ~ de cheval/de vélo** to fall off *ou* tumble off *ou* come off a horse/bicycle; **faire une mauvaise** ~ to have a bad fall; **faire une ~ mortelle** to fall to one's death; **loi de la ~ des corps** law of gravity; ~ **libre** free fall; **faire du parachutisme en ~ libre** to skydive, do skydiving; **économie en ~ libre** plummeting economy; *[ventes]* **être en ~ libre** to take a nose dive; **attention, ~ de pierres** danger, falling rocks; *voir* **point**[1].
b *[cheveux]* loss; *[feuilles]* fall(ing). **lotion contre la ~ des cheveux** lotion which prevents hair loss *ou* prevents hair from falling out.
c (*fig: ruine*) *[empire]* fall, collapse; *[commerce]* collapse; *[roi, ministère]* (down)fall; *[femme séduite]* downfall; (*Mil*) *[ville]* fall; (*Fin*) *[monnaie, cours]* fall, drop (*de* in); (*Théât*) *[pièce, auteur]* failure. (*Rel*) **la** ~ the Fall; **il a entraîné le régime dans sa** ~ he dragged the régime down with him (in his fall); **plus dure sera la** ~ the harder the fall.
d (*Géog*) fall. ~ **d'eau** waterfall; **les ~s du Niagara/Zambèze** the Niagara/Victoria Falls; (*Élec*) **barrage de basse/moyenne/haute** ~ dam with a low/medium/high head; **de fortes ~s de pluie/neige** heavy falls of rain/snow, heavy rainfalls/snowfalls.
e (*baisse*) *[température, pression]* drop, fall (*de* in). (*Élec*) ~ **de tension** voltage drop, drop in voltage.
f (*déchet*) *[papier, tissu]* offcut, scrap; *[bois]* offcut.
g *[toit]* pitch, slope; *[vers]* cadence. **la ~ des reins** the small of the back; ~ **du jour** nightfall.
h (*Cartes*) **faire 3 (plis) de** ~ to be 3 (tricks) down.
i *[histoire drôle]* punchline.
chuter [ʃyte] 1 **vi** a (*tomber*) to fall; (*fig: échouer*) to come a cropper* (*Brit*), fall on one's face; (*lit, fig*) **faire ~ qn** to bring sb down. b (*Théât*) to flop. c (*Cartes*) ~ **de deux (levées)** to go down two.
chyle [ʃil] **nm** (*Physiol*) chyle.
chyme [ʃim] **nm** (*Physiol*) chyme.
Chypre [ʃipʀ] **n** Cyprus. **à** ~ in Cyprus.
chypriote [ʃipʀiɔt] = **cypriote**.
ci [si] 1 **adv** a (*dans l'espace*) **celui-~, celle-~** this one; **ceux-~** these (ones); **ce livre-~** this book; **cette table-~** this table; **cet enfant-~** this child; **ces livres-/tables-~** these books/tables.
b (*dans le temps*) **à cette heure-~** (*à une heure déterminée*) at this time; (*à une heure indue*) at this hour of the day, at this time of night; (*à l'heure actuelle*) by now, at this moment; **ces jours-~** (*avenir*) one of these days, in the next few days; (*passé*) these past few days, in the last few days; (*présent*) these days; **ce dimanche-~/cet après-midi-~ je ne suis pas libre** I'm not free this Sunday/this afternoon; **non, je pars cette nuit-~** no, it's tonight I'm leaving.
c **de ~ de là** here and there; *voir* **comme, par-ci par-là**.
2 **comp** ►**ci-après** (*gén*) below; (*Jur*) hereinafter ►**ci-contre** opposite ►**ci-dessous** below ►**ci-dessus** above ►**ci-devant** **adv** formerly ◊ **nmf** (*Hist*) ci-devant, *aristocrat who lost his title in the French Revolution* ►**ci-gît** here lies ►**ci-inclus** enclosed; **ci-inclus une enveloppe** envelope enclosed ►**l'enveloppe ci-incluse** the enclosed envelope ►**ci-joint: vous trouverez ci-joint les papiers que vous avez demandés** you will find enclosed the papers which you asked for; **les papiers ci-joints** the enclosed papers.
CIA [seia] **nf** (**abrév de Central Intelligence Agency**) CIA.
cibiche* [sibiʃ] **nf** (*cigarette*) fag* (*Brit*), ciggy*.
cibiste [sibist] **nmf** CB enthusiast.
cible [sibl] **nf** (*Mil, Écon*) target. ~ **mouvante** moving target; (*lit, fig*) **être la ~ de, servir de ~ à** to be a target for, be the target of; (*lit, fig*) **prendre pour** ~ to take as one's target; *voir* **langue**.
cibler [sible] 1 **vt** to target (*sur* at).
ciboire [sibwaʀ] **nm** (*Rel*) ciborium (*vessel*).
ciboule [sibul] **nf** (*Bot*) (larger) chive; (*Culin*) chives (*pl*).
ciboulette [sibulɛt] **nf** (*Bot*) (smaller) chive; (*Culin*) chives (*pl*).
ciboulot‡ [sibulo] **nm** (*tête, cerveau*) head, nut*. **il s'est mis dans le ~ de** ... he got it into his head *ou* nut* to ...; **en avoir dans le** ~ to have brains; **fais marcher ton ~!** use your loaf‡ (*Brit*) *ou* your brain!
cicatrice [sikatʀis] **nf** (*lit, fig*) scar.
cicatriciel, -ielle [sikatʀisjɛl] **adj** cicatricial (*SPÉC*), scar (*épith*); *voir* **tissu**[1].
cicatrisant, e [sikatʀizɑ̃, ɑ̃t] 1 **adj** healing. 2 **nm** healing substance.
cicatrisation [sikatʀizasjɔ̃] **nf** *[égratignure]* healing; *[plaie profonde]* closing up, healing.
cicatriser [sikatʀize] 1 1 **vt** (*lit, fig*) to heal (over). **sa jambe est cicatrisée** his leg has healed. 2 **vi** (*[plaie]* to heal (up), form a scar, cicatrize (*SPÉC*); *[personne]* to heal (up). **Marc cicatrise mal** Marc doesn't heal very easily. 3 **se cicatriser** **vpr** to heal (up), form a scar, cicatrize (*SPÉC*).
Cicéron [siseʀɔ̃] **nm** Cicero.
cicérone [siseʀɔn] **nm** (*hum*) guide, cicerone. **faire le** ~ to act as a guide *ou* cicerone.
cicéronien, -ienne [siseʀɔnjɛ̃, jɛn] **adj** *éloquence, discours* Ciceronian.
ciclosporine [siklospɔʀin] **nf** cyclosporin-A.
CIDEX [sidɛks] **nm** (**abrév de courrier individuel à distribution exceptionnelle**) *special post office sorting service for individual clients.*
CIDJ [seidʒi] **nm** (**abrév de centre d'information et de documentation de la jeunesse**) *voir* **centre**.
cidre [sidʀ] **nm** cider. ~ **bouché** *fine bottled cider;* ~ **doux/sec** sweet/dry cider.
cidrerie [sidʀəʀi] **nf** (*industrie*) cider-making; (*usine*) cider factory.
Cie (**abrév de compagnie**) Co.
ciel [sjɛl] 1 **nm** a (*espace: pl littér* **cieux**) sky, heavens (*pl, littér*). **il resta là, les bras tendus/les yeux tournés vers le** ~ he remained there, (with) his arms stretched out/gazing towards the sky *ou* heavenwards (*littér*); **haut dans le** ~ *ou* (*littér*) **dans les cieux** high (up) in the sky, high in the heavens; **suspendu entre ~ et terre** *personne, objet* suspended in mid-air; *village* suspended between sky and earth; **sous un ~ plus clément, sous des cieux plus cléments** (*littér: climat*) beneath more clement skies *ou* a more clement sky; (*fig hum: endroit moins dangereux*) in *ou* into healthier climes; **sous d'autres cieux** (*littér*) beneath other skies; (*hum*) in other climes; **sous le ~ de Paris/de Provence** beneath the Parisian/Provençal sky; *voir* **remuer, septième, tomber**.
b (*paysage, Peinture: pl* **ciels**) sky. **les ~s de Grèce** the skies of Greece; **les ~s de Turner** Turner's skies.
c (*séjour de puissances surnaturelles: pl* **cieux**) heaven. **il est au** ~ he is in heaven; **le royaume des cieux** the kingdom of heaven; **notre Père qui es aux cieux** our Father which art in heaven.
d (*divinité, providence*) heaven. **le ~ a écouté leurs prières** heaven heard their prayers; ~**!, juste ~!** good heavens!; **le ~ m'est témoin que**

... heaven knows that ...; **le ~ soit loué!** thank heavens!; **c'est le ~ qui vous envoie!** you're heaven-sent!

e **à ~ ouvert** *égout* open; *piscine* open-air; *mine* opencast (*Brit*), open cut (*US*).

2 **comp ►ciel de carrière** quarry ceiling **►ciel de lit** canopy, tester.

cierge [sjɛʀʒ] **nm** (*Rel*) candle; (*Bot*) cereus; *voir* **brûler.**

cieux [sjø] **nmpl de ciel.**

cigale [sigal] **nf** cicada.

cigare [sigaʀ] **nm** (*lit*) cigar; (* *fig: tête*) head, nut*.

cigarette [sigaʀɛt] **nf** cigarette. **~ (à) bout filtre** filter tip, (filter-)tipped cigarette; **la ~ du condamné** the condemned man's last smoke *ou* cigarette.

cigarillo [sigaʀijo] **nm** cigarillo.

cigogne [sigɔɲ] **nf** (*Orn*) stork; (*Tech*) crank brace.

ciguë [sigy] **nf** (*Bot, poison*) hemlock. **grande ~** giant hemlock.

cil [sil] **nm** (*Anat*) eyelash. (*Bio*) **~s vibratiles** cilia.

ciliaire [siljɛʀ] **adj** (*Anat*) ciliary.

cilice [silis] **nm** hair shirt.

cillement [sijmɑ̃] **nm** blinking.

ciller [sije] [1] **vi: ~ (des yeux)** to blink (one's eyes); (*fig*) **il n'a pas cillé** he didn't bat an eyelid; (*fig*) **personne n'ose ~ devant lui** nobody dares move a muscle in his presence.

cimaise [simɛz] **nf** (*Peinture*) picture rail, picture moulding; (*Archit*) cyma; *voir* **honneur.**

cime [sim] **nf** *[montagne]* summit; (*pic*) peak; *[arbre]* top; (*fig*) *[gloire]* peak, height.

ciment [simɑ̃] **nm** cement. **~ armé** reinforced concrete; **~ (à prise) rapide** quick-setting cement.

cimenter [simɑ̃te] [1] **vt** **a** (*Constr*) *sol* to cement, cover with concrete; *bassin* to cement, line with cement; *piton, anneau, pierres* to cement. **b** (*fig*) *amitié, accord, paix* to cement. **l'amour qui cimente leur union** the love which binds them together.

cimenterie [simɑ̃tʀi] **nf** cement works.

cimeterre [simtɛʀ] **nm** scimitar.

cimetière [simtjɛʀ] **nm** *[ville]* cemetery; *[église]* graveyard, churchyard. **~ de voitures** scrapyard.

cimier [simje] **nm** *[casque]* crest; *[arbre de Noël] decorative Christmas ball for the top of the Christmas tree.*

cincle [sɛ̃kl] **nm** (*Orn*) **~ (plongeur)** dipper.

ciné [sine] **1** **nm** (*) (**abrév de cinéma**) (*art, procédé*) flicks* (*Brit*), pictures (*Brit*), movies (*US*); (*salle*) cinema, movie theater (*US*). **aller au ~** to go to the flicks* (*Brit*) *ou* pictures (*Brit*) *ou* movies (*US*).

2 **comp ►ciné-club nm (pl ciné-clubs)** film society *ou* club **►ciné-parc** (*Can*) **nm (pl ciné-parcs)** drive-in (cinema) **►ciné-roman nm (pl ciné-romans)** film story.

cinéaste [sineast] **nmf** film-maker, moviemaker (*US*).

cinéma [sinema] **1** **nm** **a** (*procédé, art, industrie*) cinema; (*salle*) cinema, movie theater (*US*). **roman adapté pour le ~** novel adapted for the cinema *ou* the screen; **faire du ~** to be a film *ou* movie (*US*) actor (*ou* actress); **de ~** *technicien, producteur, studio, plateau* film (*épith*); *projecteur, écran* cinema (*épith*); **acteur/vedette de ~** film *ou* movie (*US*) actor/star; **être dans le ~** to be in the film *ou* movie (*US*) business *ou* in films *ou* movies (*US*); **le ~ français/italien** French/Italian cinema; **le ~ de Carné** Carné films; **aller au ~** to go to the cinema *ou* pictures (*Brit*) *ou* movies (*US*).

b (* *fig: frime*) **c'est du ~** it's all put on*, it's all an act; **arrête ton ~** cut out the acting*; **faire tout un ~** to put on a great act*.

c (*: *embarras, complication*) fuss. **c'est toujours le même ~** it's always the same old to-do *ou* business; **tu ne vas pas nous faire ton ~!** you're not going to make a fuss *ou* a great scene *ou* a song and dance* about it!

2 **comp ►le cinéma d'animation** the cartoon film **►cinéma d'art et d'essai** avant-garde *ou* experimental films *ou* cinema; (*salle*) arts cinema **►cinéma muet** silent films *ou* movies (*US*) **►cinéma parlant** talking films *ou* pictures, talkies* **►cinéma permanent** continuous performance **►cinéma-vérité nm inv** cinéma-vérité, ciné vérité.

Cinémascope [sinemaskɔp] **nm** ® Cinemascope ®.

cinémathèque [sinematɛk] **nf** film archives *ou* library; (*salle*) film theatre, movie theater (*US*).

cinématique [sinematik] **nf** kinematics (*sg*).

cinématographe [sinematɔgʀaf] **nm** cinematograph.

cinématographie [sinematɔgʀafi] **nf** film-making, movie-making (*US*), cinematography.

cinématographier [sinematɔgʀafje] [7] **vt** to film.

cinématographique [sinematɔgʀafik] **adj** film (*épith*), cinema (*épith*).

cinéphile [sinefil] **1** **adj public ~** cinema-going public; **il est (très) ~** he's a (real) film *ou* cinema enthusiast, he's a (real) film buff* *ou* movie buff* (*US*). **2** **nmf** film *ou* cinema enthusiast, film buff*, movie buff* (*US*).

cinéraire [sineʀɛʀ] **1** **adj** *vase* cinerary. **2** **nf** (*Bot*) cineraria.

Cinérama [sineʀama] **nm** ® Cinerama®.

cinétique [sinetik] **1** **adj** kinetic. **2** **nf** kinetics (*sg*).

cing(h)alais, e [sɛ̃galɛ, ɛz] **1** **adj** Sin(g)halese.

2 **nm** (*Ling*) Sin(g)halese.

3 **nm,f: C~(e)** Sin(g)halese.

cinglant, e [sɛ̃glɑ̃, ɑ̃t] **adj** *vent* biting, bitter; *pluie* lashing, driving; *propos, ironie* biting, scathing, cutting.

cinglé, e* [sɛ̃gle] (**ptp de cingler**) **adj** nutty*, screwy*, cracked*. **c'est un ~** he's a crackpot* *ou* a nut*.

cingler [sɛ̃gle] [1] **1** **vt** *[personne] corps, cheval* to lash; *[vent, pluie, branche] visage, jambe* to sting, whip (against); *[pluie] vitre* to lash (against); (*fig*) to lash, sting. **il cingla l'air de son fouet** he lashed the air with his whip. **2** **vi** (*Naut*) **~ vers** to make for.

cinoche* [sinɔʃ] **nm** (*art*) flicks* (*Brit*), pictures* (*Brit*), movies* (*US*); (*salle*) cinema, movie theater (*US*). **aller au ~** to go to the pictures* (*Brit*) *ou* movies* (*US*).

cinoque‡ [sinɔk] **adj** = **sinoque**‡.

cinq [sɛ̃k] **adj, nm** five. **dire les ~ lettres** to use bad language; (*euph*) **je lui ai dit les ~ lettres** I told him where to go (*euph*); **en ~ sec*** in a flash, in two ticks* (*Brit*), before you could say Jack Robinson*; *pour autres loc voir* **recevoir, six.**

cinq-dix-quinze†‡ [sɛ̃diskɛ̃z] **nm** (*Can*) cheap store, dime store (*US, Can*), five-and-ten (*US, Can*).

cinquantaine [sɛ̃kɑ̃tɛn] **nf** (*âge, nombre*) about fifty.

cinquante [sɛ̃kɑ̃t] **adj inv, nm inv** fifty; *pour loc voir* **six.**

cinquantenaire [sɛ̃kɑ̃tnɛʀ] **1** **adj** *arbre etc* fifty-year-old (*épith*), fifty years old (*attrib*). **il est ~** it *ou* he is fifty years old. **2** **nm** (*anniversaire*) fiftieth anniversary, golden jubilee.

cinquantième [sɛ̃kɑ̃tjɛm] **adj, nmf** fiftieth; *pour loc voir* **sixième.**

cinquantièmement [sɛ̃kɑ̃tjɛmmɑ̃] **adv** in the fiftieth place.

cinquième [sɛ̃kjɛm] **1** **adj, nmf** fifth. **je suis la ~ roue du carrosse*** I'm treated like a nonentity; **~ colonne** fifth column; *pour autres loc voir* **sixième.** **2** **nf** (*Scol*) second form *ou* year (*Brit*), seventh grade (*US*).

cinquièmement [sɛ̃kjɛmmɑ̃] **adv** in the fifth place.

cintrage [sɛ̃tʀaʒ] **nm** *[tôle, bois]* bending.

cintre [sɛ̃tʀ] **nm** **a** (*Archit*) arch; *voir* **voûte.** **b** (*porte-manteau*) coat hanger. **c** (*Théât*) **les ~s** the flies.

cintré, e [sɛ̃tʀe] (**ptp de cintrer**) **adj** *porte, fenêtre* arched; *galerie* vaulted, arched; *veste* waisted; (‡ *fig: fou*) nuts*, crackers*. **chemise ~e** close- *ou* slim-fitting shirt.

cintrer [sɛ̃tʀe] [1] **vt** (*Archit*) *porte* to arch, make into an arch; *galerie* to vault, give a vaulted *ou* arched roof to; (*Tech*) to bend, curve; (*Habillement*) to take in at the waist.

CIO [seio] **nm** **a** (**abrév de centre d'information et d'orientation**) *voir* **centre.** **b** (**abrév de Comité international olympique**) IOC.

cirage [siʀaʒ] **nm** **a** (*produit*) (shoe) polish. **b** (*action*) *[souliers]* polishing; *[parquets]* polishing, waxing. **c** (*fig*) **être dans le ~*** (*après anesthésie*) to be a bit groggy* *ou* woozy*; (*mal réveillé*) to be a bit woozy*, be half-asleep; (*ne rien comprendre*) to be in a fog* *ou* all at sea*; (*arg Aviat*) to be flying blind; **quand il est sorti du ~*** when he came to *ou* round; *voir* **noir.**

circa [siʀka] **adv** circa.

circoncire [siʀkɔ̃siʀ] [37] **vt** to circumcize.

circoncis [siʀkɔ̃si] (**ptp de circoncire**) **adj** circumcized.

circoncision [siʀkɔ̃sizjɔ̃] **nf** circumcision.

circonférence [siʀkɔ̃feʀɑ̃s] **nf** circumference.

circonflexe [siʀkɔ̃flɛks] **adj: accent ~** circumflex.

circonlocution [siʀkɔ̃lɔkysjɔ̃] **nf** circumlocution. **employer des ~s pour annoncer qch** to announce sth in a roundabout way.

circonscription [siʀkɔ̃skʀipsjɔ̃] **nf** (*Admin, Mil*) district, area. **~ (électorale)** *[député]* constituency (*Brit*), district (*US*); *[conseiller municipal]* district, ward.

circonscrire [siʀkɔ̃skʀiʀ] [39] **vt** *feu, épidémie* to contain, confine; *territoire* to mark out; *sujet* to define, delimit. (*Math*) **~ un cercle/carré à** to draw a circle/square round; **le débat s'est circonscrit à** *ou* **autour de cette seule question** the debate limited *ou* restricted itself to *ou* was centred round that one question; **les recherches sont circonscrites au village** the search is being limited *ou* confined to the village.

circonspect, e [siʀkɔ̃spɛ(kt), ɛkt] **adj** *personne* circumspect, cautious, wary; *silence, remarque* prudent, cautious.

circonspection [siʀkɔ̃spɛksjɔ̃] **nf** caution, wariness, circumspection.

circonstance [siʀkɔ̃stɑ̃s] **nf** **a** (*occasion*) occasion. **en la ~** in this case, on this occasion, given the present circumstances; **en pareille ~** in such a case, in such circumstances; **il a profité de la ~ pour me rencontrer** he took advantage of the occasion to meet me; *voir* **concours.**

b (*situation*) **~s** circumstances; (*Écon*) **~s économiques** economic circumstances; **être à la hauteur des ~s** to be equal to the occasion; **du fait** *ou* **en raison des ~s, étant donné les ~s** in view of *ou* given the circumstances; **dans ces ~s** under *ou* in these circumstances; **dans les ~s présentes** *ou* **actuelles** in the present circumstances; **il a honteusement profité des ~s** he took shameful advantage of the situation.

c *[crime, accident]* circumstance. (*Jur*) **~s atténuantes** mitigating *ou* extenuating circumstances; **~ aggravante** aggravating circumstance, aggravation; **il y a une ~ troublante** there's one disturbing circumstance *ou* point; **dans des ~s encore mal définies** in circumstances

which are still unclear.
d **de ~** *parole, mine, conseil* appropriate, apt, fitting; *œuvre, poésie* occasional (*épith*); *habit* appropriate, suitable.
circonstancié, e [siʀkɔ̃stɑ̃sje] adj *rapport* detailed.
circonstanciel, -ielle [siʀkɔ̃stɑ̃sjɛl] adj adverbial. **complément ~ de lieu/temps** adverbial phrase of place/time.
circonvenir [siʀkɔ̃v(ə)niʀ] 22 vt (*frm*) *personne* to circumvent (*frm*), get round.
circonvoisin, e [siʀkɔ̃vwazɛ̃, in] adj (*littér*) surrounding, neighbouring.
circonvolution [siʀkɔ̃vɔlysjɔ̃] nf (*Anat*) convolution; *[rivière, itinéraire]* twist. **décrire des ~s** *[rivière]* to meander, twist and turn; *[route]* to twist and turn; **~ cérébrale** cerebral convolution.
circuit [siʀkɥi] 1 nm a (*itinéraire touristique*) tour, (round) trip. **~ d'autocar** coach (*Brit*) tour *ou* trip, bus trip; **on a fait un grand ~ à travers la Bourgogne** we did a grand tour of *ou* a great (*Brit*) *ou* long trip through Burgundy; **il y a un très joli ~ (à faire) à travers bois** there's a very nice trip *ou* run (one can go) through the woods; **faire le ~ (touristique) des volcans d'Auvergne** to tour *ou* go on a tour of the volcanoes in Auvergne.
b (*parcours compliqué*) roundabout *ou* circuitous route. **il faut emprunter un ~ assez compliqué pour y arriver** you have to take a rather circuitous *ou* roundabout route *ou* you have to go a rather complicated way to get there; **l'autre grille du parc était fermée et j'ai dû refaire tout le ~ en sens inverse** the other park gate was shut and I had to go right back round the way I'd come *ou* make the whole journey back the way I'd come.
c (*Sport: piste, série de compétitions*) circuit. **~ automobile** (motor-)racing circuit; **course sur ~** circuit racing; **sur le ~ international** on the international circuit.
d (*Élec*) circuit. **couper/rétablir le ~** to break/restore the circuit; **mettre qch en ~** to connect sth up; *[machine]* **tous les ~s ont grillé** all the fuses have blown, there's been a burnout.
e (*Écon*) circulation.
f (*enceinte*) *[ville]* circumference.
g (*Ciné*) circuit.
h (**loc*) **être dans le ~** to be around; **est-ce qu'il est toujours dans le ~?** is he still around?, is he still on the go?* (*Brit*); **se remettre dans le ~** to get back into circulation; **mettre qch dans le ~** to put sth into circulation, feed sth into the system.
2 comp ▸**circuit de distribution** (*Comm*) distribution network *ou* channels ▸**circuit électrique** (*Élec*) electric(al) circuit; *[train ou voiture miniature]* (electric) track ▸**circuit fermé** (*Élec, fig*) closed circuit; **vivre en circuit fermé** to live in a closed world; **ces publications circulent en circuit fermé** this literature has a limited *ou* restricted circulation ▸**circuit hydraulique** (*Aut*) hydraulic circuit ▸**circuit imprimé** printed circuit ▸**circuit intégré** integrated circuit ▸**circuit de refroidissement** cooling system.
circulaire [siʀkylɛʀ] adj, nf (*gén*) circular; *voir* **billet**.
circulairement [siʀkylɛʀmɑ̃] adv in a circle.
circularité [siʀkylaʀite] nf circularity.
circulation [siʀkylasjɔ̃] nf *[air, sang, argent]* circulation; *[marchandises]* movement; *[nouvelle]* spread; *[trains]* running; (*Aut*) traffic. **la ~ (du sang)** the circulation; **la libre ~ des travailleurs** the free movement of labour; (*Aut*) **pour rendre la ~ plus fluide** to improve traffic flow; **route à grande ~** major road, main highway (*US*); (*Fin*) **en ~** in circulation; **mettre en ~** *argent* to put into circulation; *livre, journal, produit* to bring *ou* put out, put on the market; *voiture* to put on the market, bring *ou* put out; *fausse nouvelle* to circulate, spread (about); **mise en ~** *[argent]* circulation; *[livre, produit, voiture]* marketing; *[fausse nouvelle]* spreading, circulation; **retirer de la ~** *argent* to take out of *ou* withdraw from circulation; *médicament, produit, livre* to take off the market, withdraw; *publicité, film, document* to withdraw; (*euph*) *personne* to get rid of; **~ aérienne** air traffic; (*Anat*) **~ générale** systemic circulation; (*Fin*) **~ monétaire** money *ou* currency circulation; (*Aut*) **"~ interdite"** "no vehicular traffic"; (*fig*) **disparaître de la ~** to drop out of sight, disappear from the scene; *voir* **accident, agent.**
circulatoire [siʀkylatwaʀ] adj circulation (*épith*), circulatory. **avoir des troubles ~s** to have trouble with one's circulation, have circulatory trouble.
circuler [siʀkyle] 1 vi a *[sang, air, marchandise, argent]* to circulate; *[rumeur]* to circulate, go round *ou* about, make *ou* go the rounds. **l'information circule mal entre les services** communication between departments is bad; **il circule bien des bruits à son propos** there's a lot of gossip going round about him, there's a lot being said about him; **faire ~** *air, sang* to circulate; *marchandises* to put into circulation; *argent, document* to circulate; **faire ~ des bruits au sujet de** to put rumours about concerning, spread rumours concerning.
b *[voiture]* to go, move; *[train]* to go, run; *[passant]* to walk; *[foule]* to move (along); *[plat, bonbons, lettre]* to be passed *ou* handed round. **un bus sur 3 circule** one bus in 3 is running; **~ à droite/à gauche** to drive on the right/on the left; **circulez!** move along!; **faire ~** *voitures, piétons* to move on; *plat, bonbons, document, pétition* to hand *ou* pass round.
circumnavigation [siʀkɔmnavigasjɔ̃] nf circumnavigation.
circumpolaire [siʀkɔmpɔlɛʀ] adj circumpolar.
cire [siʀ] nf (*gén*) wax; (*pour meubles, parquets*) polish; (*Méd*) *[oreille]* (ear)wax. **~ d'abeille** beeswax; **~ à cacheter** sealing wax; **personnage en ~** waxwork dummy; *voir* **musée.**
ciré [siʀe] nm (*Habillement*) oilskin.
cirer [siʀe] 1 vt to polish. **j'en ai rien à ~‡** I don't give a damn‡; *voir* **toile.**
cireur, -euse [siʀœʀ, øz] 1 nm,f (*personne*) *[souliers]* shoe-shiner, bootblack†; *[planchers]* (floor) polisher. 2 **cireuse** nf (*appareil*) floor polisher.
cireux, -euse [siʀø, øz] adj *matière* waxy; *teint* waxen.
ciron [siʀɔ̃] nm (*littér, Zool*) mite.
cirque [siʀk] nm a (*spectacle*) circus. b (*Antiq: arène*) amphitheatre; *voir* **jeu.** c (*Géog*) cirque. d (*‡: complication, embarras*) **quel ~ il a fait quand il a appris la nouvelle** what a scene *ou* to-do he made when he heard the news; **quel ~ pour garer sa voiture ici!** what a carry-on* (*Brit*) *ou* performance* to get the car parked here! e (**: désordre*) chaos. **c'est un vrai ~ ici aujourd'hui** it's absolute chaos here today, this place is like a bear garden today (*Brit*) *ou* is a real circus today (*US*).
cirrhose [siʀoz] nf cirrhosis. **~ du foie** cirrhosis of the liver.
cirro-cumulus [siʀokymylys] nm cirrocumulus.
cirro-stratus [siʀostʀatys] nm cirrostratus.
cirrus [siʀys] nm cirrus.
cisaille nf, **cisailles** nfpl [sizɑj] *[métal]* shears; *[fil métallique]* wire cutters; *[jardinier]* (gardening) shears.
cisaillement [sizɑjmɑ̃] nm (*voir* **cisailler**) cutting; clipping, pruning; shearing off.
cisailler [sizɑje] 1 vt a (*couper*) *métal* to cut; *arbuste* to clip, prune. b (*user*) *rivet* to shear off. c (**: tailler maladroitement*) *tissu, planche, cheveux* to hack. d (**: empêcher la promotion*) *personne* to cripple the career of; *carrière* to cripple.
cisalpin, e [sizalpɛ̃, in] adj cisalpine.
ciseau, pl **~x** [sizo] nm a **(paire de) ~x** (*gén*) *[tissu, papier]* (pair of) scissors; *[métal, laine]* shears; *[fil métallique]* wire cutters; **~x de brodeuse** embroidery scissors; **~x de couturière** dressmaking shears *ou* scissors; **~x à ongles** nail scissors; **en un coup de ~x** with a snip of the scissors; **donner des coups de ~x dans un tissu** to cut out a piece of cloth; (*fig*) **donner des coups de ~x dans un texte*** to make cuts in a text. b (*Sculp, Tech*) chisel. **~ à froid** cold chisel. c (*Sport: prise*) scissors (hold *ou* grip); (*Ski*) **montée en ~x** herringbone climb; (*Catch*) **~ de jambes** leg scissors; **faire des ~x** to do the scissors; *voir* **sauter.**
ciselage [siz(ə)laʒ] nm chiselling.
ciseler [siz(ə)le] 5 vt (*lit*) *pierre* to chisel, carve; *métal* to chase, chisel; (*fig*) *style* to polish. (*fig*) **les traits finement ciselés de son visage** his finely chiselled features.
ciseleur [siz(ə)lœʀ] nm (*voir* **ciselure**) carver; engraver.
ciselure [siz(ə)lyʀ] nf a *[bois, marbre]* carving, chiselling; *[orfèvrerie]* engraving, chasing. b (*dessin*) *[bois]* carving; *[orfèvrerie]* engraved *ou* chased pattern *ou* design, engraving.
Cisjordanie [sisʒɔʀdani] nf: **la ~** the West Bank (of Jordan).
cistercien, -ienne [sistɛʀsjɛ̃, jɛn] 1 adj, nm Cistercian. 2 nm Cistercian monk.
citadelle [sitadɛl] nf (*lit, fig*) citadel.
citadin, e [sitadɛ̃, in] 1 adj (*gén*) town (*épith*), urban; *[grande ville]* city (*épith*), urban. 2 nm,f city dweller, urbanite (*US*).
citation [sitasjɔ̃] nf *[auteur]* quotation; (*Jur*) summons. (*Jur*) **~ à comparaître** (*à accusé*) summons to appear; (*à témoin*) subpoena; (*Mil*) **~ à l'ordre du jour** *ou* **de l'armée** mention in dispatches.
cité [site] 1 nf (*littér*) (*Antiq, grande ville*) city; (*petite ville*) town; (*immeubles*) estate (*esp Brit*), project (*US*). **la C~ du Vatican** the Vatican City; *voir* **droit³.** 2 comp ▸**cité-dortoir** nf (pl **cités-dortoirs**) dormitory town ▸**cité-jardin** nf (pl **cités-jardins**) garden city ▸**cité ouvrière** ≃ (workers') housing estate (*Brit*) *ou* development (*US*) ▸**cité de transit** ≃ halfway house *ou* hostel, (temporary) hostel for homeless families ▸**cité universitaire** (student) hall(s) of residence.
citer [site] 1 vt a (*rapporter*) *texte, exemples, faits* to quote, cite. **~ (du) Shakespeare** to quote from Shakespeare; **il n'a pas pu ~ 3 pièces de Sartre** he couldn't name *ou* quote 3 plays by Sartre. b **~ (en exemple)** *personne* to hold up as an example; **il a été cité (en exemple) pour son courage** he has been held up as an example for his courage; (*Mil*) **~ un soldat (à l'ordre du jour** *ou* **de l'armée)** to mention a soldier in dispatches. c (*Jur*) to summon. **~ (à comparaître)** *accusé* to summon to appear; *témoin* to subpoena.
citerne [sitɛʀn] nf tank; (*à eau*) water tank; *voir* **camion.**
cithare [sitaʀ] nf zither; (*Antiq*) cithara.
citoyen, -yenne [sitwajɛ̃, jɛn] 1 nm,f citizen. **~/~ne d'honneur d'une ville** freeman/freewoman of a city *ou* town. 2 nm (**: type*) bloke* (*Brit*), guy*. **drôle de ~** oddbod*, oddball* (*US*).
citoyenneté [sitwajɛnte] nf citizenship.
citrique [sitʀik] adj citric.
citron [sitʀɔ̃] 1 nm (*fruit*) lemon; (*‡: tête*) nut*. **un** *ou* **du ~ pressé** a (fresh) lemon juice; **~ vert** lime; *voir* **thé.** 2 adj inv lemon(-coloured).
citronnade [sitʀɔnad] nf lemon squash (*Brit*), still lemonade (*Brit*),

lemonade (*US*).

citronné, e [sitʀɔne] adj *goût, odeur* lemony; *gâteau* lemon(-flavoured); *liquide* with lemon juice added, lemon-flavoured; *eau de toilette* lemon-scented.

citronnelle [sitʀɔnɛl] nf (*Bot, huile*) citronella; (*liqueur*) lemon liqueur.

citronnier [sitʀɔnje] nm lemon tree.

citrouille [sitʀuj] nf pumpkin; (‡ *hum: tête*) nut*.

citrus [sitʀys] nm citrus.

cive [siv] nf (*Bot*) chive; (*Culin*) chives (*pl*).

civet [sivɛ] nm stew. **un lièvre en** ~, **un** ~ **de lièvre** ≃ jugged hare.

civette¹ [sivɛt] nf (*Zool*) civet (cat); (*parfum*) civet.

civette² [sivɛt] nf (*Bot*) chive; (*Culin*) chives (*pl*).

civière [sivjɛʀ] nf stretcher.

civil, e [sivil] 1 adj a (*entre citoyens, Jur*) *guerre, mariage* civil; *voir* **code, partie²**. b (*non militaire*) civilian. c (*littér: poli*) civil, courteous. 2 nm a (*non militaire*) civilian. **se mettre en** ~ *[soldat]* to dress in civilian clothes, wear civvies*; *[policier]* to dress in plain clothes; **policier en** ~ plain-clothes policeman, policeman in plain clothes; **soldat en** ~ soldier in civvies* *ou* mufti *ou* in civilian clothes; **dans le** ~ in civilian life, in civvy street*. b (*Jur*) **poursuivre qn au** ~ to take civil ac- tion against sb, sue sb in the civil courts.

civilement [sivilmɑ̃] adv a (*Jur*) **poursuivre qn** ~ to take civil action against sb, sue sb in the (civil) courts; **être** ~ **responsable** to be legally responsible; **se marier** ~ to have a civil wedding, ≃ get married in a registry office (*Brit*) *ou* be married by a judge (*US*). b (*littér*) civilly.

civilisable [sivilizabl] adj civilizable.

civilisateur, -trice [sivilizatœʀ, tʀis] 1 adj civilizing. 2 nm,f civilizer.

civilisation [sivilizasjɔ̃] nf civilization.

civiliser [sivilize] [1] 1 vt *peuple*, (*) *personne* to civilize. 2 **se civiliser** vpr *[peuple]* to become civilized; (*) *[personne]* to become more civilized.

civilité [sivilite] nf (*politesse*) civility. (*frm: compliments*) ~**s** civilities; **faire** *ou* **présenter ses** ~**s à** to pay one's compliments to.

civique [sivik] adj civic. **avoir le sens** ~ to have a sense of civic responsibility; *voir* **éducation, instruction**.

civisme [sivism] nm public-spiritedness. **cours de** ~ civics (*sg*).

cl (abrév de **centilitre**) cl.

clabaudage [klabodaʒ] nm gossip; *[chien]* yapping.

clabauder [klabode] [1] vi (*médire*) to gossip; *[chien]* to yap. ~ **contre qn** to make denigrating remarks about sb.

clabauderie [klabodʀi] nf = **clabaudage**.

clabaudeur, -euse [klabodœʀ, øz] 1 adj (*médisant*) gossiping; (*aboyant*) yapping. 2 nm,f (*cancanier*) gossip.

clac [klak] excl *[porte]* slam!; *[élastique, stylo etc* snap!;*[fouet]* crack!; *voir* **clic**.

clafoutis [klafuti] nm clafoutis (*type of fruit cake, often cherry cake*).

claie [klɛ] nf *[fruit, fromage]* rack; (*crible*) riddle; (*clôture*) hurdle.

clair, e¹ [klɛʀ] 1 adj a (*lumineux*) *pièce* bright, light; *ciel* clear; *couleur, flamme* bright. **par temps** ~ on a clear day, in clear weather.

b (*pâle*) *teint, couleur* light; *tissu, robe* light-coloured. **bleu/vert** ~ light blue/green.

c (*lit, fig: limpide*) *eau, son, conscience, voyelle* clear. **d'une voix** ~**e** in a clear voice; **des vitres propres et** ~**es** clean and sparkling *ou* clean bright windows.

d (*peu consistant*) *sauce, soupe* thin; *tissu usé* thin; *tissu peu serré* light, thin; *blés* sparse.

e (*sans ambiguïté*) *exposé, pensée, position, attitude* clear. **voilà qui est** ~! well, that's clear anyway!; **cette affaire n'est pas** ~**e** there's something slightly suspicious *ou* not quite clear about this affair; **avoir un esprit** ~ to be a clear thinker; **je serai** ~ **avec vous** I'll be frank with you.

f (*évident*) clear, obvious, plain. **le plus** ~ **de l'histoire** the most obvious thing in the story; **il est** ~ **qu'il se trompe** it is clear *ou* obvious *ou* plain that he's mistaken; **son affaire est** ~**e, il est coupable** it's quite clear *ou* obvious that he's guilty; **c'est** ~ **comme le jour** *ou* **comme de l'eau de roche** it's as clear as daylight, it's crystal-clear; **il passe le plus** ~ **de son temps à rêver** he spends most of his time daydreaming; **il dépense le plus** ~ **de son argent en cigarettes** he spends the better part of his money on cigarettes.

2 adv *parler, voir* clearly. **il fait** ~ it is daylight; **il ne fait guère** ~ **dans cette pièce** it's not very light in this room; **il fait aussi** ~ *ou* **on voit aussi** ~ **qu'en plein jour** it's as bright as daylight; **elle ne voit plus très** ~ she can't see very well any more.

3 nm a (*loc*) **tirer qch au** ~ to clear sth up, clarify sth; **en** ~ (*c'est-à-dire*) to put it plainly; (*non codé*) *message* in clear; **le journal de 13 heures est en** ~ you don't need a decoder to see the 1 o'clock news; **mettre ses idées au** ~ to organize one's thoughts; **mettre un brouillon au** ~ to copy out a rough draft; **mettre les choses au** ~ to make things clear; **mettre les choses au** ~ **avec qn** to get things straight with sb; *voir* **sabre**.

b (*partie usée d'une chaussette*) ~**s** worn parts, thin patches.

c (*Art*) ~**s** light (*NonC*), light areas; **les** ~**s et les ombres** the light and shade.

4 comp ▸**clair de lune** moonlight; **au clair de lune** in the moonlight; **promenade au clair de lune** moonlight saunter, stroll in the moonlight ▸**clair-obscur** nm (pl **clairs-obscurs**) (*Art*) chiaroscuro; (*gén*) twilight ▸**claire-voie** nf (pl **claires-voies**) (*clôture*) openwork fence; *[église]* clerestory; **à claire-voie** openwork (*épith*).

claire² [klɛʀ] nf (*parc*) oyster bed. **(huître de)** ~ fattened oyster; *voir* **fine²**.

Claire [klɛʀ] nf Cla(i)re.

clairement [klɛʀmɑ̃] adv clearly.

clairet, -ette [klɛʀɛ, ɛt] 1 adj *soupe* thin; *voix* high-pitched. **(vin)** ~ light red wine. 2 **clairette** nf light sparkling wine.

clairière [klɛʀjɛʀ] nf clearing, glade.

clairon [klɛʀɔ̃] nm (*instrument*) bugle; (*joueur*) bugler; *[orgue]* clarion (stop).

claironnant, e [klɛʀɔnɑ̃, ɑ̃t] adj *voix* strident, resonant, like a foghorn.

claironner [klɛʀɔne] [1] 1 vt *succès, nouvelle* to trumpet, shout from the rooftops. 2 vi (*parler fort*) to speak at the top of one's voice.

clairsemé, e [klɛʀsəme] adj *arbres, maisons, applaudissements, auditoire* scattered; *blés, gazon, cheveux* thin, sparse; *population* sparse, scattered.

clairvoyance [klɛʀvwajɑ̃s] nf (*discernement*) *[personne]* clear-sightedness, perceptiveness; *[esprit]* perceptiveness.

clairvoyant, e [klɛʀvwajɑ̃, ɑ̃t] adj a (*perspicace*) *personne* clear-sighted, perceptive; *œil, esprit* perceptive. b (*doué de vision*) **les aveugles et les** ~**s** the blind and the sighted.

clam [klam] nm (*Zool*) clam.

clamecer‡ [klamse] [3] vi (*mourir*) to kick the bucket‡, snuff it‡ (*Brit*).

clamer [klɑme] [1] vt to shout out, proclaim. ~ **son innocence/son indignation** to proclaim one's innocence/one's indignation.

clameur [klɑmœʀ] nf clamour. **les** ~**s de la foule** the clamour of the crowd; (*fig*) **les** ~**s des mécontents** the protests of the discontented.

clamser‡ [klamse] [1] vi = **clamecer‡**.

clan [klɑ̃] nm (*lit, fig*) clan.

clandé [klɑ̃de] nm (*arg Crime*) (*maison close*) knocking-shop‡ (*Brit*), brothel; (*maison de jeu*) gambling joint.

clandestin, e [klɑ̃dɛstɛ̃, in] 1 adj *réunion* secret, clandestine; *revue, mouvement* underground (*épith*); *commerce* clandestine, illicit; *travailleur* illegal. 2 nm (*ouvrier*) illegal worker. **(passager)** ~ stowaway.

clandestinement [klɑ̃dɛstinmɑ̃] adv (*voir* **clandestin**) secretly; clandestinely; illicitly; illegally.

clandestinité [klɑ̃dɛstinite] nf a *[activité]* secret nature. **dans la** ~ (*en secret*) *travailler, imprimer* in secret, clandestinely; (*en se cachant*) *vivre* underground; **entrer dans la** ~ to go underground; **le journal interdit a continué de paraître dans la** ~ the banned newspaper went on being published underground *ou* clandestinely. b (*Hist: la Résistance*) **la** ~ the Resistance.

clap [klap] nm (*Ciné*) clapperboard.

clapet [klapɛ] nm a (*Tech*) valve; (*Élec*) rectifier. (*Aut*) ~ **d'admission/d'échappement** induction/exhaust valve. b (‡: *bouche*) **ferme ton** ~ hold your tongue*, shut up*; **quel** ~! what a chatterbox! *ou* gasbag!*

clapier [klapje] nm a (*cabane à lapins*) hutch; (*péj: logement surpeuplé*) dump‡, hole*. b (*éboulis*) scree.

clapotement [klapɔtmɑ̃] nm lap(ping) (*NonC*).

clapoter [klapɔte] [1] vi *[eau]* to lap.

clapotis [klapɔti] nm lap(ping) (*NonC*).

clappement [klapmɑ̃] nm click(ing) (*NonC*).

clapper [klape] [1] vi: ~ **de la langue** to click one's tongue.

claquage [klakaʒ] nm (*action*) pulling *ou* straining (of a muscle); (*blessure*) pulled *ou* strained muscle. **se faire un** ~ to pull *ou* strain a muscle.

claquant, e* [klakɑ̃, ɑ̃t] adj (*fatigant*) killing*, exhausting.

claque¹ [klak] nf a (*gifle*) slap. **donner** *ou* **flanquer*** *ou* **filer* une** ~ **à qn** to slap sb, give sb a slap *ou* clout*; (*fig:humiliation*) **il a pris une** ~ **aux dernières élections** the last election was a slap in the face for him; (*fig: choc*) **elle a pris une** ~ **quand son mari est parti*** il was a real blow to her when her husband left; **mes économies ont pris une** ~ **pendant les vacances** the holidays made a hole in my savings; *voir* **tête**. b (*loc*) **il en a sa** ~* (*excédé*) he's fed up to the back teeth* (*Brit*) *ou* to the teeth* (*US*); (*épuisé*) he's dead beat* *ou* all in*. c (*Théât*) claque.

claque² [klak] adj, nm: **(chapeau)** ~ opera hat.

claque³‡ [klak] nm knocking-shop‡ (*Brit*), brothel, whorehouse†*.

claqué, e* [klake] (ptp de **claquer**) adj (*fatigué*) all in*, dead beat*, bushed*.

claquement [klakmɑ̃] nm (*bruit répété*) *[porte]* banging (*NonC*), slamming (*NonC*); *[fouet]* cracking (*NonC*); *[langue]* clicking (*NonC*); *[doigts]* snap(ping) (*NonC*); *[talons]* click(ing) (*NonC*); *[dents]* chattering (*NonC*); *[drapeau]* flapping (*NonC*); (*bruit isolé*) *[porte]* bang, slam; *[fouet]* crack; *[langue]* click. **la corde cassa avec un** ~ **sec** the rope broke with a sharp snap.

claquemurer [klakmyʀe] [1] **1** vt to coop up. **il reste claquemuré dans son bureau toute la journée** he stays shut up *ou* shut away in his office all day. **2 se claquemurer** vpr to shut o.s. away *ou* up.

claquer [klake] [1] **1** vi **a** *[porte, volet]* to bang; *[drapeau]* to flap; *[fouet]* to crack; *[coup de feu]* to ring out. **faire ~ une porte** to bang *ou* slam a door; **faire ~ son fouet** to crack one's whip.
b ~ des doigts, faire ~ ses doigts to click *ou* snap one's fingers; (*Mil*) **~ des talons** to click one's heels; (*fig*) **~ du bec‡** to be famished; **il claquait des dents** his teeth were chattering; **faire ~ sa langue** to click one's tongue.
c (*‡: mourir*) to snuff it‡ (*Brit*), kick the bucket‡; (**: tomber hors d'usage*) *[télévision, moteur, lampe électrique]* to conk out‡, go phut* (*Brit*), pack in*; *[ficelle, élastique]* to snap. **~ dans les mains** *ou* **les doigts de qn** *[malade]* to die on sb; *[élastique]* to snap in sb's hands; *[appareil]* to bust* *ou* go phut* (*Brit*) in sb's hands; *[entreprise, affaire]* to go bust on sb*; **il a claqué d'une crise cardiaque** a heart attack finished him off.
2 vt **a** (*gifler*) *enfant* to slap.
b (*refermer avec bruit*) *livre* to snap shut. (*lit, fig*) **~ la porte** to slam the door (*de* on); **il m'a claqué la porte au nez** (*lit*) he slammed the door in my face; (*fig*) he refused to listen to me.
c (**: fatiguer*) *[travail]* to exhaust, tire out. **le voyage m'a claqué** I felt whacked* (*Brit*) *ou* dead tired after the journey; **~ son cheval** to wear out *ou* exhaust one's horse; **ne travaille pas tant, tu vas te ~** don't work so hard or you'll knock *ou* wear yourself out *ou* kill yourself.
d (**: casser*) to bust*. (*Sport*) **se ~ un muscle** to pull *ou* strain a muscle.
e (*‡: dépenser*) *argent* to blow*, blue* (*Brit*).

claquette [klakɛt] nf **a** (*Danse*) **~s** tap-dancing; **faire des ~s** to tap-dance; *voir* **danseur**. **b** (*claquoir*) clapper; (*Ciné*) clapperboard.

claquoir [klakwaʀ] nm clapper.

clarification [klaʀifikasjɔ̃] nf (*lit, fig*) clarification.

clarifier vt, **se clarifier** vpr [klaʀifje] [7] (*lit, fig*) to clarify. **la situation se clarifie** the situation is clarifying itself *ou* is becoming clear(er).

clarine [klaʀin] nf cowbell.

clarinette [klaʀinɛt] nf clarinet.

clarinettiste [klaʀinetist] nmf clarinettist.

clarté [klaʀte] nf **a** (*gén: lumière*) light; *[lampe, crépuscule, astre]* light. **~ douce/vive/faible** soft/bright/weak light; **~ de la lune** light of the moon, moonlight; **à la ~ de la lampe** in the lamplight, in *ou* by the light of the lamp.
b (*transparence, luminosité*) *[flamme, pièce, jour, ciel]* brightness; *[eau, son, verre]* clearness; *[teint]* (*pureté*) clearness; (*pâleur*) lightness.
c (*fig: netteté*) *[explication, pensée, attitude, conférencier]* clarity. **~ d'esprit** clear thinking.
d (*fig: précisions*) **~s: avoir des ~s sur une question** to have some (further *ou* bright) ideas on a subject; **cela projette quelques ~s sur la question** this throws some light on the subject.

clash [klaʃ] nm clash.

classe [klɑs] **1** nf **a** (*catégorie sociale*) class. (*Démographie*) **~s creuses** *age groups depleted by war deaths or low natality;* **les ~s moyennes** the middle classes; **les basses/hautes ~s (sociales)** the lower/upper (social) classes; **la ~ laborieuse** *ou* **ouvrière** the working class; **la ~ politique** the political community; **selon sa ~ sociale** according to one's social status *ou* social class; **(société) sans ~** classless (society).
b (*gén, Sci: espèce*) class; (*Admin: rang*) grade. **cela s'adresse à toutes les ~s d'utilisateurs** it is aimed at every category of user; (*fig*) **il est vraiment à mettre dans une ~ à part** he's really in a class of his own *ou* a class apart; (*Admin*) **cadre de première/deuxième ~** first/second grade manager; (*Comm*) **hôtel de première ~** first class hotel; (*Gram*) **~ grammaticale** *ou* **de mots** grammatical category, part of speech; **~ d'âge** age group; **établissement de ~** high-class establishment; **de ~ internationale** of international standing.
c (*Aviat, Rail*) class. **compartiment/billet de 1re/2e ~** 1st/2nd class compartment/ticket; **voyager en 1re ~** to travel 1st class; (*Aviat*) **~ affaires/club/touriste** business/club/economy class.
d (*gén, Sport: valeur*) class. **liqueur/artiste de (grande) ~** liqueur/artist of great distinction; **de ~ internationale** of international class; **elle a de la ~** she's got class; **ils ne sont pas de la même ~, ils n'ont pas la même ~** they're not in the same class; **la ~!*** classy!*; **ils sont descendus au Ritz — la ~ quoi!*** they stayed at the Ritz — classy, eh?*
e (*Scol: ensemble d'élèves*) form (*Brit*), class; (*division administrative*) form; (*année d'études secondaires*) year. **les grandes ~s, les ~s supérieures** the senior school (*Brit*), the high school (*US*), the upper forms (*Brit*) *ou* classes (*US*); **les petites ~s** the junior school (*Brit*), grade school (*US*), the lower forms (*Brit*) *ou* classes (*US*); **~ préparatoire aux grandes écoles** *class preparing for entrance to the grandes écoles;* **il est en ~ de 6e** he is in the 1st year (*Brit*) *ou* 5th grade (*US*); **toutes les ~s de première** all the 6th forms (*Brit*), all the 6th year; **monter de ~** to go up a class; **il est (le) premier/(le) dernier de la ~** he is top/bottom of the form (*Brit*) *ou* class; **~ enfantine** playschool; **~ de solfège/de danse** musical theory/dancing lesson; **partir en ~ verte** *ou* **de nature** ≃ to go to the country with the school; **partir en ~ de neige/de mer** ≃ to go skiing/to the seaside with the school; *voir* **redoubler**.
f (*Scol*) (*cours, leçon*) class. (*l'école*) **la ~** school; **la ~ d'histoire/de français** the history/French class; **aller en ~** to go to school; **pendant/après la ~** *ou* **les heures de ~** during/after school *ou* school hours; **à l'école primaire la ~ se termine** *ou* **les élèves sortent de ~ à 16 heures** school finishes *ou* classes finish at 4 o'clock in primary school; **il est en ~** (*en cours*) *[professeur]* he is in class, he is teaching; *[élève]* he is in class *ou* at lessons; (*à l'école*) *[élève]* he is at school; **faire la ~: c'est M. X qui leur fait la ~** (*habituellement*) Mr X is their (primary school) teacher, Mr X takes them at (primary) school; (*en remplacement*) Mr X is their replacement (primary school) teacher.
g (*Scol: salle*) classroom; (*d'une classe particulière*) form room (*Brit*), homeroom (*US*). **il est turbulent en ~** he's disruptive in class *ou* in the classroom; **les élèves viennent d'entrer en ~** the pupils have just gone into class.
h (*Mil*) (*rang*) **militaire** *ou* **soldat de 1re ~** (*armée de terre*) ≃ private (*Brit*), private first class (*US*); (*armée de l'air*) ≃ leading aircraftman (*Brit*), airman first class (*US*); **militaire** *ou* **soldat de 2e ~** (*terre*) private (soldier); (*air*) aircraftman (*Brit*), airman basic (*US*); (*contingent*) **la ~ de 1987** the 1987 class, the class of '87; **ils sont de la même ~** they were called up at the same time; **faire ses ~s** (*lit*) to do one's recruit training; (*fig*) to learn the ropes*, serve one's apprenticeship (*fig*).
2 adj inv* *fille, vêtements, voiture* classy*. **ça fait ~** it adds a touch of class*.

classé, e [klɑse] adj *bâtiment, monument* listed, with a preservation order on it; *vins* classified. **joueur ~** ≃ (*Tennis*) officially graded player; (*Bridge*) graded *ou* master player.

classement [klɑsmɑ̃] nm **a** (*rangement*) *[papiers]* filing; *[livres]* classification; *[fruits]* grading. **faire un ~ par ordre de taille** to grade by size; **faire un ~ par sujet** to classify by subject matter; **j'ai fait du ~ toute la journée** I've spent all day filing *ou* classifying; **~ alphabétique** alphabetical classification; **j'ai fait un peu de ~ dans mes factures** I've put my bills into some kind of order.
b (*classification*) *[fonctionnaire, élève]* grading; *[joueur]* grading, ranking; *[hôtel]* grading, classification. **on devrait supprimer le ~ des élèves** they ought to stop grading pupils.
c (*rang*) *[élève]* place (*Brit*) *ou* rank (*US*) (in class), position in class; *[coureur]* placing. **avoir un bon/mauvais ~** *[élève]* to get a high/low place in class (*Brit*), be ranked high/low in class (*US*); *[coureur]* to be well/poorly placed; **le ~ des coureurs à l'arrivée** the placing of the runners at the finishing line.
d (*liste*) *[élèves]* class list (in order of merit); *[coureurs]* finishing list; *[équipes]* league table. **je vais vous lire le ~** I'm going to read you your (final) placings (in class); (*Cyclisme*) **~ général** overall placings; **premier au ~ général/au ~ de l'étape** first overall/for the stage.
e (*clôture*) *[affaire]* closing.

classer [klɑse] [1] **1** vt **a** (*ranger*) *papiers* to file; *livres* to classify; *documents* to file, classify. **~ des livres par sujet** to classify books by *ou* according to subject (matter); **~ des factures par année/client** to file invoices according to the year/the customer's name.
b (*Sci: classifier*) *animaux, plantes* to classify.
c (*hiérarchiser*) *employé, fruits* to grade; *élève, joueur, copie* to grade; *hôtel* to grade, classify. **~ des copies de composition (par ordre de mérite)** to arrange *ou* grade exam papers in order of merit; **X, que l'on classe parmi les meilleurs violonistes** X, who ranks among the top violinists.
d (*clore*) *affaire, dossier* to close. **c'est une affaire classée maintenant** that matter is closed now.
e (*péj: cataloguer*) *personne* to size up*, categorize.
2 se classer vpr: **se ~ premier/parmi les premiers** to be *ou* come (*Brit*) *ou* come in (*US*) first/among the first; (*Courses*) **le favori s'est classé 3e** the favourite finished *ou* came (in) 3rd; **ce livre se classe au nombre des grands chefs-d'œuvre littéraires** this book ranks among the great works of literature.

classeur [klɑsœʀ] nm (*meuble*) filing cabinet; (*dossier*) (loose-leaf) file.

classicisme [klasisism] nm (*Art*) classicism; (*gén: conformisme*) conventionality.

classificateur, -trice [klasifikatœʀ, tʀis] **1** adj *procédé, méthode* classifying; (*fig: méthodique*) *esprit* methodical, orderly. **obsession ~trice** mania for categorizing *ou* classifying things. **2** nm,f classifier.

classification [klasifikasjɔ̃] nf classification.

classifier [klasifje] [7] vt to classify.

classique [klasik] **1** adj **a** (*Art*) *auteur, genre, musique* classical; (*Ling*) *langue* classical. **il préfère le ~** he prefers classical music (*ou* literature, painting).
b (*sobre*) *coupe, vêtement, ameublement, décoration* classic, classical. **j'aime mieux le ~ que tous ces meubles modernes** I prefer a classic *ou* classical style of furniture to any of these modern styles.
c (*habituel*) *argument, réponse, méthode* standard, classic; *conséquence* usual; *symptôme* usual, classic. **c'est ~!** it's the usual *ou* classic situation!; **c'est le coup ~!*** it's the usual thing; **c'est la**

question/la plaisanterie ~ dans ces cas-là it's the classic question/joke on those occasions; **son mari buvait, alors elle l'a quitté, c'est ~** her husband drank, so she left him – it's the usual *ou* classic situation; **le cambriolage s'est déroulé suivant le plan ~** the burglary followed the standard *ou* recognized pattern.

d (*banal*) *situation, maladie* classic, standard. **grâce à une opération maintenant ~, on peut guérir cette infirmité** thanks to an operation which is now quite usual *ou* standard, this disability can be cured.

e (*Scol: littéraire*) **faire des études ~s** to do classical studies, study classics; **il est en section ~** he's in the classics stream; *voir* **lettre**.

2 nm a (*auteur*) (*Antiq*) classical author; (*classicisme français*) classic, classicist. (*grand écrivain*) **(auteur) ~** classic (author).

b (*ouvrage*) classic. **un ~ du cinéma** a classic of the cinema; **c'est un ~ du genre** it's a classic of its kind; (*hum*) **je connais mes ~s!*** I know my classics!

3 nf (*Sport*) classic; (*Cyclisme*) one-day road race.

classiquement [klasikmɑ̃] adv classically.

claudication [klodikasjɔ̃] nf (*littér*) limp.

claudiquer [klodike] [1] vi (*littér*) to limp.

clause [kloz] nf (*Gram, Jur*) clause. **~ dérogatoire** escape clause; **~ pénale** penalty clause; **~ de style** standard *ou* set clause; **~ résolutoire** resolutive clause.

claustral, e, mpl **-aux** [klostʀal, o] adj monastic.

claustration [klostʀasjɔ̃] nf confinement.

claustrer [klostʀe] [1] 1 vt (*enfermer*) to confine. 2 **se claustrer** vpr to shut o.s. up *ou* away. (*fig*) **se ~ dans** to wrap *ou* enclose o.s. in.

claustrophobe [klostʀɔfɔb] adj, nmf claustrophobic.

claustrophobie [klostʀɔfɔbi] nf claustrophobia.

clausule [klozyl] nf clausula.

clavecin [klav(ə)sɛ̃] nm harpsichord. **le ~ bien tempéré** The Well-tempered Klavier.

claveciniste [klav(ə)sinist] nmf harpsichordist.

clavette [klavɛt] nf (*Tech*) [*boulon*] key, cotter pin.

clavicorde [klavikɔʀd] nm clavichord.

clavicule [klavikyl] nf collarbone, clavicle (*SPÉC*).

clavier [klavje] nm (*lit*) keyboard; (*fig: registre*) range. *orgue, clavecin* **à un/deux ~(s)** single-/double-manual (*épith*); **~ AZERTY/QWERTY** AZERTY/QWERTY keyboard.

claviste [klavist] nmf keyboard operator.

clayette [klɛjɛt] nf (*étagère*) wicker *ou* wire rack; (*cageot à fruits*) tray; [*réfrigérateur*] shelf.

clayon [klɛjɔ̃] nm (*étagère*) rack; (*plateau*) tray.

clé [kle] = **clef**.

clean* [klin] adj inv a *homme* clean-cut; *femme* squeaky-clean*; *vêtements* smart; *décor* stark. **c'est vraiment ~ chez eux** their place is really starkly decorated (*ou* furnished). b (*arg Drogue*) clean.

clébard* [klebaʀ] nm, **clebs*** [klɛps] nm (*péj: chien*) dog, hound (*hum*), mutt‡.

clef [kle] 1 nf a [*serrure, pendule, boîte de conserve*] key; [*poêle*] damper; (*fig*) [*mystère, réussite, code, rêve*] key (*de* to); (*position stratégique*) key. **la ~ de la porte d'entrée** the (front) door key; **la ~ est sur la porte** the key is in the door; **Avignon, ~ de la Provence** Avignon, the key to Provence; **la ~ des songes** the interpretation of dreams; **la préface nous fournit quelques ~s** the preface offers a few clues; *voir* **enfant, fermer, tour²**.

b (*Tech*) spanner (*Brit*), wrench. **un jeu de ~s** a set of spanners *ou* wrenches.

c (*Mus*) [*guitare, violon*] peg; [*clarinette*] key; [*gamme*] clef; [*accordeur*] key. **~ de fa/de sol/d'ut** bass *ou* F/treble *ou* G/alto *ou* C clef; **il y a trois dièses à la ~** the key signature has 3 sharps; **avec une altération à la ~** with a change in the key signature.

d (*loc*) **personnage à ~s** real-life character disguised under a fictitious name; **roman** *ou* **livre à ~s** roman à clef, *novel in which actual persons appear as fictitious characters;* (*Comm*) **acheter un appartement ~s en main** to buy a flat ready for immediate occupation *ou* with immediate entry; **prix ~s en main** [*voiture*] price on the road, on-the-road price (*Brit*), sticker price (*US*); [*appartement*] price with immediate entry *ou* possession *ou* occupation; (*fig*) **à la ~*: il y a une récompense à la ~** there's a reward at the end of it all *ou* at the end of the day; **je vais les mettre en retenue, avec un devoir à la ~** I'll keep them behind, and give them an exercise into the bargain; **mettre sous ~** (*à l'abri, en prison*) to put under lock and key; **mettre la ~ sous la porte** *ou* **le paillasson** (*faire faillite*) to shut up shop; (*s'enfuir*) to do a bunk‡ (*Brit*), clear out; **prendre la ~ des champs** [*criminel*] to take to the country, clear out; (*gén*) to run away *ou* off; **donner la ~ des champs à qn/un animal** to let sb/an animal go, give sb/an animal his/its freedom; **les ~s du Paradis** the keys to the Kingdom; **les ~s de saint Pierre** St Peter's keys.

2 adj inv key (*épith*). **position-/industrie-~** key position/industry; *voir* **mot**.

3 comp ► **clef anglaise** = **clef à molette** ► **clef de contact** (*Aut*) ignition key ► **clef dynamométrique** torque wrench ► **clef forée** pipe key ► **clef à molette** adjustable wrench *ou* spanner (*Brit*), monkey wrench ► **clef à pipe** box spanner (*Brit*), box wrench (*US*) ► **clef plate** spanner (*Brit*), wrench (*US*) ► **clef de voûte** (*Archit, fig*) keystone ► **clef en croix** wheel brace.

clématite [klematit] nf clematis.

clémence [klemɑ̃s] nf (*douceur*) [*temps*] mildness, clemency (*frm*); (*indulgence*) [*juge*] clemency, leniency.

clément, e [klemɑ̃, ɑ̃t] adj (*doux*) *temps* mild, clement (*frm*); (*indulgent*) *juge etc* lenient. **se montrer ~** to show clemency; *voir* **ciel**.

clémentine [klemɑ̃tin] nf clementine (*Brit*), Algerian tangerine (*US*).

clenche [klɑ̃ʃ] nf latch.

Cléopâtre [kleɔpɑtʀ] nf Cleopatra.

cleptomane [klɛptɔman] nmf = **kleptomane**.

cleptomanie [klɛptɔmani] nf = **kleptomanie**.

clerc [klɛʀ] nm a [*notaire*] clerk; *voir* **pas¹**. b (*Rel*) cleric. c (††: *lettré*) (learned) scholar. **être (grand) ~ en la matière** to be an expert on the subject; **on n'a pas besoin d'être grand ~ pour deviner ce qui s'est passé!** you don't need to be a genius to guess what happened!

clergé [klɛʀʒe] nm clergy.

clérical, e, mpl **-aux** [kleʀikal, o] 1 adj (*Rel*) clerical. 2 nm,f clerical, supporter of the clergy.

cléricalisme [kleʀikalism] nm clericalism.

clic [klik] nm click. **le ~-clac des sabots de cheval** the clip(pety)-clop of the horses' hooves; **le ~-clac de talons sur le parquet** the tap *ou* the clickety-clack of heels on the wooden floor.

cliché [kliʃe] nm (*lieu commun*) cliché; (*Phot*) negative; (*Typ*) plate.

client, cliente [klijɑ̃, klijɑ̃t] nm,f a [*magasin, restaurant*] customer; [*coiffeur*] client, customer; [*avocat*] client; [*hôtel*] guest, patron; [*médecin*] patient; [*taxi*] fare. **être ~ d'un magasin** to patronize a shop, be a regular customer at a shop; **le boucher me sert bien parce que je suis (une) ~e** the butcher gives me good service as I'm a regular customer (of his) *ou* as I'm one of his regulars; (*Écon*) **la France est un gros ~ de l'Allemagne** France is a large trading customer of Germany; (*fig*) **je ne suis pas ~*** it's not my thing* *ou* my cup of tea*.

b (* *péj: individu*) bloke* (*Brit*), guy*. **c'est un drôle de ~** he's an odd customer *ou* bloke*; **pour le titre de champion du monde, X est un ~ sérieux** X is a hot contender for *ou* X is making a strong bid for the world championship.

c (*Antiq: protégé*) client.

clientèle [klijɑ̃tɛl] nf a (*ensemble des clients*) [*restaurant, hôtel, coiffeur*] clientèle; [*magasin*] customers, clientèle; [*avocat, médecin*] practice; [*taxi*] fares. **le boucher a une nombreuse ~** the butcher has a large clientèle *ou* has many customers; (*Pol, fig*) **le candidat a conservé sa ~ électorale au 2e tour** the candidate held on to his voters at the second round; **la ~ d'un parti politique** the supporters of a political party.

b (*fait d'être client*) custom, business. **accorder sa ~ à qn** to give sb one's custom *ou* business, patronize sb; **retirer sa ~ à qn** to withdraw one's custom from sb, take one's business away from sb.

c (*Antiq: protégés*) clients.

clientélisme [klijɑ̃telism] nm (*péj*) vote-catching. **c'est du ~** it's just a vote-catching gimmick.

clignement [kliɲ(ə)mɑ̃] nm blinking (*NonC*). **cela l'obligeait à des ~s d'yeux continuels** it made him blink continually; **un ~ d'œil** a wink.

cligner [kliɲe] [1] vt, vt indir: **~ les** *ou* **des yeux** (*clignoter*) to blink; (*fermer à moitié*) to screw up one's eyes; **~ de l'œil** to wink (*en direction de* at).

clignotant, e [kliɲɔtɑ̃, ɑ̃t] 1 adj *lumière* (*vacillant*) flickering; (*intermittent, pour signal*) flashing, winking. 2 nm (*Aut*) indicator; (*Écon fig: indice de danger*) warning light (*fig*). (*Aut*) **mettre son ~ (pour tourner)** to indicate (that one is about to turn); (*fig*) **tous les ~s sont allumés** all the warning signs *ou* danger signals are flashing.

clignotement [kliɲɔtmɑ̃] nm (*voir* **clignoter**) blinking; twinkling; flickering; flashing, winking. **les ~s de la lampe** the flickering of the lamplight.

clignoter [kliɲɔte] [1] vi [*yeux*] to blink; [*étoile*] to twinkle; [*lumière*] (*vaciller*) to flicker; (*vu de loin*) to twinkle; (*pour signal*) to flash, wink. **~ des yeux** to blink.

climat [klima] nm (*lit, fig*) climate; (*littér: contrée*) clime (*littér*).

climatique [klimatik] adj climatic; *voir* **station**.

climatisation [klimatizasjɔ̃] nf air conditioning.

climatiser [klimatize] [1] vt *pièce, atmosphère* to air-condition; (*Tech*) *appareil* to adapt for use in severe conditions.

climatiseur [klimatizœʀ] nm air conditioner.

climatologie [klimatɔlɔʒi] nf climatology.

climatologique [klimatɔlɔʒik] adj climatological.

clin [klɛ̃] nm: **~ d'œil** (pl **~s d'œil** *ou* **d'yeux**) (*lit*) wink; (*fig: dans un roman/film*) allusion, veiled reference; (*fig*) **c'est un ~ d'œil aux Marx Brothers** it's a nod in the direction of the Marx Brothers; **c'est un ~ d'œil au lecteur** it is a veiled message to the reader; **faire un ~ d'œil** (*lit*) to wink (*à* at); (*fig*) to make a veiled reference (*à* to); **en un ~ d'œil** in a flash, in the twinkling of an eye.

clinfoc [klɛ̃fɔk] nm flying jib.

clinicien, -ienne [klinisjɛ̃, jɛn] nm,f clinician.

clinique [klinik] 1 adj clinical; *voir* **mort**. 2 nf a (*établissement*) nursing home, private hospital, private clinic; (*section d'hôpital*) clinic.

~ **d'accouchement** maternity home; *voir* **chef¹**. **b** (*enseignement*) clinic.

cliniquement [klinikmɑ̃] **adv** clinically.

clinquant, e [klɛ̃kɑ̃, ɑ̃t] **1** **adj** *bijoux, décor, langage* flashy. **2** **nm** (*lamelles brillantes*) tinsel; (*faux bijoux*) imitation *ou* tawdry jewellery; (*fig*) *[opéra, style]* flashiness.

clip [klip] **nm** **a** (*broche*) brooch. **b** (*boucle d'oreilles*) clip-on. **b** **(vidéo)** ~ (promo) video.

clique [klik] **nf** **a** (*péj: bande*) clique, set. **b** (*Mil: orchestre*) band (of bugles and drums). **c** **prendre ses ~s et ses claques (et s'en aller)** to pack up (and go), pack one's bags (and leave).

cliquer [klike] [1] **vi** to click.

cliquet [klikɛ] **nm** pawl.

cliqueter [klik(ə)te] [4] **vi** *[monnaie]* to jingle, clink, chink; *[dés]* to rattle; *[vaisselle]* to clatter; *[verres]* to clink, chink; *[chaînes]* to clank; *[ferraille]* to jangle; *[mécanisme]* to go clickety-clack; *[armes]* to clash; (*Aut*) *[moteur]* to pink, knock. **j'entends quelque chose qui cliquette** I (can) hear something clinking.

cliquetis [klik(ə)ti] **nm** *[clefs]* jingle (*NonC*), clink (*NonC*), jingling (*NonC*), clinking (*NonC*); *[vaisselle]* clatter (*NonC*); *[verres]* clink (*NonC*), clinking (*NonC*); *[chaînes]* clank (*NonC*), clanking (*NonC*); *[ferraille]* jangle (*NonC*), jangling (*NonC*); *[mécanisme]* clickety-clack (*NonC*); *[armes]* clash (*NonC*); (*Aut*) *[moteur]* pinking *ou* knocking sound, pinking (*NonC*); *[machine à écrire]* rattle (*NonC*), clicking (*NonC*). **on entendait un ~ *ou* des ~ de vaisselle** we could hear the clatter of dishes; **des ~ se firent entendre** clinking noises could be heard; **un ~ de mots** a jingle of words.

cliquettement [klikɛtmɑ̃] **nm** = **cliquetis**.

clisse [klis] **nf** **a** *[fromage]* wicker tray. **b** *[bouteille]* wicker covering.

clisser [klise] [1] **vt** *bouteille* to cover with wicker(work).

clitoridien, -ienne [klitɔʀidjɛ̃, jɛn] **adj** clitoral.

clitoris [klitɔʀis] **nm** clitoris.

clivage [klivaʒ] **nm** (*Géol: fissure*) cleavage; (*Minér*) (*action*) cleaving; (*résultat*) cleavage; (*fig*) *[groupes]* cleavage, split, division; *[idées]* distinction, split (*de* in).

cliver **vt**, **se cliver** **vpr** [klive] [1] (*Minér*) to cleave.

cloaque [klɔak] **nm** (*lit, fig: lieu de corruption*) cesspool, cesspit; (*Zool*) cloaca; (*fig: endroit sale*) pigsty (*Brit*), dump*, tip* (*Brit*).

clochard, e [klɔʃaʀ, aʀd] **nm,f** down-and-out, tramp.

clochardiser [klɔʃaʀdize] [1] **1** **vt** *personne* to turn into a down-and-out *ou* a tramp. **2** **se clochardiser** **vpr** *[personne]* to turn into a down-and-out *ou* a tramp. **la ville se clochardise** more and more down-and-outs *ou* tramps are appearing in the town.

cloche [klɔʃ] **1** **nf** **a** *[église]* bell. **en forme de ~** bell-shaped; **courbe en ~** bell-shaped curve; *voir* **son²**. **b** (*couvercle*) *[plat]* dishcover, lid; *[plantes, légumes]* cloche. **c** (*) (*imbécile*) clot* (*Brit*), idiot; (*clochard*) tramp, down-and-out. **la ~** (*les clochards*) (the) down-and-outs; (*l'existence de clochard*) a tramp's life. **d** (*Chim*) bell jar. **2** **adj** **a** (*évasé*) *jupe* bell-shaped. **chapeau ~** cloche hat. **b** (*: *idiot*) idiotic, silly. **qu'il est ~ ce type!** what a (silly) clot* (*Brit*) *ou* idiot he is! **3** **comp** ►**cloche à fromage** cheese cover ►**cloche à plongeur** diving bell.

cloche-pied [klɔʃpje] **adv**: **à ~** hopping; **il partit (en sautant) à ~** he hopped away *ou* off.

clocher¹ [klɔʃe] **nm** **a** (*Archit*) (*en pointe*) steeple; (*quadrangulaire*) church tower. **b** (*fig: paroisse*) **revoir son ~** to see one's home town *ou* native heath (*Brit*) again; **de ~** *mentalité* parochial, small-town (*épith*); *rivalités* local, parochial; *voir* **esprit**.

clocher² [klɔʃe] [1] **vi** **a** (*: *être défectueux*) *[raisonnement]* to be cock-eyed*. **qu'est-ce qui cloche donc?** what's up (with you)?*; **pourvu que rien ne cloche** provided nothing goes wrong *ou* there are no hitches; **il y a quelque chose qui cloche (dans ce qu'il dit)** there's something which doesn't quite fit *ou* something not quite right in what he says; **il y a quelque chose qui cloche dans le moteur** there's something not quite right *ou* there's something up* with the engine. **b** (*rare: boiter*) to limp.

clocheton [klɔʃtɔ̃] **nm** (*Archit*) pinnacle.

clochette [klɔʃɛt] **nf** (small) bell; (*Bot*) (*partie de fleur*) bell; (*fleur*) bellflower.

clodo* [klodo] **nm** tramp, bum* (*US*).

cloison [klwazɔ̃] **nf** **a** (*Constr*) partition (wall). **b** (*Anat, Bot*) septum, partition. **c** (*Naut*) bulkhead. **~ étanche** (*lit*) watertight compartment; (*fig*) impenetrable barrier. **d** (*fig*) barrier. **les ~s entre les différentes classes sociales** the barriers between the different social classes.

cloisonnage [klwazɔnaʒ] **nm** partitioning.

cloisonné, e [klwazɔne] (**ptp de cloisonner**) **adj**: **être ~** *[sciences, services administratifs]* to be (highly) compartmentalized, be cut off from one another; **se sentir ~** to feel shut *ou* cut off; **nous vivons dans un monde ~** we live in a compartmentalized world.

cloisonnement [klwazɔnmɑ̃] **nm** (*voir* **cloisonner**: *action, résultat*) dividing up; partitioning (off); compartmentalization.

cloisonner [klwazɔne] [1] **vt** *maison* to divide up, partition; *tiroir* to divide up; (*fig: compartimenter*) *activités, secteurs* to compartmentalize.

cloître [klwatʀ] **nm** cloister.

cloîtrer [klwatʀe] [1] **1** **vt** (*enfermer*) to shut away (*dans* in); (*Rel*) to cloister. **~ une jeune fille** (*lit*) to put a girl in a convent; (*fig*) to keep a girl shut away (from the rest of society); **couvent/religieux cloîtré** enclosed order/monk. **2** **se cloîtrer** **vpr** (*s'enfermer*) to shut o.s. up *ou* away, cloister o.s. (*dans* in); (*Rel*) to enter a convent *ou* monastery. **il est resté cloîtré dans sa chambre pendant 2 jours** he stayed shut up *ou* away in his room for 2 days; **ils vivent cloîtrés chez eux sans jamais voir personne** they cut themselves off from the world *ou* they live cloistered lives and never see anyone.

clonage [klonaʒ] **nm** cloning.

clone [klon] **nm** clone.

cloner [klone] [1] **vt** to clone.

clope* [klɔp] **nm** *ou* **f** fag* (*Brit*), cig*, smoke*.

clopin-clopant [klɔpɛ̃klɔpɑ̃] **adv** **a** (*en boitillant*) **marcher ~** to hobble along; **il vint vers nous ~** he hobbled towards us; **sortir/entrer ~** to hobble out/in. **b** (*fig*) **les affaires allaient ~** business was struggling along *ou* was just ticking over (*Brit*); **comment ça va? – ~** how are things? – so-so*.

clopiner [klɔpine] [1] **vi** (*boitiller*) to hobble *ou* limp along. **~ vers** to hobble *ou* limp to(wards).

clopinettes* [klɔpinɛt] **nfpl**: **des ~** peanuts*; **travailler pour des ~** to work for peanuts*.

cloporte [klɔpɔʀt] **nm** (*Zool*) woodlouse; (*fig péj*) creep*.

cloque [klɔk] **nf** *[peau, peinture]* blister; (*Bot*) peach leaf curl *ou* blister. **être en ~**‡ to be in the club‡ (*Brit*) *ou* knocked up (*US*); **il l'a mise en ~**‡ he got her in the club‡ (*Brit*), he knocked her up‡.

cloqué, e [klɔke] (**ptp de cloquer**) **1** **adj**: **étoffe ~e** seersucker (*NonC*). **2** **nm** (*Tex*) seersucker.

cloquer [klɔke] [1] **1** **vi** *[peau, peinture]* to blister. **2** **vt** *étoffe* to crinkle.

clore [klɔʀ] [45] **vt** **a** (*clôturer*) *liste, débat* to close; *livre, discours* to end, conclude; (*Fin*) *compte* to close. **la séance est close** the meeting is closed *ou* finished; **l'incident est clos** the matter is closed; **le débat s'est clos sur cette remarque** the discussion ended *ou* closed with that remark.

b (*être la fin de*) *spectacle, discours* to end, conclude; *livre* to end. **une description clôt le chapitre** the chapter closes *ou* ends *ou* concludes with a description.

c († *ou littér: conclure*) *accord, marché* to conclude.

d (*littér: entourer*) *terrain, ville* to enclose (*de* with).

e (*littér: fermer*) *porte, volets* to close, shut; *lettre* to seal; *chemin, passage* to close off, seal off. (*fig*) **~ le bec*** *ou* **la bouche à qn** to shut sb up*, make sb be quiet.

clos, close [klo, kloz] (**ptp de clore**) **1** **adj** *système, ensemble* closed; *espace* enclosed. **les yeux ~ *ou* les paupières ~es, il ...** with his eyes closed *ou* shut, he ...; *voir* **huis, maison**. **2** **nm** (*pré*) (enclosed) field; (*vignoble*) vineyard. **un ~ de pommiers** an apple orchard; (*Jur*) **donner *ou* fournir le ~ et le couvert** to provide food and shelter.

Clotilde [klɔtild] **nf** Clotilda.

clôture [klotyʀ] **nf** **a** (*enceinte*) (*en planches*) fence, paling; (*en fil de fer*) (wire) fence; (*haies, arbustes etc*) hedge; (*en ciment*) wall. **mur/grille de ~** outer *ou* surrounding wall/railing; *voir* **bris**.

b (*fermeture*) *[débat, liste, compte]* closing, closure; *[bureaux, magasins]* closing. (*Ciné, Théât*) **~ annuelle** annual closure; **il faut y aller avant la ~** (*du festival*) we must go before it ends *ou* is over; (*d'une pièce*) we must go before it closes *ou* ends; (*du magasin*) we must go before it closes *ou* shuts; **séance/date de ~** closing session/date; (*Bourse*) **cours de ~** closing price; **combien valait le dollar en ~?** what did the dollar close at?; **débat de ~** adjournment debate.

c *[monastère]* enclosure.

clôturer [klotyʀe] [1] **1** **vt** **a** *jardin, champ* to enclose, fence. **b** *débats, liste, compte* to close; *inscriptions* to close (the list of). **2** **vi** (*Bourse*) to close. **la séance a clôturé en baisse** prices were down at the close of dealing; **le dollar a clôturé à 5.95F** the dollar closed at 5.95 francs.

clou [klu] **1** **nm** **a** (*gén*) nail; (*décoratif*) stud. **fixe-le avec un ~** nail it up (*ou* down *ou* on); **pendre son chapeau à un ~** to hang one's hat on a nail.

b *[chaussée]* stud. **traverser aux *ou* dans les ~s, prendre les ~s (pour traverser)** to cross at the pedestrian *ou* zebra (*Brit*) crossing *ou* at the crosswalk (*US*).

c (*Méd*) boil.

d (*attraction principale*) *[spectacle]* star attraction *ou* turn. **le ~ de la soirée** the highlight *ou* the star turn of the evening.

e (*: *mont-de-piété*) pawnshop. **mettre sa montre au ~** to pawn one's watch, put one's watch in hock*.

f (*: *vieil instrument*) ancient machine *ou* implement. **(vieux) ~** (*voiture*) old banger‡ (*Brit*) *ou* crock* (*Brit*) *ou* jalopy*; (*vélo*) old boneshaker* (*Brit*).

g (*arg Mil: prison*) clink (*arg*), cooler (*arg*). **mettre qn au ~** to put sb in (the) clink *ou* in the cooler.

h (*loc*) **des ~s!**‡ no way!*, nothing doing!*; **il lui a tout expliqué mais des ~s!*** he explained everthing to him but he was just wasting his breath!; **je l'ai fait pour des ~s*** I did it all for nothing, I was just wasting my time; **j'y suis allé pour des ~s*** it was a wild-goose chase; (*Prov*) **un ~ chasse l'autre** one man goes and another steps in *ou* another takes his place; *voir* **valoir**.

2 *comp* ►**clou à crochet** hook ►**clou de girofle** (*Culin*) clove ►**clou à souliers** tack ►**clou de tapissier** (upholstery) tack ►**clou sans tête** brad ►**clou en U** staple.

clouer [klue] [1] *vt* a *planches, couvercle, caisse* to nail down; *tapis* to tack *ou* nail down; *tapisserie* to nail up. **il l'a cloué au sol d'un coup d'épée** he pinned him to the ground with a thrust of his sword.

b (*fig: immobiliser*) *ennemi, armée* to pin down. *[étonnement, peur]* **~ qn sur place** to nail *ou* root *ou* glue sb to the spot; *[maladie]* **~ qn au lit** to keep sb stuck in bed* *ou* confined to bed; **~ au sol** *personne* to pin down (*to the ground*); *avion* to ground; **je le maintenais cloué au sol** I kept him pinned to the ground; (*Échecs*) **~ une pièce** to pin a piece; **être** *ou* **rester cloué de stupeur** to be glued *ou* rooted to the spot with amazement; **~ le bec à qn*** to shut sb up*.

clouté, e [klute] *adj* *ceinture, porte etc* studded; *souliers* hobnailed; *voir* **passage**.

clouterie [klutʀi] *nf* nail factory.

clovisse [klɔvis] *nf* clam.

clown [klun] *nm* clown. **faire le ~** to clown (about), play the fool; **c'est un vrai ~** he's a real comic; **~ blanc** whiteface clown.

clownerie [klunʀi] *nf* clowning (*NonC*), silly trick. **faire des ~s** to clown (about), play the fool; **arrête tes ~s** stop your (silly) antics.

clownesque [klunɛsk] *adj* *comportement* clownish; *situation* farcical.

club [klœb] 1 *nm* (*société, crosse de golf*) club. **~ d'investissement** investment club; **~ de vacances** holiday village. 2 *adj* **sandwich ~** ham salad sandwich, ≃ club sandwich; **cravate ~** (diagonally) striped tie; *voir* **fauteuil**.

cluse [klyz] *nf* (*Géog*) transverse valley (in the Jura), cluse (*SPÉC*).

Clytemnestre [klitɛmnɛstʀ] *nf* Clytemnestra.

CM [seɛm] *nm* (*abrév de* **cours moyen**) *voir* **cours**.

cm (*abrév de* **centimètre**) cm.

CNAM [knam] *nm* (*abrév de* **Conservatoire national des arts et métiers**) *voir* **conservatoire**.

CNC [seɛnse] *nm* a (*abrév de* **Centre national de cinématographie**) ≃ *BFI* (*Brit*); *voir* **centre**. b (*abrév de* **Comité national de la consommation**) ≃ National Consumer Council (*Brit*), ≃ CA (*Brit*), ≃ CPSC (*US*).

CNCL [seɛnseɛl] *nf* (*abrév de* **Commission nationale de la communication et des libertés**) ≃ IBA (*Brit*), ≃ FCC (*US*).

CNDP [seɛndepe] *nm* (*abrév de* **Centre national de documentation pédagogique**) *voir* **centre**.

CNED [knɛd] *nm* (*abrév de* **Centre national d'enseignement à distance**) *voir* **centre**.

CNIT [knit] *nm* (*abrév de* **Centre national des industries et des techniques**) *voir* **centre**.

CNPF [seɛnpeɛf] *nm* (*abrév de* **Conseil national du patronat français**) ≃ CBI (*Brit*); *voir* **conseil**.

CNRS [seɛnɛʀɛs] *nm* (*abrév de* **Centre national de la recherche scientifique**) ≃ SERC (*Brit*), ≃ NSF (*US*).

CNTE [seɛnteə] (*abrév de* **Centre national de télé-enseignement**) *voir* **centre**.

CO (*abrév de* **conseiller d'orientation**) *voir* **conseiller**.

coaccusé, e [koakyze] *nm,f* codefendant, co-accused.

coacquéreur [koakeʀœʀ] *nm* joint purchaser.

coadjuteur [koadʒytœʀ] *nm* coadjutor.

coadjutrice [koadʒytʀis] *nf* coadjutress.

coadministrateur, -trice [koadministʀatœʀ, tʀis] *nm,f* (*Comm*) codirector; (*Jur*) co-trustee.

coagulable [kɔagylabl] *adj* which can coagulate.

coagulant, e [kɔagylɑ̃, ɑ̃t] 1 *adj* coagulative. 2 *nm* coagulant.

coagulateur, -trice [kɔagylatœʀ, tʀis] *adj* coagulative.

coagulation [kɔagylasjɔ̃] *nf* coagulation.

coaguler *vti*, **se coaguler** *vpr* [kɔagyle] [1] to coagulate; *[sang]* to coagulate (*SPÉC*), clot, congeal; *[lait]* to curdle.

coalisé, e [kɔalize] (*ptp de* **coaliser**) *adj* (*allié*) *pays* allied; (*conjoint*) *efforts, sentiments* united. **les ~s** the members of the coalition.

coaliser [kɔalize] [1] 1 *vt* to unite (in a coalition). 2 **se coaliser** *vpr* (*se liguer*) (*gén*) to unite; *[pays]* to form a coalition, unite (in a coalition). **deux des commerçants se sont coalisés contre un troisième** two of the shopkeepers joined forces *ou* united against a third; (*fig*) **tout se coalise contre moi!** everything seems to be stacked against me!, everything is conspiring against me!

coalition [kɔalisjɔ̃] *nf* coalition. (*Pol*) **ministère de ~** coalition government.

coaltar [koltaʀ] *nm* (*lit*) coal tar. (*fig*) **être dans le ~⁑** to be in a daze *ou* stupor.

coassement [kɔasmɑ̃] *nm* croaking (*NonC*).

coasser [kɔase] [1] *vi* to croak.

coassocié, e [koasɔsje] *nm,f* copartner.

coassurance [koasyʀɑ̃s] *nf* mutual assurance.

coauteur [kootœʀ] *nm* a (*Littérat*) (*homme*) co-author, joint author; (*femme*) co-authoress, joint authoress. b (*Jur*) accomplice.

coaxial, e, *mpl* **-aux** [koaksjal, jo] *adj* coaxial.

COB [kɔb] *nf* (*abrév de* **Commission des opérations de Bourse**) (*French stock exchange regulatory body*) ≃ SIB (*Brit*), ≃ SEC (*US*).

cobalt [kɔbalt] *nm* cobalt.

cobaye [kɔbaj] *nm* (*lit, fig*) guinea-pig. **servir de ~ à** to act as *ou* be used as a guinea-pig for.

cobelligérant, e [kobeliʒeʀɑ̃, ɑ̃t] *adj* cobelligerent. **les ~s** the cobelligerent nations *ou* states *etc*.

Cobol [kɔbɔl] *nm* (*Ordin*) COBOL.

cobra [kɔbʀa] *nm* cobra.

coca [kɔka] 1 *nm* a (*) (*abrév de* **Coca-Cola** ®) Coke ®. b (*aussi nf*) (*Bot: arbrisseau*) coca. 2 *nf* (*substance*) coca extract.

cocagne [kɔkaɲ] *nf voir* **mât, pays**[1].

cocaïne [kɔkain] *nf* cocaine.

cocaïnomane [kɔkainɔman] *nmf* cocaine addict.

cocard* [kɔkaʀ] *nm* shiner* (*Brit*), black eye.

cocarde [kɔkaʀd] *nf* (*en tissu*) rosette; (*Hist: sur la coiffure*) cockade; *[avion]* roundel. (*sur voiture officielle etc*) **~ (tricolore)** ≃ official sticker; (*fig*) **changer de ~** to change sides.

cocardier, -ière [kɔkaʀdje, jɛʀ] 1 *adj* jingoist(ic), chauvinistic. 2 *nm,f* jingo(ist), chauvinist.

cocasse [kɔkas] *adj* comical, funny.

cocasserie [kɔkasʀi] *nf* comicalness, funniness; (*histoire*) comical *ou* funny story. **c'était d'une ~!** it was so funny! *ou* comical!

coccinelle [kɔksinɛl] *nf* ladybird.

coccyx [kɔksis] *nm* coccyx.

coche [kɔʃ] *nm* (*diligence*) (stage)coach. (*Hist*) **~ d'eau** horse-drawn barge; (*fig*) **louper** *ou* **manquer** *ou* **rater le ~** to miss the boat* (*fig*) *ou* one's chance; *voir* **mouche**.

cochenille [kɔʃnij] *nf* cochineal.

cocher[1] [kɔʃe] [1] *vt* (*au crayon*) to tick (off) (*Brit*), check off; (*d'une entaille*) to notch.

cocher[2] [kɔʃe] *nm* coachman, coach driver; *[fiacre]* cabman, cabby*.

cochère [kɔʃɛʀ] *adj f voir* **porte**.

Cochinchine [kɔʃɛ̃ʃin] *nf* Cochin China.

cochon[1] [kɔʃɔ̃] *nm* a (*animal*) pig; (*: *viande*) pork (*NonC*). **~ d'Inde** guinea-pig; **~ de lait** (*gén*) piglet; (*Culin*) sucking-pig; *voir* **manger**. b (*loc*) (*hum*) **(et) ~ qui s'en dédit*** let's shake (hands) on it, cross my heart (and hope to die)*; **un ~ n'y retrouverait pas ses petits** it's like a pigsty in there, it's a real mess in there; **tout homme a dans son cœur un ~ qui sommeille** there's a bit of the animal in every man; *voir* **confiture, copain**.

cochon[2]**, -onne** [kɔʃɔ̃, ɔn] 1 *adj* a (⁑: *obscène*) *chanson, histoire* dirty, blue, smutty; *personne* dirty-minded. b **c'est pas ~!⁑** (*c'est bon*) it's not at all bad; (*il n'y en a pas beaucoup*) there's precious little there. 2 *nm,f* (⁑ *péj: personne*) **c'est un ~!** (*sale, vicieux*) he's a dirty pig⁑ *ou* beast⁑; (*salaud*) he's a bastard*⁑ *ou* swine⁑; **tu es une vraie petite ~ne, va te laver!** you're a dirty little pig⁑, go and get washed!; **ce ~ de voisin/de commerçant** that swine⁑ of a neighbour/shopkeeper; **quel ~ de temps!** *ou* **temps de ~!** what lousy *ou* filthy weather!*; (*: *terme amical*) **eh bien, mon ~, tu l'as échappé belle!** you had a narrow escape, you old devil!*

cochonceté* [kɔʃɔ̃ste] *nf*: **~s** (*obscénités*) filth (*NonC*), smut (*NonC*); (*plaisanteries*) smutty *ou* dirty jokes; (*saletés*) **faire des ~s** to make a mess; **arrête de dire des ~s** stop talking dirty*.

cochonnaille* [kɔʃɔnaj] *nf* (*charcuterie*) pork. **assiette de ~** selection of cold pork *ou* ham.

cochonner* [kɔʃɔne] [1] *vt* (*mal faire*) *travail* to botch (up), bungle; (*salir*) *vêtements* to mess up*, make filthy.

cochonnerie* [kɔʃɔnʀi] *nf* (*nourriture*) disgusting *ou* foul food, pigswill* (*NonC*); (*marchandise*) rubbish (*NonC*), trash (*NonC*); (*plaisanterie*) smutty *ou* dirty joke; (*tour*) dirty *ou* low trick; (*saleté*) filth (*NonC*), filthiness (*NonC*). **faire une ~ à qn** to play a dirty trick on sb; **ne fais pas de ~s dans la cuisine, elle est toute propre** don't make a mess in the kitchen, it's clean.

cochonnet [kɔʃɔnɛ] *nm* (*Zool*) piglet; (*Boules*) jack.

cocker [kɔkɛʀ] *nm* cocker spaniel.

cockpit [kɔkpit] *nm* cockpit.

cocktail [kɔktɛl] *nm* (*réunion*) cocktail party; (*boisson*) cocktail; (*fig*) mixture, potpourri. **~ Molotov** Molotov cocktail, petrol bomb.

coco[1] [koko] *nm* a (*langage enfantin: œuf*) eggie (*langage enfantin*). b (*terme d'affection*) pet, darling, poppet* (*Brit*). **oui, mon ~** yes, darling. c (⁑ *péj: type*) bloke* (*Brit*), guy*. **un drôle de ~** an odd bloke* (*Brit*) *ou* guy*, an oddbod* (*Brit*) *ou* oddball* (*US*). d (*péj *: communiste*) commie*. e (⁑: *estomac*) **n'avoir rien dans le ~** to have an empty belly⁑. f (*poudre de réglisse*) liquorice powder; (*boisson*) liquorice water. g (†: *noix*) coconut. **beurre/lait de ~** coconut butter/milk; *voir* **noix**. h (*haricot*) *small white haricot bean*.

coco[2] [koko] *nf* (*arg Drogue: cocaïne*) snow (*arg*), coke (*arg*).

cocon [kɔkɔ̃] *nm* (*lit, fig*) cocoon.

cocorico [kɔkɔʀiko] 1 *nm* *[coq]* cock-a-doodle-do; (*fig*) cheer of victory. **pousser un ~, faire ~** *[coq]* to crow; (*fig*) to crow (over one's victory); **ils ont fait ~ un peu trop tôt** their victory celebrations were premature *ou* came too soon, they started celebrating a bit too soon.

2 excl *[coq]* cock-a-doodle-do; (*fig*) three cheers (for France), hooray (for France).
cocoter‡ [kɔkɔte] 1 vi (*sentir mauvais*) to pong‡ (*Brit*), stink.
cocotier [kɔkɔtje] nm coconut palm *ou* tree; *voir* **secouer**.
cocotte [kɔkɔt] 1 nf a (*langage enfantin: poule*) hen, cluck-cluck (*langage enfantin*). b (* *péj: femme*) tart*. c (*à un cheval*) **allez ~!, hue ~!** gee up! d (*terme d'affection*) **ma ~*** pet, sweetie*. e (*marmite*) casserole. **faire un poulet à la ~** to casserole a chicken; **poulet/veau (à la) ~** casserole of chicken/veal; *voir* **œuf**. f (‡: *parfum*) cheap scent. **ça sent** *ou* **pue la ~** it smells like a scent factory. 2 comp ►**Cocotte Minute** ® pressure cooker ►**cocotte en papier** paper shape.
cocotter* [kɔkɔte] = **cocoter**.
cocu, e‡ [kɔky] 1 adj cuckold†. **elle l'a fait ~** she was unfaithful to him, she cuckolded him†. 2 nm,f cuckold†; *voir* **veine**.
cocuage‡ [kɔkɥaʒ] nm cuckoldry.
cocufier‡ [kɔkyfje] 7 vt to cuckold†, be unfaithful to.
coda [kɔda] nf (*Mus*) coda.
codage [kɔdaʒ] nm coding, encoding.
code [kɔd] 1 nm a (*Jur*) code. **le ~ civil** the civil code, ≃ common law; **~ pénal** penal code; **le ~ maritime/de commerce** maritime/commercial law; (*de procédure*) **~ du travail** labour regulations *ou* laws; (*Aut*) **~ de la route** highway code; (*Aut*) **il a eu le ~, mais pas la conduite** he passed on the highway code but not on the driving.
b (*fig: règles*) code. **~ de la politesse/de l'honneur** code of politeness/honour.
c *[message]* (*gén, Sci*) code. **~ (secret)** (secret) code; **écrire qch en ~** to write sth in code; **mettre qch en ~** to code *ou* encode sth, put sth in code.
d (*Aut*) **(phares) ~** dipped (head)lights (*Brit*), low beams (*US*); **mettre ses ~s, se mettre en ~** to dip one's (head)lights (*Brit*), put on the low beams (*US*); **rouler en ~** to drive on dipped (head)lights (*Brit*) *ou* low beams (*US*).
2 comp ►**code ASCII** ASCII code ►**code-barres** *ou* **code à barres** bar code ►**code génétique** genetic code ►**code postal** postcode (*Brit*), zip code (*US*).
codébiteur, -trice [kodebitœʀ, tʀis] nm,f joint debtor.
codéine [kɔdein] nf codeine.
codemandeur, -eresse [kod(ə)mɑ̃dœʀ, dʀɛs] nm,f joint plaintiff.
coder [kɔde] 1 vt to code.
codétenteur, -trice [kodetɑ̃tœʀ, tʀis] nm,f (*Jur, Sport*) joint holder.
codétenu, e [kodet(ə)ny] nm,f prisoner, inmate. **avec ses ~s** with his fellow prisoners *ou* inmates.
CODEVI [kodevi] nm (abrév de **compte pour le développement industriel**) *voir* **compte**.
codex [kɔdɛks] nm: **C~** (officially approved) pharmacopoeia.
codicillaire [kɔdisilɛʀ] adj (*Jur*) codicillary.
codicille [kɔdisil] nm (*Jur*) codicil.
codificateur, -trice [kɔdifikatœʀ, tʀis] 1 adj *tendance, esprit* codifying. 2 nm,f codifier.
codification [kɔdifikasjɔ̃] nf codification.
codifier [kɔdifje] 7 vt (*Jur, systématiser*) to codify.
codirecteur, -trice [kodiʀɛktœʀ, tʀis] nm,f co-director, joint manager (*ou* manageress).
coéditer [koedite] 1 vt to co-publish.
coéditeur, -trice [koeditœʀ, tʀis] nm,f co-publisher.
coédition [koedisjɔ̃] nf co-edition.
coefficient [kɔefisjɑ̃] nm (*Math, Phys*) coefficient. **~ d'erreur** margin of error; **~ de sécurité** safety margin; **~ d'élasticité** modulus of elasticity; **~ de dilatation** coefficient of expansion; **~ d'occupation des sols** planning density; **~ de marée** tidal range; (*Aut*) **~ de pénétration dans l'air** drag coefficient *ou* factor; (*Scol*) **cette matière est affectée d'un ~ trois** marks in this subject are weighted by a factor of three.
cœlacanthe [selakɑ̃t] nm cœlacanth.
cœlialgie [seljalʒi] nf coeliac disease.
cœlioscopie [seljɔskɔpi] nf coelioscopy.
cœnesthésie [senɛstezi] nf = **cénesthésie**.
coéquipier, -ière [koekipje, jɛʀ] nm,f team mate.
coercibilité [kɔɛʀsibilite] nf coercibility.
coercible [kɔɛʀsibl] adj coercible.
coercitif, -ive [kɔɛʀsitif, iv] adj coercive.
coercition [kɔɛʀsisjɔ̃] nf coercion.
cœur [kœʀ] nm a (*Anat*) heart. (*lit, hum*) **c'est une chance que j'ai le ~ solide** it's a good thing I haven't got a weak heart; **il faut avoir le ~ bien accroché pour risquer ainsi sa vie** you need guts* *ou* a strong stomach to risk your life like that; **serrer** *ou* **presser qn contre** *ou* **sur son ~** to hold *ou* clasp *ou* press sb to one's heart *ou* breast; **opération à ~ ouvert** open-heart operation; **on l'a opéré à ~ ouvert** he had an open-heart operation; **maladie de ~** heart complaint *ou* trouble; **avoir le ~ malade** to have a weak heart *ou* a heart condition; *voir* **battement, greffe**[1].
b (*fig: estomac*) **avoir mal au ~** to feel sick; **cela me soulève le ~** it nauseates me, it makes me (feel) sick; **ça vous fait mal au ~ de penser que** it is sickening to think that; **une odeur/un spectacle qui soulève le ~** a nauseating *ou* sickening smell/sight; **j'avais le ~ sur les lèvres** I thought I was going to be sick (any minute); *voir* **haut**.
c (*siège des sentiments, de l'amour*) heart. (*forme d'adresse*) **mon ~** sweetheart; **avoir un** *ou* **le ~ sensible** to be sensitive *ou* tender-hearted; **un dur au ~ tendre** someone whose bark is worse than his bite; **elle lui a donné son ~** she has lost her heart to him *ou* given him her heart; **mon ~ se serre/se brise** *ou* **se fend à cette pensée** my heart sinks/breaks at the thought; **chagrin qui brise le ~** heartbreaking grief *ou* sorrow; **un spectacle à vous fendre le ~** a heartrending *ou* heart-breaking sight; **avoir le ~ gros** *ou* **serré** to have a heavy heart; **il avait la rage au ~** he was inwardly seething with anger; **cela m'a réchauffé le ~ de les voir** it did my heart good *ou* it was heartwarming to see them; **ce geste lui est allé (droit) au ~** he was (deeply) moved *ou* touched by this gesture, this gesture went straight to his heart; **avoir un coup de ~ pour qch** to fall in love with sth; **nos coups de ~ parmi les livres du mois** our favourites among this month's new books; *voir* **affaire, courrier**.
d (*bonté, générosité*) **avoir bon ~** to be kind-hearted; **à votre bon ~!** thank you kindly!; **avoir le ~ sur la main** to be open-handed; **manquer de ~** to be unfeeling *ou* heartless; **il a du ~** he is a good-hearted man, his heart is in the right place; **c'est un (homme) sans ~, il n'a pas de ~** he is a heartless man; **il a** *ou* **c'est un ~ de pierre/d'or** he has a heart of stone/gold; **un homme/une femme de ~** a noble-hearted man/woman.
e (*humeur*) **avoir le ~ gai** *ou* **joyeux/léger/triste** to feel happy/light-hearted/sad *ou* sad at heart; **je n'ai pas le ~ à rire/à sortir** I don't feel like laughing/going out, I'm not in the mood for laughing/going out; **il n'a plus le ~ à rien** his heart isn't in anything any more; **si le ~ vous en dit** if you feel like it, if you're in the mood.
f (*âme, pensées intimes*) **c'est un ~ pur** *ou* **candide** he is a candid soul; **la noirceur de son ~** his blackness of heart; **la noblesse de son ~** his noble-heartedness; **connaître le fond du ~ de qn** to know sb's inner-most feelings; **des paroles venues (du fond) du ~** words (coming) from the heart, heartfelt words; **dévoiler son ~ à qn** to open one's heart to sb; **elle a vidé son ~** she poured out her heart; **au fond de son ~** in his heart of hearts; **nous nous sommes parlé ~ à ~** we had a heart-to-heart; **il m'a parlé à ~ ouvert** he had a heart-to-heart talk with me; *voir* **cri**.
g (*courage, ardeur*) heart, courage. **le ~ lui manqua (pour faire)** his heart *ou* courage failed him (when it came to doing); **mettre tout son ~ dans qch/à faire qch** to put all one's heart into sth/into doing sth; **comment peut-on avoir le ~ de refuser?** how can one have *ou* find the heart to refuse?; **donner du ~ au ventre à qn*** to buck sb up*; **avoir du ~ au ventre*** to have guts*; **avoir du ~ à l'ouvrage** to put one's heart into one's work; **il travaille mais le ~ n'y est pas** he does the work but his heart isn't in it; **cela m'a redonné du ~** that gave me new heart.
h (*partie centrale*) *[chou]* heart; *[arbre, bois]* heart, core; *[fruit, pile atomique]* core; *[problème, ville]* heart. **au ~ de** *région, ville, forêt* in the heart of; **aller au ~ du sujet** to get to the heart of the matter; **au ~ de l'été** in the height of summer; **au ~ de l'hiver** in the depth *ou* heart of winter; **fromage fait à ~** fully ripe cheese; **~ de palmier** heart of palm; (*lit*) **~ d'artichaut** artichoke heart; (*fig*) **c'est** *ou* **il a un ~ d'artichaut** he falls in love with every girl he meets.
i (*objet*) heart. **en (forme de) ~** heart-shaped; **volets percés de ~s** shutters with heart-shaped holes; *voir* **bouche**.
j (*Cartes*) heart. **valet/as de ~** knave/ace of hearts; **avez-vous du ~?** have you any hearts?; *voir* **atout, joli**.
k (*loc*) **par ~** *réciter, apprendre* by heart; **je la connais par ~** I know her inside out, I know her like the back of my hand; **dîner/déjeuner par ~**† to have to do without dinner/lunch; **sur le ~: ce qu'il m'a dit, je l'ai sur le ~** *ou* **ça m'est resté sur le ~** what he told me still rankles with me, I still feel sore about what he told me; **je vais lui dire ce que j'ai sur le ~** I'm going to tell him what's on my mind; **à ~ joie** to one's heart's content; **de tout mon ~** with all my heart; **je vous souhaite de tout mon ~ de réussir** I wish you success with all my heart *ou* from the bottom of my heart; **être de tout ~ avec qn dans la joie/une épreuve** to share (in) sb's happiness/sorrow; **je suis de tout ~ avec vous** I DO sympathize with you; **ne pas porter qn dans son ~** to have no great liking for sb; **je veux en avoir le ~ net** I want to be clear in my own mind (about it); **avoir à ~ de faire** to want *ou* be keen to do; **prendre les choses à ~** to take things to heart; **prendre à ~ de faire** to set one's heart on doing; **ce voyage me tient à ~** I have set my heart on this journey; **ce sujet me tient à ~** this subject is close to my heart; **trouver un ami selon son ~** to find a friend after one's own heart; *voir* **bon 1q, donner**.
coexistence [kɔɛgzistɑ̃s] nf coexistence. **~ pacifique** peaceful coexistence.
coexister [kɔɛgziste] 1 vi to coexist.
coffrage [kɔfʀaʒ] nm (*pour protéger, cacher*) boxing (*NonC*); *[galerie, tranchée]* (*dispositif, action*) coffering (*NonC*); *[béton]* (*dispositif*) form, formwork (*NonC*), shuttering; (*action*) framing.
coffre [kɔfʀ] 1 nm a (*meuble*) chest. **~ à linge/à outils** linen/tool chest. b (*Aut*) boot (*Brit*), trunk (*US*). **~ avant/arrière** front/rear boot *ou* trunk. c (*coffrage*) (*gén*) case; *[piano]* case; *[radio]* cabinet. d (*Banque, hôtel*) safe; (*Hist, fig: cassette*) coffer. **les ~s de l'État** the coffers of the state; (*Banque*) **la salle des ~s** the strongroom. e (*:

poitrine) **le** ~ the chest; **il a du** ~ he's got a lot of puff* (*Brit*) *ou* blow*. 2 **comp** ►**coffre-fort nm** (**pl coffres-forts**) safe ►**coffre à jouets** toybox ►**coffre de nuit** night safe ►**coffre de voyage**† trunk.

coffrer [kɔfʀe] 1 **vt** a (*: *emprisonner*) to throw *ou* put inside*. **se faire** ~ to get put inside*. b (*Tech*) *béton* to place a frame *ou* form for; *tranchée, galerie* to coffer.

coffret [kɔfʀɛ] **nm** casket. ~ **à bijoux** jewel box, jewellery case; ~ **de luxe**, ~**-cadeau** presentation box.

cofinancement [kofinɑ̃smɑ̃] **nm** co-financing.

cofondateur, -trice [kɔfɔ̃datœʀ, tʀis] **nm,f** cofounder.

cogérant [koʒeʀɑ̃] **nm** joint manager.

cogérante [koʒeʀɑ̃t] **nf** joint manageress.

cogestion [koʒɛstjɔ̃] **nf** co-management, joint management.

cogitation [kɔʒitasjɔ̃] **nf** (*hum*) cogitation.

cogiter [kɔʒite] 1 1 **vi** (*hum: réfléchir*) to cogitate. 2 **vt: qu'est-ce qu'il cogite?** what's he thinking up?

cognac [kɔɲak] **nm** cognac, (French) brandy.

cognassier [kɔɲasje] **nm** quince (tree), japonica.

cogne‡ [kɔɲ] **nm** (*policier*) cop*. **les** ~**s** the cops*, the fuzz‡.

cognée [kɔɲe] **nf** felling axe; *voir* **jeter**.

cognement [kɔɲmɑ̃] **nm** (*voir* **cogner**) banging; knocking; rapping; (*Aut*) knocking.

cogner [kɔɲe] 1 1 **vt** a (*heurter*) to knock. **fais attention à ne pas** ~ **les verres** mind you don't knock the glasses against anything; **quelqu'un m'a cogné en passant** somebody knocked (into) me as he went by.

b (‡: *battre*) to beat up. **ils se sont cognés** they had a punch-up* (*Brit*) *ou* fist fight.

2 **vi** a *[personne]* (*taper*) ~ **sur** *clou, piquet* to hammer; *mur* to bang *ou* knock on; (*fort*) to hammer *ou* rap on; ~ **du poing sur la table** to bang *ou* thump one's fist on the table; ~ **à la porte/au plafond** to knock at the door/on the ceiling; (*fort*) to bang *ou* rap at the door/on the ceiling.

b *[volet, battant]* to bang (*contre* against). *[objet lancé, caillou]* ~ **contre** to hit, strike; **un caillou est venu** ~ **contre le pare-brise** a stone hit the windscreen; **il y a un volet qui cogne (contre le mur)** there's a shutter banging (against the wall); (*Aut*) **le moteur cogne** the engine's knocking.

c (*) *[boxeur, bagarreur]* to hit out; (*fig*) *[soleil]* to beat down. **ça va** ~ **à la manif*** there's going to be some rough stuff at the demo*; **ce boxeur-là, il cogne dur** that boxer's a hard hitter, that boxer hits hard; *[soleil]* **ça cogne!** it's scorching!*

d (‡: *sentir mauvais*) to pong‡ (*Brit*), to stink to high heaven*.

3 **se cogner vpr: se** ~ **contre un mur** to bang o.s. on *ou* against a wall; **se** ~ **la tête/le genou contre un poteau** to bang one's head/knee on *ou* against a post; (*fig*) **c'est à se** ~ **la tête contre les murs** it's enough to drive you up the wall.

cogneur* [kɔɲœʀ] **nm** (*bagarreur, boxeur*) bruiser*.

cogniticien, -ienne [kɔgnitisjɛ̃, jɛn] **nm,f** cognitive scientist.

cognitif, -ive [kɔgnitif, iv] **adj** cognitive.

cognition [kɔgnisjɔ̃] **nf** cognition.

cohabitation [kɔabitasjɔ̃] **nf** *[couple]* cohabitation (*frm*), living together; *[plusieurs personnes]* living under the same roof; (*Pol*) cohabitation. **le caractère de son mari rendait la** ~ **impossible** her husband's character made living together *ou* living under the same roof impossible.

cohabiter [kɔabite] 1 **vi** *[couple]* to cohabit (*frm*), live together; *[plusieurs personnes]* to live under the same roof; (*Pol*) to cohabit. **la crise du logement les oblige à** ~ **avec leurs grands-parents** the shortage of accommodation forces them to live with their grandparents.

cohérence [kɔeʀɑ̃s] **nf** (*voir* **cohérent**) coherence; consistency. **la** ~ **de l'équipe laisse à désirer** the team is not as well-knit as one would like.

cohérent, e [kɔeʀɑ̃, ɑ̃t] **adj** *ensemble, arguments* coherent, consistent; *conduite, roman* consistent; *équipe* well-knit.

cohéritier [koeʀitje] **nm** joint heir, coheir.

cohéritière [koeʀitjɛʀ] **nf** joint heiress, coheiress.

cohésif, -ive [kɔezif, iv] **adj** cohesive.

cohésion [kɔezjɔ̃] **nf** cohesion.

cohorte [kɔɔʀt] **nf** (*groupe*) troop; (*Hist Mil*) cohort.

cohue [kɔy] **nf** (*foule*) crowd; (*bousculade*) crush.

coi, coite [kwa, kwat] **adj: se tenir** ~, **rester** ~ to remain silent; **en rester** ~ to be rendered speechless.

coiffant, e [kwafɑ̃, ɑ̃t] **adj m** *voir* **gel, mousse**.

coiffe [kwaf] **nf** a *[costume régional, religieuse]* headdress. b *[chapeau]* lining; (*Tech*) *[fusée]* cap; (*Anat*) *[nouveau-né]* caul.

coiffé, e [kwafe] (**ptp de coiffer**) **adj** a (*peigné*) **est-ce que tu es** ~**?** have you done your hair?; **comment était-elle** ~**e?** what was her hair like?, how did she have her hair?; **il est toujours mal/bien** ~ his hair always looks untidy/nice; **être** ~ **en brosse** to have a crew-cut; **être** ~ **en chien fou** to have dishevelled hair; **il était** ~ **en arrière** he had his hair brushed *ou* combed back; *voir* **né**. b (*couvert*) **(il était)** ~ **d'un béret** (he was) wearing a beret; **le clown entra** ~ **d'une casserole** the clown came in with a saucepan on his head. c (†: *entiché*) **être** ~ **de** to be infatuated with.

coiffer [kwafe] 1 1 **vt** a (*arranger les cheveux de*) ~ **qn** to do sb's hair; **X coiffe bien** X is a good hairdresser; **cheveux difficiles à** ~ unmanageable hair; **(aller) se faire** ~ to (go and) have one's hair done.

b (*couvrir la tête de*) ~ **(la tête d')un bébé d'un bonnet** to put a bonnet on a baby's head; **sa mère la coiffe de chapeaux ridicules** her mother makes her wear ridiculous hats; **ce chapeau la coiffe bien** that hat suits her; **le béret qui la coiffait** the beret she had on *ou* was wearing; **elle allait bientôt** ~ **Sainte-Catherine** she would soon be 25 and still unmarried.

c (*fournir en chapeaux*) **c'est Mme X qui la coiffe** Mrs X makes her hats, her hats come from Mrs X.

d (*mettre*) *chapeau* to put on. ~ **la mitre/la tiare** to be mitred/made Pope; ~ **la couronne** to be crowned (king *ou* queen).

e (*surmonter*) **de lourds nuages coiffaient le sommet** heavy clouds covered the summit, the summit was topped with heavy clouds; **pic coiffé de neige** snow-capped peak.

f (*être à la tête de*) *organismes, services* to head up, have overall responsibility for.

g (*: *dépasser*) ~ **qn à l'arrivée** *ou* **au poteau** to pip sb at the post* (*Brit*), nose sb out* (*US*).

2 **se coiffer vpr** a (*arranger ses cheveux*) to do one's hair. **elle se coiffe toujours mal** she never manages to do anything nice with her hair.

b (*mettre comme coiffure*) **se** ~ **d'une casquette** to put on a cap; **d'habitude, elle se coiffe d'un chapeau de paille** she usually wears a straw hat.

c (*se fournir en chapeaux*) **se** ~ **chez X** to buy one's hats from X.

d († *péj: s'enticher de*) **se** ~ **de qn** to become infatuated with sb.

coiffeur [kwafœʀ] **nm** *[dames]* hairdresser; *[hommes]* hairdresser, barber.

coiffeuse [kwaføz] **nf** (*personne*) hairdresser; (*meuble*) dressing table.

coiffure [kwafyʀ] **nf** (*façon d'être peigné*) hairstyle, hairdo*; (*chapeau*) hat, headgear* (*NonC*). (*métier*) **la** ~ hairdressing; *voir* **salon**.

coin [kwɛ̃] **nm** a (*angle*) *[objet, chambre]* corner. **armoire/place de** ~ corner cupboard/seat; (*Scol*) **va au** ~**!** go and stand in the corner!; (*Scol*) **envoyer** *ou* **mettre un enfant au** ~ to send a child to stand in the corner, put a child in the corner; (*Rail*) ~**(-)fenêtre/(-)couloir** seat by the window/by the door, window/corridor seat.

b *[rue]* corner. **au** ~ **(de la rue)** at *ou* on the corner (of the street); **la blanchisserie fait le** ~ the laundry is right on the corner; **le magasin du** ~ the corner shop; **le boucher du** ~ the butcher('s) at *ou* round the corner; **à tous les** ~**s de rue** on every street corner.

c *[yeux, bouche]* corner. **sourire en** ~ half smile; **regard en** ~ side glance; **regarder/surveiller qn du** ~ **de l'œil** to look at/watch sb out of the corner of one's eye.

d (*espace restreint*) *[plage, village, maison]* corner. (*dans un journal, magasin*) **le** ~ **du bricoleur** the handyman's corner; **un** ~ **de terre/ciel bleu** a patch of land/blue sky; **rester dans son** ~ to keep to oneself; **laisser qn dans son** ~ to leave sb alone; **dans un** ~ **de sa mémoire** in a corner of her memory; **dans quel** ~ **l'as-tu mis?** where on earth did you put it?; **je l'ai mis dans un** ~**, je ne sais plus où** I put it somewhere but I can't remember where; **cette maison est pleine de** ~**s et de recoins** this house is full of nooks and crannies; **j'ai cherché dans tous les** ~**s (et recoins)** I looked in every nook and cranny; ~**-bureau/-cuisine/-repas** work/kitchen/dining area; *voir* **petit**.

e (*lieu de résidence*) area. **dans quel** ~ **habitez-vous?** whereabouts do you live?; **vous êtes du** ~**?** do you live locally? *ou* round here? *ou* in the area?; **je ne suis pas du** ~ I'm not from around here, I'm a stranger here; **l'épicier du** ~ the local grocer; **un** ~ **perdu** *ou* **paumé*** a place miles from anywhere; **un** ~ **de Paris/de la France que je connais bien** an area of Paris/of France that I know well; **il y a beaucoup de pêche dans ce** ~**-là** there's a lot of fishing in that area; **on a trouvé un petit** ~ **pas cher/tranquille pour les vacances** we found somewhere nice and cheap/nice and quiet for the holidays, we found a nice inexpensive/quiet little spot for the holidays; **de tous les** ~**s du monde** from every corner of the world; **de tous les** ~**s du pays** from all over the country.

f (*objet triangulaire*) *[reliure, cartable, sous-main]* corner (piece); (*pour coincer, écarter*) wedge; (*pour graver*) die; (*poinçon*) hallmark. (*Typ*) ~ **(de serrage)** quoin; (*fig*) **frappé** *ou* **marqué au** ~ **du bon sens** bearing the stamp of commonsense.

g (*loc*) **je n'aimerais pas le rencontrer au** ~ **d'un bois** I wouldn't like to meet him on a dark night; **au** ~ **du feu** by the fireside, in the chimney corner; **causerie/rêverie au** ~ **du feu** fireside chat/daydream; *voir* **boucher, quatre**.

coinçage [kwɛ̃saʒ] **nm** wedging.

coincé, e* [kwɛ̃se] **adj** *personne* hung up*.

coincement [kwɛ̃smɑ̃] **nm** jamming (*NonC*).

coincer [kwɛ̃se] 3 1 **vt** a (*bloquer*) (*intentionnellement*) to wedge; (*accidentellement*) *tiroir, fermeture éclair* to jam. **le tiroir est coincé** the drawer is stuck *ou* jammed; **(le corps de) l'enfant était coincé sous le camion** the child('s body) was pinned under the lorry; **il se trouva coincé contre un mur par la foule** he was pinned against a wall by the crowd; **il m'a coincé entre deux portes pour me dire ...** he cornered me to tell me ...; **nous étions coincés dans le couloir/dans l'ascenseur** we were stuck *ou* jammed in the corridor/in the lift; (*fig*) **je suis coincé à**

la maison/au bureau I'm stuck at home/at the office; **ils ont coincé l'armoire en voulant la faire passer par la porte** they got the wardrobe jammed *ou* stuck trying to get it through the door.

b (* *fig: attraper*) *voleur* to pinch*, nab*; *faussaire, fraudeur* to catch up with. **je me suis fait ~** *ou* **ils m'ont coincé sur cette question** they got me on *ou* caught me out on that question, I was caught out on that question; **coincé entre son désir et la peur** caught between his desire and fear; **nous sommes coincés, nous ne pouvons rien faire** we are stuck *ou* cornered *ou* in a corner and we can't do anything; **~ la bulle**‡ to bum around*.

2 **vi** *[porte]* to stick. (*fig*) **ça coince au niveau de la direction*** there are problems at management level.

3 **se coincer vpr** *[fermeture, tiroir]* to jam, stick, get jammed *ou* stuck. **se ~ le doigt dans une porte** to catch one's finger in a door; **se ~ un nerf*** to trap *ou* pinch a nerve; **se ~ une vertèbre*** to trap a nerve in one's spine.

coinceur [kwɛ̃sœʀ] **nm** (*Alpinisme*) nut.

coïncidence [kɔɛ̃sidɑ̃s] **nf** (*gén, Géom*) coincidence.

coïncident, e [kɔɛ̃sidɑ̃, ɑ̃t] **adj** *surfaces, faits* coincident.

coïncider [kɔɛ̃side] 1 **vi** *[surfaces, opinions, dates]* to coincide (*avec* with); *[témoignages]* to tally. **faire ~ l'extrémité de deux conduits** to make the ends of two pipes meet exactly; **nous sommes arrivés à faire ~ nos dates de vacances** we've managed to get the dates of our holidays to coincide.

coin-coin [kwɛ̃kwɛ̃] **nm inv** *[canard]* quack. **~!** quack! quack!

coïnculpé, e [koɛ̃kylpe] **nm,f** co-defendant, co-accused.

coing [kwɛ̃] **nm** quince (*fruit*).

coït [kɔit] **nm** coitus, coition. **~ interrompu** coitus interruptus.

coite [kwat] **adj f** *voir* **coi.**

coke[1] [kɔk] **nm** (*combustible*) coke.

coke[2] [kɔk] **nf** (*arg Drogue: cocaïne*) coke (*arg*).

cokéfaction [kɔkefaksjɔ̃] **nf** coking.

cokéfier [kɔkefje] 7 **vt** to coke.

cokerie [kɔkʀi] **nf** cokeworks, coking works.

col [kɔl] 1 **nm** a *[chemise, manteau]* collar. **ça bâille du ~** it gapes at the neck; **pull à ~ roulé/rond** polo-/round-neck pullover *ou* jumper (*Brit*); *voir* **faux**[2].

b (*Géog*) pass. **le ~ du Simplon** the Simplon pass.

c (*partie étroite*) *[carafe, vase]* neck. **~ du fémur/de la vessie** neck of the thighbone/of the bladder; **elle s'est cassé le col du fémur** she has broken her hip; **~ de l'utérus** neck of the womb, cervix.

d († *ou littér: encolure, cou*) neck. **un homme au ~ de taureau** a man with a neck like a bull, a bull-necked man.

2 **comp ►col blanc** (*personne*) white-collar worker **►col bleu** (*ouvrier*) blue-collar worker; (*marin*) bluejacket **►col cassé** wing collar **►col châle** shawl collar **►col cheminée** turtleneck (*Brit*), high round neck **►col chemisier** shirt collar **►col Claudine** Peter Pan collar **►col-de-cygne nm (pl cols-de-cygne)** *[plomberie]* swan neck; *[mobilier]* swan('s) neck **►col dur** stiff collar **►col Mao** Mao collar **►col marin** sailor's collar **►col mou** soft collar **►col officier** mandarin collar **►col polo** polo shirt collar **►col roulé** roll neck (*Brit*), polo neck (*Brit*), turtleneck (*US*) **►col (en) V** V-neck.

cola [kɔla] **nm** cola, kola.

colback‡ [kɔlbak] **nm: attraper** *ou* **prendre qn par le ~** to grab sb by the collar.

colchique [kɔlʃik] **nm** autumn crocus, meadow saffron, colchicum (SPÉC).

colégataire [kolegatɛʀ] **nmf** joint legatee.

coléoptère [kɔleɔptɛʀ] **nm** coleopteron (SPÉC), coleopterous insect (SPÉC), beetle. **~s** coleoptera (SPÉC).

colère [kɔlɛʀ] 1 **nf** a (*irritation*) anger. **la ~ est mauvaise conseillère** anger is a bad counsellor; **être en ~** to be angry; **se mettre en ~** to get angry; **mettre qn en ~** to make sb angry; **passer sa ~ sur qn** to work off *ou* take out one's anger on sb; **en ~ contre moi-même** angry with myself, mad at myself*; **dit-il avec ~** he said angrily.

b (*accès d'irritation*) (fit of) rage. **il fait des ~s terribles** he has terrible fits of anger *ou* rage; **il est entré dans une ~ noire** he flew into a white rage; **faire** *ou* **piquer une ~** to throw a tantrum.

c (*littér*) wrath. **la ~ divine** divine wrath; **la ~ des flots/du vent** the rage *ou* wrath of the sea/of the wind.

2 **adj inv** (†) (*coléreux*) irascible; (*en colère*) irate.

coléreux, -euse [kɔleʀø, øz] **adj**, **colérique** [kɔleʀik] **adj** *caractère* quick-tempered, irascible; *enfant* quick-tempered, easily angered; *vieillard* quick-tempered, peppery, irascible.

colibacille [kɔlibasil] **nm** colon bacillus.

colibacillose [kɔlibasiloz] **nf** colibacillosis.

colibri [kɔlibʀi] **nm** hummingbird.

colifichet [kɔlifiʃɛ] **nm** (*bijou fantaisie*) trinket, bauble; (*babiole*) knickknack.

colimaçon [kɔlimasɔ̃] **nm** (†) snail. (*fig*) **escalier en ~** spiral staircase.

colin [kɔlɛ̃] **nm** (*merlu*) hake; (*lieu noir*) saithe, coalfish, coley.

colineau, pl ~x [kɔlino] **nm** = **colinot.**

colin-maillard [kɔlɛ̃majaʀ] **nm** blind man's buff.

colinot [kɔlino] **nm** codling.

colique [kɔlik] **nf** a (*diarrhée*) diarrhoea. **avoir la ~** (*lit*) to have diarrhoea; (*fig: avoir peur*) to be scared stiff. b (*gén pl: douleur intestinale*) stomach pain, colic pain, colic (*NonC*). **être pris de violentes ~s** to have violent stomach pains; **~ hépatique/néphrétique** biliary/renal colic; **quelle ~!**‡ (*personne*) what a pain in the neck!‡; (*chose*) what a drag!‡

colis [kɔli] **nm** parcel. **envoyer/recevoir un ~ postal** to send/receive a parcel through the post (*Brit*) *ou* mail; **par ~ postal** by parcel post; **~ piégé** parcel bomb (*Brit*), mail bomb.

Colisée [kɔlize] **nm: le ~** the Coliseum.

colistier, -ière [kolistje, jɛʀ] **nm,f** (*Pol*) fellow candidate.

colite [kɔlit] **nf** colitis.

collaborateur, -trice [kɔ(l)labɔʀatœʀ, tʀis] **nm,f** *[personne]* colleague; *[journal, revue]* contributor; *[livre, publication]* collaborator; (*Pol*) *[ennemi]* collaborateur, collaborationist, quisling.

collaboration [kɔ(l)labɔʀasjɔ̃] **nf** (*Pol, à un travail, un livre*) collaboration (*à* on); (*à un journal*) contribution (*à* to). **s'assurer la ~ de qn** to enlist the services of sb; **en ~ avec** in collaboration with.

collaborer [kɔ(l)labɔʀe] 1 **vi** a **~ avec qn** to collaborate *ou* work with sb; **~ à** *travail, livre* to collaborate on; *journal* to contribute to. b (*Pol*) to collaborate.

collage [kɔlaʒ] **nm** a (*à la colle forte*) sticking, gluing; (*à la colle blanche*) pasting; *[étiquettes etc]* sticking. **~ de papiers peints** paperhanging; **~ d'affiches** billposting. b (*Art*) collage. c (*apprêt*) *[vin]* fining; *[papier]* sizing. d (*péj: concubinage*) affair. **c'est un ~** they're having an affair.

collagène [kɔlaʒɛn] **nm** collagen.

collant, e [kɔlɑ̃, ɑ̃t] 1 **adj** (*ajusté*) *vêtement* skintight, tight-fitting, clinging; (*poisseux*) sticky. (*importun*) **être ~*** to cling, stick like a leech; *voir* **papier.** 2 **nm** a (*maillot*) *[femme]* body stocking; *[danseur, acrobate]* leotard. b (*bas*) (*gén*) tights *pl* (*Brit*), pantyhose (*US*); *[danseuse]* tights *pl* . 3 **collante nf** (*arg Scol*) (*convocation*) notification; (*feuille de résultats*) results slip.

collapsus [kɔlapsys] **nm** *[malade, organe]* collapse.

collatéral, e, mpl -aux [kɔ(l)lateʀal, o] **adj** *parent, artère* collateral. **(nef) ~e** (side) aisle; **les ~aux** (*parents*) collaterals; (*Archit*) (side) aisles.

collation [kɔlasjɔ̃] **nf** a (*repas*) light meal, light refreshment, collation; (*goûter*) snack. b (*voir* **collationner**) collation; checking. c (*frm*) *[titre, grade]* conferment.

collationnement [kɔlasjɔnmɑ̃] **nm** (*voir* **collationner**) collation; checking.

collationner [kɔlasjɔne] 1 **vt** (*comparer*) *manuscrits etc* to collate (*avec* with); (*vérifier*) *liste* to check; (*Typ*) to collate.

colle [kɔl] **nf** a (*gén*) glue; *[papiers peints]* wallpaper paste; (*apprêt*) size. **~ (blanche** *ou* **d'écolier** *ou* **de pâte)** paste; **~ (forte)** (strong) glue, adhesive; **~ (gomme)** gum (*Brit*), rubber cement (*US*); **~ à bois** wood glue; **~ de bureau** glue; **~ de poisson** fish glue; (*fig*) **ce riz, c'est de la vraie ~ (de pâte)** this rice is like paste *ou* is a gluey *ou* sticky mass; *voir* **chauffer, pot.**

b (*: *question*) poser*, teaser. **poser une ~ à qn** to set sb a poser*; **là, vous me posez une ~** you've stumped me there*.

c (*arg Scol*) (*examen blanc*) mock oral exam; (*retenue*) detention. **mettre une ~ à qn** to give sb detention; **j'ai eu 3 heures de ~** I was kept in for 3 hours.

d (‡) **vivre** *ou* **être à la ~** to live together, shack up together‡.

collecte [kɔlɛkt] **nf** (*quête*) collection; (*Rel: prière*) collect.

collecter [kɔlɛkte] 1 **vt** to collect.

collecteur, -trice [kɔlɛktœʀ, tʀis] 1 **nm,f** (*personne*) collector. **~ d'impôts** tax collector; **~ de fonds** fund raiser. 2 **nm** (*Aut*) manifold; (*Élec*) commutator. (*Rad*) **~ d'ondes** aerial; **(égout) ~, (grand) ~** main sewer.

collectif, -ive [kɔlɛktif, iv] 1 **adj** *travail, responsabilité, punition* collective; *billet, réservation* group (*épith*); *hystérie, licenciements* mass (*épith*); *installations* public; (*Ling*) *terme, sens* collective. **faire une démarche ~ive auprès de qn** to approach sb collectively *ou* as a group; **immeuble ~** (large) block (of flats) (*Brit*), apartment building (*US*); *voir* **convention, ferme**[2]. 2 **nm** (*Gram: mot*) collective noun; (*groupe de travail*) collective. (*Fin*) **~ budgétaire** minibudget.

collection [kɔlɛksjɔ̃] **nf** a *[timbres, papillons]* collection; (*Comm*) *[échantillons]* line; (*hum: groupe*) collection. **objet/timbre de ~** collector's item/stamp; **faire (la) ~ de** to collect; **voiture de ~** classic car. b (*Mode*) collection. c (*Presse: série*) series, collection. **notre ~ "jeunes auteurs"** our "young authors" series *ou* collection; **il a toute la ~ des œuvres de X** he's got the complete collection *ou* set of X's works.

collectionner [kɔlɛksjɔne] 1 **vt** (*gén, hum*) to collect.

collectionneur, -euse [kɔlɛksjɔnœʀ, øz] **nm,f** collector.

collectivement [kɔlɛktivmɑ̃] **adv** (*gén*) collectively; *démissionner, protester* in a body, collectively.

collectivisation [kɔlɛktivizasjɔ̃] **nf** collectivization.

collectiviser [kɔlɛktivize] 1 **vt** to collectivize.

collectivisme [kɔlɛktivism] **nm** collectivism.

collectiviste [kɔlɛktivist] **adj, nmf** collectivist.

collectivité [kɔlɛktivite] **nf** a (*groupement*) group. (*le public, l'ensemble des citoyens*) **la ~** the community; **la ~ nationale** the Nation (as a community); (*Admin*) **les ~s locales** ≃ the local communities; **~s professionnelles** professional bodies *ou* organizations; **la ~ des habitants/des citoyens** the inhabitants/the citizens as a whole *ou* a body. b (*vie en communauté*) **la ~** community life *ou* living; **vivre en ~** to live in a community. c (*possession commune*) collective ownership.

collège [kɔlɛʒ] **nm** a (*école*) school; (*privé*) private school. **~ (d'enseignement secondaire)** middle school, secondary school (*Brit*), junior high school (*US*); **~ expérimental/technique** experimental/technical school; (*Can*) **C~ d'enseignement général et professionnel** general and vocational college (*Can*). b (*Pol, Rel: assemblée*) college. **~ électoral** electoral college; *voir* **sacré**.

collégial, e, **mpl -iaux** [kɔleʒjal, jo] **adj** (*Rel*) collegiate; (*Pol*) collegial, collegiate. **(église) ~e** collegiate church.

collégialité [kɔleʒjalite] **nf** (*Pol*) collegial administration; (*Rel*) collegiality.

collégien [kɔleʒjɛ̃] **nm** schoolboy. (*fig: novice*) **c'est un ~** he's an innocent.

collégienne [kɔleʒjɛn] **nf** schoolgirl.

collègue [kɔ(l)lɛg] **nmf** colleague; *voir* **Monsieur**.

coller [kɔle] [1] 1 **vt** a (*à la colle forte*) to stick, glue; (*à la colle blanche*) to paste; *étiquette, timbre* to stick; *affiche* to stick up (*à, sur* on); *enveloppe* to stick down; *papier peint* to hang; *film* to splice. **colle-la** (*étiquette*) stick it on; (*affiche*) stick it up; (*enveloppe*) stick it down; **~ 2 morceaux (ensemble)** to stick *ou* glue *ou* paste 2 pieces together; **~ qch à** *ou* **sur qch** to stick sth on(to) sth; **les cheveux collés de sang** his hair stuck together *ou* matted with blood; **les yeux encore collés de sommeil** his eyes still half-shut with sleep.

b (*appliquer*) **~ son oreille à la porte/son nez contre la vitre** to press one's ear to *ou* against the door/one's nose against the window; **il colla l'armoire contre le mur** he stood the wardrobe right against the wall; **il se colla contre le mur pour les laisser passer** he pressed himself against the wall to let them pass; (*Mil*) **ils l'ont collé au mur** they stuck him up against the wall.

c (**: mettre*) to stick, shove*. **colle tes valises dans un coin** stick *ou* plonk* *ou* shove* *ou* dump* your bags in a corner; **il en colle des pages** he writes reams; **dans ses devoirs il colle n'importe quoi** he puts *ou* sticks *ou* shoves* any old thing (down) in his homework; **il se colla devant moi** he plonked* *ou* planted himself in front of me; **ils se collent devant la télé dès qu'ils rentrent** they're glued to the TV as soon as they come in, they plonk themselves* in front of the TV as soon as they come in; **se ~ un chapeau sur la tête** to stick *ou* shove a hat on one's head*; **ils l'ont collé ministre** they've gone and made him a minister*; *voir* **poing**.

d (**: donner*) **on m'a collé une fausse pièce** I've been palmed off with a dud coin; **il m'a collé une contravention/une punition/une gifle** he gave me a fine/a punishment/a clout; **on lui a collé 3 ans de prison** they've stuck him in prison *ou* sent him down* for 3 years, they've given him 3 years; **on lui a collé la responsabilité/la belle-mère** he's got (himself) stuck* *ou* landed* *ou* lumbered⁑ (*Brit*) with the responsibility/his mother-in-law.

e (*arg Scol*) (*consigner*) to put in detention, keep in; (*recaler, ajourner*) to fail, flunk* (*US*). **se faire ~** (*en retenue*) to be put in detention, be given a detention; (*à l'examen*) to be failed, be flunked* (*US*).

f (**: embarrasser par une question*) to catch out.

g (**: suivre*) *personne* to cling to. **la voiture qui nous suit nous colle de trop près** the car behind is sticking too close *ou* is sitting right on our tail*; **il m'a collé (après) toute la journée** he clung to me all day.

h (*apprêter*) *vin* to fine; *papier* to size.

2 **vi** a (*être poisseux*) to be sticky; (*adhérer*) to stick (*à* to).

b (*fig*) to cling to. **le cycliste collait au peloton de tête** the cyclist clung *ou* stuck close to the leaders; **robe qui colle au corps** tight-fitting *ou* clinging dress; **ils nous collent au derrière*** they're right on our tail*; **voiture qui colle à la route** car that grips the road; **un rôle qui lui colle à la peau** a part tailor-made for him, a part which fits him like a glove; **~ au sujet** to stick to the subject; **ce roman colle à la réalité** this novel sticks *ou* is faithful to reality; **mot qui colle à une idée** word which fits an idea closely.

c (**: bien marcher*) **ça colle?** OK?*; **ça ne colle pas entre eux/nous** they/we aren't hitting it off* *ou* getting on together; **il y a quelque chose qui ne colle pas** there's something wrong *ou* not right here; **ça ne colle pas, je ne suis pas libre** that's no good *ou* that won't do, I am not free; **son histoire ne colle pas** his story doesn't hold together *ou* doesn't gibe (*US*).

d (*jeux d'enfants*) **c'est à toi de ~** it's your turn to be it, you're it now.

3 **se coller vpr** a (*⁑: subir*) *tâche, personne* to be *ou* get stuck with*, be *ou* get landed with*, be *ou* get lumbered with⁑ (*Brit*). **il va falloir se ~ la belle-mère pendant 3 jours!** we'll have to put up with the mother-in-law for 3 days!

b (*⁑: se mettre à*) **se ~ à (faire) qch** to get stuck into (doing) sth*, get down to (doing) sth, set about (doing) sth.

c (*s'accrocher à*) **se ~ à qn** *[danseur]* to press o.s. against sb, cling to sb; *[importun]* to stick to sb like glue *ou* like a leech; **elle dansait collée à lui** she was dancing tightly pressed against him *ou* clinging tight to him; **ces deux-là sont toujours collés ensemble⁑** those two *ou* that pair always go around together *ou* are never apart.

d (*⁑: se mettre en concubinage*) **se ~ ensemble** to live together, shack up together⁑; **ils sont collés ensemble depuis 2 mois** they've been living together *ou* shacking up⁑ together *ou* shacked up⁑ together for 2 months.

collerette [kɔlʀɛt] **nf** (*col*) collaret; (*Hist: fraise*) ruff; (*Bot*) *[champignon]* ring, annulus; (*Tech*) *[tuyau]* flange.

collet [kɔlɛ] **nm** (*piège*) snare, noose; (*petite cape*) short cape; *[dent]* neck; (*Boucherie*) neck; (*Tech*) collar, flange; (*Bot*) neck. **prendre** *ou* **saisir qn au ~** to seize sb by the collar; (*fig*) **mettre la main au ~ de qn** to get hold of sb, collar sb; **elle est très ~ monté** she's very strait-laced *ou* stuffy.

colleter [kɔlte] [4] 1 **vt** *adversaire* to seize by the collar, grab by the throat. **il s'est fait ~ (par la police) en sortant du bar*** he was collared (by the police) as he came out of the bar. 2 **se colleter* vpr** (*se battre*) to have a tussle, tussle. (*lit, fig*) **se ~ avec** to wrestle *ou* grapple *ou* tussle with.

colleur, -euse [kɔlœʀ, øz] 1 **nm,f** a **~ d'affiches** billsticker, billposter; **~ de papiers peints** wallpaperer. b (*arg Scol*) *mock oral examiner.* 2 **colleuse nf** (*Ciné*) splicer; (*Phot*) mounting press.

colley [kɔlɛ] **nm** collie.

collier [kɔlje] **nm** a *[femme]* necklace; *[chevalier, maire]* chain; *[chien, cheval, chat]* (*courroie, pelage*) collar; (*Boucherie*) collar. **~ de fleurs** garland, chain of flowers; **~ de misère** yoke of misery; **reprendre le ~*** to get back into harness; **donner un coup de ~** to put backs into it*; *voir* **franc**[1]. b (*barbe*) **~ (de barbe)** beard (*along the line of the jaw*). c (*Tech*) **~ de serrage** clamp collar.

collimateur [kɔlimatœʀ] **nm** (*lunette*) collimator. (*lit, fig*) **avoir qn/qch dans son** *ou* **le ~** to have sb/sth in one's sights.

colline [kɔlin] **nf** hill.

collision [kɔlizjɔ̃] **nf** *[véhicules, bateaux]* collision; (*fig*) *[intérêts, manifestants]* clash. **entrer en ~** to collide (*avec* with); (*Aut*) **~ en chaîne** pile-up.

collocation [kɔlɔkasjɔ̃] **nf** (*Jur*) *classification of creditors in order of priority;* (*Ling*) collocation.

collodion [kɔlɔdjɔ̃] **nm** collodion.

colloïdal, e, mpl -aux [kɔlɔidal, o] **adj** (*Chim*) colloidal.

colloïde [kɔlɔid] **nm** (*Chim*) colloid.

colloque [kɔ(l)lɔk] **nm** colloquium, symposium; (*hum*) confab*.

collusion [kɔlyzjɔ̃] **nf** (*complicité*) collusion.

collutoire [kɔlytwaʀ] **nm** (*Méd*) oral medication (*NonC*); (*en bombe*) throat spray.

collyre [kɔliʀ] **nm** eye lotion, collyrium (*SPÉC*).

colmatage [kɔlmataʒ] **nm** (*voir* **colmater**) sealing(-off); plugging; filling-in; closing; warping.

colmater [kɔlmate] [1] **vt** a *fuite* to seal (off), plug; *fissure, trou* to fill in, plug; (*fig*) *déficit* to make good, make up. (*fig, Mil*) **~ une brèche** to seal *ou* close a gap; **la fissure s'est colmatée toute seule** the crack has filled itself in *ou* sealed itself. b (*Agr*) *terrain* to warp.

colo* [kɔlo] **nf abrév de colonie de vacances.**

colocataire [kolɔkatɛʀ] **nmf** *[locataire]* fellow tenant, co-tenant; *[logement]* tenant, co-tenant, joint tenant.

Cologne [kɔlɔɲ] **n** Cologne; *voir* **eau**.

Colomb [kɔlɔ̃] **nm: Christophe ~** Christopher Columbus.

colombage [kɔlɔ̃baʒ] **nm** half-timbering. **maison à ~** half-timbered house.

colombe [kɔlɔ̃b] **nf** (*Orn, fig Pol*) dove.

Colombie [kɔlɔ̃bi] **nf** Colombia. **C~ britannique** British Columbia.

colombien, -ienne [kɔlɔ̃bjɛ̃, jɛn] 1 **adj** Colombian. 2 **nm,f: C~(ne)** Colombian.

colombier [kɔlɔ̃bje] **nm** dovecote.

colombin⁑ [kɔlɔ̃bɛ̃] **nm** (*étron*) turd⁑.

Colombine [kɔlɔ̃bin] **nf** (*Théât*) Columbine.

Colombo [kɔlɔ̃bo] **n** Colombo.

colombophile [kɔlɔ̃bɔfil] 1 **adj** pigeon-fancying, pigeon-fanciers'. 2 **nmf** pigeon fancier.

colombophilie [kɔlɔ̃bɔfili] **nf** pigeon fancying.

colon [kɔlɔ̃] **nm** a (*pionnier*) settler, colonist. b (*enfant*) *[colonie]* child, boarder; *[pénitencier]* child, inmate. c (*arg Mil*) colonel. **eh bien, mon ~!*** heck!*, blimey!* (*Brit*).

côlon [kolɔ̃] **nm** (*Anat*) colon.

colonel [kɔlɔnɛl] **nm** (*armée de terre*) colonel; (*armée de l'air*) group captain (*Brit*), colonel (*US*).

colonelle [kɔlɔnɛl] **nf** (*voir* **colonel**) colonel's wife; group captain's wife.

colonial, e, mpl -iaux [kɔlɔnjal, jo] 1 **adj** colonial; *voir* **casque.** 2 **nm** (*soldat*) soldier of the colonial troops; (*habitant*) colonial. 3 **nf: la coloniale** the (French) Colonial Army.

colonialisme [kɔlɔnjalism] **nm** colonialism.

colonialiste [kɔlɔnjalist] **adj, nmf** colonialist.

colonie [kɔlɔni] **nf** (*gén*) colony. **~ de vacances** ≃ (children's) holiday camp (*Brit*); ≃ summer camp (*US*); **~ pénitentiaire** penal settlement

ou colony.
colonisateur, -trice [kɔlɔnizatœʀ, tʀis] 1 **adj** colonizing (*épith*). 2 **nm,f** colonizer.
colonisation [kɔlɔnizasjɔ̃] **nf** colonization, settlement.
coloniser [kɔlɔnize] 1 **vt** to colonize, settle. **les colonisés** the colonized peoples.
colonnade [kɔlɔnad] **nf** colonnade.
colonne [kɔlɔn] 1 **nf** (*gén*) column; (*Archit*) column, pillar. **en ~ par deux** *[enfants]* in twos, in a crocodile* (*Brit*); *[soldats]* in twos; **mettez-vous en ~ par huit** get into eights; (*Presse*) *[nouvelle]* **faire cinq ~s à la une** to be *ou* make front-page *ou* headline news; *voir* **cinquième, titre, titrer.** 2 **comp** ►**colonne d'air** airstream ►**colonne barométrique** barometric column ►**colonne blindée** armoured column ►**colonne de direction** (*Aut*) steering column ►**les Colonnes d'Hercule** the Pillars of Hercules ►**colonne montante** rising main ►**colonne Morris** (pillar-shaped) billboard ►**colonne de secours** rescue party ►**colonne vertébrale** spine, spinal *ou* vertebral column (*SPÉC*).
colonnette [kɔlɔnɛt] **nf** small column.
colopathie [kolopati] **nf** colitis, colonitis.
colophane [kɔlɔfan] **nf** rosin.
coloquinte [kɔlɔkɛ̃t] **nf** (*Bot*) colocynth (*SPÉC*), bitter apple; (*‡†: tête*) nut*, bonce‡ (*Brit*).
Colorado [kɔlɔʀado] **nm** Colorado.
colorant, e [kɔlɔʀɑ̃, ɑ̃t] **adj, nm** colouring.(*sur étiquette*) **"sans ~s artificiels"** "(contains) no artificial colouring"; *voir* **shampooing.**
coloration [kɔlɔʀasjɔ̃] **nf** a (*voir* **colorer**) colouring; dyeing; staining. b (*couleur, nuance*) colouring, colour, shade; *[peau]* colouring; (*fig*) *[voix, ton]* coloration; (*fig*) *[discours]* complexion. **~ politique** *[journal, mouvement]* political complexion.
colorature [kɔlɔʀatyʀ] **nf** coloratura.
coloré, e [kɔlɔʀe] (**ptp de colorer**) **adj** *teint* florid, ruddy; *objet* coloured; *foule* colourful; *style, description, récit* vivid, colourful.
colorer [kɔlɔʀe] 1 1 **vt** a (*teindre*) *substance* to colour; *tissu* to dye; *bois* to stain. **~ qch en bleu** to colour (*ou* dye *ou* stain) sth blue; (*littér*) **le soleil colore les cimes neigeuses** the sun tinges the snowy peaks with colour. b (*littér: enjoliver*) *récit, sentiments* to colour (*de* with). 2 **se colorer vpr** a (*prendre de la couleur*) *[tomate]* to turn red; *[raisin]* to turn red (*ou* green). **le ciel se colore de rose** the sky takes on a rosy tinge *ou* colour; **son teint se colora** her face became flushed, her colour rose. b (*être empreint de*) **se ~ de** to be coloured *ou* tinged with.
coloriage [kɔlɔʀjaʒ] **nm** (*action*) colouring (*NonC*); (*dessin*) coloured drawing.
colorier [kɔlɔʀje] 7 **vt** *carte, dessin* to colour (in). **images à ~** pictures to colour (in); *voir* **album.**
coloris [kɔlɔʀi] **nm** (*gén*) colour, shade; *[visage, peau]* colouring. (*Comm*) **carte de ~** shade card.
colorisation [kɔlɔʀizasjɔ̃] **nf** colourization (*Brit*), colorization (*US*).
coloriser [kɔlɔʀize] 1 **vt** to colourize (*Brit*), colorize (*US*).
coloriste [kɔlɔʀist] 1 **nmf** (*peintre*) colourist; (*enlumineur*) colourer. 2 **nf** (*coiffeuse*) hairdresser (specializing in tinting and rinsing).
coloscopie [kɔlɔskɔpi] **nf** colonoscopy.
colossal, e, mpl -aux [kɔlɔsal, o] **adj** colossal, huge.
colossalement [kɔlɔsalmɑ̃] **adv** colossally, hugely.
colosse [kɔlɔs] **nm** (*personne*) giant (*fig*); (*institution, état*) colossus, giant. **le ~ de Rhodes** the Colossus of Rhodes; **~ aux pieds d'argile** idol with feet of clay.
colostrum [kɔlɔstʀɔm] **nm** colostrum.
colportage [kɔlpɔʀtaʒ] **nm** *[marchandises, ragots]* hawking, peddling; *voir* **littérature.**
colporter [kɔlpɔʀte] 1 **vt** *marchandises, ragots* to hawk, peddle.
colporteur, -euse [kɔlpɔʀtœʀ, øz] **nm,f** (*vendeur*) hawker, pedlar. **~ de fausses nouvelles** newsmonger; **~ de rumeurs** *ou* **ragots*** gossip-monger.
colt [kɔlt] **nm** (*revolver*) gun, Colt®.
coltiner [kɔltine] 1 1 **vt** *fardeau, colis* to carry, hump* (*Brit*) *ou* lug* around. 2 **se coltiner* vpr** *colis* to hump* (*Brit*) *ou* lug* around, carry; (‡) *travail, personne* to be *ou* get stuck* *ou* landed* with. **il va falloir se ~ ta sœur pendant toutes les vacances‡** we'll have to put up with your sister for the whole of the holidays*.
columbarium [kɔlɔ̃baʀjɔm] **nm** (*cimetière*) columbarium.
colvert [kɔlvɛʀ] **nm** mallard.
colza [kɔlza] **nm** rape(seed), colza.
coma [kɔma] **nm** (*Méd*) coma. **être/entrer dans le ~** to be in/go into a coma; **dans un ~ dépassé** brain-dead.
comateux, -euse [kɔmatø, øz] **adj** comatose. **état ~** state of coma; **un ~** a patient in a coma.
combat [kɔ̃ba] 1 **nm** a (*bataille*) fight, fighting (*NonC*). **~s aériens** air-battles; **~s d'arrière-garde** rearguard fighting; **aller au ~** to go into battle, enter the fray (*littér*); **les ~s continuent** the fighting goes on; *voir* **branle-bas, char, hors.**
b (*genre de bataille*) **~ défensif/offensif** defensive/offensive action; **~ aérien** aerial combat (*NonC*), dogfight; **~ naval** naval action; (*lit, fig*) **~ d'arrière-garde/de retardement** rearguard/delaying action.
c (*fig: lutte*) fight (*contre* against, *pour* for). **des ~s continuels entre parents et enfants** endless fighting between parents and children; **engager le ~ contre la vie chère** to take up the fight against the high cost of living; **la vie est un ~ de tous les jours** life is a daily struggle; **"étudiants, professeurs même ~!"** "students and teachers fighting together", "students and teachers united"; **"fascisme, racisme même ~!"** "fight fascism! fight racism!"; **élever 5 enfants, quel ~!** bringing up 5 children is such a struggle!; **quel ~ pour le faire manger!** it's such a struggle getting him to eat!
d (*Sport*) match, fight. **~ de boxe/de catch** boxing/wrestling match.
e (*littér: concours*) **ce fut entre eux un ~ de générosité/d'esprit** they vied with each other in generosity/wit.
2 **comp** ►**combat de coqs** cockfight, cockfighting (*NonC*) ►**combat de gladiateurs** gladiatorial combat *ou* contest ►**combat rapproché** close combat ►**combat de rues** street fighting (*NonC*), street battle ►**combat singulier** single combat.
combatif, -ive [kɔ̃batif, iv] **adj** *troupes, soldat* ready to fight; *personne* of a fighting spirit; *esprit, humeur* fighting (*épith*). **les troupes fraîches sont plus ~ives** fresh troops show greater readiness to fight; **c'est un ~** he's a battler *ou* fighter.
combativité [kɔ̃bativite] **nf** *[troupe]* readiness to fight; *[personne]* fighting spirit.
combattant, e [kɔ̃batɑ̃, ɑ̃t] 1 **adj** *troupe* fighting (*épith*), combatant (*épith*). 2 **nm,f** *[guerre]* combatant; *[bagarre]* brawler; *voir* **ancien.**
combattre [kɔ̃batʀ] 41 1 **vt** *incendie, adversaire* to fight; *théorie, politique, inflation, vice* to combat, fight (against); *maladie [malade]* to fight against; *[médecin]* to fight, combat. 2 **vi** to fight (*contre* against, *pour* for).
combe [kɔ̃b] **nf** (*Géog*) coomb, comb(e).
combien [kɔ̃bjɛ̃] 1 **adv** a **~ de** (*quantité*) how much; (*nombre*) how many; **~ de lait/de bouteilles as-tu acheté/achetées?** how much milk/many bottles have you bought?; **~ y en a-t-il (en moins)?** (*quantité*) how much (less) is there (of it)?; (*nombre*) how many (fewer) are there (of them)?; **~ de temps?** how long?; **tu en as pour ~ de temps?** how long will you be?; **depuis ~ de temps travaillez-vous ici?** how long have you been working here?; **~ de fois?** (*nombre*) how many times?; (*fréquence*) how often?
b **~ (d'entre eux)** how many (of them); **~ n'ouvrent jamais un livre!** how many (people) never open a book!; **~ sont-ils?** how many (of them) are there?, how many are they?
c (*frm: à quel point, comme*) **si tu savais ~/~ plus je travaille maintenant!** if you (only) knew how much/how much more I work now!; **~ peu d'argent** how little money; **~ peu de gens** how few people; **tu vois ~ il est paresseux/inefficace** you can see how lazy/inefficient he is; **c'est étonnant de voir ~ il a changé** it is surprising to see how changed he is *ou* how (much) he has changed; **~ précieux m'est ce souvenir** how dear to me this memory is; **~ vous avez raison!** how right you are!; († *ou hum*) **il est bête, ô ~!** he is stupid, (oh) so stupid!; **~ d'ennui je vous cause** what a lot of trouble I'm causing you.
d (*tellement*) **~ peu de gens** how few people; **~ moins de gens/d'argent** how many fewer people/how much less money; **~ plus de gens/d'argent** how many more people/how much more money; **c'est plus long à faire mais ~ meilleur!** it takes (a lot) longer to do but how much better it is!
e (*quelle somme, distance*) **~ est-ce?, ~ ça coûte?, ça fait ~?*** how much is it?; **~ pèses-tu?** *ou* **fais-tu?** how heavy are you?, how much do you weigh?; **~ pèse ce colis?** how much does this parcel weigh?, how heavy is this parcel?; **~ mesure-t-il?** *[personne]* how tall is he?; *[colis]* how big is it?; **~ cela mesure-t-il?** (*gén*) how big is it?; (*longueur*) how long is it?, what length is it?; **vous le voulez en ~ de large?** what width do you want (it)?, how wide do you want it?; **ça va augmenter de ~?** how much more will it go up? *ou* be?; **ça va faire une différence de ~?** what will the difference be?; **~ y a-t-il d'ici à la ville?** how far is it from here to the town?; **~ cela mesure-t-il en hauteur/largeur?, ça a** *ou* **fait ~ de hauteur/largeur?** how high/wide is it?, what height/width is it?; (*Sport*) **il a fait ~ aux essais?** what was his time at the trial run?
2 **nm** (*) (*rang*) **le ~ êtes-vous?** where did you come?*, where were you placed?; (*date*) **le ~ sommes-nous?** what's the date?, what date is it?; (*fréquence*) *[trains]* **il y en a tous les ~?** how often do they come? *ou* go? *ou* run?
combientième* [kɔ̃bjɛ̃tjɛm] 1 **adj: Lincoln était le ~ président des USA?** what number president of the USA was Lincoln?*; **c'est le ~ accident qu'il a eu en 2 ans?** that's how many accidents he's had in 2 years?; **c'est la ~ fois que ça arrive!** how many times has that happened now!
2 **nmf** a (*rang*) **il est le ~?** where was he placed?; **ce coureur est arrivé le ~?** where did this runner come (in)?
b (*énumération*) **encore un attentat, c'est le ~ depuis le début du mois?** another attack, how many does that make *ou* is that since the beginning of the month?; **donne-moi le troisième — le ~?** give me the third one — which one did you say?
c (*date*) **on est le ~ aujourd'hui?** what's the date today?, what date is it today?
combinaison [kɔ̃binɛzɔ̃] **nf** a (*action*) combining; (*Math*) *[éléments, sons, chiffres]* combination. (*Pol*) **~ (ministérielle)** government; (*Chim*)

~ **(chimique)** (*entre plusieurs corps*) combination; (*corps composé*) compound. b *[coffre-fort, loto]* combination. c (*vêtement*) *[femme]* slip; *[aviateur]* flying suit; *[mécanicien]* boiler suit (*Brit*), (one-piece) overalls (*US*); (*Ski*) ski-suit. ~ **de plongée (sous-marine)** (underwater) diving suit. d (*astuce*) device; (*manigance*) scheme. **des ~s louches** shady schemes *ou* scheming (*NonC*).

combinard, e* [kɔ̃binaʀ, aʀd] **adj, nm,f** (*péj*) **il est ~, c'est un ~** (*astuces, trucs*) he knows all the tricks; (*manigances*) he's a schemer, he's on to all the fiddles*.

combinat [kɔ̃bina] **nm** (industrial) complex.

combinatoire [kɔ̃binatwaʀ] **adj** (*Ling*) combinative; (*Math*) combinatorial, combinatory.

combine* [kɔ̃bin] **nf** (*astuce, truc*) trick (*pour faire* to do). (*péj: manigance*) **la ~** scheming; **il est dans la ~** he knows (all) about it, he's in on it*; **entrer dans la ~** to play the game; **ça sent la ~** I smell a rat; **toutes leurs ~s** all their little schemes, all their fiddles*.

combiné [kɔ̃bine] **nm** (*Chim*) compound; *[téléphone]* receiver, handset. (*vêtement*) ~ **(gaine-soutien-gorge)** corselette; (*Rad*) ~ **(radio-tourne-disque)** radiogram; (*Tech*) ~ **(batteur-mixeur)** mixer and liquidizer *ou* blender; (*Aviat*) ~ **(avion-hélicoptère)** convertible helicopter, converti-plane; (*Ski*) ~ **alpin/nordique** alpine/nordic combination; **il est 3e au ~** he's 3rd overall.

combiner [kɔ̃bine] 1 1 **vt** a (*grouper*) *éléments, sons, chiffres* to combine. **opération combinée** joint *ou* combined operation; **l'oxygène combiné à l'hydrogène** oxygen combined with hydrogen; **l'oxygène et l'hydrogène combinés** oxygen and hydrogen combined; **l'inquiétude et la fatigue combinées** a combination of anxiety and tiredness. b (*méditer, élaborer*) *affaire, mauvais coup, plan* to devise, work out, think up; *horaire, emploi du temps* to devise, plan. **bien combiné** well devised. 2 **se combiner vpr** *[éléments]* to combine (*avec* with).

comble [kɔ̃bl] 1 **adj** *salle, autobus* packed (full), jam-packed*; *voir* **mesure, salle.**

2 **nm** a (*degré extrême*) height. **c'est le ~ du ridicule!** that's the height of absurdity!; **être au ~ de la joie** to be overjoyed; **elle était au ~ du désespoir** she was in the depths of despair; *[joie, colère]* **être (porté) à son ~** to be at its peak *ou* height; **ceci mit le ~ à sa fureur/son désespoir** this brought his anger/his despair to its climax *ou* a peak; **cela mit le ~ à sa joie** at that his joy knew no bounds.

b (*loc*) **c'est le ~!, c'est un ~!** that's the last straw!, that beats all!*, that takes the cake!* *ou* biscuit!* (*Brit*); **le ~, c'est qu'il est parti sans payer** what beats all* was that he left without paying; **pour ~ de malheur il ...** to cap *ou* crown it all he ...; **et pour ~, il est parti sans payer** and to cap *ou* crown it all, he left without paying.

c (*charpente*) roof trussing (*SPÉC*), roof timbers. ~ **mansardé** mansard roof; **les ~s** the attic, the loft; **loger (dans une chambre) sous les ~s** to live in a garret *ou* an attic; *voir* **fond.**

combler [kɔ̃ble] 1 **vt** a (*boucher*) *trou, fente* to fill in. (*fig*) **ça comblera un trou dans nos finances** that'll fill a gap in our finances.

b (*résorber*) *déficit* to make good, make up; *lacune, vide* to fill. ~ **son retard** to make up lost time.

c (*satisfaire*) *désir, espoir* to fulfil; *besoin* to fulfil, fill; *personne* to gratify. **parents comblés par la naissance d'un fils** parents overjoyed at the birth of a son; **c'est une femme comblée** she has all that she could wish for.

d (*couvrir qn de*) ~ **qn de** *cadeaux, honneurs* to shower sb with; **il mourut comblé d'honneurs** he died laden with honours; **vous me comblez d'aise *ou* de joie** you fill me with joy; **vraiment, vous nous comblez!** really you're too good to us!

combustibilité [kɔ̃bystibilite] **nf** combustibility.

combustible [kɔ̃bystibl] 1 **adj** combustible. 2 **nm** fuel. **les ~s** fuels, kinds of fuel; ~ **fossile** fossil fuel; ~ **irradié** spent fuel; ~ **nucléaire** nuclear fuel; ~ **organique** biofuel, organic fuel.

combustion [kɔ̃bystjɔ̃] **nf** combustion. **poêle à ~ lente** slow-burning stove.

come-back [kɔmbak] **nm inv** comeback. **faire son ~** to make a come-back.

COMECON [kɔmekɔn] **nm** (**abrév de Conseil pour l'aide mutuelle économique**) COMECON.

comédie [kɔmedi] 1 **nf** a (*Théât*) comedy. ~ **de mœurs/d'intrigue** comedy of manners/of intrigue; ~ **de caractères** character comedy; ~ **de situation** situation comedy, sitcom* (*Brit*); **de ~** *personnage, situation* (*Théât*) comedy (*épith*); (*fig*) comic. b (*fig: simulation*) playacting. **c'est de la ~** it's all an act, it's all sham; **jouer la ~** to put on an act. c (*) palaver, fuss. **c'est toujours la même ~** it's always the same palaver; **allons, pas de ~** come on, no nonsense *ou* fuss; **faire la ~** to make a fuss *ou* a scene. 2 **comp ►la Comédie-Française** (*Théât*) the Comédie-Française **►la comédie humaine** the comédie humaine **►comédie musicale** musical.

comédien, -ienne [kɔmedjɛ̃, jɛn] 1 **nm,f** a (*fig: hypocrite*) sham. **être ~** to be a sham. b (*fig: pitre*) show-off. 2 **nm** (*acteur*) actor; (*acteur comique*) comedy actor, comedian. 3 **comédienne nf** (*actrice*) actress; (*actrice comique*) comedy actress, comedienne.

comédon [kɔmedɔ̃] **nm** blackhead.

comestible [kɔmɛstibl] 1 **adj** edible. 2 **nmpl: ~s** (fine) foods, delicatessen; **magasin de ~s** ≈ delicatessen (shop).

comète [kɔmɛt] **nf** (*Astron*) comet; *voir* **plan[1].**

cométique [kɔmetik] **nm** (*Can*) Eskimo sledge, komatik (*US, Can*).

comice [kɔmis] 1 **nm: ~(s) agricole(s)†** agricultural show *ou* meeting. 2 **nf** Comice pear.

comique [kɔmik] 1 **adj** (*Théât*) *acteur, film, genre* comic; (*fig*) *incident, personnage* comical; *voir* **opéra.**

2 **nm** a (*NonC*) *[situation]* comic aspect; *[habillement]* comic look *ou* appearance. **c'est d'un ~ irrésistible** it's hilariously *ou* irresistibly funny; **le ~ de la chose, c'est que ...** the funny *ou* amusing thing about it is that ....

b (*Littérat*) **le ~** comedy; ~ **de caractère/de situation** character/situation comedy; ~ **de répétition** comedy of repetition; ~ **troupier** coarse comedy; **avoir le sens du ~** to have a sense of the comic.

c (*artiste, amuseur*) comic, comedian; (*dramaturge*) comedy writer.

3 **nf** (*artiste, amuseuse*) comedienne, comic; (*dramaturge*) comedy writer.

comiquement [kɔmikmɑ̃] **adv** comically.

comité [kɔmite] 1 **nm** (*groupement, ligue*) committee; (*permanent, élu*) board, committee. ~ **central/consultatif/exécutif/restreint** central/advisory/executive/select committee; **se grouper en ~ pour faire** to form a committee to do; (*fig*) **se réunir en petit ~** (*gén*) to meet in a select group; (*petite réception*) to have a small get-together.

2 **comp ►comité directeur** management committee **►comité d'entreprise** workers' *ou* works council **►comité des fêtes** gala *ou* festival committee **►comité de gestion** board of management **►comité de lecture** reading panel *ou* committee **►Comité national de la consommation** ≈ National Consumer Council (*Brit*), ≈ Consumers' Association (*Brit*), ≈ Consumer Product Safety Council (*US*).

commandant [kɔmɑ̃dɑ̃] 1 **nm** a (*armée de terre*) major; (*armée de l'air*) squadron leader (*Brit*), major (*US*); (*gén: dans toute fonction de commandement*) commander, commandant. b (*Aviat, Naut*) captain.

2 **comp ►commandant de bord** (*Aviat*) captain **►commandant en chef** commander-in-chief **►commandant en second** second in command.

commandante [kɔmɑ̃dɑ̃t] **nf** (*voir* **commandant**) major's wife; squadron leader's wife; commander's wife; captain's wife.

commande [kɔmɑ̃d] **nf** a (*Comm*) order. **passer (une) ~** to put in an order (*de* for); **on vous livrera vos ~s jeudi** your order will be delivered to you on Thursday; **payable à la ~** cash with order; **cet article est en ~** the article is on order; **fait sur ~** made to order; **carnet/bulletin de ~s** order book/form.

b *[artiste]* commission. **passer une ~ à qn** to commission sb; **travailler sur ~** to work to order; **ouvrage écrit/composé sur ~** commissioned work/composition.

c (*Aviat, Tech: gén pl*) (*action*) control (*NonC*), controlling (*NonC*); (*dispositif*) controls. **les organes *ou* leviers de ~, les ~s** the controls; ~ **à distance** remote control; ~ **numérique** numerical control; **à ~ vocale** voice-activated; (*Aut*) **~s à main** hand controls; **câble de ~** control cable; **véhicule à double ~** dual control vehicle, vehicle with dual controls; **se mettre aux ~s, prendre les ~s** (*lit*) to take control, take (over) the controls; (*fig*) to take control; (*lit, fig*) **passer les ~s à qn** to hand over control to sb, hand over the controls to sb; **être aux ~s, tenir les ~s** (*lit*) to be in control, be at the controls; (*fig*) to be in control; *voir* **levier, tableau.**

d (*loc*) **de ~** *sourire* forced, affected; *zèle* affected; **agir sur ~** to act on orders; **je ne peux pas jouer ce rôle/m'amuser sur ~** I can't act the role/enjoy myself to order.

commandement [kɔmɑ̃dmɑ̃] **nm** a (*direction*) *[armée, navire]* command. **avoir/prendre le ~ de** to be in *ou* have/take command of; **sur un ton de ~** in a commanding tone; **avoir l'habitude du ~** to be used to being in command; *voir* **poste[2].** b (*état-major*) command. **le ~ a décidé que ...** it has been decided at higher command that ...; *voir* **haut.** c (*Rel*) commandment. d (*ordre*) command. (*Mil*) **à mon ~, marche!** on my command, march!; **avoir ~ de faire qch†** to have orders to do sth. e (*Jur*) *[huissier]* summons.

commander [kɔmɑ̃de] 1 1 **vt** a (*ordonner*) *obéissance, attaque* to order, command. ~ **à qn de faire** to order *ou* command sb to do; **il me commanda le silence** he ordered *ou* commanded me to keep quiet; **l'amitié ne se commande pas** you can't make friends to order; **l'amour ne se commande pas** you don't choose who you love; **je ne peux pas le sentir, ça ne se commande pas** I can't stand him — you can't help these things; **le devoir commande** duty calls.

b (*imposer*) ~ **le respect/l'admiration** to command *ou* compel respect/admiration.

c (*requérir*) *[événements, circonstances]* to demand. **la prudence commande que ...** prudence demands that ... .

d (*Comm*) *marchandise, repas* to order; (*Art*) *tableau, œuvre* to commission. (*au café*) **avez-vous déjà commandé?** has your order been taken?, have you ordered?; **qu'as-tu commandé pour Noël?** what have you asked for for Christmas?; (*hum*) **nous avons commandé le soleil** we've ordered the sun to shine (*hum*).

e (*diriger*) *armée, navire, expédition, attaque* to command; (*emploi absolu*) to be in command, be in charge. (*Mil*) ~ **le feu** to give the order to shoot *ou* to (open) fire; **c'est lui qui commande ici** he's in charge here; **je n'aime pas qu'on me commande** I don't like to be ordered about *ou* to be given orders; **à la maison, c'est elle qui commande** she's the boss at home, she is the one who gives the orders at home.

f (*contrôler*) to control. **ce bouton commande la sirène** this switch controls the siren; **forteresse qui commande l'entrée du détroit** fortress which commands the entrance to the straits.

2 **commander à** vt indir *passions, instincts* to have command *ou* control over. **il ne commande plus à sa jambe gauche** he no longer has any control over his left leg; **il ne sait pas se ~** he cannot control himself.

3 **se commander** vpr (*communiquer*) *[pièces, chambres]* to connect, lead into one another.

commandeur [kɔmɑ̃dœʀ] nm commander (*of an Order*).

commanditaire [kɔmɑ̃ditɛʀ] nm (*Comm*) limited *ou* sleeping (*Brit*) *ou* silent (*US*) partner; *[exposition]* sponsor. **les ~s d'un meurtre** the people behind a murder.

commandite [kɔmɑ̃dit] nf (*Comm*) (*fonds*) share (*of limited partner*). **(société en) ~** limited partnership.

commandité, e [kɔmɑ̃dite] nm,f active *ou* acting *ou* ordinary partner.

commanditer [kɔmɑ̃dite] 1 vt (*Comm: financer*) to finance; *exposition etc* to sponsor.

commando [kɔmɑ̃do] nm commando (group). **les membres du ~** the commando members, the commandos.

comme [kɔm] 1 conj a (*temps*) as. **elle entra (juste) ~ le rideau se levait** she came in (just) as the curtain was rising.

b (*cause*) as, since, seeing that. **~ il pleut, je prends la voiture** I'll take the car seeing that it's raining *ou* as *ou* since it's raining; **~ il est lâche, il n'a pas osé parler** being a coward *ou* coward that he is *ou* as he is a coward, he did not dare speak out.

c (*comparaison*) as, like (*devant n et pron*); (*avec idée de manière*) as, the way*. **elle a soigné son chien ~ elle aurait soigné un enfant** she nursed her dog as she would have done a child; **il pense ~ nous** he thinks as we do *ou* like us; **c'est un homme ~ lui qu'il nous faut** we need a man like him *ou* such as him; **ce pantalon est pratique pour le travail ~ pour les loisirs** these trousers are practical for work as well as leisure; **il s'ennuie en ville ~ à la campagne** he gets bored both in town and in the country, he gets bored in town as he does in the country; (*Rel*) **sur la terre ~ au ciel** on earth as it is in heaven; **il écrit ~ il parle** he writes as *ou* the way he speaks; **c'est une excuse ~ une autre** it's as good an excuse as any; **c'est un client ~ un autre** he's just another customer; **tu n'es jamais ~ les autres** *ou* **tout le monde** you always have to be different; **il voudrait une moto ~ son frère*** *ou* **celle de son frère/la mienne** he would like a motorbike like his brother's/mine; **il voudrait une moto, ~ son frère** he would like a motorbike (just) like his brother; **le héros du film n'agit pas ~ dans la pièce** the hero in the film does not act as he does *ou* the way he does in the play; **si, ~ nous pensons, il a oublié** if, as we think (he did), he forgot; **faites ~ vous voulez** do as you like; **choisissez ~ pour vous** choose as you would for yourself, choose as if it were for yourself; **dur ~ du fer** (as) hard as iron; **il y eut ~ une hésitation/lueur** there was a sort *ou* kind of hesitation/light.

d (*en tant que*) as. **nous l'avons eu ~ président** we had him as (our) president; **~ étudiant, il est assez médiocre** as a student, he is rather poor.

e (*tel que*) like, such as. **les fleurs ~ la rose et l'œillet sont fragiles** flowers such as *ou* like roses and carnations *ou* such flowers as roses and carnations are fragile; **bête ~ il est ...** stupid as he is ...; **elle n'a jamais vu de maison ~ la nôtre** she's never seen a house like ours *ou* such as ours.

f (*devant adj, ptp*) as though, as if. **il était ~ fasciné par ces oiseaux** it was as though *ou* as if he were fascinated by these birds, he was as though *ou* as if fascinated by these birds; **il était ~ fou** he was like a madman; **il était ~ perdu dans cette foule** it was as though *ou* as if he were lost in this crowd; **~ se parlant à lui-même** as if *ou* as though talking to himself.

g **~ si** as if, as though; **~ pour faire** as if to do; **~ quoi** (*disant que*) to the effect that; (*d'où il s'ensuit que*) which goes to show that, which shows that; **il se conduit ~ si de rien n'était** he behaves as if *ou* as though nothing had happened; **~ si nous ne savions pas!** as if we didn't know!; **ce n'est pas ~ si on ne l'avait pas prévenu!** it's not as if *ou* as though he hadn't been warned!; **tu n'es pas gai mais tu peux faire ~ si*** you're not happy but you can pretend (to be); **il fit un geste ~ pour la frapper** he made (a gesture) as if to strike her; **il écrit une lettre ~ quoi il retire sa candidature** he is writing a letter to the effect that he is withdrawing his candidature; **~ quoi il ne fallait pas l'écouter** which shows *ou* goes to show that you shouldn't have listened to him.

h **~ cela, ~ ça** like that; **~ ci ~ ça** so-so, (fair to) middling; **vous aimeriez une robe ~ ça?** would you like a dress like that?, would you like that sort of dress?; **alors, ~ ça, vous nous quittez?** so you're leaving us just like that?; **je l'ai enfermé, ~ ça il ne peut pas nous suivre** I locked him in, so he can't follow us, I locked him in – like that *ou* that way he can't follow us; **il a pêché un saumon ~ ça!** he caught a salmon that *ou* this size! *ou* a salmon like that! *ou* this!; **comment l'as-tu trouvé? – ~ ça** *ou* **~ ci ~ ça** how did you find him? – so-so *ou* (fair to) middling; **c'est ~ ça, un point c'est tout** that's the way it is, and that's all there is to it; **il m'a dit ~ ça qu'il n'était pas d'accord*** he told me just like that that he didn't agree; (*admiratif*) **~ ça!*** fantastic!*, terrific!*

i (*loc*) **~ il vous plaira** as you wish; **~ de juste** naturally, needless to say; (*iro*) **~ par hasard, il était absent** he just HAPPENED to be away (*iro*); (*Prov*) **~ on fait son lit, on se couche** you have made your bed, now you must lie on it; **~ il faut** properly; **mange/tiens-toi ~ il faut** eat/sit up properly; († *ou hum*) **une personne très ~ il faut** a decent well-bred person; **elle est mignonne ~ tout** she's as sweet as can be; **c'est facile ~ tout** it's as easy as can be *ou* as easy as winking; **c'était amusant ~ tout** it was terribly funny *ou* as funny as can be; **il est menteur ~ tout** he's a terrible *ou* dreadful liar; **~ dit l'autre*** as they say; **~ qui dirait*** as you might say; *voir* **tout.**

2 adv how. **~ ces enfants sont bruyants!** how noisy these children are!, these children are so noisy!; **~ il fait beau!** what a lovely day!, what lovely weather!; **tu sais ~ elle est** you know how she is *ou* what she is like; **écoute ~ elle chante bien** listen (to) how beautifully she sings; **~ vous y allez, vous!*** (now) hold on a minute!*, don't get carried away!; *voir* **voir.**

commémoratif, -ive [kɔmemɔʀatif, iv] adj *cérémonie, plaque* commemorative (*épith*), memorial (*épith*); *service* memorial (*épith*). **monument ~** memorial.

commémoration [kɔmemɔʀasjɔ̃] nf commemoration. **en ~ de** in commemoration of.

commémorer [kɔmemɔʀe] 1 vt to commemorate.

commençant, e [kɔmɑ̃sɑ̃, ɑ̃t] 1 adj beginning (*épith*). 2 nm,f (*débutant*) beginner. **grand ~** late beginner.

commencement [kɔmɑ̃smɑ̃] nm a (*début*) beginning, commencement (*frm*); (*départ*) start. **il y a eu un ~ d'incendie** there has been the beginning(s) of a fire; **un bon/mauvais ~** a good/bad start *ou* beginning; (*Jur*) **~ d'exécution** *initial steps in the commission of a crime;* (*Jur*) **~ de preuve** prima facie evidence; **au/dès le ~** in/from the beginning, at/from the outset *ou* start; **du ~ à la fin** from beginning to end, from start to finish; **c'est le ~ de la fin** it's the beginning of the end; **il y a un ~ à tout** you've (always) got to start somewhere, there's always a beginning.

b **~s** *[science, métier]* (*premiers temps*) beginnings; (*rudiments*) basic knowledge; **les ~s ont été durs** the beginning was hard.

commencer [kɔmɑ̃se] 3 1 vt a (*entreprendre*) *travail, opération, repas* to begin, start, commence (*frm*). **ils ont commencé les travaux de l'autoroute** they've started *ou* begun work on the motorway; **j'ai commencé un nouveau chapitre** I have started *ou* begun (on) a new chapter; **quelle façon de ~ l'année!** what a way to begin *ou* start the (new) year!; **commençons par le commencement** let's begin at the beginning.

b (*Scol*) **~ un élève (en maths)** to start a pupil (off) (in maths), ground a pupil (in maths).

c *[chose]* to begin. **mot/phrase qui commence un chapitre** word/sentence which begins a chapter, opening word/sentence of a chapter; **une heure de prières commence la journée** the day begins *ou* starts with an hour of prayers.

2 vi a (*débuter*) to begin, start, commence (*frm*). **le concert va ~** the concert is about to begin *ou* start *ou* commence (*frm*); **tu ne vas pas ~!*, ne commence pas!*** don't start!*; (*lit, iro*) **ça commence bien!** that's a good start!, we're off to a good start!; **pour ~** (*lit*) to begin *ou* start with; (*fig*) to begin *ou* start with, for a start; **elle commence demain chez X** she starts (work) tomorrow at X's; **c'est lui qui a commencé!*** he started it!*

b **~ à (*ou* de) faire** to begin *ou* start to do, begin *ou* start doing; **il commençait à neiger** it was beginning *ou* starting to snow, snow was setting in; **il commençait à s'inquiéter/à s'impatienter** he was getting *ou* beginning to get nervous/impatient; **je commence à en avoir assez*** I've had just about enough (of it); **ça commence à bien faire*** it's getting a bit much*.

c **~ par qch** to start *ou* begin with sth; **~ par faire qch** to start *ou* begin by doing sth; **par quoi voulez-vous ~?** what would you like to begin *ou* start with?; **commence par faire tes devoirs, on verra après** do your homework for a start, and then we'll see; **à ~ par qch/qn** starting with sth/sb; **à ~ par faire ...** by doing ... for a start; **ils m'ont tous déçu, à ~ par Jean** they all let me down, especially Jean; **il faut apporter du changement, à ~ par trouver de nouveaux locaux** we have to make some changes, and the first thing to do is to find new premises.

commensal, e, mpl **-aux** [kɔmɑ̃sal, o] nm,f (*littér: personne*) companion at table, table companion; (*Zool*) commensal.

commensalisme [kɔmɑ̃salism] nm (*Zool*) commensalism.

commensurable [kɔmɑ̃syʀabl] adj commensurable.

comment [kɔmɑ̃] 1 adv a (*de quelle façon*) how; (*rare: pourquoi*) how is that?, how come?* **~ a-t-il fait?** how did he do it?, how did he manage that?; **je ne sais pas ~ il a fait cela** I don't know how he did it; **~ a-t-il osé!** how did he dare!; **~ s'appelle-t-il?** what's his name?; **~ appelles-tu cela?** what do you call that?; **~ allez-vous?** *ou* **vas-tu?** how are you?; **~ est-il, ce type?*** what sort of fellow* is he?, what's that fellow* like?; **~ va-t-il?** how is he?; **~ faire?** how shall we do it? *ou* go about it?; ~ **se fait-il que ...?** how is it that ...?, how come that ...?*; ~ **se peut-il que ...?** how can it be that ... ?

b (*excl*) ~? (I beg your) pardon?, pardon me? (*US*), sorry?, what?*; ~ **cela?** what do you mean?; ~, **il est mort?** what! is he dead?; **vous avez assez mangé? — et** ~! have you had enough to eat? — we (most) certainly have! *ou* I should say so! *ou* and how!*; **avez-vous bien travaillé? — et** ~! did you work well? — I should say so! *ou* not half!* *ou* and how!*; ~ **donc!** by all means!, of course!

2 **nm**: **le** ~ the how; **les** ~**(s)** the hows; *voir* **pourquoi**.

commentaire [kɔmɑ̃tɛʀ] **nm** a (*remarque*) comment (*sur* on). **quel a été son** ~ *ou* **quels ont été ses** ~**s sur ce qui s'est passé?** what was his comment *ou* what were his comments on what happened?; ~**s de presse** press comments; **je vous dispense de vos** ~**s** I can do without your comments *ou* remarks, I don't want (to hear) any comments *ou* remarks from you; **tu feras comme je te l'ordonne, et pas de** ~**s!** you will do as I say and no arguments! *ou* and that's final! *ou* and that's all there is to it!; **son attitude/une telle action se passe de** ~**s** *ou* **est sans** ~ his attitude/such an action speaks for itself; **vous avez entendu ce qu'il a dit! — sans** ~! did you hear him! — enough said! *ou* no comment!

b (*péj*) ~**s** comments; **sa conduite donne lieu à bien des** ~**s!** his behaviour gives rise to a lot of comment!; **ils vont faire des** ~**s sur ce qui se passe chez nous** they'll have a lot to say *ou* a lot of comments to make about what's going on at home.

c (*exposé*) commentary (*de* on); (*Rad, TV*) commentary. (*Littérat: mémoires*) **les "C**~**s" de César** Caesar's "Commentaries"; **un bref** ~ **de la séance** a brief commentary *ou* some brief comments on the meeting.

d (*Littérat: explication*) commentary. **faire le** ~ **d'un texte** to do *ou* give a commentary on *ou* comment (on) a text; **édition avec** ~**(s)** annotated edition.

commentateur, -trice [kɔmɑ̃tatœʀ, tʀis] **nm,f** (*glossateur, Rad, TV*) commentator.

commenter [kɔmɑ̃te] 1 **vt** *poème* to comment (on), do *ou* give a commentary on; *conduite* to make comments on, comment upon; (*donner ses opinions*) *événement, actualité* to comment on *ou* upon; (*Rad, TV*) *match* to commentate on; *cérémonie officielle* to provide the commentary for. **le match sera commenté par X** the commentary on the match will be given by X, X will be commentating on the match.

commérage [kɔmeʀaʒ] **nm** piece of gossip. ~**s** gossip (*NonC*), gossiping (*NonC*).

commerçant, e [kɔmɛʀsɑ̃, ɑ̃t] 1 **adj** a *nation* trading (*épith*), commercial; *ville* commercial; *rue, quartier* shopping (*épith*). **rue très** ~**e** busy shopping street, street with many shops. b (*habile*) *personne, procédé* commercially shrewd. **il est très** ~ he's got good business sense; **ce n'est pas très** ~ it's not a very good way to do business. 2 **nm** shopkeeper, tradesman, merchant (*US*), storekeeper (*US*). ~ **en détail** shopkeeper, retail merchant; ~ **en gros** wholesale dealer; **les** ~**s du quartier** (the) local tradesmen *ou* shopkeepers *ou* merchants. 3 **commerçante nf** shopkeeper, storekeeper (*US*).

commerce [kɔmɛʀs] **nm** a (*activités commerciales*) **le** ~ trade, commerce; (*affaires*) **le** ~ business, trade; **le** ~ **n'y est pas encore très développé** commerce *ou* trade isn't very highly developed there yet; **depuis quelques mois le** ~ **ne marche pas très bien** business *ou* trade has been bad for a few months; **opération/maison/traité de** ~ commercial operation/firm/treaty; ~ **en** *ou* **de gros/détail** wholesale/retail trade; ~ **intérieur/extérieur** domestic *ou* home/foreign trade *ou* commerce; **faire du** ~ **(avec)** to trade (with); **être dans le** ~ to be in trade; **faire** ~ **de**† to trade in; (*fig péj*) **faire** ~ **de ses charmes/son nom** to trade on one's charms/name; *voir* **effet**.

b (*circuit commercial*) *objet* **dans le** ~ in the shops (*Brit*) *ou* stores (*US*); **vendu hors** ~ sold direct to the public.

c (*commerçants*) **le** ~ tradespeople (*Brit*), traders, shopkeepers, merchants (*US*); **le petit** ~ small shopkeepers *ou* traders; **le monde du** ~ the commercial world, trading *ou* commercial circles.

d (*boutique*) business. **tenir** *ou* **avoir un** ~ **d'épicerie** to have a grocery business; **un gros/petit** ~ a big/small business.

e († *ou littér*) (*fréquentation*) (social) intercourse; (*compagnie*) company; (*rapport*) dealings. **être d'un** ~ **agréable** to be pleasant company; **avoir** ~ **avec qn** to have dealings with sb.

commercer [kɔmɛʀse] 3 **vi** to trade (*avec* with).

commercial, e, **mpl -iaux** [kɔmɛʀsjal, jo] 1 **adj** (*gén*) commercial; *activité, société, port* commercial, trading (*épith*). **accord** ~ trade *ou* trading agreement; (*péj*) **sourire** ~ phoney professional smile. 2 **nm** marketing man. **l'un de nos** ~**iaux** one of our marketing people. 3 **commerciale nf** (*véhicule*) estate car (*Brit*), station wagon (*US*).

commercialement [kɔmɛʀsjalmɑ̃] **adv** commercially.

commercialisable [kɔmɛʀsjalizabl] **adj** marketable, tradable.

commercialisation [kɔmɛʀsjalizasjɔ̃] **nf** *[produit]* marketing.

commercialiser [kɔmɛʀsjalize] 1 **vt** *brevet, produit, idée* to market.

commère [kɔmɛʀ] **nf** (*péj: bavarde*) gossip.

commérer† [kɔmeʀe] 6 **vi** to gossip.

commettant [kɔmetɑ̃] **nm** (*Jur, Fin*) ~ **et agent** principal and agent.

commettre [kɔmɛtʀ] 56 1 **vt** a (*perpétrer*) *crime, faute, injustice* to commit; *erreur* to make. (*hum*) **il a commis 2 ou 3 romans** he's perpetrated 2 or 3 novels (*hum*).

b (*littér: confier*) ~ **qch à qn** to commit sth to sb, entrust sth to sb.

c (*frm: nommer*) ~ **qn à une charge** to appoint *ou* nominate sb to an office; (*Jur*) ~ **un arbitre** to nominate *ou* appoint an arbitrator; **avocat commis d'office** barrister (*Brit*) *ou* counselor (*US*) appointed by the court.

d (†: *compromettre*) *réputation* to endanger, compromise.

2 **se commettre vpr** (*péj, frm*) to endanger one's reputation, lower o.s. **se** ~ **avec des gens peu recommandables** to associate with rather undesirable people.

comminatoire [kɔminatwaʀ] **adj** *ton, lettre* threatening; (*Jur*) *appointing a penalty for non-compliance*.

commis [kɔmi] **nm** (*gén: vendeur*) (shop *ou* store (*US*)) assistant. ~ **de bureau** office clerk; ~ **aux écritures** book-keeper; ~**-greffier** assistant to the clerk of the court; ~ **de magasin** shop assistant (*Brit*), store clerk (*US*); (*Naut*) ~ **aux vivres** ship's steward; ~ **voyageur** commercial traveller; *voir* **grand**.

commisération [kɔmizeʀasjɔ̃] **nf** commiseration.

commissaire [kɔmisɛʀ] 1 **nm** a ~ **(de police)** ≃ (police) superintendent (*Brit*), (police) captain (*US*); ~ **principal**, ~ **divisionnaire** ≃ chief superintendent (*Brit*), police chief (*US*); ~ **de police judiciaire** detective superintendent (*Brit*), (police) captain (*US*).

b (*surveillant*) *[rencontre sportive, fête]* steward. (*Aut*) ~ **de courses** marshal.

c (*envoyé*) representative; *voir* **haut**.

d *[commission]* commission member, commissioner.

2 **comp** ▸**commissaire de l'Air** chief administrator (*in Air Force*) ▸**commissaire du bord** (*Naut*) purser ▸**commissaire aux comptes** (*Fin*) auditor ▸**commissaire du gouvernement** government commissioner ▸**Commissaire aux langues officielles** (*Can*) Commissioner of Official Languages (*Can*) ▸**commissaire de la Marine** chief administrator ▸**commissaire-priseur nm** (*pl* **commissaires-priseurs**) auctioneer.

commissariat [kɔmisaʀja] **nm** a (*poste*) ~ **(de police)** police station. b (*Admin: fonction*) commissionership. ~ **du bord** pursership; ~ **aux comptes** auditorship. c (*corps*) ~ **de la marine** ≃ Admiralty Board (*Brit*); **C**~ **à l'énergie atomique** Atomic Energy Commission; *voir* **haut**.

commission [kɔmisjɔ̃] 1 **nf** a (*bureau nommé*) commission; (*comité restreint*) committee. (*Pol*) **la** ~ **du budget** the Budget committee; **les membres sont en** ~ the members are in committee; **travail en** ~ work in committee; (*Pol*) **renvoi d'un texte en** ~ committal of a bill.

b (*message*) message. **est-ce qu'on vous a fait la** ~**?** did you get *ou* were you given the message?

c (*course*) errand. **faire des** ~**s (pour)** to run errands (for); **on l'a chargé d'une** ~ he was sent on an errand; (*fig: langage enfantin*) **la petite/grosse** ~ number one/two (*langage enfantin*).

d (*emplettes*) ~**s** shopping; **faire les/des** ~**s** to do the/some shopping; **partir en** ~**s** to go shopping; **l'argent des** ~**s** the shopping money.

e (*pourcentage*) commission. **toucher 10% de** ~ to get 10% commission (*sur* on); **travailler à la** ~ to work on commission.

f (*Comm, Jur: mandat*) commission. **avoir la** ~ **de faire** to be empowered *ou* commissioned to do.

2 **comp** ▸**commission d'arbitrage** arbitration committee ▸**commission d'armistice** armistice council ▸**commission d'enquête** committee *ou* commission of inquiry ▸**commission d'examen** board of examiners ▸**commission interparlementaire** ≃ joint (parliamentary) committee ▸**commission militaire** army exemption tribunal ▸**Commission nationale de la communication et des libertés** *broadcasting regulatory body*, Independent Broadcasting Authority (*Brit*), ≃ Federal Communications Commission (*US*) ▸**Commission des opérations de Bourse** *French stock exchange regulatory body*, Securities and Investment Board (*Brit*), Securities and Exchange Commission (*US*) ▸**commission paritaire** joint commission (with equal representation of both sides) ▸**commission parlementaire** parliamentary commission, parliamentary committee ▸**commission permanente** standing committee, permanent commission ▸**commission rogatoire** (*Jur*) letters rogatory ▸**commission temporaire** ad hoc committee.

commissionnaire [kɔmisjɔnɛʀ] **nm** a (*livreur*) delivery boy, (*adulte*) delivery man; (*messager*) messenger boy, (*adulte*) messenger; (*chasseur*) page (boy), (*adulte*) commissionaire. b (*intermédiaire*) agent, broker. ~ **en douane** customs agent *ou* broker; ~ **de transport** forwarding agent; ~ **de roulage** carrier, haulage contractor (*Brit*), haulier (*Brit*).

commissionner [kɔmisjɔne] 1 **vt** (*Comm, Jur: mandater*) to commission.

commissure [kɔmisyʀ] **nf** *[bouche]* corner; (*Anat, Bot*) commissure.

commode [kɔmɔd] 1 **adj** a (*pratique*) *appartement, meuble* convenient; *outil* handy (*pour* for, *pour faire* for doing); *itinéraire* handy, convenient. b (*facile*) easy. **ce n'est pas** ~ it's not easy (*à faire* to do); **ce serait trop** ~! that would be too easy! c *morale* easy-going; (†) *caractère* easy-going. ~ **à vivre** easy to get on with (*Brit*) *ou* get along with; **il n'est pas** ~ he is an awkward customer. 2 **nf** (*meuble*) chest of drawers.

commodément [kɔmɔdemɑ̃] adv *porter* conveniently; *s'asseoir* comfortably.

commodité [kɔmɔdite] nf **a** (*agrément, confort*) convenience. **pour plus de ~** for greater convenience; **les ~s de la vie moderne** the conveniences *ou* comforts of modern life. **b** (††: *toilettes*) **~s** toilets.

commotion [kɔmosjɔ̃] nf (*secousse*) shock. (*Méd*) **~ cérébrale** concussion; (*fig*) **les grandes ~s sociales** the great social upheavals.

commotionner [kɔmosjɔne] 1 vt *[secousse, nouvelle]* **~ qn** to give sb a shock, shake sb; **être fortement commotionné par qch** to be badly *ou* severely shocked *ou* shaken by sth.

commuable [kɔmɥabl] adj *peine* commutable.

commuer [kɔmɥe] 1 vt *peine* to commute (*en* to).

commun, e[1] [kɔmœ̃, yn] **1** adj **a** (*collectif, de tous*) common; (*fait ensemble*) *effort, réunion* joint (*épith*). **pour le bien ~** for the common good; **dans l'intérêt ~** in the common interest; **ils ont une langue ~e qui est l'anglais** they have English as a common language; **d'un ~ accord** of a common accord, of one accord; *voir* **sens**.
b (*partagé*) *élément* common; *pièce, cuisine* communal, shared; (*Math*) *dénominateur, facteur, angle* common (*à* to). **ces deux maisons ont un jardin ~** these two houses have a shared garden; *[chose]* **être ~ à** to be shared by; **le jardin est ~ aux deux maisons** the garden is common to *ou* shared by the two houses; **tout est ~ entre eux** they share everything; **un ami ~** a mutual friend; **la vie ~e** *[couple]* conjugal life, life together; *[communauté]* communal life; *voir* **point**.
c (*comparable*) *goût, intérêt, caractère* common (*épith*). **ils n'ont rien de ~** they have nothing in common; **ce métal n'a rien de ~ avec l'argent** this metal has nothing in common with *ou* is nothing like silver; **il n'y a pas de ~e mesure entre eux** there's no possible comparison between them; *voir* **nom**.
d en ~ in common; **faire la cuisine/les achats en ~** to share (in) the cooking/the shopping; **vivre en ~** to live communally; **faire une démarche en ~** to take joint steps; **mettre ses ressources en ~** to share *ou* pool one's resources; **tout mettre en ~** to share everything; **ces plantes ont en ~ de pousser sur les hauteurs** these plants have in common the fact that they grow at high altitudes.
e (*habituel, ordinaire*) *accident, erreur* common; *opinion* commonly held, widespread; *métal* common. **peu ~** out of the ordinary, uncommon; **il est d'une force peu ~e pour son âge** he is unusually *ou* uncommonly strong for his age; **il est ~ de voir des daims traverser la route** it is quite common *ou* quite a common thing to see deer crossing the road; *voir* **lien**.
f (*péj: vulgaire*) *manière, voix, personne* common.
2 nm **a le ~ des mortels** the common run of people; **cet hôtel n'est pas pour le ~ des mortels** this hotel is not for ordinary mortals like myself (*ou* ourselves) *ou* is not for the common run of people; († *péj*) **le ~, les gens du ~** the common people *ou* herd; **hors du ~** out of the ordinary.
b (*bâtiments*) **les ~s** the outbuildings, the outhouses.
3 commune nf *voir* **commune**[2].

communal, e, mpl **-aux** [kɔmynal, o] adj *dépenses* council (*épith*) (*Brit*), community (*épith*) (*US*); *fête, aménagements [ville]* local (*épith*); *[campagne]* village (*épith*). **l'école ~e, la ~e*** the local (primary) school (*Brit*), the local grade *ou* elementary school (*US*).

communard, e [kɔmynaʀ, aʀd] **1** adj (*Hist*) of the Commune. **2** nm,f (*Hist*) communard; (*péj: communiste*) red (*péj*), commie* (*péj*).

communautaire [kɔmynotɛʀ] adj community (*épith*); (*Pol*) *droit, politique* Community (*épith*).

communauté [kɔmynote] nf **a** (*identité*) *[idées, sentiments]* identity; *[intérêts, culture]* community. (*Ling*) **~ linguistique** speech community.
b (*Pol, Rel etc: groupe*) community. **servir la ~** to serve the community; **~ urbaine** urban community; **vivre en ~** to live communally; **mettre qch en ~** to pool sth.
c (*Jur: entre époux*) **biens qui appartiennent à la ~** joint estate (*of husband and wife*); **mariés sous le régime de la ~ (des biens)** married with a communal estate settlement; **~ légale** communal estate; **~ réduite aux acquêts** communal estate comprising only property acquired after marriage.
d (*Pol*) **la C~ économique européenne** the European Economic Community; **la C~ européene de l'énergie atomique** the European Atomic Energy Community; **les pays de la C~** the members of the Community; **C~ des États indépendants** Commonwealth of Independent States.

commune[2] [kɔmyn] nf **a** (*ville*) town; (*village*) village. (*territoire*) **sur toute l'étendue de la ~** throughout the entire district *ou* parish (*Brit*); **~ rurale/urbaine** rural/urban district; **les travaux sont à la charge de la ~** the district council (*Brit*) *ou* the community (*US*) is responsible for the cost of the work. **b** (*Hist*) **la C~** the Commune. **c** (*Pol Brit*) **la Chambre des C~s, les C~s** the (House of) Commons.

communément [kɔmynemɑ̃] adv commonly.

communiant, e [kɔmynjɑ̃, jɑ̃t] nm,f (*Rel*) communicant. **(premier) ~** child making his first communion; **me voici en première ~e** this is me in my communion dress.

communicable [kɔmynikabl] adj *expérience, sentiment* which can be communicated; (*Jur*) *droit* transferable; *dossier* which may be made available. **ces renseignements ne sont pas ~s par téléphone** this information cannot be given over the telephone.

communicant, e [kɔmynikɑ̃, ɑ̃t] adj *pièces, salles* communicating (*épith*); *voir* **vase**[1].

communicateur, -trice [kɔmynikatœʀ, tʀis] **1** adj (*Tech*) *fil, pièce* connecting (*épith*). **2** nmf communicator.

communicatif, -ive [kɔmynikatif, iv] adj *rire, ennui* infectious; *personne* communicative.

communication [kɔmynikasjɔ̃] nf **a** (*gén, Philos: relation*) communication. **la ~ est très difficile avec lui, il est si timide** communication (with him) is very difficult because he's so shy; **être en ~ avec** *ami, société savante* to be in communication *ou* contact with; *esprit* to communicate *ou* be in communication with; **mettre qn en ~ avec qn** to put sb in touch *ou* in contact with sb; **théorie des ~s** communications theory.
b (*fait de transmettre*) *[fait, nouvelle]* communication; *[dossier]* transmission. **avoir ~ d'un fait** to be informed of a fact; **demander ~ d'un dossier/d'un livre** to ask for a file/a book; **donner ~ d'une pièce (à qn)** to communicate a document (to sb).
c (*message*) message, communication; (*Univ: exposé*) paper. **faire une ~** to read *ou* give a paper.
d ~ (téléphonique) (telephone) call, (phone) call. **être en ~** to be on the (tele)phone; **être en ~ avec qn** to be on the (tele)phone to sb, to be talking to sb on the (tele)phone; **entrer en ~ avec qn** to get through to sb on the (tele)phone; **mettre qn en ~ (avec)** to put sb through (to), connect sb (with); **~ interurbaine** trunk call (*Brit*), inter-city call; **~ à longue distance** long-distance call; **~ en PCV** reverse charge call (*Brit*), collect call (*US*); **~ avec préavis** personal call (*Brit*), person(-to-person) call (*US*); **vous avez la ~** you are through, I am connecting you now; **je n'ai pas pu avoir la ~** I couldn't get through.
e (*moyen de liaison*) communication. **porte de ~** communicating door; **les (voies de) ~s ont été coupées par les chutes de neige** communications *ou* the lines of communication were cut off by the snow(fall); **moyens de ~** means of communication.
f (*relations publiques*) **la ~** public relations.

communier [kɔmynje] 7 vi (*Rel*) to receive communion. **~ sous les deux espèces** to receive communion under both kinds; (*fig*) **~ dans** *sentiment* to be united in; (*fig*) **~ avec** *sentiment* to share.

communion [kɔmynjɔ̃] nf (*Rel, fig*) communion. **faire sa (première) ~** *ou* **sa ~ privée** to make one's first communion; **faire sa ~ solennelle** to make one's solemn communion; **pour la (première) ~ de ma fille, il pleuvait** it rained on the day of my daughter's first communion; (*fig*) **être en ~ avec** *personne* to be in communion with; *sentiments* to be in sympathy with; **être en ~ d'idées avec qn** to be in sympathy with sb's ideas; **être en ~ d'esprit avec qn** to be of the same intellectual outlook as sb; **nous sommes en ~ d'esprit** we are of the same (intellectual) outlook, we are kindred spirits; **la ~ des saints** the communion of the saints.

communiqué [kɔmynike] nm communiqué. **~ de presse** press release.

communiquer [kɔmynike] 1 **1** vt **a** *nouvelle, renseignement, demande* to pass on, communicate, convey (*à* to); *dossier, document* (*donner*) to give (*à* to); (*envoyer*) to send, transmit (*à* to). **~ un fait à qn** to inform sb of a fact; **se ~ des renseignements** to pass on information to one another.
b *enthousiasme, peur* to communicate, pass on (*à* to); (*Méd*) *maladie* to pass on, give (*à qn* to sb).
c *[chose] mouvement* to communicate, transmit, impart (*à* to); *[soleil] lumière, chaleur* to transmit (*à* to).
2 vi **a** (*correspondre*) to communicate (*avec* with). **les sourds-muets communiquent par signes** deaf-mutes communicate by signs; **~ avec qn par lettre/téléphone** to communicate with sb by letter/phone.
b *[pièces, salles]* to communicate (*avec* with). **des pièces qui communiquent** communicating rooms, rooms which communicate with one another; **couloir qui fait ~ les chambres** corridor that links *ou* connects the rooms.
3 se communiquer vpr (*se propager*) *[feu, maladie]* **se ~ à** to spread to.

communisant, e [kɔmynizɑ̃, ɑ̃t] **1** adj communistic. **2** nm,f communist sympathizer, fellow traveller (*fig*).

communisme [kɔmynism] nm communism.

communiste [kɔmynist] adj, nmf communist.

commutable [kɔmytabl] adj = **commuable**.

commutateur [kɔmytatœʀ] nm (*Élec*) (changeover) switch, commutator; (*Téléc*) commutation switch; (*bouton*) (light) switch.

commutatif, -ive [kɔmytatif, iv] adj (*Jur, Ling, Math*) commutative.

commutation [kɔmytasjɔ̃] nf (*Jur, Math*) commutation; (*Ling*) substitution, commutation. (*Ordin*) **~ des messages** message switching.

commutativité [kɔmytativite] nf *[élément]* commutative property, commutability; *[addition]* commutative nature.

commuter [kɔmyte] 1 vt (*Math*) *éléments* to commute; (*Ling*) *termes* to substitute, commute.

Comores [kɔmɔʀ] nfpl: **les (îles) ~** the Comoro Islands, the Comoros.

comorien, -ienne [kɔmɔʀjɛ̃, jɛn] **1** adj of *ou* from the Comoros. **2**

C~(ne) nm,f inhabitant *ou* native of the Comoros.

compacité [kɔ̃pasite] nf (*voir* **compact**) density; compactness.

compact, e [kɔ̃pakt] 1 adj (*dense*) *foule, substance* dense; *quartier* closely *ou* densely built-up; (*de faible encombrement*) *véhicule, appareil* compact; *poudre* pressed. **disque ~, C~ Disc** ® compact disc; (*Pol*) **une majorité ~e** a solid majority; *voir* **chaîne**. 2 nm a (*Audiovisuel*) (*chaîne hi-fi*) music centre; (*disque*) compact disc. b [*poudre*] powder compact.

compactage [kɔ̃paktaʒ] nm (*compression*) compaction; (*Ordin*) compression, squeezing.

compacter [kɔ̃pakte] [1] vt to compact.

compagne [kɔ̃paɲ] nf (*camarade, concubine, littér: épouse*) companion; (*maîtresse*) (lady) friend; [*animal*] mate. **~ de classe** classmate; **~ de jeu** playmate.

compagnie [kɔ̃paɲi] 1 nf a (*présence, société*) company. **il n'a pour toute ~ que sa vieille maman** he has only his old mother for company; **ce n'est pas une ~ pour lui** he (*ou* she) is no company for him; **en ~ de** *personne* in the company of, in company with; *chose* alongside, along with; **il n'est heureux qu'en ~ de ses livres** he's only happy when (he's) surrounded by his books; **en bonne/mauvaise/joyeuse ~** in good/bad/cheerful company; **tenir ~ à qn** to keep sb company; **être d'une ~ agréable** to be pleasant company; **être de bonne ~** to be good company; **nous voyageâmes de ~** we travelled together *ou* in company; **ça va de ~ avec** it goes hand in hand with; *voir* **fausser**.

b (*réunion*) gathering, party, company. **bonsoir la ~!** goodnight all!

c (*Comm*) company; (*groupe de savants, écrivains*) body. **~ d'assurances/théâtrale/aérienne** insurance/theatrical/airline company; **la banque X et ~** the X and company bank, the bank of X and company; **tout ça, c'est voleurs et ~*** they're all a bunch* *ou* a lot of thieves; **la ~, l'illustre ~** the French Academy.

d (*Mil*) company.

2 comp ▸**compagnie de discipline** (*Mil*) punishment company (*made up of convicted soldiers*) ▸**la Compagnie des Indes** (*Hist*) the East India Company ▸**la Compagnie de Jésus** (*Rel*) the Society of Jesus ▸**compagnie de perdreaux** (*Chasse*) covey of partridges ▸**compagnies républicaines de sécurité** (*Police*) *state security police force in France*.

compagnon [kɔ̃paɲɔ̃] 1 nm a (*camarade, concubin, littér: époux*) companion; (*écuyer*) companion. **~ d'études/de travail** fellow student/worker; **~ d'exil/de misère/d'infortune** companion in exile/in suffering/in misfortune.

b (*ouvrier*) journeyman.

c (*franc-maçon*) companion.

2 comp ▸**compagnon d'armes** companion- *ou* comrade-in-arms ▸**compagnon de bord** shipmate ▸**compagnon de jeu** playmate ▸**compagnon de route** fellow traveller (*lit*) ▸**compagnon de table** companion at table, table companion ▸**compagnon de voyage** travelling companion, fellow traveller (*lit*) ▸**compagnon du Tour de France, compagnon du voyage** (*Hist*) journeyman (*touring France after his apprenticeship*).

compagnonnage [kɔ̃paɲɔnaʒ] nm (*Hist: association d'ouvriers*) ≃ (trade) guild.

comparable [kɔ̃paʀabl] adj *grandeur, élément* comparable (*à* to, *avec* with). **ce n'est pas ~** there's (just) no comparison.

comparaison [kɔ̃paʀɛzɔ̃] nf a (*gén*) comparison (*à* to, *avec* with). **mettre qch en ~ avec** to compare sth with; **faire une ~ entre X et Y** to make a comparison between X and Y; **vous n'avez qu'à faire la ~** you only need to compare them; **il n'y a pas de ~ (possible) (entre)** there is no (possible) comparison; **ça ne soutient pas la ~** that doesn't bear *ou* stand comparison.

b (*Gram*) comparison. **adjectif/adverbe de ~** comparative adjective/adverb.

c (*Littérat*) simile, comparison.

d (*loc*) **en ~ (de)** in comparison (with); **par ~** by comparison (*avec, à* with); **il est sans ~ le meilleur** he is far and away the best; **c'est sans ~ avec** it cannot be compared with; (*Prov*) **~ n'est pas raison** comparisons are misleading.

comparaître [kɔ̃paʀɛtʀ] [57] vi (*Jur*) to appear. (*fig littér*) **il fait ~ dans ses nouvelles toutes sortes de personnages** he brings all sorts of characters into his short stories; *voir* **citation, citer**.

comparatif, -ive [kɔ̃paʀatif, iv] 1 adj comparative. **essai ~** comparison test; **la publicité ~e** comparative advertising. 2 nm comparative. (*Gram*) **au ~** in the comparative; **~ d'infériorité/de supériorité** comparative of lesser/greater degree.

comparatiste [kɔ̃paʀatist] nmf (*Ling*) specialist in comparative linguistics; (*Littérat*) specialist in comparative literature.

comparativement [kɔ̃paʀativmɑ̃] adv comparatively, by comparison. **~ à** by comparison with, compared to *ou* with.

comparé, e [kɔ̃paʀe] (ptp de **comparer**) adj *étude, littérature* comparative.

comparer [kɔ̃paʀe] [1] vt a (*confronter*) to compare (*à, avec* with). **~ deux choses (entre elles)** to compare two things; **vous n'avez qu'à ~** you've only to compare; **compare des choses comparables!** that's not a valid comparison!; **comparé à** compared to. b (*identifier*) to compare, liken (*à* to). **Molière peut se ~** *ou* **être comparé à Shakespeare** Molière can be compared *ou* likened to Shakespeare; **c'est un bon écrivain mais il ne peut quand même pas se ~ à X** he's a good writer but he still can't compare with X; **il ose se ~ à Picasso** he dares to compare himself with Picasso; **ça ne se compare pas** there's no comparison, they can't be compared.

comparse [kɔ̃paʀs] nmf (*Théât*) supernumerary, walk-on; (*péj*) associate, stooge*. **rôle de ~** (*Théât*) walk-on part; (*péj, fig*) minor part; **nous n'avons là que les ~s, il nous faut le vrai chef** we've only the small fry here, we want the real leader.

compartiment [kɔ̃paʀtimɑ̃] nm (*casier, Rail*) compartment; [*damier*] square; [*parterre*] bed; [*connaissances*] compartment. (*Sport*) **dans tous les ~s du jeu** in every area of the game.

compartimentage [kɔ̃paʀtimɑ̃taʒ] nm [*armoire*] partitioning, compartmentation; [*administration, problème*] compartmentalization.

compartimenter [kɔ̃paʀtimɑ̃te] [1] vt *armoire* to partition, divide into compartments, put compartments in; *problème, administration* to compartmentalize.

comparution [kɔ̃paʀysjɔ̃] nf (*Jur*) appearance; *voir* **non**.

compas [kɔ̃pɑ] 1 nm (*Géom*) (pair of) compasses; (*Naut*) compass. (*fig*) **avoir le ~ dans l'œil** to have an accurate eye; *voir* **naviguer**. 2 comp ▸**compas d'épaisseur** spring-adjusting callipers ▸**compas à pointes sèches** dividers ▸**compas quart de cercle** wing compass.

compassé, e [kɔ̃pɑse] (ptp de **compasser**) adj (*guindé*) formal, stuffy, starchy.

compasser [kɔ̃pɑse] [1] vt (*littér*) *attitude, démarche* to control rigidly, make (seem) stiff and unnatural.

compassion [kɔ̃pɑsjɔ̃] nf compassion. **avec ~** compassionately.

compatibilité [kɔ̃patibilite] nf compatibility.

compatible [kɔ̃patibl] adj compatible.

compatir [kɔ̃patiʀ] [2] vi to sympathize. **~ à la douleur de qn** to sympathize *ou* share *ou* commiserate with sb in his grief.

compatissant, e [kɔ̃patisɑ̃, ɑ̃t] adj compassionate, sympathetic.

compatriote [kɔ̃patʀijɔt] 1 nm compatriot, fellow countryman. 2 nf compatriot, fellow countrywoman.

compensable [kɔ̃pɑ̃sabl] adj a *perte* that can be compensated for (*par* by). b *chèque* **~ à Paris** to be cleared in Paris.

compensateur, -trice [kɔ̃pɑ̃satœʀ, tʀis] 1 adj *indemnité, élément, mouvement* compensatory, compensating (*épith*). 2 nm: **(pendule) ~** compensation pendulum.

compensation [kɔ̃pɑ̃sasjɔ̃] nf a (*dédommagement*) compensation. **donner qch en ~ d'autre chose** to give sth in compensation for sth else, make up for sth with sth else; **en ~ (des dégâts), à titre de ~ (pour les dégâts)** in compensation *ou* by way of compensation (for the damage); **c'est une piètre ~ de le savoir** it's not much (of a) compensation to know that; **il y en a peu mais en ~ c'est bon** there's not much of it but what there is is good *ou* but on the other hand *ou* but to make up for that it's good.

b (*équilibre*) balance; (*neutralisation*) balancing; (*Phys*) [*forces*] compensation; (*Méd*) [*maladie, infirmité*] compensation; (*Naut*) [*compas*] correction; (*Psych*) compensation; (*Fin*) [*dette*] set-off (*Brit*), offsetting; [*chèques*] clearing. **il y a ~ entre gains et pertes** the gains and losses cancel each other out; (*Math*) **loi de ~** law of large numbers; (*Jur*) **~ des dépens** division *ou* sharing of the costs; *voir* **chambre**.

compensatoire [kɔ̃pɑ̃satwaʀ] adj compensatory, compensating. (*Fin*) **droits ~** countervailing duties; *voir* **montant**.

compensé, e [kɔ̃pɑ̃se] (ptp de **compenser**) adj *gouvernail* balanced; *horloge* compensated. **chaussures à semelles ~es** platform shoes, shoes with platform soles.

compenser [kɔ̃pɑ̃se] [1] vt to make good, compensate for, offset; *perte, dégâts* to compensate for, make up for; (*Méd*) *infirmité* to compensate (for); (*Naut*) *compas* to correct; (*Fin*) *dette* to set off. **~ une peine par une joie** to make up for a painful experience with a happy one; **ses qualités et ses défauts se compensent** his qualities compensate for *ou* make up for his faults; **pour ~** to compensate, to make up for it, as a compensation; (*Jur*) **~ les dépens** to divide *ou* share the costs, tax each party for its own costs; (*Phys*) **forces qui se compensent** compensating forces; *voir* **ceci**.

compère [kɔ̃pɛʀ] nm a (*gén: complice*) accomplice; (*aux enchères*) puffer. b (†) (*ami*) crony*, comrade; (*personne, type*) fellow.

compère-loriot, pl **compères-loriots** [kɔ̃pɛʀlɔʀjo] nm (*Méd: orgelet*) sty(e); (*Orn*) golden oriole.

compétence [kɔ̃petɑ̃s] nf a (*expérience, habileté*) competence. **~s** abilities; **avoir de la ~** to be competent; **manquer de ~** to lack competence; **faire qch avec ~** to do sth competently; **faire appel à la ~** *ou* **aux ~s d'un spécialiste** to call (up)on the skills *ou* the skilled advice of a specialist; **savoir utiliser les ~s** to know how to put people's skills *ou* abilities to the best use.

b (*rayon d'activité*) scope of activities, domain; (*Jur*) competence. **c'est de la ~ de ce tribunal** it's within the competence of this court; **ce n'est pas de ma ~, cela n'entre pas dans mes ~s** that's not (in) my sphere *ou* domain, that falls outside the scope of my activities.

compétent, e [kɔ̃petɑ̃, ɑ̃t] adj a (*capable, qualifié*) competent, capable. ~ **en** competent in; ~ **en la matière** competent in the subject; **il est très ~ en législation du travail** he is very well-versed in *ou* conversant with labour legislation. b (*concerné*) *service* relevant, concerned (*attrib*); (*Jur*) competent. **adressez-vous à l'autorité ~e** apply to the authority concerned; *[tribunal]* **être ~ pour faire qch** to have the jurisdiction to do sth.

compétiteur, -trice [kɔ̃petitœʀ, tʀis] nm,f competitor.

compétitif, -ive [kɔ̃petitif, iv] adj competitive.

compétition [kɔ̃petisjɔ̃] nf a (*Sport: activité*) **la ~** competitive sport; **faire de la ~** to go in for competitive sport; **la ~ automobile** motor racing; **abandonner la ~** to retire from competitive sport, stop going in for competitions; **sport de ~** competitive sport. b (*Sport: épreuve*) event. **~ sportive** sporting event; **une ~ automobile** a motor racing event. c (*gén, Sport: rivalité, concurrence*) competition (*NonC*); (*Comm, Pol*) rivalry, competition. **entrer en ~ avec** to compete with; **être en ~** to be competing, be in competition (*avec* with).

compétitivité [kɔ̃petitivite] nf competitiveness.

compilateur, -trice [kɔ̃pilatœʀ, tʀis] 1 nm,f (*souvent péj*) compiler. 2 nm (*Ordin*) compiler. **~ croisé** cross compiler.

compilation [kɔ̃pilasjɔ̃] nf (*action*) compiling, compilation; (*souvent péj: ouvrage*) compilation.

compiler [kɔ̃pile] 1 vt to compile.

complainte [kɔ̃plɛ̃t] nf (*Littérat, Mus*) lament.

complaire [kɔ̃plɛʀ] 54 1 **complaire à** vt indir to (try to) please. 2 **se complaire** vpr: **se ~ dans qch/à faire qch** to take pleasure in sth/in doing sth, delight *ou* revel in sth/in doing sth.

complaisamment [kɔ̃plɛzamɑ̃] adv (*voir* **complaisant**) obligingly, kindly; accommodatingly; smugly, complacently.

complaisance [kɔ̃plɛzɑ̃s] nf a (*obligeance*) kindness (*envers* to, towards); (*esprit accommodant*) accommodating attitude. (*frm*) **il a eu la ~ de m'accompagner** he was kind *ou* good enough to *ou* he was so kind as to accompany me; **par ~** out of kindness.
b (*indulgence coupable*) indulgence, leniency; (*connivence malhonnête*) connivance; (*servilité*) servility, subservience; *[conjoint trompé]* tacit consent. **avoir des ~s pour qn** to treat sb indulgently; **sourire de ~** polite smile; **certificat** *ou* **attestation de ~** medical *ou* doctor's certificate (*issued for non-genuine illness to oblige a patient*); (*Comm*) **billet de ~** accommodation bill; *voir* **pavillon**.
c (*fatuité*) self-satisfaction, complacency. **il parlait avec ~ de ses succès** he spoke smugly about his successes.

complaisant, e [kɔ̃plɛzɑ̃, ɑ̃t] adj a (*obligeant*) kind, obliging, complaisant; (*arrangeant*) accommodating. b (*trop indulgent*) indulgent, lenient; (*trop arrangeant*) over-obliging; (*servile*) servile, subservient. **c'est un mari ~** he turns a blind eye to his wife's goings-on; **prêter une oreille ~e à qn/qch** to listen to sb/sth readily, lend a willing ear to sb/sth. c (*fat*) self-satisfied, smug, complacent.

complément [kɔ̃plemɑ̃] nm a (*gén, Bio, Math*) complement; (*reste*) rest, remainder. **~ d'information** supplementary *ou* further *ou* additional information (*NonC*). b (*Gram*) (*gén*) complement; (*complément d'objet*) object. **~ circonstanciel de lieu/de temps** *etc* adverbial phrase of place/time *etc*; **~ (d'objet) direct/indirect** direct/indirect object; **~ d'agent** agent; **~ de nom** possessive phrase.

complémentaire [kɔ̃plemɑ̃tɛʀ] adj (*gén, Math*) complementary; (*additionnel*) supplementary. **pour tout renseignement ~** for any supplementary *ou* further *ou* additional information (*NonC*); *voir* **cours**.

complémentarité [kɔ̃plemɑ̃taʀite] nf complementarity, complementary nature.

complet, -ète [kɔ̃plɛ, ɛt] 1 adj a (*exhaustif, entier*) (*gén*) complete, full; *rapport, analyse* comprehensive, full. **procéder à un examen ~ de qch** to make a full *ou* thorough examination of sth; **il reste encore 3 tours/jours ~s** there are still 3 complete *ou* full laps/days to go; **il a fait des études ~ètes de pharmacien** he has done a complete *ou* full course in pharmacy; **pour vous donner une idée ~ète de la situation** to give you a complete *ou* full idea of the situation; **les œuvres ~ètes de Voltaire** the complete works of Voltaire; **le dossier est-il ~?** is the file complete?; **il en possède une collection très ~ète** he has a very full collection (of it *ou* them); **la lecture ~ète de ce livre prend 2 heures** it takes 2 hours to read this book right through *ou* from cover to cover; **pain ~** ≃ granary *ou* wholemeal bread; *voir* **aliment, pension, riz**.
b (*total*) *échec, obscurité* complete, total, utter; *découragement* complete, total. **dans la misère la plus ~ète** in the most abject poverty.
c (*consommé, achevé: après n*) *homme, acteur* complete. **c'est un athlète ~** he's an all-round athlete, he's the complete athlete.
d (*plein*) *autobus, train* full, full up (*attrib*). (*écriteau*) "~" *[hôtel]* "no vacancies"; *[parking]* "full (up)"; *[cinéma]* "full house"; *[match]* "ground full"; **le théâtre affiche ~ tous les soirs** the theatre has a full house every evening.
e (***) **eh bien! c'est ~!** well, that's the end! *ou* the limit!, that's all we needed!
2 nm a **au (grand) ~: maintenant que nous sommes au ~** now that we are all here; **la famille au grand ~ s'était rassemblée** the whole *ou* entire family had got together.
b (*costume*) suit. **~-veston** suit.

complètement [kɔ̃plɛtmɑ̃] adv a (*en entier*) *démonter, nettoyer, repeindre* completely; *lire un article etc* right through; *lire un livre* from cover to cover; *citer* in full. **~ nu** completely *ou* stark naked; **~ trempé/terminé** completely soaked/finished; **écouter ~ un disque** to listen to a record right through, listen to the whole of a record. b (*absolument*) **~ fou** completely mad, absolutely crazy; **~ faux** completely *ou* absolutely *ou* utterly false; **~ découragé** completely *ou* totally discouraged. c (*à fond*) *étudier qch, faire une enquête* fully, thoroughly.

compléter [kɔ̃plete] 6 1 vt a (*terminer, porter au total voulu*) *somme, effectifs* to make up; *mobilier, collection, dossier* to complete. **pour ~ votre travail/l'ensemble ...** to complete your work/the whole ...; **il compléta ses études en suivant un cours de dactylographie** he completed *ou* rounded off *ou* finished off his studies by taking a course in typing; **un délicieux café compléta le repas** a delightful cup of coffee rounded off the meal; (*fig*) **sa dernière gaffe complète le tableau: il est vraiment incorrigible** his latest blunder crowns it – he never learns; (*fig*) **et pour ~ le tableau, il arriva en retard!** and to crown it all *ou* as a finishing touch he arrived late!
b (*augmenter, agrémenter*) *études, formation* to complement, supplement; *connaissances, documentation, collection* to supplement, add to; *mobilier, garde-robe* to add to. **sa collection se complète lentement** his collection is slowly building up.
2 **se compléter** vpr *[caractères, partenaires, fonctions]* to complement one another.

complétif, -ive [kɔ̃pletif, iv] 1 adj substantival. 2 **complétive** nf: **(proposition) ~ive** noun *ou* substantival clause.

complexe [kɔ̃plɛks] 1 adj (*gén: compliqué*) complex, complicated; (*Ling, Math*) *nombre, quantité, phrase* complex. **sujet ~** compound subject. 2 nm a (*Psych*) complex. **~ d'Œdipe/d'infériorité/de supériorité** Oedipus/inferiority/superiority complex; **être bourré de ~s*** to have loads of hang-ups*, be full of complexes; (*hum*) **il est vraiment sans ~** he's got no hang-ups*, he's got no shame (*péj*); **c'est une équipe de France sans ~ qui va jouer ce soir** the French team are in a very relaxed frame of mind for tonight's match. b (*Écon*) *industriel, universitaire* complex. c (*Chim, Math*) complex.

complexer [kɔ̃plɛkse] 1 vt: **ça le complexe terriblement** it gives him a terrible complex; **être très complexé** to have awful complexes, be very hung-up* *ou* mixed up* (*par* about).

complexion†† [kɔ̃plɛksjɔ̃] nf (*constitution*) constitution; (*teint*) complexion; (*humeur*) disposition, temperament.

complexité [kɔ̃plɛksite] nf complexity, intricacy; *[calcul]* complexity.

complication [kɔ̃plikasjɔ̃] nf (*complexité*) complexity, intricacy; (*ennui*) complication. (*Méd*) **~s** complications; **faire des ~s** to make life difficult *ou* complicated.

complice [kɔ̃plis] 1 adj a **être ~ de qch** to be (a) party to sth. b *regard* knowing (*épith*); *attitude* conniving. (*littér*) **la nuit ~ protégeait leur fuite** the friendly night conspired to shelter their flight (*littér*). 2 nmf a (*criminel*) accomplice. **être (le) ~ de qn** to be sb's accomplice, be in collusion with sb; **~ par instigation/par assistance** accessory before/after the fact. b (*adultère*) (*Jur*) co-respondent; (*amant*) lover; (*maîtresse*) mistress.

complicité [kɔ̃plisite] nf (*Jur, fig*) complicity. **agir en ~ avec** to act in complicity *ou* collusion with; **accusé de ~ de vol** accused of aiding and abetting a theft *ou* of being an accessary to theft.

complies [kɔ̃pli] nfpl compline.

compliment [kɔ̃plimɑ̃] nm a (*félicitations*) **~s** congratulations; **recevoir les ~s de qn** to receive sb's congratulations, be congratulated by sb; **faire des ~s à qn (pour)** to compliment *ou* congratulate sb (on); (*lit, iro*) **(je vous fais) mes ~s!** congratulations!, let me congratulate you!
b (*louange*) compliment. **elle rougit sous le ~** she blushed at the compliment; **faire des ~s à qn sur sa bonne mine, faire ~ à qn de sa bonne mine** to compliment sb on how well they look; **il lui fait sans cesse des ~s** he's always paying her compliments.
c (*formule de politesse*) **~s** compliments; **faites-lui mes ~s** give him my compliments *ou* regards; **avec les ~s de la direction** with the compliments of the management.
d (*petit discours*) congratulatory speech.

complimenter [kɔ̃plimɑ̃te] 1 vt to congratulate, compliment (*pour, sur, de* on).

complimenteur, -euse [kɔ̃plimɑ̃tœʀ, øz] 1 adj obsequious. 2 nm,f complimenter; (*péj*) flatterer.

compliqué, e [kɔ̃plike] (ptp de **compliquer**) adj *mécanisme* complicated, intricate; *affaire, explication, phrase* complicated, involved; *histoire, esprit* tortuous; *personne* complicated; (*Méd*) *fracture* compound (*épith*). **ne sois pas si ~!** don't be so complicated!; **puisque tu refuses, ce n'est pas ~, moi je pars** since you refuse, there's no problem *ou* that makes it easy *ou* that simplifies the problem – I'm leaving; **il ne m'écoute jamais, c'est pas ~!*** it's quite simple, he never listens to a word I say!

compliquer [kɔ̃plike] 1 1 vt to complicate. **il nous complique l'existence** he DOES make life difficult *ou* complicated for us; **se ~ l'existence** to make life difficult *ou* complicated for o.s. 2 **se compliquer** vpr to become *ou* get complicated. **ça se complique** things are getting more and more complicated; **la maladie se complique** complications have set in.

complot [kɔ̃plo] nm (*conspiration*) plot. **mettre qn dans le ~*** to let sb in on the plot*.

comploter [kɔ̃plɔte] 1 vti to plot (*de faire* to do, *contre* against). **qu'est-ce que vous complotez?*** what are you hatching?

comploteur, -euse [kɔ̃plɔtœʀ, øz] nm,f plotter.

componction [kɔ̃pɔ̃ksjɔ̃] nf (*péj*) (affected) gravity; (*Rel*) contrition. **avec ~** solemnly, with a great show of dignity.

componentiel, -ielle [kɔ̃pɔnɑ̃sjɛl] adj (*Ling*) componential.

comportement [kɔ̃pɔʀtəmɑ̃] nm (*gén*) behaviour (*envers, avec* towards); *[matériel, pneus]* performance.

comportemental, e, mpl **-aux** [kɔ̃pɔʀtəmɑ̃tal, o] adj behavioural (*Brit*), behavioral (*US*).

comportementalisme [kɔ̃pɔʀtəmɑ̃talism] nm behaviourism.

comportementaliste [kɔ̃pɔʀtəmɑ̃talist] adj, nmf behaviourist.

comporter [kɔ̃pɔʀte] 1 **1** vt **a** (*consister en*) to be composed of, be made up of, consist of, comprise. **ce roman comporte 2 parties** this novel is made up of *ou* is composed of *ou* comprises 2 parts; **la maison comporte 5 pièces et une cuisine** the house comprises 5 rooms and a kitchen.

b (*être muni de*) to have, include. **son livre comporte une préface** his book has *ou* includes a preface; **cette machine ne comporte aucun dispositif de sécurité** this machine is equipped with *ou* has no safety mechanism, there is no safety mechanism built into this machine; **cette règle comporte des exceptions** this rule has *ou* includes certain exceptions.

c (*impliquer*) *risques* to entail, involve. **je dois accepter cette solution, avec tout ce que cela comporte (de désavantages/d'imprévu)** I must accept this solution with all (the disadvantages/unexpected consequences) that it entails *ou* involves.

2 se comporter vpr **a** (*se conduire*) to behave. **se ~ en** *ou* **comme un enfant gâté** to behave like a spoilt child; **il s'est comporté d'une façon odieuse (avec sa mère)** he behaved in a horrible way (towards his mother).

b (*réagir*) *[personne]* to behave; *[machine, voiture]* to perform. **comment s'est-il comporté après l'accident?** how did he behave after the accident?; **notre équipe s'est très bien comportée hier** our team played *ou* acquitted itself very well yesterday, our team put up a good performance yesterday; **comment le matériel s'est-il comporté en altitude?** how did the equipment stand up to the high altitude? *ou* perform at high altitude?; **ces pneus se comportent très bien sur chaussée glissante** these tyres behave *ou* perform very well on slippery roads.

composant, e [kɔ̃pozɑ̃, ɑ̃t] **1** adj, nm component, constituent. **~s électroniques** electronic components. **2 composante** nf (*gén, Phys*) component. (*Pol*) **les diverses ~es du parti** the various elements in the party.

composé, e [kɔ̃poze] (ptp de **composer**) **1** adj **a** (*Chim, Gram, Math, Mus*) compound (*épith*); (*Bot*) *fleur* composite (*épith*); *feuille* compound (*épith*); *voir* **passé**. **b** (*guindé, affecté*) *maintien, attitude* studied. **2** nm (*Chim, Gram*) compound. (*fig*) **c'est un ~ étrange de douceur et de violence** he's a strange combination *ou* mixture of gentleness and violence. **3 composée** nf (*Bot*) plant of the family Compositae (*SPÉC*), composite. **~s** Compositae (*SPÉC*), composites.

composer [kɔ̃poze] 1 **1** vt **a** (*confectionner*) *plat, médicament* to make (up); *équipe de football etc* to select; *assemblée, équipe scientifique* to form, set up.

b (*élaborer*) *poème, lettre, roman* to write, compose; *symphonie* to compose; *tableau* to paint; *numéro de téléphone* to dial; *projet, programme* to work out, draw up.

c (*disposer*) *bouquet* to arrange, make up; *vitrine* to arrange, lay out.

d (*constituer*) *ensemble, produit, groupe* to make up; *assemblée* to form, make up. **pièces qui composent une machine** parts which (go to) make up a machine; **composé à 50% de papier recyclé** made of 50% recycled paper; **ces objets composent un ensemble harmonieux** these objects form *ou* make a harmonious group; *voir aussi* **3**.

e (*Typ*) to set.

f (*frm: étudier artificiellement*) **~ son visage** to compose one's features; **~ ses gestes** to use affected gestures; **attitudes/allures composées** studied behaviour/manners; **il s'était composé un personnage de dandy** he had established his image as that of a dandy; **se ~ un visage de circonstance** to assume a suitable expression.

2 vi **a** (*Scol*) **~ en anglais** to sit (*surtout Brit*) *ou* take an English test; **les élèves sont en train de ~** the pupils are (in the middle of) doing a test *ou* an exam.

b (*traiter*) to compromise. **~ avec** *adversaire etc* to come to terms with, compromise with.

3 se composer vpr (*consister en*) **se ~ de** *ou* **être composé de** to be composed of, be made up of, consist of, comprise; **la vitrine se compose** *ou* **est composée de robes** the window display is made up of *ou* composed of dresses; **notre équipe est composée à 70% de femmes** our team is 70% women, 70% of our team are women.

composite [kɔ̃pozit] **1** adj **a** (*hétérogène*) *éléments, mobilier, matériau, groupe* composite, heterogeneous; *public* mixed; *foule* motley (*épith*). **b** (*Archit*) composite. **2** nm (*Archit*) composite order; (*matériau*) composite.

compositeur, -trice [kɔ̃pozitœʀ, tʀis] nm,f (*Mus*) composer; (*Typ*) compositor, typesetter; *voir* **amiable**.

composition [kɔ̃pozisjɔ̃] nf **a** (*confection*) *[plat, médicament]* making(-up); *[assemblée]* formation, setting-up; *[équipe sportive]* selection; *[équipe de chercheurs]* setting-up; *[bouquet, vitrine]* arranging. **les boissons qui entrent dans la ~ du cocktail** the drinks that go into the cocktail; *voir* **rôle**.

b (*élaboration*) *[roman, lettre, poème]* writing, composition; *[symphonie]* composition; (*Ling*) composition, compounding; *[tableau]* painting. **une œuvre de ma ~** a work of my own composition, one of my own compositions.

c (*œuvre*) (*musicale, picturale*) composition; (*architecturale*) structure.

d (*structure*) *[plan, ensemble]* structure. **quelle est la ~ du passage?** what is the structure of the passage?; **la répartition des masses dans le tableau forme une ~ harmonieuse** the distribution of the masses in the picture forms *ou* makes a harmonious composition.

e (*constituants*) *[mélange]* composition; *[équipe, assemblée]* composition, line-up. **quelle est la ~ du gâteau?** what is the cake made of?, what ingredients go into the cake?; **la nouvelle ~ du Parlement européen** the new line-up in the European Parliament.

f (*Scol: examen*) **~s trimestrielles** end-of-term tests, term exams (*Brit*), final exams (*US*); **~ de français** (*en classe*) French test *ou* exam; (*à l'examen*) French paper; (*rédaction*) **~ française** French essay *ou* composition.

g (*Typ*) typesetting, composition.

h (*loc*) **venir à ~** to come to terms; **amener qn à ~** to get sb to come to terms; **être de bonne ~** to have a nice nature; *voir* **bon**[1].

compost [kɔ̃pɔst] nm compost.

compostage [kɔ̃pɔstaʒ] nm (*voir* **composter**) (date) stamping; punching.

composter [kɔ̃pɔste] 1 vt (*dater*) to (date) stamp; (*poinçonner*) to punch.

composteur [kɔ̃pɔstœʀ] nm (*timbre dateur*) date stamp; (*poinçon*) ticket machine; (*Typ*) composing stick.

compote [kɔ̃pɔt] nf (*Culin*) stewed fruit, compote. **~ de pommes/de poires** stewed apples/pears, compote of apples/pears; (*fig*) **j'ai les jambes en ~*** (*de fatigue*) my legs are aching (all over); (*par l'émotion, la maladie*) my legs are like jelly *ou* cotton wool; **il a le visage en ~*** his face is black and blue *ou* is a mass of bruises.

compotier [kɔ̃pɔtje] nm fruit dish *ou* bowl.

compréhensibilité [kɔ̃pʀeɑ̃sibilite] nf *[texte]* comprehensibility.

compréhensible [kɔ̃pʀeɑ̃sibl] adj (*clair*) comprehensible, easily understood; (*concevable*) understandable.

compréhensif, -ive [kɔ̃pʀeɑ̃sif, iv] adj (*tolérant*) understanding; (*logique*) comprehensive.

compréhension [kɔ̃pʀeɑ̃sjɔ̃] nf (*indulgence*) understanding; (*fait ou faculté de comprendre*) understanding, comprehension; (*clarté*) understanding, intelligibility; (*Logique*) comprehension; (*Scol*) aural comprehension. **exercice de ~** aural comprehension exercise.

comprendre [kɔ̃pʀɑ̃dʀ] 58 vt **a** (*être composé de*) to be composed of, be made up of, consist of, comprise; (*être muni de, inclure*) to include. **ce manuel comprend 3 parties** this textbook is composed of *ou* is made up of *ou* comprises 3 parts; **cet appareil comprend en outre un flash** this camera also has *ou* comes with* a flash, (also) included with this camera is a flash; **le loyer ne comprend pas le chauffage** the rent doesn't include *ou* cover (the) heating, the rent is not inclusive of heating; **je n'ai pas compris là-dedans les frais de déménagement** I haven't included the removal expenses in that.

b *problème, langue* to understand; *plaisanterie* to understand, get*; *personne* (*ce qu'elle dit ou écrit*) to understand, comprehend. **je ne le comprends pas/je ne comprends pas ce qu'il dit, il parle trop vite** I can't understand him/I can't make out what he says, he speaks too quickly; **vous m'avez mal compris** you've misunderstood me; **il ne comprend pas l'allemand** he doesn't understand German; **~ la vie/les choses** to understand life/things; **il ne comprend pas la plaisanterie** he can't take a joke; **il ne comprend rien à rien** he hasn't a clue about anything, he doesn't understand a thing (about anything); **c'est à n'y rien ~** it's completely baffling *ou* puzzling, it (just) baffles me, it's beyond me, I (just) can't understand it; **se faire ~** to make o.s. understood; **il est difficile de bien se faire ~** it's difficult to get one's ideas across (*de qn* to sb); **j'espère que je me suis bien fait ~** *ou* **que c'est compris** I hope I've made myself quite clear; **il comprend vite** he's quick, he catches on quickly*; **tu comprends, ce que je veux c'est ...** you see, what I want is ...; **il a bien su me faire ~ que je le gênais** he made it quite clear *ou* plain to me that I was annoying him; **dois-je ~ que ...?** am I to take it *ou* understand that ...?

c (*être compréhensif envers*) *personne* to understand. **j'espère qu'il comprendra** I hope he'll understand; **~ les jeunes/les enfants** to understand young people/children; **je le comprends, il en avait assez** I (can) understand him *ou* I know (just) how he feels *ou* felt – he'd had enough.

d (*concevoir*) *attitude, point de vue* to understand. **il ne veut pas ~ mon point de vue** he refuses to *ou* he won't understand *ou* see my point of view; **je comprends mal son attitude** I find it hard to understand his attitude; **c'est comme ça que je comprends les vacances** that's what I understand by *ou* think of as holidays; **c'est comme ça que je comprends le rôle de Hamlet** that's how I see *ou* understand the role of Hamlet; **ça se comprend, il voulait partir** it's quite understandable *ou* it's perfectly natural, he wanted to go; **nous comprenons vos difficultés mais nous ne pouvons rien faire** we understand *ou* appreciate your difficulties but there's nothing we can do.

e (*se rendre compte de, saisir*) to realize, understand (*pourquoi* why, *comment* how). **il n'a pas encore compris la gravité de son acte** he hasn't yet realized *ou* understood *ou* grasped the seriousness of his action; **j'ai compris ma douleur*** I realized what I had let myself in for*; **il m'a fait ~ que je devais faire attention** he made me realize that I should be careful; **il a enfin compris qu'elle ne voulait pas revenir** he realized *ou* understood at last that she didn't want to come back.

comprenette* [kɔ̃pʀənɛt] **nf: il est dur** *ou* **lent à la ~, il a la ~ difficile** *ou* **dure** he's slow on the uptake*, he's slow to catch on*.

compresse [kɔ̃pʀɛs] **nf** compress.

compresser [kɔ̃pʀese] [1] **vt** (*gén*) to squash; (*Tech*) to compress. **des vêtements compressés dans une valise** clothes squashed *ou* crammed into a suitcase.

compresseur [kɔ̃pʀesœʀ] **nm** compressor; *voir* **rouleau**.

compressibilité [kɔ̃pʀesibilite] **nf** (*Phys*) compressibility. (*Fin*) **la ~ des dépenses** the extent to which expenses can be reduced *ou* cut.

compressible [kɔ̃pʀesibl] **adj** (*Phys*) compressible; *dépenses* reducible. (*Fin*) **ces dépenses ne sont pas ~s à l'infini** these costs cannot be reduced *ou* cut down indefinitely.

compressif, -ive [kɔ̃pʀesif, iv] **adj** (*Méd*) compressive; († *fig*) repressive.

compression [kɔ̃pʀesjɔ̃] **nf** a (*action de comprimer*) *[gaz, substance]* compression; *[dépenses, personnel]* reduction, cutback, cutting-down (*de* in). **procéder à des ~s de crédits** to set up credit restrictions *ou* a credit squeeze; **des ~s budgétaires** cutbacks in spending, budget restrictions *ou* cuts; **~ des profits** squeeze on profits, reduction in profits; **~ des coûts** cost-cutting (*NonC*); **des mesures de ~ sont nécessaires** restrictions *ou* cutbacks are needed. b (*Aut, Phys: pression*) compression. **pompe de ~** compression pump; **meurtri par ~** bruised by crushing.

comprimé [kɔ̃pʀime] **nm** (*Pharm*) tablet.

comprimer [kɔ̃pʀime] [1] **vt** a (*presser*) *air, gaz* to compress; *artère* to compress; *substance à emballer etc* to press *ou* pack tightly together *ou* into blocks *etc.* **sa ceinture lui comprimait l'estomac** his belt was pressing *ou* digging into his stomach; **nous étions tous comprimés dans la voiture** we were all jammed together* *ou* packed tightly together in the car; *voir* **air¹**. b (*réduire*) *dépenses, personnel* to cut down *ou* back, reduce. c (*contenir*) *larmes* to hold back; *colère, sentiments* to hold back, repress, restrain, suppress.

compris, e [kɔ̃pʀi, iz] (**ptp de comprendre**) **adj** a (*inclus*) **10 F emballage ~** 10 francs inclusive of *ou* including packaging, 10 francs packaging included; **10 F emballage non ~** 10 francs exclusive of *ou* excluding *ou* not including packaging; (*sur menu etc*) **service ~** service included; **service non ~** service not included, service extra; **tout ~** all inclusive, everything included; **c'est 10 F tout ~** it's 10 francs all inclusive *ou* all in*; **il va vendre ses terres, la ferme ~e/non ~e** he's selling his land including/excluding the farm.

b **y ~: 100 F y ~ l'électricité** *ou* **l'électricité y ~e** 100 francs including electricity *ou* counting (the) electricity *ou* electricity included; **y ~ moi** myself included, including me *ou* myself; **y ~ Jean** including Jean, Jean included.

c (*situé*) **être ~ entre** to be contained between *ou* by, be bounded by; **la zone ~e entre les falaises et la mer** the area (lying) between the cliffs and the sea, the area contained between *ou* bounded by the cliffs and the sea; **il possède la portion de terrain ~e entre ces deux rues** he owns the piece of ground between these two streets *ou* contained between *ou* bounded by these two streets; **lisez tous les chapitres qui sont ~ entre les pages 12 et 145** read all the chapters (which are) contained *ou* included in pages 12 to 145.

d (*d'accord*) **(c'est) ~!** (it's) agreed!; **alors c'est ~, on se voit demain** so it's agreed then, we'll see each other tomorrow; **tu vas aller te coucher tout de suite, ~!** you're going to go to bed immediately, understand? *ou* is that understood *ou* clear?

compromettant, e [kɔ̃pʀɔmetɑ̃, ɑ̃t] **adj** compromising. **signer cette pétition, ce n'est pas très ~** you won't commit yourself to very much by signing this petition, there's no great commitment involved in signing this petition; (*péj*) **un homme ~** an undesirable associate.

compromettre [kɔ̃pʀɔmɛtʀ] [56] 1 **vt** *personne, réputation* to compromise; *avenir, chances, santé* to compromise, jeopardize. 2 **se compromettre vpr** (*s'avancer*) to commit o.s.; (*se discréditer*) to compromise o.s.

compromis, e [kɔ̃pʀɔmi, iz] (**ptp de compromettre**) 1 **adj: être ~** *[personne, réputation]* to be compromised; *[avenir, projet, chances]* to be jeopardized *ou* in jeopardy; **notre sortie/collaboration me semble bien** *ou* **très ~e** our trip/continuing collaboration looks very doubtful (to me). 2 **nm** compromise. **solution de ~** compromise solution; **~ de vente** (provisional) sales agreement.

compromission [kɔ̃pʀɔmisjɔ̃] **nf** dishonest compromise, shady deal. **c'est là une ~ avec votre conscience** now you're compromising with your conscience.

comptabilisation [kɔ̃tabilizasjɔ̃] **nf** (*Fin*) posting.

comptabiliser [kɔ̃tabilize] [1] **vt** (*Fin*) to post; (*compter*) to count.

comptabilité [kɔ̃tabilite] **nf** (*science*) accountancy, accounting; (*d'une petite entreprise*) book-keeping; (*comptes*) accounts, books; (*bureau, service*) accounts office *ou* department; (*profession*) accountancy. **il s'occupe de la ~ de notre entreprise** he does the accounting *ou* keeps the books for our firm; **~ publique** public finance; **~ à partie simple/double** single-/double-entry book-keeping; **~ industrielle** industrial book-keeping; *voir* **chef¹**.

comptable [kɔ̃tabl] 1 **adj** a (*Fin*) *règles etc* accounting, book-keeping. **il manque une pièce ~** one of the accounts is missing; (*Ling*) **nom ~** countable *ou* count noun; *voir* **machine³**. b (*responsable*) accountable (*de* for). 2 **nmf** accountant. **~ agréé** chartered accountant; **~ du Trésor** *local official of the Treasury;* **chèque adressé au ~ du Trésor** cheque addressed to the Treasury; *voir* **chef¹**, **expert**.

comptage [kɔ̃taʒ] **nm** (*action*) counting. **faire un ~ rapide** to do a quick count (*de* of).

comptant [kɔ̃tɑ̃] 1 **adv** *payer* cash, in cash; *acheter, vendre* for cash. **verser 100 F ~** to pay 100 francs down, put down 100 francs. 2 **nm** (*argent*) cash. **au ~** *payer* cash; *acheter, vendre* for cash; **achat/vente au ~** cash purchase/sale; *voir* **argent**.

compte [kɔ̃t] 1 **nm** a (*calcul*) count. **faire le ~ des prisonniers** to count (up) the prisoners, make a count of the prisoners, keep a tally of the prisoners; **l'as-tu inclus dans le ~?** have you counted *ou* included him?, did you include him in the count?; **faire le ~ des dépenses/de sa fortune** to calculate *ou* work out the expenditure/one's wealth.

b (*nombre exact*) (right) number. **le ~ y est** (*paiement*) that's the right amount; (*inventaire*) that's the right number, they're all there; **ça ne fait pas le ~** (*paiement*) that's not the right amount; (*inventaire*) there's (still) something missing, they're not all there; **j'ai ajouté 3 cuillerées/15 F pour faire le ~** I've added 3 spoonfuls/15 francs to make up the full amount; **ça devrait faire (largement) le ~** that should be (more than) enough; **avez-vous le bon** *ou* **votre ~ de chaises?** have you got the right number of chairs? *ou* the number of chairs you want?; **cela fait un ~ rond** it makes a round number *ou* figure; **je n'arrive jamais au même ~** I never get the same figure *ou* number *ou* total twice; **nous sommes loin du ~** we are a long way short of the target; (*Comm*) **faire bon ~** to make up the amount.

c (*Comptabilité*) account. **faire ses ~s** to do one's accounts *ou* books; **tenir les ~s du ménage** to keep the household accounts; **tenir les ~s d'une firme** to keep the books *ou* accounts of a firm; **publier à ~ d'auteur** to publish at the author's expense; (*hum*) **~s d'apothicaire** complicated accounting; **nous sommes en ~** we have business to settle; **approuver/liquider un ~** to approve/clear *ou* settle an account; **passer en ~** to place *ou* pass to account; *voir* **laissé-pour-compte, ligne¹**.

d (*Banque*) **~ (en banque** *ou* **bancaire)** (bank) account; **avoir de l'argent en ~** to have money in an account; **~ courant** *ou* **de chèques** *ou* **de dépôt** current *ou* checking (*US*) account; **~ sur livret** deposit account; **porter une somme au ~ débiteur/créditeur de qn** to debit/credit a sum to sb's account; **avoir un ~ dans une banque/à la Banque de France** to have an *ou* be in account with a bank/with the Banque de France.

e (*dû*) **donner** *ou* **régler son ~ à un employé** (*lit*) to settle up with an employee; (*fig: renvoyer*) to give an employee his cards* (*Brit*) *ou* books* (*Brit*) *ou* pink slip* (*US*); (*fig*) **il avait son ~*** (*fatigué*) he'd had as much as he could take; (*mort*) he'd had it*, he was done for; (*soûl*) he'd had more than he could hold; (*fig*) **son ~ est bon** his number's up*, he's had it*, he's for it* (*Brit*); *voir* **régler**.

f (*Comm: facture, addition*) (*gén*) account, invoice, bill; *[hôtel, restaurant]* bill (*Brit*), check (*US*). **pourriez-vous me faire mon ~?** would you make me out my bill?; **mettez-le sur mon ~** (*au restaurant, à l'hôtel*) put it on my bill; (*dans un magasin*) charge it to *ou* put it on my account.

g (*explications, justifications*) **~s** explanation; **devoir des ~s à qn** to owe sb an explanation; **demander** *ou* **réclamer des ~s à qn** to ask sb for an explanation; **il me doit des ~s à propos de cette perte** he owes me an explanation for this loss, he will have to account to me for this loss; *voir* **rendre**.

h (*avantage, bien*) **cela fait mon ~** that suits me; **il y a trouvé son ~** he's got something out of it, he did well out of it; **chacun y trouve son ~** it has got *ou* there is something in it for everybody.

i (*loc*) (*Boxe*) **envoyer qn/aller au tapis** *ou* **à terre pour le ~** to floor sb/go down for the count; **tenir ~ de qch/qn** to take sth/sb into account; **il n'a pas tenu ~ de nos avertissements** he didn't take any notice of our warnings, he disregarded *ou* ignored our warnings; **~ tenu de** considering, in view of; **tenir ~ à qn de son dévouement** to take sb's devotion into account; **on lui a tenu ~ de son passé** they took his past into account *ou* consideration; **en prendre pour son ~*** to take a hiding (*Brit*) *ou* beating; **prendre qch à son ~** (*payer*) to pay for sth; (*en assumer la responsabilité*) to take responsibility for sth; **je reprends cette maxime à mon ~** I shall make that saying my motto; **il a repris la boutique à son ~** he's taken over the shop on his own account *ou* in his own name; **être/s'établir** *ou* **se mettre** *ou* **s'installer à son ~** to be/set up in business for o.s., have/set up one's own business; **travailler à son ~** to be self-employed; **à ce ~-là** (*dans ce cas*) in this case; (*à ce train-là*) at this rate; **tout ~ fait** all things considered, when all is said and done; **mettre qch sur le ~ de** to put sth down to, attribute *ou* ascribe sth to; **dire/apprendre qch sur le ~ de qn** to say/learn sth about sb; **pour le ~ de** (*au nom de*) on behalf of; **pour mon ~ (personnel)** (*en ce qui me concerne*) personally; (*pour mon propre usage*) for my own use; **comment fais-tu ton ~ pour dépenser tant?/te perdre?** how do you manage to spend so much?/get lost?; *voir* **bon**.

2 **comp ►compte bloqué** (*Fin*) escrow account **►compte chèque postal** *post office bank account*, ≃ National Girobank account (*Brit*) **►compte d'épargne en actions** stock market investment savings account **►compte d'épargne logement** *house purchase savings account giving the saver a reduced mortgage rate*, ≃ building society account (*Brit*) **►compte joint** (*Fin*) joint account **►compte numéroté** *ou* **à numéro** (*Fin*) numbered account **►compte pour le développement industriel** (*Fin*) industrial development savings account **►compte des profits et pertes** (*Fin*) profit and loss account **►compte à rebours** (*Espace, fig*) countdown **►compte rendu** (*rapport*) (*gén*) account, report; *[livre, film]* review; (*sur travaux en cours*) progress report; **compte rendu d'audience** court record; **faire le compte rendu d'un match/d'une réunion** to give an account *ou* a report of a match/meeting, give a rundown of a match/meeting.

compte- [kɔ̃t] **préf** *voir* **compter**.

compter [kɔ̃te] [1] **1 vt a** (*calculer*) *choses, personnes, argent, jours* to count. **combien en avez-vous compté?** how many did you count?, how many did you make it?; **40 cm? j'avais compté 30** 40 cm? I made it 30; **il a 50 ans bien comptés** he's a good 50 (years old); **~ qch de tête** to work sth out *ou* calculate sth in one's head; **on peut ~ (sur les doigts de la main) les auditeurs qui comprennent vraiment** you can count (on the fingers of one hand) the members of the audience who really understand; **on ne compte plus ses gaffes, ses gaffes ne se comptent plus** we've lost (all) count of *ou* we can't keep count of his blunders; **~ les jours/les minutes** to count the days/the minutes; **~ les points** (*lit*) to count (up) the points; (*fig*) **pendant qu'ils se disputaient moi je comptais les points** I just sat back and watched while they argued; **pendant qu'ils se battaient je comptais les coups** I just sat back and watched while they fought; (*fig*) **~ les moutons** to count sheep; (*Boxe*) **il a été compté 7** he took a count of 7.

b (*escompter, prévoir*) to allow, reckon. **combien as-tu compté qu'il nous fallait de chaises?** how many chairs did you reckon we'd need?; **j'ai compté qu'il nous en fallait 10** I reckoned we'd need 10; **combien de temps/d'argent comptez-vous pour finir les travaux?** how much time/money do you reckon it'll take to finish the work?, how much time/money are you allowing to finish the work?; **il faut (bien) ~ 10 jours/10 F** you must allow (a good) 10 days/10 francs, you must reckon on it taking (a good) 10 days/10 francs; **j'ai compté 90 cm pour le frigo, j'espère que ça suffira** I've allowed 90 cm for the fridge, I hope that'll do.

c (*tenir compte de*) to take into account; (*inclure*) to include. **on te comptera ta bonne volonté** your goodwill *ou* helpfulness will be taken into account; **cela fait un mètre en comptant l'ourlet** that makes one metre counting *ou* including *ou* if you include the hem; **t'es-tu compté?** did you count *ou* include yourself?; **ne me comptez pas** don't include me; **nous étions 10, sans ~ l'instituteur** we were 10, not counting the teacher; **ils nous apportèrent leurs connaissances, sans ~ leur bonne volonté** they gave us their knowledge, not to mention *ou* to say nothing of their goodwill *ou* helpfulness; **sans ~ que** (*et de plus ...*) not to mention that; (*d'autant plus que*) **il aurait dû venir, sans ~ qu'il n'avait rien à faire** he ought to have come especially since he had nothing to do.

d (*facturer*) to charge for. **~ qch à qn** to charge sb for sth, charge sth to sb; **ils n'ont pas compté le café** they didn't charge for the coffee; **combien vous ont-ils compté le café?** how much did they charge you for the coffee?; **ils nous l'ont compté trop cher/10 F/au prix de gros** they charged us too much/10 francs/the wholesale price for it.

e (*avoir*) to have. **la ville compte quelques très beaux monuments** the town has some very beautiful monuments; **il compte 2 ans de règne/de service** he has been reigning/in the firm for 2 years; **il ne compte pas d'ennemis** he has no enemies; **cette famille compte trois musiciens parmi ses membres** this family has *ou* boasts three musicians among its members.

f (*classer, ranger*) to consider. **on compte ce livre parmi les meilleurs de l'année** this book is considered (to be) *ou* ranks among the best of the year; **il le compte au nombre de ses amis** he considers him one of his friends, he numbers him among his friends.

g (*verser*) to pay. **le caissier va vous ~ 600 F** the cashier will pay you 600 francs; **vous lui compterez 1000 F pour les heures supplémentaires** you will pay him 1,000 francs' overtime.

h (*donner avec parcimonie*) **il compte chaque sou qu'il nous donne** he counts every penny he gives us; **les permissions leur sont comptées** their leave is rationed; **il ne compte pas sa peine** he spares no trouble; **ses jours sont comptés** his days are numbered; **mon temps (m')est compté** my time is precious; (*fig*) **~ ses pas** to plod along.

i (*avoir l'intention de*) to intend, plan, mean (*faire* to do); (*s'attendre à*) to reckon, expect. **ils comptent partir demain** they plan *ou* mean to go tomorrow, they reckon on going tomorrow; **je compte recevoir la convocation demain** I'm expecting to receive the summons tomorrow; **~ que: je ne compte pas qu'il vienne aujourd'hui** I am not expecting him to come today.

2 **vi a** (*calculer*) to count. **il sait ~ (jusqu'à 10)** he can count (up to 10); **comment est-ce que tu as compté?** how did you work it out?; **~ sur ses doigts** to count on one's fingers; **~ de tête** to count in one's head; **tu as mal compté** you counted wrong, you miscounted; **à ~ de** (starting *ou* as) from.

b (*être économe*) to economize. **avec la montée des prix, il faut ~ sans cesse** with the rise in prices you have to watch every penny (you spend); **dépenser sans ~** (*être dépensier*) to spend extravagantly; (*donner généreusement*) to give without counting the cost; **il s'est dépensé sans ~ pour cette cause** he spared no effort in supporting that cause, he gave himself wholeheartedly to that cause.

c (*avoir de l'importance*) to count, matter. **c'est le résultat/le geste qui compte** it's the result/the gesture that counts *ou* matters; **35 ans de mariage, ça compte!** 35 years of marriage, that's quite something!; **c'est un succès qui compte** it's an important success; **ce qui compte c'est de savoir dès maintenant** the main thing is to find out right away; **sa mère compte beaucoup pour lui** his mother is very important to him; **ça ne compte pas** that doesn't count; *voir aussi* **2e**.

d (*tenir compte de*) **~ avec qch** to reckon with sth, take account of sth, allow for sth; **il faut ~ avec l'opinion** you've got to reckon with *ou* take account of public opinion; **il faut ~ avec le temps incertain** you have to allow for changeable weather; **un nouveau parti avec lequel il faut ~** a new party to be reckoned with; **on avait compté sans la grève** we hadn't reckoned on there being a strike, we hadn't allowed for the strike.

e (*figurer*) **~ parmi** to be *ou* rank among; **~ au nombre de** to be one of; **~ pour: il compte pour 2** he's worth 2 men; **il compte pour 4 quand il s'agit de bagages/manger** he takes enough luggage/eats enough for four; **cela compte pour beaucoup dans sa réussite/dans sa décision** that has a lot to do with his success/his decision, that is a big factor in his success/his decision; **cela ne compte pour rien dans sa réussite/dans sa décision** that has nothing to do with his success/his decision, that has no bearing on his success/his decision; **cela compte pour (du) beurre*** that counts for nothing, that doesn't count.

f (*valoir*) to count. **pour la retraite, les années de guerre comptent double** for the purposes of retirement, war service counts double; **après 60 ans les années comptent double** after 60 every year counts double.

g (*se fier à*) **~ sur** to count on, rely on; **~ sur la discrétion/la bonne volonté de qn** to count on *ou* rely on sb's discretion/goodwill; **nous comptons sur vous (pour) demain** we're expecting you (to come) tomorrow, we're relying on your coming tomorrow; **j'y compte bien!** I should hope so!, so I should hope!; **n'y comptez pas trop, ne comptez pas trop là-dessus** don't bank on it, don't count too much on it; **je compte sur vous** I'm counting *ou* relying on you; **vous pouvez ~ là-dessus** you can depend upon it; **ne comptez pas sur moi** (you can) count me out; **tu peux ~ sur lui pour le répéter partout!** you can bet (your life) he'll go and tell everyone!, you can count on him to go and tell everyone!; **compte (là-)dessus et bois de l'eau (fraîche)!**⁑ you've got a hope! (*Brit*), you haven't a prayer! (*US*), you'll be lucky!, you've got a fat chance!*

3 **comp ►compte-fils** (*Tech*) **nm inv** linen tester **►compte-gouttes nm inv** (*pipette*) dropper; **au compte-gouttes** (*fig*) *distribuer, dépenser* sparingly, in dribs and drabs; *rembourser* in dribs and drabs, in driblets; *entrer, sortir* in dribs and drabs **►compte-tours nm inv** (*Aut*) rev *ou* revolution counter, tachometer; (*Tech*) rev *ou* revolution counter.

compteur [kɔ̃tœʀ] **nm** meter. **~ d'eau/d'électricité/à gaz** water/electricity/gas meter; **~ Geiger** Geiger counter; **~ (kilométrique)** milometer (*Brit*), odometer (*US*); **~ (de vitesse)** speedometer.

comptine [kɔ̃tin] **nf** (*gén: chanson*) nursery rhyme; (*pour compter*) counting rhyme *ou* song.

comptoir [kɔ̃twaʀ] **nm a** *[magasin]* counter; *[bar]* bar. **b** (*colonial*) trading post. **c** (*Comm: cartel*) syndicate (*for marketing*). **d** (*Fin: agence*) branch.

compulsation [kɔ̃pylsasjɔ̃] **nf** consultation.

compulser [kɔ̃pylse] [1] **vt** to consult.

comte [kɔ̃t] **nm** count; (*britannique*) earl.

comté [kɔ̃te] **nm a** (*Hist*) earldom; (*Admin Brit, Can*) county. **b** (*fromage*) comté (*kind of gruyère cheese*).

comtesse [kɔ̃tɛs] **nf** countess.

comtois, e [kɔ̃twa, waz] **1 adj** of *ou* from Franche-Comté. **2 nm,f: C~(e)** inhabitant *ou* native of Franche-Comté. **3 comtoise nf** ≃ grandfather clock.

con, conne [kɔ̃, kɔn] **1 adj (f aussi inv)** (⁑: *stupide*) bloody*⁑ (*Brit*) *ou* damned⁑ stupid. **qu'il est ~!** what a stupid bastard*⁑ *ou* bloody fool (he is)!; **il est ~ comme la lune** *ou* **comme un balai** he's a bloody** (*Brit*) *ou* damned* fool *ou* idiot; **c'est pas ~ comme idée** (it's) not a bad idea*. 2 **nm,f** (*: *crétin*) damn fool*, bloody (*Brit*) idiot*, wally*, schmuck* (*US*). **quel ~ ce mec** what a wally* *ou* damn fool* *ou* bloody idiot* this guy* is; **bande de ~s** load of cretins* *ou* bloody idiots*; **faire le ~** to mess around*, muck about* (*Brit*), piss about**; **dispositif/gouvernement à la ~** lousy* *ou* crummy* device/government. 3 **nm** (**: *vagin*) cunt**.

Conakry [kɔnakʀi] **n** Conakry.

conard* [kɔnaʀ] **nm = connard***.

conarde* [kɔnaʀd] **nf = connarde***.

conasse* [kɔnas] **nf = connasse***.

concassage [kɔ̃kɑsaʒ] **nm** (*voir* **concasser**) crushing; grinding.

concasser [kɔ̃kɑse] [1] **vt** *pierre, sucre, céréales* to crush; *poivre* to grind.

concasseur [kɔ̃kɑsœʀ] 1 **adj m** crushing. 2 **nm** crusher.

concaténation [kɔ̃katenasjɔ̃] **nf** concatenation.

concave [kɔ̃kav] **adj** concave.

concavité [kɔ̃kavite] **nf** (*Opt*) concavity; (*gen: cavité*) hollow, cavity. **les ~s d'un rocher** the hollows *ou* cavities in a rock.

concédant [kɔ̃sedɑ̃] **nm** (*Écon*) licensor.

concéder [kɔ̃sede] [6] **vt** *privilège, droit, exploitation* to grant; *point* to concede; (*Sport*) *but, corner* to concede, give away. **je vous concède que** I'll grant you that.

concélébrant [kɔ̃selebʀɑ̃] **nm** concelebrant.

concélébrer [kɔ̃selebʀe] [1] **vt** to concelebrate.

concentration [kɔ̃sɑ̃tʀasjɔ̃] **nf** a (*gén, Chim*) concentration. **les grandes ~s urbaines des Midlands** the great conurbations of the Midlands; *voir* **camp**. b (*fusion*) **la ~ des entreprises** the merging of businesses; **~ horizontale/verticale** horizontal/vertical integration. c **~ (d'esprit)** concentration.

concentrationnaire [kɔ̃sɑ̃tʀasjɔnɛʀ] **adj** of *ou* in concentration camps, concentration camp (*épith*).

concentré, e [kɔ̃sɑ̃tʀe] (**ptp de concentrer**) 1 **adj** a *acide* concentrated; *lait* condensed. b *candidat, athlète* in a state of concentration, concentrating hard (*attrib*). 2 **nm** (*chimique*) concentrated solution; (*bouillon*) concentrate, extract. **~ de tomates** tomato purée; (*fig*) **ce livre est un ~ d'absurdités/d'obscénités** this book is full of nonsense/obscenities.

concentrer [kɔ̃sɑ̃tʀe] [1] 1 **vt** (*gén*) to concentrate. **~ son attention sur** to concentrate *ou* focus one's attention on. 2 **se concentrer vpr** *[foule, troupes]* to concentrate. **le candidat se concentra avant de répondre** the candidate gathered his thoughts *ou* thought hard before replying; **je me concentre!** I'm concentrating!; **se ~ sur un problème** to concentrate on a problem; **les regards se concentrèrent sur moi** everybody's gaze was fixed *ou* focused on me, all eyes turned on me.

concentrique [kɔ̃sɑ̃tʀik] **adj** *cercle* concentric.

concentriquement [kɔ̃sɑ̃tʀikmɑ̃] **adv** concentrically.

concept [kɔ̃sɛpt] **nm** concept.

concepteur, -trice [kɔ̃sɛptœʀ, tʀis] **nm,f** (*Ind, Comm*) designer. **~ de réseaux** network designer; **~ publicitaire** advertising designer.

conception [kɔ̃sɛpsjɔ̃] **nf** a (*Bio*) conception; *voir* **immaculé**. b (*action*) *[idée]* conception, conceiving; (*Ind, Comm*) design. **la ~ d'un tel plan est géniale** it is a brilliantly conceived plan; **voilà quelle est ma ~ de la chose** this is how I see it; **machine d'une ~ révolutionnaire** machine conceived on revolutionary lines, machine of revolutionary design; **~ assistée par ordinateur** computer-aided *ou* computer-assisted design. c (*idée*) notion, idea; (*réalisation*) creation.

conceptualisation [kɔ̃sɛptɥalizasjɔ̃] **nf** conceptualization.

conceptualiser [kɔ̃sɛptɥalize] [1] **vt** to conceptualize.

conceptuel, -elle [kɔ̃sɛptɥɛl] **adj** conceptual.

concernant [kɔ̃sɛʀnɑ̃] **prép** a (*se rapportant à*) concerning, relating to, regarding. **des mesures ~ ce problème seront bientôt prises** steps will soon be taken concerning *ou* relating to *ou* regarding this problem. b (*en ce qui concerne*) with regard to, as regards. **~ ce problème, des mesures seront bientôt prises** with regard to this problem *ou* as regards this problem *ou* as far as this problem is concerned, steps will soon be taken to resolve it.

concerner [kɔ̃sɛʀne] [1] **vt** to affect, concern. **cela ne vous concerne pas** it's no concern of yours, it doesn't concern *ou* affect you; **en ce qui concerne cette question** with regard to this question, concerning this question, as far as this question is concerned; **en ce qui me concerne** as far as I'm concerned; (*Admin*) **pour affaire vous concernant** to discuss a matter which concerns you *ou* a matter concerning you; **il ne se sent pas concerné** (*directement impliqué*) he's not affected (*par* by); (*moralement intéressé*) he's not concerned (*par* about); **je ne me sens pas concerné par sa remarque/son rapport** his remark/report doesn't apply to *ou* concern me.

concert [kɔ̃sɛʀ] **nm** a (*Mus*) concert. **~ spirituel** concert of sacred music; (*fig*) **~ de louanges/de lamentations/d'invectives** chorus of praise/lamentation(s)/invective; **on entendit un ~ d'avertisseurs** a chorus of horns started up; *voir* **café, salle**.

b (*littér*) (*harmonie*) chorus; (*accord*) entente, accord. **un ~ de voix** a chorus of voices; **le ~ des grandes puissances** the entente *ou* accord between the great powers.

c **de ~** (*ensemble*) *partir* together; *rire* in unison; *agir* together, in unison; (*d'un commun accord*) *décider* unanimously; *agir* in concert; **ils ont agi de ~ pour éviter** ... they took concerted action to avoid ...; **de ~ avec** (*en accord avec*) in cooperation *ou* conjunction with; (*ensemble*) together with.

concertant, e [kɔ̃sɛʀtɑ̃, ɑ̃t] **adj** *voir* **symphonie**.

concertation [kɔ̃sɛʀtasjɔ̃] **nf** (*échange de vues, dialogue*) dialogue; (*rencontre*) meeting. (*principe*) **la ~** dialogue; **suggérer une ~ des pays industriels** to suggest setting up *ou* creating a dialogue between industrial nations; **sans ~ préalable** without preliminary consultation(s).

concerté, e [kɔ̃sɛʀte] (**ptp de concerter**) **adj** concerted.

concerter [kɔ̃sɛʀte] [1] 1 **vt** (*organiser*) *plan, entreprise, projet* to devise. 2 **se concerter vpr** (*délibérer*) to consult (each other), take counsel together.

concertina [kɔ̃sɛʀtina] **nm** concertina.

concertino [kɔ̃sɛʀtino] **nm** concertino.

concertiste [kɔ̃sɛʀtist] **nmf** concert artiste *ou* performer.

concerto [kɔ̃sɛʀto] **nm** concerto. **~ pour piano (et orchestre)** piano concerto, concerto for piano and orchestra.

concessif, -ive [kɔ̃sesif, iv] (*Gram*) 1 **adj** concessive. 2 **concessive nf** concessive clause.

concession [kɔ̃sesjɔ̃] **nf** a (*faveur*) concession (*à* to). **faire des ~s** to make concessions. b (*cession*) *[terrain, exploitation]* concession. **faire la ~ d'un terrain** to grant a piece of land. c (*exploitation, terrain, territoire*) concession; *[cimetière]* plot. **~ minière** mining concession; **~ à perpétuité** plot held in perpetuity.

concessionnaire [kɔ̃sesjɔnɛʀ] 1 **adj**: **la société ~** the concessionary company. 2 **nmf** (*marchand agréé*) agent, dealer, franchise holder; (*bénéficiaire d'une concession*) concessionaire, concessionary. **disponible chez votre ~** available from your dealer.

concevable [kɔ̃s(ə)vabl] **adj** (*compréhensible*) conceivable. **il est très ~ que** it's quite conceivable that.

concevoir [kɔ̃s(ə)vwaʀ] [28] 1 **vt** a (*penser*) to imagine; *fait, concept, idée* to conceive of. **je n'arrive pas à ~ que c'est fini** I can't conceive *ou* believe that it's finished.

b (*élaborer, étudier*) *solution, projet, moyen* to conceive, devise, think up. **leur maison est bien/mal conçue** their house is well/badly designed *ou* planned.

c (*envisager*) *question* to see, view. **voilà comment je conçois la chose** that's how I see it *ou* view it *ou* look at it; **ils concevaient la question différemment** they viewed the question differently.

d (*comprendre*) to understand. **je conçois sa déception** *ou* **qu'il soit déçu** I can understand his disappointment *ou* his being disappointed; **cela se conçoit facilement** it's quite understandable, it's easy to understand; **il ne conçoit pas qu'on puisse souffrir de la faim** he cannot imagine *ou* conceive that people can suffer from starvation; **on concevrait mal qu'il puisse refuser** they would find it difficult to understand his refusal; **ce qui se conçoit bien s'énonce clairement** what is clearly understood can be clearly expressed.

e (*rédiger*) *lettre, réponse* to compose. **ainsi conçu, conçu en ces termes** expressed *ou* couched in these terms.

f (*littér: éprouver*) **je conçois des doutes quant à son intégrité** I have *ou* feel some doubts as to his integrity; **il en conçut une terrible jalousie** he conceived a terrible feeling of jealousy (*littér*); **il conçut de l'amitié pour moi** he took a liking to me.

g (*engendrer*) to conceive.

2 **vi** (*engendrer*) to conceive.

concierge [kɔ̃sjɛʀʒ] **nmf** *[immeuble]* caretaker, manager (of an apartment building) (*US*); *[hôtel]* porter; (*en France*) concierge. (*fig*) **c'est un(e) vrai(e) ~** he (*ou* she) is a real gossip.

conciergerie [kɔ̃sjɛʀʒəʀi] **nf** *[lycée, château]* caretaker's lodge; (*Can*) apartment house. (*Hist*) **la C~** the Conciergerie.

concile [kɔ̃sil] **nm** (*Rel*) council. **~ œcuménique** ecumenical council; **le ~ de Trente** the Council of Trent.

conciliable [kɔ̃siljabl] **adj** (*compatible*) reconcilable.

conciliabule [kɔ̃siljabyl] **nm** a (*entretien*) consultation, confab*. (*iro*) **tenir de grands ~s** to have great consultations *ou* confabs*. b (†: *réunion*) secret meeting.

conciliaire [kɔ̃siljɛʀ] **adj** conciliar. **les pères ~s** the fathers of the council.

conciliant, e [kɔ̃siljɑ̃, jɑ̃t] **adj** conciliatory, conciliating.

conciliateur, -trice [kɔ̃siljatœʀ, tʀis] 1 **adj** conciliatory, conciliating. 2 **nm,f** (*médiateur*) conciliator.

conciliation [kɔ̃siljasjɔ̃] **nf** (*gén*) conciliation, reconciliation; (*entre époux*) reconciliation. **esprit de ~** spirit of conciliation; **comité de ~** arbitration committee; **la ~ d'intérêts opposés** the reconciliation *ou* reconciling of conflicting interests; **tentative de ~** (*gén, Pol*) attempt at (re)conciliation; (*entre époux*) attempt at reconciliation; *voir* **procédure**.

conciliatoire [kɔ̃siljatwaʀ] **adj** (*Jur*) conciliatory.

concilier [kɔ̃silje] [7] 1 **vt** a (*rendre compatible*) *exigences, opinions, sentiments* to reconcile (*avec* with). b (*ménager, attirer*) to win, gain. **sa bonté lui a concilié les électeurs** his kindness won *ou* gained him the support of the voters *ou* won over the voters. c (*littér, Jur: réconcilier*) *ennemis* to reconcile, conciliate. 2 **se concilier** vpr (*se ménager, s'attirer*) to win, gain. **se ~ les bonnes grâces de qn** to win *ou* gain sb's favour.

concis, e [kɔ̃si, iz] adj concise. **en termes ~** concisely.

concision [kɔ̃sizjɔ̃] nf concision, conciseness, succinctness.

concitoyen, -yenne [kɔ̃sitwajɛ̃, jɛn] nm,f fellow citizen.

conclave [kɔ̃klav] nm (*Rel*) conclave.

concluant, e [kɔ̃klyɑ̃, ɑ̃t] adj conclusive.

conclure [kɔ̃klyʀ] 35 1 vt a (*signer*) *affaire, accord* to conclude. **~ un marché** to conclude *ou* clinch a deal; **marché conclu!** it's a deal!

b (*terminer*) *débat, discours, texte* to conclude, end. **et pour ~** and to conclude; **on vous demande de ~** will you please bring *ou* draw your discussion *etc* to a close, will you please wind up your discussion *etc*; **il conclut par ces mots/en disant ...** he concluded with these words/by saying ...; (*Jur*) **~ sa plaidoirie** to rest one's case.

c (*déduire*) to conclude (*qch de qch* sth from sth). **j'en conclus que** I therefore conclude that.

2 vi a **~ à: ils ont conclu à son innocence/au suicide** they concluded that he was innocent/that it was suicide, they pronounced him to be innocent/that it was suicide; **les juges ont conclu à l'acquittement** the judges decided on an acquittal.

b (*Jur*) **~ contre qn** [*témoignage*] to convict sb.

conclusif, -ive [kɔ̃klyzif, iv] adj concluding (*épith*).

conclusion [kɔ̃klyzjɔ̃] nf (*gén*) conclusion; [*discours*] close. **~s** (*Jur*) [*demandeur*] pleadings, submissions; [*avocat*] summing-up; [*jury*] findings, conclusions; **déposer des ~s auprès d'un tribunal** to file submissions with a court; **en ~** in conclusion; **~*, il n'est pas venu** the net result was that he didn't come; **~*, on s'était trompé** in other words, we had made a mistake.

concocter* [kɔ̃kɔkte] 1 vt (*élaborer*) *breuvage, mélange, discours, loi* to concoct.

concoction* [kɔ̃kɔksjɔ̃] nf concoction.

concombre [kɔ̃kɔ̃bʀ] nm cucumber.

concomitamment [kɔ̃kɔmitamɑ̃] adv concomitantly.

concomitance [kɔ̃kɔmitɑ̃s] nf concomitance.

concomitant, e [kɔ̃kɔmitɑ̃, ɑ̃t] adj concomitant.

concordance [kɔ̃kɔʀdɑ̃s] nf a (*gén*) agreement. **la ~ de 2 témoignages** the agreement of 2 testimonies, the fact that 2 testimonies tally *ou* agree; **la ~ de 2 résultats/situations** the similarity of *ou* between 2 results/situations; **mettre ses actes en ~ avec ses principes** to act in accordance with one's principles. b (*index*) [*Bible*] concordance; (*Géol*) conformability. (*Gram*) **~ des temps** sequence of tenses; (*Phys*) **~ de phases** synchronization of phases.

concordant, e [kɔ̃kɔʀdɑ̃, ɑ̃t] adj *faits* corroborating; (*Géol*) conformable. **2 témoignages ~s** 2 testimonies which agree *ou* which are in agreement *ou* which tally.

concordat [kɔ̃kɔʀda] nm (*Rel*) concordat; (*Comm*) composition; [*faillite*] winding-up arrangement.

concorde [kɔ̃kɔʀd] nf (*littér: harmonie*) concord.

concorder [kɔ̃kɔʀde] 1 vi [*faits, dates, témoignages*] to agree, tally; [*idées*] to coincide, match; [*caractères*] to match. **faire ~ des chiffres** to make figures agree *ou* tally; **ses actes concordent-ils avec ses idées?** is his behaviour in accordance with his ideas?

concourant, e [kɔ̃kuʀɑ̃, ɑ̃t] adj (*convergent*) *droites* convergent; *efforts* concerted (*épith*), united, cooperative.

concourir [kɔ̃kuʀiʀ] 11 1 vi a [*concurrent*] to compete (*pour* for). **les films qui concourent au festival** the films competing (for a prize) at the festival. b (*Math: converger*) to converge (*vers* towards, on). 2 **concourir à** vt indir (*coopérer pour*) **~ à qch/à faire qch** to work towards sth/towards doing sth; **tout concourt à notre réussite** everything is working in our favour; **son manque de flexibilité a concouru à sa baisse de popularité** his inflexibility contributed to *ou* was a factor in the decline in his popularity.

concours [kɔ̃kuʀ] nm a (*gén: jeu, compétition*) competition; (*Scol: examen*) competitive examination. **~ agricole** agricultural show; **~ hippique** (*Sport*) showjumping (*NonC*); (*épreuve*) **un ~ hippique** a horse show; (*Admin*) **promotion par (voie de) ~** promotion by (competitive) examination; **~ de beauté** beauty contest; (*Scol*) **~ d'entrée (à)** (competitive) entrance examination (for); **~ de recrutement** competitive entry examination; (*Scol*) **~ général** *competitive examination with prizes, open to secondary school children;* voir **hors**.

b (*participation*) aid, help. **prêter son ~ à qch** to lend one's support to sth; **avec le ~ de** (*participation*) with the participation of; (*aide*) with the support *ou* help *ou* assistance of; **il a fallu le ~ des pompiers** the firemen's help was needed.

c (*rencontre*) **~ de circonstances** combination of circumstances; **un grand ~ de peuple**† a large concourse† *ou* throng of people.

concret, -ète [kɔ̃kʀɛ, ɛt] 1 adj (*tous sens: réel*) concrete. **esprit ~** down-to-earth mind; **il en a tiré des avantages ~s** he got *ou* it gave him certain real *ou* positive advantages; voir **musique**. 2 nm: **le ~ et l'abstrait** the concrete and the abstract; **ce que je veux, c'est du ~** I want something concrete.

concrètement [kɔ̃kʀɛtmɑ̃] adv in concrete terms. **je me représente très ~ la situation** I can visualize the situation very clearly; **~, à quoi ça va servir?** what practical use will it have?, in concrete terms, what use will it be?

concrétion [kɔ̃kʀesjɔ̃] nf (*Géol, Méd*) concretion.

concrétisation [kɔ̃kʀetizasjɔ̃] nf [*promesse etc*] realization.

concrétiser [kɔ̃kʀetize] 1 1 vt to give concrete expression to. 2 vi (*Sport: marquer*) to score. 3 **se concrétiser** vpr [*espoir, projet, rêve*] to materialize. **ses promesses/menaces ne se sont pas concrétisées** his promises/threats didn't come to anything *ou* didn't materialize; **le projet commence à se ~** the project is beginning to take shape.

concubin, e [kɔ̃kybɛ̃, in] 1 nm,f (*Jur*) cohabitant, co-habitee. 2 **concubine** nf (†: *maîtresse*) concubine†.

concubinage [kɔ̃kybinaʒ] nm cohabitation; concubinage†. **ils vivent en ~** they're living together *ou* as husband and wife; (*Jur*) **~ notoire** common-law marriage.

concupiscence [kɔ̃kypisɑ̃s] nf concupiscence.

concupiscent, e [kɔ̃kypisɑ̃, ɑ̃t] adj concupiscent.

concurremment [kɔ̃kyʀamɑ̃] adv a (*conjointement*) conjointly. **il agit ~ avec le président** he acts conjointly with *ou* in conjunction with the president. b (*en même temps*) concurrently.

concurrence [kɔ̃kyʀɑ̃s] nf a (*gén, Comm: compétition*) competition. **un prix défiant toute ~** an absolutely unbeatable price, a rock-bottom price; **~ déloyale** unfair trading *ou* competition; **faire ~ à qn, être en ~ avec qn** to be in competition with sb, compete with sb. b (*limite*) **jusqu'à ~ de ...** up to ..., to a limit of ... .

concurrencer [kɔ̃kyʀɑ̃se] 3 vt to compete with. **il nous concurrence dangereusement** he is a serious threat *ou* challenge to us; **leurs produits risquent de ~ les nôtres** their products could well pose a serious threat *ou* challenge to ours *ou* could well seriously challenge ours.

concurrent, e [kɔ̃kyʀɑ̃, ɑ̃t] 1 adj a (*rival*) rival, competing. b (†: *concourant*) *forces, actions* concurrent, cooperative. 2 nm,f (*Comm, Sport*) competitor; (*Scol*) [*concours*] candidate.

concurrentiel, -elle [kɔ̃kyʀɑ̃sjɛl] adj (*Écon*) competitive.

concussion [kɔ̃kysjɔ̃] nf misappropriation of public funds.

condamnable [kɔ̃dɑnabl] adj *action, opinion* reprehensible, blameworthy. **il n'est pas ~ d'avoir pensé à ses intérêts** he cannot be blamed for having thought of his own interests.

condamnation [kɔ̃dɑnasjɔ̃] nf a (*Jur*) [*coupable*] (*action*) sentencing (*à* to, *pour* for); (*peine*) sentence. **il a 3 ~s à son actif** he (already) has 3 convictions; **~ à mort** death sentence, sentence of death, capital sentence; **~ à une amende** imposition of a fine; **~ à 5 ans de prison** 5-year (prison) sentence; **~ (aux travaux forcés) à perpétuité** life sentence (of hard labour); **~ aux dépens** order to pay the costs; **~ par défaut/par contumace** decree by default/in one's absence; **~ pour meurtre** sentence for murder.

b (*interdiction, punition*) [*livre, délit*] condemnation, condemning.

c (*blâme*) [*conduite, idée*] condemnation.

d (*faillite*) [*espoir, théorie, projet*] end. **c'est la ~ du petit commerce** it means the end of *ou* it spells the end for the small trader.

e (*Aut*) (*action*) locking; (*système*) locking device. **~ electromagnétique des serrures** central locking device.

condamné, e [kɔ̃dɑne] (ptp de **condamner**) nm,f sentenced person, convict; (*à mort*) condemned person. **un ~ à mort s'est échappé** a man under sentence of death *ou* a condemned man has escaped; **les malades ~s** the terminally ill; voir **cigarette**.

condamner [kɔ̃dɑne] 1 vt a (*Jur*) *coupable* to sentence (*à* to, *pour* for). **~ à mort** to sentence to death; **~ qn à une amende** to fine sb, impose a fine on sb; **~ qn à 5 ans de prison** to sentence sb to 5 years' imprisonment, pass a 5-year (prison) sentence on sb; **être condamné aux dépens** to be ordered to pay costs; **~ qn par défaut/par contumace** to sentence sb by default/in his absence *ou* in absentia; **~ pour meurtre** to sentence for murder; **X, plusieurs fois condamné pour vol ...** X, several times convicted of theft ... .

b (*interdire, punir*) *délit, livre* to condemn. **la loi condamne l'usage de stupéfiants** the law condemns the use of drugs; **ces délits sont sévèrement condamnés** these offences carry heavy sentences *ou* penalties.

c (*blâmer*) *action, idées,* (*Ling*) *impropriété* to condemn. **il ne faut pas le ~ d'avoir fait cela** you mustn't condemn *ou* blame him for doing that.

d (*accuser*) to condemn. **sa rougeur le condamne** his blushes condemn him.

e (*Méd*) *malade* to give up (hope for); (*fig*) *théorie, espoir* to put an end to. **ce projet est maintenant condamné** this project is now doomed; **il était condamné depuis longtemps** there had been no hope for him *ou* he had been doomed for a long time; **il est condamné par les médecins** the doctors have given up hope (for him).

f (*obliger, vouer*) **~ à: ~ qn au silence/à l'attente** to condemn sb to silence/to waiting; **je suis condamné** *ou* **ça me condamne à me lever tôt** I'm condemned to get up early; **c'est condamné à sombrer dans l'oubli** it's doomed to sink into oblivion.

g *porte, fenêtre* (*gén*) to fill in, block up; (*avec briques*) to brick up; (*avec planches etc*) to board up; *pièce* to lock up; *portière de voiture* to lock. (*fig*) **~ sa porte à qn** to bar one's door to sb.

condé [kɔ̃de] nm (arg Police: policier) cop‡.
condensable [kɔ̃dɑ̃sabl] adj condensable.
condensateur [kɔ̃dɑ̃satœʀ] nm (Élec) capacitor, condenser; (Opt) condenser.
condensation [kɔ̃dɑ̃sasjɔ̃] nf condensation.
condensé [kɔ̃dɑ̃se] nm (Presse) digest.
condenser [kɔ̃dɑ̃se] 1 1 vt gaz, vapeur to condense; exposé, pensée to condense, compress; voir lait. 2 se condenser vpr [vapeur] to condense.
condenseur [kɔ̃dɑ̃sœʀ] nm (Opt, Phys) condenser.
condescendance [kɔ̃desɑ̃dɑ̃s] nf condescension. avec ~ condescendingly.
condescendant, e [kɔ̃desɑ̃dɑ̃, ɑ̃t] adj condescending.
condescendre [kɔ̃desɑ̃dʀ] 41 vi: ~ à to condescend to; ~ à faire to condescend ou deign to do.
condiment [kɔ̃dimɑ̃] nm condiment (including pickles, spices, and any other seasoning).
condisciple [kɔ̃disipl] nm (Scol) schoolfellow, schoolmate; (Univ) fellow student.
condition [kɔ̃disjɔ̃] nf a (circonstances) ~s conditions; ~s atmosphériques/sociologiques atmospheric/sociological conditions; ~s de travail/vie working/living conditions; dans ces ~s, je refuse under these conditions, I refuse; dans les ~s actuelles in ou under (the) present conditions; améliorer la ~ des travailleurs émigrés to improve the lot of foreign workers.
b (stipulation) [traité] condition; (exigence) [acceptation] condition, requirement. ~ préalable prerequisite; la ~ nécessaire et suffisante pour que ... the necessary and sufficient condition for ...; l'endurance est une ~ essentielle endurance is an essential requirement; ~ sine qua non sine qua non condition; ~s d'un traité conditions of a treaty; l'honnêteté est la ~ du succès honesty is the (prime) requirement for ou condition of success; dicter/poser ses ~s to state/lay down one's conditions; il ne remplit pas les ~s requises (pour le poste) he doesn't fulfil the requirements (for the job); ~s d'admission (dans une société) terms ou conditions of admission ou entry (to a society); sans ~(s) (adj) unconditional; (adv) unconditionally.
c (Comm) term. ~s de vente/d'achat terms of sale/of purchase; ~s de paiement terms (of payment); obtenir des ~s intéressantes to get favourable terms; faire ses ~s to make ou name one's (own) terms; acheter/envoyer à ou sous ~ to buy/send on approval; dans les ~s normales du commerce in the ordinary course of business.
d (état) en bonne ~ aliments, envoi in good condition; en bonne ou grande ~ (physique) in condition, fit; en mauvaise ~ (physique) out of condition, unfit; mettre en ~ (physique) to get into condition, make ou get fit; (mentale) to get into condition ou form; (psychologique) to condition; la mise en ~ des téléspectateurs the conditioning of television viewers; se mettre en ~ to get fit, get into condition ou form.
e (rang social) station, condition. vivre selon sa ~ to live according to one's station; un étudiant de ~ modeste a student from a modest home ou background; ce n'est pas pour un homme de sa ~ it doesn't befit a man of his station; personne de ~†† person of quality; la ~ ouvrière the position of the workers; la ~ de prêtre (the) priesthood; la ~ d'artisan/d'intellectuel the situation of the craftsman/intellectual.
f (loc) entrer en/être de ou en ~ chez qn†† to enter sb's service/be in service with sb; à une ~ on one condition; je viendrai, à ~ d'être prévenu à temps I'll come provided (that) ou providing (that) I'm told in time; je le ferai, à la seule ~ que toi aussi tu fasses un effort I'll do it but only on one condition - you (have to) make an effort as well; tu peux rester, à ~ d'être sage ou à ~ que tu sois sage you can stay provided (that) ou providing (that) ou on condition that you're good; sous ~ conditionally.
conditionnel, -elle [kɔ̃disjɔnɛl] adj, nm (gén) conditional. (Ling) au ~ in the conditional; cette information est à mettre au ~ this information has still to be confirmed.
conditionnellement [kɔ̃disjɔnɛlmɑ̃] adv conditionally.
conditionnement [kɔ̃disjɔnmɑ̃] nm (emballage) packaging; [air, personne, textile, blé] conditioning.
conditionner [kɔ̃disjɔne] 1 vt (emballer) to package, prepack; (influencer) to condition; textiles, blé to condition. ceci conditionne notre départ our departure is dependent on ou conditioned by this, this affects our departure; voir air¹, réflexe.
conditionneur, -euse [kɔ̃disjɔnœʀ, øz] 1 nm,f (emballeur) packer. 2 nm [denrées] packaging machine; [air] air conditioner; [pour cheveux] conditioner.
condoléances [kɔ̃dɔleɑ̃s] nfpl condolences. offrir ou faire ses ~ à qn to offer sb one's sympathy ou condolences; toutes mes ~ (please accept) all my condolences ou my deepest sympathy; une lettre de ~ a letter of condolence.
condom [kɔ̃dɔm] nm condom.
condominium [kɔ̃dɔminjɔm] nm condominium.
condor [kɔ̃dɔʀ] nm condor.
conductance [kɔ̃dyktɑ̃s] nf conductance.
conducteur, -trice [kɔ̃dyktœʀ, tʀis] 1 adj (Élec) conductive, conducting; voir fil. 2 nm,f (Aut, Rail) driver; [machine] operator. ~ de bestiaux herdsman, drover; ~ d'engins heavy plant driver; ~ d'hommes leader; ~ de travaux clerk of works. 3 nm (Élec) conductor.
conductibilité [kɔ̃dyktibilite] nf conductivity.
conductible [kɔ̃dyktibl] adj conductive.
conduction [kɔ̃dyksjɔ̃] nf (Méd, Phys) conduction.
conduire [kɔ̃dɥiʀ] 38 1 vt a (emmener) ~ qn quelque part to take sb somewhere; (en voiture) to take ou drive sb somewhere; ~ un enfant à l'école/chez le docteur to take a child to school/to the doctor; ~ la voiture au garage to take the car to the garage; ~ les bêtes aux champs to take ou drive the animals to the fields; ~ qn à la gare (en voiture) to take ou drive sb to the station; (à pied) to walk ou see sb to the station; il me conduisit à ma chambre he showed me ou took me to my room.
b (guider) to lead. il conduisit les hommes à l'assaut he led the men into the attack; le guide nous conduisait the guide was leading us; il nous a conduits à travers Paris he guided us through Paris.
c (piloter) véhicule to drive; embarcation to steer; avion to pilot; cheval [cavalier] to ride; [cocher] to drive. ~ un cheval par la bride to lead a horse by the bridle.
d (Aut: emploi absolu) to drive. il conduit bien/mal he is a good/bad driver, he drives well/badly; voir permis.
e (mener) ~ qn quelque part [véhicule] to take sb somewhere; [route, traces] to lead ou take sb somewhere; [études, événement] to lead sb somewhere; la sociologie ne conduit à rien sociology doesn't lead to anything ou leads nowhere; où cela va-t-il nous ~? where will all this lead us?; cela nous conduit à penser que that leads us to think that; cet escalier conduit à la cave this staircase leads (down) to the cellar; où ce chemin conduit-il? where does this road lead ou go?; (littér) ~ ses pas vers to bend one's steps towards; ses dérèglements l'ont conduit en prison his profligacy landed him in prison.
f (diriger) affaires to run, manage; travaux to supervise; pays to run, lead; négociations, enquête to lead, conduct; orchestre [chef d'orchestre] to conduct; [premier violon] to lead. les fouilles sont conduites par X the excavation is being led ou directed by X.
g (transmettre) chaleur, électricité to conduct; (transporter) to carry. un aqueduc conduit l'eau à la ville an aqueduct carries water to the town.
2 se conduire vpr to behave. il sait se ~ (en société) he knows how to behave (in polite company); ce ne sont pas des façons de se ~ that's no way to behave; conduisez-vous comme il faut! behave properly!; il s'est mal conduit he behaved badly.
conduit [kɔ̃dɥi] 1 nm a (Tech) conduit, pipe. ~ de fumée flue; ~ d'air ou de ventilation ventilation shaft; ~ d'alimentation supply pipe; ~ d'aération air duct. b (Anat) duct, canal, meatus (SPÉC). 2 comp ►conduit auditif auditory canal ►conduit lacrymal lachrymal (SPÉC) ou tear duct ►conduit urinaire ureter, urinary canal.
conduite [kɔ̃dɥit] 1 nf a (pilotage) [véhicule] driving; [embarcation] steering; [avion] piloting. la ~ d'un gros camion demande de l'habileté driving a big truck takes a lot of skill; ~ en état d'ivresse driving while under the influence of alcohol (frm); en Angleterre la ~ est à gauche in England, you drive on the left; voiture avec ~ à gauche/à droite left-hand-drive/right-hand-drive car; faire un brin de ~ à qn* to go ou walk part of the way with sb, walk along with sb for a bit*.
b (direction) [affaires] running, management; [travaux] supervision; [pays] running, leading; [négociations, enquête] leading, conducting; (Littérat) [intrigue] conducting. sous la ~ de homme politique, capitaine, guide under the leadership of; instituteur under the supervision of; chef d'orchestre under the baton ou leadership of.
c (comportement) behaviour; (Scol) conduct. avoir une ~ bizarre to behave strangely; quelle ~ adopter? what course of action shall we take?; (Scol) zéro de ~ no marks (Brit) ou zero for conduct; (Scol) tu as combien en ou pour la ~? what did you get for conduct?; (Prison) relâché pour bonne ~ released for good conduct; voir acheter, écart, ligne¹.
d (tuyau) pipe. ~ d'eau/de gaz water/gas main.
2 comp ►conduite d'échec (Psych) defeatist behaviour ►conduite forcée (Hydro-Électricité) pressure pipeline ►conduite intérieure (Aut) saloon (car) (Brit), sedan (US) ►conduite montante rising main ►conduite de refus consumer resistance.
condyle [kɔ̃dil] nm (Anat) condyle.
cône [kon] nm (Anat, Bot, Math, Tech) cone; [volcan] cone. en forme de ~ cone-shaped; ~ de déjection alluvial cone; ~d'ombre/de lumière cone of shadow/light.
confection [kɔ̃fɛksjɔ̃] nf a (exécution) [appareil, vêtement] making; [repas] making, preparation, preparing. b (Habillement) la ~ the clothing industry, the rag trade*; être dans la ~ to be in the ready-made clothes business; vêtement de ~ ready-made garment; il achète tout en ~ he buys everything off-the-peg (surtout Brit) ou ready-to-wear; voir magasin.
confectionner [kɔ̃fɛksjɔne] 1 vt mets to prepare, make; appareil, vêtement to make.
confédéral, e, mpl **-aux** [kɔ̃fedeʀal, o] adj confederal.
confédération [kɔ̃fedeʀasjɔ̃] nf confederation, confederacy.
confédéré, e [kɔ̃fedeʀe] (ptp de confédérer) 1 adj nations confeder-

ate. 2 **nmpl** (*US Hist*) **les C~s** the Confederates.

confédérer [kɔ̃fedeʀe] 6 **vt** to confederate.

conférence [kɔ̃feʀɑ̃s] **nf** a (*exposé*) lecture. **faire une ~ sur qch** to lecture on sth, give a lecture on sth; *voir* **salle, maître.** b (*réunion*) conference, meeting. **être en ~** to be in conference *ou* in a *ou* at a meeting; **~ au sommet** summit (conference); **~ de presse** press conference. c (*poire*) conference pear.

conférencier, -ière [kɔ̃feʀɑ̃sje, jɛʀ] **nm,f** speaker, lecturer.

conférer [kɔ̃feʀe] 6 1 **vt** a (*décerner*) *dignité* to confer (*à* on); *baptême, ordres sacrés* to give; (*frm: donner*) *prestige, autorité* to impart (*à* to). **~ un certain sens/aspect à qch** to endow sth with a certain meaning/look, give sth a certain meaning/look; **ce titre lui confère un grand prestige** that title confers great prestige on him. b (*collationner*) to collate, compare. 2 **vi** (*s'entretenir*) to confer (*sur* on, about).

confesse [kɔ̃fɛs] **nf: être/aller à ~** to be at/go to confession.

confesser [kɔ̃fese] 1 1 **vt** a (*avouer, Rel*) *péchés, erreur* to confess. **~ que** to confess that; **~ sa foi** to confess one's faith. b **~ qn** (*Rel*) to hear sb's confession, confess sb; (**: faire parler*) to draw the truth out of sb, make sb talk; **l'abbé X confesse de 4 à 6** Father X hears confession from 4 to 6. 2 **se confesser vpr** (*Rel*) to go to confession. **se ~ à** *prêtre* to confess to, make confession to; *ami* to confess to; **se ~ de** *péchés,* (*littér*) *méfait* to confess.

confesseur [kɔ̃fesœʀ] **nm** confessor.

confession [kɔ̃fesjɔ̃] **nf** (*aveu*) confession; (*acte du prêtre*) hearing of confession; (*religion*) denomination; *voir* **donner.**

confessionnal, pl **-aux** [kɔ̃fesjɔnal, o] **nm** confessional.

confessionnel, -elle [kɔ̃fesjɔnɛl] **adj** denominational. **querelle ~le** interdenominational dispute; **école ~le** denominational *ou* sectarian school; **non ~** nondenominational, nonsectarian.

confetti [kɔ̃feti] **nm** confetti (*NonC*). (*fig*) **tu peux en faire des ~s!*** (*contrat, chèque*) it's not worth the paper it's written on!; (*excuse, promesse, chose inutile*) that's no use to me!; (*espoir*) you can forget it!

confiance [kɔ̃fjɑ̃s] **nf** (*en l'honnêteté de qn*) confidence, trust; (*en la valeur de qn, le succès de qch, la solidité d'un appareil*) confidence, faith (*en* in). **avoir ~ en** *ou* **dans, faire ~ à** to have confidence *ou* faith in, trust; **c'est quelqu'un en qui on peut avoir ~** he's (*ou* she's) a person you can rely on; **je l'aurai, tu peux me faire ~!** I'll get it – believe me!; (*Pol*) **voter la ~ (au gouvernement)** to pass a vote of confidence (in the government); **il faut avoir ~** one must have confidence; **je n'ai pas ~ dans leur matériel** I've no faith *ou* confidence in their equipment; **il a toute ma ~** he has my complete trust *ou* confidence; **mettre qn en ~** to win sb's trust; **placer** *ou* **mettre sa ~ dans** to place one's confidence in; **avec ~** *se confier* trustingly; *espérer* confidently; **en (toute) ~, de ~** *acheter* with confidence; **de ~** *homme, maison* trustworthy, reliable; **un poste de ~** a position of trust; **~ en soi** self-confidence; *voir* **abus, inspirer, question.**

confiant, e [kɔ̃fjɑ̃, jɑ̃t] **adj** a (*assuré, plein d'espoir*) confident; (*en soi-même*) (self-)confident, (self-)assured. b (*sans défiance*) *caractère, regard* confiding.

confidence [kɔ̃fidɑ̃s] **nf** (*secret*) confidence, little (personal) secret. **faire une ~ à qn** to confide sth to sb, trust sb with a secret; **faire des ~s à qn** to share a secret with sb, confide in sb; **en ~** in confidence; **mettre qn dans la ~** to let sb into the secret; **sur le ton de la ~** in a confidential tone (of voice); **~s sur l'oreiller** intimate confidences, pillow talk.

confident [kɔ̃fidɑ̃] **nm** confidant.

confidente [kɔ̃fidɑ̃t] **nf** confidante.

confidentialité [kɔ̃fidɑ̃sjalite] **nf** confidentiality.

confidentiel, -ielle [kɔ̃fidɑ̃sjɛl] **adj** (*secret*) confidential; (*sur une enveloppe*) private (and confidential); (*pour public limité*) *roman* for a narrow readership; *film* for a limited audience; *voir* **ultra.**

confidentiellement [kɔ̃fidɑ̃sjɛlmɑ̃] **adv** confidentially.

confier [kɔ̃fje] 7 1 **vt** a (*dire en secret*) to confide (*à* to). **il me confie ses projets** he confides his projects to me, he tells me about his projects; **il me confie tous ses secrets** he shares all his secrets with me; **dans ce livre il confie ses joies et ses peines** in this book he tells of *ou* reveals his sorrows and his joys.

b (*laisser aux soins de qn*) to confide, entrust (*à* to). **~ qn/qch aux soins/à la garde de qn** to confide *ou* entrust sb/sth to sb's care/safekeeping; **je vous confie le soin de le faire** I entrust you with the task of doing it.

2 **se confier vpr** a (*dire un secret*) **se ~ à qn** to confide in sb; **ils se confièrent l'un à l'autre leur chagrin** they confided their grief to each other; (*littér*) **qu'il est doux de se ~!** what delight to unburden one's heart! (*littér*).

b (*frm: se fier à*) **se ~ à** *ou* **en qn** to place o.s. in sb's hands.

configuration [kɔ̃figyʀasjɔ̃] **nf** a (general) shape, configuration. **la ~ des lieux** the layout of the premises; **suivant la ~ du terrain** following the lie of the land. b (*Ordin*) configuration. **~ multipostes** multi-user system.

configurer [kɔ̃figyʀe] 1 **vt** (*Ordin*) to configure.

confiné, e [kɔ̃fine] (**ptp de confiner**) **adj** a (*enfermé*) **vivre ~ chez soi** to live shut away in one's own home. b (*renfermé*) *atmosphère* enclosed; *air* stale.

confinement [kɔ̃finmɑ̃] **nm** (*voir* **confiner**) confining.

confiner [kɔ̃fine] 1 1 **vt** (*enfermer*) **~ qn à** *ou* **dans** to confine sb to *ou* in. 2 **confiner à vt indir** (*toucher à*) (*lit*) to border on, adjoin; (*fig*) to border *ou* verge on. 3 **se confiner vpr** to confine o.s. (*à* to) **se ~ chez soi** to confine o.s. to the house, shut o.s. up at home.

confins [kɔ̃fɛ̃] **nmpl** (*frontières*) borders; (*partie extrême*) fringes. **aux ~ de la Bretagne et de la Normandie/du rêve et de la réalité** on the borders of Brittany and Normandy/dream and reality; **aux ~ de la Bretagne/la science** at the outermost *ou* furthermost bounds of Brittany/science.

confire [kɔ̃fiʀ] 37 **vt** (*au sucre*) to preserve, conserve; (*au vinaigre*) to pickle; (*dans de la graisse*) to preserve; *voir* **confit.**

confirmand, e [kɔ̃fiʀmɑ̃, ɑ̃d] **nm,f** confirmand (*SPÉC*), confirmation candidate.

confirmation [kɔ̃fiʀmasjɔ̃] **nf** (*gén, Rel*) confirmation. **en ~ de** confirming, in confirmation of; **apporter ~ de** to confirm, provide confirmation of; **c'est la ~ de** it confirms, it provides *ou* is confirmation of; **j'en attends ~** I'm waiting for confirmation of it.

confirmer [kɔ̃fiʀme] 1 **vt** (*gén, Rel*) to confirm. **il m'a confirmé que** he confirmed to me that; (*dans une lettre*) **je souhaite ~ ma réservation du** ... I wish to confirm my reservation of ...; **cela l'a confirmé dans ses idées** it confirmed *ou* strengthened him in his ideas; **~ qn dans ses fonctions** to confirm sb's appointment; **la nouvelle se confirme** the news has been confirmed, there is some confirmation of the news; *voir* **exception.**

confiscable [kɔ̃fiskabl] **adj** liable to confiscation *ou* seizure, confiscable.

confiscation [kɔ̃fiskasjɔ̃] **nf** confiscation, seizure.

confiserie [kɔ̃fizʀi] **nf** (*magasin*) confectioner's (shop), sweetshop (*Brit*), candy store (*US*); (*métier*) confectionery; (*bonbons*) confectionery (*NonC*), sweets (*Brit*), candy (*NonC*) (*US*). **manger une ~/des ~s** to eat a sweet/sweets (*Brit*) *ou* candy (*US*).

confiseur, -euse [kɔ̃fizœʀ, øz] **nm,f** confectioner.

confisquer [kɔ̃fiske] 1 **vt** (*gén, Jur*) to confiscate, seize.

confit, e [kɔ̃fi, it] (**ptp de confire**) 1 **adj** *fruit* crystallized,candied; *cornichon* pickled. (*fig*) **~ de** *ou* **en dévotion** steeped in piety. 2 **nm: ~ d'oie/de canard** conserve of goose/duck.

confiture [kɔ̃fityʀ] **nf** jam. **~ de prunes/d'abricots** plum/apricot jam; **~ d'oranges** (orange) marmalade; **~ de citrons** lemon marmalade; **veux-tu de la ~?** *ou* **des ~s?** do you want (some) jam?; (*fig*) **donner de la ~ aux cochons** to throw pearls before swine.

confiturerie [kɔ̃fityʀʀi] **nf** jam factory.

conflagration [kɔ̃flagʀasjɔ̃] **nf** (*frm: conflit*) cataclysm.

conflictuel, -elle [kɔ̃fliktɥɛl] **adj** *pulsions, intérêts* conflicting. **situation ~le** situation of conflict; **avoir des rapports ~s avec qn** to have a relationship of conflict with sb.

conflit [kɔ̃fli] **nm** (*gén, Mil*) conflict, clash; (*Psych*) conflict; (*Ind: grève*) dispute; (*Jur*) conflict. **pour éviter le ~** to avoid (a) conflict *ou* a clash; **entrer en ~ avec qn** to come into conflict with sb, clash with sb; **être en ~ avec qn** to be in conflict with sb, clash with sb; **~ d'intérêts** conflict *ou* clash of interests; **le ~ des générations** the generation gap; **~ armé** armed conflict; **~ social** industrial dispute; **~s internes** infighting; **le ~ israélo-arabe** the Arab-Israeli wars.

confluence [kɔ̃flyɑ̃s] **nf** (*action*) *[cours d'eau]* confluence, flowing together; (*fig*) mingling, merging.

confluent [kɔ̃flyɑ̃] **nm** (*Géog*) confluence. (*fig*) **au ~ de deux cultures** at the bridge of two cultures, where two cultures meet; (*fig*) **au ~ du rêve et de la réalité** where dream meets reality.

confluer [kɔ̃flye] 1 **vi** *[cours d'eau]* to join, flow together; (*littér*) *[foule, troupes]* to converge (*vers* on). **~ avec** to flow into, join.

confondant, e [kɔ̃fɔ̃dɑ̃, ɑ̃t] **adj** astounding.

confondre [kɔ̃fɔ̃dʀ] 41 1 **vt** a (*mêler*) *choses, dates* to mix up, confuse. **on confond toujours ces deux frères** people always mix up *ou* confuse these two brothers *ou* get these two brothers mixed up *ou* muddled up (*Brit*); **les deux sœurs se ressemblent au point qu'on les confond** the two sisters are so alike that you take *ou* mistake one for the other; **il confond toujours le Chili et** *ou* **avec le Mexique** he keeps mixing up *ou* confusing Chile and *ou* with Mexico; **~ qch/qn avec qch/qn d'autre** to mistake sth/sb for sth/sb else; **elle a confondu sa valise avec la mienne** she mistook my case for hers; **je croyais que c'était son frère, j'ai dû ~** I thought it was his brother but I must have made a mistake *ou* I must have been mistaken; **mes réserves ne sont pas de la lâcheté, il ne faudrait pas ~** my reservations aren't cowardice, let there be no mistake about that *ou* you shouldn't confuse the two.

b (*déconcerter*) to astound. **il me confondit par l'étendue de ses connaissances** he astounded me with the extent of his knowledge; **son insolence a de quoi vous ~** his insolence is astounding *ou* is enough to leave you speechless; **je suis confondu devant** *ou* **de tant d'amabilité** I'm overcome *ou* overwhelmed by such kindness; **être confondu de reconnaissance** to be overcome with gratitude.

c (*démasquer*) *détracteur, ennemi, menteur* to confound.

d (*réunir, fusionner*) to join, meet. **deux rivières qui confondent leurs eaux** two rivers which flow together *ou* join.

2 **se confondre vpr** a (*ne faire plus qu'un*) to merge; (*se rejoin-*

dre) to meet. **les silhouettes se confondaient dans la brume** the silhouettes merged (together) in the mist; **les couleurs se confondent de loin** the colours merge in the distance; **tout se confondait dans sa mémoire** everything became confused in his memory; **les deux événements se confondirent (en un seul) dans sa mémoire** the two events merged into one in his memory, the two events became confused (as one) in his memory; **nos intérêts se confondent** our interests are one and the same; **les deux fleuves se confondent à cet endroit** the two rivers flow together *ou* join here.

b **se ~ en excuses** to apologize profusely; **se ~ en remerciements** to offer profuse thanks, be effusive in one's thanks; **il se confondit en remerciements** he thanked me (*ou* them *etc*) profusely *ou* effusively.

conformation [kɔ̃fɔʀmasjɔ̃] **nf** conformation; *voir* **vice**.

conforme [kɔ̃fɔʀm] **adj** a (*semblable*) true (*à* to). **~ à l'original/au modèle** true to the original/pattern; **c'est ~ à l'échantillon** it matches the sample; **c'est peu ~ à ce que j'ai dit** it bears little resemblance to what I said; **ce n'est pas ~ à** *accord, commande, normes* it does not comply with; **ce n'est pas ~ à l'original** it does not match the original; **cette copie est bien ~, n'est-ce pas?** it's a true *ou* good replica, isn't it?; *voir* **copie**.

b (*fidèle*) in accordance (*à* with). **l'exécution des travaux est ~ au plan prévu** the work is being carried out in accordance with the agreed plan; **~ à la loi** in accordance *ou* conformity with the law; **~ à la règle/à la norme** in accordance with the rule/norm; **être ~ aux normes de sécurité** to conform to safety standards.

c (*en harmonie avec*) **~ à** in keeping with, consonant with; **un niveau de vie ~ à nos moyens** a standard of living in keeping *ou* consonant with (*frm*) our means; **il a des vues ~s aux miennes** his views are in keeping with mine, we have similar views.

conformé, e [kɔ̃fɔʀme] (**ptp de conformer**) **adj** *corps, enfant* **bien/mal ~** well/ill-formed; **bizarrement ~** strangely shaped *ou* formed.

conformément [kɔ̃fɔʀmemɑ̃] **adv ~ à** a (*en respectant*) in conformity with, in accordance with. **~ à la loi, j'ai décidé que** in accordance *ou* conformity with the law, I have decided that; **les travaux se sont déroulés ~ au plan prévu** the work was carried out in accordance with *ou* according to the proposed plan; **ce travail a été exécuté ~ au modèle/à l'original** this piece of work was done to conform to the pattern/original *ou* to match the pattern/original exactly. b (*suivant*) in accordance with. **~ à ce que j'avais promis/prédit** in accordance with what I had promised/predicted.

conformer [kɔ̃fɔʀme] 1 1 **vt** (*calquer*) **~ qch à** to model sth on; **~ sa conduite à celle d'une autre personne** to model one's (own) conduct on somebody else's; **~ sa conduite à ses principes** to match one's conduct to one's principles. 2 **se conformer vpr: se ~ à** to conform to.

conformisme [kɔ̃fɔʀmism] **nm** (*gén, Rel*) conformism.

conformiste [kɔ̃fɔʀmist] **adj, nmf** (*gén, Rel*) conformist.

conformité [kɔ̃fɔʀmite] **nf** a (*identité*) similarity, correspondence (*à* to). **la ~ de deux choses** the similarity of *ou* between two things, the close correspondence of *ou* between two things; **en ~ avec le modèle** in accordance with the pattern.

b (*fidélité*) faithfulness (*à* to). **~ à la règle/aux ordres reçus** compliance with the rules/orders received; **en ~ avec le plan prévu/avec les ordres reçus** in accordance *ou* conformity with the proposed plan/orders received.

c (*harmonie*) conformity, agreement (*avec* with). **la ~ de nos vues sur la question, notre ~ de vues sur la question** the agreement of our views on the question; **sa conduite est en ~ avec ses idées** his conduct is in keeping *ou* in conformity *ou* in agreement with his ideas.

confort [kɔ̃fɔʀ] **nm** comfort. **appartement tout ~** *ou* **avec (tout) le ~ moderne** flat with all mod cons (*Brit*) *ou* modern conveniences; **il aime le** *ou* **son ~** he likes his creature comforts *ou* his comfort; **dès que ça dérange son ~ personnel il refuse de nous aider** as soon as it inconveniences him *ou* puts him out he refuses to help us; **~ d'écoute** sound quality; **médicament de ~** non-essential medicine (*for which the Social Security will not give a refund*).

confortable [kɔ̃fɔʀtabl] **adj** a (*douillet*) *appartement* comfortable, snug, cosy; *vêtement, vie* comfortable, comfy*; (*: *bien installé*) comfortable, comfy*. **fauteuil peu ~** rather uncomfortable armchair; **être dans une situation peu ~** to be in a rather uncomfortable *ou* awkward position. b (*opulent*) *fortune, retraite* comfortable; *métier, situation* comfortable, cushy*. c (*important*) comfortable (*épith*). **prendre une avance ~ sur ses rivaux** to get a comfortable lead over one's rivals.

confortablement [kɔ̃fɔʀtabləmɑ̃] **adv** comfortably. **vivre ~** (*dans le confort*) to live in comfort; (*dans la richesse*) to live very comfortably, lead a comfortable existence.

conforter [kɔ̃fɔʀte] 1 **vt** to reinforce, confirm.

confraternel, -elle [kɔ̃fʀatɛʀnɛl] **adj** brotherly, fraternal.

confraternité [kɔ̃fʀatɛʀnite] **nf** brotherliness.

confrère [kɔ̃fʀɛʀ] **nm** *[profession]* colleague; *[association]* fellow member; (*journal*) (fellow) newspaper. **mon cher ~** dear colleague.

confrérie [kɔ̃fʀeʀi] **nf** brotherhood.

confrontation [kɔ̃fʀɔ̃tasjɔ̃] **nf** *[opinions, personnes]* confrontation; *[textes]* comparison, collation.

confronter [kɔ̃fʀɔ̃te] 1 **vt** (*opposer*) *opinions, personnes* to confront; (*comparer*) *textes* to compare, collate. **être confronté à** to be confronted with.

confucéen, -enne [kɔ̃fyseɛ̃, ɛn] **adj** Confucian.

confucianisme [kɔ̃fysjanism] **nm** Confucianism.

confucianiste [kɔ̃fysjanist] 1 **adj** Confucian. 2 **nmf** Confucian, Confucianist.

Confucius [kɔ̃fysjys] **n** Confucius.

confus, e [kɔ̃fy, yz] **adj** a (*peu clair*) *bruit, texte, souvenir* confused; *esprit, personne* confused, muddled; *mélange, amas d'objets* confused. **cette affaire est très ~e** this business is very confused *ou* muddled. b (*honteux*) *personne* ashamed, embarrassed. **il était ~ d'avoir fait cela** he was embarrassed at having done that; **vous avez fait des folies, nous sommes ~!** you've been far too kind, we're quite overwhelmed! *ou* you make us feel quite ashamed!; **je suis tout ~ de mon erreur** I'm terribly ashamed of my mistake, I don't know what to say about my mistake.

confusément [kɔ̃fyzemɑ̃] **adv** *distinguer* vaguely; *comprendre, ressentir* vaguely, in a confused way; *parler* unintelligibly, confusedly.

confusion [kɔ̃fyzjɔ̃] **nf** a (*honte*) embarrassment; (*trouble, embarras*) confusion. **à ma grande ~** to my great embarrassment; to my great confusion.

b (*erreur*) *[noms, personnes, dates]* confusion (*de* in). **vous avez fait une ~** you've made a mistake, you've got things confused.

c (*désordre*) *[esprits, idées]* confusion; *[assemblée, pièce, papiers]* confusion, disorder (*de* in). **c'était dans une telle ~** it was in such confusion *ou* disorder; **mettre** *ou* **jeter la ~ dans les esprits/l'assemblée** to throw people/the audience into confusion *ou* disarray.

d (*Jur*) **~ des dettes** confusion; **~ de part** *ou* **de paternité** doubt over paternity; **~ des peines** concurrency of sentences; **~ des pouvoirs** *non-separation of legislature, executive and judiciary.*

confusionnisme [kɔ̃fyzjɔnism] **nm** (*Psych*) *confused thinking of a child;* (*Pol*) *policy of spreading confusion in people's minds.*

congé [kɔ̃ʒe] 1 **nm** a (*vacances*) holiday (*Brit*), vacation (*US*); (*Mil: permission*) leave. **3 jours de ~ pour** *ou* **à Noël** 3 days' holiday (*Brit*) *ou* vacation (*US*) *ou* 3 days off at Christmas; **c'est son jour de ~** it's his day off; **en ~** *écolier, employé* on holiday (*Brit*) *ou* vacation (*US*); *soldat* on leave; **avoir ~: quel jour avez-vous ~?** which day do you have off?, which day are you off?; **quand avez-vous ~ en été?** when are you off *ou* when do you get a holiday (*Brit*) *ou* vacation (*US*) in the summer?; **avoir ~ le mercredi** to have Wednesdays off, be off on Wednesdays *ou* on a Wednesday; **il me reste 3 jours de ~ à prendre** I've got 3 days (holiday) still to come.

b (*arrêt momentané de travail*) time off (*NonC*), leave (*NonC*). **prendre/donner du ~** to take/give time off *ou* some leave; **prendre un ~ d'une semaine** to take a week off *ou* a week's leave; **~ sans traitement** *ou* **solde** unpaid leave, time off without pay; **demander à être mis en ~ sans traitement** *ou* **solde pendant un an** to ask for a year's unpaid leave, ask for a year off without pay.

c (*avis de départ*) notice; (*renvoi*) notice (to quit *ou* leave). **donner son ~** *[employé]* to hand in *ou* give in one's notice (*à* to); *[locataire]* to give notice (*à* to); **donner (son) ~ à un locataire/employé** to give a lodger/an employee (his) notice; **il faut donner ~ 8 jours à l'avance** one must give a week's notice; **il a demandé son ~** he has asked to leave.

d (*adieu*) **prendre ~ (de qn)** to take one's leave (of sb); **donner ~ à qn à la fin d'un entretien** to dismiss (*frm*) sb at the end of a conversation.

e (*Admin: autorisation*) clearance certificate; *[transports d'alcool]* release (*of wine etc from bond*). (*Naut*) **~ (de navigation)** clearance.

2 **comp ►congé annuel** annual holiday (*Brit*) *ou* vacation (*US*) *ou* leave **►congé pour convenance personnelle** ≃ compassionate leave **►congé de conversion** retraining period **►congé formation** training leave **►congé de longue durée** extended *ou* prolonged leave of absence **►congé (de) maladie** sick leave; **congé de longue maladie** prolonged *ou* extended sick leave **►congé (de) maternité** maternity leave **►congé parental (d'éducation)** (unpaid) extended maternity (*ou* paternity) leave **►les congés payés** (*vacances*) (annual) paid holidays (*Brit*) *ou* vacation (*US*) *ou* leave; (*péj: vacanciers*) the rank and file (holiday-makers (*Brit*) *ou* vacationers (*US*)) **►congés scolaires** school holidays (*Brit*) *ou* vacation (*US*).

congédiable [kɔ̃ʒedjabl] **adj** (*Mil*) due for discharge; (*gén*) able to be dismissed. **le personnel non titulaire est ~ à tout moment** non-tenured staff can be dismissed at any time.

congédier [kɔ̃ʒedje] 7 **vt** to dismiss.

congelable [kɔ̃ʒlabl] **adj** which can be easily frozen.

congélateur [kɔ̃ʒelatœʀ] **nm** (*meuble*) freezer, deep-freeze; (*compartiment*) freezer compartment. **~ armoire** upright freezer; **~ bahut** chest freezer.

congélation [kɔ̃ʒelasjɔ̃] **nf** *[eau, aliments]* freezing; *[huile]* congealing. **sac de ~** freezer bag; *voir* **point¹**.

congeler [kɔ̃ʒ(ə)le] 5 1 **vt** *eau, huile* to freeze; *aliments* to (deep-)freeze. **les produits congelés** (deep-)frozen foods, deep-freeze foods. 2 **se congeler vpr** to freeze.

congénère [kɔ̃ʒenɛʀ] 1 **adj** congeneric. 2 **nmf** (*semblable*) fellow, fellow creature. **toi et tes ~s** you and the likes of you.

congénital, e, mpl **-aux** [kɔ̃ʒenital, o] adj congenital.

congère [kɔ̃ʒɛʀ] nf snowdrift.

congestif, -ive [kɔ̃ʒɛstif, iv] adj congestive.

congestion [kɔ̃ʒɛstjɔ̃] nf congestion. ~ **(cérébrale)** stroke; ~ **(pulmonaire)** congestion of the lungs.

congestionner [kɔ̃ʒɛstjɔne] 1 vt *rue* to congest; *personne, visage* to flush, make flushed. **être congestionné** *[personne, visage]* to be flushed; *[rue]* to be congested.

conglomérat [kɔ̃glɔmeʀa] nm (*Écon, Géol*) conglomerate; (*fig: amalgame*) conglomeration.

conglomération [kɔ̃glɔmeʀasjɔ̃] nf conglomeration.

conglomérer [kɔ̃glɔmeʀe] 6 vt to conglomerate.

Congo [kɔ̃go] nm: **le** ~ (*pays, fleuve*) the Congo.

congolais, e [kɔ̃gɔlɛ, ɛz] 1 adj Congolese. 2 nm,f: **C~(e)** Congolese. 3 nm (*gâteau*) coconut cake.

congratulations [kɔ̃gʀatylasjɔ̃] nfpl († *ou hum*) congratulations.

congratuler [kɔ̃gʀatyle] 1 vt († *ou hum*) to congratulate.

congre [kɔ̃gʀ] nm conger (eel).

congrégation [kɔ̃gʀegasjɔ̃] nf (*Rel*) congregation; (*fig*) assembly.

congrès [kɔ̃gʀɛ] nm (*gén*) congress; (*Pol: conférence*) conference. (*US Pol*) **le C~** Congress; **membre du C~** (*gén*) member of Congress; (*homme*) congressman; (*femme*) congresswoman.

congressiste [kɔ̃gʀesist] nmf (*gén*) participant at a congress; (*Pol*) participant at a conference.

congru, e [kɔ̃gʀy] adj a *voir* **portion.** b = **congruent.**

congruence [kɔ̃gʀyɑ̃s] nf (*Math*) congruence.

congruent, e [kɔ̃gʀyɑ̃, ɑ̃t] adj (*Math*) congruent.

conifère [kɔnifɛʀ] nm conifer.

conique [kɔnik] 1 adj conical. **de forme** ~ cone-shaped, coniform. 2 nf conic (section).

conjectural, e, mpl **-aux** [kɔ̃ʒɛktyʀal, o] adj conjectural.

conjecturalement [kɔ̃ʒɛktyʀalmɑ̃] adv conjecturally.

conjecture [kɔ̃ʒɛktyʀ] nf conjecture. **se perdre en ~s quant à qch** to lose o.s. in conjectures about sth; **nous en sommes réduits aux ~s** we can only conjecture *ou* guess (about this).

conjecturer [kɔ̃ʒɛktyʀe] 1 vt to conjecture. **on ne peut rien ~ sur cette situation** one can't conjecture anything about that situation.

conjoint, e [kɔ̃ʒwɛ̃, wɛ̃t] 1 adj *démarche, action,* (*Fin*) *débiteurs, legs* joint (*épith*); *problèmes* linked, related. **financement** ~ joint financing. 2 nm,f (*Admin: époux*) spouse. **lui et sa ~e** he and his spouse; **le maire a félicité les ~s** the mayor congratulated the couple; **les (deux) ~s** the husband and wife; **les futurs ~s** the bride and groom to be.

conjointement [kɔ̃ʒwɛ̃tmɑ̃] adv jointly. ~ **avec** together with; **la notice explicative vous sera expédiée ~ (avec l'appareil)** the explanatory leaflet will be enclosed (with the machine); (*Jur*) ~ **et solidairement** jointly and severally.

conjonctif, -ive [kɔ̃ʒɔ̃ktif, iv] 1 adj (*Gram*) conjunctive; (*Anat*) connective. 2 **conjonctive** nf (*Anat*) conjunctiva.

conjonction [kɔ̃ʒɔ̃ksjɔ̃] nf a (*Astron, Gram*) conjunction. (*Ling*) ~ **de coordination/de subordination** coordinating/subordinating conjunction. b (*frm: union*) union, conjunction.

conjonctivite [kɔ̃ʒɔ̃ktivit] nf conjunctivitis.

conjoncture [kɔ̃ʒɔ̃ktyʀ] nf (*circonstances*) situation, circumstances. **dans la ~ (économique) actuelle** in the present (economic) situation *ou* circumstances; **crise de** ~ economic crisis (due to a number of factors); **étude de** ~ study of the overall economic climate *ou* of the present state of the economy.

conjoncturel, -elle [kɔ̃ʒɔ̃ktyʀɛl] adj: **crises/fluctuations ~les** economic crises/fluctuations arising out of certain economic conditions.

conjoncturiste [kɔ̃ʒɔ̃ktyʀist] nmf economic analyst.

conjugable [kɔ̃ʒygabl] adj which can be conjugated.

conjugaison [kɔ̃ʒygɛzɔ̃] nf (*Bio, Gram*) conjugation; (*frm: union*) union, uniting. **grâce à la ~ de nos efforts** by our joint efforts.

conjugal, e, mpl **-aux** [kɔ̃ʒygal, o] adj *amour, union* conjugal. **vie ~e** married *ou* conjugal life; *voir* **domicile, foyer.**

conjugalement [kɔ̃ʒygalmɑ̃] adv: **vivre** ~ to live (together) as a (lawfully) married couple.

conjugué, e [kɔ̃ʒyge] (ptp de **conjuguer**) 1 adj (*Bot, Math*) conjugate; *efforts, actions* joint, combined. 2 nfpl (*Bot*) **conjuguées** conjugatae.

conjuguer [kɔ̃ʒyge] 1 1 vt (*Gram*) to conjugate; (*combiner*) to combine. 2 **se conjuguer** vpr *[efforts]* to combine. **ce verbe se conjugue avec avoir** this verb is conjugated with avoir.

conjuration [kɔ̃ʒyʀasjɔ̃] nf (*complot*) conspiracy; (*rite*) conjuration. **c'est une véritable ~!*** it's a conspiracy!, it's all a big plot!

conjuré, e [kɔ̃ʒyʀe] (ptp de **conjurer**) nm,f conspirator.

conjurer [kɔ̃ʒyʀe] 1 1 vt a (*éviter*) *danger, échec* to avert. b (*littér: exorciser*) *démons, diable* to ward off, cast out. **essayer de ~ le sort** to try to ward off *ou* evade ill fortune. c (*prier, implorer*) ~ **qn de faire qch** to beseech *ou* entreat *ou* beg sb to do sth; **je vous en conjure** I beseech *ou* entreat *ou* beg you. d (††: *conspirer*) *mort, perte de qn* to plot. ~ **contre qn** to plot *ou* conspire against sb. 2 **se conjurer** vpr (*s'unir*) *[circonstances]* to conspire; *[conspirateurs]* to plot, conspire (*contre* against). (*frm, hum*) **vous vous êtes tous conjurés contre moi!** you're all conspiring against me!, you're all in league against me!

connaissable [kɔnɛsabl] adj knowable. **le** ~ the knowable.

connaissance [kɔnɛsɑ̃s] nf a (*savoir*) **la ~ de qch** (the) knowledge of sth; **la** ~ knowledge; **la ~ intuitive/expérimentale** intuitive/experimental knowledge; **sa ~ de l'anglais** his knowledge of English, his acquaintance with English; **il a une bonne ~ des affaires** he has a good *ou* sound knowledge of business matters; **une profonde ~ du cœur humain** a deep understanding of *ou* insight into the human heart; **la ~ de soi** self-knowledge.

b (*choses connues, science*) ~s knowledge; **faire étalage de ses ~s** to display one's knowledge *ou* learning; **approfondir/enrichir ses ~s** to deepen *ou* broaden/enhance one's knowledge; **avoir** *ou* **posséder des ~s de** to have some knowledge of; **c'est un garçon qui a des ~s** he's a knowledgeable fellow; **il a de bonnes/vagues ~s en anglais** he has a good command of/a smattering of English; **il a de vagues ~s de physique** he has a vague knowledge of *ou* a nodding acquaintance with physics.

c (*personne*) acquaintance. **c'est une vieille/simple** ~ he is an old/a mere acquaintance; **faire de nouvelles ~s** to make new acquaintances, meet new people; **il a de nombreuses ~s** he has many acquaintances, he knows a great number of people.

d (*conscience, lucidité*) consciousness. **être sans** ~ to be unconscious; **perdre** ~ to lose consciousness; **reprendre** ~ to regain consciousness, come round* (*Brit*) *ou* to.

e (*loc*) **à ma/sa/leur** ~ to (the best of) my/his/their knowledge, as far as I know/he knows/they know; **pas à ma** ~ not to my knowledge, not as far as I know; **venir à la ~ de qn** to come to sb's knowledge; **donner ~ de qch à qn** to inform *ou* notify sb of sth; **porter qch à la ~ de qn** to notify sb of sth, bring sth to sb's attention; **avoir ~ d'un fait** to be aware of a fact; **en ~ de cause** with full knowledge of the facts; **nous sommes parmi gens de** ~ we are among familiar faces; **un visage de** ~ a familiar face; **en pays de** ~ (*gens qu'on connaît*) among familiar faces; (*branche, sujet qu'on connaît*) on familiar ground *ou* territory; **il avait amené quelqu'un de sa** ~ he had brought along an acquaintance of his *ou* someone he knew; **faire ~ avec qn, faire la ~ de qn** (*rencontrer*) to meet sb, make sb's acquaintance; (*apprendre à connaître*) to get to know sb; **prendre ~ de qch** to read *ou* peruse sth; **nous avons fait ~ à Paris** we met in Paris; **je leur ai fait faire** ~ I introduced them (to each other).

connaissement [kɔnɛsmɑ̃] nm (*Comm*) bill of lading. ~ **sans réserves** clean bill of lading.

connaisseur, -euse [kɔnɛsœʀ, øz] 1 adj *coup d'œil, air* expert. 2 nm,f connoisseur. **être ~ en vins** to be a connoisseur of wines; **il juge en** ~ his opinion is that of a connoisseur.

connaître [kɔnɛtʀ] 57 1 vt a *date, nom, adresse* to know; *fait* to know, be acquainted with; *personne* (*gén*) to know, be acquainted with; (*rencontrer*) to meet; (††: *sens biblique*) to know. **connaît-il la nouvelle?** has he heard *ou* does he know the news?; **connais-tu un bon restaurant près d'ici?** do you know of a good restaurant near here?; ~ **qn de vue/nom/réputation** to know sb by sight/by name/by repute; **chercher à ~ qn** to try to get to know sb; **apprendre à ~ qn** to get to know sb; **il l'a connu à l'université** he met *ou* knew him at university; **je l'ai connu enfant** *ou* **tout petit** I knew him when he was a child; (*je le vois encore*) I have known him since he was a child; **vous connaissez la dernière (nouvelle)?** have you heard the latest (news)?; (*hum*) **si tu te conduis comme ça je ne te connais plus!** if you behave like that (I'll pretend) I'm not with you; **je ne lui connaissais pas ce chapeau/ces talents** I didn't know he had that hat/these talents; **je ne lui connais pas de défauts/d'ennemis** I'm not aware of his having any faults/enemies.

b *langue, science* to know; *méthode, auteur, texte* to know, be acquainted with. ~ **les oiseaux/les plantes** to know about birds/plants; **tu connais la mécanique/la musique?** do you know anything *ou* much about engineering/music?; ~ **un texte** to know a text, be familiar with a text; **il connaît son affaire** he knows what he's talking about; **il connaît son métier** he (really) knows his job; **il en connaît un bout*** *ou* **un rayon*** he knows a thing or two about it*; **un poète qui connaît la vie/l'amour** a poet who knows what life/love is *ou* knows (about) life/love; **elle attendit longtemps de ~ l'amour** she waited a long time to discover what love is; **tu connais ce village? — si je connais*! j'y suis né!** do you know this village? — do I know it! I was born here!; **il ne connaît pas grand-chose à cette machine** he doesn't know (very) much about this machine; **elle n'y connaît rien** she doesn't know anything *ou* a thing about it, she hasn't a clue about it*; **je ne connais pas bien les coutumes du pays** I'm not really familiar with *ou* I'm not (very) well acquainted with the customs of the country, I'm not very well up on the customs of the country*; (*fig*) **je connais la chanson** *ou* **la musique*** I've heard it all before; **il ne connaît pas sa force** he doesn't know *ou* realize his own strength; **il ne connaît pas son bonheur** *ou* **sa chance** he doesn't know how lucky he is; **il ne connaît que son devoir** duty first is his motto.

c (*éprouver*) *faim, privations* to know, experience; *crise, événement* to experience. **il ne connaît pas la pitié** he knows no pity; **ils ont connu des temps meilleurs** they have known *ou* seen better days; **nous connaissons de tristes heures** we are going through sad times; **le pays connaît une crise économique grave** the country is going through *ou* experiencing a serious economic crisis.

d (*avoir*) *succès* to enjoy, have; *sort* to experience. ~ **un échec** to fail; **sa patience ne connaît pas de bornes** his patience knows no bounds; **cette règle ne connaît qu'une exception** there is only one exception to this rule; **l'histoire de ce pays ne connaît qu'une tentative de coup d'État** in the history of this country there has only been one attempted coup.

e **faire** ~ *idée, sentiment* to make known; *décision* to announce, make public; **faire ~ qn** *[pièce, livre]* to make sb's name *ou* make sb known; *[personne]* to make sb known, make a name for sb; **faire ~ qn à qn** to introduce sb to sb; **il m'a fait ~ les joies de la pêche** he introduced me to *ou* initiated me in(to) the joys of fishing; **se faire ~** (*par le succès*) to make a name for o.s., make one's name; (*aller voir qn*) to introduce o.s., make o.s. known.

f (*loc*) **ça le/me connaît!*** he knows/I know all about it!; **je ne connais que lui/que ça!** do I know him/it!*, don't I know him/it!*; **une bonne tasse de café après le repas, je ne connais que ça** there's nothing like a good cup of coffee after a meal; **je ne le connais ni d'Eve ni d'Adam** I don't know him from Adam.

2 **se connaître** vpr a **se ~ (soi-même)** to know o.s.; **connais-toi toi-même** know thyself; (*fig*) **il ne se connaît plus** he's beside himself (*with joy or rage etc*).

b (*se rencontrer*) to meet. **ils se sont connus en Grèce** they met *ou* became acquainted in Greece.

c **s'y ~** *ou* **se ~†** **à** *ou* **en qch** to know (a lot) about sth, be well up on* *ou* well versed in sth; **il s'y connaît en voitures** he knows (all) about cars, he's an expert on cars; **c'est de l'or ou je ne m'y connais pas*** unless I'm very much mistaken, this is gold; **quand il s'agit d'embêter les autres, il s'y connaît!*** when it comes to annoying people he's an expert!*.

3 **connaître de** vt indir (*Jur*) to take cognizance of.

connard‡ [kɔnaʀ] nm (silly) bugger‡ (*Brit*), damn fool‡, jackass‡ (*US*).

connarde‡ [kɔnaʀd] nf, **connasse** [kɔnas] nf (silly) bitch‡ *ou* cow*‡.

conne [kɔn] *voir* **con**.

connecter [kɔnɛkte] 1 vt to connect.

connecteur [kɔnɛktœʀ] nm (*Logique, Ling*) connective.

Connecticut [kɔnɛktikət] nm Connecticut.

connectique [kɔnɛktik] nf connector industry.

connerie‡ [kɔnʀi] nf a (*NonC*) bloody (*Brit*) *ou* damned stupidity‡. b (*remarque, acte*) bloody (*Brit*) *ou* damned stupid thing to say *ou* do‡; (*livre, film*) bullshit*‡ (*NonC*), bloody (*Brit*) *ou* damned rubbish‡ (*NonC*). **arrête de dire des ~s** stop talking (such) bullshit*‡ *ou* such bloody (*Brit*) *ou* damned rubbish‡; **il a encore fait une ~** he's gone and done another damned stupid thing‡; **c'est de la ~!** (a load of) cobblers!‡ (*Brit*) *ou* bullshit!*‡.

connétable [kɔnetabl] nm (*Hist*) constable.

connexe [kɔnɛks] adj (closely) related.

connexion [kɔnɛksjɔ̃] nf (*gén*) link, connection; (*Élec*) connection.

connivence [kɔnivɑ̃s] nf connivance. **être/agir de ~ avec qn** to be/act in connivance with sb; **un sourire de ~** a smile of complicity; **ils sont de ~** they're in league with each other.

connotatif, -ive [kɔ(n)nɔtatif, iv] adj (*Ling*) *sens* connotative.

connotation [kɔ(n)nɔtasjɔ̃] nf connotation.

connoter [kɔ(n)nɔte] 1 vt to connote, imply; (*Ling*) to connote.

connu, e [kɔny] (ptp de **connaître**) adj (*non ignoré*) *terre, animal* known; (*répandu, courant*) *idée, méthode* widely-known, well-known; (*fameux*) *auteur, livre* well-known. **(bien) ~** well-known; **très ~** very well-known, famous; **ces faits sont mal ~s** these facts are not well-known *ou* widely-known; **il est ~ comme le loup blanc** everybody knows him; (*Statistiques etc*) **chiffres non encore ~s** figures not yet available; *voir* **ni**.

conque [kɔ̃k] nf (*coquille*) conch; (*Anat*) concha. (*littér*) **la main en ~** cupping his hand round *ou* to his ear.

conquérant, e [kɔ̃keʀɑ̃, ɑ̃t] 1 adj *pays, peuple* conquering; *ardeur* masterful; *air, regard* swaggering. 2 nm,f conqueror.

conquérir [kɔ̃keʀiʀ] 21 vt *pays, place forte, montagne* to conquer; *part de marché* to capture; (*littér*) *femme, cœur* to conquer (*littér*), win; (*littér*) *estime, respect* to win, gain; (*littér*) *supérieur, personnage influent* to win over. **conquis à une doctrine** won over *ou* converted to a doctrine; *voir* **pays**[1].

conquête [kɔ̃kɛt] nf conquest. **faire la ~ de** *pays, montagne* to conquer; *femme* to conquer (*littér*), win; *supérieur, personnage influent* to win over; **s'élancer** *ou* **partir à la ~ de** (*gén*) to set out to conquer; *record* to set out to break; (*hum*) **faire des ~s** to make a few conquests, break a few hearts.

conquis, e [kɔ̃ki, iz] ptp de **conquérir**.

conquistador [kɔ̃kistadɔʀ] nm conquistador.

consacré, e [kɔ̃sakʀe] (ptp de **consacrer**) adj a (*béni*) *hostie, église* consecrated; *lieu* consecrated, hallowed. b (*habituel, accepté*) *coutume* established, accepted; *itinéraire, visite* traditional; *écrivain* established, recognized. **c'est l'expression ~e** it's the accepted way of saying it. c (*destiné à*) **~ à** given over to; **talents ~s à faire le bien** talents given over to *ou* dedicated to doing good.

consacrer [kɔ̃sakʀe] 1 vt a **~ à** (*destiner, dédier à*) to devote to, dedicate to, consecrate to; (*affecter à, utiliser pour*) to devote to, give (over) to; **~ sa vie à Dieu** to devote *ou* dedicate *ou* consecrate one's life to God; **il consacre toutes ses forces/tout son temps à son travail** he devotes all his energies/time to his work, he gives all his energies/time (over) to his work; **pouvez-vous me ~ un instant?** can you give *ou* spare me a moment?; **se ~ à une profession/à Dieu** to dedicate *ou* devote o.s. to a profession/God, give o.s. to a profession/God.

b (*Rel*) *reliques, lieu* to consecrate, hallow (*littér*); *église, évêque, hostie* to consecrate. **temple consacré à Apollon** temple consecrated *ou* dedicated to Apollo; (*littér*) **leur mort a consacré cette terre** their death has made this ground hallowed.

c (*entériner*) *coutume, droit* to establish; *abus* to sanction. **expression consacrée par l'usage** expression sanctioned by use *ou* which has become accepted through use; **consacré par le temps** time-honoured (*épith*); **la fuite de l'ennemi consacre notre victoire** the enemy's flight makes our victory complete.

consanguin, e [kɔ̃sɑ̃gɛ̃, in] 1 adj: **frère ~** half-brother (*on the father's side*); **mariage ~** intermarriage, marriage between blood relations; **les mariages ~s sont à déconseiller** marriages between blood relations should be discouraged, intermarrying *ou* inbreeding should be discouraged. 2 nmpl: **les ~s** blood relations.

consanguinité [kɔ̃sɑ̃g(ɥ)inite] nf (*du même père, d'ancêtre commun*) consanguinity; (*Bio: union consanguine*) intermarrying, inbreeding.

consciemment [kɔ̃sjamɑ̃] adv consciously, knowingly.

conscience [kɔ̃sjɑ̃s] nf a (*faculté psychologique*) **la ~ de qch** the awareness *ou* consciousness of sth; (*Philos, Psych*) **la ~** consciousness; **~ de soi** self-awareness; **~ collective/de classe** collective/class consciousness; **~ politique/linguistique** political/linguistic awareness; **avoir ~ que** to be aware *ou* conscious that; **avoir ~ de sa faiblesse/de l'importance de qch** to be aware *ou* conscious of one's own weakness/of the importance of sth; **prendre ~ de qch** to become aware of sth, realize sth, awake to sth; **il prit soudain ~ d'avoir dit ce qu'il ne fallait pas** he was suddenly aware that *ou* he suddenly realized that he had said something he shouldn't have; **cela lui a donné** *ou* **fait prendre ~ de son importance** it made him aware of his importance, it made him realize how important he was; *voir* **pris**.

b (*état de veille, faculté de sensation*) consciousness. **perdre/reprendre ~** to lose/regain consciousness.

c (*faculté morale*) conscience. **avoir la ~ tranquille/chargée** to have a clear/guilty conscience; **il n'a pas la ~ tranquille** he has a guilty *ou* an uneasy conscience, his conscience is troubling him; **avoir qch sur la ~** to have sth on one's conscience; **avoir bonne/mauvaise ~** to have a good *ou* clear/bad *ou* guilty conscience; **donner bonne ~ à qn** to ease sb's conscience; **donner mauvaise ~ à qn** to give sb a guilty *ou* bad conscience; **agir selon sa ~** to act according to one's conscience *ou* as one's conscience dictates; **sans ~** without conscience; **en (toute) ~** in all conscience *ou* honesty; **étouffer les ~s** to stifle consciences *ou* people's conscience; (*fig*) **il a sorti tout ce qu'il avait sur la ~** he came out with all he had on his conscience; (*fig*) **son déjeuner lui est resté sur la ~ *** his lunch is lying heavy on his stomach; *voir* **acquit, objecteur**.

d **~ (professionnelle)** conscientiousness; **faire un travail avec beaucoup de ~** to do a piece of work conscientiously.

consciencieusement [kɔ̃sjɑ̃sjøzmɑ̃] adv conscientiously.

consciencieux, -ieuse [kɔ̃sjɑ̃sjø, jøz] adj conscientious.

conscient, e [kɔ̃sjɑ̃, jɑ̃t] adj (*non évanoui*) conscious; (*lucide*) *personne* lucid; *mouvement, décision* conscious. **~ de** conscious *ou* aware of.

conscription [kɔ̃skʀipsjɔ̃] nf conscription, draft (*US*).

conscrit [kɔ̃skʀi] nm conscript, draftee (*US*). **se faire avoir comme un ~†*** to be taken in like a newborn babe *ou* like a real sucker*.

consécration [kɔ̃sekʀasjɔ̃] nf *[lieu, église, artiste]* consecration; *[coutume, droit]* establishment; *[abus]* sanctioning. **la ~ d'un temple à un culte** the consecration *ou* dedication of a temple to a religion; **la ~ du temps** time's sanction; **la ~ d'une œuvre par le succès** the consecration of a work by its success *ou* by the success it has; (*Rel*) **la ~** the consecration.

consécutif, -ive [kɔ̃sekytif, iv] adj consecutive. **pendant trois jours ~s** for three days running, for three consecutive days; **elle a eu 3 succès ~s** she had 3 hits in a row; **sa blessure est ~ive à un accident** his injury is the result of an accident; *voir* **proposition**.

consécution [kɔ̃sekysjɔ̃] nf consecutiveness.

consécutivement [kɔ̃sekytivmɑ̃] adv consecutively. **elle eut ~ deux accidents** she had two consecutive accidents, she had two accidents in a row *ou* one after the other; **~ à** following upon.

conseil [kɔ̃sɛj] 1 nm a (*recommandation*) piece of advice, advice (*NonC*), counsel; (*simple suggestion*) hint. **donner des ~s à qn** to give sb some advice; **écouter/suivre le ~ de qn** to listen to/follow sb's advice; **demander ~ à qn** to ask *ou* seek sb's advice, ask sb for advice; **prendre ~ de qn** to take advice from sb; **je lui ai donné le ~ d'attendre** I advised *ou* counselled him to wait; **un petit ~** a word *ou* a few words *ou* a bit of advice, a hint *ou* tip; **ne pars pas, c'est un ~ d'ami** don't go — that's (just) a friendly piece of advice; **écoutez mon ~** take my advice, listen to my advice; **un bon ~** a sound piece of advice; **ne suivez pas les ~s de la colère** don't let yourself be guided by the promptings *ou* dictates of anger; **les ~s que nous donne l'expérience** everything that experience teaches us; (*littér*) **un homme de bon ~** a good counsellor, a man of sound advice; (*Admin, Comm*) **~s à ...** advice to ...; **~s à la ménagère/au débutant** hints *ou* tips for the housewife/the beginner; *voir* **nuit.**

b (*personne*) consultant, adviser (*en* in). **~ en brevets d'invention** patent engineer; **~ fiscal** tax consultant; (*Jur*) **~ en propriété industrielle** patent lawyer *ou* attorney (*US*); **ingénieur-~** consulting engineer; **avocat-/esthéticienne-~** legal/beauty consultant.

c (*groupe, assemblée*) *[entreprise]* board; *[organisme politique ou professionnel]* council, committee; (*séance, délibération*) meeting. **tenir ~** (*se réunir*) to hold a meeting; (*délibérer*) to deliberate.

2 **comp ►conseil d'administration** *[société anonyme etc]* board of directors; *[hôpital, école]* board of governors **►conseil de classe** (*Scol*) staff meeting (*to discuss the progress of individual members of a class*) **►conseil communal** (*Belgique*) ≃ local council **►conseil de discipline** (*Scol, Univ*) disciplinary committee **►Conseil d'établissement** (*Scol*) ≃ governing board (*Brit*), ≃ board of education (*US*) **►Conseil d'État** (*Jur*) Council of State **►Conseil européen pour la recherche nucléaire** European Organization for Nuclear Research **►conseil de fabrique** (*Rel*) fabric committee **►conseil de famille** (*Jur*) board of guardians **►conseil général** (*Admin*) regional council **►conseil de guerre** (*Mil*) (*réunion*) war council; (*tribunal*) court-martial; **passer en conseil de guerre** to be court-martialled; **faire passer qn en conseil de guerre** to court-martial sb **►Conseil des ministres** (*personnes*) (*en Grande-Bretagne*) Cabinet; (*en France*) (French) Cabinet, council of ministers; (*réunion*) Cabinet meeting **►conseil municipal** (*Admin*) town council **►Conseil national du patronat français** *French national employers' federation,* ≃ Confederation of British Industry (*Brit*) **►Conseil œcuménique des Églises** World Council of Churches **►conseil de l'Ordre** *[avocats] lawyers' governing body,* ≃ Bar Council (*Brit*); *[médecins] doctors' governing body,* ≃ British Medical Authority (*Brit*) **►conseil des prud'hommes** (*Jur*) industrial arbitration court, ≃ industrial tribunal (*with wide administrative and advisory powers*) **►conseil régional** ≃ county council (*Brit*), ≃ county commission (*US*) **►conseil de révision** (*Mil*) recruiting board, draft board (*US*) **►Conseil de sécurité** Security Council **►Conseil supérieur de l'audiovisuel** *French broadcasting regulatory body,* ≃ Independent Broadcasting Authority (*Brit*), ≃ Federal Communications Commission (*US*) **►conseil d'U.E.R.** (*Univ*) departmental (management) committee **►conseil d'université** university management committee, ≃ Senate (*Brit*), ≃ Board of Trustees *ou* Regents (*US*).

conseiller[1] [kɔ̃seje] [1] **vt** a (*recommander*) *prudence, méthode, bonne adresse* to recommend (*à qn* to sb). (*Comm*) **prix conseillé** recommended price; **il m'a conseillé ce docteur** he advised me to go to this doctor, he recommended this doctor to me; **~ à qn de faire qch** to advise sb to do sth; **je vous conseille vivement de ...** I strongly advise you to ...; **la peur/prudence lui conseilla de ...** fear/prudence prompted him to ...; **il est conseillé de s'inscrire à l'avance** it is advisable to enrol in advance; **il est conseillé aux parents de ...** parents are advised to ... .

b (*guider*) to advise, give advice to, counsel. **~ un étudiant dans ses lectures** to advise *ou* counsel a student in his reading; **il a été bien/mal conseillé** he has been given good/bad advice, he has been well/badly advised.

conseiller[2]**, -ère** [kɔ̃seje, ɛʀ] 1 **nm,f** a (*expert*) consultant, adviser (*en* in); (*guide, personne d'expérience*) counsellor, adviser. **~ juridique/technique** legal/technical adviser; (*fig*) **que ta conscience soit ta ~ère** may your conscience be your guide; *voir* **colère.**

b (*Admin, Pol: fonctionnaire*) council member, councillor.

2 **comp ►conseiller d'État** senior member of the Council of State **►conseiller en image** image consultant **►conseiller matrimonial** marriage guidance counsellor **►conseiller municipal** town councillor (*Brit*), city council man (*US*) **►conseiller d'orientation** (*Scol*) careers adviser (*Brit*), (school) counselor (*US*), guidance counselor (*US*) **►conseiller pédagogique** educational adviser **►conseiller (principal) d'éducation** year head (*Brit*), dean (*US*) **►conseiller pédagogique de maths/français** French/Maths adviser.

conseilleur, -euse [kɔ̃sɛjœʀ, øz] **nm,f** (*péj*) dispenser of advice. (*Prov*) **les ~s ne sont pas les payeurs** givers of advice don't pay the price.

consensuel, -elle [kɔ̃sɑ̃sɥɛl] **adj** *politique* consensus (*épith*); (*Jur*) *accord* consensual.

consensus [kɔ̃sɛ̃sys] **nm** consensus (of opinion).

consentant, e [kɔ̃sɑ̃tɑ̃, ɑ̃t] **adj** *amoureuse* willing; (*frm*) *personnes, parties* in agreement, agreeable; (*Jur*) *parties, partenaire* consenting. **le mariage ne peut avoir lieu que si les parents sont ~s** the marriage can only take place with the parents' consent *ou* if the parents consent to it.

consentement [kɔ̃sɑ̃tmɑ̃] **nm** consent. **divorce par ~ mutuel** divorce by consent; **son ~ à leur mariage était nécessaire** his consent to their marriage was needed; **donner son ~ à qch** to consent to sth, give one's consent to sth; (*littér*) **le ~ universel** universal *ou* common assent.

consentir [kɔ̃sɑ̃tiʀ] [16] 1 **vi** (*accepter*) to agree, consent (*à* to). **~ à faire qch** to agree to do(ing) sth; **~ (à ce) que qn fasse qch** to consent *ou* agree to sb's doing sth; **espérons qu'il va (y) ~** let's hope he'll agree *ou* consent to it; *voir* **qui.** 2 **vt** (*accorder*) *permission, délai, prêt* to grant (*à* to). **~ une dérogation** to grant *ou* accord exemption (*à* to).

conséquemment [kɔ̃sekamɑ̃] **adv** (*littér: par suite*) consequently; († *ou littér: avec cohérence, logique*) consequentially. **~ à** as a result of, following on.

conséquence [kɔ̃sekɑ̃s] **nf** a (*effet, résultat*) result, outcome (*NonC*), consequence. **cela pourrait avoir** *ou* **entraîner des ~s graves pour ...** this could have serious consequences for *ou* repercussions on ...; **cela a eu pour ~ de l'obliger à réfléchir** the result *ou* consequence of this was that he was forced to think; **accepter/subir les ~s de ses actions** to accept/suffer the consequences of one's actions; **incident gros** *ou* **lourd de ~s** incident fraught with consequences; **avoir d'heureuses ~s** to have a happy outcome *ou* happy results.

b (*Philos: suite logique*) consequence; *voir* **proposition, voie.**

c (*conclusion, déduction*) inference, conclusion (*de* to be drawn from). **tirer les ~s** to draw conclusions *ou* inferences (*de* from).

d (*loc*) **de ~** *affaire, personne* of (some) consequence *ou* importance; **en ~** (*par suite*) consequently; (*comme il convient*) accordingly; **en ~ de** (*par suite de*) in consequence of, as a result of; (*selon*) according to; **sans ~** (*sans suite fâcheuse*) without repercussions; (*sans importance*) of no consequence *ou* importance; **cela ne tire pas à ~** it's of no consequence, that's unlikely to have any repercussions.

conséquent, e [kɔ̃sekɑ̃, ɑ̃t] 1 **adj** a (*logique*) logical, rational; (*doué d'esprit de suite*) consistent. (*littér*) **~ à** consistent with, in keeping *ou* conformity with; **~ avec soi-même** consistent (with o.s.); **~ dans ses actions** consistent in one's actions. b (**: important*) sizeable. c (*Géol*) *rivière, percée* consequent. d (*Mus*) **(partie) ~e** consequent, answer. 2 **nm** (*Ling, Logique, Math*) consequent; (*Mus*) consequent, answer. **par ~** consequently, therefore.

conservateur, -trice [kɔ̃sɛʀvatœʀ, tʀis] 1 **adj** (*gén*) conservative; (*Brit Pol*) Conservative, Tory. (*Can*) **le parti ~** the Progressive-Conservative Party (*Can*). 2 **nm,f** a (*gardien*) *[musée]* curator; *[bibliothèque]* librarian. **~ des eaux et forêts** ≃ forestry commissioner; **~ des hypothèques** ≃ land registrar. b (*Pol*) conservative; (*Brit Pol*) Conservative, Tory; (*Can*) Conservative (*Can*). 3 **nm** (*produit chimique*) preservative; (*réfrigérateur*) frozen food compartment, freezer compartment.

conservation [kɔ̃sɛʀvasjɔ̃] **nf** a (*action*) *[aliments]* preserving; *[monuments]* preserving, preservation; *[archives]* keeping; *[accent, souplesse]* retention, retaining, keeping; *[habitudes]* keeping up; *voir* **instinct, lait.** b (*état*) *[aliments, monuments]* preservation. **en bon état de ~** *fruits* well-preserved; *monument* well-preserved, in a good state of preservation. c (*Admin: charge*) **~ des eaux et forêts** ≃ Forestry Commission; **~ des hypothèques** ≃ Land Registry.

conservatisme [kɔ̃sɛʀvatism] **nm** conservatism.

conservatoire [kɔ̃sɛʀvatwaʀ] 1 **adj** (*Jur*) protective; *voir* **saisie.** 2 **nm** school, academy (*of music, drama etc*). **le C~ (de musique et de déclamation)** the (Paris) Conservatoire; **le C~ des arts et métiers** the Conservatoire *ou* Conservatory of Arts and Crafts.

conserve [kɔ̃sɛʀv] 1 **nf: les ~s** tinned (*Brit*) *ou* canned food(s); **~s en bocaux** bottled preserves; **~s de viande/poisson** tinned (*Brit*) *ou* canned meat/fish; **l'industrie de la ~** the canning industry; **en ~** canned, tinned (*Brit*); **mettre en ~** to can; **se nourrir de ~s** to live out of tins (*Brit*) *ou* cans; **faire des ~s de haricots** to bottle beans; (*fig*) **tu ne vas pas en faire des ~s!*** you're not going to hoard it away for ever!; *voir* **boîte.** 2 **adv** (*ensemble*) **de ~** *naviguer* in convoy; *agir* in concert.

conserver [kɔ̃sɛʀve] [1] 1 **vt** a (*garder dans un endroit*) *objets, papiers* to keep. **"~ à l'abri de la lumière"** "keep *ou* store away from light".

b (*ne pas perdre*) (*gén*) to retain, keep; *usage, habitude* to keep up; *espoir* to retain; *qualité, droits* to conserve, retain; (*Sport*) *titre* to retain, hold on to*; *son calme, ses amis, ses cheveux* to keep. **ça conserve tout son sens** it retains its full meaning; **~ la vie** to conserve life; **il a conservé toute sa tête** (*lucidité*) he still has his wits about him, he's still all there*; (*Naut*) **~ l'allure** to maintain speed; (*Naut*) **~ sa position** to hold one's position; (*Mil*) **~ ses positions** to stand fast.

c (*maintenir en bon état*) *aliments, santé, monument* to preserve. **la vie au grand air, ça conserve!*** (the) open-air life keeps you young; **bien conservé pour son âge** well-preserved for one's age.

d (*Culin*) to preserve, can. **~ (dans du vinaigre)** to pickle; **~ en bocal** to bottle.

2 **se conserver vpr** *[aliments]* to keep.

conserverie [kɔ̃sɛʀvəʀi] **nf** (*usine*) canning factory; (*industrie*) canning industry.

considérable [kɔ̃sideʀabl] **adj** *somme, foule, retard, travail* sizeable, considerable; *rôle, succès, changement* considerable, significant; *dégâts, surface* considerable, extensive; († *ou littér*) *personnage, situation* eminent, important. **saisi d'une émotion ~** considerably *ou* deeply moved.

considérablement [kɔ̃sideʀabləmɑ̃] **adv** (*voir* **considérable**) considerably; significantly; extensively. **ceci nous a ~ retardés** this delayed us considerably; **ceci a ~ modifié la situation** this modified the situation to a considerable *ou* significant extent, this modified the situation considerably *ou* significantly.

considérant [kɔ̃sideʀɑ̃] **nm** *[loi, jugement]* preamble.

considération [kɔ̃sideʀasjɔ̃] **nf** **a** (*examen*) *[problème etc]* consideration. **ceci mérite ~** this is worth considering *ou* consideration *ou* looking into; **prendre qch en ~** to take sth into consideration *ou* account, make allowances for sth.

b (*motif, aspect*) consideration, factor, issue. **n'entrons pas dans ces ~s** don't let's go into these considerations; **c'est une ~ dont je n'imagine pas qu'il faille se préoccuper** it's a question *ou* factor *ou* issue I don't think we need bother ourselves with.

c (*remarques, observations*) **~s** reflections; **il se lança dans des ~s interminables sur la crise politique** he launched into lengthy reflections *ou* observations on the political crisis.

d (*respect*) esteem, respect. **jouir de la ~ de tous** to enjoy everyone's esteem *ou* respect; (*formule épistolaire*) **"veuillez agréer l'assurance de ma ~ distinguée"** "yours faithfully" (*Brit*), "yours truly" (*US*).

e (*loc*) (*en raison de*) **en ~ de son âge** because of *ou* given his age; (*par rapport à*) **en ~ de ce qui aurait pu se passer** considering what could have happened; **sans ~ de** *dangers, conséquences, prix* heedless *ou* regardless of; **sans ~ de personne** without taking personalities into account *ou* consideration; **par ~ pour** out of respect *ou* regard for.

considérer [kɔ̃sideʀe] 6 **vt** **a** (*envisager*) *problème etc* to consider. **il faut ~ (les) avantages et (les) inconvénients** one must consider *ou* take into account the advantages and disadvantages; **~ le pour et le contre** to consider the pros and cons; **considère bien ceci** think about this carefully, consider this well; **il ne considère que son intérêt** he only thinks about *ou* considers his own interests; **tout bien considéré** all things considered, taking everything into consideration *ou* account; **c'est à ~** (*pour en tenir compte*) this has to be considered *ou* borne in mind *ou* taken into account; (*à étudier*) this must be gone into *ou* examined.

b (*assimiler à*) **~ comme** to look upon as, regard as, consider (to be); **je le considère comme mon fils** I look upon him as *ou* regard him as my son, I consider him (to be) my son; **il se considère comme un personnage important** he sees himself as an important person, he considers himself (to be) an important person.

c (*juger*) to consider, deem (*frm*). **je le considère intelligent** I consider him intelligent, I deem him to be intelligent (*frm*); **je considère qu'il a raison** I consider that he is right; **c'est très mal considéré (d'agir ainsi)** it's very bad form (to act like that); **considérant que** (*gén*) considering that; (*Jur*) whereas.

d (*frm: regarder*) to consider, study.

e (*respecter: gén ptp*) to respect, have a high regard for. **il est hautement considéré, on le considère hautement** he is highly regarded *ou* respected, he is held in high regard *ou* high esteem; **le besoin d'être considéré** the need to have people's respect *ou* esteem.

consignataire [kɔ̃siɲatɛʀ] **nm** (*Comm*) *[biens, marchandises]* consignee; *[navire]* consignee, forwarding agent; (*Jur*) *[somme]* depositary.

consignation [kɔ̃siɲasjɔ̃] **nf** (*Jur: dépôt d'argent*) deposit; (*Comm: dépôt de marchandise*) consignment. **la ~ d'un emballage** charging a deposit on a container; *voir* **caisse**.

consigne [kɔ̃siɲ] **nf** **a** (*instructions*) orders. **donner/recevoir/observer la ~** to give/get *ou* be given/obey orders; **c'est la ~** those are the orders. **b** (*punition*) (*Mil*) confinement to barracks; (*Scol* †) detention. **c** (*pour les bagages*) left-luggage (office) (*Brit*), checkroom (*US*). **~ automatique** (left-luggage) lockers. **d** (*Comm: somme remboursable*) deposit. **il y a 2 F de ~** *ou* **une ~ de 2 F sur la bouteille** there's a 2-franc deposit *ou* a deposit of 2 francs on the bottle, you get 2 francs back on the bottle.

consigné, e [kɔ̃siɲe] (**ptp de consigner**) **adj** (*Comm*) *bouteille, emballage* returnable. **non ~** non-returnable.

consigner [kɔ̃siɲe] 1 **vt** **a** *fait, pensée, incident* to record. **~ qch par écrit** to put sth down in writing *ou* on paper.

b (*interdire de sortir à*) *troupe, soldat* to confine to barracks; *élève* to give detention to, keep in (after school); (*interdire l'accès de*) *salle, établissement* to bar entrance to. **consigné à la caserne** confined to barracks; **établissement consigné aux militaires** establishment out of bounds to troops.

c (*mettre en dépôt*) *somme, marchandise* to deposit; *navire* to consign; *bagages* to deposit *ou* put in the left-luggage (office) (*Brit*) *ou* checkroom (*US*).

d (*facturer provisoirement*) *emballage, bouteille* to put a deposit on. **les bouteilles sont consignées 80 centimes** there is a deposit of 80 centimes on the bottles; **je vous le consigne** I'm giving it to you on a deposit.

consistance [kɔ̃sistɑ̃s] **nf** *[sauce, neige, terre]* consistency; (*fig*) *[caractère]* strength. **~ sirupeuse/élastique** syrupy/elastic consistency; **manquer de ~** (*sauce*) to lack consistency; *[idée, personnage, texte, film]* to lack substance; *nouvelle, rumeur* to be unsupported by evidence; **donner de la ~ à** *pâte* to give body to; *rumeur* to give strength to; *idée, théorie* to give substance to; **prendre ~** *[liquide]* to thicken; *[idée, projet, texte, personnage]* to take shape; **sans ~** *caractère* spineless, colourless; *nouvelle, rumeur* ill-founded, groundless; *substance* lacking in consistency (*attrib*); **cette rumeur prend de la ~** this rumour is gaining ground.

consistant, e [kɔ̃sistɑ̃, ɑ̃t] **adj** *repas* solid (*épith*), substantial; *nourriture* solid (*épith*); *mélange, peinture, sirop* thick; (*fig*) *rumeur* well-founded; (*fig*) *argument* solid, sound.

consister [kɔ̃siste] 1 **vi** **a** (*se composer de*) **~ en** to consist of, be made up of; **le village consiste en 30 maisons et une église** the village consists of *ou* is made up of 30 houses and a church; **en quoi consiste votre travail?** what does your work consist of? **b** (*résider dans*) **~ dans** to consist in; **le salut consistait dans l'arrivée immédiate de renforts** their salvation consisted *ou* lay in the immediate arrival of reinforcements; **~ à faire** to consist in doing.

consistoire [kɔ̃sistwaʀ] **nm** consistory.

consœur [kɔ̃sœʀ] **nf** (*hum*) (lady) colleague.

consolable [kɔ̃sɔlabl] **adj** consolable.

consolant, e [kɔ̃sɔlɑ̃, ɑ̃t] **adj** consoling, comforting.

consolateur, -trice [kɔ̃sɔlatœʀ, tʀis] **1 adj** consolatory. **2 nm,f** (*littér*) comforter.

consolation [kɔ̃sɔlasjɔ̃] **nf** (*action*) consoling, consolation; (*réconfort*) consolation (*NonC*), comfort (*NonC*), solace (*NonC: littér*). **nous prodiguant ses ~s** offering us comfort; **paroles de ~** words of consolation *ou* comfort; **elle est sa ~** she is his consolation *ou* comfort *ou* solace (*littér*); **enfin, il n'y a pas de dégâts, c'est une ~** anyway, (at least) there's no damage, that's one consolation *ou* comfort; **lot** *ou* **prix de ~** consolation prize.

console [kɔ̃sɔl] **nf** **a** (*table*) console (table); (*Archit*) console. **b** (*Mus*) *[harpe]* neck; *[orgue]* console; (*Ordin, Tech: d'enregistrement*) console. (*Ordin*) **~ de visualisation** visual display unit, VDU; (*Mus*) **~ de mixage** mixing desk.

consoler [kɔ̃sɔle] 1 **1 vt** *personne* to console; *chagrin* to soothe. **ça me consolera de mes pertes** that will console me for my losses; **je ne peux pas le ~ de sa peine** I cannot console *ou* comfort him in his grief; **si ça peut te ~ ...** if it is of any consolation *ou* comfort to you ...; **le temps console** time heals.

2 se consoler vpr to console o.s., find consolation. **se ~ d'une perte/de son échec** to be consoled for *ou* to get over a loss/one's failure; (*hum*) **il s'est vite consolé avec une autre** he soon consoled himself with another woman, he soon found comfort *ou* consolation with another woman; **il ne s'en consolera jamais** he'll never be consoled, he'll never get over it.

consolidation [kɔ̃sɔlidasjɔ̃] **nf** (*voir* **consolider, se consolider**) (*gén*) strengthening; reinforcement; consolidation; knitting; (*Fin*) funding. **~ de la dette** debt consolidation.

consolidé, e [kɔ̃sɔlide] (**ptp de consolider**) (*Fin*) **1 adj** funded. **2 consolidés nmpl** consols.

consolider [kɔ̃sɔlide] 1 **1 vt** **a** *maison, table* to strengthen, reinforce; (*Méd*) *fracture* to set. **b** *accord, amitié, parti, fortune* to consolidate; (*Écon*) *monnaie* to strengthen. **c** (*Fin*) *rente, emprunt* to guarantee. **dettes consolidées** consolidated debts; **rentes consolidées** funded income. **d** (*Sport*) *avance* to extend. **2 se consolider vpr** *[régime, parti]* to strengthen *ou* consolidate its position; *[fracture]* to knit, set. **la position de la gauche/droite s'est encore consolidée** the position of the left/right has been further consolidated *ou* strengthened.

consommable [kɔ̃sɔmabl] **1 adj** *solide* edible; *liquide* drinkable. **cette viande n'est ~ que bouillie** this meat can only be eaten boiled. **2 nm** (*gén, Ordin*) consumable.

consommateur, -trice [kɔ̃sɔmatœʀ, tʀis] **nm,f** (*acheteur*) consumer; (*client d'un café*) customer.

consommation [kɔ̃sɔmasjɔ̃] **nf** **a** *[nourriture, gaz, matière première, essence]* consumption. **faire une grande ~ de** *papier* to get through* *ou* use (up) a lot of; *crayons* to get through* a lot of; (*Aut*) **~ aux 100 km** (fuel) consumption per 100 km, ≃ miles per gallon (*Brit*), ≃ gas mileage (*US*); *voir* **produit**. **b** (*Écon*) **la ~** consumption; **de ~** *biens, société* consumer (*épith*); **~ ostentatoire** conspicuous consumption; **produit de ~** consumable. **c** (*dans un café*) drink. **le garçon prend les ~s** the waiter takes the orders. **d** (*frm*) *[mariage]* consummation; *[ruine]* confirmation; *[crime]* perpetration, committing. (*littér*) **jusqu'à la ~ des siècles** until the end of time.

consommatique [kɔ̃sɔmatik] **nf** consumer research.

consommé, e [kɔ̃sɔme] (**ptp de consommer**) **1 adj** *habileté* consummate (*épith*); *écrivain etc* accomplished. **tableau qui témoigne d'un art ~** picture revealing consummate artistry. **2 nm** consommé. **~ de poulet** chicken consommé, consommé of chicken.

consommer [kɔ̃sɔme] 1 **vt** **a** *nourriture* to eat, consume (*frm*); *boissons* to drink, consume (*frm*). **on consomme beaucoup de fruits chez nous** we eat a lot of fruit in our family; **la France est le pays où l'on consomme** *ou* **où il se consomme le plus de vin** France is the country with the greatest wine consumption *ou* where the most wine is consumed *ou* drunk; **il est interdit de ~ à la terrasse** drinks are not allowed *ou* drinking is not allowed *ou* drinks may not be consumed outside.

b *combustible, matière première* to use, consume. **cette machine consomme beaucoup d'eau** this machine uses (up) *ou* goes through* a lot of water; **gâteau qui consomme beaucoup de farine** a cake which uses *ou* takes *ou* needs a lot of flour; (*Aut*) **combien consommez-vous aux 100 km?** how much (petrol) do you use per 100 km?, what's your petrol consumption?, ≈ how many miles per gallon do you get? (*Brit*), ≈ what's your gas mileage? (*US*); (*Aut*) **elle consomme beaucoup d'essence/d'huile** it's heavy on petrol/oil, it uses a lot of petrol/oil.

c (*frm: accomplir*) *acte sexuel* to consummate; *crime* to perpetrate, commit. **le mariage n'a pas été consommé** the marriage has not been consummated; **cela a consommé sa ruine** this finally confirmed his downfall; **ce qui a consommé la rupture** ... what put the seal on the break-up ... .

consomption [kɔ̃sɔ̃psjɔ̃] **nf** († *ou littér: dépérissement*) wasting; (†: *tuberculose*) consumption†.

consonance [kɔ̃sɔnɑ̃s] **nf** consonance (*NonC*). **nom aux ~s étrangères/douces** foreign-/sweet-sounding name.

consonant, e [kɔ̃sɔnɑ̃, ɑ̃t] **adj** consonant.

consonantique [kɔ̃sɔnɑ̃tik] **adj** consonantal, consonant (*épith*). **groupe ~** consonant cluster.

consonantisme [kɔ̃sɔnɑ̃tism] **nm** consonant system.

consonne [kɔ̃sɔn] **nf** consonant. **~ d'appui** intrusive consonant; **~ de liaison** linking consonant.

consort [kɔ̃sɔʀ] 1 **adj** *voir* **prince**. 2 **nmpl** (*péj*) **X et ~s** (*acolytes*) X and company, X and his bunch* (*péj*); (*pareils*) X and his like (*péj*).

consortial, e, mpl -iaux [kɔ̃sɔʀsjal, jo] **adj** *prêt* syndicated.

consortium [kɔ̃sɔʀsjɔm] **nm** consortium. **former un ~ (de prêt)** to syndicate a loan, form a loan consortium.

conspirateur, -trice [kɔ̃spiʀatœʀ, tʀis] 1 **adj** conspiratorial. 2 **nm,f** conspirer, conspirator, plotter.

conspiration [kɔ̃spiʀasjɔ̃] **nf** conspiracy.

conspirer [kɔ̃spiʀe] [1] 1 **vi** (*comploter*) to conspire, plot (*contre* against). 2 **conspirer à vt indir** (*concourir à*) **~ à faire** to conspire to do; **tout semblait ~ à notre succès** everything seemed to be conspiring to bring about our success. 3 **vt** (†) *mort, ruine de qn* to conspire († *ou littér*), plot.

conspuer [kɔ̃spɥe] [1] **vt** to boo, shout down.

constamment [kɔ̃stamɑ̃] **adv** (*sans trêve*) constantly, continuously; (*très souvent*) constantly, continually.

constance [kɔ̃stɑ̃s] **nf** a (*permanence*) consistency, constancy. b (*littér: persévérance, fidélité*) constancy, steadfastness. **travailler avec ~** to work steadfastly; (*iro*) **vous avez de la ~!** you don't give up easily (I'll say that for you)! c (†: *courage*) fortitude, steadfastness.

Constance [kɔ̃stɑ̃s] **n** (*Géog*) Constance. **le lac de ~** Lake Constance.

constant, e [kɔ̃stɑ̃, ɑ̃t] 1 **adj** a (*invariable*) constant; (*continu*) constant, continuous; (*très fréquent*) constant, continual. (*Fin*) **francs ~s** inflation-adjusted francs, constant francs. b (*littér: persévérant*) *effort* steadfast; *travail* constant. **être ~ dans ses efforts** to be steadfast *ou* constant in one's efforts. 2 **constante nf** (*Math*) constant; (*fig: caractéristique*) permanent feature.

Constantin [kɔ̃stɑ̃tɛ̃] **nm** Constantine.

Constantinople [kɔ̃stɑ̃tinɔpl] **n** Constantinople.

constat [kɔ̃sta] **nm**: **~ (d'huissier)** affidavit drawn up by a bailiff; **~ (d'accident)** (accident) report; **~ (à l')amiable** *jointly-agreed statement for insurance purposes;* **~ d'adultère** recording of adultery; (*fig*) **~ d'échec/d'impuissance** acknowledgement of failure/impotence.

constatation [kɔ̃statasjɔ̃] **nf** a (*NonC: voir* **constater**) noting; noticing; seeing; taking note; recording; certifying. b (*gén*) observation. **~s** *[enquête]* findings; (*Police*) **procéder aux ~s d'usage** to make a *ou* one's routine report.

constater [kɔ̃state] [1] **vt** a (*remarquer*) *fait* to note, notice; *erreur* to see, notice; *dégâts* to note, take note of. **il constata la disparition de son carnet** he noticed *ou* saw that his notebook had disappeared; **je ne critique pas: je ne fais que ~** I'm not criticizing, I'm merely stating a fact *ou* I'm merely making a statement (of fact) *ou* an observation; **je constate que vous n'êtes pas pressé de tenir vos promesses** I see *ou* notice *ou* note that you aren't in a hurry to keep your promises; **vous pouvez ~ par vous-même les erreurs** you can see the mistakes for yourself.

b (*frm: consigner*) *effraction, état de fait, authenticité* to record; *décès* to certify. **le médecin a constaté le décès** the doctor certified that death had taken place *ou* occurred.

constellation [kɔ̃stelasjɔ̃] **nf** (*Astron*) constellation. (*fig littér*) **~ de** *lumières, poètes* constellation *ou* galaxy of.

constellé, e [kɔ̃stele] (**ptp de consteller**) **adj**: **~ (d'étoiles)** star-studded, star-spangled; **~ de** *astres, joyaux, lumières* spangled *ou* studded with; *taches* spotted *ou* dotted with.

consteller [kɔ̃stele] [1] **vt**: **des lumières constellaient le ciel** the sky was spangled *ou* studded with lights; **des taches constellaient le tapis** the carpet was spotted *ou* dotted with marks.

consternant, e [kɔ̃stɛʀnɑ̃, ɑ̃t] **adj** dismaying, disquieting.

consternation [kɔ̃stɛʀnasjɔ̃] **nf** consternation, dismay.

consterner [kɔ̃stɛʀne] [1] **vt** to dismay, fill with consternation *ou* dismay. **air consterné** air of consternation *ou* dismay.

constipation [kɔ̃stipasjɔ̃] **nf** constipation.

constipé, e [kɔ̃stipe] (**ptp de constiper**) **adj** (*Méd*) constipated. (*péj: guindé*) **avoir l'air** *ou* **être ~** to look stiff *ou* ill-at-ease, be stiff.

constiper [kɔ̃stipe] [1] **vt** to constipate.

constituant, e [kɔ̃stitɥɑ̃, ɑ̃t] 1 **adj** a *élément* constituent. b (*Pol*) **assemblée ~e** constituent assembly; (*Hist*) **l'assemblée ~e, la C~e** the Constituent Assembly; (*Hist*) **les ~s** the members of the Constituent Assembly. 2 **nm** (*Jur, Fin*) settlor; (*Gram*) constituent. **~ immédiat** immediate constituent; **analyse en ~s immédiats** constituent analysis; **~ ultime** ultimate constituent. 3 **constituante nf** (*Québec*) *[université]* branch.

constitué, e [kɔ̃stitɥe] (**ptp de constituer**) **adj** a (*Méd*) **bien/mal ~** of sound/unsound constitution. b (*Pol*) *voir* **corps**.

constituer [kɔ̃stitɥe] [1] 1 **vt** a (*fonder*) *comité, ministère, gouvernement, société anonyme* to set up, form; *bibliothèque* to build up; *collection* to build up, put together; *dossier* to make up, put together.

b (*composer*) to make up, constitute, compose. **les pièces qui constituent cette collection** the pieces that (go to) make up *ou* that constitute this collection; **sa collection est surtout constituée de porcelaines** his collection is made up *ou* is composed *ou* consists mainly of pieces of porcelain.

c (*être, représenter*) to constitute. **ceci constitue un délit/ne constitue pas un motif** that constitutes an offence/does not constitute a motive; **ce billet de 10 F constitue toute ma fortune** this 10-franc note constitutes *ou* represents my entire fortune; **ils constituent un groupe homogène** they make up *ou* form a well-knit group.

d (*Jur: établir*) *rente, pension, dot* to settle (*à* on); *avocat* to retain. **~ qn son héritier** to appoint sb one's heir; **~ qn à la garde des enfants** to appoint sb *ou* take sb on to look after one's children.

2 **se constituer vpr** a **se ~ prisonnier** to give o.s. up; **se ~ témoin** to come forward as a witness; **se ~ partie civile** *to bring an independent action for damages.*

b (*Comm*) **se ~ en société** to form o.s. into a company.

constitutif, -ive [kɔ̃stitytif, iv] **adj** constituent, component.

constitution [kɔ̃stitysjɔ̃] **nf** a (*NonC: voir* **constituer**) setting-up, formation, forming; building-up; putting together; making-up; settlement, settling; retaining. (*Jur*) **~ de partie civile** *independent action for damages;* **~ de stocks** stockpiling. b (*éléments, composition*) *[substance]* composition, make-up; *[ensemble, organisation]* make-up, composition; *[équipe, comité]* composition. c (*Méd: conformation, santé*) constitution. **il a une robuste ~** he has a sturdy constitution. d (*Pol: charte*) constitution.

constitutionnaliser [kɔ̃stitysjɔnalize] [1] **vt** to constitutionalize.

constitutionnalité [kɔ̃stitysjɔnalite] **nf** constitutionality.

constitutionnel, -elle [kɔ̃stitysjɔnɛl] **adj** constitutional; *voir* **droit**[3].

constitutionnellement [kɔ̃stitysjɔnɛlmɑ̃] **adv** constitutionally.

constricteur [kɔ̃stʀiktœʀ] **adj m, nm** (*Anat*) **(muscle) ~** constrictor (muscle); *voir* **boa**.

constrictif,-ive [kɔ̃stʀiktif, iv] **adj** (*Phon*) constricted.

constriction [kɔ̃stʀiksjɔ̃] **nf** constriction.

constrictor [kɔ̃stʀiktɔʀ] **adj, nm: (boa) ~** (boa) constrictor.

constructeur, -trice [kɔ̃stʀyktœʀ, tʀis] 1 **adj** (*Zool*) home-making (*épith*); (*fig*) *imagination* constructive. 2 **nm** (*fabricant*) maker; (*bâtisseur*) builder, constructor. **~ d'automobiles** car manufacturer; **~ de navires** shipbuilder.

constructible [kɔ̃stʀyktibl] **adj**: **terrain ~** building land; **zone/terrain non ~** *area/land where no building is permitted.*

constructif, -ive [kɔ̃stʀyktif, iv] **adj** constructive.

construction [kɔ̃stʀyksjɔ̃] **nf** a (*action: voir* **construire**) building; construction. **la ~ de l'immeuble/du navire a pris 2 ans** building the flats/ship *ou* the construction of the flats/ship took 2 years, it took 2 years to build the flats/ship; **c'est de la ~ robuste** it is solidly built, it is of solid construction; **les ~s navales/aéronautiques européennes sont menacées** European shipbuilding *ou* the European shipbuilding industry/the European aircraft industry is threatened; **cela va bien dans la ~** things are going well in the building trade (*Brit*) *ou* construction business; **matériaux de ~** building materials; **de ~ française/anglaise** *bateau, voiture* French/British built; **en ~** under construction, in the course of construction; *voir* **jeu**.

b (*structure*) *[roman, thèse]* construction; *[phrase]* structure. **c'est une simple ~ de l'esprit** it's (a) pure hypothesis.

c (*édifice, bâtiment*) building, construction.

d (*Ling: expression, tournure*) construction, structure.

e (*Géom: figure*) figure, construction.

constructivisme [kɔ̃stʀyktivism] **nm** constructivism.

constructiviste [kɔ̃stʀyktivist] **adj, nmf** constructivist.

construire [kɔ̃stʀɥiʀ] [38] **vt** *machine, bâtiment, route, navire, chemin de fer* to build, construct; *figure géométrique* to construct; *théorie, phrase, intrigue* to construct, put together, build up; *famille* to start. **~ un couple** to build a relationship; **on a** *ou* **ça s'est beaucoup construit ici depuis la guerre** there's been a lot of building here since the war; (*Ling*) **ça se construit avec le subjonctif** it takes the subjunctive, it takes a subjunctive construction.

consubstantialité [kɔ̃sypstɑ̃sjalite] **nf** consubstantiality.

consubstantiation [kɔ̃sypstɑ̃sjasjɔ̃] nf consubstantiation.

consubstantiel, -elle [kɔ̃sypstɑ̃sjɛl] adj consubstantial (*à, avec* with).

consul [kɔ̃syl] nm consul. ~ **général** consul general; ~ **de France** French Consul.

consulaire [kɔ̃sylɛʀ] adj consular.

consulat [kɔ̃syla] nm a (*bureaux*) consulate; (*charge*) consulate, consulship. b (*Hist française*) **le C~** the Consulate.

consultable [kɔ̃syltabl] adj (*disponible*) *ouvrage, livre* available for consultation, which may be consulted. (*utilisable*) **cette carte est trop grande pour être aisément ~** this map is too big to be used easily.

consultant, e [kɔ̃syltɑ̃, ɑ̃t] adj *avocat* consultant (*épith*). **(médecin) ~** consulting physician.

consultatif, -ive [kɔ̃syltatif, iv] adj consultative, advisory. **à titre ~** in an advisory capacity.

consultation [kɔ̃syltasjɔ̃] nf a (*action*) consulting, consultation. **pour faciliter la ~ du dictionnaire/de l'horaire** to make the dictionary/timetable easier *ou* easy to consult; **après ~ de son agenda** (after) having consulted his diary; **ouvrage de référence d'une ~ difficile** reference work that is difficult to use *ou* consult; **~ électorale** (*élection*) election; (*référendum*) referendum; **faire une ~ électorale** to ask the electorate's opinion, go to the country (*Brit*).

b (*séance: chez le médecin, un expert*) consultation. (*Méd*) **aller à la ~** to go to the surgery (*Brit*) *ou* doctor's office (*US*); **donner une ~/des ~s gratuites** to give a consultation/free consultations; (*Méd*) **les heures de ~** surgery (*Brit*) *ou* consulting hours; (*Méd*) **il y avait du monde à la ~** there were a lot of people at the surgery (*Brit*) *ou* doctor's office (*US*); **service (hospitalier) de ~ externe** outpatients' clinic.

c (*échange de vues*) consultation. **être en ~ avec des spécialistes** to be in consultation with specialists.

d (*frm: avis donné*) professional advice (*NonC*).

consulter [kɔ̃sylte] [1] 1 vt *médecin* to consult; *expert, avocat, parent* to consult, seek advice from; *dictionnaire, livre, horaire* to consult, refer to; *boussole, baromètre* to consult. **ne ~ que sa raison/son intérêt** to be guided only by one's reason/self-interest, look only to one's reason/self-interest. 2 vi *[médecin]* (*recevoir*) to hold surgery (*Brit*), be in (the office) (*US*); (*conférer*) to hold a consultation. 3 **se consulter** vpr (*s'entretenir*) to confer, consult each other. **ils se consultèrent du regard** they looked questioningly at each other.

consumer [kɔ̃syme] [1] 1 vt a (*brûler*) to consume, burn. **l'incendie a tout consumé** the fire consumed *ou* wiped out everything; **des débris à demi consumés** charred debris; **une bûche se consumait dans l'âtre** a log was burning in the hearth; **le bois s'est consumé entièrement** the wood was completely destroyed *ou* wiped out (by fire).

b (*fig: dévorer*) *[fièvre, mal]* to consume, devour. **consumé par l'ambition** consumed with *ou* devoured by ambition.

c (*littér: dépenser*) *forces* to expend; *fortune* to squander. **il consume sa vie en plaisirs frivoles** he fritters away his life in idle pleasures.

2 **se consumer** vpr (*littér: dépérir*) to waste away. (*se ronger de*) **se ~ de chagrin/de désespoir** to waste away with sorrow/despair; **il se consume à petit feu** he is slowly wasting away.

consumérisme [kɔ̃symeʀism] nm consumerism.

consumériste [kɔ̃symeʀist] adj, nmf consumerist.

contact [kɔ̃takt] nm a (*toucher*) touch, contact. **le ~ de 2 surfaces** contact between *ou* of 2 surfaces; **un ~ très doux** a very gentle touch; (*Méd*) **ça s'attrape par le ~** it's contagious, it can be caught by contact; **le ~ de la soie est doux** silk is soft to the touch; **au point de ~ des deux lignes** at the point of contact *ou* the meeting point of the two lines; *voir* **verre**.

b (*Aut, Élec*) contact. (*Aut*) **mettre/couper le ~** to switch on/off the ignition; **~ électrique** electrical contact; **appuyer sur le ~** to press the contact button *ou* lever; **~!** (*Aviat*) contact!; (*auto-école*) switch on the ignition!; (*machine*) switch on!; **avoir un** *ou* **être en ~ radio avec qn** to be in radio contact with sb; *voir* **clef**.

c (*rapport*) contact. **il a beaucoup de ~s (avec l'étranger)** he has got a lot of contacts *ou* connections (abroad); **notre ~ à Moscou** our contact in Moscow; **dès le premier ~, ils** ... from their first meeting, they ...; **en ~ étroit avec** in close touch *ou* contact with; **garder le ~ avec qn** to keep in touch *ou* contact with sb; **elle a besoin de ~ humain** she needs human contact; **j'ai un bon/mauvais ~ avec eux** my relations with them are good/bad, I have a good/bad relationship with them; **être de ~ facile/difficile** to be easy/not very easy to talk to; (*Mil*) **établir/rompre le ~ (avec)** to make/break off contact (with).

d (*loc*) **prendre ~, entrer en ~** (*Aviat, Mil, Rad*) to make contact (*avec* with); (*rapport d'affaires*) to get in touch *ou* contact (*avec* with); **rester/être en ~** (*Aviat, Mil, Rad*) to remain in/be in contact (*avec* with); (*rapport d'affaires*) to remain in/be in touch (*avec* with), remain in/be in contact (*avec* with); **se mettre en ~ avec la tour de contrôle/qn** to make contact with *ou* to contact the control tower/sb; **entrer/être en ~** *[objets]* to come into/be in contact; *[fils électriques]* to make/be making contact; **mettre en ~** *objets* to bring into contact; *relations d'affaires* to put in touch; (*Aviat, Rad*) to put in contact; **prise de ~** (*première entrevue*) first meeting; (*Mil*) first contact; **au ~ de: au ~ de sa main** at the touch of his hand; **au ~ de ces jeunes gens il a acquis de l'assurance** through his contact *ou* association with these young people he has gained self-assurance; **métal qui s'oxyde au ~ de l'air/de l'eau** metal that oxydises in contact with air/water.

contacter [kɔ̃takte] [1] vt to contact, get in touch with.

contagieux, -ieuse [kɔ̃taʒjø, jøz] adj *maladie* (*gén*) infectious, catching (*attrib*); (*par le contact*) contagious; *personne* infectious; contagious; (*fig*) *enthousiasme, peur, rire* infectious, contagious, catching (*attrib*). **l'isolement des ~** the isolation of contagious patients *ou* cases *ou* of patients with contagious diseases.

contagion [kɔ̃taʒjɔ̃] nf (*Méd*) contagion, contagiousness; (*fig*) infectiousness, contagion. **être exposé à la ~** to be in danger of becoming infected; **les ravages de la ~ parmi les vieillards** the ravages of the disease among the old.

container [kɔ̃tɛnɛʀ] nm (freight) container.

contamination [kɔ̃taminasjɔ̃] nf (*voir* **contaminer**) infection; contamination.

contaminer [kɔ̃tamine] [1] vt *personne* to infect, contaminate; *cours d'eau* to contaminate; (*fig: influencer*) (*négatif*) to contaminate; (*positif*) to infect.

conte [kɔ̃t] nm (*récit*) tale, story; († *ou littér: histoire mensongère*) (tall) story. (*lit, fig*) **~ de fée** fairy tale *ou* story.

contemplateur, -trice [kɔ̃tɑ̃platœʀ, tʀis] nm,f contemplator.

contemplatif, -ive [kɔ̃tɑ̃platif, iv] adj *air, esprit* contemplative, meditative; (*Rel*) *ordre* contemplative. (*Rel*) **un ~** a contemplative.

contemplation [kɔ̃tɑ̃plasjɔ̃] nf (*action*) contemplation. **la ~** (*Philos*) contemplation, meditation; (*Rel*) contemplation.

contempler [kɔ̃tɑ̃ple] [1] vt (*regarder*) to contemplate, gaze at, gaze upon (*littér*); (*envisager*) to contemplate, envisage.

contemporain, e [kɔ̃tɑ̃pɔʀɛ̃, ɛn] 1 adj a (*de la même époque*) *personne* contemporary; *événement* contemporaneous, contemporary (*de* with). b (*actuel*) *problème* contemporary, present-day (*épith*); *art, mobilier* contemporary. 2 nm contemporary.

contemporanéité [kɔ̃tɑ̃pɔʀaneite] nf contemporaneousness.

contempteur, -trice [kɔ̃tɑ̃ptœʀ, tʀis] nm,f (*littér*) denigrator.

contenance [kɔ̃t(ə)nɑ̃s] nf a (*capacité*) *[bouteille, réservoir]* capacity; *[navire]* (carrying) capacity. **avoir une ~ de 45 litres** to have a capacity of 45 litres, take *ou* hold 45 litres. b (*attitude*) bearing, attitude. **~ humble/fière** humble/proud bearing; **~ gênée** embarrassed attitude; **il fumait pour se donner une ~** he was smoking to give an impression of composure *ou* to disguise his lack of composure; **faire bonne ~ (devant)** to put on a bold front (in the face of); **perdre ~** to lose one's composure.

contenant [kɔ̃t(ə)nɑ̃] nm: **le ~ (et le contenu)** the container (and the contents).

conteneur [kɔ̃t(ə)nœʀ] nm container.

contenir [kɔ̃t(ə)niʀ] [22] 1 vt a (*avoir une capacité de*) *[récipient]* to hold, take; *[cinéma, avion, autocar]* to seat, hold.

b (*renfermer*) *[récipient, livre, minerai]* to contain. **ce minerai contient beaucoup de fer** this ore contains a lot of iron *ou* has a lot of iron in it; **discours contenant de grandes vérités** speech containing *ou* embodying great truths.

c (*maîtriser*) *surprise* to contain; *colère* to contain, suppress; *sanglots, larmes* to contain, hold back; *foule* to contain, restrain, hold in check; *inflation* to control, curb. (*Mil*) **~ l'ennemi** to contain the enemy, hold the enemy in check.

2 **se contenir** vpr to contain o.s., control one's emotions.

content, e [kɔ̃tɑ̃, ɑ̃t] 1 adj a (*heureux, ravi*) pleased, glad, happy. **l'air ~** with a pleased expression; **je serais ~ que vous veniez** I'd be pleased *ou* glad *ou* happy if you came; **je suis ~ d'apprendre cela** I'm pleased *ou* glad about this news, I'm pleased *ou* glad *ou* happy to hear this news; **il était très ~ de ce changement** he was very pleased *ou* glad about *ou* at the change; **je suis très ~ ici** I'm very happy *ou* contented here; **voilà, c'est cassé, tu es ~?** there, it's broken, are you happy *ou* satisfied now?

b (*satisfait de*) **~ de** *élève, voiture, situation* pleased *ou* happy with; **être ~ de peu** to be content with little, be easily satisfied; **être ~ de soi** to be pleased with o.s.

c **non ~ d'être/d'avoir fait** ... not content with being/with having done ... .

2 nm: **avoir (tout) son ~ de qch** to have had one's fill of sth.

contentement [kɔ̃tɑ̃tmɑ̃] nm (*action de contenter*) satisfaction, satisfying; (*état*) contentment, satisfaction. **éprouver un profond ~ à la vue de ...** to feel great contentment *ou* deep satisfaction at the sight of ...; **~ d'esprit** spiritual contentment; **~ de soi** self-satisfaction; (*Prov*) **~ passe richesse** happiness is worth more than riches.

contenter [kɔ̃tɑ̃te] [1] 1 vt *personne, besoin, envie, curiosité* to satisfy. **facile à ~** easy to please, easily pleased *ou* satisfied; **cette explication l'a contenté** he was satisfied *ou* happy with this explanation, this explanation satisfied him; **il est difficile de ~ tout le monde** it's difficult to please *ou* satisfy everyone.

2 **se contenter** vpr: **se ~ de qch/de faire qch** to content o.s. with sth/with doing sth; **se ~ de peu/de ce qu'on a** to make do with very little/with what one has (got); **il a dû se ~ d'un repas par jour/de manger les restes** he had to content himself *ou* make do with one meal

a day/with eating the left-overs; **contentez-vous d'écouter/de regarder** just listen/watch; **il se contenta d'un sourire/de sourire** he merely gave a smile/smiled.

contentieux, -ieuse [kɔ̃tɑ̃sjø, jøz] 1 **adj** (*Jur*) contentious. 2 **nm** (*litige*) dispute, disagreement; (*Comm*) litigation; (*service*) legal department. ~ **administratif/commercial** administrative/commercial actions *ou* litigation.

contention [kɔ̃tɑ̃sjɔ̃] **nf** (*Méd*) (*procédé*) *[membre, dents]* support; (*appareil*) brace. *collant, chaussettes* **de** ~ support (*épith*).

contenu, e [kɔ̃t(ə)ny] (**ptp de contenir**) 1 **adj** *colère, sentiments* restrained, suppressed. 2 **nm** *[récipient, dossier]* contents; *[loi, texte]* content; (*Ling*) content. **la table des matières indique le ~ du livre** the table shows the contents of the book; **le ~ subversif de ce livre** the subversive content of this book.

conter [kɔ̃te] 1 **vt** a (*littér*) *histoire* to recount, relate. (*hum*) **contez-nous vos malheurs** let's hear your problems, tell us all about your problems. b (*loc*) **que me contez-vous là?** what are you trying to tell me?, what yarn are you trying to spin me?*; **il lui en a conté de belles!** he really spun him some yarns!* *ou* told him some incredible stories!; **elle ne s'en laisse pas ~** she's not easily taken in, she doesn't let herself be taken in (easily); **il ne faut pas lui en ~** it's no use trying it on with him* (*Brit*), don't bother trying those stories on him; († *ou hum*) ~ **fleurette à qn** to murmur sweet nothings to sb († *ou hum*).

contestable [kɔ̃tɛstabl] **adj** *théorie, idée* questionable, disputable; *raisonnement* questionable, doubtful.

contestataire [kɔ̃tɛstatɛʀ] 1 **adj** *journal, étudiants, tendances* anti-establishment, anti-authority. 2 **nmf: c'est un ~** he's anti-establishment *ou* anti-authority; **les ~s ont été expulsés** the protesters were expelled.

contestateur, -trice [kɔ̃tɛstatœʀ, tʀis] **adj** contentious.

contestation [kɔ̃tɛstasjɔ̃] **nf** a (*NonC: voir* **contester**) contesting; questioning; disputing. b (*discussion*) dispute. **sans ~ possible** beyond dispute; **élever une ~** to raise an objection (*sur* to); **il y a matière à ~** there are grounds for contention *ou* dispute. c (*gén, Pol: opposition*) **la ~** anti-establishment *ou* anti-authority activity; **faire de la ~** to (actively) oppose the establishment, protest (against the establishment).

conteste [kɔ̃tɛst] **nf: sans ~** unquestionably, indisputably.

contester [kɔ̃tɛste] 1 1 **vt** (*Jur*) *succession, droit, compétence* to contest; *fait, raisonnement, vérité* to question, dispute, contest. **je ne conteste pas que vous ayez raison** I don't dispute that you're right; **je ne lui conteste pas ce droit** I don't question *ou* dispute *ou* contest his right; **ce roman/cet écrivain est très contesté** this novel/writer is very controversial.

2 **vi** to take issue (*sur* over); (*Pol etc*) to protest. **il ne conteste jamais** he never takes issue over anything; **il conteste toujours sur des points de détail** he's always taking issue over points of detail; **maintenant les jeunes ne pensent qu'à ~** young people nowadays think only about protesting.

conteur, -euse [kɔ̃tœʀ, øz] **nm,f** (*écrivain*) storywriter; (*narrateur*) storyteller.

contexte [kɔ̃tɛkst] **nm** context. **pris hors ~** taken out of context (*attrib*).

contextuel, -elle [kɔ̃tɛkstɥɛl] **adj** (*Ling*) contextual.

contexture [kɔ̃tɛkstyʀ] **nf** *[tissu, organisme]* texture; *[roman, œuvre]* structure.

contigu, -uë [kɔ̃tigy] **adj** *choses* adjoining, adjacent, contiguous (*frm*); (*fig*) *domaines, sujets* (closely) related. **être ~ à qch** to be adjacent *ou* next to sth.

contiguïté [kɔ̃tigɥite] **nf** *[choses]* proximity, contiguity (*frm*); (*fig*) *[sujets]* relatedness. **la ~ de nos jardins est très commode** it's very handy that our gardens are next to each other *ou* adjacent *ou* adjoining; **la ~ de ces deux sujets** the fact that these two subjects are (closely) related, the relatedness of these two subjects.

continence [kɔ̃tinɑ̃s] **nf** continence, continency.

continent¹, e [kɔ̃tinɑ̃, ɑ̃t] **adj** continent.

continent² [kɔ̃tinɑ̃] **nm** (*gén, Géog*) continent; (*par rapport à une île*) mainland.

continental, e, **mpl -aux** [kɔ̃tinɑ̃tal, o] 1 **adj** continental. 2 **nm,f** Continental.

contingence [kɔ̃tɛ̃ʒɑ̃s] **nf** a (*Philos*) contingency. b **les ~s** contingencies; **les ~s de tous les jours** (little) everyday occurrences *ou* contingencies; **les ~s de la vie** the (little) chance happenings of life; **tenir compte des ~s** to take account of all contingencies *ou* eventualities.

contingent, e [kɔ̃tɛ̃ʒɑ̃, ɑ̃t] 1 **adj** contingent. 2 **nm** a (*Mil: groupe*) contingent. (*en France*) **le ~** *the conscripts called up for national service*, the draft (*US*). b (*Comm: quota*) quota. c (*part, contribution*) share.

contingentement [kɔ̃tɛ̃ʒɑ̃tmɑ̃] **nm: le ~ des exportations/importations** the fixing *ou* establishing of export/import quotas, the placing of quotas on exports/imports.

contingenter [kɔ̃tɛ̃ʒɑ̃te] 1 **vt** (*Comm*) *importations, exportations* to place *ou* fix a quota on; *produits, matière première* to distribute by a system of quotas.

continu, e [kɔ̃tiny] 1 **adj** *mouvement, série, bruit* continuous; (*Math*) continuous; *ligne, silence* unbroken, continuous; *effort* continuous, unremitting; *souffrance* endless; *voir* **jet¹, journée, travail.** 2 **nm** (*Math, Philos, Phys*) continuum; (*Élec*) direct current. **utilisation en ~** continuous use; **faire qch en ~ pendant 5 heures** to do sth continuously *ou* non-stop for 5 hours, do sth for 5 hours non-stop; (*Ordin*) **papier (en) ~** continuous stationery. 3 **continue nf** (*Phon*) continuant.

continuateur, -trice [kɔ̃tinɥatœʀ, tʀis] **nm,f** *[œuvre littéraire]* continuator; *[innovateur, précurseur]* successor. **les ~s de cette réforme** those who carried on (*ou* carry on *etc*) the reform.

continuation [kɔ̃tinɥasjɔ̃] **nf** continuation. **nous comptons sur la ~ de cette entente** we count on the continuation of this agreement *ou* on this agreement's continuing; *voir* **bon¹**.

continuel, -elle [kɔ̃tinɥɛl] **adj** (*continu*) continuous; (*qui se répète*) continual, constant.

continuellement [kɔ̃tinɥɛlmɑ̃] **adv** (*voir* **continuel**) continuously; continually, constantly.

continuer [kɔ̃tinɥe] 1 1 **vt** a (*poursuivre*) *démarches, politique* to continue (with), carry on with; *tradition* to continue, carry on; *travaux, études* to continue (with), carry on with, go on with. ~ **son chemin** to continue on *ou* along one's way, go on one's way; ~ **l'œuvre de son maître** to carry on *ou* continue the work of one's master; **Pompidou continua de Gaulle** Pompidou carried on *ou* continued where de Gaulle left off.

b (*prolonger*) *droite, route* to continue.

2 **vi** a *[bruit, spectacle, guerre]* to continue, go on. **la route (se) continue jusqu'à la gare** the road goes (on) *ou* continues as far as the station.

b *[voyageur]* to go on, continue on one's way.

c ~ **de** *ou* **à marcher/manger** *etc* to go on *ou* keep on *ou* continue walking/eating *etc,* continue to walk/eat *etc,* walk/eat *etc* on; **je continuerai par le saumon** I'll have the salmon to follow; **"mais" continua-t-il** "but" he went on *ou* continued; **dis-le, continue!** go on, say it!; **s'il continue, je vais ...*** if he goes on *ou* keeps on *ou* continues, I'm going to ...; **si ça continue, je vais ...** if this keeps up *ou* continues I'm going to ... .

continuité [kɔ̃tinɥite] **nf** *[politique, tradition]* continuation; *[action]* continuity. **assurer la ~ d'une politique** to ensure continuity in applying a policy, ensure the continuation of a policy; *voir* **solution.**

continûment [kɔ̃tinymɑ̃] **adv** continuously.

continuum [kɔ̃tinɥɔm] **nm** continuum. **le ~ espace-temps** the four-dimensional *ou* space-time continuum.

contondant, e [kɔ̃tɔ̃dɑ̃, ɑ̃t] **adj** *instrument* blunt. **arme ~e** blunt instrument.

contorsion [kɔ̃tɔʀsjɔ̃] **nf** contortion.

contorsionner (se) [kɔ̃tɔʀsjɔne] 1 **vpr** (*lit*) *[acrobate]* to contort o.s.; (*fig, péj*) to contort o.s. **il se contorsionnait pour essayer de se défaire de ses liens** he was writhing about *ou* contorting himself in an attempt to free himself from his bonds.

contorsionniste [kɔ̃tɔʀsjɔnist] **nmf** contortionist.

contour [kɔ̃tuʀ] **nm** a *[objet]* outline; *[montagne, visage, corps]* outline, line, contour. b *[route, rivière]* ~**s** windings.

contourné, e [kɔ̃tuʀne] (**ptp de contourner**) **adj** (*péj*) *raisonnement, style* tortuous; (*péj*) *colonne, pied de table* (over)elaborate.

contournement [kɔ̃tuʀnəmɑ̃] **nm: autoroute** *f* **de ~** bypass.

contourner [kɔ̃tuʀne] 1 **vt** a *ville* to skirt round, bypass; *montagne* to skirt round, walk (*ou* drive *etc*) round; *mur, véhicule* to walk (*ou* drive *etc*) round; (*fig*) *règle, difficulté* to circumvent, bypass, get round. b (*façonner*) *arabesques* to trace (out); *vase* to fashion. c (*déformer*) to twist, contort.

contraceptif, -ive [kɔ̃tʀasɛptif, iv] **adj, nm** contraceptive.

contraception [kɔ̃tʀasɛpsjɔ̃] **nf** contraception.

contractant, e [kɔ̃tʀaktɑ̃, ɑ̃t] 1 **adj** (*Jur*) contracting. 2 **nm,f** contracting party.

contracté, e [kɔ̃tʀakte] (**ptp de contracter**) **adj** a (*Ling*) contracted. b *personne* tense, tensed up; *muscle* tense.

contracter¹ [kɔ̃tʀakte] 1 1 **vt** a (*raidir*) *muscle* to tense, contract; *traits, visage* to tense; (*fig*) *personne* to make tense. **la peur lui contracta la gorge** fear gripped his throat; **l'émotion lui contracta la gorge** his throat tightened with emotion; **les traits contractés par la souffrance** his features tense with suffering; **un sourire forcé contracta son visage** his face stiffened into a forced smile.

b (*Phys: réduire*) ~ **un corps/fluide** to make a body/fluid contract.

2 **se contracter vpr** *[muscle]* to tense (up), contract; *[gorge]* to tighten; *[traits, visage]* to tense (up); *[cœur]* to contract; (*fig*) *[personne]* to become tense, get tensed up; (*Phys*) *[corps]* to contract; (*Ling*) *[mot, syllabe]* to be (able to be) contracted.

contracter² [kɔ̃tʀakte] 1 **vt** a *dette, obligation* to contract, incur; *alliance* to contract, enter into. ~ **une assurance** to take out an insurance policy; (*Admin*) ~ **mariage avec** to contract (a) marriage with. b *maladie* to contract; *manie, habitude* to acquire, contract.

contractile [kɔ̃tʀaktil] **adj** contractile.

contractilité [kɔ̃tʀaktilite] **nf** contractility.

contraction [kɔ̃tʀaksjɔ̃] **nf** a (*NonC: action*) *[corps, liquide]* contraction; *[muscle]* tensing, contraction. b (*NonC: état*) *[muscles, traits, visage]* tenseness. c (*spasme*) contraction. d (*Scol*) ~ **de texte**

summary, précis.

contractuel, -elle [kɔ̃tʀaktɥɛl] 1 adj obligation contractual; emploi under contract (attrib); clause contract (épith), in the contract (attrib). 2 nm (agent) ~ (gén) contract worker (working for local authority); (stationnement) ≃ traffic warden (Brit), ≃ traffic policeman (US); (sortie d'école) ≃ lollipop man* (Brit), crossing guard (US). 3 contractuelle nf (gén) contract worker (working for local authority); (stationnement) ≃ traffic warden (Brit), ≃ meter maid* (US); (sortie d'école) ≃ lollipop lady* (Brit), crossing guard (US).

contractuellement [kɔ̃tʀaktɥɛlmɑ̃] adv by contract, contractually.

contracture [kɔ̃tʀaktyʀ] nf (Archit) contracture; (Physiol) spasm, (prolonged) contraction. ~ musculaire cramp.

contradicteur [kɔ̃tʀadiktœʀ] nm opponent, contradictor.

contradiction [kɔ̃tʀadiksjɔ̃] nf a (NonC: contestation) porter la ~ dans un débat to introduce counter-arguments in a debate, add a dissenting voice to a debate; je ne supporte pas la ~ I can't bear to be contradicted; voir esprit.

b (discordance) contradiction, inconsistency. texte plein de ~s text full of contradictions ou inconsistencies; le monde est plein de ~s the world is full of contradictions; ~ dans les termes contradiction in terms; il y a ~ entre ... there is a contradiction between ...; être en ~ avec soi-même to contradict o.s.; il est en ~ avec ce qu'il a dit précédemment he's contradicting what he said before; leurs témoignages sont en ~ their testimonies contradict each other.

c (Jur) fact of hearing all parties to a case.

contradictoire [kɔ̃tʀadiktwaʀ] adj idées, théories, récits contradictory, conflicting. débat ~ debate; réunion politique ~ political meeting with an open debate; ~ à in contradiction to, in conflict with; (Jur) arrêt/jugement ~ order/judgment given after due hearing of the parties.

contradictoirement [kɔ̃tʀadiktwaʀmɑ̃] adv (Jur) after due hearing of the parties.

contraignant, e [kɔ̃tʀɛɲɑ̃, ɑ̃t] adj horaire restricting, constraining; obligation, occupation restricting.

contraindre [kɔ̃tʀɛ̃dʀ] [52] 1 vt: ~ qn à faire qch to force ou compel sb to do sth; contraint à démissionner forced ou compelled ou constrained to resign; il/cela m'a contraint au silence/au repos he/this forced ou compelled me to be silent/to rest; (Jur) ~ par voie de justice to constrain by law (to pay debt). 2 se contraindre vpr to restrain o.s. se ~ à être aimable to force o.s. to be polite, make o.s. be polite.

contraint, e[1] [kɔ̃tʀɛ̃, ɛ̃t] (ptp de contraindre) adj a (gêné) constrained, forced. d'un air ~ with an air of constraint, constrainedly. b ~ et forcé under constraint ou duress.

contrainte[2] [kɔ̃tʀɛ̃t] nf a (violence) constraint. (littér) vivre dans la ~ to live in bondage; par ~ ou sous la ~ under constraint ou duress; empêcher qn d'agir par la ~ to prevent sb from acting by force, forcibly prevent sb from acting. b (gêne) constraint, restraint; (Ling) constraint. sans ~ unrestrainedly, unconstrainedly, without restraint ou constraint. c (Jur) ~ par corps civil imprisonment. d (Phys) stress.

contraire [kɔ̃tʀɛʀ] 1 adj a (opposé, inverse) sens, effet, avis opposite; (Naut) vent contrary, adverse; (contradictoire) opinions conflicting, opposite; propositions, intérêts conflicting; mouvements, forces opposite; voir avis.

b (nuisible) vent, forces, action contrary; destin adverse. l'alcool m'est ~ alcohol doesn't agree with me; le sort lui fut ~ fate was against him ou opposed him; ~ à la santé bad for the health, injurious ou prejudicial to the health (frm).

2 nm a [mot, concept] opposite. c'est le ~ de son frère he's the opposite ou the antithesis of his brother; et pourtant c'est tout le ~ and yet it's just the reverse ou opposite; il fait toujours le ~ de ce qu'on lui dit he always does the opposite ou contrary of what he's told; je ne vous dis pas le ~ I'm not saying anything to the contrary, I'm not disputing ou denying it.

b au ~, bien au ~, tout au ~ on the contrary; au ~ des autres unlike the others, as opposed to the others.

contrairement [kɔ̃tʀɛʀmɑ̃] adv: ~ à contrary to; (dans une comparaison) ~ aux autres ... unlike the others ... .

contralto [kɔ̃tʀalto] nm contralto.

contrapuntique [kɔ̃tʀapɔ̃tik] adj (Mus) contrapuntal.

contrariant, e [kɔ̃tʀaʀjɑ̃, jɑ̃t] adj personne perverse, contrary; incident tiresome, annoying, irksome.

contrarier [kɔ̃tʀaʀje] [7] vt a (irriter) to annoy; (ennuyer) to bother. il cherche à vous ~ he's trying to annoy you. b (gêner) projets to frustrate, thwart; amour to thwart. (Naut) ~ la marche d'un bateau to impede a ship's progress; (Mil) ~ les mouvements de l'ennemi to impede the enemy's movements; forces qui se contrarient forces which act against each other; pour lui, la cuisine a été un don contrarié his gift for cooking was never given a chance to develop. c (contraster) to alternate (for contrast). d gaucher to force to write with his (ou her) right hand.

contrariété [kɔ̃tʀaʀjete] nf (irritation) annoyance, vexation. éprouver une ~ to feel annoyed ou vexed; un geste de ~ a gesture of annoyance; toutes ces ~s l'ont rendu furieux all these annoyances ou vexations made him furious.

contrastant, e [kɔ̃tʀastɑ̃, ɑ̃t] adj couleurs, figures, effets contrasting (épith).

contraste [kɔ̃tʀast] nm (gén, TV) contrast. par ~ by contrast; faire ~ avec to contrast with; en ~ avec in contrast to; mettre en ~ to contrast.

contrasté, e [kɔ̃tʀaste] (ptp de contraster) adj composition, photo, style with some contrast. une photographie trop/pas assez ~e a photograph with too much/not enough contrast; couleurs très ~es strongly contrasting colours.

contraster [kɔ̃tʀaste] [1] 1 vt éléments, caractères to contrast; photographie to give contrast to, put contrast into. ce peintre contraste à peine son sujet this painter hardly brings out his subject (at all) ou hardly makes his subject stand out. 2 vi to contrast (avec with).

contrastif, -ive [kɔ̃tʀastif, iv] adj (Ling) contrastive.

contrat [kɔ̃tʀa] nm (convention, document) contract, agreement; (fig: accord, pacte) agreement. ~ à durée déterminée fixed-term contract; ~ à durée indéterminée permanent ou open-ended contract (of employment); ~ d'apprentissage apprenticeship contract; ~ de mariage marriage contract; ~ de travail work contract; ~ verbal verbal agreement; ~ collectif collective agreement; ~ administratif public service contract; ~ d'assurance contract of insurance; ~ de garantie guarantee, warranty; (Hist, Pol) ~ social social contract; (Jur) ~ aléatoire aleatory contract; (Jur, Fin) ~ de louage d'ouvrage contract for services; (Jur) ~ conclu dans les conditions normales du commerce arm's length agreement; passer un ~ (avec qn) to sign a contract (with sb); être employé sous ~ to be employed on contract; réaliser ou remplir son ~ (Bridge) to make one's contract; (fig: Pol etc) to fulfil one's pledges; voir bridge.

contravention [kɔ̃tʀavɑ̃sjɔ̃] nf a (Aut) (pour infraction au code) fine; (pour stationnement interdit) (amende) (parking) fine; (procès-verbal) parking ticket. dresser ~ (à qn) (stationnement interdit) to write out ou issue a parking ticket (for sb); (autres infractions) to fine sb, book sb* (Brit), take down sb's particulars; donner ou filer* une ~ à qn to book sb* (Brit) for parking, give sb a parking ticket; to fine sb, book sb* (Brit). b (Jur: infraction) ~ à contravention ou infraction of; être en (état de) ~ to be contravening the law; être en ~ à to be in contravention of.

contre [kɔ̃tʀ] 1 prép a (contact, juxtaposition) against. se mettre ~ le mur to (go and) stand against the wall; s'appuyer ~ un arbre to lean against a tree; la face ~ terre face downwards; son bateau est amarré ~ le mien his boat is moored alongside mine; appuyez-vous ~ lean ou press against ou on it; serrer qn ~ sa poitrine ou son cœur to hug sb (to one), hug ou clasp sb to one's breast ou chest; pousse la table ~ la fenêtre push the table (up) against the window; son garage est juste ~ notre maison his garage is built onto our house; elle se blottit ~ sa mère she nestled ou cuddled up to her mother; elle s'assit (tout) ~ lui she sat down (right) next to ou beside him; il s'est cogné la tête ~ le mur he banged his head against ou on the wall; joue ~ joue cheek to cheek; les voitures étaient pare-chocs ~ pare-chocs the cars were bumper to bumper; voir ci.

b (opposition, hostilité) against. se battre/voter ~ qn to fight/vote against sb; se battre ~ la montre to fight against the clock; course ou épreuve ~ la montre (Sport) race against the clock, time-trial; (fig) race against time; (Sport) le ~ la montre individuel/par équipe individual/team time-trial; (fig) ils sont engagés dans une course ~ la montre they are in a race against time; (Sport) Poitiers ~ Lyon Poitiers versus Lyons; être furieux/en colère ~ qn to be furious/angry with sb; jeter une pierre ~ la fenêtre to throw a stone at the window; agir ~ l'avis/les ordres de qn to act against ou contrary to ou counter to sb's advice/orders; aller/nager ~ le courant to go/swim against the current; acte ~ nature unnatural act, act contrary to ou against nature; je n'ai rien ~ (cela) ou (frm) là ~ I have nothing against it; il a les ouvriers ~ lui he's got the workers against him; je suis (tout à fait) ~! I'm (completely) against it!; voir envers[1], gré, vent.

c (défense, protection) s'abriter ~ le vent/la pluie to take shelter from the wind/rain; des comprimés ~ la grippe flu tablets, tablets for flu; sirop ~ la toux cough mixture ou syrup; s'assurer ~ les accidents/l'incendie to insure (o.s.) against ou for accidents/fire.

d (échange) for. échanger ou troquer qch ~ to exchange ou swap* sth for; donner qch ~ to give sth (in exchange) for; il a cédé ~ la promesse/l'assurance que ... he agreed in return for the promise/assurance that ...; voir mauvais.

e (proportion, rapport) il y a un étudiant qui s'intéresse ~ neuf qui bâillent for every one interested student there are nine who are bored; 9 voix ~ 4 9 votes to 4; à 100 ~ 1 at 100 to 1.

f (loc: contrairement à) ~ toute attente ou toute prévision contrary to (all) expectations, contrary to expectation; ~ toute apparence despite (all) appearances to the contrary; par ~ on the other hand.

2 adv: appuyez-vous ~ lean against ou on it.

3 nm a voir pour.

b (fig: riposte) counter, retort; (Billard) rebound; (Sport: contre-attaque) counterattack; (Cartes) double. (Rugby) faire un ~ to charge down a kick; l'art du ~ the art of repartee.

4 comp ▸ **contre-accusation** nf (pl contre-accusations) countercharge, counter-accusation ▸ **contre-alizé** nm (pl contre-alizés) anti-trade (wind)

► **contre-allée** nf (pl contre-allées) (*en ville*) service road (*Brit*), frontage road (*US*); (*dans un parc*) side path (*running parallel to the main drive*) ► **contre-amiral** nm (pl contre-amiraux) rear admiral ► **contre-analyse** nf (pl contre-analyses) second analysis, counter-analysis ► **contre-attaque** nf (pl contre-attaques) counter-attack ► **contre-attaquer** vi to counter-attack ► **contre-autopsie** nf (pl contre-autopsies) control autopsy, second autopsy ► **contre-avion(s)** adj *voir* défense[1] ► **contre-boutant** nm (pl contre-boutants) (*en bois*) shore; (*en pierre*) buttress ► **contre-braquage** nm (pl contre-braquages) steering into the skid (*NonC*); **grâce à ce contre-braquage instantané** thanks to his having immediately steered into the skid ► **contre-braquer** vi to steer into the skid ► **contre-butement** nm (pl contre-butements) = contre-boutant ► **contre-chant** nm (pl contre-chants) counter-point ► **contre-choc** nm (pl contre-chocs): **subir** *ou* **ressentir le contre-choc** to feel the repercussions *ou* after-effects ► **contre-courant** nm (pl contre-courants) *[cours d'eau]* counter-current; **à contre-courant** (*lit*) upstream, against the current; (*fig*) against the current *ou* tide ► **contre-écrou** nm (pl contre-écrous) lock nut ► **contre-électromotrice** adj f *voir* force ► **contre-enquête** nf (pl contre-enquêtes) counter-inquiry ► **contre-épreuve** nf (pl contre-épreuves) (*Typ*) counter-proof; (*vérification*) countercheck ► **contre-espionnage** nm counter-espionage ► **contre-essai** nm (pl contre-essais) control test, counter test ► **contre-étude** nf (pl contre-études) control study ► **contre-exemple** nm (pl contre-exemples) counter-example ► **contre-expert** nm (pl contre-experts) *[dommages]* second assessor; *[antiquité, bijou]* second valuer ► **contre-expertise** nf (pl contre-expertises) *[dommages]* second assessment; *[antiquité, bijou]* second valuation; *[circonstances]* double check ► **contre-fenêtre** nf (pl contre-fenêtres) inner window (*of a double window*) ► **contre-fer** nm (pl contre-fers) iron cap ► **contre-feu** nm (pl contre-feux) (*plaque*) fire-back; (*feu*) backfire ► **contre-fil:** (*Menuiserie*) **à contre-fil** against the grain ► **contre-filet** nm (pl contre-filets) sirloin ► **contre-fugue** nf (pl contre-fugues) counter-fugue ► **contre-gouvernement** nm (pl contre-gouvernements) (*administration*) shadow government, opposition; (*cabinet*) shadow cabinet (*surtout Brit*), opposition ► **contre-haut:** **en contre-haut** adj, adv (up) above; **en contre-haut de** prép above ► **contre-indication** nf (pl contre-indications) (*Méd, Pharm*) contraindication ► **contre-indiqué, e** adj (*Méd*) contraindicated; (*déconseillé*) unadvisable, ill-advised ► **contre-indiquer** vt to contraindicate ► **contre-insurgé** nm (pl contre-insurgés) counterinsurgent ► **contre-insurrection** nf (pl contre-insurrections) counterinsurgency ► **contre-interrogatoire** nm (pl contre-interrogatoires) cross-examination; **faire subir un contre-interrogatoire à qn** to cross-examine sb ► **contre-jour** nm (pl contre-jours) (*éclairage*) backlighting (*NonC*), contre-jour (*NonC*); (*photographie*) backlit *ou* contre-jour shot; **à contre-jour** *se profiler, se détacher* against the sunlight; *photographier* into the light; *travailler, lire* with one's back to the light ► **contre-manifestant, e** nm,f (mpl contre-manifestants) counter demonstrator ► **contre-manifestation** nf (pl contre-manifestations) counter demonstration ► **contre-manifester** vi to hold a counter demonstration ► **contre-mesure** nf (pl contre-mesures) (*action*) counter-measure; (*Mus*) **à contre-mesure** against the beat, off-beat ► **contre-offensive** nf (pl contre-offensives) counter-offensive ► **contre-offre** nf (pl contre-offres) counterbid, counter offer ► **contre-OPA** nf inv counterbid, counter offer (*in a takeover battle*) ► **contre-ordre** nm (pl contre-ordres) counter order; **sauf contre-ordre** unless otherwise directed ► **contre-pas** nm inv half pace ► **contre-pente** nf (pl contre-pentes) opposite slope ► **contre-performance** nf (pl contre-performances) (*Sport*) below-average *ou* substandard performance ► **contre-pied** nm (pl contre-pieds) *[opinion, attitude]* (exact) opposite; **prendre le contre-pied de** *opinion* to take the opposing *ou* opposite view of; *action* to take the opposite course to; **il a pris le contre-pied de ce qu'on lui demandait** he did the exact opposite of what he was asked; (*Sport*) **à contre-pied** on the wrong foot; **prendre qn à contre-pied** (*lit*) to wrong foot sb; (*fig*) to catch sb on the wrong foot ► **contre-plaqué** nm plywood ► **contre-plongée** nf (pl contre-plongées) low-angle shot; **filmer en contre-plongée** to film from below ► **contre-poil:** **à contre-poil** adv (*lit, fig*) the wrong way ► **contre-porte** nf (pl contre-portes) inner door ► **contre-pouvoir** nm (pl contre-pouvoirs) opposition force ► **contre-projet** nm (pl contre-projets) counterplan ► **contre-propagande** nf counter-propaganda ► **contre-proposition** nf (pl contre-propositions) counterproposal ► **contre-publicité** nf (pl contre-publicités) adverse publicity; **ça leur fait de la contre-publicité** that gives them bad *ou* adverse publicity ► **contre-rail** nm (pl contre-rails) check-rail (*Brit*), guard-rail ► **contre-réforme** nf Counter-Reformation ► **contre-révolution** nf (pl contre-révolutions) counter-revolution ► **contre-révolutionnaire** adj, nmf (pl contre-révolutionnaires) counter-revolutionary ► **contre-ténor** nm (pl contre-ténors) countertenor ► **contre-terrorisme** nm counter-terrorism ► **contre-terroriste** adj, nmf (pl contre-terroristes) counter-terrorist ► **contre-torpilleur** nm (pl contre-torpilleurs) destroyer ► **contre-ut** nm inv top *ou* high C ► **contre-valeur** nf (pl contre-valeurs) exchange value ► **contre-vérité** nf (pl contre-vérités) untruth, falsehood ► **contre-visite** nf (pl contre-visites) second (medical) opinion ► **contre-voie:** **à contre-voie** adv (*en sens inverse*) on the wrong track; (*du mauvais côté*) on the wrong side (of the train).

contrebalancer [kɔ̃tʀəbalɑ̃se] [3] 1 vt *[poids]* to counterbalance; (*fig: égaler, compenser*) to offset. 2 **se contrebalancer**‡ vpr: **se ~ de** not to give a darn* about; **je m'en contrebalance** I don't give a darn* (about it), I couldn't care a hoot* (about it).

contrebande [kɔ̃tʀəbɑ̃d] nf (*activité*) contraband, smuggling; (*marchandises*) contraband, smuggled goods. **faire de la ~** to do some smuggling; **faire la ~ du tabac** to smuggle tobacco; **produits de ~** contraband, smuggled goods.

contrebandier, -ière [kɔ̃tʀəbɑ̃dje, jɛʀ] nm,f smuggler. **navire ~** smugglers' ship.

contrebas [kɔ̃tʀəbɑ] nm: **en ~** (down) below; **en ~ de** below.

contrebasse [kɔ̃tʀəbɑs] nf (*instrument*) (double) bass; (*musicien*) (double) bass player.

contrebassiste [kɔ̃tʀəbɑsist] nmf (double) bass player.

contrebasson [kɔ̃tʀəbɑsɔ̃] nm contrabassoon, double bassoon.

contrecarrer [kɔ̃tʀəkaʀe] [1] vt *projets*, (†) *personne* to thwart.

contrechamp [kɔ̃tʀəʃɑ̃] nm (*Ciné*) reverse shot.

contrechâssis [kɔ̃tʀəʃɑsi] nm double (window) frame.

contreclef [kɔ̃tʀəkle] nf stone adjoining the keystones.

contrecœur[1] [kɔ̃tʀəkœʀ] adv: **à ~** (be)grudgingly, reluctantly.

contrecœur[2] [kɔ̃tʀəkœʀ] nm a (*fond de cheminée*) fire-back. b (*Rail*) guard-rail, checkrail (*Brit*).

contrecoup [kɔ̃tʀəku] nm (*ricochet*) ricochet; (*répercussions*) repercussions, indirect consequence. **le ~ d'un accident** the repercussions of an accident; **la révolution a eu des ~s en Asie** the revolution has had (its) repercussions in Asia; **par ~** as an indirect consequence.

contredanse [kɔ̃tʀədɑ̃s] nf a (*) (*gén*) fine; (*pour stationnement interdit*) (parking) ticket. b (††: *danse, air*) quadrille.

contredire [kɔ̃tʀədiʀ] [37] 1 vt *[personne]* to contradict; *[faits]* to be at variance with, refute. 2 **se contredire** vpr *[personne]* to contradict o.s.*[témoins, témoignages]* to contradict each other.

contredit [kɔ̃tʀədi] nm (*frm*) **sans ~** unquestionably, without question.

contrée [kɔ̃tʀe] nf (*littér*) (*pays*) land; (*région*) region.

contrefaçon [kɔ̃tʀəfasɔ̃] nf a (*NonC: voir* **contrefaire**) counterfeiting; forgery, forging. **~ involontaire d'un brevet** innocent infringement of a patent. b (*faux*) (*édition etc*) unauthorized *ou* pirated edition; (*produit*) imitation; (*billets, signature*) forgery, counterfeit. (*Comm*) **méfiez-vous des ~s** beware of imitations.

contrefacteur [kɔ̃tʀəfaktœʀ] nm (*Jur*) forger, counterfeiter.

contrefaire [kɔ̃tʀəfɛʀ] [60] vt a (*littér: imiter*) to imitate; (*ridiculiser*) to mimic, imitate. b (*déguiser*) *voix* to disguise. c (*falsifier*) *argent, signature* to counterfeit, forge; *produits, édition* to counterfeit; *brevet* to infringe. d (†: *feindre*) to feign († *ou littér*), counterfeit. e (†: *rendre difforme*) to deform.

contrefait, e [kɔ̃tʀəfɛ, ɛt] (ptp de **contrefaire**) adj (*difforme*) misshapen, deformed.

contreficher (se)* [kɔ̃tʀəfiʃe] [1] vpr: **je m'en contrefiche** I couldn't care a hoot* (about it), I don't give a darn* (about it).

contrefort [kɔ̃tʀəfɔʀ] nm a (*Archit*) *[voûte, terrasse]* buttress. b *[soulier]* stiffener. c (*Géog*) *[arête]* spur. *[chaîne]* **~s** foothills.

contrefoutre (se)‡ [kɔ̃tʀəfutʀ] vpr: **je m'en contrefous** I don't give a damn‡ (about it).

contremaître [kɔ̃tʀəmɛtʀ] nm foreman.

contremaîtresse [kɔ̃tʀəmɛtʀɛs] nf forewoman.

contremarche [kɔ̃tʀəmaʀʃ] nf a (*Mil*) countermarch. b *[marche d'escalier]* riser.

contremarque [kɔ̃tʀəmaʀk] nf a (*Comm: marque*) countermark. b (*Ciné, Théât: ticket*) passout ticket.

contrepartie [kɔ̃tʀəpaʀti] nf a (*lit, fig: compensation*) compensation. **en ~** (*en échange, en retour*) in return; (*en revanche*) in compensation, to make up for it; (*Jur, Fin*) **moyennant ~ valable** ≃ for a good and valuable consideration; **obtenir de l'argent en ~** to get money in compensation; **prendre qch sans ~** to take sth without offering compensation; (*en revanche*) **en ~ il est gentil** on the other hand he's nice. b (*littér: contre-pied*) opposing view. c (*Comm*) (*registre*) duplicate register; (*écritures*) counterpart entries.

contrepet [kɔ̃tʀəpɛ] nm, **contrepèterie** [kɔ̃tʀəpɛtʀi] nf spoonerism.

contrepoids [kɔ̃tʀəpwɑ] nm (*lit*) counterweight, counterbalance; *[acrobate]* balancing-pole. **faire ~** to act as a counterbalance; **porter un panier à chaque main pour faire ~** to carry a basket in each hand to balance oneself; (*fig*) **servir de ~ à, apporter un ~ à** to counterbalance.

contrepoint [kɔ̃tʀəpwɛ̃] nm counterpoint. (*Mus, fig*) **en ~** (adj) contrapuntal; (adv) contrapuntally.

contrepoison [kɔ̃tʀəpwazɔ̃] nm antidote, counterpoison.

contrer [kɔ̃tʀe] [1] 1 vt a *personne, menées* to counter. b (*Cartes*) to double. (*Rugby*) **~ un coup de pied** to charge down a kick. 2 vi (*Cartes*) to double.

contrescarpe [kɔ̃tʀɛskaʀp] nf (*Mil*) counterscarp.

contreseing [kɔ̃tʀəsɛ̃] nm (*Jur*) countersignature.

contresens [kɔ̃tʀəsɑ̃s] nm (*erreur*) misinterpretation; (*de traduction*) mistranslation; (*absurdité*) nonsense (*NonC*), piece of nonsense. **à ~** (*Aut*) the wrong way; (*Couture*) against the grain; **à ~ de** against; **il a pris mes paroles à ~, il a pris le ~ de mes paroles** he misinterpreted what I said; **le traducteur a fait un ~** the translator has made a mistake in translation *ou* has been guilty of a mistranslation.

contresigner [kɔ̃tʀəsiɲe] [1] vt to countersign.

contretemps [kɔ̃tʀətɑ̃] nm a (*complication, retard*) hitch, contretemps. b (*Mus*) off-beat rhythm. c **à ~** (*Mus*) off the beat; (*fig*) at an inopportune moment.

contrevenant, e [kɔ̃tʀəv(ə)nɑ̃, ɑ̃t] (*Jur*) 1 adj offending. 2 nm,f offender.

contrevenir [kɔ̃tʀəv(ə)niʀ] [22] **contrevenir à** vt indir (*Jur, littér*) *loi, règlement* to contravene.

contrevent [kɔ̃tʀəvɑ̃] nm a (*volet*) shutter. b *[charpente]* brace, strut.

contrevirage [kɔ̃tʀəviʀaʒ] nm (*Ski*) counter-turn.

contribuable [kɔ̃tʀibɥabl] nmf taxpayer.

contribuer [kɔ̃tʀibɥe] [1] **contribuer à** vt indir *résultat, effet* to contribute to(wards); *effort, dépense* to contribute towards. **de nombreux facteurs ont contribué au déclin de .../à réduire le ...** numerous factors contributed to(wards) the decline in .../to(wards) the reduction in the ... *ou* to reducing the ... .

contributif, -ive [kɔ̃tʀibytif, iv] adj (*Jur*) *part* contributory.

contribution [kɔ̃tʀibysjɔ̃] nf a (*participation*) contribution. **mettre qn à ~** to call upon sb's services, make use of sb; **mettre qch à ~** to make use of sth; **apporter sa ~ à qch** to make one's contribution to sth. b (*impôts*) **~s** (*à la commune*) rates (*Brit*), (local) taxes (*US*); (*à l'état*) taxes; **~s directes/indirectes** direct/indirect taxation; **~ sociale généralisée** *supplementary social security contribution in aid of underprivileged.* c (*administration*) **~s** tax office, ≃ Inland Revenue (*Brit*), ≃ Internal Revenue (*US*); **travailler aux ~s** to work for *ou* in the Inland Revenue (*Brit*) *ou* Internal Revenue (*US*), work in the tax office.

contrister [kɔ̃tʀiste] [1] vt (*littér*) to grieve, sadden.

contrit, e [kɔ̃tʀi, it] adj contrite.

contrition [kɔ̃tʀisjɔ̃] nf contrition; *voir* **acte**.

contrôlable [kɔ̃tʀolabl] adj *opération* that can be checked; *affirmation* that can be checked *ou* verified, verifiable; *sentiment* that can be controlled, controllable. **un billet ~ à l'arrivée** a ticket that is inspected *ou* checked on arrival.

contrôle [kɔ̃tʀol] nm a (*vérification: voir* **contrôler**) checking (*NonC*), check; inspecting (*NonC*), inspection; controlling (*NonC*), control; verifying (*NonC*), verification. (*Police*) **~ d'identité** identity check; **~ fiscal** tax inspection; **le ~ des passeports** passport control; (*Comm*) **~s de qualité** quality checks *ou* controls; (*Scol*) **~ continu** continuous assessment; **~ des connaissances** pupil *ou* student assessment, checking of standards; **(exercice de) ~** (written) test; *voir* **visite**.

b (*surveillance: voir* **contrôler**) controlling; supervising, supervision; monitoring. **exercer un ~ sévère sur les agissements de qn** to maintain strict control over sb's actions; **sous ~ étranger** *firme* foreign-owned; *territoire* under foreign control; **sous ~ militaire** under military control; **avoir une région sous son ~** to be in control of a region, have a region under one's control; (*Fin*) **~ des changes** exchange control; (*Fin*) **~ économique** *ou* **des prix** price control; (*organisme*) ≃ Prices Board; (*Sociol*) **~ des naissances** birth control; (*Aut*) **~ radar** radar speed trap.

c (*maîtrise*) control. **~ de soi-même** self-control; **garder le ~ de sa voiture** to remain in control of one's vehicle.

d (*bureau*) (*gén*) office; (*Théât*) (advance) booking office (*surtout Brit*), reservation office (*US*).

e (*Mil: registres*) **~s** rolls, lists; **rayé des ~s de l'armée** removed from the army lists.

f (*poinçon*) hallmark.

contrôler [kɔ̃tʀole] [1] 1 vt a (*vérifier*) *billets, passeports* to inspect, check; *comptes* to check, inspect, control; *texte, traduction* to check (*sur* against); *régularité de qch* to check; *qualité de qch* to control, check; *affirmations* to check, verify; (*Scol*) *connaissances* to test.

b (*surveiller*) *opérations, agissements, gestion* to control, supervise; *subordonnés, employés* to supervise; *prix, loyers* to monitor, control.

c (*maîtriser*) *colère, réactions, nerfs* to control; (*Mil*) *zone, pays* to be in control of; (*Écon*) *secteur, firme* to control; (*Sport*) *ballon, skis, jeu* to control. **nous contrôlons cette société à 80%** we have an 80% (controlling) stake in this company.

d (*Orfèvrerie*) to hallmark.

2 **se contrôler** vpr to control o.s. **il ne se contrôlait plus** he was no longer in control of himself, he could control himself no longer.

contrôleur, -euse [kɔ̃tʀolœʀ, øz] nm,f a (*dans le train, le métro, le bus*) (ticket) inspector; (*Rail: sur le quai*) ticket collector. **~ de la navigation aérienne** air traffic controller. b (*Fin*) *[comptabilité]* auditor; *[contributions]* inspector. c (*Tech*) regulator. **~ de ronde** time-clock.

contrordre [kɔ̃tʀɔʀdʀ] nm counter-order, countermand. **ordres et ~s** orders and counter-orders; **il y a ~** there has been a change of orders; **sauf ~** unless orders to the contrary are given, unless otherwise directed.

controuvé, e [kɔ̃tʀuve] adj (*littér*) *fait, nouvelle* fabricated; *histoire, anecdote* fabricated, concocted.

controverse [kɔ̃tʀɔvɛʀs] nf controversy. **prêter à ~** to be debatable.

controversé, e [kɔ̃tʀɔvɛʀse] adj *théorie, question* much debated.

contumace [kɔ̃tymas] 1 adj (*rare*) in default, defaulting. 2 nf (*Jur*) **par ~** in absentia, in his (*ou* her *etc*) absence.

contusion [kɔ̃tyzjɔ̃] nf bruise, contusion (*SPÉC*).

contusionner [kɔ̃tyzjɔne] [1] vt to bruise, contuse (*SPÉC*). **son corps était tout contusionné** his body was covered in bruises.

conurbation [kɔnyʀbasjɔ̃] nf conurbation.

convaincant, e [kɔ̃vɛ̃kɑ̃, ɑ̃t] adj convincing.

convaincre [kɔ̃vɛ̃kʀ] [42] vt a *sceptique* to convince (*de qch* of sth); *hésitant* to persuade (*de faire qch* to do sth). **je ne suis pas convaincu par son explication** I'm not convinced by his explanation; **je ne demande qu'à me laisser ~** I'm open to persuasion *ou* conviction; **il m'a finalement convaincu de renoncer à cette idée** he finally persuaded me to give up that idea, he finally talked me into giving up that idea, he finally convinced me (that) I should give up that idea; **se laisser ~** to let o.s. be persuaded. b (*déclarer coupable*) **~ qn de meurtre/trahison** to prove sb guilty of *ou* convict sb of murder/treason.

convaincu, e [kɔ̃vɛ̃ky] (ptp de **convaincre**) adj convinced. **d'un ton ~** in a tone of conviction, with conviction.

convalescence [kɔ̃valesɑ̃s] nf convalescence. **être en ~** to be convalescing; **entrer en ~** to start one's convalescence; **période de ~** (period of) convalescence; **maison de ~** convalescent home.

convalescent, e [kɔ̃valesɑ̃, ɑ̃t] adj, nm,f convalescent.

convecteur [kɔ̃vɛktœʀ] nm convector (heater).

convection [kɔ̃vɛksjɔ̃] nf convection.

convenable [kɔ̃vnabl] adj a (*approprié*) *parti* fitting, suitable; *moment, endroit* fitting, suitable, appropriate. b (*décent*) *manières* acceptable, correct, proper; *vêtements* decent, respectable; *invité, jeune homme* acceptable. **peu ~** *manières* improper, unseemly; *vêtements* unsuitable; **ne montre pas du doigt, ce n'est pas ~** don't point – it's not polite, it's bad manners to point. c (*acceptable*) *devoir* adequate, passable; *salaire, logement* decent, acceptable, adequate. **salaire à peine ~** scarcely acceptable *ou* adequate salary.

convenablement [kɔ̃vnabləmɑ̃] adv *placé, choisi* suitably, appropriately; *s'exprimer* properly; *payé, logé* adequately, decently. **tout ce que je vous demande c'est de travailler ~** all I'm asking of you is to work adequately *ou* in an acceptable fashion; **s'habiller ~** (*décemment*) to dress respectably *ou* properly; (*en fonction du temps*) to dress appropriately.

convenance [kɔ̃vnɑ̃s] nf a (*ce qui convient*) (*frm*) **consulter les ~s de qn** to consult sb's preferences; **trouver qch à sa ~** to find sth to one's liking, find sth suitable; **la chambre est-elle à votre ~?** is the room to your liking?; **le service est-il à votre ~?** is the service to your satisfaction?; **choisissez un jour à votre ~** choose a day to suit your convenience; **pour des raisons de ~(s) personnelle(s), pour ~s personnelles** for personal reasons; *voir* **mariage**.

b (*normes sociales*) **les ~s** propriety, the proprieties; **contraire aux ~s** contrary to the proprieties.

c (*littér*) (*harmonie*) *[goûts, caractères]* affinity; (†: *caractère adéquat*) *[terme, équipement]* appropriateness, suitability.

convenir [kɔ̃vniʀ] [22] 1 **convenir à** vt indir (*être approprié à*) to suit, be suitable for; (*être utile à*) to suit, be convenient for; (*être agréable à*) to be agreeable to, suit. **ce chapeau ne convient pas à la circonstance** this hat is not suitable for the occasion *ou* does not suit the occasion; **le climat ne lui convient pas** the climate does not suit him *ou* does not agree with him; **oui, cette chambre me convient très bien** yes, this room suits me very well; **cette maison convient à une personne seule** this house is suitable for a person living on their own; **j'irai si cela me convient** I'll go if it is convenient (for me); (*ton péremptoire*) I'll go if it suits me; **si l'heure/la date (vous) convient** if the time/date is convenient (for you) *ou* is agreeable to you *ou* suits you; **c'est tout à fait ce qui me convient** this is exactly what I need *ou* want; **j'espère que cela vous conviendra** I hope you will find this acceptable, I hope this will be acceptable to you.

2 **convenir de** vt indir a (*avouer, reconnaître*) to admit (to), acknowledge. **il convint d'avoir été un peu brusque** he admitted (to) having been a little abrupt, he acknowledged (that) he'd been a bit abrupt; **tu as eu tort, conviens-en** you were wrong, admit it.

b (*s'accorder sur*) to agree upon. **~ d'une date/d'un lieu** to agree upon a date/place; **une date a été convenue** a date has been agreed upon.

3 vt: **~ que** (*avouer, reconnaître*) to admit that, acknowledge the fact that; (*s'accorder sur*) to agree that; **il est convenu que nous nous réunissons demain** it is agreed that we (shall) meet tomorrow.

4 vb impers: **il convient de faire** (*il vaut mieux*) it's advisable to do; (*il est bienséant de*) it would be proper to do; **il convient d'être prudent** caution is advised, it is advisable to be prudent; **il convient qu'elle remercie ses hôtes de leur hospitalité** it is proper *ou* right for her to thank her host and hostess for their hospitality; (*frm*) **il convient de faire remarquer** we should point out.

5 **se convenir** vpr *[personnes]* to be well-suited (to each other).

convention [kɔ̃vɑ̃sjɔ̃] nf a (*pacte*) (*gén*) agreement, covenant (*frm, Admin*); (*Pol*) convention. (*Ind*) **~ collective** collective agreement; **cela n'entre pas dans nos ~s** that doesn't enter into our agreement. b (*accord tacite*) (*gén*) understanding; (*Art, Littérat*) convention. **les ~s (sociales)** convention, social conventions; (*Littérat, Théât*) **décor/**

personnage/langage de ~ conventional set/character/language; **mots/amabilité de ~** conventional words/kindness. c (*assemblée*) (*US Pol*) convention. (*Hist*) **la C~** the Convention.

conventionné, e [kɔ̃vɑ̃sjɔne] **adj** *établissement, médecin* ≃ National Health (*Brit*) (*épith*), *linked to the state health scheme; prix* government-regulated; *prêt* subsidized, low-interest (*épith*).

conventionnel, -elle [kɔ̃vɑ̃sjɔnɛl] 1 **adj** (*gén*) conventional; (*Jur*) *acte, clause* contractual. 2 **nm** (*Hist*) **les ~s** the members of the Convention.

conventionnellement [kɔ̃vɑ̃sjɔnɛlmɑ̃] **adv** conventionally.

conventionnement [kɔ̃vɑ̃sjɔnmɑ̃] **nm** ≃ National Health (*Brit*) contract, *state health service contract*.

conventuel, -elle [kɔ̃vɑ̃tɥɛl] **adj** *vie, règle [moines]* monastic; *[nonnes]* convent (*épith*), conventual; *bâtiment* monastery (*épith*); convent (*épith*); *simplicité, sérénité* monastic; convent-like.

convenu, e [kɔ̃vny] (**ptp de convenir**) **adj** a (*décidé*) *heure, prix, mot* agreed. **comme ~** as agreed. b (*littér péj: conventionnel*) conventional.

convergence [kɔ̃vɛʀʒɑ̃s] **nf** convergence.

convergent, e [kɔ̃vɛʀʒɑ̃, ɑ̃t] **adj** convergent.

converger [kɔ̃vɛʀʒe] 3 **vi** *[lignes, rayons, routes]* to converge. *[regards]* **~ sur** to focus on; **nos pensées convergent vers la même solution** our thoughts are leading towards *ou* converging on the same solution.

convers, e [kɔ̃vɛʀ, ɛʀs] **adj** (*Rel*) lay (*épith*).

conversation [kɔ̃vɛʀsasjɔ̃] **nf** a (*entretien*) (*gén*) conversation, chat*; (*politique, diplomatique*) talk. **la ~** conversation; **lors d'une ~ téléphonique** during a telephone conversation *ou* a chat* on the telephone; **les ~s téléphoniques sont surveillées** telephone conversations are tapped; **en (grande) ~ avec** (deep) in conversation with; **faire la ~ à** to make conversation with; *voir* **frais**[2].

b (*art de parler*) **il a une ~ brillante** he is a brilliant conversationalist; **avoir de la ~** to be a good conversationalist; **il n'a pas de ~** he's got no conversation.

c (*langage familier*) **dans la ~ courante** in informal *ou* conversational talk *ou* speech; **employer le style de la ~** to use a conversational style.

conversationnel, -elle [kɔ̃vɛʀsasjɔnɛl] **adj** (*Ordin*) conversational.

converser [kɔ̃vɛʀse] 1 **vi** to converse (*avec* with).

conversion [kɔ̃vɛʀsjɔ̃] **nf** a (*voir* **convertir**) conversion (*à* to, *en* into); winning over (*à* to); (*voir* **se convertir**) conversion (*à* to). **faire une ~ de fractions en ...** to convert fractions into ... . b (*demi-tour*) (*Mil*) wheel; (*Ski*) kick turn.

converti, e [kɔ̃vɛʀti] (**ptp de convertir**) 1 **adj** converted. 2 **nm,f** convert; *voir* **prêcher**.

convertibilité [kɔ̃vɛʀtibilite] **nf** (*Fin*) convertibility.

convertible [kɔ̃vɛʀtibl] 1 **adj** convertible (*en* into). 2 **nm** (*avion*) convertiplane; (*canapé*) bed-settee (*Brit*), sofa bed.

convertir [kɔ̃vɛʀtiʀ] 2 1 **vt** a (*rallier*) (*à une religion*) to convert (*à* to); (*à une théorie*) to win over, convert (*à* to). b (*transformer*) **~ en** (*gén, Fin, Math*) to convert into. 2 **se convertir vpr** (*Rel; à une théorie etc*) to be converted (*à* to).

convertissage [kɔ̃vɛʀtisaʒ] **nm** (*Métal*) conversion.

convertissement [kɔ̃vɛʀtismɑ̃] **nm** (*Fin*) conversion.

convertisseur [kɔ̃vɛʀtisœʀ] **nm** (*Élec, Métal*) converter. **~ Bessemer** Bessemer converter; (*Élec*) **~ d'images** image converter; (*Aut*) **~ de couple** torque converter; (*Ordin*) **~ numérique** digitizer.

convexe [kɔ̃vɛks] **adj** convex.

convexion [kɔ̃vɛksjɔ̃] **nf** = **convection**.

convexité [kɔ̃vɛksite] **nf** convexity.

conviction [kɔ̃viksjɔ̃] **nf** a (*certitude*) conviction, (firm) belief. **j'en ai la ~** I'm convinced of it; **parler avec ~** to speak with conviction. b (*sérieux, enthousiasme*) conviction. **faire qch avec/sans ~** to do sth with/without conviction; **manquer de ~** to lack conviction. c (*opinions*) **~s** beliefs, convictions. d *voir* **pièce**.

convier [kɔ̃vje] 7 **vt** (*frm*) **~ à** *soirée etc* to invite to; **~ qn à faire qch** (*pousser*) to urge sb to do sth; (*inviter*) to invite sb to do sth; **la chaleur conviait à la baignade** the hot weather was an invitation to swim.

convive [kɔ̃viv] **nmf** guest (*at a meal*).

convivial, e, mpl -iaux [kɔ̃vivjal, jo] **adj** (*gén*) *ambiance* convivial; (*Ordin*) user-friendly.

convivialité [kɔ̃vivjalite] **nf** (*rapports*) social interaction; (*jovialité*) conviviality; (*Ordin*) user-friendliness.

convocation [kɔ̃vɔkasjɔ̃] **nf** a (*NonC: voir* **convoquer**) convening, convoking; inviting; summoning. **la ~ des membres doit se faire longtemps à l'avance** members must be invited a long time in advance; **cette ~ chez le directeur l'intriguait** this summons to appear before the director intrigued him; **la ~ des membres/candidats doit se faire par écrit** members/candidates must be given written notification to attend. b (*lettre, carte*) (written) notification to attend; (*Jur*) summons. **je n'ai pas encore reçu ma ~** I haven't had notification yet.

convoi [kɔ̃vwa] **nm** a (*cortège funèbre*) funeral procession. b (*train*) train. **~ de marchandises** goods train. c (*suite de véhicules, navires, prisonniers*) convoy. d (*Aut*) **~ exceptionnel** ≃ wide (*ou* long *ou* dangerous) load.

convoiement [kɔ̃vwamɑ̃] **nm** (*voir* **convoyer**) escorting; convoying.

convoiter [kɔ̃vwate] 1 **vt** *héritage, objet* to covet, lust after; *personne* to lust after; *poste* to covet. **poste très convoité** highly-coveted job.

convoitise [kɔ̃vwatiz] **nf** (*NonC: désir*) (*gén*) covetousness; (*pour une personne*) lust, desire. **la ~ des richesses** the lust for wealth; **la ~ de la chair** the lusts of the flesh; **l'objet de sa ~** the object of his desire; **regarder avec ~** *objet* to cast covetous looks on; *personne* to cast lustful looks on; **un regard brillant de ~** a covetous (*ou* lustful) look; **l'objet des ~s de tous** the object of everyone's desire.

convoler [kɔ̃vɔle] 1 **vi** († *ou hum*) **~ (en justes noces)** to be wed († *ou hum*).

convoquer [kɔ̃vɔke] 1 **vt** *assemblée* to convene, convoke; *membre de club etc* to invite (*à* to); *candidat* to ask to attend; *témoin, prévenu, subordonné* to summon. **~ qn (pour une entrevue)** to call *ou* invite sb for an interview; **il va falloir ~ les membres** we're going to have to call a meeting of the members *ou* call the members together; **as-tu été convoqué pour l'assemblée annuelle?** have you been invited to (attend) the AGM?; **j'ai été convoqué à 10 heures (pour mon oral)** I've been asked to attend at 10 o'clock (for my oral); **le chef m'a convoqué** I was summoned by *ou* called before the boss; **le chef m'a convoqué dans son bureau** the boss called *ou* summoned me to his office; **le juge m'a convoqué** I was summoned to appear before the judge, I was called before the judge.

convoyage [kɔ̃vwajaʒ] **nm** = **convoiement**.

convoyer [kɔ̃vwaje] 8 **vt** (*gén*) to escort; (*Mil, Naut*) to escort, convoy.

convoyeur [kɔ̃vwajœʀ] **nm** (*navire*) convoy, escort ship; (*personne*) escort; (*Tech*) conveyor. **~ de fonds** (mobile) security guard (*transferring banknotes etc*).

convulser [kɔ̃vylse] 1 **vt** *visage* to convulse, distort; *corps* to convulse. **la douleur lui convulsa le visage** his face was distorted *ou* convulsed by *ou* with pain; **son visage se convulsait** his face was distorted.

convulsif, -ive [kɔ̃vylsif, iv] **adj** convulsive.

convulsion [kɔ̃vylsjɔ̃] **nf** (*gén, Méd, fig*) convulsion.

convulsionnaire [kɔ̃vylsjɔnɛʀ] **nmf** convulsionary.

convulsionner [kɔ̃vylsjɔne] 1 **vt** to convulse. **visage convulsionné** distorted *ou* convulsed face.

convulsivement [kɔ̃vylsivmɑ̃] **adv** convulsively.

coobligé, e [kɔɔbliʒe] **nm,f** (*Jur*) joint obligor.

cooccurrence [kɔɔkyʀɑ̃s] **nf** (*Ling*) co-occurrence.

cool* [kul] **adj** cool*.

coolie [kuli] **nm** coolie.

coopé [kɔpe] **nf** a **abrév de coopération.** b (**abrév de coopérative**) co-op.

coopérant, e [kɔɔpeʀɑ̃, ɑ̃t] 1 **adj** cooperative. 2 **coopérant nm** ≃ *person serving on Voluntary Service Overseas* (*Brit*) *ou in the Peace Corps* (*US*).

coopérateur, -trice [kɔɔpeʀatœʀ, tʀis] 1 **adj** cooperative. 2 **nm,f** a (*associé*) collaborator, cooperator. b (*membre d'une coopérative*) member of a cooperative, cooperator.

coopératif, -ive [kɔɔpeʀatif, iv] 1 **adj** cooperative. 2 **coopérative nf** (*organisme*) cooperative; (*magasin*) co-op. **~ scolaire** school fund.

coopération [kɔɔpeʀasjɔ̃] **nf** a (*gén: collaboration*) cooperation. **apporter sa ~ à une entreprise** to cooperate *ou* collaborate in an undertaking. b (*Pol*) ≃ Voluntary Service Overseas (*Brit*), VSO (*Brit*), Peace Corps (*US*) (*usually as form of military service*). **il a été envoyé en Afrique comme professeur au titre de la ~** ≃ he was sent to Africa as a VSO teacher (*Brit*), he was sent to Africa by the Peace Corps to be a teacher (*US*).

coopératisme [kɔɔpeʀatism] **nm** (*Écon*) cooperation.

coopérer [kɔɔpeʀe] 6 1 **vi** to cooperate. 2 **coopérer à vt indir** to cooperate in.

cooptation [kɔɔptasjɔ̃] **nf** coopting, cooptation.

coopter [kɔɔpte] 1 **vt** to coopt.

coordinateur, -trice [kɔɔʀdinatœʀ, tʀis] = **coordonnateur**.

coordination [kɔɔʀdinasjɔ̃] **nf** (*gén, Ling*) coordination; **~ ouvrière/étudiante** workers'/students' committee; *voir* **conjonction**.

coordonnant [kɔɔʀdɔnɑ̃] **nm** (*Ling*) co-ordinating conjunction.

coordonnateur, -trice [kɔɔʀdɔnatœʀ, tʀis] 1 **adj** coordinating. 2 **nm,f** coordinator.

coordonné, e [kɔɔʀdɔne] (**ptp de coordonner**) 1 **adj** coordinated. (*Ling*) **(proposition) ~e** coordinate clause; **papiers peints ~s** matching *ou* coordinated wallpapers. 2 **nmpl** (*Habillement*) **~s** coordinates. 3 **coordonnées nfpl** (*Math*) coordinates. **donnez-moi vos ~es*** can I have your details please?

coordonner [kɔɔʀdɔne] 1 **vt** to coordinate.

copain*, copine* [kɔpɛ̃, kɔpin] **nm,f** pal*, friend, mate* (*surtout Brit*), buddy* (*US*). **de bons ~s** good friends, great pals*; **il est très ~ avec le patron** he's (very) pally‡ (*Brit*) with the boss, he's really in with the boss*; **avec eux, c'est *ou* on est ~ ~** we're dead pally‡ (*Brit*) *ou* dead chummy* *ou* great buddies* with them; **ils sont ~s comme cochons** they are great buddies*, they're as thick as thieves; (*péj*) **les meilleurs postes sont toujours pour les petits ~s** they always give the best jobs to their cronies*, it's always jobs for the boys*.

coparticipant, e [kopaʀtisipɑ̃, ɑ̃t] (*Jur*) 1 **adj** in copartnership *ou*

joint account. 2 nm,f copartner.
coparticipation [kopartisipasjɔ̃] **nf** (*Jur*) copartnership. ~ **aux bénéfices** profit-sharing.
copeau, pl ~x [kɔpo] **nm** *[bois]* shaving; *[métal]* turning. **brûler des ~x** to burn wood shavings; (*pour emballage*) **~x de bois** wood wool *ou* shavings.
Copenhague [kɔpənag] **n** Copenhagen.
Copernic [kɔpernik] **nm** Copernicus.
copiage [kɔpjaʒ] **nm** (*gén*) copying; (*Scol*) copying, cribbing (*arg Scol*).
copie [kɔpi] **nf** a (*NonC: voir* **copier**) copying; reproduction. **la ~ au net de cette traduction m'a pris du temps** it took me a lot of time to do the fair copy of this translation.
b (*reproduction, exemplaire*) *[diplôme, film etc]* copy; *[tableau]* copy, reproduction; *[sculpture]* copy, reproduction, replica. (*Admin*) **~ certifiée conforme** certified copy; (*Admin*) **pour ~ conforme** certified accurate; (*Ciné*) **~ étalon** master print; (*Ciné*) **~ d'exploitation** release print; (*Ordin*) **~ papier** hard copy; **je veux la ~ au net de vos traductions demain** I want the fair copy of your translations tomorrow; **prendre ~ de** to make a copy of; **œuvre qui n'est que la pâle ~ d'une autre** work which is only a pale imitation of another; **c'est la ~ de sa mère** she's the replica *ou* (spitting) image of her mother.
c (*Scol*) (*feuille de papier*) sheet (of paper), paper; (*devoir*) exercise; (*composition, examen*) paper, script. **~ simple/double** single/double sheet (of paper); **~ d'examen** examination script; (*examen*) **rendre** *ou* **remettre ~ blanche** to hand in a blank sheet of paper; *voir* **mal**.
d (*Typ*) copy.
e (*Presse*) copy, material; *voir* **pisseur**.
copier [kɔpje] 7 1 **vt** a (*recopier*) *écrit, texte,* (*Jur*) *acte* to copy, make a copy of; *tableau, sculpture* to copy, reproduce; *musique* to copy. **~ qch au propre** *ou* **au net** to make a fair copy of sth, copy sth out neatly; **~ une leçon 3 fois** to copy out a lesson 3 times; **vous me la copierez*** well, I won't forget that in a hurry!* b (*Scol: tricher*) to copy, crib (*arg Scol*). **~ (sur) le voisin** to copy *ou* crib from one's neighbour. c (*imiter*) *style, démarche, auteur* to copy. 2 **vi** (*Scol*) to copy, crib (*arg Scol*) (*sur* from).
copieur, -ieuse [kɔpjœr, jøz] 1 **nm,f** (*Scol*) copier, cribber (*arg Scol*). 2 **nm** (*machine*) copier.
copieusement [kɔpjøzmɑ̃] **adv** *manger, boire* copiously, heartily. **un repas ~ arrosé** a meal generously washed down with wine; **on s'est fait ~ arroser/engueuler‡** we got thoroughly *ou* well and truly soaked/told off*; **~ illustré/annoté** copiously illustrated/annotated.
copieux, -ieuse [kɔpjø, jøz] **adj** *repas* copious, hearty; *portion* generous; *notes, exemples* copious.
copilote [kopilɔt] **nmf** (*Aviat*) co-pilot; (*Aut*) navigator.
copin* [kɔpɛ̃] **nm = copain***.
copinage* [kɔpinaʒ] **nm = copinerie***.
copine* [kɔpin] **nf** *voir* **copain***.
copiner* [kɔpine] 1 **vi** to be pally‡ (*Brit*) *ou* great buddies* (*avec* with).
copinerie* [kɔpinri] **nf** (*péj*) pally* (*Brit*) *ou* buddy-buddy* (*US*) relationship. **obtenir qch par ~** to get sth through friendly contacts.
copiste [kɔpist] **nmf** (*Hist, Littérat*) copyist, transcriber.
coposséder [kopɔsede] 6 **vt** to own jointly, be co-owner *ou* joint owner of.
copossession [kopɔsesjɔ̃] **nf** co-ownership, joint ownership.
copra(h) [kɔpra] **nm** copra.
coprésidence [koprezidɑ̃s] **nf** co-presidency, co-chairmanship.
coprésident [koprezidɑ̃] **nm** co-president, co-chairman.
coprin [kɔprɛ̃] **nm** ink cap, coprinus (*SPÉC*).
coproducteur, -trice [koprɔdyktœr, tris] **nm,f** coproducer.
coproduction [koprɔdyksjɔ̃] **nf** (*Ciné, TV*) coproduction, joint production. **une ~ franco-italienne** a joint French-Italian production.
coproduire [koprɔdɥir] 38 **vt** to coproduce.
copropriétaire [koprɔprijetɛr] **nmf** co-owner, joint owner.
copropriété [koprɔprijete] **nf** (*statut*) co-ownership, joint ownership; (*propriétaires*) co-owners. **immeuble en ~** block of flats (*Brit*) *ou* apartment building (*US*) in co-ownership, condominium (*US*).
copte [kɔpt] 1 **adj** Coptic. 2 **nm** (*Ling*) Coptic. 3 **nmf: C~** Copt.
copulatif, -ive [kɔpylatif, iv] **adj** (*Ling*) copulative.
copulation [kɔpylasjɔ̃] **nf** copulation.
copule [kɔpyl] **nf** (*Ling*) copulative verb, copula.
copuler [kɔpyle] 1 **vi** to copulate.
copyright [kɔpirajt] **nm** copyright.
coq¹ [kɔk] 1 **nm** *[basse-cour]* cock, rooster. (*oiseau mâle*) **~ faisan/de perdrix** cock pheasant/partridge; **jeune ~** cockerel; (*Boxe*) **~, poids ~** bantam-weight; **être comme un ~ en pâte** to be *ou* live in clover, live the life of Riley; (*fig*) **jambes** *ou* **mollets de ~** wiry legs; *voir* **chant¹**, **rouge**.
2 **comp** ►**coq-à-l'âne** **nm inv** abrupt change of subject; **sauter** *ou* **passer du coq à l'âne** to jump from one subject to another ►**coq de bruyère** (*grand*) capercaillie, (*petit*) black grouse ►**coq de clocher** weather cock ►**coq de combat** fighting cock ►**le coq gaulois** the French cockerel (*emblem of the Frenchman's fighting spirit*) ►**coq nain** bantam cock ►**coq de roche** cock of the rock ►**coq du village** (*fig*) the local swell* *ou* ladykiller ►**coq au vin** (*Culin*) coq au vin.
coq² [kɔk] **nm** (*Naut*) (ship's) cook.
coquart‡ [kɔkar] **nm** black eye, shiner‡.
coque [kɔk] **nf** a *[bateau]* hull; *[avion]* fuselage; *[auto]* shell, body. (*embarcation légère*) **~ de noix** skiff. b *[noix, amande],* (†) *[œuf]* shell. (*Culin*) **à la ~** (soft-)boiled. c (*mollusque*) cockle.
coquelet [kɔklɛ] **nm** (*Culin*) cockerel.
coquelicot [kɔkliko] **nm** poppy; *voir* **rouge**.
coqueluche [kɔklyʃ] **nf** (*Méd*) whooping cough. (*fig*) **être la ~ de** to be the idol *ou* darling of.
coquemar [kɔkmar] **nm** cauldron, big kettle.
coquerico [kɔk(ə)riko] = **cocorico**.
coquerie [kɔkri] **nf** (*Naut*) (*à bord*) (ship's) galley, caboose (*Brit*); (*à terre*) cookhouse.
coquet, -ette [kɔkɛ, ɛt] **adj** a (*bien habillé*) smart, well turned-out; (*soucieux de son apparence*) appearance-conscious, clothes-conscious, interested in one's appearance (*attrib*). **homme trop ~** man who takes too much interest in *ou* who is too particular about his appearance *ou* who is too clothes-conscious. b (†: *flirteur*) flirtatious. **c'est une ~ette** she's a coquette *ou* a flirt, she's very coquettish *ou* flirtatious. c *ville* pretty, charming; *logement* smart, charming, stylish; *robe* smart, stylish. d (*: *intensif*) *somme d'argent, revenu* tidy* (*épith*).
coquetier [kɔk(ə)tje] **nm** (*godet*) egg cup. **gagner** *ou* **décrocher le ~*†** to hit the jackpot*.
coquettement [kɔkɛtmɑ̃] **adv** *sourire, regarder* coquettishly; *s'habiller* smartly, stylishly; *meubler* prettily, stylishly.
coquetterie [kɔkɛtri] **nf** a (*goût d'une mise soignée*) *[personne]* interest in one's appearance, consciousness of one's appearance; *[toilette, coiffure]* smartness, stylishness. b (*galanterie*) coquetry, flirtatiousness (*NonC*). (*littér: amour propre*) **il mettait sa ~ à marcher sans canne/parler sans notes** he prided himself on *ou* made a point of walking without a stick/talking without notes. c **avoir une ~ dans l'œil*** to have a cast (in one's eye).
coquillage [kɔkijaʒ] **nm** (*mollusque*) shellfish (*NonC*); (*coquille*) shell.
coquille [kɔkij] 1 **nf** a *[mollusque, œuf, noix]* shell. (*fig*) **rentrer dans/sortir de sa ~** to go *ou* withdraw into/come out of one's shell. b (*récipient*) (shell-shaped) dish, scallop. (*Culin: mets*) **~ de poisson/crabe** scallop of fish/crab, fish/crab served in scallop shells. c (*décorative*) scallop; *[épée]* coquille, shell. d (*Typ*) misprint. e (*Sport: protectrice*) box; (*Méd: plâtre*) spinal bed. 2 **comp** ►**coquille de beurre** shell of butter ►**coquille de noix*** (*Naut*) cockleshell ►**coquille d'œuf** **adj inv** eggshell (*épith*) ►**coquille Saint-Jacques** (*animal*) scallop; (*carapace*) scallop shell.
coquillettes [kɔkijɛt] **nfpl** pasta shells.
coquillier, ière [kɔkije, jɛr] 1 **adj** conchiferous (*SPÉC*). 2 **nm** (†) shell collection.
coquin, e [kɔkɛ̃, in] 1 **adj** a (*malicieux*) *enfant* mischievous, rascally; *air* mischievous, roguish. **~ de sort!*** the devil!*, the deuce!*† b (*polisson*) *histoire, regard* naughty, suggestive. 2 **nm,f** (*enfant*) rascal, mischief. **tu es un petit ~!** you're a little monkey! *ou* rascal! 3 **nm** (††: *gredin*) rascal, rogue, rascally fellow†. 4 **coquine††** **nf** (*débauchée*) loose woman, strumpet††.
coquinerie [kɔkinri] **nf** a (*NonC: caractère*) *[enfant]* mischievousness, roguishness; *[gredin]* roguery. b (*action*) *[enfant]* mischievous trick; *[personne peu honnête]* low-down *ou* rascally trick.
cor¹ [kɔr] **nm** (*Mus*) horn. **~ anglais** cor anglais (*Brit*), English horn (*US*); **~ de chasse** hunting horn; **~ d'harmonie** French horn; **~ à pistons** valve horn; **~ de basset** basset horn; (*fig*) **réclamer** *ou* **demander qch/qn à ~ et à cri** to clamour for sth/sb.
cor² [kɔr] **nm** (*Méd*) **~ (au pied)** corn.
cor³ [kɔr] **nm** *[cerf]* tine. **un (cerf) 10 ~s** a 10-point stag, a 10-pointer.
corail, pl -aux [kɔraj, o] 1 **nm** coral. 2 **adj inv** a (*couleur*) coral (pink). b **(train) ~** ® ≃ express (train), ≃ inter-city train (*Brit*).
corallien, -ienne [kɔraljɛ̃, jɛn] **adj** coralline (*littér*), coral (*épith*).
coran [kɔrɑ̃] **nm** Koran; (*fig rare: livre de chevet*) bedside reading (*NonC*).
coranique [kɔranik] **adj** Koranic.
corbeau, pl ~x [kɔrbo] **nm** a (*oiseau*) (*terme générique*) crow. **(grand) ~** raven; **~ freux** rook; **~ corneille** crow. b († *péj: prêtre*) black-coat († *péj*), priest. c (*Archit*) corbel. d (*: *diffamateur*) writer of poison-pen letters.
corbeille [kɔrbɛj] 1 **nf** a (*panier*) basket. b (*Théât*) (dress) circle. c (*Archit*) *[chapiteau]* bell, basket. d (*Bourse*) stockbrokers' central enclosure (*in Paris Stock Exchange*). 2 **comp** ►**corbeille d'argent** (*Bot*) sweet alyssum ►**corbeille à courrier** mail tray ►**corbeille de mariage** (*fig*) wedding presents; **sa femme a apporté une fortune dans la corbeille de mariage** his wife brought him a fortune when she married him ►**corbeille d'or** (*Bot*) golden alyssum ►**corbeille à ouvrage** workbasket ►**corbeille à pain** breadbasket ►**corbeille à papier(s)** wastepaper basket *ou* bin.
corbillard [kɔrbijar] **nm** hearse.
cordage [kɔrdaʒ] **nm** a (*corde, lien*) rope. **~s** (*gén*) ropes, rigging;

(*Naut: de voilure*) rigging. b (*NonC*) *[raquette de tennis]* stringing.

corde [kɔʀd] 1 **nf** a (*gén: câble, cordage*) rope. (*fig*) **la ~†** hanging, the gallows, the hangman's rope; (*fig*) **mériter la ~†** to deserve to be hanged; **attacher qn avec une ~ *ou* de la ~** to tie up sb with a (piece of) rope; **attacher *ou* lier qn à un arbre avec une ~** to rope sb to a tree, tie sb to a tree with a (piece of) rope; **en ~, de ~** *tapis* whipcord (*épith*); **sandales à semelle de ~** rope-soled sandals; **grimper *ou* monter à la ~** to shin up *ou* climb a rope, pull o.s. up a rope; *voir* **danseur, sauter**.

b (*Mus*) string. **les instruments à ~s** the stringed instruments; **les ~s** the strings; **orchestre/quatuor à ~s** string orchestra/quartet; **~ à vide** open string; **à ~s croisées** *piano* overstrung.

c (*Sport*) *[raquette, arc]* string. (*Boxe*) **~s** ropes; (*Boxe*) **être envoyé dans les ~s** to be thrown against the ropes.

d (*Courses*) rails. **à la ~** (*gén: sur piste*) on the inside; (*Courses*) on the rails *ou* the inside; **prendre/tenir la ~** (*gén: sur piste*) to get on/be on the inside; (*Courses*) to get close to/be on the rails, get on/be on the inside; **prendre un virage à la ~** to hug a bend, take a bend on the inside.

e (*trame d'un tissu*) thread; *voir* **user**.

f (*Math*) chord.

g (*†: mesure*) cord.

h (*loc*) **avoir/se mettre la ~ au cou** to have/put one's head in the noose; (*lit, fig*) **être *ou* marcher *ou* danser sur la ~ raide** to walk a tightrope; **politique de la ~ raide** brinkmanship; (*fig*) **parler de (la) ~ dans la maison du pendu** to bring up a sore point, make a tactless remark; **avoir plus d'une ~ *ou* plusieurs ~s à son arc** to have more than one string to one's bow; **c'est dans ses ~s** it's right up his street, it's in his line, it's his bag*; **ce n'est pas dans mes ~s** it's not my line (of country); **tirer sur la ~** to push one's luck a bit*, go too far; **toucher *ou* faire vibrer la ~ sensible** to touch the right chord; **il pleut *ou* il tombe des ~s*** it's bucketing (down)* (*Brit*) *ou* raining cats and dogs*; *voir* **sac¹**.

2 **comp** ►**corde cervicale** cervical nerve ►**corde dorsale** spinal cord ►**corde à linge** clothes line, washing line ►**corde lisse** (*Sport*) (climbing) rope ►**corde à nœuds** (*Sport*) knotted climbing rope ►**corde à piano** piano wire ►**corde raide** tightrope ►**corde à sauter** skipping rope, jump rope (*US*) ►**corde du tympan** chorda tympani ►**cordes vocales** vocal cords.

cordeau, pl ~x [kɔʀdo] **nm** a (*corde*) string, line. **~ de jardinier** gardener's line; (*fig*) **fait *ou* tiré au ~** as straight as a die. b (*mèche*) fuse. **~ Bickford** Bickford fuse, safety fuse; **~ détonant** detonator fuse.

cordée [kɔʀde] **nf** a *[alpinistes]* rope, roped party; *voir* **premier**. b *[bois]* cord.

cordelette [kɔʀdəlɛt] **nf** cord.

Cordelier [kɔʀdəlje] **nm** (*religieux*) Cordelier.

cordelière [kɔʀdəljɛʀ] **nf** a (*corde*) cord. b (*Archit*) cable moulding. c (*religieuse*) **C~** Franciscan nun.

corder [kɔʀde] 1 **vt** a (*Tech*) *chanvre, tabac* to twist. b (*lier*) *malle* to tie up (with rope), rope up. c (*mesurer*) *bois* to cord. d *raquette* to string.

corderie [kɔʀd(ə)ʀi] **nf** (*industrie*) ropemaking industry; (*atelier*) rope factory.

cordial, e, mpl -iaux [kɔʀdjal, jo] 1 **adj** *accueil* hearty, warm, cordial; *sentiment, personne* warm; *manières* cordial; *antipathie, haine* cordial, hearty; *voir* **entente**. 2 **nm** heart tonic, cordial.

cordialement [kɔʀdjalmɑ̃] **adv** (*voir* **cordial**) heartily; warmly; cordially. **haïr qn ~** to detest sb cordially *ou* heartily; (*en fin de lettre*) **~ (vôtre)** kind regards.

cordialité [kɔʀdjalite] **nf** (*voir* **cordial**) heartiness; warmth; cordiality.

cordier [kɔʀdje] **nm** a (*fabricant*) ropemaker. b (*Mus*) tailpiece.

cordillère [kɔʀdijɛʀ] **nf** mountain range, cordillera. **la ~ des Andes** the Andes cordillera; **la ~ australienne** the Great Dividing Range.

cordite [kɔʀdit] **nf** cordite.

cordon [kɔʀdɔ̃] 1 **nm** a *[sonnette, rideau]* cord; *[tablier]* tie; *[sac, bourse]* string; *[souliers]* lace. **~ de sonnette** bell-pull; (*fig*) **tenir les ~s de la bourse** to hold the purse strings; **tenir les ~s du poêle** to be a pallbearer.

b *[soldats]* cordon.

c (*Archit*) string-course, cordon.

d (*décoration*) sash. **~ du Saint-Esprit** the ribbon of the order of the Holy Ghost; **~ de la Légion d'honneur** sash *ou* cordon of the Légion d'Honneur.

2 **comp** ►**cordon Bickford** Bickford fuse, safety fuse ►**cordon-bleu nm (pl cordons-bleus)** (*Culin* *) cordon-bleu cook; (*décoration*) cordon bleu ►**cordon littoral** offshore bar ►**cordon médullaire** spinal cord ►**cordon ombilical** (*lit, fig*) umbilical cord; (*fig*) **couper *ou* rompre le cordon (ombilical)** to cut *ou* sever the umbilical cord ►**cordon sanitaire** (*Méd, Pol*) quarantine line, cordon sanitaire.

cordonner [kɔʀdɔne] 1 **vt** *soie, cheveux* to twist.

cordonnerie [kɔʀdɔnʀi] **nf** (*boutique*) shoe-repairer's (shop), shoemender's (shop), cobbler's (shop); (*métier*) shoe-repairing, shoemending, cobbling.

cordonnet [kɔʀdɔnɛ] **nm** (*petit cordon*) braid (*NonC*), cord (*NonC*); (*pour boutonnière*) buttonhole twist (*NonC*).

cordonnier, -ière [kɔʀdɔnje, jɛʀ] **nm,f** (*réparateur*) shoe-repairer, shoemender, cobbler; (*†: fabricant*) shoemaker. (*Prov*) **les ~s sont toujours les plus mal chaussés** shoemaker's children are the worst shod.

cordouan, e [kɔʀduɑ̃, an] **adj** Cordovan.

Cordoue [kɔʀdu] **n** Cordoba.

coréalisateur, -trice [koʀealizatœʀ, tʀis] **nm,f** (*Ciné, TV*) codirector.

Corée [kɔʀe] **nf** Korea. **C~ du Sud/du Nord** South/North Korea.

coréen, -enne [kɔʀeɛ̃, ɛn] 1 **adj** Korean. 2 **nm** (*Ling*) Korean. 3 **nm,f**: **C~(ne)** Korean.

coreligionnaire [koʀ(ə)liʒjɔnɛʀ] **nmf** *[Arabe, Juif etc]* fellow Arab *ou* Jew *etc*, co-religionist.

Corfou [kɔʀfu] **n** Corfu.

coriace [kɔʀjas] **adj** (*lit, fig*) tough. **il est ~ en affaires** he's a hard-headed *ou* tough businessman.

coriandre [kɔʀjɑ̃dʀ] **nf** coriander.

coricide [kɔʀisid] **nm** (*Pharm*) corn remover.

corindon [kɔʀɛ̃dɔ̃] **nm** corundum.

Corinthe [kɔʀɛ̃t] **n** Corinth; *voir* **raisin**.

corinthien, -ienne [kɔʀɛ̃tjɛ̃, jɛn] **adj** Corinthian.

Coriolan [kɔʀjɔlɑ̃] **nm** Coriolanus.

cormier [kɔʀmje] **nm** (*arbre*) service tree; (*bois*) service wood.

cormoran [kɔʀmɔʀɑ̃] **nm** cormorant. **~ huppé** shag.

cornac [kɔʀnak] **nm** *[éléphant]* mahout, elephant driver.

cornaquer* [kɔʀnake] 1 **vt** to show around. **il m'a cornaqué à travers la ville** he showed me round the town.

cornard‡ [kɔʀnaʀ] **nm** cuckold†.

corne [kɔʀn] 1 **nf** a *[escargot, vache]* horn; *[cerf]* antler. **à ~s** horned; **donner un coup de ~ à qn** to butt sb; **blesser qn d'un coup de ~** to gore sb; (*fig*) **avoir *ou* porter des ~s*** to be (a) cuckold†; **sa femme lui fait porter des ~s*** his wife is unfaithful to him; (*fig*) **faire les ~s à qn** to make a face at sb, make a jeering gesture at sb; *voir* **bête, taureau**.

b (*NonC: substance*) horn.

c (*instrument*) horn; (*Chasse*) hunting horn; (*Aut †: avertisseur*) hooter†, horn.

d (*coin*) *[page]* dog-ear. **faire une ~ à la page d'un livre** to turn down the corner of the page in a book.

e (** NonC: peau dure*) **avoir de la ~** to have patches of hard skin, have calluses.

2 **comp** ►**corne d'abondance** horn of plenty, cornucopia ►**corne de brume** foghorn ►**corne à chaussures** shoehorn.

cornée [kɔʀne] **nf** cornea.

cornéen, -enne [kɔʀneɛ̃, ɛn] **adj** corneal; *voir* **lentille**.

corneille [kɔʀnɛj] **nf** crow. **~ mantelée** hooded crow; **~ noire** carrion crow; *voir* **bayer**.

cornélien, -ienne [kɔʀneljɛ̃, jɛn] **adj** (*Littérat*) Cornelian; (*fig*) *situation where love and duty conflict; héros who puts duty before everything*.

cornemuse [kɔʀnəmyz] **nf** bagpipes. **joueur de ~** bagpiper.

corner¹ [kɔʀne] 1 1 **vt** a *livre, carte* to make *ou* get dog-eared; *page* to turn down the corner of. b (*rare: claironner*) *nouvelle* to blare out. **arrête de nous ~ (cette nouvelle) aux oreilles*** stop deafening* us (with your news). 2 **vi** *[chasseur]* to sound *ou* wind (*Brit*) a horn; *[†: automobiliste]* to hoot (*Brit*) *ou* sound one's horn; *[sirène]* to sound. **les oreilles me cornent** my ears are ringing.

corner² [kɔʀnɛʀ] **nm** (*Ftbl*) corner (kick). **tirer un ~** to take a corner (kick).

cornet [kɔʀnɛ] 1 **nm** a (*récipient*) **~ (de papier)** paper cone; **~ de dragées/de frites** cornet *ou* paper cone of sweets/chips, ≈ bag of sweets/chips; **~ de glace** ice-cream cone *ou* cornet (*Brit*); **mettre sa main en ~** to cup one's hand to one's ear. b (*Suisse: sachet*) (paper *ou* plastic) bag. c (*Mus*) *[orgue]* cornet stop. 2 **comp** ►**cornet acoustique** ear trumpet ►**cornet à dés** dice cup ►**cornets du nez** (*Anat*) turbinate bones ►**cornet (à pistons)** (*Mus*) cornet ►**cornet de poste *ou* de postillon** posthorn.

cornette [kɔʀnɛt] **nf** *[religieuse]* cornet; (*Naut: pavillon*) burgee.

cornettiste [kɔʀnetist] **nmf** cornet player.

corniaud [kɔʀnjo] **nm** (*chien*) mongrel; (*‡: imbécile*) nitwit*, nincompoop*, twit* (*Brit*).

corniche¹ [kɔʀniʃ] **nf** a (*Archit*) cornice. b (*Alpinisme*) ledge. **(route en) ~** coast road, cliff road. c (*neigeuse*) cornice.

corniche² [kɔʀniʃ] **nf** (*arg Scol*) *class preparing for the school of Saint-Cyr*.

cornichon [kɔʀniʃɔ̃] **nm** (*concombre*) gherkin; (**: personne*) nitwit*, greenhorn, nincompoop*; (*arg Scol*) *pupil in the class preparing for Saint-Cyr*.

cornière [kɔʀnjɛʀ] **nf** (*pièce métallique*) corner iron; (*d'écoulement*) valley.

cornique [kɔʀnik] 1 **adj** (*rare*) Cornish. 2 **nm** (*Ling*) Cornish.

corniste [kɔʀnist] **nmf** horn player.

Cornouailles [kɔʀnwaj] **nf** Cornwall.

cornouiller [kɔʀnuje] **nm** dogwood.

cornu, e [kɔʀny] 1 **adj** *animal, démon* horned. 2 **cornue nf** (*récipient*) retort; (*Tech: four*) retort.

corollaire [kɔʀɔlɛʀ] **nm** (*Logique, Math*) corollary; (*gén: conséquence*) consequence, corollary. **et ceci a pour ~ ...** and this has as a consequence ..., and the corollary of this is ... .

corolle [kɔʀɔl] nf corolla.

coron [kɔʀɔ̃] nm (*maison*) mining cottage; (*quartier*) mining village.

coronaire [kɔʀɔnɛʀ] adj (*Anat*) coronary.

corossol [kɔʀɔsɔl] nm soursop.

corporatif, -ive [kɔʀpɔʀatif, iv] adj *mouvement, système* corporative; *esprit* corporate.

corporation [kɔʀpɔʀasjɔ̃] nf *[notaires, médecins]* corporate body; (*Hist*) guild. **dans notre ~** in our profession.

corporatisme [kɔʀpɔʀatism] nm corporatism.

corporatiste [kɔʀpɔʀatist] adj corporatist.

corporel, -elle [kɔʀpɔʀɛl] adj *châtiment* corporal; *besoin* bodily. (*Jur*) **bien ~** corporeal property; **art ~** body art.

corps [kɔʀ] 1 nm a (*Anat*) body; (*cadavre*) corpse, (dead) body. **frissonner** *ou* **trembler de tout son ~** to tremble all over; **jusqu'au milieu du ~** up to the waist; **je n'ai rien dans le ~** I've eaten nothing; **robe près du ~** close-fitting dress; *voir* **contrainte**[2], **diable** *etc.*

b (*Chim, Phys: objet, substance*) body. **~ simples/composés** simple/compound bodies; *voir* **chute**.

c (*partie essentielle*) body; *[bâtiment, lettre, article, ouvrage]* (main) body; *[meuble]* main part, body; *[pompe]* barrel; (*Typ*) body.

d *[vêtement]* body, bodice; *[armure]* cors(e)let.

e (*consistance*) *[étoffe, papier, vin]* body. **ce vin a du ~** this wine is full-bodied *ou* has (got) body.

f (*groupe de personnes*) body, corps; (*Mil*) corps. **~ de sapeurs-pompiers** fire brigade; *voir* **esprit**.

g (*recueil de textes*) corpus, body. **~ de doctrines** body of doctrines.

h (*loc*) **se donner ~ et âme à qch** to give o.s. heart and soul to sth; **perdu ~ et biens** lost with all hands; **s'élancer** *ou* **se jeter à ~ perdu dans une entreprise** to throw o.s. headlong into an undertaking; **donner ~ à qch** to give substance to sth; **faire ~** *[idées]* to form one body (*avec* with); *[choses concrètes]* to be joined (*avec* to); **prendre ~** to take shape; **s'ils veulent faire cela, il faudra qu'ils me passent sur le ~** if they want to do that, they'll have to do it over my dead body; **pour avoir ce qu'il veut, il vous passerait sur le ~** he'd trample you underfoot to get his own way; **faire qch à son ~ défendant** to do sth against one's will *ou* unwillingly; **mais qu'est-ce qu'il a dans le ~?** whatever's got into him?; **j'aimerais bien savoir ce qu'il a dans le ~** I'd like to know what makes him tick; *[aliment]* **tenir au ~** to be filling.

2 comp ▸**corps d'armée** army corps ▸**corps de ballet** corps de ballet ▸**corps de bâtiment** main body (of a building) ▸**corps caverneux** erectile tissue (of the penis) ▸**corps céleste** celestial *ou* heavenly body ▸**corps constitués** constituent bodies ▸**corps consulaire** consular corps ▸**corps à corps** adv hand-to-hand ◊ nm clinch; **se battre au corps à corps** to fight hand-to-hand ▸**corps du délit** (*Jur*) corpus delicti ▸**corps diplomatique** diplomatic corps ▸**corps électoral** electorate ▸**le corps enseignant** (*gén*) the teaching profession, teachers; *[lycée, collège]* the teaching staff ▸**corps étranger** (*Méd*) foreign body ▸**corps expéditionnaire** task force ▸**corps franc** irregular force ▸**corps de garde** (*Mil*) (*local*) guard-room; (*rare: troupe*) guard; (*péj*) **plaisanteries de corps de garde** barrack-room *ou* guardroom jokes ▸**corps gras** greasy substance, glyceride (*SPÉC*) ▸**corps jaune** (*Physiol*) yellow body, corpus luteum (*SPÉC*) ▸**corps législatif** legislative body ▸**corps de logis** main building, central building ▸**le corps médical** the medical profession ▸**corps de métier** trade association, guild ▸**corps mort** (*Naut*) mooring; (*poids mort*) dead weight ▸**corps noir** (*Phys*) black body ▸**corps politique** body politic ▸**corps de troupe** unit (of troops) ▸**corps vitré** (*Anat*) vitreous body.

corpulence [kɔʀpylɑ̃s] nf stoutness, corpulence. **(être) de forte/moyenne ~** (to be) of stout/medium build.

corpulent, e [kɔʀpylɑ̃, ɑ̃t] adj stout, corpulent.

corpus [kɔʀpys] nm (*Jur: recueil, Ling*) corpus.

corpusculaire [kɔʀpyskylɛʀ] adj (*Anat, Phys*) corpuscular.

corpuscule [kɔʀpyskyl] nm (*Anat, Phys*) corpuscle.

correct, e [kɔʀɛkt] adj a (*exact*) *plan, copie* accurate; *phrase* correct, right; *emploi, fonctionnement* proper, correct. (*en réponse*) **~!** correct!, right! b (*convenable*) *tenue* proper, correct; *conduite, personne* correct. **il est ~ en affaires** he's very correct in business matters. c (**: acceptable*) *repas, hôtel, salaire* reasonable, decent.

correctement [kɔʀɛktəmɑ̃] adv (*voir* **correct**) accurately; correctly; properly; reasonably, decently.

correcteur, -trice [kɔʀɛktœʀ, tʀis] 1 adj *dispositif* corrective; *voir* **verre**. 2 nm,f *[examen]* examiner, marker (*Brit*), grader (*US*); (*Typ*) proofreader. 3 nm (*Tech: dispositif*) corrector. **~ de tonalité** tone control; (*Ordin*) **~ d'orthographe** *ou* **orthographique** spellchecker; **~ liquide** correcting fluid.

correctif, -ive [kɔʀɛktif, iv] 1 adj *gymnastique,* (*Pharm*) *substance* corrective. 2 nm (*lit, fig: médicament*) corrective (*à* to); (*mise au point*) qualifying statement. **apporter un ~ à qch** (*corriger*) to rectify *ou* correct an error in sth; (*ajouter une précision*) to qualify sth.

correction [kɔʀɛksjɔ̃] nf a (*NonC*) *[erreur, abus]* correction, putting right; *[manuscrit]* correction, emendation; *[mauvaise habitude]* correction; *[épreuves]* correction, (proof)reading; *[compas]* correction; *[trajectoire]* correction; *[examen]* correcting, marking, correction, grading (*US*); (*Ordin*) *[programme]* patching; *[mise au point]* debugging. **apporter une ~ aux propos de qn** to amend what sb has said; **j'ai fait la ~ du devoir avec les élèves** I went through the pupils' homework with them; *voir* **maison**.

b (*châtiment*) (corporal) punishment, thrashing. **recevoir une bonne ~** to get a good hiding *ou* thrashing.

c (*surcharge, rature*) correction. (*Typ*) **~s d'auteur** author's corrections *ou* emendations.

d (*NonC; voir* **correct**) accuracy; correctness; propriety.

correctionnel, -elle [kɔʀɛksjɔnɛl] 1 adj (*Jur*) **peine ~le** penalty (*imposed by courts*); **tribunal (de police) ~** ≃ magistrate's court (*dealing with criminal matters*). 2 **correctionnelle** nf ≃ magistrate's court. **passer en ~le** to go before the magistrate.

Corrège [kɔʀɛʒ] n: **le ~** Correggio.

corrélatif, -ive [kɔʀelatif, iv] adj, nm correlative.

corrélation [kɔʀelasjɔ̃] nf correlation. **être en ~ étroite avec** to be closely related to *ou* connected with, be in close correlation with; **mettre en ~** to correlate.

corréler [kɔʀele] 6 vt to correlate.

correspondance [kɔʀɛspɔ̃dɑ̃s] nf a (*conformité*) correspondence, conformity; (*Archit: symétrie*) balance. **~ de goûts/d'idées entre 2 personnes** conformity of 2 people's tastes/ideas; **être en parfaite ~ d'idées avec X** to have ideas that correspond perfectly to X's *ou* that are perfectly in tune with X's.

b (*Math*) relation. **~ biunivoque** one-to-one mapping, bijection.

c (*échange de lettres*) correspondence. **avoir** *ou* **entretenir une longue ~ avec qn** to engage in *ou* keep up a lengthy correspondence with sb; **être en ~ commerciale avec qn** to have a business correspondence with sb; **nous avons été en ~** we have corresponded, we have been in correspondence; **être en ~ téléphonique avec qn** to be in touch by telephone with sb; **par ~** *cours* correspondence (*épith*); **il a appris le latin par ~** he learned Latin by *ou* through a correspondence course.

d (*ensemble de lettres*) mail, post (*Brit*), correspondence; (*Littérat*) *[auteur]* correspondence; (*Presse*) letters to the Editor. **il reçoit une volumineuse ~** he receives large quantities of mail *ou* a heavy post (*Brit*); **dépouiller/lire sa ~** to go through/read one's mail *ou* one's correspondence.

e (*transports*) connection. **~ ferroviaire/d'autobus** rail/bus connection; **attendre la ~** to wait for the connection; **l'autobus n'assure pas la ~ avec le train** the bus does not connect with the train.

correspondancier, -ière [kɔʀɛspɔ̃dɑ̃sje, jɛʀ] nm,f correspondence clerk.

correspondant, e [kɔʀɛspɔ̃dɑ̃, ɑ̃t] 1 adj (*gén: qui va avec, par paires*) corresponding; (*Géom*) *angles* corresponding. **ci-joint un chèque ~ à la facture** enclosed a cheque in respect of (*Brit*) *ou* in the amount of the invoice.

2 nm,f a (*gén, Presse*) correspondent; (*Scol*) penfriend, correspondent; (*banque*) correspondent bank; (*Téléc*) (*appelé*) person one is calling; (*appelant*) caller. **~ de guerre** war correspondent; **(membre) ~ de l'institut** corresponding member of the institute; (*Téléc*) **le numéro de votre ~ a changé** the number you dialled has been changed; (*Téléc*) **nous recherchons votre ~** we are trying to connect you *ou* to put you through.

b (*Scol: responsable d'un interne*) guardian (*for child at boarding school*).

correspondre [kɔʀɛspɔ̃dʀ] 41 1 **correspondre à** vt indir a (*s'accorder avec*) *goûts* to suit; *capacités* to fit; *description* to correspond to, fit. **sa version des faits ne correspond pas à la réalité** his version of the facts doesn't square *ou* tally with what happened in reality.

b (*être l'équivalent de*) *système, institutions, élément symétrique* to correspond to. **le yard correspond au mètre** the yard corresponds to the metre.

2 vi a (*écrire*) to correspond (*avec* with).

b (*communiquer*) *[mers]* to be linked; *[chambres]* to communicate (*avec* with).

c (*Transport*) **~ avec** to connect with.

3 **se correspondre** vpr *[chambres]* to communicate (with one another); *[éléments d'une symétrie]* to correspond.

corrida [kɔʀida] nf bullfight; (** fig: désordre*) carry-on* (*Brit*), to-do*. (*fig*) **ça va être la (vraie) ~!*** all hell will break loose*, there'll be a great carry-on*. (*Brit*).

corridor [kɔʀidɔʀ] nm corridor, passage. (*Géog, Hist*) **le ~ polonais** the Polish Corridor.

corrigé [kɔʀiʒe] nm (*Scol*) *[exercice]* correct version; *[traduction]* fair copy. **~s** (*en fin de manuel*) key to exercises; (*livre du professeur*) answer book; *[examens]* past papers.

corriger [kɔʀiʒe] 3 1 vt a (*repérer les erreurs de*) *manuscrit* to correct, emend; (*Typ*) *épreuves* to correct, (proof)read; (*Scol*) *examen, dictée* (*repérer les erreurs de*) to correct; (*en notant*) to mark.

b (*rectifier*) *erreur, défaut* to correct, put right; *théorie, jugement* to put right; *abus* to remedy, put right; *manières* to improve; (*Naut*) *compas* to correct, adjust; (*Aviat, Mil*) *trajectoire* to correct; (*Méd*) *vue, vision* to correct. ~ **ses actions** to mend one's ways; (*frm*) ~ **une remontrance par un sourire** to soften a remonstrance with a smile; (*frm*) ~ **l'injustice du sort** to mitigate the injustice of fate, soften the blows of unjust Fate (*littér*); (*fig*) **corrigé des variations saisonnières** seasonally adjusted; *voir* **tir**.

c (*guérir*) ~ **qn de** *défaut* to cure *ou* rid sb of; **tu ne le corrigeras pas à son âge** it's too late to make him change his ways now, he is a lost cause.

d (*punir*) to thrash.

2 **se corriger** vpr (*devenir raisonnable*) to mend one's ways. **se** ~ **de** *défaut* to cure *ou* rid o.s. of.

corrigible [kɔʀiʒibl] adj rectifiable, which can be put right.

corroboration [kɔʀɔbɔʀasjɔ̃] nf corroboration.

corroborer [kɔʀɔbɔʀe] 1 vt to corroborate.

corrodant, e [kɔʀɔdɑ̃, ɑ̃t] adj, nm corrosive.

corroder [kɔʀɔde] 1 vt to corrode, eat into; (*fig littér*) to erode.

corrompre [kɔʀɔ̃pʀ] 4 1 vt a (*soudoyer*) *témoin, fonctionnaire* to bribe, corrupt. b (*frm: altérer*) *mœurs, jugement, jeunesse, texte* to corrupt; *langage* to debase. **mots corrompus par l'usage** words corrupted *ou* debased by usage. c *air, eau, aliments* to taint; (*Méd*) *sang* to contaminate. 2 **se corrompre** vpr *[mœurs, jeunesse]* to become corrupt; *[goût]* to become debased; *[aliments etc]* to go off (*Brit*), go bad, become tainted.

corrompu, e [kɔʀɔ̃py] (ptp de **corrompre**) adj corrupt.

corrosif, -ive [kɔʀozif, iv] 1 adj *acide, substance* corrosive; (*fig*) *ironie, œuvre, écrivain* caustic, scathing. 2 nm corrosive.

corrosion [kɔʀozjɔ̃] nf (*lit*) *[métaux]* corrosion; *[rochers]* erosion; (*fig*) *[volonté etc]* erosion.

corroyage [kɔʀwajaʒ] nm *[cuir]* currying; *[métal]* welding.

corroyer [kɔʀwaje] 8 vt *cuir* to curry; *métal* to weld; *bois* to trim.

corroyeur [kɔʀwajœʀ] nm currier.

corrupteur, -trice [kɔʀyptœʀ, tʀis] 1 adj (*littér*) *spectacle, journal* corrupting. 2 nm,f (*soudoyeur*) briber; (*littér: dépravateur*) corrupter.

corruptible [kɔʀyptibl] adj (*littér*) *juges etc* corruptible; (†) *matière* perishable.

corruption [kɔʀypsjɔ̃] nf a *[juge, témoin]* bribery, corruption. ~ **de fonctionnaire** bribery of a public official. b (*dépravation: voir* **corrompre**) (*action*) corruption; debasing; (*résultat*) corruption; debasement. c (*décomposition*) *[aliments etc]* decomposition; *[sang]* contamination.

corsage [kɔʀsaʒ] nm (*chemisier*) blouse; *[robe]* bodice.

corsaire [kɔʀsɛʀ] nm a (*Hist: marin, navire*) privateer. b (*pirate*) pirate, corsair. c **(pantalon)** ~ breeches.

Corse [kɔʀs] nf Corsica.

corse [kɔʀs] 1 adj Corsican. 2 nm (*Ling*) Corsican. 3 nmf: **C**~ Corsican.

corsé, e [kɔʀse] (ptp de **corser**) adj a *vin* full-bodied; *café* (*parfumé*) full-flavoured; (*trop fort*) too strong; *mets, sauce* spicy. b (*scabreux*) *histoire* spicy. c (*: *intensif*) *addition* high, steep* (*attrib*); *exercice, problème* tough. **une intrigue** ~**e** a really lively intrigue.

corselet [kɔʀsəlɛ] nm a (*cuirasse*) cors(e)let; (*vêtement*) corselet. b (*Zool*) corselet.

corser [kɔʀse] 1 vt a *repas* to make spicier, pep up*; *vin* to strengthen; *boisson* to spike; *assaisonnement* to pep up*. b *difficulté* to intensify, aggravate; *histoire, intrigue, récit* to liven up. **l'histoire** *ou* **l'affaire se corse** the plot thickens! (*hum*); **le premier exercice est facile mais après ça se corse** the first exercise is easy but then it gets much tougher; **les choses ont commencé à se** ~ **quand il a voulu discuter le prix** things started to hot up* *ou* get lively* when he tried to haggle.

corset [kɔʀsɛ] nm (*sous-vêtement*) corset; (*pièce de costume*) bodice. ~ **orthopédique** *ou* **médical** surgical corset.

corseter [kɔʀsəte] 5 vt (*lit*) to corset; (*fig: enserrer*) to constrain, constrict.

corsetier, -ière [kɔʀsətje, jɛʀ] nm,f corset-maker.

corso [kɔʀso] nm: ~ **(fleuri)** procession of floral floats.

cortège [kɔʀtɛʒ] nm *[fête, célébration]* procession; *[prince etc]* cortège, retinue. ~ **nuptial** bridal procession; ~ **funèbre** funeral procession *ou* cortège; ~ **de manifestants/grévistes** procession of demonstrators/strikers; (*fig littér*) ~ **de malheurs/faillites** trail of misfortunes/bankruptcies; ~ **de visions/souvenirs** succession of visions/memories; **la faillite et son** ~ **de licenciements** bankruptcy and the accompanying redundancies.

cortex [kɔʀtɛks] nm cortex.

cortical, e, mpl **-aux** [kɔʀtikal, o] adj (*Anat, Bot*) cortical.

corticoïde [kɔʀtikɔid] nm (*Anat*) corticoid.

corticosurrénale [kɔʀtikɔsyʀenal] nf adrenal cortex.

cortisone [kɔʀtizɔn] nf cortisone.

corvéable [kɔʀveabl] adj (*Hist*) liable to the corvée; *voir* **taillable**.

corvée [kɔʀve] nf a (*Mil*) (*travail*) fatigue (duty); (*rare: soldats*) fatigue party. **être de** ~ to be on fatigue (duty); ~ **de vaisselle** (*Mil*) cookhouse fatigue; (*hum*) dishwashing duty; ~ **de ravitaillement** supply duty; ~ **de pommes de terre** *ou* **de patates*** spud-bashing (*arg Mil*) (*NonC*); **être de** ~ **de pommes de terre** *ou* **de patates*** to be on spud duty*. b (*toute tâche pénible*) chore, drudgery (*NonC*). **quelle** ~! what drudgery!, what an awful chore! c (*Hist*) corvée (*statute labour*). d (*Can*) voluntary work, bee* (*US, Can*).

corvette [kɔʀvɛt] nf corvette; *voir* **capitaine**.

coryphée [kɔʀife] nm (*Théât*) coryphaeus.

coryza [kɔʀiza] nm (*Méd*) coryza (*SPÉC*), cold in the head.

COS [kɔs] nm (abrév de **coefficient d'occupation des sols**) *voir* **coefficient**.

cosaque [kɔzak] nm cossack.

cosécante [kosekɑ̃t] nf cosecant.

cosignataire [kosiɲatɛʀ] adj, nmf cosignatory.

cosigner [kosiɲe] 1 vt *document [une personne]* to be a joint signatory to (*frm*); *[deux personnes]* to be joint signatories to (*frm*), sign jointly. **un document cosigné par X et Y** a document signed jointly by X and Y.

cosinus [kɔsinys] nm cosine.

cosmétique [kɔsmetik] adj, nm cosmetic.

cosmétologie [kɔsmetɔlɔʒi] nf beauty care.

cosmétologue [kɔsmetɔlɔg] nmf cosmetics expert.

cosmique [kɔsmik] adj cosmic; *voir* **rayon**.

cosmogonie [kɔsmɔgɔni] nf cosmogony.

cosmographie [kɔsmɔgʀafi] nf cosmography.

cosmographique [kɔsmɔgʀafik] adj cosmographic.

cosmologie [kɔsmɔlɔʒi] nf cosmology.

cosmonaute [kɔsmɔnot] nmf cosmonaut.

cosmopolite [kɔsmɔpɔlit] adj cosmopolitan.

cosmopolitisme [kɔsmɔpɔlitism] nm cosmopolitanism.

cosmos [kɔsmos] nm (*univers*) cosmos; (*Aviat: espace*) (outer) space.

cossard, e* [kɔsaʀ, aʀd] 1 adj lazy. 2 nm,f lazybones.

cosse [kɔs] nf a *[pois, haricots]* pod, hull. b (*Élec*) terminal spade tag. (*Aut*) ~ **de batterie** battery lead connection. c (*: *flemme*) lazy mood. **avoir la** ~ to feel as lazy as anything, be in a lazy mood.

cossu, e [kɔsy] adj *personne* well-off, well-to-do; *maison* rich-looking, opulent(-looking).

costal, e, mpl **-aux** [kɔstal, o] adj (*Anat*) costal.

costar(d)‡ [kɔstaʀ] nm suit.

Costa Rica [kɔstaʀika] nm Costa Rica.

costaricien, -ienne [kɔstaʀisjɛ̃, jɛn] 1 adj Costarican. 2 nm,f: **C**~**(ne)** Costarican.

costaud, e* [kɔsto, od] 1 adj (*gén*) strong, sturdy; *vin* strong. **une voiture** ~ *ou* ~**e** a sturdy car. 2 nm a (*homme*) strong *ou* sturdy *ou* strapping man. b **c'est du** ~ *[alcool, tissu]* it's strong stuff; *[maison]* it's strongly built. 3 **costaude** nf strong *ou* sturdy *ou* strapping woman.

costume [kɔstym] 1 nm a (*régional, traditionnel etc*) costume, dress. ~ **national** national costume *ou* dress; (*hum*) **en** ~ **d'Adam/d'Ève** in his/her birthday suit (*hum*). b (*Ciné, Théât*) costume. c (*complet*) suit. ~ **deux/trois pièces** two-piece/three-piece suit. 2 comp ▸**costume de bain** bathing costume (*Brit*) *ou* suit ▸**costume de cérémonie** ceremonial dress (*NonC*) ▸**costume de chasse** hunting gear (*NonC*).

costumer [kɔstyme] 1 1 vt: ~ **qn en Indien** *etc* to dress sb up as a Red Indian *etc*. 2 **se costumer** vpr (*porter un déguisement*) to put on fancy dress; *[acteur]* to get into costume. **se** ~ **en Indien** *etc* to dress up as a Red Indian *etc*; *voir* **bal**.

costumier [kɔstymje] nm (*fabricant, loueur*) costumier, costumer; (*Théât: employé*) wardrobe master.

costumière [kɔstymjɛʀ] nf (*Théât*) wardrobe mistress.

cosy(-corner), pl **cosys** *ou* **cosy-corners** [kozi(kɔʀnœʀ)] nm corner divan (with shelves attached).

cotangente [kotɑ̃ʒɑ̃t] nf cotangent.

cotation [kɔtasjɔ̃] nf *[valeur boursière]* quotation; *[timbre, voiture]* valuation; *[devoir scolaire]* marking (*Brit*), grading (*US*). **la** ~ **en Bourse de sa société** *ou* **des actions de sa société** the quoting of his firm *ou* his firm's shares on the stock exchange.

cote [kɔt] 1 nf a (*fixation du prix*) *[valeur boursière]* quotation; *[timbre, voiture d'occasion]* quoted value. (*Bourse: liste*) **consulter la** ~ to look at the share prices; **inscrit à la** ~ quoted (*Brit*) *ou* listed (*US*) on the stock exchange list; *voir* **hors**.

b (*évaluation*) *[devoir scolaire]* mark; (*Courses*) *[cheval]* odds (*de* on). *[film]* ~ **(morale)** rating; **la** ~ **de Lucifer est de 7 contre 1** the odds on Lucifer are 7 to 1.

c (*popularité*) rating, standing. **avoir une bonne** *ou* **grosse** ~ to be (very) highly thought of, be highly rated (*auprès de* by), have a high standing (*auprès de* with); **avoir la** ~* to be very popular (*auprès de* with), be very well thought of *ou* highly rated (*auprès de* by); **sa** ~ **(de popularité) est en baisse** his popularity is on the decline *ou* wane.

d (*sur une carte: altitude*) spot height; (*sur un croquis: dimension*) dimensions. **il y a une** ~ **qui est effacée** one of the dimensions has got rubbed out; **l'ennemi a atteint la** ~ **215** the enemy reached hill 215; **les explorateurs ont atteint la** ~ **4.550/-190** the explorers reached the 4,550-metre mark above sea level/190-metre mark below ground.

e (*marque de classement*) (*gén*) classification mark, serial number *ou* mark; *[livre de bibliothèque]* class(ification) mark (*Brit*) *ou* number (*US*), shelf mark, pressmark (*Brit*).

f (*part*) (*Fin*) ~ **mobilière/foncière** property/land assessment; *voir* **quote-part**.

2 comp ▸**cote d'alerte** (*lit*) *[rivière]* danger mark *ou* level, flood level; (*fig*) *[prix]* danger mark; (*fig*) *[situation]* crisis point ▸**cote d'amour: ce politicien a la cote d'amour** this politician has the highest popularity rating *ou* stands highest in the public's affection ▸**cote mal taillée** (*fig*) rough-and-ready settlement.

côte [kot] nf a (*Anat*) rib. (*Anat*) **~s flottantes** floating ribs; (*Anat*) **vraie/fausse ~** true/false rib; **on peut lui compter les ~s, on lui voit les ~s** he's all skin and bone; (*fig*) **avoir les ~s en long** to feel stiff; (*fig*) **se tenir les ~s (de rire)** to split one's sides (with laughter); **~ à ~** side by side; *voir* **caresser**.

b (*Boucherie*) *[bœuf]* rib; *[veau, agneau, mouton, porc]* chop. **~ première** loin chop; *voir* **faux**[2].

c (*nervure*) *[chou, tricot, coupole]* rib. **veste à ~s** ribbed jacket.

d (*pente*) *[colline]* slope, hillside; (*Aut*) *[route]* hill. **il a dû s'arrêter dans la ~** he had to stop on the hill; **ne pas dépasser au sommet d'une ~** do not overtake on the brow of a hill (*Brit*) *ou* on an uphill slope (*US*); (*Aut*) **en ~** on a hill; *voir* **course, démarrage**.

e (*littoral*) coast; (*ligne du littoral*) coastline. **les ~s de France** the French coast(s) *ou* coastline; **la C~ (d'Azur)** the (French) Riviera; **la ~ d'Émeraude** the northern coast of Brittany; **la C~-d'Ivoire** the Ivory Coast; **la ~-de-l'Or** (†) the Gold Coast; **~ rocheuse/découpée/basse** rocky/indented/low coastline; **sur la ~ *ou* les ~s, il fait plus frais** it is cooler along *ou* on *ou* at the coast; **la route qui longe la ~** the coast road; (*Naut*) **aller à la ~** to run ashore; (*fig*) **être à la ~**† to be down to *ou* have hit rock-bottom, be on one's beam-ends.

coté, e [kɔte] (ptp de **coter**) adj: **être bien ~** to be highly thought of *ou* rated *ou* considered; **être mal ~** not to be thought much of, not to be highly thought of *ou* rated *ou* considered; **historien (très) ~** historian who is (very) highly thought of *ou* rated *ou* considered, historian who is held in high esteem; **vin (très) ~** highly-rated wine.

côté [kote] 1 nm a (*partie du corps*) side. **être blessé au ~** to be wounded in the side; **l'épée au ~** (with) his sword by his side; **être couché sur le ~** to be lying on one's side; **à son ~** at his side, beside him; **aux ~s de** by the side of; *voir* **point**[1].

b (*face, partie latérale*) *[objet, route, feuille]* side. **de chaque ~ *ou* des deux ~s de la cheminée** on each side *ou* on both sides of the fireplace; **il a sauté de l'autre ~ du mur/du ruisseau** he jumped over the wall/across the stream; **le bruit vient de l'autre ~ de la rivière/de la pièce** the sound comes from across *ou* over the river *ou* from the other side of the river/from the other side of the room; **de l'autre ~ de la forêt il y a des prés** on the other side of the forest *ou* beyond the forest there are meadows; (*fig*) **de l'autre ~ de la barricade *ou* de la barrière** on the other side of the fence; (*Sport*) **le ~ fermé, le petit ~** the inside; (*Sport*) **le ~ ouvert, le grand ~** the outside; (*Naut*) **un navire sur le ~** a ship on her beam-ends.

c (*aspect*) side, point. **le ~ pratique/théorique** the practical/theoretical side; **les bons et les mauvais ~s de qn/de qch** the good and bad sides *ou* points of sb/sth; **il a un ~ sympathique** there's a likeable side to him; **son attitude/ce film a un ~ pervers** there's something perverse about his attitude/this film; **prendre qch du bon/mauvais ~** to take sth well/badly; **prendre qn par son ~ faible** to attack sb's weak spot; **par certains ~s** in some respects *ou* ways; **de ce ~(-là)** in that respect; **d'un ~ ... d'un autre ~ ...** (*alternative*) on (the) one hand ... on the other hand ...; (*hésitation*) in one respect *ou* way ... in another respect *ou* way ...; **(du) ~ santé tout va bien*** healthwise* *ou* as far as health is concerned everything is fine.

d (*parti, branche familiale*) side. **se ranger *ou* se mettre du ~ du plus fort** to side with the strongest; **du ~ paternel** on his father's side.

e (*précédé de "de": direction*) way, direction, side. **de ce ~-ci/-là** this/that way; **de l'autre ~** the other way, in the other direction; **nous habitons du ~ de la poste** we live in the direction of the post office; **le vent vient du ~ de la mer/du ~ opposé** the wind is blowing from the sea/from the opposite direction; **ils se dirigeaient du ~ des prés/du ~ opposé** they were heading towards the meadows/in the opposite direction; **venir de tous ~s** to come from all directions; **assiégé de tous ~s** besieged on *ou* from all sides; **chercher qn de tous ~s** to look for sb everywhere *ou* all over the place, search high and low for sb; (*fig*) **je l'ai entendu dire de divers ~s** I've heard it from several quarters *ou* sources; **de ~ et d'autre** here and there; (*fig*) **de mon ~, je ferai tout pour l'aider** for my part, I'll do everything I can to help him; **renseigne-toi de ton ~, je me renseignerai du mien** you find out what you can and I'll do the same; (*fig*) **voir de quel ~ vient le vent** to see which way the wind is blowing; **~ du vent** windward side; **~ sous le vent** leeward side; **ils ne sont pas partis du bon ~** they didn't go the right way *ou* in the right direction.

f (*Théât*) **~ cour** prompt side (*Brit*), stage left; **~ jardin** opposite prompt side (*Brit*), stage right; **un salon ~ jardin/~ rue** a room overlooking the garden/overlooking the street.

2 **à côté** adv a (*proximité*) nearby; (*pièce ou maison adjacente*) next door. **la maison/les gens (d')à ~** the house/the people next door; **nos voisins d'à ~** our next-door neighbours; **à ~ de** next to, beside; **l'hôtel est (tout) à ~** the hotel is just close by.

b (*en dehors du but*) **ils ont mal visé, les bombes sont tombées à ~** their aim was bad and the bombs went astray *ou* fell wide; **à ~ de la cible** off target, wide of the target; (*fig*) **il a répondu à ~ de la question** (*sans le faire exprès*) his answer was off the point; (*intentionnellement*) he avoided the question; **on passe à ~ de beaucoup de choses en ne voyageant pas** you miss a lot by not travelling; **être à ~ de la plaque**⁑ to misjudge things, be wide of the mark, have got it all wrong*.

c (*en comparaison*) by comparison. **à ~ de** compared to, by comparison with, beside; **leur maison est grande à ~ de la nôtre** their house is big compared to ours; **il est paresseux, à ~ de ça il aime son travail*** he is lazy, but on the other hand he does like his work.

3 **de côté** adv a (*de travers*) *marcher, regarder, se tourner* sideways. **un regard de ~** a sidelong look; **porter son chapeau de ~** to wear one's hat (tilted) to *ou* on one side.

b (*en réserve*) *mettre, garder* aside. **mettre de l'argent de ~** to put money by *ou* aside.

c (*à l'écart*) **se jeter de ~** to leap aside *ou* to the *ou* one side; **laisser qn/qch de ~** to leave sb/sth aside *ou* to one side *ou* out.

coteau, pl ~x [kɔto] nm (*colline*) hill; (*versant*) slope, hillside; *voir* **flanc**.

côtelé, e [kot(ə)le] adj ribbed; *voir* **velours**.

côtelette [kotlɛt] nf a (*Culin*) *[porc, agneau, mouton, veau]* cutlet. b (*favoris*) **~s***† mutton chops.

coter [kɔte] 1 vt a *valeur boursière* to quote; *timbre-poste, voiture d'occasion* to quote the market price of; *cheval* to put odds on; (*Scol*) *devoir* to mark; *film, roman* to rate. **coté en Bourse** quoted on the stock exchange; **voiture trop vieille pour être cotée à l'Argus** car which is too old to be listed (*in the secondhand car book*) *ou* in the Blue Book (*US*).

b *carte* to put spot heights on; *croquis* to mark in the dimensions on.

c *pièce de dossier* to put a classification mark *ou* serial number *ou* serial mark on; *livre de bibliothèque* to put a class(ification) mark (*Brit*) *ou* number (*US*) *ou* shelf-mark *ou* pressmark (*Brit*) on.

2 vi (*Bourse*) **valeur qui cote 500 F** share quoted at 500 francs.

coterie [kɔtʀi] nf (*gén péj*) set. **~ littéraire** literary coterie *ou* clique *ou* set.

cothurne [kɔtyʀn] nm buskin.

côtier, -ière [kotje, jɛʀ] adj *pêche* inshore; *navigation, région, fleuve* coastal. **un (bateau) ~** a coaster.

cotillon [kɔtijɔ̃] nm a (*serpentins etc*) **accessoires de ~, ~s** party novelties (*confetti, streamers, paper hats etc*). b (††: *jupon*) petticoat; *voir* **courir**. c (*danse*) cotillion, cotillon.

cotisant, e [kɔtizɑ̃, ɑ̃t] nm,f (*voir* **cotisation**) subscriber; contributor. **seuls les ~s ont ce droit** only those who pay their subscriptions (*ou* dues *ou* contributions) have this right.

cotisation [kɔtizasjɔ̃] nf (*quote-part*) *[club]* subscription; *[syndicat]* subscription, dues; *[sécurité sociale, pension]* contributions. **la ~ est obligatoire** one must pay one's subscription (*ou* dues *ou* contributions).

cotiser [kɔtize] 1 1 vi (*voir* **cotisation**) to subscribe, pay one's subscription; to pay one's contributions (*à* to). 2 **se cotiser** vpr to club together.

côtoiement [kotwamɑ̃] nm a (*voir* **côtoyer**) **ces ~s quotidiens avec les artistes l'avaient rendu plus sensible** this daily mixing *ou* these daily encounters with artists had made him more sensitive; **ces ~s quotidiens avec la mort/l'illégalité l'avaient rendu intrépide** these daily brushes with death/illegality had made him fearless. b (*voir* **se côtoyer**) **le ~ de la farce et du tragique** the meeting *ou* closeness of farce and tragedy.

coton [kɔtɔ̃] 1 nm a (*plante, fil*) cotton. **~ à broder** embroidery thread; **~ à repriser** darning thread *ou* cotton; **~ hydrophile** cotton wool (*Brit*), absorbent cotton (*US*). b (*tampon*) (cotton-wool (*Brit*) *ou* cotton (*US*)) swab. **mets un ~ dans ton nez** put some *ou* a bit of cotton wool (*Brit*) *ou* cotton (*US*) in your nose. c (*loc*) **avoir du ~ dans les oreilles*** to be deaf, have cloth ears* (*Brit*); **j'ai les bras/jambes en ~** my arms/legs feel like jelly *ou* cotton wool (*Brit*); **c'est ~*** it's tricky*; *voir* **élever, filer**. 2 comp ▸**Coton-tige** ® nm (pl **Cotons-tiges**) cotton bud.

cotonnade [kɔtɔnad] nf cotton fabric.

cotonner (se) [kɔtɔne] 1 vpr *[lainage]* to fluff up, lint (*US*).

cotonneux, -euse [kɔtɔnø, øz] adj a *fruit, feuille* downy. b (*fig*) *brouillard* wispy; *nuage* fluffy, fleecy, cotton-wool (*Brit*) (*épith*); *bruit* muffled.

cotonnier, -ière [kɔtɔnje, jɛʀ] 1 adj cotton (*épith*). 2 nm (*Bot*) cotton plant.

côtoyer [kotwaje] 8 1 vt a (*être à côté de*) to be next to; (*fréquenter*) to mix with, rub shoulders with. **~ le danger** to rub shoulders with danger.

b (*longer*) (*en voiture, à pied etc*) to drive (*ou* walk *etc*) along *ou* alongside; *[rivière]* to run *ou* flow alongside; *[route]* to skirt, run along *ou* alongside.

c (*fig: frôler*) *[personne]* to be close to; *[procédé, situation]* to be bordering *ou* verging on. **cela côtoie la malhonnêteté** that is bordering *ou* verging on dishonesty; **il aime à ~ l'illégalité** he likes to do things that verge on illegality *ou* that come close to being illegal.

2 **se côtoyer** vpr *[individus]* to mix, rub shoulders; *[genres, extrêmes]* to meet, come close.

cotre [kɔtʀ] nm (*Naut*) cutter.

cottage [kɔtɛdʒ] nm cottage.

cotte [kɔt] nf a (*Hist*) ~ **de mailles** coat of mail; ~ **d'armes** coat of arms, *surcoat*. b (*salopette*) (pair of) dungarees (*Brit*), overalls; (††: *jupe*) petticoat.

cotutelle [kotytɛl] nf joint guardianship.

cotuteur, -trice [kotytœʀ, tʀis] nm,f joint guardian.

cotylédon [kɔtiledɔ̃] nm (*Anat, Bot*) cotyledon.

cou [ku] 1 nm (*Anat, Couture, de bouteille*) neck. **porter qch au** ~ *ou* **autour du** ~ to wear sth round one's neck; **jusqu'au** ~ (*lit: enlisé*) up to one's neck; (*fig*) **endetté jusqu'au** ~ up to one's eyes in debt, in debt up to the hilt; **être impliqué jusqu'au** ~ **dans un scandale** to be heavily implicated in a scandal; **il est impliqué jusqu'au** ~ he's in it up to his neck*; **sauter** *ou* **se jeter au** ~ **de qn** to throw one's arms around sb's neck, fall on sb's neck; *voir* **bride, casser, taureau** *etc*. 2 comp ►**cou-de-pied** nm (pl **cous-de-pied**) instep.

couac [kwak] nm (*Mus*) *[instrument]* false note, goose note (*Brit*); *[voix]* false note. (*fig*) **il y a eu des ~s pendant les discussions avec les syndicats** there were moments of discord during the talks with the unions.

couard, couarde [kwaʀ, kwaʀd] (*frm*) 1 adj cowardly. **il est trop** ~ **pour cela** he's too cowardly *ou* too much of a coward for that. 2 nm,f coward.

couardise [kwaʀdiz] nf (*frm*) cowardice.

couchage [kuʃaʒ] nm a (*lit*) bed. (*installation pour la nuit*) **il faudra organiser le** ~ **en route** we'll have to organize our sleeping arrangements on the way; **matériel de** ~ sleeping equipment, bedding; **pour** ~ **90/135** for mattress size 90/135 cm; *voir* **sac**[1]. b (*péj: gén pl*) = **coucherie**.

couchant [kuʃɑ̃] 1 adj: **soleil** ~ setting sun; **au soleil** ~ at sundown (*US*) *ou* sunset; *voir* **chien**. 2 nm (*ouest*) west; (*aspect du ciel, à l'ouest*) sunset.

couche [kuʃ] nf a (*épaisseur*) *[peinture]* coat; *[beurre, fard, bois, neige]* layer; (*Culin*) layer. **ils avaient une** ~ **épaisse de crasse** they were thickly covered in *ou* coated with dirt, they were covered in a thick layer of dirt; (*fig*) **en tenir** *ou* **avoir une** ~* to be really thick* (*Brit*) *ou* dumb*.

b (*Horticulture*) hotbed; *voir* **champignon**.

c (*zone superposée*) layer, stratum; (*catégories sociales*) level, stratum. **la** ~ **d'ozone** the ozone layer; **~s de l'atmosphère** layers *ou* strata of the atmosphere; (*Bot*) **~s ligneuses** woody *ou* ligneous layers; **dans toutes les ~s de la société** at all levels of society, in every social stratum.

d *[bébé]* nappy (*Brit*), diaper (*US*). **~-culotte** disposable nappy (*Brit*) *ou* diaper (*US*).

e (*Méd: accouchement*) **~s** confinement; **mourir en ~s** to die in childbirth; **une femme en ~s** a woman in labour; **elle a eu des ~s pénibles** she had a difficult confinement *ou* labour; *voir* **faux**[2], **retour**.

f (*littér: lit*) bed. **une** ~ **de feuillage** a bed of leaves.

couche- [kuʃ] préf *voir* **coucher**.

couché, e [kuʃe] (ptp de **coucher**) adj a (*étendu*) lying (down); (*au lit*) in bed. **Rex,** ~**!** lie down, Rex! b (*penché*) *écriture* sloping, slanting. c *voir* **papier**.

coucher [kuʃe] [1] 1 vt a (*mettre au lit*) to put to bed; (*donner un lit*) to put up. **on peut vous** ~ we can put you up, we can offer you a bed; **nous pouvons** ~ **4 personnes** we can put up *ou* sleep 4 people; **on peut** ~ **à 5 dans le bateau/la maison** the boat/the house sleeps 5; *voir* **nom**.

b (*étendre*) *blessé* to lay out; *échelle etc* to lay down; *bouteille* to lay on its side. **il y a un arbre couché en travers de la route** there's a tree lying across the road; **la rafale a couché le bateau** the gust of wind made the boat keel over *ou* keeled the boat over; **le vent a couché les blés** the wind has flattened the corn; *voir* **joue**.

c (*frm: inscrire*) to inscribe. ~ **qn dans un testament** to name sb in a will; ~ **qn sur une liste** to inscribe *ou* include sb's name on a list; ~ **un article dans un contrat** to insert a clause into a contract.

d (*Horticulture*) *branches* to layer.

2 vi a (*passer la nuit, séjourner*) to sleep. **nous avons couché à l'hôtel/chez des amis** we spent the night at a hotel/with friends, we slept (the night) *ou* put up at a hotel/at friends'; **nous couchions à l'hôtel/chez des amis** we were staying in a hotel/with friends; ~ **sous la tente** to sleep under canvas; **il faudra qu'il couche par terre** he'll have to sleep on the floor; **ma voiture couche dehors*** my car stays outside at night; *voir* **beau**.

b (*: *se coucher*) to go to bed. **cela nous a fait** ~ **très tard** that kept us up very late.

c (*: *avoir des rapports sexuels*) ~ **avec qn** to sleep *ou* go to bed with sb; **ils couchent ensemble** they sleep together; **c'est une fille sérieuse, qui ne couche pas** she's a sensible girl and she doesn't sleep around.

3 **se coucher** vpr a to go to bed. **se** ~ **comme les poules** to go to bed early *ou* when the sun goes down; *voir* **comme**.

b (*s'étendre*) to lie down. **va te** ~**!*** clear off!*; **il m'a envoyé (me)** ~* he sent me packing; **il se coucha sur l'enfant pour le protéger** he lay on top of the child to protect him; (*Sport*) **se** ~ **sur les avirons/le guidon** to bend over the oars/the handlebars; **un poteau s'est couché au travers de la route** there is a post lying across the road.

c *[soleil, lune]* to set, go down.

d (*Naut*) *[bateau]* to keel over.

e (*s'incliner*) (*Cartes*) (*gén*) to throw in one's hand; (*Poker*) to fold.

4 nm a (*moment*) **surveiller le** ~ **des enfants** to see the children into bed; **le** ~ **était toujours à 9 heures** bedtime was always at 9 o'clock.

b (†: *logement*) accommodation. **le** ~ **et la nourriture** board and lodging; (*Hist*) **le** ~ **du roi** the king's going-to-bed ceremony.

c **(au)** ~ **du soleil** (at) sunset *ou* sundown (*US*); **le soleil à son** ~ the setting sun.

5 comp ►**couche-tard*** nmf inv night owl* ►**couche-tôt*** nmf inv: **c'est un couche-tôt*** he's an early-bedder* (*Brit*), he always goes to bed early.

coucherie [kuʃʀi] nf (*gén pl: péj*) sleeping around (*NonC*).

couchette [kuʃɛt] nf (*Rail*) couchette, berth; (*Naut*) *[voyageur]* couchette, berth; *[marin]* bunk.

coucheur [kuʃœʀ] nm *voir* **mauvais**.

couci-couça* [kusikusa] adv so-so*.

coucou [kuku] 1 nm a (*oiseau*) cuckoo; (*pendule*) cuckoo clock; (*péj: avion*) (old) crate*. b (*fleur*) cowslip. 2 excl: ~ **(me voici)!** peek-a-boo!

coude [kud] nm a (*Anat, partie de la manche*) elbow. **~s au corps** (*lit*) (with one's) elbows in; (*fig: courir*) at the double; (*fig*) **se tenir** *ou* **serrer les ~s** to show great solidarity, stick together; **coup de** ~ nudge; **prendre un coup de** ~ **dans la figure** to get an elbow in the face; **écarter qn d'un coup de** ~ to elbow sb out of the way; **d'un coup de** ~ **il attira son attention** he nudged him to attract his attention; **donner un coup de** ~ **à qn** (*légèrement*) to give sb a nudge, nudge sb; (*plus brutalement*) to elbow sb; ~ **à** ~ *travailler* shoulder to shoulder, side by side; *[coureurs, candidats]* **être au** ~ **à** ~ to be neck and neck; **j'ai** *ou* **je garde votre dossier sous le** ~ I am holding on to your file; **j'ai toujours ce dictionnaire sous le** ~ I always keep this dictionary handy; *voir* **doigt, huile** *etc*.

b *[route, rivière]* bend; *[tuyau, barre]* bend.

coudé, e [kude] (ptp de **couder**) adj *tuyau, barre* angled, bent at an angle, with a bend in it.

coudée [kude] nf (††) cubit††. (*fig*) **avoir ses** *ou* **les ~s franches** to have elbow room; (*fig*) **dépasser qn de cent ~s**† to stand head and shoulders above sb, be worth a hundred times more than sb.

couder [kude] [1] vt *tuyau, barre de fer* to put a bend in, bend (at an angle).

coudoiement [kudwamɑ̃] nm (close) contact, rubbing shoulders, mixing.

coudoyer [kudwaje] [8] vt *gens* to rub shoulders with, mix with, come into contact with. (*fig*) **dans cet article, la stupidité coudoie la mesquinerie la plus révoltante** in this article, stupidity stands side by side with the most despicable pettiness.

coudre [kudʀ] [48] vt *pièces de tissu* to sew (together); *pièce, bouton* to sew on; *vêtement* to sew up, stitch up; (*Reliure*) *cahiers* to stitch; (*Méd*) *plaie* to sew up, stitch (up). ~ **un bouton/une pièce à une veste** to sew a button/patch on a jacket; ~ **une semelle (à l'empeigne)** to stitch a sole (to the upper); ~ **à la main/à la machine** to sew by hand/by machine; *voir* **dé, machine**[3].

coudrier [kudʀije] nm hazel tree.

couenne [kwan] nf a *[lard]* rind. b (‡) (*peau*) hide*. c (*Méd*) *[sang]* buffy coat; *[peau]* membrane.

couenneux, -euse [kwanø, øz] adj *voir* **angine**.

couette [kwɛt] nf a *[cheveux]* **~s** bunches. b (*Tech*) bearing; (*Naut*) ways (*pl*). c *[lit]* continental quilt, duvet.

couffin [kufɛ̃] nm *[bébé]* Moses basket; (†: *cabas*) (straw) basket.

coug(o)uar [kugwaʀ] nm cougar.

couic [kwik] excl erk!, squeak! **je n'y comprends que** ~* I don't understand a blooming* (*Brit*) *ou* darn* (*US*) thing.

couille⁑ [kuj] nf a (*testicule*) (*gén pl*) ball⁑. **~s** balls⁑, bollocks⁑; ~ **molle** gutless individual; (*fig: courage*) **avoir des ~s** to have balls⁑. b (*erreur*) balls-up⁑ (*Brit*), ball-up⁑ (*US*). **faire une** ~ to screw up‡, fuck up⁑. c (*empêchement, problème*) **il y a une** ~ something has cropped up; **ça part** *ou* **se barre en ~s, son affaire** his business is going down the drain*.

couillon‡ [kujɔ̃] nm bloody (*Brit*) *ou* damn idiot‡ *ou* cretin‡.

couillonnade‡ [kujɔnad] nf (*action*) boob‡; (*propos*) bullshit⁑ (*NonC*).

couillonner‡ [kujɔne] [1] vt to do* (*Brit*), con‡. **on t'a couillonné, tu t'es fait** ~ you've been had* *ou* done* (*Brit*) *ou* conned‡.

couinement [kwinmɑ̃] nm (*voir* **couiner**) squealing (*NonC*), squeal; whining (*NonC*), whine.

couiner [kwine] [1] vi *[animal]* to squeal; (*péj*) *[enfant]* to whine.

coulage [kulaʒ] nm a *[cire, ciment]* pouring; *[statue, cloche]* casting. b (*Écon*) (*gaspillage*) waste; (*vol*) pilferage.

coulant, e [kulɑ̃, ɑ̃t] 1 adj a *pâte* runny; (*fig*) *vin* smooth; (*fig*) *style* (free-)flowing, smooth; *voir* **nœud**. b (*: *indulgent*) *personne* easy-going. 2 nm a *[ceinture]* sliding loop. b (*Bot*) runner.

coule [kul] nf a (‡) **être à la ~** to know the ropes, know the tricks of the trade. b (*capuchon*) cowl.

coulé, e [kule] (ptp de **couler**) 1 adj *voir* **brasse.** 2 nm (*Mus*) slur; (*Danse*) glide; (*Billard*) follow. 3 **coulée** nf *[métal]* casting. **~e de lave** lava flow; **~e de boue/neige** mud/snowslide; *[peinture]* **il y a une ~e** the paint has run; **il y a des/3 ~s** the paint has run (in several places)/in 3 places.

coulemelle [kulmɛl] nf parasol mushroom.

couler [kule] [1] 1 vi a *[liquide]* to run, flow; *[sang]* to flow; *[larmes]* to run down, flow; *[sueur]* to run down; *[fromage, bougie]* to run; *[rivière]* to flow. **la sueur coulait sur son visage** perspiration was running down *ou* (*plus fort*) pouring down his face; **~ à flots** *[vin, champagne]* to be flowing freely; (*fig*) **le sang a coulé** blood has been shed.

b **faire ~** *eau* to run; **faire ~ un bain** to run a bath, run water for a bath; (*fig*) **faire ~ le sang** to cause bloodshed; (*fig*) **ça a fait ~ beaucoup d'encre** it caused much ink to flow; (*fig*) **ça fera ~ de la salive** that'll cause some tongue-wagging *ou* set (the) tongues wagging.

c *[robinet]* to run; (*fuir*) to leak; *[récipient, stylo]* to leak. **ne laissez pas ~ les robinets** don't leave the taps running *ou* the taps on; **il a le nez qui coule** his nose is running, he has a runny *ou* running nose.

d *[paroles]* to flow; *[roman, style]* to flow (along). **~ de source** (*être clair*) to be obvious; (*s'enchaîner*) to follow naturally.

e *[vie, temps]* to slip by, slip past.

f *[bateau, personne]* to sink; *[entreprise]* to go under, fold. **~ à pic** to sink straight to the bottom.

2 vt a *cire, ciment* to pour; *métal* to cast; *statue, cloche* to cast. (*Aut*) **~ une bielle** to run a big end.

b (*passer*) **~ une existence paisible/des jours heureux** to enjoy a peaceful existence/happy days.

c *bateau* to sink, send to the bottom; (*fig*) (*discréditer*) *personne* to discredit; (**: faire échouer*) *candidat* to bring down; *entrepreneur, firme* to wreck, ruin. **c'est son accent/l'épreuve de latin qui l'a coulé*** it was his accent/the Latin paper that brought him down.

d (*glisser*) *regard, sourire* to steal; *pièce de monnaie* to slip.

e (*filtrer*) *liquide* to pour.

3 **se couler** vpr a (*se glisser*) **se ~ dans/à travers** to slip into/through; (*fig*) *[personne]* **se ~ dans un moule** to conform to a norm.

b **se la ~ douce*** to have it easy*, have an easy time (of it)*.

couleur [kulœʀ] 1 nf a colour; (*nuance*) shade, tint, hue (*littér*). **les ~s fondamentales/complémentaires** the primary/complementary colours; **une robe de ~ claire/sombre/bleue** a light-/dark-coloured/blue dress; **une belle ~ rouge** a beautiful shade of red, a beautiful red tint; **aux ~s délicates** delicately coloured, with delicate colours; **film/cartes en ~s** colour film/postcards; **vêtements noirs ou de ~** dark or colourful clothes; (*linge de couleur*) **la ~, les ~s** coloureds; **je n'aime pas les ~s de son appartement** I don't like the colour scheme *ou* the colours in his flat; **se faire faire sa** *ou* **une ~** to have one's hair coloured; *voir* **goût.**

b (*peinture*) paint. **~s à l'eau/à l'huile** watercolours/oil colours, water/oil paint; **boîte de ~s** paintbox, box of paints; *voir* **crayon, marchand.**

c (*carnation*) **~s** colour; **avoir des ~s** to have a good colour; **perdre ses/(re)prendre des ~s** to lose/get back one's colour; (*bronzage*) **tu as pris des ~s** you've caught the sun; *voir* **changer, haut.**

d (*NonC: vigueur*) colour. **ce récit a de la ~** this tale is colourful; **sans ~** colourless.

e (*caractère*) colour, flavour. **le poème prend soudain une ~ tragique** the poem suddenly takes on a tragic colour *ou* note.

f (*Pol: étiquette*) colour. **on ne connaît guère la ~ de ses opinions** hardly anything is known about the colour of his opinions.

g (*Cartes*) suit; *voir* **annoncer.**

h (*Sport*) *[club, écurie]* **~s** colours; **les ~s** (*drapeau*) the colours.

i **~ locale** local colour; **ces costumes font très ~ locale** these costumes give plenty of local colour.

j (*loc*) **homme/femme de ~** coloured man/woman; **sous ~ de qch** under the guise of sth; **sous ~ de faire** while pretending to do; **montrer/présenter qch sous de fausses ~s** to show/present sth in a false light; **décrire** *ou* **peindre qch sous les plus sombres/vives ~s** to paint the darkest/rosiest picture of sth, paint sth in the darkest/rosiest colours; **l'avenir se présente sous les plus sombres ~s** the future looms very dark *ou* looks very gloomy; **elle n'a jamais vu la ~ de son argent*** she's never seen the colour of his money*; **il m'a promis un cadeau mais je n'en ai jamais vu la ~*** he promised me a present but I've yet to see it; *voir* **voir.**

2 adj inv: **des yeux ~ d'azur** sky-blue eyes; **tissu ~ cyclamen/mousse** cyclamen-coloured/moss-green material; **~ chair** flesh-coloured, flesh (*épith*); **~ paille** straw-coloured.

couleuvre [kulœvʀ] nf: **~ (à collier)** grass snake; **~ lisse** smooth snake; **~ vipérine** viperine snake; *voir* **avaler.**

couleuvrine [kulœvʀin] nf (*Hist*) culverin.

coulis [kuli] 1 adj m *voir* **vent.** 2 nm a (*Culin*) **~ de framboise/de cassis** ≃ raspberry/blackcurrant sauce; **~ de tomates** ≃ tomato purée; **~ d'écrevisses** crayfish bisque. b (*Tech*) (*mortier*) grout; (*métal*) molten metal (*filler*).

coulissant, e [kulisɑ̃, ɑ̃t] adj *porte, panneau* sliding (*épith*).

coulisse [kulis] nf a (*Théât: gén pl*) wings. **en ~, dans les ~s** (*Théât*) in the wings; (*fig*) behind the scenes; (*fig*) **les ~s de la politique** what goes on behind the political scene(s); (*fig*) **rester dans la ~** to work behind the scenes. b *[porte, tiroir]* runner; *[rideau]* top hem; *[robe]* casing; (*panneau mobile*) sliding door; (*Tech: glissière*) slide. **porte à ~** sliding door; (*fig*) **regard en ~** sidelong glance *ou* look; *voir* **pied, trombone.** c (*Bourse*) unofficial Stock Market.

coulisseau, pl **~x** [kuliso] nm *[tiroir]* runner; (*Tech*) slide.

coulisser [kulise] [1] 1 vt *tiroir, porte* to provide with runners; *rideau* to hem (the top of). **jupe coulissée** skirt with a draw-string waist. 2 vi *[porte, rideau, tiroir]* to slide, run.

coulissier [kulisje] nm unofficial broker.

couloir [kulwaʀ] nm *[bâtiment]* corridor, passage; *[wagon]* corridor; *[appareil de projection]* channel, track; (*Athlétisme, Natation*) lane; (*Géog*) gully, couloir (*SPÉC*); (*Tennis*) alley, tramlines (*Brit*); (*pour bus, taxi*) lane. **~ aérien** air (traffic) lane; **~ de navigation** shipping lane; (*Géog*) **~ d'avalanches** avalanche corridor; (*Pol*) **bruits de ~(s)** rumours; (*Pol*) **intrigues de ~(s)** backstage manoeuvring.

coulpe [kulp] nf (*littér, hum*) **battre sa ~** to repent openly.

coulure [kulyʀ] nf a (*processus*) *[métal]* running out; *[fruit]* failure (*due to washing off of pollen*); *[peinture]* running. b (*trace*) *[métal]* runoff. *[peinture]* **il y a une ~** the paint has run; **il y a des/3 ~s** the paint has run (in several places)/in 3 places.

coup [ku] nm a (*heurt, choc*) knock; (*affectif*) blow, shock. **se donner un ~ à la tête/au bras** to knock *ou* hit *ou* bang one's head/arm; **la voiture a reçu un ~** the car has had a knock (*Brit*) *ou* bang *ou* bump; **donner des ~s dans la porte** to bang *ou* hammer at the door; **donner un ~ sec pour dégager qch** to give sth a sharp rap *ou* knock to release it; **ça a porté un ~ sévère à leur moral** it dealt a severe blow to their morale; **en prendre un ~*** *[carosserie]* to have a bash* (*Brit*) *ou* bang; *[personne, confiance, moral]* to take a blow *ou* knock; **ça lui a fait un ~*** it's given him a (bit of a) shock, it was a bit of a blow (for him); *voir* **accuser, marquer.**

b (*marquant l'agression*) blow. **il m'a donné un ~** he hit me; **en venir aux ~s** to come to blows; **les ~s tombaient dru** *ou* **pleuvaient** blows rained down *ou* fell thick and fast; (*Jur*) **~s et blessures** assault and battery, aggravated assault.

c *[arme à feu]* shot. **à 6 ~s** six-shot (*épith*); **il jouait avec le fusil quand le ~ est parti** he was playing with the rifle when it went off; *voir* **tirer.**

d (*mouvement du corps*) **jeter** *ou* **lancer un ~ d'œil à qn** to glance at sb, look quickly at sb; **jeter un ~ d'œil à** *texte, exposition* to have a quick look at, glance at; **allons jeter un ~ d'œil** let's go and have a look; **il y a un beau ~ d'œil d'ici** there's a lovely view from here; **un ~ d'œil lui suffit** one glance *ou* one quick look was enough; **ça vaut le ~ d'œil** it's worth seeing.

e (*habileté*) **avoir le ~** to have the knack; **avoir le ~ de main** to have the touch; **avoir le ~ d'œil** to have a good eye; **attraper le ~** to get the knack; **avoir un bon ~ de crayon** to be good at sketching.

f (*action de manier un instrument*) **~ de crayon/de plume** stroke of a pencil/pen; **~ de marteau** blow of a hammer; **d'un ~ de pinceau** with a stroke of his brush; **donner un ~ de lime à qch** to run a file over sth, give sth a quick file; **donner** *ou* **passer un ~ de chiffon/d'éponge à qch** to give sth a wipe (with a cloth/sponge), wipe sth (with a cloth/sponge), go over sth with a cloth/sponge; **donner un ~ de brosse/de balai à qch** to give sth a brush/a sweep, brush/sweep sth; **donner un ~ de fer à qch** to run the iron over sth, give sth a press; **donner un ~ de pinceau/de peinture à un mur** to give a wall a touch/a coat of paint; **donne un ~ d'aspirateur à la chambre** go over the room with the vacuum cleaner; **donne-toi un ~ de peigne** run a comb through your hair; **donner** *ou* **passer un ~ de téléphone** *ou* **de fil* à qn** to make a phone call to sb, give sb a ring *ou* call *ou* buzz*, ring sb up (*Brit*), call sb up, phone sb; **il faut que je donne un ~ de téléphone** I must make a phone call, I've got to give somebody a ring *ou* call; **recevoir un ~ de téléphone** *ou* **de fil* (de qn)** to have a (phone)call (from sb); **un ~ de volant maladroit a causé l'accident** a clumsy turn of the wheel caused the accident.

g (*Sport: geste*) (*Cricket, Golf, Tennis*) stroke; (*Tir*) shot; (*Boxe*) blow, punch; (*Échecs*) move. (*Tennis*) **~ droit** drive; (*Tennis*) **~ droit croisé** cross court drive; (*Tennis*) **~ droit de dos** backhand drive; (*Tennis*) **~ droit de face** forehand drive; **~ par ~** blow by blow; (*Boxe, fig*) **~ bas** blow *ou* punch below the belt; **~ franc** (*Ftbl, Rugby*) free kick; (*Basketball*) free throw shot; (*fig*) **tous les ~s sont permis** no holds barred; **faire ~ double** (*Chasse*) to do a right and left; (*fig*) to kill two birds with one stone; *voir* **discuter, marquer,** *etc.*

h (*bruit*) **sonner 3 ~s** to ring 3 times; **les douze ~s de midi** the twelve strokes of noon; **sur le ~ de midi** at the stroke of noon; (*Théât*) **frapper les trois ~s** to sound the three knocks (*in French theatres, before the curtain rises*); **il y eut un ~ à la porte** there was a knock at the door.

i (*événement fortuit*) **~ du sort** *ou* **du destin** blow dealt by fate; **~ de chance** *ou* **de veine*, ~ de pot‡** stroke *ou* piece of luck; **~ de déveine*** rotten luck (*NonC*); **~ dur** hard blow; **c'est un sale ~** it's a dreadful blow.

j (*: *action concertée, hasardeuse*) *[cambrioleurs]* job*. **il est sur un ~** he's up to something; **c'est un ~ à faire** *ou* **tenter** it's worth (having) a go* *ou* a bash* (*Brit*); **tenter le ~** to try one's luck, have a go*; **réussir un beau ~** to pull it off; **être dans le ~/hors du ~** to be/not to be in on it; *voir* **manquer, monter[2], valoir.**

k (*contre qn*) trick. **c'est bien un ~ à lui** that's just like him *ou* typical of him; **faire un sale ~ à qn** to play a (dirty) trick on sb; **tu ne vas pas nous faire le ~ d'être malade** you're not going to go and be ill on us*; **il nous fait le ~ chaque fois** he never fails to do that; **un ~ en vache⁑** *ou* **de salaud⁑** a dirty trick⁑; **un ~ en traître** a stab in the back; **faire un ~ en vache à qn⁑** to do the dirty on sb⁑; **~ monté** set up.

l (*: *quantité bue*) **boire un ~** to have a drink (*gen of wine*); **je te paie un ~ (à boire)** I'll buy you a drink; **donner** *ou* **verser un ~ de cidre/de rouge à qn** to pour sb a drink of cider/of red wine; **vous boirez bien un ~ avec nous?** (you'll) have a drink with us?; **il a bu un ~ de trop, il a un ~ dans le nez*** he's had one too many*.

m (*: *fois*) time. **à tous (les) ~s, à chaque** *ou* **tout ~** every time; **du premier ~** first time *ou* go*, right off the bat* (*US*); **pour un ~** for once; **du même ~** at the same time; **pleurer/rire un bon ~** to have a good cry/laugh; **au ~ par ~** *agir* on an ad hoc basis; *embaucher, acheter* as and when the need arises; **~ sur ~** one straight after the other.

n (*moyen*) **à ~(s) de: enfoncer des clous à ~s de marteau** to hammer nails in; **détruire qch à ~s de hache** to hack sth to pieces; **tuer un animal à ~s de bâton** to beat an animal to death; **traduire un texte à ~ de dictionnaire** to translate a text relying heavily on a dictionary; **réussir à ~ de publicité** to succeed through repeated advertising *ou* through a massive publicity drive.

o (*effet*) **sous le ~ de** *surprise, émotion* in the grip of; **sous le ~ d'une forte émotion** in a highly emotional state, in the grip of a powerful emotion; (*Admin*) **être sous le ~ d'une condamnation** to have a current conviction; (*Admin*) **être sous le ~ d'une mesure d'expulsion** to be under an expulsion order; (*Admin*) **tomber sous le ~ de la loi** *[activité, acte]* to be a statutory offence.

p (*loc*) **à ~ sûr** definitely; **après ~** afterwards, after the event; **~ sur ~** in quick succession, one after the other; **du ~** as a result; **c'est pour le ~ qu'il se fâcherait** then he'd really get angry, then he'd get all the angrier; **sur le ~** (*instantanément*) outright; **mourir sur le ~** (*assassinat*) to be killed outright; (*accident*) to die *ou* be killed instantly; **sur le ~ je n'ai pas compris** at the time I didn't understand; **d'un seul ~** at one go; **tout à ~, tout d'un ~** all of a sudden, suddenly, all at once; **un ~ pour rien** (*lit*) a go for nothing, a trial go; (*fig*) a waste of time; **il en met un sacré ~*** he's really going at it; **en mettre un ~** to really put one's back into it, pull out all the stops*; **en prendre un (vieux) ~*** to take a hammering*; **tenir le ~** to hold out; **c'est encore un ~ de 1 000 F*** that'll be another 1,000 francs to fork out*; **c'est un ~ à se dégoûter!*** it's enough to make you sick!*; **c'est un ~ à se tuer*/à se faire virer!*** you can get yourself killed (doing that)/fired* (for doing that)!; **sur le ~ des 10-11 heures** around 10 or 11; *voir* **cent[1], quatre.**

coupable [kupabl] 1 *adj* a (*fautif*) *personne* guilty (*de* of); *voir* **non, plaider.** b (*blâmable*) *désirs, amour* guilty (*épith*); *action, négligence* culpable, reprehensible; *faiblesse* reprehensible. 2 *nmf* (*d'un méfait, d'une faute*) culprit, guilty party (*frm, hum*). **le grand ~ c'est le jeu** the real culprit is gambling, gambling is chiefly to be blamed.

coupage [kupaʒ] *nm [vin]* (*avec un autre vin*) blending (*NonC*); (*avec de l'eau*) dilution (*NonC*), diluting (*NonC*). **ce sont des ~s, ce sont des vins de ~** these are blended wines.

coupant, e [kupɑ̃, ɑ̃t] *adj* (*lit*) *lame, brin d'herbe* sharp(-edged); (*fig*) *ton, réponse* sharp.

coupe[1] [kup] *nf* a (*à fruits, dessert*) dish; (*contenu*) dish(ful); (*à boire*) goblet. **une ~ de champagne** a goblet of champagne; *voir* **loin.** b (*Sport: objet, épreuve*) cup. **la ~ de France de football** the French football cup.

coupe[2] [kup] *nf* a (*Couture*) (*action*) cutting(-out); (*pièce de tissu*) length; (*façon d'être coupé*) cut. **leçon de ~** lesson in cutting out; **robe de belle ~/de ~ sobre** beautifully/simply cut dress; **~ nette** *ou* **franche** clean cut.

b (*Sylviculture*) (*action*) cutting (down); (*étendue de forêt*) felling area; (*surface, tranche*) section. **~ claire** radical thinning (out) (*allowing a lot more light to enter the forest*); **~ sombre** (slight) thinning (out); **~ d'ensemencement** thinning (out) (*to allow space for sowing new trees*); **~ réglée** periodic felling; *voir aussi* **h.**

c *[cheveux]* cutting. **~ (de cheveux)** (hair)cut; **~ au rasoir** razor-cut.

d (*pour examen au microscope*) section. **~ histologique** histological section.

e (*dessin, plan*) section. **le navire vu en ~** a (cross) section of the ship; **~ transversale** cross *ou* transversal section; **~ longitudinale** longitudinal section.

f (*Littérat*) *[vers]* break, caesura.

g (*Cartes*) cut, cutting (*NonC*). **jouer sous la ~ de qn** to lead (after sb has cut).

h (*loc*) **être sous la ~ de qn** *[personne]* (*être dominé*) to be under sb's thumb; (*hiérarchiquement*) to be under sb; *[firme, organisation]* to be under sb's control; **tomber sous la ~ de qn** to fall prey to sb, fall into sb's clutches; **faire des ~s sombres** *ou* **claires dans** to make drastic cuts in; **il y a eu des ~s sombres dans le personnel** there have been severe staff reductions *ou* cutbacks; **mettre en ~ réglée** to bleed systematically (*fig*).

coupe- [kup] *préf voir* **couper.**

coupé, e[1] [kupe] (*ptp de* **couper**) 1 *adj* a *vêtement* **bien/mal ~** well/badly cut. b *communications, routes* cut off. c *vin* blended. d (*Vét: castré*) neutered. 2 *nm* (*Aut, Danse*) coupé.

coupée[2] [kupe] *nf* (*Naut*) gangway (*opening, with ladder*); *voir* **échelle.**

coupelle [kupɛl] *nf* a (*petite coupe*) (small) dish. b (*Chim*) cupel.

couper [kupe] [1] 1 *vt* a (*gén*) to cut; *bois* to chop; *arbre* to cut down, fell; (*séparer*) to cut off; (*découper*) *rôti* to carve, cut up; (*partager*) *gâteau* to cut, slice; (*entailler*) to slit; (*fig*) *[vent]* to sting. **~ qch en (petits) morceaux** to cut sth up, cut sth into (little) pieces; **~ en tranches** to slice, cut into slices; (*lit*) **~ en deux** to cut in two *ou* in half; (*fig*) **le parti est coupé en deux** the party is split *ou* divided; (*Météo*) **le pays sera coupé en deux** weather-wise, the country will be split in two; **~ la gorge à qn** to slit *ou* cut sb's throat; **~ la tête à qn** to cut *ou* chop sb's head off; **~ (les pages d')un livre** to slit open *ou* cut the pages of a book; **livre non coupé** book with pages uncut; **il a coupé le ruban trop court** he has cut the ribbon too short; **coupez-lui une tranche de pain** cut him a slice of bread; **se ~ les cheveux/les ongles** to cut one's hair/nails; **se faire ~ les cheveux** to get one's hair cut, have a haircut; *voir* **six, tête, vif.**

b (*Couture*) *vêtement* to cut out; *étoffe* to cut.

c (*raccourcir*) *émission* to cut (down); (*retrancher*) *passages inutiles* to cut (out), take out, delete.

d (*arrêter*) *eau, gaz* to cut off; (*au compteur*) to turn off; (*Élec*) *courant etc* to cut off; (*au compteur*) to switch off, turn off; *communications, route, pont* to cut off; *relations diplomatiques* to cut off, break off; (*Téléc*) to cut off; *crédits* to cut off; (*Ciné*) *prise de vues* to cut. (*Ciné*) **coupez!** cut!; (*Aut*) **~ l'allumage** *ou* **le contact** to switch off the ignition; **~ le vent** to cut out the wind; **~ la faim à qn** to take the edge off sb's hunger; **~ la fièvre à qn** to bring down sb's fever; **~ le chemin** *ou* **la route à qn** to cut sb off, cut in front of sb; **~ la route d'un véhicule** to cut a vehicle off, cut a vehicle's path off; **~ l'appétit à qn** to spoil sb's appetite, take away sb's appetite, take the edge off sb's appetite; **~ la retraite à qn** to cut *ou* block off sb's line of retreat; **~ les vivres à qn** to cut off sb's means of subsistence; **~ les ponts avec qn** to break off communications with sb.

e (*interrompre*) *voyage* to break; *journée* to break up. **nous nous arrêterons à X pour ~ le voyage** we'll stop at X to break the journey, we'll break the journey at X.

f (*fig: isoler*) **~ qn de** to cut sb off from.

g (*traverser*) *[ligne]* to intersect, cut; *[route]* to cut across, cross. **le chemin de fer coupe la route en 2 endroits** the railway cuts across *ou* crosses the road at 2 points; **une cloison coupe la pièce** a partition cuts the room in two; (*fig*) **l'électorat était coupé en deux** the voters were split down the middle.

h (*Cartes*) *jeu* to cut; (*prendre avec l'atout*) to trump.

i (*Sport*) *balle* to slice.

j (*mélanger*) *lait etc, vin* (*à table*) to dilute, add water to; *vin* (*à la production*) to blend. **vin coupé d'eau** wine diluted with water.

k (*Vét: castrer*) to neuter.

l (*loc*) **~ les bras** *ou* **bras et jambes à qn** *[travail]* to wear sb out; *[nouvelle]* to knock sb for six* (*Brit*) *ou* for a loop* (*US*); **j'en ai les jambes coupées** I'm stunned by it; **~ la poire en deux** to meet halfway; **~ les cheveux en quatre** to split hairs, quibble; **~ ses effets à qn** to steal sb's thunder; **~ l'herbe sous le pied à qn** to cut the ground from under sb's feet; **~ la parole à qn** *[personne]* to cut sb short; *[émotion]* to leave *ou* render sb speechless; **~ le sifflet*** *ou* **la chique⁑ à qn** to shut sb up*, take the wind out of sb's sails; **ça te la coupe!⁑** that shuts you up!*; **~ la respiration** *ou* **le souffle à qn** (*lit*) to wind sb; (*fig*) to take sb's breath away; (*fig*) **j'en ai eu le souffle coupé** it (quite) took my breath away; **c'est à vous ~ le souffle** it's breathtaking; **~ court à** *conversation* to cut short; **un accent à ~ au couteau** an accent you could cut with a knife; **un brouillard à ~ au couteau** a real pea souper*, a fog you could cut with a knife; *voir* **herbe.**

2 **couper à** *vt indir* a (*échapper à*) *corvée* to get out of. **tu n'y couperas pas d'une amende** you won't get away with it without paying a fine, you won't get out of paying a fine; **tu n'y couperas pas** you won't get out of it.

b **~ court à** to cut short.

3 *vi* a *[couteau, verre]* to cut; *[vent]* to be biting. **ce couteau coupe bien** this knife cuts well *ou* has a good cutting edge.

b (*prendre un raccourci*) **~ à travers champs** to cut across country *ou* the fields; **~ au plus court** to take the quickest way; **~ par un sentier** to cut through by way of *ou* cut along a path.

c (*Cartes*) (*diviser le jeu*) to cut; (*jouer atout*) to trump. **~ à trèfle/à carreau** *etc* to trump with a club/diamond *etc.*

4 **se couper** *vpr* a to cut o.s. **se ~ à la jambe** to cut one's leg; (*fig*) **se ~ en quatre pour (aider) qn** to bend over backwards to help sb.

b (*) to give o.s. away.

5 *comp* ►**coupe-choux*** *nm inv* (*épée*) short sword; (*rasoir*) open

razor ▸**coupe-cigare(s)** nm inv cigar cutter ▸**coupe-circuit** nm inv cut-out, circuit breaker ▸**coupe-coupe** nm inv machete ▸**coupe-faim** nm inv appetite suppressant ▸**coupe-feu** nm inv firebreak ▸**coupe-file** nm inv pass ▸**coupe-frites** nm inv chip-cutter *ou* -slicer (*Brit*), french-fry-cutter *ou* -slicer (*US*) ▸**coupe-gorge** nm inv dangerous back alley ▸**coupe-jarret** († *ou hum*) nm (pl **coupe-jarrets**) cut-throat ▸**coupe-légumes** nm inv vegetable-cutter ▸**coupe-œufs** nm inv egg-slicer ▸**coupe-ongles** nm inv (*pince*) nail clippers; (*ciseaux*) nail scissors ▸**coupe-papier** nm inv paper knife ▸**coupe-pâte** nm inv pastry-cutter ▸**coupe-tomates** nm inv tomato-slicer ▸**coupe-vent** nm inv (*haie*) windbreak; (*vêtement*) windbreaker (*US*), windcheater (*Brit*).

couperet [kupʀɛ] nm *[boucher]* chopper, cleaver; *[guillotine]* blade, knife.

couperose [kupʀoz] nf blotches (*on the face*), rosacea (*SPÉC*).

couperosé, e [kupʀoze] adj blotchy, affected by rosacea (*attrib*) (*SPÉC*).

coupeur, -euse [kupœʀ, øz] nm,f (*Couture*) cutter. **un ~ de cheveux en quatre** a hairsplitter, a quibbler.

couplage [kuplaʒ] nm (*Élec, Tech*) coupling.

couple [kupl] 1 nm a (*époux, amoureux, danseurs*) couple; (*patineurs, animaux*) pair. **ils ont des problèmes de ~, leur ~ a des problèmes** they have problems with their relationship; (*Patinage*) **l'épreuve en** *ou* **par ~s** the pairs (event). b (*Phys*) couple. **~ moteur** torque; **~ de torsion** torque. c (*Naut*) (square) frame; (*Aviat*) frame; *voir* **nage**. 2 nf ou nm (†: *deux*) **un** *ou* **une ~ de** a couple of. 3 nf (*Chasse*) couple.

couplé [kuple] nm: (**pari**) **~** first and second place double (*on two horses in the same race*).

coupler [kuple] 1 vt a (*Chasse*) to couple (together), leash together. b (*Tech*) to couple together *ou* up; (*Ordin*) to interface (*avec* with). (*Phot*) **télémètre couplé** coupled rangefinder; (*Rail*) **bielles couplées** coupling rods.

couplet [kuplɛ] nm (*strophe*) verse; (*péj*) tirade. (*chanson*) **~s satiriques** satirical song; **y aller de son ~ sur qch** to give one's little speech about sth.

coupleur [kuplœʀ] nm (*Élec*) coupler. (*Ordin*) **~ acoustique** acoustic coupler.

coupole [kupɔl] nf a (*Archit*) dome. **petite ~** cupola, small dome; **être reçu sous la C~** to become *ou* be made a member of the Académie française. b (*Mil*) *[char d'assaut]* revolving gun turret.

coupon [kupɔ̃] 1 nm a (*Couture, Tex*) (*reste*) remnant; (*rouleau*) roll. b (*Fin*) **~ (de dividende)** coupon; **avec ~ attaché/détaché** cum-/ex-dividend; **~ de rente** income coupon. c (*billet, ticket*) coupon. **~ de théâtre** theatre ticket; (*Transport*) **~ hebdomadaire/mensuel** ≃ weekly/monthly season ticket. d (*Comm*) coupon, voucher. **~ de réduction** coupon, cash premium voucher. 2 comp ▸**coupon-réponse** nm (pl **coupons-réponse**) reply coupon; **coupon-réponse international** international reply coupon.

coupure [kupyʀ] nf (*blessure, brèche, Ciné*) cut; (*fig: fossé*) break; (*billet de banque*) note. **~ (de presse** *ou* **de journal)** (newspaper) cutting, (newspaper) clipping; **~ (de courant)** power cut; (*Banque*) **petites/grosses ~s** small/big notes, notes of small/big denomination; **il y aura des ~s ce soir** (*électricité*) there'll be power cuts tonight; (*gaz, eau*) the gas (*ou* water) will be cut off tonight.

cour [kuʀ] 1 nf a *[bâtiment]* yard, courtyard. **être sur (la) ~** to look onto the (back)yard; **la ~ de la caserne** the barracks square; **~ de cloître** cloister garth; **~ d'école** schoolyard, playground; **~ de ferme** farmyard; **la ~ de la gare** the station forecourt; **~ d'honneur** main courtyard; **~ d'immeuble** (back)yard of a block of flats (*Brit*) *ou* an apartment building (*US*); **~ de récréation** playground; *voir* **côté**.

b (*Jur*) court. **Messieurs, la C~!** ≃ be upstanding in court! (*Brit*), all rise!; **la C~ suprême** the Supreme Court; *voir* **haut**.

c *[roi]* court; (*fig*) *[personnage puissant, célèbre]* following. **vivre à la ~** to live at court; **faire sa ~ à** *roi* to pay court to; *supérieur, femme* to pay one's respects to; **être bien/mal en ~** to be in/out of favour (*auprès de qn* with sb); **homme/noble de ~** court gentleman/nobleman; **gens de ~** courtiers, people at court; **c'est la ~ du roi Pétaud** it's absolute bedlam*.

d *[femme]* (*soupirants*) following; (*essai de conquête*) wooing (*NonC*), courting (*NonC*). **faire la ~ à une femme** to woo *ou* court a woman; **faire un brin de ~ à une femme*** to flirt a little with a woman.

2 comp ▸**cour d'appel** ≃ Court of Appeal, ≃ appellate court (*US*) ▸**cour d'assises** ≃ Crown Court (*Brit*), court of assizes ▸**cour de cassation** Court of Cassation, (*final*) Court of Appeal ▸**cour des comptes** revenue court, ≃ Government Accounting Office (*US*) ▸**cour de justice** court of justice ▸**cour martiale** (*Mil*) court martial; **passer en cour martiale** to be tried by court martial ▸**la Cour des Miracles** (*Hist*) *area of Paris famed for its disreputable population;* (*fig*) **chez eux c'est une vraie cour des miracles** their place is always full of shady characters; **ce quartier est une vraie cour des miracles** this is a very unsavoury area ▸**Cour de sûreté de l'État** state security court.

courage [kuʀaʒ] nm a (*bravoure*) courage, bravery, guts*. **~ physique/moral** physical/moral courage; **se battre avec ~** to fight courageously *ou* with courage *ou* bravely; **s'il y va, il a du ~!** if he goes, he'll have guts!*; **vous n'aurez pas le ~ de lui refuser** you won't have the heart to refuse him.

b (*ardeur*) will, spirit. **entreprendre une tâche/un travail avec ~** to undertake a task/job with a will; **je voudrais finir ce travail, mais je ne m'en sens pas** *ou* **je n'en ai pas le ~** I'd like to get this work finished, but I don't feel up to it; **je n'ai pas beaucoup de ~ ce soir** I don't feel up to much this evening; **il se lève tous les jours à 5 heures? — quel ~!/il a du ~!** he gets up at 5am every day? – what willpower!/he must have willpower!; **un petit verre pour vous donner du ~*** just a small one to buck you up*.

c (*loc*) **~! nous y sommes presque!** cheer up! *ou* take heart! we're almost there!; **avoir le ~ de ses opinions** to have the courage of one's convictions; **prendre son ~ à deux mains** to take one's courage in both hands; **perdre ~** to lose heart, become discouraged; **reprendre ~** to take fresh heart.

courageusement [kuʀaʒøzmɑ̃] adv bravely, courageously. **entreprendre ~ une tâche** to tackle a task with a will.

courageux, -euse [kuʀaʒø, øz] adj brave, courageous. **il n'est pas très ~ pour l'étude** he hasn't got much will for studying; **je ne suis pas très ~ aujourd'hui** I don't feel up to very much today.

couramment [kuʀamɑ̃] adv a (*aisément*) fluently. **parler le français ~** to speak French fluently *ou* fluent French. b (*souvent*) commonly. **ce mot s'emploie ~** this word is in current usage; **ça se dit ~** it's a common *ou* an everyday expression; **cela arrive ~** it's a common occurrence; **cela se fait ~** it's quite a common thing to do, it's quite common practice.

courant, e [kuʀɑ̃, ɑ̃t] 1 adj a (*normal, habituel*) *dépenses* everyday, standard, ordinary; (*Comm*) *modèle, taille, marque* standard. **l'usage ~** everyday *ou* ordinary *ou* standard usage; **en utilisant les procédés ~s on gagne du temps** it saves time to use the normal *ou* ordinary *ou* standard procedures; **il nous suffit pour le travail ~** he'll do us for the routine *ou* everyday business *ou* work; *voir* **vie**.

b (*fréquent*) common. **ce procédé est ~, c'est un procédé ~** it's quite common practice *ou* quite a common procedure, it's quite commonplace; **ce genre d'incident est très ~ ici** this kind of incident is very common here, this kind of thing is a common occurrence here.

c (*en cours, actuel*) *année, semaine* current, present; (*Comm*) inst. *ou* instant (*Brit*). (*Comm*) **votre lettre du 5 ~** your letter of the 5th inst. *ou* instant (*Brit*) *ou* of the 5th of this month; *voir* **expédier, monnaie** *etc.*

d (*qui court*) *voir* **chien, compte, eau**.

2 nm a *[cours d'eau, mer, atmosphère]* current. **~ (atmosphérique)** airstream, current; *[cours d'eau]* **le ~** the current; **~ d'air** draught; (*Mét*) **~ d'air froid/chaud** cold/warm airstream; (*fig*) **c'est un vrai ~ d'air** one minute he is there, the next he has gone; **il y a trop de ~** the current's too strong; (*lit*) **suivre/remonter le ~** to go with/against the current; (*fig*) **suivre le ~** to go with the stream, follow the crowd; (*fig*) **remonter le ~** to get back on one's feet, climb back up.

b (*déplacement*) *[population, échanges commerciaux]* movement. **~s de population** movements *ou* shifts of (the) population; **établir une carte des ~s d'immigration et d'émigration** to draw up a map of migratory movement(s).

c (*mouvement*) (*gén*) movement; *[opinion, pensée]* trend, current. **les ~s de l'opinion** the trends of public opinion; **un ~ de scepticisme/de sympathie** a wave of scepticism/sympathy; **le ~ romantique/surréaliste** the romantic/surrealist movement.

d (*Élec*) current, power. **~ continu/alternatif** direct/alternating current; **couper le ~** to cut off the power; **rétablir le ~** to put the power back on; (*fig*) **on s'est rencontré un soir et le ~ est tout de suite passé** we met one evening and hit it off straight away*; (*fig*) **le ~ ne passe pas entre nous** we don't get on; (*fig*) **entre ce chanteur et le public le ~ passe** this singer really gets through to his audience; *voir* **coupure, pris**.

e (*cours*) **dans le ~ de la semaine/du mois** in the course of the week/month; **je dois le voir dans le ~ de la semaine** I'm to see him some time during the week; **dans le ~ de la conversation** in the course of the conversation, as the conversation was (*ou* is) going on; **le projet doit être fini ~ mai** the project is due to finish some time in May.

f **au ~: être au ~** (*savoir la nouvelle*) to know (about it); (*bien connaître la question*) to be well-informed; **tu m'as l'air très** *ou* **bien au ~ de ce qu'il fait!** you seem to know a lot about *ou* to be very well-informed about what he is doing!; **être au ~ de** *incident, accident, projets* to know about; *méthodes, théories nouvelles* to be well up on*, be up to date on; **mettre qn au ~ de** *faits, affaire* to tell sb (about), put sb in the picture about*, fill sb in on*; *méthodes, théories* to bring sb up to date on; **il s'est vite mis au ~ dans son nouvel emploi** he soon got the hang of things* in his new job; **tenir qn au ~ de** *faits, affaire* to keep sb informed of *ou* posted about*; *méthodes, théories* to keep sb up to date on; **si jamais ça recommence, tenez-moi au ~** if it happens again let me know; **s'abonner à une revue scientifique pour se tenir au ~** to subscribe to a science magazine to keep o.s. up to date (on things) *ou* abreast of things.

3 **courante** nf a (**⁑**: *diarrhée*) **la ~** the runs⁑.

b (*Mus: danse, air*) courante, courant.

courbatu, e [kuʀbaty] adj (stiff and) aching, aching all over.

courbature [kuʀbatyʀ] nf ache. **ce match de tennis m'a donné des ~s** this tennis match has made me ache *ou* made me stiff *ou* has given me aches and pains; **être plein de ~s** to be aching all over.

courbaturé, e [kuʀbatyʀe] adj aching (all over).

courbe [kuʀb] 1 adj *trajectoire, ligne, surface* curved; *branche* curved, curving. 2 nf (*gén, Géom*) curve. **le fleuve fait une ~** the river makes a curve, the river curves; (*Cartographie*) **~ de niveau** contour line; (*Méd*) **~ de température** temperature curve.

courber [kuʀbe] [1] 1 vt a (*plier*) *branche, tige, barre de fer* to bend. **branches courbées sous le poids de la neige** branches bowed down with *ou* bent under *ou* bent with the weight of the snow; **l'âge l'avait courbé** he was bowed *ou* bent with age.
b (*pencher*) **~ la tête** to bow *ou* bend one's head; **courbant le front sur son livre** his head bent over *ou* his head down over a book; (*fig*) **~ la tête** *ou* **le front** *ou* **le dos** to submit (*devant* to); *voir* **échine.**
2 vi to bend. **~ sous le poids** to bend under the weight.
3 **se courber** vpr a *[arbre, branche, poutre]* to bend, curve.
b *[personne]* (*pour entrer, passer*) to bend (down), stoop; (*signe d'humiliation*) to bow down; (*signe de déférence*) to bow (down). **il se courba pour le saluer** he greeted him with a bow; **se ~ en deux** to bend (o.s.) double.
c (*littér: se soumettre*) to bow down (*devant* before).

courbette [kuʀbɛt] nf a (*salut*) low bow. (*fig*) **faire des ~s à** *ou* **devant qn** to kowtow to sb, bow and scrape to sb. b *[cheval]* curvet.

courbure [kuʀbyʀ] nf *[ligne, surface]* curvature. **~ rentrante/sortante/en S** inward/outward/S curve; **~ du nez/des reins** curve of the nose/the back.

courette [kuʀɛt] nf small (court)yard.

coureur, -euse [kuʀœʀ, øz] 1 nm,f (*Athlétisme*) runner; (*Cyclisme*) cyclist, competitor; (*Aut*) driver, competitor. **~ de fond/de demi-fond** long-distance/middle-distance runner; **~ de 110 mètres haies** 110 metres hurdler.
2 nm a (*Zool*) **(oiseaux) ~s** running birds.
b (*péj: amateur de*) **c'est un ~ de cafés/de bals** he hangs round *ou* around cafés/dances; **c'est un ~ (de filles** *ou* **femmes** *ou* **jupons)** he's a wolf *ou* a womanizer *ou* a woman-chaser; **il est assez ~** he's a bit of a womanizer.
3 **coureuse** nf (*péj: débauchée*) manhunter. **elle est un peu ~euse** she's a bit of a manhunter.
4 comp ►**coureur automobile** racing(-car) driver ►**coureur de** *ou* **des bois** (*Can Hist*) trapper, coureur de bois (*US, Can*) ►**coureur cycliste** racing cyclist ►**coureur de dot** (*péj*) fortune-hunter ►**coureur motocycliste** motorcycle *ou* motorbike racer.

courge [kuʀʒ] nf a (*plante, fruit*) gourd, squash (*US, Can*); (*Culin*) marrow (*Brit*), squash (*US, Can*). b (⁑) idiot, nincompoop*, berk⁑ (*Brit*).

courgette [kuʀʒɛt] nf courgette (*Brit*), zucchini (*US*), summer squash (*US*).

courir [kuʀiʀ] [11] 1 vi a (*gén, Athlétisme*) to run; (*Aut, Cyclisme*) to race; (*Courses*) to run, race. **entrer/sortir en courant** to run in/out; **se mettre à ~** to break into a run, start to run, start running; **~ sur Lotus aux Vingt-Quatre Heures du Mans** to race with Lotus in the Le Mans 24 hours; **~ à toutes jambes, ~ à perdre haleine** to run as fast as one's legs can carry one, run like the wind; **~ comme un dératé*** *ou* **ventre à terre** to run flat out; **elle court comme un lapin** *ou* **lièvre** she runs *ou* can run like a hare *ou* the wind; **le voleur court encore** *ou* **toujours** the thief is still at large; **faire ~ un cheval** to race *ou* run a horse; **il ne fait plus ~** he doesn't race *ou* run horses any more; **un cheval trop vieux pour ~** a horse too old to race *ou* to be raced.
b (*se précipiter*) to rush. **~ chez le docteur/chercher le docteur** to rush *ou* run to the doctor's/for the doctor; **je cours l'appeler** I'll go *ou* run and call him straight away (*Brit*) *ou* right away (*US*); **spectacle qui fait ~ tout Paris** *ou* **tous les Parisiens** show that all Paris is rushing *ou* running to see; **faire qch en courant** to do sth in a rush *ou* hurry; **elle m'a fait ~** she had me running all over the place; **elle est toujours en train de ~** she's always rushing about; **un petit mot en courant** just a (rushed) note *ou* a few hurried lines; **~ partout pour trouver qch** to hunt everywhere for sth; **tu peux toujours ~!*** you can whistle for it!*
c (*avec à, après, sur*) **~ à l'échec/à une déception** to be heading *ou* headed for failure/a disappointment; **~ à sa perte** *ou* **ruine** to be on the road to ruin; **~ à la catastrophe** to rush headlong into disaster; **~ après qch** to chase after sth; **gardez cet argent pour l'instant, il ne court pas après** keep this money for now as he's not in any hurry *ou* rush for it *ou* he's not desperate for it; (*lit, fig*) **~ après qn** to run after sb; **~ après les femmes** to be a woman-chaser, chase women; **~ sur ses 20/30 ans** to be approaching 20/30; **~ sur ses 60/70 ans** to be approaching *ou* pushing* *ou* getting on for 60/70; **~ sur le système** *ou* **le haricot à qn⁑** to get on sb's nerves *ou* wick⁑ (*Brit*).
d *[nuages etc]* to speed, race, scud (*littér*); *[ombres, reflets]* to speed, race; *[eau]* to rush; *[chemin]* to run. **une onde courait sur les blés** a wave passed through the corn; **un frisson lui courut par tout le corps** a shiver went *ou* ran through his body; **sa plume courait sur le papier** his pen was running *ou* racing across the paper; **faire** *ou* **laisser ~ sa plume** to let one's pen flow *ou* run (on *ou* freely); **laisser ~ ses doigts sur un clavier** to tinkle away at a piano.
e (*se répandre*) **faire ~ un bruit/une nouvelle** to spread a rumour/a piece of news; **le bruit court que ...** rumour has it that ..., there is a rumour that ..., the rumour is that ...; **le bruit a récemment couru que ...** rumour recently had it that ..., the rumour has recently gone round that ...; **il court sur leur compte de curieuses histoires** there are some strange stories going round about them.
f (*se passer*) **l'année/le mois qui court** the current *ou* present year/month; **par le(s) temps qui cour(en)t** (with things as they are *ou* things being as they are) nowadays; **laisser ~*** to let things alone; **laisse ~*** forget it*, drop it*.
g (*Naut*) to sail.
h (*Fin*) *[intérêt]* to accrue; *[bail]* to run.
2 vt a (*Sport*) *épreuve* to compete in. **~ un 100 mètres** to run (in) *ou* compete in a 100 metres race; **~ le Grand Prix** to race in the Grand Prix.
b (*Chasse*) **~ le cerf/le sanglier** to hunt the stag/the boar, go staghunting/boarhunting; *voir* **lièvre.**
c (*rechercher*) *honneurs* to seek avidly. (*s'exposer à*) **~ de grands dangers** to be in great danger; **~ les aventures** *ou* **l'aventure** to seek adventure; **~ un (gros) risque** to run a (high *ou* serious) risk; **~ sa chance** to try one's luck; **il court le risque d'être accusé** he runs the risk of being accused; **c'est un risque à ~** it's a risk we'll have to take *ou* run; (*Théât*) **~ le cachet** to chase after any sort of work.
d (*parcourir*) *les mers, le monde* to roam, rove; *la campagne, les bois* to roam *ou* rove (through); (*faire le tour de*) *les magasins, les bureaux* to go round. **j'ai couru les agences toute la matinée** I've been going round the agencies all morning, I've been going from agency to agency all morning; **~ les rues** (*lit*) to wander *ou* roam the streets; (*fig*) to be run-of-the-mill, be nothing out of the ordinary; **le vrai courage ne court pas les rues** real courage is hard to find; **des gens comme lui, ça ne court pas les rues*** people like him are not thick on the ground* (*Brit*) *ou* are few and far between.
e (*fréquenter*) **~ les théâtres/les bals** to do the rounds of (all) the theatres/dances; **~ les filles** to chase the girls; **~ la gueuse†** to go wenching†; **~ le guilledou†** *ou* **la prétentaine†** *ou* **le cotillon** to go gallivanting†, go wenching†.
f (⁑) **~ qn** to get up sb's nose⁑ (*Brit*) *ou* on sb's wick⁑ (*Brit*), bug sb⁑.

courlis [kuʀli] nm curlew.

couronne [kuʀɔn] nf a *[fleurs]* wreath, circlet. **~ funéraire** *ou* **mortuaire** (funeral) wreath; **~ de fleurs d'oranger** orange-blossom headdress, circlet of orange-blossom; **~ de lauriers** laurel wreath, crown of laurels; **~ d'épines** crown of thorns; **en ~** in a ring; *voir* **fleur.**
b (*diadème*) *[roi, pape]* crown; *[noble]* coronet.
c (*autorité royale*) **la ~** the Crown; **la ~ d'Angleterre/de France** the crown of England/of France, the English/French crown; **aspirer/prétendre à la ~** to aspire to/lay claim to the throne *ou* the crown; **de la ~** *joyaux, colonie* crown (*épith*).
d (*objet circulaire*) crown; (*pain*) ring-shaped loaf; *[dent]* crown; (*Archit, Astron*) corona. (*Aut*) **~ dentée** crown wheel; **la grande/petite ~** the outer/inner suburbs (of Paris).
e (*monnaie*) crown.

couronnement [kuʀɔnmɑ̃] nm a *[roi, empereur]* coronation, crowning. b *[édifice, colonne]* top, crown; *[mur]* coping; *[toit]* ridge. c (*fig*) *[carrière, œuvre, recherche]* crowning achievement.

couronner [kuʀɔne] [1] 1 vt a *souverain* to crown. **on le couronna roi** he was crowned king, they crowned him king; *voir* **tête.**
b *ouvrage, auteur* to award a prize to; (*Hist*) *lauréat, vainqueur* to crown with a laurel wreath.
c (*littér: orner, ceindre*) to crown; *[diadème] front* to encircle. **couronné de fleurs** wreathed *ou* encircled with flowers; **remparts qui couronnent la colline** ramparts which crown the hill; **un pic couronné de neige** a peak crowned with snow, a snow-capped peak.
d (*parachever*) to crown. **cela couronne son œuvre/sa carrière** that is the crowning achievement of his work/his career; (*iro*) **et pour ~ le tout** and to crown it all; **ses efforts ont été couronnés de succès** his efforts were crowned with success.
e *dent* to crown.
2 **se couronner** vpr: **se ~ (le genou)** *[cheval, personne]* to graze its (*ou* one's) knee.

courre [kuʀ] vt *voir* **chasse¹.**

courrier [kuʀje] nm a (*lettres reçues*) mail, post (*Brit*), letters; (*lettres à écrire*) letters. **le ~ de 11 heures** the 11 o'clock post (*Brit*) *ou* mail; (*fig*) **avoir** *ou* **recevoir un ~ de ministre** to have a huge postbag* (*Brit*), be inundated with mail *ou* letters; (*Ordin*) **~ électronique** electronic mail; *voir* **retour.** b (†) (*avion, bateau*) mail; (*Mil: estafette*) courier; (*de diligence*) post. **l'arrivée du ~ de Bogota** the arrival of the Bogota mail; *voir* **long, moyen.** c (*Presse*) (*rubrique*) column; (*nom de journal*) ≃ Mail. **~ du cœur** problem page, (women's) advice column; **~ des lecteurs** letters to the Editor; **~ littéraire** literary column; **~ économique** financial page.

courriériste [kuʀjeʀist] nmf columnist.

courroie [kuRwa] nf (*attache*) strap; (*Tech*) belt. (*Tech*) ~ **de transmission** driving belt; (*fig*) **je ne suis qu'une simple ~ de transmission** I'm just a cog in the machine *ou* wheel; (*Aut*) ~ **de ventilateur** fan belt.

courroucé, e [kuRuse] (ptp de **courroucer**) adj (*littér*) wrathful, incensed.

courroucer [kuRuse] [3] (*littér*) 1 vt to anger, incense. 2 **se courroucer** vpr to become incensed.

courroux [kuRu] nm (*littér*) ire (*littér*), wrath.

cours [kuR] 1 nm a (*déroulement, Astron*) course; *[événements]* course, run; *[saisons]* course, progression; *[guerre, maladie]* progress, course; *[pensées, idées]* course; *voir* **suivre**.

b *[rivière]* (*cheminement*) course; (*écoulement*) flow. **avoir un ~ rapide/régulier** to be fast-/smooth-flowing; **sur une partie de son ~** on *ou* along part of its course; **descendre le ~ de la Seine** to go down the Seine.

c (*Fin*) *[monnaie]* currency; *[valeurs, matières premières]* price; *[devises]* rate. ~ **légal** legal tender; (*Bourse*) ~ **d'ouverture/de clôture** opening/closing price; ~ **des devises** *ou* **du change** foreign exchange rate; **au ~ (du jour)** at the price of the day; **au ~ du marché** at (the) market price; **le ~ des voitures d'occasion** the (selling) price of second-hand cars.

d (*leçon*) class; (*Univ: conférence*) lecture; (*série de leçons*) course; (*manuel*) coursebook, textbook. ~ **de solfège/de danse** musical theory/dancing lesson; ~ **de chimie** (*leçon*) chemistry class *ou* lesson; (*conférence*) chemistry lecture; (*enseignement*) chemistry course; (*manuel*) chemistry coursebook *ou* textbook; (*notes*) ~ **de droit** law (course) notes; **faire** *ou* **donner un ~ sur** to give a class *ou* lecture on; to give a course on; **il donne des ~ en fac*** he lectures at (the) university; **qui vous fait ~ en anglais?** who takes you for English?, who have you got for English?; **je ne ferai pas ~ demain** I won't be teaching tomorrow; **j'ai (un) ~ d'histoire à 2 heures** I've got a history class at 2 o'clock; ~ **du soir** (pl) evening classes; ~ **par correspondance** correspondence course; ~ **de vacances** holiday course (*Brit*), summer school (*US*); ~ **intensif** crash course (*de, en* in); **donner/prendre des ~ particuliers** to give/have private lessons; **~s particuliers de piano** private piano lessons.

e (*Scol: établissement*) school. ~ **privé** private school; ~ **de jeunes filles** girls' school *ou* college; ~ **de danse** dancing school.

f (*Scol: enseignement primaire*) class. ~ **préparatoire** first-year infants (class) (*Brit*), nursery school (*US*); ~ **élémentaire/moyen** primary/intermediate classes (*of primary school*); (*Hist*) ~ **complémentaire** *final year in elementary school.*

g (*avenue*) walk.

h (*loc*) **avoir ~** *[monnaie]* to be legal tender; (*fig*) to be current, be in current use; **ne plus avoir ~** *[monnaie]* to be no longer legal tender *ou* currency, be out of circulation; *[expression]* to be obsolete, be no longer in use *ou* no longer current; **ces plaisanteries n'ont plus ~ ici** jokes like that are no longer appreciated here; **en ~** *année* current (*épith*); *affaires* in hand, in progress; *essais* in progress, under way; **en ~ de** in the process of; **en ~ de réparation/réfection** in the process of being repaired/rebuilt; (*Jur*) **brevet en ~ d'agrément** patent pending; **en ~ de route** on the way; **au ~ de** in the course of, during; **donner (libre) ~ à** *imagination* to give free rein to; *douleur* to give free expression to; *joie, sentiment* to give vent to, give free expression to; **il donna (libre) ~ à ses larmes** he let his tears flow freely.

2 comp ►**cours d'eau** *generic term for streams, rivers and waterways;* **le confluent de deux cours d'eau** the confluence of two rivers; **un petit cours d'eau traversait cette vallée** a stream ran across this valley.

course [kuRs] 1 nf a (*action de courir*) running. **la ~ et la marche** running and walking; **prendre sa ~** to start running; **le cheval, atteint d'une balle en pleine ~** the horse, hit by a bullet in mid gallop; **il le rattrapa à la ~** he ran after him and caught him (up); **quelle ~ pour attraper le bus!** I had to rush like mad to catch the bus*; *voir* **pas**[1].

b (*discipline*) (*Athlétisme*) running; (*Aut, Courses, Cyclisme*) racing. **faire de la ~ pour s'entraîner** to go running to get fit; (*Aut, Cyclisme*) **tu fais de la ~?** do you race?; ~ **de fond/demi-fond** long-distance/middle-distance running; ~ **sur piste/route** track/road racing; (*fig*) **la ~ aux armements** the arms race; (*fig*) **la ~ au pouvoir** the race for power; **faire la ~ avec qn** to race with sb; **allez, on fait la ~** let's have a race, I'll give you a race, I'll race you; *voir* **champ, écurie**.

c (*épreuve*) race. ~ **de fond/sur piste** long-distance/track race; (*Courses*) **les ~s** the races; **parier aux ~s** to bet on the races; (*lit*) **être/ne plus être dans la ~** to be in the running/out of the running; (*fig*) **il n'est plus dans la ~*** he's out of touch; *voir* **contre**.

d (*voyage*) *[autocar]* trip, journey; *[taxi]* journey. **payer le prix de la ~, payer la ~** to pay the fare; *[taxi]* **il n'a fait que 3 ~s hier** he only picked up *ou* had 3 fares yesterday.

e (*fig*) *[projectile]* flight; *[navire]* rapid course; *[nuages, ombres]* racing, swift passage; *[temps]* swift passage, swift passing (*NonC*).

f (*excursion*) (*à pied*) hike; (*ascension*) climb.

g (*au magasin*) shopping (*NonC*); (*commission*) errand. **faire les ~s** to do the shopping; **elle est sortie faire des ~s** she has gone out to do *ou* get some shopping; **j'ai quelques ~s à faire** I've a bit of shopping to do, I've one or two things to buy; **faire une ~** to (go and) get something from the shop(s) (*Brit*) *ou* store(s) (*US*); to run an errand.

h (*Tech*) *[pièce mobile]* movement; *[piston]* stroke. **à bout de ~** (*Tech*) at full stroke; (*fig: usé*) *machine* worn out, on its last legs*; *personne* on one's last legs*; **à mi-~** at half-stroke; *voir* **fin**.

i (*Naut*) privateering. **faire la ~** to privateer, go privateering; *voir* **guerre**.

2 comp ►**course attelée** harness race ►**course automobile** motor race ►**course de chevaux** horse-race ►**course de côte** (*Sport Aut*) hill climb ►**course contre la montre** (*Sport*) race against the clock, time-trial; (*fig*) race against the clock ►**course par étapes** stage race ►**course de haies** hurdling; **faire de la course de haies** to hurdle ►**course d'obstacles** obstacle race ►**course d'orientation** orienteering race ►**course-poursuite** nf (pl **courses-poursuites**) (*Cyclisme*) pursuit; (*après voleur*) chase ►**course de relais** relay race ►**course en sac** sack race ►**course de taureaux** bullfight ►**course au trésor** treasure hunt ►**course de trot** trotting race ►**course au trot attelé** harness race ►**course de vitesse** sprint.

courser* [kuRse] [1] vt to chase *ou* hare* after.

coursier[1] [kuRsje] nm (*littér: cheval*) charger (*littér*), steed (*littér*).

coursier[2]**, -ière** [kuRsje, jɛR] nm,f messenger, courier.

coursive [kuRsiv] nf (*Naut*) gangway (*connecting cabins*).

court[1]**, e** [kuR, kuRt] 1 adj a (*gén*) *objet, récit, durée, mémoire* short; *introduction, séjour* short, brief. **il a été** *ou* **il a fait* très ~** he was very brief; **je suis pressé, il faut faire ~*** I'm in a hurry, we'll have to make it quick*; **de ~e durée** *enthousiasme, ardeur* short-lived; **c'est plus ~ par le bois** it's quicker *ou* shorter through the wood; **il connaît un chemin plus ~** he knows a shorter way; **la journée m'a paru ~e** the day has passed *ou* seemed to pass quickly, it has been a short day; **avoir l'haleine** *ou* **la respiration ~e** *ou* **le souffle ~** to be quickly out of breath, be short-winded; *voir* **idée, manche**[1]**, mémoire**[1].

b (*insuffisant*) **il lui a donné 10 jours, c'est ~** he's given him 10 days, which is (a bit) on the short side *ou* which isn't very long; **100 F pour le faire, c'est ~*** 100 francs to do it – that's not very much *ou* that's a bit stingy*.

c (*loc*) **tirer à la ~e paille** to draw lots (*Brit*) *ou* straws (*US*); **à sa ~e honte** to his humiliation; **être à ~ d'argent/d'arguments** to be short of money/arguments; **prendre au plus ~** to go the shortest way; (*fig*) **aller au plus ~** to cut corners; **prendre qn de ~** to catch sb unawares *ou* on the hop* (*Brit*).

2 adv a *coiffer, habiller* short. **les cheveux coupés ~** with short(-cut) hair, with hair cut short.

b **s'arrêter ~** to stop short; **demeurer** *ou* **se trouver ~** to be at a loss; *voir* **couper, pendre, tourner**.

3 comp ►**court-bouillon** (*Culin*) nm (pl **courts-bouillons**) court-bouillon ►**court-circuit** (*Élec*) nm (pl **courts-circuits**) short(-circuit) ►**court-circuiter** vt (*lit*) to short(-circuit); (*fig*) to bypass, short-circuit ►**courte échelle** leg up (*Brit*), boost (*US*); **faire la courte échelle à qn** to give sb a leg up (*Brit*) *ou* a boost (*US*) ►**court-jus*** nm inv short-circuit ►**court-métrage** (*Ciné*) nm (pl **courts-métrages**) short film, one-reeler (*US*) ►**court-vêtu, e** adj (mpl **court-vêtus**) short-skirted.

court[2] [kuR] nm (tennis) court. ~ **central** centre court.

courtage [kuRtaʒ] nm brokerage.

courtaud, e [kuRto, od] adj a *personne* dumpy, squat. **un ~** a dumpy *ou* squat little man. b **un (chien/cheval) ~** a docked and crop-eared dog/horse.

courtepointe [kuRtəpwɛ̃t] nf counterpane.

courtier, -ière [kuRtje, jɛR] nm,f broker. ~ **en vins** wine-broker; ~ **maritime** ship-broker.

courtine [kuRtin] nf curtain.

courtisan [kuRtizɑ̃] nm (*Hist*) courtier; (*fig*) sycophant. **des manières de ~** sycophantic manners.

courtisane [kuRtizan] nf (*Hist, littér*) courtesan, courtezan.

courtiser [kuRtize] [1] vt († *ou littér*) *femme* to woo, court, pay court to; (*flatter*) to pay court to, fawn on (*péj*).

courtois, e [kuRtwa, waz] adj courteous; (*Littérat*) courtly.

courtoisement [kuRtwazmɑ̃] adv courteously.

courtoisie [kuRtwazi] nf courtesy, courteousness. (*Jur*) ~ **internationale** comity of nations.

couru, e [kuRy] (ptp de **courir**) adj a *restaurant, spectacle* popular. b **c'est ~ (d'avance)*** it's a (dead) cert* (*Brit*), it's a sure thing*, it's a foregone conclusion.

couscous [kuskus] nm (*Culin*) couscous.

couscoussier [kuskusje] nm couscous-maker.

cousette [kuzɛt] nf (†: *ouvrière*) dressmaker's apprentice; (*nécessaire*) sewing kit.

couseuse [kuzøz] nf stitcher, sewer.

cousin[1]**, e** [kuzɛ̃, in] nm,f cousin. ~ **germain** first cousin; **~s issus de germains** second cousins; **~s au 3e/4e degré** 3rd/4th cousins; **ils sont un peu ~s** they are related (in some way) *ou* are distant relations; *voir* **mode**[1]**, roi**.

cousin[2] [kuzɛ̃] nm (*Zool*) mosquito.

cousinage† [kuzinaʒ] **nm** (*entre germains*) cousinhood, cousinship; (*vague parenté*) relationship.
cousiner† [kuzine] 1 **vi** to be on familiar terms (*avec* with).
coussin [kusɛ̃] **nm** *[siège]* cushion; (*Tech*) *[collier de cheval]* padding; (*Belgique: oreiller*) pillow. ~ **d'air** air cushion.
coussinet [kusinɛ] **nm** a *[siège, genoux]* (small) cushion; *[animal]* pad. b (*Tech*) bearing. ~ **de tête de bielle** *[arbre de transmission]* big end bearing; *[rail]* chair.
cousu, e [kuzy] (**ptp de coudre**) **adj** sewn, stitched. (*fig*) **être (tout) ~ d'or** to be rolling in riches; (*fig*) **c'est ~ de fil blanc** it's blatant, it sticks out a mile, it's a dead give-away* (*US*); ~ **main** (*lit*) handsewn, handstitched; (* *fig*) **c'est du ~ main** it's top quality stuff; ~ **machine** machine-sewn; *voir* **bouche, motus.**
coût [ku] **nm** (*lit, fig*) cost. **le ~ de la vie** the cost of living; ~ **d'acquisition** original cost; **~s de base** baseline costs; ~ **du crédit** credit charges; ~ **de distribution** distribution cost; ~ **d'investissement** capital cost; ~ **de production** production cost; ~ **salarial** wage(s) bill; ~ **d'utilisation** cost-in-use; *voir* **indice.**
coûtant [kutɑ̃] **adj m: prix ~** cost price; **vendre à prix ~** to sell at cost (price).
couteau, **pl ~x** [kuto] 1 **nm** a (*pour couper*) knife; *[balance]* knife edge; (*coquillage*) razor-shell (*Brit*), razor clam (*US*). ~ **à beurre/dessert/fromage/poisson** butter/dessert/cheese/fish knife; *voir* **lame, second.**
b (*loc*) **vous me mettez le ~ sous** *ou* **sur la gorge** you're holding a gun at my head; **être à ~(x) tiré(s)** to be at daggers drawn (*avec* with); **remuer** *ou* **retourner le ~ dans la plaie** to twist the knife in the wound, rub it in*.
2 **comp ▸couteau de chasse** hunting knife **▸couteau à cran d'arrêt** flick-knife **▸couteau de cuisine** kitchen knife **▸couteau à découper** carving knife **▸couteau électrique** electric knife **▸couteau à éplucher, couteau éplucheur, couteau à légumes** (potato) peeler **▸couteau à pain** breadknife **▸couteau à palette** *ou* **de peintre** (*Peinture*) palette knife **▸couteau pliant** *ou* **de poche** pocket knife **▸couteau-scie nm (pl couteaux-scies)** serrated knife **▸couteau de table** table knife.
coutelas [kutlɑ] **nm** (*couteau*) large (kitchen) knife; (*épée*) cutlass.
coutelier, -ière [kutəlje, jɛʀ] **nmf** (*fabricant, marchand*) cutler.
coutellerie [kutɛlʀi] **nf** (*industrie*) cutlery industry; (*atelier*) cutlery works; (*magasin*) cutlery shop, cutler's (shop); (*produits*) cutlery.
coûter [kute] 1 **vti** a to cost. **combien ça coûte?** how much is it?, how much does it cost?; **ça coûte cher?** is it expensive?, does it cost a lot?; **ça m'a coûté 10 F** it cost me 10 francs; **les vacances, ça coûte*!** holidays are expensive *ou* cost a lot!; **ça coûte une fortune** *ou* **les yeux de la tête*** it costs a fortune *ou* the earth*, it costs an arm and a leg; **ça coûte la peau des fesses**‡ it costs a damn‡ fortune; **ça va lui ~ cher** (*lit*) it'll cost him a lot; (*fig: erreur, impertinence*) he'll pay for that, it will cost him dear(ly) (*Brit*); **ça coûtera ce que ça coûtera*** never mind the expense *ou* cost, blow the expense*; **tu pourrais le faire, pour ce que ça te coûte!** you could easily do it – it wouldn't make any difference to you *ou* it wouldn't put you to any trouble; **ça ne coûte rien d'essayer** it costs nothing to try.
b (*fig*) **cet aveu/ce renoncement m'a coûté** this confession/renouncement cost me dear; **cette démarche me coûte** this is a painful step for me (to take); **il m'en coûte de refuser** it pains *ou* grieves me to have to refuse; **ça m'a coûté bien des mois de travail** it cost me many months' work; **ça lui a coûté la tête/la vie** it cost him his head/life; *voir* **premier.**
c **coûte que coûte** at all costs, no matter what; **il faut y arriver coûte que coûte** we must get there at all costs.
coûteusement [kutøzmɑ̃] **adv** expensively.
coûteux, -euse [kutø, øz] **adj** costly, expensive; (*fig*) *aveu, renoncement* painful. **ce fut une erreur ~euse** it was a costly mistake *ou* a mistake that cost him (*ou* us *etc*) dear (*Brit*).
coutil [kuti] **nm** *[vêtements]* drill, twill; *[matelas]* ticking.
coutre [kutʀ] **nm** coulter (*Brit*), colter (*US*).
coutume [kutym] **nf** a (*usage: gén, Jur*) custom; (*Jur: recueil*) customary. b (*habitude*) **avoir ~ de** to be in the habit of; **plus/moins que de ~** more/less than usual; **comme de ~** as usual; **selon sa ~** as is his custom *ou* wont (*littér*), following his usual custom; *voir* **fois.**
coutumier, -ière [kutymje, jɛʀ] 1 **adj** customary, usual. (*gén péj*) **il est ~ du fait** that is what he usually does, that's his usual trick*; *voir* **droit**[3]. 2 **nm** (*Jur*) customary.
couture [kutyʀ] **nf** a (*action, ouvrage*) sewing; (*profession*) dressmaking. **faire de la ~** to sew; **veste/robe ~** designer jacket/dress; *voir* **haut, maison, point**[2]. b (*suite de points*) seam. **sans ~(s)** seamless; **faire une ~ à grands points** to tack *ou* baste a seam; ~ **apparente** *ou* **sellier** topstitching, overstitching; ~ **anglaise/plate** *ou* **rabattue** French/flat seam; **examiner** *ou* **regarder qch/qn sous toutes les ~s** to examine sth/sb from every angle; *voir* **battre.** c (*cicatrice*) scar. d (*suture*) stitches.
couturé, e [kutyʀe] **adj** *visage* scarred.
couturier [kutyʀje] **nm** a (*personne*) couturier, fashion designer. **grand ~** grand couturier, big designer. b (*Anat*) **(muscle) ~** sartorial muscle, sartorius.
couturière [kutyʀjɛʀ] **nf** a (*personne*) dressmaker; (*en atelier etc*) dressmaker, seamstress†. b (*Théât*) *rehearsal preceding the full dress rehearsal, when alterations are made to the costumes.*
couvain [kuvɛ̃] **nm** (*œufs*) brood; (*rayon*) brood cells.
couvaison [kuvɛzɔ̃] **nf** (*période*) incubation; (*action*) brooding, sitting.
couvée [kuve] **nf** *[poussins]* brood, clutch; *[œufs]* clutch; (*fig*) (*enfants*) brood; *voir* **naître.**
couvent [kuvɑ̃] **nm** a *[sœurs]* convent, nunnery†; *[moines]* monastery. **entrer au ~** to enter a convent. b (*internat*) convent (school).
couventine [kuvɑ̃tin] **nf** (*religieuse*) conventual; (*jeune fille élevée au couvent*) convent schoolgirl.
couver [kuve] 1 1 **vi** *[feu, incendie]* to smoulder; *[haine, passion]* to smoulder, simmer; *[émeute]* to be brewing; *[complot]* to be hatching. ~ **sous la cendre** (*lit*) to smoulder under the embers; (*fig*) *[passion]* to smoulder, simmer; *[émeute]* to be brewing.
2 **vt** a *œufs [poule]* to sit on; *[appareil]* to hatch. **la poule était en train de ~** the hen was sitting on her eggs *ou* was brooding.
b (*fig*) *enfant* to be overcareful with, cocoon; *maladie* to be sickening for, be getting, be coming down with; *vengeance* to brew, plot; *révolte* to plot. **enfant couvé par sa mère** child brought up by an overcautious *ou* overprotective mother; ~ **qn/qch des yeux** *ou* **du regard** (*tendresse*) to look lovingly at sb/sth; (*convoitise*) to look covetously *ou* longingly at sb/sth.
couvercle [kuvɛʀkl] **nm** *[casserole, boîte à biscuits, bocal]* lid; *[bombe aérosol]* cap, top; (*qui se visse*) (screw-)cap, (screw-)top; (*Tech*) *[piston]* cover.
couvert, e[1] [kuvɛʀ, ɛʀt] (**ptp de couvrir**) 1 **adj** a (*habillé*) covered (up). **il est trop ~ pour la saison** he's too wrapped up *ou* he's wearing too many clothes for the time of year; **cet enfant ne reste jamais ~ au lit** this child will never keep himself covered up in bed *ou* will never keep his bedcovers *ou* bedclothes on (him); **il est resté ~ dans l'église** he kept his hat on inside the church.
b ~ **de** covered in *ou* with; **il a le visage ~ de boutons** his face is covered in *ou* with spots; **des pics ~s de neige** snow-covered *ou* snow-clad (*littér*) peaks; ~ **de chaume** *toit* thatched; *maison* thatch-roofed, thatched; **le rosier est ~ de fleurs** the rosebush is a mass of *ou* is covered in flowers.
c (*voilé*) *ciel* overcast, clouded over (*attrib*). **par temps ~** when the sky is overcast; *voir* **mot.**
d *rue, allée, cour* covered; *piscine, court de tennis* indoor (*épith*), indoors (*attrib*). *voir* **marché.**
e (*protégé par un supérieur*) covered.
f *syllabe* closed.
2 **nm** a (*ustensiles*) place setting. **une ménagère de 12 ~s** a canteen of 12 place settings; **leurs ~s sont en argent** their cutlery is silver; **j'ai sorti les ~s en argent** I've brought out the silver cutlery.
b (*à table*) **mettre le ~** to lay *ou* set the table; **mettre 4 ~s** to lay *ou* set 4 places, lay *ou* set the table for 4; **table de 4 ~s** table laid *ou* set for 4; **mets un ~ de plus** lay *ou* set another *ou* an extra place; **il a toujours son ~ mis chez nous** he can come and eat with us at any time, there's always a place for him at our table; **le vivre** *ou* **gîte et le ~** board and lodging (*Brit*), bed *ou* room and board.
c (*au restaurant*) cover charge.
d (*abri*) (*littér*) **sous le ~ d'un chêne** under the shelter of an oak tree; **à ~ de la pluie** sheltered from the rain; (*Mil*) **(être) à ~** (to be) under cover; (*Mil*) **se mettre à ~** to get under *ou* take cover.
e (*loc*) **se mettre à ~ (contre des réclamations)** to cover *ou* safeguard o.s. (against claims); **être à ~ des soupçons** to be safe from suspicion; **sous (le) ~ de** *prétexte* under cover of; **ils l'ont fait sous le ~ de leurs supérieurs** they did it by hiding behind the authority of their superiors; **sous (le) ~ de la plaisanterie** while trying to appear to be joking, under the guise of a joke; **Monsieur le Ministre sous ~ de Monsieur le Recteur** the Minister through the person of the Director of Education.
couverte[2] [kuvɛʀt] **nf** (*Tech*) glaze.
couverture [kuvɛʀtyʀ] **nf** a (*literie*) blanket. ~ **de laine/chauffante** wool *ou* woollen/electric blanket; ~ **de voyage** travelling rug; (*fig*) **amener** *ou* **tirer la ~ à soi** (*s'attribuer tout le succès*) to take (all) the credit, get unfair recognition; (*monopoliser la parole*) to turn the meeting into a one-man show.
b (*toiture*) roofing. ~ **de chaume** thatched roofing; ~ **en tuiles** tiled roofing.
c *[cahier, livre]* cover; (*jaquette*) dust cover. **en ~** on the cover.
d (*Mil*) cover; (*fig: prétexte, paravent*) cover. **troupes de ~** covering troops; ~ **aérienne** aerial cover.
e (*Fin*) cover, margin. ~ **sociale** Social Security cover.
f (*Journalisme*) coverage. **assurer la ~ d'un événement** to provide coverage of an event.
couveuse [kuvøz] **nf** a (*poule*) broody hen. ~ **(artificielle)** incubator. b *[bébé]* incubator. **être en ~** to be in an incubator.
couvrant, e [kuvʀɑ̃, ɑ̃t] 1 **adj** *peinture* that covers well. 2 **couvrante*** **nf** blanket, cover.
couvre- [kuvʀ] **préf** *voir* **couvrir.**
couvreur [kuvʀœʀ] **nm** roofer.

couvrir [kuvʀiʀ] 18 1 **vt** a (*gén*) *livre, meuble, sol, chargement* to cover (*de, avec* with); *casserole, récipient* to cover (*de, avec* with), put the lid on. ~ **un toit d'ardoises/de chaume/de tuiles** to slate/thatch/tile a roof; **des tableaux couvraient tout un mur** pictures covered a whole wall; ~ **le feu** to bank up the fire.

b (*habiller*) to cover. **couvre bien les enfants** wrap the children up well, cover the children up well; **une cape lui couvrait tout le corps** *ou* **le couvrait tout entier** he was completely covered in a cape; **un châle lui couvrait les épaules** her shoulders were covered with *ou* by a shawl, she had a shawl around *ou* over her shoulders.

c (*recouvrir de, parsemer de*) ~ **qch/qn de** (*gén*) to cover sth/sb with *ou* in; **la rougeole l'avait couverte de boutons** she was covered in spots from the measles; **son mari l'avait couverte de bleus** her husband had bruised her all over *ou* had covered her in *ou* with bruises; ~ **une femme de cadeaux** to shower a woman with gifts, shower gifts upon a woman; ~ **qn de caresses/baisers** to cover *ou* shower sb with caresses/kisses; ~ **qn d'injures/d'éloges** to shower sb with insults/praises, heap insults/praise upon sb; **cette aventure l'a couvert de ridicule** this affair has covered him with ridicule; *voir* **boue**.

d (*cacher, masquer*) *son, voix* to drown; *mystère, énigme* to conceal. **le bruit de la rue couvrait la voix du conférencier** the noise from the street drowned the lecturer's voice; (*lit, fig*) ~ **son jeu** to hold *ou* keep one's cards close to one's chest; **sa frugalité couvre une grande avarice** his frugality conceals great avarice; ~ **qch du nom de charité** to pass sth off as charity, label sth charity.

e (*protéger*) to cover. ~ **qn de son corps** to cover *ou* shield sb with one's body; (*Mil*) ~ **la retraite** to cover one's retreat; (*fig*) ~ **qn/les fautes de qn** to cover up for *ou* shield sb/cover up for sb's mistakes.

f (*Fin*) *frais, dépenses* to cover; *[assurance]* to cover. (*Admin*) **pourriez-vous nous** ~ **de la somme de 1000 F** would you remit to us the sum of 1,000 francs.

g (*parcourir*) *kilomètres, distance* to cover.

h (*Zool*) *jument etc* to cover.

i (*Journalisme*) *événement* to cover.

2 **se couvrir vpr** a *[arbre etc]* **se** ~ **de fleurs/feuilles au printemps** to come into bloom/leaf in the spring; **les prés se couvrent de fleurs** the meadows are becoming a mass of flowers; *[personne]* **se** ~ **de taches** to cover o.s. in splashes, get covered in splashes; **se** ~ **de boutons** to become covered in *ou* with spots; **se** ~ **de gloire** to cover o.s. with glory; **se** ~ **de honte/ridicule** to bring shame/ridicule upon o.s., cover o.s. with shame/ridicule.

b (*s'habiller*) to cover up, wrap up; (*mettre son chapeau*) to put on one's hat. **il fait froid, couvrez-vous bien** it's cold so wrap *ou* cover (yourself) up well.

c *[ciel]* to become overcast, cloud over. **le temps se couvre** the sky is *ou* it's becoming very overcast.

d (*Boxe, Escrime*) to cover. (*fig*) **pour se** ~ **il a invoqué ...** to cover *ou* shield himself he referred to ... .

3 **comp** ▸**couvre-chef** (*hum*) **nm** (**pl couvre-chefs**) hat, headgear (*NonC: hum*) ▸**couvre-feu nm** (**pl couvre-feux**) curfew ▸**couvre-lit nm** (**pl couvre-lits**) bedspread, coverlet ▸**couvre-livre nm** (**pl couvre-livres**) book cover ▸**couvre-pied(s) nm** (**pl couvre-pieds**) quilt ▸**couvre-plat nm** (**pl couvre-plats**) dish cover.

cow-boy, **pl cow-boys** [kobɔj] **nm** cowboy.

coxalgie [kɔksalʒi] **nf** coxalgia.

coyote [kɔjɔt] **nm** coyote, prairie wolf.

CP [sepe] **nm** (**abrév de cours préparatoire**) *voir* **cours**.

CPAM [sepeaɛm] **nf** (**abrév de caisse primaire d'assurance maladie**) *voir* **caisse**.

CPGE [sepeʒeə] **nf** (**abrév de classe préparatoire aux grandes écoles**) *voir* **classe**.

CPR [sepeɛʀ] **nm abrév de Centre pédagogique régional. stagiaire de** ~ trainee teacher; **faire son** ~ **à Paris** to do one's teacher training in Paris.

CQFD [sekyɛfde] (**abrév de ce qu'il fallait démontrer**) QED.

crabe [kʀɑb] **nm** a (*Zool*) crab. **marcher en** ~ to walk crabwise *ou* crabways; *voir* **panier**. b (*véhicule*) caterpillar-tracked vehicle.

crac [kʀak] **excl** *[bois, glace etc]* crack; *[étoffe]* rip.

crachat [kʀaʃa] **nm** a spit (*NonC*), spittle (*NonC*). **trottoir couvert de** ~**s** pavement spattered with spittle; **il a reçu un** ~ **dans l'œil** someone has spat in his eye. b (*†: *plaque, insigne*) decoration.

craché, e* [kʀaʃe] (**ptp de cracher**) **adj**: **c'est son père tout** ~ he's the spitting image of his father; **c'est lui tout** ~ that's just like him, that's him all over*.

crachement [kʀaʃmɑ̃] **nm** a (*expectoration*) spitting (*NonC*). ~ **de sang** spitting of blood; ~**s de sang** spasms of spitting blood *ou* of blood-spitting. b (*projection*) *[flammes, vapeur]* burst; *[étincelles]* shower. c (*bruit*) *[radio, mitrailleuses]* crackling (*NonC*), crackle.

cracher [kʀaʃe] 1 1 **vi** a (*avec la bouche*) to spit. **rincez-vous la bouche et crachez** rinse (out) your mouth and spit (it) out; ~ **sur qn** (*lit*) to spit at sb; (*fig*) to spit on sb; **il ne crache pas sur le caviar*** he doesn't turn his nose up at caviar; **il ne faut pas** ~ **sur cette offre*** this offer is not to be sneezed at; **il ne faut pas** ~ **dans la soupe*** you shouldn't turn your nose up at it; **c'est comme si je crachais en l'air*** I'm banging *ou* it's like banging my head against a brick wall; ~ **au bassinet*** to cough up*.

b *[stylo, plume]* to splutter, splotch; *[micro]* to crackle.

2 **vt** a *[personne] sang etc* to spit; *bouchée* to spit out; (*fig*) *injures* to spit (out); (*) *argent* to cough up*, stump up* (*Brit*). ~ **ses poumons*** to cough up one's lungs*; *voir* **venin**.

b *[canon] flammes* to spit (out); *projectiles* to spit out; *[cheminée, volcan, dragon]* to belch (out). **le moteur crachait des étincelles** the engine was sending out showers of sparks; **le robinet crachait une eau brunâtre** the tap was spitting out dirty brown water.

crachin [kʀaʃɛ̃] **nm** drizzle.

crachiner [kʀaʃine] 1 **vi** to drizzle.

crachoir [kʀaʃwaʀ] **nm** spittoon, cuspidor (*US*). (*fig*) **tenir le** ~* to hold the floor; (*fig*) **j'ai tenu le** ~ **à ma vieille tante tout l'après-midi** I had to (sit and) listen to my old aunt spouting all afternoon*.

crachotement [kʀaʃɔtmɑ̃] **nm** (*voir* **crachoter**) crackling (*NonC*), crackle; spluttering.

crachoter [kʀaʃɔte] 1 **vi** *[haut-parleur, téléphone]* to crackle; *[robinet]* to splutter.

crachouiller [kʀaʃuje] 1 **vi** *[personne]* to splutter.

crack[1] [kʀak] **nm** a (*poulain*) crack *ou* star horse. b (*: *as*) ace. **un** ~ **en informatique** an ace *ou* a wizard* at computing; **c'est un** ~ **au saut en longeur** he's an ace *ou* a first-class long jumper.

crack[2] [kʀak] **nm** (*arg Drogue*) crack.

cracking [kʀakiŋ] **nm** (*Chim*) cracking.

cracra* [kʀakʀa] **adj inv**, **crade*** [kʀad] **adj inv**, **cradingue*** [kʀadɛ̃g] **adj**, **crado*** [kʀado] **adj inv** grotty* (*Brit*), shabby.

craie [kʀɛ] **nf** (*substance, bâtonnet*) chalk. ~ **de tailleur** tailor's chalk, French chalk; **écrire qch à la** ~ **sur un mur** to chalk sth up on a wall.

craignos* [kʀɛɲos] **adj inv** *personne, quartier* dodgy* (*Brit*), shady*.

craindre [kʀɛ̃dʀ] 52 1 **vt** a *[personne]* to fear, be afraid *ou* scared of. **je ne crains pas la mort/la douleur** I do not fear *ou* I'm not afraid of *ou* I have no fear of death/pain; **ne craignez rien** don't be afraid *ou* frightened; **oui, je le crains!** yes, I'm afraid so! **il sait se faire** ~ he knows how to make himself feared *ou* how to make people fear him.

b ~ **de faire qch** to be afraid of doing sth; **il craint de se faire mal** he's afraid of hurting himself; **je ne crains pas de dire que ...** I am not afraid of saying that ...; **je crains d'avoir bientôt à partir** I fear *ou* I'm afraid I may have to leave soon; **craignant de manquer le train, il se hâta** he hurried along, afraid of missing *ou* afraid (that) he might miss the train, he made haste lest he miss (*frm*) *ou* for fear of missing the train.

c ~ **que: je crains qu'il (n')attrape froid** I'm afraid that *ou* I fear that he might catch cold; **ne craignez-vous pas qu'il arrive?** aren't you afraid he'll come? *ou* he might come?; **je crains qu'il (ne) se soit perdu** I'm afraid that he might *ou* may have got lost; **il est à** ~ **que ...** it is to be feared that ...; (*iro*) **je crains que vous (ne) vous trompiez, ma chère** I fear you are mistaken, my dear; **elle craignait qu'il ne se blesse** she feared *ou* was afraid that he would *ou* might hurt himself.

d ~ **pour** *vie, réputation, personne* to fear for.

e *[aliment, produit]* ~ **le froid/l'eau bouillante** to be easily damaged by (the) cold/by boiling water; **"craint l'humidité/la chaleur"** "keep *ou* store in a dry place/cool place", "do not expose to a damp atmosphere/ to heat"; **c'est un vêtement qui ne craint rien** it's a hard-wearing *ou* sturdy garment; **c'est un vieux tapis, ça ne craint rien** don't worry, it's an old carpet **ces animaux craignent la chaleur** these animals can't stand heat.

2 **vi** (*) *[personne, endroit]* to be dodgy* (*Brit*) *ou* shady*. **il n'y a pas de bus, ça craint** there're no buses, what the hell am I (*ou* are we *etc*) going to do (now)?*.

crainte [kʀɛ̃t] **nf** a fear. **la** ~ **de la maladie** *ou* **d'être malade l'arrête** fear of illness *ou* of being ill stops him; **il a la** ~ **du gendarme** he is in fear of the police, he is afraid of *ou* he fears the police; **soyez sans** ~, **n'ayez** ~ have no fear, never fear; **j'ai des** ~**s à son sujet** I'm worried about him; **sans** ~ (**adj**) without fear, fearless; (**adv**) without fear, fearlessly; **avec** ~ fearfully, full of fear; **la** ~ **qu'on ne les entende** the fear that they might be overheard; (*Prov*) **la** ~ **est le commencement de la sagesse** only the fool knows no fear.

b (*loc*) **dans la** ~ **de**, **par** ~ **de** for fear of; **de** ~ **d'une erreur** for fear of (there being) a mistake, lest there be a mistake (*frm*); (**par**) ~ **d'être suivi, il courut** he ran for fear of being followed *ou* fearing that he might be followed (*frm*); **de** ~ **que** for fear that, fearing that; **de** ~ **qu'on ne le suive, il courut** he ran for fear of being followed *ou* fearing that he might be followed.

craintif, -ive [kʀɛ̃tif, iv] **adj** *personne, animal, caractère* timorous, timid; *regard, ton, geste* timid.

craintivement [kʀɛ̃tivmɑ̃] **adv** *agir, parler* timorously, timidly.

cramé, e* [kʀame] 1 **adj** burnt. 2 **nm ça sent le** ~ (*lit*) I (can) smell burning; (*fig*) there's trouble brewing; **ça a un goût de** ~ it tastes burnt; **ne mange pas le** ~ don't eat the burnt bit(s).

cramer* [kʀame] 1 1 **vi** *[maison]* to burn down, go up in flames; *[mobilier]* to go up in flames *ou* smoke; *[tissu, papier]* to burn. 2 **vt** (*gén*) to burn; *maison* to burn down; *mobilier* to send up in flames.

cramoisi, e [kʀamwazi] **adj** crimson.

crampe [kRɑ̃p] nf cramp. **avoir une ~ au mollet** to have cramp (*Brit*) *ou* a cramp (*US*) in one's calf; **~ d'estomac** stomach cramp; (*hum*) **la ~ de l'écrivain** writer's cramp (*hum*).

crampon [kRɑ̃pɔ̃] nm **a** (*Tech*) cramp (iron), clamp. **b** *[chaussures de football]* stud; *[chaussures de course]* spike; *[fer à cheval]* calk. *[alpiniste]* **~ (à glace)** crampon. **c** (*Bot*) tendril. **d** (**: personne*) leech. **elle est ~** she clings like a leech, you can't shake her off.

cramponnage [kRɑ̃pɔnaʒ] nm (*Alpinisme*) crampon technique, cramponning.

cramponner [kRɑ̃pɔne] [1] **1** vt **a** (*Tech*) to cramp (together), clamp (together). **b** (** fig*) to cling to. **2 se cramponner** vpr (*pour ne pas tomber*) to hold on, hang on; (*fig: dans son travail*) to stick at it*, hang on in there*. (*fig*) **elle se cramponne** (*ne vous lâche pas*) she clings like a leech, you can't shake her off; (*ne veut pas mourir*) she's holding on (to life); **se ~ à** *branche, volant, bras* to cling (on) to, clutch, hold on to; *personne* (*lit*) to cling (on) to; (*fig*) *vie, espoir, personne* to cling to.

cran [kRɑ̃] nm **a** (*pour accrocher, retenir*) *[pièce dentée, crémaillère]* notch; *[arme à feu]* catch; *[ceinture, courroie]* hole. **hausser un rayon de plusieurs ~s** to raise a shelf a few notches *ou* holes; **~ de sécurité** *ou* **de sûreté** safety catch; **(couteau à) ~ d'arrêt** flick-knife.
b (*servant de repère*) (*Couture, Typ*) nick. **~ de mire** bead.
c *[cheveux]* wave. **le coiffeur lui avait fait un ~** *ou* **des ~s** the hairdresser had put her hair in waves.
d (**: courage*) guts*. **il a un drôle de ~*** he's got a lot of bottle‡ *ou* guts‡.
e (*loc*) **monter/descendre d'un ~** (*dans la hiérarchie*) to move up/come down a rung *ou* peg; **il est monté/descendu d'un ~ dans mon estime** he has gone up/down a notch *ou* peg in my estimation; **être à ~** to be very edgy; **ne le mets pas à ~** don't make him mad*.

crâne[1] [kRɑn] nm (*Anat*) skull, cranium (*SPÉC*); (*fig*) head. **avoir mal au ~*** to have an awful head*; (*fig*) **avoir le ~ dur*** to be thick(skulled)*; *voir* **bourrage, bourrer, fracture.**

crâne[2]† [kRɑn] adj gallant.

crânement† [kRɑnmɑ̃] adv gallantly.

crâner* [kRɑne] [1] vi to swank* (*Brit*), put on the dog* (*US*), show off*. **ce n'est pas la peine de ~** it's nothing to swank* (*Brit*) *ou* show off* about.

crânerie† [kRɑnRi] nf gallantry.

crâneur, -euse* [kRɑnœR, øz] nm,f swank* (*Brit*), show-off*. **faire le ~** to swank* (*Brit*) *ou* show off*; **elle est un peu ~euse** she's a bit of a show-off*.

crânien, -ienne [kRɑnjɛ̃, jɛn] adj cranial; *voir* **boîte.**

craniologie [kRanjɔlɔʒi] nf craniology.

cranter [kRɑ̃te] [1] vt (*Tech*) *pignon, roue* to put notches in. **tige crantée** notched stem.

crapahuter [kRapayte] [1] vi (*arg Mil*) to trudge over difficult ground.

crapaud [kRapo] **1** nm **a** (*Zool*) toad; *voir* **bave, fauteuil, piano. b** (**: gamin*) brat*. **c** *[diamant]* flaw. **2** comp ▸**crapaud de mer** angler(-fish).

crapaudine [kRapodin] nf *[tuyau]* grating.

crapouillot [kRapujo] nm (*Hist Mil*) trench mortar.

crapule [kRapyl] nf (*personne*) villain; (*††: racaille*) riffraff, scum*.

crapulerie [kRapylRi] nf **a** (*rare: caractère*) villainy, vile nature. **b** (*acte*) villainy.

crapuleusement [kRapyløzmɑ̃] adv *agir* with villainy.

crapuleux, -euse [kRapylø, øz] adj *action* villainous; *vie* dissolute; *voir* **crime.**

craquage [kRakaʒ] nm (*Chim*) cracking.

craquant, e* [kRakɑ̃, ɑ̃t] adj *femme, objet, enfant* gorgeous, lovely.

craque‡ [kRak] nf whopper‡, whopping lie*.

craqueler [kRakle] [4] **1** vt *vernis, faïence, terre [usure, âge]* to crack; (*Tech*) *[artisan]* to crackle. **2 se craqueler** vpr *[vernis, faïence, terre]* to crack.

craquellement [kRakɛlmɑ̃] nm cracking.

craquelure [kRaklyR] nf *[porcelaine]* crackle (*NonC*); *[tableau]* craquelure (*NonC*). **couvert de ~s** covered in cracks.

craquement [kRakmɑ̃] nm (*bruit*) *[arbre, branche qui se rompt]* crack, snap; *[plancher, boiserie]* creak; *[feuilles sèches, neige]* crackle, crunch; *[chaussures]* squeak. **le ~ continuel des arbres/de la banquise** the constant creak of the trees/icefield.

craquer [kRake] [1] **1** vi **a** (*produire un bruit*) *[parquet]* to creak, squeak; *[feuilles mortes]* to crackle; *[neige]* to crunch; *[chaussures]* to squeak; *[biscuit]* to crunch. **faire ~ ses doigts** to crack one's fingers; **faire ~ une allumette** to strike a match.
b (*céder*) *[bas]* to rip, go* (*Brit*); *[bois, couche de glace]* to crack; *[branche]* to crack, snap. **veste qui craque aux coutures** jacket which is coming apart at the seams; *voir* **plein.**
c (*s'écrouler*) *[entreprise, gouvernement]* to be falling apart (at the seams), be on the verge of collapse; *[athlète]* to collapse; *[accusé, malade]* to break down, collapse. **ils ont craqué en deuxième mi-temps** they gave way in the second half; **je craque*** (*je n'en peux plus*) I've had enough; (*je deviens fou*) I'm cracking up*; *voir* **nerf.**
d (**: être enthousiasmé*) **j'ai craqué** I couldn't resist it (*ou* them *ou* him *etc*).
2 vt **a** *pantalon* to rip, split. **~ un bas*** to rip *ou* tear a stocking. **b ~ une allumette** to strike a match.

crash* [kRaʃ] nm *[avion]* crash; (*à l'atterrissage*) crash landing; *[voiture, moto, train]* crash.

crasher (se)* [kRaʃe] [1] vpr *[avion]* to crash; (*à l'atterrissage*) to crash-land; *[voiture, train]* to crash; *[chauffeur, motard]* to have a crash. **il s'est crashé contre un arbre** he crashed into *ou* hit a tree; **se ~ en moto/voiture** to have a motorbike/car crash.

crassane [kRasan] nf = **passe-crassane.**

crasse [kRas] **1** nf **a** (*saleté*) grime, filth. **b** (**: sale tour*) dirty trick*. **faire une ~ à qn** to play a dirty trick on sb*. **c** (*Tech*) (*scorie*) dross, scum, slag; (*résidus*) scale. **2** adj *ignorance, bêtise* crass; *paresse* unashamed. **être d'une ignorance ~** to be abysmally ignorant *ou* pig ignorant‡.

crasseux, -euse [kRasø, øz] adj grimy, filthy.

crassier [kRasje] nm slag heap.

cratère [kRatɛR] nm crater.

cravache [kRavaʃ] nf (riding) crop. **donner un coup de ~ à** *cheval* to use the crop on; *personne* to strike (with a riding crop); (*fig*) to spur on*. (*fig*) **mener qn à la ~** to drive sb ruthlessly.

cravacher [kRavaʃe] [1] **1** vt *cheval* to use the crop on; *personne* to strike with a riding crop; (*rouer de coups*) to horsewhip. **2** vi (*) (*foncer*) to belt along*; (*pour finir un travail*) to work like mad*, pull out all the stops*.

cravate [kRavat] nf **a** *[chemise]* tie. (*hum*) **~ de chanvre** hangman's rope; **~ de commandeur de la Légion d'honneur** ribbon of commander of the Legion of Honour; *voir* **épingle, jeter. b** (*Lutte*) headlock. **c** (*Naut*) sling.

cravater [kRavate] [1] vt **a** (*lit*) *personne* to put a tie on. **cravaté de neuf** wearing a new tie; **se ~** to put one's *ou* a tie on. **b** (*prendre au collet*) (*gén*) to grab round the neck, collar; (*Lutte*) to put in a headlock; (**: arrêter*) to collar. **se faire ~ par un journaliste** to be collared *ou* buttonholed by a journalist.

crave [kRav] nm: **~ à bec rouge** chough.

crawl [kRol] nm crawl (*swimming*). **nager le ~** to do *ou* swim the crawl.

crawler [kRole] [1] vi to do *ou* swim the crawl. **dos crawlé** backstroke.

crayeux, -euse [kRɛjø, øz] adj *terrain, substance* chalky; *teint* chalk-white.

crayon [kRɛjɔ̃] **1** nm **a** (*pour écrire etc*) pencil. **écrire au ~** to write with a pencil; **écrivez cela au ~** write that in pencil; **notes au ~** pencilled notes; **avoir le ~ facile** to be a good drawer, be good at drawing; **avoir un bon coup de ~** to be good at sketching.
b (*bâtonnet*) pencil.
c (*Art: dessin*) pencil drawing, pencil sketch.
2 comp ▸**crayon à bille** ballpoint pen, Biro ® (*Brit*) ▸**crayon de couleur** crayon, colouring pencil ▸**crayon-feutre** nm (pl **crayons-feutres**) felt-tip pen ▸**crayon gras** soft lead pencil ▸**crayon hémostatique** styptic pencil ▸**crayon à lèvres** lip pencil ▸**crayon lithographique** litho pen ▸**crayon au nitrate d'argent** silver-nitrate pencil, caustic pencil ▸**crayon noir** *ou* **à papier** lead pencil ▸**crayon optique** light pen ▸**crayon à sourcils** eyebrow pencil ▸**crayon pour les yeux** eyeliner pencil.

crayonnage [kRɛjɔnaʒ] nm (*gribouillage*) scribble, doodle; (*dessin*) (pencil) drawing, sketch.

crayonner [kRɛjɔne] [1] vt **a** *notes* to scribble, jot down (in pencil); *dessin* to sketch. **b** (*péj: gribouiller*) *traits* to scribble; *dessins* to doodle.

CRDP [seɛRdepe] nm (abrév de **Centre régional de documentation pédagogique**) *voir* **centre.**

créance [kReɑ̃s] nf **a** (*Fin, Jur*) (financial) claim, debt (*seen from the creditor's point of view*); (*titre*) letter of credit. **~ hypothécaire** mortgage loan (*seen from the creditor's point of view*); (*Fin*) **~s** accounts receivable; **~ irrécouvrable** bad debt; *voir* **lettre. b** († *ou littér: crédit, foi*) credence. **donner ~ à qch** (*rendre croyable*) to lend credibility to sth; (*ajouter foi à*) to give *ou* attach credence to sth (*littér*).

créancier, -ière [kReɑ̃sje, jɛR] nm,f creditor. **~-gagiste** lienor; **~ privilégié** preferential creditor.

créateur, -trice [kReatœR, tRis] **1** adj creative. **2** nm,f (*gén, Rel*) creator. **~ de mode** fashion designer; **~ publicitaire** commercial artist; **le C~** the Creator.

créatif, -ive [kReatif, iv] **1** adj creative, inventive. **2** nm designer.

créatine [kReatin] nf creatine, creatin.

créatinine [kReatinin] nf creatinine.

création [kReasjɔ̃] nf **a** (*voir* **créer**) creation, creating; first production. **b** (*chose créée*) (*Théât: représentation*) first production; (*Comm*) product; (*Art, Haute Couture*) creation. (*Rel*) **la C~** the Creation; **cette ~ de Topaze par Jouvet est vraiment remarquable** Jouvet's creation of the role of Topaze is truly remarkable; (*Scol, Ind, etc*) **il y a deux ~s de poste** two new posts have been created; (*Phys*) **théorie de la ~ continue** steady-state theory.

créativité [kReativite] nf creativeness, creativity; (*Ling*) creativity.

créature [kReatyR] nf (*gén, péj*) creature.

crécelle [kʀesɛl] nf rattle; *voir* **voix**.

crécerelle [kʀes(ə)ʀɛl] nf kestrel.

crèche [kʀɛʃ] nf a (*Rel: de Noël*) crib. b (*établissement*) crèche, day nursery, day-care centre, child care center (*US*). ~ **familiale** *crèche in the home of a registered child minder.* c (‡: *chambre, logement*) pad‡.

crécher‡ [kʀeʃe] 6 vi to hang out‡. **je ne sais pas où ~ cette nuit** I don't know where I'm going to kip down‡ *ou* crash‡ tonight.

crédence [kʀedɑ̃s] nf a (*desserte*) credence. b (*Rel*) credence table, credenza.

crédibiliser [kʀedibilize] 1 vt (*histoire*) to back up, give credibility to; *candidature, situation financière* to support.

crédibilité [kʀedibilite] nf credibility.

crédible [kʀedibl] adj credible.

crédit [kʀedi] nm a (*paiement échelonné, différé*) credit. **12 mois de ~** 12 months' credit; **faire ~ à qn** to give sb credit; **faites-moi ~, je vous paierai la semaine prochaine** let me have (it on) credit – I'll pay you next week; **"la maison ne fait pas (de) ~"** "we are unable to give credit to our customers", "no credit is given here"; **acheter/vendre qch à ~** to buy/sell sth on credit; **possibilités de ~** credit (terms) available; **ces gens qui achètent tout à ~** these people who buy everything on credit *ou* on H.P. (*Brit*) *ou* on time (*US*); **vente à ~** selling on easy terms *ou* on credit; *voir* **carte**.
b (*prêt*) credit. **~ d'appoint** standby credit; **établissement de ~** credit institution; **l'ouverture d'un ~** the granting of credit; **~ bancaire** bank credit; **~ à la consommation** consumer credit; **~ documentaire** documentary (letter of) credit; **~ fournisseur** supplier credit; **~ gratuit** (interest-)free credit; **~ hypothécaire** mortgage; **~-bail** (*système*) leasing; (*contrat*) lease, leasing agreement; (*Scol Admin*) **~s d'enseignement** government grant (to each school); **~ à l'exportation** export credit; **~ d'impôt** tax credit; **~s non garantis** *ou* **en blanc** loans without security; **~ municipal** state-owned pawnshop *ou* pawnbroker's; *voir* **lettre**.
c (*dans une raison sociale*) bank.
d (*excédent d'un compte*) credit. **porter une somme au ~ de qn** to credit sb *ou* sb's account with a sum, credit a sum to sb *ou* sb's account.
e (*Pol: gén pl: fonds*) **~s** funds; **~s budgétaires** budget allocation; **~s extraordinaires** extraordinary funds.
f (*Can Univ: unité de valeur*) credit.
g (*prestige, confiance*) credit. **firme/client qui a du ~** creditworthy firm/client; **cette théorie connaît un grand ~** this theory is very widely accepted (*auprès de* by); **ça donne du ~ à ce qu'il affirme** that lends credit to what he says; **faire ~ à l'avenir** to put one's trust in the future, have faith in the future; **bonne action à mettre** *ou* **porter au ~ de qn** good deed which is to sb's credit *ou* which counts in sb's favour; **perdre tout ~ auprès de qn** to lose all credit with sb, lose sb's confidence; **trouver ~ auprès de qn** *[racontars]* to find credence with sb (*frm*); *[personne]* to win sb's confidence; **il a utilisé son ~ auprès de lui (pour)** he used his credit with him (to).

créditer [kʀedite] 1 vt a (*Fin*) **~ qn/un compte de** *somme* to credit sb/an account with. b (*Sport*) **être crédité de** *temps* to be credited with.

créditeur, -trice [kʀeditœʀ, tʀis] 1 adj in credit (*attrib*). **compte/solde ~** credit account/balance. 2 nm,f customer in credit.

credo [kʀedo] nm a (*Rel*) **le C~** the (Apostle's) Creed. b (*principes*) credo, creed.

crédule [kʀedyl] adj credulous, gullible.

crédulité [kʀedylite] nf credulity, gullibility.

créer [kʀee] 1 vt a (*gén*) to create. **le pouvoir/la joie de ~** the power/joy of creation; **se ~ une clientèle** to build up a clientèle; **~ des ennuis/difficultés à qn** to create problems/difficulties for sb, cause sb problems/difficulties; *voir* **fonction**. b (*Théât*) *rôle* to create; *pièce* to produce (for the first time).

crémaillère [kʀemajɛʀ] nf a *[cheminée]* trammel; *voir* **pendre**. b (*Rail, Tech*) rack. **chemin de fer à ~** rack railway, cog railway; **engrenage/direction à ~** rack-and-pinion gear/steering.

crémant [kʀemɑ̃] adj m, nm *champagne* cremant.

crémation [kʀemasjɔ̃] nf cremation.

crématoire [kʀematwaʀ] 1 adj crematory; *voir* **four**. 2 nm crematorium, crematory (*furnace*).

crématorium [kʀematɔʀjɔm] nm crematorium.

crème [kʀɛm] 1 nf a (*Culin*) (*produit laitier*) cream; (*peau sur le lait*) skin; (*entremets*) cream dessert. (*potage*) **~ d'asperges/de champignons/de tomates** cream of asparagus/of mushroom/of tomato (soup); (*liqueur*) **~ de bananes/cacao** crème de bananes/cacao; **fraises à la ~** strawberries and cream; **gâteau à la ~** cream cake; *voir* **chou**[1], **fromage** *etc*.
b (*produit pour la toilette, le nettoyage*) cream. **~ de beauté** beauty cream; **~ pour le visage** face cream; **~ pour les chaussures** shoe cream (*Brit*) *ou* polish; **les ~s de (la maison) X** beauty creams from *ou* by X.
c (*fig: les meilleurs*) **la ~** the (real) cream, the crème de la crème; **c'est la ~ des pères** he's the best of (all) fathers; **ses amis ce n'est pas la ~** his friends aren't exactly the cream of society *ou* the crème de la crème.
2 adj inv cream(-coloured).
3 nm (*café au lait*) white coffee (*Brit*), coffee with milk *ou* cream. **un grand/petit ~** a large/small cup of white coffee.
4 comp ▸**crème anglaise** (egg) custard ▸**crème anti-rides** anti-wrinkle cream ▸**crème au beurre** butter cream ▸**crème brûlée** crème brûlée ▸**crème (au) caramel** crème caramel, caramel cream *ou* custard ▸**crème Chantilly** crème Chantilly, (sweetened) whipped cream ▸**crème démaquillante** cleansing cream, make-up removing cream ▸**crème fleurette** ≃ single cream (*Brit*), light cream (*US*) ▸**crème fond de teint** fluid foundation *ou* makeup ▸**crème fouettée** (sweetened) whipped cream ▸**crème fraîche** crème fraîche; **crème fraîche épaisse** ≃ double cream (*Brit*), heavy cream (*US*) ▸**crème glacée** ice cream ▸**crème grasse** dry-skin cream ▸**crème de gruyère** ≃ cheese spread ▸**crème hydratante** moisturizing cream, moisturizer ▸**crème pâtissière** confectioner's custard ▸**crème à raser** shaving cream ▸**crème renversée** cream mould (*Brit*), cup custard (*US*).

crémerie [kʀɛmʀi] nf (*magasin*) dairy. **changeons de ~*** let's push off* somewhere else, let's take our custom (*Brit*) *ou* business (*US*) elsewhere! (*hum*).

crémeux, -euse [kʀemø, øz] adj creamy.

crémier [kʀemje] nm dairyman.

crémière [kʀemjɛʀ] nf dairywoman.

crémone [kʀemɔn] nf espagnolette bolt.

créneau, pl **~x** [kʀeno] nm a *[rempart]* crenel, crenelle; (*Mil*) *[tranchée]* slit. **les ~s** (*forme*) the crenelations; (*chemin de ronde*) the battlements; *voir* **monter**. b (*Aut*) **faire un ~** to reverse into a parking space (*between two cars*) (*Brit*), parallel park (*US*); **j'ai raté mon ~** I've parked badly. c (*Comm*) gap, niche; *[emploi du temps]* gap. (*TV*) **~ (horaire)** (time) slot; **~ publicitaire** advertising slot; **il y a un ~ pour les voitures économiques** there is a niche *ou* a ready market for fuel-efficient cars.

crénelage [kʀen(ə)laʒ] nm (*Tech*) milling.

crénelé, e [kʀen(ə)le] (ptp de **créneler**) adj *mur, arête* crenellated; *feuille, bordure* scalloped, crenate (*Bot*).

créneler [kʀen(ə)le] 4 vt a *muraille* to crenellate, crenel; *tranchée* to make a slit in. b *roue* to notch; *pièce de monnaie* to mill.

crénom [kʀenɔ̃] excl: **~ de nom!†** confound it!, dash it all! (*surtout Brit*).

créole [kʀeɔl] 1 adj *accent, parler* creole; *voir* **riz**. 2 nm (*Ling*) Creole. 3 nmf Creole. 4 nf (*boucle d'oreille*) large hoop earring.

créosote [kʀeɔzɔt] nf creosote.

crêpage [kʀɛpaʒ] nm a (*voir* **crêper**) backcombing; crimping. b **~ de chignon*** set-to* (*Brit*), dust-up*, free-for-all (*US*).

crêpe[1] [kʀɛp] nf (*Culin*) pancake. **faire sauter une ~** to toss a pancake; **~ Suzette** crêpe suzette; *voir* **dentelle, pâte, retourner**.

crêpe[2] [kʀɛp] nm a (*Tex*) crepe, crêpe, crape. **~ de Chine** crepe de Chine; **~ georgette** georgette (crepe). b (*noir: de deuil*) black mourning crepe. **voile de ~** mourning veil; **porter un ~** (*au bras*) to wear a black armband; (*autour du chapeau*) to wear a black hatband; (*aux cheveux, au revers*) to wear a black ribbon. c (*matière*) **semelles (de) ~** crepe (rubber) soles.

crêper [kʀepe] 1 1 vt a *cheveux* to backcomb. b (*Tex*) to crimp. 2 **se crêper** vpr *[cheveux]* to crimp, frizz. **se ~ le chignon*** to tear each other's hair out, have a set-to* (*Brit*) *ou* dust-up*.

crêperie [kʀɛpʀi] nf pancake restaurant.

crépi, e [kʀepi] (ptp de **crépir**) adj, nm roughcast.

crêpière [kʀepjɛʀ] nf pancake griddle.

Crépin [kʀepɛ̃] nm Crispin.

crépine [kʀepin] nf (*Aut*) oil sump filter.

crépir [kʀepiʀ] 2 vt to roughcast.

crépissage [kʀepisaʒ] nm roughcasting.

crépitation [kʀepitasjɔ̃] nf *[feu, électricité]* crackling. (*Méd*) **~ osseuse** crepitus; **~ pulmonaire** crepitations.

crépitement [kʀepitmɑ̃] nm (*voir* **crépiter**) crackling (*NonC*); sputtering (*NonC*), spluttering (*NonC*); rattle (*NonC*); patter (*NonC*).

crépiter [kʀepite] 1 vi *[feu, électricité]* to crackle; *[chandelle, friture]* to sputter, splutter; *[mitrailleuse]* to rattle out; *[grésil]* to rattle, patter. **les applaudissements crépitèrent** a ripple of applause broke out.

crépon [kʀepɔ̃] nm ≃ seersucker; *voir* **papier**.

crépu, e [kʀepy] adj *cheveux* frizzy, woolly, fuzzy. **elle est toute ~e** her hair's all frizzy.

crépusculaire [kʀepyskylɛʀ] adj (*littér, Zool*) crepuscular. **lumière ~** twilight glow.

crépuscule [kʀepyskyl] nm (*lit*) twilight, dusk; (*fig*) twilight.

crescendo [kʀeʃɛndo] 1 adv a (*Mus*) crescendo. b **aller ~** *[vacarme, acclamations]* to rise in a crescendo, grow louder and louder, crescendo; *[colère, émotion]* to grow *ou* become ever greater. 2 nm (*Mus*) crescendo. **le ~ de sa colère/de son émotion** the rising tide of his anger/emotion.

cresson [kʀesɔ̃] nm: **~ (de fontaine)** watercress.

cressonnière [kʀesɔnjɛʀ] nf watercress bed.

Crésus [kʀezys] n Croesus; *voir* **riche**.

crétacé, e [kʀetase] 1 adj Cretaceous. 2 nm: **le ~** the Cretaceous period.

crête [kʀɛt] nf a (*Zool*) *[coq]* comb; *[oiseau]* crest; *[batracien]* horn. **~ de coq** cockscomb. b (*arête*) *[mur]* top; *[toit]* ridge; *[montagne]* ridge, crest; *[vague]* crest; *[graphique]* peak. **la ~ du tibia** the edge *ou* crest (*SPÉC*) of the shin, the shin; (*Géog*) **(ligne de) ~** watershed.

Crète [kʀɛt] nf Crete.

crétin, e [kʀetɛ̃, in] 1 adj (*péj*) cretinous*, idiotic, moronic*. 2 nm,f (*péj*) idiot, moron*, cretin*, wally‡.

crétinerie* [kʀetinʀi] nf a (*NonC*) idiocy, stupidity. b idiotic *ou* stupid thing, idiocy.

crétiniser [kʀetinize] 1 vt to turn into a moron *ou* half-wit.

crétinisme [kʀetinism] nm (*Méd*) cretinism; (*péj*) idiocy, stupidity.

crétois, e [kʀetwa, waz] 1 adj Cretan. 2 nm (*Ling*) Cretan. 3 nm,f: **C~(e)** Cretan.

cretonne [kʀətɔn] nf cretonne.

creusage [kʀøzaʒ] nm, **creusement** [kʀøzmɑ̃] nm *[fondations]* digging; *[canal]* digging, cutting.

creuser [kʀøze] 1 1 vt a (*évider*) *bois, falaise* to hollow (out); *sol, roc* to make *ou* dig a hole in, dig out; (*au marteau-piqueur*) to drill a hole in. **~ la neige de ses mains nues** to dig out the snow with one's bare hands; **il a fallu ~ beaucoup *ou* profond** we (*ou* he *etc*) had to dig deep.

b *puits* to sink, bore; *fondations, mine* to dig; *canal* to dig, cut; *tranchée, fosse* to dig (out); *sillon* to plough (*Brit*), plow (*US*); *trou* (*gén*) to dig, make; (*au marteau-piqueur*) to drill, bore; *tunnel* to make, bore, dig. **~ un tunnel sous une montagne** to bore *ou* drive a tunnel under a mountain; (*fig*) **~ sa propre tombe** to dig one's own grave; (*fig*) **ça a creusé un abîme *ou* un fossé entre eux** that has created *ou* thrown a great gulf between them; (*fig*) **~ son sillon**† to plough (*Brit*) *ou* plow (*US*) one's own furrow.

c (*fig: approfondir*) *problème, sujet, idée* to go into (deeply *ou* thoroughly), look into (closely). **c'est une idée à ~** it's something to be gone into (more deeply *ou* thoroughly), it's an idea we (*ou* they *etc*) should pursue.

d (*fig*) **la mer se creuse** there's a swell coming on; **la fatigue lui creusait les joues** his face looked gaunt *ou* hollow with tiredness; **visage creusé de rides** face furrowed with wrinkles; **~ les reins** to draw o.s. up, throw out one's chest; **la promenade, ça creuse (l'estomac)*** walking gives you a real appetite; **se ~ (la cervelle *ou* la tête)*** to rack *ou* cudgel one's brains; **il ne s'est pas beaucoup creusé!*** he didn't overtax himself!, he hasn't knocked himself out!*; (*lit, fig*) **~ l'écart** to establish a convincing lead (*par rapport à* over); (*lit, fig*) **l'écart se creuse entre eux** the gap between them is widening.

2 vi: **~ dans la terre/la neige** to dig *ou* burrow into the soil/snow.

creuset [kʀøzɛ] nm a (*Chim, Ind*) crucible. **le ~ d'un haut fourneau** the heart *ou* crucible of a blast furnace; **~ de verrerie** glassmaker's crucible. b (*fig*) (*lieu de brassage*) melting pot; (*littér: épreuve*) crucible (*littér*), test. **le ~ de la souffrance** the test of suffering.

creux, creuse [kʀø, kʀøz] 1 adj a (*évidé*) *arbre, tige, dent* hollow; (*fig*) *toux, voix* hollow, deep; *son* hollow; *estomac* empty. (*fig*) **j'ai la tête *ou* la cervelle ~euse** my mind's a blank, I feel quite empty-headed; **travailler le ventre *ou* l'estomac ~** to work on an empty stomach; **avoir l'estomac *ou* le ventre ~** to feel *ou* be hungry; *voir* **nez, sonner.**

b (*concave*) *surface* concave, hollow; *yeux* deep-set, sunken; *joue* gaunt, hollow; *visage* gaunt. **aux yeux ~** hollow-eyed; *voir* **assiette, chemin.**

c (*vide de sens*) *paroles* empty, hollow, meaningless; *idées* barren, futile; *raisonnement* weak, flimsy.

d **les jours ~** slack days; **les heures ~euses** (*gén*) slack periods; (*métro, électricité, téléphone*) off-peak periods; **période creuse** (*gén*) slack period; (*Tourisme*) low season; *voir* **classe.**

2 nm a (*cavité*) *[arbre]* hollow, hole; *[rocher, dent]* cavity, hole. (*fig*) **avoir un ~ (dans l'estomac)*** to feel *ou* be hungry; **j'ai un petit ~*** I'm a bit peckish* (*Brit*), I feel a little hungry.

b (*dépression*) hollow. **être plein de ~ et de bosses** to be full of bumps and holes *ou* hollows; **le ~ de la main** the hollow of one's hand; **des écureuils qui mangent dans le ~ de la main** squirrels which eat out of one's hand; **le ~ de l'aisselle** the armpit; **le ~ de l'estomac** the pit of the stomach; **le ~ de l'épaule** the hollow of one's shoulder; **au ~ des reins** in the small of one's back; *voir* **gravure.**

c (*fig: activité réduite*) slack period. **après Noël, les ventes connaissent le ~ de janvier** after Christmas, there's a slackening-off in sales in January *ou* sales go through the January slack period.

d (*Naut*) *[voile]* belly; *[vague]* trough. **il y avait des ~ de 10 mètres** there were 10-metre-high waves, the waves were 10 metres high; (*fig*) **il est dans le ~ de la vague** his fortunes are at their lowest ebb.

crevaison [kʀəvɛzɔ̃] nf (*Aut*) puncture, flat.

crevant, e* [kʀəvɑ̃, ɑ̃t] adj (*fatigant*) killing*, gruelling; (*amusant*) priceless*, killing*. **ce travail est ~** this work is killing* *ou* really wears you out; **c'était ~!** it was priceless!* *ou* a scream!*

crevard, e‡ [kʀəvaʀ, aʀd] nm,f (*goinfre*) guzzler‡, greedy beggar*; (*crève-la-faim*) down-and-out. (*moribond*) **c'est un ~** he's a goner*.

crevasse [kʀəvas] nf *[mur, rocher]* crack, fissure, crevice; *[sol]* crack, fissure; *[glacier]* crevasse; *[peau]* break (in the skin), crack. **avoir des ~s aux mains** to have chapped hands.

crevassé, e [kʀəvase] (ptp de **crevasser**) adj *sol* fissured, with cracks; *mains, peau* chapped. **glacier très ~** glacier with a lot of crevasses.

crevasser [kʀəvase] 1 1 vt *sol* to cause cracks *ou* fissures in, crack; *mains* to chap. 2 **se crevasser** vpr *[sol]* to crack, become cracked; *[mains]* to chap, become *ou* get chapped.

crève‡ [kʀɛv] nf (*rhume*) (bad) cold. **attraper la ~** to catch one's death* (of cold).

crève- [kʀɛv] préf *voir* **crever.**

crevé, e [kʀəve] (ptp de **crever**) 1 adj a *pneu* burst, punctured. b (‡) (*mort*) dead; (*fatigué*) fagged out‡ (*Brit*), bushed*, dead*, dead-beat*. 2 nm (*Couture*) slash. **des manches à ~s** slashed sleeves.

crever [kʀəve] 5 1 vt a (*percer*) *pneu* to burst, puncture; *barrage, ballon* to burst. **~ les yeux à qn** (*intentionnellement*) to gouge (out) *ou* put out sb's eyes; (*accidentellement*) to blind sb (in both eyes); **des débris de verre lui ont crevé un œil** broken glass blinded him in one eye; **j'ai un pneu (de) crevé** I've got a flat (tyre) *ou* a puncture; **le prix a crevé le plafond** the price has broken (through) the ceiling; (*fig*) **~ le cœur à qn** to break sb's heart; (*fig*) **cela crève les yeux** it's as plain as the nose on your face; (*fig*) **cela te crève les yeux!** it's staring you in the face!; **cet acteur crève l'écran** this actor has tremendous presence on the screen.

b (*: *exténuer*) **~ qn** *[personne]* to wear sb out, work sb to death*; *[tâche, marche]* to wear sb out, fag sb out‡, kill sb*; **~ un cheval** to ride *ou* work a horse into the ground *ou* to death; **se ~ la santé *ou* la peau‡ (à faire)** to wear o.s. to a shadow (doing), ruin one's health (doing); **se ~ (au travail)** (*gén*) to work o.s. to death; *[ménagère etc]* to work one's fingers to the bone*.

c (‡) **~ la faim *ou* la dalle** to be starving* *ou* famished*; **on la crève ici!** they starve us here!

2 vi a (*s'ouvrir*) *[fruit, sac, abcès]* to burst. **les nuages crevèrent** the clouds burst, the heavens opened; (*Culin*) **faire ~ du riz** to boil rice until the grains burst *ou* split.

b (*péj: être plein de*) **~ de santé** to be bursting with health; **~ d'orgueil** to be bursting *ou* bloated with pride; **~ de jalousie** to be full of jealousy, be bursting with jealousy; **il en crevait de dépit** he was full of resentment about it; **~ d'envie de faire qch** to be dying to do sth*; *voir* **rire.**

c (*mourir*) *[animal, plante]* to die (off); (‡) *[personne]* to die, kick the bucket‡, snuff it‡ (*Brit*). **un chien crevé** a dead dog; **~ de faim/froid‡** to starve/freeze to death; (*fig*) **on crève de froid ici*** we'll catch our death of cold, it's perishing (*Brit*) *ou* freezing cold here*; **on crève de chaud ici*** it's boiling in here*; **je crève de faim*** I'm starving* *ou* famished* *ou* ravenous; **je crève de soif*** I'm dying of thirst*, I'm parched*; **~ d'ennui*** to be bored to tears *ou* death, be bored out of one's mind*; **tu veux nous faire ~!*** you want to kill us!; **faire ~ qn de soif** *etc* to make sb die of thirst *etc.*

d (*Aut*) *[pneu, automobiliste]* to have a puncture, have a burst *ou* flat tyre. **faire 10 000 km sans ~** to drive 10,000 km without a puncture *ou* flat.

3 comp ▸**crève-cœur** nm inv heartbreak ▸**crève-la-faim** nmf inv down-and-out.

crevette [kʀəvɛt] nf: **~ (rose)** prawn; **~ grise** shrimp; *voir* **filet.**

crevettier [kʀəvetje] nm (*filet*) shrimp net; (*bateau*) shrimp boat.

cri [kʀi] 1 nm a (*éclat de voix: voir* **crier 1a**) cry; shout; scream; screech, squeal, shriek; yell. **le ~ du nouveau-né** the cry of the newborn babe; **~ de surprise** cry *ou* exclamation of surprise; **~ aigu *ou* perçant** piercing cry *ou* scream, shrill cry; *[animal]* squeal; **~ sourd *ou* étouffé** muffled cry *ou* shout; **~ de colère** shout of anger, cry of rage; **jeter *ou* pousser des ~s** to shout (out), cry out; **elle jeta un ~ de douleur** she cried out in pain, she gave a cry of pain; **pousser des ~s de paon** to give *ou* make piercing screams, scream, shriek; *voir* **étouffer.**

b (*exclamation*) cry, shout. **~ d'alarme/d'approbation** cry *ou* shout of alarm/approval; **le ~ des marchands ambulants** the hawkers' cries; **marchant au ~ de "liberté"** marching to shouts *ou* cries of "freedom"; (*fig*) **le ~ des opprimés** the cries of the oppressed; (*fig*) **ce poème est un véritable ~ d'amour** this poem is a cry of love; (*fig*) **le ~ de la conscience** the voice of conscience; *voir* **dernier, haut.**

c *[oiseau]* call; *[canard]* quack; *[cochon]* squeal (*pour autres cris voir* **crier 1b**). (*terme générique*) **le ~ du chien est l'aboiement** a dog's cry is its bark, the noise a dog makes is called barking *ou* a bark; **quel est le ~ de la grenouille?** what noise does a frog make?

d (*littér: crissement*) squeal, screech.

2 comp ▸**cri du cœur** heartfelt cry, cry from the heart, cri de cœur ▸**cri de guerre** (*lit*) war cry; (*fig*) slogan, war cry ▸**cri primal** primal scream.

criaillement [kʀijajmɑ̃] nm a (*gén pl*) *[oie]* squawking (*NonC*); *[paon]* squawking (*NonC*), screeching (*NonC*); *[bébé]* bawling (*NonC*), squalling (*NonC*). b = **criailleries.**

criailler [kʀijaje] 1 vi a *[oie]* to squawk; *[paon]* to squawk, screech; *[bébé]* to bawl, squall. b (*rouspéter*) to grouse*, grumble; (*houspiller*) to nag.

criailleries [kʀijajʀi] nfpl (*rouspétance*) grousing* (*NonC*), grumbling

(*NonC*); (*houspillage*) nagging (*NonC*).

criailleur, -euse [kʀijɑjœʀ, øz] 1 **adj** squawking, scolding. 2 **nm,f** (*rouspéteur*) grouser*.

criant, e [kʀijɑ̃, ɑ̃t] **adj** *erreur* glaring (*épith*); *injustice* rank (*épith*), blatant, glaring (*épith*); *preuve* striking (*épith*), glaring (*épith*); *contraste, vérité* striking (*épith*). **portrait ~ de vérité** portrait strikingly true to life.

criard, e [kʀijaʀ, aʀd] **adj** (*péj*) *enfant* yelling, squalling; *femme* scolding; *oiseau* squawking; *son, voix* piercing; (*fig*) *couleurs, vêtement* loud, garish. (*fig*) **dette ~e** pressing debt.

criblage [kʀiblaʒ] **nm** (*voir* **cribler**) sifting; grading; riddling; screening; jigging.

crible [kʀibl] **nm** (*à main*) riddle; (*Ind, Min*) screen, jig, jigger. **~ mécanique** screening machine; **passer au ~** (*lit*) to riddle, put through a riddle; (*fig*) *idée, proposition* to examine closely; *déclaration, texte* to go through with a fine-tooth comb.

criblé, e [kʀible] (**ptp de cribler**) **adj: ~ de** *balles, flèches, trous* riddled with; *taches* covered in; **visage ~ de boutons** face covered in spots *ou* pimples, spotty face; **~ de dettes** crippled with debts, up to one's eyes in debt.

cribler [kʀible] [1] **vt** a (*tamiser*) *graines* to sift; *fruits* to grade; *sable* to riddle, sift; *charbon* to riddle, screen; *minerai* to screen, jig. b (*percer*) **~ qch/qn de** *balles, flèches* to riddle sth/sb with; **~ qn de** *questions* to bombard sb with.

cribleur, -euse [kʀiblœʀ, øz] 1 **nm,f** (*voir* **cribler:** *ouvrier*) sifter; grader; riddler; screener; jigger. 2 **cribleuse nf** (*machine*) sifter, sifting machine.

cric [kʀik] **nm: ~ (d'automobile)** (car) jack; **soulever qch au ~** to jack sth up; **~ hydraulique** hydraulic jack; **~ à vis** screw jack.

cric-crac [kʀikkʀak] **excl, nm** (*gén*) creak; (*bruit de clé*) click.

cricket [kʀikɛt] **nm** (*Sport*) cricket.

cricoïde [kʀikɔid] 1 **adj** (*Anat*) cricoid. 2 **nm: le ~** the cricoid cartilage.

cri-cri [kʀikʀi] **nm** (*cri du grillon*) chirping; (**: grillon*) cricket.

criée [kʀije] **nf: (vente à la) ~** (sale by) auction; **vendre qch à la ~** to auction sth (off), sell sth by auction; **salle des ~s** auction room, salesroom.

crier [kʀije] [7] 1 **vi** a [*personne*] to shout, cry (out); (*ton aigu*) to scream, screech, squeal, shriek; (*pleurer*) to cry, scream; (*de douleur, peur*) to cry out, scream, yell (out) (*de* with). **~ de douleur** to give a yell *ou* scream *ou* cry of pain, cry *ou* yell *ou* scream out in pain; **~ à tue-tête** *ou* **comme un sourd** to shout one's head off, bellow away; **~ comme un veau** to bawl one's head off; **~ comme un putois** to shout *ou* scream one's head off (in protest); **tu ne peux pas parler sans ~?** do you have to shout?, can't you talk without shouting?

b [*oiseau*] to call; [*canard*] to quack; [*cochon*] to squeal; [*dindon*] to gobble; [*hibou, singe*] to call, screech, hoot; [*mouette*] to cry; [*oie*] to honk; [*perroquet*] to squawk; [*souris*] to squeak.

c (*grincer*) [*porte, plancher, roue*] to creak, squeak; [*frein*] to squeal, screech; [*soulier, étoffe*] to squeak; (*fig*) [*couleur*] to scream, shriek. **faire ~ la craie sur le tableau** to make the chalk squeak on the blackboard.

d (*avec prép*) **~ contre** *ou* **après* qn** to nag (at) *ou* scold sb, go on at sb*; **tes parents vont ~** your parents are going to make a fuss; **~ contre qch** to shout about sth; **elle passe son temps à lui ~ après*** *ou* **dessus*** she's forever going on at him*; **~ à la trahison/au scandale** to call it treason/a scandal, start bandying words like treason/scandal about; **~ au miracle** to hail (it as) a miracle, call it a miracle; **~ à l'assassin** *ou* **au meurtre** to shout "murder"; **~ au loup/au voleur** to cry wolf/thief; **quand il a demandé une augmentation de 50 % son patron a crié au fou** when he asked for a 50 % rise his boss called him a madman *ou* said he was crazy.

2 **vt** a *ordre, injures* to shout (out), yell (out); (*proclamer*) *mépris, indignation* to proclaim; *innocence* to protest. **elle cria qu'elle venait de voir un rat dans la cave** she shouted *ou* (*plus fort*) screamed (out) that she'd just seen a rat in the cellar; **~ à qn de se taire** *ou* **qu'il se taise** to shout at sb to be quiet; **~ qch sur les toits** to shout *ou* proclaim sth from the rooftops.

b (*pour vendre*) **~ les journaux dans la rue** to sell newspapers in the street; **on entendait les marchandes ~ leurs légumes** you could hear the vegetable sellers crying *ou* shouting their wares, you could hear the shouts of the women selling their vegetables; **au coin de la rue, un gamin criait les éditions spéciales** at the street corner a kid was shouting out *ou* calling out the special editions.

c (*pour avertir, implorer*) **~ casse-cou** to warn of (a) danger; **sans ~ gare** without a warning; **~ grâce** (*lit*) to beg for mercy; (*fig*) to beg for peace *ou* mercy *ou* a respite; **quand j'ai parlé de me lancer tout seul dans l'entreprise, ils ont crié casse-cou** when I spoke of going into the venture on my own they were quick to point out the risks; **~ famine** *ou* **misère** to complain that the wolf is at the door, cry famine; **~ vengeance** to cry out for vengeance; *voir* **victoire**.

crieur, -euse [kʀijœʀ, øz] **nm,f: ~ de journaux** newspaper seller; (*Hist*) **~ public** town crier.

crime¹ [kʀim] **nm** a (*meurtre*) murder. **il s'agit bien d'un ~** it's definitely a case of murder; **retourner sur les lieux du ~** to go back to the scene of the crime; **la victime/l'arme du ~** the murder victim/weapon; **~ crapuleux** foul crime; **~ passionnel** crime passionnel; **~s de guerre** war crimes; **~ de lèse-majesté** crime of lèse-majesté; **~ (à motif) sexuel** sex murder *ou* crime; **le ~ parfait** the perfect crime.

b (*Jur: délit grave*) crime, offence, ≃ felony (*US*). **~ contre l'État** offence *ou* crime against the state; **~ contre les mœurs** sexual offence, offence against public decency; **~ contre la paix** crime against peace; **~ contre un particulier** crime against a private individual; **~ contre nature** unnatural act, crime against nature; **~ contre l'humanité** crime against humanity; (*Prov*) **le ~ ne paie pas** crime doesn't pay (*Prov*); *voir* **syndicat**.

c (*sens affaibli*) crime. **c'est un ~ de faire** it's criminal *ou* a crime to do; **il est parti avant l'heure? ce n'est pas un ~!** he went off early? well, it's not a crime!

d († *ou littér: péché, faute*) sin, crime.

crime² [kʀim] **nf** (**abrév de brigade criminelle**) *voir* **brigade**.

Crimée [kʀime] **nf: la ~** the Crimea, the Crimean peninsula; **la guerre de ~** the Crimean War.

criminalisation [kʀiminalizasjɔ̃] **nf** criminalization.

criminaliser [kʀiminalize] [1] **vt** (*Jur*) to criminalize.

criminaliste [kʀiminalist] **nmf** specialist in criminal law.

criminalité [kʀiminalite] **nf** a (*actes criminels*) criminality, crime. **la ~ juvénile** juvenile criminality; **la grande/petite ~** serious/petty crime. b (*rare*) [*acte*] criminal nature, criminality.

criminel, -elle [kʀiminɛl] 1 **adj** (*gén, Jur*) *acte, personne, procès* criminal. (*sens affaibli*) **il serait ~ de laisser ces fruits se perdre** it would be criminal *ou* a crime to let this fruit go to waste; *voir* **incendie**. 2 **nm,f** (*voir* **crime**) murderer (*ou* murderess); criminal. **~ de guerre** war criminal; (*hum: coupable*) **voilà le ~** there's the culprit *ou* the guilty party. 3 **nm** (*juridiction*) **avocat au ~** criminal lawyer; **poursuivre qn au ~** to take criminal proceedings against sb, prosecute sb in a criminal court.

criminellement [kʀiminɛlmɑ̃] **adv** *agir* criminally. (*Jur*) **poursuivre qn ~** to take criminal proceedings against sb, prosecute sb in a criminal court.

criminologie [kʀiminɔlɔʒi] **nf** criminology.

criminologiste [kʀiminɔlɔʒist] **nmf** criminologist.

crin [kʀɛ̃] **nm** a (*poil*) [*cheval*] hair (*NonC*); [*matelas, balai*] horse hair. **~ végétal** vegetable (horse)hair; *voir* **gant**. b **à tous ~s, à tout ~** *conservateur, républicain* diehard, dyed-in-the-wool; **révolutionnaire à tout ~** out-and-out revolutionary.

crincrin* [kʀɛ̃kʀɛ̃] **nm** (*péj*) (*violon*) squeaky fiddle; (*son*) squeaking, scraping.

crinière [kʀinjɛʀ] **nf** a [*animal*] mane. b [**: personne*] shock *ou* mop of hair, (flowing) mane. **il avait une ~ rousse** he had a mop of red hair. c [*casque*] plume.

crinoline [kʀinɔlin] **nf** crinoline petticoat. **robe à ~** crinoline (dress).

crique [kʀik] **nf** creek, inlet.

criquet [kʀikɛ] **nm** (*Zool*) locust; (*gén: grillon, sauterelle*) grasshopper.

crise [kʀiz] 1 **nf** a (*Méd*) [*rhumatisme, goutte*] attack; [*épilepsie, apoplexie*] fit. **~ de toux** fit *ou* bout of coughing.

b (*accès*) outburst, fit; (*lubie*) fit, mood. **~ de colère/de rage/de dégoût/de jalousie** fit of anger/of rage/of disgust/of jealousy; **~ de rire** laughing fit; **être pris d'une ~ de rire** to be in fits (of laughter); **la ~ (de rire)!*** what a scream!*; **elle est prise d'une ~ de nettoyage** she's felt *ou* got a sudden urge to do a spring-clean, she's in a spring-cleaning mood; *travailler* **par ~s** in fits and starts; **je vais au cinéma/je lis par ~s** I go through phases when I go to the cinema/I read a lot.

c (**: colère*) rage, tantrum. **piquer** *ou* **faire une ~** to throw a tantrum *ou* a fit*, fly off the handle.

d (*bouleversement*) (*moral, Pol*) crisis; (*Écon*) crisis, slump. **en période de ~, il faut ...** in time(s) of crisis *ou* times of trouble we must ...; **pays/économie en (état de) ~** country/economy in a (state of) crisis.

e (*pénurie*) shortage. **~ de main-d'œuvre** shortage of manpower.

2 **comp** ►**crise d'appendicite** appendicitis attack ►**crise d'asthme** attack of asthma ►**crise cardiaque** heart attack ►**crise de confiance** crisis of confidence ►**crise de conscience** crisis of conscience ►**crise économique** economic crisis, slump ►**crise d'épilepsie** epileptic fit ►**crise de foi** = **crise religieuse** ►**crise de foie** bilious *ou* liverish (*Brit*) attack ►**crise d'identité** identity crisis ►**crise de larmes** fit of crying *ou* tears, crying fit ►**crise du logement** housing shortage ►**crise ministérielle** cabinet crisis ►**crise de nerfs** attack of nerves, fit of hysterics ►**crise du pétrole** oil crisis ►**crise du pouvoir** leadership crisis ►**crise de la quarantaine** midlife crisis ►**crise religieuse** crisis of belief.

crispant, e [kʀispɑ̃, ɑ̃t] **adj** (*énervant*) irritating, aggravating*, annoying. **ce qu'il est ~!*** he really gets on my nerves!*, he's a real pain in the neck!*

crispation [kʀispasjɔ̃] **nf** a (*contraction*) [*traits, visage*] tensing; [*muscles*] contraction; [*cuir*] shrivelling-up. b (*spasme*) twitch. **des ~s nerveuses** nervous twitches *ou* twitching; **une ~ douloureuse de la main** a painful twitching of the hand; (*fig*) **donner des ~s à qn** to get on sb's nerves*. c (*nervosité*) state of tension.

crispé, e [kʀispe] (ptp de crisper) adj *sourire* nervous, strained, tense; *personne* tense, on edge (*attrib*).

crisper [kʀispe] [1] 1 vt a (*plisser, rider*) *cuir* to shrivel (up). **le froid crispe la peau** the cold makes one's skin feel taut *ou* tight.
b (*contracter*) *muscles, membres* to tense, flex; *poings* to clench. **la douleur crispait les visages** their faces were contorted *ou* tense with grief; **les mains crispées sur le volant** clutching the wheel tensely, with hands clenched on the wheel.
c (*: *agacer*) ~ **qn** to get on sb's nerves*.
2 **se crisper** vpr *[visage]* to tense; *[sourire]* to become strained *ou* tense; *[poing]* to clench; (*fig*) *[personne]* to get edgy* *ou* tense. **ses mains se crispèrent sur le manche de la pioche** his hands tightened on the pickaxe, he clutched the pickaxe tensely.

crispin [kʀispɛ̃] nm: **gants à** ~ gauntlets.

criss [kʀis] nm kris, creese.

crissement [kʀismɑ̃] nm (*voir* **crisser**) crunch(ing) (*NonC*); screech(ing) (*NonC*), squeal(ing) (*NonC*); whisper(ing) (*NonC*), rustling (*NonC*), rustle (*NonC*). **s'arrêter dans un** ~ **de pneus** to screech to a halt.

crisser [kʀise] [1] vi *[neige, gravier]* to crunch; *[pneus, freins]* to screech, squeal; *[soie, taffetas]* to whisper, rustle; *[cuir]* to squeak.

cristal, pl -aux [kʀistal, o] nm a (*Chim, Min*) crystal. ~ **(de roche)** rock crystal (*NonC*), quartz (*NonC*); ~ **(de plomb)** (lead) crystal; ~ **aux de givre** (*sur arbre*) ice-crystals; (*sur vitre*) ice-patterns; **affichage à ~aux liquides** liquid crystal display; **de** *ou* **en** ~ crystal (*épith*); (*fig littér*) **le** ~ **de sa voix, sa voix de** ~ his crystal-clear voice, the crystal-clear quality of his voice; ~ **de Bohème** Bohemian crystal; ~ **d'Islande** Iceland spar; *voir* **boule**[1]. b (*objet: gén pl*) crystal(ware) (*NonC*), piece of crystal(ware), fine glassware (*NonC*). **les ~aux du lustre** the crystal droplets of the chandelier. c (*pour le nettoyage*) **~aux (de soude)** washing soda.

cristallerie [kʀistalʀi] nf (*fabrication*) crystal (glass-)making; (*fabrique*) (crystal) glassworks; (*objets*) crystal(ware), fine glassware.

cristallier [kʀistalje] nm (*Hist*) (*chercheur*) crystal seeker; (*ouvrier*) crystal engraver.

cristallin, e [kʀistalɛ̃, in] 1 adj (*Min*) crystalline; *son, voix* crystal-clear; *eau* crystalline. 2 nm (*Anat*) crystalline lens.

cristallisation [kʀistalizasjɔ̃] nf (*lit, fig*) crystallization.

cristalliser vti, **se cristalliser** vpr [kʀistalize] [1] (*lit, fig*) to crystallize.

cristallisoir [kʀistalizwaʀ] nm crystallizing dish.

cristallographie [kʀistalɔgʀafi] nf crystallography.

cristallomancie [kʀistalomɑ̃si] nf crystal-gazing, crystallomancy.

critère [kʀitɛʀ] nm (*preuve*) criterion; (*pierre de touche*) measure, criterion. **ceci n'est pas un ~ suffisant pour prouver l'authenticité du document** this is not a good enough criterion on which to prove the document's authenticity; **la richesse matérielle n'est pas un ~ de succès** material wealth is not a criterion of success; **ceci constituera un ~ de sa bonne foi** this will be a test of his good faith; **le style n'est pas le seul ~ pour juger de la valeur d'un roman** style is not the only measure *ou* criterion by which one can judge the value of a novel; **son seul ~ est l'avis du parti** his only criterion is the opinion of the party; **selon des ~s politiques/raciaux** along political/racial lines, according to political/racial criteria.

critérium [kʀiteʀjɔm] nm a (*Cyclisme*) rally; (*Natation*) gala. b (†) = **critère**.

critiquable [kʀitikabl] adj open to criticism (*attrib*).

critique[1] [kʀitik] adj (*en crise, alarmant*) *situation, période* critical; (*décisif, crucial*) *moment, phase* crucial, decisive, critical; *situation, période* crucial, critical; (*Sci*) *pression, vitesse* critical. **dans les circonstances ~s, il perd la tête** in critical situations *ou* in emergencies *ou* in a crisis, he loses his head; **ils étaient dans une situation ~** they were in a critical situation *ou* a tight spot*; *voir* **âge**.

critique[2] [kʀitik] 1 adj a (*qui juge ou fait un choix*) *jugement, notes, édition* critical. **avoir l'esprit ~** to have a critical mind; *voir* **apparat**.
b (*défavorable*) critical, censorious (*frm*). **d'un œil ~** with a critical eye; **il s'est montré très ~ (au sujet de ...)** he was very critical (of ...); **esprit ~** criticizing *ou* critical mind.
2 nf a (*blâme*) criticism. **il ne supporte pas la ~ ou les ~s** he can't tolerate criticism; **les nombreuses ~s qui lui ont été adressées** the many criticisms that were levelled at him; **faire une ~ à (l'endroit de) qch/qn** to criticize sth/sb; **une ~ que je lui ferais est qu'il ...** one criticism I would make of him is that he ...; **la ~ est aisée** it's easy to criticize.
b (*analyse*) *[texte, œuvre]* appreciation, critique; *[livre, spectacle]* review. (*art de juger*) **la ~** criticism; **la ~ littéraire/musicale** literary/music criticism; **faire la ~ de** *livre sorti de presse, concert* to review, write a crit of* (*Brit*), do a write-up on; *poème* to write an appreciation *ou* a critique of; **une ~ impartiale** an impartial *ou* unbiased review; (*Littérat*) **la nouvelle ~** the new (French) criticism.
c (*personnes*) **la ~** the critics; **la ~ a bien accueilli sa pièce** his play was well received by the critics.
3 nmf (*commentateur*) critic. ~ **de théâtre/de musique/d'art/de cinéma** drama/music/art/cinema *ou* film critic; ~ **littéraire** literary critic.

critiquer [kʀitike] [1] vt a (*blâmer*) to criticize. **il critique tout/tout le monde** he finds fault with *ou* criticizes everything/everybody. b (*juger*) *livre, œuvre* to assess, make an appraisal of; (*examiner*) to examine (critically).

croassement [kʀɔasmɑ̃] nm caw, cawing (*NonC*).

croasser [kʀɔase] [1] vi to caw.

croate [kʀɔat] 1 adj Croatian. 2 nm (*Ling*) Croat, Croatian. 3 nmf: **C~** Croat, Croatian.

Croatie [kʀɔasi] nf Croatia.

croc [kʀo] nm a (*dent*) fang. **montrer les ~s** *[animal]* to bare its teeth, show its teeth *ou* fangs; (*) *[personne]* to show one's teeth; **avoir les ~s*** to be starving*, be famished*. b (*grappin*) hook; (*fourche*) hook. ~ **de boucherie/de marinier** meat/boat hook; ~ **à fumier** muck rake.

croc-en-jambe, pl crocs-en-jambe [kʀɔkɑ̃ʒɑ̃b] nm: **faire un ~ à qn** (*lit*) to trip sb (up); (*fig*) to trip sb up, pull a fast one on sb*; **un ~ me fit perdre l'équilibre** somebody tripped me (up) and I lost my balance, I was tripped (up) and lost my balance; (*fig*) **méfiez-vous des crocs-en-jambe de vos collaborateurs** mind your colleagues don't pull a fast one on you* *ou* don't try and do you down* (*Brit*).

croche [kʀɔʃ] nf (*Mus*) quaver (*Brit*), eighth (note) (*US*). **double ~** semiquaver (*Brit*), sixteenth (note) (*US*); **triple/quadruple ~** demisemi-/hemidemisemiquaver (*Brit*), thirty-second/sixty-fourth note (*US*).

croche-patte, pl croche-pattes [kʀɔʃpat] nm = **croc-en-jambe**.

croche-pied, pl croche-pieds [kʀɔʃpje] nm = **croc-en-jambe**.

crochet [kʀɔʃɛ] 1 nm a (*fer recourbé*) (*gén*) hook; *[chiffonnier]* spiked stick; *[patte de pantalon etc]* fastener, clip, fastening; *[cambrioleur, serrurier]* picklock. (*Rail*) ~ **d'attelage** coupling; ~ **de boucherie** *ou* **de boucher** meat hook; ~ **à boutons** *ou* **bottines** buttonhook.
b (*aiguille*) crochet hook; (*technique*) crochet. **couverture au ~** crocheted blanket; **faire du ~** to crochet; **faire qch au ~** to crochet sth.
c (*Boxe*) ~ **du gauche/du droit** left/right hook.
d (*détour*) *[véhicule]* sudden swerve; *[route]* sudden turn; *[voyage, itinéraire]* detour. **il a fait un ~ pour éviter l'obstacle** he swerved to avoid the obstacle; **faire un ~ par une ville** to make a detour through a town.
e (*Typ*) **~s** square brackets; **entre ~s** in square brackets.
f *[serpent]* fang.
g (*Archit*) crocket.
h (*loc*) **vivre aux ~s de qn** to live off *ou* sponge on* sb.
2 comp ▸ **crochet radiophonique** talent show.

crochetage [kʀɔʃtaʒ] nm *[serrure]* picking.

crocheter [kʀɔʃte] [5] vt a *serrure* to pick; *porte* to pick the lock on. b (*faire un croc-en-jambe à*) to trip (up). c (*Tricot*) to crochet.

crocheteur [kʀɔʃtœʀ] nm (*voleur*) picklock.

crochu, e [kʀɔʃy] adj *nez* hooked; *mains, doigts* claw-like. **au nez ~** hook-nosed; *voir* **atome, doigt**.

croco* [kʀɔko] nm (abrév de **crocodile**) crocodile skin. **en ~** crocodile (*épith*).

crocodile [kʀɔkɔdil] nm (*Zool, peau*) crocodile. **sac en ~** crocodile(-skin) handbag; *voir* **larme**.

crocus [kʀɔkys] nm crocus.

croire [kʀwaʀ] [44] 1 vt a *personne, fait, histoire* to believe. **je n'arrive pas à ~ qu'il a réussi** I (just) can't believe he has succeeded; **auriez-vous cru cela de lui?** would you have believed it possible of him *ou* expected it of him?; **je te crois sur parole** I'll take your word for it; **le croira qui voudra, mais ...** believe it or not (but) ...; **je veux bien le ~** I can quite (well) believe it; **je n'en crois rien** I don't believe (a word of) it; **croyez-m'en** believe me; ~ **qch dur comme fer*** to believe sth firmly, be absolutely convinced of sth.
b (*avec infin ou que: penser, estimer*) to believe, think; (*déduire*) to believe, assume, think. **nous croyons qu'il a dit la vérité** we believe *ou* think that he told the truth; **elle croyait avoir perdu son sac** she thought she had lost her bag; **il a bien cru manquer son train** he really thought he would miss his train; **on a cru préférable de refuser** we thought it preferable for us to refuse, we thought that it would be better for us to refuse; **il n'y avait pas de lumière, j'ai cru qu'ils étaient couchés** there was no light so I thought *ou* assumed they had gone to *ou* were in bed; **il a cru bien faire** he meant well, he thought he was doing the right thing *ou* acting for the best; **je crois que oui** I think so; **je crois que non** I think not, I don't think so; **il n'est pas là? — je crois que si** isn't he in? — (yes) I think he is; **on ne croyait pas qu'il viendrait** we didn't think he'd come; **elle ne croit pas/elle ne peut pas ~ qu'il mente** she doesn't think/can't believe he is lying.
c (*avec adj, adv*) (*juger, estimer*) to think, believe, consider; (*supposer*) to think, believe. **croyez-vous cette réunion nécessaire?** do you think *ou* believe this meeting is necessary?, do you consider this meeting (to be) necessary?; **on l'a cru mort** he was believed *ou* presumed (to be) dead; **on les croyait en France** they were believed *ou* thought to be in France; **je la croyais ailleurs/avec vous** I thought she was somewhere else/with you; **il n'a pas cru utile** *ou* **nécessaire de me prévenir** he didn't think it necessary to warn me; **tu ne crois pas si bien dire!** you don't know how right you are!
d **en ~** (*s'en rapporter à*): **à l'en ~** to listen to *ou* hear him, if you

(were to) go by *ou* listen to what he says; **s'il faut en ~ les journaux** if we (are to) go by what the papers say, if we are to believe the papers, if the papers are anything to go by; **vous pouvez m'en ~, croyez en mon expérience** (you can) take it from me, take it from one who knows; **si vous m'en croyez** if you want my opinion; **il n'en croyait pas ses oreilles/ses yeux** he couldn't believe his ears/his eyes.

e (*loc*) **c'est à ~ qu'il est sourd** you'd think he was deaf; **c'est à n'y pas ~!** it's beyond belief!, it's unbelievable!, it's hardly credible!; (*frm*) **il est à ~ que** it is to be supposed *ou* presumed that; **il faut ~ que** it would seem that, one must assume that, it must be assumed that; **~ de son devoir de faire** to think *ou* feel it one's duty to do; **il ne croyait pas si bien dire!** he didn't know how right he was!, he never spoke a truer word!; **on croirait une hirondelle** it looks as though it could be *ou* it looks like a swallow; **on croirait (entendre) une clarinette** it sounds like *ou* it could be a clarinet (playing); **on croirait entendre son père** it could (almost) be his father talking, you'd think it was his father talking; **on croirait qu'elle ne comprend pas** she doesn't seem to understand, you might almost think she didn't understand; **tu ne peux pas ~** *ou* (*frm*) **vous ne sauriez ~ combien il nous manque** you cannot (begin to) imagine how much we miss him; **non, mais qu'est-ce que vous croyez?*** what do you imagine?; **je vous** *ou* **te crois!*** you bet!*, rather!; **je ne suis pas celle que vous croyez!** I'm not THAT sort of person!; **faut pas ~!*** make no mistake (about it); **on croit rêver!*** I don't BELIEVE it!, it's mind-blowing!*, the mind boggles!*

2 **vi** (*Rel: avoir la foi*) to believe, be a believer.

3 **croire à vt indir** *innocence de qn, vie éternelle, Père Noël* to believe in; *justice, médecine* to have faith *ou* confidence in, believe in; *promesses* to believe (in), have faith in. **il ne croit plus à rien** he no longer believes in anything; **on a cru d'abord à un accident** at first they took it for an accident *ou* to be an accident, at first they believed it was *ou* it to be an accident; **pour faire ~ à un suicide** to make people think it was suicide, to give the impression *ou* appearance of (a) suicide; **il ne croit pas à la guerre** (*pense qu'elle n'aura pas lieu*) he doesn't think *ou* believe *ou* reckon there will be a war; (*pense qu'elle ne sert à rien*) he doesn't believe in war; **non, mais tu crois au Père Noël!** well, you really DO live in cloud-cuckoo land! (*Brit*), you must believe in Santa Claus too!; (*frm*) **"veuillez ~ à mes sentiments dévoués"** "yours sincerely", "I am, sir, your devoted servant" (*frm*).

4 **croire en vt indir** to believe in. **~ en Dieu** to believe in God; **~ en qn** to have faith *ou* confidence in sb; **il croit trop en lui-même** he is too self-confident, he is overconfident, he has an over-inflated opinion of himself.

5 **se croire vpr** a (*avec attribut*) **se ~ fort/malin** to think one is strong/(very) clever; **il se croit un acteur** he thinks he's a good *ou* a great* actor; (*avec complément*) **on se croirait en vacances** I feel as if I was on holiday; **on se croirait en Bretagne/été** it could almost be Brittany/summer.

b (*être prétentieux*) **qu'est-ce qu'il se croit, celui-là?** who does he think he is?*; (*péj*) **s'y ~*** to think one is really something*.

c (*penser que c'est arrivé*) (*péj*) **le patron lui a dit qu'elle avait un espoir de promotion et elle s'y croit déjà*** the boss told her she had a chance of promotion and she acts as if she'd already got it.

croisade [kʀwazad] **nf** (*Hist, fig*) crusade. **la ~ des Albigeois** the Albigensian Crusade.

croisé¹, e¹ [kʀwaze] (**ptp de croiser**) 1 **adj** *veste* double-breasted; *rimes, vers* alternate. **race ~e** crossbreed; **tissu ~** twill; *voir* **bras, feu¹, mot.** 2 **nm** (*Tex*) twill.

croisé² [kʀwaze] **nm** (*Hist*) crusader.

croisée² [kʀwaze] **nf** a **~ de chemins** crossroads, crossing; (*fig*) **à la ~ des chemins** at the crossroads, at the parting of the ways; (*Archit*) **~ d'ogives** intersecting ribs; (*Archit*) **~ du transept** transept crossing. b (*littér: fenêtre*) window, casement (*littér*).

croisement [kʀwazmɑ̃] **nm** a *[fils, brins]* crossing. **l'étroitesse de la route rendait impossible le ~ des véhicules** the narrowness of the road made it impossible for vehicles to pass (one another); *voir* **feu.**

b (*Bio, Zool*) *[races, espèces, plantes]* crossing (*NonC*), crossbreeding (*NonC*), interbreeding (*NonC*) (*avec* with). **faire des ~s de race** to rear *ou* produce crossbreeds, cross(breed); **est-ce un ~?** *ou* **le produit d'un ~?** is it a cross(breed)?

c (*carrefour*) crossroads, junction. **au ~ de la route et de la voie ferrée, il y a un passage à niveau** where the road and the railway cross, there is a level crossing; **le ~ des deux voies ferrées se fait sur deux niveaux** the two railway lines cross at two levels; **au ~ des chemins, ils s'arrêtèrent** they stopped where the paths crossed *ou* at the junction of the paths.

croiser [kʀwaze] [1] 1 **vt** a *bras* to fold, cross; *jambes* to cross; *fourchettes, fils, lignes* to cross. **elle croisa son châle sur sa poitrine** she folded her shawl across *ou* over her chest; **les jambes croisées** cross-legged; **~ les doigts** (*lit*) to cross one's fingers; (*fig*) to keep one's fingers crossed; (*fig*) **croisons les doigts!** fingers crossed!; **je croise les doigts pour qu'il fasse beau** I'm keeping my fingers crossed that the weather will be good; (*lit, fig*) **~ le fer** to cross swords (*avec* with); (*fig*) **se ~ les bras** to lounge around, sit around idly.

b (*intersecter, couper*) *route* to cross, cut across; *ligne* to cross, cut across, intersect.

c (*passer à côté de*) *véhicule, passant* to pass. **notre train a croisé le rapide** our train passed the express going in the other direction; **son regard croisa le mien** his eyes met mine; **je l'ai croisé plusieurs fois dans des réunions** I've seen him several times at meetings; **j'ai croisé Jean dans la rue hier** I bumped into *ou* saw Jean in the street yesterday.

d (*accoupler, mâtiner*) *races, animaux, plantes* to cross(breed), interbreed (*avec* with). **l'âne peut se ~ avec le cheval** the ass can (inter)breed with the horse; (*croisement contrôlé*) the ass can be crossed with the horse.

e (*Sport*) *tir, coup droit* to angle. **passe croisée** diagonal pass.

2 **vi** a (*Habillement*) **cette veste croise bien** that jacket has got a nice *ou* good overlap; **cette saison les couturiers font ~ les vestes** this season fashion designers are making jackets double-breasted; **il avait tellement grossi qu'il ne pouvait plus (faire) ~ sa veste** he'd got so fat that he couldn't get his jacket to fasten over *ou* across *ou* that his jacket wouldn't fasten across any more.

b (*Naut*) to cruise.

3 **se croiser vpr** a *[chemins, lignes]* to cross, cut (across) each other, intersect. **deux chemins qui se croisent à angle droit** two roads which cross at right angles *ou* which cut (across) each other at right angles; **nos regards** *ou* **nos yeux se croisèrent un instant** our eyes met for a moment.

b *[personnes, véhicules]* to pass each other. (*fig*) **ma lettre s'est croisée avec la tienne, nos lettres se sont croisées** my letter crossed yours (in the post), our letters crossed (in the post); **nous nous sommes croisés hier** we bumped into each other yersterday; **nous nous sommes croisés plusieurs fois dans des réunions** we've seen each other several times at meetings.

c (*Hist*) to take the cross, go on a crusade.

croiseur [kʀwazœʀ] **nm** cruiser (*warship*).

croisière [kʀwazjɛʀ] **nf** cruise. **partir en ~, faire une ~** to go on a cruise; **ils sont en ~ dans le Pacifique** they're on a cruise in the Pacific; **ce voilier est idéal pour la ~** this boat is ideal for cruising; **allure** *ou* **régime** *ou* **rythme** *ou* **vitesse de ~** cruising speed.

croisiériste [kʀwazjeʀist] **nmf** cruise passenger.

croisillon [kʀwazijɔ̃] **nm** *[croix, charpente]* crosspiece, crossbar; *[église]* transept. **~s** *[fenêtre]* lattice work; *[tarte]* criss-cross; *voir* **fenêtre.**

croissance [kʀwasɑ̃s] **nf** *[enfant, embryon, ville, industrie]* growth, development; *[plante]* growth. **~ autonome** self-sustained growth; **~ économique** economic growth *ou* development; **~ zéro** zero (economic) growth; **arrêté dans sa ~** arrested in his growth *ou* development; **maladie de ~** growth disease.

croissant¹ [kʀwasɑ̃] **nm** a (*forme*) crescent. **~ de lune** crescent of the moon; **en ~** crescent-shaped. b (*Culin*) croissant.

croissant², e [kʀwasɑ̃, ɑ̃t] **adj** *nombre, tension* growing, increasing, rising; *chaleur* rising; *froid* increasing. **aller ~** *[peur, enthousiasme]* to grow; *[bruit]* to grow *ou* get louder; **le rythme ~ des accidents** the increasing rate of accidents, the rising accident rate.

croissanterie [kʀwasɑ̃tʀi] **nf** croissant shop.

croître [kʀwatʀ] [55] **vi** a *[enfant, plante]* to grow; *[ville]* to grow, increase in size. **~ en beauté/sagesse** to grow in beauty/wisdom; **~ dans l'estime de qn** to rise *ou* grow in sb's esteem; **vallon où croissent de nombreuses espèces** valley where many species of plant grow.

b *[ambition, bruit, quantité]* to grow, increase. **les jours croissent** the days are getting longer *ou* are lengthening; **~ en nombre/volume** to increase in number/size *ou* volume; **l'inquiétude sur son état de santé ne cessait de ~** there was increasing anxiety over the state of his health; **son enthousiasme ne cessa de ~** he grew more and more enthusiastic (about it); **la chaleur ne faisait que ~** the heat got more and more intense, the temperature kept on rising.

c *[rivière]* to swell, rise; *[lune]* to wax; *[vent]* to rise. **les pluies ont fait ~ la rivière** the rains have swollen the river, the river waters have swollen *ou* risen after the rains.

d (*loc*) (*Bible*) **croissez et multipliez!** be fruitful and multiply!; (*iro*) **ça ne fait que ~ et embellir** (things are getting) better and better! (*iro*).

croix [kʀwa] 1 **nf** a (*gén, Hér, Rel*) cross. **~ celtique/grecque/latine** Celtic/Greek/Latin cross; **~ de Malte/de Saint-André** Maltese/St Andrew's cross; (*Hér*) **~ ancrée/fleuretée** cross moline/fleury *ou* flory; **en ~** crosswise, in the form of a cross; **mettre des bâtons en ~** to lay sticks crosswise, criss-cross sticks; **les pétales des crucifères sont disposés en ~** the petals of the Cruciferae form a cross *ou* are arranged crosswise; **chemins qui se coupent en ~** paths which cut each other at right angles *ou* crosswise; **mettre en ~, mettre à mort sur la ~** to crucify; **mise en ~** crucifixion; **mettre les bras en ~** to stretch out one's arms at the sides; **pour le faire sortir, c'est la ~ et la bannière*** it's the devil's own job *ou* a devil of a job to get him to go out*; **~ de bois ~ de fer (, si je mens je vais en enfer)** ≃ cross my heart (and hope to die); *voir* **chemin, grand, signe.**

b (*décoration*) cross; (*Scol: récompense*) prize, medal.

c (*marque*) cross. **faire** *ou* **mettre une ~ devant un nom** to put a cross in front of *ou* by a name; **(appeler) les noms marqués d'une ~** (to call out) the names which have a cross against (*Brit*) them *ou* with a cross against (*Brit*) *ou* by (*US*) them; (*fig*) **tes vacances, tu peux faire une ~ dessus*** you might just as well forget all about your holidays *ou* write your holidays off*; (*fig*) **si tu lui prêtes ton livre, tu peux faire une ~ dessus!*** if you lend him your book, you can say goodbye to it!* *ou* you can kiss it goodbye!*; (*fig, iro*) **il faut faire une ~ à la cheminée** *ou* **sur le calendrier** it is a red-letter day.

d (*fig: souffrance, épreuve*) cross, burden. **chacun a** *ou* **porte sa ~** each of us has his (own) cross to bear.

2 comp ►**croix de fer** (*Gym*) crucifix ►**croix gammée** swastika ►**Croix de guerre** (*Mil*) Military Cross ►**croix de Lorraine** cross of Lorraine ►**Croix-Rouge** Red Cross ►**Croix-du-Sud** Southern Cross.

cromorne [kʀɔmɔʀn] nf krumhorn.

croquant[1]† [kʀɔkɑ̃] nm (*péj*) yokel, (country) bumpkin.

croquant[2]**, e** [kʀɔkɑ̃, ɑ̃t] 1 adj crisp, crunchy. 2 nm *[volaille]* gristle. **le ~ de l'oreille** the cartilage in the ear.

croque* [kʀɔk] nm abrév de **croque-monsieur**.

croque au sel [kʀɔkosɛl] loc adv: **à la ~** with salt (and nothing else), with a sprinkling of salt.

croque-madame [kʀɔkmadam] nm inv *toasted cheese sandwich with ham and fried egg.*

croquembouche [kʀɔkɑ̃buʃ] nm *pyramid of cream-filled choux pastry balls.*

croque-mitaine, pl **croque-mitaines** [kʀɔkmitɛn] nm bog(e)y man, ogre (*fig*). **ce maître est un vrai ~** this schoolmaster is a real ogre.

croque-monsieur [kʀɔkməsjø] nm inv *toasted cheese sandwich with ham.*

croque-mort, pl **croque-morts*** [kʀɔkmɔʀ] nm undertaker's (*Brit*) *ou* mortician's (*US*) assistant. **avoir un air de ~** to have a funereal look *ou* a face like an undertaker.

croquenot* [kʀɔkno] nm clodhopper*.

croquer [kʀɔke] [1] 1 vt a (*manger*) *biscuits, noisettes, bonbons* to crunch; *fruits* to munch. **pastille à laisser fondre dans la bouche sans (la) ~** pastille to be sucked slowly and not chewed *ou* crunched; **~ le marmot***† to hang around (waiting)*, kick one's heels* (*Brit*); *voir* **chocolat.**

b (*: *dépenser, gaspiller*) **~ de l'argent** to squander money, go through money like water*; **~ un héritage** to squander *ou* go through an inheritance.

c (*dessiner*) to sketch. **être (joli) à ~** to be as pretty as a picture. **tu es à ~ avec ce chapeau** you look good enough to eat in this hat.

d (*camper*) *personnage* to sketch, outline, give a thumbnail sketch of.

2 vi a *[fruit]* to be crunchy, be crisp; *[salade]* to be crisp. **le sucre croque sous la dent** sugar is crunchy to eat *ou* when you eat it; **des pommes qui croquent** crunchy apples.

b **~ dans une pomme** to bite into an apple.

croquet [kʀɔkɛ] nm (*Sport*) croquet.

croquette [kʀɔkɛt] nf (*Culin*) croquette. **~s de chocolat** chocolate croquettes; **~s pour chiens/chats** dry dogfood/catfood.

croqueuse [kʀɔkøz] nf: **~ de diamants** gold digger, fortune-hunter.

croquignolet, -ette* [kʀɔkiɲɔlɛ, ɛt] adj (*mignon*) (rather) sweet, cute*, dinky* (*Brit*).

croquis [kʀɔki] nm (*dessin*) (rough) sketch; (*fig: description*) sketch. **faire un ~ de qch** to sketch sth, make a (rough) sketch of sth; (*fig*) **faire un rapide ~ de la situation** to give a rapid outline *ou* thumbnail sketch of the situation; (*fig*) **~ d'audience** court-room sketches.

crosne [kʀon] nm Chinese artichoke.

cross(-country) [kʀɔs(kuntʀi)] nm (*course*) (*à pied*) cross-country race *ou* run; (*Équitation*) cross-country race; (*sport*) (*à pied*) cross-country racing *ou* running; (*Équitation*) cross-country racing. (*à pied*) **faire du ~** to do cross-country running.

crosse [kʀɔs] nf a (*poignée*) *[fusil]* butt; *[revolver]* grip. **frapper qn à coups de ~** to hit sb with the butt of one's rifle; **mettre** *ou* **lever la ~ en l'air*** (*se rendre*) to show the white flag (*fig*), lay down one's arms; (*se mutiner*) to mutiny, refuse to fight.

b (*bâton*) (*Rel*) crook, crosier, crozier. (*Sport*) **~ de golf** golf club; **~ de hockey** hockey stick.

c (*partie recourbée*) *[violon]* head, scroll. **~ de piston** cross-head; **~ de l'aorte** arch of the aorta, aortic arch; **~ de fougère** crosier (*fern*).

d **chercher des ~s à qn*** to pick a quarrel with sb; **s'il me cherche des ~s*** if he's looking for a chance to make trouble *ou* to pick a quarrel with me.

e (*Culin*) **~ de bœuf** knuckle of beef.

crotale [kʀɔtal] nm rattlesnake, rattler* (*US*).

crotte [kʀɔt] nf a (*excrément*) *[brebis, lapin]* droppings. **~ de cheval** horse droppings *ou* manure (*NonC*) *ou* dung (*NonC*); **~ de nez‡** bog(e)y‡ (*Brit*), booger‡ (*US*); **son chien a déposé une ~ sur le palier** his dog has messed *ou* done its business on the landing; **c'est plein de ~(s) de chien** it's covered in dog's dirt; **~!***† blast (it)!* (*Brit*), oh heck!*; **c'est de la ~ de bique*** it's a load of (old) rubbish*; **c'est pas de la ~*** it's not cheap rubbish; **il ne se prend pas pour une ~*** he thinks he's a big shot*; (*terme d'affection*) **ma (petite) ~*** my little sausage*. b (*bonbon*) **~ de chocolat** chocolate whirl. c (†: *boue*) mud.

crotter [kʀɔte] [1] 1 vt to muddy, dirty, cover in mud. **souliers tout crottés** muddy shoes, shoes covered in mud. 2 vi *[chien]* to do its business, mess.

crottin [kʀɔtɛ̃] nm a **~ (de cheval/d'âne)** (horse/donkey) droppings *ou* dung (*NonC*) *ou* manure (*NonC*). b (*fromage*) (small round) cheese (*made of goat's milk*).

crouillat‡ [kʀuja] , **crouille‡** [kʀuj] nm (*péj*) wog*‡ (*péj*), North African.

croulant, e [kʀulɑ̃, ɑ̃t] 1 adj *mur* crumbling, tumbledown (*épith*); *maison* ramshackle, tumbledown (*épith*), crumbling; (*fig*) *autorité, empire* crumbling, tottering. 2 nm (‡) old fogey‡. **les ~s** the old folk, the old ones*, the old fogeys‡.

crouler [kʀule] [1] vi a (*s'écrouler*) *[maison, mur]* to collapse, tumble down, fall down; *[masse de neige]* to collapse; *[terre]* to give (way), collapse; (*fig*) *[empire]* to collapse. **le mur a croulé sous la force du vent** the wall collapsed *ou* caved in under the force of the wind; **la terre croula sous ses pas** the ground gave (way) *ou* caved in *ou* collapsed under his feet; **le tremblement de terre a fait ~ les maisons** the earthquake has brought the houses down *ou* has demolished the houses; (*fig*) **la salle croulait sous les applaudissements** the audience brought the house down *ou* raised the roof with their applause; (*fig*) **se laisser ~ dans un fauteuil** to collapse into an armchair.

b (*menacer de s'écrouler, être délabré*) **une maison qui croule** a ramshackle *ou* tumbledown *ou* crumbling house, a house which is falling into ruin *ou* going to rack and ruin; **un mur qui croule** a crumbling *ou* tumbledown wall; (*fig*) **~ sous le poids de qch** to collapse under the weight of sth; (*fig*) **une civilisation qui croule** a tottering *ou* crumbling civilization.

croup [kʀup] nm (*Méd*) croup. **faux ~** spasmodic croup.

croupe [kʀup] nf a *[cheval]* croup, crupper, rump, hindquarters. **monter en ~** to ride pillion; **il monta en ~ et ils partirent** he got on behind and off they went; **il avait son ami en ~** he had his friend behind him (on the pillion). b *[*: personne]* rump*. **~ (d'une colline)** hilltop.

croupetons [kʀuptɔ̃] adv: **se tenir** *ou* **être à ~** to be crouching, be squatting, be (down) on one's haunches *ou* hunkers* (*Brit*); **se mettre à ~** to crouch *ou* squat down, go down on one's haunches.

croupi, e [kʀupi] (ptp de **croupir**) adj *eau* stagnant.

croupier, -ière[1] [kʀupje, jɛʀ] nm,f croupier.

croupière[2] [kʀupjɛʀ] nf (*harnais*) crupper. **tailler des ~s à qn**† to put a spoke in sb's wheel.

croupion [kʀupjɔ̃] nm (*Orn*) rump; (*Culin*) parson's nose, pope's nose (*US*); (‡ *hum*) *[personne]* rear (end)*, backside*. (*péj*) **un parlement ~*** a rump parliament; **un parti ~** a rump party.

croupir [kʀupiʀ] [2] vi *[eau]* to stagnate. **feuilles qui croupissent dans la mare** leaves which rot in the pond; (*fig*) *[personne]* **~ dans son ignorance/dans l'oisiveté/dans le vice** to wallow *ou* remain sunk in (one's own) ignorance/in idleness/in vice; **je n'ai pas envie de ~ dans ce bled*/cette boîte!** I don't want to (stay and) rot in this dump*/this company!; **ils l'ont laissé ~ en prison** they left him to rot in prison.

croupissant, e [kʀupisɑ̃, ɑ̃t] adj *eau* stagnant. (*fig*) **une vie ~e** a dead-end life.

CROUS [kʀus] nm (abrév de **centre régional des œuvres universitaires et scolaires**) *voir* **centre.**

croustade [kʀustad] nf croustade.

croustillant, e [kʀustijɑ̃, ɑ̃t] adj a (*voir* **croustiller**) crusty; crisp; crunchy. b (*fig: grivois*) spicy.

croustiller [kʀustije] [1] vi *[pain, pâte]* to be crusty; *[croissant, galette, chips]* to be crisp *ou* crunchy.

croûte [kʀut] 1 nf a *[pain, pâte]* crust; *[fromage]* rind; *[vol-au-vent]* case. **à la ~!*** (*venez manger*) come and get it!*, grub's up!‡ (*Brit*), grub's on!‡ (*US*); (*allons manger*) let's go and get it!* *ou* eat!; *voir* **casser, gagner, pâté.**

b (*à la surface d'un liquide*) **~ de glace** layer of ice; (*dans un pot*) **~ de peinture** skin of paint.

c (*sédiment, sécrétion durcie*) *[plaie]* scab. **couvert d'une ~ de glace** crusted with ice, covered with a crust of ice; **~ calcaire** *ou* **de tartre** layer of scale *ou* fur; **une ~ de tartre s'était formée sur les parois de la chaudière** the sides of the boiler were covered in scale *ou* had furred up, a layer of scale had collected on the sides of the boiler; **gratter des ~s de peinture/cire sur une table** to scrape lumps of paint/wax off a table.

d (*fig: vernis*) **~ de culture** veneer of culture; **~ de bêtise** (thick) layer of stupidity.

e **~ (de cuir)** undressed leather *ou* hide; **sac en ~** hide bag.

f (*péj: tableau*) daub.

2 comp ►**croûte aux champignons** (*Culin*) mushrooms on toast ►**croûte au fromage** (*Culin*) cheese on toast, toasted cheese, ≃ Welsh rarebit *ou* rabbit ►**croûte de pain** crust of bread; **croûtes de pain** (*péj*) old crusts; (*quignons*) hunks *ou* chunks of bread ►**la croûte terrestre** (*Géol*) the earth's crust.

croûté,e [kʀute] adj (*Ski*) **neige ~e** crusted snow.

croûter‡ [kʀute] [1] vi to nosh‡ (*Brit*), have some grub‡.

croûteux, -euse [kʀutø, øz] adj scabby, covered with scabs.

croûton [kʀutɔ̃] nm a (*bout du pain*) crust; (*Culin*) crouton. b (*péj: personne*) fuddy-duddy*, old fossil*.

croyable [kʀwajabl] adj: **ce n'est pas ~!** it's unbelievable!, it's incredible!

croyance [kʀwajɑ̃s] nf a (*NonC*) **~ à** *ou* **en** belief in, faith in. b (*opinion*) belief. **~s religieuses** religious beliefs; **la ~ populaire** folk *ou* conventional wisdom.

croyant, e [kʀwajɑ̃, ɑ̃t] 1 adj: **être ~** to be a believer; **ne pas être ~** to be a non-believer. 2 nm,f believer. **les ~s** the faithful.

CRS [seɛʀɛs] (abrév de **Compagnie républicaine de sécurité**) 1 nm *member of the state security police*. **après l'intervention des ~** after the state security police had intervened. 2 nf company of the state security police.

cru[1], e[1] [kʀy] adj a (*non cuit*) *aliments* raw, uncooked. **lait ~** milk straight from the cow; (*fig*) **avaler** *ou* **manger qn tout ~** to eat sb alive (*fig*), have sb for breakfast* (*fig*); (*fig*) **je l'aurais avalée** *ou* **mangée toute ~e*** (*j'étais furieux*) I could have strangled *ou* murdered her*; (*elle était belle à croquer*) she looked good enough to eat*.
b (*Tech: non apprêté*) *soie* raw; *chanvre, toile* raw, untreated; *métal* crude, raw. **cuir ~** untreated *ou* raw leather, rawhide.
c *lumière, couleur* harsh, garish.
d (*franc, réaliste*) *mot* forthright, blunt; *description* raw, blunt. **une réponse ~e** a straight *ou* blunt *ou* forthright reply; **je vous le dis tout ~** I'll tell you straight out*, I'll give it to you straight*.
e (*choquant*) *histoire, chanson, langage* crude, coarse. **parler ~** to speak coarsely *ou* crudely.
f (*loc*) **à ~**: **construire à ~** to build without foundations; (*Équitation*) **monter à ~** to ride bareback; († *ou littér*) **être chaussé à ~** to wear one's boots (*ou* shoes) without (any) socks.

cru[2] [kʀy] nm a (*terroir, vignoble*) vineyard. **un vin d'un bon ~** a good vintage; (*lit, fig*) **du ~** local; **les gens du ~** the locals. b (*vin*) wine. **un grand ~** a famous *ou* great wine *ou* vintage; *voir* **bouilleur**. c (*loc*) **de son (propre) ~** of his own invention *ou* devising.

cruauté [kʀyote] nf a [*personne, destin*] cruelty (*envers* to); [*bête sauvage*] ferocity. b act of cruelty, cruel act, cruelty.

cruche [kʀyʃ] nf a (*récipient*) pitcher, (earthenware) jug; (*contenu*) jug(ful). b (*‡: imbécile*) ass*, twit‡ (*Brit*).

cruchon [kʀyʃɔ̃] nm (*récipient*) small jug; (*contenu*) small jug(ful).

crucial, e, mpl **-iaux** [kʀysjal, jo] adj *question, année, problème* crucial.

crucifère [kʀysifɛʀ] adj cruciferous.

crucifiement [kʀysifimɑ̃] nm crucifixion. (*fig*) **le ~ de la chair** the crucifying of the flesh.

crucifier [kʀysifje] 7 vt (*lit, fig*) to crucify.

crucifix [kʀysifi] nm crucifix.

crucifixion [kʀysifiksjɔ̃] nf crucifixion.

cruciforme [kʀysifɔʀm] adj cruciform. **tournevis ~** Phillips screwdriver ®; **vis ~** Phillips screw ®.

cruciverbiste [kʀysivɛʀbist] nmf crossword-puzzle enthusiast.

crudité [kʀydite] nf a (*NonC*) [*langage*] crudeness, coarseness; [*description*] bluntness; [*lumière, couleur*] harshness, garishness. b (*propos*) **~s** coarse remarks, coarseness (*NonC*); **dire des ~s** to make coarse remarks. c (*Culin*) **~s** crudités.

crue[2] [kʀy] nf (*montée des eaux*) rise in the water level; (*inondation*) flood. **en ~** in spate; **les ~s du Nil** the Nile floods; **la fonte des neiges provoque des ~s subites** the spring thaw produces a sudden rise in river levels.

cruel, -elle [kʀyɛl] adj a (*méchant*) *personne, acte, paroles* cruel; *animal* ferocious. b (*douloureux*) *perte* cruel; *destin, sort* cruel, harsh; *remords, froid* cruel, bitter; *nécessité* cruel, bitter. **cette ~le épreuve, courageusement supportée** this cruel ordeal, borne with courage.

cruellement [kʀyɛlmɑ̃] adv (*voir* **cruel**) cruelly; ferociously; harshly; bitterly. **l'argent fait ~ défaut** the lack of money is sorely felt; **c'est ~ vrai** it's sadly true; **~ éprouvé par ce deuil** sorely *ou* grievously distressed by this bereavement, sadly bereaved.

cruiser [kʀuzœʀ] nm (*bateau de plaisance*) cruiser.

crûment [kʀymɑ̃] adv *dire, parler* (*nettement*) bluntly, forthrightly, plainly; (*grossièrement*) crudely, coarsely. **éclairer ~** to cast a harsh *ou* garish light over.

crustacé [kʀystase] nm (*Zool*) shellfish (*pl inv*) (*crabs, lobsters and shrimps*), member of the lobster family, crustacean (SPÉC). (*Culin*) **~s** seafood, shellfish.

cryobiologie [kʀijɔbjɔlɔʒi] nf cryobiology.

cryochirurgie [kʀijɔʃiʀyʀʒi] nf cryosurgery.

cryoconservation [kʀijokɔ̃sɛʀvasjɔ̃] nf cryogenic preservation.

cryologie [kʀijɔlɔʒi] nf cryogenics (*sg*).

cryptage [kʀiptaʒ] nm [*message, émission de télévision*] encoding.

crypte [kʀipt] nf crypt.

crypter [kʀipte] 1 vt *message, émission de télévision* to encode, scramble. **chaîne/émission cryptée** channel/programme for which one needs a decoder.

cryptocommuniste [kʀiptokɔmynist] nmf crypto-communist.

cryptogame [kʀiptɔgam] 1 adj cryptogamic. 2 nm ou f cryptogam.

cryptogramme [kʀiptɔgʀam] nm cryptogram.

cryptographie [kʀiptɔgʀafi] nf cryptography.

cryptographique [kʀiptɔgʀafik] adj cryptographic.

cryptologie [kʀiptɔlɔʒi] nf cryptology.

crypton [kʀiptɔ̃] nm = **krypton**.

CSA [seɛsa] nm (abrév de **Conseil supérieur de l'audiovisuel**) *voir* **conseil**.

CSG [seɛsʒe] nf (abrév de **contribution sociale généralisée**) *voir* **contribution**.

CSM [seɛsɛm] nm (abrév de **Conseil supérieur de la magistrature**) *French magistrates' council (which also hears appeals)*.

Cuba [kyba] nf Cuba. **à ~** in Cuba.

cubage [kybaʒ] nm a (*action*) cubage. b (*volume*) cubage, cubature, cubic content. **~ d'air** air space.

cubain, e [kybɛ̃, ɛn] 1 adj Cuban. 2 nm,f: **C~(e)** Cuban.

cube [kyb] 1 nm (*Géom, Math, gén*) cube; [*jeu*] building block, (wooden) brick. (*Math*) **le ~ de 2 est 8** 2 cubed is 8, the cube of 2 is 8; **élever au ~** to cube; **gros ~** big bike*. 2 adj: **centimètre/mètre ~** cubic centimetre/metre; *voir* **cylindrée**.

cuber [kybe] 1 1 vt *nombre* to cube; *volume, solide* to cube, measure the volume of; *espace* to measure the cubic capacity of. 2 vi [*récipient*] **~ 20 litres** to have a cubic capacity of 20 litres; (*fig*) **avec l'inflation leurs dépenses vont ~*** with inflation their expenses are going to mount up.

cubique [kybik] 1 adj cubic; *voir* **racine**. 2 nf (*Math: courbe*) cubic.

cubisme [kybism] nm cubism.

cubiste [kybist] adj, nmf cubist.

Cubitainer [kybitɛnɛʀ] nm ® square plastic container (*for holding liquids*).

cubital, e, mpl **-aux** [kybital, o] adj ulnar.

cubitus [kybitys] nm ulna.

cucul* [kyky] adj: **~ (la praline)** silly.

cucurbitacée [kykyʀbitase] nf cucurbitaceous plant (SPÉC), *plant of the melon and marrow family*.

cueillette [kœjɛt] nf a (*voir* **cueillir**) picking; gathering; (*Ethnologie*) gathering. **la ~ du houblon/des pommes** hop-/apple-picking; **cette tribu pratique la ~** the people of this tribe are gatherers. b (*fruits etc*) harvest (of fruit), crop (of fruit). **elle me montra sa ~** she showed me the (bunch of) flowers she'd picked; **mûres, myrtilles en abondance: quelle ~!** brambles, bilberries galore: what a harvest! *ou* crop! c (*Can*) [*données*] collection.

cueilleur, -euse [kœjœʀ, øz] nm,f gatherer.

cueillir [kœjiʀ] 12 vt a *fleurs* to pick, gather; (*séparément*) to pick, pluck; *pommes, poires etc* to pick; *fraises, mûres* to gather, pick. b (*fig: attraper*) *ballon* to catch; *baiser* to snatch *ou* steal; (*) *voleur* to nab*, catch. **~ les lauriers de la victoire** to win *ou* bring home the laurels (of victory); **il est venu nous ~ à la gare*** he came to collect *ou* get us *ou* pick us up at the station; **il m'a cueilli à froid** (*bagarre, débat*) he caught me off guard *ou* on the hop* (*Brit*).

cuesta [kwɛsta] nf cuesta.

cui-cui [kɥikɥi] excl, nm tweet-tweet. **faire ~** to go tweet-tweet.

cuiller, cuillère [kɥijɛʀ] 1 nf a (*ustensile*) spoon; (*contenu*) spoonful. **prenez une ~ à café de sirop** take a teaspoonful of cough mixture; **petite ~** (*à thé, à dessert*) ≃ teaspoon; (*Tennis*) **service à la ~** underarm serve; **servir à la ~** to serve underarm; *voir* **dos, ramasser**.
b (*‡: main*) **serrer la ~ à qn** to shake sb's paw*.
c (*Pêche*) spoon, spoonbait. **~ tournante** spinner; **pêche à la ~** spoonbait fishing, fishing with a spoon(bait).
d (*Tech*) [*grenade*] (safety) catch.
2 comp ►**cuiller de bois** (*Rugby, gén*) wooden spoon ►**cuiller à café** coffee spoon, ≃ teaspoon ►**cuiller à dessert** dessertspoon ►**cuiller à moka** (small) coffee spoon ►**cuiller à moutarde** mustard spoon ►**cuiller à pot** ladle; **en 2** *ou* **3 coups de cuiller à pot*** in two shakes of a lamb's tail*, in a flash, in no time (at all) ►**cuiller à soupe** soupspoon, ≃ tablespoon ►**cuiller de verrier** (glassblower's) ladle.

cuillerée [kɥijʀe] nf spoonful. (*Culin*) **~ à soupe** ≃ tablespoonful; (*Culin*) **~ à café** ≃ teaspoonful.

cuir [kɥiʀ] 1 nm a (*peau apprêtée*) leather; (*: *blouson*) leather jacket. **ceinture/semelles de ~** leather belt/soles; **objets** *ou* **articles en ~** leather articles *ou* goods; (*collectivement*) leathercraft, leatherwork; *voir* **relié, rond, tanner**.
b (*sur l'animal vivant, avant tannage*) hide; (*) [*personne*] hide*. [*personne*] **avoir le ~ dur** (*gén: être résistant*) to be as tough as nails; (*insensible à la critique*) to be thick-skinned.
c (*: *faute de liaison*) false liaison (*intrusive z- or t-sound*).
d (*Ftbl*) ball.
2 comp ►**cuir bouilli** cuir-bouilli ►**cuir brut** rawhide ►**cuir chevelu** (*Anat*) scalp ►**cuir de crocodile** crocodile skin ►**cuir en croûte** undressed leather ►**cuir à rasoir** (barber's *ou* razor) strop ►**cuir suédé** suede, suède ►**cuir de vache** cowhide ►**cuir de veau** calfskin ►**cuir verni** patent leather ►**cuir vert** = **cuir brut**.

cuirasse [kɥiʀas] nf (*Hist*) [*chevalier*] breastplate; (*Naut*) armour(-plate *ou* -plating); (*Zool*) cuirass; (*fig*) armour; *voir* **défaut**.

cuirassé, e [kɥiʀase] (ptp de **cuirasser**) 1 adj *soldat* breastplated; *navire* armour-plated, armoured. (*fig*) **être ~ contre qch** to be hardened against sth, be proof against sth. 2 nm battleship.

cuirasser [kɥiʀase] 1 **1** vt *chevalier* to put a breastplate on; *navire* to armour-plate; (*fig: endurcir*) to harden (*contre* against). **2** **se cuirasser** vpr **a** *[chevalier]* to put on a breastplate. **b** (*fig: s'endurcir*) to harden o.s. (*contre* against) **se ~ contre la douleur/l'émotion** to harden o.s. against suffering/emotion.

cuirassier [kɥiʀasje] nm (*Hist*) cuirassier; (*Mil*) (*soldat*) (armoured) cavalryman. (*régiment*) **le 3e ~** the 3rd (armoured) cavalry.

cuire [kɥiʀ] 38 **1** vt **a** (*aussi* **faire ~**) *plat, dîner* to cook. **~ à feu doux** *ou* **doucement** to cook gently *ou* slowly; **~ à petit feu** to simmer; **laisser** *ou* **faire ~ à feu doux** *ou* **à petit feu pendant 20 minutes** (allow to) simmer *ou* cook gently for 20 minutes; **~ au bain-marie** ≃ to heat in a double boiler, heat in a bain-marie; **~ à la broche** to cook *ou* roast on the spit, spit-roast; **~ au four** *pain, gâteau, pommes* to bake; *viande* to roast; *pommes de terre* to roast, bake; **~ à la vapeur/au gril/à la poêle/à l'eau/à la casserole** to steam/grill/fry/boil/stew; **~ au beurre/à l'huile** to cook in butter/in oil; **~ au gaz/à l'électricité** to cook on *ou* with gas/by *ou* on electricity; **faire** *ou* **laisser ~ qch pendant 15 minutes** to cook (*ou* boil *ou* roast) sth for 15 minutes; **faites-le ~ dans son jus** cook *ou* stew it in its own juice; **faire bien/peu ~ qch** to cook sth thoroughly *ou* well/slightly *ou* lightly; **faire trop ~ qch** to overcook sth; **ne pas faire assez ~ qch** to undercook sth; **il l'a fait ~ à point** he cooked it to a turn; *voir* **carotte, cuit, dur.**

b **four qui cuit mal la viande** oven which cooks *ou* does meat badly *ou* unevenly.

c (*Boulangerie*) *pain* to bake.

d *briques, porcelaine* to fire; *voir* **terre.**

e **à ~** *chocolat* cooking (*épith*); *prunes, poires* stewing (*épith*); **pommes à ~** cooking apples, cookers* (*Brit*).

2 vi **a** *[aliment]* to cook. **~ à gros bouillon(s)** to boil hard *ou* fast; **le dîner cuit à feu doux** *ou* **à petit feu** the dinner is cooking gently *ou* is simmering *ou* is on low; **~ dans son jus** to cook in its own juice, stew.

b (*fig*) *[personne]* **~ au soleil** to roast in the sun; **~ dans son jus*** (*avoir très chaud*) to be boiling* *ou* roasting*; (*se morfondre*) to stew in one's own juice; **on cuit ici!*** it's boiling (hot)* *ou* roasting* in here!

c (*brûler, picoter*) **les mains/yeux me cuisaient** my hands/eyes were smarting *ou* stinging; **mon dos me cuit** my back is burning.

d (*frm*) **il lui en a cuit** he suffered for it, he had good reason to regret it; **il vous en cuira** you'll rue the day (you did it) (*frm*), you'll live to rue it (*frm*).

cuisant, e [kɥizɑ̃, ɑ̃t] adj **a** (*physiquement*) *douleur* smarting, sharp, burning; *blessure* burning, stinging; *froid* bitter, biting. **b** (*moralement*) *remarque* caustic, stinging; *échec, regret* bitter.

cuiseur [kɥizœʀ] nm large pan; (*pour la cuisine à l'eau*) boiling pan. **~ électrique** large pressure cooker.

cuisine [kɥizin] **1** nf **a** (*pièce*) kitchen; (*Naut*) galley. **les ~s** the kitchens; **table/couteau de ~** kitchen table/knife; *voir* **batterie, latin, livre[1]** *etc.*

b (*art culinaire*) cookery, cooking; (*préparation*) cooking; (*nourriture apprêtée*) cooking, food. **faire la ~ au beurre/à l'huile** to cook with butter/oil; **je ne supporte pas la ~ au beurre/à l'huile** I can't stand things cooked in butter/oil; **apprendre la ~** to learn cookery (*Brit*) *ou* cooking; **la ~ prend du temps** cooking takes time; **une ~ épicée** hot *ou* spicy dishes *ou* food; **une ~ soignée** carefully prepared dishes *ou* food; **aimer la bonne ~** to like good cooking *ou* food; **il est en train de faire la ~** he's busy cooking *ou* making the meal; **chez eux, c'est le mari qui fait la ~** the husband does the cooking *ou* the husband is the cook in their house; **savoir faire la~, faire de la bonne ~** to be a good cook, be good at cooking; *voir* **nouveau.**

c (*personnel*) *[maison privée]* kitchen staff; *[cantine etc]* kitchen *ou* catering staff.

d (*fig péj*) **~ électorale** electoral schemings *ou* jiggery-pokery* (*Brit*); **je n'aime pas beaucoup sa petite ~** I'm not very fond of his little fiddles (*Brit*) *ou* his underhand tricks; **faire sa petite ~** to do one's own thing.

2 comp ▸**cuisine bourgeoise** (good) plain cooking *ou* fare; **faire une cuisine bourgeoise** to do (good) plain cooking ▸**cuisine de cantine** canteen food ▸**la cuisine française** French cooking *ou* cuisine ▸**cuisine de restaurant** restaurant meals *ou* food ▸**cuisine roulante** (*Mil*) field kitchen.

cuisiner [kɥizine] 1 vt **a** *plat* to cook. **il cuisine bien** he's a good cook; **ne la dérange pas quand elle cuisine** don't bother her when she's cooking. **b** (* *fig*) *personne* to grill*, pump for information *etc,* give the third degree to*.

cuisinette [kɥizinɛt] nf kitchenette.

cuisinier, -ière [kɥizinje, jɛʀ] **1** nm,f (*personne*) cook. **2** **cuisinière** nf (*à gaz, électrique*) cooker (*Brit*), stove; (*à bois*) (kitchen) range, wood-burning stove (*US*). **~-ière à gaz** gas cooker *ou* stove; **~-ière à charbon** solid-fuel stove, coal-fired cooker (*Brit*), coal-burning stove (*US*); (*vieux modèle*) kitchen range (*Brit*), stove (*US*).

cuissage [kɥisaʒ] nm *voir* **droit[3]**.

cuissard [kɥisaʀ] nm *[armure]* cuisse; *[cycliste]* (*cycling*) shorts.

cuissardes [kɥisaʀd] nfpl *[pêcheur]* waders; (*mode féminine*) thigh boots.

cuisse [kɥis] **1** nf (*Anat*) thigh. (*Culin*) **~ de mouton** leg of mutton *ou* lamb; **~ de poulet** chicken leg, (chicken) drumstick; **~s de grenouilles** frogs' legs; (*fig*) **se croire sorti de la ~ de Jupiter*** to think a lot of o.s., think no small beer of o.s. (*Brit*); **tu te crois sorti de la ~ de Jupiter!*** you think you're God's gift to mankind!*; **elle a la ~ légère*** she is generous with her favours (*euph*). **2** comp ▸**cuisse-madame** nf (pl **cuisses-madame**) (*poire*) cuisse madam pear.

cuisseau, pl **~x** [kɥiso] nm haunch (of veal).

cuisson [kɥisɔ̃] nf *[aliments]* cooking; *[pain, gâteau]* baking; *[gigot]* roasting; *[briques]* firing. (*Culin*) **ceci demande une longue ~** this needs to be cooked (*ou* baked) for a long time; (*Culin*) **temps de ~** cooking time.

cuissot [kɥiso] nm haunch (of venison *ou* wild boar).

cuistance‡ [kɥistɑ̃s] nf (*préparation de nourriture*) cooking, preparing the grub‡; (*nourriture*) nosh‡ (*Brit*), grub‡.

cuistot* [kɥisto] nm cook.

cuistre† [kɥistʀ] nm prig, priggish pedant.

cuistrerie† [kɥistʀəʀi] nf priggish pedantry.

cuit, e[1] [kɥi, kɥit] (ptp de **cuire**) adj **a** *aliment, plat* cooked, ready (*attrib*); *pain, viande* ready (*attrib*), done (*attrib*). **bien ~** well cooked *ou* done; **trop ~** overdone; **pas assez ~** underdone; **~ à point** (*peu saignant*) medium-cooked; (*parfaitement*) done to a turn; *voir* **terre.** **b** (*loc*) **c'est du tout ~*** it's *ou* it'll be a cinch*, it's *ou* it'll be a walkover*; **il attend toujours que ça lui arrive** *ou* **tombe tout ~ (dans le bec)*** he expects everything to be handed to him on a plate; **il est ~*** (*il va se faire prendre*) he's done for, his goose is cooked*; (*il va perdre*) it's all up (*Brit*) *ou* over (*US*) for him, he's had it*; **c'est ~ (pour ce soir)*** we've had it (for tonight)*.

cuite[2] [kɥit] nf **a** (‡) **prendre une ~** to get plastered‡ *ou* canned‡; **il a pris une sacrée ~** he got really plastered‡, he was really rolling drunk*. **b** (*Tech: cuisson*) firing.

cuiter (se)‡ [kɥite] 1 vpr to get plastered‡ *ou* canned‡.

cuivre [kɥivʀ] nm **a** **~ (rouge)** copper; **~ jaune** brass; **~ blanc** white copper; **objets** *ou* **articles en ~** copperware; **casseroles à fond ~** copper-bottomed pans; *voir* **gravure.** **b** (*Art*) copperplate. **c** (*ustensiles*) **~s** (*de cuivre*) copper; (*de cuivre et laiton*) brasses; **faire (briller) les ~s** to do the brass *ou* the brasses. **d** (*Mus*) brass instrument. **les ~s** the brass (section); **orchestre de ~s** brass band.

cuivré, e [kɥivʀe] (ptp de **cuivrer**) adj *reflets* coppery; *peau, teint* bronzed. **voix ~e** resonant *ou* sonorous voice; **cheveux aux reflets ~s** hair with auburn glints *ou* copper lights in it.

cuivrer [kɥivʀe] 1 vt (*Tech*) to copper(plate), cover with copper; *peau, teint* to bronze.

cuivreux, -euse [kɥivʀø, øz] adj (*Chim*) *métal* cuprous. **oxyde ~** cuprous oxide, cuprite.

cul [ky] **1** nm **a** (****** *Anat*) backside*, bum‡ (*Brit*), arse** , ass** (*US*). **il est tombé le ~ dans l'eau** he fell arse first in the water** (*Brit*), he fell on his ass in the water** (*US*); **un coup de pied au ~** a kick *ou* boot up the arse**, a kick in the ass** (*US*); (*fig*) **gros ~*** (*camion*) heavy lorry *ou* truck, rig; (*tabac*) ≃ shag; *voir* **faux, feu[1], tirer, trou** *etc.*

b (*Hist Habillement*) **(faux) ~** bustle.

c (*fig: fond, arrière*) *[bouteille]* bottom. **faire un cendrier d'un ~ de bouteille** to make an ashtray with *ou* from the bottom of a bottle; **~ de verre/de pot** glass-/jug-bottom; **pousser une voiture au ~*** to give a car a shove.

d (******: *amour physique*) **le ~** sex; **film de ~** porn movie*, skinflick‡; **revue** *ou* **magazine de ~** girlie mag*, porn mag*, pussy mag**; **une histoire de ~** a dirty joke; **il nous a raconté ses histoires de ~** he told us all about his sexual exploits.

e (*loc*) **faire ~ sec** to down one's drink in a oner‡ (*Brit*) *ou* at one go*; **allez, ~ sec!** right, bottoms up!*; **renverser ~ par-dessus tête** to turn head over heels; **on l'a dans le ~**** that's really screwed us (up)**; (*être fatigué*) **être sur le ~‡** to be dead-beat*, be knackered‡ (*Brit*); **en tomber** *ou* **rester sur le ~*** to be taken aback, be flabbergasted; **être comme ~ et chemise*** to be as thick as thieves (*avec* with); **tu peux te le mettre** *ou* **foutre au ~!**** go and stuff yourself!‡ (*Brit*) *ou* fuck yourself!**; **mon ~!**** my arse!**, my ass!** (*US*); **avoir le ~ bordé de nouilles**, avoir du ~**** to be a jammy (*Brit*) *ou* lucky bastard‡.

2 comp ▸**cul-de-basse-fosse** nm (pl **culs-de-basse-fosse**) dungeon ▸**cul-béni** nm (pl **culs-bénis**) religious nut* ▸**cul-blanc** (*Orn*) nm (pl **culs-blancs**) wheatear ▸**cul-de-jatte** nm (pl **culs-de-jatte**) legless cripple ▸**cul-de-lampe** nm (pl **culs-de-lampe**) (*Archit*) cul-de-lampe; (*Typ*) tailpiece ▸**cul-rouge** (*Orn*) nm (pl **culs-rouges**) great spotted woodpecker ▸**cul-de-sac** nm (pl **culs-de-sac**) (*rue*) cul-de-sac, dead end; (*fig*) blind alley ▸**cul-terreux** (*fig péj*) nm (pl **culs-terreux**) yokel, country bumpkin, hick* (*US*).

3 adj inv (‡: *stupide*) silly. **quel ~, ce type!** he's a real twerp‡ *ou* wally‡, that guy!

culasse [kylas] nf **a** *[moteur]* cylinder head; *voir* **joint.** **b** *[canon, fusil]* breech. **~ (mobile)** breechblock; *voir* **bloc.**

culbute [kylbyt] nf **a** (*cabriole*) somersault; (*chute*) tumble, fall. **faire une ~** (*cabriole*) to (turn a) somersault; (*chute*) to (take a) tumble, fall (head over heels). **b** (* *fig: faillite*) *[ministère]* collapse, fall; *[banque]* collapse. **faire la ~** *(spéculation, banque)* to collapse; *[entreprise]* to go bust*; **ce spéculateur a fait la ~** (*a doublé ses gains*) this speculator has doubled his money; (*a été ruiné*) this speculator has taken a tumble *ou* come a cropper* (*Brit*).

culbuter [kylbyte] [1] **1 vi** *[personne]* to (take a) tumble, fall (head over heels); *[chose]* to topple (over), fall (over); *[voiture]* to somersault, turn a somersault, overturn. **il a culbuté dans l'étang** he tumbled *ou* fell into the pond. **2 vt** *chaise etc* to upset, knock over; *personne* to knock over; (*fig*) *ennemi* to overwhelm; (*fig*) *ministère* to bring down, topple; (‡) *femme* to lay‡, screw*‡.

culbuteur [kylbytœʀ] **nm a** (*Tech*) *[moteur]* rocker arm. **b** *[benne]* tipper. **c** (*jouet*) tumbler.

culer [kyle] [1] **vi** (*Naut*) *[bateau]* to go astern; *[vent]* to veer astern. **brasser à ~** to brace aback.

culinaire [kylinɛʀ] **adj** culinary. **l'art ~** culinary art, the art of cooking.

culminant, e [kylminɑ̃, ɑ̃t] **adj** *voir* **point¹**.

culminer [kylmine] [1] **vi a** *[sommet, massif]* to tower (*au-dessus de* above). **~ à** to reach its highest point at; **le Massif central culmine à 1 886 mètres au Puy de Sancy** the Massif Central reaches its highest point of 1,886 metres at the Puy de Sancy; **le Mont-Blanc culmine à 4 807 mètres** Mont Blanc reaches 4,807 metres at its highest point. **b** (*fig*) *[colère]* to reach a peak, come to a head. **c** (*Astron*) to reach its highest point.

culot [kylo] **nm a** (*: *effronterie*) cheek*. **il a du ~** he has a lot of nerve *ou* cheek* (*Brit*), he has a brass neck‡; **tu ne manques pas de ~!** you've got a nerve!* *ou* a cheek!* (*Brit*). **b** *[ampoule]* cap; *[cartouche]* cap, base; *[bougie]* body; *[obus, bombe]* base. **c** (*résidu*) *[pipe]* dottle; (*Ind*) *[creuset]* residue.

culottage [kylɔtaʒ] **nm** *[pipe]* seasoning.

culotte [kylɔt] **1 nf a** (*slip*) *[femme]* panties, knickers; *[homme]* underpants. *[femme]* **petite ~** panties (*pl*); **acheter 3 ~s** to buy 3 pairs of panties (*ou* underpants).

b (*pantalon*) trousers (*Brit*), pants (*US*); (*Hist*) breeches; (*short*) shorts. **boutons de ~** trouser buttons.

c (*Boucherie*) rump.

d (*loc*) **baisser (sa) ~‡** (*lit*) to pull *ou* take one's knickers (*Brit*) *ou* panties down; (*fig*) to back down; **chez eux c'est elle qui porte la ~** she wears the trousers in their house; **prendre une ~*** (*au jeu*) to come a cropper* (*Brit*), lose one's shirt, lose heavily; (*fig*) **trembler** *ou* **faire dans sa ~‡, mouiller sa ~‡** to wet oneself‡ (*fig*), pee one's pants‡ (*fig*), shake in one's shoes.

2 comp ►**culotte de bain**† (swimming *ou* bathing) trunks ►**culotte(s) bouffante(s)** jodhpurs; (†) bloomers ►**culotte(s) de cheval** (*lit*) riding breeches; (*fig*) **avoir une culotte de cheval** to have jodhpur thighs *ou* saddlebags ►**culotte(s) courte(s)** short trousers (*Brit*) *ou* pants (*US*); (*fig*) **j'étais encore en culotte(s) courte(s)** I was still in short trousers (*Brit*) *ou* short pants (*US*) ►**culotte de golf** plus fours, knickerbockers ►**culotte(s) longue(s)** long trousers (*Brit*) *ou* pants (*US*) ►**culotte de peau**: (*péj Mil*) **une (vieille) culotte de peau** a colonel Blimp.

culotté, e [kylɔte] (**ptp de culotter**) **adj a** (*) cheeky* (*Brit*), sassy* (*US*). **b** *pipe* seasoned; *cuir* mellowed.

culotter [kylɔte] [1] **1 vt a** *pipe* to season. **b** (*rare*) *petit garçon* to put trousers on. **2 se culotter vpr a** *[pipe]* to season. **b** (*rare*) *[enfant]* to put one's trousers on.

culottier, -ière† [kylɔtje, jɛʀ] **nm,f** trouser maker, breeches maker†.

culpabilisation [kylpabilizasjɔ̃] **nf** (*action*) making guilty; (*état*) guilt.

culpabiliser [kylpabilize] [1] **1 vt**: **~ qn** to make sb feel guilty. **2 vi** to feel guilty.

culpabilité [kylpabilite] **nf** guilt, culpability; *voir* **sentiment**.

culte [kylt] **1 nm a** (*vénération*) cult, worship. **le ~ de Dieu** the worship of God; **le ~ du feu/du soleil** fire-/sun-worship; **avoir le ~ de** *justice* to make a cult *ou* religion of; *argent* to worship; **avoir un ~ pour qn** to (hero-)worship sb; **rendre** *ou* **vouer un ~ à qn/la mémoire de qn** to worship sb/sb's memory; **~ de la personnalité** personality cult, cult of personality.

b (*pratiques*) cult; (*religion*) religion. **abandonner le/changer de ~** to give up/change one's religion; **le ~ catholique** the Catholic form of worship; **les objets du ~** liturgical objects; *voir* **denier, liberté, ministre**.

c (*office protestant*) (church) service. **assister au ~** to attend the (church) service.

2 adj *film, livre* cult (*épith*).

cultivable [kyltivabl] **adj** *terrain* suitable for cultivation, cultivable.

cultivateur, -trice [kyltivatœʀ, tʀis] **1 adj** *peuple* agricultural, farming (*épith*). **2 nm,f** farmer. **3 nm** (*machine*) cultivator.

cultivé, e [kyltive] (**ptp de cultiver**) **adj** (*instruit*) *homme, esprit* cultured, cultivated. **peu ~** with *ou* of little culture.

cultiver [kyltive] [1] **1 vt a** *jardin, champ* to cultivate. **~ la terre** to cultivate the soil, till *ou* farm the land; **des terrains cultivés** cultivated lands, lands under cultivation.

b *céréales, légumes, vigne* to grow, cultivate.

c (*exercer*) *goût, mémoire, don* to cultivate. **~ son esprit** to improve *ou* cultivate one's mind.

d (*pratiquer*) *art, sciences, genre* to cultivate. (*iro*) **il cultive la grossièreté/le paradoxe** he goes out of his way to be rude/to do the unexpected.

e (*fréquenter*) *personne* to cultivate. **c'est une relation à ~** it's a connection which should be cultivated; **~ l'amitié de qn** to cultivate sb's friendship.

2 se cultiver vpr to improve *ou* cultivate one's mind.

cultuel, -elle [kyltɥɛl] **adj**: **édifices ~s** places of worship; (*Admin*) **association ~le** religious organization.

culture [kyltyʀ] **nf a** *[champ, jardin]* cultivation; *[légumes]* growing, cultivating, cultivation. **méthodes de ~** farming methods, methods of cultivation; **~ mécanique** mechanized farming; **~ intensive/extensive** intensive/extensive farming; **pays de moyenne/grande ~** country with a medium-scale/large-scale farming industry; **~ maraîchère/fruitière** vegetable/fruit farming; **~ de rapport, ~ commerciale** cash crop; **~ vivrière** food crop.

b (*terres cultivées*) **~s** land(s) under cultivation, arable land.

c *[esprit]* improvement, cultivation. **la ~** culture; **la ~ occidentale** western culture; **~ scientifique/générale** scientific/general knowledge *ou* education; **~ classique** classical culture *ou* education; **~ de masse** mass culture; **~ d'entreprise** organizational culture, house style.

d ~ physique physical culture *ou* training, P.T. (*Brit*); **faire de la ~ physique** to do physical training.

e (*Bio*) **~ microbienne/de tissus** microbe/tissue culture; *voir* **bouillon**.

culturel, -elle [kyltyʀɛl] **adj** cultural.

culturisme [kyltyʀism] **nm** body-building.

culturiste [kyltyʀist] **nmf** body-builder.

cumin [kymɛ̃] **nm** (*Culin*) caraway, cumin.

cumul [kymyl] **nm a** *[fonctions, charges]* plurality; *[avantages]* amassing; *[traitements]* concurrent drawing. **le ~ de fonctions est interdit** it is forbidden to hold more than one office at the same time *ou* concurrently; **le ~ de la pension de retraite et de cette allocation est interdit** it is forbidden to draw the retirement pension and this allowance at the same time *ou* concurrently. **b** (*Jur*) *[droits]* accumulation. **avec ~ de peines** sentences to run consecutively; **~ d'infractions** combination of offences.

cumulable [kymylabl] **adj** *fonctions* which may be held concurrently *ou* simultaneously; *traitements* which may be drawn concurrently *ou* simultaneously.

cumulard [kymylaʀ] **nm** (*péj*) *holder of several remunerative positions.*

cumulatif, -ive [kymylatif, iv] **adj** cumulative.

cumulativement [kymylativmɑ̃] **adv** *exercer des fonctions* simultaneously, concurrently; (*Jur*) *purger des peines* consecutively.

cumuler [kymyle] [1] **vt a** *fonctions* to hold concurrently *ou* simultaneously; *traitements* to draw concurrently *ou* simultaneously. **~ 2 traitements** to draw 2 separate salaries; **~ les fonctions de directeur et de comptable** to act simultaneously as manager and accountant, hold concurrently the positions of manager and accountant. **b** (*Jur*) *droits* to accumulate. (*Fin*) **calcul des intérêts cumulés** calculation of the interests accrued.

cumulo-nimbus [kymylonɛ̃bys] **nm** cumulonimbus.

cumulus [kymylys] **nm** cumulus (*SPÉC*). **~ de beau temps** (*pl*) fine-weather clouds; **~ d'orage** (*pl*) storm clouds.

cunéiforme [kyneifɔʀm] **adj a** *écriture, caractère* wedge-shaped, cuneiform (*SPÉC*). **b** (*Anat*) **les (os) ~s** the cuneiform bones (*of the tarsus*).

cunnilingus [kynilɛ̃gys] **nm** cunnilingus, cunnilinctus.

cupide [kypid] **adj** *air* greedy, filled with greed (*attrib*); *personne* grasping, greedy, moneygrubbing.

cupidement [kypidmɑ̃] **adv** greedily.

cupidité [kypidite] **nf** (*caractère: voir* **cupide**) greed(iness). (*défaut*) **la ~** cupidity (*littér*), greed.

Cupidon [kypidɔ̃] **nm** Cupid.

cuprifère [kypʀifɛʀ] **adj** copper-bearing, cupriferous (*SPÉC*).

cupule [kypyl] **nf** (*Bot*) cupule; *[gland]* (acorn) cup.

curabilité [kyʀabilite] **nf** curability.

curable [kyʀabl] **adj** curable.

curaçao [kyʀaso] **nm** curaçao.

curage [kyʀaʒ] **nm** *[fossé, égout]* clearing- *ou* cleaning-out; *[puits]* cleaning-out.

curaillon* [kyʀajɔ̃] **nm** (*péj*) priest.

curare [kyʀaʀ] **nm** curare.

curatelle [kyʀatɛl] **nf** (*voir* **curateur**) guardianship; trusteeship.

curateur, -trice [kyʀatœʀ, tʀis] **nm,f** *[mineur, aliéné]* guardian; *[succession]* trustee.

curatif, -ive [kyʀatif, iv] **adj** curative.

cure¹ [kyʀ] **nf a** (*traitement*) course of treatment. **une ~ (thermale)** ≃ a course of treatment *ou* a cure at a spa; **faire une ~ (thermale) à Vichy** to take the waters at Vichy; **suivre une ~ d'amaigrissement** to go on a slimming course (*Brit*), have reducing treatment (*US*); **faire une ~ de sommeil** to have sleep therapy; *voir* **désintoxication**. **b** (*grande consommation de*) **~ de**: **une ~ de fruits/de légumes/de lait** a fruit/

vegetable/milk cure, a fruit-/vegetable-/milk-only diet; ~ **de repos** rest cure; **nous avons fait une ~ de théâtre, cet hiver** we had a positive orgy of theatregoing this winter.

cure[2] [kyʀ] **nf** (*littér, hum*) **n'avoir ~ de qch** to care little about sth, pay no attention to sth; **il n'en a ~** he's not worried about that, he pays no attention to that; **je n'ai ~ de ces formalités** I've no time for these formalities.

cure[3] [kyʀ] **nf** (*Rel*) (*fonction*) cure; (*paroisse*) cure, ≃ living (*Brit*); (*maison*) presbytery, ≃ vicarage. **~ de village** village living *ou* cure.

cure- [kyʀ] **préf** *voir* **curer.**

curé [kyʀe] **nm** parish priest. **~ de campagne** country priest; **se faire ~*** to go in for the priesthood; (*péj*) **les ~s** clerics; **il n'aime pas les ~s** he hates clerics; **élevé chez les ~s** brought up by clerics; *voir* **bouffer**[2], **Monsieur.**

curée [kyʀe] **nf** a (*Chasse*) quarry. **donner la ~ aux chiens** to give the quarry to the hounds. b (*fig: ruée*) scramble (for the spoils). **se ruer** *ou* **aller à la ~** to scramble for the spoils.

curer [kyʀe] 1 1 **vt** a *fossé, égout* to clear *ou* clean out; *puits* to clean out; *pipe* to clean out, scrape out. b **se ~ les dents/le nez** to pick one's teeth/nose; **se ~ les ongles/oreilles** to clean one's nails/ears.
2 **comp** ► **cure-dent nm** (**pl cure-dents**) toothpick ► **cure-ongles nm inv** nail-cleaner ► **cure-oreille nm** (**pl cure-oreilles**) earpick ► **cure-pipe nm** (**pl cure-pipes**) pipe cleaner.

curetage [kyʀtaʒ] **nm** curetting, curettage.

cureter [kyʀte] 5 **vt** to curette.

cureton [kyʀtɔ̃] **nm** (*péj*) priestling.

curette [kyʀɛt] **nf** (*Tech*) scraper; (*Méd*) curette.

curie[1] [kyʀi] **nf** (*Hist romaine*) curia; (*Rel*) Curia.

curie[2] [kyʀi] **nm** (*Phys*) curie.

curieusement [kyʀjøzmɑ̃] **adv** strangely, curiously, oddly, peculiarly.

curieux, -ieuse [kyʀjø, jøz] 1 **adj** a (*intéressé*) **esprit ~** inquiring mind; **~ de tout** curious about everything; **il est particulièrement ~ de mathématiques** he's especially interested in *ou* keen on (*Brit*) mathematics; **~ d'apprendre** keen to learn; **je serais ~ de voir/savoir** I'd be interested *ou* curious to see/know.
b (*indiscret*) curious, inquisitive, nosey*. **lancer un regard ~ sur qch** to glance inquisitively *ou* nosily* *ou* curiously at sth.
c (*bizarre*) *coïncidence, individu, réaction* strange, curious, funny. **ce qui est ~, c'est que ...** the funny *ou* strange *ou* curious thing is that ...; *voir* **bête, chose.**
2 **nm** (*NonC: étrangeté*) **le ~, dans cette affaire** the funny *ou* strange thing in *ou* about this business; **le plus ~ de la chose** the funniest *ou* strangest thing *ou* the most curious thing about it.
3 **nm,f** a (*indiscret*) inquisitive person, nosey-parker* (*Brit*), busybody*. **petite ~euse!** little nosey-parker!* (*Brit*) *ou* Nosy Parker* (*US*), nosey little thing!*
b (*gén mpl: badaud*) (inquisitive) onlooker, bystander. **éloigner les ~** to move the bystanders along; **venir en ~** to come (just) for a look *ou* to have a look.

curiosité [kyʀjozite] **nf** a (*NonC: intérêt*) curiosity. **~ intellectuelle** intellectual curiosity; **cette ~ de tout** this curiosity about (knowing) everything; **ayant eu la ~ d'essayer cette méthode ...** having been curious enough to try this method ... .
b (*NonC: indiscrétion*) curiosity, inquisitiveness, nosiness*. **des ~s malsaines** unhealthy curiosity; **par (pure) ~** out of (sheer) curiosity; **poussé par la ~** spurred on by curiosity; **la ~ est un vilain défaut** curiosity killed the cat.
c (*site, monument etc*) curious *ou* unusual sight *ou* feature; (*bibelot*) curio. **les ~s de la ville** the (interesting *ou* unusual) sights of the town; **un magasin de ~s** a curio *ou* curiosity shop; **cet objet n'a qu'une valeur de ~** this object has only a curiosity value; **ce timbre est une ~ pour les amateurs** this stamp has a curiosity value for collectors.

curiste [kyʀist] **nmf** person taking the waters (*at a spa*).

curium [kyʀjɔm] **nm** curium.

curling [kœʀliŋ] **nm** curling.

curriculum (vitae) [kyʀikylɔm(vite)] **nm inv** curriculum vitae.

curry [kyʀi] **nm** curry. **poulet au ~** curried chicken, chicken curry.

curseur [kyʀsœʀ] **nm** [*règle à calculer*] slide, cursor; [*fermeture éclair*] slider; [*ordinateur*] cursor.

cursif, -ive [kyʀsif, iv] **adj** a (*lié*) *écriture, lettre* cursive. **écrire en ~-ive** to write in cursive script. b (*rapide*) *lecture, style* cursory.

cursus [kyʀsys] **nm** (*Univ*) ≃ degree course; [*carrière*] career path.

curule [kyʀyl] **adj: chaise ~** curule chair.

curviligne [kyʀviliɲ] **adj** curvilinear.

custom [kœstɔm] **nm inv** (*voiture*) custom(ized) car; (*moto*) custom(ized) bike.

cutané, e [kytane] **adj** skin (*épith*), cutaneous (SPÉC). **affection ~e** skin trouble; *voir* **sous.**

cuti* [kyti] **nf abrév de cuti-réaction.**

cuticule [kytikyl] **nf** (*Bot, Zool*) cuticle.

cuti-réaction [kytiʀeaksjɔ̃] **nf** skin test. **faire une ~** to take a skin test; *voir* **virer.**

cutter [kœtœʀ] **nm** (*petit*) craft knife; (*gros*) Stanley knife ®.

cuvage [kyvaʒ] **nm, cuvaison** [kyvɛzɔ̃] **nf** [*raisins*] fermentation (*in a vat*).

cuve [kyv] **nf** [*fermentation, teinture*] vat; [*brasserie*] mash tun; [*mazout*] tank; [*eau*] cistern, tank; [*blanchissage*] laundry vat. (*Phot*) **~ de développement** developing tank.

cuvée [kyve] **nf** (*contenu*) vatful; (*produit de toute une vigne*) vintage; (*fig*) [*étudiants, films*] crop. **tonneaux d'une même ~** barrels of the same vintage; **vin de la première ~** wine from the first vintage; **la ~ 1937** the 1937 vintage; **1991 a été une excellente/mauvaise ~ pour notre université** 1991 was an excellent/a bad year for our university; *voir* **tête.**

cuver [kyve] 1 1 **vt: ~ (son vin)*** to sleep it off*; **~ sa colère** to sleep off *ou* work off one's anger. 2 **vi** [*vin, raisins*] to ferment.

cuvette [kyvɛt] **nf** a (*récipient portatif*) (*gén*) basin, bowl; (*pour la toilette*) washbowl; (*Phot*) dish. **~ de plastique** plastic bowl. b (*partie creuse*) [*lavabo*] washbasin, basin; [*évier*] basin; [*W.-C.*] pan. c (*Géog*) basin. d [*baromètre*] cistern, cup. e [*montre*] cap.

CV [seve] **nm** a (**abrév de curriculum vitae**) CV. b (**abrév de cheval-vapeur**) hp.

cyanose [sjanoz] **nf** (*Méd*) cyanosis.

cyanosé, e [sjanɔze] **adj** cyanotic (SPÉC). **avoir le visage ~** to be blue in the face.

cyanure [sjanyʀ] **nm** cyanide.

cybernéticien, -ienne [sibɛʀnetisjɛ̃, jɛn] **nm,f** cyberneticist.

cybernétique [sibɛʀnetik] **nf** cybernetics (*sg*).

cyclable [siklabl] **adj: piste ~** cycle track *ou* path (*Brit*).

cyclamate [siklamat] **nm** cyclamate.

cyclamen [siklamɛn] **nm** cyclamen.

cycle[1] [sikl] **nm** a (*révolution, Astron, Bio, Élec, Écon*) cycle.
b (*Littérat*) cycle. **le ~ breton** the Breton cycle; **~ de chansons** song cycle.
c (*Scol*) **~ (d'études)** academic cycle; (*Scol*) **~ long** *studies leading to the baccalauréat;* (*Scol*) **~ court** *studies leading to vocational training instead of the baccalauréat;* (*Scol*) **premier/deuxième ~** middle/upper school; (*Univ*) **premier ~** ≃ first and second year; (*Univ*) **deuxième ~** ≃ Final Honours; **~ élémentaire** ≃ first five years of primary school (*Brit*), ≃ grades one through five (*US*); **troisième ~** ≃ postgraduate studies; **diplôme de troisième ~** ≃ postgraduate degree, Ph.D.; **étudiant de troisième ~** ≃ postgraduate *ou* Ph.D. student; **~ d'orientation** ≃ middle school (*transition classes*).

cycle[2] [sikl] **nm** (*bicyclette*) cycle. **l'industrie du ~** the cycle industry; **magasin de ~s** cycle shop; **marchand de ~s** bicycle merchant *ou* seller; **tarif: ~s 10 F, automobiles 45 F** charge: cycles and motorcycles 10 francs, cars 45 francs.

cyclique [siklik] **adj** cyclic(al).

cycliquement [siklikmɑ̃] **adv** cyclically.

cyclisme [siklism] **nm** cycling.

cycliste [siklist] 1 **adj: course/champion ~** cycle race/champion; **coureur ~** racing cyclist. 2 **nmf** cyclist. 3 **nm** (*short*) cycling shorts (*pl*).

cyclo-cross [siklokʀɔs] **nm** (*Sport*) cyclo-cross; (*épreuve*) cyclo-cross race.

cycloïdal, e, mpl -aux [siklɔidal, o] **adj** cycloid(al).

cycloïde [siklɔid] **nf** cycloid.

cyclomoteur [siklomɔtœʀ] **nm** moped, motorized bike *ou* bicycle.

cyclomotoriste [siklomɔtɔʀist] **nmf** moped rider.

cyclonal, e, mpl -aux [siklɔnal, o] **adj** cyclonic.

cyclone [siklon] **nm** (*Mét: typhon*) cyclone; (*Mét: zone de basse pression*) zone of low pressure; (*vent violent*) hurricane; (*fig*) whirlwind. **entrer comme un ~** to sweep *ou* come in like a whirlwind; *voir* **œil.**

cyclonique [siklonik] **adj** = **cyclonal.**

cyclope [siklɔp] **nm** (*Myth*) **C~** Cyclops; **travail de ~** Herculean task.

cyclopéen, -enne [siklɔpeɛ̃, ɛn] **adj** (*Myth*) cyclopean. **travail ~** Herculean task.

cyclosporine [siklospɔʀin] **nf** = **ciclosporine.**

cyclothymie [siklotimi] **nf** manic-depression, cyclothymia (SPÉC).

cyclothymique [siklotimik] **adj, nmf** manic-depressive, cyclo-thymic (SPÉC).

cyclo-tourisme [siklotuʀism] **nm** bicycle touring. **pour les vacances nous allons faire du ~** we're going on a cycling tour during the holidays, we're going on a cycling holiday.

cyclotron [siklɔtʀɔ̃] **nm** cyclotron.

cygne [siɲ] **nm** swan. **jeune ~** cygnet; **~ mâle** cob; *voir* **bec, chant**[1], **col.**

cylindre [silɛ̃dʀ] **nm** a (*Géom*) cylinder. **~ droit/oblique** right (circular)/oblique (circular) cylinder; **~ de révolution** cylindrical solid of revolution. b (*rouleau*) roller; [*rouleau-compresseur*] wheel, roller. **~ d'impression** printing cylinder; *voir* **bureau, presse, serrure.** c [*moteur*] cylinder. **moteur à 4 ~s en ligne** straight-4 engine; **moteur à 6 ~s en V** V6 engine; **moteur à 2 ~s opposés** flat-2 engine; **une 6 ~s** a 6-cylinder (car).

cylindrée [silɛ̃dʀe] **nf** [*moteur, cylindres*] capacity. **avoir une ~ de 1 600 cm³** to have a capacity of 1,600 ccs; **une (voiture de) grosse/petite ~** a big-/small-engined car; **les petites ~s consomment peu** cars with small engines *ou* small-engined cars don't use much (petrol).

cylindrer [silɛ̃dʀe] 1 **vt** (*former en cylindre*) *métal* to roll; *papier* to roll

(up); (*presser, aplatir*) *linge* to press; *route* to roll.
cylindrique [silẽdʀik] adj cylindrical.
cymbale [sɛ̃bal] nf cymbal; *voir* **coup**.
cymbalier [sɛ̃balje] nm cymbalist.
cynégétique [sineʒetik] 1 adj cynegetic. 2 nf cynegetics (*sg*).
cynique [sinik] 1 adj cynical; (*Philos*) Cynic. 2 nm cynic; (*Philos*) Cynic.
cyniquement [sinikmɑ̃] adv cynically.
cynisme [sinism] nm cynicism; (*Philos*) Cynicism.
cynocéphale [sinosefal] nm dog-faced baboon, cynocephalus (*SPÉC*).
cynodrome [sinodʀom] nm greyhound track.
cynor(r)hodon [sinɔʀɔdɔ̃] nm rosehip.
cyprès [sipʀɛ] nm cypress.
cypriote [sipʀijɔt] 1 adj Cypriot. 2 nmf: C~ Cypriot.
cyrillique [siʀilik] adj Cyrillic.
cystite [sistit] nf cystitis (*NonC*).
Cythère [sitɛʀ] nf Cythera.
cytise [sitiz] nm laburnum.
cytologie [sitɔlɔʒi] nf cytology.
cytologique [sitɔlɔʒik] adj cytological.
cytoplasme [sitɔplasm] nm cytoplasm.
czar [tsaʀ] nm = **tsar**.
czarewitch [tsaʀevitʃ] nm = **tsarévitch**.
czariste [tsaʀist] adj = **tsariste**.

D

D, d [de] nm (*lettre*) D, d; *voir* **système**.
d' [d] *voir* **de¹, de²**.
da [da] *voir* **oui**.
DAB [dab] nm (abrév de **distributeur automatique de billets**) ATM.
dab‡ [dab] nm (*père*) old man*, father.
Dacca† [dakа] n Dacca†.
d'abord [dabɔʀ] loc adv *voir* **abord**.
dacquois, e [dakwa, waz] 1 adj of *ou* from Dax. 2 nm,f: **D~(e)** inhabitant *ou* native of Dax.
Dacron [dakʀɔ̃] nm ® Dacron ®.
dactyle [daktil] nm (*Poésie*) dactyl; (*Bot*) cocksfoot.
dactylique [daktilik] adj dactylic.
dactylo [daktilo] nf abrév de **dactylographe, dactylographie**.
dactylographe [daktilɔgʀaf] nf typist.
dactylographie [daktilɔgʀafi] nf typing, typewriting. **elle apprend la ~** she's learning to type, she's learning typing.
dactylographier [daktilɔgʀafje] 7 vt to type (out).
dactylographique [daktilɔgʀafik] adj typing (*épith*).
dactyloscopie [daktilɔskɔpi] nf fingerprinting methods.
dada¹ [dada] nm a (*langage enfantin: cheval*) horsy, gee-gee (*Brit langage enfantin*). **viens faire du ~ ou à ~** come and ride the gee-gee *ou* the horsy. b (*fig: marotte*) hobby-horse (*fig*). **enfourcher son ~** to get on one's hobby-horse, launch o.s. on one's pet subject.
dada² [dada] adj (*Art, Littérat*) Dada, dada.
dadais [dadɛ] nm: **(grand) ~** awkward lump (of a youth) (*péj*); **espèce de grand ~!** you great lump! (*péj*).
dadaïsme [dadaism] nm dadaism.
dadaïste [dadaist] adj, nmf dadaist.
DAF [daf] nm (abrév de **directeur administratif et financier**) *voir* **directeur**.
dague [dag] nf a (*arme*) dagger. b *[cerf]* spike.
daguerréotype [dageʀeɔtip] nm (*procédé*) daguerreotype; (*instrument*) daguerre photographic device.
daguet [dage] nm young stag, brocket.
dahlia [dalja] nm dahlia.
dahoméen, -enne [daɔmeɛ̃, ɛn] 1 adj Dahomean. 2 nm,f: **D~(ne)** Dahomean.
Dahomey [daɔme] nm Dahomey.
daigner [deɲe] 1 vt to deign, condescend. **il n'a même pas daigné nous regarder** he did not even deign to look at us; (*frm*) **daignez nous excuser** be so good as to excuse us.
daim [dɛ̃] nm (*gén*) (fallow) deer; (*mâle*) buck; (*peau*) buckskin, doeskin; (*cuir suédé*) suede. **chaussures en ~** suede shoes.
daine [dɛn] nf doe.
dais [dɛ] nm canopy.
Dakar [dakaʀ] n Dakar.
Dakota [dakɔta] nm: **~ du Nord/du Sud** North/South Dakota.
dalaï-lama [dalailama] nm Dalai Lama.
Dalila [dalila] nf Delilah.
dallage [dalaʒ] nm (*NonC: action*) paving, flagging; (*surface, revêtement*) paving, pavement.
dalle [dal] nf a *[trottoir]* paving stone, flag(stone). **une ~ de pierre** a stone slab; **~ funéraire** tombstone. b *[paroi de rocher]* slab. c (‡) **que ~** damn all‡ (*Brit*); **je n'y pige ou n'entrave que ~** I don't get it*, I can understand damn all‡ (*Brit*); **je n'y vois que ~** I can't see a ruddy‡ (*Brit*) *ou* damn‡ thing; **avoir la ~ en pente** to be a bit of a boozer‡; *voir* **rincer**. d (*: *faim*) **avoir ou crever la ~** to be starving* *ou* famished*.
daller [dale] 1 vt to pave, lay paving stones *ou* flagstones on.
dalleur [dalœʀ] nm flag layer, paviour.
dalmate [dalmat] 1 adj Dalmatian. 2 nm (*Ling*) Dalmatian. 3 nmf: **D~** Dalmatian.
Dalmatie [dalmasi] nf Dalmatia.
dalmatien, -ienne [dalmasjɛ̃, jɛn] nm,f (*chien*) Dalmatian.
daltonien, -ienne [daltɔnjɛ̃, jɛn] adj colour-blind.
daltonisme [daltɔnism] nm colour-blindness, daltonism (SPÉC).
dam [dɑ̃] nm: **au (grand) ~ de** (*au détriment de*) (much) to the detriment of; (*au déplaisir de*) to the (great) displeasure of.
damas [dama(s)] nm (*tissu*) damask; (*acier*) Damascus steel, damask; (*prune*) damson.
Damas [dama] n Damascus; *voir* **chemin**.
damasquinage [damaskinaʒ] nm damascening.
damasquiner [damaskine] 1 vt to damascene.
damassé, e [damase] (ptp de **damasser**) 1 adj *tissu* damask. 2 nm damask cloth.
damasser [damase] 1 vt to damask.
damassure [damasyʀ] nf damask design, damask effect.
dame [dam] 1 nf a (*gén: femme*) lady; (*: *épouse*) wife. **il y a une ~ qui vous attend** there is a lady waiting for you; **votre ~ m'a dit que*** ... your wife told me that ...; **alors ma petite ~!*** now then, dear!; **vous savez, ma bonne ~!*** you know, my dear!; (*Jur*) **la ~ X** Mrs X; **pour ~s** *coiffeur, liqueur* ladies'; **de ~** *sac, manteau* lady's.
b (*de haute naissance*) lady. **une grande ~** (*noble*) a highborn *ou* great lady; (*artiste*) a great lady (*de* of); **jouer les grandes ~s** to play the fine lady; **les belles ~s des beaux quartiers** the fashionable *ou* fine ladies of the best districts; (*hum*) **la ~ de ses pensées** his lady-love (*hum*); *voir* **premier**.
c (*Cartes, Échecs*) queen; (*Dames*) crown; (*Jacquet*) piece, man. **le jeu de ~s, les ~s** draughts (*Brit*), checkers (*US*); **aller à ~** (*Dames*) to make a crown; (*Échecs*) to make a queen; **la ~ de pique** the queen of spades.
d (*Tech: hie*) beetle, rammer; (*Naut*) rowlock.
2 excl (†) **~ oui/non!** why yes/no!, indeed yes/no!
3 comp ▸**dame catéchiste** catechism mistress, ≃ Sunday school teacher ▸**dame de charité** benefactress ▸**dame de compagnie** (lady's) companion ▸**dame d'honneur** lady-in-waiting ▸**dame-jeanne** nf (pl **dames-jeannes**) demijohn ▸**Dame Nature** Mother Nature ▸**dame patronnesse** patroness ▸**dame pipi‡** lady toilet attendant.
damer [dame] 1 vt a *terre* to ram *ou* pack down; *neige* (*à ski*) to tread (down), pack (down); (*avec un rouleau*) to roll, pack (down). (*Ski*) **c'est bien damé** it's well pisted down. b *pion* (*Dames*) to crown; (*Échecs*) to queen. (*fig*) **~ le pion à qn** to get the better of sb, checkmate sb.
damier [damje] nm (*Dames*) draughtboard (*Brit*), checkerboard (*US*); (*dessin*) check (pattern). **en ou à ~** chequered; **les champs formaient un ~** the fields were laid out like a draughtboard (*Brit*) *ou* like patchwork.
damnable [danabl] adj (*Rel*) damnable; *passion, idée* despicable, abominable.
damnation [danasjɔ̃] nf damnation. **~!†** damnation!, tarnation!† (*US*); *voir* **enfer**.
damné, e [dane] (ptp de **damner**) 1 adj (*: *maudit*) cursed*, confounded*†; *voir* **âme**. 2 nm,f damned person. **les ~s** the damned; **mener une vie de ~** to live the life of the damned; *voir* **souffrir**.
damner [dane] 1 1 vt to damn. **faire ~ qn*** to drive sb mad*, drive sb to drink*; (*hum*) **c'est bon à faire ~ un saint*** it's so good it's wicked‡; (*hum*) **elle est belle à faire ~ un saint*** she's so lovely she would tempt a saint (in heaven)*. 2 **se damner** vpr to damn o.s. **se ~ pour qn** to risk damnation for sb.
Damoclès [damɔklɛs] nm Damocles; *voir* **épée**.
damoiseau, pl **~x** [damwazo] nm (*Hist*) page, squire; (†, *hum*) young beau†.
damoiselle [damwazɛl] nf (*Hist*) damsel††.
dan [dan] nm (*Judo*) dan. **il est deuxième ~** he's a second dan.
Danaïdes [danaid] nfpl *voir* **tonneau**.
dancing [dɑ̃siŋ] nm dance hall.
dandinement [dɑ̃dinmɑ̃] nm (*voir* **dandiner**) waddle, waddling; lolloping about (*Brit*).
dandiner (se) [dɑ̃dine] 1 vpr *[canard]* to waddle; *[personne]* to lollop from side to side (*Brit*), waddle. **avancer ou marcher en se dandinant** to

waddle along.

dandy† [dɑ̃di] nm dandy.

dandysme [dɑ̃dism] nm (*Hist*) dandyism.

Danemark [danmaʀk] nm Denmark.

danger [dɑ̃ʒe] nm a danger. **être en ~** to be in danger; **ses jours sont en ~** his life is in danger; **mettre en ~** *personne* to put in danger; *vie, espèce* to endanger; *chances, réputation, carrière* to jeopardize; **en ~ de** in danger of; **il est en ~ de mort** he is in danger *ou* peril of his life; **courir un ~** to run a risk; **en cas de ~** in case of emergency; **ça n'offre aucun ~, c'est sans ~** it doesn't present any danger (*pour* to), it is quite safe (*pour* for); **il y a (du) ~ à faire cela** it is dangerous to do that, there is a danger in doing that; **il est hors de ~** he is out of danger; **cet automobiliste est un ~ public** that driver is a public menace; **les ~s de la route** road hazards; **sans ~** (adj) safe; (adv) safely; **attention ~!** look out!
b (*) **(il n'y a) pas de ~!** no way!*, no fear!*; **pas de ~ qu'il vienne!** there's no fear *ou* risk *ou* danger that he'll come *ou* of his coming.

dangereusement [dɑ̃ʒʀøzmɑ̃] adv dangerously.

dangereux, -euse [dɑ̃ʒʀø, øz] adj *chemin, ennemi, doctrine, animal* dangerous (*pour* to); *entreprise* dangerous, hazardous, risky. **zone ~euse** danger zone.

dangerosité [dɑ̃ʒʀozite] nf dangerousness.

Daniel [danjɛl] nm Daniel.

danois, e [danwa, waz] 1 adj Danish. 2 nm a (*Ling*) Danish. b (*chien*) **(grand) ~** Great Dane. 3 nm,f: **D~(e)** Dane.

dans [dɑ̃] prép a (*lit, fig: lieu*) in; (*changement de lieu*) into, to; (*à l'intérieur de*) in, inside; (*dans des limites*) within. **il habite ~ l'Est/le Jura** he lives in the East/the Jura; **il n'habite pas ~ Londres même, mais en banlieue** he doesn't live in London itself, but in the suburbs; **le ministère est ~ la rue de Rivoli** the ministry is in the rue de Rivoli; **courir ~ l'herbe/les champs** to run around in *ou* run through the grass/fields; **il a plu ~ toute la France** it rained throughout France *ou* in all parts of France; **s'enfoncer/pénétrer ~ la forêt** to make one's way deep into/go into *ou* enter the forest; **ils sont partis ~ la montagne** they have gone off to the mountains; **elle erra ~ la ville/les rues/la campagne** she wandered through *ou* round *ou* about the town/the streets/the countryside; **ne marche pas ~ l'eau** don't walk in *ou* through the water; **il est tombé ~ la rivière** he fell into *ou* in the river; **~ le périmètre/un rayon très restreint** within the perimeter/a very restricted radius; **vous êtes ~ la bonne direction** you are going the right way *ou* in the right direction; **ils ont voyagé ~ le même train/avion** they travelled on the same train/plane; **mettre qch ~ un tiroir** to put sth in a drawer; **cherche** *ou* **regarde ~ la boîte** look inside *ou* in the box; **verser du vin ~ les verres** to pour wine into the glasses; **jeter l'eau sale ~ l'évier** to pour the dirty water down the sink; **~ le fond/le bas/le haut de l'armoire** at *ou* in the back/the bottom/the top of the wardrobe; **elle fouilla ~ ses poches/son sac** she went through her pockets/bag; **il reconnut le voleur ~ la foule/l'assistance** he recognized the thief in *ou* among the crowd/among the spectators; **il a reçu un coup de poing ~ la figure/le dos** he was punched *ou* he got a punch in the face/back; **il l'a lu ~ le journal/(l'œuvre de) Gide** he read it in the newspaper/in (the works of) Gide; **l'idée était ~ l'air depuis un moment** the idea had been in the air for some time; **qu'est-ce qui a bien pu se passer ~ sa tête?** what can have got into his head?, what can he have been thinking of?; **ce n'est pas ~ ses projets** he's not planning to do *ou* on doing that, that's not one of his plans; **il avait ~ l'idée** *ou* **l'esprit** *ou* **la tête que** he had a feeling that, he had it on his mind that; **elle avait ~ l'idée** *ou* **la tête de faire** she had a mind to do; **il y a de la tristesse ~ son regard/sourire** there's a certain sadness in his eyes/smile.
b (*lieu: avec idée d'extraction*) out of, from. **prendre qch ~ un tiroir** to take sth out of *ou* from a drawer; **boire du café ~ une tasse/un verre** to drink coffee out of *ou* from a cup/glass; **la chèvre lui mangeait ~ la main** the goat ate out of his hand; **le chien a mangé ~ mon assiette** the dog ate off my plate; **bifteck ~ le filet** fillet steak; **il l'a appris/copié ~ un livre** he learnt/copied it from *ou* out of a book.
c (*temps: gén*) in. **il est ~ sa 6e année** he's in his 6th year; **~ ma jeunesse** *ou* **mon jeune temps** in my youth, in my younger days; **~ les siècles passés** in previous centuries; **~ les mois à venir** in the months to come *ou* the coming months; **~ le cours** *ou* **le courant de l'année** in the course of the year; *voir* **temps**[1], **vie**.
d (*temps futur*) in; (*dans des limites*) within, inside, in (the course of). **il part ~ 2 jours/une semaine** he leaves in 2 days *ou* 2 days' time/a week *ou* a week's time; **~ combien de temps serez-vous prêt?** how long will it be before you are ready?; **il arrive** *ou* **il sera là ~ une minute** *ou* **un instant** he'll be here in a minute; **cela pourrait se faire ~ le mois/la semaine** it could be done within the month/week *ou* inside a month/week; **il mourut ~ l'heure qui suivit** he died within the hour; **je l'attends ~ la matinée/la nuit** I'm expecting him some time this morning/some time tonight, I'm expecting him (some time) in the course of the morning/night.
e (*état, condition, manière*) in. **être ~ les affaires/l'industrie/les textiles** to be in business/industry/textiles; **faire les choses ~ les règles** to work within the rules; **vivre ~ la misère/l'oisiveté/la peur** to live in poverty/idlness/fear; **être assis/couché ~ une mauvaise position** to be sitting/lying in an awkward position; **je l'aime beaucoup ~ cette robe/ce rôle** I really like her in that dress/part; **il était plongé ~ la tristesse/une profonde méditation** he was plunged in grief/plunged deep in thought; **ses idées sont ~ la plus grande confusion** his ideas are as confused as can be, his ideas are in a state of great confusion; **et ~ tout cela, qu'est-ce que vous devenez?** and with all this going on *ou* in the meantime, how are things with you?; **il est difficile de travailler ~ ce bruit/ces conditions** it's difficult to work in this noise/these conditions; **~ le brouillard/l'obscurité** in fog/darkness, in the fog/the dark; **le camion passa ~ un bruit de ferraille** the lorry rattled past; **elles sortirent ~ un frou-frou de soie** they left in a rustle of silk; **il est ~ une mauvaise passe** he's going through a bad patch (*Brit*); **il n'est pas ~ le complot/le secret** he's not in on the plot/secret; **elle n'est pas ~ un bon jour** it's not one of her good days, she's having *ou* it's one of her off days.
f (*situation, cause*) in, with. **~ sa peur, elle poussa un cri** she cried out in fright *ou* fear; **elle partit tôt, ~ l'espoir de trouver une place** she left early in the hope of finding *ou* hoping to find a seat; **~ ces conditions** *ou* **ce cas-là, je refuse** in that case *ou* if that's the way it is* I (shall) refuse; **il l'a fait ~ ce but** he did it with this aim in view; **~ sa hâte il oublia son chapeau** in his haste he forgot his hat.
g (*approximation*) **~ les** (*prix*) (round) about, (something) in the region of; (*temps, grandeur*) (round) about, something like, some; **cela vaut/coûte ~ les 50 F** it is worth/costs in the region of 50 francs *ou* (round) about 50 francs; **il faut compter ~ les 3 ou 4 mois (pour terminer)** we'll have to allow something like 3 or 4 months *ou* some 3 or 4 months (to finish off); **il vous faut ~ les 3 mètres de tissu** you'll need something like 3 metres of fabric *ou* about *ou* some 3 metres of fabric; **cette pièce fait ~ les 8 m²** this room is about *ou* some 8 m²; **il a ~ les 30 ans** he's about 30, he's 30 or thereabouts; **l'un ~ l'autre il s'y retrouve** all in all he manages to break even.
h (*introduisant un complément*) **mettre son espoir ~ qn/qch** to pin one's hopes on sb/sth; **avoir confiance ~ l'honnêteté de qn/le dollar** to have confidence in sb's honesty/the dollar; **c'est ~ votre intérêt de le faire** it's in your own interest to do it.

dansant, e [dɑ̃sɑ̃, ɑ̃t] adj *mouvement, lueur* dancing; *musique* lively. **thé ~** (early evening) dance, thé dansant; **soirée ~e** dance.

danse [dɑ̃s] nf a (*valse, tango etc*) dance. **la ~** (*art*) dancing, dance; (*action*) dancing; **~ folklorique** folk *ou* country dance; **~ du ventre** belly dance; **~ de guerre** war dance; **~ classique** ballet dancing; **ouvrir la ~** to open the dancing; **avoir la ~ de Saint-Guy** (*Méd*) to have St Vitus's dance; (*fig*) to have the fidgets; **de ~** *professeur, leçon* dancing; *musique* dance; (*lit*) **entrer dans la ~** to join in the dance *ou* dancing; (*fig*) **si ton mari entre dans la ~ ...** if your husband decides to get involved *ou* to join in ...; *voir* **mener, piste**. b (‡: *volée*) belting‡, (good) hiding.

danser [dɑ̃se] 1 1 vi (*gén*) to dance; *[ombre, flamme]* to flicker, dance; *[flotteur, bateau]* to bob (up and down), dance. **faire ~ qn** to (have a) dance with sb; **après dîner il nous a fait ~** after dinner he got us dancing; **voulez-vous ~ (avec moi)?, vous dansez?** shall we dance?, would you like to dance?; (*fig*) **~ devant le buffet*** to have to sing for one's supper (*fig*); **~ de joie** to dance for joy. 2 vt to dance.

danseur [dɑ̃sœʀ] nm (*gén*) dancer; (*partenaire*) partner. **~ (classique** *ou* **de ballet)** ballet dancer; (*Opéra*) **~ étoile** principal dancer; **~ de corde** tightrope walker; **~ de claquettes** tap dancer; **~ mondain** host.

danseuse [dɑ̃søz] nf (*gén*) dancer; (*partenaire*) partner. **~ (classique** *ou* **de ballet)** ballet dancer; (*Opéra*) **~ étoile** prima ballerina; **~ de cabaret** cabaret dancer; (*à vélo*) **en ~** standing on the pedals; (*lit*) **entretenir une ~** to keep a mistress; (*fig*) **l'État ne peut pas se permettre d'entretenir des ~s** the state cannot afford to support unprofitable ventures; *voir* **premier**.

dantesque [dɑ̃tɛsk] adj Dantesque, Dantean.

Danube [danyb] nm Danube.

danubien, -ienne [danybjɛ̃, jɛn] adj Danubian.

DAO [deao] nm (abrév de **dessin assisté par ordinateur**) CAD.

dard [daʀ] nm *[animal]* sting; (*Mil* †) javelin, spear.

Dardanelles [daʀdanɛl] nfpl: **les ~** the Dardanelles.

darder [daʀde] 1 vt a (*lancer*) *flèche* to shoot. **le soleil dardait ses rayons sur la maison** the sun's rays beat down on the house; **il darda un regard haineux sur son rival** he shot a look full of hate at his rival. b (*dresser*) *piquants, épines* to point. **le clocher dardait sa flèche vers le ciel** the spire of the church tower thrust upwards into the sky.

dare-dare* [daʀdaʀ] loc adv double-quick*, like the clappers‡ (*Brit*). **accourir ~** to come belting up‡ (*Brit*), come running up double-quick* *ou* at the double.

darne [daʀn] nf *[poisson]* steak.

dartre [daʀtʀ] nf sore.

darwinien, -ienne [daʀwinjɛ̃, jɛn] adj Darwinian.

darwinisme [daʀwinism] nm Darwinism.

darwiniste [daʀwinist] adj, nmf Darwinist.

DASS [das] nf (abrév de **Direction de l'action sanitaire et sociale**) *voir* **direction**.

datable [databl] adj dat(e)able. **manuscrit facilement ~** manuscript which can easily be dated.

datation [datasjɔ̃] nf *[contrat, manuscrit]* dating. **~ au carbone 14** carbon dating.

date [dat] nf date. ~ **de naissance/mariage/paiement** date of birth/ marriage/payment; ~ **d'exigibilité** due *ou* maturity date; ~ **de péremption/clôture** expiry/closing date; ~ **butoir** *ou* **limite** deadline; ~ **limite de consommation** use-by date; ~ **limite de fraîcheur** best-before date; ~ **limite de vente** sell-by date; *[chèque]* ~ **de valeur** *date on which a cheque is debited from or credited to an account;* **pourriez-vous faire ce virement avec ~ de valeur le 15 juin?** could you process this payment on 15th June?; **à quelle ~ cela s'est-il produit?** on what date did that occur?; **à cette ~-là il était déjà mort** by that time *ou* by then he was already dead; **lettre en ~ du 23 mai** letter dated May 23rd; **à cette ~ il ne le savait pas encore** at that time he did not yet know about it; **j'ai pris ~ avec lui pour le 18 mai** I have set *ou* fixed a date with him for May 18th; **cet événement fait ~ dans l'histoire** this event stands out in *ou* marks a milestone in history; **sans ~** undated; **le premier en ~** the first *ou* earliest; **le dernier en ~** the latest *ou* most recent; **de longue** *ou* **vieille ~** *amitié* long-standing; *ami* old, long-time; **de fraîche ~** *ami* recent; **connaître qn de longue** *ou* **vieille/fraîche ~** to have known sb for a long/short time.

dater [date] [1] **1** vt *lettre, événement* to date. **lettre datée du 6/de Paris** letter dated the 6th/from Paris; **non daté** undated. **2** vi **a** (*remonter à*) ~ **de** to date back to, date from; **ça ne date pas d'hier** *[maladie]* it has been going a long time; *[amitié, situation]* it goes back a long way, it has a long history; *[objet]* it's as old as the hills; **à ~ de demain** as from tomorrow, from tomorrow onwards; **de quand date votre dernière rencontre?** when did you last meet? **b** (*faire date*) **événement qui date dans l'histoire** event which stands out in *ou* marks a milestone in history. **c** (*être démodé*) to be dated. **ça commence à ~** it's beginning to date.

dateur [datœʀ] nm *[montre]* date indicator. (*tampon*) **(timbre) ~** date stamp.

datif, -ive [datif, iv] adj, nm dative. **au ~** in the dative.

dation [dasjɔ̃] nf payment in kind.

datte [dat] nf (*Bot, Culin*) date.

dattier [datje] nm date palm.

daube [dob] nf (*viande*) stew, casserole. **faire une ~** *ou* **de la viande en ~** to make a (meat) stew *ou* casserole; **bœuf en ~** casserole of beef, beef stew, bœuf en daube.

dauber [dobe] [1] vi (††, *littér*) to jeer.

dauphin [dofɛ̃] nm **a** (*Zool*) dolphin. **b** (*Hist*) **le D~** the Dauphin. **c** (*fig: successeur*) heir apparent.

Dauphine [dofin] nf Dauphine, Dauphiness.

dauphinois, e [dofinwa, waz] adj of *ou* from the Dauphiné; *voir* **gratin**.

daurade [dɔʀad] nf gilt-head, sea bream. ~ **rose** red sea bream.

davantage [davɑ̃taʒ] adv **a** (*plus*) *gagner, acheter* more; (*négatif*) any more; (*interrogatif*) (any) more. **bien/encore/même ~** much/still/ even more; **je n'en sais pas ~** I don't know any more (about it), I know no more *ou* nothing further (about it); **il s'approcha ~** he drew closer *ou* nearer; **en veux-tu ~?** do you want (any *ou* some) more?

b (*plus longtemps*) longer; (*négatif, interrogatif*) any longer. **sans s'attarder/rester ~** without lingering/staying any longer.

c (*de plus en plus*) more and more. **les prix augmentent chaque jour ~** prices go up more and more every day.

d ~ **de** (some) more; (*négatif*) any more; **vouloir ~ de pain/temps** to want (some) more bread/time; **veux-tu ~ de viande?** do you want (any *ou* some) more meat?; **il n'en a pas voulu ~** he didn't want any more (of it).

e ~ **que** (*plus*) more than; (*plus longtemps*) longer than; **tu te crois malin mais il l'est ~ (que toi)** you think you're sharp but he is more so than you *ou* but he is sharper (than you).

David [david] nm David.

davier [davje] nm (*Chirurgie*) forceps; (*Menuiserie*) cramp.

db (abrév de **décibel**) dB, db.

DCA [desea] nf (abrév de **Défense contre avions**) anti-aircraft defence.

DDT [dedete] nm (abrév de **Dichloro-Diphényl Trichloréthane**) DDT.

de[1] [də] prép (*d' devant voyelle ou h muet, contraction avec le, les:* **du, des**) **a** (*copule introduisant compléments après vb, loc verbale, adj, n*) **décider ~ faire** to decide to do, decide on doing; **éviter d'aller à Paris** to avoid going to Paris; **empêcher qn ~ faire** to prevent sb (from) doing; **il est fier ~ parler 3 langues** he is proud of being able *ou* of his ability to speak 3 languages; **c'est l'occasion ~ protester** this is an opportunity for protesting *ou* to protest; **avoir l'habitude ~ qch/~ faire** to be used to sth/to doing; **je ne vois pas l'intérêt d'écrire** I don't see the point of *ou* in writing; **content ~ faire qch/~ qch** pleased to do sth/with sth; **il est pressé ~ partir** he is in a hurry to go; **se souvenir/se servir ~ qch** to remember/use *ou* make use of sth; **il est difficile/impossible/agréable ~ faire cela** it is difficult/impossible/pleasant to do that; **il est amoureux d'elle** he is in love with her; **le bombardement ~ Londres** the bombing of London; **et elle ~ se moquer de nos efforts!** and she made fun of our efforts!; **et lui d'ajouter: "jamais!"** "never!" he added.

b (*déplacement, provenance*) from, out of, of; (*localisation*) in, on. **être/provenir/s'échapper ~** to be/come/escape from; **sauter du toit** to jump from *ou* off the roof; **en sortant ~ la maison** coming out of the house, on leaving the house; **~ sa fenêtre elle voit la mer** she can see the sea from her window; **il arrive du Japon** he has just arrived from Japan; **il y a une lettre ~ Paul** there's a letter from Paul; **nous recevons des amis du Canada** we have friends from Canada staying (with us); **(ce sont) des gens ~ la campagne/la ville** (they are) country folk/townsfolk, (they are) people from the country/town; **on apprend ~ Londres que ...** we hear *ou* it is announced from London that ...; **les magasins ~ Londres/Paris** the London/Paris shops, the shops in London/ Paris; **des pommes ~ notre jardin** apples from our garden; **~ lui** *ou* **sa part, rien ne m'étonne** nothing he does (ever) surprises me; **le train/ l'avion ~ Londres** (*provenance*) the train/plane from London; (*destination*) the London train/plane, the train/plane for London; **les voisins du 2e (étage)** the neighbours on the 2nd floor; **né ~ parents pauvres** born of poor parents; **~ 6 qu'ils étaient (au départ) ils ne sont plus que 2** of *ou* out of the original 6 there are only 2 left; **le Baron ~ la Roche** Baron de la Roche; *voir* **côté, près** *etc.*

c (*appartenance*) of, *souvent traduit par cas génitif.* **la maison ~ David/~ notre ami/~ nos amis/~ l'actrice** David's/our friend's/our friends'/the actress's house; **le mari ~ la reine d'Angleterre** the Queen of England's husband; **la patte du chien** the dog's paw; **le pied ~ la table** the leg of the table, the table leg; **le bouton ~ la porte** the door knob; **le pouvoir ~ l'argent** the power of money; **un ~ mes amis** a friend of mine, one of my friends; **un ami ~ mon père/des enfants** a friend of my father's/of the children's; **un ami ~ la famille** a friend of the family, a family friend; **il n'est pas ~ notre famille** he is no relation of ours; **le roi ~ France** the King of France; **l'attitude du Canada** Canada's attitude, the Canadian attitude; **un roman ~ Wells** a novel by Wells, a novel of Wells'; **la boutique du fleuriste/boulanger** the florist's/baker's shop; **un programmeur d'IBM** *ou* **~ chez IBM** a programmer with IBM; **ses collègues ~** *ou* **du bureau** his colleagues at work; **l'homme le plus riche du monde** the richest man in the world; **quel est le nom ~ cette fleur/cette rue/cet enfant?** what is this flower/street/child called?, what's the name of this flower/street/child?; **il a la ruse du renard** he's as cunning as a fox, he's got the cunning of a fox; **c'est bien ~ lui de sortir sans manteau** it's just like him *ou* it's typical of him to go out without a coat (on).

d (*gén sans article: caractérisation*) *gén rendu par des composés.* **vase ~ cristal** crystal vase; **robe ~ soie** silk dress; **robe ~ soie pure** dress of pure silk; **sac ~ couchage** sleeping bag; **permis ~ conduire** driving (*Brit*) *ou* driver's (*US*) licence; **une fourrure ~ prix** a costly *ou* an expensive fur; **la société ~ consommation** the consumer society; **un homme ~ goût/d'une grande bonté** a man of taste/great kindness; **un homme d'affaires** a businessman; **les journaux d'hier/du dimanche** yesterday's/the Sunday papers; **le professeur d'anglais** the English teacher, the teacher of English; **la route ~ Tours** the Tours road, the road for Tours; **une heure d'attente** an hour's wait, a wait of one hour; **les romanciers du 20e siècle** 20th-century novelists; **il est d'une bêtise!** he's so stupid! *ou* incredibly stupid!; **il est ~ son temps** he's a man of his time, he moves with the time; **il est l'homme du moment** he's the man of the moment *ou* of the hour; **être ~ taille** *ou* **force à faire qch** to be equal to doing sth, be up to doing sth*; **regard ~ haine/dégoût** look of hate/disgust; **3 jours ~ libres** 3 free days, 3 days free; **quelque chose ~ beau/cher** something lovely/expensive; **rien ~ neuf/d'intéressant** nothing new/interesting *ou* of interest; **le plus grand ~ sa classe** the biggest in his class; **le seul ~ mes collègues** the only one of my colleagues; **il y a 2 verres ~ cassés** there are 2 broken glasses *ou* glasses broken.

e (*gén sans article: contenu*) of. **une bouteille ~ vin/lait** a bottle of wine/milk; **une tasse ~ thé** a cup of tea; **une pincée/cuillerée ~ sel** a pinch/spoonful of salt; **une poignée ~ gens** a handful of people; **une collection ~ timbres** a stamp collection; **une boîte ~ bonbons** a box of sweets; **un car ~ touristes/d'enfants** a coachload (*Brit*) *ou* busload (*US*) *ou* coachful (*Brit*) of tourists/children.

f (*temps*) **venez ~ bonne heure** come early; **~ nos jours** nowadays, these days, in this day and age; **du temps où** in the days when, at a time when; **d'une minute/d'un jour à l'autre** (*incessamment*) any minute/day now; (*progressivement*) from one minute/day to the next; **~ jour** by day, during the day; **travailler ~ nuit** to work at night, work nights*; **cette semaine il est ~ nuit** this week he's on nightshift *ou* he's on nights*; **elle reçoit ~ 6 à 8** she's at home (to visitors) from 6 to 8; **3 heures du matin/~ l'après-midi** 3 (o'clock) in the morning/afternoon, 3 a.m./p.m.; **il n'a rien fait ~ la semaine/l'année** he hasn't done a thing all week/year; **~ (toute) ma vie je n'ai entendu pareilles sottises** I've never heard such nonsense in (all) my life; **~ mois en mois/jour en jour** from month to month/day to day; *voir* **ici, suite.**

g (*mesure*) **une pièce ~ 6 m²** a room (measuring) 6 m²; **un enfant ~ 5 ans** a 5-year-old (child); **un bébé ~ 6 mois** a 6-month(-old) baby, a baby of 6 months; **elle a acheté 2 kg ~ pommes** she bought 2 kg of apples; **une table ~ 2 mètres ~ large** a table 2 metres wide *ou* in width; **un rôti ~ 2 kg** a 2-kg joint, a joint weighing 2 kg; **une côtelette ~ 10 F** a chop costing 10 francs; **un chèque ~ 100 dollars** a cheque to the value of $100 (*Brit*), a check in the amount of $100 (*US*); **ce poteau a 5 mètres ~ haut** *ou* **hauteur/~ long** *ou* **longueur** this post is 5 metres high *ou* in height/long *ou* in length; **elle est plus grande que lui** *ou* **elle le dépasse ~ 5 cm** she is 5 cm taller than he is, she is taller than him by 5 cm; **une attente ~ 2 heures** a 2-hour wait; **un voyage ~ 3 jours** a 3-day journey, a 3 days' journey; **une promenade ~ 3 km/3 heures** a 3-km/3-hour walk; **il gagne 90 F ~ l'heure** he earns 90 francs an hour *ou* per hour; **ça coûte 30 F du mètre** it costs 30 francs a metre.

h (*moyen*) with, on, by. **frapper/faire signe ~ la main** to strike/make a sign with one's hand; **s'aider des deux mains/~ sa canne pour se lever** to help o.s. up with (the aid of) both hands/one's stick, get up with the help of both hands/one's stick; **je l'ai fait ~ mes propres mains** I did it with my own two hands; **vivre ~ charité/~ rien** to live on charity/nothing at all; **se nourrir ~ racines/fromage** to live on roots/cheese; **il vit ~ sa peinture** he lives by (his) painting; **faire qch ~ rien/d'un bout de bois** to make sth out of nothing/a bit of wood; **il fit "non" ~ la tête** he shook his head.

i (*manière*) with, in, *souvent traduit par adv.* **aller** *ou* **marcher d'une allure paisible/d'un bon pas** to walk (along) unhurriedly/briskly; **connaître qn ~ vue/nom** to know sb by sight/name; **citer qch ~ mémoire** to quote sth from memory; **parler d'une voix émue/ferme** to speak emotionally/firmly *ou* in an emotional/a firm voice; **regarder qn d'un air tendre** to look at sb tenderly, give sb a tender look; **il me regarda ~ ses yeux doux** he looked at me with his gentle eyes; **il est pâle ~ teint** *ou* **visage** he has a pale complexion.

j (*cause, agent*) with, in, from. **mourir d'une pneumonie/~ vieillesse** to die of pneumonia/old age; **pleurer/rougir ~ dépit/~ honte** to weep/blush with vexation/with *ou* for shame; **~ colère, il la gifla** he slapped her in anger; **~ crainte** *ou* **peur de faire** for fear of doing; **être surpris/étonné ~ qch/~ voir** to be surprised/astonished at sth/at seeing *ou* to see; **être fatigué du voyage/~ répéter** to be tired from the journey/of repeating; **s'écrouler ~ fatigue** to be dropping (with fatigue); **elle rit ~ le voir si maladroit** she laughed to see him *ou* on seeing him so clumsy; **heureux d'avoir réussi** happy to have succeeded; **contrarié ~ ce qu'il se montre si peu coopératif** annoyed at his being so uncooperative.

k (*copule: apposition*) of, *souvent non traduit.* **la ville ~ Paris** the town of Paris; **le jour ~ Pâques** Easter Sunday *ou* Day; **le jour ~ Noël** Christmas Day; **le mois ~ juin** the month of June; **le prénom ~ Paul n'est plus si populaire** the name Paul is not so popular these days; **le terme ~ "franglais"** the word "franglais"; **ton idiot ~ fils** that stupid son of yours, your clot of a son*; **ce cochon ~ temps nous gâche nos vacances** this rotten weather is spoiling our holiday; **un ~ plus/~ moins/~ trop** one more/less/too many.

de[2] [də] (*d' devant voyelle ou h muet, contraction avec le, les:* **du, des**) 1 **art** *partitif* a (*dans affirmation*) some (*souvent omis*); (*dans interrogation, hypothèse*) any, some; (*avec nég*) any, no. **boire du vin/~ la bière/~ l'eau** to drink wine/beer/water; **il but ~ l'eau au robinet** he drank some water from the tap; **si on prenait ~ la bière/du vin?** what about some beer/wine?; **acheter des pommes/~ bonnes pommes** to buy some apples/some good apples; **il y a des gens qui aiment la poésie** some people like poetry; **cela demande du courage/~ la patience** this requires courage/patience; **il faut manger du pain avec du fromage** you should eat bread with cheese; **donnez-nous ~ vos nouvelles** drop us a line, tell us what you're up to; **je n'ai pas eu ~ ses nouvelles depuis** I haven't had (any) news from *ou* of him *ou* I haven't heard from *ou* of him since; **au déjeuner, nous avons eu du poulet** we had chicken for lunch; **vous ne voulez vraiment pas ~ vin?** don't you really want any wine?; **voudriez-vous du thé?** would you like some tea?; **voulez-vous du thé ou du café?** would you like tea or coffee?; **voulez-vous du pain/des œufs/~ la farine?** do you need (any) bread/eggs/flour?; **avez-vous du pain/des œufs/~ la farine à me passer?** do you have any bread/eggs/flour you could let me have?, I wonder if you could let me have some bread/eggs/flour?; **on peut acheter ~ la laine chez Dupont** you can buy wool at Dupont's; **j'ai acheté ~ la laine** I bought some wool; **il n'y a plus d'espoir** there is no hope left; **il a joué du Chopin/des valses ~ Chopin** he played (some) Chopin/some Chopin waltzes; **si j'avais ~ l'argent, je prendrais des vacances** if I had any *ou* some money, I'd take a holiday; **ça, c'est du chantage/du vol!** that's blackmail/robbery!; **ça, c'est ~ la veine!*** what a piece *ou* stroke of luck!

b (*loc*) a, an. **faire du bruit/des histoires** to make a noise/a fuss; **avoir ~ l'humour** to have a sense of humour; **avoir du courage** to have courage, be brave; **donnez-moi du feu** give me a light; **on va faire du feu** let's light the *ou* a fire; **il y a ~ la lumière, donc il est chez lui** there's a light on, so he must be in.

2 **art indéf pl** a **des, de** some (*souvent omis*); (*nég*) any, no; **des enfants ont cassé les carreaux** some children have broken the window panes; **elle élève des chats mais pas de chiens** she breeds cats but not dogs; **j'ai des voisins charmants** *ou* **de charmants voisins** I have charming neighbours; **je n'ai pas de voisins** I haven't (got) any neighbours, I have no neighbours; **avoir des doutes sur** to have doubts about.

b (*intensif*) **elle est restée des mois et des mois sans nouvelles** she was without (any) news for months and months, she went for months and months without (any) news; **j'ai attendu des heures** I waited (for) hours; **nous n'avons pas fait des kilomètres** we didn't exactly walk miles; **ils en ont cueilli des kilos (et des kilos)** they picked pounds (and pounds); **il y en a des qui exagèrent*** some people do exaggerate.

dé [de] **nm** a **~ (à coudre)** thimble; (*fig: petit verre*) tiny glass; (*fig*) **ça tient dans un ~ à coudre** it will fit into a thimble. b (*Jeux*) **~ (à jouer)** die, dice; **~s** dice; **jouer aux ~s** to play dice; **les ~s sont jetés** the die is cast; (*Culin*) **couper des carottes en ~s** to dice carrots; (*lit*) **coup de ~s** throw of the dice; (*fig*) **jouer son avenir/sa fortune sur un coup de ~s** to (take a) gamble with one's future/all one's money.

DEA [deɑa] **nm** (**abrév de diplôme d'études approfondies**) *voir* **diplôme**.

dealer[1] [dile] [1] **vi** (*arg Drogue*) to push drugs*.

dealer[2] [dilœʀ] **nm** (*arg Drogue*) drug pusher* *ou* dealer.

déambulatoire [deɑ̃bylatwaʀ] **nm** ambulatory.

déambuler [deɑ̃byle] [1] **vi** to stroll, wander, saunter (about *ou* along).

déb* [dɛb] **nf** (**abrév de débutante**) deb*.

débâcle [debɑkl] **nf** *[armée]* rout; *[régime]* collapse; *[glaces]* breaking up. **c'est une vraie ~!** it's a complete disaster!; **la ~ de la livre (face au dollar)** the collapse of the pound (against the dollar).

déballage [debalaʒ] **nm** a (*action*) *[objets]* unpacking. b *[marchandises]* display (*of loose goods*). c (*: *paroles, confession*) outpouring.

déballer [debale] [1] **vt** *affaires* to unpack; *marchandises* to display, lay out; (*) *vérité, paroles* to let out; (*) *sentiments* to pour out, give vent to; (* *péj*) *savoir* to air (*péj*).

déballonner (se)‡ [debalɔne] [2] **vpr** to chicken out*.

débandade [debɑ̃dad] **nf** (*déroute*) headlong flight; (*dispersion*) scattering. (*fig: fuite*) **c'est la ~ générale** it's a general exodus; **en ~, à la ~** in disorder; **tout va à la ~** everything's going to rack and ruin *ou* to the dogs*.

débander [debɑ̃de] [1] 1 **vt** a (*Méd*) to unbandage, take the bandage(s) off. **~ les yeux de qn** to remove a blindfold from sb's eyes. b *arc, ressort* to relax, slacken (off). 2 **vi** (**‡**: *sexuellement*) to go limp. **travailler 10 heures sans ~**‡ to work 10 hours without letting up*. 3 **se débander vpr** *[armée, manifestants]* to scatter, break up; *[arc, ressort]* to relax, slacken.

débaptiser [debatize] [1] **vt** to change the name of, rename.

débarbouillage [debaʀbujaʒ] **nm** *[visage]* quick wash, cat-lick*.

débarbouiller [debaʀbuje] [1] 1 **vt** *visage* to give a quick wash *ou* cat-lick* to. 2 **se débarbouiller vpr** to give one's face a quick wash *ou* cat-lick*.

débarbouillette [debaʀbujɛt] **nf** (*Can*) face cloth, flannel (*Brit*).

débarcadère [debaʀkadɛʀ] **nm** landing stage.

débardage [debaʀdaʒ] **nm** unloading, unlading.

débarder [debaʀde] [1] **vt** (*Naut*) to unload, unlade.

débardeur [debaʀdœʀ] **nm** (*ouvrier*) docker, stevedore; (*vêtement*) slipover (*Brit*), tank top.

débarquement [debaʀkəmɑ̃] **nm** (*voir* **débarquer**) landing; unloading. **navire** *ou* **péniche de ~** landing craft (*inv*); (*Hist: en Normandie*) **le ~** the Normandy landing.

débarquer [debaʀke] [1] 1 **vt** a *marchandises* to unload, land; *passagers* to land; (*Mil*) to land. b (*: *congédier*) to sack*, turf* out (*Brit*), kick out*. **se faire ~** to get the push*, get kicked out*, get turfed out* (*Brit*). 2 **vi** *[passagers]* to disembark, land; (*Mil*) to land. **il a débarqué chez mes parents hier soir*** he turned up at my parents' place last night; **tu débarques!*** where have you been?*; **je n'en sais rien, je débarque*** I don't know, that's the first I've heard of it.

débarras [debaʀɑ] **nm** a (*pièce*) lumber room, junk room, boxroom (*Brit*); (*placard, soupente*) junk hole* (*Brit*), glory hole (*Brit*), junk closet (*US*). b **bon ~!** good riddance!; **il est parti, quel ~!** thank goodness he has gone!

débarrasser [debaʀɑse] [1] 1 **vt** a *local* to clear (*de* of). **~ (la table)** to clear the table; **débarrasse le plancher*** hop it!* (*Brit*), make yourself scarce!*, beat it!* b **~ qn de** *fardeau, manteau, chapeau* to relieve sb of; *habitude* to break *ou* rid sb of; *ennemi, mal* to rid sb of; *liens* to release sb from. 2 **se débarrasser vpr: se ~ de** *objet, personne* to get rid of, rid o.s. of; *sentiment* to rid o.s. of, get rid of, shake off; *mauvaise habitude* to break o.s. of, rid o.s. of; (*ôter*) *vêtement* to take off, remove; **débarrassez-vous!** put your things (*ou* coat *etc*) down.

débat [deba] **nm** (*discussion*) discussion, debate; (*polémique*) debate. **~ intérieur** inner struggle; **dîner-~** dinner debate; (*TV*) **émission-~** televised *ou* television debate; (*Jur, Pol: séance*) **~s** proceedings, debates; (*Jur*) **~s à huis clos** hearing in camera; (*Parl*) **~ de clôture** ≃ adjournment debate.

débâter [debate] [1] **vt** *bête de somme* to unsaddle.

débâtir [debatiʀ] [2] **vt** (*Couture*) to take out *ou* remove the tacking *ou* basting in.

débatteur [debatœʀ] **nm** debater.

débattre [debatʀ] [41] 1 **vt** *problème, question* to discuss, debate; *prix, traité* to discuss. **le prix reste à ~** the price has still to be discussed; **à vendre 1 000 F à ~** for sale (for) 1,000 francs or nearest offer. 2 **débattre de vt indir** *question* to discuss, debate. 3 **se débattre vpr** (*contre un adversaire*) to struggle (*contre* with); (*contre le courant*) to struggle (*contre* against); (*contre les difficultés*) to struggle (*contre* against, with), wrestle (*contre* with). **se ~ comme un beau diable** *ou* **comme un forcené** to struggle like the very devil *ou* like one possessed.

débauchage [deboʃaʒ] **nm** (*licenciement*) laying off, dismissal; (*embauche d'un salarié d'une autre entreprise*) hiring away, poaching.

débauche [deboʃ] **nf** a (*vice*) debauchery. **mener une vie de ~** to lead a debauched life *ou* a life of debauchery; **scène de ~** scene of debauchery; **partie de ~** orgy; *voir* **excitation, lieu.** b (*abondance*) ~ **de** profusion *ou* abundance *ou* wealth of; ~ **de couleurs** riot of colour.

débauché, e [deboʃe] (ptp de **débaucher**) 1 adj *personne, vie* debauched. 2 nm,f (*viveur*) debauched person. **c'est un ~** he leads a debauched life.

débaucher [deboʃe] 1 1 vt a (†: *corrompre*) to debauch, corrupt; (*: *inviter à s'amuser*) to entice away, tempt away. b (*inviter à la grève*) to incite to strike; (*licencier*) to lay off, make redundant; (*embaucher un salarié d'une autre entreprise*) to hire away, poach (*de* from). 2 **se débaucher** vpr to turn to (a life of) debauchery, become debauched.

débaucheur [deboʃœʀ] nm (*voir* **débaucher**) debaucher; tempter; strike agitator.

débaucheuse [deboʃøz] nf (*voir* **débaucher**) debaucher; temptress; strike agitator.

débecter‡, débéqueter‡ [debɛkte] 1 vt (*dégoûter*) to disgust. **ça me débecte** it's disgusting, it makes me sick*.

débile [debil] adj *corps, membre* weak, feeble; *esprit* feeble; *santé* frail, poor; *enfant* sickly, weak; (*) *film, discours* pathetic*, stupid; (*) *raisonnement* moronic*. **c'est un ~ mental** (*lit*) he is subnormal *ou* mentally deficient, he is a mental defective; (*péj*) he's a moron (*péj*).

débilitant, e [debilitɑ̃, ɑ̃t] adj (*voir* **débiliter**) debilitating; enervating; demoralizing.

débilité [debilite] nf (†: *faiblesse*) debility; (*péj*) *[propos, attitude]* stupidity. ~ **mentale** mental deficiency; **enfant atteint d'une ~ légère** mildly mentally-handicapped child.

débiliter [debilite] 1 vt *[climat]* to debilitate, enervate; *[milieu]* to enervate; *[propos]* to demoralize.

débinage* [debinaʒ] nm knocking*, slamming*, running down.

débine* [debin] nf: **être dans la ~** to be on one's uppers* (*Brit*), be hard up; **tomber dans la ~** to fall on hard times.

débiner* [debine] 1 1 vt (*dénigrer*) *personne* to knock*, run down. 2 **se débiner** vpr (*se sauver*) to do a bunk‡ (*Brit*), clear off*.

débineur, -euse* [debinœʀ, øz] nm,f backbiter*.

débit [debi] 1 nm a (*Fin*) debit; *[relevé de compte]* debit side. **mettre** *ou* **porter 100 F au ~ de qn** to debit sb *ou* sb's account with 100 francs, charge 100 francs to sb's account; **pouvez-vous me faire le** *ou* **mon ~?** can I pay for it please?

b (*Comm: vente*) turnover (of goods), sales. **article qui a un bon/faible ~** article which sells well/poorly; **n'achète pas ton fromage dans cette boutique, il n'y a pas assez de ~** don't buy your cheese in this shop, there isn't a quick enough turnover; **cette boutique a du ~** this shop has a quick turnover (of goods).

c *[fleuve]* (rate of) flow; *[gaz, électricité]* output; *[pompe]* flow, outflow; *[tuyau]* discharge; *[machine]* output; *[moyen de transport: métro, téléphérique]* passenger flow. **il n'y a pas assez de ~ au robinet** there is not enough flow out of the tap *ou* pressure in the tap.

d (*élocution*) delivery. **un ~ rapide/monotone** a rapid/monotonous delivery; **elle a un sacré ~*** she is a real chatterbox, she's a great talker*.

e (*Menuiserie*) cutting up, sawing up. ~ **d'un arbre en rondins** sawing up of a tree into logs.

2 comp ▸**débit de boissons** (*petit bar ou café*) bar; (*Admin: terme générique*) drinking establishment ▸**débit de tabac** tobacconist's (shop) (*Brit*), tobacco *ou* smoke shop (*US*).

débitable [debitabl] adj *bois* which can be sawn *ou* cut up.

débitant, e [debitɑ̃, ɑ̃t] nm,f: ~ **(de boissons)** ≃ licensed grocer; ~ **(de tabac)** tobacconist (*Brit*), tobacco dealer (*US*).

débiter [debite] 1 vt a (*Fin*) *personne, compte* to debit. **pouvez-vous me ~ cet article?** can I pay for this item? b (*Comm*) *marchandises* to retail, sell. c *[usine, machine]* to produce. **ce fleuve/tuyau débite tant de m³ par seconde** the flow of this river/through this pipe is so many m³ per second. d (*péj: dire*) *âneries* to utter, mouth; *insultes* to pour forth; *sermon* to spout, spiel off* (*US*); *[acteur] rôle* to churn out. **il me débita tout cela sans s'arrêter** he poured all that out to me without stopping. e (*tailler*) *bois* to cut up, saw up; *viande* to cut up.

débiteur, -trice [debitœʀ, tʀis] 1 adj (*Fin*) *solde* debit (*épith*); *personne, organisme* debtor (*épith*). **mon compte est ~ (de 50 F)** my account has a debit balance (of 50 francs) *ou* is (50 francs) in the red*. 2 nm,f (*Fin, fig*) debtor. (*Jur*) **~-gagiste** lienee; (*lit, fig*) **être le ~ de qn** to be indebted to sb, be in sb's debt.

déblai [deblɛ] nm a (*nettoyage*) clearing; (*Tech: terrassement*) earthmoving, excavations. b **~s** (*gravats*) rubble, debris (*sg*); (*terre*) earth.

déblaiement [deblɛmɑ̃] nm *[chemin, espace]* clearing.

déblatérer* [deblateʀe] 6 vi a (*médire*) ~ **contre** *ou* **sur** to go *ou* rant on about*. b (*dire des bêtises*) to drivel (on)*, talk twaddle* (*Brit*) *ou* rot* *ou* drivel*.

déblayage [deblɛjaʒ] nm a = **déblaiement.** b (*fig*) **le ~ d'une question** (doing) the spadework on a question.

déblayer [debleje] 8 vt a *décombres* to clear away, remove; *chemin, porte, espace* to clear; *pièce* to clear up, tidy up; (*Tech*) *terrain* to level off. b *travail* to prepare, do the spadework on. (*fig: préparer*) ~ **le terrain** to clear the ground *ou* the way; (*déguerpir*) **déblaye (le terrain)!*** push off!* (*Brit*), get lost!*

déblocage [deblɔkaʒ] nm (*voir* **débloquer**) freeing; releasing; unfreezing; unjamming; unblocking.

débloquer [deblɔke] 1 1 vt a (*Fin*) *compte* to free, release; (*Écon*) *stocks, marchandises, crédits* to release; *prix, salaires* to unfreeze, free. **pour ~ la situation** in order to get things moving again. b (*Tech*) *machine* to unjam; *écrou, freins* to release; *route* to unblock. c ~ **qn** (*le rendre moins timide*) to bring sb out of his shell; (*: *le débarrasser de ses complexes*) to rid sb of his complexes *ou* inhibitions. 2 vi (‡) (*dire des bêtises*) to talk twaddle* (*Brit*) *ou* rot* *ou* drivel*; (*être fou*) to be off one's rocker‡.

débobiner [debɔbine] 1 vt (*Couture*) to unwind, wind off; (*Élec*) to unwind, uncoil.

déboguer [debɔge] 1 vt (*Ordin*) to debug.

déboires [debwaʀ] nmpl (*déceptions*) disappointments, heartbreaks; (*échecs*) setbacks, reverses; (*ennuis*) trials, difficulties.

déboisement [debwazmɑ̃] nm *[montagne, endroit]* deforestation; *[forêt]* clearing.

déboiser [debwaze] 1 vt *montagne, endroit* to deforest; *forêt* to clear of trees.

déboîtement [debwatmɑ̃] nm (*Méd*) dislocation; (*Aut: voir* **déboîter**) pulling out; changing lanes.

déboîter [debwate] 1 1 vt *membre* to dislocate; *porte* to take off its hinges; *tuyaux* to disconnect; *objet* to dislodge, knock out of place. **se ~ l'épaule** to dislocate one's shoulder. 2 vi (*Aut*) (*du trottoir*) to pull out; (*d'une file*) to change lanes, pull out; (*Mil*) to break rank.

débonnaire [debɔnɛʀ] adj (*bon enfant*) easy-going, good-natured; (†: *trop bon, faible*) soft, weak. **air ~** kindly appearance.

débordant, e [debɔʀdɑ̃, ɑ̃t] adj *activité* exuberant; *enthousiasme, joie* overflowing, unbounded; *imagination* overactive. (*Mil*) **mouvement ~** outflanking manoeuvre.

débordé, e [debɔʀde] (ptp de **déborder**) adj overburdened. ~ **de travail** snowed under with work, up to one's eyes in work.

débordement [debɔʀdəmɑ̃] nm a *[rivière, liquide]* overflowing (*NonC*); *[liquide en ébullition]* boiling over (*NonC*); (*Mil, Sport*) outflanking (*NonC*). (*manifestation*) **afin d'éviter les ~s** to prevent demonstrators from getting out of hand. b *[joie]* outburst; *[paroles, injures]* torrent, rush; *[activité]* explosion. ~ **de vie** bubbling vitality. c (*débauches*) **~s** excesses; **devant les ~s de son fils, il lui coupa les vivres** confronted with his son's excesses, he cut off his allowance.

déborder [debɔʀde] 1 1 vi a *[récipient, liquide]* to overflow; *[fleuve, rivière]* to burst its banks, overflow; *[liquide bouillant]* to boil over. **les pluies ont fait ~ le réservoir** the rains caused the reservoir to overflow; **faire ~ le café** to let the coffee boil over; **tasse/boîte pleine à ~** cup/box full to the brim *ou* to overflowing (*de* with); **l'eau a débordé du vase/de la casserole** the water has overflowed the vase/has boiled over the saucepan; **les vêtements qui débordaient de la valise** the clothes spilling out of the suitcase; **la foule débordait sur la chaussée** the crowd was overflowing onto the roadway; (*fig*) **cela a fait ~ le vase, c'est la goutte qui a fait ~ le vase** that was the last straw, that was the straw that broke the camel's back; (*fig*) **son cœur débordait, il fallait qu'il parle** his heart was (full to) overflowing and he just had to speak.

b (*en coloriant, en mettant du rouge à lèvres*) to go over the edge.

c (*fig*) ~ **de santé** to be bursting with health; ~ **de vitalité/joie** to be bubbling *ou* brimming over with vitality/joy, be bursting with vitality/joy; **son cœur débordait de reconnaissance** his heart was overflowing *ou* bursting with gratitude; ~ **de richesses** to be overflowing with riches; ~ **d'imagination** to have an overactive imagination.

2 vt a (*dépasser*) *enceinte, limites* to extend beyond; (*Mil, Pol, Sport*) *ennemi* to outflank. **leur maison déborde les autres** their house juts out from the others; **la nappe doit ~ la table** the tablecloth should hang over *ou* overhang the edge of the table; **le conférencier/cette remarque déborde le cadre du sujet** the lecturer/that remark goes beyond the bounds of the subject; **il a débordé (le temps imparti)** he has run over (the allotted time); (*Mil, Pol, Sport*) **se laisser ~ sur la droite** to allow o.s. to be outflanked on the right.

b *couvertures, lit* to untuck. ~ **qn** to untuck sb *ou* sb's bed; **il s'est débordé en dormant** he *ou* his bed came untucked in his sleep.

c (*Couture*) *jupe, rideau* to remove the border from.

débotté [debɔte] nm (*frm*) **je ne peux pas répondre au ~** I can't answer off the cuff; **donner une réponse au ~** to give an off-the-cuff reply.

débotter [debɔte] 1 1 vt: ~ **qn** to take off sb's boots. 2 **se débotter** vpr to take one's boots off.

débouchage [debuʃaʒ] nm *[bouteille]* uncorking, opening; *[tuyau]* unblocking.

débouché [debuʃe] nm a (*gén pl*) (*Comm: marché*) outlet; (*carrière*) opening, prospect. b *[défilé]* opening. **au ~ de la vallée (dans la plaine)** where the valley opens out (into the plain); **il s'arrêta au ~ de la rue** he stopped at the end of the street; **la Suisse n'a aucun ~ sur la mer** Switzerland has no outlet to the sea.

déboucher [debuʃe] 1 1 vt a *lavabo, tuyau* to unblock.

b *bouteille de vin* to uncork, open; *carafe, flacon* to unstopper, take the stopper out of; *tube* to uncap, take the cap *ou* top off.

2 vi to emerge, come out. ~ **de** *[personne, voiture]* to emerge from,

come out of; ~ **sur** *ou* **dans** *[rue]* to run into, open onto *ou* into; *[personne, voiture]* to come out onto *ou* into, emerge onto *ou* into; **sur quoi ces études débouchent-elles?** what does this course lead on to?; (*fig*) **cette discussion débouche sur une impasse** this discussion is approaching stalemate *ou* is leading up a blind alley; ~ **sur des mesures concrètes** to result in *ou* lead to concrete measures; **ne** ~ **sur rien** to end inconclusively.

3 **se déboucher** **vpr** *[bouteille]* to come uncorked; *[tuyau]* to unblock, come unblocked.

déboucheur [debuʃœʀ] **nm** caustic cleaner.

débouchoir [debuʃwaʀ] **nm** *[lavabo]* plunger, plumber's helper (*US*).

déboucler [debukle] 1 **vt** *ceinture* to unbuckle, undo. **je suis toute bouclée** my hair has all gone straight *ou* has gone quite straight, the curl has come out of my hair.

déboulé [debule] **nm** (*Danse*) déboulé; (*Courses*) charge. (*Chasse*) **au** ~ on breaking cover.

débouler [debule] 1 1 **vi** a (*Chasse*) *[lapin]* to bolt. b (*dégringoler*) to tumble down. (*arriver*) ~ **chez qn*** to land on sb. 2 **vt** (*: *dévaler*) to belt down* (*Brit*), charge down. ~ **l'escalier** to come belting down (*Brit*) *ou* charging down the stairs*.

déboulonnage [debulɔnaʒ] **nm**, **déboulonnement** [debulɔnmɑ̃] **nm** (*voir* **déboulonner**) removal of bolts (*de* from); sacking*, firing; discrediting, debunking.

déboulonner [debulɔne] 1 **vt** a *machine* to remove the bolts from, take the bolts out of. b (*) *haut fonctionnaire* (*renvoyer*) to sack*, fire; (*discréditer*) to discredit, bring down, debunk*; *député* to unseat.

débourber [debuʀbe] 1 **vt** *fossé* to clear of mud, clean out; *canal* to dredge; *véhicule* to pull out of the mud.

débourrer [debuʀe] 1 **vt** *cheval* to break in.

débours [debuʀ] **nm** (*dépense*) outlay. **pour rentrer dans ses** ~ to recover one's outlay; **sans** ~ **d'argent** without any financial outlay.

déboursement [debuʀsəmɑ̃] **nm** laying out, disbursement (*frm*).

débourser [debuʀse] 1 **vt** to pay out, lay out, disburse (*frm*). **sans** ~ **un sou** without paying *ou* laying out a penny, without being a penny out of pocket.

déboussoler* [debusɔle] 1 **vt** to disorientate. **il est complètement déboussolé** he is completely at sea, he is completely lost *ou* disorientated.

debout [d(ə)bu] **adv, adj inv** a *personne* (*en position verticale*) standing (up); (*levé*) up. **être** *ou* **se tenir** ~ to stand; **être** ~ (*levé*) to be up; (*guéri*) to be up (and about); **se mettre** ~ to stand up, get up; **il préfère être** *ou* **rester** ~ he prefers to stand *ou* remain standing; **voulez-vous, je vous prie, rester** ~ will you please remain standing; **hier, nous sommes restés** ~ **jusqu'à minuit** yesterday we stayed up till midnight; **leur enfant se tient** ~ **maintenant** their child can stand (up) now; **il l'aida à se (re)mettre** ~ he helped him (back) up, he helped him (back) to his feet; ~, **il paraît plus petit** he looks smaller standing (up); **la pièce est si petite qu'on ne peut pas se tenir** ~ the room is so small that it's impossible to stand upright; **il est si fatigué, il tient à peine** ~ he is so tired he can hardly stand; **elle est** ~ **toute la journée** she is on her feet all day; **ces gens** ~ **nous empêchent de voir** we can't see for *ou* because of the people standing in front of us; ~! get up!, on your feet!; ~ **là-dedans!*** get up, you lot!*; *voir* **dormir, magistrature**.

b *bouteille, meuble* (*position habituelle*) standing up(right); (*position inhabituelle*) standing (up) on end. **mettre qch** ~ to stand sth up(right); to stand sth (up) on end; **les tables,** ~ **le long du mur** the tables, standing (up) on end along the wall; **mets les bouteilles** ~ stand the bottles up(right).

c *édifice, mur* standing (*attrib*). (*fig*) **ces institutions sont** *ou* **tiennent encore** ~ these institutions are still going; **cette théorie/ce record est encore** ~ this theory/record still stands *ou* is still valid; **cette théorie tient** ~ **après tout** this theory holds up *ou* good after all; **ça ne tient pas** ~ **ce que tu dis** what you say doesn't stand up; **son histoire ne tient pas** ~ his story doesn't hold water.

débouté [debute] **nm** (*Jur*) ≃ nonsuit.

déboutement [debutmɑ̃] **nm** (*Jur*) ≃ nonsuiting.

débouter [debute] 1 **vt** (*Jur*) ≃ to nonsuit. ~ **qn de sa plainte** ≃ to nonsuit a plaintiff; **être débouté de sa demande** to be ruled out of court, see one's case dismissed by the court, ≃ to be nonsuited.

déboutonner [debutɔne] 1 1 **vt** to unbutton, undo. 2 **se déboutonner** **vpr** a *[personne]* to unbutton *ou* undo one's jacket (*ou* coat *etc*), unbutton *ou* undo o.s. *[habit]* to come unbuttoned *ou* undone. b (*: *se confier*) to open up*.

débraillé, e [debʀaje] (**ptp de débrailler**) 1 **adj** *tenue, personne* untidy, slovenly-looking; *manières* slovenly; *style* sloppy, slipshod. 2 **nm** *[tenue, manières]* slovenliness; *[style]* sloppiness. **être en** ~ to be half-dressed.

débrailler (se)* [debʀaje] 1 **vpr** to loosen one's clothing.

débranchement [debʀɑ̃ʃmɑ̃] **nm** (*voir* **débrancher**) disconnecting; unplugging; cutting (off); splitting up.

débrancher [debʀɑ̃ʃe] 1 **vt** (*gén*) to disconnect; *appareil électrique* to unplug, disconnect; *téléphone* to cut off, disconnect; *courant* to cut (off), disconnect; (*Rail*) *wagons* to split up.

débrayage [debʀɛjaʒ] **nm** a (*objet*) (*Aut*) clutch; *[appareil-photo]* release button. b (*action*) *[moteur]* declutching, disengagement of the clutch; *[appareil-photo]* releasing. c (*grève*) stoppage.

débrayer [debʀeje] 8 1 **vi** a (*Aut*) to declutch (*Brit*), disengage the clutch; (*Tech*) to operate the release mechanism. b (*faire grève*) to stop work, come out on strike. **le personnel a débrayé à 4 heures** the staff stopped work at 4 o'clock. 2 **vt** (*Tech*) to release.

débridé, e [debʀide] (**ptp de débrider**) **adj** unbridled, unrestrained.

débridement [debʀidmɑ̃] **nm** *[instincts]* unbridling, unleashing; *[plaie]* lancing, incising.

débrider [debʀide] 1 **vt** *cheval* to unbridle; *volaille* to untruss; *plaie* to lance, incise. (*fig*) **sans** ~ non-stop.

débris [debʀi] **nm** a (*pl: morceaux*) fragments, pieces; (*décombres*) debris (*sg*); (*détritus*) rubbish (*NonC*). **des** ~ **de verre/de vase** fragments *ou* pieces of glass/of a vase; **des** ~ **de métal** scraps of metal. b (*pl: fig littér: restes*) *[mort]* remains; *[plat, repas]* left-overs, scraps; *[armée, fortune]* remains, remnants; *[état]* ruins; *[édifice]* ruins, remains. c (*éclat, fragment*) fragment. d (*péj: personne*) (**vieux**) ~ old wreck, old dodderer.

débronzer [debʀɔ̃ze] 1 **vi** to lose one's tan.

débrouillage [debʀujaʒ] **nm** (*voir* **débrouiller**) disentangling; untangling; sorting out; unravelling.

débrouillard, e* [debʀujaʀ, aʀd] 1 **adj** (*malin*) smart*, resourceful. 2 **nm,f** coper*, survivor.

débrouillardise* [debʀujaʀdiz] **nf**, **débrouille** [debʀuj] **nf** smartness*, resourcefulness.

débrouillement [debʀujmɑ̃] **nm** = **débrouillage**.

débrouiller [debʀuje] 1 1 **vt** a (*démêler*) *fils* to disentangle, untangle; *papiers* to sort out; *problème* to sort out, untangle; *mystère* to unravel, disentangle.

b (*: *éduquer*) ~ **qn** (*gén*) to teach sb how to look after himself (*ou* herself); (*à l'école*) to teach sb the basics; ~ **qn en anglais/en informatique** to teach sb the basics *ou* give sb a grounding in English/computing.

2 **se débrouiller** **vpr** to manage. **débrouillez-vous** you'll have to manage on your own *ou* sort things out yourself; **il m'a laissé me** ~ **(tout seul) avec mes ennemis** he left me to cope (alone) with my enemies; **il s'est débrouillé pour obtenir la permission d'y aller** he somehow managed to get permission to go, he wangled* permission to go; **c'est toi qui as fait l'erreur, maintenant débrouille-toi pour la réparer** you made the mistake so now sort it out yourself*; **il faudra bien nous en** ~ we'll have to sort it out; **elle se débrouille en allemand** she has a working knowledge of German, she can get by in German.

débroussaillement [debʀusajmɑ̃] **nm** *[terrain]* clearing (*de* of); *[problème]* spadework (*de* on).

débroussailler [debʀusaje] 1 **vt** *terrain* to clear (of brushwood); *problème* to do the spadework on.

débusquer [debyske] 1 **vt** *lièvre, cerf* to flush out, drive out (from cover); *personne* to drive out, chase out, flush out.

débudgétisation [debydʒetizasjɔ̃] **nf** debudgeting.

débudgétiser [debydʒetize] 1 **vt** to debudget.

début [deby] **nm** a *[semaine, livre, action]* beginning, start; *[discours]* beginning, opening. **du** ~ **à la fin** from beginning to end, from start to finish; **les scènes du** ~ **sont très belles** the opening scenes are very beautiful; **salaire de** ~ starting salary; **dès le** ~ from the outset *ou* the start *ou* the (very) beginning; **au** ~ at first, in *ou* at the beginning; ~ **février** in early February; **au** ~ **du mois prochain** early next month, at the beginning of next month; (*hum*) **il y a** *ou* **il faut un** ~ **à tout** there's a first time for everything.

b ~**s**: **ses** ~**s furent médiocres** he made an indifferent start; **à mes** ~**s (dans ce métier)** when I started (in this job); **ce projet en est encore à ses** ~**s** the project is still in its early stages *ou* at the early stages; **faire ses** ~**s dans le monde** to make one's début in society; **faire ses** ~**s sur la scène** to make one's début *ou* one's first appearance on the stage.

débutant, e [debytɑ̃, ɑ̃t] 1 **adj** novice (*épith*). 2 **nm** (*gén*) beginner, novice; (*Théât*) debutant actor. **leçon d'anglais pour** ~**s** English lesson for beginners; **grand/faux** ~ **en anglais** absolute/virtual beginner in English. 3 **débutante** **nf** (*gén*) beginner, novice; (*Théât*) debutant actress; *[haute société]* debutante.

débuter [debyte] 1 1 **vi** a *[personne]* to start (out). ~ **bien/mal** to make a good/bad start, start well/badly; **il a débuté (dans la vie) comme livreur** he started (life) as a delivery boy; **elle a débuté dans "Autant en emporte le vent"** she made her début *ou* her first appearance in "Gone with the Wind"; **il débute (dans le métier), soyez indulgent** he is just starting (in the business) so don't be too hard on him; **l'orateur a débuté par des excuses** the speaker started (off) *ou* began *ou* opened by apologizing; ~ **dans le monde** to make one's début in society, come out; **pour** ~ to start (off) with.

b *[livre, concert, manifestation]* to start, begin, open (*par, sur* with).

2 **vt** (*) *semaine, réunion, discours* to start, begin, open (*par, sur* with). **il a bien débuté l'année** he has begun *ou* started the year well.

déca [deka] 1 **préf** deca. 2 **nm** (*: *café*) decaffeinated coffee, decaf*.

deçà [dəsa] **adv** a **en** ~ **de** (on) this side of; (*fig*) short of; **en** ~ **du fleuve/de la montagne** this side of the river/of the mountain; **en** ~ **de ses moyens** within his means; **en** ~ **d'une certaine intensité, on ne peut**

plus rien entendre below a certain intensity, one can no longer hear anything; **ce qu'il dit est très en ~ de la vérité** what he says is well short of the truth; **tu vois la rivière, sa maison se trouve en ~** you see the river – his house is this side of it; **au ~ de††** (on) this side of. **b** (*littér*) **~, delà** here and there, on this side and that.

décachetage [dekaʃtaʒ] **nm** unsealing, opening.

décacheter [dekaʃ(ə)te] [4] **vt** *lettre* to unseal, open; *colis* to break open.

décade [dekad] **nf** (*décennie*) decade; (*dix jours*) period of ten days.

décadenasser [dekadnase] [1] **vt** *porte* to unpadlock, remove the padlock from.

décadence [dekadɑ̃s] **nf** (*processus*) decline, decadence, decay; (*état*) decadence. **la ~ de l'empire romain** the decline of the Roman empire; **tomber en ~** to fall into decline; *voir* **grandeur**.

décadent, e [dekadɑ̃, ɑ̃t] **1 adj** (*gén*) decadent, declining, decaying; (*Art*) decadent. **2 nm,f** decadent.

décaèdre [dekaɛdʀ] **1 adj** decahedral. **2 nm** decahedron.

décaféiner [dekafeine] [1] **vt** to decaffeinate. **(café) décaféiné** decaffeinated coffee, caffeine-free coffee.

décagonal, e, **mpl -aux** [dekagɔnal, o] **adj** decagonal.

décagone [dekagon] **nm** decagon.

décagramme [dekagʀam] **nm** decagram(me).

décaissement [dekɛsmɑ̃] **nm** payment, disbursement.

décaisser [dekese] [1] **vt** *objet* to uncrate, unpack; *argent* to pay out.

décalage [dekalaʒ] **nm a** (*écart*) gap, interval; (*entre deux concepts*) gap, discrepancy; (*entre deux actions successives*) interval, time-lag (*entre* between). **le ~ entre le rêve et la réalité** the gap between dream and reality; **il y a un ~ entre le coup de feu et le bruit de la détonation** there is an interval *ou* a time-lag between the shot and the sound of the detonation; **le ~ horaire entre l'est et l'ouest des USA** the time difference between the east and west of the USA; (*en avion*) **(fatigue due au) ~ horaire** jet lag; **mal supporter le ~ horaire** to suffer from jet lag. **b** (*déplacement d'horaire*) move forward *ou* back. **il y a un ~ d'horaire/de date** (*avance*) the timetable/date is brought forward; (*retard*) the timetable/date is put back. **c** (*dans l'espace*) (*avancée*) jutting out; (*retrait*) standing back; (*déplacement*) *[meuble, objet]* shifting forward *ou* back.

décalaminage [dekalaminaʒ] **nm** decarbonization, decoking (*Brit*), decoke* (*Brit*).

décalaminer [dekalamine] [1] **vt** to decarbonize, decoke (*Brit*).

décalcification [dekalsifikasjɔ̃] **nf** decalcification.

décalcifier **vt,** **se décalcifier** **vpr** [dekalsifje] [7] to decalcify.

décalcomanie [dekalkɔmani] **nf** (*procédé, image*) transfer, decal. **faire de la ~** to do transfers.

décaler [dekale] [1] **vt a** *horaire, départ, repas* (*avancer*) to bring *ou* move forward; (*retarder*) to put back. **décalé d'une heure** (*avancé*) brought *ou* moved forward an hour; (*retardé*) put back an hour. **b** *pupitre, meuble* (*avancer*) to move *ou* shift forward; (*reculer*) to move *ou* shift back. **décalez-vous d'un rang** move forward (*ou* back) a row; **une série d'immeubles décalés par rapport aux autres** a row of buildings out of line with *ou* jutting out from the others. **c** (*déséquilibrer*) *meuble, objet* to unwedge.

décalitre [dekalitʀ] **nm** decalitre.

décalogue [dekalɔg] **nm** Decalogue.

décalotter [dekalɔte] [1] **vt** (*gén*) to take the top off; (*Méd*) to pull back the foreskin of.

décalquage [dekalkaʒ] **nm** (*voir* **décalquer**) tracing; transferring.

décalque [dekalk] **nm** (*dessin: voir* **décalquer**) tracing; transfer; (*fig: imitation*) reproduction, copy.

décalquer [dekalke] [1] **vt** (*avec papier transparent*) to trace; (*par pression*) to transfer.

décamètre [dekamɛtʀ] **nm** decametre.

décamper* [dekɑ̃pe] [1] **vi** (*déguerpir*) to clear out* *ou* off*, decamp*. **décampez d'ici!** clear off!*, scram!‡; **faire ~ qn** to chase sb out (*de* from).

décan [dekɑ̃] **nm** (*Astrol*) decan.

décanal, e, **mpl -aux** [dekanal, o] **adj** decanal.

décanat [dekana] **nm** (*dignité, durée*) deanship.

décaniller‡ [dekanije] [1] **vi** (*partir*) to clear out* *ou* off*, decamp*. **il nous a fait ~** he sent us packing* (*de* from).

décantage [dekɑ̃taʒ] **nm,** **décantation** [dekɑ̃tasjɔ̃] **nf** (*voir* **décanter, se décanter**) settling (and decanting); clarification.

décanter [dekɑ̃te] [1] **1 vt** *liquide, vin* to settle, allow to settle (and decant). (*fig*) **~ ses idées** to allow the dust to settle around one's ideas; **il faut laisser ~ ce liquide pendant une nuit** this liquid must be allowed to settle overnight. **2 se décanter vpr** *[liquide, vin]* to settle; (*fig*) *[idées]* to become clear. **il faut laisser les choses se ~, après on verra** we'll have to let things clarify themselves *ou* we'll have to allow the dust to settle and then we'll see; **attendre que la situation se décante** to wait until the situation becomes clearer.

décanteur [dekɑ̃tœʀ] **nm** decanter (*Tech: apparatus*).

décapage [dekapaʒ] **nm** (*voir* **décaper**) cleaning, cleansing; scouring; pickling; scrubbing; sanding; sandblasting; burning off; stripping.

décapant [dekapɑ̃] **1 adj** (*lit*) *produit* abrasive, caustic; (*fig*) *humour* caustic, biting, cutting. **2 nm** (*acide*) pickle, acid solution; (*abrasif*) scouring agent, abrasive; (*pour peinture*) paint stripper.

décaper [dekape] [1] **vt** (*gén*) to clean, cleanse; (*à l'abrasif*) to scour; (*à l'acide*) to pickle; (*à la brosse*) to scrub; (*au papier de verre*) to sand; (*à la sableuse*) to sandblast; (*au chalumeau*) to burn off; (*enlever la peinture*) to strip. **d'abord il faut bien ~ la surface de toute rouille** first you must clean the surface of any rust.

décapitation [dekapitasjɔ̃] **nf** *[personne]* beheading.

décapiter [dekapite] [1] **vt** *personne* to behead; (*accidentellement*) to decapitate; *arbre* to top, cut the top off. (*fig*) **à la suite de l'attentat le parti s'est trouvé décapité** the party was left leaderless *ou* without a leader as a result of the attack.

décapode [dekapɔd] **nm** decapod. **~s** Decapoda.

décapotable [dekapɔtabl] **adj, nf: (voiture) ~** convertible.

décapoter [dekapɔte] [1] **vt: ~ une voiture** to put down the roof (*Brit*) *ou* top (*US*) of a car.

décapsuler [dekapsyle] [1] **vt** to take the cap *ou* top off.

décapsuleur [dekapsylœʀ] **nm** bottle-opener.

décarcasser (se)* [dekaʀkase] [1] **vpr** to flog o.s. to death*, slog one's guts out‡, go to a hell of a lot of trouble* (*pour faire* to do; *pour qn* for sb).

décarreler [dekaʀle] [4] **vt** to take the tiles up from.

décarrer‡ [dekaʀe] [1] **vi** to split‡, make tracks*, hit the road *ou* trail*.

décasyllabe [dekasi(l)lab] **1 adj** decasyllabic. **2 nf** decasyllable.

décasyllabique [dekasi(l)labik] = **decasyllabe**.

décathlon [dekatlɔ̃] **nm** decathlon.

décathlonien, -ienne [dekatlɔnjɛ̃, jɛn] **nm,f** decathlete.

décati, e [dekati] **adj** (*péj*) *vieillard* decrepit, broken-down; *visage* aged; *beauté* faded; *immeuble, façade* shabby-looking.

décavé, e [dekave] **adj a** (*ruiné*) *joueur* ruined, cleaned out*; (*) *banquier* ruined. **b** (*: *hâve*) *visage* haggard, drawn.

décéder [desede] [6] **vi** (*frm*) to die. **M. X, décédé le 14 mai** Mr X, who died on May 14th; **il est décédé depuis 20 ans** he died 20 years ago, he's been dead 20 years; **les biens des personnes décédées** the property of deceased persons *ou* of those who have died.

décelable [des(ə)labl] **adj** detectable, discernible.

déceler [des(ə)le] [5] **vt a** (*trouver*) to discover, detect. **on a décelé des traces de poison** traces of poison have been detected; **on peut ~ dans ce poème l'influence germanique** the Germanic influence can be discerned *ou* detected in this poem. **b** (*montrer*) to indicate, reveal.

décélération [deseleʀasjɔ̃] **nf** deceleration.

décélérer [deseleʀe] [1] **vi** to decelerate.

décembre [desɑ̃bʀ] **nm** December; *pour loc voir* **septembre**.

décemment [desamɑ̃] **adv** *se conduire* decently. **j'arrivais à jouer ~ (du piano)** I managed to play (the piano) reasonably well *ou* quite decently; **je ne peux pas ~ l'accepter** I cannot decently *ou* properly accept it.

décence [desɑ̃s] **nf** (*bienséance*) decency, propriety; (*réserve*) (sense of) decency. **il aurait pu avoir la ~ de ...** he could *ou* might have had the decency to ... .

décennal, e, **mpl -aux** [desenal, o] **adj** decennial.

décennie [deseni] **nf** decade.

décent, e [desɑ̃, ɑ̃t] **adj** (*bienséant*) decent, proper; (*discret, digne*) proper; (*acceptable*) reasonable, decent. **je vais changer de robe pour être un peu plus ~e** I am going to change my dress to look a bit more decent; **il eût été plus ~ de refuser** it would have been more proper to refuse.

décentrage [desɑ̃tʀaʒ] **nm** decentration.

décentralisateur, -trice [desɑ̃tʀalizatœʀ, tʀis] **1 adj** decentralizing (*épith*), decentralization (*épith*). **2 nm,f** advocate of decentralization.

décentralisation [desɑ̃tʀalizasjɔ̃] **nf** decentralization.

décentraliser [desɑ̃tʀalize] [1] **1 vt** *administration* to decentralize; *bureaux* to relocate (*away from town centres*). **2 se décentraliser vpr** *[usine]* to be decentralized.

décentrement [desɑ̃tʀəmɑ̃] **nm,** **décentration** [desɑ̃tʀasjɔ̃] **nf** (*Opt*) decentration; (*action*) decentring, throwing off centre.

décentrer [desɑ̃tʀe] [1] **1 vt** to decentre, throw off centre. **2 se décentrer vpr** to move off centre.

déception [desɛpsjɔ̃] **nf** disappointment, let-down*. **~ sentimentale** unhappy love affair.

décérébrer [deseʀebʀe] [6] **vt** to decerebrate.

décernement [desɛʀnəmɑ̃] **nm** awarding.

décerner [desɛʀne] [1] **vt a** *prix, récompense* to give, award. **b** (*Jur*) to issue.

décès [desɛ] **nm** death, decease (*frm*). **"fermé pour cause de ~"** "closed owing to bereavement"; *voir* **acte**.

décevant, e [des(ə)vɑ̃, ɑ̃t] **adj a** *résultat, spectacle, personne* disappointing. **b** (††: *trompeur*) deceptive, delusive.

décevoir [des(ə)vwaʀ] [28] **vt a ~ qn** to disappoint sb, let sb down. **b** (††: *tromper*) to deceive, delude.

déchaîné, e [deʃene] (**ptp de déchaîner**) **adj** *passions, flots, éléments* raging, unbridled, unleashed; *enthousiasme* wild, unbridled; *personne* wild; *foule* raging, wild; *opinion publique* furious. **il est ~ contre moi** he is furious *ou* violently angry with me.

déchaînement [deʃɛnmɑ̃] nm a (voir se déchaîner) bursting out; explosion; breaking (out); eruption; flying into a rage. b (état agité, violent) [flots, éléments, passions] fury, raging. un ~ d'idées/d'injures a torrent of ideas/of abuse. c (colère) (raging) fury. un tel ~ contre son fils such an outburst of fury at his son.

déchaîner [deʃene] 1 1 vt a tempête, violence, passions, colère to unleash; enthousiasme to arouse; opinion publique to rouse; campagne to give rise to. ~ l'hilarité générale to give rise to general hilarity; ~ les huées/les cris/les rires to raise a storm of booing/shouting/laughter. b chien to unchain, let loose. 2 se déchaîner vpr [fureur, passions] to burst out, explode; [rires] to break out; [tempête] to break, erupt; [personne] to fly into a rage (contre against), loose one's fury (contre upon). la tempête se déchaînait the storm was raging furiously; la presse se déchaîna contre lui the press loosed its fury on him.

déchant [deʃɑ̃] nm (Mus) descant.

déchanter [deʃɑ̃te] 1 vi to become disillusioned. maintenant, il commence à ~ he is now becoming (somewhat) disillusioned.

décharge [deʃaʀʒ] nf a (Elec) ~ (électrique) electrical discharge; il a pris une ~ (électrique) dans les doigts he got an electric shock in his fingers; (Physiol) ~ d'adrénaline release of adrenalin.
b (salve) volley of shots, salvo. on entendit le bruit de plusieurs ~s a volley of shots was heard; il a reçu une ~ de chevrotines dans le dos he was hit in the back by a volley of buckshot.
c (Jur) discharge; (Comm: reçu) receipt; (Hôpital) (action) discharge; (document) discharge form. (Scol) ~ (de service) reduction in teaching load; il faut me signer la ~ pour ce colis you have to sign the receipt for this parcel for me; (fig) il faut dire à sa ~ que ... it must be said in his defence that ...; voir témoin.
d (dépôt) ~ (publique ou municipale) rubbish tip ou dump (Brit), garbage dump (US).
e (Typ) offset sheet.
f (Archit) voûte/arc de ~ relieving ou discharging vault/arch.

déchargement [deʃaʀʒəmɑ̃] nm [cargaison, véhicule, arme] unloading. commencer le ~ d'un véhicule to start unloading a vehicle.

décharger [deʃaʀʒe] 3 1 vt a véhicule, animal to unload; bagages, marchandises to unload (de from). je vais vous ~: donnez-moi vos sacs/votre manteau let me unload ou unburden you – give me your bags/your coat.
b (soulager) conscience, cœur to unburden, disburden (auprès de to). ~ sa colère ou bile to vent one's anger ou spleen (sur qn (up)on sb).
c (Jur) ~ un accusé to discharge an accused person.
d ~ qn de dette to release sb from; impôt to exempt sb from; responsabilité, travail, tâche to relieve sb of, release sb from; se ~ de ses responsabilités to pass off one's responsibilities (sur qn onto sb); il s'est déchargé sur moi du soin de prévenir sa mère he loaded onto me ou handed over to me the job of telling his mother.
e arme (enlever le chargeur) to unload; (tirer) to discharge, fire. il déchargea son revolver sur la foule he fired ou discharged his revolver into the crowd.
f (Elec) to discharge. la batterie s'est déchargée pendant la nuit the battery has run down ou gone flat ou lost its charge overnight.
g (Tech) bassin to drain off the excess of; support, étai to take the load ou weight off.
2 vi a [tissu] to lose its colour.
b (‡) to come‡.

décharné, e [deʃaʀne] (ptp de décharner) adj corps, membre all skin and bone (attrib), emaciated; doigts bony, fleshless; visage fleshless, emaciated; squelette fleshless; (fig) paysage bare.

décharner [deʃaʀne] 1 vt (amaigrir) to emaciate; (rare: ôter la chair) to remove the flesh from. cette maladie l'a complètement décharné this illness has left him mere skin and bone ou has left him completely emaciated.

déchaussé, e [deʃose] (ptp de déchausser) adj personne barefoot(ed); pied bare; dent loose; mur exposed.

déchaussement [deʃosmɑ̃] nm [dent] loosening.

déchausser [deʃose] 1 1 vt arbre to expose ou lay bare the roots of; mur to lay bare the foundations of. ~ un enfant to take a child's shoes off, take the shoes off a child; ~ ses skis to take one's skis off. 2 vi (Ski) to lose one's skis. 3 se déchausser vpr [personne] to take one's shoes off; [dents] to come ou work loose.

dèche‡ [dɛʃ] nf: on est dans la ~, c'est la ~ we're flat broke*, we're on our uppers* (Brit).

déchéance [deʃeɑ̃s] nf a (morale) decay, decline, degeneration; (physique) degeneration; (Rel) fall; [civilisation] decline, decay. b (Pol) [souverain] deposition, dethronement. (Jur) ~ de la puissance paternelle loss of parental rights. c (Fin) remboursement par ~ du terme repayment by acceleration.

déchet [deʃɛ] nm a (restes, résidus) ~s [viande, tissu] scraps, waste (NonC); (épluchures) peelings; (ordures) refuse (NonC), rubbish (NonC); ~s de viande/de métal scraps of meat/metal; ~s domestiques/industriels kitchen/industrial waste (Brit) ou wastes (US); ~s nucléaires/radioactifs nuclear/radioactive waste; va jeter les ~s à la poubelle go and throw the rubbish in the dustbin (Brit), go and throw the trash in the garbage can (US).
b (reste) [viande, tissu, métal] scrap, bit.
c (gén, Comm: perte) waste, loss. il y a du ~ (dans une marchandise etc) there is some waste ou wastage (Brit); (fig: dans un examen) there are (some) failures, there is (some) wastage (of students); [viande] il y a du ~ ou des ~s there's a lot of waste; ~ de route loss in transit.
d (péj) (raté) failure, wash-out*, dead loss*; (épave) wreck, deadbeat*. les ~s de l'humanité the dregs ou scum of humanity.

déchetterie [deʃɛtʀi] nf ® waste collection centre ou site.

déchiffonner [deʃifɔne] 1 vt to smooth out, uncrease. sa robe s'est déchiffonnée toute seule the creases have come out of her dress (on their own).

déchiffrable [deʃifʀabl] adj message decipherable; code decodable, decipherable; écriture decipherable, legible.

déchiffrage [deʃifʀaʒ] nm, **déchiffrement** [deʃifʀəmɑ̃] nm (voir déchiffrer) deciphering; decoding; sight-reading; unravelling, fathoming; reading.

déchiffrer [deʃifʀe] 1 vt message, hiéroglyphe to decipher; code to decode; écriture to make out, decipher; (Mus) to sight-read; énigme to unravel, fathom; sentiment to read, make out.

déchiffreur, -euse [deʃifʀœʀ, øz] nm,f [code] decoder; [inscriptions, message] decipherer.

déchiqueté, e [deʃik(ə)te] (ptp de déchiqueter) adj montagne, relief, côte jagged, ragged; feuille jagged(-edged); corps mutilated.

déchiqueter [deʃik(ə)te] 4 vt (lit) to tear ou cut ou pull to pieces ou shreds, shred; (fig) to pull ou tear to pieces. la malheureuse victime fut déchiquetée par le train/l'explosion the unfortunate victim was cut to pieces ou crushed by the train/blown to pieces by the explosion; déchiqueté par un lion mauled ou savaged by a lion.

déchiqueture [deʃik(ə)tyʀ] nf [tissu] slash; [feuille] notch. ~s [côte, montagne] jagged ou ragged outline.

déchirant, e [deʃiʀɑ̃, ɑ̃t] adj drame heartbreaking, heartrending; cri, spectacle heartrending, harrowing; douleur agonizing, searing; adieux heartbreaking.

déchirement [deʃiʀmɑ̃] nm a [tissu] tearing, ripping; [muscle, tendon] tearing. b (peine) wrench, heartbreak. c (Pol: divisions) ~s rifts, splits.

déchirer [deʃiʀe] 1 1 vt a (mettre en morceaux) papier, lettre to tear up, tear to pieces; (faire un accroc à) vêtement to tear, rip; (arracher) page to tear out (de from); (ouvrir) sac, enveloppe to tear open; bande de protection to tear off; (mutiler) corps to tear to pieces. ~ un papier/tissu en deux to tear a piece of paper/cloth in two ou in half.
b (fig) leurs cris déchirèrent l'air/le silence their cries rent the air/pierced the silence; ce bruit me déchire les oreilles that noise is ear-splitting; cette toux lui déchirait la poitrine his chest was racked by this cough; un spectacle qui déchire (le cœur) a heartrending ou harrowing sight; elle est déchirée par le remords/la douleur she is torn by remorse/racked by pain; les dissensions continuent à ~ le pays the country continues to be torn (apart) by dissension, dissension is still tearing the country apart; ~ qn à belles dents to tear ou pull sb to pieces.
2 se déchirer vpr [vêtement] to tear, rip; [sac] to burst. (fig) le brouillard s'est déchiré the fog has broken up; attention, tu vas te ~* be careful, you'll tear your coat (ou dress etc); se ~ un muscle to tear a muscle; se ~ les mains to graze ou skin one's hands; (fig) son cœur se déchira his heart broke; (fig) ces 2 êtres ne cessent de se ~ these 2 people are constantly tearing each other apart.

déchirure [deʃiʀyʀ] nf [tissu] tear, rip, rent; [ciel] break ou gap in the clouds. ~ musculaire torn muscle; se faire une ~ musculaire to tear a muscle.

déchoir [deʃwaʀ] 25 vi (frm) a [personne] to lower o.s., demean o.s. ce serait ~ que d'accepter you would be lowering ou demeaning yourself if you accepted; ~ de son rang to fall from rank. b [réputation, influence] to decline, wane.

déchristianisation [dekʀistjanizasjɔ̃] nf dechristianization.

déchristianiser [dekʀistjanize] 1 vt to dechristianize.

déchu, e [deʃy] (ptp de déchoir) adj roi deposed, dethroned; (Rel) ange, humanité fallen. (Jur) être ~ de ses droits to be deprived of one's rights, forfeit one's rights.

décibel [desibɛl] nm decibel.

décidé, e [deside] (ptp de décider) adj a (résolu) maintenant je suis ~ now I have made up my mind; il est ~ à agir he is determined to act; il est ~ à tout he is prepared to do anything; il était ~ à ce que je parte he was determined that I should leave; j'y suis tout à fait ~ I am quite determined (to do it). b (volontaire) air, ton determined, decided; personne determined; (net, marqué) goût decided, definite. c (fixé) question settled, decided. bon, c'est ~ right, that's settled ou decided then; c'est une chose ~e the matter is settled.

décidément [desidemɑ̃] adv (en fait) certainly, undoubtedly, indeed. oui, c'est ~ une question de chance yes, it is certainly ou undoubtedly ou indeed a matter of luck; (intensif) ~, je perds toujours mes affaires! I'm ALWAYS losing my things, I lose EVERYTHING!; ~, tu m'ennuies aujourd'hui you're really annoying me today, you ARE annoying me today; ~, **il est cinglé*** he's really crazy *ou* touched*, there's no doubt about it – he's crazy *ou* touched*.

décider [deside] [1] **1 vt a** *[personne]* (*déterminer, établir*) ~ **qch** to decide on sth; **il a décidé ce voyage au dernier moment** he decided on this trip at the last moment; ~ **que** to decide that; ~ **de faire qch** to decide to do sth; **comment ~ qui a raison?** how is one to decide who is right?; **c'est à lui de ~** it's up to him to decide; **elle décida qu'elle devait démissionner** she decided *ou* came to the decision that she must resign; **les ouvriers ont décidé la grève/de faire grève/de ne pas faire grève** the workers decided on a strike/to go on strike/against a strike *ou* not to go on strike; **les mesures sont décidées en conseil des ministres** the measures are decided in the council of ministers.
b (*persuader*) *[personne]* to persuade; *[conseil, événement]* to decide, convince. ~ **qn à faire** to persuade *ou* induce sb to do; **c'est moi qui l'ai décidé à ce voyage** I'm the one who persuaded *ou* induced him to go on this journey; **la bonne publicité décide les clients éventuels** good publicity convinces possible clients.
c *[chose]* (*provoquer*) to cause, bring about. **ces scandales ont finalement décidé le renvoi du directeur** these scandals finally brought about *ou* caused the manager's dismissal.
2 décider de vt indir (*être l'arbitre de*) to decide; (*déterminer*) to decide, determine. ~ **de l'importance/de l'urgence de qch** to decide on the *ou* as to the importance/urgency of sth, decide how important/urgent sth is; **les résultats de son examen décideront de sa carrière** the results of his exam will decide *ou* determine his career; **le sort en a décidé autrement** fate has decided *ou* ordained *ou* decreed otherwise.
3 se décider vpr a *[personne]* to come to *ou* make a decision, make up one's mind. **se ~ à qch** to decide on sth; **se ~ à faire qch** to make up one's mind to do sth, make the decision to do sth; **je ne peux pas me ~ à lui mentir** I cannot bring myself to lie to him, I cannot make up my mind to lie to him; **se ~ pour qch** to decide on *ou* in favour of sth, plump for sth.
b *[problème, affaire]* to be decided *ou* settled *ou* resolved. **la question se décide aujourd'hui** the question is being decided *ou* settled *ou* resolved today; **leur départ s'est décidé très vite** they very quickly decided to leave.
c (*) *[temps]* **est-ce qu'il va se ~ à faire beau?** do you think it'll turn out fine after all?; **ça ne veut pas se ~** it won't make up its mind*; **la voiture ne se décide pas à partir** the car just won't start.

décideur, -euse [desidœʀ, øz] **nm,f** decision-maker. **avoir un rôle de ~** to have a decision-making role.

décigramme [desigʀam] **nm** decigram(me).

décilitre [desilitʀ] **nm** decilitre.

décimal, e, mpl -aux [desimal, o] **adj, nf** decimal.

décimalisation [desimalizasjɔ̃] **nf** decimalization.

décimaliser [desimalize] [1] **vt** to decimalize.

décimation [desimasjɔ̃] **nf** decimation.

décimer [desime] [1] **vt** to decimate.

décimètre [desimɛtʀ] **nm** decimetre; *voir* **double**.

décisif, -ive [desizif, iv] **adj** *argument, combat* decisive, conclusive; *intervention, influence* decisive; *moment* decisive, critical; *ton* decisive, authoritative. (*fig*) **tournant** ~ watershed (*fig*); **le facteur ~** the deciding factor; **porter un coup ~ au terrorisme** to deal terrorism a decisive blow; (*Tennis: en fin de set*) **jeu ~** tie-break, tiebreaker.

décision [desizjɔ̃] **nf a** (*choix*) decision. ~ **collégiale** group *ou* collective decision; **arriver à** *ou* **prendre une ~** to come to *ou* reach a decision; **prendre la ~ de faire qch** to take the decision to do sth; **la ~ appartient à X** the decision is X's; **soumettre qch à la ~ de qn** to submit sth to sb for his decision; *voir* **pouvoir**[2].
b (*verdict*) decision. ~ **administrative/gouvernementale** administrative/government decision; (*Sport*) **faire la ~** to win the match; **par ~ judiciaire** by court order; **nommé à un poste de ~** appointed to a decision-making job; **organe de ~** décision-making body.
c (*qualité*) decision, decisiveness. **montrer de la ~** to show decision *ou* decisiveness; **avoir l'esprit de ~** to be decisive.

décisionnaire [desizjɔnɛʀ] **1 adj** *pouvoir* decision-making (*épith*), to decide (*attrib*). **2 nmf** decision-maker.

décisionnel, -elle [desizjɔnɛl] **adj** *rôle, responsabilité* decision-making.

déclamateur, -trice [deklamatœʀ, tʀis] (*péj*) **1 adj** ranting, declamatory. **2 nm,f** ranter, declaimer.

déclamation [deklamasjɔ̃] **nf** (*art*) declamation (*NonC*); (*péj*) ranting (*NonC*), spouting (*NonC*). **toutes leurs belles ~s** all their grand ranting.

déclamatoire [deklamatwaʀ] **adj a** (*péj*) *ton* ranting, bombastic, declamatory; *style* bombastic, turgid. **b** (*littér*) *rythme* declamatory.

déclamer [deklame] [1] **1 vt** to declaim; (*péj*) to spout. **2 vi** (*péj*) to rant. (*littér*) ~ **contre** to inveigh *ou* rail against.

déclarable [deklaʀabl] **adj** (*Douane*) *marchandise* declarable, dutiable; (*Impôts*) *revenus* declarable.

déclarant, e [deklaʀɑ̃, ɑ̃t] **nm,f** (*Jur*) informant.

déclaratif, -ive [deklaʀatif, iv] **adj** (*Jur*) declaratory; (*Ling*) declarative.

déclaration [deklaʀasjɔ̃] **nf a** (*manifeste, proclamation*) declaration; (*discours, commentaire*) statement; (*aveu*) admission; (*révélation*) revelation. **dans une ~ télévisée** in a televised statement; **le ministre n'a fait aucune ~** the minister did not make a statement; **je n'ai aucune ~ à faire** I have no comment to make; **selon sa propre ~, il était ivre** he himself admits that he was drunk, by his own admission he was drunk.
b (*amoureuse*) ~ **(d'amour)** declaration of love; **faire une** *ou* **sa ~ à qn** to make a declaration of love to sb, declare one's love to sb.
c (*Jur*) *[naissance, décès]* registration, notification; *[vol, perte, changement de domicile]* notification. **envoyer une ~ de changement de domicile** to send notification of change of address; **faire une ~ d'accident** (*à l'assurance*) to file an accident claim; (*à la police*) to report an accident; ~ **en douane** customs declaration; **D~ des droits de l'homme** declaration of the rights of man, human rights declaration; ~ **de faillite** declaration of bankruptcy; ~ **de guerre** declaration of war; ~ **d'impôts** tax declaration, statement of income; (*formulaire*) tax return; **faire sa ~ d'impôts** to make out one's statement of income *ou* one's tax return, fill in one's tax return; (*Hist US*) **D~ d'indépendance** Declaration of Independence; ~ **de principe** statement *ou* declaration of principle; ~ **publique** public statement; ~ **d'utilité publique** public notice; ~ **de revenus** statement of income; (*formulaire*) tax return; ~ **sous serment** statement under oath.

déclaratoire [deklaʀatwaʀ] **adj** (*Jur*) declaratory.

déclaré, e [deklaʀe] (**ptp de déclarer**) **adj** *opinion* professed; *athée, révolutionnaire* declared, self-confessed; *ennemi* sworn, avowed; *intention* avowed, declared; *travailleur* registered, declared. **revenus non ~s** undeclared income.

déclarer [deklaʀe] [1] **1 vt a** (*annoncer*) to announce, state, declare; (*proclamer*) to declare; (*avouer*) to admit, confess to. ~ **son amour (à qn)** to declare one's love (to sb), make a declaration of one's love (to sb); ~ **la guerre à une nation/à la pollution** to declare war on a nation/on pollution; **le président déclara la séance levée** the chairman declared the meeting closed; ~ **qn coupable/innocent** to find sb guilty/innocent.
b ~ que ... to declare *ou* say that ...; **je vous déclare que je n'y crois pas** I tell you I don't believe it; **ils ont déclaré que nous avions menti** they claimed that we had lied.
c (*Admin*) *marchandises, revenus, employés* to declare; *naissance, décès* to register, notify. **le père doit aller ~ l'enfant à la mairie** the father has to go and register the child at the town hall; ~ **qn en faillite** to declare sb bankrupt; (*Douane*) **avez-vous quelque chose à ~?** have you anything to declare?; ~ **qch au-dessus/au-dessous de sa valeur** to overvalue/undervalue sth; **rien à ~** nothing to declare.
2 se déclarer vpr a (*se prononcer*) to declare *ou* state one's opinion. **se ~ en faveur de l'intégration raciale** to declare o.s. *ou* profess o.s. in favour of racial integration; **se ~ pour/contre qch** to come out in favour of/against sth; **il s'est déclaré l'auteur de ces poèmes/crimes** he stated that he had written the poems/committed the crimes; **se ~ satisfait** to declare o.s. satisfied; **il s'est déclaré offensé** he said he was offended; (*Jur*) **se ~ incompétent** to decline a jurisdiction.
b (*apparaître*) *[incendie, épidémie]* to break out.
c *[amoureux]* to make a declaration of one's love, declare *ou* avow (*littér*) one's love.

déclassé, e [deklɑse] (**ptp de déclasser**) **adj a** *coureur* relegated (*in the placing*); *billet, wagon* re-classed; *hôtel, vin* downgraded. (*Bourse*) **valeurs ~es** displaced stocks *ou* securities. **b** *fiche, livre* out of order (*attrib*).

déclassement [deklɑsmɑ̃] **nm** (*voir* **déclasser**) fall *ou* drop in status; relegation (*in the placing*); change of class; downgrading; displacement; getting out of order.

déclasser [deklɑse] [1] **vt a** (*socialement, dans une hiérarchie*) to lower in status. **il se déclassait par de telles fréquentations** he was lowering himself socially *ou* demeaning himself by keeping such company; **il estimait qu'on l'avait déclassé en le mettant dans l'équipe B** he felt that he had suffered a drop in status *ou* that he had been downgraded by being put in the B team. **b** (*rétrograder*) (*Sport: au classement*) *coureur* to relegate (*in the placing*); (*Rail*) *voyageur* to change the class of; (*Admin*) *hôtel* to downgrade; (*Bourse*) *valeur* to displace. **c** (*déranger*) *fiches, livres* to get out of order, put back in the wrong order.

déclenchement [deklɑ̃ʃmɑ̃] **nm** (*voir* **déclencher**) release; setting off; triggering off; activating; launching; starting; opening.

déclencher [deklɑ̃ʃe] [1] **1 vt a** (*actionner*) *ressort, mécanisme* to release; *sonnerie* to set off, trigger off, activate; *appareil-photo* to work. **ce bouton déclenche l'ouverture/la fermeture de la porte** this button activates the opening/closing of the door.
b (*provoquer*) *insurrection* to launch, start; *catastrophe, guerre, crise politique, réaction nerveuse* to trigger off; *violence* to loose. **c'est ce mot qui a tout déclenché** this is the word which triggered everything off; ~ **une grève** *[meneur]* to launch *ou* start a strike; *[incident]* to trigger off a strike.
c (*Mil*) *tir* to open; *attaque* to launch. ~ **l'offensive** to launch the offensive.
2 se déclencher vpr *[ressort, mécanisme]* to release itself; *[sonnerie]* to go off; *[attaque, grève]* to start, begin; *[catastrophe, crise, réaction nerveuse]* to be triggered off.

déclencheur [deklɑ̃ʃœʀ] **nm** (*Tech*) release mechanism. (*Phot*) ~ **sou-**

ple cable release.

déclic [deklik] **nm** (*bruit*) click; (*mécanisme*) trigger mechanism. (*mentalement*) **ça a été le ~** it triggered something in my (*ou* his *etc*) mind.

déclin [deklɛ̃] **nm** a (*affaiblissement: voir* **décliner 2**) decline; deterioration; waning; fading; falling off (*de* in). **le ~ du jour** the close of day; (*littér*) **au ~ de la vie** at the close of life, in the twilight of life (*littér*). b (*loc*) **être à son ~** *[soleil]* to be setting; *[lune]* to be on the wane, be waning; **être sur le** *ou* **son ~** *[malade]* to be deteriorating *ou* on the decline; *[acteur, homme politique]* to be on the decline *ou* on the wane; **être en ~** *[talent, prestige]* to be on the decline *ou* on the wane; *[forces, intelligence, civilisation, art]* to be in decline *ou* on the wane.

déclinable [deklinabl] **adj** declinable.

déclinaison [deklinɛzɔ̃] **nf** (*Ling*) declension; (*Astron, Phys*) declination.

déclinant, e [deklinɑ̃, ɑ̃t] **adj** (*qui s'affaiblit: voir* **décliner 2**) declining; deteriorating; waning; fading; falling off.

décliner [dekline] 1 1 **vt** a (*frm: refuser*) *offre, invitation, honneur* to decline, turn down, refuse. **la direction décline toute responsabilité en cas de perte ou de vol** the management accepts no responsibility *ou* refuses to accept responsibility for loss or theft of articles; (*Jur*) **~ la compétence de qn** to refuse to recognize sb's competence.

b (*Ling*) to decline. **ce mot ne se décline pas** this word does not decline.

c (*frm: réciter*) **~ son identité** to give one's personal particulars; **déclinez vos nom, prénoms, titres et qualités** state your name, forenames, qualifications and status.

d (*Comm*) *produit* to offer in a variety of forms.

2 **vi** a (*gén: s'affaiblir*) to decline; *[malade, santé]* to deteriorate, go downhill; *[talent, forces, beauté, sentiment]* to wane, fade; *[vue]* to deteriorate; *[prestige, popularité]* to wane, fall off.

b (*baisser*) *[jour]* to draw to a close; *[soleil, lune]* to be setting, go down; *[astre]* to set; (*Tech*) *[aiguille aimantée]* to deviate.

3 **se décliner vpr** (*Comm*) *[produit]* to come in a variety of forms.

déclive [dekliv] **adj** inclined.

déclivité [deklivite] **nf** slope, incline, declivity (*frm*).

décloisonnement [deklwazɔnmɑ̃] **nm** decompartmentalization.

décloisonner [deklwazɔne] 1 **vt** to decompartmentalize.

déclouer [deklue] 1 **vt** *caisse* to open; *planche* to remove.

déco [deko] **adj inv**; *voir* **art**.

décocher [dekɔʃe] 1 **vt** a *flèche* to shoot, fire; *coup de pied* to give, deliver; *coup de poing* to throw; *ruade* to let fly. b (*fig*) *œillade, regard* to shoot, flash, dart; *sourire* to flash; *remarque* to fire, let fly.

décoction [dekɔksjɔ̃] **nf** decoction.

décodage [dekɔdaʒ] **nm** (*voir* **décoder**) decoding; cracking*; deciphering.

décoder [dekɔde] 1 **vt** *code* to decode, crack*; (*TV, Ordin*) to decode; *message* to decipher.

décodeur [dekɔdœʀ] **nm** (*voir* **décoder**) decoder; decipherer.

décoiffer [dekwafe] 1 **vt** a (*ébouriffer*) **~ qn** to disarrange sb's hair; **il s'est/le vent l'a décoiffé** he/the wind has disarranged *ou* messed up* his hair; **je suis toute décoiffée** my hair is in a mess *ou* is (all) messed up*; (*fig*) **ça décoiffe!*** that's really impressive!, that's really something! b (*ôter le chapeau*) **~ qn** to take sb's hat off; **il se décoiffa** he took his hat off. c (*Tech*) *obus* to uncap.

décoincement [dekwɛ̃smɑ̃] **nm** (*gén*) unjamming, loosening (*de* of); (*Tech*) removal of the wedge (*de* from).

décoincer [dekwɛ̃se] 3 1 **vt** (*gén*) to unjam, loosen. (*Tech*) **~ qch** to remove the wedge from sth; **~ qn*** to help sb (to) shake off his (*ou* her) hang-ups*. 2 **se décoincer vpr** *[*: personne]* to shake off one's hang-ups*.

décolérer [dekɔleʀe] 6 **vi**: **ne jamais ~** to be always in a temper; **il ne décolère pas depuis hier** he hasn't calmed down *ou* cooled off* since yesterday, he's still angry from yesterday.

décollage [dekɔlaʒ] **nm** a *[avion]* takeoff; *[fusée]* lift-off. **au ~** at take off; at lift-off; (*fig*) **depuis le ~ économique de la région** since the region's economy took off; **le ~ de l'informatique n'a pas été facile** information technology had difficulty in getting off the ground. b *[timbre]* unsticking.

décollation [dekɔlasjɔ̃] **nf** decapitation, beheading.

décollement [dekɔlmɑ̃] **nm** *[timbre]* unsticking; (*Méd*) *[rétine]* detachment. (*Coiffure*) **se faire faire un ~ de racines** to have one's hair volumized.

décoller [dekɔle] 1 1 **vt** a (*gén*) to unstick; (*en trempant*) *timbre* to soak off; (*à la vapeur*) *timbre* to steam off; *lettre* to steam open. **~ qn de*** *livre, télévision etc* to drag sb away from; *voir* **oreille**.

b (**: se débarrasser de*) *créanciers, poursuivants* to shake off. **quel raseur, je ne suis pas arrivé à m'en ~!** *ou* **le ~!** what a bore — I couldn't manage to shake him off! *ou* get rid of him!

2 **vi** a *[avion, pays]* to take off; *[fusée]* to lift off (*de* from); *[industrie]* to take off, get off the ground.

b (**: maigrir*) to lose weight.

c (**: partir*) *[gêneur]* to budge, shift; *[drogué]* to get off*. **ce casse-pieds n'a pas décollé (d'ici) pendant deux heures** that so-and-so sat *ou* stayed here for two solid hours without budging*; (*Sport*) **~ du peloton** (*en avant*) to pull away from *ou* ahead of the bunch; (*en arrière*) to fall *ou* drop behind the bunch.

3 **se décoller vpr** *[timbre]* to come unstuck; (*Méd*) *[rétine]* to become detached.

décolletage [dekɔltaʒ] **nm** a *[robe]* (*action*) cutting out of the neck; (*forme*) (low-cut) neckline, décolletage. b (*Agr*) topping; (*Tech*) cutting (from the bar).

décolleté, e [dekɔlte] (**ptp de décolleter**) 1 **adj** *robe* low-necked, low-cut, décolleté; *femme* wearing a low-cut dress, décolleté (*attrib*); *chaussure* low-cut. **robe ~e dans le dos** dress cut low at the back. 2 **nm** *[robe]* low neck(line), décolletage; *[femme]* (bare) neck and shoulders; (*plongeant*) cleavage. 3 **comp** ▸**décolleté bateau** bateau *ou* boat neck ▸**décolleté plongeant** plunging neckline ▸**décolleté en pointe** V-neck ▸**décolleté rond** round-neck.

décolleter [dekɔlte] 4 1 **vt** a *personne* to bare *ou* reveal the neck and shoulders of; *robe* to cut out the neck of. b (*Agr*) to top; (*Tech*) to cut (from the bar). 2 **se décolleter vpr** to wear a low-cut dress.

décolonisateur, -trice [dekɔlɔnizatœʀ, tʀis] 1 **adj** decolonization (*épith*), decolonizing (*épith*). 2 **nm,f** decolonizer.

décolonisation [dekɔlɔnizasjɔ̃] **nf** decolonization.

décoloniser [dekɔlɔnize] 1 **vt** to decolonize.

décolorant, e [dekɔlɔʀɑ̃, ɑ̃t] 1 **adj** decolorizing (*épith*), bleaching (*épith*), decolorant (*épith*). 2 **nm** bleaching agent.

décoloration [dekɔlɔʀasjɔ̃] **nf** (*voir* **décolorer**) decoloration; bleaching, lightening; fading. **se faire faire une ~** to have one's hair bleached.

décoloré, e [dekɔlɔʀe] (**ptp de décolorer**) **adj** *vêtement* faded; *cheveux* bleached, lightened; *teint, lèvres* pale, colourless.

décolorer [dekɔlɔʀe] 1 1 **vt** *liquide, couleur* to decolour, decolorize; *cheveux* to bleach, lighten; *tissu* (*au soleil*) to fade; (*au lavage*) to take the colour out of, fade. 2 **se décolorer vpr** *[liquide, couleur]* to lose its colour; *[tissu]* to fade, lose its colour. **elle s'est décolorée, elle s'est décoloré les cheveux** she has bleached *ou* lightened her hair.

décombres [dekɔ̃bʀ] **nmpl** rubble, debris (*sg*).

décommander [dekɔmɑ̃de] 1 1 **vt** *marchandise* to cancel (an order for); *invités* to put off; *invitation* to cancel. 2 **se décommander vpr** to cancel one's appointment.

décomplexer [dekɔ̃plɛkse] 1 **vt** to rid of complexes.

décomposable [dekɔ̃pozabl(ə)] **adj** (*voir* **décomposer**) that can be split up; that can be broken up; that can be factorized; decomposable; resoluble; that can be analysed *ou* broken down.

décomposer [dekɔ̃poze] 1 1 **vt** a (*analyser*) (*gén*) to split up *ou* break up into its component parts; (*Math*) *nombre* to factorize, express as a product of prime factors; (*Chim*) to decompose; (*Phys*) *lumière* to break up, split up; (*Tech*) *forces* to resolve; (*Ling*) *phrase* to analyse, break down, split up; *problème, idée* to dissect, break down. **l'athlète décomposa le mouvement devant nous** the athlete broke the movement up for us *ou* went through the movement slowly for us; **la phrase se décompose en 3 propositions** the sentence can be broken down *ou* split up *ou* analysed into 3 clauses.

b (*défaire*) *visage* to contort, distort. **l'horreur décomposa son visage** his face contorted *ou* was distorted with horror; **il était décomposé** he was looking very drawn.

c (*altérer*) *viande* to cause to decompose *ou* rot. **la chaleur décomposait les cadavres** the heat was causing the corpses to decompose *ou* to decay.

2 **se décomposer vpr** a (*pourrir*) *[viande]* to decompose, rot; *[cadavre]* to decompose, decay.

b *[visage]* to change dramatically. **à cette nouvelle il se décomposa** when he heard this news his face *ou* expression changed dramatically.

décomposition [dekɔ̃pozisjɔ̃] **nf** a (*voir* **décomposer**) splitting up; factorization; decomposition; breaking up; resolution; analysis; breaking down; dissection. b (*bouleversement*) *[visage]* contortion. c (*pourriture*) decomposition, decay. **cadavre en ~** corpse in a state of decomposition *ou* decay; **société/système en ~** society/system in decay.

décompresser [dekɔ̃pʀese] 1 1 **vt** (*Tech*) to decompress. 2 **vi** (*) to unwind.

décompresseur [dekɔ̃pʀesœʀ] **nm** decompression tap; (*Aut*) decompressor.

décompression [dekɔ̃pʀesjɔ̃] **nf** decompression.

décomprimer [dekɔ̃pʀime] 1 **vt** to decompress.

décompte [dekɔ̃t] **nm** (*compte*) detailed account, breakdown (of an account); (*déduction*) deduction. **faire le ~** des points to count up *ou* tot up* (*surtout Brit*) the points; **vous voulez faire mon ~?** will you make out my bill? (*Brit*) *ou* check? (*US*); (*Assurances*) **~ de primes** premium statement.

décompter [dekɔ̃te] 1 1 **vt** (*défalquer*) to deduct (*de* from). 2 **vi** *[horloge]* to strike *ou* chime at the wrong time.

déconcentration [dekɔ̃sɑ̃tʀasjɔ̃] **nf** (*Admin*) devolution, decentralization; (*Ind*) dispersal.

déconcentré, e [dekɔ̃sɑ̃tʀe] (**ptp de déconcentrer**) **adj** a (*Admin*) devolved, decentralized; (*Ind*) dispersed. b *personne* who has lost concentration.

déconcentrer [dekɔ̃sɑ̃tʀe] 1 1 **vt** (*Admin*) to devolve, decentralize;

(*Ind*) to disperse. 2 **se déconcentrer** vpr *[personne]* to lose (one's) concentration.

déconcertant, e [dekɔ̃sɛʀtɑ̃, ɑ̃t] adj disconcerting.

déconcerter [dekɔ̃sɛʀte] 1 vt (*décontenancer*) to disconcert, confound, throw (out)*; (††: *déjouer*) to thwart, frustrate.

déconfit, e [dekɔ̃fi, it] adj a (*dépité*) *personne, air, mine* crestfallen, downcast. **avoir la mine ~e** to look downcast *ou* crestfallen. b (††: *battu*) defeated, discomfited†.

déconfiture* [dekɔ̃fityʀ] nf (*déroute*) (*gén*) failure, collapse, defeat; *[parti, armée]* defeat; (*financière*) (financial) collapse, ruin.

décongélation [dekɔ̃ʒelasjɔ̃] nf defrosting, unfreezing.

décongeler [dekɔ̃ʒ(ə)le] 5 vt to defrost, unfreeze.

décongestionner [dekɔ̃ʒɛstjɔne] 1 vt (*Méd*) *poumons* to decongest, relieve congestion in; *malade* to relieve congestion in; (*fig*) *rue* to relieve congestion in; *service, aéroport, université, administration* to relieve the pressure on.

déconnecter [dekɔnɛkte] 1 vt to disconnect.

déconner⁑ [dekɔne] 1 vi *[personne]* to mess around*, fool around*; *[machine]* to be on the blink*. **sans ~, c'était super!** no joke*, it was great!

déconneur⁑ [dekɔnœʀ] nm fun-loving* *ou* crazy* guy.

déconneuse⁑ [dekɔnøz] nf fun-loving* *ou* crazy* girl.

déconnexion [dekɔnɛksjɔ̃] nf disconnection.

déconseiller [dekɔ̃seje] 1 vt to advise against. **~ qch à qn/à qn de faire qch** to advise sb against sth/sb against doing sth; **c'est déconseillé** it's not advisable, it's inadvisable.

déconsidération [dekɔ̃sideʀasjɔ̃] nf discredit, disrepute.

déconsidérer [dekɔ̃sideʀe] 6 vt to discredit. **il s'est déconsidéré en agissant ainsi** he has discredited himself *ou* brought discredit upon himself by acting thus.

déconsigner [dekɔ̃siɲe] 1 vt a *valise* to collect from the left luggage (*Brit*) *ou* baggage checkroom (*US*); *bouteille* to return the deposit on. b *troupes* to release from "confinement to barracks".

décontamination [dekɔ̃taminasjɔ̃] nf decontamination.

décontaminer [dekɔ̃tamine] 1 vt to decontaminate.

décontenancer [dekɔ̃t(ə)nɑ̃se] 3 vt to disconcert, discountenance (*frm*).

décontract* [dekɔ̃tʀakt] adj inv laid-back*, cool*.

décontractant, e [dekɔ̃tʀaktɑ̃, ɑ̃t] 1 adj *personne, ambiance* relaxing; *massage, médicament* soothing, relaxing. 2 nm relaxant.

décontracté, e [dekɔ̃tʀakte] (ptp de **décontracter**) adj (*détendu*) relaxed; (*insouciant*) relaxed, cool*, laid-back*.

décontracter vt, **se décontracter** vpr [dekɔ̃tʀakte] 1 to relax.

décontraction [dekɔ̃tʀaksjɔ̃] nf (*voir* **décontracté**) relaxation; coolness, cool*.

déconvenue [dekɔ̃v(ə)ny] nf (*déception*) disappointment.

décor [dekɔʀ] nm a (*Théât*) **le ~, les ~s** the scenery (*NonC*), the décor (*NonC*); **~ de cinéma** film set; **on dirait un ~ *ou* des ~s de théâtre** it looks like a stage setting *ou* a theatre set, it looks like scenery for a play; *[véhicule, conducteur]* **aller** *ou* **entrer dans le ~*** *ou* **les ~s*** to drive off the road, drive into a ditch (*ou* tree *ou* hedge *etc*); **envoyer qn dans le ~*** *ou* **les ~s*** to force sb off the road; *voir* **changement**.
b (*paysage*) scenery; (*arrière-plan*) setting; (*intérieur de maison*) décor (*NonC*), decorations. **~ de montagnes** mountain scenery; **dans un ~ sordide de banlieue** in a sordid suburban setting; **dans un ~ de verdure** amid green scenery, in a setting of greenery; **photographié dans son ~ habituel** photographed in his usual setting *ou* surroundings.

décorateur, -trice [dekɔʀatœʀ, tʀis] nm,f a (*d'intérieurs*) (interior) decorator; *voir* **ensemblier, peintre**. b (*Théât*) (*architecte*) stage *ou* set designer; (*exécutant, peintre*) set artist.

décoratif, -ive [dekɔʀatif, iv] adj *ornement* decorative, ornamental; *arts* decorative; (*péj*) *personne* decorative.

décoration [dekɔʀasjɔ̃] nf a (*action*) decoration. b (*gén pl: ornement*) decorations; (*ensemble des ornements*) decoration. **~s de Noël** Christmas decorations; **j'admirais la ~ de cette église** I was admiring the decoration of the church. c (*médaille*) decoration. **poitrine bardée de ~s** chest weighed down with medals *ou* decorations.

décorder (se) [dekɔʀde] 1 vpr (*Alp*) to unrope.

décorer [dekɔʀe] 1 vt a (*embellir*) (*gén*) to decorate; *robe* to trim. **~ une maison pour Noël** to decorate a house for Christmas; **l'ensemblier qui a décoré leur appartement** the designer who did the (interior) decoration of their flat; (*fig*) **~ qch du nom de** to dignify sth with the name of. b (*médailler*) to decorate (*de* with). **on va le ~** (*gén*) he is to be decorated; (*Légion d'honneur*) he is to be made a member of the Legion of Honour; **un monsieur décoré** a gentleman with *ou* wearing a decoration.

décorner [dekɔʀne] 1 vt *page* to smooth out; *animal* to dehorn; *voir* **vent**.

décorticage [dekɔʀtikaʒ] nm (*voir* **décortiquer**) shelling; hulling, husking; dissection.

décortication [dekɔʀtikasjɔ̃] nf *[arbre]* cleaning of the bark; (*Méd*) decortication.

décortiquer [dekɔʀtike] 1 vt a *crevettes, amandes* to shell; *riz* to hull, husk; (*fig*) *texte* to dissect (in minute detail). b (*Méd*) *cœur* to decorticate. c (*Sylviculture*) to remove the bark of.

décorum [dekɔʀɔm] nm: **le ~** (*convenances*) the proprieties, decorum; (*étiquette*) etiquette.

décote [dekɔt] nf (*Fin*) *[devises, valeur]* below par rating; *[impôts]* tax relief.

découcher [dekuʃe] 1 vi to stay out all night, spend the night away from home.

découdre [dekudʀ] 48 1 vt a *vêtement* to unpick (*Brit*), take the stitches out of; *bouton* to take off; *couture* to unpick (*Brit*), take out. b **en ~** (*littér, hum: se battre*) to fight, do battle. 2 **se découdre** vpr *[robe]* to come unstitched; *[bouton]* to come off; *[couture]* to come apart.

découler [dekule] 1 vi (*dériver*) to ensue, follow (*de* from). **il découle de cela que** ... it ensues *ou* follows from this that ... .

découpage [dekupaʒ] nm a *[papier, gâteau]* cutting up; *[viande]* carving; *[image, métal]* cutting out. b (*image*) cut-out. **un cahier de ~s** a cut-out book; **faire des ~s** to make cut-out figures. c (*Ciné*) cutting. d (*Pol*) **~ électoral** division into constituencies, distribution of constituencies (*Brit*), ≃ apportionment (*US*).

découpe [dekup] nf a (*Couture*) (*coupe*) cut; (*coupure*) cut-out. b *[bois]* cutting off (of upper part of tree).

découpé, e [dekupe] (ptp de **découper**) adj *relief, sommets, côte* jagged, indented; *feuille* jagged, serrate (*SPÉC*).

découper [dekupe] 1 vt a (*Culin*) *viande, volaille* to carve, cut (up); *gâteau* to cut (up). **couteau/fourchette à ~** carving knife/fork. b *papier, tissu* to cut up; *bois* to jigsaw; *images, métal* to cut out. **~ un article dans un magazine** to cut an article out of a magazine; *voir* **scie**. c (*fig littér*) to indent. **les indentations qui découpent la côte** the indentations which cut into the coastline; **la montagne découpe ses aiguilles sur le ciel** the mountain's peaks stand out (sharp) against the sky; **sa silhouette se découpe dans la lumière** his figure stands out *ou* is outlined against the light.

découpeur, -euse [dekupœʀ, øz] 1 nm,f (*personne*) *[viande]* carver; *[métal]* cutter; *[bois]* jigsaw operator. 2 **découpeuse** nf (*machine*) (*gén*) cutting machine; *[bois]* fretsaw, jigsaw.

découplé, e [dekuple] adj *athlète etc* **bien ~** well-built, well-proportioned.

découpure [dekupyʀ] nf a (*forme, contour*) jagged *ou* indented outline. **la ~ de la côte est régulière** the coastline is evenly indented. b (*échancrures*) **~s** *[côte]* indentations; *[arête]* jagged *ou* indented edge *ou* outline; *[dentelle, guirlande]* scalloped edge. c (*morceau*) bit *ou* piece cut out. **~s de papier** cut-out bits of paper.

décourageant, e [dekuʀaʒɑ̃, ɑ̃t] adj *nouvelle* disheartening, discouraging; *élève, travail, situation* disheartening.

découragement [dekuʀaʒmɑ̃] nm discouragement, despondency.

décourager [dekuʀaʒe] 3 1 vt a (*démoraliser*) to discourage, dishearten. **il ne faut pas se laisser ~ par un échec** one must not be discouraged *ou* disheartened by a setback. b (*dissuader*) to discourage, put off. **sa froideur décourage la familiarité** his coldness discourages familiarity; **pour ~ les malfaiteurs** to deter wrongdoers; **~ qn de qch/de faire qch** to discourage sb from sth/from doing sth, put sb off sth/doing sth; **~ qn d'une entreprise** to discourage *ou* deter sb from an undertaking, put sb off an undertaking. 2 **se décourager** vpr to lose heart, become disheartened *ou* discouraged.

découronner [dekuʀɔne] 1 vt *roi* to dethrone, depose. (*fig*) **arbre découronné par la tempête** tree that has had its top *ou* its topmost branches blown off by the storm.

décousu, e [dekuzy] (ptp de **découdre**) 1 adj (*Couture*) unstitched; *style* disjointed, rambling, desultory; *idées* disconnected, unconnected; *dissertation, travail* scrappy, disjointed; *paroles, conversation* disjointed, desultory. **couture ~e** seam that has come unstitched *ou* unsewn; **ourlet ~** hem that has come down *ou* come unstitched *ou* come unsewn. 2 nm *[style]* disjointedness, desultoriness; *[idées, raisonnement]* disconnectedness.

découvert, e [dekuvɛʀ, ɛʀt] (ptp de **découvrir**) 1 adj a (*mis à nu*) *corps, tête* bare, uncovered; *voir* **visage**.
b (*sans protection*) *lieu* open, exposed. **en terrain ~** in open country *ou* terrain; **allée ~e** open avenue.
2 nm a (*Fin*) *[firme, compte]* overdraft; *[caisse]* deficit; *[objet assuré]* uncovered amount *ou* sum. **~ du Trésor** Treasury deficit; **~ bancaire** bank overdraft; **~ budgétaire** budget deficit; **~ de trésorerie** cash deficit; **tirer de l'argent à ~** to overdraw one's account; **mon compte est/je suis à ~** my account is/I am overdrawn; **crédit à ~** unsecured credit; **vendre à ~** to sell short; **vente à ~** short sale.
b (*loc*) **à ~**: **être à ~ dans un champ** to be exposed *ou* without cover in a field; **la plage laissée à ~ par la marée** the beach left exposed by the tide; (*fig*) **parler à ~** to speak frankly *ou* openly; **agir à ~** to act openly; **mettre qch à ~** to expose sth, bring sth into the open.
3 **découverte** nf a (*action*) discovery; (*objet*) find, discovery. **aller *ou* partir à la ~e** to go off in a spirit of discovery; **aller *ou* partir à la ~e de** to go in search of; **faire une ~** to make a discovery; **faire la ~ de** to discover; **ce n'est pas une ~!*** that's hardly news!, so what's new*?
b (*Art, Phot*) background.

découvreur, -euse [dekuvʀœʀ, øz] **nm,f** discoverer.

découvrir [dekuvʀiʀ] [18] 1 **vt** a (*trouver*) *trésor, loi scientifique, terre inconnue* to discover; *indices, complot* to discover, unearth; *cause, vérité* to discover, find out, unearth; *personne cachée* to discover, find. **~ que** to discover *ou* find out that; **il veut ~ comment/pourquoi c'est arrivé** he wants to find out *ou* discover how/why it happened; **je lui ai découvert des qualités insoupçonnées** I have discovered some unsuspected qualities in him; **elle s'est découvert un cousin en Amérique/un talent pour la peinture** she found out *ou* discovered she had a cousin in America/a gift for painting; **c'est dans les épreuves qu'on se découvre** one finds out about oneself *ou* one finds *ou* discovers one's true self in testing situations; **il craint d'être découvert** (*percé à jour*) he is afraid of being found out; (*trouvé*) he is afraid of being found *ou* discovered; **quand ils découvriront le pot aux roses*** when they find out what's been going on.

b (*enlever ce qui couvre, protège*) *plat, casserole* to take the lid *ou* cover off; *voiture* to open the roof of; *statue* to unveil; (*Échecs*) *roi* to uncover; (*Mil*) *frontière* to expose, uncover; *corps* to uncover; *membres, poitrine, épaules, tête* to bare, uncover; (*mettre à jour*) *ruines* to uncover. **elle enleva les housses et découvrit les meubles** she removed the dust sheets and uncovered the furniture; **il découvrit son torse/avant-bras** he bared *ou* uncovered his torso/forearm; **il resta découvert devant elle** he kept his hat off in her presence; (*Mil*) **ils découvrirent leur aile gauche** they exposed their left wing, they left their left wing open to attack.

c (*laisser voir*) to reveal. **une robe qui découvre le dos** a dress which reveals the back; **son sourire découvre des dents superbes** when he smiles he shows his beautiful teeth.

d (*voir*) to see, have a view of; (*Naut*) *terre* to sight. **du haut de la falaise on découvre toute la baie** from the top of the cliff you have a view of the whole bay.

e (*révéler, dévoiler*) *projets, intentions, motifs* to reveal, disclose (*à qn* to sb). **se ~ à qn** to lay bare *ou* open one's heart to sb, confide in sb; **~ son cœur** to lay bare *ou* open one's heart; (*lit, fig*) **~ son jeu** to show one's hand.

2 **se découvrir vpr** a *[personne]* (*chapeau*) to take off one's hat; (*habits*) to undress, take off one's clothes; (*couvertures*) to throw off the bedclothes, uncover o.s. **en altitude on doit se ~ le moins possible** at high altitudes you must keep covered up as much as possible; *voir* **avril**.

b (*Boxe, Escrime*) to leave o.s. open; (*Mil, fig*) to expose o.s., leave o.s. open to attack.

c *[ciel, temps]* to clear. **ça va se ~** it will soon clear.

décrassage [dekʀasaʒ] **nm, décrassement** [dekʀasmɑ̃] **nm** (*voir* **décrasser**) cleaning; cleaning-out; cleaning-up. (**: toilette*) **un bon ~** a good scrubbing-down *ou* clean-up.

décrasser [dekʀase] [1] **vt** a *objet boueux, graisseux* to clean, get the mud (*ou* grease *etc*) off; (*en frottant*) to scrub; (*en trempant*) to soak the dirt out of; *chaudière* to clean out, clean; (*Aut*) *bougie* to clean (up). **se ~** to give o.s. a good scrubbing(-down) *ou* clean-up, get the muck off (o.s.) (*Brit*); **se ~ le visage/les mains** to give one's face/hands a scrub, clean up one's face/hands; **le bon air, ça décrasse les poumons** fresh air cleans out the lungs; **rouler à 160 à l'heure, ça décrasse le moteur** driving at 100 mph gives the engine a good decoking (*Brit*) *ou* decarbonization (*US*). b (*fig: dégrossir*) *rustre* to take the rough edges off.

décrêper [dekʀepe] [1] **vt** *cheveux* to straighten.

décrépir [dekʀepiʀ] [2] 1 **vt** *mur* to remove the roughcast from. **façade décrépie** peeling façade. 2 **se décrépir vpr** *[mur]* to peel.

décrépit, e [dekʀepi, it] **adj** *personne* decrepit; *maison* dilapidated, decrepit.

décrépitude [dekʀepityd] **nf** *[personne]* decrepitude; *[nation, institution, civilisation]* decay. **tomber en ~** *[personne]* to become decrepit; *[nation]* to decay.

decrescendo [dekʀeʃɛndo] 1 **adv** (*Mus*) decrescendo. (*fig*) **sa réputation va ~** his reputation is declining *ou* waning. 2 **nm** (*Mus*) decrescendo.

décret [dekʀɛ] **nm** (*Pol, Rel*) decree. **~-loi** statutory order, ≃ Order in Council; (*fig littér*) **les ~s de la Providence** the decrees of Providence; (*fig*) **les ~s de la mode** the dictates of fashion.

décréter [dekʀete] [6] **vt** *mobilisation* to order; *état d'urgence* to declare; *mesure* to decree. **le président a décrété la nomination d'un nouveau ministre** the president ordered the appointment of a new minister; **~ que** (*Pol*) *[patron, chef]* to decree *ou* order that; (*Rel*) to ordain *ou* decree that; **il a décrété qu'il ne mangerait plus de betteraves** he decreed that he wouldn't eat beetroot any more; **j'ai décrété que je n'irai pas** I have decided that I won't go.

décrier [dekʀije] [7] **vt** *œuvre, mesure, principe* to decry (*littér*), disparage, discredit, downcry (*US*). **la chasteté, une vertu si décriée de nos jours** chastity, a much disparaged *ou* discredited virtue nowadays; **ces auteurs maintenant si décriés par la critique** these authors now so disparaged by the critics; (*littér*) **il décria fort ma conduite** he (strongly) censured my behaviour.

décriminaliser [dekʀiminalize] [1] **vt** to decriminalize.

décrire [dekʀiʀ] [39] **vt** a (*dépeindre*) to describe. b (*parcourir*) *trajectoire* to follow. **l'oiseau/l'avion décrivait des cercles au-dessus de nos têtes** the bird/plane flew in circles overhead; **la route décrit une courbe** the road makes *ou* follows a curve; **le satellite décrit une ellipse** the satellite follows *ou* makes *ou* describes an elliptical orbit; **le bras de la machine décrivit une ellipse** the arm of the machine described an ellipse.

décrispation [dekʀispasjɔ̃] **nf** (*Pol*) detente. **être partisan de la ~** to be in favour of improved relations (*entre* between).

décrisper [dekʀispe] [1] **vt** *situation* to defuse, de-escalate; *personne* to relax. **pour ~ les relations** to make relations less strained, take the heat out of relations.

décrochage [dekʀɔʃaʒ] **nm** a *[rideaux]* taking down, unhooking; *[wagon]* uncoupling. b (*Mil*) **opérer un ~** to disengage, break off the action. c (*Rad, TV*) handover.

décroché [dekʀɔʃe] **nm** (*Constr*) recess. **dans le mur il y a un ~** the wall is recessed.

décrochement [dekʀɔʃmɑ̃] **nm** a *[wagon]* uncoupling. b (*Géol*) thrust fault, slide. c = **décroché**.

décrocher [dekʀɔʃe] [1] 1 **vt** a (*détacher*) *tableau* to take down; *rideau* to take down, unhook; *vêtement* to take down, take off the hook *ou* peg; *fermoir* to undo, unclasp; *poisson* to unhook; *wagon* to uncouple; *téléphone* (*pour répondre*) to pick up, lift; (*pour l'empêcher de sonner*) to take off the hook. **il n'a pas pu ~ son cerf-volant qui s'était pris dans l'arbre** he couldn't free *ou* unhook his kite which had got caught in the tree; **le téléphone est décroché** the telephone is off the hook; (*Sport*) **~ le reste du peloton** to leave the pack behind; *voir* **bâiller**.

b (**: obtenir*) *prix, contrat, poste, récompense* to get, land*. **il a décroché une belle situation** he's landed (himself) a fine job*; (*lit, fig*) **~ le gros lot** *ou* **la timbale** to hit the jackpot.

2 **vi** a (*Téléc*) to pick up *ou* lift the receiver.

b (*Mil*) to pull back, break off the action; *[coureur]* to fall behind.

c (**: abandonner*) (*ne pas suivre*) to fall by the wayside (*fig*), fail to keep up; (*se désintéresser*) to drop out, opt out; (*cesser d'écouter*) to switch off*.

d (*arg Drogue*) to come off.

3 **se décrocher vpr** *[tableau, vêtement]* to fall down *ou* off; *[rideau]* to fall down, come unhooked; *[fermoir]* to come undone; *[poisson]* to get unhooked; *[wagon]* to come uncoupled. **le cerf-volant pris dans l'arbre s'est finalement décroché** the kite which had been caught in the tree finally came free.

décroiser [dekʀwɑze] [1] **vt** *jambes* to uncross; *bras* to unfold; *fils* to untwine, untwist.

décroissance [dekʀwasɑ̃s] **nf** (*diminution*) decline, decrease, fall (*de* in).

décroissant, e [dekʀwasɑ̃, ɑ̃t] **adj** (*gén*) decreasing, diminishing, declining; *bruit* fading; *vitesse* decreasing, falling. **par ordre ~** in decreasing *ou* descending order.

décroissement [dekʀwasmɑ̃] **nm** *[jours]* shortening; *[lune]* waning.

décroît [dekʀwɑ] **nm** *[lune]* **dans** *ou* **sur son ~** in its last quarter.

décroître [dekʀwɑtʀ] [55] **vi** *[nombre, population, intensité, pouvoir]* to decrease, diminish, decline; *[eaux, fièvre]* to subside, go down; *[popularité]* to decline, drop; *[vitesse]* to drop, fall off; *[force]* to decline, diminish, fail; *[revenus]* to get less, diminish; *[lune]* to wane; *[jours]* to get shorter; *[silhouette]* to get smaller and smaller; *[bruit]* to die away, fade; *[lumière]* to fade, grow fainter *ou* dimmer. **ses forces vont (en) décroissant** his strength is failing *ou* gradually diminishing *ou* declining; **cette ville a beaucoup décru en importance** this town has greatly declined in importance.

décrotter [dekʀɔte] [1] **vt** *chaussures* to get the mud off; (*fig*) *rustre* to take the rough edges off.

décrottoir [dekʀɔtwaʀ] **nm** (*lame*) mud-scraper, shoescraper; (*paillasson*) wire (door)mat.

décrue [dekʀy] **nf** *[eaux, rivière]* fall *ou* drop in level (*de* of); (*fig*) *[popularité]* decline, drop (*de* in). **la ~ des eaux atteint 2 mètres** the water level *ou* flood-level has fallen *ou* dropped by 2 metres; **au moment de la ~** when the water level drops.

décryptage [dekʀiptaʒ] **nm** deciphering.

décrypter [dekʀipte] [1] **vt** (*décoder*) to decipher.

déçu, e [desy] (**ptp de décevoir**) **adj** disappointed. (*iro*) **elle ne va pas être ~e du voyage!*** she is going to be over the moon* (*iro*).

déculottée‡ [dekylɔte] **nf** (*défaite*) clobbering‡, hammering‡. **prendre** *ou* **recevoir une ~** to get a hammering‡ *ou* clobbering‡.

déculotter [dekylɔte] [1] 1 **vt: ~ qn** to take off *ou* down sb's trousers. 2 **se déculotter vpr** (*lit*) to take off *ou* down one's trousers; (‡ *fig*) (*céder*) to grovel; (*reculer*) to funk it* (*Brit*), lose one's nerve.

déculpabiliser [dekylpabilize] [1] **vt: ~ qn** to rid sb of his (*ou* her) guilt.

décuple [dekypl] 1 **adj** tenfold. **un revenu ~ du mien** an income ten times as large as mine. 2 **nm: 20 est le ~ de 2** 20 is ten times 2; **il gagne le ~ de ce que je gagne** he earns ten times what I earn; **il me l'a rendu au ~** he paid me back tenfold.

décuplement [dekypləmɑ̃] **nm** (*lit*) tenfold increase. (*fig*) **grâce au ~ de nos forces** thanks to our greatly increased strength.

décupler [dekyple] [1] **vti** to increase tenfold. (*fig*) **la colère décuplait ses forces** anger gave him the strength of ten.

dédaignable [dedɛɲabl] **adj: ce n'est pas ~** it is not to be despised.

dédaigner [dedeɲe] [1] **vt** **a** (*mépriser*) *personne* to despise, look down on, scorn; *honneurs, richesse* to scorn, despise, disdain. **il ne dédaigne pas de rire avec ses subordonnés** he doesn't consider it beneath him to joke with his subordinates; **il ne dédaigne pas un verre de vin de temps à autre** he's not averse to the occasional glass of wine.
b (*négliger*) *offre, adversaire* to spurn, think nothing of; *menaces, insultes* to disregard, discount. **ce n'est pas à ~** (*honneur, offre*) it's not to be sniffed at *ou* despised; (*danger, adversaire*) it can't just be shrugged off; (*littér*) **il dédaigna de répondre/d'y aller** he did not deign to reply/go.

dédaigneusement [dedeɲøzmɑ̃] **adv** disdainfully, scornfully, contemptuously.

dédaigneux, -euse [dedɛɲø, øz] **adj** *personne, air* scornful, disdainful, contemptuous. **~ de** contemptuous *ou* scornful *ou* disdainful of; (*littér*) **il est ~ de plaire** he scorns to please.

dédain [dedɛ̃] **nm** contempt, scorn, disdain (*de* for). **sourire de ~** disdainful *ou* scornful smile.

dédale [dedal] **nm** *[rues, idées]* maze. (*Myth*) **D~** Daedalus.

dedans [dədɑ̃] **1 adv** **a** (*à l'intérieur*) inside; (*pas à l'air libre*) indoors, inside. **voulez-vous dîner dehors ou ~?** do you want to have dinner outside or inside? *ou* outdoors or indoors?; **au-~** inside; **la maison est laide, mais ~** *ou* **au-~ c'est très joli** it's an ugly-looking house but it's lovely inside; **nous sommes restés ~ toute la journée** we stayed in *ou* inside *ou* indoors all day; **elle cherche son sac, tout son argent est ~** she is looking for her bag – all her money is in it; **prenez ce fauteuil, on est bien ~** have this chair, you'll be comfortable in it *ou* you'll find it comfortable; **de** *ou* **du ~ on n'entend rien** you can't hear a sound from inside; **rentrons ~** *ou* **au-~, il fera plus chaud** let's go in *ou* inside *ou* indoors, it will be warmer; **passez par ~ pour aller au jardin** go through the house to get to the garden; *voir* **là, pied.**
b (*loc*) **marcher les pieds en ~** to walk with one's toes *ou* feet turned in, walk pigeon-toed; **il n'en pense pas moins en ~** *ou* **au-~ (de lui)** he still has private reservations about it, deep down he's still not sure about it; **un bus lui est rentré ~*** a bus hit him *ou* ran into him; **il a dérapé, il y avait un arbre, il est rentré** *ou* **entré ~*** he skidded, there was a tree and he ran *ou* went *ou* crashed straight into it; **il s'est fichu*** *ou* **foutu‡ ~** he got it all wrong*; **mettre*** *ou* **ficher*** *ou* **foutre‡ qn ~** to get sb confused, make sb get it wrong*; **il s'est fait mettre ~‡** he got himself put away‡ *ou* put inside‡; (*Cartes*) **être ~** to lose (*de* by); *voir* **rentrer.**
2 nm *[objet, bâtiment etc]* inside. **le coup a été préparé du ~** it's an inside job.

dédicace [dedikas] **nf** **a** (*imprimée*) dedication; (*manuscrite*) *[livre, photo]* dedication, inscription (*à* to). **b** *[église]* consecration, dedication.

dédicacer [dedikase] [3] **vt** *livre, photo* to sign, autograph (*à qn* for sb), inscribe (*à qn* to sb).

dédicatoire [dedikatwaʀ] **adj** dedicatory, dedicative.

dédié, e [dedje] (**ptp de dédier**) **adj** (*Ordin*) dedicated.

dédier [dedje] [7] **vt: ~ à** (*Rel*) to consecrate to, dedicate to; **~ ses efforts à** to devote *ou* dedicate one's efforts to; **~ un livre à** to dedicate a book to.

dédire (se) [dediʀ] [37] **vpr** **a** (*manquer à ses engagements*) to go back on one's word. **se ~ d'une promesse** to go back on a promise. **b** (*se rétracter*) to retract, recant. **se ~ d'une affirmation** to withdraw a statement, retract (a statement); *voir* **cochon[1].**

dédit [dedi] **nm** **a** (*Comm: somme*) forfeit, penalty. **un ~ de 30.000 F** a 30,000 franc penalty. **b** (*rétractation*) retraction; (*manquement aux engagements*) failure to keep one's word; (*non-paiement*) default. **en cas de ~ il faut payer un supplément** in case of default a supplement must be paid.

dédommagement [dedɔmaʒmɑ̃] **nm** compensation. **en ~, je lui ai donné une bouteille de vin** in compensation *ou* to make up for it, I gave him a bottle of wine; **en ~ des dégâts** *ou* **à titre de ~ pour les dégâts, on va me donner 500 F** they will give me 500 francs in compensation for the damage; **en ~ du mal que je vous donne** to make up for the trouble I'm causing you.

dédommager [dedɔmaʒe] [3] **vt** (*indemniser*) **~ qn** to compensate sb (*de* for), give sb compensation (*de* for); **je l'ai dédommagé en lui donnant une bouteille de vin** I gave him a bottle of wine in compensation *ou* to make up for it; **~ qn d'une perte** to compensate sb for a loss, make good sb's loss; **comment vous ~ du dérangement que je vous cause?** how can I ever repay you *ou* make up for the trouble I'm causing?; **le succès le dédommage de toutes ses peines** his success is compensation *ou* compensates for all his troubles.

dédorer [dedɔʀe] [1] **vt** to remove the gilt from. **bijou dédoré** piece of jewellery that has lost its gilt.

dédouanement [dedwanmɑ̃] **nm** (*Comm*) clearing *ou* clearance through customs, customs clearance.

dédouaner [dedwane] [1] **vt** (*Comm*) to clear through customs; (** fig*) *personne* to clear (the name of), put in the clear*. **se ~** to clear one's name; **marchandises dédouanées** duty-paid goods.

dédoublement [dedubləmɑ̃] **nm** *[classe]* dividing *ou* splitting in two. **le ~ d'un train** the running *ou* putting-on of a relief train; (*Psych*) **le ~ de la personnalité est un trouble grave** having a split personality is a serious illness; **souffrir d'un ~ de la personnalité** to suffer from a split *ou* dual personality.

dédoubler [deduble] [1] **1 vt** **a** *manteau* to remove the lining of. **b** *classe* to split *ou* divide in two; *ficelle* to separate the strands of. **~ un train** to run *ou* put on a relief train; **pour Noël on a dû ~ tous les trains** at Christmas they had to run additional trains on all services. **c** *couverture* to unfold, open out. **2 se dédoubler vpr** (*se déplier*) to unfold, open out. (*Psych*) **sa personnalité se dédoublait** he suffered from a split *ou* dual personality; **je ne peux pas me ~*** I can't be in two places at once; **l'image se dédoublait dans l'eau** there was a double outline reflected in the water.

dédramatiser [dedʀamatize] [1] **vt** *examen, opération* to make less alarming *ou* awesome. **~ la mort** to take the drama out of dying; **il faut ~ la situation** you mustn't overdramatize the situation.

déductible [dedyktibl] **adj** (*Fin*) *frais, somme* deductible (*de* from). **~ du revenu imposable** tax-deductible; **dépenses non ~s** non-deductible expenses.

déductif, -ive [dedyktif, iv] **adj** deductive.

déduction [dedyksjɔ̃] **nf** **a** (*Comm*) deduction. **~ forfaitaire** standard deduction; **~ faite de** after deducting, after deduction of; **ça entre en ~ de ce que vous nous devez** that's deductible from what you owe us, that'll be taken off what you owe us. **b** (*forme de raisonnement*) deduction, inference; (*conclusion*) conclusion, inference.

déduire [dedɥiʀ] [38] **vt** (*Comm*) to deduct (*de* from); (*conclure*) to deduce, infer (*de* from). **tous frais déduits** after deduction of expenses.

déesse [deɛs] **nf** goddess.

de facto [defakto] **loc adv: reconnaître qch ~** to give de facto recognition to sth.

défaillance [defajɑ̃s] **1 nf** **a** (*évanouissement*) blackout; (*faiblesse physique*) feeling of weakness *ou* faintness; (*faiblesse morale*) weakness, failing. **avoir une ~** (*évanouissement*) to faint, have a blackout; (*faiblesse*) to feel faint *ou* weak; **l'athlète a eu une ~ au troisième kilomètre** the athlete seemed to be in difficulty *ou* to be weakening at the third kilometre; **il a eu plusieurs ~s ces derniers jours** he has had several weak spells these last few days; **faire son devoir sans ~** to do one's duty without flinching.
b (*mauvais fonctionnement*) (mechanical) fault, failure, breakdown (*de* in). **l'accident était dû à une ~ de la machine** the accident was caused by a fault in the machine.
c (*insuffisance*) weakness. **élève qui a des ~s (en histoire)** pupil who has certain shortcomings *ou* weak points (in history); **devant la ~ du gouvernement** faced with the weakness of the government *ou* the government's failure to act; **mémoire sans ~** faultless memory.
d (*Jur*) default.
2 comp ▸défaillance cardiaque heart failure **▸défaillance mécanique** mechanical fault **▸défaillance de mémoire** lapse of memory.

défaillant, e [defajɑ̃, ɑ̃t] **adj** **a** (*affaibli*) *forces* failing, declining; *santé, mémoire, raison* failing; *courage, volonté* faltering, weakening; *cœur* weak. **b** (*tremblant*) *voix, pas* unsteady, faltering; *main* unsteady. **c** (*près de s'évanouir*) *personne* weak, faint (*de* with). **d** (*Jur*) *partie, témoin* defaulting. **candidat ~** candidate who fails to appear.

défaillir [defajiʀ] [13] **vi** **a** (*s'évanouir*) to faint. **elle défaillait de bonheur/de faim** she felt faint with happiness/hunger. **b** *[forces]* to weaken, fail; *[courage, volonté]* to falter, weaken; *[mémoire]* to fail. **faire son devoir sans ~** to do one's duty without flinching.

défaire [defɛʀ] [60] **1 vt** **a** *échafaudage etc* to take down, dismantle; *installation électrique etc* to dismantle.
b *couture, tricot* to undo, unpick (*Brit*); *écheveau* to undo, unravel, unwind; *corde, nœud, ruban* to undo, untie; *courroie, fermeture, robe* to undo, unfasten; *valise* to unpack; *cheveux, nattes* to undo. **~ ses bagages** to unpack (one's luggage).
c ~ le lit (*pour changer les draps*) to strip the bed; (*pour se coucher*) to untuck the bed *ou* sheets, pull back the sheets; (*mettre en désordre*) to unmake *ou* rumple the bed.
d *mariage* to break up; *contrat, traité* to break. **cela défit tous nos plans** it ruined all our plans; **il (faisait et) défaisait les rois** he (made and) unmade kings; **elle se plaît à ~ tout ce que j'essaie de faire pour elle** she takes pleasure in undoing everything I try to do for her.
e (*miner*) **la maladie l'avait défait** his illness had left him shattered; **la douleur défaisait ses traits** pain distorted his features.
f (*littér*) *ennemi, armée* to defeat.
g (*littér*) **~ qn de** *liens, gêneur* to rid sb of, relieve sb of, deliver sb from (*littér*); *habitude* to break sb of, cure sb of, rid sb of; *défaut* to cure sb of, rid sb of.
2 se défaire vpr **a** *[nœud, ficelle, coiffure]* to come undone; *[couture]* to come undone *ou* apart; *[légumes, viande]* (*à la cuisson*) to fall to pieces, disintegrate; *[mariage, amitié]* to break up.
b (*se déformer*) **ses traits se défirent, son visage se défit** his face

crumpled, his face twisted with grief (*ou* pain *etc*).
c **se ~ de** (*se débarrasser de*) *gêneur, vieillerie, odeur* to get rid of; *image, idée* to put *ou* get out of one's mind; *habitude* to break *ou* cure o.s. of, get rid of; *défaut* to cure o.s. of; (*se séparer de*) *souvenir* to part with.

défait, e[1] [defɛ, ɛt] (**ptp de défaire**) **adj** a *visage* ravaged, haggard; *cheveux* tousled, ruffled, dishevelled. b *lit* unmade, rumpled, disarranged. c *armée* defeated.

défaite[2] [defɛt] **nf** (*Mil*) defeat; (*fig*) defeat, failure. **la ~ de notre équipe** our team's defeat; **~ électorale** defeat at the polls *ou* election.

défaitisme [defetism] **nm** defeatism.

défaitiste [defetist] **adj, nmf** defeatist.

défalcation [defalkasjɔ̃] **nf** deduction. **~ faite des frais** after deduction of expenses.

défalquer [defalke] [1] **vt** to deduct.

défausse [defos] **nf** discarding, throwing out *ou* away.

défausser (se) [defose] [1] **vpr** (*Cartes*) to discard, throw out *ou* away. **se ~ (d'une carte)** to discard; **il s'est défaussé à trèfle** he discarded a club.

défaut [defo] 1 **nm** a *[pierre précieuse, métal]* flaw; *[étoffe, verre]* flaw, fault; *[machine]* defect, fault; *[bois]* blemish; *[roman, tableau, système]* flaw, defect; (*Ordin*) bug. **sans ~** flawless, faultless.
b *[personne]* fault, failing; *[caractère]* defect, fault, failing (*de* in). **chacun a ses petits ~s** we've all got our little faults *ou* our shortcomings *ou* failings; **il n'a aucun ~** he's perfect, he hasn't a single failing; **la gourmandise n'est pas un gros ~** greediness isn't such a bad fault, it isn't a (great) sin to be greedy; *voir* **curiosité**.
c (*désavantage*) drawback. **ce plan/cette voiture a ses ~s** this plan/car has its drawbacks; **le ~ de *ou* avec* cette voiture, c'est que ...** the trouble *ou* snag *ou* drawback with this car is that ... .
d (*manque*) **~ de** *raisonnement* lack of; *main-d'œuvre* shortage of.
e (*loc*) **faire ~** *[temps, argent, talent]* to be lacking; (*Jur*) *[prévenu, témoin]* to default; **la patience/le temps lui fait ~** he lacks patience/time; **le courage lui a finalement fait ~** his courage failed him in the end; **ses amis lui ont finalement fait ~** his friends let him down in the end; **à ~ de** for lack *ou* want of; **à ~ de vin, il boira du cidre** if there's no wine *ou* for want of wine, he'll drink cider; **elle cherche une table ovale, ou, à ~, ronde** she is looking for an oval table, or, failing that, a round one (will do); **être en ~** to be at fault *ou* in the wrong; **se mettre en ~** to put o.s. in the wrong; **prendre qn en ~** to catch sb out; **si ma mémoire ne me fait pas ~** if my memory serves me right; **c'est votre mémoire qui est en ~** it's your memory that's at fault; (*Jur*) **condamner/juger qn par ~** to sentence/judge sb in his absence; (*Math*) **calculer qch par ~** to calculate sth to the nearest decimal point; **il pèche par ~** he doesn't try hard enough.
2 **comp** ►**défaut de comparution** (*Jur*) default, non-appearance, failure to appear ►**défaut-congé** **nm** (**pl défaut-congés**) (*Jur*) *dismissal of case through non-appearance of plaintiff* ►**le défaut de la cuirasse** (*lit, fig*) the chink in the armour ►**défaut d'élocution** = **défaut de prononciation** ►**le défaut de l'épaule** the hollow beneath the shoulder ►**défaut de fabrication** manufacturing defect ►**défaut de masse** (*Phys*) mass defect ►**défaut de paiement** (*Jur*) default in payment, non-payment ►**défaut de prononciation** speech impediment *ou* defect.

défaveur [defavœʀ] **nf** disfavour (*auprès de* with). **être en ~** to be out of favour, be in disfavour; **s'attirer la ~ de** to incur the disfavour of.

défavorable [defavɔʀabl] **adj** unfavourable (*à* to). **voir qch d'un œil ~** to view sth with disfavour.

défavorablement [defavɔʀabləmɑ̃] **adv** unfavourably.

défavoriser [defavɔʀize] [1] **vt** (*désavantager*) *[décision, loi]* to penalize; *[défaut, timidité]* to put at a disadvantage; *[examinateur, patron]* to put at an unfair disadvantage. **il a défavorisé l'aîné** he treated the eldest less fairly (than the others); **j'ai été défavorisé par rapport aux autres candidats** I was put at an unfair disadvantage with respect to *ou* compared with the other candidates; **aider les couches les plus défavorisées de la population** to help the most underprivileged *ou* disadvantaged sections of the population.

défécation [defekasjɔ̃] **nf** (*Physiol*) defecation; (*Chim*) defecation, purification.

défectif, -ive [defɛktif, iv] **adj** *verbe* defective.

défection [defɛksjɔ̃] **nf** *[amis, alliés politiques]* desertion, defection, failure to (give) support; *[troupes]* failure to give *ou* lend assistance *ou* to assist; *[candidats]* failure to attend *ou* appear; *[invités]* failure to appear. **faire ~** *[partisans]* to fail to lend support; *[invités]* to fail to appear *ou* turn up; **il y a eu plusieurs ~s** (*membres d'un parti*) a number of people have withdrawn their support, there has been a marked drop in support; (*invités, candidats*) several people failed to appear, there were several non-appearances.

défectueux, -euse [defɛktɥø, øz] **adj** faulty, defective.

défectuosité [defɛktɥozite] **nf** (*état*) defectiveness, faultiness; (*défaut*) imperfection, (slight) defect *ou* fault (*de* in).

défendable [defɑ̃dabl] **adj** (*Mil*) *ville* defensible; (*soutenable*) *conduite* defensible, justifiable; *position* tenable, defensible.

défendant [defɑ̃dɑ̃] *voir* **corps**.

défendeur, -deresse [defɑ̃dœʀ, dʀɛs] **nm,f** (*Jur*) defendant. **~ en appel** respondent.

défendre [defɑ̃dʀ] [41] 1 **vt** a (*protéger: gén, Jur, Mil*) to defend; (*soutenir*) *personne, opinion* to stand up for, defend (*contre* against); *cause* to champion, defend (*contre* against). **ville défendue par 2 forts** town defended *ou* protected by 2 forts; **manteau qui (vous) défend du froid** coat that protects you from *ou* against the cold; (*Tennis*) **~ son service** to hold one's serve *ou* service; (*fig*) **~ son bifteck** to guard one's patch, defend one's territory; *voir* **corps**.
b (*interdire*) **~ qch à qn** to forbid sb sth; **~ à qn de faire *ou* qu'il fasse** to forbid sb to do; **le médecin lui défend le tabac/la mer** the doctor has forbidden him *ou* won't allow him to smoke/to go to the seaside; **il m'en a défendu l'accès** he forbade me access to it, he didn't allow me in; **~ sa porte à qn** to bar one's door to sb, refuse to allow sb in; **ne fais pas ça, c'est défendu** don't do that, it's not allowed *ou* it's forbidden; **il est défendu de fumer** smoking is prohibited *ou* not allowed; **il est défendu de parler** speaking is not allowed; *voir* **fruit**[1].
2 **se défendre** **vpr** a (*se protéger: gén, Jur, Mil*) to defend o.s. (*contre* against); (*contre brimades, critiques*) to stand up for o.s., defend o.s. (*contre* against). **se ~ du froid/de la pluie** to protect o.s. from the cold/rain.
b (**: se débrouiller*) to manage, get along *ou* by. **elle se défend au tennis/au piano** she's not bad at tennis/on the piano; **il se défend bien/mal en affaires** he gets on *ou* does quite well/he doesn't do very well in business; **il se défend** he gets along *ou* by, he can hold his own (quite well).
c (*se justifier*) **se ~ d'avoir fait qch** to deny doing *ou* having done sth; **il se défendit d'être vexé/jaloux** he denied being *ou* that he was annoyed/jealous; **sa position/son point de vue se défend** his position/point of view is quite defensible; *[raisonnement]* **ça se défend!** it holds *ou* hangs together; **il dit que ce serait trop cher, ça se défend** he says it would be too expensive and he has a point *ou* it's a fair point.
d (*s'empêcher de*) **se ~ de** to refrain from; **il ne pouvait se ~ d'un sentiment de pitié/gêne** he couldn't help feeling pity/embarrassment; **elle ne put se ~ de sourire** she could not refrain from smiling, she couldn't suppress a smile.

défenestration [defənɛstʀasjɔ̃] **nf** defenestration.

défenestrer [defənɛstʀe] [1] **vt** to defenestrate.

défense[1] [defɑ̃s] **nf** a (*protection: gén, Mil, Sport*) defence (*Brit*), defense (*US*). (*fortifications etc*) **~s** defences; **~ nationale/antiaérienne *ou* contre avions/passive** national/anti-aircraft/civil defence; **une entreprise travaillant pour la D~ nationale** a firm working for the Ministry of Defence; **un contrat concernant la ~ nationale** a defence contract; **les ~s d'une frontière** border defences; **la ~ du pays** the country's defence *ou* protection; **la ~ des opprimés est notre cause** our cause is the defence *ou* protection of the oppressed; **ligne de ~** line of defence; **ouvrage de ~** fortification; **aller à la ~ de qn** to go *ou* rally to sb's defence; **prendre la ~ de qn** to stand up for sb, defend sb; (*Sport*) **~ de zone** zone defence.
b (*résistance*) defence (*Brit*), defense (*US*). **opposer une ~ courageuse** to put up a brave defence; (*Physiol, Psych*) **mécanisme/instinct de ~** defence mechanism/instinct; **moyens de ~** means of defence; **~s immunitaires** immune defence system; **sans ~** (*trop faible*) defenceless; (*non protégé*) unprotected; **sans ~ contre les tentations** helpless *ou* defenceless against temptation; *voir* **légitime**.
c (*Jur*) defence (*Brit*), defense (*US*); (*avocat*) counsel for the defence (*Brit*), defense attorney (*US*). **assurer la ~ d'un accusé** to conduct the case for the defence; **la parole est à la ~** (the counsel for) the defence may now speak; **qu'avez-vous à dire pour votre ~?** what have you to say in your defence?
d (*interdiction*) **~ d'entrer** no entrance, no entry, no admittance; **propriété privée, ~ d'entrer** private property, no admittance *ou* keep out; **danger: ~ d'entrer** danger — keep out; **~ de fumer/stationner** no smoking/parking, smoking/parking prohibited; **~ d'afficher** (stick *ou* post) no bills; **j'ai oublié la ~ qu'il m'a faite de faire cela†** I forgot that he forbade me to do that; **~ d'en parler à quiconque** it is forbidden to speak of it to anyone.

défense[2] [defɑ̃s] **nf** *[éléphant, morse, sanglier]* tusk.

défenseur [defɑ̃sœʀ] **nm** (*gén, Mil*) defender; *[cause]* champion, defender; *[doctrine]* advocate; (*Jur*) counsel for the defence (*Brit*), defense attorney (*US*). **l'accusé et son ~** the accused and his counsel; **~ de l'environnement** conservationist, preservationist.

défensif, -ive [defɑ̃sif, iv] 1 **adj** (*Mil, fig*) defensive. 2 **défensive** **nf**: **la ~ive** the defensive; **être *ou* se tenir sur la ~ive** to be on the defensive.

déféquer [defeke] [6] 1 **vt** (*Chim*) to defecate, purify. 2 **vi** (*Physiol*) to defecate.

déférence [defeʀɑ̃s] **nf** deference. **par ~ pour** in deference to.

déférent, e [defeʀɑ̃, ɑ̃t] **adj** deferential, deferent; *voir* **canal**.

déférer [defeʀe] [6] **vt** a (*Jur*) *affaire* to refer to the court. **~ un coupable à la justice** to hand a guilty person over to the law. b (*céder*) to defer (*à* to). c (*†: conférer*) to confer (*à* on, upon).

déferlante [defɛʀlɑ̃t] **adj f, nf: (vague) ~** breaker.

déferlement [defɛʀləmɑ̃] **nm** *[vagues]* breaking; *[violence]* surge, spread; *[véhicules, touristes]* flood. **ils étaient impuissants devant le ~**

des troupes they were powerless before the advancing tide of the troops; **ce ~ d'enthousiasme le prit par surprise** this sudden wave of enthusiasm took him by surprise; **le ~ de haine/des sentiments anti-catholiques dans tout le pays** the hatred/anti-Catholic feeling which has engulfed the country *ou* swept through the country.

déferler [defɛʀle] [1] **1** **vi** *[vagues]* to break. (*fig*) **la violence/haine déferla sur le pays** violence/hatred swept *ou* surged through the country; (*fig*) **les touristes déferlaient sur les plages** tourists were streaming towards the beaches; (*fig*) **la foule déferla dans la rue/sur la place** the crowd surged *ou* flooded into the street/over the square. **2** **vt** *voile, pavillon* to unfurl.

défi [defi] **nm** challenge; (*fig: bravade*) defiance. **lancer un ~ à qn** to challenge sb; **relever un ~** to take up *ou* accept a challenge; **mettre qn au ~** to defy sb (*de faire* to do); **c'est un ~ au bon sens** it defies common sense, it goes against common sense; **d'un air/ton de ~** defiantly.

défiance [defjɑ̃s] **nf** mistrust, distrust. **avec ~** with mistrust *ou* distrust, distrustingly, mistrustingly; **sans ~** **(adj)** unsuspecting; **(adv)** unsuspectingly; **mettre qn en ~** to arouse sb's mistrust *ou* suspicions, make sb suspicious.

défiant, e [defjɑ̃, jɑ̃t] **adj** mistrustful, distrustful.

déficeler [defis(ə)le] [4] **1** **vt** to untie. **2** **se déficeler** **vpr** *[paquet]* to come untied *ou* undone.

déficience [defisjɑ̃s] **nf** (*Méd, fig*) deficiency. **~ musculaire** muscular insufficiency; **~ immunologique** immunodeficiency; **~ de mémoire** lapse of memory; **~ mentale** mental deficiency; **~ intellectuelle** mental retardation.

déficient, e [defisjɑ̃, jɑ̃t] **1** **adj** (*Méd*) *force, intelligence* deficient; (*fig*) *raisonnement* weak. **enfant ~** (*intellectuellement*) mentally deficient child; (*physiquement*) child with a physical disability, physically disabled *ou* handicapped child. **2** **nm,f: ~ mental/visuel** mentally/visually handicapped person; **~ moteur** person with motor deficiencies.

déficit [defisit] **nm** (*Fin*) deficit. **être en ~** to be in deficit; **le ~ budgétaire** the budget deficit; **le ~ de notre commerce extérieur** the deficit in our foreign trade; **~ de la balance des paiements** balance of payments deficit; **~ commercial/d'exploitation** trade/operating deficit; **~ de trésorerie** cash deficit; **~ de ressources** resource(s) gap; **~ psychologique/intellectuel** psychological/mental defect; **~ immunitaire** immunodeficiency.

déficitaire [defisitɛʀ] **adj** (*Fin*) in deficit (*attrib*); *récolte* poor; *année* poor (*en* in), bad (*en* for). **~ en** *main-d'œuvre* deficient in, short of.

défier [defje] [7] **1** **vt** **a** *adversaire* to challenge (*à* to). **~ qn en combat singulier** to challenge sb to single combat; **~ qn du regard** to give sb a challenging look.

b *mort, adversité* to defy, brave; *opinion publique* to fly in the face of, defy; *autorité* to defy, challenge. **ça défie l'imagination!** the mind boggles!*; **à des prix qui défient toute concurrence** at absolutely unbeatable prices.

c **~ qn de faire qch** to defy *ou* challenge sb to do sth; **je t'en défie!** I dare *ou* challenge you (to)!

2 **se défier** **vpr** (*littér*) **se ~ de** to distrust, mistrust; **je me défie de moi-même** I don't trust myself; **défie-toi de ton caractère impulsif** be on your guard against *ou* beware of your impulsiveness; **défie-toi de lui!** beware of him!, be on your guard against him!

défigurement [defigyʀmɑ̃] **nm** *[vérité]* distortion; *[texte, tableau]* mutilation; *[visage]* disfigurement.

défigurer [defigyʀe] [1] **vt** **a** *[blessure, maladie]* to disfigure; *[bouton, larmes] visage* to spoil. **l'acné qui la défigurait** the acne which marred *ou* spoiled her looks. **b** (*altérer*) *pensée, réalité, vérité* to distort; *texte, tableau* to mutilate, deface; *monument* to deface; *paysage* to disfigure, mar, spoil.

défilé [defile] **nm** **a** (*cortège*) procession; (*manifestation*) march; (*Mil*) march-past, parade. **~ de mode** *ou* **de mannequins** fashion parade. **b** (*succession*) *[visiteurs]* procession, stream; *[voitures]* stream; *[impressions, pensées]* stream, succession. **c** (*Géog*) (narrow) gorge, narrow pass, defile.

défilement [defilmɑ̃] **nm** *[film]* projection; *[bande magnétique]* unreeling, unwinding; (*Ordin*) scrolling. (*Ciné*) **vitesse de ~** projection speed; (*Ordin*) **~ horizontal/vertical** horizontal/vertical scrolling.

défiler [defile] [1] **1** **vt** **a** *aiguille, perles* to unthread; *chiffons* to shred.

b (*Mil*) *troupes* to put under cover (*from the enemy's fire*).

2 **vi** (*Mil*) to march past, parade; *[manifestants]* to march (*devant* past). (*Ordin*) **faire ~ un document** to scroll a document; **les souvenirs défilaient dans sa tête** a constant stream of memories passed through his mind; **les visiteurs défilaient devant le mausolée** the visitors filed past the mausoleum; **la semaine suivante tous les voisins défilèrent chez nous** the following week we were visited by all the neighbours one after the other; **nous regardions le paysage qui défilait devant nos yeux** we watched the scenery pass by *ou* (*plus vite*) flash by.

3 **se défiler** **vpr** **a** *[aiguille]* to come unthreaded; *[perles]* to come unstrung *ou* unthreaded.

b (*Mil*) to take cover (*from the enemy's fire*).

c (** fig*) (*s'éclipser*) to slip away *ou* off, crayfish* (*US*). (*se dérober*) **il s'est défilé** he wriggled *ou* ducked out of it.

défini, e [defini] (**ptp de définir**) **adj** **a** (*déterminé*) *but* definite, precise. **terme bien ~** well-defined term. **b** (*Gram*) *article* definite. **passé ~** preterite.

définir [definiʀ] [2] **vt** *idée, sentiment, position* to define; (*Géom, Gram*) to define; *personne* to define, characterize; *conditions* to specify, define. **il se définit comme un humaniste** he describes *ou* defines himself as a humanist; **notre politique se définit comme étant avant tout pragmatique** our policies can be defined *ou* described as being essentially pragmatic.

définissable [definisabl(ə)] **adj** definable.

définitif, -ive [definitif, iv] **1** **adj** **a** (*final*) *résultat, destination, résolution* final; *mesure, installation, victoire, fermeture* permanent, definitive; *solution* definitive, final, permanent; *étude, édition* definitive. **son départ était ~** he was leaving for good, his departure was final. **b** (*sans appel*) *décision* final; *refus* definite, decisive; *argument* conclusive. **un jugement ~** a final judgment; **et c'est ~!** and that's that! *ou* that's final! **2** **définitive nf: en ~ive** (*à la fin*) eventually; (*somme toute*) in fact, when all is said and done.

définition [definisjɔ̃] **nf** *[concept, mot]* definition; *[mots croisés]* clue; (*TV*) definition. **par ~** by definition; **~ de poste** job description; *voir* **haut**.

définitivement [definitivmɑ̃] **adv** *partir* for good; *résoudre* conclusively, definitively; *exclure, s'installer* for good, permanently, definitively; *refuser, décider, savoir* definitely, positively; *nommer* on a permanent basis, permanently.

définitoire [definitwaʀ] **adj** (*Ling*) *vocabulaire* defining (*épith*).

défiscalisation [defiskalizasjɔ̃] **nf** tax exemption.

défiscaliser [defiskalize] [1] **vt** to exempt from tax(ation).

déflagration [deflagʀasjɔ̃] **nf** (*gén*) explosion; (*Chim*) deflagration.

déflagrer [deflagʀe] [1] **vi** to deflagrate.

déflation [deflasjɔ̃] **nf** deflation.

déflationniste [deflasjɔnist] **1** **adj** *politique* deflationist; *mesures etc* deflationary. **2** **nmf** deflationist.

déflecteur [deflɛktœʀ] **nm** (*Aut*) quarter-light; (*Tech*) jet deflector; (*Naut*) deflector.

défleurir [deflœʀiʀ] [2] (*littér*) **1** **vt** *fleur* to remove the flower of; *buisson* to remove the blossom of. **2** **vi** to shed its flower *ou* its blossom.

déflexion [deflɛksjɔ̃] **nf** deflection.

défloraison [deflɔʀɛzɔ̃] **nf** (*Bot, littér*) falling of blossoms.

défloration [deflɔʀasjɔ̃] **nf** *[jeune fille]* defloration.

déflorer [deflɔʀe] [1] **vt** *jeune fille* to deflower; (*littér*) *sujet, moments* to take the bloom off (*littér*), spoil the charm of.

défoliant [defɔljɑ̃] **nm** defoliant.

défoliation [defɔljasjɔ̃] **nf** defoliation.

défolier [defɔlje] [7] **vti** to defoliate.

défonçage [defɔ̃saʒ] **nm, défoncement** [defɔ̃smɑ̃] **nm** (*voir* **défoncer**) staving in; smashing in *ou* down; breaking; ripping *ou* ploughing *ou* breaking up; deep-ploughing.

défonce [defɔ̃s] **nf** (*arg Drogue*) high*. **~ à la colle** *ou* **aux solvants** glue-sniffing.

défoncer [defɔ̃se] [3] **1** **vt** *caisse, barque* to stave in, knock *ou* smash the bottom out of; *porte, clôture* to smash in *ou* down, stave in; *sommier, fauteuil* to break *ou* burst the springs of; *route, terrain [bulldozers, camions]* to rip *ou* plough *ou* break up; (*Agr*) to plough deeply, deep-plough. **un vieux fauteuil tout défoncé** an old sunken armchair; **la route défoncée par les pluies** the road broken up by the rains, the road full of potholes *ou* ruts after the rains.

2 **se défoncer** **vpr** **a** (*: *travailler dur*) to work like a dog*. **se ~ (la caisse) pour qn/pour faire qch** to beat one's brains out *ou* work like a dog* for sb/to do sth.

b (*arg Drogue*) to get high*, get stoned*.

déforestation [defɔʀɛstasjɔ̃] **nf** deforestation.

déformant, e [defɔʀmɑ̃, ɑ̃t] **adj** *miroir* distorting.

déformation [defɔʀmasjɔ̃] **nf** **a** (*voir* **déformer**) bending (out of shape); putting out of shape; deformation; distortion; misrepresentation; warping; corruption. **par une curieuse ~ d'esprit, il poussait tout au macabre** by a strange twist in his character, he would take everything to gruesome extremes; **~ professionnelle** job conditioning; **c'est de la ~ professionnelle** he's (*ou* you are *etc*) completely conditioned by his (*ou* your *etc*) job; **par ~ professionnelle** as a result of being so conditioned by one's job. **b** (*voir* **se déformer**) loss of shape. **c** (*Méd*) deformation.

déformer [defɔʀme] [1] **1** **vt** *objet, bois, métal* to bend (out of shape); *chaussures, vêtements* to put out of shape; *corps* to deform; *visage, image, vision* to distort; *vérité, pensée* to distort, misrepresent; *esprit, goût* to warp, corrupt. **un vieillard au corps déformé** an old man with a deformed *ou* misshapen body; **veste déformée** jacket which has lost its shape *ou* has gone out of shape; **pantalon (tout) déformé** baggy trousers; **traits déformés par la douleur** features contorted *ou* distorted by pain; **mes propos ont été déformés** (*involontairement*) I've been misquoted; (*volontairement*) my words have been twisted; (*fig*) **il est déformé par son métier** he has been conditioned by his job; **chaussée déformée** uneven road surface.

2 **se déformer** **vpr** *[objet, bois, métal]* to be bent (out of shape), lose

its shape; *[vêtement]* to lose its shape.
défoulement [defulmɑ̃] **nm** *[instincts, sentiments]* (psychological) release. **moyen de ~** (psychological) outlet *ou* means of release; **après les examens on a besoin de ~** after the exams you need some kind of (psychological) release *ou* you need to let off steam* *ou* to unwind.
défouler (se) [defule] 1 **vpr** to work off one's frustrations *ou* tensions, release one's pent-up feelings, let off steam*, unwind (*en faisant* by doing). **ça (vous) défoule de courir** running helps you unwind *ou* relax.
défourner [defuʀne] 1 **vt** *pain* to take out of the oven; *poteries* to take out of the kiln.
défraîchir [defʀeʃiʀ] 2 **1 vt** to take the freshness from. **2 se défraîchir vpr** *[fleur, couleur]* to fade; *[tissu]* (*passer*) to fade; (*s'user*) to become worn. **articles défraîchis** shop-soiled items.
défraiement [defʀɛmɑ̃] **nm** payment *ou* settlement of expenses.
défrayer [defʀeje] 8 **vt a** (*payer*) **~ qn** to pay *ou* settle *ou* meet sb's expenses. **b** (*être en vedette*) **~ la conversation** to be the main topic of conversation; **~ la chronique** to be widely talked about, be in the news, be the talk of the town (*fig*).
défrichage [defʀiʃaʒ] **nm**, **défrichement** [defʀiʃmɑ̃] **nm** *[forêt, terrain]* clearing (*for cultivation*). (*fig*) **~ d'un sujet** spadework (done) on a subject.
défricher [defʀiʃe] 1 **vt** *forêt, terrain* to clear (*for cultivation*); (*fig*) *sujet, question* to open up (*fig*), do the spadework on. (*fig*) **~ le terrain** to prepare the ground *ou* way (*fig*), clear the way (*fig*).
défricheur [defʀiʃœʀ] **nm** (*lit*) land-clearer; (*fig*) pioneer.
défriper [defʀipe] 1 **vt** to smooth out.
défriser [defʀize] 1 **vt** *cheveux* to uncurl; (*‡: contrarier*) *personne* to annoy, madden*. **ce qui me défrise*** what bugs‡ *ou* gets* me; **et alors! ça te défrise?*** so (what)?*, what's it to you?*
défroisser [defʀwase] 1 **vt** to smooth out.
défroque [defʀɔk] **nf** (*frusques*) old cast-offs; *[moine]* effects (*left by a dead monk*).
défroqué, e [defʀɔke] (**ptp de défroquer**) **1 adj** unfrocked, defrocked. **2 nm** unfrocked *ou* defrocked priest *ou* monk.
défroquer [defʀɔke] 1 **1 vt** to defrock, unfrock. **2 vi, se défroquer vpr** to give up the cloth, renounce one's vows.
défunt, e [defœ̃, œ̃t] **1 adj** (*frm*) *personne* late (*épith*); (*littér*) *espoir, année* which is dead and gone; (*littér*) *assemblée, projet* defunct. **son ~ père, ~ son père** his late father. **2 nm,f** deceased.
dégagé, e [degaʒe] (**ptp de dégager**) **adj a** *route* clear; *ciel* clear, cloudless; *espace, site* open, clear; *vue* wide, open; *front, nuque* bare. **c'est un peu trop ~ autour des oreilles** it's a bit short around the ears. **b** *allure, manières* casual, jaunty; *ton* airy, casual.
dégagement [degaʒmɑ̃] **nm a** (*action de libérer: voir* **dégager**) freeing; extricating; relief; redemption; release; clearing. (*Aut*) **voie de ~** slip road; (*Aut*) **itinéraire de ~** alternative route (*to relieve traffic congestion*). **b** *[obligation]* freeing *ou* releasing o.s. (*de* from) **le ~ d'une promesse** going back on a promise. **c** (*émanation*) *[fumée, gaz, chaleur]* emission, emanation; *[parfum]* emanation. **un ~ de vapeurs toxiques** a discharge *ou* an emission of toxic fumes. **d** (*Escrime*) disengagement; (*Ftbl, Rugby*) clearance. **e** (*espace libre*) *[forêt]* clearing; *[appartement]* passage; (*Tech*) *[camion]* clearance, headroom (*de* above).
dégager [degaʒe] 3 **1 vt a** (*libérer*) *personne* to free, extricate; *objet, main* to free; (*Mil*) *troupe, ville* to relieve, bring relief to; (*Ftbl, Rugby*) *ballon* to clear, kick *ou* clear downfield; (*Escrime*) *épées* to disengage; (*Fin*) *crédits, titres* to release (*for a specific purpose*); *objet en gage* to redeem, take out of pawn. **cela devrait se ~ facilement** it should come free easily; **après l'accident on a dû ~ les blessés au chalumeau** after the accident the injured had to be cut loose *ou* free (from the wreckage); (*fig*) **~ qn de sa promesse/d'une obligation** to release *ou* free sb from his promise/an obligation; (*fig*) **~ sa responsabilité d'une affaire** to disclaim *ou* deny (all) responsibility in a matter; (*fig*) **~ sa parole** to go back on one's word; **être dégagé de ses obligations militaires** to have been discharged from the army, have done one's military service; (*Sport*) **l'arrière dégagea en touche** the back cleared *ou* kicked the ball into touch; (*Habillement*) **col/robe qui dégage le cou/les épaules** collar/dress which leaves the neck/shoulders bare.
b *place, passage, table* to clear (*de* of); (*Méd*) *gorge, nez, poitrine* to clear; *[coiffeur] oreilles, nuque* to cut it short around. **~ la place des manifestants** to clear the demonstrators off the square, clear the square of demonstrators; (*fig*) **~ son esprit d'idées fausses** to free *ou* rid one's mind of false ideas; **allons, dégagez!*** right, clear off!*; **dégage!‡** clear off!‡, buzz off!‡ (*Brit*); **toutes ces vieilleries, à ~!*** chuck (out)* all this old-fashioned stuff!
c (*exhaler*) *odeur, fumée, gaz, chaleur* to give off, emit; (*fig*) *enthousiasme* to radiate. **le paysage dégageait une impression de tristesse** the landscape had a sad look about it.
d (*extraire*) *conclusion* to draw; *idée, sens* to bring out. **quelles impressions as-tu dégagées de ton voyage?** what impressions have you gained *ou* can you single out from your trip?; (*Math*) **~ l'inconnue** to isolate the unknown quantity; **l'idée principale qu'on peut ~ de ce rapport** the main idea that can be drawn *ou* derived *ou* extracted from this report; **je vous laisse ~ la morale de cette histoire** I'll let you extract the moral from *ou* unearth the moral of this story; **~ la vérité de l'erreur** to separate truth from untruth.
2 se dégager vpr a *[personne]* to free *ou* extricate o.s., get free; (*Mil*) *[troupe]* to extricate itself (*de* from). (*fig*) **se ~ de** *dette* to free o.s. of; *obligation* to free *ou* release o.s. from; *affaire* to get *ou* back out of; *promesse* to go back on; (*fig*) **j'ai une réunion mais je vais essayer de me ~** I have a meeting but I'll try to get out of it; **se ~ de préjugés** to free o.s. *ou* shake o.s. free of prejudice; **il s'est dégagé d'une situation très délicate** he extricated himself from a very tricky situation.
b *[ciel, rue, nez]* to clear. **le Mont-Blanc/la silhouette se dégagea du brouillard** Mont Blanc/the outline loomed up out of the fog.
c *[odeur, fumée, gaz, chaleur]* to emanate, be given off; *[enthousiasme]* to emanate, radiate; *[impression d'ennui ou de tristesse]* to emanate (*de* from). **la rumeur qui se dégage de la foule** the murmur rising from the crowd; **une telle vitalité se dégage d'elle** she exudes such vitality.
d *[conclusion]* to be drawn; *[impression, idée, sens]* to emerge; *[morale]* to be drawn, emerge (*de* from). **il se dégage de tout cela que** ... from all this it emerges that ... .
dégaine* [degɛn] **nf** (*démarche*) gawky walk (*NonC*), gawkiness (*NonC*); (*air, accoutrement*) gawky look, gawkiness (*NonC*). **quelle ~!** what a gawky sight!, what a loon!* *ou* a gawk!*
dégainer [degene] 1 **1 vt** *épée* to unsheathe, draw; *pistolet* to draw. **2 vi** to draw one's sword (*ou* gun).
déganter (se) [degɑ̃te] 1 **vpr** to take off one's gloves. **sa main dégantée** his ungloved hand.
dégarni, e [degaʀni] (**ptp de dégarnir**) **adj** *front, arbre, salle, rayon* bare; *compte en banque* low; *portefeuille* empty; *magasin* low in stock; *tête, personne* balding.
dégarnir [degaʀniʀ] 2 **1 vt** *maison, salle, vitrine* to empty, clear; *arbre de Noël* to strip (of decorations); *compte en banque* to drain, draw heavily on; (*Mil*) *ville, place* to withdraw troops from. **2 se dégarnir vpr** *[salle]* to empty; *[tête, personne]* to go bald; *[arbre]* to lose its leaves; *[bois]* to become sparse; (*Comm*) *[rayons]* to be cleaned out *ou* cleared; (*Comm*) *[stock]* to run out, be cleaned out, become depleted.
dégât [degɑ] **nm** damage (*NonC*). **causer *ou* faire beaucoup de ~(s)** *[grêle]* to cause lot of damage; *[alcool]* to do a lot of *ou* great harm; (*Assurances*) **~ des eaux** water damage; *voir* **limiter.**
dégauchir [degoʃiʀ] 2 **vt** *bois* to surface; *pierre* to dress.
dégauchissement [degoʃismɑ̃] **nm**, **dégauchissage** [degoʃisaʒ] **nm** (*voir* **dégauchir**) surfacing; dressing.
dégauchisseuse [degoʃisøz] **nf** surface-planing machine.
dégel [deʒɛl] **nm** (*lit, fig*) thaw; *voir* **barrière.**
dégelée* [deʒ(ə)le] **nf** (*coups*) thrashing, hiding, beating. **une ~ de coups** a hail *ou* shower of blows; **recevoir une ~** to get a hiding.
dégeler [deʒ(ə)le] 5 **1 vt a** *lac, terre* to thaw (out); *glace* to thaw, melt; (*) *pieds, mains* to warm up, get warmed up. **b** (* *fig*) *invité, réunion* to thaw (out); *atmosphère* to unfreeze. **c** (*Fin*) to unfreeze. **2 vi a** *[neige, lac]* to thaw (out). **b** (*Culin*) **faire ~** to thaw, leave to thaw. **3 vb impers: ça dégèle** it's thawing. **4 se dégeler vpr** *[personne]* (*lit*) to warm up, get o.s. warmed up; (*fig*) to thaw (out).
dégénéré, e [deʒeneʀe] (**ptp de dégénérer**) **1 adj** (*abâtardi*) degenerate; (*Psych* †) defective. **2 nm,f** degenerate; (*Psych* †) defective.
dégénérer [deʒeneʀe] 6 **vi a** (*s'abâtardir*) *[race]* to degenerate; *[qualité]* to deteriorate. **b** (*mal tourner*) to degenerate (*en* into). **leur dispute a dégénéré en rixe** their quarrel degenerated into a brawl; **un coup de froid qui dégénère en grippe** a chill which develops into flu; *[manifestation]* **ça a rapidement dégénéré** it soon got out of hand.
dégénérescence [deʒeneʀesɑ̃s] **nf a** *[personne]* (*morale*) degeneracy; (*physique, mentale*) degeneration. **b** *[moralité, race]* degeneration, degeneracy; *[qualité]* deterioration (*de* in). **c** (*Méd*) *[cellule]* degeneration.
dégénérescent, e [deʒeneʀɛsɑ̃, ɑ̃t] **adj** (*Méd*) degenerating, deteriorating.
dégermer [deʒɛʀme] 1 **vt** to degerm, remove the germ from.
dégingandé, e* [deʒɛ̃gɑ̃de] **adj** gangling, lanky.
dégivrage [deʒivʀaʒ] **nm** (*voir* **dégivrer**) defrosting; de-icing.
dégivrer [deʒivʀe] 1 **vt** *réfrigérateur* to defrost; *avion, pare-brise* to de-ice.
dégivreur [deʒivʀœʀ] **nm** (*voir* **dégivrer**) defroster; de-icer.
déglaçage [deglasaʒ] **nm**, **déglacement** [deglasmɑ̃] **nm** (*voir* **déglacer**) deglazing; removal of the glaze (*de* from); removal of the ice (*de* from), melting of the ice (*de* on).
déglacer [deglase] 3 **vt** (*Culin*) to deglaze; *papier* to remove the glaze from; (*dégeler*) *surface* to remove the ice from, melt the ice on.
déglinguer* [deglɛ̃ge] 1 **1 vt** *objet, appareil* to bust*. **ce fauteuil est tout déglingué** this armchair is falling *ou* coming apart *ou* is (all) falling to pieces. **2 se déglinguer vpr** *[appareil]* to be on the blink*; *[chaise]* to fall to pieces, fall *ou* come apart; *[serrure, robinet]* to go bust*.
déglutir [deglytiʀ] 2 **vti** (*Méd*) to swallow.
déglutition [deglytisjɔ̃] **nf** (*Méd*) swallowing, deglutition (*SPÉC*).
dégobiller‡ [degɔbije] 1 **vti** (*vomir*) to throw up‡, spew (up)‡, puke‡.

dégoiser* [degwaze] [1] **1 vt** *boniments, discours* to spout*. **qu'est-ce qu'il dégoise?** what is he rattling on about?* **2 vi** (*parler*) to rattle on*, go on (and on)*. (*médire*) ~ **sur le compte de qn** to tittle-tattle about sb.

dégommage‡ [degɔmaʒ] **nm** (*voir* **dégommer**) **le ~ de qn** the demoting of sb; the unseating of sb; giving the push to sb*, the sacking (*Brit*) *ou* firing of sb*.

dégommer‡ [degɔme] [1] **vt a** (*dégrader*) to demote; (*détrôner*) to unseat; (*renvoyer*) to give the push to*, sack* (*Brit*), fire. **se faire ~** to be demoted; to be unseated; to get the push*, be sacked* *ou* fired*. **b** *avion* to down*, zap*; *quille* to knock flying*.

dégonflage‡ [degɔ̃flaʒ] **nm a** *[pneu]* deflating. **b** (*lâcheté*) chickening out*, backing out. **j'appelle ça du ~!** that's what I call being chicken* *ou* yellow(-bellied)‡, that's what I call chickening out*.

dégonflard, e‡ [degɔ̃flaʀ, aʀd] **nm,f** (*lâche*) chicken*, yellow-belly‡.

dégonflé, e [degɔ̃fle] (**ptp de dégonfler**) **1 adj a** *pneu* flat. **b** (‡: *lâche*) chicken* (*attrib*), yellow(-bellied)‡. **2 nm,f** yellow-belly‡. **c'est un ~** he's a yellow-belly‡, he's chicken* *ou* yellow*.

dégonflement [degɔ̃fləmɑ̃] **nm** *[ballon, pneu]* deflation; *[enflure]* reduction.

dégonfler [degɔ̃fle] [1] **1 vt** *pneu* to let down, let the air out of, deflate; *ballon* to deflate, let the air out of; *enflure* to reduce, bring down; (*fig*) *mythe* to debunk. **2 se dégonfler vpr a** *[ballon, pneu]* to deflate, go down; *[enflure]* to go down. **b** (*: *avoir peur*) to chicken out*, back out.

dégonfleur, -euse‡ [degɔ̃flœʀ, øz] = **dégonflard‡**.

dégorgement [degɔʀʒəmɑ̃] **nm a** (*débouchage*) *[évier, égout]* clearing out. **b** (*évacuation*) *[eau, bile]* discharge. **c** (*écoulement*) *[égout, rivière]* discharge; *[gouttière]* discharge, overflow. **d** (*Tech: lavage*) *[cuir]* cleaning, cleansing; *[laine]* scouring.

dégorgeoir [degɔʀʒwaʀ] **nm** (*conduit d'évacuation*) overflow duct *ou* pipe; (*Pêche*) disgorger.

dégorger [degɔʀʒe] [3] **1 vt a** *évier, égout* to clear out. **b** *[tuyau] eau* to discharge, pour out; (*fig*) *[rue, train] voyageurs* to disgorge, pour forth *ou* out (*dans* into). **c** (*Tech: laver*) *cuir, étoffe* to clean, cleanse; *laine* to scour. **2 vi a** *[étoffe]* to soak (*to release impurities*); (*Culin*) *[viande]* to soak; *[escargots, concombres]* to sweat. **faire ~** *étoffe* to soak; *viande* to soak; *escargots, concombres* to (leave to) sweat. **b ~ dans** *[égout, gouttière]* to discharge into; *[rivière]* to discharge itself into. **3 se dégorger vpr** *[eau]* to be discharged, pour out (*dans* into); (*fig*) *[voyageurs]* to pour forth *ou* out (*dans* into).

dégot(t)er* [degɔte] [1] **vt** (*trouver*) to dig up*, unearth, find.

dégoulinade [degulinad] **nf** trickle.

dégoulinement [degulinmɑ̃] **nm** (*voir* **dégouliner**) trickling; dripping.

dégouliner [deguline] [1] **vi** (*en filet*) to trickle; (*goutte à goutte*) to drip. **ça me dégouline dans le cou** it's dripping *ou* trickling down my neck.

dégoulinure [degulinyʀ] = **dégoulinade**.

dégoupiller [degupije] [1] **vt** *grenade* to take the pin out of.

dégourdi, e* [deguʀdi] (**ptp de dégourdir**) **1 adj** (*malin*) smart, resourceful, bright. **il n'est pas très ~** he's not really on the ball*, he's not all that smart *ou* bright, he's pretty clueless* (*Brit*). **2 nm,f: c'est un ~** he's a smart one *ou* a fly one*, he knows what's what*, he's on the ball*; (*iro*) **quel ~ tu fais!** you're a bright spark!* (*Brit*) *ou* a smart one! *ou* a bright one! (*iro*).

dégourdir [deguʀdiʀ] [2] **1 vt** *eau* to warm (up); *membres* (*ankylosés*) to bring the circulation back to; (*gelés*) to warm up; (*fig*) *provincial* to knock the rough edges off, teach a thing or two to*. **le service militaire/habiter à Paris le dégourdira** military service/living in Paris will knock him into shape *ou* teach him a thing or two*; **~ qn en anglais/en physique** to teach sb the basics of English/physics.

2 se dégourdir vpr: il est sorti pour se ~ un peu (les jambes) he went out to stretch his legs a bit; (*fig*) **elle s'est un peu dégourdie depuis l'an dernier** she seems to have learnt a thing or two* *ou* lost some of her rough edges since last year.

dégoût [degu] **nm a** (*NonC: répugnance*) disgust (*NonC*), distaste (*NonC*) (*pour, de* for). **j'éprouve un certain ~ pour son comportement** I feel somewhat disgusted at his behaviour; **avoir du ~ pour** to feel (a sense of) disgust *ou* distaste for; **il fit une grimace de ~** he screwed up his face in disgust *ou* distaste; **ce ~ de la vie m'étonnait** such world-weariness *ou* such weariness of life surprised me. **b** dislike. **nos goûts et nos ~s** our likes and dislikes.

dégoûtamment [degutamɑ̃] **adv** *manger, se conduire* disgustingly.

dégoûtant, e [degutɑ̃, ɑ̃t] **adj** disgusting, revolting. **espèce de vieux ~!*** (*sale*) you messy old pig‡; (*vicieux*) you disgusting *ou* filthy (old) beast!‡, you dirty old man!‡

dégoûtation* [degutasjɔ̃] **nf** (*dégoût*) disgust. (*saleté*) **quelle ~!** what a disgusting *ou* filthy mess!

dégoûté, e [degute] (**ptp de dégoûter**) **adj: je suis ~!** (*scandalisé*) I'm disgusted!; (*lassé*) I'm sick and tired of it!; **c'est un homme ~ maintenant que tous ses projets ont échoué** he is sick at heart *ou* fed up* now that all his plans have failed; **être ~ de** to be sick of; **il fait le ~** (*devant un mets, une offre*) he turns his nose up (at it) in distaste; **ne fais pas le ~!** don't be so fussy!; **il mange des sauterelles/il sort avec cette femme, il n'est pas ~!** he eats grasshoppers/he goes out with that woman – he's not (too) fussy! *ou* choosy!*

dégoûter [degute] [1] **1 vt a** (*répugner à*) to disgust. **cet homme me dégoûte** that man disgusts me *ou* fills me with disgust, I find that man disgusting *ou* revolting; **ce plat me dégoûte** I find this dish disgusting *ou* revolting; **la vie me dégoûte** I'm weary of life, I'm sick *ou* weary of living, I'm fed up with life*.

b ~ qn de qch (*ôter l'envie de*) to put sb (right) off sth; (*remplir de dégoût pour*) to make sb feel disgusted with; **c'est à vous ~ d'être honnête** it's enough to put you (right) off being honest; **si tu n'aimes pas ça, n'en dégoûte pas les autres** if you don't like it, don't put the others off; **dégoûté de la vie** weary *ou* sick of life *ou* living; **je suis dégoûté par ces procédés** I'm disgusted *ou* revolted by this behaviour.

2 se dégoûter vpr: se ~ de qn/qch to get sick of sb/sth*; **il se dégoûte dans cette maison sale** he's sick of this dirty house*, he dislikes it (intensely) in this dirty house.

dégoutter [degute] [1] **vi** to drip. **dégouttant de sueur** dripping with sweat; **l'eau qui dégoutte du toit** the water dripping (down) from *ou* off the roof; **manteau dégouttant de pluie** dripping wet coat.

dégradant, e [degʀadɑ̃, ɑ̃t] **adj** degrading.

dégradation [degʀadasjɔ̃] **nf a** (*voir* **dégrader**) degradation; debasement; defiling; damaging; erosion; defacing; shading-off. (*dégâts*) **~s** damage (*NonC*); (*Jur*) **~ civique** loss of civil rights; **les ~s causées au bâtiment** the damage caused to the building. **b** (*voir* **se dégrader**) degradation; debasement; loss of one's (physical) powers; deterioration; decline; weakening; worsening; shading-off. (*Phys*) **la ~ de l'énergie** the degradation *ou* dissipation of energy; (*Ordin*) **la ~ des données** the corruption of the data.

dégradé [degʀade] **nm** *[couleurs]* gradation; *[lumière]* (gradual) moderation; (*Ciné*) grading; (*Coiffure*) layers (*pl*), layered cut. **couper en ~** to layer; **un ~ de couleurs** a gradation of colours, a colour gradation.

dégrader [degʀade] [1] **1 vt a** (*Mil*) *officier* to degrade.

b *personne* to degrade, debase.

c *qualité* to debase; *beauté* to defile, debase.

d *mur, bâtiment [vandales]* to damage, cause damage to; *[pluie]* to erode, cause to deteriorate; *monument, façade* to deface, damage; (*Géol*) *roches* to erode, wear away. **les mauvais ouvriers dégradent le matériel** bad workers damage the equipment.

e (*Art*) *couleurs* to shade off; *lumière* to subdue. **couleurs dégradées** colours which shade into each other *ou* shade off gradually.

f *cheveux* to layer, cut in layers.

2 se dégrader vpr a *[personne]* (*s'avilir moralement*) to degrade o.s., debase o.s., become degraded *ou* debased; (*s'affaiblir physiquement*) to lose one's physical powers.

b *[relation, situation, qualité, santé, bâtiment]* to deteriorate; *[valeurs morales, intérêt, forces]* to decline; *[monnaie]* to grow weaker. **le temps se dégrade** the weather is beginning to break, there's a change for the worse in the weather.

c (*Sci*) *[énergie]* to become dissipated *ou* degraded; (*Art*) *[couleurs]* to shade off; *[lumière]* to become subdued.

dégrafer [degʀafe] [1] **1 vt** *vêtement* to unfasten, unhook, undo; *ceinture* to unbuckle, unfasten, undo; *personne* to unfasten, unhook, undo. **2 se dégrafer vpr** *[robe, bracelet]* to come undone *ou* unfastened; *[personne]* to unfasten *ou* unhook *ou* undo one's dress *etc*.

dégraissage [degʀɛsaʒ] **nm a le ~ d'un vêtement** removal of the grease marks from a piece of clothing; **le ~ du bouillon** skimming the fat off the broth; **"~ et nettoyage à sec"** "dry cleaning". **b** (*Écon*) *[effectifs]* cutback, rundown (*de* in). **opérer un ~ ou des ~s dans le secteur industriel** to slim down *ou* cut back the workforce in the industrial sector.

dégraissant [degʀɛsɑ̃] **nm** (*produit*) spot remover.

dégraisser [degʀese] [1] **vt a** *vêtement* to take the grease marks out of. **b** (*Culin*) *bouillon* to skim (the fat off); *viande* to remove the fat from, cut the fat off. **c** (*Menuiserie*) *bois* to trim the edges of. **d** (*Écon*) *personnel, effectifs* to cut back, slim down.

degré [dəgʀe] **nm a** (*gén: niveau*) degree; (*stade de développement*) stage, degree; (*Admin: échelon*) grade; (*littér: marche*) step. **le ~ zéro de la civilisation/culture** the dawn of civilization/the birth of culture; **haut ~ de civilisation** high degree *ou* level of civilization; **à un ~ avancé de** at an advanced stage of; (*Alpinisme*) **mur de 6e ~** grade 6 wall; (*fig*) **les ~s de l'échelle sociale** the rungs of the social ladder (*fig*); **avare au plus haut ~** miserly in the extreme, miserly to a degree; **jusqu'à un certain ~** to some *ou* a certain extent *ou* degree, to a degree; **par ~(s)** by degrees; *voir* **dernier, troisième**.

b (*Gram, Mus, Sci*) degree. **équation du 1er/2e ~** equation of the 1st/2nd degree; **il fait 20 ~s dans la chambre** it's 20 degrees (centigrade) in the room; **la température a baissé/est montée de 2 ~s** there has been a 2-degree drop/rise in temperature, the temperature has gone down *ou* dropped/gone up *ou* risen 2 degrees; **~ d'alcool d'une boisson** proof of an alcoholic drink; **~ en alcool d'un liquide** percentage of alcohol in a liquid; **alcool à 90 ~s** 90% proof alcohol, surgical spirit (*Brit*); **du cognac à 40 ~s** 70° proof cognac (*Brit*); **vin de 11 ~s** 11° wine (*on Gay-Lussac scale = 19° Sykes (Brit) and 22° proof (US)*); **ce vin**

fait (du) 11 ~s this wine is 11°; ~ centigrade/Fahrenheit/Baumé degree centigrade/Fahrenheit/Baumé.

c (*Méd*) ~ de brûlure degree of burns; brûlure du premier/deuxième ~ first/second degree burn; (*Scol*) enseignement du premier/second ~ primary/secondary education; enseignant du premier/second ~ primary/secondary schoolteacher; (*Sociol*) ~ de parenté degree of (family) relationship *ou* of kinship (*frm*); cousins au premier ~ first cousins; cousins au second ~ second cousins, first cousins once removed; parents au premier/deuxième ~ relatives of the first/second degree; prendre qch au premier ~ to take sth literally; prendre qch au deuxième *ou* second ~ to look below the surface of sth.

dégressif, -ive [degʀesif, iv] adj: appliquer un tarif ~ to use a sliding scale of charges.

dégressivité [degʀesivite] nf *[impôt]* degression.

dégrèvement [degʀɛvmɑ̃] nm a bénéficier d'un ~ fiscal *ou* de ~s fiscaux to be granted tax exemption *ou* tax relief; le ~ d'un produit the reduction of the tax(es) on a product; le ~ d'une industrie the reduction of the tax burden on an industry; le ~ d'un contribuable the granting of tax relief to a taxpayer. b (*Jur: d'hypothèque*) disencumbrance.

dégrever [degʀəve] 5 vt *produit* to reduce the tax(es) on; *industrie* to reduce the tax burden on; *contribuable* to grant tax relief to; *immeuble* to disencumber.

dégriffé, e [degʀife] 1 adj: robe ~e unlabelled designer dress. 2 nm: magasin de ~s designer seconds store; ils vendent du ~ they sell designer seconds.

dégringolade [degʀɛ̃gɔlad] nf (*voir* dégringoler) tumbling (down); tumble. la ~ du dollar face aux monnaies européennes the collapse of the dollar against European currencies.

dégringoler [degʀɛ̃gɔle] 1 1 vi *[personne, objet]* to tumble (down); *[monnaie]* to collapse, take a tumble; *[prix, firme, réputation]* to tumble. il a dégringolé jusqu'en bas he tumbled all the way down, he came *ou* went tumbling *ou* crashing down; elle a essayé de prendre un livre et elle a fait ~ toute la pile she tried to get a book and toppled the whole pile over *ou* brought the whole pile (crashing) down. 2 vt *escalier, pente* to rush *ou* leap down.

dégrippant [degʀipɑ̃] nm penetrating oil.

dégripper [degʀipe] 1 vt to unblock, unchoke.

dégrisement [degʀizmɑ̃] nm (*lit, fig*) sobering up.

dégriser [degʀize] 1 1 vt (*lit*) to sober up; (*fig*) to sober up *ou* down, bring back down to earth. 2 se dégriser vpr (*lit*) to sober up; (*fig*) to sober up, come back down to earth.

dégrossir [degʀosiʀ] 2 vt a *bois, planche* to trim, cut down to size; *marbre* to rough-hew. b (*fig*) *projet, travail* to rough out, work out roughly, do the spadework on. c (*) *personne* to knock the rough edges off, polish up. individu mal dégrossi coarse *ou* unpolished *ou* unrefined individual; il s'est un peu dégrossi he has lost some of his rough edges.

dégrossissage [degʀosisaʒ] nm (*voir* dégrossir) trimming; rough-hewing; roughing-out. le ~ d'une personne knocking the rough edges off a person, polishing up *ou* refining a person.

dégrouiller (se)* [degʀuje] 1 vpr (*se dépêcher*) to hurry up, get a move on*. allez, dégrouille(-toi)! come on, hurry up! *ou* get a move on!*; se ~ de *ou* pour faire qch to hurry to do sth.

dégroupement [degʀupmɑ̃] nm putting *ou* dividing into groups.

dégrouper [degʀupe] 1 vt to put *ou* divide into groups.

déguenillé, e [deg(ə)nije] 1 adj ragged, tattered. 2 nm,f ragamuffin.

déguerpir* [degɛʀpiʀ] 2 vi (*s'enfuir*) to clear off*, scarper‡ (*Brit*). faire ~ *ennemi* to scatter; *voleur* to chase *ou* drive off.

dégueu‡ [degø] adj abrév de dégueulasse.

dégueulasse‡ [degœlas] adj (*mauvais, injuste*) lousy‡, rotten‡; (*crasseux, vicieux*) filthy. c'est ~ de faire ça that's a lousy‡ *ou* rotten‡ thing to do; c'est pas ~ that's not bad; c'est un ~ he's a lousy *ou* rotten swine‡, he's a filthy dog‡.

dégueulasser‡ [degœlase] 1 vt *vêtement, feuille etc* to muck up*, mess up*, make mucky*.

dégueuler‡ [degœle] 1 vti (*vomir*) to throw up‡, spew (up)‡, puke (up)‡. c'est à ~ it's enough to make you throw up‡ *ou* spew (up)‡ *ou* puke (up)‡.

dégueulis‡ [degœli] nm puke‡.

déguisé, e [degize] (ptp de déguiser) adj a (*pour tromper*) in disguise (*attrib*), disguised; (*pour s'amuser*) in fancy dress, in costume (*US*), dressed up. b (*fig*) *voix, écriture, dévaluation* disguised; *ambition, sentiment* disguised, masked, veiled; *prêt, accord* backdoor (*épith*). non ~ unconcealed, undisguised.

déguisement [degizmɑ̃] nm (*pour tromper*) disguise; (*pour s'amuser*) fancy dress, costume (*US*), disguise. (*littér*) sans ~ without disguise, openly.

déguiser [degize] 1 1 vt (*gén*) *voix, écriture, visage* to disguise; *pensée, ambition, vérité* to disguise, mask, veil; *poupée, enfant* to dress up (*en* as). (*littér*) je ne puis vous ~ ma surprise I cannot conceal my surprise from you. 2 se déguiser vpr (*pour tromper*) to disguise o.s.; (*pour s'amuser*) to dress up. se ~ en Peau-Rouge to dress up as a Red Indian; se ~ en courant d'air* to make o.s. scarce*.

dégurgiter [degyʀʒite] 1 vt *nourriture* to vomit *ou* bring back (up); *leçon* to parrot out, regurgitate.

dégustateur, -trice [degystatœʀ, tʀis] nm,f wine taster.

dégustation [degystasjɔ̃] nf *[coquillages, fromages]* sampling. ~ de vin(s) wine-tasting session; ici, ~ d'huîtres à toute heure oysters available *ou* served at all times.

déguster [degyste] 1 1 vt *vins* to taste; *coquillages, fromages* to sample; *repas, café*, (*fig*) *spectacle* to enjoy, savour. as-tu fini ton café? non, je le déguste have you finished your coffee? — no I'm enjoying it *ou* savouring it. 2 vi (*: *souffrir*) qu'est-ce qu'il a dégusté! (*coups*) he didn't half catch it!* *ou* cop it!*; (*douleur*) he didn't half have a rough time!*; j'ai une rage de dents, je déguste! I've got toothache and I'm in agony* *ou* and it's killing me*.

déhanché, e [deɑ̃ʃe] (ptp de se déhancher) adj *démarche [femme etc]* swaying; *[infirme]* lop-sided.

déhanchement [deɑ̃ʃmɑ̃] nm (*voir* déhanché) (*mouvement*) swaying walk; lop-sided walk.

déhancher (se) [deɑ̃ʃe] 1 vpr a (*en marchant*) to sway one's hips. b (*immobile*) to stand with *ou* lean one's weight on one hip.

dehors [dəɔʀ] 1 adv a (*à l'extérieur*) outside; (*à l'air libre*) outside, outdoors, out of doors; (*pas chez soi*) out. attendez-le ~ wait for him outside; je serai ~ toute la journée I shall be out all day; par beau temps, les enfants passent la journée ~ when it's fine, the children spend the day outdoors *ou* out of doors *ou* outside; il fait plus frais dedans que ~ it is cooler inside than out(side) *ou* indoors than out(doors); cela ne se voit pas de ~ it can't be seen from (the) outside; passez par ~ pour aller au jardin go round the outside (of the house) to get to the garden; dîner ~ (*dans le jardin*) to eat out of doors *ou* outside; (*au restaurant*) to eat *ou* dine out; jeter *ou* mettre *ou* ficher* *ou* foutre‡ qn ~ (*gén*) to throw *ou* kick‡ *ou* chuck‡ sb out; *[patron]* to sack* *ou* fire* sb; mettre le nez *ou* le pied ~ to set foot outside; il fait un temps à ne pas mettre le nez ~ it's weather for staying indoors.

b (*loc*) en ~ de (*lit*) outside; (*fig*) (*sans rapport avec*) outside, irrelevant to; (*excepté*) apart from; ce passage est en ~ du sujet this passage is outside the subject *ou* is irrelevant (to the subject); marcher les pieds en ~ to walk with one's feet *ou* toes turned out; en ~ de cela, il n'y a rien de neuf apart from that *ou* beyond that *ou* otherwise there's nothing new; cette tâche est en ~ de ses possibilités this task is beyond his capabilities; (*fig*) il a voulu rester en ~ he wanted to stay uninvolved; au ~, elle paraît calme, mais c'est une nerveuse outwardly she looks relaxed, but she is highly strung; au ~, la situation est tendue outside the country, the situation is tense.

2 nm a (*extérieur*) outside. on n'entend pas les bruits du ~ you can't hear the noise from outside; nos employés sont honnêtes, ce sont des gens du ~ qui ont commis ce vol our employees are honest — it must be outsiders *ou* people from outside who are responsible for the theft.

b (*apparences: pl*) les ~ sont trompeurs appearances are deceptive; sous des ~ aimables, il est dur under a friendly exterior, he is a hard man.

c (*Patinage*) faire des ~ to skate on the outside edge.

déhoussable [deusabl] adj with loose covers (*attrib*).

déicide [deisid] 1 adj deicidal. 2 nmf deicide. 3 nm (*crime*) deicide.

déictique [deiktik] nm (*Ling*) deictic.

déification [deifikasjɔ̃] nf deification.

déifier [deifje] 7 vt to deify.

déisme [deism] nm deism.

déiste [deist] 1 adj deistic, deist. 2 nmf deist.

déité [deite] nf (*littér*) (mythological) deity.

déjà [deʒa] adv a already. il a ~ fini he has finished already, he has already finished; est-il ~ rentré? has he come home yet?; (*surprise*) has he come home already?; à 3 heures il avait ~ écrit 3 lettres he'd already written 3 letters by 3 o'clock; ~ à cette époque as far back as then, already *ou* even at that time; j'aurais ~ fini si tu ne me dérangeais pas tout le temps I would have finished by now *ou* already if you didn't keep bothering me all the time; je l'aurais ~ dit si je n'avais pas craint de le vexer I would have said it before now *ou* by now *ou* already if I hadn't been afraid of offending him; c'est ~ vieux tout ça! all that's already out of date!, all that's old hat!*.

b (*auparavant*) before, already. je suis sûr de l'avoir ~ rencontré I'm sure I've met him before, I'm sure I've already met him; j'ai ~ fait ce genre de travail I've done that sort of work before, I've already done that sort of work; c'est du ~-vu we've seen it all before, it's old hat*; impression de ~-vu sense *ou* feeling of déjà vu.

c (*intensif*) 1 000 F, c'est ~ pas mal* 1,000 francs, that's not bad at all; 30 tonnes, c'est ~ un gros camion 30 tons, that's quite a big truck *ou* that's a fair-sized truck; il est ~ assez paresseux he's lazy enough as it is; enfin, c'est ~ quelque chose! anyway, it's better than nothing! *ou* it's a start!; ~ que je ne suis pas riche*, s'il faut encore payer une amende ... as it is I'm not rich *ou* I'm not rich as it is but if I (should) have to pay a fine as well ... .

d (*: *interrogatif*) qu'est-ce qu'il a dit, ~? what was it he said again?, what did he say again?; c'est combien, ~? how much is it again?, how much did you say it was again?; *voir* ores.

déjanter [deʒɑ̃te] 1 1 vt *[pneu]* to remove from its rim. 2 vi (‡:

devenir fou) to go off one's rocker‡ (*Brit*) *ou* trolley‡ (*Brit*). **non mais tu déjantes!** you must be off your rocker!‡ *ou* trolley!‡ 3 **se déjanter** vpr *[pneu]* to come off its rim.

déjection [deʒɛksjɔ̃] nf a (*Méd*) evacuation. **~s** dejecta (*SPÉC*), faeces, excrement. b (*Géol*) **~s** ejecta (*SPÉC*), ejectamenta (*SPÉC*); *voir* **cône**.

déjeté, e [deʒ(ə)te] adj *position, mur, arbre, infirme* lop-sided, crooked; *colonne vertébrale* twisted. **il est tout ~** he's all lop-sided *ou* misshapen.

déjeuner [deʒœne] 1 1 vi a (*gén: à midi*) to (have) lunch. **nous avons déjeuné de fromage et de pain** we had bread and cheese for lunch, we lunched on bread and cheese; **inviter qn à ~** to invite sb to lunch; **rester à ~ chez qn** to stay and have lunch with sb, stay to lunch at sb's; **viens ~ avec nous demain** come and have lunch with us tomorrow, come to lunch with us tomorrow; **nous avons déjeuné sur l'herbe** we had a picnic lunch; **ne pars pas sans ~** don't go before you've had your lunch.
b (*Belgique, Suisse: le matin*) to (have) breakfast; *voir* **petit, pouce**.
2 nm a (*repas de midi*) (*gén*) lunch, luncheon (*frm*). **~ d'affaires** business lunch; **~ de travail** working lunch, lunch meeting; **~ sur l'herbe** picnic lunch; **prendre son ~** to have lunch; **j'ai eu du poulet à ~** I had chicken for lunch; **j'ai ma mère à ~** I've got my mother coming for lunch.
b (*Belgique, Suisse: du matin*) breakfast.
c (*tasse et soucoupe*) breakfast cup and saucer.
d **ça a été un vrai ~ de soleil** (*vêtement*) it didn't take long to fade; (*objet*) it soon gave up the ghost*, it didn't last long; (*résolution*) it was a flash in the pan, it didn't last long, it was short-lived.

déjouer [deʒwe] 1 vt *complot* to foil, thwart; *plan* to thwart, frustrate; *ruse* to outsmart; *surveillance* to elude. **~ les plans de l'ennemi** to frustrate the enemy in his plans, confound the enemy's plans; **j'ai déjoué ses plans** I thwarted his plans, I outwitted him.

déjuger (se) [deʒyʒe] 3 vpr to go back on *ou* reverse one's decision.

delà [dəla] 1 adv a **au-~** beyond; **au-~ il y a l'Italie** beyond (that) is Italy; **il a eu ce qu'il voulait et bien au-~** he had all he wanted and more (besides); **vous avez droit à 10 bouteilles et pas au-~/mais au-~ vous payez une taxe** you're entitled to 10 bottles and no more/but above that you pay duty; (*somme, prix*) **n'allez pas au-~** don't go beyond *ou* over that figure (*ou* sum *etc*), don't exceed that figure; **mes connaissances ne vont pas au-~** that's as far as my knowledge goes, that's the extent of my knowledge; *voir* **au-delà**.
b **par ~, par-~** beyond; **devant eux il y a le pont et par(-)~ l'ennemi** in front of them is the bridge and beyond (that) the enemy *ou* and on the other *ou* far side (of it), the enemy.
c **en ~** beyond, outside; **la clôture était à 20 mètres et il se tenait un peu en ~** the fence was 20 metres away and he was standing just beyond it *ou* outside it.
d (*littér*) **de ~ les mers** from beyond *ou* over the seas; *voir* **deçà**.
2 prép a **au ~ de** *lieu, frontière* beyond, on the other side of; *somme, limite* over, above; (*littér*) **au ~ des mers** overseas, beyond *ou* over the seas; **ceci va au ~ de tout ce que nous espérions** this goes (far) beyond anything we hoped for; **au ~ de la conscience/douleur** beyond consciousness/pain; **aller au ~ de ses forces/moyens** to go beyond *ou* exceed one's strength/means.
b (*gén littér*) **par ~** beyond; **par ~ les mers** overseas, beyond *ou* over the seas; **par ~ les apparences** beneath appearances; **par ~ les siècles** across the centuries.

délabré, e [delabʀe] (ptp de **délabrer**) adj *maison* dilapidated, ramshackle (*épith*), tumbledown (*épith*); *mobilier, matériel* broken-down; *santé* impaired, broken (*épith*); *mur* falling down (*épith*), crumbling, in ruins (*attrib*); *affaires* in a poor *ou* sorry state (*attrib*); *fortune* depleted.

délabrement [delabʀəmɑ̃] nm *[maison]* dilapidation, decay, ruin; *[santé, affaires]* poor *ou* sorry state; *[vêtements]* raggedness; *[mobilier, matériel, mur]* decay, ruin; *[fortune]* depletion. **état de ~** dilapidated state, state of decay *ou* ruin.

délabrer [delabʀe] 1 1 vt *maison* to ruin; *mobilier, matériel* to spoil, ruin; *santé* to ruin, impair. 2 **se délabrer** vpr *[maison, mur, matériel]* to fall into decay; *[santé]* to break down; *[affaires]* to go to rack and ruin.

délacer [delase] 3 1 vt *chaussures* to undo (the laces of); *corset* to unlace. 2 **se délacer** vpr *[chaussures]* to come undone.

délai [delɛ] 1 nm a (*temps accordé*) time limit. **c'est un ~ trop court pour ...** it's too short a time for ...; **je vous donne 3 mois, c'est un ~ impératif** I'll give you 3 months and that's an absolute deadline; **avant l'expiration du ~** before the deadline; **dans le ~ imparti** *ou* **prescrit** within the allotted *ou* prescribed time, within the time laid down *ou* allotted; **dans un ~ de 6 jours** within (a period of) 6 days; (*sur facture*) **livrable dans un ~ de 15 jours** allow two weeks for delivery; **un ~ de 10 jours pour payer est insuffisant** (a period of) 10 days to pay is not enough; **observer** *ou* **respecter** *ou* **tenir les ~s** *[travail]* to keep *ou* meet the deadline; *[livraison]* to keep *ou* meet delivery dates; **prolonger un ~** to extend a time limit *ou* a deadline; **lundi prochain, c'est le dernier ~** next Monday is the absolute deadline.
b (*période d'attente*) waiting period. **il faut compter un ~ de 8 jours** you'll have to allow a week, there'll be a week's delay.
c (*sursis*) extension of time. **un dernier ~ de 10 jours** a final extension of 10 days; **accorder des ~s successifs** to allow further extensions (of time); **il va demander un ~ pour achever le travail** he's going to ask for more time to finish off the job.
d (*loc*) **dans le(s) plus bref(s) ~(s)** as soon *ou* as quickly as possible; **ce sera fait dans les ~s** it'll be done within the time limit *ou* allotted time; **à bref ~** *prévenir* at short notice; (*très bientôt*) shortly, very soon; **sans ~** without delay, immediately.
2 comp ▸**délai de carence** (*Fin, Jur*) grace period ▸**délai-congé** nm (pl **délais-congés**) term *ou* period of notice ▸**délai d'exécution** (*pour un travail*) turnaround time ▸**délai de forclusion** (*Jur*) time limit ▸**délai de grâce** (*Fin, Jur*) grace period; **un délai de grâce de 5 jours** 5 days' grace ▸**délai de livraison** delivery time *ou* period ▸**délai de paiement** term of payment, time for payment ▸**délai de préavis** = **délai-congé** ▸**délai de réflexion** (*avant réponse*) time for consideration, time to think; (*avant sanctions*) cooling-off period ▸**délai de rigueur: à remettre avant le 15 mai, délai de rigueur** to be handed in before the final deadline of May 15th.

délaissement [delɛsmɑ̃] nm (*action*) abandonment, desertion; (*état*) neglect, state of neglect *ou* abandonment; (*Jur*) relinquishment *ou* renunciation (*of a right*).

délaisser [delese] 1 vt a (*abandonner*) *famille, ami, travail* to abandon, quit, give up. **épouse délaissée** deserted wife; **enfant délaissé** abandoned child. b (*négliger*) *famille, ami, travail* to neglect. **épouse/fillette délaissée** neglected wife/little girl. c (*Jur*) *droit* to relinquish.

délassant, e [delɑsɑ̃, ɑ̃t] adj *bain* relaxing, refreshing; *lecture* diverting, entertaining.

délassement [delɑsmɑ̃] nm (*état*) relaxation, rest; (*distraction*) relaxation, diversion.

délasser [delɑse] 1 1 vt (*reposer*) *membres* to refresh; (*divertir*) *personne, esprit* to divert, entertain. **un bon bain, ça délasse** a good bath is relaxing *ou* refreshing; **c'est un livre qui délasse** it's an entertaining *ou* a relaxing sort of book. 2 **se délasser** vpr (*se détendre*) to relax (*en faisant qch* by doing sth).

délateur, -trice [delatœʀ, tʀis] nm,f (*frm*) informer.

délation [delasjɔ̃] nf (*frm*) denouncement, informing. **une atmosphère de ~** an incriminatory atmosphere; **faire une ~** to inform.

délavage [delavaʒ] nm (*Tech: voir* **délaver**) watering down; fading; waterlogging.

délavé, e [delave] (ptp de **délaver**) adj a *tissu, jeans* faded, prefaded; *inscription* washed-out. **un ciel ~ après la pluie** a watery *ou* washed-out (blue) sky after rain. b *terre* waterlogged.

délaver [delave] 1 vt a *aquarelle* to water down; *tissu, inscription* to (cause to) fade (*by the action of water*). b *terre* to waterlog.

Delaware [dəlawɛʀ] nm Delaware.

délayage [delɛjaʒ] nm (*voir* **délayer**) thinning down; mixing; dragging-out, spinning-out; padding-out. (*péj*) **faire du ~** *[personne, écrivain]* to waffle* (*surtout Brit*); **son commentaire est un pur ~** his commentary is pure waffle* *ou* padding.

délayer [deleje] 8 vt *couleur* to thin down; (*Culin*) *farine, poudre* to mix (*to a certain consistency*) (*dans* with); (*fig péj*) *idée* to drag out, spin out; *texte* to pad out; *exposé* to pad out, spin out. **~ 100 grammes de farine dans un litre d'eau** mix 100 grammes of flour and *ou* with a litre of water; **quelques idées habilement délayées** a few ideas cleverly spun out.

Delco [dɛlko] nm ® distributor; *voir* **tête**.

délectable [delɛktabl] adj delectable.

délectation [delɛktasjɔ̃] nf delight, delectation (*littér*); (*Rel*) delight. **~ morose** delectatio morosa.

délecter [delɛkte] 1 1 vt (*littér*) to delight. 2 **se délecter** vpr: **se ~ de qch/à faire** to delight *ou* revel *ou* take delight in sth/in doing; **il se délectait** he was revelling in it, he took great delight in it, he was thoroughly enjoying it.

délégataire [delegatɛʀ] nmf proxy.

délégation [delegasjɔ̃] nf a (*groupe*) delegation; (*commission*) commission. **nous venons en ~ voir le patron** we have come as a delegation to see the boss.
b (*mandat*) delegation. **quand il est absent, sa secrétaire signe le courrier par ~** when he is away his secretary signs his letters on his authority; **il agit par ~** *ou* **en vertu d'une ~** he is acting on somebody's authority; (*Jur*) **~ de créance** assignment *ou* delegation of debt; **~ de pouvoirs** delegation of powers; (*Mil*) **~ de solde** assignment of pay (*to relatives*).
c (*Admin: succursale*) branch, office(s). **D~ générale à la recherche scientifique et technique** *bureau for technical and scientific research*.

délégué, e [delege] (ptp de **déléguer**) 1 adj delegated (*à* to). **membre ~** delegate; (*Écon*) **administrateur ~** managing director; (*Ciné*) **producteur ~** associate producer; (*Pol*) **ministre ~** ministerial delegate; **ministre ~ à la Culture** minister with special responsibility for the arts. 2 nm,f (*représentant*) delegate, representative. (*Scol*) **~ rectoral** ≃ temporary teacher; (*Scol*) **~ de classe** class representative; (*Scol*) **~ des parents** parents' representative; **~ du personnel** staff representative; **~ syndical** union representative, shop steward.

déléguer [delege] 6 vt *pouvoirs, personne* to delegate (*à* to); (*Jur*) *créance* to assign, delegate.

délestage [delɛstaʒ] nm (*Élec*) power cut; (*Aut*) diversion; *[ballon, navire]* removal of ballast (*de* from), unballasting. **établir un itinéraire de ~** to set up a relief route.

délester [delɛste] 1 1 vt *navire, ballon* to remove ballast from, unballast; (*Élec*) to cut off power from. (*Aut*) **on a délesté la RN4** a diversion has been set up on the RN4 to relieve traffic congestion; (*fig*) **~ qn d'un fardeau** to relieve sb of a burden; (*: *voler*) **~ qn de qch** to relieve sb of sth. 2 **se délester** vpr *[bateau, ballon]* to jettison ballast. (*Aviat*) **se ~ de ses bombes** (*en cas de panne*) to jettison its bombs; (*sur l'objectif*) to release its bombs; (*fig*) **elle se délesta de ses colis** she unloaded *ou* dropped her parcels.

délétère [deletɛʀ] adj *émanations, gaz* noxious, deleterious; (*fig*) *influence, propagande* pernicious, deleterious.

Delhi [dɛli] n Delhi.

déliassage [deljasaʒ] nm (*Ordin*) decollation.

déliasser [deljase] 1 vt (*Ordin*) to decollate.

délibérant, e [delibeʀɑ̃, ɑ̃t] adj deliberative.

délibération [delibeʀasjɔ̃] nf a (*débat*) deliberation, debate. **~s** proceedings, deliberations; **mettre une question en ~** to debate *ou* deliberate (over *ou* upon) an issue; **après ~ du jury** after the jury's due deliberation. b (*réflexion*) deliberation, consideration. c (*décision*) decision, resolution. **~s** resolutions; **par ~ du jury** on the jury's recommendation.

délibérative [delibeʀativ] adj f: **avoir voix ~** to have voting rights.

délibéré, e [delibeʀe] (ptp de **délibérer**) 1 adj (*intentionnel*) deliberate; (*assuré*) resolute, determined; *voir* **propos**. 2 nm (*Jur*) deliberation (*of court at end of trial*). **mettre une affaire en ~** to deliberate on a matter.

délibérément [delibeʀemɑ̃] adv (*volontairement*) deliberately, intentionally; (*après avoir réfléchi*) with due consideration; (*résolument*) resolutely.

délibérer [delibeʀe] 6 1 vi (*débattre*) (*gén*) to deliberate, confer, debate; *[jury]* to confer, deliberate; (*réfléchir*) to deliberate, consider. **après avoir mûrement délibéré** after having pondered the matter, after duly considering the matter; **~ sur une question** to deliberate (over *ou* upon) an issue. 2 **délibérer de** vt indir (*décider*) **~ de qch** to deliberate sth; **~ de faire qch** to decide *ou* resolve to do sth (after deliberation).

délicat, e [delika, at] adj a (*fin*) *dentelle, parfum, forme, couleur* delicate; *fil, voile, facture, travail* fine; *mets* dainty. **un objet gravé de facture ~e** a finely engraved object.
b (*fragile*) *tissu, fleur, enfant, santé* delicate. **il a la peau très ~e** he has very tender *ou* delicate skin; **lotion pour peaux ~es** lotion for sensitive skins.
c (*difficile*) *situation, question,* (*Méd*) *opération* delicate, tricky. **c'est ~!** it's rather delicate! *ou* tricky!; **un sujet ~** a delicate *ou* sensitive subject.
d (*gén nég*) (*scrupuleux*) *personne, conscience* scrupulous. **des procédés peu ~s** unscrupulous *ou* dishonest methods; **il ne s'est pas montré très ~ envers vous** he hasn't behaved very fairly *ou* decently towards you.
e (*raffiné*) *sentiment, goût, esprit, style* refined, delicate; *attention* thoughtful; *geste* delicate, thoughtful. **ces propos conviennent peu à des oreilles ~es** this conversation isn't suitable for delicate *ou* sensitive ears; **avoir le palais ~** to have a discerning palate.
f (*précis*) *nuance* subtle, fine, delicate; *oreille* sensitive, fine; *travail* fine, delicate.
g (*léger*) *toucher, touche* gentle, delicate. **prendre qch d'un geste ~** to take sth gently *ou* delicately.
h (*plein de tact*) tactful (*envers* to, towards).
i (*exigeant*) fussy, particular. **cet enfant est ~ pour manger** this child is fussy *ou* particular about his food; **faire le ~** (*nourriture*) to be particular *ou* fussy; (*spectacle*) to be squeamish; (*propos*) to act easily shocked.

délicatement [delikatmɑ̃] adv a (*finement*) **tableau ~ coloré** finely *ou* delicately coloured painting; **dentelle ~ ouvragée** finely *ou* delicately worked lace; **mets ~ préparé** daintily *ou* delicately prepared dish. b (*avec précision*) **exécuter un travail ~** to do a piece of work delicately *ou* finely; **nuance ~ exprimée** subtly *ou* finely *ou* delicately expressed shade of meaning. c (*avec légèreté*) **prendre qch ~ entre ses mains** to take sth gently *ou* delicately in one's hands. d (*avec raffinement*) **sentiment ~ exprimé** delicately expressed feeling.

délicatesse [delikatɛs] nf a (*finesse*) *[dentelle, parfum, couleur, forme]* delicacy; *[mets]* daintiness; *[fil, voile, facture, travail]* fineness.
b (*fragilité*) *[peau]* tenderness, delicacy; *[tissu]* delicacy.
c (*scrupules*) *[personne, procédés]* scrupulousness. **sa manière d'agir manque de ~** his behaviour is somewhat unscrupulous.
d (*raffinement*) *[sentiment, goût, esprit, style]* refinement, delicacy; *[geste]* delicacy.
e (*gén: tact*) tact; (*attentions*) thoughtfulness. **par ~ il se retira** he withdrew tactfully *ou* out of politeness.
f (*précision*) *[nuance]* subtlety, fineness, delicacy; *[oreille]* sensitivity, fineness; *[travail]* fineness, delicacy.
g (*légèreté*) gentleness. **il prit le vase avec ~** he picked up the vase gently *ou* delicately.
h (*caractère complexe*) *[situation, question],* (*Méd*) *[opération]* delicacy.
i (*prévenances: gén pl*) consideration (*NonC*), (kind) attentions. **avoir des ~s pour qn** to show attentions to sb, show consideration for sb.

délice [delis] nm (*plaisir*) delight. **quel ~ de s'allonger au soleil!** what a delight to lie in the sun!; **se plonger dans l'eau avec ~** to jump into the water with sheer delight; **ce dessert est un vrai ~** this dessert is quite delightful *ou* delicious.

délices [delis] nfpl (*plaisirs*) delights. **les ~ de l'étude** the delights of study; **toutes les ~ de la terre se trouvaient réunies là** every worldly delight was to be found there; **faire ses ~ de qch** to take delight in sth; **cette vie rustique ferait les ~ de mon père** this country life would be the delight of my father; **ce livre ferait les ~ de mon père** this book would be a delight to *ou* would delight my father, my father would revel in this book.

délicieusement [delisjøzmɑ̃] adv delightfully, exquisitely. **elle chante ~ (bien)** she sings delightfully (well); **c'est ~ beau** it's exquisitely beautiful; **une poire ~ parfumée** a deliciously *ou* delightfully scented pear; **s'enfoncer ~ dans les couvertures** to snuggle down under the covers with delight.

délicieux, -ieuse [delisjø, jøz] adj *fruit* delicious; *goût* delicious, delightful; *lieu, personne, sensation, anecdote* charming, delightful.

délictueux, -euse [deliktɥø, øz] adj (*Jur*) criminal. **fait ~** criminal act.

délié, e [delje] (ptp de **délier**) 1 adj a (*agile*) *doigts* nimble, agile; *esprit* astute, penetrating. **avoir la langue ~e** to have a ready tongue. b (*fin*) *taille* slender; *fil, écriture* fine. 2 nm *[lettre]* (thin) upstroke. **les pleins et les ~s** the downstrokes and the upstrokes (*in handwriting*); (*Mus*) **avoir un bon ~** to have a flowing *ou* an even touch.

délier [delje] 7 1 vt a *corde, paquet, prisonnier* to untie; *gerbe* to unbind. **déliez-lui les mains** untie his hands; (*fig*) **~ la langue de qn** to loosen sb's tongue; *voir* **bourse**. b **~ qn de** *obligation, serment* to free *ou* release sb from; (*Rel*) *péché* to absolve sb from. 2 **se délier** vpr a *[lien]* to come untied; *[prisonnier]* to untie o.s., get (o.s.) free; *[langue]* to loosen. **sous l'effet de l'alcool les langues se délient** as alcohol starts to take effect tongues are loosened. b **se ~ d'un serment** to free *ou* release o.s. from an oath.

délimitation [delimitasjɔ̃] nf (*voir* **délimiter**) demarcation; delimitation; definition; determination.

délimiter [delimite] 1 vt *terrain, frontière* to demarcate, delimit; *sujet, rôle* to define (the scope of), delimit; *responsabilités, attributions* to determine.

délinquance [delɛ̃kɑ̃s] nf criminality. **~ juvénile** juvenile delinquency.

délinquant, e [delɛ̃kɑ̃, ɑ̃t] 1 adj delinquent. **la jeunesse ~e** juvenile delinquents *ou* offenders. 2 nm,f delinquent, offender. **~ primaire** first offender.

déliquescence [delikesɑ̃s] nf a (*Chim: action*) deliquescence. b (*fig*) decay. **tomber en ~** to fall into decay.

déliquescent, e [delikesɑ̃, ɑ̃t] adj a (*Chim*) deliquescent. b (*fig*) *personne* decrepit; *esprit* enfeebled; *régime, mœurs, société* decaying; *atmosphère* devitalizing.

délirant, e [deliʀɑ̃, ɑ̃t] adj *idée, architecture* extraordinary, wild.

délire [deliʀ] 1 nm a (*Méd*) delirium. **dans un accès de ~** in a fit of delirium; **c'est du ~!*** it's sheer madness! *ou* lunacy!
b (*frénésie*) frenzy. **sa passion allait jusqu'au ~** his passion was almost frenzied; **dans le ~ de son imagination** in his wild *ou* frenzied imagination; **acclamé par une foule en ~** acclaimed by a crowd gone wild *ou* berserk *ou* by a frenzied crowd; **quand l'acteur parut, ce fut le *ou* du ~*** when the actor appeared there was a frenzy of excitement.
2 comp ▸**délire alcoolique** alcoholic mania ▸**délire de grandeur** delusions of grandeur ▸**délire hallucinatoire** hallucinatory delirium ▸**délire de persécution** persecution mania ▸**délire poétique** (*Littérat*) poetic frenzy.

délirer [deliʀe] 1 vi (*Méd*) to be delirious. **~ de joie** to be in a frenzy of delight, be delirious with joy; **il délire!*** he's raving!*, he's out of his mind!*

délirium tremens [deliʀjɔmtʀemɛ̃s] nm delirium tremens.

délit [deli] nm (*gén*) crime, offence; (*Jur*) (criminal) offence, misdemeanour (*US*). **~ de fuite** failure to report an accident; **~ de presse** violation of the press laws; **être poursuivi pour ~ d'opinion** to be prosecuted for one's beliefs *ou* convictions; **~ d'initié** insider dealing *ou* trading; *voir* **corps, flagrant**.

déliter (se) [delite] 1 vpr (*lit*) to disintegrate (*because of exposure to moisture*); (*fig*) to disintegrate.

délivrance [delivʀɑ̃s] nf a *[prisonniers]* release; *[pays]* deliverance, liberation. b (*fig: soulagement*) relief. **il est parti, quelle ~!** he's gone – what a relief! c *[passeport, reçu]* issue, delivery; *[ordonnance]* issue; *[lettre, marchandise]* delivery. (*Jur*) **~ d'un brevet** issue of a patent. d (*littér: accouchement*) delivery, confinement.

délivrer [delivʀe] 1 1 vt a *prisonnier, esclave* to set free. **~ qn de**

rival to relieve *ou* rid sb of; *liens, obligation* to free sb from, relieve sb of; *crainte* to relieve sb of; **être** *ou* **se sentir délivré d'un grand poids** to be *ou* feel relieved of a great weight. **b** *passeport, reçu* to issue, deliver; *lettre, marchandise* to deliver; *ordonnance* to give, issue. **2 se délivrer** vpr *[prisonnier etc]* to free o.s. (*de* from); (*fig*) to get relief (*de* from).

délocalisation [delɔkalizasjɔ̃] nf relocation.

délocaliser [delɔkalize] 1 vt (*gén*) to relocate; (*à l'étranger*) to offshore.

déloger [delɔʒe] 3 **1** vt *locataire* to turn *ou* throw out; *fugitif* to flush out; *lièvre* to start; *objet, ennemi* to dislodge (*de* from). **2** vi to move out (*in a hurry*). **délogez de là!** clear out of there!*

déloquer (se)‡ [delɔke] 1 vpr (*se déshabiller*) to peel off*.

déloyal, e, mpl **-aux** [delwajal, o] adj *ami* unfaithful, disloyal (*envers* towards); *adversaire* underhand; *conduite* disloyal, underhand; *procédé* unfair; (*Sport*) *coup* foul (*épith*), dirty (*épith*). (*Comm*) **concurrence ~e** unfair competition.

déloyalement [delwajalmɑ̃] adv disloyally.

déloyauté [delwajote] nf **a** (*NonC: voir* **déloyal**) disloyalty; unfairness. **b** (*action*) disloyal act.

Delphes [dɛlf] n Delphi.

delta [dɛlta] nm (*Géog, Ling*) delta. **le ~ du Mékong** the Mekong delta; (*Aviat*) **à ailes (en) ~** delta-winged.

deltaïque [dɛltaik] adj deltaic, delta (*épith*).

deltaplane [dɛltaplan] nm ® (*appareil*) hang-glider; (*sport*) hang gliding. **faire du ~** to hang glide, go hang gliding.

deltoïde [dɛltɔid] adj, nm (*Méd*) deltoid.

déluge [delyʒ] nm (*pluie*) downpour, deluge; *[larmes, paroles, injures]* flood; *[compliments, coups]* shower. (*Bible*) **le ~** the Flood, the Deluge; **ça date du ~, ça remonte au ~** it's ancient history; *voir* **après**.

déluré, e [delyʀe] (ptp de **délurer**) adj **a** (*débrouillard*) smart, resourceful. **b** (*impertinent*) (*gén*) forward, pert; *fille* saucy, sassy* (*US*).

délurer [delyʀe] 1 **1** vt (*dégourdir*) to make smart *ou* resourceful, teach a thing or two to*; (*péj*) to make forward *ou* pert. **2 se délurer** vpr (*se dégourdir*) to become smart *ou* resourceful; (*péj*) to become forward *ou* pert. **il s'est déluré au régiment** he became something of a smart lad *ou* he learnt a thing or two* in the army.

démagnétisation [demaɲetizasjɔ̃] nf demagnetization.

démagnétiser [demaɲetize] 1 vt to demagnetize.

démago* [demago] **1** adj abrév de **démagogique**. **2** nmf abrév de **démagogue**.

démagogie [demagɔʒi] nf demagogy, demagoguery.

démagogique [demagɔʒik] adj *discours, réforme* popularity-seeking, demagogic.

démagogue [demagɔg] **1** nm demagogue. **2** adj: **être ~** to be a demagogue.

démaillage [demɑjaʒ] nm *[bas]* laddering (*Brit*); *[tricot]* undoing, unravelling.

démailler [demɑje] 1 **1** vt *bas* to ladder (*Brit*); *filet* to undo (the mesh of); *tricot* to undo (the stitches of), unravel; *chaîne* to unlink, separate the links of. **ses bas sont démaillés** her stockings are laddered (*Brit*) *ou* have got ladders (*Brit*) in them. **2 se démailler** vpr *[bas]* to ladder (*Brit*), run; *[tricot, filet]* to unravel, come unravelled. **la chaîne s'est démaillée** the links of the chain have come apart.

démailloter [demajɔte] 1 vt *enfant* to take off the nappy of (*Brit*) *ou* diaper of (*US*).

demain [d(ə)mɛ̃] adv tomorrow. **~ matin** tomorrow morning; **~ soir** tomorrow evening *ou* night; **~ en huit/en quinze** a week/two weeks tomorrow; **à dater** *ou* **à partir de ~** (as) from tomorrow, from tomorrow on; **~ il fera jour** tomorrow is another day; **ce n'est pas ~ la veille*, ce n'est pas pour ~*** it's not just around the corner, it's not going to happen in a hurry; **~ on rase gratis!*** tomorrow never comes!; **~ est jour férié** tomorrow is a holiday; **à ~** (*gén*) see you tomorrow; (*je téléphonerai*) I'll talk to you tomorrow; **d'ici (à) ~ tout peut changer** everything might be different by tomorrow; (*fig*) **le monde de ~** the world of tomorrow, tomorrow's world; *voir* **après, remettre**.

démanché, e [demɑ̃ʃe] (ptp de **démancher**) **1** adj *bras* out of joint (*attrib*), dislocated; (*) *objet* loose; *meuble* rickety. **le marteau est ~** the hammer has no handle *ou* has lost its handle. **2** nm (*Mus*) shift.

démancher [demɑ̃ʃe] 1 **1** vt *outil* to take the handle off; (*: *disloquer*) *meuble* to knock a leg off; *bras* to put out of joint, dislocate. **2** vi (*Mus*) to shift. **3 se démancher** vpr **a** *[outil]* to lose its handle; *[bras]* to be put out of joint, be dislocated; (*) *[meuble, objet]* to fall to bits. **se ~ le bras** to dislocate one's arm, put one's arm out of joint. **b** (*: *se mettre en quatre*) to go out of one's way, move heaven and earth (*pour faire* to do).

demande [d(ə)mɑ̃d] nf **a** (*requête*) request (*de qch* for sth); (*revendication*) claim, demand (*de* for); (*Admin*) *[emploi, autorisation, naturalisation]* application (*de* for); *[remboursement, dédommagement]* claim (*de* for); *[renseignement]* enquiry; (*Écon: opposé à offre*) demand; (*Cartes*) bid. (*gén*) **faire une ~** to make a request; **faire une ~ d'emploi/de naturalisation** to apply for a post/for naturalization; (*formulaire*) **remplir une ~** to fill in a claim form (*de* for); (*annonces*) **"~s d'emploi"** "situations wanted"; **~ d'adhésion** application for membership; *[ravisseurs]* **faire une ~ de rançon** to make a ransom demand; **faire une ~ de remboursement** to put in *ou* make a request for reimbursement (*à qn* to sb), request reimbursement (*à qn* from sb); (*Écon*) **pour répondre à la ~ (de pétrole/de fruits)** to meet the demand (for oil/fruit); **et maintenant, à la ~ générale ...** and now, by popular request ...; (*Admin*) **adressez votre ~ au ministère** apply to the ministry; **~ (en mariage)** proposal (of marriage); **faire sa ~ (en mariage)** to propose; **à** *ou* **sur la ~ de qn** at sb's request; **à la ~, sur ~** on request; (*Admin*) on application.

b (*Jur*) **~ en divorce** divorce petition; **~ en renvoi** request for remittal; **~ principale/accessoire/subsidiaire** chief/secondary/contingency petition; **introduire une ~ reconventionnelle** to bring a counterclaim.

c (*besoins*) *[malade, enfant]* needs (*pl*). **~ d'affection** need for affection.

d (†: *question*) question.

demandé, e [d(ə)mɑ̃de] (ptp de **demander**) adj (*Comm etc*) in demand. **cet article est très ~** this item is (very) much in demand, there is a great demand for this item; *[médecin, chanteur]* **il est très ~** he is (very) much in demand *ou* sought after.

demander [d(ə)mɑ̃de] 1 **1** vt **a** (*solliciter*) *chose, conseil, réponse, entrevue* to ask for, request (*frm*); *volontaire* to call for, ask for; (*Admin, Jur*) *délai, emploi, divorce* to apply for; *indemnité, remboursement* to claim; *réunion, enquête* to call for, ask for. **~ qch à qn** to ask sb for sth; **~ un service** *ou* **une faveur à qn** to ask sb a favour; (*Mil*) **~ une permission** to ask for *ou* request (*frm*) leave; **~ la permission de faire** to ask *ou* request (*frm*) permission to do; **~ à voir qn/à parler à qn** to ask to see sb/to speak to sb; **~ à qn de faire** *ou* **qu'il fasse qch** to ask *ou* request (*frm*) sb to do sth; **il a demandé à partir plus tôt** he has asked to leave early *ou* earlier; **~ la paix** to sue for peace; **puis-je vous ~ (de me passer) du pain?** may I trouble you for some bread?, would you mind passing me some bread?; **vous n'avez qu'à ~, il n'y a qu'à ~** you only have to ask.

b (*appeler*) *médecin, prêtre, plombier* to send for. **il va falloir ~ un médecin** we'll have to send for *ou* call (for) a doctor; **le blessé demande un prêtre** the injured man is asking *ou* calling for a priest.

c (*au téléphone, au bureau etc*) *personne, numéro* to ask for. (*au téléphone*) **demandez-moi M. X** get me Mr X; **qui demandez-vous?** who do you wish to speak to?; **on le demande au bureau/au téléphone** he is wanted at the office/on the phone, someone is asking for him at the office/on the phone; **le patron vous demande** the boss wants to see you *ou* speak to you *ou* is asking to see you.

d (*désirer*) to be asking for, want. **ils demandent 50 F de l'heure et une semaine de congé** they are asking (for) 50 francs an hour and a week's holiday; **il demande à partir plus tôt** he wants to *ou* is asking to leave early *ou* earlier; **il demande qu'on le laisse partir** he wants us to *ou* is asking us to let him go; **il ne demande qu'à apprendre/à se laisser convaincre** all he wants is to learn/to be convinced, he's more than willing to learn/be convinced; **le chat miaule, il demande son lait** the cat's mewing — he's asking for his milk; **je ne demande pas mieux!** *ou* **que ça!** that's exactly *ou* just what I'd like!, I'll be *ou* I'm only too pleased!; **il ne demandera pas mieux que de vous aider** he'll be only too pleased to help you; **je demande à voir!*** that I must see!; **tout ce que l'on demande c'est qu'il fasse beau** all (that) we ask is that we have good weather.

e (*s'enquérir de*) *heure, nom, chemin* to ask. **~ l'heure à qn** to ask sb the time; **~ un renseignement à qn** to ask sb for some information; **je lui ai demandé son nom** I asked him his name; **~ quand/comment/pourquoi c'est arrivé** to ask when/how/why it happened; **~ des nouvelles de qn, ~ après qn*** to enquire *ou* ask after sb; **va ~!** go and ask!; **je ne t'ai rien demandé** I didn't ask you; **je ne te demande rien** I'm not asking you; **on ne t'a pas demandé l'heure (qu'il était)*** *ou* **ton avis*** who asked you?, who rattled your cage?‡; (*excl*) **je vous le demande!, je vous demande un peu!*** honestly!*, what do you think of that!

f (*nécessiter*) *[travail, décision etc]* to require, need. **cela demande un effort** it requires an effort; **ces plantes demandent beaucoup d'eau/à être arrosées** these plants need *ou* require a lot of water/watering; **ce travail va (lui) ~ six heures** this job will take (him) 6 hours *ou* will require 6 hours, he'll need 6 hours to do this job; **cette proposition demande réflexion** this proposal needs thinking over; **cette proposition demande toute votre attention** this proposal calls for *ou* requires your full attention.

g (*exiger*) **~ qch de** *ou* **à qn** to ask sth of sb; **il demande de ses employés qu'ils travaillent bien** he asks *ou* requires of his employees that they work well; **~ beaucoup à** *ou* **de la vie/de ses élèves** to ask a lot of life/of one's pupils; **il ne faut pas trop lui en ~!** you mustn't ask too much of him!

h (*Comm*) **ils (en) demandent 50 F** they are asking *ou* want 50 francs (for it); **ils m'en ont demandé 50 F** they asked (me) for 50 francs for it; **"on demande une vendeuse"** "shop assistant required *ou* wanted"; **ils demandent 3 vendeuses** they are advertising for *ou* they want 3 shop assistants; **on demande beaucoup de vendeuses en ce moment** shop assistants are very much in demand *ou* are in great demand just now; **comme vous l'avez demandé dans votre lettre du 25**

janvier as requested in your letter of 25th January.

i (*loc*) ~ **aide et assistance** to request aid (*à* from); ~ **audience** to request an audience (*à, auprès de* with); ~ **l'aumône** *ou* **la charité** to ask *ou* beg for charity; ~ **grâce** to ask for mercy; ~ **l'impossible** to ask the impossible; ~ **pardon à qn** to apologize to sb (*de qch* for sth); **je vous demande pardon** I apologize, I'm sorry; (*fig*) **je vous demande pardon, mais ...!** I beg your pardon but ...!; ~ **la lune** to ask for the moon; ~ **la parole** to ask to be allowed to speak; **il l'a demandée en mariage** he asked if he could marry her; ~ **la main de qn** to ask for sb's hand (in marriage); **il est parti sans ~ son reste** he left without a murmur; (*hum*) **que demande le peuple?** what more could you ask for?

2 **se demander** vpr (*hésiter, douter*) to wonder. **on peut vraiment se ~ ou c'est à se ~ s'il a perdu la tête** one may well wonder *ou* ask if he isn't out of his mind; **il se demande où aller/ce qu'il doit faire** he is wondering where to go/what to do; **il se demanda: suis-je vraiment aussi bête?** he asked himself *ou* wondered: am I really so stupid?; **ils se demandent bien pourquoi il a démissionné** they can't think why he resigned, they really wonder why he resigned; **cela ne se demande pas!** that's a stupid question!

demandeur[1], -deresse [d(ə)mɑ̃dœʀ, dʀɛs] nm,f (*Jur*) plaintiff, complainant; (*en divorce*) petitioner. ~ **en appel** appellant; **la partie demanderesse** the moving party.

demandeur[2], -euse [d(ə)mɑ̃dœʀ, øz] nm,f (*Téléc*) caller. **ils sont très ~s (de nos produits)** they are eager buyers (of our goods); **s'il existe un bon dictionnaire, je suis ~** if there is such a thing as a good dictionary I'm interested; ~ **d'emploi** person looking for work, job-seeker; (*Admin*) **le nombre des ~s d'emploi a baissé** the number of those seeking work has fallen.

démangeaison [demɑ̃ʒɛzɔ̃] nf itching (*NonC*), itching sensation. **avoir des ~s** to be itching; **j'ai des ~s dans le dos** my back is itching; **j'ai une ~** I've got an itch.

démanger [demɑ̃ʒe] 3 vt: **son dos/son coup de soleil le** *ou* **lui démange** his back/sunburn itches *ou* is itching; **où est-ce que ça (vous) démange?** where does it *ou* do you itch?, where is it *ou* are you itching?; **ça (me) démange** it itches, it's itching, it makes me itch; (*fig*) **le poing le démange** he's itching* for a fight; (*fig*) **la main me démange** I'm itching* *ou* dying to hit him (*ou* her *etc*); (*fig*) **la langue me démange** I'm itching* *ou* dying to speak; (*fig*) **ça me démange de faire ..., l'envie me démange de faire ...** I'm dying to do ... .

démantèlement [demɑ̃tɛlmɑ̃] nm (*voir* **démanteler**) demolition, demolishing; breaking up; bringing down; cracking; dismantling.

démanteler [demɑ̃t(ə)le] 5 vt (*Mil*) *forteresse, remparts* to demolish; *organisation, gang* to break up; (*fig*) *empire, monarchie* to bring down; *réseau d'espionnage* to crack; *compagnie, service* to dismantle.

démantibuler* [demɑ̃tibyle] 1 1 vt *objet* to demolish, break up. 2 **se démantibuler** vpr to fall apart. **se ~ le bras** to dislocate one's arm.

démaquillage [demakijaʒ] nm removal of make-up. **le ~ d'un acteur** the removal of an actor's make-up; **l'acteur commença son ~** the actor started to take off *ou* remove his make-up; **crème pour le ~** make-up remover, make-up removing cream.

démaquillant, e [demakijɑ̃, ɑ̃t] 1 adj make-up removing (*épith*). 2 nm make-up remover.

démaquiller [demakije] 1 1 vt *yeux, visage* to remove the make-up from, take the make-up off. ~ **un acteur** to take off *ou* remove an actor's make-up. 2 **se démaquiller** vpr to take one's make-up off, remove one's make-up.

démarcage [demaʀkaʒ] = **démarquage**.

démarcatif, -ive [demaʀkatif, iv] adj demarcating.

démarcation [demaʀkasjɔ̃] nf demarcation (*de, entre* between); *voir* **ligne[1]**.

démarchage [demaʀʃaʒ] nm (*Comm*) door-to-door *ou* doorstep selling, canvassing. (*Pol*) ~ **électoral** canvassing; **faire du ~** (*Comm*) to do door-to-door selling; (*Pol*) to canvass.

démarche [demaʀʃ] nf a (*façon de marcher*) gait, walk. **avoir une ~ pesante/gauche** to have a heavy/an awkward gait *ou* walk, walk heavily/awkwardly. b (*intervention*) step, move. **faire une ~ auprès de qn (pour obtenir qch)** to approach sb (to obtain sth); **toutes nos ~s se sont trouvées sans effet** none of the steps we took was effective; **les ~s nécessaires pour obtenir qch** the necessary *ou* required procedures *ou* steps *ou* moves to obtain sth; **l'idée de (faire) cette ~ m'effrayait** I was frightened at the idea of (taking) this step *ou* of (making) this move. c (*cheminement*) *[raisonnement, pensée]* processes. ~ **intellectuelle** thought processes.

démarcher [demaʀʃe] 1 vt *clients* to canvass; *produit* to sell door-to-door.

démarcheur [demaʀʃœʀ] nm (*vendeur*) door-to-door *ou* doorstep salesman, canvasser; (*Pol*) (door-to-door) canvasser.

démarcheuse [demaʀʃøz] nf (*vendeuse*) door-to-door saleswoman; (*pour un parti etc*) (door-to-door) canvasser.

démarier [demaʀje] 7 vt (*Agr*) to thin out.

démarquage [demaʀkaʒ] nm *[linge, argenterie]* removal of the identifying mark(s) (*de* on); *[auteur, œuvre]* copying (*de* from). (*Sport*) **le ~ d'un joueur** the drawing away of a player's marker; **cet ouvrage est un ~ grossier** this work is a crude plagiarism *ou* copy.

démarque [demaʀk] nf (*Comm*) *[article]* markdown, marking-down. ~ **inconnue** shortfall (*in stock*).

démarqué, e [demaʀke] (ptp de **démarquer**) adj (*Sport*) *joueur* unmarked. **robe ~e** unlabelled designer dress.

démarquer [demaʀke] 1 1 vt a *linge, argenterie* to remove the (identifying) mark(s) from; (*Comm*) *article* to mark down. b *œuvre, auteur* to plagiarize, copy. c (*Sport*) *joueur* to draw a marker away from. 2 **se démarquer** vpr (*Sport*) to lose *ou* shake off one's marker. (*fig*) **se ~ de** to distinguish *ou* differentiate o.s. from.

démarrage [demaʀaʒ] 1 nm a (*départ*) *[véhicule]* moving off (*NonC*). ~ **en trombe** shooting off (*NonC*); **il a calé au ~** he stalled as he moved off; **secoués à chaque ~ du bus** shaken about every time the bus moved off.

b (*fig*) *[affaire, campagne, élève, débutant]* start. **l'excellent/le difficile ~ de la campagne électorale** the excellent/difficult start to the electoral campaign.

c (*Sport: accélération*) *[coureur]* pulling away (*NonC*). **il a placé un ~ à 100 m de l'arrivée** he put on a burst of speed *ou* he pulled away 100 metres from the finishing line.

d (*Naut*) casting off, unmooring.

e (*mise en marche*) *[véhicule]* starting. **le ~ d'une affaire/campagne** getting an affair/a campaign going.

2 comp ▸**démarrage en côte** hill start ▸**démarrage à la manivelle** crank-starting.

démarrer [demaʀe] 1 1 vi a *[moteur, conducteur]* to start (up); *[véhicule]* to move off; (*fig*) *[affaire, campagne]* to get moving, get off the ground; *[élève, débutant]* to start off. **l'affaire a bien démarré** the affair got off to a good *ou* fast start *ou* started off well; ~ **en trombe** to shoot off; **faire ~** *affaire, campagne* to get moving, get off the ground; **l'économie va-t-elle enfin ~?** is the economy at last going to take off? *ou* get moving? *ou* going to get off the ground?; **il a bien démarré en latin** he has got off to a good start in Latin, he started off well in Latin; *voir* **froid**.

b (*Sport: accélérer*) *[coureur]* to pull away.

c (*Naut*) to cast off, unmoor.

2 **démarrer de** vt indir (*démordre de*) *idée, projet* to let go of. **il ne veut pas ~ de son idée** he just won't let go of his idea.

3 vt *véhicule* to start, get started; (*Naut*) *embarcation* to cast off, unmoor; (* *fig*) *affaire, travail* to get going on*. ~ **qn en anglais** to get sb started at English.

démarreur [demaʀœʀ] nm (*Aut*) starter.

démasquer [demaske] 1 1 vt a (*dévoiler*) *imposteur, espion, hypocrisie* to unmask; *plan* to unveil, uncover. ~ **ses batteries** (*Mil*) to unmask one's guns; (*fig*) to show one's hand, lay one's cards on the table. b (*enlever le masque de*) to unmask. 2 **se démasquer** vpr *[imposteur]* to drop one's mask; *[enfant déguisé]* to take off one's mask.

dématage [demataʒ] nm (*voir* **démâter**) dismasting; losing its masts.

démâter [demate] 1 1 vt to dismast. 2 vi to lose its masts, be dismasted.

d'emblée [dɑ̃ble] *voir* **emblée**.

démêlage [demɛlaʒ] nm (*lit, fig*) disentangling, untangling.

démêlant, e [demɛlɑ̃, ɑ̃t] 1 adj (hair) conditioning. 2 nm (hair) conditioner.

démêlé [demele] nm (*dispute*) dispute, quarrel. (*ennuis*) ~**s** problems; **il a eu des ~s avec la justice** he has fallen foul of the law *ou* has had some problems *ou* trouble with the law, he has had a brush with the law; **il risque d'avoir des ~s avec l'administration** he's likely to come up against the authorities.

démêler [demele] 1 1 vt a *ficelle, écheveau* to disentangle, untangle; *cheveux* to untangle, comb out; (*fig*) *problème, situation* to untangle, sort out; (*fig*) *intentions, machinations* to unravel, get to the bottom of. ~ **qch d'avec** *ou* **de** to distinguish *ou* tell sth from; ~ **le vrai du faux** to sort the truth out from the lies *ou* falsehood. b (*littér: débattre*) ~ **qch avec qn** to dispute sth with sb; **je ne veux rien avoir à ~ avec lui** I do not wish to have to contend with him. 2 **se démêler** vpr (†, *littér: se tirer de*) **se ~ de** *embarras, difficultés* to disentangle o.s. from, extricate o.s. from.

démêloir [demɛlwaʀ] nm (large-toothed) comb.

démêlures [demelyʀ] nfpl combings.

démembrement [demɑ̃bʀəmɑ̃] nm (*voir* **démembrer**) dismemberment; slicing up.

démembrer [demɑ̃bʀe] 1 vt *animal* to dismember; *domaine, pays conquis* to slice up, carve up.

déménagement [demenaʒmɑ̃] nm a *[meubles]* removal (*Brit*), moving (*US*); *[pièce]* emptying (of furniture) (*NonC*). **camion de ~** removal (*Brit*) *ou* moving (*US*) van; **le ~ du mobilier s'est bien passé** moving the furniture *ou* the removal of the furniture went off well; **le ~ du bureau/laboratoire a posé des problèmes** moving the furniture out of the office/laboratory *ou* emptying the office/laboratory of (its) furniture proved (to be) no easy matter; **ils ont fait 4 ~s en 3 jours** they did 4 removals in 3 days.

b (*changement de domicile*) move, moving (house) (*NonC*). **faire un ~** to move (house); **on a dû perdre ça pendant le ~** we must have lost that during the move; **3 ~s en une année, c'est trop** 3 moves in one year is too much, moving (house) 3 times in one year is too much.

déménager [demenaʒe] 3 1 vt *meubles, affaires* to move, remove (*Brit*); *maison, pièce* to move the furniture out of, empty (of furniture). 2 vi a to move (house). ~ **à la cloche de bois** to do a moonlight flit* (*Brit*), sneak off in the middle of the night. b (‡) (*partir*) to clear off‡; (*aller très vite*) to shift*. **allez, déménage!** buzz off!*, hop it!*; **il nous a fait** ~ he sent us packing*. c (‡: *être fou*) to be off one's rocker‡. d **ça déménage!*** it's brilliant* *ou* great* *ou* fantastic!

déménageur [demenaʒœʀ] nm (*entrepreneur*) furniture remover; (*ouvrier*) removal man (*Brit*), (furniture) mover (*US*).

démence [demɑ̃s] nf (*Méd*) dementia; (*Jur*) mental disorder; (*gén*) madness, insanity. (*fig*) **c'est de la** ~ it's (sheer) madness *ou* lunacy, it's insane; (*Méd*) ~ **précoce** dementia praecox.

démener (se) [dem(ə)ne] 5 vpr (*se débattre*) to thrash about, struggle (violently); (*se dépenser*) to exert o.s. **se** ~ **comme un beau diable** (*pour se sauver*) to thrash about *ou* struggle violently; (*pour obtenir qch*) to make a tremendous effort, go to great lengths; **si on se démène un peu on aura fini avant la nuit** if we put our back(s) into it a bit* *ou* if we exert ourselves a bit we'll finish before nightfall; **ils se démenèrent tant et si bien que ...** they exerted themselves to such an extent that ..., they made such a great effort that ... .

dément, e [demɑ̃, ɑ̃t] 1 adj (*fou*) mad, insane, crazy; (*incroyable*) incredible, unbelievable; (*: *extravagant*) *type, musique* way-out*, weird*; *prix, projet* mad, crazy. 2 nm,f (*Méd*) lunatic, demented person.

démenti [demɑ̃ti] nm (*déclaration*) denial, refutation; (*fig: apporté par les faits, les circonstances*) refutation. **opposer un** ~ **à** *nouvelle, allégations, rumeurs* to deny formally; **publier un** ~ to publish a denial; **sa version des faits reste sans** ~ his version of the facts remains uncontradicted *ou* unchallenged; (*fig*) **son expression opposait un** ~ **à ses paroles** his expression belied his words.

démentiel, -ielle [demɑ̃sjɛl] adj *projet, prix* insane.

démentir [demɑ̃tiʀ] 16 1 vt a *[personne] nouvelle, rumeur* to refute, deny; *personne* to contradict. ~ **(formellement) que ...** to deny absolutely that ...; **il dément ses principes par son attitude** his attitude contradicts his principles.

b *[faits] témoignage* to refute; *apparences* to belie; *espoirs* to disappoint. **la douceur de son sourire est démentie par la dureté de son regard** the hardness in her eyes belies the sweetness of her smile; **les résultats ont démenti les pronostics des spécialistes** the results have contradicted the predictions of the specialists.

2 **se démentir** vpr (*nég: cesser*) **son amitié/sa fidélité ne s'est jamais démentie** his friendship/loyalty has never failed; **roman dont le succès ne s'est jamais démenti** novel which has always maintained its popularity; **leur intérêt pour ces mystères, qui ne s'est jamais démenti** their unfailing *ou* never-failing interest in these mysteries.

démerdard‡ [demɛʀdaʀ] 1 nm shrewd customer*. 2 adj m: **il est** ~ he's a shrewd customer*, there are no flies on him (*Brit*); **il n'est pas** ~ **pour deux sous** he's bloody clueless‡ (*Brit*), he hasn't (got) a clue*; **dans la vie il faut être** ~ you have to learn to look after yourself in life.

démerder (se)‡ [demɛʀde] 1 vpr a (*se débrouiller*) to manage. **il sait se** ~ **dans la vie** he knows how to look after himself all right*, he knows his way around all right*; **elle se démerde (pas mal) au ski/en peinture** she gets by (all right) in skiing/in painting; **si je m'étais mieux démerdé, j'aurais gagné** if I'd known how to handle things better, I'd have won; **il s'est démerdé pour avoir une permission** he wangled himself some leave*, he wangled it so that he got some leave*.

b (*se tirer d'affaire*) to get out of the shit*‡ *ou* a mess. **il a voulu y aller, maintenant qu'il se démerde tout seul** he wanted to go so now he can get out of his own bloody (*Brit*) *ou* damn mess‡.

démerdeur‡ [demɛʀdœʀ] = **démerdard‡**.

démérite [demeʀit] nm (*littér*) demerit (*littér*), fault. **où est son** ~, **dans ce cas?** where is he at fault *ou* wherein lies his fault in this matter? (*littér*); **son** ~ **fut d'avoir ...** his fault *ou* demerit was to have ... .

démériter [demeʀite] 1 1 **démériter de** vt indir *patrie, institution* to show o.s. unworthy of. 2 vi (*Rel*) to deserve to fall from grace. (*gén*) ~ **auprès de qn** *ou* **aux yeux de qn** to come down in sb's eyes; **en quoi a-t-il démérité?** how was he to blame?; **il n'a jamais démérité** he has never been guilty of an unworthy action; **l'équipe perdante n'a cependant pas démérité** the losing team nevertheless put up a creditable performance.

démesure [dem(ə)zyʀ] nf *[personnage]* excessiveness, immoderation; *[propos, exigences, style]* outrageousness, immoderateness.

démesuré, e [dem(ə)zyʀe] adj *orgueil, ambition, prétentions,* inordinate, immoderate; *taille* disproportionate; *territoire, distances* vast, enormous; *membres* enormous.

démesurément [dem(ə)zyʀemɑ̃] adv *exagérer* immoderately, inordinately; *augmenter* disproportionately. **territoire qui s'étendait** ~ territory of vast *ou* inordinate proportions; ~ **long** disproportionately *ou* inordinately long.

démettre [demɛtʀ] 56 1 vt a (*disloquer*) *articulation* to dislocate. **se** ~ **le poignet/la cheville** to dislocate one's wrist/ankle, put one's wrist/ankle out of joint. b (*révoquer*) ~ **qn de ses fonctions/son poste** to dismiss sb from his duties/post. c (*Jur*) ~ **qn de son appel** to dismiss sb's appeal. 2 **se démettre** vpr (*frm: démissionner*) to resign, hand in one's resignation. **se** ~ **de ses fonctions/son poste** to resign (from) one's duties/post, hand in one's resignation.

demeurant [d(ə)mœʀɑ̃] nm: **au** ~ incidentally.

demeure [d(ə)mœʀ] nf a (*maison*) residence; (*littér: domicile*) residence, dwelling place (*littér*); *voir* **dernier**. b (*loc*) **à** ~ *installations* permanent; *domestique* live-in, resident. **s'installer à** ~ **dans la ville** to make one's permanent home *ou* set o.s. up permanently in the town; **il ne faudrait pas qu'ils y restent à** ~ they mustn't stay there permanently; **mettre qn en** ~ **de faire qch** to instruct *ou* order sb to do sth; (*Jur*) **mettre qn en** ~ **de payer/de partir** to give sb notice to pay/to quit *ou* leave; *voir* **mise[2]**.

demeuré, e [d(ə)mœʀe] (ptp de **demeurer**) 1 adj half-witted. 2 nm,f half-wit.

demeurer [d(ə)mœʀe] 1 vi a (*avec aux avoir*) ~ **quelque part** (*habiter*) to live somewhere; (*séjourner*) to stay somewhere; **il demeure au 24 rue d'Ulm** he lives at number 24 (in the) rue d'Ulm.

b (*frm: avec aux être*) (*avec attrib, adv de lieu: rester*) to remain; (*subsister*) to remain. ~ **fidèle/quelque part** to remain faithful/somewhere; **il lui faut** ~ **couché** he must remain in bed; **l'odeur demeurait dans la pièce** the smell lingered in the room; **la conversation en est demeurée là** the conversation was taken no further *ou* was left at that.

c (*frm: être transmis*) ~ **à qn** to be left to sb; **la maison leur est demeurée de leur mère** the house was left to them by their mother, they inherited the house from their mother.

demi[1] [d(ə)mi] adv: ~ **plein/nu** half-full/-naked; **il n'était qu'à** ~ **rassuré** he was only half reassured; **il ne te croit qu'à** ~ he only half believes you; **il a fait le travail à** ~ he has (only) done half the work, he has (only) half done the work; **je ne fais pas les choses à** ~ I don't do things by halves; **ouvrir la porte à** ~ to half open the door, open the door halfway.

demi[2], e [d(ə)mi] 1 adj a (*avant n: inv, avec trait d'union*) **une ~-livre/-douzaine/-journée** half a pound/dozen/day, a half-pound/half-dozen/half-day; **un ~-tour de clef** half a turn of the key, a half turn of the key; *voir* **demi-**.

b (*après n: avec et, nominal*) **une livre/heure et ~e** one and a half pounds/hours, a pound/an hour and a half; **un centimètre/kilo et** ~ one and a half centimetres/kilos, one centimetre/kilo and a half; **à six heures et ~e** at half past six; **2 fois et ~e plus grand/autant** 2 and a half times greater/as much; *voir* **malin**.

2 nm,f (*fonction pronominale*) **un** ~ (a) half; **une bouteille? — non, une ~e** one bottle? — no, (a) half *ou* no, half a bottle *ou* no, a half-bottle; **est-ce qu'un** ~ **suffira, ou faut-il deux tiers?** will (a) half do, or do we need two-thirds?; **deux ~s font un entier** two halves make a whole.

3 **demie** nf (*à l'horloge*) **la ~e** the half-hour; **la ~e a sonné** the half-hour has struck; **c'est déjà la ~e** it's already half past; **on part à la ~e** we'll leave at half past; **le bus passe à la ~e** the bus comes by at half past (the hour), the bus comes by on the half-hour; **la pendule sonne les heures et les ~es** the clock strikes the hours and the halves *ou* the half-hours.

4 nm a (*bière*) glass of beer, ≃ half-pint (*Brit*), half*. **garçon, un** ~ a glass of beer, please, a half-pint *ou* a half, please. b (*Sport*) half-back. ~ **gauche/droit** left/right half; (*Rugby*) ~ **de mêlée** scrum half; (*Rugby*) ~ **d'ouverture** stand-off half.

5 comp ▸**demi-additionneur** (*Ordin*) nm (pl **demi-additionneurs**) half-adder ▸**demi-bas** nm inv kneesock ▸**demi-botte** nf (pl **demi-bottes**) ankle-boot, short boot ▸**demi-bouteille** nf (pl **demi-bouteilles**) half-bottle ▸**demi-cercle** nm (pl **demi-cercles**) (*figure*) semicircle; (*instrument*) protractor; **en demi-cercle** semicircular; **se mettre en demi-cercle** to make a semi-circle, stand in a semi-circle ▸**demi-colonne** nf (pl **demi-colonnes**) semi-column, demi-column, half-column ▸**demi-deuil** nm half-mourning (*voir* **poularde**) ▸**demi-dieu** nm (pl **demi-dieux**) demigod ▸**demi-douzaine** nf (pl **demi-douzaines**) half-a-dozen, half-dozen; **une demi-douzaine d'œufs** half-a-dozen eggs, a half-dozen eggs; **une demi-douzaine suffit** a half-dozen *ou* half-a-dozen will do; **cette demi-douzaine d'apéritifs m'a coupé les jambes** those half-a-dozen drinks knocked me off my feet ▸**demi-droite** (*Géom*) nf (pl **demi-droites**) half-line, half-ray ▸**demi-fin, e** adj *petit pois* small; *aiguille* medium; *or* 12-carat ▸**demi-finale** (*Sport*) nf (pl **demi-finales**) semifinal ▸**demi-finaliste** (*Sport*) nmf (pl **demi-finalistes**) semifinalist ▸**demi-fond** nm (pl **demi-fonds**) (*discipline*) medium-distance *ou* middle-distance running; (*épreuve*) medium-distance *ou* middle-distance race; **coureur de demi-fond** medium-distance *ou* middle-distance runner ▸**demi-frère** nm (pl **demi-frères**) half-brother ▸**demi-gros** (*Comm*) nm wholesale trade ▸**demi-heure** nf (pl **demi-heures**): **une demi-heure** half an hour, a half-hour; **la première demi-heure passe très lentement** the first half-hour goes very slowly ▸**demi-jour** nm (pl **demi-jour(s)**) (*gén*) half-light; (*le soir*) twilight ▸**demi-journée** nf (pl **demi-journées**): **une demi-journée** half a day, a half-day; **faire des demi-journées de nettoyage/couture** to work half-days cleaning/sewing; **travailler par demi-journées** to work half-days ▸**demi-litre** nm (pl **demi-litres**): **un demi-litre (de)** half a litre

(of), a half-litre (of); **ce demi-litre de lait** this half-litre of milk ▸**demi-longueur** (*Sport*) **nf (pl demi-longueurs): une demi-longueur** half a length, a half-length; **la demi-longueur d'avance qui lui a valu le prix** the half-length lead that won him the prize ▸**demi-lune nf (pl demi-lunes)** (*Mil*) demilune; (*Rail*) relief line; **en demi-lune** semicircular, half-moon (*épith*) ▸**demi-mal nm: il n'y a que** *ou* **ce n'est que demi-mal** it could have been worse, there's no great harm done ▸**demi-mesure nf (pl demi-mesures)** half-measure; (*Habillement*) **la demi-mesure** semi-finished clothing; **s'habiller en demi-mesure** to buy semi-finished clothing ▸**demi-mondaine nf (pl demi-mondaines)** demi-mondaine ▸**demi-monde nm** demi-monde ▸**demi-mot nm: à demi-mot** without having to spell things out; **se faire comprendre à demi-mot** to make o.s. understood without having to spell it out; **ils se comprenaient à demi-mot** they didn't have to spell things out to each other ▸**demi-pause** (*Mus*) **nf (pl demi-pauses)** minim (*Brit*) *ou* half-note (*US*) rest ▸**demi-pension nf** (*à l'hôtel*) half-board (*Brit*), bed and breakfast with an evening meal (*Brit*), lodging, breakfast and one main meal (*US*); (*Scol*) half-board; (*Scol*) **être en demi-pension** to take school lunches ▸**demi-pensionnaire nmf (pl demi-pensionnaires)** day pupil; **être demi-pensionnaire** to take school lunches ▸**demi-place nf (pl demi-places)** (*Transport*) half-fare; (*Ciné, Théât etc*) half-price ticket *ou* seat ▸**demi-portion** (*péj*) **nf (pl demi-portions)** weed* (*péj*), weedy* person (*péj*) ▸**demi-queue nm inv: (piano) demi-queue** baby grand ▸**demi-reliure nf (pl demi-reliures)** half-binding ▸**demi-saison nf** spring (*ou* autumn), cool season; **un manteau de demi-saison** a spring (*ou* an autumn) coat ▸**demi-sang nm inv** (*cheval*) half-breed (horse) ▸**demi-sel adj inv** *beurre* slightly salted; **(fromage) demi-sel** (slightly salted) cream cheese ◊ **nm (pl demi-sels)** *arg Crime* small-time pimp ▸**demi-sœur nf (pl demi-sœurs)** half-sister ▸**demi-solde nf (pl demi-soldes)** (*Mil*) half-pay ▸**demi-sommeil nm** half-sleep ▸**demi-soupir nm (pl demi-soupirs)** (*Mus*) quaver (*Brit*) *ou* eighth note (*US*) rest ▸**demi-tarif nm** half-price; (*Transport*) half-fare; **billet** *etc* **(à) demi-tarif** half-price ticket *etc;* **voyager à demi-tarif** to travel at half-fare ▸**demi-teinte** (*Art, fig*) **nf (pl demi-teintes)** half-tone ▸**demi-ton** (*Mus*) **nm (pl demi-tons)** semitone, half tone (*US*) ▸**demi-tonneau** (*Aviat*) **nm (pl demi-tonneaux)** half flick (*Brit*) *ou* snap (*US*) roll ▸**demi-tour** (*lit, fig*) **nm (pl demi-tours)** about-turn, U-turn; (*Aut*) U-turn; (*lit*) **faire un demi-tour** to make an about-turn *ou* a U-turn; (*fig*) **faire demi-tour** to do a U-turn, make an about-turn ▸**demi-vie** *[radiation]* **nf** half-life ▸**demi-vierge nf (pl demi-vierges)** virgin in name only ▸**demi-volée** (*Sport*) **nf (pl demi-volées)** half-volley.

demiard [dəmjaʀ] **nm** (*Can*) half-pint (*Brit*), 0,284 litre.

démilitarisation [demilitaʀizasjɔ̃] **nf** demilitarization.

démilitariser [demilitaʀize] [1] **vt** to demilitarize.

déminage [deminaʒ] **nm** *[terrain]* mine clearance; *[eaux]* minesweeping. **opérations de ~** mineclearing operations.

déminer [demine] [1] **vt** to clear of mines.

déminéralisation [demineʀalizasjɔ̃] **nf** (*Tech*) demineralization.

déminéraliser [demineʀalize] [1] **1 vt** (*Tech*) to demineralize; (*Méd*) to make deficient in essential minerals. **eau déminéralisée** distilled *ou* demineralized water. **2 se déminéraliser vpr** (*Méd*) to become deficient in essential minerals.

démineur [deminœʀ] **nm** bomb disposal expert.

démis, e [demi, iz] (**ptp de démettre**) **adj** *membre* dislocated.

démission [demisjɔ̃] **nf** (*lit*) resignation; (*fig*) abdication. **donner sa ~** to hand in *ou* tender (*frm*) one's resignation; **la ~ des parents modernes** the abdication of parental responsibilities on the part of modern parents.

démissionnaire [demisjɔnɛʀ] **1 adj** resigning, who has resigned. **2 nmf** person resigning.

démissionner [demisjɔne] [1] **1 vi** to resign, hand in one's notice; (*fig*) *[parents, enseignants]* to give up. **2 vt** (*iro*) **~ qn*** to give sb his cards* (*Brit*) *ou* his pink slip* (*US*); **on l'a démissionné** they persuaded him to resign (*iro*).

démiurge [demjyʀʒ] **nm** demiurge.

démobilisateur, -trice [demɔbilizatœʀ, tʀis] **adj** *discours, mesure* demobilising, disarming.

démobilisation [demɔbilizasjɔ̃] **nf** (*Mil*) demobilization, demob* (*Brit*); (*apathie*) apathy, demobilization.

démobiliser [demɔbilize] [1] **vt** (*Mil*) to demobilize, demob* (*Brit*); (*fig*) to demobilize. **se ~** to become demobilized *ou* apathetic.

démocrate [demɔkʀat] **1 adj** democratic. **2 nmf** democrat.

démocrate-chrétien, -ienne, mpl démocrates-chrétiens [demɔkʀatkʀetjɛ̃, jɛn] **adj, nm,f** Christian Democrat.

démocratie [demɔkʀasi] **nf** democracy. **~ directe/représentative** direct/representative democracy; **~ populaire** people's democracy.

démocratique [demɔkʀatik] **adj** democratic. **la République démocratique de ...** the Democratic Republic of ...; (*Can*) **le Nouveau Parti D~** the New Democratic Party.

démocratiquement [demɔkʀatikmɑ̃] **adv** democratically.

démocratisation [demɔkʀatizasjɔ̃] **nf** democratization.

démocratiser [demɔkʀatize] [1] **1 vt** to democratize. **2 se démocratiser vpr** to become (more) democratic.

démodé, e [demɔde] (**ptp de se démoder**) **adj** *vêtement, manières, institution* old-fashioned, out-of-date; *procédé, théorie* outmoded, old-fashioned.

démoder (se) [demɔde] [1] **vpr** (*voir* **démodé**) to become old-fashioned, go out of fashion; to become outmoded.

démographe [demɔgʀaf] **nmf** demographer, demographist.

démographie [demɔgʀafi] **nf** demography. **~ galopante** massive population growth, ≃ population explosion.

démographique [demɔgʀafik] **adj** demographic. **poussée ~** increase in population, population increase.

demoiselle [d(ə)mwazɛl] **1 nf a** (*frm, hum: jeune*) young lady; (*d'un certain âge*) single lady, maiden lady. (*dial: fille*) **votre ~*** your daughter. **b** (*Hist: noble*) damsel††. **c** (*Zool*) dragonfly. **d** (*Tech*) rammer. **2 comp** ▸**demoiselle de compagnie** (lady's) companion ▸**demoiselle d'honneur** (*à un mariage*) bridesmaid; (*d'une reine*) maid of honour.

démolir [demɔliʀ] [2] **vt a** (*lit*) *maison, quartier* to demolish, pull down. **on démolit beaucoup dans le quartier** they are pulling down *ou* demolishing a lot of houses *ou* they are doing a lot of demolition in this area.

b (*abîmer*) *jouet, radio, voiture* to wreck, demolish, smash up*. **cet enfant démolit tout!** that child wrecks *ou* demolishes everything!; **ces boissons vous démolissent l'estomac/la santé*** these drinks play havoc with *ou* ruin your stomach//health.

c (*fig: détruire*) *autorité* to overthrow, shatter, bring down; *influence* to overthrow, destroy; *doctrine* to demolish, crush; *espoir* to crush, shatter; *foi* to shatter, destroy.

d (*fig*) *personne* (*: *épuiser*) to do for*, do in*; (*: *cogner*) to bash up*, duff up* (*Brit*); (*: *critiquer*) to slate* (*Brit*), tear to pieces, demolish. **ce travail/cette maladie l'avait démoli** this work/this illness had just about done for him*; **les critiques l'ont démoli/ont démoli sa pièce** the critics tore him/his play to pieces, he/his play was slated* (*Brit*) *ou* demolished* by the critics; **je vais lui ~ le portrait‡** I'm going to smash his face in‡; **ces 40 kilomètres de marche m'ont démoli** that 40-kilometre walk has done for me* *ou* shattered me*, I'm whacked* (*Brit*) *ou* shattered* after that 40-kilometre walk.

démolissage* [demɔlisaʒ] **nm** (*critique*) slating* (*Brit*), panning*.

démolisseur, -euse [demɔlisœʀ, øz] **nm,f** (*ouvrier*) demolition worker; (*entrepreneur*) demolition contractor; (*fig*) *[doctrine]* demolisher.

démolition [demɔlisjɔ̃] **nf a** *[immeuble, quartier]* demolition, pulling down; (*fig*) *[doctrine etc]* demolition, crushing. **la ~, ça rapporte** there's money in the demolition business, demolition is a profitable business; **entreprise de ~** demolition contractor(s); **l'immeuble est en ~** the building is (in the course of) being demolished; *voir* **chantier**. **b** (*décombres*) **~s** debris (*sg*), ruins.

démon [demɔ̃] **nm a** (*Rel*) demon, fiend; (*fig*) (*harpie*) harpy; (*séductrice*) evil woman; (*enfant*) devil, demon. **le ~** the Devil; **le ~ de midi** middle-aged lust; **le ~ du jeu** a passion for gambling; **le ~ de la luxure/de l'alcool/de la curiosité** the demon lechery/drink/curiosity; *voir* **possédé**. **b** (*Myth*) genius, daemon. **écoutant son ~ familier/son mauvais ~** listening to his familiar/evil spirit.

démonétisation [demɔnetizasjɔ̃] **nf** (*Fin*) demonetization, demonetarization.

démonétiser [demɔnetize] [1] **vt** (*Fin*) to demonetize, demonetarize.

démoniaque [demɔnjak] **1 adj** diabolical, fiendish. **2 nmf** person possessed by the devil *ou* by an evil spirit.

démonologie [demɔnɔlɔʒi] **nf** demonology.

démonstrateur, -trice [demɔ̃stʀatœʀ, tʀis] **nm,f** demonstrator (*of commercial products*).

démonstratif, -ive [demɔ̃stʀatif, iv] **adj a** *personne, caractère* demonstrative. **peu ~** undemonstrative. **b** *argument, preuve* demonstrative, illustrative. **c** (*Gram*) demonstrative. **les ~s** the demonstratives.

démonstration [demɔ̃stʀasjɔ̃] **nf a** (*gén, Math*) *[vérité, loi]* demonstration; *[théorème]* proof. **cette ~ est convaincante** this demonstration is convincing; **~ par l'absurde** reductio ad absurdum. **b** (*Comm*) *[fonctionnement, appareil]* demonstration. **faire une ~** to give a demonstration; **faire la ~ d'un appareil** to demonstrate an appliance; **un appareil de ~** a demonstration model; (*Ordin*) **disquette de ~** demo disk. **c** (*manifestation*) *[joie, tendresse]* demonstration, show, display. **accueillir qn avec des ~s d'amitié** to welcome sb with a great show of friendship; (*Mil*) **~ de force** show of force; (*Mil*) **~ aérienne/navale** display of air/naval strength.

démontable [demɔ̃tabl] **adj** (*gén*) that can be dismantled. **armoire ~** cupboard that can be dismantled *ou* taken to pieces.

démontage [demɔ̃taʒ] **nm** (*voir* **démonter**) taking down; dismantling; stripping; taking to pieces; taking apart; taking off. **pièces perdues lors de ~s successifs** pieces lost during successive dismantling operations; **c'était un ~ difficile** it was a difficult dismantling job *ou* operation, the dismantling was a difficult job *ou* operation.

démonté, e [demɔ̃te] (**ptp de démonter**) **adj** (*houleux*) *mer* raging, wild.

démonte-pneu, pl démonte-pneus [demɔ̃t(ə)pnø] **nm** tyre lever (*Brit*), tire iron (*US*).

démonter [demɔ̃te] [1] **1 vt a** (*démanteler*) *installation, échafaudage,*

étagères, tente to take down, dismantle; *moteur* to strip down, dismantle; *armoire, appareil, horloge, arme* to dismantle, take to pieces, take apart; *circuit électrique* to dismantle.
b (*détacher*) *rideau* to take down; *pneu, porte* to take off.
c (*déconcerter*) to disconcert. **ça m'a complètement démonté** I was completely taken aback by that, that really disconcerted me; **il ne se laisse jamais ~** he never gets flustered, he's never flustered, he always remains unruffled.
d (*Équitation*) *cavalier* to throw, unseat.
2 **se démonter** vpr a *[assemblage, pièce]* (*accidentellement*) to come apart *ou* to pieces. **est-ce que ça se démonte?** can it be dismantled *ou* taken apart?
b (*perdre son calme: gén nég*) to lose countenance. **répondre sans se ~** to reply without losing countenance; **il ne se démonte pas pour si peu** he's not that easily flustered, it takes more than that to make him lose countenance.

démontrable [demɔ̃tʀabl] adj demonstrable.

démontrer [demɔ̃tʀe] [1] vt (*prouver*) *loi, vérité* to demonstrate; *théorème* to prove; (*expliquer*) *fonctionnement* to demonstrate; (*faire ressortir*) *urgence, nécessité* to show, demonstrate. **~ l'égalité de 2 triangles** to demonstrate *ou* prove *ou* show that 2 triangles are equal; **~ qch (à qn) par A plus B** to prove sth conclusively (to sb); **sa hâte démontrait son inquiétude** his haste clearly indicated his anxiety; **tout cela démontre l'urgence de ces réformes** all this shows *ou* demonstrates the urgency of these reforms.

démoralisant, e [demɔʀalizɑ̃, ɑ̃t] adj demoralizing.

démoralisateur, -trice [demɔʀalizatœʀ, tʀis] adj demoralizing.

démoralisation [demɔʀalizasjɔ̃] nf demoralization.

démoraliser [demɔʀalize] [1] 1 vt to demoralize. 2 **se démoraliser** vpr to lose heart, become demoralized.

démordre [demɔʀdʀ] [41] vi: **il ne démord pas de son avis/sa décision** he is sticking to his opinion/decision, he won't give up his opinion/decision; **il ne veut pas en ~** he won't budge an inch, he is sticking to his guns.

Démosthène [demɔstɛn] nm Demosthenes.

démotivation [demɔtivasjɔ̃] nf lack of motivation.

démotiver [demɔtive] [1] vt to demotivate.

démoucheté, e [demuʃte] adj *fleuret* unbuttoned.

démoulage [demulaʒ] nm (*voir* **démouler**) removal from the mould; turning out.

démouler [demule] [1] vt *statue* to remove from the mould; *flan, gâteau* to turn out.

démoustication [demustikasjɔ̃] nf clearing *ou* ridding of mosquitoes (*de* from).

démoustiquer [demustike] [1] vt to clear *ou* rid of mosquitoes.

démultiplicateur, -trice [demyltiplikatœʀ, tʀis] 1 adj reduction (*épith*), reducing (*épith*). 2 nm reduction system.

démultiplication [demyltiplikasjɔ̃] nf (*procédé*) reduction; (*rapport*) reduction ratio.

démultiplier [demyltiplije] [7] vt to reduce, gear down.

démuni, e [demyni] (ptp de **démunir**) adj a (*sans ressources*) destitute. **nous sommes ~s** (*sans argent*) we are destitute; (*sans défense*) we are powerless (*devant* in the face of). b (*privé de*) **~ de** without, lacking in; **~ d'ornements** unornamented, unadorned; **~ de protection** unprotected; **~ de défenses** undefended; **~ de talents/d'attraits** without talent/attraction, untalented/unattractive; **~ d'intérêt** devoid of *ou* without interest, uninteresting; **~ de tout** destitute; **~ d'argent** penniless, without money; **~ de papiers d'identité** without identity papers.

démunir [demyniʀ] [2] 1 vt: **~ qn de** *vivres* to deprive sb of; *ressources, argent* to divest *ou* deprive sb of; **~ qch de** to divest sth of. 2 **se démunir** vpr (*financièrement*) to part with one's money. (*se défaire de*) **se ~ de** to part with, give up.

démystification [demistifikasjɔ̃] nf enlightenment, demystification.

démystifier [demistifje] [7] vt to enlighten, disabuse, demystify.

démythification [demitifikasjɔ̃] nf demythification.

démythifier [demitifje] [7] vt to demythologize, demythify.

dénasalisation [denazalizasjɔ̃] nf denasalization.

dénasaliser [denazalize] [1] vt to denasalize.

dénatalité [denatalite] nf fall *ou* decrease in the birth rate.

dénationalisation [denasjɔnalizasjɔ̃] nf denationalization.

dénationaliser [denasjɔnalize] [1] vt to denationalize.

dénatter [denate] [1] vt *cheveux* to unplait.

dénaturation [denatyʀasjɔ̃] nf (*Tech*) denaturation.

dénaturé, e [denatyʀe] (ptp de **dénaturer**) adj a (*Tech*) *alcool, sel* denatured. b *goût, mœurs, parents* unnatural.

dénaturer [denatyʀe] [1] vt a *vérité, faits* to distort, misrepresent. b (*Tech*) *alcool, substance alimentaire* to denature; (*altérer*) *goût, aliment* to alter completely, change the nature of.

dénazification [denazifikasjɔ̃] nf denazification.

dénégation [denegasjɔ̃] nf (*gén, Jur*) denial.

déneigement [denɛʒmɑ̃] nm snow-clearing (operation), snow removal.

déneiger [deneʒe] [3] vt to clear of snow, clear the snow from.

déni [deni] nm denial. (*Jur*) **~ de justice** denial of justice.

déniaiser [denjeze] [1] vt: **~ qn** (*dégourdir*) to teach sb a thing or two; (*dépuceler*) to take away sb's innocence; **se ~** to learn about life; to lose one's innocence.

dénicher [deniʃe] [1] 1 vt a (**: trouver*) *objet* to unearth*; *bistro* to discover; *personne* to track *ou* hunt down. b (*débusquer*) *fugitif, animal* to drive out (of hiding), flush out. c (*enlever du nid*) *œufs, oisillons* to take out of the nest. 2 vi *[oiseau]* to leave the nest.

dénicheur, -euse [deniʃœʀ, øz] nm,f a (*hum*) **~ de** *antiquités, trouvailles* unearther of (*hum*). b (*d'oiseaux*) bird's-nester.

denier [dənje] 1 nm a (*monnaie*) (*Hist romaine*) denarius; (*Hist française*) denier. **ça ne leur a pas coûté un ~†** it didn't cost them a farthing (*Brit*) *ou* a cent (*US*); **l'ayant payé de ses propres ~s** having paid for it out of his own pocket; **les trente ~s de Judas** Judas's thirty pieces of silver. b (*Tex: unité de poids*) denier. **bas de 30 ~s** 30-denier stockings. 2 comp ▸**le denier du culte** the contribution to parish costs (*paid yearly*) ▸**les deniers publics** *ou* **de l'État** public monies.

dénier [denje] [7] vt a *responsabilité* to deny, disclaim; *faute* to deny. b (*refuser*) **~ qch à qn** to deny *ou* refuse sb sth.

dénigrement [denigʀəmɑ̃] nm denigration, defamation.

dénigrer [denigʀe] [1] vt to denigrate, run down.

denivelé nm, **dénivelée** nf [deniv(ə)le] difference in height (*entre* between).

déniveler [deniv(ə)le] [4] vt (*rendre inégal*) to make uneven; (*abaisser*) to lower, put on a lower level.

dénivellation [denivelasjɔ̃] nf, **dénivellement** [denivɛlmɑ̃] nm a (*NonC: voir* **déniveler**) making uneven; lowering, putting on a lower level. b (*pente*) slope; (*cassis, creux*) unevenness (*NonC*), dip. c (*différence de niveau*) difference in level *ou* altitude. **la dénivellation** *ou* **le dénivellement entre deux points** the difference in height *ou* level between two points.

dénombrable [denɔ̃bʀabl] adj countable. (*Ling*) **nom ~** countable *ou* count noun.

dénombrement [denɔ̃bʀəmɑ̃] nm counting. **~ de la population** census of population.

dénombrer [denɔ̃bʀe] [1] vt (*compter*) to count; (*énumérer*) to enumerate, list.

dénominateur [denɔminatœʀ] nm (*Math*) denominator. (*Math, fig*) **~ commun** common denominator; **plus petit ~ commun** lowest common denominator.

dénominatif, -ive [denɔminatif, iv] adj, nm denominative.

dénomination [denɔminasjɔ̃] nf (*nom*) designation, appellation (*frm*), denomination (*frm*); (*action*) denomination (*frm*), naming.

dénommé, e [denɔme] (ptp de **dénommer**) adj (*parfois péj*) **le ~ X** a certain X, the man called X; **on m'a présenté un ~ Dupont** I was introduced to a certain Mr Dupont, I was introduced to someone *ou* a man by the name of Dupont *ou* who called himself Dupont.

dénommer [denɔme] [1] vt (*frm*) (*donner un nom à*) to denominate (*frm*), name; (*désigner*) to designate, denote; (*Jur*) to name.

dénoncer [denɔ̃se] [3] 1 vt a (*révéler*) *coupable* to denounce; *forfait, abus* to expose. (*fig*) **sa hâte le dénonça** his haste gave him away *ou* betrayed him; **~ qn à la police** to inform against sb, give sb away to the police. b (*signaler publiquement*) *abus, danger, injustice* to denounce. c (*annuler*) *contrat, traité* to denounce. d (*littér: dénoter*) to announce, indicate. 2 **se dénoncer** vpr *[criminel]* to give o.s. up, come forward. **se ~ à la police** to give o.s. up to the police.

dénonciateur, -trice [denɔ̃sjatœʀ, tʀis] 1 adj denunciatory, accusatory. 2 nm,f a *[criminel]* denouncer, informer; *[forfait]* exposer. b **~ de** *injustices etc* denouncer of.

dénonciation [denɔ̃sjasjɔ̃] nf *[criminel]* denunciation; *[forfait, abus]* exposure (*NonC*); *[traité]* denunciation, denouncement; *[contrat]* termination. **emprisonné sur la ~ de qn** imprisoned on the strength of a denunciation by sb.

dénotatif, -ive [denɔtatif, iv] adj (*Ling*) denotative.

dénotation [denɔtasjɔ̃] nf (*Ling*) denotation.

dénoter [denɔte] [1] vt (*révéler*) to indicate, denote; (*Ling*) to denote.

dénouement [denumɑ̃] nm (*Théât*) dénouement; *[affaire, aventure, intrigue]* outcome, conclusion.

dénouer [denwe] [1] 1 vt a *nœud, lien* to untie, undo; *cheveux* to let down, loose, undo. **les cheveux dénoués** with her hair (falling) loose. b *situation* to untangle, resolve; *difficultés, intrigue* to untangle, clear up, resolve, unravel. 2 **se dénouer** vpr a *[lien, nœud]* to come untied, come undone; *[cheveux]* to come loose, come undone, come down; *voir* **langue**. b *[intrigue, situation]* to be resolved.

dénoûment [denumɑ̃] = **dénouement**.

dénoyautage [denwajotaʒ] nm *[fruit]* stoning (*Brit*), pitting (*US*).

dénoyauter [denwajote] [1] vt *fruit* to stone (*Brit*), pit (*US*).

dénoyauteur [denwajotœʀ] nm stoner (*Brit*), pitter (*US*).

denrée [dɑ̃ʀe] nf a commodity, foodstuff, produce (*NonC*). **~s alimentaires** foodstuffs; **~s de base** basic foods; **~s de consommation courante** basic consumer goods; **~s périssables** perishable foods *ou* foodstuffs; **~s coloniales** colonial produce. b (*fig*) commodity. **l'honnêteté devient une ~ rare** honesty is becoming a rare commodity.

dense [dɑ̃s] adj (*Phys*) dense; *foule* dense, tightly packed; *feuillage, brouillard* dense, thick; *style* compact, condensed.
densimètre [dɑ̃simɛtʀ] nm densimeter.
densité [dɑ̃site] nf (*Démographie, Phys*) density; *[brouillard]* denseness, thickness; (*rare*) *[foule]* denseness. **région à forte/faible ~ (de population)** densely/sparsely populated area, area with a high/low population density; (*Ordin*) **~ d'implantation** packing density.
dent [dɑ̃] 1 nf a *[homme, animal]* tooth. **~s du haut/du bas/de devant/du fond** upper/lower/front/back teeth; **~ de lait/de sagesse** milk (*Brit*) *ou* baby/wisdom tooth; **~ de remplacement** permanent *ou* second tooth; **~ gâtée/creuse** bad/hollow tooth; **mal** *ou* **rage de ~** toothache (*NonC*); **donner un coup de ~ à** to bite into, take a bite at; *voir* **arracher, brosse, faux²** *etc.*
b *[herse, fourche, fourchette]* prong; *[râteau]* tooth, prong; *[scie, peigne]* tooth; *[roue, engrenage]* tooth, cog; *[feuille]* serration; *[arête rocheuse]* jag; *[timbre]* perforation. **en ~s de scie** *couteau* serrated; *montagne* jagged; **graphique/carrière en ~s de scie** switchback graph/career.
c (*loc*) **avoir la ~*** to be hungry; **avoir la ~ dure** to be scathing in one's comments (*envers* about); **avoir/garder une ~ contre qn** to have/hold a grudge against sb; **avoir les ~s longues** (†: *faim*) to be ravenous *ou* starving; (*fig: être ambitieux*) to have one's sights fixed high; **être sur les ~s** (*fébrile*) to be keyed up; (*très occupé*) to be under great pressure; **faire** *ou* **percer ses ~s** to teethe, cut (one's) teeth; **il vient de percer une ~** he has just cut a tooth; **croquer/manger qch à belles ~s** to bite into sth/eat sth with gusto; **manger du bout des ~s** to eat half-heartedly, pick at one's food; **parler/marmotter entre ses ~s** to talk/mumble between one's teeth; **ils n'ont rien à se mettre sous la ~** they have nothing to eat; **on voudrait bien quelque chose à se mettre sous la ~** we wouldn't say no to a bite (to eat) *ou* something to eat; **il mange tout ce qui lui tombe sous la ~** he eats everything he can lay his hands on; *voir* **armé, casser** *etc.*
2 comp ▸**dent-de-lion** nf (pl **dents-de-lion**) dandelion.
dentaire [dɑ̃tɛʀ] adj dental; *voir* **formule, prothèse.**
dental, e, mpl **-aux** [dɑ̃tal, o] (*Ling*) 1 adj dental. 2 **dentale** nf dental.
denté, e [dɑ̃te] adj (*Tech*) toothed; (*Bot*) dentate; *voir* **roue.**
dentelé, e [dɑ̃t(ə)le] (ptp de **denteler**) adj *arête* jagged; *timbre* perforated; *contour, côte* indented, jagged; (*Bot*) dentate; (*Anat*) serrate.
denteler [dɑ̃t(ə)le] 4 vt (*Tech*) *timbre-poste* to perforate. (*fig: découper*) **l'érosion avait dentelé la côte** erosion had indented the coastline *ou* had given the coast a jagged outline; **les pics qui dentelaient l'horizon** the peaks that stood in a jagged line along the horizon.
dentelle [dɑ̃tɛl] nf lace (*NonC*). **col de ~** lace collar; **~ à l'aiguille** *ou* **au point** needle-point lace; **~ au(x) fuseau(x)** bobbin lace; **~ de papier** lacy paper; **crêpe ~** thin pancake; (*fig*) **ne pas faire dans la ~*** not to be particular about details.
dentellerie [dɑ̃tɛlʀi] nf (*fabrication*) lacemaking; (*Comm*) lace manufacture.
dentellier, -ière [dɑ̃təlje, jɛʀ] 1 adj *industrie* lace (*épith*). 2 nm,f lacemaker. 3 **dentellière** nf (*machine*) lacemaking machine.
dentelure [dɑ̃t(ə)lyʀ] nf *[timbre-poste]* perforations; *[feuille]* serration; *[côte, arête]* jagged outline. **les ~s d'une côte** the indentations *ou* jagged outline of a coastline.
dentier [dɑ̃tje] nm denture, dental plate.
dentifrice [dɑ̃tifʀis] 1 nm toothpaste, dentifrice. 2 adj: **eau ~** mouthwash; **poudre ~** tooth powder; **pâte ~** toothpaste.
dentine [dɑ̃tin] nf (*Anat*) dentine.
dentiste [dɑ̃tist] nmf dentist; *voir* **chirurgien.**
dentisterie [dɑ̃tistəʀi] nf dentistry.
dentition [dɑ̃tisjɔ̃] nf (*dents*) teeth (*pl*); (*croissance*) dentition.
denture [dɑ̃tyʀ] nf (*humaine*) teeth (*pl*), set of teeth, dentition (*SPÉC*); (*Tech*) *[roue]* teeth (*pl*), cogs.
dénudé, e [denyde] (ptp de **dénuder**) adj (*gén*) bare; *crâne* bald; *colline* bare, bald.
dénuder [denyde] 1 1 vt a (*Tech*) *fil* to bare, strip; (*Méd*) *os* to strip. b *arbre, sol, colline* to bare, strip. c *bras, dos [robe]* to leave bare; *[mouvement]* to bare. 2 **se dénuder** vpr a *[personne]* to strip (off). b *[colline, arbre]* to become bare, be bared; *[crâne]* to be balding, be going bald.
dénué, e [denɥe] (ptp de **dénuer**) adj: **~ de** devoid of; **~ de bon sens** senseless, devoid of sense; **~ d'intérêt** devoid of interest; **~ de talent/d'imagination** lacking in *ou* without talent/imagination, untalented/unimaginative; **~ de tout** destitute; **~ de tout fondement** completely unfounded *ou* groundless, entirely without foundation.
dénuement [denymɑ̃] nm *[personne]* destitution; (*littér*) *[logement]* bareness. (*fig littér*) **~ moral** moral deprivation.
dénuer (se) [denɥe] 1 vpr (*littér*) to deprive o.s. (*de* of).
dénûment [denymɑ̃] nm = **dénuement.**
dénutrition [denytʀisjɔ̃] nf undernutrition, undernourishment.
déodorant [deɔdɔʀɑ̃] adj m, nm: **(produit) ~** deodorant; **~ (corporel)** deodorant.
déontologie [deɔ̃tɔlɔʒi] nf professional code of ethics, deontology (*SPÉC*).
déontologique [deɔ̃tɔlɔʒik] adj ethical, deontological (*SPÉC*).
dép. (abrév de **département**) = **dépt.**
dépailler [depɑje] 1 vt *chaise* to remove the straw seating from.
dépannage [depanaʒ] nm (*voir* **dépanner**) fixing; repairing; helping out. **camion de ~** breakdown lorry (*Brit*), tow truck (*US*); **service de ~** breakdown service; **ils ont fait 3 ~s aujourd'hui** they've fixed 3 breakdowns today; **partir pour un ~** to go out on a repair *ou* breakdown job.
dépanner [depane] 1 vt *véhicule, poste de télévision* to get going (again), fix, repair; *automobiliste* to fix the car of; (*: *tirer d'embarras*) *personne* to help out, tide over.
dépanneur [depanœʀ] nm (*gén*) repairman; (*Aut*) breakdown mechanic; (*TV*) television engineer, television repairman.
dépanneuse [depanøz] nf breakdown lorry (*Brit*), tow truck (*US*), wrecker (*US*).
dépaqueter [depak(ə)te] 4 vt to unpack.
déparasiter [depaʀazite] 1 vt *poste de radio* to fit a suppressor to.
dépareillé, e [depaʀeje] (ptp de **dépareiller**) adj *collection* incomplete; *objet* odd (*épith*). (*Comm*) **articles ~s** oddments; (*Comm*) **couverts ~s** odd cutlery.
dépareiller [depaʀeje] 1 vt *collection, service de table* to make incomplete, spoil. **en cassant cette assiette tu as dépareillé le service** you've spoilt the set now you've broken that plate.
déparer [depaʀe] 1 vt *paysage* to spoil, disfigure, mar; *visage* to disfigure; *beauté, qualité* to detract from, mar. **cette pièce ne ~ait pas ma collection** this piece would not disgrace my collection; **cette lampe ne ~ait pas dans la chambre** this lamp would go well with *ou* would not look bad in the bedroom.
déparié, e [depaʀje] (ptp de **déparier**) adj *chaussures, gants* odd (*épith*).
déparier [depaʀje] 7 vt *gants, chaussures* to split up.
départ¹ [depaʀ] nm a *[voyageur, véhicule, excursion]* departure; (*endroit*) point of departure. **observer le ~ du train** to watch the train leave; **le ~ est à 8 heures** the train (*ou* coach *etc*) leaves at 8 o'clock; **fixer l'heure/le jour de son ~** to set a time/day for one's departure; **être sur le ~** to be about to leave *ou* go; **excursions au ~ de Chamonix** excursions (leaving *ou* departing) from Chamonix, (day) trips from Chamonix; (*Rail*) "**~ des grandes lignes**" "main-line departures"; **dès son ~ j'ai ...** as soon as he had left I ...; **mon ~ de l'hôtel** my departure from *ou* my leaving the hotel; **peu après mon ~ de l'hôtel** soon after I had left the hotel, soon after my departure from the hotel; **c'est bientôt le ~ en vacances** we'll soon be off on holiday (*Brit*) *ou* vacation (*US*), we'll soon be leaving on our holidays (*Brit*) *ou* on vacation (*US*); **alors, c'est pour bientôt le grand ~?** well then, how soon is the great departure?; **le ~ du train/bateau est imminent** the train/boat is leaving any time now *ou* is about to depart; **son ~ précipité** his hasty departure; **la levée du matin est à 7 heures et le ~ du courrier se fait à 9 heures** the morning collection is at 7 and the mail leaves town at 9 o'clock; *voir* **tableau.**
b (*Sport*) start. **un bon ~** a good start; (*lit, fig*) **un faux ~** a false start; **donner le ~ aux coureurs** to give the runners the starting signal, start the race; **les coureurs se rassemblent au ~** the runners are assembling at the start; **~ lancé/arrêté** flying/standing start; **~ décalé** staggered start.
c *[employé, ministre]* leaving (*NonC*), departure. **le ~ du ministre a fait l'effet d'une bombe** the minister's leaving *ou* departure was something of a bombshell; **le ministre annonça son ~** the minister announced that he was going to quit *ou* that he was leaving; **demander le ~ d'un fonctionnaire** to demand the resignation of a civil servant; **réduire le personnel par ~s naturels** to reduce the staff gradually by natural wastage; **indemnité de ~** severance pay; **~ en préretraite** early retirement; **~ à la retraite** retirement; **~ volontaire** resignation.
d (*origine*) *[processus, transformation]* start. (*fig*) **au ~** at the start *ou* outset; **de ~** *hypothèse* initial; **salaire de ~** starting salary; **la substance de ~** the original substance; **de la langue de ~ à la langue d'arrivée** from the source language to the target language; *voir* **point¹.**
départ² [depaʀ] nm (*littér*) **faire le ~ entre le vrai et le faux** to draw *ou* make a distinction between truth and falsehood.
départager [depaʀtaʒe] 3 vt *concurrents* to decide between; *votes* to settle, decide; (*littér*) *opinions* to decide between; (*littér*) *camps opposés* to separate. **~ l'assemblée** to settle the voting in the assembly.
département [depaʀtəmɑ̃] nm *[organisme, entreprise]* department; (*division du territoire*) department, *one of the 95 main administrative divisions of France,* ≃ county (*Brit*). **~ (ministériel)** ministry, department; (*aux USA*) **le ~ d'État** the State Department; **~ d'outre-mer** overseas region of France.
départemental, e, mpl **-aux** [depaʀtəmɑ̃tal, o] adj (*voir* **département**) departmental; ministerial. **(route) ~e** secondary road, ≃ B-road (*Brit*).
départir [depaʀtiʀ] 16 1 vt (†, *littér: attribuer*) *tâche* to assign; *faveur* to accord (*frm*). 2 **se départir** vpr (*gén nég: abandonner*) **se ~ de** *ton, attitude* to abandon, depart from; *sourire* to drop.
dépassé, e [depɑse] (ptp de **dépasser**) adj (*périmé*) outmoded, old-fashioned, out of date; (*: *désorienté*) out of one's depth (*attrib*).
dépassement [depɑsmɑ̃] nm a (*Aut*) overtaking (*Brit: NonC*), passing (*NonC*). **tout ~ est dangereux** overtaking is always dangerous, it is

always dangerous to overtake; **"~ interdit"** "no overtaking"; **après plusieurs ~s dangereux** ... after perilously overtaking several vehicles ... .

b *[limite, prix]* (*action*) exceeding; (*excès*) excess. **~ d'honoraires** charge exceeding the statutory fee; **faire des ~s d'honoraires** to charge more than the statutory fee.

c (*Fin*) **~ (de crédit)** overspending (*NonC*); **un ~ de crédit de 5 millions** overspending by 5 million francs; **~ budgétaire** overspend on budget, overspending.

d **~ (de soi-même)** surpassing of oneself.

dépasser [depɑse] 1 1 vt a (*aller plus loin que*) *endroit* to pass, go past; (*Aviat*) *piste* to overshoot; (*distancer*) *véhicule, personne* to overtake (*Brit*), pass. **dépassez les feux et prenez la première rue à gauche** go through *ou* pass the lights and take the first (on the) left.

b (*déborder de*) *alignement* (*horizontalement*) to jut out over, overhang; (*verticalement*) to jut out above, stand higher than. **son succès a dépassé les frontières** his success has reached beyond *ou* transcended national boundaries.

c (*excéder*) *limite, quantité mesurable* to exceed. **~ qch en hauteur/largeur** to be higher *ou* taller/wider than sth, exceed sth in height/width; **il a dépassé son père (de 10 cm) maintenant** he's (10 cm) taller than his father now; **cette plante a dépassé l'autre** this plant has outgrown the other *ou* is now taller than the other; **~ en nombre** to outnumber; **tout colis qui dépasse 20 kg/la limite (de poids)** all parcels in excess of *ou* exceeding *ou* over 20 kg/the (weight) limit; **~ le nombre prévu** to be more than expected; **la réunion ne devrait pas ~ trois heures** the meeting shouldn't go on longer than *ou* last longer than 3 hours, the meeting shouldn't exceed 3 hours (in length); **il ne veut pas ~ 500 F** he won't go above *ou* over 500 francs; **ça va ~ 100 F** it'll be more than *ou* over 100 francs; **elle a dépassé la quarantaine** she is over forty, she has turned forty; (*Méd*) **"ne pas ~ la dose prescrite"** "it is dangerous to exceed the prescribed dose"; **le prix de cette maison dépasse nos moyens** this house is beyond our means *ou* is more than we can afford.

d (*surpasser*) *valeur, prévisions* to exceed; *réputation* to outshine; *rival* to outmatch, outstrip. **~ qn en violence/intelligence** to surpass sb in violence/intelligence; **pour la paresse/l'appétit il dépasse tout le monde** he beats everybody for laziness/appetite; **il dépasse tous ses camarades** he is ahead of *ou* he surpasses all his friends; **sa bêtise dépasse tout ce qu'on peut imaginer** his stupidity goes beyond all imagining *ou* goes beyond anything you could imagine *ou* beggars the imagination; **l'homme doit se ~** man must try to transcend himself *ou* surpass himself; **les résultats ont dépassé notre attente** the results exceeded *ou* surpassed our expectations; **cela dépasse toutes mes espérances** it is beyond my wildest dreams, it is better than anything I had ever hoped for.

e (*outrepasser*) *moyens, instructions* to go beyond; *attributions* to go beyond, overstep; *crédits* to exceed. **cela dépasse les bornes** *ou* **les limites** *ou* **la mesure** that's the absolute limit, that's going too far; **il a dépassé les bornes** *ou* **la mesure** *ou* **la dose*** he has really gone too far *ou* overstepped the mark *ou* passed over the bounds (*US*); **cela a dépassé le stade de la plaisanterie** it has gone beyond a joke; **les mots ont dû ~ sa pensée** he must have been carried away (to have said that); **cela dépasse mes forces/ma compétence** it's beyond my strength/capabilities; **cela me dépasse** it's beyond me; **il a dépassé ses forces** he has overtaxed himself *ou* overdone it.

f (***: *dérouter*) cela/cet argument me dépasse!** it/this argument is beyond me!; **être dépassé (par les événements)** to be overtaken (by events).

2 vi a (*Aut*) to overtake (*Brit*), pass. **"défense de ~"** "no overtaking" (*Brit*), "no passing".

b (*faire saillie*) *[bâtiment, tour]* to stick out; *[planche, balcon, rocher]* to stick out, jut out, protrude; *[clou]* to stick out; *[jupon]* to show (*de, sous* below); *[chemise]* to be hanging out (*de* of), be untucked. **il y a quelque chose qui dépasse du tiroir** something's sticking *ou* hanging out of the drawer; **leur chien a toujours un bout de langue qui dépasse** their dog always has the end of his tongue hanging out.

3 **se dépasser** vpr to surpass o.s., excel o.s.

dépassionner [depasjɔne] 1 vt *débat* to take the heat out of.

dépatouiller (se)* [depatuje] 1 vpr: **se ~ de** *situation difficile* to get out of; **laisse-le se ~!** leave him to *ou* let him get out of it on his own!; **savoir se ~** (to manage) to get by.

dépavage [depavaʒ] nm removal of the cobbles *ou* cobblestones (*de* from).

dépaver [depave] 1 vt to dig up the cobbles *ou* cobblestones from.

dépaysé, e [depeize] (ptp de **dépayser**) adj like a fish out of water (*attrib*), disoriented. **je me sens très ~ ici** I feel very much like a fish out of water here, I feel very disoriented here, I don't feel at home at all here.

dépaysement [depeizmɑ̃] nm (*changement salutaire*) change of scenery; (*désorientation*) disorientation, feeling of strangeness. **aimer le ~** to like a change of scenery.

dépayser [depeize] 1 vt (*désorienter*) to disorientate; (*changer agréablement*) to give a change of scenery to, give a welcome change of surroundings to. **ce séjour m'a dépaysé** this stay has given me a change of scenery *ou* a welcome change of surroundings.

dépeçage [depəsaʒ] nm, **dépècement** [depɛsmɑ̃] nm (*voir* **dépecer**) jointing (*Brit*), cutting up; dismembering; carving up.

dépecer [depəse] 5 vt *animal [boucher]* to joint (*Brit*), cut up; *[lion]* to dismember, tear limb from limb; (*fig*) *territoire, état* to carve up, dismember.

dépêche [depɛʃ] nf dispatch. **~ (télégraphique)** telegram, wire; **~ diplomatique** diplomatic dispatch.

dépêcher [depeʃe] 1 1 vt to dispatch, send (*auprès de* to). 2 **se dépêcher** vpr to hurry. **il se dépêchait** (*il marchait etc*) he was hurrying (along); (*il travaillait*) he was hurrying; **dépêche-toi!** hurry (up)!, (be) quick!; **se ~ de faire qch** to hurry (in order) to do sth; **il se dépêchait de finir son travail** he was hurrying (in order) to get his work finished *ou* to finish his work; **dépêche-toi de les commander, il n'y en aura bientôt plus** hurry up and order them or there soon won't be any left.

dépeigner [depeɲe] 1 vt: **~ qn** to make sb's hair untidy, ruffle sb's hair; **dépeigné par le vent** with windswept hair; **elle entra toute dépeignée** she came in with tousled *ou* dishevelled hair.

dépeindre [depɛ̃dʀ] 52 vt to depict.

dépenaillé, e [dep(ə)naje] adj *personne, vêtements* (*débraillé*) messy; (*en haillons*) tattered, ragged; *drapeau, livre* tattered.

dépénaliser [depenalize] 1 vt to decriminalize.

dépendance [depɑ̃dɑ̃s] nf a (*interdépendance*) dependence (*NonC*), dependency. **la ~ de qch vis-à-vis de qch d'autre** the dependence of sth (up)on sth else; **un réseau subtil de ~s** a subtle network of dependencies *ou* interdependencies. b (*asservissement, subordination*) subordination. **la ~ de qn vis-à-vis de qn d'autre** the subordination of sb to sb else; **être sous** *ou* **dans la ~ de qn** to be subordinate to sb. c (*bâtiment*) *[hôtel, château, ferme]* outbuilding. d (*Hist Pol: territoire*) dependency. e (*Drogue*) dependence, dependency. f (*Ling*) dependency.

dépendanciel, -ielle [depɑ̃dɑ̃sjɛl] adj (*Ling*) **grammaire ~ielle** dependency grammar.

dépendant, e [depɑ̃dɑ̃, ɑ̃t] adj (*voir* **dépendre de**) **~ de** answerable to, responsible to; dependent (up)on.

dépendre [depɑ̃dʀ] 41 1 **dépendre de** vt indir a *[employé]* to be answerable to, be responsible to; *[organisation]* to be dependent (up)on; *[territoire]* to be dependent (up)on, be a dependency of. **~ (financièrement) de ses parents** to be financially dependent (up)on one's parents; **ce pays dépend économiquement de la France** this country is economically dependent (up)on France; **je ne veux ~ de personne** I don't wish to be dependent (up)on anyone *ou* to have to depend (up)on anyone; **ce terrain dépend de leur domaine** this piece of land is part of *ou* belongs to their property; **ne ~ que de soi-même** to be answerable only to oneself, be one's own boss*.

b *[décision, résultat, phénomène]* to depend (up)on, be dependent (up)on. **ça va ~ du temps** it'll (all) depend on the weather; **— ça dépend** — it (all) depends; **il dépend de vous/de ceci que** ... it depends *ou* rests (up)on you/this whether ...; **il ne dépend que de vous que** ... it depends *ou* rests entirely (up)on you whether ..., it's entirely up to you whether ...; **il dépend de toi de réussir** (your) success depends on you, it depends on you *ou* it's up to you whether you succeed (or not).

2 vt *lustre, guirlandes* to take down.

dépens [depɑ̃] nmpl a (*Jur*) costs. **être condamné aux ~** to be ordered to pay costs, have costs awarded against one. b **aux ~ de** at the expense of; **rire aux ~ de qn** to (have a) laugh at sb's expense; **je l'ai appris à mes ~** I learnt this to my cost.

dépense [depɑ̃s] nf a (*argent dépensé, frais*) spending (*NonC*), expense, expenditure (*NonC*); (*sortie*) outlay, expenditure (*NonC*). **une ~ de 1.000 F** an outlay *ou* expenditure of 1,000 francs; **les ~s du ménage** household expenses; **contrôler les ~s de qn** to control sb's expenditure *ou* spending; **je n'aurais pas dû faire cette ~** I should not have incurred that expense (*frm*) *ou* spent that money; **j'hésite, c'est une grosse ~** I'm hesitating, it's a large outlay *ou* it's a lot to lay out; **calculer ~s et recettes** to calculate expenditure and receipts; **~s diverses** sundries; **~s publiques** public *ou* government expenditure *ou* spending; **~ d'investissement** *ou* **d'équipement** capital expenditure (*NonC*); **pousser qn à la ~** to make sb spend some money *ou* incur an expense (*frm*); **faire la ~ d'une voiture** to lay out money *ou* spend money on a car; **ne pas regarder à la ~** to spare no expense.

b (*fig*) *[électricité, essence]* consumption. **~s d'imagination** expenditure of imagination; **~ physique** (physical) exercise; **~ de temps** spending of time (*NonC*), time spent (*NonC*).

dépenser [depɑ̃se] 1 1 vt a *argent* to spend; (*fig*) *électricité, essence* to use. **~ sans compter** to spend without counting the cost, spend lavishly; **elle dépense peu pour la nourriture** she doesn't spend much on food, she spends little on food.

b (*fig*) *forces, énergie* to expend, use up; *temps, jeunesse* to spend, use up. **~ son trop-plein d'énergie** to use up one's surplus energy; **vous dépensez inutilement votre salive** you're wasting your breath.

2 **se dépenser** vpr to exert o.s. **se ~ en démarches inutiles** to waste one's energies in useless procedures; **pour ce projet il s'est dépensé sans compter** he has put all his energy *ou* energies into this project; **il**

faut que les enfants se dépensent children have to let off steam.

dépensier, -ière [depɑ̃sje, jɛʀ] 1 *adj* extravagant. **c'est une ~ière, elle est ~ière** she's a spendthrift. 2 *nm,f* (*trésorier de couvent*) bursar.

déperdition [depɛʀdisjɔ̃] *nf* (*Sci, gén*) loss.

dépérir [depeʀiʀ] [2] *vi* [*personne*] to fade away, waste away; [*santé, forces*] to fail, decline; [*plante*] to wither; [*commerce*] to (be on the) decline, fall off; [*affaire*] to (be on the) decline, go downhill.

dépérissement [depeʀismɑ̃] *nm* (*voir* **dépérir**) fading away, wasting away; failing; decline; withering; falling off.

dépersonnalisation [depɛʀsɔnalizasjɔ̃] *nf* depersonalization.

dépersonnaliser [depɛʀsɔnalize] 1 *vt* to depersonalize. 2 **se dépersonnaliser** *vpr* [*relations etc*] to become impersonal, become depersonalized; (*Psych*) to become depersonalized.

dépêtrer [depetʀe] [1] 1 *vt*: **~ qn de** (*lit*) *bourbier, ronces, harnachement* to extricate sb from, free sb from; (*fig*) *situation* to extricate sb from, get sb out of. 2 **se dépêtrer** *vpr* (*lit, fig*) to extricate o.s., free o.s. **se ~ de** *ronces, situation* to extricate *ou* free o.s. from, get out of; (*fig*) *liens* to free o.s. from; *gêneur* to get free of, get rid of.

dépeuplement [depœpləmɑ̃] *nm* (*voir* **dépeupler**) depopulation; emptying of people (*ou* fish *ou* wildlife); clearing (of trees *etc*). **le ~ tragique de ces forêts** the tragic disappearance of wildlife from these forests.

dépeupler [depœple] [1] 1 *vt* *région, ville* to depopulate; (*temporairement*) *salle, place* to empty (of people); *rivière* to empty of fish; *région* to empty of wildlife; *écuries etc* to empty; *forêt* to clear (of trees, plants *etc*). 2 **se dépeupler** *vpr* (*voir* **dépeupler**) to be depopulated; to be emptied of people (*ou* fish *ou* wildlife); to be emptied; to be cleared (of trees *etc*).

déphasage [defɑzaʒ] *nm* (*Phys*) phase difference; (* *fig: perte de contact*) being out of touch. **il y a ~ entre les syndicats et leurs dirigeants** the unions and their leaders are out of phase *ou* step.

déphasé, e [defɑze] (*ptp de* **déphaser**) *adj* (*Phys*) out of phase; (*: *désorienté*) out of phase *ou* step (*attrib*), not with it* (*attrib*).

déphaser* [defɑze] [1] *vt* (*désorienter*) to put out of touch.

dépiauter* [depjote] [1] *vt* *animal* to skin; *paquet* to undo; *texte* to pull to pieces.

dépigmentation [depigmɑ̃tasjɔ̃] *nf* depigmentation.

dépilation [depilasjɔ̃] *nf* (*voir* **dépiler**) hair loss.

dépilatoire [depilatwaʀ] 1 *adj* depilatory, hair-removing (*épith*). 2 *nm* depilatory *ou* hair-removing cream.

dépiler [depile] [1] *vt* (*Méd*) to cause hair loss to; (*Tech*) *peaux* to grain.

dépiquer [depike] [1] *vt* (*Couture*) to unpick (*Brit*), unstitch; (*Agr*) *laitue etc* to transplant; *blé* to thresh; *riz* to hull.

dépistage [depistaʒ] *nm* (*voir* **dépister**) tracking down; detection; unearthing. **centre de ~ anticancéreux** cancer screening unit.

dépister [depiste] [1] *vt* a *gibier, criminel* to track down; *maladie* to detect; *influence, cause* to unearth, detect. b (*semer*) **~ qn** to throw sb off the scent, give sb the slip*.

dépit [depi] *nm* a pique, (great) vexation. **causer du ~ à qn** to vex sb greatly, cause sb much heartache; **il en a conçu du ~** he was very piqued at it; **il l'a fait par ~** he did it out of pique *ou* in a fit of pique; **par ~ amoureux elle a épousé le premier venu** she married the first man she met on the rebound*. b **en ~ de** in spite of, despite; **faire qch en ~ du bon sens** to do sth any old how.

dépité, e [depite] (*ptp de* **dépiter**) *adj* (greatly) vexed, piqued.

dépiter [depite] [1] *vt* (*littér*) to vex greatly, frustrate greatly.

dépitonner [depitɔne] [1] *vti* (*Alpinisme*) to depeg.

déplacé, e [deplase] (*ptp de* **déplacer**) *adj* *présence* uncalled-for; *intervention, scrupule* misplaced, out of place (*attrib*); *remarque, propos* uncalled-for, out of place (*attrib*); *voir* **personne**.

déplacement [deplasmɑ̃] 1 *nm* a (*action*) (*voir* **déplacer**) moving; shifting; displacement; transfer; (*voir* **se déplacer**) movement; displacement. **ça vaut le ~** it's worth going.
b (*voyage*) trip, travel (*NonC*), travelling (*NonC*). **les ~s coûtent cher** travelling *ou* travel is expensive; **être en ~ (pour affaires)** to be on a (business) trip; *voir* **frais**[2].
c (*Naut*) displacement. **~ de 10.000 tonnes** 10,000 tons' displacement.
2 *comp* ▸**déplacement d'air** displacement of air ▸**déplacement d'organe** organ displacement ▸**déplacement de troupes** movement of troops ▸**déplacement de vertèbre** slipped disc ▸**déplacement d'enfant(s)** (*Jur*) child abduction; (*Jur*) **loi sur les déplacements d'enfants** ≃ Child Abduction Act.

déplacer [deplase] [3] 1 *vt* a *objet, meuble, élève* to move, shift; (*Méd*) *articulation, os* to displace. **se ~ une articulation** to put a joint out, displace a joint; **se ~ une vertèbre** to slip a disc; (*hum*) **il déplace beaucoup d'air** he's all talk (and no action).
b *usine, fonctionnaire* to transfer, move; *collectivité* to move, shift; *rendez-vous* to change.
c (*fig*) *problème, question* to shift the emphasis of.
d (*Naut*) to displace. **navire qui déplace 10.000 tonnes** ship with a 10,000-ton displacement.
2 **se déplacer** *vpr* a [*pièce mobile*] to move; [*air, substance*] to move, be displaced.
b [*animal*] to move (along); [*personne*] (*se mouvoir*) to move, walk; (*circuler*) to move (around); (*voyager*) to travel; (*se rendre chez qn*) [*médecin, réparateur etc*] to come out. **il ne se déplace qu'avec peine** he can get around *ou* about *ou* he can move only with difficulty; **il est interdit de se ~ pendant la classe** no moving around during class; **pouvez-vous vous ~ sur la droite?** can you move (over) to the right?; **il ne se déplace qu'en avion** he travels only by air; **il se déplace fréquemment** he's a frequent traveller, he travels a lot.

déplafonnement [deplafɔnmɑ̃] *nm* (*voir* **déplafonner**) derestriction; removal of the ceiling (*de* from).

déplafonner [deplafɔne] [1] *vt* *crédit* to derestrict; *cotisations* to remove the ceiling on.

déplaire [deplɛʀ] [54] 1 *vt* a (*n'être pas aimé de*) **il déplaît à tout le monde** he is disliked by everyone; **cette mode/ville/femme me déplaît** I dislike *ou* I don't like *ou* I don't care for this fashion/town/woman; **au bout d'un moment, cela risque de ~** after a while it can become disagreeable *ou* irksome *ou* unpleasant; **ça ne me déplairait pas (de le faire)** I wouldn't mind doing it; (*frm*) **il me déplaît de faire ...** I dislike doing ...; (*frm*) **il me déplairait d'avoir à vous renvoyer** I should not care *ou* I should be sorry to have to dismiss you.
b (*irriter*) **~ à qn** to displease sb; **il fait tout pour nous ~** he does all he can to displease us; **ceci a profondément déplu** this gave profound *ou* great displeasure; **il cherche à ~** he is trying to be disagreeable *ou* unpleasant.
c (†, *hum*) **elle est, n'en déplaise à son mari, bien moins intelligente que sa sœur** whether her husband likes it or not *ou* agrees or not, she is far less intelligent than her sister; **j'irai la voir, n'en déplaise à votre père** whatever your father's views on the matter, I shall go and see her.
2 **se déplaire** *vpr*: **elle se déplaît ici/à la campagne** she dislikes it *ou* doesn't like it here/in the country; **se ~ dans son nouvel emploi** to be unhappy in one's new job, dislike one's new job.

déplaisant, e [deplɛzɑ̃, ɑ̃t] *adj* disagreeable, unpleasant.

déplaisir [deplezir] *nm* (*contrariété*) displeasure, annoyance. **je le ferai sans ~** I'm quite willing *ou* happy to do it, I don't mind doing it; **faire qch avec (le plus grand) ~** to do sth with (the greatest) displeasure.

déplantage [deplɑ̃taʒ] *nm*, **déplantation** [deplɑ̃tasjɔ̃] *nf* (*voir* **déplanter**) transplanting; digging up; pulling out.

déplanter [deplɑ̃te] [1] *vt* *plante* to transplant; *plate-bande* to dig up; *piquet* to pull out.

déplâtrage [deplɑtʀaʒ] *nm* (*Constr*) **le ~ d'un mur** stripping the plaster off a wall, stripping a wall of its plaster; (*Méd*) **le ~ d'un membre** taking a limb out of plaster *ou* out of its plaster cast, taking a plaster cast off a limb.

déplâtrer [deplɑtʀe] [1] *vt* (*Constr*) to strip the plaster off; (*Méd*) to take out of plaster, take the plaster cast off.

dépliage [deplijaʒ] *nm* (*voir* **déplier**) unfolding; opening out.

dépliant, e [deplijɑ̃, ijɑ̃t] 1 *adj* extendible. 2 *nm* (*prospectus*) leaflet, folder; (*grande page*) fold-out page.

dépliement [deplimɑ̃] *nm* = **dépliage**.

déplier [deplije] [7] 1 *vt* a *serviette, vêtement* to unfold; *carte, journal, canapé-lit* to open out, unfold; (*fig*) *jambes* to stretch out. b (†: *déballer*) *paquet* to open out, open up. **~ sa marchandise** to spread out one's wares. 2 **se déplier** *vpr* [*carte, journal*] to come unfolded, open out; [*vêtement, serviette*] to come unfolded; [*feuille d'arbre*] to open out, unfold. **ça peut se ~, ça se déplie** it unfolds *ou* opens out, it can be unfolded.

déplissage [deplisaʒ] *nm* (*voir* **déplisser**) [*étoffe*] taking the pleats out of; flattening (out); smoothing (out).

déplisser [deplise] [1] 1 *vt* *étoffe plissée* to take the pleats out of; *étoffe avec faux plis* to flatten (out), smooth (out); (*littér*) *front* to smooth. 2 **se déplisser** *vpr* [*jupe*] to come unpleated, lose its pleats.

déploiement [deplwamɑ̃] *nm* [*voile, drapeau*] unfurling; [*ailes*] spreading; [*troupes*] deployment; [*richesses, forces, amabilité, talents*] display. **~ de force** deployment of troops (*ou* police).

déplomber [deplɔ̃be] [1] *vt* *colis, compteur* to unseal; *dent* to remove the filling from, take the filling out of.

déplorable [deplɔʀabl] *adj* deplorable, disgraceful.

déplorablement [deplɔʀabləmɑ̃] *adv* deplorably, disgracefully.

déplorer [deplɔʀe] [1] *vt* (*trouver fâcheux*) to deplore; (*littér: s'affliger de*) to lament.

déployer [deplwaje] [8] 1 *vt* a *carte, tissu* to open out, spread out; *voile, drapeau* to unfurl; *ailes* to spread.
b *troupes* to deploy; *assortiment, échantillons* to spread out, lay out. **ils ont déployé d'importantes forces de police** they laid on *ou* deployed a huge number of police, they put a large police force into action; **~ en éventail** *troupes* to fan out; **il déploie tout un assortiment dans sa vitrine** he displays a wide variety of goods in his window.
c *richesses, fastes* to make a display of, display; *talents, ressources, forces* to display, exhibit.
d **~ beaucoup d'activité** to be very active, engage in great activity; **~ beaucoup d'efforts/d'énergie** to expend a lot of effort/energy; *voir* **rire**.
2 **se déployer** *vpr* [*voile, drapeau*] to unfurl; [*ailes*] to spread;

[troupes] to deploy; *[cortège]* to spread out.

déplumer [deplyme] 1 **1 vt** (†) to pluck. **2 se déplumer vpr** *[oiseau]* to moult, lose its feathers; (**: perdre ses cheveux*) to go bald, lose one's hair.

dépoétiser [depɔetize] 1 **vt** to take the romance out of, make prosaic.

dépoitraillé, e [depwatʀɑje] **adj** (*péj*) **quelle tenue, il est tout ~!** what a sight he is, with his shirt all undone at the front showing his chest!

dépolarisant, e [depɔlaʀizɑ̃, ɑ̃t] **1 adj** depolarizing. **2 nm** depolarizer.

dépolarisation [depɔlaʀizasjɔ̃] **nf** depolarization.

dépolariser [depɔlaʀize] 1 **vt** to depolarize.

dépoli, e [depɔli] (**ptp de dépolir**) **adj** *voir* **verre**.

dépolir [depɔliʀ] 2 **1 vt** *argent, étain* to tarnish; *verre* to frost. **2 se dépolir vpr** to tarnish.

dépolissage [depɔlisaʒ] **nm** (*voir* **dépolir**) tarnishing; frosting.

dépolitisation [depɔlitizasjɔ̃] **nf** depoliticization.

dépolitiser [depɔlitize] 1 **vt** to depoliticize.

dépolluer [depɔlɥe] 1 **vt** to clean up, rid *ou* clear of pollution.

dépollution [depɔlysjɔ̃] **nf** getting rid of pollution (*de* from). **la ~ des plages souillées par le mazout** the cleaning (up) of oil-polluted beaches.

déponent, e [depɔnɑ̃, ɑ̃t] **1 adj** (*Ling*) deponent. **2 nm** deponent (verb).

dépopulation [depɔpylasjɔ̃] **nf** depopulation.

déportation [depɔʀtasjɔ̃] **nf** (*exil*) deportation, transportation; (*internement*) imprisonment (in a concentration camp).

déporté, e [depɔʀte] (**ptp de déporter**) **nm,f** (*exilé*) deportee; (*interné*) prisoner (in a concentration camp).

déportement [depɔʀtəmɑ̃] **nm a** (*embardée*) **~ vers la gauche** swerve to the left. **b** (†*: écarts de conduite*) **~s** misbehaviour, excesses.

déporter [depɔʀte] 1 **vt a** *personne* (*exiler*) to deport, transport; (*interner*) to send to a concentration camp. **b** (*faire dévier*) to carry off course. **le vent l'a déporté** the wind carried *ou* blew him off course; (*Aut*) **se ~ sur la gauche** to swerve to the left.

déposant, e [depozɑ̃, ɑ̃t] **nm,f** (*épargnant*) depositor; (*Jur*) bailor; (*témoin*) deponent.

dépose [depoz] **nf** *[tapis]* lifting, taking up; *[serrure, moteur]* taking out, removal; *[rideau]* taking down.

déposer [depoze] 1 **1 vt a** (*poser*) to lay down, put down, set down; *ordures* to dump. **~ une gerbe** (*sur une tombe etc*) to lay a wreath; **"défense de ~ des ordures"** "dumping of rubbish is prohibited", "no tipping" (*Brit*), "no dumping"; (*fig*) **~ les armes** to lay down (one's) arms; (*littér*) **~ un baiser sur le front de qn** to plant a kiss on sb's forehead.

b (*laisser*) *chose* to leave; *personne* to drop, set down. **~ sa carte** to leave one's card; **on a déposé une lettre/un paquet pour vous** somebody left a letter/parcel for you, somebody dropped a letter/parcel in for you; **~ une valise à la consigne** to deposit *ou* leave a suitcase at the left-luggage (office); **je te dépose à la gare** I'll drop you (off) at the station, I'll set you down at the station; **l'autobus le déposa à la gare** the bus dropped him at the station; **est-ce que je peux vous ~ quelque part?** can I give you a lift anywhere?, can I drop you anywhere?

c (*Fin*) *argent, valeur* to deposit. **~ de l'argent sur un compte** to put money into an account, deposit money in an account.

d (*Admin, Jur etc*) *plainte* to lodge; *réclamation* to file; *conclusions* to present; *brevet, marque de fabrique* to register; *projet de loi* to bring in, table; *rapport* to send in, file. **~ son bilan** to go into (voluntary) liquidation; *voir* **marque**.

e (*destituer*) *souverain* to depose.

f *[eau, vin] sable, lie* to deposit.

g (*démonter*) *tenture* to take down; *tapis* to take up, lift; *serrure, moteur* to take out, remove.

2 vi a *[liquide]* to form a sediment, form a deposit. **laisser ~** to leave to settle.

b (*Jur*) to give evidence, testify.

3 se déposer vpr *[poussière, lie]* to settle.

dépositaire [depozitɛʀ] **nmf a** *[objet confié]* depository; (*fig*) *[secret, vérité]* possessor, guardian; (*Jur*) bailee. (*Jur*) **~ public** ≃ authorized depository; (*Fin*) **~ légal** escrow agent. **b** (*Comm: agent*) agent (*de* for). **~ exclusif** sole agent (*de* for); **nous ne sommes pas ~s** we are not agents for them, it's not a line we carry.

déposition [depozisjɔ̃] **nf a** (*Jur*) (*à un procès*) evidence (*NonC*); (*écrite*) (sworn) statement, deposition. **signer sa ~** to sign one's statement *ou* deposition. **b** *[souverain]* deposition, deposing. **c** (*Art*) **~ de croix** Deposition.

déposséder [depɔsede] 6 **vt: ~ qn de** *terres* to dispossess sb of; *place, biens* to deprive sb of; *charge* to divest *ou* deprive sb of; **ils se sentaient dépossédés** they felt dispossessed.

dépossession [depɔsesjɔ̃] **nf** (*voir* **déposséder**) dispossession; deprivation; divesting. **leur sentiment de ~** their feeling of being dispossessed.

dépôt [depo] **1 nm a** (*action de déposer*) *[argent, valeurs]* deposit(ing). **le ~ des manteaux au vestiaire est obligatoire** (all) coats must be left *ou* deposited in the cloakroom; **le ~ d'une marque de fabrique** the registration of a trademark; **~ de bilan** (voluntary) liquidation; (*Jur*) **~ légal** registration of copyright; (*Fin*) **en ~ fiduciaire** in escrow; *voir* **mandat**.

b (*garde*) **avoir qch en ~** to hold sth in trust; **confier qch en ~ à qn** to entrust sth to sb.

c (*chose confiée*) **restituer un ~** to return what has been entrusted to one; **~ sacré** sacred trust; (*Fin*) **~ (bancaire)** (bank) deposit; (*Fin*) **~ à vue** deposit on current account (*Brit*), checking deposit (*US*); **~ à terme** fixed term deposit; *voir* **banque, compte**.

d (*garantie*) deposit. **~ préalable** advance deposit; **verser un ~** to put down *ou* pay a deposit.

e (*sédiment*) *[liquide, lie]* sediment, deposit. **~ de sable** silt (*NonC*); **~ de tartre** fur (*Brit: NonC*), layer of sediment; **l'eau a formé un ~ calcaire dans la bouilloire** the water has formed a layer of sediment on the kettle *ou* has furred up the kettle (*Brit*).

f (*entrepôt*) warehouse, store; *[autobus]* depot, garage; *[trains]* depot, shed; (*Mil*) depot.

g (*Comm: point de vente*) **il n'y a pas de boulangerie/laiterie mais un ~ de pain/de lait à l'épicerie** there is no baker's/dairy but bread/milk can be bought at the grocer's *ou* but the grocer supplies *ou* sells bread/milk.

h (*prison*) jail, prison. **il a passé la nuit au ~** he spent the night in the cells *ou* in jail.

2 comp ▸dépôt d'essence (*Aut*) petrol (*Brit*) *ou* gasoline (*US*) depot **▸dépôt de marchandises** goods (*Brit*) *ou* freight (*US*) depot *ou* station **▸dépôt de munitions** ammunition dump **▸dépôt d'ordures** (rubbish) dump *ou* tip (*Brit*), garbage dump (*US*) **▸dépôt-vente nm** (**pl dépôts-ventes**) sale or return shop.

dépotage [depɔtaʒ] **nm**, **dépotement** [depɔtmɑ̃] **nm** (*voir* **dépoter**) transplanting; decanting.

dépoter [depɔte] 1 **vt** *plante* to take out of the pot, transplant; *liquide* to decant.

dépotoir [depɔtwaʀ] **nm a** (*lit, fig: décharge*) dumping ground, (rubbish) dump *ou* tip (*Brit*), garbage dump (*US*). **b** (*usine*) sewage works.

dépouille [depuj] **nf a** (*peau*) skin, hide; (*Zool: de mue*) cast; *[serpent]* slough. **b** (*littér: cadavre*) **~ (mortelle)** (mortal) remains. **c** (*littér: butin*) **~s** plunder, spoils.

dépouillé, e [depuje] (**ptp de dépouiller**) **adj** *décor* bare; *style* bald. **~ de** *poésie* lacking in; *ornements* shorn *ou* stripped of.

dépouillement [depujmɑ̃] **nm a** (*examen: voir* **dépouiller a**) perusal; going through; studying. **le ~ du courrier a pris trois heures** going through the mail *ou* the perusal of the mail took 3 hours, it took 3 hours to go through *ou* peruse the mail; **le ~ du scrutin** counting the votes; **lors du ~** when the votes are (*ou* were *etc*) being counted, during the count. **b** (*ascèse, pauvreté*) voluntary deprivation; (*sobriété*) lack of ornamentation. **c** (*spoliation*) stripping.

dépouiller [depuje] 1 **1 vt a** (*examiner en détail*) *comptes, journal, courrier, ouvrage* to go through, peruse; *auteur* to go through, study (in detail). **~ un scrutin** to count the votes.

b (*écorcher*) to skin; (*écorcer*) to bark, strip the bark from.

c (*enlever à*) **~ qn de** *vêtements, économies, honneurs* to strip *ou* divest *ou* deprive sb of.

d (*dégarnir*) **~ qch de** *ornements* to strip *ou* divest *ou* denude sth of; *feuilles, fleurs* to strip *ou* denude sth of; **un livre qui dépouille l'amour de son mystère** a book that strips *ou* divests love of its mystery.

e (*littér: dénuder*) to strip, denude. **le vent dépouille les arbres** the wind strips *ou* denudes the trees (of their leaves); **l'hiver dépouille les champs** winter lays bare the fields; **~ un autel** to remove the ornaments from an altar, strip an altar (of its ornaments); (*fig*) **~ son style** to strip one's style of ornaments.

f (*littér: spolier*) **~ un voyageur** to despoil (*littér*) *ou* strip a traveller of his possessions; **~ un héritier** to deprive *ou* divest an heir of his inheritance; **ce père avare a dépouillé ses enfants** this tight-fisted father has deprived *ou* stripped his children of everything; (*fig*) **~ Pierre pour habiller Paul** to rob Peter to pay Paul; **ils ont dépouillé le pays** they have plundered the country *ou* laid the country bare.

g (*littér: se défaire de*) *vêtement* to shed, divest o.s. of; (*Zool*) *peau* to cast off, shed; *prétention, orgueil* to cast off, cast aside.

2 se dépouiller vpr a (*littér*) **se ~ de** *vêtements* to shed, divest o.s. of; *possessions* to divest *ou* deprive o.s. of; (*fig*) *arrogance* to cast off *ou* aside, divest o.s. of; *[arbre] feuilles, fleurs* to shed; *[prés etc] verdure, fleurs* to become stripped *ou* denuded of. **les arbres se dépouillent (de leurs feuilles)** the trees are shedding their leaves; **la campagne se dépouille (de son feuillage *ou* de sa verdure)** the countryside is losing *ou* shedding its greenery; **son style s'était dépouillé de toute redondance** his style had been stripped *ou* shorn of all unnecessary repetition.

b *[animal qui mue]* to cast off *ou* shed its skin.

dépourvu, e [depuʀvy] **1 adj: ~ de** (*gén*) lacking *ou* wanting in, without; *intérêt, qualités, bon sens* devoid of, lacking *ou* wanting in; *méchanceté, mauvaises intentions* devoid of, without; **~ d'ornements** unornamented, bare of ornaments; **~ d'argent** penniless, without money; **ce récit n'est pas ~ d'intérêt/de qualités** this story is not devoid of interest/qualities *ou* not without interest/its qualities; **des gens ~s (de**

tout) destitute people. 2 **nm: prendre qn au ~** to catch sb unprepared, catch sb napping; **il a été pris au ~ par cette question inattendue** he was caught off his guard *ou* on the hop* by this unexpected question.

dépoussiérage [depusjeʀaʒ] **nm** removal of dust (*de* from). **techniques de ~** dust removal techniques.

dépoussiérant [depusjeʀɑ̃] **nm** anti-static furniture polish.

dépoussiérer [depusjeʀe] 6 **vt** (*lit*) to remove dust from; (*fig*) *texte, institution* to blow *ou* brush away the cobwebs from.

dépravation [depʀavasjɔ̃] **nf** (*état*) depravity.

dépravé, e [depʀave] (**ptp de dépraver**) 1 **adj** depraved. 2 **nm,f** degenerate.

dépraver [depʀave] 1 **vt** to deprave. **les mœurs se dépravent** morals are becoming depraved.

dépréciateur, -trice [depʀesjatœʀ, tʀis] **nm,f** disparager, belittler.

dépréciatif, -ive [depʀesjatif, iv] **adj** *propos, jugement* depreciatory, disparaging; *mot, sens* derogatory, disparaging.

dépréciation [depʀesjasjɔ̃] **nf** depreciation.

déprécier [depʀesje] 7 1 **vt** (*faire perdre de la valeur à*) to depreciate; (*dénigrer*) to belittle, disparage, depreciate. 2 **se déprécier vpr** *[monnaie, objet]* to depreciate; *[personne]* to belittle *ou* disparage o.s., be self-depreciating.

déprédateur, -trice [depʀedatœʀ, tʀis] (*voir* **déprédation**) 1 **adj** plundering (*épith*). 2 **nm,f** plunderer; embezzler.

déprédation [depʀedasjɔ̃] **nf** a (*gén pl*) (*pillage*) plundering (*NonC*), depredation (*frm*); (*dégâts*) damage (*NonC*), depredation (*frm*). **commettre des ~s** to cause damage. b (*Jur: détournement*) misappropriation, embezzlement.

déprendre (se) [depʀɑ̃dʀ] 58 **vpr** (*littér*) **se ~ de** to lose one's fondness for.

dépressif, -ive [depʀesif, iv] **adj** depressive.

dépression [depʀesjɔ̃] **nf** a **~ (de terrain)** depression; **le village était dans une ~** the village was in a depression; **la maison était dans une ~** the house stood in a dip. b **~ (atmosphérique)** (atmospheric) depression; **une ~ centrée sur le nord de la France** a trough of low pressure over northern France. c (*Psych*) (*état*) depression. **~ (nerveuse)** (nervous) breakdown; **elle fait de la ~** she is having a bad fit of depression. d **~ (économique)** (economic) depression *ou* slump.

dépressionnaire [depʀesjɔnɛʀ] **adj: zone ~** trough of low pressure.

dépressurisation [depʀesyʀizasjɔ̃] **nf** (*Astron, Aviat*) depressurization. **en cas de ~ de la cabine** should the pressure drop in the cabin.

dépressuriser [depʀesyʀize] 1 **vt** (*Aviat, Astron*) to depressurize.

déprimant, e [depʀimɑ̃, ɑ̃t] **adj** (*moralement*) depressing; (*physiquement*) enervating, debilitating.

déprime* [depʀim] **nf** depression. **faire de la ~** to have (a fit of) the blues*; **c'est la ~ dans les milieux financiers** financial circles are depressed; **période de ~** low period.

déprimé, e [depʀime] (**ptp de déprimer**) **adj** a (*moralement*) depressed, low (*attrib*). b *terrain* low-lying.

déprimer [depʀime] 1 1 **vt** a (*moralement*) to depress; (*physiquement*) to debilitate, enervate. b (*enfoncer*) to depress. 2 **vi** (*) to have (a fit of) the blues*, be depressed.

De profundis [depʀɔfɔ̃dis] **nm** de profundis.

déprogrammation [depʀɔgʀamasjɔ̃] **nf** cancellation.

déprogrammer [depʀɔgʀame] 1 **vt** (*TV*) (*définitivement*) to take off the air; (*temporairement*) to cancel; *rendez-vous, visite* to cancel.

dépt. (**abrév de département**) a *[organisme, entreprise]* dept. b (*division du territoire*) *voir* **département**.

dépucelage‡ [depys(ə)laʒ] **nm: ~ d'une fille** taking of a girl's virginity.

dépuceler‡ [depys(ə)le] 4 **vt** *fille*, (*hum*) *garçon* to take the virginity of. **elle s'est fait ~ à 13 ans** she lost it when she was 13‡; **c'est lui qui l'a dépucelée** she lost it to him‡; **c'est avec elle que je me suis dépucelé** it was with her that I had it for the first time‡, she gave me my first experience.

depuis [dəpɥi] 1 **prép** a (*point de départ dans le temps*) since, ever since (*intensif*). **il attend ~ hier/ce matin** he has been waiting (ever) since yesterday/this morning; **il attendait ~ lundi/le 3 mars** he had been waiting (ever) since Monday/since March 3rd; **~ leur dispute ils ne se parlent/parlaient plus** they haven't/hadn't spoken to each other (ever) since their quarrel *ou* (ever) since they quarrelled; **ils ont toujours habité la même maison ~ leur mariage** they've lived in the same house ever since they were married, they've always lived in the same house since they were married; **je ne l'ai pas vue ~ qu'elle/~ le jour où elle s'est cassé la jambe** I haven't seen her since she/since the day she broke her leg; **elle joue du violon ~ son plus jeune âge** she has played the violin since *ou* from early childhood, she has been playing *ou* has played the violin (ever) since she was very small; **~ cette affaire il est très méfiant** (ever) since that affair he has been very suspicious; **~ quand le connaissez-vous?** (for) how long have you known him?, how long is it that you've known him?; **~ quelle date êtes-vous ici?** since when have you been here?, when did you arrive here?; **~ cela**, (*littér*) **~ lors** since then *ou* that time, from that time forward (*littér*), ever since; (*iro*) **~ quand es-tu (devenu) expert sur la question?** since when have you been an expert on the matter? (*iro*); **~ le matin jusqu'au soir** from morning till night.

b (*durée*) for. **il est malade ~ une semaine** he has been ill for a week (now); **~ combien de temps êtes-vous/travaillez-vous ici? — je suis/travaille ici ~ 5 ans** how long have you been here/been working here? — I've been here/been working here (for) 5 years *ou* for the last 5 years; **il est parti/mort ~ 2 ans** he has been gone/dead (for) 2 years; **~ ces derniers jours/mois il a bien changé** he has changed a great deal in *ou* over the last *ou* past few days/months; **elle cherche du travail ~ plus d'un mois** she's been looking for a job for over *ou* more than a month; **il dormait ~ une heure quand le réveil sonna** he had been sleeping *ou* asleep for an hour when the alarm went off; **mort ~ longtemps** long since dead; **tu le connais ~ longtemps? — ~ toujours** have you known him long? *ou* for a long time? — I've known him all my life *ou* I've always known him; **je la connaissais ~ peu quand elle est partie** I hadn't known her long *ou* I had known her (for) only a short time *ou* I had only known her a little while when she left; **nous n'avons pas été au théâtre ~ des siècles** we haven't been to the theatre for *ou* in ages; **~ peu elle a recommencé à sortir** lately *ou* recently *ou* of late she has started going out again.

c (*lieu: à partir de*) since, from. **nous roulons/roulions sous la pluie ~ Londres** it's been raining/it rained all the way from London; **~ Nice il a fait le plein 3 fois** he's filled up 3 times since Nice; **le concert est retransmis ~ Paris/nos studios** the concert is broadcast from Paris/our studios; **il sera bientôt possible de téléphoner ~ la lune** it'll soon be possible to telephone from the moon.

d (*rang, ordre, quantité*) from. **~ le simple soldat jusqu'au général** from private (right up) to general; **~ le premier jusqu'au dernier** from the first to the last; **robes ~ 100 F jusqu'à ...** dresses from 100 francs to ..., dresses starting at 100 francs (and) going up to ...; **~ 5 grammes jusqu'à ...** from 5 grammes (up) to ...; **ils ont toutes les tailles ~ le 36** they have all sizes from 36 upwards, they have all sizes starting at 36.

e **~ que, ~ le temps que: ~ qu'il habite ici, il n'a cessé de se plaindre** he hasn't stopped complaining (ever) since he's lived here; **~ qu'il est ministre il ne nous parle plus** now that he is *ou* since he became a minister he doesn't speak to us any more; **~ qu'il avait appris son succès il désirait** *ou* **il avait désiré la féliciter** he had wanted to congratulate her ever since he had heard of her success; **~ le temps qu'il apprend le français, il devrait pouvoir le parler** considering how long *ou* for all the time he's been learning French, he ought to be able to speak it; **~ le temps qu'il est ici, il ne nous a jamais dit un mot** in all the time he has been here he has never said a word to us; **~ le temps que nous ne nous étions vus!** it's ages since we (last) saw each other!, long time no see!*; **~ le temps que je voulais voir ce film!** I had been wanting to see that film for ages! *ou* for such a long time!; **~ le temps que je dis que je vais lui écrire!** I've been saying I'll write to him for ages!; **~ que le monde est monde** from time immemorial.

2 **adv** ever since, since (then). **~, nous sommes sans nouvelles** we have been without news ever since; **nous étions en vacances ensemble, je ne l'ai pas revu ~** we were on holiday together and I haven't seen him since (then).

dépuratif, -ive [depyʀatif, iv] **adj, nm** depurative.

députation [depytasjɔ̃] **nf** (*envoi, groupe*) deputation, delegation; (*mandat de député*) position of deputy. **candidat à la ~** parliamentary candidate; **se présenter à la ~** to stand (*Brit*) *ou* run (*US*) for parliament.

député [depyte] **nm** a (*au parlement*) deputy, ≃ member of Parliament (*Brit*), ≃ representative (*US*). **elle a été élue ~ de Metz** she has been elected (as) deputy *ou* member for Metz; **~ au parlement européen** member of the European Parliament; **le ~-maire de Rouen** the deputy and mayor of Rouen; **~ en exercice** present incumbent, sitting member (*Brit*). b (*envoyé d'un prince*) envoy; (*envoyé d'une assemblée*) delegate.

députer [depyte] 1 **vt: ~ qn pour faire/aller** to delegate sb to do/go; **~ qn à** *ou* **auprès d'une assemblée/auprès de qn** to send sb (as representative) to an assembly/to sb.

déqualification [dekalifikasjɔ̃] **nf** deskilling.

déqualifier [dekalifje] 7 **vt** *personnel, emploi* to deskill.

der* [dɛʀ] **nf** (*Cartes*) very last (one). (*guerre de 1914-1918*) **la ~ des ~s** the war to end all wars.

déracinable [deʀasinabl] **adj** *préjugé* eradicable. **difficilement ~** difficult to eradicate.

déracinement [deʀasinmɑ̃] **nm** (*voir* **déraciner**) uprooting; eradication.

déraciner [deʀasine] 1 **vt** *arbre, personne* to uproot; *erreur* to eradicate; *préjugé* to root out, eradicate.

déraillement [deʀɑjmɑ̃] **nm** derailment.

dérailler [deʀɑje] 1 **vi** *[train]* to be derailed, go off *ou* leave the rails; (*: *divaguer*) to rave*, talk twaddle* (*Brit*); (*: *mal fonctionner*) to be up the spout* (*Brit*), be on the blink*. **faire ~ un train** to derail a train; **tu dérailles!*** (*être fou*) you're nuts!*, you're off your rocker!‡; (*se tromper*) you're talking through your hat!*; (*être gâteux, délirer*) **son père déraille complètement*** his dad's quite gaga* *ou* off his head*.

dérailleur [deʀɑjœʀ] **nm** *[bicyclette]* dérailleur gears; (*Rail*) derailer, derailing stop.

déraison [deʀɛzɔ̃] **nf** (*littér*) insanity.

déraisonnable [deʀɛzɔnabl] **adj** unreasonable.

déraisonnablement [deʀɛzɔnabləmɑ̃] adv unreasonably.
déraisonner [deʀɛzɔne] [1] vi (*littér*) (*dire des bêtises*) to talk nonsense; (*être fou*) to rave.
dérangeant, e [deʀɑ̃ʒɑ̃, ɑ̃t] adj disturbing.
dérangement [deʀɑ̃ʒmɑ̃] nm a (*gêne*) trouble. **(toutes) mes excuses pour le ~** my apologies for the trouble I'm causing *ou* for the inconvenience. b (*déplacement*) **pour vous éviter un autre ~** to save you another trip; **voilà 10 F pour votre ~** here's 10 francs for coming *ou* for taking the trouble to come. c (*bouleversement*) *[affaires, papiers]* disorder (*de* in). **en ~** *machine, téléphone* out of order; **~ d'esprit†** mental derangement *ou* disturbance.
déranger [deʀɑ̃ʒe] [3] 1 vt a (*déplacer*) *papiers* to disturb, mix *ou* muddle up; *vêtements, coiffure* to disarrange, ruffle.
b (*gêner, importuner*) to trouble, bother; (*surprendre*) *animal, cambrioleur* to disturb. **je ne vous dérange pas?** am I disturbing you?, I trust I'm not disturbing you?; **les cambrioleurs ont été dérangés** the burglars were disturbed; **elle viendra vous voir demain, si cela ne vous dérange pas** she'll come and see you tomorrow, if that's all right by you* *ou* if that's no trouble to you; **elle ne veut pas ~ le docteur inutilement** she doesn't want to bother the doctor unnecessarily; **ne me dérangez pas toutes les cinq minutes** don't come bothering me every five minutes; **~ qn dans son sommeil** to disturb sb's sleep; **on le dérange toutes les nuits en ce moment** he is disturbed every night at the moment; **ça vous dérange si je fume?** do you mind *ou* will it bother you if I smoke?; **cela vous dérangerait-il de venir?** would you mind coming?; **alors, ça te dérange?*** what does it matter to you?; (*pancarte*) **"ne pas ~"** "do not disturb"; **ses films dérangent** his films are disturbing.
c (*dérégler*) *projets, routine* to disrupt, upset; *machine* to put out of order. **les essais atomiques ont dérangé le temps** the nuclear tests have unsettled *ou* upset the weather; **ça lui a dérangé l'esprit** this has disturbed his mind; **il a le cerveau dérangé, il est dérangé** he *ou* his mind is deranged *ou* unhinged; **il a l'estomac dérangé** his stomach is upset, he has an upset stomach *ou* a stomach upset; **il est (un peu) dérangé** he has (a bit of) diarrhoea, his bowels are (a bit) loose.
2 **se déranger** vpr a *[médecin, réparateur]* to come out.
b (*pour une démarche, une visite*) to go along, come along. **sans vous ~, sur simple appel téléphonique, nous vous renseignons** without leaving your home, you can obtain information simply by telephoning us; **je me suis dérangé pour rien, c'était fermé** it was a waste of time going (along) *ou* it was a wasted journey *ou* trip because it was closed.
c (*changer de place*) to move. **il s'est dérangé pour me laisser passer** he moved *ou* stepped aside to let me pass; **surtout, ne vous dérangez pas pour moi** please don't put yourself out *ou* go to any inconvenience on my account.
dérapage [deʀapaʒ] nm *[véhicule]* skid; (*Ski*) side-slipping. **faire un ~** to skid; **faire un ~ contrôlé** to do a controlled skid; (*Ski*) **piste de ~** skidpad; (*fig*) **~ de l'indice des prix** unexpected increase in the price index; (*fig*) **~ verbal** verbal faux pas.
déraper [deʀape] [1] vi a *[véhicule]* to skid; *[piéton, semelles, échelle]* to slip. b *[ancre]* to be atrip *ou* aweigh; *[bateau]* to trip her anchor. c (*fig*) *[prix, salaires]* to get out of hand, soar; *[conversation]* to slide onto sticky ground.
dératé, e [deʀate] nm,f *voir* **courir.**
dératisation [deʀatizasjɔ̃] nf rat extermination.
dératiser [deʀatize] [1] vt: **~ un lieu** to exterminate the rats in a place, rid a place of rats.
derby [dɛʀbi] nm (*Ftbl, Rugby*) derby; (*Équitation*) Derby.
derechef [dəʀəʃɛf] adv (*†† ou littér*) once more, once again.
déréglé, e [deʀegle] (ptp de **dérégler**) adj (*voir* **dérégler**) out of order (*attrib*); upset; unsettled; dissolute. **les élucubrations de son imagination ~e** the ravings of his wild *ou* disordered imagination.
dérèglement [deʀɛgləmɑ̃] nm *[machine, mécanisme]* disturbance; *[pouls, estomac, temps]* upset; *[esprit]* unsettling (*NonC*); *[mœurs]* dissoluteness (*NonC*). (*littér: dépravations*) **~s** dissoluteness.
déréglementation [deʀɛgləmɑ̃tasjɔ̃] nf deregulation.
déréglementer [deʀɛgləmɑ̃te] [1] vt to deregulate.
dérégler [deʀegle] [6] 1 vt a *mécanisme* to throw out (of order), disturb; *machine* to disturb the mechanism of, put out of order; *esprit* to unsettle; *habitudes, temps* to upset, unsettle; *estomac, appétit, pouls* to upset. b *vie, mœurs* to make dissolute. 2 **se dérégler** vpr *[mécanisme, machine, appareil]* to go wrong; *[pouls, estomac, temps]* to be upset; *[esprit]* to become unsettled; *[mœurs]* to become dissolute. **cette montre se dérègle tout le temps** this watch keeps going wrong.
dérider [deʀide] [1] 1 vt *personne* to brighten up; *front* to uncrease. 2 **se dérider** vpr *[personne]* to cheer up; *[front]* to uncrease.
dérision [deʀizjɔ̃] nf derision, mockery. **par ~** derisively, mockingly; **de ~** *parole, sourire* of derision, derisive; **c'est une ~!** it's derisory!; *voir* **tourner.**
dérisoire [deʀizwaʀ] adj (*gén*) derisory, pathetic, laughable. **pour une somme ~** for a nominal *ou* derisory sum.
dérisoirement [deʀizwaʀmɑ̃] adv pathetically.
dérivatif, -ive [deʀivatif, iv] 1 adj derivative. 2 nm distraction. **il a son travail comme ~ à sa douleur** he has his work to take his mind off *ou* to distract him from his sorrow.
dérivation [deʀivasjɔ̃] nf a *[rivière]* diversion; *voir* **canal.** b (*Ling, Math*) derivation. **~ régressive** back formation. c (*Élec*) shunt. d (*Aviat, Naut*) drift, deviation.
dérive [deʀiv] nf a (*déviation*) drift, leeway. **~ sur bâbord** drift to port; **navire en ~** ship adrift; **~ des continents** continental drift; **~ nord-atlantique** North Atlantic Drift; (*lit*) **à la ~** adrift; (*fig*) **tout va à la ~** everything is going to the dogs *ou* is going downhill; **partir à la ~** to go drifting off. b (*dispositif*) (*Aviat*) fin, vertical stabilizer (*US*); (*Naut*) centre-board.
dérivé, e [deʀive] (ptp de **dériver**) 1 adj (*gén, Chim, Math*) derived. 2 nm (*Chim, Ling, Math*) derivative; (*produit*) by-product. 3 **dérivée** nf (*Math*) derivative.
dériver [deʀive] [1] 1 vt a *rivière* to divert; (*Chim, Ling, Math*) to derive; (*Élec*) to shunt. b (*Tech: dériveter*) to unrivet. 2 **dériver de** vt indir to derive *ou* stem from; (*Ling*) to derive from, be derived from, be a derivative of. 3 vi (*Aviat, Naut*) to drift; (*fig*) *[orateur]* to wander *ou* drift (away) from the subject.
dériveur [deʀivœʀ] nm (*voile*) storm sail; (*bateau*) sailing dinghy (*with centre-board*).
dermatite [dɛʀmatit] nf = **dermite.**
dermatologie [dɛʀmatɔlɔʒi] nf dermatology.
dermatologique [dɛʀmatɔlɔʒik] adj dermatological.
dermatologiste [dɛʀmatɔlɔʒist] nmf, **dermatologue** [dɛʀmatɔlɔg] nmf dermatologist.
dermatose [dɛʀmatoz] nf dermatosis.
derme [dɛʀm] nm dermis.
dermique [dɛʀmik] adj dermic, dermal.
dermite [dɛʀmit] nf dermatitis.
dernier, -ière [dɛʀnje, jɛʀ] 1 adj a (*dans le temps, l'espace*) (*gén*) last; *étage* top (*épith*); *rang* back (*épith*); *branche* upper (*épith*), highest. **arriver (bon) ~** to come in last (a long way behind the others); **la ~ière marche de l'escalier** (*en bas*) the bottom step; (*en haut*) the top step; **prends le ~ mouchoir de la pile** (*dessus*) take the top handkerchief in the pile; (*dessous*) take the bottom handkerchief in the pile; (*Presse*) **en ~ière page** on the back page; **les 100 ~ières pages** the last 100 pages; (*Sport*) **être en ~ière position** to be in (the) last place, bring up the rear; **durant les ~s jours du mois** in the last few days of the month, as the month was drawing to a close; **l'artiste, dans ses ~ières œuvres** ... the artist, in his final *ou* last works ...; **les ~ières années de sa vie** the last few years of his life; **il faut payer avant le 15, ~ délai** it must be paid by the 15th at the latest, the 15th is the deadline for payment; **15 octobre, ~ délai pour les inscriptions** 15th October is the closing *ou* final date for registration, registration must be completed by 15th October at the latest; **il faut partir à midi, ~ carat*** we have to leave by midday at the latest; *voir* **jugement, premier.**
b (*en mérite*) *élève* bottom, last. **être reçu ~** to come last *ou* bottom (*à* in); **il est toujours ~ (en classe)** he's always bottom (of the class), he's always last (in the class); **c'est bien la ~ière personne à qui je demanderais!** he's the last person I'd ask!
c (*gén avant n: le plus récent*) last, latest. **le ~ roman de X** X's latest *ou* last novel; **ces ~s mois/jours** (during) the last *ou* past couple of *ou* few months/days; **ces ~s incidents/événements** these latest *ou* most recent incidents/events; **ces ~s temps** lately, of late; **aux ~ières nouvelles, il était à Paris** the last I (*ou we etc*) heard (of him) he was in Paris, the latest news was that he was in Paris; **voici les ~ières nouvelles concernant l'accident** here is the latest news of the accident, here is an up-to-the-minute report on the accident; **nouvelles de ~ière heure** *ou* **minute** stop-press news; (*fig*) **collaborateur/combattant de la ~ière heure** last-minute helper/fighter; (*Presse*) **~ière édition** (late) final; **c'est le ~ cri** *ou* **la ~ière mode** it's the very latest thing *ou* fashion; **un ordinateur ~ cri** a state-of-the-art computer; (*péj*) **c'est le salon où l'on cause** what a lot of chatterboxes (you are)!*
d (*extrême*) **il s'est montré grossier au ~ point** *ou* **degré** he was extremely rude; **il a protesté avec la ~ière énergie** he protested most vigorously *ou* with the utmost vigour; **examiner qch dans les ~s détails** to study sth in the most minute *ou* in the minutest detail; **le ~ degré de perfection** the height *ou* summit of perfection; **le ~ degré de la souffrance** the depths of suffering; **c'est du ~ ridicule** it's utterly ridiculous, it's ridiculous in the extreme; **c'est du ~ chic** it's the last word in elegance; **c'est de la ~ière importance** it is of the utmost importance; **il est du ~ bien avec le patron** he's on the best of terms with his boss.
e (*pire*) *qualité* lowest, poorest. **de ~ ordre** very inferior; **vendre des morceaux de ~ choix** to sell the poorest quality *ou* most inferior cuts of meat; **c'était la ~ière chose à faire!** that was the last thing to do!; **faire subir les ~s outrages à une femme** to ravish *ou* violate a woman.
f (*évoquant la mort*) last. **ses ~s moments** *ou* **instants** his last *ou* dying moments; **être à sa ~ière heure** to be on one's deathbed; **jusqu'à mon ~ jour** until the day I die, until my dying day; **je croyais que ma ~ière heure était venue** I thought my last *ou* final hour had come; **dans les ~s temps il ne s'alimentait plus** towards the end he stopped eating; (*littér*) **rendre le ~ soupir** to breathe one's last (*littér*); (*frm*) **rendre les ~s devoirs** to pay one's last respects (*à* to); (*Rel*) **les ~s sacrements** the last sacraments *ou* rites.

g (*précédent*) last, previous. **les ~s propriétaires sont partis à l'étranger** the last *ou* previous owners went abroad; **le ~ détenteur du record était américain** the last *ou* previous holder of the record was an American; **l'an/le mois ~** last year/month.

h (*final, ultime*) *échelon, grade* top, highest. **après un ~ regard/effort** after one last *ou* final look/effort; **quel est votre ~ prix?** (*pour vendre*) what's the lowest you'll go?; (*pour acheter*) what's your final offer?; (*pour une offre*) **c'est votre ~ mot?** is that your final offer?; **avoir le ~ mot** to have the last word; **je n'ai pas dit mon ~ mot** you (*ou* they *etc*) haven't heard the last of me; (*Bourse*) **~s cours** closing prices, latest quotations; **en ~ière analyse** in the final *ou* last analysis; **en ~ lieu** finally; **mettre la ~ière main à qch** to put the finishing touches to sth; **en ~ ressort** *ou* **recours** as a last resort; **les ~ières volontés de qn** the last wishes of sb; **les ~ières dispositions du défunt** the deceased's last will and testament; **accompagner qn à sa ~ière demeure** to accompany sb to his final resting place; **y laisser jusqu'à son ~ sou** to lose one's last buck on it*.

2 **nm,f** a last (one). **parler/sortir le ~** to speak/leave last; **les ~s arrivés n'auront rien** the last ones to arrive *ou* the last arrivals will get nothing; **le ~ venu** (*lit*) the last to come; (*fig péj*) just anybody; **~ entré, premier sorti** last in, first out; **tu seras servi le ~** you'll be served last, you'll be the last to get served; **il est le ~ de sa classe/de la liste** he's at the bottom of the class/list; **voilà le ~ de la classe** there's the one *ou* boy who's bottom of the class *ou* last in the class; **il a été reçu dans les ~s** he was nearly bottom among those who passed the exam; **elle a tendance à gâter son (petit) ~** she's inclined to spoil her youngest (child); **il est le ~ à pouvoir** *ou* **qui puisse faire cela** he's the last person to be able to do that; **c'est le ~ de mes soucis** it's the least of my worries; **ils ont été tués jusqu'au ~** they were all killed (right down) to the last man, every single one of them was killed; **c'est la ~ière à qui vous puissiez demander un service** she's the last person you can ask a favour of.

b (*péj*) **le ~ des imbéciles** an absolute imbecile, a complete and utter fool; **le ~ des filous** an out-and-out scoundrel; **c'est le ~ des ~s!** he's the lowest of the low.

c **ce ~, cette ~ière** (*de deux*) the latter; (*de plusieurs*) this last, the last-mentioned.

3 **nm** (*étage*) top floor *ou* storey (*Brit*) *ou* story (*US*). **acheter qch/arriver en ~** to buy sth/arrive last.

4 **dernière nf** (*Théât*) last performance. **vous connaissez la ~ière?*** have you heard the latest?

5 **comp ▸dernier-né, dernière-née nm,f (mpl derniers-nés)** last-born, youngest child; (*fig: œuvre*) latest *ou* most recent creation.

dernièrement [dɛʀnjɛʀmɑ̃] **adv** (*il y a peu de temps*) recently; (*ces derniers temps*) lately, recently, of late.

dérobade [deʀɔbad] **nf** side-stepping (*NonC*), equivocation, evasion; (*Équitation*) refusal. **~ fiscale** tax evasion.

dérobé, e [deʀɔbe] (**ptp de dérober**) 1 **adj** *escalier, porte* secret, hidden. 2 **dérobée nf: à la ~** secretly, surreptitiously; **regarder qn à la ~** to give sb a surreptitious *ou* stealthy glance.

dérober [deʀɔbe] [1] 1 **vt** a (*voler*) to steal. **~ qch à qn** to steal sth from sb; **~ un baiser (à qn)** to steal a kiss (from sb).

b (*cacher*) **~ qch à qn** to hide *ou* conceal sth from sb; **une haie dérobait la palissade aux regards** a hedge hid *ou* screened the fence from sight, a hedge concealed the fence; **~ qn à la justice/au danger/à la mort** to shield sb from justice/danger/death.

c (*littér: détourner*) *regard, front* to turn away.

2 **se dérober vpr** a (*refuser d'assumer*) to shy away. **se ~ à son devoir/à ses obligations** to shy away from *ou* shirk one's duty/obligations; **se ~ à une discussion** to shy away from a discussion; **je lui ai posé la question mais il s'est dérobé** I put the question to him but he evaded *ou* side-stepped it.

b (*se cacher de*) to hide, conceal o.s. **se ~ aux regards** to hide from view; **se ~ à la justice** to hide from justice; **pour se ~ à la curiosité dont il était l'objet** in order to escape the curiosity surrounding him.

c (*se libérer*) to slip away. **se ~ à l'étreinte de qn** to slip out of sb's arms; **il voulut la prendre dans ses bras mais elle se déroba** he tried to take her in his arms but she shrank *ou* slipped away.

d (*s'effondrer*) *[sol]* to give way. **ses genoux se dérobèrent (sous lui)** his knees gave way (beneath him).

e (*Équitation*) to refuse.

dérogation [deʀɔgasjɔ̃] **nf** (special) dispensation. **ceci constitue une ~ par rapport à la loi** this constitutes a departure from the law; **aucune ~ ne sera permise** no departure from this will be permitted, no special dispensation will be allowed; **certaines ~s sont prévues dans le règlement** certain special dispensations are allowed for in the rules; **il a obtenu ceci par ~** he obtained this by special dispensation.

dérogatoire [deʀɔgatwaʀ] **adj** dispensatory, exceptional. **appliquer un régime ~ à** to apply exceptional arrangements to *ou* in respect of; **à titre ~** by special dispensation.

déroger [deʀɔʒe] [3] **vi** a (*déchoir*) (*gén*) to lower o.s., demean o.s.; (*Hist*) to lose rank and title. b (*enfreindre*) **~ à qch** to go against sth, depart from sth; **~ aux règles** to depart from the rules; **ce serait ~ à la règle établie** that would go against the established order *ou* procedure.

dérouillée‡ [deʀuje] **nf** thrashing, belting‡. **recevoir une ~** (*coups*) to get a thrashing; (*défaite*) to get a hammering*.

dérouiller [deʀuje] [1] 1 **vt** a *métal* to remove the rust from. (*fig*) **je vais me ~ les jambes** I'm going to stretch my legs. b (‡: *battre*) to give a thrashing *ou* belting‡ to, thrash. 2 **vi** (‡) (*souffrir*) to go through it* (*surtout Brit*), have a hard time of it; (*se faire battre*) to cop it‡ (*Brit*), catch it*. **j'ai une rage de dents, qu'est-ce que je dérouille!** I've got toothache, it's agony!* *ou* it's driving me mad! *ou* it's killing me!*

déroulement [deʀulmɑ̃] **nm** a *[match, cérémonie]* progress; *[action, histoire]* development, unfolding, progress. **pendant le ~ des opérations** during the course of (the) operations, while the operations were in progress; **pendant le ~ du film** while the film was on, during the film; **rien n'est venu troubler le ~ de la manifestation** the demonstration went off *ou* passed without incident, nothing happened to disturb the course of the demonstration. b (*voir* **dérouler**) unwinding; uncoiling; unrolling.

dérouler [deʀule] [1] 1 **vt** *fil, bobine* to unwind; *cordage* to uncoil; *nappe, carte, papier* to unroll; *tapis* to roll out; (*Tech*) *tronc d'arbre* to peel a veneer from. **il déroula dans son esprit les événements de la veille** in his mind he went over *ou* through the events of the previous day; (*littér*) **la rivière déroule ses méandres** the river snakes *ou* winds along its tortuous course; (*hum*) **~ le tapis rouge** to roll out the red carpet.

2 **se dérouler vpr** a (*lit*) *[fil, bobine]* to unwind, come unwound; *[ruban]* to unwind, uncoil, come unwound; *[carte, drapeau]* to unroll, come unrolled.

b (*se produire*) (*comme prévu*) to take place; (*accidentellement*) to happen, occur; (*se situer*) to take place. **la ville où la cérémonie s'est déroulée** the town where the ceremony took place; **c'est là que toute ma vie s'est déroulée** it was there that my whole life was spent.

c (*se développer*) *[histoire, faits]* to progress, develop, unfold. **la manifestation s'est déroulée dans le calme** the demonstration went off peacefully; **comment s'est déroulé le match?** how did the match go (off)?; **à mesure que l'histoire se déroulait** as the story unfolded *ou* developed *ou* progressed; **son existence se déroulait, calme et morne** his life went on, calm and drab; **le paysage se déroulait devant nos yeux** the landscape unfolded before our eyes.

dérouleur [deʀulœʀ] **nm** *[papier]* roller. (*Ordin*) **~ de bande magnétique** magnetic tape drive.

dérouleuse [deʀuløz] **nf** (*Tech*) winding machine.

déroutant, e [deʀutɑ̃, ɑ̃t] **adj** disconcerting.

déroute [deʀut] **nf** rout. **armée en ~** routed army; **mettre en ~** to rout, put to rout *ou* flight.

déroutement [deʀutmɑ̃] **nm** (*Aviat, Naut*) rerouting, diversion.

dérouter [deʀute] [1] **vt** *avion, navire* to reroute, divert; *candidat, orateur* to disconcert, throw (out)*, put out; *poursuivants, police, recherches* to throw *ou* put off the scent.

derrick [deʀik] **nm** derrick.

derrière [dɛʀjɛʀ] 1 **prép** a (*à l'arrière de, à la suite de*) behind. **il se cache ~ le fauteuil** he's hiding behind the armchair; **il avait les mains ~ le dos** he had his hands behind his back; **sors de ~ le lit** come out from behind the bed; **passe (par) ~ la maison** go round the back of *ou* round behind the house; **marcher l'un ~ l'autre** to walk one behind the other; (*lit, fig*) **il a laissé les autres loin ~ lui** he left the others far *ou* a long way behind (him); **disparaître ~ une colline** to disappear behind a hill.

b (*fig*) behind. **il faut chercher ~ les apparences** one must look beneath (outward) appearances; **~ sa générosité se cache l'intérêt le plus sordide** behind his generosity lurks *ou* his generosity hides the most sordid self-interest; **faire qch ~ (le dos de) qn** to do sth behind sb's back; **dire du mal ~ le dos de qn** to say (unkind) things behind sb's back; **il a laissé 3 enfants ~ lui** he left 3 children; **le président avait tout le pays ~ lui** the president had the whole country behind him *ou* had the backing of the whole country; **ayez confiance, je suis ~ vous** take heart, I'll support you *ou* back you up *ou* I'm on your side; **il faut toujours être ~ lui** *ou* **son dos** you've always got to keep an eye *ou* a watch on him; **un vin de ~ les fagots*** an extra-special (little) wine; **une bouteille de ~ les fagots*** a bottle of the best; *voir* **idée**.

c (*Naut*) (*dans le bateau*) abaft; (*sur la mer*) astern of.

2 **adv** a behind. **vous êtes juste ~** you're just *ou* right behind it (*ou* us *etc*); **on l'a laissé (loin) ~** we (have) left him (far *ou* a long way) behind; **il est assis 3 rangs ~** he's sitting 3 rows back *ou* 3 rows behind (us *ou* them *etc*); **il a pris des places ~** he has got seats at the back; (*Aut*) **il a préféré monter ~** he preferred to sit in the back; **chemisier qui se boutonne (par) ~** blouse which buttons up *ou* does up at the back; **passe le plateau ~** pass the tray back; **regarde ~, on nous suit** look behind (you) *ou* look back – we're being followed; **il est ~** he's behind (us *ou* them *etc*); **regarde ~** (*au fond de la voiture*) look in the back; (*derrière un objet*) look behind (it); **arrêtez de pousser, ~!** stop pushing back there!, you behind *ou* back there, stop pushing!; (*fig*) **tu peux être sûr qu'il y a quelqu'un ~** you can be sure that there's somebody at the back of it (all) *ou* behind it (all).

b **par-~: c'est fermé, entre** *ou* **passe par-~** it's locked, go in by the back *ou* go in (by) the back way; **attaquer par-~** *ennemi* to attack from behind *ou* from the rear; *adversaire* to attack from behind; **dire du mal**

de qn par-~ to say (unkind) things behind sb's back; **il fait tout par-~** he does everything behind people's backs *ou* in an underhand way.

c (*Naut*) (*dans le bateau*) aft, abaft; (*sur la mer*) astern.

3 **nm** a *[personne]* bottom, behind*; *[animal]* hindquarters, rump. **donner un coup de pied au ~ *ou* dans le ~ de qn** to kick sb in the behind*, give sb a kick in *ou* on the behind* *ou* in the pants‡; **quand j'ai eu 20 ans mon père m'a chassé à coups de pied dans le ~** when I was 20 my father sent me packing *ou* kicked me out*; *voir* **botter**.

b *[objet]* back; *[maison]* back, rear. **le ~ de la tête** the back of the head; **habiter sur le ~** to live at the back (of the house); **roue/porte de ~** back *ou* rear wheel/door; *voir* **patte**.

c **~s** *[édifice]* back, rear; *[armée]* rear.

derviche [dɛʀviʃ] **nm** dervish. **~ tourneur** dancing dervish.

DES [deəɛs] **nm** (**abrév de diplôme d'études supérieures**) *voir* **diplôme**.

des [de] *voir* **de**[1], **de**[2].

dès [dɛ] **prép** a (*dans le temps*) from. **dimanche il a commencé à pleuvoir ~ le matin** on Sunday it rained from the morning onwards, on Sunday it started raining (right) in the morning; **~ le 15 août nous ne travaillerons plus qu'à mi-temps** (as) from August 15th we will only be working half-time; **~ le début** from the (very) start *ou* beginning, right from the start *ou* beginning; **~ son retour il fera le nécessaire** as soon as he's back *ou* immediately upon his return he'll do what's necessary; **~ son retour il commença à se plaindre** as soon as he was back *ou* from the moment he was back he started complaining; **il se précipita vers la sortie ~ la fin du spectacle** as soon as *ou* immediately the performance was over he rushed towards the exit; **~ l'époque romaine on connaissait le chauffage central** as early as *ou* as far back as Roman times people used central heating; **~ son enfance il a collectionné les papillons** he has collected butterflies from (his) childhood *ou* ever since he was a child; **on peut dire ~ maintenant *ou* à présent** one can say (right) here and now; **~ l'abord/ce moment** from the very beginning *ou* the outset/that moment.

b (*dans l'espace*) **~ Lyon il se mit à pleuvoir** we ran into rain *ou* it started to rain as *ou* when we got to Lyons; **~ Lyon il a plu sans arrêt** it never stopped raining from Lyons onwards *ou* after Lyons; **~ l'entrée vous êtes accueillis par des slogans publicitaires** advertising slogans hit you as soon as *ou* immediately you walk in the door; **~ le seuil je sentis qu'il se passait quelque chose** (even) standing in the doorway *ou* as I walked in at the door I sensed that something was going on.

c (*dans une gradation*) **~ sa première année il brilla en anglais** he was good at English right from the first year; **~ le premier verre il roula sous la table** after the (very) first glass he collapsed under the table; **~ la troisième chanson elle se mit à pleurer** at the third song she started to cry.

d (*loc*) **~ que** as soon as, immediately; **~ qu'il aura fini il viendra** as soon as *ou* immediately he's finished he'll come; **~ lors** (*depuis lors*) from that moment (on), from that time on, from then on; (*conséquemment*) that being the case, consequently; **~ lors il ne fuma plus** from that time *ou* moment on he stopped smoking; **~ lors il décida de ne plus fumer** from that moment he decided he wouldn't smoke any more; **vous ne pouvez rien prouver contre lui, ~ lors vous devez le relâcher** you can prove nothing against him and that being the case *ou* and so you'll have to release him; **~ lors que** (*temporel*) as soon as; (*relation de conséquence*) (*si*) from the moment that; (*puisque*) since, as; **~ lors que vous décidez de partir, nous ne pouvons plus rien pour vous** from the moment (that) you choose to go, we can do nothing more for you; **~ lors qu'il a choisi de démissionner, il n'a plus droit à rien** since *ou* as he has decided to hand in his notice he is no longer entitled to anything; **peu m'importe, ~ lors qu'ils sont heureux** I don't mind so long as they are happy.

désabonnement [dezabɔnmɑ̃] **nm** non-renewal *ou* cancellation of one's subscription.

désabonner [dezabɔne] [1] 1 **vt** to cancel the subscription of. 2 **se désabonner vpr** to cancel one's subscription, not to renew one's subscription.

désabusé, e [dezabyze] (**ptp de désabuser**) **adj** *personne, air, ton* disenchanted, disillusioned; (†: *détrompé*) disabused, undeceived. **geste ~** gesture of disillusion.

désabusement [dezabyzmɑ̃] **nm** disillusionment.

désabuser [dezabyze] [1] **vt** to disabuse (*de* of), undeceive (*de* of).

désacclimater [dezaklimate] [1] **vt** to disacclimatize.

désaccord [dezakɔʀ] **nm** a (*mésentente*) discord. **être en ~ avec sa famille/son temps** to be at odds *ou* at variance with one's family/time.

b (*divergence*) (*entre personnes, points de vue*) disagreement; (*entre idées, intérêts*) conflict, clash. **le ~ qui subsiste entre leurs intérêts** their unresolved conflict *ou* clash of interests; **leurs intérêts sont en ~ avec les nôtres** their interests conflict *ou* clash with ours.

c (*contradiction*) discrepancy. **~ entre la théorie et la réalité** discrepancy between (the) theory and (the) reality; **les deux versions de l'accident sont en ~ sur bien des points** the two versions of the accident conflict *ou* diverge on many points; **ce qu'il dit est en ~ avec ce qu'il fait** what he says conflicts with what he does, there is a discrepancy between what he says and what he does.

désaccordé, e [dezakɔʀde] (**ptp de désaccorder**) **adj** *piano* out of tune.

désaccorder [dezakɔʀde] [1] 1 **vt** *piano* to put out of tune. 2 **se désaccorder vpr** to go out of tune.

désaccoupler [dezakuple] [1] **vt** *wagons* to uncouple; (*Élec*) to disconnect.

désaccoutumance [dezakutymɑ̃s] **nf**: **~ de qch** losing the habit of (doing) sth.

désaccoutumer [dezakutyme] [1] 1 **vt**: **~ qn de qch/de faire** to get sb out of the habit of sth/of doing, disaccustom sb from sth/from doing (*frm*). 2 **se désaccoutumer vpr**: **se ~ de qch/de faire** to lose the habit of sth/of doing.

désacralisation [desakʀalizasjɔ̃] **nf**: **la ~ d'une institution/profession** the removal of the sacred aura surrounding an institution/a profession.

désacraliser [desakʀalize] [1] **vt** *institution, profession* to take away its sacred aura. **la médecine se trouve désacralisée** medicine has lost its sacred aura; **il désacralise tout** he knocks* everything, nothing escapes his cynicism.

désactiver [dezaktive] [1] **vt** to deactivate.

désadapter [dezadapte] [1] **vt**: **~ qn de qch** to wean sb off sth.

désaffectation [dezafɛktasjɔ̃] **nf** *[lieu]* closing down; *[somme d'argent]* deallocation.

désaffecté, e [dezafɛkte] (**ptp de désaffecter**) **adj** disused.

désaffecter [dezafɛkte] [1] **vt** *lieu* to close down; *somme d'argent* to withdraw. **le lycée a été désaffecté pour en faire une prison** the lycée was closed down and converted (in)to a prison.

désaffection [dezafɛksjɔ̃] **nf** loss of affection *ou* fondness (*pour* for).

désaffectionner (se)† [dezafɛksjɔne] [1] **vpr**: **se ~ de** to lose one's affection *ou* fondness for.

désagréable [dezagʀeabl] **adj** unpleasant, disagreeable.

désagréablement [dezagʀeabləmɑ̃] **adv** unpleasantly, disagreeably.

désagrégation [dezagʀegasjɔ̃] **nf** (*voir* **désagréger, se désagréger**) disintegration; breaking up.

désagréger [dezagʀeʒe] [3] *et* [6] 1 **vt** (*lit, fig*) to break up, disintegrate. 2 **se désagréger vpr** (*gén : lit, fig*) to break up, disintegrate; *[foule]* to break up; *[amitié]* to break up.

désagrément [dezagʀemɑ̃] **nm** a (*gén pl: inconvénient, déboire*) annoyance, trouble (*NonC*). **malgré tous les ~s que cela entraîne** despite all the annoyances *ou* trouble it involves; **c'est un des ~s de ce genre de métier** it's one of the annoyances of *ou* part of the trouble with this kind of job; **cette voiture m'a valu bien des ~s** this car has given me a great deal of trouble. b (*frm: déplaisir*) displeasure. **causer du ~ à qn** to cause sb displeasure.

désaimantation [dezɛmɑ̃tasjɔ̃] **nf** demagnetization.

désaimanter [dezɛmɑ̃te] [1] **vt** to demagnetize.

désaltérant, e [dezalteʀɑ̃, ɑ̃t] **adj** thirst-quenching.

désaltérer [dezalteʀe] [6] 1 **vt** to quench *ou* slake the thirst of. **le vin ne désaltère pas** wine does not quench a thirst, wine is not a thirst-quenching drink. 2 **se désaltérer vpr** to quench *ou* slake one's thirst.

désambiguïsation [dezɑ̃biɡɥizasjɔ̃] **nf** desambiguation.

désambiguïser [dezɑ̃biɡɥize] [1] **vt** to disambiguate.

désamorçage [dezamɔʀsaʒ] **nm** a *[fusée, pistolet]* removal of the primer (*de* from); (*fig*) *[situation, conflit]* defusing. b *[dynamo]* failure.

désamorcer [dezamɔʀse] [3] **vt** *fusée, pistolet* to remove the primer from; *pompe* to drain; (*fig*) *situation explosive, crise* to defuse; *mouvement de revendication* to forestall, nip in the bud.

désapparié, e [dezapaʀje] **adj** (**ptp de désapparier**) = **déparié**.

désapparier [dezapaʀje] [7] **vt** = **déparier**.

désappointement [dezapwɛ̃tmɑ̃] **nm** disappointment.

désappointer [dezapwɛ̃te] [1] **vt** to disappoint.

désapprendre [dezapʀɑ̃dʀ] [58] **vt** (*littér*) to forget; (*volontairement*) to unlearn.

désapprobateur, -trice [dezapʀɔbatœʀ, tʀis] **adj** disapproving.

désapprobation [dezapʀɔbasjɔ̃] **nf** disapproval, disapprobation (*frm*).

désapprouver [dezapʀuve] [1] **vt** *acte, conduite* to disapprove of. **je le désapprouve quand il refuse de les aider** I disapprove of him for refusing to help them, I disapprove of his refusing *ou* refusal to help them; **je le désapprouve de les inviter** I disagree with his inviting them, I disapprove of his inviting them; **le public désapprouva** the audience showed its disapproval; **elle désapprouve qu'il vienne** she disapproves of his coming.

désarçonner [dezaʀsɔne] [1] **vt** *[cheval]* to throw, unseat; *[adversaire]* to unseat, unhorse; (*fig*) *[argument]* to throw*, nonplus. **son calme/sa réponse me désarçonna** I was completely thrown* *ou* nonplussed by his calmness/reply.

désargenté, e [dezaʀʒɑ̃te] (**ptp de désargenter**) **adj** a **un métal ~** a metal with the silver worn off. b (*: *sans un sou*) broke* (*attrib*), penniless. **je suis ~ en ce moment** I'm a bit short of cash *ou* a bit tight for cash* at the moment.

désargenter [dezaʀʒɑ̃te] [1] **vt** a *métal* to rub *ou* wear the silver off. **cette fourchette se désargente** the silver is wearing off this fork. b **~ qn*** to leave sb broke* *ou* penniless.

désarmant, e [dezaʀmɑ̃, ɑ̃t] **adj** disarming.

désarmé, e [dezaʀme] (**ptp de désarmer**) **adj** *pays, personne* unarmed; (*fig: démuni*) helpless (*devant* before).

désarmement [dezaʀməmɑ̃] nm *[personne, forteresse]* disarming; *[pays]* disarmament; *[navire]* laying up. ~ **unilatéral** unilateral disarmament.

désarmer [dezaʀme] [1] [1] vt [a] *adversaire, pays* to disarm. [b] *mine* to disarm, defuse; *fusil* to unload; (*mettre le cran de sûreté*) to put the safety catch on. [c] (*Naut*) to lay up. [d] (*fig: émouvoir*) *[sourire, réponse]* to disarm. [2] vi *[pays]* to disarm; (*fig*) *[haine]* to yield, abate. **il ne désarme pas contre son fils** he is unrelenting in his attitude towards his son; **il ne désarme pas et veut intenter un nouveau procès** he will not yield and wants to start new proceedings.

désarrimage [dezaʀimaʒ] nm shifting (of the cargo).

désarrimer [dezaʀime] [1] vt to shift, cause to shift.

désarroi [dezaʀwa] nm *[personne]* (feeling of) helplessness, disarray (*littér*); *[armée, équipe]* confusion. **ceci l'avait plongé dans le ~ le plus profond** this had plunged him into a state of utter confusion; **être en plein ~** to be in (a state of) utter confusion, feel quite helpless.

désarticulation [dezaʀtikylasjɔ̃] nf *[membre]* dislocation; (*Chirurgie*) disarticulation.

désarticuler [dezaʀtikyle] [1] [1] vt *membre* (*déboîter*) to dislocate; (*Chirurgie: amputer*) to disarticulate; *mécanisme* to upset; *horaire, prévisions* to upset, disrupt. **il s'est désarticulé l'épaule** he dislocated his shoulder. [2] **se désarticuler** vpr *[acrobate]* to contort o.s.

désassemblage [dezasɑ̃blaʒ] nm dismantling.

désassembler [dezasɑ̃ble] [1] vt to dismantle, take apart. **l'étagère s'est désassemblée** the shelves are coming to bits *ou* coming apart.

désassorti, e [dezasɔʀti] (ptp de **désassortir**) adj *service de table* unmatching, unmatched; *assiettes etc* odd (*épith*); *magasin, marchand* low in stock (*attrib*).

désassortir [dezasɔʀtiʀ] [2] vt *service de table* to break up, spoil; *magasin* to clear out.

désastre [dezastʀ] nm (*lit, fig*) disaster. **courir au ~** to head straight for disaster; **les ~s causés par la tempête** the damage caused by the storm.

désastreusement [dezastʀøzmɑ̃] adv disastrously.

désastreux, -euse [dezastʀø, øz] adj *erreur, décision, récolte, influence* disastrous; *bilan, conditions, temps* terrible, appalling.

désavantage [dezavɑ̃taʒ] nm (*handicap*) disadvantage, handicap; (*inconvénient*) disadvantage, drawback. **avoir un ~ sur qn** to be at a disadvantage *ou* be handicapped in comparison with sb; **cela présente bien des ~s** it has many disadvantages *ou* drawbacks; **être/tourner au ~ de qn** to be/turn to sb's disadvantage; **voir qn à son ~** to see sb in an unfavourable *ou* in a disadvantageous light; **se montrer à son ~** to show o.s. to one's disadvantage, show o.s. in an unfavourable light; **malgré le ~ du terrain, ils ont gagné** they won even though the ground put them at a disadvantage.

désavantager [dezavɑ̃taʒe] [3] vt to disadvantage, put at a disadvantage. **cette mesure nous désavantage par rapport aux autres** this measure puts us at a disadvantage by comparison with the others; **cela désavantage surtout les plus pauvres** this puts the very poor at the greatest disadvantage, this is particularly disadvantageous *ou* detrimental to the very poor, this penalizes the very poor in particular; **nous sommes désavantagés par rapport aux USA dans le domaine économique** in the economic field we are handicapped *ou* disadvantaged *ou* at a disadvantage by comparison with the USA; **se sentir désavantagé par rapport à son frère** to feel unfavourably treated by comparison with one's brother, feel one is treated less fairly than one's brother; **les couches sociales les plus désavantagées** the most under-privileged *ou* disadvantaged sectors of society.

désavantageusement [dezavɑ̃taʒøzmɑ̃] adv unfavourably, disadvantageously.

désavantageux, -euse [dezavɑ̃taʒø, øz] adj unfavourable, disadvantageous.

désaveu [dezavø] nm (*rétractation*) retraction; (*reniement*) *[opinion, propos]* disowning, disavowal, repudiation; (*blâme*) repudiation, disowning (*NonC*); *[signature]* disclaiming, repudiation. **encourir le ~ de qn** to be disowned by sb; (*Jur*) ~ **de paternité** repudiation *ou* denial of paternity, contestation of legitimacy.

désavouer [dezavwe] [1] [1] vt [a] (*renier*) *livre, opinion, propos* to disown, disavow; *promesse* to disclaim, deny, repudiate; *signature* to disclaim; *paternité* to disclaim, deny. [b] (*blâmer*) *personne, action* to disown. [2] **se désavouer** vpr (*revenir sur ses opinions*) to retract; (*revenir sur ses paroles*) to take back what one has said, retract, withdraw one's statement *etc*.

désaxé, e [dezakse] (ptp de **désaxer**) [1] adj disordered, unhinged. [2] nm,f lunatic. **ce crime est l'œuvre d'un ~** this crime is the work of a sick *ou* disordered mind.

désaxer [dezakse] [1] vt *roue* to put out of true; *personne, esprit* to unbalance, unhinge.

descellement [desɛlmɑ̃] nm (*voir* **desceller**) freeing; unsealing, breaking the seal on *ou* of.

desceller [desele] [1] [1] vt *pierre* to (pull) free; *acte* to unseal, break the seal on *ou* of. [2] **se desceller** vpr *[objet]* to come loose.

descendance [desɑ̃dɑ̃s] nf (*enfants*) descendants, issue (*frm*); (*origine*) descent, lineage (*littér*).

descendant, e [desɑ̃dɑ̃, ɑ̃t] [1] adj *direction, chemin* downward, descending; (*Mus*) *gamme* falling, descending; (*Mil*) *garde* coming off duty (*attrib*); (*Rail*) *voie, train* down (*épith*); *bateau* sailing downstream. **marée ~e** ebb tide; **à marée ~e, à la ~e** when the tide is going out *ou* on the ebb. [2] nm,f descendant (*de* of).

descendeur, -euse [desɑ̃dœʀ, øz] [1] nm,f (*Ski, Cyclisme*) downhill specialist *ou* racer, downhiller. [2] nm (*Alpinisme*) descender, abseil device.

descendre [desɑ̃dʀ] [41] [1] vi (*avec aux être*) [a] (*aller*) to go down; (*venir*) to come down (*à vers* to, *dans* into); *[fleuve]* to flow down; *[oiseau]* to fly down; *[avion]* to come down, descend. **descends me voir** come down and *ou* to see me; **descends le prévenir** go down and warn him; **~ à pied/à bicyclette/en voiture/en parachute** to walk/cycle/drive/parachute down; **on descend par un sentier étroit** the way down is by a narrow path, you go down a narrow path; **~ en courant/en titubant** to run/stagger down; **~ en train/par l'ascenseur** to go down by train/in the lift (*Brit*) *ou* elevator (*US*); **~ par la fenêtre** to climb *ou* get *ou* come down through the window; **nous sommes descendus en dix minutes** we got down in 10 minutes; (*fig Pol*) **~ dans la rue** to take one's protest onto the streets, take to the streets; (*fig*) **~ dans l'arène** to enter the arena; (*Alpinisme*) **~ en rappel** to abseil, rope down; **~ à Marseille** to go down to Marseilles; **~ en ville** to go into town.

[b] **~ de** *toit, rocher, arbre* to climb *ou* come down from; **il descendait de l'échelle** he was climbing *ou* coming down (from) the ladder; **il est descendu de sa chambre** he came down from his room; **~ de la colline** to come *ou* climb *ou* walk down the hill; **fais ~ le chien du fauteuil** get the dog (down) off the armchair; **descends de ton nuage!*** come back (down) to earth!

[c] (*d'un moyen de transport*) **~ de voiture/du train** to get out of the car/off *ou* out of the train, alight from the car/train (*frm*); **beaucoup de voyageurs sont descendus à Lyon** a lot of people got off *ou* out at Lyons; **~ à terre** to go ashore, get off the boat; **~ de cheval** to dismount; **~ de bicyclette** to get off one's bicycle, dismount from one's bicycle.

[d] (*atteindre*) *[habits, cheveux]* **~ à** *ou* **jusqu'à** to come down to; **son manteau lui descendait jusqu'aux chevilles** his coat came down to his ankles; **ses cheveux lui descendent sur les épaules** his hair is down on his shoulders *ou* comes down to his shoulders, he has shoulder-length hair.

[e] (*loger*) **~ dans un hôtel** *ou* **à l'hôtel** to put up *ou* stay at a hotel; **~ chez des amis** to stay with friends.

[f] *[colline, route]* **~ en pente douce** to slope gently down; **~ en pente raide** to drop *ou* fall away sharply; **la route descend en tournant** *ou* **en lacets** the road winds downwards; **le puits descend à 60 mètres** the well goes down 60 metres.

[g] *[obscurité, neige]* to fall; *[soleil]* to go down, sink. **le brouillard descend sur la vallée** the fog is coming down over the valley; **le soleil descend sur l'horizon** the sun is going down on the horizon; **le soir descendait** evening was falling; **les impuretés descendent au fond** the impurities fall *ou* drop to the bottom; **la neige descend en voltigeant** the snow is fluttering down; **ça descend bien!*** *[pluie]* it's pouring, it's bucketing down!* (*Brit*) *ou* tipping it down!* (*Brit*); *[neige]* it's snowing really hard.

[h] (*baisser*) *[baromètre, température]* to fall, drop; *[mer, marée]* to go out, ebb; *[prix]* to come down, fall, drop; *[valeurs boursières]* to fall. **ma voix ne descend pas plus bas** my voice doesn't *ou* won't go any lower.

[i] (*s'abaisser*) **~ dans l'estime de qn** to go down in sb's estimation; **il est descendu bien bas/jusqu'à mendier** he has stooped very low/to begging; (*iro*) **il est descendu jusqu'à nous parler** he deigned *ou* condescended to speak to us (*iro*).

[j] (*faire irruption*) **la police est descendue dans cette boîte de nuit** the police have raided the night club, there was a police raid on the night club.

[k] (*‡*) *[vin, repas]* **ça descend bien** that goes down well, that goes down a treat* (*Brit*); **mon déjeuner ne descend pas** my lunch won't go down; **se promener pour faire ~ son déjeuner** to help one's lunch down by taking a walk; **boire un verre pour faire ~ son déjeuner** to wash *ou* help one's lunch down with a drink.

[2] **descendre de** vt indir (*avec aux être*) (*avoir pour ancêtre*) to be descended from. **l'homme descend du singe** man is descended from the ape.

[3] vt (*avec aux avoir*) [a] *escalier, colline, pente* to go down, descend (*frm*). **~ l'escalier/les marches précipitamment** to dash downstairs/down the steps; **la péniche descend le fleuve** the barge goes down the river; **~ une rivière en canoë** to go down a river in a canoe, canoe down a river; **~ la rue en courant** to run down the street; (*Mus*) **~ la gamme** to go down the scale.

[b] (*porter, apporter*) *valise* to get down, take down, bring down; *meuble* to take down, bring down. **faire ~ ses bagages** to have one's luggage brought *ou* taken down; **si tu montes descends-moi mes lunettes** if you go upstairs *ou* if you're going upstairs bring *ou* fetch me my glasses down; **il faut ~ la poubelle tous les soirs** the dustbin (*Brit*) *ou* garbage can (*US*) must be taken down every night; **~ des livres d'un rayon** to reach *ou* take books down from a shelf; **je te descends en ville** I'll take *ou* drive you into town, I'll give you a lift into town; **le**

bus me descend à ma porte the bus drops me right outside my front door.

c (*baisser*) *étagère, rayon* to lower. **descends les stores** pull the blinds down, lower the blinds; ~ **une étagère d'un cran** to lower a shelf (by) a notch, take a shelf down a notch.

d (*: *abattre*) *avion* to bring down, shoot down; (*tuer*) *personne* to do in*, bump off*; (*boire*) *bouteille* to down*. **il risquait de se faire** ~ he was liable to get himself done in* *ou* bumped off*; (*fig*) ~ **qn en flammes** to shoot sb down in flames, demolish sb.

descente [desɑ̃t] 1 **nf** a (*action*) going down (*NonC*), descent; (*Aviat*) descent; (*Alpinisme*) descent, way down. **la** ~ **dans le puits est dangereuse** going down the well is dangerous; **en montagne, la** ~ **est plus fatigante que la montée** in mountaineering, coming down *ou* the descent is more tiring than going up *ou* the climb; **le téléphérique est tombé en panne dans la** ~ the cable-car broke down on the *ou* its way down; (*Aviat*) ~ **en vol plané** gliding descent; (*Aviat*) ~ **en feuille morte** falling leaf; (*Aviat*) ~ **en tire-bouchon** spiral dive; ~ **en parachute** parachute drop; (*Ski*) **la** ~, **l'épreuve de** ~ the downhill race; ~ **en slalom** slalom descent; **la** ~ **hommes/dames** the men's/women's downhill (race); (*Alpinisme*) ~ **en rappel** abseiling, roping down; **accueillir qn à la** ~ **du train/bateau** to meet sb off the train/boat; **il m'a accueilli à ma** ~ **de voiture** he met me as I got out of the car; *voir* **tuyau**.

b (*raid, incursion*) raid. ~ **de police** police raid; **faire une** ~ **sur** *ou* **dans** to raid, make a raid on; **les enfants ont fait une** ~ **sur les provisions/dans le frigidaire*** the children have raided the larder/fridge.

c **la** ~ **des bagages prend du temps** it takes time to bring down the luggage; **s'occuper de la** ~ **d'un tonneau à la cave** to get on with taking a barrel down to the cellar.

d (*partie descendante*) (downward) slope, incline. **s'engager dans la** ~ to go off on the downward slope; **la** ~ **est rapide** it's a steep (downward) slope; **freiner dans les** ~**s** to brake going downhill *ou* on the downhill; **les freins ont lâché au milieu de la** ~ the brakes gave way *ou* went* halfway down (the slope *ou* incline); **la** ~ **de la cave** the stairs *ou* steps down to the cellar; **la** ~ **du garage** the slope down to the garage; **avoir une bonne** ~* to be fond of one's drink, be a big drinker.

2 **comp** ▸**descente de croix** (*Art, Rel*) Deposition ▸**descente aux enfers** (*Rel*) descent into Hell ▸**descente de lit** bedside rug ▸**descente d'organe** (*Méd*) prolapse of an organ.

descriptible [dɛskʀiptibl] **adj**: **ce n'est pas** ~ it is indescribable.

descriptif, -ive [dɛskʀiptif, iv] 1 **adj** descriptive. 2 **nm** (*brochure*) explanatory leaflet; *[travaux]* specifications, specification sheet; *[projet]* outline.

description [dɛskʀipsjɔ̃] **nf** description. **faire la** ~ **de** to describe.

descriptivisme [dɛskʀiptivism] **nm** (*Ling*) descriptivism.

descriptiviste [dɛskʀiptivist] **nmf** descriptivist.

désectorisation [desɛktɔʀizasjɔ̃] **nf** (*Scol*) removal of catchment area boundaries.

désectoriser [desɛktɔʀize] 1 **vt** (*Scol*) ~ **une région** to remove a region's catchment area boundaries.

déségrégation [desegʀegasjɔ̃] **nf** desegregation.

désembourber [dezɑ̃buʀbe] 1 **vt** to get out of *ou* extricate from the mud.

désembourgeoiser [dezɑ̃buʀʒwaze] 1 1 **vt** to make less bourgeois. 2 **se désembourgeoiser vpr** to become less bourgeois, lose some of one's middle-class habits *ou* attitudes.

désembouteiller [dezɑ̃buteje] 1 **vt** (*Aut*) to unblock; *lignes téléphoniques* to unjam.

désembuage [dezɑ̃bɥaʒ] **nm** demisting.

désembuer [dezɑ̃bɥe] 1 **vt** *vitre* to demist.

désemparé, e [dezɑ̃paʀe] (**ptp de désemparer**) **adj** a (*fig*) helpless, distraught. b *navire, avion* crippled.

désemparer [dezɑ̃paʀe] 1 1 **vi**: **sans** ~ without stopping. 2 **vt** (*Naut*) to cripple.

désemplir [dezɑ̃pliʀ] 2 1 **vt** to empty. 2 **vi**: **le magasin ne désemplit jamais** the shop is never empty *ou* is always full. 3 **se désemplir vpr** to empty (*de* of).

désenchaîner [dezɑ̃ʃene] 1 **vt** to unchain, unfetter.

désenchantement [dezɑ̃ʃɑ̃tmɑ̃] **nm** a disenchantment, disillusion. b (†: *action*) disenchanting.

désenchanter [dezɑ̃ʃɑ̃te] 1 **vt** a *personne* to disenchant, disillusion. b (*littér*) *activité* to dispel the charm of; (††: *désensorceler*) to free from a *ou* the spell, disenchant.

désenclavement [dezɑ̃klavmɑ̃] **nm** *[région]* opening up.

désenclaver [dezɑ̃klave] 1 **vt** to open up, make less isolated.

désencombrement [dezɑ̃kɔ̃bʀəmɑ̃] **nm** clearing.

désencombrer [dezɑ̃kɔ̃bʀe] 1 **vt** *passage* to clear.

désencrasser [dezɑ̃kʀase] 1 **vt** to clean out.

désencroûter* [dezɑ̃kʀute] 1 **vt**: ~ **qn** to get sb out of the *ou* a rut, shake sb up*; **se** ~ to get (o.s.) out of the *ou* a rut, shake o.s. up*.

désendettement [dezɑ̃dɛtmɑ̃] **nm** getting out of debt.

désendetter [dezɑ̃dete] 1 1 **vt** to get out of debt. 2 **se désendetter vpr** to get (o.s.) out of debt.

désenfiler [dezɑ̃file] 1 **vt** *aiguille* to unthread; *perles* to unstring. **mon aiguille s'est désenfilée** my needle has come unthreaded.

désenfler [dezɑ̃fle] 1 **vi** to go down, become less swollen. **l'eau salée fait** ~ **les entorses** salt water makes sprains go down.

désengagement [dezɑ̃gaʒmɑ̃] **nm** (*gén, Mil*) disengagement; (*Fin*) disinvestment.

désengager [dezɑ̃gaʒe] 3 1 **vt** *troupes* to disengage. ~ **qn d'une obligation** to free sb from an obligation. 2 **se désengager vpr** *[troupes]* to disengage; *[État etc]* to pull out (*de* from).

désengorger [dezɑ̃gɔʀʒe] 3 **vt** *tuyau etc* to unblock; *route* to relieve the traffic congestion on; *service* to relieve.

désenivrer [dezɑ̃nivʀe] 1 **vti** to sober up.

désennuyer [dezɑ̃nɥije] 8 1 **vt**: ~ **qn** to relieve sb's boredom; **la lecture désennuie** reading relieves (one's) boredom. 2 **se désennuyer vpr** to relieve the *ou* one's boredom.

désensabler [dezɑ̃sɑble] 1 **vt** *voiture* to dig out of the sand; *chenal* to dredge.

désensibilisation [desɑ̃sibilizasjɔ̃] **nf** (*Méd, Phot*) desensitization.

désensibiliser [desɑ̃sibilize] 1 **vt** (*Méd, Phot*) to desensitize.

désensorceler [dezɑ̃sɔʀsəle] 4 **vt** to free from a *ou* the spell, free from enchantment, disenchant.

désentortiller [dezɑ̃tɔʀtije] 1 **vt** to disentangle, unravel.

désentraver [dezɑ̃tʀave] 1 **vt** to unshackle.

désenvaser [dezɑ̃vɑze] 1 **vt** (*sortir*) to get out of *ou* extricate from the mud; (*nettoyer*) to clean the mud off; *port, chenal* to dredge.

désenvenimer [dezɑ̃vnime] 1 **vt** *plaie* to take the poison out of; (*fig*) *relations* to take the bitterness out of. **pour** ~ **la situation** to defuse *ou* take the heat out of the situation.

désenvoûtement [dezɑ̃vutmɑ̃] **nm** release from a *ou* the spell.

désenvoûter [dezɑ̃vute] 1 **vt** to release from a spell.

désépaissir [dezepesiʀ] 2 **vt** *cheveux* to thin (out); *sauce* to thin (down), make thinner.

déséquilibrant, e [dezekilibʀɑ̃, ɑ̃t] **adj** destabilizing.

déséquilibre [dezekilibʀ] **nm** (*dans un rapport de forces, de quantités*) imbalance (*entre* between); (*mental, nerveux*) unbalance, disequilibrium (*frm*); (*lit: manque d'assise*) unsteadiness. **l'armoire est en** ~ the cupboard is unsteady; **le budget est en** ~ the budget is not balanced; ~ **commercial** trade gap *ou* imbalance.

déséquilibré, e [dezekilibʀe] (**ptp de déséquilibrer**) 1 **adj** *budget* unbalanced; *esprit* disordered, unhinged. 2 **nm,f** unbalanced person.

déséquilibrer [dezekilibʀe] 1 **vt** (*lit*) to throw off balance; (*fig*) *esprit, personne* to unbalance; *budget* to create an imbalance in.

désert, e [dezɛʀ, ɛʀt] 1 **adj** deserted; *voir* **île**. 2 **nm** (*Géog*) desert; (*fig*) desert, wilderness (*littér*). ~ **de Gobi/du Kalahari/d'Arabie** Gobi/Kalahari/Arabian Desert; *voir* **prêcher, traversée**.

déserter [dezɛʀte] 1 **vti** (*Mil*) to desert; (*fig*) *[touristes etc]* to leave en masse.

déserteur [dezɛʀtœʀ] 1 **nm** deserter. 2 **adjm** deserting. **les soldats** ~**s** the deserters, the deserting soldiers.

désertification [dezɛʀtifikasjɔ̃] **nf** (*humaine*) population drain; (*climatique*) turning into a desert, desertification.

désertifier (se) [dezɛʀtifje] 7 **vpr** (*facteurs humains*) to become depopulated; (*facteurs climatiques*) to turn into a desert.

désertion [dezɛʀsjɔ̃] **nf** desertion.

désertique [dezɛʀtik] **adj** *lieu* desert (*épith*), barren; *climat, plante* desert (*épith*).

désertisation [dezɛʀtizasjɔ̃] **nf** = **désertification**.

désescalade [dezɛskalad] **nf** de-escalation.

désespérant, e [dezɛspeʀɑ̃, ɑ̃t] **adj** *lenteur, nouvelle, bêtise* appalling; *enfant* hopeless; *temps* maddening, sickening. **d'une naïveté** ~**e** hopelessly naïve.

désespéré, e [dezɛspeʀe] (**ptp de désespérer**) 1 **adj** *personne* in despair (*attrib*), desperate; *situation* desperate, hopeless; *cas* hopeless; *tentative* desperate. **appel/regard** ~ cry/look of despair, desperate cry/look; (*sens affaibli*) **je suis** ~ **d'avoir à le faire** I'm desperately sorry to have to do it. 2 **nm,f** desperate person, person in despair; (*suicidé*) suicide (*person*).

désespérément [dezɛspeʀemɑ̃] **adv** desperately; (*sens affaibli*) hopelessly. **salle** ~ **vide** hopelessly empty room.

désespérer [dezɛspeʀe] 6 1 **vt** (*décourager*) to drive to despair. **il désespère ses parents** he drives his parents to despair, he is the despair of his parents.

2 **vi** (*se décourager*) to despair, lose hope, give up hope. **c'est à** ~ it's despairing, it's enough to drive you to drink*.

3 **désespérer de vt indir** to despair of. **je désespère de toi/de la situation** I despair of you/of the situation; **je désespère de son succès** I despair of his being successful; ~ **de faire qch** to have lost (all) hope *ou* have given up (all) hope of doing sth, despair of doing sth; **il désespère de leur faire entendre raison** he has lost all hope of making them see reason, he despairs of making them see reason; **je ne désespère pas de les amener à signer** I haven't lost hope *ou* given up hope of getting them to sign.

4 **se désespérer vpr** to despair. **elle passe ses nuits à se** ~ her nights are given over to despair.

désespoir [dezɛspwaʀ] 1 **nm** (*perte de l'espoir*) despair; (*chagrin*) despair, despondency. **il fait le ~ de ses parents** he is the despair of his parents; **sa paresse fait mon ~** his laziness drives me to despair *ou* to desperation; **sa supériorité fait le ~ des autres athlètes** his superiority is the despair of the other athletes; **être au ~** to be in despair; (*sens affaibli*) **je suis au ~ de ne pouvoir venir** I'm desperately sorry not to be able to come; **en ~ de cause, on fit appel au médecin** in desperation, we called in the doctor. 2 **comp ▸désespoir des peintres** (*Bot*) London pride, saxifrage.

désétatisation [dezetatizasjɔ̃] **nf** denationalization.

désétatiser [dezetatize] [1] **vt** to denationalize.

déshabillage [dezabijaʒ] **nm** undressing.

déshabillé [dezabije] **nm** négligé.

déshabiller [dezabije] [1] 1 **vt** to undress; (*fig*) to reveal. 2 **se déshabiller vpr** to undress, take off one's clothes; (**: ôter son manteau etc*) to take off one's coat *ou* things. **déshabillez-vous dans l'entrée** leave your coat *ou* things in the hall.

déshabituer [dezabitɥe] [1] 1 **vt: ~ qn de (faire) qch** to get sb out of the habit of (doing) sth, break sb of the habit of (doing) sth. 2 **se déshabituer vpr: se ~ de qch/de faire qch** (*volontairement*) to break o.s. of the habit *ou* get (o.s.) out of the habit of sth/of doing sth; (*à force d'inaction etc*) to get out of *ou* lose the habit of sth/of doing sth.

désherbage [dezɛʀbaʒ] **nm** weeding.

désherbant [dezɛʀbɑ̃] **nm** weed-killer.

désherber [dezɛʀbe] [1] **vt** to weed.

déshérence [dezeʀɑ̃s] **nf** escheat. **tomber en ~** to escheat.

déshérité, e [dezeʀite] (**ptp de déshériter**) **adj** (*désavantagé*) deprived. **les ~s** the deprived, the have-nots*; **je suis un pauvre ~** I'm a poor deprived person.

déshériter [dezeʀite] [1] **vt** *héritier* to disinherit; (*désavantager*) to deprive. **déshérité par la nature** ill-favoured by nature.

déshonnête [dezɔnɛt] **adj** (*littér: impudique*) unseemly (†, *littér*), immodest.

déshonnêteté [dezɔnɛtte] **nf** (*littér: impudeur*) unseemliness (†, *littér*), immodesty.

déshonneur [dezɔnœʀ] **nm** disgrace, dishonour.

déshonorant, e [dezɔnɔʀɑ̃, ɑ̃t] **adj** dishonourable, degrading.

déshonorer [dezɔnɔʀe] [1] 1 **vt** a (*discréditer*) *profession* to disgrace, dishonour; *personne, famille* to dishonour, be a disgrace to, bring disgrace *ou* dishonour upon. **il se croirait déshonoré de travailler** he would think it beneath him to work. b (†) *femme, jeune fille* to dishonour†. 2 **se déshonorer vpr** to bring disgrace *ou* dishonour on o.s.

déshumaniser [dezymanize] [1] **vt** to dehumanize.

déshydratation [dezidʀatasjɔ̃] **nf** dehydration.

déshydrater vt, se déshydrater vpr [dezidʀate] [1] to dehydrate.

déshydrogénation [dezidʀɔʒenasjɔ̃] **nf** dehydrogenation, dehydrogenization.

déshydrogéner [dezidʀɔʒene] [6] **vt** to dehydrogenate, dehydrogenize.

déshypothéquer [dezipɔteke] [6] **vt** to free from mortgage.

desiderata [dezideʀata] **nmpl** (*souhaits*) desiderata, wishes, requirements.

design [dizajn] 1 **nm: le ~** (*activité*) design; (*style*) the contemporary look in furniture; (*mobilier*) contemporary *ou* modern furniture; **le ~ industriel** industrial design. 2 **adj inv: chaise ~** contemporary- *ou* modern-look chair.

désignation [deziɲasjɔ̃] **nf** (*appellation*) name, designation (*frm*); (*élection*) naming, appointment, designation.

designer [dizajnœʀ] **nm** (*décorateur*) designer.

désigner [deziɲe] [1] **vt** a (*montrer*) to point out, indicate. **~ qn du doigt** to point sb out; **ces indices le désignent clairement comme coupable** these signs point clearly to him *ou* make him out clearly as the guilty party; **~ qch à l'attention de qn** to draw *ou* call sth to sb's attention; **~ qch à l'admiration de qn** to point sth out for sb's admiration.

b (*nommer*) to name, appoint, designate. **le gouvernement a désigné un nouveau ministre** the government has named *ou* appointed *ou* designated a new minister; **~ qn pour remplir une mission** to designate sb to undertake a mission; **~ qn à un poste** to appoint sb to a post; **que des volontaires se désignent!** volunteers step forward!, could we have some volunteers!; **membre/successeur désigné** member/successor elect *ou* designate.

c (*qualifier*) to mark out. **sa hardiesse le désigne pour (faire) cette tentative** his boldness marks him out for this attempt; **c'était le coupable désigné/la victime désignée** he was the classic culprit/victim; **être tout désigné pour faire qch** to be cut out to do sth, be altogether suited to doing sth.

d (*dénommer*) to designate, refer to. **~ qn par son nom** to refer to sb by his name; **on désigne sous ce nom toutes les substances toxiques** this name designates all toxic substances; **ces métaphores désignent toutes le héros** these metaphors all refer to the hero; **les mots qui désignent des objets concrets** the words which denote *ou* designate concrete objects.

désillusion [dezi(l)lyzjɔ̃] **nf** disillusion.

désillusionnement [dezi(l)lyzjɔnmɑ̃] **nm** disillusionment.

désillusionner [dezi(l)lyzjɔne] [1] **vt** to disillusion.

désincarné, e [dezɛ̃kaʀne] **adj** (*lit*) disembodied. (*fig: gén péj*) **on dirait qu'il est ~** you'd think he wasn't flesh and blood.

désincrustant, e [dezɛ̃kʀystɑ̃, ɑ̃t] 1 **adj** a (*Tech*) (de)scaling. b *crème, masque* (deep) cleansing (*épith*). 2 **nm** (de)scaling agent.

désindexation [dezɛ̃dɛksasjɔ̃] **nf** deindexation.

désindexer [dezɛ̃dɛkse] [1] **vt** to deindex.

désindustrialisation [dezɛ̃dystʀijalizasjɔ̃] **nf** de-industrialization.

désindustrialiser [dezɛ̃dystʀijalize] [1] **vt** to de-industrialize.

désinence [dezinɑ̃s] **nf** (*Ling*) ending, inflexion.

désinentiel, -ielle [dezinɑ̃sjɛl] **adj** inflexional.

désinfectant, e [dezɛ̃fɛktɑ̃, ɑ̃t] **adj, nm** disinfectant. **produit ~** disinfectant.

désinfecter [dezɛ̃fɛkte] [1] **vt** to disinfect.

désinfection [dezɛ̃fɛksjɔ̃] **nf** disinfection.

désinflation [dezɛ̃flasjɔ̃] **nf = déflation.**

désinformation [dezɛ̃fɔʀmasjɔ̃] **nf** disinformation.

désinformer [dezɛ̃fɔʀme] [1] **vt** to give false information to.

désinhiber [dezinibe] [1] **vt: ~ qn** to rid sb of his (*ou* her) inhibitions.

désinsectisation [dezɛ̃sɛktizasjɔ̃] **nf** spraying *ou* treatment with insecticide, ≃ pest control.

désinsectiser [dezɛ̃sɛktize] [1] **vt** to rid of insects, spray *ou* treat with insecticide.

désintégration [dezɛ̃tegʀasjɔ̃] **nf** (*voir* **désintégrer**) splitting-up; breaking-up; splitting; disintegration; self-destructing. **la ~ de la matière** the disintegration of matter.

désintégrer [dezɛ̃tegʀe] [6] 1 **vt** *groupe* to split up, break up; *roche* to break up; *atome* to split. 2 **se désintégrer vpr** *[groupe]* to split up, break up, disintegrate; *[roche]* to disintegrate, break up; *[fusée]* to self-destruct.

désintéressé, e [dezɛ̃teʀese] (**ptp de désintéresser**) **adj** (*généreux*) disinterested, unselfish, selfless; (*impartial*) disinterested.

désintéressement [dezɛ̃teʀɛsmɑ̃] **nm** a (*générosité*) unselfishness, selflessness; (*impartialité*) disinterestedness. **avec ~** unselfishly. b (*Fin*) *[créancier]* paying off; *[associé]* buying out.

désintéresser [dezɛ̃teʀese] [1] 1 **vt** *créancier* to pay off; *associé* to buy out. 2 **se désintéresser vpr: se ~ de** to lose interest in.

désintérêt [dezɛ̃teʀɛ] **nm** disinterest, lack of interest.

désintoxication [dezɛ̃tɔksikasjɔ̃] **nf** (*voir* **désintoxiquer**) treatment for alcoholism, drying out, detoxification; treatment for drug addiction, detoxification. **faire une cure de ~** to undergo treatment for alcoholism (*ou* drug addiction).

désintoxiqué, e [dezɛ̃tɔksike] (**ptp de désintoxiquer**) **adj** *alcoolique* dried out.

désintoxiquer [dezɛ̃tɔksike] [1] **vt** *alcoolique* to treat for alcoholism, dry out, detoxify; *drogué* to treat for drug addiction, detoxify; (*fig: purifier l'organisme*) *citadin, gros mangeur* to cleanse the system of. **se faire ~** *[alcoolique]* to dry out; *[drogué]* to come off drugs.

désinvolte [dezɛ̃vɔlt] **adj** (*sans gêne*) casual, offhand, airy; (*à l'aise*) casual, relaxed, airy.

désinvolture [dezɛ̃vɔltyʀ] **nf** casualness. **avec ~** casually, in an offhand way.

désir [deziʀ] **nm** a (*souhait*) wish, desire. **le ~ de qch** the wish *ou* desire for sth; **le ~ de faire qch** the desire to do sth; **vos ~s sont des ordres** your wish is my command; **selon le ~ de qn** in accordance with sb's wishes; **prendre ses ~s pour des réalités** to indulge in wishful thinking, wish o.s. into believing things. b (*convoitise*) desire. **le ~ de qch** the desire for sth; **yeux brillants de ~** eyes shining with desire. c (*sensualité*) desire.

désirabilité [deziʀabilite] **nf** desirability.

désirable [deziʀabl] **adj** desirable. **peu ~** undesirable.

désirer [deziʀe] [1] **vt** a (*vouloir*) to want, desire. **~ faire qch** to want *ou* wish to do sth; **que désirez-vous?** (*au magasin*) what would you like?, what can I do for you?; (*dans une agence, un bureau*) what can I do for you?; **désirez-vous prendre du café?** would you care for *ou* would you like some coffee?; **Madame désire?** (*dans une boutique*) can I help you, madam?; *[maître d'hôtel etc]* you rang, madam?; **il désire que tu viennes tout de suite** he wishes *ou* wants you to come at once; **désirez-vous qu'on vous l'envoie?** would you like it sent to you?, do you wish to have it sent to you?

b (*sexuellement*) to desire.

c (*loc*) **se faire ~*** to play hard-to-get*; **la cuisine/son travail laisse à ~** the cooking/his work leaves something to be desired *ou* is not (quite) up to the mark* (*Brit*); **ça laisse beaucoup à ~** it leaves much to be desired; **la décoration ne laisse rien à ~** the decoration leaves nothing to be desired *ou* is all that one could wish.

désireux, -euse [deziʀø, øz] **adj: ~ de qch** avid for sth, desirous of sth (*frm*); **~ de faire** anxious to do, desirous of doing (*frm*).

désistement [dezistəmɑ̃] **nm** (*Jur, Pol*) withdrawal.

désister (se) [deziste] [1] **vpr** a (*Pol*) to stand down (*Brit*), withdraw (*en faveur de qn* in sb's favour). b (*Jur*) **se ~ de** *action, appel* to withdraw.

désobéir [dezɔbeiʀ] [2] **vi** to be disobedient, disobey. **~ à qn/à un ordre** to disobey sb/an order; **il désobéit sans cesse** he's always being disobedient.

désobéissance [dezɔbeisɑ̃s] **nf** disobedience (*NonC*) (*à* to).

désobéissant, e [dezɔbeisɑ̃, ɑ̃t] adj disobedient.
désobligeamment [dezɔbliʒamɑ̃] adv (*frm*) *répondre, se conduire* disagreeably.
désobligeance [dezɔbliʒɑ̃s] nf (*frm*) disagreeableness.
désobligeant, e [dezɔbliʒɑ̃, ɑ̃t] adj disagreeable.
désobliger [dezɔbliʒe] 3 vt (*frm*) to offend.
désodé, e [desɔde] adj *régime etc* sodium-free.
désodorisant, e [dezɔdɔʀizɑ̃, ɑ̃t] 1 adj *savon, filtre* deodorizing (*épith*), deodorant (*épith*). **bombe ~e** air freshener. 2 nm (*pour le corps*) deodorant; (*pour l'air*) air freshener.
désodoriser [dezɔdɔʀize] 1 vt to deodorize.
désœuvré, e [dezœvʀe] adj idle. **il restait ~ pendant des heures** he did nothing *ou* he sat idle for hours on end; **les ~s qui se promenaient dans le parc** people with nothing to do walking in the park.
désœuvrement [dezœvʀəmɑ̃] nm idleness. **aller au cinéma par ~** to go to the pictures for something to do *ou* for want of anything better to do.
désolant, e [dezɔlɑ̃, ɑ̃t] adj *nouvelle, situation* distressing. **cet enfant/le temps est vraiment ~** this child/the weather is terribly disappointing; **il est ~ qu'elle ne puisse pas venir** it's a terrible shame *ou* such a pity that she can't come.
désolation [dezɔlasjɔ̃] nf a (*consternation*) distress, grief. **être plongé dans la ~** to be plunged in grief *ou* sadness; **il fait la ~ de sa mère** he causes his mother great distress, he breaks his mother's heart. b (*dévastation*) desolation, devastation.
désolé, e [dezɔle] (ptp de **désoler**) adj a *endroit* desolate. b *personne, air* (*affligé*) distressed; (*contrit*) sorry. **(je suis) ~ de vous avoir dérangé** (I'm) sorry to have disturbed you; **~, je dois partir** (very) sorry, I have to go; **je suis ~ d'avoir appris que vous avez perdu votre mari** I am sorry to hear that you have lost your husband.
désoler [dezɔle] 1 1 vt a (*affliger*) to distress, grieve, sadden; (*contrarier*) to upset. b (*littér: dévaster*) to desolate, devastate. 2 **se désoler** vpr to be upset. **inutile de vous ~** it's no use upsetting yourself.
désolidariser (se) [desɔlidaʀize] 1 vpr: **se ~ de** to dissociate o.s. from.
désopilant, e [dezɔpilɑ̃, ɑ̃t] adj screamingly funny*, hilarious, killing*.
désordonné, e [dezɔʀdɔne] adj a *pièce, personne* untidy, disorderly; *mouvements* uncoordinated; *combat, fuite* disorderly; *esprit* muddled, disorganized. **être ~ dans son travail** to be disorganized in one's work. b (*littér*) *vie* disorderly; *dépenses, imagination* reckless, wild.
désordre [dezɔʀdʀ] nm a (*état*) *[pièce, vêtements, cheveux]* untidiness, disorderliness; *[affaires publiques, service]* disorderliness, disorder; *[esprits]* confusion. **il ne supporte pas le ~** he can't bear disorder *ou* untidiness; **mettre une pièce en ~, mettre du ~ dans une pièce** to make a room untidy; **mettre du ~ dans sa coiffure** to make one's hair untidy, mess up one's hair; **être en ~** *[pièce, affaires]* to be untidy *ou* in disorder *ou* in a mess; *[cheveux, toilette]* to be untidy *ou* in a mess; *[service administratif]* to be in a state of disorder; **jeter quelques idées en ~ sur le papier** to jot down a few disordered *ou* random ideas; **quel ~!** what a muddle! *ou* mess!; **il régnait dans la pièce un ~ indescriptible** the room was in an indescribable muddle *ou* mess, the room was indescribably untidy; **ça fait ~*** it looks out of place; *voir* **tiercé**.
b (*agitation*) disorder. **des agitateurs qui sèment le ~ dans l'armée** agitators who spread unrest in the army; **faire du ~ (dans la classe/dans un lieu public)** to cause a commotion *ou* a disturbance (in class/in a public place); **arrêté pour ~ sur la voie publique** arrested for disorderly conduct in the streets; **jeter le ~ dans les esprits** to throw people's minds into confusion; **c'est un facteur de ~** this is a disruptive influence.
c (*émeute*) **~s** disturbance, disorder (*NonC*); **de graves ~s ont éclaté** serious disturbances have broken out, there have been serious outbreaks of violence.
d (*littér: débauche*) dissoluteness, licentiousness. **mener une vie de ~** to lead a disorderly *ou* dissolute *ou* licentious life; **regretter les ~s de sa jeunesse** to regret the dissolute *ou* licentious ways *ou* the licentiousness of one's youth.
e (*Méd*) **~ fonctionnel/hépatique** functional/liver disorder.
désorganisation [dezɔʀganizasjɔ̃] nf disorganization.
désorganiser [dezɔʀganize] 1 vt (*gén*) to disorganize; *projet, service* to disrupt, disorganize. **à cause de la grève, nos services sont désorganisés** owing to the strike our services are disrupted *ou* disorganized.
désorientation [dezɔʀjɑ̃tasjɔ̃] nf disorientation.
désorienté, e [dezɔʀjɑ̃te] (ptp de **désorienter**) adj (*lit: égaré*) disorientated; (*fig: déconcerté*) bewildered, confused (*par* by).
désorienter [dezɔʀjɑ̃te] 1 vt (*voir* **désorienté**) to disorientate; to bewilder, confuse.
désormais [dezɔʀmɛ] adv in future, henceforth (†, *frm*), from now on.
désossé, e [dezɔse] (ptp de **désosser**) adj *viande* boned; (*fig*) *personne* supple; *style* flaccid.
désossement [dezɔsmɑ̃] nm *[viande]* boning.
désosser [dezɔse] 1 vt *viande* to bone; *objet, texte* to take to pieces. (*fig*) **acrobate qui se désosse** acrobat who can twist himself in every direction.
désoxydant, e [dezɔksidɑ̃, ɑ̃t] 1 adj deoxidizing. 2 nm deoxidizer.
désoxyder [dezɔkside] 1 vt to deoxidize.
désoxyribonucléique [dezɔksiʀibonykleik] adj desoxyribonucleic.
desperado [dɛspeʀado] nm desperado.
despote [dɛspɔt] 1 adj despotic. 2 nm (*lit, fig*) despot, tyrant.
despotique [dɛspɔtik] adj despotic.
despotiquement [dɛspɔtikmɑ̃] adv despotically.
despotisme [dɛspɔtism] nm (*lit, fig*) despotism, tyranny.
desquamation [dɛskwamasjɔ̃] nf desquamation.
desquamer [dɛskwame] 1 1 vt to remove (*in scales*). 2 **se desquamer** vpr to flake off, desquamate (*SPÉC*).
desquels, desquelles [dekɛl] *voir* **lequel**.
DESS [deəɛsɛs] nm (abrév de **diplôme d'études supérieures spécialisées**) *voir* **diplôme**.
dessaisir [desezir] 2 1 vt (*Jur*) **~ un tribunal d'une affaire** to remove a case from a court; (*Jur*) **être déssaisi du dossier** to be taken off the case. 2 **se dessaisir** vpr: **se ~ de** to give up, part with, relinquish.
dessaisissement [desezismɑ̃] nm a (*Jur*) **~ d'un tribunal/juge (d'une affaire)** removal of a case from a court/judge. b (*voir* **se dessaisir**) giving up, relinquishment.
dessalage [desalaʒ] nm, **dessalaison** [desalɛzɔ̃] nf *[eau de mer]* desalination; *[poisson]* soaking.
dessalé, e* [desale] (ptp de **dessaler**) adj (*déluré*) **il est drôlement ~ depuis qu'il a fait son service militaire** he has really learnt a thing or two since he did his military service*.
dessalement [desalmɑ̃] nm = **dessalage**.
dessaler [desale] 1 1 vt a *eau de mer* to desalinate, desalinize; *poisson* to soak (*to remove the salt*). **faire ~** *ou* **mettre à ~ de la viande** to put meat to soak. b (*: *délurer*) **~ qn** to teach sb a thing or two*, teach sb about life; **il s'était dessalé au contact de ses camarades** he had learnt a thing or two* *ou* learnt about life through contact with his friends. 2 vi (*arg Naut*) to turn turtle*, capsize.
dessangler [desɑ̃gle] 1 vt *cheval* to ungirth; *paquetage* to unstrap; (*détendre sans défaire*) to loosen the girths of; loosen the straps of.
dessaouler* [desule] 1 vti = **dessoûler***.
desséchant, e [deseʃɑ̃, ɑ̃t] adj *vent* parching, drying; (*fig*) *études* mind-deadening.
dessèchement [desɛʃmɑ̃] nm (*action*) drying (out *ou* up), parching; (*état*) dryness; (*fig: amaigrissement*) emaciation; (*fig: du cœur*) hardness.
dessécher [deseʃe] 6 1 vt a *terre, végétation* to dry out, parch; *plante, feuille* to wither, dry out, parch. **le vent dessèche la peau** (the) wind dries (out *ou* up) the skin; **la soif me dessèche la bouche** my mouth is dry *ou* parched with thirst.
b (*volontairement*) *aliments etc* to dry, dehydrate, desiccate.
c (*fig: racornir*) *cœur* to harden. **l'amertume/la vie lui avait desséché le cœur** bitterness/life had hardened his heart *ou* left him stony-hearted; **desséché par l'étude** dried up through study; **il s'était desséché à force d'étudier** he had become as dry as dust as a result of too much studying.
d (*amaigrir*) to emaciate. **les maladies l'avaient desséché** illness had left him wizened *ou* emaciated; **les épreuves l'avaient desséché** his trials and tribulations had worn him to a shadow.
2 **se dessécher** vpr *[terre]* to dry out, become parched; *[plante, feuille]* to wither, dry out; *[aliments]* to dry out, go dry; *[bouche, lèvres]* to go dry, become parched; *[peau]* to dry out.
dessein [desɛ̃] nm (*littér*) (*intention*) intention, design; (*projet*) plan, design. **son ~ est** *ou* **il a le ~ de faire** he intends *ou* means to do; **former le ~ de faire qch** to make up one's mind to do sth, form a plan to do sth; **avoir des ~s sur qn** to have designs on sb; **c'est dans ce ~ que** it is with this in mind *ou* with this intention that; **il est parti dans le ~ de** *ou* **à ~ de faire fortune** he went off meaning *ou* intending to make his fortune *ou* with the intention of making his fortune; **faire qch à ~** to do sth intentionally *ou* deliberately *ou* on purpose.
desseller [desele] 1 vt to unsaddle.
desserrage [deseʀaʒ] nm *[vis, écrou]* unscrewing, undoing, loosening; *[câble]* loosening, slackening; *[frein]* releasing.
desserré, e [deseʀe] (ptp de **desserrer**) adj *vis, écrou* undone (*attrib*), loose; *nœud, ficelle* loose, slack; *cravate, ceinture* loose; *frein* off (*attrib*).
desserrement [desɛʀmɑ̃] nm (*voir* **se desserrer**) slackening; loosening; releasing; relaxation.
desserrer [deseʀe] 1 1 vt *nœud, ceinture, ficelle* to loosen, slacken; *étau* to loosen, release; *étreinte* to relax, loosen; *poing, dents* to unclench; *écrou* to unscrew, undo, loosen; *frein* to release, take *ou* let off; *objets alignés, mots, lignes* to space out. **~ sa ceinture de 2 crans** to loosen *ou* slacken one's belt 2 notches, let one's belt out 2 notches; (*fig*) **il n'a pas desserré les dents** he hasn't opened his mouth *ou* lips. 2 **se desserrer** vpr *[ficelle, câble]* to slacken, come loose; *[nœud]* to come undone *ou* loose; *[écrou]* to work *ou* come loose; *[frein]* to release itself; *[étreinte]* to relax, loosen.
dessert [desɛʀ] nm dessert, pudding, sweet (*Brit*).
desserte [desɛʀt] nf a (*meuble*) sideboard. b (*service de transport*) **la ~ d'une localité par bateau** the servicing of an area by water

transport; **la ~ de la ville est assurée par un car** there is a bus service to the town. c *[prêtre]* cure.

dessertir [desɛʀtiʀ] 2 **vt** to unset, remove from its setting.

desservant [desɛʀvɑ̃] **nm** priest in charge.

desservir¹ [desɛʀviʀ] 14 **vt** a *repas, plat* to clear away. **vous pouvez ~ (la table)** you can clear away, you can clear the table. b (*nuire à*) *personne* to go against, put at a disadvantage; *intérêts* to harm. **il est desservi par sa mauvaise humeur** his bad temper goes against him *ou* puts him at a disadvantage; **il m'a desservi auprès de mes amis** he did me a disservice with my friends.

desservir² [desɛʀviʀ] 14 **vt** a (*Transport*) to serve. **le village est desservi par 3 autobus chaque jour** there is a bus service from the village *ou* a bus runs from the village 3 times daily; **le village est desservi par 3 lignes d'autobus** the village is served by *ou* has 3 bus services; **ville bien desservie** town well served by public transport. b *[porte, couloir]* to lead into. c *[prêtre]* to serve. **~ une paroisse** to minister to a parish.

dessiccatif, -ive [desikatif, iv] 1 **adj** desiccative. 2 **nm** desiccant.

dessiccation [desikasjɔ̃] **nf** (*Chim*) desiccation; *[aliments]* drying, desiccation, dehydration.

dessiller [desije] 1 **vt** (*fig*) **~ les yeux de** *ou* **à qn** to open sb's eyes (*fig*); **mes yeux se dessillèrent** my eyes were opened, the scales fell from my eyes (*Brit*).

dessin [desɛ̃] **nm** a (*image*) drawing. **il a fait un (joli) ~** he did a (nice) drawing; **il passe son temps à faire des ~s** he spends his time drawing; **il fait toujours des petits ~s sur son cahier** he's always doodling on his exercise book; **~ à la plume/au fusain/au trait** pen-and-ink/charcoal/line drawing; **~ animé** cartoon (film); **~ humoristique** cartoon (*in a newspaper etc*); **~ publicitaire/de mode** advertisement/fashion drawing; (*hum*) **il n'a rien compris, fais lui donc un ~!*** he hasn't understood a word – explain it in words of one syllable *ou* you'll have to spell it out for him; *voir* **carton**.

b (*art*) **le ~** drawing; **il est doué pour le ~** he has a gift for drawing; **école de ~** (*Art*) art school; (*technique*) technical college (for draughtsmen); **professeur de ~** art teacher; **~ technique** technical drawing; **~ de mode** fashion design; **~ industriel** draughtsmanship; **table/planche à ~** drawing table/board; **~ assisté par ordinateur** computer-aided design.

c (*motif*) pattern, design. **tissu avec des ~s jaunes** material with a yellow pattern on it; **le ~ des veines sur la peau** the pattern of the veins on the skin.

d (*contour*) outline, line. **la bouche a un joli ~** the mouth has a good line *ou* is finely delineated.

dessinateur, -trice [desinatœʀ, tʀis] **nm,f** (*artiste*) drawer; (*technicien*) draughtsman (*Brit*), draftsman (*US*). **~ humoristique** cartoonist; **~ de mode** fashion designer; **~ industriel** draughtsman (*Brit*), draftsman (*US*); **~ de publicité** commercial artist; **~-cartographe** cartographic designer, cartographer; **~ concepteur** designer.

dessiner [desine] 1 1 **vt** a to draw. **il dessine bien** he's good at drawing, he draws well; **~ qch à grands traits** to draw a broad outline of sth; **~ au pochoir** to stencil; **~ au crayon/à l'encre** to draw in pencil/ink.

b (*faire le plan, la maquette de*) *véhicule, meuble* to design; *plan d'une maison* to draw; *jardin* to lay out, landscape. (*fig*) **une bouche/oreille bien dessinée** a finely delineated mouth/ear.

c *[chose]* (*gén*) to make, form. **les champs dessinent un damier** the fields form *ou* are laid out like a checkerboard *ou* (a) patchwork; **un vêtement qui dessine bien la taille** a garment that shows off the waist well.

2 **se dessiner vpr** a *[contour, forme]* to stand out, be outlined. **des collines se dessinaient à l'horizon** hills stood out on the horizon.

b (*se préciser*) *[tendance]* to become apparent; *[projet]* to take shape. **on voit se ~ une tendance à l'autoritarisme** an emergent tendency to authoritarianism may be noted, a tendency towards authoritarianism is becoming apparent; **un sourire se dessina sur ses lèvres** a smile formed on his lips.

dessouder [desude] 1 **vt** to unsolder. **le tuyau s'est dessoudé** the pipe has come unsoldered.

dessoûler* [desule] 1 **vti** to sober up. **il n'a pas dessoûlé depuis 2 jours** he's been drunk non-stop for the past 2 days, he's been on a bender‡ for the past 2 days.

dessous [d(ə)su] 1 **adv** a (*sous*) *placé, suspendre* under, underneath, beneath; *passer* under, underneath; (*plus bas*) below. **mettez votre valise ~** put your suitcase underneath (it) *ou* under it; **soulevez ces dossiers: la liste est ~** lift up those files – the list is underneath (them) *ou* under *ou* beneath them; **passez (par) ~** go under *ou* underneath (it); **tu as mal lu, il y a une note ~** you misread it – there is a note underneath; **retirer qch de ~ le lit/la table** to get sth from under(neath) *ou* beneath the bed/table; **ils ont pris le buffet par (en) ~** they took hold of the sideboard from underneath.

b **au-~** below; **au-~ de** (*lit*) below, underneath; (*fig*) *possibilités, limite* below; (*fig: pas digne de*) beneath; **ils habitent au-~** they live downstairs *ou* underneath; **sa jupe lui descend au-~ du genou** her skirt comes down to below her knees *ou* reaches below her knees; **les enfants au-~ de 7 ans ne paient pas** children under 7 don't pay, the under-sevens don't pay; **20° au-~ (de zéro)** 20° below (zero); **des articles à 20 F et au-~** items at 20 francs and less *ou* below; **il considère que c'est au-~ de lui de faire la vaisselle** he considers it beneath him to do the dishes; (*incapable*) **il est au-~ de sa tâche** he is not up to his task; **il est au-~ de tout!** he's the absolute limit!, he's the end!; **le service est au-~ de tout** the service is hopeless *ou* a disgrace.

c **en ~** (*sous*) under(neath); (*plus bas*) below; (*hypocritement*) in an underhand (*Brit*) *ou* underhanded (*US*) manner; **en ~ de** below; **il s'est glissé en ~** he slid under(neath); **les locataires d'en ~** the people who rent the flat below *ou* downstairs; **jeter un coup d'œil en ~ à qn, regarder qn en ~** to give sb a shifty look; **faire qch en ~** to do sth in an underhand (*Brit*) *ou* underhanded (*US*) manner; **il est très en ~ de la moyenne** he's well below (the) average.

2 **nm** a *[objet]* bottom, underside; *[pied]* sole; *[main]* inside; *[avion, voiture, animal]* underside; *[tissu]* wrong side; *[tapis]* back. **du ~** *feuille, drap* bottom; **les gens/l'appartement du ~** the people/the flat downstairs (from us *ou* them *etc*), the people/flat below (us *ou* them *etc*); **le ~ de la table est poussiéreux** the table is dusty underneath; **les fruits du ~ sont moisis** the fruit at the bottom *ou* the fruit underneath is mouldy; **avoir le ~** to get the worst of it, come off worst.

b (*côté secret*) **le ~ de l'affaire** *ou* **l'histoire** the hidden side of the affair; **les ~ de la politique** the unseen *ou* hidden side of policies; **connaître le dessous des cartes**to have inside information.

c (*Habillement*) undergarment. **les ~** underwear, undies*.

3 **comp ▸dessous-de-bouteille nm inv** bottle mat **▸dessous-de-bras nm inv** dress shield **▸dessous de caisse** (*Aut*) underbody **▸dessous-de-plat nm inv** table mat (*for hot serving dishes*) **▸dessous de robe** slip, petticoat **▸dessous-de-table** (*fig*) **nm inv** backhander*, under the counter payment **▸dessous de verre** coaster, drip mat.

dessus [d(ə)sy] 1 **adv** a (*sur*) *placé, poser, monter* on top (of it); *collé, écrit, fixer* on it; *passer, lancer* over (it); (*plus haut*) above. **mettez votre valise ~** put your suitcase on top (of it); **regardez ces dossiers: la liste doit être ~** have a look at those files – the list must be on top (of them); **il n'y a pas de timbre ~** there's no stamp on it; **c'est écrit ~** it's written on it; **montez ~** (*tabouret, échelle*) get up on it; **passez (par) ~** go over it; **il a sauté par ~** he jumped over it; **ôter qch de ~ la table** to take sth (from) off the table; **il n'a même pas levé la tête de ~ son livre** he didn't even look up from his book, he didn't even take his eyes off his book; **il lui a tapé/tiré ~** he hit him/shot at him; **il nous sont arrivés** *ou* **tombés ~ à l'improviste** they dropped in on us unexpectedly.

b **au-~** above; (*à l'étage supérieur*) upstairs; (*posé sur*) on top; (*plus cher etc*) over, above; **au-~ de** (*plus haut que, plus au nord que*) above; (*sur*) on top of; (*fig*) *prix, limite* over, above; *possibilités* beyond; **la valise est au-~ de l'armoire** the suitcase is on top of the wardrobe; **les enfants au-~ de 7 ans paient** children over 7 pay, the over-sevens pay; **20° au-~ (de zéro)** 20° above (zero); **il n'y a pas d'articles au-~ de 20 F** there are no articles over 20 francs; (*prix*) **c'est au-~ de ce que je peux mettre** it's beyond my means, it's more than I can afford; **cette tâche est au-~ de ses capacités** this task is beyond his capabilities; **c'est au-~ de mes forces** it's too much for me; **il ne voit rien au-~ de son fils** he thinks no one can hold a candle to his son; **il est au-~ de ces petites mesquineries** he is above this petty meanness; **être au-~ de tout soupçon/reproche** to be above suspicion/beyond reproach; **pour le confort, il n'y a rien au-~** there's nothing to beat it for comfort.

2 **nm** a *[objet, pied, tête]* top; *[main]* back; *[tissu]* right side. **du ~** *feuille, drap* top; **le ~ de la table est en marbre** the table-top *ou* the top of the table is marble; **les gens/l'appartement du ~** the people/flat above (us *ou* them *etc*) *ou* upstairs (from us *ou* them *etc*); **les fraises du ~ sont plus belles (qu'en dessous)** the strawberries on top are nicer (than the ones underneath); (*fig*) **le ~ du panier** the pick of the bunch; (*élite sociale*) the upper crust; **elle portait 2 vestes de laine: celle du ~ était bleue** she was wearing 2 cardigans and the top one was blue.

b (*loc*) **avoir le ~** to have the upper hand; **prendre le ~** to get the upper hand; **reprendre le ~** to get over it; **il a été très malade/déprimé mais il a repris le ~ rapidement** he was very ill/depressed but he soon got over it.

3 **comp ▸dessus de cheminée** mantleshelf runner **▸dessus-de-lit** bedspread **▸dessus de table** table runner.

DEST [deəɛste] **nm** (**abrév de diplôme d'études supérieures techniques**) *voir* **diplôme**.

déstabilisant, e [destabilizɑ̃, ɑ̃t] **adj**, **déstabilisateur, -trice** [destabilizatœʀ, tʀis] **adj** *influence, événement* destabilizing.

déstabilisation [destabilizasjɔ̃] **nf** destabilization.

déstabiliser [destabilize] 1 **vt** (*Pol*) *régime* to destabilize.

déstalinisation [destalinizasjɔ̃] **nf** destalinization.

déstaliniser [destalinize] 1 **vt** to destalinize.

destin [dɛstɛ̃] **nm** (*fatalité, sort*) fate; (*existence, avenir, vocation*) destiny. **le ~ contraire** ill-fortune; **elle connut un ~ tragique** she met with a tragic end; **c'est le ~!** it was meant to be.

destinataire [dɛstinatɛʀ] **nmf** *[lettre]* addressee (*frm*); *[marchandise]* consignee; *[mandat]* payee; (*Ling*) person addressed. **remettre une let-**

tre à son ~ to hand a letter to the person it is addressed to.
destinateur [dɛstinatœʀ] **nm** (*Ling*) speaker.
destination [dɛstinasjɔ̃] **nf** **a** (*direction*) destination. **à ~ de** *avion, train* to; *bateau* bound for; *voyageur* travelling to; *lettre* sent to; **arriver à ~** to reach one's destination, arrive (at one's destination); **train/vol 702 à ~ de Paris** train number 702/flight (number) 702 to *ou* for Paris. **b** (*usage*) *[édifice, appareil, somme d'argent]* purpose. **quelle ~ comptez-vous donner à cette somme/pièce?** to what purpose do you intend to put this money/room?
destiné, e¹ [dɛstine] (**ptp de destiner**) **adj** **a** (*prévu pour*) **~ à faire qch** intended *ou* meant to do sth; **ces mesures sont ~es à freiner l'inflation** these measures are intended *ou* meant to curb inflation; **ce texte est ~ à être lu à haute voix** this text is intended *ou* meant to be read aloud; **cette pommade est ~e à guérir les brûlures** this ointment is intended for healing burns; **livre ~ aux enfants** book (intended *ou* meant) for children; **édifice ~ au culte** building intended for worship; **ce terrain est ~ à être construit** this ground is intended for construction *ou* to be built on.
b (*voué à*) **~ à qch** destined for sth; **~ à faire** destined to do; **ce livre était ~ au succès** this book was destined for success; **cette œuvre était ~e à l'échec** this work was doomed to fail *ou* to failure, it was fated that this work should be a failure; **il était ~ à une brillante carrière** he was destined for a brilliant career; **elle était ~e à mourir jeune** she was destined *ou* fated *ou* doomed to die young.
destinée² [dɛstine] **nf** (*fatalité, sort*) fate; (*existence, avenir, vocation*) destiny. **unir sa ~ à celle de qn** to unite one's destiny with sb's; **promis à de hautes ~s** destined for great things.
destiner [dɛstine] 1 **vt** **a** (*attribuer*) **~ sa fortune à qn** to intend *ou* mean sb to have one's fortune, intend that sb should have one's fortune; **il vous destine ce poste** he intends *ou* means you to have this post; **~ une allusion/un coup à qn** to intend an allusion/a blow for sb; **~ un accueil enthousiaste à qn** to reserve an enthusiastic welcome for sb; **nous destinons ce livre à tous ceux qui souffrent** this book is intended *ou* meant (by us) for all who are suffering, this book is aimed at all who are suffering; **il ne put attraper le ballon qui lui était destiné** he couldn't catch the ball meant for *ou* aimed at him; **sans deviner le sort qui lui était destiné** (*par le destin*) not knowing what fate he was destined for *ou* what fate lay *ou* was in store for him; (*par ses ennemis*) not knowing what fate lay *ou* was in store for him; **cette lettre t'était/ne t'était pas destinée** this letter was/was not meant *ou* intended for you.
b (*affecter*) **~ une somme à l'achat de qch** to intend to use a sum *ou* earmark a sum to buy sth, earmark a sum for sth; **~ un local à un usage précis** to intend a place to be used for a specific purpose, have a specific use in mind for a place; **les fonds seront destinés à la recherche** the money will be devoted to *ou* used for research.
c (*vouer*) to destine. **~ qn à une fonction** to destine sb for a post *ou* to fill a post; **~ qn à être médecin** to destine sb to be a doctor; **sa bravoure le destinait à mourir de mort violente** his boldness marked him out *ou* destined him to die a violent death; (*littér*) **je vous destine ma fille** I intend that my daughter should marry you; **il se destine à l'enseignement/à être ingénieur** he intends to go into teaching/to be an engineer, he has set his sights on teaching/being an engineer.
destituer [dɛstitɥe] 1 **vt** *ministre* to dismiss; *roi* to depose; *officier* to discharge. **~ un officier de son commandement** to relieve an officer of his command; **~ qn de ses fonctions** to relieve sb of his duties.
destitution [dɛstitysjɔ̃] **nf** *[ministre]* dismissal; *[officier]* discharge; *[fonctionnaire]* dismissal, discharge; *[roi]* deposition.
déstockage [destɔkaʒ] **nm** destocking.
déstocker [destɔke] 1 **vt** to destock.
destrier [dɛstʀije] **nm** (*Hist littér*) steed (*littér*), charger (*littér*).
destroyer [dɛstʀwaje] **nm** (*Naut*) destroyer.
destructeur, -trice [dɛstʀyktœʀ, tʀis] **1 adj** destructive. **2 nm,f** destroyer.
destructible [dɛstʀyktibl] **adj** destructible.
destructif, -ive [dɛstʀyktif, iv] **adj** destructive, destroying (*épith*).
destruction [dɛstʀyksjɔ̃] **nf** (*gén*) destruction (*NonC*); *[armée, flotte]* destroying (*NonC*), destruction (*NonC*); *[rats, insectes]* extermination (*NonC*). **les ~s causées par la guerre** the destruction caused by the war.
déstructuration [destʀyktyʀasjɔ̃] **nf** destructuring.
déstructurer [destʀyktyʀe] 1 **vt** to destructure.
désuet, -ète [dezɥɛ, ɛt] **adj** (*gén*) outdated, antiquated, outmoded; *charme* old-fashioned, quaint; *vêtement* outdated, old-fashioned; *mode* outdated.
désuétude [desɥetyd] **nf** disuse, obsolescence, desuetude (*littér*). **tomber en ~** *[loi]* to fall into abeyance; *[expression, coutume]* to become obsolete, fall into disuse.
désuni, e [dezyni] (**ptp de désunir**) **adj** *couple, famille* divided, disunited; *mouvements* uncoordinated; *coureur, cheval* off his stride (*attrib*).
désunion [dezynjɔ̃] **nf** *[couple, parti]* disunity, dissension (*de* in).
désunir [dezyniʀ] 2 **1 vt** *famille* to divide, disunite; *pierres, planches* to separate. **2 se désunir vpr** *[athlète]* to lose one's stride; *[cheval]* to lose its stride; *[équipe]* to lose its coordination.
désynchroniser [desɛ̃kʀɔnize] 1 **vt** to de-synchronize.
détachable [detaʃabl] **adj** detachable.
détachage [detaʃaʒ] **nm** (*nettoyage*) stain removal.
détachant [detaʃɑ̃] **nm** stain remover.
détaché, e [detaʃe] (**ptp de détacher**) **adj** (*indifférent, aussi Mus*) detached; *voir* **pièce**.
détachement [detaʃmɑ̃] **nm** **a** (*indifférence*) detachment (*envers, à l'égard de* from). **regarder/dire qch avec ~** to look at/say sth with (an air of) detachment; **le ~ qu'il montrait pour les biens matériels** the disregard he showed for material goods. **b** (*Mil*) detachment. **c** *[fonctionnaire]* secondment. **être en ~** to be on secondment.
détacher¹ [detaʃe] 1 **1 vt** **a** (*délier*) *chien, cheval* to untie, let loose; *prisonnier* to untie, (let) loose, unbind; *paquet, objet* to undo, untie; *wagon, remorque* to take off, detach. **~ un wagon d'un convoi** to detach a carriage (*Brit*) *ou* car (*US*) from a train; **il détacha la barque/le prisonnier/le paquet de l'arbre** he untied the boat/the prisoner/the parcel from the tree.
b (*dénouer*) *vêtement, ceinture* to undo, unfasten, loose; *lacet, nœud* to undo, untie, loose; *soulier, chaîne* to unfasten, undo. **il détacha la corde du poteau** he untied *ou* removed the rope from the post.
c (*ôter*) *peau, écorce* to remove (*de* from), take off; *papier collé* to remove, unstick (*de* from); *rideau, tableau* to take down (*de* from); *épingle* to take out (*de* of), remove; *reçu, bon* to tear out (*de* of), detach (*de* from). **l'humidité avait détaché le papier** the damp had unstuck *ou* loosened the paper; **~ des feuilles d'un bloc** to tear *ou* take some sheets out of a pad, detach some sheets from a pad; **~ un morceau de plâtre du mur** to remove a piece of plaster from the wall, take a piece of plaster from *ou* off the wall; **il détacha une pomme de l'arbre** he took an apple (down) from the tree, he picked an apple off the tree; **détachez bien les bras du corps** keep your arms well away from your body; (*fig*) **il ne pouvait ~ son regard du spectacle** he could not take his eyes off the sight; (*sur coupon etc*) **"partie à ~"** "tear off (this section)"; **"~ suivant le pointillé"** "tear off along the dotted line".
d (*envoyer*) *personne* to send, dispatch; (*Admin: affecter*) to second. **se faire ~ auprès de qn/à Londres** to be sent on secondment to sb/to London; (*Admin*) **être détaché** to be on secondment.
e (*mettre en relief*) *lettres* to separate; *syllabes, mots* to articulate, separate; (*Peinture*) *silhouette, contour* to bring out, make stand out; (*Mus*) *notes* to detach. **~ une citation** to make a quotation stand out, bring out a quotation.
f (*éloigner*) **~ qn de qch/qn** to turn sb away from sth/sb; **son cynisme a détaché de lui tous ses amis** his cynicism has turned his friends away from him.
2 se détacher vpr **a** (*se délier*) *[chien]* to free itself, get loose, loose itself (*de* from); *[prisonnier]* to free o.s., get loose (*de* from); *[paquet]* to come undone *ou* untied *ou* loose; *[barque]* to come untied, loose itself (*de* from); *[wagon]* to come off, detach itself (*de* from). **la boule s'était détachée de l'arbre de Noël** the bobble had fallen off the Christmas tree.
b (*se dénouer*) *[ceinture, soulier]* to come undone *ou* unfastened *ou* loose; *[lacet, ficelle]* to come undone *ou* untied *ou* loose.
c (*se séparer*) *[fruit, ficelle]* to come off; *[page]* to come loose, come out; *[peau, écorce]* to come off; *[papier collé]* to come unstuck, come off; *[épingle]* to come out, fall out; *[rideau]* to come down. **le papier s'était détaché à cause de l'humidité** the paper had come loose *ou* come unstuck because of the damp; **un bloc de pierre se détacha du rocher** a block of stone came off *ou* broke off *ou* detached itself from the rock; **l'écorce se détachait de l'arbre** the bark was coming off the tree *ou* was coming away from the tree; **la capsule spatiale s'est détachée de la fusée** the space capsule has separated from *ou* come away from the rocket.
d (*Sport etc*) *[coureur]* to pull *ou* break away (*de* from). **un petit groupe se détacha du reste des manifestants** a small group broke away from *ou* detached itself from the rest of the demonstrators.
e (*ressortir*) to stand out. **la forêt se détache sur le ciel clair** the forest stands out against the clear sky.
f se ~ de (*renoncer à*) to turn one's back on, renounce; (*se désintéresser de*) to grow away from; **se ~ des plaisirs de la vie** to turn one's back on *ou* renounce the pleasures of life; **ils se sont détachés l'un de l'autre** they have grown apart.
détacher² [detaʃe] 1 **vt** to remove the stains from, clean. **donner une robe à ~** to take a dress to be cleaned *ou* to the cleaner's; **~ au savon/à la benzine** to clean with soap/benzine.
détail [detaj] **nm** **a** (*particularité*) detail. **dans les (moindres) ~s** in (minute) detail; **se perdre dans les ~s** to lose o.s. in details; **entrer dans les ~s** to go into detail(s) *ou* particulars; **je n'ai pas remarqué ce ~** I didn't notice that detail *ou* point; **ce n'est qu'un ~!** that's a mere detail!; *voir* **revue**.
b (*description précise*) *[facture, compte]* breakdown. **examiner le ~ d'un compte** to examine a breakdown of *ou* the particulars of an account; **pourriez-vous nous faire le ~ de la facture/de ce que l'on vous doit?** could you give us a breakdown of the invoice/of what we owe you?; **il nous a fait le ~ de ses aventures** he gave us a detailed account *ou* a rundown* of his adventures; **en ~, dans le ~** in detail; (*fig*) **il ne fait pas de ~s!*** he doesn't make any exceptions, he doesn't discriminate.

c (*Comm*) retail. **commerce/magasin/prix de ~** retail business/shop (*Brit*) *ou* store (*US*)/price; **vendre au ~** *marchandise, vin* to (sell) retail; *articles, couverts* to sell separately; **marchand de ~** retailer, retail dealer; **il fait le gros et le ~** he deals in wholesale and retail.

détaillant, e [detajɑ̃, ɑ̃t] nm,f retailer, retail dealer.

détaillé, e [detaje] (ptp de **détailler**) adj *récit, plan, explications* detailed; *facture* itemized.

détailler [detaje] 1 vt a (*Comm*) *articles* to sell separately; *marchandise* to sell retail. **nous détaillons les services de table** we sell dinner services in separate pieces, we will split up dinner services; **est-ce que vous détaillez cette pièce de tissu?** do you sell lengths of this piece of material? b (*passer en revue*) *plan* to detail, explain in detail; *facture* to itemize; *récit* to tell in detail; *incidents, raisons* to detail, give details of. **il m'a détaillé (de la tête aux pieds)** he examined me *ou* looked me over (from head to foot).

détaler [detale] 1 vi *[lapin]* to bolt; (*) *[personne]* to take off*, clear off*. **il a détalé comme un lapin** he made a bolt for it*, he skedaddled*.

détartrage [detaʀtʀaʒ] nm (*voir* **détartrer**) scaling; descaling. **se faire faire un ~** to have one's teeth scaled (and polished).

détartrant [detaʀtʀɑ̃] nm descaling agent.

détartrer [detaʀtʀe] 1 vt *dents* to scale (and polish); *chaudière etc* to descale, remove fur (*Brit*) *ou* sediment (*US*) from.

détaxe [detaks] nf (*réduction*) reduction in tax; (*suppression*) removal of tax (*de* from); (*remboursement*) tax refund. **~ à l'exportation** duty-free for export.

détaxer [detakse] 1 vt (*réduire*) to reduce the tax on; (*supprimer*) to remove the tax on, take the tax off. **produits détaxés** tax-free goods.

détectable [detɛktabl] adj detectable, detectible.

détecter [detɛkte] 1 vt to detect.

détecteur, -trice [detɛktœʀ, tʀis] 1 adj *dispositif* detecting (*épith*), detector (*épith*); *lampe, organe* detector (*épith*). 2 nm detector. **~ d'ondes/de mines** wave/mine detector; **~ de fumée** smoke detector; **~ de faux billets** forged banknote detector; **~ de mensonges** polygraph, lie detector.

détection [detɛksjɔ̃] nf detection. **~ sous-marine/électromagnétique** underwater/electromagnetic detection.

détective [detɛktiv] nm: **~ (privé)** private detective *ou* investigator, private eye*.

déteindre [detɛ̃dʀ] 52 1 vt *[personne, produit]* to take the colour out of; *[soleil]* to fade, take the colour out of. 2 vi (*au lavage*) *[étoffe]* to run, lose its colour; *[couleur]* to run, come out; (*par l'humidité*) *[couleur]* to come off; (*au soleil*) *[étoffe]* to fade, lose its colour; *[couleur]* to fade. **~ sur** (*lit*) *[couleur]* to run into; (*fig: influencer*) *[trait de caractère]* to rub off on; **elle a déteint sur sa fille** she had an influence on her daughter; **mon pantalon a déteint sur les rideaux** some of the colour has come out of my trousers on to the curtains.

dételage [det(ə)laʒ] nm (*voir* **dételer**) unyoking; unharnessing; unhitching; uncoupling.

dételer [det(ə)le] 4 1 vt *bœufs* to unyoke; *chevaux* to unharness; *voiture* to unhitch; *wagon* to uncouple, unhitch. 2 vi (*) to leave off working*. **sans ~** *travailler, faire qch* without letting up; **on dételle à 5 heures** we knock off* at 5 o'clock; **trois heures sans ~** 3 hours on end *ou* at a go *ou* without a break.

détendeur [detɑ̃dœʀ] nm *[bouteille de gaz]* regulator; *[installation frigorifique]* regulator.

détendre [detɑ̃dʀ] 41 1 vt *ressort* to release; *corde* to slacken, loosen; (*Phys*) *gaz* to release the pressure of; *corps, esprit* to relax. **se ~ les jambes** to unbend *ou* straighten out one's legs; **ces vacances m'ont détendu** these holidays have made me more relaxed; **pour ~ un peu ses nerfs** to calm *ou* soothe his nerves a little; **pour ~ la situation/les relations internationales** to relieve *ou* ease the situation/the tension of international relations; **il n'arrivait pas à ~ l'atmosphère** he couldn't manage to ease the strained *ou* tense atmosphere.

2 **se détendre** vpr a *[ressort]* to lose its tension; *[corde]* to become slack, slacken; (*Phys*) *[gaz]* to be reduced in pressure.

b (*fig*) *[visage, esprit, corps]* to relax; *[nerfs]* to calm down; *[atmosphère]* to relax, become less tense. **aller à la campagne pour se ~** to go to the country for relaxation *ou* to unwind*; **détendez-vous!** relax!, let yourself unwind!*; **la situation internationale s'est détendue** the international situation has grown less tense *ou* has relaxed *ou* eased; **pour que leurs rapports se détendent** to make their relations less strained *ou* more relaxed.

détendu, e [detɑ̃dy] (ptp de **détendre**) adj *personne, visage, atmosphère* relaxed; *câble* slack; *ressort* unextended.

détenir [det(ə)niʀ] 22 vt a *record, grade, titres* to hold; *secret, objets volés* to hold, be in possession of, have in one's possession; *moyen* to have (in one's possession). **~ le pouvoir** to be in power, have *ou* hold the power; **il détient la clef de l'énigme** he holds the key to the enigma. b *prisonnier* to detain. **il a été détenu dans un camp** he was held prisoner in a camp.

détente [detɑ̃t] nf a (*délassement*) relaxation. **~ physique/intellectuelle** physical/intellectual relaxation; **avoir besoin de ~** to need to relax *ou* unwind*; **ce voyage a été une (bonne) ~** this trip has been (very) relaxing; **quelques instants/une semaine de ~** a few moments'/a week's relaxation.

b (*décrispation*) *[relations]* easing (*dans* of); *[atmosphère]* relaxation (*dans* in). (*Pol*) **la ~** détente.

c (*élan*) *[sauteur]* spring; *[lanceur]* thrust. **ce sauteur a de la ~** *ou* **une bonne ~** this jumper has plenty of spring *ou* a powerful spring; **d'une ~ rapide, il bondit sur sa victime** with a swift bound he leaped upon his victim.

d (*relâchement*) *[ressort, arc]* release; *[corde]* slackening, loosening.

e (*lit, fig: gâchette*) trigger; *voir* **dur**.

f (*Tech*) *[pendule]* catch; *[gaz]* reduction in pressure; *[moteur à explosion]* expansion.

détenteur, -trice [detɑ̃tœʀ, tʀis] nm,f *[secret]* possessor, holder, keeper; *[record, titres, objet volé]* holder.

détention [detɑ̃sjɔ̃] nf a (*possession*) *[armes]* possession; *[titres]* holding; (*Jur*) *[bien]* holding. b (*captivité*) detention. (*Jur*) **en ~ préventive** *ou* **provisoire** remanded in custody, on remand; **mettre en ~ préventive** to remand in custody, put on remand.

détenu, e [det(ə)ny] (ptp de **détenir**) nm,f prisoner. **~ politique** political prisoner; **~ de droit commun** ordinary prisoner.

détergent, e [detɛʀʒɑ̃, ɑ̃t] adj, nm detergent.

détérioration [deteʀjɔʀasjɔ̃] nf (*voir* **détériorer, se détériorer**) damaging (*de* of), damage (*de* to); deterioration (*de* in); worsening (*de* in).

détériorer [deteʀjɔʀe] 1 1 vt *objet, relations* to damage, spoil; *santé, bâtiment* to damage. 2 **se détériorer** vpr *[matériel, bâtiment, santé, temps]* to deteriorate; *[relations, situation]* to deteriorate, worsen.

déterminable [detɛʀminabl] adj determinable.

déterminant, e [detɛʀminɑ̃, ɑ̃t] 1 adj (*décisif*) determining (*épith*), deciding (*épith*). **ça a été ~** that was the deciding *ou* determining factor (*dans* in). 2 nm (*Ling*) determiner; (*Math*) determinant.

déterminatif, -ive [detɛʀminatif, iv] 1 adj determinative; *proposition* defining (*épith*). 2 nm determiner, determinative.

détermination [detɛʀminasjɔ̃] nf a *[cause, sens]* determining, establishing; *[date, quantité]* determination, fixing. b (*résolution*) decision, resolution. c (*fermeté*) determination. **il le regarda avec ~** he looked at him with (an air of) determination *ou* determinedly. d (*Philos*) determination.

déterminé, e [detɛʀmine] (ptp de **déterminer**) 1 adj a *personne, air* determined, resolute. b (*précis*) *but, intentions* specific, definite, well-defined; (*spécifique*) *quantité, distance, date* determined, given (*épith*). c (*Philos*) *phénomènes* predetermined. 2 nm (*Gram*) determinatum.

déterminer [detɛʀmine] 1 vt a (*préciser*) *cause, distance, sens d'un mot* to determine, establish; *date, lieu, quantité* to determine, fix. **~ par des calculs où les astronautes vont amerrir** to calculate *ou* work out where the astronauts will splash down.

b (*décider*) to decide, determine. **~ qn à faire** to decide *ou* determine sb to do; **ils se sont déterminés à agir** they have made up their minds *ou* have determined to act.

c (*motiver*) *[chose]* to determine. **conditions qui déterminent nos actions** conditions which determine our actions; **c'est ce qui a déterminé mon choix** that is what fixed *ou* determined *ou* settled my choice; **ceci a déterminé d'importants retards** this caused *ou* brought about long delays.

d (*Gram*) to determine.

déterminisme [detɛʀminism] nm determinism.

déterministe [detɛʀminist] 1 adj determinist(ic). 2 nmf determinist.

déterré, e [deteʀe] (ptp de **déterrer**) nm,f: (*péj*) **avoir une tête** *ou* **une mine de ~** to look deathly pale *ou* like death warmed up*.

déterrer [deteʀe] 1 vt *objet enfoui* to dig up, unearth; *arbre* to uproot, dig up; *mort* to dig up, disinter; (*) *vieil objet, bouquin* to dig out*, unearth.

détersif, -ive [detɛʀsif, iv] adj, nm detergent, detersive.

détersion [detɛʀsjɔ̃] nf cleaning.

détestable [detɛstabl] adj appalling, dreadful, foul, ghastly.

détestablement [detɛstabləmɑ̃] adv *jouer, chanter* appallingly badly, dreadfully badly.

détester [detɛste] 1 vt to hate, detest. **il déteste la peinture/les enfants/le fromage** he hates *ou* detests *ou* can't bear painting/children/cheese; **elle déteste attendre** she hates *ou* detests *ou* can't bear having to wait; **il ne déteste pas le chocolat** he is quite keen on (*Brit*) *ou* is rather fond of *ou* is not averse to chocolate; **il ne déteste pas (de) faire parler de lui** he's not averse to having people talk about him.

déthéiné, e [deteine] adj: **thé ~** decaffeinated tea.

détonant, e [detɔnɑ̃, ɑ̃t] adj: **mélange ~** explosive mixture.

détonateur [detɔnatœʀ] nm (*Tech*) detonator. (*fig*) **être le ~** *crise etc* to trigger off.

détonation [detɔnasjɔ̃] nf *[bombe, obus]* detonation, explosion; *[fusil]* report, bang.

détoner [detɔne] 1 vi to detonate, explode.

détonner [detɔne] 1 vi a *[couleurs]* to clash (with each other); *[meuble]* to be out of place, be out of keeping; *[personne]* to be out of place, clash. **ses manières vulgaires détonnent dans ce milieu raffiné** his vulgar manners are out of place in this refined milieu. b (*Mus*) (*sortir du ton*) to go out of tune; (*chanter faux*) to sing out of tune.

détordre [detɔʀdʀ] 41 vt to untwist, unwind. **le câble s'est détordu** the cable came untwisted *ou* unwound.

détortiller [detɔʀtije] 1 vt to untwist, unwind.

détour [detuʀ] nm a (*sinuosité*) bend, curve. **la rivière fait des ~s** the river meanders and winds about; **ce sentier est plein de ~s** this path is full of twists and turns *ou* is full of bends, this is a very winding path; **au ~ du chemin** at the bend of *ou* in the path; **on devine au ~ d'une phrase ...** one guesses as one is reading ... .
b (*déviation*) detour. **au ~ de la conversation** in the course of the conversation; **faire un ~** to make a detour (*par* via); **ça vaut le ~** it's worth seeing; *voir* **tour**[2].
c (*subterfuge*) roundabout means; (*circonlocution*) circumlocution. **explique-toi sans ~s** just say straight out what you mean, explain yourself without beating about the bush; **user de longs ~s** *ou* **prendre beaucoup de ~s pour demander qch** to ask for sth in a very roundabout way.

détourné, e [detuʀne] (ptp de **détourner**) adj *chemin* roundabout (*épith*); *moyen* roundabout (*épith*), indirect; *reproche* indirect, oblique. **je l'ai appris de façon ~e** I heard it in a roundabout way *ou* on the grapevine.

détournement [detuʀnəmɑ̃] nm *[rivière]* diversion, rerouting. **~ d'avion** hijacking, skyjacking*; **~ de fonds** embezzlement, misappropriation of funds; **~ de mineur** corruption of a minor; **~ de pouvoir** abuse of power.

détourner [detuʀne] 1 1 vt a (*dévier*) *route, ruisseau, circulation, convoi* to divert, reroute; *bus [pirate]* to hijack; *avion [pirate de l'air]* to hijack, skyjack*; *soupçon* to divert (*sur* on to); *coup* to parry, ward off. **~ l'attention de qn** to divert *ou* distract sb's attention; **~ la conversation** to turn *ou* divert the conversation, change the subject; **pour ~ leur colère** to ward off *ou* avert their anger.
b (*tourner d'un autre côté*) to turn away. **~ les yeux** *ou* **le regard** to avert one's gaze, look away, turn one's eyes away; **~ la tête** to turn one's head away.
c (*écarter*) to divert. **~ qn de sa route/de son chemin** to divert sb from his road/from *ou* off his path, take *ou* lead sb off his road/path; **~ qn d'un projet/de faire** to dissuade sb from a plan/from doing, put sb off a plan/off doing; **~ qn de qn** to put sb off sb, turn sb away from sb; **~ qn du droit chemin** to lead sb astray, lead sb off the straight and narrow; **~ qn de son devoir** to lead sb away *ou* divert sb from his duty; **pour le ~ de ses soucis** to divert him from his worries, to take his mind off his worries.
d (*voler*) *argent* to embezzle, misappropriate; *marchandises* to misappropriate.
2 **se détourner** vpr to turn away. **se ~ de sa route** (*pour aller ailleurs*) to make a detour *ou* diversion; (*par erreur*) to go off the right road; (*fig*) **il s'est détourné de tous ses amis** he has turned away *ou* aside from all his friends.

détracteur, -trice [detʀaktœʀ, tʀis] 1 adj disparaging. **~ de** disparaging of. 2 nm,f detractor, disparager, belittler.

détraqué, e [detʀake] (ptp de **détraquer**) adj *machine* broken down; (*) *personne* unhinged, cracked*; *temps* unsettled, upside-down (*attrib*), crazy; *nerfs, santé* shaky; *imagination* unbalanced. **cette horloge est ~e** this clock has gone completely wrong *ou* is bust* (*Brit*); **il a l'estomac ~** his stomach is out of order *ou* out of sorts; **avoir le cerveau ~*** to be unhinged *ou* cracked*, have a screw loose‡; **c'est un ~*** he's a headcase‡, he's off his head‡.

détraquement [detʀakmɑ̃] nm *[machine]* breakdown; *[santé, nerfs]* shakiness. **à cause du ~ de mon estomac** because of my upset stomach; **à cause du ~ du temps** because the weather is unsettled.

détraquer [detʀake] 1 1 vt *machine* to put out of order; *personne* (*physiquement*) to put out of sorts; *estomac** to put out of sorts, put out of order; *nerfs** to shake up, upset. **ces orages ont détraqué le temps** these storms have unsettled the weather *ou* caused the weather to break; **cela lui a détraqué le cerveau*, ça l'a détraqué*** that has unhinged him *ou* sent him off his head* *ou* made him go nuts*. 2 **se détraquer** vpr *[machine]* to go wrong, break down; *[estomac]* to get out of sorts, be upset. **le temps se détraque*** the weather is breaking *ou* is becoming unsettled.

détrempe [detʀɑ̃p] nf a (*Peinture*) (*substance*) tempera; (*tableau*) tempera painting. **peindre en** *ou* **à la ~** to paint in tempera. b (*Tech*) *[acier]* softening.

détremper [detʀɑ̃pe] 1 vt a (*délayer*) *terre, pain* to soak; *couleurs* to dilute, water down; *chaux* to mix with water, slake; *mortier* to mix with water, temper. **chemins détrempés** sodden *ou* waterlogged paths; **ma chemise est détrempée** my shirt is soaking (wet) *ou* soaked. b (*Tech*) *acier* to soften.

détresse [detʀɛs] nf a (*sentiment*) distress. **son cœur en ~** his anguished heart. b (*situation*) distress. **être dans la ~** to be in distress *ou* in dire straits; **bateau/avion en ~** boat/plane in distress; **entreprise en ~** business in difficulties; **envoyer un appel/un signal de ~** to send out a distress call/signal; *voir* **feu**[1].

détriment [detʀimɑ̃] nm: **au ~ de** to the detriment of.

détritique [detʀitik] adj *roche* detrital.

détritus [detʀity(s)] nmpl rubbish (*NonC*) (*Brit*), refuse (*NonC*), garbage (*NonC*).

détroit [detʀwa] nm (*Géog*) strait. **le ~ de Gibraltar/du Bosphore** the Strait of Gibraltar/of the Bosphorus; **le ~ de Magellan** the Magellan Strait.

détromper [detʀɔ̃pe] 1 1 vt *personne* to disabuse (*de* of). 2 **se détromper** vpr: **détrompez-vous, il n'est pas venu** you're quite mistaken, he didn't come; **si tu crois que je vais accepter, détrompe-toi!** if you think I'm going to accept, (I'm afraid) I'll have to disillusion you! *ou* you'll have to think again!

détrôner [detʀone] 1 vt *souverain* to dethrone, depose; (*fig*) to oust, dethrone.

détrousser [detʀuse] 1 vt († *ou hum*) **~ qn** to relieve sb of his money *ou* luggage *etc* (*hum*), rob sb.

détrousseur [detʀusœʀ] nm († *ou hum*) bandit, footpad† (*Brit*).

détruire [detʀɥiʀ] 38 vt a (*ravager*) *bâtiment, ville, document, déchets* to destroy; *avion, machines* to destroy, write off*. **un incendie a détruit l'hôtel** the hotel was burnt (*Brit*) *ou* burned (*US*) down, the hotel was destroyed by fire; **la ville a été complètement détruite** the town was wiped out *ou* razed to the ground *ou* completely destroyed; **cet enfant détruit tout** this child wrecks *ou* ruins everything *ou* smashes everything up; **la tempête a détruit les récoltes** the storm has ruined the crops.
b (*tuer*) *population, armée* to wipe out; *animaux, insectes* to destroy, exterminate. **il a essayé de se ~** he tried to do away with himself.
c (*ruiner*) *empire* to destroy; *santé, réputation* to ruin, wreck; *sentiment* to destroy, kill; *espoir, théorie, projet* to ruin, wreck, put paid to (*Brit*). **les effets se détruisent** the effects cancel each other out; **cela détruit tous ses beaux arguments** that destroys *ou* puts paid to* (*Brit*) all his fine arguments.

dette [dɛt] nf a (*Fin*) debt. **avoir des ~s** to be in debt, have debts; **faire des ~s** to get into debt, run up debts; **avoir 10.000 F de ~s** to be 10,000 francs in debt, be in debt to the tune of 10,000 francs*; **~ de jeu, ~ d'honneur** a gambling *ou* gaming debt is a debt of honour; **la ~ publique** *ou* **de l'État** the national debt; *voir* **prison, reconnaissance.** b (*morale*) debt. **~ d'amitié/de reconnaissance** debt of friendship/gratitude; **je suis en ~ envers vous** I am indebted to you; **il a payé sa ~ envers la société** he has paid his debt to society; **je vous garde une ~ de reconnaissance** I shall remain gratefully indebted to you.

DEUG [døg] nm (abrév de **diplôme d' études universitaires générales**) *voir* **diplôme**.

deuil [dœj] nm a (*perte*) bereavement. **il a eu un ~ récemment** he was recently bereaved, he recently suffered a bereavement (*frm*), there has recently been a death in his family.
b (*affliction*) mourning (*NonC*), grief. **cela nous a plongés dans le ~** it has plunged us into mourning *ou* grief; **si nous pouvons vous réconforter dans votre ~** if we can comfort you in your grief *ou* sorrow; **décréter un ~ national** to declare national mourning.
c (*vêtements*) mourning (clothes). **en grand ~** in deep mourning; **être/se mettre en ~** to be in/go into mourning; **quitter le ~** to come out of mourning; **prendre/porter le ~ d'un ami** to go into/be in mourning for a friend; (*fig*) **porter le ~ de ses espoirs/illusions** to grieve for one's lost hopes/illusions; (*littér*) **la nature/la forêt est en ~** nature/the forest is in mourning; *voir* **demi-, ongle.**
d (*durée*) mourning. **jour/semaine de ~** day/week of mourning; **le ~ du président dura un mois** the mourning for the president lasted a month.
e (*cortège*) funeral procession. **conduire** *ou* **mener le ~** to head the funeral procession, be (the) chief mourner.
f (*) **faire son ~ de qch** to kiss sth goodbye*, say goodbye to sth*; **les vacances sont annulées, j'en ai fait mon ~** the holidays have been cancelled but I am resigned to it *ou* it's no use crying about it.

deus ex machina [deusɛksmakina] nm deus ex machina.

deusio* [døzjo] adv = **deuzio**.

DEUST [døst] nm (abrév de **diplôme d'études universitaires scientifiques et techniques**) *voir* **diplôme**.

deutérium [døteʀjɔm] nm deuterium.

Deutéronome [døteʀɔnɔm] nm Deuteronomy.

deux [dø] 1 adj inv a two. **les ~ yeux/mains** *etc* both eyes/hands *etc*; **ses ~ jambes** both his legs, his two legs; **montrez-moi les ~** show me both (of them) *ou* the two of them; **~ fois** twice; **il ne peut être en ~ endroits/aux ~ endroits à la fois** he can't be in two places/in both places at once; **je les ai vus tous (les) ~** I saw them both, I saw both of them, I saw the two of them; (*lit, fig*) **à ~ tranchants** two-edged, double-edged; **inflation à ~ chiffres** double-figure *ou* two-figure inflation; **des ~ côtés de la rue** on both sides *ou* on either side of the street; **tous les ~ jours/mois** every other *ou* every second day/month, every two days/months; **habiter** *ou* **vivre à ~** to live together *ou* as a couple; **il y a ~ t dans "commettre"** there are two t's in "commettre"; (*en épelant*) **~ t/l** double t/l, tt/ll.
b (*quelques*) a couple, a few. **c'est à ~ pas/à ~ minutes d'ici** it's only a short distance/just a few minutes from here, it's only a step/only a couple of minutes from here; **pouvez-vous attendre ~ (ou trois) minutes?** could you wait two (or three) minutes? *ou* a couple of minutes?; **vous y serez en ~ secondes** you'll be there in two ticks*

(*Brit*) *ou* shakes* *ou* in no time (at all); **j'ai ~ mots à vous dire** I want to have a word with you, I've a word to say to you.

c (*deuxième*) second. **volume/acte ~** volume/act two; **le ~ janvier** the second of January; **Jacques ~** James the Second; *pour autres loc voir* **six**.

d (*Mus*) **mesure à ~-~/à ~-quatre/à ~-huit** two-two/two-four/two-eight time.

e (*loc*) **essayer et réussir, cela fait ~** to try and to succeed are two (entirely) different things, to try is one thing but to succeed is another thing altogether; **pris entre ~ feux** caught in the crossfire; **lui et les maths, ça fait ~!*** he hasn't got a clue about maths; **lui et la tendresse, ça fait ~!*** he doesn't know the meaning of tenderness; **avoir ~ poids ~ mesures** to have double standards *ou* two sets of rules; **être assis** *ou* **avoir le cul* entre ~ chaises** to be in a difficult predicament *ou* on the horns of a dilemma; **à ~ vitesses** *enseignement, justice* two-tier; **une Europe à ~ vitesses** a two-speed Europe; (*Prov*) **~ précautions valent mieux qu'une** better safe than sorry (*Prov*); **~ avis valent mieux qu'un** two heads are better than one (*Prov*); **en ~ temps, trois mouvements il l'a réparé*** he repaired it in two ticks* (*Brit*) *ou* shakes* *ou* before you could say Jack Robinson* (*hum*); **ne pas avoir les ~ pieds dans le même sabot** to be hardly bogged down*.

2 **nm inv** (*chiffre*) two. (*Cartes, Dés*) **le ~** the two, the deuce; **couper en ~/en ~ morceaux** to cut in two *ou* in half/into two pieces; **marcher ~ par ~** *ou* **à ~** to walk two by two *ou* in pairs *ou* two abreast; **à nous ~** (*parlons sérieusement*) let's have a chat; (*je m'occupe de vous*) I'm with you now; (*à un ennemi*) now let's fight it out!; (*à un appareil à réparer*) now let's see what we can do with you, now let's get you fixed; *pour autres loc voir* **six** *et* **moins, pas**[1].

3 **comp** ▸**deux-chevaux** (*Aut*) **nf inv** 2 CV (*car*) ▸**deux-mâts** (*Naut*) **nm inv** two-master ▸**deux-pattes*** = **deux-chevaux** ▸**deux-pièces nm inv** (*ensemble*) two-piece suit; (*maillot*) two-piece (swimsuit) ▸**deux pièces** (*appartement*) two-room flat (*Brit*) *ou* apartment (*US*) ▸**deux-points nm inv** colon ▸**deux-ponts adj, nm inv** (*Naut*) two-decker; (*Aviat*) double-decker ▸**deux-roues** (*Admin*) **nm inv** two-wheeled vehicle ▸**deux-temps adj** (*Aut*) two-stroke ◊ **nm inv** (*moteur*) two-stroke (engine); (*Mus*) half-common time.

deuxième [døzjɛm] 1 **adj, nmf** second; *pour loc voir* **sixième**. 2 **comp** ▸**le Deuxième Bureau** (*Admin*) the intelligence branch *ou* service ▸**deuxième classe** (*Mil*) **nm inv** *voir* **soldat**.

deuxièmement [døzjɛmmɑ̃] **adv** second(ly).

deuzio* [døzjo] **adv** secondly.

dévaler [devale] 1 1 **vt** (*courir*) to tear down, hurtle down; (*glisser, tomber*) to tumble down. **il dévala les escaliers quatre à quatre** he tore *ou* hurtled down the stairs four at a time, he came tearing *ou* hurtling down the stairs four at a time. 2 **vi** *[rochers]* to hurtle down; *[lave]* to rush down, gush down; *[terrain]* to fall away sharply. **il a dévalé dans les escaliers et s'est cassé le bras** he tumbled down the stairs and broke his arm.

dévaliser [devalize] 1 **vt** *maison* to strip, burgle (*Brit*), burglarize (*US*); *banque* to rob. **~ qn** to strip sb of what he has on him; **~ un magasin** (*lit*) *[voleurs]* to strip *ou* burgle (*Brit*) *ou* burglarize (*US*) a shop; (*fig*) *[clients]* to buy up a shop; **~ le réfrigérateur** to raid the fridge.

dévalorisation [devalɔʀizasjɔ̃] **nf** depreciation.

dévaloriser [devalɔʀize] 1 1 **vt** *marchandises, collection* to reduce the value of; *monnaie, talent, diplôme* to depreciate; *personne* to sell short, belittle. 2 **se dévaloriser vpr** *[monnaie, marchandise]* to fall in value, depreciate; *[personne]* to sell o.s. short, belittle o.s.

dévaluation [devalɥasjɔ̃] **nf** devaluation.

dévaluer [devalɥe] 1 1 **vt** to devalue, devaluate (*US*). 2 **se dévaluer vpr** *[objet]* to devalue, be devalued, fall in value; *[personne]* to devalue *ou* belittle o.s., sell o.s. short.

devancement [d(ə)vɑ̃smɑ̃] **nm**: **~ d'une échéance** (making of a) payment in advance *ou* before time; (*Mil*) **~ d'appel** enlistment before call-up.

devancer [d(ə)vɑ̃se] 3 **vt** a (*distancer*) *coureur* to get ahead of, get in front of, outstrip; *concurrent, rival* to get ahead of, forestall. **il m'a devancé de trois minutes/de 3 points** he beat me by 3 minutes/3 points, he was 3 minutes/3 points ahead of me.

b (*précéder*) to arrive before, arrive ahead of. **il m'a devancé au carrefour** he got to the crossroads before me; (*littér*) **~ son siècle** to be ahead of *ou* in advance of one's time.

c (*aller au devant de*) *question, objection, désir* to anticipate. **j'allais le faire mais il m'a devancé** I was going to do it but he did it first *ou* got there first.

d (*faire qch en avance*) (*Mil*) **~ l'appel** to enlist before call-up; (*Fin*) **~ la date d'un paiement** to make a payment before it is due.

devancier, -ière [d(ə)vɑ̃sje, jɛʀ] **nm,f** precursor.

devant [d(ə)vɑ̃] 1 **prép** a (*position: en face de*) in front of, before (*littér*); (*mouvement: le long de*) past. **ma voiture est ~ la porte** my car is (just) outside *ou* at the door; **~ nous se dressait un vieux chêne** before us *ou* in front of us stood an old oak tree; **le bateau est ancré ~ le port** the boat is anchored outside the port; **il est passé ~ moi sans me voir** he walked past me *ou* he passed me *ou* he went right by me without seeing me; **elle était assise ~ la fenêtre** she was sitting at *ou* by the window; **il est passé** *ou* **a filé ~ nous comme une flèche** he shot past us (like an arrow), he flashed past us; **va-t-en de ~ la vitrine** move away from (in front of) the window; **va-t-en de ~ la lumière** get out of the *ou* my light.

b (*lit, fig: en avant de*) (*proximité*) in front of; (*distance*) ahead of. **il marchait ~ moi** he was walking in front of *ou* ahead of me; **il est loin ~ nous** he is a long way ahead of us; **regarde ~ toi** look in front of you *ou* straight ahead (of you); **il est ~ moi en classe** (*banc*) he sits in front of me at school; (*résultats*) he is ahead of me at *ou* in school; **fuir ~ qn** to flee before *ou* from sb; **(droit) ~ nous se dressait la muraille** the wall rose up (straight) in front of *ou* ahead of us; (*fig*) **avoir du temps/de l'argent ~ soi** to have time/money in hand *ou* to spare; **il a tout l'avenir ~ lui** he has his whole future in front of *ou* before him, his whole future lies before him *ou* in front of him; **allez droit ~ vous, vous trouverez le village** go straight on *ou* ahead and you'll come to the village; (*fig*) **aller droit ~ soi (sans s'occuper des autres)** to go straight on (regardless of others); **passe ~ moi si tu es pressé** you go first *ou* in front of me if you're in a hurry; **elle est passée ~ moi chez le boucher** she pushed (in) in front of me at the butcher's.

c (*en présence de*) before, in front of. **s'incliner ~ qn** to bow before sb; **comparaître ~ ses juges** to appear before one's judges; **ne dis pas cela ~ les enfants/tout le monde** don't say that in front of the children/everyone; **cela s'est passé juste ~ nous** *ou* **nos yeux** it happened before *ou* in front of our very eyes; **imperturbable ~ le malheur d'autrui** unmoved by *ou* in the face of other people's misfortune; (*fig*) **reculer ~ ses responsabilités** to shrink from one's responsibilities; (*Jur*) **par-~ notaire/Maître X** in the presence of a notary/Maître X.

d (*fig*) (*face à*) faced with, in the face of; (*étant donné*) in view of, considering. **~ la gravité de la situation** in view of *ou* considering the gravity of the situation; **rester ferme ~ le danger** to stand fast in the face of danger; **il ne sut quelle attitude prendre ~ ces faits** he did not know what line to adopt when faced *ou* confronted with these facts; **tous égaux ~ la loi** everyone (is) equal in the eyes of the law.

2 **adv** a in front. **vous êtes juste ~** you are right in front of it; **vous êtes passé ~** you came past *ou* by it; **je suis garé juste ~** I am parked just out at the front *ou* just outside; **en passant ~, regarde si la boutique est ouverte** see if the shop is open as you go past; **corsage qui se boutonne (par-)~** blouse which buttons up *ou* does up at the front; **entre par-~, le jardin est fermé** go in (by) the front (way) because the garden is closed.

b (*en avant*) ahead, in front. **il est parti ~** he went on ahead *ou* in advance; **il est loin ~** he's a long way ahead; (*Naut*) **attention, obstacle (droit) ~** stand by, hazard ahead!; **il est assis 3 rangs ~** he's sitting 3 rows in front (of us); **passe ~, je te rejoindrai** (you) go on ahead and I'll catch up with you; **fais passer le plateau ~** pass the tray forward; **il a pris des places ~** he has got front seats *ou* seats at the front *ou* up front*; (*Aut*) **il a préféré monter ~** he preferred to sit in (the) front; **marchez ~, les enfants** walk in front, children; **passe ~, il roule trop lentement** go past him *ou* overtake him (*Brit*) *ou* get in front of him, he's going too slowly; **passez ~, je ne suis pas pressé** after you *ou* you go first *ou* you go in front of me, I'm in no hurry; *voir* **pied**.

3 **nm** a *[maison, voiture, objet]* front; *[bateau]* fore, bow(s). **habiter sur le ~** to live at the front (of the house *etc*); **de ~** *roue, porte* front; *voir* **patte, point**[2].

b **prendre le(s) ~(s)**: **voyant qu'il hésitait, j'ai pris les ~s pour lui parler** seeing that he hesitated, I made the first move *ou* took the initiative and spoke to him; **nous étions plusieurs sur cette affaire, j'ai dû prendre les ~s en offrant un contrat plus intéressant** there were several of us after the job so I had to pre-empt *ou* forestall the others and offer a more competitive contract; (*Mil*) **prendre les ~s en attaquant** to launch a pre-emptive strike *ou* attack.

c **au-~ (de)**: **je l'ai vu de loin et je suis allé au-~ (de lui)** I saw him in the distance and went (out) to meet him; **aller au-~ des désirs de qn** to anticipate sb's wishes; **courir au-~ du danger** to court danger; **aller au-~ des ennuis** *ou* **difficultés** to be asking for trouble; **en faisant cela, tu vas au-~ de bien des ennuis** you'll run into *ou* be asking for no end of trouble by doing that.

devanture [d(ə)vɑ̃tyʀ] **nf** a (*étalage*) display; (*vitrine*) (shop) window (*Brit*), (store) window (*US*). **à la ~** on display; (*dans la vitrine*) in the window. b (*façade*) (shop) front.

dévastateur, -trice [devastatœʀ, tʀis] **adj** *torrent, orage* devastating, ruinous; *passion* destructive.

dévastation [devastasjɔ̃] **nf** devastation. **les ~s de la guerre/de la tempête** the ravages of war/the storm, the devastation *ou* havoc wreaked by war/the storm.

dévasté, e [devaste] (**ptp de dévaster**) **adj** *pays, ville, cultures* devastated; *maison* ruined; *visage* ravaged.

dévaster [devaste] 1 **vt** *pays, ville, cultures* to devastate, lay waste; (*fig*) *âme* to devastate, ravage.

déveine* [devɛn] **nf** (piece of) rotten luck*. **être dans la ~** to be down on one's luck *ou* out of luck, be damned unlucky*; **avoir la ~ de** to have the rotten luck to*; **quelle ~!** what rotten luck!*

développable [dev(ə)lɔpabl] **adj** (*gén, Géom*) developable.

développateur [dev(ə)lɔpatœʀ] nm (*Phot*) developer.

développé, e [dev(ə)lɔpe] (ptp de **développer**) 1 adj developed. *membre* **bien/peu** ~ well-developed/underdeveloped. 2 nm (*Haltérophilie*) press; (*Danse*) développé.

développement [dev(ə)lɔpmɑ̃] nm a (*croissance*) *[intelligence, corps, science]* development; *[industrie, affaire, commerce]* development, expansion, growth. **une affaire en plein ~** a fast-expanding *ou* fast-developing business; **l'entreprise a connu un ~ important** the firm has expanded *ou* developed greatly *ou* has undergone a sizeable expansion; **la crise a connu un ~ inattendu** the crisis has taken an unexpected turn *ou* has developed in an unexpected way, there has been an unexpected development in the crisis; *voir* **pays**[1].
b (*conséquences*) **~s** *[affaire]* consequences.
c *[sujet]* exposition; (*Mus*) *[thème]* development. **entrer dans des ~s inutiles** to go into unnecessary details, develop the subject unnecessarily.
d (*Phot*) developing, development, processing. **appareil/photographie à ~ instantané** instant camera/photograph.
e (*Cyclisme*) **choisir un grand/petit ~** to choose a high/low gear.
f (*Géom*) *[solide]* development; (*Algèbre*) *[fonction]* development; *[expression algébrique]* simplification.

développer [dev(ə)lɔpe] [1] 1 vt a *corps, muscle, intelligence* to develop; *commerce, industrie* to develop, expand. **~ le goût de l'aventure chez les enfants** to bring out *ou* develop adventurousness in children; **il faut ~ les échanges entre les pays** exchanges between countries must be developed.
b *récit, argument, projet* to develop, enlarge (up)on, elaborate upon. **il faut ~ ce paragraphe** this paragraph needs developing *ou* expanding.
c (*Phot*) *film* to develop. **envoyer une pellicule à ~** to send (off) a film to be developed *ou* processed.
d (*déballer*) *paquet* to unwrap.
e (*déployer*) *parchemin* to unroll; *coupon de tissu* to unfold; *armée, troupes* to deploy.
f (*Géom*) *solide* to develop; (*Algèbre*) *fonction, série* to develop; *expression algébrique* to simplify.
g **vélo qui développe 6 mètres** bicycle which moves forward 6 metres for every complete revolution of the pedal.
h (*Haltérophilie*) *poids* to lift.
2 **se développer** vpr a *[personne, intelligence, plante]* to develop, grow; *[affaire]* to expand, develop, grow.
b *[armée]* to spread out.
c *[habitude]* to spread.

devenir [dəv(ə)niʀ] [22] 1 vi a to become. **~ capitaine/médecin** to become a captain/a doctor; **que veux-tu ~ dans la vie?** what do you want to do *ou* be in life?; **cet enfant maladif est devenu un homme solide** that sickly child has turned out *ou* turned into *ou* has become a strong man; **il est devenu tout rouge** he turned *ou* went (*Brit*) quite red; **il devient de plus en plus agressif** he's becoming *ou* growing *ou* getting more and more aggressive; **~ vieux/grand** to grow *ou* get old/tall; **arrête, tu deviens grossier** stop it, you're getting *ou* becoming rude *ou* starting to be rude; **c'est à ~ fou!** it's enough to drive you mad!
b (*advenir de*) **bonjour, que devenez-vous?*** hullo, how are you making out?* (*Brit*) *ou* getting on? *ou* doing?*; **qu'étais-tu devenu? nous te cherchions partout** where *ou* wherever had you got to? we have been looking for you everywhere; **que sont devenues mes lunettes?** where *ou* wherever have my glasses got to? *ou* gone?; **que sont devenus tes grands projets?** what has become of your fine plans?; **que deviendrais-je sans toi?** what(ever) would I do *ou* what(ever) would become of me without you?; **qu'allons-nous ~?** what is going to happen to us?, what will become of us?
2 nm (*progression*) evolution; (*futur*) future. **quel est le ~ de l'homme?** what is man's destiny?; **en ~** constantly evolving.

dévergondage [devɛʀgɔ̃daʒ] nm licentious *ou* loose living.

dévergondé, e [devɛʀgɔ̃de] (ptp de **se dévergonder**) adj *femme* shameless, bad; *homme* wild, bad, loose; *conversation* licentious, shameless. **vie ~e** licentious *ou* loose living; **c'est une ~e** she's a shameless hussy; **c'est un ~** he leads a wild life.

dévergonder (se) [devɛʀgɔ̃de] [1] vpr to run wild, get into bad ways.

déverrouillage [deveʀujaʒ] nm (*voir* **déverrouiller**) unbolting; unlocking, opening.

déverrouiller [deveʀuje] [1] vt *porte* to unbolt; *mécanisme* to unlock, release; *arme à feu* to release the bolt of; *train d'atterrissage* to release.

devers [dəvɛʀ] *voir* **par-devers**.

dévers [devɛʀ] nm *[route]* banking; *[mur]* slant.

déversement [devɛʀsəmɑ̃] nm (*voir* **déverser**) pouring(-out); tipping(-out); unloading. **~ accidentel de pétrole** oil spill.

déverser [devɛʀse] [1] 1 vt *liquide* to pour (out); *sable, ordures* to tip (out); *bombes* to unload. **la rivière déverse ses eaux dans le lac** the river flows into *ou* pours its waters into the lake; **il déversa toute sa colère sur moi** he poured out *ou* vented his anger upon me; **~ des injures sur qn** to shower abuse on sb; (*fig*) **le train déversa des milliers de banlieusards** the train disgorged *ou* discharged thousands of commuters; (*fig*) **~ des produits sur le marché européen** to dump *ou* unload products onto the European market.
2 **se déverser** vpr to pour (out). **la rivière se déverse dans le lac** the river flows into *ou* pours its waters into the lake; **un orifice par où se déversaient des torrents d'eaux boueuses** an opening out of which poured torrents of muddy water.

déversoir [devɛʀswaʀ] nm *[canal]* overflow; *[réservoir]* spillway, overflow; (*fig*) outlet.

dévêtir [devetiʀ] [20] 1 vt *personne, poupée* to undress. **~ un enfant** to undress a child, take a child's clothes off (him), take the clothes off a child. 2 **se dévêtir** vpr to undress, get undressed, take one's clothes off.

déviance [devjɑ̃s] nf (*Psych*) deviancy, deviance.

déviant, e [devjɑ̃, jɑ̃t] adj, nm,f deviant.

déviation [devjasjɔ̃] nf a *[projectile, navire, aiguille aimantée]* deviation; *[circulation]* diversion. b (*Aut: détour obligatoire*) diversion (*Brit*), detour (*US*). c (*Méd*) *[organe]* inversion; *[utérus]* displacement; *[colonne vertébrale]* curvature. d (*écart de conduite etc*) deviation.

déviationnisme [devjasjɔnism] nm deviationism. **faire du ~ de droite** to move to the right.

déviationniste [devjasjɔnist] adj, nmf deviationist.

dévidage [devidaʒ] nm (*voir* **dévider**) unwinding; winding.

dévider [devide] [1] vt a (*dérouler*) *pelote, bobine* to unwind. **elle m'a dévidé tout son chapelet*** she reeled off all her grievances to me*. b (*mettre en pelote*) *fil* to wind into a ball *ou* skein; *écheveau* to wind up.

dévidoir [devidwaʀ] nm *[fil, tuyau]* reel; *[câbles]* drum, reel.

dévier [devje] [7] 1 vi a *[aiguille magnétique]* to deviate; *[ballon, bateau, projectile]* to veer (off course), turn (off course). **le ballon a dévié vers la gauche** the ball veered to the left; **le poteau a fait ~ le ballon** the post deflected the ball; **le vent nous a fait ~ (de notre route)** the wind blew *ou* turned us off course *ou* made us veer off course; **nous avons dévié par rapport à notre route** we've gone off course, we're off course.
b (*fig*) *[doctrine]* to alter; *[conversation]* to turn (*sur* (on)to). **voyant que la conversation déviait dangereusement** seeing that the conversation was taking a dangerous turn *ou* was turning onto dangerous ground; **nous avons dévié par rapport au projet initial** we have moved away *ou* diverged *ou* departed from the original plan; **on m'accuse de ~ de ma ligne politique** I'm accused of deviating *ou* departing from my political line; **rien ne me fera ~ de mes principes** nothing will turn me away from my principles, nothing will make me depart *ou* swerve from my principles; **il fit ~ la conversation vers des sujets plus neutres** he turned *ou* diverted the conversation onto more neutral subjects.
2 vt *route, circulation* to divert (*Brit*), detour (*US*); *projectile, coup* to deflect, divert. **avoir la colonne vertébrale déviée** to have curvature of the spine.

devin, devineresse [dəvɛ̃, dəvin(ə)ʀɛs] nm,f soothsayer, seer. **je ne suis pas ~*** I don't have second sight, I can't see into the future.

devinable [d(ə)vinabl] adj *résultat* foreseeable; *énigme* solvable; *secret, raison* that can be guessed, guessable.

deviner [d(ə)vine] [1] vt *secret, raison* to guess; *énigme* to solve. **~ l'avenir** to foretell the future; (*littér*) **~ qn** to see into sb; **devine pourquoi/qui** guess why/who; **vous ne devinez pas?** can't you guess?; **je ne devine pas** I give up, I don't know.

devineresse [dəvin(ə)ʀɛs] nf *voir* **devin**.

devinette [d(ə)vinɛt] nf riddle, conundrum. (*lit*) **jouer aux ~s** to play at (asking) riddles; **arrête de jouer aux ~s*** stop playing guessing games *ou* talking in riddles.

déviriliser [deviʀilize] [1] vt: **~ qn** to make sb look less manly.

devis [d(ə)vi] nm estimate, quotation, quote. **~ descriptif** detailed estimate; **~ estimatif** preliminary estimate.

dévisager [devizaʒe] [3] vt to stare at, look hard at.

devise [dəviz] nf a (*Hér*) (*formule*) motto, watchword; (*figure emblématique*) device. b *[maison de commerce]* slogan; *[parti]* motto, slogan. **simplicité est ma ~** simplicity is my motto. c (*Fin: monnaie*) currency. **~ forte** hard *ou* strong currency; **~ faible** soft *ou* weak currency; **~s** (*argent*) currency; **~s étrangères** foreign currency; **~ convertible** convertible currency; *voir* **cours**.

deviser [dəvize] [1] vi (*littér*) to converse (*de* about, on).

dévissage [devisaʒ] nm (*voir* **dévisser**) unscrewing, undoing; fall.

dévisser [devise] [1] 1 vt to unscrew, undo. (*fig*) **se ~ la tête/le cou** to screw one's head/neck round. 2 vi *[alpiniste]* to fall (off).

de visu [devizy] loc adv: **s'assurer/se rendre compte de qch ~** to make sure of sth/see sth for o.s.

dévitalisation [devitalizasjɔ̃] nf: **~ d'une dent** removal of a nerve from a tooth, devitalization (*SPÉC*) of a tooth.

dévitaliser [devitalize] [1] vt *dent* to remove the nerve from, devitalize (*SPÉC*).

dévoilement [devwalmɑ̃] nm (*voir* **dévoiler**) unveiling; unmasking; disclosure; revelation. **le ~ d'un mystère** the unfolding of a mystery.

dévoiler [devwale] [1] vt *statue, visage* to unveil; *intention, secret, vérité, avenir* to unveil, disclose; *nom, date* to reveal, disclose. **le mystère s'est dévoilé** the mystery has been revealed *ou* unfolded; (*hum*) **~ ses charmes** to reveal one's charms.

devoir [d(ə)vwaʀ] [28] 1 vt a (*avoir à payer*) *chose, somme d'argent* to owe. ~ **qch à qn** to owe sb sth; **elle (lui) doit 200 F/2 jours de travail** she owes (him) 200 francs/2 days' work; **il réclame seulement ce qui lui est dû** he is asking only for what is owing *ou* due to him, he is only asking for his due(s).

b (*être redevable*) ~ **qch à qch** to owe sth to sth; ~ **qch à qn** to owe sth to sb, be indebted to sb for sth; **il ne veut rien ~ à personne** he doesn't want to be indebted to anyone *ou* to owe anyone anything; **c'est à son courage qu'elle doit la vie** she owes her life to his courage, it's thanks to his courage that she's alive; **je dois à mes parents d'avoir réussi** I have my parents to thank for my success, I owe my success to my parents; **sa réussite ne doit rien au hasard** he doesn't owe his success to luck, his success has nothing to do with *ou* is not down to luck; **c'est à Fleming que l'on doit la découverte de la pénicilline** we have Fleming to thank for the discovery of penicillin, it is to Fleming that we owe the discovery of penicillin; **je lui dois une fière chandelle** I am enormously grateful to him (*ou* her).

c (*être tenu à*) to owe. ~ **le respect/l'obéissance à qn** to owe sb respect/obedience; **il lui doit bien cela!** it's the least he can do for him!; **avec les honneurs dûs à son rang** with honours due to *ou* befitting his rank.

2 **vb aux** a (*obligation*) to have to. **elle doit (absolument) partir ce soir** she (really) has to *ou* she (really) must go tonight; **il aurait dû la prévenir** he should have *ou* ought to have warned her; **il avait promis, il devait le faire** he had promised so he had to do it; **il devrait maintenant connaître le chemin** he ought to *ou* should know the way by now; **dois-je lui écrire tout de suite?** must I *ou* do I have to *ou* have I got to write to him immediately?; **vous ne devez pas entrer sans frapper** you are not to *ou* must not come in without knocking; **non, tu ne dois pas le rembourser** no, you need not *ou* don't have to pay it back.

b (*fatalité*) **cela devait arriver un jour** it (just) had to happen *ou* it was bound to happen some time; **elle ne devait pas apprendre la nouvelle avant le lendemain** she was not to hear the news until the next day; (*littér*) **dût-il** *ou* **même s'il devait être condamné, il refuserait de parler** even if he were (to be) found guilty he would refuse to talk, were he to be found guilty *ou* should he be found guilty he would still refuse to talk; **les choses semblent ~ s'arranger/empirer** it looks as though things are *ou* things seem to be sorting themselves out/getting worse.

c (*prévision*) **il devait acheter une moto mais c'était trop cher** he was (going) to buy *ou* he was to have bought a motorbike but it was too expensive; **il doit arriver ce soir** he is due (to arrive) tonight, he is to arrive tonight; **elle doit vous téléphoner demain** she is to ring you tomorrow; **tu ne devais pas venir avant 8 heures** you were not supposed to come *ou* you were not expected before 8; **vous deviez le lui cacher** you were (supposed) to hide it *ou* to have hidden it from him.

d (*probabilité*) **il doit faire froid ici en hiver** it must be cold here in winter; **vous devez vous tromper** you must be mistaken; **il a dû se tromper** *ou* **il doit s'être trompé de chemin** he must have lost his way; **il devait être 6 heures quand il est sorti** it must have been 6 when he went out; **elle ne doit pas être bête, vous savez** she can't be stupid, you know; **il ne devait pas être loin du sommet quand il a abandonné** he can't have been far from the top when he gave up; **cela devrait pouvoir s'arranger** it should be *ou* ought to be possible to put that right, we should be able to put that right.

3 **se devoir** **vpr: se ~ à qn/qch** to have to devote o.s. to sb/sth; **une mère se doit à sa famille** a mother has to *ou* must devote herself to her family; **nous nous devons de le lui dire** it is our duty *ou* we are duty bound to tell him; **comme il se doit** (*comme il faut*) as is proper *ou* right; (*comme prévu*) as expected.

4 **nm** a (*obligation morale*) duty. **agir par ~** to act from a sense of duty; **un homme de ~** a man of conscience *ou* with a sense of duty; ~ **de réserve** duty to preserve secrecy.

b (*ce que l'on doit faire*) duty. **accomplir** *ou* **faire** *ou* **remplir son ~** to carry out *ou* do one's duty; **les ~s du citoyen/d'une charge** the duties of a citizen/post; **se faire un ~ de faire** to make it one's duty to do; **il est de mon/ton/son** *etc* **~ de faire** it is my/your/his ~ *etc* duty to do; **~s religieux** religious duties; (*frm*) **il se mit en ~ de répondre à la lettre** he proceeded to reply to the letter; **il se mit immédiatement en ~ de le faire** he set about doing it immediately.

c (*Scol*) (*à la maison*) homework (*NonC*); (*en classe*) exercise. **faire ses ~s** to do one's homework; **il n'a pas de ~ de français aujourd'hui** he has no French homework tonight; **~s de vacances** homework to be done over the holidays; ~ **sur table** *ou* **surveillé** (written) test.

d (†, *hum: hommage*) **~s** respects; **présenter ses ~s à qn** to pay one's respects to sb; *voir* **dernier**.

dévoisé, e [devwaze] **adj** (*Ling*) *consonne* devoiced.

dévoisement [devwazmɑ̃] **nm** (*Ling*) devoicing.

dévoltage [devɔltaʒ] **nm** reduction in voltage.

dévolter [devɔlte] [1] **vt** to reduce the voltage of.

dévolu, e [devɔly] 1 **adj: être ~ à qn** *[succession, droits]* to be devolved upon *ou* to sb; *[charge]* to be handed down *ou* passed on to sb; **le budget qui a été ~ à la recherche** the funds that have been allotted *ou* granted *ou* devoted to research; **la part de gâteau qui m'avait été ~e** the piece of cake that had been allotted to me; **c'est à moi qu'il a été ~ de commencer** it fell to my lot to start; **le sort qui lui sera dévolu** the fate that is in store for him. 2 **nm** *voir* **jeter**.

dévolution [devɔlysjɔ̃] **nf** devolution.

dévorant, e [devɔʀɑ̃, ɑ̃t] **adj** *faim* raging (*épith*); *curiosité, soif* burning (*épith*); *passion* devouring (*épith*), consuming (*épith*); (*littér*) *flammes* all-consuming (*littér*), ravaging (*épith*).

dévorer [devɔʀe] [1] **vt** a (*manger*) *[fauve]* to devour; *[personne]* to devour, wolf (down)*. **des limaces ont dévoré mes laitues** slugs have eaten up *ou* devoured my lettuces; **cet enfant dévore!** this child has a huge appetite!; **on est dévoré par les moustiques!** we're being eaten alive by mosquitoes!; ~ **un livre** to devour a book; ~ **qch à belles dents** to wolf sth down; ~ **qn/qch du regard** *ou* **des yeux** to eye sb/sth greedily *ou* covetously; ~ **qn de baisers** to smother sb with kisses; **l'acné/la barbe qui lui dévorait les joues** the acne/the beard which was engulfing his face; *voir* **loup**.

b (*consumer*) to consume. **le feu dévore le bâtiment** the fire is consuming *ou* devouring the building; **il a dévoré sa fortune** he has consumed his (whole) fortune; **voiture qui dévore les kilomètres** *ou* **la route** car which eats up the miles; **c'est une tâche qui dévore tous mes loisirs** it's a task which swallows up all my free time.

c (*littér*) (*tourmenter*) *[jalousie, remords, soucis]* to consume, devour; *[maladie]* to consume. **la soif le dévore** he has a burning thirst, he is consumed with thirst; **être dévoré de remords/jalousie** to be eaten up with *ou* consumed with *ou* devoured by remorse/jealousy.

d (*frm: cacher*) ~ **un affront** to swallow an affront; ~ **ses larmes** to choke back *ou* gulp back one's tears.

dévoreur, -euse [devɔʀœʀ, øz] **nm,f** devourer. (*fig*) **un ~ de livres** an avid reader; **ce projet est un gros ~ de crédits** this project takes a huge amount of money *ou* is a great drain on funds.

dévot, e [devo, ɔt] 1 **adj** (*gén*) devout, pious; (*péj: bigot*) churchy*, holier-than-thou. 2 **nm,f** deeply religious person; (*péj*) excessively pious person. (*péj*) **une vieille ~e** a churchy old woman*; *voir* **faux**[2].

dévotement [devɔtmɑ̃] **adv** devoutly, piously.

dévotion [devosjɔ̃] **nf** a (*piété*) devoutness, religious devotion; *voir* **faux**[2]. b **~s** devotions; **faire ses ~s** to perform one's devotions. c (*culte*) devotion. (*fig*) **avoir une ~ pour qn** to worship sb; **être à la ~ de qn** to be totally devoted to sb; **il avait à sa ~ plusieurs employés** he had several totally devoted employees.

dévoué, e [devwe] (**ptp de se dévouer**) **adj** *infirmière* devoted, dedicated; *femme* devoted; *ami, serviteur* devoted, faithful. **être ~ à qn/qch** to be devoted to sb/sth; (††: *formule de lettre*) **votre ~ serviteur** your devoted servant; *voir* **croire**.

dévouement [devumɑ̃] **nm** *[mère, ami, voisin]* devotion; *[infirmière, sauveteur, soldat]* devotion, dedication. ~ **à un parti** devotion to a party; **avec ~** devotedly; **avoir un ~ aveugle pour qn** to be blindly devoted to sb.

dévouer (se) [devwe] [1] **vpr** a (*se sacrifier*) to sacrifice o.s. **il se dévoue pour les autres** he sacrifices himself *ou* makes a sacrifice of himself for others; **c'est toujours moi qui me dévoue!** it's always me who makes the sacrifices!; (*hum*) **personne ne veut le manger? bon, je me dévoue** so nobody wants to eat it? all right, I'll be a martyr (*hum*). b (*se consacrer à*) **se ~ à qn/qch** to devote *ou* dedicate o.s. to sb/sth.

dévoyé, e [devwaje] (**ptp de dévoyer**) 1 **adj** delinquent. 2 **nm,f** delinquent. **une bande de jeunes ~s** a gang of young delinquents.

dévoyer [devwaje] [8] 1 **vt** to lead astray. 2 **se dévoyer vpr** to go astray.

dextérité [dɛksteʀite] **nf** skill, dexterity. **avec ~** skilfully, dextrously, with dexterity.

dextre [dɛkstʀ] **nf** (††, *hum*) right hand.

dextrine [dɛkstʀin] **nf** dextrin(e).

dey [dɛ] **nm** dey.

DG [deʒe] 1 **nm** (**abrév de directeur général**) *voir* **directeur**. 2 **nf** (**abrév de direction générale**) (*siège social*) HO; (*de la CEE*) DG.

dg **abrév de décigramme**.

DGA [deʒea] **nm** (**abrév de directeur général adjoint**) *voir* **directeur**.

DGE [deʒeə] **nf** (**abrév de dotation globale d'équipement**) *state contribution to local government budget*.

DGRST [deʒeɛʀɛste] **nf** (**abrév de Délégation générale à la recherche scientifique et technique**) *voir* **délégation**.

DGSE [deʒeɛsə] **nf** (**abrév de Direction générale de la sécurité extérieure**) ≃ MI6 (*Brit*), ≃ CIA (*US*).

Dhaka [daka] **n** Dhaka.

dia [dja] **excl** *voir* **hue**.

diabète [djabɛt] **nm** diabetes (*sg*). **avoir du ~** to have diabetes.

diabétique [djabetik] **adj, nmf** diabetic.

diable [djɑbl] **nm** a (*Myth, Rel*) devil. **le ~** the Devil; **s'agiter comme un beau ~** to thrash about like the (very) devil; **j'ai protesté comme un beau ~** I protested for all I was worth *ou* as loudly as I could; **cet enfant a le ~ au corps** this child is the very devil; **faire le ~ à quatre** to create the devil of a rumpus; **que le ~ l'emporte!** the devil take him!; **le ~ m'emporte si j'y comprends quelque chose!** the devil take me† *ou* the deuce† if I understand any of it!, I'll be damned if I understand it!*; **c'est bien le ~ si on ne trouve pas à les loger** it would be most unusual *ou* surprising if we couldn't find anywhere for them to stay; **ce n'est pas le** ~ it's not that bad; **(fait) à la** ~ (done) any old how; **tirer le** ~ **par la queue*** to live from hand to mouth, be on one's uppers (*Brit*); **se démener comme un** ~ **dans un bénitier** to be like a cat on hot bricks (*Brit*) *ou* on a hot tin roof; *voir* **avocat¹**, **île**.

b (*excl*) **D~!† c'est difficile!** it's dashed *ou* deuced difficult!†; ~ **oui/non!** good gracious yes/no!; **du** ~ **si je le sais!** the devil take me† *ou* the deuce† if I know!; **allons, du courage que** ~**!** cheer up, dash it!*; **où/quand/qui/pourquoi** ~ **...?** where/when/who/why the blazes* *ou* the devil ...?

c **au** ~**: être situé/habiter au** ~ **(vauvert)** to be situated/live miles from anywhere *ou* at the back of beyond (*Brit*); **envoyer qn au** ~ *ou* **à tous les** ~**s** to tell sb to go to the devil; **il peut aller au** ~**, qu'il aille au** ~**!** he can go to the devil!; **au** ~ **l'avarice/le percepteur!** the devil take miserliness/the tax collector!

d **du** ~**, de tous les** ~**s: il fait un froid du** ~ *ou* **de tous les** ~**s** it's fearfully *ou* fiendishly cold; **il faisait un vent du** ~ *ou* **de tous les** ~**s** there was the *ou* a devil of a wind, it was fearfully *ou* fiendishly windy; **on a eu un mal du** ~ **à le faire avouer** we had the *ou* a devil of a job making him own up.

e (†) **en** ~ deuced†, dashed†; **il est menteur en** ~ he is a deuced *ou* dashed liar†; **il est courageux/robuste en** ~ he is devilishly *ou* dashed brave/strong†.

f (*: *enfant*) devil, rogue. (*: *personne*) **pauvre** ~ poor devil *ou* wretch; **grand** ~ tall fellow; **c'est un bon/ce n'est pas un mauvais** ~ he's a nice/he's not a bad sort *ou* fellow; **leur enfant est très** ~ their child is a real little devil.

g ~ **de** wretched; **ce** ~ **d'homme** that wretched fellow; **cette** ~ **d'affaire** this wretched business; **avec ce** ~ **de temps on ne peut pas sortir** we can't go out in this wretched weather.

h (*chariot*) hand truck. (*jouet*) ~ **(à ressort)** jack-in-the-box.

i (*casserole*) earthenware braising pot.

j (*Culin*) **à la** ~ in a piquant sauce, à la diable.

diablement* [djɑbləmɑ̃] **adv** (*très*) darned*. **il y a** ~ **longtemps que** it's a heck* of a long time since; **il m'a** ~ **surpris** he gave me a heck* of a surprise.

diablerie [djɑbləʀi] **nf** a (*espièglerie*) devilment, roguishness; (*acte*) mischief (*NonC*). **leurs** ~**s me feront devenir folle** their mischief will drive me mad. b (††: *machination*) machination, evil intrigue. c (††: *sorcellerie*) devilry.

diablesse [djɑblɛs] **nf** (*diable femelle*) she-devil; (†: *mégère*) shrew, vixen; (*: *bonne femme*) wretched woman. **cette enfant est une vraie** ~ that child is a little devil.

diablotin [djɑblɔtɛ̃] **nm** (*lit, fig*) imp; (*pétard*) (Christmas) cracker (*Brit*), favor (*US*).

diabolique [djabɔlik] **adj** diabolic(al), devilish.

diaboliquement [djabɔlikmɑ̃] **adv** diabolically.

diabolo [djabɔlo] **nm** (*jouet*) diabolo. (*boisson*) ~ **grenadine/menthe** grenadine/mint (cordial) and lemonade.

diachronie [djakʀɔni] **nf** diachrony.

diachronique [djakʀɔnik] **adj** diachronic.

diaclase [djaklɑz] **nf** (*Géol*) joint (*in rock*).

diaconal, e, mpl -aux [djakɔnal, o] **adj** diaconal.

diaconat [djakɔna] **nm** diaconate.

diaconesse [djakɔnɛs] **nf** deaconess.

diacre [djakʀ] **nm** deacon.

diacritique [djakʀitik] **adj** diacritic(al). **(signe)** ~ diacritic (mark).

diadème [djadɛm] **nm** (*lit, fig: couronne*) diadem; (*bijou féminin*) tiara.

diagnostic [djagnɔstik] **nm** diagnosis.

diagnostique [djagnɔstik] **adj** diagnostic.

diagnostiquer [djagnɔstike] 1 **vt** (*lit, fig*) to diagnose.

diagonal, e, mpl -aux [djagɔnal, o] 1 **adj** diagonal. 2 **diagonale nf** diagonal. **couper un tissu dans la** ~**e** to cut a fabric on the cross (*Brit*) *ou* on the bias; **en** ~**e** diagonally, crosswise; **tirer un trait en** ~ to draw a line across the page; (*fig*) **lire en** ~**e** to skim through.

diagonalement [djagɔnalmɑ̃] **adv** diagonally.

diagramme [djagʀam] **nm** (*schéma*) diagram; (*courbe, graphique*) chart, graph. ~ **à barres** *ou* **à bâtons** *ou* **en tuyaux d'orgue** bar chart *ou* graph.

dialectal, e, mpl -aux [djalɛktal, o] **adj** dialectal, dialectic(al).

dialecte [djalɛkt] **nm** dialect.

dialecticien, -ienne [djalɛktisjɛ̃, jɛn] **nm,f** dialectician.

dialectique [djalɛktik] 1 **adj** dialectic(al); *voir* **matérialisme**. 2 **nf** dialectic.

dialectiquement [djalɛktikmɑ̃] **adv** dialectically.

dialectologie [djalɛktɔlɔʒi] **nf** dialectology.

dialogue [djalɔg] **nm** (*entre syndicats, ministres etc, Littérat*) dialogue (*Brit*), dialog (*US*); (*entre amis etc*) conversation, talk, dialogue (*Brit*), dialog (*US*). **c'est un** ~ **de sourds** it's a dialogue (*Brit*) *ou* dialog (*US*) of the deaf.

dialoguer [djalɔge] 1 1 **vt** *roman* to put into dialogue (form). 2 **vi** *[amis]* to have a conversation, converse; *[syndicats]* to have a dialogue. ~ **avec un ordinateur** to interact with a computer.

dialoguiste [djalɔgist] **nmf** dialogue writer, screen writer.

dialyse [djaliz] **nf** dialysis. **subir une** ~ to have dialysis.

dialyser [djalize] 1 **vt** to dialyse (*Brit*), dialyze (*US*). **(malade) dialysé** dialysis patient.

dialyseur [djalizœʀ] **nm** dialyser (*Brit*), dialyzer (*US*).

diamant [djamɑ̃] **nm** (*gén*) diamond; *voir* **croqueuse**.

diamantaire [djamɑ̃tɛʀ] **nm** (*tailleur*) diamond-cutter; (*vendeur*) diamond merchant.

diamantifère [djamɑ̃tifɛʀ] **adj** diamantiferous.

diamétral, e, mpl -aux [djametʀal, o] **adj** diametral, diametric(al).

diamétralement [djametʀalmɑ̃] **adv** (*Géom*) diametrally, diametrically. **points de vue** ~ **opposés** diametrically opposite *ou* opposed views.

diamètre [djamɛtʀ] **nm** *[arbre, cercle, courbe]* diameter.

diane [djan] **nf** (*Mil* †) reveille. **sonner/battre la** ~ to sound/beat the reveille.

Diane [djan] **nf** Diane, Diana. ~ **chasseresse** Diana the Huntress.

diantre [djɑ̃tʀ] **excl** (†, *hum*) by Jove! (†, *hum*), by gad! (†, *hum*) **qui/pourquoi/comment** ~ **...?** who/why/how the deuce ...?† *ou* the devil ...?

diantrement [djɑ̃tʀəmɑ̃] **adv** (†, *hum*) devilish†, deuced†.

diapason [djapazɔ̃] **nm** (*Mus*) (*registre*) compass, range, diapason; (*instrument*) tuning fork, diapason. ~ **de Scheibler** tonometer; (*fig*) **être au** ~ **d'une situation** to be in tune with a situation; (*fig*) **se mettre au** ~ **de qn** to get in tune with sb, get on to sb's wavelength; **il s'est vite mis au** ~ he soon fell *ou* got in step *ou* tune with (the ideas of) the others.

diaphane [djafan] **adj** *tissu* diaphanous, filmy; *parchemin, porcelaine* translucent; *mains* diaphanous.

diaphragme [djafʀagm] **nm** (*Anat, Bot, Tech*) diaphragm; (*contraceptif*) diaphragm, (Dutch) cap (*Brit*); (*Phot*) aperture. (*Phot*) **ouvrir de 2** ~**s** to open 2 stops.

diaphragmer [djafʀagme] 1 **vi** (*Phot*) to adjust the aperture.

diaphyse [djafiz] **nf** (*Anat*) shaft.

diapo* [djapo] **nf abrév de diapositive.**

diaporama [djapɔʀama] **nm** slide show.

diapositive [djapozitiv] **nf** slide, transparency.

diapré, e [djapʀe] (**ptp de diaprer**) **adj** mottled, variegated, many-coloured.

diaprer [djapʀe] 1 **vt** (*littér*) to mottle, variegate.

diaprure [djapʀyʀ] **nf** (*NonC: littér*) variegation, mottled effect.

diarrhée [djaʀe] **nf** diarrhoea (*Brit*) (*NonC*), diarrhea (*US*) (*NonC*). **avoir la** ~ *ou* **des** ~**s** to have diarrhoea (*Brit*) *ou* diarrhea (*US*); (*péj*) ~ **verbale*** verbal diarrhoea*.

diarrhéique [djaʀeik] **adj** diarrhoeal, diarrhoeic.

diarthrose [djaʀtʀoz] **nf** (*Anat*) hinge joint. ~ **rotatoire** pivot joint.

diaspora [djaspɔʀa] **nf** (*gén*) diaspora. **la D~ (juive)** the (Jewish) Diaspora.

diastase [djastɑz] **nf** diastase.

diastasique [djastɑzik] **adj** diastatic, diastasic.

diastole [djastɔl] **nf** diastole.

diathermie [djatɛʀmi] **nf** diathermy, diathermia.

diatomique [diatɔmik] **adj** diatomic.

diatonique [djatɔnik] **adj** diatonic.

diatoniquement [djatɔnikmɑ̃] **adv** diatonically.

diatribe [djatʀib] **nf** diatribe.

dichotomie [dikɔtɔmi] **nf** (*Bot, littér*) dichotomy.

dichotomique [dikɔtɔmik] **adj** dichotomous, dichotomic.

dichromatique [dikʀɔmatik] **adj** dichromatic.

dico* [diko] **nm abrév de dictionnaire.**

dicotylédone [dikɔtiledɔn] 1 **adj** dicotyledonous. 2 **nf** dicotyledon.

Dictaphone [diktafɔn] **nm** ® Dictaphone ®.

dictateur [diktatœʀ] **nm** dictator. (*fig*) **faire le** ~ to play the dictator; **ton/allure de** ~ dictatorial tone/manner.

dictatorial, e, mpl -iaux [diktatɔʀjal, jo] **adj** dictatorial.

dictature [diktatyʀ] **nf** dictatorship. **la** ~ **du prolétariat** dictatorship of the proletariat; ~ **militaire** military dictatorship; (*fig*) **c'est de la** ~**!** this is tyranny!

dictée [dikte] **nf** (*action*) dictating, dictation; (*exercice*) dictation. **écrire qch sous la** ~ to take down a dictation of sth; **écrire sous la** ~ **de qn** to take down sb's dictation *ou* what sb dictates; ~ **musicale** musical dictation, aural training; (*littér*) **les** ~**s de son cœur** the dictates of his heart.

dicter [dikte] 1 **vt** *lettre*, (*fig*) *condition, action* to dictate. **ils nous ont dicté leurs conditions** they laid down *ou* dictated their conditions to us; **les mesures que nous dicte la situation** the steps that the situation imposes upon us; **il m'a dicté sa volonté** he imposed his will upon me; **sa réponse (lui) est dictée par sa femme/par la peur** his wife/fear has dictated his reply; **je n'aime pas qu'on me dicte ce que je dois faire!** I won't be dictated to!; **une paix dictée par l'ennemi** peace on the enemy's terms.

diction [diksjɔ̃] **nf** (*débit*) diction, delivery; (*art*) speech production. **professeur/leçons de** ~ speech production teacher/lessons.

dictionnaire [diksjɔnɛʀ] **nm** dictionary. ~ **des synonymes** dictionary of synonyms; ~ **de langue/de rimes** language/rhyme dictionary; (*Ordin*) ~ **de données** data directory *ou* dictionary; ~ **encyclopédique/étymologique** encyclopaedic/etymological dictionary; ~ **géographique**

gazetteer; **c'est un vrai ~ *ou* un ~ vivant** he's a walking encyclopaedia.

dicton [diktɔ̃] **nm** saying, dictum. **il y a un ~ qui dit ...** there's a saying which goes ... .

didacticiel [didaktisjɛl] **nm** educational software (*NonC*), piece of educational software. **des ~s** educational software.

didactique [didaktik] **adj** *poème, exposé* didactic; *mot, terme* technical.

didactiquement [didaktikmɑ̃] **adv** didactically.

Didon [didɔ̃] **nf** Dido.

dièdre [djɛdʀ] 1 **adj** *angle* dihedral. 2 **nm** dihedron, dihedral; (*Alpinisme*) dièdre, corner.

diérèse [djeʀɛz] **nf** (*Ling*) di(a)eresis.

dièse [djɛz] **adj, nm** (*Mus*) sharp. **fa/sol ~** F/G sharp.

diesel [djezɛl] **nm** diesel. **(moteur/camion) ~** diesel engine/lorry (*Brit*) *ou* truck (*US*).

diéser [djeze] 6 **vt** (*Mus*) to sharpen, make sharp.

diète[1] [djɛt] **nf** (*Méd*) (*jeûne*) starvation diet; (*régime*) diet. **~ lactée/végétale** milk/vegetarian diet; **mettre qn à la ~** to put sb on a starvation diet; **il est à la ~** he has been put on a starvation diet.

diète[2] [djɛt] **nf** (*Hist*) diet.

diététicien, -ienne [djetetisjɛ̃, jɛn] **nm,f** dietician, dietitian.

diététique [djetetik] 1 **adj** dietary, dietetic(al). **restaurant ~** health-food *ou* organic (*US*) restaurant; **magasin *ou* centre ~** health-food shop. 2 **nf** dietetics (*sg*).

dieu, **pl ~x** [djø] **nm** a god. **les ~x de l'Antiquité** the gods of Antiquity; **le ~ Chronos** the god Chronos.

b (*dans le monothéisme*) **D~** God; **le D~ des chrétiens/musulmans** the God of the Christians/Muslims; **D~ le père** God the Father; (*hum*) **c'est D~ le père dans l'entreprise** he's God in the company; **une société/génération sans D~** a godless society/generation, a society/generation without God; **le bon D~** the good *ou* dear Lord; **donner/recevoir le bon D~** to offer/receive the Lord (in Sacrament); **on lui donnerait le bon D~ sans confession** he looks as if butter wouldn't melt in his mouth; *voir* **âme, homme**.

c (*fig: idole*) god.

d (*loc*) **mon D~!** my goodness!, goodness me!; **(grand) D~!, grands D~x!** good heavens!, goodness gracious (me)!; **D~ qu'il est beau/bête!** Heavens, he's so good-looking/stupid!; **mon D~ oui, on pourrait ...** well yes, we could ...; **D~ vous bénisse!** God bless you!; **que D~ vous assiste!** God be with you!; **à D~ ne plaise!, D~ m'en garde!** God forbid!; **D~ vous entende/aide!** may God hear/help you!; **D~ seul le sait** God only *ou* alone knows; **D~ sait s'il est généreux/si nous avons essayé!** God knows he is generous/we have tried!; **D~ sait pourquoi elle a épousé un homme si stupide** heaven *ou* God (only) knows why she married such a stupid man; **D~ merci**, (*frm*) **D~ soit loué!** thank God!, praise God! *ou* the Lord!; **D~ merci, il n'a pas plu** it didn't rain, thank goodness *ou* thank God *ou* thank heaven(s); **c'est pas D~ possible!*** that's just not possible; **à-D~-vat!** (*entreprise risquée*) well, it's in God's hands; (*départ*) God be with you; **D~ m'est témoin que je n'ai jamais ...** as God is my witness I have never ...; **tu vas te taire bon D~!**‡ for Christ's sake‡ (*Brit*) *ou* sakes‡ (*US*) will you be quiet!; *voir* **amour, grâce, plaire**.

diffamant, e [difamɑ̃, ɑ̃t] **adj** (*voir* **diffamer**) slanderous; defamatory; libellous.

diffamateur, -trice [difamatœʀ, tʀis] (*voir* **diffamer**) 1 **adj** slanderous; libellous. 2 **nm,f** slanderer.

diffamation [difamasjɔ̃] **nf** a (*NonC: voir* **diffamer**) slandering; defamation; libelling. (*Jur*) **la ~** slander; libel; (*Jur*) **un procès en ~** (*pour injures verbales*) an action for slander; (*pour injures écrites*) an action for libel; **campagne de ~** smear campaign. b (*propos*) slander (*NonC*); (*pamphlet*) libel (*NonC*). **les ~s des journaux** the libellous reports in the newspapers.

diffamatoire [difamatwaʀ] **adj** (*voir* **diffamer**) slanderous; defamatory; libellous.

diffamer [difame] 1 **vt** to slander, defame; (*Jur*) (*en paroles*) to slander; (*par écrit*) to libel.

différé, e [difeʀe] (**ptp de différer**) 1 **adj** (*TV*) (pre-)recorded. **émission en ~** (pre-)recorded programme, recording. 2 **nm** (pre-)recorded programme, recording.

différemment [difeʀamɑ̃] **adv** differently.

différence [difeʀɑ̃s] **nf** a (*gén*) difference. **~ d'opinion** difference of opinion; **~ d'âge/de prix** difference in age/price, age/price difference; **quelle ~ avec les autres!** what a difference from the others!; **ne pas faire de ~** to make no distinction (*entre* between); **faire la ~** to know the difference (*entre* between); **faire des ~s entre ses subordonnés** to discriminate between one's subordinates, treat one's subordinates differently; **tu auras à payer la ~** you will have to make up *ou* pay the difference. b (*loc*) **à la ~ de** unlike; **à la ~ *ou* à cette ~ que** except (for the fact) that.

différenciateur, -trice [difeʀɑ̃sjatœʀ, tʀis] **adj** differentiating, differential.

différenciation [difeʀɑ̃sjasjɔ̃] **nf** differentiation.

différencier [difeʀɑ̃sje] 7 1 **vt** to differentiate. 2 **se différencier vpr** (*être différent de*) to differ (*de* from); (*devenir différent*) to become differentiated (*de* from); (*se rendre différent*) to differentiate o.s. (*de* from).

différend [difeʀɑ̃] **nm** difference of opinion, disagreement; (*Jur, Fin*) controversy. **avoir un ~ avec qn** to have a difference of opinion with sb.

différent, e [difeʀɑ̃, ɑ̃t] **adj** a (*dissemblable*) different (*de* from). **dans des circonstances ~es, je vous aurais aidé** if things had been different *ou* in other *ou* different circumstances, I would have helped you; **chercher des solutions ~es** to try to find alternative *ou* other solutions. b (*pl, gén avant n: divers*) different, various. **à ~es reprises** on several different *ou* on various occasions; **à ~es heures de la journée** at different times of day; **pour ~es raisons** for various *ou* divers (*frm*) reasons.

différentiation [difeʀɑ̃sjasjɔ̃] **nf** (*Math*) differentiation.

différentiel, -ielle [difeʀɑ̃sjɛl] **adj, nm, nf** (*gén*) differential. **~ d'inflation** inflation differential.

différer [difeʀe] 6 1 **vi** a (*être dissemblable*) to differ, be different (*de* from, *en, par* in). **cette maladie ne diffère en rien de la rougeole** this illness is no different *ou* is in no way different from measles.

b (*diverger*) to differ. **elle et moi différons sur *ou* en tout** she and I differ about everything.

c (*varier*) to differ, vary. **la mode diffère de pays à pays** fashions differ *ou* vary from one country to the next.

2 **vt** *travail* to postpone, put off; *jugement, paiement, départ* to defer, postpone. **~ une décision** to defer *ou* postpone making *ou* put off making a decision; **à quoi bon ~ plus longtemps?** why delay any longer?; (*frm*) **~ de *ou* à faire qch** to delay *ou* defer *ou* postpone doing sth; *voir* **crédit**.

difficile [difisil] **adj** a (*ardu*) *travail, problème* difficult. **il nous est ~ de prendre une décision tout de suite** it is difficult *ou* hard for us *ou* we find it difficult *ou* hard to make a decision straight away; **il a eu un moment ~ lorsque sa femme est morte** he went through a difficult *ou* hard *ou* trying time when his wife died; **il a trouvé l'expédition ~** he found the expedition hard going *ou* heavy going; **~ à faire** difficult *ou* hard to do; **morceau ~ (à jouer) *ou* d'exécution ~** difficult *ou* hard piece to play.

b (*délicat*) *position, situation* difficult, awkward, tricky*. **ils ont des fins de mois ~s** they have a hard time making ends meet.

c *personne* (*contrariant*) difficult, trying; (*exigeant*) fastidious, hard *ou* difficult to please (*attrib*), fussy. **un enfant ~** a difficult child, a problem child; **elle est ~ pour ce qui est de *ou* en ce qui concerne la propreté** she's a stickler for cleanliness, she's very fussy *ou* particular about cleanliness; **être *ou* se montrer ~ sur la nourriture** to be difficult *ou* fussy *ou* finicky about one's food; **faire le *ou* la ~** to be hard to please *ou* (over-)fussy; **il ne faut pas être trop ~ *ou* (trop) faire le ~** it's no good being too fussy *ou* overfussy; **cette chambre ne vous plaît pas? vous êtes vraiment ~!** don't you like this room? you really are hard *ou* difficult to please!; *voir* **vivre**.

difficilement [difisilmɑ̃] **adv** *marcher, s'exprimer* with difficulty. **c'est ~ visible/croyable** it's difficult *ou* hard to see/believe; **il gagne ~ sa vie** he has difficulty *ou* trouble earning a living, he finds it difficult *ou* hard to earn a living.

difficulté [difikylte] **nf** a (*NonC*) difficulty. **selon la ~ du travail** according to the difficulty of the work; **faire qch avec ~** to do sth with difficulty; **avoir/éprouver de la ~ à faire qch** to have difficulty (in) doing sth, find it difficult *ou* hard to do sth; **se trouver en ~** to find o.s. in difficulty, experience *ou* have difficulty; **j'ai eu beaucoup de ~ à trouver des arguments** I had great difficulty finding *ou* I was hard put to it to find any arguments. b (*embarras, obstacle*) difficulty, problem; *[texte, morceau de musique]* difficult passage, difficulty. **avoir des ~s pour faire qch** to have some difficulty (in) doing sth; **enfant qui a des ~s (à l'école/en orthographe)** a child who has difficulty *ou* difficulties (at school/with spelling); **avoir des ~s financières** to be in financial difficulties *ou* straits; **il s'est heurté à de grosses ~s** he has come up against grave difficulties; **ils ont des ~s avec leurs enfants** they have problems *ou* trouble *ou* difficulty with their children; **cela ne fait *ou* ne présente aucune ~** that presents *ou* poses no problem; **il y a une ~** there's a problem *ou* hitch* *ou* snag*; **il a fait des ~s pour accepter nos conditions** he made *ou* raised difficulties about accepting our conditions; **il n'a pas fait de ~s pour nous suivre** he followed us without protest *ou* fuss; **c'est là la ~** that's where the trouble lies, that's the difficulty; **être en ~** to be in difficulties *ou* in trouble; **avion/navire en ~** aircraft/ship in distress; **mettre qn en ~** to put sb in a difficult position; (*Scol, Psych*) **enfant en ~** problem child; **en cas de ~** in case of difficulty; **~ du langage** speech disorder *ou* disability *ou* defect; **~s d'apprentissage** learning disabilities *ou* difficulties.

difficultueux, -euse† [difikyltɥø, øz] **adj** difficult, awkward.

difforme [difɔʀm] **adj** *corps, membre* deformed, misshapen, twisted; *visage, arbre* twisted.

difformité [difɔʀmite] **nf** (*voir* **difforme**) deformity, misshapenness; twistedness. (*Méd*) **présenter des ~s** to have deformities, be deformed.

diffracter [difʀakte] 1 **vt** to diffract.

diffraction [difʀaksjɔ̃] **nf** diffraction; *voir* **réseau**.

diffus, e [dify, yz] **adj** (*gén*) diffuse.

diffusément [difyzemɑ̃] **adv** diffusely.

diffuser [difyze] 1 **vt** *lumière, chaleur* to diffuse; *bruit, idée* to spread (abroad), circulate, diffuse; *livres* to distribute; (*Jur*) *document* to circulate; *émission* to broadcast. **programme diffusé en direct** live programme, programme broadcast live.

diffuseur [difyzœʀ] nm (*Aut, Tech: appareil*) diffuser; (*Presse: distributeur*) distributor; (*fig: propagateur*) diffuser, spreader.

diffusion [difyzjɔ̃] nf (*voir* **diffuser**) diffusion; spreading; circulation; distribution; broadcasting. *rapport* **pour ~ restreinte** (*gén*) restricted; (*secret d'État*) classified; **journal de grande ~** large *ou* high circulation paper.

digérer [diʒeʀe] [6] vt a *aliment, connaissance* to digest. **~ bien/mal** to have a good/bad digestion; (*fig*) **c'est du Marx mal digéré** it's ill-digested Marx. b (**: supporter*) *insulte, attitude* to stomach*, put up with. **si tu crois que je vais ~ ça sans protester!** if you think I'll put up with *ou* stand for that without protest!; **je ne peux plus ~ son insolence** I won't put up with *ou* stand for his insolence any longer, I can't stomach his insolence any longer*.

digeste [diʒɛst] adj *aliment* easily digested, easily digestible. **livre peu ~*** book which is heavy going, rather heavy book.

digestibilité [diʒɛstibilite] nf digestibility.

digestible [diʒɛstibl] adj easily digested, easily digestible.

digestif, -ive [diʒɛstif, iv] 1 adj digestive; *voir* **tube**. 2 nm (*Méd*) digestive; (*liqueur*) liqueur.

digestion [diʒɛstjɔ̃] nf digestion. **j'ai une ~ difficile** I have trouble with my digestion, I have digestive problems.

digital, e[1], mpl **-aux** [diʒital, o] adj (*gén*) digital; *voir* **empreinte[2]**.

digitale[2] [diʒital] nf digitalis. **~ pourprée** foxglove.

digitaline [diʒitalin] nf digitalin.

digitaliser [diʒitalize] [1] vt to digitize.

diglossie [diglɔsi] nf diglossia.

digne [diɲ] adj a (*auguste*) dignified. **il avait un air très ~** he had a very dignified air (about him).
b (*qui mérite*) **~ de** *admiration, intérêt* worthy of, deserving (of); **~ de ce nom** worthy of the name; **~ d'être remarqué** noteworthy; **~ d'éloges** praiseworthy, deserving of praise; **~ de foi** trustworthy; **~ de pitié** pitiable; **~ d'envie** enviable; **vous devez vous montrer ~s de représenter la France** you must show that you are fit *ou* worthy to represent France; **livre à peine ~ d'être lu** book which is scarcely worth reading *ou* which scarcely deserves to be read; **il n'est pas ~ de vivre** he's not fit to live; (*littér*) **je ne suis pas ~ que vous m'offriez votre soutien** I am not worthy of your offering me your support (*littér*).
c (*à la hauteur*) worthy. **son ~ fils/père/représentant** his worthy son/father/representative; (*lit, péj*) **tu es le ~ fils** *ou* **tu es ~ de ton père** you're fit to be your father's son, you take after your father; **avoir un adversaire ~ de soi** to have an opponent worthy of oneself; **œuvre ~ de son auteur** work worthy of its author; **avec une attitude peu ~ d'un juge** with an attitude little befitting a judge *ou* unworthy of a judge; **un dessert ~ d'un si fin repas** a fitting dessert for such a fine meal.

dignement [diɲ(ə)mɑ̃] adv a (*noblement*) with dignity. **garder ~ le silence** to maintain a dignified silence. b (*justement*) fittingly, justly. **être ~ récompensé** to receive a fitting *ou* just reward, be fittingly *ou* justly rewarded.

dignitaire [diɲitɛʀ] nm dignitary.

dignité [diɲite] nf a (*noblesse*) dignity. **la ~ du travail** the dignity of labour; **la ~ de la personne humaine** human dignity; **avoir de la ~** to be dignified, have dignity; **manquer de ~** to be lacking in dignity, be undignified; (*hum*) **c'est contraire à sa ~** it is beneath his dignity; **elle entra, pleine de ~** she came in with great dignity. b (*fonction*) dignity. **être élevé à la ~ de juge** to be promoted to the dignity *ou* rank of judge.

digramme [digʀam] nm digraph.

digression [digʀesjɔ̃] nf digression. **faire une ~** to digress, make a digression.

digue [dig] nf a (*lit*) (*gén*) dyke, dike; (*pour protéger la côte*) sea wall. b (*fig*) barrier.

diktat [diktat] nm diktat.

dilapidateur, -trice [dilapidatœʀ, tʀis] 1 adj spendthrift, wasteful. 2 nm,f spendthrift, squanderer. **~ des fonds publics** embezzler of public funds.

dilapidation [dilapidasjɔ̃] nf (*voir* **dilapider**) squandering, wasting; embezzlement, misappropriation.

dilapider [dilapide] [1] vt (*gaspiller*) *héritage, fortune* to squander, waste; (*détourner*) *biens, fonds publics* to embezzle, misappropriate.

dilatabilité [dilatabilite] nf dilatability.

dilatable [dilatabl] adj *corps* dilatable.

dilatant, e [dilatɑ̃, ɑ̃t], **dilatateur, -trice** [dilatatœʀ, tʀis] 1 adj dilative. 2 nm dilat(at)or, dilatant.

dilatation [dilatasjɔ̃] nf (*voir* **dilater**) dila(ta)tion; distension; expansion; swelling. **avoir une ~ d'estomac** to have a distended stomach.

dilater [dilate] [1] 1 vt *pupille, narine* to dilate; *estomac* to distend; *métal, gaz, liquide* to cause to expand, cause the expansion of; *pneu* to cause to swell, distend. (*fig*) **~ le cœur** to swell the heart, cause the heart to swell. 2 **se dilater** vpr (*voir* **dilater**) to dilate; to distend; to expand; to swell. **se ~ les poumons** to open *ou* swell one's lungs; (*fig*) **son cœur se dilate de joie** his heart is swelling with joy; **se ~ la rate*** to split one's sides (laughing)*; **ça me dilate (la rate)*** it's side-splitting*.

dilatoire [dilatwaʀ] adj: **manœuvres** *ou* **moyens ~s** delaying *ou* stalling tactics; **donner une réponse ~** to give a reply which allows one to gain time *ou* play for time.

dilemme [dilɛm] nm dilemma. **sortir du ~** to resolve the dilemma.

dilettante [dilɛtɑ̃t] nmf (*amateur d'art*) dilettante; (*péj: amateur*) dilettante, dabbler. **faire qch en ~** to dabble in sth; **faire un travail en ~** to do a piece of work in an amateurish way.

dilettantisme [dilɛtɑ̃tism] nm amateurishness. **faire qch avec ~** to do sth in an amateurish way *ou* amateurishly.

diligemment [diliʒamɑ̃] adv (*littér*) (*avec soin*) diligently; (*avec célérité*) promptly, speedily.

diligence [diliʒɑ̃s] nf a (†, *littér: empressement*) haste, dispatch. **faire ~** to make haste, hasten; **en ~** posthaste, speedily. b (*littér: soin*) diligence, conscientiousness. (*Jur*) **à la ~ du ministre** at the minister's behest (*littér*) *ou* request. c (*Hist: voiture*) diligence, stagecoach.

diligent, e [diliʒɑ̃, ɑ̃t] adj (*littér*) a (*actif*) *serviteur* speedy, prompt. b (*assidu*) *employé, travail* diligent, conscientious; *soins, attention* diligent, sedulous.

diluant [dilɥɑ̃] nm thinner.

diluer [dilɥe] [1] vt *liquide* to dilute; *peinture* to thin (down); (*fig*) *discours* to pad out; *force* to mitigate, dilute. **alcool dilué** alcohol diluted with water.

dilution [dilysjɔ̃] nf (*voir* **diluer**) dilution; thinning (down); padding out; mitigation.

diluvien, -ienne [dilyvjɛ̃, jɛn] adj *pluie* torrential; (*Bible*) *époque* diluvian.

dimanche [dimɑ̃ʃ] nm Sunday. **le ~ des Rameaux/de Pâques** Palm/Easter Sunday; **le ~ de Noël** the Sunday after Christmas; **les ~s de l'Avent/de Carême** the Sundays in Advent/Lent; **mettre son costume** *ou* **ses habits du ~** to put on one's Sunday clothes *ou* one's Sunday best; **promenade du ~** Sunday walk; (*péj*) **peintre/sportif du ~** amateur *ou* spare-time painter/sportsman; **chauffeur du ~** Sunday driver; **sauf ~ et jours fériés** Sundays and holidays excepted; *pour autres loc voir* **samedi**.

dîme [dim] nf (*Hist*) tithe. **lever une ~ sur qch** to tithe sth; **payer la ~ du vin/des blés** to pay tithes *ou* the tithe on wine/corn; (*fig*) **le grossiste/l'État prélève sa ~ (sur la marchandise)** the wholesaler takes his/the State takes its cut (on the goods).

dimension [dimɑ̃sjɔ̃] nf a (*taille*) *[pièce, terrain]* size. **avoir la même ~** to be the same size, have the same dimensions; **de grande/petite ~** large/small-sized, of large/small dimensions; **faire une étagère à la ~ d'un recoin** to make a shelf to fit (into) an alcove; (*fig*) **une faute de cette ~** a mistake of this magnitude; (*fig*) **un repas à la ~ de son appétit** a meal commensurate with one's appetite; (*fig*) **une tâche à la ~ de son talent** a task equal to *ou* commensurate with one's talent.
b (*mesures*) **~s** dimensions; **quelles sont les ~s de la pièce?** what are the dimensions *ou* measurements of the room?, what does the room measure?; **placard fait aux ~s du mur** cupboard built to the dimensions of the wall *ou* built to fit the wall; **quelles sont vos ~s?** what are your statistics? *ou* measurements?; **mesurez-le dans la plus grande ~** measure it at the widest *ou* longest point; **à 2/3 ~s** 2-/3-dimensional.
c (*Philos, Phys*) dimension.

dimensionner [dimɑ̃sjɔne] [1] vt to calculate the ideal dimensions of. **objet bien dimensionné** well-proportioned object.

diminué, e [diminɥe] (ptp de **diminuer**) adj a **il est (très)** *ou* **c'est un homme (très) ~ depuis son accident** he has (really) gone downhill *ou* he's not (at all) the man he was since his accident; **très ~ physiquement** physically very run-down; **très ~ mentalement** mentally much less alert. b (*Mus*) diminished; (*Tricot*) *vêtement* fully-fashioned; *rang* decreased.

diminuendo [diminɥɛndo] adv, nm (*Mus*) diminuendo.

diminuer [diminɥe] [1] 1 vt a (*réduire*) *longueur, largeur, vitesse* to reduce, decrease; *durée, volume, nombre, quantité* to reduce, cut down, decrease; *prix, impôts, consommation, valeur* to reduce, bring down, cut; *son* to lower, turn down; (*Tricot*) to decrease; *beauté, ardeur, courage* to lessen; *chances de succès, plaisir, intérêt* to lessen, reduce, diminish; *forces* to cut down, decrease. **~ les effectifs** to cut back on numbers, reduce *ou* cut back the numbers; **ça l'a beaucoup diminué physiquement/moralement** this has greatly undermined him physically/mentally.
b (*dénigrer*) *personne* to belittle; *mérite, talent* to belittle, depreciate. **il veut toujours se ~** he's always trying to belittle himself.
c (**: réduire le salaire de*) *employé* to cut *ou* reduce the salary of.
2 vi a *[violence, intensité]* to diminish, lessen; *[lumière]* to fade, diminish; *[bruit]* to die down, diminish, fade; *[circulation]* to die down; *[pluie]* to let up, diminish; *[orage]* to die down, die away, subside; *[intérêt, ardeur]* to die down, decrease, diminish. **l'attaque/le bruit diminue d'intensité** the attack/noise is dying down *ou* is decreasing in intensity *ou* is subsiding.
b *[effectifs, nombre, valeur, pression]* to decrease, diminish, go *ou* come down, fall, drop; *[provisions]* to diminish, run low; *[forces]* to decline, diminish. **~ de longueur/largeur** to grow shorter/narrower, decrease in length/breadth; **le (prix du) beurre a diminué** butter has gone *ou* come down *ou* dropped in price; **ça a diminué de volume** it has been reduced in volume; **les jours diminuent** the days are growing shorter *ou* drawing in (*Brit*).

diminutif, -ive [diminytif, iv] 1 adj *suffixe* diminutive. 2 nm (*Ling*) diminutive; (*petit nom*) pet name (*de* for), diminutive (*de* of).
diminution [diminysjɔ̃] nf a (*réduction: voir* **diminuer**) reduction; decreasing; cutting-down; cutting-back; bringing-down; lowering; turning-down; lessening. **il nous a consenti une petite ~** he gave *ou* allowed us a small reduction; (*Tricot*) **commencer les ~s** to begin decreasing *ou* to decrease. b (*décroissance: voir* **diminuer**) diminishing; lessening; fading; dying-down; letting-up; dying-away; subsiding; decrease (*de* in). **une ~ très nette du nombre des accidents** a marked decrease *ou* drop *ou* fall-off in the number of accidents.
dimorphe [dimɔʀf] adj dimorphous, dimorphic.
dimorphisme [dimɔʀfism] nm dimorphism.
dinanderie [dinɑ̃dʀi] nf (*commerce*) copperware trade; (*articles*) copperware.
dinandier [dinɑ̃dje] nm copperware manufacturer and retailer.
dinar [dinaʀ] nm dinar.
dînatoire [dinatwaʀ] adj (*frm*) **goûter** *ou* **buffet ~** ≃ high tea (*Brit*), supper.
dinde [dɛ̃d] nf a turkey hen; (*Culin*) turkey. **~ rôtie/de Noël** roast/Christmas turkey. b (*péj: fille stupide*) stupid little goose.
dindon [dɛ̃dɔ̃] nm a (*gén*) turkey, (*mâle*) turkey cock. b (*: *homme sot*) **être le ~ (de la farce)** to be cheated; *voir* **pavaner**.
dindonneau, pl **~x** [dɛ̃dɔno] nm turkey poult.
dîner [dine] 1 1 vi a to have dinner, dine. **~ aux chandelles** to have dinner *ou* dine by candlelight; **~ d'une tranche de pain** to have a slice of bread for dinner; **avoir qn à ~** to have sb for *ou* to dinner; *voir* **dormir**. b (*Can, Suisse, Belgique*) to have lunch, lunch. 2 nm a dinner. **ils donnent un ~ demain** they are having a dinner party tomorrow; **~ de famille/d'affaires** family/business dinner; **avant le ~** before dinner. b (*Can, Suisse, Belgique*) lunch.
dînette [dinɛt] nf a (*jeu d'enfants*) doll's tea party. **jouer à la ~** to play at having a tea party; **venez à la maison, on fera (la) ~*** come home for a meal – it'll only be a snack. b (*jouet*) **~ de poupée** doll's tea set, toy tea set.
dîneur, -euse [dinœʀ, øz] nm,f diner.
ding [diŋ] excl ding. **~ dong!** ding dong!
dingo[1] [dɛ̃go] nm (*chien*) dingo.
dingue* [dɛ̃g], **dingo**[2]*† [dɛ̃go] 1 adj *personne* nuts*, crazy*, barmy* (*Brit*); *bruit, prix* fantastic, incredible, stupendous. **tu verrais les prix, c'est ~!** you should see the prices, they're crazy *ou* incredible!; **un film ~** a really way-out* film; **un vent ~** a hell of* a wind, an incredible wind; **il est ~ de cette fille/de ce chanteur** he's crazy* *ou* nuts* about *ou* over that girl/singer, he's mad about *ou* on that girl/singer*. 2 nmf nutcase*, loony‡. **on devrait l'envoyer chez les ~s** he ought to be locked up, he ought to be sent to the loony bin‡; **c'est un ~ de la voiture/de la guitare** he's crazy* *ou* nuts* *ou* mad* about cars/guitar-playing.
dinguer* [dɛ̃ge] 1 vi: **aller ~** *[personne]* to fall flat on one's face, go sprawling; *[chose]* to go crashing down, go flying*; **les boîtes ont failli ~ par terre** the boxes nearly came crashing down; (*fig*) **envoyer ~ qn** (*faire tomber*) to send sb flying*; (*fig : chasser*) to tell sb to clear *ou* buzz off* *ou* push off*, send sb packing; **envoyer ~ qch** to send sth flying*.
dinguerie* [dɛ̃gʀi] nf craziness, stupidity. **toutes ces ~s** all these stupidities.
dinosaure [dinɔzɔʀ] nm (*Zool, fig*) dinosaur.
diocésain, e [djɔsezɛ̃, ɛn] adj, nm,f diocesan.
diocèse [djɔsɛz] nm diocese.
diode [djɔd] nf diode.
Diogène [djɔʒɛn] nm Diogenes.
dionysiaque [djɔnizjak] adj Dionysian, Dionysiac. **les ~s** the Dionysia.
Dionysos [djɔnizɔs] nm Dionysus, Dionysos.
dioptrie [djɔptʀi] nf dioptre.
dioptrique [djɔptʀik] 1 adj dioptric(al). 2 nf dioptrics (*sg*).
diorama [djɔʀama] nm diorama.
dioxine [diɔksin] nf dioxin.
dioxyde [diɔksid] nm dioxide.
diphasé, e [difaze] adj diphase, diphasic, two-phase.
diphtérie [difteʀi] nf diphtheria.
diphtérique [difteʀik] adj diphther(it)ic, diphtherial.
diphtongaison [diftɔ̃gɛzɔ̃] nf diphthongization.
diphtongue [diftɔ̃g] nf diphthong.
diphtonguer vt, **se diphtonguer** vpr [diftɔ̃ge] 1 to diphthongize.
diplodocus [diplɔdɔkys] nm diplodocus.
diplomate [diplɔmat] 1 adj diplomatic. 2 nmf (*ambassadeur*) diplomat; (*personne habile*) diplomatist. 3 nm (*Culin*) ≃ trifle. **~ au chocolat** ≃ chocolate charlotte russe.
diplomatie [diplɔmasi] nf (*Pol, fig*) diplomacy. **le personnel de la ~** the diplomatic staff; **faire preuve de ~ envers qn** to treat sb diplomatically, be diplomatic towards sb.
diplomatique [diplɔmatik] adj (*gén*) diplomatic. **c'est une maladie ~** it's a sort of "diplomatic" *ou* face-saving illness; *voir* **valise**.
diplomatiquement [diplɔmatikmɑ̃] adv (*Pol, fig*) diplomatically.
diplôme [diplom] nm (*titre*) (*gén*) diploma, certificate; (*licence*) degree. **avoir des ~s** to have qualifications; **~ d'études universitaires générales** *diploma taken after two years at university,* ≃ ordinary degree (*Brit*), ≃ Associate of Arts (*ou* Science) (*US*); **~ d'études approfondies** *post-graduate diploma taken before completing a PhD,* ≃ all but dissertation (*US*); **~ d'études supérieures** *university post-graduate degree;* **~ d'études supérieures spécialisées** *post-graduate diploma in an applied subject lasting one year;* **~ d'études supérieures techniques** *university post-graduate technical degree;* **~ d'études universitaires scientifiques et techniques** *diploma awarded after the first two years of university education in scientific and technical subjects;* **~ universitaire de technologie** *two-year diploma in a technical subject taken in a polytechnic* (*Brit*) *or technical institute* (*US*) *after the baccalauréat.*
diplômé, e [diplome] (ptp de **diplômer**) 1 adj qualified. 2 nm,f holder of a diploma.
diplômer [diplome] 1 vt to award a diploma to.
diplopie [diplɔpi] nf double vision, diplopia (SPÉC).
dipsomane [dipsɔman] 1 adj dipsomaniacal. 2 nmf dipsomaniac.
dipsomanie [dipsɔmani] nf dipsomania.
diptère [diptɛʀ] 1 adj *temple* dipteral; *insecte* dipterous, dipteran. 2 nm (*Zool*) dipteran. **les ~s** the Diptera.
diptyque [diptik] nm (*Hist: tablette, Art*) diptych; (*fig: roman*) work in two parts.
dir abrév de **direction**.
dire [diʀ] 37 1 vt a to say. **avez-vous quelque chose à ~?** have you got anything to say?; **"j'ai froid" dit-il** "I'm cold" he said; **on peut commencer: elle a dit oui** we can start – she said yes *ou* she said we could; **~ bonjour/quelques mots à qn** to say hullo/a few words to sb; **il m'a dit: "je comprends"** he said to me, "I understand"; **comment dit-on ça en anglais?** what's the English for that?, how do you say that in English?; **~ qch carrément** *ou* **crûment** to put sth (quite) bluntly, state sth (quite) plainly *ou* frankly; **comme disent les Anglais** as the English put it *ou* say; **~ ce que l'on pense** to speak one's mind, say what one thinks; **ne plus savoir quoi ~** to be at a loss for words; **il dit n'importe quoi** he talks through his hat*, he talks a load of rubbish* (*Brit*); **il n'a pas dit un mot** he hasn't said *ou* spoken *ou* uttered a (single) word; **qu'est-ce que les gens vont ~!, qu'en dira-t-on?** whatever will people *ou* they say!; **il ne croyait pas si bien ~** he didn't know how right he was, he never spoke a truer word; **ce n'est pas une chose à ~, il est préférable de ne pas le ~** it is not the sort of thing one says, it's not the sort of thing to say, it is better left unsaid; (*aux enchères*) **qui dit mieux?** any advance?; **il a au moins 70 ans, que dis-je, plutôt 80** he must be at least 70 – what am I saying? – more like 80; **où va-t-il? – il ne l'a pas dit** *ou* **il n'a pas dit*** where is he going? – he didn't say; (*Cartes*) **c'est à vous de ~** your call; *voir* **bien, mal, parler**.
b **~ que** to say that; **~ à qn que** to tell sb that, say to sb that; **il dit qu'il nous a écrit, il dit nous avoir écrit** he says that he wrote to us; **il a bien dit qu'il ne rentrerait pas** he did say that he would not be coming home; **doit-il venir? – elle dit que oui/que non** is he coming? – she says he is/he isn't *ou* she says so/not; **la radio et les journaux avaient dit qu'il pleuvrait** (both) the radio and the papers had said it would rain; **vous nous dites dans votre lettre que** you tell us in *ou* you say in your letter that; **votre lettre/la loi dit clairement que** your letter/the law says clearly that *ou* clearly states that; **l'espoir fait vivre, dit-on** you can live on hope, as the saying has it *ou* as the saying goes *ou* as they say; **on dit que ...** rumour has it that ..., they say that ..., it is said that ...; **on le dit malade/à Londres** he's rumoured to be ill/in London; **à** *ou* **d'après ce qu'il dit** according to him, according to what he says; **il sait ce qu'il dit** he knows what he's talking about; **il ne sait pas ce qu'il dit** he doesn't know what he is talking about! *ou* what he is saying!; **qu'est-ce qui me dit que c'est vrai?** how can I tell it's the truth?, how am I to know *ou* how do I know it's the truth?
c *mensonges, nouvelle, adresse, nom* to tell; *sentiment* to tell of, express. **~ qch à qn** to tell sb sth; **il m'a dit quelque chose qui m'a fait rire** he told me something *ou* he said something to me that made me laugh; **j'ai quelque chose à vous ~** there's something I want to tell you *ou* say to you; **~ des bêtises** to talk nonsense; **~ la bonne aventure/l'avenir** to tell fortunes/the future; **~ la bonne aventure à qn** to tell sb's fortune; **dis-nous-en la raison** give *ou* tell us the reason (for it); **il nous a dit toute sa joie/tout son soulagement** he told us of his great joy/relief, he told us how happy/how relieved he was; **ce nom me dit quelque chose** this name rings a bell; **cela ne me dit rien du tout** that doesn't mean a thing to me; **quelque chose me dit que ...** something tells me (that) ..., I've got the feeling (that) ...; **qu'est-ce que ça dit, ton jardin?*** how is your garden doing?*
d (*ordonner, prévenir*) to tell. **dites-lui de partir/qu'il parte ce soir** tell him to go/that he must leave tonight; **il a dit de venir de bonne heure** he said we were to come *ou* he said to come* early, he told us to come early; **fais ce qu'on te dit!** do as *ou* what you are told!; **ça suffit, j'ai dit!** I said that's enough!; **on nous a dit de l'attendre** we were told to wait for him; **"méfie-toi" me dit-il** he told me *ou* he said to me, "be cautious"; *voir* **envoyer**.
e (*objecter*) to say (*à, contre* against). **que veux-tu que je dise à** *ou* **contre ça?** what can I say against that?, how can I object to that?; **tu n'as rien à ~, tu aurais fait la même chose** YOU can't say anything! *ou*

YOU can talk! you would have done exactly the same thing!; **tais-toi, tu n'as rien à ~!** be quiet, you can't talk! *ou* you're in no position to make remarks!; **je n'ai rien à ~ sur son travail** I cannot complain about his work; **tu n'as rien à ~, tu es bien servi** you can't talk because you've done very well, you can't complain *ou* object with what you've got.

f *poèmes* to say, recite; *prière* to say; *rôle* to speak. **~ son chapelet** to say the rosary, tell one's beads†; **~ la messe** to say mass; **l'acteur a très mal dit ce passage** the actor spoke these lines very badly.

g (*plaire*) **cela vous dit de sortir?** do you feel like going out?, do you fancy (*Brit*) going out?; **cela ne me dit rien** I don't feel like it at all, it doesn't appeal to me at all, I don't fancy (*Brit*) it at all; **il y a des fraises mais ça ne me dit pas** there are strawberries but I don't fancy them (*Brit*) *ou* I'm not in the mood for them; **rien ne me dit en ce moment** I am not in the mood for anything *ou* I don't feel like doing anything just now; **si le cœur vous en dit** if you feel like it, if you feel so inclined; **cela ne me dit rien qui vaille** I don't like the look of that, that looks suspicious to me; **pour l'instant, cette robe ne dit rien†*, mais attendez qu'elle soit finie!** for the moment this dress doesn't look anything special *ou* doesn't look up to much*, but just wait until it's finished!

h [*chose*] (*indiquer*) to say, show. **ma montre dit 6 heures** my watch says 6 o'clock, it is 6 o'clock by my watch; **son visage disait sa déception** his face gave away his disappointment, disappointment was written all over his face; **son silence en dit long** his silence speaks for itself *ou* speaks volumes *ou* tells its own story.

i (*penser*) to think. **qu'est-ce que tu dis de ma robe?** what do you think of *ou* how do you like my dress?; **qu'est-ce que vous dites de la question?** what do you think *ou* how do you feel about the matter?, what are your feelings on the subject?; **qu'est-ce que vous diriez d'une promenade?** what would you say to a walk?, how about a walk?; **et ~ qu'il aurait pu se tuer!** to think he might have killed himself!; **on dirait qu'il n'aime pas cette ville** one gets the impression he does not like this town, he doesn't seem to like this town; **on dirait qu'il le fait exprès!** you'd almost think he does it on purpose!; **qui aurait dit qu'elle allait gagner?** who would have thought (that) she would win?; **on dirait qu'il va pleuvoir** it looks like rain; **on dirait qu'il va pleurer** he looks as though he is going to cry; **cette eau est noire, on dirait de l'encre** this water is black – it looks like ink; **on dirait du poulet** it tastes like *ou* it's like chicken; **on dirait du Brahms** it sounds like *ou* it's like Brahms; **on dirait du parfum** it's like *ou* it smells like perfume; **on dirait de la soie** it's like *ou* it feels like silk; **qui l'eût dit!** who would have thought it!

j (*décider*) **venez bientôt, disons demain** come soon, let's make it tomorrow *ou* (let's) say tomorrow; **tout n'est pas dit** the last word has not been said, it isn't all over yet; **c'est plus facile à ~ qu'à faire** it's easier said than done; **il est dit** *ou* **il a été dit que je ne gagnerai jamais** I'm destined *ou* fated never to win; **bon, c'est dit** *ou* **voilà qui est dit** right, it's settled *ou* it's all arranged; **ce qui est dit est dit** what's said is said; **tenez-vous-le pour dit** don't say I didn't warn you, I shan't tell you a second time; **à l'heure dite** at the appointed time *ou* hour; **au jour dit** on the appointed day; *voir* **aussitôt**.

k (*appeler*) **X, dit le Chacal** X, known as the Jackal.

l (*admettre*) to say, admit. **il faut bien ~ que** I must say *ou* admit that; **disons-le, il nous ennuie** let's be frank *ou* to be frank *ou* let's face it*, he bores us.

m (*loc*) **je ne dis pas non** I won't say no; **qui dit argent, dit problèmes** money means problems; **tu l'as dit!** quite true!, how right you are!, you('ve) said it!; **ceci dit** (*à ces mots*) thereupon, having said this; (*avec restriction*) nevertheless, having said this; (*littér*) **ce disant** so saying; **pour ainsi ~** so to speak, as it were; **comme qui dirait*** as you might say; **ou pour mieux ~ ...** or, rather ..., or, to put it another way ...; **j'entends comme qui dirait des grognements** I can hear what sounds like groans *ou* something like groans; **cette maison c'est comme qui dirait un gros cube** the house looks a bit like a huge cube; **dis donc!** (*à propos*) by the way; (*holà*) hey!, say! (*US*); **c'est joli dis donc!** my*, isn't it pretty!; **ça lui a rapporté 100.000 F – ben dis donc!** that earned him 100,000 F – I say!*, well I never!*; **tu me l'envoies, dis, cette lettre?** you will send me that letter, won't you?; **comme on dit, comme dit** *ou* **disait l'autre*** as they say, so to speak; **je suis sûr, je te dis*** I'm certain, I tell you; **pour tout ~** in fact; **~ que ...** to think that ...; **je vous l'avais bien dit!** I told you so!, didn't I tell you?; **que tu dis** (*ou* **qu'il dit** *etc*)**!**‡ that's your (*ou* his *etc*) story!, that's what you say (*ou* he says *etc*)!; **à qui le dites-vous!** *ou* **le dis-tu!** don't I know it!*, you're telling ME!*; **cela va sans ~** it goes without saying; **il va sans ~ que c'était faux** needless to say it was wrong; **à vrai ~, à ~ vrai** actually, to tell (you) the truth, in actual fact, to be (quite) truthful; **quand je vous le disais!** I told you so!, what did I tell you!; **je ne veux pas avoir à le lui ~ deux fois** I don't want to have to tell him again; **il n'y a pas à ~** there's no doubt about it, there's no denying it, there's no getting away from it; **je ne vous dis que cela!** that's all I can say!; **on a beau ~** say what you like *ou* will; **comment dirais-je ...** how shall I put it ..., what can I say ...; **que dites-vous, qu'est-ce que tu dis?** *ou* **vous dites?** (I beg your) pardon?, what did you say?; **c'est ~ s'il est content** that just shows you how pleased he is; **c'est beaucoup ~** that's saying a lot; **c'est peu ~** that's an understatement; **c'est trop ~** that's saying too much; **c'est (tout) ~** that (just) shows you; **ça dit bien ce que ça veut ~** that should tell you something, that says something; **c'est moi qui vous le dis** you take my word for it; **c'est vous qui le dites** YOU say so, that's what YOU say; **ce n'est pas pour ~, mais ...** (*se vanter*) I don't mean *ou* wish to boast, but ...; (*se plaindre*) I don't mean *ou* wish to complain, but ...; **c'est-à-~** that is (to say); **c'est-à-~ que je ne le savais pas** well actually *ou* well the thing is *ou* I'm afraid I didn't know; **qu'est-ce à ~?** what does that mean?; **est-ce à ~ que ...?** does this mean that ...?, is that to say that ...?; **entre nous soit dit, il est un peu bête** (just) between the two of us *ou* confidentially he is a bit of an idiot; **soit dit en passant** by the way, let me say in passing, incidentally.

n (*avec faire, laisser, vouloir*) **faire ~ qch à qn** to send word of sth to sb; **faire ~ à qn de venir** to send for sb; **faire ~ à qn qu'on a besoin de lui** to let sb know that he is needed; **faire ~ à qn des choses (qu'il n'a pas dites)** to put words in sb's mouth; **il ne se l'est pas fait ~ deux fois** he did not need *ou* have to be told twice; **elle partit sans se le faire ~ deux fois** she was off without a second bidding *ou* without having to be told twice; **par la torture on fait ~ aux gens ce qu'on veut** people can be made to say *ou* you can make people say anything under torture; **je ne lui ai pas fait ~** I didn't make him say it; **je ne vous le fais pas ~!** I'm not putting words into your mouth!; **laisser ~** to let people talk; **laisse ~!** let them talk!, never mind what they say!; **je me suis laissé ~ que** I heard that, I was told that; **vouloir ~** (*signifier*) to mean; **que veut ~ ce mot/sa réponse?** what does this word/his answer mean?, what is the meaning of this word/his answer?; **cette phrase ne veut rien ~** this sentence does not mean a thing; **c'est bien cela que je veux ~** that is exactly *ou* just what I mean; **cela dit bien ce que cela veut ~** it means exactly *ou* just what it says; **cela ne veut pas ~ qu'il viendra** *ou* **qu'il vienne** that does not mean (to say) that *ou* it does not follow that he will come.

2 **se dire** vpr a (*penser*) to say to o.s. **il se dit qu'il était inutile de rester** he said to himself that there was no point in staying; **je me dis que j'aurais dû l'acheter** I feel now *ou* I'm thinking now that I should have bought it; **il faut bien se ~ que** one has to realize *ou* accept that.

b (*se prétendre*) to claim to be. **il se dit malade** he claims to be ill *ou* that he is ill; **elle se dit sa cousine** she claims to be his cousin, she says she is his cousin.

c **elles se dirent au revoir** they said goodbye (to each other).

d (*sens passif*) **cela ne se dit pas en société** this word is not in polite use, it's not the sort of thing one says in company; **cela ne se dit plus en français** this expression is no longer used *ou* in use in French; **cela se dit de la même façon en anglais et en français** it's the same in English and in French, English and French use the same expression for it; **comment se dit ... en français?** what is the French for ...?, how do you say ... in French?; (*dans un dictionnaire*) **se dit d'un objet/d'une personne** *etc* of an object/a person *etc*.

e (*se croire*) **on se dirait en Grèce/au Moyen Âge** you would think you were in Greece/back in the Middle Ages.

3 nm (*déclaration*) statement. **d'après ses ~s** according to him *ou* to what he says; **au ~ de** according to; **au ~ de** *ou* **selon le ~ de tous** by all accounts; **croire aux ~s de qn** to believe what sb says; (*Jur*) **leurs ~s ne concordent pas** their statements do not agree.

direct, e [dirɛkt] 1 adj a (*sans détour*) *route* direct; *personne, reproche, regard* direct; *question* direct, straight; *allusion* direct, pointed (*épith*). **c'est le chemin le plus ~** it's the most direct route; **c'est ~ en bus** there's a bus that goes direct; **il m'a parlé de manière très ~e, il a été très ~** he spoke to me in a very direct *ou* straightforward way *ou* very frankly, he didn't beat about the bush.

b (*sans intermédiaire*) *impôt, descendant, adversaire, responsabilité* direct; *cause* immediate, direct; (*Jur*) *action* direct. **ses chefs ~s** his immediate superiors; **vente ~e (au consommateur)** direct selling; **ligne téléphonique ~e** (*privée*) private *ou* direct line; (*automatique*) automatic dialling system; **être en rapport** *ou* **contact ~** *ou* **en relations ~es avec** to deal directly *ou* be in direct contact with; **se mettre en rapport ~ avec qn** to contact sb *ou* make contact with sb directly; **il n'y a pas de rapport** *ou* **lien ~ entre les deux faits** there is no direct connection *ou* link between the two facts; **il a pris une part très ~e à cette affaire** he was directly involved in this business.

c (*absolu*) **en contradiction ~e** in direct *ou* complete contradiction.

d (*Astron*) direct; (*Ling*) *style, discours, objet* direct; (*Logique*) *proposition* positive; *voir* **complément**.

e (*Rail*) *train* fast (*épith*), non-stop (*épith*), express (*épith*); *voiture* through (*épith*). **ce train est ~ jusqu'à Lyon** this is a fast *ou* non-stop train to Lyons.

2 nm a (*Rail*) express (train), fast *ou* non-stop train. **le ~ Paris-Dijon** the Paris-Dijon express.

b (*Boxe*) jab. **~ du gauche/du droit** straight left/right; **il lui a envoyé un ~ dans l'estomac** he delivered a punch straight to his stomach.

c (*Rad, TV*) **c'est du ~** it's live; **émission en ~** live broadcast; **parler/faire un reportage en ~ (sur l'antenne) de New York** to be speaking/reporting live from New York; **ce sont les risques du ~** those are the risks of live broadcasting *ou* of broadcasting live.

3 adv (*) straight. **tu fais la traduction ~?** do you translate straight

off?

directement [diʀɛktəmɑ̃] adv a (immédiatement) straight, straight away (Brit), right away. il est ~ allé se coucher he went straight ou directly to bed, he went to bed straight (Brit) ou right away; en rentrant il est allé ~ au réfrigérateur pour voir ce qu'il y avait à manger when he came home he went straight to the fridge ou he made a beeline for the fridge to see what there was to eat.

b (sans détour) straight, directly. cette rue mène ~ à la gare this street leads straight to the station; cet escalier communique ~ avec la cave this staircase leads straight ou directly to the cellar; il est entré ~ dans le vif du sujet he came straight to the point.

c (personnellement) directly. il m'a très ~ accusé de ce crime he accused me of this crime straight out ou to my face; sa bonne foi est ~ mise en cause it's a direct challenge to his good faith; tout ceci ne me concerne pas ~ mais ... none of this concerns me directly ou personally but ..., none of this is of any direct ou immediate concern to me but ...; les secteurs de l'économie les plus ~ touchés par la crise the sectors of the economy most directly ou immediately affected by the crisis.

d (sans intermédiaire) direct, straight. adressez-vous ~ au patron apply to the boss direct ou in person, go straight to the boss; j'ai été ~ le trouver pour le lui demander I went to find him myself ou in person to ask him about it; ~ du producteur au consommateur direct ou straight from (the) producer to (the) consumer; colis expédié ~ à l'acheteur parcel sent direct to the buyer.

e (diamétralement) (lit) directly; (fig) completely, utterly, directly. la maison ~ en face the house directly ou straight opposite; ~ opposé diametrically ou utterly opposed; ~ contraire/contradictoire completely ou utterly contrary/contradictory.

directeur, -trice [diʀɛktœʀ, tʀis] 1 adj (dirigeant) directing; (fig: principal) idée leading, principal, main; principe guiding; force guiding, driving; (Tech) bielle driving; roue front; voir comité, ligne[1], plan[1].

2 nm a (responsable, gérant) [banque, usine] manager; (Admin) head; (Police) ≃ chief constable (Brit); (Ciné, TV: technicien) director. ~ commercial/général/du personnel sales/general/personnel manager; ~ général general manager, chief executive officer (US); ~ général adjoint assistant general manager; (Univ) le ~ de l'U.E.R. d'anglais the head of the English department.

b (administrateur, propriétaire) director.

c ~ (d'école) headmaster (Brit), principal (US).

3 directrice nf a [entreprise] manageress; (propriétaire) director; (Admin) head.

b ~trice (d'école/de lycée) (primary/secondary school) headmistress (Brit), principal (US).

c (Math) directrix.

4 comp ▸directeur administratif et financier financial and administrative director ▸directeur artistique artistic director ▸directeur de cabinet (d'un ministre) principal private secretary ▸directeur de conscience director, spiritual adviser ▸directeur financier financial director ▸directeur gérant managing director ▸directeur de journal newspaper editor ▸directeur de la photographie director of photography ▸directeur de prison prison governor (Brit), head warden (US) ▸directeur spirituel = directeur de conscience ▸directeur de théâtre theatre director ▸directeur de thèse (Univ) supervisor (Brit), reader (US).

directif, -ive[1] [diʀɛktif, iv] adj managerial.

direction [diʀɛksjɔ̃] nf a (lit, fig: sens) direction; (route, chemin) direction, way. vous n'êtes pas dans ou vous n'avez pas pris la bonne ~ you're not going the right way ou in the right direction, you're not on the right road; dans quelle ~ est-il parti? which way did he go? ou head?; aller dans la ~ de ou en ~ de Paris, prendre la ~ de Paris to go towards ou in the direction of Paris; train/avion en ~ de ... train/plane for ou going to ...; bateau en ~ de ... ship bound ou heading for ...; (fig) nous devons chercher dans une autre ~ we must look in some other ou a different direction, we must direct our search elsewhere; (fig) l'enquête a pris une nouvelle ~ the inquiry has taken a new turn; dans toutes les ~s in all directions; (Aut) "autres ~s" "all other routes"; "toutes ~s" "all routes".

b (action d'administrer: voir diriger) management; running; editorship; leadership; directing; supervision; conducting. il a été chargé de ou on lui a confié la ~ de l'enquête/des travaux he has been put in charge of the inquiry/the work; avoir la ~ de (gén, Admin, Ind) to run, be at the head of, be in charge of (the running of); recherches, travaux to supervise, oversee, be in charge of; prendre la ~ de (gén, Admin) to take over the running of; usine, entreprise to take over the running ou management of; équipe, travaux to take charge of, take over the supervision of; mouvement, pays to take over the leadership of; débats to take control of; journal to take over ou take on the editorship of; sous sa ~ under his leadership (ou management etc); ~ par objectifs management by objectives; prendre la ~ des opérations to take charge ou control (of the running of operations); il a travaillé sous la ~ d'un spécialiste he has worked under the supervision of an expert; il a fait ses études sous la ~ de X he studied under X; (Mus) orchestre (placé) sous la ~ de X orchestra conducted by X.

c (fonction de gérant, de responsable) post of manager, managership; (fonction de propriétaire, d'administrateur) post of director, directorship; [école] headship, post of head ou principal; [journal] editorship, post of editor. on lui a offert la ~ de l'usine/d'une équipe de chercheurs he was offered the post of factory manager/of leader ou head of a research team; on lui a donné la ~ générale he was given the director-generalship.

d (personnel dirigeant) [usine, service, équipe] management; [journal] editorial board. la ~ générale/commerciale the general/sales management; se plaindre à la ~ to make a complaint to the board ou the management; la ~ décline toute responsabilité the directors accept ou the management accepts no responsibility; voir changement.

e (bureau) [usine] manager's (ou director's) office; [école] headmaster's (ou headmistress's) office (Brit), principal's office (US); [journal] editor's office.

f (service) department. adressez-vous à la ~ du personnel apply to the personnel department; notre ~ générale est à Paris our head office is in Paris; (de la CEE) D~ Générale Directorate General; la D~ de la surveillance du territoire the counter-espionage services, ≃ MI5 (Brit), ≃ the CIA (US); D~ de l'action sanitaire et sociale department of health and social services; D~ générale des Impôts ≃ Inland Revenue (Brit), Internal Revenue (US).

g (Aut: mécanisme) steering. ~ assistée power steering; voir rupture.

directionnel, -elle [diʀɛksjɔnɛl] adj (Tech) directional.

directive[2] [diʀɛktiv] nf (gén pl) directive, order, instruction.

directoire [diʀɛktwaʀ] nm a (Comm etc) board of directors ou management. b (Hist) le D~ the Directory, the Directoire; fauteuil/table ~ Directoire chair/table; voir style.

directorial, e, mpl -iaux [diʀɛktɔʀjal, jo] adj fonction, responsabilité (Comm, Ind) managerial; (Admin) of directors; (Scol) of headmaster (ou headmistress) (Brit), of principal (US). fauteuil/bureau ~ manager's ou director's ou headmaster's (Brit) ou principal's (US) chair/office.

directrice [diʀɛktʀis] nf voir directeur.

dirigeable [diʀiʒabl] adj, nm: (ballon) ~ dirigible, airship.

dirigeant, e [diʀiʒɑ̃, ɑ̃t] 1 adj classe ruling. cadre ~ senior manager ou executive. 2 nm,f [parti, syndicat] leader; [pays] leader, ruler. ~ d'entreprise company director; (salarié) company manager.

diriger [diʀiʒe] [3] 1 vt a (administrer) (gén, Admin) to run, be head of, be in charge of; entreprise, usine, théâtre to manage, run; journal to run, edit; pays, mouvement, parti to lead; opération, manœuvre to direct, be in charge of; recherches, travaux to supervise, oversee, be in charge of; enquête, procès to conduct; débat to conduct, lead; orchestre to conduct. ~ la circulation to control ou direct the traffic; (Mil) ~ le tir to direct the firing; mal ~ une entreprise to mismanage a business, run a business badly; équipe bien/mal dirigée team under good/bad leadership ou management, well-/badly-run team; savoir ~ to know how to command ou lead, be a good manager ou leader; ils n'ont pas su ~ leurs enfants they weren't able to guide their children; a-t-il bien su ~ sa vie? did he manage to run his life properly?; cette idée dirige toute notre politique this idea guides ou determines our whole policy; l'ambition dirige tous ses actes ambition rules ou guides his every act; voir économie, loisir.

b (guider) voiture to steer; avion to pilot, fly; bateau to steer, navigate; cheval (de trait) to steer; (de selle) to guide. (fig) bien/mal ~ sa barque to run one's affairs well/badly; bateau qui se dirige facilement boat which is easy to steer.

c (acheminer) marchandises, convoi to send (vers, sur to); personnes to direct, send (sur, vers to). on m'a mal dirigé I was misdirected ou sent the wrong way.

d (orienter) ~ une arme sur to point ou level ou aim a weapon at; ~ un canon/télescope sur to train a gun/telescope on, point a gun/telescope at; ~ une lampe de poche/lumière sur to shine a torch/light on; ~ son attention sur qn/qch to turn one's attention to ou on sb/to sth; ~ son regard ou ses yeux sur ou vers qch to look towards ou in the direction of sth; le pompier dirigea sa lance vers les flammes the fireman aimed ou pointed his hose at ou trained his hose on the flames; la flèche est dirigée vers la gauche the arrow is pointing left ou to(wards) the left; ~ ses pas vers un lieu to make for ou make one's way to ou head for a place; on devrait ~ ce garçon vers les sciences we should advise this boy to specialize in science, we should guide this boy towards the sciences; cet élève a été mal dirigé this pupil has been badly advised ou guided; nous dirigeons notre enquête/nos travaux dans une voie nouvelle we are conducting ou directing our inquiry/carrying out ou directing our work along new lines; son regard se dirigea vers elle he turned his gaze towards ou on her; ~ un article/une allusion contre qn/qch to aim ou direct an article/an allusion at sb/sth; ~ une critique contre qn/qch to aim ou direct ou level a criticism at sb/sth; les poursuites dirigées contre lui the proceedings directed ou brought against him.

2 se diriger vpr a se ~ vers (aller, avancer vers) to make for, head for, make one's way towards; il se dirigea vers la sortie he made his way towards ou made for the exit; le bateau/la voiture semblait se diriger vers le port the boat/car seemed to be heading ou making for the

harbour; (*fig*) **nous nous dirigeons vers une solution/un match nul** we seem to be heading towards a solution/a draw; **l'avion se dirigea vers le nord** the plane flew *ou* headed northwards; **se ~ droit sur qch/qn** to make a beeline *ou* make straight for sth/sb.

b (*se guider*) to find one's way. **se ~ sur les étoiles/le soleil** to navigate *ou* sail by the stars/the sun; **se ~ au radar** to navigate by radar; **il n'est pas facile de se ~ dans le brouillard** it isn't easy to find one's way in the fog; (*fig, Scol*) **se ~ vers les sciences** to specialize in science; **se ~ vers les carrières juridiques** to opt for *ou* be headed for a career in law.

dirigisme [diʀiʒism] **nm** (*Écon*) interventionism, state intervention.

dirigiste [diʀiʒist] **adj, nmf** interventionist.

disant [dizɑ̃] *voir* **soi-disant**.

discal, e, **mpl -aux** [diskal, o] **adj** (*Méd*) of the intervertebral discs. **hernie ~e** herniated (*SPÉC*) *ou* slipped disc.

discernable [disɛʀnabl] **adj** discernible, detectable.

discernement [disɛʀnəmɑ̃] **nm** a (*sagesse*) discernment, judgment. **manquer de ~** to be lacking in judgment *ou* discernment; **agir sans ~** to act without proper judgment. b (*action*) distinguishing, discriminating, distinction. **sans ~** without (making a) distinction; (*littér*) **le ~ de la vérité d'avec l'erreur** distinguishing truth from error, discriminating between truth and error.

discerner [disɛʀne] 1 **vt** a (*distinguer*) *forme* to discern, make out, perceive; *bruit* to detect, hear, make out; *nuance* to discern, detect; *douleur* to feel. b (*différencier*) to distinguish, discriminate (*entre* between). **~ une couleur d'une** *ou* **d'avec une autre/le vrai du faux** to distinguish *ou* tell one colour from another/truth from falsehood.

disciple [disipl] **nm** (*élève*) disciple; (*adepte*) follower, disciple.

disciplinable [disiplinabl] **adj** disciplinable.

disciplinaire [disiplinɛʀ] **adj** disciplinary.

disciplinairement [disiplinɛʀmɑ̃] **adv** in a disciplinary way.

discipline [disiplin] **nf** a (*règle*) discipline; *voir* **compagnie, conseil.** b (*matière*) discipline, subject. **~ de base** core *ou* basic subject.

discipliné, e [disipline] (**ptp de discipliner**) **adj** (well-)disciplined.

discipliner [disipline] 1 **vt** *soldats, élèves* to discipline; *impulsions* to discipline, control; (*fig*) *cheveux* to control, keep tidy. **cheveux difficiles à ~** *[enfant]* unruly hair; *[adulte]* unmanageable hair; **il faut apprendre à se ~** one must learn self-control *ou* self-discipline *ou* to discipline oneself.

disc-jockey [disk(ə)ʒɔkɛ] **nm** disc jockey, DJ.

disco [disko] 1 **adj** *musique* disco. 2 **nm: le ~** disco music.

discobole [diskɔbɔl] **nm** discus thrower; (*Antiq*) discobolus.

discoïde [diskɔid] **adj** discoid(al), disc- *ou* disk-shaped.

discontinu, e [diskɔ̃tiny] 1 **adj** *ligne, fonction* discontinuous; (*intermittent*) *bruit, effort* intermittent; (*Ling*) discontinuous. **bande jaune** *ou* **blanche ~e** *[ligne ou route]* broken yellow *ou* white line. 2 **nm** (*Philos*) discontinuity.

discontinuer [diskɔ̃tinɥe] 1 **vti** (*littér*) to discontinue, cease, stop, break off. **sans ~** without stopping, without a break; **pendant deux heures sans ~** for 2 hours at a stretch *ou* without stopping *ou* without a break.

discontinuité [diskɔ̃tinɥite] **nf** discontinuity.

disconvenir [diskɔ̃v(ə)niʀ] 22 **vi** (*littér: nier*) **ne pas ~ de/que: je n'en disconviens pas** I don't deny it; **je ne puis ~ que ce soit vrai** I cannot deny the truth of it *ou* that it's true.

discophile [diskɔfil] **nmf** record enthusiast.

discordance [diskɔʀdɑ̃s] **nf** a *[caractères]* conflict, clash (*NonC*); *[opinions]* difference, conflict; *[sons]* discord (*NonC*), discordance, dissonance; *[couleurs]* clash (*NonC*), clashing (*NonC*). **leurs témoignages présentent des ~s graves** their evidence shows serious discrepancies, their evidence conflicts seriously. b (*Géol*) unconformability, discordance.

discordant, e [diskɔʀdɑ̃, ɑ̃t] **adj** a *caractères, opinions, témoignages* conflicting, discordant; *sons, cris, bruits* discordant, harsh; *instruments* out of tune; *couleurs* clashing, discordant. **elle a une voix ~e** she has a harsh *ou* grating voice, her voice grates. b (*Géol*) unconformable, discordant.

discorde [diskɔʀd] **nf** (*littér*) discord, dissension. **mettre** *ou* **semer la ~** to sow discord, cause dissension; *voir* **pomme**.

discorder [diskɔʀde] 1 **vi** *[sons]* to be discordant; *[couleurs]* to clash; *[témoignages]* to conflict.

discothèque [diskɔtɛk] **nf** (*collection*) record collection; (*meuble*) record cabinet; (*bâtiment*) record library; (*club*) discotheque.

discount [diskunt] 1 **nm** (*rabais*) discount. **pratiquer le ~, faire du ~** to give a discount. 2 **adj inv: magasin ~** discount store *ou* shop; **à des prix ~** at discount prices.

discounter[1] [diskunte] 1 **vt:** to discount, sell at a discount. **boutique où tout est discounté** shop *ou* store where everything is cut-price *ou* is at a discount price.

discounter[2] [diskuntœʀ] **nm** discount dealer.

discoureur, -euse [diskuʀœʀ, øz] **nm,f** (*péj*) speechifier, windbag* (*péj*).

discourir [diskuʀiʀ] 11 **vi** a (*faire un discours*) to discourse, expatiate (*sur, de* upon); (*péj*) to hold forth (*sur, de* upon), speechify. **elle le suivit sans ~** she followed him without demur *ou* without a murmur. b (*bavarder*) to talk (away).

discours [diskuʀ] **nm** a (*allocution*) speech. **~ d'ouverture/de clôture** opening/closing speech *ou* address; **~ du trône** Queen's (*ou* King's) speech, speech from the throne; (*US Pol*) **D~ sur l'état de l'Union** State of the Union Address; **faire** *ou* **prononcer un ~** to make *ou* deliver a speech; **prononcer un ~ sur la tombe de qn** to deliver a funeral oration for sb; **~-programme** keynote speech.

b (*péj*) talking (*NonC*), chatter (*NonC*). **tous ces beaux ~ n'y changeront rien** all these fine words *ou* all this fine talk won't make any difference; **suis-moi sans faire de ~!** follow me without argument *ou* any arguing!; **que de ~!** what a lot of fuss (about nothing)!; **perdre son temps en ~** to waste one's time talking *ou* in idle (chit)chat; **il m'a tenu un long ~ sur ce qui lui était arrivé** he spun me a long yarn *ou* he told me a long-drawn-out tale about what had happened to him; **elle m'a tenu des ~ à n'en plus finir** she went on and on as if she was never going to stop.

c **le ~** (*expression verbale*) speech; (*Ling*) discourse; (*Philos: raisonnement*) discursive reasoning *ou* thinking; (*Rhétorique*) discourse; (*Ling*) **(au) ~ direct/indirect** (in) direct/indirect *ou* reported speech; **les parties du ~** (*Ling*) the parts of speech; (*Rhétorique*) the parts of discourse.

d (*Philos: traité*) discourse, treatise. **le D~ de la méthode** the Discourse on Method.

discourtois, e [diskuʀtwa, waz] **adj** discourteous.

discourtoisement [diskuʀtwazmɑ̃] **adv** discourteously.

discourtoisie [diskuʀtwazi] **nf** (*littér*) discourtesy.

discrédit [diskʀedi] **nm** *[personne]* discredit, disfavour; *[idée, théorie, œuvre]* discredit, disrepute. **tomber dans le ~** to fall into disrepute; **être en ~** to be discredited *ou* in disrepute; *voir* **jeter**.

discréditer [diskʀedite] 1 1 **vt** *personne* to discredit; *théorie, œuvre* to discredit, bring into disrepute. **c'est une opinion tout à fait discréditée de nos jours** it is an opinion which has gone right out of favour *ou* which is quite discredited nowadays. 2 **se discréditer vpr** *[idée, théorie]* to become discredited, fall into disrepute; *[personne]* to bring discredit upon o.s., discredit o.s. **se ~ aux yeux de** *ou* **auprès de qn** to discredit o.s. *ou* bring discredit upon o.s. in the eyes of sb.

discret, -ète [diskʀɛ, ɛt] **adj** a (*réservé, retenu*) *personne, attitude* discreet, reserved; *allusion, reproche, compliment* discreet. **soyez ~, ne lui parlez pas de sa défaite** be tactful *ou* discreet and don't mention his defeat to him.

b (*qui n'attire pas l'attention*) *personne, manière* unassuming, unobtrusive; *parfum, maquillage* discreet, unobtrusive; *vêtement* sober, plain, simple; *couleur* quiet, restrained; *lumière* subdued; *endroit* quiet, secluded; *parole, regard* discreet. **il lui remit un paquet sous emballage ~** he handed her a plainly wrapped parcel; **"envoi ~"** "sent under plain cover"; **n'y a-t-il pas une façon plus ~ète de m'avertir?** isn't there a more discreet *ou* less conspicuous way of warning me?

c (*qui garde les secrets*) discreet.

d (*Math*) *quantité* discrete; (*Phys*) *fonction* discontinuous; (*Ling*) *unité* discrete.

discrètement [diskʀɛtmɑ̃] **adv** a *se tenir à l'écart, parler, reprocher* discreetly, quietly. **il a ~ fait allusion à** ... he made a discreet allusion to ..., he gently hinted at ... . b *se maquiller* discreetly, unobtrusively; *s'habiller* soberly, plainly, simply; (*pour ne pas être vu, entendu*) discreetly. **parler ~ à l'oreille de qn** to have a quiet *ou* discreet word in sb's ear.

discrétion [diskʀesjɔ̃] **nf** a (*art de garder un secret*) discretion. **~ assurée** discretion assured. b (*réserve*) *[personne, attitude]* discretion, tact. **sa ~ est exemplaire** he's a model of discretion *ou* tact. c (*modération*) *[maquillage]* unobtrusiveness; *[vêtement]* sobriety, plainness, simpleness. **avec ~** *s'habiller etc* soberly, plainly, simply; *se conduire* discreetly, unobtrusively; *parler* discreetly. d (*littér: discernement*) discretion. e (*loc*) **vin** *etc* **à ~** unlimited wine *etc*, as much wine *etc* as you want; (*littér*) **être à la ~ de qn** to be in sb's hands.

discrétionnaire [diskʀesjɔnɛʀ] **adj** discretionary.

discriminant [diskʀiminɑ̃] **nm** (*Math*) discriminant.

discrimination [diskʀiminasjɔ̃] **nf** discrimination.

discriminatoire [diskʀiminatwaʀ] **adj** *mesures* discriminatory, discriminating.

discriminer [diskʀimine] 1 **vt** (*littér*) to distinguish. **apprendre à ~ les méthodes** to learn how to discriminate *ou* distinguish between methods.

disculpation [diskylpasjɔ̃] **nf** exoneration, exculpation (*frm*).

disculper [diskylpe] 1 1 **vt** to exonerate, exculpate (*frm*) (*de* from). 2 **se disculper vpr** to exonerate o.s., vindicate o.s., exculpate o.s. (*frm*) (*auprès de qn* in sb's eyes).

discursif, -ive [diskyʀsif, iv] **adj** discursive.

discussion [diskysjɔ̃] **nf** a *[problème]* discussion, examination (*de* of); *[projet de loi]* debate (*de* on), discussion (*de* of). **mettre une question en ~** to bring a matter up for discussion; **le projet de loi est en ~** the bill is being debated *ou* is under discussion. b (*débat*) discussion, debate; (*pourparlers, échanges de vues*) discussion(s), talks; (*conversation*) discussion, talk. **les délégués sont en ~** the delegates are in conference; **sans ~ possible** indisputably, undoubtedly. c (*querelle*) argument, quarrel. **avoir une violente ~ avec qn** to have a violent disagreement *ou* quarrel *ou* argument with sb; **suis-moi et pas de ~s** follow me and no argument.

discutable [diskytabl] adj *solution, théorie* debatable, questionable, arguable; *goût* doubtful, questionable.

discutailler* [diskytɑje] 1 vi (*péj*) (*bavarder*) to chat (away)*, natter (away)* (*Brit*); (*débattre sans fin*) to argue (*sur* over), go on* (*sur* about), discuss; (*ergoter*) to wrangle, quibble (*sur* over). **~ dans le vide** to argue *ou* quibble over nothing.

discuter [diskyte] 1 1 vt a (*débattre*) *problème* to discuss, examine; *projet de loi* to debate, discuss; *prix* to argue about, haggle over.

b (*contester*) *ordre* to question, dispute. **~ les droits de qn** to debate *ou* question sb's rights; **ministre très discuté** much discussed *ou* very controversial minister; **question très discutée** vexed question, much debated *ou* disputed question; **théorie très discutée** very controversial theory; **ça se discute, ça peut se ~** that's debatable *ou* disputable.

c **~ le coup*** *ou* **le bout de gras‡** (*parler*) to have a chat* *ou* natter* (*Brit*) *ou* chinwag‡ (*Brit*); (*parlementer*) to argue away.

2 vi a (*être en conférence*) to have a discussion, confer (*avec* with); (*parler*) to talk (*avec* with); (*parlementer*) to argue (*avec* with). **~ de** *ou* **sur qch** to discuss sth; **~ (de) politique** *etc* to discuss *ou* talk politics *etc;* **on ne peut pas ~ avec lui!*** it's no good arguing with him!, you can't have a discussion with him!

b (*protester*) to argue. **suivez-moi sans ~** follow me and no argument; **j'en ai décidé ainsi et il n'y a pas à ~** my mind's made up about it and that's that *ou* that's final *ou* and there's nothing further to be said; **tu discutes?‡** no ifs and buts!* (*Brit*), no ifs ands or buts!* (*US*), no argument!

c (*débattre*) **~ de** *ou* **sur** *question, problème* to discuss, debate; **ensuite, nous avons discuté du prix** then we discussed the price; **~ sur le cas de qn** to discuss *ou* debate sb's case; **j'en ai discuté avec lui et il est d'accord** I have discussed the matter *ou* talked the matter over with him and he agrees; **vous discutez sur des points sans importance** you are arguing about *ou* niggling over trifles; **~ du sexe des anges*** to discuss futilities.

disert, e [dizɛʀ, ɛʀt] adj (*frm, hum, péj*) loquacious, articulate, fluent.

disette [dizɛt] nf a (*manque*) [*vivres, idées*] scarcity, shortage, dearth. b (*famine*) food shortage, scarcity (of food).

diseur, -euse [dizœʀ, øz] nm,f: **~ de bonne aventure** fortuneteller; **~ de bons mots** wit, wag.

disgrâce [disgʀɑs] nf (*défaveur, déchéance*) disgrace. **encourir** *ou* **mériter la ~ de qn** to incur sb's disfavour *ou* displeasure; **tomber en ~** to fall into disgrace; **la ~ du ministre** the minister's disgrace.

disgracié, e [disgʀasje] (**ptp de disgracier**) adj (*en disgrâce*) in disgrace, disgraced; (*laid*) ill-favoured, ugly.

disgracier [disgʀasje] 7 vt to disgrace, dismiss from favour.

disgracieux, -ieuse [disgʀasjø, jøz] adj *geste* inelegant, awkward; *démarche* inelegant, awkward, ungainly; *visage* ill-favoured; *forme, objet* unsightly.

disjoindre [disʒwɛ̃dʀ(ə)] 49 1 vt *planches, tôles, tuiles* to take apart, separate; *tuyaux* to disconnect, take apart; *pierres* to break apart; (*fig*) *problèmes* to separate, split. **ces deux questions sont disjointes** these two matters are not connected. 2 **se disjoindre** vpr [*planches, tôles, tuiles*] to come apart *ou* loose, separate; [*tuyaux, pierres*] to come apart. **planches/tuiles disjointes** planks/tiles which are coming apart *ou* loose, loose planks/tiles; **tuyaux disjoints** pipes which have come apart *ou* undone.

disjoncter [disʒɔ̃kte] 1 1 vt *courant* to cut off, disconnect. 2 vi [*disjoncteur*] to act as a curcuit-breaker *ou* cutout; (*: *fig*) to crack up*.

disjoncteur [disʒɔ̃ktœʀ] nm (*Élec*) circuit breaker, cutout.

disjonctif, -ive [disʒɔ̃ktif, iv] 1 adj disjunctive. 2 **disjonctive** nf disjunctive.

disjonction [disʒɔ̃ksjɔ̃] nf disjunction, separation.

dislocation [dislɔkasjɔ̃] nf (*voir* **disloquer**) dislocation; dismantling; smashing; breaking up; dispersal; scattering; dismemberment; dislocation; (*Géol*) fault.

disloquer [dislɔke] 1 1 vt a *bras, épaule* to dislocate, put out of joint. **avoir l'épaule disloquée** to have a dislocated shoulder.

b *machine, meuble* (*démonter*) to dismantle, take apart *ou* to pieces; (*casser*) to smash, break up. **la chaise est toute disloquée** the chair is all smashed *ou* broken.

c *rassemblement, cortège* to disperse, break up; *troupes* to disperse, scatter.

d *empire* to dismantle, dismember, break up.

2 **se disloquer** vpr a **se ~ le bras** to dislocate one's arm, put one's arm out of joint; **son épaule s'est disloquée** his shoulder has been dislocated.

b [*meuble*] to come apart, fall to pieces.

c [*troupes*] to disperse, scatter; [*cortège*] to disperse, break *ou* split up.

d [*empire*] to break up, disintegrate.

disparaître [dispaʀɛtʀ] 57 vi a (*lit: s'en aller, devenir invisible*) to disappear, vanish. **le fuyard disparut au coin de la rue/dans la foule** the fugitive disappeared *ou* vanished round the corner of the street/into the crowd; **~ discrètement** to slip away quietly; **~ furtivement** to sneak away *ou* out; **je ne veux pas le voir, je disparais** I don't want to see him so I'll just slip away *ou* disappear *ou* I'll be off; **le voilà, disparais!** there he is, make yourself scarce*!; **~ aux regards** to vanish out of sight, disappear from view; **~ à l'horizon** [*soleil*] to disappear *ou* vanish *ou* sink below the horizon; [*bateau*] to vanish *ou* disappear over the horizon; **l'arbre disparut dans le brouillard** the tree vanished *ou* was swallowed up in the fog; **le bâtiment disparaît sous le lierre** the building is (half-)hidden under a cloak of ivy.

b (*être porté manquant*) [*personne*] to go missing (*Brit*), disappear; [*objet*] to disappear. **il a disparu de son domicile** he is missing *ou* has gone missing (*Brit*) *ou* has disappeared from home; **trois camions ont disparu (du garage)** three lorries have disappeared *ou* are missing *ou* have gone (from the garage); **~ sans laisser de traces** to disappear without trace; **il a disparu de la circulation*** he seems to have vanished into thin air.

c (*passer, s'effacer*) [*joie, crainte etc*] to disappear, vanish, evaporate; [*sourire, rougeur, douleur, cicatrice*] to disappear, vanish, go away; (*graduellement*) to fade; [*jeunesse*] to vanish, be lost; [*brouillard*] to disappear, vanish, thin out.

d (*mourir*) [*race, civilisation*] to die (out), vanish; [*coutume*] to die out, disappear; [*personne*] to die; (*se perdre*) [*navire*] to sink, be lost. **si je venais à ~, tu n'aurais pas de soucis matériels** if I were to die, you wouldn't have any financial worries; **tout le charme de la Belle Époque disparaît avec elle** all the charm of the Belle Époque dies *ou* vanishes with her; **~ en mer** to be lost at sea; (*Naut*) **~ corps et biens** to go down with all hands.

e **faire ~** *objet* to remove, hide away *ou* out of sight; *document* to dispose of, get rid of; *tache, trace, obstacle, difficulté* to remove; *personne* to eliminate, get rid of, do away with*; *crainte* to dispel, eliminate; **cela a fait ~ la douleur/la rougeur** it made the pain/red mark go away, it got rid of the pain/all trace of the red mark; **faire ~ un objet** [*prestidigitateur*] to make an object vanish; **le voleur fit ~ le bijou dans sa poche** the thief concealed the jewel *ou* hid the jewel out of sight in his pocket; **il prenait de gros morceaux de pain qu'il faisait ~ dans sa bouche** he was taking large hunks of bread and cramming them into his mouth; **ils firent ~ toute trace de leur passage** they destroyed *ou* wiped out *ou* removed all trace of their visit; **faire ~ une inscription** [*temps*] to erase *ou* efface *ou* wear away an inscription; [*personne*] to erase *ou* wipe out *ou* remove an inscription.

disparate [dispaʀat] adj *éléments* disparate; *objets, mobilier* disparate, ill-assorted; *couple, couleurs* ill-assorted, badly matched.

disparité [dispaʀite] nf [*éléments, salaires*] disparity (*de* in); [*objets, couleurs*] mismatch, ill-assortedness (*NonC*) (*de* of).

disparition [dispaʀisjɔ̃] nf a [*personne*] disappearance; [*cicatrice, rougeur*] disappearance; (*graduelle*) fading; [*brouillard*] lifting, thinning; [*soleil*] sinking, setting; [*tache, obstacle*] disappearance, removal. **la ~ de la douleur sera immédiate** the pain will be relieved *ou* will go away *ou* vanish immediately. b (*mort, perte*) [*personne*] death; [*espèce*] disappearance, extinction; [*coutume, langue*] disappearance, dying out; [*objet, bateau*] loss, disappearance. **cette race est en voie de ~** this race is becoming extinct; **espèce en voie de ~** endangered species.

disparu, e [dispaʀy] (**ptp de disparaître**) 1 adj a (*révolu*) *monde, époque* bygone (*épith*), vanished; *bonheur, jeunesse* lost, departed.

b (*effacé*) **une lueur menaçante, aussitôt ~e, brilla dans ses yeux** a dangerous gleam flickered and died in his eyes, his eyes glinted dangerously for a brief moment; **un sentiment d'espoir, bientôt ~, l'anima un court instant** hope filled him for a brief moment only to fade again.

c (*mort*) *personne* dead, departed; *race, coutume, langue* vanished, dead, extinct; (*dont on est sans nouvelles*) *victime* missing. **il a été porté ~** (*Mil*) he has been reported missing; (*dans une catastrophe*) he is missing, believed dead; **marin ~ en mer** sailor lost at sea.

2 nm,f (*mort*) dead person; (*dont on a perdu la trace*) missing person. (*littér*) **le cher ~** the dear departed; **il y a 5 morts et 3 ~s dans ce naufrage** there are 5 (reported) dead and 3 missing in this shipwreck.

dispatcher [dispatʃe] 1 vt (*gén*) to dispatch.

dispendieusement [dispɑ̃djøzmɑ̃] adv (*frm*) *vivre* extravagantly, expensively.

dispendieux, -ieuse [dispɑ̃djø, jøz] adj (*frm*) *goûts, luxe* extravagant, expensive.

dispensaire [dispɑ̃sɛʀ] nm community (*Brit*) *ou* free (*US*) clinic; (†) people's dispensary.

dispensateur, -trice [dispɑ̃satœʀ, tʀis] (*littér*) 1 adj dispensing. 2 nm,f dispenser.

dispense [dispɑ̃s] nf (*exemption*) exemption (*de* from); (*permission*) special permission; (*Rel*) dispensation (*de* from). **~ du service militaire/d'un examen** exemption from military service/from an exam; **~ d'âge pour passer un examen** permission to sit an exam under the statutory age limit.

dispenser [dispɑ̃se] 1 **1** **vt** a (*exempter*) to exempt, excuse (*de faire* from doing, *de qch* from sth). (*Rel*) **~ qn d'un vœu** to release sb from a vow; **je vous dispense de vos réflexions** I can do without your comments, you can spare me your comments; (*frm, hum*) **dispensez-moi de sa vue** spare me the sight of him; (*frm*) **dispensez-moi d'en dire plus** spare me the necessity of saying any more; **se faire ~** to get exempted.

b (*littér: distribuer*) *bienfaits* to dispense; *charme* to radiate; *lumière* to dispense, give out. **~ à qn son dévouement** to bestow *ou* lavish one's devotion on sb; (*Méd*) **~ des soins à un malade** to give medical care to a patient.

2 se dispenser **vpr: se ~ de** *corvée* to avoid, get out of; *remarque* to refrain from; **se ~ de faire qch** to get out of doing sth, not to bother doing sth; **il peut se ~ de travailler** he doesn't need to work, he has no need to bother working; **je me dispenserais bien d'y aller** I would (gladly) get out of *ou* save myself the bother of going if I could; (*iro*) **il s'est dispensé de s'excuser** he didn't see any necessity for excusing himself.

dispersant [dispɛʀsɑ̃] **nm** dispersant.

dispersé, e [dispɛʀse] (**ptp de disperser**) **adj** *habitat* scattered; *esprit* unselective, undisciplined; *travail* disorganized, fragmented, bitty*. **en ordre ~** in a disorganised manner.

disperser [dispɛʀse] 1 **1** **vt** a (*éparpiller*) *papiers, feuilles* to scatter, spread about; (*dissiper*) *brouillard* to disperse, break up; (*répartir*) *personnes* to disperse, spread out; *collection* to break up; (*faire partir*) *foule, ennemi* to scatter, disperse; (*Mil: congédier*) to dismiss. **tous nos amis sont maintenant dispersés** all our friends are now scattered. b (*fig: déconcentrer*) *ses forces, ses efforts* to dissipate. **2 se disperser** **vpr** *[foule]* to scatter, disperse, break up; *[élève, artiste]* to overdiversify, dissipate one's efforts. **ne vous dispersez pas trop!** don't overdiversify!, don't try to do too many different things at once!

dispersion [dispɛʀsjɔ̃] **nf** (*voir* **disperser**) scattering; spreading about; dispersal; breaking up; dismissal; dissipation; (*Chim, Phys*) dispersion. **évitez la ~ dans votre travail** don't attempt to do too many things at once, don't overdiversify in your work.

disponibilité [dispɔnibilite] **nf** a *[choses]* availability. (*Jur*) **~ des biens** (*faculté du possesseur*) ability to transfer one's property; (*caractère des possessions*) transferability of property; **en fonction des ~s** *ou* **de la ~ de chacun** according to each person's availability. b (*Fin*) **~s** available funds, liquid assets. c **mettre en ~** *fonctionnaire* to free from duty temporarily, grant leave of absence to; *officier* to place on reserve; **mise en ~** *[fonctionnaire]* leave of absence; *[officier]* transfer to reserve duty. d *[élève, esprit, auditoire]* alertness, receptiveness. **~ d'esprit** alertness *ou* receptiveness of mind.

disponible [dispɔnibl] **1** **adj** a *livre, appartement, fonds* available. **avez-vous des places ~s pour ce soir?** are there any seats (available) for this evening?; **il n'y a plus une seule place ~** there's not a single seat left *ou* not one spare seat; **je ne suis pas ~ ce soir** I'm not free tonight; (*Jur*) **biens ~s** transferable property. b **fonctionnaire ~** civil servant on leave of absence *ou* temporarily freed from duty; **officier ~** officer on reserve. c *élève, esprit, auditoire* alert, receptive. **2** **nm** (*Fin*) available assets *ou* funds.

dispos, e [dispo, oz] **adj** *personne* refreshed, in good form (*attrib*), full of energy (*attrib*). **avoir l'esprit ~** to have a fresh mind; *voir* **frais**[1].

disposé, e [dispoze] (**ptp de disposer**) **adj** a **être ~ à faire** to be willing *ou* disposed *ou* prepared to do; **être peu ~ à faire** to be unwilling to do, not to be disposed *ou* prepared to do; **bien/mal ~** in a good/bad mood; **bien/mal ~ à l'égard de** *ou* **pour** *ou* **envers qn** well-/ill-disposed towards sb. b *terrain* situated, sited. **comment le terrain est-il ~?** what is the site like?; **pièces bien/mal ~es** well-/badly-laid-out rooms.

disposer [dispoze] 1 **1** **vt** a (*arranger*) *personnes, meubles, fleurs* to arrange; *couverts* to set, lay. **~ des troupes sur le terrain** to draw up *ou* range *ou* dispose troops on the battlefield; **~ des objets en ligne/en cercle** to place *ou* lay *ou* arrange things in a row/in a circle; **on avait disposé le buffet dans le jardin** they had laid out *ou* set out the buffet in the garden.

b **~ qn à faire/à qch** (*engager à*) to dispose *ou* incline sb to do/towards sth; (*frm: préparer à*) to prepare sb to do/for sth; **cela ne dispose pas à l'optimisme** it doesn't (exactly) incline one to optimism.

2 **vi** (*frm: partir*) to leave. **vous pouvez ~** you may leave (now), (now) you can go.

3 disposer de **vt indir** (*avoir l'usage de*) to have (at one's disposal). **~ d'une voiture** to have a car (at one's disposal), have the use of a car; **~ d'une somme d'argent** to have a sum of money at one's disposal *ou* available (for one's use); **il disposait de quelques heures pour visiter Lyon** he had a few hours free *ou* to spare in which to visit Lyons; **avec les moyens dont il dispose** with the means at his disposal *ou* available to him; **si vous voulez vous pouvez en ~** if you wish you can use it; (*Jur*) **~ d'un domaine (par testament)** to dispose of an estate (in one's will); **il dispose de ses employés/de ses amis de manière abusive** he takes advantage of his employees/friends; **droit des peuples à ~ d'eux-mêmes** right of nations to self-determination.

4 se disposer **vpr: se ~ à faire** (*se préparer à*) to prepare to do, be about to do; **il se disposait à quitter le bureau** he was about to *ou* was preparing to *ou* was getting ready to leave the office.

dispositif [dispozitif] **nm** a (*mécanisme*) device, mechanism. **~ d'alarme** alarm *ou* warning device; **~ de sûreté** safety device. b (*moyens prévus*) plan of action. (*Mil*) **~ d'attaque** plan of attack; (*Mil*) **~ de défense** defence system; **~ de contrôle** plan of control; **~ de combat** fighting plan; **tout un ~ a été établi pour enrayer l'inflation** a complete plan of action has been drawn up to eliminate inflation; **un important ~ (policier) a été mis en place pour disperser les manifestants** a large police operation was set up *ou* a large contingent of police was brought in to disperse the demonstrators. c (*Jur*) *[jugement]* pronouncement; *[loi]* purview.

disposition [dispozisjɔ̃] **nf** a (*arrangement*) (*action*) arrangement, arranging, placing; (*résultat*) arrangement, layout. **selon la ~ des pions/des joueurs** according to how the pawns/players are placed; **ils ont changé la ~ des objets dans la vitrine** they have changed the arrangement *ou* layout of the things in the window; **cela dépend de la ~ du terrain** that depends on the situation of the ground, it depends how the ground lies; **la ~ des lieux/pièces** the layout of the premises/rooms.

b (*usage*) disposal. (*Jur*) **avoir la libre ~ de qch** to have free disposal of sth, be free to dispose of sth; **mettre qch/être à la ~ de qn** to put sth/be at sb's disposal; **la maison/la bibliothèque est à votre ~** the house/library is at your disposal, you can have the run of the house/library; **les moyens (mis) à notre ~ sont insuffisants** we have insufficient means at our disposal; **je me mets** *ou* **tiens à votre entière ~ pour de plus amples renseignements** I am entirely at your disposal *ou* service should you require further information; (*Jur*) **l'inculpé a été mis à la ~ de la justice** the accused was handed over to the law.

c (*mesures*) **~s** (*préparatifs*) arrangements, preparations; (*précautions*) measures, precautions, steps; **prendre des** *ou* **ses ~s pour que qch soit fait** to make arrangements *ou* take steps to have sth done *ou* for sth to be done; **prendre ses ~s pour partir** to make arrangements for *ou* prepare for one's departure; **nous avons prévu des ~s spéciales** we have arranged for special steps *ou* measures *ou* precautions to be taken.

d (*manière d'être*) mood, humour, frame of mind. **être dans de bonnes/mauvaises ~s** to be in a good/bad mood *ou* humour; **être dans de bonnes ~s pour faire qch** to be in the right mood to do sth, be in the right frame of mind for doing sth; **être dans les meilleures ~s** to be in the best of moods; **être dans de bonnes/de mauvaises/les meilleures ~s à l'égard de qn** to feel well-disposed/ill-disposed/most kindly disposed towards sb; **est-il toujours dans les mêmes ~s à l'égard de ce projet/candidat?** does he still feel the same way *ou* have the same feelings about this plan/candidate?; **~ d'esprit** mood, state *ou* frame of mind.

e (*inclination, aptitude*) **~s** bent, aptitude, natural ability; **avoir des ~s pour la musique/les langues/le tennis** to have a special aptitude for *ou* a gift for music/languages/tennis.

f (*tendance*) *[personne]* predisposition, tendency; *[objet]* tendency (*à* to). **avoir une ~ au rhumatisme/à contracter une maladie** to have a tendency to rheumatism/to catch an illness; **ce bateau a une curieuse/fâcheuse ~ à ...** this boat has a strange/an annoying tendency to ..., this boat is prone to ... .

g (*Jur*) clause. **~s testamentaires** provisions of a will, testamentary provisions; **~s entre vifs** donation inter vivos; *voir* **dernier**.

disproportion [dispʀɔpɔʀsjɔ̃] **nf** disproportion (*de* in).

disproportionné, e [dispʀɔpɔʀsjɔne] **adj** disproportionate (*à, avec* to), out of (all) proportion (*à, avec* with). **il a une tête ~e** his head is disproportionately *ou* abnormally large; **un salaire ~ au travail** a salary which is disproportionate to *ou* out of (all) proportion with the work.

dispute [dispyt] **nf** a (*querelle*) argument, quarrel. **~ d'amoureux** lovers' tiff *ou* quarrel. b (††*: débat polémique*) debate, dispute.

disputé, e [dispyte] (**ptp de disputer**) **adj** *match* close, closely fought; *siège de député* hotly contested.

disputer [dispyte] 1 **1** **vt** a (*contester*) **~ qch/qn à qn** to fight with sb for *ou* over sth/sb; **~ la victoire/la première place à son rival** to fight for victory/for first place with one's rival, fight one's rival for victory/first place; **elle essaya de lui ~ la gloire de son invention** she tried to rob him of the glory of his invention; (*littér*) **le ~ en beauté/en grandeur à qn** to vie with *ou* rival sb in beauty/greatness; **~ le terrain** (*Mil*) to fight for every inch of ground; (*fig*) to fight every inch of the way.

b (*livrer*) *combat* to fight; *match* to play. **le match a été disputé** *ou* **s'est disputé en Angleterre** the match was played *ou* took place in England.

c (**: gronder*) to tell off*, tick off* (*Brit*). **se faire ~ par son père** to get a telling-off* *ou* ticking-off* (*Brit*) from one's father.

2 se disputer **vpr** a (*se quereller*) to quarrel, argue, have a quarrel *ou* an argument (*avec* with). **il s'est disputé avec son oncle** he quarrelled *ou* had a quarrel *ou* an argument with his uncle, he fell out with his uncle.

b (*se battre pour*) **se ~ qch** to fight over sth, contest sth; **deux chiens se disputent un os** two dogs are fighting over a bone; **deux candidats se disputent un siège à l'Académie** two candidates are contesting a seat at the Academy.

disquaire [diskɛʀ] **nm** (*commerçant*) record-dealer.

disqualification [diskalifikasjɔ̃] nf (*Sport*) disqualification.

disqualifier [diskalifje] 7 vt a (*Sport: exclure*) to disqualify. b (*fig: discréditer*) to dishonour, bring discredit on. **il s'est disqualifié aux yeux de l'opinion** he has destroyed people's trust in him *ou* people's good opinion of him.

disque [disk] nm a (*gén, Méd, Phot*) disc, disk. ~ **d'embrayage** clutch plate; ~ **de stationnement** parking disk; *voir* **frein**. b (*Sport*) discus. c (*Mus*) record, disc*. ~ **microsillon** long-playing record, L.P.; ~ **compact/laser** compact/laser disc; ~ **optique compact** compact optical disc; ~ **optique numérique** digital optical disk; ~ **vidéo** video disc. d (*Ordin*) disc, disk. ~ **dur/souple/optique/laser** hard/floppy/optical/laser disc *ou* disk.

disquette [diskɛt] nf (*Ordin*) floppy (disc *ou* disk), diskette (*US*).

dissection [disɛksjɔ̃] nf dissection. **de** ~ *instrument, table* dissecting, dissection.

dissemblable [disɑ̃blabl] adj dissimilar, different (*de* from, to).

dissemblance [disɑ̃blɑ̃s] nf dissimilarity, difference (*de* in).

dissémination [diseminasjɔ̃] nf a (*action*) *[graines]* scattering; *[troupes, maisons, usines]* scattering, spreading; *[idées]* dissemination. b (*état*) *[maisons, points de vente]* scattered layout *ou* distribution. **à cause de la** ~ **de notre famille** because our family is scattered.

disséminer [disemine] 1 1 vt *graines* to scatter; *troupes, maisons* to scatter, spread (out); *idées* to disseminate. **les points de vente sont très disséminés** the (sales) outlets are widely scattered *ou* thinly distributed. 2 **se disséminer** vpr *[graines]* to scatter; *[personnes]* to spread (out). **les pique-niqueurs se disséminèrent aux quatre coins de la forêt** the picnickers spread out *ou* scattered to the four corners of the forest.

dissension [disɑ̃sjɔ̃] nf dissension.

dissentiment [disɑ̃timɑ̃] nm disagreement, difference of opinion.

disséquer [diseke] 6 vt (*lit, fig*) to dissect.

dissertation [disɛʀtasjɔ̃] nf (*Scol, hum*) essay; (*péj*, ††: *traité*) dissertation.

disserter [disɛʀte] 1 vi a (*Scol*) ~ **sur** (*parler*) to speak on, discourse upon (*frm*); (*écrire*) to write an essay on. b (*péj*) to hold forth (*de, sur* about, on).

dissidence [disidɑ̃s] nf (*sécession*) (*Pol*) rebellion, dissidence; (*Rel*) dissent; (*dissidents*) rebels, dissidents; (*littér: divergence*) disagreement, dissidence. **entrer en** ~ to break away, rebel; **être en** ~ to have broken away; **rejoindre la** ~ to join the dissidents *ou* the rebels.

dissident, e [disidɑ̃, ɑ̃t] 1 adj (*Pol*) dissident; (*Rel*) dissenting. **groupe** ~ breakaway *ou* splinter group; **une fraction ~e de cette organisation terroriste** a dissident minority in this terrorist organization. 2 nm,f (*Pol*) rebel, dissident; (*Rel*) dissenter.

dissimilation [disimilasjɔ̃] nf (*Ling*) dissimilation.

dissimilitude [disimilityd] nf dissimilarity.

dissimulateur, -trice [disimylatœʀ, tʀis] 1 adj dissembling. 2 nm,f dissembler.

dissimulation [disimylasjɔ̃] nf (*NonC: duplicité*) dissimulation, dissembling; (*cachotterie*) dissimulation (*NonC*), dissembling (*NonC*); (*action de cacher*) concealment. **agir avec** ~ to act in an underhand way; (*Jur*) ~ **d'actif** (fraudulent) concealment of assets.

dissimulé, e [disimyle] (**ptp de dissimuler**) adj *caractère, enfant* secretive.

dissimuler [disimyle] 1 1 vt (*cacher*) *objet, personne, sentiment, difficulté* to conceal, hide (*à qn* from sb); (*Fin*) *bénéfices* to conceal; (*déguiser*) *sentiment, difficulté, défaut* to conceal, disguise. **il sait bien** ~ he's good at pretending *ou* dissembling (*frm*); **il parvenait mal à** ~ **son impatience/son envie de rire** he had great difficulty in covering up *ou* disguising *ou* hiding his annoyance/his urge to laugh; **je ne vous dissimulerai pas qu'il y a de gros problèmes** I won't disguise *ou* conceal the fact that there are serious problems.
2 **se dissimuler** vpr to conceal *ou* hide o.s. **il essaie de se** ~ **la vérité/qu'il a tort** he tries to close his eyes to the truth/to the fact that he's wrong, he tries to conceal the truth from himself/to conceal from himself the fact that he's wrong.

dissipateur, -trice [disipatœʀ, tʀis] 1 adj wasteful, extravagant, prodigal. 2 nm,f spendthrift, squanderer, prodigal.

dissipation [disipasjɔ̃] nf a (*indiscipline*) misbehaviour, unruliness; (*littér: débauche*) dissipation. **une vie de** ~ a dissipated life, a life of dissipation. b (*dilapidation*) *[fortune]* squandering, dissipation; (*folle dépense*) extravagance. c *[fumée, nuage]* dissipation, dispersal; *[brouillard]* clearing, lifting, dispersal; *[craintes]* dispelling. **après** ~ **des brouillards matinaux** after the early morning fog has lifted *ou* cleared.

dissipé, e [disipe] (**ptp de dissiper**) adj *élève* undisciplined, unruly; *vie* dissolute, dissipated.

dissiper [disipe] 1 1 vt a (*chasser*) *brouillard, fumée* to dispel, disperse, clear away; *nuage* to break up, disperse; *soupçon, crainte* to dissipate, dispel; *malentendu* to clear up.
b (*dilapider*) *fortune* to dissipate, squander, fritter away; *jeunesse* to waste, dissipate, idle away; (*littér*) *santé* to ruin, destroy.
c ~ **qn** to lead sb astray *ou* into bad ways; **il dissipe ses petits camarades en classe** he is a distracting influence on *ou* he distracts his little friends in class.
2 **se dissiper** vpr a (*disparaître*) *[fumée]* to drift away, disperse; *[nuages]* to break (up), disperse; *[brouillard]* to clear, lift, disperse; *[inquiétude]* to vanish, melt away; *[malaise, fatigue]* to disappear, go away, wear off.
b *[élève]* to become undisciplined *ou* unruly, misbehave.

dissociable [disɔsjabl] adj *molécules* dissociable, separable; *problèmes* separable.

dissociation [disɔsjasjɔ̃] nf *[molécules, problèmes]* dissociation, separation.

dissocier [disɔsje] 7 1 vt *molécules, problèmes* to dissociate. 2 **se dissocier** vpr *[éléments, groupe, équipe]* to break up, split up. **nous tenons à nous** ~ **de ces groupes/vues** we are anxious to dissociate ourselves from these groups/views.

dissolu, e [disɔly] adj dissolute.

dissolubilité [disɔlybilite] nf (*voir* **dissoluble**) dissolubility; solubility.

dissoluble [disɔlybl] adj *assemblée* dissoluble; *substance* soluble.

dissolution [disɔlysjɔ̃] nf a (*Jur*) *[assemblée, mariage]* dissolution; *[groupe, parti]* dissolution, disbanding; *[compagnie]* winding-up, dismantling. **prononcer la** ~ **de** *mariage* to dissolve; *parti, groupement* to disband. b (*désagrégation*) *[groupe, association]* breaking-up, splitting-up; *[empire]* crumbling, decay, dissolution. **l'unité nationale est en pleine** ~ national unity is crumbling *ou* disintegrating *ou* falling apart. c *[sucre etc]* dissolving. **tourner jusqu'à** ~ **complète du cachet** stir until the tablet has completely dissolved. d (*colle*) rubber solution. e (*littér: débauche*) dissoluteness, dissipation.

dissolvant, e [disɔlvɑ̃, ɑ̃t] 1 adj (*lit*) solvent, dissolvent; (*fig*) *doctrines* undermining (*épith*), demoralizing; *climat* debilitating. 2 nm (*produit*) solvent. (*pour les ongles*) ~ (**gras**) nail polish *ou* varnish remover.

dissonance [disɔnɑ̃s] nf (*Mus*) (*intervalle*) dissonance, discord; *[couleurs, styles]* mismatch; (*fig*) clash; (*manque d'harmonie*) discord, dissonance. (*fig*) **des ~s de tons dans un tableau** clashes of colour in a painting.

dissonant, e [disɔnɑ̃, ɑ̃t] adj *sons, accord* dissonant, discordant; *couleurs* clashing (*épith*).

dissoudre [disudʀ] 51 1 vt a *sel* to dissolve. **faire** ~ **du sucre** to dissolve sugar. b (*Jur, Pol*) *assemblée* to dissolve; *parti, groupement* to disband, break up; *mariage* to dissolve. 2 **se dissoudre** vpr a *[sel, sucre]* to dissolve, be dissolved. b *[association]* to disband, break up.

dissuader [disɥade] 1 vt to dissuade (*de qch* from sth, *de faire* from doing). **il m'a dissuadé d'y aller** he talked me out of going, he persuaded me not to go.

dissuasif, -ive [disɥazif, iv] adj dissuasive. **avoir un effet** ~ **sur** to have a dissuasive *ou* deterrent effect upon; **à un prix** ~ at too high a price.

dissuasion [disɥazjɔ̃] nf dissuasion; *voir* **force**.

dissyllabe [disi(l)lab] 1 adj disyllabic. 2 nm disyllable.

dissyllabique [disi(l)labik] adj disyllabic.

dissymétrie [disimetʀi] nf dissymmetry.

dissymétrique [disimetʀik] adj dissymmetric(al).

distance [distɑ̃s] nf a (*éloignement, intervalle, trajet*) distance. **à quelle** ~ **est la gare?** how far (away) is the station?, what's the distance to the station?; **parcourir de grandes/petites ~s** to cover great/small distances; (*Sport*) **il est meilleur sur les grandes ~s** he's better over long distances; **habiter à une grande ~/à quelques kilomètres de** ~ to live a great distance away *ou* a long way away/a few kilometres away (*de* from); **entendre un bruit/distinguer qch à une** ~ **de 30 mètres** to hear a noise/make out sth from a distance of 30 metres *ou* from 30 metres away; **à 2 ou 3 ans de** ~ **je m'en souviens encore** 2 or 3 years later I can still remember it; **nés à quelques années de** ~ born within a few years of one another, born a few years apart; **quelle** ~ **parcourue depuis son dernier roman!** what a long way *ou* how far he has come since his last novel!
b (*écart*) gap. **la** ~ **qui sépare deux générations/points de vue** the gap between *ou* which separates two generations/points of view; **la guerre a mis une grande** ~ **entre ces deux peuples** the war has left a great gulf between these two nations.
c (*loc*) **garder ses ~s** to keep one's distance (*vis à vis de* from); **prendre ses ~s** (*Mil*) to form open order; (*Scol etc*) to space out; (*fig*) to stand aloof (*à l'égard de* from), distance o.s. (*par rapport à* from); **les syndicats ont pris leurs ~s vis-à-vis du gouvernement** the unions have distanced themselves from the government; **tenir qn à** ~ to keep sb at a distance *ou* at arm's length; **se tenir à** ~ to keep one's distance, stand aloof; **tenir qn à une** ~ **respectueuse** to keep sb at arm's length; **se tenir à une** ~ **respectueuse de** to keep *ou* stay a respectful distance from; **tenir la** ~ *[coureur]* to go *ou* do *ou* cover the distance, last *ou* stay the course; *[conférencier]* to stay *ou* last the course; **de** ~ **en** ~ at intervals, here and there; **à** ~ (*dans l'espace*) at *ou* from a distance, from afar; (*dans le temps*) at *ou* from a distance; **le prestidigitateur fait bouger des objets à** ~ the conjurer moves objects from a distance; **mettre en marche à** ~ *appareil* to start up by remote control; (*Phot*) ~ **focale** focal length; *voir* **commande**.

distancer [distɑ̃se] 3 vt a *coureur* to outrun, outdistance, leave behind; *voiture* to outdistance, leave behind; *concurrent, élève* to outstrip, outclass, leave behind. **se laisser** *ou* **se faire** ~ to be left behind, be outdistanced (*par* by); **ne nous laissons pas ~** let's not fall behind *ou* be left behind. b (*Sport: disqualifier*) to disqualify.

distanciation [distɑ̃sjasjɔ̃] **nf** distance. **parvenir à faire une ~ par rapport à qch** to manage to distance o.s. from sth.

distancier (se) [distɑ̃sje] 7 **vpr** to distance o.s. (*de* from)

distant, e [distɑ̃, ɑ̃t] **adj** a *lieu* far-off, faraway, distant; *événement* distant, far-off. **~ d'un lieu** far away from a place; **une ville ~e de 10 km** a town 10 km away; **deux villes ~es de 10 km (l'une de l'autre)** two towns 10 km apart *ou* 10 km away from one another. b *attitude* distant, aloof. **il s'est montré très ~** he was very stand-offish.

distendre [distɑ̃dʀ] 41 1 **vt** *peau* to distend; *muscle, corde,* (*fig*) *lien* to strain. 2 **se distendre vpr** *[lien]* to slacken, become looser; *[ventre, peau]* to distend, become distended *ou* bloated.

distendu, e [distɑ̃dy] (**ptp de distendre**) **adj** *ventre* distended, bloated; *corde* slack, loose; *ressort* slack.

distension [distɑ̃sjɔ̃] **nf** *[peau, estomac]* distension; *[corde]* slackening, loosening.

distillateur [distilatœʀ] **nm** (*personne*) distiller.

distillation [distilasjɔ̃] **nf** distillation, distilling.

distiller [distile] 1 **vt** *alcool* to distil; *suc* to elaborate; (*fig*) *ennui, venin* to exude. **eau distillée** distilled water.

distillerie [distilʀi] **nf** (*usine*) distillery; (*industrie*) distilling.

distinct, e [distɛ̃(kt), ɛ̃kt] **adj** a (*indépendant*) distinct, separate (*de* from). b (*net*) distinct, clear.

distinctement [distɛ̃ktəmɑ̃] **adv** distinctly, clearly.

distinctif, -ive [distɛ̃ktif, iv] **adj** distinctive.

distinction [distɛ̃ksjɔ̃] **nf** a (*différentiation*) distinction. **faire la ~ entre** to make a distinction between; **sans ~ (de race)** without distinction (of race). b (*décoration, honneur*) distinction. c (*raffinement*) distinction, refinement. **il a de la ~** he is very distinguished *ou* refined, he has great distinction. d (*éminence*) distinction, eminence. (*frm*) **un pianiste de la plus haute ~** a pianist of the highest distinction.

distinguable [distɛ̃gabl] **adj** distinguishable.

distingué, e [distɛ̃ge] (**ptp de distinguer**) **adj** a (*élégant, bien élevé*) *personne* distinguished; *allure* elegant, refined, distinguished. **il a l'air très ~** he looks very distinguished, he has a very distinguished look about him; **ça fait très ~** it's very distinguished. b (*illustre*) distinguished, eminent. **notre ~ collègue, le professeur X** our distinguished *ou* eminent colleague, Professor X. c (*formule épistolaire*) **veuillez agréer l'expression de mes sentiments ~s** *ou* **de ma considération ~e** yours faithfully (*Brit*), yours truly, sincerely yours.

distinguer [distɛ̃ge] 1 1 **vt** a (*percevoir*) *objet, bruit* to make out, distinguish, perceive; *ironie* to distinguish, perceive. **~ qn dans la foule** to pick out *ou* spot sb in the crowd; **on commença à ~ les collines à travers la brume** the hills began to be visible through the mist, you could begin to make out the hills through the mist; **il distingue mal sans lunettes** he can't see very well without his glasses.

b (*différencier*) to distinguish. **~ une chose d'une autre** *ou* **d'avec une autre** to distinguish *ou* tell one thing from another; **savoir ~ les oiseaux/plantes** to be able to distinguish birds/plants; **les deux sœurs sont difficiles à ~ (l'une de l'autre)** the two sisters are difficult to tell apart; **~ le bien du mal/un Picasso d'un** *ou* **d'avec un Braque** to tell good from evil/a Picasso from a Braque, distinguish between good and evil/ between a Picasso and a Braque; **tu la distingueras à sa veste rouge** you will recognize her *ou* pick her out by her red jacket; **distinguons, il y a chanteur et chanteur** we must make a distinction, there are singers and singers *ou* good singers and bad singers.

c (*rendre différent*) to distinguish, set apart (*de* from), mark off. **c'est son accent qui le distingue des autres** it is his accent which distinguishes him from *ou* makes him different from the others *ou* which sets him apart.

d (*frm*) (*choisir*) to single out; (*honorer*) to honour. **on l'a distingué pour faire le discours d'adieu** he was singled out to make the farewell speech; **l'Académie Française a distingué X pour son œuvre poétique** the Académie Française has honoured X for his works of poetry.

2 **se distinguer vpr** a (*différer*) to distinguish o.s., be distinguished (*de* from). **ces objets se distinguent par** *ou* **grâce à leur couleur** these objects can be distinguished by their colour; **les deux frères se distinguent (l'un de l'autre) par leur taille** you can tell the two brothers apart by their (different) height; **il se distingue par son accent/sa démarche** his accent/his way of walking makes him stand out *ou* makes him seem quite different.

b (*se signaler, réussir*) to distinguish o.s. **se ~ (pendant une guerre) par son courage** to distinguish o.s. (in a war) by one's courage; **il s'est distingué par ses découvertes en physique** he has become famous for *ou* from his discoveries in physics, he's made a name for himself by his discoveries in physics; (*hum*) **il se distingue par son absence** he is noticeable *ou* conspicuous by his absence; **il s'est particulièrement distingué en latin** he has done particularly well *ou* he has particularly distinguished himself in Latin.

distinguo [distɛ̃go] **nm** (*nuance*) distinction.

distique [distik] **nm** distich.

distordre vt, se distordre vpr [distɔʀdʀ] 41 to twist, distort.

distorsion [distɔʀsjɔ̃] **nf** (*gén, Anat, Téléc*) distortion; (*déséquilibre*) imbalance, disequilibrium; (*Jur*) bias.

distraction [distʀaksjɔ̃] **nf** a (*inattention*) absent-mindedness, abstraction, lack of attention. **j'ai eu une ~** my concentration lapsed, my attention wandered; **cette ~ lui a coûté la vie** this one lapse in concentration cost him his life; **les ~s proverbiales des savants** the proverbial absent-mindedness of scientists. b (*passe-temps*) leisure *ou* recreational activity, pastime. **ça manque de ~** there's not much in the way of entertainment; **c'est sa seule ~** it's his only form of entertainment. c (*Jur: vol*) abstraction. **~ de fonds** misappropriation of funds.

distraire [distʀɛʀ] 50 1 **vt** a (*divertir*) to entertain, divert, amuse. b (*déranger*) to distract, divert (*de* from). **~ l'attention de qn** to distract sb's attention; (*Scol*) **il distrait ses camarades** he distracts his friends; **se laisser facilement ~ de son travail** to be easily distracted from one's work; **~ qn de son chagrin** to take sb's mind off his grief. c (*frm: voler*) to abstract (*de* from). **~ des fonds** to misappropriate funds. 2 **se distraire vpr** to amuse o.s., enjoy o.s. **j'ai envie d'aller au cinéma pour me distraire** I feel like going to the cinema – it'll take my mind off things.

distrait, e [distʀɛ, ɛt] (**ptp de distraire**) **adj** *personne, caractère* absent-minded; *attitude* inattentive, abstracted. **d'un air ~** absent-mindedly, abstractedly; **d'une oreille ~e** with only half an ear, abstractedly.

distraitement [distʀɛtmɑ̃] **adv** absent-mindedly, abstractedly.

distrayant, e [distʀɛjɑ̃, ɑ̃t] **adj** entertaining, diverting. **les romans policiers sont d'une lecture ~e** detective novels make pleasant light reading.

distribanque [distʀibɑ̃k] **nm** cash dispenser, cashomat (*US*), automated telling machine.

distribuer [distʀibɥe] 1 **vt** a (*donner*) *objets* to distribute, give out, hand out; *vivres* to distribute, share out; *courrier* to deliver; *récompense* to distribute, present; (*Fin*) *actions* to allot; *travail, rôle* to give out, allot, allocate, distribute; *argent, dividendes* to distribute, hand out; *cartes* to deal (out); *ordres* to hand out, deal out; *coups* to deal, deliver; *saluts, sourires, enseignement* to dispense (*à* to). **~ des claques à qn** to slap sb.

b (*répartir*) to distribute, arrange; (*Typ*) *caractères* to distribute. **on distribue ces plantes en 4 espèces** these plants are divided into 4 species; **savoir ~ son temps** to know how to allocate *ou* divide (up) one's time; **comment les pièces sont-elles distribuées?** how are the rooms set out? *ou* laid out?; **~ les masses dans un tableau** to arrange *ou* distribute the masses in a picture; **mon emploi du temps est mal distribué** my timetable is badly arranged.

c (*amener*) to distribute, carry. **~ l'eau dans les campagnes** to distribute *ou* carry *ou* supply water to country areas; **le sang est distribué dans tout le corps par le cœur** blood is pumped *ou* carried round the body by the heart.

d (*Comm*) *film, produit* to distribute.

distributeur, -trice [distʀibytœʀ, tʀis] 1 **nm,f** (*agent commercial*) distributor. 2 **nm** (*appareil*) machine; *[savon]* dispenser; (*Aut*) distributor. **~ automatique** vending machine, slot machine; (*Banque*) **~ automatique de billets** cash dispenser, cashomat (*US*), automatic telling machine; (*Rail*) **~ de billets** ticket machine; (*Agr*) **~ d'engrais** manure- *ou* muck-spreader.

distributif, -ive [distʀibytif, iv] **adj** distributive.

distribution [distʀibysjɔ̃] **nf** a *[objets]* distribution, giving out, handing out; *[vivres]* distribution, sharing out; *[argent, dividendes]* distribution; *[cartes]* deal; *[courrier]* delivery; (*Fin*) *[actions]* allotment. **la ~ du travail sera faite suivant l'âge** the work will be shared out *ou* allotted *ou* allocated according to age; **~ gratuite** free gifts; **~ des prix** prize giving (day).

b (*répartition*) distribution, arrangement. **la ~ des mots dans une phrase** the distribution of words in a sentence; **la ~ des meubles dans une pièce** the arrangement of the furniture in a room; **cet appartement a une bonne/mauvaise ~ (des pièces)** the flat is well/badly laid out; (*fig*) **ce résultat a conduit à une nouvelle ~ des cartes** this result has shifted *ou* altered the balance of power *ou* has given a new look to the situation.

c (*Ciné, Théât: acteurs*) cast. **~ par ordre d'entrée en scène** cast *ou* characters in order of appearance; **qui est responsable de la ~ de cette pièce?** who's in charge of casting this play?

d (*acheminement*) *[eau, électricité]* supply.

e (*Comm*) *[livres, films]* distribution. **nos réseaux de ~** our distribution network; **grande ~** mass marketing.

f (*Aut, Tech*) distribution.

distributionnel, -elle [distʀibysjɔnɛl] **adj** distributional.

distributivement [distʀibytivmɑ̃] **adv** distributively.

distributivité [distʀibytivite] **nf** distributiveness.

district [distʀikt] **nm** district.

dit [di] **nm** a (*Littérat*) story, tale. b **le ~ et le non-dit** what is said and what is left unsaid.

dithyrambe [ditiʀɑ̃b] **nm** (*poème*) dithyramb; (*éloge*) panegyric, eulogy.

dithyrambique [ditiʀɑ̃bik] **adj** *paroles* laudatory, eulogistic; *éloges* extravagant; (*Littérat*) dithyrambic. **une critique ~** a rave review.

dito [dito] **adv** (*Comm*) ditto.

DIU [deiy] nm (abrév de **dispositif intra-utérin**) IUD.
diurèse [djyʀɛz] nf (*Physiol*) diuresis.
diurétique [djyʀetik] adj, nm diuretic.
diurne [djyʀn] adj diurnal.
diva [diva] nf († *ou hum*) diva, prima donna.
divagation [divagasjɔ̃] nf (*gén pl*) (*délire*) wandering, rambling; (*bêtises*) raving.
divaguer [divage] 1 vi (*délirer*) to ramble; (**: dire des bêtises*) to rave. **il commence à ~** he is beginning to ramble, his mind is beginning to wander; **tu divagues!*** you're off your head!*
divan [divɑ̃] nm divan (*seat*); (*Hist*) divan. **~-lit** divan (bed).
divergence [divɛʀʒɑ̃s] nf (*voir* **diverger**) divergence; difference.
divergent, e [divɛʀʒɑ̃, ɑ̃t] adj (*voir* **diverger**) divergent; differing.
diverger [divɛʀʒe] 3 vi *[chemins, rayons]* to diverge; *[opinions]* to diverge, differ.
divers, e [divɛʀ, ɛʀs] adj a (*pl*) (*varié*) *couleurs, coutumes, opinions* diverse, varied; (*différent*) *sens d'un mot, moments, occupations* different, various. **frais ~, dépenses ~es** sundries, miscellaneous expenses; *voir* **fait**[1]. b (*pl: plusieurs*) various, several. **~es personnes m'en ont parlé** various *ou* several people have spoken to me about it. c (*littér: changeant*) *spectacle* varied, changing (*épith*).
diversement [divɛʀsəmɑ̃] adv in various ways, in diverse ways. **son livre a été ~ reçu** his book has had a varied *ou* mixed reception.
diversification [divɛʀsifikasjɔ̃] nf diversification.
diversifier [divɛʀsifje] 7 1 vt *méthodes, exercices* to vary; *production* to diversify. **avoir une économie/une gamme de produits diversifiée** to have a varied *ou* diversified economy/range of products; **nous devons nous ~ davantage** we must diversify (our production) more. 2 **se diversifier** vpr (*Écon*) to diversify.
diversion [divɛʀsjɔ̃] nf (*Mil, littér*) diversion. **faire ~** to create a diversion; **faire ~ au chagrin de qn** to take sb's mind off his sorrow.
diversité [divɛʀsite] nf (*grand nombre*) *[opinions, possibilités]* range, variety; (*variété*) *[sujet, spectacle]* variety, diversity; (*divergence: entre deux opinions etc*) diversity, difference, divergence.
divertir [divɛʀtiʀ] 2 1 vt a (*amuser*) to amuse, entertain, divert. b (*frm: voler*) to abstract, divert. **~ des fonds/une succession** to misappropriate funds/an inheritance. c (*††: détourner*) to distract (*de* from). **~ qn d'un projet** to distract sb's mind from a plan. 2 **se divertir** vpr to amuse o.s., enjoy o.s. **se ~ l'esprit** to occupy one's mind, amuse *ou* entertain o.s.; (*littér*) **se ~ de qn** to make fun of sb, laugh at sb.
divertissant, e [divɛʀtisɑ̃, ɑ̃t] adj amusing, entertaining, diverting.
divertissement [divɛʀtismɑ̃] nm a (*NonC: amusement*) diversion, recreation, relaxation; (*passe-temps*) distraction, entertainment, amusement, diversion. b (*Mus*) divertimento, divertissement. c (*Jur: vol*) misappropriation. d (*Philos ou* ††) distraction.
dividende [dividɑ̃d] nm (*Fin, Math*) dividend. **~ sous forme d'actions** share *ou* stock dividend; **~ prioritaire** preferential *ou* preference dividend; **avec ~** cum div(idend), dividend on (*US*); **sans ~** ex div(idend), dividend off (*US*).
divin, e [divɛ̃, in] adj a *caractère, justice, service* divine, heavenly. **le ~ Achille** the divine Achilles; **la ~e Providence** divine Providence; **notre ~ Père/Sauveur** our Holy *ou* Heavenly Father/Saviour; **l'amour ~** sacred *ou* holy *ou* divine *ou* heavenly love; **le sens du ~** the sense of the divine; *voir* **bonté, droit**[3]. b (**: excellent*) *poésie, beauté, mets, robe, temps* divine*, heavenly.
divinateur, -trice [divinatœʀ, tʀis] 1 adj divining, foreseeing. **instinct ~** instinctive foresight. 2 nm,f (††) diviner, soothsayer.
divination [divinasjɔ̃] nf divination.
divinatoire [divinatwaʀ] adj *science* divinatory.
divinement [divinmɑ̃] adv divinely.
divinisation [divinizasjɔ̃] nf deification.
diviniser [divinize] 1 vt to deify.
divinité [divinite] nf (*essence divine*) divinity; (*lit, fig: dieu*) deity, divinity.
diviser [divize] 1 1 vt a (*fractionner*) (*gén*) to divide; *tâche, ressources* to share out, split up; *gâteau* to cut up, divide up *ou* out. **~ une somme en 3/en 3 parties** to divide *ou* split a sum of money in 3/into 3 parts; **~ une somme entre plusieurs personnes** to share (out) *ou* divide (out) a sum among several people; **le pays est divisé en deux par des montagnes** the country is split *ou* divided in two by mountains; **~ un groupe en plusieurs équipes** to split a group up into several teams; **ce livre se divise en plusieurs chapitres** this book is divided into several chapters.
b (*désunir*) *famille, adversaires* to divide, set at variance. **"~ pour (mieux) régner"** "divide and rule"; **une famille divisée** a broken family; **les historiens sont très divisés à ce sujet** historians are very divided on this subject; **l'opinion est divisée en deux par cette affaire** opinion is split *ou* divided over this affair.
c (*†: séparer*) to divide, separate. **un rideau divise la chambre d'avec le salon** *ou* **du salon** a curtain separates the bedroom (off) from the drawing room.
d (*Math*) to divide. **~ 4 par 2** to divide 4 by 2.
2 **se diviser** vpr a (*se scinder*) *[groupe, cellules]* to split up, divide (*en* into).
b (*se ramifier*) *[route]* to fork, divide; *[tronc d'arbre]* to fork.
diviseur [divizœʀ] nm a (*Math*) divisor. **nombre/fraction ~** divisor number/fraction; **plus grand commun ~** highest common factor. b (*personne*) divisive force *ou* influence.
divisibilité [divizibilite] nf divisibility.
divisible [divizibl] adj divisible.
division [divizjɔ̃] nf a (*fractionnement*) division; (*partage*) sharing out, division (*en* into). **~ du travail** division of labour; **~ cellulaire** cellular division. b (*désaccord*) division. **il y a une ~ au sein du parti** there's a split *ou* rift within the party; **semer la ~** to sow discord (*entre* among). c (*Math*) division. **faire une ~** to do a division (sum). d (*section, service, circonscription*) division; (*Scol: classe*) group, section; (*Mil, Ftbl*) division. (*Mil*) **~ blindée** armoured division; *voir* **général.** e (*graduation, compartiment*) division. f (*chapitre*) *[livre, discours, exposé]* division; (*branche*) *[science]* division.
divisionnaire [divizjɔnɛʀ] 1 adj divisional. 2 nm (*Mil* †) major-general. (*Police*) **(commissaire) ~** ≃ chief superintendent (*Brit*), police chief (*US*).
divorce [divɔʀs] nm (*lit, fig*) divorce (*avec, d'avec* from). **demander le ~** to sue for (a) divorce, ask for a divorce; **obtenir le ~** to obtain *ou* get a divorce; **~ par consentement mutuel** divorce by consent (*Brit*), no-fault divorce (*US*).
divorcé, e [divɔʀse] (ptp de **divorcer**) 1 adj (*lit, fig*) divorced (*de* from). 2 nm,f divorcee.
divorcer [divɔʀse] 3 vi a (*Jur*) to get a divorce, be *ou* get divorced. **~ d'avec sa femme/son mari** to divorce one's wife/husband. b (*fig*) to break (*d'avec, de* with).
divulgateur, -trice [divylgatœʀ, tʀis] nm,f divulger.
divulgation [divylgasjɔ̃] nf disclosure, divulging, divulgence.
divulguer [divylge] 1 vt to divulge, disclose.
dix [dis] 1 adj inv, nm ten. **les ~ commandements** the Ten Commandments; **elle a eu ~ sur ~** she got ten out of ten, she got full marks; **avoir ~ dixièmes à chaque œil** to have twenty-twenty vision; **répéter/recommencer ~ fois la même chose** to repeat/start the same thing over and over (again); *pour autres loc voir* **six.** 2 comp ▸**dix-huit** adj inv, nm eighteen ▸**dix-huitième** adj, nmf eighteenth ▸**dix-huitièmement** adv in (the) eighteenth place ▸**dix-neuf** adj inv, nm nineteen ▸**dix-neuvième** adj, nmf nineteenth ▸**dix-neuvièmement** adv in (the) nineteenth place ▸**dix-sept** adj inv, nm seventeen ▸**dix-septième** adj, nmf seventeenth ▸**dix-septièmement** adv in (the) seventeenth place.
dixième [dizjɛm] adj, nmf tenth. **un ~ (de la Loterie nationale)** *a tenth share in a ticket (in the National Lottery)*.
dixièmement [dizjɛmmɑ̃] adv tenthly, in (the) tenth place.
dixit [diksit] loc verb dixit.
dizain [dizɛ̃] nm ten-line poem.
dizaine [dizɛn] nf (*dix*) ten; (*quantité voisine de dix*) about ten, ten or so; **des ~s et des ~s de fois** over and over (again), countless times, hundreds* *ou* thousands* of times.
djellaba [dʒɛ(l)laba] nf jellaba.
Djibouti [dʒibuti] nm Djibouti.
djiboutien, -ienne [dʒibusjɛ̃, jɛn] 1 adj of *ou* from Djibouti. 2 nm,f: **D~(ne)** inhabitant *ou* native of Djibouti.
djihad [dʒi(j)ad] nf jihad, jehad.
djinn [dʒin] nm jinn, djinn.
dl (abrév de **décilitre**) dl.
DM (abrév de **Deutsche Mark**) DM.
dm (abrév de **décimètre**) dm.
Dniepr [dnjɛpʀ] nm Dnieper.
do [do] nm inv (*Mus*) (*note*) C; (*en chantant la gamme*) doh. **le ~ du milieu du piano** middle C.
doberman [dɔbɛʀman] nm Doberman pinscher.
doc [dɔk] nf abrév de **documentation.**
docile [dɔsil] adj *personne, caractère* docile, meek, obedient; *animal* docile; *cheveux* manageable.
docilement [dɔsilmɑ̃] adv docilely, obediently.
docilité [dɔsilite] nf docility, obedience.
docimologie [dɔsimɔlɔʒi] nf (statistical) analysis of test *ou* exam results.
dock [dɔk] nm a (*bassin*) dock; (*cale de construction*) dockyard. **~ de carénage/flottant** dry/floating dock. b (*hangar, bâtiment*) warehouse.
docker [dɔkɛʀ] nm docker, stevedore.
docte [dɔkt] adj (*littér, hum*) learned.
doctement [dɔktəmɑ̃] adv (*littér, hum*) learnedly.
docteur [dɔktœʀ] nm (*gén, Univ*) doctor (*ès, en* of); (*Méd*) doctor. **~ en médecine** doctor of medicine; (*Méd*) **le ~ Lebrun** Dr Lebrun; (*Univ*) **maintenant que tu es ~** now you've got your doctorate *ou* Ph.D.; **Monsieur Leroux, ~ ès lettres** Dr Leroux, Ph.D.; (*Rel*) **les ~s de l'Église** the Doctors of the Church.
doctoral, e, mpl **-aux** [dɔktɔʀal, o] adj (*péj: pédantesque*) *ton* pompous, bombastic.
doctoralement [dɔktɔʀalmɑ̃] adv (*péj*) pompously, bombastically.
doctorat [dɔktɔʀa] nm doctorate (*ès, en* in). **~ de 3e cycle, ~ d'État** doctorate, ≃ Ph.D.

doctoresse [dɔktɔʀɛs] **nf** lady doctor.
doctrinaire [dɔktʀinɛʀ] 1 **adj** (*dogmatique*) doctrinaire; (*sentencieux*) pompous, sententious. 2 **nmf** doctrinarian.
doctrinal, e, **mpl -aux** [dɔktʀinal, o] **adj** doctrinal.
doctrine [dɔktʀin] **nf** doctrine, tenet.
document [dɔkymɑ̃] **nm** document. **nous avons des ~s le prouvant** we have documentary evidence (of that), we have documents to prove it; **~ de référence** *ou* **d'information** background paper; **~ d'expédition** dispatch documents.
documentaire [dɔkymɑ̃tɛʀ] 1 **adj** *intérêt* documentary. **à titre ~** for your (*ou* his *etc*) information. 2 **nm** (*film*) documentary (film).
documentaliste [dɔkymɑ̃talist] **nmf** (*Presse, TV*) researcher; (*Scol*) (assistant) librarian.
documentariste [dɔkymɑ̃taʀist] **nmf** maker of documentaries.
documentation [dɔkymɑ̃tasjɔ̃] **nf** (*brochures*) documentation, literature, information; (*Presse, TV: service*) research department.
documenter [dɔkymɑ̃te] [1] 1 **vt** *personne, livre* to document. **documenté** *personne* well-informed; *livre* well-documented, well-researched. 2 **se documenter vpr** to gather information *ou* material (*sur* on, about).
dodécaèdre [dɔdekaɛdʀ] **nm** dodecahedron.
dodécagonal, e, **mpl -aux** [dɔdekagɔnal, o] **adj** dodecagonal.
dodécagone [dɔdekagɔn] **nm** dodecagon.
Dodécanèse [dɔdekanɛz] **nm** Dodecanese.
dodécaphonique [dɔdekafɔnik] **adj** dodecaphonic.
dodécaphonisme [dɔdekafɔnism] **nm** dodecaphony.
dodelinement [dɔd(ə)linmɑ̃] **nm** *[tête]* nodding (*with sleep, age*).
dodeliner [dɔd(ə)line] [1] **vi**: **il dodelinait de la tête** his head kept nodding gently.
dodo[1] [dodo] **nm** (*langage enfantin*) (*sommeil*) beddy-byes (*langage enfantin*), sleep; (*lit*) beddy-byes (*langage enfantin*), bed. **faire ~** to have gone to beddy-byes (*langage enfantin*), be asleep; **il est temps d'aller au ~** *ou* **d'aller faire ~** it's time to go to beddy-byes (*langage enfantin*); **(fais) ~!** come on, sleepy-time!; **il fait ~** he's asleep; **un bon gros/un petit ~** a nice long/a short sleep.
dodo[2] [dodo] **nm** (*Orn*) dodo.
Dodoma [dodoma] **n** Dodoma.
dodu, e [dɔdy] **adj** *personne, poule, bras* plump; *enfant, joue* chubby.
doge [dɔʒ] **nm** doge.
dogmatique [dɔgmatik] **adj** dogmatic.
dogmatiquement [dɔgmatikmɑ̃] **adv** dogmatically.
dogmatiser [dɔgmatize] [1] **vi** to dogmatize.
dogmatisme [dɔgmatism] **nm** dogmatism.
dogme [dɔgm] **nm** (*lit, fig*) dogma. (*Rel*) **le ~** the dogma.
dogue [dɔg] **nm** (*Zool*) mastiff; *voir* **humeur**.
Doha [doa] **n** Doha.
doigt [dwa] **nm** a *[main, gant]* finger; *[animal]* digit. **~ de pied** toe; **se mettre** *ou* **se fourrer les ~s dans le nez** to pick one's nose; *voir* **bague, compter, petit** *etc*.
b (*mesure*) **raccourcir une jupe de 2/3 ~s** to shorten a skirt by 1/2 inches; **un ~ de vin** a drop of wine; **il a été à deux ~s de se tuer/de la mort/de réussir** he was within an ace *ou* an inch of being killed/of death/of succeeding; **la balle est passée à un ~ de sa tête** the bullet passed within a hair's-breadth *ou* an inch of his head.
c (*loc*) **avoir des ~s de fée** *[couturière, tricoteuse etc]* to have nimble fingers; *[infirmière]* to have gentle hands; **il ne fait rien de ses dix ~s** he's an idle *ou* a lazy good-for-nothing, he is bone idle (*Brit*); **il ne sait rien faire de ses dix ~s** he's a good-for-nothing; **faire marcher qn au ~ et à l'œil** to keep a tight rein on sb; **avec lui, ils obéissent au ~ et à l'œil** with him, they have to toe the line; **se mettre** *ou* **se fourrer le ~ dans l'œil (jusqu'au coude)*** to be kidding o.s.*; **là tu te mets** *ou* **te fourres le ~ dans l'œil*** you're completely up the pole* (*Brit*), you've got another thing coming*; **il n'a pas levé** *ou* **bougé le petit ~ pour nous aider** he didn't lift a finger to help us; **son petit ~ le lui a dit** a little bird told him; **mettre le ~ sur le problème** to put one's finger on the problem; **mettre le ~ dans l'engrenage** to get involved *ou* mixed up *ou* caught up in something; **filer** *ou* **glisser entre les ~s de qn** to slip through sb's fingers; **ils sont unis comme les (deux) ~s de la main** they're very close; **je le ferais les ~s dans le nez*** I could do it standing on my head *ou* with my eyes closed; **il a gagné les ~s dans le nez*** he won hands down*; **avoir un morceau de musique dans les ~s** to know a piece of music like the back of one's hand; **être les ~s de pied en éventail*** to have one's feet up; **être à deux ~s de faire** to come very close to doing.
doigté [dwate] **nm** *[pianiste, dactylo, chirurgien]* touch; (*Mus*) (*jeu des doigts*) fingering technique; (*position des doigts*) fingering; (*fig: tact*) diplomacy, tact.
doigter [dwate] [1] **vti** (*Mus*) to finger.
doigtier [dwatje] **nm** fingerstall.
doit [dwa] **nm** debit. **~ et avoir** debit and credit.
doléances [dɔleɑ̃s] **nfpl** (*plaintes*) complaints; (*réclamations*) grievances.
dolent, e [dɔlɑ̃, ɑ̃t] **adj** (*littér*) doleful, mournful.
doline [dɔlin] **nf** doline.
dollar [dɔlaʀ] **nm** dollar. **~ australien/canadien** Australian/Canadian dollar; **~ titre** security dollar.
dolman [dɔlmɑ̃] **nm** dolman, (*hussar's jacket*).
dolmen [dɔlmɛn] **nm** dolmen.
dolomie [dɔlɔmi] **nf**, **dolomite** [dɔlɔmit] **nf** dolomite. **les Dolomites** the Dolomites.
dolomitique [dɔlɔmitik] **adj** dolomitic.
DOM [dɔm] **nm** (**abrév de département d'outre-mer**) ≃ overseas region of France.
Dom [dɔ̃] **nm** Dom.
domaine [dɔmɛn] **nm** a (*propriété*) estate, domain, property. **le ~ de la couronne** the crown lands; (*Jur*) **le ~ (de l'État)** (*propriété*) state administered property; (*service*) state property department; **dans le ~ public/privé** in the public/private domain, in public/private ownership; **ses œuvres sont maintenant tombées dans le ~ public** his works are now out of copyright; **la salle de jeux est le ~ des enfants** the playroom is the children's domain, the playroom belongs to the children.
b (*sphère*) field, province, domain, sphere. **ce n'est pas de mon ~** it's not my field *ou* sphere; **dans tous les ~s** in every domain *ou* field; (*Gestion*) **~ d'activité stratégique** strategic business unit; (*fig*) **~ réservé** preserve.
c (*dans un dictionnaire*) field label.
domanial, e, **mpl -iaux** [dɔmanjal, jo] **adj** (*d'un domaine privé*) belonging to a private estate; (*d'un domaine public*) national (*épith*), state (*épith*).
dôme [dom] **nm** (*voûte*) dome; (*cathédrale*) cathedral. (*littér*) **le ~ du ciel** the vault of heaven; (*fig*) **un ~ de verdure** a canopy of foliage *ou* greenery; (*Géog*) **~ volcanique** volcanic dome.
domestication [dɔmɛstikasjɔ̃] **nf** (*action*) domestication, domesticating; (*résultat*) domestication.
domesticité [dɔmɛstisite] **nf** a (*condition de domestique*) domestic service. b (*personnel*) (domestic) staff, household. **une nombreuse ~** a large staff of servants. c *[animal]* domesticity.
domestique [dɔmɛstik] 1 **nmf** servant, domestic. **les ~s** the servants, the staff (of servants); **je ne suis pas ton ~!** I'm not your servant! 2 **adj** a (*ménager*) *travaux* domestic, household (*épith*); *soucis, querelle* domestic, family (*épith*). **accidents ~s** accidents in the home; **déchets ~s** kitchen waste (*Brit*) *ou* wastes (*US*); **les dieux ~s** the household gods. b (*Comm*) *marché, consommation* domestic, home (*épith*). c (*Zool*) domestic, domesticated. **le chien est un animal ~** the dog is a domestic animal; **canards ~s et canards sauvages** tame *ou* domesticated ducks and wild ducks.
domestiquer [dɔmɛstike] [1] **vt** *animal* to domesticate; *peuple* to subjugate; *vent, marée* to harness.
domicile [dɔmisil] **nm** place of residence, home, domicile (*Admin*); (*Jur*) *[société]* registered address; (*sur formulaire*) address. **~ légal** official domicile; **quitter le ~ conjugal** to leave the marital home; **sans ~,** (*Admin*) **sans ~ fixe** of no fixed abode *ou* address; **dernier ~ connu** last known address; **travailler à ~** to work at home; **il cherche du travail (à faire) à ~** he's looking for work (to do) at home; **je vous l'apporterai à ~** I'll bring it to your home; **livrer à ~** to deliver; **faire des livraisons à ~** to carry out deliveries; **"livraisons à ~"** "deliveries", "we deliver"; **vente à ~** door-to-door *ou* house-to-house selling; **"réparations à ~"** "home repairs carried out"; (*Sport*) **jouer à ~** to play at home; *voir* **élire, violation**.
domiciliaire [dɔmisiljɛʀ] **adj** domiciliary, house (*épith*).
domiciliataire [dɔmisiljatɛʀ] **nm** paying agent.
domiciliation [dɔmisiljasjɔ̃] **nf** payment by banker's order.
domicilier [dɔmisilje] [7] **vt** *facture* to pay by banker's order. **être domicilié** to be domiciled (*Admin*), have one's home (*à* in); **je me suis fait ~ à Lyon** I gave Lyons as my official address *ou* place of residence; **faire ~ ses factures** to have one's bills paid by banker's order.
dominance [dɔminɑ̃s] **nf** *[gène]* dominance.
dominant, e [dɔminɑ̃, ɑ̃t] 1 **adj** *pays, nation, rôle* dominant; *opinion, vent* prevailing (*épith*); *idée, trait* dominant, main (*épith*); *passion* ruling (*épith*); *problème, préoccupation* main (*épith*), chief (*épith*); *position* dominating (*épith*), leading (*épith*); (*Bio, Jur*) dominant. 2 **dominante nf** (*caractéristique*) dominant characteristic; (*couleur*) dominant *ou* predominant colour; (*Mus*) dominant. **tableau à ~e rouge** painting with red as the dominant *ou* predominant colour.
dominateur, -trice [dɔminatœʀ, tʀis] 1 **adj** *personne, caractère* domineering, overbearing; *voix, geste, regard* imperious; *pays* dominating (*épith*); *passion* ruling (*épith*). 2 **nm,f** (*littér*) ruler.
domination [dɔminasjɔ̃] **nf** (*Pol: autorité*) domination, dominion, rule; (*fig: emprise*) domination, influence. **la ~ de la Gaule (par Rome)** the domination of Gaul (by Rome); **la ~ de Rome (sur la Gaule)** Roman rule *ou* domination (over Gaul); **les pays sous la ~ britannique** countries under British rule *ou* domination *ou* dominion; **exercer sa ~ sur qn** to exert one's influence on sb, hold sway over sb; **exercer une ~ morale sur qn** to exert a moral influence on sb; **un besoin insatiable de ~** an insatiable need to dominate; **~ de soi-même** self-control, self-possession.
dominer [dɔmine] [1] 1 **vt** a (*être maître de*) *personne, pays* to dominate. **il voulait ~ le monde** he wanted to rule the world; **ces enfants sont dominés par leur père** these children are kept down *ou* dominated by their father; **il se laisse ~ par sa femme** he's dominated

by his wife, he's under his wife's sway; **elle ne sait pas ~ ses élèves** she can't keep her pupils in order *ou* under control, she can't keep control over her pupils.

b (*surpasser*) *adversaire, concurrent* to outclass, tower above, surpass. **il domine de loin les autres étudiants** he is miles better than *ou* way above the other students*; **écrivain qui domine son siècle** writer who dominates his century; **se faire ~ par l'équipe adverse** to be dominated *ou* outclassed by the opposing team; **parler fort pour ~ le bruit de la rue** to speak loudly to be heard above the noise from the street; **chez lui cette passion domine toutes les autres** this passion dominates *ou* overshadows all others in him; **le problème de la pollution domine tous les autres** the problem of pollution overshadows all others; (*Comm*) **~ un marché** to control a market.

c (*maîtriser*) *sentiment* to control, master, overcome; *problème* to overcome, master; *sujet* to master; *situation* to dominate, master. **elle ne put ~ son trouble** she couldn't overcome her confusion.

d (*diriger, gouverner*) to dominate, govern. **l'idée maîtresse/la préoccupation qui domine toute son œuvre** the key idea/the main concern which dominates his whole work.

e (*surplomber*) to tower above, dominate. **rocher/terrasse qui domine la mer** rock/terrace which overlooks *ou* dominates the sea; **il dominait la foule de sa haute taille** he towered above the crowd with his great height; **de là-haut on domine la vallée** from up there you overlook *ou* dominate the whole valley.

2 vi a (*être le meilleur*) *[nation]* to hold sway; *[orateur, concurrent]* to be in the dominant position; (*Sport*) *[équipe]* to be in the dominant position, be on top; *[coureur]* to be in a commanding position. **l'Angleterre a dominé sur les mers pendant des siècles** England ruled the seas *ou* held dominion over the seas for centuries; **dans les débats, il domine nettement** in debates, he clearly has the edge on everyone else *ou* he's definitely the strongest speaker; **leur équipe a dominé pendant tout le match** their team was on top throughout the match; **ce coureur a dominé pendant les premiers kilomètres** this runner was on his own *ou* was out in front for the first few kilometres; (*fig*) **~ de la tête et des épaules** to be head and shoulders above the others.

b (*prédominer*) *[caractère, défaut, qualité]* to predominate; *[idée, théorie]* to prevail; *[préoccupation, intérêt]* to be dominant, predominate; *[parfum]* to predominate; *[couleur]* to stand out, predominate. **dans cette réunion, l'élément féminin dominait** at that meeting the female element predominated *ou* was most in evidence; **c'est l'ambition qui domine chez lui** ambition is his dominant characteristic; **c'est le jaune qui domine** it is yellow which stands out *ou* which is the predominant colour.

3 **se dominer** vpr to control o.s., keep o.s. under control. **il ne sait pas se ~** he has no control over himself *ou* no self-control.

dominicain, e [dɔminikɛ̃, ɛn] 1 adj (*Géog, Rel*) Dominican. **République ~e** Dominican Republic. 2 nm,f a (*Rel*) Dominican. b (*Géog*) **D~(e)** Dominican.

dominical, e, mpl **-aux** [dɔminikal, o] adj Sunday (*épith*); *voir* **oraison, repos.**

dominion [dɔminjɔn] nm (*Brit: état*) dominion (*of the British Commonwealth*).

Dominique [dɔminik] 1 nf a (*Géog*) **la ~** Dominica. b (*prénom*) Dominica. 2 nm Dominic.

domino [dɔmino] nm (*Habillement, Jeux*) domino. (*jeu*) **les ~s** dominoes (*sg*).

dommage [dɔmaʒ] 1 nm a (*préjudice*) harm (*NonC*), injury. **causer un ~ à qn** to cause *ou* do sb harm; **pour réparer le ~ que je vous ai causé** to repair the harm I've caused you, to repair the injury I've done you; (*Jur*) **~ causé avec intention de nuire** malicious damage.

b (*ravages*) **~s** damage (*NonC*); **causer des ~s aux récoltes** to damage *ou* cause damage to the crops; **les ~s sont inestimables** there is incalculable damage.

c (*loc*) **c'est ~!, quel ~!** what a pity! *ou* shame!; **il est vraiment ~ que ...** it's such a great pity that ...; **(c'est** *ou* **quel) ~ que tu ne puisses pas venir** it's a *ou* what a pity *ou* shame (that) you can't come; (*iro*) **ça ne te plaît pas? c'est bien ~!** you don't like it? well, that really is a shame! (*iro*) *ou* pity isn't it?* (*iro*).

2 comp ►**dommage(s) corporel(s)** physical injury ►**dommages de guerre** war damages ►**dommages et intérêts, dommages-intérêts** nmpl damages ►**dommage(s) matériel(s)** material damage.

dommageable [dɔmaʒabl] adj prejudicial, harmful, injurious (*à* to).

domotique [dɔmɔtik] nf home automation.

domptable [dɔ̃(p)tabl] adj tam(e)able.

domptage [dɔ̃(p)taʒ] nm taming.

dompter [dɔ̃(p)te] 1 vt *fauve* to tame, train; *cheval* to break in; *enfant insoumis* to subdue; *rebelles* to put down, subdue; *sentiments, passions* to master, control, overcome; *nature, fleuve* to tame.

dompteur, -euse [dɔ̃(p)tœʀ, øz] nm,f (*gén*) tamer, trainer. **~ (de lions)** liontamer; **~ de chevaux** horsebreaker.

DOM-TOM [dɔmtɔm] nmpl (abrév de **départements et territoires d'outre-mer**) *French overseas departments and territories.*

Don [dɔ̃] nm a (*Géog*) Don. b (*titre*) Don.

don [dɔ̃] nm a (*aptitude*) gift, talent. **~s littéraires** literary gifts *ou* talents; **avoir un ~ pour** to have a gift *ou* talent for; **avoir le ~ des maths** to have a gift for maths; **avoir des ~s** to be gifted *ou* talented; **elle a le ~ de m'énerver** she has a knack of *ou* a genius for getting on my nerves; **cette proposition n'a pas eu le ~ de lui plaire** this proposal was not destined to *ou* didn't happen to please him.

b (*cadeau*) gift; (*offrande*) donation. **~ en argent** cash donation; **~ en nature** donation in kind; **~ d'organes** donation of organs; (*littér*) **les ~s de la terre** the gifts of the earth; **faire ~ de** *fortune, maison* to donate; **je lui ai fait ~ de ce livre** I made him a present *ou* gift of that book, I gave him that book as a gift; **cette tâche exige le ~ de soi** this task demands real self-sacrifice *ou* self-denial; **faire (le) ~ de sa vie pour sauver qn** to give one's life to save sb, lay own one's life for sb; (*fig*) **c'est un ~ du ciel** it's a godsend.

Doña [dɔɲa] nf Doña.

donataire [dɔnatɛʀ] nmf donee.

donateur, -trice [dɔnatœʀ, tʀis] nm,f donor.

donation [dɔnasjɔ̃] nf (*Jur*) ≃ settlement. **faire une ~ à qn** to make a settlement on sb; **~ entre vifs** donation inter vivos.

donc [dɔ̃k *en tête de proposition ou devant voyelle; ailleurs* dɔ̃] conj a (*par conséquent*) therefore, so, thus; (*après une digression*) so, then. **il partit ~ avec ses amis et ...** so he left with his friends and ..., he left with his friends then and ...; **je n'étais pas d'accord, ~ j'ai refusé** I didn't agree (and) so I refused *ou* and I therefore refused; **j'ai raté le train, ~ je n'ai pas pu venir** I missed the train and was thus not able to come *ou* and so I couldn't come; **si ce n'est pas la variole c'est ~ la rougeole** if it's not smallpox then it's measles.

b (*intensif: marque la surprise*) then, so. **c'était ~ un espion?** he was a spy then?, so he was a spy?; **voilà ~ ce dont il s'agissait** this is what it was (all) about then, so this is what it was (all) about.

c (*de renforcement*) **allons ~!** come on!, come now!; **écoute-moi ~** do listen to me; **demande-lui ~** go on, ask him; **tais-toi ~!** do be quiet!; **regardez ~ ça comme c'est joli** just look at that, isn't it pretty?; **pensez ~!** just imagine *ou* think!; **comment ~?** how do you mean?; **quoi ~?** what was that?, what did you say?; **dis ~, dites ~** (*introduit une question*) tell me, I say; (*introduit un avertissement, une injonction*) look (here) ...; **non mais dis ~, ne te gêne pas!** look (here) don't put yourself out; **dites ~ Jacques, où avez-vous rangé l'aspirateur?** I say, Jacques, where did you put the vacuum cleaner?; **tiens ~!** well, well!, I say!

dondon* [dɔ̃dɔ̃] nf big *ou* fat woman *ou* girl. **une grosse ~** a big lump* of a woman *ou* girl.

donjon [dɔ̃ʒɔ̃] nm keep, donjon.

don Juan [dɔ̃ʒɥɑ̃] nm Don Juan.

donjuanesque [dɔ̃ʒɥanɛsk] adj of Don Juan, typical of Don Juan.

donjuanisme [dɔ̃ʒɥanism] nm donjuanism.

donnant, e [dɔnɑ̃, ɑ̃t] adj a (†) generous, open-handed. b (*loc: emploi participial*) **avec lui, c'est ~, ~** he always wants something in return for a service; **~, ~ je te prête mon livre, tu me prêtes ton stylo** fair's fair – I lend you my book and you lend me your pen.

donne [dɔn] nf (*Cartes*) deal. **à vous la ~** your deal; **faire la ~** to deal (out) the cards; **il y a mauvaise** *ou* **fausse ~** it's a misdeal; (*fig*) **nouvelle ~** new order.

donné, e [dɔne] (ptp de **donner**) 1 adj a (*déterminé*) *lieu, date* given, fixed; *voir* **moment.** b **étant ~ la situation** in view of *ou* given *ou* considering the situation; **étant ~ que tu es parti** seeing *ou* given that you left. c (*: *pas cher*) (dirt) cheap*. 2 **donnée** nf a (*Math, Sci*) *[problème]* datum. **~es** data; **banque/base/fichier** *etc* **de ~es** data bank/database/data file *etc*; (*Econ*) **en ~es corrigées des variations saisonnières** figures adjusted for seasonal variation(s). b (*chose connue*) piece of information. **~es** facts, particulars; **manquer de ~es** to be short of facts; **modifier les ~es du problème** to refine the problem. c *[roman]* main theme, basic idea *ou* element.

donner [dɔne] 1 1 vt a (*gén: offrir*) **~ qch à qn** to give sth to sb, give sb sth; **je le lui ai donné** I gave it (to) him; **donné c'est donné** a gift is a gift; **~ son cœur/son amitié (à qn)** to give one's heart/one's friendship (to sb); **~ à manger/boire à qn** to give sb something to eat/drink; **~ son corps à la science** to donate one's body to research; **~ son sang pour un malade** to give *ou* donate one's blood for somebody who is ill; **~ son sang pour une cause** to shed one's blood for a cause; **~ sa vie/son temps pour une cause** to give up one's life/one's time for a cause; **~ qch à qn par testament** to bequeath sth to sb; **~ qch pour** *ou* **contre qch d'autre** to give sth in exchange for sth else, exchange sth for sth else; **en ~ à qn pour son argent** to give sb his money's worth; **on ne les vend pas, on les donne** we're not selling them, we're giving them away; *voir* **change, matière.**

b (*remettre, confier*) to give, hand; *copie d'examen* to hand in, give in. **~ quelque chose à faire à qn** to give sb something to do; **je donnerai la lettre au concierge** I shall hand the letter (in) to the caretaker; **donnez-moi les outils** give me *ou* hand me *ou* pass me the tools; **~ ses chaussures à ressemeler/au cordonnier** to take one's shoes (in) to be resoled/to the cobbler's, put one's shoes in to be resoled/at the mender's.

c (*céder*) *vieux vêtements* to give away. **~ sa place à une dame** to give up one's seat to a lady; **je donnerais beaucoup pour savoir** I would give a lot to know; *voir* **langue.**

d (*distribuer*) to hand out, give out; *cartes* to deal (out). (*Cartes*) **c'est à vous de ~** it's your deal.

e (*communiquer, indiquer*) *description, détails, idée, avis* to give; *sujet de devoir* to set. **il lui a donné l'ordre de partir** he has ordered him to go; **pouvez-vous me ~ l'heure?** can you tell me the time?; *voir* **alarme, alerte.**

f (*accorder*) *moyen, occasion* to give; *permission, interview* to grant, give; *prix, décoration* to award, give. **~ sa fille en mariage à qn** to give one's daughter to sb in marriage; **donnez-moi le temps d'y réfléchir** give me time to think about it; **on lui a donné 24 heures pour quitter le pays** he was given 24 hours to leave the country; **il n'est pas donné à tout le monde d'être bon en maths** not everyone is lucky enough *ou* it is not given to everyone to be good at maths; **l'intelligence n'est pas donnée à tout le monde** not everyone is gifted with intelligence; **le médecin lui donne 3 mois (à vivre)** the doctor has given him 3 months (to live); **je vous le donne en cent *ou* en mille!*** you'll never guess (in a million years)!; **se ~ un maître/un président** to choose a master/a president; (*Rel*) **~ la communion** *etc* **à** to give communion *etc* to; (*fig*) **on lui donnerait le bon Dieu sans confession** he looks as if butter wouldn't melt in his mouth.

g (*causer*) *plaisir, courage* to give (*à* to); *peine, mal* to cause, give (*à* to). **~ de l'appétit à qn** to give sb an appetite; **cela donne chaud/froid/soif/faim** this makes you (feel) hot/cold/thirsty/hungry; **~ le vertige/le mal de mer (à qn)** to make sb (feel) giddy/seasick; **cela donne des maux de tête** that causes headaches *ou* gives you headaches; **ça va vous ~ des forces** that'll give you strength *ou* put strength into you; **se ~ du mal/de la peine** to take (great) trouble/pains; **se ~ du bon temps** to have a good time, live it up*; **s'en ~ à cœur joie, s'en ~*** to have a whale of a time*, have the time of one's life; **se ~ bonne conscience** to ease *ou* soothe one's conscience.

h (*avec à + infin: faire*) **il m'a donné à penser/à sentir que** he made me think/feel that; **ces événements nous ont donné (beaucoup) à réfléchir** these events have given us (much) food for thought *ou* have set us thinking; **c'est ce qu'on m'a donné à entendre** that is what I was given to understand *ou* led to believe; **~ à rire** to give cause for laughter.

i (*organiser*) *réception, bal* to give, hold (*à* for); *film* to show; *pièce* to perform, put on. **ça se donne encore?** *[film]* is it still on? *ou* showing?; *[pièce]* is it still on?

j (*indiquant une action sur qn/qch*) **~ un baiser/un coup de pied à qn** to give sb a kiss/a kick; **~ une gifle à qn** to slap sb's face, box sb's ears; **~ une fessée à qn** to smack sb's bottom; **~ une caresse au chat** to stroke the cat; **donne-toi un coup de peigne** give your hair a quick comb, run a comb through your hair; **~ un coup de balai à la pièce** to give the room a sweep; **~ un coup de chiffon à la pièce** to flick a duster over the room, give the room a quick dust; **ils se sont donné des coups** they exchanged blows; **je me donnerais des coups!** I could kick myself!

k (*conférer*) *poids, valeur* to add, give. **le brouillard donne un air triste à la ville** the fog makes the town look dismal; **il fumait pour se ~ une contenance** he was smoking to disguise his lack of composure; **elle se donne un air de jeune fille naïve** she gives herself the appearance of an innocent young thing, she likes to appear the innocent young thing.

l (*attribuer*) **quel âge lui donnez-vous?** how old do you take him to be? *ou* would you say he was?; **je lui donne 50 ans** I'd put his age at 50, I'd say he was 50, I'd take him to be 50; **on lui donne des qualités qu'il n'a pas** he's said to have *ou* is credited with qualities which he hasn't got; *voir* **raison, tort.**

m **~ un fait pour certain** to present a fact as a certainty; **on le donne pour un homme habile** he is said *ou* made out to be a clever man; **il se donne pour un tireur d'élite** he makes himself out *ou* professes *ou* claims to be a crack shot.

n (*Mus*) *le la, la note, le ton* to give. (*fig*) **~ le ton *ou* la note** to set the tone.

o (*produire*) *fruits, récolte* to yield; *résultat* to produce. **les pommiers ont bien donné cette année** the apple trees have produced a good crop *ou* given a good yield this year; **cette vigne donne un très bon vin** this vine produces a very good wine; **elle lui a donné un fils** she gave *ou* bore him a son; (*péj*) **~ du Monsieur à qn (gros comme le bras)** to toady to sb; (*fig*) **cet écrivain donne un livre tous les ans** this writer produces a book every year; **cette méthode ne donne rien** this method is unrewarding *ou* is producing nothing; **qu'est-ce que ça donne?*** (*qu'en penses-tu*) how's that?, what do you think?; (*comment ça se passe*) how's it going?

p (*‡: dénoncer*) *complice* to squeal *ou* grass on‡, shop‡ (*Brit*), give away, finger‡.

2 **vi** a (*frapper*) **aller ~ sur les rochers** to run onto *ou* strike the rocks; **~ de la tête contre une porte** to knock *ou* bump one's head against a door; **le soleil donne en plein sur la voiture** the sun is beating down on *ou* shining right onto the car; **ne savoir où ~ de la tête*** not to know which way to turn.

b (*être la victime de*) **~ dans** *piège* to fall into; *défaut* to lapse into; **~ dans le snobisme** to be rather snobbish, have a tendency to be snobbish; *voir* **panneau.**

c (*s'ouvrir sur*) **~ sur** *[pièce, porte]* to give onto, open onto; *[fenêtre]* to overlook, open onto, look onto; **la maison donne sur la mer** the house faces *ou* looks onto the sea front.

d (*attaquer*) to attack. **l'artillerie va ~** the artillery is going to fire; **faites ~ la garde!** send in the guards!

e (*produire*) to yield. **cet arbre ne donnera pas avant 3 ans** this tree won't bear fruit for 3 years; (*fig*) **la radio donne à plein** the radio is turned right up; (*fig*) **ça donne!‡** it's cool‡ *ou* magic‡ *ou* brill!‡; **mes tomates vont bientôt ~** my tomatoes will soon be producing *ou* yielding fruit.

3 **se donner vpr: se ~ à** *cause, parti, travail* to devote o.s. to; **elle s'est donnée (à son amant)** she gave herself (to her lover); **il s'est donné à fond** he gave his all; **il se donne pour réussir dans la vie** he works hard to succeed in life; *voir* **main, rendez-vous.**

donneur, -euse [dɔnœʀ, øz] **nm,f** (*gén*) giver; (*Cartes*) dealer; (*arg Police: dénonciateur*) squealer‡, informer, grass‡; (*Méd*) donor. (*Comm*) **~ d'ordre** principal; **~ de sang** blood donor; **~ universel** universal donor; (*péj*) **~ de leçons** sermonizer (*péj*).

Don Quichotte [dɔ̃kiʃɔt] **nm** Don Quixote.

don-quichottisme [dɔ̃kiʃɔtism] **nm** quixotism.

dont [dɔ̃] **pron rel** a (*provenant d'un complément de nom: indique la possession, la qualité etc*) whose, of which; (*antécédent humain*) whose. **la femme ~ vous apercevez le chapeau** the woman whose hat you can see; **c'est un pays ~ j'aime le climat** it's a country whose climate I like *ou* which has a climate I like *ou* the climate of which I like (*frm*); **un vagabond ~ les souliers laissaient voir les doigts de pied** a tramp whose shoes revealed his toes *ou* whose toes showed through his shoes; **les enfants ~ la mère travaille sont plus indépendants** children whose mothers go out to work are more independent; **l'histoire, ~ voici l'essentiel, est ...** the story, of which these are the main points, is ... .

b (*indiquant la partie d'un tout*) **il y a eu plusieurs blessés, ~ son frère** there were several casualties, among which *ou* among whom was his brother *ou* including his brother; **des livres dont j'ai lu une dizaine environ/dont une dizaine sont reliés** books of which I have read about ten/of which about ten are bound; **ils ont 3 filles ~ 2 sont mariées** they have 3 daughters, 2 of whom are married *ou* of whom 2 are married, they have 3 daughters, 2 of them married; **il a écrit 2 romans ~ un est autobiographique** he has written 2 novels one of which is autobiographical.

c (*indique la manière, la provenance: voir aussi* **de**) **la façon ~ elle marche/s'habille** the way she walks/(in which) she dresses, her way of walking/dressing; **la pièce ~ il sort** the room (which) he is coming out of *ou* out of which he is coming; **mines ~ on extrait de l'or** mines from which gold is extracted, mines (that) gold is extracted from; **la classe sociale ~ elle est issue** the social class (which) she came from.

d (*provenant d'un complément prépositionnel d'adjectif, de verbe: voir aussi les adjectifs et verbes en question*) **l'outil ~ il se sert** the tool (which) he is using; **la maladie ~ elle souffre** the illness she suffers from *ou* from which she suffers; **le vase ~ la maison m'a fait cadeau** the vase (which) the firm gave me *ou* presented me with, the vase with which the firm presented me; **le film/l'acteur ~ elle parle tant** the film/actor she talks so much about *ou* about which/whom she talks so much; **voilà ce ~ il faut vous assurer** that is what you must make sure of *ou* about; **l'accident ~ il a été responsable** the accident he was responsible for *ou* for which he was responsible; **le collier/l'enfant ~ elle est si fière** the necklace/child she is so proud of *ou* of which/whom she is so proud.

donzelle [dɔ̃zɛl] **nf** (*péj*) young miss (*péj*).

dopage [dɔpaʒ] **nm** doping.

dopant [dɔpɑ̃] **nm** dope (*NonC*).

dope [dɔp] **nf** (*arg Drogue*) dope (*arg*).

doper [dɔpe] 1 **1 vt** to dope. **2 se doper vpr** to take stimulants, dope o.s.

doping [dɔpiŋ] **nm** (*action*) doping; (*excitant*) dope (*NonC*).

Doppler [dɔplɛʀ] **1 adj: effet ~** Doppler effect. **2 nm: (examen) ~** Doppler test; **se faire faire un ~** to have a Doppler test.

dorade [dɔʀad] **nf** = **daurade.**

Dordogne [dɔʀdɔɲ] **nf: la ~** the Dordogne.

doré, e [dɔʀe] (**ptp de dorer**) **1 adj** a (*couvert d'une dorure*) gilt, gilded. **~ sur tranche** gilt-edged, with gilded edges. b (*couleur d'or*) *peau* bronzed, tanned; *blé, cheveux, lumière* golden; *gâteau, gigot* browned. (*fig*) **des rêves ~s** golden dreams; **~ comme les blés** golden-blond, flaxen; *voir* **blouson, jeunesse. 2 nm** a (*dorure*) gilt, gilding. **le ~ du vase s'en va** the gilt *ou* gilding is coming off the vase. b (*Can*) yellow pike, wall-eyed pike. **3 dorée nf** John Dory, dory.

dorénavant [dɔʀenavɑ̃] **adv** from now on, henceforth (†, *frm*), henceforward (*frm*).

dorer [dɔʀe] 1 **1 vt** a (*couvrir d'or*) *objet* to gild. **faire ~ un cadre** to have a frame gilded; (*fig*) **~ la pilule à qn*** to gild *ou* sugar *ou* sweeten the pill for sb; **se ~ la pilule*** *voir* **c.** b (*Culin*) *gâteau* to glaze (*with egg yolk*). **le four dore bien la viande** the oven browns the meat well. c *peau* to bronze, tan. (*littér*) **le soleil dore les blés** the sun turns the corn gold; **le soleil dore les dunes** the sun tinges the dunes with gold; **se ~ au soleil, se ~ la pilule*** to lie (and get brown) in the sun, sunbathe. **2 vi** (*Culin*) *[rôti]* to brown. **faire ~ un poulet** to brown a chicken; **le poulet est bien doré cette fois** the chicken is well browned this time.

d'ores et déjà [dɔʀzedeʒa] adv *voir* **ores.**

doreur, -euse [dɔʀœʀ, øz] nm,f gilder.

dorien, -ienne [dɔʀjɛ̃, jɛn] 1 adj (*Géog*) Dorian, Doric; *dialecte* Doric; (*Mus*) *mode* Dorian. 2 nm (*Ling*) Doric (dialect).

dorique [dɔʀik] adj, nm Doric.

dorlotement [dɔʀlɔtmɑ̃] nm pampering, (molly)coddling, cosseting.

dorloter [dɔʀlɔte] [1] 1 vt to pamper, (molly)coddle, cosset. **il est trop dorloté** he's mollycoddled; **se faire ~** to be pampered *ou* (molly)coddled *ou* cosseted. 2 **se dorloter** vpr to coddle *ou* cosset o.s.

dormant, e [dɔʀmɑ̃, ɑ̃t] 1 adj *eau* still; (*Tech*) *châssis* fixed. (*Jur, Fin*) **compte ~** dead account. 2 nm *[porte, châssis]* casing, frame.

dormeur, -euse [dɔʀmœʀ, øz] 1 adj *poupée* with shutting eyes. 2 nm,f sleeper; (*péj*) sleepyhead*. **c'est un gros** *ou* **grand ~** he likes his sleep, he's a real sleepyhead*. 3 nm (*crabe*) (common *ou* edible) crab. 4 **dormeuse** nf (†: *boucle d'oreille*) earring.

dormir [dɔʀmiʀ] [16] vi a (*gén*) to sleep; (*être en train de dormir*) to be asleep, be sleeping. **~ d'un sommeil léger/lourd** to sleep lightly/heavily; **il dormait d'un sommeil agité** he was tossing about in his sleep; **je n'ai pas dormi de la nuit/de 3 jours** I haven't slept a wink (all night)/for 3 days; **avoir envie de ~** to feel sleepy; **essayez de ~ un peu** try to get some sleep; **ça m'empêche de ~** *[café]* it keeps me awake; *[soucis]* I'm losing sleep over it; **ce n'est pas ça qui va m'empêcher de ~** I'm not going to lose any sleep over that; **parler/chanter en dormant** to talk/sing in one's sleep.

b (*rester inactif*) *[eau]* to be still; *[argent, capital]* to lie idle; *[machines]* to be *ou* lie idle; *[nature, forêt]* to be still, be asleep. **tout dormait dans la maison/ville** everything was quiet *ou* still in the house/town; **la brute qui dormait en lui** the brute which lay dormant within him; **investis ton capital plutôt que de le laisser ~** invest your capital rather than leave it idle; **ce n'est pas le moment de ~!** this is no time for slacking *ou* idling; **~ sur son travail** to dawdle *ou* be slack at one's work; *voir* **pire.**

c (*loc*) **je dors debout** I'm asleep on my feet, I can't keep awake *ou* my eyes open; **une histoire à ~ debout** a cock-and-bull story; (*frm*) **~ (de) son dernier sommeil** to sleep one's last sleep; **~ comme un loir** *ou* **une marmotte** *ou* **une souche** *ou* **un sonneur** to sleep like a log; **ne ~ que d'un œil** to sleep with one eye open; **il dort à poings fermés** he is sound *ou* fast asleep, he's dead to the world*; **cette nuit je vais ~ à poings fermés** tonight I'm going to sleep very soundly; **~ du sommeil du juste** to sleep the sleep of the just; (*fig*) **~ tranquille** *ou* **sur ses deux oreilles** (*sans soucis*) to sleep soundly; (*sans danger*) to sleep safely (in one's bed); **il n'en dort pas** *ou* **plus** he's losing sleep over it, he can't sleep for thinking of it; *voir* **qui.**

dormitif, -ive [dɔʀmitif, iv] adj soporific.

dorsal, e, mpl **-aux** [dɔʀsal, o] 1 adj (*gén*) dorsal, back (*épith*); (*Ling*) dorsal; *voir* **épine, parachute.** 2 **dorsale** nf a (*Ling*) dorsal consonant. b (*Géog*) ridge. (*Mét*) **~e barométrique** ridge of high pressure.

dortoir [dɔʀtwaʀ] nm dormitory. **cité-** *ou* **ville-~** dormitory town.

dorure [dɔʀyʀ] nf a (*couche d'or*) gilt, gilding; *[gâteau]* glaze (*of egg yolk*). **uniforme couvert de ~s** uniform covered in gold decorations. b (*action*) gilding.

doryphore [dɔʀifɔʀ] nm Colorado beetle.

dos [do] 1 nm a *[être animé, main, vêtement, siège, page]* back; *[livre]* spine; *[langue]* back, upper surface; *[lame, couteau]* blunt edge. **avoir le ~ rond** to be round-shouldered; **couché sur le ~** lying on one's (*ou* its) back; **écrire au ~ d'une lettre/enveloppe** to write on the back of a letter/an envelope; **robe décolletée dans le ~** low-backed dress; **"voir au ~"** "see over *ou* overleaf"; **aller à ~ d'âne/de chameau** to ride on a donkey/a camel; **les vivres sont portés à ~ de chameau/d'homme** the supplies are carried by camel/men; **ils partirent, sac au ~** they set off, (with) their rucksacks on their backs; **porter ses cheveux dans le ~** to wear one's hair loose *ou* down one's back; **(vu) de ~ il a une allure jeune** (seen) from behind *ou* from the back he looks quite young; *voir* **gros.**

b (*nage*) **~ (crawlé)** backstroke.

c (*loc*) **être ~ à ~** to be back to back; **renvoyer 2 adversaires ~ à ~** to send away *ou* dismiss 2 opponents without pronouncing in favour of either; (*fig*) **le train/ta mère a bon ~*** (that's right) blame the train/your mother (*iro*); **il s'est mis tout le monde à ~** he has turned everybody against him; (*fig*) **j'ai toujours mon patron sur le ~** my boss is always breathing down my neck *ou* is always standing over me; **on l'a dans le ~ !*⁑** we've had it!*⁑; **mettre qch sur le ~ de qn** (*responsabilité*) to saddle sb with sth, make sb shoulder the responsibility for sth; (*accusation*) to pin sth on sb; **il s'est mis une sale affaire sur le ~** he has got himself mixed up in a nasty bit of business; **faire des affaires sur le ~ de qn** to do a bit of business at sb's expense; **il a tout pris sur le ~*** he bore the brunt of the whole thing; **je n'ai rien à me mettre sur le ~** I haven't a thing to wear; **tomber sur le ~ de qn** (*arriver à l'improviste*) to drop in on sb, pay sb an unexpected visit; (*attaquer*) (*lit*) to fall on sb, go for sb; (*fig*) to jump down sb's throat, go for sb; **faire qch dans** *ou* **derrière le ~ de qn** to do sth behind sb's back; (*fig*) **faire un enfant à qn dans le ~*** to play a dirty trick on sb*; **nous avions la mer/l'ennemi dans le ~** we had the sea/the enemy behind us *ou* at our back(s); **avoir le ~ tourné à la mer/à la porte** to have one's back to the sea/door; **dès qu'il a le ~ tourné** as soon as his back is turned; **il n'y va pas avec le ~ de la cuiller*** he certainly doesn't go in for half-measures*, there are no half-measures with him; *voir* **froid, plein.**

2 comp ▶**dos-d'âne** nm inv humpback (*Brit*), hogback, hogsback (*US*); **pont en dos-d'âne** humpback bridge.

dosage [dozaʒ] nm (*action: voir* **doser**) measuring out; correct proportioning; (*mélange*) mixture. **se tromper dans le ~ d'un cocktail/d'une solution chimique** to mix a cocktail/a chemical solution in the wrong proportions; (*fig*) **dans ce domaine, tout est question de ~** it's all a matter of striking a balance *ou* the right balance in this area; (*fig*) **un ~ réussi de romanesque et de description historique** a well-balanced mixture of romance and historical description, a good balance between romance and historical description.

dose [doz] nf a (*Pharm*) dose. **~ mortelle** lethal dose; **absorber une ~ excessive de barbituriques** to take an overdose of barbiturates; **s'en tenir à la ~ prescrite** to keep to the prescribed dose *ou* dosage.

b (*gén: proportion*) *[ingrédient, élément]* amount, quantity. (*hum*) **il a bu sa ~ quotidienne** he has drunk *ou* had his daily dose (*hum*); **en avoir sa ~*** to have had more than one's share of it; (*fig*) **forcer la ~** to overdo it, overstep the mark; (*fig*) **introduire une petite ~ d'ironie dans un récit** to introduce a touch of irony into a story; **il faut pour cela une ~ peu commune de courage/de mauvaise foi** for that you need an above-average amount of courage/bad faith; **affligé d'une forte ~ de stupidité** afflicted with more than one's fair share of stupidity; **j'aime bien la poésie/ce chanteur mais seulement par petites ~s** *ou* **à petites ~s** I like poetry/that singer all right but only in small doses; (*hum*) **le travail, c'est bien mais à ~s homéopathiques** work's fine but only in minute doses.

doser [doze] [1] vt a (*Chim, gén*) *ingrédient, élément* to measure out; *remède* to measure out a dose of; *mélange* to proportion correctly, mix in the correct proportions. **mal ~ un cocktail/une solution chimique** to mix a cocktail/a chemical solution in the wrong proportions.

b (*fig: mêler, combiner*) to strike a balance between. **savoir ~ compréhension et sévérité** to be good at striking a balance *ou* the right balance between understanding and severity.

c (*mesurer*) *exercices, difficultés* to grade. **savoir ~ ses efforts** to know how much effort to expend; **cet auteur sait ~ l'ironie** this author has a gift for using irony in just the right amounts.

doseur [dozœʀ] nm measure. **bouchon ~** measuring cap.

dossard [dosaʀ] nm (*Sport*) number (*worn by competitor*). **avec le ~ numéro 9** wearing number 9.

dosseret [dosʀɛ] nm headboard.

dossier [dosje] nm a *[siège]* back. b (*documents*) file, dossier; (*Jur: affaire*) case. **constituer un ~ sur qn** to draw up a file on sb; (*Presse*) **"le ~ africain/du pétrole"** "the African/oil question"; **~ en béton*** cast-iron case*; (*fig*) **ouvrir/fermer un ~** to open/close a case; **connaître** *ou* **posséder ses ~s** to know what one is about, know what's what; **~ scolaire** school record (*Brit*), student file (*US*); **être sélectionné sur ~** to be selected on the basis of *ou* according to one's qualifications; **~ de presse** press kit; **~ médical** medical records. c (*classeur*) file, folder.

Dostoïevski [dɔstɔjɛvski] nm Dostoyevsky.

dot [dɔt] nf *[mariage]* dowry; (*Rel*) (spiritual) dowry. **apporter qch en ~** to bring a dowry of sth, bring sth as one's dowry; *voir* **coureur.**

dotal, e, mpl **-aux** [dɔtal, o] adj dotal, dowry (*épith*).

dotation [dɔtasjɔ̃] nf (*Jur*) *[institution]* endowment; (*Hist*) *[fonctionnaire, dignitaire]* emolument; (*Admin: allocation*) grant.

doté, e [dɔte] (ptp de **doter**) adj (*pourvu*) **~ de** *équipement, matériel, dispositif* equipped with; *talent, courage, pouvoir* endowed with.

doter [dɔte] [1] vt a (*Jur*) *fille à marier* to provide with a dowry, dower; *institution* to endow; (*Hist*) *fonctionnaire, dignitaire* to endow with an emolument; (*Admin*) *université, organisme* to grant money to, give a grant to. **~ richement sa fille** to provide one's daughter with a large dowry. b (*pourvoir de*) **~ une armée d'un équipement moderne** to equip an army with modern equipment; **la nature l'avait doté d'un grand talent** nature had endowed him with great talent, nature had bestowed great talent upon him.

douaire [dwɛʀ] nm dower.

douairière [dwɛʀjɛʀ] nf dowager.

douane [dwan] nf a (*service*) Customs. **il est employé aux ~s** *ou* **à la ~** he is employed by *ou* in the Customs (department); **marchandises (entreposées) en ~** bonded goods, goods in bond; **zone/port sous ~** zone/port under the authority of the Customs. b (*à la frontière*) **(poste** *ou* **bureau de) ~** customs house, customs; (*à l'aéroport etc*) **passer (à) la ~** to go through (the) customs; (*dans le train*) **la visite de la ~** the customs check. c **(droits de) ~** customs dues *ou* duty, duty; **exempté de ~** duty-free, non-dutiable.

douanier, -ière [dwanje, jɛʀ] 1 adj custom(s) (*épith*); *voir* **barrière, union.** 2 nm,f customs officer.

doublage [dublaʒ] nm a *[fil]* doubling; *[revêtement]* doubling, laying double; *[couverture]* doubling, folding (in half). b *[film]* dubbing. **le ~ d'un acteur** *[voix]* dubbing an actor; *[rôle]* using a double for an actor.

c *[vêtement, paroi, boîte, tableau]* lining; (*Naut*) *[coque]* sheathing. d *[somme, quantité, lettre]* doubling.

double [dubl] 1 **adj** a *consonne, longueur, épaisseur* double; *fleur* double, multifoliate (*SPÉC*); *inconvénient, avantage* double, twofold. **feuille** ~ folded A4 (*ou* A3) sheet (of paper); ~ **whisky** double *ou* large whisky; **le prix est** ~ **de ce qu'il était** the price is double *ou* twice what it was; **vous avez fait une** ~ **erreur** you have made two mistakes; **faire qch en** ~ **exemplaire** to make two copies of sth, do sth in duplicate; **dispositif/machine à** ~ **effet** double-action *ou* dual-action device/machine; **ustensile à** ~ **usage** dual-purpose utensil; **faire** ~ **emploi** to be redundant; **cet appareil fait maintenant** ~ **emploi avec l'ancien** this apparatus now duplicates the old one *ou* makes the old one redundant; **à vendre voiture, cause** ~ **emploi** for sale: car, surplus to requirements; **fermer une porte à** ~ **tour** to double-lock a door; **enfermer qn à** ~ **tour** to put sb under lock and key; **à** ~ **tranchant** (*lit, fig*) double-edged, two-edged; **boîte/valise à** ~ **fond** box/case with a false bottom; ~ **nationalité** dual nationality; **foyer à** ~ **revenu** dual-income *ou* double-income household; **mettre un fil (en)** ~ to use a double thread, use a thread double(d); **mettre une couverture (en)** ~ to put a blanket on double; **en** ~ **aveugle** double blind; *voir* **bouchée, coup**.

b (*qui a des aspects opposés*) *vie, aspect* double. **à** ~ **face** *tissu* reversible; (*fig*) two-faced; **accusé de jouer un** ~ **jeu** accused of double-dealing *ou* of playing a double game (*Brit*); **phrase à** ~ **sens** *ou* **entente** sentence with a double meaning; **avoir le don de** ~ **vue** to have the gift of second sight; **personnage à personnalité** ~ person with a dual personality *ou* a Jekyll-and-Hyde personality; *voir* **agent**.

2 **nm** a (*quantité*) **manger/gagner le** ~ **(de qn)** to eat/earn twice as much (as sb) *ou* double the amount (that sb does); **il pèse le** ~ **de vous** he weighs *ou* is twice your weight, he weighs twice as much as you do; **4 est le** ~ **de 2** 4 is two times *ou* twice 2; **c'est le** ~ **du prix normal** it is twice *ou* double the normal price; **c'est le** ~ **de la distance Paris-Lyon** it's twice *ou* double the distance from Paris to Lyons; **hier il a mis le** ~ **de temps à faire ce travail** yesterday he took twice as long *ou* double the time to do this job; **nous attendons le** ~ **de gens** we expect twice as many people *ou* double the number of people; **plier qch en** ~ to fold sth in half *ou* in two; *voir* **quitte**.

b (*copie, duplicata*) *[facture, acte]* copy; *[timbre]* duplicate, double, swap*; *[personne]* double; *[objet d'art]* replica, exact copy. **se faire faire un** ~ **de clef** to have a second key cut; **avoir des timbres en** ~ to have swaps* *ou* duplicates *ou* doubles *ou* two of a stamp; **il a tous les documents/toutes les photos en** ~ he has copies of all the documents/all the photos; **on a tout en** ~**, pour plus de sûreté** we have two of everything to be on the safe side.

c (*Sport*) doubles. **le** ~ **dames/messieurs/mixte** the ladies'/men's/mixed doubles; **faire un** ~**, jouer en** ~ to play a doubles match.

d (*Jeux*) *[dés, dominos]* double. **faire un** ~ to throw a double; ~**-six** double six; ~**-blanc** double blank.

3 **adv** *payer, compter* double; *voir* **voir**.

4 **comp** ►**double allumage** (*Tech*) **nm** dual ignition ►**double barre** (*Mus*) **nf** double bar ►**double commande** (*Tech*) **nf** dual controls; **voiture à double commande** dual-control car, car with dual controls ►**doubles cordes** (*Mus*) **nfpl** double stopping ►**double-crème** **nm inv** cream cheese ►**double croche** (*Mus*) **nf** semiquaver (*Brit*), sixteenth note (*US*) ►**double-débrayage: faire un double-débrayage** (*Aut*) to double-declutch ►**double-décimètre nm (pl double-décimètres)** (20-cm) ruler ►**double dièse** (*Mus*) **nm** double sharp ►**double-fenêtre nf (pl double-fenêtres)** double window ►**double mètre nm** two-metre rule ►**double nœud nm** double knot ►**double page nf** double page (spread) ►**doubles rideaux nmpl** double curtains (*Brit*) *ou* drapes (*US*).

doublé, e [duble] (**ptp de doubler**) 1 **adj** a *vêtement* lined (*de* with). ~ **de cuir/cuivre** *boîte, paroi* lined with leather/copper; **non** ~ unlined; ~ **de fourrure** fur-lined; ~ **(de) coton/nylon** cotton/nylon-lined, lined with cotton/nylon. b *film, acteur* dubbed. 2 **nm** a (*victoire, réussite: Sport, fig*) double; (*coup double: Chasse*) right and left. b (*Orfèvrerie*) rolled gold. c (*Mus*) turn.

doublement [dubləmɑ̃] 1 **adv** (*pour deux raisons*) for a double reason, for two reasons; (*à un degré double*) doubly. 2 **nm** a *[somme, quantité, lettre]* doubling. b *[feuille]* doubling, folding (in half); *[fil]* doubling. c *[véhicule]* overtaking (*Brit*), passing.

doubler [duble] [1] 1 **vt** a (*augmenter*) *fortune, dose, longueur* to double. ~ **le pas** to quicken one's pace, speed up; ~ **le salaire de qn** to double sb's salary; **il a doublé son poids** he has doubled his weight.

b (*mettre en double*) *fil, ficelle* to use double, double; *revêtement* to double, lay double; *couverture* to double, fold (in half). **il faut** ~ **le fil pour que ce soit plus solide** you'll have to use the thread double(d) *ou* double the thread to make it stronger.

c (*Scol*) *classe, année* to repeat.

d *film, acteur* to dub.

e (*revêtir*) *boîte, paroi, tableau, veste* to line (*de* with). ~ **de fourrure une veste** to line a jacket with fur.

f (*dépasser*) *véhicule* to overtake (*Brit*), pass; (*Naut*) *cap* to double, round. (*fig*) **il a doublé ce cap important** he has got over this important hurdle *ou* turned this important corner; ~ **le cap des 50 ans** to turn 50, pass the 50 mark.

g (**: tromper*) ~ **qn** to pull a fast one on sb*.

2 **vi** a (*augmenter*) *[nombre, quantité, prix]* to double, increase twofold. ~ **de poids/valeur** to double in weight/value; **le nombre des crimes a doublé** the number of crimes has doubled *ou* increased twofold.

b (*Aut*) to overtake (*Brit*), pass.

3 **se doubler vpr: se** ~ **de** to be coupled with; **chez lui le sens de l'honneur se double de courage** with him a sense of honour is coupled with *ou* goes hand in hand with courage; **ce dispositif se double d'un système d'alarme** this device works *ou* functions in conjunction with an alarm system; **c'est un savant doublé d'un pédagogue** he is a teacher as well as a scholar.

doublet [dublɛ] **nm** a (*Ling*) doublet. b (*Orfèvrerie*) doublet.

doublon [dublɔ̃] **nm** a (*monnaie*) doubloon. b (*Typ*) double.

doublure [dublyʀ] **nf** a (*étoffe*) lining. b (*Théât*) understudy; (*Ciné*) stand-in; (*pour scènes dangereuses*) stuntman (*ou* stuntwoman).

douce [dus] *voir* **doux**.

douce-amère, pl douces-amères [dusamɛʀ] **nf** (*Bot*) woody nightshade, bittersweet.

douceâtre [dusɑtʀ] **adj** *saveur* sickly sweet; (*péj*) *air, sourire* sickly sweet, mawkish.

doucement [dusmɑ̃] 1 **adv** a (*légèrement*) *toucher, prendre, soulever* gently; *frapper, parler* gently, softly; *éclairer* softly. **marcher** ~ to tread carefully *ou* softly; **allez-y** ~*! easy *ou* gently does it!*, go easy*!

b (*graduellement*) *monter, progresser* gently, gradually; (*lentement*) *rouler, avancer* slowly; (*en douceur*) *démarrer* smoothly. **la route monte/descend** ~ the road climbs/descends gradually *ou* goes gently up/down; **la température monte/descend** ~ the temperature is slowly *ou* gradually rising/falling.

c (**: plus ou moins bien*) so-so*. **comment allez-vous? — (tout)** ~ how are you? — so-so*.

d (**: en cachette*) **s'amuser** ~ **de voir qn dans l'embarras** to have a quiet laugh* (to o.s.) at seeing sb in difficulties; **ça me fait** ~ **rigoler!** it doesn't half make me laugh!*

2 **excl:** ~! gently!, easy!; ~ **avec le whisky!** go easy on the whisky!*, careful with the whisky!; ~ **les basses!**‡ take it easy!*, go easy!*

doucereux, -euse [dus(ə)ʀø, øz] **adj** *goût, saveur* sickly sweet; (*péj*) *ton, paroles* sugary, honeyed; (*péj*) *personne, manières* suave, smooth*.

doucet, -ette [dusɛ, ɛt] 1 **adj** (†) meek, mild. 2 **doucette nf** (*Bot*) corn-salad, lamb's lettuce.

doucettement* [dusɛtmɑ̃] **adv** *commencer, avancer* gently; *vivre* quietly.

douceur [dusœʀ] **nf** a (*caractère: voir* **doux**) softness; smoothness; mildness; gentleness; sweetness. ~ **angélique** angelic sweetness; **prendre qn par la** ~ to deal gently with sb, use gentleness with sb; ~ **de vivre** gentle way of life; **les** ~**s de l'amitié** the (sweet) pleasures of friendship; *voir* **plus**. b (*gén pl*) (*sucrerie*) sweet; (*flatterie*) sweet talk (*NonC*). c **en** ~ *démarrage* smooth; *démarrer* smoothly; *commencer, manœuvrer* gently; **il faut y aller en** ~ we must go about it gently; **ça s'est passé en** ~ it went off smoothly.

Douchanbé [duʃɑ̃be] **n** Douchanbe.

douche [duʃ] 1 **nf** a (*jet, système*) shower. **prendre une** ~ to have *ou* take a shower; **passer à la** ~ to go for a shower; **il est sous la** ~ he's in the *ou* having a shower. b (*salle*) ~**s** shower room, showers. c (** fig*) (*déception*) let-down*, bummer* (*US*); (*réprimande*) (good) telling-off* *ou* ticking-off* (*Brit*); (**: averse, arrosage*) soaking, drenching. **on a pris une bonne** ~* we got drenched *ou* soaked; **ça nous a fait l'effet d'une** ~ **(froide) quand nous l'avons appris** it was a real let-down* when we found out. 2 **comp** ►**douche écossaise** (*lit*) alternately hot and cold shower; (** fig*) **ça a été la douche écossaise** it came as a bit of a blow *ou* shock.

doucher [duʃe] [1] 1 **vt** (*voir* **douche**) ~ **qn** to give sb a shower; to let sb down (with a bump)*; to give sb a (good) telling-off* *ou* ticking-off* (*Brit*); to soak *ou* drench sb; **on s'est fait** ~ (*par l'averse*) we got soaked *ou* drenched; (*par le tuyau d'arrosage*) we got sprayed *ou* soaked *ou* drenched. 2 **se doucher vpr** to have *ou* take a shower.

douchette [duʃɛt] **nf** shower rose.

doudou* [dudu] **nf** (*Antilles*) lady*.

doudoune [dudun] **nf** a (*anorak*) down jacket. b (**: sein*) boob‡.

doué, e [dwe] (**ptp de douer**) **adj** a (*talentueux*) gifted, talented (*en* in). **être** ~ **pour** to have a gift for; (*iro*) **il n'est pas** ~* he's not exactly bright *ou* clever (*iro*); ~ **sur le plan scolaire** academically able.

b (*pourvu de*) ~ **de** *vie, raison* endowed with; *intelligence, talent, mémoire* blessed with, endowed with.

douer [dwe] [1] **vt:** ~ **qn de** *vie, raison* to endow sb with; *intelligence, talent, mémoire* to bless sb with, endow sb with.

douille [duj] **nf** *[cartouche]* (cartridge) case, cartridge; *[fil électrique]* (electric light) socket; *[manche]* socket.

douiller‡ [duje] [1] **vi** (*payer cher*) to pay through the nose*, fork out* a lot. **ça douille** it's damn expensive‡, it's damn pricy‡.

douillet, -ette [dujɛ, ɛt] 1 **adj** a (*péj: à la douleur*) *personne* soft (*péj*). b *maison, atmosphère* cosy, snug; *nid, lit* soft, cosy; *vie* soft, cosy. 2 **douillette nf** *[ecclésiastique]* (clerical) overcoat; *[bébé]* quilted

coat.
douillettement [dujɛtmɑ̃] adv cosily, snugly.
douilletterie [dujɛtʀi] nf (*péj*) softness (*péj*).
douleur [dulœʀ] nf a (*physique*) pain. **~s rhumatismales** rheumatic pains; **~s dorsales** backache (*NonC*), back pains; **les ~s (de l'accouchement)** labour pains; **j'ai une ~ dans le bras** I have a sore arm, I have a pain in my arm, my arm hurts; **mes vieilles ~s me font souffrir** my old aches and pains are bothering me; *voir* **accouchement**.
b (*morale*) grief, distress. **il a eu la ~ de perdre son frère** he had the distress of *ou* had to suffer the grief of losing his brother; **"nous avons la ~ de vous faire part du décès de"** "it is our sad duty to tell you *ou* it is with great sorrow that we have to tell you of the death of"; **"nous avons la ~ d'apprendre que ..."** "it was with great sorrow that we learned that ..."; *voir* **grand**.
douloureusement [duluʀøzmɑ̃] adv (*physiquement*) painfully; (*moralement*) grievously.
douloureux, -euse [duluʀø, øz] 1 adj a *sensation, maladie, opération, membre* painful. b *perte* grievous, distressing; *décision, spectacle* painful, distressing, harrowing; *séparation, circonstances, moment* painful, distressing; *regard, expression* sorrowful. 2 **douloureuse*** nf (*hum*) (*addition*) bill (*Brit*), check (*US*); (*facture*) bill. **apportez-nous la ~euse** let's hear the worst*, what's the damage?*
doute [dut] nm a (*état d'incertitude*) doubt, uncertainty; (*Philos, Rel*) doubt. **être dans le ~** to be doubtful *ou* uncertain; **laisser qn dans le ~** to leave sb in (a state of) uncertainty; **être dans le ~ au sujet de qch** to be in doubt *ou* doubtful *ou* uncertain about sth; **le ~ l'envahit** he was invaded by doubt; **le ~ n'est plus permis quant à** there is no more room for doubt concerning; **le ~ subsiste quant à** there is still room for doubt concerning; **un air de ~** a doubtful air.
b (*soupçon, perplexité*) doubt. **je n'ai pas le moindre ~ à ce sujet** I haven't the slightest doubt about it; **avoir des *ou* ses ~s sur *ou* au sujet de qch/qn** to have misgivings *ou* (one's) doubts about sth/sb; **malgré tout, j'ai des ~s** nevertheless, I have my doubts; **il a émis des ~s à propos de ...** he expressed (his) doubts *ou* misgivings about ...; **un ~ plane sur l'affaire** a certain amount of *ou* an element of doubt hangs over the matter.
c (*loc*) (*Prov*) **dans le ~, abstiens-toi** when in doubt, don't!; **sans ~** (*vraisemblablement*) doubtless, no doubt, probably; **sans (nul *ou* aucun) ~** (*incontestablement*) without (a) doubt; **sans ~ s'est-il trompé** he is doubtless *ou* no doubt mistaken; **il ne fait aucun ~ que ...** there is (absolutely) no doubt that ..., there is no question that ...; **ceci ne fait aucun ~** there is no doubt *ou* question about it; **mettre en ~** *affirmation, honnêteté de qn* to question, challenge, cast doubt on; **mettre en ~ que** to question whether; *voir* **hors, ombre**[1].
douter [dute] 1 1 **douter de** vt indir a (*sentiment d'incertitude*) *identité, authenticité, existence de qch* to doubt, question, have doubts as to; *réussite* to be doubtful of. **je doute de l'authenticité de ce document** I doubt *ou* question the authenticity of this document, I have doubts as to the authenticity of this document; **au débat il le croyait, maintenant il doute** in the debate he believed it, now he's questioning it *ou* now he's doubting it; **il le dit mais j'en doute** he says so but I have my doubts *ou* but I doubt it; **il a dit la vérité, n'en doutez pas** he is telling the truth, you can be sure of that *ou* there's no doubt about that; **je doute d'avoir jamais fait/dit cela** I doubt that I ever did/said that; **je n'ai jamais douté du résultat** I never had any doubts about *ou* as to the result; **je doute qu'il vienne** I doubt if *ou* whether he'll come; **je ne doute pas qu'il le fera *ou* ne le fasse** I don't doubt *ou* I dare say that he'll do it; **à n'en pas ~** (*sans aucun doute*) without (a) doubt; (*vraisemblablement*) doubtless, no doubt; (*littér*) **~ si** to doubt whether.
b (*Philos, Rel: esprit de réfutation*) **~ de** *dogme philosophique ou religieux* to have *ou* entertain (*frm*) doubts about, doubt; **mieux vaut ~ que tout accepter** it is better to doubt than to accept everything.
c (*sentiment de méfiance*) **~ de** *allié, sincérité de qn* to have (one's) doubts about, doubt; **je n'ai jamais douté de vous** I never doubted you, I never had any doubts about you; **~ de la parole de qn** to doubt sb's word; **il ne doute de rien!*** he's got some nerve!*; **il doute de lui(-même)** he has doubts about himself.
2 **se douter** vpr: **se ~ de qch** to suspect sth; **je me doute de son inquiétude quand il apprendra la nouvelle** I can (just) imagine his anxiety when he learns the news; **je ne m'en suis jamais douté** I never guessed *ou* suspected it for a moment; **ça, je m'en doutais depuis longtemps** I've thought so *ou* thought as much *ou* suspected as much for a long time; **j'étais (bien) loin de me ~ que ...** little did I know that ...; **se ~ que** to suspect that, have an idea that; **il ne se doutait pas qu'elle serait là** he had no idea *ou* hadn't suspected (that) she would be there; **je me doute qu'il a dû accepter** I expect *ou* imagine that he must have accepted; **qu'il soit fâché, je m'en doute** I can well imagine that he's angry; **on s'en serait douté!*** surprise, surprise! (*iro*).
douteux, -euse [dutø, øz] adj a (*incertain*) *fait* doubtful, questionable, uncertain; *résultat, issue* doubtful, uncertain; *sens, date, réponse* doubtful. **il est ~ que** it is doubtful *ou* questionable that *ou* whether; **il n'est pas ~ que** there is no doubt that; **d'origine ~euse** of uncertain *ou* doubtful origin. b (*péj*) (*médiocre*) *raisonnement, propreté, qualité, mœurs* doubtful, dubious, questionable; (*peu solide ou peu propre*) *vêtements, individu, aliment* dubious-looking; *amarrage, passerelle* shaky, dubious-looking. **d'un goût ~** *décoration, cravate, plaisanterie* in doubtful *ou* questionable *ou* dubious taste.
douve [duv] nf a (*Agr*) drainage ditch; (*Équitation*) water jump. *[château]* **~(s)** moat. b *[tonneau]* stave. c (*Vét, Zool*) fluke. **~ du foie** liver fluke.
Douvres [duvʀ] n Dover.
doux, douce [du, dus] 1 adj a (*lisse*) *peau, tissu* soft, smooth; (*souple, moelleux*) *matelas, suspension, brosse* soft; *voir* **fer, lime**.
b *eau* (*non calcaire*) soft; (*non salé*) fresh.
c (*clément*) *temps, climat, température* mild; *brise, chaleur* gentle; (*Culin*) *feu* gentle, low.
d (*au goût*) (*sucré*) *fruit, saveur, liqueur* sweet; (*pas fort*) *moutarde, fromage, tabac, piment* mild. **~ comme le miel** as sweet as honey; *voir* **orange**.
e (*à l'ouïe, la vue*) *son, musique, accents* sweet, gentle; (*Phon*) *consonne* soft; *lumière, couleur* soft, mellow, subdued. **un nom aux consonances douces** a sweet-sounding name.
f (*modéré, peu brusque*) *pente, montée* gentle, gradual; *démarrage* smooth; *voiture, moteur* smooth-running. **en pente douce** gently sloping.
g (*patient, tolérant*) *personne, caractère, manières* mild, gentle; *sourire* gentle; (*non brutal*) *geste, personne, voix* gentle; *reproche* gentle, mild; *punition* mild. **il est ~ comme un agneau** he's as meek (*Brit*) *ou* gentle as a lamb; *voir* **œil**.
h (*gén avant nom: agréable*) *victoire, revanche, repos, tranquillité* sweet; *parfum, souvenirs, pensées* sweet, agreeable, pleasant. **se faire une douce violence** to inflict a pleasant burden upon o.s.; **cette pensée lui était douce** this thought gave him great pleasure; **qu'il m'était ~ de repenser à ces moments** what pleasure it gave me *ou* how pleasant *ou* agreeable for me to think over those moments; *pensées, souvenirs* **~-amer** bittersweet; *voir* **billet, couler**.
i *drogue* soft; *médecine* alternative.
j (*loc*) **en douce*** on the quiet.
2 adv: **ça va tout ~*** things are going so-so*; († *ou hum*) **tout ~!** gently (now)!, careful (now)!; *voir* **filer**.
3 nm,f (*parfois péj: personne douce*) mild(-natured) person.
4 nm: **le ~** sweet tastes *ou* things; **préférer le ~ à l'amer** to prefer sweet tastes *ou* things to bitter.
5 **douce** nf († *ou hum: amoureuse*) sweetheart†.
douzain [duzɛ̃] nm (*Poésie*) twelve-line poem; (*Hist: monnaie*) douzain, *obsolete French coin*.
douzaine [duzɛn] nf (*douze*) dozen. (*environ douze*) **une ~** about *ou* roughly twelve, a dozen (or so); **une ~ d'huîtres/d'œufs** a dozen oysters/eggs; **une ~ d'années** roughly *ou* about twelve years, a dozen years (or so); **vendre qch à la ~** to sell sth by the dozen; (*fig*) **il y en a à la ~** there are dozens of them; *voir* **treize**.
douze [duz] 1 adj inv twelve. (*Comm*) **~ douzaines** a gross, twelve dozen; *pour autres loc voir* **six**. 2 nm inv twelve; *pour autres loc voir* **six**.
douzième [duzjɛm] adj, nmf twelfth; *pour loc voir* **sixième**.
douzièmement [duzjɛmmɑ̃] adv in twelfth place, twelfthly.
doyen, -enne [dwajɛ̃, jɛn] nm,f (*Rel, Univ* †) ≃ dean; *[équipe, groupe]* most senior member. *[assemblée, corps constitué]* **~ (d'âge)** most senior member, doyen; **le ~ des Français** France's oldest citizen.
doyenné [dwajene] 1 nm (*Rel*) (*circonscription*) deanery; (*charge*) deanery, deanship. 2 nf (*poire*) **~ (du comice)** comice (pear).
DPLG [depeɛlʒe] (abrév de **diplômé par le gouvernement**) **ingénieur ~** (state) certified engineer.
Dr (abrév de **docteur**) Dr.
drachme [dʀakm] nf drachma.
draconien, -ienne [dʀakɔnjɛ̃, jɛn] adj *loi* excessively severe, draconian; *mesure* drastic, stringent, draconian; *régime alimentaire* strict.
dragage [dʀagaʒ] nm (*Tech: voir* **draguer**) dredging; dragging. **~ des mines** minesweeping.
dragée [dʀaʒe] nf a (*friandise*) sugared almond, dragée; (*Méd*) sugar-coated pill, dragée (*SPÉC*). b (*plomb de chasse*) small shot; (**: balle*) slug*, bullet. c (*Agr*) dredge. d (*loc*) **tenir la ~ haute à qn** to hold out on sb.
dragéifier [dʀaʒeifje] 7 vt to sugar, coat with sugar. **comprimé dragéifié** sugared *ou* sugar-coated tablet.
drageon [dʀaʒɔ̃] nm (*Bot*) sucker.
dragon [dʀagɔ̃] nm a (*Myth, fig*) dragon. (*fig*) **un ~ de vertu** a dragon of virtue. b (*Hist Mil*) dragoon.
dragonnade [dʀagɔnad] nf (*Hist*) dragonnade.
dragonne [dʀagɔn] nf *[épée]* sword-knot; *[parapluie]* loop (*for wrist*); *[bâton de ski]* wrist-strap; (*Alpinisme*) wrist loop.
dragonnier [dʀagɔnje] nm dragon tree.
drague [dʀag] nf a (*Pêche*) dragnet. b (*Tech*) (*machine*) dredge; (*navire, ponton*) dredger. c (**: pour séduire*) **la ~** chatting people up* (*Brit*), sweet-talking people* (*US*).
draguer [dʀage] 1 1 vt a (*Pêche*) to fish with a dragnet. b (*Tech*) (*pour nettoyer*) to dredge; (*pour trouver qch*) to drag; *mines* to sweep. c (*Naut*) *[ancre]* **~ (le fond)** to drag. d (**: pour séduire*) **~ qn** to chat sb up* (*Brit*), try and pick sb up*, try and get off with sb* (*Brit*). 2

vi (*: *pour séduire*) to chat up* girls (*ou* boys) (*Brit*), try and pick up* girls (*ou* boys).

dragueur[1] [dʀagœʀ] nm (*pêcheur*) dragnet fisherman; (*ouvrier*) dredger; (*bateau*) dredger. ~ **de mines** minesweeper.

dragueur[2], **-euse*** [dʀagœʀ, øz] nm,f: **c'est un sacré ~/une sacrée dragueuse** he's a great one for trying to pick up* girls/boys.

drain [dʀɛ̃] nm (*Agr*) (underground) drain; (*Méd*) drain.

drainage [dʀɛnaʒ] nm (*voir* **drainer**) drainage; tapping, draining off. (*Méd*) ~ **lymphatique** lymphatic drainage.

draine [dʀɛn] nf mistlethrush.

drainer [dʀene] 1 vt (*Agr, Méd*) to drain; (*fig*) *main-d'œuvre, capitaux* to drain (off), tap.

draisienne [dʀɛzjɛn] nf (*Hist*) dandy horse.

draisine [dʀezin] nf (*Rail*) track motorcar (*Brit*), gang car (*US*), hand-car (*US*).

Dralon [dʀalɔ̃] nm ® Dralon ®.

dramatique [dʀamatik] 1 adj a (*Théât*) *spectacle, artiste* dramatic; *voir* **art**. b (*passionnant, épique*) dramatic; (*tragique*) tragic. **ce n'est pas ~!** it's not a tragedy! 2 nf (*TV*) ~ (television) play *ou* drama.

dramatiquement [dʀamatikmɑ̃] adv (*de façon épique*) dramatically; (*tragiquement*) tragically.

dramatisation [dʀamatizasjɔ̃] nf dramatization.

dramatiser [dʀamatize] 1 vt to dramatize. **il ne faut pas ~ (la situation)** you shouldn't dramatize things.

dramaturge [dʀamatyʀʒ] nmf dramatist, playwright.

dramaturgie [dʀamatyʀʒi] nf (*art*) dramatic art; (*traité*) treatise on dramatic art.

drame [dʀam] nm a (*Théât*) drama. **l'histoire du ~** the history of (the) drama; ~ **lyrique** lyric drama. b (*événement tragique*) drama, tragedy. ~ **de la jalousie** drama *ou* tragedy of jealousy; **la farce tournait au ~** the joke was going tragically wrong; **faire un ~ de qch** to make a drama out of sth; **n'en faites pas un ~** don't make such a fuss *ou* to-do* about it; **ce n'est pas un ~!** it's not a tragedy!

drap [dʀa] nm a (*tissu*) woollen cloth. b (*pièce de tissu*) ~ **(de lit)** sheet; **~s de soie/nylon** silk/nylon sheets; ~ **de dessus/dessous** top/bottom sheet; **~-housse** fitted sheet; ~ **de bain** bath sheet; ~ **de plage** beach towel; ~ **mortuaire** *ou* **funéraire** pall; **être entre deux** *ou* **dans les ~s** to be between the sheets; (*fig*) **mettre qn dans de beaux** *ou* **sales** *ou* **vilains ~s** to land sb in a fine mess *ou* a nice pickle*.

drapé, e [dʀape] (ptp de **draper**) 1 adj draped. **tambours ~s** muffled drums. 2 nm: **le ~ d'un rideau** *etc* the hang *ou* drape of a curtain *etc*.

drapeau, pl **~x** [dʀapo] nm a (*gén*) flag. **le ~ tricolore** the tricolour; **le ~ blanc/rouge** the white/red flag; (*Golf*) ~ **de trou** pin; **le respect du ~** respect for the flag; **être sous les ~x** to be doing one's military service; **le ~ de la liberté** the flag of liberty; **mettre son ~ dans sa poche** to keep one's views well hidden. b (*Naut*) **en ~** feathered; **mettre une hélice en ~** to feather a propeller.

draper [dʀape] 1 1 vt to drape; (*Tex*) *laine* to process. **un foulard de soie drapait ses épaules** a silk scarf was draped over her shoulders, her shoulders were draped in a silk scarf. 2 **se draper** vpr: **se ~ dans** to drape o.s. in; (*fig péj*) **se ~ dans sa dignité** to stand on one's dignity; (*fig péj*) **se ~ dans sa vertu/son honnêteté** to cloak o.s. in one's virtue/honesty.

draperie [dʀapʀi] nf (*tenture*) drapery, hanging; (*Comm*) drapery, cloth; (*Art*) drapery.

drapier, -ière [dʀapje, jɛʀ] 1 adj: **industrie ~ière** clothing industry; **ouvrier ~** cloth-worker. 2 nm (*fabricant*) (woollen) cloth manufacturer. **(marchand) ~** draper (*Brit*), clothier.

drastique [dʀastik] adj (*Méd, gén*) drastic.

drave* [dʀav] nf (*Can Hist*) [*bois*] drive, rafting.

draver* [dʀave] 1 vt (*Can Hist*) *bois* to drive, raft.

draveur* [dʀavœʀ] nm (*Can Hist*) (log *ou* timber) driver, raftsman.

dravidien, -ienne [dʀavidjɛ̃, jɛn] adj Dravidian.

drenne [dʀɛn] nf = **draine**.

dressage [dʀesaʒ] nm a (*domptage*: *voir* **dresser**) taming; breaking in; training; knocking *ou* licking into shape*. b [*tente*] pitching; [*échafaudage*] erection.

dresser [dʀese] 1 1 vt a (*établir*) *inventaire, liste* to draw up, make out; *plan, carte* to draw up. (*Jur*) ~ **un acte** to draw up an act; ~ **(un) procès-verbal** *ou* **(une) contravention à qn** to report sb, book sb*; **il a dressé un bilan encourageant de la situation** he gave an encouraging review of the situation *ou* an encouraging run-down* on the situation.

b (*ériger*) *monument, statue, échafaudage* to put up, erect; *barrière, échelle* to put up, set up; *tente* to pitch, put up, erect; *mât* to raise, put up, erect; *lit* to put up. **nous avons dressé un buffet dans le jardin** we set *ou* laid out a buffet in the garden; ~ **le couvert** *ou* **la table** to lay *ou* set the table.

c (*inciter*) ~ **qn contre** to set sb against.

d *tête* to raise, lift; *menton* to stick out, jut out. (*fig*) ~ **l'oreille** to prick up one's ears; [*chien*] ~ **l'oreille** *ou* **ses oreilles** to prick up *ou* cock (up) its ears; **faire ~ les cheveux sur la tête à qn** to make sb's hair stand on end; **une histoire à faire ~ les cheveux sur la tête** a hair-raising story.

e (*dompter*) *animal sauvage* to tame; *cheval* to break (in); (*pour le cirque etc*) *chien, cheval* to train; (*) *recrue* to knock *ou* lick into shape*. ~ **un chien à rapporter** to train a dog to retrieve; **ça le dressera!*** that will knock *ou* lick him into shape*; ~ **le poil à qn*** to teach sb a lesson*; ~ **un enfant*** to teach a child his place; **les enfants/les élèves, ça se dresse!*** children/pupils should be taught their place; **enfant mal dressé*** badly brought-up child.

2 **se dresser** vpr a [*personne*] (*debout*) to stand up (straight), draw o.s. up; (*assis*) to sit up (straight). **se ~ sur la pointe des pieds** to stand up on tiptoe; **se ~ de toute sa taille** to draw o.s. up to one's full height; **se ~ sur ses pattes de derrière** [*animal*] to rise (up) on(to) *ou* stand up on its hind legs; [*cheval*] to rear (up); *voir* **ergot**.

b [*cheveux*] to stand on end; [*oreille*] to prick up.

c [*statue, bâtiment, obstacle*] to stand; (*avec grandeur, menace*) to tower (up). **un navire se dressa soudain dans le brouillard** a ship suddenly loomed (up) out of the fog.

d (*s'insurger*) to rise up (*contre, face à* against). **se ~ en justicier** to set o.s. up as dispenser of justice.

dresseur, -euse [dʀesœʀ, øz] nm,f trainer, tamer (*of animals*). ~ **de lions** lion tamer; ~ **de chevaux** horsebreaker.

dressing [dʀesiŋ] nm dressingroom.

dressoir [dʀeswaʀ] nm dresser (*Brit*).

dreyfusard, e [dʀefyzaʀ, aʀd] 1 adj (*Hist*) supporting *ou* defending Dreyfus. 2 nm,f supporter *ou* defender of Dreyfus.

dribble [dʀibl] nm (*Ftbl*) dribble.

dribbler [dʀible] 1 (*Ftbl*) 1 vi to dribble. 2 vt *ballon* to dribble; *joueur* to dribble past *ou* round.

drill[1] [dʀil] nm (*Zool*) drill.

drill[2] [dʀil] nm (*Scol etc: exercice*) drill.

drille [dʀij] 1 nm (†) **bon** *ou* **joyeux ~** cheerful character*. 2 nf (*Tech*) hand-drill.

dring [dʀiŋ] excl, nm ding, ding-a-ling.

drisse [dʀis] nf (*Naut*) halyard.

drive [dʀajv] nm (*Golf, Ordin*) drive.

driver[1] [dʀajve] 1 1 vt [*jockey*] to drive. 2 vi (*Golf*) to drive.

driver[2] [dʀajvœʀ] nm (*jockey, Golf*) driver.

drogue [dʀɔg] nf a (*stupéfiant*) drug. **la ~** drugs; **une ~ dure/douce** a hard/soft drug; *voir* **trafic**. b (*Pharm †, fig*) drug; (*péj*) patent medicine, quack remedy (*péj*).

drogué, e [dʀɔge] (ptp de **droguer**) nm,f drug addict.

droguer [dʀɔge] 1 1 vt a *malade* (*péj*) to dose up (*péj*); (*Méd †*) to give drugs to. b *victime* to drug. 2 **se droguer** vpr a (*péj: de médicaments*) to dose o.s. (up) (*de* with). b (*de stupéfiants*) to take drugs. **il se drogue** he's on drugs, he's taking drugs; **se ~ à la cocaïne** to be on *ou* take cocaine.

droguerie [dʀɔgʀi] nf (*commerce*) hardware trade; (*magasin*) hardware shop.

droguet [dʀɔgɛ] nm (*Tex*) drugget.

droguiste [dʀɔgist] nmf owner *ou* (*gérant*) keeper of a hardware shop.

droit[1], **e**[1] [dʀwa, dʀwat] 1 adj (*après nom: contraire de gauche*) *main, bras, jambe* right; *poche, soulier* right (-hand). **du côté ~** on the right-hand side; *voir* **bras, centre, main**.

2 nm (*Boxe*) (*coup*) right. (*poing*) **direct du ~** straight right; **crochet du ~** right hook.

3 **droite** nf a **la ~e** the right (side), the right-hand side; **à ~e** on the right; (*direction*) to the right; **3e rue à ~e** 3rd street on the right; **à ma/sa ~e** on my/his right (hand), on my/his right(-hand) side; **le tiroir/chemin de ~e** the right-hand drawer/path; **il ne connaît pas sa ~e de sa gauche** he can't tell (his) right from (his) left; **à ~e de la fenêtre** to the right of the window; **de ~e à gauche** from right to left; **à ~e et à gauche, de ~e et de gauche** this way and that; **il a couru à ~e et à gauche pour se renseigner** he tried everywhere *ou* all over the place to get some information; **c'est ce qu'on entend dire de ~e et de gauche** that's what one hears from all sides *ou* quarters.

b (*Aut*) **la ~e** the right; **rouler à ~e** to drive on the right; **garder** *ou* **tenir sa ~e** to keep to the right; *voir* **conduite**.

c (*Pol*) **la ~e** the right (wing); **candidat/idées de ~e** right-wing candidate/ideas; **un homme de ~e** a man of the right; **membre de la ~e** right-winger; **elle est très à ~e** she's very right-wing *ou* very much on the right; **la ~e est divisée** the right wing is split; *voir* **extrême**.

d (*Boxe*) (*coup*) right.

droit[2], **e**[2] [dʀwa, dʀwat] 1 adj a (*sans déviation, non courbe*) *barre, ligne, route, nez* straight. **ça fait 4 km en ligne ~e** it's 4 km as the crow flies; (*fig*) **cela vient en ~e ligne de ...** that comes straight *ou* direct from ...; (*Rel*) **le ~ chemin** the straight and narrow (way); (*Couture*) ~ **fil** straight grain; (*fig*) **cette décision s'inscrit dans le ~ fil d'une politique** this decision is totally in keeping with *ou* in line with a policy; *voir* **coup**.

b (*vertical, non penché*) *arbre, mur* upright, straight; (*Géom*) *prisme, cylindre, cône* right; *écriture* upright. **ce tableau n'est pas ~** this picture isn't (hanging) straight; **est-ce que mon chapeau est ~?** is my hat (on) straight?; **jupe ~e** straight skirt; **veston ~** single-breasted jacket; **tiens ta tasse ~e** hold your cup straight *ou* level; (*péj, hum*) **être ~ comme un pieu** *ou* **un piquet** to be as stiff as a poker *ou* ramrod (*péj*); **être ~ comme un i** to have a very upright posture, hold o.s. very erect; **se tenir ~ comme un i** to stand bolt upright *ou* very erect; **tiens-toi ~** (*debout*) stand up (straight); (*assis*) sit up (straight); *voir* **angle.**

c (*honnête, loyal*) *personne* upright, straight(forward); *conscience* honest, straightforward.

d (*judicieux*) *jugement* sound, sane.

2 **droite** nf (*Géom*) **(ligne) ~e** straight line.

3 adv *viser, couper, marcher* straight. **aller/marcher ~ devant soi** to go/walk straight ahead; **écrire ~** to have (an) upright handwriting; **c'est ~ devant vous** it's straight ahead of you *ou* right in front of you; **aller ~ à la faillite** to be making *ou* heading *ou* headed straight for bankruptcy; (*fig*) **aller ~ au but** *ou* **au fait** to go straight to the point; (*fig*) **cela lui est allé ~ au cœur** it went straight to his heart; *voir* **marcher.**

droit[3] [dʀwa] 1 nm a (*prérogative*) right. **avoir des ~s sur qn/qch** to have rights over sb/sth; **il n'a aucun ~ sur ce terrain** he has no right to this land; **~ de pêche/chasse** fishing/hunting rights; (*fig*) **les ~s du sang** rights of kinship; **l'humour ne perd jamais ses ~s** there is always a place for humour; **c'est bien votre ~** you've every right to do so, you are perfectly entitled to do so, you're perfectly within your rights; **de quel ~ est-il entré?** what right had he *ou* what gave him the right to come in?; **avoir le ~ de vie ou de mort sur** to have (the) power of life and death over; **avoir ~ de regard sur** to have the right to examine *ou* to inspect; (*Fin, Jur*) **avoir ~ de regard dans la comptabilité** to be entitled to have access to the books and records; **avoir le ~ de faire** (*gén: simple permission, possibilité*) to be allowed to do; (*Admin, Jur: autorisation*) to have the right to do; **être en ~ de faire** to have a *ou* the right to do, be entitled to do; (*fig*) **on est en ~ de se demander pourquoi ...** one has every right *ou* one is entitled to wonder why ...; **cette carte vous donne ~ à des places gratuites** this card entitles you to free seats; **avoir ~ à** *allocation* to be entitled to, be eligible for; *critique* to come in for; (*hum*) **il a eu ~ à une bonne râclée/réprimande*** he got *ou* earned himself a good hiding/telling-off*; **être dans son (bon) ~** to be (quite) within one's rights; **c'est à lui de (plein) ~** it's his by right(s) *ou* as of right, it is rightfully his; **membre de (plein) ~** ex officio member; **le ~ du plus fort** the law of the jungle; **faire ~ à** *requête* to grant, accede to; **avoir le ~ pour soi** to have right on one's side; **de ~ comme de fait** both legitimately and effectively; **monarque de ~ divin** monarch by divine right; **le ~ des peuples à disposer d'eux-mêmes** the right of peoples to self-determination; *voir* **bon**[1]**, force, qui.**

b (*Jur*) **le ~** law; (*Univ*) **faire son ~** *ou* **le ~** to study law; **~ civil/pénal** civil/criminal law; **~ constitutionnel/international** constitutional/international law; **~ canon** canon law; **~ romain** Roman law; **~ privé/public** private/public law; **~ coutumier/écrit** customary/statute law; **~ administratif/commercial/fiscal/du travail** administrative/commercial/tax/employment law; **le ~ des gens** the law of nations; **étudier le ~ de la famille** to study family law.

c (*gén pl*) (*taxe*) duty, tax; (*d'inscription etc*) fee, fees. **~ d'entrée** entrance (fee); **~s d'inscription/d'enregistrement** enrolment/registration fee(s); (*Comm*) **~s portuaires** *ou* **de port** harbour fees *ou* dues; **exempt de ~s** duty-free; **passible de ~s** liable to duty.

2 comp ▸**droit d'accise** excise duty ▸**droit d'aînesse** birthright ▸**droit d'asile** right of asylum ▸**droits d'auteur** royalties ▸**droit de cité:** (*fig*) **avoir droit de cité parmi/dans** to be established among/in ▸**droits civils** civil rights ▸**droits civiques** civic rights ▸**droit commun: un condamné/délit de droit commun** a common law criminal/crime ▸**droits compensatoires** (*Fin*) countervailing duties ▸**droit de cuissage** (*Hist*) droit du seigneur; (*hum*) *employer's right to subject employees to sexual harassment* ▸**droits de douane** customs duties ▸**droit de gage** (*Jur*) lien ▸**droit de grâce** right of reprieve ▸**le droit de grève** the right to strike ▸**les droits de l'homme** human rights ▸**droit d'initiative** (*Pol*) *citizens' right to initiate legislation (in Switzerland etc)* ▸**droit de mutation** (*Fin*) transfer tax ▸**les droits naturels** natural rights ▸**droit de passage** right of way, easement (*US*) ▸**droit réel** (*Jur*) title ▸**droits de reproduction** reproduction rights; **"tous droits (de reproduction) réservés"** "all rights reserved" ▸**droit de souscription** application right ▸**droits de succession** inheritance tax ▸**droit de timbre** stamp duty ▸**droits de tirage spéciaux** special drawing rights ▸**droit d'usage** (*Jur*) right of user ▸**droit de visite** (*Jur*) (right of) access ▸**le droit de vote** the right to vote, the vote, the franchise.

droitement [dʀwatmɑ̃] adv *agir, parler* uprightly, honestly; *juger* soundly.

droitier, -ière [dʀwatje, jɛʀ] 1 adj right-handed; (*rare: Pol*) right-wing. 2 nm,f right-handed person; (*rare: Pol*) right-winger. (*Tennis etc*) **c'est un ~** he's a right-handed player *ou* a right-hander.

droiture [dʀwatyʀ] nf *[personne]* uprightness, straightness, straightforwardness; *[conscience]* honesty. **~ de caractère** uprightness, rectitude (of character).

drolatique [dʀɔlatik] adj (*littér*) comical, droll.

drôle [dʀol] 1 adj a (*amusant*) *situation, accoutrement* funny, comical, amusing; (*spirituel*) *personne* funny, amusing. **je ne trouve pas ça ~** I don't find that funny *ou* amusing; **la vie n'est pas ~** life's no joke; *voir* **histoire.**

b (*bizarre*) funny, peculiar, strange. **c'est ~, j'aurais juré l'avoir rangé** that's funny *ou* peculiar *ou* strange, I could have sworn I had put it away; **avoir un ~ d'air** to look funny *ou* peculiar *ou* strange; **un ~ de type** a strange *ou* peculiar fellow, a queer fish*, an oddbod*; **c'est un ~ de numéro** he's a bit of a character; **une ~ d'idée/d'odeur** a funny *ou* strange *ou* peculiar idea/smell; **il a fait une ~ de tête!** he pulled a wry *ou* funny face!; **la ~ de guerre** the phoney war; **se sentir tout ~** to feel funny *ou* strange *ou* peculiar; **ça me fait (tout) ~ (de le voir)*** it gives me a funny *ou* strange *ou* odd feeling (to see him); **tu es ~, je ne pouvais pourtant pas l'insulter!*** you must be joking *ou* kidding – I really couldn't insult him.

c (*: *intensif*) **un ~ d'orage** a fantastic* *ou* terrific* storm; **de ~s de muscles/progrès** fantastic *ou* terrific muscles/progress*; **une ~ de correction** a hell of a punishment*.

2 nm (*dial: enfant*) child, kid*; († *péj*) scamp, rascal.

drôlement [dʀolmɑ̃] adv a (*voir* **drôle**) funnily; comically; amusingly; peculiarly; strangely. b (*: *intensif*) **~ bon/sage** awfully *ou* terribly *ou* tremendously good/well-behaved; **il fait ~ froid** it's terribly *ou* awfully *ou* dreadfully cold*, it isn't half cold*; **il est ~ musclé** he's awfully *ou* terribly muscular*, he's got an awful lot of muscle*; **il est ~ culotté** he's got some cheek*, he hasn't half got a cheek*; **il a ~ changé** he really has changed, he's changed an awful lot*.

drôlerie [dʀolʀi] nf a (*NonC*) funniness, comicalness, drollness. **la ~ de la situation m'échappe** I don't see *ou* I fail to see what's so funny *ou* amusing. b (*propos, action*) funny *ou* comical *ou* amusing thing (to say *ou* do).

drôlesse† [dʀolɛs] nf (*péj*) hussy† (*péj*).

dromadaire [dʀɔmadɛʀ] nm dromedary.

drop [dʀɔp] nm: **~(-goal)** drop-kick; **passer un ~** to score a drop goal.

drosophile [dʀozɔfil] nf (*Zool*) fruit fly, drosophila (*SPÉC*).

drosser [dʀɔse] 1 vt (*Naut*) *[vent, courant]* to drive (*contre* onto, against).

dru, e [dʀy] 1 adj *herbe* thick, dense; *barbe* thick, bushy; *haie* thickset, dense; *pluie* heavy. 2 adv *pousser* thickly, densely; *tomber [pluie]* heavily, fast; *[coups]* thick and fast.

drug(-)store, pl **drug(-)stores** [dʀœgstɔʀ] nm drugstore.

druide [dʀɥid] nm druid.

druidique [dʀɥidik] adj druidic.

druidisme [dʀɥidism] nm druidism.

drupe [dʀyp] nf drupe.

dryade [dʀijad] nf (*Myth*) dryad, wood-nymph; (*Bot*) dryas.

DST [deɛste] nf (abrév de **Direction de la surveillance du territoire**) ≃ MI5 (*Brit*), ≃ CIA (*US*).

DT [dete] (abrév de **diphtérie, tétanos**) DT.

DTP [detepe] abrév de **diphtérie, tétanos, polio.**

DTTAB [deteteabe] (abrév de **diphtérie, tétanos, typhoïde A et B**) TABDT.

du [dy] 1 art partitif *voir* **de**[2]. 2 prép + art déf = **de**[1]**+ le.**

dû, due [dy] (ptp de **devoir**) 1 adj a (*à restituer*) owing, owed; (*arrivé à échéance*) due. **la somme due** the sum owing *ou* owed, the sum due; **la somme qui lui est due** the sum owing *ou* owed *ou* due to him; *voir* **chose, port**[2]. b **~ à** due to; **ces troubles sont ~s à ...** these troubles are due to ... . c (*Admin, Jur*) **en (bonne et) due forme** in due form.

2 nm due; (*somme d'argent*) dues.

dualisme [dɥalism] nm dualism.

dualiste [dɥalist] 1 adj dualistic. 2 nmf dualist.

dualité [dɥalite] nf duality.

Dubaï, Dubay [dybaj] n Dubai.

dubitatif, -ive [dybitatif, iv] adj doubtful, dubious, dubitative.

dubitativement [dybitativmɑ̃] adv doubtfully, dubiously, dubitatively.

Dublin [dyblɛ̃] n Dublin.

duc [dyk] nm duke; *voir* **grand.**

ducal, e, mpl **-aux** [dykal, o] adj ducal.

ducat [dyka] nm ducat.

duché [dyʃe] nm (*fonction*) dukedom; (*territoire*) dukedom, duchy.

duchesse [dyʃɛs] nf a duchess. (*péj*) **elle fait la** *ou* **sa ~** she's playing the grand lady *ou* putting on airs. b **(poire) ~** Duchesse pear.

ductile [dyktil] adj ductile.

ductilité [dyktilite] nf ductility.

duègne [dɥɛɲ] nf duenna.

duel[1] [dɥɛl] nm duel. **provoquer qn en ~** to challenge sb to a duel; **se battre en ~** to fight a duel (*avec* with); **~ oratoire** verbal duel *ou* battle; **~ d'artillerie** artillery battle.

duel[2] [dɥɛl] nm (*Ling*) dual (number).

duelliste [dɥelist] nm duellist.

duettiste [dɥetist] nmf duettist.

duffel-coat, pl **duffel-coats** [dœfœlkot] nm duffel coat.

dulcinée [dylsine] nf († *ou hum*) lady-love († *ou hum*).

dum-dum [dumdum] nf inv: **(balle) ~** dum-dum (bullet).

dûment [dymɑ̃] adv duly.

dumping [dœmpiŋ] nm (*Écon*) dumping. **faire du ~** to dump goods.

dune [dyn] nf dune. **~ de sable** sand dune.

dunette [dynɛt] nf (*Naut*) poop deck.

Dunkerque [dœ̃kɛʀk] n Dunkirk.

duo [dɥo] nm (*Mus*) duet; (*Théât*) duo; (*fig: plaisantins*) pair, duo; (*fig: dialogue*) exchange. **~ d'injures** slanging match* (*surtout Brit*),

exchange of insults.
duodécimal, e, mpl **-aux** [dɥɔdesimal, o] adj duodecimal.
duodénal, e, mpl **-aux** [dɥɔdenal, o] adj duodenal.
duodénum [dɥɔdenɔm] nm duodenum.
duopole [dɥɔpɔl] nm duopoly.
dupe [dyp] 1 nf dupe. **prendre pour ~** to fool, take in, dupe; **être la ~ de qn** to be taken in *ou* fooled by sb; *voir* **jeu, marché.** 2 adj: **être ~ (de)** to be taken in (by), be fooled (by); **je ne** *ou* **n'en suis pas ~** I'm not taken in (by it), he (*ou* it *etc*) doesn't fool me.
duper [dype] 1 vt to dupe, deceive, fool. **se ~ (soi-même)** to deceive o.s.
duperie [dypʀi] nf (*tromperie*) dupery (*NonC*), deception.
duplex [dyplɛks] 1 adj inv (*Téléc*) duplex, two-way. (*Rad, TV*) **émission ~** link-up. 2 nm (*appartement*) split-level apartment, duplex (*US*); (*Can*) duplex (house), maisonette. (*Téléc*) **(émission en) ~** link-up.
duplicata [dyplikata] nm inv (*Admin, Jur*) duplicate.
duplicateur [dyplikatœʀ] nm duplicator, duplicating machine.
duplication [dyplikasjɔ̃] nf (*Math*) duplication; (*Bio*) doubling; (*Téléc*) installation of a duplex system.
duplicité [dyplisite] nf duplicity.
dupliquer [dyplike] 1 vt to duplicate.
dur, e [dyʀ] 1 adj a (*ferme, résistant*) *roche, métal, lit, peau, crayon* hard; *carton, col, brosse* stiff; *viande* tough; *porte, serrure, levier* stiff. **être ~ d'oreille, être ~ de la feuille*, avoir l'oreille ~e** to be hard of hearing; **~ comme le roc** as hard as (a) rock; *voir* **œuf.**
b (*difficile*) *problème, travail, parcours* hard, stiff, tough. **~ à manier/digérer/croire** hard to handle/digest/believe; **être ~ à la détente*** to be tight-fisted*; **leur fils est un enfant très ~** their son is a very difficult child.
c (*pénible*) *climat, lumière, punition, combat* harsh, hard; (*âpre*) *vin, cidre* harsh, bitter; (*calcaire*) *eau* hard. **il lui est ~ d'avoir à partir** it's hard for him to have to leave; **ce sont des vérités ~es à avaler*** these are hard truths to take; (*souvent hum*) **la vie est ~e** it's a hard life, life's no bed of roses; (*souvent hum*) **les temps sont ~s** times are hard; *voir* **coup, drogue.**
d (*sévère*) *personne, voix, regard* hard, harsh, severe; *traits, visage* hard; *loi, critique* harsh, severe. **être ~ avec** *ou* **pour** *ou* **envers qn** to be tough *ou* harsh with sb, be hard on sb; *voir* **école.**
e (*insensible, cruel*) *personne, regard* hard(-hearted). **c'est un cœur ~, il a le cœur ~** he's a hard-hearted man, he has a heart of stone.
f (*endurant*) **être ~ au mal** *ou* **à la douleur** to be tough, be stoical about pain; **être ~ à la peine** *ou* **à l'ouvrage** to be a tireless worker.
2 adv (*) *travailler, frapper* hard. **le soleil tape ~** the sun is beating down; **croire à qch ~ comme fer** to have a blind belief in sth; **le vent souffle ~** the wind is blowing hard *ou* strongly.
3 nm a (*) (*résistant*) tough one; (*meneur, casseur*) tough nut*, tough guy*, hard one; (*gén Pol: intransigeant*) hard-liner. **un ~ à cuire*** a hard nut to crack*; **jouer les ~s** to act the tough guy*, act tough.
b **construire en ~** to build a permanent structure; **une construction en ~** a permanent structure; **c'est du ~*** it's solid *ou* tough stuff, it's sturdy.
4 **dure** nf a (*) (*résistante*) tough one; (*meneuse*) hard one.
b **être élevé à la ~e** to be brought up the hard way; **vivre à la ~e** to live rough; **coucher sur la ~e** to sleep rough (*surtout Brit*), sleep on the ground.
c (*) **en dire de ~es à qn** to give sb a good telling-off* *ou* ticking-off* (*Brit*); **en entendre de ~es** (*reproches*) to get a good telling-off* *ou* ticking-off* (*Brit*); **en faire voir de ~es à qn** to give sb a hard *ou* tough time (of it)*; **en voir de ~es** to have a hard *ou* tough time (of it)*.
durabilité [dyʀabilite] nf (*gén*) durability; *[produit]* life span.
durable [dyʀabl] adj *bonheur, monument, souvenir, lien* lasting; *étoffe* durable, long-lasting.
durablement [dyʀabləmɑ̃] adv *s'installer* on a long-term basis. **bâtir ~** to build something to last; **bâti ~** built to last.
duraille* [dyʀaj] adj *problème* tough, hard; *matelas, viande* hard.
duralumin [dyʀalymɛ̃] nm duralumin.
durant [dyʀɑ̃] prép (*gén: pendant*) for; (*au cours de*) during, in the course of. **il peut rêvasser ~ des heures** *ou* **des heures ~** he can daydream for hours (on end); **2 heures ~** for (a full *ou* whole) 2 hours; **des années ~** for years (and years); **sa vie ~** throughout his life, for as long as he lived (*ou* lives); **~ le spectacle** during the show; **il a plu ~ la nuit** it rained in (the course of) *ou* during the night.
duratif, -ive [dyʀatif, iv] adj durative.
Durban [dyʀban] n Durban.
durcir [dyʀsiʀ] 2 1 vt to harden. **~ ses positions** to take a tougher stand; **~ un mouvement de grève** to step up strike action. 2 vi, **se durcir** vpr (*gén*) to harden; *[mouvement de grève]* to become more firmly entrenched.
durcissement [dyʀsismɑ̃] nm hardening. **~ des mouvements de grève** stepping up of strike action.
durcisseur [dyʀsisœʀ] nm hardener.
durée [dyʀe] nf a *[spectacle, opération]* duration, length; *[bail]* term; *[prêt]* period; *[matériau, pile, ampoule]* life; (*Mus*) *[note]* value, length, duration. **la ~ d'une mode dépend de ...** how long a fashion lasts depends on ...; **je m'étonne de la ~ de ce spectacle** I'm amazed at the length of this show; **pour une ~ illimitée** for an unlimited length of time, for an unlimited period; **pendant une ~ d'un mois** for (the period of) one month; **pour la ~ des négociations** while negotiations continue, for the duration of the negotiations; **pendant la ~ des réparations** for the duration of repairs, while repairs are being carried out; **de courte ~** *séjour* short; *bonheur, répit* short-lived; **de longue ~** *effet* long-lasting; *pile* long-life (*épith*), long-lasting; **~ de vie utile** useful life; *voir* **disque.** b (*permanence*) continuance. **il n'osait croire à la ~ de cette prospérité** he did not dare to believe that this prosperity would last *ou* to believe in the continuance of this prosperity. c (*Philos*) duration.
durement [dyʀmɑ̃] adv (*voir* **dur**) (*péniblement*) harshly; severely; (*sévèrement*) harshly, severely; (*cruellement*) hard-heartedly. **~ éprouvé** sorely tried; **élever qn ~** to bring sb up harshly *ou* the hard way.
durer [dyʀe] 1 vi a to last. **combien de temps cela dure-t-il?** how long does it last?; **l'effet dure 2 minutes/mois** the effect lasts (for) 2 minutes/months; **le festival dure (pendant) 2 semaines** the festival lasts (for) 2 weeks. b (*se prolonger*) *[mode, maladie, tempête]* to last. **la fête a duré toute la nuit/jusqu'au matin** the party went on *ou* lasted all night/until morning; **sa maladie dure depuis 2 mois** he has been ill for 2 months (now), his illness has lasted for 2 months (now); **ça fait 2 mois que ça dure** it has been going on *ou* it has lasted for 2 months (now); **ça n'a que trop duré!** it's gone on too long already!; **ça va ~ longtemps, cette plaisanterie?** how much longer is this joke going to go on? *ou* continue?; **ça durera ce que ça durera** I don't know if it'll last, it might last and it might not; **ça ne peut plus ~!** this can't go on (any longer)!; **faire ~ un travail** to spin out* (*Brit*) *ou* prolong a job; (*gén iro*) **faire ~ le plaisir** to prolong the agony; (*littér*) **le temps me dure** time hangs heavy on me *ou* on my hands; (*littér*) **l'inaction me dure** I am growing impatient at this inactivity; *voir* **pourvu²**. c (*littér: subsister*) *[coutume]* to linger on; (*péj*) *[mourant]* to hang on (*péj*), linger on. d (*se conserver*) *[matériau, vêtement, outil]* to last. **faire ~ des chaussures** to make shoes last; **cette somme doit te ~ un mois** the sum will have to last you a month.
dureté [dyʀte] nf (*voir* **dur**) hardness; stiffness; toughness; harshness; severity. **~ (de cœur)** hard-heartedness.
durillon [dyʀijɔ̃] nm (*aux mains*) callus, hard skin (*NonC*); (*aux pieds*) callus, corn.
durit, durite [dyʀit] nf ® (*Aut*) (radiator) hose.
DUT [deyte] nm (abrév de **diplôme universitaire de technologie**) *voir* **diplôme.**
duvet [dyvɛ] nm a *[oiseau, fruit, joues]* down. b (*sac de couchage*) (down-filled) sleeping bag.
duveter (se) [dyv(ə)te] 5 vpr to become downy. **duveté** downy.
duveteux, -euse [dyv(ə)tø, øz] adj downy.
dynamique [dinamik] 1 adj (*Phys, gén*) dynamic. 2 nf (*Phys, Mus*) dynamics (*sg*). **s'inscrire dans la ~ en cours** to fit into the dynamic current; (*Sociol*) **la ~ de groupe** group dynamics.
dynamiquement [dinamikmɑ̃] adv dynamically.
dynamisant, e [dinamizɑ̃, ɑ̃t] adj *personne, atmosphère etc* motivating.
dynamisation [dinamizasjɔ̃] nf energization.
dynamiser [dinamize] 1 vt *personnel etc* to energize; (*Méd*) *médicament* to potentiate (*SPÉC*).
dynamisme [dinamism] nm (*Philos, gén*) dynamism.
dynamitage [dinamitaʒ] nm dynamiting.
dynamite [dinamit] nf (*lit, fig*) dynamite.
dynamiter [dinamite] 1 vt to dynamite, blow up with dynamite.
dynamiteur, -euse [dinamitœʀ, øz] nm,f dynamiter.
dynamo [dinamo] nf dynamo.
dynamo-électrique [dinamoelɛktʀik] adj dynamoelectric.
dynamogène [dinamɔʒɛn] adj, **dynamogénique** [dinamɔʒenik] adj dynamogenic.
dynamographe [dinamɔgʀaf] nm dynamograph.
dynamomètre [dinamɔmɛtʀ] nm dynamometer.
dynamométrique [dinamɔmetʀik] adj dynamometric; *voir* **clef.**
dynastie [dinasti] nf dynasty.
dynastique [dinastik] adj dynastic, dynastical.
dyne [din] nf dyne.
dysenterie [disɑ̃tʀi] nf dysentery.
dysentérique [disɑ̃teʀik] adj dysenteric.
dysfonctionnement [disfɔ̃ksjɔnmɑ̃] nm dysfunction.
dysgraphie [disgʀafi] nf dysgraphia.
dyslexie [dislɛksi] nf dyslexia, word-blindness.
dyslexique [dislɛksik] adj, nmf dyslexic.
dysménorrhée [dismenɔʀe] nf dysmenorrhoea.
dyspepsie [dispɛpsi] nf dyspepsia.
dyspepsique [dispɛpsik] adj, nmf, **dyspeptique** [dispɛptik] adj, nmf dyspeptic.
dysphasie [disfazi] nf dysphasia.
dysprosium [dispʀozjɔm] nm dysprosium.
dystrophie [distʀɔfi] nf: **~ musculaire progressive** muscular dystrophy.

E

E¹, e [ə] **nm** (*lettre*) E, e. **~ dans l'o** e and o joined together.
E² (**abrév de Est**) E.
EAO [əao] **nm** (**abrév de enseignement assisté par ordinateur**) CAI, CAL.
eau, **pl ~x** [o] 1 **nf** a (*gén, Bijouterie, Méd*) water; (*pluie*) rain. **sans ~** *alcool* neat, straight; **cuire à l'~** to boil; **se passer les mains à l'~** to rinse one's hands, give one's hands a quick wash; **passer qch sous l'~** to give sth a quick rinse; **diamant de la plus belle ~** diamond of the first water; **escroc de la plus belle ~** thoroughgoing thief; **la Compagnie** *ou* **le Service des E~x** ≈ the Water Board; *[fleuve]* **basses/hautes ~x** low/high water; *voir* **déminéralisé, mort², ville** *etc.*
b (*loc*) **tout cela apporte de l'~ à son moulin** all that is grist to his mill; (*Méd*) **aller aux ~x, prendre les ~x** to take the waters; (*Naut*) **aller sur l'~** (*flotter*) to be buoyant; (*naviguer*) to sail; **aller à l'~** to go for a dip*; **j'en avais l'~ à la bouche** my mouth was watering, it made my mouth water; (*Naut*) **être dans les ~x d'un navire** to be in the wake of a ship; **être en ~** to be bathed in perspiration *ou* sweat; (*Naut, Rail*) **faire de l'~** to take on (a supply of) water; **faire ~ (de toutes parts)** to leak (like a sieve); (*Naut*) **mettre à l'~** to launch; **mise à l'~** launch, launching; **se mettre à l'~** (*nager*) to get into the water; (*être sobre*) to go on the wagon*, keep off drink; **mettre de l'~ dans son vin** (*lit*) to water down one's wine; (*fig*) to climb down; (*Méd*) **elle a perdu les ~x** her waters have broken; *[chaussures]* **prendre l'~** to leak, let in water; **il passera beaucoup d'~ sous les ponts** much water will have flowed under the bridge; **dans ces ~x-là*** or thereabouts; (*Prov*) **porter de l'~ à la rivière** to carry coals to Newcastle (*Prov*); (*Prov*) **l'~ va à la rivière** money makes money, to him that has shall more be given; **s'en aller en ~ de boudin*** to flop; **notre projet est (tombé) à l'~** our project fell through; **il y a de l'~ dans le gaz*** things aren't running too smoothly; (*fig*) **nager** *ou* **naviguer en ~x troubles** to move in shady circles.
2 **comp** ►**eau bénite** holy water ►**eau de Cologne** eau de Cologne ►**eau courante** running water ►**eau douce** fresh water ►**eau d'érable** maple sap (*Can*) ►**eau-forte** (*Art*) etching; (*Chim*) aqua fortis ►**eau gazeuse** sparkling (mineral) water ►**eau de javel** bleach ►**eau lourde** heavy water ►**eaux ménagères** waste (household) water ►**eau de mer** sea water ►**eau minérale** mineral water ►**eaux minérales** minerals (*Brit*), mineral waters (*US*) ►**eau oxygénée** hydrogen peroxide ►**eau de parfum** eau de parfum ►**eau plate** plain *ou* still water ►**eau de pluie** rainwater ►**eau potable** drinking water ►**eau de rose** rose water; **roman/histoire à l'eau de rose** mawkish *ou* sentimental *ou* soppy* *ou* schmaltzy* novel/story ►**eau rougie** wine and water ►**eau salée** salt water ►**eau savonneuse** soapy water ►**eau de Seltz** soda (water), seltzer water (*US*) ►**eau de source** spring water ►**eau sucrée** sugar water ►**eaux territoriales** territorial waters; **dans les eaux territoriales françaises** in French waters ►**eaux thermales** thermal springs *ou* waters ►**eau de toilette** toilet water, eau de toilette ►**eaux usées** liquid waste ►**eau de vaisselle** dishwater, washing-up (*Brit*) water ►**eau-de-vie (de prune/poire** *etc*) (plum/pear *etc*) brandy; **cerises à l'eau-de-vie** cherries in brandy.
EAU [əay] **nmpl** (**abrév de Émirats arabes unis**) UAE.
ébahi, e [ebai] (**ptp de ébahir**) **adj** dumbfounded, flabbergasted, astounded.
ébahir [ebaiʀ] [2] **vt** to dumbfound, flabbergast, astound. **s'~** to gawp (*Brit*), wonder (*de voir* at seeing).
ébahissement [ebaismɑ̃] **nm** astonishment, amazement.
ébarber [ebaʀbe] [1] **vt** *papier, métal, poisson* to trim; *plante* to clip, trim.
ébats [eba] **nmpl** frolics, gambols. **~ amoureux** lovemaking; **prendre ses ~ = s'ébattre.**
ébattre (s') [ebatʀ] [41] **vpr** *[animaux]* to frolic, frisk, gambol (about); *[enfants]* to play *ou* romp about, frolic.
ébaubi, e [ebobi] (**ptp de s'ébaubir**) **adj** (†, *hum*) bowled over, flabbergasted (*de* at). **être tout ~** to be agog (*devant* at).
ébaubir (s') [ebobiʀ] [2] **vpr** (†, *hum*) to gawp (*Brit*), wonder (*de voir* at seeing).
ébauche [eboʃ] **nf** a (*action: voir* **ébaucher**) sketching out, roughing out; rough-hewing; starting up; opening up. b (*résultat*) *[livre]* skeleton, outline; *[statue]* rough shape; *[projet]* (rough) outline. **l'~ d'une amitié** the beginnings of a friendship; **l'~ de relations futures** the first steps towards future relationships; **une ~ de sourire** the ghost *ou* flicker *ou* glimmer of a smile; **l'~ d'un geste** the hint of a gesture; **ce n'est que la première ~** this is just a rough draft; **c'est encore à l'état d'~** it's still in the early stages.
ébaucher [eboʃe] [1] 1 **vt** *livre, plan, tableau* to sketch *ou* rough out; *statue* to rough-hew; *amitié, conversation* to start up; *relations* to open up. **~ un sourire** to give a faint smile, give a flicker *ou* glimmer *ou* ghost of a smile; **~ un geste** to give a hint of a movement, start to make a movement. 2 **s'ébaucher** **vpr** *[plan]* to form, take shape *ou* form; *[livre]* to take shape *ou* form; *[amitié]* to form; *[conversation]* to start up; *[relations]* to open up. **une solution s'ébauche lentement** a solution is gradually evolving *ou* taking shape; **une idée à peine ébauchée** the bare bones *ou* the mere outline of an idea.
ébaudir **vt, s'ébaudir** **vpr** [ebodiʀ] [2] (†, *hum*) to rejoice (*de, à* over, at).
ébène [ebɛn] **nf** ebony. **cheveux/table d'~** ebony hair/table; *voir* **bois.**
ébénier [ebenje] **nm** ebony (tree); *voir* **faux².**
ébéniste [ebenist] **nm** cabinetmaker.
ébénisterie [ebenist(ə)ʀi] **nf** (*métier*) cabinetmaking; (*façon, meuble*) cabinetwork.
éberluer [ebɛʀlɥe] [1] **vt** (*gén ptp*) to astound, flabbergast, dumbfound.
éblouir [ebluiʀ] [2] **vt** (*lit, fig*) to dazzle, bedazzle.
éblouissant, e [ebluisɑ̃, ɑ̃t] **adj** (*lit, fig*) dazzling. **~ de talent/de beauté** dazzlingly talented/beautiful.
éblouissement [ebluismɑ̃] **nm** a *[lampe]* dazzle. b (*émerveillement*) bedazzlement; (*spectacle*) dazzling sight. c (*Méd: étourdissement*) **avoir un ~** to take *ou* have a dizzy turn.
ébonite [ebɔnit] **nf** vulcanite, ebonite.
éborgner [ebɔʀɲe] [1] **vt**: **~ qn** to blind sb in one eye, put *ou* poke sb's eye out; **j'ai failli m'~ contre la cheminée*** I nearly put *ou* poked my eye out on the corner of the mantelpiece.
éboueur [ebwœʀ] **nm** dustman (*Brit*), dustbinman (*Brit*), garbage collector (*US*), sanitation man (*US*), refuse collector (*Brit Admin*).
ébouillanter [ebujɑ̃te] [1] 1 **vt** (*gén*) to scald; *légumes* to scald, blanch; *théière* to warm. 2 **s'ébouillanter** **vpr** to scald o.s.
éboulement [ebulmɑ̃] **nm** a (*action: voir* **s'ébouler**) crumbling; collapsing; falling in, caving in; fall. **~ de rochers** rock fall; **~ de terre** fall of earth, landslide, landslip. b (*amas*) heap *ou* mass of rocks (*ou* earth *etc*).
ébouler [ebule] [1] 1 **vt** (*aussi:* **faire ~**) to cause to collapse *ou* crumble, bring down. 2 **vi, s'ébouler** **vpr** *[pente, falaise]* (*progressivement*) to crumble; (*soudainement*) to collapse; *[mur, toit]* to fall in, cave in, crumble; *[sable]* to fall; *[terre]* to fall, slip, slide.
éboulis [ebuli] **nm** mass of fallen rocks (*ou* earth *etc*). **pente couverte d'~** scree-covered slope.
ébouriffant, e* [ebuʀifɑ̃, ɑ̃t] **adj** *vitesse, prix* hair-raising.
ébouriffer [ebuʀife] [1] **vt** a *cheveux* to tousle, ruffle, dishevel; *plumes, poil* to ruffle. **il était tout ébouriffé** his hair was all tousled *ou* ruffled. b (**: surprendre*) to amaze, astound.
ébrancher [ebʀɑ̃ʃe] [1] **vt** to prune, lop.
ébranchoir [ebʀɑ̃ʃwaʀ] **nm** billhook.
ébranlement [ebʀɑ̃lmɑ̃] **nm** (*voir* **ébranler**) shaking; weakening; disturbance, unhinging. **l'~ provoqué par cette nouvelle** the shock caused by this news.
ébranler [ebʀɑ̃le] [1] 1 **vt** *vitres* to shake, rattle; *mur, sol* (*faire trembler*) to shake; (*affaiblir*) to weaken, make unsound; *nerfs* to shake; *santé* to weaken; *esprit* to disturb, unhinge; *résolution, confiance, gouvernement* to shake, weaken. **ça a fortement ébranlé ses nerfs/sa santé** it has shattered his nerves/health; **le monde entier a été ébranlé**

par cette nouvelle the whole world was shaken *ou* shattered by the news; **ces paroles l'ont ébranlé** these words shook him; **se laisser ~ par des prières** to allow o.s. to be swayed by pleas. 2 **s'ébranler** vpr *[véhicule, cortège]* to move off, set off.

ébrécher [ebʀeʃe] 6 vt *assiette* to chip; *lame* to nick; *fortune [personne]* to break into; *[achat]* make a hole *ou* dent in.

ébréchure [ebʀeʃyʀ] nf *[assiette]* chip; *[lame]* nick.

ébriété [ebʀijete] nf (*frm*) intoxication; *voir* **état**.

ébrouement [ebʀumɑ̃] nm *[cheval]* snort.

ébrouer (s') [ebʀue] 1 vpr a (*souffler*) *[cheval]* to snort. b (*se secouer*) *[personne, chien]* to shake o.s.

ébruitement [ebʀɥitmɑ̃] nm (*voir* **ébruiter**) spreading; disclosing; divulging.

ébruiter [ebʀɥite] 1 vt *nouvelle, rumeur* to disclose, spread (about); *secret* to divulge, disclose. **pour que rien ne s'ébruite** so that nothing leaks out.

ébullition [ebylisjɔ̃] nf *[eau]* boiling; (*fig: agitation*) turmoil, ferment. **porter à (l')~** to bring to the boil; **au moment de/avant l'~** as/before boiling point is reached, as/before it begins to boil; **être en ~** *[liquide]* to be boiling; *[ville, maison]* to be in turmoil, be in an uproar, be in a state of ferment; *[pays]* to be seething with unrest; *[personne]* (*par la surexcitation*) to be bubbling over, be simmering with excitement; (*par la colère*) to be seething *ou* simmering with anger; *voir* **point**[1].

écaillage [ekajaʒ] nm (*voir* **écailler**) scaling; opening; chipping; flaking, peeling.

écaille [ekaj] nf *[poisson, reptile]* scale; *[tortue, huître]* shell; *[oignon]* layer, scale; *[peinture sèche]* flake. **lunettes (à monture) d'~** horn-rimmed spectacles; **peigne en ~** tortoiseshell comb; **meuble en ~** piece of furniture in tortoiseshell; (*frm*) **les ~s lui sont tombées des yeux** the scales fell from his eyes.

écailler[1] [ekaje] 1 1 vt *poisson* to scale; *huîtres* to open; *peinture etc* to chip. 2 **s'écailler** vpr *[peinture]* to flake (off), peel (off).

écailler[2], **-ère** [ekaje, ɛʀ] nm,f oyster seller.

écailleux, -euse [ekajø, øz] adj *poisson, peau* scaly; *peinture* flaky, flaking.

écaillure [ekajyʀ] nf (*morceau de peinture*) chip, flake; (*surface écaillée*) chipped *ou* flaking patch.

écale [ekal] nf *[noix]* shell.

écaler [ekale] 1 vt *noix* to shell.

écarlate [ekaʀlat] adj, nf scarlet. (*fig: de honte*) **devenir ~** to turn scarlet *ou* crimson (*de* with).

écarquiller [ekaʀkije] 1 vt: **~ les yeux** to stare wide-eyed (*devant* at).

écart [ekaʀ] 1 nm a *[objets]* distance, space, gap; *[dates]* interval, gap; *[chiffres, températures]* difference; *[opinions, points de vue]* difference, divergence; *[explications]* discrepancy, disparity (*entre* between). **~ par rapport à la règle** deviation *ou* departure from the rule; **il y a un ~ important de prix entre** there's a big difference in price between; (*lit, fig*) **réduire l'~ entre** to narrow *ou* close the gap between; (*Sport*) **réduire l'~ à la marque** to narrow *ou* close the gap between the scores.

b **faire un ~** *[cheval apeuré]* to shy; *[voiture folle]* to swerve; *[personne surprise]* to jump out of the way, leap aside; **faire un ~ de régime** to allow o.s. an occasional break *ou* lapse in one's diet; (*Danse*) **faire le grand ~** to do the splits.

c **à l'~: être à l'~** *[hameau]* to be out-of-the-way *ou* remote *ou* isolated; **tirer qn à l'~ pour lui dire qch** to take sb aside *ou* on one side to say sth to him; **mettre** *ou* **tenir qn à l'~** (*fig: empêcher de participer*) to keep sb in the background, keep sb out of things; (*lit: empêcher d'approcher*) to keep *ou* hold sb back; **se tenir** *ou* **rester à l'~** (*s'isoler*) to hold o.s. aloof, stand apart, keep (o.s.) to o.s.; (*ne pas approcher*) to stay in the background, keep out of the way; (*fig: ne pas participer*) to stay on the sidelines, keep out of things.

d **à l'~ de: la maison est à l'~ de la route** the house is (well) off the road *ou* is off the beaten track; **tenir qn à l'~ d'un lieu** to keep sb (well) away from a place; **tenir qn à l'~ d'une affaire** to keep sb out of a deal; **se tenir** *ou* **rester à l'~ des autres** to keep out of the way of *ou* well away from other people, hold (o.s.) aloof from others; **se tenir** *ou* **rester à l'~ d'une affaire/de la politique** to steer clear of *ou* keep out of an affair/out of politics.

e (*Cartes*) discard.

f (*Admin: hameau*) hamlet.

2 comp ▸**écart de conduite** misdemeanour, misbehaviour (*NonC*) ▸**écart d'inflation** inflation differential ▸**écart de jeunesse** youthful misdemeanour ▸**écart de langage** strong *ou* bad language (*NonC*) ▸**écart type** standard deviation.

écarté, e [ekaʀte] (ptp de **écarter**) 1 adj *lieu, hameau* remote, isolated, out-of-the-way. **chemin ~** lonely road. 2 nm (*Cartes*) écarté.

écartèlement [ekaʀtɛlmɑ̃] nm (*supplice*) quartering; (*fig: déchirement*) agonizing struggle.

écarteler [ekaʀtəle] 5 vt (*Hist: supplicier*) to quarter; (*fig: tirailler*) to tear apart. **écartelé entre ses obligations familiales et professionnelles** torn between family and professional obligations.

écartement [ekaʀtəmɑ̃] nm space, distance, gap (*de, entre* between). (*Rail*) **~ (des rails)** gauge; (*Aut*) **~ des essieux** wheelbase.

écarter [ekaʀte] 1 1 vt a (*séparer*) *objets* to move apart, move away from each other, separate; *bras, jambes* to open, spread; *doigts* to spread (open), part; *rideaux* to draw (back). **il écarta la foule pour passer** he pushed his way through the crowd, he cut a path through the crowd; **avoir les dents écartées** to have gaps between one's teeth; **il se tenait debout, les jambes écartées/les bras écartés** he stood with his legs *ou* feet apart/with his arms outspread *ou* with outspread arms.

b (*exclure*) *objection, solution* to dismiss, set *ou* brush aside; *idée* to dismiss, rule out; *candidature* to dismiss, turn down; *personne* (*d'une liste*) to remove, strike off; (*d'une équipe*) to remove, exclude (*de* from).

c (*éloigner*) *meuble* to move away, push away *ou* back; *foule, personne* to push back (*de* from), push aside. (*fig: brouiller*) **elle essaie d'~ son mari de ses parents** she tries to cut her husband off from *ou* estrange her husband from his parents; **~ qn de la tentation** to keep sb (away) from temptation; **tout danger est maintenant écarté** there is no further risk of danger; **ce chemin nous écarte du village** this road takes *ou* leads us away from the village; **ça nous écarte de notre propos** this is taking *ou* leading us off the subject *ou* away from the issue; **ça l'écarte de l'étude** it distracts him from his studies.

d (*Cartes*) to discard.

2 **s'écarter** vpr a (*se séparer*) to draw aside, part. **la foule s'écarta pour le laisser passer** the crowd drew aside *ou* parted to let him through; **les nuages s'écartèrent pour montrer le soleil** the clouds parted and the sun shone through.

b (*s'éloigner*) to withdraw, move away, step back (*de* from). **le mur s'écarte dangereusement de la verticale** the wall is dangerously out of plumb; **la foule s'écarta du lieu de l'accident** the crowd moved away from the scene of the accident; **écartez-vous!** (move) out of the way!; **s'~ de sa route** to stray *ou* wander from one's path; **avec ce chemin nous nous écartons** this path is taking us out of our way; **les deux routes s'écartent l'une de l'autre** the two roads diverge; (*fig*) **s'~ du droit chemin** to wander from the straight and narrow; **s'~ de la norme** to deviate *ou* depart from the norm; **s'~ d'un sujet** to stray *ou* wander from a subject; **nous nous écartons!** we are getting away from the point!

écarteur [ekaʀtœʀ] nm (*Méd*) retractor.

ecchymose [ekimoz] nf bruise, ecchymosis (*SPÉC*).

Ecclésiaste [eklezjast] nm: **(le livre de) l'~** (the Book of) Ecclesiastes.

ecclésiastique [eklezjastik] 1 adj *vie, charge* ecclesiastical; *revenus* church (*épith*); *voir* **habit**. 2 nm ecclesiastic, clergyman.

écervelé, e [esɛʀvəle] 1 adj (*étourdi*) scatterbrained, hare-brained, birdbrained (*US*). 2 nm,f scatterbrain, hare-brain, birdbrain (*US*).

échafaud [eʃafo] nm a scaffold. **monter à l'~** to mount the scaffold; (*lit*) **finir sur l'~** to die on the scaffold; (*fig*) **il finira sur l'~** he'll come to a sorry end; **il risque l'~** he's risking his neck. b (††: *estrade*) platform, stand.

échafaudage [eʃafodaʒ] nm a (*Constr*) scaffolding (*NonC*). **ils ont mis un ~** they have put up some scaffolding. b (*empilement*) *[objets]* heap, pile; *[idées]* frail structure. c (*élaboration*) *[fortune]* building up, amassing; *[théorie]* building up, construction.

échafauder [eʃafode] 1 1 vt a *fortune* to build (up), amass; *projets* to construct, build; *théorie* to construct. b (*empiler*) to pile up, stack up. 2 vi (*Tech*) to put up *ou* erect scaffolding.

échalas [eʃala] nm (*perche*) stake, pole; (*: *personne*) spindleshanks* (*Brit*), beanpole*.

échalier [eʃalje] nm (*échelle*) stile; (*clôture*) gate.

échalote [eʃalɔt] nf shallot.

échancré, e [eʃɑ̃kʀe] (ptp de **échancrer**) adj *côte* indented; *feuille* serrated, jagged. **robe très ~e sur le devant** dress with a plunging neckline; **robe ~e dans le dos** dress with a low neckline at the back.

échancrer [eʃɑ̃kʀe] 1 vt *robe* (*devant*) to cut (out) a V-neckline *ou* round neckline in; (*dans le dos*) to cut (out) a low neckline at the back of; *manche* to widen the top of, widen at the top; *côte* to indent.

échancrure [eʃɑ̃kʀyʀ] nf *[robe]* (*ronde*) round neckline; (*en V*) V-neckline; *[côte]* indentation; *[feuille]* serration.

échange [eʃɑ̃ʒ] nm a (*gén, Échecs, Sci, Sport*) exchange; (*troc*) swap, trade off (*entre* between). (*Écon*) **le volume des ~s** the volume of trade; **~s culturels** cultural exchanges; **~ de vues** exchange of views; **~s de coups avec la police** scuffles with the police; **de vifs ~s entre les orateurs** heated exchanges between the speakers; **~ de bons procédés** exchange of friendly services; **~s commerciaux** trade, trading; (*Aut*) **faire l'~ standard d'un moteur** to replace an engine by a factory reconditioned one.

b **en ~** (*par contre*) on the other hand; (*en guise de troc*) in exchange; (*pour compenser*) to make up for it; **en ~ de** in exchange for, in return for.

c **faire (l')~ de qch** to swap *ou* exchange sth; **on a fait ~** we've done a swap *ou* an exchange; **ils ont fait (l')~ de leur appartement** they've changed flats with each other, they've swapped flats; (*Échecs*) **faire ~** to exchange pieces.

d (*Tennis*) rally.

échangeabilité [eʃɑ̃ʒabilite] nf exchangeability.

échangeable [eʃɑ̃ʒabl] adj exchangeable.

échanger [eʃɑ̃ʒe] 3 vt a (*troquer*) to exchange, swap (*contre* for, *avec* with). (*Comm*) **articles ni repris ni échangés** goods can neither be returned nor exchanged; (*fig*) **~ son cheval borgne contre un aveugle** to make a bad bargain. **b** *idées, regards, lettres, coups* to exchange; *injures* to bandy. **ils ont échangé des remerciements** they thanked one another.

échangeur [eʃɑ̃ʒœʀ] **nm** **a** (*Aut: route*) interchange. **b** (*Tech*) *[chaleur]* heat exchanger.

échangisme [eʃɑ̃ʒism] **nm** (*gén*) partner-swapping; (*d'épouses*) wife-swapping.

échangiste [eʃɑ̃ʒist] **adj**: **couple ~** couple who swap partners.

échanson [eʃɑ̃sɔ̃] **nm** (*Hist*) cupbearer; (*hum*) wine waiter.

échantillon [eʃɑ̃tijɔ̃] **nm** (*lit*) sample; (*fig*) example, sample.

échantillonnage [eʃɑ̃tijɔnaʒ] **nm** (*action*) sampling; (*collection*) range *ou* selection of samples. **un ~ d'outils/de tissus** a selection of tools/fabrics; **~ par couches** *ou* **par strates** stratified sampling.

échantillonner [eʃɑ̃tijɔne] 1 **vt** to sample.

échappatoire [eʃapatwaʀ] **nf** (*faux-fuyant*) evasion, way out, let-out.

échappé, e [eʃape] (**ptp de échapper**) **1 nm,f** **a** (*Sport*) breakaway. **les ~s** the breakaway group. **b** (†† *ou hum*) **~ de l'asile** bedlamite††. **2 échappée nf** **a** (*Sport*) breakaway. **faire une ~ de 100 km** to be ahead of the pack for 100 km. **b** (*vue*) vista; (*rayon de soleil*) gleam. **une ~ sur la plaine entre deux montagnes** a vista *ou* glimpse of the plain between two mountains.

échappement [eʃapmɑ̃] **nm** **a** (*Aut*) exhaust. **~ libre** cutout; **soupape/tuyau d'~** exhaust valve/pipe; *voir* **pot**. **b** (*Horlogerie, Tech*) escapement.

échapper [eʃape] 1 **1 vi** **a ~ à** *danger, destin, punition* to escape; *poursuivants* (*en fuyant*) to escape (from), get away from; (*par ruse*) to evade, elude; *obligations, responsabilités* to evade; *corvée* to get out of; *ennuis* to avoid; **~ aux recherches** to escape detection; **~ à la mort** to escape death; (*Écon*) **~ à l'impôt** (*par privilège*) to be exempt from taxation; (*illégalement*) to evade *ou* dodge* income tax, avoid paying income tax; **~ à la règle** to be an exception to the rule; **cela échappe à toute tentative de définition** it baffles *ou* eludes all definition; **il échappe à tout contrôle** he is beyond (any) control; (*Jur*) **cela échappe à notre juridiction** it is outside *ou* beyond our jurisdiction; **tu ne m'échapperas pas!** (*lit*) you won't get away from me!; (*fig*) you won't get off as easily as that!, I'll get you yet!; (*fig*) **son fils lui échappe** (*gén*) her son is slipping from her clutches; (*en grandissant*) her son is growing away from her; (*hum*) **nous n'échapperons pas à une tasse de thé** we won't get away without having (to have) a cup of tea; **essaie d'~ pour quelques jours à ton travail** try and escape *ou* get away from work for a few days; **~ à la vue** *ou* **aux regards de qn** to escape sb's notice.

b ~ à l'esprit de qn to escape *ou* elude sb; **son nom m'échappe** his name escapes me *ou* has slipped my mind; **ce détail m'avait échappé** this detail had escaped me, I had overlooked this detail; **ce détail ne lui a pas échappé** this detail was not lost on him; **ce qu'il a dit m'a échappé** (*je n'ai pas entendu*) I did not catch what he said; (*je n'ai pas compris*) I did not understand *ou* get* *ou* grasp what he said; **ça a échappé à mon attention** it escaped my notice; **l'opportunité d'une telle mesure m'échappe** I can't see *ou* I fail to see the point *ou* the use of such a measure; **rien ne lui échappe** (*il voit tout*) nothing escapes him, he doesn't miss a thing.

c ~ des mains de qn to slip out of *ou* slip from sb's hands; **~ des lèvres de qn** *[cri, parole]* to burst from sb's lips; **un cri de douleur lui échappa** he let out *ou* gave a cry of pain; **un gros mot lui a échappé** he let slip *ou* let out a swearword; **je ne voulais pas le dire mais ça m'a échappé** I didn't mean to say it but it just slipped out.

d il l'a échappé belle he had a narrow escape, that was a close shave (for him).

e laisser ~ *gros mot* to let out, let slip; *cri* to let out, utter; *objet* to let slip, drop; *secret* to let drop, let out; *occasion* to let slip, let go; *détail, faute* to overlook; **laisser ~ un prisonnier** to let a prisoner escape *ou* get away.

f faire ~ un prisonnier to help a prisoner (to) escape *ou* get out.

2 s'échapper vpr **a** *[prisonnier]* to escape (*de* from), break out (*de* of); *[cheval]* to escape (*de* from), get out (*de* of); *[oiseau]* to fly away; *[cri]* to escape, burst (*de* from). **la voiture réussit à s'~ malgré la foule** the car got away in spite of the crowd; (*fig*) **je m'échappe un instant pour préparer le dîner** I'll slip away for a moment *ou* I must leave you for a moment to get dinner ready; (*fig*) **j'ai pu m'~ du bureau de bonne heure** I managed to get away *ou* slip out early from the office; (*Sport*) **le coureur s'échappe dans la côte** the runner draws ahead *ou* pulls away on the uphill stretch.

b *[gaz]* to escape, leak; *[odeur, lumière etc]* to come, issue (*littér*) (*de* from). **la fumée s'échappe de la cheminée** smoke is coming from *ou* out of the chimney; **l'eau s'est échappée de la casserole** the water boiled over in the pan; **des flammes s'échappaient du toit** flames were darting *ou* coming out of the roof.

écharde [eʃaʀd] **nf** splinter *ou* sliver (of wood).

écharpe [eʃaʀp] **nf** *[femme]* scarf; *[maire]* sash; (*bandage*) sling. **porter** *ou* **avoir le bras en ~** to have one's arm in a sling; **prendre en ~** *voiture* to hit broadside *ou* sideways on (*Brit*).

écharper [eʃaʀpe] 1 **vt** (*lit, fig*) to tear to pieces. **se faire ~** to be torn to pieces.

échasse [eʃas] **nf** (*objet, oiseau*) stilt. (*hum*) **être monté sur des ~s** to be long in the leg, have long legs.

échassier [eʃasje] **nm** wader (*bird*).

échauder [eʃode] 1 **vt** **a** (*fig: faire réfléchir*) **~ qn** to teach sb a lesson; **se faire ~** to burn one's fingers, get one's fingers burnt; *voir* **chat**. **b** (*laver à l'eau chaude*) to wash in hot water; (*ébouillanter*) to scald. **~ la théière** to warm the teapot.

échauffant, e [eʃofɑ̃, ɑ̃t] **adj** (†: *constipant*) constipating.

échauffement [eʃofmɑ̃] **nm** **a** (*Sport*) warm-up. **b** *[terre]* heating; *[moteur]* overheating. **c** (*Méd* †) (*constipation*) constipation; (*inflammation*) inflammation; *[sang]* overheating.

échauffer [eʃofe] 1 **1 vt** **a** *moteur, machine* to overheat, make hot; (*Sport*) *coureur* to make hot. **il était échauffé par la course, la course l'avait échauffé** *[coureur, cheval]* he was hot after the race.

b *imagination* to fire, excite. **cette intervention a échauffé le débat** the discussion became fiercer *ou* more heated after this speech; **après une heure de discussion les esprits étaient très échauffés** after arguing for an hour people were getting very heated *ou* worked up*; **tu commences à m'~* (les oreilles** *ou* **la bile†)** you're getting my goat*, you're putting me in a temper.

c (*Méd* †) **~ le sang** to overheat the blood; **~ la peau** to inflame the skin; **je suis un peu échauffé** I'm a bit constipated.

2 s'échauffer vpr **a** (*Sport*) to warm up.

b (*s'animer*) *[personne]* to become heated, get worked up*.

échauffourée [eʃofuʀe] **nf** (*avec la police*) brawl, clash; (*Mil*) skirmish.

échauguette [eʃogɛt] **nf** bartizan, watchtower.

èche [ɛʃ] **nf** (*Pêche*) bait.

échéance [eʃeɑ̃s] **nf** **a** (*date limite*) *[délai]* expiry (*Brit*) *ou* expiration (*US*) date; *[bon, action]* maturity date; *[traite, emprunt]* redemption date; *[loyer]* date of payment; *[facture, dette]* settlement date; (*Bourse*) settling day. (*fig*) **~s politiques** elections; (*fig*) **l'~ fatale** the day of reckoning, the fatal date; (*Jur, Fin, Comm*) **payable à l'~** payable when due; **venir à ~** to fall due.

b (*règlements à effectuer*) **l'~ de fin de mois** the end-of-month payments; **faire face à ses ~s** to meet one's financial obligations *ou* commitments; **avoir de lourdes ~s** to be heavily committed, have heavy financial commitments.

c (*laps de temps*) term. **à longue/courte ~** *traite* long-/short-term (*épith*); *bon* long-/short-dated; (*fig*) **à longue ~** in the long run; (*fig*) **à courte** *ou* **brève ~** before long.

échéancier [eʃeɑ̃sje] **nm** *[effets]* billbook; *[emprunt]* schedule of repayments.

échéant, e [eʃeɑ̃, ɑ̃t] **adj** *voir* **cas**.

échec¹ [eʃɛk] **nm** **a** (*insuccès*) failure; (*défaite*) defeat; (*revers*) setback. **subir un ~** (*gén*) to fail, suffer a setback; (*Mil*) to suffer a defeat *ou* setback; **son troisième ~ dans une élection** his third defeat in an election; **l'~ des pourparlers** the breakdown in *ou* the failure of the talks; **après l'~ des négociations** after negotiations broke down; **sa tentative s'est soldée par un ~** his attempt has failed *ou* has ended in failure; **voué à l'~** bound to fail, doomed to failure; **l'~ scolaire** academic failure. **b** (*loc*) **tenir qn en ~** to hold sb in check; **faire ~ à qn** to foil *ou* frustrate *ou* thwart sb *ou* sb's plans.

échec² [eʃɛk] **nm** (*Jeux*) **les ~s** chess; **jeu d'~s** (*échiquier*) chessboard; (*pièces*) chessmen; **jouer aux ~s** to play chess; **mettre/être en ~** to put/be in check; **faire ~ au roi** to check the king; **~ au roi!** check!; **~ et mat** checkmate; **faire ~ et mat** to checkmate.

échelle [eʃɛl] **1 nf** **a** (*objet*) ladder. (*fig*) **il a grimpé à** *ou* **est monté à l'~*** he fell for it, he was taken in (by it); (*fig*) **il n'y a plus qu'à tirer l'~** we may as well give it up, there's no point trying to take it further; *voir* **court¹**.

b (*dimension*) scale. **carte à grande ~** large-scale map; **croquis à l'~** scale drawing; (*fig*) **sur une grande ~** on a large scale; **à l'~ nationale/mondiale** on a national/world scale; **un monde à l'~ de l'homme** a world fitted to man; **à l'~ de la firme** (*et non d'une seule usine*) at the level of the firm as a whole; (*en rapport avec son importance*) in proportion to the firm's size (*ou* requirements *etc*).

c *[bas, collant]* ladder (*Brit*), run.

d (*dans les cheveux*) **faire des ~s à qn** to cut sb's hair all unevenly.

e (*gradation, Mus*) scale; (*fig: hiérarchie*) ladder, scale. **être au sommet de l'~** (*poste*) to be at the top of the ladder; (*salaire*) to be at the top of the scale.

2 comp ►**échelle de Beaufort** Beaufort scale ►**échelle de corde** rope ladder ►**échelle des couleurs** range of colours ►**échelle coulissante** extending *ou* extension ladder ►**échelle de coupée** accommodation ladder ►**échelle d'incendie** = **échelle des pompiers** ►**échelle double** high stepladder ►**l'échelle de Jacob** (*Bible*) Jacob's ladder ►**les Échelles du Levant** the Ports of the Levant ►**échelle de meunier** (wooden) step ladder ►**échelle mobile** *[pompier]* extending ladder; (*Écon*) sliding scale ►**échelle de Richter** Richter scale ►**échelle des salaires** salary scale ►**échelle à saumons** salmon ladder ►**échelle sociale** social scale *ou* ladder ►**échelle des traitements** = **échelle des salaires** ►**échelle des**

valeurs scale of values; *voir* **grand 5.**

échelon [eʃ(ə)lɔ̃] nm a *[échelle]* rung; *[hiérarchie]* step, grade. (*Admin*) **fonctionnaire au 8e ~** official on grade 8 (of the salary scale); (*Admin*) **être au dernier/premier ~** to be on the highest *ou* top grade/on the lowest *ou* bottom grade; **monter d'un ~ dans la hiérarchie** to go up one step *ou* grade *ou* rung in the hierarchy; **grimper rapidement les ~s** to get ahead fast, get quick promotion. b (*Admin: niveau*) level. **à l'~ national/du régiment** at the national/at regimental level; (*lit, fig*) **à tous les ~s** at every level. c (*Mil: troupe*) echelon.

échelonnement [eʃ(ə)lɔnmɑ̃] nm (*voir* **échelonner**) spacing out, spreading out; spreading; staggering; grading; gradual introduction; disposing in echelons.

échelonner [eʃ(ə)lɔne] 1 vt a *objets* to space out, spread out, place at intervals (*sur* over). **les bouées sont échelonnées à 50 mètres l'une de l'autre** the buoys are spaced *ou* placed 50 metres apart; **les membres du service d'ordre sont échelonnés tout au long du parcours** the police are positioned *ou* stationed at intervals all along the route; **les bâtiments s'échelonnent sur 3 km** the buildings stretch over a distance of 3 km *ou* are spaced out over 3 km.

b *paiements* to spread (out) (*sur* over); *congés, vacances* to stagger (*sur* over).

c *exercices, difficultés* (*dans la complexité*) to grade; (*dans le temps*) to introduce gradually.

d (*Mil*) to place in echelon, echelon.

échenilloir [eʃ(ə)nijwaʀ] nm billhook, pruning hook.

écheveau, pl **~x** [eʃ(ə)vo] nm skein, hank; (*fig*) tangle, web.

échevelé, e [eʃəv(ə)le] (ptp de **écheveler**) adj *personne* tousled, dishevelled; *course, danse, rythme* wild, frenzied.

écheveler [eʃəv(ə)le] 4 vt (*littér*) *personne* to ruffle *ou* tousle *ou* dishevel the hair of.

échevin [ɛʃ(ə)vɛ̃] nm (*Hist*) alderman, principal county magistrate; (*Belgique*) deputy burgomaster; (*Can*) municipal councillor, alderman.

échiffer* [eʃife] 1 vt (*Can*) to tease, unravel.

échine [eʃin] nf a backbone, spine; (*Culin*) loin, chine. (*fig*) **il a l'~ souple** he kowtows to his superiors, he's a bit of a doormat; **plier** *ou* **courber l'~** to submit (*devant* to). b (*Archit*) echinus.

échiner (s') [eʃine] 1 vpr (*fig*) to work o.s. to death *ou* into the ground, nearly kill o.s. (*à faire qch* doing sth). **s'~ à répéter/écrire qch** to wear o.s. out repeating/writing sth.

échiquier [eʃikje] nm (*Échecs*) chessboard. (*fig*) **l'~ politique/économique** the political/economic scene; **notre place sur l'~ mondial** our place in the field *ou* on the scene of world affairs; **en ~** in a chequered pattern; (*Brit Pol*) **l'É~** the Exchequer.

écho [eko] nm a (*lit*) echo. **~ simple** echo; **~ multiple** reverberations; **il y a de l'~** there is an echo.

b (*fig*) (*rumeur*) rumour, echo; (*témoignage*) account, report; (*réponse*) response. **avez-vous eu des ~s de la réunion?** did you get any inkling of what went on at the meeting?, did anything come back to you from the meeting?; **se faire l'~ de** *souhaits, opinions, inquiétudes* to echo, repeat; *rumeurs* to repeat, spread; **sa proposition est restée sans ~** his suggestion wasn't taken up, nothing further came of his suggestion; **l'~ donné par les médias à cette nouvelle** the coverage *ou* publicity given to this news item by the media; **cette nouvelle n'a eu aucun ~ dans la presse** this item got no coverage *ou* was not mentioned in the press.

c (*Presse : nouvelle*) miscellaneous news item, item of gossip. **(rubrique des) ~s** gossip column, news (items) in general.

échographie [ekogʀafi] nf (*technique*) ultrasound. (*examen*) **passer une ~** to have a scan.

échographier [ekogʀafje] 1 vt: **~ qn** to give sb a scan.

échoir [eʃwaʀ] vi a (*littér*) **~ (en partage) à qn** to fall to sb's share *ou* lot; **il vous échoit de faire** it falls to you to do. b *[loyer, dettes]* to fall due; *[délai]* to expire.

échoppe†† [eʃɔp] nf (*boutique*) workshop; (*sur un marché*) stall, booth.

échotier† [ekɔtje] nm gossip columnist.

échouage [eʃwaʒ] nm, **échouement** [eʃumɑ̃] nm (*Naut*) (*état*) state of being aground; (*action*) grounding, running aground.

échouer [eʃwe] 1 1 vi a *[personne]* to fail. **~ à un examen/dans une tentative** to fail an exam/in an attempt.

b *[tentative, plan]* to fail, miscarry, fall through.

c **faire ~** *complot* to foil; *projet* to wreck, ruin; **faire ~ les plans de l'ennemi** to foil the enemy's plans, frustrate *ou* thwart the enemy in his plans; **on a fait ~ leur tentative d'enlèvement du directeur** they were foiled in their attempt to kidnap the manager.

d (*aboutir*) to end up. **nous avons finalement échoué dans un petit hôtel** we finally landed up *ou* ended up in a small hotel.

e (*Naut: aussi* **s'~**) *[bateau]* to run aground; *[débris d'épave]* to be washed up. **le bateau s'est échoué** *ou* **a échoué sur un écueil** the boat ran onto a reef; **le bateau s'est échoué** *ou* **a échoué sur un banc de sable** the boat ran aground on *ou* ran onto a sandbank; **bateau échoué** (*dans un port de marée*) boat lying high and dry; (*dans la vase*) boat sunk in the mud.

2 vt (*Naut*) (*accidentellement*) to ground; (*volontairement*) to beach. **il a échoué sa barque sur un écueil** he ran his boat onto a reef.

3 **s'échouer** vpr *voir* **1e.**

écimer [esime] 1 vt *arbre* to pollard, poll.

éclaboussement [eklabusmɑ̃] nm splash.

éclabousser [eklabuse] 1 vt to splash, spatter. **~ de sang** to spatter *ou* splash with blood; **ils ont été éclaboussés par le scandale** their good name has been smeared *ou* sullied *ou* tarnished by the scandal; **~ qn de son luxe** (*éblouir*) to dazzle sb with a show of wealth, show off one's wealth to sb; (*humilier*) to overwhelm sb with a show of wealth.

éclaboussure [eklabusyʀ] nf *[boue]* splash; *[sang]* spatter; (*fig: sur la réputation*) stain, smear, blot. **il y a des ~s sur la glace** there are smears *ou* spots on the mirror.

éclair [eklɛʀ] 1 nm a (*Mét*) flash of lightning; (*Phot*) flash. **il y a des ~s dans le lointain** it's lightning *ou* there's lightning in the distance; **~s de chaleur** summer lightning; **~ de magnésium** magnesium flash.

b **~ d'intelligence/de génie** flash *ou* spark of intelligence/of genius; **~ de malice** mischievous glint.

c (*loc*) **passer comme un ~** *[coureur]* to dart *ou* flash past *ou* by; *[moment]* to fly *ou* flash past *ou* by; **comme un ~** like a flash, like greased lightning*; **en un ~** in a flash, in a split second; *voir* **rapide.**

d (*Culin*) éclair.

2 adj inv *attaque, visite,* (*Échecs*) *partie* lightning (*épith*). **voyage ~** flying visit; **raid ~** (*Aviat*) blitz raid; (*Mil*) hit-and-run raid; *voir* **fermeture, guerre.**

éclairage [eklɛʀaʒ] nm (*intérieur*) lighting; (*luminosité extérieure*) light (level); (*fig*) light. **~ à l'électricité** electric lighting; **~ direct/indirect/d'ambiance** direct/indirect *ou* concealed/subdued lighting; (*lit, fig*) **sous cet ~** in this light; (*fig*) **changement d'~** shift of emphasis; (*fig*) **donner un nouvel ~ à qch** to shed *ou* cast new light on sth.

éclairagiste [eklɛʀaʒist] nm (*Théât*) electrician; (*Ciné*) lighting engineer.

éclairant, e [eklɛʀɑ̃, ɑ̃t] adj (*fig*) illuminating, enlightening; (*lit*) *pouvoir, propriétés* lighting (*épith*); *voir* **fusée.**

éclaircie [eklɛʀsi] nf a bright interval, sunny spell. **une ~ dans les nuages** a break in the clouds. b (*fig littér*) bright spot *ou* interval, ray of sunshine. **une vie monotone et sans ~** a life of cheerless monotony; **ce fut une ~ dans sa vie** it was a ray of sunshine in his life.

éclaircir [eklɛʀsiʀ] 2 1 vt a *teinte* to lighten; *pièce* to brighten up, make brighter. **~ le teint** to improve one's complexion.

b (*désépaissir*) *soupe* to make thinner, thin (down); *plantes* to thin (out); *arbres, cheveux* to thin.

c *mystère* to clear up, solve, explain; *question, pensée, situation* to clarify, make clear; (†) *doutes* to dispel; *meurtre* to solve. **pouvez-vous nous ~ sur ce point?** can you enlighten us on this point?

2 **s'éclaircir** vpr a *[ciel]* to clear; *[temps]* to clear up. **s'~ la voix** *ou* **la gorge** to clear one's throat.

b *[arbres, foule]* to thin out; *[cheveux]* to thin, get *ou* grow thin *ou* thinner. **les rangs de leurs alliés se sont éclaircis** their allies are becoming thin on the ground.

c *[idées, situation]* to grow *ou* become clearer; *[mystère]* to be solved *ou* explained; (†) *[doutes]* to vanish.

éclaircissant, e [eklɛʀsisɑ̃, ɑ̃t] adj: **shampooing ~** shampoo for lightening the hair.

éclaircissement [eklɛʀsismɑ̃] nm a *[mystère]* solution, clearing up; *[texte obscur]* clarification; (*explication*) explanation. **j'exige des ~s sur votre attitude** I demand some explanation of your attitude; (*Jur*) **demande d'~** request for clarification. b *[cheveux]* **se faire faire un ~** to have one's hair lightened.

éclairé, e [ekleʀe] (ptp de **éclairer**) adj *minorité, avis* enlightened.

éclairement [eklɛʀmɑ̃] nm (*Phys*) illumination.

éclairer [ekleʀe] 1 1 vt a *[lampe]* to light (up); *[soleil]* to shine (down) on. **une seule fenêtre était éclairée** there was a light in only one window, only one window was lit up; **une grande baie éclairait l'entrée** a large bay window gave light to the hall; **ce papier peint éclaire le couloir** this wallpaper makes the passage look lighter *ou* brighter; (*littér*) **deux grands yeux éclairaient son visage** her large eyes seemed to light up her face; **un sourire éclaira son visage** his face lit up in a smile; **bien/mal éclairé** well-/badly-lit.

b *problème, situation* to throw *ou* shed light on, clarify, explain; *auteur, texte* to throw light on. **~ qch d'un jour nouveau** to shed *ou* cast new light on sth.

c **~ qn** (*lit: montrer le chemin*) to light the way for sb; (*fig: renseigner*) to enlighten sb (*sur* about); **~ la lanterne de qn** to put sb in the picture*.

d (*Mil*) **~ le terrain** to reconnoitre the area, scout out the ground; **~ un régiment** to reconnoitre for a regiment; **~ la route** (*Mil*) to scout out the route; (*Aut*) to show the way, go on ahead.

2 vi: **~ bien/mal** to give a good/poor light.

3 **s'éclairer** vpr a *[rue]* to be lit; (*fig*) *[visage]* to light up, brighten (up).

b *[situation]* to get clearer; *[question]* to be cleared up *ou* clarified. **tout s'éclaire!** everything's becoming clear *ou* plain!, the light is beginning to dawn!*

c **s'~ à l'électricité** to have electric light; **il a fallu s'~ à la bougie** we had to use candlelight; **prends une lampe pour t'~** take a lamp to light the way.

éclaireur [eklɛʀœʀ] **nm** a (*Mil*) scout. **avion ~** reconnaissance plane; (*lit, fig*) **partir en ~** to go off and scout around. b (*Scoutisme*) (boy) scout.

éclaireuse [eklɛʀøz] **nf** (girl) guide (*Brit*), girl scout (*US*).

éclat [ekla] **nm** a *[os, verre]* splinter, fragment; *[bois]* splinter, sliver; *[grenade, pierre]* fragment. **un ~ d'obus** a piece of shrapnel; **des ~s d'obus** shrapnel; *voir* **voler**.
b *[lumière, métal, soleil]* brightness, brilliance; (*aveuglant*) glare; *[diamant, pierreries]* flash, brilliance, sparkle; *[couleur]* brightness, vividness; *[braise]* glow; *[vernis]* shine, gloss; *[satin, bronze]* sheen; *[perle]* lustre. (*Aut*) **l'~ des phares** the glare of the headlights; (*Théât*) **l'~ (des lumières) de la rampe** the blaze *ou* glare of the footlights.
c *[yeux]* brightness, sparkle; *[teint, beauté]* radiance. **dans tout l'~ de sa jeunesse** in the full radiance *ou* bloom of her youth; **perdre son ~** to lose one's sparkle.
d *[gloire, cérémonie]* glamour, splendour; *[nom]* fame; *[richesse, époque]* brilliance, glamour; *[personnage]* glamour. **donner de l'~ à qch** to lend glamour to sth; **réception donnée avec ~** sumptuous *ou* dazzling reception; **ça s'est déroulé sans ~** it passed off quietly *ou* without fuss; (*exploit*) **coup** *ou* **action d'~** (glorious) feat; *voir aussi* **e**.
e (*scandale*) fuss (*NonC*), commotion (*NonC*). **faire un ~** *ou* **un coup d'~** to make *ou* cause a fuss, create a commotion.
f **~s de voix** shouts; **sans ~ de voix** without voices being raised; **avec un soudain ~ de colère** in a sudden blaze of anger; **~ de rire** roar *ou* burst of laughter; **on l'accueillit avec des ~s de rire** his arrival was greeted with roars *ou* shouts of laughter *ou* with a burst of laughter; **comme un ~ de tonnerre†** like a peal of thunder, like a thunderclap.

éclatant, e [eklatɑ̃, ɑ̃t] **adj** a *lumière* bright, brilliant; (*aveuglant*) glaring; *couleur* bright, vivid; *feu, soleil* blazing; *blancheur* dazzling. b *teint* blooming, radiant; *beauté* radiant, dazzling. **~ de santé** radiant with health. c *succès* dazzling, resounding; *revanche* shattering, devastating; *victoire* resounding; *gloire* shining; *vérité* manifest, self-evident; *exemple* striking, shining; *mensonge* blatant, flagrant, glaring. **il a des dons ~s** he is brilliantly gifted. d *rire, bruit* loud; *voix* loud, ringing; *musique* blaring (*péj*), loud.

éclaté, e [eklate] 1 **adj** *initiatives, marché* fragmented; *paysage politique* confused, fragmented. 2 **nm** exploded view.

éclatement [eklatmɑ̃] **nm** *[bombe, mine]* explosion; *[obus]* bursting, explosion; *[pneu, ballon]* bursting; *[veine]* rupture (*de* of); *[parti]* break-up, split (*de* in). **à cause de l'~ d'un pneu** as a result of a burst tyre; **l'~ d'une bombe/d'un obus le couvrit de terre** an exploding bomb/shell covered him with earth.

éclater [eklate] [1] 1 **vi** a *[mine, bombe]* to explode, blow up; *[obus]* to burst, explode; *[veine]* to rupture; *[bourgeon]* to burst open; *[pneu, chaudière]* to burst; *[verre]* to splinter, shatter; *[parti, ville, services, structures familiales]* to break up. **j'ai cru que ma tête allait ~** I thought my head would burst.
b *[incendie, épidémie, guerre]* to break out; *[orage, scandale, nouvelle]* to break. **la nouvelle a éclaté comme un coup de tonnerre** the news came like a thunderbolt *ou* like a bolt from the blue, the news burst like a bombshell.
c (*retentir*) **des cris ont éclaté** shouts were raised; **une détonation éclata** there was the blast of an explosion; **une fanfare éclata** there was a sudden flourish of trumpets, trumpet notes rang out; **un coup de fusil a éclaté** there was the crack of a rifle; **un coup de tonnerre éclata** there was a sudden peal of thunder; **des rires/des applaudissements ont éclaté** there was a roar of laughter/a burst of applause, laughter/applause broke out.
d (*se manifester*) *[vérité, bonne foi]* to shine out, shine forth (*littér*); *[mauvaise foi]* to be blatant. **sa joie** *ou* **la joie éclate dans ses yeux/sur son visage** joy shines in his eyes/on his face, his eyes are/face is shining with joy.
e **~ de rire** to burst out laughing; **il éclata (de rage)** he exploded (with rage); **~ en menaces** *ou* **en reproches** to inveigh (*contre* against), rail (*contre* at, against); **~ en sanglots** to burst into tears; **~ en applaudissements** to break *ou* burst into applause; **nous avons éclaté en protestations devant sa décision** we broke out in angry protest at his decision.
f **faire ~** *mine* to detonate, blow up; *bombe, obus* to explode; *poudrière* to blow up; *pétard* to let *ou* set off; *ballon* to burst; *tuyau* to burst, crack; *verre* to shatter, splinter; **cette remarque l'a fait ~ (de colère)** he blew up* at this remark; **faire** *ou* **laisser ~ sa joie** to give free rein to one's joy; **faire** *ou* **laisser ~ sa colère** to give vent *ou* give free rein to one's anger.
2 **s'éclater‡ vpr** (*se défouler*) to have a ball‡. **s'~ à faire** *ou* **en faisant qch** to get one's kicks* out of doing sth.

éclateur [eklatœʀ] **nm** (*Élec*) spark gap.

éclectique [eklɛktik] **adj** eclectic.

éclectisme [eklɛktism] **nm** eclecticism.

éclipse [eklips] **nf** (*Astron, fig*) eclipse. **carrière à ~s** career which goes by fits and starts; **personnalité à ~s** public figure who comes and goes, figure who is in and out of the public eye.

éclipser [eklipse] [1] 1 **vt** (*Astron*) to eclipse; *[événement, gloire]* to eclipse, overshadow; *[personne]* to eclipse, overshadow, outshine. 2 **s'éclipser* vpr** to slip away, slip out.

écliptique [ekliptik] **adj, nm** ecliptic.

éclisse [eklis] **nf** (*Méd*) splint; (*Rail*) fishplate.

éclisser [eklise] [1] **vt** (*Méd*) to splint, put in splints; (*Rail*) to join with fishplates.

éclopé, e [eklɔpe] 1 **adj** *personne* limping, lame; *cheval* lame. 2 **nm,f** (*hum*) (*dans une bagarre*) (slightly) wounded person; (*dans un accident*) (slightly) injured person.

éclore [eklɔʀ] [45] **vi** a *[œuf]* to hatch, be hatched; *[poussin]* to hatch (out); (*littér*) *[fleur]* to open out; *[amour, talent, jour]* to be born, dawn. (*littér*) **fleur à peine éclose/fraîche éclose** budding/fresh-blown flower. b **faire ~** *œuf* to hatch; (*littér*) *sentiment* to kindle; *qualités* to draw forth.

éclosion [eklozjɔ̃] **nf** (*voir* **éclore**) hatching; opening; birth, dawn.

écluse [eklyz] **nf** (*Naut*) lock. (*fig*) **lâcher** *ou* **ouvrir les ~s*** to turn on the waterworks*.

éclusée [eklyze] **nf** sluicing water.

écluser [eklyze] [1] **vt** a (‡: *boire*) to down*, knock back‡. **qu'est-ce qu'il a éclusé!** what a hell of a lot he knocked back!‡. b (*Tech*) *canal* to close the locks in.

éclusier, -ière [eklyzje, jɛʀ] **nm,f** lock keeper.

écodéveloppement [ekodevlɔpmɑ̃] **nm** ecodevelopment.

écœurant, e [ekœʀɑ̃, ɑ̃t] **adj** *conduite* disgusting, sickening; *personne* disgusting, loathsome; *gâteau, boisson* sickly (sweet); *goût* sickly, cloying; (*péj: excessif*) *richesse* obscene; *talent, succès* sickening. **elle a une chance ~e** she is so lucky it would make you sick *ou* it makes you sick *ou* it's sickening; **~ de banalité** painfully trivial.

écœurement [ekœʀmɑ̃] **nm** (*dégoût*) (*lit*) nausea; (*fig*) disgust; (*lassitude*) disillusionment, discouragement. **manger/boire jusqu'à ~** to eat/drink o.s. sick; **manger de la crème jusqu'à ~** to eat cream until one is sick.

écœurer [ekœʀe] [1] **vt: ~ qn** *[gâteau, boisson]* to make sb feel sick; *[conduite, personne]* to disgust sb, nauseate sb, make sb sick; *[avantage, chance]* to make sb sick, sicken sb; *[échec, déception]* to discourage sb, sicken sb.

école [ekɔl] 1 **nf** a (*établissement, secte*) school. **avion-/navire-~** training plane/ship; **ferme-~** teaching farm; **l'~ reprend dans une semaine** school starts again in a week's time; **aller à l'~** (*en tant qu'élève*) to go to school; (*en tant que visiteur*) to go to the school; **querelle d'~s** petty quarrel between factions; **son œuvre est une ~ de courage/de vertu** his work is an excellent schooling in courage/virtue.
b (*enseignement*) schooling. **l'~ en France** the French school system; **les partisans de l'~ laïque** the supporters of non-denominational state education; **elle fait l'~ depuis 15 ans** she's been teaching for 15 years.
c (*loc*) **être à bonne ~** to be in good hands; **il a été à dure** *ou* **rude ~** he learned about life the hard way; **à l'~ de qn** under sb's guidance; **apprendre la vie à l'~ de la pauvreté** to be schooled by poverty; **faire l'~ buissonnière** to play truant (*Brit*), play hooky (*US*); **faire ~** *[personne]* to collect a following; *[théorie]* to gain widespread acceptance.
2 **comp** ► **école de l'air** flying school ► **école d'application** (*Mil*) officers' training school ► **école des Beaux-Arts** ≃ art college ► **école de conduite** driving school ► **école confessionnelle** sectarian *ou* denominational school ► **école de danse** (*gén*) dancing school; (*classique*) ballet school ► **école de dessin** art school ► **école d'escalade** (*Alpinisme*) practice cliff, crag ► **école élémentaire** elementary school ► **école hôtelière** catering school, hotel management school ► **école libre** = **école confessionnelle** ► **école maternelle** nursery school ► **école militaire** military academy ► **École nationale d'administration** *college for senior civil servants* ► **École nationale supérieure de chimie** *national college of chemical engineering* ► **École nationale supérieure d'ingénieurs** national college of engineering ► **école de neige** ski school ► **École normale** ≃ teachers' training college ► **École normale supérieure** *grande école for training of teachers* ► **école de pensée** school of thought ► **école de police** police academy ► **École polytechnique** École Polytechnique ► **école primaire** primary *ou* elementary school, grade school (*US*) ► **école de secrétariat** secretarial college ► **École supérieure des sciences économiques et sociales** *grande école for management and business students* *voir* **grand, haut, mixte** *etc.*

écolier [ekɔlje] **nm** schoolboy; (††) scholar††; (*fig: novice*) novice. **papier (format) ~** exercise (book) paper; *voir* **chemin**.

écolière [ekɔljɛʀ] **nf** schoolgirl.

écolo* [ekɔlo] 1 **adj** green (*épith*), environmentalist. 2 **nmf** Green, environmentalist.

écologie [ekɔlɔʒi] **nf** ecology.

écologique [ekɔlɔʒik] **adj** ecological. **mouvement ~** ecomovement.

écologisme [ekɔlɔʒism] **nm** environmentalism.

écologiste [ekɔlɔʒist] 1 **adj** environmentalist, green (*épith*). 2 **nmf** ecologist, environmentalist.

écomusée [ekomyze] **nm** museum of man and the environment (*pedagogically orientated*).

éconduire [ekɔ̃dɥiʀ] [38] **vt** *visiteur* to dismiss; *soupirant* to reject;

solliciteur to put off.
éconocroques* [ekɔnɔkʀɔk] nfpl savings.
économat [ekɔnɔma] nm (*fonction*) bursarship, stewardship; (*bureau*) bursar's office, steward's office; (*magasin*) staff cooperative *ou* store.
économe [ekɔnɔm] 1 adj thrifty. **être ~ de son temps/ses efforts** *etc* to be sparing of one's time/efforts *etc.* 2 nmf bursar, steward. 3 nm: **(couteau) ~** paring knife.
économétricien, ienne [ekɔnɔmetʀisjɛ̃, jɛn] nm,f econometrician.
économétrie [ekɔnɔmetʀi] nf econometrics (*sg*).
économétrique [ekɔnɔmetʀik] adj econometric.
économie [ekɔnɔmi] nf a (*science*) economics (*sg*); (*Pol: système*) economy. **~ politique** political economy; **~ de troc** barter economy; **~ dirigée** state-controlled *ou* centrally-planned economy; **~ monétaire** cash economy; **~ de marché** free market *ou* free enterprise economy; (*Scol*) **~ domestique** home economics.
b (*NonC: épargne*) economy, thrift. **par ~** for the sake of economy; **ménagère qui a le sens de l'~** careful *ou* thrifty housewife.
c (*gain*) saving. **faire une ~ de temps/d'argent** to save time/money; **représenter une ~ de temps** to represent a saving in time; **procédé permettant une ~ de temps/de main-d'œuvre** time-saving/labour-saving process; **elle fait l'~ d'un repas par jour** she goes *ou* does without one meal a day; **j'ai fait l'~ d'une visite** I've saved myself a visit; **avec une grande ~ de moyens** with very restricted *ou* limited means.
d (*gains*) **~s** savings; **avoir des ~s** to have (some) savings, have some money saved up; **faire des ~s** to save up, save money, put money by; **faire des ~s de chauffage** to economize on heating; **les ~s d'énergie sont nécessaires** energy conservation is essential; **réaliser d'importantes ~s d'énergie** to make significant energy savings *ou* make significant savings on one's fuel *ou* heating bills; **il n'y a pas de petites ~s** take care of the pennies and the pounds will take care of themselves, every little (bit) helps; (*fig péj*) **faire des ~s de bouts de chandelle** to make footling (*Brit*) *ou* cheeseparing economies.
e *[livre]* arrangement; *[projet]* organization.
économique [ekɔnɔmik] adj (*Écon*) economic; (*bon marché*) economical; (*Aut*) fuel-efficient. *[machine à laver]* **cycle ~** economy cycle.
économiquement [ekɔnɔmikmɑ̃] adv economically. (*Admin*) **les ~ faibles** the lower-income groups.
économiser [ekɔnɔmize] 1 vt *électricité* to economize on, save on; *énergie* to conserve, save; *temps* to save; *argent* to save up, put aside. **~ ses forces** to save one's strength; **~ sur le chauffage** to economize on *ou* cut down on heating; **économise ta salive** *ou* **tes paroles** don't waste your breath.
économiseur [ekɔnɔmizœʀ] nm (*Aut*) **~ (de carburant)** fuel-saving device.
économiste [ekɔnɔmist] nmf economist.
écope [ekɔp] nf (*Naut*) bale(r).
écoper [ekɔpe] 1 vti a (*Naut*) to bale (out). b (*fig*) **~ (d')une punition*** to cop it* (*Brit*), catch it*; **~ de 3 ans de prison*** to get a 3-year gaol sentence, get sentenced to 3 years; **c'est moi qui ai écopé** it was me *ou* I was the one who got it in the neck* *ou* who took the rap*; **il a écopé pour les autres** he took the rap for the others*.
écorce [ekɔʀs] nf *[arbre]* bark; *[orange]* peel, skin. (*Géol*) **l'~ terrestre** the earth's crust; (*Can*) **canot d'~** bark canoe.
écorcer [ekɔʀse] 3 vt *fruit* to peel; *arbre* to bark, strip the bark from.
écorché [ekɔʀʃe] nm (*Anat*) écorché; (*Tech*) cut-away (diagram). (*fig*) **c'est un ~ vif** he's a tormented soul.
écorchement [ekɔʀʃəmɑ̃] nm *[animal]* skinning.
écorcher [ekɔʀʃe] 1 vt a (*dépecer*) *animal* to skin; *criminel* to flay. **écorché vif** flayed alive. b (*égratigner*) *peau, visage* to scratch, graze; *genoux* to graze, scrape. **il s'est écorché les mollets** he grazed *ou* barked his shins. c (*par frottement*) to chafe, rub; *cheval* to gall. d (*fig*) *mot, nom* to mispronounce. **il écorche l'allemand** he speaks broken German. e (*fig : ruiner*) **~ le client** to fleece* one's customers; **vous m'écorchez!** you're bleeding me white!; **se faire ~** to get fleeced*. f **~ les oreilles de qn** *[bruit]* to grate on sb's ears; *[personne]* to hurt sb's ears.
écorcheur, -euse [ekɔʀʃœʀ, øz] nm,f *[animal]* skinner; (* *fig: hôtelier*) fleecer*, extortioner.
écorchure [ekɔʀʃyʀ] nf (*voir* **écorcher**) scratch; graze; scrape.
écorner [ekɔʀne] 1 vt *meuble* to chip the corner of; *livre* to turn down the corner of; (*fig*) *fortune* to make a hole in. **laisser une fortune bien écornée** to leave a greatly depleted fortune; **vieux livre tout écorné** old dog-eared book.
écornifler*† [ekɔʀnifle] 1 vt to cadge, scrounge (*chez qn* from sb).
écornifleur, -euse*† [ekɔʀniflœʀ, øz] nm,f cadger, scrounger.
écossais, e [ekɔsɛ, ɛz] 1 adj *temps, caractère* Scottish, Scots (*épith*); *whisky, confiture* Scotch; *tissu* tartan, check; *voir* **douche.** 2 nm a **É~** Scot, Scotsman; **les É~** the Scots. b (*Ling*) (*dialecte anglais*) Scots; (*dialecte gaélique*) Gaelic. c (*tissu*) tartan (cloth). 3 **Écossaise** nf Scot, Scotswoman.
Écosse [ekɔs] nf Scotland; *voir* **nouveau.**
écosser [ekɔse] 1 vt to shell, pod. **petits pois/haricots à ~** peas/beans in the pod, unshelled peas/beans.
écosystème [ekosistɛm] nm ecosystem.
écot [eko] nm share (of a bill). **chacun de nous a payé son ~** we went Dutch*, we all paid our share.
écoulement [ekulmɑ̃] nm a *[eau]* flow. **tuyau/fossé d'~** drainage pipe/ditch. b *[humeur, pus]* discharge. **~ de sang** flow of blood, bleeding. c (*fig*) *[foule]* dispersal; *[temps]* passage, passing. **l'~ des voitures** the flow of traffic. d (*Comm*) selling, passing. **articles d'~ facile** quick-selling *ou* fast-moving articles.
écouler [ekule] 1 1 vt a (*Comm*) to sell. **~ des faux billets** to get rid of *ou* dispose of counterfeit money; **on n'arrive pas à ~ ce stock** this stock isn't moving *ou* selling; **nous avons écoulé tout notre stock** we've cleared all our stock.
b **faire ~** *eau* to let out, run off.
2 **s'écouler** vpr a *[liquide]* (*suinter*) to seep *ou* ooze (out); (*fuir*) to leak (out); (*couler*) to flow (out); (*Méd*) *[pus]* to ooze out. **s'~ à grands flots** to pour out.
b *[temps]* to pass (by), go by; *[argent]* to disappear, melt away; *[foule]* to disperse, drift away. **en réfléchissant sur sa vie écoulée** thinking over his past life; **10 ans s'étaient écoulés** 10 years had passed *ou* had elapsed *ou* had gone by; **les fonds s'écoulent vite** (the) funds are soon spent *ou* exhausted.
c (*Comm*) to sell. **marchandise qui s'écoule bien** quick-selling item *ou* line; **nos produits se sont bien écoulés** our products have sold well.
écourter [ekuʀte] 1 vt *bâton* to shorten; *visite, attente, supplice, adieux* to cut short, shorten, curtail; *texte, discours* to shorten, cut down; *queue* to dock.
écoute [ekut] nf a **être aux ~s** to be listening (*de* to); (*péj : épier*) to listen in, eavesdrop (*de* on); (*fig: être aux aguets*) to be on the look-out (*de* for), keep one's ears open (*de* for).
b (*Rad*) listening (*de* to). **être à l'~ de** (*Rad*) to be tuned in to, be listening to; (*fig*) to be in touch with, listen to; **se mettre à** *ou* **prendre l'~** to tune in; **nous restons à l'~** we are staying tuned in; **reprendre l'~** to retune; **heures de grande ~** (*Rad*) peak listening hours; (*TV*) peak viewing hours; (*Rad, TV*) **avoir une grande ~** to have a large audience; **avoir une grande ~ féminine** to have a large female audience *ou* a large number of women listeners (*Rad*) *ou* viewers (*TV*); **l'indice d'~ d'une émission** the ratings of a programme.
c (*Mil, Police*) **les ~s téléphoniques** phone-tapping; **ils sont sur ~** their phone is tapped; *voir* **table.**
d (*Naut*) sheet.
e *[sanglier]* **~s** ears.
écouter [ekute] 1 1 vt a *discours, chanteur* to listen to, hear; *radio, disque* to listen to. **écoute!** listen!; (*au téléphone*) **(allô, oui) j'écoute** hello!; **j'ai été ~ sa conférence** I went to hear his lecture; **écoutons ce qu'il dit** let's listen to *ou* hear what he has to say; **~ qn jusqu'au bout** to hear sb out; **~ qch/qn secrètement** to listen in on *ou* to sth/sb; **~ qn parler** to hear sb speak; **savoir ~** to be a good listener; **~ aux portes** to eavesdrop; **~ de toutes ses oreilles** to be all ears, listen with both ears; **n'~ que d'une oreille** to listen with (only) half an ear; **faire ~ un disque à qn** to play a record to sb.
b *justification, confidence* to listen to; (*Jur, Rel*) to hear. **écoute-moi au moins!** at least listen to *ou* hear what I have to say!
c *conseil* to listen to, take notice of. **écoute-moi** listen to me, take my advice; **refuser d'~ un conseil** to turn a deaf ear to advice, disregard (a piece of) advice; **bon, écoute!** look!, listen!; **aide-moi, écoute!** come on — help me!; **écoute, c'est bien simple** look *ou* listen — it's quite simple; **ses conseils sont très écoutés** his advice is greatly valued *ou* greatly sought after; **il se fait ~ du ministre** he has the ear of the minister; **quelqu'un de très écouté** someone whose opinion is highly valued.
d (*obéir à*) to listen to, obey. **~ ses parents** to listen to *ou* obey one's parents; **vas-tu (m')~!** will you listen to me!; **faire ~ qn** to get sb to listen *ou* obey *ou* behave; **son père saura le faire ~** his father will teach him how to behave; **il sait se faire ~** he knows how to make himself obeyed, he's good at getting people to do what he says; **n'écoutant que son courage** letting (his) courage be his only guide.
2 **s'écouter** vpr *[malade]* **elle s'écoute trop** she coddles herself; **si je m'écoutais je n'irais pas** if I were to take my own advice I wouldn't go; **s'~ parler** to savour one's words; **il aime s'~ parler** he loves the sound of his own voice.
écouteur, -euse [ekutœʀ, øz] 1 nm,f (*littér: personne*) (*attentif*) listener; (*indiscret*) eavesdropper. 2 nm *[téléphone]* earpiece. (*Rad*) **~s** earphones, headphones.
écoutille [ekutij] nf (*Naut*) hatch(way).
écouvillon [ekuvijɔ̃] nm *[fusil]* swab; *[bouteilles]* (bottle-)brush; *[boulanger]* scuffle.
écouvillonner [ekuvijɔne] 1 vt *fusil* to swab; *bouteille, four* to clean.
écrabouiller* [ekʀabuje] 1 vt to squash, crush. **se faire ~ par une voiture** to get flattened *ou* crushed by a car.
écran [ekʀɑ̃] nm a (*gén*) screen. **ce mur fait ~ et nous isole du froid/du bruit** this wall screens *ou* shields us from the cold/noise, this wall acts as a screen *ou* shield (for us) against the cold/noise; **faire ~ à qn** (*abriter*) to screen *ou* shelter sb; (*gêner*) to get in the way of sb; (*éclipser*) to stand in the way of sb; **son renom me fait ~** his fame puts

me in the shade; ~ **de fumée/de protection** smoke/protective screen; ~ **de verdure** screen of greenery; (*Ordin*) ~ **à haute définition/à fenêtres** high-resolution/split screen; (*Ordin*) ~ **pleine page** full page display; ~ **de contrôle** monitor screen; ~ **tactile** touch-sensitive screen; ~ **cathodique** cathode-ray screen; ~ **publicitaire** advertising slot; (*crème solaire*) ~ **total** total sunblock; *voir* **petit**.

b ~ **(de cinéma)** (*toile*) screen; (*salle*) cinema; ~ **de projection** projector screen; **vedette de l'~** film *ou* movie (*US*) star; **prochainement sur vos ~s** coming soon to a cinema near you; **porter un roman à l'~** to screen a novel, adapt a novel for the screen; **ce film sera la semaine prochaine sur les ~s londoniens** this film will open *ou* be showing next week in London.

écrasant, e [ekʀazɑ̃, ɑ̃t] **adj** *impôts, mépris, poids* crushing; *preuve, responsabilité, nombre* overwhelming; *travail* gruelling, back-breaking; *victoire, défaite, superiorité* crushing, overwhelming; *chaleur* overpowering, overwhelming. (*Pol*) **majorité/victoire ~e** landslide *ou* crushing majority/victory.

écrasé, e [ekʀaze] (**ptp de écraser**) **adj** *nez* flat, squashed; *perspective, relief* dwarfed.

écrasement [ekʀazmɑ̃] **nm** (*voir* **écraser**) crushing; swatting; stubbing out; mashing; grinding; pounding; squeezing; flattening; trampling down; running over; suppressing.

écraser [ekʀaze] [1] **1 vt a** (*gén*) to crush; *mouche* to swat; *mégot* to stub out; (*en purée*) to mash; (*en poudre*) to grind (*en* to); (*au pilon*) to pound; (*pour le jus*) to squeeze; (*en aplatissant*) to flatten (out); (*en piétinant*) to trample down; (*Tennis*) *balle* to flatten, kill. ~ **sous la dent** *biscuit* to crunch; *noix* to crush between one's teeth; **écrasé par la foule** squashed *ou* crushed in the crowd; **aïe, vous m'écrasez les pieds** ouch, you're standing *ou* treading on my feet; ~ **le champignon*** to put one's foot hard down (on the accelerator) (*Brit*), step on the gas*; ~ **le frein** to stamp on *ou* slam on the brakes; ~ **le coup*** (*se taire*) to drop the subject; (*rester discret*) to keep it quiet, shut up* about it; (*abandonner*) to give up (trying).

b (*tuer*) *[voiture]* to run over; *[avalanche]* to crush. **la voiture l'a écrasé** the car ran him over (*Brit*) *ou* ran over him; **il s'est fait ~ par une voiture** he was run over by a car.

c (*fig: accabler*) to crush. **les impôts nous écrasent, nous sommes écrasés d'impôts** we are overburdened *ou* crushed by taxation; **il nous écrase de son mépris** he crushes *ou* withers us with his scorn; **écrasé de chaleur** overcome by the heat; **écrasé de sommeil/de douleur** overcome by sleep/with grief; **écrasé de travail** snowed under with* *ou* overloaded with work.

d (*vaincre*) *ennemi* to crush; *rébellion* to crush, suppress, put down. **notre équipe a été écrasée** *ou* **s'est fait ~ par les adversaires** we were beaten hollow (*Brit*) *ou* we were hammered* by the opposing team; **il écrase tout le monde** he outstrips *ou* outdoes everyone; **en maths il écrase tout le monde** he outshines *ou* outdoes everyone at maths.

e (*Ordin*) *données, fichiers* to delete.

2 **vi a** (*: *ne pas insister*) (*verbalement*) to drop the subject; (*abandonner*) to give up (trying); (*se taire*) to keep it quiet, pipe down, shut up. **oh écrase!** oh shut up!* *ou* belt up!‡ (*Brit*).

b **en ~‡** to sleep like a log*.

3 **s'écraser vpr a** *[avion, auto]* to crash (*contre* into, against, *sur* on); *[objet, corps]* to be dashed *ou* smashed *ou* crushed (*contre* on, against).

b *[foule]* (*dans le métro*) to be *ou* get crushed (*dans* in). **on s'écrase pour en acheter** they're falling over each other *ou* they're rushing to buy them; **on s'écrase devant les cinémas** there's a great crush to get into the cinemas.

c (‡: *se taire*) to pipe down*. **écrasons-nous, ça vaut mieux!** we'd better pipe down!*.

écraseur, -euse* [ekʀazœʀ, øz] **nm,f** roadhog*.

écrémage [ekʀemaʒ] **nm** (*voir* **écrémer**) skimming, creaming; creaming off.

écrémer [ekʀeme] [6] **vt** *lait* to skim, cream; (*fig*) to cream off the best from. **lait écrémé** skimmed milk.

écrémeuse [ekʀemøz] **nf** creamer, (cream) separator.

écrêter [ekʀete] [1] **vt** (*niveler*) to lop.

écrevisse [ekʀəvis] **nf** (freshwater) crayfish, crawfish. **avancer** *ou* **marcher comme une ~** to take one step forward and two steps backward; *voir* **rouge**.

écrier (s') [ekʀije] [7] **vpr** to exclaim, cry out.

écrin [ekʀɛ̃] **nm** case, box (*for silver, jewels*), casket†. (*littér*) **niché dans un ~ de verdure** nestling in a bosky bower (*littér*).

écrire [ekʀiʀ] [39] **1 vt a** (*gén*) *mots, livres* to write; (*orthographier*) to spell; (*inscrire, marquer*) to write down. **je lui ai écrit que je viendrais** I wrote and told him I would be coming; ~ **des commentaires au crayon** to pencil in comments, make notes *ou* comments in pencil.

b (*loc*) **c'était écrit** it was bound to happen, it was inevitable; **il est écrit que je ne pourrai jamais y arriver!** I'm fated *ou* doomed never to succeed!; **c'est écrit sur sa figure** it's stamped *ou* written all over his face; **c'est écrit noir sur blanc** *ou* **en toutes lettres** it's written in black and white.

2 **vi** (*gén*) to write; (*être écrivain*) to be a writer, write. **vous écrivez trop mal** your writing is really bad; ~ **gros/fin** *[personne]* to have large/small (hand)writing; *[stylo]* to have a thick/fine nib; ~ **au crayon/à l'encre** to write in pencil/in ink.

3 **s'écrire vpr** *[personnes]* to write to each other. **comment ça s'écrit?** how do you spell it *ou* write it?; **ça s'écrit comme ça se prononce** it's spelt how it sounds, you write it the same way as you pronounce it.

écrit [ekʀi] **nm** (*ouvrage*) piece of writing, written work; (*examen*) written exam *ou* paper; (*Jur*) document. **par ~** in writing; (*Scol*) **être bon à l'~** to be good *ou* do well at the written papers.

écriteau, pl ~x [ekʀito] **nm** notice, sign.

écritoire [ekʀitwaʀ] **nf** writing case.

écriture [ekʀityʀ] **nf a** (*à la main*) (hand)writing (*NonC*). **il a une belle ~** he has beautiful (hand)writing, he writes a good hand; ~ **de chat** spidery (hand)writing.

b (*alphabet*) writing (*NonC*), script. ~ **hiéroglyphique** hieroglyphic writing; ~ **phonétique** phonetic script.

c (*littér: style*) writing (*NonC*), style.

d (*rédaction*) writing. **se consacrer à l'~ (de romans)** to devote one's time to writing (novels); (*Poésie*) ~ **automatique** automatic writing.

e (*Comm*) **~s** accounts, entries, books; **employé aux ~s** ledger clerk; **tenir les ~s** to do the book-keeping *ou* the accounts *ou* the books.

f (*Fin*) entry. **passer une ~** to make an entry.

g (*Rel*) **les (Saintes) É~s, l'É~ (sainte)** Scripture, the Scriptures, (the) Holy Writ.

écrivailler [ekʀivaje] [1] **vi** (*péj*) to scribble.

écrivailleur, -euse [ekʀivajœʀ, øz] **nm,f**, **écrivaillon** [ekʀivajɔ̃] **nm** (*péj*) scribbler.

écrivain [ekʀivɛ̃] **nm** (*homme*) writer. **(femme-)~** woman writer; ~ **public** (public) letter-writer.

écrivassier, -ière [ekʀivasje, jɛʀ] **nm,f** = **écrivailleur.**

écrou [ekʀu] **nm** (*Tech*) nut; *voir* **levée**[2].

écrouelles†† [ekʀuɛl] **nfpl** scrofula.

écrouer [ekʀue] [1] **vt** (*incarcérer*) to imprison, lock away (in prison). ~ **qn sous le numéro X** to enter sb on the prison register under the number X.

écroulé, e [ekʀule] (**ptp de s'écrouler**) **adj a à moitié ~** *maison, mur* half-ruined, tumbledown (*épith*), dilapidated. **b être ~ (de rire)** to be doubled up with laughter.

écroulement [ekʀulmɑ̃] **nm** (*voir* **s'écrouler**) fall; collapse; caving in; crumbling; crash.

écrouler (s') [ekʀule] [1] **vpr a** *[mur]* to fall (down), collapse; *[rocher]* to fall; *[toit]* to collapse, cave in, fall in; (*Rugby*) *[mêlée]* to collapse; *[empire]* to collapse, crumble; *[empire financier, entreprise]* to fall, collapse, crash; *[prix, cours]* to collapse, plummet; *[espoir, projet, théorie]* to collapse, crumble; *[personne]* (*tomber*) to collapse *ou* crumble (to the ground); (*: *s'endormir*) to fall fast asleep. **être près de s'~** to be on the verge of collapse; **tous nos projets s'écroulent** all our plans are crumbling *ou* falling apart, this is the collapse of all our plans; **s'~ de sommeil/de fatigue** to be overcome with *ou* collapse with sleepiness/weariness; **il s'écroula dans un fauteuil*** he flopped down *ou* slumped down *ou* collapsed into an armchair.

b (*fig*) *[coureur, candidat]* to collapse; *[accusé]* to break down.

écru, e [ekʀy] **adj** *tissu* raw, in its natural state; *couleur* ecru, natural-coloured. **toile ~e** unbleached linen; **soie ~e** raw silk (*before dyeing*).

ectoplasme [ektoplasm] **nm** ectoplasm.

écu [eky] **nm** (*monnaie ancienne, papier*) crown; (*monnaie de la CEE*) ecu; (*Hér, Hist: bouclier*) shield. ~ **dur** hard ecu.

écubier [ekybje] **nm** hawse-hole.

écueil [ekœj] **nm** (*lit*) reef, shelf; (*fig*) (*pierre d'achoppement*) stumbling block; (*piège, danger*) pitfall.

écuelle [ekɥɛl] **nf** (*pour chien*) bowl; (*assiette creuse*) bowl, porringer††; (*Hist*) platter; (*contenu*) bowlful.

éculé, e [ekyle] (**ptp de éculer**) **adj** *soulier* down-at-heel; *plaisanterie* hackneyed, worn.

éculer [ekyle] [1] **1 vt** *souliers* to wear down at the heel. **2 s'éculer vpr** *[plaisanterie]* to become hackneyed, wear thin.

écumage [ekymaʒ] **nm** skimming.

écume [ekym] **nf** *[mer]* foam; *[bouche]* froth; *[bière]* foam, froth; *[métal]* dross; *[confiture, bouillon]* scum; *[savon, cheval]* lather. **pipe en ~ de mer** meerschaum pipe; (*fig*) **l'~ de la société** the scum *ou* dregs of society.

écumer [ekyme] [1] **1 vt a** *bouillon* to skim; *confiture* to take the scum off, skim; *métal* to scum. **b** (*piller*) to clean out, plunder. ~ **les mers** to scour the seas; ~ **la ville à la recherche de** to scour the town in search of. **2 vi** *[mer, confiture]* to foam; *[métal]* to scum; *[bouche, liquide]* to froth; *[cheval]* to lather. (*fig*) ~ **(de rage)** to foam *ou* boil with rage.

écumeur [ekymœʀ] **nm** (*Hist, hum*) ~ **des mers** pirate, buccaneer.

écumeux, -euse [ekymø, øz] **adj** foamy, frothy.

écumoire [ekymwaʀ] **nf** skimmer. **troué comme une ~** riddled with holes.

écureuil [ekyʀœj] **nm** squirrel.

écurie [ekyʀi] **nf** *[chevaux, cyclistes etc]* stable; (*fig: endroit sale*) pigsty. **mettre un cheval à l'~** to stable a horse; ~ **de course** racing stable; **~s**

d'Augias Augean stables; *voir* **sentir.**

écusson [ekysɔ̃] **nm** (*insigne*) badge; (*Hér*) escutcheon; *[serrure]* escutcheon. (*Agr*) **(greffe en)** ~ shield-graft.

écuyer [ekɥije] **nm** a (*cavalier*) rider, horseman; (*professeur d'équitation*) riding master. ~ **de cirque** circus rider. b (*Hist*) (*d'un chevalier*) squire; (*à la cour*) equerry.

écuyère [ekɥijɛʀ] **nf** rider, horsewoman. ~ **de cirque** circus rider.

eczéma [ɛgzema] **nm** eczema. **avoir** *ou* **faire de l'~** to have eczema.

eczémateux, -euse [ɛgzematø, øz] **adj** eczematous.

edelweiss [edɛlvajs] **nm** edelweiss.

Éden [edɛn] **nm: l'~, le jardin d'~** (the garden of) Eden.

édénique [edenik] **adj** Edenic.

édenté, e [edɑ̃te] (**ptp de édenter**) 1 **adj** (*totalement*) toothless; (*partiellement*) with (some) teeth missing. 2 **nmpl: les É~s** the Edentata, edentate mammals.

édenter [edɑ̃te] [1] **vt** to break the teeth of.

EDF [ədeɛf] **nf** (**abrév de Electricité de France**) French Electricity Board ≃ CEGB (*Brit*).

édicter [edikte] [1] **vt** *loi* to enact, decree; *peine* to decree.

édicule [edikyl] **nm** (*hum: cabinets*) public lavatory (*Brit*) *ou* convenience (*Brit*), rest room (*US*); (*kiosque*) kiosk (*Brit*).

édifiant, e [edifjɑ̃, jɑ̃t] **adj** *livre, conduite* edifying.

édification [edifikasjɔ̃] **nf** *[bâtiment]* erection, construction; *[esprit]* edification, enlightenment.

édifice [edifis] **nm** edifice, building. ~ **public** public building; **l'~ social** the social structure *ou* fabric.

édifier [edifje] [7] **vt** a *maison* to build, construct, erect; *fortune, empire* to build (up). b (*moralement*) to edify; (*iro*) to enlighten, edify.

édile [edil] **nm** (*frm, hum*) (town) councillor.

Édimbourg [edɛ̃buʀ] **n** Edinburgh.

édit [edi] **nm** (*Hist*) edict.

éditer [edite] [1] **vt** (*publier*) to publish; *disques* to produce; (*annoter, commenter*) to edit.

éditeur, -trice [editœʀ, tʀis] **nm,f** (*voir* **éditer**) publisher; editor. ~ **de disques** record producer; (*Ordin*) ~ **de textes** text editor.

édition [edisjɔ̃] **nf** a (*action de publier*) publishing; *[disques]* production. **travailler dans l'~** to be in publishing *ou* in the publishing business.
b (*livre, journal*) edition. ~ **spéciale** (*journal*) special edition; (*magazine*) special issue; (*journal*) ~ **de 5 heures** five o'clock edition; (*Rad, TV: informations*) **notre** ~ **de 13 heures** our 1 o'clock news bulletin; (*iro*) **deuxième/troisième** ~! for the second/third time! c (*annotation*) editing; (*texte*) edition. **établir l'~ critique d'un texte** to produce a critical edition of a text; ~ **revue et corrigée/revue et augmentée** revised and corrected/revised and enlarged edition. d (*Ordin*) editing.

édito* [edito] **abrév de éditorial.**

éditorial, e, **mpl -iaux** [editɔʀjal, jo] 1 **nm** leading article, leader, editorial. 2 **adj** *politique etc* editorial.

éditorialiste [editɔʀjalist] **nmf** leader *ou* editorial writer.

Edmond [ɛdmɔ̃] **nm** Edmund.

Édouard [edwaʀ] **nm** Edward. ~ **le Confesseur** Edward the Confessor.

édredon [edʀədɔ̃] **nm** eiderdown.

éducable [edykabl] **adj** educable, teachable.

éducateur, -trice [edykatœʀ, tʀis] 1 **adj** educational. 2 **nm,f** (*gén*) teacher; (*prison*) tutor, instructor; (*théoricien*) educationalist. ~ **spécialisé** teacher of children with learning difficulties.

éducatif, -ive [edykatif, iv] **adj** educational, educative. **jeu** ~ educational game; **système** ~ education system.

éducation [edykasjɔ̃] **nf** a (*enseignement*) education. **les problèmes de l'~** educational problems; **il faut faire l'~ politique des masses** the masses must be educated politically; **j'ai fait mon ~ à Paris** I was educated *ou* I went to school in Paris; **j'ai fait mon ~ musicale à Paris** I studied music in Paris; **il a reçu une bonne ~** he is well-educated *ou* well-read; ~ **manuelle et technique** technical education (*Brit*), industrial arts (*US*); **l'É~ nationale** (*système*) the state education system; (*ministère*) the Ministry (*Brit*) *ou* Department (*US*) of Education; ~ **religieuse** religious education; ~ **permanente** continuing education; ~ **professionnelle** professional training; ~ **physique** physical training *ou* education, P.E.; ~ **sexuelle** sex education; *voir* **maison, ministère.**
b (*discipline familiale*) upbringing. **une** ~ **spartiate** a Spartan upbringing; **avoir de l'~** (*bonnes manières*) to be well-mannered *ou* well-bred *ou* well brought up; **manquer d'~** to be ill-mannered *ou* ill-bred, be badly brought up; **sans** ~ ill-bred, uncouth.
c *[goût, volonté]* training.

édulcorant, e [edylkɔʀɑ̃, ɑ̃t] 1 **adj** sweetening. 2 **nm** sweetener.

édulcorer [edylkɔʀe] [1] **vt** a (*expurger*) *doctrine, propos* to water down; *texte osé* to tone down, bowdlerize. b (*Pharm*) to sweeten.

éduquer [edyke] [1] **vt** *enfant* (*à l'école*) to educate; (*à la maison*) to bring up, rear, raise; *peuple* to educate; *goût, volonté* to train. **bien éduqué** well-mannered, well-bred, well brought up; **mal éduqué** ill-mannered, ill-bred, badly brought up.

effaçable [efasabl] **adj** *inscription* erasable.

effacé, e [efase] (**ptp de effacer**) **adj** a *teinte, couleur* (*qui a passé*) faded; (*sans éclat*) subdued. b *personne, manières* retiring, unassuming, self-effacing; *vie* retiring; *rôle* unobtrusive. c *menton* receding; *poitrine* flat. (*Escrime*) **en position ~e** sideways (on).

effacement [efasmɑ̃] **nm** a *[inscription, faute, souvenir]* obliteration, effacing; *[bande magnétique]* erasing; *[craintes]* dispelling; (*Ling*) deletion. (*Escrime*) ~ **du corps/des épaules** drawing o.s./one's shoulders in.
b *[personne]* (*par sa modestie*) retiring *ou* self-effacing manner; (*devant un rival*) eclipse. **vivre dans l'~** to live a retiring life; **son ~ progressif au profit du jeune sous-directeur** the gradual erosion of his position *ou* the way in which he was gradually being eclipsed by the young deputy director.

effacer [efase] [3] 1 **vt** a (*lit: enlever*) *inscription, traces* to obliterate, efface, erase; *bande magnétique* to erase; *écran d'ordinateur* to clear; *tableau noir* to clean; (*à la gomme*) to rub out (*Brit*), erase; (*à l'éponge*) to wipe off, sponge off; (*en lavant*) to wash off *ou* out; (*au chiffon*) to wipe off; (*au grattoir*) to scratch out; (*Ling*) to delete. **cette gomme efface bien** this is a good rubber (*Brit*) *ou* eraser (*US*), this rubber (*Brit*) *ou* eraser (*US*) works well; **prends un chiffon pour ~** use a cloth to rub it out *ou* wipe it off; **efface le tableau** clean *ou* wipe the blackboard; **un chemin à demi effacé** a hardly distinguishable track.
b (*fig: faire disparaître*) *mauvaise impression, souvenir* to erase, efface; *faute* to erase, obliterate; *craintes* to dispel. **on efface tout et on recommence** (*oublier le passé*) we'll let bygones be bygones, we'll wipe the slate clean (and make a fresh start); (*reprendre à zéro*) let's go back to square one, let's make a fresh start; **tenter d'~ son passé** to try to live down *ou* blot out one's past; **le temps efface tout** everything fades with time.
c (*éclipser*) to outshine, eclipse.
d ~ **le corps** (*Escrime*) to stand sideways on; (*gén*) to draw o.s. in; **effacez les épaules!** shoulders back!; **effacez le ventre!** stomach in!
2 **s'effacer** **vpr** a *[inscription]* to wear away, wear off, become obliterated; *[couleurs]* to fade; *[sourire]* to fade, die. **le crayon s'efface mieux que l'encre** it is easier to rub out (*Brit*) *ou* erase pencil than ink, pencil rubs out (*Brit*) *ou* erases more easily than ink; **tableau noir qui s'efface bien/mal** blackboard which is easy/hard to clean.
b *[crainte, impression, souvenir]* to fade, diminish. **tout s'efface avec le temps** everything fades in *ou* with time; **un mauvais souvenir qui s'efface difficilement** an unpleasant memory which (it) is hard to forget *ou* which is slow to fade.
c (*lit: s'écarter*) to move aside, step back *ou* aside; (*fig: se tenir en arrière*) to keep in the background; (*se retirer*) to withdraw. **l'auteur s'efface derrière ses personnages** the author hides behind his characters; **elle s'efface le plus possible** she keeps (herself) in the background as much as possible.

effaceur [efasœʀ] **nm** (ink) eraser pen.

effarant, e [efaʀɑ̃, ɑ̃t] **adj** *prix* outrageous, mind-blowing*; *vitesse* alarming, breathtaking; *bêtise* stunning, abysmal.

effaré, e [efaʀe] (**ptp de effarer**) **adj** alarmed (*attrib*) (*de* by, at), aghast (*attrib*) (*de* at). **son regard** ~ his wild eyes, his look of alarm.

effarement [efaʀmɑ̃] **nm** alarm, trepidation.

effarer [efaʀe] [1] **vt** to alarm, fill with trepidation. (*sens affaibli: stupéfier*) **cette bêtise/hausse des prix m'effare** I find such stupidity/this rise in prices most alarming *ou* extremely worrying, I am aghast at *ou* appalled by such stupidity/this rise in prices.

effaroucher [efaʀuʃe] [1] 1 **vt** (*alarmer*) *animal* to frighten away *ou* off, scare away *ou* off; *personne timide etc* to frighten, scare; (*choquer*) to shock, upset. 2 **s'effaroucher** **vpr** (*par timidité*) *[animal, personne]* to shy (*de* at), take fright (*de* at); (*par pudeur*) to be shocked *ou* upset (*de* by).

effectif, -ive [efɛktif, iv] 1 **adj** *aide* real (*épith*), positive (*épith*); *travail* effective, actual (*épith*), real (*épith*); (*Fin*) *capital* real (*épith*). **le couvre-feu sera ~ à partir de 22 heures** the curfew will take effect *ou* become effective as from 10 p.m.
2 **nm** *[armée]* strength (*NonC*); *[classe]* size, complement, (total) number of pupils; *[parti]* size, strength; *[entreprise]* staff, workforce. (*fig: troupes: Mil, Pol*) **~s** numbers, strength; **le lycée n'a jamais atteint son ~** *ou* **l'~ prévu** the (total) number of pupils in the school has never reached its projected level, the school has never reached its full complement; **l'~ de la classe a triplé en 2 ans** the (total) number of pupils in the class has *ou* the (size of the) class has trebled in 2 years; (*Mil*) **l'~ est au complet** we are at full strength *ou* up to strength; **augmenter ses ~s** *[parti, lycée]* to boost its numbers; *[entreprise]* to increase its workforce; **l'usine a un ~ de 70 personnes** the factory has 70 people on the payroll *ou* has a staff *ou* workforce of 70; (*Ind*) **maintenir le niveau des ~s** to keep up manning levels.

effectivement [efɛktivmɑ̃] **adv** a (*concrètement*) *aider, travailler* effectively. **contribuer ~ à qch** to make a real *ou* positive contribution to sth. b (*réellement*) actually, really. **je répète que cet incident s'est ~ produit** I repeat that this incident did actually *ou* really happen. c (*en effet*) actually, in fact. **c'est ~ plus rapide** it's actually faster, it is in fact faster; **n'y a-t-il pas risque de conflit? — ~!** is there not a risk of conflict? — quite (so)! *ou* there is indeed!; **~, quand ce phénomène se produit ...** indeed *ou* in fact, when this phenomenon occurs ... .

effectuer [efɛktɥe] [1] 1 **vt** *manœuvre, opération, mission, réparation* to carry out; *expérience* to carry out, perform, make; *mouvement, geste* to make, execute; *paiement* to make, effect; *trajet* to make, complete; *reprise économique etc* to undergo, stage. **le franc/le coureur a effectué une remontée spectaculaire** the franc/the runner made *ou* staged a spectacular recovery.

2 **s'effectuer** vpr: **le trajet s'effectue en 2 heures** the journey takes 2 hours (to complete); **le paiement peut s'~ de 2 façons** payment may be made in 2 ways; **le rapatriement des prisonniers s'est effectué sans incident** the repatriation of the prisoners went off without a hitch; **la rentrée scolaire s'est effectuée dans de bonnes conditions** the new school year got off to a good start.

efféminé, e [efemine] (ptp de **efféminer**) adj effeminate.

efféminement [efeminmɑ̃] nm effeminacy.

efféminer [efemine] [1] vt (*littér*) *personne* to make effeminate; *peuple, pensée* to emasculate. **s'~** to become effeminate.

effervescence [efɛʀvesɑ̃s] nf (*lit*) effervescence; (*fig*) agitation. **mettre la ville en ~** to set the town astir, put the town in a turmoil; **être en ~** to be in a turmoil (of excitement), be simmering with excitement; **l'~ révolutionnaire** the stirrings of revolution.

effervescent, e [efɛʀvesɑ̃, ɑ̃t] adj (*lit*) effervescent; (*fig*) agitated, in a turmoil (*attrib*).

effet [efɛ] nm a (*résultat*) *[action, médicament]* effect. **c'est un ~ de son inexpérience** it is because of *ou* a result of his inexperience; **c'est l'~ du hasard** it is quite by chance, it is the result of chance; **avoir *ou* produire beaucoup d'~/l'~ voulu** to have *ou* produce a considerable effect/the desired effect; **ces livres ont un ~ nocif sur la jeunesse** these books have a harmful effect on young people; **créer un ~ de surprise** to create an effect of surprise; **en faisant cela il espérait créer un ~ de surprise** by doing this he was hoping to surprise them (*ou* us *etc*); **être *ou* rester sans ~** to be ineffective, have no effect; **ces mesures sont demeurées sans ~** these measures had no effect *ou* were ineffective *ou* were of no avail; **avoir pour ~ de faire** to have the effect of doing; **avoir pour ~ une augmentation/diminution de** to result in an increase/a decrease in; *[médicament]* **faire ~** to take effect; **ce médicament (me) fait de l'~/a fait son ~** this medicine is effective *ou* works (on me)/has taken effect *ou* has worked; **~ de serre** greenhouse effect; **~ pervers** opposite effect; (*Phys*) **~ tunnel** tunnel effect; *voir* **relation**.

b (*impression*) impression. **faire *ou* produire un ~ considérable/déplorable (sur qn)** to make *ou* have a great/dreadful impression (on sb); **il a fait *ou* produit son petit ~** he managed to cause a bit of a stir *ou* a minor sensation; **il aime faire de l'~** he likes to create a stir; **c'est tout l'~ que ça te fait?** is that all it means to you?, is that all you feel about it?; **quel ~ ça te fait d'être revenu?** how does it feel *ou* what does it feel like being back? **faire bon/mauvais ~ sur qn** to make a good/bad impression on sb; **il m'a fait bon ~** he made a good impression on me, I was favourably impressed by him; **ce tableau fait bon ~/beaucoup d'~ ici** this picture is quite/very effective here; **il me fait l'~ d'(être) une belle crapule** he strikes me as (being) a real crook, he seems like a real crook to me; **il me fait l'~ d'un renard** he puts me in mind of a fox (*Brit*), he reminds me of a fox; **cette déclaration a fait l'~ d'une bombe** this statement came as a bombshell; **cela m'a fait de l'~, de le voir dans cet état** it really affected me *ou* it gave me quite a turn to see him in that state; *voir* **bœuf**.

c (*artifice, procédé*) effect. **~ de contraste/de style/comique** contrasting/stylistic/comic(al) effect; **~ de perspective/d'optique** 3-D *ou* 3-dimensional/visual effect; **~ facile** facile *ou* trite effect; **~ de lumière** (*au théâtre*) lighting effect; (*naturel, sur l'eau*) play of light (*NonC*), effects of light; (*Ciné*) **~s spéciaux** special effects; **rechercher les ~s *ou* l'~** to strive for effect; **soigner ses ~s** to take great trouble over one's effects; **elle lui a coupé ses ~s** she stole his thunder; **manquer *ou* rater son ~** *[personne]* to spoil one's effect; *[plaisanterie]* to fall flat, misfire; **faire des ~s de voix** to use one's voice to dramatic effect, make dramatic use of one's voice; **cet avocat fait des ~s de manches** this barrister flourishes his arms *ou* waves his arms about in a most dramatic fashion.

d (*Tech*) **~ Doppler(-Fizeau)** Doppler effect; **machine à simple/double ~** single-/double-effect machine.

e (*Sport*) *[balle]* spin. **donner de l'~ à une balle** to spin a ball.

f (*Admin, Jur*) **augmentation de salaire avec ~ rétroactif au 1er janvier** payrise backdated to the 1st January, retrospective payrise from 1st January; **prendre ~ à la date de** to take effect from, be operative from.

g (*Comm: valeur*) **~ de commerce, ~ bancaire** bill of exchange; **~ à vue** sight bill, demand note; **~ au porteur** bill payable to bearer; **~s à payer** notes payable; **~s à recevoir** bills receivable; **~s publics** government securities.

h (†: *affaires, vêtements*) **~s** things, clothes; **~s personnels** personal effects.

i **en ~**: (*introduit une explication*) **cette voiture me plaît beaucoup, en ~, elle est rapide et confortable** I like this car very much because it's fast and comfortable; (*dans une réponse*) **étiez-vous absent, mardi dernier? — en ~, j'avais la grippe** were you absent last Tuesday? — yes (I was) *ou* that's right, I had flu; **cela me plaît beaucoup, en ~** yes (indeed), I like it very much; **c'est en ~ plus rapide** it's actually faster, it is in fact faster.

j (*loc*) **mettre à ~** to put into operation *ou* effect; **à cet ~** to that effect *ou* end; **sous l'~ de** *alcool* under the effect(s) *ou* influence of; *drogue* under the effect(s) of; **sous l'~ de la colère il me frappa** in his anger he hit me, he hit me in anger; **il était encore sous l'~ de la colère** his anger had not yet worn off, he was still angry.

effeuillage [efœjaʒ] nm a (*Agr*) thinning-out of leaves. b (*hum*) striptease.

effeuiller [efœje] [1] 1 vt *arbre, branche [arboriculteur]* to thin out the leaves of; *[vent]* to blow the leaves off. (*par jeu*) **~ une branche/une fleur** to pull *ou* pick the leaves off a branch/the petals off a flower; **~ la marguerite** to play "she-loves-me, she-loves-me-not". 2 **s'effeuiller** vpr *[arbre]* to shed *ou* lose its leaves.

effeuilleuse [efœjøz] nf (*hum: femme*) stripper.

efficace [efikas] adj *remède, mesure* effective, efficacious, effectual; *personne, machine* efficient; *voir* **grâce**.

efficacement [efikasmɑ̃] adv (*voir* **efficace**) effectively, efficaciously, effectually; efficiently.

efficacité [efikasite] nf (*voir* **efficace**) effectiveness, efficacy, efficiency.

efficience [efisjɑ̃s] nf efficiency.

efficient, e [efisjɑ̃, jɑ̃t] adj efficient.

effigie [efiʒi] nf effigy. **à l'~ de** bearing the effigy of; **en ~** in effigy.

effilé, e [efile] (ptp de **effiler**) 1 adj *doigt, silhouette* slender, tapering; *pointe, outil* highly-sharpened; *carrosserie* streamlined; *tissu* frayed. **amandes ~es** split almonds; **poulet ~** prepared roasting fowl. 2 nm *[jupe, serviette]* fringe.

effiler [efile] [1] 1 vt a *objet* to taper; *lignes, forme* to streamline. b *étoffe* to fray; *cheveux* to thin (out). 2 **s'effiler** vpr *[objet]* to taper; *[étoffe]* to fray.

effilochage [efilɔʃaʒ] nm fraying.

effilocher [efilɔʃe] [1] 1 vt *tissu* to fray. 2 **s'effilocher** vpr to fray. **veste effilochée** frayed jacket.

efflanqué, e [eflɑ̃ke] adj raw-boned. **c'était un cheval ~** the horse was mere skin and bones, the horse was a raw-boned creature.

effleurement [eflœʀmɑ̃] nm (*frôlement*) light touch. **elle sentit sur son bras l'~ d'une main** she felt the light touch of a hand on her arm, she felt a hand brush against her arm.

effleurer [eflœʀe] [1] vt (*frôler*) to touch lightly, brush (against); (*érafler*) to graze; (*fig*) *sujet* to touch (lightly) upon, skim over. **les oiseaux effleuraient l'eau** the birds skimmed (across) the water; **une idée lui effleura l'esprit** an idea crossed his mind; **ça ne m'a pas effleuré** it didn't cross my mind, it didn't occur to me; (*littér*) **ayant oublié le désir qui l'avait effleuré** having forgotten his fleeting desire.

efflorescence [eflɔʀesɑ̃s] nf (*Bot, Chim*) efflorescence.

efflorescent, e [eflɔʀesɑ̃, ɑ̃t] adj (*Bot, Chim*) efflorescent.

effluve [eflyv] nm (*littér*) **~s** (*agréables*) fragrance, exhalation(s); (*désagréables*) effluvia, exhalations, smell.

effondré, e [efɔ̃dʀe] (ptp de **s'effondrer**) adj (*abattu*) shattered, crushed (*de* by). **~ de douleur** prostrate with grief; **les parents ~s** the grief-stricken parents.

effondrement [efɔ̃dʀəmɑ̃] nm a (*voir* **s'effondrer**) collapse; caving-in; falling-in; falling-down; falling-away; breaking-down. b (*abattement*) utter dejection.

effondrer [efɔ̃dʀe] [1] 1 vt (*Rugby*) *mêlée* to cause to collapse. 2 **s'effondrer** vpr a *[toit, plancher]* to collapse, cave in, fall in; *[mur]* to collapse, fall down; *[terre]* to fall away, collapse; *[pont]* to collapse, cave in; (*Rugby*) *[mêlée]* to collapse. b (*fig*) *[empire, projets]* to collapse, fall in ruins; *[prix, marché]* to collapse, plummet; *[argument]* to collapse, fall down (completely). c *[personne]* to collapse; (*fig*) *[accusé]* to break down. (*fig*) **elle s'est effondrée en larmes** she dissolved *ou* collapsed into tears, she broke down and wept; **effondré sur sa chaise** slumped on his chair.

efforcer (s') [efɔʀse] [3] vpr: **s'~ de faire** to try hard *ou* endeavour to do, do one's best to do; (*littér*) **il s'efforçait à une politesse dont personne n'était dupe** he was striving to remain polite but he convinced nobody; (†, *littér*) **ils s'efforçaient en vain** they were striving in vain.

effort [efɔʀ] nm a (*physique, intellectuel*) effort. **après bien des ~s** after much exertion *ou* effort; **la récompense de nos ~s** the reward for our efforts; **nécessiter un (gros) ~ financier** to require a (large) financial outlay; **~ de guerre** war effort; **faire un ~ financier en faveur des petites entreprises** to give financial help to small businesses; **l'~ financier de la France dans le domaine de l'énergie** France's investment in the field of energy (production); **~ de volonté** effort of will; **cela demande un ~ de réflexion** that requires careful thought; **faire un ~ de mémoire** to make an effort *ou* try hard to remember; **cela demande un ~ d'attention** you have to make an effort to concentrate (on that); **tu dois faire un ~ d'imagination** you should (make an effort and) try to use your imagination.

b (*Tech*) stress, strain. **~ de torsion** torsional stress; **~ de traction** traction, pull; **l'~ que subissent les fondations** the strain on the foundations.

c (*loc*) **faire un ~** to make an effort; **faire de gros ~s pour réussir** to make a great effort *ou* great efforts to succeed, try very hard to succeed; **faire un ~ sur soi-même pour rester calme** to make an effort *ou* force o.s. to stay calm, try to keep calm; **faire l'~ de** to make the effort to; **plier sous l'~** to bend with the effort; (*Sport*) **il est resté en deçà de son ~** he did not go all out, he didn't stretch himself to his limit; **encore un ~** just one more go, just a little more effort; **sans ~** effortlessly, easily; **avec ~** with an effort; *voir* **moindre**.

effraction [efʀaksjɔ̃] **nf** (*Jur*) breaking and entering (*Jur*) breaking(-in). **entrer par ~** to break in; **ils sont entrés par ~ dans la maison** they broke into the house; **~ informatique** (computer) hacking; *voir* **vol**[2].

effraie [efʀɛ] **nf: (chouette) ~** barn-owl.

effrangé, e [efʀɑ̃ʒe] (**ptp de effranger**) **adj** fringed; (*effiloché*) frayed.

effranger [efʀɑ̃ʒe] [3] **1 vt** to fringe (*by fraying*). **2 s'effranger vpr** to fray. **ces manches s'effrangent** these sleeves are fraying (at the edges).

effrayant, e [efʀɛjɑ̃, ɑ̃t] **adj** frightening, fearsome; (*sens affaibli*) frightful, dreadful.

effrayer [efʀeje] [8] **1 vt** to frighten, scare. **2 s'effrayer vpr** to be frightened *ou* scared (*de* by), take fright (*de* at), be afraid (*de* of).

effréné, e [efʀene] **adj** *course* wild, frantic; *passion, luxe* unbridled, unrestrained, wild.

effritement [efʀitmɑ̃] **nm** (*voir* **s'effriter**) crumbling(-away); disintegration; erosion; dwindling; disintegration.

effriter [efʀite] [1] **1 vt** *biscuit, sucre* to crumble; *roche, falaise* to cause to crumble. **2 s'effriter vpr** *[roche]* to crumble (away); *[valeurs morales]* to crumble (away), disintegrate; *[majorité électorale]* to crumble; *[monnaie]* to be eroded, decline in value; *[fortune, valeurs boursières]* to dwindle; *[relation]* to disintegrate, fall apart.

effroi [efʀwa] **nm** (*littér*) terror, dread.

effronté, e [efʀɔ̃te] **adj** *personne, air, réponse* cheeky (*Brit*), insolent, impudent; *mensonge, menteur* barefaced (*épith*), brazen, shameless. **l'~!** (*enfant*) (the) impudent *ou* insolent *ou* cheeky (*Brit*) child!; (*adulte*) (the) insolent fellow!

effrontément [efʀɔ̃temɑ̃] **adv** (*voir* **effronté**) insolently, impudently; barefacedly, brazenly, shamelessly; cheekily (*Brit*).

effronterie [efʀɔ̃tʀi] **nf** *[réponse, personne]* cheek (*Brit*), insolence, impudence, effrontery; *[mensonge]* shamelessness, effrontery.

effroyable [efʀwajabl] **adj** horrifying, appalling.

effroyablement [efʀwajabləmɑ̃] **adv** appallingly, horrifyingly.

effusion [efyzjɔ̃] **nf** *[tendresse, sentiment]* burst. **après ces ~s** after these effusions *ou* emotional demonstrations; **remercier qn avec ~** to thank sb effusively; **~ de sang** bloodshed.

égaiement [egɛmɑ̃] **nm** (*voir* **égayer**) cheering-up; brightening-up; amusement; enlivenment; merrymaking.

égailler (s') [egaje] [1] **vpr** to scatter, disperse.

égal, e, mpl -aux [egal, o] **1 adj a** (*de même valeur*) equal (*à* to). **de poids ~** of equal weight; **à poids ~** weight for weight; **à nombre/prix ~** for the same number/price; **égaux en nombre** of equal numbers, equal in numbers; **à ~e distance de deux points** equidistant *ou* exactly halfway between two points; **Orléans est à ~e distance de Tours et de Paris** Orléans is equidistant from Tours and Paris *ou* is the same distance from Tours as from Paris; **Tours et Paris sont à ~e distance d'Orléans** Tours and Paris are the same distance from Orléans *ou* Tours and Paris are equidistant from Orléans; **d'adresse/d'audace ~e** of equal skill/boldness, equally skilful/bold; **toutes choses ~es par ailleurs** other things being equal; *voir* **signe**.

b (*sans variation*) *justice* even, unvarying; *climat* equable, unchanging; *terrain* even, level; *bruit, rumeur* steady, even; *vent* steady. **de caractère ~** even-tempered, equable(-tempered); **marcher d'un pas ~** to walk with a regular *ou* an even step.

c (*loc*) **ça m'est ~** (*je n'y attache pas d'importance*) I don't mind, I don't feel strongly (about it); (*je m'en fiche*) I don't care; **tout lui est ~** he doesn't feel strongly about anything; **c'est ~, il aurait pu m'écrire** all the same *ou* be that as it may, he might have written (to me); **la partie n'est pas ~e (entre eux)** they are not evenly matched; **sa probité n'a d'~e que sa générosité** his integrity is matched *ou* equalled only by his generosity; **rester ~ à soi-même** to remain true to form, be still one's old self; *voir* **arme, jeu**.

2 nm,f a (*personne*) equal. **il ne fréquente que ses égaux** he only associates with his equals.

b (*loc*) **il a traité d'~ à ~ avec moi** he treated me as his *ou* an equal; **nous parlions d'~ à ~** we talked to each other as equals; (*égal à*) **sa probité est à l'~ de sa générosité** his generosity is equalled *ou* matched by his integrity; (*comme*) **c'est une vraie mégère à l'~ de sa mère** she's a real shrew just like her mother; **sans ~** *beauté, courage* matchless, unequalled, peerless.

égalable [egalabl] **adj: difficilement ~** difficult to equal *ou* match.

également [egalmɑ̃] **adv** (*sans aspérités*) evenly; (*sans préférence*) equally; (*aussi*) also, too, as well. **elle lui a ~ parlé** (*elle aussi*) she also *ou* too spoke to him; (*à lui aussi*) she spoke to him as well *ou* too.

égaler [egale] [1] **1 vt a** *personne, record* to equal (*en* in). (*Math*) **2 plus 2 égalent 4** 2 plus 2 equals 4; **personne ne l'a encore égalé en adresse** so far there has been no one to equal *ou* match his skill, so far no one has equalled him in skill *ou* matched him for skill; **son intégrité égale sa générosité** his generosity is matched *ou* equalled by his integrity, his integrity matches *ou* equals his generosity.

b (*comparer*) **~ qn à** to rank sb with; **c'est un bon compositeur mais je ne l'égalerais pas à Ravel** he's a good composer but I wouldn't rank him with *ou* put him beside Ravel.

c (†: *rendre égal*) **la mort égale tous les êtres** death makes all men equal *ou* levels all men.

2 s'égaler vpr: s'~ à (*se montrer l'égal de*) to equal, be equal to; (*se comparer à*) to liken o.s. to, compare o.s. to.

égalisateur, -trice [egalizatœʀ, tʀis] **adj** equalizing. (*Sport*) **le but ~** the equalizer (*Brit*), the tying goal (*US*); (*Tennis*) **le jeu ~** the game which evened (up) the score.

égalisation [egalizasjɔ̃] **nf** (*Sport*) equalization (*Brit*), tying (*US*); *[sol, revenus]* levelling. (*Sport*) **c'est l'~** they've scored the equalizer (*Brit*) *ou* the equalizing (*Brit*) *ou* tying (*US*) goal, they've equalized (*Brit*) *ou* tied (*US*).

égaliser [egalize] [1] **1 vt** *chances* to equalize, make equal; *cheveux* to straighten up; *sol, revenus* to level (out). **2 vi** (*Sport*) to equalize (*Brit*), tie (*US*). **3 s'égaliser vpr** *[chances]* to become (more) equal; *[sol]* to level (out), become (more) level.

égaliseur [egalizœʀ] **nm: ~ graphique** graphic equalizer.

égalitaire [egalitɛʀ] **adj** egalitarian.

égalitarisme [egalitaʀism] **nm** egalitarianism.

égalitariste [egalitaʀist] **adj, nmf** egalitarian.

égalité [egalite] **nf** *[chances, hommes]* equality; (*Math*) identity; *[climat]* equableness, equability; *[pouls]* regularity; *[surface]* evenness, levelness; (*Tennis*) deuce. **obtenir l'~** to manage to get a draw (*Brit*) *ou* tie (*US*); **~ d'humeur** evenness of temper, equableness, equanimity; **~ d'âme** equanimity; **à ~ de qualification on prend le plus âgé** in the case of equal qualifications we take the oldest; **~ des chances** equality of opportunity; (*Sport*) **être à ~** (*après un but*) to be equal; (*fin du match*) to draw (*Brit*), tie (*US*); (*Tennis: à 40/40*) to be at deuce; *voir* **pied**.

égard [egaʀ] **nm a** (*respect*) **~s** consideration; **il la reçut avec de grands ~s** he welcomed her with every *ou* great consideration; **il a beaucoup d'~s pour sa femme** he shows great consideration for his wife, he's very considerate to(wards) his wife; **manquer d'~s envers qn** to be inconsiderate to(wards) sb, show a lack of consideration for sb; **vous n'avez aucun ~ pour votre matériel** you have no respect for your equipment.

b à l'~ de: (*envers*) **aimable à l'~ des enfants** friendly towards children; (*contre*) **des mesures ont été prises à son ~** measures have been taken concerning him *ou* with regard to him; (*en ce qui concerne*) **à l'~ de ce que vous me dites ...** concerning *ou* regarding *ou* with regard to what you tell me ...; (†: *en comparaison de*) **il est médiocre à l'~ de l'autre** he is mediocre in comparison with *ou* compared with the other.

c (*loc*) **par ~ pour** out of consideration for; **sans ~ pour** without regard for, without considering; **à tous ~s** in all respects; **à certains ~s** in certain respects; **à cet/aucun ~** in this/no respect; (*frm*) **eu ~ à** in view of, considering; **avoir ~ à qch** to take sth into account *ou* consideration.

égaré, e [egaʀe] (**ptp de égarer**) **adj a** *voyageur* lost; *animal* stray (*épith*), lost; *obus* stray (*épith*); *voir* **brebis**. **b** *air, regard* distraught, wild.

égarement [egaʀmɑ̃] **nm a** (*littér: trouble affectif*) distraction. **un ~ de l'esprit** mental distraction; **dans un moment d'~** in a moment of madness. **b** (*littér: dérèglements*) **~s** aberrations; **revenir de ses ~s** to return to the straight and narrow.

égarer [egaʀe] [1] **1 vt a** *voyageur* to lead out of his way; *enquêteurs* to mislead; (*moralement*) *jeunes, esprits* to lead astray. (*frm*) **la douleur vous égare** you are distraught *ou* distracted with grief.

b *objet* to mislay.

2 s'égarer vpr a *[voyageur]* to lose one's way, get lost, lose o.s.*[colis, lettre]* to get lost, go astray; *[discussion, auteur]* to wander from the point. **ne nous égarons pas!** let's stick to the point!, let's not wander from the point!; **il s'égare dans des détails** he loses himself *ou* he gets lost in details; **une espèce d'original égaré dans notre siècle** an eccentric sort of fellow who seems lost *ou* who seems out of place in the age we live in; (*fig, Rel*) **s'~ du droit chemin** to wander *ou* stray from the straight and narrow; **quelques votes socialistes se sont égarés sur ce candidat d'extrême droite** a few Socialist votes have been lost to the candidate of the far right.

b (*perdre la raison*) to lose one's reason. **mon esprit s'égare à cette pensée** the thought of it makes me feel quite distraught.

égayement [egɛjmɑ̃] **nm = égaiement.**

égayer [egeje] [8] **1 vt** *personne* (*remonter*) to cheer up*, brighten up; (*divertir*) to amuse, cheer up*; *pièce* to brighten up; *conversation* to enliven, liven up, brighten up. **2 s'égayer vpr** to make merry. **s'~ aux dépens de qn** to amuse o.s. at sb's expense, make sb an object of fun; **s'~ à voir ...** to be highly amused *ou* entertained at seeing ... .

Égée [eʒe] **adj: la mer ~** the Aegean Sea; **îles de la mer ~** Aegean Islands.

égéen, -enne [eʒeɛ̃, ɛn] **adj** *peuples* Aegean.

Égérie [eʒeʀi] **nf** (*Hist*) Egeria. **é~** (*fig*) *[poète]* oracle; *[voleurs]* mastermind; **la police a arrêté l'é~ de la bande** the police have arrested the woman (*ou* girl) who masterminded the gang *ou* who was the brains *ou* driving force behind the gang.

égide [eʒid] **nf: sous l'~ de** under the aegis of.

églantier [eglɑ̃tje] **nm** wild *ou* dog rose(bush).

églantine [eglɑ̃tin] **nf** wild *ou* dog rose, eglantine.

églefin [egləfɛ̃] **nm = aiglefin.**

église [egliz] **nf** a (*bâtiment*) church. **~ abbatiale** abbey church; **~ paroissiale** parish church; **aller à l'~** to go to church; **il est à l'~** (*pour l'office*) he's at *ou* in church; (*en curieux*) he's in the church; **se marier à l'~** to get married in church, have a church wedding. b (*secte, clergé*) **l'É~** the Church; **l'É~ militante/triomphante** the Church militant/triumphant; **l'É~ anglicane** the Church of England, the Anglican Church; **l'É~ catholique** the Church of Rome, the Roman Catholic Church; **l'É~ réformée** the Reformed Church; **l'É~ orthodoxe** the Greek Orthodox Church; **l'É~ de France** The Church of France; *voir* **gens, hommes.**

églogue [eglɔg] **nf** eclogue.

ego [ego] **nm** (*Philos, Psych*) ego.

égocentrique [egosɑ̃tʀik] 1 **adj** egocentric, self-centred. 2 **nmf** egocentric *ou* self-centred person.

égocentrisme [egosɑ̃tʀism] **nm** (*gén*) egocentricity, self-centredness; (*Psych*) egocentricity.

égocentriste [egosɑ̃tʀist] **adj, nmf = égocentrique.**

égoïne [egɔin] **nf: (scie)~** hand-saw.

égoïsme [egɔism] **nm** selfishness, egoism.

égoïste [egɔist] 1 **adj** selfish, egoistic. 2 **nmf** selfish person, egoist.

égoïstement [egɔistəmɑ̃] **adv** selfishly, egoistically.

égorgement [egɔʀʒəmɑ̃] **nm: l'~ d'un mouton/prisonnier** slitting *ou* cutting of a sheep's/prisoner's throat.

égorger [egɔʀʒe] [3] **vt** (*lit*) to slit *ou* cut the throat of; (* *fig*) *débiteur, client* to bleed white.

égorgeur, -euse [egɔʀʒœʀ, øz] **nm,f** cut-throat.

égosiller (s') [egozije] [1] **vpr** (*crier*) to shout o.s. hoarse; (*chanter fort*) to sing at the top of one's voice (*Brit*) *ou* lungs (*US*).

égotisme [egɔtism] **nm** egotism.

égotiste [egɔtist] 1 **adj** (*littér*) egotistic(al). 2 **nmf** egotist.

égout [egu] **nm** sewer. **réseau** *ou* **système d'~s** sewerage system; **eaux d'~** sewage; *[eaux usées]* **aller à l'~** to go down the drain; **~ pluvial** storm drain *ou* sewer; *voir* **tout.**

égoutier [egutje] **nm** sewer worker.

égoutter [egute] [1] 1 **vt** *légumes* (*avec une passoire*) to strain; *linge* (*en le tordant*) to wring out; *fromage* to drain. 2 **vi** *[vaisselle]* to drain, drip; *[linge, eau]* to drip. **faire ~ l'eau** to drain off the water; **mettre le linge à ~** to hang up the washing to drip; **"laver à la main et laisser ~"** "wash by hand and drip dry". 3 **s'égoutter vpr** *[arbre, linge, eau]* to drip; *[vaisselle]* to drain, drip.

égouttoir [egutwaʀ] **nm** *[vaisselle]* (*intégré dans l'évier*) draining (*Brit*) *ou* drain (*US*) board; (*mobile*) draining rack (*Brit*), drainer (*US*); *[légumes]* strainer, colander.

égratigner [egʀatiɲe] [1] **vt** *peau* to scratch, graze; *genou* to graze, scrape; (*fig*) *adversaire* to have a dig at. **le film/l'auteur s'est fait ~ par la critique** the film/the author was given a bit of a rough ride by the critics.

égratignure [egʀatiɲyʀ] **nf** (*voir* **égratigner**) scratch; graze; scrape. **il s'en est sorti sans une ~** he came out of it without a scratch *ou* unscathed; **ce n'était qu'une ~ faite à son amour-propre** it was only a dig at his self-esteem.

égrènement [egʀɛnmɑ̃] **nm: l'~ des heures/minutes** marking out the hours/minutes; **l'~ des hameaux le long de la vallée** the hamlets dotted along the valley.

égrener [egʀəne] [5] 1 **vt** a (*lit*) *pois* to shell, pod; *blé, maïs, épi* to shell; *coton* to gin; *grappe* to pick grapes off. **~ des raisins** to pick grapes off the bunch. b (*fig*) **~ son chapelet** to tell one's beads (†, *littér*), say the rosary; **la pendule égrène les heures** the clock marks out the hours. 2 **s'égrener vpr** *[raisins]* to drop off the bunch; *[blé]* to drop off the stalk; (*fig*) *[rire]* to ripple out. **les maisons s'égrenaient le long de la route** the houses were dotted along the road; **les notes cristallines du piano s'égrenaient dans le silence** the crystal notes of the piano fell one by one on the silence.

égreneuse [egʀənøz] **nf** *[céréales]* corn-sheller; *[coton]* gin.

égrillard, e [egʀijaʀ, aʀd] **adj** *ton, regard* ribald; *plaisanterie, rire, propos* ribald, bawdy.

Égypte [eʒipt] **nf** Egypt.

égyptien, -ienne [eʒipsjɛ̃, jɛn] 1 **adj** Egyptian. 2 **nm,f: É~(ne)** Egyptian.

égyptologie [eʒiptɔlɔʒi] **nf** Egyptology.

égyptologue [eʒiptɔlɔg] **nmf** Egyptologist.

eh [e] **excl** hey! **~ oui!/non!** I'm afraid so!/not!; **~ bien** well.

éhonté, e [eɔ̃te] **adj** *action* shameless, brazen; *menteur, mensonge* shameless, barefaced, brazen.

eider [ɛdɛʀ] **nm** eider.

einsteinien, -ienne [ɛnstajnjɛ̃, ɛn] **adj** Einsteinian.

einsteinium [ɛnstɛnjɔm] **nm** einsteinium.

Eire [ɛʀ] **nf** Eire.

éjaculation [eʒakylasjɔ̃] **nf** (*Physiol*) ejaculation. **~ précoce** premature ejaculation.

éjaculatoire [eʒakylatwaʀ] **adj** (*Physiol*) ejaculatory.

éjaculer [eʒakyle] [1] **vi** (*Physiol*) to ejaculate.

éjectable [eʒɛktabl] **adj** *voir* **siège¹.**

éjecter [eʒɛkte] [1] 1 **vt** (*Tech*) to eject; *personne* to throw out; (*: *congédier*) to kick out*, chuck out‡. **se faire ~** (*dans un accident*) to get thrown out; (*: *être congédié*) to get o.s. kicked* *ou* chucked‡ out. 2 **s'éjecter vpr** *[pilote]* to eject.

éjection [eʒɛksjɔ̃] **nf** (*Tech*) ejection; kicking-out*, chucking-out‡.

élaboration [elabɔʀasjɔ̃] **nf** (*voir* **élaborer**) (careful) working-out; elaboration; development.

élaborer [elabɔʀe] [1] **vt** *plan, système* to work out (carefully), elaborate, develop, map out; *bile, sève, aliments* to elaborate.

élagage [elagaʒ] **nm** (*lit, fig*) pruning.

élaguer [elage] [1] **vt** (*lit, fig*) to prune.

élagueur, -euse [elagœʀ, øz] **nm,f** pruner.

élan¹ [elɑ̃] **nm** (*Zool*) elk, moose.

élan² [elɑ̃] **nm** a (*début de course*) run up. **prendre son ~** to take a run up; **saut avec/sans ~** running/standing jump; **ils ont couru jusque chez eux d'un seul ~** they dashed home without stopping (once); (*fig*) **l'~ du clocher vers le ciel** the thrust of the steeple towards the sky, the soaring steeple pointing heavenwards.

b (*vitesse acquise*) momentum. **prendre de l'~** *[coureur]* to gather speed; **perdre son ~** to lose one's momentum; **il a continué dans ou sur son ~** he continued to run at the same pace *ou* speed; **rien ne peut arrêter son ~** nothing can check *ou* stop his pace *ou* momentum; **emporté par son propre ~** (*lit*) carried along by his own impetus *ou* momentum; (*fig*) carried away on *ou* by the tide of his own enthusiasm.

c (*poussée, transport*) **~ de** *enthousiasme, colère* surge *ou* rush *ou* burst of; **dans un ~ de générosité** in a fit of generosity; **les ~s de l'imagination** flights of fancy; **les rares ~s (de tendresse) qu'il avait vers elle** the few surges *ou* rushes of affection he felt for her; **les ~s lyriques de l'orateur** the lyrical outbursts of the speaker; **maîtriser les ~s de son cœur** to quell the ardent impulses of one's heart; **dire qch avec ~** to say sth with fervour *ou* passion.

d (*ardeur*) vigour, spirit, élan. **~ patriotique** patriotic fervour; **l'~ des troupes** the vigour *ou* spirit *ou* élan of the troops.

e (*dynamisme*) boost. **redonner de l'~** *ou* **donner un nouvel ~ à une politique/une institution/l'économie** to give a fresh boost* to a policy/an institution/the economy.

élancé, e [elɑ̃se] (**ptp de élancer**) **adj** *clocher, colonne, taille* slender.

élancement [elɑ̃smɑ̃] **nm** (*Méd*) shooting *ou* sharp pain. (*littér*) **~ de l'âme** yearning of the soul.

élancer¹ [elɑ̃se] [3] **vi** *[blessure]* to give shooting *ou* sharp pains. **mon doigt m'élance** I get shooting *ou* sharp pains in my finger.

élancer² [elɑ̃se] [3] 1 **vt** (*littér*) **le clocher élance sa flèche vers le ciel** the church steeple soars up *ou* thrusts upwards into the sky.

2 **s'élancer vpr** a (*se précipiter*) to rush forward; (*prendre son élan*) to take a run up. **s'~ au-dehors** to rush *ou* dash outside; **s'~ comme une flèche vers** to dart towards; **s'~ d'un bond sur** to leap onto; **s'~ au secours de qn** to rush *ou* dash to help sb; **s'~ à la poursuite de qn** to hurl o.s. in pursuit of sb, hurl o.s. *ou* dash after sb; **s'~ vers qn** to leap *ou* dash towards sb; **s'~ sur qn** to hurl *ou* throw o.s. at sb, rush at sb; **s'~ à l'assaut d'une montagne/forteresse** to launch an attack on a mountain/fortress.

b (*littér: se dresser*) to soar *ou* thrust (upwards). **la tour s'élance vers le ciel** the tower soars *ou* thrusts up into the sky.

élargir [elaʀʒiʀ] [2] 1 **vt** a *rue* to widen; *robe* to let out; *souliers* to stretch, widen; (*fig*) *débat, connaissances* to broaden, widen. (*Pol*) **majorité élargie** increased majority; **ça lui élargit la taille** that makes her waist look fatter; **une veste qui élargit les épaules** a jacket that makes the shoulders look broader *ou* wider; **~ son horizon** to enlarge *ou* widen one's horizons. b (*Jur: libérer*) to release, free. 2 **s'élargir vpr** *[vêtement]* to stretch, get wider *ou* broader; *[route]* to widen, get wider; (*fig*) *[esprit, débat]* to broaden; *[idées]* to broaden, widen.

élargissement [elaʀʒismɑ̃] **nm** (*voir* **élargir**) widening; letting-out; stretching; broadening; release, freeing.

élasticité [elastisite] **nf** (*voir* **élastique**) elasticity; spring, buoyancy; flexibility; accommodating nature.

élastine [elastin] **nf** elastin.

élastique [elastik] 1 **adj** *objet* elastic; *démarche* springy, buoyant; *sens, esprit, principes* flexible; (*péj*) *conscience* accommodating; *règlement* elastic, flexible; (*Écon*) *offre, demande* elastic. (*Couture*) **taille ~** elasticated waist. 2 **nm** (*de bureau*) elastic *ou* rubber band; (*pour couture, jeu etc*) elastic (*NonC*). **en ~** elasticated, elastic; *voir* **lâcher, saut.**

élastomère [elastɔmɛʀ] **nm** elastomer.

Elbe [ɛlb] **nf: l'île d'~** (the isle of) Elba; (*fleuve*) **l'~** the Elbe.

Eldorado [ɛldɔʀado] **nm** El Dorado.

électeur, -trice [elɛktœʀ, tʀis] **nm,f** a (*Pol*) (*gén*) voter, elector; (*dans une circonscription*) constituent. **le député et ses ~s** ≃ the member of parliament and his constituents; (*corps électoral*) **les ~s** the electorate, the voters; *voir* **grand.** b (*Hist*) **É~** Elector; **É~trice** Electress.

électif, -ive [elɛktif, iv] adj (*Pol*) elective.

élection [elɛksjɔ̃] nf a (*Pol, gén*) election. **jour des ~s** polling *ou* election day; **se présenter aux ~s** to stand *ou* run (*US*) as a candidate (in the election); **l'~ présidentielle** the presidential election; **~ partielle** ≃ by-election; **~s législatives** ≃ general election; **~s municipales** municipal elections; **~s régionales** ≃ local (government) elections; **~s cantonales** cantonal elections. b (*littér: choix*) choice. **lieu/patrie d'~** place/country of one's (own) choosing *ou* choice; **la France est une patrie** *ou* **terre d'~ pour les poètes** France is a country much favoured by poets; (*Jur*) **~ de domicile** choice of residence.

électoral, e, mpl **-aux** [elɛktɔʀal, o] adj *affiche, réunion* election (*épith*). **campagne ~e** election *ou* electoral campaign; **pendant la période ~e** during election time, during the run-up to the election; **il m'a promis son soutien ~** he promised me his backing in the election; *voir* **agent, circonscription, corps.**

électoralisme [elɛktɔʀalism] nm electioneering.

électoraliste [elɛktɔʀalist] adj electioneering.

électorat [elɛktɔʀa] nm a (*électeurs*) electorate; (*dans une circonscription*) constituency; (*droit de vote*) franchise. **l'~ socialiste** the voters for the Socialist party, the socialist vote. b (*Hist: principauté*) electorate.

Électre [elɛktʀ] nf Electra.

électricien, -ienne [elɛktʀisjɛ̃, jɛn] nm,f electrician.

électricité [elɛktʀisite] nf electricity. **allumer l'~** to turn *ou* switch *ou* put the light on; **ça marche à l'~** it runs on electricity, it's electrically operated; **refaire l'~** to rewire the house (*ou* shop *etc*); (*fig*) **il y a de l'~ dans l'air*** the atmosphere is electric; *voir* **panne.**

électrification [elɛktʀifikasjɔ̃] nf electrification.

électrifier [elɛktʀifje] 7 vt to electrify. **~ un village** to bring electricity *ou* electric power to a village.

électrique [elɛktʀik] adj (*lit*) electric(al); (*fig*) electric.

électriquement [elɛktʀikmɑ̃] adv electrically.

électrisable [elɛktʀizabl] adj *foule* easily roused; *substance* chargeable, electrifiable.

électrisant, e [elɛktʀizɑ̃, ɑ̃t] adj (*fig*) *discours, contact* electrifying.

électrisation [elɛktʀizasjɔ̃] nf *[substance]* charging, electrifying.

électriser [elɛktʀize] 1 vt *substance* to charge, electrify; *audience* to electrify, rouse.

électro-aimant, pl **électro-aimants** [elɛktʀoɛmɑ̃] nm electromagnet.

électrocardiogramme [elɛktʀokaʀdjɔgʀam] nm electrocardiogram.

électrocardiographe [elɛktʀokaʀdjɔgʀaf] nm electrocardiograph.

électrocardiographie [elɛktʀokaʀdjɔgʀafi] nf electrocardiography.

électrochimie [elɛktʀoʃimi] nf electrochemistry.

électrochimique [elɛktʀoʃimik] adj electrochemical.

électrochoc [elɛktʀoʃɔk] nm (*procédé*) electric shock treatment, electroconvulsive therapy (*SPÉC*). **on lui a fait des ~s** he was given electric shock treatment *ou* ECT.

électrocuter [elɛktʀɔkyte] 1 1 vt to electrocute. 2 **s'électrocuter** vpr to electrocute o.s.

électrocution [elɛktʀɔkysjɔ̃] nf electrocution.

électrode [elɛktʀɔd] nf electrode.

électrodynamique [elɛktʀodinamik] 1 adj electrodynamic. 2 nf electrodynamics (*sg*).

électro-encéphalogramme, pl **électro-encéphalogrammes** [elɛktʀoɑ̃sefalɔgʀam] nm electroencephalogram.

électro-encéphalographie [elɛktʀoɑ̃sefalɔgʀafi] nf electroencephalography.

électrogène [elɛktʀɔʒɛn] adj (*Zool*) electric; *voir* **groupe.**

électrolyse [elɛktʀɔliz] nf electrolysis.

électrolyser [elɛktʀɔlize] 1 vt to electrolyse.

électrolyseur [elɛktʀɔlizœʀ] nm electrolyser.

électrolyte [elɛktʀɔlit] nm electrolyte.

électrolytique [elɛktʀɔlitik] adj electrolytic(al).

électromagnétique [elɛktʀomaɲetik] adj electromagnetic.

électromagnétisme [elɛktʀomaɲetism] nm electromagnetism.

électromécanique [elɛktʀomekanik] 1 adj electromechanical. 2 nf electromechanical engineering.

électroménager [elɛktʀomenaʒe] 1 adj *appareil* (household *ou* domestic) electrical. 2 nm household *ou* domestic (electrical) appliances.

électrométallurgie [elɛktʀometalyʀʒi] nf electrometallurgy.

électrométallurgique [elɛktʀometalyʀʒik] adj electrometallurgical.

électromètre [elɛktʀɔmɛtʀ] nm electrometer.

électromoteur, -trice [elɛktʀomɔtœʀ, tʀis] 1 adj electromotive. 2 nm electric motor, electromotor.

électron [elɛktʀɔ̃] nm electron.

électronégatif, -ive [elɛktʀonegatif, iv] adj electronegative.

électronicien, -ienne [elɛktʀɔnisjɛ̃, jɛn] nm,f electronics engineer.

électronique [elɛktʀɔnik] 1 adj (*gén*) electronic; *optique, téléscope, microscope* electron (*épith*). 2 nf electronics (*sg*).

électronucléaire [elɛktʀonykleɛʀ] 1 adj nuclear power (*épith*). 2 nm nuclear power.

électrophone [elɛktʀɔfɔn] nm record player.

électropositif, -ive [elɛktʀopozitif, iv] adj electropositive.

électrostatique [elɛktʀostatik] 1 adj electrostatic. 2 nf electrostatics (*sg*).

électrotechnique [elɛktʀotɛknik] nf electrotechnics (*sg*), electrotechnology, electrical engineering. **institut ~** institute of electrical engineering.

électrothérapie [elɛktʀoteʀapi] nf electrotherapy.

élégamment [elegamɑ̃] adv elegantly.

élégance [elegɑ̃s] nf (*voir* **élégant**) elegance; stylishness, smartness; generosity, handsomeness; neatness. **~s (de style)** ornaments (of style); **perdre avec ~** to be a graceful loser; **l'~ féminine** feminine elegance; **il aurait pu avoir l'~ de s'excuser** he might have had the good grace to apologize.

élégant, e [elegɑ̃, ɑ̃t] 1 adj *personne, toilette* elegant, stylish, smart; *conduite* generous, handsome; *solution* elegant, neat. **user de procédés peu ~s** to use crude methods; **c'était une façon ~e de le remettre à sa place** it was a neat way of putting him in his place. 2 nm (†: *dandy*) elegant *ou* stylish man, man of fashion. 3 **élégante** nf (†) elegant *ou* stylish woman, woman of fashion.

élégiaque [eleʒjak] adj elegiac.

élégie [eleʒi] nf elegy.

élément [elemɑ̃] nm a (*composante*) *[structure, ensemble]* element, component; *[problème]* element; *[mélange]* ingredient, element; *[réussite]* factor, element; *[machine, appareil]* part, component. **~ comique (d'un roman)** comic element (of a novel); **l'~ révolutionnaire était bien représenté** the revolutionary element was well represented; **~s de rangement** storage units; **~s de cuisine/de bibliothèque** kitchen/bookshelf units; (*Mil*) **~s blindés/aéroportés** armoured/airborne units.
b (*Chim*) element. (*Chim*) **l'~ hydrogène** the element hydrogen.
c (*Tech*) *[pile]* cell.
d (*fait*) fact. **nous manquons d'~s** we lack information *ou* facts; **aucun ~ nouveau n'est survenu** there have been no new developments, no new facts have come to light; (*Mil*) **~s de tir** range data.
e (*individu*) **c'est le meilleur ~ de ma classe** he's the best pupil in my class; **bons et mauvais ~s** good and bad elements; **~s subversifs/ennemis** subversive/hostile elements.
f (*rudiments*) **~s** basic principles, rudiments, elements; **il a quelques ~s de chimie** he has some elementary knowledge of chemistry; (*titre d'ouvrage*) **"É~s de Mécanique"** "Elements of *ou* Elementary Mechanics".
g (*milieu*) element. **les quatre ~s** the four elements; (*littér*) **les ~s (naturels)** the elements (*littér*); (*littér*) **l'~ liquide** the liquid element (*littér*); **quand on parle d'électronique il est dans son ~*** when you talk about electronics he's in his element; **parmi ces artistes il ne se sentait pas dans son ~*** he didn't feel at home *ou* he felt like a fish out of water among those artists.

élémentaire [elemɑ̃tɛʀ] adj a (*facile*) *problème* elementary; (*de base*) *notion* elementary, basic; *forme* rudimentary, basic; (*Scol*) *cours, niveau* elementary; (*évident*) *précaution* elementary, basic. **c'est ~!** it's elementary!; **la plus ~ courtoisie/discrétion veut que ...** elementary *ou* basic *ou* simple courtesy/discretion demands that ... . b (*Chim*) elemental.

Éléonore [eleɔnɔʀ] nf Eleanor.

éléphant [elefɑ̃] nm elephant. **~ femelle** cow elephant; **~ d'Asie/d'Afrique** Indian/African elephant; **~ de mer** sea elephant, elephant seal; **comme un ~ dans un magasin de porcelaine** like a bull in a china shop.

éléphanteau, pl **~x** [elefɑ̃to] nm baby elephant.

éléphantesque [elefɑ̃tɛsk] adj (*énorme*) elephantine, gigantic.

éléphantiasis [elefɑ̃tjazis] nm elephantiasis.

élevage [el(ə)vaʒ] nm a *[bétail]* rearing, breeding; *[porcs, chevaux, vers à soie, vin]* breeding. **l'~ (du bétail)** cattle breeding *ou* rearing; **l'~ des abeilles** beekeeping; **faire de l'~** to breed *ou* rear cattle; **faire l'~ de** to rear, to breed, to keep; **région** *ou* **pays d'~** cattle-rearing *ou* -breeding area; **truite/saumon d'~** farmed trout/salmon. b (*ferme*) cattle farm. **~ de poulets/de truites** poultry/trout farm.

élévateur, -trice [elevatœʀ, tʀis] adj, nm,f: **(muscle) ~** elevator; **(appareil) ~** elevator; (*Élec*) **(appareil** *ou* **transformateur) ~ de tension** step-up transformer; *voir* **chariot.**

élévation [elevasjɔ̃] nf a (*action d'élever*) *[rempart, statue]* putting up, erection; *[objet, niveau]* raising; *[fonctionnaire]* raising, elevation; (*fig*) *[pensée, âme]* elevation. (*Math*) **~ d'un nombre au carré** squaring of a number; (*Math*) **~ d'un nombre à une puissance** raising of a number to a power; **son ~ au rang de** his being raised *ou* elevated to the rank of, his elevation to the rank of. b (*action de s'élever*) *[température, niveau]* rise (*de* in). c (*Rel*) **l'~** the Elevation. d (*tertre*) elevation, mound. **~ de terrain** rise (in the ground). e (*Archit, Géom: coupe, plan*) elevation. f (*noblesse*) *[pensée, style]* elevation, loftiness.

élève [elɛv] nmf (*gén*) pupil, student; *[Grande École]* student; (*Mil*) cadet. **~ professeur** student teacher, trainee teacher; **~ infirmière** student nurse; **~ officier** officer cadet; **~-officier de réserve** officer cadet.

élevé, e [el(ə)ve] (ptp de **élever**) adj a *prix, niveau* high; *pertes* heavy.

peu ~ *prix, niveau* low; *pertes* slight; (*Jur*) **dommages-intérêts ~s** substantial damages. b *cime, arbre* tall, lofty; *colline* high, lofty. c *rang, grade* high, elevated. (*frm*) **être de condition ~e** to be of high birth; **occuper une position ~e** to hold a high position, be high-ranking. d (*noble*) *pensée, style* elevated, lofty; *conception* exalted, lofty; *principes* high (*épith*). e **bien ~** well-mannered; **mal ~** (*rustre*) bad-mannered, ill-mannered; (*impoli*) rude, impolite; **espèce de mal ~!** you rude creature!; **c'est mal ~ de parler en mangeant** it's bad manners *ou* it's rude to talk with your mouth full.

élever [el(ə)ve] 5 1 **vt** a (*éduquer*) *enfant* to bring up, raise (*US*). **il a été élevé dans du coton/selon des principes vertueux** he was given a sheltered/very moral upbringing; **son fils est élevé maintenant** his son is grown-up now.

b (*faire l'élevage de*) *bétail* to rear, breed; *porcs, chevaux, vers à soie* to breed; *abeilles* to keep; *vin* to produce.

c (*dresser*) *rempart, mur, statue* to put up, erect, raise. (*littér*) **la maison élevait sa masse sombre** the dark mass of the house rose up *ou* reared up (*littér*); (*fig*) **~ des objections/des protestations** to raise objections/a protest; (*fig*) **~ des critiques** to make criticisms.

d (*hausser*) *édifice* to raise, make higher. **~ la maison d'un étage** to raise the house by one storey, make the house one storey higher.

e (*lever, mettre plus haut*) *poids, objet* to lift (up), raise; *niveau, taux, prix* to raise; *voix* to raise; (*littér*) *yeux, bras* to raise, lift (up). **pompe qui élève l'eau** pump which raises water.

f *débat* to raise the tone of. **~ sa pensée jusqu'aux grandes idées** to raise one's thoughts to *ou* set one's thoughts on higher things; **musique qui élève l'âme** elevating *ou* uplifting music; (*Rel*) **élevons nos cœurs vers le Seigneur** let us lift up our hearts unto the Lord.

g (*promouvoir*) to raise, elevate. **il a été élevé au grade de** he was raised *ou* elevated to the rank of; **chez eux l'abstinence est élevée à la hauteur d'une institution** they've give abstinence the status of an institution, they have made abstinence a way of life.

h (*Math*) **~ une perpendiculaire** to raise a perpendicular; **~ un nombre à la puissance 5** to raise a number to the power of 5; **~ un nombre au carré** to square a number.

2 **s'élever vpr** a (*augmenter*) [*température, niveau, prix*] to rise, go up. **le niveau des élèves/de vie s'est élevé** the standard of the pupils/of living has risen *ou* improved.

b (*se dresser*) [*montagne, tour*] to rise. **la tour s'élève à 50 mètres au-dessus du sol** the tower rises *ou* stands 50 metres above the ground; **un mur s'élevait entre ces deux jardins** a wall stood between these two gardens; **la cime s'élève majestueusement au-dessus des forêts** the peak rises (up) *ou* towers majestically above the forests.

c (*monter*) [*avion*] to go up, ascend; [*oiseau*] to fly up, ascend. **l'avion s'élevait regulièrement** the plane was climbing *ou* ascending regularly; **la pensée s'élève vers l'absolu** thought soars *ou* ascends towards the Absolute; **l'âme s'élève vers Dieu** the soul ascends to(wards) God; **le ton s'élève, les voix s'élèvent** voices are beginning to rise.

d [*discussions*] to arise; [*objections, doutes*] to be raised, arise. **sa voix s'éleva dans le silence** his voice broke the silence; **aucune voix ne s'éleva en sa faveur** not a (single) voice was raised in his favour.

e (*dans la société*) to rise. **s'~ jusqu'au sommet de l'échelle** to climb to the top of the ladder; **s'~ à la force du poignet/par son seul travail** to work one's way up unaided/by the sweat of one's (own) brow; **s'~ au-dessus des querelles** to rise above (petty) quarrels.

f (*protester*) **s'~ contre** to rise up against.

g (*se bâtir*) to go up, be put up *ou* erected. **la maison s'élève peu à peu** the house is going up bit by bit *ou* is gradually going up.

h (*se monter*) **s'~ à** [*prix, pertes*] to total, add up to, amount to.

éleveur, -euse [el(ə)vœʀ, øz] 1 **nm,f** stockbreeder. **~ (de bétail)** cattle breeder *ou* rearer; **~ de chevaux/porcs** horse/pig breeder; **~ de vers à soie** silkworm breeder, sericulturist (*SPÉC*); **~ d'abeilles** beekeeper; *voir* **propriétaire.** 2 **éleveuse nf** (*pour poussins*) brooder.

elfe [ɛlf] **nm** elf.

élider vt, s'élider vpr [elide] 1 to elide.

Élie [eli] **nm** Elijah.

éligibilité [eliʒibilite] **nf** (*Pol*) eligibility.

éligible [eliʒibl] **adj** (*Pol*) eligible.

élimer [elime] 1 1 **vt** *vêtement, tissu* to wear thin. 2 **s'élimer vpr** [*vêtement, tissu*] to wear thin, become threadbare. **chemise élimée au col/aux coudes** shirt worn (thin) *ou* wearing thin *ou* (which is) threadbare at the collar/elbows.

élimination [eliminasjɔ̃] **nf** (*gén*) elimination.

éliminatoire [eliminatwaʀ] 1 **adj** *épreuve* eliminatory (*épith*); *note,* (*Sport*) *temps* disqualifying (*épith*). 2 **nf** (*Sport*) (eliminating *ou* preliminary) heat.

éliminer [elimine] 1 **vt** (*gén, Math, Méd*) to eliminate; *possibilité* to rule out, eliminate, dismiss; *données secondaires* to discard, eliminate. (*Pol*) **éliminé au second tour** eliminated in the second ballot; (*Scol*) **être éliminé à l'oral** to be eliminated *ou* to fail in the oral; (*Jeux*) **éliminé!** you're out!; **éliminé en quart de finale** knocked out *ou* eliminated in the quarter finals; **les petits exploitants seront éliminés du marché** small farmers will be forced out of the market.

élire [eliʀ] 43 **vt** to elect. **il a été élu président** he was elected president, he was voted in as president; **~ domicile** to take up residence (*à, dans* in).

Élisabeth [elizabɛt] **nf** = **Élizabeth.**

élisabéthain, e [elizabetɛ̃, ɛn] 1 **adj** Elizabethan. 2 **nm,f: É~(e)** Elizabethan.

Élisée [elize] **nm** Elisha.

élision [elizjɔ̃] **nf** elision.

élite [elit] **nf** elite, élite. **l'~ de** the cream *ou* elite of; **nature** *ou* **âme d'~** noble soul; **sujet d'~** first-rate person; (*Mil*) **corps/cavalerie d'~** crack corps/cavalry; **les ~s (de la nation)** the elite (of the nation); (*Imprimerie*) **caractères ~** elite (type); *voir* **tireur.**

élitisme [elitism] **nm** elitism. **faire de l'~** to be elitist.

élitiste [elitist] **adj, nmf** elitist.

élixir [eliksiʀ] **nm** elixir. **~ de longue vie** elixir of life; **~ parégorique** paregoric (elixir).

Élizabeth [elizabɛt] **nf** Elizabeth.

elle [ɛl] **pron pers f** a (*fonction sujet*) (*personne, nation*) she; (*chose*) it; (*animal, bébé*) she, it. **~s** they; **~ est couturière** she is a dressmaker; **prends cette chaise, ~ est plus confortable** have this chair — it is more comfortable; **je me méfie de sa chienne, ~ mord** I don't trust his dog because she *ou* it bites; **la fourmi emmagasine ce qu'~ trouve** the ant stores what it finds; **~, furieuse, a refusé** furious, she refused; **la Suisse a décidé qu'~ resterait neutre** Switzerland decided that she would remain neutral; **qu'est-ce qu'ils ont dit? — ~, rien** what did they say? — SHE said nothing; **il est venu mais pas ~/~s** he came but she/they didn't, he came but not her*/them*; **~ partie, j'ai pu travailler** with her gone *ou* after she had gone I was able to work; **~, ~ n'aurait jamais fait ça** SHE would never have done that; **~ renoncer? ce n'est pas son genre** HER give up? it wouldn't be like her; *voir aussi* **même.**

b (*fonction objet, souvent emphatique*) (*personne, nation*) her; (*animal*) her, it; (*chose*) it. **~s** them; **il n'admire qu'~** he only admires her, she's the only one he admires; **je l'ai bien vue ~** I saw HER all right, I definitely saw HER; **je les ai bien vus, ~ et lui** I definitely saw both *ou* the two of them; **la revoir ~? jamais!** see HER again? never!

c (*emphatique avec qui, que*) **c'est ~ qui me l'a dit** she told me herself, it's she who told me; (*iro*) **c'est ~s qui le disent** that's THEIR story!, that's what THEY say!; (*frm*) **ce fut ~ qui lança le mouvement des suffragettes** it was she *ou* she it was (*frm*) who launched the suffragette movement; **voilà la pluie, et ~ qui est sortie sans manteau!** here comes the rain and to think she has gone out without a coat! *ou* and there she is out without a coat!; **chasse cette chienne, c'est ~ qui m'a mordu** chase that dog away, it's the one that bit me; **c'est ~ que j'avais invitée** it's *ou* it was her I had invited; **c'est à ~ que je veux parler** it's HER I want to speak to, I want to speak to HER; **il y a une chouette dans le bois, c'est ~ que j'ai entendue cette nuit** there's a screech owl in the wood and that's what I heard last night.

d (*avec prép*) (*personne*) her; (*animal*) her, it; (*chose*) it. **ce livre est à ~** this book belongs to her *ou* is hers; **ces livres sont à ~s** these books belong to them *ou* are theirs; **c'est à ~ de décider** it's up to her to decide, it's her decision; **c'est gentil à ~ d'avoir écrit** it was kind of her to write; **un ami à ~** a friend of hers, one of her friends; **elle ne pense qu'à ~** she only thinks of herself; **elle a une maison à ~** she has a house of her own; **ses enfants à ~** her children; **qu'est-ce qu'il ferait sans ~** what (on earth) would he do without her; **ce poème n'est pas d'~** this poem is not one of hers *ou* not one that she wrote; **il veut une photo d'~** he wants a photo of her; **vous pouvez avoir confiance en ~** (*femme*) she is thoroughly reliable, you can have complete confidence in her; (*machine*) it is thoroughly reliable.

e (*dans comparaisons*) (*sujet*) she; (*objet*) her. **il est plus grand qu'~/~s** he is taller than she is/they are *ou* than her/them; **je le connais aussi bien qu'~** (*aussi bien que je la connais*) I know him as well as (I know) her; (*aussi bien qu'elle le connaît*) I know him as well as she does *ou* as well as her*; **ne faites pas comme ~** don't do as *ou* what she does, don't do like her*.

f (*interrog, emphatique: gén non traduit*) **Alice est-~ rentrée?** is Alice back?; **sa lettre est-~ arrivée?** has his letter come?; **les infirmières sont-~s bien payées?** are nurses well paid?; **~ est loin, notre jeunesse!** it's so long since we were young!; **tu sais, ta tante, ~ n'est pas très aimable!** you know your aunt *ou* that aunt of yours isn't very nice!

ellébore [elebɔʀ] **nm** hellebore.

elle-même, pl elles-mêmes [ɛlmɛm] **pron** *voir* **même.**

ellipse [elips] **nf** (*Géom*) ellipse; (*Ling*) ellipsis.

ellipsoïdal, e, mpl -aux [elipsɔidal, o] **adj** ellipsoidal.

ellipsoïde [elipsɔid] 1 **nm** ellipsoid. 2 **adj** (*Géom*) elliptical.

elliptique [eliptik] **adj** (*Géom*) elliptic(al); (*Ling*) elliptical.

elliptiquement [eliptikmɑ̃] **adv** (*Ling*) elliptically.

élocution [elɔkysjɔ̃] **nf** (*débit*) delivery; (*clarté*) diction. **défaut d'~** speech impediment; **professeur d'~** elocution *ou* speech production (*Brit*) teacher.

éloge [elɔʒ] **nm** a (*louange*) praise. **couvert d'~s** showered with praise(s); **digne d'~** praiseworthy, commendable; **faire des ~s à qn** to praise sb (to his face); *voir* **tarir.** b **faire l'~ de** to praise, speak (very) highly of; **son ~ n'est plus à faire** I do not need to add to his praise;

c'est le plus bel ~ à lui faire it's the highest praise one can give him; **faire son propre ~** to sing one's own praises, blow one's own trumpet* (*Brit*) *ou* horn* (*US*); **l'~ que vous avez fait de cette œuvre** your praise *ou* commendation of this work. c (*littér: panégyrique*) eulogy. **prononcer l'~ funèbre de qn** to deliver a funeral oration in praise of sb.

élogieusement [elɔʒjøzmɑ̃] **adv** very highly, most favourably.

élogieux, -ieuse [elɔʒjø, jøz] **adj** laudatory, eulogistic(al). **parler de qn en termes ~** to speak very highly of sb, speak of sb in the most laudatory terms.

éloigné, e [elwaɲe] (**ptp de éloigner**) **adj** a (*dans l'espace*) distant, remote, far-off, faraway. **est-ce très ~ de la gare? — oui, c'est très ~** is it very far *ou* a long way (away) from the station? – yes, it's a long way; **~ de 3 km** 3 km away; **le village est trop ~ pour qu'on puisse y aller à pied** the village is too far away *ou* too far off for one to be able to walk there.

b (*dans le temps*) *époque, événement, échéance* distant (*de* from), remote (*de* from). **le passé ~** the distant *ou* remote past; **l'avenir ~** the distant *ou* far-off *ou* remote future; **dans un avenir peu ~** in the not-too-distant future, in the near future.

c *parent* distant; *ancêtre* remote. **la famille ~e** distant relatives.

d (*fig*) **être ~ de** to be far from, be a long way from; **sa version est très ~e de la vérité** his version is very far from (being) the truth; **un sentiment pas très ~ de la haine** an emotion not far removed from hatred; **rien n'est plus ~ de mes pensées** nothing is *ou* could be farther from my thoughts; **je ne suis pas très ~ de le croire** I almost believe him, I'm not far from believing him; **je suis fort ~ de ses positions** my point of view is very far removed from his.

e **tenir ~ de** to keep away from; **cette conférence m'a tenu ~ de chez moi** the conference kept me away from home; **se tenir ~ du feu** to keep away from *ou* clear of the fire; **se tenir ~ du danger/des querelles** to steer *ou* keep clear of danger/of quarrels, keep *ou* stay out of the way of danger/quarrels.

éloignement [elwaɲmɑ̃] **nm** a (*action d'éloigner*) *[personne indésirable]* taking away, removal; *[soupçons]* removal, averting; *[échéance]* putting off, postponement. **l'~ des objets obtenu au moyen d'une lentille spéciale** the distancing of objects by means of a special lens; **leur ~ de la cour, ordonné par le roi** their having been ordered away *ou* their banishment from the court by the king.

b (*action de s'éloigner*) *[être aimé]* estrangement. **son ~ des affaires** his progressive disinvolvement with business.

c (*état: spatial, temporel*) distance. **l'~ rapetisse les objets** distance makes objects (look) smaller; **notre ~ de Paris complique le travail** our being so far from Paris *ou* our distance from Paris complicates the work; **en amour, l'~ rapproche** absence makes the heart grow fonder (*Prov*); **bruit étouffé par l'~** noise muffled by distance; **avec l'~, on juge mieux les événements** one can judge events better after a lapse of time *ou* from a distance.

éloigner [elwaɲe] 1 **1 vt** a *objet* to move away, take away (*de* from). **éloigne ce coussin du radiateur** move *ou* take that cushion away from the radiator; **une lentille qui éloigne les objets** a lens that distances objects *ou* that makes objects look distant.

b *personne* (*lit*) to take away, remove (*de* from); (*fig: exiler, écarter*) to send away (*de* from). **~ les curieux du lieu de l'accident** to move the onlookers *ou* bystanders away from the scene of the accident; **allumer du feu pour ~ les bêtes sauvages** to light a fire to keep off the wild animals; (*fig*) **~ qn de** *être aimé, compagnons* to estrange sb from; *activité* to take sb away from; *tentations, carrière* to take sb away from, remove sb from; **son penchant pour la boisson éloigna de lui ses amis** his inclination for drink lost him his friends *ou* made his friends drift away from him; **ce chemin nous éloigne du village** this path takes *ou* leads us away from the village.

c *souvenir, idée* to banish, dismiss; *crainte* to remove, dismiss; *danger* to ward off, remove; *soupçons* to remove, avert (*de* from).

d *chose à faire, échéance, visite* to put off, postpone.

e (*espacer*) *visites* to make less frequent, space out.

2 **s'éloigner vpr** a *[tout objet en mouvement]* to move away; *[orage]* to go away, pass; *[bruit]* to go away, grow fainter. **le village s'éloignait et finit par disparaître dans la brume** the village got further (and further) away *ou* grew more and more distant and finally disappeared in the mist.

b *[personne]* (*par prudence etc*) to go away (*de* from); (*par pudeur, discrétion*) to go away, withdraw (*de* from). **s'~ en courant/en hâte** to run/hurry away *ou* off; **éloignez-vous, les enfants, ça risque d'éclater!** move away *ou* back, children, *ou* stand *ou* get back, children, it might explode!; **ne t'éloigne pas (trop) (de la voiture)** don't go (too) far *ou* don't go (too) far away (from the car); (*fig*) **s'~ de** *être aimé, compagnons* to become estranged from, grow away from; *sujet traité* to wander from; *position prise* to move away from; *devoir* to swerve *ou* deviate from; **là vous vous éloignez (du sujet)** you're wandering from *ou* getting off the point *ou* subject; **je la sentais s'~ (de moi)** I felt her becoming estranged *ou* growing away from me, I felt her becoming more (and more) distant; **s'~ du droit chemin** to stray *ou* wander from the straight and narrow; **s'~ de la vérité** to wander from the truth.

c *[souvenir, échéance]* to grow more (and more) distant *ou* remote; *[danger]* to pass, go away; *[craintes]* to go away, retreat.

élongation [elɔ̃gasjɔ̃] **nf** a (*Méd*) strained *ou* pulled muscle. **les ~s font très mal** straining *ou* pulling a muscle is very painful, a pulled muscle is very painful; **se faire une ~** to strain *ou* pull a muscle. b (*Astron*) elongation; (*Phys*) displacement.

éloquemment [elɔkamɑ̃] **adv** eloquently.

éloquence [elɔkɑ̃s] **nf** eloquence. **il m'a fallu toute mon ~ pour la convaincre** I needed all the eloquence I could summon up *ou* muster to convince her; (*fig*) **l'~ de ces chiffres rend tout commentaire superflu** these figures speak for themselves *ou* need no comment.

éloquent, e [elɔkɑ̃, ɑ̃t] **adj** *orateur, discours, geste* eloquent. (*fig*) **ces chiffres sont ~s** these figures speak for themselves; **une étreinte plus ~e que toute parole** an embrace that spoke louder than any word(s), an embrace more eloquent *ou* meaningful than any word(s); **un silence ~** a silence that speaks volumes, a meaningful *ou* an eloquent silence.

élu, e [ely] (**ptp de élire**) **1 adj** (*Rel*) chosen; (*Pol*) elected. **2 nm,f** a (*Pol*) (*député*) elected member, ≃ member of parliament, M.P. (*Brit*); (*conseiller*) elected representative, councillor. **les nouveaux ~s** the newly elected members; the newly elected councillors; **les ~s locaux** the local *ou* town councillors; **les citoyens et leurs ~s** the citizens and their elected representatives. b (*hum: fiancé*) **l'~ de son cœur** her heart's desire (*hum*), her beloved; **quelle est l'heureuse ~e?** who's the lucky girl? c (*Rel*) **les É~s** the Chosen ones, the Elect; **être l'~ de Dieu** to be chosen by God.

élucidation [elysidasjɔ̃] **nf** elucidation.

élucider [elyside] 1 **vt** to clear up, elucidate.

élucubrations [elykybʀasjɔ̃] **nfpl** (*péj*) wild imaginings.

élucubrer [elykybʀe] 1 **vt** (*péj*) to dream up.

éluder [elyde] 1 **vt** *difficulté* to evade, elude; *loi, problème* to evade, dodge, fudge.

élusif, -ive [elyzif, iv] **adj** (*frm*) elusive.

Élysée [elize] **nm** (*Myth*) **l'~** the Elysium; **(le palais de) l'~** the Elysee palace, *official residence of the President of the French Republic;* **les Champs ~s** (*Myth*) the Elysian Fields; (*à Paris*) the Champs Élysées.

élyséen, -enne [elizeɛ̃, ɛn] **adj** Elysian.

élytre [elitʀ] **nm** (hard) outer wing, elytron (*SPÉC*).

émaciation [emasjasjɔ̃] **nf** emaciation.

émacier [emasje] 7 **1 vt** to emaciate. **2 s'émacier vpr** to become emaciated *ou* wasted. **visage émacié** emaciated *ou* haggard *ou* wasted face.

émail, pl -aux [emaj, o] **nm** (*substance*) enamel. **en** *ou* **d'~** enamel(led); **des ~aux décoraient la pièce** the room was decorated with pieces of enamel work; **cendrier en ~aux** enamelled ashtray.

émaillage [emajaʒ] **nm** enamelling.

émaillé, e [emaje] (**ptp de émailler**) **adj** a (*lit*) enamelled. b (*fig: parsemé de*) **~ de** *étoiles* spangled *ou* studded with; *fautes, citations* peppered *ou* dotted with; **voyage ~ d'incidents** journey punctuated by unforeseen incidents.

émailler [emaje] 1 **vt** a (*lit*) to enamel. b (*fig: parsemer*) *[étoiles]* to stud, spangle. **~ un texte de citations/d'erreurs** to pepper a text with quotations/errors.

émanation [emanasjɔ̃] **nf** a (*odeurs*) **~s** smells, emanations; **~s fétides** fetid emanations; **~s volcaniques** volatiles; **~s toxiques** toxic fumes. b (*fig*) product. **le pouvoir est l'~ du peuple** power issues from the people, power is a product of the will of the people. c (*Phys*) emanation; (*Rel*) procession.

émancipateur, -trice [emɑ̃sipatœʀ, tʀis] **1 adj** liberating, emancipatory. **2 nm,f** liberator, emancipator.

émancipation [emɑ̃sipasjɔ̃] **nf** (*Jur*) emancipation; *[colonie, femme]* liberation, emancipation.

émancipé, e [emɑ̃sipe] (**ptp de émanciper**) **adj** liberated.

émanciper [emɑ̃sipe] 1 **1 vt** (*Jur*) to emancipate; *femme* to emancipate, liberate; *esprit* to liberate, (set) free. **2 s'émanciper vpr** *[femme]* to become emancipated *ou* liberated, liberate o.s.; *[esprit, art]* to become liberated, liberate *ou* free itself.

émaner [emane] 1 émaner de **vt indir** (*Pol, Rel*) *[pouvoir etc]* to issue from; *[ordres, note]* to come from, be issued by; *[chaleur, lumière, odeur]* to emanate *ou* issue *ou* come from; (*fig*) *[charme]* to emanate from, be radiated by.

émargement [emaʀʒəmɑ̃] **nm** a (*NonC: voir* **émarger**) signing; annotating. **feuille d'~** (*feuille de paye*) paysheet; (*feuille de présence*) attendance sheet. b (*signature*) signature; (*annotation*) annotation.

émarger [emaʀʒe] 3 **1 vt** a (*frm*) (*signer*) to sign; (*mettre ses initiales*) to initial; (*annoter*) to annotate. b (*Typ*) to trim. **2 vi** a (*†: toucher son salaire*) to draw one's salary. **à combien émarge-t-il par mois?** what is his monthly salary? b **~ d'une certaine somme à un budget** to receive a certain sum out of a budget.

émasculation [emaskylasjɔ̃] **nf** emasculation.

émasculer [emaskyle] 1 **vt** to emasculate.

emballage [ɑ̃balaʒ] **nm** a (*action d'emballer*) (*dans un carton etc*) packing(-up); (*dans du papier*) wrapping(-up), doing-up. **papier d'~** packing paper; wrapping paper. b (*Comm*) (*boîte, carton etc*) package, packaging (*NonC*); (*papier*) wrapping (*NonC*). (*Comm*) **~ perdu/consigné** non-returnable *ou* one-way/returnable bottle (*ou* jar

etc); ~ **promotionnel** flash pack.
emballement [ɑ̃balmɑ̃] **nm** a (*) (*enthousiasme*) flight of enthusiasm; (*colère*) flash of anger. (*passade*) **méfiez-vous de ses ~s** beware of his (sudden) crazes*. b *[moteur]* racing; *[cheval]* bolting. c (*Écon*) **cela a provoqué l'~ du dollar/de l'économie** that caused the dollar/the economy to race out of control.
emballer [ɑ̃bale] 1 1 **vt** a (*empaqueter*) (*dans un carton, de la toile etc*) to pack (up); (*dans du papier*) to wrap (up), do up.
b (‡: *arrêter*) to nick‡ (*Brit*), run in*.
c *moteur* to race.
d (*: *enthousiasmer*) *[idée, film]* to thrill to bits*. **je n'ai pas été très emballé par ce film** I wasn't exactly carried away* by that film, that film didn't exactly thrill me to bits*.
e (‡: *séduire*) to pick up*, get off with*.
2 **s'emballer vpr** a (*) *[personne]* (*enthousiasme*) to get *ou* be carried away*, get worked up*; (*colère*) to fly off the handle*, go off (at) the deep end*.
b *[moteur]* to race; *[cheval]* to bolt. **cheval emballé** runaway *ou* bolting horse.
c *[économie, monnaie]* to race out of control.
emballeur, -euse [ɑ̃balœʀ, øz] **nm,f** packer.
embarbouiller* [ɑ̃baʀbuje] 1 1 **vt** (*troubler*) to confuse, get mixed up*. 2 **s'embarbouiller vpr** to get mixed up (*dans* in).
embarcadère [ɑ̃baʀkadɛʀ] **nm** landing stage, pier.
embarcation [ɑ̃baʀkasjɔ̃] **nf** (small) boat, (small) craft (*pl inv*).
embardée [ɑ̃baʀde] **nf** (*Aut*) swerve; (*Naut*) yaw. **faire une ~** (*Aut*) to swerve; (*Naut*) to yaw.
embargo [ɑ̃baʀgo] **nm** embargo. **mettre l'~ sur qch** to impose *ou* put an embargo on sth, embargo sth; **lever l'~ (mis sur)** to lift *ou* raise the embargo (on).
embarquement [ɑ̃baʀkəmɑ̃] **nm** *[marchandises]* loading; *[passagers]* (*en bateau*) embarkation, boarding; (*en avion*) boarding.
embarquer [ɑ̃baʀke] 1 1 **vt** a *passagers* to embark, take on board. **je l'ai embarqué dans le train*** I saw him onto the train, I put him on the train.
b *cargaison* (*en train, gén*) to load; (*en bateau*) to load, ship. (*Naut*) **le navire embarque des paquets d'eau** the boat is taking in *ou* shipping water.
c (‡) (*emporter*) to cart off*, lug off*; (*voler*) to pinch*, nick‡ (*Brit*); (*pour emprisonner*) to cart off* *ou* away*. **se faire ~ par la police** to get picked up by the police*.
d (*: *entraîner*) **~ qn dans** to get sb mixed up in* *ou* involved in, involve sb in; **il s'est laissé ~ dans une sale histoire** he has got (himself) mixed up in* *ou* involved in a nasty bit of business; **une affaire bien/mal embarquée** an affair that has got off to a good/bad start.
2 **vi** a (*aussi s'~: partir en voyage*) to embark. **il a embarqué *ou* il s'est embarqué hier pour le Maroc** he sailed for Morocco yesterday.
b (*monter à bord*) to board, go aboard *ou* on board.
c (*Naut*) **le navire embarque, la mer embarque** we are *ou* the boat is shipping water.
3 **s'embarquer vpr** a = **2a**.
b **s'~ dans*** *aventure, affaire* to embark (up)on, launch into; *affaire louche* to get mixed up in *ou* involved in.
embarras [ɑ̃baʀa] **nm** a (*ennui*) trouble. **cela constitue un ~ supplémentaire** that's yet another problem; **je ne veux pas être un ~ pour vous** I don't want to be a nuisance *ou* trouble to you, I don't want to bother you *ou* get in your way; **causer *ou* faire toutes sortes d'~ à qn** to give *ou* cause sb no end* of trouble *ou* bother; **ne vous mettez pas dans l'~ pour moi** don't put yourself out *ou* go to any trouble for me.
b (*gêne*) confusion, embarrassment. **dit-il avec ~** he said in some confusion *ou* with (some) embarrassment; **il remarqua mon ~ pour répondre** he noticed that I was at a loss for a reply *ou* at a loss how to reply *ou* that I was stuck* for a reply.
c (*situation délicate*) predicament, awkward position. **mettre *ou* plonger qn dans l'~** to put sb in an awkward position *ou* on the spot*; **tirer qn d'~** to get *ou* help sb out of an awkward position *ou* out of a predicament. **être dans l'~** (*en mauvaise position*) to be in a predicament *ou* an awkward position; (*dans un dilemme*) to be in a quandary *ou* in a dilemma.
d (*gêne financière*) **~ (d'argent *ou* financiers)** financial difficulties, money worries; **être dans l'~** to be in financial straits *ou* difficulties, be short of money.
e (*Méd*) **~ gastrique** upset stomach, stomach upset.
f (†: *encombrement*) **~ de circulation *ou* de voitures** (road) congestion (*NonC*), traffic holdup; **les ~ de Paris** the congestion of the Paris streets.
g (*chichis, façons*) **faire des ~** to (make a) fuss, make a to-do; **c'est un faiseur d'~** he's a fusspot*, he's always making a fuss.
h **elle a l'~ du choix, elle n'a que l'~ du choix** her only problem is that she has too great a choice, her only difficulty is that of choosing *ou* deciding; **~ de richesses**† embarrassment of riches.
embarrassant, e [ɑ̃baʀasɑ̃, ɑ̃t] **adj** a *situation* embarrassing, uncomfortable; *problème* awkward, thorny. b *paquets* cumbersome, awkward. **ce que cet enfant peut être ~!** what a hindrance this child is!, this child is always in the way!
embarrassé, e [ɑ̃baʀase] (**ptp de embarrasser**) **adj** a (*gêné*) *personne* embarrassed, ill-at-ease (*attrib*), self-conscious; *sourire* embarrassed, uneasy. **être ~ de sa personne** to be awkward *ou* ill-at-ease; **il était tout timide et ~** he was very shy and ill-at-ease *ou* embarrassed; **je serais bien ~ de choisir entre les deux** I should really be at a loss (if I had) *ou* I should be hard put (to it) to choose between the two. b (*peu clair*) *explication, phrase* muddled, confused. c (*Méd*) **avoir l'estomac ~** to have an upset stomach; **j'ai la langue ~e** my tongue is coated. d (*encombré*) *table, corridor* cluttered (up). **j'ai les mains ~es** my hands are full.
embarrasser [ɑ̃baʀase] 1 1 **vt** a (*encombrer*) *[paquets]* to clutter (up); *[vêtements]* to hinder, hamper. **enlève ce manteau qui t'embarrasse** take that coat off – it's in your way *ou* it's hampering your movements; **je ne t'embarrasse pas au moins?** are you sure I'm not bothering you? *ou* I'm not in your way?
b (*désorienter*) **~ qn** to put sb in a predicament *ou* an awkward position; **~ qn par des questions indiscrètes** to embarrass sb with indiscreet questions; **sa demande m'embarrasse** his request puts me in a predicament *ou* an awkward position *ou* on the spot*; **ça m'embarrasse de te le dire mais ...** I don't like to tell you this but ...; **il y a quelque chose qui m'embarrasse là-dedans** there's something about it that bothers *ou* worries me.
c (*Méd*) **~ l'estomac** to lie heavy on the stomach.
2 **s'embarrasser vpr** a (*s'encombrer*) **s'~ de** *paquets, compagnon* to burden o.s. with.
b (*fig: se soucier*) to trouble o.s. (*de* about), be troubled (*de* by). **sans s'~ des détails** without troubling *ou* worrying about the details; **en voilà un qui ne s'embarrasse pas de scrupules** there's one person for you who doesn't burden *ou* trouble himself with scruples.
c (*s'emmêler: dans un vêtement etc*) to get tangled *ou* caught up (*dans* in). (*fig*) **il s'embarrasse dans ses explications** he gets in a muddle with his explanations, he ties himself in knots with his explanations*.
embastillement [ɑ̃bastijmɑ̃] **nm** (††, *hum*) imprisonment.
embastiller [ɑ̃bastije] 1 **vt** (††, *hum*) to imprison.
embauche [ɑ̃boʃ] **nf** (*action d'embaucher*) taking-on, hiring; (*travail disponible*) vacancy. **est-ce qu'il y a de l'~?** are there any vacancies?, are you taking anyone on? *ou* hiring anyone?; **bureau d'~** employment office.
embaucher [ɑ̃boʃe] 1 **vt** to take on, hire. **s'~ comme peintre** to get o.s. taken on *ou* hired as a painter.
embaucheur, -euse [ɑ̃boʃœʀ, øz] **nm,f** labour (*Brit*) *ou* employment contractor.
embauchoir [ɑ̃boʃwaʀ] **nm** shoetree.
embaumé, e [ɑ̃bome] (**ptp de embaumer**) **adj** *air* fragrant, balmy (*littér*).
embaumement [ɑ̃bommɑ̃] **nm** embalming.
embaumer [ɑ̃bome] 1 1 **vt** a *cadavre* to embalm. b (*littér: parfumer*) **le lilas embaumait l'air** the scent of lilac hung heavy in the air; **l'air embaumait le lilas** the air was fragrant *ou* balmy (*littér*) with the scent of lilac. 2 **vi** to give out a fragrance, be fragrant.
embaumeur, -euse [ɑ̃bomœʀ, øz] **nm,f** embalmer.
embellie [ɑ̃beli] **nf** *[temps]* slight improvement (*de* in); *[économie]* slight improvement *ou* upturn (*de* in).
embellir [ɑ̃beliʀ] 2 1 **vt** *personne, jardin* to beautify, make (more) attractive; *ville* to smarten up (*Brit*), give a face lift to*; *vérité, récit* to embellish. 2 **vi** *[personne]* to grow lovelier *ou* more attractive, grow in beauty (*littér*).
embellissement [ɑ̃belismɑ̃] **nm** *[récit, vérité]* embellishment. **ce nouveau luminaire dans l'entrée est un ~** this new light fitting in the hall is a nice decorative touch *ou* is an improvement; **les récents ~s de la ville** the recent smartening-up (*Brit*) of the town *ou* improvements to the town, the recent face lift the town has been given*.
emberlificoter* [ɑ̃bɛʀlifikɔte] 1 1 **vt** (*enjôler*) to get round*; (*embrouiller*) to mix up*, muddle (up); (*duper*) to hoodwink*, bamboozle*. 2 **s'emberlificoter vpr** (*dans un vêtement*) to get tangled *ou* caught up (*dans* in). **il s'emberlificote dans ses explications** he gets in a terrible muddle *ou* he gets himself tied up in knots with his explanations*.
embêtant, e [ɑ̃bɛtɑ̃, ɑ̃t] **adj** (*gén*) annoying; *situation, problème* awkward, tricky. **c'est ~!** (*ennuyeux*) what a nuisance!, how annoying!; (*alarmant*) it's worrying!
embêtement [ɑ̃bɛtmɑ̃] **nm** problem, trouble. **causer des ~s à qn** to make trouble for sb.
embêter [ɑ̃bete] 1 1 **vt** (*gêner, préoccuper*) to bother, worry; (*importuner*) to pester, bother; (*irriter*) to annoy, get on one's nerves*; (*lasser*) to bore. 2 **s'embêter vpr** a (*se morfondre*) to be bored, be fed up*. **qu'est-ce qu'on s'embête ici!** what a drag it is here!*, it's so boring here! b (*s'embarrasser*) to bother o.s. (*à faire* doing). **ne t'embête pas avec ça** don't bother *ou* worry about that; **il ne s'embête pas!** he does all right for himself!*; **pourquoi s'~ à le réparer?** why go to all the trouble *ou* bother of repairing it?, why bother yourself repairing it?

emblaver [ɑ̃blave] [1] **vt** to sow (with a cereal crop).
emblavure [ɑ̃blavyʀ] **nf** field (sown with a cereal crop).
emblée [ɑ̃ble] **adv: d'~** straightaway, right away, at once; **détester qn d'~** to detest sb on sight, take an instant dislike to sb.
emblématique [ɑ̃blematik] **adj** *(lit)* emblematic; *(fig)* symbolic.
emblème [ɑ̃blɛm] **nm** *(lit)* emblem; *(fig)* symbol, emblem.
embobiner* [ɑ̃bɔbine] [1] **vt** *(enjôler)* to get round*; *(embrouiller)* to mix up*, muddle (up); *(duper)* to hoodwink*, bamboozle*. **elle sait ~ son père** she can twist her father round her little finger, she knows how to get round her father.
emboîtement [ɑ̃bwatmɑ̃] **nm** fitting, interlocking.
emboîter [ɑ̃bwate] [1] 1 **vt** a *pièces, parties* to fit together, fit into each other. **~ qch dans** to fit sth into. b **~ le pas à qn** *(lit)* to follow close behind sb *ou* close on sb's heels; *(fig: imiter)* to follow suit. 2 **s'emboîter vpr** *[pièces]* to fit together, fit into each other. **ces 2 pièces s'emboîtent exactement** these 2 parts fit together exactly; **des chaises qui peuvent s'~ pour le rangement** chairs that can be stacked (together) when not in use.
embolie [ɑ̃bɔli] **nf** embolism. **~ gazeuse/pulmonaire** gaseous/pulmonary embolism.
embonpoint [ɑ̃bɔ̃pwɛ̃] **nm** stoutness, portliness. **avoir/prendre de l'~** to be/become rather stout.
embossage [ɑ̃bɔsaʒ] **nm** fore and aft mooring.
embosser [ɑ̃bɔse] [1] **vt** a *(Naut)* to moor fore and aft. b *carte* to emboss.
emboucher [ɑ̃buʃe] [1] **vt** *instrument* to raise to one's lips; *voir* **mal**.
embouchure [ɑ̃buʃyʀ] **nf** *[fleuve]* mouth; *[mors]* mouthpiece; *(Mus)* mouthpiece, embouchure.
embourber [ɑ̃buʀbe] [1] 1 **vt** *voiture* to get stuck in the mud. 2 **s'embourber vpr** *[voiture]* to get stuck in the mud, get bogged down (in the mud). **notre voiture s'est embourbée dans le marais** our car got stuck in *ou* got bogged down in the marsh; *(fig)* **s'~ dans** *détails* to get bogged down in; *monotonie* to sink into.
embourgeoisement [ɑ̃buʀʒwazmɑ̃] **nm** *[personne, parti]* trend towards a middle-class outlook.
embourgeoiser [ɑ̃buʀʒwaze] [1] 1 **s'embourgeoiser vpr** *[parti, personne]* to become middle-class, adopt a middle-class outlook; *[quartier]* to become middle-class. 2 **vt** *personne* to make middle-class (in outlook).
embout [ɑ̃bu] **nm** *[canne]* tip, ferrule; *[tuyau]* nozzle.
embouteillage [ɑ̃butɛjaʒ] **nm** *(Aut)* traffic jam, (traffic) holdup; *(†: mise en bouteilles)* bottling.
embouteiller [ɑ̃buteje] [1] **vt** *(Aut)* to jam, block; *(Téléc) lignes* to block; (†) *vin, lait* to bottle. **les routes sont très embouteillées** the roads are very congested.
emboutir [ɑ̃butiʀ] [2] **vt** *métal* to stamp; *(Aut fig)* to crash *ou* run into. **avoir une aile emboutie** to have a dented *ou* damaged wing; **il s'est fait ~ par un camion** he was hit by a lorry, his car was dented by a lorry.
embranchement [ɑ̃bʀɑ̃ʃmɑ̃] **nm** a *[voies, routes, tuyaux]* junction. **à l'~ des 2 routes** at the fork in the roads, where the roads fork. b *(route)* side road, branch road; *(Rail: voie)* branch line; *(tuyau)* branch pipe; *(rivière)* embranchment. c *(Bot, Zool: catégorie)* branch.
embrancher [ɑ̃bʀɑ̃ʃe] [1] 1 **vt** *tuyaux, voies* to join (up). **~ qch sur** to join sth (up) to. 2 **s'embrancher vpr** *[tuyaux, voies]* to join (up). **s'~ sur** to join (up) to.
embrasement [ɑ̃bʀazmɑ̃] **nm** *(†: incendie)* fire, conflagration; *[pays]* uprising, rebellion. **ce qui a provoqué l'~ de la maison** what set the house on fire; **l'~ du ciel au couchant** *(état)* the blazing *ou* fiery sky at sunset; *(action)* the flaring-up *ou* blazing-up of the sky at sunset; *(lueurs)* **des ~s soudains** sudden blazes of light; **l'~ des esprits** the stirring *ou* rousing of people's passions.
embraser [ɑ̃bʀaze] [1] 1 **vt** *(littér) maison, forêt etc* to set ablaze, set fire to; *(fig) ciel* to inflame, set aglow *ou* ablaze; *cœur* to kindle, fire. 2 **s'embraser vpr** *[maison]* to blaze up, flare up; *[ciel]* to flare up, be set ablaze *(de* with); *[cœur]* to become inflamed, be fired *(de* with); *[pays en révolte]* to rise up in arms.
embrassade [ɑ̃bʀasad] **nf** *(gén pl)* hugging and kissing *(NonC)*.
embrasse [ɑ̃bʀas] **nf** curtain loop, tieback *(US)*. **rideaux à ~s** looped curtains.
embrassement [ɑ̃bʀasmɑ̃] **nm** *(littér)* = **embrassade**.
embrasser [ɑ̃bʀase] [1] 1 **vt** a *(donner un baiser)* to kiss. **~ qn à pleine bouche** to kiss sb (full) on the lips; *(en fin de lettre)* **je t'embrasse (affectueusement)** with love. b *(frm ou †: étreindre)* to embrace; *voir* **rime**. c *(frm: choisir) doctrine, cause* to embrace *(frm)*, espouse *(frm)*; *carrière* to take up, enter upon. d *(couvrir) problèmes, sujets* to encompass, embrace. *(littér)* **il embrassa la plaine du regard** his eyes took in the plain, he took in the plain at a glance. 2 **s'embrasser vpr** to kiss (each other).
embrasure [ɑ̃bʀazyʀ] **nf** *(Constr, créneau)* embrasure. **il se tenait dans l'~ de la porte/la fenêtre** he stood in the doorway/the window.
embrayage [ɑ̃bʀɛjaʒ] **nm** a *(mécanisme)* clutch. b *(action) (Aut, Tech)* letting in *ou* engaging the clutch.
embrayer [ɑ̃bʀeje] [8] 1 **vt** *(Aut, Tech)* to put into gear. 2 **vi** *(Aut)* to let in *ou* engage the clutch. *(fig)* **~ sur** to switch to.
embrigadement [ɑ̃bʀigadmɑ̃] **nm** *(voir* **embrigader***)* indoctrination; dragooning.
embrigader [ɑ̃bʀigade] [1] **vt** *(péj) (endoctriner)* to indoctrinate; *(de force)* to dragoon *(dans* into).
embringuer‡ [ɑ̃bʀɛ̃ge] [1] **vt** to mix up*, involve. **il s'est laissé ~ dans une sale histoire** he got (himself) mixed up* *ou* involved in some nasty business.
embrocation [ɑ̃bʀɔkasjɔ̃] **nf** embrocation.
embrocher [ɑ̃bʀɔʃe] [1] **vt** *(Culin) (sur broche)* to spit, put on a spit; *(sur brochette)* to skewer. *(fig)* **~ qn** to run sb through.
embrouillage [ɑ̃bʀujaʒ] **nm** = **embrouillement**.
embrouillamini* [ɑ̃bʀujamini] **nm** muddle, jumble.
embrouille* [ɑ̃bʀuj] **nf: il y a de l'~ là-dessous** there's some hanky-panky* *ou* something funny at the bottom of this; **toutes ces ~s** all this carry-on*.
embrouillé, e [ɑ̃bʀuje] **(ptp de embrouiller) adj** *style, problème, idées* muddled, confused; *papiers* muddled, mixed-up.
embrouillement [ɑ̃bʀujmɑ̃] **nm** *(voir* **embrouiller***) (action)* tangling; muddling up; mixing up; confusion; *(état)* tangle; muddle; confusion. **essayant de démêler l'~ de ses explications** trying to sort out his muddled explanations *ou* the confusion of his explanations.
embrouiller [ɑ̃bʀuje] [1] 1 **vt** a *ficelle* to tangle (up), snarl up; *objets, papiers* to muddle up, mix up; *affaire* to muddle (up), tangle up, confuse; *problème* to muddle (up), confuse. b *personne* to muddle (up), confuse, mix up; *voir* **ni**. 2 **s'embrouiller vpr** a *[idées, style, situation]* to become muddled *ou* confused. b *[personne]* to get in a muddle, become confused *ou* muddled. **s'~ dans un discours/ses explications** to get in a muddle with *ou* tie o.s. up in knots* in a speech/with one's explanations; **s'~ dans ses dates** to get one's dates muddled (up) *ou* mixed up.
embroussaillé, e [ɑ̃bʀusaje] **adj** *chemin* overgrown; *barbe, sourcils, cheveux* bushy, shaggy.
embrumer [ɑ̃bʀyme] [1] **vt** *(littér)* to mist over, cloud over *(de* with); *(fig)* to cloud *(de* with). **à l'horizon embrumé** on the misty *ou* hazy horizon; **l'esprit embrumé par l'alcool** his mind fuddled *ou* clouded with drink.
embruns [ɑ̃bʀœ̃] **nmpl** sea spray *(NonC)*, spindrift *(NonC)*.
embryologie [ɑ̃bʀijɔlɔʒi] **nf** embryology.
embryologique [ɑ̃bʀijɔlɔʒik] **adj** embryologic(al).
embryologiste [ɑ̃bʀijɔlɔʒist] **nmf** embryologist.
embryon [ɑ̃bʀijɔ̃] **nm** embryo.
embryonnaire [ɑ̃bʀijɔnɛʀ] **adj** *(Méd)* embryonic, embryonal; *(fig)* embryonic. *(fig)* **à l'état ~** in embryo, in an embryonic state.
embûche [ɑ̃byʃ] **nf** pitfall, trap. **semé d'~s** treacherous, full of pitfalls *ou* traps.
embuer [ɑ̃bɥe] [1] **vt** to mist (up), mist over. **vitre embuée** misted(-up) window pane; **yeux embués de larmes** eyes misted (over) *ou* clouded with tears.
embuscade [ɑ̃byskad] **nf** ambush. **être *ou* se tenir en ~** to lie in ambush; **tendre une ~ à qn** to set (up) *ou* lay an ambush for sb; **tomber dans une ~** *(Mil)* to fall into an ambush; *(tendue par des brigands)* to fall into an ambush, be waylaid.
embusqué, e [ɑ̃byske] **(ptp de embusquer)** 1 **adj: être ~** *[soldats]* to lie *ou* wait in ambush. 2 **nm** *(arg Mil)* shirker.
embusquer (s') [ɑ̃byske] [1] **vpr** to take cover, lie *ou* wait in ambush.
éméché, e* [emeʃe] **adj** tipsy*, merry*.
émeraude [em(ə)ʀod] **nf, adj inv** emerald.
émergence [emɛʀʒɑ̃s] **nf** *(gén)* emergence. **(point d')~ d'une source** source of a spring.
émergent, e [emɛʀʒɑ̃, ɑ̃t] **adj** *rocher, (Phys)* emergent.
émerger [emɛʀʒe] [3] **vi** a *(apparaître) [rocher, cime]* to emerge, rise up; *[vérité, astre]* to emerge, come out; *[fait, artiste]* to emerge; *[personne] (de sa chambre)* to emerge. **le sommet émergea du brouillard** the summit rose out of *ou* emerged from the fog. b *(faire saillie) [rocher, fait, artiste]* to stand out. **des rochers qui émergent** rocks that stand out, salient rocks *(SPÉC)*. c *(d'une situation difficile)* to begin to see light at the end of the tunnel.
émeri [em(ə)ʀi] **nm** emery. **toile *ou* papier ~** emery paper; *voir* **bouché**.
émerillon [em(ə)ʀijɔ̃] **nm** *(Orn)* merlin; *(Tech)* swivel.
émérite [emeʀit] **adj** *(chevronné)* highly skilled. **professeur ~** professor emeritus, emeritus professor.
émersion [emɛʀsjɔ̃] **nf** emersion.
émerveillement [emɛʀvɛjmɑ̃] **nm** *(sentiment)* wonder; *(vision, sons etc)* wonderful thing, marvel.
émerveiller [emɛʀveje] [1] 1 **vt** to fill with wonder. 2 **s'émerveiller vpr** to be filled with wonder. **s'~ de** to marvel at, be filled with wonder at.
émétique [emetik] **adj, nm** emetic.
émetteur, -trice [emetœʀ, tʀis] 1 **adj** a *(Rad)* transmitting; *voir* **poste**[2], **station**. b *(Fin)* issuing *(épith)*. 2 **nm** transmitter. **~-récepteur** transmitter-receiver, transceiver. 3 **nm,f** *(Fin)* issuer.
émettre [emɛtʀ] [56] **vt** a *lumière [lampe]* to give (out), send out; *(Phys)* to emit; *son, radiation, liquide* to give out, send out, emit; *odeur* to give off. b *(Rad, TV)* to transmit. *(Rad)* **~ sur ondes courtes** to

broadcast *ou* transmit on shortwave. c (*Fin*) *monnaie, actions* to issue; *emprunt* to issue, float; *chèque* to draw; (*fig*) *idée, hypothèse* to voice, put forward, venture; *vœux* to express.

émeu [emø] nm emu.

émeute [emøt] nf riot. **~s** riots, rioting.

émeutier, -ière [emøtje, jɛʀ] nm,f rioter.

émiettement [emjɛtmɑ̃] nm (*voir* **émietter**) crumbling; breaking up, splitting up; dispersion; dissipation; frittering away. **un ~ de petites parcelles de terre** a scattering of little plots of land.

émietter [emjete] [1] 1 vt *pain, terre* to crumble; *territoire* to break up, split up; *pouvoir, responsabilités* to disperse; *énergie, effort,* (*littér*) *temps* to dissipate. 2 **s'émietter** vpr *[pain, terre]* to crumble; *[pouvoir]* to disperse; *[énergie, existence]* to dissipate; *[fortune]* to be frittered *ou* whittled away.

émigrant, e [emigʀɑ̃, ɑ̃t] nm,f emigrant.

émigration [emigʀasjɔ̃] nf emigration.

émigré, e [emigʀe] (ptp de **émigrer**) nm,f (*Hist*) émigré; (*Pol*) expatriate, émigré. (*Écon*) **(travailleur) ~** migrant worker.

émigrer [emigʀe] [1] vi to emigrate; (*Zool*) to migrate.

émincé [emɛ̃se] nm (*plat*) émincé; (*tranche*) sliver, thin slice. **un ~ de veau/de foie de veau** an émincé of veal/calves' liver.

émincer [emɛ̃se] [3] vt to slice thinly, cut into slivers *ou* thin slices.

éminemment [eminamɑ̃] adv eminently.

éminence [eminɑ̃s] nf a *[terrain]* knoll, hill; (*Méd*) protuberance. b *[qualité, rang]* distinction, eminence. c (*cardinal*) Eminence. **Son/Votre É~** his/your Eminence; (*fig*) **~ grise** éminence grise.

éminent, e [eminɑ̃, ɑ̃t] adj distinguished, eminent. (*frm*) **mon ~ collègue** my learned *ou* distinguished colleague.

éminentissime [eminɑ̃tisim] adj (*hum*) most distinguished *ou* eminent; (*Rel*) most eminent.

émir [emiʀ] nm emir.

émirat [emiʀa] nm emirate. **les É~s arabes unis** the United Arab Emirates.

émissaire [emisɛʀ] nm (*gén*) emissary; *voir* **bouc**.

émission [emisjɔ̃] nf a (*action: voir* **émettre**) giving out, sending out; emission; giving off; transmission; broadcast(ing); issue; flotation; drawing; voicing, putting forward, venturing; expression. (*Physiol*) **~ d'urine/de sperme** emission of urine/semen; (*Fin*) **monopole d'~** monopoly of issue; (*Fin*) **cours d'~** issue par; (*Fin*) **prix d'~** offering price; (*Phys*) **source d'~ (de lumière/chaleur)** (emitting) source (of light/heat); (*Phonétique*) **~ de voix** emission of sound (by the voice); *voir* **banque**.
b (*Rad, TV: spectacle*) programme (*Brit*), program (*US*), broadcast. **dans une ~ télévisée/radiophonique** in a television/radio programme *ou* broadcast; **~ en direct/différé** live/(pre-)recorded programme *ou* broadcast; **~ (de télévision) par câble** cablecast; **as-tu le programme des ~s de la semaine?** have you got (the list of) this week's programmes?; **"nos ~s sont terminées"** "that's the end of today's broadcasts *ou* programmes *ou* broadcasting".

emmagasiner [ɑ̃magazine] [1] vt (*gén: amasser*) to store up, accumulate; *chaleur* to store; *souvenirs, connaissances* to amass, accumulate; (*Comm*) to store, put into store, warehouse.

emmaillotement [ɑ̃majɔtmɑ̃] nm (*voir* **emmailloter**) binding up, bandaging; wrapping up.

emmailloter [ɑ̃majɔte] [1] vt *doigt, pied* to bind (up), bandage, wrap up; *enfant* to wrap up.

emmanchement [ɑ̃mɑ̃ʃmɑ̃] nm *[outil]* fitting of a handle (*de* to, on, onto).

emmanché, e‡ [ɑ̃mɑ̃ʃe] (ptp de **emmancher**) nm,f (*crétin*) twit‡, berk‡ (*Brit*).

emmancher [ɑ̃mɑ̃ʃe] [1] vt *pelle* to fix *ou* put a handle on. **~ une affaire*** to get a deal going, set up a deal; **l'affaire s'emmanche mal*** things are getting off to a bad start; **une affaire bien/mal emmanchée*** a deal which has got off to a good/bad start.

emmanchure [ɑ̃mɑ̃ʃyʀ] nf armhole.

Emmanuel [emanɥɛl] nm Emmanuel, Immanuel.

Emmanuelle [emanɥɛl] nf Emmanuelle.

emmêlement [ɑ̃mɛlmɑ̃] nm (*action*) tangling; (*état*) tangle, muddle. **un ~ de tuyaux** a tangle of pipes.

emmêler [ɑ̃mele] [1] 1 vt *cheveux* to tangle (up), knot; *fil* to tangle (up), entangle, muddle up; (*fig*) *affaire* to confuse, muddle. (*fig*) **tu emmêles tout** you're confusing everything, you're getting everything mixed up *ou* muddled (up) *ou* confused. 2 **s'emmêler** vpr to tangle, get in a tangle. **la corde s'est emmêlée** the rope has got tangled; **s'~ les pieds dans le tapis** to get one's feet caught in the carpet, catch one's feet in the carpet; **s'~ dans ses explications** to get in a muddle with one's explanations; **s'~ les crayons*** *ou* **les pinceaux*** *ou* **les pédales*** to get in a right muddle*.

emménagement [ɑ̃menaʒmɑ̃] nm moving in (*NonC*). **au moment de leur ~ dans la nouvelle maison** at the time of their move into the new house.

emménager [ɑ̃menaʒe] [3] vi to move in. **~ dans** to move into.

emmener [ɑ̃m(ə)ne] [5] vt a *personne* (*comme otage*) to take away; (*comme invité, compagnon*) to take (along). **~ qn au cinéma** to take sb to the cinema; **~ qn en prison** to take sb (away *ou* off) to prison; **~ qn faire une balade en voiture** to take sb for a run in the *ou* one's car; **~ promener qn** *ou* **~ qn faire une promenade** to take sb (off) for a walk; **~ déjeuner qn** to take sb out to *ou* for lunch; **voulez-vous que je vous emmène? (en voiture)** shall I give you a lift (*Brit*) *ou* ride (*US*)?, would you like a lift (*Brit*) *ou* ride (*US*)?
b (*: *emporter*) *chose* to take. **tu vas ~ cette grosse valise?** are you going to take that great suitcase (with you)?
c (*Mil, Sport: guider*) *équipe, troupe* to lead.

emment(h)al [emɛ̃tal] nm Emmenthal (cheese).

emmerdant, e‡ [ɑ̃mɛʀdɑ̃, ɑ̃t] adj (*irritant*) bloody (*Brit*) *ou* damned annoying‡; (*lassant*) bloody (*Brit*) *ou* damned boring‡. **qu'est-ce qu'il est ~ avec ses histoires** what a bloody (*Brit*) *ou* damned nuisance‡ *ou* pain (in the neck)‡ he is with his stories; **c'est vraiment ~ qu'il ne puisse pas venir** it's bloody (*Brit*) *ou* damned annoying‡ *ou* a hell of a nuisance‡ that he can't come.

emmerde‡ [ɑ̃mɛʀd] nf = **emmerdement**.

emmerdement‡ [ɑ̃mɛʀdəmɑ̃] nm: **quel ~!** what a bloody‡ (*Brit*) *ou* damned nuisance!‡; **j'ai eu tellement d'~s avec cette voiture** that car gave me so much bloody (*Brit*) *ou* damned trouble‡, I had so many bloody (*Brit*) *ou* damned problems with that car‡.

emmerder‡ [ɑ̃mɛʀde] [1] 1 vt: **~ qn** (*irriter*) to get on sb's wick‡ (*Brit*), give sb a pain in the neck*, bug sb*; (*préoccuper, contrarier*) to bug sb*, bother sb; (*lasser*) to bore the pants off sb‡, bore sb stiff* *ou* to death*; (*mettre dans l'embarras*) to get sb into trouble, land sb in the soup; **on n'a pas fini d'être emmerdé avec ça** we've not heard the last of that; **je suis drôlement emmerdé** I'm in deep trouble*, I'm really in the soup*; **arrête de nous ~ avec tes histoires!** stop being such a bloody (*Brit*) *ou* damned nuisance‡ *ou* pain (in the neck)‡ with your stories; **il m'emmerde à la fin, avec ses questions** he really bugs me* *ou* gets up my nose‡ (*Brit*) with his questions; **ça m'emmerde qu'il ne puisse pas venir** it's a damned nuisance‡ *ou* a hell of a nuisance‡ that he can't come; **je les emmerde!** to hell with them!‡, bugger them!*‡ (*Brit*).
2 **s'emmerder** vpr (*s'ennuyer*) to be bored stiff* *ou* to death*; (*s'embarrasser*) to put o.s. out. **ne t'emmerde pas avec ça** don't bother *ou* worry about that; **je me suis emmerdé à réparer ce poste, et maintenant il ne le veut plus!** I really put myself out repairing this damned radio and now he doesn't even want it!‡; **tu ne t'emmerdes pas!** you've got a damn‡ nerve *ou* cheek!; **elle a trois voitures — dis donc, elle ne s'emmerde pas!** she has three cars — (it's) alright for some!*.

emmerdeur, -euse‡ [ɑ̃mɛʀdœʀ, øz] nm,f damned nuisance‡, pain in the neck‡.

emmitoufler [ɑ̃mitufle] [1] vt to wrap up (warmly), muffle up. **s'~ (dans un manteau)** to wrap o.s. up (warmly) *ou* get muffled up (in a coat).

emmouscailler‡ [ɑ̃muskaje] [1] vt: **~ qn** (*irriter*) to bug sb*; (*préoccuper*) to bother sb; (*mettre qn dans l'embarras*) to land sb in the soup*; **être bien emmouscaillé** to be in deep trouble* *ou* in a real mess; **s'~ à faire qch** to go to the bother of doing sth.

emmurer [ɑ̃myʀe] [1] vt to wall up, immure.

émoi [emwa] nm (*littér*) (*trouble*) agitation, emotion; (*de joie*) excitement; (*tumulte*) commotion. **doux ~** pleasant agitation; **dit-elle non sans ~** she said with some confusion *ou* a little flustered; **en ~** *cœur* in a flutter (*attrib*); *sens* agitated, excited; **la rue était en ~** the street was in turmoil *ou* in a commotion.

émollient, e [emɔljɑ̃, jɑ̃t] adj, nm emollient.

émoluments [emɔlymɑ̃] nmpl (*Admin*) remuneration, emolument (*frm*).

émondage [emɔ̃daʒ] nm pruning, trimming.

émonder [emɔ̃de] [1] vt *arbre* to prune, trim; *amandes* to blanch.

émondeur, -euse [emɔ̃dœʀ, øz] nm,f pruner (*person*).

émondoir [emɔ̃dwaʀ] nm pruning hook.

émotif, -ive [emɔtif, iv] 1 adj emotional; (*Ling*) emotive. 2 nm,f emotional person.

émotion [emosjɔ̃] nf (*vif sentiment*) emotion; (*peur*) fright; (*sensibilité*) emotion, feeling; (†: *tumulte*) commotion. **ils ont évité l'accident mais l'~ a été grande** they avoided the accident but it really gave them a bad fright; **donner des ~s à qn*** to give sb a (nasty) turn* *ou* fright.

émotionnel, -elle [emosjɔnɛl] adj *choc, réaction* emotional.

émotionner* [emosjɔne] [1] 1 vt to upset. **j'en suis encore tout émotionné** it gave me quite a turn*, I'm still all upset about it. 2 **s'émotionner** vpr to get worked up*, get upset (*de* about).

émotivité [emɔtivite] nf emotionalism.

émoulu, e [emuly] adj *voir* **frais**.

émoussé, e [emuse] (ptp de **émousser**) adj *couteau, tranchant* blunt; *goût, sensibilité* blunted, dulled.

émousser [emuse] [1] vt *lame, couteau, appétit* to blunt, take the edge off; *sentiment, souvenir, désir* to dull. **son talent s'est émoussé** his talent has lost its fine edge.

émoustillant, e* [emustijɑ̃, ɑ̃t] adj *présence* tantalizing, titillating; *propos* titillating.

émoustiller* [emustije] [1] vt to titillate, tantalize.

émouvant, e [emuvɑ̃, ɑ̃t] **adj** (*nuance de compassion*) moving, touching; (*nuance d'admiration*) stirring.

émouvoir [emuvwaʀ] 27 **1 vt a** *personne* (*gén*) to move, disturb, stir; (*indigner*) to rouse (the indignation of); (*effrayer*) to disturb, worry, upset. **leur attitude ne l'émut/leurs menaces ne l'émurent pas le moins du monde** their attitude/threats didn't disturb *ou* worry *ou* upset him in the slightest; **plus ému qu'il ne voulait l'admettre par ce baiser/ces caresses** more (a)roused than he wished to admit by this kiss/these caresses; **le spectacle/leur misère l'émouvait profondément** the sight/their wretchedness moved him deeply *ou* upset him greatly; **~ qn jusqu'aux larmes** to move sb to tears; **cet auteur s'attache à ~ le lecteur** this author sets out to move *ou* stir the reader; **se laisser ~ par des prières** to be moved by entreaties, let o.s. be swayed by entreaties; **encore tout ému d'avoir frôlé l'accident/de cette rencontre** still very shaken *ou* greatly upset at having been so close to an accident/over that encounter.

b (*littér*) *pitié, colère* to (a)rouse. **~ la pitié de qn** to move sb to pity, (a)rouse sb's pity.

2 s'émouvoir vpr (*voir* **émouvoir**) to be moved; to be disturbed; to be stirred; to be *ou* get worried, be *ou* get upset. **il ne s'émeut de rien** nothing upsets *ou* disturbs him; **dit-il sans s'~** he said calmly *ou* impassively *ou* quite unruffled; **s'~ à la vue de** to be moved at the sight of; **le pays entier s'est ému de l'affaire** the whole country was roused by the affair, the affair (a)roused the indignation of the whole country; **le gouvernement s'en est ému** the government was roused to action.

empailler [ɑ̃pɑje] 1 **vt** *animal* to stuff; *chaise* to bottom (with straw).

empailleur, -euse [ɑ̃pɑjœʀ, øz] **nm,f** *[chaise]* chair-bottomer; *[animal]* taxidermist.

empalement [ɑ̃palmɑ̃] **nm** impalement.

empaler [ɑ̃pale] 1 **vt** to impale. **s'~** to impale o.s.

empan [ɑ̃pɑ̃] **nm** (*Hist: mesure*) span.

empanaché, e [ɑ̃panaʃe] **adj** plumed.

empanner [ɑ̃pane] 1 **vi** to gibe (*Brit*), jibe (*US*).

empaquetage [ɑ̃paktaʒ] **nm** (*voir* **empaqueter**) packing, packaging; parcelling up (*Brit*), wrapping up.

empaqueter [ɑ̃pakte] 4 **vt** to parcel up (*Brit*), wrap up; (*Comm: conditionner*) to pack, package.

emparer (s') [ɑ̃paʀe] 1 **vpr a** *[personne]* **s'~ de** *objet* to seize *ou* grab (hold of), snatch up; *butin* to seize, grab; *personne* (*comme otage etc*) to seize; (*fig*) *conversation, sujet* to take over; (*fig*) *prétexte* to seize (up)on; (*Mil*) *ville, territoire, ennemi* to seize; **s'~ des moyens de production/de l'information** to take over *ou* seize the means of production/the information networks; **ils se sont emparés de la ville par surprise** they seized *ou* took the town by surprise; **ils se sont emparés du caissier et l'ont assommé** they grabbed (hold of) *ou* laid hold of the cashier and knocked him out; (*Rugby*) **s'~ du ballon** to get possession of the ball; (*fig*) **son confesseur s'est emparé de son esprit** her confessor has gained *ou* got a hold over her; (*fig*) **les journaux se sont emparés de l'affaire** the papers picked up the story.

b s'~ de *[jalousie, colère, remords]* to take possession of, take *ou* lay *ou* seize hold of; **cette obsession s'empara de son esprit** this obsession took possession of his mind, his mind was taken over by this obsession; **une grande peur/le remords s'empara d'elle** she was seized with a great fear/remorse.

empâtement [ɑ̃pɑtmɑ̃] **nm** (*voir* **s'empâter**) thickening-out, fattening-out; thickening.

empâter [ɑ̃pɑte] 1 **1 vt** *langue, bouche* to coat, fur (up) (*Brit*); *traits* to thicken, coarsen. **la maladie l'a empâté** his illness has made him thicken out *ou* put on weight. **2 s'empâter vpr** *[personne, silhouette, visage]* to thicken out, fatten out; *[traits]* to thicken, grow fleshy; *[voix]* to become thick.

empathie [ɑ̃pati] **nf** empathy.

empattement [ɑ̃patmɑ̃] **nm** (*Constr*) footing; (*Aut*) wheelbase; (*Typ*) serif.

empêché, e [ɑ̃peʃe] (**ptp de empêcher**) **adj a** (*retenu*) detained, held up. **le professeur, ~, ne peut pas faire son cours** the teacher has been detained *ou* held up and is unable to give the class; **~ par ses obligations, il n'a pas pu venir** his commitments prevented him from coming, he was prevented from coming by his commitments. **b** (*embarrassé*) **avoir l'air ~** to look *ou* seem embarrassed *ou* ill-at-ease. **c** (†) **tu es bien ~ de me le dire** you seem at a (complete) loss to know what to tell me; **je serais bien ~ de vous le dire** I'd be hard put (to it) to tell you, I'd be at a loss to know what to tell you.

empêchement [ɑ̃pɛʃmɑ̃] **nm** (*obstacle*) (unexpected) obstacle *ou* difficulty, hitch, holdup; (*Jur*) impediment. **il n'est pas venu, il a eu un ~** something unforeseen cropped up which prevented him from coming; **en cas d'~** if there's a hitch, should you be prevented from coming.

empêcher [ɑ̃peʃe] 1 **1 vt a** *chose, action* to prevent, stop. **~ que qch (ne) se produise, ~ qch de se produire** to prevent sth from happening, stop sth happening; **~ que qn (ne) fasse** to prevent sb from doing, stop sb (from) doing.

b ~ qn de faire to prevent sb from doing, stop sb (from) doing; **rien ne nous empêche de partir** there's nothing stopping us (from) going *ou* preventing us from going *ou* preventing our going; **~ qn de sortir/d'entrer** to prevent sb from going out/coming in, keep sb in/out; **s'il veut le faire, on ne peut pas l'en ~** *ou* **l'~** if he wants to do it, we can't prevent him (from doing it) *ou* stop him (doing it); **ça ne m'empêche pas de dormir** (*lit*) it doesn't prevent me from sleeping *ou* stop me sleeping *ou* keep me awake; (*fig*) I don't lose any sleep over it.

c (*loc*) **qu'est-ce qui empêche (qu'on le fasse)?** what's there to stop us (doing it)? *ou* to prevent us (from doing it)?, what's stopping us (doing it)?*; **qu'est-ce que ça empêche?*** what odds* *ou* difference does that make?; **ça n'empêche rien*** it makes no odds* *ou* no difference; **ça n'empêche qu'il vienne*** that won't stop him coming, he's still coming anyway*; **il n'empêche qu'il a tort*** nevertheless *ou* be that as it may, he is wrong; **n'empêche qu'il a tort** all the same *ou* it makes no odds*, he's wrong; **j'ai peut-être tort, n'empêche, il a un certain culot de dire ça!*** maybe I'm wrong, but all the same *ou* even so he has got some cheek *ou* nerve saying that!*; *voir* **empêcheur**.

2 s'empêcher vpr a (*littér*) **s'~ de faire** to stop o.s. (from) doing, refrain from doing; **par politesse, il s'empêcha de bâiller** out of politeness he stifled a yawn *ou* he stopped himself yawning.

b il n'a pas pu s'~ de rire he couldn't help laughing, he couldn't stop himself (from) laughing; **je ne peux m'~ de penser que** I cannot help thinking that; **je n'ai pu m'en ~** I could not help it, I couldn't stop myself.

empêcheur, -euse [ɑ̃pɛʃœʀ, øz] **nm,f: ~ de danser** *ou* **de tourner en rond** spoilsport; (*hum*) **un ~ de travailler/de s'amuser en rond** a spoilsport as far as work/enjoyment is concerned.

empeigne [ɑ̃pɛɲ] **nf** *[soulier]* upper.

empennage [ɑ̃penaʒ] **nm** (*Aviat*) stabilizer, tailplane (*Brit*); *[flèche]* feathering.

empenner [ɑ̃pene] 1 **vt** *flèche* to feather.

empereur [ɑ̃pʀœʀ] **nm** emperor.

empesé, e [ɑ̃pəze] (**ptp de empeser**) **adj** *col* starched; (*fig*) stiff, starchy.

empeser [ɑ̃pəze] 5 **vt** to starch.

empester [ɑ̃pɛste] 1 **vt** (*sentir*) *odeur, fumée* to stink of, reek of; (*empuantir*) *pièce* to stink out (*de* with), make stink (*de* of); (*fig littér: empoisonner*) to poison, taint (*de* with). **ça empeste ici** it stinks in here, it smells foul in here, there's a stink *ou* foul smell in here.

empêtrer (s') [ɑ̃petʀe] 1 **vpr a** (*lit*) **s'~ dans** to get tangled up in, get entangled in, get caught up in. **b** (*fig*) **s'~ dans** *mensonges* to get o.s. tangled up in; *affaire* to get (o.s.) involved in, get (o.s.) mixed up in; **s'~ dans des explications** to tie o.s. up in knots trying to explain*, get tangled up in one's explanations; **s'~ de qn** to get (o.s.) landed *ou* lumbered* with sb.

emphase [ɑ̃fɑz] **nf a** (*pomposité*) bombast, pomposity. **avec ~** bombastically, pompously; **sans ~** in a straightforward manner, simply. **b** (†: *force d'expression*) vigour.

emphatique [ɑ̃fatik] **adj a** (*grandiloquent*) bombastic, pompous. **b** (*Ling*) emphatic.

emphatiquement [ɑ̃fatikmɑ̃] **adv** bombastically, pompously.

emphysémateux, -euse [ɑ̃fizematø, øz] **1 adj** emphysematous. **2 nm,f** emphysema sufferer.

emphysème [ɑ̃fizɛm] **nm** emphysema.

empiècement [ɑ̃pjɛsmɑ̃] **nm** *[corsage]* yoke.

empierrement [ɑ̃pjɛʀmɑ̃] **nm a** (*action: voir* **empierrer**) metalling, gravelling; ballasting; lining with stones. **b** (*couche de pierres*) road metal (*Brit*), roadbed; *[chemin de fer]* ballast.

empierrer [ɑ̃pjeʀe] 1 **vt** *route* to metal (*Brit*), gravel (*US*); *voie de chemin de fer* to ballast; *bassin, cour, fossé* to line with stones.

empiètement [ɑ̃pjɛtmɑ̃] **nm** (*voir* **empiéter**) **~ (sur)** encroachment (upon); overlapping (onto); trespassing (on).

empiéter [ɑ̃pjete] 6 **vi: ~ sur** *[territoire, état]* to encroach (up)on; *[mer]* to cut into, encroach (up)on; *[terrain]* to overlap into *ou* onto, encroach (up)on; *[route]* to run into *ou* onto, encroach (up)on; *[personne] droit, liberté* to encroach (up)on; *attributions* to trespass on; *[activité] attributions, activité* to encroach (up)on; *temps* to encroach (up)on, cut into.

empiffrer (s')‡ [ɑ̃pifʀe] 1 **vpr** to stuff one's face‡, stuff o.s.* (*de* with).

empilage [ɑ̃pilaʒ] **nm**, **empilement** [ɑ̃pilmɑ̃] **nm** (*action*) piling-up, stacking-up; (*pile*) pile, stack.

empiler [ɑ̃pile] 1 **1 vt a** to pile (up), stack (up). **b** (‡: *voler*) to do‡ (*Brit*), rook‡. **se faire ~** to be had* *ou* done‡ (*Brit*) (*de* out of). **2 s'empiler vpr a** (*s'amonceler*) to be piled up (*sur* on). **b** (*s'entasser*) **s'~ dans** *local, véhicule* to squeeze *ou* pack *ou* pile into.

empileur, -euse [ɑ̃pilœʀ, øz] **nm,f** (*ouvrier*) stacker; (‡: *escroc*) swindler.

empire [ɑ̃piʀ] **1 nm a** (*Pol, fig*) empire. **premier/second E~** First/Second Empire; **pas pour un ~!** not for all the tea in China!, not for (all) the world!; **commode/pendule E~** Empire commode/clock.

b (*emprise*) influence, authority. **avoir de l'~ sur** to have influence *ou* a hold on *ou* over, hold sway over; **prendre de l'~ sur** to gain influence *ou* a hold over; **exercer son ~ sur** to exert one's authority over, use one's influence on *ou* over; **sous l'~ de** *peur, colère* in the grip of; *jalousie* possessed by; **sous l'~ de la boisson** under the influence of

drink, the worse for drink; ~ **sur soi-même** self-control, self-command.
2 comp ►**l'Empire d'Occident** the Western Empire ►**l'Empire d'Orient** the Byzantine Empire ►**l'Empire du Soleil-Levant** the Land of the Rising Sun.

empirer [ɑ̃piʀe] [1] 1 vi to get worse, deteriorate. 2 vt to make worse, worsen.

empirique [ɑ̃piʀik] 1 adj (*Philos, Phys*) empirical; (*Méd* ††) empiric. 2 nm (*Méd* ††) empiric.

empiriquement [ɑ̃piʀikmɑ̃] adv empirically.

empirisme [ɑ̃piʀism] nm empiricism.

empiriste [ɑ̃piʀist] adj, nmf (*Philos, Phys*) empiricist; (*Méd* ††) empiric.

emplacement [ɑ̃plasmɑ̃] nm (*gén : endroit*) place; (*site*) site; (*pour construire*) site, location. **à** ou **sur l'~ d'une ancienne cité romaine** on the site of an ancient Roman city; **quelques pieux qui dépassaient de la neige indiquaient l'~ du chemin** a few posts sticking up above the snow showed the location of the path ou showed where the path was; ~ **publicitaire** (*sur un mur*) advertising site; (*dans un journal*) advertising space (*NonC*).

emplafonner‡ [ɑ̃plafɔne] [1] vt to slam* ou smash* into. **il s'est fait ~ par un camion** a lorry slammed* ou smashed* into his car ou him.

emplâtre [ɑ̃plɑtʀ] nm (*Méd*) plaster; (*Aut*) patch; (**: personne*) (great) lump*, clot*. **ce plat vous fait un ~ sur l'estomac*** this dish lies heavy on ou lies like a (solid) lump in your stomach; voir **jambe**.

emplette† [ɑ̃plɛt] nf purchase. **faire l'~ de** to purchase; **faire des** ou **quelques ~s** to do some shopping, make some purchases.

emplir [ɑ̃pliʀ] [2] 1 vt (†, *littér*) a *verre, récipient* to fill (up) (*de* with). b *[foule, meubles]* to fill. 2 **s'emplir** vpr: **s'~ de** to fill with; **la pièce s'emplissait de lumière/de gens** the room was filling with light/people.

emploi [ɑ̃plwa] nm a (*usage*) use. **je n'en ai pas l'~** I have no use for it; **l'~ qu'il fait de son argent/temps** the use he makes of his money/time, the use to which he puts his money/time; **sans ~** unused; **son ~ du temps** his timetable, his schedule; **un ~ du temps chargé** a heavy ou busy timetable, a busy schedule; voir **double, mode²**.
b (*mode d'utilisation*) *[appareil, produit]* use; *[mot, expression]* use, usage. **un ~ nouveau de cet appareil** a new use for this piece of equipment; **appareil à ~s multiples** multi-purpose implement; **divers ~s d'un mot** different uses of a word; **c'est un ~ très rare de cette expression** it's a very rare use ou usage of this expression.
c (*poste, travail*) job, employment (*NonC*). (*Écon*) **l'~** employment; **créer de nouveaux ~s** to create new jobs; **être sans ~** to be unemployed; (*Écon*) **la situation de l'~** the employment situation; (*Écon*) **plein-~** full employment; **sous-~** underemployment; **avoir le physique** ou **la tête de l'~*** to look the part; voir **demande, offre**.
d (*rare Théât: rôle*) role, part.

employé, e [ɑ̃plwaje] (ptp de **employer**) nm,f employee. ~ **de banque** bank employee ou clerk; ~ **de commerce** business employee; ~ **de bureau** office worker ou clerk; ~ **des postes/des chemins de fer/du gaz** postal/railway (*Brit*) ou railroad (*US*)/gas worker; **on a sonné: c'est l'~ du gaz** there's someone at the door – it's the gas man; ~ **de maison** domestic employee; **les ~s de cette firme** the staff ou employees of this firm.

employer [ɑ̃plwaje] [8] 1 vt a (*utiliser*) *appareil, produit, mot, force, moyen* to use, employ; *temps* to spend, use, employ. ~ **toute son énergie à faire qch** to apply ou devote all one's energies to doing sth; ~ **son temps à faire qch/à qch** to spend one's time doing sth/on sth; ~ **son argent à faire qch/à qch** to spend ou use one's money doing sth/on sth; **bien ~** *temps, argent* to put to good use, make good use of, use properly; *mot, expression* to use properly ou correctly; **mal ~** *temps, argent* to misuse; *mot, expression* to misuse, use wrongly ou incorrectly; **ce procédé emploie énormément de matières premières** this process uses (up) huge amounts of raw materials.
b (*faire travailler*) *main-d'œuvre, ouvrier* to employ. **ils l'emploient comme vendeur/à trier le courrier** they employ him as a salesman/to sort the mail; **cet ouvrier est mal employé à ce poste** this workman has been given the wrong sort of job ou is not suited to the post; **il est employé par cette société** he is employed by that firm, he works for that firm, he is on the staff of that firm.
2 **s'employer** vpr: **s'~ à faire qch/à qch** to apply ou devote o.s. to doing sth/to sth; **s'~ pour†** ou **en faveur de†** to go to great lengths ou exert o.s. on behalf of.

employeur, -euse [ɑ̃plwajœʀ, øz] nm,f employer.

emplumé, e [ɑ̃plyme] adj feathered, plumed.

empocher* [ɑ̃pɔʃe] [1] vt to pocket.

empoignade [ɑ̃pwaɲad] nf row*, set-to*.

empoigne [ɑ̃pwaɲ] nf voir **foire**.

empoigner [ɑ̃pwaɲe] [1] 1 vt a to grasp, grab (hold of). b (*émouvoir*) to grip. 2 **s'empoigner*** vpr (*se colleter*) to have a set-to*, have a go at one another*.

empois [ɑ̃pwa] nm starch (*for linen etc*).

empoisonnant, e* [ɑ̃pwazɔnɑ̃, ɑ̃t] adj (*irritant*) irritating; (*contrariant*) annoying, aggravating*. **oh, il est ~ avec ses questions** he's so irritating ou he's a darned nuisance* ou such a pain* with his questions.

empoisonnement [ɑ̃pwazɔnmɑ̃] nm a (*lit*) poisoning. b (**: ennui*) darned nuisance* (*NonC*), bother (*NonC*). **tous ces ~s** all this bother.

empoisonner [ɑ̃pwazɔne] [1] 1 vt a ~ **qn** *[assassin]* to poison sb; *[aliments avariés]* to give sb food poisoning; **flèches empoisonnées** poisoned arrows; (*fig*) **des propos empoisonnés** poisonous words.
b (*fig*) *relations* to poison; *air* to stink out.
c (*) ~ **qn** *[gêneur, casse-pieds]* to get on sb's nerves*; *[contretemps]* to annoy sb, bug sb*; *[corvée, travail]* to drive sb mad*, drive sb up the wall*; **ça m'empoisonne d'avoir à le dire mais ...** I hate to have to say this but ..., I don't like saying this but ...; **il m'empoisonne avec ses jérémiades** he gets on my nerves* ou drives me up the wall* with his complaints; **il est bien empoisonné maintenant** he's in a real mess now*, he's really in the soup now*.
2 **s'empoisonner** vpr a (*lit*) to poison o.s.; (*par intoxication alimentaire*) to get food poisoning.
b (**: s'ennuyer*) to be bored stiff* ou to death. **qu'est-ce qu'on s'empoisonne** what a drag this is*, this is driving us mad* ou up the wall*; (*s'embarrasser*) **s'~ (l'existence) à faire qch** to go to the trouble of doing sth.

empoisonneur, -euse [ɑ̃pwazɔnœʀ, øz] nm,f a (*lit*) poisoner. b (*) pain in the neck* (*NonC*), nuisance, bore.

empoissonner [ɑ̃pwasɔne] [1] vt to stock with fish.

emporté, e [ɑ̃pɔʀte] (ptp de **emporter**) adj *caractère, personne* quick-tempered, hot-tempered; *ton, air* angry.

emportement [ɑ̃pɔʀtəmɑ̃] nm fit of anger, rage, anger (*NonC*). **avec ~** angrily; (*littér*) **aimer qn avec ~** to love sb passionately, be wildly in love with sb.

emporte-pièce [ɑ̃pɔʀtəpjɛs] nm inv a (*Tech*) punch. b **à l'~** *caractère* incisive; *formule, phrase* incisive, sharp.

emporter [ɑ̃pɔʀte] [1] 1 vt a (*prendre comme bagage*) *vivres, vêtements etc* to take. **emportez des vêtements chauds** take warm clothes (with you); **j'emporte de quoi écrire** I'm taking something to write with; **si vous gagnez, vous pouvez l'~ (avec vous)** if you win, you can take it away (with you); **plats chauds/boissons à ~** take-away hot meals/drinks (*Brit*), hot meals/drinks to go (*US*); (*fig*) ~ **un bon souvenir de qch** to take ou bring away a pleasant memory of sth; (*fig*) ~ **un secret dans la tombe** to take a secret ou carry a secret to the grave; (*fig*) **il ne l'emportera pas en** ou **au paradis!** he'll soon be smiling on the other side of his face!
b (*enlever*) *objet inutile* to take away, remove; *prisonniers* to take away; *blessés* to carry ou take away; (**: dérober*) to take. **emportez ces papiers/vêtements, nous n'en avons plus besoin** take those papers/clothes away ou remove those papers/clothes because we don't need them any more; **ils ont emporté l'argenterie!** they've made off with* ou taken the silver!; voir **diable**.
c (*entraîner*) *[courant, vent]* to sweep along, carry along; *[navire, train]* to carry along; (*fig*) *[imagination, colère]* to carry away; *[enthousiasme]* to carry away ou along, sweep along. **le courant emportait leur embarcation** the current swept ou carried their boat along; **emporté par son élan** carried ou borne along by his own momentum ou impetus; **emporté par son imagination/enthousiasme** carried along ou away by his imagination/enthusiasm; **se laisser ~ par la colère** to (let o.s.) give way to one's anger, let o.s. be carried away by one's anger; **le train qui m'emportait vers de nouveaux horizons** the train which carried ou swept me along ou bore me away towards new horizons.
d (*arracher*) *jambe, bras* to take off; *cheminée, toit* to blow away ou off; *pont, berge* to wash away, carry away; (*euph: tuer*) *[maladie]* to carry off. **l'obus lui a emporté le bras gauche** the shell blew off ou took off his left arm; **pont emporté par le torrent** bridge swept ou carried away by the flood; **la vague a emporté 3 passagers** the wave washed ou swept 3 passengers overboard; (*fig*) **plat qui emporte la bouche** ou **la gueule‡** dish that takes the roof off your mouth*; (*fig*) **cette maladie l'a emporté à l'âge de 30 ans** this illness carried him off at the age of 30.
e (*gagner*) *prix* to carry off; (*Mil*) *position* to take, win. ~ **la décision** to carry ou win the day.
f **l'~ (sur)** *[personne]* to gain ou get the upper hand (of); *[solution, méthode]* to prevail (over); **il a fini par l'~** he finally gained ou got the upper hand, he finally came out on top; **il va l'~ sur son adversaire** he's going to gain ou get the better of ou the upper hand of his opponent; **la modération/cette solution finit par l'~** moderation/this solution prevailed in the end, moderation/this solution finally won the day; **cette méthode l'emporte sur l'autre** this method has the edge on the other one ou is more satisfactory than the other one; **cette voiture l'emporte sur ses concurrents sur tous les plans** this car outperforms its competitors on every score; **il l'emporte sur ses concurrents en adresse** he outmatches his opponents in skill, his opponents can't match ou rival him for skill; **il l'emporte de justesse (sur l'autre) en force** he has the edge (on the other one) as far as strength goes.
2 **s'emporter** vpr a (*de colère*) to lose one's temper (*contre* with), flare up (*contre* at), blow up* (*contre* at).
b (*s'emballer*) *[cheval]* to bolt. **faire (s')~ son cheval** to make one's horse bolt.

empoté, e* [ɑ̃pɔte] 1 adj awkward, clumsy. 2 nm,f (*péj*) awkward lump*.

empourprer [ɑ̃puʀpʀe] 1 **1** vt *visage* to flush, (turn) crimson; *ciel* to (turn) crimson. **2 s'empourprer** vpr *[visage]* to flush, turn crimson; *[ciel]* to turn crimson.

empoussiérer [ɑ̃pusjeʀe] 6 vt to cover with dust, make dusty.

empreindre [ɑ̃pʀɛ̃dʀ] 52 (*littér*) **1** vt (*imprimer*) to imprint; (*fig*) (*marquer*) to stamp; (*nuancer*) to tinge (*de* with). **2 s'empreindre** vpr: **s'~ de** to be imprinted with; to be stamped with; to be tinged with.

empreint, e[1] [ɑ̃pʀɛ̃, ɛ̃t] (ptp de **empreindre**) adj: **~ de** *regret, jalousie* tinged with; *bonté, autorité* marked *ou* stamped with; *menaces* fraught *ou* heavy with.

empreinte[2] [ɑ̃pʀɛ̃t] nf **a** (*lit*) (*gén*) imprint, impression; *[animal]* track. **~ (de pas)** footprint; **~s (digitales)** (finger)prints; **~ génétique** genetic fingerprint; **~ vocale** voiceprint; **prendre l'~ d'une dent** to take the impression of a tooth. **b** (*fig*) stamp, mark. **laisser une ~ indélébile sur (la vie de) qn** to make a lasting impression on sb; **son œuvre laissera son ~ dans ce siècle** his work will leave its mark on this century.

empressé, e [ɑ̃pʀese] (ptp de **s'empresser**) adj **a** (*prévenant*) *infirmière* attentive; *serveur* attentive, willing; *aide* willing; (*souvent péj*) *admirateur* assiduous, overzealous; *prétendant* assiduous, overattentive; *subordonné* overanxious to please (*attrib*), overzealous. (*péj*) **faire l'~ (auprès d'une femme)** to be overattentive (towards a woman), fuss around (a woman) (trying to please). **b** (*littér: marquant de la hâte*) eager. **~ à faire** eager *ou* anxious to do.

empressement [ɑ̃pʀɛsmɑ̃] nm **a** (*prévenance: voir* **empressé**) attentiveness; willingness; overzealousness, assiduity, assiduousness; overattentiveness. **son ~ auprès des femmes** his fussing around women, his overattentiveness towards women; **elle me servait avec ~** she waited upon me attentively. **b** (*hâte*) eagerness, anxiousness. **son ~ à partir me paraît suspect** his eagerness *ou* anxiousness to leave seems suspicious to me; **il montrait peu d'~ à ...** he showed little desire to ..., he was obviously not anxious to ...; **il s'exécuta avec ~** he complied eagerly *ou* with alacrity.

empresser (s') [ɑ̃pʀese] 1 vpr **a** (*s'affairer*) to bustle about; (*péj*) to fuss about *ou* around (*péj*), bustle about *ou* around. **s'~ auprès** *ou* **autour de** *blessé* to surround with attentions; *nouveau venu, invité* to be attentive toward(s), surround with attentions; *femme courtisée* to dance attendance upon, fuss round; **ils s'empressèrent autour de la victime** they rushed to help *ou* assist the victim; **ils s'empressaient auprès de l'actrice** they surrounded the actress with attentions. **b** (*se hâter*) **s'~ de faire** to hasten to do.

emprise [ɑ̃pʀiz] nf hold, ascendancy (*sur* over). **avoir beaucoup d'~ sur qn** to have a great hold *ou* have great ascendancy over sb; **sous l'~ de** la colère in the grip of anger, gripped by anger.

emprisonnement [ɑ̃pʀizɔnmɑ̃] nm imprisonment. **condamné à l'~ à perpétuité** sentenced to life imprisonment; **condamné à 10 ans d'~** sentenced to 10 years in prison, given a 10-year prison sentence.

emprisonner [ɑ̃pʀizɔne] 1 vt **a** (*en prison*) to imprison, put in prison *ou* jail, jail; (*fig: dans une chambre, un couvent*) to shut up, imprison. **b** (*fig*) *[vêtement]* to confine; *[doctrine, milieu]* to trap. **ce corset lui emprisonne la taille** this corset grips her (too) tightly around the waist *ou* really confines her waist; **~ qn dans un système/un raisonnement** to trap sb within a system/by a piece of reasoning; **emprisonné dans ses habitudes/la routine** imprisoned within *ou* a prisoner of his habits/routine.

emprunt [ɑ̃pʀœ̃] nm **a** (*action d'emprunter*) *[argent, objet]* borrowing. **l'~ de sa voiture était la seule solution** borrowing his car was the only solution, the only solution was to borrow his car; **ce n'était pas un vol, mais seulement un ~** it (*ou* I *ou* he *etc*) wasn't really stealing, only borrowing, I (*ou* he *etc*) was really just borrowing it, not stealing; (*Fin*) **recourir à l'~** to resort to borrowing *ou* to a loan.

b (*demande, somme*) loan. **ses ~s successifs l'ont mis en difficulté** successive borrowing has *ou* his successive loans have put him in difficulty; (*Fin*) **~ d'État/public** Government/public loan (*with government etc as borrower*); (*Fin*) **~ à 5 %** loan at 5 % (interest); (*Fin*) **faire un ~ d'un million à une banque** to raise a loan of a million from a bank; **faire un ~ pour payer sa voiture** to borrow money *ou* take out a loan to pay for one's car.

c (*littéraire etc*) borrowing; (*terme*) loan word, borrowed word, borrowing. **c'est un ~ à l'anglais** it's a loan word *ou* borrowing from English.

d (*loc*) **d'~** *nom, autorité* assumed; *matériel* borrowed.

emprunté, e [ɑ̃pʀœ̃te] (ptp de **emprunter**) adj **a** (*gauche*) *air, personne* ill-at-ease (*attrib*), self-conscious, awkward. **b** (*artificiel*) *gloire, éclat* sham, feigned.

emprunter [ɑ̃pʀœ̃te] 1 vt **a** *argent, objet* to borrow (*à* from); *idée* to borrow, take (*à* from); *chaleur* to derive, take (*à* from); *mot, expression* (*directement*) to borrow, take (*à* from); (*par dérivation*) to derive, take (*à* from); *nom, autorité* to assume, take on. **~ un langage noble** to use *ou* adopt a noble style (of language); **cette pièce emprunte son sujet à l'actualité** this play is based on a topical subject; (*Ling*) **mot emprunté à l'anglais** loan word from English. **b** *route* to take; *itinéraire* to follow.

emprunteur, -euse [ɑ̃pʀœ̃tœʀ, øz] nm,f borrower.

empuantir [ɑ̃pɥɑ̃tiʀ] 2 vt to stink out (*de* with).

EMT [əɛmte] nf (abrév de **éducation manuelle et technique**) *voir* **éducation**.

ému, e [emy] (ptp de **émouvoir**) adj *personne* (*compassion*) moved; (*gratitude*) touched; (*joie*) excited; (*timidité, peur*) nervous, agitated; *air* filled with emotion; *voix* emotional, trembling with emotion; *souvenirs* tender, touching. **~ jusqu'aux larmes devant leur misère** moved to tears by their poverty; **très ~ lors de son premier rendez-vous amoureux/la remise des prix** very excited *ou* agitated on his first date/at the prize giving; **encore tout ~, il la remercia** still quite overcome *ou* still (feeling) very touched, he thanked her; **dit-il d'une voix ~e** he said with emotion, he said in a voice trembling with emotion; **trop ~ pour les remercier/leur annoncer la nouvelle** too overcome to thank them/announce the news to them.

émulateur [emylatœʀ] nm (*Ordin*) emulator.

émulation [emylasjɔ̃] nf (*gén, Ordin*) emulation. **esprit d'~** spirit of competition, competitive spirit.

émule [emyl] nmf (*littér*) (*imitateur*) emulator; (*égal*) equal. (*péj*) **ce fripon et ses ~s** this scoundrel and his like; **être l'~ de qn** to emulate sb; **il fait des ~s** people emulate him.

émuler [emyle] 1 vt (*Ordin*) to emulate.

émulsif, -ive [emylsif, iv] adj (*Pharm*) emulsive; (*Chim*) emulsifying.

émulsifiant, e [emylsifjɑ̃, jɑ̃t] **1** adj emulsifying. **2** nm emulsifier.

émulsion [emylsjɔ̃] nf emulsion.

émulsionner [emylsjɔne] 1 vt to emulsify.

en[1] [ɑ̃] prép **a** (*lieu*) in; (*changement de lieu*) to. **vivre ~ France/Normandie** to live in France/Normandy; **aller ~ Angleterre/Normandie** to go to England/Normandy; **aller de pays ~ pays/ville ~ ville** to go from country to country/town to town; **il voyage ~ Grèce/Corse** he's travelling around Greece/Corsica; **il habite ~ province/banlieue/ville** he lives in the provinces/the suburbs/the town; **être ~ ville** to be in town; **aller ~ ville** to go (in)to town; **avoir des projets ~ tête** to have plans, have something in mind; **les objets ~ vitrine** the items in the window; **~ lui-même, il n'y croit pas** deep down *ou* in his heart of hearts he doesn't believe it; **je n'aime pas ~ lui cette obstination** I don't like this stubbornness of his, what I don't like about him is his stubbornness; *voir* **âme, tête**.

b (*temps: date, durée*) in; (*progression, périodicité*) to. **~ semaine** in *ou* during the week; **~ automne/été/mars/1976** in autumn/summer/March/1976; **il peut le faire ~ 3 jours** he can do it in 3 days; **~ 6 ans je lui ai parlé deux fois** in (all of) 6 years I've spoken to him twice; **de jour ~ jour** from day to day, daily; **d'année ~ année** from year to year, yearly; **son inquiétude grandissait d'heure ~ heure** hour by hour *ou* as the hours went by he grew more (and more) anxious, he grew hourly more anxious.

c (*moyen de transport*) by. **~ taxi/train/avion** *etc* by taxi/train *ou* rail/air *etc;* **aller à Londres ~ avion** to fly to London; **faire une promenade ~ barque/voiture** to go for a ride *ou* trip in a boat/car, go for a boat-/car-trip; **ils y sont allés ~ voiture** they went by car *ou* in a car; **ils sont arrivés ~ voiture** they arrived in a car *ou* by car; **ils ont remonté le fleuve ~ pirogue** they canoed up the river, they rowed up the river in a canoe.

d (*état, manière*) in, on; (*disposition*) in. **~ bonne santé** in good health; **il était ~ sang** he was covered in *ou* with blood; **être ~ sueur** to be bathed in sweat; **partir ~ vacances/voyage** to go on holiday/on a journey; **faire qch ~ hâte/~ vitesse*** to do sth in a hurry *ou* hurriedly/quick* *ou* right away*; **elle est ~ rage** she is furious *ou* in a rage; **le toit est ~ flammes** the roof is on fire *ou* in flames *ou* ablaze; **il a laissé le bureau ~ désordre** he left the office untidy *ou* in (a state of) disorder *ou* in a mess; **être ~ noir/blanc** to be (dressed) in black/white, be wearing black/white; **elle est arrivée ~ manteau de fourrure** she arrived wearing *ou* in a fur coat *ou* with a fur coat on; **il était ~ chemise/pyjama** he was in his *ou* wearing his shirt/pyjamas; **elle était ~ bigoudis** she was in her rollers; **être ~ guerre** to be at war; **télévision/carte ~ couleur** colour television/card; **ils y vont ~ groupe/bande*** they are going in a group/bunch*; **~ cercle/rang** in a circle/row; *voir* **état, haillon**.

e (*transformation*) into. **se changer ~** to change into; **se déguiser ~** to disguise o.s. as, dress up as; **traduire ~ italien** to translate into Italian; **convertir/transformer qch ~** to convert/transform sth into; **casser qch ~ morceaux** to break sth in(to) pieces; **couper/casser ~ deux** to cut/break in two; **partir ~ fumée** to end *ou* go up in smoke, fizzle out; **entrer** *ou* **tomber ~ disgrâce** to fall into disgrace; *voir* **éclater, larmes**.

f (*copule avec comp, adv etc*) in. **c'est son père ~ plus jeune/petit** he's just like his father only younger/smaller, he's a younger/smaller version of his father; **je veux la même valise ~ plus grand** I want the same suitcase only bigger *ou* only in a bigger size, I want a bigger version of the same suitcase; **nous avons le même article ~ vert** we have *ou* do the same item in green; *voir* **général, grand, gros**.

g (*conformité*) as. **~ tant que** as; **~ tant qu'ami** *ou* **~ (ma) qualité d'ami de la famille** as a family friend; **agir ~ tyran/lâche** to act like a tyrant/coward; **~ bon politicien/~ bon commerçant (qu'il est), il est très rusé** good politician/tradesman that he is *ou* like all good politicians/tradesmen, he's very cunning; **je le lui ai donné ~ cadeau/souvenir** I gave it to him as a present/souvenir; *voir* **qualité**.

h (*composition*) made of; (*présentation*) in. **le plat est ~ or/argent** the dish is made of gold/silver; **une bague ~ or/argent** a gold/silver ring; **une table ~ acajou** a mahogany table; **l'escalier sera ~ marbre** the staircase will be (in *ou* made of) marble; **une jupe ~ soie imprimée** a printed silk skirt, a skirt made (out) of printed silk; **~ quoi est-ce (que c'est) fait?, c'est ~ quoi?*** what's it made of? *ou* out of?; **l'œuvre de Proust ~ 6 volumes** Proust's works in 6 volumes; **une pièce ~ 3 actes** a 3-act play; **c'est écrit ~ anglais/vers/prose/lettres d'or** it is written in English/verse/prose/gold lettering.

i (*matière*) in, at, of. **~ politique/art/musique** in politics/art/music; **être bon** *ou* **fort ~ géographie** to be good at geography; **~ affaires, il faut de l'audace** you have to be bold in business; **licencié/docteur ~ droit** bachelor/doctor of law; *voir* **expert, matière.**

j (*mesure*) in. **mesurer ~ mètres** to measure in metres; **compter ~ francs** to reckon in francs; **ce tissu se fait ~ 140 (cm)** this material comes in 140-cm widths *ou* is 140 cm wide; **~ long** lengthways, lengthwise; **~ large** widthways, widthwise; **~ hauteur/profondeur** in height/depth; **nous avons ce manteau ~ 3 tailles** we have *ou* do this coat in 3 sizes; **cela se vend ~ boîtes de 12** this is sold in boxes of 12; *voir* **long, saut.**

k (*avec gérondif: manière, moyen etc*) **monter/entrer ~ courant** to run up/in; **sortir ~ rampant/boitant** to crawl/limp out; **se frayer un chemin/avancer ~ jouant des coudes** to elbow one's way through/forward; **elle est arrivée ~ chantant** she arrived singing, she was singing when she arrived; **endormir un enfant ~ le berçant** to rock a child to sleep; **vous ne le ferez obéir qu'~ le punissant** you'll only get him to obey by punishing him; **il s'est coupé ~ essayant d'ouvrir une boîte** he cut himself trying to open a tin; **il a fait une folie ~ achetant cette bague** it was very extravagant of him to buy this ring; **je suis allé jusqu'à la poste ~ me promenant** I went for *ou* took a walk as far as the post office; **ils ont réussi à lui faire signer la lettre ~ lui racontant des histoires** they talked him into signing the letter, they got him to sign the letter by spinning him some yarn.

l (*avec gérondif: simultanéité, durée*) **~ apprenant la nouvelle, elle s'est évanouie** she fainted at the news *ou* when she heard the news *ou* on hearing the news; **il a buté ~ montant dans l'autobus** he tripped getting into *ou* as he got into the bus; **j'ai écrit une lettre (tout) ~ vous attendant** I wrote a letter while I was waiting for you; **il s'est endormi ~ lisant le journal** he fell asleep (while) reading the newspaper, he fell asleep over the newspaper; **fermez la porte ~ sortant** shut the door as you go out; **il est sorti ~ haussant les épaules/~ criant au secours** he left shrugging his shoulders/shouting for help *ou* with a shrug of his shoulders/a cry for help.

m (*introduisant compléments*) in. **croire ~ Dieu** to believe in God; **avoir confiance/foi ~ qn** to have confidence/faith in sb.

en² [ɑ̃] **pron** a (*lieu*) **quand va-t-il à Nice? — il ~ revient** when is he off to Nice? — he's just (come) back (from there); **elle était tombée dans une crevasse, on a eu du mal à l'~ sortir** she had fallen into a crevasse and they had difficulty *ou* trouble (in) getting her out (of it); **le bénéfice qu'il ~ a tiré** the profit he got out of it *ou* from it; **il faut ~ tirer une conclusion** we must draw a conclusion from it; (*fig*) **où ~ sommes-nous?** (*livre, leçon*) where have we got (up) to?, where are we now?; (*situation*) where do we stand?

b (*cause, agent, instrument*) **je suis si inquiet que je n'~ dors pas** I can't sleep for worrying, I am so worried that I can't sleep; **il saisit sa canne et l'~ frappa** he seized his stick and struck her with it; **ce n'est pas moi qui ~ perdrai le sommeil** I won't lose any sleep over it; **quelle histoire! nous ~ avons beaucoup ri** what a business! we had a good laugh over *ou* about it; **il a été gravement blessé, il pourrait ~ rester infirme** he has been seriously injured and could remain crippled (as a result *ou* because of it); **~ mourir** (*maladie*) to die of it; (*blessure*) to die because of it *ou* as a result of it; **elle ~ est aimée/très blessée** she is loved by him/very hurt by it.

c *complément de vb, d'adj, de n*) **rendez-moi mon projecteur, j'~ ai besoin** give me back my projector — I need it; **qu'est-ce que tu ~ feras?** what will you do with it (*ou* them)?; **on lui apprend des mots faciles pour qu'il s'~ souvienne** he is taught easy words so that he will remember *ou* retain them; **c'est une bonne classe, les professeurs ~ sont contents** they are a good class and the teachers are pleased with them; **elle, mentir? elle ~ est incapable** she couldn't lie if she tried; **elle a réussi et elle n'~ est pas peu fière** she has been successful and she is more than a little proud of herself *ou* of it; **il ne fume plus, il ~ a perdu l'habitude** he doesn't smoke any more — he has got out of *ou* has lost the habit; **sa décision m'inquiète car j'~ connais tous les dangers** her decision worries me because I am aware of all the dangers (of it) *ou* of all its possible dangers; **je t'~ donne/offre 10 F** I'll give/offer you 10 francs for it.

d (*quantitatif, indéf*) of it, of them (*souvent omis*). **si vous aimez les pommes, prenez-~ plusieurs** if you like apples, take several; **il avait bien des lettres à écrire mais il n'~ a pas écrit la moitié/beaucoup** he had a lot of letters to write but he hasn't written half of them/many (of them); **le vin est bon mais il n'y ~ a pas beaucoup** the wine is good but there isn't much (of it); **si j'~ avais** if I had any; **voulez-vous du pain/des pommes? il y ~ a encore** would you like some bread/some apples? we have still got some (left); **il n'y ~ a plus** (*pain*) there isn't any left, there's none left; (*pommes*) there aren't any left, there are none left; **si vous cherchez un crayon, vous ~ trouverez des douzaines/un dans le tiroir** if you are looking for a pencil you will find dozens (of them)/one in the drawer; **élevé dans le village, j'~ connaissais tous les habitants** having been brought up in the village I knew all its inhabitants; **a-t-elle des poupées? — oui, elle ~ a 2/trop/de belles** has she any dolls? — yes, she has 2/too many/some lovely ones; **nous avons du vin, j'~ ai acheté une bouteille hier** we have some wine because I bought a bottle yesterday; **j'~ ai assez/ras le bol*̲*** I've had enough (of it)/a bellyful*̲* (of it); **des souris ici? nous n'~ avons jamais vu(es)** mice here? we've never seen any; **il ~ aime une autre** he loves another (*littér*), he loves somebody else; **~ voilà/voici un** there/here is one (of them) now.

e (*renforcement*) *non traduit.* **il s'~ souviendra de cette réception** he'll certainly remember that party; **je n'~ vois pas, moi, de places libres** well (I must say), I don't see any empty seats; **tu ~ as eu de beaux jouets à Noël!** well you did get some lovely toys *ou* what lovely toys you got for Christmas!

f (*loc verbales*) *non traduit.* **~ être quitte pour la peur** to get off with a fright; **~ venir aux mains** to come to blows; **ne pas ~ croire ses yeux/ses oreilles** not to believe one's eyes/ears; **~ être réduit à faire** to be reduced to doing; **il ~ est** *ou* **il ~ arrive à penser que** he has come to think that; **je ne m'~ fais pas** I don't worry *ou* care, I don't get het up*; **ne vous ~ faites pas** don't worry, never mind; **il ~ est** *ou* **il ~ va de même pour** the same goes for, the same may be said for; *voir* **accroire, assez, entendre.**

E.N. (**abrév de Éducation nationale**) *voir* **éducation.**

ENA [ena] **nf** (**abrév de École nationale d'administration**) *voir* **école.**

enamouré, e [enamuʀe] (**ptp de s'enamourer**) **adj** *regard* infatuated.

enamourer (s')†† [enamuʀe] 1 **vpr: s'~ de** to become enamoured of.

énarque [enaʀk] **nmf** énarque, *student or former student of the École nationale d'administration.*

énarthrose [enaʀtʀoz] **nf** socket joint.

en-avant [ɑ̃navɑ̃] **nm inv** (*Rugby*) forward pass, knock on.

en-but [ɑ̃by(t)] **nm inv** (*Rugby*) in-goal area.

encablure [ɑ̃kablyʀ] **nf** cable's length. **à 3 ~s de** 3 cables' length away from.

encadré [ɑ̃kadʀe] (**ptp de encadrer**) **nm** (*emplacement*) box; (*texte*) boxed piece of text.

encadrement [ɑ̃kadʀəmɑ̃] **nm** a (*NonC: voir* **encadrer**) framing; training, supervision. **"tous travaux d'~"** "all framing (work) undertaken". b (*embrasure*) *[porte, fenêtre]* frame. **il se tenait dans l'~ de la porte** he stood in the doorway. c (*cadre*) frame. **cet ~ conviendrait mieux au sujet** this frame would be more appropriate to the subject. d (*Admin: instructeurs*) training personnel; (*cadres*) managerial staff. e (*Écon*) **~ du crédit** credit restriction *ou* squeeze.

encadrer [ɑ̃kadʀe] 1 **vt** a *tableau* to frame. (*iro*) **c'est à ~!** that's priceless!, that's one to remember!

b (*instruire*) *étudiants, débutants, recrues* to train (and supervise); (*contrôler*) *enfant* to take in hand; *équipe sportive* to manage.

c (*fig: entourer*) *cour, plaine, visage* to frame, surround; *prisonnier* to surround; (*par 2 personnes*) to flank. **les collines qui encadraient la plaine** the hills that framed *ou* surrounded the plain; **encadré de ses gardes du corps** surrounded by his bodyguards; **l'accusé, encadré de 2 gendarmes** the accused, flanked by 2 policemen.

d (*̲*: gén nég: supporter*) to stick*, stand*. **je ne peux pas l'~** I can't stick* *ou* stand* *ou* abide him.

e (*Mil*) *objectif* to straddle.

f (*Aut*) **il s'est fait ~*** he got his his car badly dented, someone smashed into his car.

encadreur [ɑ̃kadʀœʀ] **nm** (picture) framer.

encager [ɑ̃kaʒe] 3 **vt** *animal, oiseau* to cage (up); (*fig*) *personne* to cage in, cage up.

encaissable [ɑ̃kɛsabl] **adj** encashable (*Brit*), cashable.

encaisse [ɑ̃kɛs] **nf** cash in hand, cash balance. **~ métallique** gold and silver reserves; **~ or** gold reserves.

encaissé, e [ɑ̃kese] (**ptp de encaisser**) **adj** *vallée* deep, steep-sided; *rivière* hemmed in by steep banks *ou* hills; *route* hemmed in by steep hills.

encaissement [ɑ̃kɛsmɑ̃] **nm** a (*voir* **encaisser**) collection; receipt; receipt of payment for; cashing. b *[vallée]* depth, steep-sidedness. **l'~ de la route/rivière faisait que le pont ne voyait jamais le soleil** the steep hills hemming in the road/river *ou* which reared up from the road/river stopped the sun from ever reaching the bridge.

encaisser [ɑ̃kese] 1 **vt** a *argent, loyer* to collect, receive; *facture* to receive payment for; *chèque* to cash; *effet de commerce* to collect.

b (*) *coups, affront, défaite* to take. **savoir ~** *[boxeur]* to be able to take a lot of beating *ou* punishment (*fig*); (*fig: dans la vie*) to be able to stand up to *ou* take a lot of beating *ou* buffeting; **qu'est-ce qu'il a encaissé!** (*coups*) what a hammering he got!*, what a beating he took!; (*injures, réprimande*) what a hammering he got!*, he certainly got what for!*; **qu'est-ce qu'on encaisse avec ces cahots** we're taking a real hammering on these bumps*.

c (*̲*: gén nég: supporter*) **je ne peux pas ~ ce type** I can't stick*

(*Brit*) *ou* stand* *ou* abide that guy; **il n'a pas encaissé cette décision** he couldn't stomach* that decision; **il n'a pas encaissé cette remarque** he didn't appreciate that remark one little bit*.
d (*Tech*) *route, fleuve, voie ferrée* to embank. **les montagnes qui encaissent la vallée** the mountains which enclose the valley; **la route s'encaisse entre les collines** the road is hemmed in by the hills.
e *objets* to pack in(to) boxes; *plantes* to plant in boxes *ou* tubs.

encaisseur [ɑ̃kɛsœʀ] **nm** collector (*of debts etc*).

encan [ɑ̃kɑ̃] **nm: mettre** *ou* **vendre à l'~** to sell off by auction.

encanaillement [ɑ̃kanɑjmɑ̃] **nm** (*voir* **s'encanailler**) mixing with the riffraff, slumming it*.

encanailler (s') [ɑ̃kanɑje] 1 **vpr** (*hum*) to mix with the riffraff, slum it*. **son style/langage s'encanaille** his style/language is taking a turn for the worse *ou* is becoming vulgar.

encapuchonner [ɑ̃kapyʃɔne] 1 **vt:** ~ **un enfant** to put a child's hood up; **la tête encapuchonnée** hooded; **un groupe de bambins encapuchonnés** a group of toddlers snug in their hoods.

encart [ɑ̃kaʀ] **nm** (*Typ*) insert, inset. ~ **publicitaire** publicity *ou* advertising insert.

encarter [ɑ̃kaʀte] 1 **vt** (*Typ*) to insert, inset.

en-cas [ɑ̃kɑ] **nm** (*nourriture*) snack.

encaserner [ɑ̃kazɛʀne] 1 **vt** to quarter *ou* lodge in barracks.

encastrable [ɑ̃kastʀabl] **adj** slot-in (*épith*).

encastrement [ɑ̃kastʀəmɑ̃] **nm** *[interrupteur]* flush fitting; *[armoire, rayonnage]* recessed fitting.

encastrer [ɑ̃kastʀe] 1 **vt** (*dans un mur*) to embed (*dans* in(to)), sink (*dans* into); *interrupteur* to fit flush (*dans* with); *rayonnages, armoire* to recess (*dans* into), embed (*dans* into); (*dans un boîtier, une pièce de mécanisme*) *pièce* to fit (*dans* into). **tous les boutons sont encastrés dans le mur** all the switches are flush with the wall *ou* are embedded in *ou* sunk in the wall; **armoire à pharmacie encastrée (dans le mur)** medicine cabinet recessed into the wall; **four encastré** built-in *ou* recessed oven; **de gros blocs encastrés dans la neige/le sol** great blocks sunk in *ou* embedded in the snow/ground; (*fig*) **la voiture s'est encastrée sous l'avant du camion** the car jammed itself underneath the front of the lorry; **cette pièce s'encastre exactement dans le boîtier** this part fits exactly into the case; **ces pièces s'encastrent exactement l'une dans l'autre** these parts fit exactly into each other.

encaustique [ɑ̃kostik] **nf** polish, wax.

encaustiquer [ɑ̃kostike] 1 **vt** to polish, wax.

enceindre [ɑ̃sɛ̃dʀ] 52 **vt** (*gén ptp*) to encircle, surround (*de* with). **enceint de** encircled *ou* surrounded by.

enceinte[1] [ɑ̃sɛ̃t] **adj f** pregnant (*de qn* by sb), expecting* (*attrib*). **femme** ~ pregnant woman, expectant mother; ~ **de cinq mois** five months pregnant, five months gone* (*Brit*); **je suis ~e de Paul** I'm pregnant by Paul; ~ **de quintuplés** pregnant with *ou* expecting quintuplets.

enceinte[2] [ɑ̃sɛ̃t] **nf** a (*mur*) wall; (*palissade*) enclosure, fence. **une ~ de fossés défendait la place** the position was surrounded by defensive ditches *ou* was defended by surrounding ditches; **une ~ de pieux protégeait le camp** the camp was protected by an enclosure made of stakes; **mur d'~** surrounding wall. b (*espace clos*) enclosure; *[couvent]* precinct. **dans l'~ de la ville** within *ou* inside the town; **dans l'~ du tribunal** in(side) the court room; **dans l'~ de cet établissement** within *ou* in(side) this establishment; ~ **militaire** military area *ou* zone. c (*Élec*) ~ **(acoustique)** (loud)speaker.

encens [ɑ̃sɑ̃] **nm** incense. (*fig*) **l'~ des louanges/de leur flatterie** the heady wine of praise/of their flattery.

encensement [ɑ̃sɑ̃smɑ̃] **nm** (*voir* **encenser**) (in)censing; praising (*NonC*) to the skies.

encenser [ɑ̃sɑ̃se] 1 **vt** to (in)cense; (*fig*) to heap *ou* shower praise(s) upon, praise to the skies.

encenseur [ɑ̃sɑ̃sœʀ] **nm** (*Rel*) thurifer, censer-bearer; (*fig* †) flatterer.

encensoir [ɑ̃sɑ̃swaʀ] **nm** censer, thurible. (*fig péj*) **manier l'~** to pour out flattery, heap on the praise; (*fig*) **coups d'~** excessive flattery.

encéphale [ɑ̃sefal] **nm** encephalon.

encéphalique [ɑ̃sefalik] **adj** encephalic.

encéphalite [ɑ̃sefalit] **nf** encephalitis.

encéphalogramme [ɑ̃sefalɔgʀam] **nm** encephalogram.

encerclement [ɑ̃sɛʀkləmɑ̃] **nm** (*voir* **encercler**) surrounding; encircling.

encercler [ɑ̃sɛʀkle] 1 **vt** *[murs]* to surround, encircle; *[armée, police]* to surround. (*littér*) **il encercla sa taille de ses bras puissants** he encircled her waist with his powerful arms.

enchaîné [ɑ̃ʃene] **nm** (*Ciné*) change; *voir* **fondu**.

enchaînement [ɑ̃ʃɛnmɑ̃] **nm** a (*suite logique*) *[épisodes, preuves]* linking. **l'~ de la violence** the spiral of violence. b *[scènes, séquences]* (*action*) linking; (*résultat*) link. c (*série*) ~ **de circonstances** sequence *ou* series *ou* string of circumstances; ~ **d'événements** chain *ou* series *ou* string *ou* sequence of events. d (*Danse*) enchaînement. (*Mus*) ~ **des accords** chord progression.

enchaîner [ɑ̃ʃene] 1 1 **vt** a (*lier*) *animal* to chain up; *prisonnier* to put in chains, chain up. ~ **un animal/prisonnier à un arbre** to chain an animal/a prisoner (up) to a tree; ~ **2 prisonniers l'un à l'autre** to chain 2 prisoners together.
b (*fig littér*) *[secret, souvenir, sentiment]* to bind. **l'amour enchaîne les cœurs** love binds hearts (together); **ses souvenirs l'enchaînaient à ce lieu** his memories tied *ou* bound *ou* chained him to this place.
c (*fig: asservir*) *peuple* to enslave; *presse* to muzzle, gag. ~ **la liberté** to put freedom in chains.
d (*assembler*) *faits, épisodes, séquences* to connect, link (together *ou* up); *paragraphes, pensées, mots* to link (together *ou* up), put together, string together. **incapable d'~ deux pensées/paragraphes** incapable of linking *ou* putting *ou* stringing two thoughts/paragraphs together; (*Ciné*) ~ **(la scène suivante)** to change to *ou* move on to the next scene; (*Ciné*) **on va ~ les dernières scènes** we'll carry on with the last scenes, we'll go on to the last scenes.
2 **vi** (*Ciné, Théât*) to carry on (*Brit*) *ou* move on (to the next scene). **sans laisser à Anne le temps de répondre, Paul enchaîna: "d'abord ...** without giving Anne the time to reply, Paul went on *ou* continued: "first ...; **on enchaîne, enchaînons** (*Ciné, Théât*) let's carry on (*Brit*) *ou* keep going; (*: *dans un débat etc*) let's go on *ou* carry on (*Brit*), let's continue.
3 **s'enchaîner vpr** *[épisodes, séquences]* to follow on from each other, be linked (together); *[preuves, faits]* to be linked (together). **tout s'enchaîne** it's all linked *ou* connected, it all ties up; **des paragraphes/raisonnements qui s'enchaînent bien** well-linked paragraphs/pieces of reasoning, paragraphs/pieces of reasoning that are well strung *ou* put together.

enchanté, e [ɑ̃ʃɑ̃te] (**ptp de enchanter**) **adj** a (*ravi*) enchanted (*de* by), delighted (*de* with), enraptured (*de* by). (*frm*) ~ **(de vous connaître)** how do you do?, (I'm) very pleased to meet you. b (*magique*) *forêt, demeure* enchanted.

enchantement [ɑ̃ʃɑ̃tmɑ̃] **nm** a (*action*) enchantment; (*effet*) (magic) spell, enchantment. **comme par ~** as if by magic. b (*ravissement*) delight, enchantment. **ce spectacle fut un ~** the sight of this was an absolute delight *ou* was enchanting *ou* delightful; **être dans l'~** to be enchanted *ou* delighted *ou* enraptured.

enchanter [ɑ̃ʃɑ̃te] 1 1 **vt** a (*ensorceler*) to enchant, bewitch. b (*ravir*) to enchant, delight, enrapture. **ça ne m'enchante pas beaucoup** I'm not exactly taken with it, it doesn't exactly appeal to me *ou* fill me with delight. 2 **s'enchanter vpr** (*littér*) to rejoice (*de* at).

enchanteur, -teresse [ɑ̃ʃɑ̃tœʀ, tʀɛs] 1 **adj** enchanting, bewitching. 2 **nm** (*sorcier*) enchanter; (*fig*) charmer. 3 **enchanteresse nf** enchantress.

enchâssement [ɑ̃ʃɑsmɑ̃] **nm** a *[pierre]* setting (*dans* in). b (*Ling*) embedding.

enchâsser [ɑ̃ʃɑse] 1 1 **vt** (*gén*) to set (*dans* in); (*Ling*) to embed. (*littér*) ~ **une citation dans un texte** to insert a quotation into a text. 2 **s'enchâsser vpr: s'~ (l'un dans l'autre)** to fit exactly together; **s'~ dans** to fit exactly into.

enchère [ɑ̃ʃɛʀ] **nf** a (*Comm: offre*) bid. **faire une ~** to bid, make a bid; **faire monter les ~s** (*lit*) to raise the bidding; (*fig*) to raise *ou* up the ante; *voir* **vente**. b (*Comm: vente*) **~s: mettre aux ~s** to put up for auction; **vendre aux ~s** to sell by auction; **acheté aux ~s** bought at an auction (sale). c (*Cartes*) bid. **le système des ~s** the bidding system.

enchérir [ɑ̃ʃeʀiʀ] 2 **vi** a (*Comm*) ~ **sur une offre** to make a higher bid; **il a enchéri sur mon offre** he bid higher than I did, he made a bid higher than mine; ~ **sur qn** to bid higher than sb, make a higher bid than sb; ~ **sur une somme** to go higher than *ou* above *ou* over an amount. b (*fig*) ~ **sur** to go further than, go beyond, go one better than. c (†: *augmenter*) to become more expensive.

enchérissement† [ɑ̃ʃeʀismɑ̃] **nm** = **renchérissement**.

enchérisseur, -euse [ɑ̃ʃeʀisœʀ, øz] **nm,f** bidder.

enchevêtrement [ɑ̃ʃ(ə)vɛtʀəmɑ̃] **nm** *[ficelles, branches]* entanglement; (*fig*) *[idées, situation]* confusion. **l'~ de ses idées** the confusion *ou* muddle his ideas were in; **un ~ de branches barrait la route** a tangle of branches blocked the way.

enchevêtrer [ɑ̃ʃ(ə)vetʀe] 1 1 **vt** *ficelle* to tangle (up), entangle, muddle up; (*fig*) *idées, intrigue* to confuse, muddle. 2 **s'enchevêtrer vpr** a *[ficelles]* to get in a tangle, become entangled, tangle; *[branches]* to become entangled. **s'~ dans des cordes** to get caught up *ou* tangled up in ropes. b *[situations, paroles]* to become confused *ou* muddled. **mots qui s'enchevêtrent les uns dans les autres** words that get confused together *ou* that run into each other; **s'~ dans ses explications** to tie o.s. up in knots* explaining (something), get tangled up in one's explanations.

enchifrené, e [ɑ̃ʃifʀəne] **adj** *nez* blocked up.

enclave [ɑ̃klav] **nf** (*lit, fig*) enclave.

enclavement [ɑ̃klavmɑ̃] **nm** (*action*) enclosing, hemming in. (*état*) **l'~ d'un département dans un autre** one department's being enclosed by another; **cette province souffre de son ~** this province suffers from its isolation *ou* from its hemmed-in position.

enclaver [ɑ̃klave] 1 **vt** a (*entourer*) to enclose, hem in. **terrain complètement enclavé dans un grand domaine** piece of land completely enclosed within *ou* hemmed in by a large property; **pays enclavé** landlocked country. b (*encastrer*) ~ **(l'un dans l'autre)** to fit together, interlock; ~ **dans** to fit into. c (*insérer*) ~ **entre** to insert between.

enclenchement [ɑ̃klɑ̃ʃmɑ̃] nm (*action*) engaging; (*état*) engagement; (*dispositif*) interlock.

enclencher [ɑ̃klɑ̃ʃe] [1] 1 vt *mécanisme* to engage; (*fig*) *affaire* to set in motion, get under way. **l'affaire est enclenchée** the business is under way. 2 **s'enclencher** vpr *[mécanisme]* to engage.

enclin, e [ɑ̃klɛ̃, in] adj: ~ **à qch/à faire qch** inclined *ou* prone to sth/to do sth.

enclore [ɑ̃klɔʀ] [45] vt to enclose, shut in. ~ **qch d'une haie/d'une palissade/d'un mur** to hedge/fence/wall sth in.

enclos [ɑ̃klo] nm (*gén: terrain, clôture*) enclosure; *[chevaux]* paddock; *[moutons]* pen, fold.

enclume [ɑ̃klym] nf anvil; (*Aut*) engine block; (*Anat*) anvil (bone), incus (SPÉC). (*fig*) **entre l'~ et le marteau** between the devil and the deep blue sea.

encoche [ɑ̃kɔʃ] nf (*gén*) notch; *[flèche]* nock. **faire une ~ à** *ou* **sur qch** to notch sth, make a notch in sth.

encocher [ɑ̃kɔʃe] [1] vt (*Tech*) to notch; *flèche* to nock.

encodage [ɑ̃kɔdaʒ] nm encoding.

encoder [ɑ̃kɔde] [1] vt to encode.

encodeur [ɑ̃kɔdœʀ] nm encoder.

encoignure [ɑ̃kɔɲyʀ] nf a (*coin*) corner. b (*meuble*) corner cupboard.

encoller [ɑ̃kɔle] [1] vt to paste.

encolure [ɑ̃kɔlyʀ] nf *[cheval, personne, robe]* neck; (*Comm: tour de cou*) collar size. (*Équitation*) **battre d'une ~** to beat by a neck.

encombrant, e [ɑ̃kɔ̃bʀɑ̃, ɑ̃t] 1 adj (*lit*) *paquet* cumbersome, unwieldy, bulky; (*fig*) *présence* burdensome, inhibiting. **cet enfant est très ~** (*agaçant*) this child is a real nuisance *ou* pest*; (*indésirable*) this child is in the way *ou* is a nuisance. 2 nmpl: **les ~s** (*objets*) (unwanted) junk; (*: *service*) junk removal service.

encombre [ɑ̃kɔ̃bʀ] nm: **sans ~** without mishap *ou* incident.

encombré, e [ɑ̃kɔ̃bʀe] (ptp de **encombrer**) adj *couloir* cluttered (up), obstructed; *passage* obstructed; *lignes téléphoniques* blocked; *profession, marché* saturated. **table ~e de papiers** table cluttered *ou* littered with papers; (*Aut*) **le boulevard est très ~** the traffic is very heavy on the boulevard, the boulevard is very congested.

encombrement [ɑ̃kɔ̃bʀəmɑ̃] nm a (*obstruction*) *[lieu]* congestion. **à cause de l'~ des lignes téléphoniques** because of the telephone lines being blocked; **l'~ du couloir rendait le passage malaisé** the state of congestion *ou* clutter in the corridor *ou* all the clutter in the corridor made it difficult to get through; **un ~ de vieux meubles** a clutter *ou* jumble of old furniture; **les ~s qui ralentissent la circulation** the obstructions *ou* holdups that slow down the traffic; (*Aut*) **être pris dans un ~** *ou* **dans les ~s** to be stuck in a traffic jam *ou* in the traffic jams. b (*volume*) bulk; (*taille*) size. **objet de faible ~** small object.

encombrer [ɑ̃kɔ̃bʀe] [1] 1 vt *pièce* to clutter (up); *couloir* to clutter (up), obstruct, congest; (*fig*) *mémoire* to clutter (up), encumber; *profession* to saturate; (*Téléc*) *lignes* to block; (*Comm*) *marché* to glut. **ces paquets encombrent le passage** these packages block the way *ou* are an obstruction; **ces boîtes m'encombrent** (*je les porte*) I'm loaded down with these boxes; (*elles gênent le passage*) these boxes are in my way. 2 **s'encombrer** vpr: **s'~ de** *paquets* to load o.s. with; *enfants* to burden *ou* saddle* o.s. with; **il ne s'encombre pas de scrupules** he's not overburdened with scruples, he's not overscrupulous.

encontre [ɑ̃kɔ̃tʀ] 1 prép: **à l'~ de** (*contre*) against, counter to; (*au contraire de*) contrary to; **aller à l'~ de** *[décision, faits]* to go against, run counter to; **je n'irai pas à l'~ de ce qu'il veut/fait** I shan't go against his wishes/what he does; **cela va à l'~ du but recherché** it's counterproductive, it defeats the purpose; **action qui va à l'~ du but recherché** self-defeating *ou* counterproductive action; **à l'~ de ce qu'il dit, mon opinion est que ...** contrary to what he says, my opinion is that ... . 2 adv (*rare*) **à l'~** in opposition, against it; **je n'irai pas à l'~** I shan't go against it, I shan't act in opposition.

encor [ɑ̃kɔʀ] adv (††, *Poésie*) = **encore**.

encorbellement [ɑ̃kɔʀbɛlmɑ̃] nm (*Archit*) corbelled construction. **fenêtre en ~** oriel window; **balcon en ~** corbelled balcony.

encorder [ɑ̃kɔʀde] [1] 1 vt to rope up. 2 **s'encorder** vpr to rope up. **les alpinistes s'encordent** the climbers rope themselves together *ou* rope up.

encore [ɑ̃kɔʀ] adv a (*toujours*) still. **il restait ~ quelques personnes** there were still a few people left; **il en était ~ au brouillon** he was still working on the draft; (*péj*) **il en est ~ au stade de la règle à calculer/du complet cravate** he hasn't got past the slide rule/the collar and tie stage yet, he's still at the slide rule/the collar and tie stage; (*péj*) **tu en es ~ là!** haven't you got beyond *ou* past that yet!; **il n'est ~ qu'en première année/que caporal** he's only in first year/a corporal as yet, he's still only in first year/a corporal; **il n'est ~ que 8 heures** it's (still) only 8 o'clock; **ce malfaiteur court ~** the criminal is still at large.

b **pas ~** not yet; **il n'est pas ~ prêt** he's not ready yet, he's not yet ready; **ça ne s'était pas ~ vu, ça ne s'était ~ jamais vu** that had never been seen before.

c (*pas plus tard que*) only. **~ ce matin** *ou* **ce matin ~, il semblait bien portant** only this morning he seemed quite well; **il me le disait ~ hier** *ou* **hier ~** he was saying that to me only yesterday.

d (*de nouveau*) again. **~ une fois** (once) again, once more, one more time; **~ une fois, je n'affirme rien** but there again, I'm not absolutely positive about it; **~ une fois non!** how many times do I have to tell you – no!; **ça s'est ~ défait** it has come undone (yet) again *ou* once more; **il a ~ laissé la porte ouverte** he has left the door open (yet) again; **elle a ~ acheté un nouveau chapeau** she has bought yet another new hat; **~ vous!** (not) you again!; **quoi ~?, qu'y a-t-il ~?, que te faut-il ~?** what's the matter with you this time?, what is it THIS time?

e (*de plus, en plus*) more. **~ un!** yet another!, one more!; **~ un rhume** (yet) another cold; **~ une tasse?** another cup?; **vous prendrez bien ~ quelque chose?** *ou* **quelque chose ~?** surely you'll have something more? *ou* something else?; **~ un peu de thé?** a little more tea?, (any) more tea?; **~ quelques gâteaux?** (some *ou* any) more cakes?; **j'en veux ~** I want some more; **~ un mot, avant de terminer** (just) one more word before I finish; **que te faut-il ~?** what else *ou* more do you want?; **qu'est-ce que j'oublie ~?** what else have I forgotten?; **qui y avait-il ~?** who else was there?; **pendant ~ 2 jours** for another 2 days, for 2 more days, for 2 days more; **il y a ~ quelques jours avant de partir** there are a few (more) days to go before we leave; **~ un fou du volant!** (yet) another roadhog!; **en voilà ~ 2** here are 2 more *ou* another 2; **mais ~?** is that all?, what else?; *voir* **non**.

f (*avec compar*) even, still, yet (*littér*). **il fait ~ plus froid qu'hier** it's even *ou* still colder than yesterday; **il fait ~ moins chaud qu'hier** it's even less warm than it was yesterday; **il est ~ plus grand que moi** he is even taller than I am; **ils veulent l'agrandir ~ (plus)** they want to make it even *ou* still larger, they want to enlarge it even further; **~ pire, pire ~** even *ou* still worse, worse and worse; **~ autant** as much again (*que* as).

g (*aussi*) too, also, as well. **tu le bats non seulement en force, mais ~ en intelligence** you beat him not only in strength but also in intelligence, not only are you stronger than he is but you are more intelligent too *ou* also *ou* as well.

h (*valeur restrictive*) even then, even at that. **~ ne sait-il pas tout** even then he doesn't know everything, and he doesn't even know everything (at that); **~ faut-il le faire** you still have to do it, you have to do it even so; (*iro*) **~ une chance** *ou* **~ heureux qu'il ne se soit pas plaint au patron** (still) at least he didn't complain to the boss, let's think ourselves lucky that he didn't complain to the boss; **on t'en donnera peut-être 10 F, et ~** they'll give you perhaps 10 francs for it, if that *ou* and perhaps not even that; **c'est passable, et ~!** it's passable but only just!; **et ~, ça n'a pas été sans mal** and even that wasn't easy; **si ~** if only; **si ~ je savais où ça se trouve, j'irais bien,** (*frm*) **~ irais-je bien si je savais où ça se trouve** if only I knew where it was, I would willingly go.

i (*littér*) **~ que** (*quoique*) even though; **~ qu'il eût mal, il voulut y aller** even though he felt ill he wanted to go.

encorner [ɑ̃kɔʀne] [1] vt to gore.

encornet [ɑ̃kɔʀnɛ] nm squid.

encourageant, e [ɑ̃kuʀaʒɑ̃, ɑ̃t] adj encouraging.

encouragement [ɑ̃kuʀaʒmɑ̃] nm encouragement.

encourager [ɑ̃kuʀaʒe] [3] vt (*gén*) to encourage (*à faire* to do); *équipe* to cheer. **~ qn au meurtre** to encourage sb to commit murder, incite sb to murder; **~ qn à l'effort** to encourage sb to make an effort; **~ qn du geste et de la voix** to cheer sb on; **encouragé par ses camarades, il a joué un vilain tour au professeur** egged on *ou* encouraged by his classmates, he played a nasty trick on the teacher.

encourir [ɑ̃kuʀiʀ] [11] vt (*littér*) *amende, frais* to incur; *mépris, reproche, punition* to bring upon o.s., incur.

encours, en-cours [ɑ̃kuʀ] nm inv outstanding discounted bills.

encrage [ɑ̃kʀaʒ] nm inking.

encrassement [ɑ̃kʀasmɑ̃] nm (*voir* **encrasser**) fouling (up); sooting up; clogging (up), choking (up).

encrasser [ɑ̃kʀase] [1] 1 vt a *arme* to foul (up); *cheminée,* (*Aut*) *bougie* to soot up; *piston, poêle, tuyau, machine* to clog (up), choke (up), foul up. b (*salir*) to make filthy, (make) dirty. **ongles encrassés de cambouis** nails encrusted *ou* filthy with engine grease. 2 **s'encrasser** vpr (*voir* **encrasser**) to foul (up); to soot up; to clog (up), get choked (up).

encre [ɑ̃kʀ] 1 nf ink. **écrire à l'~** to write in ink; (*fig*) **de sa plus belle ~** in his best style; *voir* **bouteille, couler** *etc.* 2 comp ►**encre de Chine** Indian ink ►**encre d'imprimerie** printing ink ►**encre sympathique** invisible ink.

encrer [ɑ̃kʀe] [1] vt to ink.

encreur [ɑ̃kʀœʀ] 1 adj m *rouleau, tampon* inking. 2 nm inker.

encrier [ɑ̃kʀije] nm inkwell, inkpot (*Brit*).

encroûté, e* [ɑ̃kʀute] (ptp de **encroûter**) adj: **être ~** to stagnate, be in a rut; **quel ~ tu fais!** you're really stagnating!, you're really in a rut!

encroûtement [ɑ̃kʀutmɑ̃] nm a *[personne]* getting into a rut. **essayons de le tirer de son ~** let's try and get him out of his rut; **l'~ dans certaines habitudes** gradually becoming entrenched in certain habits. b *[objet]* encrusting, crusting over.

encroûter [ɑ̃kʀute] [1] 1 vt (*entartrer*) to encrust, crust over. 2 **s'encroûter** vpr a (*) *[personne]* to stagnate, get into a rut. **s'~ dans** *habitudes, préjugés* to become entrenched in; **s'~ dans la vie de province**

to get into the rut of provincial life. b *[objet]* to crust over, form a crust.
enculé** [ɑ̃kyle] nm sod**, bugger**.
enculer** [ɑ̃kyle] 1 vt to bugger** **va te faire ~!** fuck off!**; *(fig)* **ils enculent les mouches** they are nit-picking*.
encyclique [ɑ̃siklik] adj, nf: **(lettre)** ~ encyclical.
encyclopédie [ɑ̃siklɔpedi] nf encyclopaedia.
encyclopédique [ɑ̃siklɔpedik] adj encyclopaedic.
encyclopédiste [ɑ̃siklɔpedist] nmf *(Hist)* encyclopaedist.
endémie [ɑ̃demi] nf endemic disease.
endémique [ɑ̃demik] adj *(Méd, fig)* endemic.
endetté, e [ɑ̃dete] (ptp de **endetter**) adj in debt *(attrib)*. **très ~** heavily *ou* deep in debt; *(fig)* **(très) ~ envers qn** (greatly) indebted to sb.
endettement [ɑ̃dɛtmɑ̃] nm *(action)* indebtedness; *(résultat)* debt. **notre ~ extérieur** our foreign debt; **causer l'~ de l'entreprise** to put the company in debt; **le montant de notre ~ envers la banque** the amount of our indebtedness to the bank.
endetter vt, **s'endetter** vpr [ɑ̃dete] 1 *[particulier, entreprise]* to get into debt.
endeuiller [ɑ̃dœje] 1 vt *personne, pays (toucher par une mort)* to plunge into mourning; *(attrister)* to plunge into grief; *épreuve sportive, manifestation* to cast a (tragic) shadow over; *(littér) paysage* to make *ou* render dismal, give a dismal aspect to. **course endeuillée par la mort d'un pilote** race over which a tragic shadow was cast by the death of a driver.
endiablé, e [ɑ̃djɑble] adj *danse, rythme* boisterous, furious; *course* furious, wild; *personne* boisterous, turbulent.
endigage [ɑ̃digaʒ] nm, **endiguement** [ɑ̃digmɑ̃] nm *(voir* **endiguer***)* dyking (up); holding back; containing; checking; curbing. **politique d'~** policy of containment.
endiguer [ɑ̃dige] 1 vt a *fleuve* to dyke (up). b *(fig) foule, invasion* to hold back, contain; *révolte* to check, contain; *sentiments, progrès* to check, hold back; *inflation, chômage* to curb.
endimanché, e [ɑ̃dimɑ̃ʃe] (ptp de **s'endimancher**) adj (all done up) in one's Sunday best; *(fig) style* fancy, florid. *(péj)* **il a l'air ~** he looks terribly stiff in his Sunday best.
endimancher (s') [ɑ̃dimɑ̃ʃe] 1 vpr to put on one's Sunday best.
endive [ɑ̃div] nf chicory *(NonC)*. **5 ~s** 5 pieces *ou* heads of chicory.
endocarde [ɑ̃dɔkaʀd] nm endocardium.
endocardite [ɑ̃dɔkaʀdit] nf endocarditis.
endocarpe [ɑ̃dɔkaʀp] nm endocarp.
endocrine [ɑ̃dɔkʀin] adj: **glande ~** endocrine (gland).
endocrinien, -ienne [ɑ̃dɔkʀinjɛ̃, jɛn] adj endocrinal, endocrinous.
endocrinologie [ɑ̃dɔkʀinɔlɔʒi] nf endocrinology.
endocrinologue [ɑ̃dɔkʀinɔlɔg] nmf, **endocrinologiste** [ɑ̃dɔkʀinɔlɔʒist] nmf endocrinologist.
endoctrinement [ɑ̃dɔktʀinmɑ̃] nm indoctrination.
endoctriner [ɑ̃dɔktʀine] 1 vt to indoctrinate.
endoderme [ɑ̃dɔdɛʀm] nm endoderm.
endogamie [ɑ̃dɔgami] nf endogamy.
endogène [ɑ̃dɔʒɛn] adj endogenous.
endolori, e [ɑ̃dɔlɔʀi] (ptp de **endolorir**) adj painful, aching, sore. **~ par un coup** made tender by a blow.
endolorir [ɑ̃dɔlɔʀiʀ] 2 vt *(gén ptp)* to make painful *ou* sore.
endolymphe [ɑ̃dɔlɛ̃f] nf endolymph.
endomètre [ɑ̃dɔmɛtʀ] nm endometrium.
endommagement [ɑ̃dɔmaʒmɑ̃] nm damaging.
endommager [ɑ̃dɔmaʒe] 3 vt to damage.
endormant, e [ɑ̃dɔʀmɑ̃, ɑ̃t] adj (deadly) boring, deadly dull, deadly*.
endormeur, -euse [ɑ̃dɔʀmœʀ, øz] nm,f *(péj: trompeur)* beguiler.
endormi, e [ɑ̃dɔʀmi] (ptp de **endormir**) adj a *(lit) personne* sleeping, asleep *(attrib)*. b *(fig) (apathique)* sluggish, languid; *(engourdi)* numb; *(assoupi) passion* dormant; *facultés* dulled; *ville, rue* sleepy, drowsy. **j'ai la main tout ~e** my hand has gone to sleep *ou* is completely numb *ou* dead; **à moitié ~** half asleep; **quel ~** what a sleepyhead (he is).
endormir [ɑ̃dɔʀmiʀ] 16 1 vt a *[somnifère, discours]* to put *ou* send to sleep; *[personne] (en berçant etc)* to send *ou* lull to sleep. **elle chantait pour l'~** she used to sing him to sleep.
b (* *fig: ennuyer*) to send to sleep*, bore stiff*. **tu nous endors avec tes histoires!** you're sending us to sleep* *ou* boring us stiff* with your stories!
c **~ qn** *(anesthésier)* to put sb to sleep*, put sb under*, anaesthetize sb; *(hypnotiser)* to hypnotise sb, put sb under*.
d *(dissiper) douleur* to deaden; *soupçons* to allay, lull.
e *(tromper)* to beguile. **se laisser ~ par des promesses** to let o.s. be beguiled by promises, (let o.s.) be lulled into a false sense of security by promises.
2 **s'endormir** vpr a *[personne]* to go to sleep, fall asleep, drop off to sleep.
b *(fig: se relâcher)* to let up, slack off. **ce n'est pas le moment de nous ~** now is not the time to slow up *ou* slacken off; **allons, ne vous endormez pas!** come on, don't go to sleep on the job!*; *voir* **laurier**.
c *[rue, ville]* to grow calm, fall asleep; *[passion, douleur]* to subside, die down; *[facultés]* to go to sleep*.
d (*euph: mourir*) to pass away.
endormissement [ɑ̃dɔʀmismɑ̃] nm: **médicament qui facilite l'~** medicine which helps one to sleep, sleep-inducing medicine; **au moment de l'~** as one falls asleep.
endorphine [ɑ̃dɔʀfin] nf endorphin.
endos [ɑ̃do] nm endorsement.
endoscope [ɑ̃dɔskɔp] nm endoscope.
endoscopie [ɑ̃dɔskɔpi] nf endoscopy.
endoscopique [ɑ̃dɔskɔpik] adj endoscopic.
endosmose [ɑ̃dɔsmoz] nf endosmosis.
endossable [ɑ̃dosabl] adj *(Fin)* endorsable.
endossataire [ɑ̃dosatɛʀ] nmf endorsee.
endossement [ɑ̃dosmɑ̃] nm endorsement.
endosser [ɑ̃dose] 1 vt a *(revêtir) vêtement* to put on. *(fig)* **~ l'uniforme/la soutane** to enter the army/the Church. b *(assumer) responsabilité* to take, shoulder *(de* for). **il a voulu me faire ~ son erreur** he wanted to load his mistake onto me*, he wanted me to take *ou* shoulder the responsibility for his mistake. c *(Fin)* to endorse.
endosseur [ɑ̃dosœʀ] nm endorser.
endothermique [ɑ̃dotɛʀmik] adj endothermic.
endroit [ɑ̃dʀwa] nm a *(localité, partie du corps)* place, spot; *(lieu de rangement, partie d'un objet)* place. **un ~ idéal pour le pique-nique/une usine** an ideal spot *ou* place for a picnic/a factory; **je l'ai mis au même ~** I put it in the same place; **manteau usé à plusieurs ~s** coat worn in several places, coat with several worn patches; **les gens de l'~** the local people, the locals*; *voir* **petit**.
b *[livre, récit]* passage, part. **le plus bel ~ du film** the finest point in *ou* part of the film; **il arrêta sa lecture à cet ~** he stopped reading at that point.
c **à l'~ où** (at the place) where; **c'est à cet ~ que** *(ici)* it's here that; *(là)* it's there that; **de/vers l'~ où** from/to (the place) where; **en** *ou* **à quel ~?** where(abouts)?, where exactly?; **en quelque ~ que ce soit** wherever it may be.
d *(loc)* **en plusieurs ~s** in several places; **par ~s** in places; **au bon ~** in *ou* at the right place; *(littér)* **à l'~ de** *(à l'égard de)* regarding, with regard to.
e *(bon côté)* right side. **à l'~** *vêtement* right side out, the right way out; *objet posé* the right way round; **remets tes chaussettes à l'~** turn your socks right side out *ou* the right way out; *(Tricot)* **une maille à l'~, une maille à l'envers** knit one – purl one, one plain – one purl; **tout à l'~** knit every row.
enduire [ɑ̃dɥiʀ] 38 vt a *[personne, appareil]* **~ une surface de** *peinture, vernis, colle* to coat a surface with; *huile, boue* to coat *ou* smear a surface with; **ces émanations enduisaient de graisse les vitres** these fumes coated the panes with grease; **~ ses cheveux de brillantine** to grease one's hair with brilliantine, plaster brilliantine on one's hair; **surface enduite d'une substance visqueuse** surface coated *ou* smeared with a sticky substance; **s'~ de crème** to cover o.s. with cream. b *[substance]* to coat. **la colle qui enduit le papier** the glue coating the paper.
enduit [ɑ̃dɥi] nm coating.
endurable [ɑ̃dyʀabl] adj endurable, bearable.
endurance [ɑ̃dyʀɑ̃s] nf *(moral)* endurance; *(physique)* stamina, endurance. **coureur qui a de l'~** runner with stamina *ou* staying power.
endurant, e [ɑ̃dyʀɑ̃, ɑ̃t] adj tough, hardy. (*†: *patient*) **peu** *ou* **pas très ~ (avec)** not very patient (with).
endurci, e [ɑ̃dyʀsi] (ptp de **endurcir**) adj *cœur* hardened; *personne* hardened, hard-hearted. **un criminel ~** a hardened criminal; **un célibataire ~** a confirmed bachelor.
endurcir [ɑ̃dyʀsiʀ] 2 1 vt *corps* to toughen; *âme* to harden. 2 **s'endurcir** vpr *(physiquement)* to become tough; *(moralement)* to harden, become hardened. **il faut t'~ à la douleur** you must become hardened *ou* inured to pain.
endurcissement [ɑ̃dyʀsismɑ̃] nm *(voir* **s'endurcir***)* *(action)* toughening; hardening; *(état)* toughness; hardness. **~ à la douleur** being hardened to pain.
endurer [ɑ̃dyʀe] 1 vt to endure, bear. **~ de faire** to bear to do; **il fait froid, on endure un pull** it's cold, one needs a jersey.
enduro [ɑ̃dyʀo] nm enduro, trial.
Énée [ene] nm Aeneas.
Énéide [eneid] nf: **l'~** the Aeneid.
énergéticien, -ienne [enɛʀʒetisjɛ̃, jɛn] nm,f energetics specialist.
énergétique [enɛʀʒetik] 1 adj *ressources, théorie* energy *(épith)*, of energy; *aliment* energy-giving, energizing. *(Physiol)* **dépense ~** energy expenditure; *(Écon)* **nos dépenses ~s** the nation's fuel *ou* energy bill. 2 nf energetics *(sg)*.
énergie [enɛʀʒi] nf a *(force physique)* energy. **dépenser beaucoup d'~ à faire qch** to expend a great deal of energy doing sth; **un effort pour lequel il avait besoin de toute son ~** an effort for which he needed all his energy *ou* energies; **nettoyer/frotter avec ~** to clean/rub energetically; **être** *ou* **se sentir sans ~** to be *ou* feel lacking in energy, be *ou* feel unenergetic; **avec l'~ du désespoir** with the strength born of despair.
b *(fermeté, ressort moral)* spirit, vigour. **protester/refuser avec ~** to protest/refuse energetically *ou* vigorously *ou* forcefully; **cet individu**

sans ~ leur a cédé this feeble individual has given in to them; (*littér*) **l'~ du style/d'un terme** the vigour *ou* energy of style/of a term.

c (*Phys*) energy; (*Tech*) power, energy. (*Tech*) **~ électrique/mécanique/nucléaire/éolienne** electrical/mechanical/nuclear/wind power *ou* energy; (*Phys*) **~ cinétique/potentielle** kinetic/potential energy; **les ~s douces** alternative energy; **les ~s renouvelables** renewable energy; **~s fossiles** fossil fuels; **réaction qui libère de l'~** reaction that releases energy; **l'~ fournie par le moteur** the power supplied by the motor; **dépense** *ou* **consommation d'~** power consumption; **la consommation d'~ est moindre si l'on utilise ce modèle de radiateur électrique** power consumption is reduced by the use of this type of electric radiator; **les diverses sources d'~** the different sources of energy; **transport d'~** conveying of power.

énergique [enɛʀʒik] adj a (*physiquement*) *personne* energetic; *mouvement, geste, effort* vigorous, energetic. b (*moralement*) *personne, style, voix* vigorous, energetic; *refus, protestation, intervention* forceful, vigorous; *mesures* drastic, stringent; *punition* severe, harsh; *médicament* powerful, strong.

énergiquement [enɛʀʒikmɑ̃] adv (*voir* **énergique**) energetically; vigorously; forcefully; drastically; severely, harshly; powerfully, strongly.

énergisant, e [enɛʀʒizɑ̃, ɑ̃t] adj energizing.

énergumène [enɛʀgymɛn] nmf firebrand.

énervant, e [enɛʀvɑ̃, ɑ̃t] adj (*voir* **énerver**) irritating; annoying; enervating.

énervé, e [enɛʀve] (ptp de **énerver**) adj (*agacé*) irritated, annoyed; (*agité*) nervous, nervy* (*Brit*), edgy*.

énervement [enɛʀvəmɑ̃] nm (*voir* **énervé**) irritation, annoyance; nervousness, nerviness*, edginess*. **après les ~s du départ** after the upsets of the departure.

énerver [enɛʀve] 1 1 vt a **~ qn** (*agiter*) to overstimulate *ou* overexcite sb; (*agacer*) to irritate sb, annoy sb, get on sb's nerves*; **cela m'énerve** it gets (to) me*; **le vin blanc énerve** white wine is bad for your nerves. b (*littér: débiliter*) to enervate. 2 **s'énerver** vpr to get excited*, get worked up. **ne t'énerve pas!** don't get excited!*, don't get (all) worked up *ou* edgy*!, take it easy!; **ne t'énerve pas pour cela** don't let it get to you*.

enfance [ɑ̃fɑ̃s] nf a (*jeunesse*) childhood; *[garçon]* boyhood; *[fille]* girlhood; (*petite enfance*) infancy; (*fig: début*) infancy. **science encore dans son ~** science still in its infancy; **c'est l'~ de l'art** it's child's play *ou* kid's stuff*; *voir* **retomber**. b (*enfants*) children (*pl*). **la naïveté de l'~** the naïvety of children *ou* of childhood; **~ déshéritée** deprived children.

enfant [ɑ̃fɑ̃] 1 nmf a (*gén*) child; (*garçon*) (little) boy; (*fille*) (little) girl. **quand il était ~, il aimait grimper aux arbres** when he was a child *ou* a (little) boy *ou* as a child he liked climbing trees; **il se souvenait que, tout ~, il avait une fois ...** he remembered that, while still *ou* only a child, he had once ...; (*fig*) **c'est un grand ~** he's such a child; **il est resté très ~** he has remained very childlike, he has never really grown up; **faire l'~** to behave childishly, behave like a child; **ne faites pas l'~** don't be (so) childish, stop behaving like a child; *voir* **bon**[1], **bonne**[2], **jardin**.

b (*descendant*) child. **sans ~** childless; **M. X, décédé sans ~** Mr X who died childless *ou* without issue (*SPÉC*); **faire un ~ à une femme*** to get a woman pregnant; (*fig*) **il nous a fait un ~ dans le dos*** he stabbed us in the back; (*fig*) **ce livre est son ~** this book is his baby; *voir* **attendre, marier, petit.**

c (*originaire*) **c'est un ~ du pays/de la ville** he's a native of these parts/of the town; **~ de l'Auvergne/de Paris** child of the Auvergne/of Paris; **un ~ du peuple** a (true) child of the people.

d (**: adulte*) **les ~s!** folks*, kids*; **bonne nouvelle, les ~s!** good news, folks!* *ou* kids!*

2 comp ▸**enfant de l'amour** love child ▸**enfant de la balle** child of the theatre (*ou* circus *etc*) ▸**enfant bleu** (*Méd*) blue baby ▸**enfant de chœur** (*Rel*) altar boy; (*ingénu*) **il me prend pour un enfant de chœur!*** he thinks I'm still wet behind the ears!*; (*ange*) **ce n'est pas un enfant de chœur!*** he's no angel* ▸**enfant gâté** spoilt child ▸**l'Enfant Jésus** (*Rel*) the baby Jesus ▸**enfants de Marie** (*Rel*) children of Mary; **c'est une enfant de Marie** (*lit*) she's in the children of Mary; (**: ingénue*) she's a real innocent; **ce n'est pas une enfant de Marie!** she's no cherub!*, she's no innocent! ▸**enfant naturel** natural child ▸**enfant prodige** child prodigy ▸**enfant prodigue** (*Bible, fig*) prodigal son ▸**enfant terrible** (*lit*) unruly child; (*fig*) enfant terrible ▸**enfant de troupe** child reared by the army ▸**enfant trouvé** foundling ▸**enfant unique: il est enfant unique** he is an only child; **famille à enfant unique** one-child family, family with one child.

enfantement [ɑ̃fɑ̃tmɑ̃] nm (†, *Bible: accouchement*) childbirth; (*littér, fig*) *[œuvre]* giving birth (*de* to).

enfanter [ɑ̃fɑ̃te] 1 1 vt (†, *Bible: mettre au monde*) to give birth to, bring forth (*littér, Bible*); (*littér, fig: élaborer*) to give birth to (*littér*). 2 vi to give birth, be delivered (*littér, Bible*).

enfantillage [ɑ̃fɑ̃tijaʒ] nm childishness (*NonC*). **se livrer à des ~s** to do childish things, behave childishly; **c'est de l'~, arrête ces ~s!** do grow up!, don't be so childish!, you're just being childish.

enfantin, e [ɑ̃fɑ̃tɛ̃, in] adj (*typique de l'enfance*) *joie, naïveté, confiance* childlike, childish; (*puéril*) *attitude, réaction* childish, infantile. (*facile*) **c'est un travail ~** it's simple, it's dead easy* (*Brit*), it's child's play*; (*propre à l'enfant*) **rire/jeu ~** child's laugh/game; *voir* **classe, langage.**

enfariné, e [ɑ̃faʀine] adj (*lit*) dredged with flour; (*fig: poudré*) powdered. **arriver la gueule ~e*̣** *ou* **le bec ~*** to turn up breezily, turn up all bright and unsuspecting*.

enfer [ɑ̃fɛʀ] 1 nm a (*Rel*) **l'~** hell, Hell; (*Myth*) **les E~s** Hell, the Underworld; (*Prov*) **l'~ est pavé de bonnes intentions** the road to hell is paved with good intentions (*Prov*).

b (*fig*) **cette vie/usine est un ~** this life/factory is (absolute) hell *ou* is (a) hell; **l'~ de la guerre/de l'alcoolisme** the purgatory of war/alcoholism; **vivre un véritable ~** to live a life of hell.

c *[bibliothèque]* forbidden books department.

d **d'~: bruit/vision d'~** hellish *ou* infernal noise/vision; **feu d'~** raging fire; (*Jeux*) **jouer un jeu d'~** to play for high stakes; **chevaucher à un train d'~** to ride hell (*Brit*) *ou* hellbent (*US*) for leather*; **rouler à un train d'~** to tear along at breakneck speed; **c'est d'~!** it's magic!*; **sa copine est d'~*** his girlfriend's smashing* (*Brit*) *ou* cute* (*surtout US*).

2 excl: **~ et damnation!*** hell and damnation!*

enfermement [ɑ̃fɛʀməmɑ̃] nm confinement.

enfermer [ɑ̃fɛʀme] 1 1 vt a (*mettre sous clef*) *enfant puni, témoin gênant* to shut up, lock up; (*par erreur*) to lock in; *prisonnier* to shut up *ou* away, lock up; (***) *aliéné* to lock up*; *objet précieux* to lock away *ou* up; *animaux* to shut up (*dans* in). **~ qch dans** *coffre* to lock sth away *ou* up in; *boîte, sac* to shut sth up *ou* away in; **il est bon à ~ (à l'asile)*** he ought to be locked up* *ou* certified* (*Brit*), he's certifiable* (*Brit*); **il était dans un tel état qu'ils ont dû l'~ à clef dans sa chambre** he was in such a state that they had to lock him in his room; **il faudra l'~ à clef (pour qu'il ne puisse pas sortir)** he'll have to be locked in (so that he can't get out); **ne reste pas enfermé par ce beau temps** don't stay indoors *ou* inside in this lovely weather.

b (*fig littér*) **~ la culture dans une définition trop rigide** to confine *ou* imprison culture within an over-rigid definition; **~ qn dans un dilemme/un cercle vicieux/ses contradictions** to trap sb in a dilemma/in a vicious circle/in his (self-)contradictions; **l'école enferme la créativité dans un carcan de conventions** school traps *ou* imprisons *ou* confines creativity in the strait jacket of convention; **~ le savoir dans des livres inaccessibles** to shut *ou* lock knowledge away in inaccessible books.

c (*littér: contenir, entourer*) to enclose, shut in. **les collines qui enfermaient le vallon** the hills that shut in *ou* enclosed the valley; (*littér*, †) **cette remarque enferme une certaine ironie** this remark contains an element of irony.

d (*Sport*) *concurrent* to hem *ou* box in.

2 **s'enfermer** vpr a (*lit*) to shut o.s. up *ou* in. **il s'est enfermé dans sa chambre** he shut himself away *ou* up in his room; **s'~ à clef** to lock o.s. away *ou* up *ou* in; **zut, je me suis enfermé!** (*à l'intérieur*) dash it, I've locked myself in!; (*à l'extérieur*) dash it, I've locked myself out!; **il s'est enfermé à clef dans son bureau** he has locked himself (away *ou* up) in his office; **ils se sont enfermés dans le bureau pour discuter** they have closeted themselves in the office *ou* shut themselves away in the office to have a discussion; **elle s'enferme toute la journée** she stays shut up indoors all day long.

b (*fig*) **s'~ dans un mutisme absolu** to retreat into absolute silence; **s'~ dans un rôle/une attitude** to stick to a role/an attitude; **s'~ dans sa décision/position** to keep *ou* stick stubbornly *ou* rigidly to one's decision/position; **s'~ dans un système** to lock o.s. into a rigid pattern of behaviour.

enferrer (s') [ɑ̃fere] 1 vpr a (*s'embrouiller*) to tie o.s. up in knots*. **s'~ dans ses contradictions/ses mensonges** to tie *ou* tangle o.s. up in one's own contradictions/one's lies, ensnare o.s. in the mesh of one's own contradictions/lies; **s'~ dans une analyse/une explication** to tie o.s. up in knots* trying to make an analysis/trying to explain; **il s'enferre de plus en plus** he's getting himself in more and more of a mess *ou* into deeper and deeper water. b (*s'empaler*) **s'~ sur** to spike o.s. on.

enfiévré, e [ɑ̃fjevʀe] (ptp de **enfiévrer**) adj feverish.

enfiévrer [ɑ̃fjevʀe] 6 vt a *imagination* to fire, stir up; *esprits* to rouse; *assistance* to inflame, rouse. b *malade* to make feverish; *visage, joues* to inflame.

enfilade [ɑ̃filad] nf (*série*) **une ~ de maisons** a row *ou* string of houses; **une ~ de colonnes/couloirs** a row *ou* series of columns/corridors; (*fig littér*) **une ~ de phrases/lieux communs** a string of sentences/commonplaces; **pièces/couloirs en ~** series of linked rooms/corridors; **maisons en ~** houses in a row; **prendre en ~** *boulevards* to go from one to the next; (*Mil*) *objectif* to rake, enfilade (*SPÉC*).

enfiler [ɑ̃file] 1 1 vt a *aiguille* to thread; *perles* to string, thread. **on n'est pas là pour ~ des perles*** let's get on with it*, let's get down to it* *ou* to business; **~ des anneaux sur une tringle** to slip rings onto a rod.

b (**: passer*) *vêtement* to slip on, put on.

c (**: fourrer*) **~ un objet dans** to stick* *ou* shove* an object into.

d (*s'engager dans*) *ruelle, chemin* to take; *corridor* to enter, take. **au carrefour il tourna à gauche et enfila la rue de la Gare** at the crossroads he turned left into Rue de la Gare *ou* he turned left and took the Rue de la Gare.

e (**: *sexuellement*) to screw**, shag** (*Brit*).

2 **s'enfiler** vpr a (*s'engager dans*) **s'~ dans** *escalier, couloir, ruelle* to disappear into.

b (*: *s'envoyer*) *verre de vin* to knock back*, down*; *nourriture* to guzzle*, down*; *corvée* to land o.s. with*, get lumbered with* (*Brit*) *ou* landed with*.

enfin [ɑ̃fɛ̃] adv a (*à la fin, finalement*) at last, finally. **il y est ~ arrivé** he has at last *ou* finally succeeded, he has succeeded at last; **quand va-t-il ~ y arriver?** when is he finally going to *ou* when on earth is he going to manage it?; **~, après bien des efforts, ils y arrivèrent** at (long) last *ou* at length *ou* eventually, after much effort, they managed it, after much effort they finally *ou* eventually managed it; **~ seuls!** alone at last!; **~, ils se sont décidés!** they've made up their minds at last!; **~ ça va commencer!** at long last it's going to begin!

b (*en dernier lieu*) lastly, finally. **on y trouvait des fougères, des noisetiers, des framboisiers, ~ des champignons de toutes sortes** there were ferns, hazel trees, raspberry bushes and lastly *ou* finally all kinds of fungi; **... ensuite des manuels et des ouvrages de référence, ~ et surtout, des dictionnaires** ... and next manuals and reference works, and last but not least *ou* and last but by no means least, dictionaries.

c (*en conclusion*) in short, in a word. **rien n'était prêt, tous les invités se bousculaient, ~ (bref), la vraie pagaïe!** nothing was ready, the guests were all jostling each other – in short *ou* in a word, it was absolute chaos! *ou* it was absolute chaos, in fact!

d (*restrictif: disons, ou plutôt*) well. **elle était assez grosse, ~, potelée** she was rather fat, well (let's say *ou* at least), chubby; **pas exactement, ~, dans un sens, oui** not exactly, well – in a way, yes.

e (*somme toute*) after all. **c'est un élève qui, ~, n'est pas bête et pourrait** ... this pupil is not stupid, after all, and could ...; **c'est une méthode qui, ~, a fait ses preuves, et j'estime que** ... it is, after all, a well-tried method, and I believe that ... .

f (*toutefois*) still. **~, si ça vous plaît/si vous le voulez, prenez-le** still, if you like it/if you want it, take it; **moi je veux bien, ~ ...!** I don't mind, but ...! *ou* still ...!

g (*valeur exclamative*) **~! que veux-tu y faire!** anyway *ou* still, what can you do!; **~, tu aurais pu le faire!** all the same *ou* even so, you could have done it!; **(mais) ~! je viens de te le dire!** but I've just told you!, (but) for goodness sake*, I've just told you!; **~! un grand garçon comme toi!** come now *ou* come, come, a big boy like you!; **c'est son père, ~!** he is his father, after all!

h **mais ~** but; **j'irai, mais ~ ce ne sera pas de gaieté de cœur** I'll go, but not willingly; **car ~** because; **je ne pense pas qu'il voudra sortir ce soir, car ~ il vient juste d'arriver** I don't think he'll want to go out tonight, since *ou* because (after all) he has only just arrived.

enflammé, e [ɑ̃flɑme] (ptp de **enflammer**) adj a *allumette, torche, paille* burning, blazing, ablaze (*attrib*); *ciel* ablaze (*attrib*), blazing, flaming. b *visage, yeux* blazing, ablaze (*attrib*); *caractère* fiery, ardent, passionate; *esprit* afire (*attrib*), burning, on fire (*attrib*); *paroles* inflamed, fiery, ardent; *déclaration* impassioned, passionate, ardent. c *plaie* inflamed.

enflammer [ɑ̃flɑme] [1] 1 vt a (*mettre le feu à*) *bois* to set on fire, set fire to; *allumette* to strike; (*fig littér*) *ciel* to set ablaze. b (*exciter*) *visage, regard* to set ablaze; *colère, désir, foule* to inflame; *imagination* to fire, kindle; *esprit* to set on fire. c *plaie* to inflame. 2 **s'enflammer** vpr a (*prendre feu*) *[bois]* to catch fire, ignite. **le bois sec s'enflamme bien** dry wood catches fire *ou* ignites *ou* kindles easily.

b (*fig*) *[visage, regard]* to blaze; *[sentiment, désir]* to flare up; *[imagination]* to be fired; *[orateur]* to become inflamed *ou* impassioned. **s'~ (de colère)** to flare up (in anger).

enflé, e [ɑ̃fle] (ptp de **enfler**) 1 adj a (*lit*) swollen. b (*fig*) *style* bombastic, turgid. c († *fig*) **~ d'orgueil** puffed up *ou* swollen with pride. 2 nm,f (*: *imbécile*) twit*, clot* (*Brit*), jerk*.

enfler [ɑ̃fle] [1] 1 vt a *membre* to cause to swell (up), make swell (up); (*littér*) *voiles* to fill, swell; (*littér*) *fleuve* to (cause to) swell; *voix* to raise; *addition, facture* to inflate. **~ son style** to adopt a bombastic *ou* turgid style. b (*: *voler*) **~ qn** to diddle* *ou* do* sb (*de* out of); **se faire ~ de 10 F*** to be done out of 10 francs*. 2 vi (*lit*) *[membre]* to become swollen, swell (up); (*: *prendre du poids*) to fill out. 3 **s'enfler** vpr a *[voix]* to rise; *[style]* to become bombastic *ou* turgid; *[son]* to swell. b (*littér*) *[fleuve]* to swell, become swollen; *[vagues]* to surge, swell; *[voiles]* to fill (out), swell (out).

enflure [ɑ̃flyʀ] nf a (*Méd*) swelling. b *[style]* turgidity. c (*: *imbécile*) twit* (*Brit*), clot* (*Brit*), jerk* (*US*).

enfoiré, e* [ɑ̃fwaʀe] nm,f silly sod*, bungling idiot.

enfoncé, e [ɑ̃fɔ̃se] (ptp de **enfoncer**) adj *yeux* deep-set; *recoin* deep. **il avait la tête ~e dans les épaules** his head was sunk between his shoulders.

enfoncement [ɑ̃fɔ̃smɑ̃] nm a (*action d'enfoncer*) *[pieu]* driving in; *[porte]* breaking down *ou* open; *[lignes ennemies]* breaking through. (*Méd*) **il souffre d'un ~ de la cage thoracique/de la boîte crânienne** he has crushed ribs/a fractured skull. b (*action de s'enfoncer*) *[sol]* giving way; *[fondations]* sinking. **cet ~ progressif dans le vice/la misère** this gradual sinking into vice/poverty. c (*recoin*) *[mur]* recess, nook. **dissimulé dans un ~ de la muraille** hidden in a recess *ou* nook in the wall; **chalet enfoui dans un ~ du vallon** chalet tucked away in a corner of the valley.

enfoncer [ɑ̃fɔ̃se] [3] 1 vt a (*faire pénétrer*) *pieu, clou* to drive (well) in; *épingle, punaise* to stick (well) in, push (well) in. **~ un pieu dans** to drive a stake in(to); **~ une épingle dans** to stick *ou* push a pin in(to); **~ un couteau/une épée dans** to thrust *ou* plunge a knife/a sword into; **~ qch à coups de marteau** to hammer sth in, knock sth in with a hammer; (*fig*) **~ le clou** to hammer it in, din it in* (*Brit*), drive the point home.

b (*mettre*) **~ les mains dans ses poches** to thrust *ou* dig one's hands (deep) into one's pockets; **~ son chapeau jusqu'aux yeux** to ram *ou* pull one's hat (right) down over one's eyes; **il lui enfonça sa canne dans les côtes** he prodded *ou* poked *ou* stuck him in the ribs with his walking stick; (*fig*) **qui a bien pu lui ~ ça dans le crâne?** *ou* **la tête?** who on earth put *ou* got that into his head?; **~ qn dans la misère/le désespoir** to plunge sb into poverty/despair; **ça les a enfoncés davantage dans les frais** that involved them in *ou* plunged them into even greater expense.

c (*défoncer*) *porte* to break open *ou* down; *devant, arrière d'un véhicule* to smash in; (*fig*) *lignes ennemies* to break through. **~ le plancher** to make the floor give way *ou* cave in, cause the floor to give way *ou* cave in; **le choc lui a enfoncé la cage thoracique/les côtes** the blow smashed his rib cage/his ribs; **il a eu les côtes enfoncées** he had his ribs broken, his ribs were broken *ou* smashed; **le devant de sa voiture a été enfoncé** the front of his car has been smashed *ou* bashed* in; (*fig*) **~ une porte ouverte** *ou* **des portes ouvertes** to labour an obvious point; **c'est ~ une porte ouverte que d'affirmer** ... it's a statement of the obvious to say ... .

d (*) (*battre*) to beat hollow*, hammer*; (*surpasser*) to lick*. **ils se sont fait ~!** they got beaten hollow!*, they got hammered!*; **il les enfonce tous** he has got them all licked*; (*causer la perte de*) **elle a cherché à ~ son complice** she tried to put all the blame on her accomplice; **l'examinateur a voulu ~ le candidat** the examiner tried to destroy the candidate.

2 vi a (*pénétrer*) to sink in. **attention, on enfonce ici** careful, you'll sink in here; **on enfonçait dans la neige jusqu'aux cuisses** we sank up to our thighs in *ou* sank thigh-deep in(to) the snow.

b (*céder*) *[sol]* to yield. **ça enfonce sous le poids du corps** it yields beneath the weight of the body.

3 **s'enfoncer** vpr a *[lame, projectile]* **s'~ dans** to plunge *ou* sink into; **la lame s'enfonça dans sa poitrine** the blade plunged *ou* sank into his chest; **l'éclat d'obus s'enfonça dans le mur** the shell fragment embedded itself in the wall.

b (*disparaître*) (*dans l'eau, la vase etc*) to sink (*dans* into, in). (*fig*) **s'~ dans** *forêt, rue, l'ombre* to disappear into; *fauteuil, coussins* to sink deep into, sink back in(to); *misère* to sink into, be plunged into; *vice, rêverie* to plunge into, sink into; **il s'enfonça dans la brume** he disappeared into the mist; **chemin qui s'enfonce dans les bois** path which disappears into the woods; **je le regardais s'~, impuissant à le secourir** I watched him sinking (in), powerless to help him; **s'~ sous les couvertures** to bury o.s. under *ou* snuggle down under the covers; **il s'est enfoncé jusqu'au cou dans une sale histoire** he's up to his neck in a nasty bit of business; **à mentir, tu ne fais que t'~ davantage** by lying, you're just getting yourself into deeper and deeper water *ou* into more and more of a mess.

c (*céder*) to give way. **le sol s'enfonce sous nos pas** the ground is giving way *ou* caving in beneath us; **les coussins s'enfoncent sous son poids** the cushions sink under his weight.

d (*faire pénétrer*) **s'~ une arête dans la gorge** to get a bone stuck in one's throat; **s'~ une aiguille dans la main** to stick *ou* run a needle into one's hand; **enfoncez-vous bien ça dans le crâne*** now get this firmly into your head.

enfonceur, -euse [ɑ̃fɔ̃sœʀ, øz] nm,f (*hum*) **c'est un ~ de porte(s) ouverte(s)** he's always labouring the obvious.

enfouir [ɑ̃fwiʀ] [2] 1 vt to bury (*dans* in). **il l'a enfoui dans sa poche** he tucked it (away) in his pocket; **chalet enfoui dans la neige** chalet buried away in the snow. 2 **s'enfouir** vpr: **s'~ dans/sous** to bury o.s. (*ou* itself) in/under; **s'~ sous les draps** to bury o.s. *ou* burrow beneath the covers.

enfouissement [ɑ̃fwismɑ̃] nm burying.

enfourcher [ɑ̃fuʀʃe] [1] vt *cheval* to mount; *bicyclette* to mount, get astride. (*fig*) **~ son dada** to get on one's hobby-horse.

enfourner [ɑ̃fuʀne] [1] 1 vt a *aliment* to put in the oven; *poterie* to put in the kiln. b (*: *avaler*) to guzzle down, put away*. c (*: *enfoncer*) **~ qch dans** to shove* *ou* stuff* sth into. 2 **s'enfourner** vpr: **s'~ dans** *[personne]* to dive into; *[foule]* to rush into.

enfreindre [ɑ̃fʀɛ̃dʀ] [52] vt (*frm*) to infringe, break.

enfuir (s') [ɑ̃fɥiʀ] [17] vpr (*se sauver*) to run away, run off, flee (*littér*) (*chez, dans* to); (*s'échapper*) to run away, escape (*de* from); (*littér*) *[temps, souffrance]* to fly away (*littér*), flee (*littér*).

enfumer [ɑ̃fyme] [1] vt *pièce* to fill with smoke; *personne, renard, ruche* to smoke out. **atmosphère/pièce enfumée** smoky atmosphere/room; **tu nous enfumes avec ta cigarette** you're smoking us out.

enfutailler [ɑ̃fytaje], **enfûter** [ɑ̃fyte] [1] vt to cask.

engagé, e [ɑ̃gaʒe] (ptp de **engager**) 1 adj a *écrivain, littérature* committed. (*Pol*) **non ~** uncommitted. b (*Archit*) *colonne* engaged. 2 nm a (*Mil*) (*soldat*) enlisted man. **~ volontaire** volunteer. b (*Sport*) (*coureur*) entrant, competitor; (*cheval*) runner.

engageant, e [ɑ̃gaʒɑ̃, ɑ̃t] adj *air, sourire* engaging, winning, appealing, prepossessing; *proposition* attractive, appealing, tempting; *repas, gâteau* tempting, inviting. **il eut des paroles ~es** he spoke winningly.

engagement [ɑ̃gaʒmɑ̃] nm a (*promesse*) agreement, commitment, promise. **sans ~ de votre part** without obligation *ou* commitment on your part; **signer un ~** to sign an agreement; **prendre l'~ de** to make a commitment to, undertake to; **manquer à ses ~s** to fail to honour one's agreements, fail to keep one's promises; **faire face à ses ~s** to fulfil one's commitments *ou* promises.
b (*Théât: contrat*) engagement. **artiste sans ~** out of work artist(e).
c (*embauche*) *[ouvrier]* taking on, engaging.
d (*Fin*) *[capitaux]* investing; *[dépenses]* incurring. **~s financiers** financial commitments *ou* liabilities; **cela a nécessité l'~ de nouveaux frais** this meant committing further funds; **faire face à ses ~s (financiers)** to meet one's (financial) commitments.
e (*amorce*) *[débat, négociations]* opening, start.
f (*Sport*) (*inscription*) entry; (*coup d'envoi*) kick-off; (*Boxe*) attack; (*Escrime*) engagement. **réclamer un grand ~ physique** to be physically very demanding.
g (*Mil*) *[recrues]* enlistment; *[combat]* engaging; *[troupes fraîches]* throwing in, engaging. **tué dans un ~** killed in an engagement.
h (*Littérat, Pol: prise de position*) commitment (*dans* to). **politique de non-~** policy of non-commitment.
i (*mise en gage*) *[montre etc]* pawning.
j (*encouragement*) encouragement. **c'est un ~ à persévérer** it encourages one to persevere.
k (*introduction*) *[clef]* introduction, insertion (*dans* in, into); *[voiture]* entry (*dans* into).
l (*Méd*) *[fœtus]* engagement.

engager [ɑ̃gaʒe] 3 1 vt a (*lier*) to bind, commit. **nos promesses nous engagent** we are bound to honour our promises, our promises are binding on us; **ça l'engagerait trop** that would commit him too far; **ça n'engage à rien** it doesn't commit you to anything; **~ sa parole *ou* son honneur** to give *ou* pledge (*frm*) one's word (of honour).
b (*embaucher*) *ouvrier* to take on, hire; *artiste* to engage. **je vous engage (à mon service)** you've got the job, I'm taking you on, you're hired.
c (*entraîner*) to involve. **ça l'a engagé dans de gros frais** that involved him in great expense; **ils l'ont engagé dans une affaire douteuse** they got him involved in a shady deal; **le pays est engagé dans une politique d'inflation** the country is pursuing an inflationary policy.
d (*encourager*) **~ qn à faire qch** to urge *ou* encourage sb to do sth; **je vous engage à la circonspection** I advise you to be (very) cautious.
e (*introduire*) to insert (*dans* in, into); (*Naut*) *ancre* to foul. **il engagea sa clef dans la serrure** he fitted *ou* inserted his key into the lock; **~ sa voiture dans une ruelle** to enter a lane, drive into a lane; (*Aut*) **c'était à lui de passer puisqu'il était engagé** it was up to him to go since he had already pulled out.
f (*amorcer*) *discussion* to open, start (up), get under way; *négociations* to enter into *ou* upon; (*Jur*) *procédure, poursuites* to institute (*contre* against). **~ la conversation** to engage in conversation, start up a conversation (*avec* with); **l'affaire semble bien/mal engagée** things seem to have got off to a good/bad start.
g (*Fin*) (*mettre en gage*) to pawn, put in pawn; (*investir*) to invest, lay out.
h (*Sport*) *concurrents* to enter. **15 chevaux sont engagés dans cette course** 15 horses are running in this race; **~ la partie** to begin the match; **la partie est bien engagée** the match is well under way.
i (*Mil*) *recrues* to enlist; *troupes fraîches* to throw in, engage. **~ le combat contre l'ennemi** to engage the enemy, join battle with the enemy†; **~ toutes ses forces dans la bataille** to throw all one's troops into the battle.
2 **s'engager** vpr a (*promettre*) to commit o.s. **s'~ à faire** to commit o.s. to doing, undertake *ou* promise to do; **il n'a pas voulu s'~ trop** he didn't want to commit himself (too far), he didn't want to stick his neck out too far; **sais-tu à quoi tu t'engages?** do you know what you're letting yourself in for?, do you know what you're committing yourself to?
b (*s'embaucher*) to take a job (*chez* with). **il s'est engagé comme garçon de courses** he took a job as an errand boy, he got himself taken on as an errand boy.
c **s'~ dans** *frais* to incur; *discussion, pourparlers* to enter into; *affaire, entreprise* to become involved in; **le pays s'engage dans une politique dangereuse** the country is embarking on a dangerous policy *ou* is steering a dangerous course.
d (*s'emboîter*) **s'~ dans** to engage into, fit into; (*pénétrer*) **s'~ dans** *[véhicule]* to enter, turn into; *[piéton]* to take, turn into; **s'~ sur la chaussée** to step (out) onto the road; **la voiture s'engagea sous le pont** the car drove under the bridge; **j'avais la priorité puisque j'étais engagé (dans la rue)** I had (the) right of way since I had already pulled out *ou* drawn out (into the main street).
e (*s'amorcer*) *[pourparlers]* to begin, start (up), get under way. **une conversation s'engagea entre eux** they started up a conversation.
f (*Sport*) to enter (one's name) (*dans* for).
g (*Mil*) *[recrues]* to enlist. **s'~ dans l'armée de l'air** to join the air force; **le combat s'engagea avec vigueur** the fight began briskly; **des troupes fraîches s'engagèrent dans la bataille** fresh troops were thrown into the battle *ou* were brought in.
h (*Littérat, Pol: prendre position*) to commit o.s.

engazonner [ɑ̃gɑzɔne] 1 vt *terrain* to turf.

engeance† [ɑ̃ʒɑ̃s] nf (*péj*) mob, crew.

engelure [ɑ̃ʒlyʀ] nf chilblain.

engendrement [ɑ̃ʒɑ̃dʀəmɑ̃] nm *[enfant]* begetting, fathering.

engendrer [ɑ̃ʒɑ̃dʀe] 1 vt a (*frm*) *enfant* to beget, father. b (*Ling, Math, Phys*) to generate. c *colère, dispute* to breed, create; *malheurs* to breed, create, engender (*frm*). **ils/ses films n'engendrent pas la mélancolie** they/his films are (always) a good laugh*.

engin [ɑ̃ʒɛ̃] 1 nm (*machine*) machine; (*outil*) instrument, tool; (*Aut*) heavy vehicle; (*Aviat*) aircraft; (*: *objet*) contraption*, gadget. **attention sortie d'~s** heavy plant crossing, beware lorries turning (*Brit*). 2 comp ►**engin balistique** ballistic missile ►**engin blindé** armoured vehicle ►**engin explosif** explosive device ►**engins de guerre†** engines of war († *ou littér*) ►**engin non identifié** unidentified flying object ►**engins (spéciaux)** missiles ►**engin de terrassement** earth-mover.

englober [ɑ̃glɔbe] 1 vt (*inclure*) to include, encompass (*dans* in); (*annexer*) to take in, annexe, incorporate.

engloutir [ɑ̃glutiʀ] 2 1 vt *nourriture* to gobble up, gulp *ou* wolf down; *navire* to engulf, swallow up; *fortune [personne]* to devour, run through; *[dépenses]* to eat *ou* swallow up. **qu'est-ce qu'il peut ~!*** it's amazing what he puts away!*, the amount of food he stuffs in is quite incredible!*; **la ville a été engloutie par un tremblement de terre** the town was swallowed up *ou* engulfed in *ou* by an earthquake. 2 **s'engloutir** vpr *[navire]* to be engulfed.

engloutissement [ɑ̃glutismɑ̃] nm (*voir* **engloutir**) gobbling up; engulfing; devouring.

engluer [ɑ̃glye] 1 1 vt *arbre, oiseau* to lime. 2 **s'engluer** vpr *[oiseau]* to get caught *ou* stuck in (bird) lime. **s'~ les doigts** to get one's fingers sticky; (*fig*) **s'~ dans ses problèmes/une situation** to get bogged down in one's problems/a situation.

engoncer [ɑ̃gɔ̃se] 3 vt (*gén ptp*) to restrict, cramp. **ce manteau l'engonce** he looks cramped in that coat, that coat restricts his movements; **engoncé dans ses vêtements** (looking) cramped in his clothes; **le cou engoncé dans un gros col** his neck (stiffly) encased in a big collar.

engorgement [ɑ̃gɔʀʒəmɑ̃] nm *[tuyau]* obstruction, clogging, blocking (*de* of); (*Méd*) engorgement; (*Comm*) glut (*de* in).

engorger [ɑ̃gɔʀʒe] 3 1 vt *tuyau* to obstruct, clog, block; (*Méd*) to engorge; (*Comm*) to glut. 2 **s'engorger** vpr *[tuyau]* to become blocked; (*Comm*) *[marché]* to become glutted.

engouement [ɑ̃gumɑ̃] nm (*pour qn*) infatuation, fancy (*pour* for); (*pour qch*) fad, craze (*pour* for). **~ passager** passing fancy; brief craze.

engouer (s') [ɑ̃gwe] 1 vpr: **s'~ de *ou* pour qch** to develop a passion for sth; **s'~ de qn** to become infatuated with sb.

engouffrer [ɑ̃gufʀe] 1 1 vt *charbon* to shovel (*dans* into); (*) *fortune* to swallow up, devour; (*) *nourriture* to gobble up, gulp down, wolf down; *navire* to swallow up, engulf. **qu'est-ce qu'il peut ~!*** it's amazing what he puts away!* *ou* stuffs in!* 2 **s'engouffrer** vpr *[vent]* to rush, sweep; *[flot, foule]* to surge, rush; *[personne]* to rush, dive; *[navire]* to sink (*dans* into).

engoulevent [ɑ̃gulvɑ̃] nm: **~ (d'Europe)** nightjar; **~ (d'Amérique)** nighthawk.

engourdi, e [ɑ̃guʀdi] (ptp de **engourdir**) adj *membre* numb; *esprit* dull, dulled.

engourdir [ɑ̃guʀdiʀ] 2 1 vt a *membres* to numb, make numb. **être engourdi par le froid** *membre* to be numb with cold; *animal* to be sluggish with the cold; **j'ai la main engourdie** my hand is numb *ou* has gone to sleep *ou* gone dead. b *esprit* to dull, blunt; *douleur* to deaden, dull. **la chaleur et le vin l'engourdissaient** the heat and the wine were making him sleepy *ou* drowsy. 2 **s'engourdir** vpr *[corps]* to become *ou* go numb; *[bras, jambe]* to become *ou* go numb, go to sleep, go dead; *[esprit]* to grow dull *ou* sluggish.

engourdissement [ɑ̃guʀdismɑ̃] nm a (*état*) *[membre, corps]* numbness; *[esprit]* (*torpeur*) sleepiness, drowsiness; (*affaiblissement*) dullness. b (*action: voir* **engourdir**) numbing; dulling.

engrais [ɑ̃gʀɛ] nm a (*chimique*) fertilizer; (*animal*) manure. **~ vert** green manure; **~ azoté** nitrate fertilizer, nitrate. b (*engraissement*) **mettre un animal à l'~** to fatten up an animal.

engraissement [ɑ̃gʀɛsmɑ̃] nm, **engraissage** [ɑ̃gʀɛsaʒ] nm *[bœufs]* fattening (up); *[volailles]* cramming.

engraisser [ɑ̃gʀese] 1 1 vt *volailles* to cram; *bétail* to fatten (up); *terre* to manure, fertilize; (‡) *personne* to fatten up. **quel pique-assiette, c'est nous qui devons l'~‡** we seem to be expected to feed this scrounger* *ou* provide for this scrounger*; **l'État s'engraisse sur le dos du contribuable** the state grows fat at the taxpayer's expense; ~ **l'État*** to enrich the state. 2 **vi** (*) *[personne]* to get fat(ter), put on weight.

engrangement [ɑ̃gʀɑ̃ʒmɑ̃] **nm** *[foin]* gathering in, garnering (*littér*).

engranger [ɑ̃gʀɑ̃ʒe] 3 **vt** *foin, moisson* to gather *ou* get in, garner (*littér*); *bénéfices* to reap, rake in*; *connaissances* to amass, store (up).

engrenage [ɑ̃gʀənaʒ] **nm** gears, gearing; (*fig: d'événements*) chain. ~ **à chevrons** double helical gearing; (*fig*) **quand on est pris dans l'~** when one is caught up in the system; **l'~ de la violence** the spiral of violence; *voir* **doigt**.

engrener [ɑ̃gʀəne] 5 1 **vt** a *roues dentées* to engage; (*fig*) *personne* to catch up (*dans* in), draw (*dans* into). (*fig*) ~ **l'affaire** to set the thing going *ou* in motion. b (*remplir de grain*) to feed *ou* fill with grain. 2 **s'engrener vpr** *[roues dentées]* to mesh (*dans* with), gear (*dans* into).

engrosser‡ [ɑ̃gʀose] 1 **vt:** ~ **qn** to knock sb up**, get sb pregnant; **se faire** ~ to get (o.s.) knocked up**, get (o.s.) pregnant (*par* by).

engueulade‡ [ɑ̃gœlad] **nf** (*dispute*) row*, slanging match* (*Brit*); (*réprimande*) bawling out‡, rocket‡ (*Brit*). **passer une** ~ **à qn** to bawl sb out‡, give sb a rocket‡ (*Brit*); **avoir une** ~ **avec qn** to have a row* *ou* slanging match* (*Brit*) with sb; **lettre d'~** stinking letter‡.

engueuler‡ [ɑ̃gœle] 1 1 **vt:** ~ **qn** to give sb a rocket‡ (*Brit*), bawl sb out‡; **se faire** ~ to get bawled out‡, get a rocket‡ (*Brit*); *voir* **poisson**. 2 **s'engueuler vpr** to have a slanging match* (*Brit*) *ou* row* (*avec* with).

enguirlander [ɑ̃giʀlɑ̃de] 1 **vt** a (*) ~ **qn** to give sb a telling-off* *ou* ticking-off*, tear sb off a strip‡ (*Brit*); **se faire** ~ to get a telling-off* *ou* ticking-off*, get torn off a strip‡ (*Brit*). b (*orner*) to garland.

enhardir [ɑ̃aʀdiʀ] 2 1 **vt** to make bolder. **enhardi par** emboldened by. 2 **s'enhardir vpr** to become *ou* get bolder. **s'~ (jusqu')à dire** to make so bold as to say, be bold enough to say.

enharmonique [ɑ̃naʀmɔnik] **adj** enharmonic.

énième [ɛnjɛm] **adj** = **nième**.

énigmatique [enigmatik] **adj** enigmatic.

énigmatiquement [enigmatikmɑ̃] **adv** enigmatically.

énigme [enigm] **nf** (*mystère*) enigma, riddle; (*jeu*) riddle, puzzle. **tu es une** ~ **pour moi** you are an enigma to *ou* for me; **trouver la clef** *ou* **le mot de l'~** to find the key *ou* clue to the puzzle *ou* riddle; **parler par ~s** to speak in riddles.

enivrant, e [ɑ̃nivʀɑ̃, ɑ̃t] **adj** *parfum, vin, succès* heady, intoxicating; *beauté* intoxicating; *vitesse* intoxicating, dizzying.

enivrement [ɑ̃nivʀəmɑ̃] **nm** *[personne]* (†: *ivresse*) intoxication; (*fig: exaltation*) elation, exhilaration. **l'~ du succès** the intoxication of success.

enivrer [ɑ̃nivʀe] 1 1 **vt** (*lit*) to intoxicate, make drunk; (*fig*) to intoxicate. **le parfum m'enivrait** I was intoxicated by the perfume. 2 **s'enivrer vpr** (*lit*) to get drunk (*de* on), become intoxicated (*de* with); (*fig*) to become intoxicated (*de* with). **il passe son temps à s'~** he spends all his time getting drunk; **s'~ de mots** to get drunk on words; **enivré de succès** intoxicated with *ou* by success.

enjambée [ɑ̃ʒɑ̃be] **nf** stride. **d'une** ~ in a stride; **faire de grandes ~s** to stride out, take big *ou* long strides; **il allait à grandes ~s vers ...** he was striding (along) towards ... .

enjambement [ɑ̃ʒɑ̃bmɑ̃] **nm** (*Littérat*) enjambement.

enjamber [ɑ̃ʒɑ̃be] 1 **vt** *obstacle* to stride *ou* step over; *fossé* to step *ou* stride across; *[pont]* to span, straddle, stretch across. **il enjamba la rampe et s'assit dessus** he sat down astride the banister.

enjeu, pl **~x** [ɑ̃ʒø] **nm** *[pari, guerre]* stake, stakes (*de* in). **quel est l'~ de la bataille?** what is at stake in the battle?, what are the battle stakes?

enjoindre [ɑ̃ʒwɛ̃dʀ] 49 **vt** (*frm*) ~ **à qn de faire** to enjoin *ou* charge sb to do (*frm*).

enjôlement [ɑ̃ʒolmɑ̃] **nm** bewitching.

enjôler [ɑ̃ʒole] 1 **vt** (*ensorceler*) to bewitch; (*amadouer*) get round. **elle a si bien su l'~ qu'il a accepté** she coaxed *ou* wheedled *ou* cajoled him into accepting it.

enjôleur, -euse [ɑ̃ʒolœʀ, øz] 1 **adj** *sourire, paroles* coaxing, wheedling, winning. 2 **nm,f** (*charmeur*) coaxer, wheedler; (*escroc*) twister. 3 **enjôleuse nf** (*séductrice*) wily woman.

enjolivement [ɑ̃ʒɔlivmɑ̃] **nm** (*voir* **enjoliver**) (*action*) ornamenting, embellishment, adornment; embroidering; (*détail*) ornament, embellishment, adornment. **les ~s apportés aux faits par le narrateur** the embellishments lent to the facts by the narrator.

enjoliver [ɑ̃ʒɔlive] 1 **vt** *objet* to ornament, embellish, adorn; *réalité, récit* to embroider, embellish, dress up.

enjoliveur [ɑ̃ʒɔlivœʀ] **nm** (*Aut*) hub cap.

enjolivure [ɑ̃ʒɔlivyʀ] **nf** = **enjolivement**.

enjoué, e [ɑ̃ʒwe] **adj** cheerful. **d'un ton** ~ cheerfully, in a cheerful way.

enjouement [ɑ̃ʒumɑ̃] **nm** cheerfulness.

enkystement [ɑ̃kistəmɑ̃] **nm** encystment.

enkyster (s') [ɑ̃kiste] 1 **vpr** to encyst.

enlacement [ɑ̃lasmɑ̃] **nm** (*étreinte*) embrace; (*enchevêtrement*) intertwining, interlacing.

enlacer [ɑ̃lase] 3 1 **vt** a (*étreindre*) to embrace, clasp, hug. **le danseur enlaça sa cavalière** the dancer put his arm round his partner's waist.
b (*enchevêtrer*) *fils* to intertwine, interlace.
c (*entourer*) *[lianes]* to wind round, enlace, entwine.
2 **s'enlacer vpr** a *[amants]* to embrace, hug each other; *[lutteurs, guerriers]* to take hold of each other, clasp each other. **amoureux enlacés** lovers clasped in each other's arms *ou* clasped in a fond embrace.
b (*s'entrecroiser*) to intertwine, interlace. **fils inextricablement enlacés** hopelessly tangled *ou* intertwined threads; **des petites rues qui s'enlacent** side streets which twine *ou* wind in and out of each other.
c *[lianes]* **s'~ autour de** to twine round, wind round.

enlaidir [ɑ̃lediʀ] 2 1 **vt** to make ugly. **cette coiffure l'enlaidit** that hair style makes her look very plain *ou* rather ugly. 2 **vi** *[personne]* to become ugly.

enlaidissement [ɑ̃ledismɑ̃] **nm: l'~ du paysage par les usines** the ruining *ou* defacing of the countryside by factories.

enlevé, e [ɑ̃l(ə)ve] (**ptp de enlever**) **adj** *récit* spirited; *scène, morceau de musique* played with spirit *ou* brio; *voir* **trot**.

enlèvement [ɑ̃lɛvmɑ̃] **nm** a *[personne]* kidnapping, abduction. ~ **de bébé** babysnatching; **l'~ des Sabines** the Rape of the Sabine Women. b *[meuble, objet]* removal, taking *ou* carrying away; (*Méd*) *[organe]* removal; *[ordures]* collection, clearing (away); *[bagages, marchandises]* collection. c (*Mil*) *[position]* capture, taking.

enlever [ɑ̃l(ə)ve] 5 1 **vt** a (*gén*) to remove; *couvercle* to remove, lift (off); *meuble* to remove, take away; *étiquette* to remove, take off; *tache* to remove, take off, take out; (*en brossant ou lavant etc*) to brush *ou* wash *etc* out *ou* off; *tapis* to take up, remove; *lustre, tableau* to take down; *peau de fruit* to take off, peel off, remove; (*Méd*) *organe* to remove, take out. **enlève tes mains de tes poches/de là** take your hands out of your pockets/off there, remove your hands from your pockets/ from there; ~ **le couvert** to clear the table; **enlève tes coudes de la table** take your elbows off the table.
b *vêtements* to take off, remove. **il enleva son chapeau pour dire bonjour** he took his hat off *ou* raised his hat in greeting; **j'enlève ma robe pour mettre quelque chose de plus confortable** I'll just slip out of this dress into something more comfortable, I'll just take off this dress and put on something more comfortable.
c ~ **à qn** *courage* to rob sb of; *espoir* to deprive sb of, rob sb of; *objet, argent* to take (away) from sb; **on lui a enlevé son commandement** he was relieved of his command; **on lui a enlevé la garde de l'enfant** the child was taken *ou* removed from his care; **ça lui enlèvera peut-être le goût de recommencer** perhaps that'll cure him of trying that again, perhaps that'll make him think twice before he does it again; **ça n'enlève rien à son mérite** that doesn't in any way detract from his worth; **pour vous ~ tout scrupule** in order to allay your scruples, in order to dispel your misgivings.
d (*emporter*) *objet, meuble* to take away, carry away, remove; *ordures* to collect, clear (away). **il a fait ~ ses vieux meubles** he had his old furniture taken away; **il fut enlevé dans les airs** he was borne (up) *ou* lifted (up) into the air; (*frm*) **il a été enlevé par un mal foudroyant** he was borne off by a sudden illness; (*littér*) **la mort nous l'a enlevé** death has snatched *ou* taken him from us.
e (*kidnapper*) to kidnap, abduct. **se faire ~ par son amant** to elope with one's lover, be carried off by one's lover; (*hum*) **je vous enlève votre femme pour quelques instants** I'll just steal *ou* borrow your wife for a moment (if I may) (*hum*).
f (*remporter*) *victoire* to win; (*Mil*) *position* to capture, take. **il a facilement enlevé la course** he won the race easily, the race was a walkover* for him; **il l'a enlevé de haute lutte** he won it in a worthy fight; **elle enlève tous les suffrages** she wins everyone's sympathies, she wins everyone over; ~ **la décision** to carry the day; ~ **une affaire** (*tractation*) to pull off a deal; (*commande*) to get *ou* secure an order; (*marchandise*) to carry off *ou* get away with a bargain; **ça a été vite enlevé** (*marchandise*) it sold *ou* went quickly, it was snapped up; (*: *travail*) it was done in no time, it was done in a jiffy*.
g (*Mus*) *morceau, mouvement* to play with spirit *ou* brio.
h (*Sport*) *cheval* to urge on.
i (*enthousiasmer*) *public* to fill with enthusiasm.
2 **s'enlever vpr** a *[tache]* to come out, come off; (*en brossant ou lavant etc*) to brush *ou* wash *etc* out *ou* off; *[peinture, peau, écorce]* to peel off, come off. **enlève-toi de là*** get out of the way*, mind out of the way!* (*Brit*); **comment est-ce que ça s'enlève?** *[étiquette]* how does one remove it *ou* take it off?; *[vêtement]* how does one get out of it *ou* take it off?
b (*Comm*) to sell. **ça s'enlève comme des petits pains*** it's selling *ou* going like hot cakes*.
c (*Sport: sauter*) *[cheval]* to take off. **le cheval s'enlève sur l'obstacle** the horse takes off to clear the obstacle.

enlisement [ɑ̃lizmɑ̃] **nm: causer l'~ d'un bateau** to cause a ship to get stuck in the mud (*ou* sand *etc*).

enliser [ɑ̃lize] 1 1 **vt:** ~ **sa voiture** to get one's car stuck in the mud (*ou* sand *etc*). 2 **s'enliser vpr** a (*dans le sable etc*) *[personne]* to sink (*dans* into), be sucked down (*dans* into), get stuck (*dans* in); *[bateau, voiture]* to sink (*dans* into), get stuck (*dans* in). b (*fig*) (*dans les détails*) to get bogged down (*dans* in). **s'~ (dans la monotonie)** to sink into *ou* get bogged down in a monotonous routine; **en mentant, tu t'enlises davantage** you're getting in deeper and deeper with your lies.

enluminer [ɑ̃lymine] 1 **vt** *manuscrit* to illuminate.

enlumineur, -euse [ɑ̃lyminœʀ, øz] **nm,f** illuminator.

enluminure [ɑ̃lyminyʀ] **nf** illumination.

enneigé, e [ɑ̃neʒe] **adj** *pente, montagne* snowy, snow-covered; *sommet* snow-capped; *maison* snowbound, snowed up (*attrib*); *col, route* blocked by snow, snowed up (*attrib*), snowbound.

enneigement [ɑ̃nɛʒmɑ̃] **nm** snow coverage. **à cause du faible ~** because of the poor snow coverage; **bulletin d'~** snow report; **les conditions d'~** the snow conditions.

ennemi, e [ɛnmi] 1 **adj** (*Mil*) enemy (*épith*); (*hostile*) hostile. **en pays ~** in enemy territory. 2 **nm,f** a enemy, foe († *ou littér*). **se faire des ~s** to make enemies (for o.s.); **se faire un ~ de qn** to make an enemy of sb; **passer à l'~** to go over to the enemy; **~ public numéro un** public enemy number one. b **être ~ de qch** *[personne]* to be opposed to sth, be against sth; **être ~ de la poésie/de la musique** to be strongly averse to poetry/music; **la hâte est l'~e de la précision** speed and accuracy don't mix *ou* don't go together; *voir* **mieux**.

ennième [ɛnjɛm] **adj** = **nième**.

ennoblir [ɑ̃nɔbliʀ] 2 **vt** (*moralement*) to ennoble.

ennoblissement [ɑ̃nɔblismɑ̃] **nm** (*moral*) ennoblement.

ennuager (s') [ɑ̃nɥaʒe] 3 **vpr** (*littér*) *[ciel]* to cloud over. **ennuagé** cloudy, clouded.

ennui [ɑ̃nɥi] **nm** a (*désœuvrement*) boredom; (*littér: spleen*) ennui (*littér*), world-weariness (*littér*); (*monotonie*) tedium, tediousness. **écouter avec ~** to listen wearily; **c'est à mourir d'~** it's enough to bore you to tears *ou* death *ou* to bore you stiff*.

b (*tracas*) trouble, worry, problem. **avoir des ~s** to have problems, be in difficulty; **il a eu des ~s avec la police** he's been in trouble with the police; **avoir des ~s de santé** to be troubled with bad health, have problems with one's health; **avoir des ~s d'argent** to have money worries; **elle a des tas d'~s** she has a great many worries, she has more than her share of troubles; **faire** *ou* **créer** *ou* **causer des ~s à qn** to make trouble for sb; **se préparer des ~s** to be looking for *ou* asking for trouble; **ça peut lui attirer des ~s** that could get him into trouble *ou* hot water*; **j'ai eu un ~ avec mon électrophone** I had some trouble *ou* bother with my record-player, something went wrong with my record-player; **si ça vous cause le moindre ~** if it is in any way inconvenient to you; **l'~, c'est que ...** the trouble *ou* the hitch is that ...; **quel ~!** what a nuisance!, bother it!* (*Brit*).

c (*littér, ††: peine*) grief.

ennuyé, e [ɑ̃nɥije] (**ptp de ennuyer**) **adj** (*préoccupé*) worried, bothered (*de* about); (*contrarié*) annoyed, put out (*de* at, about).

ennuyer [ɑ̃nɥije] 8 1 **vt** a (*lasser*) to bore, weary (†, *littér*). **ce spectacle m'a profondément ennuyé** I was thoroughly bored by the show; **cela (vous) ennuie à force** it palls (on you) *ou* it becomes boring in the long run.

b (*préoccuper*) to worry; (*importuner*) to bother, put out. **il y a quelque chose qui m'ennuie là-dedans** there's something that worries *ou* bothers me about it; **ça m'ennuierait beaucoup de te voir fâché** I should be really upset to see you cross; **ça m'ennuie de te le dire, mais ...** I'm sorry to have to tell you but ..., I hate to say it but ...; **ça m'ennuierait beaucoup d'y aller** it would really put me out *ou* annoy me to go; **si cela ne vous ennuie pas trop** if it wouldn't put you to any trouble *ou* inconvenience, if you wouldn't mind; **je ne voudrais pas vous ~** I don't want to put you to any trouble *ou* inconvenience, I don't want to bother you *ou* put you out; **ça m'ennuie, ce que tu me demandes de faire** what you're asking me to do is rather awkward *ou* a nuisance.

c (*irriter*) **~ qn** to annoy sb, get on sb's nerves; **tu m'ennuies avec tes jérémiades** I'm getting fed up with* *ou* tired of your constant complaints, you're getting on my nerves with your constant complaints.

2 **s'ennuyer vpr** a (*se morfondre*) to be bored (*de, à* with). **il s'ennuie à faire un travail monotone** he's getting bored doing a humdrum job; **s'~ à mourir** to be bored to tears *ou* to death, be bored stiff*; **on ne s'ennuie jamais avec lui** you're never bored when you're with him.

b **s'~ de qn** to miss sb.

ennuyeux, -euse [ɑ̃nɥijø, øz] **adj** a (*lassant*) *personne, spectacle, livre* boring, tedious; *travail* boring, tedious, wearisome. *personne, film etc* **~ comme la pluie** dull as ditchwater (*Brit*), deadly dull. b (*qui importune*) annoying, tiresome; (*préoccupant*) worrying. **ce qui t'arrive est bien ~** this is a very annoying *ou* tiresome thing to happen to you.

énoncé [enɔ̃se] **nm** a (*termes*) (*Scol*) *[sujet]* exposition; *[problème]* terms; (*Jur*) *[loi]* terms, wording. b (*Ling*) utterance. c *[faits, décision]* statement. (*Scol*) **pendant l'~ du sujet** while the subject is being read out.

énoncer [enɔ̃se] 3 **vt** *idée* to express; *faits, conditions* to state, set out, set forth. (*littér*) **pour m'~ plus clairement**† to express myself more clearly, to put it more clearly; *voir* **concevoir**.

énonciatif, -ive [enɔ̃sjatif, iv] **adj** (*Ling*) *phrase* enunciative.

énonciation [enɔ̃sjasjɔ̃] **nf** *[faits]* statement; (*Ling*) enunciation.

enorgueillir [ɑ̃nɔʀgœjiʀ] 2 1 **vt** to make proud. 2 **s'enorgueillir vpr: s'~ de** (*être fier de*) to pride o.s. on, boast about; (*avoir*) to boast; **la ville s'enorgueillit de 2 opéras et un théâtre** the town boasts 2 opera houses and a theatre.

énorme [enɔʀm] **adj** enormous, tremendous, huge, terrific*. **mensonge ~** enormous *ou* whopping* lie, whopper*; **ça lui a fait un bien ~** it's done him a world *ou* a power* (*Brit*) *ou* a great deal of good; **il a accepté, c'est déjà ~** he has accepted and that's quite something; **c'est un type ~!*** he's a terrific* *ou* a tremendous* *ou* a great* guy!

énormément [enɔʀmemɑ̃] **adv** a enormously, tremendously, hugely, terrifically*. **ça m'a ~ amusé** I was greatly *ou* hugely amused by it; **ça m'a ~ déçu** it greatly disappointed me, I was tremendously *ou* greatly disappointed by it; **il boit ~** he drinks a tremendous *ou* an enormous *ou* a huge *ou* a terrific* amount. b **~ d'argent/d'eau/de bruit** a tremendous *ou* an enormous *ou* a huge *ou* a terrific* amount of money/water/noise, a great deal of money/water/noise; **~ de gens/de voitures** a tremendous *ou* an enormous *ou* a huge *ou* a terrific* number of people/cars, a great many people/cars.

énormité [enɔʀmite] **nf** a (*NonC*) *[poids, somme]* hugeness; *[demande, injustice]* enormity. b (*propos inconvenant*) outrageous remark; (*erreur*) big blunder, howler*.

enquérir (s') [ɑ̃keʀiʀ] 21 **vpr** to inquire, ask (*de* about). **s'~ (de la santé) de qn** to ask *ou* inquire after sb *ou* after sb's health; **je m'en suis enquis auprès de lui/à la mairie** I enquired of him/at the town hall about it.

enquête [ɑ̃kɛt] **nf** (*gén, Jur*) inquiry; (*après un décès*) inquest; (*Police*) investigation; (*Comm, Sociol: sondage*) survey, (opinion) poll. (*Jur*) **ouvrir une ~** to set up *ou* open an inquiry; **faire une ~** (*Police*) to make an investigation, make investigations, investigate; (*Comm, Sociol*) to do *ou* conduct a survey (*sur* on); (*Police*) **mener** *ou* **conduire une ~** to be in charge of *ou* lead an investigation; **j'ai fait** *ou* **mené ma petite ~** I've done a little investigating (myself), I've done a little private investigation; **~ administrative** public inquiry (*into planning proposals etc*); **~ parlementaire** parliamentary inquiry (*by parliamentary committee*); **~ statistique** statistical survey; **faire une ~-reportage sur** to do a (newspaper) report on; (*Presse*) **"notre grande ~: les jeunes et la drogue"** "our big investigation *ou* survey: youth and drugs".

enquêter [ɑ̃kete] 1 **vi** (*Jur*) to hold an inquiry (*sur* on); (*Police*) to investigate; (*Comm, Sociol*) to conduct a survey (*sur* on). **ils vont ~ sur l'origine de ces fonds** they'll investigate the origin of these funds *ou* carry out an investigation into the origin of these funds.

enquêteur [ɑ̃kɛtœʀ] **nm** a (*Police*) officer in charge of *ou* (who is) leading the investigation. **les ~s poursuivent leurs recherches** the police are continuing their investigations; **les ~s sont aidés par la population du village** the police are being helped in their investigations by the people of the village; **un des ~s a été abattu** one of the officers involved in the investigation was shot dead.

b (*Comm, Sociol etc*) investigator; (*pour sondages*) pollster. **des ~s sont venus à la porte poser toutes sortes de questions sur l'emploi de nos loisirs** some people doing *ou* conducting a survey came to the door asking all sorts of questions about what we do in our spare time; **il travaille comme ~ pour un institut de sondages** he works as an investigator *ou* interviewer for a poll organization, he does *ou* conducts surveys for a poll organization.

enquêteuse [ɑ̃kɛtøz] **nf** (*Police*) officer in charge of *ou* leading an investigation; (*Sociol*) *voir* **enquêtrice**.

enquêtrice [ɑ̃kɛtʀis] **nf** (*Comm, Sociol*) investigator; (*pour sondages*) pollster; *voir aussi* **enquêteur**.

enquiquinant, e* [ɑ̃kikinɑ̃, ɑ̃t] **adj** (*qui importune*) annoying, irritating; (*préoccupant*) worrying; (*lassant*) boring.

enquiquinement* [ɑ̃kikinmɑ̃] **nm: quel ~!** what a flipping (*Brit*) *ou* darned nuisance!*; **j'ai eu tellement d'~s avec cette voiture** that car gave me so much flipping (*Brit*) *ou* darned trouble*, I had so many flipping (*Brit*) *ou* darned problems with that car*.

enquiquiner* [ɑ̃kikine] 1 1 **vt** (*importuner*) to annoy, irritate, bother; (*préoccuper*) to bother, worry; (*lasser*) to bore. 2 **s'enquiquiner vpr** (*se morfondre*) to be fed up*, be bored. (*se donner du mal*) **s'~ à faire** to go to a heck of a lot of trouble to do*, put o.s. out to do.

enquiquineur, -euse* [ɑ̃kikinœʀ, øz] **nm,f** pest*, darned nuisance*. **c'est un ~** he's a pest* *ou* a darned nuisance*, he's a pain in the neck*.

enracinement [ɑ̃ʀasinmɑ̃] **nm** (*voir* **enraciner, s'enraciner**) implanting, entrenchment; taking root; settling.

enraciner [ɑ̃ʀasine] 1 1 **vt** *idée* to implant, entrench, root; *arbre* to root. **solidement enraciné** *préjugé* deep-rooted, firmly *ou* deeply entrenched, deeply implanted; *famille* firmly rooted *ou* fixed; *bavard* firmly entrenched; *arbre* strongly rooted. 2 **s'enraciner vpr** *[arbre, préjugé]* to take root; *[bavard]* to settle o.s. down; *[immigrant]* to put down roots, settle.

enragé, e [ɑ̃ʀaʒe] (**ptp de enrager**) **adj** a (*: *passionné*) *chasseur, joueur* keen. **être ~ de** to be mad keen on* (*Brit*), be mad* *ou* crazy about*; **c'est un ~ de la voiture** he's mad keen on cars* (*Brit*), he's mad* *ou* crazy about cars*, he's a car fanatic. b (*en colère*) furious. **les ~s de mai 68** the rebels of May '68. c (*Vét*) rabid; *voir* **vache**.

enrager [ɑ̃ʀaʒe] 3 vi a **faire ~ qn*** (*taquiner*) to tease sb; (*importuner*) to pester sb. b (*frm*) to be furious, be in a rage. **j'enrage d'avoir fait cette erreur** I'm furious at having made this mistake; **il enrageait dans son coin** he was fretting and fuming.

enrayage [ɑ̃ʀɛjaʒ] nm *[machine, arme]* jamming.

enrayer [ɑ̃ʀeje] 8 1 vt *maladie, évolution* to check, stop; *chômage, inflation* to check, curb; *machine, arme* to jam. 2 **s'enrayer** vpr *[machine, arme]* to jam.

enrégimenter [ɑ̃ʀeʒimɑ̃te] 1 vt a (*péj: dans un parti*) to enlist, enrol. **se laisser ~ dans** *parti* to let o.s. be dragooned into. b (*Mil* †) to enlist.

enregistrement [ɑ̃ʀ(ə)ʒistʀəmɑ̃] nm a *[fait, son, souvenir]* recording. b (*disque, bande*) recording. **~ magnétique** tape recording; **~ magnétoscopique** video recording. c (*Jur*) *[acte]* registration. **l'E~** the Registration Department (*for legal transactions*); **droits** *ou* **frais d'~** registration fees. d **~ des bagages** (*à l'aéroport*) check-in; (*à la gare*) registration of luggage; **se présenter à l'~** to go to the check-in desk; **comptoir d'~** check-in desk.

enregistrer [ɑ̃ʀ(ə)ʒistʀe] 1 vt *souvenir, voix, musique* to record; (*sur bande*) to tape(-record); (*sur magnétoscope*) to video(-tape); (*Jur*) *acte, demande, réclamation* to register; (*Comm*) *commande* to enter, record; *constatation* to note. **d'accord, j'enregistre*** *ou* **c'est enregistré*** all right, I'll make *ou* I've made a mental note of it, all right, I'll bear it in mind; **cet enfant enregistre tout ce qu'on dit** this child takes in *ou* retains *ou* registers everything one says; **(faire) ~ ses bagages** (*à l'aéroport*) to check in (one's luggage); (*à la gare*) to register one's luggage; (*Télec*) **vous écoutez un message enregistré** this is a recorded message; **nous avons enregistré de bonnes ventes** we've rung up good sales; **la plus forte hausse/température enregistrée** the greatest rise/highest temperature recorded.

enregistreur, -euse [ɑ̃ʀ(ə)ʒistʀœʀ, øz] 1 adj *appareil* recording; *voir* **caisse**. 2 nm *[température etc]* recorder, recording machine *ou* device.

enrhumer [ɑ̃ʀyme] 1 1 vt to give a cold to. **être enrhumé** to have a cold. 2 **s'enrhumer** vpr to catch a cold.

enrichi, e [ɑ̃ʀiʃi] (ptp de **enrichir**) adj a (*péj*) nouveau riche. b *pain* enriched; *lessive* improved (*de* with). **shampooing formule ~e** enriched formula shampoo; *voir* **uranium**.

enrichir [ɑ̃ʀiʃiʀ] 2 1 vt *œuvre, esprit, langue, collection* to enrich; *catalogue* to expand; *[financièrement]* to make rich. 2 **s'enrichir** vpr *[financièrement]* to get *ou* grow rich; *[esprit]* to grow richer (*de* in); *[collection]* to be enriched (*de* with). **leur collection s'enrichit d'année en année** their collection is becoming richer from year to year.

enrichissant, e [ɑ̃ʀiʃisɑ̃, ɑ̃t] adj enriching.

enrichissement [ɑ̃ʀiʃismɑ̃] nm enrichment (*NonC*).

enrobage [ɑ̃ʀɔbaʒ] nm, **enrobement** [ɑ̃ʀɔbmɑ̃] nm coating.

enrober [ɑ̃ʀɔbe] 1 vt *bonbon* to coat (*de* with); *paroles* to wrap up (*de* in). (*hum*) **il est un peu enrobé** he's a bit podgy *ou* plump, he's on the podgy *ou* plump side.

enrochement [ɑ̃ʀɔʃmɑ̃] nm rocks (*protecting a jetty etc*).

enrôlé [ɑ̃ʀole] nm recruit.

enrôlement [ɑ̃ʀolmɑ̃] nm (*voir* **enrôler**) enlistment; signing on; enrolment.

enrôler vt, **s'enrôler** vpr [ɑ̃ʀole] 1 (*Mil*) to enlist, sign on, enrol; (*dans un parti*) to enrol, sign on.

enroué, e [ɑ̃ʀwe] (ptp de **enrouer**) adj: **être ~** to be hoarse, have a hoarse *ou* husky voice; **j'ai la voix ~e** my voice is hoarse *ou* husky.

enrouement [ɑ̃ʀumɑ̃] nm hoarseness, huskiness.

enrouer [ɑ̃ʀwe] 1 1 vt *[froid, cris]* to make hoarse. 2 **s'enrouer** vpr (*par le froid etc*) to go hoarse *ou* husky; (*en criant*) to make o.s. hoarse. **s'~ à force de chanter** to sing o.s. hoarse.

enroulement [ɑ̃ʀulmɑ̃] nm a (*NonC: voir* **enrouler**) rolling-up; coiling-up; winding(-up). b (*Archit, Art*) volute, scroll, whorl; (*Élec*) coil.

enrouler [ɑ̃ʀule] 1 1 vt *tapis* to roll up; *cheveux* to coil up; *corde, ruban* to wind up, coil up, roll up; *fil* to wind (*sur, autour de* round); *bobine* to wind. **~ une feuille autour de/dans** to roll a sheet of paper round/up in. 2 **s'enrouler** vpr *[serpent]* to coil up; *[film, fil]* to wind. **s'~ dans une couverture** to wrap *ou* roll o.s. up in a blanket.

enrouleur, -euse [ɑ̃ʀulœʀ, øz] 1 adj *mécanisme, cylindre* winding. 2 nm *[tuyau d'arrosage]* drum; *voir* **ceinture**.

enrubanner [ɑ̃ʀybane] 1 vt to decorate *ou* trim with ribbon(s) *ou* a ribbon; (*en attachant*) to tie up *ou* do up with (a) ribbon.

ENS [əɛnɛs] nf (abrév de **École normale supérieure** *et de* **École nationale supérieure**) *voir* **école**.

ensablement [ɑ̃sɑbləmɑ̃] nm a (*voir* **ensabler**) silting-up; choking *ou* blocking (with sand); stranding; sinking into the sand. b (*tas de sable*) (*formé par le vent*) (sand) dune; (*formé par l'eau*) sandbank.

ensabler [ɑ̃sɑble] 1 1 vt *port* to silt up, sand up; *tuyau* to choke *ou* block with sand; *bateau* to strand (on a sandbank); *voiture* to get stuck in the sand. 2 **s'ensabler** vpr *[port]* to silt up; *[bateau, voiture]* to get stuck in the sand. **je m'étais ensablé jusqu'aux essieux** my car had sunk in the sand up to the axles.

ensacher [ɑ̃saʃe] 1 vt to bag, pack (into bags).

ensanglanter [ɑ̃sɑ̃glɑ̃te] 1 vt *visage* to cover with blood; *vêtement* to soak with blood. **manche ensanglantée** blood-soaked sleeve; **~ un pays** to bathe a country in blood; **l'accident qui a ensanglanté la course** the accident which cast a tragic shadow over the race; **l'attentat qui a ensanglanté la visite du président** the terrorist attack which brought a note of bloodshed to the president's visit.

enseignant, e [ɑ̃sɛɲɑ̃, ɑ̃t] 1 adj teaching; *voir* **corps**. 2 nm,f teacher. **~-chercheur** teacher-cum-researcher; **poste d'~** teaching position *ou* post *ou* job.

enseigne [ɑ̃sɛɲ] 1 nf a (*Comm*) (shop) sign. **~ lumineuse** neon sign; **(restaurant) à l'~ du Lion Noir** the Black Lion (restaurant); **loger à l'~ du Lion Noir**†† to put up at (the sign of) the Black Lion††. b (*Mil, Naut*) ensign. **(défiler) ~s déployées** (to march) with colours flying. c (*littér*) **à telle(s) ~(s) que** so much so that. 2 nm a (*Hist*) ensign. b **~ de vaisseau** (*de 1re classe*) lieutenant; (*de 2e classe*) sub-lieutenant (*Brit*), ensign (*US*).

enseignement [ɑ̃sɛɲ(ə)mɑ̃] nm a (*Admin*) education. **~ général** general education; **~ libre** denominational education; **~ ménager** home economics (*sg*); **~ mixte** coeducation; **~ par correspondance** tuition by correspondence; **~ primaire** *ou* **du premier degré** primary education; **~ secondaire** *ou* **du second degré/supérieur** *ou* **universitaire** secondary/higher *ou* university education; **~ privé/public** private/state education; **~ professionnel** professional *ou* vocational training; **~ programmé** programmed learning; **~ technique** technical education, industrial arts (*US*); **~ spécialisé** special education *ou* schooling; **~ court/long** full-time education to the age of 16/18; **on l'a orienté vers l'~ court/long** he was advised to leave school at 16/to go on to further education; **~ assisté par ordinateur** computer-aided instruction, computer-assisted learning; **établissement d'~** educational establishment; **l'~ en France** (the system of) education in France.

b (*art d'enseigner*) teaching. **~ moderne** modern (methods of) teaching.

c (*carrière*) teaching profession. **être dans l'~** to be a teacher, be a member of the teaching profession.

d (*leçon donnée par l'expérience*) teaching, lesson. **on peut en tirer plusieurs ~s** it has taught us several things, we can draw many lessons from it; **les ~s du Christ** the teachings of Christ.

enseigner [ɑ̃seɲe] 1 vt to teach. **~ qch à qn** to teach sb sth; **~ à qn à faire qch** to teach sb (how) to do sth.

ensemble [ɑ̃sɑ̃bl] 1 adv a (*l'un avec l'autre*) together. **ils sont partis ~** they left together; **tous ~** all together.

b (*simultanément*) (*deux personnes*) together, both at once; (*plusieurs*) together, at the same time. **ils ont répondu ~** (*deux*) they both answered together *ou* at once; (*plusieurs*) they all answered together *ou* at the same time, they answered all together.

c (*littér: à la fois*) **tout ~** (*deux*) both, at once; (*plus de deux*) at (one and) the same time; **il était tout ~ triste et joyeux** he was both *ou* at once sad and happy.

d **aller ~: les deux serre-livres vont ~** the two book ends are sold together; **ces deux idées vont ~** these two ideas go together *ou* go hand in hand; **je trouve qu'ils vont bien ~** I think they make a good couple *ou* that they go together well; **ces crapules vont bien ~** (*deux*) they make a pretty *ou* fine pair (of rascals); (*plus de deux*) they make a fine bunch of rascals; **l'armoire et la table ne vont pas (bien) ~** *ou* **vont mal ~** the wardrobe and the table don't go (very well) together, the wardrobe doesn't go (very well) with the table.

e *[personnes]* **être bien ~** to be on good terms, get on well (together), hit it off*; **ils sont mal ~** they don't get on (well) (together), they don't hit it off*.

2 nm a (*unité*) unity. **œuvre qui manque d'~** work which lacks unity; **avec ~, avec un parfait ~** simultaneously, as one man, with one accord; **ils répondirent avec un ~ touchant** they answered with a touching unanimity.

b (*totalité*) whole. **former un ~ harmonieux** to form a harmonious whole; **l'~ du personnel** the entire *ou* whole staff; **on reconnaît cette substance à l'~ de ses propriétés** you can identify this substance from all its various properties; **dans l'~** on the whole, in the main, by and large; **dans l'~ nous sommes d'accord** basically we agree; **les spectateurs dans leur ~** the audience as a whole; **examiner la question dans son ~** to examine the question in its entirety *ou* as a whole.

c **d'~** *vue, étude* overall, comprehensive, general; *impression* overall, general; **mouvement d'~** ensemble movement.

d (*groupement*) *[personnes]* set, group, body; *[objets, poèmes]* set, collection; *[faits]* set, series; *[meubles]* suite; *[lois]* body, corpus; (*Mus*) ensemble.

e (*zone résidentielle*) (housing) scheme *ou* development (*Brit*), housing project (*US*); *voir* **grand**.

f (*Math*) set. **~ vide** empty set; **théorie des ~s** set theory.

g (*Couture*) ensemble, outfit, suit. **~ de ville** town suit; **~ de voyage** travelling outfit; **~ de plage** beach ensemble *ou* outfit; **~ pantalon** trouser suit (*Brit*), pantsuit.

h (*Aut*) **~ chemise-pistons** cylinder block.

ensemblier [ɑ̃sɑ̃blije] nm (*décorateur*) interior designer; (*Ciné*) set designer; (*entreprise*) factory design consultancy.

ensemencement [ɑ̃s(ə)məsmɑ̃] nm sowing.

ensemencer [ɑ̃s(ə)mɑ̃se] [3] vt (*Agr*) to sow; (*Bio*) to culture.

enserrer [ɑ̃seʀe] [1] vt *[vêtement]* to hug tightly. **son col lui enserre le cou** his collar is too tight; **il l'enserre dans ses bras** he holds *ou* clasps her in his arms; **vallée enserrée par des montagnes** valley shut in *ou* hemmed in by mountains.

ensevelir [ɑ̃səv(ə)liʀ] [2] vt (*frm: enterrer*) to bury; (*d'un linceul*) to shroud (*de* in); (*fig*) *peine, honte* to hide, bury; *[avalanche, décombres]* to bury. **enseveli sous la neige/la lave** buried beneath the snow/lava; **il est allé s'~ dans sa province** he has gone to hide himself away *ou* to bury himself in his native country; **la nuit l'a enseveli** he was swallowed up in the darkness.

ensevelissement [ɑ̃səv(ə)lismɑ̃] nm (*dans la terre, sous une avalanche*) burying; (*dans un linceul*) shrouding.

ENSI [ɛnsi] nf (abrév de **École nationale supérieure d'ingénieurs**) *voir* **école**.

ensilage [ɑ̃silaʒ] nm ensilage.

ensiler [ɑ̃sile] [1] vt to ensilage, ensile.

en-soi [ɑ̃swa] nm (*Philos*) en-soi.

ensoleillé, e [ɑ̃sɔleje] (ptp de **ensoleiller**) adj sunny.

ensoleillement [ɑ̃sɔlɛjmɑ̃] nm (*durée*) period *ou* hours of sunshine. **la région reçoit un ~ de 10 heures par jour** the region gets 10 hours of sunshine per day; **l'~ est meilleur sur le versant est de la montagne** there is more sun(shine) on the eastern side of the mountain, the eastern side of the mountain gets more sun(shine).

ensoleiller [ɑ̃sɔleje] [1] vt (*lit*) to fill with *ou* bathe in sunshine *ou* sunlight; (*fig*) to brighten, light up.

ensommeillé, e [ɑ̃sɔmeje] adj sleepy, drowsy. **il a les yeux ~s** he is heavy-eyed with sleep, he is drowsy- *ou* sleepy-eyed, his eyes are (still) heavy with sleep.

ensorceler [ɑ̃sɔʀsəle] [4] vt (*lit, fig*) to bewitch, put *ou* cast a spell on *ou* over.

ensorceleur, -euse [ɑ̃sɔʀsəlœʀ, øz] 1 adj bewitching, spellbinding. 2 nm (*lit*) sorcerer, enchanter; (*fig*) charmer. 3 **ensorceleuse** nf (*lit*) witch, enchantress, sorceress; (*fig*) (*femme*) enchantress; (*hum: enfant*) charmer.

ensorcellement [ɑ̃sɔʀsɛlmɑ̃] nm (*action*) bewitching, bewitchment; (*charme*) charm, enchantment.

ensuite [ɑ̃sɥit] adv (*puis*) then, next; (*par la suite*) afterwards, later. **il nous dit ~ que** then *ou* next he said that; **d'accord mais ~?** all right but what now? *ou* what next? *ou* then what?; **il se mit à crier, ~ de quoi il claqua la porte** he started shouting, after which *ou* and after that he slammed the door; **je le reçois d'abord et je vous verrai ~** I'll meet him first and I'll see you after *ou* afterwards.

ensuivre (s') [ɑ̃sɥivʀ] [40] vpr to follow, ensue. **il s'ensuit que** it follows that; **et tout ce qui s'ensuit** and all that goes with it; **torturé jusqu'à ce que mort s'ensuive** tortured to death.

entablement [ɑ̃tabləmɑ̃] nm entablature.

entacher [ɑ̃taʃe] [1] vt *honneur* to soil, sully, taint; *joie* to taint, blemish. (*Jur*) **entaché de nullité** null and void; **entaché d'erreurs** spoilt *ou* marred by mistakes.

entaille [ɑ̃taj] nf a (*sur le corps*) (*gén*) cut; (*profonde*) gash; (*petite*) nick. **se faire une ~** to cut o.s. b (*sur un objet*) notch; (*allongée*) groove; (*dans une falaise*) gash.

entailler [ɑ̃taje] [1] vt (*voir* **entaille**) to cut; to gash; to nick; to notch. **carrière qui entaille la colline** quarry which cuts a gash in the hill; **s'~ la main** to cut *ou* gash one's hand.

entame [ɑ̃tam] nf (*tranche*) first slice; (*Cartes*) first card.

entamer [ɑ̃tame] [1] vt a *pain, jambon* to start (upon); *tonneau* to broach, tap; *bouteille, boîte, sac* to start, open; *tissu* to cut into; *patrimoine* to make a hole in, dip into.

b (*inciser*) *chair, tissu* to cut (into); *métal* to cut *ou* bite into.

c (*amorcer*) *journée, livre* to start; *travail* to start on; *négociations, discussion* to start, open; *poursuites* to institute, initiate. **la journée est déjà bien entamée** we are already well into the day, the day is already quite far advanced.

d (*ébranler*) *résistance* to wear down, break down; *conviction* to shake, weaken; *optimisme, moral* to wear down.

e (*porter atteinte à*) *réputation, honneur* to damage, harm, cast a slur on.

f (*Cartes: commencer*) **~ la partie** to open the game; **c'est à toi d'~** it's you to open.

entartrage [ɑ̃taʀtʀaʒ] nm (*voir* **entartrer**) furring-up (*Brit*); scaling.

entartrer [ɑ̃taʀtʀe] [1] 1 vt *chaudière, tuyau* to fur up (*Brit*), scale; *dents* to scale. 2 **s'entartrer** vpr to fur up (*Brit*), to scale.

entassement [ɑ̃tasmɑ̃] nm a (*action*) *[objets]* piling up, heaping up; *[personnes]* cramming in, packing together. b (*tas*) pile, heap.

entasser [ɑ̃tase] [1] 1 vt a (*amonceler*) *objets, arguments* to pile up, heap up (*sur* onto); *argent* to hoard, amass. b (*tasser*) **~ des objets/personnes dans** to cram *ou* pack objects/people into; **entassons-les là** let's cram *ou* pack them in there. 2 **s'entasser** vpr (*s'amonceler*) *[déchets, erreurs]* to pile up. **s'~ dans** *[voyageurs]* to cram *ou* pack into; **ils s'entassent à 10 dans cette pièce** there are 10 of them crammed *ou* packed into that room; **s'~ sur la plage** to pack onto the beach.

ente [ɑ̃t] nf (*Agr*) graft.

entendement [ɑ̃tɑ̃dmɑ̃] nm (*Philos*) understanding. **cela dépasse l'~** that's beyond all understanding *ou* comprehension; (*frm*) **perdre l'~** to lose one's reason.

entendeur [ɑ̃tɑ̃dœʀ] nm: **à bon ~, salut** a word to the wise is enough.

entendre [ɑ̃tɑ̃dʀ] [41] 1 vt a *voix etc* to hear. **il entendit du bruit** he heard a noise; **il entendit parler qn** he heard sb speak(ing); **j'entendais quelqu'un parler** *ou* **parler quelqu'un, j'entendais qu'on parlait** I heard *ou* could hear somebody speaking; **il entend mal de l'oreille droite** he can't hear very well with his right ear; (*fig*) **il ne l'entend pas de cette oreille** he's not prepared to accept that; **qu'est-ce que j'entends?** what did you say?, am I hearing right?; **tu vas être sage, tu entends!** you're to be good, do you hear (me)!; **ce qu'il faut ~ tout de même!*** really – the things you hear! *ou* the things people say!

b (*écouter*) to hear, listen to. **le patron a entendu les syndicats pendant une heure** the boss listened to *ou* heard the unions for an hour; **j'ai entendu son discours jusqu'au bout** I listened right to the end of his speech; **à l'~ c'est lui qui a tout fait** to hear him talk *ou* to listen to him you'd think he had done everything; **il ne veut rien ~** he doesn't want to hear *ou* know about it, he just won't listen; (*Jur*) **~ les témoins** to hear the witnesses; (*Rel*) **~ la messe** to hear *ou* attend mass; **~ raison** to listen to *ou* see reason; **comment lui faire ~ raison?** how do we make him see sense? *ou* reason?

c (*frm: comprendre*) to understand. **oui, j'entends bien, mais ...** yes, I fully *ou* quite understand but ...; **je vous entends** I see what you mean, now I understand (you); **en peinture, il n'y entend strictement rien** he doesn't know the first thing *ou* he doesn't have the first idea about painting; **il n'entend pas la plaisanterie** he can't take a joke, he doesn't know how to take a joke; **laisser ~ à qn que, donner à ~ à qn que** (*faire comprendre à qn que*) to give sb to understand that; (*donner l'impression que*) to let it be understood that, give sb the impression that; *voir* **pire**.

d (*frm: avec infin: vouloir*) to intend, mean. **j'entends bien y aller** I certainly intend *ou* mean to go (there); **faites comme vous l'entendez** do as you see fit *ou* think best; **j'entends être obéi** *ou* **qu'on m'obéisse** I intend *ou* mean to be obeyed, I WILL be obeyed; **j'entends n'être pas commandé, je n'entends pas être commandé** I will not take orders from anyone, I will not be ordered about.

e (*vouloir dire*) to mean. **qu'entendez-vous par là?** what do you mean by that?; **entendez-vous par là que ...?** are you trying to say that ...?, do you mean that ...?; *voir* **malice**.

f (*loc*) **~ parler de** to hear of *ou* about; **j'en ai vaguement entendu parler** I did vaguely hear something about *ou* of it; **on n'entend plus parler de lui** you don't hear anything of him these days, you never hear of him any more; (*fig*) **il ne veut pas en ~ parler** he won't hear of it; **~ dire que** to hear it said that; **d'après ce que j'ai entendu dire** from what I have heard, by all accounts; **on entend dire que** it is said *ou* rumoured that, rumour has it that; **on entend dire des choses étranges** there are strange rumours going about; **je l'ai entendu dire que** I heard him say that; **elle fit ~ sa voix mélodieuse, sa voix mélodieuse se fit ~** her sweet voice was heard; **il a pu faire ~ sa voix dans le débat, sa voix a pu se faire ~ dans le débat** he was able to make himself heard in the debate; **on entendrait voler une mouche** you could hear a pin drop.

2 **s'entendre** vpr a (*être d'accord*) to agree; (*s'accorder*) to get on. **ils se sont entendus sur plusieurs points** they have agreed on several points; **ces collègues ne s'entendent pas** these colleagues don't get on (*Brit*) *ou* along (together *ou* with each other); **s'~ comme larrons en foire** to be as thick as thieves; **ils s'entendent à merveille** they get on (*Brit*) *ou* along extremely well (together *ou* with each other), they get on like a house on fire (*Brit*).

b (*s'y connaître*) **il s'y entend pour le faire** he's very good at it, he knows how to do it; **il s'y entend!** he knows what he's doing!, he knows his onions!* (*Brit*) *ou* stuff!*

c (*se comprendre*) **quand je dis magnifique, je m'entends, disons que c'est très joli** when I say it's magnificent, what I'm really saying *ou* what I really mean *ou* what I mean to say is that it's very attractive; **il le fera, moyennant finances, (cela) s'entend** he will do it, for a fee it's understood *ou* of course *ou* naturally; **entendons-nous bien!** let's be quite clear about *ou* on this, let's make quite sure we understand one another; **ça peut s'~ différemment suivant les contextes** that can be taken to mean different things depending on the context.

d (*être entendu*) **on ne s'entend plus ici** you can't hear yourself think in here; **le bruit s'entendait depuis la route** the noise could be heard *ou* was audible from the road; **tu ne t'entends pas!, tu n'entends pas ce que tu racontes!** you don't know what you are saying!; (*fig*) **cette expression ne s'entend plus guère** that phrase is hardly ever used *ou* heard nowadays, you hardly ever hear that phrase nowadays; **je me suis entendu à la radio** I heard myself on the radio.

entendu, e [ɑ̃tɑ̃dy] (ptp de **entendre**) adj a (*convenu*) agreed. **étant ~ que** it being understood *ou* agreed that, since; **il est bien ~ que vous n'en dites rien** of course it's understood *ou* it must be understood that you make no mention of it; **c'est (bien) ~, n'est-ce pas?** that's (all) agreed, isn't it?; **(c'est) ~!** right!, agreed!, right-oh!* (*Brit*).

b (*évidemment*) **bien ~!** of course!; **bien ~ *ou* comme de bien ~* tu dormais!** as I might have known *ou* expected (you to be), you were asleep!

c (*concessif*) all right, granted, so we all agree. **c'est ~ *ou* c'est une affaire ~e, il t'a poussé** all right, so he pushed you.

d (*complice*) *sourire, air* knowing. **oui, fit-il d'un air ~** yes, he said with a knowing look *ou* knowingly.

e (††: *habile*) competent.

entente [ɑ̃tɑ̃t] **nf** a (*amitié*) harmony, understanding; (*alliance*) understanding. **politique d'~ avec un pays** policy of friendship with a country; **l'E~ cordiale** the Entente Cordiale; **l'E~ *ou* la Triple E~** the Triple Alliance; **vivre en bonne ~** to live in harmony *ou* harmoniously; **vivre en bonne ~ avec les voisins** to be on good terms with the neighbours. b (*accord*) agreement, understanding; (*Écon: cartel*) combine. **~s illicites** illegal agreements *ou* arrangements; (*Jur, Fin*) **~ entre enchérisseurs** knock-out agreement. c (*rare: connaissance*) grasp, understanding; (*habileté*) skill; *voir* **double**.

enter [ɑ̃te] 1 **vt** (*Agr*) to graft.

entérinement [ɑ̃teʀinmɑ̃] **nm** ratification, confirmation.

entériner [ɑ̃teʀine] 1 **vt** to ratify, confirm.

entérite [ɑ̃teʀit] **nf** enteritis.

enterrement [ɑ̃tɛʀmɑ̃] **nm** a (*action*) *[mort]* burial; *[projet]* laying aside, forgetting about; *[espoir]* end, death. b (*cérémonie*) funeral, burial (service); (*convoi*) funeral procession. **~ civil/religieux** non-religious/religious burial (service) *ou* funeral; **faire *ou* avoir une tête *ou* mine d'~*** to look down in the mouth*, look gloomy *ou* glum; (*hum*) **~ de première classe** glorious send-off.

enterrer [ɑ̃teʀe] 1 **vt** a (*inhumer*) to bury, inter (*frm*). **hier il a enterré sa mère** yesterday he attended his mother's burial *ou* funeral; **on l'enterre ce matin** he is being buried this morning; **tu nous enterreras tous!** you'll outlive us all!; (*fig*) **s'~ dans un trou perdu** to bury o.s. in the back of beyond (*Brit*) *ou* in the sticks.

b (*enfouir*) *os, trésor* to bury; *plante* to plant.

c (*oublier*) *projet* to lay aside, forget about; *scandale* to hush up; *espoir* to forget about. **enterrons cette querelle** (let's) let bygones be bygones; **c'est une querelle enterrée depuis longtemps** that quarrel has long since been buried and forgotten (about) *ou* dead and buried; **~ son passé** to put one's past behind one; **~ sa vie de garçon** to have *ou* throw a stag party (before one's wedding).

entêtant, e [ɑ̃tɛtɑ̃, ɑ̃t] **adj** *vin, parfum* heady (*épith*), which goes to the head.

en-tête, **pl en-têtes** [ɑ̃tɛt] **nm** heading; (*Ordin*) header. **papier à lettres à ~** headed notepaper.

entêté, e [ɑ̃tete] (**ptp de entêter**) 1 **adj** stubborn, pigheaded*. 2 **nm,f** mule, stubborn individual. **quel ~ tu fais!** what a stubborn thing you are!

entêtement [ɑ̃tɛtmɑ̃] **nm** stubbornness, pigheadedness*.

entêter [ɑ̃tete] 1 1 **vt** *[vin, parfum]* to go to the head of. **ce parfum entête** this perfume goes to your head. 2 **s'entêter vpr** to persist (*dans qch* in sth, *à faire qch* in doing sth).

enthousiasmant, e [ɑ̃tuzjasmɑ̃, ɑ̃t] **adj** *spectacle, livre, idée* exciting, exhilarating.

enthousiasme [ɑ̃tuzjasm] **nm** enthusiasm. **avec ~** enthusiastically, with enthusiasm; **avoir des ~s soudains** to have sudden fits of enthusiasm *ou* sudden crazes.

enthousiasmer [ɑ̃tuzjasme] 1 1 **vt** to fill with enthusiasm. 2 **s'enthousiasmer vpr** to be enthusiastic (*pour* about, over). **il s'enthousiasma tout de suite pour ...** he was immediately enthusiastic about *ou* over ..., he enthused straight away over ...; **c'est quelqu'un qui s'enthousiasme facilement** he's easily carried away (*pour* by).

enthousiaste [ɑ̃tuzjast] 1 **adj** enthusiastic (*de* about, over). 2 **nmf** enthusiast.

entichement [ɑ̃tiʃmɑ̃] **nm** (*pour une femme*) infatuation (*pour, de* for, with); (*pour une activité, théorie*) passion, craze (*de, pour* for).

enticher (s') [ɑ̃tiʃe] 1 **vpr** (*frm, péj*) **s'~ de** *femme* to become besotted (*Brit*) *ou* infatuated with; *activité, théorie* to get completely hooked on; **il est entiché de vieux livres** he has a passion for old books.

entier, -ière [ɑ̃tje, jɛʀ] 1 **adj** a (*dans sa totalité*) *quantité, prix* whole, full; *surface, endroit, année* whole, entire. **boire une bouteille ~-ière** to drink a whole *ou* full bottle; **payer place ~-ière** (*Théât*) to pay the full price; (*Rail*) to pay the full fare *ou* price; **une heure ~-ière** a whole hour; **des heures ~-ières** for hours (on end *ou* together); **dans le monde ~** in the whole *ou* entire world, in the whole of the world, throughout the world; **dans la France ~-ière** throughout France, in the whole of France; *voir* **nombre**.

b **tout ~** entirely, completely; **se donner tout ~ à une tâche** to devote o.s. wholeheartedly *ou* entirely *ou* wholly to a task; **il était tout ~ à son travail** he was completely wrapped up in *ou* engrossed in his work.

c (*intact*) *objet, vertu* intact; (*Vét: non châtré*) entire. **aucune assiette n'était ~-ière** there wasn't one unbroken plate; **la question reste ~-ière** the question still remains unresolved; **c'est un miracle qu'il en soit sorti ~** it's a miracle he escaped unscathed *ou* in one piece.

d (*absolu*) *liberté, confiance* absolute, complete. **mon accord plein et ~** my full *ou* entire (and) wholehearted agreement; **donner ~-ière satisfaction** to give complete satisfaction.

e (*sans demi-mesure*) *personne, caractère* unyielding, unbending; *opinion* strong, positive.

f (*Culin*) **lait ~** full-cream milk (*Brit*), whole milk.

2 **nm** a (*Math*) whole, integer; (*Ordin*) integer. **deux demis font un ~** two halves make a whole.

b **en ~** totally, in its entirety; **occupé en ~ par des bureaux** totally occupied by offices, occupied in its entirety by offices; **boire une bouteille en ~** to drink a whole *ou* an entire bottle; **lire/voir qch en ~** to read/see the whole of sth, read/watch sth right through; **la nation dans son ~** the nation as a whole, the entire nation.

entièrement [ɑ̃tjɛʀmɑ̃] **adv** entirely, completely, wholly. **je suis ~ d'accord avec vous** I fully *ou* entirely agree with you; **la ville a été ~ détruite** the town was wholly *ou* entirely destroyed.

entièreté [ɑ̃tjɛʀte] **nf** entirety.

entité [ɑ̃tite] **nf** entity.

entoiler [ɑ̃twale] 1 **vt** *estampe* to mount on canvas; *vêtement* to stiffen (with canvas).

entôler‡ [ɑ̃tole] 1 **vt** to con‡, do‡ (*Brit*) (*de* out of), fleece‡ (*de* of).

entomologie [ɑ̃tɔmɔlɔʒi] **nf** entomology.

entomologique [ɑ̃tɔmɔlɔʒik] **adj** entomological.

entomologiste [ɑ̃tɔmɔlɔʒist] **nmf** entomologist.

entonner [ɑ̃tɔne] 1 **vt**: **~ une chanson** to break into song, strike up a song, start singing; **~ des louanges au sujet de qn** to start singing sb's praises; **~ un psaume** to strike up a psalm, start singing a psalm.

entonnoir [ɑ̃tɔnwaʀ] **nm** (*Culin*) funnel; (*Géog*) swallow hole, doline; (*trou*) *[obus]* shell-hole; *[bombe]* crater. *forme, conduit* **en ~** funnel-shaped.

entorse [ɑ̃tɔʀs] **nf** a (*Méd*) sprain. **se faire une ~ au poignet** to sprain one's wrist. b *[loi]* infringement (*à* of). **faire une ~ à la vérité** to twist the truth; **faire une ~ à ses habitudes** to break one's habits; **faire une ~ au règlement** to bend *ou* stretch the rules; **faire une ~ à son régime** to break one's diet.

entortillement [ɑ̃tɔʀtijmɑ̃] **nm** (*action*) twisting, winding, twining; (*état*) entwinement.

entortiller [ɑ̃tɔʀtije] 1 1 **vt** a *ruban* to twist, twine, wind; *bonbons* to wrap (up); (*fig*) *paroles* to make long and involved, complicate. b (*) (*enjôler*) to get round, wheedle, cajole; (*embrouiller*) to mix up, muddle (up); (*duper*) to hoodwink*. 2 **s'entortiller vpr** *[liane]* to twist, wind, twine. (*fig*) **s'~ dans ses réponses** to get (all) mixed up in one's answers, get in a muddle with one's answers, tie o.s. in knots* with one's answers; **s'~ dans les couvertures** (*volontairement*) to wrap *ou* roll o.s. up in the blankets; (*involontairement*) to get caught up *ou* tangled up *ou* entangled in the blankets.

entour [ɑ̃tuʀ] **nm** (*littér*) **les ~s de qch** the surroundings of sth; **à l'~ de qch** around sth.

entourage [ɑ̃tuʀaʒ] **nm** a (*famille*) family circle; (*compagnie, familiers*) (*gén*) set, circle; *[roi, président]* entourage. **les gens de son ~/dans l'~ du président** people around him/the president. b (*bordure, cadre*) *[sculpture, fenêtre]* frame, surround (*Brit*); *[massif floral]* border, surround (*Brit*).

entouré, e [ɑ̃tuʀe] (**ptp de entourer**) **adj** a (*admiré*) popular. **cette jeune femme est très ~e** this young woman is the centre of attraction; (*soutenu*) **pendant cette épreuve il était très ~** during this difficult time many people rallied round (him). b **~ de** surrounded with *ou* by.

entourer [ɑ̃tuʀe] 1 1 **vt** a (*mettre autour*) **~ qch de** *clôture, arbres* to surround sth with; (*fig*) *mystère* to surround sth with, wrap sth in; **~ qn de** *gardes, soins* to surround sb with; **~ un champ d'une clôture** to put a fence round a field, surround a field with a fence; **il entoura ses épaules d'une couverture/d'un châle** he put *ou* wrapped a blanket/shawl (a)round her shoulders; **~ qn de ses bras** to put one's arms (a)round sb; **~ ses pieds d'une couverture** to put *ou* wrap a blanket round one's feet.

b (*être autour*) *[arbres, foule, clôture]* to surround; *[cadre]* to frame, surround; *[couverture, écharpe]* to be round; *[soldats]* to surround, encircle; *[admirateurs, cour,* (*fig*) *dangers, mystères]* to surround. **tout ce qui nous entoure** everything around us *ou* round about us; **le monde qui nous entoure** the world around *ou* about us, the world that surrounds us; **ils entourèrent les manifestants** they surrounded the demonstrators.

c (*soutenir*) *personne souffrante* to rally round. **~ qn de toute son affection** to surround sb with love; **ils ont su admirablement l'~ après la mort de sa mère** they really rallied round him after his mother's death; (*Bourse*) **ce titre est très entouré** buyers are rallying round this security.

2 **s'entourer vpr**: **s'~ de** *amis, gardes du corps, luxe* to surround o.s. with; **s'~ de mystère** to surround o.s. with *ou* shroud o.s. in mystery; **s'~ de précautions** to take elaborate precautions; **nous voulons nous ~ de toutes les garanties** we wish to have *ou* avail ourselves of all possible guarantees.

entourloupe* [ɑ̃tuʀlup] **nf**, **entourloupette*** [ɑ̃tuʀlupɛt] **nf** mean trick, rotten trick*. **faire une ~ à qn** to play a (rotten* *ou* mean) trick on sb.

entournure [ɑ̃tuʀnyʀ] **nf** armhole; *voir* **gêné**.

entracte [ɑ̃tʀakt] nm (*au théâtre, au concert*) interval, interlude; (*Ciné*) interval, intermission; (*Théât: divertissement*) entr'acte, interlude; (*fig: interruption*) interlude, break.

entraide [ɑ̃tʀɛd] nf mutual aid. (*Jur*) ~ **judiciaire internationale** international judicial cooperation; (*Admin*) **service d'~** support service.

entraider (s') [ɑ̃tʀede] [1] vpr to help one another *ou* each other.

entrailles [ɑ̃tʀɑj] nfpl a *[animaux]* entrails, guts. b (*littér*) *[personne]* entrails; (*ventre maternel*) womb. (*fig*) **sans ~** heartless, unfeeling; **la faim le mordait aux ~** hunger gnawed at him *ou* at his guts; **spectacle qui vous prend aux ~** *ou* **qui vous remue les ~** sight that shakes your very soul *ou* shakes you to the core. c (*littér*) *[édifice, terre]* bowels, depths.

entrain [ɑ̃tʀɛ̃] nm *[personne]* spirit, drive; *[réunion]* spirit, liveliness, go. **avec ~** *répondre* with gusto; *travailler* spiritedly, with spirit *ou* plenty of drive; *manger* with gusto, heartily; **faire qch sans ~** to do sth half-heartedly *ou* unenthusiastically; **être sans ~** to feel dispirited, have no energy; **être plein d'~, avoir de l'~** to have plenty of *ou* be full of drive *ou* go; **ça manque d'~** *[soirée]* it's dragging, it's not exactly lively, it's a bit dead*.

entraînant, e [ɑ̃tʀɛnɑ̃, ɑ̃t] adj *paroles, musique* stirring, rousing; *rythme* brisk, lively.

entraînement [ɑ̃tʀɛnmɑ̃] nm a (*action d'entraîner*) *[roue, bielle etc]* driving; *[athlète]* training, coaching; *[cheval]* training. **~ à chaîne** chain drive. b (*impulsion, force*) *[passions]* (driving) force, impetus; *[habitude]* force. **des ~s dangereux** dangerous impulses. c (*Sport: préparation, exercice*) training (*NonC*). **deux heures d'~ chaque matin** 2 hours of training every morning; **course/terrain d'~** training course/ground; **manquer d'~** to be out of training; **il a de l'~** he's highly trained, he's really fit; **il est à l'~** he's in a training session, he's training; **il s'est blessé à l'~** he hurt himself at *ou* while training *ou* during a training session.

entraîner [ɑ̃tʀene] [1] 1 vt a (*lit*) (*charrier*) *épave, objets arrachés* to carry *ou* drag along; (*Tech: mouvoir*) *bielle, roue, machine* to drive; (*tirer*) *wagons* to pull. **le courant les entraîna vers les rapides** the current carried *ou* dragged *ou* swept them along towards the rapids; **la locomotive entraîne une vingtaine de wagons** the locomotive pulls *ou* hauls twenty or so carriages; **le poids de ses habits l'entraîna vers le fond** the weight of his clothes dragged him (down) towards the bottom; **il entraîna son camarade dans sa chute** he pulled *ou* dragged his friend down in his fall; **danseur qui entraîne sa cavalière** dancer who carries his partner along (with him); (*fig*) **il l'entraîna (avec lui) dans la ruine** he dragged her down (with him) in his downfall.

b (*emmener*) *personne* to take (off) (*vers* towards). **il m'entraîna vers la sortie/dans un coin** he dragged *ou* took me (off) towards the exit/into a corner; **il les entraîna à sa suite vers ...** he took them (along *ou* off) with him towards ... .

c (*fig: influencer*) to lead. **~ qn à voler qch** to get sb to steal sth; **~ ses camarades à boire/dans la débauche** to lead one's friends into drinking/bad ways; **se laisser ~ par ses camarades** to let o.s. be led by one's friends; **cela l'a entraîné à de grosses dépenses** that meant great expense for him, that led him into great expense.

d (*causer*) to bring about, lead to; (*impliquer*) to entail, mean. **ceci a entraîné des compressions budgétaires/dépenses imprévues** this has brought about *ou* led to budgetary restraints/unexpected expense; **si je vous comprends bien, ceci entraîne la perte de nos avantages** if I understand you, this means *ou* will mean *ou* will entail the loss of our advantages.

e (*emporter*) *[rythme]* to carry along; *[passion, enthousiasme, éloquence]* to carry away. **son éloquence entraîna les foules** his eloquence carried the crowds along (with him); **son enthousiasme l'a entraîné trop loin/au-delà de ses intentions** his enthusiasm carried him too far/further than he intended; (*fig*) **se laisser ~ (par l'enthousiasme/ses passions/un rythme)** to (let o.s.) get *ou* be carried away (by enthusiasm/one's passions/a rhythm).

f (*préparer*) *athlète* to train, coach; *cheval* to train (*à* for).

2 **s'entraîner** vpr a (*Sport*) to train. **il est indispensable de s'~ régulièrement** one must train regularly; **où est-il? — il s'entraîne au stade** where is he? — he's (doing some) training at the stadium; **s'~ à la course/au lancer du poids/pour le championnat** to get in training *ou* to train for running/for the shot put *ou* for putting the shot/for the championship; **s'~ à faire un certain mouvement** to practise a certain movement, work on a certain movement.

b (*gén*) **s'~ à faire qch** to train o.s. to do sth; **s'~ à la discussion/à l'art de la discussion** to train o.s. for discussion/in the art of discussion; **il s'entraîne à parler en public** he is training himself to speak in public.

entraîneur [ɑ̃tʀɛnœʀ] nm *[cheval]* trainer; *[équipe, coureur, boxeur]* coach, trainer. (*fig littér*) **un ~ d'hommes** a leader of men.

entraîneuse [ɑ̃tʀɛnøz] nf *[bar]* hostess; (*Sport*) coach, trainer.

entrapercevoir [ɑ̃tʀapɛʀsəvwaʀ] [28] vt to catch a (brief) glimpse of.

entrave [ɑ̃tʀav] nf a (*fig: obstacle*) hindrance (*à* to). **~ à la circulation** hindrance to traffic; **~ à la liberté d'expression** constraint upon *ou* obstacle to freedom of expression; *liberté, bonheur* **sans ~** unbridled. b *[animal]* hobble, fetter, shackle. *[prisonnier]* **~s** chains, fetters (*littér*); (*fig littér*) **se débarrasser des ~s de la rime** to free o.s. from the shackles *ou* fetters of rhyme (*littér*).

entraver [ɑ̃tʀave] [1] vt a (*gêner*) *circulation* to hold up; *action, plans* to hinder, hamper, get in the way of. **~ la carrière de qn** to hinder sb in his career. b *animal* to hobble, shackle, fetter; *prisonnier* to chain (up), fetter (*littér*). c (‡: *comprendre*) to get‡. **je n'y entrave que couic** *ou* **que dalle** I just don't get it‡, I don't twig (it) at all‡ (*Brit*). d (*Ling*) **voyelle entravée** checked vowel.

entre [ɑ̃tʀ] prép a (*à mi-chemin de, dans l'intervalle de*) *objets, dates, opinions* between. **~ guillemets/parenthèses** in inverted commas (*Brit*) *ou* quotation marks/brackets *ou* parentheses; (*fig*) **mettons nos querelles ~ parenthèses** let's put our disagreements behind us; (*fig*) **~ parenthèses, ce qu'il dit est faux** by the way, what he says is wrong; **~ le vert et le jaune** between green and yellow; **~ la vie et la mort** between life and death; **~ ciel et terre** between heaven and earth; **vous l'aimez saignant, à point ou ~ les deux?** do you like it rare, medium or between the two? *ou* or in-between?; **la vérité est ~ les deux** the truth is somewhere *ou* something between the two; *voir* **lire**[1].

b (*entouré par*) *murs* within, between; *montagnes* among, between. (*fig*) **enfermé ~ quatre murs** shut in; **encaissé ~ les hautes parois** enclosed between the high walls.

c (*au milieu de, parmi*) *pierres, objets épars, personnes* among, amongst. **il aperçut un objet brillant ~ les pierres** he saw an object shining among(st) the stones; **choisir ~ plusieurs choses** to choose from among several things, choose between several things; **il hésita ~ plusieurs routes** he hesitated between several roads; **brave ~ les braves†** bravest of the brave†; (*frm*) **je le compte ~ mes amis** I number him among my friends; **lui, ~ autres, n'est pas d'accord** he, for one *ou* among others, doesn't agree; **~ autres (choses)** among other things; **~ autres (personnes)** among others; **l'un d'~ eux** one of them; **plusieurs d'~ nous** several of us, several of our number (*frm*); **il est intelligent ~ tous** he is supremely intelligent; **problème difficile ~ tous** inordinately *ou* particularly difficult problem; **cette heure ~ toutes** this (hour) of all hours; **je le reconnaîtrais ~ tous** I would know *ou* recognize him anywhere; **c'est le meilleur ~ tous mes amis** he's the best friend I have; **il l'a partagé ~ tous ses amis** he shared it out among all his friends.

d (*dans*) in, into. (*fig*) **ma vie est ~ vos mains** my life is *ou* lies in your hands; **j'ai eu ce livre ~ les mains** I had that book in my (very) hands; **prendre ~ ses bras** to take in one's arms; **tomber ~ les mains de l'ennemi/d'escrocs** to fall into the hands of the enemy/of crooks.

e (*à travers*) through, between. **le poisson/le prisonnier m'a filé ~ les doigts** the fish/the prisoner slipped through my fingers; **je l'ai aperçu ~ les branches** I saw it through *ou* between the branches.

f (*indiquant une relation*) (*deux choses*) between; (*plus de deux*) among. **rapports ~ deux personnes/choses** relationship between two people/things; **nous sommes ~ nous** *ou* **~ amis** we're all friends here, we're among friends; **~ nous** between you and me, between ourselves; **~ nous c'est à la vie, à la mort** we are *ou* shall be friends for life; **~ eux 4** among the 4 of them; **qu'y a-t-il exactement ~ eux?** what exactly is there between them?; **il n'y a rien de commun ~ eux** they have nothing in common *ou* no common ground; **ils se marient ~ eux** they intermarry; **ils préfèrent rester ~ eux** they prefer to keep (themselves) to themselves *ou* to be on their own; (*fig*) **ils se dévorent ~ eux** they are (constantly) at each other's throats; **ils se sont entendus ~ eux** they reached a mutual agreement; **entendez-vous ~ vous** sort it out among yourselves; **ils se sont disputés ~ eux** they have quarrelled (with each other *ou* with one another); **laissons-les se battre ~ eux** let's leave them to fight it out (between *ou* among themselves); **on ne va pas se battre ~ nous** we're not going to fight (among ourselves).

g (*loc*) **~ chien et loup** when the shadows are falling, at dusk; **~ deux âges** middle-aged; (*fig*) **~ deux portes** briefly, quickly; (*lit*) **~ deux eaux** just below the surface; (*fig*) **nager ~ deux eaux** to keep a foot in both camps; **pris ~ deux feux** caught in the crossfire; **~ quatre-z-yeux*** in private; **parler ~ ses dents** to mumble; (*fig*) **être assis** *ou* **avoir le cul‡ ~ deux chaises** to be caught between two stools.

entrebâillement [ɑ̃tʀəbɑjmɑ̃] nm: **l'~ de la porte le fit hésiter** the door's being half-open *ou* ajar made him hesitate, he hesitated on seeing the door half-open *ou* ajar; **dans/par l'~ de la porte** in/through the half-open door.

entrebâiller [ɑ̃tʀəbɑje] [1] vt to half-open. **la porte est entrebâillée** the door is ajar *ou* half-open.

entrebâilleur [ɑ̃tʀəbɑjœʀ] nm door chain.

entrechat [ɑ̃tʀəʃa] nm (*Danse*) entrechat; (*hum: saut*) leap, spring. **faire des ~s** to leap about.

entrechoquement [ɑ̃tʀəʃɔkmɑ̃] nm (*voir* **entrechoquer, s'entrechoquer**) knocking, banging; clinking; chattering; clashing.

entrechoquer [ɑ̃tʀəʃɔke] [1] 1 vt (*gén*) to knock *ou* bang together; *verres* to clink *ou* chink (together). 2 **s'entrechoquer** vpr (*gén*) to knock *ou* bang together; *[verres]* to clink *ou* chink (together); *[dents]* to chatter; *[épées]* to clash *ou* clang together; (*fig*) *[idées, mots]* to jostle together.

entrecôte [ɑ̃tʀəkot] nf entrecôte steak, rib steak.

entrecouper [ɑ̃tʀəkupe] [1] 1 vt: **~ de** *citations* to intersperse *ou* pepper with; *rires, sarcasmes* to interrupt with; *haltes* to interrupt with, break with. **voix entrecoupée de sanglots** voice broken with sobs; **parler d'une voix entrecoupée** to speak in a broken voice, have a catch in one's voice as one speaks. 2 **s'entrecouper** vpr *[lignes]* to intersect, cut across each other.

entrecroisement [ɑ̃tʀəkʀwazmɑ̃] nm (*voir* **entrecroiser**) intertwining; intersecting.

entrecroiser vt, **s'entrecroiser** vpr [ɑ̃tʀəkʀwaze] [1] *fils* to intertwine; *lignes, routes* to intersect.

entre-déchirer (s') [ɑ̃tʀədeʃiʀe] [1] vpr (*littér*) to tear one another *ou* each other to pieces.

entre-deux [ɑ̃tʀədø] nm inv a (*intervalle*) intervening period, period in between. b (*Sport*) jump ball. c (*Couture*) ~ **de dentelle** lace insert.

entre-deux-guerres [ɑ̃tʀədøgɛʀ] nm inv: **l'~** the interwar years *ou* period; **pendant l'~** between the wars, in *ou* during the interwar years *ou* period.

entre-dévorer (s') [ɑ̃tʀədevɔʀe] [1] vpr (*littér*) to tear one another *ou* each other to pieces.

entrée [ɑ̃tʀe] 1 nf a (*arrivée*) *[personne]* entry, entrance; *[véhicule, bateau, armée occupante]* entry. **à son ~, tous se sont tus** as he came *ou* walked in *ou* entered, everybody fell silent; **à son ~ dans le salon** as he came *ou* walked into *ou* entered the lounge; **faire une ~ remarquée** to be noticed as one enters; **faire une ~ discrète** to make a discreet entry *ou* entrance, enter discreetly; **faire son ~ dans le salon** to enter the lounge; **l'~ en gare du train/au port du navire** the train's/ship's entry into the station/port; (*Admin*) **à son ~ en fonctions** when he took up office; (*Théât*) **faire son ~** to make one's entry *ou* entrance; (*Théât*) **rater son ~** (*sur scène*) to fluff one's entrance; (*première réplique*) to fluff one's cue.

b (*accès*) entry, admission (*de, dans* to). (*sur pancarte*) "**~**" "way in"; "**~ libre**" (*dans boutique*) "come in and look round"; (*dans musée*) "admission free"; "**~ interdite**" "no admittance", "no entry"; "**~ interdite à tout véhicule**" "vehicles prohibited"; **l'~ est gratuite/payante** there is no charge/there is a charge for admission; **on lui a refusé l'~ de la salle** he was refused admission *ou* entrance *ou* entry to the hall; **cette porte donne ~ dans le salon** this door leads into the lounge *ou* gives access to the lounge.

c (*Comm*) *[marchandises]* entry; (*Fin*) *[capital]* inflow. **droits d'~** import duties.

d (*Tech: pénétration*) *[pièce, clou]* insertion; *[fluide, air]* entry.

e (*fig: fait d'adhérer etc*) **~ dans un club** joining a club, admission to a club; **~ dans une famille** becoming part of a family; **~ au couvent/à l'hôpital** going into a convent/into hospital; **~ à l'université** university entrance; **depuis son ~ à l'université** since his entrance to university, since he went to university; **se voir refuser son ~ dans un club/une école** to be refused admission *ou* entry to a club/school, be rejected by a club/school; **faire son ~ dans le monde** *[bébé]* to come into the world; *[débutante]* to enter society, make one's début in society.

f (*fig*) **au moment de l'~ en fusion/ébullition** *etc* when melting/boiling *etc* point is reached.

g (*billet*) ticket. **j'ai pris 2 ~s** I got 2 tickets; **billet d'~** entrance ticket; **les ~s couvriront tous les frais** the receipts *ou* takings will cover all expenses; **ils ont fait 10 000 ~s** they sold 10,000 tickets.

h (*porte, portail etc*) entry, entrance; *[tunnel, port, grotte]* entry, entrance, mouth. (*Théât*) **~ des artistes** stage door; **~ de service** service entrance; *[villa]* tradesmen's entrance; **~ principale** main entrance.

i (*vestibule*) entrance (hall).

j (*fig littér: début*) outset; (*Mus: motif*) entry. **à l'~ de l'hiver/de la belle saison** as winter/the warm weather set (*ou* sets *etc*) in, at the onset *ou* beginning of winter/the warm weather; **à l'~ de la vie** at life's outset.

k (*Culin: mets*) entrée.

l (*Comm, Statistique*) entry; (*Lexicographie*) (*mot*) headword (*Brit*), entry word (*US*); (*article*) entry. **tableau à double ~** double entry table.

m (*Ordin*) input. **~-sortie** input-output.

n (*loc*) **d'~, d'~ de jeu** from the outset.

2 **entrées** fpl: **avoir ses ~s auprès de qn** to have free *ou* easy access to sb; **il a ses ~s au ministère** he comes and goes freely in the ministry.

3 comp ▸**entrée d'air** (*Tech*) air inlet ▸**entrée de ballet** (*Théât*) entrée de ballet ▸**entrée en matière** introduction ▸**entrée en scène** entrance ▸**entrée en vigueur** coming into force *ou* application; *voir* **concours, date, examen.**

entre-égorger (s') [ɑ̃tʀegɔʀʒe] [3] vpr to cut each other's *ou* one another's throats.

entrefaites [ɑ̃tʀəfɛt] nfpl: **sur ces ~** (*à ce moment-là*) at that moment, at this juncture.

entrefer [ɑ̃tʀəfɛʀ] nm air-gap.

entrefilet [ɑ̃tʀəfilɛ] nm (*petit article*) paragraph.

entregent [ɑ̃tʀəʒɑ̃] nm savoir-faire. **avoir de l'~** to have a good manner with people.

entre-jambes [ɑ̃tʀəʒɑ̃b] nm inv (*Couture*) crotch.

entrelacement [ɑ̃tʀəlasmɑ̃] nm (*action, état*) intertwining, interlacing. **un ~ de branches** a network *ou* crisscross of branches.

entrelacer vt, **s'entrelacer** vpr [ɑ̃tʀəlase] [3] to intertwine, interlace.

entrelacs [ɑ̃tʀəlɑ] nm (*Archit*) interlacing (*NonC*); (*Peinture*) interlace (*NonC*).

entrelardé, e [ɑ̃tʀəlaʀde] (ptp de **entrelarder**) adj (*gras*) *viande* streaked with fat.

entrelarder [ɑ̃tʀəlaʀde] [1] vt (*Culin*) to lard. (*fig*) **~ de citations** to interlard *ou* intersperse with quotations.

entremêler [ɑ̃tʀəmele] [1] 1 vt a *choses* to (inter)mingle, intermix. **~ des scènes tragiques et des scènes comiques** to (inter)mingle *ou* intermix tragic and comic scenes. b (*truffer de*) **~ un récit de** to intersperse *ou* pepper a tale with. 2 **s'entremêler** vpr *[branches, cheveux]* to become entangled (*à* with); *[idées]* to become intermingled.

entremets [ɑ̃tʀəmɛ] nm (cream) sweet (*Brit*) *ou* dessert.

entremetteur [ɑ̃tʀəmɛtœʀ] nm a (*péj*) (*gén*) go-between; (*proxénète*) procurer, go-between. b (*intermédiaire*) mediator, go-between.

entremetteuse [ɑ̃tʀəmɛtøz] nf (*péj*) (*gén*) go-between; (*proxénète*) procuress, go-between.

entremettre (s') [ɑ̃tʀəmɛtʀ] [56] vpr a (*dans une querelle*) to act as mediator, mediate, intervene (*dans* in); (*péj*) to interfere (*dans* in). b (*intercéder*) to intercede (*auprès de* with).

entremise [ɑ̃tʀəmiz] nf intervention. **offrir son ~** to offer to act as mediator *ou* to mediate; **grâce à son ~** thanks to his intervention; **apprendre qch par l'~ de qn** to hear about sth through sb.

entrepont [ɑ̃tʀəpɔ̃] nm (*Naut*) steerage. **dans l'~** in steerage.

entreposage [ɑ̃tʀəpozaʒ] nm storing, storage.

entreposer [ɑ̃tʀəpoze] [1] vt (*gén*) to store, put into storage; (*en douane*) to put in a bonded warehouse.

entrepôt [ɑ̃tʀəpo] nm (*gén*) warehouse; (*Douane*) bonded warehouse; (*ville, port*) entrepôt.

entreprenant, e [ɑ̃tʀəpʀənɑ̃, ɑ̃t] adj (*gén*) enterprising; (*avec les femmes*) forward.

entreprendre [ɑ̃tʀəpʀɑ̃dʀ] [58] vt a (*commencer*) (*gén*) to begin *ou* start (upon), embark upon; *travail, démarche* to set about; *voyage* to set out (up)on; *procès* to start up; (*se lancer dans*) *voyage, travail* to undertake, embark upon, launch upon. **~ de faire qch** to undertake to do sth; **la peur d'~** the fear of undertaking things. b *personne* (†: *courtiser*) to woo†, court†; (*pour raconter une histoire etc*) to buttonhole, collar*; (*pour poser des questions*) to tackle. **il m'entreprit sur le sujet de ...** he tackled me on the question of ... .

entrepreneur, -euse [ɑ̃tʀəpʀənœʀ, øz] nm,f a (*en menuiserie etc*) contractor. **~ (en bâtiment)** building contractor; **~ de transports** haulage contractor (*Brit*), trucker (*US*); **~ de pompes funèbres** undertaker (*Brit*), funeral director (*Brit*), mortician (*US*). b (*brasseur d'affaires*) entrepreneur.

entrepreneurial, e, mpl **-iaux** [ɑ̃ntʀəpʀənøʀjal, jo] adj entrepreneurial.

entreprise [ɑ̃tʀəpʀiz] nf a (*firme*) firm, company. **petite/grosse ~** small/big firm *ou* concern; **~ de construction/camionnage** building firm/haulage firm (*Brit*) *ou* trucker (*US*); **~ de déménagement** removal (*Brit*) *ou* moving (*US*) firm; **~ de pompes funèbres** undertaker's (*Brit*), funeral director's (*Brit*), funeral parlor (*US*); **~ de travaux publics** civil engineering firm; *voir* **chef[1], concentration.** b (*dessein*) undertaking, venture, enterprise; *voir* **esprit, libre.** c (*hum: envers une femme*) **~s** advances.

entrer [ɑ̃tʀe] [1] 1 vi (*avec aux être*) a (*lit*) (*gén*) (*aller*) to go in, get in, enter; (*venir*) to come in, enter; (*à pied*) to walk in; (*en voiture*) to drive in; *[véhicule]* to drive in, go *ou* come in, enter. **~ dans** *pièce, jardin* to go *ou* come into, enter; *voiture* to get in(to); *région, pays [voyageurs]* to go *ou* come into, enter; *[armée]* to enter; **~ chez qn** to come (*ou* go) into sb's house; **~ en gare/au port** to come into *ou* enter the station/harbour; **~ en courant** to run in, come running in; **~ en boitant** to limp in, come limping in, come in limping; **il entra discrètement** he came in *ou* entered discreetly, he slipped in; **~ en coup de vent** to burst in, come bursting in, come in like a whirlwind; **~ sans payer** to get in without paying; **entrez sans frapper** come *ou* go *ou* walk straight in (without knocking); **frappez avant d'~** knock before you go in *ou* enter; **entrez!** come in!; **entre donc!** come on in!; **qu'il entre!** tell him to come in, show him in; **entrons voir** let's go in and see; **je ne fais qu'~ et sortir** I'm only stopping for a moment; **les gens entraient et sortaient** people were going *ou* coming in and out; **~ en scène** (*lit*) to come (*ou* go) on (to the stage); (*fig*) to come on *ou* enter the scene; (*Théât*) "**entre la servante**" "enter the maid"; (*Théât*) "**entrent 3 gardes**" "enter 3 guards"; **~ par la porte de la cave/par la fenêtre** to go *ou* get in *ou* enter by the cellar door/the window; **je suis entré chez eux** I called in *ou* dropped in at their house; **je suis entré chez le boucher** I went to *ou* I called in at the butcher's; **on y entre comme dans un moulin** you can just walk in.

b (*Comm*) *[marchandises, devises]* to enter. **tout ce qui entre (dans le pays) est soumis à une taxe** everything entering (the country) is subject to duty.

c (*s'enfoncer*) **la boule est entrée dans le trou** the ball went into the hole; **l'objet n'entre pas dans la boîte** the object doesn't *ou* won't go into *ou* fit (into) the box; **le tenon entre dans la mortaise** the tenon fits into the mortice; **ça n'entre pas** it doesn't fit, it won't go *ou* fit in; **la balle est entrée dans le poumon gauche/le montant de la porte** the bullet went into *ou* lodged itself in the left lung/the doorframe; **son coude m'entrait dans les côtes** his elbow was digging into my ribs; **l'eau entre (à l'intérieur)/par le toit** the water gets inside/gets *ou* comes in through the roof; **l'air/la lumière entre dans la pièce** air/light comes into *ou* enters the room; **pour que l'air/la lumière puisse ~** to allow air/light to enter *ou* get in; **le vent entre de partout** the wind comes *ou* gets in from all sides *ou* blows in everywhere; **~ dans l'eau** *[baigneur]* to get into the water; (*en marchant*) to wade into the water; *[embarcation]* to enter the water; **~ dans le bain** to get into the bath; **~ dans le brouillard** *[randonneurs, avion]* to enter *ou* hit* fog; **nous n'entrerons jamais tous dans ta voiture** we're never all going to get *ou* fit into your car; **la rage/jalousie est entrée dans son cœur** his heart filled with rage/jealousy; **l'argent entre dans les caisses** money is coming in; **à force d'explications ça finira par ~*** explain it for long enough and it'll sink in*; **alors ces maths, ça entre?*** are you getting the hang of maths then?*; **c'est entré comme dans du beurre*** it went like a (hot) knife through butter.

d (*fig: devenir membre*) **~ dans** *club, parti, firme* to join; *groupe, famille* to go *ou* come into; *métier* to go into; **~ dans la magistrature** to become a magistrate, enter the magistracy; **~ à l'hôpital/à l'asile** to go into hospital/an asylum; **~ dans l'armée** to join the army; **~ dans les affaires** to go into business; **~ dans la profession médicale** to enter the medical profession; **~ dans les ordres** to take orders; **~ en religion/au couvent** to enter the religious life/a convent; **on l'a fait ~ comme serveur/sous-chef** he's been found a job as *ou* they got him taken on as a waiter/deputy chief clerk; (*Scol*) **elle entre en dernière année** she's just going into her final year; **~ à l'université** to enter *ou* go to university *ou* college; **~ au service de qn** to enter sb's service; **~ dans l'histoire** to go down in history; **~ dans la légende** to become a legend; **~ dans l'usage courant** *[mot]* to come into *ou* enter common use; *voir* **jeu, scène.**

e (*heurter*) **~ dans** *arbre, poteau* to go into; (*Aut*) **quelqu'un lui est entré dedans*** someone banged into him.

f (*partager*) **~ dans** *vues, peines de qn* to share; (*frm*) **~ dans les sentiments de qn** to share sb's *ou* enter into sb's feelings, sympathize with sb.

g (*être une composante de*) **~ dans** *catégorie* to fall into, come into; *mélange* to go into; **les substances qui entrent dans ce mélange** the substances which go into *ou* make up this mixture; **on pourrait faire ~ ceci dans la catégorie suivante** one might put this into the following category; **tous ces frais entrent dans le prix de revient** all these costs (go to) make up the cost price; **il y entre un peu de jalousie** a bit of jealousy comes into it; **votre avis est entré pour beaucoup dans sa décision** your opinion counted for a good deal in his decision; **il n'entre pas dans mes intentions de le faire** I don't have any intention of doing so; *voir* **ligne[1]**.

h (*fig: commencer*) **~ dans** *phase, période* to enter (into *ou* (up)on); **~ dans une profonde rêverie/une colère noire** to go (off) into a deep daydream/a towering rage; **~ dans la vie active** to embark on *ou* enter active life; **~ dans la cinquantaine** to turn fifty; *voir* **danse.**

i (*fig: aborder*) **~ dans** *sujet, discussion* to enter into; **~ dans le vif du sujet** to get to *ou* reach the heart of the subject; **il s'agit d'~ véritablement dans la discussion** one must enter into the discussion properly; **sans ~ dans les détails/ces considérations** without going into details/these considerations; **il entra dans des considérations futiles** he went off into some futile considerations.

j (*devenir*) **~ en convalescence** to begin convalescence; **~ en effervescence** to reach a state of effervescence (*frm*), begin to effervesce; **~ en ébullition** to reach boiling point, begin to boil; **~ en guerre** to enter the war; *voir* **contact, fonction, vigueur.**

k **laisser ~** *visiteur, intrus* to let in; *lumière, air* to let in, allow in; (*involontairement*) *eau, air, poussière* to let in; **ne laisse ~ personne** don't let anybody in; **laisser ~ qn dans** *pièce* to let sb into; *pays* to let sb into *ou* enter, allow sb into *ou* to enter; **on t'a laissé ~ au parti/club/dans l'armée** they've let you into *ou* let you join the party/club/army.

l **faire ~** (*introduire*) *invité, visiteur, client* to show in; *pièce, tenon, objet à emballer* to fit in; (*en fraude*) *marchandises, immigrants* to smuggle in, take *ou* bring in; *accusé, témoin* to bring in, call; **faire ~ la voiture dans le garage** to get the car into the garage; **faire ~ une clef dans la serrure** to insert *ou* fit a key in the lock; **il m'a fait ~ dans leur club/au jury** (*m'a persuadé*) he had me join *ou* got me to join their club/the panel; (*a fait jouer son influence*) he got me into their club/onto the panel, he helped me join their club/the panel; (*m'a contraint*) he made me join their club/the panel; **il me fit ~ dans la cellule** he showed me into the cell; **faire ~ qch de force dans un emballage** to force *ou* stuff sth into a package.

2 **vt** (*avec aux avoir; plus gén* **faire ~**) a *marchandises* (*par la douane*) to take *ou* bring in, import; (*en contrebande*) to take *ou* bring in, smuggle in.

b (*faire pénétrer*) **~ les bras dans les manches** to put one's arms into the sleeves; **ne m'entre pas ta canne dans les côtes** stop digging your stick into my ribs.

c (*faire s'ajuster*) *pièce* to make fit (*dans qch* in sth). **comment allez-vous ~ cette armoire dans la chambre?** how are you going to get that wardrobe into the bedroom?

d (*Ordin*) *données* to key in.

entresol [ɑ̃tʀəsɔl] **nm** entresol, mezzanine (*between ground and first floor*).

entre-temps [ɑ̃tʀətɑ̃] **adv** (*aussi* **dans l'~†**) meanwhile, (in the) meantime.

entretenir [ɑ̃tʀət(ə)niʀ] 22 1 **vt** a (*conserver en bon état*) *propriété, bâtiment* to maintain, see to the upkeep of, look after; *vêtement* to look after; *route, machine* to maintain. **~ un jardin** to look after *ou* see to the upkeep of a garden; **ce meuble s'entretient facilement** it is easy to keep this piece of furniture in good condition *ou* to look after this piece of furniture.

b (*faire vivre*) *famille* to support, keep, maintain; *maîtresse* to keep, support; *armée* to keep, maintain; *troupe de théâtre etc* to support. **se faire ~ par qn** to be kept *ou* supported by sb.

c (*faire durer*) *souvenir* to keep alive; *haine, amitié* to keep alive, keep going, foster; *espoir* to cherish, keep alive, foster. **~ l'inquiétude de qn** to keep sb feeling uneasy, keep sb in a state of anxiety; **~ des rapports suivis avec qn** to be in constant contact with sb; **~ une correspondance suivie avec qn** to keep up a regular correspondence with sb, correspond regularly with sb; **l'air marin entretient une perpétuelle humidité** the sea air maintains a constant state of humidity; **~ le feu** to keep the fire going *ou* burning; **il m'a entretenu dans l'erreur** he didn't disabuse me (of it); **j'entretiens des craintes à son sujet** I am somewhat anxious about him; **~ sa forme, s'~ (en bonne forme)** to keep o.s. in (good) shape, keep (o.s.) fit.

d (*frm: converser*) **~ qn** to converse with *ou* speak to sb; **il m'a entretenu pendant une heure** we conversed for an hour, he conversed with me for an hour; **il a entretenu l'auditoire de ses voyages** he addressed the audience *ou* spoke to the audience about his travels.

2 **s'entretenir vpr** a (*converser*) **s'~ avec qn** to converse with *ou* speak to sb (*de* about); **ils s'entretenaient à voix basse** they were conversing in hushed tones.

b (*pourvoir à ses besoins*) to support o.s., be self-supporting. **il s'entretient tout seul maintenant** he is completely self-supporting now, he supports himself entirely on his own now.

entretenu, e [ɑ̃tʀət(ə)ny] (**ptp de entretenir**) **adj** *femme* kept (*épith*). **jardin bien/mal ~** well-/badly-kept garden, well-/badly-tended garden.

entretien [ɑ̃tʀətjɛ̃] **nm** a (*conservation*) *[jardin, maison]* upkeep; *[route]* maintenance, upkeep; *[machine]* maintenance. **cher à l'~** expensive to maintain; **d'un ~ facile** *surface* easy to clean; *voiture, appareil* easy to maintain; **visite d'~** service; *voir* **produit.**

b (*aide à la subsistance*) *[famille, étudiant]* keep, support; *[armée, corps de ballet]* maintenance, keep. **pourvoir à l'~ de** *famille* to keep, support; *armée* to maintain.

c (*discussion privée*) discussion, conversation; (*accordé à qn*) interview; (*débat public*) discussion. (*Pol*) **~(s)** talks, discussions; **~ télévisé** televised interview; **demander un ~ à son patron** to ask one's boss for an interview; **nous aurons un ~ à Francfort avec nos collègues allemands** we shall be having a meeting *ou* having discussions in Frankfurt with our German colleagues.

entre-tuer (s') [ɑ̃tʀətɥe] 1 **vpr** to kill one another *ou* each other.

entrevoir [ɑ̃tʀəvwaʀ] 30 **vt** a (*voir indistinctement*) to make out; (*fig: pressentir*) *objections, solutions, complications* to foresee, anticipate; *amélioration* to glimpse. **je commence à ~ la vérité** I have an inkling of the truth, I'm beginning to see the truth; (*fig*) **~ la lumière au bout du tunnel** to see (the) light at the end of the tunnel. b (*apercevoir brièvement*) (*gén*) to catch a glimpse of, catch sight of; *visiteur* to see briefly. **vous n'avez fait qu'~ les difficultés** you have only half seen the difficulties.

entrevue [ɑ̃tʀəvy] **nf** (*discussion*) meeting; (*audience*) interview; (*Pol*) talks *(pl)*, discussions *(pl)*, meeting. **venir/se présenter à** *ou* **pour une ~** to come for *ou* to an interview.

entrisme [ɑ̃tʀism] **nm** entryism.

entriste [ɑ̃tʀist] **adj, nmf** entryist.

entrouvert, e [ɑ̃tʀuvɛʀ, ɛʀt] (**ptp de entrouvrir**) **adj** (*gén*) half-open; *fenêtre, porte* ajar (*attrib*), half-open; *abîme* gaping. **ses lèvres ~es** her parted lips.

entrouvrir [ɑ̃tʀuvʀiʀ] 18 1 **vt** to half-open. 2 **s'entrouvrir vpr** (*gén*) to half-open; *[abîme]* to gape; *[lèvres]* to part.

entuber⁑ [ɑ̃tybe] 1 **vt** (*duper*) to do⁑ (*Brit*), con⁑. **se faire ~** to be done⁑ (*Brit*) *ou* conned⁑.

enturbanné, e [ɑ̃tyʀbane] **adj** turbaned.

énucléation [enykleasjɔ̃] **nf** (*Méd*) enucleation.

énucléer [enyklee] 1 **vt** (*Méd*) to enucleate.

énumératif, -ive [enymeʀatif, iv] **adj** enumerative.

énumération [enymeʀasjɔ̃] **nf** enumeration, listing.

énumérer [enymeʀe] 6 **vt** to enumerate, list.

énurésie [enyʀezi] **nf** enuresis.

énurétique [enyʀetik] **adj** enuretic.

env (**abrév de environ**) approx.

envahir [ɑ̃vaiʀ] 2 **vt** a (*Mil, gén*) to invade, overrun; *[douleur,* *sentiment]* to overcome, sweep through. **le sommeil l'envahissait** he was overcome by sleep, sleep was creeping *ou* stealing over him; **le jardin est envahi par les orties** the garden is overrun *ou* overgrown with nettles; **la foule envahit la place** the crowd swarmed *ou* swept into the square. **b** (*gén hum: déranger*) ~ **qn** to invade sb's privacy, intrude on sb's privacy.

envahissant, e [ɑ̃vaisɑ̃, ɑ̃t] **adj** *personne* interfering, intrusive; *enfant* demanding; *passion* invading (*épith*), invasive (*épith*); *odeur, goût* strong, pervasive; *herbes* which overrun everything.

envahissement [ɑ̃vaismɑ̃] **nm** invasion.

envahisseur [ɑ̃vaisœʀ] **1** **adj m** invading. **2** **nm** invader.

envasement [ɑ̃vɑzmɑ̃] **nm** *[port]* silting up.

envaser [ɑ̃vɑze] [1] **1** **vt** *port* to silt up. **2** **s'envaser** **vpr** *[port]* to silt up; *[bateau]* to stick in the mud; *[épave]* to sink in(to) the mud.

enveloppant, e [ɑ̃v(ə)lɔpɑ̃, ɑ̃t] **adj** enveloping (*épith*); (*Mil*) surrounding (*épith*), encircling (*épith*). **mouvement** ~ encircling movement.

enveloppe [ɑ̃v(ə)lɔp] **nf** **a** (*pli postal*) envelope. ~ **gommée/autocollante** *ou* **auto-adhésive** stick-down/self-seal envelope; ~ **rembourrée** padded bag; ~ **à fenêtre** window envelope; **sous** ~ *envoyer* under cover; **mettre une lettre sous** ~ to put a letter in an envelope.
b (*emballage*) (*gén*) covering; (*en papier, toile*) wrapping; (*en métal*) casing; (*gaine*) *[graine]* husk; *[organe]* covering membrane; *[pneu]* cover, casing; *[dirigeable]* envelope; *[chaudière]* lagging, jacket. **dans une** ~ **de métal** in a metal casing.
c (*apparence*) outward appearance, exterior. **un cœur d'or sous une rude** ~ a heart of gold beneath a rough exterior.
d (*littér: corps*) **il a quitté son** ~ **mortelle** he has cast off his earthly *ou* mortal frame (*littér*) *ou* shroud (*littér*).
e (*Math*) envelope.
f (*fig: somme d'argent*) sum of money; (*crédits*) budget. **toucher une** ~ (*pot-de-vin*) to get a bribe; (*gratification*) to get a bonus; (*départ en retraite*) to get a golden handshake; ~ **de départ** gratuity; ~ **budgétaire** budget; **l'**~ **de la recherche** the research budget; **le projet a reçu une** ~ **de 10 millions** the project was budgeted at 10 million.

enveloppement [ɑ̃v(ə)lɔpmɑ̃] **nm** **a** (*Méd*) pack. **b** (*Mil*) *[ennemi]* surrounding, encirclement. **manœuvre d'**~ pincer *ou* encircling movement.

envelopper [ɑ̃v(ə)lɔpe] [1] **vt** **a** *objet, enfant* to wrap (up). ~ **un membre de bandages** to wrap *ou* swathe a limb in bandages; **il s'enveloppa dans une cape** he wrapped *ou* swathed himself in a cape; (*fig hum*) **il s'enveloppa dans sa dignité** he donned an air of dignity; (*fig*) ~ **qn de son affection** to envelop sb in one's affection, surround sb with one's affection; (*hum*) **elle est assez enveloppée** she's well-padded* (*hum*).
b (*voiler*) *pensée, parole* to veil.
c (*gén littér: entourer*) *[brume]* to envelop, shroud. **le silence enveloppe la ville** the town is wrapped *ou* shrouded in silence; **la lumière enveloppe la campagne** the countryside is bathed in light; **événement enveloppé de mystère** event shrouded *ou* veiled in mystery; ~ **qn du regard** to envelop sb with one's gaze; **il l'enveloppa d'un regard tendre** he gave her a long loving look; **il enveloppa la plaine du regard** he took in the plain with his gaze; ~ **dans sa réprobation**† to include in one's disapproval.
d (*Mil*) *ennemi* to surround, encircle.

envenimement [ɑ̃v(ə)nimmɑ̃] **nm** *[plaie]* poisoning; *[querelle]* embittering; *[situation]* worsening.

envenimer [ɑ̃v(ə)nime] [1] **1** **vt** *plaie* to make septic, poison; *querelle* to inflame, fan the flame of; *situation* to inflame, aggravate. **2** **s'envenimer** **vpr** *[plaie]* to go septic, fester; *[querelle, situation]* to grow more bitter *ou* acrimonious.

envergure [ɑ̃vɛʀgyʀ] **nf** **a** *[oiseau, avion]* wingspan; *[voile]* breadth. **b** *[personne]* calibre; *[entreprise]* scale, scope; *[intelligence]* scope, range. **esprit de large** ~ wide-ranging mind; **entreprise de grande** ~ large-scale enterprise; **entreprendre des travaux de grande** ~ to embark upon an ambitious programme of building; **prendre de l'**~ *[entreprise, projet]* to expand; **manquer d'**~ *[personne]* to be low calibre.

envers[1] [ɑ̃vɛʀ] **prép** towards, to. **cruel/traître** ~ **qn** cruel/a traitor to sb; ~ **et contre tous** in the face of *ou* despite all opposition; **son attitude** ~ **moi** his attitude towards *ou* to me; **son dédain** ~ **les biens matériels** his disdain for *ou* of material possessions; **sa patience** ~ **elle** his patience with her.

envers[2] [ɑ̃vɛʀ] **nm** **a** *[étoffe]* wrong side; *[vêtement]* wrong side, inside; *[papier]* back; *[médaille]* reverse (side); *[feuille d'arbre]* underside; *[peau d'animal]* inside. **l'**~ **et l'endroit** the wrong (side) and the right side; (*fig*) **quand on connaît l'**~ **du décor** *ou* **du tableau** when you know what is going on underneath it all, when you know the other side of the picture.
b **à l'**~ *vêtement* inside out; *objet* (*à la verticale*) upside down, wrong side up; (*à l'horizontale*) the wrong way round, back to front; (*mouvement*) in the wrong way; **il a mis la maison à l'**~* he turned the house upside down *ou* inside out; (*fig*) **tout marche** *ou* **va à l'**~ everything is haywire *ou* is upside down, things are going all wrong; (*fig*) **faire qch à l'**~ (*à rebours*) to do sth the wrong way round; (*mal*) to do sth all wrong; (*fig*) **elle avait la tête à l'**~ her mind was in a whirl; (*Tricot*) **une maille à l'endroit, une maille à l'**~ knit one – purl one, one plain – one purl; *voir* **monde**.

envi [ɑ̃vi] **adv**: **imiter qn à l'**~ to vie with one another in imitating sb; **plats appétissants à l'**~ dishes each more appetizing *ou* mouth-watering than the last.

enviable [ɑ̃vjabl] **adj** enviable.

envie [ɑ̃vi] **nf** **a** ~ **de qch/de faire** (*désir de*) desire for sth/to do; (*grand désir de*) craving *ou* longing for sth/to do; (*besoin de*) need for sth/to do; **avoir** ~ **de** *objet, changement, ami* to want; (*sexuellement*) *personne* to desire, want; **avoir** ~ **de faire qch** to want to do sth, feel like doing sth; **j'ai** ~ **de ce livre, ce livre me fait** ~ I want *ou* should like that book; **avoir une** ~ **de chocolat** to have a craving *ou* longing for chocolate; **ce gâteau me fait** ~ I like the look of that cake, I fancy (*Brit*) that cake; **cette** ~ **de changement lui passa vite** he soon lost this desire *ou* craving *ou* longing for change; **j'ai** ~ **d'y aller** I feel like going, I should like to go; **il lui a pris l'**~ **d'y aller** he suddenly felt like *ou* fancied (*Brit*) going there, he suddenly felt the urge to go there; **je vais lui faire passer l'**~ **de recommencer*** I'll make sure he won't feel like doing that again in a hurry; **avoir bien/presque** ~ **de faire qch** to have a good *ou* great mind/half a mind to do sth; **j'ai** ~ **qu'il s'en aille** I would like him to go away, I wish he would go away; **avoir** ~ **de rire** to feel like laughing; **avoir** ~ **de vomir** to feel sick *ou* like vomiting; **cela lui a donné (l')**~ **de rire** it made him want to laugh; **avoir** ~* (*d'aller aux toilettes*) to need the loo* *ou* the toilet; **être pris d'une** ~ **pressante** to have a sudden urge for the toilet; *voir* **mourir**.
b (*convoitise*) envy. **mon bonheur lui fait** ~ he envies my happiness, my happiness makes him envious (of me); **ça fait** ~ it makes you envious; **regarder qch avec (un œil d')**~, **jeter des regards d'**~ **sur qch** to look enviously at sth, cast envious eyes on sth; **digne d'**~ enviable.
c (*Anat*) (*sur la peau*) birthmark; (*autour des ongles*) hangnail.

envier [ɑ̃vje] [7] **vt** *personne, bonheur etc* to envy, be envious of. **je vous envie votre maison** I envy you your house, I wish I had your house *ou* a house like yours, I'm envious of your house; **je vous envie (de pouvoir le faire)** I envy you *ou* I'm envious of you (being able to do it); **ce pays n'a rien à** ~ **au nôtre** (*il est mieux*) that country has no cause to be jealous of us; (*il est aussi mauvais*) that country is just as badly off as we are, there's nothing to choose between that country and ours.

envieusement* [ɑ̃vjøzmɑ̃] **adv** enviously.

envieux, -ieuse [ɑ̃vjø, jøz] **adj** envious. **faire des** ~ to excite *ou* arouse envy.

environ [ɑ̃viʀɔ̃] **1** **adv** about, or thereabouts, or so. **c'est à 100 km d'ici** it's about 100 km from here, it's 100 km or so from here; **il était** ~ **3 heures** it was about 3 o'clock, it was 3 o'clock or thereabouts. **2** **nmpl**: **les** ~**s** the surroundings; **aux** ~**s de 3 heures** (round) about 3 o'clock, 3 o'clock or thereabouts; **aux** ~**s de 10 F** (round) about *ou* in the region of 10 francs, 10 francs or thereabouts *ou* or so; **aux** ~**s** *ou* **dans les** ~**s du château** in the vicinity of *ou* neighbourhood of the castle; **qu'y a-t-il à voir dans les** ~**s?** what is there to see round about here?

environnant, e [ɑ̃viʀɔnɑ̃, ɑ̃t] **adj** surrounding.

environnement [ɑ̃viʀɔnmɑ̃] **nm** environment. **le ministère de l'E**~ ≃ the Department of the Environment (*Brit*), the Environmental Protection Agency (*US*).

environnemental, e, **pl -aux** [ɑ̃viʀɔnmɑ̃tal, o] **adj** environmental.

environnementaliste [ɑ̃viʀɔnmɑ̃talist(ə)] **nmf** environmentalist.

environner [ɑ̃viʀɔne] [1] **vt** to surround, encircle. **s'**~ **d'experts** to surround o.s. with experts.

envisageable [ɑ̃vizaʒabl] **adj** conceivable.

envisager [ɑ̃vizaʒe] [3] **vt** (*considérer*) to view, envisage, contemplate. **il envisage l'avenir de manière pessimiste** he views *ou* contemplates the future with pessimism, he has a pessimistic view of the future; **nous envisageons des transformations** we are thinking of *ou* envisaging changes; **nous n'avions pas envisagé cela** we hadn't counted on *ou* envisaged that; ~ **de faire** to be thinking of doing, consider *ou* contemplate doing.

envoi [ɑ̃vwa] **nm** **a** (*NonC: voir* **envoyer**) sending (off); dispatching; shipment; remittance. **faire un** ~ **de vivres** to send (a consignment of) supplies; **faire un** ~ **de fonds** to remit cash; ~ **contre remboursement** cash on delivery; **l'**~ **des couleurs** the hoisting of the colours; **coup d'**~ (*Sport*) kick-off; *[festival]* start, opening; *[série d'événements]* start, beginning. **b** (*colis*) parcel. ~ **de bouteilles** consignment of bottles; "~ **en nombre**" "mass mailing". **c** (*Littérat*) envoi.

envol [ɑ̃vɔl] **nm** *[oiseau]* taking flight *ou* wing; *[avion]* takeoff, taking off; *[âme, pensée]* soaring, flight. **prendre son** ~ *[oiseau]* to take flight *ou* wing; *[pensée]* to soar, take off.

envolée [ɑ̃vɔle] **nf**: ~ **oratoire/poétique** flight of oratory/poetry; **l'**~ **des prix** the explosion in prices; **l'**~ **du dollar** the soaring rise in *ou* of the dollar.

envoler (s') [ɑ̃vɔle] [1] **vpr** *[oiseau]* to fly away; *[avion]* to take off; *[chapeau]* to blow off, be blown off; *[feuille, papiers]* to blow away; *[temps]* to fly (past *ou* by); *[espoirs]* to vanish (into thin air); *[prix]* to soar; (*: *disparaître*) *[portefeuille, personne]* to disappear *ou* vanish (into thin air). **je m'envole pour Tokyo dans 2 heures** my flight leaves *ou* I take off for Tokyo in 2 hours; **il s'est envolé dans les sondages** his popularity rating has soared in the opinion polls.

envoûtant, e [ɑ̃vutɑ̃, ɑ̃t] **adj** entrancing, bewitching, spellbinding.

envoûtement [ɑ̃vutmɑ̃] **nm** bewitchment.

envoûter [ɑ̃vute] 1 **vt** to bewitch, cast a spell on. **être envoûté par qn** to be under sb's spell.

envoûteur [ɑ̃vutœʀ] **nm** sorcerer.

envoûteuse [ɑ̃vutøz] **nf** witch, sorceress.

envoyé, e [ɑ̃vwaje] (**ptp de envoyer**) 1 **adj** *remarque, réponse* **(bien)** ~ well-aimed, sharp; **ça, c'est ~!** well said!, well done! 2 **nm,f** (*gén*) messenger; (*Pol*) envoy; (*Presse*) correspondent. (*Presse*) **notre ~ spécial** our special correspondent; **un ~ du Ministère** a government official.

envoyer [ɑ̃vwaje] 8 1 **vt** a (*expédier*) *colis, lettre* to send (off); *vœux, amitiés, message radio* to send; (*Comm*) *marchandises* to dispatch, send off; (*par bateau*) to ship; *argent* to send, remit (*Admin*). **~ sa démission** to send in *ou* give in one's resignation; **~ sa candidature** to send in one's *ou* an application; **n'envoyez pas d'argent par la poste** do not send money by post; **envoie-moi un mot** drop me a line*.

b *personne* (*gén*) to send; (*en vacances, en commissions*) to send (off) (*chez, auprès de* to); (*en mission*) *émissaire, troupes* to dispatch, send out. **envoie le petit à l'épicerie/aux nouvelles** send the child to the grocer's/to see if there's any news; **ils l'avaient envoyé chez sa grand-mère pour les vacances** they had sent him (off) *ou* packed him off* to his grandmother's for the holidays; (*fig*) **~ qn à la mort** to send sb to his death; **~ qn dans l'autre monde** to dispatch sb, dispose of sb.

c (*lancer*) *objet* to throw, fling; (*avec force*) to hurl; *obus* to fire; *signaux* to send (out); (*Sport*) *ballon* to send. **~ des baisers à qn** to blow sb kisses; **~ des sourires à qn** to smile at sb, give sb smiles; **~ des œillades à qn** to ogle (at) sb, make eyes at sb; **~ des coups de pied/poing à qn** to kick/punch sb; **ne m'envoie pas ta fumée dans les yeux** don't blow (your) smoke in(to) my eyes; **il le lui a envoyé dans les dents‡** *ou* **les gencives‡** he really let him have it!*; **~ balader une balle sous le buffet*** to send a ball flying under the sideboard; (*Ftbl*) **~ le ballon au fond des filets** to put *ou* send the ball into the back of the net; **~ qn à terre** *ou* **au tapis** to knock sb down, knock sb to the ground, floor sb; **~ un homme sur la Lune** to send a man to the moon; (*Naut*) **~ par le fond** to send down *ou* to the bottom.

d (*Mil*) **~ les couleurs** to run up *ou* hoist the colours.

e (*loc*) **~ chercher qn/qch** to send for sb/sth; **~ promener qn*** *ou* **balader qn***, **~ qn coucher***, **~ qn sur les roses*** to send sb packing*, send sb about his business; **~ valser** *ou* **dinguer qch*** to send sth flying*; **il a tout envoyé promener*** he has chucked (up) everything‡, he has chucked the whole thing up‡ (*Brit*); **il ne le lui a pas envoyé dire*** he gave it to him straight*, he told him straight to his face.

2 **s'envoyer‡ vpr** (*subir, prendre*) *corvée* to get stuck* *ou* landed* with; *bouteille* to knock back*; *nourriture* to scoff*. **je m'enverrais des gifles*** I could kick myself*; **s'~ une fille/un mec*‡** to have it off with a girl/a guy‡ (*Brit*), make it with a girl/a guy‡; **s'~ en l'air*‡** to have it off‡ (*Brit*), have it‡, get some‡ (*US*).

envoyeur, -euse [ɑ̃vwajœʀ, øz] **nm,f** sender; *voir* **retour**.

enzyme [ɑ̃zim] **nm ou f** enzyme.

Éole [eɔl] **nm** Aeolus.

éolien, -ienne [eɔljɛ̃, jɛn] 1 **adj** wind (*épith*), aeolian (*littér*); *voir* **énergie, harpe.** 2 **éolienne nf** windmill, windpump.

EOR [eoœʀ] **nm** (**abrév de élève-officier de réserve**) *voir* **élève**.

éosine [eozin] **nf** eosin.

épagneul, e [epaɲœl] **nm,f** spaniel. **~ breton** Brittany spaniel.

épais, -aisse [epɛ, ɛs] 1 **adj** a (*gén*) *chevelure, peinture* thick; *neige* thick, deep; *barbe* bushy, thick; *silence* deep; *personne, corps* thickset; *nuit* pitch-black. **cloison ~-aisse de 5 cm** partition 5 cm thick; **j'ai la langue ~-aisse** my tongue is furred up (*Brit*) *ou* coated; **au plus ~ de la forêt** in the thick *ou* the depths of the forest; **tu n'es pas bien ~** you're not exactly fat. b (*péj: inhabile*) *esprit* dull; *personne* dense, thick(headed); *mensonge, plaisanterie* clumsy. 2 **adv: semer ~** to sow thick *ou* thickly; **il n'y en a pas ~!‡** there's not much of it!

épaisseur [epɛsœʀ] **nf** a (*gén*) thickness; [*neige, silence*] depth; (*péj*) [*esprit*] dullness. **la neige a un mètre d'~** there is a metre of snow, the snow is a metre deep; **prenez deux ~s de tissu** take two thicknesses *ou* a double thickness of material; **plier une couverture en double ~** to fold a blanket double; **dans l'~ de la nuit** in the depths of the night. b (*couche*) layer. c (*fig: richesse*) substance.

épaissir [epesiʀ] 2 1 **vt** *substance* to thicken; *mystère* to deepen. **l'air était épaissi par les fumées** the air was thick with smoke; **l'âge lui épaissit les traits** his features are becoming coarse with age; **ce manteau m'épaissit beaucoup** this coat makes me look much broader *ou* fatter.

2 **vi** to get thicker, thicken. **il a beaucoup épaissi** he has thickened out a lot.

3 **s'épaissir vpr** [*substance, brouillard*] to thicken, get thicker; [*chevelure, feuillage*] to get thicker; [*ténèbres*] to deepen. **sa taille s'épaissit** his waist is getting thicker, he's getting stouter around the waist; **le mystère s'épaissit** the mystery deepens, the plot thickens.

épaississant, e [epesisɑ̃, ɑ̃t] 1 **adj** thickening. 2 **nm** thickener.

épaississement [epesismɑ̃] **nm** thickening.

épanchement [epɑ̃ʃmɑ̃] **nm** [*sang*] effusion; [*sentiments*] outpouring. (*Méd*) **avoir un ~ de synovie** to have water on the knee.

épancher [epɑ̃ʃe] 1 1 **vt** *sentiments* (*irrités*) to give vent to, vent; (*tendres*) to pour forth. 2 **s'épancher vpr** [*personne*] to open one's heart, pour out one's feelings (*auprès de* to); [*sang*] to pour out.

épandage [epɑ̃daʒ] **nm** (*Agr*) manure spreading, manuring. **champ d'~** sewage farm.

épandre [epɑ̃dʀ] 41 1 **vt** (†, *littér*) *liquide, tendresse* to pour forth (*littér*); (*Agr*) *fumier* to spread. 2 **s'épandre vpr** (*littér*) to spread.

épanoui, e [epanwi] (**ptp de épanouir**) **adj** *fleur* in full bloom (*attrib*), full *ou* right out (*attrib*); *visage, sourire* radiant, beaming (*épith*); *corps* in full bloom (*attrib*); *personne* totally fulfilled (*attrib*).

épanouir [epanwiʀ] 2 1 **vt** (*littér*) *fleur* to open out; *branches, pétales* to open *ou* spread out; *visage* to light up. 2 **s'épanouir vpr** [*fleur*] to bloom, come out, open up *ou* out; [*visage*] to light up; [*personne*] to blossom (out), bloom; [*vase etc*] to open out, curve outwards. **à cette nouvelle il s'épanouit** his face lit up at the news.

épanouissant, e [epanwisɑ̃, ɑ̃t] **adj** totally fulfilling.

épanouissement [epanwismɑ̃] **nm** (*voir* **s'épanouir**) blooming; opening out; lighting up; blossoming (out); coming out; opening up. **en plein ~** in full bloom.

épargnant, e [epaʀɲɑ̃, ɑ̃t] **nm,f** saver, investor.

épargne [epaʀɲ] **nf** (*somme*) savings. (*vertu*) **l'~** saving; **~ de temps/d'argent** saving of time/money; **~ forcée** forced savings; **~-logement** home-buyers' savings scheme; **~-retraite** retirement savings scheme; *voir* **caisse, compte, plan.**

épargner [epaʀɲe] 1 **vt** a (*économiser*) *argent, nourriture, temps* to save. **~ 10 F sur une somme** to save 10 francs out of a sum; **~ sur la nourriture** to save *ou* make a saving on food; **ils n'ont pas épargné le poivre*** they haven't stinted on *ou* spared the pepper!; **~ pour ses vieux jours** to save (up) for one's old age, put something aside for one's old age; **je n'épargnerai rien pour le faire** I'll spare nothing to get it done.

b (*éviter*) **~ qch à qn** to spare sb sth; **pour t'~ des explications inutiles** to save giving you *ou* to spare you useless explanations; **~ à qn la honte/le spectacle de** to spare sb the shame/the sight of; **pour m'~ la peine de venir** to save *ou* spare myself the bother of coming.

c (*ménager*) *ennemi etc* to spare. **l'épidémie a épargné cette région** that region was spared the epidemic.

éparpillement [epaʀpijmɑ̃] **nm** (*action: voir* **éparpiller**) scattering; dispersal; distribution; dissipation; (*état*) [*troupes, succursales*] dispersal. **l'~ des maisons rendait les communications très difficiles** the houses being so scattered made communications difficult.

éparpiller [epaʀpije] 1 1 **vt** *objets* to scatter; *troupes* to disperse; *points de vente* to distribute, scatter; *efforts, talent* to dissipate. 2 **s'éparpiller vpr** (*gén*) to scatter. **maisons qui s'éparpillent dans la campagne** houses that are dotted about the countryside; **c'est un homme qui s'éparpille beaucoup trop** he's a man who spreads himself too thin; **tu t'es trop éparpillé dans tes lectures/recherches** you've spread yourself too thin in your reading/research.

épars, e [epaʀ, aʀs] **adj** (*littér*) scattered.

épatamment*† [epatamɑ̃] **adv** capitally*† (*Brit*), splendidly*.

épatant, e*† [epatɑ̃, ɑ̃t] **adj** splendid*, capital*† (*Brit*).

épate* [epat] **nf** (*péj*) **l'~** showing off*; **faire de l'~** to show off*.

épaté, e [epate] (**ptp de épater**) **adj** *vase etc* flat-bottomed; *nez* flat.

épatement [epatmɑ̃] **nm** a [*nez*] flatness. b (*: *surprise*) amazement.

épater [epate] 1 1 **vt** (*) (*étonner*) to amaze, stagger*; (*impressionner*) to impress. **pour ~ le bourgeois** to shake *ou* shock middle-class attitudes; **pour ~ la galerie** to impress people, create a sensation; **ça t'épate, hein!** how about that!*, what do you think of that! 2 **s'épater vpr** [*objet, colonne*] to spread out.

épaulard [epolaʀ] **nm** killer whale.

épaule [epol] **nf** (*Anat, Culin*) shoulder. **large d'~s** broad-shouldered; **~ d'agneau** shoulder of lamb; **donner un coup d'~ à qn** to knock *ou* bump sb with one's shoulder; *voir* **changer, hausser, tête.**

épaulé, e [epole] (**ptp de épauler**) **adj** *vêtement* with padded shoulders.

épaulé-jeté, pl **épaulés-jetés** [epoleʒ(ə)te] **nm** clean-and-jerk. **il soulève 150 kg à l'~** he can do a clean-and-jerk using 150 kg.

épaulement [epolmɑ̃] **nm** (*mur*) retaining wall; (*rempart*) breast-work, epaulement; (*Géol*) escarpment.

épauler [epole] 1 **vt** a *personne* to back up, support. **il faut s'~ dans la vie** people must help *ou* support each other in life. b *fusil* to raise (to the shoulder). **il épaula puis tira** he took aim *ou* he raised his rifle and fired. c (*Tech*) *mur* to support, retain. d (*Couture*) *vêtement* to add shoulder pads to.

épaulette [epolɛt] **nf** (*Mil*) epaulette; (*bretelle*) shoulder strap; (*rembourrage d'un vêtement*) shoulder pad.

épave [epav] **nf** a (*navire, voiture*) wreck; (*débris*) piece of wreckage, wreckage (*NonC*); (*déchets*) flotsam (and jetsam) (*NonC*). b (*Jur: objet perdu*) derelict. c (*fig*) (*restes*) ruin; (*loque humaine*) human wreck. **des ~s d'une civilisation autrefois florissante** ruins of a once-flourishing civilization.

épée [epe] **nf** a sword. **~ de Damoclès** Sword of Damocles; **l'~ nue** *ou* **à la main** with drawn sword; *voir* **cape, noblesse.** b (†: *escrimeur*) swordsman. **bonne ~** good swordsman.

épéiste [epeist] **nmf** swordsman *(m)*, swordswoman *(f)*.

épeler [ep(ə)le] 4 *ou* 5 **vt** *mot* to spell; *texte* to spell out.

épépiner [epepine] **vt** to deseed, seed. **raisins épépinés** seedless grapes.

éperdu, e [epɛʀdy] **adj** **a** *personne* distraught, overcome. **~ (de douleur/de terreur)** distraught *ou* frantic *ou* out of one's mind with grief/terror; **~ (de joie)** overcome *ou* beside o.s. with joy. **b** *gratitude* boundless; *regard* wild, distraught; *amour* passionate; *fuite* headlong, frantic. **désir/besoin ~ de bonheur** frantic desire for/need of happiness.

éperdument [epɛʀdymɑ̃] **adv** *crier, travailler* frantically, desperately; *aimer* passionately, madly. **je m'en moque ~** I couldn't care less.

éperlan [epɛʀlɑ̃] **nm** (*Zool*) smelt.

éperon [epʀɔ̃] **nm** *[cavalier, coq, montagne]* spur; (*Naut*) *[galère]* ram; *[pont]* cutwater. **~ rocheux** rocky outcrop *ou* spur.

éperonner [epʀɔne] 1 **vt** *cheval* to spur (on); *navire* to ram; (*fig*) *personne* to spur on. **botté et éperonné** booted and spurred, wearing boots and spurs.

épervier [epɛʀvje] **nm** **a** (*Orn*) sparrowhawk. **b** (*filet*) cast(ing) net.

éphèbe [efɛb] **nm** (*Hist*) ephebe; (*iro, péj*) beautiful young man.

éphémère [efemɛʀ] **1 adj** *bonheur, succès* ephemeral, fleeting, short-lived, transient; *moment* fleeting, short-lived; *règne, publication* short-lived. **2 nm** mayfly, ephemera (*SPÉC*).

éphéméride [efemeʀid] **nf** **a** (*calendrier*) block calendar, tear-off calendar. **b** (*Astron: tables*) **~s** ephemeris *(sg)*.

Éphèse [efɛz] **n** Ephesus.

Éphésien, -ienne [efezjɛ̃, jɛn] **1 adj** Ephesian. **2 nm,f: ~(ne)** Ephesian.

épi [epi] **1 nm** **a** *[blé, maïs]* ear; *[fleur]* spike; *[cheveux]* tuft. **les blés sont en ~s** the corn is in the ear. **b** (*jetée*) groin, groyne. **c être garé en ~** to be parked at an angle to the kerb. **2 comp ▸ épi de faîtage** finial.

épice [epis] **nf** spice. **quatre ~s** allspice; *voir* **pain**.

épicé, e [epise] (**ptp de épicer**) **adj** *viande, plat* highly spiced, spicy; *goût* spicy; (*fig*) *histoire* spicy, juicy*.

épicéa [episea] **nm** spruce.

épicentre [episɑ̃tʀ] **nm** epicentre.

épicer [epise] 3 **vt** to spice; (*fig*) to add spice to.

épicerie [episʀi] **nf** (*voir* **épicier**) (*magasin*) grocer's (shop (*Brit*) *ou* store (*US*)), greengrocer's; (*nourriture*) groceries, greengroceries (*Brit*); (*métier*) grocery trade, greengrocery trade (*Brit*). (*Supermarché*) **rayon ~** grocery stand *ou* counter; **aller à l'~** to go to the grocer's *ou* grocery; **~ fine** ≃ delicatessen.

épicier, -ière [episje, jɛʀ] **nm,f** (*Comm*) (*gén*) grocer; (*en fruits et légumes*) greengrocer (*Brit*), grocer (*US*). (*fig, péj*) **d'~** *idées, mentalité* small-town, parochial.

Épicure [epikyʀ] **nm** Epicurus.

épicurien, -ienne [epikyʀjɛ̃, jɛn] **adj, nm,f** **a** (*gourmet*) epicurean. **b** (*Philos*) **É~(ne)** Epicurean.

épicurisme [epikyʀism] **nm** epicureanism.

épidémie [epidemi] **nf** epidemic.

épidémiologie [epidemjɔlɔʒi] **nf** epidemiology.

épidémiologique [epidemjɔlɔʒik] **adj** epidemiological.

épidémique [epidemik] **adj** (*lit*) epidemic; (*fig*) contagious, catching (*attrib*).

épiderme [epidɛʀm] **nm** epidermis (*SPÉC*), skin. **elle a l'~ délicat** she has a delicate skin.

épidermique [epidɛʀmik] **adj** **a** (*Anat*) skin (*épith*), epidermal (*SPÉC*), epidermic (*SPÉC*). **blessure ~** (surface) scratch. **b** (*fig*) **ce sujet provoque en lui une réaction ~** he has a gut reaction to *ou* he always has the same immediate reaction to that subject.

épididyme [epididim] **nm** epididymis.

épier [epje] 7 **vt** *personne* to spy on; *geste* to watch closely; *bruit* to listen out for; *occasion* to be on the look-out for, look (out) for, watch for.

épigastre [epigastʀ] **nm** epigastrium.

épiglotte [epiglɔt] **nf** epiglottis.

épigone [epigɔn] **nm** (*Littérat*) epigone.

épigramme [epigʀam] **nf** epigram.

épigraphe [epigʀaf] **nf** epigraph. **mettre un vers en ~** to use a line as an epigraph.

épigraphique [epigʀafik] **adj** epigraphic.

épilation [epilasjɔ̃] **nf** removal of (unwanted) hair; *[sourcils]* plucking.

épilatoire [epilatwaʀ] **adj** depilatory, hair-removing (*épith*).

épilepsie [epilɛpsi] **nf** epilepsy. **crise d'~** epileptic fit.

épileptique [epilɛptik] **adj, nmf** epileptic.

épiler [epile] 1 **vt** *jambes* to remove the hair from; *sourcils* to pluck. **elle s'épilait les jambes** she was removing the hair(s) from her legs; **crème à ~** hair-removing *ou* depilatory cream.

épilogue [epilɔg] **nm** (*littér*) epilogue; (*fig*) conclusion, dénouement.

épiloguer [epilɔge] 1 **vi** (*parfois péj*) to hold forth (*sur* on), go on* (*sur* about), expatiate (*frm, hum*) (*sur* upon).

épinard [epinaʀ] **nm** (*Bot*) spinach. (*Culin*) **~s** spinach (*NonC*); *voir* **beurre**.

épine [epin] **nf** **a** *[buisson]* thorn, prickle; *[hérisson, oursin]* spine, prickle; *[porc-épic]* quill. **~ dorsale** backbone; **vous m'enlevez une belle ~ du pied** you have got me out of a spot*. **b** (*arbre*) thorn bush. **~ blanche** hawthorn; **~ noire** blackthorn.

épinette [epinɛt] **nf** **a** (*Mus*) spinet. **b** (*Can*) spruce. **~ blanche** white spruce; **~ noire** black spruce; **~ rouge** tamarack, hackmatack.

epinettière [epinɛtjɛʀ] **nf** (*Can*) spruce *ou* tamarack grove.

épineux, -euse [epinø, øz] **1 adj** *plante* thorny, prickly; *problème* thorny, tricky, ticklish; *situation* tricky, ticklish, sensitive; *caractère* prickly, touchy. **2 nm** prickly shrub *ou* bush.

épinglage [epɛ̃glaʒ] **nm** pinning.

épingle [epɛ̃gl] **nf** pin. **~ à chapeau** hatpin; **~ à cheveux** hairpin; **virage en ~ à cheveux** hairpin bend (*Brit*) *ou* turn (*US*); **~ de cravate** tie clip, tiepin; **~ à linge** clothes peg (*Brit*) *ou* pin (*US*); **~ de nourrice** *ou* **de sûreté** safety pin, (*grand modèle*) nappy (*Brit*) *ou* diaper (*US*) pin; **tirer son ~ du jeu** (*bien manœuvrer*) to play one's game well; (*s'en sortir à temps*) to extricate o.s.; *voir* **monter**.

épingler [epɛ̃gle] 1 **vt** **a** (*attacher*) to pin (on) (*à, sur* to). **~ ses cheveux** to pin up one's hair; (*Couture*) **~ une robe** to pin up a dress. **b** (*‡: arrêter*) to nick‡ (*Brit*), nab*. **se faire ~** to get nicked‡ (*Brit*) *ou* nabbed*.

épinière [epinjɛʀ] **adj f** *voir* **moelle**.

épinoche [epinɔʃ] **nf** stickleback.

Épiphanie [epifani] **nf: l'~** Epiphany, Twelfth Night; **à l'~** at Epiphany, on *ou* at Twelfth Night.

épiphénomène [epifenɔmɛn] **nm** epiphenomenon.

épiphyse [epifiz] **nf** epiphysis.

épique [epik] **adj** (*lit, fig*) epic; (*hum*) epic, dramatic.

épiscopal, e, mpl -aux [episkɔpal, o] **adj** episcopal.

épiscopat [episkɔpa] **nm** episcopate, episcopacy.

épiscope [episkɔp] **nm** episcope (*Brit*), opaque projector (*US*).

épisiotomie [epizjɔtɔmi] **nf** episiotomy.

épisode [epizɔd] **nm** episode. **roman/film à ~s** serial, serialized novel/film.

épisodique [epizɔdik] **adj** **a** (*occasionnel*) *événement* occasional; *rôle* fleeting, transitory. **de façon ~** sporadically, on and off. **b** (*secondaire*) *événement* minor, of secondary importance; *personnage* minor, secondary.

épisodiquement [epizɔdikmɑ̃] **adv** (*voir* **épisodique**) occasionally; fleetingly.

épisser [epise] 1 **vt** to splice.

épissoir [episwaʀ] **nm** marlin(e) spike.

épissure [episyʀ] **nf** splice.

épistémologie [epistemɔlɔʒi] **nf** (*Philos*) epistemology; (*Sci*) epistemics *(sg)*.

épistémologique [epistemɔlɔʒik] **adj** epistemological.

épistolaire [epistɔlɛʀ] **adj** *style* epistolary. **être en relations ~s avec qn** to correspond with sb, exchange letters *ou* correspondence with sb.

épistolier, -ière [epistɔlje, jɛʀ] **nm,f** (*littér*) letter writer.

épitaphe [epitaf] **nf** epitaph.

épithélial, e, mpl -iaux [epiteljal, jo] **adj** epithelial.

épithélium [epiteljɔm] **nm** epithelium.

épithète [epitɛt] **nf** **a** (*Gram*) attribute. **adjectif ~** attributive adjective. **b** (*qualificatif*) epithet.

épître [epitʀ] **nf** epistle.

éploré, e [eplɔʀe] **adj** (*littér*) *visage* bathed in tears; *personne* tearful, weeping, in tears (*attrib*); *voix* tearful.

éployé, e [eplwaje] **adj** (*littér, Hér*) spread (out).

épluchage [eplyʃaʒ] **nm** (*voir* **éplucher**) cleaning; peeling; unwrapping; dissection.

épluche-légumes [eplyʃlegym] **nm inv** potato peeler.

éplucher [eplyʃe] 1 **vt** **a** *salade, radis* to clean; *fruits, légumes, crevettes* to peel; *bonbon* to unwrap. **b** *texte, comptes* to go over with a fine-tooth comb, dissect.

épluchette [eplyʃɛt] **nf** (*Can*) corn-husking bee *ou* party.

éplucheur, -euse [eplyʃœʀ, øz] **nm,f** (automatic potato) peeler; (*péj*) faultfinder.

épluchure [eplyʃyʀ] **nf: ~ de pomme de terre** *etc* piece of potato *etc* peeling; **~s** peelings.

épointer [epwɛ̃te] 1 **vt** *aiguille etc* to blunt. **crayon épointé** blunt pencil.

éponge [epɔ̃ʒ] **nf** **a** (*Zool, gén*) sponge. **passer un coup d'~ sur qch** to give sth a (quick) sponge; (*fig*) **passons l'~!** let's let bygones be bygones!, let's forget all about it!; **passons l'~ sur cette vieille querelle!** let's forget all about that old quarrel!, let's put that old quarrel behind us; **~ métallique** scouring pad, scourer; **~ végétale** loofah (*Brit*), luffa (*US*); **quelle ~!*** what a drunk* *ou* drunkard!; *voir* **boire, jeter**. **b** (*Tex*) **(tissu) ~** (terry) towelling.

éponger [epɔ̃ʒe] 3 **vt** *liquide* to mop *ou* sponge up; *plancher, visage,* to mop; (*Fin*) *dette etc* to soak up, absorb. **s'~ le front** to mop one's brow.

épopée [epɔpe] **nf** (*lit, fig*) epic.

époque [epɔk] **nf** **a** (*gén*) time. **j'étais jeune à l'~** I was young at the time; **être de son ~** to be in tune with one's time; **quelle ~!** what times these are!; **à l'~ où nous sommes** in this day and age. **b** (*Hist*) age, era, epoch. **l'~ révolutionnaire** the revolutionary era *ou* age *ou* epoch; **à l'~ des Grecs** at the time of *ou* in the age of the Greeks; **la Belle É~** the

Belle Époque, ≃ the Edwardian Age *ou* Era; **cette invention a fait ~** it was an epoch-making invention. c (*Géol*) period. **à l'~ glaciaire** in the glacial period *ou* epoch. d (*Art: style*) period. **tableaux de la même ~** pictures of *ou* from the same period; **meuble d'~** genuine antique, piece of period furniture.

épouiller [epuje] 1 **vt** to delouse.

époumoner (s') [epumɔne] 1 **vpr** (*lit, fig*) to shout *etc* o.s. hoarse. **il s'époumonait à chanter** he was singing himself hoarse.

épousailles [epuzɑj] **nfpl** († *ou hum*) nuptials († *ou hum*).

épouse [epuz] **nf** wife, spouse (*frm ou hum*).

épousée [epuze] **nf** († *ou dial*) bride.

épouser [epuze] 1 **vt** a *personne* to marry, wed†; *idée* to embrace, espouse (*frm*); *cause* to espouse (*frm*), take up. **~ une grosse fortune** to marry into money. b *[robe]* to fit; *[route, tracé]* to follow; (*étroitement*) to hug.

épouseur† [epuzœʀ] **nm** suitor†, wooer†.

épousseter [epuste] 4 **vt** (*nettoyer*) to dust; (*enlever*) to dust *ou* flick off.

époustouflant, e* [epustuflɑ̃, ɑ̃t] **adj** staggering, amazing.

époustoufler* [epustufle] 1 **vt** to stagger, flabbergast.

épouvantable [epuvɑ̃tabl] **adj** terrible, appalling, dreadful.

épouvantablement [epuvɑ̃tabləmɑ̃] **adv** terribly, appallingly, dreadfully.

épouvantail [epuvɑ̃taj] **nm** a (*à oiseaux*) scarecrow. b (*péj: personne*) scruff*; (*chose*) bugbear.

épouvante [epuvɑ̃t] **nf** terror, (great) fear. **saisi d'~** terror-stricken; **il voyait arriver ce moment avec ~** with dread he saw the moment approaching; **roman/film d'~** horror story/film.

épouvanter [epuvɑ̃te] 1 **vt** to terrify, appal, frighten. **s'~ de qch** to get frightened at sth.

époux [epu] **nm** husband, spouse (*frm ou hum*). **les ~** the (married) couple, the husband and wife.

époxy [epɔksi] **adj inv** epoxy.

époxyde [epɔksid] **nm** epoxide.

éprendre (s') [epʀɑ̃dʀ] 58 **vpr** (*littér*) **s'~ de** to fall in love with, become enamoured of (*littér*).

épreuve [epʀœv] **nf** a (*essai*) test. **~ de résistance** resistance test; **résister à l'~ (du temps)** to stand the test (of time); (*fig*) **~ de force** showdown, confrontation; **~ de vérité** litmus test; **mettre à l'~** to put to the test; (*Tech*) **faire l'~ d'un métal** to test a metal; (*Jur*) **mise à l'~** ≃ probation; *voir* **rude**.
b (*malheur*) ordeal, trial, hardship. **subir de rudes ~s** to suffer great hardships, undergo great trials *ou* ordeals; **savoir réagir dans l'~** to react well in the face of adversity.
c (*Scol*) test. **corriger les ~s d'un examen** to mark the examination papers; **~ orale** oral test; **~ écrite** written test *ou* paper.
d (*Sport*) event. **~ de sélection** heat; **~ contre la montre** time trial; **~s sur piste** track events; **~ d'endurance** *[personne]* test of endurance, endurance test; (*Aut*) endurance test.
e (*Typ*) proof. **première ~** galley proof; **dernière ~** final proof; **corriger les ~s d'un livre** to proofread a book, correct the proofs of a book.
f (*Phot*) print; (*gravure*) proof. **~ (par) contact** contact print; (*Ciné*) **~s (de tournage)** rushes.
g (*Hist, initiatique*) ordeal. **~s d'initiation** initiation ordeals *ou* rites; **~ du feu** ordeal by fire.
h **à l'~ de**: **gilet à l'~ des balles** bulletproof vest; **à l'~ du feu** fireproof; (*fig*) **à toute ~** *amitié, foi* staunch; *mur* solid as a rock; **il a un courage à toute ~** he has unfailing courage, his courage is equal to anything.

épris, e [epʀi, iz] (**ptp de s'éprendre**) **adj** (*frm*) (*d'une femme*) smitten† (*de* with), enamoured (*de* of) (*littér*), in love (*de* with). **~ de** *idée* in love with.

éprouvant, e [epʀuvɑ̃, ɑ̃t] **adj** *travail, climat* trying, testing. **~ pour les nerfs** nerve-racking.

éprouvé, e [epʀuve] (**ptp de éprouver**) **adj** (*sûr*) *moyen, remède* well-tried, proven; *spécialiste, qualités* (well-)proven; *ami* staunch, true, steadfast.

éprouver [epʀuve] 1 **vt** a (*ressentir*) *sensation, sentiment* to feel, experience. b (*subir*) *perte* to suffer, sustain; *difficultés* to meet with, experience. c (*tester*) *métal* to test; *personne* to put to the test, test. d (*frm: affliger*) to afflict, distress. **très éprouvé par la maladie** sorely afflicted by illness (*frm*).

éprouvette [epʀuvɛt] **nf** test tube; *voir* **bébé**.

EPS [əpeɛs] **nf** (**abrév de éducation physique et sportive**) PE, PT.

epsilon [ɛpsilɔn] **nm** epsilon.

épuisant, e [epɥizɑ̃, ɑ̃t] **adj** exhausting.

épuisé, e [epɥize] (**ptp de épuiser**) **adj** *personne, cheval, corps* exhausted, worn-out; *énergie* spent; (*Comm*) *article* sold out (*attrib*); *stocks* exhausted (*attrib*); *livre* out of print. **~ de fatigue** exhausted, tired out, worn-out.

épuisement [epɥizmɑ̃] **nm** (*gén*) exhaustion. **devant l'~ de ses finances** seeing that his money was exhausted *ou* had run out; (*Comm*) **jusqu'à ~ des stocks** while stocks last; **jusqu'à l'~ du filon** until the vein is (*ou* was) worked out; **faire marcher qn jusqu'à (l')~** to make sb walk till he drops (with exhaustion); **dans un grand état d'~** in a completely *ou* an utterly exhausted state, in a state of complete *ou* utter exhaustion.

épuiser [epɥize] 1 1 **vt** *personne* to exhaust, tire out, wear out; *terre, sujet* to exhaust; *réserves, munitions* to use up, exhaust; *filon* to exhaust, work out; *patience* to wear out, exhaust. 2 **s'épuiser vpr** *[réserves]* to run out; *[source]* to dry up; *[personne]* to exhaust o.s., wear o.s. out, tire o.s. out (*à faire qch* doing sth). **les stocks s'étaient épuisés** the stocks had run out; **ses forces s'épuisent peu à peu** his strength is gradually failing; **je m'épuise à vous le répéter** I'm wearing myself out repeating this (to you).

épuisette [epɥizɛt] **nf** (*Pêche*) landing net; (*à crevettes*) shrimping net.

épurateur [epyʀatœʀ] **nm** (*Tech*) purifier.

épuration [epyʀasjɔ̃] **nf** (*voir* **épurer**) purification; refinement, refining; purge.

épure [epyʀ] **nf** working drawing.

épurer [epyʀe] 1 **vt** *eau, huile* to purify; *langue, goût* to refine; (*Pol*) to purge.

équarrir [ekaʀiʀ] 2 **vt** a *pierre, tronc* to square (off). **poutre mal équarrie** rough-hewn beam. b *animal* to quarter.

équarrissage [ekaʀisaʒ] **nm** (*voir* **équarrir**) squaring (off); quartering. **envoyer à l'~** to send to the knacker's yard (*Brit*).

équarrisseur [ekaʀisœʀ] **nm** knacker (*Brit*).

équateur [ekwatœʀ] **nm** equator. **sous l'~** at *ou* on the equator; **(la république de) l'É~** Ecuador.

équation [ekwasjɔ̃] **nf** equation. **~ du premier degré** simple equation; **~ du second degré** quadratic equation.

équatorial, e, **mpl -iaux** [ekwatɔʀjal, jo] **adj** equatorial.

équatorien, -ienne [ekwatɔʀjɛ̃, jɛn] 1 **adj** Ecuadorian. 2 **nm,f**: **É~(-ienne)** Ecuadorian.

équerre [ekɛʀ] **nf** (*pour tracer*) (set) square; (*de soutien*) brace. **double ~** T-square; **en ~** at right angles; **ce tableau n'est pas d'~** this picture isn't straight *ou* level.

équestre [ekɛstʀ] **adj** equestrian. **centre ~** riding school.

équeuter [ekøte] 1 **vt** *cerises* to remove the stalk from, pull the stalk off; *fraises* to hull.

équi [ekɥi] **préf** equi. **~ probable/possible** equally probable/possible.

équidé [ekide] **nm** member of the horse family. **les ~s** the Equidae (*SPÉC*).

équidistance [ekɥidistɑ̃s] **nf** equidistance.

équidistant, e [ekɥidistɑ̃, ɑ̃t] **adj** equidistant (*de* between).

équilatéral, e, **mpl -aux** [ekɥilateʀal, o] **adj** (*lit*) equilateral. **ça m'est ~**‡ I don't give a damn‡.

équilibrage [ekilibʀaʒ] **nm** (*Aut*) *[roues]* balancing.

équilibrant, e [ekilibʀɑ̃, ɑ̃t] **adj** stabilizing (*épith*). **shampooing ~** shampoo which restores the hair's natural balance.

équilibre [ekilibʀ] **nm** a (*gén*) *[corps, objet]* balance, equilibrium. **perdre/garder l'~** to lose/keep one's balance; **avoir le sens de l'~** to have a (good) sense of balance; **se tenir** *ou* **être en ~ (sur)** *[personne]* to balance (on); *[objet]* to be balanced (on); **mettre qch en ~** to balance sth (*sur* on); **en ~ instable sur le bord du verre** precariously balanced on the edge of the glass; **exercice/tour d'~** balancing exercise/act.
b **~ (mental)** (mental) equilibrium, (mental) stability; **il a su garder (tout) son ~** he managed to remain quite cool-headed; **il manque d'~** he is rather unstable.
c (*harmonie*) *[couple]* harmony; *[activités]* balance, equilibrium.
d (*Écon, Pol*) *[course aux armements]* parity. **~ budgétaire/économique** balance in the budget/economy; **budget en ~** balanced budget; **atteindre l'~ financier** to break even (financially); **~ des pouvoirs** balance of power; **~ politique** political balance; **l'~ du monde** the world balance of power; **~ de la terreur** balance of terror.
e (*Sci*) equilibrium. (*Chim*) **solution en ~** balanced solution.
f (*Archit, Mus, Peinture*) balance.

équilibré, e [ekilibʀe] (**ptp de équilibrer**) **adj** *personne* stable, well-balanced, level-headed; *régime alimentaire* (well-)balanced; *esprit* well-balanced; *vie* well-regulated, regular. **mal ~** unstable, unbalanced.

équilibrer [ekilibʀe] 1 **vt** a (*contrebalancer*) *forces, poids, poussée* to counterbalance. **les avantages et les inconvénients s'équilibrent** the advantages and the disadvantages counterbalance each other *ou* cancel each other out. b (*mettre en équilibre*) *balance* to equilibrate, balance; *charge, embarcation, avion, roues* to balance; (*Archit, Art*) to balance. c (*harmoniser*) *emploi du temps, budget, pouvoirs* to balance. (*fig*) **~ qn** to restore sb's mental equilibrium.

équilibriste [ekilibʀist] **nmf** (*funambule*) tightrope walker.

équille [ekij] **nf** sand eel.

équinoxe [ekinɔks] **nm** equinox. **marée d'~** equinoctial tide; **~ de printemps/d'automne** spring/autumn equinox.

équipage [ekipaʒ] **nm** a (*Aviat*) (air)crew; (*Naut*) crew; *voir* **homme, rôle**. b (*: *attirail*) gear* (*NonC*). c (†) *[seigneur, chevaux]* equipage†. **~ à deux chevaux** carriage and pair; **~ à quatre chevaux** carriage and four; **en grand ~** in state, in great array. d (*Tech*) equipment (*NonC*), gear (*NonC*).

équipe [ekip] **nf** a (*Sport*) (*gén*) team; *[rameurs]* crew. **jeu** *ou* **sport d'~** team game; **jouer en** *ou* **par ~s** to play in teams; **l'~ de France a donné le coup d'envoi** the French team *ou* side kicked off; *voir* **esprit.** b (*groupe*) team. **~ de chercheurs** research team, team of researchers; **~ de sauveteurs** *ou* **de secours** rescue party *ou* squad *ou* team; **~ pédagogique** teaching staff; (*Ind*) **l'~ de jour/de 8 heures** the day/8 o'clock shift; **travailler en** *ou* **par ~s** to work in teams; (*sur un chantier*) to work in gangs; (*Ind*) to work in shifts; **travailler en ~** to work as a team; **faire ~ avec** to team up with; *voir* **chef¹.** c (**, parfois péj: bande*) bunch*, crew*.

équipée [ekipe] **nf** *[prisonnier]* escape, flight; *[aventurier]* undertaking, venture; *[promeneur, écolier]* jaunt.

équipement [ekipmɑ̃] **nm** a (*NonC: voir* **équiper**) equipment; fitting out; kitting out (*Brit*) (*de* with). b (*matériel*) equipment, kit (*Brit*). **l'~ complet du skieur** all skiing equipment, the complete skier's kit (*Brit*), "everything for the skier". c (*aménagement*) equipment. **l'~ électrique d'une maison** the electrical fittings of a house; **l'~ hôtelier d'une région** the hotel facilities *ou* amenities of a region; **l'~ industriel d'une région** the industrial plant of a region; (*Admin*) **les ~s collectifs** community facilities *ou* amenities; **prime** *ou* **subvention d'~** equipment grant.

équipementier [ekipmɑ̃tje] **nm**: **~ (automobile)** parts manufacturer.

équiper [ekipe] 1 **vt** *troupe* to equip; *local* to equip, fit out; *usine* to tool up; *sportif* to equip, kit out (*Brit*), fit out (*de* with). **cuisine tout équipée** fully equipped kitchen; **~ industriellement une région** to bring industry into a region; **~ une machine d'un dispositif de sécurité** to fit a machine out with a safety device; **s'~** *[usine]* to tool up; *[sportif]* to equip o.s., kit o.s. out (*Brit*), get o.s. kitted out (*Brit*).

équipier, -ière [ekipje, jɛʀ] **nm,f** (*Sport*) team member.

équitable [ekitabl] **adj** *partage, jugement* equitable, fair; *personne* impartial, fair(-minded).

équitablement [ekitabləmɑ̃] **adv** equitably, fairly.

équitation [ekitasjɔ̃] **nf** (horse-)riding, equitation (*frm*). **faire de l'~** to go horse-riding.

équité [ekite] **nf** equity. **avec ~** equitably, fairly.

équivalence [ekivalɑ̃s] **nf** equivalence. **à ~ de prix, ce produit est meilleur** for the equivalent *ou* same price this is the better product; (*Univ*) **diplômes étrangers admis en ~** recognized foreign diplomas; **demande d'~** *request for an equivalent rating of one's degree.*

équivalent, e [ekivalɑ̃, ɑ̃t] 1 **adj** equivalent (*à* to). **ces solutions sont ~es** these solutions are equivalent; **à prix ~, ce produit est meilleur** for the same *ou* equivalent price this is the better product. 2 **nm** equivalent (*de* of). **vous ne trouverez l'~ nulle part** you won't find the *ou* its like *ou* equivalent anywhere; **~ pétrole** fuel oil equivalent.

équivaloir [ekivalwaʀ] 29 **vi** (*lit*) *[quantité etc]* to be equivalent (*à* to); (*fig*) *[effet etc]* to be equivalent (*à* to), amount (*à* to). **ça équivaut à dire que** ... it amounts to *ou* is equivalent to saying that ... .

équivoque [ekivɔk] 1 **adj** (*ambigu*) equivocal, ambiguous; (*louche*) dubious, questionable. 2 **nf** (*ambiguïté*) equivocation, ambiguity; (*incertitude*) doubt; (*malentendu*) misunderstanding. **conduite sans ~** unequivocal *ou* unambiguous behaviour; **pour lever l'~** to remove any doubt (on the matter).

érable [eʀabl] **nm** maple.

érablière [eʀablijɛʀ] **nf** maple grove.

éradication [eʀadikasjɔ̃] **nf** eradication.

éradiquer [eʀadike] 1 **vt** to eradicate.

éraflement [eʀɑfləmɑ̃] **nm** scratching.

érafler [eʀɑfle] 1 **vt** *peau, genou* to scratch, graze; *surface* to scratch, scrape.

éraflure [eʀɑflyʀ] **nf** (*sur peau*) scratch, graze; (*sur objet*) scratch, scrape (mark).

éraillé, e [eʀɑje] (**ptp de érailler**) **adj** *voix* rasping, hoarse, croaking (*épith*).

éraillement [eʀɑjmɑ̃] **nm** *[voix]* hoarseness.

érailler [eʀɑje] 1 **vt** *voix* to make hoarse; (*rayer*) *surface* to scratch. **s'~ la voix** to make o.s. hoarse.

Érasme [eʀasm] **nm**: **~ (de Rotterdam)** Erasmus.

erbium [ɛʀbjɔm] **nm** erbium.

ère [ɛʀ] **nf** era. **400 avant notre ~** 400 B.C.; **en l'an 1600 de notre ~** in the year of our Lord 1600, in the year 1600 A.D.; **~ secondaire/tertiaire** secondary/tertiary era; **les ~s géologiques** the geological eras.

érectile [eʀɛktil] **adj** erectile.

érection [eʀɛksjɔ̃] **nf** a *[monument]* erection, raising; (*fig*) establishment, setting-up. b (*Physiol*) erection. **avoir une ~** to have an erection.

éreintant, e* [eʀɛ̃tɑ̃, ɑ̃t] **adj** *travail* exhausting, backbreaking.

éreintement* [eʀɛ̃tmɑ̃] **nm** (*épuisement*) exhaustion; (*critique*) savage attack (*de* on), slating* (*Brit*), panning*.

éreinter [eʀɛ̃te] 1 **vt** a (*épuiser*) *animal* to exhaust; (*) *personne* to shatter*, wear out. **être éreinté*** to be shattered* *ou* all in* *ou* worn out; **s'~ à faire qch** to wear o.s. out doing sth. b (*critiquer*) *auteur, œuvre* to pull to pieces, slate* (*Brit*), pan*, slam*.

érésipèle [eʀezipɛl] **nm = érysipèle.**

Erevan [əʀəvɑ̃] **n** Yerevan.

erg [ɛʀg] **nm** (*Géog, Phys*) erg.

ergatif, -ive [ɛʀgatif, iv] **adj** *construction* ergative.

ergol [ɛʀgɔl] **nm** propellant.

ergonome [ɛʀgɔnɔm] **nmf** ergonomist.

ergonomie [ɛʀgɔnɔmi] **nf** ergonomics (*sg*).

ergonomique [ɛʀgɔnɔmik] **adj** ergonomic(al).

ergonomiste [ɛʀgɔnɔmist] **nmf** ergonomist.

ergot [ɛʀgo] **nm** a *[coq]* spur; *[chien]* dewclaw. (*fig*) **monter** *ou* **se dresser sur ses ~s** to get one's hackles up. b *[blé etc]* ergot. c (*Tech*) lug.

ergotage [ɛʀgɔtaʒ] **nm** quibbling (*NonC*), cavilling (*NonC*), petty argument.

ergoter [ɛʀgɔte] 1 **vi** to quibble (*sur* about), cavil (*sur* at).

ergoteur, -euse [ɛʀgɔtœʀ, øz] **nm,f** quibbler, hairsplitter*.

ergothérapeute [ɛʀgɔteʀapøt] **nmf** occupational therapist.

Érié [eʀje] **n**: **le lac ~** Lake Erie.

ériger [eʀiʒe] 3 **vt** (*frm*) *monument, bâtiment* to erect; *société etc* to set up, establish. **~ ses habitudes en doctrine** to raise one's habits to the status of a doctrine; **~ un criminel en héros** to set a criminal up as a hero; **il s'érige en maître** he sets himself up as a master.

ermitage [ɛʀmitaʒ] **nm** (*d'ermite*) hermitage; (*fig*) retreat.

ermite [ɛʀmit] **nm** hermit.

éroder [eʀɔde] 1 **vt** to erode.

érogène [eʀɔʒɛn] **adj** erogenous.

Éros [eʀos] **nm** (*Myth*) Eros. (*Psych*) **l'é~** Eros.

érosif, -ive [eʀozif, iv] **adj** erosive.

érosion [eʀozjɔ̃] **nf** (*lit, fig*) erosion. **~ monétaire** (monetary) depreciation.

érotique [eʀɔtik] **adj** erotic.

érotiquement [eʀɔtikmɑ̃] **adv** erotically.

érotisation [eʀɔtizasjɔ̃] **nf** eroticization.

érotiser [eʀɔtize] 1 **vt** to eroticize.

érotisme [eʀɔtism] **nm** eroticism.

érotomane [eʀɔtɔman] **nmf** erotomaniac.

errance [eʀɑ̃s] **nf** (*littér*) wandering, roaming.

errant, e [eʀɑ̃, ɑ̃t] 1 **adj** (*gén*) wandering. **chien ~** stray dog; *voir* **chevalier, juif.** 2 **nm,f** (*littér*) wanderer, rover.

errata [eʀata] **nm inv** errata.

erratique [eʀatik] **adj** (*Géol, Méd*) erratic.

erratum [eʀatɔm] **nmsg** erratum.

errements [ɛʀmɑ̃] **nmpl** (*littér*) erring ways, bad habits.

errer [eʀe] 1 **vi** (*littér*) a *[voyageur]* to wander, roam; *[regard]* to rove, roam, wander (*sur* over); *[pensée]* to wander, stray. **un sourire errait sur ses lèvres** a smile hovered on *ou* flitted across his lips. b (*se tromper*) to err.

erreur [eʀœʀ] **nf** a (*gén*) mistake, error; (*Statistique*) error. **~ matérielle** *ou* **d'écriture** clerical error; **~ de calcul** mistake in calculation, miscalculation; **~ de date** mistake in the date; **faire une ~ de date** to make a mistake in *ou* be mistaken about the date; **~ d'impression, ~ typographique** misprint, typographical error; **~ de sens** wrong meaning; **~ de traduction** mistranslation; **~ (de) tactique** tactical error; **~ de fait/de jugement** error of fact/of judgment.

b (*loc*) **par suite d'une ~** due to an error *ou* a mistake; **sauf ~** unless I'm (very much) mistaken; **sauf ~ ou omission** errors and omissions excepted; **par ~** by mistake; **~ profonde!, grave ~!** that's (just) where you're (*ou* he's *etc*) wrong!, you are (*ou* he is *etc*) very much mistaken (there)!; **commettre** *ou* **faire une ~** to make a mistake *ou* an error (*sur* about); **faire ~, tomber dans l'~** to be wrong *ou* mistaken; **être dans l'~** to be mistaken, be under a misapprehension *ou* delusion; **il y a ~, ce n'est pas lui** there's been a mistake *ou* there's some mistake – it isn't him; **il n'y a pas d'~ (possible)** I'm telling you!, there's no mistake!; **ce serait une ~ de croire que** ... it would be a mistake *ou* be wrong to think that ..., you would be mistaken in thinking that ...; **l'~ est humaine** to err is human; **il y a ~ sur la personne** you've *etc* got the wrong person.

c (*dérèglements*) **~s** errors, lapses; **~s de jeunesse** mistakes of youth, youthful indiscretions; **retomber dans les ~s du passé** to lapse (back) into bad habits.

d (*Jur*) **~ judiciaire** miscarriage of justice.

erroné, e [eʀɔne] **adj** erroneous.

ersatz [ɛʀzats] **nm** (*lit, fig*) ersatz, substitute. **~ de café** ersatz coffee.

erse¹ [ɛʀs] **nm, adj** (*Ling*) Erse.

erse² [ɛʀs] **nf** (*Naut*) grommet.

éructation [eʀyktasjɔ̃] **nf** (*frm*) eructation (*frm*).

éructer [eʀykte] 1 **vi** (*frm*) to eructate (*frm*).

érudit, e [eʀydi, it] 1 **adj** erudite, learned, scholarly. 2 **nm,f** erudite *ou* learned person, scholar.

érudition [eʀydisjɔ̃] **nf** erudition, scholarship.

éruptif, -ive [eʀyptif, iv] **adj** eruptive.

éruption [eʀypsjɔ̃] **nf** eruption. **~ de boutons** outbreak of spots *ou* pimples; **entrer en ~** to erupt.

érysipèle [eʀizipɛl] **nm** erysipelas.

érythème [eʀitɛm] **nm** rash. **~ fessier** nappy (*Brit*) *ou* diaper (*US*) rash.

érythrocyte [eRitRɔsit] **nm** erythrocyte.
ès [ɛs] **prép: licencié ~ lettres/sciences** ≃ Bachelor of Arts/Science; **docteur ~ lettres** ≃ Ph.D.; **membre ~-qualités** ex officio member.
Ésaü [ezay] **nm** Esau.
esbigner (s')‡† [ɛsbiɲe] 1 **vpr** to skedaddle*, clear off*.
esbroufe* [ɛsbRuf] **nf: faire de l'~** to shoot a line‡; **il essaie de nous la faire à l'~** he's shooting us a line‡, he's bluffing.
esbroufeur, -euse* [ɛsbRufœR, øz] **nm,f** hot air merchant‡ (*Brit*), big talker*.
escabeau, pl **~x** [ɛskabo] **nm** (*tabouret*) (wooden) stool; (*échelle*) stepladder, pair of steps (*Brit*). **tu me prêtes ton ~?** may I borrow your steps (*Brit*)? *ou* your stepladder?
escadre [ɛskadR] **nf** (*Naut*) squadron. (*Aviat*) **~ (aérienne)** wing.
escadrille [ɛskadRij] **nf** (*Aviat*) flight, ≃ squadron. **~ de chasse** fighter squadron.
escadron [ɛskadRɔ̃] **nm** (*Mil*) squadron; (*fig: bande*) bunch*, crowd. **~ de gendarmerie** platoon of gendarmes; **~ de la mort** death squad.
escalade [ɛskalad] **nf** a (*action: voir* **escalader**) climbing; scaling. **partir faire l'~ d'une montagne** to set off to climb a mountain. b (*Sport*) **l'~** (rock) climbing; **une belle ~** a beautiful (rock) climb; **faire de l'~** to go (rock) climbing. c (*Pol, gén: aggravation*) escalation. **l'~ de la violence** an escalation of violence; **pour éviter l'~** to avoid an escalation.
escalader [ɛskalade] 1 **vt** *montagne* to climb; *mur* to climb, scale; (*Hist*) *forteresse* to scale.
escalator [ɛskalatɔR] **nm** escalator.
escale [ɛskal] **nf** a (*endroit*) (*Naut*) port of call; (*Aviat*) stop. **faire ~ à** (*Naut*) to call at, put in at; (*Aviat*) to stop over at. b (*temps d'arrêt*) (*Naut*) call; (*Aviat*) stop(over); (*brève*) touchdown. **vol sans ~** nonstop flight; **faire une ~ de 5 heures à Marseille** (*Naut*) to put in at Marseilles for 5 hours; (*Aviat*) to stop (over) at Marseilles for 5 hours; (*Aviat*) **~ technique** refuelling stop.
escalier [ɛskalje] **nm** (*marches*) stairs; (*à l'extérieur*) stairs, steps; (*cage*) staircase, stairway. **assis dans l'~** *ou* **les ~s** sitting on the stairs; **~ d'honneur** main staircase *ou* stairway, main stairs; **~ de service** backstairs; **l'~ de service donne sur la cour** the backstairs come out into the yard; **~ mécanique** *ou* **roulant** escalator; **~ en colimaçon** spiral staircase; **~ de secours** fire escape; (*Ski*) **montée en ~** sidestepping (*NonC*); (*fig*) **il m'a fait des ~s dans les cheveux*** he's cut my hair all unevenly; *voir* **dérobé, esprit**.
escalope [ɛskalɔp] **nf** escalope.
escamotable [ɛskamɔtabl] **adj** *train d'atterrissage, antenne* retractable; *lit, siège* collapsible, foldaway (*épith*); *escalier* foldaway (*épith*).
escamotage [ɛskamɔtaʒ] **nm** (*voir* **escamoter**) conjuring away; evading; getting *ou* skirting round; dodging; skipping; filching*, pinching*; retraction.
escamoter [ɛskamɔte] 1 **vt** a (*faire disparaître*) *cartes etc* to conjure away. b (*fig*) *difficulté* to evade, get round, skirt round; *question* to dodge, evade; *mot* to skip. c (*: *voler*) *portefeuille* to filch*, pinch*. d *train d'atterrissage* to retract.
escamoteur, -euse [ɛskamɔtœR, øz] **nm,f** (*prestidigitateur*) conjurer.
escampette* [ɛskɑ̃pɛt] **nf** *voir* **poudre**.
escapade [ɛskapad] **nf** *[écolier]* **faire une ~** to run away *ou* off, do a bunk‡ (*Brit*); **on a fait une petite ~ pour le week-end** we went off on a jaunt for the weekend.
escarbille [ɛskaRbij] **nf** bit of grit.
escarboucle [ɛskaRbukl] **nf** (*pierre*) carbuncle.
escarcelle [ɛskaRsɛl] **nf** (††: *portefeuille*) moneybag. (*hum*) **tomber dans l'~ de qn** *[argent, prime]* to wind up in sb's pocket; *[entreprise]* to get caught in sb's net.
escargot [ɛskaRgo] **nm** (*Zool*) snail; (*: *lambin*) slowcoach* (*Brit*), slowpoke* (*US*). **avancer comme un ~** *ou* **à une allure d'~** to go at a snail's pace; (*manifestation*) **opération ~** lorry drivers' go-slow.
escargotière [ɛskaRgɔtjɛR] **nf** (*parc*) snailery; (*plat*) snail-dish.
escarmouche [ɛskaRmuʃ] **nf** (*lit, fig*) skirmish.
escarpé, e [ɛskaRpe] **adj** steep.
escarpement [ɛskaRpəmɑ̃] **nm** (*côte*) steep slope, escarpment (*SPÉC*); (*raideur*) steepness. (*Géol*) **~ de faille** fault scarp.
escarpin [ɛskaRpɛ̃] **nm** low-fronted shoe, court shoe (*Brit*).
escarpolette† [ɛskaRpɔlɛt] **nf** (*balançoire*) swing; (*Alpinisme*) etrier (*Brit*), stirrup (*US*).
escarre, eschare [ɛskaR] **nf** bedsore.
Escaut [ɛsko] **nm: l'~** the Scheldt.
Eschyle [eʃil] **nm** Aeschylus.
escient [esjɑ̃] **nm: à bon ~** advisedly; **à mauvais ~** ill-advisedly.
esclaffer (s') [ɛsklafe] 1 **vpr** (*frm, hum*) to burst out laughing, guffaw.
esclandre [ɛsklɑ̃dR] **nm** (*scandale*) scene. **faire** *ou* **causer un ~** to make a scene.
esclavage [ɛsklavaʒ] **nm** (*lit*) (*état*) slavery, bondage (*littér*); (*système, fig*) slavery. **réduire en ~** to enslave; **tomber en ~** to become enslaved; (*fig*) **c'est de l'~!** it's sheer slavery.
esclavagisme [ɛsklavaʒism] **nm** proslavery.
esclavagiste [ɛsklavaʒist] 1 **adj** proslavery (*épith*). **États ~s** slave states. 2 **nmf** proslaver.
esclave [ɛsklav] **nmf** slave (*de qn/qch* to sb/sth). **vie d'~** slave's life, life of slavery; **être ~ de la mode** to be a slave of fashion; **être l'~ d'une habitude** to be a slave to habit; **devenir l'~ d'une femme** to become enslaved to a woman; **se rendre ~ de qch** to become a slave to sth.
escogriffe [ɛskɔgRif] **nm: (grand) ~** (great) beanpole*.
escomptable [ɛskɔ̃tabl] **adj** (*Banque*) discountable.
escompte [ɛskɔ̃t] **nm** (*Banque*) discount.
escompter [ɛskɔ̃te] 1 **vt** (*Banque*) to discount; (*fig*) to expect. **~ faire qch** to expect to do sth, reckon *ou* count on doing sth.
escompteur [ɛskɔ̃tœR] **nm** discounter.
escopette† [ɛskɔpɛt] **nf** blunderbuss.
escorte [ɛskɔRt] **nf** (*gén, Mil, Naut*) escort; (*suite*) escort, retinue. (*fig*) **(toute) une ~ de** a whole train *ou* suite of; **sous bonne ~** under escort; **faire ~ à** to escort.
escorter [ɛskɔRte] 1 **vt** to escort.
escorteur [ɛskɔRtœR] **nm** escort (ship).
escouade [ɛskwad] **nf** (*Mil*) squad; *[ouvriers]* gang, squad; (*fig: groupe de gens*) group, squad.
escrime [ɛskRim] **nf** fencing. **faire de l'~** to fence.
escrimer (s')* [ɛskRime] 1 **vpr: s'~ à faire qch** to wear *ou* knock* o.s. out doing sth; **s'~ sur** qch to struggle away at sth.
escrimeur, -euse [ɛskRimœR, øz] **nm,f** (*Sport*) fencer.
escroc [ɛskRo] **nm** crook, swindler, shark, con man‡.
escroquer [ɛskRɔke] 1 **vt** to swindle, con‡. **~ qch à qn** to swindle sb out of sth, swindle *ou* con‡ sth out of sb.
escroquerie [ɛskRɔkRi] **nf** (*gén*) swindle, swindling (*NonC*); (*Jur*) fraud. **être victime d'une ~** to be a victim of fraud; **c'est de l'~** it's a rip-off‡ *ou* a swindle.
escudo [ɛskydo] **nm** escudo.
Esculape [ɛskylap] **nm** Aesculapius.
ESEU [əɛsəy] **nm** (**abrév de examen spécial d'entrée à l'université**) *voir* **examen**.
esgourde†‡ [ɛsguRd] **nf** ear, lug‡ (*Brit*).
Ésope [ezɔp] **nm** Aesop.
ésotérique [ezɔteRik] **adj** esoteric.
ésotérisme [ezɔteRism] **nm** esotericism.
espace [ɛspas] **nm** (*Art, Philos, Phys, Typ, gén*) space. (*Phys*) **~-temps** space-time; **~ de temps** space of time, interval (of time); **avoir assez d'~ pour bouger/vivre** to have enough room to move/live; **manquer d'~** to lack space, be short of space *ou* room, be cramped for space; **laisser de l'~ (entre)** to leave some space (between); **laisser un ~ (entre)** to leave a space *ou* gap (between); **en l'~ de 3 minutes** within the space of 3 minutes; **~ parcouru** distance covered; **~s verts** parks, green spaces *ou* areas; **~ vital** living space; **dans l'~ intersidéral** in deep space; **l'~ aérien** air space; **~ publicitaire** advertising site; (*Ordin*) **~ disque** disk space.
espacement [ɛspasmɑ̃] **nm** (*action*) spacing out; (*résultat*) spacing. **devant l'~ de ses visites** since his visits were (*ou* are *etc*) becoming more infrequent *ou* spaced out, in view of the increasing infrequency of his visits.
espacer [ɛspase] 3 1 **vt** *objets* to space out; *visites* to space out, make less frequent. 2 **s'espacer vpr** *[visites, symptômes]* to become less frequent.
espadon [ɛspadɔ̃] **nm** swordfish.
espadrille [ɛspadRij] **nf** rope-soled sandal, espadrille.
Espagne [ɛspaɲ] **nf** Spain; *voir* **château, grand**.
espagnol, e [ɛspaɲɔl] 1 **adj** Spanish. 2 **nm** (*Ling*) Spanish. 3 **nm: E~** Spaniard; **les E~s** the Spanish, the Spaniards. 4 **Espagnole nf** Spanish woman, Spaniard.
espagnolette [ɛspaɲɔlɛt] **nf** (window) catch (*as on a continental casement window*). **fenêtre fermée à l'~** window half-shut (resting on the catch).
espalier [ɛspalje] **nm** (*Agr*) espalier; (*Sport*) wall bars. **arbre en ~** espalier (tree).
espar [ɛspaR] **nm** (*Naut*) spar.
espèce [ɛspɛs] **nf** a (*Bio*) species. **~s** species; **~ humaine** human race; *voir* **propagation**.
b (*sorte*) sort, kind, type. **de toute ~** of all kinds *ou* sorts *ou* types; **ça n'a aucune ~ d'importance** that is of absolutely no importance *ou* not of the slightest importance; **c'était une ~ d'église** it was a kind *ou* sort of church, it was a church of sorts (*péj*); **formant des ~s de guirlandes** making (up) sort of *ou* kind of festoons, making (up) something resembling *ou* like festoons; **un voyou de la plus belle ~** *ou* **de la pire ~** a hoodlum of the worst kind *ou* sort.
c (*péj*) **une** *ou* **un ~ d'excentrique est venu*** some eccentric turned up; **qu'est-ce que c'est que cette** *ou* **cet ~ de crétin?*** who's this stupid twit?‡ *ou* idiot?; **~ de maladroit!** you clumsy clot* (*Brit*) *ou* oaf!*
d (*Fin*) **~s** cash; **versement en ~s** payment in cash *ou* in specie (*SPÉC*); (†, *hum*) **en ~s sonnantes et trébuchantes** in coin of the realm (*hum*).
e (*Philos, Rel*) species. **les Saintes E~s** the Eucharistic *ou* sacred species; *voir* **communier**.
f (*frm, littér*) **en l'~** in the case in point; *voir* **cas**.

espérance [ɛspeʀɑ̃s] nf a (*espoir*) hope, expectation(s). (*Rel, gén*) **l'~** hope; **dans** *ou* **avec l'~ de vous voir bientôt** hoping to see you soon, in the hope of seeing you soon; **contre toute ~** against all expectations *ou* hope, contrary to expectation(s); **~s trompeuses** false hopes; **donner de grandes ~s** to be very promising, show great promise; **avoir de grandes ~s** to have great prospects; **les plus belles ~s lui sont ouvertes** he has excellent prospects; **bâtir** *ou* **fonder des ~s sur** to build *ou* found one's hopes on; **mettre son ~** *ou* **ses ~s en** *ou* **dans** to put one's hopes in, pin one's hopes on; **avoir l'~ de pouvoir** ... to be hopeful that one will be able to ..., be hopeful of being able to ...; **garder l'~ de pouvoir** ... to remain hopeful of being able to ..., remain hopeful that one will be able to ..., hold on to the hope of being able to ... .

b (*sujet d'espoir*) hope. **c'est là toute mon ~** that is my greatest hope, it's what I hope for most, that's what I'm pinning all my hopes on; **vous êtes toute mon ~** you are my only hope.

c (*Sociol*) **~ de vie** life expectancy, expectation of life.

d († *ou hum: financières*) **~s** expectations; **il a de belles ~s du côté de sa tante** he has great expectations of an inheritance from his aunt.

espérantiste [ɛspeʀɑ̃tist] adj, nmf Esperantist.

espéranto [ɛspeʀɑ̃to] nm Esperanto.

espérer [ɛspeʀe] 6 1 vt (*souhaiter*) *succès, récompense, aide* to hope for. **~ réussir** to hope to succeed; **~ que** to hope that; **nous ne vous espérions plus** we'd given up (all) hope of seeing you *ou* of your coming; **je n'en espérais pas tant** I wasn't hoping *ou* I hadn't dared to hope for as much; **viendra-t-il? — je l'espère (bien)** *ou* **j'espère (bien)** will he come? — I (certainly) hope so; **ceci (nous) laisse** *ou* **fait ~ un succès rapide** this gives us hope *ou* makes us hopeful of quick success *ou* allows us to hope for quick success; **n'espérez pas qu'il change d'avis** there is no point in hoping he'll change his mind; **j'espère bien n'avoir rien oublié** I hope I haven't forgotten anything.

2 vi (*avoir confiance*) to have faith. **il faut ~** you must have faith; **~ en** *Dieu, honnêteté de qn, bienfaiteur* to have faith in, trust in.

esperluette [ɛspɛʀlɥɛt] nf ampersand.

espiègle [ɛspjɛgl] 1 adj *enfant* mischievous, impish; *air* roguish, mischievous. 2 nmf imp, monkey*.

espièglerie [ɛspjɛgləʀi] nf a (*caractère: voir* **espiègle**) mischievousness; impishness; roguishness. b (*tour*) piece of mischief, prank, monkey trick (*Brit*).

espion, -ionne [ɛspjɔ̃, jɔn] nm,f spy.

espionite [ɛspʒɔnit] nf spy mania.

espionnage [ɛspjɔnaʒ] nm espionage, spying. **film/roman d'~** spy film/novel *ou* thriller; **~ industriel** industrial espionage.

espionner [ɛspjɔne] 1 vt *personne, actions* to spy (up)on, keep a close watch on. **~ pour le compte de qn** to spy for sb.

espionnite = **espionite**.

esplanade [ɛsplanad] nf esplanade.

espoir [ɛspwaʀ] nm a (*espérance*) hope. **~s chimériques** wild hopes; **dans l'~ de vous voir bientôt** hoping to see you soon, in the hope of seeing you soon; **avoir l'~/le ferme ~ que** to be hopeful/very hopeful that; **il n'y a plus d'~ (de faire)** all hope is lost *ou* there's no longer any hope (of doing); **avoir bon ~ de faire/que** to have great hopes of doing/that, be confident of doing/that; **reprendre ~** to (begin to) feel hopeful again, take heart once more; **sans ~** *amour, situation* hopeless; **aimer sans ~** to love without hope; *voir* **lueur, rayon**.

b (*sujet d'espérance*) hope. **vous êtes mon dernier ~** you are my last hope; **les jeunes ~s du ski/de la chanson** the young hopefuls of the skiing/singing world; **un des grands ~s de la boxe française** one of the great hopes in French boxing, one of France's great boxing hopes.

esprit [ɛspʀi] 1 nm a (*gén: pensée*) mind. **l'~ humain** the mind of man, the human mind *ou* intellect; **se reporter en ~** *ou* **par l'~ à** to cast one's mind back to; **avoir l'~ large/étroit** to be broad-/narrow-minded; **avoir l'~ vif** to be quick-witted, have a lively mind; **à l'~ lent** slow-witted; **vivacité/lenteur d'~** quickness/slowness of wit *ou* mind; **avoir l'~ clair** to have a clear head *ou* mind; **avoir l'~ mal tourné** to have a dirty mind; **avoir l'~ d'escalier** *voir* **2**; **il a l'~ ailleurs** his mind is elsewhere *ou* on other things; **où ai-je l'~?** I'm miles away!, what am I thinking of?; **j'ai l'~ plus libre maintenant** my mind is freer now; **il n'a pas l'~ à ce qu'il fait** his mind is not on what he's doing; **je n'ai pas l'~ à rire** I'm not in the mood for laughing; **dans mon ~ ça voulait dire** to my mind it meant; (*hum*) **l'~ est fort** *ou* **prompt, mais la chair est faible** the spirit is willing but the flesh is weak; **il m'est venu à l'~ que** it crossed my mind that, it occurred to me that; (*Prov*) **un ~ sain dans un corps sain** mens sana in corpore sano, a sound mind in a healthy body; *voir* **disposition, état, faible**.

b (*humour*) wit. **avoir de l'~** to be witty; **faire de l'~** to try to be witty *ou* funny; **manquer d'~** to lack sparkle *ou* wit; *voir* **femme, mot, trait**.

c (*être humain*) **son pouvoir sur les ~s/jeunes ~s** his power over people's minds/young minds, his power over people/young people; **c'est un ~ subtil** he is a shrewd man, he has a shrewd mind; **un de nos plus grands ~s** one of our greatest minds; *voir* **beau, grand, mauvais**.

d (*Rel, Spiritisme*) spirit. **~, es-tu là?** is (there) anybody there?; **je ne suis pas un pur ~** I'm flesh and blood (and I have to eat); **il joue les ~s forts** he claims to be a rational man.

e [*loi, époque, texte*] spirit.

f (*aptitude*) **avoir l'~ mathématique/d'analyse/d'entreprise** to have a mathematical/an analytical/an enterprising mind; **avoir l'~ des affaires** to have a good head for business; **avoir l'~ critique** to be critical, take a critical attitude; **avoir l'~ de critique** to like criticizing for its own sake; **avoir l'~ de synthèse** to have an analytical mind; **avoir le bon ~ de** to have enough sense to, have the (good) sense to.

g (*attitude*) spirit. **l'~ de cette classe** *ou* **qui règne dans cette classe me déplaît** I do not like the (general) attitude of this class; **~ de révolte/sacrifice** spirit of rebellion/sacrifice; **dans un ~ de conciliation** in a spirit of conciliation; **avoir mauvais ~** to have a negative personality; **faire preuve de mauvais ~** to be a disruptive *ou* disturbing influence; **comprenez l'~ dans lequel je le dis** you must understand the spirit in which I say it.

h (*Ling*) **~ doux/rude** smooth/rough breathing.

2 comp ► **esprits animaux**† (*Méd*) animal spirits ► **esprit d'à-propos** ready wit ► **esprit-de-bois** wood alcohol ► **esprit de caste** class consciousness ► **esprits chagrins** (*péj*) faultfinders ► **esprit de chapelle** cliquishness ► **esprit de clan** clannishness ► **esprit de clocher** parochialism ► **esprit de compétition** competitive spirit ► **esprit de contradiction** argumentativeness ► **esprit de corps** esprit de corps ► **esprit d'équipe** team spirit ► **esprit d'escalier: tu as l'esprit d'escalier** you never think of an answer until it's too late ► **esprit de famille** family feeling; (*péj*) clannishness ► **esprit frappeur** spirit-rapper ► **esprit malin** *ou* **du mal** evil spirit ► **l'Esprit saint** (*Rel*) the Holy Spirit *ou* Ghost ► **esprit-de-sel** spirits of salt ► **esprit de suite** consistency (*of thought*) ► **esprit de système** methodical *ou* systematic mind ► **esprit-de-vin** spirits of wine.

esquif [ɛskif] nm (*littér*) skiff. **frêle ~** frail barque (*littér*).

esquille [ɛskij] nf splinter (of bone).

esquimau, -aude, mpl **~x** [ɛskimo, od] 1 adj Eskimo. **chien ~** husky. 2 nm (*Ling*) Eskimo; (*glace* ®) choc-ice (*Brit*), Eskimo (*US*); (*chien*) husky. 3 nm,f: **E~(-aude)** Eskimo.

esquintant, e* [ɛskɛ̃tɑ̃, ɑ̃t] adj exhausting. **un travail ~** an exhausting job, a job that (really) takes it out of you*.

esquinter* [ɛskɛ̃te] 1 1 vt a (*abîmer*) *objet* to mess up*; *yeux, santé* to do in*, ruin; *adversaire* to beat up, bash up*; *voiture* to smash up. **se faire ~ par une voiture** [*automobiliste*] to have *ou* get one's car bashed* *ou* smashed into by another; [*cycliste, piéton*] to get badly bashed up* by a car; (*Aut*) **aile esquintée** damaged *ou* dented wing; **vieux rateau tout esquinté** battered old rake.

b (*critiquer*) *film, livre* to pull to pieces, slate* (*Brit*), pan*, slam*.

2 **s'esquinter** vpr to tire *ou* knock* o.s. out. **s'~ à travailler** to work o.s. to death, work o.s. into the ground; **s'~ à étudier** to beat one's brains out* studying, work o.s. into the ground studying; **s'~ les yeux (à lire)** to strain ones eyes (reading).

esquisse [ɛskis] nf (*Peinture*) sketch; (*fig*) [*projet*] outline, sketch; [*geste, sourire*] beginnings, suggestion.

esquisser [ɛskise] 1 vt (*Peinture*) to sketch (out); (*fig*) *projet* to outline, sketch. **~ un geste** to make the merest suggestion of a gesture, half-make a gesture; **~ un pas de danse** to have a quick dance, have a quick twirl*; **un sourire à peine esquissé** the ghost of a smile, the faintest of smiles; **un certain progrès commence à s'~** one can begin to detect some progress.

esquive [ɛskiv] nf (*Boxe*) dodge; (*fig: en politique etc*) evasion, sidestepping (*NonC*). (*fig*) **passé maître dans l'art de l'~** past master in the art of sidestepping *ou* dodging his opponents *ou* the issue.

esquiver [ɛskive] 1 1 vt *coup, question, personne* to dodge, evade, elude; *obligation* to shirk, dodge; *difficulté* to evade, get round, skirt round. 2 **s'esquiver** vpr to slip *ou* sneak away.

essai [esɛ] nm a (*mise à l'épreuve*) [*produit*] testing; [*voiture*] trying out, testing. (*Aut, Aviat: tests techniques*) **~s** trials; **~s de résistance** resistance tests; (*Course automobile*) **~s** practice; **venez faire l'~ de notre nouveau modèle** come and test drive *ou* try (out) our new model; **prendre qn à l'~** to take sb on for a trial period *ou* on a trial basis; **mettre à l'~** to test (out), put to the test; *voir* **balance, banc, bout**.

b (*première utilisation*) **l'~ de ce produit n'a pas été convaincant** this product didn't prove very satisfactory when it was tried out; **faire l'~ d'un produit** to try out a product.

c (*tentative*) attempt, try; (*Sport*) attempt. **~ raté** failed attempt; **faire plusieurs ~s** to have several tries, make *ou* have several attempts; **faire des ~s infructueux** to make fruitless attempts; **où en sont tes ~s de plantations?** how are your efforts at growing things *ou* your attempts in the garden progressing?; **ce n'est pas mal pour un premier ~** that's not bad for a first try *ou* attempt *ou* go *ou* shot; [*compagnie pétrolière*] **se livrer à des forages d'~** to test drill; **coup d'~** first attempt.

d (*Rugby*) try. **marquer un ~** to score a try.

e (*Littérat*) essay.

f (*Tech*) [*or, argent*] assay.

essaim [esɛ̃] nm (*lit, fig*) swarm. (*fig*) **~ de jeunes filles/de vieilles femmes** bevy *ou* gaggle of girls/of old women.

essaimage [esɛmaʒ] nm (*voir* **essaimer**) swarming; scattering; spreading, expansion.

essaimer [eseme] vi (*lit*) to swarm; (*fig*) *[famille]* to scatter; *[firme]* (*se développer*) to spread, expand; (*se séparer*) to hive off.

essayage [esɛjaʒ] nm (*Couture*) fitting, trying on; *voir* **cabine, salon.**

essayer [eseje] 8 1 vt a (*mettre à l'épreuve*) *produit* to test (out), try (out); *voiture* to test; *[client]* to test drive, try (out). **venez ~ notre nouveau modèle** come and test drive *ou* try (out) our new model; (*fig*) **~ sa force/son talent** to try *ou* test one's strength/skill.
b (*utiliser pour la première fois*) *voiture, produit* to try (out). **avez-vous essayé le nouveau boucher?*** have you tried the new butcher('s)?
c *vêtement* to try on. **il faut que je vous l'essaie** I must try it on you.
d (*tenter*) *méthode* to try. **~ de faire** to try *ou* attempt to do; **as-tu essayé les petites annonces?** have you tried the classified ads?; **essaie de le faire** try to do it, try and do it; **il a essayé de s'échapper** he attempted *ou* tried to run away; **je vais ~** I'll try, I'll have a go *ou* a try *ou* a shot (at it); **essaie un coup*** have a crack at it*, have a bash (at it)*; **essaie un peu pour voir** (*si tu y arrives*) have a try *ou* a go and see; (*: *si tu l'oses*) just you try!*, just let me see you try it!; **n'essaie pas de ruser avec moi** don't try being clever with me, don't try it on with me* (*Brit*).
e (*Tech*) *or, argent* to assay.
2 **s'essayer** vpr: **s'~ à qch/à faire** to try one's hand at sth/at doing, have a go at sth/at doing.

essayeur, -euse [esɛjœʀ, øz] nm,f (*Couture*) fitter; (*Tech*) assayer.

essayiste [esejist] nmf essayist.

esse [ɛs] nf (*crochet*) hook; (*goupille*) linchpin; *[violon]* sound-hole.

ESSEC [esɛk] nf (**abrév de École supérieure des sciences économiques et commerciales**) *voir* **école.**

essence¹ [esɑ̃s] nf a (*carburant*) petrol (*Brit*), gas(oline) (*US*); (*solvant*) spirit. **~ minérale** mineral oil; **~ ordinaire** two-star petrol (*Brit*), regular gas (*US*); **~ sans plomb** lead-free *ou* unleaded petrol (*Brit*), unleaded gas (*US*); **~ de térébenthine** turpentine; **à ~** petrol-driven (*Brit*), gasoline-powered (*US*); *voir* **distributeur, panne.** b (*extrait*) *[plantes]* essential oil, essence; *[aliments]* essence. **~ de violette/de café** violet/coffee essence, essence of violet/coffee; **~ de citron/de rose** lemon/rose oil; **~ de lavande** lavender essence, essence of lavender, lavender oil, oil of lavender.

essence² [esɑ̃s] nf (*fondement*) *[conversation, question, doctrine]* gist, essence; *[livre, ouvrage]* gist; (*Philos*) essence. (*littér*) **par ~** in essence, essentially.

essence³ [esɑ̃s] nf (*espèce*) *[arbres]* species. **~ à feuilles persistantes** evergreen species; (*fig littér*) **se croire d'une ~ supérieure** to think of o.s. as a superior being *ou* as of a superior species.

essentiel, -elle [esɑ̃sjɛl] 1 adj a (*indispensable*) essential. **ces formalités sont ~elles** these formalities are essential (*à* to, *pour* for).
b (*de base*) essential, basic, main (*épith*). **~ à** essential to.
2 nm a **l'~** the main thing; (*objets nécessaires*) the basic essentials; (*points principaux*) the essentials, the essential *ou* basic points; **tant qu'on a la santé, c'est l'~** as long as you have your health, that's the main thing; **l'~ est de ...** the main *ou* important thing is to ... .
b **l'~ de** *conversation* the main part of; *fortune* the best *ou* main part of, the bulk of; **l'~ de ce qu'il dit** most of what he says; **ils passaient l'~ de leur temps à faire ...** they spent the best part of their time doing ... .

essentiellement [esɑ̃sjɛlmɑ̃] adv (*gén*) basically, essentially, mainly; (*Philos*) essentially. **nous tenons ~ à ...** we are concerned above all with ... .

esseulé, e [esœle] adj (*littér*) forsaken (*littér*), forlorn (*littér*).

essieu, pl ~x [esjø] nm axle(-tree).

essor [esɔʀ] nm (*frm: envol*) *[oiseau, imagination]* flight; (*croissance*) *[entreprise, pays]* rapid development *ou* expansion; *[art, civilisation]* blossoming. **entreprise en plein ~** firm in full expansion; **prendre son ~** *[oiseau]* to fly up *ou* off; *[société]* to develop *ou* expand rapidly; **le cinéma connaît un nouvel ~** the cinema is enjoying a new boom.

essorage [esɔʀaʒ] nm (*voir* **essorer**) wringing, mangling; wringing out; spin-drying. (*sur machine à laver*) **mettre sur la position "~"** to put on "spin"; **3 ~s** 3 spins.

essorer [esɔʀe] 1 vt (*avec essoreuse à rouleaux*) to wring, mangle; (*à la main*) to wring out; (*par la force centrifuge*) to spin-dry.

essoreuse [esɔʀøz] nf (*à rouleaux*) wringer, mangle; (*à tambour*) spin-dryer.

essoufflement [esufləmɑ̃] nm breathlessness (*NonC*), shortness of breath (*NonC*); (*fig*) *[mouvement]* running out of steam.

essouffler [esufle] 1 1 vt to make breathless, wind. **il était essoufflé** he was out of breath *ou* winded *ou* puffed* (*Brit*). 2 **s'essouffler** vpr *[coureur]* to get out of breath, get puffed* (*Brit*); (*fig*) *[roman, travail]* to tail off, fall off; *[romancier]* to exhaust o.s. *ou* one's talent, dry up*; *[reprise économique, mouvement de grève]* to run out of steam.

essuie [esɥi] nm (*Belgique*) (*pour les mains*) hand towel; (*serviette de bain*) bath towel; (*torchon*) cloth.

essuie- [esɥi] préf *voir* **essuyer.**

essuyage [esɥijaʒ] nm (*voir* **essuyer**) (*gén*) wiping; drying; mopping; cleaning; dusting; wiping up, mopping up.

essuyer [esɥije] 8 1 vt a (*nettoyer*) *objet mouillé, assiettes* to wipe, dry; *sol, surface mouillée* to wipe, mop; *tableau noir* to clean, wipe; *surface poussiéreuse* to dust; *eau* to wipe up, mop up. **s'~ les mains** to wipe one's hands (dry), dry one's hands; **s'~ la bouche** to wipe one's mouth; **essuie-toi les pieds** *ou* **essuie tes pieds avant d'entrer** wipe your feet before you come *ou* go in; **s'~ le torse/les pieds après un bain** to dry one's body/feet after a bath; **~ la vaisselle** to wipe *ou* dry up, do the drying-up (*Brit*), dry the dishes; **le tableau est mal essuyé** the blackboard has been badly cleaned *ou* hasn't been cleaned *ou* wiped properly; **nous avons essuyé les plâtres*** we had all the initial problems to put up with.
b (*subir*) *pertes, reproches, échec* to suffer; *insultes* to endure, suffer; *refus* to meet with; *tempête* to weather, ride out. **~ le feu de l'ennemi** to come under enemy fire; **~ un coup de feu** to be shot at.
2 **s'essuyer** vpr *[baigneur]* to dry o.s.
3 comp ▸**essuie-glace** nm inv windscreen (*Brit*) *ou* windshield (*US*) wiper; **essuie-glace à balayage intermittent** intermittent wiper ▸**essuie-mains** nm inv hand towel ▸**essuie-meubles** nm inv duster ▸**essuie-tout** nm inv kitchen paper ▸**essuie-verres** nm inv glass cloth.

est¹ [ɛ] *voir* **être.**

est² [ɛst] 1 nm a (*point cardinal*) east. **le vent d'~** the east wind; **un vent d'~** an east(erly) wind, an easterly (*Naut*); **le vent tourne/est à l'~** the wind is veering east(wards) *ou* towards the east/is blowing from the east; **regarder vers l'~** *ou* **dans la direction de l'~** to look east(wards) *ou* towards the east; **à l'~** (*situation*) in the east; (*direction*) to the east, east(wards); **le soleil se lève à l'~** the sun rises in the east; **à l'~ de** east of, to the east of; **l'appartement est (exposé) à l'~/exposé plein ~** the flat faces (the) east *ou* eastwards/due east, the flat looks east(wards)/due east.
b (*régions orientales*) east. (*Pol*) **l'E~** the East; **la France de l'E~, l'~ (de la France)** the East (of France); **les pays de l'E~** the Eastern countries; **le bloc de l'E~** the Eastern bloc; **l'Europe de l'E~** Eastern Europe; **l'Allemagne de l'E~** East Germany.
2 adj inv *région, partie* eastern; *entrée, paroi* east; *versant, côte* east(ern); *côté* east(ward); *direction* eastward, easterly; *voir* **longitude.**
3 comp ▸**est-allemand, e** adj East German ▸**Est-Allemand, e** nm,f (**mpl Est-Allemands**) East German ▸**est-nord-est** nm, adj inv east-north-east ▸**est-sud-est** nm, adj inv east-south-east.

estacade [ɛstakad] nf landing stage.

estafette [ɛstafɛt] nf (*Mil*) courier; (®*: camionnette*) van.

estafilade [ɛstafilad] nf gash, slash.

estaminet† [ɛstaminɛ] nm tavern; (*péj*) pothouse† (*péj*), (low) dive (*péj*).

estampage [ɛstɑ̃paʒ] nm (*voir* **estamper**) fleecing, swindling, diddling* (*Brit*); stamping. **c'est de l'~‡** it's a plain swindle.

estampe [ɛstɑ̃p] nf (*image*) engraving, print; (*outil*) stamp. (*euph*) **venez voir mes ~s japonaises** you must let me show you my etchings.

estamper [ɛstɑ̃pe] 1 vt (‡*: voler*) to fleece, swindle, diddle* (*Brit*); (*Tech*) to stamp.

estampeur, -euse [ɛstɑ̃pœʀ, øz] nm,f (‡) swindler, shark*; (*Tech*) stamper.

estampillage [ɛstɑ̃pijaʒ] nm stamping, marking.

estampille [ɛstɑ̃pij] nf stamp.

estampiller [ɛstɑ̃pije] 1 vt to stamp.

estarie [ɛstaʀi] nf (*Naut*) lay-days.

este [ɛst] adj *voir* **estonien.**

ester¹ [ɛste] vi (*Jur*) **~ en justice** to go to court, appear (*as plaintiff or defendant*).

ester² [ɛstɛʀ] nm (*Chim*) ester.

Esther [ɛstɛʀ] nf Esther.

esthète [ɛstɛt] nmf aesthete.

esthéticien, -ienne [ɛstetisjɛ̃, jɛn] nm,f (*maquillage*) beautician; (*Art*) aesthetician.

esthétique [ɛstetik] 1 adj *jugement, sentiment* aesthetic; *pose, carrosserie* attractive, aesthetically pleasing; *voir* **chirurgie, soin.** 2 nf *[visage, pose]* aesthetic quality, attractiveness. (*discipline*) **l'~** aesthetics (*sg*); **l'~ industrielle** industrial design.

esthétiquement [ɛstetikmɑ̃] adv aesthetically.

esthétisant, e [ɛstetizɑ̃, ɑ̃t] adj favouring aestheticism.

esthétisme [ɛstetism] nm aestheticism.

estimable [ɛstimabl] adj a (*frm: digne d'estime*) estimable (*frm*), highly considered *ou* respected; (*assez bon*) honest, sound. b (*déterminable*) assessable, calculable. **ces dégâts sont difficilement ~s** it is difficult to assess the extent of this damage.

estimatif, -ive [ɛstimatif, iv] adj: **devis ~** estimate; **état ~** estimated statement.

estimation [ɛstimasjɔ̃] nf a (*action*) *[objet]* appraisal, valuation; *[dégâts, prix]* assessment, estimation; *[distance, quantité]* estimation, reckoning; *[propriété]* valuation, assessment. b (*chiffre donné*) estimate, estimation. **d'après mes ~s** according to my estimations *ou* reckonings; **~ injuste** unfair estimate; **~ des coûts** cost estimate; (*sondage d'opinion, vote*) **~s** projections.

estime [ɛstim] nf a (*considération*) esteem, respect, regard. **jouir d'une grande ~** to be highly respected *ou* regarded, be held in high esteem *ou* regard; **il a baissé dans mon ~** he has sunk in my estimation; **ce succès mérite l'~ de tous** this success deserves the respect of everyone; **avoir de l'~ pour** to have (a) great esteem *ou* respect *ou* great regard for; **tenir en piètre ~** to have little regard *ou* respect for; *voir* **succès. b naviguer à l'~** (*Naut*) to sail by dead reckoning; (*fig*) to sail in the dark.

estimer [ɛstime] 1 **vt a** (*évaluer*) *objet, propriété* to appraise, value, evaluate, assess; *dégâts, prix* to assess, estimate, evaluate (*à* at); *distance, quantité* to estimate, reckon. **faire ~ un bijou** to have a piece of jewellery appraised *ou* valued; **cette bague est estimée à 3 000 F** this ring is valued at 3,000 francs; **les pertes sont estimées à 2 000 morts** 2,000 people are estimated to have died, an estimated 2,000 people have died, the number of those dead is estimated at *ou* put at 2,000; **j'estime sa vitesse à 80 km/h** I reckon his speed to be 80 km/h, I would put his speed at 80 km/h.

b (*respecter*) *personne* to esteem, hold in esteem *ou* high esteem *ou* regard, respect. **estimé de tous** respected *ou* esteemed *ou* highly regarded by everyone; **savoir se faire ~** to know how to win people's respect *ou* regard *ou* esteem.

c (*faire cas de*) *qualité* to value highly *ou* greatly, prize, rate highly, appreciate. **~ qch à sa juste valeur** to recognize the true worth *ou* value of sth; **il faut savoir ~ un service rendu** one must know how to appreciate a favour; **j'estime beaucoup sa loyauté** I greatly value his loyalty, I set great store by his loyalty; **c'est un plat très estimé** this dish is considered a great delicacy.

d (*considérer*) **~ que ...** to consider *ou* judge *ou* deem† that ...; **j'estime qu'il est de mon devoir de** I consider it *ou* judge it *ou* deem it† (to be) my duty to; **il estime que vous avez tort de faire cela** he considers it wrong for you to do that; **il estime avoir raison** he considers he is right *ou* in the right; **nous estimons nécessaire de dire/que** we consider it *ou* judge it *ou* deem it† necessary to say/that; **~ inutile de faire** to see no point in doing, consider it pointless to do; **s'~ heureux d'avoir/d'un résultat/que** to consider o.s. fortunate to have/with a result/that.

estivage [ɛstivaʒ] **nm** summering of cattle on mountain pastures.

estival, e, **mpl -aux** [ɛstival, o] **adj** (*lit*) summer (*épith*); (*fig: agréable*) summery.

estivant, e [ɛstivɑ̃, ɑ̃t] **nm,f** holiday-maker (*Brit*), vacationer (*US*), summer visitor.

estoc [ɛstɔk] **nm** *voir* **frapper.**

estocade [ɛstɔkad] **nf** (*Tauromachie*) death-blow, final thrust. **donner l'~ à un taureau** to deal a bull the death-blow; (*fig*) **donner l'~ à une personne/un projet** to give *ou* deal the finishing blow to a person/a plan.

estomac [ɛstɔma] **nm a** stomach. **avoir mal à l'~** to have (a) stomach ache *ou* tummy ache*; **partir l'~ creux** to set off on an empty stomach; **avoir l'~ creux** *ou* **vide/bien rempli** *ou* **garni** to feel *ou* be empty/full (up); **j'ai l'~ dans les talons** I'm starving *ou* famished; **avoir un ~ d'autruche** to have a cast-iron digestive system *ou* a stomach of cast-iron; **prendre de l'~*** to develop a paunch; *voir* **aigreur, creux, rester. b** (‡) **avoir de l'~** (*du culot*) to have a nerve; (*du courage*) to have guts*; **il la lui a fait à l'~** he bluffed *ou* hoodwinked him, he pulled a fast one on him*.

estomaquer* [ɛstɔmake] 1 **vt** to flabbergast, stagger.

estompe [ɛstɔ̃p] **nf** stump (*Art*).

estompé, e [ɛstɔ̃pe] (**ptp de estomper**) **adj** *couleurs, image* blurred, soft.

estomper [ɛstɔ̃pe] 1 **vt** (*Art*) *dessin* to stump (*SPÉC*), shade off (*with a stump*); (*fig: voiler*) *contours, souvenir* to blur, dim, soften. **la côte s'estompait dans la brume du soir** the coastline became blurred *ou* hazy *ou* indistinct in the evening mist.

Estonie [ɛstɔni] **nf** Estonia.

estonien, -ienne [ɛstɔnjɛ̃, jɛn] **1 adj** Estonian. **2 nm** (*Ling*) Estonian. **3 nm,f: E~(-ienne)** Estonian.

estouffade [ɛstufad] **nf:** (*Culin*) **~ de bœuf** ≃ beef stew; (*fig*) **c'est de l'~** it's very stodgy.

estourbir* [ɛstuʀbiʀ] 2 **vt** (*assommer*) to stun; (*tuer*) to do in‡, bump off‡ (*Brit*).

estrade [ɛstʀad] **nf** platform, rostrum, dais.

estragon [ɛstʀagɔ̃] **nm** tarragon.

estrapade [ɛstʀapad] **nf** strappado (torture).

estrogène [ɛstʀɔʒɛn] **nm** *voir* **œstrogène.**

estropié, e [ɛstʀɔpje] (**ptp de estropier**) **nm,f** cripple, maimed person.

estropier [ɛstʀɔpje] 7 **vt** *personne* to cripple, disable, maim; (*fig*) *texte, citation* to twist, distort, mangle; *nom* to mutilate, mangle; *langue étrangère, morceau de musique* to mangle, murder.

estuaire [ɛstɥɛʀ] **nm** estuary; (*en Écosse*) firth. **l'~ de la Seine** the Seine estuary.

estudiantin, e [ɛstydjɑ̃tɛ̃, in] **adj** student (*épith*).

esturgeon [ɛstyʀʒɔ̃] **nm** sturgeon.

et [e] **conj a** (*lie des termes, des subordonnées*) and. **c'est vert ~ rouge** it's green and red; **la clarinette ~ le trombone sont des instruments de musique** the clarinet and the trombone are musical instruments; **il est travailleur ~ ne boit pas** he works hard and (he) doesn't drink; (*Mus*) **pour piano ~ orchestre** for piano and orchestra; **lui ~ moi nous nous entendons bien** he and I get along well; **~ lui ~ vous l'avez dit** he and you have both said so, both he and you have said so; **2 ~ 2 font 4** 2 and 2 make 4; **j'aime beaucoup ça, ~ vous?** I'm very fond of that, aren't you? *ou* what about you?, I like that very much – do you?; **je n'aime pas ça ~ lui non plus** I don't like that and nor does he *ou* and he doesn't either; **je n'ai rien vu, ~ toi?** I didn't see anything, did you? *ou* what about you?; **il ne peut ~ ne doit pas y aller** he cannot and must not go; (*répétition*) **il a ri ~ ri/pleuré ~ pleuré** he laughed and laughed/cried and cried; (*littér*) **Charles y alla, ~ Jules** Charles went, as did Jules; **une belle ~ grande maison** a beautiful, big house; (*littér*) **un homme noble ~ pur ~ généreux** a noble, pure and generous man; **il y a mensonge ~ mensonge** there are lies and lies, there's lying and lying; **il y a erreur ~ erreur** there are mistakes and mistakes; **je ne l'approuve pas ~ ne l'approuverai jamais** I don't approve of it and (I) never shall *ou* will; **plus j'en mange ~ plus j'en ai envie** the more of it I eat the more I want.

b (*lie des principales: simultanéité, succession, conséquence*) and. **je suis né à Genève ~ mes parents aussi** I was born in Geneva and so were my parents, I was born in Geneva, as were my parents; **j'ai payé ~ je suis parti** I paid and left.

c (*valeur emphatique*) **~ alors/ensuite/après?** and so/then/afterwards?; **~ alors?** (*peu importe*) so (what)?*; **~ moi alors?** (and) what about me then?; **~ puis** and then; **~ puis?, ~ puis après?*** so (what)?*; **~ moi, je peux venir?** can I come too?; (*indignation*) **~ vous osez revenir?** and you dare (to) come back?; **~ lui alors qu'est-ce qu'il va dire?** what's he going to have to say?; **~ ces livres que tu devais me prêter?** what about these books (then) *ou* and what's happened to these books that you were supposed to lend me?; **~ vous, vous y allez?** and what about you, are you going?; **~ si nous y allions aussi?** what about (us) going as well?, why don't we go too?; **~ voilà!** and there you are!; **~ voilà que le voisin revient ...** and then the next-door neighbour comes back ...; **~ voici que s'amène notre ami** (and) along comes our friend; **~ alors eux, voyant cela, ils sont partis** (and) so, seeing that, they left; (*littér*) **~ lui de sourire/se fâcher** whereupon he smiled/grew angry; **~ d'un ... ~ de deux** for one thing ... and for another; **il est bête, ~ d'un, ~ il est méchant, ~ de deux** he's stupid for one thing and for another he's a nasty character.

d vingt/trente *etc* **~ un** twenty-/thirty- *etc* one; **à midi/deux heures ~ quart** at (a) quarter past twelve/two; **le vingt ~ unième** the twenty-first; *voir* **mille[1]**.

ETA [əteа] **nf** (**abrév de Euzkadi Ta Askatasuna**) ETA.

êta [ɛta] **nm** eta.

étable [etabl] **nf** cowshed.

établi [etabli] **nm** (work) bench.

établir [etabliʀ] 2 **1 vt a** (*installer dans un lieu*) *immeuble* to put up, erect; *usine, liaisons, communications* to establish, set up; *empire* to build, found. **~ son domicile** *ou* **sa demeure à** to set up house in, make one's home in; **l'ennemi a établi son camp/son quartier général dans le village** the enemy has pitched camp/has set up its headquarters in the village.

b (*instaurer*) *usage* to establish, institute; *gouvernement* to form, set up; *impôt* to introduce, bring in; *règlement* to lay down, establish, institute.

c (*donner un emploi*) to set up, establish. **~ un fonctionnaire dans une charge** to set a civil servant up in a position; **il a cinq enfants à ~** he has five children to settle; **il lui reste deux filles à ~** he has still two daughters to marry off *ou* get established; **il a établi son fils médecin** he has set his son up *ou* established his son in medical practice.

d (*asseoir*) *démonstration* to base; *réputation* to found, base; *droits* to establish; *fortune* to found (*sur* on). **~ son pouvoir sur la force** to found *ou* base one's power on force.

e (*faire régner*) *autorité, paix* to establish (*sur* over). **~ son pouvoir sur le pays** to get control of the country, establish control over the country.

f (*dresser*) *liste* to draw up, make out; *programme* to arrange; *facture, chèque* to make out; *plans* to draw up, draft; *prix* to fix, work out.

g (*montrer*) *fait, comparaison* to establish. **~ l'innocence de qn** to establish sb's innocence; **il est établi que** it's an established fact that.

h (*nouer*) *relations* to establish. **ils ont établi une amitié solide** they have established a firm friendship.

i (*Sport*) **~ un record** to set (up) *ou* establish a record.

2 s'établir vpr a (*s'installer dans un lieu*) *[jeune couple]* to settle. **une nouvelle usine s'est établie dans le village** a new factory has been set up *ou* they've set up a new factory in the village; **l'ennemi s'est établi sur la colline** the enemy has taken up position on the hill; **les Anglais se sont solidement établis dans leurs colonies** the English established *ou* settled themselves firmly in their colonies.

b (*s'instaurer*) *[usage]* to become customary *ou* common practice. **l'usage s'est établi de faire ...** it has become customary to do ..., it has become established custom to do ... .

c (*prendre un emploi*) **s'~ boulanger** to set o.s. up as a baker; **il s'est établi médecin** he has established himself *ou* set himself up in medical practice; **s'~ à son compte** to set up in business on one's own account.

d (*régner*) *[pouvoir, régime]* to become established. **son pouvoir s'est établi sur le pays** his rule has become (firmly) established throughout the country; **un grand silence s'établit, il s'établit un grand silence** there

was a great silence, a great silence fell.
e (*se nouer*) *[amitié, contacts]* to develop, be established. **une amitié solide s'est établie entre eux, il s'est établi entre eux une solide amitié** a firm friendship has developed *ou* has been established between them.

établissement [etablismɑ̃] **nm** a (*voir* **établir**) putting-up, erecting; setting-up; establishing; building, founding; institution; forming; introduction, bringing-in; laying-down; basing; drawing-up; making-out; arranging; drafting; fixing, working-out.
b (*voir* **s'établir**) settling; setting-up; establishment; development.
c (*bâtiment*) establishment. ~ **scolaire** school, educational establishment (*frm*); ~ **d'enseignement secondaire** secondary school (*Brit*), high school (*US*); ~ **d'enseignement privé** independent *ou* private school; ~ **scolaire spécialisé** special school; ~ **hospitalier** hospital; ~ **thermal** hydropathic establishment; ~ **religieux** religious institution; ~ **commercial** commercial establishment; ~ **financier** financial institution; ~ **industriel** industrial plant, factory; **avec les compliments des ~s X** with the compliments of X and Co. *ou* of the firm of X; (*Fin, Jur*) ~ **public autonome** government-owned corporation; ~ **de soins** health care centre; (*Jur*) ~ **stable** fixed place of business.
d (*colonie*) settlement.

étage [etaʒ] **nm** a *[bâtiment]* floor, storey (*Brit*), story (*US*). **au premier** ~ (*en France*) on the first floor (*Brit*), on the second floor (*US*); (*au Canada*) on the ground floor; **maison à** *ou* **de deux ~s** three-storeyed (*Brit*) *ou* -storied (*US*) house, house with three floors; **grimper les ~s** to go *ou* climb upstairs; **monter à l'~** to go upstairs; **monter à l'~ supérieur** to go to the next floor up; **il grimpa 3 ~s** he went up *ou* walked up 3 floors *ou* flights; **les 3 ~s de la tour Eiffel** the 3 levels of the Eiffel Tower; *voir* **bas**[1].
b *[fusée]* stage; *[mine]* level; *[jardin]* terrace, level; *[gâteau]* tier. (*Géog*) **~s de végétation** levels of vegetation; (*Tech*) ~ **de pression** pressure stage.

étagement [etaʒmɑ̃] **nm** *[vignobles]* terracing.

étager [etaʒe] ③ 1 **vt** *objets* to set out in tiered rows, lay out in tiers.
2 **s'étager vpr** *[jardins, maisons]* to rise in tiers *ou* terraces. **la foule s'étage sur les gradins** the crowd is gathered on the terracing *ou* the steps; **vignobles étagés sur la colline** vines in terraced rows on the hillside.

étagère [etaʒɛʀ] **nf** (*tablette, rayon*) shelf; (*meuble*) shelves.

étai [etɛ] **nm** (*support*) stay, prop, strut; (*Naut: cordage*) stay.

étaiement [etɛmɑ̃] **nm** *voir* **étayage**.

étain [etɛ̃] **nm** (*Min*) tin; (*Orfèvrerie*) (*matière*) pewter; (*objet*) piece of pewterware, pewterware (*NonC*). **pot en** *ou* **d'~** pewter pot; *voir* **papier**.

étal, pl **~s** [etal] **nm** *[boucherie, marché]* stall.

étalage [etalaʒ] **nm** a (*Comm*) (*action*) display, displaying; (*devanture*) shop window, show window, display window; (*tréteaux*) stall, stand; (*articles exposés*) display. **présentation de l'~** window dressing; **disposer l'~** to dress the window, do the window display; **chemise qui a fait l'~** shop-soiled shirt; **droit d'~** stallage; *voir* **vol**[2]. b (*déploiement*) *[luxe, connaissances]* display, show. **faire ~ de** to make a show of, show off, parade; ~ **de force** show of strength. c (*Métal*) **~s** bosh.

étalagiste [etalaʒist] **nmf** (*décorateur*) window dresser; (†: *marchand*) stallkeeper.

étale [etal] 1 **adj** *mer, situation* slack; *vent* steady. **navire ~** ship which makes no headway, becalmed ship. 2 **nm ou f** *[mer]* slack (water).

étalement [etalmɑ̃] **nm** (*voir* **étaler**) spreading; strewing; spreading-out; displaying; laying-out; application; staggering.

étaler [etale] ① 1 **vt** a (*déployer*) *papiers, objets* to spread, strew (*sur* over); *journal, tissu* to spread out (*sur* on); (*Comm*) *marchandise* to display, lay out, spread out (*sur* on). (*Cartes*) ~ **son jeu** *ou* **ses cartes** to display *ou* lay down one's hand *ou* one's cards.
b (*étendre*) *beurre* to spread (*sur* on); *peinture* to apply, put on; *crème solaire* to apply, smooth on.
c (*répartir*) *paiements* to spread, stagger (*sur* over); *vacances* to stagger (*sur* over); *travaux, opération* to spread (*sur* over). (*Poste*) **étalez vos envois** space out your consignments; **les vacances/paiements s'étalent sur 4 mois** holidays/payments are staggered *ou* spread over a period of 4 months.
d (*fig*) *luxe, savoir* to parade, flaunt; *malheurs* to make a show of; *secrets* to give away, disclose. **il aime à en ~*** he likes to cause a stir.
e (*: *frapper*) to floor, lay out.
2 **s'étaler vpr** a *[plaine, cultures]* to stretch out, spread out.
b *[richesse, vanité]* to be flaunted, flaunt itself; *[vaniteux]* to flaunt o.s. *[titre de journal]* **s'~ sur** to be splashed on *ou* across; **son ignominie s'étale au grand jour**his ignominy is plain for all to see.
c (*se vautrer*) **s'~ sur un divan** to sprawl *ou* lounge on a divan; **étalé sur le tapis** sprawling on *ou* stretched out on the carpet.
d (*: *tomber*) **s'~ (par terre)** to come a cropper* (*Brit*), fall flat on the ground; **attention, tu vas t'~!** look out, you're going to fall flat on your face*!

étalon[1] [etalɔ̃] **nm** (*cheval*) stallion.

étalon[2] [etalɔ̃] **nm** (*mesure: Comm, Fin*) standard; (*fig*) yardstick. **kilogramme/balance ~** standard kilogram/scales; (*Écon*) **~-or** gold standard; (*Écon*) ~ **de change-or** gold exchange standard; **c'est devenu l'~ de la beauté** it has become the yardstick by which we measure beauty; (*Ciné*) **copie ~** master print; *voir* **mètre**.

étalonnage [etalɔnaʒ] **nm**, **étalonnement** [etalɔnmɑ̃] **nm** (*voir* **étalonner**) calibration; standardization.

étalonner [etalɔne] ① **vt** (*graduer*) *instrument* to calibrate; (*vérifier*) to standardize.

étambot [etɑ̃bo] **nm** stern-post.

étamer [etame] ① **vt** (*gén*) to tin, tinplate; *glace* to silver.

étameur [etamœʀ] **nm** tinsmith.

étamine [etamin] **nf** (*Bot*) stamen; (*tissu*) muslin; (*pour égoutter, cribler*) cheesecloth, butter muslin (*Brit*).

étanche [etɑ̃ʃ] **adj** *vêtements, chaussures, montre* waterproof; *bateau, compartiment* watertight; (*fig*) watertight. ~ **à l'air** airtight; **enduit ~** sealant; *voir* **cloison**.

étanchéité [etɑ̃ʃeite] **nf** (*voir* **étanche**) waterproofness; watertightness; airtightness.

étancher [etɑ̃ʃe] ① **vt** a *sang* to staunch, stem; (*littér*) *larmes* to dry, stem; (*littér*) *soif* to quench, slake; (*Naut*) *voie d'eau* to stop (up). b (*rendre étanche*) to make watertight; *écoulement, source* to dam up, stem.

étançon [etɑ̃sɔ̃] **nm** (*Tech*) stanchion, shore, prop.

étançonner [etɑ̃sɔne] ① **vt** to shore up, prop up.

étang [etɑ̃] **nm** pond.

étant [etɑ̃] **prp de être**.

étape [etap] **nf** a (*trajet: gén, Sport*) stage, leg; (*lieu d'arrêt*) (*gén*) stop, stopping place; (*Sport*) stopover point, staging point. **faire ~ à** to break the journey at, stop off at; **par petites ~s** in easy stages; ~ **de ravitaillement** staging post. b (*fig*) (*phase*) stage; (*palier*) stage, step; *voir* **brûler**.

état [eta] 1 **nm** a (*condition physique*) *[personne]* state, condition. **dans un tel ~ d'épuisement** in such a state of exhaustion; **bon ~ général** good general state of health; ~ **(de santé)** health; **en ~ d'ivresse** *ou* **d'ébriété** under the influence (of drink); **il n'est pas en ~ de le faire** he's in no condition *ou* (fit) state to do it; **dans quel ~ es-tu! tu saignes!** what a state you're in! you're bleeding!; **être dans un triste ~** to be in a sad *ou* sorry state.
b (*condition psychique*) state. **dans un grand ~ d'épuisement** in a considerable state of exhaustion; **il ne faut pas te mettre dans un ~ pareil** *ou* **des ~s pareils** you mustn't get yourself into such a state; **être dans tous ses ~s** to be beside o.s. (with anger *ou* anxiety *etc*), be all worked up*, be in a terrible state; **ça l'a mis dans tous ses ~s** that got him all worked up* *ou* into a terrible state; **il n'était pas dans son ~ normal** he wasn't his usual *ou* normal self; **être dans un ~ second** to be spaced out*; **je ne suis pas en ~ de le recevoir** I'm in no fit state to receive him.
c *[chose abstraite]* state; (*Chim*) *[corps]* state. **dans l'~ actuel de nos connaissances** in the present state of our knowledge, as our knowledge stands at (the) present; **réduit à l'~ de cendres** reduced to cinders; **quel est l'~ de la question?** where *ou* how do things stand in the matter?, what stage have things reached?
d *[objet, article d'occasion]* condition, state. **en bon/mauvais ~** in good/poor *ou* bad condition; **en ~** in (working) order; (*Naut*) **en ~ de naviguer** sea-worthy; **en ~ de marche** in working order; **remettre en ~** *voiture* to repair, renovate, do up* (*Brit*); *maison* to renovate, do up* (*Brit*); **tenir en ~** *voiture* to maintain in good order, keep in good repair; *maison* to keep in good repair, look after; **hors d'~** out of order; **sucre/pétrole à l'~ brut** sugar/oil in its raw *ou* unrefined *ou* crude state; **à l'~ (de) neuf** as good as new; **remettre qch en l'~** to put sth back *ou* leave sth as it was *ou* in the state it was when one found it.
e (*nation*) **É~** state; **être un É~ dans l'É~** to be a law unto itself; **l'É~-patron** the state as an employer; **l'É~-providence** the welfare state; **les É~s pontificaux** *ou* **de l'Église** the Papal States; **coup d'É~** coup (d'État); *voir* **affaire, chef**[1], **coup** *etc*.
f (†: *métier*) profession, trade; (*statut social*) station. **l'~ militaire** the military profession; **boucher/tailleur de son ~** butcher/tailor by *ou* to trade; **donner un ~ à qn** to find sb a post *ou* trade; **honteux de son ~** ashamed of his station in life†.
g (*registre, comptes*) statement, account; (*inventaire*) inventory. **faire un ~ des recettes** *etc* to draw up a statement *ou* an account of the takings *etc*; ~ **appréciatif** evaluation, estimation; ~ **vérifié des comptes** audited statement of accounts.
h (*Ling*) **verbe d'~** stative verb; **grammaire à ~s finis** finite state grammar.
i (*loc*) **faire ~ de** *ses services etc* to instance; *craintes, intentions* to state; *conversation, rumeur* to report; **(mettre) en ~ d'arrestation** (to put) under arrest; **en tout ~ de cause** in any case, whatever the case; **c'est un ~ de fait** it is an established *ou* irrefutable fact; (*hum*) **dans un ~ intéressant** in an interesting condition, in the family way*; (*gén, Bio, Psych*) **à l'~ latent** in a latent state; (*Rel*) **en ~ de péché (mortel)** in a state of (mortal) sin.
2 **comp ▸ état d'alerte** (*Mil*) state of alert **▸ état d'âme** mood, frame of mind; **avoir des états d'âme** to have uncertainties **▸ état d'apesanteur** weightlessness; **en état d'apesanteur** weightless;

expérience en état d'apesanteur experiment carried out under conditions of weightlessness ▸ **état de choc: être en état de choc** to be in (a state of) shock ▸ **état de choses** state of affairs, situation ▸ (**bureau de**) **l'état civil** (*Admin*) registry office ▸ **état de conscience** (*Psych*) state of consciousness ▸ **état de crise** state of crisis ▸ **état d'esprit** frame *ou* state of mind ▸ **les états** *ou* **États généraux** (*Hist*) the States General ▸ **état de grâce** (*Rel*) state of grace; **en état de grâce** (*fig*) inspired ▸ **état de guerre** (*Pol*) state of war ▸ **état des lieux** (*Jur*) inventory of fixtures ▸ **l'état de nature** (*Philos*) the natural state ▸ **états de service** (*Mil*) service record ▸ **état de siège** state of siege ▸ **État tampon** (*Pol*) buffer state ▸ **état d'urgence** (*Pol*) state of emergency ▸ **état de veille** (*Psych*) waking state.

étatique [etatik] adj *système, doctrine* of state control.

étatisation [etatizasjɔ̃] nf (*doctrine*) state *ou* government control. ~ **d'une entreprise** placing of a concern under direct state *ou* government control, takeover of a concern by the state.

étatiser [etatize] 1 vt to establish state *ou* government control over, put *ou* bring under state *ou* government control. **économie/entreprise étatisée** state-controlled economy/firm.

étatisme [etatism] nm state socialism, state *ou* government control.

étatiste [etatist] 1 adj *système, doctrine* of state *ou* government control. 2 nmf partisan of state *ou* government control, state socialist.

état-major, pl **états-majors** [etamaʒɔʀ] nm a (*Mil*) (*officiers*) staff (*inv*); (*bureaux*) staff headquarters. **officier d'~** staff officer; *voir* **chef**. b (*fig*) *[parti politique]* administrative staff (*inv*); *[entreprise]* top *ou* senior management.

États barbaresques [etabaʀbaʀɛsk] nmpl: **les ~** the Barbary States.

États-Unis [etazyni] nmpl: **les ~ (d'Amérique)** the United States (of America); **les ~ d'Europe** the United States of Europe.

étau, pl **~x** [eto] nm (*Tech*) vice. ~ **limeur** shaper; (*fig*) **l'~ se resserre (autour des coupables)** the noose is tightening (round the guilty men); **se trouver pris (comme) dans un ~** to find o.s. caught in a stranglehold.

étayage [etɛjaʒ] nm, **étayement** [etɛjmɑ̃] nm (*voir* **étayer**) propping-up; shoring-up; support(ing); backing-up.

étayer [eteje] 8 vt *mur* to prop up, shore up; (*fig*) *théorie* to support, back up; *régime, société* to support, prop up.

etc [ɛtseteʀa] loc (**abrév de et caetera**) etc.

et caetera, et cetera [ɛtseteʀa] loc etcetera, etc, and so on (and so forth).

été [ete] nm summer(time). ~ **de la Saint-Martin** Indian summer; ~ **indien** *ou* (*Can*) **des Indiens** Indian summer; ~ **comme hiver** summer and winter alike; **en ~** in (the) summer, in (the) summertime.

éteignoir [etɛɲwaʀ] nm a *[bougie]* extinguisher. b (*personne*) wet blanket, killjoy.

éteindre [etɛ̃dʀ] 52 1 vt a *incendie, poêle* to put out, extinguish; *bougie* to blow out, snuff out, extinguish; *cigarette* to stub out, put out, extinguish. **laisse le feu éteint** leave the fire out.
b *gaz, lampe* to switch off, put out, turn off; *électricité, chauffage, radio* to turn off, switch off. **éteins dans la cuisine** put the kitchen light(s) out, switch out *ou* off the light in the kitchen; **tous feux éteints** without lights.
c *pièce, endroit* to put out *ou* turn off the lights in. **sa fenêtre était éteinte** his window was dark, there was no light at *ou* in his window.
d *colère* to subdue, quell; *amour, envie* to kill; *soif* to quench, slake.
e (*Jur*) *dette* to extinguish.
2 **s'éteindre** vpr a *[agonisant]* to pass away, die. **famille qui s'est éteinte** family which has died out.
b *[colère]* to abate, evaporate; *[amour, envie]* to die, fade.
c *[cigarette, feu, gaz etc]* to go out. **la fenêtre s'est éteinte** the light at the window went out, the window went dark.

éteint, e [etɛ̃, ɛ̃t] (**ptp de éteindre**) adj *couleur* faded; *race, volcan* extinct; *regard* dull, lacklustre; *voix* feeble, faint, dying; (*: *épuisé*) exhausted, tired out. **chaux ~e** slaked lime; **c'est un homme ~ maintenant** his spirit is broken now, he's a broken man now.

étendard [etɑ̃daʀ] nm (*lit, fig*) standard. **brandir** *ou* **lever l'~ de la révolte** to raise the standard of revolt.

étendoir [etɑ̃dwaʀ] nm (*corde*) clothes *ou* washing line; (*sur pied*) clotheshorse.

étendre [etɑ̃dʀ] 41 1 vt a (*déployer*) *journal, tissu* to spread out, open out; *tapis* to roll out; (*étaler*) *beurre* to spread; (*Culin*) *pâte* to roll out; *bras, jambes* to stretch out; *ailes* to spread; (*Ling*) *sens* to stretch, extend. ~ **du linge** (*sur un fil*) to hang out *ou* hang up the washing; **veux-tu ~ le bras pour me passer ...** would you mind stretching your arm and passing me ...; ~ **un blessé** to stretch out a wounded man; **le cadavre, étendu sur le sol** the corpse, stretched (out) *ou* spreadeagled on the ground.
b (*) *adversaire* (*frapper*) to floor, lay out; (*vaincre*) to thrash*, knock out; *candidat* (*Scol*) to fail, clobber‡; (*Pol*) to hammer*. **se faire ~** *[adversaire]* to be laid out cold, be flattened*; *[candidat]* to be failed, be clobbered‡; (*Pol*) to be hammered*.
c (*agrandir*) *pouvoirs* to extend, widen, expand, increase (*sur* over); *affaires, fortune* to extend, increase, expand; *connaissances, domaine, cercle d'amis* to widen, extend, expand, increase; *recherches* to extend *ou* broaden (the field of), increase the scope of. ~ **son action à d'autres domaines** to extend *ou* widen one's action to other fields; ~ **une idée à une autre** to extend one idea to (cover) another, apply one idea to another.
d (*diluer*) *vin* to dilute, let down; *sauce* to thin, let down (*de* with). **étendu d'eau** watered down.
2 **s'étendre** vpr a *[personne]* (*s'allonger*) to stretch out (*sur* on); (*se reposer*) to have a lie down (*Brit*), lie down; (*fig: en expliquant*) to elaborate. **s'~ sur son lit** to stretch out *ou* lie down on one's bed; **s'~ sur un sujet** to elaborate on *ou* enlarge on a subject.
b (*occuper un espace, une période*) *[côte, forêt]* to stretch (out), extend; *[cortège]* to stretch (out) (*jusqu'à* as far as, to); (*fig*) *[vacances, travaux]* to stretch, extend (*sur* over). **la plaine s'étendait à perte de vue** the plain stretched (away) as far as the eye could see.
c (*fig: augmenter*) *[brouillard, épidémie]* to spread; *[parti politique]* to expand; *[ville]* to spread, expand; *[pouvoirs, domaine, fortune]* to increase, expand; *[cercle d'amis]* to expand, widen; *[recherches]* to broaden in scope; *[connaissances, vocabulaire]* to increase, widen.
d (*s'appliquer*) *[loi, avis]* to apply (*à* to). **sa bonté s'étend à tous** his kindness extends to everyone; **cette mesure s'étend à tous les citoyens** this measure applies *ou* is applicable to *ou* covers all citizens.
e (*s'étaler*) *[substance]* to spread. **cette peinture s'étend facilement** this paint goes on *ou* spreads easily.

étendu, e [etɑ̃dy] (**ptp de étendre**) 1 adj a (*vaste*) *ville* sprawling (*épith*), spread out (*attrib*); *domaine* extensive, large; *connaissances, pouvoirs* extensive, wide, wide-ranging; *vue* wide, extensive; *vocabulaire* wide, large, extensive; *sens d'un mot* broad (*épith*), wide; *dégâts* extensive, widespread; *famille* extended.
b (*allongé*) *personne, jambes* stretched out. ~ **sur l'herbe** lying *ou* stretched out on the grass.
2 **étendue** nf a (*surface*) *[plaine]* area, expanse. **pays d'une grande ~** country with a large surface area *ou* which covers a large area; **sur une ~ de 16 km** over an expanse *ou* area of 16 km; **sur toute l'~ de la province** throughout the whole province, throughout the length and breadth of the province; **grande ~ de sable** large stretch *ou* expanse of sand; **surpris par l'~ de ce territoire** amazed at the sheer size *ou* extent of the territory.
b (*durée*) *[vie]* duration, length. **sur une ~ de trois ans** over a period of three years.
c (*importance*) *[pouvoir, dégâts]* extent; *[affaires, connaissances, recherches]* range, scope, extent. **pouvoir/culture d'une grande ~** wide *ou* extensive power/culture, wide-ranging power/culture; **devant l'~ du désastre** faced with the scale of the disaster.
d (*Mus*) *[voix]* compass, range.
e (*Philos*) *[matière]* extension, extent.

éternel, -elle [etɛʀnɛl] 1 adj a (*Philos, Rel*) eternal.
b (*sans fin*) eternal, everlasting, endless, unending. **ma reconnaissance sera ~elle** I shall be grateful (to you) for evermore, I'll be eternally grateful; **soucis ~s** never-ending *ou* endless worries; *voir* **neige**.
c (*perpétuel*) perpetual, eternal. **c'est un ~ insatisfait** he is never happy with anything, he is perpetually *ou* eternally dissatisfied.
d (*: *inamovible: avant n*) inevitable. **son ~ chapeau sur la tête** the inevitable hat on his head.
2 nm a (*Rel*) **l'É~** the Eternal, the Everlasting; (*Bible*) the Lord; (*hum*) **grand joueur devant l'É~** great *ou* inveterate gambler.
b **l'~ féminin** the eternal feminine *ou* woman.

éternellement [etɛʀnɛlmɑ̃] adv (*voir* **éternel**) eternally; everlastingly; endlessly; perpetually.

éterniser [etɛʀnize] 1 1 vt a *débats, supplice, situation* to drag out, draw out. b (*littér*) *nom, mémoire* to immortalize, perpetuate. 2 **s'éterniser** vpr *[situation, débat, attente]* to drag on, go on and on; *[visiteur]* to stay *ou* linger too long, linger on. **le jury s'éternise** the jury is taking ages; **on ne peut pas s'~ ici** we can't stay here for ever.

éternité [etɛʀnite] nf eternity. (*fig*) **cela fait une ~** *ou* **des ~s que je ne l'avais rencontré** it's ages *ou* donkey's years* (*Brit*) since I'd met him, I hadn't met him in ages; **il y a des ~s que tu m'as promis cela** you promised me that ages ago, it's ages since you promised me that; **ça a duré une ~** it lasted for ages; **ça va durer une ~** it'll take forever; **de toute ~** from the beginning of time, from time immemorial; **pour l'~** to all eternity, eternally.

éternuement [etɛʀnymɑ̃] nm sneeze.

éternuer [etɛʀnɥe] 1 vi to sneeze.

étêter [etete] 1 vt *arbre* to pollard, poll; *clou, poisson* to cut the head off.

éthane [etan] nm ethane.

éthanol [etanɔl] nm ethanol.

éther [etɛʀ] nm (*Chim, Poésie*) ether.

éthéré, e [eteʀe] adj (*Chim, littér*) ethereal.

éthéromane [eteʀɔman] nm ether addict.

éthéromanie [eteʀɔmani] nf addiction to ether.

Éthiopie [etjɔpi] nf Ethiopia.

éthiopien, -ienne [etjɔpjɛ̃, jɛn] 1 adj Ethiopian. 2 nm,f: **É~(ne)** Ethiopian.

éthique [etik] 1 adj ethical. 2 nf (*Philos*) ethics (*sg*); (*code moral*)

moral code, code of ethics.

ethmoïde [ɛtmɔid] nm ethmoid.

ethnie [ɛtni] nf ethnic group.

ethnique [ɛtnik] adj ethnic(al). **minorité ~** ethnic minority.

ethnographe [ɛtnɔgʀaf] nmf ethnographer.

ethnographie [ɛtnɔgʀafi] nf ethnography.

ethnographique [ɛtnɔgʀafik] adj ethnographic(al).

ethnolinguistique [ɛtnolɛ̃gɥistik] nf ethnolinguistics *(sg)*.

ethnologie [ɛtnɔlɔʒi] nf ethnology.

ethnologique [ɛtnɔlɔʒik] adj ethnologic(al).

ethnologue [ɛtnɔlɔg] nmf ethnologist.

éthologie [etɔlɔʒi] nf ethology.

éthologique [etɔlɔʒik] adj ethological.

éthologiste [etɔlɔʒist] nmf ethologist.

éthyle [etil] nm ethyl.

éthylène [etilɛn] nm ethylene.

éthylique [etilik] nmf alcoholic.

éthylisme [etilism] nm alcoholism. **crise d'~** alcoholic fit.

éthylomètre [etilɔmɛtʀ] nm = **éthylotest**.

éthylotest [etilɔtɛst] nm Breathalyser ® (*Brit*), Breathalyzer ® (*US*).

étiage [etjaʒ] nm (*débit*) low water (*NonC*) (*of a river*); (*marque*) low-water mark.

Étienne [etjɛn] nm Stephen, Steven.

étincelant, e [etɛ̃s(ə)lɑ̃, ɑ̃t] adj (*voir* **étinceler**) sparkling; glittering; gleaming; twinkling; flashing; shining. **conversation ~e** scintillating *ou* brilliant conversation; **il a été ~** he was brilliant.

étinceler [etɛ̃s(ə)le] [4] vi a *[lame]* to sparkle, glitter, gleam; *[étoile, diamant]* to glitter, gleam, twinkle, sparkle. **la mer étincelle au soleil** the sea sparkles *ou* glitters in the sun. b *[yeux, regard]* **~ de colère** to glitter *ou* flash with anger; **~ de joie** to sparkle *ou* shine with joy. c *[conversation, esprit, intelligence]* to sparkle; *[beauté]* to sparkle, shine. d (*littér*) **~ de mille feux** *[soleil, nuit]* to glitter with a myriad lights (*littér*).

étincelle [etɛ̃sɛl] nf a (*parcelle incandescente*) spark. **~ électrique** electric spark; **jeter des ~s** to throw out sparks; (*fig*) **c'est l'~ qui a mis le feu aux poudres** it was this which touched off *ou* sparked off the incident; (*fig: se distinguer*) **faire des ~s*** to scintillate, shine; (*fig: exploser*) **ça va faire des ~s*** sparks will fly. b *[lame, regard]* flash, glitter. **jeter** *ou* **lancer des ~s** *[diamant, regard]* to flash fire. c *[raison, intelligence]* gleam, flicker, glimmer. **~ de génie** spark *ou* flash of genius.

étincellement [etɛ̃sɛlmɑ̃] nm (*voir* **étinceler**) sparkle (*NonC*); glitter (*NonC*); gleam (*NonC*); twinkling (*NonC*); flash (*NonC*); shining (*NonC*).

étiolement [etjɔlmɑ̃] nm (*voir* **étioler, s'étioler**) blanching, etiolation (*SPÉC*); weakening; wilting; decline; withering.

étioler [etjɔle] [1] 1 vt a *plante* to blanch, etiolate (*SPÉC*). b *personne* to weaken, make sickly. 2 **s'étioler** vpr *[plante]* to wilt, grow weak; *[personne]* to languish, decline; *[intelligence]* to wither, become dull.

étiologie [etjɔlɔʒi] nf etiology.

étiologique [etjɔlɔʒik] adj etiological.

étique [etik] adj skinny, bony.

étiquetage [etik(ə)taʒ] nm *[paquet]* labelling; *[prix]* marking, labelling.

étiqueter [etik(ə)te] [4] vt *paquet* to label; *prix* to mark, label; (*fig*) *personne* to label, classify (*comme* as).

étiquette [etikɛt] nf a (*sur paquet, Ordin*) label; (*de prix*) ticket, label. **~ autocollante/collante** self-stick *ou* self-adhesive/stick-on label; **~ politique** political label; (*fig*) **mettre une ~ à qn** to label sb, stick a label on sb. b (*protocole*) **l'~** etiquette.

étirer [etiʀe] [1] 1 vt *peaux* to stretch; *métal, verre* to draw (out). **~ ses membres** to stretch one's limbs. 2 **s'étirer** vpr *[personne]* to stretch; *[vêtement]* to stretch; *[convoi]* to stretch out; *[route]* to stretch out *ou* away.

Etna [ɛtna] nm: **l'~** Etna, Mount Etna.

étoffe [etɔf] nf a (*de laine etc*) material, fabric; (*fig: d'un livre*) material, stuff. b (*fig*) **avoir l'~ de** to have the makings of, be cut out to be; **avoir l'~ d'un héros** to be of the stuff heros are made of, have the makings of a hero; **il a de l'~** *[personne]* he has a strong personality; *[roman]* it is something you can really get your teeth into, it is really meaty; **manquer d'~** *[personne]* to lack personality; *[roman]* to lack substance, have nothing you can really get your teeth into.

étoffer [etɔfe] [1] 1 vt *style* to enrich; *discours, personnage* to fill out, flesh out. **voix étoffée** rich *ou* deep *ou* sonorous voice; **discours étoffé** meaty speech. 2 **s'étoffer** vpr *[personne]* to fill out.

étoile [etwal] nf a (*Astron*) star. **~ filante** shooting star; **~ polaire** pole star, north star; **~ du berger** *ou* **du soir** evening star; **~ de David** star of David; **semé d'~s** starry, star-studded; **sans ~** starless; **à la clarté des ~s** by starlight; **dormir** *ou* **coucher à la belle ~** to sleep out (in the open), sleep under the stars.

b (*dessin, objet*) star. **général à deux ~s** two-star general; **(hôtel) trois ~s** three-star hotel; **moteur en ~** radial engine.

c (*Ciné, Danse*) star. **~ du cinéma** film star (*Brit*), movie star (*US*); **~ de la danse** dancing star; **~ montante** rising *ou* up-and-coming star.

d (*destinée*) **avoir foi en son ~** to trust one's lucky star, trust to one's luck; **être né sous une bonne/mauvaise ~** to be born under a lucky/an unlucky star; **son ~ a pâli** his star has set.

e **~ de mer** starfish.

étoiler [etwale] [1] 1 vt a (*parsemer*) to stud (*de* with). **nuit étoilée** starry *ou* starlit night; **ciel étoilé** starry *ou* star-studded sky. b (*fêler*) to crack. **le pare-brise est étoilé** the windscreen is crazed. 2 vpr *[pare-brise]* to craze.

étole [etɔl] nf (*Rel, gén*) stole.

étonnamment [etɔnamɑ̃] adv surprisingly, amazingly, astonishingly.

étonnant, e [etɔnɑ̃, ɑ̃t] 1 adj a (*surprenant*) surprising, amazing, astonishing. **rien d'~ à cela, cela n'a rien d'~** no wonder, there's nothing (so) surprising about that; **vous êtes ~** you're incredible *ou* amazing, you're the absolute limit*. b (*remarquable*) *personne* amazing, fantastic*, incredible. 2 nm: **l'~ est que** the astonishing *ou* amazing thing *ou* fact is that, what is astonishing *ou* amazing is that.

étonnement [etɔnmɑ̃] nm surprise, amazement, astonishment.

étonner [etɔne] [1] 1 vt to surprise, amaze, astonish. **ça m'étonne que** I am surprised that, it surprises me that; **ça ne m'étonne pas (que)** I'm not surprised (that), I don't wonder (that), it doesn't surprise me (that); **ça m'étonnerait** I should be very surprised; (*iro*) **tu m'étonnes!*** you don't say!* (*iro*). 2 **s'étonner** vpr to be amazed, wonder, marvel (*de qch* at sth, *de voir* at seeing). **je m'étonne que** I am surprised that, it surprises me that; **il ne faut pas s'~ si** it's hardly surprising that.

étouffant, e [etufɑ̃, ɑ̃t] adj stifling.

étouffe-chrétien* [etufkʀetjɛ̃] nm inv: **c'est de l'~** *ou* **un ~** it's stodgy.

étouffée [etufe] nf: **à l'~** *poisson, légumes* steamed; *viande* braised; **cuire à l'~** to steam; to braise.

étouffement [etufmɑ̃] nm a (*mort*) suffocation. **tuer qn par ~** to kill sb by suffocating *ou* smothering him; **mourir d'~** to die of suffocation. b (*Méd*) **sensation d'~** feeling of suffocation *ou* breathlessness; **avoir des ~s** to have fits of breathlessness. c (*action: NonC*) *[scandale]* hushing-up; *[rumeurs]* suppression, stifling; *[révolte]* quelling, suppression; *[scrupules]* stifling, overcoming. d *[pas]* muffling.

étouffer [etufe] [1] 1 vt a *[assassin]* to suffocate, smother; *[chaleur, atmosphère]* to suffocate, stifle; *[sanglots, colère, aliment]* to choke; (*fig*) to stifle, suffocate. **le bébé s'est étouffé dans ses draps** the baby suffocated in its sheets; **s'~ en mangeant** to choke whilst eating; **~ qn de baisers** to smother sb with kisses; **les scrupules ne l'étouffent pas** he isn't hampered *ou* overburdened by scruples, he doesn't let scruples cramp his style; **ça l'étoufferait de dire merci** it would kill him to say thank you; (*Agr*) **plantes qui étouffent les autres** plants which choke *ou* smother others.

b *bruit* to muffle, deaden; *bâillement* to stifle, smother, suppress; *sanglots, cris* to smother, choke back, stifle. **rires étouffés** suppressed *ou* smothered laughter; **dit-il d'une voix étouffée** he said in a low *ou* hushed tone; **voix étouffées** (*discrètes*) subdued voices; (*confuses*) muffled voices.

c *scandale* to hush up, smother, keep quiet; *rumeurs, scrupules, sentiments* to smother, suppress, stifle; *révolte* to put down, quell, suppress.

d *flammes* to smother, extinguish, quench (*littér*). **~ un feu** to put out *ou* smother a fire.

e (†*: *voler*) to pinch*.

2 vi (*mourir étouffé*) to die of suffocation, suffocate to death; (*fig: être mal à l'aise*) to feel stifled, suffocate. **~ de colère/de rire** to choke with anger/with laughter; **~ de chaleur** to be stifling, be overcome with the heat; **on étouffe dans cette pièce** it's stifling in here, the heat is suffocating *ou* overpowering in here.

étouffoir [etufwaʀ] nm (*Mus*) damper.

étoupe [etup] nf (*de lin, chanvre*) tow; (*de cordages*) oakum.

étourderie [etuʀdəʀi] nf (*caractère*) absent-mindedness; (*faute*) careless mistake. **agir par** *ou* **avec ~** to act without thinking *ou* carelessly.

étourdi, e [etuʀdi] (ptp de **étourdir**) 1 adj *personne, action* scatter-brained, absent-minded. 2 nm,f scatterbrain. **agir en ~** to act without thinking *ou* carelessly.

étourdiment [etuʀdimɑ̃] adv carelessly, rashly.

étourdir [etuʀdiʀ] [2] 1 vt a (*assommer*) to stun, daze.

b **~ qn** *[bruit]* to deafen; *[altitude, vin]* to make sb dizzy *ou* giddy; *[succès, parfum, vin]* to go to sb's head. **l'altitude m'étourdit** heights make me dizzy *ou* giddy, I've no head for heights (*Brit*); **ce vacarme m'étourdit** this row is deafening; **ce mouvement m'étourdit** this movement makes my head spin *ou* makes me feel quite dizzy.

2 **s'étourdir** vpr: **il s'étourdit par la boisson** he drowns his sorrows in drink; **il s'étourdit par les plaisirs** he tries to forget *ou* to deaden his sorrows by living a life of pleasure; **il s'étourdit pour oublier** he keeps up a whirl of activity to forget; **s'~ de paroles** to get drunk on words, be carried away by the sound of one's own voice.

étourdissant, e [etuʀdisɑ̃, ɑ̃t] adj *bruit* deafening, earsplitting; *succès* staggering, stunning; *beauté* stunning. **à un rythme ~** at a tremendous *ou* breakneck pace; **~ de beauté** stunningly beautiful.

étourdissement [etuʀdismɑ̃] nm a (*syncope*) blackout; (*vertige*) dizzy spell, fit of giddiness. **ça me donne des ~s** it makes me feel dizzy, it makes my head swim*. b (*littér: surprise*) surprise. c (*littér: griserie*) exhilaration, intoxication.

étourneau, pl ~x [eturno] nm a (*Orn*) starling. b (*: *distrait*) scatterbrain, featherbrain (*Brit*), birdbrain (*US*).

étrange [etʀɑ̃ʒ] adj strange, odd, queer, peculiar, weird, funny. **et chose** ~ (and) strange to say, strangely enough, the odd thing is; **aussi** ~ **que cela puisse paraître** strange as it may seem; **cela n'a rien d'**~ there is nothing strange about *ou* in that.

étrangement [etʀɑ̃ʒmɑ̃] adv (*bizarrement*) strangely, oddly, peculiarly; (*étonnamment*) surprisingly, amazingly. **ressembler** ~ **à** to be surprisingly *ou* amazingly *ou* suspiciously like.

étranger, -ère [etʀɑ̃ʒe, ɛʀ] 1 adj a (*d'un autre pays*) foreign; (*Pol*) *politique, affaires* foreign. **être** ~ **au pays** to be a foreigner; **visiteurs** ~**s** foreign visitors, visitors from abroad.

b (*d'un autre groupe*) strange, unknown (*à* to). **être** ~ **à un groupe** not to belong to a group, be an outsider; **il est** ~ **à notre famille** he is not a relative of ours, he is not a member of our family; **entrée interdite à toute personne** ~**ère (à l'établissement** *ou* **au service)** no entry for unauthorized persons, no unauthorized entry.

c (*inconnu*) *nom, usage, milieu* strange, unfamiliar (*à* to); *idée* strange, odd. **son nom/son visage ne m'est pas** ~ his name/face is not unknown *ou* not unfamiliar to me; **la chimie lui est** ~**ère** chemistry is a closed book to him, he has no knowledge of chemistry; **cette personne/technique lui est** ~**ère** this person/technique is unfamiliar *ou* unknown to him, he is unfamiliar *ou* unacquainted with this person/technique; **ce sentiment ne lui est pas** ~ this feeling is not unknown to him, it is not unknown for him to feel this way; *voir* **corps.**

d (*extérieur*) *donnée, fait* extraneous (*à* to). ~ **au sujet** irrelevant (to the subject), beside the point; **être** ~ **à un complot** not to be involved *ou* mixed up in a plot, have nothing to do with a plot.

2 nm,f a (*d'un autre pays*) foreigner; (*péj, Admin*) alien. **une** ~**ère** a foreign lady *ou* woman; **c'est une** ~**ère** she's a foreigner.

b (*inconnu*) stranger; (*à un groupe*) outsider, stranger.

3 nm (*pays*) **l'**~ foreign countries, foreign parts; **vivre/voyager à l'**~ to live/travel abroad; **rédacteur pour l'**~ foreign editor.

étrangeté [etʀɑ̃ʒte] nf (*caractère*) *[conduite]* strangeness, oddness, queerness; (*fait ou événement etc bizarre*) odd *ou* strange fact (*ou* event *etc*).

étranglement [etʀɑ̃gləmɑ̃] nm a *[victime]* strangulation; (*Hist: supplice*) garotting; (*fig*) *[presse, libertés]* stifling. b *[vallée]* neck; *[rue]* bottleneck, narrowing; *[taille, tuyau]* constriction. c *[voix]* strain, tightness. d (*Méd*) strangulation.

étrangler [etʀɑ̃gle] [1] 1 vt a (*tuer*) *personne* to strangle, choke, throttle; *poulet* to wring the neck of; (*Hist: supplicier*) to garotte. **mourir étranglé (par son écharpe)** to be strangled (by one's scarf); **cette cravate m'étrangle** this tie is choking *ou* throttling me.

b *[rage etc]* to choke. **la fureur l'étranglait** he was choking with rage; **voix étranglée par l'émotion** voice choking *ou* strained *ou* tight with emotion.

c *presse, libertés* to strangle, stifle. **taxes qui étranglent les commerçants** taxes which cripple the traders.

d (*resserrer*) to squeeze (tightly). **taille étranglée** tightly constricted *ou* tightly corseted waist.

2 **s'étrangler** vpr a *[personne]* to strangle o.s. **elle s'est étranglée accidentellement** she was strangled accidentally, she accidentally strangled herself; **s'**~ **de rire/colère** to choke with laughter/anger; **s'**~ **en pleurant** to choke with tears; **s'**~ **en mangeant** to choke whilst eating.

b *[voix, sanglots]* to catch in one's throat. **un cri s'étrangla dans sa gorge** a cry caught *ou* died in his throat.

c *[rue, couloir]* to narrow (down), make a bottleneck.

d (*Méd*) **hernie étranglée** strangulated hernia.

étrangleur, -euse [etʀɑ̃glœʀ, øz] nm,f strangler.

étrave [etʀav] nf (*Naut*) stem.

être [ɛtʀ] [61] 1 vb *copule* a (*gén*) to be. **le ciel est bleu** the sky is blue; **elle veut** ~ **médecin** she wants to be a doctor; **soyez sages!** be good!; **tu n'es qu'un enfant** you are only a child; **si j'étais vous, je lui parlerais** if I were you I should *ou* would speak to her; **nous sommes 10 à vouloir partir** there are 10 of us wanting *ou* who want to go; *voir* **ailleurs, ce, que.**

b (*pour indiquer la date*) **nous sommes** *ou* **on est le 12 janvier** it is January 12th; **on était en juillet** it was (in) July; **quel jour sommes-nous?** (*date*) what's the date today?, what's today's date?; (*jour*) what day is it (today)?

c (*avec à, de: appartenir*) **à qui est ce livre? — il est à moi** whose book is this? — it's mine *ou* it belongs to me; **je suis à vous** what can I do for you?; **c'était à elle de protester** it was up to her to protest, it was her job to protest; **nous sommes de la même religion** we are of the same faith; ~ **de la fête/de l'expédition** to take part in the celebration/expedition; ~ **de noce/de baptême** *etc* to be at a wedding/christening *etc;* **vous en êtes?** are you taking part?, are you in on this?*; (*péj*) **il en est‡, c'en est une‡** (*un homosexuel*) he's one of them* (*péj*); **je ne pourrai pas** ~ **des vôtres jeudi** I shan't *ou* won't be able to join you on Thursday.

d (*avec complément introduit par préposition: indiquant l'état, le fait, l'opinion etc; voir aussi prép et noms en question*) to be. ~ **en colère/de bonne humeur** to be angry/in a good mood; ~ **pour la paix/contre la violence** to be for *ou* in favour of peace/against *ou* opposed to violence; **il est/n'est pas à son travail** his attention *ou* mind is/is not on his work; **il est au travail** he is working; **le livre est à la reliure** the book is (away) being bound; **elle était en chemise de nuit** she was in her nightdress; **il est pour beaucoup dans sa nomination** he is largely responsible for his appointment, he had a lot to do with his being appointed; **elle n'y est pour rien** it's not her responsibility, it's not her fault, it has nothing to do with her; **je suis pour dormir ici** I am for sleeping here*, I am in favour of sleeping here; **au bal, elle sera en Bretonne** she will be dressed as a Breton girl at the dance.

2 vb aux a (*formant les temps composés actifs*) **il est passé hier** he came yesterday; **nous étions montés** we had gone upstairs; **elle serait tombée** she would *ou* might have fallen; **il n'est pas passé** he hasn't been; **nous nous sommes promenés** we had a walk, we went for a walk; **vous vous seriez bien trompés** you would have been greatly mistaken; **il s'est assis** he sat down; **elle s'est laissée aller** she has let herself go; **ils se sont écrit** they wrote to each other.

b (*formant le passif*) ~ **donné/fabriqué par ...** to be given/made by ...; **il est soutenu par son patron** he is backed up by his boss, he has the support *ou* the backing of his boss; **il a été blessé dans un accident** he was injured in an accident.

c (*avec à + infin: indiquant une obligation*) **ce livre est à lire/relier** this book must be read/bound; **le poisson est à manger tout de suite** the fish is to be eaten *ou* must be eaten at once; **cet enfant est à tuer!** I could kill *ou* murder that child!; **tout est à refaire** it's all got to be done again; **ces journaux sont à brûler** these papers are for burning.

d (*avec à + infin: indiquant un état en cours*) **il est à travailler** he is (busy) working; **ma robe est à nettoyer*** my dress is being cleaned *ou* is at the cleaners'; **elle est toujours à le taquiner** she keeps teasing him, she's forever teasing him.

3 vi a (*exister*) to be. **je pense donc je suis** I think, therefore I am; **le meilleur homme qui soit** the kindest man that ever was, the kindest man living; **elle n'est plus** she is no more; **le temps n'est plus où ...** the time is past when ...; **que la lumière soit** let there be light; **un menteur s'il en est** a liar if ever there was one.

b (*se trouver, habiter*) **il est maintenant à Lille** he now lives *ou* he is now in Lille; **le village est à 10 km d'ici** the village is 10 km away from here; **j'y suis j'y reste** here I am and here I stay; **elle n'y est pour personne** she is not at home to anyone, she is not available (to anyone).

c (*: *avoir été = être allé*) **il n'avait jamais été à Londres** he'd never been to London; **avez-vous jamais été à l'étranger? — oui j'ai été en Italie l'an dernier** have you ever been abroad? — yes I went to Italy *ou* I was in Italy last year.

d (*littér*) **il s'en fut la voir** he went (forth) to see her.

4 vb impers a **il est** + *adj* it is + *adj*; **il serait très agréable de voyager** it would be very pleasant to travel; **il n'est pas nécessaire qu'il vienne** it is not necessary for him to come, it is not necessary that he should come, he need not come.

b (*pour dire l'heure*) **quelle heure est-il?** what time is it?; **il est 10 heures** it is 10 o'clock; **il serait temps de partir** it is time (for us) to go, it's time we went.

c (*littér: il y a*) **il est des gens qui** there are people who; **il était une fois ...** once upon a time there was ... .

d (*avoir atteint*) **en** ~ **à la page 9** to be at page 9, have reached page 9; **où en est-il de** *ou* **dans ses études?** how far has he got with his studies?, what point has he reached in his studies?; **il en est à sa première année de médecine** he has reached his first year in medicine; **l'affaire en est là** that's how the matter stands, that's as far as it's got; (*fig*) **je ne sais plus où j'en suis** I don't know whether I am coming or going.

e (*se voir réduit à*) **j'en suis à me demander si** I'm beginning to wonder if, I've come to wonder if, I've got to wondering if*; **il en est à mendier** he has come down to *ou* stooped to begging, he has been reduced to begging.

f (*loc*) **il en est de sa poche** he is out of pocket; **en** ~ **pour ses frais** *ou* **sa peine/son argent** to get nothing for one's trouble *ou* pains/money; **il n'en est rien** it's nothing of the sort, that's not it at all; **tu y es?*** (*tu es prêt*) are you ready?; (*comprends-tu*) do you follow me?, are you with me?; **tu n'y es pas du tout!** you haven't got it at all!*

g (*avec ce: pour présenter un être, une chose*) **ce sera une belle cérémonie** it will be a beautiful ceremony; **c'est un docteur, il est docteur** he is a doctor.

h (*pour mettre en relief gén non traduit*) **c'est lui qui me l'a dit/qui vous le dira** he (is the one who) told me/(is the one who) will tell you; **c'est elle qui a voulu** she wanted it; **c'est mon père et moi qui devons payer** my father and I must pay; **c'est à qui dira son mot** they all want to have their say; **c'est moi qu'on attendait** I was the one they were waiting for, it was me they were waiting for; **c'est pour eux que je l'ai fait** I did it for their sake; **c'est que je le connais bien!** I know him so well!; **c'est qu'elle n'a pas d'argent** it's because *ou* just that she has no money; (*exclamatif*) but she has no money!; **ce n'est pas qu'il soit beau!** it's not that he's good-looking!

i (*est-ce que: forme interrogative*) **est-ce que vous saviez?** did you know?; **est-ce que c'est toi qui l'as battu?** was it you who beat him?

j **n'est-ce pas: il fait beau, n'est-ce pas?** isn't it a lovely day?, it's a lovely day isn't it?; **vous viendrez, n'est-ce pas?** you will come, won't you?, you are coming, aren't you?; **n'est-ce pas qu'il a promis?** he did promise, didn't he?

k (*pour exprimer la supposition*) **si ce n'était** were it not for, if it were not for, but for; (*littér*) **n'était son orgueil** were it not for *ou* but for his pride, if it were not for his pride; **ne serait-ce que pour quelques jours** if (it were) only for a few days; **ne serait-ce que pour nous ennuyer** if only to annoy us; **comme si de rien n'était** as if nothing had happened; (*Math*) **soit une droite XY** let XY be a straight line, take a straight line XY.

5 **nm** a (*gén, Sci*) being. **~ humain/animé/vivant** human/animate/living being.

b (*individu*) being, person. **les ~s qui nous sont chers** our loved ones, those who are dear to us; **un ~ cher** a loved one; **c'était un ~ merveilleux** he was a wonderful person; (*péj*) **quel ~!** what a character!

c (*âme*) heart, soul, being. **il l'aimait de tout son ~** he loved her with all his heart; **au plus profond de notre ~** deep down in our souls; **tout son ~ se révoltait** his whole being rebelled.

d (*Philos*) **l'~** being; **l'~ et le néant** being and nothingness; **l'E~ suprême** the Supreme Being.

étreindre [etʀɛ̃dʀ] 52 **vt** a (*frm*) (*dans ses bras*) *ami* to embrace, hug, clasp in one's arms; *ennemi* to seize, grasp; (*avec les mains*) to clutch, grip, grasp. **les deux amis s'étreignirent** the two friends embraced each other; *voir* **qui**. b (*fig*) *[douleur]* to grip.

étreinte [etʀɛ̃t] **nf** (*frm*) *[ami]* embrace, hug; *[ennemi]* stranglehold, grip; *[main, douleur]* clutch, grip, grasp. (*Mil*) **l'armée resserre son ~ autour de ...** the army is tightening its grip round ... .

étrenne [etʀɛn] **nf** (*gén pl*) (*à un enfant*) New Year's gift; (*au facteur etc*) ≃ Christmas box. **que veux-tu pour tes ~s?** what would you like for Christmas? *ou* as a Christmas present?; **donner ses ~s à la femme de ménage** to give a Christmas box to one's daily help.

étrenner [etʀene] 1 1 **vt** to use (*ou* wear *etc*) for the first time. 2 **vi** (†*: *écoper*) to catch it*, cop it‡ (*Brit*), get it*.

étrier [etʀije] **nm** (*gén, Méd*) stirrup. **boire le coup de l'~*** to have one for the road*; *voir* **pied, vider**.

étrille [etʀij] **nf** (*brosse*) currycomb; (*crabe*) velvet swimming crab.

étriller [etʀije] 1 **vt** *cheval* to curry; (†, *hum: rosser*) to trounce†.

étripage [etʀipaʒ] **nm** gutting.

étriper [etʀipe] 1 1 **vt** *lapin* to disembowel, gut; *volaille* to draw; *poisson* to gut; (‡ *fig*) *adversaire* to cut open, hack about (*Brit*). 2 **s'étriper‡** **vpr** to make mincemeat of each other*, tear each other's guts out‡.

étriqué, e [etʀike] (**ptp de étriquer**) **adj** *habit* skimpy, tight; *esprit* narrow; *vie* narrow, cramped. **il fait tout ~ dans son manteau** he looks cramped in his coat, he looks as though he's bursting out of his coat.

étriquer [etʀike] 1 **vt: ce vêtement l'étrique** this garment is too tight-fitting for him.

étrivière [etʀivjɛʀ] **nf** stirrup leather.

étroit, e [etʀwa, wat] **adj** a (*lit*) (*gén*) *rue, fenêtre, ruban* narrow; *espace* narrow, restricted, cramped, confined; *vêtement, chaussure* tight.

b (*littér: serré*) *nœud, étreinte* tight.

c (*fig: borné*) *vues* narrow, limited. **à l'esprit ~** narrow-minded.

d (*fig: intime*) *amitié* close (*épith*); *liens* close (*épith*), intimate (*épith*). **en collaboration ~e avec** in close collaboration with.

e (*fig: strict*) *surveillance* close (*épith*), strict (*épith*); (*littér*) *obligations* strong (*épith*), strict (*épith*); *coordination* close (*épith*); *soumission, subordination* strict (*épith*).

f (*Ling*) *acception* narrow (*épith*), strict (*épith*), restricted. **au sens ~ du terme** in the narrow *ou* strict sense of the term.

g **à l'~** cramped; **vivre *ou* être logé à l'~** to live in cramped *ou* confined conditions; **être à l'~ dans ses vêtements** to wear clothes which are too small, be cramped in one's clothes, be bursting out of one's clothes.

étroitement [etʀwatmɑ̃] **adv** *lier, unir* closely; *obéir* strictly; *surveiller* closely, strictly; *tenir* tightly. **être ~ logé** to live in cramped *ou* confined conditions.

étroitesse [etʀwatɛs] **nf** (*voir* **étroit**) narrowness; crampedness; tightness; closeness. **l'~ de ce logement** the cramped accommodation; **~ (d'esprit)** narrow-mindedness.

étron [etʀɔ̃] **nm** (†, *hum*) turd**.

Étrurie [etʀyʀi] **nf** Etruria.

étrusque [etʀysk] 1 **adj** Etruscan. 2 **nm** (*Ling*) Etruscan. 3 **nmf: É~** Etruscan.

étude [etyd] **nf** a (*action*) (*gén*) study. (*Mus*) **l'~ d'un instrument** the study of an instrument, learning to play an instrument; **ce projet est à l'~** this project is under consideration *ou* is being studied; **mettre un projet à l'~, procéder à l'~ d'un projet** to investigate *ou* go into *ou* study a project; **avoir le goût de l'~** to like study *ou* studying; **une ~ gratuite de vos besoins** a free assessment of your needs; **voyage/frais d'~** study trip/costs; (*Écon*) **~ de marché** market research (*NonC*); **~ de cas** case study; (*Fin*) **~ complémentaire** follow-up study; *voir* **bureau**.

b (*Scol, Univ*) **~s** studies; **faire ses ~s à Paris** to study in Paris, be educated in Paris; **travailler pour payer ses ~s** to work to pay for one's education; **faire des ~s de droit** to study law; **a-t-il fait des ~s?** has he studied at all?, has he been to university? *ou* college?; **~s secondaires/supérieures** secondary/higher education.

c (*ouvrage*) study; (*Écon, Sci*) paper, study; (*Littérat*) study, essay. (*Art*) **~s de fleurs** studies of flowers; (*Mus*) **~s pour piano** studies *ou* études for (the) piano.

d (*Scol*) **(salle d')~** study *ou* prep room, private study room (*Brit*), study hall (*US*); **l'~ (du soir)** preparation, prep* (*Brit*); **~ surveillée** (supervised) study period (*Brit*), study hall (*US*); **être en ~** to have a study period; **mettre des élèves en ~** to leave pupils to study on their own.

e (*Jur*) (*bureau*) office; (*charge, clientèle*) practice.

étudiant, e [etydjɑ̃, jɑ̃t] 1 **adj** *vie, problèmes, allures* student (*épith*). 2 **nm,f** student. **~ en médecine/en lettres** medical/arts student; **~ de première année** first-year student *ou* undergraduate; **~ de troisième cycle** post-graduate (student).

étudié, e [etydje] (**ptp de étudier**) **adj** a (*calculé*) *jeu de scène* studied; *coupe, conception* carefully designed; (*Comm*) *prix* competitive, keen (*épith*) (*Brit*). **à des prix très ~s** at the keenest (*Brit*) *ou* the lowest possible prices; **maison d'une conception très ~e** very carefully *ou* thoughtfully designed house. b (*affecté*) *allure* studied; *sentiments* affected, assumed.

étudier [etydje] 7 1 **vt** a (*apprendre*) *matière* (*gén*) to study; (*Univ*) to read (*Brit*), study; *instrument* to study, learn to play; (*Scol*) *leçon* to learn; *texte, auteur* to study. **s'amuser au lieu d'~** to have a good time instead of studying.

b (*examiner*) *projet* to study, examine, go into; *dossier, cas* to study, examine, scrutinize (*frm*). **~ les prix** to do a study of prices, compare prices; **~ les possibilités** to study *ou* examine *ou* go into the possibilities; **~ une proposition sous tous ses aspects** to explore a proposal; **~ qch de près** to study sth closely, make a close study of sth, take a close look at sth.

c (*observer*) *terrain, adversaire* to study, observe closely; *visage* to study, examine. **au début, je sentais qu'il m'étudiait constamment** at the start I sensed that he was observing me all the time.

d (*concevoir*) *procédé, dispositif* to devise; *machine, coupe* to design.

e (*calculer*) *gestes, ton, effets* to study, calculate.

2 **s'étudier** **vpr** a (*s'analyser*) to analyse o.s., be introspective; (*s'examiner*) to study o.s. *ou* one's appearance. **les deux adversaires s'étudiaient** the two opponents studied *ou* observed each other closely.

b (†) **s'~ à faire** to strive *ou* try to do.

étui [etɥi] **nm** *[lunettes, violon, cigares]* case; *[revolver]* holster.

étuve [etyv] **nf** (*bains*) steamroom; (*de désinfection*) sterilizer; (*incubateur*) incubator; (*fig*) oven.

étuvée [etyve] **nf** (*Culin*) **à l'~** *poisson* steamed; *viande* braised.

étuver [etyve] 1 **vt** *poisson* to steam; *viande* to braise.

étymologie [etimɔlɔʒi] **nf** etymology.

étymologique [etimɔlɔʒik] **adj** etymological.

étymologiquement [etimɔlɔʒikmɑ̃] **adv** etymologically.

étymologiste [etimɔlɔʒist] **nmf** etymologist.

étymon [etimɔ̃] **nm** etymon.

eu, e [y] **ptp de avoir**.

E.-U.(A.) (**abrév de États-Unis (d'Amérique)**) US(A).

eucalyptus [økaliptys] **nm** eucalyptus.

eucharistie [økaʀisti] **nf: l'E~** the Eucharist, the Lord's Supper.

eucharistique [økaʀistik] **adj** eucharistic.

Euclide [øklid] **nm** Euclid.

euclidien, -ienne [øklidjɛ̃, jɛn] **adj** Euclidean.

eudiomètre [ødjɔmɛtʀ] **nm** eudiometer.

Eugène [øʒɛn] **nm** Eugene.

eugénique [øʒenik] 1 **nf** eugenics (*sg*). 2 **adj** eugenic.

eugénisme [øʒenism] **nm** eugenics (*sg*).

euh [ø] **excl** er!

eunuque [ønyk] **nm** eunuch.

euphémique [øfemik] **adj** euphemistic(al).

euphémiquement [øfemikmɑ̃] **adv** euphemistically.

euphémisme [øfemism] **nm** euphemism.

euphonie [øfɔni] **nf** euphony.

euphonique [øfɔnik] **adj** euphonious, euphonic.

euphoniquement [øfɔnikmɑ̃] **adv** euphoniously, euphonically.

euphonium [øfɔnjɔm] **nm** euphonium.

euphorbe [øfɔʀb] **nf** euphorbia, spurge.

euphorie [øfɔʀi] **nf** euphoria.

euphorique [øfɔʀik] **adj** euphoric.

euphorisant, e [øfɔʀizɑ̃, ɑ̃t] 1 **adj** *nouvelle* exhilarating. 2 **nm (médicament)** anti-depressant, pep pill*.

euphoriser [øfɔʀize] 1 **vt** to make exhilarated.

Euphrate [øfʀat] **nm: l'~** the Euphrates.

eurafricain, e [øʀafʀikɛ̃, ɛn] 1 adj Eurafrican. 2 nm,f: **E~(e)** Eurafrican.
eurasiatique [øʀazjatik] adj Eurasiatic.
Eurasie [øʀazi] nf Eurasia.
eurasien, -ienne [øʀazjɛ̃, jɛn] 1 adj Eurasian. 2 nm,f: **E~(ne)** Eurasian.
EURATOM [øʀatɔm] (abrév de **European Atomic Energy Commission**) EURATOM.
eurêka [øʀeka] excl eureka!
eurent [yʀ] *voir* **avoir**.
Euripide [øʀipid] nm Euripides.
euristique [øʀistik] = **heuristique**.
eurocheque [øʀɔʃɛk] nm Eurocheque.
eurocommunisme [øʀɔkɔmynism] nm Eurocommunism.
eurocrate [øʀɔkʀat] nmf Eurocrat.
eurodevises [øʀɔdəviz] nfpl Eurocurrency.
eurodollar [øʀodɔlaʀ] nm Eurodollar.
euromissile [øʀomisil] nm European missile.
euro-obligations [øʀoɔbligasjɔ̃] nfpl Euro-bonds.
Europe [øʀɔp] nf Europe. **l'~ Centrale** central Europe; **l'~ des douze** the Twelve (Common Market countries); **l'~ politique** Europe as a single political entity; **l'~ de l'espace** the joint European space venture; **l'~ verte** European *ou* Community agriculture.
européanisation [øʀɔpeanizasjɔ̃] nf Europeanization.
européaniser [øʀɔpeanize] 1 vt to Europeanize.
européen, -enne [øʀɔpeɛ̃, ɛn] 1 adj European. 2 nm,f: **E~(ne)** European.
europium [øʀɔpjɔm] nm europium.
Eurovision [øʀɔvizjɔ̃] nf Eurovision.
Eurydice [øʀidis] nf Eurydice.
eurythmie [øʀitmi] nf eurhythmics *(sg)*.
Eustache [østaʃ] nm Eustace; *voir* **trompe**.
eut [y] *voir* **avoir**.
euthanasie [øtanazi] nf euthanasia.
eutrophisation [øtʀɔfizasjɔ̃] nf eutrophication.
eux [ø] pron pers a (*sujet*) they; (*objet*) them. **~ et toi, vous ne manquez pas d'aplomb** they and you are certainly sure of yourselves; **si j'étais ~** if I were *ou* was them *ou* they (*frm*); **il n'obéit qu'à ~** they are the only ones he obeys, he'll only obey them; **nous y allons, ~ non** *ou* **pas ~** we are going but they aren't *ou* they're not *ou* not them; **~ mentir? ce n'est pas possible** them tell a lie? I can't believe it; **ce sont ~ qui répondront** they are the ones who will reply, they'll reply; **~ ils n'ont rien à dire** they've got nothing to say; **ils l'ont bien fait, ~** they did it all right; **les aider, ~? jamais!** help them? never!; **~, pauvres innocents, ne l'ont jamais su** they, poor fools, never knew.
b (*avec prép*) **à ~ tout seuls, ils ont tout acheté** they bought everything all on their own; **cette maison est-elle à ~?** does this house belong to them?, is this house theirs?; **ils ont cette grande maison à ~ seuls** they have this big house all to themselves; **ils ne pensent qu'à ~, ces égoïstes** these selfish people only think of themselves; *voir* **aussi, moi, toi**.
E.V. [əve] (abrév de **en ville**) "by hand".
évacuateur, -trice [evakɥatœʀ, tʀis] 1 adj evacuation (*épith*). 2 nm sluice.
évacuation [evakɥasjɔ̃] nf *[pays, personnes]* evacuation; *[liquide]* draining, emptying; (*Méd*) evacuation.
évacué, e [evakɥe] (ptp de **évacuer**) nm,f evacuee.
évacuer [evakɥe] 1 vt *pays, ville, population* to evacuate; *salle, maison* to evacuate, clear; (*Méd*) to evacuate, discharge; *liquide* to drain (off); (*) *problème* to dispose of. **faire ~** *salle, bâtiment* to clear.
évadé, e [evade] (ptp de **s'évader**) nm,f escaped prisoner.
évader (s') [evade] 1 vpr (*lit, fig*) to escape (*de* from). **faire ~ qn** to help sb (to) escape.
évaluable [evalɥabl] adj assessable. **difficilement ~** difficult to assess *ou* evaluate.
évaluation [evalɥasjɔ̃] nf (*voir* **évaluer**) appraisal; evaluation; assessment; valuation; estimation.
évaluer [evalɥe] 1 vt a (*expertiser*) *maison, bijou* to appraise, evaluate, assess, value (*à* at); *dégâts, prix* to assess, evaluate (*à* at). **faire ~ qch par un expert** to have sth valued *ou* appraised by an expert.
b (*juger approximativement*) *fortune, nombre, distance* to estimate, assess (*à* at). **on évalue à 60 000 le nombre des réfugiés qui auraient traversé la frontière** an estimated 60,000 refugees have crossed the border, the number of refugees crossing the border is estimated at *ou* put at 60,000.
évanescent, e [evanesɑ̃, ɑ̃t] adj (*littér*) evanescent.
évangélique [evɑ̃ʒelik] adj evangelic(al).
évangélisateur, -trice [evɑ̃ʒelizatœʀ, tʀis] 1 adj evangelistic. 2 nm,f evangelist.
évangélisation [evɑ̃ʒelizasjɔ̃] nf evangelization.
évangéliser [evɑ̃ʒelize] 1 vt to evangelize.
évangélisme [evɑ̃ʒelism] nm evangelicalism, evangelism.
évangéliste [evɑ̃ʒelist] nm evangelist; (*Bible*) Evangelist.
évangile [evɑ̃ʒil] nm a (*Rel*) **É~** gospel; (*Rel*) **l'~ du jour** the day's gospel (reading), the day's reading from the gospel; **les É~s synoptiques** the synoptic Gospels. b (*fig*) gospel. **ce n'est pas l'~, ce n'est pas parole d'~** it's not gospel.
évanoui, e [evanwi] (ptp de **s'évanouir**) adj *blessé* unconscious. **tomber ~** to faint, pass out.
évanouir (s') [evanwiʀ] 2 vpr *[personne]* to faint (*de* from), pass out (*de* with), black out*; (*fig*) *[rêves, apparition, craintes]* to vanish, disappear, fade.
évanouissement [evanwismɑ̃] nm a (*syncope*) fainting fit, blackout. b (*fig*) *[rêves, apparition, craintes]* disappearance, fading.
évaporation [evapɔʀasjɔ̃] nf evaporation.
évaporé, e [evapɔʀe] (ptp de **évaporer**) 1 adj (*péj*) *personne* giddy, scatterbrained, featherbrained (*Brit*). 2 nm,f scatterbrain, featherbrain (*Brit*), birdbrain (*US*).
évaporer [evapɔʀe] 1 1 vt (*gén faire ~*) to evaporate. 2 **s'évaporer** vpr (*lit*) to evaporate; (*: *disparaître*) to vanish *ou* disappear (into thin air).
évasé, e [evɑze] (ptp de **évaser, s'évaser**) adj *vallée, conduit* which widens *ou* opens out; *jambes, manches, jupe* flared. **verre à bords ~s** glass with a curving *ou* bell-shaped rim.
évasement [evɑzmɑ̃] nm a (*voir* **évaser**) widening- *ou* opening-out; flaring. b (*voir* **s'évaser**) opening-out; flare.
évaser [evɑze] 1 1 vt *tuyau, ouverture* to widen, open out; (*Couture*) *jupe, poignets* to flare. 2 **s'évaser** vpr *[passage, tuyau]* to open out; *[manches]* to flare.
évasif, -ive [evazif, iv] adj evasive.
évasion [evazjɔ̃] nf (*lit, fig: fuite*) escape. (*fig: tendance*) **l'~** escapism; (*fig*) **littérature d'~** escapist literature; (*fig*) **besoin d'~** need to escape; (*Écon*) **~ des capitaux** flight of capital; (*Admin*) **~ fiscale** tax evasion.
évasivement [evazivmɑ̃] adv evasively.
Ève [ɛv] nf Eve. (*hum*) **en tenue d'~** in the altogether*, in one's birthday suit; *voir* **connaître**.
évêché [eveʃe] nm (*région*) bishopric; (*palais*) bishop's palace; (*ville*) cathedral town.
éveil [evɛj] nm (*littér*) *[dormeur, intelligence]* awakening; *[amour]* awakening, dawning; *[soupçons, jalousie]* arousing. **être en ~** *[personne]* to be on the alert *ou* on the qui vive; *[sens]* to be alert *ou* wide awake, be aroused; **donner l'~** to raise the alarm *ou* alert; **mettre qn en ~, donner l'~ à qn** to alert *ou* arouse sb's suspicions, put sb on his guard; (*Scol*) **activités d'~** early-learning games *etc*.
éveillé, e [eveje] (ptp de **éveiller**) adj (*alerte*) *enfant, esprit, air* alert, sharp, bright; (*à l'état de veille*) (wide-)awake.
éveiller [eveje] 1 1 vt a (*littér: réveiller*) to awaken, waken. **tenir qn éveillé** to keep sb awake; *voir* **rêve**.
b (*fig: faire naître*) *curiosité, sentiment, soupçons, souvenirs* to arouse, awaken; *passion* to kindle, arouse. **pour ne pas ~ l'attention** so as not to arouse attention.
c (*développer*) *esprit, intelligence* to stimulate. **~ l'intelligence de l'enfant** to awaken the child's intelligence, stimulate the child's interest.
2 **s'éveiller** vpr a (*se réveiller*) (*lit*) to wake up, awaken, waken; (*fig*) *[ville, nature]* to come to life, wake (up).
b (*fig: naître*) *[sentiment, curiosité, soupçons]* to be aroused; *[amour]* to dawn, be aroused *ou* born.
c (*se développer*) *[intelligence, esprit]* to develop.
d (*littér: ressentir*) **s'~ à** *amour* to awaken to.
événement, évènement [evɛnmɑ̃] nm event, occurrence. (*Pol*) **~s** events, incidents; **c'est un véritable ~ quand il dit merci** it's quite an event *ou* occasion when he says thank you; **semaine chargée en ~s** eventful week, action-packed week; **l'~ de la semaine** the main story *ou* news of the week; *voir* **dépasser, heureux, tournure**.
événementiel, -ielle [evɛnmɑ̃sjɛl] adj factual. **histoire ~ielle** factual history.
évent [evɑ̃] nm (*Zool*) *[baleine]* blowhole, spout (hole), spiracle (*SPÉC*).
éventail [evɑ̃taj] nm (*instrument*) fan; (*fig: gamme*) range. **en (forme d')~** *objet* fan-shaped; **en ~** fan-shaped; *plusieurs objets* fanned out, splayed out; (*Mil*) **se déployer en ~** to fan out; **~ des salaires** salary range, wage range *ou* spread (*US*); **l'~ politique** the political spectrum; *voir* **déployer, doigt, voûte**.
éventaire [evɑ̃tɛʀ] nm (*corbeille*) tray, basket; (*étalage*) stall, stand.
éventé, e [evɑ̃te] (ptp de **éventer, s'éventer**) adj *parfum, vin* stale, musty; *bière* stale, flat.
éventer [evɑ̃te] 1 1 vt a (*rafraîchir*) to air; (*avec un éventail*) to fan. **rue très éventée** very windy *ou* exposed street. b (*fig: découvrir*) *secret, complot* to discover, lay open. **le secret est éventé** the secret is out; **c'est un truc éventé** it's a well-known *ou* a rather obvious *ou* a pretty well-worn trick. 2 **s'éventer** vpr a *[bière]* to go flat; *[vin, parfum]* to go stale *ou* musty. b (*avec éventail*) to fan o.s. **s'~ avec un journal** to fan o.s. with a newspaper.
éventration [evɑ̃tʀasjɔ̃] nf (*Méd*) rupture.
éventrer [evɑ̃tʀe] 1 vt a (*avec un couteau*) to disembowel; (*d'un coup de corne*) to gore. **il s'est éventré sur son volant** he ripped himself open *ou* eviscerated himself on his steering wheel. b *boîte, sac* to tear

open; *muraille, coffre* to smash open; *matelas* to rip open.

éventualité [evɑ̃tɥalite] nf a (*NonC*) possibility. b eventuality, contingency, possibility. **pour parer à toute ~** to guard against all eventualities *ou* possibilities *ou* contingencies; **dans cette ~** if this happens, should that arise; **dans l'~ d'un refus de sa part** should he refuse, in the event of his refusal.

éventuel, -elle [evɑ̃tɥɛl] adj possible.

éventuellement [evɑ̃tɥɛlmɑ̃] adv possibly. **~, nous pourrions ...** we could possibly *ou* perhaps ...; **~ je prendrais ma voiture** if need be *ou* if necessary I'd take my car.

évêque [evɛk] nm bishop. **(~) suffragant** suffragan (bishop).

évertuer (s') [evɛʀtɥe] 1 vpr a (*s'efforcer de*) **s'~ à faire** to strive *ou* do one's utmost *ou* struggle hard *ou* make strenuous efforts to do. b (*frm, †: se dépenser*) to strive, struggle. **je m'évertue à t'expliquer** I'm doing by best *ou* my utmost to explain to you; **s'~ contre qch** to struggle against sth.

éviction [eviksjɔ̃] nf (*Jur*) eviction; *[rival]* ousting, supplanting. **procéder à l'~ de** *locataires* to evict.

évidage [evidaʒ] nm, **évidement** [evidmɑ̃] nm hollowing-out, scooping-out.

évidemment [evidamɑ̃] adv (*bien sûr*) of course, obviously; (*frm: d'une manière certaine*) obviously.

évidence [evidɑ̃s] nf a (*caractère*) obviousness, evidence. **c'est l'~ même!** it's quite *ou* perfectly evident *ou* patently obvious; **se rendre à l'~** to bow *ou* yield to facts *ou* the evidence, face facts *ou* the evidence; **nier l'~** to deny the obvious *ou* the facts.

b (*fait*) obvious fact. **trois ~s se dégagent de ce discours** this speech brings three obvious facts to light; **c'est une ~ que de dire** it's a statement of the obvious *ou* it's stating the obvious to say.

c (*loc*) **(être) en ~** *[personne]* (to be) conspicuous *ou* in evidence; *[objet]* (to be) conspicuous *ou* in evidence, (be) in a conspicuous *ou* prominent position; **mettre en ~** *personne* to bring to the fore; *fait* (*souligner*) to bring to the fore, give prominence to, underscore; (*révéler*) to reveal; *objet* to put in a prominent *ou* conspicuous position; **se mettre en ~** to make o.s. conspicuous, make one's presence felt; **la lettre était bien en ~ sur la table** the letter was (lying) there for all to see *ou* was lying conspicuously on the table; **de toute ~, à l'~†** quite obviously *ou* evidently.

évident, e [evidɑ̃, ɑ̃t] adj obvious, evident, self-evident. **il est ~ que** it is obvious *ou* evident that, it is plain for all to see that; **ce n'est pas ~!*** it's not that easy *ou* simple!

évider [evide] 1 vt to hollow out, scoop out.

évier [evje] nm sink. **~ (à) un bac/deux bacs** single/double sink; *voir* **bloc**.

évincement [evɛ̃smɑ̃] nm *[rival]* ousting, supplanting.

évincer [evɛ̃se] 3 vt *concurrent* to oust, supplant; (*Jur*) *locataire* to evict.

évitable [evitabl] adj avoidable.

évitage [evitaʒ] nm (*Naut: mouvement*) swinging; (*espace*) swinging room.

évitement [evitmɑ̃] nm (*Transport*) **voie d'~** loop line; **gare d'~** station with a loop line; (*Aut, Aviat*) **manœuvre d'~** avoidance action.

éviter [evite] 1 1 vt a *coup, projectile* to avoid, dodge; *obstacle, danger, maladie, situation* to avoid, steer clear of; *gêneur, créancier* to avoid, keep clear of, evade; *regard* to avoid, evade. **ils s'évitaient depuis quelque temps** they had been avoiding each other *ou* keeping clear of each other for some time; **~ qu'une situation n'empire** to avoid *ou* prevent the worsening of a situation, prevent a situation from getting worse; **~ d'être repéré** to escape detection, avoid being detected.

b *erreur, mensonge, méthode* to avoid. **~ de faire qch** to avoid doing sth; **on lui a conseillé d'~ le sel** he has been advised to avoid *ou* keep off salt; **on lui a conseillé d'~ la mer/la marche** he has been advised to avoid the sea/walking; **évite le mensonge** *ou* **de mentir** avoid lying, shun lies (*littér*).

c **~ qch à qn** to spare *ou* save sb sth; **ça lui a évité d'avoir à se déplacer** that spared *ou* saved him the bother *ou* trouble of going; **s'~ toute fatigue** to spare o.s. any fatigue, save o.s. from getting at all tired.

2 vi (*Naut*) to swing.

évocateur, -trice [evɔkatœʀ, tʀis] adj evocative, suggestive (*de* of).

évocation [evɔkasjɔ̃] nf a *[souvenirs, faits]* evocation, recalling; *[scène, idée]* conjuring-up, evocation. **ces ~s la faisaient s'attendrir** she became more tender as she recalled these memories; **pouvoir d'~ d'un mot** evocative *ou* suggestive power of a word. b (*littér*) *[démons]* evocation, calling-up, conjuring-up.

évolué, e [evɔlɥe] (ptp de **évoluer**) adj *peuple, civilisation* (highly) developed, advanced; *personne* broad-minded, enlightened; *procédé* advanced. **une jeune fille très ~e** a girl with very progressive *ou* liberated views *ou* a very independent attitude.

évoluer [evɔlɥe] 1 vi a (*changer*) *[idées, civilisation, science]* to evolve, develop, advance; *[personne, goûts, maladie, tumeur]* to develop; *[situation]* to develop, evolve. **il a beaucoup évolué** his ideas have *ou* he has developed a great deal, he has come a long way (in his ideas). b (*se mouvoir*) *[danseur]* to move about; *[avion]* to manœuvre; *[troupes]* to manœuvre, wheel about. **le monde dans lequel il évolue** the world in which he moves.

évolutif, -ive [evɔlytif, iv] adj (*gén, Bio*) evolutionary, evolutional; (*Méd*) progressive; *poste* with potential (for advancement *ou* promotion); *voir* **ski**.

évolution [evɔlysjɔ̃] nf a (*changement*) *[idées, civilisation, science]* evolution, development, advancement; *[personne, goûts, maladie, situation]* development. (*Bio*) **théorie de l'~** theory of evolution. b (*mouvements*) **~s** movements; **il regardait les ~s du danseur/de l'avion** he watched the dancer as he moved about gracefully/the plane as it wheeled *ou* circled overhead; **suivre à la jumelle les ~s des troupes** to watch troop manœuvres through field glasses.

évolutionnisme [evɔlysjɔnism] nm evolutionism.

évolutionniste [evɔlysjɔnist] 1 adj evolutionary. 2 nmf evolutionist.

évoquer [evɔke] 1 vt a (*remémorer*) *souvenirs* to recall, call up, evoke; *fait, événement* to evoke, recall; *mémoire d'un défunt* to recall. b (*faire penser à*) *scène, idée* to call to mind, evoke, conjure up. **ça évoque mon enfance** it reminds me of *ou* recalls my childhood. c (*effleurer*) *problème, sujet* to touch on, mention. d (*littér: invoquer*) *démons* to evoke, call up, conjure up.

evzone [ɛvzon] nm evzone.

ex.[1] (abrév de **exemple**) eg, e.g.

ex[2]* [ɛks] nmf ex*.

ex- [ɛks] préf ex-.

exacerbation [ɛgzasɛʀbasjɔ̃] nf exacerbation.

exacerber [ɛgzasɛʀbe] 1 vt to exacerbate, aggravate. **sensibilité exacerbée** exaggerated sensitivity.

exact, exacte [ɛgza(kt), ɛgzakt(ə)] adj a (*fidèle*) *reproduction, compte rendu* exact, accurate, true. **est-il ~ que?** is it right *ou* correct *ou* true that?; **c'est l'~e vérité** that's the absolute *ou* exact truth; **ce n'est pas tout à fait ~** that's not quite right *ou* accurate, that's not altogether correct; **~!*** quite right!, absolutely!, exactly!

b (*correct*) *définition, raisonnement* correct, exact; *réponse, calcul* correct, right.

c (*précis*) *dimension, nombre, valeur* exact, precise; *donnée* accurate, precise, correct; *pendule* accurate, right. **l'heure ~e** the right *ou* exact *ou* correct time; *voir* **science**.

d (*ponctuel*) punctual, on time. **c'est quelqu'un de très ~ d'habitude** he's normally always on time, he's normally very punctual; **être ~ à un rendez-vous** to arrive at an appointment on time, arrive punctually for an appointment; **~ à payer ses dettes** punctual *ou* prompt in paying one's debts.

e (*littér*) *discipline* exact, rigorous, strict; *obéissance* rigorous, strict, scrupulous.

exactement [ɛgzaktəmɑ̃] adv (*voir* **exact**) exactly; accurately; correctly; precisely; rigorously; strictly; scrupulously. **c'est ~ ce que je pensais** it's exactly *ou* just *ou* precisely what I was thinking; **oui, ~!** yes exactly *ou* precisely!

exaction [ɛgzaksjɔ̃] nf exaction.

exactitude [ɛgzaktityd] nf a (*NonC: voir* **exact**) exactness, exactitude (*frm*); accuracy; correctness; precision. **calculer qch avec ~** to calculate sth exactly *ou* accurately. b (*ponctualité*) punctuality. **l'~ est la politesse des rois** punctuality is the politeness of kings. c (*littér: minutie*) exactitude.

ex æquo [ɛgzeko] 1 adj inv (*Scol, Sport*) equally placed, placed equal. **avoir le premier prix ~, être classé premier ~** to be placed first equal *ou* joint first, to tie for first place; **les ~** the pupils (*ou* players *etc*) who are placed equal; **il y a deux ~ pour la deuxième place** there is a tie for second place. 2 adv *classer* equal.

exagération [ɛgzaʒeʀasjɔ̃] nf (*gén*) exaggeration. **on peut dire sans ~ que** ... one can say without any exaggeration *ou* without exaggerating that ...; **il est sévère sans ~** he's severe without taking it to extremes.

exagéré, e [ɛgzaʒeʀe] (ptp de **exagérer**) adj (*amplifié*) exaggerated; (*excessif*) excessive. **venir se plaindre après ça, c'est un peu ~** to come and complain after all that, it's a bit much* (*Brit*) *ou* too much; **il n'est pas ~ de dire** it is not an exaggeration *ou* an overstatement *ou* it's not going too far to say.

exagérément [ɛgzaʒeʀemɑ̃] adv excessively, exaggeratedly.

exagérer [ɛgzaʒeʀe] 6 1 vt (*gén*) to exaggerate; *attitude* to exaggerate, take too far, overdo; *qualités* to exaggerate, overemphasize. **sans ~, ça a duré 3 heures** without any exaggeration *ou* I'm not exaggerating *ou* kidding* it lasted 3 hours; **quand même il exagère** really he goes too far *ou* oversteps the mark; **joue le personnage plus passionné, mais sans ~** make the character more passionate but don't overdo it *ou* but don't exaggerate. 2 **s'exagérer** vpr *difficultés* to exaggerate; *plaisirs, avantages* to exaggerate, overrate.

exaltant, e [ɛgzaltɑ̃, ɑ̃t] adj exalting, elating, exhilarating.

exaltation [ɛgzaltasjɔ̃] nf a (*surexcitation: gén*) intense excitement. **~ joyeuse** elation, rapturous joy; **~ mystique** exaltation. b (*glorification*) extolling, praising, exalting.

exalté, e [ɛgzalte] (ptp de **exalter**) 1 adj *personne, sentiments* elated; *imagination* wild, vivid; *esprit* excited. 2 nm,f (*impétueux*) hothead; (*fanatique*) fanatic.

exalter [ɛgzalte] 1 vt a (*surexciter*) *imagination, esprit, courage* to fire, excite. **exalté par cette nouvelle** (*très excité*) excited by *ou* keyed up with excitement over this piece of news; (*euphorique*) elated *ou* overjoyed by *ou* at this piece of news; **il s'exalte facilement en lisant des romans** he is easily carried away when he reads novels. b (*glorifier*) to exalt, glorify, praise.

exam* [ɛgzam] **nm** (**abrév de examen 1 c**) exam.

examen [ɛgzamɛ̃] 1 **nm** a (*action d'étudier, d'analyser*) (*gén*) examination; *[situation]* examination, survey; *[question, demande, cas]* examination, consideration, investigation; *[appartement]* looking-round (*Brit*), looking-over. **~ détaillé** scrutiny, detailed *ou* close examination; **la question est à l'~** the matter is under consideration *ou* scrutiny; (*Comm*) **à l'~** on approval.

b (*Méd*) **~ (médical)** (medical) examination *ou* test; **se faire faire des ~s** to have some tests done *ou* taken; **subir un ~ médical complet** to undergo *ou* have a complete *ou* thorough checkup, have a thorough medical examination.

c (*Scol*) exam, examination. **~ écrit/oral** written/oral examination; **~ spécial d'entrée à l'université** university entrance examination.

2 **comp** ►**examen blanc** (*Scol*) mock exam (*Brit*), practise test (*US*) ►**examen de conscience** self-examination; (*Rel*) examination of conscience; **faire son examen de conscience** to examine one's conscience, take stock of o.s ►**examen partiel** (*Univ*) class exam (*Brit*), mid-term exam ►**examen de passage** (*Scol*) end-of-year exam (*Brit*), final exam (*US*) ►**examen prénuptial** (*Méd*) pre-marital examination ►**examen spectroscopique** (*Sci*) spectroscopic examination ►**examen de la vue** (*Méd*) sight test; **passer un examen de la vue** to have one's sight *ou* eyes tested.

examinateur, -trice [ɛgzaminatœʀ, tʀis] **nm,f** examiner. **~ extérieur/à l'oral** external/oral examiner.

examiner [ɛgzamine] 1 **vt** a (*analyser*) (*gén*) to examine; *situation* to examine, survey; *possibilité, faits* to examine, go into; *question, demande, cas* to examine, consider, investigate, scrutinize, look into; *comptes, dossier* to examine, go through; *notes, documents* to examine, have a close look at. **~ dans le** *ou* **en détail** to scrutinize, examine closely; **~ une question de près** to go closely into a question, take a close look at a question; **~ qch de plus près** to take a closer *ou* a second look at sth; (*fig*) **~ qch à la loupe** to go through sth with a fine-tooth comb, look into *ou* examine sth in the greatest detail.

b (*regarder*) *objet, personne, visage* to examine, study; *ciel, horizon* to scan; *appartement, pièce* to have a (close) look round (*Brit*), look over. **~ les lieux** to have a look round (*Brit*), look over the place; **~ qch au microscope/à la loupe** to examine *ou* look at sth under a microscope/with a magnifying glass; **~ qn de la tête aux pieds** to look sb up and down (contemptuously); **s'~ devant la glace** to look at o.s. *ou* examine o.s. in the mirror.

c (*Méd*) *malade* to examine. **se faire ~ par un spécialiste** to be examined by a specialist, have o.s. examined by a specialist.

d (*Scol*) *étudiant* to examine.

exanthème [ɛgzɑ̃tɛm] **nm** exanthem.

exarque [ɛgzaʀk] **nm** exarch.

exaspérant, e [ɛgzaspeʀɑ̃, ɑ̃t] **adj** exasperating.

exaspération [ɛgzaspeʀasjɔ̃] **nf** exasperation.

exaspérer [ɛgzaspeʀe] 6 **vt** a (*irriter*) to exasperate. b (*littér: aviver*) to exacerbate, aggravate.

exaucement [ɛgzosmɑ̃] **nm** fulfilment, granting.

exaucer [ɛgzose] 3 **vt** *vœu* to fulfil, grant; (*Rel*) *prière* to grant, answer. **~ qn** to grant sb's wish, answer sb's prayer.

ex cathedra [ɛkskatedʀa] **adv** ex cathedra.

excavateur [ɛkskavatœʀ] **nm** (*machine*) excavator, mechanical digger (*Brit*), steam shovel (*US*).

excavation [ɛkskavasjɔ̃] **nf** (*trou*) excavation. **~ naturelle** natural hollow (*ou* cave *etc*); (*creusement*) excavation.

excavatrice [ɛkskavatʀis] **nf** = **excavateur**.

excaver [ɛkskave] 1 **vt** to excavate.

excédant, e [ɛksedɑ̃, ɑ̃t] **adj** (*énervant*) exasperating, infuriating.

excédent [ɛksedɑ̃] **nm** surplus (*sur* over). **~ de poids/bagages** excess weight/luggage *ou* baggage; **~ de la balance des paiements** balance of payments surplus; **il y a 2 kg d'~** *ou* **en ~** it's 2 kg over (weight); **budget en ~** surplus budget; **~ budgétaire** budget surplus; **payer 3 F d'~** to pay 3 francs excess charge.

excédentaire [ɛksedɑ̃tɛʀ] **adj** *production* excess (*épith*), surplus (*épith*). **budget ~** surplus budget; **la production est ~** production is over target; **ils ont une balance commerciale ~** they have an active trade balance.

excéder [ɛksede] 6 **vt** a (*dépasser*) *longueur, temps, prix* to exceed, be greater than. **le prix excédait (de beaucoup) ses moyens** the price was (way *ou* far) beyond *ou* far exceeded his means; **les avantages excèdent les inconvénients** the advantages outweigh the disadvantages; **l'apprentissage n'excède pas 3 ans** the apprenticeship doesn't last more than 3 years *ou* lasts no more than *ou* does not exceed 3 years.

b (*outrepasser*) *pouvoir, droits* to overstep, exceed, go beyond; *forces* to overtax.

c (*accabler: gén pass*) to exhaust, weigh down, weary. **excédé de fatigue** overcome by tiredness, exhausted, tired out; **excédé de travail** overworked.

d (*agacer: gén pass*) to exasperate, irritate, infuriate. **je suis excédé** I'm furious; **tu m'excèdes avec tes jérémiades!** your whining irritates me!, you exasperate me with your moaning!

excellemment [ɛkselamɑ̃] **adv** (*littér*) excellently.

excellence [ɛkselɑ̃s] **nf** a excellence. **il est le poète surréaliste par ~** he is the surrealist poet par excellence; **il aime la musique par ~** he loves music above all else. b **Son E~** His (*ou* Her) Excellency; **merci (Votre) E~** thank you, Your Excellency.

excellent, e [ɛkselɑ̃, ɑ̃t] **adj** excellent.

exceller [ɛksele] 1 **vi** to excel (*dans ou en qch* at *ou* in sth, *à faire* in doing).

excentré, e [ɛksɑ̃tʀe] **adj** *quartier, région* outlying (*épith*).

excentricité [ɛksɑ̃tʀisite] **nf** eccentricity.

excentrique [ɛksɑ̃tʀik] 1 **adj** *personne,* (*Math*) *cercle* eccentric; *quartier* outlying (*épith*). 2 **nmf** eccentric, crank (*péj*).

excentriquement [ɛksɑ̃tʀikmɑ̃] **adv** (*gén*) eccentrically.

excepté, e [ɛksɛpte] (**ptp de excepter**) 1 **adj**: **il n'a plus de famille sa mère ~e** he has no family left apart from *ou* aside from (*US*) *ou* except his mother, excluding his mother he has no family left. 2 **prép** except, but for, apart from, aside from (*US*). **~ quand** except *ou* apart from when; **~ que** except that; **tous ~ sa mère** everyone but his mother, everyone except for *ou* aside from (*US*) his mother.

excepter [ɛksɛpte] 1 **vt** to except (*de* from), make an exception of. **sans ~ personne** without excluding anyone, no one excepted.

exception [ɛksɛpsjɔ̃] **nf** a (*dérogation*) exception. **à quelques (rares) ~s près** with a (very) few exceptions; **c'est l'~ qui confirme la règle** it's the exception which proves the rule; **d'~** *tribunal* special; *régime, mesure* special, exceptional; (*Jur*) **~ péremptoire** ≃ demurrer. b (*loc*) **faire une ~ à** *règle* to make an exception to; **faire ~ (à la règle)** to be an exception (to the rule); **faire ~ de** to make an exception of; **~ faite de, à l'~ de** except for, apart from, aside from (*US*), with the exception of; **sauf ~** allowing for exceptions; *voir* **titre**.

exceptionnel, -elle [ɛksɛpsjɔnɛl] **adj** exceptional. (*Comm*) **offre ~le** special offer (*Brit*), special (*US*).

exceptionnellement [ɛksɛpsjɔnɛlmɑ̃] **adv** (*à titre d'exception*) in this particular instance, in particular instances; (*très: avec adj*) exceptionally. **ils se sont réunis ~ un dimanche** contrary to their general practice *ou* in this particular instance they met on a Sunday; **le magasin sera ~ ouvert dimanche** the store will open on Sunday just for this week *ou* for this week only; **~ doué** exceptionally *ou* outstandingly gifted.

excès [ɛksɛ] 1 **nm** a (*surplus*) *[argent]* excess, surplus; *[marchandises, produits]* glut, surplus. **il y a un ~ d'acide** (*il en reste*) there is some acid left over *ou* some excess acid; (*il y en a trop*) there is too much acid; **~ de précautions** excessive care *ou* precautions; **~ de zèle** overzealousness; *voir* **pécher**.

b (*gén, Méd, Pol: abus*) excess. **des ~ de langage** extreme *ou* immoderate language; **tomber dans l'~ inverse** to go to the opposite extreme; **~ (*pl*) de boisson** overindulgence in drink, intemperance; **~ (*pl*) de table** overindulgence at (the) table, surfeit of (good) food; **faire des ~ de table** to overindulge, eat too much; **se laisser aller à des ~** to go overboard*.

c (*loc*) (*littér*) **à l'~, jusqu'à l'~** to excess, excessively, inordinately; **généreux à l'~** inordinately generous, overgenerous, generous to a fault; **avec ~** to excess, excessively; **il fait tout avec ~** he does everything to excess, he is excessive in everything he does; **boire avec ~** to drink excessively *ou* to excess; **dépenser avec ~** to be excessive in one's spending.

2 **comp** ►**excès de pouvoir** (*Jur*) abuse of power, actions ultra vires (*SPÉC*) ►**excès de vitesse** (*Aut*) breaking *ou* exceeding the speed limit, speeding; **coupable de plusieurs excès de vitesse** guilty of having broken *ou* exceeded the speed limit on several occasions.

excessif, -ive [ɛksesif, iv] **adj** (*gén*) excessive; *prix, fierté* excessive, inordinate. **c'est une femme ~ive (en tout)** she's a woman of extremes, she takes everything to extremes *ou* too far; **30 F, c'est ~!** 30 francs, that's far too much! *ou* that's excessive!

excessivement [ɛksesivmɑ̃] **adv** excessively; inordinately.

exciper [ɛksipe] 1 **exciper de vt indir** (*frm*) *bonne foi, précédent* to plead.

excipient [ɛksipjɑ̃] **nm** excipient.

exciser [ɛksize] 1 **vt** to excise.

excision [ɛksizjɔ̃] **nf** excision.

excitabilité [ɛksitabilite] **nf** (*Bio*) excitability.

excitable [ɛksitabl] **adj** excitable, easily excited.

excitant, e [ɛksitɑ̃, ɑ̃t] 1 **adj** (*gén*) exciting; (*sexuellement*) arousing, sexy. 2 **nm** stimulant.

excitation [ɛksitasjɔ̃] **nf** a (*Méd*) *[nerf, muscle]* excitation, stimulation; (*Élec*) *[électro-aimant]* excitation. b (*Jur: incitation*) **~ à** incitement to; **~ des mineurs à la débauche** incitement of minors to immoral behaviour. c (*enthousiasme*) excitement, exhilaration; (*désir sexuel*) (sexual) excitement *ou* arousal. **dans un état de grande ~** in a state of great excitement.

excité, e [ɛksite] (**ptp de exciter**) **nm,f** (*impétueux*) hothead; (*fanatique*) fanatic. **une poignée d'~s** a bunch of hotheads; **ne fais pas attention, c'est un ~** don't take any notice — he gets carried away.

exciter [ɛksite] 1 **1** vt **a** (*provoquer*) *ardent désir* to arouse, waken, excite; *rire* to cause; *pitié* to rouse; *curiosité* to rouse, excite, whet; *imagination* to stimulate, fire, stir; *appétit* to whet, excite.
b (*aviver*) *colère, douleur, ardeur* to intensify, increase. **cela ne fit qu'~ sa colère** that only increased *ou* intensified his anger, that only made him even more angry.
c (*enthousiasmer*) *personne* to thrill, excite, exhilarate. **il était tout excité** he was all excited; **il ne semble pas très excité par son nouveau travail*** he doesn't seem very thrilled about *ou* by *ou* wild* about his new job; **excitant pour l'esprit** mentally stimulating.
d (*rendre nerveux*) *personne* to arouse, make tense; *chien, cheval* to pester, tease, excite; (*sexuellement*) to arouse *ou* excite (sexually). **le café m'exciterait trop** coffee would just act as a stimulant on me *ou* would make me too wakeful; **tous ses sens étaient excités** all his senses were aroused; **il est arrivé tout excité** he was all wound up* *ou* in quite a state when he arrived.
e (*: *irriter*) to irritate, exasperate, annoy. **il commence à m'~** he's getting on my nerves.
f (*encourager*) to urge on, spur on. **excitant ses chiens de la voix** urging on *ou* spurring on his dogs with shouts, shouting to urge on his dogs; **~ qn contre qn** to set sb against sb.
g (*inciter*) **~ à** to exhort to, incite to, urge to; **~ qn à faire qch** to push sb into doing sth, provoke *ou* urge sb to do sth; **~ des soldats au combat** to incite *ou* exhort soldiers to combat *ou* battle.
h (*Méd*) *nerf, muscle* to stimulate, excite; (*Élec*) *électro-aimant* to excite.
2 s'exciter (*: *s'enthousiasmer*) to get excited *ou* wound up* (*sur, à propos de* about, over); (*devenir nerveux*) to get worked up*, get in a flap*; (*sexuellement*) to become (sexually) excited, be (sexually) aroused; (*: *se fâcher*) to get angry *ou* annoyed, get hot under the collar*.

exclamatif, -ive [ɛksklamatif, iv] adj exclamatory.

exclamation [ɛksklamasjɔ̃] nf exclamation; *voir* **point**[1].

exclamer (s') [ɛksklame] 1 vpr to exclaim. **"dommage!" s'exclama-t-il** "what a pity!" he exclaimed; (*littér*) **s'~ de colère/d'admiration** to exclaim *ou* cry out in anger/admiration; (*littér: protester*) **s'~ sur qch** to shout *ou* make a fuss about sth.

exclu, e [ɛkskly] nm,f: **les ~s de la société** social outcasts; **les ~s de la croissance économique** those left out of the economic boom.

exclure [ɛksklyʀ] 35 vt **a** (*chasser*) (*d'une salle*) to turn *ou* put out; (*d'un parti politique*) (*gén*) to expel; *chef* to expel, oust; (*d'une école*) to expel, exclude; (*temporairement*) to suspend, exclude; (*d'une université*) to send down (*Brit*), expel (*de* from). **se faire ~ de** to get o.s. put out *ou* expelled *ou* sent down (*Brit*) from.
b (*écarter*) *solution* to exclude, rule out; *hypothèse* to dismiss, turn down. **~ qch de son régime** to cut sth out of one's diet; **~ qch d'une somme** to exclude sth from a sum, leave sth out of a sum; **je tiens à être exclu de cette affaire** count me out of this business; **c'est tout à fait exclu** it's quite out of the question, it's just not on* (*Brit*); **il n'est pas exclu que ...** it is possible *ou* it is not impossible that ...; **idées qui s'excluent mutuellement** ideas which are mutually exclusive.

exclusif, -ive[1] [ɛksklyzif, iv] adj **a** *sentiment, reportage* exclusive. **il a un caractère (trop) ~** he's (too) exclusive in his relationships; **très ~ dans ses amitiés** very selective *ou* exclusive in his friendships; **très ~ dans ses goûts** very selective in his tastes. **b** *droit* exclusive (*de qch* of sth, *de faire* to do). **dans le but ~ d'une amélioration/de faire ...** with the sole *ou* exclusive aim of making an improvement/of doing ... . **c** (*Comm*) *droits, distributeur* sole (*épith*), exclusive (*épith*); *représentant* sole (*épith*); *fabrication* exclusive (*épith*).

exclusion [ɛksklyzjɔ̃] nf **a** (*expulsion*) (*d'une salle*) exclusion; (*d'un parti politique*) expulsion; (*d'une école*) exclusion, expulsion (*de* from). **~ temporaire** *[étudiant]* exclusion, suspension. **b à l'~ de** (*en écartant*) to the exclusion of; (*sauf*) with the exclusion *ou* exception of; **aimer les pommes à l'~ de tous les autres fruits** to love apples to the exclusion of all other fruit; **il peut manger de tous les fruits à l'~ des pommes** he can eat any fruit excluding apples *ou* with the exclusion *ou* exception of apples.

exclusive[2] [ɛksklyziv] nf (*frm*) bar, debarment. **tous sans ~** with none debarred; **frapper qn d'~, prononcer l'~ contre qn** to debar sb.

exclusivement [ɛksklyzivmɑ̃] adv **a** (*seulement*) exclusively, solely. **~ réservé au personnel** reserved for staff only. **b** (*non inclus*) **du 10 au 15 du mois ~** from the 10th to the 15th exclusive. **c** (*littér: de manière entière ou absolue*) exclusively.

exclusivité [ɛksklyzivite] nf **a** (*Comm*) exclusive rights. **avoir l'~ d'un reportage** to have (the) exclusive coverage of an event; (*fig*) **il n'en a pas l'~*** he's not the only one to have it, he hasn't (got) a monopoly on it*. **b** (*Ciné*) **ce film passe en ~ à** this film is showing only *ou* exclusively at; **cinéma d'~** cinema with exclusive showing rights on new releases. **c** *[sentiment]* exclusiveness.

excommunication [ɛkskɔmynikasjɔ̃] nf excommunication.

excommunier [ɛkskɔmynje] 7 vt to excommunicate.

excrément [ɛkskʀemɑ̃] nm excrement (*NonC*). **~s** excrement, faeces.

excrémenteux, -euse [ɛkskʀemɑ̃tø, øz] adj, **excrémentiel, -elle** [ɛkskʀemɑ̃sjɛl] adj excremental.

excréter [ɛkskʀete] 6 vt to excrete.

excréteur, -trice [ɛkskʀetœʀ, tʀis] adj excretory.

excrétion [ɛkskʀesjɔ̃] nf excretion. **~s** excreta.

excrétoire [ɛkskʀetwaʀ] adj = **excréteur.**

excroissance [ɛkskʀwasɑ̃s] nf (*surtout Méd*) excrescence, outgrowth; (*fig*) outgrowth, development.

excursion [ɛkskyʀsjɔ̃] nf (*en car etc*) excursion, (sightseeing) trip; (*à pied*) walk, hike. **~ de 3 jours à travers le pays** 3-day tour *ou* (sightseeing) trip around the country; **~s d'un jour en autocar** day trips by coach; **partir en ~** (*en car etc*) to go on an excursion *ou* trip; (*à pied*) to go on a walk *ou* hike, go walking *ou* hiking.

excursionner [ɛkskyʀsjɔne] 1 vi (*voir* **excursion**) to go on excursions *ou* trips; to go on walks, go hiking; to go touring. **station idéale pour ~** resort ideal for walks *ou* hiking, resort ideal as a base for touring.

excursionniste [ɛkskyʀsjɔnist] nmf (*en car etc*) (day) tripper (*Brit*), traveler (*US*); (*à pied*) hiker, walker.

excusable [ɛkskyzabl] adj excusable, forgivable.

excuse [ɛkskyz] nf **a** (*prétexte*) excuse. **bonne ~** good excuse; **mauvaises ~s** poor excuses; **sans ~** inexcusable; **il a pris pour ~ qu'il avait à travailler** he made *ou* gave the excuse that he had work to do, he used his work as an excuse; *voir* **mot. b** (*regret*) **~s** apology; **faire des ~s, présenter ses ~s** to apologize, offer one's apologies; **je vous dois des ~s** I owe you an apology; **exiger des ~s** to demand an apology; **mille ~s** do forgive me, I'm so sorry. **c faites ~**‡ excuse me, 'scuse me*. **d** (*tarot*) Excuse.

excuser [ɛkskyze] 1 **1** vt **a** (*pardonner*) *personne, faute* to excuse, forgive. **veuillez ~ mon retard** please excuse my being late *ou* my lateness, I do apologize for being late; **je vous prie de l'~** please excuse *ou* forgive him; (*frm*) **veuillez m'~, je vous prie de m'~** I beg your pardon, please forgive me (*pour avoir fait* for having done); **excusez-moi** excuse me, I'm sorry; **je m'excuse*** I'm sorry, sorry; **excusez-moi de vous le dire mais ...** excuse *ou* forgive *ou* pardon my saying so but ...; **excusez-moi de ne pas venir** excuse my not coming, I'm sorry I can't come; **vous êtes tout excusé** please don't apologize, you are quite forgiven; (*hum*) **ils ont invité 500 personnes, excusez du peu!*** they invited 500 people if you please!*; (*hum*) **vous invitez 500 personnes? excusez du peu!*** you're inviting 500 people? is that all? (*iro*).
b (*justifier*) to excuse. **cette explication n'excuse rien** this explanation is no excuse.
c (*dispenser*) to excuse. **il a demandé à être excusé pour la réunion de demain** he asked to be excused from tomorrow's meeting; **se faire ~** to ask to be excused; **"M. Dupont: (absent) excusé"** "Mr Dupont has sent an apology", "apologies for absence received from Mr Dupont".
2 s'excuser vpr: **s'~ de qch** to apologize for sth; **(aller) s'~ auprès de qn** to apologize to sb.

exécrable [ɛgzekʀabl] adj atrocious, execrable.

exécrablement [ɛgzekʀabləmɑ̃] adv atrociously, execrably.

exécration [ɛgzekʀasjɔ̃] nf **a** (*littér: haine*) execration, loathing. **avoir qch en ~** to hold sth in abhorrence. **b** (††: *imprécation*) curse.

exécrer [ɛgzekʀe] 6 vt to loathe, abhor, execrate.

exécutable [ɛgzekytabl] adj *tâche* possible, manageable; *projet* workable, feasible.

exécutant, e [ɛgzekytɑ̃, ɑ̃t] nm,f (*Mus*) performer, executant; (*fig péj: agent*) underling. **il n'est qu'un ~** he just carries out (his) orders, he's just an underling.

exécuter [ɛgzekyte] 1 **1** vt **a** (*accomplir*) *plan, ordre, mouvements* to execute, carry out; *projet, mission* to execute, carry out, accomplish; *promesse* to fulfil, carry out; *travail* to do, execute; *tâche* to execute, discharge, perform. **il a fait ~ des travaux dans sa maison** he had some work done on his house.
b (*confectionner*) *objet* to produce, make; *tableau* to paint, execute; *commande* to fulfil, carry out.
c *ordonnance* to make up. **il a fait ~ l'ordonnance par le pharmacien** he had the prescription made up by the chemist.
d (*Mus*) *morceau* to perform, execute. **brillamment exécuté** brilliantly executed *ou* played.
e (*tuer*) to execute, put to death; (*fig*) *[boxeur etc]* to dispose of, eliminate, wipe out; *[critique] film, acteur etc* to demolish.
f (*Jur*) *traité, loi, décret* to enforce; *contrat* to perform.
g (*Ordin*) *programme* to run.
2 s'exécuter vpr (*en s'excusant etc*) to comply; (*en payant*) to pay up. **je lui demandai de s'excuser — à contrecœur il finit par s'~** I asked him to apologize and finally he reluctantly complied *ou* did so; **vint le moment de l'addition, il s'exécuta de mauvaise grâce** when the time came to settle the bill he paid up with bad *ou* ill grace.

exécuteur, -trice [ɛgzekytœʀ, tʀis] **1** nm,f *[arrêt, décret]* enforcer. **2** nm (*Hist*) **~ (des hautes œuvres)** executioner; (*Jur*) **~ (testamentaire)** (*homme*) executor; (*femme*) executrix.

exécutif, -ive [ɛgzekytif, iv] adj, nm: **pouvoir ~** executive power; **l'~** the executive.

exécution [ɛgzekysjɔ̃] nf **a** (*voir* **exécuter**) execution; carrying out; accomplishment; fulfilment; discharge; performance; production; making; painting; making up; enforcement. **mettre à ~** *projet, idées* to put into operation, execute, carry out; *menaces* to carry out; *loi* to enforce; "~!" "(get) on with it!*"; **l'~ des travaux a été ralentie** the work has been slowed down, there have been delays *ou* hold-ups with the work; (*Mus*) **d'une ~ difficile** difficult to play; (*Jur*) **en ~ de la loi** in compliance *ou* accordance with the law; *voir* **voie.** b *[condamné]* execution. **~ capitale** capital execution. c (*Jur*) *[débiteur]* execution of a writ (*de* against). **~ forcée** execution of a writ.

exécutoire [ɛgzekytwaʀ] **adj** (*Jur*) executory, enforceable. **mesure ~ pour chaque partie contractante** measure binding on each contracting party.

exégèse [ɛgzeʒɛz] **nf** exegesis.

exégète [ɛgzeʒɛt] **nm** exegete.

exemplaire [ɛgzɑ̃plɛʀ] 1 **adj** *mère* model, exemplary; *punition* exemplary. **infliger une punition ~ à qn** to make an example of sb (by punishing him). 2 **nm** a *[livre, formulaire]* copy. **en deux ~s** in duplicate; **en trois ~s** in triplicate; **25 ~s de cet avion ont été vendus** 25 aeroplanes of this type have been sold. b (*échantillon*) specimen, example.

exemplairement [ɛgzɑ̃plɛʀmɑ̃] **adv** exemplarily.

exemplarité [ɛgzɑ̃plaʀite] **nf** exemplary nature.

exemple [ɛgzɑ̃pl] **nm** a (*modèle*) example. **l'~ de leur faillite/de sa sœur lui sera bien utile** their failure/his sister will be a useful example for him; **il est l'~ de la vertu/l'honnêteté** he sets an example of virtue/honesty, he is a model of virtue/honesty; **citer qn/qch en ~** to quote sb/sth as an example; **donner l'~ de l'honnêteté/de ce qu'il faut faire** to give *ou* set an example of honesty/of what to do; **donner l'~** to set an example; **suivre l'~ de qn** to follow sb's example; **prendre ~ sur qn** to take sb as a model; **à l'~ de son père** just like his father, following in his father's footsteps; **faire un ~ de qn** (*punir*) to make an example of sb; **il faut absolument faire un ~** we must make an example of somebody; **il faut les punir pour l'~** they must be punished as an example *ou* as a deterrent to others; *voir* **prêcher.**

b (*cas, spécimen*) example. **voici un ~ de leur avarice** here is an example *ou* instance of their meanness; **voici un bel ~ du gothique flamboyant** this is a fine example of flamboyant gothic; **ce pays fournit un ~ typique de monarchie constitutionnelle** this country provides a typical example of a constitutional monarchy; **le seul ~ que je connaisse** the only example *ou* instance I know of *ou* am aware of; **être d'une bêtise/avarice sans ~** to be of unparalleled stupidity/meanness; **il en existe plusieurs: ~, le rat musqué** there are several, for example the muskrat.

c (*Lexicographie*) example, illustrative phrase.

d **par ~** (*explicatif*) for example *ou* instance; **(ça) par ~!** (*surprise*) my word!; (*indignation*) oh really!; (*‡: par contre*) **c'est assez cher, par ~ on y mange bien** it's pretty expensive but on the other hand *ou* but there again the food is good.

exemplification [ɛgzɑ̃plifikasjɔ̃] **nf** exemplification.

exemplifier [ɛgzɑ̃plifje] 7 **vt** to exemplify.

exempt, e [ɛgzɑ̃, ɑ̃(p)t] 1 **adj** a (*dispensé de*) **~ de** *service militaire, corvée, impôts* exempt from; **~ de taxes** tax-free, duty-free; **~ de TVA** zero-rated for VAT. b (*dépourvu de*) **~ de** *vent, dangers, arrogance, erreurs* free from; **entreprise ~e de dangers** danger-free undertaking, undertaking free from all danger; **d'un ton qui n'était pas ~ d'humour** in a voice which was not without humour, with the faintest tinge of humour in his voice. 2 **nm** (*Hist: Mil, Police*) exempt.

exempter [ɛgzɑ̃(p)te] 1 **vt** a (*dispenser*) to exempt (*de* from). b (*préserver de*) **~ qn de** *soucis* to save sb from.

exemption [ɛgzɑ̃psjɔ̃] **nf** exemption.

exerçant, e [ɛgzɛʀsɑ̃, ɑ̃t] **adj: médecin ~** practising doctor.

exercé, e [ɛgzɛʀse] (**ptp de exercer**) **adj** *yeux, oreilles* keen, trained.

exercer [ɛgzɛʀse] 3 1 **vt** a (*pratiquer*) *métier* to carry on, ply; *profession* to practise, exercise; *fonction* to fulfil, exercise; *talents* to exercise; (*littér*) *charité, hospitalité* to exercise, practise. *[médecin, avocat]* **il exerce encore** he's still practising *ou* in practice.

b *droit, pouvoir* to exercise (*sur* over); *contrôle, influence* to exert, exercise (*sur* over); *représailles* to take (*sur* on); *poussée, pression* to exert (*sur* on). **~ des pressions sur qn** to bring pressure to bear on sb, exert pressure on sb; **~ ses sarcasmes contre qn** to use one's sarcasm on sb, make sb the butt of one's sarcasm; **ses sarcasmes s'exerçaient impitoyablement contre elle** she was the butt of his pitiless sarcasm; **les forces qui s'exercent sur le levier** the force exerted on *ou* brought to bear on the lever; (*Jur*) **~ des poursuites contre qn** to bring an action against sb.

c (*aguerrir*) *corps, esprit* to train, exercise (*à* to, for); *mémoire, jugement, facultés* to exercise. **~ des élèves à lire** *ou* **à la lecture** to exercise pupils in reading, get pupils to practise their reading; **~ un chien à rapporter le journal** to train a dog to bring back the newspaper.

d (*éprouver*) *sagacité, habileté* to tax; *patience* to try, tax.

2 **s'exercer vpr** *[pianiste, sportif]* to practise. **s'~ à** *technique, mouvement* to practise; **s'~ à la patience** to train o.s. to be patient; **s'~ à faire qch** to train o.s. to do sth.

exercice [ɛgzɛʀsis] 1 **nm** a (*voir* **exercer**) *[métier, profession]* practice; *[droit]* exercising; *[facultés]* exercise. **l'~ du pouvoir** the exercise of power; **l'~ du culte ne se fait plus dans ce batiment** religious services are no longer conducted in this building; **après 40 ans d'~** after 40 years in practice; **condamné pour ~ illégal de la médecine** sentenced for practising medicine illegally *ou* for the illegal practice of medicine; **dans l'~ de ses fonctions** in the exercise *ou* execution *ou* discharge of his duties; **être en ~** *[médecin]* to be in practice; *[juge, fonctionnaire]* to be in *ou* hold office; **juge en ~** sitting judge; **président en ~** serving chairman; **entrer en ~** to take up *ou* assume one's duties.

b (*voir* **s'exercer**) practice, practising.

c (*activité physique*) **l'~** exercise; **prendre** *ou* **faire de l'~** to take some exercise.

d (*Mil*) **l'~** exercises, drill; **aller à l'~** to go on exercises; **faire l'~** to drill, be at drill.

e (*Mus, Scol, Sport: petit travail d'entraînement*) exercise. **~ pour piano** piano exercise; **~ d'application** practise *ou* application exercise; (*Gym*) **~s au sol** floor exercises; (*Incendie*) **~ d'évacuation** fire drill; *voir* **cahier.**

f (*Admin, Fin: période*) **l'~ 1986** the 1986 fiscal year.

2 **comp ►exercices d'assouplissement** limbering up exercises, bending and stretching exercises **►exercice budgétaire** (*Fin*) budgetary year **►exercice comptable** accounting year **►exercices phonétiques** phonetic drills **►exercices spirituels** (*Rel*) spiritual exercises **►exercices structuraux** structure drills **►exercice de style** (*Littérat*) stylistic composition **►exercices de tir** (*Mil*) shooting drill *ou* practice.

exerciseur [ɛgzɛʀsizœʀ] **nm** (*gén*) exercise machine; (*pour poitrine*) chest expander.

exergue [ɛgzɛʀg] **nm: en ~:** (*lit*) **cette médaille porte en ~ l'inscription** ... this medal is inscribed below ...; **le chapitre portait en ~ une citation de X** the chapter bore in epigraph a quotation from X, a quotation from X provided the epigraph to the chapter *ou* headed the chapter; **mettre une citation en ~ à un chapitre** to head a chapter with a quotation, put in a quotation as (an) epigraph to a chapter; **mettre un proverbe en ~ à un tableau** to inscribe a painting with a proverb; (*fig: en évidence*) **mettre une idée/une phrase en ~** to bring out *ou* underline an idea/a sentence.

exfoliant, e [ɛksfɔljɑ̃, jɑ̃t] **adj** exfoliating (*épith*).

exhalaison [ɛgzalɛzɔ̃] **nf** (*littér*) (*désagréable*) exhalation; (*agréable*) fragrance, exhalation.

exhalation [ɛgzalasjɔ̃] **nf** (*Physiol*) exhalation.

exhaler [ɛgzale] 1 1 **vt** (*littér*) a *odeur, vapeur* to exhale, give off. b *soupir* to breathe; *plainte* to utter, give forth (*littér*); *joie, douleur* to give vent *ou* expression to. c (*Physiol: souffler*) to exhale. 2 **s'exhaler vpr** *[odeur]* to rise (up) (*de* from). **un soupir s'exhala de ses lèvres** a sigh rose from his lips.

exhaussement [ɛgzosmɑ̃] **nm** raising.

exhausser [ɛgzose] 1 **vt** *construction* to raise (up). **~ une maison d'un étage** to add a floor to a house.

exhaustif, -ive [ɛgzostif, iv] **adj** exhaustive.

exhaustivement [ɛgzostivmɑ̃] **adv** exhaustively.

exhaustivité [ɛgzostivite] **nf** exhaustiveness.

exhiber [ɛgzibe] 1 1 **vt** (*péj*) *savoir, richesse* to display, show off, flaunt; *chiens savants etc* to show, exhibit; (*frm*) *document, passeport* to present, show, produce; *partie du corps* to show off, display. 2 **s'exhiber vpr** a (*péj*) to show o.s. off (in public), parade. b (*outrage à la pudeur*) to expose o.s.

exhibition [ɛgzibisjɔ̃] **nf** a (*voir* **exhiber**) display; flaunting; show, exhibition; presentation, production. **que signifient ces ~s?** what do you mean by this exhibitionism? b (*spectacle forain*) show, display.

exhibitionnisme [ɛgzibisjɔnism] **nm** exhibitionism.

exhibitionniste [ɛgzibisjɔnist] **nmf** exhibitionist. **il est un peu ~** he's a bit of an exhibitionist.

exhortation [ɛgzɔʀtasjɔ̃] **nf** exhortation.

exhorter [ɛgzɔʀte] 1 **vt** to exhort (*à faire* to do, *à qch* to sth), urge (*à faire* to do).

exhumation [ɛgzymasjɔ̃] **nf** (*voir* **exhumer**) exhumation; excavation; unearthing, digging up *ou* out, disinterring; recollection, recalling.

exhumer [ɛgzyme] 1 **vt** *corps* to exhume; *ruines, vestiges* to excavate; (*fig*) *faits, vieux livres* to unearth, dig up *ou* out, disinter; *souvenirs* to recollect, recall.

exigeant, e [ɛgziʒɑ̃, ɑ̃t] **adj** *client, hôte* particular (*attrib*), demanding, hard to please (*attrib*); *enfant, amant* demanding, hard to please (*attrib*); *parents, patron, travail, amour* demanding, exacting. **je ne suis pas ~*, donnez-moi 100 F** I'm not asking for much – give me 100 francs.

exigence [ɛgziʒɑ̃s] **nf** a (*caractère*) *[client]* particularity; *[maître]* strictness. **il est d'une ~ insupportable** he's impossibly demanding *ou* particular; **son ~ de rigueur** his requirement *ou* demand for accuracy.

b (*gén pl: revendication, condition*) demand, requirement. **produit satisfaisant à toutes les ~s** product which meets all requirements.

exiger [ɛgziʒe] 3 **vt** a (*réclamer*) to demand, require (*qch de qn* sth of *ou* from sb), insist on (*qch de qn* sth from sb). **j'exige de le faire** I insist on doing it, I demand to do it; **j'exige que vous le fassiez** I insist on your doing it, I demand *ou* insist that you do it; **j'exige (de vous) des excuses** I demand an apology (from you), I insist on an apology (from you); **la loi l'exige** the law requires *ou* demands it; **des titres**

universitaires sont exigés pour ce poste university degrees are required *ou* needed *ou* are a requirement for this post; **trop ~ de ses forces** to overtax one's strength, ask *ou* demand too much of one's strength.
b (*nécessiter*) to require, call for, demand. **cette plante exige beaucoup d'eau** this plant needs *ou* requires a lot of water.
exigibilité [ɛgziʒibilite] **nf** *[dette]* payability. **~s** current liabilities.
exigible [ɛgziʒibl] **adj** *dette* payable, due for payment.
exigu, -uë [ɛgzigy] **adj** *lieu* cramped, exiguous (*littér*); *ressources* scanty, meagre, exiguous (*littér*); *délais* short.
exiguïté [ɛgzigɥite] **nf** (*voir* **exigu**) crampedness; exiguity (*littér*); scantiness, meagreness; shortness.
exil [ɛgzil] **nm** exile. *personne* **en ~** in exile (*attrib*), exiled.
exilé, e [ɛgzile] (**ptp de exiler**) **nm,f** exile.
exiler [ɛgzile] 1 1 **vt** (*Pol*) to exile; (*fig littér*) to banish. **se sentir exilé (loin de)** to feel like an outcast *ou* exile (far from); (*fig*) **une note importante exilée en bas de page** an important note tucked away at the bottom of the page. 2 **s'exiler vpr** (*Pol*) to go into exile. (*fig*) **s'~ à la campagne** to bury o.s. in the country; (*fig*) **s'~ en Australie** to exile o.s. to Australia, take o.s. off to Australia; (*fig*) **s'~ loin du monde** to cut o.s. off from the world.
existant, e [ɛgzistɑ̃, ɑ̃t] **adj** *coutume, loi, prix* existing, in existence.
existence [ɛgzistɑ̃s] **nf** a (*Philos, Rel: présence*) existence. b (*vie quotidienne*) existence, life. **dans l'~** in life; *voir* **moyen**.
existentialisme [ɛgzistɑ̃sjalism] **nm** existentialism.
existentialiste [ɛgzistɑ̃sjalist] **adj, nmf** existentialist.
existentiel, -ielle [ɛgzistɑ̃sjɛl] **adj** existential.
exister [ɛgziste] 1 **vi** a (*vivre*) to exist. (*péj*) **il se contente d'~** he is content with just getting by *ou* just existing.
b (*être réel*) to exist, be. **pour lui, la peur n'existe pas** there is no such thing as fear *ou* fear doesn't exist as far as he is concerned; **quoi que vous pensiez, le bonheur ça existe** whatever you may say, there is such a thing as happiness.
c (*se trouver*) to be, be found. **la vie existe-t-elle sur Mars?** is there life on Mars?; **produit qui existe en magasin** product (to be) found in shops; **ce modèle existe-t-il en rose?** is this model available in pink?; **le costume régional n'existe plus guère** regional dress is scarcely ever (to be) found *ou* seen these days; **les dinosaures n'existent plus/existent encore** dinosaurs are extinct/are still in existence; **les bateaux à aubes n'existent plus/existent encore** paddle steamers no longer/still exist; **il existe encore une copie** there is still one copy extant *ou* in existence; **pourquoi monter à pied? les ascenseurs ça existe!** why walk up? there are lifts, you know! *ou* lifts have been invented!
d (*il y a*) **il existe** there is, there are; **il n'existe pas de meilleur exemple** there is no better example; **il existe des bégonias de plusieurs couleurs** begonias come *ou* are found in several colours.
ex nihilo [ɛksniilo] **adv** ex nihilo.
exocet [ɛgzɔsɛ] **nm** (*poisson*) flying fish; ® (*missile*) exocet ®.
exode [ɛgzɔd] **nm** (*lit, fig*) exodus. (*Bible*) **l'E~** the Exodus; **(le livre de) l'E~** (the Book of) Exodus; **~ rural** drift from the land; **~ des cerveaux** brain drain; **~ des capitaux** outflow of capital.
exogène [ɛgzɔʒɛn] **adj** exogenous.
exonération [ɛgzɔneʀasjɔ̃] **nf** (*Fin*) exemption (*de* from). **~ d'impôt** tax exemption.
exonérer [ɛgzɔneʀe] 6 **vt** (*Fin*) to exempt (*de* from).
exorbitant, e [ɛgzɔʀbitɑ̃, ɑ̃t] **adj** *prix, demande, prétention* exorbitant, inordinate, outrageous.
exorbité, e [ɛgzɔʀbite] **adj** *yeux* bulging (*de* with).
exorcisation [ɛgzɔʀsizasjɔ̃] **nf** exorcizing.
exorciser [ɛgzɔʀsize] 1 **vt** to exorcize.
exorciseur [ɛgzɔʀsizœʀ] **nm** exorcizer.
exorcisme [ɛgzɔʀsism] **nm** exorcism.
exorciste [ɛgzɔʀsist] **nm** exorcist.
exorde [ɛgzɔʀd] **nm** introduction, exordium (*SPÉC*).
exosmose [ɛgzɔsmoz] **nf** exosmosis.
exotique [ɛgzɔtik] **adj** *pays, plante* exotic.
exotisme [ɛgzɔtism] **nm** exoticism. **aimer l'~** to love all that is exotic.
expansé, e [ɛkspɑ̃se] **adj** expanded. **polystyrène ~** expanded polystyrene.
expansibilité [ɛkspɑ̃sibilite] **nf** expansibility.
expansible [ɛkspɑ̃sibl] **adj** expansible.
expansif, -ive [ɛkspɑ̃sif, iv] **adj** (*de caractère*) expansive, out-going. **il s'est montré peu ~** he was not very forthcoming *ou* communicative.
expansion [ɛkspɑ̃sjɔ̃] **nf** a (*extension*) expansion. **l'~ d'une doctrine** the spreading of a doctrine; **notre économie est en pleine ~** our economy is booming, we have a booming *ou* fast-expanding economy; **univers** *etc* **en ~** expanding universe *etc*. b (*effusion*) expansiveness (*NonC*), effusiveness (*NonC*). **avec de grandes ~s** expansively, effusively.
expansionnisme [ɛkspɑ̃sjɔnism] **nm** expansionism.
expansionniste [ɛkspɑ̃sjɔnist] **adj, nmf** expansionist.
expansivité [ɛkspɑ̃sivite] **nf** expansiveness.
expatriation [ɛkspatʀijasjɔ̃] **nf** expatriation.
expatrié, e [ɛkspatʀije] (**ptp de expatrier**) **nm,f** expatriate.
expatrier [ɛkspatʀije] 7 1 **vt** to expatriate. 2 **s'expatrier vpr** to expatriate o.s., leave one's country.
expectative [ɛkspɛktativ] **nf** (*incertitude*) state of uncertainty; (*attente prudente*) cautious approach. **être** *ou* **rester dans l'~** (*incertitude*) to be still waiting *ou* hanging on (to hear *ou* see *etc*); (*attente prudente*) to hold back, wait and see.
expectorant, e [ɛkspɛktɔʀɑ̃, ɑ̃t] **adj, nm** expectorant.
expectoration [ɛkspɛktɔʀasjɔ̃] **nf** expectoration.
expectorer [ɛkspɛktɔʀe] 1 **vti** to expectorate.
expédient, e [ɛkspedjɑ̃, jɑ̃t] 1 **adj** (*frm*) expedient. 2 **nm** expedient, makeshift. **vivre d'~s** *[personne]* to live by one's wits; *[pays]* to resort to short-term measures.
expédier [ɛkspedje] 7 **vt** a *lettre, paquet* to send, dispatch. **~ par la poste** to send through the post (*Brit*) *ou* mail; **~ par le train** to send by rail *ou* train; **~ par bateau** *lettres, colis* to send surface mail; *matières premières* to ship, send by sea; (*fig*) **je l'ai expédié en vacances chez sa grand-mère*** I sent *ou* packed* him off to his grandmother's for the holidays; (*fig hum*) **~ qn dans l'autre monde** to bump sb off* (*Brit*), do sb in‡.
b (*) *client, visiteur* to dispose of. **~ une affaire** to dispose of *ou* dispatch a matter, get a matter over with; **~ son déjeuner en 5 minutes** to polish off* one's lunch in 5 minutes.
c (*Admin*) **~ les affaires courantes** to deal with *ou* dispose of day-to-day matters.
expéditeur, -trice [ɛkspeditœʀ, tʀis] 1 **adj** dispatching, forwarding. 2 **nm,f** *[courrier]* sender, addresser, addressor; *[marchandises]* consignor, shipper; *voir* **retour**.
expéditif, -ive [ɛkspeditif, iv] **adj** quick, expeditious.
expédition [ɛkspedisjɔ̃] **nf** a (*action*) *[lettre, vivres, renforts]* dispatch; (*par bateau*) shipping. b (*paquet*) consignment; (*par bateau*) shipment. c (*Mil, Sport, Sci*) expedition. **~ de police** police raid; (*fig*) **quelle ~!** what an expedition!, what a palaver! d (*Admin*) **l'~ des affaires courantes** the dispatching of day-to-day matters. e (*Jur*) exemplified copy.
expéditionnaire [ɛkspedisjɔnɛʀ] 1 **adj** (*Mil*) expeditionary. 2 **nmf** (*Comm*) forwarding agent; (*Admin*) copyist.
expéditivement [ɛkspeditivmɑ̃] **adv** expeditiously.
expérience [ɛkspeʀjɑ̃s] **nf** a (*pratique*) experience. **avoir de l'~** to have experience, be experienced (*en* in); (*frm*) **avoir l'~ du monde** to have experience of the world, know the ways of the world; **sans ~** inexperienced; **il est sans ~ de la vie** he has no experience of life; **savoir par ~** to know by *ou* from experience; **il a une longue ~ de l'enseignement** he has a lot of teaching experience.
b (*aventure humaine*) experience. **~ amoureuse** love affair; **tente l'~, tu verras bien** try it and see; **faire l'~ de qch** to experience sth; **ils ont fait une ~ de vie communautaire** they experimented with communal living.
c (*essai scientifique*) experiment. **vérité** *ou* **fait d'~** experimental truth *ou* fact; **faire une ~ sur un cobaye** to do *ou* carry out an experiment on a guinea-pig.
expérimental, e, mpl -aux [ɛkspeʀimɑ̃tal, o] **adj** experimental.
expérimentalement [ɛkspeʀimɑ̃talmɑ̃] **adv** experimentally.
expérimentateur, -trice [ɛkspeʀimɑ̃tatœʀ, tʀis] **nm,f** (*gén*) experimenter; (*Sci*) bench scientist.
expérimentation [ɛkspeʀimɑ̃tasjɔ̃] **nf** experimentation.
expérimenté, e [ɛkspeʀimɑ̃te] (**ptp de expérimenter**) **adj** experienced.
expérimenter [ɛkspeʀimɑ̃te] 1 **vt** *appareil* to test; *remède* to experiment with, try out; *méthode* to test out, try out. **~ en laboratoire** to experiment *ou* do experiments in a laboratory.
expert, e [ɛkspɛʀ, ɛʀt] 1 **adj** expert, skilled (*en* in, *à* at). **être ~ en la matière** to be skilled *ou* (an) expert in the subject. 2 **nm** (*connaisseur*) expert (*en* in, at), connoisseur (*en* in, of); (*spécialiste*) expert; (*d'assurances*) (*après dégâts*) assessor; (*d'objet de valeur*) valuer, assessor; (*Naut*) surveyor. **médecin** *etc* **~** medical *etc* expert. 3 **comp ▸expert-comptable nm (pl experts-comptables)** independent auditor, ≃ chartered accountant (*Brit*), ≃ certified public accountant (*US*).
expertement [ɛkspɛʀtəmɑ̃] **adv** expertly.
expertise [ɛkspɛʀtiz] **nf** a (*voir* **expertiser**) (*évaluation*) expert evaluation *ou* appraisal; (*rapport*) valuer's *ou* assessor's *ou* expert's report. **~ d'avarie** damage survey. b (*compétence*) expertise.
expertiser [ɛkspɛʀtize] 1 **vt** *bijou* to value, appraise, assess, evaluate; *dégâts* to assess, appraise, evaluate. **faire ~ un diamant** to have a diamond valued.
expiable [ɛkspjabl] **adj** expiable.
expiation [ɛkspjasjɔ̃] **nf** expiation (*de* of), atonement (*de* for). **en ~ de ses crimes** in expiation of *ou* atonement for his crimes.
expiatoire [ɛkspjatwaʀ] **adj** expiatory.
expier [ɛkspje] 7 **vt** *péchés, crime* to expiate, atone for. (*fig*) **~ une imprudence** to pay for an imprudent act.
expirant, e [ɛkspiʀɑ̃, ɑ̃t] **adj** dying.
expiration [ɛkspiʀasjɔ̃] **nf** a (*terme*) expiration, expiry (*Brit*). **venir à ~** to expire; **à l' ~ du délai** at the expiry (*Brit*) *ou* expiration (*US*) of the deadline, when the deadline expires. b (*respiration*) expiration, exhalation. **une profonde ~** a complete exhalation.

expirer [ɛkspiʀe] [1] 1 vt *air* to breathe out, expire (*SPÉC*). **expirez lentement!** breathe out slowly! 2 vi (*mourir, prendre fin*) to expire. **le contrat/la carte expire le 5 mai** the contract/the card expires on May 5th.

explétif, -ive [ɛkspletif, iv] 1 adj expletive, expletory. 2 nm expletive.

explicable [ɛksplikabl] adj explicable, explainable.

explicatif, -ive [ɛksplikatif, iv] adj explanatory, explicative. (*Gram*) **proposition relative ~ive** non-restrictive relative clause.

explication [ɛksplikasjɔ̃] nf a *[phénomène]* explanation (*de* for); *[méthode]* explanation (*de* of). **les ~s sont écrites au dos** the explanations *ou* instructions are written on the back. b (*justification*) explanation (*de qch* for sth). **votre conduite demande des ~s** your conduct requires some explanation; **j'exige des ~s** I demand an explanation. c (*discussion*) discussion; (*dispute*) argument; (*bagarre*) fight. d (*Scol*) *[auteur, passage]* commentary (*de* on), analysis (*de* of). **~ de texte** critical analysis *ou* appreciation of a text, interpretation (of a text).

explicite [ɛksplisit] adj explicit.

explicitement [ɛksplisitmɑ̃] adv explicitly.

expliciter [ɛksplisite] [1] vt to explain, clarify.

expliquer [ɛksplike] [1] 1 vt a (*faire comprendre*) to explain. **il m'a expliqué comment faire** he told me *ou* explained to me how to do it; **je lui ai expliqué qu'il avait tort** I pointed out to him *ou* explained to him that he was wrong; **explique-moi comment/pourquoi** explain how/why, tell me how/why.

b (*rendre compte de*) to account for, explain. **cela explique qu'il ne soit pas venu** that explains why he didn't come, that accounts for his not coming.

c (*Scol*) *texte* to comment on, criticize, analyse. **~ un passage de Flaubert** to give a critical analysis *ou* a critical appreciation *ou* a critical interpretation of a passage from Flaubert.

2 **s'expliquer** vpr a (*donner des précisions*) to explain o.s., make o.s. clear. **je m'explique** let me explain, let me make myself clear; **le président s'explique** the president gives his reasons; **s'~ sur ses projets** to talk about *ou* explain one's plans; **s'~ devant qn** to justify o.s. to sb, explain one's actions to sb.

b (*comprendre*) to understand. **je ne m'explique pas bien qu'il soit parti** I can't see *ou* understand *ou* it isn't at all clear to me why he should have left.

c (*être compréhensible*) **son retard s'explique par le mauvais temps** his lateness is explained by the bad weather, the bad weather accounts for *ou* explains his lateness; **leur attitude s'explique: ils n'ont pas reçu notre lettre** that explains their attitude: they didn't get our letter; **tout s'explique!** it's all clear now!, I see it all now!

d (*parler clairement*) **s'~ bien/mal** to express *ou* explain o.s. well/badly; **je me suis peut-être mal expliqué** perhaps I have explained *ou* expressed myself badly, perhaps I didn't make myself (quite) clear.

e (*discuter*) **s'~ avec qn** to explain o.s. to sb, have it out with sb*; **va t'~ avec lui** go and sort it out with him, go and explain yourself to him; **après s'être longuement expliqués ils sont tombés d'accord** after having discussed the matter *ou* after having talked the matter over for a long time they finally reached an agreement; **ils sont allés s'~ dehors*** they went to fight it out outside *ou* to finish it off outside; **s'~ à coups de fusil** to shoot it out.

exploit [ɛksplwa] nm exploit, feat, achievement. **quel ~!** what a feat! *ou* achievement!; **il a réussi l'~ d'arriver le premier** his great achievement was to come first; (*Jur*) **~ d'huissier** writ.

exploitable [ɛksplwatabl] adj (*gén*) exploitable.

exploitant, e [ɛksplwatɑ̃, ɑ̃t] nm,f a (*fermier*) **~ (agricole)** farmer; **petit ~ (agricole)** smallholder (*Brit*), small farmer. b (*Ciné*) (*propriétaire*) cinema owner; (*gérant*) cinema manager.

exploitation [ɛksplwatasjɔ̃] nf a (*action: voir* **exploiter**) working; exploitation; running, operating. **mettre en ~** *domaine, ressources* to exploit, develop; **l'~ de l'homme par l'homme** man's exploitation of man *ou* of his fellow man; **frais/méthodes d'~** running *ou* operating costs/methods; (*Ciné*) **copie d'~** release print. b (*entreprise*) concern. **~ (agricole)** farm; **petite ~ (agricole)** smallholding (*Brit*), small farm; **~ commerciale/industrielle** business/industrial concern; **~ minière/forestière** mining/forestry development.

exploiter [ɛksplwate] [1] vt *mine, sol* to work, exploit; *entreprise* to run, operate; *ressources* to exploit; *idée, situation* to exploit, make the most of; *personne, bonté* to exploit. **pouvoir ~ un avantage** to be able to capitalize on an advantage *ou* exploit an advantage; **nous sommes des exploités** we are exploited.

exploiteur, -euse [ɛksplwatœʀ, øz] nm,f exploiter.

explorateur, -trice [ɛksplɔʀatœʀ, tʀis] nm,f (*personne*) explorer.

exploration [ɛksplɔʀasjɔ̃] nf (*voir* **explorer**) exploration; investigation; examination.

exploratoire [ɛksplɔʀatwaʀ] adj exploratory.

explorer [ɛksplɔʀe] [1] vt (*gén*) to explore; *possibilité, problème* to investigate, examine, explore.

exploser [ɛksploze] [1] vi *[bombe, chaudière]* to explode, blow up; *[gaz]* to explode; *[colère]* to explode, burst out. **il explosa (de colère)** he flared up, he exploded with *ou* in anger; **faire ~** *bombe* to explode, detonate; *bâtiment* to blow up; (*fig*) **cette remarque le fit ~** he blew up *ou* flared up at that remark.

explosible [ɛksplozibl] adj *mélange* explosive.

explosif, -ive [ɛksplozif, iv] adj, nm explosive.

explosion [ɛksplozjɔ̃] nf *[bombe, gaz, chaudière]* explosion. **faire ~** *[bombe, poudrière]* to explode, blow up; **~ de colère** angry outburst, explosion of anger; **~ de joie** outburst *ou* explosion of joy; *voir* **moteur**[1].

exponentiel, -ielle [ɛkspɔnɑ̃sjɛl] adj exponential.

exponentiellement [ɛkspɔnɑ̃sjɛlmɑ̃] adv exponentially.

export [ɛkspɔʀ] nm (**abrév de exportation**) export.

exportable [ɛkspɔʀtabl] adj exportable.

exportateur, -trice [ɛkspɔʀtatœʀ, tʀis] 1 adj export (*épith*), exporting. **pays ~** exporting country; **être ~ de** to export, be an exporter of. 2 nm,f exporter. **~ de pétrole** oil exporter.

exportation [ɛkspɔʀtasjɔ̃] nf (*action*) export, exportation; (*produit*) export. **faire de l'~** to export, be in the export business.

exporter [ɛkspɔʀte] [1] vt to export.

exposant, e [ɛkspozɑ̃, ɑ̃t] 1 nm,f *[foire, salon]* exhibitor. 2 nm (*Math*) exponent.

exposé [ɛkspoze] nm (*action*) account, statement, exposition (*frm*); (*conférence: gén, Scol*) talk. **faire un ~ sur** to give a talk on; **faire un ~ de la situation** to give an account *ou* overview of the situation; (*Jur*) **~ des motifs** preamble (*in bill, stating grounds for its adoption*).

exposer [ɛkspoze] [1] 1 vt a (*exhiber*) *marchandises* to put on display, display; *tableaux* to exhibit, show. **ce peintre expose dans cette galerie** that painter shows *ou* exhibits at that gallery; **c'est resté exposé pendant 3 mois** it has been on display *ou* on show for 3 months; (*frm*) **son corps est exposé dans l'église** he is lying in state in the church.

b (*expliquer*) (*gén*) to explain, state; *faits, raisons* to expound, set out, make known; *griefs* to air, make known; *théories, idées* to expound, explain, set out, put forward. **il nous exposa la situation** he explained the situation to us.

c (*mettre en danger*) (*gén*) *personne, objet* to expose (*à* to); (*Hist*) *condamné, enfant* to expose; *vie, réputation* to risk. **c'est une personnalité très exposée** his position makes him an easy target for criticism; **sa conduite l'expose à des reproches** his behaviour lays him open to censure.

d (*orienter, présenter*) to expose; (*Phot*) to expose. **~ au soleil/aux regards** to expose to sunlight/to view; **maison exposée au sud** house facing (due) south, house with a southern aspect; **maison bien exposée** well-situated house; **endroit très exposé** (*au vent, à l'ennemi*) very exposed place.

e (*Littérat*) *action* to set out; (*Mus*) *thème* to introduce.

2 **s'exposer** vpr to expose o.s. **s'~ à** *danger, reproches* to expose o.s. to, lay o.s. open to; **s'~ à des poursuites** to run the risk of prosecution, lay o.s. open to *ou* expose o.s. to prosecution; **s'~ au soleil** to stay out in the sun.

exposition [ɛkspozisjɔ̃] nf a *[marchandises]* display; *[faits, raisons, situation, idées]* exposition; *[condamné, enfant]* exposure; (*au danger, à la chaleur*) exposure (*à* to). (*Comm*) **grande ~ de blanc** special linen week *ou* event. b (*foire, salon*) exhibition, show. **l'E~ universelle** the World Fair. c (*Phot*) exposure. d (*Littérat, Mus*) exposition. **scène d'~** expository *ou* introductory scene. e (*orientation*) *[maison]* aspect.

exprès[1] [ɛkspʀɛ] adv (*spécialement*) specially; (*intentionnellement*) on purpose, deliberately, intentionally. **venir (tout) ~ pour** to come specially to; **il l'a fait ~** he did it on purpose *ou* deliberately *ou* intentionally; **il ne l'a pas fait ~** he didn't do it on purpose, he didn't mean to do it; **c'est fait ~** it's meant to be like that, it's deliberate; **et par *ou* comme un fait ~ il l'avait perdu** by some (almost) deliberate coincidence he had lost it, it would have to happen that he had lost it.

exprès[2]**, -esse** [ɛkspʀɛs] adj a *interdiction, ordre* formal, express; (*Jur*) *clause* express. b (inv) **(lettre/colis) ~** express (*Brit*) *ou* special delivery (*US*) letter/parcel; **(messager) ~**† express messenger; **envoyer qch en ~** to send sth by express post (*Brit*) *ou* special delivery (*US*), send sth express (*Brit*).

express [ɛkspʀɛs] adj, nm inv: **(train) ~** fast train; **(café) ~** espresso (coffee).

expressément [ɛkspʀesemɑ̃] adv (*formellement*) expressly; (*spécialement*) specially.

expressif, -ive [ɛkspʀesif, iv] adj *geste, regard,* expressive, meaningful; *physionomie* expressive; *langage* expressive, vivid.

expression [ɛkspʀesjɔ̃] nf a (*gén*) expression. **au-delà de toute ~** beyond (all) expression, inexpressible; **veuillez agréer l'~ de mes sentiments les meilleurs** yours faithfully (*Brit*), yours truly (*US*); **visage plein d'~/sans ~** expressive/expressionless face; **jouer avec beaucoup d'~** to play with great feeling *ou* expression; **~ corporelle** self-expression through movement; **journal d'~ française/anglaise** French/English-language newspaper; *voir* **liberté, moyen, réduire.**

b (*Math: formule*) expression; (*Gram: locution*) phrase, expression. **~ figée** set *ou* fixed expression, set phrase; **~ toute faite** cliché, hack phrase; **~ nominale** nominal; (*fig*) **réduit à sa plus simple ~** reduced to its simplest terms *ou* expression.

expressionnisme [ɛkspʀesjɔnism] nm expressionism.

expressionniste [ɛkspʀesjɔnist] 1 adj expressionist (*épith*), expressionistic. 2 nmf expressionist.

expressivement [ɛkspʀesivmɑ̃] adv expressively.

expressivité [ɛkspʀesivite] nf expressiveness.

exprimable [ɛkspʀimabl] adj expressible.

exprimer [ɛkspʀime] 1 1 vt a (*signifier*) to express; *pensée* to express, give expression *ou* utterance to (*frm*); *opinion* to voice, express. **mots qui expriment un sens** words which express *ou* convey a meaning; **regards qui expriment la colère** looks which express *ou* indicate anger; **œuvre qui exprime parfaitement l'artiste** work which expresses the artist completely.
b (*Écon, Math*) to express. **somme exprimée en francs** sum expressed in francs; **le signe + exprime l'addition** the sign + indicates *ou* stands for addition.
c (*littér*) *jus* to press out.
2 **s'exprimer** vpr to express o.s. **s'~ par gestes** to use gestures to express o.s.; **je me suis peut-être mal exprimé** perhaps I have expressed myself badly, perhaps I have put it badly *ou* not made myself clear; **si je peux m'~ ainsi** if I may put it like that; (*fig*) **il faut permettre au talent de s'~** talent must be allowed free expression *ou* to express itself; **la joie s'exprima sur son visage** (his) joy showed in his expression, his face expressed his joy.

expropriation [ɛkspʀɔpʀijasjɔ̃] nf (*action*) expropriation, compulsory purchase (*Brit*); (*arrêté*) expropriation order, compulsory purchase order (*Brit*).

exproprier [ɛkspʀɔpʀije] 7 vt *propriété* to expropriate, place a compulsory purchase order on (*Brit*). **ils ont été expropriés** their land has been expropriated, they have had a compulsory purchase order made on their land.

expulser [ɛkspylse] 1 vt (*gén*) *élève* to expel (*de* from); *étranger* to deport, expel (*de* from); *locataire* to evict (*de* from), throw out (*de* of); (*Ftbl*) *joueur* to send off; *manifestant* to eject (*de* from), throw out, turn out (*de* of); (*Anat*) *déchets* to evacuate, excrete.

expulsion [ɛkspylsjɔ̃] nf (*voir* **expulser**) expulsion; deportation; eviction; throwing out; ejection; turning out; sending off; evacuation, excretion (*de* from).

expurger [ɛkspyʀʒe] 3 vt to expurgate, bowdlerize. **version expurgée** sanitized *ou* expurgated *ou* bowdlerized version.

exquis, -ise [ɛkski, iz] adj *plat, choix, politesse* exquisite; *personne, temps* delightful.

exsangue [ɛksɑ̃g] adj *visage, lèvres* bloodless; (*fig*) *littérature* anaemic. **les guerres/impôts ont laissé le pays ~** wars/taxes have bled the country white.

exsudation [ɛksydasjɔ̃] nf (*frm*) exudation (*frm*).

exsuder [ɛksyde] vti (*frm*) (*lit*) to exude. (*fig*) **son visage exsude la joie** his face radiates joy.

extase [ɛkstɑz] nf (*Rel*) ecstasy; (*sexuelle*) climax; (*fig*) ecstasy, rapture. **il est en ~ devant sa fille** he is rapturous about his daughter, he goes into raptures over his daughter; **tomber/rester en ~ devant un tableau** to go into ecstasies at/stand in ecstasy before a painting.

extasié, e [ɛkstɑzje] (ptp **de s'extasier**) adj ecstatic, enraptured.

extasier (s') [ɛkstɑzje] 7 vpr to go into ecstasies *ou* raptures (*devant, sur* over).

extatique [ɛkstatik] adj ecstatic, enraptured.

extenseur [ɛkstɑ̃sœʀ] 1 adj: **(muscle) ~** extensor. 2 nm (*Sport*) chest expander.

extensibilité [ɛkstɑ̃sibilite] nf extensibility.

extensible [ɛkstɑ̃sibl] adj *matière* extensible; *définition* extendable.

extensif, -ive [ɛkstɑ̃sif, iv] adj (*Agr*) *culture* extensive; *sens* wide, extensive.

extension [ɛkstɑ̃sjɔ̃] nf a (*étirement*) *[membre, ressort]* stretching; (*Méd*) *[membre]* traction. **le ressort atteint son ~ maximum** the spring is fully stretched *ou* is stretched to its maximum. b (*augmentation*) *[épidémie, grève, incendie]* extension, spreading; *[commerce, domaine]* expansion; *[pouvoirs]* extension, expansion. **prendre de l'~** *[épidémie]* to spread, extend, develop; *[entreprise]* to expand. c (*élargissement*) *[loi, mesure, sens d'un mot]* extension (*à* to); (*Logique*) extension. **par ~ (de sens)** by extension.

exténuant, e [ɛkstenyɑ̃, ɑ̃t] adj exhausting.

exténuer [ɛkstenɥe] 1 1 vt to exhaust, tire out. 2 **s'exténuer** vpr to exhaust o.s., tire o.s. out (*à faire qch* doing sth).

extérieur, e [ɛksteʀjœʀ] 1 adj a (*à un lieu*) *paroi* outer, outside, exterior; *escalier, W.-C.* outside; *quartier, cour, boulevard* outer; *bruit* external, outside; *décoration* exterior, outside; *collaborateur* outside. **apparence ~e** *[personne]* outward appearance; *[maison]* outside.
b (*à l'individu*) *monde, influences* external, outside; *activité, intérêt* outside; *réalité* external. **signes ~s de richesse** outward signs of wealth; **manifestation ~e de colère** outward show *ou* display of anger.
c (*étranger*) *commerce, vente* external, foreign; *politique, nouvelles* foreign.
d (*superficiel*) *amabilité* surface (*épith*), superficial. **sa gaieté est toute ~e** his gaiety is all on the surface *ou* all an outward display.
e (*sans relation avec*) **être ~ à une question/un sujet** to be external to *ou* outside a question/a subject, be beyond the scope of a question/a subject; **c'est tout à fait ~ à moi** it has nothing to do with me, it doesn't concern me in the least; **rester ~ à un conflit/une affaire** to stay *ou* keep out of a conflict/matter; **"interdit à toute personne ~e à l'usine/au chantier"** "factory employees/site workers only", "no entry for unauthorised personnel".
f (*Géom*) *angle* exterior.
2 nm a *[objet, maison]* outside, exterior; *[piste, circuit etc]* outside. *[joueur]* **il l'a débordé par l'~** he overtook him on the outside.
b **à l'~** (*au dehors*) outside; (*Sport*) away; **c'est à l'~ (de la ville)** it's outside (the town); (*fig*) **juger qch de l'~** (*d'après son apparence*) to judge sth by appearances; (*en tant que profane*) to judge sth from the outside.
c (*pays etc*) **l'~** (*gén*) the outside world; (*pays étrangers*) foreign countries; **entretenir de bonnes relations avec l'~** to have good foreign relations; **vendre beaucoup à l'~** to sell a lot abroad *ou* to foreign countries; **recevoir des nouvelles de l'~** to have news from abroad; **cellule sans communication avec l'~** cell without communication with the outside world.
d (*Ciné*) **~s** location shots; **prises de vues/tourner en ~** shots taken/to shoot on location; **les ~s ont été tournés à Paris** the shots on location were taken in Paris.
e (*frm: apparence*) exterior, (outward) appearance.

extérieurement [ɛksteʀjœʀmɑ̃] adv a (*du dehors*) on the outside, externally. b (*en apparence*) on the surface, outwardly.

extériorisation [ɛksteʀjɔʀizasjɔ̃] nf *[joie etc]* display, outward expression; (*Psych*) externalization, exteriorization.

extérioriser [ɛksteʀjɔʀize] 1 vt *joie etc* to show, express; (*Psych*) to exteriorize, externalize. **les enfants ont besoin de s'~** (*personnalité*) children need to express themselves.

extériorité [ɛksteʀjɔʀite] nf (*Philos*) exteriority.

exterminateur, -trice [ɛkstɛʀminatœʀ, tʀis] 1 adj exterminating; *voir* **ange**. 2 nm,f exterminator.

extermination [ɛkstɛʀminasjɔ̃] nf extermination; *voir* **camp**.

exterminer [ɛkstɛʀmine] 1 vt (*lit, fig*) to exterminate, wipe out.

externat [ɛkstɛʀna] nm (*Scol*) day school. (*Méd*) **faire son ~ à** to be a non-resident student *ou* an extern (*US*) at.

externe [ɛkstɛʀn] 1 adj *surface etc* external, outer; *angle* exterior. **à usage ~** for external use only, not to be taken (internally). 2 nmf (*Scol*) day pupil. (*Méd*) **~ (des hôpitaux)** non-resident student at a teaching hospital, extern (*US*).

exterritorialité [ɛksteʀitɔʀjalite] nf exterritoriality.

extincteur, -trice [ɛkstɛ̃ktœʀ, tʀis] 1 adj extinguishing. 2 nm (fire) extinguisher.

extinction [ɛkstɛ̃ksjɔ̃] nf *[incendie, lumières]* extinction, extinguishing, putting out; (*fig*) *[peuple]* extinction, dying out; (*Jur*) *[dette, droit]* extinguishment. **~ de voix** loss of voice, aphonia (*SPÉC*); **avoir une ~ de voix** to lose one's voice; (*Mil, fig*) **avant l'~ des feux** before lights out; **espèce en voie d'~** endangered species.

extirpation [ɛkstiʀpasjɔ̃] nf (*voir* **extirper**) eradication; extirpation; rooting out; pulling up, pulling out.

extirper [ɛkstiʀpe] 1 vt (*littér*) *abus, vice* to eradicate, extirpate, (*littér*) root out; (*Chirurgie*) to extirpate; *herbes* to root out, pull up, pull out. **impossible de lui ~ une parole*** it's impossible to drag *ou* get a word out of him!; **~ qn de son lit*** to drag *ou* haul sb out of bed; **s'~ de son manteau** to extricate o.s. from one's coat.

extorquer [ɛkstɔʀke] 1 vt to extort (*à qn* from sb).

extorqueur, -euse [ɛkstɔʀkœʀ, øz] nm,f extortioner.

extorsion [ɛkstɔʀsjɔ̃] nf extortion. **~ de fonds** extortion of money.

extra [ɛkstʀa] 1 nm inv (*domestique*) extra servant *ou* help; (*gâterie*) (special) treat. **s'offrir un ~** to give o.s. a treat, treat o.s. to something special.
2 adj inv (*Comm: supérieur*) *fromage, vin* first-rate, extra-special; *tissu* top-quality; (*: *excellent*) *film, week-end, personne* fantastic*, terrific*, great*. (*Comm*) **de qualité ~** of the finest *ou* best quality.
3 comp ▸**extra-fin, e** adj *haricots, petits pois* superfine; *aiguille* extra fine ▸**extra-fort, e** adj *carton, moutarde* extra strong ◊ nm (*Couture*) bias binding ▸**extra-légal, e** adj extra-legal ▸**extra-linguistique** adj extralinguistic ▸**(voyante) extra-lucide** clairvoyant ▸**extra-muros** adj, adv outside the town ▸**extra-parlementaire** adj extra-parliamentary ▸**extra-sensible** adj extra-sensible ▸**extra-sensoriel, -elle** adj *perception* extrasensory ▸**extra-terrestre** adj, nmf extra-terrestrial ▸**extra-territorialité** nf extraterritoriality ▸**extra-utérin, e** adj extra-uterine.

extraconjugal, e, mpl **-aux** [ɛkstʀakɔ̃ʒygal, o] adj extramarital.

extracteur [ɛkstʀaktœʀ] nm extractor.

extractif, -ive [ɛkstʀaktif, iv] adj *industrie etc* extractive, mining.

extraction [ɛkstʀaksjɔ̃] nf a *[pétrole]* extraction; *[charbon]* mining; *[marbre]* quarrying. b (*Math, Méd*) extraction. c (*††: origine*) **de haute/basse ~** of noble/mean extraction *ou* descent, of high/low birth.

extrader [ɛkstʀade] 1 vt to extradite.

extradition [ɛkstʀadisjɔ̃] nf extradition.

extraire [ɛkstʀɛʀ] 50 vt a *minerai, pétrole* to extract; *charbon* to mine; *marbre* to quarry. b *gaz, jus* to extract. **~ un liquide en pressant/en tordant** *etc* to squeeze out/wring out *etc* a liquid. c *dent* to extract, pull out; *clou* to pull out; (*Math*) *racine* to extract; *balle* to extract, remove (*de* from). **d** ~ **de** *poche, placard* to take *ou* bring *ou* dig* out of; *prison, avalanche* to rescue from, get out of; **passage extrait d'un livre** extract from a book, passage taken from a book; **s'~ de son manteau*** to extricate o.s. from one's coat; **s'~ de sa voiture** to climb out of one's car.

extrait [ɛkstʀɛ] **nm** *[discours, journal]* extract; *[livre, auteur]* extract, excerpt; (*Admin*) extract (*de* from). ~ **de lavande** *etc* essence *ou* extract of lavender *etc*; ~ **de viande** beef extract; ~ **de naissance** *etc* birth *etc* certificate; (*Fin*) ~ **de compte** abstract of accounts.

extraordinaire [ɛkstʀaɔʀdinɛʀ] **adj** **a** (*étrange*) *événement, costume, opinions* extraordinary. **l'~ est que** the extraordinary thing is that. **b** (*exceptionnel*) *beauté* exceptional; *succès, force* extraordinary, exceptional. **c'est un acteur** ~ he's an extraordinary *ou* a remarkable actor; **ce roman n'est pas** ~ this novel isn't up to much*, there's nothing particularly good *ou* very special about this novel. **c** (*Pol*) *moyens, mesures, assemblée* special; *voir* **ambassadeur**. **d** **si par** ~ if by some unlikely chance; **quand par** ~ on those rare occasions when.

extraordinairement [ɛkstʀaɔʀdinɛʀmɑ̃] **adv** (*exceptionnellement*) extraordinarily, exceptionally; (*d'une manière étrange*) extraordinarily.

extraplat, e [ɛkstʀapla, at] **adj** *télévision, montre etc* flat.

extrapolation [ɛkstʀapɔlasjɔ̃] **nf** extrapolation.

extrapoler [ɛkstʀapɔle] [1] **vti** to extrapolate (*à partir de* from).

extrascolaire [ɛkstʀaskɔlɛʀ] **adj** *activités* extracurricular.

extravagance [ɛkstʀavagɑ̃s] **nf** **a** (*caractère*) *[costume, conduite]* eccentricity, extravagance. **b** (*acte*) eccentric *ou* extravagant behaviour (*NonC*). **dire des ~s** to talk wildly *ou* extravagantly.

extravagant, e [ɛkstʀavagɑ̃, ɑ̃t] **adj** *idée, théorie* extravagant, wild, crazy; *prix* excessive, extravagant.

extraversion [ɛkstʀavɛʀsjɔ̃] **nf** = **extroversion**.

extraverti, e [ɛkstʀavɛʀti] **adj, nm,f** = **extroverti**.

extrême [ɛkstʀɛm] **1** **adj** **a** (*le plus éloigné*) extreme, furthest. **à l'~ bout de la table** at the far *ou* furthest end of the table, at the very end of the table; **dans son ~ jeunesse** in his very young days, in his earliest youth; **à l'~ opposé** at the opposite extreme (*de* of); (*Pol*) **l'~-droite** the far right.
b (*le plus intense*) extreme, utmost. **dans la misère ~** in extreme *ou* the utmost poverty; **c'est avec un plaisir ~ que** it is with the greatest *ou* the utmost pleasure that; **il m'a reçu avec une ~ amabilité** he received me in the friendliest possible way *ou* with the utmost kindness; **il fait une chaleur ~** it is extremely hot; **d'une pâleur/difficulté ~** extremely pale/difficult; *voir* **rigueur, urgence**.
c (*après n: excessif, radical*) *théories, moyens* extreme. **ça l'a conduit à des mesures ~s** that drove him into taking drastic *ou* extreme steps; **il a un caractère ~** he tends to go to extremes, he is an extremist by nature.
2 **nm** **a** (*opposé*) extreme. **les ~s se touchent** extremes meet; **passer d'un ~ à l'autre** to go from one extreme to the other *ou* to another.
b (*Math*) ~s extremes.
c **à l'~, jusqu'à l'~** in the extreme, to a degree; **cela lui répugnait à l'~** he was extremely loath to do it; **noircir une situation à l'~** to paint the blackest possible picture of a situation; **scrupuleux à l'~** scrupulous to a fault.
3 **comp** ►**extrême droite/gauche** extreme right/left (wing), far right/left ►**extrême-onction** **nf** Extreme Unction ►**Extrême-Orient** **nm** Far East ►**extrême-oriental, e** (**mpl extrême-orientaux**) **adj** far eastern, oriental; **les Extrêmes Orientaux** Orientals.

extrêmement [ɛkstʀɛmmɑ̃] **adv** extremely, exceedingly.

extrémisme [ɛkstʀemism] **nm** extremism.

extrémiste [ɛkstʀemist] **adj, nmf** extremist.

extrémité [ɛkstʀemite] **nf** **a** (*bout*) (*gén*) end; *[aiguille]* point; *[objet mince]* tip; *[village, île]* extremity, limit; *[lac, péninsule]* head.
b (*frm: situation critique*) plight, straits. **être dans la pénible ~ de devoir** to be in the unfortunate necessity of having to; **réduit à la dernière ~** in the most dire plight *ou* straits; **être à toute ~, être à la dernière ~** to be on the point of death.
c (*frm: action excessive*) extremes, extreme lengths. **se porter à une ~** *ou* **à des ~s** to go to extremes; **pousser qn à une ~** *ou* **à des ~s** to push *ou* drive sb to extremes *ou* into taking extreme action; **se livrer à des ~s (sur qn)** to assault sb; **d'une ~ dans l'autre** from one extreme to another.
d (*Anat: pieds et mains*) ~s extremities.

extroversion [ɛkstʀɔvɛʀsjɔ̃] **nf** extroversion.

extroverti, e [ɛkstʀɔvɛʀti] **adj, nm,f** extrovert.

extruder [ɛkstʀyde] [1] **vt** to extrude.

extrusion [ɛkstʀyzjɔ̃] **nf** extrusion.

exubérance [ɛgzybeʀɑ̃s] **nf** (*caractère*) exuberance (*NonC*); (*action*) exuberant behaviour (*NonC*) (*ou* talk (*NonC*) *etc*). **parler avec ~** to speak exuberantly.

exubérant, e [ɛgzybeʀɑ̃, ɑ̃t] **adj** (*gén*) exuberant.

exultation [ɛgzyltasjɔ̃] **nf** exultation.

exulter [ɛgzylte] [1] **vi** to exult.

exutoire [ɛgzytwaʀ] **nm** outlet, release (*à* of).

ex-voto [ɛksvɔto] **nm inv** thanksgiving *ou* commemorative plaque.

eye-liner [ajlajnœʀ] **nm** eyeliner.

Ézéchiel [ezekjɛl] **nm** Ezekiel. **(le livre d')** ~ (the Book of) Ezekiel.

F1, f [ɛf] **nm** (*lettre*) F, f. (**abrév de franc**) **F** F, fr; (*appartement*) **un F2** a 2-roomed flat (*Brit*) *ou* apartment (*US*).

F2 a (**abrév de Fahrenheit**) F. b **abrév de frère**.

fa [fɑ] **nm inv** (*Mus*) F; (*en chantant la gamme*) fa; *voir* **clef**.

FAB [ɛfabe] (**abrév de franco à bord**) FOB.

fable [fɑbl] **nf** (*genre*) fable; (*légende*) fable, legend; (*mensonge*) tale, story, fable. **quelle ~ va-t-il inventer?** what yarn *ou* tale will he spin?; **être la ~ de toute la ville**† to be the laughing stock of the whole town.

fabliau, **pl ~x** [fɑblijo] **nm** fabliau.

fablier [fɑblije] **nm** book of fables.

fabricant, e [fabʀikɑ̃, ɑ̃t] **nm,f** manufacturer. **~ de papier** paper manufacturer *ou* maker; **~ d'automobiles** car manufacturer; **~ de pneus** tyre-maker.

fabricateur, -trice [fabʀikatœʀ, tʀis] **nm,f**: **~ (de fausse monnaie)** counterfeiter, forger; **~ (de fausses nouvelles)** fabricator, spinner of yarns; **~ (de faux papiers)** forger (of documents), counterfeiter.

fabrication [fabʀikasjɔ̃] **nf** a (*industrielle*) manufacture, manufacturing; (*artisanale, personnelle*) making. **la ~ industrielle/en série** factory *ou* industrial/mass production; **~ par lots** batch production; **de ~ française** made in France, French-made, of French make; **de ~ étrangère** of foreign make *ou* manufacture; **de ~ artisanale** produced *ou* made on a small scale; **bombe de ~ artisanale** home-made bomb; **de bonne ~** well-made, of good *ou* high-quality workmanship; **~ assistée par ordinateur** computer-assisted *ou* computer-aided manufacturing; **un romancier réduit à la ~ en série** a novelist reduced to churning out novels by the dozen *ou* to mass-producing his works; **une robe de sa ~** a dress of her own making, a dress she has (*ou* had *etc*) made herself; *voir* **défaut, secret**.
b *[faux]* forging; *[fausses nouvelles]* fabricating, making up. **~ de fausse monnaie** counterfeiting *ou* forging money.

fabrique [fabʀik] **nf** a (*établissement*) factory. **~ de gants** glove factory; **~ de papier** paper mill; *voir* **marque, prix**. b (*littér: fabrication, facture*) workmanship. **de bonne ~** well-made, of good *ou* high-quality workmanship. c (*Rel*) **la ~** the fabric.

fabriquer [fabʀike] 1 **vt** a *meuble, outil, chaussures* (*industriellement*) to manufacture; (*de façon artisanale, chez soi*) to make; *faux* to forge; *fausses nouvelles* to fabricate, make up; *incident, histoire* to fabricate, invent, make up. **~ de la fausse monnaie** to counterfeit *ou* forge money; **~ en série** to mass-produce; **~ industriellement** to manufacture, produce industrially; **~ sur commande** *ou* **sur mesure** to make to order; **~ de façon artisanale** to handcraft, make *ou* produce on a small scale; **c'est une histoire fabriquée de toutes pièces** this story is all made up *ou* is a complete fabrication from start to finish; **il s'est fabriqué un personnage de prophète** he created *ou* invented a prophet-like character for himself; **il s'est fabriqué un poste de radio/une cabane** he built *ou* made himself a radio set/a shed.
b (*: *faire*) **qu'est-ce qu'il fabrique?** what (on earth) is he doing? *ou* is he up to?*; **des fois, je me demande ce que je fabrique ici!** sometimes I really wonder what the heck I'm doing here!*

fabulateur, -trice [fabylatœʀ, tʀis] 1 **adj** (*d'imagination*) **faculté ~trice** faculty for fantasizing; (*de mythomanie*) **tendance ~trice** tendency to fabricate *ou* spin stories. 2 **nm,f** storyteller.

fabulation [fabylasjɔ̃] **nf** (*fait d'imaginer*) fantasizing; (*fait de mentir*) storytelling; (*fable*) tale, fable; (*mensonge*) story, yarn, tale.

fabuler [fabyle] 1 **vi** to fantasize.

fabuleusement [fabyløzmɑ̃] **adv** fabulously, fantastically.

fabuleux, -euse [fabylø, øz] **adj** a (*littér*) (*des temps anciens, de la mythologie*) mythical, legendary; (*de la légende, du merveilleux*) fabulous. b (*intensif: prodigieux*) *richesse, exploits, vitesse* fabulous, fantastic.

fabuliste [fabylist] **nm** writer of fables *ou* tales.

fac [fak] **nf** (*arg Univ*) **abrév de faculté**.

façade [fasad] **nf** a (*devant de maison*) (*gén*) façade, front, frontage; (*Archéol*) façade; (*côté de maison*) side; *[magasin]* front, frontage. **~ latérale** side wall; **~ ouest** west side *ou* wall; **la ~ arrière de la maison** the back of the house; **les ~s des magasins** the shop fronts; **3 pièces en ~** 3 rooms at *ou* facing the front.
b (*fig*) (*apparence*) façade, appearance; (*couverture*) cover. **~ d'honnêteté/de vertu** façade *ou* outward show *ou* appearance of honesty/virtue; **ce n'est qu'une ~** it's just a front *ou* façade, it's a mere pretence; **de ~** *luxe, vertu, foi* sham; **ce restaurant est une ~ qui cache un tripot clandestin** this restaurant is a cover for an illegal dive.
c (⁑: *figure*) **se refaire la ~** (*se maquiller*) to redo one's face*; (*se faire faire un lifting*) to have a face-lift, have a face job*; **il va te démolir la ~** he's going to smash your mug *ou* face in⁑.

face [fas] 1 **nf** a (*frm, Méd: visage*) face. **les blessés de la ~** people with facial injuries; **tomber ~ contre terre** to fall flat on the ground *ou* flat on one's face; **se prosterner ~ contre terre** to prostrate o.s. with one's face to the ground; **~ de rat/de singe⁑** rat/monkey face⁑; **sauver/perdre la ~** to save/lose face; **opération destinée à sauver la ~** face-saving move; *voir* **voiler1**.
b (*côté*) *[disque, objet]* side; *[médaille, pièce de monnaie]* front, obverse; (*Math*) *[cube, figure]* side, face; (*Alpinisme*) face, wall. **la ~ cachée de la lune** the hidden face *ou* side of the moon; **mets l'autre ~ (du disque)** put on *ou* play the other side (of the record), turn the record over; (*fig*) **question à double ~** two-sided question; (*lit, fig*) **examiner un objet/une question sous** *ou* **sur toutes ses ~s** to examine an object/a problem from all sides; **la pièce est tombée sur ~** *ou* **côté ~** the coin fell face up; (*jeu de pile ou face*) **~!** heads!; *voir* **pile**.
c (*aspect*) face. **la ~ changeante des choses** the changing face of things; **le monde a changé de ~** (the face of) the world has changed.
d (*littér: surface*) **la ~ de la terre** *ou* **du globe** the face of the earth; **la ~ de l'océan** the surface *ou* face of the ocean.
e (*loc*) **faire ~** to face (up to) things; **faire ~ à** *lieu, objet, personne* to face, be opposite; *épreuve, adversaire, obligation* to face up to, face; *dette, engagement* to meet; **se faire ~** *[maisons]* to be facing *ou* opposite each other; *[adversaires]* to be face to face; **il a dû faire ~ à des dépenses élevées** he has been faced with *ou* he has had to face considerable expense.
f **à la ~ de: il éclata de rire à la ~ de son professeur** he burst out laughing in his teacher's face; **proclamer à la ~ de l'univers** *ou* **du monde** to proclaim to the universe *ou* to the whole world *ou* to the world at large.
g **en ~ de** (*en vis à vis de*) opposite; (*en présence de*) in front of; **au banquet, on les a mis l'un en ~ de l'autre** *ou* **en ~ l'un de l'autre** at the banquet, they were placed opposite each other *ou* facing each other; **les deux ennemis étaient maintenant l'un en ~ de l'autre** the two enemies now stood facing each other *ou* face to face *ou* were now face to face; **il n'ose rien dire en ~ de son patron** he daren't say anything in front of his boss; **ne te mets pas en ~ de moi/de ma lumière** don't stand in my way/in my light; (*fig*) **se trouver en ~ d'un danger/problème** to be confronted *ou* faced with a danger/problem; (*fig*) **en ~ de cela** on the other hand.
h **en ~** (*directement, ouvertement*): **regarder qn (bien) en ~** to look sb (straight) in the face; **il lui a dit en ~ ce qu'il pensait de lui** he told him to his face what he thought of him; **regarder la mort en ~** to look death in the face; **il faut voir les choses en ~** one must see things as they are, one must face facts; **avoir le soleil en ~** to have the sun in one's eyes.
i **en ~** (*de l'autre côté de la rue*) across the street, opposite, over the road; **j'habite en ~** I live across the street *ou* over the road *ou* opposite; **la maison d'en ~** the house across the street *ou* over the road *ou* opposite; **le trottoir d'en ~** the opposite pavement, the pavement on the other *ou* opposite side; **la dame d'en ~** the lady (from) across the street *ou* (from) over the road, the lady opposite.
j **de ~** *portrait* fullface; *nu, portrait en pied* frontal; *attaque* frontal; *place* (*au théâtre*) in the centre, facing the front of the stage; (*dans le train etc*) facing the engine; **voir qn de ~** to see sb face on; **attaquer de**

~ to make a frontal attack (on), attack from the front; **un personnage/cheval de** ~ the front view of a person/horse; **avoir une vue de** ~ **sur qch** to have a front view of sth; **assis de** ~ **dans l'autobus** sitting facing the front of the bus, sitting facing forward in the bus; **avoir le vent de** ~ to have the wind in one's face.

k ~ **à** facing; **il se dressa** ~ **à l'ennemi** he positioned himself facing the enemy; ~ **à ces problèmes, il se sentait impuissant** faced with *ou* in the face of such problems, he felt helpless; ~ **à** ~ *lieux, objets* opposite *ou* facing each other; *personnes, animaux* face to face, facing each other; ~ **à** ~ **avec** *lieu, objet* opposite, facing; *personne, animal* face to face with; ~ **à** ~ **avec une difficulté** faced with *ou* up against a difficulty.

2 **comp** ▸**face à face nm inv** (*rencontre, gén, TV*) encounter, interview ▸**face-à-main nm (pl faces-à-main)** lorgnette.

facétie [fasesi] **nf** (*drôlerie*) joke; (*farce*) prank, trick. **faire des** ~**s** to play pranks *ou* tricks; **dire des** ~**s** to crack jokes.

facétieusement [fasesjøzmɑ̃] **adv** (*voir* **facétieux**) facetiously, impishly, mischievously; humorously.

facétieux, -ieuse [fasesjø, jøz] **adj** (*espiègle*) facetious, impish, mischievous; (*comique*) humorous.

facette [fasɛt] **nf** (*lit, fig*) facet. **à** ~**s** *pierre* faceted; *caractère, personnage* many-faceted, many-sided; (*Bio*) **yeux à** ~**s** compound eyes.

facetter [fasete] [1] **vt** to facet.

fâché, e [fɑʃe] (**ptp de fâcher**) **adj** a (*en colère, mécontent*) angry, cross (*contre* with). **elle a l'air** ~**(e)** she looks cross *ou* angry; **tu n'es pas** ~**, au moins?** you're not angry *ou* cross with me, are you?

b (*brouillé*) **ils sont** ~**s** they have fallen out, they are on bad terms; **elle est** ~**e avec moi** she has fallen out with me; (*hum*) **il est** ~ **avec les chiffres** he's hopeless with numbers; (*hum*) **il est** ~ **avec l'orthographe** he can't spell to save himself.

c (*contrarié*) sorry (*de qch* about sth). (*frm*) **je suis** ~ **de ne pas pouvoir vous aider** I am sorry that I cannot help you; **je ne suis pas** ~ **d'avoir fini ce travail** I'm not sorry to have finished this job; (*hum*) **je ne serais pas** ~ **que vous me laissiez tranquille** I wouldn't mind being left alone *ou* in peace, I wouldn't object to a bit of peace and quiet.

fâcher [fɑʃe] [1] 1 **vt** a (*mettre en colère*) to anger, make angry, vex. **tu ne réussiras qu'à le** ~ **davantage** you will only make him more angry *ou* angrier.

b (*frm: contrarier*) to grieve (*frm*), distress. **cette triste nouvelle me fâche beaucoup** this sad news grieves me (*frm*) *ou* greatly distresses me.

2 **se fâcher vpr** a (*se mettre en colère*) to get angry, lose one's temper. **se** ~ **contre qn/pour** *ou* **au sujet de qch** to get angry *ou* annoyed with sb/about *ou* over sth; (*hum*) **se** ~ **tout rouge*** to get really cross, blow one's top* (*hum*) (*contre qn* at sb); (*hum*) **si tu continues, je vais me** ~ **tout rouge*** if you go on like that, I'll get really cross *ou* you'll make me really cross.

b (*se brouiller*) to quarrel, fall out (*avec* with). **ils se sont fâchés à mort à propos d'une femme** they quarrelled bitterly over a woman.

fâcherie [fɑʃʀi] **nf** (*brouille*) quarrel.

fâcheusement [fɑʃøzmɑ̃] **adv** *survenir* (most) unfortunately *ou* awkwardly. ~ **surpris** (most) unpleasantly surprised.

fâcheux, -euse [fɑʃø, øz] 1 **adj** (*blâmable*) *exemple, influence, décision* deplorable, regrettable, unfortunate; (*ennuyeux*) *coïncidence, incident, situation* unfortunate, awkward, regrettable, tiresome. **il est** ~ **qu'il ait cru devoir s'abstenir** it's unfortunate *ou* a pity that he felt it necessary to abstain; **le** ~ **dans tout ça c'est que ...** the unfortunate *ou* annoying *ou* tiresome thing about it (all) is that ... . 2 **nm,f** (*littér: importun*) bore.

facho* [faʃo] **nmf** (**abrév de fasciste**) (*péj*) fascist. **il est un peu** ~ he's a bit of a fascist.

facial, e, mpl ~**s** *ou* **-iaux** [fasjal, jo] **adj** facial; *voir* **angle**.

faciès [fasjɛs] **nm** a (*visage*) features; (*Ethnologie, Méd*) facies. b (*Bot, Géog*) facies.

facile [fasil] 1 **adj** a (*aisé*) *travail, problème* easy (*à faire* to do). ~ **d'accès, d'accès** ~ easy to reach *ou* get to, of easy access; **avoir la vie** ~ to live *ou* have an easy life; **ils ne lui rendent pas la vie** ~ they don't make life easy for him; **plus** ~ **à dire qu'à faire** easier said than done; **c'est trop** ~ **de s'indigner** it's too easy to get indignant; **ce n'est pas si** ~ it's not as simple as that; ~ **comme tout***, ~ **comme bonjour*** (as) easy as pie*, dead easy* (*Brit*).

b (*spontané*) **avoir la parole** ~ (*parler aisément*) to be a fluent *ou* an articulate speaker, have a fluent tongue; (*parler volontiers*) to have a ready tongue *ou* the gift of the gab*; **il a la plume** ~ (*écrire aisément*) he has an eloquent pen; (*être toujours prêt à écrire*) he finds it easy to write, writing comes easily to him; **avoir la larme** ~ to be quick to shed a tear, be easily moved to tears; **il a l'argent** ~* he's very casual about money, money just slips through his fingers; **avoir la gachette** ~ to be trigger-happy; **il a le couteau** ~ he's all too quick to use his knife, he's very ready with his knife.

c (*péj*) (*superficiel*) **effet/ironie** ~ facile effect/irony; **littérature** ~ cheap literature.

d *caractère* easy-going. **il est d'humeur** ~ he is easy-going; **il est** ~ **à vivre/contenter** he's easy to get on with (*Brit*) *ou* along with/to please; **il n'est pas** ~ **tous les jours** he's not always easy to get on with (*Brit*) *ou* along with; **c'est un bébé très** ~ he's a very easy baby.

e (*péj*) *femme* loose (*épith*), of easy virtue. **une fille** ~ a woman of easy virtue.

2 **adv** (*) (*facilement*) easily; (*au moins*) at least, easily. **il y est arrivé** ~ he managed it easily; **il fait du 200 km/h** ~ he's doing at least *ou* easily 200 km/h; **elle a 50 ans** ~ she's easily 50, she's 50 anyway*.

facilement [fasilmɑ̃] **adv** (*gén*) easily. **médicament** ~ **toléré par l'organisme** medicine easily *ou* readily tolerated by the body; **il se fâche** ~ he loses his temper *ou* gets cross easily, he's quick-tempered; **on met** ~ **10 jours*** it takes 10 days easily *ou* at least 10 days.

facilité [fasilite] **nf** a (*simplicité*) *[devoir, problème, travail]* easiness. **aimer la** ~ to like things that are easy *ou* simple; **tâche d'une grande** ~ extremely easy *ou* straightforward task.

b (*aisance*) *[succès, victoire]* ease; *[expression, style]* fluency, ease. **il a choisi la** ~ **en ne venant pas** he took the easy way out by not coming; **réussir qch avec** ~ to manage sth with ease; **la** ~ **avec laquelle il a appris le piano** the ease with which he learnt the piano, the ease he had in learning the piano; **il travaille avec** ~ he works with ease; **il s'exprime avec** ~ *ou* **avec une grande** ~ **de parole** he expresses himself with (great) fluency *ou* ease *ou* (very) articulately *ou* fluently; *voir* **solution**.

c (*aptitude*) ability, aptitude. **cet élève a beaucoup de** ~ this pupil has great ability *ou* aptitude; **il a beaucoup de** ~ **pour les langues** he has a great aptitude *ou* talent for languages.

d (*gén pl: possibilité*) facility. **avoir la** ~**/toutes (les)** ~**s de** *ou* **pour faire qch** to have the/every opportunity to do sth *ou* of doing sth; ~**s de transport** transport facilities; (*Comm*) ~**s de crédit** credit facilities *ou* terms; (*Comm*) ~**s de paiement** easy terms.

e (*tendance*) tendency. **il a une certaine** ~ **à se mettre en colère** he has a tendency to lose his temper; **la** ~ **avec laquelle il se met en colère m'inquiète** his quick-temperedness worries me.

f (*littér: complaisance*) readiness. **il a une grande** ~ **à croire ce que l'on raconte/à se plier à une règle** he has a great readiness *ou* is very ready to believe what people tell him/to comply with a rule.

faciliter [fasilite] [1] **vt** (*gén*) to make easier, facilitate. **ça ne va pas** ~ **les choses** that's not going to make matters *ou* things (any) easier, that's not going to ease matters; **pour lui** ~ **sa mission/tâche** to make his mission/work easier, make the mission/work easier for him.

FACOB [fakɔb] **nm** (**abrév de facultatif obligatoire**) open cover.

façon [fasɔ̃] **nf** a (*manière*) way. **voilà la** ~ **dont il procède** this is how *ou* the way he does it; **il s'y prend de** *ou* **d'une** ~ **curieuse** he sets about things in a peculiar way *ou* fashion (*frm*); **de quelle** ~ **est-ce arrivé?** how did it happen?; **il faut le faire de la** ~ **suivante** you must do it in the following way *ou* as follows; **je le ferai à ma** ~ I shall do it my own way; **à la** ~ **d'un enfant** like a child, as a child would do; **sa** ~ **d'agir/de répondre** *etc* the way he behaves/answers *etc*, his way of behaving/answering *etc*; **c'est une** ~ **de parler** it's just a figure of speech; **je vais lui dire ma** ~ **de penser** (*point de vue*) I'll tell him what I think about it *ou* how I feel about it; (*colère*) I'll give him a piece of my mind, I'll tell him what I think about it; **c'est une** ~ **de voir (les choses)** it's one way of seeing things *ou* of looking at things; (*Prov*) **la** ~ **de donner vaut mieux que ce qu'on donne** it's the thought that counts.

b (*loc*) **rosser qn de (la) belle** ~†† to give sb a sound thrashing; **d'une certaine** ~**, c'est vrai** it is true in a way *ou* in some ways; **d'une** ~ **générale** generally speaking, as a general rule; **de toute(s)** ~**(s)** in any case, at any rate, anyway; **de cette** ~ (in) this way; **d'une** ~ **ou d'une autre** somehow or other, one way or another; **en aucune** ~ in no way; **de quelque** ~ **qu'il s'y prenne** however *ou* no matter how he goes about it; **je vais lui jouer un tour de ma** ~ I'm going to play a trick of my own on him; **un poème de ma** ~ a poem written by me; **un plat de ma** ~ a dish of my own making *ou* made by me; **de** ~ **à ne pas le déranger** so as not to disturb him; **de** ~ **à ce qu'il puisse regarder, de (telle)** ~ **qu'il puisse regarder** so that he can see.

c **sans** ~**: accepter sans** ~ to accept without fuss; **il est sans** ~ he is unaffected; **merci, sans** ~ no thanks really *ou* honestly; **repas sans** ~ simple *ou* unpretentious meal; **et sans plus de** ~**s** and without further ado.

d ~**s** manners, behaviour; **ses** ~**s me déplaisent profondément** I find his manners extremely unpleasant, I don't like his behaviour at all; **en voilà des** ~**s!** what sort of behaviour is this!, that's no way to behave!; **faire des** ~**s** (*minauderies*) to put on airs and graces; (*chichis*) to make a fuss.

e (*Couture*) *[robe]* cut, making-up (*Brit*). **robe d'une bonne** ~† well-cut dress; **payer la** ~ to pay for the tailoring *ou* making-up (*Brit*); **travailler à** ~ to (hand) tailor *ou* make up (*Brit*) customers' own material; **le travail à** ~ **est mal rémunéré** tailoring *ou* dressmaking is badly paid.

f (*imitation*) **veste** ~ **daim/cuir** jacket in imitation suede/leather; **bijoux** ~ **antique** old-fashioned *ou* antique style jewellery; **gigot** ~ **chevreuil** leg of lamb cooked like *ou* done like venison.

g (†*: genre*) **une** ~ **de maître d'hôtel** a head waiter of sorts; **une** ~ **de roman** a novel of sorts.

h (*Agr*) **donner une** ~ **à la terre** to till the land.

faconde [fakɔ̃d] nf (*littér*) volubility, loquaciousness. **avoir de la ~** to be very voluble *ou* loquacious.

façonnage [fasɔnaʒ] nm (*voir* **façonner**) shaping; fashioning; modelling; hewing; tilling; manufacturing; making; crafting; moulding; forming.

façonnement [fasɔnmɑ̃] nm *[esprits, caractère]* moulding, shaping, forming.

façonner [fasɔne] 1 vt a (*travailler*) (*gén*) to shape, fashion; *argile* to model, shape, fashion; *tronc d'arbre, bloc de pierre* to hew, shape; *terre, sol* to till. b (*fabriquer*) *pièce, clef* (*industriellement*) to manufacture; (*artisanalement*) to make, craft; *chapeau, robe, statuette* to fashion, make. c (*former*) *caractère, personne* to mould, shape, form. (*littér*) ~ **qn à** *travail, violence* to train sb for.

façonnier, -ière [fasɔnje, jɛʀ] adj (*maniéré*) affected, over-refined. **elle est ~ière** she puts on airs and graces, she's affected.

fac-similé, pl **fac-similés** [faksimile] nm facsimile.

factage [faktaʒ] nm (*transport*) cartage, forwarding. **entreprise de ~** parcel delivery company, transport company; **frais de ~** cartage, delivery charge, carriage.

facteur [faktœʀ] nm a (*Poste*) postman (*Brit*), mailman (*US*); *voir* **factrice**. b (*élément, Math*) factor. **le ~ chance/prix** the chance/price factor; **~ de risque** risk factor; (*Math*) **mettre en ~s** to factorize; (*Math*) **mise en ~s** factorization; (*Méd*) **~ Rhésus** Rhesus *ou* Rh factor. c (*fabricant*) **~ de pianos** piano maker; **~ d'orgues** organ builder.

factice [faktis] adj *marbre, beauté* artificial; *cuir, bijou* imitation (*épith*), artificial; *barbe* false; *bouteilles, articles exposés* dummy (*épith*); *enthousiasme, amabilité* false, artificial, feigned, sham. **tout semblait ~, le marbre du sol et la civilité des employés** everything seemed phoney* *ou* artificial, from the marble floor to the politeness of the employees; **ces livres sont ~s** these books are dummies.

facticement [faktismɑ̃] adv artificially.

factieux, -ieuse [faksjø, jøz] 1 adj factious, seditious. 2 nm,f seditionary.

faction [faksjɔ̃] nf a (*groupe factieux*) faction. b (*garde*) *[sentinelle]* sentry (duty), guard (duty); *[soldat, guetteur]* guard (duty); (*fig*) *[personne qui attend]* long watch. **être de** *ou* **en ~** *[soldat, guetteur]* to be on guard (duty), stand guard; *[sentinelle]* to be on guard (duty) *ou* (sentry) duty, stand guard; (*fig*) *[personne qui attend]* to keep *ou* stand watch; **mettre qn de ~** to put sb on guard (duty).

factionnaire [faksjɔnɛʀ] nm (*sentinelle, garde*) sentry *ou* guard (on duty).

factitif, -ive [faktitif, iv] adj (*Ling*) factitive, causative.

factoriel, -ielle [faktɔʀjɛl] 1 adj (*Math*) factorial. **analyse ~le** factor analysis. 2 **factorielle** nf (*Math*) factorial.

factoring [faktɔʀiŋ] nm factoring.

factorisation [faktɔʀizasjɔ̃] nf factorization.

factoriser [faktɔʀize] 1 vt to factorize.

factotum [faktɔtɔm] nm (*homme à tout faire*) odd-job man, general handyman, (general) factotum (*hum*); (*péj: larbin*) (general) dogsbody (*Brit péj*).

factrice [faktʀis] nf (*Poste*) postwoman (*Brit*), mailwoman (*US*).

factuel, -elle [faktɥɛl] adj factual.

factum [faktɔm] nm (*littér*) lampoon.

facturation [faktyʀasjɔ̃] nf (*opération*) invoicing; (*bureau*) invoice office.

facture [faktyʀ] nf a (*note*) (*gén*) bill; (*Comm*) invoice. (*Écon*) **notre ~ pétrolière** the nation's oil bill; **fausse ~** forged *ou* faked invoice; **~ pro forma** pro forma invoice, interim invoice (*US*). b (*manière, style*) *[œuvre d'art]* construction; *[artiste]* technique. **poème de ~ délicate/gauche** sensitively/awkwardly constructed poem; **meubles de bonne ~** well-made furniture, furniture of good workmanship. c (*Tech*) *[piano, orgue etc]* making.

facturer [faktyʀe] 1 vt (*établir une facture pour*) to invoice; (*compter*) to charge (for), put on the bill, include in the bill. **~ qch 20 F (à qn)** to charge *ou* bill (sb) 20 francs for sth; **ils ont oublié de ~ l'emballage** they've forgotten to charge for the packing, they've forgotten to include the packing in the bill.

facturette [faktyʀɛt] nf credit card slip.

facturier [faktyʀje] nm (*registre*) invoice register; (*employé*) invoice clerk.

facturière [faktyʀjɛʀ] nf (*employée*) invoice clerkess *ou* clerk; (*machine*) invoicing machine, biller (*US*).

facultatif, -ive [fakyltatif, iv] adj *travail, examen, cours* optional; *halte, arrêt* request (*épith*). **matière ~ive** optional subject, elective (subject) (*US*).

facultativement [fakyltativmɑ̃] adv optionally.

faculté [fakylte] nf a (*Univ*) faculty. **la ~ des Lettres/de Médecine** the Faculty of Arts/Medicine, the Arts/Medical Faculty (*Brit*), the School *ou* College of Arts/Medicine (*US*); (*Can*) **F~ des Arts/Sciences** Faculty of Arts/Science; (*Québec*) **F~ des études supérieures** graduate and postgraduate studies; (*arg Univ: université*) **quand j'étais en ~** *ou* **à la ~** when I was at university *ou* college *ou* school (*US*); **professeur de ~** university lecturer (*Brit*), professor (*US*); (*hum*) **la F~ me défend le tabac** I'm not allowed to smoke on doctor's orders; **il osait s'attaquer à la F~** he dared to attack the medical profession.

b (*don*) faculty; (*pouvoir*) power; (*propriété*) property. **avoir une grande ~ de concentration** to have great powers of concentration *ou* a great faculty for concentration; **avoir une grande ~ de mémoire** to have great powers of memory; **avoir la ~ de marcher/de la préhension** to have the ability to walk/grasp *ou* power of walking/of grasping; (*pl: aptitudes intellectuelles*) **~s** faculties; **ce problème dépasse mes ~s** this problem is beyond my powers; **jouir de** *ou* **avoir toutes ses ~s** to be in (full) possession of all one's faculties.

c (*droit*) right, option; (*possibilité*) power, freedom, possibility. **le propriétaire a la ~ de vendre son bien** the owner has the right to sell *ou* the option of selling his property; **je te laisse la ~ de choisir** I'll give you the freedom to choose *ou* the possibility *ou* option of choosing; (*frm*) **le Premier ministre a la ~ de révoquer certains fonctionnaires** the Prime Minister has the faculty *ou* power of dismissing certain civil servants; (*Jur, Fin, Comm*) **l'acheteur aura la ~ de décider** the buyer shall have the option to decide.

fada* [fada] 1 adj (*dial: fou*) cracked*, crackers* (*attrib*), barmy* (*Brit*). 2 nm crackpot*.

fadaise [fadɛz] nf (*littér: gén pl*) (*bagatelle*) trifle. (*platitude*) **dire des ~s** to mouth insipid *ou* empty phrases.

fadasse [fadas] adj (*péj*) *plat, boisson* tasteless, insipid; *couleur, style, propos* wishy-washy, insipid.

fade [fad] adj *soupe, cuisine* tasteless, insipid; *goût* insipid, flat, bland; *lumière, teinte* dull; *compliment, plaisanterie* tame, insipid; *décor, visage, individu* insipid, dull; *conversation, style* dull, insipid, vapid; *politesses, amabilité* insipid, conventional. **l'odeur ~ du sang** the sickly smell of blood; **la beauté ~ de certaines blondes** the insipid beauty of some blondes.

fadé, e‡ [fade] adj (*iro*) first-class, priceless, sensational (*iro*). **il est drôlement ~** he's a prize specimen*.

fader (se)‡ [fade] 1 vpr *corvée, personne* to get landed with*, get lumbered with* (*Brit*).

fadeur [fadœʀ] nf a (*voir* **fade**) tastelessness; insipidness; flatness, blandness; dullness; tameness; vapidness, vapidity; conventionality; sickliness. b (*platitudes*) **~s** sweet nothings, insipid *ou* bland compliments; **dire des ~s à une dame** to say sweet nothings to *ou* pay insipid *ou* bland compliments to a lady.

fading [fadiŋ] nm (*Rad*) fading.

faf* [faf] adj, nmf (abrév de **fasciste**) (*péj*) fascist.

fafiots‡† [fafjo] nmpl (*billets*) (bank)notes.

fagot [fago] nm bundle of sticks *ou* firewood; *voir* **derrière, sentir**.

fagoter [fagɔte] 1 1 vt (*péj: accoutrer*) *enfant* to dress up, rig out*. **il est drôlement fagoté** (*déguisé*) he's wearing a peculiar getup* *ou* rig-out*; (*mal habillé*) he's really oddly dressed. 2 **se fagoter** vpr to rig o.s. out*, dress o.s. (*en* as a)

Fahrenheit [faʀɛnajt] adj, nm Fahrenheit. **32 degrés ~** 32 degrees Fahrenheit.

faiblard, e* [fɛblaʀ, aʀd] 1 adj (*péj*) (*gén*) weak; *élève, personne* (*en classe*) weak, on the slow *ou* weak side (*attrib*); (*physiquement*) (rather) weakly; *argument, démonstration* feeble, weak, on the weak side (*attrib*). 2 nm,f weakling.

faible [fɛbl] 1 adj a (*gén*) *personne, esprit, support, pays* weak; *monnaie* weak, soft. **je me sens encore très ~ (des jambes)** I still feel very weak *ou* shaky (on my legs); **être ~ du cœur/des jambes** to have a weak heart/weak legs; **avoir la vue ~** *ou* **les yeux ~s** to have weak *ou* poor eyesight, have weak eyes; (*hum, iro*) **une ~ femme** one of the weaker sex; **il est trop ~ avec elle/ses élèves** he is too soft with her/with his pupils; **il est ~ de caractère** he has a weak character; *voir* **économiquement, sexe**.

b (*maigre*) (*Écon*) *rendement, revenu* low, poor; *demande* light, slack, low, poor; *intensité* low; *résistance, protestation* mild, weak; *somme* low, small; *quantité* small, slight; *écart, différence* slight, small; *espoir* faint, slight, slender; *avantage* slight. **il a une ~ attirance pour le travail** he has very little urge to work; **il a de ~s chances de s'en tirer** (*optimiste*) he has a slight chance of pulling through; (*pessimiste*) his chances of pulling through are slight *ou* slim, he has a poor chance of pulling through; **vous n'avez qu'une ~ idée de sa puissance** you have only a slight *ou* faint idea *ou* the merest inkling of his power; **à une ~ hauteur** at low height, not very high up; **à une ~ profondeur** not far below the surface, (at) a slight depth beneath the surface; (*Pol*) **à une ~ majorité** by a narrow *ou* slight majority; (*Naut*) **navire de ~ tirant d'eau** ship with a shallow draught.

c *voix, pouls* weak, faint, feeble; *lumière* dim, weak, faint; *bruit, odeur* faint, slight; *vent* light, faint. (*Mét*) **vent ~ à modéré** wind light to moderate; **~ en alcool** low in alcoholic content *ou* in alcohol; **de ~ teneur en sucre/cuivre** of low sugar/copper content.

d (*médiocre*) *élève* weak, slow; *expression, devoir, style* weak, poor; *raisonnement, argument* weak, poor, feeble, lame. **il est ~ en français** he's weak *ou* poor at *ou* in French; **c'est un escroc, et le terme est ~** he's a crook, and that's putting it mildly *ou* and that's an understatement; **le côté ~ de ce raisonnement** the weak side of this argument; *voir* **esprit, point**[1], **temps**[1].

2 **nm** a (*sans défense*) **les ~s et les opprimés** the weak *ou* feeble and the oppressed.

b (*sans volonté*) weakling. **c'est un ~, elle en fait ce qu'elle veut** he's a weakling – she does what she wants with him.

c (*littér*) (*déficience*) weak point. **le ~ de ce livre, ce sont les dialogues** the dialogues are the weak point in this book; **le ~ chez moi, c'est la mémoire** my weak point is my memory.

d (*penchant*) weakness, partiality. **il a un ~ pour le chocolat** he has a weakness *ou* a partiality for chocolate; **il a un ~ pour sa fille** he has a soft spot for his daughter.

3 **comp** ▸**faible d'esprit** **adj** feeble-minded ◊ **nmf** feeble-minded person.

faiblement [fɛbləmɑ̃] **adv** (*voir* **faible**) weakly; mildly; faintly; feebly; dimly; slightly; lightly. **le vent soufflait ~ vers la terre** the wind blew lightly landwards, a light wind blew landwards; (*Écon*) **la demande reprend ~** demand is picking up slightly; **~ alcoolisé/gazéifié** slightly alcoholic/gaseous; **~ éclairé** dimly *ou* poorly lit.

faiblesse [fɛblɛs] **nf** a (*NonC: voir* **faible**) weakness; mildness; faintness; feebleness; dimness; lightness. **la ~ de la demande** the light *ou* slack *ou* low *ou* poor demand; **la ~ du revenu** the low *ou* poor income, the smallness of the income; **~ du dollar** weakness of the dollar; **~ à l'égard de qn** softness *ou* weakness towards sb; **sa ~ de constitution** his weak *ou* frail constitution, the weakness *ou* frailty of his constitution; **sa ~ de caractère** his weak character, his weakness of character; **~ d'esprit** feeble-mindedness; **avoir la ~ d'accepter** to be weak enough to accept.

b (*syncope*) sudden weakness, dizzy spell; (*défaillance coupable*) (moment's) weakness; (*insuffisance, préférence*) weakness. **il a une ~ dans le bras gauche** he has a weakness in his left arm; **chacun a ses petites ~s** we all have our little foibles *ou* weaknesses *ou* failings.

faiblir [fɛbliʀ] 2 **vi** a *[malade, branche]* to get weaker, weaken; *[cœur, vue, intelligence]* to fail; *[forces, courage]* to fail, flag, give out; *[influence]* to wane, fall off; *[résolution, autorité]* to weaken. **elle a faibli à la vue du sang/à sa vue** she felt weak *ou* faint when she saw the blood/at the sight of him; **il a faibli devant leurs prières** he weakened *ou* relented in the face of their pleas; **pièce qui faiblit au 3e acte** play that falls off *ou* weakens in the 3rd act; (*Mil*) **la première ligne a faibli sous le choc** the front line weakened under the impact; **ce n'est pas le moment de ~!** don't give up now!

b *[voix]* to weaken, get weaker *ou* fainter; *[bruit, protestation]* to die out *ou* down; *[lumière]* to dim, get dimmer *ou* fainter; *[pouls]* to weaken, fail; *[vent]* to slacken, abate, drop; *[rendement]* to slacken (off); *[intensité, espoir]* to diminish; *[résistance, demande]* to weaken, slacken; *[chances]* to weaken, run out. **l'écart faiblit entre eux** the gap is closing *ou* narrowing between them.

faïence [fajɑ̃s] **nf** (*substance*) (glazed) earthenware; (*objets*) crockery (*NonC*), earthenware (*NonC*); (*vase, objet*) piece of earthenware, earthenware (*NonC*). **assiette en/carreau de ~** earthenware plate/tile; **~ fine** china; **~ de Delft** delft, delftware; *voir* **chien**.

faïencerie [fajɑ̃sʀi] **nf** earthenware factory.

faignant, e [fɛɲɑ̃, ɑ̃t] = **fainéant**.

faille[1] [faj] **nf** (*Géol*) fault; (*fig*) (*point faible*) flaw, weakness; (*cassure*) rift. **il y a une ~ dans votre raisonnement** there's a flaw in your argument; **ce qui a causé une ~ dans leur amitié ...** what caused a rift in their friendship ... *ou* a rift between them ...; *voir* **ligne**[1].

faille[2] [faj] *voir* **falloir**.

failli[1] [faji] **ptp de faillir**.

failli[2]**, e** [faji] **adj, nm,f** (*Comm*) bankrupt.

faillibilité [fajibilite] **nf** fallibility.

faillible [fajibl] **adj** fallible.

faillir [fajiʀ] **vi** a (*manquer*) **j'ai failli tomber/réussir** I almost *ou* very nearly fell/succeeded, I all but fell/succeeded; **j'ai bien failli me laisser tenter** I almost *ou* very nearly let myself be tempted; **il a failli se faire écraser** he almost *ou* very nearly got run over, he narrowly missed getting run over; (*iro*) **j'ai failli attendre** I hope you didn't rush on my account (*iro*). b (*frm: manquer à*) **~ à** *engagement, devoir* to fail in; *promesse, parole* to fail to keep; **son cœur/courage lui faillit†** his heart/courage failed him; **il résista jusqu'au bout sans ~** he resisted unfailingly *ou* unflinchingly to the end. c (*†: fauter*) to lapse.

faillite [fajit] 1 **nf** a (*Comm*) bankruptcy. b (*fig: échec*) *[espoir, tentative, méthode, gouvernement]* collapse, failure. **la ~ du gouvernement en matière économique** the government's failure on the economic front. c (*loc*) **être en ~** (*Comm*) to be bankrupt *ou* in a state of bankruptcy; (*fig*) to be in a state of collapse; **faire ~** (*Comm*) to go bankrupt; (*fig*) to collapse; **faire une ~ de 800 000 F** to go bankrupt with debts of 800,000 F; **déclarer/mettre qn en ~** to declare/make sb bankrupt. 2 **comp** ▸**faillite frauduleuse** fraudulent bankruptcy ▸**faillite simple** bankruptcy.

faim [fɛ̃] **nf** hunger. **avoir (très) ~** to be (very) hungry; **manger sans ~** (*sans besoin réel*) to eat for the sake of eating; (*sans appétit*) to pick at one's food, toy with one's food; **ça m'a donné ~** it made me hungry; **manger à sa ~** to eat one's fill; (*fig*) **avoir ~ de** *honneur, tendresse, justice* to hunger for, crave (for); **sa ~ de richesses/d'absolu** his yearning for wealth/the absolute; **j'ai une ~ de loup** *ou* **une ~ canine** I'm ravenous *ou* famished, I could eat a horse; (*fig*) **son discours a laissé les journalistes sur leur ~** his speech left the journalists unsatisfied *ou* hungry for more; (*Prov*) **la ~ fait sortir** *ou* **chasse le loup du bois** hunger will drive him out; *voir* **crever, mourir, rester** *etc.*

faîne [fɛn] **nf** beechnut.

fainéant, e [fɛneɑ̃, ɑ̃t] 1 **adj** lazy, idle, bone idle; *voir* **roi**. 2 **nm,f** idler, loafer, lazybones.

fainéanter [fɛneɑ̃te] 1 **vi** to idle *ou* loaf about.

fainéantise [fɛneɑ̃tiz] **nf** laziness, idleness.

faire [fɛʀ] 60 1 **vt** a (*fabriquer*) *meuble, voiture, confiture, vin* to make; *mur, maison, nid* to build; *pain, gâteau* to make, bake. **cette école fait de bons ingénieurs*** this school turns out* *ou* produces good engineers.

b (*être l'auteur de*) *faute, déclaration, promesse, offre* to make; *discours, film* to make; *liste* to make, draw up; *chèque* to make out, write; *conférence, cours, réception* to give; *livre, dissertation* to write, produce; *tableau* to paint; *dessin, carte* to draw; *compliment, visite* to pay; *faveur* to do; *farce, tour* to play. **il lui a fait 3 enfants*** he got her pregnant 3 times*, she had 3 children by him.

c (*avoir une activité, une occupation*) *bonne action, travail, jardinage, service militaire* to do; *tennis, rugby* to play. **que faites-vous dans la vie?, quel métier faites-vous?** what do you do (for a living)?, what is your job?, what job do you do?; **qu'est-ce que tu fais ce soir?** what are you doing tonight?; **j'ai beaucoup/je n'ai rien à ~** I have a lot/nothing to do; **ils sont en retard, qu'est-ce qu'ils peuvent bien ~?** they are late – what on earth are they doing? *ou* are they up to?*; **~ du théâtre** (*professionnel*) to be on the stage, be an actor; (*amateur*) to do a bit of acting; **il ne fait pas de sport** he doesn't do any sport, he doesn't take part in any sport; **~ de la voiture** to drive, go driving; **il fait beaucoup de voiture/de bicyclette** he does a lot of driving/cycling; **~ du tricot** to knit; **~ un peu de tricot/de couture** to do a bit of knitting/sewing; **~ de la photographie** to go in for *ou* do photography; **~ du bricolage** to do odd jobs.

d (*étudier*) *examen* to do, take; (*Scol* *) *roman, comédie* to do. **~ des études** to study; **~ du** *ou* **son droit/sa médecine** to do *ou* study law/medicine; **~ de la recherche** to do research; **~ du français** to study *ou* do *ou* take French, be learning French; **~ du piano/du violon** to play *ou* learn the piano/violin; **va ~ ton piano*** go and practise your piano, go and do your piano practice; **~ l'école hôtelière/navale** to be *ou* study at catering school/naval college.

e (*préparer*) *repas* to make, cook, prepare; *soupe, sauce, dessert* to make; *salade* to prepare. **~ du thé/du café** to make (some) tea/(some) coffee; **elle fait un rôti/du lapin** she is doing *ou* cooking a roast/a rabbit.

f (*mettre en ordre, nettoyer*) *lit* to make; *pièce* to clean, do; *argenterie* to polish, clean, do; *chaussures* to clean, do, polish; *valise* to pack. **~ le ménage** to do the housework, clean the house; **~ les carreaux** to clean the windows; **~ le jardin** to do the gardening; **~ la vaisselle** to do the dishes, do the washing-up (*Brit*), wash up (*Brit*).

g (*accomplir une action*) *match* to play; *compte, problème* to do; *projet* to make; *rêve, chute, sieste* to have; *geste* to make; *pas, bond* to take; *sourire, sursaut, secousse* to give. **~ un voyage** to go on a journey, take a trip; **~ une promenade** to go for *ou* take a walk; **~ une réparation** to do a repair (job) (*à* on); **~ un tournoi** *[participant]* to go in for *ou* enter *ou* play in a tournament; *[organisateur]* to organize a tournament; **~ une coupe/un shampooing à qn** to cut/shampoo sb's hair; **~ de l'essence*** to fill up with petrol; **~ de l'eau** *[train, bateau]* to take on water; **~ la vidange** to change the oil; **je vais ~ le plein** I'm going to fill it up; **~ de l'herbe pour (nourrir) les lapins** to cut grass for the rabbits.

h (*Méd*) *diabète, tension* to have, suffer from; *grippe* to get, come *ou* go (*Brit*) down with. **~ de la fièvre** to have *ou* run a temperature; **~ des complexes** to have a complex, have hang-ups*; **~ une dépression nerveuse** to have a nervous breakdown.

i (*besoins naturels*) **~ ses (petits) besoins** *[personne]* to go to the toilet; *[animal]* to make a mess; **le chat a fait (ses ordures** *ou* **ses saletés** *ou* **sa crotte) dans la cuisine** the cat has made a mess in the kitchen; (*langage enfantin*) **~ pipi** to go and spend a penny* (*Brit*), go to the john* (*US*), do a wee-wee* (*Brit*); **~ caca** to do a pooh (*langage enfantin*).

j (*parcourir, visiter*) to do. **~ un long trajet** to travel a long way, have a long journey; **~ 10 km** to do *ou* cover 10 km; **~ (une moyenne de) 100 km/h, ~ du cent** to do *ou* average 100 km/h; **~ Rome/la Grèce en 2 jours** to do Rome/Greece in 2 days; **~ Lyon-Paris en cinq heures** to get from Lyons to Paris in 5 hours; **~ tous les magasins pour trouver qch** to do all *ou* comb the stores *ou* try every store in search of sth; **il a fait toute la ville pour trouver ...** he has been all over *ou* he has combed the town looking for ...; **~ les bistros/les boîtes de nuit** to do the round of the cafés/night clubs; **commerçant qui fait les foires** tradesman who does *ou* goes the round of the markets.

k (*Comm*) *l'épicerie, les légumes* to sell, deal in; (*Agr*) *blé, betteraves* to grow, produce. **~ le gros/le détail** to be a wholesale dealer/a retailer, be in the wholesale/retail trade; **nous ne faisons pas les boutons/cette marque** we do not stock *ou* carry *ou* keep buttons/this make; **cet hôtel fait aussi restaurant** this hotel is also run as a restaurant.

l (*mesurer, peser, coûter*) **cette cuisine fait 6 mètres de large sur 3 de long** this kitchen is 6 metres wide by 3 metres long; **il fait 23 degrés** it is 23 degrees; **ce rôti fait bien 3 kg** this joint weighs a good 3 kg; **ça fait encore loin jusqu'à Paris** it is still quite a long way *ou* quite far to Paris; **combien fait cette chaise?** how much is this chair?; **cette table fera un bon prix** this table will go for *ou* will fetch a high price; **je vous fais ce fauteuil 700 F** I'll let you have *ou* I'll give you this armchair for 700 francs; **ça nous fera 1 000 F** (*dépense*) that will cost us 1,000 francs; (*gain*) that will give *ou* bring us 1,000 francs.

m (*imiter l'apparence de*) **~ le malade/le mort** to feign *ou* sham illness/death; **~ le sourd** *ou* **la sourde oreille/le timide** to feign deafness/shyness, pretend to be deaf/shy; **~ l'innocent/la bête** to play *ou* act the innocent/the fool; **~ le dictateur** to act the dictator; **~ l'imbécile** *ou* **le pitre** to play *ou* act the fool; **ne fais pas l'enfant/l'idiot** don't be so childish/so stupid, don't behave so childishly/so stupidly.

n (*tenir un rôle, faire fonction de*) (*Théât*) to play the part of, be. **il fait le fantôme dans "Hamlet"** he plays (the part of) the ghost in "Hamlet"; **~ le Père Noël** to be Father Christmas (*Brit*) *ou* Santa Claus; **leur fils fait le jardinier pendant les vacances*** their son's being the gardener *ou* acting as gardener during the holidays; **quel idiot je fais!** what a fool I am! *ou* I look!; **ils font un beau couple** they make a fine couple.

o (*transformer*) to make. **la vie a fait de lui un aigri** life has made him *ou* turned him into a bitter man, life has embittered him; **il a fait d'une grange une demeure agréable** he has transformed *ou* turned *ou* made a barn into a comfortable home; **elle a fait de son neveu son héritier** she made her nephew her heir; **il veut en ~ un avocat** he wants to make a lawyer of him, he wants him to be a lawyer; **se ~ moine/marin** to become a monk/a sailor.

p (*représenter*) **on le fait plus riche qu'il n'est** he's made out *ou* people make him out to be richer than he is; **ne faites pas les choses plus sombres qu'elles ne sont** don't paint things blacker *ou* don't make things out to be worse than they are.

q (*causer, avoir un effet sur*) **~ du bien/du mal à ...** to do good/harm to ...; **~ du chagrin** *ou* **de la peine à qn** to cause grief to sb, make sb unhappy; **~ le malheur/le bonheur de qn** to make sb very unhappy/happy; **~ la joie de qn** to delight sb; **cela fait la richesse du pays** that's what makes the country rich; **qu'est-ce que cela peut bien te ~?** what does it matter to you?, what difference can it possibly make to you?; **qu'est-ce que ça fait?*** so what?*; **la mort de son père ne lui a rien fait** his father's death didn't affect him, he was unaffected by his father's death; **cela ne vous ferait rien de sortir?** would you mind going out?; **~ des piqûres/rayons à qn** to give sb injections/X-rays; **qu'est-ce qu'on lui fait à l'hôpital?** what are they doing to him in hospital?; **qu'est-ce qu'on t'a donc fait!** whatever have they done to you!; **ils ne peuvent rien me ~** they can't do anything to me, they can't hurt me; **ça ne fait rien** it doesn't matter, it's of no importance; **l'épidémie a fait 10 victimes** the epidemic has claimed 10 victims *ou* lives.

r (*servir de*) to serve as, be used as, do duty as. **la cuisine fait salle à manger** the kitchen serves as *ou* is used as a dining room.

s **qu'avez-vous fait de votre sac/de vos enfants?** what have you done with *ou* where have you left your bag/your children?; **qu'ai-je bien pu ~ de mes lunettes?** where on earth have I put *ou* left my glasses?; what on earth have I done with my glasses?

t (*dans un calcul*) **24 en tout, ce qui en fait 2 chacun** 24 altogether, which gives *ou* makes 2 each; (*addition*) **deux et deux font quatre** two and two make *ou* are four; **cela fait combien en tout?** how much does that make altogether?

u (*loc*) **pour ce qu'on en fait!** for all that we (*ou* you *etc*) do with it!, for all the good it is to us (*ou* you *etc*)!; **n'en faites rien** do nothing of the sort; **n'avoir que ~ de** to have no need of; **~ tant (et si bien) que** to finish *ou* end up by; **ne ~ que** (*faire constamment*): **ne ~ que de protester** to keep on and on *ou* be constantly *ou* continually protesting; **il ne fait que bavarder** he won't stop chattering, he does nothing but chatter; **je ne fais que d'arriver** I've only just come; **je ne fais que dire la vérité** I'm only telling the truth *ou* saying what's true; **je ne fais que passer** I am just passing by; **la ~ à qn au sentiment*** to take sb in by appealing to his emotions.

2 **vi** a (*agir, procéder*) to act, do. **~ vite** to act quickly; **faites vite!** be quick about it!, make it quick!; **il a bien fait** he did the right thing; **il a bien fait de partir** he was quite right *ou* he did right to go; **tu as mal fait** you behaved badly; **~ de son mieux** to do one's best; **on ferait bien/mieux de le prévenir** it would be a good/better idea *ou* safer/much safer to warn him; **ça commence à bien ~*!** this has gone on quite long enough!, this is getting beyond a joke!; **faites comme vous voulez** do as you please, please yourself; **faites comme chez vous** make yourself at home; **que voulez-vous qu'on y fasse?** what do you expect us to do (about it)?; **il n'y a rien à ~** (*gén*) there's nothing we can do, there's nothing to be done; (*c'est inutile*) it's useless *ou* hopeless; **il sait y ~** he's good at getting things his own way; **pour bien ~ il faudrait partir maintenant** the best thing would be to leave now.

b (*dire*) to say. **"vraiment?" fit-il** "really?" he said; **il fit un "ah" de surprise** he gave a surprised "ah"; **le chat fait miaou** the cat goes *ou* says miaow.

c (*durer*) **ce chapeau (me) fera encore un hiver** this hat will last me *ou* will do me another winter.

d (*paraître*) to look. **ce vase fait bien sur la table** the vase looks nice on the table; **~ vieux/jeune** to look old/young (for one's age); **elle fait très femme** she's very womanly(-looking) *ou* grown-up looking for her age.

e (*gén au futur: devenir*) to make; [*personne*] to make, have the makings of. **cette branche fera une belle canne** this branch will make a fine walking stick; **cet enfant fera un bon musicien** this child has the makings of *ou* will make a good musician; **il veut ~ médecin** he wants to be a doctor.

f (*besoins naturels*) to go. **as-tu fait ce matin?** have you been this morning?; **~ dans sa culotte** (*lit*) to dirty one's pants; (**: avoir peur*) to wet one's pants*, be scared stiff.

3 **vb impers** a **il fait jour/nuit/clair/sombre** it is daylight/dark/light/dull; **il fera beau demain** it *ou* the weather will be fine tomorrow, tomorrow will be fine; **il fait du soleil** the sun is shining, it is sunny; **il fait lourd** it *ou* the weather is close *ou* thundery; **il fait faim/soif*** we are hungry/thirsty.

b (*exprimant le temps écoulé*) **cela fait 2 ans/très longtemps que je ne l'ai pas vu** it is 2 years/a very long time since I last saw him, I haven't seen him for 2 years/for a very long time; **ça fait 3 ans qu'il est parti** it's 3 years since he left, he left 3 years ago, he has been gone 3 years.

c **il fait bon** + *infin* it is nice *ou* pleasant; **il fait bon se promener** it is nice *ou* pleasant to go for a walk; **il ne fait pas bon le contredire** it is unwise to *ou* it's better not to contradict him; **il fait bon vivre** life is good.

d (*) **cela fait que nous devons partir** the result is that we must leave, as a result *ou* so we must leave.

4 **vb** *substitut* to do. **ne manquez pas le train comme nous l'avons fait** don't miss the train as we did; **il travaille mieux que je ne fais** he works better than I do; **as-tu payé la note? — non, c'est lui qui l'a fait** did you pay the bill? — no, he did; **puis-je téléphoner? — faites, je vous en prie** may I phone? — (yes) please do *ou* (yes) by all means.

5 **se faire vpr** a **se ~ les ongles** to do one's nails; **se ~ une robe** to make o.s. a dress; **il se fait sa cuisine** he does his own cooking; **il se fait 8 000 F par mois*** he earns *ou* gets *ou* makes 8,000 francs a month; **il s'est fait beaucoup d'amis/d'ennemis** he has made himself a great many friends/enemies; **se ~ une fille‡** to have* *ou* pull‡ a girl.

b **se ~ une idée** to get some idea; **se ~ des idées** to imagine things, have illusions; **s'en ~** to worry; **il ne s'en fait pas** he does not worry, he is not the worrying type; (*excl*) he's got a nerve!; *voir* **bile, raison** *etc.*

c (*se former*) [*fromage*] to ripen, mature; [*vin*] to mature. (*fig*) **il s'est fait tout seul** he is a self-made man.

d (+ *attribut: devenir*) to become, get. **se ~ vieux** to be getting old; **il se faisait tard** it was getting late; (*littér*) **il se fit violent sous l'insulte** he turned *ou* became violently angry at the insult; **ça ne se fera pas** it won't happen.

e (+ *adj: devenir volontairement*) **se ~ beau** to make o.s. beautiful; **se ~ tout petit** to make o.s. small.

f **se ~ à** to become used to, get used to; **il ne peut pas se ~ au climat** he can't get used to the climate; **il faut se le ~!‡** (*travail*) it's a hell of a chore!*, it's really heavy going!‡; (*personne*) he's a real pain in the neck!*

g **cela ne se fait pas** it's not done; **les jupes longues se font beaucoup cette année** long skirts are in this year *ou* are being worn a lot this year.

h (*impers*) **il peut/il pourrait se ~ qu'il pleuve** it may/it might (well) rain; **comment se fait-il qu'il soit absent?** how is it (that) he is absent?, how does he happen to be absent?, how come he's absent?*

i **se ~ mal** to hurt o.s.; **se ~ peur** to give o.s. a fright; **se ~ violence** to force o.s.

j **se ~** + *infin* : **elle s'est fait opérer** she was operated on, she had an operation; **tu vas te ~ gronder** you'll get yourself into trouble *ou* told off*; **il s'est fait remettre le document** he had the document handed over to him; **il s'est fait ouvrir par le voisin** he got the neighbour to let him in; **fais-toi vite vomir: c'est du poison** quick, make yourself vomit *ou* be sick — it's poisonous; **elle s'en est fait montrer le fonctionnement** she had a demonstration of *ou* she was shown how it worked.

6 **vb aux** + *infin* a (*être la cause de*) **la pluie fait pousser l'herbe** the rain makes the grass grow; **mon voisin fait pousser des dahlias** my neighbour grows dahlias; **j'ai fait démarrer la voiture** I made the car start, I got the car going *ou* started; **elle a fait lire les enfants** she made the children read, she got the children to read; **elle a fait opérer sa fille** she had her daughter operated on; **il lui a fait lire Stendhal** he made him read Stendhal; **il lui a fait boire un grog** he gave her some grog to drink.

b (*aider à*) **~ traverser la rue à un aveugle** to help a blind man across the road; **~ faire ses devoirs à un enfant** to help a child with his homework, see that a child does his homework; **~ manger un invalide** to (help to) feed an invalid; **on a dû les ~ sortir par la fenêtre** they had to help *ou* get them out through the window.

c (*inviter à*) ~ **entrer/monter qn** to show *ou* ask sb in/up(stairs); ~ **venir** *employé* to send for; *docteur* to send for, fetch.

d (*donner une tâche à exécuter*) ~ **faire qch par qn** to have sth done *ou* made by sb; ~ **faire qch à qn** to have sb do *ou* make sth; **(se) ~ faire une robe** to have a dress made; ~ **réparer une voiture/une montre** to have a car/a watch repaired; ~ **faire la vaisselle à qn** to have sb do *ou* get sb to do the dishes.

e (*laisser*) ~ **entrer/sortir le chien** to let the dog in/out; **faites entrer le public** let the public in; **elle a fait tomber une tasse** she dropped a cup.

f (*forcer*) to make. **il lui a fait ouvrir le coffre-fort** he made him open *ou* forced him to open the safe.

7 **comp ▸faire-part nm inv** announcement (of birth *ou* marriage *ou* death); **faire-part de mariage** wedding announcement, ≃ wedding invitation **▸faire-valoir nm inv** (*Agr*) exploitation, farming, working (of land); (*personne*) foil; **faire-valoir direct/indirect** farming by the owner/tenant.

fair-play [fɛʀplɛ] 1 **nm inv** fair play. 2 **adj: être ~** to play fair; **c'est un joueur ~** he plays fair.

faisabilité [fəzabilite] **nf** feasibility. **étude de ~** feasibility study.

faisable [fəzabl] **adj** feasible. **est-ce ~ en 2 jours?** can it be done in 2 days?; **est-ce ~ à pied?** can it be done on foot?, is it quite feasible on foot?

faisan [fəzɑ̃] **nm** a (*oiseau*) (*gén*) pheasant; (*mâle*) cock pheasant. ~ **doré** golden pheasant; *voir* **faisane.** b (†: *escroc*) shark.

faisandé, e [fəzɑ̃de] (**ptp de faisander**) **adj** a (*Culin*) *gibier, goût* high. **je n'aime pas le ~** I don't like high game; **viande trop ~e** meat which has hung for too long. b (*péj*) *littérature, société* corrupt, decadent; *milieux* crooked.

faisandeau, pl ~x [fəzɑ̃do] **nm** young pheasant.

faisander [fəzɑ̃de] [1] **vt** (*Culin*) **(faire *ou* laisser) ~** to hang.

faisanderie [fəzɑ̃dʀi] **nf** pheasantry.

faisandier [fəzɑ̃dje] **nm** pheasant breeder.

faisane [fəzan] **nf, adj f: (poule) ~** hen pheasant.

faisceau, pl ~x [fɛso] 1 **nm** a (*fagot*) bundle. (*réseau*) ~ **de preuves/faits** body *ou* network of proofs/facts; **nouer en ~** to tie in a bundle; **nouer en ~x** to tie into bundles. b (*Mil*) **~x (d'armes)** stack (of arms); **mettre en ~x** *fusils* to stack; **former/rompre les ~x** to stack/unstack arms. c (*rayons*) beam. ~ **convergent/divergent** convergent/divergent beam. d (*Antiq, Hist*) **~x** fasces. 2 **comp ▸faisceau d'électrons** electron beam **▸faisceau hertzien** electro-magnetic wave **▸faisceau lumineux** beam of light **▸faisceau musculaire/nerveux** fasciculus *ou* fascicule of muscle/nerve fibres.

faiseur, -euse [fəzœʀ, øz] 1 **nm,f: ~ de**† *monuments, meubles* maker of; (*hum, péj*) *romans, tableaux, opéras* producer of. 2 **nm** (†) (*péj: hâbleur*) show-off; (*escroc*) shark. (*frm: tailleur*) **(bon) ~** good tailor. 3 **comp ▸faiseuse d'anges** backstreet abortionist **▸faiseur de bons mots** (*péj*) punster, wag **▸faiseur d'embarras** fusspot **▸faiseur d'intrigues** (*péj*) schemer **▸faiseur de littérature** (*péj*) scribbler **▸faiseur de marché** (*Bourse*) market maker **▸faiseur de mariages** (*péj*) matchmaker **▸faiseur de miracles** (*péj*) miracle-worker **▸faiseur de phrases** (*péj*) speechifier **▸faiseur de projets** (*péj*) schemer **▸faiseur de vers** (*péj*) poetaster (*péj*), versifier.

faisselle [fɛsɛl] **nf** cheese strainer.

fait¹ [fɛ] 1 **nm** a (*événement*) event, occurrence; (*donnée*) fact; (*phénomène*) phenomenon. **il s'agit d'un ~ courant/rare** this is a common/rare occurrence *ou* event; **aucun ~ nouveau n'est survenu** no new development has taken place, no new fact has come to light; **il me faut des ~s concrets** I must have concrete facts *ou* evidence; (*Jur*) **reconnaissez-vous les ~s?** do you accept the facts?; (*Jur*) **les ~s qui lui sont reprochés** the charges against him; **ces ~s remontent à 3 ans** these events go back 3 years; **il s'est produit un ~ curieux** a strange thing has happened; **s'incliner devant les ~s** to bow to (the) facts; **les ~s sont là *ou* sont têtus** there's no denying the facts, the facts speak for themselves; *voir* **erreur, point¹.**

b (*acte*) **le ~ de manger/bouger** the fact of eating/moving, eating/moving; (*Jur, Mil*) **être puni pour ~ d'insoumission** to be punished for (an act of) insubordination; *voir* **haut.**

c (*cause*) **c'est le ~ du hasard** it's the work of fate; **c'est le ~ de son inexpérience** it's because of *ou* owing to his inexperience, it comes of his inexperience; **par le ~ même que/de** by the very fact that/of; **par le (simple) ~ de** by the simple fact of; **par le ~ même de son obstination** because of *ou* by his very obstinacy, by the very fact of his obstinacy.

d (*loc*) **au ~** (*à propos*) by the way; **au ~!** (*à l'essentiel*) come to the point!; **aller droit/en venir au ~** to go straight/get to the point; **au ~ de** (*au courant*) conversant *ou* acquainted with, informed of; **est-il au ~?** does he know?, is he informed?; **mettre qn au ~ (d'une affaire)** to acquaint *ou* familiarize sb with (the facts of) a matter, inform sb of (the facts of) a matter; **de ~** (*de facto*) *gouvernement, dictature* de facto; (*en fait*) in fact; **il est de ~ que** it is a fact that; **de ce ~** therefore, for this reason; **du ~ de qch** on account *ou* as a result of sth; **du ~ qu'il a démissionné** on account of *ou* as a result of his having resigned; **en ~** in (actual) fact, in point of fact, as a matter of fact; **en ~ de** (*en guise de*) by way of; (*en matière de*) as regards, in the way of; **en ~ de repas on a eu droit à un sandwich** we were allowed a sandwich by way of a meal; **en ~ de spécialiste, c'est plutôt un charlatan!** as for being a specialist! charlatan more like!*; **le ~ est que** the fact is that; **le ~ que** the fact that; **le ~ est là** that's the fact of the matter; **être le ~ de** (*être typique de*) to be typical *ou* characteristic of; (*être le résultat de*) to be the result of; **par le ~** in fact; **par ce ~** by this very fact; **par le ~ même** by this very *ou* selfsame fact; **par son (propre) ~** through *ou* by his (own) doing; **c'est un ~** that's a fact; **c'est un ~ que** it's a fact that; **dire son ~ à qn** to tell sb what's what, talk straight to sb, give sb a piece of one's mind; **prendre ~ et cause pour qn** to fight for sb's cause, take up the cudgels for sb, take sides with sb; **comme par un ~ exprès** almost as if on purpose; *voir* **sur, sûr, tout, voie.**

2 **comp ▸fait accompli** fait accompli; **mettre qn devant le fait accompli, pratiquer avec qn la politique du fait accompli** to present sb with a fait accompli **▸fait d'armes** feat of arms **▸fait divers** (*nouvelle*) (short) news item; (*événement insignifiant*) trivial event; (*rubrique*) **"faits divers"** "(news) in brief" **▸faits et gestes** actions, doings; **épier les moindres faits et gestes de qn** to spy on sb's slightest actions *ou* movements **▸faits de guerre** acts of war **▸fait de langue** (*Ling*) fait de langue, language event **▸fait de parole** (*Ling*) fait de parole, speech event **▸le fait du prince** (*Hist*) the imperial fiat; (*Assurance*) government action; (*fig*) **c'est le fait du prince** there's no going against authority **▸faits de résistance** acts of resistance.

fait², faite [fɛ, fɛt] (**ptp de faire**) **adj** a **être ~ pour** to be suitable *ou* made *ou* meant for; **voitures ~es pour la course** cars (specially) made *ou* designed *ou* conceived for racing; **ces souliers ne sont pas ~s pour la marche** these are not proper walking shoes, these shoes are not suitable *ou* designed for walking in; **c'est ~ pour*** that's what it's for; **ce que tu lui as dit l'a énervé — c'était ~ pour*** what you said annoyed him — it was meant to; **ceci n'est pas ~ pour lui plaire** this is not going to *ou* is not calculated to *ou* likely to please him; **ce discours n'est pas ~ pour le rassurer** this is not the kind of speech to reassure him, this sort of speech isn't likely to reassure him; **il est ~ pour être médecin** he's cut out to be a doctor; **ils sont ~s l'un pour l'autre** they are made for each other, they make a perfect couple.

b (*fini*) **c'en est ~ de notre vie calme** that's the end of our quiet life, it's goodbye to peace and quiet in our life!; **c'en est ~ de moi** I am done for, it's all up with me*; **c'est toujours ça de ~** that's one job done, that's one thing out of the way.

c (*constitué*) **avoir la jambe/main bien ~e** to have shapely *ou* nice legs/pretty *ou* nice hands; **une femme bien ~e** a good-looking woman; **un homme bien ~** a good-looking *ou* handsome man; **le monde est ainsi ~** that's the way of the world; **les gens sont ainsi ~s que** people are such that; **comment est-il ~?** what is he like?, what does he look like?; **regarde comme tu es ~!*** look at the way you're dressed!, look what a sight you are!

d (*mûr*) *personne* mature; *fromage* ripe. **fromage ~ à cœur** fully ripened cheese.

e (*maquillé*) made-up. **avoir les yeux ~s** to have one's eyes made up; **avoir les ongles ~s** to have painted nails.

f **tout ~** ready made; **acheter des vêtements tout ~s** to buy ready-made *ou* ready-to-wear clothes; **phrase toute ~e** ready-made phrase.

g (*loc*) **il est ~ (comme un rat)*** he's in for it now*, he's cornered!; **c'est bien ~ pour toi!** you asked for it!*, you got what you deserved!; **c'est bien ~!** it serves them (*ou* him *etc*) right!; **ce n'est ni ~ ni à faire** it's a botched job*; *voir* **vite.**

faîtage [fɛtaʒ] **nm** (*poutre*) ridgepole; (*couverture*) roofing; (*littér: toit*) roof.

faîte [fɛt] **nm** a (*poutre*) ridgepole. b (*sommet*) [*montagne*] summit; [*arbre*] top; [*maison*] rooftop. ~ **du toit** rooftop; *voir* **ligne¹.** c (*fig: summum*) ~ **de la gloire** pinnacle *ou* height of glory; **parvenu au ~ des honneurs** having attained the highest honours.

faîtière [fɛtjɛʀ] **adj f, nf: (tuile) ~** ridge tile; **lucarne ~** skylight.

faitout nm, fait-tout nm inv [fɛtu] stewpot.

faix [fɛ] **nm** (*littér: lit, fig*) burden. **sous le ~ (de)** under the weight *ou* burden (of).

fakir [fakiʀ] **nm** (*Rel*) fakir; (*Music-Hall*) wizard.

fakirisme [fakiʀism] **nm** (*Rel*) practice of a fakir. (*fig*) **c'est du ~!** (*divination*) it's prophecy!; (*pouvoir magique*) it's wizardry!

falaise [falɛz] **nf** cliff.

falbalas [falbala] **nmpl** frills and flounces, furbelows; (*péj*) frippery (*NonC*) (*péj*), furbelows (*péj*).

fallacieusement [fa(l)lasjøzmɑ̃] **adv** *promettre* deceptively.

fallacieux, -ieuse [fa(l)lasjø, jøz] **adj** *promesse, apparence, appellation* deceptive; *arguments, raisonnement* fallacious; *espoir* illusory, delusive.

falloir [falwaʀ] [29] 1 **vb impers** a (*besoin*) **il va ~ 10 000 F** we're going to need 10,000 francs, it's going to take 10,000 francs; **il doit ~ du temps/de l'argent pour faire cela** it must take time/money *ou* you must need time/money to do that; **il faut du courage pour le faire!** it takes some courage to do it!; **il me le faut à tout prix** I must have it at all costs, I desperately need it; **il lui faut quelqu'un pour l'aider** he needs *ou* wants somebody to help him; **il vous faut tourner à gauche** you have *ou* need *ou* want to turn left; **faut-il aussi de l'ail?** do we need *ou* want garlic as well?; **c'est juste ce qu'il faut** (*outil etc*) that's just what we need *ou* want, that's exactly what's required; (*assaisonnement*) there's *ou* that's just the right amount; (*au magasin*) **qu'est-ce qu'il vous faut?** what are you looking for?; **il n'en faut pas beaucoup pour qu'il se mette à pleurer** it doesn't take much to make him cry; **c'est plus qu'il n'en faut** that's more than we need, that's more than is needed; **il faudrait avoir plus de temps** we'd have to have more time, we'd need more time.

b (*obligation*) ~ **faire: il va ~ le faire** it'll have to be done, we'll have to do it; **il va ~ y aller** we'll have to go; **il ne fallait pas faire ça, c'est tout** you shouldn't have done that and that's all there is to it; **que vous fallait-il faire?** what did you have to do?; **il m'a fallu obéir** I had to comply; **s'il le faut** (*besoin*) if need be; (*obligation*) if I (*ou* we *etc*) have to, if I (*ou* we *etc*) must; **que faut-il leur dire?** what shall I (*ou* we *etc*) tell them?; **le faut-il? — il le faut** do I (*ou* we) have to? — yes you do; **il a bien fallu!** I (*ou* we *etc*) HAD to!

c (*obligation*) ~ **que: il va ~ qu'il parte** he'll have to *ou* he has got to go; **il faut qu'il le fasse** he'll have to *ou* he has got to do it, he must do it; **il faudrait qu'il parte** he ought to *ou* should go; **il faut qu'il soit malade pour qu'il s'arrête de travailler** he has to be ill before he stops working.

d (*intensif*) **il fallait me le dire** you should have told me; **il faut voir ce spectacle** this show is a must, you must see this show; **faut voir ça, quel luxe!*** you should see the luxury of it!; — **il ne fallait pas!** — you shouldn't have!; **va pas ~ traîner*** we can't afford to mess about*; **faudrait pas qu'il essaie*** he'd better not try*; **fallait-il vraiment le dire?** did you really have to say it?; **il ne faudrait surtout pas lui en parler** don't speak to him about it whatever you do; **(il) faut dire qu'il est culotté*** you've got to admit he's got a nerve.

e (*probabilité*) **il faut que tu te sois trompé** you must have made a mistake; **s'il est absent, il faut qu'il soit malade** if he's absent he must be ill *ou* it must be because he's ill; **il faut être fou pour parler comme ça** you must be mad to talk like that; **il ne faut pas être intelligent pour dire ça** that's a pretty stupid thing to say; **faut-il donc être bête!** some people are so *ou* really stupid!; **faut-il qu'il soit bête!** he must be so *ou* really stupid!; **faut (pas) être gonflé*** it takes some nerve*.

f (*fatalité*) **il a fallu qu'elle l'apprenne** she WOULD have to hear about it; **faut-il donc abandonner si près du but?** do we have to give up when we're so near to the goal?; **il faut toujours qu'elle se trouve des excuses** she always has to find some excuse; **il faut toujours que ça tombe sur moi!** it always has to happen to me!

g (*loc*) (*hum*) **elle a ce qu'il faut*** she's got what it takes*; **il faut ce qu'il faut*** you've got to do things properly *ou* in style; **(il) faut le faire!** (*admiratif*) that takes some doing!; (**: péj*) that takes some beating!; **(il) faut se le faire!‡** (*personne*) he's a real pain in the neck!*; (*travail*) it's a hell of a chore!‡ (*Brit*), it's really heavy going; **(il) faut voir** (*réserve*) we'll have to see; (*admiration*) you should see!; **faudrait voir à voir*** steady on!, not so fast!; **(il) faudrait voir à faire/ne pas faire*** ... you'd better mind (*Brit*) *ou* make sure you do/don't do ...; **il ne faut pas y songer** it's out of the question; **il faut bien vivre/manger** you have to live/eat; **il faut vous dire que** ... I must *ou* I have to tell you (confidentially) that ...; **il faut de tout pour faire un monde** it takes all sorts to make a world; **il ne faut jamais remettre au lendemain ce qu'on peut faire le jour même** never put off till tomorrow what you can do today, procrastination is the thief of time (*Prov*); **(il) faut le voir pour le croire** it needs *ou* has to be seen to be believed; **ce qu'il faut entendre!** the things you hear!; *voir* **comme**.

2 **s'en falloir** *vpr* (*frm*) **s'en ~ de: tu n'es pas à l'heure, il s'en faut de cinq minutes** you're not on time, by a matter of 5 minutes; **il ne s'en fallait que de 100 F pour qu'il ait la somme** he was only *ou* just 100 francs short of the full amount; **il s'en faut de beaucoup** not by a long way *ou* chalk (*Brit*), far from it; **il s'en faut de beaucoup qu'il soit heureux** he is far from being happy, he is by no means happy; **il s'en est fallu d'un cheveu qu'il ne soit pris** he was within a hair's breadth *ou* a whisker *ou* an ace of being caught; **il a fini, ou peu s'en faut** he has as good as finished, he has just about finished; **il ne s'en est guère fallu pour que** *ou* **il s'en est fallu de peu (pour) que ça (n')arrive** this came very close to happening, this very nearly happened, it wouldn't have taken much for this to happen; **et il s'en faut!, tant s'en faut!** far from it!, not by a long way! *ou* chalk! (*Brit*); **ça m'a coûté 50 F ou peu s'en faut** that cost me the best part of 50 francs, that cost me very nearly 50 francs; **peu s'en est fallu (pour) qu'il pleure** he all but *ou* he almost wept; *voir* **entendre, se fier, voir**.

falot[1] [falo] *nm* lantern.

falot[2]**, e** [falo, ɔt] *adj personne* colourless; *lueur, lumière* wan, pale.

falsificateur, -trice [falsifikatœʀ, tʀis] *nm,f* falsifier.

falsification [falsifikasjɔ̃] *nf* (*voir* **falsifier**) falsification; doctoring; alteration; adulteration.

falsifier [falsifje] [7] *vt comptes, faits* to falsify, doctor, alter; *document, signature* to falsify, alter, tamper with; *aliment* to doctor, adulterate.

falzar‡ [falzaʀ] *nm* bags* (*Brit*), (pair of) trousers (*Brit*), (pair of) pants (*US*).

famé, e [fame] *adj voir* **mal**.

famélique [famelik] *adj* scrawny, scraggy, rawboned.

fameusement [famøzmɑ̃] *adv* (**: très*) remarkably, really. **c'est ~ bon** it's remarkably *ou* really good.

fameux, -euse [famø, øz] *adj* a (**: après n: bon*) *mets, vin* first-rate, first-class.

b **pas ~*** *mets, travail, temps* not too good, not so great*; *roman, auteur* not up to much* (*Brit*), no great shakes*; **et le temps pour demain? — pas ~** and tomorrow's weather? — not all that good *ou* not all that fine *ou* not up to much* (*Brit*); **il n'est pas ~ en latin/en maths** he's not too good *ou* not all that good at Latin/maths.

c (*avant n: intensif*) **c'est un ~ trajet/problème/travail** it's a real *ou* it's quite a *ou* some journey/problem/piece of work; **c'est une ~euse erreur/migraine/raclée** it's quite a *ou* it's a real mistake/headache/thrashing; **c'est un ~ salaud‡** he's a downright *ou* an out-and-out *ou* a real bastard‡; **c'est une ~euse assiettée** that's a huge *ou* great plateful; **c'est un ~ gaillard** (*bien bâti*) he's a strapping fellow; (*chaud lapin*) he's a bit of a lad *ou* a randy fellow*.

d (*avant n: bon*) *idée, voiture* first-rate, great*, fine. **c'est une ~euse aubaine** it's a real *ou* great stroke of luck; **il a fait un ~ travail** he's done a first-class *ou* first-rate *ou* fine job; **elle était ~euse, ton idée!** what a bright *ou* great* idea you had!

e (**: avant n: fonction de référence*) **quel est le nom de cette ~euse rue?** what's the name of that (famous) street?; **ah, c'est ce ~ Paul dont tu m'as tant parlé** so this is the famous Paul you've told me so much about; **c'est ça, sa ~euse honnêteté** so this is his much-vaunted honesty.

f (*après n: célèbre*) famous (*pour* for).

familial, e, *mpl* **-iaux** [familjal, jo] 1 *adj ennui, problème* family (*épith*), domestic (*épith*); *liens, vie, entreprise* family (*épith*); *boîte, paquet* family-size(d); *modèle de voiture* family (*épith*); *voir* **aide, allocation.** 2 **familiale** *nf* family estate car (*Brit*), station wagon (*US*).

familiarisation [familjaʀizasjɔ̃] *nf* familiarization.

familiariser [familjaʀize] [1] 1 *vt*: **~ qn avec** to familiarize sb with, get sb used to. 2 **se familiariser** *vpr* to familiarize o.s. **se ~ avec** *lieu, personne, méthode, langue* to familiarize o.s. with, get to know, become acquainted with; *bruit, danger* to get used *ou* accustomed to; **peu familiarisé avec cette maison** unfamiliar with this house; **ses pieds, peu familiarisés avec le sol rocailleux** his feet, unused *ou* unaccustomed to the stony ground.

familiarité [familjaʀite] *nf* a (*bonhomie*) familiarity; (*désinvolture*) offhandedness, (over)familiarity. b (*privautés*) **~s** familiarities; **cessez ces ~s** stop these familiarities, stop taking liberties. c (*habitude de*) **~ avec** *langue, auteur, méthode* familiarity with. d (*atmosphère amicale*) informality. (*littér*) **dans la ~ de** on familiar terms *ou* terms of familiarity with.

familier, -ière [familje, jɛʀ] 1 *adj* a (*bien connu*) *technique, problème, spectacle, objet, voix* familiar. **sa voix/cette technique m'est ~ière** I'm familiar with his voice/this technique, his voice/this technique is familiar *ou* well-known to me; **la langue anglaise lui est devenue ~ière** he has become (thoroughly) familiar with *ou* at home with the English language.

b (*routinier*) *tâche* familiar. **cette attitude lui est ~ière** this is a familiar *ou* customary attitude of his; **le mensonge lui était devenu ~** lying had become quite a habit of his *ou* had become almost second nature to him.

c (*amical*) *entretien, atmosphère* informal, friendly, casual.

d (*désinvolte*) *personne* (over)familiar; *surnom* familiar; *ton, remarque* (over)familiar, offhand; *attitude, manières* offhand. **il devient vite ~** he soon gets too familiar; **(trop) ~ avec ses supérieurs/clients** overfamiliar with his superiors/customers; **être ~ avec les femmes** to be overfamiliar with women.

e (*non recherché*) *mot, expression* familiar, colloquial; *style, registre* familiar, conversational, colloquial. **expression ~ière** colloquialism, colloquial phrase *ou* expression.

f *divinités* household (*épith*); *voir* **démon.**

2 *nm* [*club, théâtre*] regular visitor (*de* to). **le crime a été commis par un ~ (de la maison)** the crime was committed by a very good friend of the household *ou* by a regular visitor to the house.

familièrement [familjɛʀmɑ̃] *adv* (*amicalement*) *s'entretenir* informally; (*cavalièrement*) *se conduire, s'adresser à qn* familiarly; (*sans recherche*) *parler, s'exprimer* familiarly, colloquially. **comme on dit ~** as you say familiarly *ou* colloquially *ou* in conversation; **il te parle un peu (trop) ~** he's speaking to you a bit too familiarly.

famille [famij] *nf* a (*gén*) family. **~ éloignée/proche** distant/close family *ou* relations *ou* relatives; **avez-vous de la ~?** have you any family?; **avez-vous de la ~ à Londres?** have you any family *ou* relations *ou* relatives in London?; **on a prévenu la ~** the relatives *ou* the next of kin (*frm*) have been informed; **~ nombreuse** large family; **~ monoparentale** single-parent *ou* one-parent family; **elle promenait (toute) sa petite ~*** she was taking her (entire) brood* for a walk; **elle fait partie de la ~, elle est de la ~** she is part *ou* one of the family; (*Sociol*) **la ~ étendue/nucléaire** the extended/nuclear family; *voir* **beau.**

b (*fig*) [*plantes, langues*] family. (*Mus*) **la ~ des cuivres** the brass family; (*Ling*) **~ de mots** word family; **ils sont de la même ~ politique** they're of the same political persuasion.

c (*loc*) **de** ~ *possessions, réunion, dîner* family (*épith*); **c'est un tableau de** ~ this painting is a family heirloom; *voir* **air**[2], **caveau, chef**[1] *etc.*

d **c'est de** ~, **ça tient de** ~ it runs in the family; **en** ~ (*avec la famille*) with the family; (*comme une famille*) as a family; **tout se passe en** ~ it's all kept in the family; **passer ses vacances en** ~ to spend one's holidays with the family; **il est sans** ~ he has no family; **un (petit) bridge des** ~**s*** a quiet *ou* cosy little game of bridge; **il est très** ~* he's very family-oriented, he's a real family man.

famine [famin] nf (*épidémie*) famine; (*littér: privation*) starvation. **nous allons à la** ~ we are heading for starvation, we are going to starve; *voir* **crier, salaire.**

fan* [fan] nm (*admirateur*) fan.

fana* [fana] (abrév de **fanatique**) 1 adj crazy* (*de* about), mad keen* (*de* on, about). 2 nmf: ~ **de l'ordinateur** *etc* computer *etc* enthusiast *ou* fanatic *ou* buff* *ou* freak*.

fanage [fanaʒ] nm tossing, turning, tedding.

fanal, pl -aux [fanal, o] nm (*feu*) *[train]* headlight, headlamp; *[mât]* lantern; (*phare*) beacon, lantern; (*lanterne à main*) lantern, lamp.

fanatique [fanatik] 1 adj fanatical (*de* about). 2 nmf (*gén, Sport*) fanatic; (*Pol, Rel*) fanatic, zealot. ~ **du ski/du football/des échecs** skiing/football/chess fanatic.

fanatiquement [fanatikmɑ̃] adv fanatically.

fanatisation [fanatizasjɔ̃] nf rousing to fanaticism, fanaticization (*frm*).

fanatiser [fanatize] [1] vt to rouse to fanaticism, fanaticize (*frm*).

fanatisme [fanatism] nm fanaticism.

faner [fane] [1] 1 vi (*littér*) to make hay. 2 vt a *herbe* to toss, turn, ted. **on fane (l'herbe) après la fauchaison** the tossing *ou* turning of the hay *ou* the tedding is done after the mowing. b (*littér*) *fleur, couleur, beauté* to fade. **femme (que l'âge a) fanée** woman whose looks have faded. 3 **se faner** vpr *[plante]* to fade, wither, wilt; *[peau]* to wither; *[teint, beauté, couleur]* to fade.

faneur, -euse [fanœʀ, øz] 1 nm,f (*ouvrier*) haymaker. 2 **faneuse** nf (*machine*) tedder.

fanfare [fɑ̃faʀ] nf a (*orchestre*) brass band. **la** ~ **du régiment** the regimental band. b (*musique*) fanfare. ~ **de clairons** fanfare of bugles; ~ **de trompettes** flourish *ou* fanfare of trumpets; **des** ~**s éclatèrent** brassy music rang forth (from every side); (*fig*) **cette alliance a été annoncée par les** ~**s de la presse** this alliance was blazoned *ou* trumpeted forth by the press. c (*fig*) **en** ~ *réveil, départ* clamorous, tumultuous; *réveiller, partir* noisily, with great commotion; **il est arrivé en** ~ (*avec bruit*) he came in noisily *ou* with great commotion; (*fièrement*) he came in triumphantly; **annoncer en** ~ *réforme etc* to blazon *ou* trumpet forth, publicize widely.

fanfaron, -onne [fɑ̃faʀɔ̃, ɔn] 1 adj *personne, attitude* boastful; *air, propos* bragging, boastful. **il avait un petit air** ~ he was quite full of himself, he looked very pleased with himself. 2 nm,f braggart. **faire le** ~ to brag, boast, go around bragging *ou* boasting.

fanfaronnade [fɑ̃faʀɔnad] nf bragging (*NonC*), boasting (*NonC*), boast. **arrête tes** ~**s** stop boasting.

fanfaronner [fɑ̃faʀɔne] [1] vi to brag, boast.

fanfreluche [fɑ̃fʀəlyʃ] nf (*sur rideau etc*) trimming. **robe ornée de** ~**s** dress trimmed with frills and flounces.

fange [fɑ̃ʒ] nf (*littér*) mire (*littér*); *voir* **traîner, vautrer.**

fangeux, -euse [fɑ̃ʒø, øz] adj (*littér*) miry (*littér*).

fanion [fanjɔ̃] nm *[vélo, club, bateau]* pennant; (*Rugby*) flag; (*Ski*) pennant. (*Mil*) ~ **de commandement** commanding officer's pennant.

fanon [fanɔ̃] nm a *[baleine]* plate of baleen; (*matière*) whalebone (*NonC*). b *[cheval]* fetlock. c *[bœuf]* dewlap; *[dindon]* wattle.

fantaisie [fɑ̃tezi] nf a (*caprice*) whim. **elle se plie à toutes ses** ~**s, elle lui passe toutes ses** ~**s** she gives in to his every whim; **s'offrir une** ~ **en allant** *ou* **s'offrir la** ~ **d'aller au restaurant** to give o.s. a treat by having a meal out *ou* by eating out; **je me suis payé une petite** ~ (*bijou etc*) I bought myself a little present.

b (*extravagance*) extravagance. **cette guerre est une** ~ **coûteuse** this war is a wasteful extravagance; **ces** ~**s vestimentaires** such extravagance *ou* extravagances of dress.

c (*littér: bon plaisir*) **agir selon sa** ~**/vivre à sa** ~**/n'en faire qu'à sa** ~ to behave/live/do as the fancy takes one; **il lui a pris la** ~ **de faire** he took it into his head to do; **à votre** ~ as it may please you.

d (*imagination*) fancy, imagination. **être plein de** ~ to be full of imagination *ou* very fanciful *ou* imaginative; **manquer de** ~ *[vie]* to be monotonous *ou* uneventful; *[personne]* to be lacking in imagination; **c'est de la** ~ **pure** that is sheer *ou* pure fantasy *ou* fancy *ou* imagination.

e **boucles d'oreille (de)** ~ fancy *ou* novelty earrings; **rideaux** ~ fancy curtains; **boutons** ~ fancy *ou* novelty buttons; **kirsch** ~ kirsch-flavoured brandy.

f (*œuvre*) (*Littérat*) fantasy; (*Mus*) fantasia.

fantaisiste [fɑ̃tezist] 1 adj a *nouvelle, explication* fanciful, whimsical. b *personne* (*fumiste*) fanciful; (*bizarre*) eccentric, unorthodox; (*farceur*) whimsical, clownish, comical. 2 nmf a (*Théât*) variety artist *ou* entertainer. b (*original*) eccentric; (*fumiste*) phoney*.

fantasmagorie [fɑ̃tasmagɔʀi] nf phantasmagoria.

fantasmagorique [fɑ̃tasmagɔʀik] adj phantasmagorical.

fantasmatique [fɑ̃tasmatik] adj *rêve, vision* fantastical.

fantasme [fɑ̃tasm] nm fantasy. **il vit dans ses** ~**s** he lives in a fantasy world.

fantasmer [fɑ̃tasme] [1] vi to fantasize (*sur* about).

fantasque [fɑ̃task] adj (*littér*) *personne, humeur* whimsical, capricious; *chose* weird, fantastic.

fantassin [fɑ̃tasɛ̃] nm foot soldier, infantryman. **2 000** ~**s** 2,000 foot *ou* infantry.

fantastique [fɑ̃tastik] 1 adj a (*étrange*) *atmosphère* uncanny, weird, eerie; *événement* uncanny, fantastic; *rêve* weird, fantastic. **conte** ~ tale of fantasy *ou* of the supernatural; **roman** ~ novel of the fantastic, gothic novel; **film** ~ fantasy film; (*genre*) **le cinéma** *ou* **le film** ~ fantasy films (*pl*). b (*) (*excellent*) fantastic*, terrific*, great*; (*énorme, incroyable*) fantastic*, incredible. 2 nm: **le** ~ the fantastic, the uncanny; (*Littérat*) (*gén*) the literature of fantasy *ou* of the fantastic; (*de l'âge romantique*) gothic literature; (*Ciné*) the fantastic.

fantastiquement [fɑ̃tastikmɑ̃] adv (*voir* **fantastique**) uncannily; weirdly; eerily; fantastically*; terrifically*; incredibly.

fantoche [fɑ̃tɔʃ] nm, adj puppet. **gouvernement** ~ puppet government.

fantomatique [fɑ̃tomatik] adj ghostly.

fantôme [fɑ̃tom] 1 nm (*spectre*) ghost, phantom. (*fig*) **c'est un** ~ **de ministre** he is minister in name only; **les** ~**s de l'imagination** the ghosts of the imagination. 2 adj *firme, administrateur* bogus. **bateau** ~ ghost *ou* phantom ship; (*Pol*) **cabinet** ~ shadow cabinet; *voir* **vaisseau.**

fanzine [fɑ̃zin] nm fanzine.

FAO [ɛfao] nf a (abrév de **fabrication assistée par ordinateur**) CAM. b (abrév de **Food and Agriculture Organization**) FAO.

faon [fɑ̃] nm (*Zool*) fawn.

faquin†† [fakɛ̃] nm wretch, rascal.

farad [faʀad] nm farad.

faraday [faʀadɛ] nm faraday.

faramineux, -euse* [faʀaminø, øz] adj *bêtise etc* staggering*, fantastic*, mind-boggling*; *prix* colossal, astronomical*, sky-high* (*attrib*). **toi et tes idées** ~**euses!** you and your brilliant ideas!

farandole [faʀɑ̃dɔl] nf (*danse*) farandole.

faraud, e† [faʀo, od] 1 adj boastful. **tu n'es plus si** ~ you are no longer quite so boastful *ou* full of yourself *ou* pleased with yourself. 2 nm,f braggart. **faire le** ~ to brag, boast.

farce[1] [faʀs] nf a (*tour*) (practical) joke, prank, hoax. **faire une** ~ **à qn** to play a (practical) joke *ou* a prank *ou* a hoax on sb; ~**s (et) attrapes** (*objets*) (assorted) tricks; **magasin de** ~**s-attrapes** joke (and novelty) shop. b (*Théât, fig*) farce. **grosse** ~ slapstick comedy; **ce procès est une** ~ this trial is a farce; *voir* **dindon.**

farce[2] [faʀs] nf (*gén*) stuffing; (*à la viande*) forcemeat.

farceur, -euse [faʀsœʀ, øz] adj, nm,f (*espiègle*) (practical) joker; (*blagueur*) joker, wag; (*péj: fumiste*) clown (*péj*). **il est très** ~ (*gén*) he's quite a (practical) joker, he likes playing tricks *ou* (practical) jokes; *[enfant]* he's very mischievous.

farcir [faʀsiʀ] [2] 1 vt a (*Culin*) to stuff. **tomates farcies** stuffed tomatoes.

b (*fig péj: surtout ptp*) ~ **de** to stuff *ou* cram *ou* pack with; **c'est farci de fautes** it's crammed *ou* packed with mistakes; **j'en ai la tête farcie** I've as much as I can take, I've got a headful of it* (*Brit*).

2 **se farcir** vpr a (*péj*) **se** ~ **la mémoire de** to cram *ou* pack one's memory with.

b (‡) *lessive, travail, personne* to get stuck *ou* landed with*; *bouteille* to knock back*, polish off*; *gâteaux* to scoff* (*Brit*), gobble down*, guzzle*; (**‡) *fille* to have it off with‡ (*Brit*), make it with‡. **il faudra se** ~ **la belle-mère pendant 3 jours** we'll have to put up with the mother-in-law for 3 days; **il faut se le** ~**!** (*importun, bavard*) he's a real pain (in the neck)!*; (*livre*) it's really *ou* hellish heavy going!‡.

fard [faʀ] nm (*maquillage*) make-up; (†: *poudre*) rouge†, paint; *[acteur]* greasepaint. ~ **à joues** blusher; ~ **à paupières** eye shadow; (*fig*) **sans** ~ *parler* openly; *élégance* unpretentious, simple; *voir* **piquer.**

fardage [faʀdaʒ] nm *[bilan, marchandise]* dressing-up.

fardeau, pl ~**x** [faʀdo] nm (*lit*) load, burden (*littér*); (*fig*) burden. **sous le** ~ **de** under the weight *ou* burden of; **il a traîné** *ou* **porté ce** ~ **toute sa vie** he carried *ou* bore this burden all his life.

farder [faʀde] [1] 1 vt a (*Théât*) *acteur* to make up; (††) *visage* to rouge†, paint; (*littér*) *vérité* to disguise, mask, veil. b *bilan, marchandise* to dress up. 2 **se farder** vpr (*se maquiller*) to make (o.s.) up; (†: *se poudrer*) to paint one's face†; *[acteur]* to make up. **femme outrageusement fardée** woman wearing heavy make-up, heavily made-up woman; **se** ~ **les yeux** to put on eye make-up.

farfadet [faʀfadɛ] nm sprite, elf.

farfelu, e* [faʀfəly] 1 adj *idée, projet* cranky, scatty* (*Brit*), harebrained; *personne, conduite* cranky, scatty* (*Brit*), eccentric. 2 nm,f eccentric.

farfouiller* [faʀfuje] [1] vi to rummage about (*dans* in).

faribole [faʀibɔl] nf (*littér*) (piece of) nonsense. **conter des** ~**s** to talk nonsense *ou* twaddle (*Brit*); ~**s (que tout cela)!** (stuff and) nonsense!, fiddlesticks!†

farine [faʀin] 1 nf [blé] flour. **de même ~††** of the same ilk. 2 comp ▸**farine d'avoine** oatmeal ▸**farine complète** wholemeal (*Brit*) *ou* whole wheat flour ▸**farine de froment** wheat *ou* wheaten flour ▸**farine lactée** baby cereal ▸**farine de lin** linseed meal ▸**farine de maïs** cornflour (*Brit*), cornstarch (*US*) ▸**farine de moutarde** mustard powder; *voir* **fleur, rouler.**

fariner [faʀine] [1] vt to flour.

farineux, -euse [faʀinø, øz] 1 adj *consistance, aspect, goût* floury, chalky; *chocolat* powdery, chalky; *fromage* chalky; *pomme de terre* floury; *pomme* dry, mushy. 2 nm: **(aliment) ~** starchy *ou* farinaceous (*SPÉC*) food.

farniente [faʀnjɛnte] nm idle life, idleness. **faire du ~ sur la plage** to lounge on the beach.

farouche [faʀuʃ] adj a (*timide*) *personne, animal* shy, timid; (*peu sociable*) *voisin etc* unsociable. **ces daims ne sont pas ~s** these deer are not a bit shy *ou* timid *ou* are quite tame; (*iro*) **c'est une femme peu ~** she doesn't exactly keep you at arm's length (*iro*). b (*hostile*) fierce. **ennemi ~** bitter enemy *ou* foe. c (*opiniâtre*) *volonté* unshakeable, inflexible; *résistance* unflinching, fierce; *énergie* irrepressible. d (*indompté*) savage, wild.

farouchement [faʀuʃmɑ̃] adv fiercely. **nier ~ qch** to deny sth fiercely *ou* heatedly.

fart [faʀt] nm (ski) wax. **~ de montée** climbing wax.

fartage [faʀtaʒ] nm waxing (*of skis*).

farter [faʀte] [1] vt to wax (*skis*).

Far-West [faʀwɛst] nm: **le ~** the Wild West.

fascicule [fasikyl] nm part, instalment, fascicle (*SPÉC*). **ce livre est vendu avec un ~ d'exercices** this book is sold with a manual of exercises.

fascinant, e [fasinɑ̃, ɑ̃t] adj (*gén*) fascinating; *beauté* bewitching, fascinating.

fascination [fasinasjɔ̃] nf fascination. **exercer une grande ~** to exert (a) great fascination (*sur* on, over), have (a) great fascination (*sur* for).

fascine [fasin] nf (*fagot*) faggot (*of brushwood*); (*Constr*) fascine.

fasciner[1] [fasine] [1] vt (*gén*) to fascinate; (*soumettre à son charme*) to bewitch. **se laisser ~ par des promesses** to allow o.s. to be bewitched by promises; **être fasciné par le pouvoir** to be fascinated *ou* mesmerized by power.

fasciner[2] [fasine] [1] vt (*Constr*) to line with fascines.

fascisant, e [faʃizɑ̃, ɑ̃t] adj fascistic.

fascisme [faʃism] nm fascism.

fasciste [faʃist] adj, nmf fascist.

faste[1] [fast] nm splendour, pomp.

faste[2] [fast] adj (*littér*) *année* (*de chance*) lucky; (*prospère*) good. **jour ~** lucky day.

fastfood [fastfud] nm (*restaurant*) fast food restaurant; (*restauration*) fast food.

fastidieusement [fastidjøzmɑ̃] adv tediously, tiresomely, boringly.

fastidieux, -ieuse [fastidjø, jøz] adj tedious, tiresome, boring.

fastoche‡ [fastɔʃ] adj dead easy*. **c'est vachement ~!** it's a dead cinch!‡.

fastueusement [fastɥøzmɑ̃] adv sumptuously, luxuriously. **recevoir qn ~** (*pour dîner*) to entertain sb lavishly; (*à son arrivée*) to give sb a lavish reception.

fastueux, -euse [fastɥø, øz] adj sumptuous, luxurious. **réception ~euse** lavish reception; **mener une vie ~euse** to lead a sumptuous *ou* luxurious existence, live a life of great luxury.

fat† [fa(t), fat] 1 adj conceited, smug. 2 nm conceited *ou* smug person.

fatal, e, mpl **~s** [fatal] adj a (*funeste*) *accident, issue* fatal; *coup* fatal, deadly. **erreur ~e!** grievous *ou* fatal error!; **être ~ à qn** [*chute, accident*] to kill sb; [*erreur, bêtise*] to prove fatal *ou* disastrous for *ou* to sb. b (*inévitable*) inevitable. **c'était ~!** it was inevitable, it was fated *ou* bound to happen; **il était ~ qu'elle le fasse** she was bound *ou* fated to do it, it was inevitable that she should do it. c (*marqué par le destin*) *instant* fatal, fateful; *air, ton* fateful, fated; *voir* **femme.**

fatalement [fatalmɑ̃] adv (*inévitablement*) **~, il est tombé!** inevitably, he fell!; **au début, ce fut ~ mauvais** at the beginning, it was inevitably *ou* unavoidably bad; **ça devait ~ arriver** it was bound *ou* fated to happen.

fatalisme [fatalism] nm fatalism.

fataliste [fatalist] 1 adj fatalistic. 2 nmf fatalist.

fatalité [fatalite] nf a (*destin*) fate, fatality (*littér*). **être poursuivi par la ~** to be pursued by fate. b (*coïncidence*) fateful coincidence. **par quelle ~ se sont-ils rencontrés?** by what fateful coincidence did they meet?; **ce serait vraiment une ~ si je ne le vois pas** something really extraordinary would have to happen to stop me seeing him. c (*inévitabilité*) inevitability. **la ~ de la mort/de cet événement** the inevitability of death/this event.

fatidique [fatidik] adj (*lourd de conséquences*) *décision, paroles, date* fateful; (*crucial*) *moment* fatal, fateful.

fatigant, e [fatigɑ̃, ɑ̃t] adj (*épuisant*) tiring; (*agaçant*) *personne* annoying, tiresome, tedious; *conversation* tiresome, tedious. **c'est ~ pour la vue** it's tiring *ou* a strain on the eyes; **c'est ~ pour le cœur** it's a strain on the heart; **tu es vraiment ~ avec tes questions** you really are annoying *ou* tiresome *ou* a nuisance with your questions; **c'est ~ de devoir toujours tout répéter** it's annoying *ou* tiresome *ou* a nuisance to have to repeat everything all the time.

fatigue [fatig] nf (*gén*) tiredness (*NonC*), fatigue (*NonC*); (*Méd, Tech*) fatigue. **la ~ des métaux** metal fatigue; **tomber** *ou* **être mort de ~** to be dead tired, be dead beat*, be all in*; **il a voulu nous épargner cette ~** he wanted to save *ou* spare us the strain; **elle avait de soudaines ~s** she had sudden bouts of fatigue *ou* periods of tiredness; **se remettre des ~s du voyage** to get over the wear and tear *ou* the strain *ou* the tiring effects of the journey; **pour se reposer de la ~ du voyage** to rest after the tiring journey *ou* the weary journey; **cette ~ dans le bras gauche** this weakness in the left arm; **~ des yeux** eyestrain; *voir* **recru.**

fatigué, e [fatige] (ptp de **fatiguer**) adj a *personne* tired, weary, fatigued (*frm*); *voix, traits, membres* tired, weary; *cœur* strained, overworked; *cerveau* overtaxed, overworked; *estomac, foie* upset. **il a les bras ~s** his arms are tired *ou* weary; **avoir les yeux ~s** to have eyestrain *ou* strained eyes; **à trente ans, ils ont déjà l'organisme ~** by thirty their bodies are already tired *ou* overworked; **~ par le voyage** travel-worn, travel-weary, tired *ou* weary through *ou* after travelling; (*péj*) **il est né ~** he's bone-lazy *ou* bone-idle (*Brit*). b **~ de** *jérémiades, voiture, femme* tired of; **~ de vivre** tired of living. c *poutre, joint, moteur, habits* worn.

fatiguer [fatige] [1] 1 vt a (*physiquement*) **~ qn** [*maladie, effort, études*] to make sb tired *ou* weary, tire sb; [*professeur, patron*] to overwork sb; **ces efforts fatiguent, à la longue** all this effort tires *ou* wears you out in the end; **ça fatigue les yeux/le cœur/les bras/l'organisme** it is *ou* puts a strain on the eyes/heart/arms/whole body; **se ~ les yeux/le cœur/les bras** to strain one's eyes/heart/arms.

b *bête de somme* [*effort, montée*] to tire, put a strain on; [*propriétaire*] to overwork; *moteur, véhicule* [*effort, montée*] to put (a) strain on, strain; [*propriétaire*] to overwork, strain; *poutre, pièce, joint* to put strain on; *outil, chaussures, vêtement* to wear out; *terre, sol* to exhaust, impoverish; *arbre* to impoverish.

c (*fig: agacer*) to annoy; (*lasser*) to wear out. **tu commences à me ~** you're beginning to annoy me; **avec ses sermons il fatigue, à la longue** in the end he wears you out with his sermons, after a while he becomes a bit wearisome with his sermons.

d *salade* to toss.

2 vi [*moteur*] to labour, strain; [*poutre, pièce, joint*] to become strained, show (signs of) strain; [*personne*] to tire, grow tired *ou* weary. **je commence à ~** I'm starting to get tired.

3 **se fatiguer** vpr a to get tired. **se ~ à faire qch** to tire o.s. out doing sth; (*iro*) **il ne s'est pas trop fatigué** he didn't overdo it *ou* overwork (*iro*), he didn't kill himself*.

b (*se lasser de*) **se ~ de qch/de faire** to get tired *ou* weary of sth/of doing.

c (*s'évertuer à*) **se ~ à répéter/expliquer** to wear o.s. out repeating/explaining; **ne te fatigue pas*** *ou* **pas la peine de te ~*, il est borné** he's just dim so don't bother to *ou* there's no need to wear yourself out *ou* no point wearing yourself out, he's just dim so don't waste your time *ou* your breath.

fatras [fatʀɑ] nm [*choses*] jumble; [*idées*] hotchpotch, jumble.

fatuité [fatɥite] nf self-complacency, self-conceit.

faubourg [fobuʀ] nm (inner) suburb. **avoir l'accent des ~s** to have a Paris working-class accent.

faubourien, -ienne [fobuʀjɛ̃, jɛn] adj *accent, manières* Paris working-class.

fauchage [foʃaʒ] nm (*voir* **faucher**) reaping; mowing; scything; cutting.

fauchaison [foʃɛzɔ̃] nf a (*époque*) [*pré*] mowing (time), reaping (time); [*blés*] reaping (time). b (*action*) = **fauchage.**

fauche [foʃ] nf a (‡: *vol*) pinching* (*Brit*), swiping*, nicking‡ (*Brit*). **il y a beaucoup de ~** there's a lot of thieving; **lutter contre la ~ dans les supermarchés** to combat shoplifting *ou* thieving in supermarkets. b (††) = **fauchaison.**

fauché, e* [foʃe] (ptp de **faucher**) adj (*sans argent*) (stony-)broke* (*Brit*), flat *ou* dead broke* (*attrib*), hard up*. **il est ~ comme les blés** he hasn't got a bean* (*Brit*) *ou* a brass farthing (*Brit*), he hasn't a penny to his name; **c'est un éternel ~** he's permanently broke*, he never has a penny; (*iro*) **avec toi, on n'est pas ~!** you're a fat lot of goods!*, you're a dead loss!*

faucher [foʃe] [1] 1 vt a *blé* to reap; *champs, prés* to mow, reap; *herbe* (*avec une faux*) to scythe, mow, cut; (*mécaniquement*) to mow, cut. **on va ~ demain** we're mowing *ou* reaping tomorrow.

b (*fig: abattre*) [*vent*] to flatten; [*véhicule*] to knock over *ou* down, mow down; [*tir*] to mow down; [*explosion*] to flatten, blow over; (*Ftbl*) to bring down. **la mort l'a fauché en pleine jeunesse** death cut him down in the prime of (his) youth; **avoir un bras fauché par l'explosion** to have an arm blown off by the explosion; **avoir une jambe fauchée par le train** to have a leg cut off *ou* taken off by the train.

c (‡: *voler*) *portefeuille, femme* to pinch* (*Brit*), swipe*, nick‡ (*Brit*).

2 vi [*cheval*] to dish.

faucheur, -euse [foʃœʀ, øz] 1 nm,f (*personne*) mower, reaper. 2

nm = faucheux. 3 **faucheuse** nf (*machine*) reaper, mower. (*littér: mort*) **la F~** the (Grim) Reaper.

faucheux [foʃø] nm harvestman (*Brit*), harvest-spider, daddy-long-legs (*US*).

faucille [fosij] nf sickle. **la ~ et le marteau** the hammer and sickle.

faucon [fokɔ̃] nm (*lit*) falcon, hawk; (*fig: personne*) hawk. **~ pèlerin** peregrine falcon; **chasser au ~** to hawk.

fauconneau, pl ~x [fokɔno] nm young falcon *ou* hawk.

fauconnerie [fokɔnʀi] nf (*art*) falconry; (*chasse*) hawking, falconry; (*lieu*) hawk house.

fauconnier [fokɔnje] nm falconer, hawker.

faufil [fofil] nm tacking *ou* basting thread.

faufilage [fofilaʒ] nm tacking, basting.

faufiler [fofile] 1 1 vt to tack, baste. 2 **se faufiler** vpr (*dans un passage étroit*) **se ~ dans** to worm *ou* inch *ou* edge one's way into; (*entre des obstacles, des personnes*) **se ~ entre** to dodge in and out of, thread one's way through; **se ~ par un sentier étroit** to thread *ou* edge one's way along a narrow path; **se ~ parmi la foule** to worm *ou* inch *ou* thread one's way through the crowd, slip through the crowd; **se ~ entre les** *ou* **au milieu des voitures** to nip *ou* dodge in and out of the traffic, thread one's way through the traffic; **il se faufila à l'intérieur/au dehors** he wormed *ou* inched *ou* edged his way in/out.

faufilure [fofilyʀ] nf (*Couture*) tacked *ou* basted seam; (*action*) tacking, basting.

faune[1] [fon] nm (*Myth*) faun.

faune[2] [fon] nf (*Zool*) wildlife, fauna (*SPÉC*); (*péj: personnes*) set, mob. **~ marine** marine animal-life; **~ des Alpes** Alpine wildlife *ou* fauna (*SPÉC*).

faunesque [fonɛsk] adj faunlike.

faussaire [fosɛʀ] nmf forger.

fausse [fos] adj f *voir* **faux**[2].

faussement [fosmɑ̃] adv *accuser* wrongly, wrongfully; *croire* wrongly, erroneously, falsely. **~ modeste** falsely modest; **~ intéressé** superficially *ou* falsely interested; **d'un ton ~ indifférent** in a tone of feigned indifference, in a deceptively detached tone of voice.

fausser [fose] 1 vt a *calcul, statistique, fait* to distort, alter; *réalité, pensée* to distort, pervert; *sens d'un mot* to distort; *esprit* to unsettle, disturb; *jugement* to distort, disturb. b *clef* to bend; *serrure* to break; *poulie, manivelle, charnière* to buckle, bend; *essieu, volant, hélice, lame* to warp, buckle, bend. **soudain il se troubla, sa voix se faussa** suddenly he became flustered and his voice became strained. c (*loc*) **~ compagnie à qn** to give sb the slip, slip *ou* sneak away from sb; **vous nous avez de nouveau faussé compagnie hier soir** you gave us the slip again last night, you sneaked *ou* slipped off again last night.

fausset[1] [fosɛ] nm falsetto (voice). **d'une voix de ~** in a falsetto voice.

fausset[2] [fosɛ] nm *[tonneau]* spigot.

fausseté [foste] nf a *[idée, accusation, dogme]* falseness, falsity. b *[caractère, personne]* duplicity, deceitfulness. c (†: *propos mensonger*) falsity†, falsehood.

Faust [fost] nm Faust.

faustien, -ienne [fostjɛ̃, jɛn] adj Faustian, of Faust.

faut [fo] *voir* **falloir**.

faute [fot] 1 nf a (*erreur*) mistake, error. **faire** *ou* **commettre une ~** to make a mistake *ou* an error; **~ de grammaire** grammatical mistake *ou* error; **~ de ponctuation** mistake in punctuation, error of punctuation; **candidat qui a fait un sans ~*** candidate who hasn't put a foot wrong.

b (*mauvaise action*) misdeed; (*Jur*) offence; (†: *péché de chair*) lapse (from virtue), sin (of the flesh). **commettre une ~** (*gén*) to commit a misdeed *ou* misdemeanour; (†: *péché de chair*) to sin; **une ~ contre** *ou* **envers la religion** a sin *ou* transgression against religion; **commettre une ~ professionnelle grave** to commit a serious professional misdemeanour; **renvoyé pour ~ professionnelle** dismissed for professional misconduct.

c (*Sport*) (*Ftbl etc*) foul; (*Tennis*) fault. **le joueur a fait une ~** the player committed a foul; **faire une ~ sur qn** to foul sb; (*Volleyball*) **faire une ~ de filet** to make contact with the net; **faire une ~ de main** to handle the ball; (*Basketball*) **~ personnelle** personal foul; **faire une ~ de pied** to foot fault; (*Tennis*) **faire une double ~ (de service)** to serve a double fault, double-fault; **~!** (*pour un joueur*) foul!; (*Tennis: pour la balle*) fault!; (*Tennis*) **la balle est ~** the ball was out.

d (*responsabilité*) fault. **par la ~ de Richard/sa ~** because of Richard/him; **c'est de la ~ de Richard/de sa ~** it's Richard's fault/his fault; **c'est la ~ à Richard/sa ~*** it's because of Richard/him, it's through Richard/him*; **la ~ lui en revient** the fault lies with him; **à qui la ~?** whose fault is it?, who is to blame?

e (*loc*) **être/se sentir en ~** to be/feel at fault *ou* in the wrong; **prendre qn en ~** to catch sb out; **il ne se fait pas ~ de faire** he doesn't shy from *ou* at doing, he doesn't fail to do; **ce livre perdu lui fait bien ~†** he really misses that lost book; **~ de** for *ou* through lack of; **~ d'argent** for want of *ou* through lack of money; **~ de temps** for *ou* through lack of time; **~ de mieux** for lack of *ou* want of anything better, failing anything better; **~ de quoi** failing which, otherwise; **relâché ~ de preuves** released for *ou* through lack of evidence; **~ de réponse sous huitaine** failing a reply within a week, if we receive no reply within a week; **~ d'avis contraire** unless advised to the contrary, unless otherwise informed; **~ d'y être allé, je ...** since I didn't go, I ...; **je n'y suis pas arrivé, mais ce n'est pas ~ d'avoir essayé** I didn't manage to do it but it wasn't for want *ou* lack of trying; **le combat cessa ~ de combattants** the battle died down, there being nobody left to carry on the fight; (*Prov*) **~ de grives, on mange des merles** you have to cut your coat according to your cloth (*Prov*), beggars can't be choosers (*Prov*); (*Prov*) **~ avouée est à demi pardonnée** a sin confessed is a sin half pardoned; *voir* **sans**.

2 comp ►**faute d'accord** (*Ling*) mistake in (the) agreement ►**faute de calcul** miscalculation, error in calculation ►**faute de carres** (*Ski*) edging mistake ►**faute civile** (*Jur*) civil wrong ►**faute de conduite** (*Aut*) (*erreur*) driving error; (*infraction*) driving offence ►**faute d'étourderie** = **faute d'inattention** ►**faute de français** grammatical mistake (*in French*) ►**faute de frappe** typing error ►**faute de goût** error of taste ►**faute d'impression** misprint ►**faute d'inattention** careless *ou* thoughtless mistake ►**faute lourde** *[employé]* gross misconduct (*NonC*) ►**faute d'orthographe** spelling mistake ►**faute pénale** (*Jur*) criminal offence ►**faute professionnelle** professional misconduct (*NonC*) ►**faute de service** (*Admin*) act of (administrative) negligence.

fauter† [fote] 1 vi *[jeune fille]* to sin.

fauteuil [fotœj] 1 nm (*gén*) armchair; (*avec dos rembourré, moderne*) easy chair, armchair; *[président]* chair; *[théâtre, académicien]* seat. (*siéger comme président*) **occuper le ~** to be in the chair; (*fig*) **il est arrivé dans un ~*** he walked it* (*Brit*), he romped home*.

2 comp ►**fauteuil de balcon** (*Théât*) balcony seat; seat in the dress circle ►**fauteuils de balcon** (*région de la salle*) dress circle ►**fauteuil à bascule** rocking chair ►**fauteuil club** (big) leather easy chair ►**fauteuil crapaud** squat armchair ►**fauteuil de dentiste** dentist's chair ►**fauteuil de jardin** garden chair ►**fauteuil d'orchestre** (*Théât*) seat in the front *ou* orchestra stalls (*Brit*) *ou* the orchestra (*US*) ►**fauteuils d'orchestre** (*région de la salle*) front *ou* orchestra stalls (*Brit*), orchestra (*US*) ►**fauteuil pivotant** swivel chair ►**fauteuil pliant** folding chair ►**fauteuil roulant** wheelchair ►**fauteuil tournant** = **fauteuil pivotant**.

fauteur [fotœʀ] nm: **~ de troubles** *ou* **de désordre** troublemaker, mischief-maker, agitator; **~ de guerre** warmonger.

fautif, -ive [fotif, iv] 1 adj a *conducteur* at fault (*attrib*), in the wrong (*attrib*); *élève, enfant* guilty. **il se sentait ~** he felt (he was) at fault *ou* in the wrong *ou* guilty. b *texte, liste, calcul* faulty, incorrect; *citation* incorrect, inaccurate; (*littér*) *mémoire* poor, faulty. 2 nm,f: **c'est moi le ~** I'm the one to blame *ou* the guilty one *ou* the culprit.

fautivement [fotivmɑ̃] adv by mistake, in error.

fauve [fov] 1 adj a *tissu, couleur* tawny, fawn(-coloured); (*littér*) *odeur* musky; *voir* **bête**. b (*Art*) **période ~** Fauvist period. 2 nm a (*animal*) wildcat. **les ~s** the big cats; **ça sent le ~ ici*** there's a strong smell of B.O. in here*, it really stinks (of sweat) here*. b (*couleur*) fawn. c (*Art*) Fauvist, painter of the Fauvist school. **les F~s** the Fauvists *ou* Fauves.

fauverie [fovʀi] nf big-cat house.

fauvette [fovɛt] nf warbler. **~ d'hiver** *ou* **des haies** hedgesparrow, durnock; **~ des marais** sedge warbler.

faux[1] [fo] nf scythe.

faux[2], **fausse** [fo, fos] 1 adj a (*imité*) *argent, billet* forged, fake; *marbre, bijoux, meuble* (*en toc*) imitation; (*pour duper*) false, fake; *documents, signature* false, fake; *tableau* fake. **fausse pièce** forged *ou* fake coin, dud*; **une fausse carte** a trick card; **~ papiers** forged identity papers; **fausse monnaie** forged currency; **fausse perle** artificial *ou* imitation pearl.

b (*postiche*) *dent, nez* false.

c (*simulé*) *bonhomie, colère, désespoir, modestie* feigned. **un ~ air de prude/de bonhomie** an air of false prudery/good-naturedness; **fausse dévotion** false piety.

d (*mensonger*) *déclaration, promesse, prétexte* false, spurious (*frm*). **c'est ~** it's wrong *ou* untrue.

e (*pseudo*) *savant, écrivain* bogus, sham (*épith*).

f (*fourbe*) *personne, attitude* false, deceitful; *regard* deceitful.

g (*inexact*) *calcul, numéro, rue* wrong; *idée* mistaken, wrong; *affirmation, faits* wrong, untrue; *instrument de mesure, raisonnement* wrong, inaccurate, faulty; *instrument de musique, voix* out of tune; *vers* faulty. **c'est ~** *[résultat]* that's wrong; *[fait]* that's wrong *ou* untrue; **il est ~ (de dire) qu'il y soit allé** it's wrong *ou* incorrect to say that he went, it's not true (to say) that he went; **dire quelque chose de ~** to say something (that's) wrong *ou* untrue; **faire fausse route** (*lit*) to go the wrong way, take the wrong road; (*fig*) to be on the wrong track; **faire un ~ pas** (*lit*) to trip, stumble; (*fig*) to make a foolish mistake; (*par manque de tact*) to make a faux pas.

h (*non fondé*) *espoir, rumeur, soupçons, principe* false. **avoir de fausses craintes** to have groundless *ou* ill-founded fears.

i (*gênant, ambigu*) *position, situation, atmosphère* awkward, false.

2 nm a (*mensonge, Philos*) **le ~** falsehood; *voir* **vrai**.

b (*contrefaçon*) forgery; (*tableau, meuble, document*) fake, forgery.

faire un ~ to commit a forgery; (*Jur*) **pour ~ et usage de ~** for forgery and the use of forgeries; **~ en écriture** false entry; *voir* **inscrire**.

3 **adv** a *chanter, jouer* out of tune, off key. **sonner ~** *[rire, paroles]* to have a false *ou* hollow ring, sound false; **avoir tout ~*** (*gén: avoir tort*) to get it all wrong; (*à un examen*) to get everything wrong.

b **tomber à ~** to come at the wrong moment; **accuser qn à ~** to accuse sb unjustly *ou* wrongly; *voir* **porter**.

4 **comp ▸faux acacia** locust tree, false acacia **▸fausse alerte** false alarm **▸faux ami** (*traître*) false friend; (*Ling*) false friend, faux ami, deceptive cognate **▸faux bond: faire faux bond à qn** to let sb down, leave sb in the lurch **▸faux-bourdon nm (pl faux-bourdons)** (*Mus*) faux bourdon **▸faux bourdon** (*Entomologie*) faux bourdon, drone **▸faux bruit** false rumour **▸faux chignon** hairpiece **▸fausse clef** skeleton key **▸faux col** *[chemise]* detachable collar; *[bière]* head **▸fausses côtes** false ribs **▸fausse couche** miscarriage; **faire une fausse couche** to have a miscarriage **▸faux cul‡** (*homme*) two-faced bastard‡; (*femme*) two-faced bitch‡ **▸faux départ** (*lit, fig*) false start **▸faux dévôt, fausse dévote nm,f** pharisee **▸faux ébénier** laburnum **▸fausse fenêtre** blind window **▸faux-filet nm (pl faux-filets)** sirloin **▸faux frais pl** extras, incidental expenses **▸faux frère** false friend **▸faux-fuyant nm (pl faux-fuyants)** prevarication, evasion, equivocation; **assez de faux-fuyants** stop dodging *ou* evading the issue, stop hedging *ou* prevaricating; **user de faux-fuyants** to equivocate, prevaricate, evade the issue **▸faux jeton*** phoney* **▸fausse joie** vain joy **▸faux jour** (*lit*) deceptive light; (*fig*) **sous un faux jour** in a false light **▸fausse manœuvre** (*lit*) wrong movement; (*fig*) wrong move **▸faux-monnayeur nm (pl faux-monnayeurs)** forger, counterfeiter **▸faux mouvement** clumsy *ou* awkward movement **▸faux nom** false *ou* assumed name **▸fausse note** (*Mus*) wrong note; (*fig*) sour note; (*fig*) **sans une fausse note** without a sour note, smoothly **▸fausse nouvelle** false report **▸faux ourlet** false hem **▸fausse piste** (*lit, fig*) wrong track **▸faux plafond** false ceiling **▸faux plat** (*montée*) slight incline; (*creux*) dip (in the road) **▸faux pli** crease **▸faux(-)pont** (*Naut*) **(pl faux(-)ponts)** orlop deck **▸fausse porte** false door **▸faux problème** non-problem, non-issue **▸fausse pudeur** false modesty **▸faux seins** falsies* **▸faux-semblant nm (pl faux-semblants)** sham, pretence; **user de faux-semblants** to put up a pretence **▸faux-sens (pl faux-sens)** misinterpretation **▸faux serment** false oath **▸fausse sortie** (*Théât*) sham exit; (*fig*) **il a fait une fausse sortie** he made a pretence of leaving **▸faux témoignage** (*déposition mensongère*) false evidence (*NonC*); (*délit*) perjury **▸faux témoin** lying witness **▸faux-titre** (*Typ*) **nm (pl faux-titres)** half-title, bastard title.

faveur[1] [favœʀ] **nf** a (*frm: gentillesse*) favour. **faites-moi la ~ de ...** would you be so kind as to ...; **fais-moi une ~** do me a favour; **obtenir qch par ~** to get sth as a favour; **par ~ spéciale (de la direction)** by special favour (of the management).

b (*considération*) (*littér, hum*) **avoir la ~ du ministre** to be in favour with the minister; **gagner/perdre la ~ du public** to win/lose public favour, find favour/fall out of favour with the public; (*littér*) **être en ~** to be in favour (*auprès de qn* with sb).

c (*littér, hum*) **~s** favours; **elle lui a refusé ses ~s** she refused him her favours; **elle lui a accordé ses dernières ~s** she bestowed her (ultimate) favours upon him (*littér, hum*).

d **de ~** preferential, special; **billet de ~** complimentary ticket; **prix/taux de ~** preferential *ou* special price/rate; **régime *ou* traitement de ~** preferential treatment.

e **en ~ de** (*à cause de*) in consideration of, on account of; (*au profit de*) in favour of, for; (*dans un but charitable*) in aid of, on behalf of, for; **en ma/sa ~** in my/his (*ou* her) favour.

f **à la ~ de** thanks to, owing to; **à la ~ de la nuit** under cover of darkness.

faveur[2] [favœʀ] **nf** (*ruban*) ribbon, favour.

favorable [favɔʀabl] **adj** a *moment, occasion* right, favourable; *terrain, position, vent* favourable. **par temps ~** in favourable weather; **avoir un préjugé ~ envers** to be biased in favour of, be favourably disposed towards; **jouir d'un préjugé ~** to be favourably considered; **recevoir un accueil ~** to meet with a favourable reception; **se montrer sous un jour ~** to show o.s. in a favourable light; **prêter une oreille ~ à** to lend a sympathetic *ou* kindly ear to; **voir qch d'un œil ~** to view sth favourably *ou* with a favourable eye; **le change nous est ~** the exchange rate is in our favour. b *[personne]* **être ~ à** to be favourable to.

favorablement [favɔʀabləmɑ̃] **adv** favourably.

favori, -ite [favɔʀi, it] 1 **adj** favourite. 2 **nm** a (*préféré, gagnant probable*) favourite. **cet acteur est un ~ du public** this actor is a favourite with the public; **le ~ des jeunes** the favourite with *ou* of young people; (*Sport*) **ils sont partis ~s** they started off favourites; **c'est le grand ~ de la course** he's the firm favourite for the race. b (*Hist*) king's favourite. 3 **favorite nf** favourite; (*Hist*) king's favourite *ou* mistress.

favoris [favɔʀi] **nmpl** side whiskers, sideboards* (*Brit*), sideburns*.

favoriser [favɔʀize] 1 **vt** a (*avantager, encourager*) *candidat, ambitions, commerce, parti* to favour. **les événements l'ont favorisé** events favoured him *ou* were to his advantage; **la fortune le favorise** fortune favours him; **les classes les plus favorisées** the most fortunate *ou* favoured classes. b (*faciliter*) to further, favour. **ceci a favorisé la rébellion/sa fuite** this furthered *ou* favoured the rebellion/his escape.

favorite [favɔʀit] *voir* **favori**.

favoritisme [favɔʀitism] **nm** favouritism.

fax [faks] **nm** fax. **envoyer par ~** to send by fax, fax.

faxer [fakse] 1 **vt** to fax.

fayot [fajo] **nm** a (**: Culin*) bean. b (*‡ péj: lèche-bottes*) bootlicker, crawler*, brown-nose‡ (*US*).

fayo(t)tage‡ [fajɔtaʒ] **nm** boot-licking, crawling*, brown-nosing‡ (*US*).

fayo(t)ter‡ [fajɔte] 1 **vi** (*faire du zèle*) to crawl*, suck up‡, brown-nose‡ (*US*).

FB (**abrév de franc belge**) *voir* **franc**.

FBI [ɛfbiaj] **nm** (**abrév de Federal Bureau of Investigation**) FBI.

Fco abrév de franco.

féal, e, mpl -aux [feal, o] 1 **adj** (††) loyal, trusty. 2 **nm,f** (*littér, hum*) loyal supporter.

fébrifuge [febʀifyʒ] **adj, nm** febrifuge (*SPÉC*), antipyretic.

fébrile [febʀil] **adj** (*lit, fig*) feverish, febrile (*frm*).

fébrilement [febʀilmɑ̃] **adv** feverishly.

fébrilité [febʀilite] **nf** feverishness.

fécal, e, mpl -aux [fekal, o] **adj** faecal. **matières ~es** faeces.

fèces [fɛs] **nfpl** faeces.

FECOM [fekɔm] **nm** (**abrév de Fonds européen de coopération monétaire**) EMCF.

fécond, e [fekɔ̃, ɔ̃d] **adj** a (*non stérile*) *femelle, fleur* fertile. b (*prolifique*) prolific. c (*fertile*) *sujet, idée* fruitful; *esprit* creative, fertile; (*littér*) *terre* fruitful, rich, fecund (*littér*). **journées/vacances ~es en mésaventures/événements** days/holidays rich in *ou* abounding in mishaps/events.

fécondable [fekɔ̃dabl(ə)] **adj** *ovule* capable of being fertilized; *femme, femelle* capable of becoming pregnant.

fécondateur, -trice [fekɔ̃datœʀ, tʀis] **adj** (*littér*) fertilizing.

fécondation [fekɔ̃dasjɔ̃] **nf** a (*NonC: voir* **féconder**) impregnation; insemination; pollination; fertilization. b (*acte, moment*) **la ~** fertilization; **la ~ artificielle** artificial insemination; **~ in vitro** in vitro fertilization; **le mystère de la ~** the mystery of fertilization.

féconder [fekɔ̃de] 1 **vt** *femme* to make pregnant, impregnate (*frm*); *animal* to inseminate, fertilize; *fleur* to pollinate, fertilize; (*littér*) *terre* to make fruitful; (*fig*) *esprit* to enrich.

fécondité [fekɔ̃dite] **nf** fertility, fecundity (*littér*); (*fig*) *[terre, sujet, idée]* fruitfulness, richness, fecundity (*littér*).

fécule [fekyl] **nf** starch. **~ (de pommes de terre)** potato flour.

féculent, e [fekylɑ̃, ɑ̃t] 1 **adj** starchy. 2 **nm** starchy food.

FED [ɛfəde] **nm** (**abrév de Fonds européen de développement**) EDF.

fédéral, e, mpl -aux [fedeʀal, o] **adj** federal.

fédéraliser [fedeʀalize] 1 **vt** to federalize.

fédéralisme [fedeʀalism] **nm** federalism.

fédéraliste [fedeʀalist] **adj, nmf** federalist.

fédérateur, -trice [fedeʀatœʀ, tʀis] 1 **adj** federative. 2 **nm, f** unifier.

fédératif, -ive [fedeʀatif, iv] **adj** federative.

fédération [fedeʀasjɔ̃] **nf** federation. **~ syndicale** trade union; **F~ syndicale mondiale** World Federation of Trade Unions.

fédéré, e [fedeʀe] (**ptp de fédérer**) **adj** federate.

fédérer [fedeʀe] 6 **vt** to federate.

fée [fe] **nf** fairy. **la ~ du logis** the perfect homemaker; **la ~ Carabosse** the (wicked) fairy Carabossa; *voir* **conte, doigt**.

feed-back [fidbak] **nm inv** feedback.

feeder [fidœʀ] **nm** (*Tech*) feeder.

feeling [filiŋ] **nm** feeling. **faire qch au ~** to do sth intuitively.

féerie [fe(e)ʀi] **nf** a (*Ciné, Théât*) extravaganza, spectacular (*incorporating features from pantomime*). b (*littér: vision enchanteresse*) **~ des soirées d'été/d'un ballet** enchantment of summer evenings/of a ballet; **la ~ à jamais perdue de l'enfance** the irretrievable fairytale world of childhood.

féerique [fe(e)ʀik] **adj** magical, fairy (*épith*).

feignant, e [fɛɲɑ̃, ɑ̃t] = **fainéant.**

feindre [fɛ̃dʀ] 52 1 **vt** (*simuler*) *enthousiasme, ignorance, innocence* to feign. **~ la colère** to pretend to be angry, feign anger; **~ d'être/de faire** to pretend to be/do; **il feint de ne pas comprendre** he pretends not to understand; **~ de dormir** to feign sleep, pretend to be asleep. 2 **vi** (*frm*) to dissemble, dissimulate. **inutile de ~ (avec moi)** no use pretending (with me).

feint, e[1] [fɛ̃, fɛ̃t] (**ptp de feindre**) **adj** a *émotion, maladie* feigned, affected. b (*Archit*) *fenêtre etc* false.

feinte[2] [fɛ̃t] **nf** a (*manœuvre*) (*gén*) dummy move; (*Ftbl, Rugby*) dummy (*Brit*), fake (*US*); (*Boxe, Escrime*) feint. (*Rugby*) **faire une ~** to dummy; (*Rugby*) **~ de passe** dummy pass. b (*littér: ruse*) sham (*NonC*), pretence. **agir/parler sans ~** to act/speak without dissimulation.

feinter [fɛ̃te] 1 1 **vt** a (*Ftbl, Rugby*) to dummy (*Brit*) *ou* fake (*US*) (one's way past); (*Boxe, Escrime*) to feint at. b (*‡: duper, avoir*) to trick, have*, take in. **j'ai été feinté** I've been had* *ou* taken in. 2 **vi** (*Escrime*) to feint.

feldspath [fɛldspat] **nm** fel(d)spar.

fêler [fele] 1 1 **vt** to crack. **avoir le cerveau fêlé*** *ou* **la tête fêlée*, être**

fêlé* to be a bit cracked*. 2 **se fêler** vpr to crack. **se ~ le bras** to crack a bone in one's arm; **voix fêlée** cracked voice.

félicitations [felisitasjɔ̃] nfpl congratulations (*pour* on). **~!** congratulations!; **faire ses ~ à qn de** *ou* **sur qch** to congratulate sb on sth; (*Scol, Univ*) **avec les ~ du jury** highly commended, summa cum laude.

félicité [felisite] nf (*littér, Rel*) bliss (*NonC*).

féliciter [felisite] 1 1 vt to congratulate (*qn de ou sur qch* sb on sth). (*iro*) **je vous félicite!** congratulations! (*iro*), well done! (*iro*); **eh bien je ne vous félicite pas** you don't get any praise for that. 2 **se féliciter** vpr to congratulate o.s. (*de* on), be very glad *ou* pleased (*de* about). **je n'y suis pas allé et je m'en félicite** I didn't go and I'm glad *ou* very pleased I didn't; **il se félicitait d'avoir refusé d'y aller** he was congratulating himself on having *ou* patting himself on the back* for having refused to go.

félidés [felide] nmpl (*Zool*) **les ~** the Felidae (*SPÉC*), the cat family.

félin, e [felɛ̃, in] 1 adj *race* feline; *allure, grâce* feline, catlike. 2 nm feline. **les ~s** the (big) cats.

fellah [fela] nm fellah.

fellation [felasjɔ̃] nf fellatio(n).

félon, -onne [felɔ̃, ɔn] (*frm*) 1 adj perfidious (*frm*), disloyal, treacherous. 2 nm (*aussi hum*) traitor. 3 **félonne** nf (*aussi hum*) traitress.

félonie [felɔni] nf (*frm*) (*NonC*) perfidy (*frm*), disloyalty; (*acte*) act of treachery, perfidy.

felouque [fəluk] nf felucca.

fêlure [felyʀ] nf (*lit, fig*) crack.

femelle [fəmɛl] 1 adj (*Bot, Tech, Zool*) female; *animal* (*gén*) she-, female; *oiseau* hen-, female; *baleine, éléphant* cow-, female. 2 nf (*Zool*) female; (‡ *péj: femme*) female‡ (*péj*).

féminin, e [feminɛ̃, in] 1 adj (*gén, Ling*) feminine; *hormone, population, sexe* female; *mode, revendications, vêtements,* (*Sport*) *épreuve, équipe* women's. **elle est peu ~e** she's not very feminine; **elle est déjà très ~e** she's already quite a young woman; **il a des traits assez ~s** he has rather feminine *ou* womanish features; *voir* **éternel, intuition, rime** *etc.* 2 nm (*Ling*) feminine. **au ~** in the feminine.

féminisant, e [feminizɑ̃, ɑ̃t] adj feminizing.

féminisation [feminizasjɔ̃] nf feminization.

féminiser [feminize] 1 1 vt (*Bio*) to feminize; (*Ling*) to make feminine, put in the feminine; (*rendre efféminé*) to make effeminate. **~ une profession** to increase the number of women in a profession; **profession féminisée** largely female profession. 2 **se féminiser** vpr (*Bio*) to feminize; (*devenir efféminé*) to become effeminate. **la profession de juriste se féminise** an increasing number of women are entering the legal profession.

féminisme [feminism] nm feminism.

féministe [feminist] adj, nmf feminist.

féminité [feminite] nf femininity.

femme [fam] 1 nf a (*individu*) woman. (*espèce*) **la ~** woman; **une jeune ~** a young woman *ou* lady; **les droits de la ~ mariée** the rights of married women *ou* a married woman; **la ~ de sa vie** the only woman for him; **elle n'est pas ~ à faire ceci** she's not the type (of woman) to do that; **ce que ~ veut ...** what a woman wants ...; **les ~s et les enfants d'abord!** women and children first!; *voir* **bon[1], bout, chercher** *etc.*

b (*épouse*) wife. **demander qn pour ~**† to ask (for) sb's hand (in marriage)†; **prendre qn pour ~**† to take sb as one's wife (†, *hum*), take sb to wife (*littér*); **chercher/prendre ~** to seek/take a wife (*littér*).

c (*profession*) **~ médecin/professeur** (woman *ou* lady) doctor/teacher.

d (*Jur*) **la ~ X** the wife of X, the woman X.

2 adj inv a **être/devenir ~** (*nubile*) to have reached *ou* attained/reach *ou* attain womanhood; (*n'être plus vierge*) to be/become a woman; **être très ~** (*féminine*) to be very much a woman, be very womanly.

b **professeur/médecin ~** woman *ou* lady teacher/doctor.

3 comp ►**femme d'affaires** businesswoman ►**femme auteur** authoress ►**femme de chambre** chambermaid ►**femme de charge** housekeeper ►**femme entretenue**† (*péj*) kept woman ►**femme d'esprit** woman of wit and learning ►**femme fatale** femme fatale ►**la femme au foyer** the housewife, the woman who stays at home ►**femme d'intérieur** housewife; **être femme d'intérieur** to be homely (*Brit*) *ou* houseproud ►**femme de lettres** woman of letters ►**femme de mauvaise vie**† loose woman ►**femme de ménage** domestic help, cleaning lady ►**femme du monde** society woman ►**la femme-objet** woman as a sex object ►**femme de petite vertu**† woman of easy virtue ►**femme de service** (*nettoyage*) cleaner; (*cantine*) dinner lady ►**femme soldat** woman soldier ►**femme de tête** strong-minded intellectual woman.

femmelette [famlɛt] nf (*péj*) (*homme*) weakling; (*femme*) frail female.

fémoral, e, mpl **-aux** [femɔʀal, o] adj femoral.

fémur [femyʀ] nm thighbone, femur (*SPÉC*); *voir* **col.**

F.E.N. [fɛn] nf (abrév de **Fédération de l'éducation nationale**) *confederation of teachers' unions.*

fenaison [fənɛzɔ̃] nf (*époque*) haymaking time; (*action*) haymaking.

fendant [fɑ̃dɑ̃] nm Swiss white wine (*from the Valais region*).

fendard[1]‡ [fɑ̃daʀ] nm bags* (*Brit*), (pair of) trousers (*Brit*), (pair of) pants (*US*).

fendard[2], e‡ [fɑ̃daʀ, aʀd] adj hilarious. **ce film est vraiment ~** that film is a real scream*.

fendart‡ [fɑ̃daʀ] nm = **fendard[1].**

fendillé, e [fɑ̃dije] (ptp de **fendiller**) adj (*voir* **fendiller**) crazed; sprung; chapped.

fendillement [fɑ̃dijmɑ̃] nm (*voir* **fendiller**) crazing; springing; chapping.

fendiller [fɑ̃dije] 1 1 vt *glace, plâtre, porcelaine, terre, vernis* to craze; *bois* to spring; *lèvres, peau* to chap. 2 **se fendiller** vpr to craze (over); to spring; to chap.

fendoir [fɑ̃dwaʀ] nm chopper, cleaver.

fendre [fɑ̃dʀ] 41 1 vt a *[personne]* (*couper en deux*) *bûche, ardoise* to split; *tissu* to slit, slash. **~ du bois** to chop wood; **il lui fendit le crâne d'un seul coup de son arme** he cleft open *ou* he split his skull with a single blow of his weapon.

b *[éléments, cataclysme, accident] rochers* to cleave; *mur, plâtre, meuble* to crack. **cette chute lui a fendu le crâne** this fall cracked *ou* split his skull open; **le séisme fendit la colline dans le sens de la longueur** the earthquake split *ou* cleft the hill lengthwise *ou* along its length; *voir* **geler.**

c (*pénétrer*) to cut *ou* slice through, cleave through (*littér*). **~ les flots/l'air** to cleave through (*littér*) the waves/air; **le soc fend la terre** the ploughshare cuts through the earth; (*fig*) **~ la foule** to push *ou* cleave (*littér*) one's way through the crowd.

d (*Habillement*) *jupe* to put a slit in; *veste* to put a vent in; *manche* to put a slash in.

e (*loc*) **ce récit me fend le cœur** *ou* **l'âme** this story breaks my heart *ou* makes my heart bleed; **des soupirs à ~ l'âme** heartrending *ou* heartbreaking sighs.

2 **se fendre** vpr a (*se fissurer*) to crack.

b **il s'est fendu le crâne** he has cracked his skull; **se ~ la lèvre** to cut one's lip; **se ~ la pipe‡** *ou* **la pêche‡** *ou* **la poire‡** *ou* **la gueule‡** (*rire*) to laugh one's head off, split one's sides*; (*s'amuser*) to have a good laugh.

c (*Escrime*) to lunge.

d (‡) **se ~ de** *somme* to shell out*; *bouteille, cadeau* to lash out on*; **il ne s'est pas fendu!** he didn't exactly break himself!*

fendu, e [fɑ̃dy] (ptp de **fendre**) adj a *crâne* cracked; *lèvre* cut; *manche* slashed; *veste* with a vent; *jupe* slit. **la bouche ~e jusqu'aux oreilles** with a grin (stretching) from ear to ear. b (*: *hilare*) **j'étais ~** I was creased up*, I fell about (laughing)*.

fenestrage [fənɛstʀaʒ] nm = **fenêtrage.**

fenestration [fənɛstʀasjɔ̃] nf (*Archit, Méd*) fenestration.

fenêtrage [fənɛtʀaʒ] nm (*Archit*) windows, fenestration (*SPÉC*).

fenêtre [f(ə)nɛtʀ] nf a (*Archit*) window. **regarder/sauter par la ~** to look out of *ou* through/jump out of the window; (*dans un train*) **coin** *ou* **place côté ~** window seat, seat by the window; **~ à guillotine** sash window; **~ à battants/à meneaux** casement/mullioned window; **~ treillisée, ~ à croisillons** lattice window; **~ mansardée** dormer window; **~ en saillie** bow window, bay window; **~ à tabatière** skylight; **~ borgne** dim and viewless window; (*Ciné*) **~ d'observation** port, (projectionist's) window; *voir* **faux[2], porte** *etc.* b *[enveloppe, ordinateur]* window. **laisser une ~ sur un formulaire** to leave a space on a form. c (*Anat: dans l'oreille*) fenestra.

fenêtrer [fənetʀe] 1 vt (*Archit*) to make windows in.

fenil [fəni(l)] nm hayloft.

fennec [fenɛk] nm fennec.

fenouil [fənuj] nm fennel.

fente [fɑ̃t] nf a (*fissure*) *[mur, terre, rocher]* crack, fissure, cleft; *[bois]* crack, split. b (*interstice*) (*dans un volet, une palissade*) slit; (*dans une boîte à lettres*) slot, opening; (*dans une tirelire etc*) slit, slot; (*dans la tête d'une vis*) groove, slot; (*dans une jupe*) slit; (*dans un veston*) vent; (*dans une pèlerine etc*) slit, armhole.

fenugrec [fənygʀɛk] nm fenugreek.

féodal, e, mpl **-aux** [feɔdal, o] 1 adj feudal. 2 nm feudal lord.

féodaliser [feɔdalize] 1 vt to feudalize.

féodalisme [feɔdalism] nm feudalism.

féodalité [feɔdalite] nf (*Hist*) feudal system, feudalism.

fer [fɛʀ] 1 nm a (*métal*) iron. (*lit, fig*) **de ~** iron (*épith*); **volonté de ~** will of iron, iron will; *voir* **âge, chemin, fil** *etc.*

b (*barre, poutre*) iron girder. **~ en T/U** T/U girder.

c (*embout*) *[cheval]* shoe; *[soulier]* steel tip; *[club de golf]* iron; *[flèche, lance]* head, point; *[rabot]* blade, iron. **avoir** *ou* **tenir plusieurs ~s au feu** to have several irons in the fire; *voir* **plaie, quatre.**

d (*outil*) *[relieur]* blocking stamp; *[tailleur]* iron.

e (*fig: arme*) (*Escrime*) **engager/croiser le ~** to engage/cross swords; **par le ~ et par le feu** by fire and by sword.

f (††: *chaînes*) **~s** chains, fetters, irons; **mettre un prisonnier aux ~s** to clap a prisoner in irons; (*fig littér*) **être dans les ~s** to be in chains *ou* irons.

g (*Méd* ††) **~s** forceps.

2 comp ▸**fer-blanc** nm (pl **fers-blancs**) tin(plate) ▸**fer à cheval** (*lit, fig*) horseshoe; **en fer à cheval** in a semicircle ▸**fer doux** soft iron ▸**fer forgé** wrought iron ▸**fer à friser** curling tongs ▸**fer à gaufrer** goffering iron ▸**fer de lance** (*fig*) spearhead ▸**fer à repasser** (*électrique*) (electric) iron; (*ancien modèle*) (flat)iron; (*: *pour cartes bancaires*) credit card machine; **donner un coup de fer (à repasser) à qch** to run the iron over sth; (*plus soigneusement*) to press sth ▸**fer rouge** red-hot iron; **marquer au fer rouge** to brand ▸**fer à souder** soldering iron ▸**fer à vapeur** steam iron.

ferblanterie [fɛʀblɑ̃tʀi] nf (*métier*) tinplate making; (*produit*) tinware; (*commerce*) tin trade; (*boutique*) ironmonger's (shop) (*Brit*), hardware store (*US*).

ferblantier [fɛʀblɑ̃tje] nm tinsmith. **ouvrier** ~ tinplate worker.

Ferdinand [fɛʀdinɑ̃] nm Ferdinand.

féria [feʀja] nf feria, *Spanish and Southern French festival*.

férié, e [feʀje] adj: **jour** ~ public holiday, official holiday; **le lundi suivant est** ~ the following Monday is a holiday.

férir [feʀiʀ] vt: **sans coup** ~ without meeting *ou* encountering any opposition.

ferler [fɛʀle] 1 vt (*Naut*) to furl.

fermage [fɛʀmaʒ] nm (*procédé*) tenant farming; (*loyer*) (farm) rent.

fermail†† , pl **-aux** [fɛʀmaj, o] nm (metal) clasp.

ferme[1] [fɛʀm] 1 adj a (*lit*) *chair, fruit* firm; *sol* firm, solid. **cette viande est un peu** ~ this meat is a bit tough; *voir* **terre**.

b (*assuré*) *main, écriture* steady, firm; *voix* firm; *style, exécution, trait* confident, assured. **être** ~ **sur ses jambes** to be steady on one's legs *ou* feet; **marcher d'un pas** ~ to walk with a firm stride *ou* step; **rester** ~ **dans l'adversité** to remain steadfast in adversity; *voir* **attendre**.

c (*déterminé*) *personne, ton* firm; *décision, résolution* firm, definite. **avec la** ~ **intention de faire** with the firm intention of doing.

d (*Comm*) *achat, vente* firm; *acheteur, vendeur* firm, definite; (*Bourse*) *marché, cours* steady, buoyant. **prix** ~**s et définitifs** firm prices; **ces prix sont** ~**s** these prices are binding; (*Bourse*) **les mines d'or sont restées** ~**s en clôture** gold mines closed firm.

2 adv a (*intensif*) *travailler, cogner* hard. **boire** ~ to drink hard; **discuter** ~ to discuss vigorously; **s'ennuyer** ~* to be bored rigid* *ou* stiff; *voir* **tenir**.

b (*Comm*) *acheter, vendre* definitely.

ferme[2] [fɛʀm] nf a (*domaine*) farm; (*habitation*) farmhouse. ~ **collective** collective farm; ~ **d'élevage** cattle(-breeding) farm; ~ **marine** fish farm; *voir* **cour, fille, valet**. b (*Jur: contrat*) farm lease; (*Hist: perception*) farming (*of taxes*). **donner à** ~ *terres* to let, farm out; **prendre à** ~ *terres* to farm (on lease).

ferme[3] [fɛʀm] nf (*Constr*) roof timbers, truss.

ferme[4] [fɛʀm] excl: **la** ~!‡ shut up!‡, shut your mouth!‡, pipe down!*; *voir aussi* **fermer**.

fermé, e [fɛʀme] (ptp de **fermer**) adj a *porte, magasin, valise* shut, closed; *col, route* closed; *espace* closed-in; *voiture* shut (up), locked; *angle* narrow; *voyelle* close(d), high; *syllabe* closed; *série, ensemble* closed; *robinet* off (*attrib*); *chemise* fastened (*attrib*), done up (*attrib*). **la porte est** ~**e à clef** the door is locked; (*Ftbl*) **pratiquer un jeu** ~ to play a tight game.

b *milieu, club* exclusive, select. **cette carrière lui est** ~**e** this career is not open to him *ou* is closed to him; **économie** ~**e** closed economy.

c *visage, air* inscrutable, impassive, impenetrable; *caractère* impassive, uncommunicative; *personne* uncommunicative.

d **être** ~ **à** *sentiment, qualité* to be impervious to *ou* untouched by *ou* closed to; *science, art* to have no appreciation of, have no feeling for.

fermement [fɛʀməmɑ̃] adv (*lit, fig*) firmly.

ferment [fɛʀmɑ̃] nm (*lit*) ferment, fermenting agent, leaven (*NonC*); (*fig*) ferment (*NonC*).

fermentation [fɛʀmɑ̃tasjɔ̃] nf fermentation. (*fig*) ~ **(des esprits)** stirring people up; **en** ~ (*lit*) fermenting; (*fig*) in a ferment.

fermenter [fɛʀmɑ̃te] 1 vi (*lit*) to ferment, work; (*fig littér*) *[esprits]* to be in a ferment.

fermer [fɛʀme] 1 1 vt a *porte, fenêtre, tiroir, paquet* to close, shut; *rideaux* to draw (to), close, shut; *store* to pull down, draw (down), close, shut; *magasin, café, musée* (*le soir*) to shut, close; (*pour cause de vacances*) to shut (up), close. ~ **à clef** *porte* to lock; *chambre* to lock (up); ~ **au verrou** to bolt; **il ferma violemment la porte** he slammed the door (shut); ~ **(la porte) à double tour** to double-lock (the door); ~ **la porte au nez de qn** to shut *ou* slam the door in sb's face; (*fig*) ~ **sa porte** *ou* **sa maison à qn** to close one's door to sb; (*fig*) **maintenant, toutes les portes lui sont fermées** all doors are closed to him now; (*fig*) ~ **la porte aux abus** to close the door to abuses; **va** ~ go and close *ou* shut the door; **on ferme!** (it's) closing time!, the shop (*ou* pub *etc*) is closing (now); **on ferme en juillet** we close *ou* shut down in July, we're closed *ou* shut in July; **on ferme un jour par semaine** we close *ou* shut one day a week, we are closed *ou* shut one day a week; *voir* **parenthèse**.

b *yeux, bouche, paupières* to close, shut. **ferme ta gueule**‡ shut your trap‡ *ou* face‡; **la ferme**‡, **ferme-la**‡ shut *ou* belt up‡, wrap up‡ (*Brit*), shut your mouth‡, pipe down*; **je n'ai pas fermé l'œil de la nuit** I didn't get a wink of sleep *ou* I didn't sleep a wink all night; (*fig*) ~ **les yeux** to turn a blind eye, look the other way; ~ **les yeux sur** *misère, scandale* to close *ou* shut one's eyes to; *abus, fraude, défaut* to turn a blind eye to; **s'ils sont d'accord pour** ~ **les yeux, bon** if they don't mind turning a blind eye, all well and good; (*fig*) ~ **son cœur à la pitié** to close one's heart to pity.

c *couteau, livre, éventail* to close, shut; *lettre* to close; *parapluie* to put down, close, shut; *main, poing* to close; *manteau, gilet* to do up, fasten.

d (*boucher*) *chemin, passage* to block, bar; *accès* to shut off, close off. **des montagnes ferment l'horizon** mountains hem in the horizon; **le champ/jardin était fermé par une haie** the field/garden was closed in *ou* enclosed by a hedge; (*Sport*) ~ **le jeu** to tighten up play.

e (*interdire l'accès de*) *frontière, col, route* to close; *aéroport* to close (down), shut (down).

f (*cesser l'exploitation de*) *magasin, restaurant, école* to close (down), shut (down). ~ **boutique** to shut up shop, close down; **obliger qn à** ~ **(boutique)** to put sb out of business; **ils ont dû** ~ **pour des raisons financières** they had to close down *ou* shut up shop *ou* cease trading because of financial difficulties.

g (*arrêter*) *liste, souscription, compte en banque, débat* to close. ~ **la marche** to bring up the rear; ~ **le cortège** to bring up the rear of the procession.

h *gaz, électricité, radio* to turn off, switch off, put off; *eau, robinet* to turn off; *lumière* to turn off *ou* out, switch off, put off; *vanne* to close.

2 vi a *[fenêtre, porte, boîte]* to close, shut. **cette porte/boîte ferme mal** this door/box doesn't close *ou* shut properly; **ce robinet ferme mal** this tap doesn't turn off properly.

b *[magasin]* (*le soir*) to close, shut; (*définitivement, pour les vacances*) to close down, shut down. **ça ferme à 7 heures** they close *ou* shut at 7 o'clock, closing time is 7 o'clock.

c *[vêtement]* to do up, fasten. **ça ferme par devant** it does up *ou* fastens at the front.

3 **se fermer** vpr a *[porte, fenêtre, livre]* to close, shut; *[fleur, coquillage]* to close (up); *[blessure]* to close (up); *[paupières, yeux]* to close, shut. **cela se ferme par devant** it does up *ou* fastens at the front; **l'avenir se fermait devant lui** the future was closing before him; **quand on essaie de lui expliquer cela, son esprit se ferme** when you try to explain that to him he closes his mind to it; **son cœur se fermait à la vue de cette misère** he refused to be moved *ou* touched by *ou* to let his heart *ou* feelings be touched by the sight of this poverty; **son visage se ferma** his face became expressionless; **pays qui se ferme aux produits étrangers** country which closes its markets to foreign produce.

b *[personne]* **se** ~ **à la pitié/l'amour** to close one's heart *ou* mind to pity/love; **il se ferme tout de suite, dès qu'on le questionne d'un peu près** he clams up* *ou* closes up immediately one tries to question him closely.

fermeté [fɛʀməte] nf (*voir* **ferme**[1]) firmness; solidness; steadiness; confidence; assurance; steadfastness. **avec** ~ firmly, resolutely; (*Bourse*) ~ **des cours** price stability.

fermette [fɛʀmɛt] nf (small) farmhouse.

fermeture [fɛʀmətyʀ] nf a (*action: voir* **fermer**) closing; shutting; drawing; pulling down; locking; bolting; blocking; shutting off; closing off; closing down; shutting down; turning off; switching off; switching out. (*Comm*) ~ **annuelle** (*gén*) annual closure; (*sur la devanture*) closed for holidays; (*Comm*) ~ **définitive** permanent closure; **à (l'heure de) la** ~ at closing time; "~ **pour (cause de) travaux**" "closed for repairs (*ou* redecoration *ou* refurbishment *etc*)"; ~ **d'un compte** closing of an account; **"ne pas gêner la** ~ **des portes"** "do not obstruct the doors (when closing)".

b (*mécanisme*) *[coffre-fort]* catch, latch; *[vêtement]* fastener, fastening; *[sac]* fastener, catch, clasp. ~ **à glissière**, ~ **éclair** ® zip (fastener) (*Brit*), zipper.

fermier, -ière [fɛʀmje, jɛʀ] 1 adj: **poulet** ~ ≃ free-range chicken, farm chicken; **beurre** ~ dairy butter. 2 nm a (*cultivateur*) farmer. b (*Hist*) ~ **général** farmer general. 3 **fermière** nf farmer's wife; (*indépendante*) (woman) farmer.

fermium [fɛʀmjɔm] nm fermium.

fermoir [fɛʀmwaʀ] nm *[livre, collier, sac]* clasp.

féroce [feʀɔs] adj *animal, regard, personne* ferocious, fierce, savage; *répression, critique* fierce, savage; *envie* savage, raging; *appétit* ferocious, ravenous; *concurrence* fierce, harsh, cut-throat. **avec une joie** ~ with (a) savage joy; *voir* **bête**.

férocement [feʀɔsmɑ̃] adv (*voir* **féroce**) ferociously; fiercely; savagely.

férocité [feʀɔsite] nf (*voir* **féroce**) ferocity, ferociousness; fierceness; savagery.

Féroé [feʀɔe] nm: **les îles** ~ the Fa(e)roe Islands.

ferrage [feʀaʒ] nm *[cheval]* shoeing.

ferraillage [feʀɑjaʒ] nm (*Constr*) (iron) framework.

ferraille [feʀɑj] nf a (*déchets de fer*) scrap (iron), old iron. **tas de** ~ scrap heap; **bruit de** ~ clanking *ou* rattling noise; **mettre une voiture à la** ~ to scrap a car, send a car for scrap; **la voiture n'était plus qu'un amas de** ~ the car was no more than a heap of twisted metal. b (*: *monnaie*) small *ou* loose change.

ferrailler†† [feʀɑje] 1 vi (*péj*) to clash swords.

ferrailleur [feʀɑjœʀ] nm a scrap (metal) merchant. b (†† *péj*)

swashbuckler.
Ferrare [fɛʀaʀ] nf Ferrara.
ferrate [fɛʀat] nm ferrate.
ferré, e [fɛʀe] (ptp de **ferrer**) adj **a** *canne, bâton* steel-tipped; *soulier* hobnailed; *lacet* tagged; *cheval* shod; *roue* steel-rimmed; *voir* **voie**. **b** (*: *calé*) well up* (*sur, en* in), clued up* (*en, sur* about). **être ~ sur un sujet** to be well up* in a subject *ou* hot* at a subject, know a subject inside out.
ferrement [fɛʀmɑ̃] nm **a** (*garniture*) iron fitment. **b** = **ferrage**.
ferrer [fɛʀe] 1 vt **a** *cheval* to shoe; *roue* to rim with steel; *soulier* to nail; *lacet* to tag; *bâton* to tip, fit a metal tip to; *porte* to fit with iron corners. **b** *poisson* to strike.
ferret [fɛʀɛ] nm **a** *[lacet]* (metal) tag. **b** (*Minér*) **~ d'Espagne** red haematite.
ferreux, -euse [fɛʀø, øz] adj m ferrous.
ferrique [fɛʀik] adj ferric.
ferrite [fɛʀit] nf ferrite.
ferro- [fɛʀɔ] préf (*Chim, Phys*) ferro-.
ferro-alliage, pl **ferro-alliages** [fɛʀɔaljaʒ] nm iron alloy.
ferronnerie [fɛʀɔnʀi] nf (*atelier*) ironworks; (*métier*) ironwork; (*objets*) ironwork, ironware. **faire de la ~ d'art** to be a craftsman in wrought iron; **une grille en ~** a wrought-iron gate; **c'est un beau travail de ~** that's a fine piece of wrought iron work.
ferronnier [fɛʀɔnje] nm (*artisan*) craftsman in (wrought) iron; (*commerçant*) ironware merchant. **~ d'art** craftsman in wrought iron.
ferroutage [fɛʀʀutaʒ] nm (*Rail*) piggyback.
ferrouter [fɛʀʀute] 1 vt (*Rail*) to piggyback.
ferroviaire [fɛʀɔvjɛʀ] adj *réseau, trafic* railway (*épith*) (*Brit*), railroad (*épith*) (*US*), rail (*épith*); *transport* rail.
ferrugineux, -euse [fɛʀyʒinø, øz] adj ferruginous.
ferrure [fɛʀyʀ] nf **a** *[porte]* (ornamental) hinge. **b** *[cheval]* shoeing.
ferry, pl **ferries** [fɛʀi] nm abrév de **ferry-boat**.
ferry-boat, pl **ferry-boats** [fɛʀibot] nm *[voitures]* (car) ferry; *[trains]* (train) ferry.
fertile [fɛʀtil] adj *sol, région* fertile, fruitful, productive; *esprit, imagination* fertile. **affaire ~ en rebondissements** affair which triggers off *ou* which spawns a whole series of new developments; **journée ~ en événements/en émotions** eventful/emotion-packed day.
fertilisable [fɛʀtilizabl] adj fertilizable.
fertilisant, e [fɛʀtilizɑ̃, ɑ̃t] adj fertilizing.
fertilisation [fɛʀtilizasjɔ̃] nf fertilization.
fertiliser [fɛʀtilize] 1 vt to fertilize.
fertilité [fɛʀtilite] nf (*lit, fig*) fertility.
féru, e [feʀy] adj (*frm*) **être ~ de** to be keen on (*Brit*) *ou* passionately interested in.
férule [feʀyl] nf (*Hist Scol*) ferula. (*fig*) **être sous la ~ de qn** to be under sb's (firm *ou* iron) rule.
fervent, e [fɛʀvɑ̃, ɑ̃t] **1** adj fervent, ardent. **2** nm,f devotee. **~ de musique** music lover, devotee of music.
ferveur [fɛʀvœʀ] nf fervour, ardour. **avec ~** fervently, ardently.
fesse [fɛs] nf **a** (*Anat*) buttock. **les ~s** the buttocks, the bottom, the bum‡ (*Brit hum*), the backside*; **coup de pied aux ~s*** kick in the backside* *ou* in the pants*; **le bébé a les ~s rouges** the baby's got a bit of nappy (*Brit*) *ou* diaper (*US*) rash, the baby's got a sore bottom; **on a les flics aux ~s*** the cops are on our tail*; *voir* **pousser, serrer**. **b** (**‡: *femmes*) **film où il y a de la ~** film with lots of (bare) bums (*Brit*) *ou* ass (*US*) and tits in it**‡; **magazine de ~s** girlie magazine*; **histoire de ~s** dirty story; **il y avait de la ~ à ce bal** there were some really smart *ou* sexy pieces‡ *ou* there was some lovely crumpet‡ (*Brit*) at that dance.
fessée [fese] nf spanking, smack on the bottom. **je vais te donner une ~** I'm going to smack your bottom.
fesse-mathieu††, pl **fesse-mathieux** [fɛsmatjø] nm skinflint.
fesser [fese] 1 vt to give a spanking to, spank.
fessier, -ière [fesje, jɛʀ] **1** adj *muscles* buttock (*épith*), gluteal (SPÉC). **2** nm (*Anat*) gluteus (SPÉC); (‡) behind, backside*, ass‡ (*US*).
fessu, e* [fesy] adj with a big bottom (*attrib*), big-bottomed.
festif, -ive [fɛstif, iv] adj festive.
festin [fɛstɛ̃] nm feast. **c'était un vrai ~** it was a real feast.
festival, pl **~s** [fɛstival] nm (*Mus, Théât*) festival. (*fig*) **ce fut un vrai ~ (de talent)!** what a feast *ou* brilliant display (of talent) it was!
festivalier, -ière [fɛstivalje, jɛʀ] nm,f festival-goer.
festivités [fɛstivite] nfpl (*gén*) festivities; (*: *repas joyeux*) festivities, merrymaking.
festoiement [fɛstwamɑ̃] nm feasting.
feston [fɛstɔ̃] nm (*guirlande, Archit*) festoon; (*Couture*) scallop. **à ~** scalloped; *voir* **point²**.
festonner [fɛstɔne] 1 vt *façade* to festoon; *robe* to scallop.
festoyer [fɛstwaje] 8 vi to feast.
fêtard, e* [fɛtaʀ, aʀd] nm,f (*péj*) high liver, roisterer. **réveillé par une bande de ~s** woken up by a band of merrymakers *ou* roisterers.
fête [fɛt] **1** nf **a** (*commémoration*) (*religieuse*) feast; (*civile*) holiday. **la Toussaint est la ~ de tous les saints** All Saints' Day is the feast of all the saints; **le 11 novembre est la ~ de la Victoire** November 11th is the day we celebrate *ou* for celebrating the Victory (in the First World War); **Noël est la ~ des enfants** Christmas is the festival for children.
b (*jour du prénom*) saint's day, name day. **la ~ de la Saint-Jean** Saint John's day; **souhaiter sa *ou* bonne ~ à qn** to wish sb a happy saint's day.
c (*congé*) holiday. **les ~s (de fin d'année)** the (Christmas and New Year) celebrations *ou* holidays; **demain c'est ~** tomorrow is a holiday.
d (*foire*) fair; (*kermesse*) fête, fair; (*exposition, salon*) festival, show. **~ paroissiale/communale** parish/local fête *ou* fair; **~ de la bière/du jambon** beer/ham festival; **~ de l'aviation** air show; **la ~ de la moisson** the harvest festival; **~ de la vendange** festival of the grape harvest; **c'est la ~ au village** the fair is on in the village; **la ~ de la ville a lieu le premier dimanche de mai** the town festival takes place on the first Sunday in May; **la foule en ~** the festive crowd; **air/atmosphère de ~** festive air/atmosphere; *voir* **comité, jour** *etc*.
e (*réception*) **donner une ~ dans son château/parc** to put on a lavish entertainment in one's château/grounds; **donner une petite ~ pour célébrer sa nomination** to hold a little party to celebrate one's appointment; **faire une ~ (pour son anniversaire** *etc***)** to have a (birthday *etc*) party; **les ~s en l'honneur d'un souverain étranger** the celebrations in honour of a foreign monarch.
f (*allégresse collective*) **la ~** celebration; **c'est la ~!** everyone's celebrating!, everyone's in a festive mood!; **c'est la ~ chez nos voisins** our neighbours are celebrating.
g (*loc*) **hier il était à la ~** he had a field day yesterday, it was his day yesterday; **je n'étais pas à la ~** it was no picnic (for me)*, I was feeling pretty uncomfortable; **il n'avait jamais été à pareille ~** he'd never had such a fine time; **être de la ~** to be one of the party; **ça va être ta ~‡** you've got it coming to you*, you're going to get it in the neck‡; **faire sa ~ à qn‡** to bash sb up‡; **faire la ~*** to live it up*, have a wild time; **faire ~ à qn** to give sb a warm welcome *ou* reception; **le chien fit ~ à son maître** the dog fawned on *ou* made up to its master; **elle se faisait une ~ d'y aller/de cette rencontre** she was really looking forward to going/to this meeting.
2 comp ▸**fête carillonnée** great feast day ▸**fête de charité** charity bazaar *ou* fair ▸**Fête-Dieu** nf (pl **Fêtes-Dieu**) Corpus Christi ▸**fête de famille** family celebration ▸**fête fixe** fixed festival ▸**fête foraine** fun fair ▸**la fête du Grand Pardon** the Day of Atonement ▸**fête légale** public holiday ▸**la fête des Mères** Mother's Day, Mothering Sunday (*Brit*) ▸**fête mobile** movable feast ▸**la fête des Morts** All Souls' Day ▸**fête nationale** national holiday *ou* festival; (*Can*) **le jour de la Fête nationale** Confederation Day ▸**la fête des Pères** Father's Day ▸**la fête des Rois** Twelfth Night ▸**la fête du travail** Labour Day, first of May ▸**fête de village** village fête.
fêter [fete] 1 vt *anniversaire, victoire* to celebrate; *personne* to fête. **~ un ami qui revient d'un long voyage** to have a celebration for a friend who is back from a long journey.
fétiche [fetiʃ] nm (*lit*) fetish; (*fig: mascotte*) mascot.
fétichisme [fetiʃism] nm fetishism.
fétichiste [fetiʃist] adj, nmf fetishist.
fétide [fetid] adj fetid.
fétidité [fetidite] nf fetidness.
fétu [fety] nm: **~ (de paille)** wisp of straw.
feu¹ [fø] **1** nm **a** (*source de chaleur*) fire. **~ de bois/tourbe** wood/peat fire; **allumer/faire un ~** to light/make a fire; **faire du ~** to have *ou* make a fire; **jeter qch au ~** to throw sth on the fire; **un ~ d'enfer brûlait dans la cheminée** a fire blazed brightly *ou* a hot fire blazed in the fireplace; (*pour une cigarette*) **avez-vous du ~?** do you have a light?; (*pour une cigarette*) **donner du ~ à qn** to give sb a light; **condamné au (supplice du) ~** condemned to be burnt at the stake; (*Hist*) **juger par le ~** to try by fire (*Hist*); **sur un ~ de braises** on glowing embers.
b (*incendie*) fire. **prendre ~** to catch fire; **mettre le ~ à qch** to set fire to sth, set sth on fire; **le ~ a pris dans la grange** fire has broken out in the barn; **en ~** on fire; **il y a le ~** there's a fire; (*fig*) **il n'y a pas le ~ (au lac)!*** there's no panic*!, take your time!; **au ~!** fire!
c (*signal lumineux*) (*Aut, Aviat, Naut*) light. **le ~ était (au) rouge** the lights were at red; **s'arrêter au(x) feu(x)** to stop at the lights; **naviguer tous ~x éteints** to sail without lights; **les ~x de la côte** the lights of the shore.
d (*Culin*) (*brûleur*) burner; (*plaque électrique*) ring (*Brit*), burner. **cuisinière à 3 ~x** stove with 3 rings (*Brit*) *ou* burners; **mettre qch/être sur le ~** to put sth/be on the stove; **plat qui va sur le ~ *ou* au ~** fireproof dish; **faire cuire à ~ doux/vif** to cook over a slow/fast *ou* brisk heat; (*au four*) to cook in a slow/fast *ou* hot oven; **faire cuire à petit ~** to cook gently; (*fig*) **faire mourir qn à petit ~** to kill sb by inches.
e (*Mil*) (*combat*) action; (*tir*) fire. **aller au ~** to go to the firing line; **tué au ~** killed in action; **faire ~** to fire; **~!** fire!; **~ à volonté!** fire at will!; **sous le ~ de l'ennemi** under enemy fire; **~ nourri/rasant/roulant** sustained/grazing/running fire; (*fig*) **un ~ roulant de questions** a running fire of questions; **des ~x croisés** crossfire; **~ en rafales** firing in bursts; **coup de ~** (gun)shot; **il a reçu un coup de ~** he has been shot; **faire le coup de ~ avec qn** to fight alongside sb; *voir aussi* **m**.
f (*arg Crime: revolver*) gun, gat‡, rod‡.

g (††: *maison*) hearth†, homestead. **un hameau de 15 ~x** a hamlet of 15 homesteads; **sans ~ ni lieu†** with neither hearth nor home†.

h (*ardeur*) fire. **plein de ~** full of fire; **parler avec ~** to speak with fire; **dans le ~ de l'action/de la discussion** in the heat of (the) action/the discussion; **le ~ de son éloquence** the fire of his eloquence; **il prend facilement ~ dans la discussion** he easily gets heated in discussion; **un tempérament de ~** a fiery temperament; **dans le ~ de la colère, il ...** in the heat of his anger, he ...; **avoir du ~ dans les veines** to have fire in one's blood.

i (*sensation de brûlure, de chaleur*) **j'ai le ~ au visage** my face is burning; **j'ai la gorge/les joues en ~** my throat is/my cheeks are burning; **le poivre met la bouche en ~** pepper makes your mouth burn; **le ~ lui monta au visage** the blood rushed to his face; **le ~ du rasoir** shaving rash; **le ~ d'un whisky** the fire *ou* the fiery taste of a whisky; **le ~ de la fièvre** the heat of fever.

j (*éclairage*) light. **être sous le ~ des projecteurs** (*lit*) to be in the glare of the spotlights; (*fig*) to be in the limelight; **mettre pleins ~x sur qn/qch** to put the spotlight on sb/sth; **pleins ~x sur** spotlight on; **les ~x de la rampe** the footlights; **les ~x de l'actualité sont dirigés sur eux** the spotlight is on them, the full glare of the media is on them.

k (*littér: éclat*) **les ~x d'une pierre précieuse** the fire of a precious stone; **ce diamant jette mille ~x** this diamond flashes *ou* sparkles brilliantly; **le ~ de son regard** the fire in his gaze, his fiery gaze.

l (*littér: lumière*) **les ~x de la nuit** the lights in the night; **les ~x du couchant** the fiery glow of sunset; **le ~ du ciel** the fire of heaven; **les ~x de la ville** the lights of the town; (*chaleur*) **les ~x de l'été** the summer heat.

m (*loc*) **avoir le ~ sacré** to burn with zeal; **faire ~ de tout bois** to make the most of what one has, turn everything to account; **mettre le ~ aux poudres** to touch off an explosion *ou* a crisis; **avoir le ~ au derrière*** *ou* **au cul**** (*être pressé*) to run like the blazes* *ou* like hell*; be in a devil of a hurry*; (*être sexuellement chaud*) to be horny*; **mettre une ville à ~ et à sang** to put a town to fire and the sword; **mettre à ~ une fusée** to fire off a rocket; **au moment de la mise à ~** at the moment of blast-off; **jeter** *ou* **lancer ~ et flammes** to breathe fire and fury, be in a towering rage; **être tout ~ tout flamme** to be wildly enthusiastic; **une soirée du ~ de Dieu*** a fantastic evening*; (*précipitation*) **c'est le coup de ~** it's all go*; **ma pizza a eu un coup de ~** my pizza's a bit burnt; *voir* **arme, baptême, coin.**

2 **adj inv: rouge ~** flame red; **de couleur ~** flame-coloured; **chien noir et ~** black and tan dog.

3 **comp** ►**feux anti-brouillard** = **feux de brouillard** ►**feu arrière** rear light (*Brit*), tail light ►**feu d'artifice** firework display, fireworks; **un beau feu d'artifice** beautiful fireworks ►**feu de Bengale** Bengal light ►**feux de brouillard** fog lights *ou* lamps ►**feu de brousse** bush fire ►**feu de camp** campfire ►**feu de cheminée** chimney fire ►**feux clignotants** flashing lights ►**feux de croisement** dipped headlights (*Brit*), low beams (*US*) ►**feux de détresse** hazard warning lights ►**feu follet** will-o'-the-wisp ►**feu grégeois** Greek fire ►**feu de joie** bonfire ►**feu orange** orange light, amber (light) ►**feu de paille** (*fig*) flash in the pan ►**feu de pinède** (pine) forest fire ►**feu de position** sidelight ►**feux de recul** reversing lights ►**feu rouge** (*couleur*) red light; (*objet*) traffic light; **tournez au prochain feu rouge** turn at the next set of traffic lights ►**feux de route** headlamps *ou* headlights on full beam ►**feux de signalisation** traffic lights ►**feux de stationnement** parking lights ►**feu de stop** stop *ou* brake light ►**feux tricolores** traffic lights ►**feu vert** green light; (*fig*) **donner le feu vert à qch/qn** to give sth/sb the green light *ou* the go-ahead.

feu², e [fø] **adj** (*inv devant art ou adj poss*) (*frm*) **~ ma tante, ma ~e tante** my late aunt.

feuillage [fœjaʒ] **nm** (*sur l'arbre*) foliage (*NonC*); (*coupé*) greenery (*NonC*). **les oiseaux gazouillaient dans le ~** *ou* **les ~s** the birds were twittering among the leaves *ou* the foliage.

feuillaison [fœjɛzɔ̃] **nf** leafing, foliation (*SPÉC*). **à l'époque de la ~** when the trees come into leaf.

feuille [fœj] 1 **nf** a [*arbre, plante*] leaf; (*littér: pétale*) petal. **à ~s caduques/persistantes** deciduous/evergreen; *voir* **trèfle, trembler.**

b [*papier, bois, ardoise, acier*] sheet. **les ~s d'un cahier** the leaves of an exercise book; **or en ~s** gold leaf; **doré à la ~ d'or** gilded with gold leaf.

c (*bulletin*) slip; (*formulaire*) form; (*journal*) paper; (*: *oreille*) ear, lug* (*Brit*). **~ à scandales** scandal sheet; (*Scol*) **~ d'appel** daily register (sheet) (*Brit*), attendance sheet (*US*); **dur de la ~*** hard of hearing.

d (*Ordin*) **~ de programmation** work *ou* coding sheet.

2 **comp** ►**feuille de chêne** (*Bot*) oak-leaf; (*Mil fig*) general's insignia ►**feuille de chou** (*péj: journal*) rag (*voir* **oreille**) ►**feuille de garde** endpaper ►**feuille d'impôt** tax form *ou* slip ►**feuille de maladie** *form supplied by doctor to patient for forwarding to the Social Security* ►**feuille morte** dead leaf; (*Aviat*) **descendre en feuille morte** to do the falling leaf ►**feuille-morte** (*couleur*) **adj inv** russet ►**feuille de paye** pay slip ►**feuille de présence** attendance sheet ►**feuille de route** (*Mil*) travel warrant ►**feuille de température** temperature chart ►**feuilles de thé** tea leaves ►**feuille de vigne** (*Bot, Culin*) vine leaf; (*Sculp*) fig leaf ►**feuille volante** loose sheet.

feuillet [fœjɛ] **nm** a [*cahier, livre*] leaf, page; [*bois*] layer. b [*ruminants*] omasum, manyplies.

feuilleté, e [fœjte] (**ptp de feuilleter**) 1 **adj** *roche* foliated; *verre* laminated. **pâte ~e** puff pastry, flaky pastry; **pare-brise ~** laminated windscreen (*Brit*) *ou* windshield (*US*). 2 **nm** (*pâtisserie*) ≃ Danish pastry. **~ au jambon/aux amandes** ham/almond pastry.

feuilleter [fœjte] [4] **vt** a *pages, livre* to leaf through; (*fig: lire rapidement*) to leaf *ou* skim *ou* glance through. b (*Culin*) **~ de la pâte** to turn and roll (puff *ou* flaky) pastry; **cette pâte n'est pas assez feuilletée** this pastry hasn't been turned and rolled enough.

feuilleton [fœjtɔ̃] **nm** (*Presse, Rad*) (*histoire à suivre*) serial; (*histoire complète*) series (*sg*). **~ télévisé** television serial (*gén*), soap (opera)* (*péj*); **publié en ~** serialized; (*fig*) **ses amours, c'est un véritable ~** his love life is like a soap opera; *voir* **roman¹.**

feuilletoniste [fœjtɔnist] **nmf** serial writer.

feuillette [fœjɛt] **nf** cask, barrel (*containing 114-140 litres*).

feuillu, e [fœjy] 1 **adj** leafy. 2 **nm** broad-leaved tree.

feuillure [fœjyʀ] **nf** rebate, rabbet.

feulement [følmɑ̃] **nm** growl.

feuler [føle] [1] **vi** to growl.

feutrage [føtʀaʒ] **nm** felting.

feutre [føtʀ] **nm** (*Tex*) felt; (*chapeau*) felt hat, trilby (*Brit*), fedora (*US*); (*stylo*) felt-tip (pen), felt pen.

feutré, e [føtʀe] (**ptp de feutrer**) **adj** a *étoffe, surface* felt-like, felt (*épith*); *lainage* matted. b (*fig*) *atmosphère, bruit* muffled. **marcher à pas ~s** to walk with a muffled tread, pad along *ou* about.

feutrer [føtʀe] [1] 1 **vt** to line with felt, felt; *lainage* to mat; (*fig: amortir*) to muffle. 2 **vi** to felt. 3 **se feutrer vpr** to felt, mat. **mon pull-over s'est feutré** my pullover has gone all matted *ou* has felted.

feutrine [føtʀin] **nf** (lightweight) felt.

fève [fɛv] **nf** a (*Bot*) broad bean. b charm (*hidden in cake for Twelfth Night*). c (*: *Can*) bean. **~s jaunes** wax beans; **~s vertes** string *ou* French beans; **~s au lard** pork and beans, (baked) beans.

février [fevʀije] **nm** February; *pour loc voir* **septembre.**

fez [fɛz] **nm** fez.

FF (**abrév de franc français**) *voir* **franc.**

F.F. a (**abrév de Fédération française de ...**) French Federation of .... b **abrév de frères.**

F.F.I. [ɛfɛfi] **nfpl** (**abrév de Forces françaises de l'intérieur**) *French army of the Resistance, operating within France during World War II.*

F.F.L. [ɛfɛfɛl] **nfpl** (**abrév de Forces françaises libres**) Free French Army.

FG abrév de faubourg.

fi [fi] **excl** (††, *hum*) bah!, pooh! **faire ~ de** to snap one's fingers at.

fiabilité [fjabilite] **nf** [*chiffres*] accuracy, reliability; [*personnel*] reliability, dependability; [*machine*] reliability.

fiable [fjabl] **adj** *chiffres* accurate, reliable; *personnel* reliable, dependable; *machine* reliable.

fiacre [fjakʀ] **nm** (hackney) cab *ou* carriage, hackney.

fiançailles [fjɑ̃saj] **nfpl** engagement, betrothal (*littér*).

fiancé, e [fjɑ̃se] (**ptp de fiancer**) 1 **adj** engaged. 2 **nm** (*homme*) fiancé. (*couple*) **les ~s** the engaged couple. 3 **fiancée nf** fiancée.

fiancer [fjɑ̃se] [3] 1 **vt** to betroth (*littér*) (*avec, à* to). 2 **se fiancer vpr** to become *ou* get engaged *ou* betrothed (*littér*) (*avec, à* to).

fiasco [fjasko] **nm** fiasco. **faire un ~** to be *ou* turn out a fiasco.

fiasque [fjask] **nf** wine flask.

fibranne [fibʀan] **nf** bonded fibre.

fibre [fibʀ] **nf** a (*lit: gén*) fibre. **dans le sens des ~s** with the grain; **~ de bois/carbone** wood/carbon fibre; **~s musculaires** muscle fibres; **~s nerveuses** nerve fibres; **~ de verre** fibreglass (*Brit*), fiberglass (*US*), Fiberglas ® (*US*); **~ optique** (*câble*) optical fibre; (*procédé*) fibre optics; **câble en ~s optiques** fibre-optic cable; **riche en ~s (alimentaires)** high in (dietary) fibre. b (*fig: âme*) **avoir la ~ maternelle/militaire** to be a born mother/soldier, have a strong maternal/military streak in one; **faire jouer la ~ patriotique** to play on *ou* stir patriotic feelings.

fibreux, -euse [fibʀø, øz] **adj** *texture* fibrous; *viande* stringy.

fibrillation [fibʀijasjɔ̃] **nf** fibrillation.

fibrille [fibʀij] **nf** fibril, fibrilla.

fibrine [fibʀin] **nf** fibrin.

fibrinogène [fibʀinɔʒɛn] **nm** fibrinogen.

fibrociment [fibʀosimɑ̃] **nm** ® fibrocement.

fibromateux, -euse [fibʀɔmatø, øz] **adj** fibromatous.

fibrome [fibʀom] **nm** fibroid, fibroma.

fibroscope [fibʀɔskɔp] **nm** fibrescope (*Brit*), fiberscope (*US*).

fibroscopie [fibʀɔskɔpi] **nf** *endoscopy produced by fibroscope.*

ficelage [fis(ə)laʒ] **nm** (*action*) tying (up); (*liens*) string.

ficeler [fis(ə)le] [4] **vt** a *paquet, rôti, prisonnier* to tie up. **ficelé comme un saucisson** tied up like a parcel *ou* in a bundle. b (*: *habiller*) to rig out* (*Brit*), get up*. **ta mère t'a drôlement ficelé!** that's some rig-out* (*Brit*) *ou* get-up* your mother has put you in!; **être bien/mal ficelé** [*personne*] to be well/badly rigged out* (*Brit*) *ou* got up*; [*texte, histoire*] to be well *ou* tightly-structured/badly-structured.

ficelle [fisɛl] **nf** a (*matière*) string; (*morceau*) piece *ou* length of string; (*pain*) stick (of French bread); (*arg Mil*) stripe (*of officer*).

b (*loc*) **tirer les ~s** to pull the strings; **connaître les ~s du métier** to know the tricks of the trade, know the ropes; **la ~ est un peu grosse** you can see right through it.

fichage [fiʃaʒ] **nm: le ~ de la population** filing *ou* recording information on the population.

fiche[1] [fiʃ] **nf** a (*carte*) (index) card; (*feuille*) sheet, slip; (*formulaire*) form. **~ client** (*gén*) customer card; *[hôtel]* guest history card; **~ d'état civil** *record of civil status,* ≈ birth and marriage certificate; **~ perforée** perforated card; **~ de paye** pay slip; (*Police*) **~ signalétique** identification sheet; **mettre en ~** to index. b (*cheville*) pin, peg; (*Élec*) (*broche*) pin; (*prise*) plug.

fiche[2]* [fiʃ] **vb** *voir* **ficher**[2]*.

ficher[1] [fiʃe] [1] 1 **vt** a (*mettre en fiche*) *renseignements* to file; *suspects* to put on file, data (*US*). **tous les meneurs sont fichés à la police** the police have files on all subversives. b (*enfoncer*) to stick in, drive in. **~ qch en terre** to drive sth into the ground. 2 **se ficher vpr** to stick. **la flèche s'est fichée dans la cible** the arrow embedded itself in the target; **j'ai une arête fichée dans le gosier** I've got a fishbone stuck in my throat, a fishbone has got stuck in my throat.

ficher[2]* [fiʃe] [1] (**ptp courant fichu**) 1 **vt** a (*faire*) to do. **qu'est-ce qu'il fiche, il est déjà 8 heures** what on earth *ou* what the heck* is he doing *ou* is he up to* – it's already 8 o'clock; **qu'est-ce que tu as fichu aujourd'hui?** what have you been up to* *ou* what have you done today?; **il n'a rien fichu de la journée** he hasn't done a darned* *ou* blinking* (*Brit*) thing all day, he hasn't done a stroke (*Brit*) all day*, he hasn't lifted a finger all day; **(pour) ce que j'en ai à fiche, de leurs histoires** what's it to me, all this carry-on* of theirs?

b (*donner*) **~ une trempe** *ou* **raclée à qn** to give sb a walloping*; **ça me fiche la trouille** it gives me the jitters* *ou* the willies*; **ce truc me fiche la migraine** this darned* *ou* blinking* (*Brit*) thing gives me a headache; **fiche-moi la paix!** leave me alone!; **eux, faire ça? je t'en fiche!** you think they'd do that? not a hope*! *ou* you'll be lucky*!; **ça va nous ~ la poisse** that'll bring us bad luck *ou* put a jinx* on us; **je vous fiche mon billet que ...** I bet you anything (you like) *ou* my bottom dollar* that ...; **qui est-ce qui m'a fichu un idiot pareil!** of all the blinking (*Brit*) idiots*!, how stupid can you get!*

c (*mettre*) to put. **fiche-le dans le tiroir** bung* (*Brit*) *ou* stick* it in the drawer; **~ qn à la porte** to chuck* *ou* kick* *ou* boot* sb out; **se faire ~** *ou* **fiche à la porte** to get o.s. chucked* *ou* kicked* out, get the push* *ou* the sack*; **~ qch par la fenêtre/à la corbeille** to chuck* sth out of the window/in the wastebasket; **ce médicament me fiche à plat** this medicine knocks me right out* *ou* knocks me for six* (*Brit*); **~ qch par terre** to send sth flying; (*fig*) **ça fiche tout par terre** that mucks* *ou* messes everything up; **~ qch en l'air** to mess sth up, get sth in a mess; **tout ~ en l'air** (*envoyer promener*) to chuck everything up*; **~ qn dedans** (*emprisonner*) to put sb inside*; (*faire se tromper*) to drop sb in it*; **ça m'a fichu en colère** that really made me (hopping) mad*.

d **~ le camp** to clear off!*, shove off!‡, push off*; **fiche-moi le camp!** clear off!*, shove off!‡, push off!*, beat it!*, scram!‡

2 **se ficher vpr** a (*se mettre*) **attention, tu vas te ~ ce truc dans l'œil** careful, you're going to stick that thing in your eye; (*fig*) **se ~ qch dans le crâne** to get sth into one's head *ou* noddle*; (*fig*) **je me suis fichu dedans** I (really) boobed‡; **se ~ par terre** to go sprawling, come a cropper* (*Brit*); **il s'est fichu en l'air avec sa bagnole de sport** he smashed himself up* in his sports car.

b (*se gausser*) **se ~ de qn** to pull sb's leg; **se ~ de qch** to make fun of sth; (*être indifférent*) **se ~ de qn/de qch/de faire qch** not to give a darn about sb/about sth/about doing sth*, not to care two hoots about sb/about sth/about doing sth*; (*dépasser les bornes*) **se ~ de qn** to mess sb about* (*Brit*); **laisse-le tomber, tu vois bien qu'il se fiche de toi** drop him – it's perfectly obvious that he's leading you on* *ou* he couldn't care less about you; **il s'en fiche pas mal** he couldn't care less *ou* give a darn* (about it); **ah ça ils se fichent de nous, 50 F pour une bière!** what (on earth) do they take us for *ou* they really must think we're idiots, 50 francs for a beer!; **il se fiche de nous, c'est la troisième fois qu'il se décommande** he's really messing us about* (*Brit*) *ou* he's giving us the runaround* – that's the third time he has cancelled his appointment; **ce garagiste se fiche du monde!** that garage man is the absolute limit!* *ou* has got a flipping (*Brit*) *ou* darned nerve!*, who the heck* does that garage man think he is!; **là, ils ne se sont vraiment pas fichus de nous** they really did us proud!; **il s'en fiche comme de sa première chemise** *ou* **comme de l'an quarante** he couldn't care two hoots* *ou* tuppence* (*Brit*) (about it), what the heck does he care!*

c (‡) **va te faire fiche!** get lost!*, go to blazes!*, take a running jump!*; **j'ai essayé, mais va te faire ~! ça n'a pas marché** I did try but blow me* (*Brit*), it didn't work, I did try but I'll be darned if it worked* (*US*).

fichier [fiʃje] **nm** file; *[bibliothèque]* catalogue. **~ d'adresses** mailing list; **~ (informatisé)** data file; (*Ordin*) **~ maître** master file; (*Ordin*) **~ de travail** scratch *ou* work file.

fichiste [fiʃist(ə)] **nmf** filing clerk.

fichtre†* [fiʃtʀ] **excl** gosh!*

fichtrement†* [fiʃtʀəmɑ̃] **adv** dashed* (*Brit*), darned*. **ça a coûté ~ cher** it was dashed (*Brit*) *ou* darned expensive*.

fichu[1] [fiʃy] **nm** (head)scarf; (*Hist: couvrant le corsage*) fichu.

fichu[2], **e*** [fiʃy] (**ptp de ficher**[2]) **adj** a (*avant n*) (*sale*) *temps, métier, idée* darned*, wretched*; (*mauvais*) rotten*, lousy*, foul*; (*sacré*) one heck of a*, a heck of a*. **avec ce ~ temps on ne peut rien faire** with this darned* *ou* wretched* weather we can't do a thing; **il fait un ~ temps** the weather's rotten* *ou* lousy* *ou* foul*, what rotten* *ou* lousy* *ou* foul* weather; **il a un ~ caractère** he's got a rotten* *ou* lousy* temper, he's a nasty piece of work* (*Brit*); **il y a une ~e différence** there's one heck of a *ou* a heck of a difference*.

b (*après n: perdu, détruit*) *malade, vêtement* done for*; *appareil* done for*, bust*. **il/ce veston est ~** he/this jacket has had it* *ou* is done for*; **avec ce temps, le pique-nique est ~** with weather like this, we've had it for the picnic* *ou* the picnic has had it*.

c (*habillé*) rigged out* (*Brit*), got up*. **regarde comme il est ~!** look at the way he's rigged out* (*Brit*) *ou* got up*; **~ comme l'as de pique** looking like a scarecrow.

d (*bâti, conçu*) **elle est bien ~e** she's a smart piece‡, she's a bit of all right‡ (*Brit*); **cet appareil/ce livre est bien ~** this is a clever little job/book*; **cet appareil/ce livre est mal ~** this gadget/book is badly put together *ou* is hopeless; **il est tout mal ~** he's a fright; **comment c'est ~ ce truc?** how does this thing work?

e *[malade]* **être mal ~** *ou* **pas bien ~** to feel rotten*, be under the weather* *ou* out of sorts*.

f (*capable*) **il est ~ d'y aller, tel que je le connais** knowing him, he's quite likely *ou* liable to go *ou* it's quite on the cards (*Brit*) that he'll go; **il n'est (même) pas ~ de réparer ça** he hasn't even got the gumption to mend the thing*, he can't even mend the blinking (*Brit*) *ou* darned thing*.

fictif, -ive [fiktif, iv] **adj** a (*imaginaire*) *personnage, exemple* imaginary. **naturellement tout ceci est ~** of course this is all imagined *ou* imaginary. b (*faux*) *nom* false, assumed, fictitious; *adresse* fictitious, false; *promesse, sentiment* false. **créer une concurrence ~ive en lançant une sous-marque** to stimulate artificial competition by launching a sub-brand. c (*Fin*) fictitious.

fiction [fiksjɔ̃] **nf** a (*imagination*) fiction, imagination. **cette perspective est encore du domaine de la ~** this prospect still belongs in the realms of fiction; **livre de ~** work of fiction. b (*fait imaginé*) invention; (*situation imaginaire*) fiction; (*roman*) (work of) fiction, fictional work; (*mythe*) illusion, myth. **heureusement, ce que je vous décris est une ~** fortunately all that I've been telling you is imaginary.

fictivement [fiktivmɑ̃] **adv** in fiction.

ficus [fikys] **nm** ficus.

fidéicommis [fideikɔmi] **nm** (*Jur*) (*régime*) trust; (*fonction*) trusteeship.

fidéicommissaire [fideikɔmisɛʀ] **nm** (*Jur*) trustee.

fidèle [fidɛl] 1 **adj** a (*loyal*) faithful, loyal; *époux* faithful. **~ serviteur/épée** trusty *ou* loyal servant/sword; (*lit, fig*) **demeurer ~ au poste** to be loyal *ou* faithful to one's post, stay at one's post; **rester ~ à** *ami, femme* to remain faithful *ou* true to; *promesse* to be *ou* remain faithful to, keep; *principe, idée* to remain true *ou* faithful to, stand by; *habitude, mode* to keep to; *marque, produit* to remain loyal to, stay *ou* stick* with; **être ~ à soi-même** to be true to o.s.; **~ à lui-même** *ou* **à son habitude, il est arrivé en retard** true to form *ou* true to character he arrived late.

b (*habituel*) *lecteur, client* regular, faithful. **nous informons nos ~s clients que ...** we wish to inform our customers that ... .

c (*exact*) *historien, narrateur, son, reproduction* faithful; *souvenir, récit, portrait, traduction* faithful, accurate; *mémoire, appareil, montre* accurate, reliable. **sa description est ~ à la réalité** his description is a true *ou* an accurate picture of the situation.

2 **nmf** a (*Rel*) believer. **les ~s** (*croyants*) the faithful; (*assemblée*) the congregation.

b (*client*) regular (customer); (*lecteur*) regular (reader). **je suis un ~ de votre émission depuis 10 ans** I have been a regular listener to your programme for 10 years.

c (*adepte*) *[doctrine, mode, écrivain]* follower, devotee.

fidèlement [fidɛlmɑ̃] **adv** a (*loyalement*) faithfully, loyally. b (*régulièrement*) faithfully, regularly. **j'écoute ~ vos émissions depuis 10 ans** I have been listening to your programmes regularly *ou* I have been a regular listener to your programmes for the past 10 years. c (*scrupuleusement*) faithfully. d (*conformément à la réalité*) faithfully, accurately. **combat ~ décrit dans un livre** fight which is accurately described in a book.

fidélisation [fidelizasjɔ̃] **nf: ~ de la clientèle** development of customer loyalty.

fidéliser [fidelize] [1] **vt: ~ sa clientèle/son personnel** to establish *ou* develop customer/staff loyalty.

fidélité [fidelite] **nf** (*voir* **fidèle**) faithfulness; loyalty; accuracy; reliability; (*Comm: à un produit*) loyalty, fidelity. **la ~ (conjugale)** marital fidelity; *voir* **haut, jurer**.

Fidji [fidʒi] **nfpl: les îles ~** Fiji, the Fiji Islands.

fidjien, -ienne [fidʒjɛ̃, jɛn] 1 **adj** Fiji, Fijian. 2 **nm,f: F~(ne)** Fiji, Fijian.

fiduciaire [fidysjɛʀ] 1 **adj** fiduciary. **circulation ~** fiduciary circulation;

monnaie ~ paper currency; **héritier** ~ heir, trustee; **monnaie** ~ fiat money; **société** ~ trust company. 2 **nm** (*Jur*) trustee.

fiducie [fidysi] **nf** trust. **société de** ~ trust company.

fief [fjɛf] **nm** (*Hist*) fief; (*fig: zone d'influence*) *[firme, organisation]* preserve; *[parti, secte]* stronghold; (*hum: domaine*) private kingdom. ~ **(électoral)** electoral stronghold; (*hum*) **ce bureau est son** ~ this office is his kingdom.

fieffé, e [fjefe] **adj** *menteur* arrant.

fiel [fjɛl] **nm** (*lit, fig*) gall, venom. **propos pleins de** ~ words filled with venom *ou* gall.

fielleux, -euse [fjelø, øz] **adj** venomous, rancorous, spiteful.

fiente [fjɑ̃t] **nm** *[oiseau]* droppings (*pl*).

fienter [fjɑ̃te] [1] **vi** to make *ou* leave droppings.

fier, fière [fjɛʀ] **adj** a (*arrogant*) proud, haughty. ~ **comme Artaban** *ou* **comme un coq** (as) proud as a peacock; **trop** ~ **pour accepter** too proud to accept; **faire le** ~ (*être méprisant*) to be aloof, give o.s. airs; (*faire le brave*) to be full of o.s.; **c'est quelqu'un de pas** ~* he's not stuck-up*; **devant le danger, il n'était plus si** ~ when he found himself faced with danger, he wasn't so full of himself any more; *voir* **fier-à-bras.**

b (*littér: noble*) *âme, démarche* proud, noble. **avoir fière allure** to cut a fine figure, cut a dash.

c ~ **de qch/de faire qch** proud of sth/to do sth; **elle est fière de sa beauté** she's proud of her beauty; **toute fière de sortir avec son papa** as proud as can *ou* could be to be going out with her daddy; **il n'y a pas de quoi être** ~ there's nothing to feel proud about *ou* to be proud of *ou* to boast about; **je n'étais pas** ~ **de moi** I didn't feel very proud of myself, I felt pretty small*; **elle est fière qu'il ait réussi** she's proud he has succeeded.

d (*intensif: avant n*) ~ **imbécile** first-class *ou* prize* *ou* egregious idiot; **fière canaille** out-and-out *ou* downright scoundrel; **il a un** ~ **toupet** he has the devil of a cheek* (*Brit*) *ou* nerve; **je te dois une fière chandelle** I'm terribly indebted to you.

e (*littér: fougueux*) *cheval* mettlesome. **le** ~ **Aquilon** the harsh *ou* chill north wind.

fier (se) [fje] [7] **vpr** a (*question de loyauté*) **se** ~ **à** *allié, promesses, discrétion* to trust; **on ne peut pas se** ~ **à lui** one cannot trust him, he's not to be trusted, he can't be trusted; **ne vous fiez pas aux apparences/à ce qu'il dit** don't go by *ou* trust appearances/what he says; **il a l'air calme mais il ne faut pas s'y** ~ he looks calm but you can't trust that *ou* go by that. b (*question de fiabilité*) **se** ~ **à** *appareil, collaborateur, instinct, mémoire* to trust, rely on; *destin, hasard* to trust to. **ne te fie pas à ta mémoire, prends des notes** don't trust to memory, make notes.

fier-à-bras, **pl fiers-à-bras** [fjɛʀabʀɑ] **nm** braggart.

fièrement [fjɛʀmɑ̃] **adv** (*dignement*) proudly; (*†: *extrêmement*) devilishly*†.

fiérot, e* [fjeʀo, ɔt] **adj** cocky*. **faire le** ~ to show off; **tout** ~ **(d'avoir gagné/de son succès)** as pleased as Punch (about winning/about *ou* at his success).

fierté [fjɛʀte] **nf** (*gén*) pride; (*péj: arrogance*) pride, haughtiness. **tirer** ~ **de** to get a sense of pride from; **sa** ~ **est d'avoir réussi tout seul** he takes pride in having succeeded all on his own; **son jardin est sa** ~ his garden is his pride and joy; **je n'ai pas accepté son aide, j'ai ma** ~**!** I didn't accept his help — I have my pride!

fiesta* [fjɛsta] **nf** rave-up*. **faire la** *ou* **une** ~ to have a rave-up*.

fieu [fjø] **nm** († *ou dial*) son, lad.

fièvre [fjɛvʀ] **nf** a (*température*) fever, temperature. **avoir un accès de** ~ to have a bout of fever; **avoir (de) la** ~**/beaucoup de** ~ to have *ou* run a temperature/a high temperature; **avoir 39 de** ~ to have a temperature of 104(°F) *ou* 39(°C); **une** ~ **de cheval*** a raging fever; **il a les yeux brillants de** ~ his eyes are bright with fever.

b (*maladie*) fever. ~ **jaune/typhoïde** yellow/typhoid fever; ~ **aphteuse** foot-and-mouth disease; ~ **quarte** quartan fever *ou* ague; **avoir les** ~**s** to have marsh fever.

c (*fig: agitation*) fever, excitement. **parler avec** ~ to speak excitedly; **dans la** ~ **du départ** in the heat of departure, in the excitement of going away; **la** ~ **de l'or/des élections** gold/election fever.

d (*fig: envie*) fever. **être pris d'une** ~ **d'écrire** to be seized with a frenzied *ou* feverish urge to write.

fiévreusement [fjevʀøzmɑ̃] **adv** feverishly, excitedly.

fiévreux, -euse [fjevʀø, øz] **adj** (*Méd, fig*) feverish.

FIFA [fifa] **nf** (**abrév de Fédération internationale de football association**) FIFA.

fifille†* [fifij] **nf** little girl. (*péj*) ~ **à sa maman** mummy's (*Brit*) *ou* mommy's (*US*) little girl.

fifre [fifʀ] **nm** (*instrument*) fife; (*joueur*) fife player.

fifrelin† [fifʀəlɛ̃] **nm: ça ne vaut pas un** ~ that's not worth a farthing (*Brit*) *ou* nickel (*US*).

figaro† [figaʀo] **nm** (*hum*) barber.

figé, e [fiʒe] (**ptp de figer**) **adj** *style* stilted, fixed; *manières* stiff, constrained; *société, mœurs* rigid, ossified; *attitude, sourire* set, fixed; (*Ling*) *forme, phrase* fossilized. **être** ~ **dans des structures anciennes** to be set rigidly in outdated structures; (*Ling*) **expression** ~**e** set expression.

figement [fiʒmɑ̃] **nm** (*voir* **figer**) congealing; clotting, coagulation.

figer [fiʒe] [3] 1 **vt** *huile, sauce* to congeal; *sang* to clot, coagulate, congeal. **le cri le figea sur place** the cry froze *ou* rooted him to the spot; **figé par la peur** terror-stricken; **histoire à vous** ~ **le sang** bloodcurdling story, story to make one's blood run cold; **figé par la mort** rigid in death. 2 **vi** *[huile]* to congeal; *[sang]* to clot, coagulate, congeal. 3 **se figer vpr** *[sauce, huile]* to congeal; *[sang]* to clot, coagulate, congeal; *[sourire, regard]* to freeze; *[visage]* to stiffen, freeze. **il se figea au garde-à-vous** he stood rigidly *ou* he froze to attention; (*fig*) **son sang se figea dans ses veines** his blood froze in his veins.

fignolage* [fiɲɔlaʒ] **nm** touching up, polishing up.

fignoler* [fiɲɔle] [1] **vt** (*soigner*) to polish up, put the finishing touches to. **ça c'est du travail fignolé** that's a really neat job*; **c'est une voiture fignolée** this car is nicely finished off.

fignoleur, -euse [fiɲɔlœʀ, øz] **nm,f** meticulous worker.

figue [fig] **nf** (*Bot*) fig. ~ **de Barbarie** prickly pear; *voir* **mi-**.

figuier [figje] **nm** fig tree. ~ **de Barbarie** prickly pear.

figurant, e [figyʀɑ̃, ɑ̃t] **nm,f** (*Ciné*) extra; (*Théât*) walk-on, supernumerary; (*fig*) (*pantin*) puppet, cipher; (*complice*) stooge. **avoir un rôle de** ~ (*dans un comité, une conférence*) to be a puppet *ou* cipher, play a minor part, be a mere onlooker; (*dans un crime etc*) to be a stooge; (*Ciné*) to be an extra; (*Théât*) to have a walk-on part.

figuratif, -ive [figyʀatif, iv] 1 **adj** a *art, peinture* representational, figurative; *peintre, tableau* representational. b *plan, écriture* figurative. 2 **nm,f** representational artist.

figuration [figyʀasjɔ̃] **nf** a (*Théât*) (*métier*) playing walk-on parts; (*rôle*) walk-on (part); (*figurants*) walk-on actors; (*Ciné*) (*métier*) working as an extra; (*rôle*) extra part; (*figurants*) extras. **faire de la** ~ (*Théât*) to do walk-on parts; (*Ciné*) to work as an extra. b (*représentation*) representation.

figurativement [figyʀativmɑ̃] **adv** diagrammatically.

figure [figyʀ] 1 **nf** a (*visage*) face; (*mine*) face, countenance (*frm*). **sa** ~ **s'allongea** his face fell; *voir* **casser, chevalier.**

b (*personnage*) figure. ~ **équestre** equestrian figure; **les grandes** ~**s de l'histoire** the great figures of history; (*Cartes*) **les** ~**s** the court *ou* face cards.

c (*image*) illustration, picture; (*Danse, Ling, Patinage*) figure; (*Math: tracé*) diagram, figure. ~ **géométrique** geometrical figure; **faire une** ~ to draw a diagram.

d (*loc*) **faire** ~ **de favori** to be generally thought of as the favourite, be looked on as the favourite; **faire** ~ **d'idiot** to look a fool; **faire** ~ **dans le monde††** to cut a figure in society†; **faire bonne** ~ to put up a good show; **faire triste** ~ **à** to give a cool reception to, greet unenthusiastically; **faire triste** *ou* **piètre** ~ to cut a sorry figure, look a sorry sight; **il n'a plus** ~ **humaine** he is disfigured beyond recognition.

2 **comp** ▶**figure de ballet** balletic figure ▶**figure chorégraphique** choreographic figure ▶**figures imposées** (*Patinage*) compulsory figures ▶**figures libres** freestyle (skating) ▶**figure mélodique** (*Mus*) figure ▶**figure de proue** (*Naut*) figurehead; (*fig: chef*) key figure, figurehead ▶**figure de rhétorique** rhetorical figure ▶**figure de style** stylistic device.

figuré, e [figyʀe] (**ptp de figurer**) **adj** *langage, style, sens* figurative, metaphorical; *prononciation* symbolized; *plan, représentation* diagrammatic. **mot employé au** ~ word used figuratively *ou* in the figurative; **au propre comme au** ~ in the literal as well as the metaphorical *ou* figurative sense.

figurément [figyʀemɑ̃] **adv** figuratively, metaphorically.

figurer [figyʀe] [1] 1 **vt** to represent. **le peintre l'avait figuré sous les traits de Zeus** the painter had shown *ou* represented him in the guise of Zeus; **la scène figure un palais** the scene is a palace; **la balance figure la justice** scales are the symbol of justice.

2 **vi** a (*être mentionné*) to appear. **mon frère figure parmi les gagnants** my brother is listed among the winners *ou* is in the list of the winners; **son nom figure en bonne place/ne figure pas parmi les gagnants** his name is high up amongst/does not appear amongst the winners; ~ **sur une liste/dans l'annuaire** to appear on a list/in the directory; **cet article ne figure plus sur votre catalogue** this item is no longer featured *ou* listed in your catalogue.

b (*Théât*) to have a walk-on part; (*Ciné*) to be an extra.

3 **se figurer vpr** to imagine. **figurez-vous une grande maison** picture *ou* imagine a big house; **si tu te figures que tu vas gagner** if you fancy *ou* imagine you're going to win; **figurez-vous que j'allais justement vous téléphoner** would you believe it *ou* it so happens I was just about to phone you; **je ne tiens pas à y aller, figure-toi!** I'm not particularly keen on going, believe you me*, believe it or not, I've no particular desire to go; **tu ne peux pas te** ~ **comme il est bête** you can't (begin to) believe *ou* imagine how stupid he is.

figurine [figyʀin] **nf** figurine.

fil [fil] 1 **nm** a (*brin*) *[coton, nylon]* thread; *[laine]* yarn; *[cuivre, acier]* wire; *[haricots, marionnette]* string; *[araignée]* thread; *[bouilloire, rasoir électrique]* cord. (*fig*) **les** ~**s d'une affaire** the ins and outs of an affair, the threads of an affair; **il tient dans sa main tous les** ~**s de l'affaire** he has his hands on all the strings; (*Tex*) ~ **de trame/de chaîne** weft/warp yarn; **tu as tiré un** ~ **à ton manteau** you have pulled a thread in your coat; **ramasser un** ~ to pick up a thread; (*fig: téléphone*) **j'ai ta mère**

au bout du ~ I have your mother on the line *ou* phone; **coup de** ~* (phone) call; **donner** *ou* **passer un coup de** ~ **à qn*** to give sb a ring *ou* call *ou* buzz*; **téléphone sans** ~ cordless phone; **haricots pleins de** ~**s/sans** ~**s** stringy/stringless beans; *voir* **inventer** *etc.*

b (*Tex: matière*) linen. **chemise de** ~ linen shirt; **chaussettes pur** ~ **(d'Écosse)** lisle socks.

c (*sens*) *[bois, viande]* grain. **couper dans le sens du** ~ to cut with the grain; **dans le sens contraire du** ~ against the grain; *voir* **droit**[2].

d (*tranchant*) edge. **donner du** ~ **à un rasoir** to give an edge to a razor; (*fig*) **être sur le** ~ **du rasoir** to be on the razor's edge *ou* on a razor-edge; **passer un prisonnier au** ~ **de l'épée** to put a prisoner to the sword.

e (*cours*) *[discours, pensée]* thread. **suivre/interrompre le** ~ **d'un discours/de ses pensées** to follow/interrupt the thread of a speech/one's thoughts; **tu m'as interrompu et j'ai perdu le** ~ you've interrupted me and I've lost the thread; **au** ~ **des jours/des ans** with the passing days/years, as the days/years go (*ou* went) by; **raconter sa vie au** ~ **de ses souvenirs** to tell one's life story as the memories drift back; **suivre le** ~ **de l'eau** to follow the current; **le bateau/papier s'en allait au** ~ **de l'eau** the boat/paper was drifting away with *ou* on the stream *ou* current.

f (*loc*) **maigre** *ou* **mince comme un** ~ as thin as a rake; **donner du** ~ **à retordre à qn** to give sb a headache, make life difficult for sb; **avoir un** ~ **à la patte*** to be tied down; **ne tenir qu'à un** ~ to hang by a thread; **de** ~ **en aiguille** one thing leading to another, gradually.

2 comp ►**fil d'Ariane** (*Myth*) Ariadne's clue (*Brit*) *ou* clew (*US*); (*fig*) vital lead ►**fil conducteur** *[enquête]* vital lead; *[récit]* main theme *ou* thread ►**fil à coudre** (sewing) thread ►**fil à couper le beurre** cheesewire ►**fil dentaire** dental floss ►**fil électrique** electric wire ►**fil de fer** wire; (*fig*) **avoir les jambes comme des fils de fer** to have legs like matchsticks ►**fil de fer barbelé** barbed wire ►**fil-de-fériste** nmf (pl **fil-de-féristes**) high-wire artiste ►**fil-à-fil** (*Tex*) nm inv pepper and salt ►**fil (à linge)** (washing *ou* clothes) line ►**fil (à pêche)** (fishing) line ►**fil à plomb** plumbline ►**fil de soie dentaire** = **fil dentaire** ►**fil à souder** soldering wire ►**fil de terre** earth wire (*Brit*), ground wire (*US*) ►**fils de la vierge** gossamer (*NonC*), gossamer threads.

filage [filaʒ] nm *[laine]* spinning; (*Ciné*) ghost image; (*Théât*) run-through.

filament [filamɑ̃] nm (*Bio, Élec*) filament; *[glu, bave]* strand, thread.

filamenteux, -euse [filamɑ̃tø, øz] adj filamentous.

filandière [filɑ̃djɛʀ] nf (hand-)spinner.

filandreux, -euse [filɑ̃dʀø, øz] adj *viande* stringy; *discours, explication* long-winded.

filant, e [filɑ̃, ɑ̃t] adj *liquide* free-running; *voir* **étoile**.

filasse [filas] 1 nf tow. 2 adj inv: **cheveux (blonds)** ~ tow-coloured hair.

filateur [filatœʀ] nm mill owner.

filature [filatyʀ] nf a (*Tex*) (*action*) spinning; (*usine*) mill. b (*surveillance*) shadowing (*NonC*), tailing* (*NonC*). **prendre qn en** ~ to shadow sb, put a tail on sb*.

file [fil] nf *[personnes, objets]* line. ~ **(d'attente)** queue (*Brit*), line (*US*); ~ **de voitures** (*en stationnement*) line of cars; (*roulant*) line *ou* stream of cars; (*Aut*) **se mettre sur** *ou* **prendre la** ~ **de gauche/droite** to move into the left-hand/right-hand lane; **se garer en double** ~ to double-park; **se mettre en** ~ to line up; **se mettre à la** ~, **prendre la** ~ to join the queue (*Brit*) *ou* the line (*US*); **marcher à la** ~ *ou* **en** ~ to walk in line; **entrer/sortir en** ~ *ou* **à la** ~ to file in/out; **en** ~ **indienne** in single *ou* Indian file; **chanter plusieurs chansons à la** ~ to sing several songs in succession *ou* one after the other; *voir* **chef**[1].

filer [file] [1] 1 vt a *laine, coton, acier, verre* to spin; *[araignée, chenille]* to spin. (*fig*) ~ **un mauvais coton** (*au physique*) to be in a bad way; (*au moral*) to get into bad ways; **verre filé** spun glass.

b (*prolonger*) *image, comparaison* to spin out; *son, note* to draw out. (*fig*) ~ **le parfait amour** to spin out love's sweet dream; **métaphore filée** long-drawn-out metaphor; ~ **une pièce de théâtre** to run through a play.

c (*Police etc: suivre*) to shadow, tail*.

d (*Naut*) *amarre* to veer out. **navire qui file 20 nœuds** ship which does 20 knots.

e (*‡: donner*) ~ **à qn de l'argent/un objet** to slip sb some money/an object; ~ **à qn une maladie** to land sb with an illness*, pass on an illness to sb; ~ **à qn un coup de poing** to punch sb, give sb a punch; **file-toi un coup de peigne** run a comb through your hair.

f (*démailler*) *bas, collant* to ladder (*Brit*), get a run in.

2 vi a *[liquide, sirop]* to run, trickle; *[fromage]* to run; *[lampe, flamme]* to smoke. **il faisait** ~ **du sable entre ses doigts** he was running *ou* trickling sand through his fingers.

b (*: *courir, passer*) *[personne]* to fly* by *ou* past, dash by *ou* past; *[train, voiture]* to fly by; *[cheval, temps]* to fly (by). ~ **bon train/comme le vent/à toute allure** to go at a fair speed/like the wind/at top speed; **il fila comme une flèche devant nous** he darted *ou* zoomed* straight past us; ~ **à la poste/voir qn** to dash to the post office/to see sb.

c (*: *s'en aller*) to go off. **le voleur avait déjà filé** the thief had already made off*; **il faut que je file** I must dash *ou* fly*; **file dans ta chambre** off to your room with you; **allez, file, garnement!** clear off, pest!*; ~ **à l'anglaise** to take French leave (*Brit*), run off *ou* away; ~ **entre les doigts de qn** *[poisson]* to slip between sb's fingers; *[voleur, fig: argent]* to slip through sb's fingers; **les billets de 100 F, ça file vite** 100 F notes disappear in no time; ~ **doux** to behave (o.s. nicely), keep a low profile*.

d (*se démailler*) *[maille]* to run; *[bas, collant]* to ladder (*Brit*), run.

e *[monnaie]* to slide, slip. **laisser** ~ **le dollar** to let the dollar slide.

filet [filɛ] nm a (*petite quantité*) *[eau, sang]* dribble, trickle; *[fumée]* wisp; *[lumière]* (thin) shaft *ou* streak; *[trait]* thin line. **il avait un** ~ **de voix** his voice was very thin; **mettez un** ~ **de vinaigre** add a drop *ou* a dash of vinegar.

b *[poisson]* fillet; *[viande]* fillet (*Brit*) *ou* filet (*US*) steak. **un rôti dans le** ~ a roasting joint (from rump and sirloin) (*Brit*), a roast (*US*); ~ **mignon** fillet (*Brit*) *ou* filet (*US*) mignon.

c (*nervure*) *[langue]* frenum; *[pas de vis]* thread; (*Typ*) rule. ~**s nerveux** nerve endings.

d (*Pêche, Sport*) net. ~ **(à provisions)** string bag; ~ **(à bagages)** (luggage) rack; ~ **à crevettes/à papillons/à cheveux/à poissons** *ou* **de pêche** shrimping/butterfly/hair/fishing net; (*Ftbl*) **envoyer la balle au fond des** ~**s** to send the ball into the back of the net; (*Tennis*) **envoyer la balle dans le** ~ to put the ball into the net, net the ball; (*Tennis*) **monter au** ~ to get up to the net; **travailler sans** ~ *[acrobates]* to perform without a safety net; (*fig*) to be out on one's own; **tendre un** ~ *[chasseur]* to set a snare; *[police]* to set a trap; **le** ~ **se resserre** the net is closing in *ou* tightening; (*fig*) **coup de** ~ haul; (*fig*) **attirer qn dans ses** ~**s** to ensnare sb.

filetage [filtaʒ] nm (*action*) threading; *[pas de vis]* thread.

fileter [filte] [5] vt *vis, tuyau* to thread.

fileur, -euse [filœʀ, øz] nm,f spinner.

filial, e, mpl **-iaux** [filjal, jo] 1 adj filial. 2 **filiale** nf (*Comm*) subsidiary (company). ~**e commune** joint venture; ~**e à cent pour cent** wholly-owned subsidiary.

filialement [filjalmɑ̃] adv with filial devotion.

filiation [filjasjɔ̃] nf *[personnes]* filiation; *[idées, mots]* relation. **être issu de qn par** ~ **directe** to be a direct descendant of sb.

filière [filjɛʀ] nf a *[carrière]* path(way); *[administration]* channels, procedures; *[recel, drogue]* network. (*métier*) **la** ~ **électronique** careers in electronics; (*Univ*) **les nouvelles** ~**s** new subjects; **la** ~ **administrative** the administrative procedures *ou* channels; **passer par** *ou* **suivre la** ~ **pour devenir directeur** to work one's way up to become a director; **de nouvelles** ~**s sont offertes aux jeunes ingénieurs** new paths are open to young engineers; **les policiers ont réussi à remonter toute la** ~ the police have managed to trace the network right through to the man at the top; **on a découvert de nouvelles** ~**s pour le passage de la drogue** new channels for drug trafficking have been discovered.

b (*Tech*) (*pour étirer*) drawplate; (*pour fileter*) screwing die.

filiforme [filifɔʀm] adj *antenne, patte* threadlike, filiform (SPÉC); (*) *jambes* spindly; (*) *corps* spindly, lanky; (*Méd*) *pouls* thready.

filigrane [filigʀan] nm *[papier, billet]* watermark; *[objet]* filigree. **en** ~ (*lit*) as a watermark; filigree (*épith*); (*fig*) just beneath the surface; **sa haine apparaissait en** ~ **dans ses paroles** there was veiled hatred in his words.

filigraner [filigʀane] [1] vt *papier, billet* to watermark; *objet* to filigree.

filin [filɛ̃] nm rope.

fille [fij] 1 nf a (*opp de* **fils**) daughter. **la** ~ **de la maison** the daughter of the house; (*souvent péj*) **la** ~ **Martin** the Martin girl*; (*littér*) **la peur,** ~ **de la lâcheté** fear, the daughter of cowardice; (*Rel*) **oui, ma** ~ yes, my child; *voir* **jouer, petit**.

b (*opp de* **garçon**) (*enfant*) girl; (*femme*) woman; (†: *vierge*) maid†. **c'est une grande/petite** ~ she's a big/little girl; **elle est belle** ~ she's a good-looking girl; **c'est une bonne** *ou* **brave** ~ she's a nice girl *ou* a good sort; **elle n'est pas** ~ **à se laisser faire** she's not the type to let herself *ou* the type of girl who lets herself be messed about; **être encore/rester** ~† to be still/stay unmarried; **mourir** ~† to die an old maid; *voir* **beau, jeune, vieux**.

c (*servante*) ~ **de ferme** farm girl; ~ **d'auberge/de cuisine** serving/kitchen maid; **ma** ~†† my girl.

d († *péj: prostituée*) whore. ~ **en carte** registered prostitute.

2 comp ►**fille d'Ève*** daughter of Eve ►**fille d'honneur** (*Hist*) maid of honour ►**fille de joie** loose woman ►**fille-mère** (*péj*) nf (pl **filles-mères**) unmarried mother ►**fille publique** streetwalker ►**fille des rues** streetwalker ►**fille de salle** (*restaurant*) waitress; (*hôpital*) ward orderly ►**fille à soldats** (*péj* †) soldiers' whore.

fillette [fijɛt] nf a (little) girl. **rayon** ~**s** girls' department. b (*bouteille*) (half-)bottle.

filleul [fijœl] nm godson, godchild. ~ **de guerre** adoptive son (*in wartime*).

filleule [fijœl] nf goddaughter.

film [film] nm a (*Ciné*) (*pellicule*) film; (*œuvre*) film, picture*, movie*. **le grand** ~† the feature film, the main picture; (*genre*) **le** ~ **fantastique/d'avant-garde** fantasy/avant-garde films; ~ **d'animation** cartoon film; ~ **doublé** dubbed film; ~ **muet/parlant** silent/talking film; ~ **en version originale** film with the original soundtrack; ~ **à succès** box-office success, blockbuster*; ~ **à sketches** film made up of sketches; ~ **d'horreur** horror film; ~ **publicitaire** (*publicité*) advertising

film; (*film promotionnel*) promotional film; (*fig*) **repasser le ~ des événements (de la journée)** to go over the sequence of the day's events.
b (*mince couche*) film. **~ alimentaire** clingfilm; **~ plastique de congélation** freezer film.

filmage [filmaʒ] nm (*Ciné*) filming; shooting.

filmer [filme] 1 vt *personne, paysage* to film; *film, scène* to film, shoot. **théâtre filmé** drama on film.

filmique [filmik] adj film (*épith*), cinematic. **l'œuvre ~ de Renoir** Renoir's film work.

filmographie [filmɔgʀafi] nf filmography.

filmologie [filmɔlɔʒi] nf film studies.

filoguidé, e [filogide] adj wire-guided.

filon [filɔ̃] nm (*Minér*) vein, seam, lode; (**: combine*) cushy number*. (*fig*) **trouver le ~** to strike it lucky *ou* rich; **on n'a pas fait de recherches sur ce sujet, c'est un ~ qu'il faudrait exploiter** no research has been done on that subject — it's a line worth developing; **il exploite ce ~ depuis des années** he's worked that seam for years, that (theme *ou* line) has been a real money-spinner for him for years; **être dans l'immobilier c'est un bon ~** it's a cushy number* *ou* a soft option* dealing in property *ou* real estate.

filou [filu] nm (*escroc*) rogue, swindler; (*enfant espiègle*) rogue.

filouter* [filute] 1 1 vt *personne* to cheat, do* (*Brit*), diddle* (*Brit*) (*hum*); *argent, objets* to snaffle*, filch*. **il m'a filouté (de) 10 F** he has cheated *ou* diddled (*Brit*) me out of 10 francs*. 2 vi (*tricher*) to cheat. **il est difficile de ~ avec le fisc** it's hard to diddle (*Brit*) *ou* cheat the taxman*.

filouterie [filutʀi] nf fraud (*NonC*), swindling (*NonC*).

fils [fis] 1 nm son. **le ~ de la maison** the son of the house; **M. Martin ~** young Mr Martin; (*Comm*) **Martin ~** Mr Martin junior; (*Comm*) **Martin et F~** Martin and Son (*ou* Sons); **le ~ Martin** the Martin boy; **elle est venue avec ses 2 ~** she came with her 2 sons *ou* boys; **c'est bien le ~ de son père** he's very much his father's son, he's a chip off the old block; (*frm*) **les ~ de la France/de Charlemagne** the sons of France/of Charlemagne; (*frm*) **être le ~ de ses œuvres** to be a self-made man; (*Rel*) **oui, mon ~** yes, my son; (*Rel*) **le F~ de l'homme/de Dieu** the Son of Man/of God; **~ de garce!**‡† son of a bitch!‡
2 comp ▸**fils de famille** young man of means *ou* with money ▸**fils à papa** (*péj*) daddy's boy ▸**fils spirituel** spiritual son.

filtrage [filtʀaʒ] nm *[liquide]* filtering; *[nouvelles, spectateurs]* screening.

filtrant, e [filtʀɑ̃, ɑ̃t] adj *substance* filtering (*épith*); *pouvoir* of filtration; *verre* filter (*épith*). **virus ~** filterable virus.

filtrat [filtʀa] nm filtrate.

filtration [filtʀasjɔ̃] nf *[liquide]* filtering, filtration.

filtre [filtʀ] nm (*gén, Chim, Élec, Opt*) filter; *[cafetière]* filter; *[cigarette]* filter tip. **papier-~** filter paper; **(café-)~** (filter) coffee; **cigarette avec ~** filter-tipped cigarette; **"avec ou sans ~?"** "tipped or plain?"; *[voiture]* **~ à air/huile** air/oil filter.

filtrer [filtʀe] 1 1 vt *liquide, lumière, son* to filter; *nouvelles, spectateurs* to screen. 2 vi *[liquide]* to filter (through), seep through; *[lumière, son]* to filter through; *[nouvelles]* to leak out, filter through.

fin[1], fine[1] [fɛ̃, fin] 1 adj a (*mince*) *tranche, couche, papier, tissu* thin; *cheveux, sable, poudre, papier de verre* fine; *pointe, pinceau* fine; *bec d'oiseau* thin, pointed; *lame* sharp, keen; *écriture* small, fine; *taille, doigt, jambe* slender, slim. **plume fine** fine pen; **petits pois ~s/très ~s/extra ~s** high-quality/top-quality/superfine (graded) garden peas; **une petite pluie fine** a fine drizzle; *voir* **peigne, sel.**
b (*raffiné, supérieur*) *lingerie, porcelaine, travail* fine, delicate; *traits, visage* fine; *silhouette, membres* neat, shapely; *produits, aliments* high-class, top-quality; *mets* choice, exquisite; *souliers* fine-leather; *or, pierres* fine. **faire un repas ~** to have a superb *ou* an exquisite meal; **vins ~s** fine wines; **perles fines** real pearls; **fine fleur de froment** finest wheat flour; **la fine fleur de l'armée française** the pride *ou* flower of the French army; **le ~ du ~** the last word *ou* the ultimate (*de* in); *voir* **épicerie, partie[2].**
c (*très sensible*) *vue, ouïe* sharp, keen; *goût, odorat* fine, discriminating. **avoir l'oreille** *ou* **l'ouïe fine** to have a keen ear, have keen hearing; *voir* **nez.**
d (*subtil*) *personne* subtle, astute; *esprit, observation* shrewd, sharp; *allusion, nuance* subtle; *sourire* wise, shrewd. **faire des plaisanteries fines sur qch** to joke wittily about sth; **il n'est pas très ~** he's not very bright; **ce n'est pas très ~ de sa part** it's not very clever of him; (*iro*) **comme c'est ~!** that really is clever! (*iro*); (*iro*) **c'est ~ ce que tu as fait!** that was clever of you! (*iro*); **il se croit plus ~ que les autres** he thinks he's smarter than everybody else; **bien ~ qui pourrait le dire** it would take a shrewd man to say that; **tu as l'air ~!** you look a prize idiot!*; **jouer au plus ~ avec qn** to try to outsmart sb.
e (*avant n: très habile, connaisseur*) expert. **~ connaisseur** connoisseur; **fine cuisinière** skilled cook; **~ gourmet, fine gueule*** gourmet, epicure; **fine lame** expert swordsman; **~ stratège** expert strategist; **~ tireur** crack shot; **~ voilier** fast yacht; *voir* **bec.**
f (*avant n: intensif*) **au ~ fond de la campagne** right in the heart of the country, in the depths of the country; **au ~ fond du tiroir** right at the back of the drawer; **du ~ fond de ma mémoire** from the depths *ou* recesses of my memory; **savoir le ~ mot de l'histoire** to know the real story (behind it all).
2 adv *moudre, tailler* finely. **écrire ~** to write small; **~ prêt** quite *ou* all ready; **~ soûl** dead *ou* blind drunk*.
3 comp ▸**fines herbes** (sweet) herbs, fines herbes ▸**fin limier** (keen) sleuth ▸**fine mouche, fin renard** sharp customer; *voir aussi* **1e.**

fin[2] [fɛ̃] 1 nf a (*gén*) end; *[année, réunion]* end, close; *[compétition]* end, finish, close. *[film, roman]* **(F)~** The End; **vers** *ou* **sur la ~** towards the end; **le quatrième en partant de** *ou* **en commençant par la ~** the fourth from the end, the last but three (*Brit*); **~ juin, à la ~ (de) juin** at the end of June; (*Comm*) **~ courant** at the end of the current month; **jusqu'à la ~** to the very end; **jusqu'à la ~ des temps** *ou* **des siècles** until the end of time; **la ~ du monde** the end of the world; **avoir des ~s de mois difficiles** to have difficulty making ends meet at the end of the month, run short of money at the end of the month; **en ~ de semaine** towards *ou* at the end of the week; **on n'en verra jamais la ~** we'll never see the end of this; **à la ~ il a réussi à se décider** he eventually managed *ou* in the end he managed to make up his mind; **tu m'ennuies, à la ~!*** you're getting on my nerves now!, you're beginning to get on my nerves!; **en ~ d'après-midi** towards the end of the afternoon, in the late afternoon; **en ~ de liste** at the end of the list; **en ~ de compte** (*tout bien considéré*) when all is said and done, in the end, at the end of the day, in the last analysis; (*en conclusion*) in the end, finally; **sans ~** (adj) endless; (adv) endlessly; **arriver en ~ de course** *[vis]* to screw home; *[piston]* to complete its stroke; *[batterie]* to wear out; (*) *[personne]* to be worn out, come to the end of the road; (*Bourse*) **en ~ de séance** at the close; **chômeur en ~ de droits** *unemployed person who is no longer entitled to receive unemployment benefit;* **prendre ~** *[réunion]* to come to an end; *[contrat]* to terminate, expire (*le* on); **être sur sa ~, toucher à** *ou* **tirer à sa ~** to be coming to an end, be drawing to a close; **on arrive à la ~ du spectacle** it's getting near the end of the show, the show is coming to an end; **mettre ~ à** to put an end to, end; **mettre ~ à ses jours** to put an end to one's life; **mener qch à bonne ~** to pull sth off, bring sth to a successful conclusion, deal successfully with sth, carry sth off successfully; **faire une ~** to settle down; *voir* **début, mot** *etc.*
b (*ruine*) end. **c'est la ~ de tous mes espoirs** that's the end of all my hopes; **c'est la ~ de tout*** *ou* **des haricots*** that's the last straw!
c (*mort*) end, death. **avoir une ~ tragique** to die a tragic death, meet a tragic end; **il a eu une belle ~** he had a fine end; **la ~ approche** the end is near *ou* nigh.
d (*but*) end, aim, purpose; (*Philos*) end. **~ en soi** end in itself; (*Prov*) **la ~ justifie les moyens** the end justifies the means; **il est arrivé** *ou* **parvenu à ses ~s** he achieved his aim *ou* ends; **à cette ~** to this end, with this end *ou* aim in view; **à quelle ~ faites-vous cela?** what is your purpose *ou* aim in doing that?; **c'est à plusieurs ~s** it has a variety of purposes *ou* uses; **à seule ~ de faire** for the sole purpose of doing; (*frm*) **à toutes ~s utiles** for your information, on a point of information; (*Jur*) **aux ~s de la présente loi** for the purposes of this Act; *voir* **qui.**
2 comp ▸**fin d'exercice** (*Comptabilité*) end of the financial year ▸**fin de non-recevoir** (*Jur*) demurrer, objection; (*fig*) blunt refusal ▸**fin de race** (*péj*) adj inv degenerate ▸**fin de section** *[autobus]* stage limit, fare stage ▸**fin de semaine** (*Can*) weekend ▸**fin de série** (*Comm*) oddment ▸**fin de siècle** (*péj*) adj inv decadent, fin de siècle.

final, e[1], mpl ~s *ou* -aux [final, o] 1 adj a (*terminal*) final; *voir* **point[1].** b (*marquant la finalité: Ling, Philos*) final. (*Ling*) **proposition ~e** purpose *ou* final clause. 2 nm (*Mus*) finale. 3 **finale** nf a (*Sport*) final. **quart de ~e** quarterfinal; **demi-~e** semifinal. b (*syllabe*) final *ou* last syllable; (*voyelle*) final *ou* last vowel.

finale[2] [final] nm (*Mus*) finale.

finalement [finalmɑ̃] adv (*gén*) in the end, finally, eventually, ultimately. (*fig: après tout*) **ce n'est pas si mal ~** it's not so bad after all; **~ je ne suis pas plus avancé** in the end *ou* finally I'm no further on.

finaliser [finalize] 1 vt a (*achever*) to finalize. b (*orienter*) to target.

finalisme [finalism] nm finalism.

finaliste [finalist] 1 adj (*Philos*) finalist. 2 nmf (*Philos, Sport*) finalist.

finalité [finalite] nf (*but*) end, aim; (*fonction*) purpose, function.

finance [finɑ̃s] nf a (*Pol*) (*recettes et dépenses*) **~s** finances; (*administration*) **les F~s** the Ministry of Finance, ≃ the Treasury, the Exchequer (*Brit*), the Treasury Department (*US*); **il est aux F~s** *[employé]* he works at the Ministry of Finance *ou* at the Treasury (*Brit*) *ou* at the Treasury Department (*US*); *[ministre]* he is Minister of Finance *ou* Chancellor of the Exchequer (*Brit*) *ou* Secretary of the Treasury (*US*); **l'état de mes ~s*** the state of my finances, my financial state; **les** *ou* **mes ~s sont à sec*** (my) funds are exhausted; *voir* **loi, ministre.**
b (*Fin*) finance. **la (haute) ~** (*activité*) (high) finance; (*personne*) (top) financiers; **il est dans la ~** he's in banking *ou* finance; *voir* **moyennant.**

financement [finɑ̃smɑ̃] nm financing. **plan de ~** financial plan; **~ à court/long terme** short/long-term financing; **~-relais** bridge *ou* interim financing; **~ à taux fixe** fixed-rate financing.

financer [finɑ̃se] 3 1 vt to finance, back (*with money*), put up the money for. 2 vi (*) to fork out*.

financier, -ière [finɑ̃sje, jɛʀ] 1 adj a (*Fin*) financial. **soucis ~s** money *ou* financial worries; *voir* **place**. b (*Culin*) **(sauce) ~ière** sauce financière; **quenelles (sauce) ~ière** quenelles sauce financière. 2 nm financier.

financièrement [finɑ̃sjɛʀmɑ̃] adv financially.

finasser* [finase] [1] vi to use trickery. **inutile de ~ avec moi!** there's no point trying to use your tricks on me!

finasserie* [finasʀi] nf trick, dodge*, ruse.

finassier, -ière [finasje, jɛʀ] nm,f trickster, dodger*.

finaud, e [fino, od] 1 adj wily. 2 nm wily bird. **c'est un petit ~** he's as crafty as they come*, there are no flies on him*, he's nobody's fool. 3 **finaude** nf crafty minx.

finauderie [finodʀi] nf (*caractère*) wiliness, guile; (*action*) wile, dodge* (*Brit*).

fine[2] [fin] nf a (*alcool*) liqueur brandy. **~ Champagne** fine champagne; *voir* **fin**[1]. b (*huître*) **~ de claire** green oyster.

finement [finmɑ̃] adv *ciselé, brodé* finely, delicately; *faire remarquer* subtly; *agir, manœuvrer* cleverly, shrewdly.

finesse [finɛs] nf a (*minceur*) *[cheveux, poudre]* fineness; *[pointe]* fineness, sharpness; *[lame]* keenness, sharpness; *[écriture]* smallness, neatness; *[taille]* slenderness, slimness; *[couche, papier]* thinness.
b (*raffinement*) *[broderie, porcelaine, travail, traits]* delicacy, fineness; *[aliments, mets]* delicacy, choiceness. **son visage est d'une grande ~** he has very refined *ou* delicate features.
c (*sensibilité*) *[sens]* sharpness, sensitivity; *[vue, odorat, goût, ouïe]* sharpness, keenness.
d (*subtilité*) *[personne]* sensitivity; *[esprit, observation, allusion]* subtlety.
e **~s** *[langue, art]* niceties, finer points; *[affaire]* ins and outs; **il connaît toutes les ~s** he knows all the tricks *ou* the ins and outs.

finette [finɛt] nf brushed cotton.

fini, e [fini] (ptp de **finir**) 1 adj a (*terminé*) finished, over. **tout est ~ entre nous** it's all over between us, we're finished, we're through*; **~e la rigolade!*** the party* *ou* the fun is over!; **(c'est) ~ de rire maintenant** the fun *ou* joke is over now.
b (*) *acteur, homme politique* finished; *chose* finished, done (*attrib*). **il est ~** he is finished, he is a has-been*.
c (*usiné, raffiné*) finished. **produits ~s** finished goods *ou* articles; **costume bien/mal ~** well-/badly-finished suit.
d (*péj: complet*) *menteur, escroc, ivrogne* utter, out-and-out.
e (*Math, Philos, Ling*) finite. **grammaire à états ~s** finite state grammar.
2 nm *[ouvrage]* finish. **ça manque de ~** it needs a few finishing touches.

finir [finiʀ] [2] 1 vt a (*achever*) *travail, études, parcours* to finish, complete; (*clôturer*) *discours, affaire* to finish, end, conclude. **finis ton travail *ou* de travailler avant de partir** finish your work before you leave; **il a fini ses jours à Paris** he ended his days in Paris; **~ son verre** to finish one's glass, drink up; **finis ton pain!** finish your bread!, eat up your bread!; **il finira (d'user) sa veste en jardinant** he can wear out his old jacket (doing the) gardening; **il a fini son temps** *[soldat, prisonnier]* he has done *ou* served his time.
b (*arrêter*) to stop (*de faire* doing). **finissez donc!** do stop it!; **finissez de vous plaindre!** stop complaining!; **vous n'avez pas fini de vous chamailler?** haven't you done enough squabbling?, can't you stop your squabbling?
c (*parachever*) *œuvre d'art, meuble, mécanisme* to put the finishing touches to.
2 vi a (*se terminer*) to finish, end. **le cours finit à 2 heures** the class finishes *ou* ends at two; **les vacances finissent demain** the holidays end *ou* are over tomorrow; **la réunion/le jour finissait** the meeting/the day was drawing to a close; **le sentier finit ici** the path ends *ou* comes to an end here *ou* tails off here; **il est temps que cela finisse** it is time it (was) stopped; **ce film finit bien** this film has a happy ending; **tout cela va mal ~** it will all have a sorry end, it will all end in disaster; *voir* **beauté**.
b *[personne]* to finish up, end up. **il finira mal** he will come to a bad end; **il a fini directeur** he ended up as (a) director; **il finira en prison** he will end up in prison; **~ dans la misère** to end one's days in poverty, end up in poverty.
c (*mourir*) to die. **il a fini dans un accident de voiture** he died in a car accident.
d **~ en qch** to end in sth; **ça finit en pointe/en chemin de terre** it ends in a point/in a path.
e **~ par remarquer/trouver** to notice/find in the end *ou* eventually; **~ par une dispute/un concert** to end in an argument/with a concert; **il a fini par se décider** he finally *ou* eventually made up his mind, he made up his mind in the end; **tu finis par m'ennuyer** you're beginning to annoy me; *voir* **queue**.
f **en ~ avec qch/qn** to have *ou* be done with sth/sb; **il faut en ~ avec cette situation** we'll have to put an end to this situation; **nous en aurons bientôt fini** we'll soon be finished with it, we'll soon have it over and done with; **quand en auras-tu fini avec tes jérémiades?** when will you ever stop moaning?; **je vais lui parler pour qu'on en finisse** I'll talk to him so that we can get the matter settled; **pour vous en ~** to cut a long story short; **qui n'en finit pas, à n'en plus ~** *route, discours, discussions* never-ending, endless; **elle n'en finit pas de se préparer** she takes an age to get ready, her preparations are a lengthy business; **on n'en aurait jamais fini de raconter ses bêtises** you could go on for ever recounting the stupid things he has done; **il a des jambes qui n'en finissent pas** he's all legs*.

finish [finiʃ] nm (*Sport*) finish. **combat au ~** fight to the finish.

finissage [finisaʒ] nm (*Couture, Tech*) finishing.

finisseur, -euse [finisœʀ, øz] nm,f a (*Couture, Tech*) finisher. b (*Sport*) good *ou* strong finisher.

finition [finisjɔ̃] nf (*action*) finishing; (*résultat*) finish. **la ~ est parfaite** the finish is perfect; (*Couture*) **faire les ~s** to put the finishing touches; (*Constr*) **travaux de ~** finishing off.

finlandais, e [fɛ̃lɑ̃dɛ, ɛz] 1 adj Finnish. 2 nm,f: **F~(e)** Finn.

Finlande [fɛ̃lɑ̃d] nf Finland.

finlandisation [fɛ̃lɑ̃dizasjɔ̃] nf Finlandization.

finnois, e [finwa, waz] 1 adj Finnish. 2 nm (*Ling*) Finnish.

finno-ougrien, -ienne [finougʀijɛ̃, ijɛn] adj, nm (*Ling*) Finno-Ugric, Finno-Ugrian.

fiole [fjɔl] nf phial, flask; (*‡: tête*) face, mug‡.

fiord [fjɔʀ(d)] nm = **fjord**.

fioriture [fjɔʀityʀ] nf *[dessin]* flourish; (*Mus*) fioritura. **~s de style** flourishes *ou* embellishments of style.

fioul [fjul] nm = **fuel**.

firmament [fiʀmamɑ̃] nm (*littér*) firmament (*littér*). (*fig*) **au ~ de** at the height of.

firme [fiʀm] nf firm.

fisc [fisk] nm tax department, ≃ Inland Revenue (*Brit*), ≃ Internal Revenue (*US*). **agent du ~** official of the tax department, ≃ Inland Revenue official (*Brit*), ≃ Collector of Internal Revenue (*US*).

fiscal, e, mpl **-aux** [fiskal, o] adj fiscal, tax (*épith*). **l'année ~e** the tax *ou* fiscal year; **timbre ~** revenue *ou* fiscal stamp; **politique ~e** tax *ou* fiscal policy; **allègements *ou* dégrèvements ~aux** tax relief; **abattement ~** tax allowance; **avantage ~** tax break; **charges ~es** taxes, taxation; **l'Administration ~e** the tax authority; *voir* **abri, fraude**.

fiscalement [fiskalmɑ̃] adv fiscally.

fiscalisation [fiskalizasjɔ̃] nf *[revenus]* making subject to tax; *[prestation sociale]* funding by taxation.

fiscaliser [fiskalize] [1] vt *revenus* to make subject to tax; *prestation sociale* to fund by taxation.

fiscalité [fiskalite] nf (*système*) tax system; (*impôts*) taxation.

fish-eye [fiʃaj] nm,pl **fish-eyes** fish-eye lens.

fissa* [fisa] adv: **faire ~** to get a move on*.

fissible [fisibl] adj fissile, fissionable.

fissile [fisil] adj (*Géol*) tending to split; (*Phys*) fissile, fissionable.

fission [fisjɔ̃] nf fission. **~ de l'atome** atomic fission.

fissuration [fisyʀasjɔ̃] nf fissuring, cracking, splitting.

fissure [fisyʀ] nf (*lit*) crack, fissure; (*fig*) crack; (*Anat*) fissure.

fissurer [fisyʀe] [1] 1 vt to crack, fissure; (*fig*) to split. 2 **se fissurer** vpr to crack, fissure.

fiston* [fistɔ̃] nm son, lad, junior (*US*). **dis-moi, ~** tell me, son *ou* sonny* *ou* laddie* (*Brit*).

fistulaire [fistylɛʀ] adj fistular.

fistule [fistyl] nf fistula.

fistuleux, -euse [fistylø, øz] adj fistulous.

FIV [ɛfive] nf (abrév de **fécondation in vitro**) IVF.

five o'clock [fajvɔklɔk] nm (†, *hum*) (afternoon) tea.

fivète [fivɛt] nf in vitro fertilization.

fixage [fiksaʒ] nm (*Art, Phot, Tex, Fin*) fixing.

fixateur [fiksatœʀ] nm (*Art*) fixative spray; (*Coiffure*) (*laque*) hair spray; (*crème*) hair cream; (*avant la mise en plis*) setting lotion; (*Phot*) fixer. **bain ~** fixing bath.

fixatif [fiksatif] nm fixative; (*Can: laque*) hair spray.

fixation [fiksasjɔ̃] nf a (*Chim, Psych, Zool*) fixation; (*Phot*) fixing. (*Psych*) **faire une ~ sur qch** to be obsessed with *ou* by sth. b (*attache*) fastening. (*Ski*) **~ (de sécurité)** (safety) binding; (*Ski*) **~s de randonnée** touring bindings. c *[peuple]* settling. d *[salaires, date]* fixing.

fixe [fiks] 1 adj a (*immobile*) *point, panneau* fixed; *personnel* permanent; *emploi* permanent, steady; *regard* vacant, fixed. **regarder qn les yeux ~s** to gaze *ou* look fixedly *ou* intently at sb, fix an unblinking gaze *ou* stare on sb; (*commandement*) **~!** attention!; *voir* **barre, domicile**. b (*prédéterminé*) *revenu* fixed; *jour, date* fixed, set. **à heure ~** at a set time, at set times; *voir* **prix**. c (*inaltérable*) *couleur* fast, permanent. **encre bleu ~** permanent blue ink; *voir* **idée**. 2 nm basic *ou* fixed salary.

fixe-chaussette, pl **fixe-chaussettes** [fiksəʃosɛt] nm garter, suspender (*Brit*).

fixer [fikse] [1] 1 vt a (*attacher*) to fix, fasten (*à, sur* to). (*fig*) **~ qch dans sa mémoire** to fix sth firmly in one's memory.
b (*décider*) *date* to fix, arrange, set. **~ la date/l'heure d'un rendez-vous** to arrange *ou* set *ou* fix the date/the time for a meeting; (*fig*) **~ son choix sur qch** to decide *ou* settle on sth; **mon choix s'est fixé sur cet article** I settled *ou* decided on this article; (*fig*) **je ne suis pas encore**

fixé sur ce que je ferai I haven't made up my mind what to do yet, I haven't got any fixed plans in mind yet; **avez-vous fixé le jour de votre départ?** have you decided what day you are leaving (on)?; **à l'heure fixée** at the agreed *ou* appointed time; **au jour fixé** on the appointed day.

c *regard, attention* to fix. ~ **les yeux sur qn/qch,** ~ **qn/qch du regard** to stare at sb/sth; **il le fixa longuement** he looked hard at him, he stared at him; ~ **son attention sur** to focus *ou* fix one's attention on; **mon regard se fixa sur lui** I fixed my gaze on him, my gaze fastened on him.

d (*déterminer*) *prix, impôt, délai* to fix, set; *règle, principe* to lay down, determine; *idées* to clarify, sort out; *conditions* to lay down, set. **les droits et les devoirs fixés par la loi** the rights and responsibilities laid down *ou* determined by law; ~ **ses idées sur le papier** to set one's ideas down on paper; (*Ling*) **mot fixé par l'usage** word fixed by usage; (*Ling*) **l'orthographe s'est fixée** spelling has become fixed.

e (*renseigner*) ~ **qn sur qch*** to put sb in the picture about sth*, enlighten sb as to sth; **être fixé sur le compte de qn** to be wise to sb*, have sb weighed up* (*Brit*) *ou* sized up* *ou* taped* (*Brit*); **alors, es-tu fixé maintenant?*** have you got the picture now?*

f ~ **qn** to make sb settle (down); **seul le mariage pourra le** ~ marriage is the only thing that will make him settle down.

g (*Phot*) to fix.

2 **se fixer** vpr a (*s'installer*) to settle. **il s'est fixé à Lyon** he settled in Lyons.

b (*s'assigner*) **se** ~ **un objectif** to set o.s. a target; **je me suis fixé fin mai pour terminer** I've set myself a deadline of the end of May (to finish).

fixing [fiksiŋ] nm (*Fin*) fixing.

fixité [fiksite] nf *[opinions]* fixedness; *[regard]* fixedness, steadiness.

fjord [fjɔʀ(d)] nm fiord, fjord.

Fl (abrév de **florin**) fl.

flac [flak] excl splash!

flaccidité [flaksidite] nf flabbiness, flaccidity.

flacon [flakɔ̃] nm (small, stoppered) bottle; (*Chim*) flask. ~ **à parfum** perfume bottle.

flafla* [flafla] nm: **faire des ~s** to show off.

flagada* [flagada] adj inv: **être** ~ to be dog-tired* *ou* washed-out*.

flagellateur, -trice [flaʒelatœʀ, tʀis] nm,f flogger, scourger, flagellator (*frm*).

flagellation [flaʒelasjɔ̃] nf (*gén*) flogging; (*Rel*) scourging; (*pratique sexuelle*) flagellation.

flagelle [flaʒɛl] nm flagellum.

flagellé, e [flaʒele] (ptp de **flageller**) adj, nm (*Zool*) flagellate.

flageller [flaʒele] 1 vt to flog, scourge, flagellate (*frm*); (*Rel*) to scourge; (*fig*) to flay. ~ **le vice** to castigate vice.

flageolant, e [flaʒɔlɑ̃, ɑ̃t] adj shaky.

flageoler [flaʒɔle] 1 vi: ~ **(sur ses jambes), avoir les jambes qui flageolent** (*de faiblesse*) to be sagging at the knees; (*de peur*) to quake at the knees.

flageolet [flaʒɔlɛ] nm a (*Mus*) flageolet. b (*Bot*) flageolet, dwarf kidney bean.

flagorner [flagɔʀne] 1 vt (*frm, hum*) to toady to, fawn upon.

flagornerie [flagɔʀnəʀi] nf (*frm, hum*) toadying (*NonC*), fawning (*NonC*), sycophancy (*NonC*).

flagorneur, -euse [flagɔʀnœʀ, øz] (*frm, hum*) 1 adj toadying, fawning, sycophantic. 2 nm,f toady, fawner, sycophant.

flagrant, e [flagʀɑ̃, ɑ̃t] adj *mensonge* blatant; *erreur, injustice* flagrant, blatant, glaring. **prendre qn en** ~ **délit** to catch sb red-handed *ou* in the act *ou* in flagrante delicto (*SPÉC*); **pris en** ~ **délit de mensonge** caught out blatantly lying.

flair [flɛʀ] nm *[chien]* sense of smell, nose; (*fig*) sixth sense, intuition. **avoir du** ~ to have a good nose; to have intuition.

flairer [fleʀe] 1 vt a to smell (at), sniff (at); (*Chasse*) to scent. b (*fig*) to scent, sense, smell. ~ **quelque chose de louche** to smell *ou* scent something fishy, smell a rat; ~ **le danger** to sense *ou* scent danger; ~ **le vent** to see which way the wind is blowing, read the wind (*US*).

flamand, e [flamɑ̃, ɑ̃d] 1 adj Flemish. 2 nm a **F~** Fleming; **les F~s** the Flemish. b (*Ling*) Flemish. 3 **Flamande** nf Fleming, Flemish woman.

flamant [flamɑ̃] nm flamingo. ~ **rose** (pink) flamingo.

flambage [flɑ̃baʒ] nm a *[volaille]* singeing; *[instrument]* sterilizing (*with flame*). b (*Tech*) buckling.

flambant, e [flɑ̃bɑ̃, ɑ̃t] adj (*qui brûle*) burning; (*: *superbe*) great*. ~ **neuf** brand new.

flambart*†, **flambard***† [flɑ̃baʀ] nm swankpot*. **faire le** *ou* **son** ~ to swank*.

flambé, e¹‡ [flɑ̃be] (ptp de **flamber**) adj *personne* finished. **il est ~!** he has had it!*; **l'affaire est ~e!** it's up the spout!*

flambeau, pl **~x** [flɑ̃bo] nm a (flaming) torch; *voir* **retraite**. b (*fig, frm*) torch. **passer le** ~ **à qn** to pass on *ou* hand on the torch to sb. c (*chandelier*) candlestick.

flambée² [flɑ̃be] nf a (*feu*) (quick) blaze. b (*fig*) *[violence]* outburst; *[cours, prix]* surge, explosion. ~ **de colère** angry outburst, flare-up; **la** ~ **des prix** the explosion in prices.

flambement [flɑ̃bmɑ̃] nm (*Tech*) buckling.

flamber [flɑ̃be] 1 1 vi a *[bois]* to burn; *[feu]* to blaze, flame; *[incendie]* to blaze. **la maison a flambé en quelques minutes** in a few minutes the house was burnt to the ground. b (*: *être joueur*) to be a big-time gambler. c *[cours, prix]* to shoot up, rocket. 2 vt a (*Culin*) to flambé. **bananes flambées** bananas flambé. b *volaille, cheveux* to singe; (*Méd*) *aiguille, instrument de chirurgie* to sterilize (*in a flame*).

flambeur, -euse* [flɑ̃bœʀ, øz] nm,f big-time gambler.

flamboiement [flɑ̃bwamɑ̃] nm *[flammes]* blaze, blazing; *[lumière]* blaze; *[yeux]* flash, gleam. **dans un** ~ **de couleurs** in a blaze of colour.

flamboyant, e [flɑ̃bwajɑ̃, ɑ̃t] 1 adj a *feu, lumière* blazing; *yeux* flashing, blazing; *couleur* flaming; *regard* fiery; *ciel, soleil* blazing; *épée, armure* gleaming, flashing. b (*Archit*) flamboyant. 2 nm (*Archit*) flamboyant style.

flamboyer [flɑ̃bwaje] 8 vi *[flamme]* to blaze (up), flame (up); *[yeux]* to flash, blaze; *[soleil, ciel]* to blaze; *[couleur]* to flame; *[épée, armure]* to gleam, flash.

flamingant, e [flamɛ̃gɑ̃, ɑ̃t] 1 adj Flemish-speaking. 2 nm,f: **F~(e)** Flemish speaker; (*Pol*) Flemish nationalist.

flamme [flɑm] nf a (*lit*) flame. **être en ~s, être la proie des ~s** to be on fire *ou* ablaze; (*Aviat, fig*) **descendre (qch/qn) en ~s** to shoot (sth/sb) down in flames; **dévoré par les ~s** consumed by fire *ou* the flames; **la** ~ **olympique** the Olympic flame; **les ~s de l'enfer** the flames *ou* fires of hell. b (*fig: ardeur*) fire, fervour. **discours plein de** ~ passionate *ou* fiery speech; **jeune homme plein de** ~ young man full of fire. c (*fig: éclat*) fire, brilliance. **la** ~ **de ses yeux** *ou* **de son regard** his flashing eyes. d (*littér: amour*) love, ardour. e (*drapeau*) pennant, pennon. f (*Poste*) postal logo *ou* slogan.

flammé, e [flɑme] adj *céramique* flambé.

flammèche [flamɛʃ] nf (flying) spark.

flan [flɑ̃] nm a (*Culin*) custard tart. b (*Tech*) *[imprimeur]* flong; *[monnaie]* blank, flan; *[disque]* mould. c (*) **il en est resté comme deux ronds de** ~ you could have knocked him down with a feather*; **c'est du** ~ it's a load of waffle!* (*Brit*) *ou* hooey*.

flanc [flɑ̃] nm a *[personne]* side; *[animal]* side, flank. (†, *littér*) **l'enfant qu'elle portait dans son** ~ the child she was carrying in her womb; **être couché sur le** ~ to lie *ou* be lying on one's side; **tirer au ~*** to skive‡, swing the lead*; **être sur le** ~ (*malade*) to be laid up; (*fatigué*) to be all in*; **cette grippe m'a mis sur le** ~ that bout of flu has knocked me out*; *voir* **battre**. b *[navire]* side; *[armée]* flank; *[montagne]* slope, side. **à** ~ **de coteau** *ou* **de colline** on the hillside; **prendre de** ~ (*Naut, fig*) to catch broadside on; (*Mil*) to attack on the flank; *voir* **prêter**.

flancher* [flɑ̃ʃe] 1 vi *[cœur]* to give out, pack up* (*Brit*); *[troupes]* to quit. **sa mémoire a flanché** his memory failed him; **c'est le moral qui a flanché** he lost his nerve; **il a flanché en math** he fell down *ou* came down in maths; **sans** ~ without flinching; **ce n'est pas le moment de** ~ this is no time for weakening *ou* weakness.

flanchet [flɑ̃ʃɛ] nm (*Boucherie*) flank.

Flandre [flɑ̃dʀ] nf: **la** ~, **les ~s** Flanders.

flandrin [flɑ̃dʀɛ̃] nm (††, *péj*) **grand** ~ great gangling fellow.

flanelle [flanɛl] nf (*Tex*) flannel.

flâner [flɑne] 1 vi to stroll, saunter; (*péj*) to hang about, lounge about. **va chercher du pain, et sans ~!** go and get some bread, and get a move on!*

flânerie [flɑnʀi] nf stroll, saunter. (*péj*) **perdre son temps en ~s** to waste one's time lounging about.

flâneur, -euse [flɑnœʀ, øz] 1 adj idle. 2 nm,f stroller; (*péj*) idler, lounger, loafer.

flanquer¹ [flɑ̃ke] 1 vt to flank. **la boutique qui flanque la maison** the shop adjoining *ou* flanking the house; **flanqué de ses gardes du corps** flanked by his bodyguards; (*péj*) **il est toujours flanqué de sa mère** he always has his mother in tow* *ou* at his side.

flanquer²* [flɑ̃ke] 1 1 vt a (*jeter*) ~ **qch par terre** (*lit*) to fling sth to the ground; (*fig*) to put paid to sth (*Brit*), knock sth on the head*; ~ **qn par terre** to fling sb to the ground; ~ **qn à la porte** to chuck sb out‡; (*licencier*) to sack sb* (*Brit*), give sb the sack* (*Brit*), fire sb; ~ **tout en l'air** to pack it all in* (*Brit*), chuck it all up‡. b (*donner*) ~ **une gifle à qn** to cuff sb round the ear, give sb a clout*; ~ **la trouille à qn** to give sb a scare, put the wind up sb*. 2 **se flanquer‡** vpr: **se** ~ **par terre** to fall flat on one's face, measure one's length (*Brit*).

flapi, e* [flapi] adj dog-tired*, dead-beat*.

flaque [flak] nf: ~ **de sang/d'eau** *etc* pool of blood/water *etc;* (*petite flaque*) ~ **d'eau** puddle.

flash [flaʃ] nm a (*Phot*) flash(light). **au** ~ by flash(light). b (*Rad, TV*) newsflash; (*Ciné*) flash. (*Rad*) ~ **publicitaire** commercial(s).

flash-back [flaʃbak] nm flashback.

flasher* [flaʃe] 1 vi: **j'ai flashé pour** *ou* **sur cette robe** I fell in love with this dress at first sight; **à chaque fois que je le vois je flashe** *ou* **il me fait** ~ every time I see him I go weak at the knees *ou* my heart skips a beat.

flashmètre [flaʃmɛtʀ] nm flash meter.

flasque¹ [flask] adj *peau* flaccid, flabby; (*fig*) *personne* spineless, spirit-

less; *style* limp.
flasque[2] [flask] **nf** (*bouteille*) flask.
flatté, e [flate] (**ptp de flatter**) **adj** *portrait* flattering.
flatter [flate] 1 **1 vt a** (*flagorner*) to flatter. ~ **servilement qn** to fawn upon sb; (*fig*) **cette photo la flatte** this photo flatters her; **sans vous** ~ without flattering you.
b (*faire plaisir*) *[compliment, décoration]* to flatter, gratify. **je suis très flatté de cet honneur** I am most flattered by this honour; **cela le flatte dans son orgueil, cela flatte son orgueil** it flatters his vanity.
c (*frm: favoriser*) *manie, goûts* to pander to; *vice, passion* to encourage.
d (*littér: tromper*) ~ **qn d'un espoir** to hold out false hopes to sb; ~ **qn d'une illusion** to delude sb.
e (*frm: charmer*) *oreille, regard* to delight, charm, be pleasing to; *goût* to flatter. ~ **le palais** to delight the taste buds.
f (*frm: caresser*) to stroke, pat.
2 se flatter vpr (*frm*) **a** (*prétendre*) **se** ~ **de faire** to claim *ou* profess to be able to do; **il se flatte de tout comprendre** he professes to understand everything; **je me flatte de le persuader en dix minutes** I flatter myself that I can persuade him in 10 minutes.
b (*s'enorgueillir*) **se** ~ **de qch** to pride o.s. on sth; **elle se flatte de son succès** she prides herself on her success; **et je m'en flatte!** and I'm proud of it!
c (*se leurrer*) to delude o.s. **se** ~ **d'un vain espoir** to cherish a forlorn hope; **s'il croit réussir, il se flatte!** if he thinks he can succeed, he is deluding himself!
flatterie [flatʀi] **nf** flattery (*NonC*). (*littér, hum*) **vile** ~ base flattery.
flatteur, -euse [flatœʀ, øz] **1 adj** flattering. **comparaison** ~**euse** flattering comparison; **faire un tableau** ~ **de la situation** to paint a rosy picture of the situation; **ce n'est pas** ~! it's not very flattering. **2 nm,f** flatterer. (*littér, hum*) **c'est un vil** ~ he's a base flatterer.
flatteusement [flatøzmɑ̃] **adv** flatteringly.
flatulence [flatylɑ̃s] **nf** wind, flatulence.
flatulent, e [flatylɑ̃, ɑ̃t] **adj** flatulent.
flatuosité [flatɥozite] **nf** (*Méd*) flatus (*SPÉC*). **avoir des** ~**s** to have wind.
fléau, pl ~**x** [fleo] **nm a** (*calamité*) scourge, curse; (* *fig*) plague, bane. **b** *[balance]* beam; (*Agr*) flail.
fléchage [fleʃaʒ] **nm** arrowing, signposting (with arrows).
flèche[1] [flɛʃ] **1 nf a** arrow, shaft (*littér*). ~ **en caoutchouc** rubber-tipped dart; (*fig*) **les** ~**s de l'Amour** *ou* **de Cupidon** Cupid's darts *ou* arrows; **monter en** ~ (*lit*) to rise like an arrow; (*fig*) to soar, rocket; **c'est un acteur qui monte en** ~ this actor is shooting to the top *ou* rocketing to fame; **les prix sont montés en** ~ prices have shot up *ou* rocketed; **partir comme une** ~ to set off like a shot; **il est passé devant nous comme une** ~ he shot past us; **se trouver en** ~ *ou* **prendre une position en** ~ **dans un conflit** to take up an extreme position in a conflict.
b (*fig: critique*) **diriger ses** ~**s contre qn** to direct one's shafts against sb; **la** ~ **du Parthe** the Parthian shot; **faire** ~ **de tout bois** to use all means available to one; **il fait** ~ **de tout bois** it's all grist to his mill, he'll use any means he can.
c (*direction*) (direction) arrow, pointer.
d *[église]* spire; *[grue]* jib; *[mât]* pole; *[affût, canon]* trail; *[balance]* pointer, needle; *[charrue]* beam; *[attelage]* pole. **atteler en** ~ to drive tandem; **cheval de** ~ lead horse.
2 comp ▸**flèche lumineuse** (*sur l'écran*) arrow; (*torche*) arrow pointer.
flèche[2] [flɛʃ] **nf** (*Culin*) flitch.
flécher [fleʃe] 1 **vt** to arrow, mark (with arrows). **parcours fléché** arrowed course, course marked *ou* signposted with arrows.
fléchette [fleʃɛt] **nf** dart. **jouer aux** ~**s** to play darts.
fléchir [fleʃiʀ] 2 **1 vt a** (*plier*) to bend; (*Méd*) *articulation* to flex; (*fig*) to bend. ~ **le genou devant qn** to bend *ou* bow the knee to *ou* before sb.
b (*fig: apaiser*) *personne* to sway; *colère* to soothe.
2 vi a (*gén*) to bend; *[planches]* to sag, bend; *[armées]* to give ground, yield; *[genoux]* to sag; *[volonté]* to weaken; *[attention]* to flag; *[recettes, talent, nombre]* to fall off; (*Bourse*) *[cours]* to ease, drop; *[monnaie]* to weaken, drop. **ses jambes** *ou* **ses genoux fléchirent** his knees sagged; **la courbe de l'inflation fléchit** there is a downturn in inflation; (*Bourse*) **les pétrolières ont fléchi en début de séance** oils were down *ou* dropped slightly in early trading.
b (*s'apaiser*) to yield, soften, be moved. **il fléchit devant leurs prières** he yielded to *ou* was moved by their entreaties; **il s'est laissé** ~ he allowed himself to be won round *ou* persuaded *ou* swayed.
c (*Ling*) **forme fléchie** inflected form.
fléchissement [fleʃismɑ̃] **nm** (*voir* **fléchir**) bending; flexing; bowing; soothing; sagging; yielding; weakening; flagging; falling off; easing off, drop; softening; swaying.
fléchisseur [fleʃisœʀ] **adj m, nm** (*Anat*) **(muscle)** ~ flexor.
flegmatique [flɛgmatik] **adj** phlegmatic.
flegmatiquement [flɛgmatikmɑ̃] **adv** phlegmatically.
flegme [flɛgm] **nm** composure, phlegm. **il perdit son** ~ he lost his composure *ou* cool*.
flémingite* [flemɛ̃ʒit] **nf** (*hum*) bone idleness. **il a une** ~ **aiguë** he's suffering from acute inertia.
flemmard, e* [flemaʀ, aʀd] **1 adj** bone-idle* (*Brit*), workshy. **2 nm,f** idler, slacker, lazybones.
flemmarder* [flemaʀde] 1 **vi** to loaf about, lounge about.
flemmardise* [flemaʀdiz] **nf** laziness, idleness.
flemme* [flɛm] **nf** laziness. **j'ai la** ~ **de le faire** I can't be bothered doing it; **tirer sa** ~ to idle around, loaf about.
fléole [fleɔl] **nf:** ~ **des prés** timothy.
flet [flɛ] **nm** flounder.
flétan [fletɑ̃] **nm** halibut.
flétrir[1] [fletʀiʀ] 2 **1 vt** (*faner*) to wither, fade. **l'âge a flétri son visage** age has withered his face. **2 se flétrir vpr** *[fleur]* to wither, wilt; *[beauté]* to fade; *[peau]* to wither; (*fig*) *[cœur]* to wither.
flétrir[2] [fletʀiʀ] 2 **vt a** (*stigmatiser*) *personne, conduite* to condemn; *réputation* to blacken. **b** (*Hist*) to brand.
flétrissure[1] [fletʀisyʀ] **nf** *[fleur, peau]* withered state; *[teint]* fading.
flétrissure[2] [fletʀisyʀ] **nf a** *[réputation, honneur]* stain, blemish (*à* on). **b** (*Hist*) brand.
fleur [flœʀ] **1 nf a** (*Bot*) flower; *[arbre]* blossom, bloom. **en** ~**(s)** in bloom, in blossom, in flower; **papier à** ~**s** flowered *ou* flower-patterned *ou* flowery paper; **assiette à** ~**s** flower-patterned *ou* flowery plate; **chapeau à** ~**s** flowery hat; **"ni** ~**s ni couronnes"** "no flowers by request".
b (*le meilleur*) **la** ~ **de** the flower of; **à** *ou* **dans la** ~ **de l'âge** in the prime of life, in one's prime; (†, *hum*) **perdre sa** ~ to lose one's honour (†, *hum*); *voir* **fin**[1].
c (*loc*) **comme une** ~* hands down*, without trying; **il est arrivé le premier comme une** ~ he won hands down*, he romped home (to win); **à** ~ **de terre** just above the ground; **un écueil à** ~ **d'eau** a reef just above the water *ou* which just breaks the surface of the water; **j'ai les nerfs à** ~ **de peau** I'm all on edge, my nerves are all on edge; **il a une sensibilité à** ~ **de peau** he's very touchy ; **faire une** ~ **à qn*** to do sb a favour *ou* a good turn; (*fig*) **lancer des** ~**s à qn, couvrir qn de** ~**s** to shower praise on sb; **s'envoyer des** ~**s** (*réfléchi*) to pat o.s. on the back*; (*réciproque*) to pat each other on the back*; (*hum*) ~ **bleue** naïvely sentimental; **il est resté** ~ **bleue en vieillissant** even in his old age he is still a bit of a romantic.
2 comp ▸**fleur de farine** fine wheaten flour ▸**fleurs de givre** frost patterns ▸**fleur de lis** (*Hér*) fleur-de-lis ▸**fleurs d'oranger** orange blossom ▸**fleurs de rhétorique/de soufre/de vin** flowers of rhetoric/sulphur/wine.
fleuraison [flœʀɛzɔ̃] **nf** = **floraison.**
fleurdelisé, e [flœʀdəlize] **adj** decorated with fleurs-de-lis.
fleurer [flœʀe] 1 **vt** (*littér*) to have the scent of, smell sweetly of. **ça fleure bon le pain grillé** there's a lovely smell of toast; ~ **bon la lavande** to smell (sweetly) of *ou* have the scent of lavender.
fleuret [flœʀɛ] **nm** (*épée*) foil. **propos à** ~**s mouchetés** discussion full of barbed remarks.
fleurette [flœʀɛt] **nf** (†, *hum*) floweret; *voir* **conter.**
fleuri, e [flœʀi] (**ptp de fleurir**) **adj a** *fleur* in bloom; *branche* in blossom; *jardin, pré* in flower *ou* bloom; *tissu, papier* flowered, flowery; *appartement* decorated *ou* decked out with flowers; *table* decorated *ou* decked with flowers. **à la boutonnière** ~**e** (*avec une fleur*) wearing *ou* sporting a flower in his buttonhole; (*avec une décoration*) wearing a decoration in his buttonhole. **b** *nez d'ivrogne* red; *teint* florid; (*fig*) *style* flowery, florid. (*hum*) **une barbe** ~**e** a flowing white beard.
fleurir [flœʀiʀ] 2 **1 vi a** *[arbre]* to blossom, (come into) flower; *[fleur]* to flower, (come into) bloom; (*hum*) *[menton d'adolescent]* to grow downy, begin to sprout a beard; *[visage]* to come out in spots *ou* pimples; (*littér*) *[qualité, sentiment]* to blossom (*littér*). **un sourire fleurit sur ses lèvres** his lips broke into a smile.
b (imparfait florissait, prp florissant) *[commerce, arts]* to flourish, prosper, thrive.
2 vt *salon* to decorate with *ou* deck out with flowers. ~ **une tombe/un mort** to put flowers on a grave/on sb's grave; (*frm*) ~ **une femme** to offer a flower to a lady; ~ **sa boutonnière** to put a flower in one's buttonhole; **un ruban fleurissait (à) sa boutonnière** he was wearing a decoration on his lapel; **fleurissez-vous, mesdames, fleurissez-vous!** treat yourselves to some flowers, ladies!, buy yourselves a buttonhole (*Brit*) *ou* boutonnière (*US*), ladies!
fleuriste [flœʀist] **nmf** (*personne*) florist; (*boutique*) florist's (shop), flower shop.
fleuron [flœʀɔ̃] **nm** *[couronne]* floweret; *[bâtiment]* finial; (*fig*) *[collection]* jewel; (*Écon*) flagship. (*fig*) **c'est le plus beau** ~ **de ma collection** it's the finest jewel *ou* piece in my collection; **l'un des** ~**s de l'industrie française** a flagship French industry.
fleuve [flœv] **1 nm** (*lit*) river. ~ **de boue/de lave** river of mud/of lava; ~ **de larmes** flood of tears; ~ **de sang** river of blood; **le** ~ **Jaune** the Yellow River. **2 adj inv** marathon (*épith*), interminable; *voir* **roman**[1].
flexibilité [flɛksibilite] **nf** flexibility. **la** ~ **de l'emploi** flexibility in employment.
flexible [flɛksibl] **1 adj** *métal* flexible, pliable, pliant; *branche, roseau*

pliable, pliant; *caractère* (*accommodant*) flexible, adaptable; (*malléable*) pliant, pliable. 2 **nm** (*câble*) flexible coupling; (*tuyau*) flexible tubing *ou* hose.

flexion [flɛksjɔ̃] **nf** a (*courbure*) *[ressort, lame d'acier]* flexion, bending; *[poutre, pièce]* bending, sagging. **résistance à la ~** bending strength. b *[membre, articulation]* flexing (*NonC*), bending (*NonC*); (*Ski*) knee-bend. **faire plusieurs ~s du bras/du corps** to flex the arm/bend the body several times. c (*Ling*) inflection, inflexion. **langue à ~** inflecting *ou* inflected language.

flexionnel, -elle [flɛksjɔnɛl] **adj** *désinence* inflexional, inflectional, inflected. **langue ~** inflecting *ou* inflected language.

flexueux, -euse [flɛksɥø, øz] **adj** flexuous, flexuose.

flexuosité [flɛksɥozite] **nf** flexuosity.

flexure [flɛksyʀ] **nf** flexure.

flibuste [flibyst] **nf** (*piraterie*) freebooting, buccaneering; (*pirates*) freebooters, buccaneers.

flibustier [flibystje] **nm** (*pirate*) freebooter, buccaneer; (*†: *escroc*) swindler, crook.

flic* [flik] **nm** cop*, copper*, policeman. **les ~s** the cops*, the Old Bill* (*Brit*), the police.

flicage‡ [flikaʒ] **nm** *[quartier]* heavy policing. **le ~ des ouvriers par la direction** the management keeping tabs on workers*.

flicaille‡ [flikɑj] **nf: la ~** the fuzz‡, the pigs‡, the filth‡ (*Brit*).

flicard‡ [flikaʀ] **nm** cop*, pig‡.

flic flac [flikflak] **excl** splash! **ses chaussures font ~ dans la boue** his shoes slop in the mud *ou* go splash splash through the mud.

flingue [flɛ̃g] **nm** gun, rifle.

flinguer‡ [flɛ̃ge] 1 **vt** to gun down, put a bullet in, shoot up* (*US*). (*fig*) **il y a de quoi se ~!** it's enough to make you want to end it all! *ou* make you shoot yourself!

flingueur‡ [flɛ̃gœʀ] **nm** (*tueur à gages*) hitman*, contract killer. **c'est un ~** he's trigger-happy*.

flingueuse‡ [flɛ̃gøz] **nf** contract killer.

flint(-glass) [flint(glas)] **nm** flint glass.

flippant, e‡ [flipɑ̃, ɑ̃t] **adj** *situation, film* grim*, depressing; *personne* depressing.

flipper[1] [flipœʀ] **nm** (*billard électrique*) pin-ball machine.

flipper[2]‡ [flipe] 1 **vi** (*gén, Drogue*) (*être déprimé*) to feel low*; (*être exalté*) to get high‡, flip‡ (*US*).

fliqué, e‡ [flike] **adj** *endroit* crawling with cops*.

flirt [flœʀt] **nm** a (*action*) flirting (*NonC*); (*amourette*) brief romance. **avoir un ~ avec qn** to have a brief romance with sb. b (*amoureux*) boyfriend (*ou* girlfriend).

flirter [flœʀte] 1 **vi** to flirt. (*fréquenter*) **~ avec qn** to go about with sb; (*fig*) **~ avec** *idée, parti* to flirt with.

flirteur, -euse [flœʀtœʀ, øz] **nm,f** flirt.

FLN [ɛfɛlɛn] **nm** (**abrév de Front de libération nationale**) FLN, *Algerian Freedom Fighters*.

FLNC [ɛfɛlɛnse] **nm** (**abrév de Front de libération nationale de la Corse**) *Corsican national liberation front*.

floc [flɔk] **nm, excl** plop, splash.

flocon [flɔkɔ̃] **nm** *[écume]* fleck; *[laine]* flock. **~ de neige** snowflake; **~s d'avoine** oat flakes, rolled oats; **~s de maïs** cornflakes; **la neige tombe à gros ~s** the snow is falling in big flakes; **purée en ~s** dehydrated potato flakes.

floconneux, -euse [flɔkɔnø, øz] **adj** *nuage, étoffe* fluffy; *écume, substance, liquide* frothy.

flonflons [flɔ̃flɔ̃] **nmpl** blare. **les ~ de la musique foraine** the pom-pom of the fairground music.

flop* [flɔp] **nm** flop*. **sa tournée a fait un ~** his tour was a real flop*.

flopée* [flɔpe] **nf: une ~ de** loads of*, masses of; **il y a une** *ou* **des ~(s) de touristes** there are masses of tourists; **elle a une ~ d'enfants** she has a whole brood of children.

floraison [flɔʀɛzɔ̃] **nf** a (*lit*) (*épanouissement*) flowering, blossoming; (*époque*) flowering time. **rosiers qui ont plusieurs ~s** rosebushes which have several flowerings. b (*fig*) *[talents]* flowering, blossoming; *[affiches, articles]* rash, crop.

floral, e, **mpl -aux** [flɔʀal, o] **adj** a *art, composition* floral; *exposition* flower (*épith*). **parc ~** floral garden. b (*Bot*) *enveloppe, organes* floral.

floralies [flɔʀali] **nfpl** flower show.

flore [flɔʀ] **nf** (*plantes*) flora; (*livre*) plant guide. **~ intestinale** intestinal flora.

floréal [flɔʀeal] **nm** Floreal (*eighth month in the French Republican calendar*).

Florence [flɔʀɑ̃s] **n** (*ville*) Florence.

florentin, e [flɔʀɑ̃tɛ̃, in] 1 **adj** Florentine. 2 **nm** (*Ling*) Florentine dialect. 3 **nm,f: F~(e)** Florentine.

florès [flɔʀɛs] **nm** (*littér, hum*) **faire ~** *[personne]* to shine, enjoy (great) success; *[théorie]* to enjoy (great) success, be in vogue.

floriculture [flɔʀikyltyʀ] **nf** flower-growing, floriculture (*SPÉC*).

Floride [flɔʀid] **nf** Florida.

florifère [flɔʀifɛʀ] **adj** (*qui a des fleurs*) flower-bearing; (*qui porte beaucoup de fleurs*) which is a prolific flowerer.

florilège [flɔʀilɛʒ] **nm** anthology.

florin [flɔʀɛ̃] **nm** florin.

florissant, e [flɔʀisɑ̃, ɑ̃t] **adj** *pays, économie, théorie* flourishing; *santé, teint* blooming.

flot [flo] **nm** a (*littér*) *[lac, mer]* **~s** waves; **les ~s** the waves; **voguer sur les ~s bleus** to sail the ocean blue; (*fig*) **les ~s de sa chevelure** her flowing locks *ou* mane (*littér*).

b (*fig: grande quantité*) *[boue, lumière]* stream; *[véhicules, visiteurs, insultes]* flood, stream; *[larmes, lettres]* flood, spate. **un** *ou* **des ~(s) de rubans/dentelle** a cascade of ribbons/lace.

c (*marée*) **le ~** the floodtide, the incoming tide.

d (*loc*) **à (grands) ~s** in streams *ou* torrents; **l'argent coule à ~s** money flows like water; **la lumière entre à ~s** light is streaming in *ou* flooding in *ou* pouring in; **être à ~** (*lit*) *[bateau]* to be afloat; (*fig*) *[personne, entreprise]* to be on an even keel; *[personne]* to have one's head above water; **remettre à ~** *bateau* to refloat; *entreprise* to bring back onto an even keel; (*lit, fig*) **mettre à ~** to launch; **la mise à ~ d'un bateau** the launching of a ship.

flottabilité [flɔtabilite] **nf** buoyancy.

flottable [flɔtabl] **adj** *bois, objet* buoyant; *rivière* floatable.

flottage [flɔtaʒ] **nm** floating (of logs down a river).

flottaison [flɔtɛzɔ̃] **nf** (*Fin*) flotation, floatation; *voir* **ligne**.

flottant, e [flɔtɑ̃, ɑ̃t] 1 **adj** a *bois, glace, mine* floating; *brume* drifting; *voir* **île, virgule**. b *cheveux, cape* (loose and) flowing; *vêtement* loose. c (*Fin, Pol*) floating; *effectifs* fluctuating. **dette ~e** floating debt. d *caractère, esprit* irresolute, vacillating. **rester ~** to be unable to make up one's mind (*devant* when faced with). e *côte, rein* floating. 2 **nm** a (*short*) shorts. **son ~ est usé** his shorts are worn out; **acheter 2 ~s** to buy 2 pairs of shorts. b (*Fin*) float.

flotte [flɔt] **nf** a (*Aviat, Naut*) fleet. **~ aérienne/de guerre/de commerce** air/naval/merchant navy fleet. b (*) (*pluie*) rain; (*eau*) water. c (*flotteur*) float.

flottement [flɔtmɑ̃] **nm** a (*hésitation*) wavering, hesitation. **on observa un certain ~ dans la foule** certain parts of the crowd were seen to waver *ou* hesitate; **il y a eu un ~ électoral important** there was strong evidence *ou* a strong element of indecision among voters. b (*Mil: dans les rangs*) swaying, sway. c (*relâchement*) (*dans une œuvre, copie*) vagueness, imprecision; (*dans le travail*) unevenness (*dans* in). **le ~ de son esprit/imagination** his wandering mind/roving imagination. d (*ondulation*) *[fanion]* fluttering. **le ~ du drapeau dans le vent** the fluttering *ou* flapping of the flag in the wind. e (*Fin*) floating.

flotter [flɔte] 1 1 **vi** a (*lit: sur l'eau*) to float. **faire ~ qch sur l'eau** to float sth on the water.

b (*fig: au vent*) *[brume]* to drift, hang; *[parfum]* to hang; *[cheveux]* to stream (out); *[drapeau]* to fly, flap; *[fanion]* to flutter. *[cape, écharpe]* **~ au vent** to flap *ou* flutter in the wind; **un drapeau flottait sur le bâtiment** a flag was flying over *ou* from the building.

c (*être trop grand*) *[vêtement]* to hang loose. **il flotte dans ses vêtements** his clothes hang baggily *ou* loosely about him, his clothes are too big for him.

d (*littér: errer*) *[pensée, imagination]* to wander, rove. **un sourire flottait sur ses lèvres** a smile hovered on *ou* played about his lips.

e (*fig: hésiter*) to waver, hesitate.

f (*Fin*) *[devise]* to float. **faire ~** to float.

2 **vb impers** (*: *pleuvoir*) to rain.

3 **vt** *bois* to float (down a waterway).

flotteur [flɔtœʀ] **nm** *[filet, hydravion, carburateur]* float; *[chasse d'eau]* ballcock (*Brit*), floater (*US*).

flottille [flɔtij] **nf** *[bateaux, bateaux de guerre]* flotilla; *[avions]* squadron.

flou, e [flu] 1 **adj** a *dessin, trait, contour* blurred; *image* hazy, vague; *photo* blurred, fuzzy, out of focus; *couleur* soft. b *robe* loose(-fitting); *coiffure* soft, loosely waving. c *idée, pensée, théorie* woolly, vague. 2 **nm** *[photo, tableau]* fuzziness, blurredness; *[couleur]* softness; *[robe]* looseness; *[contours]* blurredness. **le ~ de son esprit** the vagueness *ou* woolliness (*péj*) of his mind; **le ~ artistique** (*lit*) soft focus; (*fig*) (deliberate) vagueness.

flouer*† [flue] 1 **vt** (*duper*) to diddle* (*Brit*), swindle. **se faire ~** to be taken in, be had*.

flouse‡, flouze‡ [fluz] **nm** (*argent*) bread‡, dough‡, lolly‡.

fluctuant, e [flyktɥɑ̃, ɑ̃t] **adj** *prix, monnaie* fluctuating; *humeur* changing.

fluctuation [flyktɥasjɔ̃] **nf** *[prix]* fluctuation; *[opinion publique]* swing, fluctuation (*de* in). **~s du marché** market fluctuations *ou* ups and downs.

fluctuer [flyktɥe] 1 **vi** to fluctuate.

fluet, -ette [flyɛ, ɛt] **adj** *corps* slight, slender; *personne* slightly built, slender; *taille, membre, doigt* slender, slim; *voix* thin, reedy, piping.

fluide [flɥid] 1 **adj** *liquide, substance* fluid; *style* fluid, flowing; *ligne, silhouette* flowing; (*Écon*) *main-d'œuvre* flexible. **la circulation est ~** traffic flows freely; **la situation politique reste ~** the political situation remains fluid. 2 **nm** (*gaz, liquide*) fluid; (*fig: pouvoir*) (mysterious) power. **il a du ~, il a un ~ magnétique** he has mysterious powers.

fluidification [flɥidifikasjɔ̃] **nf** fluidification, fluxing.

fluidifier [flɥidifje] 7 **vt** to fluidify, flux.

fluidité [flɥidite] nf *[liquide, style]* fluidity; *[ligne, silhouette]* flow; *[circulation]* free flow; (*Écon*) *[main-d'œuvre]* flexibility.

fluo* [flyo] adj inv (abrév de fluorescent) fluorescent.

fluor [flyɔʀ] nm fluorine.

fluoré, e [flyɔʀe] adj *dentifrice* fluoride (*épith*); *eau* fluoridated.

fluorescéine [flyɔʀesein] nf fluorescein.

fluorescence [flyɔʀesɑ̃s] nf fluorescence.

fluorescent, e [flyɔʀesɑ̃, ɑ̃t] adj fluorescent. écran/tube ~ fluorescent screen/lamp.

fluorine [flyɔʀin] nf fluorspar, fluorite, calcium fluoride.

fluorure [flyɔʀyʀ] nm fluoride.

flush [flœʃ] nm (*Cartes*) flush.

flûte [flyt] 1 nf a (*instrument*) flute; (*verre*) flute, flute glass; (*pain*) French stick. (*Mus*) petite ~ piccolo; (*jambes*) ~s* pins* (*Brit*), gams* (*US*); se tirer les ~s‡ to skip off*, do a bunk‡; *voir* bois, jouer. b (*Hist: navire*) store ship. 2 excl (*) drat it!*, dash it!* (*Brit*) 3 comp ▸flûte à bec recorder ▸La Flûte enchantée The Magic Flute ▸flûte de Pan panpipes, Pan's pipes ▸flûte traversière flute.

flûté, e [flyte] adj *voix* flute-like, fluty.

flûteau, pl ~x [flyto] nm, **flutiau**, pl ~x [flytjo] nm (*flûte*) penny whistle, reed pipe; (*mirliton*) kazoo.

flûtiste [flytist] nmf flautist, flutist (*US*).

fluvial, e, mpl -iaux [flyvjal, jo] adj *eaux, pêche, navigation* river (*épith*); *érosion* fluvial (*épith*).

fluvio-glaciaire [flyvjoglasjɛʀ] adj fluvioglacial.

flux [fly] nm a (*grande quantité*) *[argent]* flood; *[paroles, récriminations]* flood, spate. (*Écon*) ~ de capitaux capital flow; ~ monétaire flow of money; ~ de trésorerie cash flow. b (*marée*) le ~ the floodtide, the incoming tide; le ~ et le reflux the ebb and flow. c (*Phys*) flux, flow. ~ électrique/magnétique/lumineux electric/magnetic/luminous flux. d (*Méd*) ~ de sang flow of blood; ~ menstruel menstrual flow.

fluxion [flyksjɔ̃] nf (*Méd*) swelling, inflammation; (*dentaire*) gumboil. ~ de poitrine pneumonia.

FM [ɛfɛm] 1 nm (abrév de fusil-mitrailleur) MG. 2 nf (abrév de fréquence modulée) FM.

FMI [ɛfɛmi] nm (abrév de Fonds monétaire international) IMF.

FN [ɛfɛn] nm (abrév de Front national) *French political party.*

FNE [ɛfɛnə] nm (abrév de Fonds national de l'emploi) *voir* fonds.

FNSEA [ɛfɛnɛsəa] nf (abrév de Fédération nationale des syndicats d'exploitants agricoles) Farmers' Union, ≃ NFU (*Brit*).

FO [ɛfo] nf (abrév de Force ouvrière) *French trade union.*

foc [fɔk] nm jib. grand/petit ~ outer/inner jib; ~ d'artimon mizzen-topmast staysail.

focal, e, mpl -aux [fɔkal, o] 1 adj focal. 2 **focale** nf (*Géom, Opt*) focal distance *ou* length.

focaliser [fɔkalize] [1] 1 vt (*Phys, fig*) to focus (*sur* on). 2 **se focaliser** vpr to be focused (*sur* on).

foehn [føn] nm foehn.

foène, foëne [fwɛn] nf pronged harpoon, fish gig.

fœtal, e, mpl -aux [fetal, o] adj foetal, fetal.

fœtus [fetys] nm foetus, fetus.

fofolle [fɔfɔl] adj f *voir* fou-fou.

foi [fwa] nf a (*croyance*) faith. avoir la ~ to have (a religious) faith; perdre la ~ to lose one's faith; il faut avoir la ~!* you've got to be (really) dedicated!; il n'y a que la ~ qui sauve! faith is a marvellous thing!; la ~ du charbonnier blind (and simple) faith; sans ~ ni loi fearing neither God nor man; *voir* article, profession.

b (*confiance*) faith, trust. avoir ~ en Dieu to have faith *ou* trust in God; avoir ~ en qn/qch/l'avenir to have faith in sb/sth/the future; digne de ~ *témoin* reliable, trustworthy; *témoignage* reliable; *voir* ajouter.

c (*assurance*) (pledged) word. respecter la ~ jurée to honour one's (sworn *ou* pledged) word; ~ d'honnête homme! on my word as a gentleman!, on my word of honour!; cette lettre en fait ~ this letter proves *ou* attests it; les réponses doivent être envoyées avant le 10 janvier à minuit, le cachet de la poste faisant ~ replies must be postmarked no later than midnight January 10th; (*Jur*) les deux textes feront ~ both texts shall be deemed authentic; sous la ~ du serment under *ou* on oath; sur la ~ de vagues rumeurs on the strength of vague rumours; sur la ~ des témoins on the word *ou* testimony of witnesses; en ~ de quoi j'ai décidé ... (*gén*) on the strength of which I have decided ...; (*Jur*) in witness whereof I have decided ...; être de bonne/mauvaise ~ *[personne]* to be in good/bad faith, be sincere/insincere, be honest/dishonest; c'était de bonne ~ it was done (*ou* said *etc*) in good faith; faire qch en toute bonne ~ to do sth in all good faith; en toute bonne ~ je l'ignore honestly I don't know.

d ma ~ ... well ...; ma ~, c'est comme ça, mon vieux well, that's how it is, old man; ça, ma ~, je n'en sais rien well, I don't know anything about that; c'est ma ~ vrai que ... well it's certainly *ou* undeniably true that ... .

foie [fwa] nm liver. ~ de veau/de volaille calf's/chicken liver; ~ gras foie gras; avoir mal au ~ to have a stomach ache; avoir une crise de ~ to have a bad stomach upset; avoir les ~s‡ to be scared to death*.

foin¹ [fwɛ̃] nm hay. faire les ~s to make hay; à l'époque des ~s in the haymaking season; ~ d'artichaut choke; faire du ~* (*faire un scandale*) to kick up* a fuss *ou* row *ou* shindy* (*Brit*); (*faire du bruit*) to make a row *ou* racket; *voir* rhume.

foin² [fwɛ̃] excl (††, *hum*) ~ des soucis d'argent/des créanciers! a plague on money worries/creditors!, the devil take money worries/creditors!

foire [fwaʀ] nf a (*marché*) fair; (*exposition commerciale*) trade fair; (*fête foraine*) fun fair. ~ agricole agricultural show; ~ aux bestiaux cattle fair *ou* market; *voir* larron. b (*loc*) avoir la ~†‡ to have the runs* *ou* skitters‡ (*Brit*); faire la ~* to whoop it up*, go on a spree; c'est la ~ ici!, c'est une vraie ~!* it's bedlam in here!, it's a proper madhouse!*; c'est une ~ d'empoigne it's a free-for-all.

foirer [fwaʀe] [1] 1 vi (*) *[vis]* to slip; *[obus]* to hang fire; (‡) *[projet]* to fall through, bomb* (*US*). 2 vt (‡: *rater*) to flunk‡. j'ai foiré les maths I flunked maths‡.

foireux, -euse‡ [fwaʀø, øz] adj (*peureux*) yellow(-bellied)‡, chicken‡ (*attrib*); (*raté*) *idée, projet* useless. ce projet/film est ~ this project/film is a washout*.

fois [fwa] nf a time. une ~ once; deux ~ twice; trois ~ three times; (*aux enchères*) une ~, deux ~, trois ~, adjugé going, going, gone!; pour la toute première ~ for the very first time; quand je l'ai vu pour la première/dernière ~ when I first/last saw him, the first/last time I saw him; c'est bon *ou* ça va pour cette ~ I'll let you off this time *ou* (just) this once; de ~ à autre† from time to time, now and again; plusieurs ~ several times, a number of times; peu de ~ on few occasions; bien des ~, maintes (et maintes) ~ many a time, many times; autant de ~ que as often as, as many times as; y regarder à deux *ou* à plusieurs ~ avant d'acheter qch to think twice *ou* very hard before buying sth; s'y prendre à *ou* en deux/plusieurs ~ pour faire qch to take two/several attempts *ou* goes to do sth; payer en plusieurs ~ to pay in several instalments; frapper qn par deux/trois ~ to hit sb twice/three times; *voir* autre, cent, encore, merci, regarder *etc*.

b (*dans un calcul*) une ~ once; deux ~ twice, two times; trois/quatre *etc* ~ three/four *etc* times; une ~ tous les deux jours once every two days, once every other *ou* second day; 3 ~ par an, 3 ~ l'an† 3 times a year; 9 ~ sur 10 9 times out of 10; 4 ~ plus d'eau/de voitures 4 times as much water/as many cars; quatre ~ moins d'eau four times less water, a quarter as much water; quatre ~ moins de voitures a quarter as many cars; (*Math*) 3 ~ 5 (font 15) 3 times 5 (is *ou* makes 15); il avait deux ~ rien *ou* trois ~ rien (*argent*) he had absolutely nothing, he hadn't a bean* (*Brit*); (*blessure*) he had the merest scratch, he had nothing at all wrong with him; et encore merci! — oh, c'est deux ~ rien *ou* trois ~ rien and thanks again! — oh, please don't mention it!

c une ~ once; il était une ~, il y avait une ~ once upon a time there was; (*Prov*) une ~ n'est pas coutume just the once will not hurt, once (in a while) does no harm; pour une ~! for once!; en une ~ at *ou* in one go; une (bonne) ~ pour toutes once and for all; une ~ (qu'il sera) parti once he has left; une ~ qu'il n'était pas là once *ou* on one occasion when he wasn't there.

d (*) des ~ (*parfois*) sometimes; des ~, il est très méchant he can be very nasty at times *ou* on occasion, sometimes he's pretty nasty; si des ~ vous le rencontrez if you should happen *ou* chance to meet him; non mais, des ~! (*scandalisé*) do you mind!; (*en plaisantant*) you must be joking!; non mais des ~ pour qui te prends-tu? look here, who do you think you are!; des ~ que (just) in case; attendons, des ~ qu'il viendrait let's wait in case he comes; allons-y, des ~ qu'il resterait des places let's go — there may be some seats left, let's go in case there are some seats left.

e à la ~ at once, at the same time; ne répondez pas tous à la ~ don't all answer at once; il était à la ~ grand et gros he was both tall and fat; il était à la ~ grand, gros et fort he was tall, fat and strong as well; faire deux choses à la ~ to do two things at once *ou* at the same time.

foison [fwazɔ̃] nf: il y a du poisson/des légumes à ~ there is an abundance of fish/vegetables, there is fish/are vegetables in plenty, there are fish/vegetables galore; il y en avait à ~ au marché there was plenty of it *ou* there were plenty of them at the market.

foisonnement [fwazɔnmɑ̃] nm a (*épanouissement*) burgeoning; (*abondance*) profusion, abundance, proliferation. b *[chaux]* expansion.

foisonner [fwazɔne] [1] vi a *[idées, erreurs]* to abound, proliferate; *[gibier]* to abound. pays qui foisonne de *ou* en matières premières country which abounds in raw materials; pays qui foisonne de *ou* en talents country which has a profusion *ou* an abundance of talented people *ou* is teeming with talented people; texte foisonnant d'idées/de fautes text teeming with ideas/mistakes. b *[chaux]* to expand.

fol [fɔl] *voir* fou.

folâtre [fɔlɑtʀ] adj *enfant* playful, frisky, frolicsome; *gaieté, jeux* lively, jolly; *caractère* lively, sprightly. (*frm, hum*) il n'est pas d'humeur ~ he's not in a playful mood.

folâtrer [fɔlɑtʀe] [1] vi *[enfants]* to frolic, romp; *[chiots, poulains]* to gambol, frolic, frisk. au lieu de ~ tu ferais mieux de travailler instead of fooling around you would do better to work.

folâtrerie [fɔlɑtʀəʀi] nf (*littér*) (*NonC: caractère*) playfulness, sprightliness; (*action*) frolicking (*NonC*), romping (*NonC*), gambolling (*NonC*).

foliacé, e [fɔljase] adj foliated, foliaceous.

foliation [fɔljasjɔ̃] nf (*développement*) foliation, leafing; (*disposition*) leaf arrangement.

folichon, -onne* [fɔliʃɔ̃, ɔn] adj (*gén nég*) pleasant, interesting, exciting. **aller à ce dîner, ça n'a rien de ~** going to this dinner won't be much fun *ou* won't be very exciting; **la vie n'est pas toujours ~ne avec ma belle-mère** life's not always fun with my mother-in-law.

folie [fɔli] nf a (*maladie*) madness, lunacy, insanity; (*gén*) madness, lunacy. **il a un petit grain de ~*** there's a streak of eccentricity in his character; (*Méd*) **~ furieuse** raving madness; (*fig*) **c'est de la ~ douce** *ou* **pure** *ou* **furieuse** it's utter madness *ou* lunacy, it's sheer folly *ou* lunacy; **~ meurtrière** killing frenzy; **avoir la ~ des grandeurs** to have delusions of grandeur; **il a la ~ des timbres-poste** he is mad about stamps, he is stamp-mad*; **aimer qn à la ~** to be madly in love with sb, love sb to distraction; **il a eu la ~ de refuser** he was mad enough (*Brit*) *ou* crazy enough to refuse, he had the folly *ou* madness to refuse; **les soldats en ~ ont tout saccagé** the soldiers went mad and ransacked the place.

b (*bêtise, erreur, dépense*) extravagance. **il a fait des ~s dans sa jeunesse** he had his fling *ou* a really wild time in his youth; **des ~s de jeunesse** follies of youth, youthful indiscretions *ou* extravagances; **ils ont fait une ~ en achetant cette voiture** they were mad (*Brit*) *ou* crazy to buy that car; **vous avez fait des ~s en achetant ce cadeau** you have been far too extravagant in buying this present; **il ferait des ~s pour elle** he would do anything for her; **il ferait des ~s pour la revoir** he'd give anything to see her again; (*hum*) **je ferais des ~s pour un morceau de fromage** I would give *ou* do anything for a piece of cheese; **une nouvelle ~ de sa part** (*dépense*) another of his extravagances; (*projet*) another of his hare-brained schemes.

c (*Hist: maison*) pleasure house, ≃ country house.

d **les F~s-Bergère** the Folies Bergères.

folié, e [fɔlje] adj foliate.

folingue* [fɔlɛ̃g] adj nuts*, crazy*.

folio [fɔljo] nm folio.

foliole [fɔljɔl] nf (*Bot*) leaflet.

folioter [fɔljɔte] 1 vt to folio.

folk [fɔlk] 1 nm abrév de **folk song**. 2 adj: **chanteur/musique ~** folk singer/music.

folklo* [fɔlklo] adj (abrév de **folklorique**) (*excentrique*) weird. **c'est un peu ~ chez lui** his house (*ou* apartment *etc*) is a bit weird.

folklore [fɔlklɔʀ] nm folklore.

folklorique [fɔlklɔʀik] adj a *chant, costume* folk. b (*: *excentrique*) *personne, tenue, ambiance* outlandish. **la réunion a été assez ~** the meeting was a rather weird *ou* quaint affair.

folk song [fɔlksɔ̃g] nm folk music.

folle [fɔl] adj f, nf *voir* **fou**.

follement [fɔlmɑ̃] adv a *espérer, dépenser* madly. **~ amoureux** madly *ou* wildly in love, head over heels in love; **il se lança ~ à leur poursuite** he dashed after them in mad pursuit; **avant de te lancer ~ dans cette aventure** before rushing headlong into *ou* jumping feet first into this business. b (*énormément*) *drôle, intéressant* madly, wildly. **on s'est ~ amusé** we had a fantastic* time; **il désire ~ lui parler** he is dying* to speak to her, he wants desperately to speak to her.

follet, -ette [fɔlɛ, ɛt] adj (*étourdi*) scatterbrained; *voir* **feu[1], poil**.

folliculaire [fɔlikylɛʀ] adj follicular.

follicule [fɔlikyl] nm follicle.

folliculine [fɔlikylin] nf oestrone.

fomentateur, -trice [fɔmɑ̃tatœʀ, tʀis] nm,f troublemaker, agitator, fomenter.

fomentation [fɔmɑ̃tasjɔ̃] nf fomenting, fomentation.

fomenter [fɔmɑ̃te] 1 vt (*lit, fig*) to foment, stir up.

foncé, e [fɔ̃se] (ptp de **foncer**) adj *couleur* (*gén*) dark; (*tons pastels*) deep. **à la peau ~e** dark-skinned.

foncer[1] [fɔ̃se] 3 vi a (*: *aller à vive allure*) *[conducteur, voiture]* to tear* *ou* belt* (*Brit*) *ou* hammer* along; *[coureur]* to charge* *ou* tear* along; (*dans un travail*) to get a move on*. **maintenant, il faut que je fonce** I must dash *ou* fly* now; **fonce le chercher** go and fetch him straight away (*Brit*) *ou* right away (*US*).

b (*: *être dynamique*) to have drive.

c (*se précipiter*) to charge (*vers* at, *dans* into). **~ sur** *ou* **vers l'ennemi/l'obstacle** to charge at *ou* make a rush at the enemy/obstacle; **le camion a foncé sur moi** the truck came charging straight at me; (*lit, fig*) **~ sur un objet** to make straight for *ou* make a beeline for an object; **~ dans la foule** *[camion, taureau, police]* to charge into the crowd; **~ (tête baissée) dans la porte/dans le piège** to walk straight into the door/straight *ou* headlong into the trap; (*fig*) **~ dans le brouillard** to forge ahead regardless, forge ahead in the dark; **la police a foncé dans le tas** the police charged in.

foncer[2] [fɔ̃se] 3 1 vt *couleur* to make darker. 2 vi *[liquide, couleur, cheveux]* to turn *ou* go darker.

foncer[3] [fɔ̃se] 3 vt *tonneau* to bottom; *puits* to sink, bore; (*Culin*) *moule* to line.

fonceur, -euse* [fɔ̃sœʀ, øz] nm,f go-ahead type. **c'est un ~** he's got tremendous drive.

foncier, -ière [fɔ̃sje, jɛʀ] 1 adj a *impôt, revenu* land (*épith*); *noblesse, propriété* landed (*épith*); *problème, politique* (relating to) land ownership. **crédit/impôt ~** land *ou* property loan/tax; **propriétaire ~** landowner. b *qualité, différence* fundamental, basic. **la malhonnêteté ~ière de ces pratiques** the fundamental *ou* basic dishonesty of these practices; **être d'une ~ière malhonnêteté** to have an innate streak of dishonesty, be fundamentally dishonest. 2 nm: **le ~** land *ou* property tax.

foncièrement [fɔ̃sjɛʀmɑ̃] adv fundamentally, basically.

fonction [fɔ̃ksjɔ̃] nf a (*métier*) post, office. (*tâches*) **~s** office, duties; **entrer en ~s** *[employé]* to take up one's post; *[maire, président]* to come into *ou* take office, take up one's post; **ça n'entre pas dans mes ~s** it's not part of my duties; **de par ses ~s** by virtue of his office; **être en ~** to be in office; **la ~ publique** the public *ou* state *ou* civil (*Brit*) service; **logement de ~** accommodation which goes with a post; **avoir une voiture de ~** (*gén*) to have a car with one's post; (*firme privée*) to have a company car; *voir* **démettre, exercice**.

b (*gén, Gram: rôle*) function. **~ biologique** biological function; **remplir une ~** to fulfil a function; **cet organe a pour ~ de, la ~ de cet organe est de** the function of this organ is to; (*Gram*) **avoir** *ou* **faire ~ de sujet** to function *ou* act as a subject; (*fig, hum*) **c'est la ~ qui crée l'organe** ≃ needs must where the devil drives (*Prov*).

c (*Math*) **~ (algébrique)** (algebraic) function; (*Chim*) **~ acide** acid(ic) function; (*Math*) **être ~ de** to be a function of.

d (*loc*) **faire ~ de directeur/d'ambassadeur** to act as a manager/as an ambassador; **il n'y a pas de porte, ce rideau en fait ~** there is no door but this curtain serves the purpose *ou* does instead; **sa réussite est ~ de son travail** his success depends on how well he works; **salaire en ~ des diplômes** salary commensurate with qualifications; **en ~ de** according to.

fonctionnaire [fɔ̃ksjɔnɛʀ] nmf (*gén*) state servant *ou* employee; (*dans l'administration*) *[ministère]* government official, civil servant (*Brit*); *[municipalité]* local government officer *ou* official. **haut ~** high-ranking *ou* top civil servant, senior official; **petit ~** minor (public) official; **les ~s de l'enseignement** state-employed teachers; **~ de (la) police** police officer, officer of the law.

fonctionnalité [fɔ̃ksjɔnalite] nf (*gén*) practicality; (*Ordin*) functionality.

fonctionnarisation [fɔ̃ksjɔnaʀizasjɔ̃] nf: **la ~ de la médecine** the state takeover of medicine; **le gouvernement propose la ~ des médecins** the government proposes taking doctors into the public service *ou* making doctors employees of the state.

fonctionnariser [fɔ̃ksjɔnaʀize] 1 vt: **~ qn** to make sb an employee of the state; (*dans l'administration*) to take sb into the public service; **~ un service** to take over a service (to be run by the state).

fonctionnarisme [fɔ̃ksjɔnaʀism] nm (*péj*) officialdom. **c'est le règne du ~** bureaucracy rules, officialdom has taken over.

fonctionnel, -elle [fɔ̃ksjɔnɛl] 1 adj functional. (*Ling*) **mot ~** function word. 2 nm staff manager. **les ~s et les opérationnels** managers and operatives, staff and line.

fonctionnellement [fɔ̃ksjɔnɛlmɑ̃] adv functionally.

fonctionnement [fɔ̃ksjɔnmɑ̃] nm *[appareil, entreprise, institution]* working, functioning, operation, running; (*Méd*) *[organisme]* functioning. **en état de bon ~** in good working order; **pour assurer le (bon) ~ de l'appareil** to keep the machine in (good) working order; **pour assurer le (bon) ~ du service** to ensure the smooth running of the service; **panne due au mauvais ~ du carburateur** breakdown due to a fault *ou* a malfunction in the carburettor; **pendant le ~ de l'appareil** while the machine is in operation *ou* is running; **budget de ~** operating budget; **frais de ~** running *ou* upkeep costs.

fonctionner [fɔ̃ksjɔne] 1 vi *[mécanisme, machine]* to work, function; *[entreprise]* to function, operate, run; *[*: personne]* to function, operate. **faire ~** *machine* to operate; **il n'a jamais vraiment compris comment je fonctionne*** he has never really understood what makes me tick*; **notre téléphone/télévision fonctionne mal** there's something wrong with our phone/television, our phone/television isn't working properly; **le courrier fonctionne mal** the mail isn't reliable; **ça ne fonctionne pas** it's out of order, it's not working; **sais-tu faire ~ la machine à laver?** can you operate *ou* do you know how to work the washing machine?

fond [fɔ̃] 1 nm a *[récipient, vallée etc]* bottom; *[armoire]* back; *[jardin]* bottom, far end; *[pièce]* far end, back; *[utérus]* fundus. (*Min*) **le ~** the (coal) face; **être/tomber au ~ de l'eau** to be at/fall to the bottom of the water; (*Min*) **travailler au ~** to work at *ou* on the (coal) face; (*Naut*) **envoyer par le ~** to send to the bottom; **y a-t-il beaucoup de ~?** is it very deep?; **l'épave repose par 10 mètres de ~** the wreck is lying 10 metres down; (*Naut*) **à ~ de cale** (down) in the hold; **le ~ de la gorge/l'œil** the back of the throat/eye; **au ~ du couloir** down the corridor, at the far end of the corridor; **au ~ de la boutique** at the back of the shop; **ancré au ~ de la baie** anchored at the (far) end of the bay; **village perdu au ~ de la province** village in the depths *ou* heart *ou* wilds of the country; **sans ~** (*lit, fig*) bottomless; *voir* **bas[1], double, fin[1]** *etc*.

b (*fig: tréfonds*) **le ~ de son cœur est pur** deep down his heart is pure; **savoir lire au ~ des cœurs** to be able to see deep (down) into people's hearts; **merci du ~ du cœur** I thank you from the bottom of my heart; **il pensait au ~ de son cœur** *ou* **de lui(-même) que** deep down he thought that, in his heart of hearts he thought that; **vous avez deviné/je vais vous dire le ~ de ma pensée** you have guessed/I shall tell you what I really think *ou* what my feelings really are; **regarder qn au ~ des yeux** to look deep into sb's eyes; **il a un bon ~, il n'a pas un mauvais ~** he's basically a good person, he's a good person at heart *ou* bottom; **il y a chez lui un ~ d'honnêteté/de méchanceté** there's a streak of honesty/maliciousness in him; **il y a un ~ de vérité dans ce qu'il dit** there's an element *ou* a grain of truth in what he says; **toucher le ~ de la douleur/misère** to plumb the depths of sorrow/misery.

c (*essentiel*) *[affaire, question, débat]* heart. **c'est là le ~ du problème** that's the heart *ou* root *ou* core of the problem; **aller au ~ du problème** to get to the heart *ou* root of the problem; **ce qui compose le ~ de son discours/de sa nourriture** what forms the basis of his speech/diet; **il faut aller jusqu'au ~ de cette histoire** we must get to the root of this business; **débat de ~** background discussion; **ouvrage de ~** basic work; (*Presse*) **article de ~** feature article.

d (*Littérat, gén: contenu*) content; (*Jur*) substance. **le ~ et la forme** content and form; (*Jur*) **le ~ de l'affaire** the substance of the case.

e (*arrière-plan*) *[tableau, situation]* background. **avec ~ sonore** *ou* **musical** with background music, with music in the background; **blanc sur ~ noir** white on a black background; **ceci tranchait sur le ~ assez sombre de la conversation** this contrasted with the general gloom of the conversation; **avec cette sombre perspective pour ~** with this gloomy prospect in the background; *voir* **bruit, toile.**

f (*petite quantité*) drop. **versez-m'en juste un ~ (de verre)** pour me just a drop; **ils ont vidé les ~s de bouteilles** they emptied what was left in the bottles *ou* the dregs from the bottles; **il va falloir racler** *ou* **gratter** *ou* **faire les ~s de tiroirs** we'll have to fish around* *ou* scrape around for pennies.

g (*lie*) sediment, deposit.

h (*Sport*) **de ~** *épreuves, course, coureur* long-distance (*épith*); *voir* **demi-, ski.**

i *[chapeau]* crown; *[pantalon]* seat. (*fig*) **c'est là que j'ai usé mes ~s de culotte** that's where I spent my early school years.

j (*loc*) **le ~ de l'air est frais*** it's a bit chilly, there's a nip in the air; **au ~, dans le ~** (*sous les apparences*) basically, at bottom; (*en fait*) basically, really, in fact; **il n'est pas méchant au ~** he's not a bad sort basically *ou* at heart; **il fait semblant d'être désolé, mais dans le ~ il est bien content** he makes out he's upset but he's quite pleased really *ou* but deep down he's quite pleased; **dans le ~** *ou* **au ~, ça ne change pas grand-chose** basically *ou* really, that makes no great difference; **ce n'est pas si stupide, au ~** it's not such a bad idea after all; **étudier une question à ~** to study a question thoroughly *ou* in depth; **il est soutenu à ~ par ses amis** he is backed up to the hilt by his friends; **visser un boulon à ~** to screw a bolt (right) home; **respirer à ~** to breathe deeply; **à ~ de train, à ~ la caisse*, à ~ les manettes*** hell for leather* (*Brit*), full tilt; **de ~ en comble** *fouiller* from top to bottom; *détruire* completely, utterly; **ce retard bouleverse mes plans de ~ en comble** this delay throws my plans right out, this delay completely overturns my plans.

2 comp ▸**fond d'artichaut** artichoke heart ▸**fond de magasin** (*invendus*) shop's leftover stock ▸**les fonds marins** the sea bed ▸**fond d'œil** fundus; **faire un fond d'œil à qn** to do a funduscopic examination, perform a funduscopy ▸**fond de portefeuille** (*Bourse*) portfolio base ▸**fond de robe** (full-length) slip *ou* petticoat ▸**fond de tarte** (*pâte*) pastry base; (*crème*) custard base ▸**fond de teint** foundation (cream).

fondamental, e, mpl **-aux** [fɔ̃damɑ̃tal, o] 1 adj (*essentiel*) *question, recherche, changement* fundamental, basic; *vocabulaire* basic; (*foncier*) *égoïsme, incompréhension* basic, inherent, fundamental. **son ~, note ~e** fundamental (note); (*Scol*) **matière ~e** basic subject, core subject (*Brit*); **c'est ~** it's a basic necessity *ou* truth. 2 **fondamentale** nf (*Mus*) root, fundamental (note).

fondamentalement [fɔ̃damɑ̃talmɑ̃] adv *vrai, faux* inherently, fundamentally; *modifier, opposer* radically, fundamentally. **~ méchant/généreux** basically *ou* fundamentally malicious/generous; **cela vient ~ d'un manque d'organisation** that arises from a basic *ou* an underlying lack of organization.

fondamentalisme [fɔ̃damɑ̃talism] nm fundamentalism.

fondamentaliste [fɔ̃damɑ̃talist] adj, nmf fundamentalist.

fondant, e [fɔ̃dɑ̃, ɑ̃t] 1 adj *neige* thawing, melting; *fruit* that melts in the mouth. **température de la glace ~e** temperature of melting ice; **bonbon ~** fondant; **chocolat ~** high-quality plain chocolate. 2 nm (*Culin, bonbon*) fondant; (*Chim*) flux.

fondateur, -trice [fɔ̃datœʀ, tʀis] nm,f founder; (*Jur, Fin*) *[société]* incorporator. **membre ~** founder member.

fondation [fɔ̃dasjɔ̃] nf (*action*) foundation; (*institut*) foundation. (*Constr*) **~s** foundations.

fondé, e [fɔ̃de] (ptp de **fonder**) 1 adj a *crainte, réclamation* well-founded, justified. **bien ~** well-founded, fully justified; **mal ~** ill-founded, groundless; **ce qu'il dit n'est pas ~** what he says has no foundation, there are no grounds for what he says; **~ sur des ouï-dire** based on hearsay. b **être ~ à faire/croire/dire** to have good reason to do/believe/say, have (good) grounds for doing/believing/saying. 2 nm: **~ (de pouvoir)** (*Jur*) authorized representative; (*cadre bancaire*) senior banking executive.

fondement [fɔ̃dmɑ̃] nm a foundation. (*Jur*) **~ d'une action en justice** cause of action; **sans ~** without foundation, unfounded, groundless; **jeter les ~s de** to lay the foundations of. b (*hum: derrière*) fundament† (*hum*), backside; (*fond de pantalon*) trouser seat.

fonder [fɔ̃de] [1] 1 vt a (*créer*) *ville, parti, prix littéraire* to found; *commerce* to set up, found (*frm*); *famille* to start. **~ un foyer** to start a home and family; (*Comm*) **"maison fondée en 1850"** "Established 1850". b (*baser*) to base, found (*sur* on). **~ sa richesse sur** to build one's wealth on; **~ une théorie sur** to base a theory on; **~ tous ses espoirs sur** to place *ou* pin all one's hopes on. c (*justifier*) *réclamation* to justify; *voir* **fondé.** 2 **se fonder** vpr: **se ~ sur** *[personne]* to go by, go on, base o.s. on; *[théorie, décision]* to be based on; **sur quoi vous fondez-vous pour l'affirmer?** what grounds do you have for maintaining this?

fonderie [fɔ̃dʀi] nf a (*usine d'extraction*) smelting works; (*atelier de moulage*) foundry. b (*action*) founding, casting.

fondeur, -euse [fɔ̃dœʀ, øz] 1 nm,f (*Ski*) long-distance skier, langlauf specialist. 2 nm (*Métal*) caster.

fondre [fɔ̃dʀ] [41] 1 vt a (*liquéfier*) *substance* to melt; *argenterie, objet de bronze* to melt down; *minerai* to smelt; *neige* to melt, thaw; (*fig*) *dureté, résolution* to melt.

b (*couler*) *cloche, statue* to cast, found.

c (*réunir*) to combine, fuse together, merge (*en* into).

d (*Peinture*) *couleur, ton* to merge, blend.

2 vi a (*à la chaleur*) (*gén*) to melt; *[neige]* to melt, thaw; (*dans l'eau*) to dissolve. **faire ~** *beurre* to melt; *sel, sucre* to dissolve; *neige* to melt, thaw; **ce fruit/bonbon fond dans la bouche** this fruit/sweet melts in your mouth.

b (*fig*) *[colère, résolution]* to melt away; *[provisions, réserves]* to vanish. **~ comme neige au soleil** to melt away *ou* vanish like the snow; **l'argent fond entre ses mains** money runs through his fingers; **cela fit ~ sa colère** at that his anger melted (away); **~ en larmes** to dissolve *ou* burst into tears.

c (**: maigrir*) to slim down. **j'ai fondu de 5 kg** I've lost 5 kg.

d (**: s'attendrir*) **j'ai fondu** my heart melted.

e (*s'abattre*) **~ sur qn** *[vautour, ennemi]* to swoop down on sb; *[malheurs]* to sweep down on sb.

3 **se fondre** vpr a *[cortèges, courants]* to merge (*en* into).

b **se ~ dans la nuit/brume** to fade (away) *ou* merge into the night/mist.

fondrière [fɔ̃dʀijɛʀ] nf pothole, rut, hole.

fonds [fɔ̃] nm a **~ (de commerce)** business; **il possède le ~ mais pas les murs** he owns the business but not the property; **vendre son ~** to sell up; **~ de terre** land (*NonC*).

b (*ressources*) *[musée, bibliothèque]* collection; *[œuvre d'entraide]* fund. **~ de secours/de solidarité/d'amortissement** relief/solidarity/sinking fund; **~ de garantie** guarantee fund; **~ de caisse** cash in hand; **F~ national de l'emploi** *French state fund to provide retraining and redundancy payments for the unemployed;* **F~ européen de coopération monétaire** European Monetary Cooperation Fund; **F~ européen de développement** European Development Fund; **F~ social européen** European Social Fund; **le F~ monétaire international** the International Monetary Fund; (*fig*) **ce pays a un ~ folklorique très riche** this country has a rich fund of folklore *ou* a rich folk heritage.

c (*Fin: pl*) (*argent*) sums of money, money; (*capital*) funds, capital; (*pour une dépense précise*) funds. **pour transporter les ~** to transport the money; **investir des ~ importants dans** to invest large sums of money *ou* a large amount of capital in; **réunir les ~ nécessaires à un achat** to raise the necessary funds for a purchase; **mise de ~ initiale** initial (capital) outlay; **ne pas être/être en ~** to be out of/be in funds; **je lui ai prêté de l'argent, ça a été à ~ perdus** I lent him money, but I never saw it again *ou* but I never got it back; **~ de roulement** working capital; **~ bloqués** frozen assets; **~ disponibles** liquid assets; **~ d'État** government securities; **~ publics** (*Bourse*) government stock *ou* securities; (*recettes de l'État*) public funds *ou* money; **~ secrets** secret funds; *voir* **appel, bailleur, détournement.**

fondu, e [fɔ̃dy] (ptp de **fondre**) 1 adj a (*liquide*) *beurre* melted; *métal* molten. **neige ~e** slush; *voir* **fromage.** b (*Métal: moulé*) **statue de bronze ~** cast bronze statue. c (*fig*) *contours* blurred, hazy; *couleurs* blending. 2 nm a (*Peinture*) *[couleurs]* blend. **le ~ de ce tableau me plaît** I like the way the colours blend in this picture. b (*Ciné*) **~ (enchaîné)** dissolve, fade in-fade out; **fermeture en ~, ~ en fermeture** fade-out; **ouverture en ~, ~ en ouverture** fade-in. 3 **fondue** nf (*Culin*) **~ savoyarde** (cheese) fondue; **~ bourguignonne** fondue bourguignonne, meat fondue.

fongible [fɔ̃ʒibl] adj fungible.

fongicide [fɔ̃ʒisid] 1 adj fungicidal. 2 nm fungicide.

fontaine [fɔ̃tɛn] nf (*ornementale*) fountain; (*naturelle*) spring; (*murale*) fountain. (*fig*) **~ de** fountain of; (*hum*) **cette petite, c'est une vraie ~*** this child turns on the taps at anything, she's a real little crybaby; (*Prov*) **il ne faut pas dire ~ je ne boirai pas de ton eau** don't burn your bridges *ou* your boats.

fontanelle [fɔ̃tanɛl] **nf** fontanel(le).

fonte [fɔ̃t] **nf** a (*action*) *[substance]* melting; *[argenterie, objet de bronze]* melting down; *[minerai]* smelting; *[neige]* melting, thawing; *[cloche, statue]* casting, founding. **à la ~ des neiges** when the thaw comes, when the snow melts *ou* thaws. b (*métal*) cast iron. **~ brute** pig-iron; **en ~** *tuyau, radiateur* cast-iron (*épith*). c (*Typ*) fount.

fontes [fɔ̃t] **nfpl** holsters (*on saddle*).

fonts [fɔ̃] **nmpl**: **~ baptismaux** (baptismal) font.

foot* [fut] **nm abrév de football.**

football [futbol] **nm** football, soccer. **~ américain** American football (*Brit*), football (*US*); **jouer au ~** to play football; *voir* **ballon.**

footballeur, -euse [futbolœʀ, øz] **nm,f** footballer, football *ou* soccer player.

footing [futiŋ] **nm** jogging (*NonC*). **faire du ~** to go jogging; **faire un (petit) ~** to go for a (little) jog.

for [fɔʀ] **nm**: **dans** *ou* **en son ~ intérieur** in one's heart of hearts, deep down inside.

forage [fɔʀaʒ] **nm** *[roche, paroi]* drilling, boring; *[puits]* sinking, boring. **se livrer à des ~s d'essai** to test-drill.

forain, e [fɔʀɛ̃, ɛn] 1 **adj** fairground (*épith*); *voir* **baraque, fête.** 2 **nm** (*acteur*) (fairground) entertainer. **(marchand) ~** stallholder.

forban [fɔʀbɑ̃] **nm** (*Hist: pirate*) pirate; (*fig: escroc*) shark, crook.

forçage [fɔʀsaʒ] **nm** (*Agr*) forcing.

forçat [fɔʀsa] **nm** (*bagnard*) convict; (*galérien, fig*) galley slave. **travailler comme un ~** to work like a (galley) slave; **c'est une vie de ~** it's (sheer) slavery.

force [fɔʀs] 1 **nf** a *[personne]* (*vigueur*) strength. **avoir de la ~** to have strength, be strong; **avoir de la ~ dans les bras** to be strong in the arm; **je n'ai plus la ~ de parler** I've no strength left to talk; **il ne connaît pas sa ~** he doesn't know his own strength; **à la ~ des bras** by the strength of one's arms; **à la ~ du poignet** (*lit*) (*grimper*) by the strength of one's arms; (*fig*) (*obtenir qch, réussir*) by the sweat of one's brow; **cet effort l'avait laissé sans ~** the effort had left him drained (of strength); **c'est une ~ de la nature** he is a mighty figure; **dans la ~ de l'âge** in the prime of life; **~ morale/intellectuelle** moral/intellectual strength; (*fig*) **c'est ce qui fait sa ~** that is where his great strength lies; *voir* **bout, union.**

b *[personne]* (*violence*) force. **recourir/céder à la ~** to resort to/give in to force; **employer la ~ brutale** *ou* **brute** to use brute force; **la ~ prime le droit** might is right.

c *[personne]* (*ressources physiques*) **~s** strength; **reprendre des ~s** to get one's strength back, regain one's strength; **ses ~s l'ont trahi** his strength failed *ou* deserted him; **au-dessus de mes ~s** too much for me, beyond me; **frapper de toutes ses ~s** to hit as hard as one can *ou* with all one's might; **désirer qch de toutes ses ~s** to want sth with all one's heart.

d *[coup, vent, habitude]* force; *[argument]* strength, force; *[sentiment]* strength; *[alcool, médicament]* strength. **vent de ~ 4** force 4 wind; **dans toute la ~ du terme** in the fullest *ou* strongest sense of the word; **la ~ de l'évidence** the weight of evidence; **la ~ de l'habitude** force of habit; **par la ~ des choses** by force of circumstance(s); **les ~s naturelles** *ou* **de la nature** the forces of nature; **les ~s aveugles du destin** the blind forces of fate; **les ~s vives du pays** the living strength of a country; **avoir ~ de loi** to have force of law; *voir* **cas, idée, ligne**[1].

e (*Mil*) strength. **~s** forces; **notre ~ navale** our naval strength; (*Pol*) **les ~s de l'opposition** the opposition forces; **d'importantes ~s de police** large contingents *ou* numbers of police; **armée d'une ~ de 10 000 hommes** army with a strength of 10,000 men; **être dans une position de ~** to be in a position of strength.

f (*valeur*) **les deux joueurs sont de la même ~** the two players are evenly *ou* well matched; **ces deux cartes sont de la même ~** these two cards have the same value; **il est de première ~ au bridge** he's a first-class bridge player, he's first-rate at bridge; **il est de ~ à le faire** he's equal to it, he's up to (doing) it*; **tu n'es pas de ~ à lutter avec lui** you're no match for him; **à ~s égales, à égalité de ~s** on equal terms.

g (*Phys*) force. (*Élec*) **la ~** ≃ 30-amp circuit; **~ de gravité** force of gravity; **~ centripète/centrifuge** centripetal/centrifugal force; (*Élec*) **faire installer la ~** to have a 30-amp *ou* cooker (*ou* immerser *etc*) circuit put in.

h (*loc*) **attaquer/arriver en ~** to attack/arrive in force; **ils étaient venus en ~** they had come in strength; (*Sport*) **passer un obstacle en ~** to get past an obstacle by sheer effort; **faire entrer qch de ~ dans** to cram *ou* force sth into; **faire entrer qn de ~** *ou* **par la ~ dans** to force sb to enter; **enlever qch de ~ à qn** to remove sth forcibly from sb, take sth from sb by force; **entrer de ~ chez qn** to force one's way into *ou* force an entry into sb's house; **être en position de ~ pour négocier** to bargain from a position of strength; **coup de ~** takeover by force; **~ nous est/lui est d'accepter** we have/he has no choice but to accept, we are/he is forced to accept; **~ m'est de reconnaître que ...** I am forced *ou* obliged to recognize that ...; **affirmer avec ~** to insist, state firmly; **insister avec ~ sur un point** to insist strongly on a point; **vouloir à toute ~** to want absolutely *ou* at all costs; **obtenir qch par ~** to get sth by *ou* through force; **à ~ d'essayer, il a réussi** by dint of trying he succeeded; **à ~ de gentillesse** by dint of kindness; **à ~, tu vas le casser*** you'll end up breaking it; (*Naut*) **faire ~ de rames** to ply the oars; (*Naut*) **faire ~ de voiles** to cram on sail; *voir* **tour.**

2 **adv** († *hum*) many, a goodly number of (*hum*). **boire ~ bouteilles** to drink a goodly number of bottles; **avec ~ remerciements** with profuse thanks.

3 **comp** ►**force d'âme** fortitude, moral strength ►**la force armée** the army, the military ►**les forces armées** the armed forces ►**force de caractère** strength of character ►**force contre-électromotrice** (*Élec*) back electromotive force ►**force de dissuasion** deterrent power ►**les Forces françaises libres** the Free French (Forces) ►**force de frappe** strike force ►**force d'inertie** force of inertia ►**forces d'intervention** (*Mil, Police*) rapid deployment force ►**forces de maintien de la paix** peace-keeping force(s) ►**force nucléaire stratégique** strategic nuclear force ►**les forces de l'ordre** the police ►**la force publique** the police ►**Force d'urgence des Nations Unies** United Nations Emergency Forces ►**force de vente** sales force.

forcé, e [fɔʀse] (**ptp de forcer**) **adj** a (*imposé*) *cours, mariage* forced; (*poussé*) *comparaison* forced. **atterrissage ~** forced *ou* emergency landing; **prendre un bain ~** to take an unintended dip; **conséquence ~e** inevitable consequence; *voir* **marche**[1], **travail**[1]. b (*feint*) *rire, sourire* forced; *amabilité* affected, put-on. c (*) **c'est ~** there's no way round it, it's inevitable; **je suis malade — c'est ~, tu as mangé des kilos de chocolats!** I'm ill — of course you are, you've eaten kilos of chocolates!; **c'est ~ que tu sois en retard** it's obvious you're going to be late.

forcement [fɔʀsəmɑ̃] **nm** forcing.

forcément [fɔʀsemɑ̃] **adv** inevitably. **ça devait ~ arriver** it was bound to happen, it was inevitable; **il le savait ~ puisqu'on le lui a dit** he must have known since he was told; **il est enrhumé — ~, il ne se couvre pas** he's got a cold — of course (he has), he doesn't wear warm clothes; **c'est voué à l'échec — pas ~** it's bound to fail — not necessarily.

forcené, e [fɔʀsəne] 1 **adj** (*fou*) deranged, out of one's wits (*attrib*) *ou* mind (*attrib*); (*acharné*) *ardeur, travail* frenzied; (*fanatique*) *joueur, travailleur* frenzied; *partisan, critique* fanatical. 2 **nm,f** maniac. **travailler comme un ~** to work like a maniac*; (*hum*) **~ du travail** demon for work, workaholic*; (*hum*) **les ~s du vélo/de la canne à pêche** cycling/angling fanatics.

forceps [fɔʀsɛps] **nm** pair of forceps, forceps (*pl*).

forcer [fɔʀse] 3 1 **vt** a (*contraindre*) to force, compel. **~ qn à faire qch** to force sb to do sth, make sb do sth; **il est forcé de garder le lit** he is forced to stay in bed; **il a essayé de me ~ la main** he tried to force my hand; **~ qn au silence/à des démarches/à la démission** to force sb to keep silent/to take action/to resign.

b (*faire céder*) *coffre, serrure* to force; *porte, tiroir* to force (open); *blocus* to run; *barrage* to force; *ville* to take by force. **~ le passage** to force one's way through; (*fig*) **~ la porte de qn** to force one's way in; **~ la consigne** to bypass orders; **sa conduite force le respect/l'admiration** his behaviour commands respect/admiration; (*Sport*) **il a réussi à ~ la décision** he managed to settle *ou* decide the outcome.

c (*traquer*) *cerf, lièvre* to run *ou* hunt down; *ennemi* to track down. **la police a forcé les bandits dans leur repaire** the police tracked the gangsters down to their hideout.

d (*pousser*) *cheval* to override; *fruits, plantes* to force; *talent, voix* to strain; *allure* to increase; (*fig*) *destin* to tempt, brave. **votre interprétation force le sens du texte** your interpretation stretches *ou* twists the meaning of the text; **~ sa nature** (*timidité*) to overcome one's shyness; (*volonté*) to force o.s.; **~ le pas** to quicken one's pace; (*fig*) **il a forcé la dose*** *ou* **la note*** he overdid it.

2 **vi** to overdo it, force it. **j'ai voulu ~, et je me suis claqué un muscle** I overdid it and pulled a muscle; **il a gagné sans ~*** he had no trouble winning, he won easily; **ne force pas, tu vas casser la corde** don't force it or you'll break the rope; **arrête de tirer, tu vois bien que ça force** stop pulling — can't you see it's jammed?; **~ sur ses rames** to strain at one's oars; **il force un peu trop sur l'alcool*** he overdoes the drink a bit*.

3 **se forcer vpr** to force o.s., make an effort (*pour faire* to do). **il se force à travailler** he forces himself to work, he makes himself work; **elle se force pour manger** she forces herself to eat.

forcing [fɔʀsiŋ] **nm** (*Boxe*) pressure. **faire le ~** to pile on the pressure; **on a dû faire le ~ pour avoir le contrat** we had to put on a lot of pressure to get the contract; **négociations menées au ~** negotiations conducted under pressure.

forcir [fɔʀsiʀ] 2 **vi** *[personne]* to broaden out; *[vent]* to strengthen.

forclore [fɔʀklɔʀ] 45 **vt** (*Jur*) to debar.

forclusion [fɔʀklyzjɔ̃] **nf** (*Jur*) debarment.

forer [fɔʀe] 1 **vt** *roche, paroi* to drill, bore; *puits* to drill, sink, bore.

forestier, -ière [fɔʀɛstje, jɛʀ] 1 **adj** *région, végétation, chemin* forest (*épith*). **exploitation ~ière** (*activité*) forestry, lumbering; (*lieu*) forestry site; *voir* **garde**[2]. 2 **nm** forester.

foret [fɔʀɛ] **nm** drill.

forêt [fɔʀɛ] **nf** (*lit, fig*) forest. **~-galerie** gallery forest; **~ vierge** virgin forest; **~ domaniale** national *ou* state-owned forest; **la Forêt-Noire** the Black Forest; **gâteau de la Forêt-Noire** Black Forest gâteau; *voir* **arbre,**

eau.

foreuse [fɔʀøz] **nf** drill.

forfaire [fɔʀfɛʀ] [60] **vi** (*frm*) ~ **à qch** to be false to sth, betray sth; ~ **à l'honneur** to forsake honour.

forfait [fɔʀfɛ] **nm** a (*Comm*) (*prix fixe*) fixed *ou* set price; (*prix tout compris*) all-inclusive price; (*ensemble de prestations*) package. **travailler au** ~ to work for a flat rate *ou* a fixed sum; **notre nouveau ~-vacances** our new package holiday; ~ **hôtelier** hotel package; **~-skieur(s)** ski-pass; **à** ~ for a fixed sum; **nous payons un ~ qui comprend la location et les réparations éventuelles** we pay a set *ou* fixed price which includes the hire and any repairs; *[impôts]* **être au (régime du)** ~ to be taxed on estimated income.
b (*Sport: abandon*) withdrawal, scratching. **gagner par** ~ to win by default, win by a walkover; **déclarer** ~ to withdraw.
c (*littér: crime*) infamy (*littér*).

forfaitaire [fɔʀfɛtɛʀ] **adj** (*fixe*) fixed, set; (*tout compris*) inclusive. **montant** ~ lump *ou* fixed sum; **indemnité** ~ inclusive payment, lump sum payment; **prix** ~ contract *ou* fixed *ou* set *ou* all-inclusive price.

forfaitairement [fɔʀfɛtɛʀmɑ̃] **adv** *payer, évaluer* on an inclusive basis, inclusively.

forfaiture [fɔʀfɛtyʀ] **nf** (*Jur*) abuse of authority; (*Hist*) felony; (*littér: crime*) act of treachery.

forfanterie [fɔʀfɑ̃tʀi] **nf** (*caractère*) boastfulness; (*acte*) bragging (*NonC*).

forge [fɔʀʒ] **nf** (*atelier*) forge, smithy; (*fourneau*) forge. (†: *fonderie*) **~s** ironworks; *voir* **maître.**

forger [fɔʀʒe] [3] **vt** a *métal* to forge; (*fig*) *caractère* to form, mould. (*littér*) ~ **des liens** to forge bonds; (*Prov*) **c'est en forgeant qu'on devient forgeron** practice makes perfect (*Prov*); **il s'est forgé une réputation d'homme sévère** he has won *ou* earned himself the reputation of being a stern man; **se ~ un idéal** to create an ideal for o.s.; **se ~ des illusions** to build up illusions; *voir* **fer.** b (*inventer*) *mot* to coin; *exemple, prétexte* to contrive, make up; *histoire, mensonge, plan* to concoct. **cette histoire est forgée de toutes pièces** this story is a complete fabrication.

forgeron [fɔʀʒəʀɔ̃] **nm** blacksmith, smith; *voir* **forger.**

formalisation [fɔʀmalizasjɔ̃] **nf** formalization.

formaliser [fɔʀmalize] [1] **1 vt** to formalize. **2 se formaliser vpr** to take offence (*de* at).

formalisme [fɔʀmalism] **nm** a (*péj*) formality. **pas de ~ ici** we don't stand on ceremony here; **s'encombrer de** ~ to weigh o.s. down with formalities. b (*Art, Philos*) formalism.

formaliste [fɔʀmalist] **1 adj** a (*péj*) formalistic. b (*Art, Philos*) formalist. **2 nmf** formalist.

formalité [fɔʀmalite] **nf** (*Admin*) formality. (*fig*) **ce n'est qu'une** ~ it's a mere formality; (*fig*) **sans autre** ~ without any more *ou* further ado.

formant [fɔʀmɑ̃] **nm** (*Ling, Phon*) formant.

format [fɔʀma] **nm** *[livre]* format, size; *[papier, objet]* size. **en ~ de poche** in pocket format; **papier ~ international** A4 paper.

formatage [fɔʀmataʒ] **nm** formatting.

formater [fɔʀmate] [1] **vt** to format.

formateur, -trice [fɔʀmatœʀ, tʀis] **1 adj** *élément, expérience* formative; *stage* training. **2 nm,f** trainer.

formatif, -ive [fɔʀmatif, iv] **1 adj** *langue* inflected, flexional; *préfixe* formative. **2 formative nf** (*Ling*) formative.

formation [fɔʀmasjɔ̃] **nf** a (*développement*) *[gouvernement, croûte, fruits]* formation, forming. **à (l'époque de) la** ~ *[adolescent]* at puberty; *[fruit]* when forming; **parti en voie** *ou* **en cours de** ~ party in the process of formation; **la ~ des mots** word formation.
b (*apprentissage*) training. **la ~ du caractère** the forming *ou* moulding of character; ~ **d'ingénieur** training as an engineer; **il a reçu une ~ littéraire** he received a literary education; ~ **des maîtres,** ~ **pédagogique** teacher training (*Brit*), teacher education (*US*); **stage de ~ accélérée** crash course; **centre de** ~ training centre; ~ **alternée** *ou* **en alternance** part-time *ou* sandwich course; ~ **sur le tas** in-house *ou* on-site *ou* on-the-job training; ~ **professionnelle** vocational training; ~ **permanente** continuing education; ~ **continue (au sein de l'entreprise)** (in-house) training; **je suis juriste de** ~ I was trained as a lawyer.
c (*gén, Mil: groupe*) formation. (*Aviat*) **voler en** ~ to fly in formation; ~ **musicale** music group; ~ **politique** political grouping *ou* formation.

forme [fɔʀm] **nf** a (*contour, apparence*) form, shape. **cet objet est de ~ ronde/carrée** this object is round/square *ou* is round/square in shape; **en ~ de poire/cloche** pear-/bell-shaped; **elle a des ~s gracieuses** she has a graceful form *ou* figure; **elle prend des ~s** she's filling out *ou* getting rounder; **vêtement qui moule les ~s** clinging *ou* figure-hugging garment; **une ~ apparut dans la nuit** a form *ou* figure *ou* shape appeared out of the darkness; **n'avoir plus ~ humaine** to be unrecognizable; **sans** ~ *chapeau* shapeless; *pensée* formless; **prendre la ~ d'un rectangle** to take the form *ou* shape of a rectangle; **prendre la ~ d'un entretien** to take the form of a talk; *[statue, projet]* **prendre** ~ to take shape; **sous ~ de comprimés** in tablet form; **sous la ~ d'un vieillard** in the guise of *ou* as an old man; **sous toutes ses ~s** in all its forms.
b (*genre*) *[civilisation, gouvernement]* form. **les ~s d'énergie** the forms of energy; ~ **de vie** (*présence effective*) form of life, life form; (*coutumes*) way of life; **une ~ de pensée différente de la nôtre** a different way of thinking from our own; **les animaux ont-ils une ~ d'intelligence?** do animals have a form of intelligence?
c (*Art, Jur, Littérat, Philos*) form. **soigner la** ~ to be careful about form; **poème à ~ fixe** fixed-form poem; **poème en ~ d'acrostiche** poem forming an acrostic; *aide, soutien* **de pure** ~ token (*épith*), nominal; **remarques de pure** ~ purely formal remarks; **pour la** ~ as a matter of form, for form's sake; **en bonne (et due)** ~ (*gén*) in due form; (*fig*) **sans autre ~ de procès** without further ado; **faites une réclamation en** ~ put in a formal request; *voir* **fond, vice.**
d (*convenances*) **~s** proprieties, conventions; **respecter les ~s** to respect the proprieties *ou* conventions; **refuser en y mettant des ~s** to decline as tactfully as possible; **faire une demande dans les ~s** to make a request in the correct form.
e (*Ling*) form. **mettre à la ~ passive** to put in the passive; ~ **contractée** contracted form; ~ **de base** base form.
f (*moule*) mould; (*Typ*) forme; *[cordonnier]* last; *[couturier]* (dress) form; (*partie de chapeau*) crown; *voir* **haut.**
g (*Sport: gén*) form; (*condition physique*) fitness. **être en (pleine** *ou* **grande)** ~, **tenir la** ~* (*gén*) to be in (great) form; (*condition physique*) to be (really) fit, be in (really) good shape; **il n'est pas en** ~, **il n'a pas la** ~* he is not on form, he is off form *ou* out of form, he doesn't feel too good*; **retour de** ~ (*gén*) return to form; (*condition physique*) return to fitness; **baisse de** ~ (*gén*) loss of form; (*condition physique*) loss of fitness; **retrouver la** ~ (*gén*) to get back *ou* come back on form; (*condition physique*) to get back into shape, get fit again; **la ~ revient** (*gén*) his (*ou* her *etc*) form is coming back; (*condition physique*) he's (*ou* she's *etc*) getting fitter again; **ce n'est pas la grande** ~* I'm (*ou* he's *etc*) not feeling too good*.
h (*Mus*) ~ **sonate** sonata form.

formel, -elle [fɔʀmɛl] **adj** a (*catégorique*) definite, positive. **dans l'intention ~le de refuser** with the definite intention of refusing; **il a l'obligation ~le de le faire** it is mandatory upon him to do so; **je suis** ~! I'm absolutely sure! b (*Art, Philos*) formal. c (*extérieur*) *politesse* formal.

formellement [fɔʀmɛlmɑ̃] **adv** a (*catégoriquement*) positively. b (*Art, Philos*) formally.

former [fɔʀme] [1] **1 vt** a *gouvernement* to form; *compagnie* to form, establish; *équipe* to set up; *liens d'amitié* to form, create; *croûte, dépôt* to form. **il s'est formé des liens entre nous** bonds have formed *ou* been created between us; **le cône que forme la révolution d'un triangle** the cone formed by the revolution of a triangle.
b *collection* to form, build up; *convoi* to form; *forme verbale, phrase* to form, make up. ~ **correctement ses phrases** to form *ou* make up correct sentences; **phrase bien formée** well-formed sentence; **le train n'est pas encore formé** they haven't made up the train yet.
c (*être le composant de*) to make up, form. **article formé de 3 paragraphes** article made up of *ou* consisting of 3 paragraphs; **ceci forme un tout** this forms a whole.
d (*dessiner*) to make, form. **ça forme un rond** it makes *ou* forms a circle; **la route forme des lacets** the road winds; **il forme bien/mal ses lettres** he forms his letters well/badly.
e (*éduquer*) *soldats, ingénieurs* to train; *intelligence, caractère, goût* to form, develop. **les voyages forment la jeunesse** travel broadens *ou* develops the mind of the young.
f ~ **l'idée** *ou* **le projet de faire qch** to form *ou* have the idea of doing sth; **nous formons des vœux pour votre réussite** we wish you every success.
2 se former vpr a (*se rassembler*) to form, gather. **des nuages se forment à l'horizon** clouds are forming *ou* gathering on the horizon; **se ~ en cortège** to form a procession; **l'armée se forme en carré** *ou* **forma le carré** the army took up a square formation.
b *[dépôt, croûte]* to form.
c (*apprendre un métier etc*) to train o.s.; (*éduquer son goût, son caractère*) to educate o.s.
d (*se développer*) *[goût, caractère, intelligence]* to form, develop; *[fruit]* to form. **les fruits commencent à se ~ sur l'arbre** fruit begins to form on the tree; **une jeune fille qui se forme** a girl who is maturing *ou* developing; **son jugement n'est pas encore formé** his judgment is as yet unformed; **cette jeune fille est formée maintenant** this girl is fully developed now.

Formica [fɔʀmika] **nm** ® Formica ®.

formidable [fɔʀmidabl] **adj** a (*très important*) *coup, obstacle, bruit* tremendous. b (*: *très bien*) fantastic*, great*, tremendous*. c (*: *incroyable*) incredible. **c'est tout de même ~ qu'on ne me dise jamais rien!** all the same it's a bit much* that nobody ever tells me anything!; **il est** ~: **il convoque une réunion et il est en retard!** he's marvellous (*iro*) *ou* incredible – he calls a meeting and then he's late! d (*littér: effrayant*) fearsome.

formidablement [fɔʀmidabləmɑ̃] **adv** (*voir* **formidable**) tremendously*, fantastically*. **on s'est ~ amusé** we had a fantastic time*; **comment ça a marché? –** ~! how did it go? – great!* *ou* fantastic!*

formique [fɔʀmik] **adj** formic.

formol [fɔʀmɔl] nm formalin.

formosan, e [fɔʀmozɑ̃, an] 1 adj Formosan. 2 nm,f: **F~(e)** Formosan.

Formose [fɔʀmoz] nf Formosa.

formulable [fɔʀmylabl] adj which can be formulated.

formulaire [fɔʀmylɛʀ] nm a *(à remplir)* form. b *[pharmaciens, notaires]* formulary.

formulation [fɔʀmylasjɔ̃] nf *(voir* **formuler***)* formulation; wording; expression; drawing up. **il faudrait changer la ~ de votre demande** you should change the way your application is formulated, you should change the wording on your application.

formule [fɔʀmyl] nf a *(Chim, Math)* formula. **~ dentaire** dentition, dental formula.
b *(expression)* phrase, expression; *(magique, prescrite par l'étiquette)* formula. **~ heureuse** happy turn of phrase; **~ de politesse** polite phrase; *(en fin de lettre)* letter ending; **~ publicitaire** advertising slogan; **~ toute faite** ready-made phrase; **~ incantatoire** incantation.
c *(méthode)* system, way. **~ de paiement** method of payment; **~ de vacances** holiday programme *ou* schedule; **trouver la bonne ~** to hit on *ou* find the right formula; *(dans un restaurant)* **~ à 89 F** 89 F menu.
d *(formulaire)* form. **~ de chèque/de télégramme** cheque/telegram form.
e *(Aut)* **la ~ un** Formula One; **voiture de ~ un** Formula-One car.

formuler [fɔʀmyle] 1 1 vt *plainte, requête* to formulate, set out, word; *sentiment* to formulate, express; *ordonnance, acte notarié* to draw up; *(Chim, Math)* to formulate. 2 **se formuler** vpr to be expressed (in words). **ça ne se formule pas** words can't express it.

fornicateur, -trice [fɔʀnikatœʀ, tʀis] nm,f fornicator.

fornication [fɔʀnikasjɔ̃] nf fornication.

forniquer [fɔʀnike] 1 vi to fornicate.

fors†† [fɔʀ] prép save, except.

forsythia [fɔʀsisja] nm forsythia.

fort, e [fɔʀ, fɔʀt] 1 adj a *(puissant) personne, état, motif, lunettes* strong. **il est ~ comme un bœuf** *ou* **un Turc** he's as strong as an ox *ou* a horse; **il est de ~e constitution** he has a strong constitution; **le dollar est une monnaie ~e** the dollar is a strong *ou* hard currency; *(Mil)* **une armée ~e de 20 000 hommes** an army 20,000 strong; *(Cartes)* **la dame est plus ~e que le valet** the queen is higher than the jack; **avoir affaire à ~e partie** to have a strong *ou* tough opponent; **user de la manière ~e** to use strong-arm methods; *voir* **homme, main.**
b *(euph: gros) personne* stout, large; *hanches* broad, wide, large; *jambe* heavy, large; *poitrine* large, ample. **il s'habille au rayon (pour) hommes ~s** he gets his clothes from the outsize department; **elle est un peu ~e des hanches** she has rather wide *ou* broad *ou* large hips, she is rather wide- *ou* large-hipped.
c *(solide, résistant) carton* strong, stout; *colle, métal* strong; *voir* **château, coffre, place.**
d *(intense) vent* strong, high; *bruit* loud; *lumière, rythme, battements* strong; *colère, douleur, chaleur* great, intense; *houle, pluie* heavy; *sentiments* strong, great, intense. **j'ai une ~e envie de le lui dire** I'm very *ou* strongly tempted to tell him; **il avait une ~e envie de rire/de pleurer** he very much wanted to laugh/cry; **aimer les sensations ~es** to enjoy sensational experiences *ou* big thrills.
e *(corsé) remède, café, thé, mélange* strong; *rhume* heavy; *fièvre* high.
f *(marqué) pente* pronounced, steep; *accent* marked, pronounced, strong; *dégoût, crainte* great; *impression* great, strong. **il y a de ~es chances pour qu'il vienne** there's a strong *ou* good chance he'll come, he's very likely to come; **une œuvre ~e** a work that has impact.
g *(violent) secousse, coup* hard.
h *(quantitativement) somme* large, great; *hausse, baisse, différence* great, big; *dose* large, big; *consommation, augmentation* high. **faire payer le prix ~** to charge the full *ou* the list price; **il est ~ en gueule*** he's loud-mouthed* *ou* a loudmouth‡; *voir* **temps¹.**
i *(courageux, obstiné) personne* strong. **être ~ dans l'adversité** to be strong *ou* to stand firm in (the face of) adversity; **âme ~e** steadfast soul; **esprit ~†** freethinker; **~e tête** rebel.
j *(doué)* good *(en, à* at), able. **il est ~ en histoire/aux échecs** he's good at history/at chess; **il est très ~!** he's very good (at it)!; **être ~ sur un sujet** to be well up on* *ou* good at a subject; **il a trouvé plus ~ que lui** he has found *ou* met (more than) his match *ou* someone to outmatch him; **ce n'est pas très ~ (de sa part)*** that's not very clever *ou* bright of him; **cette remarque n'était pas très ~e*** that wasn't a very intelligent *ou* clever *ou* bright thing to say; *(iro)* **quand il s'agit de critiquer, il est ~** (oh yes) he can criticize all right! *ou* he's very good at criticizing!; *voir* **point¹.**
k *(de goût prononcé) tabac, moutarde, café* strong(-flavoured); *goût, odeur* strong. **vin ~ en alcool** strong wine, wine with a high alcoholic content; **avoir l'haleine ~e** to have bad breath.
l *(Ling)* **consonne ~e** hard consonant; **forme ~e** strong form; **verbe ~** strong verb.
m *(loc)* **~ de leur assentiment/de cette garantie** fortified by their approval/this guarantee, in a strong position because of their approval/of this guarantee; **être ~ de son bon droit** to be confident of one's rights; **nos champions se font ~ de gagner** our champions are confident they will win *ou* confident of winning; **je me fais ~ de le réparer** I'm (quite) sure I can mend it, I can mend it, don't worry *ou* you'll see; **se porter ~ pour qn** to answer for sb; **au sens ~ du terme** in the strongest sense of the term; **à plus ~e raison, tu aurais dû venir** all the more reason for you to have come; **à plus ~e raison, parce que** ... the more so because ...; **c'est plus ~ que moi** I can't help it; **c'est trop ~!** that's too much!, that's going too far!; *(hum)* **c'est trop ~ pour moi** it's above *ou* beyond me; **elle est ~e celle-là!*, c'est plus ~ que l'as de pique*** *ou* **que de jouer au bouchon!*** that takes the biscuit!* *(Brit)*, that beats everything!*; **c'est un peu ~ (de café)*** that's a bit much* *ou* steep*, that's going a bit (too) far*; **et le plus ~** *ou* **et ce qu'il y a de plus ~, c'est que** ... and the best (part) of it is that ... .

2 adv a *(intensément) parler, crier* loudly, loud; *lancer, serrer, souffler* hard. **frapper ~** *(bruit)* to knock loudly; *(force)* to knock *ou* hit hard; **sentir ~** to have a strong smell, smell strong; **parlez plus ~** speak up *ou* louder; **respirez bien ~** breathe deeply, take a deep breath; **son cœur battait très ~** his heart was pounding *ou* was beating hard; **le feu marche trop ~** the fire is (up) too high *ou* is burning too fast; **tu y vas un peu ~ tout de même*** even so, you're overdoing it a bit* *ou* going a bit far*; **tu as fait ~!*** that was a bit much!*; **c'est de plus en plus ~!*** it's better and better.
b *(littér: beaucoup)* greatly. **cela me déplaît ~** that displeases me greatly *ou* a great deal; **j'en doute ~** I very much doubt it; **il y tient ~** he sets great store by it; **j'ai ~ à faire avec lui** I have a hard job with him, I've got my work cut out with him.
c *(littér: très) aimable* most; *mécontent, intéressant* most, highly. **il est ~ inquiet** he is very *ou* most anxious; **c'est ~ bon** it is very *ou* exceedingly good, it is most excellent *(frm)*; **j'en suis ~ aise** I am most pleased; **j'ai ~ envie de faire ceci** I greatly desire to do this, I am most desirous of doing this *(littér)*; **il y avait ~ peu de monde** there were very few people; **~ bien!** very good!, excellent!; **tu refuses? ~ bien tu l'auras voulu** you refuse? very well, be it on your own head; **c'est ~ bien dit** very well said; **tu le sais ~ bien** you know very well.

3 nm a *(forteresse)* fort.
b *(personne)* **le ~ l'emporte toujours contre le faible** the strong will always win against the weak; *(Scol péj)* **un ~ en thème** a swot* *(Brit)*, an egghead*; *voir* **raison.**
c *(spécialité)* strong point, forte. **l'amabilité n'est pas son ~** kindness is not his strong point *ou* his forte.
d *(littér: milieu)* **au ~ de été** at the height of; *hiver* in the depths of; **au plus ~ du combat** *(lieu)* in the thick of the battle; *(intensité)* when the battle was at its most intense, at the height of the battle.

4 comp ► **fort des Halles** market porter.

Fort-de-France [fɔʀdəfʀɑ̃s] n Fort-de-France.

forte [fɔʀte] adv *(Mus)* forte.

fortement [fɔʀtəmɑ̃] adv *conseiller* strongly; *tenir* fast, tight(ly); *frapper* hard; *serrer* hard, tight(ly). **il est ~ probable** it is highly *ou* most probable; **~ marqué/attiré** strongly marked/attracted; **il en est ~ question** it is being (very) seriously considered; **j'espère ~ que vous le pourrez** I very much hope that you will be able to; **boiter ~** to have a pronounced limp, limp badly; **il est ~ intéressé par l'affaire** he is highly *ou* most interested in the matter.

forteresse [fɔʀtəʀɛs] nf *(lit)* fortress, stronghold; *(fig)* stronghold. **~ volante** flying fortress.

fortiche* [fɔʀtiʃ] adj *personne* terrific*, great* *(en* at).

fortifiant, e [fɔʀtifjɑ̃, jɑ̃t] 1 adj *médicament, boisson* fortifying; *air* invigorating, bracing; *(littér) exemple, lecture* uplifting. 2 nm *(Pharm)* tonic.

fortification [fɔʀtifikasjɔ̃] nf fortification.

fortifier [fɔʀtifje] 7 1 vt *corps, âme* to strengthen, fortify; *position, opinion, impression* to strengthen; *ville* to fortify. **l'air marin fortifie** (the) sea air is fortifying; **cela m'a fortifié dans mes résolutions** that strengthened my resolve. 2 **se fortifier** vpr *(Mil)* to fortify itself; *[opinion, amitié, position]* to grow stronger, be strengthened; *[santé]* to grow more robust.

fortin [fɔʀtɛ̃] nm (small) fort.

fortiori [fɔʀsjɔʀi] loc adv: **a ~** all the more so, a fortiori.

fortran [fɔʀtʀɑ̃] nm Fortran, FORTRAN.

fortuit, e [fɔʀtɥi, it] adj *événement, circonstance, remarque, rencontre* fortuitous, chance *(épith)*; *coïncidence* fortuitous; *découverte* fortuitous, chance *(épith)*, accidental.

fortuitement [fɔʀtɥitmɑ̃] adv *(voir* **fortuit***)* fortuitously; by chance; accidentally.

fortune [fɔʀtyn] nf a *(richesse)* fortune. **situation de ~** financial situation; **ça vaut une ~** it's worth a fortune; **cet homme est l'une des plus grosses ~s de la région** that man has one of the largest fortunes *ou* that man is one of the wealthiest in the area; **avoir de la ~** to have private means; **faire ~** to make one's fortune; *(fig)* **le mot a fait ~** the word has really become popular, the word has really caught on; *voir* **impôt, revers.**
b *(chance)* luck *(NonC)*, fortune *(NonC)*; *(destinée)* fortune. **quelle a été la ~ de ce roman?** what were the fortunes of this novel?; **tenter** *ou* **chercher ~** to seek one's fortune; **connaître des ~s diverses** *(sujet*

pluriel) to enjoy varying fortunes; (*sujet singulier*) to have varying luck; **il a eu la (bonne) ~ de le rencontrer** he was fortunate enough to meet him, he had the good fortune to meet him; **ayant eu la mauvaise ~ de le rencontrer** having had the misfortune *ou* the ill-fortune to meet him; **faire contre mauvaise ~ bon cœur** to make the best of it; **venez dîner à la ~ du pot** come to dinner and take pot luck with us; (*Jur, Naut*) **~s de mer** sea risks, perils of the sea; (*Prov*) **la ~ sourit aux audacieux** fortune favours the brave.

c **de ~** *réparations, moyens* makeshift; *installation* makeshift, rough-and-ready; *compagnon* chance (*épith*); (*Naut*) **mât/gouvernail de ~** jury mast/rudder.

fortuné, e [fɔʀtyne] **adj** (*riche*) wealthy, well-off; (*littér: heureux*) fortunate.

forum [fɔʀɔm] **nm** (*place, colloque*) forum.

fosse [fos] **nf** (*trou*) pit; (*tombe*) grave; (*Sport*) (*pour le saut*) (sand)pit; (*Anat*) fossa. **~ d'aisances** cesspool; **~ commune** common *ou* communal grave; **~ à fumier** manure pit; (*lit, fig*) **~ aux lions** lions' den; **la ~ marine** the (ocean) deep; **~s nasales** nasal fossae; **~ d'orchestre** orchestra pit; **~ aux ours** bear pit; **~ à purin = ~ à fumier; ~ septique** septic tank.

fossé [fose] **nm** (*gén*) ditch; (*fig: écart*) gulf, gap. (*fig*) **un ~ les sépare** a gulf lies between them; **~ d'irrigation** irrigation channel *ou* ditch; **~ anti-char** anti-tank ditch; **~ culturel** cultural gap.

fossette [fosɛt] **nf** dimple.

fossile [fosil] 1 **nm** (*lit, fig*) fossil. 2 **adj** fossil (*épith*), fossilized.

fossilifère [fosilifɛʀ] **adj** fossiliferous.

fossilisation [fosilizasjɔ̃] **nf** fossilization.

fossiliser [fosilize] [1] (*lit, fig*) 1 **vt** to fossilize. 2 **se fossiliser vpr** to fossilize, become fossilized.

fossoyeur [foswajœʀ] **nm** gravedigger; (*fig*) destroyer.

fou [fu] **, fol** *devant n commençant par une voyelle ou h muet,* **folle** [fɔl] *f* 1 **adj** a (*Méd, gén,* *: *sot*) mad, crazy. **~ à lier, ~ furieux** raving mad; **il est devenu subitement ~** he suddenly went mad *ou* crazy *ou* insane; (*lit, fig*) **ça l'a rendu ~** it drove him mad *ou* crazy; **c'est à devenir ~** it's enough to drive you mad *ou* crazy, it's enough to drive you to distraction; **~ de colère/de désir/de chagrin** out of one's mind* *ou* crazed with anger/desire/grief; **~ de joie** delirious *ou* out of one's mind* with joy; **~ d'amour, (pour) amoureux ~ (de)** madly *ou* wildly in love (with); **elle est folle de lui/de ce musicien** she's mad* *ou* crazy* about *ou* she's mad keen* (*Brit*) on him/that musician; **tu es complètement ~ de refuser*** you're completely mad *ou* absolutely crazy to refuse*; **y aller? (je ne suis) pas si ~!*** go there?, I'm not that crazy!*; **pas folle, la guêpe*** he's (*ou* she's) not stupid *ou* daft* (*Brit*) you know!; *voir* **fou-fou.**

b (*insensé*) *terreur, rage, course* mad, wild; *amour, joie, espoir* mad, insane; *idée, désir, tentative, dépense* mad, insane, crazy; *audace* insane; *imagination* wild, insane; *regard, gestes* wild, crazed. **avoir le ~ rire** to have the giggles; (*Comm*) **prix ~s sur les chemises** shirts at give-away prices; (†, *hum*) **folle jeunesse** wild youth.

c (*: *énorme*) *courage, énergie, succès* fantastic*, terrific, tremendous; *peur* terrific, tremendous. **j'ai un mal de tête ~** I've got a splitting headache*, my head's killing me*; **j'ai une envie folle de chocolat/d'y aller** I've got a mad (*Brit*) *ou* wild desire for some chocolate/to go; **j'ai eu un mal ~ pour venir** I had a terrific *ou* terrible job* to get here; **tu as mis un temps ~** you've taken absolutely ages* *ou* an absolute age*; **gagner/dépenser un argent ~** to earn/spend loads *ou* pots of money*; **payer un prix ~** to pay a ridiculous *ou* an astronomical price; **rouler à une vitesse folle** to go at a fantastic* *ou* terrific *ou* tremendous speed; **il y a un monde ~** there are masses of people, there's a fantastic crowd* *ou* a huge great crowd*; **c'est ~ ce qu'il y a comme monde** it's incredible how many people there are, what a fantastic crowd*; **c'est ~ ce qu'on s'amuse** what a great *ou* fantastic time we're having!*; **c'est ~ ce qu'il a changé** it's incredible *ou* unbelievable how he has changed.

d (*déréglé*) *boussole, aiguille* erratic, wobbling all over the place (*attrib*); *camion, moteur, cheval* runaway (*épith*), out-of-control (*épith*); *mèche de cheveux* stray, unruly. **avoir les cheveux ~s** to have one's hair in a mess *ou* all over the place; **avoir une patte folle*** to have a limp *ou* a dicky leg* (*Brit*); *voir* **herbe.**

2 **nm** a (†, *hum:* **fol**) (*Méd, fig*) madman, lunatic. **courir comme un ~** to run like a madman *ou* lunatic; **travailler comme un ~** to work like mad* *ou* crazy*; **arrête de faire le ~** stop playing *ou* acting the fool; **ce jeune ~** this young lunatic *ou* fool; **espèce de vieux ~** you silly old fool, you old lunatic; *voir* **histoire, maison, plus.**

b (*Échecs*) bishop.

c (*Hist: bouffon*) jester, fool.

d (*Zool*) **~ (de Bassan)** gannet.

3 **folle nf** madwoman, lunatic. (‡ *péj: homosexuel*) **(grande) folle** queen‡, fag‡ (*US*); **cette vieille folle** that old madwoman, that mad old woman; **il faut se méfier de la folle du logis** you mustn't let your imagination run away with you *ou* run wild.

4 **comp ▸ folle avoine** wild oats.

foucade [fukad] **nf** (*littér*) caprice, whim, passing fancy; (*emportement*) outburst.

foudre[1] [fudʀ] **nf** a (*Météo*) lightning; (*Myth: attribut*) thunderbolt. **frappé par la ~** struck by lightning; **la ~ est tombée sur la maison** the house was struck by lightning; **comme la ~, avec la rapidité de la ~** like lightning, as quick as a flash; (*fig*) **ce fut le coup de ~** it was love at first sight; **j'ai eu le coup de ~ pour Julie** I fell head over heels in love with Julie; **elle a eu le coup de ~ pour l'Écosse** she fell in love with Scotland. b (*colère*) (*Rel*) **~s** anathema (*sg*); (*fig*) **s'attirer les ~s de qn** to bring down sb's wrath upon o.s.

foudre[2] [fudʀ] **nm** (†, *hum*) **~ de guerre** outstanding *ou* great leader (in war); **ce n'est pas un ~ de guerre** he's no firebrand; **~ d'éloquence** brilliant orator.

foudre[3] [fudʀ] **nm** (*tonneau*) tun; *voir* **wagon.**

foudroiement [fudʀwamɑ̃] **nm** striking (by lightning).

foudroyant, e [fudʀwajɑ̃, ɑ̃t] **adj** *progrès, vitesse, attaque* lightning (*épith*); *poison, maladie* violent (*épith*); *mort* instant; *succès* thundering (*épith*), stunning (*épith*). **une nouvelle ~e** a devastating piece of news; **il lui lança un regard ~** he looked daggers at him.

foudroyer [fudʀwaje] [8] **vt** *[foudre]* to strike; *[coup de feu, maladie, malheur]* to strike down. **la décharge électrique la foudroya** the electric shock killed her stone dead; **cette nouvelle le foudroya** he was thunderstruck *ou* transfixed by the news; **~ qn du regard** to look daggers at sb, glare at sb; **dans le champ il y avait un arbre foudroyé** in the field lay *ou* stood a tree that had been struck by lightning.

fouet [fwɛ] **nm** (*cravache*) whip; (*Culin: batteur*) whisk. **donner le ~ à qn** to give sb a whipping *ou* flogging; **coup de ~** (*lit*) lash; (*fig*) boost; **donner un coup de ~ à l'économie** to stimulate the economy, give the economy a boost, kick-start the economy; **le café/la douche froide lui a donné un coup de ~** the coffee/the cold shower perked him up; *voir* **plein.**

fouettard [fwɛtaʀ] **adj** *voir* **père.**

fouettement [fwɛtmɑ̃] **nm** *[pluie]* lashing.

fouetter [fwete] [1] 1 **vt** *personne* to whip, flog; *cheval* to whip; (*Culin*) *crème, blanc d'œuf* to whip, whisk; (*fig*) *imagination* to fire; *désir* to whip up. **la pluie fouette les vitres** the rain lashes *ou* whips the window panes; **le vent le fouettait au visage** the wind whipped his face; **l'air frais fouette le sang** fresh air whips up the blood; (*fig*) **il n'y a pas de quoi ~ un chat** it's nothing to make a fuss about; (*hum*) **fouette cocher!** don't spare the horses! (*hum*); *voir* **autre.**

2 **vi** a **la pluie fouette contre les vitres** the rain lashes *ou* whips against the window panes.

b (‡: *avoir peur*) to be scared stiff* *ou* to death*.

c (‡: *puer*) to reek, stink. **ça fouette ici!** there's one hell of a stench *ou* stink in here!‡

foufou, fofolle* [fufu, fɔfɔl] **adj** scatty* (*Brit*), crazy.

fougère [fuʒɛʀ] **nf** fern. **ces plantes sont des ~s** these plants are ferns; **clairière envahie de ~(s)** clearing overgrown with bracken; **~ arborescente** tree fern.

fougue [fug] **nf** *[personne, discours, attaque]* ardour, spirit. **plein de ~** *orateur, réponse* ardent, fiery; *cheval* mettlesome, fiery; **la ~ de la jeunesse** the hotheadedness of youth; **avec ~** with spirit, ardently.

fougueusement [fugøzmɑ̃] **adv** with spirit, ardently. **se ruer ~ sur qn** to hurl o.s. impetuously at sb.

fougueux, -euse [fugø, øz] **adj** *réponse, tempérament, orateur* fiery, ardent; *jeunesse* hotheaded, fiery; *cheval* mettlesome, fiery; *attaque* spirited.

fouille [fuj] **nf** a *[personne]* searching, frisking; *[maison, bagages]* search, searching. **~ corporelle** body search. b (*Archéol*) **~s** excavation(s), dig*; **faire des ~s dans une région** to carry out excavations in an area, excavate an area. c (*Constr*) (*action*) excavation; (*lieu*) excavation (site). d (‡: *poche*) pocket. (*gagner de l'argent*) **s'en mettre plein les ~s** to line one's pockets, make a packet*.

fouille-merde‡ [fujmɛʀd] **nmf inv** muckraker.

fouiller [fuje] [1] 1 **vt** *pièce, mémoire* to search; *personne* to search, frisk; *bagages, poches* to search, go *ou* rummage through; *région, bois* to search, scour, comb; *question* to go (deeply) into; *sol* to dig; *terrain* to excavate, dig up; *bas-relief* to undercut. **il fouillait l'horizon avec ses jumelles** he scanned *ou* searched the horizon with his binoculars; **il fouilla l'obscurité des yeux** he peered into the darkness; **il le fouilla du regard** he gave him a searching look; **étude/analyse très fouillée** very detailed study/analysis; **rinceaux très fouillés** finely detailed mouldings.

2 **vi: ~ dans** *tiroir, armoire* to rummage in, dig about in; *poches* to go through, grope in; *bagages* to go through; *mémoire* to delve into, search; **qui a fouillé dans mes affaires?** who has been through *ou* who has been rummaging *ou* digging about in my things?; **~ dans les archives** to delve into the files; **~ dans le passé de qn** to delve into sb's past.

3 **se fouiller vpr** to go through one's pockets. **tu peux toujours te ~!‡** you haven't a hope in hell!‡, nothing doing!*

fouillis [fuji] **nm** *[papiers, objets]* jumble, muddle; *[branchages]* tangle; *[idées]* jumble, hotchpotch. **faire du ~** (*dans une pièce*) *[personne]* to make a mess; *[objets]* to look a mess, look messy; **sa chambre est en ~** his room is in a dreadful muddle, his room is a jumble of bits and pieces; **il régnait un ~ indescriptible** everything was in an indescribable muddle *ou* mess; **il est très ~*** he's very untidy; **un exposé ~*** a muddled account.

fouinard, e* [fwinaʀ, aʀd] = **fouineur.**

fouine [fwin] nf (*Zool*) stone marten. (*fig*) **c'est une vraie ~** he's a real snoop(er)* (*péj*); **visage de ~** weasel face.

fouiner [fwine] [1] vi (*péj*) to nose around *ou* about. **je n'aime pas qu'on fouine dans mes affaires** I don't like people nosing *ou* ferreting about in my things; **être toujours à ~ partout** to be always poking one's nose into things.

fouineur, -euse [fwinœʀ, øz] (*péj*) 1 adj prying, nosey*. 2 nm,f nosey parker* (*Brit*), Nosey Parker* (*US*), snoop(er)*.

fouir [fwiʀ] [2] vt to dig.

fouisseur, -euse [fwisœʀ, øz] 1 adj burrowing, fossorial (*SPÉC*). 2 nm burrower, fossorial animal (*SPÉC*).

foulage [fulaʒ] nm *[raisin]* pressing; *[drap]* fulling; *[cuir]* tanning.

foulant, e* [fulɑ̃, ɑ̃t] adj: **ce n'est pas trop ~** it won't kill you (*ou* him *etc*)*; *voir* **pompe**[1].

foulard [fulaʀ] nm a (*écharpe*) (*carré*) (head)scarf; (*long*) scarf. b (*NonC: tissu*) foulard.

foule [ful] nf a (*gén*) crowd, throng (*littér*); (*péj: populace*) mob. (*le peuple*) **la ~** the masses; **une ~ hurlante** a howling mob; **la ~ et l'élite** the masses and the élite; *voir* **psychologie.**

b (*loc*) **il y avait ~ à la réunion** there were crowds at the meeting; **il n'y avait pas ~!** there was hardly anyone there!; **il y avait une ~ de gens** there was a crowd *ou* host of people, there were crowds of people; **une ~ de gens pensent que c'est faux** lots *ou* masses* of people think it's wrong; **j'ai une ~ de choses à te dire** I've got loads* *ou* masses* (of things) to tell you; **elle m'a posé une ~ de questions** she asked me masses* *ou* heaps* *ou* loads* of questions; **il y avait une ~ de livres** there were masses* *ou* loads* *ou* heaps* of books; **ils vinrent en ~ à l'exposition** they came in crowds *ou* they flocked to the exhibition; **les idées me venaient en ~** ideas were crowding into my head, I had a host *ou* a multitude of ideas.

foulée [fule] nf *[cheval, coureur]* stride. (*Sport*) **suivre qn dans la ~, être dans la ~ de qn** to follow (close) on sb's heels; (*fig*) **il travailla encore trois heures dans la ~** he worked on for another 3 hours while he was at it *ou* for another 3 hours without a break; **courir à petites ~s** to jog *ou* trot along.

fouler [fule] [1] 1 vt *raisins* to press; *drap* to full; *cuir* to tan. (*littér*) **~ le sol de sa patrie** to walk upon *ou* tread (upon) native soil; **~ aux pieds quelque chose de sacré** to trample something sacred underfoot, trample on something sacred. 2 **se fouler** vpr a **se ~ la cheville/le poignet** to sprain one's ankle/wrist. b (*: *travailler dur*) to flog o.s. to death*. **il ne se foule pas beaucoup, il ne se foule pas la rate** he doesn't exactly flog himself to death* *ou* overtax himself *ou* strain himself.

fouleur, -euse [fulœʀ, øz] nm,f *[drap]* fuller; *[cuir]* tanner.

fouloir [fulwaʀ] nm *[drap]* fulling mill; *[cuir]* tanning drum.

foulon [fulɔ̃] nm *voir* **terre.**

foulque [fulk] nf coot.

foultitude* [fultityd] nf: **une ~** heaps* *pl*, masses* *pl*; **j'ai une ~ de choses à faire** I've got a thousand and one things *ou* heaps* *ou* masses* of things to do.

foulure [fulyʀ] nf sprain.

four [fuʀ] 1 nm a *[boulangerie, cuisinière]* oven; *[potier]* kiln; *[usine]* furnace. **~ à céramique/à émaux** pottery/enamelling kiln; **cuire au ~** *gâteau* to bake; *viande* to roast; **plat allant au ~** ovenproof *ou* fireproof dish; **poisson cuit au ~** (oven-)baked fish; **il a ouvert la bouche comme un ~*** he opened his great cavern of a mouth; **je ne peux pas être au ~ et au moulin** I can't do two things at once, I can't be in two places at once; *voir* **banal**[2]**, noir, petit.**

b (*arg Théât*) flop, fiasco. **cette pièce est** *ou* **a fait un ~** this play is a flop *ou* has fallen flat.

c (*gâteau*) **(petit) ~** small cake, petit four; **petits ~s frais** miniature cakes (*ou* pastries).

2 comp ▸**four à chaux** lime kiln ▸**four crématoire** crematorium furnace ▸**four électrique** (*gén*) electric oven; (*Ind*) electric furnace ▸**four à micro-ondes** micro-wave oven ▸**four à pain** baker's oven ▸**four solaire** solar furnace.

fourbe [fuʀb] adj *personne, caractère* deceitful, false-hearted, treacherous; *air, regard* deceitful, treacherous. **c'est un ~** he is a deceitful *ou* false-hearted *ou* treacherous rogue.

fourberie [fuʀbəʀi] nf (*littér*) (*NonC*) deceitfulness, treachery; (*acte, geste*) deceit, piece of treachery. **à cause de ses ~s** because of his treachery *ou* deceits.

fourbi* [fuʀbi] nm (*attirail*) gear* (*NonC*), clobber‡ (*NonC*) (*Brit*); (*fouillis*) mess. **canne à pêche, hameçons et tout le ~** fishing rod, hooks, you name it!*, fishing rod, hooks and goodness knows what else!*; **partir en vacances avec le bébé, ça va en faire du** *ou* **un ~** going on holiday with the baby, that'll mean a whole heap of gear* *ou* clobber‡ (*Brit*).

fourbir [fuʀbiʀ] [2] vt *arme* to furbish. (*fig*) **~ ses armes** to prepare for battle, get ready for the fray.

fourbissage [fuʀbisaʒ] nm furbishing.

fourbu, e [fuʀby] adj exhausted.

fourche [fuʀʃ] nf a (*pour le foin*) pitchfork; (*pour bêcher*) fork. b *[arbre, chemin, bicyclette]* fork; *[pantalon, jambes]* crotch. **la route faisait une ~** the road forked. c (*Hist*) **les F~s Caudines** the Caudine Forks; (*fig*) **passer sous les ~s caudines** to admit defeat. d (*Belgique: temps libre*) free time.

fourcher [fuʀʃe] [1] vi *[arbre, chemin]* (†) to fork; *[cheveux]* to split (at the ends). **ma langue a fourché** I made *ou* it was a slip of the tongue.

fourchette [fuʀʃɛt] nf a (*pour manger*) fork. **~ à gâteaux/à huîtres** pastry/oyster fork; (*hum*) **manger avec la ~ d'Adam** to eat with one's fingers; **il a une bonne ~** *ou* **un bon coup de ~** he has a hearty appetite, he's a good *ou* hearty eater. b *[oiseau]* wishbone; *[cheval]* frog; (*Aut*) selector fork; (*Tech*) fork. (*Anat*) **~ vulvaire** fourchette. c (*Statistique*) margin. **la ~ se rétrécit** the margin is narrowing; **~ d'âge** age bracket; **~ d'imposition** tax bracket *ou* band; **~ de prix** price range.

fourchu, e [fuʀʃy] adj *arbre, chemin* forked; *menton* jutting (*épith*). **animal au pied ~** cloven-hoofed animal; **elle a les cheveux fourchus** she's got split ends; *voir* **langue.**

fourgon [fuʀgɔ̃] nm (*wagon*) coach, wag(g)on; (*camion*) (large) van, lorry (*Brit*); (*diligence*) coach, carriage; (*tisonnier*) poker. **~ à bagages** luggage van; **~ à bestiaux** cattle truck; **~ cellulaire** prison *ou* police van (*Brit*), patrol wagon (*US*); **~ de déménagement** removal (*Brit*) *ou* furniture van; **~ funéraire** hearse; (*Mil*) **~ de munitions** munitions wagon; **~ mortuaire = ~ funéraire; ~ postal** mail van; **~ de queue** rear brake van; (*Mil*) **~ de vivres** supply wagon.

fourgonner [fuʀgɔne] [1] 1 vt *poêle, feu* to poke, rake. 2 vi (*: *parmi des objets*) to poke about, rake about. **je l'entendais qui fourgonnait dans la cuisine/dans le placard** I heard him clattering *ou* poking about in the kitchen/cupboard.

fourgonnette [fuʀgɔnɛt] nf (small) van, delivery van.

fourguer* [fuʀge] [1] vt (*vendre*) to flog‡ (*à* to), unload* (*à* onto). (*donner*) **~ qch à qn** to unload sth onto sb*, palm sth off onto sb*.

fourme [fuʀm] nf *type of French blue-veined cheese.*

fourmi [fuʀmi] nf ant; (*fig: personne*) beaver; (*arg Drogue*) small-time dealer. **~ maçonne** builder *ou* worker ant; **avoir des ~s dans les jambes** to have pins and needles in one's legs; **vus de si haut les gens ont l'air de ~s** seen from so high up the people look like ants; **elle s'affaire comme une ~** she bustles about as busy as a bee; *voir* **travail**[1].

fourmilier [fuʀmilje] nm anteater.

fourmilière [fuʀmiljɛʀ] nf (*monticule*) ant-hill; (*intérieur*) ants' nest; (*fig*) hive of activity. **cette ville/ce bureau est une (vraie) ~** this town/office is a hive of activity.

fourmilion [fuʀmiljɔ̃] nm antlion, doodlebug (*US*).

fourmillant, e [fuʀmijɑ̃, ɑ̃t] adj *foule* milling, swarming; *cité* teeming.

fourmillement [fuʀmijmɑ̃] nm a *[insectes, personnes]* swarming. **le ~ de la rue** the swarming *ou* milling crowds in the street; **un ~ d'insectes** a mass of swarming insects; **un ~ d'idées** a welter of ideas. b (*gén pl: picotement*) **~s** pins and needles (*dans* in).

fourmiller [fuʀmije] [1] vi *[insectes, personnes]* to swarm. **dissertation où fourmillent les erreurs** essay teeming with mistakes; **~ de** *insectes, personnes* to be swarming *ou* crawling *ou* teeming with; *idées, erreurs* to be teeming with; **forêt qui fourmille de lapins, forêt où les lapins fourmillent** forest which is overrun with *ou* that teems with rabbits; (*fig*) **les pieds me fourmillent, j'ai les pieds qui fourmillent** I've got pins and needles in my feet.

fournaise [fuʀnɛz] nf (*feu*) blaze, blazing fire; (*fig: endroit surchauffé*) furnace, oven.

fourneau, pl **~x** [fuʀno] nm a (†: *cuisinière, poêle*) stove†. **être aux ~x** to do the cooking. b *[forge, chaufferie]* furnace; *[pipe]* bowl; *voir* **haut.**

fournée [fuʀne] nf (*lit, fig*) batch; *[pains]* batch (of loaves).

fourni, e [fuʀni] (ptp de **fournir**) adj *herbe* luxuriant, lush; *cheveux* thick, abundant; *barbe, sourcils* bushy, thick. **chevelure peu ~e** sparse *ou* thin head of hair; **table bien ~e** well-stocked *ou* well-supplied table; **boutique bien ~e** well-stocked shop.

fournil [fuʀni] nm bakery, bakehouse.

fourniment* [fuʀnimɑ̃] nm gear* (*NonC*). **il va falloir emporter tout un ~** we'll have to take a whole heap of gear* *ou* stuff* *ou* clobber‡ (*Brit*).

fournir [fuʀniʀ] [2] 1 vt a (*approvisionner*) *client, restaurant* to supply. **~ qn en viande/légumes** to supply sb with meat/vegetables.

b (*procurer*) *matériel, main-d'œuvre* to supply, provide; *preuves, secours* to supply, furnish; *renseignements* to supply, provide, furnish; *pièce d'identité* to produce; *prétexte, exemple* to give, supply. **~ qch à qn** to supply sb with sth, supply sth to sb, provide sb with sth, furnish sb with sth, produce sth for sb; **~ à qn l'occasion/les moyens** to provide sb with the opportunity/the means, give sb *ou* afford sb the opportunity/the means (*de faire* of doing); **~ du travail à qn** to provide sb with work; **~ le vivre et le couvert** to provide board and lodging.

c (*produire*) *effort* to put in; *prestation* to give; *récolte* to supply. **~ un gros effort** to put in a lot of effort, make a great (deal of) effort.

d (*Cartes*) **~ (une carte)** to follow suit; **~ à cœur** to follow suit in hearts.

2 **fournir à** vt indir *besoins* to provide for; *dépense, frais* to defray. **ses parents fournissent à son entretien** his parents give him his keep *ou*

provide for his maintenance; la photocopieuse/la secrétaire ne fournit plus* the photocopier/secretary can't keep up any more.

3 se fournir vpr to provide o.s. (de with). se ~ en ou de charbon to get (in) supplies of coal; je me fournis toujours chez le même épicier I always buy ou get my groceries from the same place, I always shop at the same grocer's.

fournisseur [fuʀnisœʀ] nm (*commerçant*) tradesman (*Brit*), merchant, purveyor (*frm*); (*détaillant*) stockist (*Brit*), retailer; (*Comm, Ind*) supplier. ~ exclusif sole supplier; ~ de viande/papier supplier ou purveyor (*frm*) of meat/paper, meat/paper supplier; les pays ~s de la France countries that supply France (with goods ou imports); les ~s de l'armée army contractors; chez votre ~ habituel at your local stockist('s) (*Brit*) ou retailer('s); nos ~s manquent de matière première our suppliers are out of raw materials.

fourniture [fuʀnityʀ] nf *[matériel, marchandises]* supply(ing), provision. ~s (de bureau) office supplies, stationery; ~s scolaires school stationery.

fourrage [fuʀaʒ] nm (*Agr*) fodder, forage. ~ vert silage.

fourrager [fuʀaʒe] 3 vi: ~ dans *papiers, tiroir* to rummage through, dig about in.

fourragère¹ [fuʀaʒɛʀ] adj f: plante/betterave ~ fodder plant/beet; céréales ~s feed grains.

fourragère² [fuʀaʒɛʀ] nf (*Mil*) fourragère.

fourré¹ [fuʀe] nm thicket. se cacher dans les ~s to hide in the bushes.

fourré², e [fuʀe] (ptp de fourrer) adj *bonbon, chocolat* filled; *manteau, gants* fur-lined; (*molletonné*) fleecy-lined. ~ d'hermine ermine-lined; chocolats ~s chocolate creams, chocolates; gâteau ~ à la crème cream(-filled) cake; tablette de chocolat ~ à la crème bar of cream-filled chocolate; (*fig*) coup ~ underhand trick.

fourreau, pl ~x [fuʀo] nm a *[épée]* sheath, scabbard; *[parapluie]* cover. mettre au/tirer du ~ son épée to sheathe/unsheathe one's sword. b (robe) ~ sheath dress.

fourrer [fuʀe] 1 1 vt a (*) (*enfoncer*) to stick*, shove*, stuff; (*mettre*) to stick*. où ai-je bien pu le ~? where the heck did I stick ou put it?*; ~ ses mains dans ses poches to stuff ou stick* ou shove* one's hands in one's pockets; ~ qch dans un sac to stuff ou shove* sth into a bag; qui t'a fourré ça dans le crâne? who put that (idea) into your head?; ~ son nez partout/dans les affaires des autres to poke ou stick* one's nose into everything/into other people's business; ~ qn dans le pétrin to land sb in the soup* ou in it* (*Brit*); ~ qn en prison to stick sb in prison*.

b *volaille* to stuff; *gâteau* to fill; *manteau* to line (with fur).

2 se fourrer* vpr a se ~ une idée dans la tête to get an idea into one's head; il s'est fourré dans la tête que ... he has got it into his head that ... .

b se ~ dans un coin/sous la table to get in a corner/under the table; où a-t-il encore été se ~? where has he got to now?; il ne savait plus où se ~ he didn't know where to put himself; être toujours fourré chez qn to be never off sb's doorstep, be constantly hanging around sb's house; son ballon est allé se ~ dans la niche du chien his ball ended up in ou landed in the dog's kennel; *voir* doigt, guêpier.

fourre-tout [fuʀtu] nm inv (*pièce*) lumber room (*Brit*), junk room, glory hole (*Brit*); (*placard*) junk cupboard, glory hole (*Brit*); (*sac*) holdall. sa chambre est un vrai ~* his bedroom is an absolute tip* (*Brit*) ou dump*; (*péj*) sa dissertation/son livre est un vrai ~ his essay/book is a hotch-potch of ideas ou a real jumble of ideas; un discours/une loi ~ a rag-bag of a speech/law.

fourreur [fuʀœʀ] nm furrier.

fourrier [fuʀje] nm (*Hist Mil*) (*pour le logement*) harbinger; (*pour les vivres*) quartermaster; (*fig littér*) forerunner, harbinger (*littér*); *voir* sergent¹.

fourrière [fuʀjɛʀ] nf (*gén, Aut*) pound; *[chiens]* dog pound. emmener une voiture à la ~ to tow away a car, impound a car.

fourrure [fuʀyʀ] nf (*pelage*) coat; (*matériau, manteau etc*) fur.

fourvoiement [fuʀvwamɑ̃] nm (*littér: voir* se fourvoyer) losing one's way; going astray.

fourvoyer [fuʀvwaje] 8 1 vt: ~ qn *[guide]* to get sb lost, mislead sb; *[mauvais renseignement]* to mislead sb; *[mauvais exemple]* to lead sb astray. 2 se fourvoyer vpr (*lit: s'égarer*) to lose one's way; (*fig: se tromper*) to go astray. se ~ dans un quartier inconnu to stray into an unknown district (by mistake); dans quelle aventure s'est-il encore fourvoyé? what has he got involved in now?; il s'est complètement fourvoyé en faisant son problème he has gone completely wrong ou completely off the track with his problem.

foutaise‡ [futɛz] nf: des ~s, de la ~ bullshit‡ (*NonC*), crap‡ (*NonC*); dire des ~s to talk bullshit‡ ou crap‡; se disputer pour une ~ ou des ~s to quarrel over damn all‡.

foutoir‡ [futwaʀ] nm bloody (*Brit*) ou damned shambles‡ (*sg*). sa chambre est un vrai ~ his bedroom is a pigsty ou a dump ou a bloody shambles‡ (*Brit*).

foutre‡ [futʀ] 1 vt a (*faire*) to do. qu'est-ce qu'il fout, il est déjà 8 heures what the hell‡ is he doing ou up to* – it's already 8 o'clock; il n'a rien foutu de la journée he hasn't done a bloody** (*Brit*) ou ruddy‡ (*Brit*) ou damned‡ thing all day, he's done damn all‡ ou bugger all** (*Brit*) today; j'en ai rien à ~ de leurs histoires I don't bloody (*Brit*) care** ou give a damn‡ about what they're up to; qu'est-ce que ça peut me ~? what the hell do I care?‡

b (*donner*) ~ une trempe ou raclée à qn to give sb a belting‡ (*Brit*) ou thumping‡, beat the hell out of sb‡; ~ une gifle à qn to fetch (*Brit*) ou give sb a clout‡; ça me fout la trouille it gives me the bloody (*Brit*) willies** ou creeps**; fous-moi la paix! lay off!‡, bugger off!** (*Brit*); je t'en fous! not a bloody (*Brit*) hope!**, you'll be damned lucky!‡; qu'est-ce qui m'a foutu un idiot pareil! of all the flaming idiots!‡, how bloody (*Brit*) stupid can you get!**; je t'en foutrais des amis comme ça! who the hell needs friends like that?‡

c (*mettre*) fous-le là/dans ta poche* shove* it in here/in your pocket; ~ qn à la porte to give sb the boot*, kick sb out*; il a tout foutu en l'air he chucked the whole flaming lot away‡; il a foutu le vase par terre he knocked the flaming vase off‡, he sent the bloody (*Brit*) vase flying**; ça fout tout par terre ou en l'air that buggers (*Brit*) ou screws everything up**; ça l'a foutu en rogne that really made him bloody (*Brit*) mad**; ça la fout mal it looks pretty bad*.

d ~ le camp to bugger off** (*Brit*), sod off** (*Brit*); fous-moi le camp! bugger off!**, sod off!**, get the hell out of here!‡

2 se foutre vpr a (*se mettre*) (*fig*) je me suis foutu dedans I really boobed‡; tu vas te ~ par terre you're going to fall flat on your face ou go sprawling; se ~ dans une sale affaire to get mixed up in a messy business; ils se sont foutu sur la gueule they beat (the) hell out of each other*.

b (*se gausser*) se ~ de qn/qch to get a laugh at sb/sth*, take the mickey out of sb/sth‡ (*Brit*); (*être indifférent*) not to give a damn about sb/sth‡; (*dépasser les bornes*) se ~ de qn to mess* (*Brit*) ou muck‡ sb about; 100 F pour ça, ils se foutent de nous ou du monde 100 francs for that! – they must take us for bloody idiots** (*Brit*) ou for assholes** (*US*) ou what the hell do they take us for!‡; ça, je m'en fous pas mal I couldn't give a damn‡ about that; tu te fous de ma gueule? are you taking the piss (out of me)?** (*Brit*), are you putting me on?*

c (**) va te faire ~! fuck off!**, bugger off!** (*Brit*), get stuffed!‡ (*Brit*), fuck you!**; je lui ai bien demandé, mais va te faire ~: il n'a jamais voulu I did ask him but he wouldn't fucking** ou bloody** (*Brit*) do it.

foutrement‡ [futʀəmɑ̃] adv bloody** (*Brit*), damn‡. il s'est ~ bien défendu he stood up for himself bloody well** (*Brit*) ou damn well‡.

foutriquet* [futʀikɛ] nm (*péj*) (little) nobody, little runt*.

foutu, e‡ [futy] (ptp de foutre) adj a (*avant n*) (*intensif: sale*) bloody** (*Brit*), ruddy‡ (*Brit*), damned‡, fucking**; (*mauvais*) bloody awful** (*Brit*), ruddy awful‡ (*Brit*), damned awful‡; (*sacré*) one ou a hell of a‡.

b (*après n*) *malade, vêtement* done for* (*attrib*); *appareil* buggered‡ (*Brit*), screwed up‡, bust*.

c (*habillé*) got up*, rigged out*.

d (*bâti, conçu*) cet appareil est bien ~ this device is bloody (*Brit*) ou damned clever‡; ce manuel est mal ~ this textbook's bloody** (*Brit*) ou damned‡ hopeless; une nana bien ~e a nice piece‡, a nice bit of ass‡ (*US*).

e (*malade*) être mal ~ ou pas bien ~ to feel hellish‡ ou lousy‡ ou bloody (*Brit*) awful**.

f (*capable*) il est ~ de le faire he's quite likely ou liable to go and do it; il est même pas ~ de réparer ça he can't even mend the damned thing‡.

fox-hound, pl fox-hounds [fɔksaund] nm foxhound.

fox(-terrier), pl fox(-terriers) [fɔks(tɛʀje)] nm fox terrier.

fox(-trot) [fɔks(tʀɔt)] nm inv foxtrot.

foyer [fwaje] nm a (*frm*) (*maison*) home; (*famille*) family. ~ uni close ou united family; les joies du ~ the joys of family life; quand il revint au ~ ou à son ~ when he came back home; un jeune ~ a young couple; ~ fiscal *household as defined for tax purposes;* (*revenu*) household income; *voir* femme, fonder, renvoyer.

b *[locomotive, chaudière]* firebox; (*âtre*) hearth, fireplace; (*dalle*) hearth(stone).

c (*résidence*) *[vieillards, soldats]* home; *[jeunes]* hostel; *[étudiants]* hostel, hall. ~ éducatif special (residential) school; ~ socio-éducatif community home; ~ d'étudiants students' hall (of residence) ou hostel.

d (*lieu de réunion*) *[jeunes, retraités]* club; (*Théât*) foyer. ~ des artistes greenroom; ~ des jeunes youth club.

e (*Math, Opt, Phys*) focus. à ~ variable variable-focus (*épith*); verres à double ~ bifocal lenses.

f ~ de *incendie* seat of, centre of; *lumière, infection* source of; *agitation* centre of; ~ d'extrémistes centre of extremist activities.

FP (abrév de franchise postale) *voir* franchise.

FPLP [ɛfpeɛlpe] nm (abrév de Front populaire pour la libération de la Palestine) PFLP.

FR3† [ɛfɛʀtʀwa] (abrév de France Régions 3) *3rd channel on French television, specializing in regional programmes.*

frac [fʀak] nm tails, tail coat. être en ~ to be in tails, be wearing a tail coat.

fracas [fʀaka] nm *[objet qui tombe]* crash; *[train, tonnerre, vagues]* roar; *[ville, bataille]* din. tomber avec ~ to fall with a crash, come crashing down; **annoncer une nouvelle à grand ~** to create a sensation with a piece of news; *voir* **perte.**

fracassant, e [fʀakasɑ̃, ɑ̃t] **adj** *bruit* thunderous, deafening; *nouvelle, déclaration* shattering, staggering, sensational; *succès* thundering (*épith*), sensational.

fracasser [fʀakase] 1 1 **vt** *objet, mâchoire, épaule* to smash, shatter; *porte* to smash (down), shatter. 2 **se fracasser vpr: se ~ contre** *ou* **sur** *[vagues]* to crash against; *[bateau, véhicule]* to be shattered *ou* be smashed (to pieces) against; **la voiture est allée se ~ contre l'arbre** the car smashed *ou* crashed into the tree.

fraction [fʀaksjɔ̃] **nf** (*Math*) fraction; *[groupe, somme, terrain]* part. **une ~ de seconde** a fraction of a second, a split second; **par ~ de 3 jours/de 10 unités** for every 3-day period/10 units; **une ~ importante du groupe** a large proportion of the group.

fractionnaire [fʀaksjɔnɛʀ] **adj** (*Math*) fractional.

fractionnel, -elle [fʀaksjɔnɛl] **adj** *attitude, menées* divisive.

fractionnement [fʀaksjɔnmɑ̃] **nm** splitting up, division. (*Bourse*) **~ d'actions** stock splitting.

fractionner [fʀaksjɔne] 1 1 **vt** *groupe, somme, travail* to divide (up), split up. **mon emploi du temps est trop fractionné** my timetable is too disjointed *ou* fragmented; **paiement fractionné** payment in instalments (*Brit*) *ou* installments (*US*), installment payment (*US*). 2 **se fractionner vpr** *[groupe]* to split up, divide.

fracture [fʀaktyʀ] **nf** (*Géol, Méd*) fracture. **~ du crâne** fractured skull, fracture of the skull; **~ ouverte** open fracture.

fracturer [fʀaktyʀe] 1 **vt** (*Géol, Méd*) to fracture; *serrure* to break (open); *coffre-fort, porte* to break open. **il s'est fracturé la jambe** he's fractured his leg.

fragile [fʀaʒil] **adj** *corps, vase* fragile, delicate; *organe, peau* delicate; *cheveux* brittle; *santé* fragile, delicate, frail; *construction, économie, preuve, argument* flimsy, frail; *équilibre* delicate, shaky; *bonheur, paix* frail, flimsy, fragile; *gloire* fragile; *pouvoir, prospérité* fragile, flimsy. (*sur étiquette*) **"attention ~"** "fragile, (handle) with care"; (*physiquement, affectivement*) **ne soyez pas trop brusque, elle est encore ~** don't be too rough with her – she is still (feeling) rather fragile *ou* frail; **~ comme du verre** as delicate as porcelain *ou* china; **avoir l'estomac ~, être ~ de l'estomac** to have a weak stomach.

fragilement [fʀaʒilmɑ̃] **adv: pouvoir ~ établi** power established on a flimsy *ou* shaky foundation; **argument ~ étayé** flimsily upheld argument.

fragiliser [fʀaʒilize] 1 **vt** to weaken, make fragile.

fragilité [fʀaʒilite] **nf** (*voir* **fragile**) fragility; delicacy; brittleness; flimsiness; frailty.

fragment [fʀagmɑ̃] **nm** a *[vase, roche, papier]* fragment, bit, piece; *[os, vitre]* fragment, splinter, bit; *[meuble]* piece, bit; *[cheveux]* snippet, bit. b *[conversation]* bit, snatch; *[chanson]* snatch; *[lettre]* bit, part; *[roman]* (*bribe*) fragment; (*extrait*) passage, extract. **je vais vous en lire un ~** I'll read you a bit *ou* part of it, I'll read you a passage *ou* an extract from it.

fragmentaire [fʀagmɑ̃tɛʀ] **adj** *connaissances* sketchy, patchy, fragmentary; *étude, exposé* sketchy, fragmentary; *effort, travail* sketchy, fragmented. **nous avons une vue très ~ des choses** we have only a sketchy *ou* an incomplete picture of the situation.

fragmentairement [fʀagmɑ̃tɛʀmɑ̃] **adv** in a sketchy way, sketchily.

fragmentation [fʀagmɑ̃tasjɔ̃] **nf** (*voir* **fragmenter**) fragmentation; splitting up; breaking up; division.

fragmenter [fʀagmɑ̃te] 1 1 **vt** *matière* to break up, fragment; *état, terrain* to fragment, split up, break up; *étude, travail, livre, somme* to split up, divide (up). **~ la publication d'un livre** to divide up the publication of a book; **avoir une vision fragmentée du monde** to have a fragmented view of life; **ce travail est trop fragmenté** this piece of work is too fragmented *ou* has too many subdivisions. 2 **se fragmenter vpr** *[roches]* to fragment, break up.

fragrance [fʀagʀɑ̃s] **nf** (*littér*) fragrance.

frai [fʀɛ] **nm** (*œufs*) spawn; (*alevins*) fry; (*époque*) spawning season; (*ponte*) spawning.

fraîche [fʀɛʃ] *voir* **frais¹.**

fraîchement [fʀɛʃmɑ̃] **adv** a (*récemment*) freshly, newly. **~ arrivé** freshly *ou* newly *ou* just arrived; **fruit ~ cueilli** freshly picked fruit; **amitié ~ nouée** newly-formed friendship. b (*froidement*) *accueillir* coolly. **comment ça va? – ~!*** how are you? – a bit chilly!*

fraîcheur [fʀɛʃœʀ] **nf** *[boisson]* coolness; *[aliment, sentiment, jeunesse, teint]* freshness; *[pièce]* (*agréable*) coolness; (*froid*) chilliness; *[âme]* purity; *[accueil]* coolness, chilliness; *[couleurs]* freshness, crispness. **la ~ du soir/de la nuit** the cool of the evening/of the night.

fraîchir [fʀɛʃiʀ] 2 **vi** *[temps, température]* to get cooler; (*Naut*) *[brise, vent]* to freshen.

frais¹, fraîche [fʀɛ, fʀɛʃ] 1 **adj** a (*lit*) *vent* cool, fresh; *eau, endroit* cool; (*fig*) *accueil* chilly, cool. **il fait un peu ~ ici** it's a bit chilly *ou* cool here; *voir* **fond.**

b (*fig*) *couleur* fresh, clear, crisp; *joues, teint* fresh; *parfum* fresh; *haleine* fresh, sweet; *voix* clear; *joie, âme* unsullied, pure.

c (*récent*) *plaie* fresh; *traces, souvenir* recent, fresh; *peinture* wet, fresh; *nouvelles* recent. **l'encre est encore fraîche** the ink is still wet; *voir* **date.**

d (*inaltéré, pas en conserve*) *poisson, légumes, lait* fresh; *œuf* fresh, new-laid; *pain* new, fresh. **un peu d'air ~** a breath of *ou* a little fresh air; **ses vêtements ne sont plus très ~** his clothes don't look very fresh; *voir* **chair.**

e (*jeune, reposé*) *troupes* fresh. **~ et dispos** fresh (as a daisy); **~ comme un gardon** bright as a button; **fraîche comme une rose** as fresh as a daisy; **~ comme la rosée** bright-eyed and bushy-tailed; **elle est encore très fraîche pour son âge** she's still very young- *ou* youthful-looking for her age.

f (*Comm*) **argent ~** (*disponible*) ready cash; (*à investir*) fresh money.

g (*) **être ~** to be in a fix* *ou* a nice mess*.

2 **adv** a **il fait ~** (*agréable*) it's cool; (*froid*) it's chilly; **en été, il faut boire ~** in summer you need cool *ou* cold drinks; **servir ~** serve cold *ou* chilled.

b (*récemment*) newly. **herbe ~** *ou* **fraîche coupée** newly *ou* freshly cut grass; **~ émoulu de l'université** fresh from *ou* newly graduated from university; **~ débarqué de sa province** fresh *ou* newly up from the country; **habillé/rasé de ~** freshly changed/shaven.

3 **nm: prendre le ~** to take a breath of cool air; (*lit*) **mettre (qch) au ~** to put (sth) in a cool place; (*fig*) **mettre qn au ~*** to put sb in the cooler*.

4 **fraîche nf: (sortir) à la ~** (to go out) in the cool of evening.

frais² [fʀɛ] **nmpl** a (*gén: débours*) expenses; (*facturés*) charges; (*à comptabiliser: Comm, Écon: charges*) costs; (*Admin: droits*) charges, fee(s). **~ d'agence** agency fees; **~ de déplacement/de logement** travelling/accommodation expenses *ou* costs; **~ d'entretien** *[jardin, maison]* (cost of) upkeep; *[machine, équipement]* maintenance costs; **~ d'expédition/de timbre** forwarding/stamp charges; **~ de port et d'emballage** postage and packing; **~ d'enregistrement** registration fee(s); **~ financiers** (*gén*) interest charges; *[crédit]* loan charges; **~ généraux** overheads (*Brit*), overhead (*US*); **~ généraux essentiels** basic overhead expenditure; **~ de gestion** (*charges*) running costs; (*prix d'un service*) management fees; (*Fin, Banque*) management charges; **~ bancaires** banking charges; **~ divers** miscellaneous expenses, sundries; **~ de justice** (legal) costs; **~ de main-d'œuvre** labour costs; **~ notariés** legal fees; **~ de scolarité** school fees (*Brit*), tuition (*US*); **~ de subsistance** living expenses; **~ de démarrage** start-up costs; **~ d'exploitation** running costs; **~ d'encaissement** collection charges; **~ de premier établissement** start-up costs, organization expenses; **~ de manutention** handling charges; **~ réels** expenses; **~ de représentation** entertainment allowance, expense account; **séjour tous ~ compris** holiday inclusive of all costs; **voyage d'affaires tous ~ payés** business trip with all expenses paid; (*Comm*) **tous ~ payés** after costs; **faire de grands ~** to go to great expense; **ça m'a fait beaucoup de ~** it cost me a great deal of money; **avoir de gros ~** to have heavy outgoings; *voir* **arrêter, faux².**

b (*loc*) **se mettre en ~** (*lit*) to go to great expense; (*fig*) to put o.s. out, go to great lengths; **se mettre en ~ pour qn/pour recevoir qn** to put o.s. out for sb/to entertain sb; **faire les ~ de la conversation** (*parler*) to keep the conversation going; (*en être le sujet*) to be the (main) topic of conversation; **nous ne voulons pas faire les ~ de cette erreur** we do not want to have to bear the brunt of this mistake; **rentrer dans** *ou* **faire ses ~** to recover one's expenses; **j'ai essayé d'être aimable mais j'en ai été pour mes ~** I tried to be friendly but I might just as well have spared myself the trouble *ou* but I was wasting my time; **aux ~ de la maison** at the firm's expense; **à ses ~** at one's own expense; **aux ~ de la princesse*** at the firm's (*ou* the taxpayer's *etc*) expense; **il l'a acheté à moindre/à grands ~** it didn't cost/it cost him a lot, he paid very little/a great deal for it; **à peu de ~** cheaply, at little cost; **il s'en est tiré à peu de ~** he got off lightly.

fraisage [fʀɛzaʒ] **nm** (*voir* **fraiser**) reaming; countersinking; milling.

fraise [fʀɛz] 1 **nf** a (*fruit*) strawberry. **~ des bois** wild strawberry; *voir* **ramener, sucrer.** b (*Tech*) (*pour agrandir un trou*) reamer; (*pour trou de vis*) countersink (bit); *[métallurgiste]* milling-cutter; *[dentiste]* drill. c (*Boucherie*) **~ de veau** calf's caul. d (*Hist: col*) ruff, fraise; (*Zool: caroncule*) wattle. e (*Méd*) strawberry mark. f (*: *visage*) face. 2 **adj inv** *couleur* strawberry pink.

fraiser [fʀeze] 1 **vt** (*Tech*) to ream; *trou* to countersink; *pièce* to mill. **à tête fraisée** countersunk.

fraiseur [fʀɛzœʀ] **nm** milling machine operator.

fraiseuse [fʀɛzøz] **nf** a (*machine*) milling machine. b (*ouvrière*) (woman) milling machine operator.

fraisier [fʀezje] **nm** a (*Bot*) strawberry plant. b (*Culin*) strawberry cake.

fraisure [fʀezyʀ] **nf** countersink, countersunk hole.

framboise [fʀɑ̃bwaz] **nf** (*fruit*) raspberry; (*liqueur*) raspberry liqueur.

framboisier [fʀɑ̃bwazje] **nm** a (*Bot*) raspberry bush. **~s** raspberry canes *ou* bushes. b (*Culin*) raspberry cake.

franc¹, franche [fʀɑ̃, fʀɑ̃ʃ] 1 **adj** a (*loyal*) *personne* frank, straightforward; *réponse* frank, straight(forward), plain; *regard* frank, candid, open; *gaieté* open; *entrevue* frank, candid. **pour être ~ avec vous** to be frank *ou* plain *ou* candid with you; **~ comme l'or** perfectly frank; **accord ~ et massif** unequivocal acceptance; *voir* **jouer**.

b (*net*) *situation* clear-cut, unequivocal; *différence, réaction* clear(-cut); *cassure* clean; *hostilité, répugnance* clear, definite; *couleur* clear, pure. (*Jur*) **5 jours ~s** 5 clear days.

c (*péj: entier*) *imbécile* utter, downright, absolute; *canaille* downright, out-and-out, absolute; *ingratitude* downright, sheer. **c'est une franche comédie/grossièreté** it's downright *ou* utterly hilarious/rude, it's sheer comedy/rudeness.

d (*libre*) *zone, ville* free. (*Comm*) **~ de** free of; **(livré) ~ de port** *marchandises* carriage-paid; *paquet* post-free, postage paid; **~ d'avaries** free of average; **~ d'avaries communes** free of general average; **~ d'avarie particulière** free of particular average; (*fig*) **~ du collier†** hard-working; *voir* **corps, coudée, coup.**

e (*Agr*) **(arbre) ~** cultivar; **greffer sur ~** to graft onto a cultivar.

2 **adv: à vous parler ~** to be frank *ou* plain *ou* candid with you; **je vous le dis tout ~** I'm being frank *ou* candid with you.

3 **comp ►franc-bord** (*Naut*) **nm (pl francs-bords)** freeboard **►franc-maçon nm (pl francs-maçons)** freemason **►franc-maçonnerie nf inv** freemasonry **►franc-maçonnique adj** masonic **►franc-parler nm inv** outspokenness; **avoir son franc-parler** to speak one's mind, be outspoken **►franc-tireur nm (pl francs-tireurs)** (*Mil*) irregular, franc tireur; (*fig*) independent, freelance; **faire qch/agir en franc-tireur** to do sth/act off one's own bat (*Brit*) *ou* independently.

franc² [fʀɑ̃] **nm** (*monnaie*) franc. **ancien/nouveau ~** old/new franc; **~ lourd/léger** revalued/pre-revaluation franc; **~ constant** constant *ou* inflation-adjusted franc; **~ courant** franc at the current rate; **~ CFA** CFA franc (*unit of currency used in certain African states*); **demander/obtenir le ~ symbolique** to demand/obtain token damages.

franc³, franque [fʀɑ̃, fʀɑ̃k] 1 **adj** Frankish. 2 **nm: F~** Frank. 3 **Franque nf** Frank.

français, e [fʀɑ̃sɛ, ɛz] 1 **adj** French; *voir* **jardin.** 2 **adv: acheter ~** to buy French; **boire/rouler** *etc* **~** to buy French wine/cars *etc.* 3 **nm** a **F~** Frenchman; **les F~** (*gens*) the French, French people; (*hommes*) Frenchmen; **le F~ moyen** the average Frenchman, the man in the street. b (*Ling*) French. **tu ne comprends pas le ~?*** ≃ don't you understand (plain) English?; **c'est une faute de ~** ≃ it's a grammatical mistake. 4 **Française nf** Frenchwoman.

franc-comtois, e, mpl francs-comtois [fʀɑ̃kɔ̃twa, waz] 1 **adj** of *ou* from (the) Franche-Comté. 2 **nm,f: F~(e)** inhabitant *ou* native of Franche-Comté.

France [fʀɑ̃s] **nf** France. (*TV*) **~2/3** *2nd/3rd channel on French television*; *voir* **vieux.**

Francfort [fʀɑ̃kfɔʀ] **n** Frankfurt. **~-sur-le-Main** Frankfurt am Main; *voir* **saucisse.**

franchement [fʀɑ̃ʃmɑ̃] **adv** a (*honnêtement*) *parler, répondre* frankly, plainly, candidly; *agir* openly. **pour vous parler ~** to be frank *ou* plain *ou* candid with you, to speak plainly to you; **avouez ~ que vous exagérez** admit frankly *ou* openly that you are going too far; **~ qu'en penses-tu?** what do you honestly think?; **~! j'en ai assez!** really! *ou* honestly! I've had enough!; **il y a des gens, ~!** really! *ou* honestly! some people!; **~ non** frankly no.

b (*sans hésiter*) *entrer, frapper* boldly. **il entra ~** he walked straight *ou* boldly in; **appuyez-vous ~ sur moi** don't be afraid to lean on me, lean hard on me; **allez-y ~** (*explication etc*) go straight to the point, say it straight out; (*opération, manœuvre etc*) go right ahead, go right at it.

c (*sans ambiguïté*) clearly; (*nettement*) definitely. **je lui ai posé la question ~** I put the question to him straight; **dis-moi ~ ce que tu veux** tell me straight out *ou* clearly what you want; **c'est ~ rouge** it's a clear red, it's clearly red; **c'est ~ au-dessous de la moyenne** it's definitely *ou* well below average.

d (*intensif: tout à fait*) *mauvais, laid* utterly, downright, really; *bon* really; *impossible* downright, utterly; *irréparable* utterly, absolutely. **ça m'a ~ dégoûté** it really *ou* utterly disgusted me; **ça s'est ~ mal passé** it went really badly; **on s'est ~ bien amusé** we really *ou* thoroughly enjoyed ourselves; **c'est ~ trop (cher)** it's much *ou* far too expensive.

franchir [fʀɑ̃ʃiʀ] 2 **vt** *obstacle* to clear, get over; *fossé* to clear, jump over; *rue, rivière, ligne d'arrivée* to cross; *seuil* to cross, step across; *porte* to go through; *distance* to cover; *mur du son* to break (through); *difficulté* to get over, surmount; *borne, limite* to overstep, go beyond. (*littér*) **~ les mers** to cross the sea; **~ le Rubicon** to cross the Rubicon; **il lui reste 10 mètres à ~** he still has 10 metres to go; **~ le cap de la soixantaine** to turn sixty, pass the sixty mark; **le pays vient de ~ un cap important** the country has just passed a major turning point; *[chiffres, vote]* **ne pas réussir à ~ la barre de ...** to be *ou* fall short of ...; **sa renommée a franchi les frontières** his fame has crossed frontiers; **le coureur a franchi la ligne d'arrivée** the runner crossed the finishing line; **l'historien, franchissant quelques siècles ...** the historian, passing over a few centuries ... .

franchisage [fʀɑ̃ʃizaʒ] **nm** franchising.

franchise [fʀɑ̃ʃiz] **nf** a *[personne, réponse]* frankness, straightforwardness; *[regard]* candour, openness. **en toute ~** quite frankly. b (*exemption*) (*gén*) exemption; (*Hist*) *[ville]* franchise. **~ fiscale** tax exemption; **~ (douanière)** exemption from (customs) duties; **colis en ~** duty-free parcel; **"~ postale"** ≃ "official paid"; **~ de bagages** baggage allowance. c (*Assurance*) excess (*Brit*), deductible (*US*). d (*Comm*) franchise. **agent/magasin en ~** franchised dealer/shop (*Brit*) *ou* store (*US*).

franchisé [fʀɑ̃ʃize] **nm** franchisee.

franchiser [fʀɑ̃ʃize] 1 **vt** to franchise.

franchiseur [fʀɑ̃ʃizœʀ] **nm** franchisor.

franchissable [fʀɑ̃ʃisabl] **adj** *obstacle* surmountable. **limite facilement ~** limit that can easily be overstepped.

franchissement [fʀɑ̃ʃismɑ̃] **nm** *[obstacle]* clearing; *[rivière, seuil]* crossing; *[limite]* overstepping.

franchouillard, e* [fʀɑ̃ʃujaʀ, aʀd] (*péj*) 1 **adj** typically French. 2 **nm** typically narrow-minded Frenchman. 3 **franchouillarde nf** typically narrow-minded French woman.

francisation [fʀɑ̃sizasjɔ̃] **nf** (*Ling*) gallicizing, Frenchifying.

franciscain, e [fʀɑ̃siskɛ̃, ɛn] **adj, nm,f** Franciscan.

franciser [fʀɑ̃size] 1 **vt** (*Ling*) to gallicize, Frenchify.

francium [fʀɑ̃sjɔm] **nm** francium.

franco [fʀɑ̃ko] **adv** (*Comm*) **~ (de port)** *marchandise* carriage-paid; *colis* postage paid; **~ de port et d'emballage** free of charge; **~ à bord/sur wagon** free on board/on rail; **~ (le) long du bord** free alongside ship; **~ (le long du) quai** free alongside quay; **y aller ~*** (*explication etc*) to go straight to the point, come straight out with it*; (*opération, manœuvre etc*) to go right at it*, go right ahead.

franco- [fʀɑ̃ko] **préf** franco-. **les relations ~-britanniques** Franco-British relations.

franco-canadien, -ienne [fʀɑ̃kokanadjɛ̃, jɛn] **adj, nm,f** (*Ling*) French Canadian.

franco-français, e [fʀɑ̃kofʀɑ̃sɛ, ɛz] **adj** purely French; (*péj*) typically French.

François [fʀɑ̃swa] **nm** Francis. **saint ~ d'Assise** Saint Francis of Assisi.

Françoise [fʀɑ̃swaz] **nf** Frances.

francophile [fʀɑ̃kɔfil] **adj, nmf** francophile.

francophilie [fʀɑ̃kɔfili] **nf** francomania.

francophobe [fʀɑ̃kɔfɔb] **adj, nmf** francophobe.

francophobie [fʀɑ̃kɔfɔbi] **nf** francophobia.

francophone [fʀɑ̃kɔfɔn] 1 **adj** French-speaking; (*Can*) primarily French-speaking. 2 **nmf** (native) French speaker; (*Can*) Francophone (*Can*).

francophonie [fʀɑ̃kɔfɔni] **nf** French-speaking communities.

franco-québécois [fʀɑ̃kɔkebekwa] **nm** (*Ling*) Quebec French.

frange [fʀɑ̃ʒ] **nf** *[tissu, cheveux]* fringe; (*fig*) *[conscience, sommeil]* threshold. **une ~ de lumière** a band of light; (*Opt*) **~s d'interférence** interference fringes.

franger [fʀɑ̃ʒe] 3 **vt** (*gén ptp*) to fringe (*de* with).

frangin* [fʀɑ̃ʒɛ̃] **nm** brother.

frangine* [fʀɑ̃ʒin] **nf** sister.

frangipane [fʀɑ̃ʒipan] **nf** (*Culin*) almond paste, frangipane. **gâteau fourré à la ~** frangipane (pastry).

frangipanier [fʀɑ̃ʒipanje] **nm** frangipani (tree).

franglais [fʀɑ̃glɛ] **nm** Franglais.

franque [fʀɑ̃k] *voir* **franc³.**

franquette* [fʀɑ̃kɛt] **nf: à la bonne ~** *recevoir, manger* simply, without any fuss; **venez manger, ce sera à la bonne ~** come and eat with us – it'll be a simple meal *ou* we won't go to any special trouble (for you).

franquisme [fʀɑ̃kism] **nm** Francoism.

franquiste [fʀɑ̃kist] 1 **adj** pro-Franco. 2 **nmf** Franco supporter.

frappant, e [fʀapɑ̃, ɑ̃t] **adj** striking; *voir* **argument.**

frappe [fʀap] **nf** a *[monnaie, médaille]* (*action*) striking; (*empreinte*) stamp, impression. b *[dactylo, pianiste]* touch; *[machine à écrire]* (*souplesse*) touch; (*impression*) typeface. **la lettre est à la ~** the letter is being typed (out); **c'est la première ~** it's the top copy; *voir* **faute.** c (*péj: voyou*) tough guy. d (*Sport*) *[boxeur]* punch; *[footballeur]* kick; *[joueur de tennis]* stroke. **il a une bonne ~ de la balle** *[footballeur]* he kicks the ball well, he has a good kick; *[joueur de tennis]* he strikes *ou* hits the ball very well; *voir* **force.**

frappé, e [fʀape] (**ptp de frapper**) **adj** a (*saisi*) struck. **~ de panique** panic-stricken; **~ de stupeur** thunderstruck; **(très) ~ de voir que ...** (very) struck to see that ... . b *velours* embossed. (*fig*) **vers bien ~s** neatly turned lines (of verse); *voir* **coin.** c *champagne, café* iced. **boire un vin bien ~** to drink a wine well chilled. d (**: fou*) touched* (*attrib*), crazy*.

frappement [fʀapmɑ̃] **nm** striking.

frapper [fʀape] 1 1 **vt** a (*cogner*) *personne, surface [poing, projectile]* to hit, strike; *[couteau]* to stab, strike; *cordes, clavier* to strike; *coups* to strike, deal. **~ le sol du pied** to stamp (one's foot) on the ground; **~ sec*** to hit hard; (*Hist*) **~ d'estoc et de taille** to cut and thrust; (*Théât*) **~ les trois coups** to give the three knocks (*to announce start of performance*); **la pluie/la lumière frappait le mur** the rain lashed (against)/the light fell on the wall; (*fig*) **~ un grand coup** to strike a decisive blow; **frappé à mort** fatally *ou* mortally wounded.

b (*fig*) *[malheur, maladie]* to strike (down); *[coïncidence, détail]* to strike. **frappé par le malheur** stricken by misfortune; **ce deuil le frappe cruellement** this bereavement is a cruel blow to him; **il a frappé tout le monde par son énergie, son énergie a frappé tout le monde** he amazed everybody by his energy, his energy amazed everybody, everybody was struck by his energy; **j'ai été frappé d'entendre que ...** I was amazed to hear that ...; **cela l'a frappé de stupeur** he was thunderstruck *ou* dumbfounded at this; **cette découverte le frappa de panique/d'horreur** he was panic-/horror-stricken at this discovery, this discovery filled him with panic/horror; **~ l'imagination** to catch *ou* fire the imagination; **ce qui (me) frappe** what strikes me; **ce qui a frappé mon regard/mon oreille** what caught my eye/reached my ears.

c (*fig*) *[mesures, impôts]* to hit. **ces impôts/amendes frappent les plus pauvres** these taxes/fines hit the very poor; **ces impôts frappent lourdement les petits commerçants** these taxes are hitting small businesses hard; **l'amende qui frappe les contrevenants à ce règlement** the fine imposed upon those who infringe this regulation; **~ qn d'une amende/d'un impôt** to impose a fine/a tax upon sb; **la loi doit ~ les coupables** the law must punish the guilty; **ils ont frappé la vente du tabac d'un impôt supplémentaire** they have put *ou* slammed* an extra tax on tobacco sales.

d *monnaie, médaille* to strike.

e (*glacer*) *champagne, vin* to put on ice, chill; *café* to ice.

2 **vi** to strike (*sur* on, *contre* against). **~ du poing sur la table** to bang one's fist on the table; **~ sur la table avec une règle** to tap the table *ou* (*plus fort*) to knock the table *ou* bang on the table with a ruler; **~ dans ses mains** to clap one's hands; **~ du pied** to stamp (one's foot); (*lit, fig*) **~ à la porte** to knock on *ou* at the door; **on a frappé** there's someone at the door, there was a knock at the door; **entrez sans ~** come in without knocking, come straight in; (*fig*) **~ à toutes les portes** to try every door; (*fig*) **~ à la bonne/mauvaise porte** to go to the right/wrong person *ou* place.

3 **se frapper vpr** a **se ~ la poitrine** to beat one's breast; **se ~ le front** to tap one's forehead.

b (**: se tracasser*) to get (o.s.) worked up, get (o.s.) into a state*.

frappeur [fʀapœʀ] **adj m** *voir* **esprit**.

frasil [fʀazi(l)] **nm** (*Can*) frazil (*Can*).

frasque [fʀask] **nf** (*gén pl*) escapade. **faire des ~s** to get up to mischief *ou* high jinks*; **~s de jeunesse** youthful indiscretions.

fraternel, -elle [fʀatɛʀnɛl] **adj** brotherly, fraternal. **se montrer ~ envers qn** to behave in a brotherly manner towards sb.

fraternellement [fʀatɛʀnɛlmɑ̃] **adv** in a brotherly way, fraternally.

fraternisation [fʀatɛʀnizasjɔ̃] **nf** fraternization, fraternizing. **élan de ~** surge of brotherly feeling.

fraterniser [fʀatɛʀnize] 1 **vi** *[pays, personnes]* to fraternize (*avec* with).

fraternité [fʀatɛʀnite] **nf** a (*amitié*) brotherhood (*NonC*), fraternity (*NonC*). **il y a une ~ d'esprit entre eux** there is a kinship *ou* brotherhood of spirit between them; *voir* **liberté**. b (*Rel*) fraternity, brotherhood.

fratricide [fʀatʀisid] 1 **adj** fratricidal. 2 **nmf** fratricide. 3 **nm** (*crime*) fratricide.

fraude [fʀod] **nf** (*gén*) fraud (*NonC*); (*à un examen*) cheating. **en ~** *fabriquer, vendre* fraudulently; *lire, fumer* secretly; **passer qch/faire passer qn en ~** to smuggle sth/sb in; **~ électorale** electoral fraud; **~ fiscale** tax evasion.

frauder [fʀode] 1 1 **vt** to defraud, cheat. **~ le fisc** to evade taxation. 2 **vi** (*gén*) to cheat. **~ sur la quantité/qualité** to cheat over the quantity/quality; **~ sur le poids** to cheat on the weight.

fraudeur, -euse [fʀodœʀ, øz] **nm,f** (*gén*) person guilty of fraud; (*à la douane*) smuggler; (*envers le fisc*) tax evader. (*à un examen*) **les ~s seront lourdement sanctionnés** cheating will be *ou* candidates who cheat will be severely punished; **il a un tempérament ~, il est ~** he has a tendency towards cheating.

frauduleusement [fʀodyløzmɑ̃] **adv** fraudulently.

frauduleux, -euse [fʀodylø, øz] **adj** *trafic, pratiques, concurrence* fraudulent. **sans intention ~euse de ma part** with no fraudulent intention *ou* no intention of cheating on my part.

frayer [fʀeje] 8 1 **vt** *chemin* to open up, clear. **~ le passage à qn** to clear the way for sb; (*fig*) **~ la voie** to pave the way. 2 **se frayer vpr**: **se ~ un passage (dans la foule)** to force *ou* plough *ou* elbow one's way through (the crowd); **se ~ un chemin dans la jungle** to cut a path through the jungle; (*fig*) **se ~ un chemin vers les honneurs** to work one's way up to fame. 3 **vi** a *[poisson]* to spawn. b (*fig*) **~ avec** to mix *ou* associate with.

frayeur [fʀɛjœʀ] **nf** fright. **tu m'as fait une de ces ~s!** you gave me a dreadful fright!; **cri/geste de ~** cry/gesture of fear, startled cry/gesture; **se remettre de ses ~s** to recover from one's fright.

fredaine [fʀədɛn] **nf** mischief (*NonC*), escapade, prank. **faire des ~s** to be up to mischief.

Frédéric [fʀedeʀik] **nm** Frederick.

Frédérique [fʀedeʀik] **nf** Frederica.

fredonnement [fʀədɔnmɑ̃] **nm** humming.

fredonner [fʀədɔne] 1 **vt** to hum. **elle fredonnait dans la cuisine** she was humming (away) (to herself) in the kitchen.

free-lance, **pl free-lances** [fʀilɑ̃s] **adj inv, nmf** freelance. **travailler en ~** to work freelance, do freelance work.

freesia [fʀezja] **nm** freesia.

Freetown [fʀitaʊn] **n** Freetown.

freezer [fʀizœʀ] **nm** freezer *ou* ice-making compartment, freezer (*of refrigerator*).

frégate [fʀegat] **nf** (*Hist, Mil, Naut*) frigate; (*Zool*) frigate bird; *voir* **capitaine**.

frein [fʀɛ̃] 1 **nm** *[voiture]*, (*aussi fig*) brake; *[cheval]* bit. **c'est un ~ à l'expansion** it acts as a brake upon expansion; **mets le ~** put the brake on; **mettre un ~ à** *inflation, colère, ambitions* to put a brake on, curb, check; **sans ~** *imagination, curiosité* unbridled, unchecked; **coup de ~** (*lit*) brake; (*fig*) brake, curb; **donner un brusque coup de ~** to brake suddenly *ou* sharply; **donner un coup de ~ à** *dépenses, inflation* to put a brake on, curb, slow down, check; *importations* to stem, curtail; *voir* **bloquer, ronger**.

2 **comp** ►**frein aérodynamique** air brake ►**frein à disques** disc brake ►**frein à main** handbrake ►**frein moteur** engine braking ►**frein à pied** footbrake ►**frein à tambours** drum brake.

freinage [fʀɛnaʒ] **nm** (*action*) braking; (*Écon*) *[expansion, dépenses, inflation etc]* curbing, slowing down. **dispositif de ~** braking system; **traces de ~** tyre marks (*caused by braking*); **un bon ~** good braking.

freiner [fʀene] 1 1 **vt** *véhicule* to pull up, slow down; *progression, coureur* to slow up *ou* down, hold up; *progrès, évolution* to put a brake on, check; *expansion, dépenses, inflation* to put a brake on, curb, slow down, check; *chômage* to curb, check; *enthousiasme, joie* to check, put a damper on. **il faut que je me freine** I have to cut down (*dans* on); **~ les importations** to stem *ou* curtail imports. 2 **vi** (*Aut*) to brake; (*à ski, en patins etc*) to slow down. **~ à bloc** to jam *ou* slam on the brakes; **il freina brusquement** he braked suddenly, he jammed *ou* slammed on the brakes; (*lit, fig*) **~ des quatre fers** to jam *ou* slam on the brakes.

frelater [fʀəlate] 1 **vt** *vin, aliment* to adulterate. (*fig*) **un milieu frelaté** a dubious *ou* slightly corrupt milieu.

frêle [fʀɛl] **adj** *tige, charpente* flimsy, frail, fragile; *enfant, femme, corps* frail, fragile; *voix* thin, frail. (*littér*) **de ~s espérances** frail *ou* flimsy hopes.

frelon [fʀəlɔ̃] **nm** hornet.

freluquet [fʀəlykɛ] **nm** (*péj*) whippersnapper.

frémir [fʀemiʀ] 2 **vi** a *[personne, corps]* (*de peur*) to quake, tremble, shudder; (*d'horreur*) to shudder, shiver; (*de fièvre, froid*) to shiver; (*de colère*) to shake, tremble, quiver; (*d'impatience, de plaisir, d'espoir*) to quiver, tremble (*de* with). **ça me fait ~** it makes me shudder; **il frémit de tout son être** his whole being quivered *ou* trembled; **histoire à vous faire ~** story that gives you the shivers* *ou* that makes you shudder *ou* shiver; **aux moments de suspense toute la salle frémissait** at the moments of suspense the whole audience trembled.

b *[lèvres, feuillage]* to tremble, quiver; *[narine, aile, corde]* to quiver; *[eau chaude]* to simmer, quiver. **sensibilité frémissante** quivering sensitivity.

frémissement [fʀemismɑ̃] **nm** a (*humain: voir* **frémir**) shudder; shiver; quiver. **un ~ de plaisir** a thrill *ou* quiver of pleasure; **un long ~ parcourut son corps** a shiver ran all the way through him *ou* ran the length of his body; **le ~ de son être** his quivering *ou* shivering *ou* shuddering being; **un ~ parcourut la salle** a quiver ran through the room.

b *[lèvres, feuillage]* trembling (*NonC*), quivering (*NonC*); *[narine, aile, corde]* quivering (*NonC*); *[eau chaude]* simmering, quivering.

c (*fig: regain d'activité*) **un ~ de l'économie** signs of economic recovery; **des ~s dans l'opinion publique** signs of renewed public interest; **il y a eu un ~ des valeurs françaises** French securities perked up a little.

frêne [fʀɛn] **nm** ash (tree); (*bois*) ash.

frénésie [fʀenezi] **nf** frenzy. **avec ~** *travailler, applaudir* frenetically, furiously; **aimer qn avec ~** to be wildly *ou* desperately in love with sb.

frénétique [fʀenetik] **adj** *applaudissements, rythme* frenzied, frenetic; *passion* frenzied, wild.

frénétiquement [fʀenetikmɑ̃] **adv** *aimer* wildly, desperately; *travailler, applaudir* frenetically, furiously.

Fréon [fʀeɔ̃] **nm** ® Freon ®.

fréquemment [fʀekamɑ̃] **adv** frequently, often.

fréquence [fʀekɑ̃s] **nf** (*gén*) frequency. **~ d'achat** purchase rate; *voir* **modulation**.

fréquent, e [fʀekɑ̃, ɑ̃t] **adj** frequent.

fréquentable [fʀekɑ̃tabl] **adj**: **sont-ils ~s?** are they the sort of people one can associate with?; **ils ne sont pas ~s** they aren't the sort of people one associates with, they aren't nice to know*.

fréquentatif, -ive [fʀekɑ̃tatif, iv] **adj** frequentative.

fréquentation [fʀekɑ̃tasjɔ̃] **nf** a (*action*) *[établissement]* frequenting. **la ~ des salles de cinéma augmente** the number of people going to the cinema is rising, more and more people are going to the cinema; **la ~ de ces gens** frequent contact with these people, seeing these people frequently *ou* often. b (*gén pl: relation*) company (*NonC*), associate. **des ~s douteuses** dubious company *ou* associates; **ce n'est pas une ~ pour une jeune fille bien élevée** that isn't the sort of company for a well-brought-up young lady to keep.

fréquenté, e [fʀekɑ̃te] (ptp de **fréquenter**) adj *lieu, établissement* busy. **très ~** very busy, much frequented; **établissement bien/mal ~** establishment of good/ill repute.

fréquenter [fʀekɑ̃te] 1 vt *lieu* to frequent; *voisins* to see frequently *ou* often; *jeune fille* to go around with; (*littér*) *auteurs classiques* to keep company with. **~ la bonne société** to move in fashionable circles; **il fréquente plus les cafés que la faculté** he's in cafés more often than at lectures; **il les fréquente peu** he seldom sees them; **nous nous fréquentons beaucoup** we see quite a lot of each other, we see each other quite often *ou* frequently; **ces jeunes gens se fréquentent depuis un an** those young people have been going around together for a year now.

frère [fʀɛʀ] nm a (*gén, fig*) brother. **partager en ~s** to share like brothers; **alors, vieux ~!*** well, old pal!* *ou* mate!* (*Brit*) *ou* buddy!* (*US*); (*fig*) **j'ai trouvé le ~ de ce vase chez un antiquaire*** I found the partner to this vase in an antique shop; (*Mil*) **~s d'armes** brothers in arms; (*Pol*) **partis/peuples ~s** sister parties/countries; *voir* **demi-, faux[2]**. b (*Rel*) (*égal*) brother; (*paroissien*) brother; (*moine*) brother, friar. **les hommes sont tous ~s** all men are brothers; (*Rel*) **mes (bien chers) ~s** (dearly beloved) brethren; **~ lai** lay brother; **~ mendiant** mendicant friar; **~ Antoine** Brother Antoine, Friar Antoine; **on l'a mis en pension chez les ~s** he has been sent to a Catholic boarding school.

frérot* [fʀeʀo] nm kid brother*.

fresque [fʀɛsk] nf (*Art*) fresco; (*Littérat*) portrait.

fresquiste [fʀɛskist] nmf fresco painter.

fret [fʀɛ(t)] nm (*prix*) (*Aviat, Naut*) freight(age); (*Aut*) carriage; (*cargaison*) (*Aviat, Naut*) freight, cargo; (*Aut*) load. (*Comm: affréter*) **prendre à ~** to charter.

fréter [fʀete] 6 vt (*gén: prendre à fret*) to charter; (*Naut: donner à fret*) to freight.

fréteur [fʀetœʀ] nm (*Naut*) owner. **~ et affréteur** owner and charterer.

frétillant, e [fʀetijɑ̃, ɑ̃t] adj *poisson* wriggling; *personne* frisky, lively. **chien à la queue ~e** dog with a quivering *ou* wagging tail; **~ d'impatience** fidgeting *ou* quivering with impatience.

frétillement [fʀetijmɑ̃] nm *[poisson]* wriggling (*NonC*). **un ~ d'impatience** a quiver of impatience.

frétiller [fʀetije] 1 vi *[poisson]* to wriggle; *[personne]* to wriggle, fidget. **le chien frétillait de la queue** the dog was wagging its tail; **~ d'impatience** to fidget *ou* quiver with impatience; **~ de joie** to be quivering *ou* quiver with joy; (*hum, péj*) **elle frétille de l'arrière-train** she's wiggling her bottom (*hum*).

fretin [fʀətɛ̃] nm (*poissons*) fry; (*fig*) small fry; *voir* **menu[2]**.

frette [fʀɛt] nf (*Mus*) fret.

freudien, -ienne [fʀødjɛ̃, jɛn] adj Freudian.

freudisme [fʀødism] nm Freudianism.

freux [fʀø] nm (*Orn*) rook.

friabilité [fʀijabilite] nf *[roche, sol]* crumbly nature, flakiness, friability (*SPÉC*).

friable [fʀijabl] adj *roche, sol* crumbly, flaky, friable (*SPÉC*); (*Culin*) *pâte* crumbly.

friand, friande [fʀijɑ̃, fʀijɑ̃d] 1 adj: **~ de** *lait, miel, bonbons* partial to, fond of; (*fig*) *compliments, chatteries* fond of. 2 nm (*pâté*) (minced) meat pie, ≃ sausage roll (*Brit*); (*sucré*) small almond cake. **~ au fromage** cheese puff.

friandise [fʀijɑ̃diz] nf titbit, delicacy, sweetmeat†. **c'est une ~** it's a delicacy.

fric‡ [fʀik] nm (*argent*) bread‡, dough‡, cash*, lolly‡ (*Brit*). **il a du ~** he's loaded*; **elle se fait beaucoup de ~** she makes a packet*.

fricandeau, pl **~x** [fʀikɑ̃do] nm fricandeau.

fricassée [fʀikase] nf fricassee. **~ de poulet** chicken fricassee.

fricative [fʀikativ] adj f, nf fricative.

fric-frac*, pl **fric-frac(s)** [fʀikfʀak] nm break-in.

friche [fʀiʃ] nf fallow land (*NonC*). (*lit, fig*) **en ~** (lying) fallow; (*lit, fig*) **être/laisser en ~** to lie/let lie fallow; **~ industrielle** *temporarily inactive industrial area or estate*.

frichti* [fʀiʃti] nm, **fricot*** [fʀiko] nm nosh‡ (*NonC*) (*Brit*), grub* (*NonC*). **préparer son ~** to cook up one's grub‡.

fricoter* [fʀikɔte] 1 1 vt (*lit, fig*) to cook up*. (*fig*) **qu'est-ce qu'il fricote?** what's he cooking up?*, what's he up to?* 2 vi: **~ avec qn** (*s'associer*) to knock around with sb*; (*avoir des relations sexuelles*) to sleep with sb.

friction [fʀiksjɔ̃] nf (*Phys, Tech, Ling*) friction; (*massage*) rub, rubdown; (*chez le coiffeur*) scalp massage; (*fig: conflits*) friction.

frictionner [fʀiksjɔne] 1 vt to rub. **se ~ après un bain** to rub o.s. down after a bath.

fridolin‡ [fʀidɔlɛ̃] nm (*péj: Allemand*) Kraut‡, Fritz‡, Jerry‡.

Frigidaire [fʀiʒidɛʀ] nm ® refrigerator, fridge (*Brit*).

frigide [fʀiʒid] adj frigid.

frigidité [fʀiʒidite] nf frigidity.

frigo* [fʀigo] nm fridge (*Brit*), refrigerator. **~-armoire** upright fridge *ou* refrigerator.

frigorifier [fʀigɔʀifje] 7 vt (*lit*) to refrigerate; (*fig: pétrifier*) to petrify, freeze to the spot. **être frigorifié*** (*avoir froid*) to be frozen stiff.

frigorifique [fʀigɔʀifik] adj *mélange* refrigerating (*épith*); *camion, wagon* refrigerator (*épith*); *voir* **armoire**.

frigoriste [fʀigɔʀist] nmf refrigeration engineer.

frileusement [fʀiløzmɑ̃] adv: **~ serrés l'un contre l'autre** huddled close together to keep warm *ou* against the cold; **~ enfouis sous les couvertures** huddled under the blankets to keep warm.

frileux, -euse [fʀilø, øz] adj a *personne* sensitive to (the) cold; *geste, posture* shivery. **il est très ~** he feels the cold easily, he is very sensitive to (the) cold; **elle se couvrit de son châle d'un geste ~** with a shiver she pulled her shawl around her. b (*trop prudent*) *boursier* overcautious; *marché* nervous.

frilosité [fʀilozite] nf *[boursier]* overcautiousness; *[marché]* nervousness.

frimaire [fʀimɛʀ] nm Frimaire (*third month in the French Republican calendar*).

frimas [fʀimɑ] nmpl (*littér*) wintry weather.

frime* [fʀim] nf: **c'est de la ~** that's a lot of eyewash* (*Brit*), it's all put on*; **c'est pour la ~** it's all *ou* just for show.

frimer* [fʀime] 1 vi to show off*.

frimeur, -euse [fʀimœʀ, øz] nm,f show-off*. **il est très ~** he's a real show-off*.

frimousse [fʀimus] nf (sweet) little face.

fringale* [fʀɛ̃gal] nf (*faim*) raging hunger. (*désir*) **une ~ de** a craving for; **j'ai la ~** I'm ravenous* *ou* famished* *ou* starving*.

fringant, e [fʀɛ̃gɑ̃, ɑ̃t] adj *cheval* frisky, high-spirited; *personne, allure* dashing.

fringillidé [fʀɛ̃ʒil(l)ide] nm finch.

fringué, e* [fʀɛ̃ge] (ptp de **(se) fringuer**) adj dressed, done up*. **bien/mal ~** well-/badly-dressed; **vise un peu comme elle est ~e!** look what she's got on!, look what she's done up in!*

fringuer* [fʀɛ̃ge] 1 1 **se fringuer** vpr (*s'habiller*) to get dressed; (*s'habiller élégamment*) to doll (o.s.) up*, do o.s. up*. 2 vt to dress.

fringues* [fʀɛ̃g] nfpl clothes, togs*, threads‡ (*US*). **elle a toujours de belles ~s** she always has such great clothes* *ou* such fantastic gear*.

friper [fʀipe] 1 vt to crumple (up), crush. **ça se fripe facilement** it crumples *ou* crushes easily; **des habits tout fripés** badly crumpled *ou* rumpled clothes; (*fig*) **visage tout fripé** crumpled face.

friperie [fʀipʀi] nf (*boutique*) secondhand clothes shop (*Brit*) *ou* store (*US*).

fripes* [fʀip] nfpl second-hand clothes. **vendre des ~** *ou* **de la fripe** to sell secondhand clothes.

fripier, -ière [fʀipje, jɛʀ] nm,f secondhand clothes dealer.

fripon, -onne [fʀipɔ̃, ɔn] 1 adj *air, allure, visage, yeux* roguish, mischievous, cheeky (*Brit*); *nez* cheeky (*Brit*), saucy. 2 nm,f (†: *gredin*) knave†, rascally fellow†; (*: *nuance affectueuse*) rascal, rogue. **petit ~!** you little rascal! *ou* rogue!

friponnerie [fʀipɔnʀi] nf (*acte*) piece of mischief, prank, escapade. **les ~s de ce gamin** the mischief this little imp gets up to, the pranks of the little imp.

fripouille [fʀipuj] nf (*péj*) rogue, scoundrel. (*nuance affectueuse*) **petite ~!*** you little devil!* *ou* rogue!

fripouillerie [fʀipujʀi] nf roguishness.

friqué, e‡ [fʀike] adj loaded*, filthy rich*. **je ne suis pas très ~ en ce moment** I'm not exactly loaded* at the moment, I'm a bit hard-up* at the moment.

frire [fʀiʀ] vt (*aussi* **faire ~**) to fry; *voir* **pâte, poêle[1]**.

Frisbee [fʀizbi] nm ® Frisbee ®.

frise [fʀiz] nf (*Archit, Art*) frieze; (*Théât*) border; *voir* **cheval**.

frisé, e [fʀize] (ptp de **friser**) 1 adj *cheveux* (very) curly; *personne, animal* curly-haired. **il est tout ~** he has very curly hair; **~ comme un mouton** curly-headed *ou* -haired, frizzy-haired; *voir* **chou[1]**. 2 nm (‡ *péj: Allemand*) Fritz‡, Kraut‡, Jerry‡; (*soldat*) Jerry‡. 3 **frisée** nf (*chicorée*) curly endive.

friselis [fʀizli] nm slight trembling (*NonC*).

friser [fʀize] 1 1 vt a *cheveux* to curl; *moustache* to twirl. **~ qn** to curl sb's hair; *voir* **fer**. b (*frôler*) *surface* to graze, skim; *catastrophe, mort* to be within a hair's breadth of, be within an ace of; *insolence* to border on, verge on. **~ la soixantaine** to be getting on towards sixty, be close to sixty, be pushing sixty*. 2 vi *[cheveux]* to curl, be curly; *[personne]* to have curly hair. **faire ~ ses cheveux** to make one's hair go curly; (*chez le coiffeur*) to have one's hair curled. 3 **se friser** vpr to curl one's hair. **se faire ~** (*par un coiffeur*) to have one's hair curled.

frisette [fʀizɛt] nf a (*cheveux*) little curl, little ringlet. b (*lambris*) panel. **~ de pin** pine panel.

frison[1] [fʀizɔ̃] nm little curl *ou* ringlet (*around face or neck*).

frison[2], -onne [fʀizɔ̃, ɔn] 1 adj Frisian *ou* Friesian. 2 nm (*Ling*) Frisian *ou* Friesian. 3 nm,f: **F~(ne)** Frisian *ou* Friesian. 4 **frisonne** nf: (**vache**) **~ne** Frisian *ou* Friesian (cow).

frisotter [fʀizɔte] 1 1 vt to crimp, curl tightly. 2 vi to curl tightly. **ses cheveux frisottent quand il pleut** his hair goes all curly when it rains.

frisquet, -ette* [fʀiskɛ, ɛt] adj m *vent* chilly. **il fait ~** it's chilly, there's a chill *ou* nip in the air.

frisson [fʀisɔ̃] nm *[froid, fièvre]* shiver; *[répulsion, peur]* shudder, shiver; *[volupté]* thrill, shiver, quiver. **elle fut prise** *ou* **saisie d'un ~** a sudden shiver ran through her; **la fièvre me donne des ~s** this fever is making me shiver *ou* is giving me the shivers*; **ça me donne le** ~ it gives me the creeps* *ou* the shivers*, it makes me shudder *ou* shiver; **le** ~ **des herbes sous le vent** the quivering of the grass in the wind; (*hum*) **ça a été le grand** ~ (*gén*) it was a real thrill*; (*sexuel*) the earth moved.

frissonnement [fʀisɔnmɑ̃] **nm** a (*action: voir* **frissonner**) quaking; trembling; shuddering; shivering; quivering; rustling; rippling. b (*frisson*) shiver, shudder. ~ **de volupté** thrill *ou* shiver *ou* quiver of sensual delight.

frissonner [fʀisɔne] [1] **vi** a *[personne, corps]* (*de peur*) to quake, tremble, shudder; (*d'horreur*) to shudder, shiver; (*de fièvre, froid*) to shiver; (*de volupté, désir*) to quiver, tremble (*de* with). **le vent le fit** ~ the wind made him shiver *ou* shudder. b *[feuillage]* to quiver, tremble, rustle; *[lac]* to ripple. **la lumière frissonnait sur l'eau** the light shimmered on *ou* over the water.

frit, e [fʀi, fʀit] (**ptp de frire**) 1 **adj** (*Culin*) fried. (‡: *fichu, perdu*) **ils sont ~s** they've had it*, their goose is cooked*, their number's up*; *voir* **pomme.** 2 **frite nf** (*gén pl*) **~s** chips (*Brit*), French fried potatoes, French fries, fries (*surtout US*); **un steak** *ou* **bifteck ~s** a steak and chips (*Brit*) *ou* French fries *ou* French fried potatoes *ou* fries (*surtout US*); (*fig*) **avoir la** ~‡ to be feeling cheery, be full of beans* (*Brit*).

friterie [fʀitʀi] **nf** (*boutique*) ≃ chip shop (*Brit*), ≃ hamburger stand (*US*).

friteuse [fʀitøz] **nf** chip pan (*Brit*), deep fryer. ~ **électrique** electric fryer.

friture [fʀityʀ] **nf** a (*Culin*) (*méthode*) frying; (*graisse*) (deep) fat (*for frying*); (*mets*) fried fish (*NonC ou pl*). **le docteur me déconseille les ~s** the doctor advises me against fried food; **(petite)** ~ small fish (*NonC ou pl*); **une** ~ **de goujons** (a dish of) fried gudgeon. b (*: *Rad*) crackle, crackling (*NonC*).

fritz‡ [fʀits] **nm** (*péj: Allemand*) Kraut‡, Jerry‡ (*Brit*).

frivole [fʀivɔl] **adj** *personne* frivolous, shallow; *occupation, argument* frivolous, trivial.

frivolement [fʀivɔlmɑ̃] **adv** frivolously.

frivolité [fʀivɔlite] **nf** (*voir* **frivole**) frivolity, frivolousness; shallowness; triviality; (*gén pl: bagatelle*) frivolities. (*Comm: articles*) **~s**† fancy goods.

froc [fʀɔk] **nm** a (*Rel*) frock, habit. **porter le** ~ to be a monk, wear the habit of a monk; (*fig*) **jeter le** ~ **aux orties** to leave the priesthood. b (‡: *pantalon*) bags* (*Brit*), (pair of) trousers (*Brit*), (pair of) pants (*US*).

froid, e [fʀwa, fʀwad] 1 **adj** a *personne, boisson, repas, décor, couleur* cold; *manières, accueil* cold, chilly; *détermination, calcul* cold, cool. **colère ~e** cold *ou* controlled anger; **il fait assez** ~ it is rather cold; **d'un ton** ~ coldly; **ça me laisse** ~ it leaves me cold; **garder la tête ~e** to keep cool, keep a cool head; ~ **comme le marbre** as cold as marble; *voir* **battre, sang, sueur** *etc.*

b **à** ~: **laminer à** ~ to cold-roll; **souder à** ~ to cold-weld; **démarrer à** ~ to start (from) cold; **démarrage à** ~ cold start *ou* starting (*US*); **coller à** ~ to glue without preheating; **opérer à** ~ (*Méd*) to perform cold surgery; (*fig*) to let things cool down before acting; (*fig*) **parler à** ~ **de qch** to speak coldly *ou* coolly of sth; (*fig*) **prendre** *ou* **cueillir qn à** ~* to catch sb unawares *ou* off guard; *voir* **ciseau.**

2 **nm** a **le** ~ (*gén*) the cold; (*industrie*) refrigeration; **j'ai** ~ I am cold; **j'ai** ~ **aux pieds** my feet are cold; **il fait** ~**/un** ~ **de canard*** it's cold/freezing cold *ou* perishing*; **ça me donne** ~ it makes me (feel) cold; **ça me fait** ~ **dans le dos** (*lit*) it gives me a cold back, it makes my back cold; (*fig*) it sends shivers down my spine; **prendre** *ou* **attraper (un coup de)** ~ to catch cold *ou* a chill; **vague** *ou* **coup de** ~ cold spell; **les grands ~s** the cold of winter; **n'avoir pas** ~ **aux yeux** *[homme d'affaires, aventurier]* to be venturesome *ou* adventurous; *[enfant]* to have plenty of pluck; *voir* **craindre, jeter, mourir.**

b (*brouille*) coolness (*NonC*). **malgré le** ~ **qu'il y avait entre eux** despite the coolness that existed between them; **être en** ~ **avec qn** to be on bad terms *ou* not to be on good terms with sb.

froidement [fʀwadmɑ̃] **adv** *accueillir, remercier* coldly, coolly; *calculer, réfléchir* coolly; *tuer* cold-bloodedly, in cold blood. **il me reçut** ~ I got a cold *ou* chilly reception (from him), he greeted me coldly; **meurtre accompli** ~ cold-blooded murder; (*hum*) **comment vas-tu? —** ~! how are you? — cold! (*hum*).

froideur [fʀwadœʀ] **nf** *[personne, sentiments]* coldness; *[manières, accueil]* coldness, chilliness. **recevoir qn avec** ~ to give sb a cold *ou* chilly *ou* cool reception, greet sb coldly; **contempler qch avec** ~ to contemplate sth coldly *ou* coolly; (*littér*) **la** ~ **de son cœur** her coldness of heart.

froidure†† [fʀwadyʀ] **nf** cold (*NonC*), cold season.

froissement [fʀwasmɑ̃] **nm** a *[tissu]* crumpling, creasing. b (*bruit*) rustle, rustling (*NonC*). **des ~s soyeux** the sound of rustling silk. c (*Méd*) ~ **(d'un muscle)** (muscular) strain. d (*fig littér*) **évitez tout** ~ **d'amour-propre** try to avoid hurting anyone's feelings.

froisser [fʀwase] [1] 1 **vt** *tissu* to crumple, crease; *habit* to crumple, rumple, crease; *herbe* to crush; (*fig*) *personne* to hurt, offend. **ça l'a froissé dans son orgueil** that ruffled his pride; **il froissa la lettre et la jeta** he screwed up the letter and threw it away. 2 **se froisser vpr** *[tissu]* to crease, crumple; *[personne]* to take offence, take umbrage (*de* at). (*Méd*) **se** ~ **un muscle** to strain a muscle.

frôlement [fʀolmɑ̃] **nm** (*contact*) light touch, light contact (*NonC*); (*bruit*) rustle, rustling (*NonC*). **le** ~ **des corps dans l'obscurité** the light contact of bodies brushing against each other in the darkness.

frôler [fʀole] [1] **vt** (*lit*) (*toucher*) to brush against; (*passer près de*) to skim; (*fig: confiner à*) to verge on. **le projectile le frôla** the projectile skimmed past him; **l'automobiliste frôla le trottoir/le poteau** the driver just missed the pavement (*Brit*) *ou* sidewalk (*US*)/post; (*fig*) ~ **la mort/catastrophe** to come within a hair's breadth *ou* an ace of death/a catastrophe; **ça frôle l'indécence** this verges on the indecent; **le dollar a frôlé la barre des 7 F** the dollar came very close to the 7 F mark.

fromage [fʀɔmaʒ] 1 **nm** cheese. **biscuit/omelette/soufflé au** ~ cheese biscuit/omelette/soufflé; **nouilles au** ~ pasta with cheese (sauce), ≃ macaroni cheese; (*fig*) **trouver un (bon)** ~* to find a cushy job* *ou* cushy number* (*Brit*), get on the gravy train* (*US*); **tu ne vas pas en faire (tout) un** ~!* you don't have to make such a fuss about it!*; *voir* **cloche, plateau, poire.**

2 **comp** ►**fromage blanc** fromage blanc, soft white cheese ►**fromage de chèvre** goat's milk cheese ►**fromage à la crème** cream cheese ►**fromage fermenté** fermented cheese ►**fromage fondu** cheese spread ►**fromage frais** fromage frais, soft white cheese ►**fromage gras** full-fat cheese ►**fromage maigre** low-fat cheese ►**fromage à pâte dure** hard cheese ►**fromage à pâte molle** soft cheese ►**fromage à tartiner** cheese spread ►**fromage de tête** pork brawn.

fromager, -ère [fʀɔmaʒe, ɛʀ] 1 **adj** *industrie, commerce, production* cheese (*épith*). **association ~ère** cheese producers' association. 2 **nm** a (*fabricant*) cheese maker; (*marchand*) cheesemonger (*Brit*), cheese merchant. b (*Bot*) kapok tree.

fromagerie [fʀɔmaʒʀi] **nf** cheese dairy.

froment [fʀɔmɑ̃] **nm** wheat.

from(e)ton‡ [fʀɔmtɔ̃] **nm** cheese.

fronce [fʀɔ̃s] **nf** gather. **~s** gathers, gathering (*NonC*); **faire des ~s** to gather; **jupe à ~s** gathered skirt.

froncement [fʀɔ̃smɑ̃] **nm**: ~ **de sourcils** frown.

froncer [fʀɔ̃se] [3] **vt** (*Couture*) to gather. ~ **les sourcils** to frown, knit one's brows.

frondaison [fʀɔ̃dɛzɔ̃] **nf** (*feuillage*) foliage (*NonC*).

fronde[1] [fʀɔ̃d] **nf** (*arme*) sling; (*jouet*) catapult (*Brit*), slingshot (*US*).

fronde[2] [fʀɔ̃d] **nf** (*révolte*) **esprit/vent de** ~ spirit/wind of revolt *ou* insurrection; (*Hist*) **la F~** the Fronde.

fronder [fʀɔ̃de] [1] **vt** (*railler*) to lampoon, satirize.

frondeur, -euse [fʀɔ̃dœʀ, øz] **adj** *attitude, mentalité* recalcitrant, anti-authority, rebellious; *propos* anti-authority.

front [fʀɔ̃] **nm** a (*Anat*) forehead, brow; (*fig: tête*) head; (*littér: visage*) brow (*littér*), face; (*littér*) *[bâtiment]* façade, front. **il peut marcher le** ~ **haut** he can hold his head (up) high; (*littér*) **la honte sur son** ~ the shame on his brow (*littér*) *ou* face; ~ **de mer** (sea) front; ~ **de taille** coalface; *voir* **courber, frapper.**

b (*Mét, Mil, Pol*) front. **aller** *ou* **monter au** ~ to go up to the front, go into action; **tué au** ~ killed in action; **le** ~ **ennemi** the enemy front; **le F~ populaire** the Popular Front.

c (*loc*) **attaque de** ~ frontal attack; **choc de** ~ head-on crash; **attaquer qn de** ~ (*lit*) to attack sb head-on; (*fig*) to attack sb head-on *ou* face to face; **se heurter de** ~ (*lit*) to collide head-on; (*fig*) to clash head-on; **marcher (à) trois de** ~ to walk three abreast; **mener plusieurs tâches de** ~ to have several tasks in hand *ou* on the go (at one time); **aborder de** ~ **un problème** to tackle a problem head-on; **il va falloir faire** ~ you'll (*ou* we'll *etc*) have to face up to it *ou* to things; **faire** ~ **à l'ennemi/aux difficultés** to face up *ou* stand up to the enemy/difficulties; **faire** ~ **commun contre qn/qch** to join forces against sb/sth, take a united stand against sb/sth; (*littér*) **avoir le** ~ **de faire** to have the effrontery *ou* front to do.

frontal, e, **mpl -aux** [fʀɔ̃tal, o] 1 **adj** *collision* head-on; (*Mil*) *attaque* frontal, head-on; (*Anat, Géom*) frontal. 2 **nm: (os)** ~ frontal (bone).

frontalier, -ière [fʀɔ̃talje, jɛʀ] 1 **adj** *ville, zone* border (*épith*), frontier (*épith*). **travailleurs ~s** people who cross the border every day to work. 2 **nm,f** inhabitant of the border *ou* frontier zone.

frontière [fʀɔ̃tjɛʀ] 1 **nf** (*Géog, Pol*) frontier, border. **à l'intérieur et au-delà de nos ~s** at home and abroad; ~ **naturelle** natural boundary; ~ **linguistique** linguistic boundary; (*fig*) **faire reculer les ~s du savoir/d'une science** to push back the frontiers of knowledge/of a science; (*fig*) **à la** ~ **du rêve et de la réalité** on the borders of dream and reality, on the borderline between dream and reality; *voir* **incident.** 2 **adj inv: ville/zone** ~ frontier *ou* border town/zone; *voir* **garde**[1]**, poste**[2]**.**

frontispice [fʀɔ̃tispis] **nm** frontispiece.

fronton [fʀɔ̃tɔ̃] **nm** (*Archit*) pediment; (*pelote basque*) (front) wall.

frottement [fʀɔtmɑ̃] **nm** (*action*) rubbing; (*bruit*) rubbing (*NonC*), rubbing noise, scraping (*NonC*), scraping noise; (*Tech: contact qui freine*) friction. (*fig*) **~s** friction.

frotter [fʀɔte] [1] 1 **vt** a (*gén*) *peau, membre* to rub; *cheval* to rub down. **frotte tes mains avec du savon** rub your hands with soap; ~ **son doigt sur la table** to rub one's finger on the table; ~ **une allumette** to strike a match; **pain frotté d'ail** bread rubbed with garlic.

b (*pour nettoyer*) *cuivres, meubles* to rub (up), shine; *plancher, casserole, pomme de terre* to scrub; *linge* to rub; *chaussures* (*pour cirer*) to rub (up), shine; (*pour enlever la terre*) to scrape.

c (†, *hum*) ~ **les oreilles à qn** to box sb's ears; **je vais te ~ l'échine** I'm going to beat you black and blue.

2 **vi** to rub, scrape. **la porte frotte (contre le plancher)** the door is rubbing *ou* scraping (against the floor).

3 **se frotter vpr** a (*en se lavant*) to rub o.s. (*lit, fig*) **se ~ les mains** to rub one's hands.

b **se ~ à la bonne société** to rub shoulders with high society; **se ~ à qn** to cross swords with sb; **il vaut mieux ne pas s'y ~** I wouldn't cross swords with him; *voir* **qui**.

frottis [fʀɔti] **nm** (*Méd*) smear; (*Art*) scumble. **se faire faire un ~ (cervico-)vaginal** to have a cervical smear.

frottoir [fʀɔtwaʀ] **nm** (*à allumettes*) friction strip; (*pour le parquet*) (long-handled) brush.

froufrou [fʀufʀu] **nm** rustle, rustling (*NonC*), swish (*NonC*). **faire ~** to rustle, swish; (*dentelles*) **des ~s** frills.

froufroutant, e [fʀufʀutɑ̃, ɑ̃t] **adj** rustling, swishing.

froufroutement [fʀufʀutmɑ̃] **nm** rustle, rustling (*NonC*), swish (*NonC*).

froufrouter [fʀufʀute] [1] **vi** to rustle, swish.

Frounzé [fʀunze] **n** Frounze.

froussard, e* [fʀusaʀ, aʀd] (*péj*) 1 **adj** chicken* (*attrib*), yellow-bellied‡ (*épith*). 2 **nm,f** chicken*, coward.

frousse* [fʀus] **nf** fright. **avoir la ~** to be scared (to death) *ou* scared stiff*; **quand il a sonné j'ai eu la ~** when he rang I really got a fright *ou* the wind up* (*Brit*); **ça lui a fichu la ~** that really put the wind up him* (*Brit*) *ou* gave him a fright, that really scared him (to death) *ou* scared him stiff*; **tu te rappelles la ~ que j'avais avant les examens** you remember how scared I was *ou* the funk‡ (*Brit*) I was in before the exams.

fructidor [fʀyktidɔʀ] **nm** Fructidor (*twelfth month in the French Republican calendar*).

fructifier [fʀyktifje] [7] **vi** *[arbre]* to bear fruit; *[terre]* to be productive; *[idée]* to bear fruit; *[capital, investissement]* to yield a profit. **faire ~ son argent** to make one's money yield a profit.

fructose [fʀyktoz] **nm** fructose.

fructueusement [fʀyktɥøzmɑ̃] **adv** fruitfully, profitably.

fructueux, -euse [fʀyktɥø, øz] **adj** *lectures, spéculation* fruitful, profitable; *collaboration, recherches* fruitful; *commerce* profitable.

frugal, e, mpl -aux [fʀygal, o] **adj** frugal.

frugalement [fʀygalmɑ̃] **adv** frugally.

frugalité [fʀygalite] **nf** frugality.

fruit[1] [fʀɥi] 1 **nm** a fruit (*gén sans pl*). **il y a des ~s/3 ~s dans la coupe** there is some fruit/there are 3 pieces of fruit in the bowl; **passez-moi un ~** pass me some fruit *ou* a piece of fruit; (*espèce*) **l'orange et la banane sont des ~s** the orange and the banana are kinds of fruit *ou* are fruits; *voir* **pâte, salade**.

b (*littér: produit*) fruit(s). **les ~s de la terre/de son travail** the fruits of the earth/of one's work *ou* labour; (*le résultat de*) **c'est le ~ de l'expérience/beaucoup de travail** it is the fruit of experience/of much work *ou* labour; **ils ont perdu le ~ de leur(s) travail/recherches** they lost the fruits of their work *ou* labour/research; **cet enfant est le ~ de leur union** this child is the fruit of their union (*littér*); **porter ses ~s** to bear fruit; **avec ~** fruitfully, profitably, with profit; **sans ~** fruitlessly, to no avail.

2 **comp** ►**fruits confits** candied *ou* glacé fruits ►**fruit défendu** (*Bible, fig*) forbidden fruit ►**fruits déguisés** *prunes or dates stuffed with marzipan* ►**fruits de mer** seafood(s) ►**fruit de la passion** passion fruit ►**fruits rafraîchis** fresh fruit salad (*soaked in alcohol*) ►**fruit sec** (*séché*) dried fruit (*NonC*); (*fig: raté*) failure; **pour quelques étudiants qui trouvent leur voie combien de fruits secs ou d'indifférents!** for the few students who find the right path, how many fall by the wayside or show no interest!

fruit[2] [fʀɥi] **nm** *[mur]* batter.

fruité, e [fʀɥite] **adj** fruity.

fruiterie [fʀɥitʀi] **nf** fruit (and vegetable) store, fruiterer's (shop) (*Brit*), greengrocer's (shop) (*Brit*), greengrocery (*Brit*).

fruiticulteur, -trice [fʀɥitikyltœʀ, tʀis] **nm** fruit farmer.

fruitier, -ière [fʀɥitje, jɛʀ] 1 **adj** fruit (*épith*). 2 **nm,f** fruiterer (*Brit*), greengrocer (*Brit*), fruit seller. 3 **fruitière nf** (*fromagerie*) cheese dairy (*in Savoy, Jura*).

frusques [fʀysk] **nfpl** (*péj*) (*vêtements*) gear* (*NonC*), togs*, clobber‡ (*NonC*) (*Brit*); (*vieux vêtements*) rags.

fruste [fʀyst] **adj** *art, style* crude, unpolished; *manières* unpolished, crude, uncultivated, uncouth; *personne* unpolished, uncultivated, uncouth.

frustrant, e [fʀystʀɑ̃, ɑ̃t] **adj** frustrating.

frustration [fʀystʀasjɔ̃] **nf** (*Psych*) frustration.

frustré, e [fʀystʀe] (**ptp de frustrer**) **adj** (*Psych, gén*) frustrated.

frustrer [fʀystʀe] [1] **vt** a (*priver*) ~ **qn de** *satisfaction* to frustrate *ou* deprive sb of, do sb out of*; (*Jur*) *biens* to defraud sb of; ~ **qn dans ses espoirs/efforts** to thwart *ou* frustrate sb's hopes/efforts, thwart sb in his hopes/efforts; (*Jur*) ~ **qn au profit d'un autre** to defraud one party by favouring another. b (*Psych*) to frustrate.

FS (**abrév de franc suisse**) *voir* **franc**.

FSE [ɛfɛsə] **nm** (**abrév de Fonds social européen**) ESF.

fuchsia [fyʃja] **nm** fuchsia.

fuchsine [fyksin] **nf** fuchsin(e).

fucus [fykys] **nm** wrack, fucus (*SPÉC*). ~ **vésiculeux** bladderwrack.

fuel(-oil) [fjul(ɔjl)] **nm** (*carburant*) fuel oil. ~ **(domestique)** domestic *ou* heating oil.

fugace [fygas] **adj** *parfum, impression, lueur* fleeting; *beauté, fraîcheur* fleeting, transient.

fugacité [fygasite] **nf** (*voir* **fugace**) fleetingness; transience.

fugitif, -ive [fyʒitif, iv] 1 **adj** (*en fuite*) *esclave, épouse* fugitive (*épith*), runaway (*épith*); (*fugace*) *vision, forme, émotion, impression* fleeting; *calme* momentary; *beauté, bonheur* fleeting, transient, short-lived; (*littér*) *jours, années* fleeting. 2 **nm,f** fugitive.

fugitivement [fyʒitivmɑ̃] **adv** *entrevoir* fleetingly. **il pensa ~ à son doux sourire** he thought fleetingly *ou* briefly *ou* momentarily of her sweet smile.

fugue [fyg] **nf** a (*fuite*) running away (*NonC*). **faire une ~** to run away, abscond (*Admin*); **il a fait plusieurs ~s** he ran away several times; **surveillez-le, il fait des ~s** keep an eye on him — he tends to run away *ou* he runs away (a lot); ~ **amoureuse** elopement. b (*Mus*) fugue.

fuguer* [fyge] [1] **vi** to run away *ou* off.

fugueur, -euse [fygœʀ, øz] **nm,f** absconder (*Admin*), runaway. **un élève ~** an absconding pupil.

fuir [fɥiʀ] [17] 1 **vt** a (*éviter*) *personne, coterie, danger* to avoid, shun, fight shy of, flee (*littér*); *mauvais exemple* to avoid, shun; *obligation, responsabilité* to evade, shirk. **on le fuit comme la peste** we avoid him like the plague; (*fig*) **le sommeil/la tranquillité me fuit** sleep/quiet eludes me; (*littér*) ~ **le monde** to flee society, withdraw from the world; (*littér*) **l'homme se fuit** man flees from his inner self.

b (*s'enfuir de*) *patrie, bourreaux, persécuteurs* to flee from, run away from, fly from (*littér*).

2 **vi** a (*s'enfuir*) *[prisonnier]* to run away, escape; *[troupes]* to take flight, flee (*devant* from); *[femme]* (*avec un amant*) to run off; (*pour se marier*) to elope (*avec* with). **faire ~** (*mettre en fuite*) to put to flight; (*chasser*) to chase off *ou* away; **laid à faire ~** repulsively ugly; ~ **devant** *danger, obligations* to run away from; **il a fui chez ses parents** he has fled to his parents.

b (*littér: passer rapidement*) *[esquif]* to speed along, glide swiftly along; *[heures, saison]* to fly by, slip by; *[horizon, paysage]* to recede. **l'été a fui si rapidement** summer flew *ou* slipped *ou* shot by so quickly; **les arbres semblaient ~ de part et d'autre de la route** the trees were whizzing *ou* flashing *ou* shooting past *ou* by on both sides of the road.

c (*s'échapper*) *[gaz]* to leak, escape; *[liquide]* to leak; (*n'être pas étanche*) *[récipient, robinet]* to leak.

fuite [fɥit] **nf** a *[fugitif]* flight, escape; *[prisonnier]* escape; *[amants]* flight; (*pour se marier*) elopement. (*Écon*) **la ~ des capitaux** the flight of capital; ~ **des cerveaux** brain drain; **dans sa ~ il perdit son portefeuille** he lost his wallet as he ran away *ou* in his flight; **la ~ des galaxies** the flight of the galaxies; **chercher la ~ dans le sommeil** to seek escape *ou* flight in sleep; **la ~ en avant du gouvernement dans le domaine économique** the government's relentless pursuit of the same economic policy in spite of all the evidence; (*fig*) **sa ~ devant toute responsabilité est révoltante** his evasion of all responsibility is disgusting; **prendre la ~** to take flight *ou* to one's heels; **mettre qn en ~** to put sb to flight; **les prisonniers sont en ~** the prisoners are on the run; **les voleurs en ~ n'ont pas été retrouvés** the thieves escaped and haven't been found; **renversé par une voiture qui a pris la ~** knocked down by a hit-and-run driver; *voir* **délit**.

b (*littér: passage rapide*) *[esquif]* swift passage; *[temps, heures, saisons]* (swift) passage *ou* passing.

c (*perte de liquide*) leak, leakage; (*fig: d'information*) leak. ~ **de gaz/d'huile** gas/oil leak; **avaries dues à des ~s** damage due to *ou* caused by leakage; **il y a eu des ~s à l'examen** there have been leaks in the exam, questions have been leaked in the exam.

d (*trou*) *[récipient, tuyau]* leak.

e (*Art*) **point de ~** vanishing point.

fulgurant, e [fylgyʀɑ̃, ɑ̃t] **adj** *vitesse, progrès* lightning (*épith*), dazzling; *réplique* lightning (*épith*); *regard* blazing (*épith*), flashing (*épith*). **une douleur ~e me traversa le corps** a searing pain flashed *ou* shot through my body; **une clarté ~e illumina le ciel** a blinding flash lit up the sky.

fulguration [fylgyʀasjɔ̃] **nf** (*lit*) flash (of lightning); (*fig*) flash.

fulgurer [fylgyʀe] [1] **vi** to flash.

fuligineux, -euse [fyliʒinø, øz] **adj** (*littér*) *couleur, flamme* sooty.

fuligule [fyligyl] **nm**: ~ **(morillon)** tufted duck.

fulmar [fylmaʀ] **nm** fulmar.

fulminant, e [fylminɑ̃, ɑ̃t] **adj** a *personne* enraged, livid; *lettre, réponse, regard* angry and threatening. ~ **de colère** enraged, livid (with anger). b (*détonant*) *mélange* explosive. **poudre ~e** fulminating powder; **capsule ~e** percussion cap; **sels ~s** explosive salts (*of*

fulminic acid).
fulminate [fylminat] **nm** fulminate.
fulmination [fylminasjɔ̃] **nf** a (*malédictions*) **~s** denunciations, fulminations. b (*Rel*) fulmination.
fulminer [fylmine] [1] 1 **vt** *reproches, insultes* to thunder forth; (*Rel*) to fulminate. 2 **vi** a (*pester*) to thunder forth. **~ contre** to fulminate *ou* thunder forth against. b (*Chim*) to fulminate, detonate.
fulminique [fylminik] **adj: acide ~** fulminic acid.
fumage [fymaʒ] **nm** (*Culin*) *[saucissons etc]* smoking, curing (*by smoking*); (*Agr*) *[terre]* manuring, dunging.
fumant, e [fymɑ̃, ɑ̃t] **adj** a (*chaud*) *cendres, cratère* smoking; *soupe, corps, naseaux* steaming; (*Chim*) fuming. (*fig*) **un coup ~** a master stroke. b (*en colère*) *patron* fuming* (*attrib*). **~ de colère** fuming with anger.
fumasse‡ [fymas] **adj** fuming* (*attrib*).
fume- [fym] **préf** *voir* **fumer.**
fumé, e[1] [fyme] (**ptp de fumer**) **adj** *jambon, saumon, verre* smoked. **verres ~s** tinted lenses; **aimer le ~** to like smoked food; *voir* **lard.**
fumée[2] [fyme] **nf** a *[combustion]* smoke. **~ de tabac/de cigarettes** tobacco/cigarette smoke; **la ~ ne vous gêne pas?** do you mind my smoking?; **sans ~** *combustible* smokeless; *voir* **avaler, noir, rideau.** b (*vapeur*) *[soupe, étang, corps, naseaux]* steam. (*fig*) **les ~s de l'alcool** *ou* **de l'ivresse** the vapours of alcohol. c (*loc*) **partir** *ou* **s'en aller en ~** to go up in smoke; (*Prov*) **il n'y a pas de ~ sans feu** there's no smoke without fire (*Prov*).
fumer [fyme] [1] 1 **vi** a *[volcan, cheminée, cendres, lampe]* to smoke; *[soupe, étang, corps]* to steam; *[produit chimique]* to emit *ou* give off fumes, fume. b (*: *être en colère*) to be fuming*. **il fumait de rage** he was fuming with rage*. c *[fumeur]* to smoke. **~ comme un sapeur** *ou* **un pompier** *ou* **une locomotive** to smoke like a chimney; *voir* **défense**[1]. 2 **vt** a *cigarettes, tabac* to smoke. **~ la cigarette/le cigare/la pipe** to smoke cigarettes/cigars/a pipe. b (*Culin*) *aliments* to smoke, cure (*by smoking*). c (*Agr*) *sol, terre* to manure. 3 **comp ▸fume-cigare nm inv** cigar holder **▸fume-cigarette nm inv** cigarette holder.
fumerie [fymʀi] **nf: ~ (d'opium)** opium den.
fumerolle [fymʀɔl] **nf** (*gén pl*) (*gaz*) smoke and gas (*emanating from a volcano*); (*fumée*) wisp of smoke.
fumet [fymɛ] **nm** *[plat, viande]* aroma; *[vin]* bouquet, aroma.
fumeur, -euse [fymœʀ, øz] **nm,f** smoker. (*Rail*) **(compartiment) ~s** smoking compartment (*Brit*) *ou* car (*US*), smoker; **je suis non-~** I'm a non-smoker; **(compartiment) non-~s** non-smoking compartment (*Brit*) *ou* car (*US*), non-smoker; **~ d'opium** opium smoker.
fumeux, -euse [fymø, øz] **adj** a (*confus*) *idées, explication* hazy, woolly; *esprit* woolly; *théoricien* woolly-minded. b (*avec de la fumée*) *flamme, clarté* smoky; (*avec de la vapeur*) *horizon, plaine* hazy, misty.
fumier [fymje] **nm** a (*engrais*) dung, manure. **du ~ de cheval** horse-dung *ou* -manure *ou* -muck; **tas de ~** dunghill, dung *ou* muck *ou* manure heap. b (*‡ *péj: salaud*) bastard‡, shit‡.
fumigateur [fymigatœʀ] **nm** (*appareil: Agr, Méd*) fumigator.
fumigation [fymigasjɔ̃] **nf** fumigation.
fumigatoire [fymigatwaʀ] **adj** fumigating, fumigatory.
fumigène [fymiʒɛn] **adj** *engin, grenade* smoke (*épith*). (*Agr*) **(appareil) ~** smoke apparatus.
fumiste [fymist] 1 **nm** (*réparateur-installateur*) heating mechanic; (*ramoneur*) chimney sweep. 2 **nmf** (*péj*) (*paresseux*) (*étudiant, employé*) shirker, skiver‡ (*Brit*); (*plaisantin*) (*philosophe, politicien*) phoney*, fake. 3 **adj** *attitude* (*de paresseux*) shirking; (*de plaisantin*) phoney*. **il est un peu ~ (sur les bords)** he's a bit of a shirker *ou* skiver‡ (*Brit*); he's a bit of a phoney* *ou* fake.
fumisterie [fymistəʀi] **nf** a (*péj*) **c'est une ~** it's a fraud *ou* a con‡; **ce projet est une vaste ~** this project is a massive fraud *ou* a complete con‡; **c'est de la ~** (*tromperie*) it's a fraud *ou* a con‡, it's just eyewash* (*Brit*). b (*établissement*) (heating mechanic's) workshop; (*métier*) stove-building.
fumoir [fymwaʀ] **nm** (*salon*) smoking room; (*Ind*) smokehouse.
fumure [fymyʀ] **nf** manuring; (*substance*) manure (*NonC*).
funambule [fynɑ̃byl] **nmf** tightrope walker, funambulist (*SPÉC*). **artiste ~** tightrope artiste.
funambulesque [fynɑ̃bylɛsk] **adj** (*lit*) *prouesse, art* of tightrope walking; (*fig: bizarre*) *idée, organisation* fantastic, bizarre.
funèbre [fynɛbʀ] **adj** a (*de l'enterrement*) *service, marche, décoration, oraison* funeral (*épith*); *cérémonie, éloge, discours* funeral (*épith*), funerary (*épith*). **air ~** dirge; *voir* **entrepreneur, pompe**[2]**, veillée.** b (*lugubre*) *mélodie, ton* mournful, doleful; *silence, air, allure* lugubrious, funereal; *atmosphère, couleur, décor* gloomy, dismal.
funèbrement [fynɛbʀəmɑ̃] **adv** (*littér*) funereally, lugubriously.
funérailles [fyneʀɑj] **nfpl** (*frm: enterrement*) funeral, obsequies (*littér*).
funéraire [fyneʀɛʀ] **adj** *dalle, monument, urne* funeral (*épith*), funerary (*épith*). **pierre ~** gravestone; (*Can*) **salon ~** funeral home (*US, Can*) *ou* parlor (*US, Can*).
funérarium [fyneʀaʀjɔm] **nm** *place where funeral guests gather before the service.*
funeste [fynɛst] **adj** a (*désastreux*) *erreur* disastrous, grievous; *conseil, décision* disastrous, harmful; *influence* baneful, harmful; *suite, conséquence* dire, disastrous. **loin d'imaginer les suites ~s de cet accident** far from imagining the dire *ou* disastrous *ou* tragic consequences of that accident; **le jour ~ où je l'ai rencontrée** the fateful *ou* ill-fated day upon which I met her; **politique ~ aux intérêts du pays** policy harmful to the country's interests. b (*de mort*) *pressentiment, vision* deathly (*épith*), of death. c (*littér: mortel*) *accident* fatal; *coup* fatal, lethal, deadly, mortal.
funiculaire [fynikylɛʀ] **nm** funicular (railway).
funk [fœnk] 1 **adj** funk (*épith*), funky. 2 **nm** funk.
funky [fœnki] **adj** funky.
FUNU [fyny] **nf** (**abrév de Force d'urgence des Nations Unies**) UNEF.
fur [fyʀ] **nm** a **au ~ et à mesure: classer/nettoyer qch au ~ et à mesure** to file/clean sth as one goes along; **dépenser au ~ et à mesure** to spend as fast *ou* as soon as one earns; **il vaut mieux leur donner leur argent de poche au ~ et à mesure qu'en une fois** it's better to give them their pocket money in dribs and drabs* *ou* as they need it rather than all in one go; **le frigidaire se vidait au ~ et à mesure** the fridge was emptied as fast as it was stocked up; **passe-moi les assiettes au ~ et à mesure** pass the plates to me as you go along.
b **au ~ et à mesure que: donnez-les-nous au ~ et à mesure que vous les recevez** give them to us as (soon as) you receive them; **nous dépensions tout notre argent au ~ et à mesure que nous le gagnions** we spent all our money as fast as *ou* as soon as we earned it.
c **au ~ et à mesure de: au ~ et à mesure de leur progression** as they advanced, the further they advanced; **prenez-en au ~ et à mesure de vos besoins** take some as and when you need them, help yourselves as you find you need them.
furax‡ [fyʀaks] **adj inv** (*furieux*) livid (*attrib*), hopping mad* (*attrib*).
furet [fyʀɛ] **nm** (*animal*) ferret; (*jeu*) pass-the-slipper; (†: *curieux*) pry.
furetage [fyʀ(ə)taʒ] **nm** (*voir* **fureter**) nosing *ou* ferreting *ou* prying about; rummaging (about).
fureter [fyʀ(ə)te] [5] **vi** (*regarder partout*) to nose *ou* ferret *ou* pry about; (*fouiller partout: dans un tiroir etc*) to rummage (about).
fureteur, -euse [fyʀ(ə)tœʀ, øz] 1 **adj** *regard, enfant* prying, inquisitive. 2 **nm,f** pry.
fureur [fyʀœʀ] **nf** a (*NonC: colère*) fury; (*accès de colère*) fit of rage. **crise** *ou* **accès de ~** fit of rage, furious outburst; **être pris de ~** to be seized with anger, fly into a rage (*contre qn* at sb); **être/entrer en ~** to be/become infuriated *ou* enraged; **être/entrer dans une ~ noire** to be in/go *ou* fly into a towering rage; **mettre en ~** to infuriate, enrage; **se mettre dans des ~s folles** to have mad fits of rage, fly into wild fits of anger.
b (*violence*) *[passion]* violence, fury; *[combat, attaque]* fury, furiousness; *[tempête, flots, vents]* fury.
c (*passion*) **la ~ du jeu** a passion *ou* mania for gambling; **il a la ~ de la vitesse/de lire** he has a mania for speed/reading; **la ~ de vivre** the lust *ou* passion for life.
d (*littér: transe*) **~ prophétique** prophetic frenzy; **~ poétique** poetic ecstasy *ou* frenzy.
e (*loc*) **avec ~** (*avec rage*) with rage, furiously; (*à la folie*) wildly, madly, passionately; **aimer qch/qn à la ~** to love sth/sb wildly *ou* madly *ou* passionately; **faire ~** to be all the rage.
furibard, e* [fyʀibaʀ, aʀd] **adj** hopping mad* (*attrib*), livid, mad* (*attrib*).
furibond, e [fyʀibɔ̃, ɔ̃d] **adj** *personne* hopping mad* (*attrib*), livid, mad* (*attrib*); *colère* wild, furious; *ton, voix, yeux* enraged, furious.
furie [fyʀi] **nf** a (*péj: mégère*) shrew, termagant; (*Myth*) Fury. b (*violence*) *[attaque, combat]* fury, furiousness; *[tempête, flots]* fury; *[passions]* violence, fury. c (*passion*) **la ~ du jeu** a passion *ou* mania for gambling. d (*colère*) fury. e (*loc*) **en ~** *personne* infuriated, enraged, in a rage (*attrib*); *mer* raging; *tigre* enraged; **mettre qn en ~** to infuriate sb, enrage sb.
furieusement [fyʀjøzmɑ̃] **adv** (*avec fureur*) *attaquer* furiously; *répondre* angrily; (*gén hum: extrêmement*) *ressembler* amazingly, tremendously. **j'ai ~ envie d'une glace à la fraise** I'm simply dying for* *ou* I've got a terrible hankering for a strawberry ice cream.
furieux, -ieuse [fyʀjø, jøz] **adj** a (*violent*) *combat, résistance* furious, violent; *tempête* raging, furious, violent; *voir* **folie, fou.** b (*en colère*) *personne, animal* furious (*contre* with, at); *ton, geste* furious. **elle est ~euse d'avoir refusé** she is furious at having refused; **il est ~ que je lui aie menti** he is furious with *ou* at me for having lied. c (*gén hum: fort*) *envie, coup* almighty* (*épith*), tremendous. **avoir un ~ appétit** to have an almighty* *ou* a prodigious appetite.
furoncle [fyʀɔ̃kl] **nm** boil, furuncle (*SPÉC*).
furonculose [fyʀɔ̃kyloz] **nf** (recurrent) boils, furunculosis (*SPÉC*).
furtif, -ive [fyʀtif, iv] **adj** *coup d'œil, geste* furtive, stealthy; *joie* secret; *voir* **avion.**
furtivement [fyʀtivmɑ̃] **adv** furtively, stealthily.
fusain [fyzɛ̃] **nm** (*crayon*) charcoal (crayon); (*croquis*) charcoal (drawing); (*arbrisseau*) spindle-tree. **dessiner au ~** to draw in charcoal; **tracé au ~** charcoal(-drawn), (drawn) in charcoal.
fuseau, pl ~x [fyzo] 1 **nm** a *[fileuse]* spindle; *[dentelière]* bobbin. b **(pantalon) ~, ~x** stretch ski pants. c (*loc*) **en (forme de) ~** *colonne* with a swelling; *cuisses, jambes* slender; **arbuste taillé en ~** shrub

shaped into a cone. 2 comp ▸ **fuseau horaire** time zone.

fusée [fyze] 1 nf a (*spatiale*) rocket; (*missile*) rocket, missile. ~ **air-air/sol-air** air-to-air/ground-to-air missile; *voir* **avion.** b *[feu d'artifice]* rocket; *[obus, mine]* fuse. **partir comme une** ~ to shoot *ou* whizz off like a rocket. c (*Tech*) *[essieu]* spindle; (*Aut*) stub axle; *[montre]* fusee.
2 comp ▸ **fusée antichar** anti-tank rocket ▸ **fusée de détresse** distress rocket ▸ **fusée éclairante** flare ▸ **fusée-engin** nf (pl **fusées-engins**) rocket shell ▸ **fusée à étages, fusée gigogne** multi-stage rocket ▸ **fusée interplanétaire** (interplanetary) space rocket ▸ **fusée de lancement** launch vehicle ▸ **fusée-sonde** nf (pl **fusées-sondes**) (rocket powering a) space probe.

fuselage [fyz(ə)laʒ] nm *[avion]* fuselage.

fuselé, e [fyz(ə)le] adj *colonne* swelled; *doigts* tapering, slender; *cuisses, jambes* slender.

fuséologie [fyzeɔlɔʒi] nf rocket technology.

fuser [fyze] 1 vi a *[cris, rires]* to burst forth; *[liquide]* to gush *ou* spurt out; *[étincelles]* to fly (out); *[lumière]* to stream out *ou* forth. b *[bougie]* to run; *[pile]* to sweat; *[poudre]* to burn out.

fusibilité [fyzibilite] nf fusibility.

fusible [fyzibl] 1 adj fusible. 2 nm (*fil*) fuse(-wire); (*fiche*) fuse.

fusiforme [fyzifɔʀm] adj spindle-shaped, fusiform (*SPÉC*).

fusil [fyzi] 1 nm a (*arme*) (*de guerre, à canon rayé*) rifle, gun; (*de chasse, à canon lisse*) shotgun, gun. (*fig*) **c'est un bon** ~ he's a good shot; (*Mil* †) **un groupe de 30 ~s** a group of 30 riflemen *ou* rifles; (*fig*) **changer son ~ d'épaule** to change one's plans; **coup de** ~ gun shot, rifle shot; (*fig*) **c'est le coup de** ~ the prices are extortionate, you pay through the nose*.
b (*allume-gaz*) gas lighter; (*instrument à aiguiser*) steel.
2 comp ▸ **fusil à canon rayé** rifle, rifled gun ▸ **fusil à canon scié** sawn-off (*Brit*) *ou* sawed-off (*US*) shotgun ▸ **fusil de chasse** shotgun, hunting gun ▸ **fusil à deux coups** double-barrelled *ou* twin-barrel rifle ▸ **fusil de guerre** army rifle ▸ **fusil à harpon** harpoon gun ▸ **fusil à lunette** rifle with telescopic sight ▸ **fusil-mitrailleur** (pl ~s-~s) machine gun ▸ **fusil à pompe** pump-action shotgun ▸ **fusil à répétition** repeating rifle ▸ **fusil sous-marin** (underwater) speargun.

fusilier [fyzilje] nm rifleman, fusilier; (*Hist*) fusilier. **les ~s** (*régiment*) the rifles; (*Hist*) the fusiliers; ~ **marin** marine.

fusillade [fyzijad] nf (*bruit*) fusillade (*frm*), gunfire (*NonC*), shooting (*NonC*); (*combat*) shoot-out, shooting battle; (*exécution*) shooting.

fusiller [fyzije] 1 vt a (*exécuter*) to shoot. ~ **qn du regard** to look daggers at sb. b (*: *casser*) to bust*. c (*: *dépenser*) to blow*.

fusion [fyzjɔ̃] nf a *[métal etc]* melting, fusion; *[glace]* melting, thawing. **en** ~ *métal* molten. b (*Bio, Phys*) fusion; *[atomes]* (nuclear) fusion. c (*union*) *[cœurs, esprits, races]* fusion; *[partis]* merging, combining; *[systèmes, philosophies]* blending, merging, uniting; (*Comm*) *[sociétés]* merger, amalgamation. **la ~ de l'individu en Dieu/dans la nature** the union of the individual with God/nature.

fusionnement [fyzjɔnmɑ̃] nm (*Comm*) merger, amalgamation; (*Pol*) merging, combining.

fusionner [fyzjɔne] 1 vti (*Comm*) to merge, amalgamate; (*Pol*) to merge, combine; (*Ordin*) to merge.

fustanelle [fystanɛl] nf fustanella.

fustigation [fystigasjɔ̃] nf (*littér: voir* **fustiger**) flaying; censuring, denouncing, denunciation; birching, thrashing.

fustiger [fystiʒe] 3 vt a (*littér: critiquer*) *adversaire* to flay; *pratiques, mœurs* to censure, denounce. b (††: *fouetter*) to birch, thrash.

fût [fy] nm a *[arbre]* bole, trunk; *[colonne]* shaft; *[fusil]* stock. b (*tonneau*) barrel, cask.

futaie [fytɛ] nf (*groupe d'arbres*) cluster of (tall) trees; (*forêt*) forest (*of tall trees*); (*Sylviculture*) plantation of trees (*for timber*). **haute** ~ mature (standing) timber.

futaille [fytɑj] nf (*barrique*) barrel, cask.

futaine [fytɛn] nf (*Tex*) fustian.

futal*, pl ~s [fytal] nm bags* (*Brit*), (pair of) trousers (*Brit*), (pair of) pants (*US*).

futé, e [fyte] adj wily, crafty, cunning, sly. **c'est une petite ~e** she's a crafty *ou* sly little minx.

futile [fytil] adj (*inutile*) *entreprise, tentative* futile, pointless; (*frivole*) *raison, souci, occupation, propos* trifling, trivial, futile; *personne, esprit* trivial, frivolous.

futilement [fytilmɑ̃] adv (*frivolement*) frivolously.

futilité [fytilite] nf a (*NonC: voir* **futile**) futility; pointlessness; triviality; frivolousness. b **~s** trivialities.

futur, e [fytyʀ] 1 adj (*prochain*) *génération, désastres, besoins* future (*épith*). (*Rel*) **dans la vie ~e** in the life to come, in the afterlife, in the hereafter; ~ **mari** husband-to-be; **les ~s époux** the bride and groom-to-be; **tout pour la ~e maman** everything for the mother-to-be; ~ **collègue/directeur/soldat** future colleague/director/soldier; ~ **client** intending *ou* prospective customer; (*en herbe*) **un ~ président/champion** a budding *ou* future president/champion.
2 nm a (*conjoint*) fiancé, husband-to-be, intended†.
b (*avenir*) future.
c (*Ling*) **le** ~ the future (tense); (*fig*) **parlez-en au** ~ don't count your chickens (before they're hatched); **le ~ proche** the immediate future; **le ~ simple** the future (tense); **le ~ antérieur** *ou* **du passé** the future perfect *ou* anterior.
3 **future** nf (*conjointe*) fiancée, wife-to-be, intended†.

futurisme [fytyʀism] nm futurism.

futuriste [fytyʀist] 1 nmf futurist. 2 adj futuristic.

futurologie [fytyʀɔlɔʒi] nf futurology.

futurologue [fytyʀɔlɔg] nmf futurist, futurologist.

fuyant, e [fɥijɑ̃, ɑ̃t] adj a (*insaisissable*) *regard, air* evasive; *personne, caractère* elusive, evasive. b (*en retrait*) *menton, front* receding (*épith*). c (*littér: fugitif*) *ombre, vision* fleeting (*épith*). d (*Art*) *vues, lignes* receding (*épith*), vanishing (*épith*); *perspective* vanishing (*épith*).

fuyard, e [fɥijaʀ, aʀd] nm,f runaway.

G

G, g [ʒe] **nm** (*lettre*) G, g. **le G-7** the G7 nations, the Group of Seven.

g **abrév de gramme.**

GAB (**abrév de guichet automatique de banque**) cash dispenser (*Brit*), ATM (*US*).

gabardine [gabaʀdin] **nf** (*tissu*) gabardine; (*manteau*) gabardine (raincoat).

gabarit [gabaʀi] **nm** a (*dimension*) *[objet, véhicule]* size. b (*) *[personne]* (*taille*) size, build; (*valeur*) calibre. **ce n'est pas le petit ~!** he's not exactly small!, he's rather on the large side!; **du même ~** of the same build; **il n'a pas le ~ d'un directeur commercial** he hasn't got what it takes *ou* he isn't of the right calibre to be a sales manager. c (*Tech*) (*appareil de mesure*) gauge; (*maquette*) template; *voir* **hors.**

gabegie [gabʒi] **nf** (*péj*) chaos, muddle, mess. **c'est une vraie ~!** it's a real mess!, it's total chaos!

gabelle [gabɛl] **nf** (*Hist: impôt*) salt tax, gabelle.

gabelou [gablu] **nm** (*Hist*) salt-tax collector; (*péj*) customs officer.

gabier [gabje] **nm** (*Naut*) topman.

Gabon [gabɔ̃] **nm** (the) Gabon.

gabonais, e [gabɔnɛ, ɛz] 1 **adj** Gabonese. 2 **nm,f: G~(e)** Gabonese.

Gaborone [gabɔʀɔn] **n** Gaborone.

Gabriel [gabʀijɛl] **nm** Gabriel.

Gabrielle [gabʀijɛl] **nf** Gabrielle.

gâchage [gɑʃaʒ] **nm** (*voir* **gâcher**) tempering; mixing; wasting; botching.

gâche [gɑʃ] **nf** *[maçon]* (plasterer's) trowel; *[serrure]* striking plate, strike (plate); (*Imprimerie*) spoilage.

gâcher [gɑʃe] 1 **vt** a *plâtre* to temper; *mortier* to mix. b (*gaspiller*) *argent, talent, temps* to waste, fritter away; *nourriture* to waste; (*rater*) *occasion* to waste, lose; (*bâcler*) *travail* to botch. **~ sa vie** to fritter away *ou* waste one's life; **une vie gâchée** a wasted *ou* misspent life. c (*gâter*) to spoil. **il nous a gâché le** *ou* **notre plaisir** he spoiled our pleasure (for us); **il gâche le métier** he spoils it for others (*by selling cheap or working for a low salary*).

gâchette [gɑʃɛt] **nf** *[arme]* trigger; *[serrure]* tumbler. **appuyer** *ou* **presser sur la ~** to pull the trigger; **il a la ~ facile** he's trigger-happy.

gâcheur, -euse [gɑʃœʀ, øz] 1 **adj** wasteful. 2 **nm,f** a (*de matériel*) wasteful person; (*d'argent*) spendthrift; (*de travail*) bungler, botcher. b (*péj: snob, délicat*) fusspot*, fussy person. **quel ~, il ne supporte que les cravates en soie!** what a fussy dresser — he won't wear anything but silk ties! 3 **nm** (*ouvrier*) builder's mate (*who mixes cement or tempers plaster*).

gâchis [gɑʃi] **nm** a (*désordre*) mess. **tu as fait un beau ~!** you've made a fine mess of it! b (*gaspillage*) waste (*NonC*). c (*Tech*) mortar.

gadget [gadʒɛt] **nm** (*gén: machin*) thingummy* (*Brit*), gizmo* (*US*); (*jouet, ustensile*) gadget; (*procédé, trouvaille*) gimmick.

gadgétiser [gadʒetize] 1 **vt** to equip with gadgets.

gadin* [gadɛ̃] **nm: prendre** *ou* **ramasser un ~** to come a cropper* (*Brit*), fall flat on one's face.

gadolinium [gadɔlinjɔm] **nm** gadolinium.

gadoue [gadu] **nf** (*boue*) mud, sludge; (*neige*) slush; (*engrais*) night soil.

GAEC [gaɛk] **nm** (**abrév de groupement agricole d'exploitation en commun**) *voir* **groupement.**

gaélique [gaelik] 1 **adj** Gaelic. 2 **nm** (*Ling*) Gaelic.

gaffe [gaf] **nf** a (*bévue*) blunder, boob* (*Brit*). **faire une ~** (*action*) to make a blunder *ou* a boob* (*Brit*); (*parole*) to drop a clanger* (*Brit*). b (*perche*) (*Naut*) boat hook; (*Pêche*) gaff. c (*) **faire ~** to pay attention (*à* to); **fais ~!** watch out!, be careful!; **fais ~ à toi** watch yourself.

gaffer [gafe] 1 1 **vi** (*bévue*) to blunder, boob* (*Brit*); (*paroles*) to drop a clanger* (*Brit*), put one's foot in it*. **j'ai gaffé?** have I put my foot in it?, have I made a boob*? (*Brit*). 2 **vt** a (*Naut*) to hook; (*Pêche*) to gaff. b (‡: *regarder*) **gaffe un peu la fille!** take a look at that bird!‡ (*Brit*) *ou* chick!‡ (*US*).

gaffeur, -euse [gafœʀ, øz] **nm,f** blunderer, blundering fool. **il est drôlement ~!** he's always putting his foot in it!, he's a blundering fool!

gag [gag] **nm** (*gén, Ciné, Théât*) gag.

gaga* [gaga] **adj** *vieillard* gaga*, senile. **sa fille le rend ~** he's putty in his daughter's hands, his daughter can wind him round her little finger.

gage [gaʒ] **nm** a (*à un créancier, arbitre*) security; (*à un prêteur*) pledge. **mettre qch en ~ (chez le prêteur)** to pawn sth (at the pawnbroker's); **laisser qch en ~** to leave sth as (a) security; *voir* **prêteur.**

b (*garantie*) guarantee. **sa bonne forme physique est un ~ de succès** his fitness will guarantee him success *ou* assure him of success.

c (*témoignage*) proof, evidence (*NonC*). **donner des ~s de sa sincérité/son talent** to give proof *ou* evidence of one's sincerity/talent; **donner à qn un ~ d'amour/de fidélité** to give sb a token of one's love/faithfulness; **en ~ de notre amitié/de ma bonne foi** as a token *ou* in token of our friendship/of my good faith.

d (*Jeux*) forfeit.

e (†: *salaire*) **~s** wages; **être aux ~s de qn** (*gén*) to be employed by sb; (*péj*) to be in the pay of sb; *voir* **tueur.**

gager [gaʒe] 3 **vt** a (*frm: parier*) **~ que** to wager that, bet that; **gageons que ..., je gage que ...** I bet (you) that ... . b *emprunt* to guarantee.

gageure [gaʒyʀ] **nf** a (*entreprise difficile*) **c'est une véritable ~ que de vouloir tenter seul cette ascension** it's attempting the impossible to try to do this climb alone; **il a réussi la ~ de faire cette ascension tout seul** he achieved the impossible — he managed to do the climb on his own, despite the odds he managed to do the climb on his own. b (††: *pari*) wager.

gagnable [gaɲabl] **adj** winnable.

gagnant, e [gaɲɑ̃, ɑ̃t] 1 **adj** *numéro, combinaison, point etc* winning (*épith*). **on donne ce concurrent ~** this competitor is the favourite to win *ou* is expected to win; **il joue** *ou* **part ~ dans cette affaire** he's bound to win *ou* come out on top in this deal; **tu es ~** you can't lose (out); (*Jur*) **la partie ~e** the prevailing party. 2 **nm,f** winner.

gagne- [gaɲ] **préf** *voir* **gagner.**

gagner [gaɲe] 1 1 **vt** a (*acquérir par le travail*) to earn. **~ sa vie** to earn one's living (*à faire* by doing); **elle gagne mal sa vie** she doesn't earn much; **elle gagne bien sa vie** she earns a good living; **~ son pain** to earn one's daily bread; **~ de l'argent** (*par le travail*) to earn *ou* make money; (*dans une affaire*) to make money; **~ de quoi vivre** to earn a living; **~ des mille et des cents*** to earn *ou* make a packet*; **~ sa croûte*** *ou* **son bifteck*** to earn one's crust *ou* one's bread and butter; **il gagne bien sa croûte dans cet emploi*** he earns a good wage in that job.

b (*mériter*) to earn. **il a bien gagné ses vacances** he's really earned his holiday.

c (*acquérir par le hasard*) *prix, somme* to win. (*lit, fig*) **~ le gros lot** to hit *ou* win the jackpot.

d (*obtenir*) *réputation etc* to gain. **vous n'y gagnerez rien** you'll gain nothing by it; **vous n'y gagnerez rien de bon** you'll get nothing out of it; **~ du temps** (*temporiser*) to gain time; (*économiser*) to save time; **chercher à ~ du temps** to play for time; **~ du poids** to put on *ou* gain weight; **~ de la place** to save space; **c'est toujours ça de gagné!** that's always something!; **c'est toujours 10 F de gagné** at least that's 10 francs saved *ou* that's saved us 10 francs; **l'indice CAC 40 gagne 4 points** the CAC 40 index is up 4 points; **à sortir par ce temps, vous y gagnerez un bon rhume** you'll get nothing but a bad cold going out in this weather; **ce n'est pas gagné d'avance** we (*ou* they *etc*) have not won yet.

e (*être vainqueur de*) *bataille, procès, course* to win. **le match/procès n'est pas gagné** the match/action hasn't been won yet; (†) **~ qn aux échecs** to beat sb at chess; **~ qn de vitesse** to beat sb to it*.

f (*se concilier*) *gardiens, témoins* to win over. **~ l'estime/le cœur de qn** to win sb's esteem *ou* regard/heart; **~ la confiance de qn** to win *ou* gain sb's confidence; **savoir se ~ des amis/des partisans** to know how to win friends/supporters; **se laisser ~ par les prières de qn** to be won over by sb's prayers; **~ qn à une cause** to win sb over to a cause; **~ qn à sa cause** to win sb over.

g (*envahir*) **le sommeil les gagnait** sleep was creeping over them *ou* was gradually overcoming them; **la gangrène gagne la jambe** the gangrene is spreading to his leg; **le froid les gagnait** they were beginning to feel the cold; **le feu gagna rapidement les rues voisines** the fire quickly spread to the neighbouring streets; **l'eau/l'ennemi gagne du terrain** the water/the enemy is gaining ground.

h (*atteindre*) *lieu, frontière, refuge* to reach. **~ le port** to reach port; **~ le large** (*Naut*) to get out into the open sea.

2 **vi** a (*être vainqueur*) to win. **~ aux courses** to win on the horses *ou* at the races; **il a gagné aux courses hier** he had a win at the races yesterday; **il gagne sur tous les tableaux** he's winning all the way *ou* on all fronts; (*iro*) **eh bien, tu as gagné!** well, you got what you asked for!*

b (*trouver un avantage*) **vous y gagnez** it's in your interest, it's to your advantage; **vous gagnerez à ce que personne ne le sache** it'll be to your advantage *ou* it will be better for you if nobody knows about it; **qu'est-ce que j'y gagne?** what do I get out of it? *ou* gain from it?, what's in it for me?; **vous gagneriez à partir en groupe** you'd be better off going in a group; **tu aurais gagné à te taire!** you would have done better to keep quiet!; **~ au change** to make (something) on the deal.

c (*s'améliorer*) **~ en hauteur** to increase in height; **son style gagne en force ce qu'il perd en élégance** his style gains in vigour what it loses in elegance; **ce vin gagnera à vieillir** this wine will improve with age; **il gagne à être connu** he improves on acquaintance; **ce roman gagne à être relu** this novel gains by a second reading, this novel is better at a second reading.

d (*s'étendre*) *[incendie, épidémie]* to spread, gain ground. **la mer gagne sur les falaises** the sea is encroaching *ou* advancing on the cliffs.

3 **comp** ▶**gagne-pain*** **nm inv** (*travail*) job; (*instrument*) source of income ▶**gagne-petit** **nm inv** low wage earner; **c'est un gagne-petit** he doesn't earn much (money).

gagneur, -euse [gaɲœʀ, øz] **nm,f** winner, go-getter*.

gai, e [ge] 1 **adj** a (*joyeux*) *personne, vie* cheerful, gay, happy; *voix, visage* cheery, cheerful, happy; *roman, conversation, musique* cheerful, gay; *caractère* cheerful, merry. **c'est un ~ luron** he's a cheery *ou* happy fellow; **~ comme un pinson** happy as a lark; **tu n'as pas l'air (bien) ~** you don't look too happy.

b (*euph: ivre*) merry, tipsy.

c (*riant*) *couleur, robe* bright, gay; *pièce* bright, cheerful. **on va peindre la chambre en jaune pour faire ~** we're going to paint the bedroom yellow to brighten it up.

d (*iro: amusant*) **j'ai oublié mon parapluie, c'est ~!** that's great*, I've forgotten my umbrella! (*iro*); **ça ne va pas être ~** *ou* **ça va être ~ la rentrée sur Paris, dimanche!** it's going to be great fun, going back to Paris this Sunday! (*iro*); **ça va être ~, les vacances avec lui!** I can see we're going to have a good holiday *ou* the holidays are going to be great fun with him around! (*iro*).

e (*homosexuel*) gay.

2 **nm** (*homosexuel*) gay.

gaiement [gemɑ̃] **adv** (*voir* **gai**) cheerfully; gaily; happily; cheerily; merrily. (*iro*) **allons-y ~!** come on then, let's get on with it!; (*iro*) **il va recommencer ~ à faire les mêmes bêtises** he'll blithely *ou* gaily start the same old tricks again.

gaieté [gete] **nf** *[personne, caractère]* cheerfulness, gaiety; *[couleur]* brightness, gaiety; *[conversation, pièce, roman]* cheerfulness, gaiety. **plein de ~** *fête, maison* cheerful; **ses films sont rarement d'une ~ folle** his films are not exactly cheerful; **ce n'est pas de ~ de cœur qu'il accepta** it was with no light heart *ou* with some reluctance that he accepted.

gaillard, e [gajaʀ, aʀd] 1 **adj** a (*alerte*) *personne* strong; *allure* lively, springy, sprightly. **vieillard encore ~** sprightly *ou* spry old man. b (*grivois*) *propos* bawdy, ribald. 2 **nm** a (*costaud*) **(robuste** *ou* **grand** *ou* **beau) ~** strapping *ou* hale and hearty *ou* robust fellow. b (*: *type*) fellow, chap* (*Brit*), guy*. **toi, mon ~, je t'ai à l'œil!** I've got my eye on you, chum!* *ou* mate!* (*Brit*). 3 **gaillarde nf** a (*) (*femme forte*) strapping wench* *ou* woman*. (*femme hardie*) **c'est une sacrée ~e** she's quite a woman!* b (*Mus*) galliard. 4 **comp** ▶**gaillard d'arrière** (*Hist*) quarter-deck ▶**gaillard (d'avant)** forecastle (head), fo'c'sle.

gaillardement [gajaʀdəmɑ̃] **adv** (*avec bonne humeur*) cheerfully; (*sans faiblir*) bravely, gallantly. **ils attaquèrent la côte ~** they set off energetically *ou* stoutly up the hill; **il porte ~ sa soixantaine** he's a sprightly *ou* vigorous sixty-year-old.

gaillardise [gajaʀdiz] **nf** bawdy *ou* ribald remark.

gaîment [gemɑ̃] **adv = gaiement.**

gain [gɛ̃] **nm** a (*salaire*) (*gén*) earnings; *[ouvrier]* earnings, wages, wage. **pour un ~ modeste** for a modest wage.

b (*lucre*) **le ~** gain; **pousser qn au ~** to push *ou* urge sb to make money; **l'amour du ~** the love of money.

c (*bénéfices*) **~s** *[société]* profits; (*au jeu*) winnings; (*à la Bourse*) profits; **se retirer sur son ~** (*jeu*) to pull out with one's winnings intact; (*spéculation*) to retire on one's profits *ou* with what one has made; **~s illicites** illicit gains; **compensation des ~s et des pertes** compensation of gains and losses.

d (*avantage matériel*) *[élections, guerre de conquête]* gains. **ce ~ de 3 sièges leur donne la majorité** winning *ou* gaining these 3 seats has given them a majority.

e (*avantage spirituel*) benefit. **tirer un ~ (énorme) de qch** to gain *ou* draw (great) benefit from sth.

f (*économie*) saving. **~ de temps/d'argent/de place** saving of time/of money/of space; **ce procédé permet un ~ de cinquante minutes/d'électricité** this procedure saves 50 minutes/electricity; **ça nous permet un ~ de temps** it's time-saving, it saves us time.

g (*littér: obtention*) *[bataille, procès]* winning; *[fortune, voix d'électeurs]* gaining.

h **~ de cause: avoir** *ou* **obtenir ~ de cause** (*lit*) to win the case; (*fig*) to be proved *ou* pronounced right; **on ne voulait pas me rembourser mais j'ai fini par avoir ~ de cause** they didn't want to reimburse me but in the end I won my claim; **donner ~ de cause à qn** (*Jur*) to decide the case in favour of sb; (*fig*) to pronounce sb right.

gaine [gɛn] **nf** (*Habillement*) girdle; (*Bot, fourreau*) sheath; (*piédestal*) plinth; (*enveloppe*) *[obus]* priming tube. **~ d'aération** ventilation shaft; **~ culotte** panty girdle.

gainer [gene] 1 **vt** to cover. **jambes gainées de soie** legs sheathed in silk; **objet gainé de cuir** leather-covered *ou* -cased object.

gaîté [gete] **nf = gaieté.**

gala [gala] **nm** official reception; (*pour collecter des fonds*) fund-raising reception. **de ~** *soirée, représentation* gala (*épith*); **~ de bienfaisance** reception for charity.

Galaad [galaad] **nm** Galahad.

galactique [galaktik] **adj** galactic.

galactogène [galaktɔʒɛn] **adj** galactagogue (*SPÉC*). **glande ~** milk gland.

galactomètre [galaktɔmɛtʀ] **nm** lactometer.

galactophore [galaktɔfɔʀ] **adj: canal ~** milk duct; **glande ~** milk gland.

galactose [galaktoz] **nm** galactose.

Galalithe [galalit] **nf** ® Galalith ®.

galamment [galamɑ̃] **adv** courteously, gallantly. **se conduire ~** to behave courteously *ou* gallantly *ou* in a gentlemanly fashion.

galandage [galɑ̃daʒ] **nm** (brick) partition.

galant, e [galɑ̃, ɑ̃t] 1 **adj** a (*courtois*) gallant, courteous, gentlemanly. **soyez ~, ouvrez-lui la porte** be a gentleman and open the door for her; **c'est un ~ homme** he is a gentleman. b *ton, humeur, propos* flirtatious, gallant; *scène, tableau* amorous, romantic; *conte* racy, spicy; *rendez-vous* romantic; *poésie* amorous, courtly. **en ~e compagnie** *homme* with a lady friend (*hum*); *femme* with a gentleman friend (*hum*). 2 **nm** (††, *hum: soupirant*) gallant††, suitor††, admirer (†, *hum*).

galanterie [galɑ̃tʀi] **nf** (*courtoisie*) gallantry, chivalry; (*propos*) gallant remark.

galantine [galɑ̃tin] **nf** galantine.

Galapagos [galapagɔs] **nfpl: les (îles) ~** the Galapagos (Islands).

galapiat† [galapja] **nm** (*polisson*) rapscallion†, scamp.

Galatée [galate] **nf** Galatea.

Galates [galat] **nmpl** (*Bible*) Galatians.

galaxie [galaksi] **nf** galaxy.

galbe [galb] **nm** *[meuble, visage, cuisse]* curve. **des cuisses d'un ~ parfait** shapely thighs.

galbé, e [galbe] (**ptp de galber**) **adj** *meuble* with curved outlines; *mollet* rounded. **bien ~** *corps* curvaceous, shapely; *objet* beautifully shaped.

galber [galbe] 1 **vt** to shape (*into curves*), curve.

gale [gal] **nf** a (*Méd*) scabies, itch; (*Vét*) *[chien, chat]* mange; *[mouton]* scab; (*Bot*) scab. (*hum*) **tu peux boire dans mon verre, je n'ai pas la ~!**⁑ you can drink out of my glass – you won't catch anything from me!* *ou* I'm not infectious! b (*fig: personne*) nasty character, nasty piece of work* (*Brit*). **il est mauvais** *ou* **méchant comme la ~** he's a really nasty piece of work*.

galée [gale] **nf** (*Typ*) galley.

galéjade [galeʒad] **nf** (*dial*) tall story.

galéjer [galeʒe] 6 **vi** (*dial*) to spin a yarn. **oh, tu galèjes!** that's a tall story!

galène [galɛn] **nf** galena, galenite.

galère [galɛʀ] **nf** a (*Hist: bateau*) galley. **on l'a envoyé aux ~s** they sent him to the galleys; *voir* **voguer.** b (*loc*) **qu'est-il allé faire dans cette ~?** why did he have to get involved in this business?; **dans quelle ~ me suis-je embarqué!** whatever have I let myself in for?; **quelle ~!*, c'est la ~!*** it's a real grind!*

galérer⁑ [galeʀe] 1 **vi** a (*travailler dur*) to sweat blood*, slog*. b (*rencontrer des difficultés*) to have a hassle*. **il a galéré pendant des années avant d'être reconnu** he struggled for years before gaining recognition.

galerie [galʀi] 1 **nf** a (*couloir*) (*gén*) gallery; *[mine]* gallery, level; *[fourmilière]* gallery; *[taupinière]* tunnel.

b (*Art*) (*magasin*) gallery; (*salle de musée*) room, gallery; (*rare:*

collection) collection.

c (*Théât: balcon*) circle. **premières/deuxièmes ~s** dress/upper circle; **les troisièmes ~s** the gods* (*Brit*), the gallery.

d (*public, spectateurs*) gallery, audience. **faire le pitre pour amuser la ~** to act the fool to amuse the audience; **il a dit cela pour la ~** he said that for appearances' sake.

e (*Aut*) roof rack; (*Archit: balustrade*) gallery.

2 **comp** ►**galerie d'art** art gallery ►**galerie marchande** shopping arcade, shopping mall (*US*) ►**galerie de peinture** picture gallery ►**galerie de portraits** (*Littérat*) collection of pen portraits ►**galerie de tableaux** = **galerie de peinture**.

galérien [galeʀjɛ̃] **nm** (*Hist*) galley slave. (*fig*) **travailler comme un ~** to work like a (galley) slave.

galeriste [galʀist] **nmf** gallery owner.

galet [galɛ] **nm** a (*pierre*) pebble. **~s** shingle, pebbles. b (*Tech*) wheel, roller.

galetas [galta] **nm** (*mansarde*) garret; (*taudis*) hovel.

galette [galɛt] **nf** a (*Culin*) (*gâteau*) *round, flat cake made of puff pastry;* (*crêpe*) (buckwheat) pancake; (*Naut*) ship's biscuit. **~ des Rois** *cake eaten in France on Twelfth Night; voir* **plat.** b (**‡**: *argent*) dough‡, lolly‡ (*Brit*), bread‡. **il a de la ~** he's loaded‡.

galeux, -euse [galø, øz] 1 **adj** a *personne* affected with scabies, scabious (*SPÉC*); *chien* mangy; *mouton* scabby; *plante, arbre* scabby; *plaie* caused by scabies *ou* the itch; *éruption* scabious. **il m'a traité comme un chien ~** he treated me like dirt *ou* as if I was the scum of the earth; *voir* **brebis.** b (*fig: sordide*) *murs* peeling, flaking; *pièce, quartier* squalid, dingy, seedy. 2 **nm,f** (*personne méprisable*) scabby *ou* scruffy individual. **pour lui je suis un ~, il ne veut pas me fréquenter** as far as he's concerned I'm the lowest of the low *ou* the scum of the earth and he wants nothing to do with me.

galhauban [galobɑ̃] **nm** (*Naut*) back-stay.

Galice [galis] **nf** Galicia (*in Spain*).

Galicie [galisi] **nf** Galicia (*in central Europe*).

Galien [galjɛ̃] **nm** Galen.

Galilée[1] [galile] **nm** Galileo.

Galilée[2] [galile] **nf** Galilee. **la mer de ~** the Sea of Galilee.

galiléen, -enne [galileɛ̃, ɛn] (*Géog*) 1 **adj** Galilean. 2 **nm,f: G~(ne)** Galilean.

galimatias [galimatja] **nm** (*propos*) gibberish (*NonC*); (*écrit*) tedious nonsense (*NonC*), twaddle (*Brit*) (*NonC*).

galion [galjɔ̃] **nm** galleon.

galipette* [galipɛt] **nf** somersault. **faire des ~s** to somersault, do somersaults.

galle [gal] **nf** gall. **~ du chêne, noix de ~** oak apple, oak gall.

Galles [gal] **nfpl** *voir* **pays, prince.**

gallican, e [ga(l)likɑ̃, an] **adj, nm,f** Gallican.

gallicanisme [ga(l)likanism] **nm** Gallicanism.

gallicisme [ga(l)lisism] **nm** (*idiotisme*) French idiom; (*dans une langue étrangère: calque*) gallicism.

gallinacé, e [galinase] 1 **adj** gallinaceous. 2 **nm** gallinacean.

gallique [galik] **adj** gallic.

gallium [galjɔm] **nm** gallium.

gallo- [galo] **préf** Gallo-.

gallois, e [galwa, waz] 1 **adj** Welsh. 2 **nm** a **G~** Welshman; **les G~** the Welsh. b (*Ling*) Welsh. 3 **Galloise nf** Welshwoman.

gallon [galɔ̃] **nm** gallon. (*Can*) **~ canadien** *ou* **impérial** Imperial gallon (*4,545 litres*); **~ américain** US gallon (*3,785 litres*).

gallo-romain, e [ga(l)loʀɔmɛ̃, ɛn] 1 **adj** Gallo-Roman. 2 **nm,f: G~-R~(e)** Gallo-Roman.

gallup [galœp] **nm: (sondage) ~** Gallup Poll.

galoche [galɔʃ] **nf** (*sabot*) clog; (*chaussure*) *wooden-soled shoe; voir* **menton.**

galon [galɔ̃] **nm** a (*Couture*) braid (*NonC*), piece of braid; (*Mil*) stripe. (*fig* **il a gagné ses ~s au combat** he got his stripes in battle; (*fig* **prendre du ~** to get promotion (*Brit*), get a promotion (*US*). b (*Can*) measuring tape, tape measure.

galonné, e [galɔne] (**ptp de galonner**) **adj** (*Mil*) *manche, uniforme* with stripes on. **un ~*** a brass hat*.

galonner [galɔne] 1 **vt** (*Couture*) to trim with braid.

galop [galo] **nm** a gallop. **petit ~** canter; **grand ~** (full) gallop; **~ d'essai** (*lit*) trial gallop; (*fig*) trial run; **nous avons fait un ~ de quelques minutes** we galloped for a few minutes; **cheval au ~** galloping horse; **prendre le ~, se mettre au ~** to break into a gallop; **mettre son cheval au ~** to put one's horse into a gallop; **partir au ~** [*cheval*] to set off at a gallop; [*personne*] to take off like a shot, rush off *ou* away; **aller au grand ~** to ride full gallop; **nous avons dîné au ~** we ate our dinner in a great rush; **va chercher tes affaires au ~!** go and get your things, at (*Brit*) *ou* on (*US*) the double! *ou* and look smart (about it)!; (*Mil*) **au ~! chargez!** charge!

b (*danse*) gallopade.

galopade [galɔpad] **nf** (*Équitation*) hand gallop; (*fig: course précipitée*) stampede. (*fig*) **~ effrénée** mad rush.

galopant, e [galɔpɑ̃, ɑ̃t] **adj** (*qui progresse rapidement*) *inflation* galloping, runaway. **démographie ~e** population explosion; *voir* **phtisie.**

galoper [galɔpe] 1 **vi** [*cheval*] to gallop; [*imagination*] to run wild, run riot; [*enfant*] to run. **les enfants galopent dans les couloirs** the children charge *ou* hare* (*Brit*) along the corridors; **j'ai galopé toute la journée!*** I've been haring* (*Brit*) *ou* rushing around all day!

galopin* [galɔpɛ̃] **nm** (*polisson*) urchin, ragamuffin. **petit ~!** you little rascal! *ou* ragamuffin!

galure‡ [galyʀ] **nm, galurin** [galyʀɛ̃] **nm** (*chapeau*) hat, headgear* (*NonC*).

galvanique [galvanik] **adj** galvanic.

galvanisation [galvanizasjɔ̃] **nf** galvanization.

galvaniser [galvanize] 1 **vt** (*lit, Tech*) to galvanize; (*fig: stimuler*) to galvanize (into action).

galvanisme [galvanism] **nm** (*Méd*) galvanism.

galvanomètre [galvanɔmɛtʀ] **nm** galvanometer.

galvanoplastie [galvanoplasti] **nf** (*reproduction*) electrotyping, galvanoplasty; (*dépôt*) electroplating.

galvanoplastique [galvanoplastik] **adj** galvanoplastic.

galvanotype [galvanotip] **nm** electrotype.

galvanotypie [galvanotipi] **nf** electrotyping.

galvaudage [galvodaʒ] **nm** a [*nom, réputation*] tarnishing, bringing into disrepute, sullying; [*talent*] prostituting, debasing. b (*vagabondage*) loafing about, idling around.

galvaudé, e [galvode] (**ptp de galvauder**) **adj** *expression* trite, hackneyed; *mot* overworked.

galvauder [galvode] 1 1 **vt** *réputation, nom* to tarnish, sully, bring into disrepute; *talent* to prostitute, debase; *expression* to make trite *ou* hackneyed; *mot* to overwork. 2 **se galvauder vpr** (*s'avilir*) to demean o.s., lower o.s., compromise o.s.

galvaudeux, -euse† [galvodø, øz] **nm,f** (*vagabond*) tramp; (*bon à rien*) good-for-nothing.

gambade [gɑ̃bad] **nf** leap, caper. **faire des ~s** [*personne, enfant*] to leap (about), caper (about), prance about; [*animal*] to gambol, leap (about), frisk about.

gambader [gɑ̃bade] 1 **vi** [*animal*] to gambol, leap (about), frisk about; [*personne, enfant*] to leap (about), caper (about), prance about; [*esprit*] to flit *ou* jump (from one idea to another). **~ de joie** to jump for joy.

gambas [gɑ̃bas] **nfpl** Mediterranean prawns, gambas.

gambe [gɑ̃b] **nf** *voir* **viole.**

gamberge‡ [gɑ̃bɛʀʒ] **nf** hard thought.

gamberger‡ [gɑ̃bɛʀʒe] 3 **vi** to think hard. **ça gamberge là-dedans!** your brain is really working overtime!*

gambette* [gɑ̃bɛt] **nf** leg.

Gambie [gɑ̃bi] **nf: la ~** (*pays*) The Gambia; (*fleuve*) the Gambia.

gambien, -ienne [gɑ̃bjɛ̃, jɛn] 1 **adj** Gambian. 2 **nm,f: G~(ne)** Gambian.

gambiller‡† [gɑ̃bije] 1 **vi** to dance, jig*.

gambit [gɑ̃bi] **nm** (*Échecs*) gambit.

gamelle [gamɛl] **nf** [*soldat*] mess tin (*Brit*) *ou* kit (*US*); [*ouvrier, campeur*] billy-can, billy; [*chien*] bowl, dish; (*hum: assiette*) dish, plate. (*lit, fig*) **ramasser** *ou* **prendre une ~*** to come a cropper* (*Brit*), fall flat on one's face.

gamète [gamɛt] **nm** gamete.

gamin, e [gamɛ̃, in] 1 **adj** (*espiègle*) mischievous, playful; (*puéril*) childish. 2 **nm,f** (*: *enfant*) kid*. **quand j'étais ~** when I was a kid*; **~ des rues/de Paris** street/Paris urchin.

gaminerie [gaminʀi] **nf** (*espièglerie*) playfulness (*NonC*); (*puérilité*) childishness (*NonC*). **faire des ~s** to play (mischievous) pranks; to be childish; **arrête tes ~s** stop being so childish.

gamma [ga(m)ma] **nm** gamma; *voir* **rayon.**

gamme [gam] **nf** a (*Mus*) scale. **faire des ~s** to practise scales; **~ ascendante/descendante** rising/falling scale. b (*série*) [*couleurs, articles*] range; [*sentiments*] gamut, range. **toute la ~*** the whole lot; **~ de produits** range of products; **haut/bas de ~** up-/down-market; **une voiture/maison haut/bas de ~** a car/house at the top/lower end of the range, an up-/down-market car/house.

gammée [game] **adj f** *voir* **croix.**

ganache [ganaʃ] **nf** a (*†: *imbécile*) **(vieille) ~** (old) fool, (old) duffer*. b [*cheval*] lower jaw. c (*Culin*) (crème) ganache.

Gand [gɑ̃] **n** Ghent.

gandhiste [gɑ̃dist] **adj** of Gandhi, typical of Gandhi.

gandin [gɑ̃dɛ̃] **nm** (*péj*) dandy.

gang [gɑ̃g] **nm** gang (*of crooks*).

Gange [gɑ̃ʒ] **nm: le ~** the Ganges.

gangétique [gɑ̃ʒetik] **adj** gangetic.

ganglion [gɑ̃glijɔ̃] **nm** ganglion.

ganglionnaire [gɑ̃glijɔnɛʀ] **adj** ganglionic.

gangrène [gɑ̃gʀɛn] **nf** (*Méd*) gangrene; (*fig*) corruption, canker (*fig*). **la ~ urbaine** urban decay; **la ~ de l'extrémisme** the blight of extremism.

gangrener [gɑ̃gʀɔne] 5 **vt** a (*Méd*) to gangrene. **blessure qui se gangrène** wound which is going gangrenous; **membre gangréné** gangrenous limb. b (*fig*) to corrupt, blight. **société gangrenée** society in decay.

gangreneux, -euse [gɑ̃gʀənø, øz] **adj** gangrenous.

gangster [gɑ̃gstɛʀ] **nm** gangster, mobster (*US*); (*fig*) shark, swindler, crook.

gangstérisme [gɑ̃gsteʀism] **nm** gangsterism.

gangue [gɑ̃g] **nf** *[minerai, pierre]* gangue; (*fig: carcan*) strait jacket (*fig*). **~ de boue** coating *ou* layer of mud.

ganse [gɑ̃s] **nf** (*Habillement*) braid (*NonC*).

ganser [gɑ̃se] [1] **vt** to braid.

gant [gɑ̃] 1 **nm** a glove. **~s de caoutchouc/de boxe** rubber/boxing gloves.

b (*loc*) **remettre les ~s*** to take up boxing again; **cette robe lui va comme un ~** this dress fits her like a glove; **ton idée/ce rôle lui va comme un ~** your idea/this role suits him down to the ground; **il ne s'agit pas de prendre** *ou* **mettre des ~s** there's no point using kid-glove methods *ou* trying to be as gentle as possible; **je ne vais pas prendre des ~s avec lui** I'm not going to pull my punches with him; **tu ferais mieux de prendre des ~s avec lui** you'd better handle him with kid gloves; **il va falloir prendre des ~s pour lui annoncer la nouvelle** we'll have to break the news to him gently; (*lit, fig*) **jeter/relever le ~** to throw down/take up the gauntlet; *voir* **main, retourner.**

2 **comp ►gant de crin** massage glove **►gant de cuisine** oven glove **►gant de jardinage** gardening glove **►gant de toilette** (face) flannel (*Brit*), wash glove, face cloth.

gantelet [gɑ̃t(ə)lɛ] **nm** (*Mil, Sport*) gauntlet; (*Tech*) hand leather.

ganter [gɑ̃te] [1] 1 **vt** *main, personne* to fit with gloves, put gloves on. **tu es bien ganté** these gloves look nice on you *ou* suit your hand well; **il était ganté de cuir** he was wearing leather gloves; **main gantée de cuir** leather-gloved hand. 2 **vi: ~ du 7** to take (a) size 7 in gloves. 3 **se ganter vpr** to put on one's gloves.

ganterie [gɑ̃tʀi] **nf** (*usine*) glove factory; (*magasin*) glove shop; (*commerce*) glove trade; (*industrie*) glove-making industry.

gantier, -ière [gɑ̃tje, jɛʀ] **nm,f** glover.

garage [gaʀaʒ] 1 **nm** (*Aut*) garage. **as-tu mis la voiture au ~?** have you put the car in the garage? *ou* away? 2 **comp ►garage d'autobus** bus depot *ou* garage **►garage d'avions** hangar **►garage de** *ou* **à bicyclettes** bicycle shed **►garage de canots** boathouse; *voir* **voie.**

garagiste [gaʀaʒist] **nmf** (*propriétaire*) garage owner; (*mécanicien*) garage mechanic. **le ~ m'a dit que ...** the man at the garage *ou* the mechanic told me that ... .

garance [gaʀɑ̃s] 1 **nf** (*Bot: teinture*) madder.
2 **adj inv** madder(-coloured).

garant, e [gaʀɑ̃, ɑ̃t] **nm,f** (*gén, personne, état*) guarantor (*de* for); (*chose: garantie*) guarantee (*de* of). **servir de ~ à qn** *[personne]* to stand surety for sb, act as guarantor for sb; *[honneur, parole]* to be sb's guarantee; **être** *ou* **se porter ~ de qch** (*Jur*) to be answerable *ou* responsible for sth; (*gén: assurer*) to vouch for sth, guarantee sth; **ils vont échouer, ça je m'en porte ~** they'll come to grief – I can absolutely guarantee it.

garanti, e¹ [gaʀɑ̃ti] (**ptp de garantir**) **adj** (*Comm*) guaranteed. **~ étanche/3 ans** guaranteed waterproof/for 3 years; **~ à l'usage** guaranteed for normal use; **~ pure laine** warranted *ou* guaranteed pure wool; **c'est ~ pour cinq ans** it carries a five-year guarantee, it is guaranteed for five years; (*fig*) **~ sur facture*** sure as anything, sure as heck*; **il va refuser, c'est ~*** he'll refuse – it's a cert* (*Brit*) *ou* it's for sure, you can bet your life he'll refuse*; **c'est la migraine ~e*** you're bound to get *ou* it's a surefire way of getting* a headache.

garantie² [gaʀɑ̃ti] 1 **nf** a (*Comm*) guarantee. **sous ~** under guarantee; *voir* **bon², contrat.**

b (*assurance*) guarantee, guaranty (*SPÉC*); (*gage*) security, surety; (*fig: protection*) safeguard. **ils nous ont donné leur ~ que ...** they gave us their guarantee that ...; **si on a la ~ qu'ils se conduiront bien** if we have a firm undertaking (*Brit*) *ou* a guarantee that they'll behave; **servir de ~** *[bijoux]* to act as a surety *ou* security *ou* guarantee; *[otages]* to be used as a security; *[honneur]* to be a guarantee; **donner des ~s** to give guarantees; **il faut prendre des ~s** we have to find sureties *ou* get guarantees; **cette entreprise présente toutes les ~s de sérieux** there is every indication that this firm is a reliable concern; **c'est une ~ de succès** it's a guarantee of success; **c'est une ~ contre le chômage/l'inflation** it's a safeguard against unemployment/inflation.

c (*caution*) **donner sa ~ à** to guarantee, stand security *ou* surety for, be guarantor for.

d *[police d'assurance]* cover (*NonC*).

e (*loc*) **sans ~: je vous dis ça, mais c'est sans ~** I can't vouch for what I'm telling you, I can't guarantee that what I'm telling you is right; **j'essaierai de le faire pour jeudi mais sans ~** I'll try and get it done for Thursday but I can't guarantee it *ou* I'm not making any promises; **ils ont bien voulu essayer de le faire, sans ~ de succès** they were quite willing to try and do it, but they couldn't guarantee success.

2 **comp ►garantie constitutionnelle** constitutional guarantee **►garantie d'exécution** performance bond **►garantie d'intérêt** guaranteed interest **►garantie de paiement** guarantee of payment **►garanties parlementaires** guarantee in law.

garantir [gaʀɑ̃tiʀ] [2] **vt** a (*gén: assurer*) to guarantee; *emprunt* to guarantee, secure. **~ que** to assure *ou* guarantee that; **je te garantis que ça ne se passera pas comme ça!*** I can assure you *ou* believe you me* things won't turn out like that!; **le poulet sera tendre, le boucher me l'a garanti** the chicken will be tender – the butcher assured me it would be; **je te garantis le fait** I can vouch for the fact; **il m'a garanti le succès** he guaranteed me success, he assured me I would be successful; *voir* **garanti.** b (*protéger*) **~ qch de** to protect sth from; **se ~ les yeux (du soleil)** to protect one's eyes (from the sun).

garce‡ [gaʀs] **nf** (*péj*) (*méchante*) bitch‡; (*dévergondée*) tart‡ (*Brit*), slut. **qu'est-ce que tu es ~!** you're such a bitch!‡; **~ de tondeuse!** bloody*‡ (*Brit*) *ou* damned‡ mower!; **~ de vie!‡†** what a bloody*‡ (*Brit*) *ou* damned‡ awful life!

garçon [gaʀsɔ̃] 1 **nm** a (*enfant, fils*) boy. **tu es un grand ~ maintenant** you're a big boy now; **traiter qn comme un petit ~** to treat sb like a child *ou* a little boy; **à côté d'eux, on est des petits ~s** compared with them we're only beginners; **cette fille est un ~ manqué** *ou* **un vrai ~** this girl is a real tomboy.

b (*jeune homme*) young man. (*hum*) **eh bien mon ~ ...** well my boy ...; **c'est un brave ~** he's a good sort *ou* a nice fellow; **ce ~ ira loin** that young man will go far; *voir* **mauvais.**

c (*commis*) (shop) assistant. **~ boulanger/boucher** baker's/butcher's assistant; (*jeune homme*) baker's/butcher's boy; **~ coiffeur** hairdresser's assistant *ou* junior.

d (*serveur*) waiter.

e (*†: célibataire*) bachelor. **être/rester ~** to be/remain single *ou* a bachelor; **vivre en ~** to lead a bachelor's life; *voir* **enterrer, vie, vieux.**

2 **comp ►garçon d'ascenseur** lift (*Brit*) *ou* elevator (*US*) attendant; (*jeune homme*) lift (*Brit*) *ou* elevator (*US*) boy **►garçon de bureau** office assistant; (*jeune homme*) office boy **►garçon de cabine** cabin boy **►garçon de café** waiter **►garçon de courses** messenger; (*jeune homme*) errand boy **►garçon d'écurie** stable lad (*Brit*) *ou* boy **►garçon d'étage** boots (*sg*) (*Brit*), bellhop (*US*) **►garçon de ferme** farm hand **►garçon d'honneur** best man **►garçon de laboratoire** laboratory assistant **►garçon livreur** delivery man; (*jeune homme*) delivery boy **►garçon de recettes** bank messenger **►garçon de salle** waiter.

garçonne [gaʀsɔn] **nf: à la ~** *coiffure* urchin cut; **être coiffée à la ~** to have an urchin cut.

garçonnet [gaʀsɔnɛ] **nm** small boy. **taille/rayon ~** boy's size/boys' department.

garçonnière [gaʀsɔnjɛʀ] **nf** bachelor flat (*Brit*) *ou* apartment (*US*).

Garde [gaʀd] **n: le lac de ~** Lake Garda.

garde¹ [gaʀd] 1 **nf** a (*surveillance*) **on lui avait confié la ~ des bagages/prisonniers** he had been put in charge of the luggage/the prisoners, he had been given the job of looking after *ou* of guarding the luggage/the prisoners; **il s'est chargé de la ~ des bagages/prisonniers** he undertook to look after *ou* to guard *ou* to keep an eye on the luggage/the prisoners; **la ~ des frontières est assurée par ...** the task *ou* job of guarding the frontiers is carried out by ...; **confier qch/qn à la ~ de qn** to entrust sth/sb to sb's care, leave sth/sb in sb's care; **prendre en ~** *enfant, animal* to take into one's care, look after; **il nous ont laissé leur enfant en ~** they left their child in our care; **Dieu vous ait en sa (sainte) ~** (may) God be with you; **être sous la ~ de la police** to be under police guard; **être/mettre qn sous bonne ~** to be/put sb under guard.

b (*Jur: après divorce*) custody. **l'enfant a été laissé à la ~ de la mère** the child was left in the custody of the mother; **c'est elle qui a eu la ~ des enfants** she had *ou* got *ou* was given (the) custody of the children; **~ alternée/conjointe** alternating/joint custody.

c (*veille*) *[soldat]* guard duty; *[infirmière]* ward duty; *[médecin]* duty period. **sa ~ a duré douze heures** *[soldat]* he was on guard duty for 12 hours; *[médecin, infirmier]* he was on duty for 12 hours; *[médecin]* **assurer 15 ~s par mois** to be on call *ou* on duty 15 times a month; **(être) de ~** *[infirmière, sentinelle]* (to be) on duty; *[médecin, pharmacien]* (to be) on call *ou* on duty; **pharmacie de ~** duty chemist (*Brit*) *ou* pharmacist (*US*); **quel est le médecin de ~?** who is the doctor on duty?; *voir* **chien, monter¹, poste².**

d (*groupe, escorte*) guard. (*Mil*) **~ descendante/montante** old/relief guard; *voir* **arrière, avant, corps, relever** *etc.*

e (*personne*) *[salle d'hôpital]* nurse. **~ de jour/de nuit** day/night nurse.

f (*Boxe, Escrime*) guard. (*Escrime*) **~s** positions; **en ~!** on guard!; **se mettre en ~** to take one's guard; **avoir/tenir la ~ haute** to have/keep one's guard up; **fermer/ouvrir sa ~** to close/open one's guard; **baisser sa ~** (*lit*) to lower one's guard; (*fig*) to drop one's guard.

g *[épée]* hilt, guard. (*lit*) **jusqu'à la ~** (up) to the hilt; (*fig*) **il s'est enferré jusqu'à la ~** he's in it up to his neck*.

h (*Typ*) **(page de) ~** flyleaf.

i (*Tech*) *[serrure]* **~s** wards.

j (*Aut*) **~ au toit** headroom; **laisser une ~ suffisante à la pédale** to allow enough play on the pedal; **~ d'embrayage** clutch linkage play, clutch pedal play.

k (*Cartes*) **avoir la ~ à cœur** to have a stop (*Brit*) *ou* covering card (*US*) in hearts.

l (*loc*) (*littér*) **n'avoir ~ de faire** to take good care not to do, make sure one doesn't do; **mettre qn en ~** to put sb on his guard, warn sb (*contre* against); **mise en ~** warning; **faire bonne ~** to keep a close watch; **prendre ~ de ne pas faire, prendre ~ à ne pas faire†** to be careful *ou* take care not to do; **prenez ~ de (ne pas) tomber** mind you don't fall (*Brit*), be careful *ou* take care you don't fall *ou* not to fall; **prenez ~ qu'il ne prenne pas froid** mind *ou* watch *ou* be careful he doesn't catch cold; **prends ~!** (*exhortation*) watch out!; (*menace*) watch it!*; **prends ~ à toi** watch yourself*, take care; **prends ~ aux voitures** be careful of the cars, watch out for *ou* mind the cars; **sans prendre ~ au danger** without considering *ou* heeding the danger; **sans y prendre ~** without realizing it; **être/se mettre/se tenir sur ses ~s** to be/put o.s./stay on one's guard; (*Mil*) **~-à-vous nm inv** (*action*) standing to attention (*NonC*); (*cri*) order to stand to attention; **~-à-vous (fixe)!** attention!; **ils exécutèrent des ~-à-vous impeccables** they stood to attention faultlessly; **rester/se mettre au ~-à-vous** to stand at/stand to attention.

2 **comp** ► **garde d'enfants** (*personne*) child minder; (*activité*) child minding ► **garde d'honneur** guard of honour ► **garde impériale** imperial guard ► **garde judiciaire** legal surveillance (*of impounded property*) ► **garde juridique** (*Jur*) legal liability ► **garde mobile** anti-riot police ► **garde municipale** *municipal guard* ► **garde pontificale** papal guard ► **garde républicaine** republican guard ► **garde à vue** (*Jur*) ≃ police custody; **être mis** *ou* **placé en garde à vue** ≃ to be kept in police custody, be held for questioning.

garde[2] [gaʀd] 1 **nm** a *[prisonnier]* guard; *[domaine, propriété, château]* warden; *[jardin public]* keeper.

b (*Mil: soldat*) guardsman; (*Hist*) guard, guardsman; (*sentinelle*) guard.

2 **comp** ► **garde champêtre** rural policeman ► **garde du corps** bodyguard ► **garde forestier** forest warden (*Brit*), (park) ranger (*US*), forester ► **garde impérial** imperial guard *ou* guardsman ► **garde maritime** coastguard ► **garde mobile** member of the anti-riot police ► **garde municipal** *municipal guard or guardsman* ► **garde pontifical** papal guard *ou* guardsman ► **garde républicain** republican guard *ou* guardsman, member of the Republican Guard ► **garde rouge** Red Guard ► **Garde des Sceaux** French Minister of Justice, ≃ Lord Chancellor (*Brit*), ≃ Attorney General (*US*); (*Hist*) ≃ Keeper of the Seals; *voir aussi* **garder**.

garde- [gaʀd] **préf** *voir* **garder**.

gardé, e [gaʀde] (**ptp de garder**) **adj: passage à niveau ~/non ~** manned/unmanned level crossing; (*Alpinisme, Ski*) **cabane ~e/non ~e** hut with/without resident warden; *voir* **chasse**[1], **proportion**.

Gardénal [gaʀdenal] **nm** ® phenobarbitone (*Brit*), phenobarbital (*US*), Luminal ®.

gardénia [gaʀdenja] **nm** gardenia.

garder [gaʀde] [1] 1 **vt** a (*surveiller*) *enfants, magasin* to look after, mind; *bestiaux* to look after, guard; *bagages, trésor, prisonnier* to look after, guard, watch over; (*défendre*) *frontière, passage, porte* to guard. **le chien garde la maison** the dog guards the house; (*Jur*) **~ qn à vue** ≃ to keep sb in custody; **~ des enfants (à domicile)** to baby-sit, child mind; **garde ma valise pendant que j'achète un livre** look after *ou* keep an eye on my suitcase while I buy a book; **on n'a pas gardé les cochons ensemble!*** you've a nerve to take liberties like that!*; **toutes les issues sont gardées** all the exits are guarded, a watch is being kept on all the exits; **une statue gardait l'entrée** a statue stood at the entrance *ou* guarded the entrance.

b (*ne pas quitter*) **~ la chambre** to stay in one's room; **~ le lit** to stay in bed; **un rhume lui a fait ~ la chambre** he stayed in his room because of his cold, his cold kept him at home *ou* in his room.

c *denrées, marchandises, papiers* to keep. **gardez la monnaie** keep the change; **ces fleurs ne gardent pas leur parfum** these flowers lose their scent; **il ne peut rien ~** he can't keep anything; (*: *vomir*) he can't keep anything down.

d (*conserver sur soi*) *vêtement* to keep on. **gardez donc votre chapeau** do keep your hat on.

e (*retenir*) *personne, employé, client* to keep; *[police]* to detain. **~ qn à déjeuner** to have sb stay for lunch; **~ un élève en retenue** to keep a pupil in, keep a pupil in detention; **il m'a gardé une heure au téléphone** he kept me on the phone for an hour.

f (*mettre de côté*) to keep, put aside *ou* to one side; (*réserver*) *place* (*pendant absence*) to keep (*à, pour* for); (*avant l'arrivée d'une personne*) to save, keep (*à, pour* for). **je lui ai gardé une côtelette pour ce soir** I've kept *ou* saved a chop for him for tonight; **j'ai gardé de la soupe pour demain** I've kept *ou* saved *ou* I've put aside some soup for tomorrow; **~ le meilleur pour la fin** to keep the best till the end; **~ qch pour la bonne bouche** to keep the best till last; **je lui garde un chien de ma chienne*** he's got it coming to him (from me)*; **~ une poire pour la soif** to keep something in hand, keep something for a rainy day; *voir* **dent**.

g (*maintenir*) to keep. **~ les yeux baissés/la tête haute** to keep one's eyes down/one's head up; **~ un chien enfermé/en laisse** to keep a dog shut in/on a leash.

h (*ne pas révéler*) to keep. **~ le secret** to keep the secret; **~ ses pensées pour soi** to keep one's thoughts to oneself; **gardez cela pour vous** keep this to yourself, keep it under your hat*.

i (*conserver*) *souplesse, élasticité, fraîcheur* to keep, retain; *jeunesse, droits, facultés* to retain; *habitudes* to keep up. **~ son emploi** to keep one's job; **il a gardé toutes ses facultés** *ou* **toute sa tête** he still has all his faculties, he's still in possession of all his faculties; **~ les apparences** to keep up appearances; **~ son calme** to keep *ou* remain calm; **~ la tête froide** to keep a cool head, keep one's head; **~ un bon souvenir de qch** to have *ou* retain happy memories of sth; **~ sa raison** to keep one's sanity; **~ le silence** to keep silent *ou* silence; **~ l'anonymat** to remain anonymous; **~ la ligne** to keep one's figure; **~ rancune à qn** to bear sb a grudge; **j'ai eu du mal à ~ mon sérieux** I had a job keeping *ou* to keep a straight face; **~ les idées claires** to keep a clear head.

j (*protéger*) **~ qn de l'erreur/de ses amis** to save sb from error/ from his friends; **ça vous gardera du froid** it'll protect you from the cold; **Dieu** *ou* **le Ciel vous garde** God be with you; **la châsse qui garde ces reliques** the shrine which houses these relics.

2 **se garder vpr** a *[denrées]* to keep. **ça se garde bien** it keeps well.

b **se ~ de qch** (*se défier de*) to beware of *ou* be wary of sth; (*se protéger de*) to protect o.s. from sth, guard against sth; **gardez-vous de décisions trop promptes/de vos amis** beware *ou* be wary of hasty decisions/of your own friends; **se ~ de faire qch** to be careful not to do sth; **elle s'est bien gardée de le prévenir** she was very careful not to warn him, she carefully avoided warning him; **vous allez lui parler? — je m'en garderai bien!** are you going to speak to him? — that's one thing I won't do! *ou* that's the last thing I'd do!

3 **comp** ► **garde-barrière nmf (pl gardes-barrière(s))** level-crossing keeper ► **garde-boue nm inv** mudguard ► **garde-chasse nm (pl gardes-chasse(s))** gamekeeper ► **garde-chiourme nm (pl garde(s)-chiourme(s))** (*Hist*) warder (*of galley slaves*); (*fig*) martinet ► **garde-corps nm inv** (*Naut*) lifeline, manrope; (*rambarde*) railing ► **garde-côte nm (pl garde-côte(s))** (*Mil*) coastguard ship; (*garde-pêche*) fisheries protection ship ► **garde-feu nm inv** fireguard ► **garde-fou nm (pl garde-fous)** (*en fer*) railing; (*en pierre*) parapet; (*fig*) safeguard ► **garde-frein nm (pl gardes-frein(s))** guard, brakeman ► **garde-magasin nm (pl gardes-magasin(s))** (*Mil*) ≃ quartermaster ► **garde-malade nmf (pl gardes-malades)** home nurse ► **garde-manger nm inv** (*armoire*) meat safe (*Brit*), cooler (*US*); (*pièce*) pantry, larder ► **garde-meuble nm (pl garde-meubles)** furniture depository (*Brit*), storehouse; **mettre une armoire au garde-meuble** to put a wardrobe in store (*Brit*) *ou* in storage ► **garde-nappe nm (pl garde-nappe(s))** tablemat ► **garde-pêche nm inv** (*personne*) water bailiff (*Brit*), fish (and game) warden (*US*); (*frégate*) fisheries protection ship; **une vedette garde-pêche** a fisheries protection launch ► **garde-place nm (pl garde-place(s))** holder *ou* slot (for reservation ticket) (*in a railway compartment*) ► **garde-port nm (pl gardes-port(s))** wharf *ou* harbour master ► **garde-robe nf (pl garde-robes)** (*habits*) wardrobe ► **garde-voie nm (pl gardes-voie(s))** (*Rail*) line guard; *voir aussi* **garde**[1], **garde**[2].

garderie [gaʀdəʀi] **nf: ~ (d'enfants)** (*jeunes enfants*) day nursery (*Brit*), day-care center (*US*); (*Scol*) ≃ after-school club (*Brit*), ≃ after-school center (*US*) (*child-minding service in a school, factory etc operating outside school hours while parents are working*).

gardeur [gaʀdœʀ] **nm: ~ de troupeaux** herdsman; **~ de vaches** cowherd; **~ de chèvres** goatherd; **~ de cochons** pig-keeper, swineherd†; **~ d'oies** gooseherd; **~ de dindons** turkey-keeper.

gardeuse [gaʀdøz] **nf** (*voir* **gardeur**) herdswoman; cowherd; goatherd; pig-keeper, swineherd†; goose girl; turkey-keeper.

gardian [gaʀdjɑ̃] **nm** herdsman (*in the Camargue*).

gardien, -ienne [gaʀdjɛ̃, jɛn] 1 **nm,f** *[prisonnier]* guard; *[propriété, château]* warden (*Brit*), keeper (*US*); *[usine, locaux]* guard; *[musée, hôtel]* attendant; *[cimetière]* caretaker, keeper; *[jardin public, phare, zoo]* keeper; *[réserve naturelle]* warden; (*fig: défenseur*) guardian, protector. **le ~ du troupeau** the herdsman; (*fig*) **la constitution, ~ne des libertés** the constitution, protector *ou* guardian of freedom; **les ~s de l'ordre public** the keepers of public order; *voir* **ange**.

2 **comp** ► **gardien de but** (goal)keeper ► **gardienne (d'enfants)** child minder ► **gardien d'immeuble** caretaker (*of a block of flats*) (*Brit*), (apartment house) manager (*US*) ► **gardien de musée** museum attendant ► **gardien de nuit** night watchman ► **gardien de la paix** policeman, (police) constable, patrolman (*US*) ► **gardien de phare** lighthouse keeper ► **gardien (de prison)** prison warder *ou* officer *ou* guard (*US*) ► **gardienne (de prison)** prison wardress *ou* officer *ou* guard (*US*).

gardiennage [gaʀdjenaʒ] **nm** *[immeuble]* caretaking; *[locaux]* guarding; *[port]* security; *voir* **société**.

gardon [gaʀdɔ̃] **nm** roach; *voir* **frais**[1].

gare[1] [gaʀ] 1 **nf** (*Rail*) station. **~ d'arrivée/de départ** station of arrival/ departure; **~ de marchandises/de voyageurs** goods/passenger station; **le train entre/est en ~** the train is coming in/is in; **l'express de Dijon entre en ~ sur la voie 6** the train now approaching platform 6 is the express from Dijon, the express from Dijon is now approaching platform 6; (*péj*) **littérature/roman de ~** pulp literature/novel; *voir* **chef**[1]. 2 **comp** ► **gare fluviale** canal *ou* river basin ► **gare maritime** harbour station ► **gare routière** *[camions]* haulage depot; *[autocars]* coach (*Brit*) *ou* bus (*US*) station ► **gare de triage** marshalling yard.

gare[2]* [gaʀ] **excl** (*attention*) **~ à toi!, ~ à tes fesses!**⁑ (just) watch it*!; **~ à toi** *ou* **à tes fesses si tu recommences!** you'll be for it (*Brit*) *ou* in for it if you start that again*!; **~ au premier qui bouge!** whoever makes the first move will be in trouble!, the first one to move will be for it!* (*Brit*); **et fais ce que je dis, sinon ~!** and do what I say, or else!*; **~ à ne pas recommencer** just make sure you don't do it again!; **la porte est basse, ~ à ta tête** it's a low door so mind (*Brit*) *ou* careful you don't bang your head; **~ aux conséquences/à ce type** beware of the consequences/this fellow; *voir* **crier**.

garenne[1] [garɛn] **nf** rabbit warren; *voir* **lapin**.

garenne[2] [garɛn] **nm** wild rabbit.

garer [gare] 1 1 **vt** *véhicule* to park; *train* to put into a siding; *embarcation* to dock; *récolte* to (put into) store. (*fig*) **~ son argent** *ou* **sa fortune** to put one's money *ou* fortune in a safe place; **d'habitude, je gare devant la porte** I usually park at the door. 2 **se garer vpr** a *[automobiliste]* to park. b (*se ranger de côté*) *[véhicule, automobiliste]* to draw into the side, pull over; *[piéton]* to move aside, get out of the way. c (**: éviter*) **se ~ de qch/qn** to avoid sth/sb, steer clear of sth/sb.

Gargantua [gargɑ̃tɥa] **nm** Gargantua. **appétit de ~** gargantuan *ou* gigantic appetite; **c'est un ~** he has a gargantuan *ou* gigantic appetite.

gargantuesque [gargɑ̃tɥɛsk] **adj** *appétit, repas* gargantuan.

gargariser (se) [gargarize] 1 **vpr** to gargle. (*fig péj*) **se ~ de** (*se vanter de*) to crow over *ou* about; (*se délecter de*) to lap up; **se ~ de grands mots** to revel in big words.

gargarisme [gargarism] **nm** gargle. **se faire un ~** to gargle.

gargote [gargɔt] **nf** (*péj*) cheap restaurant *ou* eating-house.

gargouille [garguj] **nf** (*Archit*) gargoyle; (*Constr*) waterspout.

gargouillement [gargujmɑ̃] **nm** = **gargouillis**.

gargouiller [garguje] 1 **vi** *[eau]* to gurgle; *[intestin]* to rumble.

gargouillis [garguji] **nm** (*gén pl*) *[eau]* gurgling (*NonC*); *[intestin]* rumbling (*NonC*). **faire des ~** *[eau]* to gurgle; *[intestin]* to rumble.

gargoulette [gargulɛt] **nf** earthenware water jug.

garnement [garnəmɑ̃] **nm** (*gamin*) (young) imp; (*adolescent*) tearaway (*Brit*), hellion (*US*). **petit ~!** you little rascal!

garni, e [garni] (**ptp de garnir**) 1 **adj** a (*rempli*) **bien ~** *réfrigérateur, bibliothèque* well-stocked; *bourse* well-lined; **un portefeuille bien ~** a wallet full of notes, a well-filled *ou* well-lined wallet; **il a encore une chevelure bien ~e** he has still got a good head of hair. b *plat, viande* (*de légumes*) served with vegetables; (*de frites*) served with chips (*Brit*) *ou* French fries (*US*). **cette entrecôte est bien ~e** this steak has a generous helping of chips (*Brit*) *ou* French fries (*US*) with it; *voir* **bouquet**[1], **choucroute**. c (*†: meublé*) *chambre* furnished. 2 **nm** (†) furnished accommodation *ou* rooms (*for letting* (*Brit*) *or renting* (*US*)).

garnir [garnir] 2 1 **vt** a *[personne]* (*protéger, équiper*) **~ de** to fit out with; **~ une porte d'acier** to fit *or* reinforce a door with steel plate; **~ une canne d'un embout** to put a tip on the end of a walking stick; **~ une muraille de canons** to range cannons along a wall; **~ une boîte de tissu** to line a box with material; **~ un mur de pointes** to arm a wall with spikes, set spikes along a wall; **mur garni de canons/pointes** wall bristling with cannons/spikes.

b *[chose]* (*couvrir*) **l'acier qui garnit la porte** the steel plate covering the door; **les canons qui garnissent la muraille** the cannons lining the wall *or* ranged along the wall; **des pointes garnissent le mur** spikes are set in the wall; **le cuir qui garnit la poignée** the leather covering the handle; **coffret garni de velours** casket lined with velvet, velvet-lined casket.

c (*approvisionner*) *boîte, caisse* to fill; *réfrigérateur, bibliothèque* to stock; *chaudière* to stoke; *hameçon* to bait (*de* with). **le cuisinier garnissait les plats de charcuterie** the cook was setting out *or* putting (slices of) cold meat on the plates; **~ de livres une bibliothèque** to stock *or* fill (the shelves of) a library with books; (*Mil*) **~ les remparts** to garrison the ramparts; **les boîtes, garnies de chocolats, partaient à l'emballage** the boxes filled with chocolates were going to be packed.

d (*remplir*) *boîte* to fill; (*recouvrir*) *surface, rayon* to cover, fill. **une foule dense garnissait les trottoirs** a dense crowd covered *or* packed the pavements; **les chocolats qui garnissaient la boîte** the chocolates which filled the box; **boîte garnie de chocolats** box full of chocolates; **plats garnis de tranches de viande** plates filled with *or* full of slices of meat.

e (*enjoliver*) *vêtement* to trim; *étagère* to decorate; *aliment* to garnish (*de* with). **~ une jupe d'un volant** to trim a skirt with a frill; **~ une table de fleurs** to decorate a table with flowers; **les bibelots qui garnissent la cheminée** the trinkets which decorate the mantelpiece; **des plats joliment garnis de charcuterie** plates nicely laid out *or* decorated with cold meat; **des côtelettes garnies de cresson/de mayonnaise** chops garnished with cress/with mayonnaise.

2 **se garnir vpr** *[salle, pièce]* to fill up (*de* with). **la salle commençait à se ~** the room was beginning to fill up.

garnison [garnizɔ̃] **nf** (*troupes*) garrison. **(ville de) ~** garrison town; **vie de ~** garrison life; **être en ~ à, tenir ~ à** to be stationed *or* garrisoned at.

garniture [garnityr] 1 **nf** a (*décoration*) *[robe, chapeau]* trimming (*NonC*); *[table]* set of table linen, place mats *etc*; *[coffret]* lining; *[aliment, plat]* garnish. (*Aut*) **la ~ intérieure de cette voiture est très soignée** the upholstery in this car *or* the interior trim in this car is well-finished.

b (*Culin*) (*légumes*) garnish (*Brit*), fixings (*US*); (*sauce à vol-au-vent*) filling. **servi avec ~** served with vegetables, vegetables included; **~ non comprise** vegetables extra *or* not included.

c (*Typ*) furniture.

d (*Tech: protection*) *[chaudière]* lagging (*NonC*); *[boîte]* covering (*NonC*). **avec ~ de caoutchouc/cuir** with rubber/leather fittings *or* fitments; **~ d'embrayage/de frein** clutch/brake lining; **changer les ~s de freins** to reline the brakes, change the brake linings.

2 **comp ► garniture de cheminée** mantelpiece ornaments **► garniture de foyer** (set of) fire irons **► garniture de lit** (set of) bed linen **► garniture périodique** sanitary towel (*Brit*) *or* napkin (*US*) **► garniture de toilette** toilet set.

Garonne [garɔn] **nf: la ~** the Garonne.

garou [garu] **nm** *voir* **loup**.

garrigue [garig] **nf** garrigue, scrubland.

garrot [garo] **nm** *[cheval]* withers; (*Méd*) tourniquet; (*supplice*) garrotte.

garrotter [garɔte] 1 **vt** to tie up; (*fig*) to muzzle. **~ qn sur** to tie *or* strap sb down to.

gars* [gɑ] **nm** (*enfant, jeune homme*) lad (*Brit*); (*fils*) lad (*Brit*), boy; (*type*) bloke* (*Brit*), guy*. **mon petit ~** my lad; **dis-moi mon ~** tell me son *or* sonny* *ou* laddie*; **au revoir les ~!** cheerio boys!* *or* fellows!*; **un ~ du milieu** a bloke* (*Brit*) *or* fellow in the underworld.

Gascogne [gaskɔɲ] **nf** Gascony; *voir* **golfe**.

gascon, -onne [gaskɔ̃, ɔn] 1 **adj** Gascon. 2 **nm** (*Ling*) Gascon. 3 **nm,f: G~(ne)** Gascon; *voir* **promesse**.

gasconnade [gaskɔnad] **nf** (*littér: vantardise*) boasting (*NonC*), bragging (*NonC*).

gasoil nm, gas-oil [gazwal, gɑzɔjl] **nm** diesel oil.

Gaspard [gaspar] **nm** Gaspar.

gaspillage [gaspijaʒ] **nm** (*voir* **gaspiller**) wasting; squandering. (*résultat*) **quel ~!** what a waste!

gaspiller [gaspije] 1 **vt** *eau, nourriture, temps, dons* to waste; *fortune* to waste, squander. **qu'est-ce que tu gaspilles!** how you waste things!, how wasteful you are!

gaspilleur, -euse [gaspijœr, øz] 1 **adj** wasteful. 2 **nm,f** *[eau, nourriture, temps, dons]* waster; *[fortune]* squanderer.

gastéropode [gasterɔpɔd] **nm** gastropod, gasteropod. **~s** Gastropoda.

gastralgie [gastralʒi] **nf** stomach pains, gastralgia (*SPÉC*).

gastralgique [gastralʒik] **adj** gastralgic.

gastrine [gastrin] **nf** gastrin.

gastrique [gastrik] **adj** gastric; *voir* **embarras**.

gastrite [gastrit] **nf** gastritis.

gastro-entérite, pl gastro-entérites [gastroɑ̃terit] **nf** gastro-enteritis (*NonC*).

gastro-entérologie [gastroɑ̃terɔlɔʒi] **nf** gastroenterology.

gastro-entérologue, pl gastro-entérologues [gastroɑ̃terɔlɔg] **nmf** gastroenterologist.

gastro-intestinal, e, mpl -aux [gastroɛ̃tɛstinal, o] **adj** gastrointestinal.

gastronome [gastrɔnɔm] **nmf** gourmet, gastronome.

gastronomie [gastrɔnɔmi] **nf** gastronomy.

gastronomique [gastrɔnɔmik] **adj** gastronomic; *voir* **menu**[1], **restaurant**.

gastropode [gastrɔpɔd] **nm** = **gastéropode**.

gâte- [gɑt] **préf** *voir* **gâter**.

gâteau, pl ~x [gɑto] 1 **nm** a (*pâtisserie*) cake; (*au restaurant*) gateau; (*en Suisse: tarte*) tart. **~ d'anniversaire/aux amandes** birthday/almond cake; **~x à apéritif** (small) savoury biscuits, appetizers; **~x secs** biscuits (*Brit*), cookies (*US*); **~ de semoule/de riz** semolina/rice pudding; *voir* **petit**.

b (*fig *: butin, héritage*) loot‡. **se partager le ~** to share out the loot‡; **vouloir sa part du ~** to want one's share of the loot‡ *or* a fair share of the cake *ou* a piece of the pie* (*US*).

c **c'est du ~*** it's a piece of cake* (*Brit*) *or* a doddle* (*Brit*), it's a walkover*, it's a snap* (*US*); **pour lui, c'est du ~*** it's a piece of cake* for him (*Brit*), that's pie* to him (*US*); **c'est pas du ~*** it's no joke*.

d (*de plâtre etc*) cake. (*Agr*) **~ de miel** *or* **de cire** honeycomb.

2 **adj inv** (**: indulgent*) soft. **c'est un papa ~** he's a real softie* of a dad.

gâter [gɑte] 1 1 **vt** a (*abîmer*) *paysage, mur, papier, visage* to ruin, spoil; *plaisir, goût* to ruin, spoil; *esprit, jugement* to have a harmful effect on. **la chaleur a gâté la viande** the heat has made the meat go bad *or* go off (*Brit*); **avoir les dents gâtées** to have bad teeth; **tu vas te ~ les dents avec ces sucreries** you'll ruin your teeth with these sweets; **et, ce qui ne gâte rien, elle est jolie** and she's pretty, which is an added bonus *or* is even better.

b (*choyer*) *enfant etc* to spoil. **nous avons été gâtés cette année, il a fait très beau** we've been really lucky this year – the weather has been lovely; (*iro*) **il pleut, on est gâté!** just our luck! (*iro*) – it's raining!; **la malheureuse n'est pas gâtée par la nature** nature hasn't been very kind to the poor girl; *voir* **enfant**.

2 **se gâter vpr** *[viande]* to go bad, go off (*Brit*); *[fruit]* to go bad; *[temps]* to change (for the worse), take a turn for the worse; (*) *[ambiance, relations]* to take a turn for the worse. **le temps va se ~** the

weather's going to change for the worse *or* going to break; **ça commence** *or* **les choses commencent à se ~ (entre eux)** things are beginning to go badly *or* wrong (between them); **mon père vient de rentrer, ça va se ~!** my father has just come in and there's going to be trouble! *or* things are going to turn nasty!
3 comp ▸ **gâte-sauce** nm inv kitchen boy; (*péj*) bad cook.

gâterie [gɑtʀi] nf little treat. **je me suis payé une petite ~** (*objet*) I've treated myself to a little something, I've bought myself a little present; (*sucrerie*) I've bought myself a little treat.

gâteux, -euse* [gɑtø, øz] 1 adj (*sénile*) *vieillard* senile, gaga*, doddering (*épith*). **il l'aime tellement qu'il en est ~** he's really quite besotted with her, he loves her so much (that) it has made him a bit soft in the head* (*Brit*); **son petit-fils l'a rendu ~** he's gone soft* over his grandson. 2 nm: **(vieux) ~** (*sénile*) dotard, doddering old man; (*péj: radoteur, imbécile*) silly old duffer*. 3 **gâteuse** nf: **(vieille) ~euse** doddering old woman; silly old woman.

gâtifier* [gɑtifje] 1 vi to go soft in the head* (*Brit*).

gâtisme [gɑtism] nm *[vieillard]* senility; *[personne stupide]* idiocy, stupidity.

GATT [gat] nm (abrév de **General Agreement on Tariffs and Trade**) GATT.

gauche[1] [goʃ] 1 adj (*après n*) *bras, soulier, côté, rive* left. **du côté ~** on the left(-hand) side; *voir* **arme, lever, main, marier.**
2 nm (*Boxe*) (*coup*) left. (*poing*) **direct du ~** straight left; **crochet du ~** left hook.
3 nf a **la ~** the left (side), the left-hand side; **à ~** on the left; (*direction*) to the left; **à ma/sa ~** on my/his left, on my/his left-hand side; **le tiroir/chemin de ~** the left-hand drawer/path; **rouler à ~** *or* **sur la ~** to drive on the left; **mettre de l'argent à ~*** to put money aside (on the quiet); *voir* **conduite, jusque** *et pour autres exemples voir* **droite**[1].
b (*Pol*) **la ~** the left (wing); **les ~s** the parties of the left; **un homme de ~** a man of the left, a left-winger; **candidat/idées de ~** left-wing candidate/ideas; **elle est très à ~** she's very left-wing; **la ~ est divisée** the left-wing is split; *voir* **extrême.**
c (*Boxe*) (*coup*) left. (*main*) **crochet de la ~** left hook.

gauche[2] [goʃ] adj a (*maladroit*) *personne, style, geste* awkward, clumsy; (*emprunté*) *air, manière* awkward, gauche. b (*tordu*) *planche, règle* warped; (*Math*) *courbe, surface* skew.

gauchement [goʃmɑ̃] adv clumsily, awkwardly.

gaucher, -ère [goʃe, ɛʀ] 1 adj left-handed. 2 nm,f left-handed person; (*Sport*) left-hander.

gaucherie [goʃʀi] nf *[allure]* awkwardness (*NonC*); *[action, expression]* clumsiness (*NonC*); (*acte*) awkward *or* clumsy behaviour (*NonC*). **une ~ de style** a clumsy turn of phrase.

gauchir [goʃiʀ] 2 1 vt (*Aviat, Menuiserie*) to warp; (*fig*) *idée, fait* to distort, misrepresent; *esprit* to warp. 2 vi to warp. 3 **se gauchir** vpr to warp.

gauchisant, e [goʃizɑ̃, ɑ̃t] adj *auteur* with left-wing *or* leftist tendencies; *théorie* with a left-wing *or* leftish bias.

gauchisme [goʃism] nm leftism.

gauchissement [goʃismɑ̃] nm (*voir* **gauchir**) warping; distortion, misrepresentation.

gauchiste [goʃist] 1 adj leftist (*épith*). 2 nmf leftist.

gaudriole* [godʀijɔl] nf a (*NonC*) *[homme]* womanizing; *[femme]* manhunting* (*fig*). **celui-là, pour la ~, il est toujours prêt!** he's always game for a spot of womanizing!*, he's a great one for the women!* b (*propos*) broad joke.

gaufrage [gofʀaʒ] nm (*voir* **gaufrer**) embossing; figuring; goffering.

gaufre [gofʀ] nf (*Culin*) waffle; (*en cire*) honeycomb; *voir* **moule**[1].

gaufrer [gofʀe] 1 vt *papier, cuir* (*en relief*) to emboss; (*en creux*) to figure; *tissu* to goffer. **sur papier gaufré** on embossed paper; *voir* **fer.**

gaufrerie [gofʀəʀi] nf (*Can*) waffle shop.

gaufrette [gofʀɛt] nf wafer.

gaufrier [gofʀije] nm waffle iron.

gaufrure [gofʀyʀ] nf (*voir* **gaufrer**) embossing (*NonC*); embossed design; figuring (*NonC*); goffering (*NonC*).

Gaule [gol] nf Gaul.

gaule [gol] nf (*perche*) (long) pole; (*Pêche*) fishing rod.

gauler [gole] 1 vt *arbre* to beat (*using a long pole to bring down the fruit or nuts*); *fruits, noix* to bring down, shake down (*with a pole*). **se faire ~*** to get caught (in the act).

gaullien, -ienne [goljɛ̃, jɛn] adj de Gaullian.

gaullisme [golism] nm Gaullism.

gaulliste [golist] adj, nmf Gaullist.

gaulois, e [golwa, waz] 1 adj a (*de Gaule*) Gallic. b (*grivois*) bawdy. **esprit ~** (broad *ou* bawdy) Gallic humour. 2 nm (*Ling*) Gaulish. 3 nm,f: **G~(e)** Gaul; *voir* **moustache.** 4 **gauloise** nf (®: *cigarette*) Gauloise.

gauloisement [golwazmɑ̃] adv bawdily.

gauloiserie [golwazʀi] nf (*propos*) bawdy story (*ou* joke); (*caractère grivois*) bawdiness.

gauss [gos] nm (*Phys*) gauss.

gausser (se) [gose] 1 vpr (*littér: se moquer*) to laugh (and make fun), mock. **vous vous gaussez!** you jest!; **se ~ de** to deride, make mock of (*littér*), poke fun at.

gavage [gavaʒ] nm (*Élevage*) force-feeding.

gave [gav] nm mountain stream (*in the Pyrenees*).

gaver [gave] 1 1 vt *animal* to force-feed; *personne* to fill up (*de* with). **je suis gavé!** I'm full (up)!, I'm full to bursting!*; (*fig*) **on les gave de connaissances inutiles** they cram them with useless knowledge; **on nous gave de séries télévisées/de publicité** we're fed a non-stop diet of television serials/advertisements.
2 **se gaver** vpr: **se ~ de** *nourriture* to stuff o.s. with; *romans* to devour; **il se gave de films** he's a glutton for films, he's a real film addict; **si tu te gaves maintenant, tu ne pourras plus rien manger au moment du dîner** if you go stuffing yourself* *ou* filling yourself up now, you won't be able to eat anything at dinner time.

gavial [gavjal] nm gavial, g(h)arial.

gavotte [gavɔt] nf gavotte.

gavroche [gavʀɔʃ] nm street urchin (*in Paris*).

gay* [gɛ] adj, nm gay.

gaz [gɑz] 1 nm inv a (*Chim*) gas; *[boisson]* fizz. **le ~ (domestique)** (domestic) gas (*NonC*); (*Mil*) **les ~** gas; **l'employé du ~** the gasman; **se chauffer au ~** to have gas(-fired) heating; **s'éclairer au ~** to have *ou* use gas lighting; **faire la cuisine au ~** to cook with gas; **cuisinière** *etc* **à ~** gas cooker *etc*; **vous avez le ~?** are you on gas?, do you have gas?; **il s'est suicidé au ~** he gassed himself; **suicide au ~** (suicide by) gassing; (*Aut*) **mettre les ~*** to step on the gas*, put one's foot down* (*Brit*); *voir* **bec, chambre, eau, plein.**
b (*euph: pet*) wind (*NonC*). **avoir des ~** to have wind.
2 comp ▸ **gaz d'admission** (*Aut*) air-fuel mixture ▸ **gaz asphyxiant** poison gas ▸ **gaz en bouteille** bottled gas ▸ **gaz carbonique** carbon dioxide ▸ **gaz de combat** poison gas (*for use in warfare*) ▸ **gaz d'échappement** (*Aut*) exhaust gas ▸ **gaz d'éclairage**† = **gaz de ville** ▸ **gaz hilarant** laughing gas ▸ **gaz des houillères** firedamp (*NonC*) ▸ **gaz lacrymogène** teargas ▸ **gaz des marais** marsh gas ▸ **gaz moutarde** (*Mil*) mustard gas ▸ **gaz naturel** natural gas ▸ **gaz neurotoxique** nerve gas ▸ **gaz parfait** perfect *ou* ideal gas ▸ **gaz de pétrole liquéfié** liquid petroleum gas ▸ **gaz poivre** pepper gas ▸ **gaz rare** rare gas ▸ **gaz sulfureux** sulphur dioxide ▸ **gaz de ville** town gas.

Gaza [gaza] n: **la bande** *ou* **le territoire de ~** the Gaza Strip.

gazage [gɑzaʒ] nm (*Mil*) gassing.

gaze [gɑz] nf gauze.

gazé, e [gɑze] (ptp de **gazer**) adj (*Mil*) gassed. **les ~s de 14-18** the (poison) gas victims of the 1914-18 war.

gazéification [gɑzeifikasjɔ̃] nf (*voir* **gazéifier**) gasification; aeration.

gazéifier [gɑzeifje] 7 vt (*Chim*) to gasify; *eau minérale* to aerate.

gazelle [gazɛl] nf gazelle; *voir* **œil.**

gazer [gɑze] 1 1 vi (*: *aller, marcher*) **ça gaze?** (*affaires, santé*) how's things?*, how goes it?*; (*travail*) how goes it?*, how's it going?*; **ça gaze avec ta belle-mère?** how's it going with your *ou* are you getting on OK with your mother-in-law?*; **ça a/ça n'a pas gazé?** did it/didn't it go OK?*; **ça ne gaze pas fort** (*santé*) I'm not feeling so *ou* too great*; (*affaires*) things aren't going too well; **il y a quelque chose qui ne gaze pas** there's something slightly fishy about it, there's something wrong somewhere. 2 vt (*Mil*) to gas.

gazetier, -ière [gɑz(ə)tje, jɛʀ] nm,f (†† *ou hum*) journalist.

gazette [gazɛt] nf (††, *hum, littér*) newspaper. (*hum*) **c'est dans la ~ locale** it's in the local rag; **c'est une vraie ~** he's a mine of information about the latest (local) gossip; **faire la ~** to give a rundown* (*de* on).

gazeux, -euse [gɑzø, øz] adj (*Chim*) gaseous; *boisson* fizzy; *voir* **eau.**

gazier, -ière [gɑzje, jɛʀ] 1 adj (*rare*) gas (*épith*). 2 nm (*employé*) gasman; (‡: *type*) geezer‡ (*Brit*), guy.

gazinière [gɑzinjɛʀ] nf gas cooker.

gazoduc [gɑzodyk] nm gas main, gas pipeline.

gazogène [gɑzɔʒɛn] nm gas producer (*plant*).

gazole [gazɔl] nm diesel oil.

gazoline [gazɔlin] nf gasoline, gasolene.

gazomètre [gɑzɔmɛtʀ] nm gasometer.

gazon [gɑzɔ̃] nm (*pelouse*) lawn. (*herbe*) **le ~** turf (*NonC*), grass (*NonC*); **motte de ~** turf, sod; (*pelouse*) **~ anglais** well-kept *ou* smooth lawn.

gazonner [gɑzɔne] 1 vt *talus, terrain* to plant with grass, turf.

gazouillement [gazujmɑ̃] nm (*voir* **gazouiller**) chirping (*NonC*), warbling (*NonC*); babbling (*NonC*); gurgling (*NonC*), gurgle.

gazouiller [gazuje] 1 vi *[oiseau]* to chirp, warble; *[ruisseau]* to babble; *[bébé]* to gurgle, babble.

gazouilleur, -euse [gazujœʀ, øz] adj (*voir* **gazouiller**) chirping, warbling; babbling; gurgling.

gazouillis [gazuji] nm *[oiseau]* chirping, warbling; *[ruisseau, bébé]* babbling.

GB [ʒebe] nf (abrév de **Grande-Bretagne**) GB.

Gdansk [gdɑ̃sk] n Gdansk.

gdb* [ʒedebe] nf (abrév de **gueule de bois**) **avoir la ~** to have a hangover.

GDF [ʒedeɛf] nm (abrév de **Gaz de France**) *French gas company.*

geai [ʒɛ] nm jay.

géant, e [ʒeɑ̃, ɑ̃t] 1 adj gigantic; *animal, plante* gigantic, giant (*épith*); *paquet, carton* giant-size (*épith*), giant (*épith*); *étoile* great (*épith*). (*fig*) **c'est ~!*** it's great *ou* magic!* **2 nm** (*lit, fig*) giant; (*Écon, Pol*) giant power; *voir* **pas¹**. **3 géante nf** giantess.

Gédéon [ʒedeɔ̃] **nm** Gideon.

géhenne [ʒeɛn] **nf** (*Bible: enfer*) Gehenna.

geignant, e [ʒɛɲɑ̃, ɑ̃t] **adj** (*voir* **geindre**) groaning; moaning; whining; complaining.

geignard, e* [ʒɛɲaʀ, aʀd] **1 adj** *personne* moaning; *voix* whingeing, whining; *musique* whining. **2 nm,f** moaner.

geignement [ʒɛɲmɑ̃] **nm** moaning (*NonC*).

geindre [ʒɛ̃dʀ] [52] **vi** (*gémir*) to groan, moan (*de* with); (*péj: pleurnicher*) to moan; *[vent]* to whine, moan. **il geint tout le temps*** he never stops *ou* he's always moaning *ou* complaining *ou* griping*; (*littér*) **le vent faisait ~ les peupliers/le gréement** the wind made the poplars/the rigging groan *ou* moan.

geisha [gɛʃa] **nf** geisha (girl).

gel [ʒɛl] **nm a** (*temps*) frost. **un jour de ~** one frosty day; **plantes tuées par le ~** plants killed by (the) frost. **b** (*glace*) frost. **"craint le ~"** "keep away from extreme cold". **c** (*Écon*) *[crédits]* freezing. **d** (*substance*) gel. **~ de silice** silica gel; **~ fixant** *ou* **coiffant** *ou* **structurant** hair gel.

gélatine [ʒelatin] **nf** gelatine.

gélatineux, -euse [ʒelatinø, øz] **adj** jelly-like, gelatinous.

gelé, e¹ [ʒ(ə)le] (**ptp de geler**) **adj** (*Théât*) *public* cold (*fig*), unresponsive.

gelée² [ʒ(ə)le] **nf a** (*gel*) frost. **~ blanche** white frost, hoarfrost. **b** (*Culin*) *[fruits]* jelly (*Brit*), Jell-O ® (*US*), jello (*US*); *[viande, volaille]* jelly. **poulet en ~** chicken in aspic *ou* jelly; **~ de framboises** raspberry jelly (*Brit*) *ou* Jell-O ® (*US*) *ou* jello (*US*); **~ royale** royal jelly.

geler [ʒ(ə)le] [5] **1 vt a** *eau, rivière* to (make) freeze *ou* ice over; *buée* to turn to ice; *sol* to freeze.

b les nuits printanières ont gelé les bourgeons the buds were blighted *ou* nipped by frost during the spring nights; **le skieur a eu les pieds gelés** the skier's feet were frostbitten, the skier had frostbite on both feet; **le froid lui a gelé les mains** he got frostbite in both hands; **ils sont morts gelés** they froze to death, they died of exposure.

c (*Fin*) *prix, crédits* to freeze; (*Pol*) *négociations* to suspend; *relations* to break off.

2 se geler* **vpr** (*avoir froid*) to freeze. **on se gèle ici** we're *ou* it's freezing here; **on se les gèle‡** it's bloody (*Brit*) *ou* damned freezing‡, it's brass monkey weather‡ (*Brit*); **vous allez vous ~, à l'attendre** you'll get frozen stiff waiting for him.

3 vi a *[eau, lac]* to freeze (over), ice over; *[sol, linge, conduit]* to freeze; *[récoltes]* to be attacked *ou* blighted *ou* nipped by frost; *[doigt, membre]* to be freezing, be frozen. **les salades ont gelé sur pied** the lettuces have frozen on their stalks.

b (*avoir froid*) to be frozen, freeze. **on gèle ici** we're *ou* it's freezing here; **j'ai les mains gelées** my hands are frozen (stiff) *ou* freezing; **je suis gelé** I'm frozen (stiff) *ou* freezing.

4 vb impers: il gèle it's freezing; **il a gelé dur** *ou* (*littér*) **à pierre fendre** it froze hard, there was a hard frost; **il a gelé blanc** there was a white icy frost.

gélifiant [ʒelifjɑ̃] **nm** jelling *ou* gelling agent.

gélifier [ʒelifje] [7] **1 vt** to make gel. **2 se gélifier vpr** to gel.

gélinotte [ʒelinɔt] **nf: ~ (des bois)** hazel grouse, hazel hen.

gélose [ʒeloz] **nf** agar-agar.

gélule [ʒelyl] **nf** (*Pharm*) capsule.

gelure [ʒ(ə)lyʀ] **nf** (*Méd*) frostbite (*NonC*).

Gémeaux [ʒemo] **nmpl** (*Astron*) Gemini. **être (des) ~** to be (a) Gemini.

gémellaire [ʒemelɛʀ] **adj** twin (*épith*).

gémination [ʒeminasjɔ̃] **nf** gemination.

géminé, e [ʒemine] **1 adj** (*Ling*) *consonne* geminate; (*Archit*) gemeled, gemel; (*Bio*) geminate. **2 géminée nf** (*Ling*) geminate.

gémir [ʒemiʀ] [2] **vi a** (*geindre*) to groan, moan (*de* with). **~ sur son sort** to bemoan one's fate; (*littér*) **~ sous l'oppression** to groan under oppression. **b** (*fig: grincer*) *[ressort, gonds, plancher]* to creak; *[vent]* to moan. **les gonds de la porte gémissaient horriblement** the door hinges made a horrible creaking noise. **c** *[colombe]* to cry plaintively, moan.

gémissant, e [ʒemisɑ̃, ɑ̃t] **adj** *voix* wailing; *gonds, plancher* creaking.

gémissement [ʒemismɑ̃] **nm** *[voix]* groan, moan; (*prolongé*) groaning (*NonC*), moaning (*NonC*); *[meuble]* creaking (*NonC*); *[vent]* moaning (*NonC*).

gemmage [ʒemaʒ] **nm** tapping (*of pine trees*).

gemmail, pl -aux [ʒemaj, o] **nm** non-leaded stained glass.

gemme [ʒɛm] **nf a** (*Minér*) gem(stone). **b** (*résine de pin*) (pine) resin; *voir* **sel**.

gemmé, e [ʒeme] (**ptp de gemmer²**) **adj** (*littér*) gemmed, studded with precious stones.

gemmer¹ [ʒeme] [1] **vt** to tap (*pine trees*).

gemmer² [ʒeme] [1] **vt** (*littér*) to decorate *ou* stud with precious stones.

gémonies [ʒemɔni] **nfpl** (*littér*) **vouer** *ou* **traîner qn aux ~** to subject sb to *ou* hold sb up to public obloquy.

gênant, e [ʒɛnɑ̃, ɑ̃t] **adj a** (*irritant*) **l'eau est coupée, c'est vraiment ~** they've cut the water off – it's a real nuisance; **il est ~ avec sa fumée** he is a nuisance with his smoke; **ce n'est pas ~** it's OK, it doesn't matter. **b** (*embarrassant*) *situation, moment, témoin* awkward, embarrassing; *révélations, regard, présence* embarrassing.

gencive [ʒɑ̃siv] **nf** (*Anat*) gum. **il a pris un coup dans les ~s‡** he got a sock on the jaw* *ou* kick in the teeth*.

gendarme [ʒɑ̃daʀm] **nm a** (*policier*) policeman, police officer; (*en France*) gendarme; (*cavalier*) (*Hist Mil*) horseman; (*soldat*) soldier, man-at-arms. (*fig*) **faire le ~** to play the role of policeman; (*hum*) **sa femme est un vrai ~** his wife's a real battle-axe*; **jouer aux ~s et aux voleurs** to play cops and robbers; **~ mobile** member of the anti-riot police; (*fig*) **~ couché** sleeping policeman (*Brit*), speed bump; *voir* **chapeau, peur**. **b** (*Zool: punaise*) fire bug; (*Alpinisme*) gendarme (*SPÉC*), pinnacle. **c** (*†: hareng*) bloater (*Brit*), salt herring (*US*).

gendarmer (se) [ʒɑ̃daʀme] [1] **vpr** to kick up a fuss* (*contre* about). **il faut se ~ pour qu'elle aille se coucher/pour la faire manger** you really have to take quite a strong line (with her) *ou* you really have to lay down the law to get her to go to bed/to get her to eat.

gendarmerie [ʒɑ̃daʀməʀi] **nf** (*corps militaire*) police force, constabulary (*in countryside and small towns*); (*en France*) Gendarmerie; (*bureaux*) police station (*in countryside and small towns*); (*caserne*) gendarmes' *ou* Gendarmerie barracks, police barracks; (*Hist Mil*) (*cavalerie*) heavy cavalry *ou* horse; (*garde royale*) royal guard. **~ mobile** anti-riot police; **~ maritime** coastguard.

gendre [ʒɑ̃dʀ] **nm** son-in-law.

gène [ʒɛn] **nm** gene.

gêne [ʒɛn] **nf a** (*malaise physique*) discomfort. **~ respiratoire** breathing *ou* respiratory problems; **il ressentait une certaine ~ à respirer** he experienced some *ou* a certain difficulty in breathing.

b (*désagrément, dérangement*) trouble, bother. **je ne voudrais vous causer aucune ~** I wouldn't like to put you to any trouble *ou* bother, I wouldn't want to be a nuisance; (*Prov*) **où il y a de la ~, il n'y a pas de plaisir** comfort comes first, there's no sense in being uncomfortable; (*péj*) some people only think of their own comfort; (*Sport*) **il y a eu ~** there was a (slight) obstruction.

c (*manque d'argent*) financial difficulties *ou* straits. **vivre dans la ~/dans une grande ~** to be in financial difficulties *ou* straits/in great financial difficulties *ou* straits.

d (*confusion, trouble*) embarrassment. **un moment de ~** a moment of embarrassment; **j'éprouve de la ~ devant lui** I feel embarrassed *ou* ill-at-ease in his presence; **il éprouva de la ~ à lui avouer cela** he felt embarrassed admitting *ou* to admit that to her; *voir* **sans**.

gêné, e [ʒene] (**ptp de gêner**) **adj a** (*à court d'argent*) short (of money) (*attrib*), hard up* (*attrib*). **être ~ aux entournures*** to be short of money *ou* hard up*. **b** (*embarrassé*) *personne, sourire, air* embarrassed, self-conscious; *silence* uncomfortable, embarrassed, awkward. **j'étais ~!** I was (so) embarrassed!, I felt (so) awkward *ou* uncomfortable. **c** (*physiquement*) uncomfortable. **êtes-vous ~ pour respirer?** do you have trouble (in) breathing?; **je suis ~e dans cette robe** I'm uncomfortable in this dress.

généalogie [ʒenealɔʒi] **nf** *[famille]* ancestry, genealogy; *[animaux]* pedigree; (*Bio*) *[espèces]* genealogy; (*sujet d'études*) genealogy. **faire** *ou* **dresser la ~ de qn** to trace sb's ancestry *ou* genealogy.

généalogique [ʒenealɔʒik] **adj** genealogical; *voir* **arbre**.

généalogiste [ʒenealɔʒist] **nmf** genealogist.

gêner [ʒene] [1] **1 vt a** (*physiquement*) *[fumée, bruit]* to bother; *[vêtement étroit, obstacle]* to hamper. **cela vous gêne-t-il si je fume?** do you mind if I smoke?, does it bother you if I smoke?; **~ le passage** to be in the way; **ça me gêne** *ou* **c'est gênant pour respirer/pour écrire** it hampers my breathing/hampers me when I write; **le bruit me gêne pour travailler** noise bothers me *ou* disturbs me when I'm trying to work; **son complet le gêne (aux entournures*)** his suit is uncomfortable *ou* constricting; **ces papiers me gênent** these papers are in my way.

b (*déranger*) *personne* to bother, put out; *projet* to hamper, hinder. **je crains de ~** I am afraid to bother people *ou* put people out, I'm afraid of being a nuisance; **je ne voudrais pas (vous) ~** I don't want to bother you *ou* put you out *ou* be in the way; **j'espère que ça ne vous gêne pas d'y aller** I hope it won't inconvenience you *ou* put you out to go; **cela vous gênerait de faire mes courses/de ne pas fumer?** would you mind doing my shopping/not smoking?; **et alors, ça te gêne?*** so what?*, what's it to you?*

c (*financièrement*) to put in financial difficulties. **ces dépenses vont les ~ considérablement** *ou* **vont les ~ aux entournures*** these expenses are really going to put them in financial difficulties *ou* make things tight for them *ou* make them hard up*.

d (*mettre mal à l'aise*) to make feel ill-at-ease *ou* uncomfortable. **ça me gêne de vous dire ça mais ...** I hate to tell you but ...; **ça me gêne de me déshabiller chez le médecin** I find it embarrassing to get undressed at the doctor's; **sa présence me gêne** his presence *ou* he makes me feel uncomfortable, he cramps my style; **son regard la gênait** his glance made her feel ill-at-ease *ou* uncomfortable; **cela le gêne qu'on fasse tout le travail pour lui** it embarrasses him to have all the work done for him, he feels awkward about having all the work done for him.

2 se gêner vpr a (*se contraindre*) to put o.s. out. **ne vous gênez pas pour moi** don't mind me, don't put yourself out for me; (*iro*) **ne vous gênez pas!** feel free!, (just) make yourself at home!; **il ne faut**

pas vous ~ avec moi don't stand on ceremony with me; **non mais! je vais me ~!** why shouldn't I!; **il y en a qui ne se gênent pas!** some people just don't care!; **il ne s'est pas gêné pour le lui dire** he told him straight out, he didn't mind telling him.

b (*dans un lieu*) **on se gêne à trois dans ce bureau** three's a crowd *ou* the three of us get in each other's way in this office, this office is too small for three of us.

général, e, mpl **-aux** [ʒeneʀal, o] 1 adj a (*d'ensemble*) *vue, tableau* general; (*vague*) general. **un tableau ~ de la situation** a general *ou* an overall picture of the situation; **avoir le goût des idées ~es** to have a preference for broad *ou* general ideas; **remarques d'ordre très ~** comments of a very general nature; **se lancer dans des considérations ~es sur le temps** to venture some general remarks about the weather; **d'une façon** *ou* **manière ~e** in a general way, generally; (*précédant une affirmation*) generally *ou* broadly speaking; *voir* **règle**.

b (*total, global*) *assemblée, grève etc* general. (*commun*) **dans l'intérêt ~** in the general *ou* common interest; **cette opinion est devenue ~e** this is now a widely shared *ou* generally held opinion; *[crise, peur]* **devenir ~** to become widespread; **la mêlée devint ~e** the fight turned into a general free-for-all; **à l'indignation/la surprise ~e** to the indignation/surprise of most *ou* many people; **à la demande ~e** in response to popular *ou* general demand; *voir* **concours, état, médecine.**

c **en ~** (*habituellement*) usually, generally, in general; (*de façon générale*) generally, in general. **je parle en ~** I'm speaking in general terms *ou* generally.

d (*Admin: principal*) general (*épith*). **conseil ~** general council; **secrétaire ~** (*gén*) general secretary; *[organisation internationale]* secretary-general; *voir* **directeur, fermier, président.**

2 nm a (*Mil*) general; *voir* **mon.**

b (*Philos*) **le ~** the general; **aller du ~ au particulier** to go from the general to the particular.

3 **générale** nf a (*épouse du général*) general's wife; *voir* **Madame.**

b (*Théât*) **(répétition) ~e** (final) dress rehearsal.

c (*Mil*) **battre** *ou* **sonner la ~e** to call to arms.

4 comp ▸**général d'armée** general; (*Aviat*) air chief marshal (*Brit*), general (*US*) ▸**général de brigade** brigadier (*Brit*), brigadier general (*US*) ▸**général de brigade aérienne** air commodore (*Brit*), brigadier general (*US*) ▸**général en chef** general-in-chief, general-in-command ▸**général de corps aérien** air marshal (*Brit*), lieutenant general (*US*) ▸**général de corps d'armée** lieutenant-general ▸**général de division** major general ▸**général de division aérienne** air vice marshal (*Brit*), major general (*US*).

généralement [ʒeneʀalmɑ̃] adv generally. **il est ~ chez lui après 8 heures** he's generally *ou* usually at home after 8 o'clock; **~ parlant** generally speaking; **coutume assez ~ répandue** fairly widespread custom.

généralisable [ʒeneʀalizabl] adj *mesure, observation* which can be applied generally.

généralisateur, -trice [ʒeneʀalizatœʀ, tʀis] adj: **tendance ~trice** tendency to generalize *ou* towards generalization; **il a un esprit ~** he is given to generalizing.

généralisation [ʒeneʀalizasjɔ̃] nf (*extension, énoncé*) generalization.

généraliser [ʒeneʀalize] [1] 1 vt a (*étendre*) to generalize; *méthode* to put *ou* bring into general *ou* widespread use. (*Méd*) **cancer généralisé** general cancer; (*Méd*) **infection généralisée** systemic infection. b (*raisonner*) to generalize. **il aime beaucoup ~** he loves to generalize. 2 **se généraliser** vpr *[infection]* to become widespread; *[procédé]* to become widespread, come into general use. **la semaine de 5 jours se généralise en France** the 5-day (working) week is becoming the norm in France.

généralissime [ʒeneʀalisim] nm generalissimo.

généraliste [ʒeneʀalist] 1 adj *radio, télévision* general-interest (*épith*); *formation* general; *ingénieur* non-specialized. 2 nm: **(médecin) ~** G.P., general *ou* family practitioner.

généralité [ʒeneʀalite] nf a (*presque totalité*) majority. **dans la ~ des cas** in the majority of cases, in most cases. b (*caractère général*) *[affirmation]* general nature. c **~s** (*introduction*) general points; (*péj: banalités*) generalities.

générateur, -trice [ʒeneʀatœʀ, tʀis] 1 adj *force* generating; *fonction* generative, generating. **~ de** (*gén*) which causes, productive of; (*Math*) which generates, generating; **~ de désordres** *ou* **de troubles** which causes trouble; **usine ~trice** generator. 2 nm (*Tech*) **~ (électrique)** (electric) generator; **~ (de vapeur)** steam boiler. 3 **génératrice** nf a (*Tech*) **~trice (d'électricité)** generator. b (*Math*) **(ligne) ~trice** generating line, generatrix.

génératif, -ive [ʒeneʀatif, iv] adj (*Ling*) generative. **grammaire ~ive** generative grammar.

génération [ʒeneʀasjɔ̃] nf (*gén*) generation. (*Bio*) **~ spontanée** spontaneous generation; **ordinateur de la première/seconde** *etc* **~** first/second *etc* generation computer.

générer [ʒeneʀe] [6] vt (*Ling*) to generate.

généreusement [ʒeneʀøzmɑ̃] adv (*voir* **généreux**) generously; nobly; magnanimously.

généreux, -euse [ʒeneʀø, øz] 1 adj a (*libéral*) generous. **être ~ de son temps** to be generous with one's time. b (*noble, désintéressé*) *acte, caractère* generous; *âme, sentiment, idée* generous, noble; *adversaire* generous, magnanimous. c (*riche*) *sol* productive, fertile, generous; *vin* generous, full-bodied. **femmes aux formes ~euses** women with generous curves. 2 nm,f: **faire le ~** to act generous*.

générique [ʒeneʀik] 1 adj generic; (*Comm*) *produit* unbranded, generic; *médicament* generic. (*Ordin*) **caractère ~** wildcard (character); (*Ling*) **terme ~** generic term. 2 nm (*Ciné*) credit titles, credits, cast (and credits) (*US*).

générosité [ʒeneʀozite] nf a (*libéralité*) *[pourboire, personne]* generosity. **avec ~** generously. b (*noblesse*) *[acte, caractère]* generosity; *[âme, sentiment]* nobility; *[adversaire]* generosity, magnanimity. **avoir la ~ de** to be generous enough to, have the generosity to. c (*largesses*) **~s** kindnesses.

Gênes [ʒɛn] n Genoa.

genèse [ʒənɛz] nf (*élaboration*) genesis. (*Bible*) **(le livre de) la G~** (the Book of) Genesis.

genet [ʒ(ə)nɛ] nm jennet.

genêt [ʒ(ə)nɛ] nm broom (*Bot*).

généticien, -ienne [ʒenetisjɛ̃, jɛn] nm,f geneticist.

génétique [ʒenetik] 1 adj genetic; *voir* **manipulation.** 2 nf genetics (*sg*).

génétiquement [ʒenetikmɑ̃] adv genetically.

gêneur, -euse [ʒɛnœʀ, øz] nm,f (*importun*) intruder. (*représentant un obstacle*) **supprimer un ~/les ~s** to do away with a person who is *ou* stands/people who are *ou* stand in one's way.

Genève [ʒ(ə)nɛv] n Geneva.

genevois, e [ʒən(ə)vwa, waz] 1 adj Genevan. 2 nm,f: **G~(e)** Genevan.

genévrier [ʒənevʀije] nm juniper.

génial, e, mpl **-iaux** [ʒenjal, jo] adj a (*inspiré*) *écrivain, invention* of genius; *plan, idée* inspired (*gén épith*). **un plan d'une conception ~e** an inspired idea, a brilliantly thought out idea. b (**: formidable*) fantastic*, great*. **c'est ~!** that's fantastic!*; **c'est un type ~!** he's a tremendous *ou* fantastic bloke* (*Brit*) *ou* guy*; **physiquement, il n'est pas ~ mais ...** he's not up to much physically but ...; **elle est ~e ton idée** that's a brilliant *ou* great idea*; **ce n'est pas ~!** *[idée]* that's not very clever!; *[film]* it's not brilliant!*

génialement [ʒenjalmɑ̃] adv a (*magistralement*) with genius, brilliantly. b (*rare: magnifiquement*) brilliantly.

génie [ʒeni] 1 nm a (*aptitude supérieure*) genius. **avoir du ~** to have genius; **éclair** *ou* **trait de ~** stroke of genius; **homme de ~** man of genius; **compositeur/idée/découverte de ~** composer/idea/discovery of genius.

b (*personne*) genius. **ce n'est pas un ~!** he's no genius!

c (*talent*) **(avoir) le ~ des maths/des affaires** (to have) a genius for maths/for business; **avoir le ~ du mal** to have an evil bent; **il a le ~ de** *ou* **pour dire ce qu'il ne faut pas** he has a genius for saying the wrong thing.

d (*caractère inné*) **le ~ latin** the Latin genius; **le ~ de la langue française** the genius of the French language.

e (*allégorie*) spirit. **le ~ de la liberté** the spirit of liberty; *[histoires arabes]* **le ~ de la lampe** the genie of the lamp; **~ des airs/des eaux** spirit of the air/waters; **être le bon/mauvais ~ de qn** to be sb's good/evil genius.

f (*Mil*) **le ~** ≃ the Engineers; **soldat du ~** sapper, engineer; **faire son service dans le ~** to do one's service in the Engineers.

2 comp ▸**génie atomique/chimique** atomic/chemical engineering ▸**génie civil** (*branche*) civil engineering; (*corps*) civil engineers ▸**génie électronique** electronic engineering ▸**génie génétique** genetic engineering ▸**génie industriel** industrial engineering ▸**génie logiciel** software engineering ▸**génie maritime** (*branche*) marine engineering; (*corps*) marine engineers (*under State command*) ▸**génie mécanique** mechanical engineering ▸**génie militaire** (*branche*) military engineering; (*corps*) ≃ Engineers; *voir* **ingénieur.**

genièvre [ʒənjɛvʀ] nm (*boisson*) Hollands (*Brit*), geneva (*Brit*), gin; (*arbre*) juniper; (*fruit*) juniper berry. **grains de ~** juniper berries.

génisse [ʒenis] nf heifer.

génital, e, mpl **-aux** [ʒenital, o] adj genital. **organes ~aux, parties ~es** genitals, genital organs, genitalia.

géniteur, -trice [ʒenitœʀ, tʀis] 1 nm,f (*hum: parent*) parent. 2 nm (*Zool: reproducteur*) sire.

génitif [ʒenitif] nm genitive (case).

génito-urinaire, pl **génito-urinaires** [ʒenitoyʀinɛʀ] adj genito-urinary.

génocide [ʒenɔsid] nm genocide.

génois, e [ʒenwa, waz] 1 adj Genoese. 2 nm,f: **G~(e)** Genoese. 3 nm (*Naut*) genoa (jib). 4 **génoise** nf (*Culin*) sponge cake.

génome [ʒenom] nm genom(e).

génotype [ʒenotip] nm genotype.

genou, pl **~x** [ʒ(ə)nu] nm a (*Anat, Habillement, Zool*) knee. **avoir les ~x cagneux** *ou* **rentrants** to be knock-kneed; **mes ~x se dérobèrent sous moi** my legs gave way under me; **avoir de la vase jusqu'aux ~x, être dans la vase jusqu'aux ~x** to be up to one's knees *ou* be knee-deep in mud.

b **à ~x: il était à ~x** he was kneeling, he was on his knees; (*fig*)

être à ~x devant qn to idolize *ou* worship sb; **se mettre à ~x** to kneel down, go down on one's knees; (*fig*) **se mettre à ~x devant qn** to go down on one's knees to sb; **c'est à se mettre à ~x!*** it's out of this world!*; **tomber/se jeter à ~x** to fall/ throw o.s. on *ou* to one's knees; **j'en suis tombé à ~x!*** I just about dropped!*; **demander qch à (deux) ~x** to ask for sth on bended knee, go down on one's knees for sth; **je te demande pardon à ~x** I beg you to forgive me.

c (*Tech*) ball and socket joint.

d (*loc*) **avoir/prendre qn sur ses ~x** to have/take sb on one's knee *ou* lap; **donner un coup de ~ à qn** to knee sb; **il me donna un coup de ~ dans le ventre** he thrust his knee into my stomach, he kneed me in the stomach; **il me donna un coup de ~ pour me réveiller** he nudged me with his knee to waken me; **faire du ~ à qn*** to play footsie with sb*; **tomber aux ~x de qn** to fall at sb's feet, go down on one's knees to sb; (*littér*) **fléchir** *ou* **plier** *ou* **ployer le ~ devant qn** to bend the knee to sb; (*littér*) **mettre (un) ~ à terre devant qn** to go down on one knee before sb; **être sur les ~x*** to be ready to drop, be on one's last legs, be on one's knees* (*Brit*); **le pays est sur les ~x*** the country is on its knees*; **ça m'a mis sur les ~x de courir à droite et à gauche** I was run off my feet dashing here, there and everywhere.

genouillère [ʒ(ə)nujɛʀ] **nf** (*Méd*) knee support; (*Sport*) kneepad, kneecap.

genre [ʒɑ̃ʀ] **nm** a (*espèce*) kind, type, sort. **~ de vie** lifestyle, way of life; **c'est le ~ de femme qui** she is the type *ou* the kind *ou* the sort of woman who; **les rousses, ce n'est pas mon ~** redheads aren't my type; **lui c'est le ~ grognon*** he's the grumpy sort*; **ce type n'est pas mal dans** *ou* **en son ~** that fellow isn't bad in his own way *ou* isn't bad of (*Brit*) *ou* for (*US*) his type; **cette maison n'est pas mauvaise en son ~** that house isn't bad of (*Brit*) *ou* for (*US*) its type; **ce qui se fait de mieux dans le ~** the best of its kind; **réparations en tout ~** *ou* **en tous ~s** all kinds of repairs *ou* repair work undertaken; **chaussures en tout ~** *ou* **en tous ~s** all kinds *ou* sorts of shoes; **quelque chose de ce ~** *ou* **du même ~** something of the kind, that sort of thing; **des remarques de ce ~** remarks *ou* comments like that *ou* of that nature; **il a écrit un ~ de roman** he wrote a novel of sorts *ou* a sort of novel; **plaisanterie d'un ~ douteux** doubtful joke; *voir* **unique**.

b (*allure*) **avoir bon ~** to look a nice sort; **avoir mauvais ~** to be coarse-looking; **je n'aime pas son ~** I don't like his style; **il a un drôle de ~** he's a bit weird; **avoir le ~ bohème/artiste** to be a bohemian/an arty type; **avoir un ~ prétentieux** to have a pretentious manner; **faire du ~** to stand on ceremony; **c'est un ~ qu'il se donne** it's (just) something *ou* an air he puts on; **il aime se donner un ~** he likes to stand out *ou* to be a bit different; **ce n'est pas son ~ de ne pas répondre** it's not like him not to answer.

c (*Art, Littérat, Mus*) genre. (*Peinture*) **tableau de ~** genre painting; **œuvre dans le ~ ancien/italien** work in the old/Italian style *ou* genre; **ses tableaux/romans sont d'un ~ un peu particulier** the style of his paintings/novels is slightly unusual.

d (*Gram*) gender. **s'accorder en ~** to agree in gender.

e (*Philos, Sci*) genus. **le ~ humain** mankind, the human race.

gens[1] [ʒɑ̃] 1 **nmpl** a people, folk*. **connais-tu ces ~?** do you know these people? *ou* folk?*; **ce sont des ~ compétents** they are competent people *ou* folk*; **il faut savoir prendre les ~** you've got to know how to handle people; **les ~ sont fous!** some people are crazy!, people are crazy (at times)!; **les ~ de la ville** townspeople, townsfolk; **les ~ du pays** *ou* **du coin*** the local people, the locals*; *voir* **droit**[3]**, jeune, monde.**

b (*loc, avec accord féminin de l'adjectif antéposé*) **ce sont de petites/de braves ~** they are people of modest means/good people *ou* folk*; **les vieilles ~ sont souvent crédules** old people *ou* folk* are often gullible; **c'est une insulte aux honnêtes ~** it's an insult to honest people; (*hum*) **écoutez bonnes ~** harken, ye people (*hum*).

c (†, *hum: serviteurs*) servants. **il appela ses ~** he called his servants.

2 **comp ▸gens d'affaires**† business people **▸gens d'armes** (*Hist*) men-at-arms† **▸les gens d'Église** the clergy **▸gens d'épée** (*Hist*) soldiers (*of the aristocracy*) **▸gens de lettres** men of letters **▸les gens de loi**† the legal profession **▸gens de maison** people in service **▸gens de mer** sailors, seafarers **▸les gens de robe** (*Hist*) the legal profession **▸gens de service** = **gens de maison ▸les gens de théâtre** the acting profession, theatrical people **▸les gens du voyage** travelling entertainers.

gens[2] [ʒɛ̃s] **nf** (*Antiq*) gens.

gent [ʒɑ̃(t)] **nf** (†† *ou hum*) race, tribe. **la ~ canine** the canine race; **la ~ féminine** the fair sex; **la ~ masculine** the male *ou* masculine sex.

gentiane [ʒɑ̃sjan] **nf** gentian.

gentil, -ille [ʒɑ̃ti, ij] 1 **adj** a (*aimable*) kind, nice (*avec, pour* to). **il a toujours un mot ~ pour chacun** he always has a kind word for everyone *ou* to say to everyone; **vous serez ~ de me le rendre** would you mind giving it back to me, would you be so kind as to give it back to me (*frm*); **c'est ~ à toi de ...** it's very kind *ou* nice *ou* good of you to ...; **tu es ~ tout plein*** you're so sweet; **tout ça, c'est bien ~ mais ...** that's (all) very nice *ou* well but ...; **elle est bien ~le avec ses histoires mais ...** what she has to say is all very well *ou* nice but ...; **ça n'est pas très ~** that's not very nice *ou* kind; **il n'est pas très ~** he's not very nice; **il a une ~le petite femme/fille** he has a nice little wife/daughter; **sois ~, va me le chercher** be a dear and go and get it for me; **va me le chercher, tu seras ~** would you mind going to get it for me.

b (*sage*) good. **il n'a pas été ~** he hasn't been a good boy; **sois ~, je reviens bientôt** be good, I'll be back soon.

c (*gracieux*) *visage, endroit* nice, pleasant. **c'est ~ comme tout chez vous** you've got a lovely little place; **c'est ~ sans plus** it's OK but it's nothing special.

d (*rondelet*) *somme* tidy, fair.

2 **nm** (*Hist, Rel*) gentile.

gentilhomme [ʒɑ̃tijɔm], **pl gentilshommes** [ʒɑ̃tizɔm] **nm** (*Hist, fig*) gentleman. **~ campagnard** country squire.

gentilhommière [ʒɑ̃tijɔmjɛʀ] **nf** (small) country seat, (small) manor house.

gentille [ʒɑ̃tij] *voir* **gentil**.

gentillesse [ʒɑ̃tijɛs] **nf** a (*NonC: amabilité*) kindness. **être d'une grande ~** to be very kind (*avec qn* to sb); **me ferez-vous la ~ de faire ...** would you be so kind as to do ..., would you do me the kindness of doing ... . b (*faveur*) favour, kindness. **remercier qn de toutes ses ~s** to thank sb for all his kindness(es); **avoir des ~s pour qn** to be kind to sb; **une ~ en vaut une autre** one good turn deserves another; **il me disait des ~s** he said kind *ou* nice things to me.

gentillet, -ette [ʒɑ̃tijɛ, ɛt] **adj** nice little (*épith*); (*péj*) nice enough.

gentiment [ʒɑ̃timɑ̃] **adv** (*aimablement*) kindly; (*gracieusement*) nicely. **ils jouaient ~** they were playing nicely *ou* like good children; (*iro*) **on m'a ~ fait comprendre que ...** they told me in the nicest *ou* kindest possible way that ... (*iro*).

gentleman [ʒɑ̃tləman], **pl gentlemen** [ʒɑ̃tləmɛn] **nm** gentleman.

génuflexion [ʒenyflɛksjɔ̃] **nf** (*Rel*) genuflexion. **faire une ~** to make a genuflexion, genuflect.

géo [ʒeo] **nf** (*arg Scol*) **abrév de géographie**.

géocentrique [ʒeosɑ̃tʀik] **adj** geocentric.

géochimie [ʒeoʃimi] **nf** geochemistry.

géode [ʒeɔd] **nf** geode.

géodésie [ʒeɔdezi] **nf** geodesy.

géodésique [ʒeɔdezik] **adj** geodesic. **point ~** triangulation point.

géodynamique [ʒeodinamik] 1 **adj** geodynamic. 2 **nf** geodynamics (*sg*).

géographe [ʒeɔgʀaf] **nmf** geographer.

géographie [ʒeɔgʀafi] **nf** geography. **~ humaine/économique** human/ economic geography.

géographique [ʒeɔgʀafik] **adj** geographic(al); *voir* **dictionnaire**.

géographiquement [ʒeɔgʀafikmɑ̃] **adv** geographically.

geôle [ʒol] **nf** (*littér*) gaol (*Brit*), jail.

geôlier, -ière [ʒolje, jɛʀ] **nm,f** (*littér*) gaoler (*Brit*), jailer.

géologie [ʒeɔlɔʒi] **nf** geology.

géologique [ʒeɔlɔʒik] **adj** geological.

géologiquement [ʒeɔlɔʒikmɑ̃] **adv** geologically.

géologue [ʒeɔlɔg] **nmf** geologist.

géomagnétique [ʒeomaɲetik] **adj** geomagnetic.

géomagnétisme [ʒeomaɲetism] **nm** geomagnetism.

géométral, e, **mpl -aux** [ʒeɔmetʀal, o] **adj** plane (*not in perspective*).

géomètre [ʒeɔmɛtʀ] **nm** (*arpenteur*) surveyor.

géométrie [ʒeɔmetʀi] **nf** (*science*) geometry; (*livre*) geometry book. **~ descriptive** descriptive geometry; **~ plane** plane geometry; **~ analytique** analytical geometry; **~ dans l'espace** solid geometry; **à ~ variable** (*Aviat*) swing-wing; *politique* which changes with the wind; **c'est une justice à ~ variable** it's one rule for one and one rule for another.

géométrique [ʒeɔmetʀik] **adj** geometric(al); *voir* **lieu, progression.**

géométriquement [ʒeɔmetʀikmɑ̃] **adv** geometrically.

géomorphologie [ʒeomɔʀfɔlɔʒi] **nf** geomorphology.

géophage [ʒeɔfaʒ] 1 **adj** geophagous. 2 **nmf** geophagist.

géophysicien, -ienne [ʒeofizisjɛ̃, jɛn] **nm,f** geophysicist.

géophysique [ʒeofizik] 1 **adj** geophysical. 2 **nf** geophysics (*sg*).

géopolitique [ʒeopɔlitik] 1 **adj** geopolitical. 2 **nf** geopolitics (*sg*).

Georges [ʒɔʀʒ] **nm** George.

Géorgie [ʒeɔʀʒi] **nf** (*URSS, USA*) Georgia. **~ du Sud** South Georgia.

géorgien, -ienne [ʒeɔʀʒjɛ̃, jɛn] 1 **adj** Georgian. 2 **nm** (*Ling*) Georgian. 3 **nm,f: G~(ne)** Georgian.

géorgique [ʒeɔʀʒik] **adj** (*Hist Littérat*) georgic.

géostationnaire [ʒeostasjɔnɛʀ] **adj** geostationary.

géosynchrone [ʒeosɛ̃kʀɔn] **adj** geosynchronous.

géosynclinal, **pl -aux** [ʒeosɛ̃klinal, o] **nm** geosyncline.

géothermie [ʒeotɛʀmi] **nf** geothermal science.

géothermique [ʒeotɛʀmik] **adj** geothermal.

gérable [ʒeʀabl] **adj** manageable. **difficilement ~** hard to handle.

gérance [ʒeʀɑ̃s] **nf** [*commerce, immeuble, appartement*] management. **il assure la ~ d'une usine** he manages a factory; **au cours de sa ~** while he was manager; **prendre un commerce en ~** to take over the management of a business; **il a mis son commerce en ~** he has appointed a manager for his business; [*entreprise*] **être en ~ libre** to be run by a manager; **~ salariée** salaried management.

géranium [ʒeʀanjɔm] **nm** geranium. **~-lierre** ivyleaf geranium.

gérant [ʒeʀɑ̃] **nm** [*usine, café, magasin, banque*] manager; [*immeuble,* *appartement]* managing agent; *[journal]* managing editor. ~ **de portefeuilles** portfolio manager.

gérante [ʒeʀɑ̃t] nf manageress.

gerbage [ʒɛʀbaʒ] nm (*voir* **gerber**) binding, sheaving; stacking, piling.

gerbe [ʒɛʀb] nf *[blé]* sheaf; *[osier]* bundle; *[fleurs]* spray; (*fig*) *[souvenirs]* collection. **déposer une ~ sur une tombe** to place a spray of flowers on a grave; **le choc provoqua une ~ d'étincelles/d'écume** the impact sent up a shower *ou* burst of sparks/a shower *ou* flurry of foam; ~ **d'eau** spray *ou* shower of water; **éclater/retomber en ~** to go up/fall in a shower *ou* burst of sparks.

gerber [ʒɛʀbe] [1] 1 vt (*Agr*) to bind into sheaves, sheave; (*Tech*) *tonneaux* to stack, pile. 2 vi (*‡: vomir*) to throw up‡, puke (up)‡.

gerbera [ʒɛʀbeʀa] nm gerbera.

gerbeur [ʒɛʀbœʀ] nm stacking *ou* pallet truck.

gerbille [ʒɛʀbij] nf gerbil.

gerboise [ʒɛʀbwaz] nf jerboa.

gercement [ʒɛʀsmɑ̃] nm (*voir* **gercer**) chapping; cracking.

gercer [ʒɛʀse] [3] 1 vt *peau, lèvres* to chap, crack; *sol* to crack. **avoir les lèvres toutes gercées** to have badly chapped lips. 2 vi, **se gercer** vpr (*voir* **gercer**) to chap; to crack.

gerçure [ʒɛʀsyʀ] nf (small) crack. **pour éviter les ~s, achetez la crème X** to avoid chapped hands *etc ou* to avoid chapping, buy X cream.

gérer [ʒeʀe] [6] vt *société, commerce, budget, temps, données* to manage; *fortune, biens* to administer, manage. **il gère bien ses affaires** he manages his affairs well; **il a mal géré son affaire** he has mismanaged his business, he has managed his business badly; (*Pol*) ~ **la crise** to manage the crisis.

gerfaut [ʒɛʀfo] nm (*Orn*) gyrfalcon.

gériatre [ʒeʀjatʀ] nmf geriatrician.

gériatrie [ʒeʀjatʀi] nf geriatrics (*sg*).

gériatrique [ʒeʀjatʀik] adj geriatric.

germain, e [ʒɛʀmɛ̃, ɛn] 1 adj a *voir* **cousin**[1]. b (*Hist*) German. 2 nm,f (*Hist*) **G~(e)** German.

Germanie [ʒɛʀmani] nf (*Hist*) Germania.

germanique [ʒɛʀmanik] 1 adj Germanic. 2 nm (*Ling*) Germanic. 3 nmf: **G~** Germanic.

germanisant, e [ʒɛʀmanizɑ̃, ɑ̃t] nm,f = **germaniste**.

germanisation [ʒɛʀmanizasjɔ̃] nf germanization.

germaniser [ʒɛʀmanize] [1] vt to germanize.

germanisme [ʒɛʀmanism] nm (*Ling*) germanism.

germaniste [ʒɛʀmanist] nmf German scholar, germanist.

germanium [ʒɛʀmanjɔm] nm germanium.

germanophile [ʒɛʀmanɔfil] adj, nmf germanophil(e).

germanophilie [ʒɛʀmanɔfili] nf germanophilia.

germanophobe [ʒɛʀmanɔfɔb] 1 adj germanophobic. 2 nmf germanophobe.

germanophobie [ʒɛʀmanɔfɔbi] nf germanophobia.

germanophone [ʒɛʀmanɔfɔn] 1 adj *personne* German-speaking; *littérature* German-language (*épith*), in German (*attrib*). 2 nmf German speaker.

germe [ʒɛʀm] nm a (*Bio*) *[embryon, graine]* germ; *[œuf]* germinal disc; *[pomme de terre]* eye; (*Méd: microbe*) germ. **~s de blé** wheatgerm; ~ **dentaire** tooth bud; *voir* **porteur**. b (*fig: source*) *[maladie, erreur, vie]* seed. ~ **d'une idée** germ of an idea; **avoir** *ou* **contenir en ~** to contain in embryo, contain the seeds of; **cette idée est en ~** the idea is beginning to take root.

germer [ʒɛʀme] [1] vi to sprout, shoot, germinate; (*fig*) *[idée, sentiment]* to germinate. **pommes de terre germées** sprouting potatoes.

germicide [ʒɛʀmisid] 1 adj germicidal. 2 nm germicide.

germinal[1]**, e,** mpl **-aux** [ʒɛʀminal, o] adj germinal.

germinal[2] [ʒɛʀminal] nm Germinal, *seventh month in the French Republican calendar.*

germinateur, -trice [ʒɛʀminatœʀ, tʀis] adj germinative.

germinatif, -ive [ʒɛʀminatif, iv] adj germinal.

germination [ʒɛʀminasjɔ̃] nf (*Bot, fig*) germination.

germoir [ʒɛʀmwaʀ] nm (*Agr*) seed tray; *[brasserie]* maltings (*sg*).

gérondif [ʒeʀɔ̃dif] nm (*Ling*) (*latin*) (*avec être*) gerundive; (*complément de nom*) gerund; (*français*) gerund.

gérontocratie [ʒeʀɔ̃tɔkʀasi] nf gerontocracy.

gérontocratique [ʒeʀɔ̃tɔkʀatik] adj gerontocratic.

gérontologie [ʒeʀɔ̃tɔlɔʒi] nf gerontology.

gérontologique [ʒeʀɔ̃tɔlɔʒik] adj gerontological.

gérontologiste [ʒeʀɔ̃tɔlɔʒist] nmf, **gérontologue** [ʒeʀɔ̃tɔlɔg] nmf gerontologist.

gérontophile [ʒeʀɔ̃tɔfil] nmf gerontophile, gerontophiliac.

gérontophilie [ʒeʀɔ̃tɔfili] nf gerontophilia.

gésier [ʒezje] nm gizzard.

gésine [ʒezin] nf (*accoucher*) **être en ~**† to be in labour.

gésir [ʒeziʀ] vi (*être étendu*) to be lying (down), lie (down). **il gît/gisait sur le sol** he is lying/was lying *ou* lay on the ground; (*fig*) **là gît le problème** therein lies the problem; *voir* **ci**.

gestaltisme [gɛʃtaltism] nm Gestalt (psychology).

gestation [ʒɛstasjɔ̃] nf gestation. **en ~** in gestation.

geste[1] [ʒɛst] nm a (*mouvement*) gesture. ~ **d'approbation/d'effroi** gesture of approval/of terror; ~ **maladroit** *ou* **malheureux** clumsy gesture *ou* movement; **pas un ~ ou je tire!** one move and I'll shoot!; **faire un ~ de la main** to gesture with one's hand, give a wave (of one's hand); **faire un ~ de la tête** (*affirmatif*) to nod (one's head), give a nod; (*négatif*) to shake one's head; **il refusa d'un ~** he made a gesture of refusal, he gestured his refusal; **il le fit entrer d'un ~ de la tête/main** he nodded/waved him in, he nodded/waved to him to come in; **il le fit entrer d'un ~** he motioned *ou* gestured to him to come in; **il lui indiqua la porte d'un ~** with a gesture he showed him the door; **s'exprimer par ~s** to use one's hands to express o.s.; **quelle précision dans le ~ de l'horloger** what precision there is in every move of the watchmaker's hand; **le ~ du service (au tennis)** the (tennis) serving action; (*fig*) **il ne fit pas un ~ pour l'aider** he didn't lift a finger *ou* make a move to help him; (*fig*) **tu n'as qu'un ~ à faire pour qu'il revienne** just say the word *ou* you only have to say the word and he'll come back; *voir* **encourager, fait**[1]**, joindre.** b (*action*) act, deed; (*action généreuse*) gesture, act, deed. ~ **lâche/méprisable** cowardly/despicable act *ou* deed; ~ **de réconciliation** gesture of reconciliation; **c'était un beau ~** it was a noble gesture *ou* deed; **faites un ~** make a gesture.

geste[2] [ʒɛst] nf (*Littérat*) *collection of epic poems centred around the same hero; voir* **chanson**.

gesticulation [ʒɛstikylasjɔ̃] nf gesticulation, gesticulating (*NonC*).

gesticuler [ʒɛstikyle] [1] vi to gesticulate.

gestion [ʒɛstjɔ̃] nf *[entreprise, emploi du temps, données]* management; *[biens]* administration, management. **mauvaise ~** mismanagement, bad management; ~ **de l'économie/budgétaire** economic/budget management; ~ **des stocks** inventory control; ~ **de ressources humaines** human resources management; ~ **de la production assistée par ordinateur** computer-assisted production management.

gestionnaire [ʒɛstjɔnɛʀ] 1 adj administrative, management (*épith*). 2 nmf administrator. 3 nm (*Ordin*) ~ **de base de données/de fichiers** database/file management.

gestuel, -elle [ʒɛstɥɛl] 1 adj gestural. 2 **gestuelle** nf body movements.

Gethsemani [ʒetsəmani] n Gethsemane.

geyser [ʒɛzɛʀ] nm geyser.

Ghana [gana] nm Ghana.

ghanéen, -enne [ganeɛ̃, ɛn] 1 adj Ghanaian. 2 nm,f: **G~(ne)** Ghanaian.

ghetto [geto] nm (*lit, fig*) ghetto.

ghilde [gild] nf = **guilde**.

GI [dʒiaj] nm (abrév de **Government Issue**) (*soldat américain*) GI.

gibbeux, -euse [ʒibø, øz] adj (*Astron, littér*) gibbous, gibbose.

gibbon [ʒibɔ̃] nm gibbon.

gibbosité [ʒibozite] nf (*Astron, littér, Méd*) hump, gibbosity (*SPÉC*).

gibecière [ʒib(ə)sjɛʀ] nf (*gén*) (leather) shoulder bag; *[chasseur]* gamebag; (†) *[écolier]* satchel.

gibelin [ʒiblɛ̃] nm (*Hist*) Ghibelline.

gibelotte [ʒiblɔt] nf *fricassee of game in wine.*

giberne [ʒibɛʀn] nf cartridge pouch.

gibet [ʒibɛ] nm gibbet, gallows. (*Hist*) **condamner au ~** to condemn to death by hanging, condemn to the gallows.

gibier [ʒibje] nm a (*Chasse*) game. **gros ~** game; **menu ~** small game; ~ **d'eau** waterfowl; ~ **à poil** game animals; ~ **à plume** game birds. b (*fig: personne*) prey. **les policiers attendaient leur ~** the policemen awaited their prey; ~ **de potence** gallows bird; **le gros ~** big game (*fig*).

giboulée [ʒibule] nf (sudden) shower, sudden downpour. ~ **de mars** ≈ April shower.

giboyeux, -euse [ʒibwajø, øz] adj *pays, forêt* abounding in game, well-stocked with game.

Gibraltar [ʒibʀaltaʀ] nm Gibraltar.

gibus [ʒibys] nm opera hat.

giclée [ʒikle] nf spurt, squirt.

giclement [ʒikləmɑ̃] nm (*voir* **gicler**) spurting, squirting.

gicler [ʒikle] [1] vi (*jaillir*) to spurt, squirt. **faire ~ de l'eau d'un robinet** to squirt water from a tap; **le véhicule a fait ~ de l'eau à son passage** the passing vehicle sent up a spray of water.

gicleur [ʒiklœʀ] nm (*Aut*) jet. ~ **de ralenti** slow-running jet (*Brit*), idle.

gidien, -ienne [ʒidjɛ̃, jɛn] adj of André Gide.

GIE [ʒeiə] nm (abrév de **groupement d'intérêt économique**) *voir* **groupement**.

gifle [ʒifl] nf (*lit*) slap (in the face), smack (on the face), box on the ear; (*fig*) slap in the face. **donner une ~ à qn** to slap sb in the face, give sb a slap in the face, box sb's ears; *voir* **paire**[2]**, tête**.

gifler [ʒifle] [1] vt to slap (in the face). ~ **qn** to slap *ou* smack sb's face, slap sb in the face; **visage giflé par la grêle** face lashed by (the) hail.

giga... [ʒiga] préf giga. **~octet/watt** gigabyte/watt.

gigantesque [ʒigɑ̃tɛsk] adj *taille* gigantic, immense; *objet, entreprise* gigantic, giant (*épith*); *bêtise* immense.

gigantisme [ʒigɑ̃tism] nm (*Méd*) gigantism; (*fig: grandeur*) gigantic size *ou* proportions. **ville/entreprise atteinte de ~** city/firm that suffers from overexpansion on a gigantic scale.

GIGN [ʒeiʒeɛn] **nm** (**abrév de Groupe d'intervention de la Gendarmerie nationale**) ≃ SAS (*Brit*).
gigogne [ʒigɔɲ] **nf** *voir* **fusée, lit, poupée, table.**
gigolette [ʒigɔlɛt] **nf** (*Culin*) ~ **(de canard)/(de dinde)** leg of duck/of turkey.
gigolo* [ʒigɔlo] **nm** gigolo.
gigot [ʒigo] **nm** (*Culin*) ~ **(de mouton)/(d'agneau)** leg of mutton/lamb; ~ **(de chevreuil)** haunch of venison; **une tranche de ~** a slice off the leg of mutton *ou* lamb *etc,* a slice off the joint; (*fig*) **elle a de bons ~s*** she has nice sturdy legs; *voir* **manche**[1].
gigoter* [ʒigɔte] [1] **vi** to wriggle (about).
gigoteuse [ʒigɔtøz] **nf** Babygro ®.
gigue [ʒig] **nf** (*Mus*) gigue; (*danse*) jig. (*jambes*) **~s*** legs; (*péj: fille*) **une grande ~** a bean-pole (of a girl)*; (*Culin*) ~ **de chevreuil** haunch of venison.
gilde [gild] **nf = guilde.**
gilet [ʒilɛ] **nm** (*de complet*) waistcoat (*Brit*), vest (*US*); (*cardigan*) cardigan. ~ **(de corps *ou* de peau)** vest (*Brit*), undershirt (*US*); ~ **pare-balles** bulletproof jacket, flak jacket*; ~ **de sauvetage** life jacket; *voir* **pleurer.**
giletier, -ière [ʒil(ə)tje, jɛʀ] **nm,f** waistcoat (*Brit*) *ou* vest (*US*) maker.
Gilles [ʒil] **nm** Giles.
gin [dʒin] **nm** gin. **~-tonic** gin and tonic.
gingembre [ʒɛ̃ʒɑ̃bʀ] **nm** ginger.
gingival, e, **mpl -aux** [ʒɛ̃ʒival, o] **adj** gingival. **pâte ~e** gum ointment.
gingivite [ʒɛ̃ʒivit] **nf** inflammation of the gums, gingivitis (*SPÉC*).
ginglyme [ʒɛ̃glim] **nm: ~ angulaire** hinge joint.
ginkgo [ʒiŋko] **nm** ginkgo, gingko.
ginseng [ʒinsɛŋ] **nm** ginseng.
girafe [ʒiʀaf] **nf** (*Zool*) giraffe; (*péj: personne*) beanpole*; (*Ciné*) boom; *voir* **peigner.**
girafeau [ʒiʀafo] **nm, girafon** [ʒiʀafɔ̃] **nm** baby giraffe.
giralducien, -ienne [ʒiʀaldysjɛ̃, jɛn] **adj** of Giraudoux.
girandole [ʒiʀɑ̃dɔl] **nf** (*chandelier*) candelabra, girandole; (*feu d'artifice*) girandole.
girasol [ʒiʀasɔl] **nm** girasol.
giration [ʒiʀasjɔ̃] **nf** gyration.
giratoire [ʒiʀatwaʀ] **adj** gyrating, gyratory; *voir* **sens.**
girelle [ʒiʀɛl] **nf** rainbow wrasse.
girl [gœʀl] **nf** chorus girl.
girofle [ʒiʀɔfl] **nm** clove; *voir* **clou.**
giroflée [ʒiʀɔfle] **nf** wallflower, gillyflower; (*vivace*) stock. (*: *gifle*) ~ **à cinq feuilles** slap in the face.
giroflier [ʒiʀɔflije] **nm** clove tree.
girolle [ʒiʀɔl] **nf** chanterelle.
giron [ʒiʀɔ̃] **nm** (*Anat: genoux*) lap; (*fig: sein*) bosom. (*fig*) **rentrer dans le ~ de l'église** to return to the fold, return to the bosom of the Church; **enfant élevé dans le ~ maternel** child reared in the bosom of his family.
girond, e* [ʒiʀɔ̃, ɔ̃d] **adj** well-padded*, plump.
Gironde [ʒiʀɔ̃d] **nf: la ~** the Gironde.
girondin, e [ʒiʀɔ̃dɛ̃, in] **1 adj** (*Géog*) from the Gironde; (*Hist*) Girondist. **2 nm,f** (*Géog*) inhabitant *ou* native of the Gironde. **3 nm** (*Hist*) Girondist.
girouette [ʒiʀwɛt] **nf** weather vane *ou* cock. (*fig*) **c'est une vraie ~** he changes (his mind) with the weather (*fig*), he changes his mind depending on which way the wind is blowing.
gisait, gisaient [ʒizɛ] *voir* **gésir.**
gisant [ʒizɑ̃] **nm** (*Art*) recumbent statue (*on tomb*).
gisement [ʒizmɑ̃] **nm** **a** (*Minér*) deposit. ~ **de pétrole** oilfield; ~ **houiller** coal seam; (*fig*) ~ **d'emplois/de clientèle** pool of jobs/customers; ~ **d'informations** mine of information. **b** (*Naut*) bearing.
gisent [ʒiz] **, gît** [ʒi] *voir* **ci, gésir.**
gitan, e [ʒitɑ̃, an] **1 adj** gipsy (*épith*). **2 nm,f: G~(e)** gipsy. **3 gitane nf** (®: *cigarette*) Gitane (*cigarette*).
gîte[1] [ʒit] **nm** **a** (*abri*) shelter; (†: *maison*) home; (*Tourisme*) gîte, self-catering cottage *ou* flat. **rentrer au ~** to return home; **ils lui donnent le ~ et le couvert** they give him room and board *ou* board and lodging (*Brit*); ~ **d'étape *ou* rural** (country) gîte, holiday cottage in the country. **b** (*Chasse*) *[lièvre]* form. **c** (*Boucherie*) ~ **(à la noix)** topside (*Brit*), bottom round (*US*); **gîte-gîte** shin (*Brit*), shank (*US*). **d** (*Minér*) deposit.
gîte[2] [ʒit] **nf** (*Naut*) (*emplacement d'épave*) bed (*of a sunken ship*). **donner de la ~** to list, heel.
gîter [ʒite] [1] **vi** (*littér*) to lodge; (*Naut*) (*pencher*) to list, heel; (*être échoué*) to be aground.
givrage [ʒivʀaʒ] **nm** (*Aviat*) icing.
givrant, e [ʒivʀɑ̃, ɑ̃t] **adj: brouillard ~** icy fog.
givre [ʒivʀ] **nm** **a** (hoar) frost, rime (*SPÉC*); *voir* **fleur.** **b** (*Chim*) crystallization.
givré, e [ʒivʀe] (**ptp de givrer**) **adj** **a** *arbre* covered in frost; *fenêtre, hélice* frosted-up, iced-up, covered in frost; *verre* frosted. **orange** *etc* **~e** orange *etc* sorbet served in the (orange *etc*) skin. **b** (*) (*ivre*) plastered‡; (*fou*) cracked‡, bonkers‡ (*Brit*), nuts‡. **devenir complètement ~** to go completely off one's head *ou* rocker‡.
givrer **vt, se givrer** **vpr** [ʒivʀe] [1] to frost up, ice up.
glabre [glɑbʀ] **adj** (*imberbe*) hairless; (*rasé*) clean-shaven; (*Bot*) glabrous.
glaçage [glasaʒ] **nm** *[viande, papier, étoffe]* glazing; *[gâteau]* (*au sucre*) icing; (*au blanc d'œuf*) glazing.
glace[1] [glas] **nf** **a** (*eau congelée*) ice (*NonC*). **cube de ~** ice cube; **seau/pince à ~** ice bucket/tongs; **le thermomètre est à la ~** the thermometer is at freezing (point); **les sports de ~** ice sports; (*lit, fig*) **briser *ou* rompre la ~** to break the ice; *voir* **crampon, hockey, saint.**
b (*Géog*) **~s** ice sheets, ice fields; **~s flottantes** drift ice, ice floes; **canal bloqué par les ~s** canal blocked with ice *ou* with ice floes; **bateau pris dans les ~s** icebound ship.
c (*fig*) **de ~** *accueil* icy, frosty, ice-cold; *expression, visage* stony, frosty; **rester de ~** to remain unmoved.
d (*Culin*) (*crème*) ice cream; (*jus de viande*) glaze; (*pour pâtisserie: glaçage*) royal icing. ~ **à l'eau** water ice (*Brit*), sherbet (*US*); ~ **à la crème** dairy ice cream (*Brit*), iced-milk ice cream (*US*); ~ **à la vanille/au café** vanilla/coffee ice cream; ~ **à l'italienne** soft ice cream; ~ **portative** ice-cream cake *ou* gateau; *voir* **sucre.**
glace[2] [glas] **nf** **a** (*miroir*) mirror. ~ **à main** hand mirror; *voir* **armoire.** **b** (*plaque de verre*) sheet of (plate) glass; plate glass (*NonC*). **la ~ d'une vitrine** the glass of a shop window. **c** *[véhicule]* (*vitre*) window; *voir* **essuyer, laver, tain.**
glacé, e [glase] (**ptp de glacer**) **adj** *neige, lac* frozen; *vent, eau, chambre* icy, freezing; *boisson* icy, ice-cold; *cuir, tissu* glazed; *fruit* glacé; *accueil, attitude, sourire* stiff, chilly. **je suis ~** I'm frozen (stiff), I'm chilled to the bone; **j'ai les mains ~es** my hands are frozen *ou* freezing; **à servir ~** to be served iced *ou* ice-cold; **café/chocolat ~** iced coffee/chocolate; *voir* **crème, marron**[1]**, papier.**
glacer [glase] [3] **1 vt** **a** *liquide* (*geler*) to freeze; (*rafraîchir*) to chill, ice. **mettre des boissons à ~** to put some drinks to chill.
b *personne, membres* to make freezing, freeze. **ce vent glace les oreilles** this wind is freezing to the ears *ou* freezes your ears; **ce vent vous glace** it's a freezing *ou* perishing (*Brit*) (cold) wind, this wind chills you to the bone.
c (*fig*) ~ **qn** (*intimider*) to turn sb cold, chill sb; (*paralyser*) to make sb's blood run cold; **cela l'a glacé d'horreur *ou* d'épouvante** he was frozen with terror at this; ~ **le sang de qn** to make sb's blood run cold, chill sb's blood; (*littér*) **cette réponse lui glaça le cœur** this reply turned his heart to ice; **son attitude vous glace** he has a chilling way about him, his attitude turns you cold.
d *viande, papier, étoffe* to glaze; *gâteau* (*au sucre*) to ice; (*au blanc d'œuf*) to glaze.
2 se glacer **vpr** *[eau]* to freeze. **mon sang se glaça dans mes veines** my blood ran cold *ou* my blood froze in my veins; **son sourire/son expression se glaça** his smile/expression froze.
glaceuse [glasøz] **nf** glazing machine.
glaciaire [glasjɛʀ] **adj** *période, calotte* ice (*épith*); *relief, régime, vallée, érosion* glacial.
glaciairiste [glasjɛʀist] **nmf = glaciériste.**
glacial, e, **mpl ~s *ou* -iaux** [glasjal, jo] **adj** **a** *froid* icy, freezing (*épith*); *nuit, pluie, vent* icy, freezing (cold); *voir* **océan.** **b** (*fig*) *accueil* icy, frosty, ice-cold; *silence, regard* frosty, icy. **c'est quelqu'un de ~** he's as cold as ice, he's a real iceberg; **"non", dit-elle d'un ton ~** "no", she said frostily *ou* icily.
glaciation [glasjasjɔ̃] **nf** glaciation.
glacier [glasje] **nm** **a** (*Géog*) glacier. **b** (*fabricant*) ice-cream maker; (*vendeur*) ice-cream man; *voir* **pâtissier.**
glacière [glasjɛʀ] **nf** icebox. **mettre qch à la ~** to put sth in the icebox; (*fig*) **c'est une vraie ~ ici!** it's like a fridge *ou* an icebox here!
glaciériste [glasjeʀist] **nmf** ice climber.
glaciologie [glasjɔlɔʒi] **nf** glaciology.
glaciologique [glasjɔlɔʒik] **adj** glaciological.
glaciologue [glasjɔlɔg] **nmf** glaciologist.
glacis [glasi] **nm** **a** (*Art*) glaze. **b** (*Archit*) weathering; (*Géog, Mil*) glacis.
glaçon [glasɔ̃] **nm** *[rivière]* block of ice; *[toit]* icicle; *[boisson]* ice cube; (*péj: personne*) iceberg. **un whisky avec des ~s** a whisky on the rocks; **mes pieds sont comme des ~s** my feet are like blocks of ice.
gladiateur [gladjatœʀ] **nm** gladiator.
glagla* [glagla] **loc adv: à ~!** it's freezing!; **les avoir à ~** to be frozen (stiff).
glaïeul [glajœl] **nm** gladiola, gladiolus.
glaire [glɛʀ] **nf** *[œuf]* white; (*Méd*) phlegm.
glaireux, -euse [glɛʀø, øz] **adj** slimy.
glaise [glɛz] **nf** clay; *voir* **terre.**
glaiseux, -euse [glɛzø, øz] **adj** clayey.
glaisière [glɛzjɛʀ] **nf** clay pit.
glaive [glɛv] **nm** two-edged sword. (*littér*) **le ~ de la justice** the sword of justice.
glanage [glanaʒ] **nm** gleaning.
gland [glɑ̃] **nm** (*Bot*) acorn; (*Anat*) glans; (*ornement*) tassel. (**‡**: *imbécile*) **quel ~!** what a prick!**‡**

glande [glɑ̃d] nf gland. (*Méd*) **avoir des ~s** to have swollen glands; **avoir les ~s‡** (*être en colère*) to be hopping mad*; (*être anxieux*) to be all wound-up*; **~ pinéale** pineal body *ou* gland.

glander‡ [glɑ̃de] [1] vi (*traînailler*) to fart around‡* (*Brit*), footle about* (*Brit*), screw around‡ (*US*); (*attendre*) to hang around*, kick one's heels* (*Brit*). **j'en ai rien à ~** I don't give *ou* care a damn‡; **qu'est-ce que tu glandes?** what the hell are you doing?‡

glandeur, -euse‡ [glɑ̃dœʀ, øz] nm,f layabout*, shirker.

glandouiller‡ [glɑ̃duje] [1] vi = **glander‡**.

glandulaire [glɑ̃dylɛʀ] adj glandular.

glaner [glane] [1] vt (*lit, fig*) to glean.

glaneur, -euse [glanœʀ, øz] nm,f gleaner.

glapir [glapiʀ] [2] vi *[renard, chien]* to yap, yelp; (*péj*) *[personne]* to yelp, squeal.

glapissement [glapismɑ̃] nm (*voir* **glapir**) yapping; yelping; squealing.

glas [glɑ] nm knell (*NonC*), toll (*NonC*). **on sonne le ~** the bell is tolling, they are tolling the knell *ou* bell; (*fig*) **sonner le ~ de** to toll *ou* sound the knell of.

glaucome [glokom] nm glaucoma.

glauque [glok] adj *yeux, eau* dull blue-green; (*: *louche*) *quartier, hôtel* shabby, run-down; *regard* shifty; *individu* shifty, shady.

glaviot‡ [glavjo] nm gob of spit‡.

glavioter‡ [glavjɔte] [1] vi to spit.

glèbe [glɛb] nf (*Hist, littér*) glebe.

glissade [glisad] nf a (*par jeu*) slide; (*chute*) slip; (*dérapage*) skid. (*Aviat*) **~ sur l'aile** sideslip; **il fit une ~ mortelle** he slipped and was fatally injured; **faire des ~s sur la glace** to slide on the ice. b (*Danse*) glissade.

glissage [glisaʒ] nm sledging (*of wood*).

glissando [glisɑ̃do] adv, nm glissando.

glissant, e [glisɑ̃, ɑ̃t] adj *sol, savon, poisson* slippery; *voir* **terrain**.

glisse [glis] nf (*Ski*) glide. **sports de ~** *sports which involve sliding or gliding (eg skiing, surfing, skating)*.

glissé, e [glise] (ptp de **glisser**) adj, nm: **(pas) ~** glissé.

glissement [glismɑ̃] nm *[porte, rideau, pièce]* sliding; *[bateau]* gliding; (*Ski, Phon*) glide; *[valeurs boursières]* downturn, downswing. **~ électoral (à gauche)** electoral swing *ou* move (to the left); **~ de sens** shift in meaning; **~ de terrain** landslide, landslip.

glisser [glise] [1] 1 vi a (*avancer*) to slide along; *[voilier, nuages, patineurs]* to glide along. **le bateau glissait sur les eaux** the boat glided over the water; (*Ski*) **avec ce fart, on glisse bien** you slide *ou* glide easily with this wax, this wax slides *ou* glides easily; **il fit ~ le fauteuil (sur le sol)** he slid the armchair (along the floor).

b (*tomber*) to slide. **ils glissèrent le long de la pente dans le ravin** they slid down the slope into the gully; **il se laissa ~ le long du mur** he slid down the wall; **une larme glissa le long de sa joue** a tear trickled *ou* slid down his cheek; **d'un geste maladroit il fit ~ le paquet dans le ravin** with a clumsy gesture he sent the parcel sliding down into the gully; **il fit ~ l'argent dans sa poche** he slipped the money into his pocket.

c (*fig: aller*) to slip. **le pays glisse vers l'anarchie** the country is slipping *ou* sliding towards anarchy; **le pays glisse vers la droite** the country is moving *ou* swinging towards the right; **il glisse dans la délinquance** he's slipping into crime.

d (*déraper*) *[personne, objet]* to slip; *[véhicule, pneus]* to skid. **il a glissé sur la glace et il est tombé** he slipped on the ice and fell; **son pied a glissé** his foot slipped.

e (*être glissant*) *[parquet]* to be slippery. **attention, ça glisse** be careful, it's slippery (underfoot).

f (*coulisser*) *[tiroir, rideau]* to slide; *[curseur, anneau]* to slide (along). **ces tiroirs ne glissent pas bien** these drawers don't slide (in and out) easily.

g (*échapper de*) **~ de la table** to slip *ou* slide off the table; **~ de la poêle/des mains** to slip *ou* slide out of the frying pan/one's hands; (*fig*) **le voleur leur a glissé entre les mains** the thief slipped (right) through their fingers.

h (*effleurer*) **~ sur: ses doigts glissaient sur les touches** his fingers slipped over the keys; **les reproches glissent sur lui (comme l'eau sur les plumes d'un canard)** reproaches roll off him (like water off a duck's back); **~ sur un sujet** to skate over a subject; **glissons!** let's not dwell on it, let's skate over that, let that pass; (*Prov*) **glissez, mortels, n'appuyez pas!** enough said!; **la balle glissa sur le blindage** the bullet glanced off the armour plating; **son regard glissa d'un objet à l'autre** he glanced from one object to another, his eyes slipped from one object to another.

2 vt (*introduire*) **~ qch sous/dans qch** to slip *ou* slide sth under/into sth; **~ une lettre sous la porte** to slip *ou* slide a letter under the door; **il me glissa un billet dans la main** he slipped a note into my hand; (*fig*) **~ un mot à l'oreille de qn** to slip *ou* drop a word in sb's ear; (*fig*) **il glisse toujours des proverbes dans sa conversation** he's always slipping proverbs into his conversation; **il me glissa un regard en coulisse** he gave me a sidelong glance; **il me glissa que ...** he whispered to me that ... .

3 **se glisser** vpr a *[personne, animal]* **se ~ quelque part** to slip somewhere; **le chien s'est glissé sous le lit/derrière l'armoire** the dog has slipped under the bed/behind the cupboard; **se ~ dans les draps** to slip *ou* slide between the sheets; **le voleur a réussi à se ~ dans la maison** the thief managed to sneak *ou* slip into the house; **il a réussi à se ~ jusqu'au premier rang** he managed to edge *ou* worm his way to the front *ou* to slip through to the front.

b *[erreur, sentiment]* **se ~ dans** to creep into; **l'inquiétude/le soupçon se glissa en lui/dans son cœur** anxiety/suspicion crept into him/into his heart; **une erreur s'est glissée dans le texte** a mistake has slipped *ou* crept into the text.

glissière [glisjɛʀ] nf slide *ou* sliding channel; (*Aut*) *[siège]* runner. **porte/panneau/système à ~** sliding door/panel/device; (*sur une route*) **~ de sécurité** crash barrier; *voir* **fermeture**.

glissoire [gliswaʀ] nf slide (*on ice or snow*).

global, e, mpl **-aux** [glɔbal, o] adj *somme* global (*épith*), total (*épith*), overall (*épith*), aggregate (*épith*); *résultat, résumé* overall (*épith*); *perspective, vue* global (*épith*), overall (*épith*), comprehensive. **méthode ~e** word recognition method (*of teaching reading*).

globalement [glɔbalmɑ̃] adv (*en bloc*) globally; (*pris dans son ensemble*) taken as a whole. **considérer un problème ~** to consider a problem from every angle; **~ nous sommes tous d'accord** overall *ou* in the main we are in agreement.

globalisant, e [glɔbalizɑ̃, ɑ̃t], **globalisateur, -trice** [glɔbalizatœʀ, tʀis] adj *vision* all-embracing.

globalité [glɔbalite] nf global nature. **regardons le problème dans sa ~** let us look at the problem from every angle.

globe [glɔb] nm a (*sphère, monde*) globe. **~ oculaire** eyeball; **le ~ terrestre** the globe, the earth; **un conflit qui pourrait s'étendre à tout le ~** a conflict which could become worldwide *ou* which could affect the whole world. b (*pour recouvrir*) glass cover, globe. (*fig*) **mettre qn/qch sous ~** to keep sb/sth in cotton wool (*Brit*), keep sb/sth in a glass case.

globe-trotter, pl **globe-trotters** [glɔbtʀɔtœʀ] nm globe-trotter.

globine [glɔbin] nf globin.

globulaire [glɔbylɛʀ] adj (*sphérique*) global; (*Physiol*) corpuscular; *voir* **numération**.

globule [glɔbyl] nm (*gén, Chim*) globule; (*Physiol*) corpuscle. **~s rouges/blancs** red/white corpuscles.

globuleux, -euse [glɔbylø, øz] adj *forme* globular; *œil* protruding.

globuline [glɔbylin] nf globulin.

glockenspiel [glɔkœnʃpil] nm glockenspiel.

gloire [glwaʀ] nf a (*renommée*) glory, fame; *[vedette]* stardom, fame. **trouver la ~ sur le champ de bataille** to win glory on the battlefield; **la ~ littéraire** literary fame; **être au sommet de la ~ ou en pleine ~** to be at the height of one's fame; **il s'est couvert de ~ à l'examen** he covered himself in glory in the exam; **elle a eu son heure de ~** she has had her hour of glory; **(faire qch) pour la ~** (to do sth) for the glory of it *ou* for love*.

b (*distinction*) **sa plus grande ~ a été de faire** his greatest distinction *ou* his greatest claim to fame was to do; **s'attribuer toute la ~ de qch** to give o.s. all the credit for sth, take all the glory for sth; **se faire** *ou* **tirer ~ de qch** to revel *ou* glory in sth.

c (*littér, Rel: éclat*) glory. **la ~ de Rome/de Dieu** the glory of Rome/God; **le trône/le séjour de ~** the throne/the Kingdom of Glory.

d (*louange*) glory, praise. **~ à Dieu** glory to God, praise be to God; **~ à tous ceux qui ont donné leur vie** glory to all those who gave their lives; **disons-le à sa ~** it must be said in praise of him; **poème/chant à la ~ de** poem/song in praise of; **célébrer** *ou* **chanter la ~ de** to sing the praises of; *voir* **rendre**.

e (*personne: célébrité*) celebrity. (*hum*) **toutes les ~s de la région étaient là** all the worthies (*hum*) *ou* notables of the region were there; **cette pièce est la ~ du musée** this piece is the pride of the museum.

f (*Art: auréole*) glory. **Christ en ~** Christ in majesty.

gloria [glɔʀja] nm inv (*Rel*) Gloria; (†: *boisson*) laced coffee, spiked coffee (*US*).

glorieusement [glɔʀjøzmɑ̃] adv gloriously.

glorieux, -ieuse [glɔʀjø, jøz] adj *exploit, mort, personne* glorious; *air, ton* self-important. (*littér, péj*) **tout ~ de sa richesse/de pouvoir dire ...** glorying in *ou* priding himself on his wealth/being able to say ... .

glorification [glɔʀifikasjɔ̃] nf glorification.

glorifier [glɔʀifje] [7] 1 vt to glorify, extol. **~ Dieu** to glorify God. 2 **se glorifier** vpr: **se ~ de** to glory in, take great pride in.

gloriole [glɔʀjɔl] nf misplaced vanity, vainglory. **faire qch par ~** to do sth out of (misplaced) vanity *ou* out of vainglory.

glose [gloz] nf (*annotation*) gloss.

gloser [gloze] [1] 1 vt to annotate, gloss. 2 vi to ramble on (*sur* about).

glossaire [glɔsɛʀ] nm glossary.

glossématique [glɔsematik] nf glossematics (*sg*).

glossine [glɔsin] nf glossina.

glossolalie [glɔsɔlali] nf glossolalia.

glottal, e, mpl **-aux** [glɔtal, o] adj glottal.

glotte [glɔt] nf glottis. **coup de ~** glottal stop.

glouglou [gluglu] nm a *[eau]* gurgling, glug-glug*. **faire ~** to gurgle,

go glug-glug*. b [dindon] gobbling, gobble-gobble. **faire ~** to gobble, go gobble-gobble.
glouglouter [gluglute] 1 vi [eau] to gurgle; [dindon] to gobble.
gloussement [glusmɑ̃] nm (voir **glousser**) chuckle; cluck.
glousser [gluse] 1 vi [personne] to chuckle; [poule] to cluck.
glouton, -onne [glutɔ̃, ɔn] 1 adj personne gluttonous, greedy; appétit voracious. 2 nm,f glutton. 3 nm (Zool) wolverine.
gloutonnement [glutɔnmɑ̃] adv manger gluttonously, greedily; lire voraciously. **avalant ~ son repas** gulping his meal down gluttonously ou greedily, guzzling (down) his meal*.
gloutonnerie [glutɔnʀi] nf gluttony, greed.
gloxinia [glɔksinja] nm gloxinia.
glu [gly] nf (pour prendre les oiseaux) birdlime. **prendre les oiseaux à la ~** to lime birds; **on dirait de la ~, c'est comme de la ~** it's like glue; (fig: personne) **quelle ~, ce type!*** what a leech the guy is!*
gluant, e [glyɑ̃, ɑ̃t] adj (substance) sticky, gummy; (fig: répugnant) personne slimy.
glucide [glysid] nm glucide.
glucose [glykoz] nm glucose.
glutamate [glytamat] nm glutamate.
gluten [glytɛn] nm gluten.
glycémie [glisemi] nf glycaemia.
glycérine [gliseʀin] nf glycerin(e), glycerol (SPÉC).
glycériner [gliseʀine] 1 vt: **joint glycériné** glycerol-coated joint.
glycérol [gliseʀɔl] nm glycerin(e), glycerol (SPÉC).
glycérophtalique [gliseʀoftalik] adj: **peinture ~** oil-based paint.
glycine [glisin] nf a (plante) wisteria, wistaria. b (acide) glycine.
glycocolle [glikokɔl] nm glycine.
glycogène [glikɔʒɛn] nm glycogen.
glycol [glikɔl] nm glycol.
GMT [ʒeɛmte] (abrév de **Greenwich Mean Time**) GMT. **à 15 heures ~** at fifteen (hundred) hours GMT.
gnangnan* [ɲɑ̃ɲɑ̃] 1 adj inv film, roman soppy*. **qu'est-ce qu'il est ~!** what a drip* ou a whinger* he is! 2 nmf whinger*, drip*.
gneiss [gnɛs] nm gneiss.
gniard‡ [ɲaʀ] nm brat*.
gniole* [ɲol] nf = **gnôle***.
GNL [ʒeɛnɛl] nm (abrév de **gaz naturel liquéfié**) LNG.
gnocchi [ɲɔki] nmpl gnocchi.
gnognote* [ɲɔɲɔt] nf: **c'est de la ~!** it's rubbish!; **c'est pas de la ~!** that's really something!*; **500 F? c'est de la ~ pour lui** 500 F? that's nothing ou peanuts* to him.
gnôle* [ɲol] nf (eau-de-vie) hooch*. **un petit verre de ~** a snifter‡, a dram*.
gnome [gnom] nm gnome.
gnomique [gnɔmik] adj gnomic.
gnon* [ɲɔ̃] nm (coup) blow, bash*; (marque) dent, bump. **prendre un ~ ou des ~s** to get bashed*; **il donnait des ~s à tout le monde** he was hitting out at everybody.
gnose [gnoz] nf gnosis.
gnosticisme [gnɔstisism] nm gnosticism.
gnostique [gnɔstik] adj, nmf gnostic.
gnou [gnu] nm gnu, wildebeest.
gnouf‡ [ɲuf] nm (arg Crime) nick‡, clink‡. **au ~** in the nick‡, in clink‡.
Go (abrév de **gigaoctet**) M6.
GO (abrév de **grandes ondes**) voir **onde**.
go [go] nm (jeu) go; voir **tout**.
goal [gol] nm goalkeeper, goalie*.
gobelet [gɔblɛ] nm [enfant, pique-nique] beaker; (en étain, verre, argent) tumbler; [dés] cup. **un ~ en plastique/papier** a plastic/paper cup.
gobe-mouches [gɔbmuʃ] nm inv (Orn) flycatcher. **~ gris** spotted flycatcher.
gober [gɔbe] 1 vt huître, œuf to swallow (whole); (fig) mensonge, histoire to swallow (hook, line and sinker). **je ne peux pas le ~*** I can't stand him; **ne reste pas là à ~ les mouches** don't just stand there gawping.
goberger (se)* [gɔbɛʀʒe] 3 vpr (faire bonne chère) to indulge o.s.; (prendre ses aises) to pamper o.s.
gobie [gɔbi] nm goby.
godailler [gɔdɑje] 1 vi = **goder**.
godasse* [gɔdas] nf shoe.
godelureau†, pl **~x** [gɔd(ə)lyʀo] nm (young) dandy; (péj) ladies' man (péj).
godemiché [gɔdmiʃe] nm dildo.
goder [gɔde] 1 vi [vêtement] to pucker, be puckered; [papier peint] to have bubbles ou bulges in it. **sa jupe godait de partout** her skirt was all puckered.
godet [gɔdɛ] nm a (gén: récipient) jar, pot; (à peinture) pot. **viens boire un ~ avec nous*** come and have a jar* (Brit) ou a drink with us. b (Couture) gore. **jupe à ~s** gored skirt. c (Tech) bucket.
godiche [gɔdiʃ] adj lumpish, oafish. **quelle ~, ce garçon!** what an awkward lump ou what a clumsy oaf that boy is!
godille [gɔdij] nf a (Sport) scull; (Ski) wedeln. **descendre en ~** to wedeln. b (*: péj) **à la ~** système dicky* (Brit), ropey* (Brit), cheesy* (US); jambe, bras dicky* (Brit), game.
godiller [gɔdije] 1 vi (Sport) to scull; (Ski) to wedeln, use the wedeln technique.
godillot* [gɔdijo] nm clodhopper, clumpy shoe.
goéland [gɔelɑ̃] nm seagull, gull. **~ cendré** common gull; **~ argenté** herring gull.
goélette [gɔelɛt] nf schooner.
goémon [gɔemɔ̃] nm wrack.
goglu [gɔgly] nm (Can) bobolink, ricebird.
gogo¹* [gɔgo] nm (personne crédule) sucker*, mug‡. **c'est bon pour les ~s** it's a con‡, it's a mug's game‡.
gogo²* [gɔgo] adv (en abondance) **à ~** galore; **on avait du vin à ~** we had wine galore.
goguenard, e [gɔg(ə)naʀ, aʀd] adj mocking.
goguenardise [gɔg(ə)naʀdiz] nf mocking.
goguenot‡‡ [gɔgno] nm, **gogues‡‡** [gɔg] nmpl (toilettes) bog‡ (Brit), loo* (Brit), john‡ (US).
goguette* [gɔgɛt] nf: **être en ~** to be on the binge* (Brit), be on a spree.
goï [gɔj] = **goy**.
goinfre* [gwɛ̃fʀ] (glouton) 1 adj piggish*. 2 nm pig*.
goinfrer (se) [gwɛ̃fʀe] 1 vpr to make a pig of o.s.*, make a beast of o.s.* **se ~ de gâteaux** to guzzle cakes*, pig o.s. on cakes*.
goinfrerie [gwɛ̃fʀəʀi] nf piggery*, piggishness*.
goitre [gwatʀ] nm goitre.
goitreux, -euse [gwatʀø, øz] 1 adj goitrous. 2 nm,f person suffering from goitre.
golden [gɔldɛn] nf inv: **(pomme) ~** Golden Delicious (apple).
golem [gɔlɛm] nm golem.
golf [gɔlf] nm (sport) golf; (terrain) golf course ou links. **~ miniature** miniature golf; **culottes ou pantalon de ~** plus fours; voir **joueur**.
golfe [gɔlf] nm gulf; (petit) bay. **le ~ de Botnie** the Gulf of Bothnia; **le ~ de Gascogne** the Bay of Biscay; **le ~ du Bengale** the Bay of Bengal; **le ~ du Lion** the Gulf of Lions; **le ~ du Mexique** the Gulf of Mexico; **le ~ Arabique** the Arabian Gulf; **le ~ Persique** the Persian Gulf; **les États du G~** the Gulf States.
golfeur, -euse [gɔlfœʀ, øz] nm,f golfer.
Golgotha [gɔlgɔta] nm: **le ~** Golgotha.
Goliath [gɔljat] nm Goliath.
gomina [gɔmina] nf ® hair cream, Brylcreem ®.
gominer (se) [gɔmine] 1 vpr to put hair cream on, Brylcreem ®. **cheveux gominés** plastered-down hair, hair plastered down with Brylcreem ®.
gommage [gɔmaʒ] nm (voir **gommer**) rubbing-out; erasing; gumming; [peau] exfoliation. **se faire un ~** (visage) to use a facial scrub, exfoliate; (corps) to use a body scrub, exfoliate.
gomme [gɔm] 1 nf (NonC: substance) gum; (Méd) gumma; (pour effacer) rubber (Brit), eraser (US). **mettre ou donner toute la ~*** to step on the gas, put one's foot right down* (Brit), give it full throttle; **à la ~*** personne, outil, système, idée pathetic*, useless; renseignement useless, hopeless; voir **boule¹**. 2 comp ►**gomme adragante** tragacanth ►**gomme arabique** gum arabic ►**gomme à encre** ink rubber (Brit) ou eraser (US) ►**gomme-gutte** nf (pl **gommes-guttes**) gambage, cambogia ►**gomme laque** lac ►**gomme à mâcher** chewing gum ►**gomme-résine** nf (pl **gommes-résines**) gum resin.
gommer [gɔme] 1 vt a (effacer) mot, trait to rub out, erase; (fig) ride, souvenir, différence to erase. b (enduire) to gum. **papier gommé** gummed paper. c (nettoyer) peau to scrub.
gommette [gɔmɛt] nf coloured sticky label.
gommeux, -euse [gɔmø, øz] 1 adj arbre gum-yielding; substance sticky, gummy. 2 nm (*†: jeune prétentieux) pretentious (young) toff*† (Brit) ou dandy.
gommier [gɔmje] nm gum tree.
Gomorrhe [gɔmɔʀ] n Gomorrah.
gonade [gɔnad] nf gonad.
gonadotrope [gɔnadɔtʀɔp] adj gonadotropic.
gonadotrophine [gɔnadotʀɔfin] nf gonadotropin.
gond [gɔ̃] nm hinge; voir **hors, sortir**.
gondolage [gɔ̃dɔlaʒ] nm (voir **gondoler**) crinkling; warping; buckling.
gondolant, e* [gɔ̃dɔlɑ̃, ɑ̃t] adj (amusant) side-splitting*, hilarious.
gondole [gɔ̃dɔl] nf (bateau) gondola; (supermarché) supermarket shelf, gondola.
gondolement [gɔ̃dɔlmɑ̃] nm = **gondolage**.
gondoler [gɔ̃dɔle] 1 1 vi [papier] to crinkle, go crinkly; [planche] to warp; [tôle] to buckle. 2 **se gondoler** vpr a [papier] to crinkle; [planche] to warp; [tôle] to buckle. b (*: rire) to split one's sides laughing*, crease up*.
gondolier, -ière [gɔ̃dɔlje, jɛʀ] nm,f gondolier.
gonfalon [gɔ̃falɔ̃] nm gonfalon.
gonfalonier [gɔ̃falɔnje] nm gonfalonier.
gonfanon [gɔ̃fanɔ̃] nm = **gonfalon**.
gonfanonier [gɔ̃fanɔnje] nm = **gonfalonier**.
gonflable [gɔ̃flabl] adj inflatable.

gonflage [gɔ̃flaʒ] **nm** inflating (*NonC*), inflation (*NonC*).

gonflant, e [gɔ̃flɑ̃, ɑ̃t] 1 **adj** a *coiffure* bouffant. b (*: *irritant*) bloody** (*Brit*) *ou* damned* irritating. **il est ~ avec ses histoires** he is a real pain (in the neck)* the way he goes on. 2 **nm: donner du ~ à ses cheveux** to give body to one's hair.

gonflé, e [gɔ̃fle] (**ptp de gonfler**) **adj** a *yeux, visage, pieds, chevilles* puffy, swollen; *ventre* (*par la maladie*) distended, swollen; (*par un repas*) blown-out, bloated. **il a les joues bien ~es** he has chubby *ou* plump cheeks; **je me sens un peu ~** I feel a bit bloated. b (* *fig*) **il est ~!** (*courageux*) he's got some nerve!*; (*impertinent*) he's got a nerve!* *ou* a cheek!* *ou* some cheek!*; **être ~ à bloc** to be raring to go*.

gonflement [gɔ̃fləmɑ̃] **nm** *[ballon, pneu]* inflation; *[visage, ventre]* swelling; *[prix, résultats]* inflation; *[effectifs]* (*augmentation*) swelling; (*exagération*) exaggeration. **le ~ de son estomac m'inquiétait** his swollen stomach worried me; **le ~ de la circulation des billets** the increase in the amount of money in circulation; **le ~ de la dette publique** the expansion of *ou* the increase in the public debt.

gonfler [gɔ̃fle] 1 1 **vt** a *pneu, ballon* (*avec une pompe*) to pump up, inflate; (*en soufflant*) to blow up, inflate; *aérostat* to inflate; *joues, narines* to puff out; *poumons* to fill (*de* with). **les pluies ont gonflé la rivière** the rain has swollen the river *ou* caused the river to swell; **le vent gonfle les voiles** the wind fills (out) *ou* swells the sails; **un paquet gonflait sa poche** his pocket was bulging with a package; **un soupir gonflait sa poitrine** he heaved a great sigh; **éponge gonflée d'eau** sponge swollen with water; **la bière me gonfle** *ou* **me fait ~ l'estomac** beer blows out my stomach, beer makes me feel bloated *ou* makes my stomach bloated; **il avait les yeux gonflés par le manque de sommeil** his eyes were puffy *ou* swollen with lack of sleep.

b (*fig: dilater*) to swell. **ses succès l'ont gonflé d'orgueil** his successes have made his head swell *ou* made him puffed up (with pride); **l'orgueil gonfle son cœur** his heart is swollen with pride; **l'espoir lui gonflait le cœur** his heart was swelling *ou* bursting with hope; **le chagrin lui gonflait le cœur** his heart was heavy with sorrow; **cœur gonflé de joie/d'indignation** heart bursting with joy/indignation; **il nous les gonfle!*** he is a pain in the neck* *ou* butt!* (*surtout US*).

c (*fig: grossir*) *prix, résultat* to inflate; *effectif* (*augmenter*) to swell; (*exagérer*) to exaggerate; *moteur* to soup up*. **on a gonflé l'importance de l'incident** the incident has been blown up out of (all) proportion, they have exaggerated the importance of the incident; **chiffres gonflés** inflated *ou* exaggerated figures.

2 **vi** (*enfler*) *[genou, cheville]* to swell (up); *[bois]* to swell; (*Culin*) *[pâte]* to rise. **faire ~ le riz/les lentilles** to leave the rice/lentils to swell (up) (in water), soak the rice/lentils.

3 **se gonfler vpr** a *[rivière]* to swell; *[poitrine]* to swell, expand; *[voiles]* to swell, fill (out).

b (*fig*) **se ~ (d'orgueil)** to be puffed up (with pride), be bloated with pride; **son cœur se gonfle (de tristesse)** his heart is heavy (with sorrow); **son cœur se gonfle d'espoir** his heart is bursting with hope.

gonflette* [gɔ̃flɛt] **nf** (*péj*) body building (exercises). **faire de la ~** to pump iron*.

gonfleur [gɔ̃flœʀ] **nm** air pump.

gong [gɔ̃(g)] **nm** (*Mus*) gong; (*Boxe*) bell.

goniomètre [gɔnjɔmɛtʀ] **nm** goniometer.

goniométrie [gɔnjɔmetʀi] **nf** goniometry.

goniométrique [gɔnjɔmetʀik] **adj** goniometric(al).

gonococcie [gɔnɔkɔksi] **nf** gonorrhoea, gonorrhea (*US*).

gonocoque [gɔnɔkɔk] **nm** gonococcus.

gonsesse*, gonzesse* [gɔ̃zɛs] **nf** (*péj*) bird* (*Brit*), chick* (*US*).

gordien [gɔʀdjɛ̃] **adj m** *voir* **nœud**.

goret [gɔʀɛ] **nm** piglet. (*à un enfant*) **petit ~!** you mucky (little) pup!* (*Brit*), you dirty little pig!*

gorge [gɔʀʒ] 1 **nf** a *[personne]* (*cou, gosier*) throat; (*littér: seins*) breast, bosom (*littér*); *[oiseau]* (*poitrine*) breast; (*gosier*) throat. (*hum*) **avoir la ~ sèche** *ou* **comme du buvard** to be parched *ou* dry; **avoir la ~ serrée** *ou* **nouée** to have a lump in one's throat; **rire à pleine ~** *ou* **à ~ déployée** to roar with laughter, laugh heartily; **chanter à pleine ~** *ou* **à ~ déployée** to sing at the top of one's voice; *voir* **chat, couper, couteau**.

b (*vallée, défilé*) gorge. **les ~s du Tarn** the gorges of the Tarn.

c (*rainure*) *[moulure, poulie]* groove; *[serrure]* tumbler.

d (*loc*) **prendre qn à la ~** *[créancier]* to put a gun to sb's head (*fig*); *[agresseur]* to grab sb by the throat; *[fumée, odeur]* to catch *ou* get in sb's throat; *[peur]* to grip sb by the throat (*fig*); **tenir qn à la ~** (*lit*) to hold sb by the throat; (*fig: avoir à sa merci*) to have a stranglehold on sb, have sb by the throat; **l'os lui est resté dans la** *ou* **en travers de la ~** the bone (got) stuck in his throat; (*fig*) **ça lui est resté dans la** *ou* **en travers de la ~** (*il n'a pas aimé*) he found it hard to take, he couldn't swallow it; (*il n'a pas osé le dire*) it *ou* the words stuck in his throat; **faire des ~s chaudes de qch** to laugh sth to scorn; **je lui enfoncerai** *ou* **ferai rentrer ses mots dans la ~** I'll make him eat his words; *voir* **rendre, tendre[1]**.

2 **comp ►gorge-de-pigeon adj inv** dapple-grey; **des (cerises) gorge-de-pigeon** *type of cherry*.

gorgée [gɔʀʒe] **nf** mouthful. **boire à petites ~s** to take little sips; **boire à grandes ~s** to drink in gulps; **boire son vin à grandes/petites ~s** to gulp down/sip one's wine; **vider un verre d'une seule ~** to empty a glass in one gulp, down a glass in one*.

gorger [gɔʀʒe] 3 1 **vt** to fill (*de* with). **~ qn de pâtisseries** to fill sb up *ou* stuff* sb with cakes; **terre/éponge gorgée d'eau** earth/sponge saturated with *ou* full of water; **fruits gorgés de soleil** fruit bursting with sunshine. 2 **se gorger vpr: se ~ (de nourriture)** to gorge o.s., stuff o.s.* (with food); **se ~ de bananes** to gorge o.s. on *ou* with bananas; **se ~ de bon air** to drink in *ou* soak up the fresh air; **éponge qui se gorge d'eau** sponge which soaks up water.

Gorgone [gɔʀgɔn] **nf** (*Myth*) Gorgon. (*Zool*) **g~** gorgonia.

gorgonzola [gɔʀgɔ̃zɔla] **nm** Gorgonzola (cheese).

gorille [gɔʀij] **nm** (*Zool*) gorilla; (*: *garde du corps*) bodyguard.

Gorki [gɔʀki] **nm** Gorky.

gosier [gozje] **nm** (*Anat*) throat; (*: *gorge*) throat, gullet. **avoir le ~ sec*** to be parched *ou* dry; **ça m'est resté en travers du ~*** (*lit*) it (got) stuck in my throat; (*fig*) I couldn't swallow it, I found it hard to take; *voir* **humecter, plein**.

gospel [gɔspɛl] **nm** gospel (music).

gosse* [gɔs] **nmf** kid*. **sale ~** little brat*; **elle est restée très ~** she's still a kid at heart*; (*péj*) **~ de riches** spoilt rich brat*; *voir* **beau**.

Goth [gɔt] **nmf** Goth.

gotha* [gɔta] **nm: le ~ de la finance/de la publicité** the financial/advertising bigwigs*.

gothique [gɔtik] **adj** *architecture, style* Gothic. **écriture ~** Gothic script.

gotique [gɔtik] **nm** (*Ling*) Gothic.

gouache [gwaʃ] **nf** (*matière*) gouache, poster paint; (*tableau*) gouache.

gouaille [gwɑj] **nf** cheeky *ou* cocky* humour.

gouailler [gwɑje] 1 **vi** to have a cheeky *ou* cocky* sense of humour. **en gouaillant** with cheeky *ou* cocky* humour.

gouailleur, -euse [gwɑjœʀ, øz] **adj** cheeky, cocky*.

gouape* [gwap] **nf** thug.

gouda [guda] **nm** Gouda (cheese).

Goudjerate [gudʒeʀat] **nm** = **Gujarât**.

goudron [gudʀɔ̃] **nm** tar. **~ de houille** coal tar; (*sur un paquet de cigarettes*) "**~s: 15 mg**" ≃ "low tar".

goudronnage [gudʀɔnaʒ] **nm** tarring.

goudronner [gudʀɔne] 1 **vt** *route* to tar.

goudronneux, -euse [gudʀɔnø, øz] **adj** tarry.

gouffre [gufʀ] **nm** a (*Géog*) abyss, gulf, chasm. b (*fig*) **le ~ de l'oubli** the depths of oblivion; **c'est un ~ d'ignorance/de bêtise** he's abysmally ignorant/utterly stupid; **cette entreprise est un vrai ~** this business just swallows up money; **cette femme est un ~** this woman is a bottomless pit where money is concerned; **nous sommes au bord du ~** we are on the brink of the abyss.

gouge [guʒ] **nf** gouge.

gougnafier* [guɲafje] **nm** bungling idiot*.

gouine* [gwin] **nf** dyke*.

goujat [guʒa] **nm** boor, churl.

goujaterie [guʒatʀi] **nf** boorishness.

goujon [guʒɔ̃] **nm** (*poisson*) gudgeon; (*Tech: cheville*) pin, bolt.

goulache, goulasch [gulaʃ] **nm ou f** goulash.

goulafre* [gulafʀ] 1 **adj** gluttonous. 2 **nmf** greedy pig*.

goulag [gulag] **nm** Gulag. **(Archipel** *m* **du) ~** Gulag Archipelago.

goule [gul] **nf** ghoul.

goulée [gule] **nf** *[liquide]* gulp; *[solide]* big mouthful. **prendre une ~ d'air frais** (*gorgée*) to take in a lungful of fresh air; (*: *bol d'air*) to get some fresh air.

goulet [gulɛ] **nm** (*Naut*) narrows, bottleneck (*at entrance of harbour*); (*Géog*) gully. **~ d'étranglement** bottleneck.

gouleyant, e [gulɛjɑ̃, ɑ̃t] **adj** very drinkable.

goulot [gulo] **nm** *[bouteille]* neck. **boire au ~** to drink straight from the bottle; **~ d'étranglement** bottleneck (*fig*).

goulu, e [guly] 1 **adj** *personne* greedy, gluttonous; *regards* greedy. 2 **nm,f** glutton.

goulûment [gulymɑ̃] **adv** greedily, gluttonously.

goupil†† [gupi(l)] **nm** fox.

goupille [gupij] **nf** (*Tech*) pin.

goupillé, e* [gupije] (**ptp de goupiller**) **adj** (*arrangé*) **bien/mal ~** *machine, plan, procédé* well/badly thought out; **comment est-ce ~, ce mécanisme?** how does this thing work?

goupiller [gupije] 1 1 **vt** a (*: *combiner*) to fix*. **il a bien goupillé son affaire** he fixed things nicely for himself*. b (*Tech*) to pin. 2 **se goupiller* vpr** (*s'arranger*) **comment est-ce que ça se goupille pour demain?** what's the setup *ou* gen (*Brit*) *ou* dope (*US*) for tomorrow?*; **ça s'est bien/mal goupillé, notre plan** our plan came off* (all right)/didn't come off*; **ça se goupille plutôt mal cette histoire de déménagement** this removal business is a bit of a shambles* *ou* cock-up*.

goupillon [gupijɔ̃] **nm** (*Rel*) (holy water) sprinkler, aspergillum; (*à bouteille*) bottle brush; *voir* **sabre**.

gourance* [guʀɑ̃s] **nf, gourante*** [guʀɑ̃t] **nf** cock-up*, boob* (*Brit*). **faire une ~** to make a cock-up*, boob* (*Brit*), goof up* (*US*).

gourbi [guʀbi] nm (*arabe*) shack; (**: taudis*) slum.
gourd, e[1] [guʀ, guʀd] adj numb (with cold).
gourde[2] [guʀd] 1 nf (*Bot*) gourd; (*à eau, alcool*) flask; (**: empoté*) clot* (*Brit*), dumbbell* (*US*). 2 adj (*) doltish.
gourdin [guʀdɛ̃] nm club, bludgeon. **assommer qn à coups de ~** to club *ou* bludgeon sb.
gourer (se)‡ [guʀe] 1 vpr to boob‡ (*Brit*), make a boob‡. **je me suis gouré de numéro** I've boobed‡ over the number (*Brit*), I got the wrong number; **je me suis gouré dans mes calculs** I made a cock-up of *ou* I goofed up (*US*) my calculations‡.
gourgandine*†† [guʀgɑ̃din] nf hussy*†.
gourmand, e [guʀmɑ̃, ɑ̃d] 1 adj (*personne*) greedy; *moto, auto* thirsty, greedy. **~ comme un chat** greedy but fussy *ou* choos(e)y; **être ~ de** *sucreries* to be fond of, be partial to; *nouveautés* to be avid for; (*Bot*) **branche ~e** sucker. 2 nm,f gourmand. 3 nm (*Agr*) sucker.
gourmander [guʀmɑ̃de] 1 vt (*littér*) to rebuke, berate (*littér*).
gourmandise [guʀmɑ̃diz] nf a greed, greediness. **elle regardait le gâteau avec ~** she looked greedily at the cake. b **~s** delicacies, sweetmeats†.
gourme [guʀm] nf (*†: Méd*) impetigo; (*Zool*) strangles (*sg*); *voir* **jeter**.
gourmé, e [guʀme] adj starchy, stiff.
gourmet [guʀmɛ] nm gourmet, epicure; *voir* **fin**[1].
gourmette [guʀmɛt] nf *[cheval]* curb chain; *[poignet]* chain bracelet.
gourou [guʀu] nm guru.
gousse [gus] nf *[vanille, petits pois]* pod. **~ d'ail** clove of garlic.
gousset [gusɛ] nm *[gilet, pantalon]* fob; *[slip]* gusset; *voir* **montre**.
goût [gu] nm a (*sens*) taste. **amer au ~** bitter to the taste; **avoir le ~ fin** to have a fine palate.

b (*saveur*) taste. **cela a un ~ de moisi** it tastes mouldy; **ça a bon ~** it tastes good, it has a nice taste; **ça a mauvais ~** it has a bad taste, it tastes nasty; **cette glace n'a pas vraiment un ~ de fraise** this ice cream doesn't really taste like strawberry *ou* hasn't really got a strawberry taste *ou* flavour; **la soupe a un ~** the soup tastes funny *ou* has a funny taste; **un plat sans ~** a tasteless *ou* flavourless dish; *[épice, condiment]* **donner du ~ à qch** to add (a bit of) flavour to sth; (*fig*) **la vie n'a plus de ~ pour lui** he has no longer any taste for life, he has lost his taste for life; (*fig*) **ses souvenirs ont un ~ amer** he has bitter memories; (*fig*) **cette rétrospective a un ~ de nostalgie** this retrospective has a nostalgic feel *ou* flavour; **ça a un ~ de revenez-y*** it makes you want seconds, it's very more-ish* (*Brit*); *voir* **arrière, avant**.

c (*jugement*) taste. **(bon) ~** (good) taste; **avoir du/manquer de ~** to have/lack taste; **avoir un ~ vulgaire** to have vulgar tastes; **le ~ ne s'apprend pas** taste is something you're born with; **faire qch sans/avec ~** to do something tastelessly/tastefully; **elle s'habille avec beaucoup de ~** she has very good *ou* a lot of taste in dress, she has very good dress sense; **à mon/son ~** for my/his liking, for my/his taste(s); **un homme/une femme de ~** a man/woman of taste; *voir* **faute**.

d *vêtement, ameublement* **de bon ~** tasteful, in good taste (*attrib*); *bijoux, plaisanterie, meubles* **de mauvais ~** tasteless, in bad *ou* poor taste (*attrib*); **garni d'un ameublement de bon/mauvais ~** furnished in good/bad taste, with tasteful/tasteless furnishings; **c'est une plaisanterie de mauvais ~** this joke is in bad taste *ou* is bad form; **il serait de mauvais ~/d'un ~ douteux de faire** it would be in bad *ou* poor/doubtful taste to do; (*iro*) **il serait de bon ~ d'y aller/qu'il se mette à travailler** it would be as well to go/if he started doing some work.

e (*penchant*) taste, liking (*de, pour* for). **salez à votre ~** salt (according) to taste; **il a peu de ~ pour ce genre de travail** this sort of work is not to his taste *ou* liking *ou* is not his cup of tea*; **il n'a aucun ~ pour les sciences** the sciences don't appeal to him, he has no taste for the sciences; **il a le ~ de l'ordre** he has a taste for order; **il a le ~ du risque** he likes taking risks; **faire qch par ~** to do sth from inclination *ou* because one has a taste for it; **prendre ~ à qch** to get *ou* acquire a taste *ou* liking for sth, get to like sth; **elle a repris ~ à la vie/la danse** she has started to enjoy life/dancing again; **il n'avait ~ à rien** he didn't feel like (doing) anything; **ce n'est pas du ~ de chacun** it's not to everybody's taste; **cela m'a mis en ~** that gave me a taste for it; **c'est tout à fait à mon ~** this is very much to my taste; **il la trouve à son ~** she suits his taste; **faire passer le ~ du pain à qn*** to wipe the smile off sb's face; *voir* **chacun**.

f (*tendances, penchants*) **~s** tastes; **avoir des ~s dispendieux/modestes** to have expensive/simple tastes; **avoir des ~s communs** to have (some) tastes in common; **ses déclarations n'ont pas été du ~ de ses alliés politiques** what he said didn't go down well with his political allies, his political allies didn't like the sound of what he said; (*Prov*) **des ~s et des couleurs (on ne discute pas)** there's no accounting for taste(s); (*Prov*) **tous les ~s sont dans la nature** it takes all sorts to make a world.

g (*style*) style. **dans le ~ classique/de X** in the classical style/the style of X; **ou quelque chose dans ce ~-là*** or something of that sort; **au ~ du jour** in keeping with the style of the day *ou* with current tastes; **il s'est mis au ~ du jour** he has brought himself into line with current tastes; **pièce de théâtre/chanson/robe remise au ~ du jour** play/song/dress brought up to date.

goûter [gute] 1 1 vt a *aliment* to taste. **goûte-le, pour voir si c'est assez salé** taste it and see if there's enough salt.

b *repos, spectacle* to enjoy, savour.

c (*littér*) *écrivain, œuvre, plaisanterie* to appreciate. **il ne goûte pas l'art abstrait** he doesn't appreciate abstract art, abstract art isn't to his taste.

d (*Belgique*) *[aliment]* to taste of.

2 **goûter à** vt indir *aliment, plaisir* to taste, sample; *indépendance, liberté* to taste. **il y a à peine goûté** he's hardly touched it; **voulez-vous ~ à mon gâteau?** would you like to try *ou* sample my cake?; **goûtez-y** (*vin*) have a sip *ou* taste, taste it; (*plat*) have a taste, taste it.

3 **goûter de** vt indir (*faire l'expérience de*) to have a taste of, taste. **il a goûté de la vie militaire/de la prison** he has had a taste of army/prison life, he has tasted army/prison life.

4 vi a (*faire une collation*) to have tea (*Brit*), have an afterschool snack (*US*). **emporter à ~** to take an afterschool snack; **inviter des enfants à ~** to ask children to tea (*Brit*), invite children for a snack (*US*).

b (*Belgique*) *[aliment]* to taste good.

5 nm (afterschool) snack. **donner un ~ d'enfants** to give *ou* have a children's (tea) party (*Brit*), invite children for a snack (*US*).
goûteur, -euse [gutœʀ, øz] nm,f: **~ d'eau** *etc* water *etc* taster.
goûteux, -euse [gutø, øz] adj *vin, viande* flavourful (*Brit*), flavorful (*US*).
goutte [gut] 1 nf a (*lit, fig*) drop. **~ de rosée** dewdrop; **~ de sueur** bead of sweat; **suer à grosses ~s** to be streaming with sweat; **pleuvoir à grosses ~s** to rain heavily; **il est tombé quelques ~s** a few spots *ou* drops of rain have fallen; **du lait? – une ~** milk? – just a drop; **savourer qch ~ à ~** to savour sth drop by drop; **tomber ~ à ~** to drip.

b (*Pharm*) **~s** drops; **~s pour les yeux/le nez** eye/nose drops.

c (**: eau-de-vie*) **on va prendre la ~ *ou* un verre de ~** we'll have a dram* (*Brit*) *ou* a nip* (*Brit*) *ou* a drop (*US*).

d (*††, hum: rien*) **je n'y vois/entends ~** I see/hear not a thing (*††, hum*).

e (*Méd*) gout.

f (*loc*) **avoir la ~ au nez** to have a dripping *ou* runny nose; **c'est une ~ d'eau dans la mer** it's a drop in the ocean (*Brit*) *ou* bucket; **c'est la ~ (d'eau) qui fait déborder le vase** it's the last straw (that breaks the camel's back); *voir* **ressembler**.

2 comp ►**goutte d'eau** (*Bijouterie*) drop, droplet ►**goutte-à-goutte** nm inv (*Méd*) drip (*Brit*), IV (*US*); **alimenter qn au goutte-à-goutte** to put sb on a drip (*Brit*) *ou* an IV (*US*), drip-feed sb (*Brit*).
gouttelette [gut(ə)lɛt] nf droplet.
goutter [gute] 1 vi to drip (*de* from).
goutteux, -euse [gutø, øz] adj gouty.
gouttière [gutjɛʀ] nf (*horizontale*) gutter; (*verticale*) drainpipe; (*Méd*) (plaster) cast; (*Anat: sur os*) groove; *voir* **chat**.
gouvernable [guvɛʀnabl] adj governable. **difficilement ~** difficult to govern, governed with difficulty.
gouvernail [guvɛʀnaj] nm (*pale*) rudder; (*barre*) helm, tiller. **~ de direction** rudder; **~ de profondeur** elevator; (*fig*) **tenir le ~** to be at the helm.
gouvernant, e [guvɛʀnɑ̃, ɑ̃t] 1 adj *parti, classe* ruling (*épith*), governing (*épith*). (*Pol*) **les ~s** those in power. 2 **gouvernante** nf (*institutrice*) governess; (*dame de compagnie*) housekeeper.
gouverne [guvɛʀn] nf a **pour ta ~** for your guidance. b (*Naut*) steering; (*Aviat*) control surface.
gouverné [guvɛʀne] nm (*gén pl*) citizen. **les ~s et les gouvernants** the governed and the governing.
gouvernement [guvɛʀnəmɑ̃] nm (*administration, régime*) government; (*cabinet*) Cabinet, Government. **former le ~** to form a government; **soutenir le ~** to back the government; **il est au ~** he's a member of the government; **les gens du ~** members of the government, government members; **sous un ~ socialiste** under socialist rule *ou* government; **ça a eu lieu sous le ~ de X** it happened during the X government *ou* during X's government.
gouvernemental, e, mpl **-aux** [guvɛʀnəmɑ̃tal, o] adj *député* of the governing party; *organe, politique* government (*épith*), governmental (*épith*); *journal* pro-government; *troupes* government (*épith*). **le parti ~** the governing *ou* ruling party, the party in office; **l'équipe ~e** the government.
gouverner [guvɛʀne] 1 1 vt a (*Pol*) to govern, rule. **le parti qui gouverne** the party in power *ou* in office, the governing *ou* ruling party; **peuple capable de se ~ lui-même** nation capable of governing its own affairs *ou* of self-government; **droit des peuples à se ~ (eux-mêmes)** right of peoples to be self-governing.

b (*littér*) to control. **savoir ~ son cœur** to have control over one's heart; **se laisser ~ par l'ambition/par qn** to let o.s. be ruled *ou* governed by ambition/by sb; **il sait fort bien se ~** he is well able to control himself; **l'intérêt gouverne le monde** self-interest rules the world.

c (*Naut*) to steer, helm. **~ vers tribord** to steer to(wards) starboard.

d (*Gram*) to govern, take.

2 vi (*Naut*) to steer. **le bateau gouverne bien/mal** the boat steers well/badly.

gouverneur [guvɛʀnœʀ] nm (*Admin, Pol*) governor. ~ **(militaire)** commanding officer; (*Can*) ~ **général** governor general; (*Can*) **lieutenant-~** lieutenant-governor.

gouzi-gouzi* [guziguzi] nm tickle, tickle*. **faire des ~s à qn** to tickle sb.

goy [gɔj] 1 adj goyish. 2 nmf goy.

goyave [gɔjav] nf (*fruit*) guava.

goyavier [gɔjavje] nm (*arbre*) guava.

GPAO [ʒepeao] nf (abrév de **gestion de la production assistée par ordinateur**) *voir* **gestion**.

GPL [ʒepeɛl] nm (abrév de **gaz de pétrole liquéfié**) LPG.

GQG [ʒekyʒe] nm (abrév de **Grand Quartier Général**) GHQ.

GR [ʒeɛʀ] nm (abrév de **(sentier de) grande randonnée**) (registered) hiking trail.

Graal [gʀɑl] nm Grail.

grabat [gʀaba] nm pallet, mean bed.

grabataire [gʀabatɛʀ] 1 adj bedridden. 2 nmf bedridden invalid.

grabuge* [gʀabyʒ] nm: **il va y avoir du ~** there'll be ructions* (*Brit*) *ou* a ruckus* (*US*) *ou* a rumpus*; **faire du ~** to create havoc *ou* mayhem.

grâce [gʀɑs] nf a (*charme*) *[personne, geste]* grace; *[chose, paysage]* charm. **plein de ~** graceful; **un visage sans ~** a plain face; **avec ~** *danser* gracefully; *s'exprimer* elegantly; **faire des ~s** to put on airs (and graces).

b (*faveur*) favour. **demander une ~ à qn** to ask a favour of sb; **accorder une ~ à qn** to grant sb a favour; (*frm, hum*) **il nous a fait la ~ d'accepter** he did us the honour of accepting (*frm, hum*); **elle nous a fait la ~ de sa présence** *ou* **d'être présente** she graced *ou* honoured us with her presence; **être dans les bonnes ~s de qn** to be in favour with sb, be in sb's good graces *ou* good books*; **être en ~** to be in favour; **rentrer en ~** to come back into favour, come in from the cold; **chercher/gagner les bonnes ~s de qn** to seek/gain sb's favour; **délai de ~** days of grace; **donner à qn une semaine de ~** to give sb a week's grace; *voir* **trouver**.

c **bonne ~** (*bonne volonté, affabilité*) good grace; **mauvaise ~** (*mauvaise volonté*) bad grace; **faire qch de** *ou* **avec bonne/mauvaise ~** to do sth with (a) good/bad grace, do sth willingly/grudgingly; **il y a mis de la mauvaise ~** he did it with (a) bad grace; **il a eu la bonne ~ de reconnaître ...** he had the grace to recognize ...; **il aurait mauvaise ~ à refuser** it would be bad form *ou* in bad taste for him to refuse.

d (*miséricorde*) mercy; (*Jur*) pardon. **la ~ royale/présidentielle** the royal/presidential pardon; **demander** *ou* **crier ~** to beg *ou* cry for mercy; **demander ~ pour qn** to appeal for clemency on behalf of sb; **~!** (have) mercy!; **de ~, laissez-le dormir** for pity's sake *ou* for goodness' sake, let him sleep; **je vous fais ~ des détails/du reste** I'll spare you the details/the rest; **coup de ~** coup de grâce, deathblow; **donner/recevoir le coup de ~** to give/receive the coup de grâce *ou* deathblow; *voir* **droit**³, **recours, trouver**.

e (*reconnaissance*) **dire les ~s** to give thanks (*after a meal*); **~ à qn/qch** thanks to sb/sth; **~ à Dieu!** thank God!, thank goodness!; *voir* **action, jour, rendre**.

f (*Rel*) grace; (*fig: don*) gift. (*Rel*) **Marie, pleine de ~** Mary, full of grace; **avoir la ~** to have a gift; (*fig*) **il a été touché par la ~** he has been inspired; (*fig*) **c'est la ~ que nous lui souhaitons** that is what we wish for him; **à la ~ de Dieu!** it's in God's hands!; **nous réussirons par la ~ de Dieu** with God's blessing we shall succeed; **~ efficace/suffisante/vivifiante** efficacious/sufficient/life-giving grace; *voir* **an, état**.

g (*déesse*) **les trois G~s** the three Graces.

h (*titre*) **Sa G~ ...** (*homme*) His Grace ...; (*femme*) Her Grace ... .

gracier [gʀasje] 7 vt to pardon.

gracieusement [gʀasjøzmɑ̃] adv (*élégamment*) gracefully; (*aimablement*) amiably, kindly; (*gratuitement*) free of charge. **ceci vous est offert par la société X** Messrs X offer you this with their compliments, please accept this with the compliments of Messrs X; **documents ~ prêtés par l'Institut X** documentation kindly loaned by the X Institute.

gracieuseté [gʀasjøzte] nf (*frm*) (*amabilité*) amiability; (*geste élégant*) graceful gesture; (*cadeau*) free gift. (*iro*) **je vous remercie de vos ~s** so kind of you to say so (*iro*).

gracieux, -ieuse [gʀasjø, jøz] adj a (*élégant*) *gestes, silhouette, personne* graceful. b (*aimable*) *sourire, abord, personne* amiable, kindly; *enfant* amiable. (*frm*) **notre ~ieuse souveraine** our gracious sovereign (*frm*). c (*frm: gratuit*) *aide, service* gratuitous (*frm*); *voir* **recours, titre**.

gracile [gʀasil] adj *personne, corps, tige* slender; *cou* slender, swanlike.

gracilité [gʀasilite] nf slenderness.

Gracques [gʀak] nmpl: **les ~** the Gracchi.

gradation [gʀadasjɔ̃] nf gradation.

grade [gʀad] nm a (*dans la hiérarchie: Admin, Mil*) rank. **monter en ~** to be promoted; **en prendre pour son ~*** to get a proper dressing-down*. b (*titre: Univ*) degree. **le ~ de licencié** the (first) degree, bachelor's degree. c (*Math*) grade. d (*Tech*) *[huile]* grade.

gradé [gʀade] nm (*Mil*) (*gén*) officer; (*subalterne*) N.C.O., non-commissioned officer; (*Police*) officer, (police) sergeant (*Brit*).

gradient [gʀadjɑ̃] nm pressure gradient.

gradin [gʀadɛ̃] nm (*Théât*) tier; *[stade]* step (of the terracing); (*Agr*) terrace. *[stade]* **les ~s** the terraces; **dans les ~s** on the terraces; **en ~s** terraced; **la colline s'élevait/descendait en ~s** the hill went up/down in steps *ou* terraces.

graduation [gʀadɥasjɔ̃] nf *[instrument]* graduation.

gradué, e [gʀadɥe] (ptp de **graduer**) adj *exercices* graded; *règle, thermomètre* graduated. **verre ~** calibrated (glass) beaker.

graduel, -elle [gʀadɥɛl] 1 adj *progression, amélioration, augmentation* gradual; *difficultés* progressive. 2 nm (*Rel*) gradual.

graduellement [gʀadɥɛlmɑ̃] adv gradually.

graduer [gʀadɥe] 1 vt *exercices* to increase in difficulty; *difficultés, efforts* to step up *ou* increase gradually; *règle, thermomètre* to graduate.

graffiter [gʀafite] 1 vt to write graffiti on.

graffiteur, -euse [gʀafitœʀ, øz] nm,f graffiti artist.

graffiti [gʀafiti] nmpl graffiti. **un ~** a piece of graffiti.

grailler [gʀɑje] 1 vi a (‡: *manger*) to nosh‡ (*Brit*), chow down‡ (*US*). b *[corneille]* to caw.

graillon [gʀɑjɔ̃] nm (*péj: déchet*) bit of burnt fat. **ça sent le ~ ici** there's a smell of burnt fat here.

graillonner* [gʀɑjɔne] 1 vi (*tousser*) to cough; (*parler*) to speak in a throaty *ou* hoarse voice.

grain [gʀɛ̃] 1 nm a *[blé, riz, maïs, sel]* grain. (*céréales*) **le(s) ~(s)** (the) grain; **donner du ~ aux poules** to give grain to chickens; **alcool** *ou* **eau-de-vie de ~(s)** grain alcohol; **le commerce des ~s** the grain trade; (*Rel*) **le bon ~** the good seed; *voir* **poulet, séparer**.

b *[café]* bean; *[moutarde]* seed. **~ de café** coffee bean; **~ de raisin** grape; **~ de poivre** peppercorn; **~ de groseille/cassis** red currant/blackcurrant (berry); **poivre en ~s** whole pepper *ou* peppercorns; **café en ~s** unground coffee, coffee beans; **mettre son ~ de sel*** to put one's oar in*.

c *[collier, chapelet]* bead; (*Méd: petite pilule*) pellet.

d (*particule*) *[sable, farine, pollen]* grain; *[poussière]* speck. (*fig*) **un ~ de fantaisie** a touch of fantasy; (*fig*) **ça a été le ~ de sable dans l'engrenage** that upset the applecart; **un ~ de bon sens** a grain *ou* an ounce of commonsense; **il n'y a pas un ~ de vérité dans ce qu'il dit** there's not a grain *ou* scrap of truth in what he says; **il a un (petit) ~*** he's a bit touched*, he's not quite all there*; **il faut parfois un petit ~ de folie** it sometimes helps to have a touch of madness *ou* to be a bit eccentric.

e (*texture*) grain. **à gros ~s** coarse-grained; **travailler dans le sens du ~** to work with the grain; *voir* **gros**.

f (*averse brusque*) heavy shower; (*Naut: bourrasque*) squall; *voir* **veiller**.

g (††: *poids*) grain; (*Can*) grain (*0,0647 gramme*).

2 comp ▸ **grain de beauté** mole, beauty spot.

graine [gʀɛn] nf (*Agr*) seed. **~s de radis** radish seeds; **tu vois ce qu'a fait ton frère, prends-en de la ~*** you've seen what your brother has done so take a leaf out of his book*; **c'est de la ~ de voleur** he has the makings of a thief; *voir* **casser, mauvais, monter**.

grainer [gʀene] 1 = **grener**.

graineterie [gʀɛntʀi] nf (*commerce*) seed trade; (*magasin*) seed shop, seed merchant's (shop).

grainetier, -ière [gʀɛntje, jɛʀ] nm,f seed merchant; (*homme*) seedsman.

graissage [gʀɛsaʒ] nm *[machine]* greasing, lubricating. **faire faire un ~ complet de sa voiture** to take one's car in for a complete lubricating job.

graisse [gʀɛs] 1 nf *[personne, animal]* fat; (*Culin*) fat; *[viande cuite]* dripping (*Brit*), drippings (*US*); (*lubrifiant*) grease. **~(s) végétale(s)/animale(s)** vegetable/animal fat; *[animal]* **prendre de la ~** to put on fat; *voir* **bourrelet, paquet**. 2 comp ▸ **graisse de baleine** (whale) blubber ▸ **graisse de phoque** seal blubber ▸ **graisse de porc** lard ▸ **graisse de viande** dripping (*Brit*), drippings (*US*).

graisser [gʀese] 1 vt (*lubrifier*) (*gén*) to grease, lubricate; *bottes* to wax; (*salir*) to get grease on, make greasy. (*fig*) **~ la patte à qn*** to grease *ou* oil sb's palm*.

graisseur [gʀɛsœʀ] nm lubricator. **dispositif ~** lubricating *ou* greasing device; **(pistolet) ~** grease gun.

graisseux, -euse [gʀɛsø, øz] adj *main, objet* greasy; *papiers* grease-stained, greasy; *nourriture* greasy, fatty; *bourrelet* fatty, of fat; *tissu, tumeur* fatty.

graminacée [gʀaminase] nf = **graminée**.

graminée [gʀamine] adj f, nf: **une (plante) ~** a grass; **les (plantes) ~s** (the) grasses, the graminae (SPÉC).

grammaire [gʀa(m)mɛʀ] nf (*science, livre*) grammar. **faute de ~** grammatical mistake; **règle de ~** grammatical rule, rule of grammar; **exercice/livre de ~** grammar exercise/book; **~ des cas** case grammar; **~ (de structure) syntagmatique** phrase structure grammar; **~ de surface** surface grammar.

grammairien, -ienne [gʀa(m)mɛʀjɛ̃, jɛn] nm,f grammarian.

grammatical, e, mpl **-aux** [gʀamatikal, o] adj (*gén*) grammatical. **exercice ~** grammar *ou* grammatical exercise; **phrase ~e** well-formed *ou* grammatical sentence; *voir* **analyse**.

grammaticalement [gʀamatikalmɑ̃] adv grammatically.

grammaticalisation [gʀamatikalizasjɔ̃] nf (*Ling*) grammaticalization.

grammaticalité [gʀamatikalite] nf grammaticality.
gramme [gʀam] nm gramme. **il n'a pas un ~ de jugeote** he hasn't an ounce of commonsense.
gramophone† [gʀamɔfɔn] nm ® gramophone†.
grand, e [gʀɑ̃, gʀɑ̃d] 1 adj a (*de haute taille*) *personne, verre* tall; *arbre, échelle* high, big, tall.
b (*plus âgé, adulte*) **son ~ frère** his big *ou* older *ou* elder brother; **il a un petit garçon et deux ~es filles** he has a little boy and two older *ou* grown-up daughters; **ils ont 2 ~s enfants** they have 2 grown-up children; **quand il sera ~** *[enfant]* when he's grown-up; *[chiot]* when it's big, when it's fully grown; **il est assez ~ pour savoir** he's big enough *ou* old enough to know; **tu es ~/~e maintenant** you're a big boy/girl now; *voir* **5**.
c (*en dimensions*) (*gén*) big, large; *hauteur, largeur* great; *bras, distance, voyage* long; *pas, enjambées* long; (*lit, fig*) *marge* wide. **aussi/plus ~ que nature** as large as/larger than life; **ouvrir de ~s yeux** to open one's eyes wide; **ouvrir la fenêtre/la bouche toute ~e** to open the window/one's mouth wide.
d (*en nombre, quantité*) *vitesse, poids, valeur, puissance* great; *nombre, quantité* large, great; *famille* large, big; *foule* large, great, big; *dépense* great; *fortune* great, large. **la ~e majorité des gens** the great *ou* vast majority of people; **une ~e partie de ce qu'il a** a great *ou* large proportion of what he has.
e (*intense, violent*) *bruit, cri* great, loud; *froid* severe, intense; *chaleur* intense; *vent* strong, high; *effort, danger, plaisir, déception* great; *pauvreté* great, dire (*épith*); *soupir* deep, big. **il fait une ~e chaleur/un ~ froid** it's extremely *ou* intensely hot/cold, we're having a particularly hot/cold spell, the heat/cold is intense; **pendant les ~s froids** during the cold season, in the depth of winter; **pendant les ~es chaleurs** during the hot season, at the height of summer; **l'incendie a causé de ~s dégâts** the fire has caused extensive damage *ou* enormous damage *ou* a great deal of damage; **avec un ~ rire** with a loud *ou* great laugh; **~ chagrin** deep *ou* great sorrow; **les ~es douleurs sont muettes** great sorrow is often silent; *voir* **frapper**.
f (*riche, puissant*) *pays, firme, banquier, industriel* leading, big. **les ~s trusts** the big trusts; **le ~ capital** big investors; **un ~ personnage** an important person; (*lit*) **un ~ seigneur** a great *ou* powerful lord; (*fig*) **faire le ~ seigneur** to play *ou* act the grand *ou* fine gentleman; **faire le ~ seigneur avec qn** to lord it over sb; **~e dame** great lady.
g (*important*) *aventure, nouvelle, progrès, intelligence* great; *difficulté, différence, appétit* great, big; *ville, travail* big. **c'est un ~ jour/honneur pour nous** this is a great day/honour for us; **son mérite est ~** it's greatly to his credit.
h (*principal*) **la ~e nouvelle/difficulté** the great *ou* main news/difficulty; **il a eu le ~ mérite d'avoir ...** to his great credit he has ..., his great merit was to have ...; **le ~ moment approche** the great moment is coming; **le ~ jour approche** the great day *ou* D-day is coming; **le ~ soir** the great evening; **les ~s points/les ~es lignes de son discours** the main points/lines of his speech; **les ~s fleuves du globe** the major *ou* main *ou* great rivers of the globe; **c'est la ~e question** (*problème*) it's the main *ou* major issue *ou* question; (*interrogation*) it's the big question *ou* the $64,000 question*.
i (*intensif*) *travailleur* great, hard; *collectionneur* great, keen; *buveur* heavy, hard; *mangeur* big; *fumeur* heavy; *ami, rêveur, menteur* great. **c'est un ~ ennemi du bruit** he cannot abide noise, he's a sworn enemy of noise; **un ~ amateur de musique** a great music lover; **~ lâche/sot!** you great coward/fool!; **~e jeunesse** extreme youth; **~ âge** great age, old age; **~e vieillesse** extreme *ou* great age; **un ~ mois/quart d'heure** a good month/quarter of an hour; **rester un ~ moment** to stay a good while; **un ~ kilomètre** a good kilometre; **un ~ verre d'eau** a nice big *ou* long glass of water; **un ~ panier de champignons** a full basket of mushrooms; **les ~s malades** the very ill *ou* sick; **un ~ invalide** a badly *ou* seriously disabled person; **à ~ ahan††** with much striving.
j (*remarquable*) *champion, œuvre, savant, civilisation* great. **un ~ vin/homme** a great wine/man; **une ~e année** a vintage *ou* great year; **le ~ Molière** the great Molière; **c'est du (tout) ~ art** it's (very) great art; **c'est du (tout) ~ Mozart*** it's Mozart at his best *ou* greatest; **les ~s esprits se rencontrent** great minds think alike; *voir* **couture, maison**.
k (*de gala*) *réception, dîner* grand. **en ~e cérémonie/pompe** with great ceremony/pomp; **en ~ apparat** in full regalia; **de ~ apparat** *habit* full-dress (*épith*).
l (*noble*) *âme* noble, great; *pensée* high, lofty; *cœur* noble, big. **se montrer ~ (et généreux)** to be big-hearted *ou* magnanimous.
m (*exagéré*) **de ~s mots** high-flown *ou* fancy words; **tout de suite les ~s mots!** you go off the deep end straight away!, you start using these high-sounding words straight away!; **voilà le ~ mot lâché!** you've come out with it at last!, that's the word I've (*ou* we've *etc*) been waiting for!; **génie! c'est un bien ~ mot!** genius! that's a big word!; **faire de ~es phrases** to trot out high-flown sentences; **prendre de ~s airs** to put on airs, give oneself airs; **faire de ~s gestes** to wave one's arms about; *voir* **cheval**.
n (*loc adv, adj*) **à ma ~e surprise/honte** much to my surprise/embarrassment, to my great surprise/shame; **de ~e classe** *produit* high-class; *œuvre, exploit* admirable; **de ~ cœur** wholeheartedly; **le groupe/bureau (était) au ~ complet** the whole group/office (was there); **à ~s cris** vociferously; **à ~e distance** *détection* long-range (*épith*), at long range; *apercevoir* from a long way off *ou* away; **à ~e eau: laver à ~e eau** *sol* to wash *ou* sluice down; *légumes* to wash thoroughly; **de ~e envergure** *opération* large-scale (*épith*); *auteur* of great stature; *réforme* far-reaching; **à ~s frais** at great expense; **au ~ galop** at full gallop; **au ~ jamais** never ever; **au ~ jour** (*lit*) in broad daylight; (*fig*) in the open; **employer les ~s moyens** to use drastic *ou* extreme measures; **de ~ matin** very early in the morning; **en ~e partie** largely, in the main; **marcher** *ou* **avancer à ~s pas** to stride along; **à ~-peine** with great difficulty; **à ~ renfort de** *publicité* with the help of much, having recourse to much; *arguments* with the help *ou* support of many; **à ~ spectacle** *revue* spectacular; **boire qch à ~s traits** to take big *ou* large gulps of sth; **à ~e vitesse** at great speed; *voir* **bandit**.
o (*loc verbales: beaucoup de*) **avoir ~ air, avoir ~e allure** to look very impressive; **~ bien: cela te fera (le plus) ~ bien** that'll do you a great deal of *ou* the world of good; **j'en pense le plus ~ bien** I think most highly of it; **~ bien vous fasse!** much good may it do you!; **faire ~ bruit** to cause quite a stir; **il n'y a pas ~ danger** there's no great danger; **il n'y a pas ~ mal** (*après accident*) (there's) no harm done; **il n'y a pas ~ mal à ce qu'il fasse** there's not much harm *ou* wrong in him doing; **il n'y a pas ~ monde** there aren't very many (people) here; **cela lui fera ~ tort** it'll do him a lot of harm; *voir* **train**.
p (*loc verbales: bien, très*) **avoir ~ avantage à** to be well advised to; **il aurait ~ avantage à** it would be very much to his advantage to, he would be well advised to; **elle avait ~e envie d'un bain/de faire** she very much wanted a bath/to do, she was longing for a bath/to do; **avoir ~ faim** to be very hungry; **il aurait ~ intérêt à ...** it would be very much in his (own) interest to ..., he would be well advised to ...; **prendre ~ intérêt à qch** to take great interest in sth; **il fait ~ jour** it's broad daylight; **avoir ~ peur** to be very frightened *ou* very much afraid; **avoir ~ peur que** to be very much afraid that; **avoir ~ soif/faim** to be very thirsty/hungry; **il est ~ temps de faire ceci** it's high time this was done *ou* we did this.
2 adv: **voir ~** to think big*, envisage things on a large scale; **il a vu trop ~** he was over-ambitious; **faire ~** to do things on a grand *ou* large scale *ou* in a big way; **ces souliers chaussent ~** these shoes are big-fitting (*Brit*) *ou* run large (*US*); **faire qch en ~** to do sth on a large *ou* big scale *ou* in a big way; **ouvrir (tout) ~ la fenêtre** to open the window wide; **la fenêtre était ~ ouverte** the window was wide open *ou* was open wide.
3 nm a (*Scol*) older *ou* bigger boy, senior boy *ou* pupil (*frm*). **jeu pour petits et ~s** game for old and young alike *ou* for the young and the not-so-young; **aller à l'école tout seul comme un ~** to go to school on one's own like a big boy.
b (*terme d'affection*) **mon ~** son, my lad (*Brit*).
c **les ~s de ce monde** men in high places; (*Pol*) **les quatre G~s** the Big Four.
d **Pierre/Alexandre/Frédéric le G~** Peter/Alexander/Frederick the Great.
4 **grande** nf a (*Scol*) older *ou* bigger girl, senior girl *ou* pupil (*frm*).
b (*terme d'affection*) **ma ~e** (my) dear.
5 comp ►**le grand air** the open air ►**grand angle** adj inv (*Phot*) wide-angle (*épith*) ◊ nm inv wide-angle lens ►**grand-angulaire** adj (*Phot*) wide-angle (*épith*) ◊ nm (pl **grand-angulaires**) wide-angle lens ►**grand argentier** (*Hum*) Minister of Finance ►**la Grande Armée** (*Hist*) the Grande Armée (*army of Napoleon*) ►**grands axes** (*Aut*) (main) trunk roads (*Brit*), main highways (*US*) ►**la Grande Baie Australienne** the Great Australian Bight ►**la grande banlieue** the outer suburbs ►**la Grande Barrière (de Corail)** the Great Barrier Reef ►**la grande Bleue** *ou* **bleue** the Med* ►**grand-bois*** nm (*Can*) virgin forest ►**la Grande-Bretagne** Great Britain ►**grand chantre** precentor ►**grand chef** big boss ►**grand-chose: on ne sait pas grand-chose à son sujet** we don't know (very) much about him; **cela ne vaut pas grand-chose** it's not worth much, it's not up to much* (*Brit*), it's no great shakes*; **es-tu blessé? — ce n'est pas grand-chose** are you hurt? — it's nothing much; **il n'y a pas grand-chose dans ce magasin** there isn't much *ou* there's nothing much in this shop; **il n'y a pas grand-chose à dire** there's not a lot to say, there's nothing much to say; **il n'en sortira pas grand-chose de bon** not much good will come (out) of this, I can't see much good coming out of this; **tu y connais grand-chose?*** do you know much about it? (*voir* **pas**[2]) ►**les grandes classes** (*Scol*) the senior forms (*Brit*), the high school grades (*US*) ►**un grand commis de l'État** a top-ranking *ou* senior civil servant ►**grand coq de bruyère** capercaillie ►**les grands corps de l'État** senior branches of the civil service ►**grand-croix** nf inv Grand Cross (*of the Légion d'honneur*) ◊ nm (pl **grands-croix**) *holder of the Grand Cross* ►**grand-duc** nm (pl **grands-ducs**) (*prince*) grand duke; (*Orn*) eagle owl (*voir* **tournée**[2]) ►**grand-duché** nm (pl **grands-duchés**) grand duchy ►**grande-duchesse** nf (pl **grandes-duchesses**) grand duchess ►**grandes eaux: les grandes eaux de Versailles** the fountains of Versailles; **regarde-le pleurer, c'est les grandes eaux!** look at him crying, he's really turned on the waterworks! ►**le grand écart** (*Danse, Gym*)

the splits; **faire le grand écart** to do the splits ►**la grande échelle (des pompiers)** the (firemen's) big (turntable) ladder ►**grande école** (*Univ*) grande école, *prestigious school of university level with competitive entrance examination, eg École Polytechnique*; (*Scol*) **être à la grande école*** to be at primary school ►**le grand écran** (*Ciné*) the big screen ►**grand électeur** (*en France*) *elector who votes in the elections for the French Senate;* (*aux USA*) presidential elector ►**grand ensemble** housing scheme (*Brit*), high-density housing (project *ou* scheme *ou* development *ou* estate) (*US*); **la vie dans les grands ensembles** life in high-rise flats (*Brit*) *ou* in multi-storey *ou* tower blocks ►**grand escalier** main staircase ►**grand d'Espagne** Spanish grandee ►**les grands fauves** the big cats ►**le grand film*** the feature *ou* main film, the big picture ►**les grands fonds** (*Naut*) the ocean deeps ►**la Grande Guerre** (*Hist*) the Great War (*Brit*), World War I (*US*) ►**Grand-Guignol nm: c'est du Grand-Guignol** it's all blood and thunder ►**grand-guignolesque adj** *situation, événement, pièce de théâtre* gruesome, bloodcurdling ►**le grand huit** *[fête foraine]* the scenic railway ►**les Grands Lacs** (*Géog*) the Great Lakes ►**le grand large** (*Naut*) the high seas ►**les grandes lignes** (*Rail, fig*) the main lines ►**grand-livre nm (pl grands-livres)** (*Comm* †) ledger ►**le Grand Londres** Greater London ►**grand magasin** department store ►**grand maître** (*Échecs, Franc-Maçonnerie*) Grand Master ►**grand-maman nf (pl grands-mamans)** granny*, grandma ►**grand manitou*** big boss* ►**grand mât** mainmast ►**grand-mère nf (pl grands-mères)** grandmother; (*: *vieille dame*) (old) granny* ►**grand-messe nf (pl grand-messes)** high mass ►**le grand monde** high society ►**la grande Muette** (*Mil*) the army ►**la Grande Muraille de Chine** the Great Wall of China ►**le Grand Nord** the far North ►**grand officier** Grand Officer ►**grand-oncle nm (pl grands-oncles)** great-uncle ►**le Grand Orient** the Grand Lodge of France ►**grand-papa nm (pl grands-papas)** grandpa, grandad* ►**grands-parents nmpl** grandparents ►**les grands patrons** (*gén*) the big bosses; (*Méd*) ≃ the top consultants ►**grand-père nm (pl grands-pères)** grandfather; (*: *vieux monsieur*) old man; (*péj*) **avance, grand-père!**⁑ get a move on, grandad!* ►**grande personne** grown-up ►**les Grandes Plaines** the Great Plains ►**grand prêtre** high priest ►**le grand public** the general public; **appareils électroniques grand public** consumer electronics ►**grande puissance** (*Pol*) major power, superpower ►**Grand Quartier Général** General Headquarters ►**la grande roue** *[fête foraine]* the big wheel (*Brit*), the Ferris Wheel (*US*) ►**grand-route nf (pl grand-routes)** main road ►**la grand-rue nf** the high *ou* main street ►**le Grand Siècle** the 17th century (*in France*), the grand siècle ►**les grands singes** the great apes ►**grande surface** hypermarket ►**grand-tante nf (pl grands-tantes)** great-aunt ►**grand teint adj inv** *couleur* fast; *tissu* colourfast, fastcolour (*épith*) ►**grand tétras** capercaillie ►**grand tourisme: voiture de grand tourisme** G.T. saloon car (*Brit*), 4-door sedan (*US*) ►**le Grand Turc** the Sultan ►**les grandes vacances** the summer holidays (*Brit*) *ou* vacation (*US*); (*Univ*) the long vacation ►**grand veneur** master of the royal hounds ►**grand-vergue nf (pl grands-vergues)** main yard ►**la grande vie** the good life; **mener la grande vie** to live in style, live the good life ►**grand-voile nf (pl grands-voiles)** mainsail ►**le grand voyage** (*littér*) the last great journey (*littér*).

grandement [gʀɑ̃dmɑ̃] **adv** a (*tout à fait*) **se tromper** ~ to be greatly mistaken; **avoir** ~ **raison/tort** to be absolutely right/wrong.

b (*largement*) *aider, contribuer* a great deal, greatly. **il a** ~ **le temps** he easily has time, he has plenty of time *ou* easily enough time; **il y en a** ~ **assez** there's plenty of it *ou* easily enough (of it); **être** ~ **logé** to have plenty of room *ou* ample room (in one's house); **nous ne sommes pas** ~ **logés** we haven't (very) much room; **je lui suis** ~ **reconnaissant** I'm deeply *ou* extremely grateful to him; **il est** ~ **temps de partir** it's high time we went.

c (*généreusement*) *agir* nobly. **faire les choses** ~ to do things lavishly *ou* in grand style.

grandeur [gʀɑ̃dœʀ] **nf** a (*dimension*) size. **c'est de la** ~ **d'un crayon** it's the size of *ou* as big as a pencil; **ils sont de la même** ~ they are the same size; ~ **nature** life-size; *voir* **haut, ordre.**

b (*importance*) *[œuvre, sacrifice, amour]* greatness. **avoir des idées de** ~ to have delusions of grandeur; *voir* **délire.**

c (*dignité*) greatness; (*magnanimité*) magnanimity. **faire preuve de** ~ to show magnanimity; **la** ~ **humaine** the greatness of man; ~ **d'âme** nobility of soul.

d (*gloire*) greatness. ~ **et décadence de** rise and fall of; **politique de** ~ politics of grandeur.

e (*Astron, Math*) magnitude. (*Math*) ~ **variable** variable magnitude; (*fig*) **gaffe de première** ~ blunder of the first order.

f (†: *titre*) **Sa G~ l'évêque de X** (the) Lord Bishop of X; **oui, Votre G~** yes, my Lord.

g (*honneurs*) ~**s** glory; *voir* **folie.**

grandiloquence [gʀɑ̃dilɔkɑ̃s] **nf** grandiloquence, bombast.

grandiloquent, e [gʀɑ̃dilɔkɑ̃, ɑ̃t] **adj** grandiloquent, bombastic.

grandiose [gʀɑ̃djoz] **adj** *œuvre, spectacle, paysage* imposing, grandiose.

grandir [gʀɑ̃diʀ] [2] 1 **vi** a *[plante, enfant]* to grow; *[ombre portée]* to grow (bigger). **il a grandi de 10 cm** he has grown 10 cm; **je le trouve grandi** he has grown *ou* he's bigger since I last saw him; **en grandissant tu verras que ...** as you grow up you'll see that ...; (*fig*) **il a grandi dans mon estime** he's gone up in my estimation, he has grown *ou* risen in my esteem; **enfant grandi trop vite** lanky *ou* gangling child.

b *[sentiment, influence, foule]* to increase, grow; *[bruit]* to grow (louder), increase; *[firme]* to grow, expand. **l'obscurité grandissait** (the) darkness thickened, it grew darker and darker; **son pouvoir va grandissant** his power grows ever greater *ou* constantly increases; ~ **en sagesse** to grow *ou* increase in wisdom.

2 **vt** a (*faire paraître grand*) *[microscope]* to magnify. ~ **les dangers/difficultés** to exaggerate the dangers/difficulties; **ces chaussures te grandissent** those shoes make you (look) taller; **il se grandit en se mettant sur la pointe des pieds** he made himself taller by standing on tiptoe.

b (*rendre prestigieux*) **cette épreuve l'a grandi** this ordeal has made him grow in stature; **il sort grandi de cette épreuve** he has come out of this ordeal with increased stature; **sa conduite ne le grandit pas à mes yeux** his behaviour doesn't raise him in my eyes.

grandissant, e [gʀɑ̃disɑ̃, ɑ̃t] **adj** *foule, bruit, sentiment* growing. **nombre/pouvoir (sans cesse)** ~ (ever-)growing *ou* (ever-)increasing number/power.

grandissement† [gʀɑ̃dismɑ̃] **nm** (*Opt*) magnification.

grandissime [gʀɑ̃disim] **adj** (*hum: très grand*) tremendous.

grange [gʀɑ̃ʒ] **nf** barn.

granit(e) [gʀanit] **nm** granite.

granité, e [gʀanite] 1 **adj** granitelike. **papier** ~ grained paper. 2 **nm** (*tissu*) pebbleweave (cloth); (*glace*) granita (*Italian ice cream*).

graniteux, -euse [gʀanitø, øz] **adj** (*Minér*) granitic.

granitique [gʀanitik] **adj** granite (*épith*), granitic.

granivore [gʀanivɔʀ] 1 **adj** grain-eating, granivorous (*SPÉC*). 2 **nm** grain-eater, granivore (*SPÉC*).

granny smith [gʀanismis] **nf inv** Granny Smith (apple).

granulaire [gʀanylɛʀ] **adj** (*Sci*) granular.

granulation [gʀanylasjɔ̃] **nf** a (*grain*) grainy effect. ~**s** granular *ou* grainy surface. b (*action: Tech*) granulation. c (*Phot*) graininess.

granule [gʀanyl] **nm** granule; (*Pharm*) small pill. ~ **homéopathique** homeopathic pill.

granulé, e [gʀanyle] (**ptp de granuler**) 1 **adj** *surface* granular. 2 **nm** granule.

granuler [gʀanyle] [1] **vt** *métal, poudre* to granulate.

granuleux, -euse [gʀanylø, øz] **adj** (*gén*) granular; *peau* grainy.

grape(-)fruit, pl grape(-)fruits [gʀɛpfʀut] **nm** grapefruit.

graphe [gʀaf] **nm** (*Écon, Math*) graph.

graphème [gʀafɛm] **nm** grapheme.

grapheur [gʀafœʀ] **nm** (*Ordin*) graphics application package, graphics software (*NonC*).

graphie [gʀafi] **nf** (*Ling*) written form. **il y a plusieurs** ~**s pour ce mot** there are several written forms of this word *ou* several ways of spelling this word; **une** ~ **phonétique** a phonetic spelling.

graphique [gʀafik] 1 **adj** graphic. (*Ordin*) **écran** ~ graphics screen. 2 **nm** (*courbe*) graph.

graphiquement [gʀafikmɑ̃] **adv** graphically.

graphisme [gʀafism] **nm** a (*technique*) (*Design*) graphics (*sg*); (*Art*) graphic arts. b (*style*) *[peintre, dessinateur]* style of drawing. c (*écriture individuelle*) hand, handwriting; (*alphabet*) script.

graphiste [gʀafist] **nmf** graphic designer.

graphitage [gʀafitaʒ] **nm** (*Tech*) graphitization.

graphite [gʀafit] **nm** graphite.

graphiter [gʀafite] [1] **vt** to graphitize. **lubrifiant graphité** graphitic lubricant.

graphiteux, -euse [gʀafitø, øz] **adj** graphitic.

graphologie [gʀafɔlɔʒi] **nf** graphology.

graphologique [gʀafɔlɔʒik] **adj** of handwriting, graphological.

graphologue [gʀafɔlɔg] **nmf** graphologist.

grappe [gʀap] **nf** *[fleurs]* cluster. ~ **de raisin** bunch of grapes; **en** *ou* **par** ~**s** in clusters; ~**s humaines** clusters of people.

grappillage [gʀapijaʒ] **nm** (*voir* **grappiller**) gleaning; fiddling* (*Brit*); picking up; gathering; lifting. **ses** ~**s se montaient à quelques centaines de francs** his pickings amounted to several hundred francs.

grappiller [gʀapije] [1] 1 **vi** (*après la vendange*) to glean (*in vineyards*); (*faire de petits profits*) to fiddle (a few pounds)* (*Brit*), pick up (a bit extra) on the side (*US*). **arrête de** ~**, prends la grappe** stop picking (at it) and take the whole bunch; **il a beaucoup grappillé chez d'autres auteurs** he has lifted a lot from other authors; **elle ne mange pas, elle grappille** she doesn't eat, she just nibbles. 2 **vt** *grains, fruits* to gather; *connaissances, nouvelles* to pick up; *renseignements, informations* to glean; *idées* to lift. ~ **quelques sous** to fiddle (*Brit*) *ou* pick up a bit extra on the side (*US*).

grappin [gʀapɛ̃] **nm** *[bateau]* grapnel; *[grue]* grab (*Brit*), drag (*US*). (*attraper*) **mettre le** ~ **sur qn*** to grab sb, collar sb*; (*pour l'épouser*) **elle lui a mis le** ~ **dessus*** she's got her claws into him*; **mettre le** ~ **sur qch*** to get one's claws on *ou* into sth*.

gras, grasse [gʀɑ, gʀɑs] 1 **adj** a *substance, aliment, bouillon* fatty. **fromage** ~ full fat cheese; **crème grasse pour la peau** rich moisturizing cream; *voir* **chou**[1]**, corps, matière.**

b (*gros*) *personne, animal, visage, main* fat; *bébé* podgy (*Brit*), pudgy (*US*); *volaille* plump. **être ~ comme un chanoine, être ~ à lard** to be as round as a barrel; *voir* **tuer, vache.**

c (*graisseux, huileux*) *mains, cheveux, surface* greasy; *peinture* oily; *pavé, rocher* slimy; *boue, sol* sticky, slimy; *voir* **houille.**

d (*épais*) *trait, contour* thick; *voir* **caractère, crayon, plante**[1].

e *toux* loose, phlegmy; *voix, rire* throaty.

f (*vulgaire*) *mot, plaisanterie* coarse, crude.

g (*abondant*) *pâturage* rich, luxuriant; *récompense* fat* (*épith*). **la paye n'est pas grasse** the pay is rather meagre, it's not much of a salary; **j'ai touché 200 F, ce n'est pas ~*** I earned 200 francs, which is hardly a fortune; **il n'y a pas ~ à manger*** there's not much to eat.

h (*loc*) **faire la grasse matinée** to have a lie in *ou* a long lie (*Brit*) *ou* a sleep in (*US*).

2 **nm** a (*Culin*) fat; *[baleine]* blubber; (*Théât*) greasepaint. **~-double** tripe; **j'ai les mains couvertes de ~** my hands are covered in grease.

b (*partie charnue*) *[jambe, bras]* **le ~ de** the fleshy part of.

c (*Typ*) **c'est imprimé en ~** it's printed in bold (type).

3 **adv** a **manger ~** to eat fatty foods; (*Rel*) **faire ~** to eat meat.

b **il tousse ~** he has a loose *ou* phlegmy cough; **parler/rire ~*** to speak/laugh coarsely.

grassement [gʀasmɑ̃] **adv** a *rétribuer* generously, handsomely. (*péj*) **vivre ~** to live off the fat of the land; **c'est ~ payé** it's highly paid, it's well paid. b *parler, rire* coarsely.

grasseyement [gʀasɛjmɑ̃] **nm** guttural pronunciation.

grasseyer [gʀaseje] [1] **vi** to have a guttural pronunciation; (*Ling*) to use a fricative *ou* uvular (Parisian) R.

grassouillet, -ette* [gʀasujɛ, ɛt] **adj** podgy (*Brit*), pudgy (*US*), plump.

gratifiant, e [gʀatifjɑ̃, jɑ̃t] **adj** *expérience, travail* rewarding, gratifying.

gratification [gʀatifikasjɔ̃] **nf** (*Admin*) bonus. **~ de fin d'année** Christmas box *ou* bonus.

gratifier [gʀatifje] [7] **vt**: **~ qn de** *récompense, avantage,* (*iro*) *amende* to present sb with; *sourire, bonjour* to favour *ou* grace sb with; (*iro*) *punition* to reward sb with (*iro*); **il nous gratifia d'un long sermon sur l'obéissance** he favoured *ou* honoured us with a long sermon on obedience.

gratin [gʀatɛ̃] **nm** a (*Culin*) (*plat*) cheese(-topped) dish, gratin (*SPÉC*); (*croûte*) cheese topping, gratin (*SPÉC*). **au ~** au gratin; **~ de pommes de terre** potatoes au gratin; **chou-fleur au ~** cauliflower cheese; **~ dauphinois** gratin Dauphinois. b **le ~** (*: *haute société*) the upper crust*, the nobs* (*Brit*), the swells* (*US*); **tout le ~ de la ville était à sa réception** all the nobs* (*Brit*) *ou* swells* (*US*) of the town were at his reception.

gratiné, e [gʀatine] (**ptp de gratiner**) 1 **adj** a (*Culin*) au gratin. b (*: *intensif*) *épreuve, amende* (really) stiff*; *aventures, plaisanterie* (really) wild*. **il m'a passé une engueulade ~e*** he didn't half give me a telling-off*, he gave me a heck of a telling-off*; **c'est un examen ~** it's a heck of an exam (to get through)*, it's a really stiff exam; **comme film érotique, c'est plutôt ~** it's pretty hot stuff* *ou* spicy for an erotic film; **comme imbécile il est ~** they don't come much dafter than him*. 2 **gratinée nf** onion soup au gratin.

gratiner [gʀatine] [1] 1 **vt** (*Culin*) *pommes de terre* to cook au gratin. 2 **vi** (*dorer*) to brown, turn golden.

gratis [gʀatis] 1 **adj** free. 2 **adv** free, for nothing.

gratitude [gʀatityd] **nf** gratitude, gratefulness.

gratouiller* [gʀatuje] [1] **vt** a (*démanger*) **~ qn** to make sb itch. b **~ sa guitare** to strum on one's guitar.

grattage [gʀataʒ] **nm** (*voir* **gratter**) scratching; scraping; scratching off; scratching out; scraping off.

gratte [gʀat] **nf** a (*: *petit bénéfice illicite*) pickings. **faire de la ~** to make a bit on the side*. b (*: *guitare*) guitar.

gratte- [gʀat] **préf** *voir* **gratter.**

grattement [gʀatmɑ̃] **nm** scratching.

gratter [gʀate] [1] 1 **vt** a *surface* (*avec un ongle, une pointe*) to scratch; (*avec un outil*) to scrape; *guitare* to strum. **gratte-moi le dos** scratch my back for me; (*fig*) **si on gratte un peu on se rend compte qu'il n'est pas très cultivé** if one scratches the surface one will realise that he is not very cultured.

b (*enlever*) *tache* to scratch off; *inscription* to scratch out; *boue, papier peint* to scrape off.

c (*irriter*) **ce drap me gratte** this sheet is making me itch; **ça (me) gratte** I've got an itch; **il y a quelque chose qui me gratte la gorge** I've got a tickly throat, my throat's tickly; (*fig*) **vin qui gratte la gorge** wine which catches in one's throat.

d (*) **~ quelques francs** to fiddle a few pounds* (*Brit*), pick up a bit extra on the side; **~ (de l'argent) sur la dépense** to scrimp on one's spending; **~ les fonds de tiroir** to raid the piggy bank (*fig*), scrape around to find enough money; **il n'y a pas grand-chose à ~** there's not much to be made on that.

e (*arg Sport: dépasser*) to overtake.

2 **vi** a *[plume]* to scratch. **j'entends quelque chose qui gratte** I can hear something scratching.

b *[drap]* (*irriter*) to be scratchy; (*démanger*) to itch, be itchy.

c (*: *économiser*) to scrimp and save.

d (*: *travailler*) to slog away* (*Brit*), slave away*.

e (*: *écrire*) to scribble.

f (*frapper*) **~ à la porte** to tap quietly *ou* softly at the door.

g (*: *jouer de*) **~ du violon** to scrape (away at) one's violin; **~ de la guitare** to strum (away on) one's guitar.

3 **se gratter vpr** to scratch (o.s.). (*fig*) **tu peux toujours te ~!*** you can whistle for it!*

4 **comp ▸gratte-ciel nm inv** skyscraper **▸gratte-cul nm** (**pl gratte-culs**) (*Bot*) rose hip **▸gratte-dos nm inv** back-scratcher **▸gratte-papier nm inv** (*péj*) penpusher (*Brit*), pencil pusher (*US*) **▸gratte-pieds nm inv** shoe-scraper.

grattoir [gʀatwaʀ] **nm** scraper.

gratton [gʀatɔ̃] **nm** a (*: *aspérité*) hold. b (*Culin*) **~s** ≃ pork scratchings (*Brit*).

grattouiller [gʀatuje] **vt** = **gratouiller.**

gratuit, e [gʀatɥi, ɥit] **adj** a (*lit: sans payer*) free. **entrée ~e** admission free; **le premier exemplaire est ~** no charge is made for the first copy, the first copy is free (of charge); (*frm*) **à titre ~** free of charge.

b (*non motivé*) *supposition, affirmation* unwarranted; *cruauté, insulte* wanton, gratuitous; *geste* gratuitous, unmotivated. c (*littér: désintéressé*) *bienveillance* disinterested.

gratuité [gʀatɥite] **nf** a (*lit: voir* **gratuit**) **la ~ de l'éducation/des soins médicaux a permis le progrès** free education/medical care has allowed progress. b (*non-motivation: voir* **gratuit**) unwarranted nature; wantonness; gratuitousness; unmotivated nature.

gratuitement [gʀatɥitmɑ̃] **adv** a (*gratis*) *entrer, participer, soigner* free (of charge). b (*sans raison*) *détruire* wantonly, gratuitously; *agir* gratuitously, without motivation. **supposer ~ que** to make the unwarranted supposition that.

gravats [gʀava] **nmpl** (*Constr*) rubble.

grave [gʀav] 1 **adj** a (*posé*) *air, ton, personne* grave, solemn; (*digne*) *assemblée* solemn.

b (*important*) *raison, opération* serious; *faute, avertissement, responsabilité* serious, grave. **c'est une ~ question que vous me posez là** that is a serious question you are asking me.

c (*alarmant*) *maladie, nouvelle, situation, danger* grave, serious; *blessure, menace, résultat* serious. **blessé ~** seriously injured man, serious casualty; **l'heure est ~** it is a serious *ou* grave moment; **ne vous en faites pas, ce n'est pas (bien) ~** never mind — there's no harm done *ou* it's not serious.

d *note* low; *son, voix* deep, low-pitched; *voir* **accent.**

2 **nm** (*Ling*) grave (accent); (*Mus*) low register. (*Rad*) **"~-aigu"** "bass-treble"; (*Rad*) **appareil qui vibre dans les ~s** set that vibrates at the bass tones; (*Mus*) **les ~s et les aigus** (the) low and high notes, the low and high registers.

graveleux, -euse [gʀav(ə)lø, øz] **adj** a (*grivois*) smutty. b *terre* gravelly; *fruit* gritty.

gravelle [gʀavɛl] **nf** (*Méd* ††) gravel††.

gravelure [gʀavlyʀ] **nf** (*rare*) smut (*NonC*).

gravement [gʀavmɑ̃] **adv** a *parler, regarder* gravely, solemnly. b (*de manière alarmante*) *blesser, offenser* seriously. **être ~ compromis** to be seriously compromised; **être ~ menacé** to be under a serious threat; **être ~ coupable** to be seriously involved in an offence *ou* crime; **être ~ malade** to be gravely *ou* seriously ill.

graver [gʀave] [1] **vt** *signe, inscription* (*sur pierre, métal, papier*) to engrave; (*sur bois*) to carve, engrave; (*fig: dans la mémoire*) to engrave, imprint (*dans* on); *médaille, monnaie* to engrave; *disque* to cut. **~ à l'eau-forte** to etch; **faire ~ des cartes de visite** to get some visiting cards printed; (*fig*) **c'est gravé sur son front** it's written all over his face; (*fig*) **c'est gravé dans sa mémoire** it's imprinted *ou* engraved on his memory.

graveur, -euse [gʀavœʀ, øz] **nm,f** (*sur pierre, métal, papier*) engraver; (*sur bois*) (wood) engraver, woodcutter. **~ à l'eau-forte** etcher.

gravide [gʀavid] **adj** *animal, utérus* gravid (*SPÉC*). **truie ~** sow in pig.

gravier [gʀavje] **nm** a (*caillou*) (little) stone, bit of gravel. b (*Géol, revêtement*) gravel (*NonC*). **allée de** *ou* **en ~** gravel *ou* gravelled path.

gravillon [gʀavijɔ̃] **nm** a (*petit caillou*) bit of grit *ou* gravel. b (*revêtement*) *[route]* (loose) chippings (*Brit*), gravel; *[jardin etc]* (fine) gravel (*NonC*). **du ~, des ~s** loose chippings (*Brit*), gravel.

gravillonner [gʀavijɔne] [1] **vt** to gravel. **~ une route** to gravel a road, put loose chippings (*Brit*) on a road.

gravimétrie [gʀavimetʀi] **nf** gravimetry.

gravimétrique [gʀavimetʀik] **adj** gravimetric(al).

gravir [gʀaviʀ] [2] **vt** *montagne* to climb (up); *escalier* to climb. **~ péniblement une côte** to struggle up a slope; **~ les échelons de la hiérarchie** to climb the rungs of the hierarchical ladder.

gravissime [gʀavisim] **adj** extremely *ou* most serious.

gravitation [gʀavitasjɔ̃] **nf** gravitation.

gravitationnel, -elle [gʀavitasjɔnɛl] **adj** gravitational.

gravité [gʀavite] **nf** a (*NonC: voir* **grave**) gravity, graveness; solemnity; seriousness. *regards, paroles* **plein de ~** very serious *ou* solemn; **c'est un accident sans ~** it was a minor accident, it wasn't a serious accident. b (*Phys, Rail*) gravity; *voir* **centre, force.**

graviter [gʀavite] 1 vi a (*tourner*) *[astre]* to revolve (*autour de* round, about); *[personne]* to hover, revolve (*autour de* round). **cette planète gravite autour du Soleil** this planet revolves around *ou* orbits the Sun; **il gravite dans les milieux diplomatiques** he moves in diplomatic circles; **pays satellite qui gravite dans l'orbite d'une grande puissance** country that is the satellite of a major power. b (*tendre vers*) *[astre]* ~ **vers** to gravitate towards.

gravois† [gʀavwa] nmpl = **gravats.**

gravure [gʀavyʀ] 1 nf a (*voir* **graver**) engraving; carving; imprinting; cutting. b (*reproduction*) (*dans une revue*) plate; (*au mur*) print. 2 comp ▸**gravure sur bois** (*technique*) woodcutting, wood engraving; (*dessin*) woodcut, wood engraving ▸**gravure en creux** intaglio engraving ▸**gravure sur cuivre** copperplate (engraving) ▸**gravure directe** hand-cutting ▸**gravure à l'eau-forte** etching ▸**gravure de mode** fashion plate.

gré [gʀe] nm a *[personnes]* **à mon/votre** ~ (*goût*) to my/your liking *ou* taste; (*désir*) as I/you like *ou* please *ou* wish; (*choix*) as I/you like *ou* prefer *ou* please; (*avis*) **c'est trop moderne, à mon** ~ it's too modern for my liking *ou* to my mind; **c'est à votre ~?** is it to your liking? *ou* taste?; **agir** *ou* **(en) faire à son** ~ to do as one likes *ou* pleases *ou* wishes; **venez à votre** ~ **ce soir ou demain** come tonight or tomorrow, as you like *ou* prefer *ou* please; **on a fait pour le mieux, au** ~ **des uns et des autres** we did our best to take everyone's wishes into account; **contre le** ~ **de qn** against sb's will.

b (*loc*) **de** ~ **à** ~ by mutual agreement; **il le fera de** ~ **ou de force** he'll do it whether he likes it or not, he'll do it willy-nilly; **de son plein** ~ of one's own free will, of one's own accord; **de bon** ~ willingly; **de mauvais** ~ reluctantly, grudgingly; *voir* **bon[1], savoir.**

c *[choses]* **au** ~ **de: flottant au** ~ **de l'eau** drifting wherever the water carries (*ou* carried) it, drifting (along) on *ou* with the current; **volant au** ~ **du vent** *chevelure* flying in the wind; *plume, feuille* carried along by the wind; *planeur* gliding wherever the wind carries (*ou* carried) it; **au** ~ **des événements** *décider, agir* according to how *ou* the way things go *ou* develop; **balloté au** ~ **des événements** tossed about by events; **il décorait sa chambre au** ~ **de sa fantaisie** he decorated his room as the fancy took him; **son humeur change au** ~ **des saisons** his mood changes with *ou* according to the seasons.

grèbe [gʀɛb] nm grebe.

grec, grecque [gʀɛk] 1 adj *île, personne, langue* Greek; *habit, architecture, vase* Grecian, Greek; *profil, traits* Grecian; *voir* **renvoyer.** 2 nm (*Ling*) Greek. 3 nm,f: **G~(que)** Greek. 4 **grecque** nf (*décoration*) (Greek) fret. (*Culin*) **champignons** *etc* **à la ~que** mushrooms *etc* à la grecque.

Grèce [gʀɛs] nf Greece.

gréco-latin, e, mpl **gréco-latins** [gʀekolatɛ̃, in] adj Gr(a)eco-Latin.

gréco-romain, e, mpl **gréco-romains** [gʀekoʀɔmɛ̃, ɛn] adj Gr(a)eco-Roman.

gredin† [gʀədɛ̃] nm (*coquin*) scoundrel†, rascal†.

gréement [gʀemɑ̃] nm (*Naut*) rigging.

green [gʀin] nm (*Golf*) green.

gréer [gʀee] 1 vt (*Naut*) to rig.

greffage [gʀefaʒ] nm (*Bot*) grafting.

greffe[1] [gʀɛf] nf a (*NonC: voir* **greffer**) transplanting; grafting. b (*opération*) (*Méd*) *[organe]* transplant; *[tissu]* graft; (*Bot*) graft. ~ **du cœur/rein** heart/kidney transplant.

greffe[2] [gʀɛf] nm Clerk's Office (*of courts*).

greffé, e [gʀefe] (ptp de **greffer**) nm,f: **un** ~ **du cœur** (*récent*) a heart transplant patient; (*ancien*) a person who has had a heart transplant.

greffer [gʀefe] 1 vt (*Méd*) *organe* to transplant; *tissu* to graft; (*Bot*) to graft. **on lui a greffé un rein** he's been given a kidney transplant; (*fig*) **là-dessus se sont greffées d'autres difficultés** further difficulties have added themselves to it.

greffier, -ière [gʀefje, jɛʀ] nm,f clerk (of the court).

greffon [gʀefɔ̃] nm (*voir* **greffer**) transplant, transplanted organ; graft.

grégaire [gʀegɛʀ] adj gregarious. **avoir l'instinct** *ou* **l'esprit** ~ to like socialising, be the sociable type; (*péj*) to go with the crowd, be easily led.

grégarisme [gʀegaʀism] nm gregariousness.

grège [gʀɛʒ] 1 adj raw; *voir* **soie[1].** 2 nm raw silk.

grégeois [gʀeʒwa] adj m *voir* **feu[1].**

Grégoire [gʀegwaʀ] nm Gregory.

grégorien, -ienne [gʀegɔʀjɛ̃, jɛn] 1 adj Gregorian. 2 nm: **(chant)** ~ Gregorian chant, plainsong.

grêle[1] [gʀɛl] adj *jambes, silhouette, tige* spindly; *personne* lanky; *son, voix* shrill; *voir* **intestin[1].**

grêle[2] [gʀɛl] nf hail. **averse de** ~ hail storm; (*fig*) ~ **de coups/de pierres** hail *ou* shower of blows/stones; *voir* **canon[1].**

grêlé, e [gʀele] (ptp de **grêler**) adj pockmarked.

grêler [gʀele] 1 1 vb impers: **il grêle** it is hailing. 2 vt: **la tempête a grêlé les vignes** the storm has left the vines damaged by (the) hail; **région qui a été grêlée** region where crops have been damaged by hail.

grêlon [gʀɛlɔ̃] nm hailstone.

grelot [gʀəlo] nm (little spherical) bell.

grelottement [gʀəlɔtmɑ̃] nm (*voir* **grelotter**) shivering; jingling.

grelotter [gʀəlɔte] 1 vi (*trembler*) to shiver (*de* with). ~ **de fièvre** to be shivery with fever, shiver with fever.

greluche‡ [gʀəlyʃ] nf (*péj*) bird‡ (*Brit*), chick‡ (*US*).

Grenade [gʀənad] 1 n (*ville*) Granada. 2 nf (*État*) Grenada.

grenade [gʀənad] nf a (*Bot*) pomegranate. b (*explosif*) grenade. ~ **à fusil/main** rifle/hand grenade; ~ **lacrymogène/fumigène** teargas/smoke grenade; ~ **sous-marine** depth charge. c (*insigne*) badge (*on soldier's uniform etc*).

grenadier [gʀənadje] nm a (*Bot*) pomegranate tree. b (*Mil*) grenadier.

grenadin, e[1] [gʀənadɛ̃, in] 1 adj Grenadian. 2 nm,f: **G~(e)** Grenadian.

grenadine[2] [gʀənadin] nf grenadine.

grenaille [gʀənɑj] nf: **de la** ~ (*projectiles*) shot; (*pour poules*) middlings; ~ **de plomb** lead shot; ~ **de fer** iron filings.

grenaison [gʀənɛzɔ̃] nf seeding.

grenat [gʀəna] 1 nm garnet. 2 adj inv dark red, garnet-coloured.

grené, e [gʀəne] (ptp de **grener**) adj *cuir, peau* grainy; *dessin* stippled.

greneler [gʀɛnle] 4 vt (*Tech*) *cuir, papier* to grain.

grener [gʀəne] 5 1 vt (*Tech*) *sel, sucre* to granulate, grain. 2 vi (*Agr*) *[plante]* to seed.

grenier [gʀənje] nm attic, garret; (*pour conserver le grain etc*) loft. ~ **à blé** (*lit*) corn loft (*Brit*), wheat loft (*US*); (*fig*) granary; ~ **à foin** hayloft.

grenouillage [gʀənujaʒ] nm (*Pol péj*) jiggery-pokery (*Brit péj*), hanky-panky (*péj*).

grenouille [gʀənuj] nf frog. (*péj*) ~ **de bénitier** Holy Joe* (*Brit péj*), churchy old man (*ou* woman) (*péj*); **c'est une vraie** ~ **de bénitier** he *ou* she is very pi* (*Brit péj*) *ou* a proper Holy Joe* (*Brit péj*) *ou* a fanatical churchgoer; **manger** *ou* **bouffer la** ~* to make off with the takings; *voir* **homme.**

grenouiller* [gʀənuje] 1 vi (*péj*) to indulge in *ou* be involved in shady dealings (*esp in political sphere*).

grenouillère [gʀənujɛʀ] nf (*pyjama*) sleepsuit.

grenu, e [gʀəny] adj (*épith*) grainy; *cuir, papier* grained; (*Géol*) *roche* granular.

grenure [gʀənyʀ] nf graining.

grès [gʀɛ] nm a (*Géol*) sandstone. b (*Poterie*) stoneware. **cruche/pot de** ~ stoneware pitcher/pot.

gréseux, -euse [gʀezø, øz] adj sandstone (*épith*).

grésil [gʀezil] nm (*Mét*) (fine) hail.

grésillement [gʀezijmɑ̃] nm (*voir* **grésiller[1]**) sizzling, sputtering; crackling; chirruping, chirping.

grésiller[1] [gʀezije] 1 vi (*crépiter*) *[huile, friture]* to sizzle, sputter; *[poste de radio, téléphone]* to crackle; *[grillon]* to chirrup, chirp.

grésiller[2] [gʀezije] 1 vb impers: **il grésille** fine hail is falling, it's hailing.

gressin [gʀesɛ̃] nm (small) bread stick.

grève [gʀɛv] 1 nf a (*arrêt du travail*) strike. **se mettre en** ~ to go on strike, strike, take industrial action; **être en** ~**, faire** ~ to be on strike, be striking; **usine en** ~ striking factory; **entreprendre une** ~ to take strike *ou* industrial action, go on strike; *voir* **briseur, droit, piquet.**

b (*rivage*) *[mer]* shore, strand (*littér*); *[rivière]* bank, strand (*littér*).

2 comp ▸**grève bouchon** partial strike (*in key areas of production*) ▸**grève de la faim** hunger strike; **faire la grève de la faim** to go (*ou* be) on hunger strike ▸**grève de l'impôt** non-payment of taxes ▸**grève patronale** lockout ▸**grève perlée** ≃ go-slow (strike) (*Brit*), ≃ slowdown (strike) (*US*); **faire une grève perlée** ≃ to go slow (*Brit*), ≃ to slowdown (*US*) ▸**grève sauvage** wildcat strike ▸**grève de solidarité** sympathy strike; **faire une grève de solidarité** to strike *ou* come out (*Brit*) in sympathy ▸**grève surprise** lightning strike ▸**grève sur le tas** sit-down strike ▸**grève totale** all-out strike ▸**grève tournante** strike by rota (*Brit*), staggered strike (*US*) ▸**grève du zèle** ≃ work-to-rule; **faire la grève du zèle** to work to rule.

grever [gʀəve] 5 vt *budget* to put a strain on; *économie, pays* to burden. **la hausse des prix grève sérieusement le budget des ménagères** the rise in prices puts a serious strain on the housewife's budget; **être grevé d'impôts** to be weighed down with *ou* crippled by taxes; **une maison grevée d'hypothèques** a house mortgaged down to the last brick.

gréviste [gʀevist] nmf striker. **les employés ~s** the striking employees; ~ **de la faim** hunger striker.

gribiche [gʀibiʃ] adj: **sauce** ~ *vinaigrette sauce with chopped boiled eggs, gherkins, capers and herbs.*

gribouillage [gʀibujaʒ] nm (*écriture*) scrawl (*NonC*), scribble; (*dessin*) doodle, doodling (*NonC*).

gribouille† [gʀibuj] nm short-sighted idiot (*fig*), rash fool.

gribouiller [gʀibuje] 1 1 vt (*écrire*) to scribble, scrawl; (*dessiner*) to scrawl. 2 vi (*dessiner*) to doodle.

gribouilleur, -euse [gʀibujœʀ, øz] nm,f (*péj*) (*écrivain*) scribbler; (*dessinateur*) doodler.

gribouillis [gʀibuji] nm = **gribouillage.**

grièche [gʀijɛʃ] adj *voir* **pie-grièche.**

grief [gʀijɛf] nm grievance. **faire** ~ **à qn de qch** to hold sth against sb;

ils me font ~ d'être parti *ou* **de mon départ** they reproach me *ou* they hold it against me for having left.

grièvement [gʀijɛvmɑ̃] adv: ~ **blessé** (very) seriously injured.

griffade [gʀifad] nf scratch.

griffe [gʀif] nf a (*Zool*) *[mammifère, oiseau]* claw. **le chat fait ses ~s** the cat is sharpening its claws; (*lit, fig*) **sortir** *ou* **montrer/rentrer ses ~s** to show/draw in one's claws; (*fig*) **tomber sous la ~/arracher qn des ~s d'un ennemi** to fall into/snatch sb from the clutches of an enemy; (*fig*) **les ~s de la mort** the jaws of death; **coup de ~** (*lit*) scratch; (*fig*) dig; **donner un coup de ~ à qn** (*lit*) to scratch sb; (*plus fort*) to claw sb; (*fig*) to have a dig at sb.
b (*marque*) *[couturier]* maker's label (*inside garment*); (*signature*) *[couturier]* signature; *[fonctionnaire]* signature stamp; (*fig: empreinte*) *[auteur, peintre]* stamp (*fig*). **l'employé a mis sa ~ sur le document** the clerk stamped his signature on the document.
c (*Bijouterie*) claw.
d (*Bot*) tendril.

griffer [gʀife] 1 vt a *[chat]* to scratch; (*avec force*) to claw; *[ronces]* to scratch. **attention, il griffe!** be careful – he scratches!; **dans sa rage, elle lui griffa le visage** in her rage she clawed *ou* scratched his face. b (*Haute Couture*) *chaussures* to put one's name to. **un manteau griffé** a coat with a famous name *ou* label.

griffon [gʀifɔ̃] nm (*chien*) griffon; (*vautour*) griffon vulture; (*Myth*) griffin.

griffonnage [gʀifɔnaʒ] nm (*écriture*) scribble; (*dessin*) hasty sketch.

griffonner [gʀifɔne] 1 1 vt (*écrire*) to scribble, jot down; (*dessiner*) to sketch hastily. 2 vi (*écrire*) to scribble; (*dessiner*) to sketch hastily.

grif(f)ton [gʀiftɔ̃] nm = **griveton**.

griffu, e [gʀify] adj (*lit, péj*) **pattes** *ou* **mains ~es** claws.

griffure [gʀifyʀ] nf scratch, claw mark.

grignotage [gʀiɲɔtaʒ] nm *[salaires, espaces verts, majorité]* (gradual) erosion, eroding, whittling away.

grignotement [gʀiɲɔtmɑ̃] nm *[souris]* nibbling, gnawing.

grignoter [gʀiɲɔte] 1 1 vt a *[personne]* to nibble (at); *[souris]* to nibble (at), gnaw (at). b (*fig*) (*réduire*) *salaires, espaces verts, libertés* to eat away (at), erode gradually, whittle away; *héritage* to eat away (at); (*obtenir*) *avantage, droits* to win gradually. ~ **du terrain** to gradually gain ground; **il a grignoté son adversaire*** he gradually made up on *ou* gained ground on his opponent; **il n'y a rien à ~ dans cette affaire** there's nothing much to be gained in that business. 2 vi (*manger peu*) to nibble (at one's food), pick at one's food. ~ **entre les repas** to nibble between meals.

grigou* [gʀigu] nm (*avare*) penny-pincher*, skinflint.

gri-gri [gʀigʀi] nm = **gris-gris**.

gril [gʀil] nm (*Culin*) steak pan, grill pan. (*supplice*) **saint Laurent a subi le supplice du ~** Saint Laurence was roasted alive; (*fig*) **être sur le ~*** to be on tenterhooks, be like a cat on hot bricks (*Brit*) *ou* on a hot tin roof (*US*); **faire cuire au ~** to grill.

grill [gʀil] *voir* **grill-room**.

grillade [gʀijad] nf (*viande*) grill.

grillage[1] [gʀijaʒ] nm (*action: voir* **griller**[1]) toasting; grilling; roasting; singeing.

grillage[2] [gʀijaʒ] nm (*treillis métallique*) (*gén*) wire netting (*NonC*); (*très fin*) wire mesh (*NonC*); *[clôture]* wire fencing (*NonC*).

grillager [gʀijaʒe] 3 vt (*voir* **grillage**[2]) to put wire netting on; to put wire mesh on; to put wire fencing on. **à travers la fenêtre grillagée on voyait le jardin** through the wire mesh covering the window we could see the garden; **on va ~ le jardin** we're going to put wire fencing around the garden.

grille [gʀij] nf a (*clôture*) railings; (*portail*) (metal) gate. b (*claire-voie*) *[cellule, fenêtre]* bars; *[comptoir, parloir]* grille; *[château-fort]* portcullis; *[égout, trou]* (metal) grate, (metal) grating; *[radiateur de voiture]* grille, grid; *[poêle à charbon]* grate. c (*répartition*) *[salaires, tarifs]* scale; *[programmes de radio]* schedule; *[horaires]* grid, schedule.
d (*codage*) (cipher *ou* code) grid. ~ **de mots croisés** crossword puzzle (grid); **appliquer une ~ de lecture freudienne/structuraliste à un roman** to interpret a novel from a Freudian/structuralist perspective. e (*Élec*) grid. f (*Sport Aut*) ~ **de départ** starting grid.

grille- [gʀij] préf *voir* **griller**[1].

grillé, e [gʀije] (ptp de **griller**) adj (*arg Crime*) **il est ~** his cover's been blown (*arg*).

griller[1] [gʀije] 1 1 vt a (*Culin*) *pain, amandes* to toast; *poisson, viande* to grill; *café, châtaignes* to roast.
b (*brûler*) *visage, corps* to burn. **se ~ les pieds devant le feu** to toast one's feet in front of the fire; **se ~ au soleil** to roast in the sun.
c *[chaleur]* to scorch. *[froid]* ~ **les bourgeons/plantes** to make the buds/plants shrivel up, blight the buds/plants.
d (*mettre hors d'usage*) *fusible, lampe* (*court-circuit*) to blow; (*trop de courant*) to burn out; *moteur* to burn out.
e (* *loc*) ~ **une cigarette, en ~ une** to have a smoke*; ~ **un feu rouge** to jump the lights*, run a stoplight (*US*); ~ **une étape** to cut out a stop; ~ **qn à l'arrivée** to pip sb at the post* (*Brit*), beat sb (out) by a nose (*US*).
f (*Tech*) *minerai* to roast; *coton* to singe.
2 vi a (*Culin*) **faire ~** *pain* to toast; *viande* to grill; *café* to roast; **on a mis les steaks à ~** we've put the steaks on to grill *ou* on the grill.
b (*fig*) ~ **(d'impatience** *ou* **d'envie) de faire** to be burning *ou* itching to do.
c (*: *brûler*) **on grille ici!** we're *ou* it's roasting *ou* boiling in here!*; **ils ont grillé dans l'incendie** they were roasted in the fire.
3 comp ▶ **grille-pain** nm inv toaster.

griller[2] [gʀije] 1 vt *fenêtre, porte* to put bars on. **fenêtre grillée** barred window.

grilloir [gʀijwaʀ] nm grill.

grillon [gʀijɔ̃] nm cricket.

grill-room [gʀilʀum] nm ≃ steakhouse.

grimaçant, e [gʀimasɑ̃, ɑ̃t] adj *visage, bouche* (*de douleur, de colère etc*) twisted, grimacing; (*sourire figé*) grinning unpleasantly *ou* sardonically.

grimace [gʀimas] nf a (*de douleur etc*) grimace; (*pour faire rire, effrayer*) grimace, (funny) face. **l'enfant me fit une ~** the child made a face at me; **s'amuser à faire des ~s** to play at making *ou* pulling (funny) faces *ou* at making grimaces; **il eut** *ou* **fit une ~ de dégoût/de douleur** he gave a grimace of disgust/pain, he grimaced with disgust/pain, his face twisted with disgust/pain; **avec une ~ de dégoût/de douleur** with a disgusted/pained expression; **il eut** *ou* **fit une ~** he pulled a wry face, he grimaced; **il fit la ~ quand il connut la décision** he pulled a long face when he learned of the decision; *voir* **apprendre, soupe**.
b (*hypocrisies*) **~s** posturings; **toutes leurs ~s me dégoûtent** I find their posturings *ou* hypocritical façade quite sickening.
c (*arg Couture: faux pli*) pucker. **faire une ~** to pucker.

grimacer [gʀimase] 3 1 vi a (*par contorsion*) ~ **(de douleur)** to grimace with pain; ~ **(de dégout)** to pull a wry face (in disgust); ~ **(sous l'effort)** to grimace *ou* screw one's face up (with the effort); **le soleil le faisait ~** the sun made him screw his face up; **à l'annonce de la nouvelle il grimaça** he pulled a wry face *ou* he grimaced when he heard the news. b (*par sourire figé*) *[personne]* to grin unpleasantly *ou* sardonically; *[portrait]* to wear a fixed grin. c (*arg Couture*) to pucker. 2 vt (*littér*) ~ **un sourire** to pull a sardonic smile; **il grimaça des remerciements** he expressed his thanks with a sardonic smile.

grimacier, -ière [gʀimasje, jɛʀ] adj (*affecté*) affected; (*hypocrite*) hypocritical.

grimage [gʀimaʒ] nm (*Théât*) (*action*) making up; (*résultat*) (stage) make-up.

grimer [gʀime] 1 1 vt (*Théât: maquiller*) to make up. **on l'a grimé en vieille dame** he was made up as an old lady. 2 **se grimer** vpr to make (o.s.) up.

grimoire [gʀimwaʀ] nm a (*écrit inintelligible*) piece of mumbo jumbo; (*illisible*) illegible scrawl (*NonC*), unreadable scribble. b (*livre de magie*) **un (vieux) ~** (magician's) book of magic spells.

grimpant, e [gʀɛ̃pɑ̃, ɑ̃t] adj: **plante ~e** climbing plant, climber; **rosier ~** climbing rose, rambling rose.

grimpe* [gʀɛ̃p] nf rock-climbing.

grimpée [gʀɛ̃pe] nf (*montée*) (steep) climb.

grimper [gʀɛ̃pe] 1 1 vi a *[personne, animal]* to climb (up); (*avec difficulté*) to clamber up. ~ **aux arbres** to climb trees; ~ **à l'échelle** to climb (up) the ladder; ~ **sur** *ou* **dans un arbre** to climb onto *ou* into a tree; ~ **le long de la gouttière** to climb up the drain pipe; **grimpé sur la table/le toit** having climbed *ou* clambered onto the table/roof. b *[route, plante]* to climb. **ça grimpe dur!** it's a hard *ou* stiff *ou* steep climb! c (*) *[fièvre]* to soar; *[prix]* to rocket, soar. 2 vt *montagne, côte* to climb (up), go up. ~ **l'escalier** to climb (up) the stairs; ~ **un étage** to climb up a *ou* one floor. 3 nm (*Athlétisme*) (rope-)climbing (*NonC*).

grimpereau, pl **~x** [gʀɛ̃pʀo] nm: ~ **(des bois)** tree creeper.

grimpette* [gʀɛ̃pɛt] nf (steep little) climb.

grimpeur, -euse [gʀɛ̃pœʀ, øz] 1 adj, nm: **(oiseaux) ~s** scansores (*SPÉC*). 2 nm,f (*varappeur*) (rock-)climber; (*cycliste*) hill-specialist, climber.

grinçant, e [gʀɛ̃sɑ̃, ɑ̃t] adj *ironie* grating; *ton, musique* grating, jarring; *charnière, essieux* grating.

grincement [gʀɛ̃smɑ̃] nm (*voir* **grincer**) grating; creaking; scratching. (*fig*) **il ne l'a pas accepté sans ~s de dents** he accepted it only with much gnashing of teeth; *voir* **pleur**.

grincer [gʀɛ̃se] 3 vi *[objet métallique]* to grate; *[plancher, porte]* to creak; *[plume]* to scratch; *[craie]* to squeak. ~ **des dents (de colère)** to grind *ou* gnash one's teeth (in anger); (*fig*) **ce bruit vous fait ~ des dents** this noise sets your teeth on edge.

grincheux, -euse [gʀɛ̃ʃø, øz] 1 adj (*acariâtre*) grumpy. **humeur ~euse** grumpiness. 2 nm,f grumpy person, misery.

gringalet [gʀɛ̃galɛ] 1 adj m (*péj: chétif*) puny. 2 nm (*péj*) **(petit) ~** puny little chap (*Brit*), (little) runt.

gringue* [gʀɛ̃g] nm: **faire du ~ à qn** to chat sb up.

griotte [gʀijɔt] nf Morello cherry.

grip [gʀip] nm (*Sport*) (*prise*) grip; (*revêtement*) overgrip.

grippage [gʀipaʒ] nm (*Tech: voir* **gripper**) jamming; seizing up.

grippal, e, mpl **-aux** [gʀipal, o] adj flu-like, influenzal (*SPÉC*). **médicament pour état ~** anti-flu drug.

grippe [gʀip] nf flu, influenza (*frm*). **avoir la ~** to have (the) flu, have influenza; **il a une petite** ~ he's got a slight touch of flu; ~ **intestinale** gastric flu; (*fig*) **prendre qn/qch en** ~ to take a sudden dislike to sb/sth.

grippé, e [gRipe] (**ptp de gripper**) **adj: il est** ~ he's got (the) flu; **rentrer** ~ to go home with (the) flu; **les** ~**s** people with *ou* suffering from flu.

grippement [gRipmɑ̃] **nm** = **grippage.**

gripper [gRipe] 1 **vti, se gripper vpr** (*Tech*) to jam. **le moteur a** *ou* **s'est grippé** the engine has seized up (*Brit*) *ou* jammed; **le système judiciaire se grippe** the court system is seizing up.

grippe-sou*, pl grippe-sous [gRipsu] **nm** (*avare*) penny pincher*, skinflint.

gris, e [gRi, gRiz] 1 **adj** a *couleur, temps* grey (*Brit*), gray (*US*). ~ **acier/ardoise/fer/perle/souris** steel/slate/iron/pearl/squirrel grey; ~**-bleu/-vert** blue-/green-grey; **cheval** ~ **pommelé** dapple-grey horse; **aux cheveux** ~ grey-haired; **il fait** ~ it's a grey *ou* dull day; *voir* **ambre, éminence, matière.** b (*morne*) *vie* colourless, dull; *pensées* grey. c (*éméché*) tipsy*. d **faire** ~**e mine à qn** to give sb a cool reception; **faire** ~**e mine** to look rather surly *ou* grumpy. 2 **nm** a (*couleur*) grey (*Brit*), gray (*US*). b (*tabac*) shag. c (*Équitation*) grey (horse).

grisaille [gRizɑj] **nf** a *[vie]* colourlessness, dullness; *[ciel, temps, paysage]* greyness (*Brit*), grayness (*US*). b (*Art*) grisaille. **peindre qch en** ~ to paint sth in grisaille.

grisant, e [gRizɑ̃, ɑ̃t] **adj** (*stimulant*) exhilarating; (*enivrant*) intoxicating.

grisâtre [gRizɑtR] **adj** greyish.

grisbi [gRizbi] **nm** (*arg Crime*) dough‡, lolly‡ (*Brit*), loot‡.

grisé [gRize] **nm** grey tint.

griser [gRize] 1 1 **vt** *[alcool]* to intoxicate, make tipsy; (*fig*) *[air, vitesse, parfum]* to intoxicate. **ce vin l'avait grisé** the wine had gone to his head *ou* made him tipsy*; **l'air de la montagne grise** the mountain air goes to your head (like wine); **se laisser** ~ **par le succès/des promesses** to let success/promises go to one's head; **se laisser** ~ **par l'ambition** to be carried away by ambition. 2 **se griser vpr** *[buveur]* to get tipsy* (*avec, de* on). **se** ~ **de** *air, vitesse* to get drunk on; *émotion, paroles* to allow o.s. to be intoxicated by *ou* carried away by.

griserie [gRizRi] **nf** (*lit, fig*) intoxication.

grisette [gRizɛt] **nf** (*Hist*) grisette.

gris-gris [gRigRi] **nm** *[indigène]* grigri; (*gén*) charm.

grison†† [gRizɔ̃] **nm** ass.

grisonnant, e [gRizɔnɑ̃, ɑ̃t] **adj** greying (*attrib*). **il avait les tempes** ~**es** he was greying *ou* going grey round *ou* at the temples.

grisonnement [gRizɔnmɑ̃] **nm** greying.

grisonner [gRizɔne] 1 **vi** to be greying, be going grey.

grisou [gRizu] **nm** firedamp. **coup de** ~ firedamp explosion.

grisoumètre [gRizumɛtR] **nm** firedamp detector.

grive [gRiv] **nf** (*Orn*) thrush. ~ **musicienne** song thrush; *voir* **faute.**

grivèlerie [gRivɛlRi] **nf** (*Jur*) *offence of ordering food or drink in a restaurant and being unable to pay for it.*

griveton* [gRivtɔ̃] **nm** soldier.

grivois, e [gRivwa, waz] **adj** saucy.

grivoiserie [gRivwazRi] **nf** (*mot*) saucy expression; (*attitude*) sauciness; (*histoire*) saucy story.

grizzli, grizzly [gRizli] **nm** grizzly bear.

grœnendael [gRɔ(n)ɛndal] **nm** Groenendael (sheepdog).

Groenland [gRɔɛnlɑ̃d] **nm** Greenland.

groenlandais, e [gRɔɛnlɑ̃dɛ, ɛz] 1 **adj** of *ou* from Greenland, Greenland (*épith*). 2 **nm,f: G**~**(e)** Greenlander.

grog [gRɔg] **nm** grog, ≃ (hot) toddy.

groggy* [gRɔgi] **adj inv** dazed; (*Boxe*) groggy.

grognard [gRɔɲaR] **nm** (*Hist*) soldier of the old guard of Napoleon I.

grognasse‡ [gRɔɲas] **nf** (*péj*) old bag‡ (*péj*), old sow‡ (*péj*).

grognasser* [gRɔɲase] 1 **vi** to grumble *ou* moan on (and on).

grogne* [gRɔɲ] **nf: la** ~ **des étudiants/patrons** the rumbling *ou* simmering discontent of students/employers.

grognement [gRɔɲmɑ̃] **nm** *[personne]* grunt; *[cochon]* grunting (*NonC*), grunt; *[sanglier]* snorting (*NonC*), snort; *[ours, chien]* growling (*NonC*), growl.

grogner [gRɔɲe] 1 1 **vi** *[personne]* to grumble, moan*; *[cochon]* to grunt; *[sanglier]* to snort; *[ours, chien]* to growl. 2 **vt** *insultes* to growl (out), grunt (out).

grognon [gRɔɲɔ̃] **adj** *air, expression, vieillard* grumpy, gruff (*épith*); *attitude* surly; *enfant* grouchy. **elle est** ~, **quelle** ~! what a grumbler! *ou* moaner!*

groin [gRwɛ̃] **nm** *[animal]* snout; (*péj*) *[personne]* ugly *ou* hideous face.

grol(l)e‡ [gRɔl] **nf** shoe.

grommeler [gRɔm(ə)le] 4 1 **vi** *[personne]* to mutter (to o.s.), grumble to o.s.; *[sanglier]* to snort. 2 **vt** *insultes* to mutter.

grommellement [gRɔmɛlmɑ̃] **nm** muttering, indistinct grumbling.

grondement [gRɔ̃dmɑ̃] **nm** (*voir* **gronder**) rumbling; growling; (angry) muttering. **le** ~ **de la colère/de l'émeute** the rumbling of mounting anger/of the threatening riot; **le train passa devant nous dans un** ~ **de tonnerre** the train thundered past us.

gronder [gRɔ̃de] 1 1 **vt** *enfant* to scold. **il faut que je vous gronde d'avoir fait ce cadeau** you're very naughty to have bought this present, I should scold you for buying this present. 2 **vi** a *[canon, train, orage, torrent]* to rumble; *[chien]* to growl; *[foule]* to mutter (angrily). b (*fig*) *[colère, émeute]* to be brewing (up). c (*littér: grommeler*) to mutter.

gronderie [gRɔ̃dRi] **nf** scolding.

grondeur, -euse [gRɔ̃dœR, øz] **adj** *ton, humeur, personne* grumbling; *vent, torrent* rumbling. **d'une voix** ~**euse** in a grumbling voice.

grondin [gRɔ̃dɛ̃] **nm** gurnard.

groom [gRum] **nm** bellboy.

gros, grosse[1] [gRo, gRos] 1 **adj** a (*dimension*) (*gén*) big, large; *peau, lèvres, corde* thick; *chaussures* big, heavy; *personne, ventre, bébé* fat, big; *pull, manteau* thick, heavy. **le** ~ **bout** the thick end; **il pleut à grosses gouttes** heavy *ou* great drops of rain are falling; **de grosses pluies** heavy rainfalls; **c'est** ~ **comme une tête d'épingle/mon petit doigt** it's the size of *ou* it's no bigger than a pinhead/my little finger; **des tomates grosses comme le poing** tomatoes as big as your fist; **un mensonge** ~ **comme une maison*** a gigantic lie, a whopper*; **je l'ai vu venir** ~ **comme une maison*** I could see it coming a mile off*.

b (*important*) *travail* big; *problème, ennui, erreur* serious, great, big; *somme* large, substantial; *firme* big, large; *soulagement, progrès* great; *dégâts* extensive, serious; (*violent*) *averse* heavy; *fièvre* high; *rhume* heavy, bad. **une grosse affaire** a large business, a big concern; **les grosses chaleurs** the height of summer, the hot season; **un** ~ **mensonge** a terrible lie, a whopper*; (*fig*) **c'est un** ~ **morceau*** (*travail*) it's a big job; (*obstacle*) it's a big hurdle (to clear) *ou* a big obstacle (to get over); **il a un** ~ **appétit** he has a big appetite; **la grosse industrie** heavy industry; **acheter par** *ou* **en grosses quantités** to bulk-buy (*Brit*), buy in bulk.

c (*houleux*) *mer* heavy. (*gonflé*) **la rivière est grosse** the river is swollen.

d (*sonore*) *voix* booming (*épith*); *soupir* deep, big. ~ **rire** guffaw.

e (*riche et important*) big. **un** ~ **industriel/banquier** a big industrialist/banker.

f (*intensif*) **un** ~ **buveur** a heavy drinker; **un** ~ **mangeur** a big eater; **un** ~ **kilo/quart d'heure** a good kilo/quarter of an hour; **tu es un** ~ **fainéant/nigaud*** you're a big *ou* great lazybones/silly* (*Brit*) *ou* ninny*.

g (*rude*) *drap, laine, vêtement* coarse; *traits du visage* thick, heavy. **le** ~ **travail, les** ~ **travaux** the heavy work; **son** ~ **bon sens est réconfortant** his down-to-earth commonsense *ou* plain commonsense is a comfort; **il aime la grosse plaisanterie** he likes obvious *ou* unsubtle *ou* inane jokes; **oser nous dire cela, c'est vraiment un peu** ~ it's a bit thick* *ou* a bit much* *ou* he's really pushing his luck*, daring to say that to us; **une grosse vérité** an obvious truth.

h ~ **de: avoir les yeux** ~ **de larmes** to have eyes filled *ou* brimming with tears; **cœur** ~ **de chagrin** heart heavy with sorrow; **regard** ~ **de menaces** threatening look, look charged with threats; **l'incident est** ~ **de conséquences** the incident is fraught with *ou* loaded with consequences.

i (†: *enceinte*) pregnant. **grosse de 6 mois** 6 months pregnant.

j (*loc*) **jouer** ~ **jeu** to play for big *ou* high stakes; **avoir le cœur** ~ to have a heavy heart, be sad at heart; **le chat fait le** ~ **dos** the cat is arching its back; **faire les** ~ **yeux (à un enfant)** to glower (at a child); **faire la grosse voix*** to speak gruffly *ou* sternly; **c'est une grosse tête*** he's brainy*, he's a brainbox* (*péj*); (*fig*) **avoir la grosse tête*** to feel thick-headed; **faire une grosse tête à qn**‡ to bash sb up*, smash sb's face in‡; (*péj*) **c'est une histoire de** ~ **sous** there's big money involved; **je la voyais venir, avec ses** ~ **sabots*** you could tell what she was getting at a mile off*, it was pretty obvious what her little game was*; **il me disait des "Monsieur"** ~ **comme le bras** he was falling over himself to be polite to me and kept addressing me as "sir" *ou* kept calling me "sir" (at two second intervals).

2 **nm** a (*personne*) (*corpulent*) fat man; (*riche*) rich man. **un petit** ~* a fat little man *ou* bloke* (*Brit*) *ou* guy*; **mon** ~* old man*, old boy*; (*péj*) **un** ~ **plein de soupe**‡ a big fat lump‡ (*péj*); **les** ~ the big bugs*, the big shots*.

b (*principal*) **le** ~ **de: le** ~ **du travail est fait** the bulk of *ou* the main part of the work is done; **le** ~ **de l'armée/de l'assistance** the main body of the army/the audience; **le** ~ **de l'orage est passé** the worst of the storm is past; **faites le plus** ~ **d'abord** do the main things *ou* the essentials first; **une évaluation en** ~ a rough *ou* broad estimate; **dites-moi, en** ~, **ce qui s'est passé** tell me roughly *ou* broadly what happened.

c (*milieu*) **au** ~ **de l'hiver** in the depth of winter; **au** ~ **de l'été/de la saison** at the height of summer/of the season.

d (*Comm*) **le (commerce de)** ~ the wholesale business; **il fait le** ~ **et le détail** he deals in *ou* trades in both wholesale and retail; **maison/prix de** ~ wholesale firm/prices; **papetier en** ~ wholesale stationer; **commande en** ~ bulk order; **acheter/vendre en** ~ to buy/sell wholesale; *voir* **demi-, marchand.**

3 **grosse nf** (*personne*) fat woman. **ma grosse*** old girl*, old thing* (*Brit*); (*péj*) **c'est une bonne grosse**‡ she's a good-natured lump of a girl*; *voir aussi* **grosse**[2].

4 **adv: écrire** ~ to write big, write in large letters; **c'est écrit en** ~ it's written in big *ou* large letters; **il risque** ~ he's risking a lot *ou* a great deal; **ça peut nous coûter** ~ it could cost us a lot *ou* a great deal; **je donnerais** ~ **pour** ... I'd give a lot *ou* a great deal to ...; **il y a** ~ **à parier que** ... it's a safe bet that ...; **en avoir** ~ **sur le cœur** *ou* **sur la**

patate‡ to be upset *ou* peeved*.

5 **comp** ►**gros-bec nm** (**pl gros-becs**) (*Orn*) hawfinch ►**gros bétail** cattle ►**gros bonnet*** bigwig*, big shot* ►**gros bras*** muscleman; **jouer les gros bras*** to play *ou* act the he-man* ►**grosse caisse** (*Mus*) big *ou* bass drum ►**(fusil de) gros calibre** large-bore shotgun ►**grosse cavalerie*** heavy stuff* ►**gros gibier** game ►**grosse-gorge‡ nf** (*Can*) goitre ►**gros-grain nm** (**pl gros-grains**) (*Tex*) petersham ►**gros intestin** large intestine ►**Gros-jean* nm: il s'est retrouvé Gros-jean comme devant** he found himself back at square one (*Brit*) *ou* back where he started ►**grosse légume*** = **gros bonnet*** ►**gros lot** (*lit, fig*) jackpot ►**gros mot** vulgarity, coarse word ►**gros mots** bad language ►**gros œuvre** (*Archit*) shell (*of a building*) ►**gros orteil** big toe ►**gros pain** large (crusty) loaf ►**gros plan** (*Phot*) close-up; **une prise de vue en gros plan** a shot in close-up, a close-up shot; (*fig: émission*) **gros plan sur** programme devoted to *ou* all about ►**gros poisson*** = **gros bonnet*** ►**(avion) gros-porteur** wide-bodied aircraft *ou* jet, jumbo jet ►**gros rouge*** (red) plonk* (*Brit*), rough (red) wine, Mountain Red (wine) (*US*) ►**gros sel** cooking salt ►**gros temps** rough weather; **par gros temps** in rough weather *ou* conditions ►**gros titre** (*Presse*) headline.

groseille [gʀozɛj] 1 **nf:** ~ **(rouge)** red currant; ~ **(blanche)** white currant; ~ **à maquereau** gooseberry. 2 **adj inv** (cherry-)red.

groseillier [gʀozeje] **nm** currant bush. ~ **rouge/blanc** red/white currant bush; ~ **à maquereau** gooseberry bush.

grosse[2] [gʀos] **nf** (*Jur*) engrossment; (*Comm*) gross.

grossesse [gʀosɛs] **nf** pregnancy. ~ **nerveuse** false pregnancy, phantom pregnancy; *voir* **robe**.

grosseur [gʀosœʀ] **nf** a *[objet]* size; *[fil, bâton]* thickness; *[personne]* weight, fatness. **être d'une** ~ **maladive** to be unhealthily fat; **as-tu remarqué sa** ~**?** have you noticed how fat he is? b (*tumeur*) lump.

grossier, -ière [gʀosje, jɛʀ] **adj** a *matière, tissu* coarse; *vin* rough; *aliment* unrefined; *ornement, instrument* crude.

b (*sommaire*) *travail* superficially done, roughly done; *imitation* crude, poor; *dessin* rough; *solution, réparation* rough-and-ready; *estimation* rough. **avoir une idée ~ière des faits** to have a rough idea of the facts.

c (*lourd*) *manières* unrefined, crude; *esprit, être* unrefined; *traits du visage* coarse, thick; *ruse* crude; *plaisanterie* unsubtle, inane; *erreur* stupid, gross (*épith*); *ignorance* crass (*épith*).

d (*bas, matériel*) *plaisirs, jouissances* base.

e (*insolent*) *personne* rude; (*vulgaire*) *plaisanterie, geste* coarse; *personne* coarse, uncouth. **il s'est montré très** ~ **envers eux** he was very rude to them; ~ **personnage!** uncouth individual!; **il est** ~ **avec les femmes** he is coarse *ou* uncouth in his dealings with women.

grossièrement [gʀosjɛʀmɑ̃] **adv** a (*de manière sommaire*) *exécuter, réparer* roughly, superficially; *façonner* crudely; *dessiner, tisser* roughly; *imiter* crudely. **pouvez-vous me dire** ~ **combien ça va coûter?** can you tell me roughly how much that will cost? b (*de manière vulgaire*) coarsely; (*insolemment*) rudely. c (*lourdement*) **se tromper** ~ to make a gross error.

grossièreté [gʀosjɛʀte] **nf** a (*NonC*) (*insolence*) rudeness; (*vulgarité*) *[personne]* coarseness, uncouthness; *[plaisanterie, geste]* coarseness. **dire des ~s** to use coarse language *ou* expressions. b (*rusticité*) *[fabrication]* crudeness; *[travail, exécution]* superficiality; *[étoffe]* coarseness. c (*littér: manque de finesse*) *[personne]* lack of refinement; *[traits]* coarseness. **la** ~ **de ses manières** his unrefined *ou* crude manners.

grossir [gʀosiʀ] [2] 1 **vi** *[personne]* (*signe de déficience*) to get fat(ter), put on weight; (*signe de santé*) to put on weight; *[fruit]* to swell, grow; *[rivière]* to swell; *[tumeur]* to swell, get bigger; *[foule]* to grow (larger), swell; *[somme, économies]* to grow, get bigger; *[bruit]* to get louder, grow (louder), swell. **l'avion grossissait dans le ciel** the plane grew larger *ou* bigger in the sky; **j'ai grossi de 3 kilos** I've put on 3 kilos.

2 **vt** a (*faire paraître plus gros*) *personne* to make look fatter. **ce genre de vêtement (vous) grossit** clothing of this sort *ou* kind makes one look fatter.

b *[microscope]* to magnify; *[lentille, lunettes]* to enlarge, magnify; (*fig*) *[imagination] dangers, importance* to magnify, exaggerate.

c (*exagérer volontairement*) *fait, événement* to exaggerate, blow up. **ils ont grossi l'affaire à des fins politiques** they've blown up the issue for political reasons.

d *cours d'eau* to swell; *voix* to raise.

e *somme* to increase, add to; *foule* to swell. ~ **les rangs/le nombre de** to add to *ou* swell the ranks/the numbers of.

grossissant, e [gʀosisɑ̃, ɑ̃t] **adj** a *lentille, verre* magnifying, enlarging. b *foule, bruit* swelling, growing.

grossissement [gʀosismɑ̃] **nm** a *[tumeur]* swelling, enlarging. *[personne]* **pour empêcher un** ~ **excessif** to prevent excessive weight-gain. b *[objet]* magnification, magnifying; (*fig*) *[dangers etc]* magnification, exaggeration; (*fig*) *[faits]* exaggeration, blowing up*; (*pouvoir grossissant*) *[microscope]* magnification, (magnifying) power; *[imagination]* magnification; (*aspect grossi*) *[objet, dangers]* magnification.

grossiste [gʀosist] **nmf** wholesaler, wholesale dealer.

grosso modo [gʀosomɔdo] **adv** a (*sans entrer dans les détails*) more or less, roughly. **je vous explique ça** ~ I'll explain the broad *ou* rough outlines of it to you. b (*tant bien que mal*) after a fashion.

grotesque [gʀɔtɛsk] 1 **adj** (*risible*) ludicrous; (*difforme*) grotesque. **il est d'un** ~ **incroyable** he's absolutely ridiculous. 2 **nm** (*Littérat*) **le** ~ the grotesque. 3 **nf** (*Art*) grotesque.

grotesquement [gʀɔtɛskəmɑ̃] **adv** (*voir* **grotesque**) ludicrously; grotesquely.

grotte [gʀɔt] **nf** (*naturelle*) cave; (*artificielle*) grotto.

grouillant, e [gʀujɑ̃, ɑ̃t] **adj** *foule, masse* milling, swarming. ~ **de** *touristes, insectes* swarming *ou* teeming *ou* crawling with; *policiers* bristling *ou* swarming with; **boulevard/café** ~ **(de monde)** street/café swarming *ou* teeming *ou* crawling with people, bustling street/café.

grouillement [gʀujmɑ̃] **nm** *[foule, touristes]* milling, swarming; *[vers, insectes]* swarming.

grouiller [gʀuje] [1] 1 **vi** *[foule, touristes]* to mill about; *[café, rue]* to be swarming *ou* teeming *ou* bustling with people. ~ **de** *touristes, insectes* to be swarming *ou* teeming *ou* crawling with. 2 **se grouiller vpr** (*) to get a move on*, stir one's stumps* (*Brit*), shake a leg* (*US*). **grouille-toi!** get your skates on!*, stir your stumps!*

grouillot [gʀujo] **nm** messenger (boy).

groupage [gʀupaʒ] **nm** (*Comm*) *[colis]* bulking.

groupe [gʀup] 1 **nm** a (*Art, Écon, Math, Pol, Sociol*) group. **le** ~ **de la majorité** the M.P.s (*Brit*) *ou* Congressmen (*US*) of the majority party; **psychologie de** ~ group psychology.

b *[personnes]* group, knot; *[touristes]* party, group; *[musiciens]* band, group. **des ~s se formaient dans la rue** groups (of people) *ou* knots of people were forming in the street; ~ **de manifestants/de curieux** group of demonstrators/onlookers; **par ~s de 3 ou 4** in groups of 3 or 4, in threes or fours; **travailler/marcher en** ~ to work/walk in *ou* as a group; **travail/billet de** ~ group work/ticket.

c *[objets]* ~ **de maisons** cluster *ou* group of houses; ~ **d'arbres** clump *ou* cluster *ou* group of trees.

d (*Ling*) group, cluster. ~ **nominal/verbal** nominal/verbal group; ~ **consonantique** consonant cluster.

2 **comp** ►**groupe d'âge** age group ►**groupe de combat** fighter group ►**groupe électrogène** generating set, generator ►**groupe hospitalier** hospital complex ►**groupe d'intervention de la Gendarmerie nationale** anti-terrorist squad ►**groupe de mots** word group, phrase ►**groupe parlementaire** parliamentary group (*M.P.s of the same party*) ►**groupe de presse** publishing conglomerate ►**groupe de pression** pressure group, ginger group (*Brit*), special interest group (*US*) ►**groupe sanguin** blood group ►**groupe de saut** *[parachutistes]* stick ►**groupe scolaire** school complex ►**le groupe des Sept (pays les plus industrialisés)** (*Écon*) the Group of Seven (most industrialized countries) ►**groupe de tête** (*Sport*) (group of) leaders; (*Scol*) top pupils (in the class); (*Écon*) (group of) leading firms ►**groupe de travail** working party.

groupement [gʀupmɑ̃] **nm** a (*action*) *[personnes, objets, faits]* grouping. ~ **de mots par catégories** grouping words by categories. b (*groupe*) group. ~ **révolutionnaire** band of revolutionaries, revolutionary band; ~ **d'achats** (commercial) bulk-buying organization; ~ **de gendarmerie** squad of Gendarmes; ~ **professionnel** professional organization; ~ **d'intérêt économique** economic interest group; ~ **agricole d'exploitation en commun** farmers' economic interest group.

grouper [gʀupe] [1] 1 **vt** a *personnes, objets, faits* to group (together); (*Comm*) *colis* to bulk; *efforts, ressources, moyens* to pool. ~ **des colis par destination** to bulk parcels according to their destination. b (*Sport*) *genoux* to tuck; *voir* **saut.** 2 **se grouper vpr** *[foule]* to gather. **les consommateurs doivent se** ~ **pour se défendre** consumers must band together to defend their interests; **se** ~ **en associations** to form associations; (*fig*) **se** ~ **autour d'un chef** to rally round a leader; **le village groupé autour de l'église** the village clustered round the church; *voir* **habitat.**

groupie [gʀupi] **nmf** *[chanteur]* groupie‡; *[*: parti]* (party) faithful.

groupusculaire [gʀupyskylɛʀ] **adj** small, diminutive.

groupuscule [gʀupyskyl] **nm** (*Pol péj*) small group.

grouse [gʀuz] **nf** grouse.

gruau [gʀyo] **nm** (*graine*) hulled grain, groats. **farine de** ~ fine wheat flour; **pain de** ~ fine wheaten bread.

grue [gʀy] **nf** a (*Tech, TV*) crane. ~ **de levage** wrecking crane. b (*Orn*) crane; *voir* **pied.** c (‡ *péj: prostituée*) tart‡ (*Brit péj*), hooker‡ (*US péj*).

gruger [gʀyʒe] [3] 1 **vt** (*littér: duper*) to dupe. **se faire** ~ to be duped, be had*. 2 **vi** (*arg Scol*) to cheat.

grumeau, pl ~x [gʀymo] **nm** *[sel, sauce]* lump. **la sauce fait des ~x** the sauce is going lumpy.

grumeler (se) [gʀym(ə)le] [5] **vpr** *[sauce]* to go lumpy; *[lait]* to curdle.

grumeleux, -euse [gʀym(ə)lø, øz] **adj** *sauce* lumpy; *lait* curdled; *fruit* gritty; *peau* bumpy, lumpy.

gruppetto [gʀupeto], **pl gruppetti** [gʀupeti] **nm** (*Mus*) gruppetto, turn.

grutier, -ière [gʀytje, jɛʀ] **nm,f** crane driver *ou* operator.

gruyère [gʀyjɛʀ] **nm** gruyère (cheese) (*Brit*), Swiss (cheese) (*US*).

Guadeloupe [gwadlup] **nf** Guadeloupe.

guadeloupéen, -enne [gwadlupeɛ̃, ɛn] 1 adj Guadelupian. 2 nm,f: **G~(ne)** inhabitant *ou* native of Guadeloupe.
Guam [gwam] nm Guam.
guano [gwano] nm *[oiseau]* guano; *[poisson]* manure.
Guatemala [gwatemala] nm Guatemala.
guatémalien, -ienne [gwatemaljɛ̃, jɛn] 1 adj Guatemalan. 2 nm,f: **G~(ne)** Guatemalan.
guatémaltèque [gwatemaltɛk] 1 adj Guatemalan. 2 nmf: **G~** Guatemalan.
gué [ge] nm ford. **passer (une rivière) à ~** to ford a river.
guéable [geabl] adj fordable.
guéer [gee] [1] vt to ford.
guéguerre* [gegɛʀ] nf squabble. **c'est la ~ entre les représentants** the representatives are squabbling amongst themselves.
guelfe [gɛlf] 1 adj Guelphic. 2 nmf Guelph.
guelte [gɛlt] nf *(Comm)* commission.
guenille [gənij] nf (piece of) rag. **~s** (old) rags; **en ~s** in rags (and tatters).
guenon [gənɔ̃] nf *(Zool)* female monkey; *(péj: laideron)* fright, (ugly) hag.
guépard [gepaʀ] nm cheetah.
guêpe [gɛp] nf wasp; *voir* **fou, taille[1]**.
guêpier [gepje] nm *(piège)* trap; *(nid)* wasp's nest. **se fourrer dans un ~*** to land o.s. in the soup* *ou* in it* *(Brit)*.
guêpière [gɛpjɛʀ] nf basque.
guère [gɛʀ] adv a *(avec adj ou adv: pas très, pas beaucoup)* hardly, scarcely. **elle ne va ~ mieux** she's hardly *ou* scarcely any better; **il n'est ~ poli** he's not very polite, he's hardly *ou* scarcely polite; **le chef, ~ satisfait de cela, ...** the boss, little *ou* hardly satisfied with that, ...; **il n'y a ~ plus de 2 km** there is barely *ou* scarcely more than 2 km to go; **ça ne fera ~ moins de 100 F** that won't be (very) much less than 100 francs.
b *(avec vb)* **ne ... ~** *(pas beaucoup)* not much *ou* really; *(pas souvent)* hardly *ou* scarcely ever; *(pas longtemps)* not (very) long; **je n'aime ~ qu'on me questionne** I don't much like *ou* really care for being questioned; **cela ne te va ~** that doesn't really suit you; **ce n'est plus ~ à la mode** that's hardly *ou* scarcely fashionable at all nowadays; **il ne vient ~ nous voir** he hardly *ou* scarcely ever comes to see us; **cela ne durera ~** that won't last (for) very long; **il ne tardera ~** he won't be (very) long now; *(frm)* **l'aimez-vous? — ~** do you like it? — not (very) much *ou* not really *ou* not particularly.
c *(avec de, que)* **il n'y a ~ de monde** there's hardly *ou* scarcely anybody there; **il n'y a ~ que lui qui ...** he's about the only one who ..., there's hardly *ou* scarcely anyone but he who ...; **il n'y a ~ que ceci que ...** there's hardly *ou* scarcely anything but this that ... .
guéret [geʀɛ] nm fallow land *(NonC)*.
guéridon [geʀidɔ̃] nm pedestal table.
guérilla [geʀija] nf guerrilla war *ou* warfare *(NonC)*. **~ urbaine** urban guerrilla warfare.
guérillero [geʀijeʀo] nm guerrilla.
guérir [geʀiʀ] [2] 1 vt *(Méd: soigner)* *malade* to cure, make better; *maladie* to cure; *membre, blessure* to heal. *(fig)* **je ne peux pas le ~ de ses mauvaises habitudes** I can't cure *ou* break him of his bad habits.
2 vi a *(Méd: aller mieux)* *[malade, maladie]* to get better, be cured; *[blessure]* to heal, mend. **sa main guérie était encore faible** his hand although healed was still weak; **il est guéri (de son angine)** he is cured (of his throat infection); **dépenser de telles sommes, j'en suis guéri!** you won't catch me spending money like that again!, that's the last time I spend money like that!
b *(fig)* *[chagrin, passion]* to heal.
3 **se guérir** vpr *[malade, maladie]* to get better, be cured. **se ~ d'une habitude** to cure *ou* break o.s. of a habit; **se ~ par les plantes** to cure o.s. by taking herbs, cure o.s. with herbs; **se ~ d'un amour malheureux** to get over *ou* recover from an unhappy love affair.
guérison [geʀizɔ̃] nf *[malade]* recovery; *[maladie]* curing *(NonC)*; *[membre, plaie]* healing *(NonC)*. **sa ~ a été rapide** he made a rapid recovery; **~ par la foi** faith healing; *voir* **voie**.
guérissable [geʀisabl] adj *malade, maladie* curable. **sa jambe/blessure est ~** his leg/injury can be healed.
guérisseur, -euse [geʀisœʀ, øz] nm,f healer; *(péj)* quack (doctor) *(péj)*.
guérite [geʀit] nf a *(Mil)* sentry box. b *(sur chantier etc)* workman's hut; *(servant de bureau)* site office.
Guernesey [gɛʀn(ə)zɛ] nf Guernsey.
guernesiais, e [gɛʀnəzjɛ, ɛz] 1 adj of *ou* from Guernsey, Guernsey *(épith)*. 2 nm,f: **G~(e)** inhabitant *ou* native of Guernsey.
guerre [gɛʀ] 1 nf a *(conflit)* war. **de ~** *correspondant, criminel* war *(épith)*; **~ civile/sainte/atomique** civil/holy/atomic war; **~ de religion/de libération** war of religion/of liberation; **~ scolaire** "school war" *(about Church and State schools)*; **entre eux c'est la ~ (ouverte)** there's open war between them.
b *(technique)* warfare. **la ~ atomique/psychologique/chimique** atomic/psychological/chemical warfare.
c *(loc)* **en ~** *(lit, fig)* at war *(avec, contre* with, against); **dans les pays en ~** in the warring countries, in the countries at war; *(Mil)* **faire la ~ à** to wage war on *ou* against; **soldat qui a fait la ~** soldier who was in the war; **ton chapeau a fait la ~*** your hat has been in the wars* *(Brit)* *ou* through the war *(US)*; *(fig)* **elle lui fait la ~ pour qu'il s'habille mieux** she is constantly battling with him to get him to dress better; **faire la ~ aux abus/à l'injustice** to wage war against *ou* on abuses/injustice; **partir en ~ contre** *(lit)* to go to war against, wage war on; *(fig)* to wage war on; **de ~ lasse elle finit par accepter** she grew tired of resisting and finally accepted; *(Prov)* **à la ~ comme à la ~** we'll just have to make the best of things, you must take things as you find them *ou* as they come; *voir* **bon[1], entrer**.
2 comp ▶**guerre bactériologique** bacteriological warfare ▶**guerre biologique** biological warfare ▶**guerre de conquête** war of conquest ▶**la guerre des Deux-Roses** the Wars of the Roses ▶**guerre éclair** blitzkrieg *(Brit)*, lightning war *(US)* ▶**guerre d'embuscade** guerrilla warfare ▶**la guerre des étoiles** Star Wars ▶**guerre d'extermination** war of extermination ▶**guerre froide** cold war ▶**guerre mondiale** world war ▶**guerre de mouvement** war of movement ▶**guerre N.B.C.** nuclear, biological and chemical warfare ▶**guerre des nerfs** war of nerves ▶**guerre nucléaire** nuclear war ▶**guerre des ondes** battle for the airwaves ▶**guerre à outrance** all-out war ▶**guerre de position** war of position ▶**guerre psychologique** psychological warfare ▶**la guerre de quatorze** the 1914-18 war ▶**la guerre de Sécession** the American Civil War ▶**guerre de succession** war of succession ▶**guerre totale** total warfare, all-out war ▶**guerre de tranchées** trench warfare ▶**la guerre de Trente Ans** the Thirty Years War ▶**la guerre de Troie** the Trojan War ▶**guerre d'usure** war of attrition.
guerrier, -ière [gɛʀje, jɛʀ] 1 adj *nation, air* warlike; *danse, chants, exploits* war *(épith)*. 2 nm,f warrior.
guerroyer [gɛʀwaje] [8] vi *(littér)* to wage war *(contre* against, on).
guet [gɛ] 1 nm a **faire le ~** to be on the watch *ou* lookout; **avoir l'œil au ~** to keep one's eyes open *ou* skinned*; **avoir l'oreille au ~** to keep one's ears open; **~ aérien** aerial surveillance. b *(Hist: patrouille)* watch. 2 comp ▶**guet-apens** nm **(pl guets-apens)** *(lit)* ambush, ambuscade; *(fig)* trap, ambush.
guêtre [gɛtʀ] nf gaiter; *voir* **traîner**.
guêtré, e [getʀe] adj *(Hist, hum)* wearing gaiters *ou* spats.
guetter [gete] [1] vt a *(épier)* *victime, ennemi* to watch (intently). b *(attendre)* *signal, personne* to watch (out) for, be on the lookout for; *(hostilement)* to lie in wait for. **~ le passage/l'arrivée de qn** to watch (out) for sb (to pass)/(to come); *(fig)* **~ l'occasion** to watch out for the opportunity, be on the lookout for the opportunity; *(fig)* **la crise cardiaque le guette** there's a heart attack lying in wait for him; *(fig)* **la faillite le guette** he is threatened by bankruptcy.
guetteur [getœʀ] nm *(Mil)* lookout; *(Hist)* watch.
gueulante‡ [gœlɑ̃t] nf: **pousser une** *ou* **sa ~** *(protestation)* to shout one's head off‡; *(acclamation)* to give an almighty cheer *ou* yell*; *(douleur)* to give an almighty yell*.
gueulard, e [gœlaʀ, aʀd] 1 adj a (‡: *braillard*) *personne* loud-mouthed; *air, musique* noisy. **bébé ~** bawling brat; **ce qu'il est ~!** isn't he a loud-mouth!* b (‡: *criard*) *couleur, vêtement* gaudy, garish. c *(gourmand)* gourmet *(épith)*. 2 nm,f a (‡: *braillard*) loud-mouth. b *(gourmand)* gourmet, foodie*. 3 nm *(Tech)* throat.
gueule [gœl] 1 nf a (‡: *bouche*) mouth. **(ferme) ta ~!** shut your trap!‡ *ou* face!‡; **ça vous emporte** *ou* **brûle la ~** it takes the roof off your mouth; **il dépense beaucoup d'argent pour la ~** he spends a lot on feeding his face*; **s'en mettre** *ou* **foutre plein la ~** to stuff o.s. *ou* one's face*; **tu peux crever la ~ ouverte** you can go to hell for all I care‡; **il nous laisserait bien crever la ~ ouverte** he wouldn't give a damn what happened to us‡; **donner un coup de ~*** to shout one's head off*; **il est connu pour ses coups de ~*** he's well known to be a loud-mouth; *voir* **fin**.
b (*: *figure*) face. **il a une bonne/sale ~** I like/I don't like the look of him; **faire la ~** to sulk; **faire la ~ à qn** to be in a huff* with sb; **faire une ~ d'enterrement** to look a real misery *(Brit)* *ou* really miserable, look really down in the mouth*; **il a fait une sale ~ quand il a appris la nouvelle‡** he didn't half pull a face when he heard the news*; **bien fait pour sa ~!‡** bully for him!‡; **cette bagnole a de la ~** that's a great-looking car!*, that's some car!*; **cette maison a une drôle de ~** that's a weird-looking house; **les vêtements achetés en boutique ont plus de ~** boutique clothes look much nicer *ou* better; **~ de raie‡** fish-face‡; *voir* **casser, foutre, soûler**.
c *[animal]* mouth. *(fig)* **se jeter** *ou* **se mettre dans la ~ du loup** to throw o.s. into the lion's jaws.
d *(ouverture)* *[four]* mouth; *[canon]* muzzle.
2 comp ▶**gueule de bois*** hangover; **avoir la gueule de bois** to have a hangover, be feeling the effects of the night before* ▶**gueule cassée** *war veteran with severe facial injuries* ▶**gueule-de-loup** nf **(pl gueules-de-loup)** *(Bot)* snapdragon ▶**gueule noire** miner.
gueulement‡ [gœlmɑ̃] nm *(cri)* bawl. **pousser des ~s** *(douleur)* to yell one's head off*; *(colère)* to shout one's head off‡.
gueuler‡ [gœle] [1] 1 vi a *(parler fort)* to bawl, bellow; *(chanter fort)* to bawl; *(hurler de douleur)* to yell (one's head off) *(de* with);

(protester) to shout, bellyache‡ *(contre* about). **ça va le faire ~** *(de douleur)* that'll make him yell*; *(de mécontentement)* that'll have him shouting his head off‡; **ça va ~** there'll be all hell let loose‡, there'll be one hell of a row‡. b *[poste de radio]* to blast out, blare out. **faire ~ sa télé** to turn one's TV up full blast*. 2 **vt** *ordres* to bawl (out), bellow (out); *chanson* to bawl.

gueules [gœl] **nm** *(Hér)* gules.

gueuleton* [gœltɔ̃] **nm** blow-out* *(Brit)*, nosh-up* *(Brit)*, chow-down‡ *(US)*.

gueuletonner* [gœltɔne] 1 **vi** to have a blow-out* *(Brit)* ou a nosh-up* *(Brit)* ou a chow-down‡ *(US)*.

gueuse [gøz] **nf** a (†, *littér*) *(mendiante)* beggarwoman; *(coquine)* rascally wench; *voir* **courir**.
b *[fonte]* pig.
c *(bière)* **~(-lambic)** gueuse beer.

gueux [gø] **nm** (†, *littér*) *(mendiant)* beggar; *(coquin)* rogue, villain.

Gugusse [gygys] **nm** *(clown)* ≃ Coco the clown; (*: *type, personne*) bloke* *(Brit)*, guy*; (*: *personne ridicule*) twit* *(Brit)*, nincompoop.

gui [gi] **nm** a *(Bot)* mistletoe.
b *(Naut)* boom.

guibol(l)e* [gibɔl] **nf** *(jambe)* leg.

guiche [giʃ] **nf** kiss curl.

guichet [giʃɛ] **nm** a *(comptoir individuel)* window. *(bureau)* **~(s)** *[banque, poste]* counter; *[théâtre]* box office, ticket office; *[gare]* ticket office, booking office *(Brit)*; **adressez-vous au ~ d'à côté** inquire at the next window; **renseignez-vous au(x) ~(s)** *(banque, poste)* go and ask at the counter; *(théâtre, gare)* go and ask at the ticket office; *(à la poste, à la banque)* "**~ fermé**" "position closed"; **~ automatique (de banque)** cash dispenser *(Brit)*, automatic telling machine *(US)*; *voir* **jouer**. b *[porte, mur]* wicket, hatch; *(grillagé)* grille.

guichetier, -ière [giʃ(ə)tje, jɛʀ] **nm,f** *[banque]* counter clerk.

guidage [gidaʒ] **nm** *(Min, Tech)* guides; *(Aviat)* guidance; *voir* **radioguidage.**

guide [gid] 1 **nm** a *(personne)* guide; *(livre)* guide(book); *(fig: idée, sentiment)* guide. **l'ambition est son seul ~** ambition is his only guide; **~ (de montagne)** (mountain) guide.
b *(Tech: glissière)* guide. **~ de courroie** belt-guide.
2 **nfpl** *(rênes)* **~s** reins.
3 **nf** *(éclaireuse)* (Catholic) girl guide *(Brit)* ou girl scout *(US)*.

guide- [gid] **préf** *voir* **guider.**

guider [gide] 1 **vt** *(conduire) voyageur, embarcation, cheval* to guide; *(fig: moralement etc)* to guide. **l'ambition le guide** he is guided by (his) ambition, ambition is his guide; **organisme qui guide les étudiants durant leur première année** organization that provides guidance for first-year students; **il m'a guidé dans mes recherches** he guided me through ou in my research; **se laissant ~ par son instinct** letting himself be guided by (his) instinct, letting (his) instinct be his guide; **se guidant sur les étoiles/leur exemple** guided by the stars/their example, using the stars/their example as a guide; **missile guidé par infrarouge** heat-seeking missile; *voir* **visite.**

guidon [gidɔ̃] **nm** a *[vélo]* handlebars. b *(drapeau)* guidon. c *[mire]* foresight, bead.

guigne¹ [giɲ] **nf** *(cerise)* *type of cherry.* *(fig)* **il s'en soucie comme d'une ~** he doesn't care a fig about it.

guigne²* [giɲ] **nf** *(malchance)* rotten luck*. **avoir la ~** to be jinxed*; **porter la ~ à qn** to put a jinx ou hoodoo on sb*; **quelle ~!** what rotten luck!*

guigner [giɲe] 1 **vt** *femme* to eye surreptitiously; *héritage, place* to have one's eye on, eye. **il guignait du coin de l'œil** he was casting surreptitious ou sidelong glances.

guignol [giɲɔl] **nm** a *(Théât)* *(marionnette)* puppet *(name of popular French glove puppet)*; *(spectacle)* puppet show (≃ *Punch and Judy show*). **aller au ~** to go to the puppet show; **c'est du ~!** it's a real farce!, it's burlesque!
b *(péj: personne)* clown. **arrête de faire le ~!** stop clowning about!, stop acting the clown!

guignolesque [giɲɔlɛsk] **adj** *(péj: grotesque)* farcical.

guignolet [giɲɔlɛ] **nm** cherry liqueur.

guignon [giɲɔ̃] **nm** = **guigne².**

guilde [gild] **nf** *(Hist)* guild.

guili-guili* [giligili] **nm** tickle, tickle*. **faire ~ à qn** to tickle sb.

Guillaume [gijom] **nm** William. **~ le Roux** William Rufus; **~ Tell** William Tell; **~ d'Orange** William of Orange; **~ le Conquérant** William the Conqueror.

guillaume [gijom] **nm** rabbet plane.

guilledou [gij(ə)du] **nm** *voir* **courir.**

guillemet [gijmɛ] **nm** inverted comma *(Brit)*, quotation mark. **ouvrez les ~s** open (the) inverted commas; **fermez les ~s** close (the) inverted commas; *(iro)* **sa digne épouse, entre ~s** his noble spouse, quote unquote ou in inverted commas *(Brit)*; **mettre un mot entre ~s** to put a word in quotation marks ou inverted commas *(Brit)* ou quotes.

guillemeter [gijmete] 4 **vt** to put in inverted commas, put in quotes.

guillemot [gijmo] **nm** guillemot.

guilleret, -ette [gijʀɛ, ɛt] **adj** a *(enjoué) personne, air* perky, bright. **être tout ~** to be full of beans*.
b *(leste) propos* saucy.

guillochage [gijɔʃaʒ] **nm** ornamentation with guilloche.

guillocher [gijɔʃe] 1 **vt** to ornament with guilloche.

guillochis [gijɔʃi] **nm** guilloche.

guillochure [gijɔʃyʀ] **nf** guilloche pattern.

guillotine [gijɔtin] **nf** guillotine; *voir* **fenêtre.**

guillotiner [gijɔtine] 1 **vt** to guillotine.

guimauve [gimov] **nf** *(Bot)* marsh mallow; *(Culin)* marshmallow. *(fig péj)* **c'est de la ~** *(mou)* it's jelly; *(sentimental)* it's mush*, it's schmaltzy*; **chanson (à la) ~** sloppy* *(Brit)* ou mushy* ou schmaltzy* song.

guimbarde [gɛ̃baʀd] **nf** *(Mus)* Jew's harp. (*: *voiture*) **(vieille) ~** old banger* *(Brit)*, old crock* *(Brit)*, jalopy.

guimpe [gɛ̃p] **nf** *(Rel)* wimple; *(corsage)* chemisette *(Brit)*, dickey *(US)*.

guincher* [gɛ̃ʃe] 1 **vi** *(danser)* to dance.

guindé, e [gɛ̃de] (**ptp de guinder**) **adj** *personne, air* stiff, starchy, uptight*; *style* stilted.

guinder [gɛ̃de] 1 1 **vt** a *style* to make stilted. **des vêtements qui le guindent** ou **qui guindent son allure** clothes that make him look stiff (and starchy).
b *(hisser) mât, charge* to raise.
2 **se guinder vpr** *[personne]* to become starchy; *[style]* to become stilted.

Guinée [gine] **nf** Guinea. **~ équatoriale** Equatorial Guinea; **~-Bissau** Guinea-Bissau; *voir* **Papouasie.**

guinée [gine] **nf** guinea.

guinéen, -enne [gineɛ̃, ɛn] 1 **adj** Guinean. 2 **nm,f: G~(ne)** native of Guinea, Guinean.

guingois [gɛ̃gwa] **adv** *(de travers)* **de ~** askew, skew-whiff* *(Brit)*; **le tableau est (tout) de ~** the picture is askew ou skew-whiff* ou lop-sided; **il se tient tout de ~ sur sa chaise** he's sitting lop-sidedly ou skew-whiff* in his chair; **marcher de ~** to walk lop-sidedly; **tout va de ~** everything's going haywire*.

guinguette [gɛ̃gɛt] **nf** *open-air café or dance hall.*

guipure [gipyʀ] **nf** guipure.

guirlande [giʀlɑ̃d] **nf** *[fleurs]* garland. **~ de Noël** tinsel garland; **~ de papier** paper chain; **~ lumineuse** string of fairy lights *(Brit)* ou Christmas tree lights.

guise [giz] **nf** a **n'en faire qu'à sa ~** to do as one pleases ou likes; **à ta ~!** as you wish! ou please! ou like! b *(loc)* **en ~ de** by way of; **en ~ de remerciement il m'a offert un livre/il m'a flanqué une gifle** by way of thanks he gave me a book/he slapped me in the face; **en ~ de chapeau il portait un pot de fleurs** he was wearing a flowerpot by way of a hat ou for a hat.

guitare [gitaʀ] **nf** guitar. **~ hawaïenne/électrique** *etc* Hawaiian/electric *etc* guitar; **~ sèche** acoustic guitar.

guitariste [gitaʀist] **nmf** guitarist, guitar player.

guitoune* [gitun] **nf** tent.

Guj(a)rât [gudʒ(a)ʀat] **nm** Gujarat.

Gulf Stream [gœlfstʀim] **nm** Gulf Stream.

guru [guʀu] **nm** = **gourou.**

gus* [gys] **nm** *(personne, type)* guy*, bloke* *(Brit)*.

gustatif, -ive [gystatif, iv] **adj** *(Bio)* gustative, gustatory; *voir* **nerf, papille.**

gustation [gystasjɔ̃] **nf** *(Bio)* gustation.

guttural, e, mpl **-aux** [gytyʀal, o] 1 **adj** *langue, son, consonne* guttural; *voix* guttural, throaty.
2 **gutturale nf** *(Phonétique)* guttural.

guyanais, e [gɥijanɛ, ɛz] 1 **adj** Guyanese.
2 **nm,f: G~(e)** Guyanese.

Guyane [gɥijan] **nf** Guiana, Guyana. **~ française** French Guiana.

guyot [gɥijo] **nf** guyot pear.

gym [ʒim] **nf** (**abrév de gymnastique**) gym, P.E.

gymkhana [ʒimkana] **nm** rally. **~ motocycliste** motorcycle scramble; *(fig)* **quelle pagaille! il faut faire du ~ pour arriver à la fenêtre** what a mess! it's like an obstacle course to get to the window.

gymnase [ʒimnɑz] **nm** *(Sport)* gymnasium, gym; *(Suisse: lycée)* secondary school *(Brit)*, high school *(US)*.

gymnaste [ʒimnast] **nmf** gymnast.

gymnastique [ʒimnastik] **nf** a *(sport)* gymnastics *(sg)*; *(Scol)* physical education, gymnastics *(sg)*. **de ~** *professeur, instrument* physical education *(épith)*, P.E. *(épith)*; **~ corrective** ou **médicale** remedial gymnastics *(sg)*; **~ oculaire** eye exercises; **~ orthopédique** orthopaedic *(Brit)* ou orthopedic *(US)* exercises; **~ rythmique** eurhythmics *(sg)*; **~ acrobatique** acrobatics *(sg)*; **~ respiratoire** breathing exercises; **~ suédoise** Swedish movements; **faire de la ~** *(sport)* to do gymnastics; *(au réveil etc)* to do exercises; *(fig)* **c'est toute une ~ pour attraper ce que l'on veut dans ce placard** it's a real juggling act ou you have to stand on your head to find what you want in this cupboard; *voir* **pas¹.**
b *(fig)* gymnastics *(sg)*. **~ intellectuelle** ou **de l'esprit** mental gymnastics *(sg)*; **j'ai dû me livrer à toute une ~ pour faire coïncider nos**

dates de vacances I had to tie myself in knots *ou* stand on my head to get our holiday dates to coincide; **quelle ~ il faut faire pour aller d'une banlieue à une autre** what a palaver* (*Brit*) *ou* a performance to get from one suburb to another.

gymnique [ʒimnik] 1 **adj** gymnastic.
2 **nf** gymnastics *(sg)*.

gynécée [ʒinese] **nm** (*Hist*) gynaeceum; (*fig*) den of females.

gynécologie [ʒinekɔlɔʒi] **nf** gynaecology (*Brit*), gynecology (*US*).

gynécologique [ʒinekɔlɔʒik] **adj** gynaecological (*Brit*), gynecological (*US*).

gynécologiste [ʒinekɔlɔʒist] **nmf**, **gynécologue** [ʒinekɔlɔg] **nmf** gynaecologist (*Brit*), gynecologist (*US*).

gypaète [ʒipaɛt] **nm** bearded vulture, lammergeyer.

gypse [ʒips] **nm** gypsum.

gypseux, -euse [ʒipsø, øz] **adj** gypseous.

gypsophile [ʒipsɔfil] **nf** gypsophila.

gyrocompas [ʒiʀokɔ̃pɑ] **nm** gyrocompass.

gyrophare [ʒiʀofaʀ] **nm** revolving *ou* flashing light (*on vehicle*).

gyroscope [ʒiʀɔskɔp] **nm** gyroscope.

gyroscopique [ʒiʀɔskɔpik] **adj** gyroscopic.

gyrostat [ʒiʀosta] **nm** gyrostat.

H

H, h [aʃ] nm (*lettre*) H, h. **h aspiré** aspirate h; **h muet** silent *ou* mute h; *voir* **bombe, heure.**

ha[1] ['a] excl oh! *[rire]* ~, ~! ha-ha!

ha[2] (abrév de **hectare**) ha.

habile [abil] adj a (*adroit*) *mains* skilful, skilled, clever; *ouvrier, chirurgien* skilful, skilled; *diplomate, tactique, démarche* skilful, clever, smart; *film, pièce de théâtre* clever. **il est ~ de ses mains** he's good *ou* clever with his hands; **être ~ à (faire) qch** to be clever *ou* skilful *ou* good at (doing) sth; **façonné d'une main ~** fashioned by a skilful *ou* skilled *ou* cunning hand; **ce n'était pas bien ~ de sa part** that wasn't very clever of him. b (*Jur*) fit (*à* to).

habilement [abilmɑ̃] adv (*voir* **habile**) skilfully; cleverly. **~ façonné** skilfully *ou* cunningly made.

habileté [abilte] nf a (*adresse: voir* **habile**) skill, skilfulness; cleverness; smartness. **~ manuelle** manual skill; **son ~ à travailler le bois** his talent for working with wood, his woodworking skills. b (*artifice, truc*) clever move, skilful move. c (*Jur*) = **habilité.**

habilitation [abilitasjɔ̃] nf (*Jur*) capacitation. (*Univ*) **~ (à diriger des recherches)** authorization *ou* accreditation to supervise research.

habilité [abilite] nf (*Jur*) fitness.

habiliter [abilite] [1] vt (*Jur*) to capacitate; (*Univ*) to authorize, accredit. **être habilité à faire qch** (*Jur, Pol*) to be empowered to do sth; (*gén*) to be entitled to do sth; (*Jur, Fin*) **représentant dûment habilité** duly authorized officer.

habillage [abijaʒ] nm a *[acteur, poupée]* dressing. b (*Tech*) *[montre]* assembly; *[bouteille]* labelling and sealing; *[marchandise]* packaging and presentation; *[machine]* casing; *[chaudière]* lagging; *[viande, volaille]* dressing. (*Aut*) **~ intérieur** interior trim.

habillé, e [abije] (ptp de **habiller**) adj a *robe* smart, dressy; *chaussures* dress (*épith*), smart; *soirée* dressy. **trop ~** *costume* too dressy, overdressy, over-smart; *personne* overdressed, too dressed up; **ça fait très ~** it looks very smart *ou* dressy *ou* posh*. b *personne* dressed. **être bien/mal ~** to be well/badly dressed; **être ~ de noir/d'un complet** to be dressed in *ou* wearing black/a suit; **se coucher tout ~** to go to bed fully dressed *ou* with all one's clothes on.

habillement [abijmɑ̃] nm (*action*) clothing; (*toilette, costume*) clothes, dress (*NonC*), outfit; (*Mil: uniforme*) outfit; (*profession*) clothing trade, rag trade* (*Brit*), garment industry (*US*).

habiller [abije] [1] 1 vt a *poupée, enfant* (*vêtir*) to dress (*de* in); (*déguiser*) to dress up (*en* as). **cette robe vous habille bien** that dress really suits you *ou* looks good on you; **un rien l'habille** she looks good in the simplest thing, she can wear anything; **~ un enfant en Peau-Rouge** to dress a child up as a Red Indian.

b (*fournir en vêtements*) *enfant, miséreux* to clothe; (*Mil*) *recrues* to provide with uniforms. **elle habille entièrement ses enfants** she makes all her children's clothes; (*Couture*) **elle se fait ~ par X, c'est X qui l'habille** she buys *ou* gets all her clothes from X's, X makes all her clothes; **ce tissu habille bien** this is good dress material (*ou* suit *etc* material).

c (*recouvrir, envelopper*) *mur, fauteuil, livre* to cover (*de* with); *bouteille* to label and seal; *marchandise* to package; *machine, radiateur* to encase (*de* in); *chaudière* to lag (*de* with). **~ un fauteuil d'une housse** to put a loose cover on a chair; **tableau de bord habillé de bois** wooden dashboard; (*fig*) **il faut ~ ce coin de la pièce qui est un peu nu** we must put something in *ou* do something with this rather bare corner of the room.

d (*Culin*) *viande, volaille* to dress; (*Horticulture*) *arbre* to trim (for planting); (*Typ*) *gravure* to set the text around.

e (*Tech*) *montre* to assemble.

2 **s'habiller** vpr a (*mettre ses habits*) to dress (o.s.), get dressed; (*se déguiser*) to dress up (*en* as). **aider qn à s'~** to help sb on with his clothes, help sb get dressed; **elle s'habille trop jeune/vieux** she wears clothes that are too young/old for her; **s'~ en Arlequin/Peau-Rouge** to dress up as Harlequin/a Red Indian; **elle s'habille long/court** she wears long/short skirts, she wears her skirts long/short; **faut-il s'~ pour la réception?** must we dress (up) for the reception?; **comment t'habilles-tu ce soir?** what are you wearing tonight?; **ne vous habillez pas, c'est en famille** don't (bother to) dress up – it's a family party; **elle ne sait pas s'~** she has no clothes sense *ou* dress sense.

b (*Couture*) **s'~ chez un tailleur/en grand magasin** to buy *ou* get one's clothes from a tailor/a department store; **s'~ sur mesure** to have one's clothes made to measure.

habilleur, -euse [abijœʀ, øz] nm,f (*Théât*) dresser.

habit [abi] 1 nm a **~s** clothes; **mettre/ôter ses ~s** to put on/take off one's clothes *ou* things; **~s de travail/du dimanche/de deuil** working/Sunday/mourning clothes; **il portait ses ~s du dimanche** he was wearing his Sunday best *ou* Sunday clothes; **il était encore en ~s de voyage** he was still in his travelling clothes *ou* in the clothes he'd worn for the journey; *voir* **brosse.**

b (*costume*) dress (*NonC*), outfit. **~ d'arlequin** Harlequin suit *ou* costume; (*Prov*) **l'~ ne fait pas le moine** appearances are (sometimes) deceptive, do not judge by appearances.

c (*jaquette*) morning coat; (*queue-de-pie*) tail coat, tails. **en ~ (de soirée)** wearing tails, in evening dress; **l'~ est de rigueur** formal *ou* evening dress must be worn; (*sur carte d'invitation*) "white tie", "dress: formal".

d (*Rel*) **prendre l'~** *[homme]* to take (holy) orders; *[femme]* to take the veil; **quitter l'~** *[homme]* to leave the priesthood; *[femme]* to leave the Church.

2 comp ▸**habit de cheval** riding habit ▸**habit de cour** (*Hist*) court dress (*NonC*) ▸**habit ecclésiastique** clerical dress (*NonC*); (*fig*) **porter l'habit ecclésiastique** to be a cleric ▸**habit de gala** formal *ou* evening dress (*NonC*) ▸**habit de lumière** bullfighter's costume ▸**habit militaire** military dress (*NonC*) ▸**habit religieux** (monk's) habit ▸**habit de soirée** = **habit de gala** ▸**habit vert** *(green coat of) member of the Académie française.*

habitabilité [abitabilite] nf *[maison]* habitability; *[voiture, ascenseur]* capacity.

habitable [abitabl] adj (in)habitable. **35 m² ~s** *ou* **de surface ~** 35 m² living space.

habitacle [abitakl] nm a (*Naut*) binnacle; (*Aviat*) cockpit; (*Aut*) passenger cell. b (*Rel, littér*) dwelling place (*littér*), abode (*littér*).

habitant, e [abitɑ̃, ɑ̃t] nm,f a *[maison]* occupant, occupier; *[ville, pays]* inhabitant. **pays/ville de 3 millions d'~s** country/town of 3 million inhabitants; **les ~s de la maison** the people who live in the house, the occupants of the house; **les ~s du village/du pays** the people who live in the village/country, the inhabitants of the village/country; **être** *ou* **loger chez l'~** *[touristes]* to stay with local people in their own homes; *[soldats]* to be billeted on the locals *ou* local people; **~s des cavernes** cave dwellers. b (*Can *: fermier*) farmer; (*Canadien français*) habitant (*Can*).

habitat [abita] nm (*Bot, Zool*) habitat; (*conditions de logement*) housing *ou* living conditions; (*Géog: mode de peuplement*) settlement. (*Géog*) **~ rural/nomade/dispersé/groupé** rural/nomadic/scattered/grouped settlement.

habitation [abitasjɔ̃] nf a (*fait de résider*) living, dwelling (*littér*). **locaux à usage d'~** dwelling houses; **conditions d'~** housing *ou* living conditions; **impropre à l'~** unfit for human habitation, uninhabitable.

b (*domicile*) residence, home, dwelling place (*littér*). **la caravane qui lui sert d'~** the caravan that serves as his home; **changer d'~** to change one's (place of) residence.

c (*logement, bâtiment*) house. **des ~s modernes** modern housing *ou* houses; **groupe d'~s** (*immeuble*) block of flats (*Brit*), apartment building (*US*); (*lotissement*) housing estate (*Brit*) *ou* development; **~ à loyer modéré** (*Admin: appartement*) ≃ council flat (*Brit*), public housing unit (*US*); **~s à loyer modéré** (*Admin: immeuble*) ≃ (block of) council flats (*Brit*), public sector housing.

habité, e [abite] (ptp de **habiter**) adj *vol, engin, station orbitale* manned.

habiter [abite] 1 1 vt *maison, appartement* to live in, occupy; *zone, planète, région* to inhabit; (*fig*) *[idée, sentiment]* to dwell in. ~ **la banlieue** to live in the suburbs; **la maison n'a pas l'air habitée** the house doesn't look lived-in *ou* occupied; **est-ce que cette maison est habitée?** does anyone live in this house?, is this house occupied?; (*fig*) **habité d'idées sombres** preoccupied by gloomy thoughts. 2 vi to live (*en, dans* in). ~ **à la campagne/chez des amis/en ville** to live in the country/with friends/in (the) town; ~ **(au) 17 (de la) rue Leblanc** to live at number 17 rue Leblanc.

habitude [abityd] nf a (*accoutumance*) habit. **avoir/prendre l'~ de faire** to be/get used to doing; **avoir pour ~** *ou* **l'~ de faire** to be in the habit of doing; **prendre de mauvaises ~s** to pick up *ou* get into bad habits; **perdre une ~** to get out of a habit; **faire perdre une ~ à qn** to break sb of a habit; **avoir une longue ~ de** to have long experience of; **ce n'est pas dans ses ~s de faire cela** he doesn't usually do that, he doesn't make a habit of (doing) that; **j'ai l'~!** I'm used to it!; **je n'ai pas l'~ de me répéter** I'm not in the habit of repeating myself; (*Prov*) **l'~ est une seconde nature** habit is second nature; **avoir ses ~s dans un restaurant** *etc* to have a familiar routine in a restaurant *etc;* **il a ses petites ~s** he has his (pet) ways *ou* habits; *voir* **esclave, question.**
b (*coutume*) **~s** customs; **les ~s d'un pays** the customs of a country; **il a des ~s de bourgeois** he has a middle-class way of life.
c (*loc*) **d'~** usually, as a rule; **c'est meilleur que d'~** it's better than usual; **par ~** out of habit, from force of habit; **comme d'~** as usual; **selon** *ou* **suivant** *ou* **comme à son ~** as he usually does, as is his wont (*frm*).

habitué, e [abitɥe] (ptp de **habituer**) nm,f *[maison]* regular visitor, habitué(e); *[café]* regular (customer), habitué(e).

habituel, -elle [abitɥɛl] adj *comportement, geste* usual, customary, habitual; *réjouissances, formule de politesse* customary, usual. **d'un geste qui lui était ~** with his usual gesture, with that typical gesture of his; **c'est l'histoire ~le** it's the usual story.

habituellement [abitɥɛlmɑ̃] adv usually, generally, as a rule.

habituer [abitɥe] 1 1 vt: **~ qn à qch/à faire** (*accoutumer, endurcir*) to accustom sb to sth/to doing, get sb used to sth/to doing; (*apprendre, entraîner*) to teach sb sth/to do; **on m'a habitué à obéir** I've been taught to obey; **être habitué à qch/à faire** to be used *ou* accustomed to sth/to doing. 2 **s'habituer** vpr: **s'~ à qch/à faire** to get *ou* grow used *ou* accustomed to sth/to doing, accustom o.s. to sth/to doing.

hâblerie ['ɑbləʀi] nf (*manière d'être*) bragging, boasting; (*propos*) boast, big talk* (*NonC*).

hâbleur, -euse ['ɑblœʀ, øz] 1 adj bragging, boasting, boastful. 2 nm,f braggart, boaster.

Habsbourg ['apsbuʀ] nmf Hapsburg.

hachage ['aʃaʒ] nm (*voir* **hacher**) chopping; mincing (*Brit*), grinding (*US*).

hache ['aʃ] nf axe. ~ **d'armes** battle-axe; (*lit*) ~ **de guerre** hatchet, axe; (*fig*) **déterrer/enterrer la ~ de guerre** to take up/bury the hatchet; (*fig*) **visage taillé à la ~** *ou* **à coups de ~** angular *ou* roughly-hewn face.

hache- ['aʃ] préf *voir* **hacher.**

haché, e ['aʃe] (ptp de **hacher**) 1 adj a *viande* minced (*Brit*), ground (*US*). **bifteck ~** minced beef *ou* steak (*Brit*), (beef *ou* steak) mince (*Brit*), ground beef (*US*), hamburger (*US*). b *style* jerky; *phrases* jerky, broken. 2 nm mince (*Brit*), minced meat (*Brit*), ground beef (*US*).

hachement ['aʃmɑ̃] nm = **hachage.**

hacher ['aʃe] 1 1 vt a (*couper*) (*au couteau etc*) to chop; (*avec un appareil*) to mince (*Brit*), grind (*US*). ~ **menu** to mince, chop finely; ~ **menu comme chair à pâté** to make mincemeat of. b (*déchiqueter*) *récolte* to slash to pieces; *soldats* to cut to pieces. **je me ferais plutôt ~ que d'accepter** I'd go through fire rather than accept; **il se ferait ~ pour vous** he'd go through fire for you. c (*interrompre*) *discours, phrases* to break up; *voir* **haché.** 2 comp ▸**hache-légumes** nm inv vegetable-chopper ▸**hache-paille** nm inv chaff-cutter ▸**hache-viande** nm inv (meat-)mincer (*Brit*), grinder (*US*).

hachette ['aʃɛt] nf hatchet.

hachis ['aʃi] nm *[légumes]* chopped vegetables; *[viande]* mince (*Brit*) (*NonC*), minced meat (*Brit*), hamburger (*US*), ground meat (*US*); (*farce*) forcemeat (*NonC*). ~ **de porc** pork mince; ~ **Parmentier** ≃ shepherd's *ou* cottage pie (*Brit*).

hachisch ['aʃiʃ] nm hashish.

hachoir ['aʃwaʀ] nm (*couteau*) *[viande]* chopper, cleaver; *[légumes]* chopper; (*planche*) chopping board; (*appareil*) (meat-)mincer (*Brit*), grinder (*US*).

hachurer ['aʃyʀe] 1 vt (*Art*) to hatch; (*Cartographie*) to hachure.

hachures ['aʃyʀ] nfpl (*Art*) hatching (*NonC*), hachures; (*Cartographie*) hachures.

haddock ['adɔk] nm smoked haddock.

Hadrien [adʀijɛ̃] nm Hadrian.

Haendel ['ɛndɛl] nm Handel.

hafnium ['afnjɔm] nm hafnium.

hagard, e ['agaʀ, aʀd] adj *yeux* wild; *visage, air, gestes* distraught, frantic, wild.

hagiographe [aʒjɔgʀaf] nmf hagiographer.

hagiographie [aʒjɔgʀafi] nf hagiography.

haie ['ɛ] nf a (*clôture*) hedge. ~ **d'aubépines** hawthorn hedge; ~ **vive** quickset hedge. b (*Sport: obstacle*) *[coureur]* hurdle; *[chevaux]* fence. **course de ~s** *[coureur]* hurdles (race); *[chevaux]* steeplechase; **110 mètres ~s** 110 metres hurdles. c (*fig: rangée*) *[spectateurs, policiers]* line, row. **faire une ~ d'honneur** to form a guard of honour; **faire la ~** to form a line.

haillon ['ɑjɔ̃] nm rag. **en ~s** in rags, in tatters.

haillonneux, -euse ['ɑjɔnø, øz] adj (*littér*) in rags, in tatters, tattered and torn.

Hainaut ['ɛno] nm: **le ~** Hainaut *ou* Hainault.

haine ['ɛn] nf hatred (*de, pour* of, for). **des ~s mesquines** petty hatreds *ou* dislikes; **prendre qn en ~** to take a violent dislike *ou* a strong aversion to sb; **avoir de la ~ pour** to feel hatred for, be filled with hate *ou* hatred for; **par ~ de** out of *ou* through hatred of.

haineusement ['ɛnøzmɑ̃] adv *dire, regarder* with hatred; *saisir* malevolently.

haineux, -euse ['ɛnø, øz] adj *parole* full of hatred; *caractère, joie* malevolent. **regard ~** look of hate *ou* hatred, look full of hate *ou* hatred.

haïr ['aiʀ] 10 vt to detest, abhor, hate. **elle me hait de l'avoir trompée** she hates me for having deceived her; **je hais ses manières affectées** I can't stand *ou* I hate *ou* I loathe her affected ways; **je hais d'être dérangé** I hate being disturbed *ou* to be disturbed; **ils se haïssent cordialement** they cordially detest one another.

haire ['ɛʀ] nf hair shirt.

haïssable ['aisabl] adj detestable, hateful.

Haïti [aiti] nf Haiti.

haïtien, -ienne [aisjɛ̃, jɛn] 1 adj Haitian. 2 nm,f: **H~(ne)** Haitian.

halage ['alaʒ] nm (*Naut*) towing. **(chemin de) ~** towpath; **cheval de ~** towhorse.

hâle ['ɑl] nm (sun)tan, sunburn.

hâlé, e ['ɑle] (ptp de **hâler**) adj (sun)tanned, sunburnt (*Brit*).

haleine [alɛn] nf a (*souffle*) breath; (*respiration*) breathing (*NonC*). **avoir l'~ courte** to be short of breath *ou* short-winded; **retenir son ~** to hold one's breath; **être hors d'~** to be out of breath, be breathless; **perdre ~** to lose one's breath, get out of breath; **reprendre ~** (*lit*) to get one's breath *ou* wind back, regain one's breath; (*fig*) to get one's breath back, take a breather; **d'une seule ~** *dire* in one breath, in the same breath; *faire* (all) at one go; **il respirait d'une ~ régulière** his breathing was regular.
b (*air expiré*) breath. **avoir l'~ fraîche** to have fresh breath; **avoir mauvaise ~** *ou* **l'~ forte** to have bad breath; **j'ai senti à son ~ qu'il avait bu** I smelt *ou* could smell drink on his breath, I could tell from his breath that he'd been drinking; (*fig*) **l'~ glaciale de la crevasse/rivière** the icy breath of the crevasse/river.
c (*loc*) **tenir qn en ~** (*attention*) to hold sb spellbound *ou* breathless; (*incertitude*) to keep sb in suspense *ou* on tenterhooks; **travail de longue ~** long-term job, long and exacting job; **rire à perdre ~** to laugh until one's sides ache *ou* until one is out of breath; *voir* **courir.**

haler ['ale] 1 vt *corde, ancre* to haul in; *bateau* to tow.

hâler ['ɑle] 1 vt to (sun)tan, sunburn.

haletant, e ['al(ə)tɑ̃, ɑ̃t] adj *personne* (*essoufflé*) panting, gasping for breath (*attrib*), out of breath (*attrib*); (*assoiffé, effrayé*) panting (*de* with); (*curieux*) breathless (*de* with); *animal* panting; *poitrine* heaving; *voix* breathless, gasping. **sa respiration était ~e** he was panting, his breath came in gasps; **être ~ d'impatience** to be gasping *ou* burning with impatience.

halètement ['alɛtmɑ̃] nm (*voir* **haleter**) panting; gasping for breath; puffing; heaving.

haleter ['al(ə)te] 5 vi a *[personne]* (*manquer d'air*) to pant, gasp for breath, puff; (*de soif, d'émotion*) to pant (*de* with); *[chien]* to pant. **son auditoire haletait** his audience listened with bated breath. b *[poitrine]* to heave; *[moteur]* to puff.

haleur, -euse ['alœʀ, øz] nm,f (boat) hauler.

Haligonien, -ienne [aligɔnjɛ̃, jɛn] 1 adj Haligonian. 2 nm,f: **~(ne)** Haligonian.

hall ['ol] nm *[hôtel, immeuble]* hall, foyer, lobby; *[gare]* arrival (*ou* departure) hall. ~ **d'accueil** reception hall; ~ **d'exposition** exhibition hall.

hallali [alali] nm (*Chasse*) (*mise à mort*) kill; (*sonnerie*) mort. **sonner l'~** to blow the mort.

halle ['al] nf (*marché*) (covered) market; (*grande pièce*) hall. (*alimentation en gros*) **~s** central food market; (*Hist*) **les H~s (de Paris)** *formerly the central food market of Paris; voir* **fort.**

hallebarde ['albaʀd] nf halberd. **il pleut** *ou* **tombe des ~s*** it's bucketing (down)*, it's raining cats and dogs*.

hallebardier ['albaʀdje] nm halberdier.

hallier ['alje] nm thicket, brush (*NonC*), brushwood (*NonC*).

Halloween [alɔwin] nf (*Can*) Hallowe'en.

hallucinant, e [a(l)lysinɑ̃, ɑ̃t] adj *spectacle, ressemblance* staggering*, incredible.

hallucination [a(l)lysinasjɔ̃] nf hallucination. **avoir des ~s** to hallucinate; **tu as des ~!*** you must be seeing things!

hallucinatoire [a(l)lysinatwaʀ] adj hallucinatory.

halluciné, e [a(l)lysine] (ptp de **halluciner**) 1 adj *malade* suffering from hallucinations. **avoir un air** ~ to look wild-eyed *ou* distracted. 2 nm,f (*Méd: malade, fou*) hallucinated person; (*: *fou, exalté*) raving lunatic*, crackpot*.
halluciner [a(l)lysine] 1 vt: ~ **qn** to make sb hallucinate.
hallucinogène [a(l)lysinɔʒɛn] 1 adj *drogue* hallucinogenic, mind-expanding. 2 nm hallucinogen, hallucinant.
halo ['alo] nm (*Astron, Tech: auréole*) halo. (*fig*) ~ **de gloire** cloud of glory.
halogène [alɔʒɛn] (*Chim*) 1 adj (*gén*) halogenous; *lampe* halogen (*épith*). 2 nm halogen.
halte ['alt] 1 nf a (*pause, repos*) stop, break; (*fig: répit*) pause. **faire** ~ to (make a) stop. b (*endroit*) stopping place; (*Rail*) halt. c (*loc*) ~! (*gén: arrêtez-vous*) stop!; (*Mil*) halt!; ~ **aux essais nucléaires!** an end to *ou* no more atomic tests!; **dire** ~ **à un conflit** to call for a stop *ou* an end to a conflict; ~**-là!** (*Mil*) halt!, who goes there?; (*fig*) just a moment!, hold on!; ~**-là! vous exagérez** hold on!, you're going too far. 2 comp ▸ **halte-garderie** nf (pl **haltes-garderies**) crèche, ≃ day nursery.
haltère [altɛʀ] nm (*à boules*) dumbbell; (*à disques*) barbell. **faire des** ~**s** to do weight lifting; *voir* **poids**.
haltérophile [alteʀɔfil] nmf weight lifter.
haltérophilie [alteʀɔfili] nf weight lifting. **faire de l'**~ to lift weights, do weight lifting.
hamac ['amak] nm hammock.
hamamélis [amamelis] nm hamamelis.
Hambourg ['ɑ̃buʀ] n Hamburg.
hamburger ['ɑ̃buʀgœʀ] nm hamburger.
hameau, pl ~**x** ['amo] nm hamlet.
hameçon [amsɔ̃] nm (fish) hook; *voir* **mordre**.
Hamilton [amiltɔn] n Hamilton.
hammam ['amam] nm hammam.
hampe[1] ['ɑ̃p] nf *[drapeau]* pole; *[lance]* shaft; *[lettre]* downstroke, upstroke; (*Bot*) scape.
hampe[2] ['ɑ̃p] nf *[cerf]* breast; *[bœuf]* flank.
hamster ['amstɛʀ] nm hamster.
han ['ɑ̃] excl oof! **il poussa un** ~ **et souleva la malle** he gave a grunt as he lifted the trunk.
hanap ['anap] nm (*Hist*) (lidded) goblet.
hanche ['ɑ̃ʃ] nf *[personne]* hip; *[cheval]* haunch; *voir* **tour**[2].
hand-ball ['ɑ̃dbal] nm handball.
handballeur, -euse ['ɑ̃dbalœʀ, øz] nm,f handball player.
Händel ['ɛndɛl] nm Handel.
handicap ['ɑ̃dikap] nm (*lit, fig*) handicap.
handicapant, e ['ɑ̃dikapɑ̃, ɑ̃t] adj crippling.
handicapé, e ['ɑ̃dikape] (ptp de **handicaper**) 1 adj handicapped. **très** ~ severely handicapped. 2 nm,f handicapped person. ~ **mental/physique** mentally/physically handicapped person; ~ **moteur** spastic.
handicaper ['ɑ̃dikape] 1 vt (*lit, fig*) to handicap.
handicapeur ['ɑ̃dikapœʀ] nm (*Courses*) handicapper.
handisport ['ɑ̃dispɔʀ] adj *tennis, basketball* wheelchair (*épith*); *natation* for the disabled.
hangar ['ɑ̃gaʀ] nm *[matériel, machines]* shed; *[fourrage]* barn; *[marchandises]* warehouse, shed; *[avions]* hangar. ~ **de locomotives** engine shed.
hanneton ['an(ə)tɔ̃] nm cockchafer, maybug; *voir* **piqué**.
Hannibal [anibal] nm Hannibal.
Hanoi [anɔj] n Hanoi.
Hanovre ['anɔvʀ] n Hanover.
hanovrien, -ienne ['anɔvʀjɛ̃, jɛn] 1 adj Hanoverian. 2 nm,f: **H**~**(ne)** Hanoverian.
hanse ['ɑ̃s] nf (*Hist*) Hanse. **la H**~ the Hanseatic League.
hanséatique [ɑ̃seatik] adj Hanseatic. **la ligue** ~ the Hanseatic League.
hanter ['ɑ̃te] 1 vt *[fantôme, personne, souvenir]* to haunt. (*fig*) ~ **les mauvais lieux** to haunt places of ill repute; **maison hantée** haunted house.
hantise ['ɑ̃tiz] nf obsessive fear. **avoir la** ~ **de la maladie** to be haunted by the fear of illness, have an obsessive fear of illness.
happement ['apmɑ̃] nm (*voir* **happer**) snapping (up); snatching (up); grabbing.
happening ['ap(ə)niŋ] nm (*Art, Théât*) happening. ~ **politique** informal question-and-answer session.
happer ['ape] 1 vt (*avec la gueule, le bec*) to snap up, snatch; (*avec la main*) to snatch (up), grab. **se faire** ~ **par une voiture** to be hit by a car; **happé par l'abîme** dragged down into the abyss.
happy end ['apiɛnd] nm, pl **happy ends** happy ending.
happy few ['apifju] nmpl: **les** ~ the privileged few.
hara-kiri ['aʀakiʀi] nm hara-kiri, hari-kiri. **(se) faire** ~ to commit hara-kiri.
harangue ['aʀɑ̃g] nf harangue.
haranguer ['aʀɑ̃ge] 1 vt to harangue, hold forth to *ou* at.
Hararo [aʀaʀɔ] n Hararo.
haras ['aʀɑ] nm stud farm.
harassant, e ['aʀasɑ̃, ɑ̃t] adj exhausting, wearing.
harassé, e ['aʀase] (ptp de **harasser**) adj exhausted, tired out, worn out. ~ **de travail** overwhelmed with work.
harassement ['aʀasmɑ̃] nm exhaustion.
harasser ['aʀase] 1 vt to exhaust.
harcèlement ['aʀsɛlmɑ̃] nm (*voir* **harceler**) harassing; plaguing; pestering; badgering; harrying; worrying. ~ **sexuel** sexual harassment.
harceler ['aʀsəle] 5 vt *personne* (*de critiques, d'attaques*) to harass, plague (*de* with); (*de questions, de réclamations*) to plague, pester, badger (*de* with); (*Mil*) *ennemi* to harass, harry; *animal* to worry, harass; *gibier* to hunt down, harry. ~ **qn pour obtenir qch** to pester sth out of sb, get sth by pestering *ou* plaguing *ou* badgering sb.
hard* ['aʀd] 1 nm a (*Mus*) hard rock. **le** ~**(-rock)** hard rock, ≃ heavy metal. b (*pornographie*) hard porn*. c (*Ordin*) hardware. 2 adj a **film** ~ blue movie, pornographic film. b (*Mus*) heavy.
harde ['aʀd] nf *[cerfs]* herd.
hardes ['aʀd] nfpl (*péj: vieux habits*) old clothes, rags.
hardi, e ['aʀdi] adj a (*audacieux*) bold, daring. b (*effronté*) *décolleté* daring; *plaisanterie* daring, audacious; *fille* bold, brazen; (†) *mensonge* brazen, barefaced (*épith*). c (*original*) *talent, imagination* bold (*épith*). d (*loc excl*) ~ **les gars!** go to it, lads! (*Brit*), come on, lads! (*Brit*) *ou* you guys! (*US*); **et** ~ **petit! les voilà qui poussent la voiture*** and heave-ho! there they are pushing the car.
hardiesse ['aʀdjɛs] nf a (*littér: audace*) boldness, daring. **avoir la** ~ **de** to be bold *ou* daring enough to, have the effrontery to; **montrer une grande** ~ to show great boldness *ou* daring. b (*effronterie*) *[personne]* audacity, effrontery, impudence; *[livre, plaisanterie]* audacity. **la** ~ **de son décolleté choqua tout le monde** everyone was shocked by her daring neckline. c (*originalité*) *[style, tableau]* boldness. **des** ~**s de style** bold turns of phrase. d (*libertés*) ~**s** *[livre, pamphlet]* bold statements; *[domestique, soupirant]* liberties; ~**s de langage** bold language (*NonC*).
hardiment ['aʀdimɑ̃] adv (*voir* **hardi**) boldly; daringly; audaciously; brazenly. **ne vous engagez pas trop** ~ don't commit yourself rashly.
hard-top, pl **hard-tops** ['aʀdtɔp] nm hard-top.
hardware ['aʀdwɛʀ] nm hardware.
harem ['aʀɛm] nm harem.
hareng ['aʀɑ̃] nm herring. ~ **saur** smoked herring, kipper, bloater; *voir* **sec, serré**.
harengère† ['aʀɑ̃ʒɛʀ] nf (*péj*) fishwife (*péj*).
harfang ['aʀfɑ̃] nm snowy owl.
hargne ['aʀɲ] nf spite (*NonC*). **j'étais dans une telle** ~! I was so angry! *ou* mad!*; **avec** ~ spitefully.
hargneusement ['aʀɲøzmɑ̃] adv (*voir* **hargneux**) aggressively; belligerently; fiercely.
hargneux, -euse ['aʀɲø, øz] adj *personne, caractère, ton* aggressive, belligerent; *chien* aggressive, fierce.
haricot ['aʀiko] nm a bean. **des** ~**s!**‡ nuts to that (*ou* him *ou* you *etc*)!‡; ~ **beurre** *type of yellow French bean*; ~ **blanc** haricot bean; ~ **grimpant** *ou* **à rame** runner bean; ~ **rouge** kidney bean; ~ **vert** French bean; ~ **sec** dried bean; ~**s à écosser** fresh beans (for shelling); *voir* **courir, fin**[1]. b (*Culin*) ~ **de mouton** haricot of mutton, mutton stew.
haridelle ['aʀidɛl] nf (*péj: cheval*) nag, jade.
harissa ['aʀisa] nf harissa, hot chilli sauce.
harki ['aʀki] nm *Algerian soldier loyal to the French.*
harle ['aʀl] nm: ~ **bièvre** goosander; ~ **huppé** red-breasted merganser.
harmonica [aʀmɔnika] nm harmonica, mouth organ.
harmonie [aʀmɔni] nf (*Littérat, Mus, gén*) harmony; (*section de l'orchestre*) wind section; (*fanfare*) wind band. (*Mus*) ~**s** harmonies; (*Littérat*) ~ **imitative** onomatopoeia; **être en** ~ **avec** to be in harmony *ou* in keeping with; **vivre en bonne** ~ to live together harmoniously *ou* in harmony; *voir* **table**.
harmonieusement [aʀmɔnjøzmɑ̃] adv harmoniously.
harmonieux, -ieuse [aʀmɔnjø, jøz] adj (*gén*) harmonious. **couleurs** ~**euses** well-matched *ou* harmonizing colours; **un couple** ~ a well-matched couple.
harmonique [aʀmɔnik] 1 adj harmonic. 2 nm (*Mus*) harmonic.
harmoniquement [aʀmɔnikmɑ̃] adv harmonically.
harmonisation [aʀmɔnizasjɔ̃] nf harmonization. (*Ling*) ~ **vocalique** vowel harmony.
harmoniser [aʀmɔnize] 1 1 vt to harmonize (*avec* with). 2 **s'harmoniser** vpr to harmonize. **s'**~ **avec** to be in harmony with, harmonize with.
harmonium [aʀmɔnjɔm] nm harmonium.
harnachement ['aʀnaʃmɑ̃] nm *[cheval, bébé, cascadeur]* (*action*) harnessing; (*objet*) harness; *[*: campeur etc]* gear*, rig-out* (*Brit*), get-up*.
harnacher ['aʀnaʃe] 1 1 vt *cheval, bébé, cascadeur* to harness. (*fig péj*) **il était drôlement harnaché** he was wearing the strangest gear* *ou* rig-out* (*Brit*) *ou* get-up*. 2 **se harnacher** vpr *[cascadeur, parachutiste]* to put one's harness on; *[*: campeur etc]* to put one's gear on*, rig o.s. out*.
harnais ['aʀnɛ] nm, **harnois**†† ['aʀnwa] nm *[cheval, bébé, cascadeur]* harness; (*armure, équipement*) equipment. ~ **(de sécurité)** (safety) harness; (*Tech*) ~ **d'engrenage** train of gear wheels.
haro ['aʀo] excl (*Jur* ††) harrow!, haro! (*fig*) **crier** ~ **sur** to inveigh *ou*

rail against.

Harold ['aʀɔld] nm Harold.

harpagon [aʀpagɔ̃] nm Scrooge.

harpe ['aʀp] nf (*Mus*) harp. **~ éolienne** aeolian *ou* wind harp.

harpie ['aʀpi] nf (*Myth, péj*) harpy; (*Zool*) harpy eagle.

harpiste ['aʀpist] nmf harpist.

harpon ['aʀpɔ̃] nm (*Pêche*) harpoon; (*Constr*) toothing stone; *voir* **fusil, pêche.**

harponnage ['aʀpɔnaʒ] nm, **harponnement** ['aʀpɔnmɑ̃] nm harpooning.

harponner ['aʀpɔne] 1 vt *baleine* to harpoon; (*) *malfaiteur* to collar*, nab*; (*) *passant, voisin* to waylay, corner.

harponneur ['aʀpɔnœʀ] nm harpooner.

hasard ['azaʀ] nm a (*événement fortuit*) **un ~ heureux/malheureux** a stroke *ou* piece of luck/bad luck, a stroke of good fortune/misfortune; **quel ~ de vous rencontrer ici!** what a coincidence meeting you here!, fancy meeting you here!*; **c'est un vrai** *ou* **pur ~ que je sois libre** it's quite by chance that I'm free, it's a pure coincidence that I'm free; **par un curieux ~** by a curious coincidence; **on l'a retrouvé par le plus grand des ~s** it was quite by chance *ou* it was a piece of sheer luck that they found him; **les ~s de la vie/de la carrière** the fortunes of life/one's career.
b (*destin*) **le ~** chance, fate, luck; (*Statistique*) chance. **les caprices du ~** the whims of fate; **le ~ fait bien les choses: nous étions dans le même hôtel** as luck would have it *ou* by a stroke of good fortune we were *ou* we happened to be in the same hotel; **faire confiance** *ou* **s'en remettre au ~** to trust to luck; **il ne laisse jamais rien au ~** he never leaves anything to chance; **faire la part du ~** (*événements futurs*) to allow for chance (to play its part); (*événements passés*) to admit that chance had a hand in it; **le ~ a voulu qu'il soit** *ou* (*littér*) **fût absent** as luck would have it he was not there, fate willed that he should be absent (*littér*); **c'est ça le ~!*** that's the luck of the draw!*; **c'est un fait du ~** it's a matter of chance; **les lois du ~** the laws of fate; *voir* **jeu.**
c (*risques*) **~s** hazards; **les ~s de la guerre** the hazards of war.
d (*loc*) **au ~** *aller* aimlessly; *agir* haphazardly, in a haphazard way; *tirer, choisir* at random; **j'ai répondu au ~** I gave an answer off the top of my head*; **voici des exemples au ~** here are some random examples *ou* some examples taken at random; **il a acheté ces livres au ~ des ventes/de ses voyages** he bought these books as he came across them by chance in the sales/on his trips; **à tout ~** (*en cas de besoin*) just in case; (*espérant trouver ce qu'on cherche*) (just) on the off chance; **on avait emporté une tente à tout ~** we had taken a tent just in case; **je suis entré à tout ~** I looked in on the off chance; **par ~** by chance, by accident; **nous nous sommes rencontrés tout à fait par ~** we met quite by chance *ou* by accident; **je passais par ~** I happened to be passing by; **tu n'aurais pas par ~ 100 F à me prêter?** you wouldn't by any chance have *ou* you wouldn't happen to have 100 francs to lend me?; **voudrais-tu par ~ m'apprendre mon métier?** you wouldn't be trying to teach me my job by any chance?; **comme par ~!** what a coincidence!; **il est arrivé comme par ~ au moment où on débouchait les bouteilles** he turned up as if by chance as we were opening the bottles; **si par ~ tu le vois** if you happen to see him, if by chance you should see him.

hasardé, e ['azaʀde] (ptp de **hasarder**) adj = **hasardeux.**

hasarder ['azaʀde] 1 1 vt *vie, réputation* to risk; *remarque, hypothèse, démarche* to hazard, venture; *argent* to gamble, risk. 2 **se hasarder** vpr: **se ~ dans un endroit dangereux** to venture into a dangerous place; **se ~ à faire** to risk doing, venture to do; **à votre place je ne m'y hasarderais pas** if I were you I wouldn't risk it.

hasardeux, -euse ['azaʀdø, øz] adj *entreprise* hazardous, risky; *hypothèse* dangerous, rash. **il serait bien ~ de** it would be dangerous *ou* risky to.

hasch ['aʃ] nm (*arg Drogue*) hash (*arg*), pot (*arg*), grass (*arg*).

haschich ['aʃiʃ] nm = **hachisch.**

hase ['ɑz] nf doe (*female hare*).

hâte ['ɑt] nf (*empressement*) haste; (*impatience*) impatience. **à la ~** hurriedly, hastily; **en (grande** *ou* **toute) ~** as fast as you (*ou* we *etc*) can, posthaste, with all possible speed; **elle est montée/descendue en toute ~** she hurried up/down the stairs; **mettre de la ~ à faire qch** to do sth speedily *ou* in a hurry *ou* hurriedly; **avoir ~ de faire** to be eager *ou* anxious to do, be in a hurry to do; **je n'ai qu'une ~, c'est d'avoir terminé ce travail** all I'm anxious to do is get this work finished; **sans ~** unhurriedly.

hâté, e ['ɑte] (ptp de **hâter**) adj *travail* hastily *ou* hurriedly done.

hâter ['ɑte] 1 1 vt *fin, développement* to hasten; *départ* to bring forward, hasten; *fruit* to bring on, force. **~ le pas** to quicken *ou* hasten one's pace *ou* step. 2 **se hâter** vpr to hurry, hasten. **se ~ de faire** to hurry *ou* hasten *ou* make haste to do; **hâtez-vous** hurry up; **je me hâte de dire que** I hasten to say that; **hâte-toi lentement** more haste, less speed (*Prov*); **ne nous hâtons pas de juger** let's not be in a hurry to judge *ou* too hasty in our judgments.

hâtif, -ive ['ɑtif, iv] adj *développement* precocious; *fruit, saison* early; *travail* hurried; *décision, jugement* hasty. **ne tirons pas de conclusions ~ives** let's not rush to conclusions.

hâtivement ['ɑtivmɑ̃] adv hurriedly, hastily.

hauban ['obɑ̃] nm (*Naut*) shroud.

haubert ['obɛʀ] nm (*Hist*) coat of mail, hauberk.

hausse ['os] nf a *[prix, niveau, température]* rise, increase (*de* in); (*Bourse*) rise (*de* in). **une ~ inattendue de la température/des prix** an unexpected increase *ou* rise in temperature/prices; **~ de salaire** (pay) rise (*Brit*) *ou* raise (*US*); **la ~ du coût de la vie** the rise in the cost of living; **être en ~** *[monnaie, prix]* to be going up *ou* rising; *[actions, marchandises]* to be going up (in price); (*Bourse*) **marché à la ~** rising market; **tendance à la ~** rising *ou* upward trend; (*fig*) **sa cote est** *ou* **ses actions sont en ~** things are looking up for him, his popularity is increasing; *[essence]* **une ~ à la pompe** a rise in pump prices; **revoir** *ou* **réviser à la ~** to scale up; *voir* **jouer.**
b *[fusil]* backsight adjuster.

haussement ['osmɑ̃] nm: **~ d'épaules** shrug; **il eut un ~ d'épaules** he shrugged (his shoulders).

hausser ['ose] 1 1 vt a (*élever*) to raise. **~ les épaules** to shrug (one's shoulders); **~ la voix** *ou* **le ton** to raise one's voice. b *mur* to heighten, raise; *maison* to heighten, make higher. **~ une maison d'un étage** to add another floor to a house. 2 **se hausser** vpr: **se ~ sur la pointe des pieds** to stand up on tiptoe; **se ~ au niveau de qn** to raise o.s. up to sb's level.

haussier, -ière ['osje, jɛʀ] 1 adj (*Bourse*) *marché* bullish. **tendance ~ière** upward trend. 2 nm (*Bourse*) bull.

haut, e ['o, 'ot] 1 adj a *mur, montagne* high; *herbe, arbre, édifice* tall, high. **un mur ~ de 3 mètres** a wall 3 metres high; **~ de plafond** with a high ceiling, high-ceilinged; **une ~e silhouette** a tall figure; **de ~e taille** tall; **des chaussures à ~s talons** high-heeled shoes; **un chien ~ sur pattes** a long-legged dog; **il a le front ~** he has a high forehead; **~ comme trois pommes*** knee-high to a grasshopper*.
b *plafond, branche, nuage, plateau* high. **le plus ~ étage** the top floor; **dans les plus ~es branches de l'arbre** in the topmost branches of the tree; **pièce ~e de plafond** room with a high ceiling; (*lit, fig*) **marcher la tête ~e** *ou* **le front ~** to walk with one's head held high; (*Naut*) **les ~es voiles** the (flying) kites; *voir* **montagne, ville.**
c *rivière, température, prix* high; (*Élec*) *fréquence, voltage* high; *note, ton* high, high-pitched. **c'est (la) marée ~e, la mer est ~e** it is high tide, the tide is in; **à marée ~e** at high tide; **en ~e mer** on the open sea, on the high seas; **pendant les ~es eaux du fleuve** while the river is high, during high water; **n'avoir jamais une parole plus ~e que l'autre** to be even-spoken; **jeter** *ou* **pousser des** *ou* **les ~s cris** to exclaim in horror *ou* indignation, raise one's hands in horror; **à voix ~e, à ~e voix** aloud, out loud; **le prix de l'or est au plus ~** the price of gold has reached a peak *ou* maximum; *voir* **verbe.**
d (*gén avant n*) (*fig: élevé, supérieur*) *qualité, rang, précision* high; *âme, pensée* lofty, noble. **avoir une ~e idée** *ou* **opinion de soi-même** to have a high *ou* an exalted opinion of o.s.; **c'est du plus ~ comique** it's highly amusing *ou* comical, it's excruciatingly funny; **~ en couleur** (*rougeaud*) with a high colour *ou* a ruddy complexion; (*coloré, pittoresque*) colourful; **avoir la ~e main sur qch** to have supreme control of sth; **discussions au plus ~ niveau** top-level discussions; (*hum*) **~s faits** heroic deeds; **de ~ rang** high-ranking; **de ~e naissance** of noble *ou* high birth; **les ~es cartes** the high cards, the picture cards; **la ~e cuisine/couture/coiffure** haute cuisine/couture/coiffure; **les ~es mathématiques** higher mathematics; **la ~e finance/société** high finance/society; **les ~s sphères du pouvoir/de la société** the highest levels of power/society; (*Mil*) **~ commandement** high command; **~ fonctionnaire** high- *ou* top-ranking civil servant; **~ personnage** high-ranking person; **un expert de ~e volée** one of the foremost experts, a top-ranking expert; **gagner qch de ~e lutte** to win sth after a well-fought battle; (*lit, fig*) **de ~e voltige** acrobatic; **la ~e bourgeoisie** the upper middle classes.
e (*ancien*) **dans la plus ~e antiquité** in earliest antiquity; **le ~ moyen âge** the Early Middle Ages; **le ~ Empire** the Early (Roman) Empire; (*Ling*) **le ~ allemand** Old High German.
f (*Géog*) **le H~ Rhin** the Upper Rhine; **la H~e Normandie** Upper Normandy; **les H~es-Terres** the highlands; (*Hist Can*) **le H~ Canada** Upper Canada; **la H~e-Volta** Upper Volta.
2 nm a *[arbre, colline, robe, armoire]* top. **dans le ~** at the top, high up; **le mur a 3 mètres de ~** the wall is 3 metres high; **au** *ou* **en ~ de l'arbre** at the top of the tree, high up in the tree; **le ~ du visage** the top part of the face; **les pièces du ~** the rooms upstairs, the upstairs rooms; **les voisins du ~** the neighbours upstairs; **l'étagère du ~** the top shelf; **en ~ de l'échelle sociale** high up the social ladder; **combien fait-il de ~?** how high is it?; (*fig*) **des ~s et des bas** ups and downs; **tenir le ~ du pavé** to take pride of place.
b **du ~ de: du ~ d'un arbre** from the top of a tree; **tomber du ~ du 5e étage** to fall from the 5th floor; **parler du ~ d'une tribune/d'un balcon** to speak from a platform/a balcony; (*fig*) **regarder qn du ~ de sa grandeur** to look down at sb from one's lofty height (*fig*).
c (*Géog*) **les H~s de Meuse/de Seine** the upper reaches of the Meuse/Seine.
d (*loc*) **voir les choses de ~** to take a detached view of things; **tomber de ~** (*lit*) to fall from a height; (*fig*) to have one's hopes dashed, come down with a crash; **tomber de tout son ~** to fall head-

long, measure one's length (*Brit*); **prendre qch de (très)** ~ to take sth in a (very) high and mighty way, react (most) indignantly *ou* disdainfully to sth; **traiter qn de** ~ to look down on sb; **regarder qn de** ~ **en bas** to look sb up and down; **frapper de** ~ **en bas** to strike downwards; **en** ~ at the top; **il habite en** ~**/tout en** ~ he lives upstairs/right at the top; **manteau boutonné jusqu'en** ~ coat buttoned right up *ou* (right) up to the top; **regarder par en** ~ to look from upstairs *ou* above; **en** ~ **de** at the top of; **les voleurs sont passés par en** ~ the burglars came (in) from upstairs *ou* from above; (*lit, fig*) **d'en** ~ from above; **des ordres qui viennent de** *ou* **d'en** ~ orders from on high *ou* from above; *voir* **bas**[1], **là**.

3 **haute** nf: **(les gens de) la** ~**e**‡ the upper crust*, the toffs‡ (*Brit*), the swells†*.

4 **adv** a *monter, sauter, voler* high. **mettez vos livres plus** ~ put your books higher up; **il a sauté le plus** ~ he jumped the highest.

b *parler* loudly. **lire/penser tout** ~ to read/think aloud *ou* out loud; **mettez la radio plus** ~ turn up the radio; **j'ose le dire bien** ~ I'm not afraid of saying it out loud; **parle plus** ~! speak up!; (*Mus*) **monter** ~ to hit the top notes; **chanter trop** ~ to sing sharp.

c (*sur un colis*) "top", "this way up", "this side up".

d (*sur le plan social*) **des gens** ~ **placés** people in high places; **arriver** ~ to reach a high position; **viser** ~ to aim high.

e (*en arrière*) **aussi** ~ **qu'on peut remonter** as far back as we can go; **"voir plus** ~**"** "see above"; **comme je l'ai dit plus** ~ as I said above *ou* previously.

f ~ **les mains!** hands up!, stick 'em up!‡; **gagner** ~ **la main** to win hands down; ~ **les cœurs!** take heart!

5 **comp** ►**haut-de-chausse(s)** (*Hist*) **nm (pl hauts-de-chausse(s))** (knee) breeches, trunk-hose ►**haut-le-cœur nm inv** retch, heave; **avoir un haut-le-cœur** to retch, heave ►**haut commissaire** high commissioner (*à* of) ►**haut commissariat** (*ministère*) high commission (*à* of); (*grade*) high commissionership ►**haute-contre** (*Mus*) **(pl hautes-contre) adj, nm:** (*chanteur*) counter tenor ◊ **nf:** (*voix*) counter tenor, alto ►**haut-le-corps nm inv** (sudden) start, jump; **avoir un haut-le-corps** to start, jump ►**Haute Cour** (*Jur*) high court (*for impeachment of French President or Ministers*) ►**haute définition** (*TV*) **nf, adj** high definition ►**haute école** (*Équitation*) haute école; (*fig*) **c'est de la haute école** it's very advanced (stuff*) ►**haute fidélité** (*Rad*) hi-fi, high fidelity ►**haut-fond** (*Naut*) **nm (pl hauts-fonds)** shallow, shoal ►**haut-de-forme nm (pl hauts-de-forme)** top hat ►**haut-fourneau nm (pl hauts-fourneaux)** blast *ou* smelting furnace ►**haut lieu: le haut lieu de la culture/musique** the Mecca of culture/music; **en haut lieu** in high places ►**haut-parleur nm (pl haut-parleurs)** (loud)speaker ►**haut-parleur aigu** tweeter ►**haut-parleur grave** woofer ►**haut-relief** (*Art*) **nm (pl hauts-reliefs)** high relief ►**haute trahison** high treason ►**haut vol, haute volée: de haut vol, de haute volée** *personne* high-flying; *projet* far-reaching; *voir* **lutte, montagne**.

hautain, e ['otɛ̃, ɛn] **adj** *personne* haughty; *air, manière* haughty, lofty.

hautainement ['otɛnmɑ̃] **adv** haughtily, loftily.

hautbois ['obwɑ] **nm** oboe. ~ **d'amour** oboe d'amore.

hautboïste ['obɔist] **nmf** oboist, oboe player.

hautement ['otmɑ̃] **adv** (*extrêmement*) highly; (*ouvertement*) openly.

hauteur ['otœʀ] **nf** a (*élévation verticale*) *[tour, montagne, arche, personne]* height; *[son]* pitch; (*Aut*) *[châssis]* ground clearance. **il se redressa de toute sa** ~ he drew himself up to his full height; **d'une** ~ **de 4 mètres** (*dimension*) 4 metres high; (*d'un point élevé*) from a height of 4 metres; (*Aut*) ~ **maximum** *ou* **libre 3 mètres** headroom 3 metres; **pièce de 3 mètres de** ~ **sous plafond** room whose ceiling height is 3 metres; **tomber de toute sa** ~ *[personne]* to measure one's length (*Brit*), fall headlong *ou* flat; *[armoire]* to come crashing down; **perdre de la** ~ to lose height; **prendre de la** ~ to climb, gain height; **à** ~ **d'appui** at leaning height; **à** ~ **des yeux** at eye level; **à** ~ **d'homme** at the right height *ou* level for a man; (*fig*) **élever l'épargne à la** ~ **d'une institution** to make saving a way of life; *voir* **saut**.

b (*Géom*) perpendicular height; (*ligne*) perpendicular; (*Astron*) altitude.

c (*plan horizontal*) **arriver à la** ~ **de qn** to draw level with sb; **la procession arrivait à sa** ~ the procession was drawing level with him; **nous habitons à la** ~ **de la mairie** we live up by the town hall; (*Naut*) **arriver à la** ~ **d'un cap** to come abreast of a cape; **un accident à la** ~ **de Tours** an accident near Tours *ou* in the vicinity of *ou* neighbourhood of Tours.

d (*fig: digne de*) **être à la** ~ **de la situation** to be equal to the situation; **il s'est vraiment montré à la** ~* he proved he was up to it*; **ne pas se sentir à la** ~* not to feel up to it*, not to feel equal to the task.

e (*colline*) height, hill. **gagner les** ~**s** to make for the heights *ou* hills.

f (*fig: noblesse*) loftiness, nobility. **la** ~ **de ses sentiments** his noble *ou* lofty sentiments, the loftiness *ou* nobility of his sentiments.

g (*fig: arrogance*) haughtiness, loftiness. **parler avec** ~ to speak haughtily *ou* loftily.

h (*Écon*) **à (la)** ~ **de 10 000 F** up to 10,000 francs.

hauturier, -ière ['otyʀje, jɛʀ] **adj: navigation** ~**ière** ocean navigation; **pêche** ~**ière** deep-sea fishing; **pilote** ~ deep-sea pilot.

havage ['avaʒ] **nm** (mechanical) cutting.

havanais, e ['avanɛ, ɛz] 1 **adj** of *ou* from Havana. 2 **nm,f: H~(e)** inhabitant *ou* native of Havana.

Havane ['avan] 1 **nf: la** ~ Havana. 2 **nm: h~** (*cigare*) Havana. 3 **adj inv: h~** (*couleur*) tobacco (brown).

hâve ['ɑv] **adj** (*émacié*) gaunt, haggard; (*pâle*) wan.

haveneau, pl ~**x** ['av(ə)no] **nm** shrimping net.

haver ['ave] [1] **vt** (*Tech*) to cut (*mechanically*).

haveuse ['avøz] **nf** cutting machine.

havrais, e ['ɑvʀɛ, ɛz] 1 **adj** from *ou* of Le Havre. 2 **nm,f: H~(e)** inhabitant *ou* native of Le Havre.

havre ['avʀ] **nm** (*littér: lit, fig*) haven. ~ **de paix** haven of peace.

havresac ['ɑvʀəsak] **nm** haversack, knapsack.

Hawaï, Hawaii [awai] **n** Hawaii. **les îles** ~ the Hawaiian Islands.

hawaïen, -ïenne [awajɛ̃, jɛn] 1 **adj** Hawaiian. 2 **nm** (*Ling*) Hawaiian. 3 **nm,f: H~(ne)** Hawaiian.

Haye ['ɛ] **nf: La** ~ The Hague.

hayon ['ɛjɔ̃] **nm** (*Aut*) ~ **(arrière)** hatchback, tailgate; **modèle avec** ~ **arrière** hatchback (model).

hé ['e] **excl** (*pour appeler*) hey!; (*pour renforcer*) well. ~! ~! well, well!, ha-ha!; ~ **non!** I should think not!

heaume ['om] **nm** (*Hist*) helmet.

hebdo* [ɛbdo] **nm abrév de hebdomadaire.**

hebdomadaire [ɛbdɔmadɛʀ] **adj, nm** weekly. ~ **d'actualité** news weekly; *voir* **repos.**

hebdomadairement [ɛbdɔmadɛʀmɑ̃] **adv** weekly.

hébergement [ebɛʀʒəmɑ̃] **nm** (*voir* **héberger**) accommodation; lodging; putting up; taking in; harbouring.

héberger [ebɛʀʒe] [3] **vt** *touristes* to accommodate, lodge; *ami* to put up; *réfugiés* to take in; *évadé* to harbour, take in. **les sinistrés ont été hébergés chez des voisins** the victims were taken in *ou* given shelter by neighbours; **pouvez-vous nous** ~? can you put us up?, can you accommodate us?

hébété, e [ebete] **(ptp de hébéter) adj** a (*étourdi*) *regard, air, personne* dazed. **être** ~ **de fatigue/de douleur** to be numbed with fatigue/pain; ~ **par l'alcool** stupefied by *ou* besotted (*Brit*) with drink. b (*: *stupide*) *regard, air* dumb*, vacant.

hébétement [ebɛtmɑ̃] **nm** stupor.

hébéter [ebete] [6] **vt** *[alcool]* to besot (*Brit*), stupefy; *[lecture, télévision]* to daze, numb; *[fatigue, douleur]* to numb.

hébétude [ebetyd] **nf** (*littér*) stupor.

hébraïque [ebʀaik] **adj** Hebrew (*épith*), Hebraic.

hébraïsant, e [ebʀaizɑ̃, ɑ̃t] **nm,f** Hebraist, Hebrew scholar.

hébraïser [ebʀaize] [1] **vt** to assimilate into Jewish culture.

hébraïsme [ebʀaism] **nm** Hebraism.

hébraïste [ebʀaist] **nmf** = **hébraïsant.**

hébreu, pl ~**x** [ebʀø] 1 **adj m** Hebrew. 2 **nm** (*Ling*) Hebrew. **pour moi, c'est de l'**~* it's all Greek *ou* double Dutch (*Brit*) to me!* 3 **nm: H~** Hebrew.

Hébrides [ebʀid] **nfpl: les** ~ the Hebrides.

HEC ['aʃese] **nf (abrév de (école des) Hautes études commerciales)** *top French business college.*

Hécate ['ekat] **nf** Hecate.

hécatombe [ekatɔ̃b] **nf** (*tuerie*) slaughter, hecatomb; (*fig: à un examen etc*) (wholesale) slaughter *ou* massacre. **faire une** ~ **de** to slaughter.

hectare [ɛktaʀ] **nm** hectare.

hectique [ɛktik] **adj** (*Méd*) hectic.

hecto [ɛkto] **nm abrév de hectogramme** *et de* **hectolitre.**

hecto... [ɛkto] **préf** hecto... .

hectogramme [ɛktɔgʀam] **nm** hectogram(me).

hectolitre [ɛktɔlitʀ] **nm** hectolitre. **3 millions d'**~**s** 300 million litres.

hectomètre [ɛktɔmɛtʀ] **nm** hectometre.

hectométrique [ɛktɔmetʀik] **adj** hectometre (*épith*).

hectopascal [ɛktopaskal] **nm** milibar.

Hector ['ɛktɔʀ] **nm** Hector.

hectowatt [ɛktɔwat] **nm** hectowatt, 100 watts (*pl*).

Hécube ['ekyb] **nf** Hecuba.

hédonisme [edɔnism] **nm** hedonism.

hédoniste [edɔnist] 1 **adj** hedonist(ic). 2 **nmf** hedonist.

hégélianisme [egeljanism] **nm** Hegelianism.

hégélien, -ienne [egeljɛ̃, jɛn] **adj, nm,f** Hegelian.

hégémonie [eʒemɔni] **nf** hegemony.

hégémonique [eʒemɔnik] **adj** hegemonic.

hégire [eʒiʀ] **nf: l'**~ the Hegira.

hein* ['ɛ̃] **excl** (*de surprise, pour faire répéter*) eh?*, what? **qu'est-ce que tu feras,** ~? what are you going to do (then), eh?*; **ça suffit,** ~! that's enough, O.K.?* *ou* all right?*; ~ **que je te l'ai dit?** didn't I tell you so?, I told you so, didn't I?; **arrête** ~! stop it will you!

hélas [elɑs] **excl** alas! ~ **non!** I'm afraid not!, unfortunately not; ~ **oui!** I'm afraid so!, yes unfortunately; **mais** ~**, ils n'ont pas pu en profiter** but unfortunately *ou* sadly they were not able to reap the benefits of it.

Hélène [elɛn] **nf** Helen, Helena, Ellen. ~ **de Troie** Helen of Troy.

héler ['ele] [6] **vt** *navire, taxi* to hail; *personne* to call, hail.

hélianthe [eljɑ̃t] nm helianthus, sunflower.
hélianthine [eljɑ̃tin] nf (*Chim*) helianthine, methyl orange.
hélice [elis] nf (*Tech*) propeller, screw(-propeller); (*Archit, Géom*) helix. **escalier en ~** spiral staircase; **~ double** double helix.
hélico* [eliko] nm whirlybird*, chopper*, copter*.
hélicoïdal, e, mpl **-aux** [elikɔidal, o] adj (*gén*) helical; (*Bot, Math*) helicoid.
hélicoïde [elikɔid] adj, nmf helicoid.
hélicon [elikɔ̃] nm helicon.
hélicoptère [elikɔptɛʀ] nm helicopter. **transporter en ~** to transport by helicopter, helicopter; **amener/évacuer par ~** to take in/out by helicopter, helicopter in/out; **plateforme pour ~s** helipad.
héligare [eligaʀ] nf heliport.
héliographe [eljɔgʀaf] nm heliograph.
héliographie [eljɔgʀafi] nf (*Typ*) heliography.
héliogravure [eljogʀavyʀ] nf heliogravure.
héliomarin, e [eljomaʀɛ̃, in] adj *cure* of sun and sea-air. **établissement ~** seaside sanatorium specializing in heliotherapy.
héliotrope [eljɔtʀɔp] nm heliotrope.
héliport [elipɔʀ] nm heliport.
héliporté, e [elipɔʀte] adj transported by helicopter.
hélitreuiller [elitʀœje] [1] vt to winch up into a helicopter.
hélium [eljɔm] nm helium.
hélix [eliks] nm helix.
hellène [elɛn] 1 adj Hellenic. 2 nmf: **H~** Hellene.
hellénique [elenik] adj Hellenic. **la République ~** the Hellenic Republic.
hellénisant, e [elenizɑ̃, ɑ̃t] adj, nm,f: **(juif) ~** hellenistic Jew; **(savant) ~** hellenist, Hellenic scholar.
hellénisation [elenizasjɔ̃] nf hellenization.
helléniser [elenize] [1] vt to hellenize.
hellénisme [elenism] nm hellenism.
helléniste [elenist] nmf = **hellénisant**.
hello* ['ɛllo] excl hello, hullo.
Helsinki [ɛlzinki] n Helsinki.
helvète [ɛlvɛt] 1 adj Helvetian. 2 nmf: **H~** Helvetian.
Helvétie [ɛlvesi] nf Helvetia.
helvétique [ɛlvetik] adj Swiss, Helvetian (*rare*).
helvétisme [ɛlvetism] nm (*Ling*) Swiss idiom.
hem ['ɛm] excl (*gén*) hem!, h'm!; (*pour appeler*) hey!
hématie [emasi] nf red (blood) corpuscle.
hématologie [ematɔlɔʒi] nf haematology.
hématologique [ematɔlɔʒik] adj haematological.
hématologiste [ematɔlɔʒist] nmf, **hématologue** [ematɔlɔg] nmf haematologist.
hématome [ematom] nm nasty bruise, haematoma (*SPÉC*).
hématopoïèse [ematopɔjɛz] nf hæmatopoiesis, hæmatosis, hæmatogenesis.
héméralope [emeʀalɔp] 1 adj night-blind, nyctalopic (*SPÉC*). 2 nmf person suffering from night-blindness *ou* nyctalopia (*SPÉC*).
héméralopie [emeʀalɔpi] nf night-blindness, nyctalopia (*SPÉC*).
hémicycle [emisikl] nm semicircle, hemicycle; (*salle*) amphitheatre; (*assemblée*) (parliamentary) assembly. **l'~ (de l'Assemblée nationale)** the benches of the French National Assembly, ≃ the benches of the Commons (*Brit*) *ou* House of Representatives (*US*).
hémiplégie [emipleʒi] nf paralysis of one side, hemiplegia (*SPÉC*).
hémiplégique [emipleʒik] 1 adj paralyzed on one side, hemiplegic (*SPÉC*). 2 nmf person paralyzed on one side, hemiplegic (*SPÉC*).
hémisphère [emisfɛʀ] nm (*gén*) hemisphere. **~ sud/nord** southern/northern hemisphere.
hémisphérique [emisfeʀik] adj hemispheric(al).
hémistiche [emistiʃ] nm hemistich.
hémoglobine [emɔglɔbin] nf haemoglobin.
hémophile [emɔfil] 1 adj haemophilic. 2 nmf haemophiliac.
hémophilie [emɔfili] nf haemophilia.
hémorragie [emɔʀaʒi] nf bleeding (*NonC*), haemorrhage. **~ cérébrale** cerebral haemorrhage; **~ interne** internal bleeding (*NonC*) *ou* haemorrhage; (*fig*) **l'~ due à la guerre** the dramatic loss of manpower through war, the sapping of a country's resources through war; (*fig*) **~ de capitaux** massive outflow *ou* drain of capital; (*fig*) **l'~ de cadres/main-d'œuvre** mass exodus of executives/labour *ou* manpower.
hémorragique [emɔʀaʒik] adj haemorrhagic.
hémorroïdaire [emɔʀɔidɛʀ] adj *malade* with haemorrhoids. **remède ~** ointment *etc* for haemorrhoids.
hémorroïdal, e, mpl **-aux** [emɔʀɔidal, o] adj haemorrhoidal.
hémorroïde [emɔʀɔid] nf (*gén pl*) haemorrhoid, pile.
hémostatique [emɔstatik] adj, nm haemostatic; *voir* **crayon**.
hendécagone [ɛ̃dekagɔn] nm (*Géom*) hendecagon.
henné ['ene] nm henna. **se faire un ~** to henna one's hair.
hennin ['enɛ̃] nm (*Hist: bonnet*) hennin.
hennir ['eniʀ] [2] vi to neigh, whinny; (*fig péj*) to bray.
hennissement ['enismɑ̃] nm neigh, whinny; (*fig péj*) braying (*NonC*).
Henri [ɑ̃ʀi] nm Henry.
hep ['ɛp] excl hey!
héparine [epaʀin] nf heparin.
hépatique [epatik] 1 adj (*Méd*) hepatic. 2 nmf person who suffers from a liver complaint. 3 nf (*Bot*) liverwort, hepatic (*SPÉC*).
hépatisme [epatism] nm hepatic symptoms (*pl*).
hépatite [epatit] nf hepatitis. **~ virale** viral hepatitis.
hépatologie [epatɔlɔʒi] nf hepatology.
heptaèdre [ɛptaɛdʀ(ə)] nm heptahedron.
heptagonal, e, mpl **-aux** [ɛptagɔnal, o] adj heptagonal.
heptagone [ɛptagɔn] nm heptagon.
heptasyllabe [ɛptasi(l)lab] 1 adj heptasyllabic. 2 nm heptasyllable.
heptathlon [ɛptatlɔ̃] nm heptathlon.
Héra [eʀa] nf Hera.
Héraclite [eʀaklit] nm Heraclitus.
héraldique [eʀaldik] 1 adj heraldic. 2 nf heraldry.
héraldiste [eʀaldist] nmf heraldist, expert on heraldry.
héraut ['eʀo] nm a (*Hist*) **~ (d'armes)** herald. b (*fig littér*) herald, harbinger (*littér*).
herbacé, e [ɛʀbase] adj herbaceous.
herbage [ɛʀbaʒ] nm (*herbe*) pasture, pasturage; (*pré*) pasture.
herbager, -ère [ɛʀbaʒe, ɛʀ] nm,f grazier.
herbe [ɛʀb] nf a (*plante*) grass (*NonC*); (*Bot: espèce*) grass; (*arg Drogue*) grass (*arg*), pot (*arg*). **dans les hautes ~s** in the long *ou* tall grass; **la moitié de leurs terres est en ~** half their estate is under grass; **arracher une ~** to pull up a blade of grass; **~s folles** wild grasses; **jardin envahi par les ~s** weed-infested garden, garden overrun with weeds; **~-aux-chats** catmint, catnip; *voir* **déjeuner, mauvais** *etc*.
b (*Culin, Méd*) herb. **~s médicinales/aromatiques/potagères** medicinal/aromatic/pot herbs; *voir* **fin**[1], **omelette**.
c (*loc*) **en ~** *blé* green, unripe; (*fig*) *avocat, mécanicien* budding (*épith*); **ce gamin est un avocat/un mécanicien en ~** this boy is a budding lawyer/mechanic *ou* has the makings of a lawyer/mechanic; **couper** *ou* **faucher l'~ sous les pieds de qn** to cut the ground from under sb's feet; *voir* **manger**.
herbeux, -euse [ɛʀbø, øz] adj grassy.
herbicide [ɛʀbisid] 1 adj herbicidal. 2 nm weed-killer, herbicide.
herbier [ɛʀbje] nm (*collection, planches*) herbarium.
herbivore [ɛʀbivɔʀ] 1 adj herbivorous. 2 nm herbivore.
herborisation [ɛʀbɔʀizasjɔ̃] nf (*action*) collection of plants.
herboriser [ɛʀbɔʀize] [1] vi to collect plants, botanize.
herboriste [ɛʀbɔʀist] nmf herbalist.
herboristerie [ɛʀbɔʀistəʀi] nf (*commerce*) herb trade; (*magasin*) herbalist('s shop).
herbu, e [ɛʀby] adj grassy.
Hercule [ɛʀkyl] nm (*Myth*) Hercules. (*fig*) **c'est un h~** he's a real Hercules; **h~ de foire** strong man.
herculéen, -enne [ɛʀkyleɛ̃, ɛn] adj Herculean.
hercynien, -ienne [ɛʀsinjɛ̃, jɛn] adj Armorican, Hercynian.
hère ['ɛʀ] nm: **pauvre ~** poor *ou* miserable wretch.
héréditaire [eʀeditɛʀ] adj hereditary.
héréditairement [eʀeditɛʀmɑ̃] adv hereditarily.
hérédité [eʀedite] nf a (*Bio*) heredity (*NonC*). **il a une lourde ~, il a une ~ chargée** his family has a history of mental (*ou* physical) illness; (*fig: culturelle etc*) **une ~ catholique/royaliste** a Catholic/Royalist heritage. b (*Jur*) (*droit*) right of inheritance; (*caractère héréditaire*) hereditary nature.
hérésie [eʀezi] nf (*Rel*) heresy; (*fig*) sacrilege, heresy. (*hum*) **servir du vin rouge avec le poisson est une véritable ~!** it's absolute sacrilege to serve red wine with fish!
hérétique [eʀetik] 1 adj heretical. 2 nmf heretic.
hérissé, e ['eʀise] (ptp de **hérisser**) adj a (*dressé*) *poils, cheveux* standing on end, bristling; *barbe* bristly. b (*garni*) **~ de poils** bristling with hairs; **~ d'épines/de clous** spiked with thorns/nails; **~ d'obstacles/de fusils** bristling with obstacles/rifles. c (*garni de pointes*) *cactus, tige* prickly.
hérisser ['eʀise] [1] 1 vt a *[animal]* **le chat hérisse ses poils** the cat bristles its coat *ou* makes its coat bristle; **le porc-épic hérisse ses piquants** the porcupine bristles its spines *ou* makes its spines bristle; **l'oiseau hérisse ses plumes** the bird ruffles its feathers.
b *[vent, froid]* **le vent hérisse ses cheveux** the wind makes his hair stand on end.
c (*armer*) **~ une planche de clous** to spike a plank with nails; **~ une muraille de créneaux** to top *ou* crown a wall with battlements; **il avait hérissé la dictée de pièges** he had put a good sprinkling of tricky points into the dictation.
d (*garnir*) **des clous hérissent la planche** the plank is spiked with nails; **les créneaux qui hérissent la muraille** the battlements crowning the wall; **de nombreuses difficultés hérissent le texte** numerous difficulties are scattered through the text.
e (*mettre en colère*) **~ qn** to put *ou* get sb's back up*, ruffle sb's feathers; **faites attention de ne pas le ~** be careful not to put his back up* *ou* to ruffle his feathers; **il y a une chose qui me hérisse, c'est le mensonge** there's one thing that gets my back up* *ou* that makes me bristle and that's lying.
2 **se hérisser** vpr a *[poils, cheveux]* to stand on end, bristle.
b *[animal]* to bristle. **le chat se hérissa** the cat's fur stood on end *ou*

bristled, the cat bristled.
c (*se fâcher*) to bristle, get one's back up*.
hérisson ['eʀisɔ̃] nm (*Zool*) hedgehog; (*Tech*) (*brosse*) (chimney sweep's) brush. (*fig*) (*mal coiffé*) **c'est un vrai ~** his hair sticks out all over the place.
héritage [eʀitaʒ] nm a (*action*) inheritance. b (*argent, biens*) inheritance, legacy; (*coutumes, système*) heritage, legacy. **faire un ~** to come into an inheritance; **laisser qch en ~ à qn** to leave sth to sb, bequeath sth to sb; **obtenir une maison par ~** to inherit a house; (*péj*) **tante/oncle à ~** wealthy *ou* rich aunt/uncle; (*fig*) **l'~ du passé** the heritage *ou* legacy of the past.
hériter [eʀite] 1 vti: **~ (de) qch de qn** to inherit sth from sb; **~ de son oncle** to inherit *ou* come into one's uncle's property; **~ d'une maison** to inherit a house; **~ d'une fortune** to come into *ou* inherit a fortune; **qui hériterait?** who would benefit from the will?, who would inherit?; **impatient d'~** eager to come into *ou* to gain his inheritance; **il a hérité d'un vieux chapeau*** he has fallen heir to *ou* he has inherited an old hat; **il a hérité d'un rhume*** he's picked up a cold.
héritier [eʀitje] nm heir. **~ naturel** heir-at-law; **~ institué** legatee; **~ légitime** legitimate heir; **il est l'~ d'une grande fortune** he is heir to a large fortune; (*hum*) **elle lui a donné un ~** she produced him an heir *ou* a son and heir; **~ présomptif de la couronne** heir apparent (to the throne).
héritière [eʀitjɛʀ] nf heiress.
hermaphrodisme [ɛʀmafʀɔdism] nm hermaphroditism.
hermaphrodite [ɛʀmafʀɔdit] 1 adj hermaphrodite, hermaphroditic(al). 2 nm hermaphrodite.
herméneutique [ɛʀmenøtik] 1 adj hermeneutic. 2 nf hermeneutics (*sg*).
Hermès [ɛʀmɛs] nm Hermes.
hermétique [ɛʀmetik] adj a (*étanche*) *boîte, joint* airtight, watertight, hermetic. **cela assure une fermeture ~ de la porte** this makes sure that the door closes tightly *ou* that the door is a tight fit. b (*fig: impénétrable*) *barrage, secret* impenetrable; *mystère* impenetrable. *visage* **~** closed *ou* impenetrable expression; **être ~ à** to be impervious to. c (*obscur*) *écrivain, livre* abstruse, obscure. (*Littérat*) **poésie/poète ~** hermetic poetry/poet. d (*Alchimie*) hermetic.
hermétiquement [ɛʀmetikmɑ̃] adv *fermer, joindre* tightly, hermetically; (*fig*) *s'exprimer* abstrusely, obscurely. **joint ~ soudé** hermetically soldered joint; **emballage ~ fermé** hermetically sealed package; **local ~ clos** sealed(-up) premises; **secret ~ gardé** closely guarded secret.
hermétisme [ɛʀmetism] nm (*péj: obscurité*) abstruseness, obscurity; (*Alchimie, Littérat*) hermetism.
hermine [ɛʀmin] nf (*fourrure*) ermine; (*animal*) ermine, stoat.
herminette [ɛʀminɛt] nf adze.
herniaire ['ɛʀnjɛʀ] adj hernial; *voir* **bandage**.
hernie ['ɛʀni] nf (*Méd*) hernia, rupture; *[pneu]* bulge. **~ discale** slipped disc; **~ étranglée** strangulated hernia.
hernié, e ['ɛʀnje] adj *organe* herniated.
Hérode [eʀɔd] nm Herod; *voir* **vieux**.
Hérodiade [eʀɔdjad] nf Herodiad.
Hérodote [eʀɔdɔt] nm Herodotus.
héroï-comique [eʀɔikɔmik] adj mock-heroic.
héroïne [eʀɔin] nf (*femme*) heroine; (*drogue*) heroin.
héroïnomane [eʀɔinɔman] nmf heroin addict.
héroïnomanie [eʀɔinɔmani] nf heroin addiction.
héroïque [eʀɔik] adj heroic. **l'époque ~** the pioneering days; **les temps ~s** the heroic age.
héroïquement [eʀɔikmɑ̃] adv heroically.
héroïsme [eʀɔism] nm heroism. **boire ces médicaments si mauvais, c'est de l'~!*** taking such nasty medicines is nothing short of heroic! *ou* is nothing short of heroism!
héron ['eʀɔ̃] nm heron.
héros ['eʀo] nm hero. **mourir en ~** to die the death of a hero *ou* a hero's death; **~ national** national hero; **le ~ du jour** the hero of the day.
herpès [ɛʀpɛs] nm (*gén*) herpes; (*autour de la bouche*) cold sore. **~ génital** genital herpes.
herpétique [ɛʀpetik] adj herpetic.
hersage ['ɛʀsaʒ] nm (*Agr*) harrowing.
herse ['ɛʀs] nf (*Agr*) harrow; *[château]* portcullis; (*Théât*) batten.
herseuse ['ɛʀsøz] nf harrow.
hertz [ɛʀts] nm hertz.
hertzien, -ienne [ɛʀtsjɛ̃, jɛn] adj Hertzian.
hésitant, e [ezitɑ̃, ɑ̃t] adj *personne, début* hesitant; *caractère* wavering, hesitant; *voix, pas* hesitant, faltering.
hésitation [ezitasjɔ̃] nf hesitation. **marquer une ~** *ou* **un temps d'~** to hesitate; **sans ~** without hesitation, unhesitatingly; **j'accepte sans ~** I accept without hesitation *ou* unhesitatingly; **après bien des ~s** after much hesitation; **il eut un moment d'~ et répondit ...** he hesitated for a moment and replied ..., after a moment's hesitation he replied ...; **je n'ai plus d'~s** I shall hesitate no longer; **ses ~s continuelles** his continual hesitations *ou* dithering.
hésiter [ezite] 1 vi a (*balancer*) to hesitate. **tu y vas? — j'hésite** are you going? — I'm not sure *ou* I'm in two minds; **il n'y a pas à ~** there are no two ways about it; **sans ~** without hesitating, unhesitatingly; **~ à faire** to hesitate to do, be unsure whether to do; **j'hésite à vous déranger** I don't like to disturb you, I hesitate to disturb you; **il hésitait sur la route à prendre** he hesitated as to which road to take, he dithered over which road to take* (*Brit*); **~ sur une date** to hesitate over a date; **~ entre plusieurs possibilités** to waver between several possibilities.
b (*s'arrêter*) to hesitate. **~ dans ses réponses** to be hesitant in one's replies; **~ en récitant sa leçon** to falter in reciting one's lesson, recite one's lesson falteringly *ou* hesitantly; **~ devant l'obstacle** to falter *ou* hesitate before an obstacle.
Hespérides [ɛspeʀid] nfpl: **les ~** the Hesperides.
hétaïre [etaiʀ] nf (*prostituée*) courtesan; (*Antiq*) hetaera.
hétéro* [eteʀo] adj, nmf (**abrév de hétérosexuel**) hetero* (*épith*), straight*.
hétéroclite [eteʀɔklit] adj (*disparate*) *ensemble, roman, bâtiment* heterogeneous; *objets* sundry, assorted; (*bizarre*) *personne* eccentric. **pièce meublée de façon ~** room filled with an ill-assorted collection of furniture.
hétérodoxe [eteʀɔdɔks] adj heterodox.
hétérodoxie [eteʀɔdɔksi] nf heterodoxy.
hétérogamie [eteʀɔgami] nf heterogamy.
hétérogène [eteʀɔʒɛn] adj heterogeneous. **c'est un groupe ~** it's a very mixed group.
hétérogénéité [eteʀɔʒeneite] nf heterogeneousness.
hétérosexualité [eteʀosɛksɥalite] nf heterosexuality.
hétérosexuel, -elle [eteʀosɛksɥɛl] adj, nm,f heterosexual.
hétérozygote [eteʀozigɔt] 1 adj heterozygous. 2 nmf heterozygote.
hêtraie ['ɛtʀɛ] nf beech grove.
hêtre ['ɛtʀ] nm (*arbre*) beech (tree); (*bois*) beech (wood).
heu ['ø] excl (*doute*) h'm!, hem!; (*hésitation*) um!, er!
heur†† [œʀ] nm good fortune. (*littér, iro*) **je n'ai pas eu l'~ de lui plaire** I did not have the good fortune to please him, I was not fortunate enough to please him.
heure [œʀ] nf a (*mesure de durée*) hour. (*Scol*) **~ (de cours)** period, class; **j'ai attendu une bonne ~/une petite ~** I waited (for) a good hour/just under an hour; **j'ai attendu 2 ~s d'horloge*** I waited 2 solid hours*; **il a parlé des ~s** he spoke for hours; (*Scol*) **~ de libre** free period; (*Scol*) **j'ai deux ~s de français aujourd'hui** I've two periods of French today; **pendant les ~s de classe/de bureau** during school/office *ou* business hours; (*Admin*) **~s de réception de 14 à 16 heures** consultations between 2 and 4 p.m.; (*Scol*) **quelles sont vos ~s de réception?** when are you available to see parents?; **gagner/coûter 80 F (de) l'~** to earn/cost 80 francs an hour *ou* per hour; (*Aut*) **faire du 100 (km) à l'~** to do 60 miles *ou* 100 km an hour *ou* per hour; **1 ~/3 ~s de travail** 1 hour's/3 hours' work; **cela représente 400 ~s de travail** it represents 400 man-hours *ou* 400 hours of work; **faire beaucoup d'~s** to put in long hours; **lutter pour la semaine de 30 ~s (de travail)** to fight for a 30-hour (working) week; **faire des/10 ~s supplémentaires** to work *ou* do overtime/10 hours' overtime; **les ~s supplémentaires sont bien payées** you get well paid for (doing) overtime, overtime hours are well-paid; **fait dans les 24 ~s** done within 24 hours.
b (*divisions de la journée*) **savoir l'~** to know what time it is, know the time; **avez-vous l'~?** have you got the time?; **quelle ~ avez-vous?** what time do you make it?; **il est 6 ~s/6 ~s 10/6 ~s moins 10/6 ~s et demie** it is 6 (o'clock)/10 past 6/10 to 6/half past 6; **10 ~s du matin/du soir** 10 (o'clock) in the morning/at night, 10 a.m./p.m.; (*frm*) **à 16 ~s 30** at 4.30 p.m., at 16.30 (*frm*); **il est 8 ~s passées** *ou* **sonnées** it's gone 8; **il était 18 ~s ~ de Paris** it was 6 o'clock Paris time; **à 4 ~s pile** *ou* **sonnant(es)** *ou* **tapant(es)*** *ou* **pétant(es)‡** at exactly 4 (o'clock), at dead on 4 (o'clock)* (*Brit*), at 4 (o'clock) on the dot*; **à 4 ~s juste(s)** at 4 sharp; **les bus passent à l'~** the buses come on the hour; **à une ~ avancée (de la nuit)** at a late hour (of the night), late on (in the night); **à une ~ indue** at an *ou* some ungodly hour; *voir* **demander**.
c (*l'heure fixée*) time. **c'est l'~** it's time; **avant l'~** before time, ahead of time, early; **à l'~ (juste)** (right *ou* exactly) on time; **après l'~** late; **venez quand vous voulez, je n'ai pas d'~** come when you like, I have no fixed timetable *ou* schedule *ou* anytime suits me; **~ de Greenwich** Greenwich mean time; **~ légale/locale** standard/local time; **nous venons de passer à l'~ d'hiver** we have just put the clocks back; **~ d'été** daylight saving time, British Summer Time (*Brit*); (*Can*) **~ avancée** daylight saving time; **passer à l'~ d'été** to go over *ou* change to summer time; **l'~ militaire** the right *ou* exact time; **votre ~ sera la mienne** name *ou* say a time; **mettre sa montre à l'~** to set *ou* put one's watch right; **ma montre/l'horloge est toujours à l'~** my watch/the clock is always right *ou* keeps good time; **ma montre n'est pas à l'~** my watch is wrong; **l'~ c'est l'~** on time is on time; **avant l'~, ce n'est pas l'~, après l'~, ce n'est plus l'~*** a minute late is a minute too late; *voir* **remettre**.
d (*moment*) time, moment. **je n'ai pas une ~ à moi** I haven't a moment to myself; (*frm*) **l'~ est venue** *ou* **a sonné** the time has come; **nous avons passé ensemble des ~s heureuses** we spent many happy hours together; **l'~ du déjeuner** lunchtime, time for lunch; **l'~ d'aller se coucher** bedtime, time for bed; **l'~ du biberon** (baby's) feeding time; **à l'~** *ou* **aux ~s des repas** at mealtime(s); **~ d'affluence** *ou* **de pointe**

(*trains, circulation*) rush hour, peak hour; (*magasin*) peak shopping period, busy period; ~ **de pointe** (*téléphone*) peak period; ~**s creuses** (*gén*) slack periods; (*pour électricité, téléphone etc*) off-peak periods; **l'~ de la sortie** *[écoliers, ouvriers]* time to go home; **travailler/rester jusqu'à l'~ de la sortie** to work/stay until it is time to go home; **les problèmes de l'~** the problems of the moment; **à l'~ H** at zero hour; **l'~ est grave** it is a grave moment; **à l'~ dite** at the appointed *ou* prearranged time; **à l'~ du danger** at the time of danger; **l'~ de vérité/de la mort** the moment *ou* hour of truth/the hour of death; **l'~ est à la concertation** it is now time for consultation and dialogue, dialogue is now the order of the day; *voir* **bon[1], dernier, premier.**

e (*avec adj poss*) **il est poète/aimable à ses ~s** he writes poetry/he can be quite pleasant when the fancy takes him *ou* when the mood is on him *ou* when he feels like it; **ce doit être Paul — c'est son ~** it must be Paul — it's his (usual) time; **elle a eu son ~ de gloire/de célébrité** she has had her hour of glory/fame; **il aura son ~** (*de gloire etc*) his hour *ou* time will come; **il attend son ~** he is biding his time *ou* waiting for the right moment; **son ~ viendra/est venue** (*de mourir*) his time will come/has come.

f (*mesure de distance*) hour. **Chartres est à plus d'une ~ de Paris** Chartres is more than an hour from Paris *ou* more than an hour's run from Paris; **c'est à 2 ~s de route** it's 2 hours away by road; **il y a 2 ~s de route/train** it's a 2-hour drive/train journey, it takes 2 hours by car/train (to get there).

g (*Rel*) **~s canoniales** canonical hours; (*Rel*) **Grandes/Petites ~s** night/daylight offices; *voir* **livre[1].**

h (*loc*) **à l'~ qu'il est il doit être arrivé** he must have arrived by now; (*fig: de nos jours*) **à l'~ qu'il est** *ou* **à cette ~** at this moment in time; **à toute ~** at any time (of the day); **repas chaud à toute ~** hot meals all day; **24 ~s sur 24** round the clock, 24 hours a day; **d'~ en ~** with each passing hour, hour by hour; **nous l'attendons d'une ~ à l'autre** we are expecting him any time now; **"Paris à l'~ écossaise"** "Paris goes Scottish"; **la France à l'~ de l'ordinateur** France in the computer age; **pour l'~†** for the time being; (*littér*) **sur l'~** at once; **tout à l'~** (*passé récent*) a short while ago, just now; (*futur proche*) in a little while, shortly.

heureusement [øʀøzmɑ̃] **adv** a (*par bonheur*) fortunately, luckily. **~, il n'y avait personne** fortunately, there was no one there. b (*tant mieux*) **il est parti, ~!** he has gone, thank goodness!; **~ pour lui!** fortunately *ou* luckily for him!; **~ qu'il est parti*** thank goodness he has gone. c (*judicieusement*) happily. **mot ~ choisi** happily chosen word; **phrase ~ tournée** cleverly turned sentence. d (*favorablement*) successfully. **l'entreprise fut ~ menée à terme** the task was successfully completed; **tout s'est ~ terminé** it all turned out well in the end.

heureux, -euse [øʀø, øz] **adj** a (*gén après n*) (*rempli de bonheur*) *personne, souvenir, vie* happy. **il a tout pour être ~** he has everything he needs to be happy *ou* to make him happy; **ils vécurent ~** they lived happily ever after; **~ comme un poisson dans l'eau** *ou* **comme un roi** happy as a sandboy (*Brit*) *ou* clam (*US*); **ces jouets vont faire des ~!** these toys will make some children very happy; *voir* **bon[1], ménage.**

b (*satisfait*) **je suis très ~ d'apprendre la nouvelle** I am very glad *ou* happy *ou* pleased to hear the news; **M. et Mme X sont ~ de vous annoncer ...** Mr and Mrs X are happy *ou* pleased to announce ...; **je suis ~ de ce résultat** I am pleased *ou* happy with this result; **je suis ~ de cette rencontre** I am pleased *ou* glad about this meeting; **il sera trop ~ de vous aider** he'll be only too glad *ou* happy *ou* pleased to help you; **~ de vous revoir** nice *ou* good *ou* pleased to see you again.

c (*gén avant n*) (*qui a de la chance*) *personne* fortunate, lucky. **~ au jeu/en amour** lucky at cards/in love; (*Prov*) **~ au jeu, malheureux en amour** lucky at cards, unlucky in love (*Prov*); **tu peux t'estimer ~ que** you can think yourself lucky *ou* fortunate that; **c'est ~ (pour lui) que** it is fortunate *ou* lucky (for him) that; **il accepte de venir — (*iro*) c'est encore ~!** he's willing to come — it's just as well! *ou* I should think so too!; **encore ~ que je m'en sois souvenu!** it's just as well *ou* it's lucky *ou* it's a good thing that I remembered!; *voir* **élu, main, mémoire.**

d (*gén avant n: optimiste, agréable*) *disposition, caractère* happy, cheerful. **il a *ou* c'est une ~euse nature** he has a happy *ou* cheerful nature.

e (*judicieux*) *décision, choix* fortunate, happy; *formule, expression, effet, mélange* happy, felicitous (*frm*).

f (*favorable*) *présage* propitious, happy; *résultat, issue* happy. **par un ~ hasard** by a fortunate coincidence; **attendre un ~ événement** to be expecting a happy event.

heuristique [øʀistik] 1 **adj** heuristic. 2 **nf** heurism.

heurt ['œʀ] **nm** (*lit: choc*) *[voitures]* collision; *[objets]* hitting together; (*fig: conflit*) clash. **sans ~s (adj)** smooth; **(adv)** smoothly; **leur amitié ne va pas sans quelques ~s** their friendship has its ups and downs, their friendship goes through occasional rough patches.

heurté, e ['œʀte] (**ptp de heurter**) **adj** *couleurs* clashing; *style, jeu* jerky, uneven; *discours* jerky, halting.

heurter ['œʀte] [1] 1 **vt** a (*lit: cogner*) *objet* to strike, hit; *personne* to collide with; (*bousculer*) to jostle. **sa tête heurta la table** his head struck the table; **la voiture heurta un arbre** the car ran into *ou* struck a tree.

b (*fig: choquer*) *préjugés* to offend; *théorie, bon goût, bon sens, tradition* to go against, run counter to; *amour-propre* to upset; *opinions* to conflict *ou* clash with. **~ qn de front** to clash head-on with sb.

2 **vi**: **~ à** to knock at *ou* on; **~ contre qch** *[personne]* to stumble against sth; *[objet]* to knock *ou* bang against sth.

3 **se heurter vpr** a (*s'entrechoquer*) *[passants, voitures]* to collide (with each other); *[objets]* to hit one another. **ses idées se heurtaient dans sa tête** his head was a jumble of ideas, ideas jostled about in his head.

b (*s'opposer*) *[personnes, opinions, couleurs]* to clash (with each other).

c **se ~ à *ou* contre qn/qch** to collide with sb/sth; **se ~ à un refus** to come up against a refusal, meet with a refusal; **se ~ à un problème** to come up against a problem.

heurtoir ['œʀtwaʀ] **nm** *[porte]* (door) knocker; (*Tech: butoir*) stop; (*Rail*) buffer.

hévéa [evea] **nm** hevea.

hexadécimal, e, **mpl -aux** [ɛgzadesimal, o] **adj** hexadecimal.

hexaèdre [ɛgzaɛdʀ] 1 **adj** hexahedral. 2 **nm** hexahedron.

hexaédrique [ɛgzaedʀik] **adj** hexahedral.

hexagonal, e, **mpl -aux** [ɛgzagɔnal, o] **adj** (*Géom*) hexagonal; (*français*) *politique, frontière etc* national; (*péj*) *conception* chauvinistic.

hexagone [ɛgzagɔn] **nm** (*Géom*) hexagon. (*fig*) **l'H~** (metropolitan) France.

hexamètre [ɛgzamɛtʀ] 1 **adj** hexameter (*épith*), hexametric(al). 2 **nm** hexameter.

HF (**abrév de haute fréquence**) HF, h.f.

hiatus ['jatys] **nm** (*Anat, Ling*) hiatus; (*fig*) break, hiatus.

hibernal, e, **mpl -aux** [ibɛʀnal, o] **adj** winter (*épith*), hibernal.

hibernation [ibɛʀnasjɔ̃] **nf** hibernation. (*Méd*) **~ artificielle** induced hypothermia.

hiberner [ibɛʀne] [1] **vi** to hibernate.

hibiscus [ibiskys] **nm** hibiscus.

hibou, **pl ~x** ['ibu] **nm** owl. (*péj*) **(vieux) ~*** crusty old bird* *ou* beggar* *ou* devil*.

hic* ['ik] **nm**: **c'est là le ~** that's the snag *ou* the trouble; **il y a un ~** there's a snag *ou* slight problem.

hic et nunc ['ikɛtnɔ̃k] **loc adv** immediately, at once, there and then.

hickory ['ikɔʀi] **nm** hickory.

hideur ['idœʀ] **nf** (*littér*) hideousness (*NonC*).

hideusement ['idøzmɑ̃] **adv** hideously.

hideux, -euse ['idø, øz] **adj** hideous.

hie ['i] **nf** rammer.

hier [jɛʀ] **adv** yesterday. **~ (au) soir** yesterday evening, last night *ou* evening; **toute la matinée d'~** all yesterday morning; **toute la journée d'~** all day yesterday; **il avait tout ~ pour se décider** he had all (day) yesterday to make up his mind; **je m'en souviens comme si c'était ~** I remember it as if it was yesterday; *voir* **dater, naître.**

hiérarchie ['jeʀaʀʃi] **nf** hierarchy.

hiérarchique ['jeʀaʀʃik] **adj** hierarchic(al). **chef *ou* supérieur ~** superior, senior in rank *ou* in the hierarchy; *voir* **voie.**

hiérarchiquement ['jeʀaʀʃikmɑ̃] **adv** hierarchically.

hiérarchisation ['jeʀaʀʃizasjɔ̃] **nf** (*action*) organization into a hierarchy; (*organisation*) hierarchical organization.

hiérarchiser ['jeʀaʀʃize] [1] **vt** to organize into a hierarchy.

hiératique ['jeʀatik] **adj** hieratic.

hiératiquement ['jeʀatikmɑ̃] **adv** hieratically.

hiéroglyphe ['jeʀɔglif] **nm** (*Ling*) hieroglyph(ic). **~s** (*plusieurs symboles*) hieroglyph(ic)s; (*système d'écriture*) hieroglyphics; (*fig péj*) hieroglyphics (*fig*).

hiéroglyphique ['jeʀɔglifik] **adj** hieroglyphic(al).

hi-fi ['ifi] **adj, nf** hi-fi.

hi-han ['iɑ̃] **excl** heehaw!

hi-hi [hihi] **excl** (*rire*) tee-hee!, hee-hee!; (*pleurs*) sniff-sniff!

hilarant, e [ilaʀɑ̃, ɑ̃t] **adj** *aventure* hilarious, side-splitting; *voir* **gaz.**

hilare [ilaʀ] **adj** *personne* smiling; *visage* beaming, smiling.

hilarité [ilaʀite] **nf** great hilarity *ou* mirth.

hile ['il] **nm** (*Anat, Bot*) hilum.

hilote [ilɔt] **nm** = **ilote.**

Himalaya [imalaja] **nm**: **l'~** the Himalayas; **escalader un sommet de l'~** to climb one of the Himalayan peaks *ou* one of the peaks in the Himalayas.

himalayen, -yenne [imalajɛ̃, jɛn] **adj** Himalayan.

hindi [indi] **nm** (*Ling*) Hindi.

hindou, e [ɛ̃du] 1 **adj** *nationalité* Indian; *coutumes, dialecte* Hindu, Hindoo. 2 **nm,f**: **H~(e)** (*citoyen*) Indian; (*croyant*) Hindu, Hindoo.

hindouisme [ɛ̃duism] **nm** Hinduism, Hindooism.

hindouiste [ɛ̃duist] **adj, nmf** Hindu, Hindoo.

Hindoustan [ɛ̃dustɑ̃] **nm** Hindustan.

hindoustani [ɛ̃dustani] **nm** (*Ling*) Hindustani.

hip ['ip] **excl**: **~ ~ ~ hourra!** hip hip hurray! *ou* hurrah!

hippie ['ipi] **adj, nmf** hippy.

hippique [ipik] **adj** horse (*épith*), equestrian. **concours ~** show-jumping event, horse show; **course ~** horse-race; **le sport ~** equestrian sport.

hippisme [ipism] nm (horse) riding, equestrianism.
hippocampe [ipɔkɑ̃p] nm (*Myth*) hippocampus; (*poisson*) sea horse.
Hippocrate [ipɔkʀat] nm Hippocrates.
hippodrome [ipodʀom] nm racecourse; (*Antiq*) hippodrome.
hippogriffe [ipogʀif] nm hippogriff *ou* hippogryph.
Hippolyte [ipɔlit] nm Hippolytus.
hippomobile [ipomɔbil] adj horse-drawn.
hippophagique [ipɔfaʒik] adj: **boucherie** ~ horse(meat) butcher's.
hippopotame [ipɔpɔtam] nm hippopotamus, hippo*. **c'est un vrai ~*** he (*ou* she) is (like) an elephant* *ou* a hippo*.
hippy, pl **hippies** ['ipi] = **hippie.**
hirondelle [iʀɔ̃dɛl] nf **a** (*Zool*) swallow. **~ de fenêtre** house martin; **~ de rivage** sand martin; **~ de mer** tern; (*Prov*) **une ~ ne fait pas le printemps** one swallow doesn't make a summer (*Prov*); *voir* **nid. b** (*†: *policier*) (bicycle-riding) policeman.
Hiroshima ['iʀɔʃima] n Hiroshima.
hirsute [iʀsyt] adj **a** (*ébouriffé*) *tête* tousled; *gamin* shaggy-haired; *barbe* shaggy. **un individu ~** a shaggy-haired *ou* hirsute individual. **b** (*Bio*) hirsute.
hirsutisme [iʀsytism] nm (*Méd*) hirsutism.
hispanique [ispanik] adj Hispanic.
hispanisant, e [ispanizɑ̃, ɑ̃t] nm,f hispanist, Spanish scholar.
hispanisme [ispanism] nm hispanicism.
hispaniste [ispanist] nmf = **hispanisant.**
hispano-américain, e, pl **hispano-américains** [ispanoameʀikɛ̃, ɛn] **1** adj Spanish-American. **2** nm,f: **Hispano-Américain(e)** Spanish-American, Hispanic (*US*). **3** nm (*Ling*) Latin American Spanish.
hispano-arabe, pl **hispano-arabes** [ispanoaʀab] adj, **hispano-mauresque,** pl **hispano-mauresques** [ispanomɔʀɛsk] adj Hispano-Moresque.
hispanophone [ispanɔfɔn] **1** adj Spanish-speaking; *littérature etc* Spanish-language (*épith*), in Spanish (*attrib*). **2** nmf Spanish-speaker.
hisse: oh hisse ['ois] excl heave ho!
hisser ['ise] [1] **1** vt (*Naut*) to hoist; (*soulever*) *objet* to hoist, haul up, heave up; *personne* to haul up, heave up. **~ les couleurs** to run up *ou* hoist the colours; **hissez les voiles!** up sails!; (*fig*) **~ qn au pouvoir** to hoist sb into a position of power. **2 se hisser** vpr to heave o.s. up, haul o.s. up. **se ~ sur un toit** to heave *ou* haul o.s. (up) onto a roof; **se ~ sur la pointe des pieds** to stand up *ou* raise o.s. on tiptoe; (*fig*) **se ~ à la première place/au pouvoir** to pull o.s. up to first place/a position of power.
histamine [istamin] nf histamine.
histaminique [istaminik] adj histaminic.
histocompatibilité [istokɔ̃patibilite] nf histocompatibility.
histogramme [istɔgʀam] nm histogram.
histoire [istwaʀ] nf **a** (*science, événements*) **l'~** history; **l'~ jugera** posterity will be the judge; **l'~ est un continuel recommencement** history is constantly being remade; **laisser son nom dans l'~** to find one's place in history; **l'~ ancienne/du Moyen Âge** ancient/medieval history; **~ naturelle†** natural history; **l'~ de France** French history, the history of France; **l'H~ sainte** Biblical *ou* sacred history; **la petite ~** the footnotes of history; **pour la petite ~** for the record; **~ romancée** fictionalized history; (*fig*) **tout cela, c'est de l'~ ancienne*** all that's ancient history*.

b (*déroulement de faits*) history, story. **l'~ du château de Windsor** the history of Windsor Castle; **raconter l'~ de sa vie** to tell one's life story *ou* the story of one's life.

c (*Scol* *) (*livre*) history book; (*leçon*) history (lesson). **une ~ de France/d'Angleterre** a history of France/England; **on a H~ à 2 heures** we have history at 2 o'clock.

d (*récit, conte*) story; (*: *mensonge*) story*, fib*. **une ~ vraie** a true story; **~s de pêche/de chasse** fishing/hunting stories; **~s de revenant** ghost stories; **~ drôle** funny story, joke; **~ marseillaise** tall story *ou* tale, fisherman's tale (*Brit*); **~ de fous** shaggy-dog story; **c'est une ~ à dormir debout** it's a cock-and-bull story *ou* a tall story; **qu'est-ce que c'est que cette ~?** what on earth is all this about?, just what is all this about?; **tout ça, ce sont des ~s** that's just a lot of fibs*, you've made all that up; **tu me racontes des ~s** you're pulling my leg, come off it!*; **le plus beau *ou* curieux de l'~ c'est que** the best part *ou* strangest part of it is that; **c'est toute une ~** it's a long story; **l'~ veut qu'il ait dit** the story goes that he said.

e (*: *affaire, incident*) business. **c'est une drôle d'~** it's a funny business; **il vient de lui arriver une curieuse ~/une drôle d'~** something odd/funny has just happened to him; **pour une ~ d'argent/de femme** because of something to do with money/a woman; **se mettre dans une sale ~, se mettre une sale ~ sur le dos** to get mixed up in some nasty business; **sa nomination va faire toute une ~** his appointment will cause a lot of fuss *ou* a great to-do, there will be quite a fuss *ou* to-do over his appointment; **c'est toujours la même ~!** it's always the same old story!; **ça, c'est une autre ~!** that's (quite) another story!; **j'ai pu avoir une place mais ça a été toute une ~** I managed to get a seat but it was a real struggle; **sans ~s** (adj) uneventful; (adv) uneventfully.

f (*: *ennui*) **~s** trouble; **faire des ~s à qn** to make trouble for sb; **elle veut nous faire des ~s*** she means to make trouble for us; **cela ne peut lui attirer *ou* lui valoir que des ~s** that's bound to get him into trouble, that will cause him nothing but trouble.

g (*: *chichis*) fuss, to-do, carry-on* (*Brit*). **faire un tas d'~s** to make a whole lot of fuss *ou* a great to-do; **quelle ~ pour si peu!** what a to-do *ou* fuss *ou* carry-on* (*Brit*) over so little!; **allez, au lit, et pas d'~s!** come along now, off to bed, and I don't want any fuss!; **il fait ce qu'on lui demande sans (faire d')~s** he does what he is told without (making) a fuss; **je ne veux pas d'~s** I don't want any fuss *ou* nonsense.

h (*) **~ de faire** just to do; **~ de prendre l'air** just for a breath of (fresh) air; **~ de rire** just for a laugh*, just for fun; **il a essayé, ~ de voir/de faire quelque chose** he had a go just to see what it was like/just for something to do *ou* just to be doing something.

i (*: *machin*) thingummyjig* (*Brit*), thingamajig* (*US*), whatsit*.
histologie [istɔlɔʒi] nf histology.
histologique [istɔlɔʒik] adj histological.
histologiste [istɔlɔʒist] nmf histologist.
historié, e [istɔʀje] adj (*Art*) historiated.
historien, -ienne [istɔʀjɛ̃, jɛn] nm,f (*savant*) historian; (*étudiant*) history student, historian.
historiette [istɔʀjɛt] nf little story, anecdote.
historiographe [istɔʀjɔgʀaf] nmf historiographer.
historiographie [istɔʀjɔgʀafi] nf historiography.
historique [istɔʀik] **1** adj *étude, vérité, roman, temps* historical; *personnage, événement, monument* historic. **2** nm history, review. **faire l'~ de** *problème, affaire* to review, make a review of; *institution, mot* to examine the history of, give the historical background to.
historiquement [istɔʀikmɑ̃] adv historically.
histrion [istʀijɔ̃] nm **a** (*Hist Théât*) (wandering) minstrel, strolling player. **b** (*péj*) buffoon; (*comédien*) ham (actor).
histrionisme [istʀijɔnism] nm (*Psych*) histrionics.
hit* [it] nm hit*.
hitlérien, -ienne [itleʀjɛ̃, jɛn] adj, nm,f Hitlerian, Hitlerite, Nazi.
hitlérisme [itleʀism] nm Hitlerism.
hit-parade, pl **hit-parades** ['itpaʀad] nm (*Mus*) **le ~** the charts; **premier au ~** number one in the charts; **être bien placé au ~** to be high up in the charts; **être *ou* figurer au ~** to be in the charts; **être en tête du ~** to be at the top of the charts; (*fig*) **être *ou* figurer au ~ du chômage** to be in the list of countries with high unemployment; **être bien placé au ~ des hommes politiques** to be one of the most popular politicians; **être bien placé au ~ de la criminalité** to be high up in the crime figures.
hittite ['itit] **1** adj Hittite. **2** nmf: **H~** Hittite.
HIV [aʃive] nm (abrév de **human immuno deficiency virus**) HIV.
hiver [ivɛʀ] nm winter. **il fait un temps d'~** it's like winter, it's wintry weather; **jardin d'~** wintergarden; **sports d'~** winter sports; **~ nucléaire** nuclear winter.
hivernage [ivɛʀnaʒ] nm *[bateau, caravane]* wintering.
hivernal, e, mpl **-aux** [ivɛʀnal, o] **1** adj (*lit: de l'hiver*) *brouillard, pluies* winter (*épith*), hibernal (*littér*); (*fig: comme en hiver*) *atmosphère, température, temps* wintry (*épith*). **il faisait une température ~e** it was as cold as (in) winter, it was like winter. **2 hivernale** nf (*Alpinisme*) winter ascent.
hivernant, e [ivɛʀnɑ̃, ɑ̃t] nm,f winter holiday-maker (*Brit*) *ou* visitor.
hiverner [ivɛʀne] [1] vi to winter.
HLA [aʃɛla] (abrév de **human leucocyte antigens**) HLA.
HLM ['aʃɛlɛm] nm ou nf (abrév de **habitation à loyer modéré**) *voir* **habitation.**
ho ['o] excl (*appel*) hey (there)!; (*surprise, indignation*) oh!
hobby, pl **hobbies** ['ɔbi] nm hobby.
hobereau, pl **~x** ['ɔbʀo] nm (*Orn*) hobby; (*péj: seigneur*) local (country) squire.
hochement ['ɔʃmɑ̃] nm: **~ de tête** (*affirmatif*) nod (of the head); (*négatif*) shake (of the head).
hochequeue ['ɔʃkø] nm wagtail.
hocher ['ɔʃe] [1] vt: **~ la tête** (*affirmativement*) to nod (one's head); (*négativement*) to shake one's head.
hochet ['ɔʃɛ] nm *[bébé]* rattle; (*fig*) toy.
hockey ['ɔkɛ] nm hockey. **~ sur glace** ice hockey (*Brit*), hockey (*US*); **~ sur gazon** field hockey.
hockeyeur, -euse ['ɔkɛjœʀ, øz] nm,f hockey player.
hoirie [waʀi] nf (††) inheritance; *voir* **avancement.**
holà ['ɔla] **1** excl (*pour attirer l'attention*) hello!; (*pour protester*) whoa (there)! **2** nm: **mettre le ~ à qch** to put a stop *ou* an end to sth.
holding ['ɔldiŋ] nm holding company.
hold-up ['ɔldœp] nm inv hold-up. **condamné pour le ~ d'une banque** sentenced for having held up a bank *ou* for a bank hold-up.
holisme ['ɔlism] nm holism.
holistique [ɔlistik] adj holistic.
hollandais, e ['ɔ(l)lɑ̃dɛ, ɛz] **1** adj Dutch; *voir* **sauce. 2** nm **a H~** Dutchman; **les H~** the Dutch. **b** (*Ling*) Dutch. **3 Hollandaise** nf Dutchwoman.
Hollande ['ɔ(l)lɑ̃d] nf Holland.
hollande ['ɔ(l)lɑ̃d] **1** nf (*toile*) holland; (*pomme de terre*) holland potato. **2** nm (*fromage*) Dutch cheese; (*papier*) Holland.
Hollywood ['ɔliwud] n Hollywood.

hollywoodien, -ienne [ˈɔliwudjɛ̃, jɛn] adj Hollywood (*épith*).

holmium [ˈɔlmjɔm] nm holmium.

holocauste [ɔlokost] nm **a** (*Rel, fig: sacrifice*) sacrifice, Holocaust. **offrir qch en ~** to offer sth up in sacrifice; (*littér*) **se donner en ~** to make a total sacrifice of one's life. **b** (*victime*) sacrifice.

hologramme [ɔlɔgʀam] nm hologram.

holographe [ɔlɔgʀaf] adj holograph (*épith*).

holographie [ɔlɔgʀafi] nf holography.

holophrastique [ˈɔlɔfʀastik] adj holophrastic.

homard [ˈɔmaʀ] nm lobster. (*Culin*) **~ à l'armoricaine/à l'américaine/thermidor** lobster à l'armoricaine/à l'américaine/thermidor.

home [ˈom] nm: **~ d'enfants** children's home.

homélie [ɔmeli] nf homily.

homéopathe [ɔmeɔpat] nmf homoeopath(ist). **médecin ~** homoeopathic doctor.

homéopathie [ɔmeɔpati] nf homoeopathy.

homéopathique [ɔmeɔpatik] adj homoeopathic. (*hum*) **il aime la musique, mais à dose ~** he likes music but in small doses.

Homère [ɔmɛʀ] nm Homer.

homérique [ɔmeʀik] adj Homeric; *voir* **rire**.

home-trainer, pl home-trainers [ˈomtʀɛnœʀ] nm exercise bike.

homicide [ɔmisid] **1** adj (†, *littér*) homicidal. **2** nmf (*littér: criminel*) homicide (*littér*), murderer (*ou* murderess). **3** nm (*Jur: crime*) homicide (*US*), murder. **~ volontaire** murder, voluntary manslaughter, first-degree murder (*US*); **~ involontaire** *ou* **par imprudence** manslaughter, second-degree murder (*US*).

hominidé [ɔminide] nm hominid. **les ~s** the Hominidae.

hominien [ɔminjɛ̃] nm hominoid.

hommage [ɔmaʒ] nm **a** (*marque d'estime*) tribute. **rendre ~ à qn/au talent de qn** to pay homage *ou* (a) tribute to sb/to sb's talent; **rendre ~ à Dieu** to pay homage to God; **rendre un dernier ~ à qn** to pay one's last respects to sb; **recevoir l'~ d'un admirateur** to accept the tribute paid by an admirer.

b (*frm: civilités*) **~s** respects; **mes ~s, Madame** my humble respects, Ma'am; **présenter ses ~s à une dame** to pay one's respects to a lady; **présentez mes ~s à votre femme** give my respects to your wife; **daignez agréer mes respectueux ~s** yours faithfully (*Brit*), yours truly (*US*).

c (*don*) **acceptez ceci comme un ~** *ou* **en ~ de ma gratitude** please accept this as a mark *ou* token of my gratitude; **faire ~ d'un livre** to give a presentation copy of a book; **~ de l'auteur/de l'éditeur** with the author's/publisher's compliments.

d (*Hist*) homage.

hommasse [ɔmas] adj mannish.

homme [ɔm] **1** nm **a** (*individu*) man. (*espèce*) **l'~** man, mankind; **un ~ fait** a grown man; **approche si tu es un ~!** come on if you're man enough *ou* if you dare!; **l'enfant devient ~** the child grows into *ou* becomes a man; **des vêtements d'~** men's clothes; (*Comm*) **rayon ~s** men's *ou* menswear department; **voilà mon ~** (*que je cherche*) there's my man; (*qu'il me faut*) that's the man for me; (**: mon mari*) here comes that man of mine*; **je suis votre ~** I'm the man you want, I'm the man for you; **elle a rencontré l'~ de sa vie** she has found Mr Right *ou* the man for her; **c'est l'~ de ma vie** he's the man of my life; **c'est l'~ du jour** he's the man of the moment *ou* hour; **c'est l'~ de la situation** he's the right man for the job; (*fig*) **l'~ fort du régime** the muscleman of the régime; *voir* **abominable, âge, mémoire** *etc*.

b (*loc*) **parler d'~ à ~** to speak man to man, have a man-to-man talk; **il n'est pas ~ à mentir** he's not one to lie *ou* a man to lie; **comme un seul ~** as one man; **il a trouvé son ~** (*un égal*) he has found his match; (*Prov*) **un ~ averti en vaut deux** forewarned is forearmed (*Prov*); (*Prov*) **l'~ propose, Dieu dispose** man proposes, God disposes (*Prov*); (*Naut*) **un ~ à la mer!** man overboard!

c (*unité*) **heure-/journée-/mois-** *etc* **~** man-hour/-day/-month *etc*.

2 comp ►**homme d'action** man of action ►**homme d'affaires** businessman ►**homme d'armes**†† man-at-arms†† ►**homme de barre** helmsman ►**homme de bien** man of property *ou* of means ►**homme à bonnes fortunes**† ladykiller, ladies' man ►**homme des cavernes** cave man ►**homme de confiance** right-hand man ►**l'homme de Cro-Magnon** Cro-Magnon man ►**homme d'église** man of the Church ►**homme d'équipage** member of a ship's crew; **navire avec 30 hommes d'équipage** ship with a crew of 30 (men) ►**homme d'esprit** man of wit ►**homme d'État** statesman ►**homme à femmes** womanizer, ladies' man ►**homme au foyer** househusband ►**homme de génie** man of genius ►**homme-grenouille** nm (pl **hommes-grenouilles**) frogman ►**homme de lettres** man of letters ►**homme lige** liege man ►**homme de loi** man of law ►**homme de main** hired man, henchman ►**homme de ménage** (male) domestic help ►**homme du monde** man about town, socialite; **c'est un parfait homme du monde** he's a real gentleman ►**homme-orchestre** nm (pl **hommes-orchestres**) (*Mus*) one-man band; (*fig*) **c'est l'homme-orchestre** he wears many hats ►**homme de paille** man of straw ►**homme de peine** workhand ►**homme du peuple** man of the people ►**l'homme de plume** man of letters, writer ►**homme politique** politician ►**homme de robe**†† legal man, lawyer ►**homme de la rue** the man in the street ►**homme-sandwich** nm (pl **hommes-sandwiches**) sandwich man ►**homme de science** man of science ►**homme de terrain** (*Pol*) grass-roots politician; (*Ind etc*) man with a practical background; **le nouveau P.-D.G. est un homme de terrain** the new managing director has done his stint at the coalface (*fig*) *ou* has a practical rather than an academic background ►**homme à tout faire** odd-job man ►**homme de troupe** (*Mil*) private.

homo* [omo] nm (abrév de **homosexuel**) gay.

homocentre [ɔmɔsɑ̃tʀ] nm common centre.

homocentrique [ɔmɔsɑ̃tʀik] adj homocentric.

homogène [ɔmɔʒɛn] adj homogeneous. (*Scol*) **c'est un groupe ~** they are all about the same level *ou* standard in that group.

homogénéisation [ɔmɔʒeneizasjɔ̃] nf homogenization.

homogénéiser [ɔmɔʒeneize] [1] vt to homogenize.

homogénéité [ɔmɔʒeneite] nf homogeneity, homogeneousness.

homographe [ɔmɔgʀaf] **1** adj homographic. **2** nm homograph.

homologation [ɔmɔlɔgasjɔ̃] nf (*Sport*) ratification; (*Jur*) approval, sanction.

homologie [ɔmɔlɔʒi] nf (*Sci*) homology; (*gén*) equivalence.

homologue [ɔmɔlɔg] **1** adj (*Sci*) homologous; (*gén*) equivalent, homologous (*de* to). **2** nm (*Chim*) homologue; (*personne*) equivalent, counterpart, opposite number.

homologuer [ɔmɔlɔge] [1] vt (*Sport*) to ratify; (*Jur*) to approve, sanction.

homoncule [ɔmɔ̃kyl] nm = **homuncule**.

homonyme [ɔmɔnim] **1** adj homonymous. **2** nm (*Ling*) homonym; (*personne*) namesake.

homonymie [ɔmɔnimi] nf homonymy.

homonymique [ɔmɔnimik] adj homonymic.

homophone [ɔmɔfɔn] **1** adj (*Ling*) homophonous; (*Mus*) homophonic. **2** nm homophone.

homophonie [ɔmɔfɔni] nf homophony.

homosexualité [ɔmɔsɛksɥalite] nf homosexuality.

homosexuel, -elle [ɔmɔsɛksɥɛl] adj, nm,f homosexual.

homozygote [omozigɔt] **1** adj homozygous. **2** nmf homozygote.

homuncule [ɔmɔ̃kyl] nm homunculus.

Honduras [ˈɔ̃dyʀas] nm: **le ~** Honduras; **le ~ britannique** British Honduras.

hondurien, -ienne [ˈɔ̃dyʀjɛ̃, jɛn] **1** adj Honduran. **2** nm,f: **H~(ne)** Honduran.

Hong-Kong [ˈɔ̃gkɔ̃g] n Hong Kong.

hongre [ˈɔ̃gʀ] **1** adj gelded. **2** nm gelding.

Hongrie [ˈɔ̃gʀi] nf Hungary.

hongrois, e [ˈɔ̃gʀwa, waz] **1** adj Hungarian. **2** nm (*Ling*) Hungarian. **3** nm,f: **H~(e)** Hungarian.

Honiara [ɔɲaʀa] n Honiara.

honnête [ɔnɛt] **1** adj **a** (*intègre*) *personne* honest, decent; *juge* honest; *conduite* decent; *procédés, intentions* honest, honourable. **ce sont d'~s gens** they are decent people *ou* folk*; **un vin ~** an honest little wine. **b** (*vertueux*) *femme* honest, decent. **c** (*juste*) *marché* fair; *prix* fair, reasonable. **d** (*satisfaisant*) *résultats* reasonable, fair; *repas* reasonable. **ce livre est ~** this book isn't bad *ou* is reasonable *ou* is fair; **rester dans une ~ moyenne** to maintain a fair average. **e** (*franc*) honest, frank. **sois ~, tu aimerais bien le renvoyer** be honest, you'd really love to sack him. **2** comp ►**honnête homme** (*Hist*) gentleman, man of breeding.

honnêtement [ɔnɛtmɑ̃] adv (*voir* **honnête**) honestly; decently; honourably; fairly; reasonably. **c'est ~ payé** it's reasonably paid, you get a fair *ou* reasonable wage for it; **gagner ~ sa vie** (*dignement*) to earn an honest penny *ou* crust; (*bien*) to make a good living; **~, vous le saviez bien!** come now, you knew!

honnêteté [ɔnɛtte] nf (*voir* **honnête**) honesty; decency; fairness. **l'~ ne paie pas** honesty doesn't pay; **en toute ~, je ne le crois pas** in all honesty, I don't believe it.

honneur [ɔnœʀ] nm **a** (*dignité morale, réputation*) honour. **l'~ m'oblige à le faire** I am in honour bound to do it; **mettre son** *ou* **un point d'~ à faire qch** to make it a point of honour to do sth; **jurer/promettre sur l'~** to swear/promise on one's honour; **homme/femme d'~** man/woman of honour, man/woman with a sense of honour; **bandit d'~** outlaw (*because of a blood feud*); **il s'en est tiré avec ~** he came out of it honourably; *voir* **dette, manquer, parole, point, tout** *etc*.

b (*mérite*) credit. **avec ~** creditably; **cette action est toute à son ~** this act does him (great) credit *ou* is much to his credit; **c'est à lui que revient l'~ d'avoir inventé ...** the credit is his for having invented ...; **faire ~ à** *ou* **être l'~ de sa famille/sa profession** to be a credit *ou* an honour to one's family/one's profession; **cette décision vous fait ~** this decision does you credit *ou* is to your credit; *voir* **tour**[2].

c (*privilège, faveur*) honour. **faire (à qn) l'~ de venir** *etc* to do sb the honour of coming *etc*; **me ferez-vous l'~ de danser avec moi?** may I have the pleasure of this dance?; **avoir l'~ de** to have the honour of; **j'ai eu l'~ de recevoir sa visite** he honoured me with a visit; **je suis ravi de vous rencontrer — tout l'~ est pour moi** delighted to meet you — the pleasure is (all) mine *ou* it is my pleasure; **qui commence à jouer? — à**

toi l'~ who is it to start? – it's you (to start); (*Admin: formule épistolaire*) **j'ai l'~ de solliciter ...** I am writing to ask ...; **j'ai l'~ de vous informer que** I am writing to inform you that, I beg to inform you that (*frm*); **garde/invité d'~** guard/guest of honour; **président/membre d'~** honorary president/member; *voir* **baroud, champ, citoyen** *etc*.

d (*marques de distinction*) **~s** honours; **aimer/mépriser les ~s** to be fond of/despise honours; **couvert d'~s** covered in honours; **avec tous les ~s dus à son rang** with all the honour due to his rank; **les derniers ~s (funèbres)** the last tribute; **~s militaires** military honours; **se rendre avec** *ou* **obtenir les ~s de la guerre** (*Mil*) to be granted the honours of war; (*fig*) to suffer an honourable defeat; (*fig*) **faire les ~s de la maison** *etc* **à qn** to (do the honours and) show sb round the house *etc;* **avoir les ~s de la première page** to make the front page; **avoir les ~s de la cimaise** to have one's works exhibited; *voir* **rendre.**

e (*Cartes*) honour.

f (*titre*) **votre H~** Your Honour.

g (*loc*) **~ aux vainqueurs!** honour to the conquerors!; **~ aux dames** ladies first; **à vous l'~** after you; **être à l'~** (*personne*) to have the place of honour; *[mode, style]* to be to the fore, be much in evidence; **être en ~** *[coutume etc]* to be the done thing; *[style, mode]* to be in favour; **remettre en ~** to reintroduce; **en l'~ de nos hôtes** in honour of our guests; **en l'~ de cet événement** in honour of this event; **à qui ai-je l'~?** to whom do I have the honour of speaking?; **que me vaut l'~ de votre visite?** to what do I owe the honour of your visit?; (*iro*) **en quel ~ toutes ces fleurs?*** what are all these flowers in aid of?*; (*iro*) **en quel ~ t'appelle-t-il "mon bijou"?** what gives him the right to call you "my love"?; **faire ~ à ses engagements/sa signature** to honour one's commitments/signature; **faire ~ à une traite** to honour *ou* meet a bill; **faire ~ à un repas** to do justice to a meal; **il a fini la partie pour l'~** he gallantly finished the game (for its own sake); *voir* **à, bras, rendre.**

honnir ['ɔniʀ] [2] **vt** (*frm*) to hold in contempt. **honni soit qui mal y pense** evil be to him who evil thinks.

honorabilité [ɔnɔʀabilite] **nf** *[personne, sentiments]* worthiness. **soucieux d'~** anxious to be thought honourable.

honorable [ɔnɔʀabl] **adj** (*lit: estimable*) *personne, buts* honourable, worthy; *sentiments* creditable, worthy; (*suffisant*) *salaire, résultats* decent, respectable. (*frm, hum*) **l'~ compagnie** this worthy company (*frm, hum*); (*frm, iro*) **mon ~ collègue** my honourable *ou* esteemed colleague (*frm, iro*); **à cet âge ~** at this grand old age; *voir* **amende.**

honorablement [ɔnɔʀabləmɑ̃] **adv** (*voir* **honorable**) honourably; worthily; creditably; decently. **~ connu dans le quartier** known and respected in the district.

honoraire [ɔnɔʀɛʀ] 1 **adj** *membre, président* honorary. **professeur ~** professor emeritus. 2 **nmpl: ~s** fee, fees, honorarium; *voir* **note.**

honorer [ɔnɔʀe] [1] 1 **vt** a (*glorifier*) *savant, Dieu* to honour. **~ la mémoire de qn** to honour the memory of sb.

b (*littér: estimer*) to hold in high regard *ou* esteem. **je l'honore à l'égal de ...** I have the same regard *ou* esteem for him as I do for ...; **mon honoré collègue** my esteemed *ou* respected colleague.

c (*gratifier*) **~ qn de qch** to honour sb with sth; **il m'honorait de son amitié/de sa présence** he honoured me with his friendship/his presence; (*iro*) **il ne m'a pas honoré d'un regard** he did not honour me with so much as a glance (*iro*), he did not (even) deign to look at me; **je suis très honoré** I am highly *ou* greatly honoured.

d (*faire honneur à*) to do credit to, be a credit to. **cette franchise l'honore** this frankness does him credit; **il honore sa profession/son pays** he's a credit *ou* an honour to his profession/country.

e *chèque, signature, promesse* to honour; *traite* to honour, meet; *médecin, notaire* to settle one's account with. (†: *lettre*) **votre honorée du ...** yours of the ...; (*hum* †) **~ sa femme** to fulfil one's conjugal duties (*hum*).

2 **s'honorer vpr: s'~ de** to pride o.s. (up)on; **pays qui s'honore de ses artistes** country which prides itself (up)on its artists.

honorifique [ɔnɔʀifik] **adj** *fonction* honorary (*Brit*), ceremonial (*US*). **à titre ~** honorary; **fonction accordée à titre ~** honorary post; **il a été nommé à titre ~** his appointment was an honorary one, he was appointed on an honorary basis.

honoris causa [ɔnɔʀiskoza] **adj: il a été nommé docteur ~** he has been awarded an honorary doctorate; **il est docteur ~ de l'université de X** he is an honorary doctor of the University of X.

honte ['ɔ̃t] **nf** a (*déshonneur, humiliation*) disgrace, shame. **couvrir qn de ~** to bring disgrace *ou* shame on sb, disgrace sb; **quelle ~** *ou* **c'est une ~ pour la famille!** what a disgrace to the family!, he brings shame upon the family!; **faire la ~** *ou* **être la ~ de la famille/profession** to be the disgrace of one's family/profession; (*littér*) **~ à celui qui ...** shame upon him who ... (*littér*); **il n'y a aucune ~ à être ...** there's no shame *ou* disgrace in being ...; **c'est une ~!** that's disgraceful! *ou* a disgrace!

b (*sentiment de confusion, gêne*) shame. **à ma (grande) ~** to my (great) shame; **sans ~** shamelessly; **sans fausse ~** quite openly; **avoir ~ (de qch/de faire)** to be *ou* feel ashamed (of sth/of doing); **faire ~ à qn** to make sb (feel) ashamed; **elle n'a aucune ~†** she is utterly shameless, she has no shame; **toute ~ bue** dead to *ou* lost to shame; **faire ~ à qn de sa lenteur** to make sb (feel) ashamed of his slowness; **il leur fait ~ par sa rapidité** he puts them to shame with his speed; *voir* **court**[1].

honteusement ['ɔ̃tøzmɑ̃] **adv** (*voir* **honteux**) shamefully; ashamedly; disgracefully.

honteux, -euse ['ɔ̃tø, øz] **adj** a (*déshonorant*) shameful; (*confus*) ashamed (*de* of). **c'est ~!** it's a disgrace!, it's disgraceful! *ou* shameful!; *voir* **maladie, partie**[2]. b (*cachant ses opinions*) **bourgeois/communiste ~** apologetic bourgeois/communist.

hooligan ['uligan] **nm** hooligan.

hooliganisme ['uliganism] **nm** hooliganism.

hop ['ɔp] **excl: ~ (là)!** (*pour faire sauter*) hup!; (*pour faire partir*) off you go!; (*après un geste maladroit*) (w)oops!

hôpital, pl -aux [ɔpital, o] **nm** hospital. **être à l'~** to be in hospital; **~ militaire/psychiatrique** military/psychiatric hospital; **c'est l'~ qui se moque de la charité!** ≃ it's the pot calling the kettle black.

hoquet ['ɔkɛ] **nm** hiccough. **avoir le ~** to have (the) hiccoughs; **il a eu un ~ de dégoût/peur** he gulped with distaste/fear.

hoqueter ['ɔk(ə)te] [4] **vi** to hiccough.

Horace [ɔʀas] **nm** Horatio; (*le poète*) Horace.

horaire [ɔʀɛʀ] 1 **adj** a *salaire, moyenne* hourly. **débit/vitesse ~** rate/speed per hour. b (*Astron*) horary; *voir* **fuseau.** 2 **nm** timetable, schedule. **pratiquer l'~ variable** *ou* **mobile** *ou* **flexible** *ou* **souple** *ou* **à la carte** to work flexitime *ou* on sliding time (*US*), have flexible working hours. 3 **nmf** employee paid by the hour.

horde ['ɔʀd] **nf** horde.

horion ['ɔʀjɔ̃] **nm** († *hum, gén pl*) blow, punch. **échanger des ~s avec la police** to exchange blows with the police.

horizon [ɔʀizɔ̃] **nm** a (*limite, ligne, Art*) horizon. **la ligne d'~** (*gén, Art*) the horizon; **un bateau sur l'~** a boat on the horizon *ou* skyline; **on voyait à l'~ ...** one could see on the horizon ...; **s'enfoncer/disparaître à l'~** to sink/disappear below the horizon.

b (*Astron*) horizon.

c (*paysage*) landscape, view. **un des plus beaux ~s qui soit** one of the most beautiful landscapes *ou* views; **on découvre un vaste ~/un ~ de collines** you come upon a vast panorama/a hilly landscape; **changer d'~** to have a change of scenery *ou* scene; **ce fond de vallon humide était tout son ~** the bottom of this damp valley was all he ever saw; **voyager vers de nouveaux ~s** to make for new horizons; (*fig*) **venir d'~s divers** to hail from different backgrounds.

d (*fig: perspective*) horizon. **ça lui a ouvert de nouveaux ~s** it opened (up) new horizons *ou* vistas for him; **l'~ politique/international** the political/international scene; **faire des prévisions pour l'~ 2020** to make forecasts for (the year) 2020; **à l'~ 2020** by the year 2020 or so; *voir* **tour**[2].

horizontal, e, mpl -aux [ɔʀizɔ̃tal, o] 1 **adj** horizontal. 2 **horizontale nf** (*gén, Géom*) horizontal. **placer qch à l'~e** to put sth horizontal *ou* in a horizontal position.

horizontalement [ɔʀizɔ̃talmɑ̃] **adv** horizontally.

horizontalité [ɔʀizɔ̃talite] **nf** horizontality, horizontalness.

horloge [ɔʀlɔʒ] **nf** (*gén, Ordin*) clock. **il a la régularité d'une ~, il est réglé comme une ~** he's as regular as clockwork; **il est 2 heures à l'~ de la chambre** it's 2 o'clock by *ou* according to the bedroom clock; **l'~ parlante** the speaking clock (*Brit*), Time (*US*); **~ normande** grandfather clock; **~ pointeuse** time clock; **~ physiologique/interne** biological/internal clock; *voir* **heure.**

horloger, -ère [ɔʀlɔʒe, ɛʀ] 1 **adj** *industrie* watch-making (*épith*), clock-making (*épith*). 2 **nm,f** watchmaker; (*horloges en particulier*) clockmaker. **~ bijoutier** jeweller (specializing in clocks and watches).

horlogerie [ɔʀlɔʒʀi] **nf** (*fabrication*) watch-making; (*horloges en particulier*) clock-making; (*objets*) time-pieces; (*magasin*) watchmaker's (shop); clockmaker's (shop); (*technique, science*) horology. **~ bijouterie** jeweller's shop (specializing in clocks and watches); **pièces d'~** clock components; *voir* **mouvement.**

hormis ['ɔʀmi] **prép** (*frm*) but, save.

hormonal, e, mpl -aux [ɔʀmɔnal, o] **adj** hormonal, hormone (*épith*).

hormone [ɔʀmɔn] **nf** hormone. **~ de croissance/sexuelle** growth/sex hormone.

horodaté, e [ɔʀɔdate] **adj** *stationnement* pay and display (*épith*); *ticket* stamped with the hour and date (*attrib*).

horodateur [ɔʀɔdatœʀ] **nm** *[parking etc]* ticket machine.

horoscope [ɔʀɔskɔp] **nm** horoscope. **faire l'~ de qn** to cast sb's horoscope.

horreur [ɔʀœʀ] **nf** a (*effroi, répulsion*) horror. **il était devenu pour elle un objet d'~** he had become a source of horror to her; **frappé** *ou* **saisi d'~** horror-stricken, horror-struck; **une vision d'~** a horrific *ou* horrendous *ou* horrifying sight; **l'~ d'agir/du risque qui le caractérise** the horror of acting/taking risks which is typical of him; **son ~ de la lâcheté** his horror *ou* loathing of cowardice; **je me suis aperçu avec ~ que ...** to my horror I realized that ... .

b (*laideur*) *[crime, guerre]* horror. **l'esclavage dans toute son ~** slavery in all its horror.

c (*chose horrible, dégoûtante*) **les ~s de la guerre** the horrors of war; **ce film/travail est une ~*** this film/piece of work is terrible *ou* awful *ou* dreadful; **ce chapeau est une ~*** this hat is a fright *ou* is hideous *ou* ghastly*; **c'est une ~*** *[femme]* she's a fright, she's hideous *ou* ghastly*; *[tableau etc]* it's hideous *ou* ghastly*; *[enfant]* **c'est une petite**

~! he (*ou* she) is a little horror!; **quelle** ~! how dreadful! *ou* awful!; *voir* **film, musée.**

d (*: *actes ou propos dégoûtants*) ~**s** dreadful *ou* terrible things; **débiter des ~s sur qn** to say dreadful *ou* terrible things about sb.

e (*loc*) **cet individu me fait** ~ that individual disgusts me; **le mensonge me fait** ~ I loathe *ou* detest lying, I have a horror of lying; **la viande me fait** ~ I can't stand *ou* bear meat, I loathe *ou* detest meat; **avoir qch/qn en** ~ to loathe *ou* detest sth/sb; **j'ai ce genre de livre en** ~ I loathe *ou* detest this type of book, I have a horror of this type of book; **prendre qch/qn en** ~ to come to loathe *ou* detest sth/sb; **avoir** ~ **de qch/de faire qch** to loathe *ou* detest sth/doing sth.

horrible [ɔʀibl] **adj** (*effrayant*) *crime, accident, blessure* horrible; (*extrême*) *chaleur, peur* terrible, dreadful; (*très laid*) *chapeau, personne, tableau* horrible, hideous, ghastly*; (*très mauvais*) *temps* terrible, ghastly*, dreadful; *travail* terrible, dreadful.

horriblement [ɔʀibləmɑ̃] **adv** (*de façon effrayante*) horribly; (*extrêmement*) horribly, terribly, dreadfully.

horrifiant, e [ɔʀifjɑ̃, jɑ̃t] **adj** horrifying.

horrifier [ɔʀifje] [7] **vt** to horrify. **elle était horrifiée par la dépense** she was horrified at the expense.

horripilant, e [ɔʀipilɑ̃, ɑ̃t] **adj** trying, exasperating.

horripiler [ɔʀipile] [1] **vt:** ~ **qn** to try sb's patience, exasperate sb.

hors ['ɔʀ] **1 prép a** (*excepté*) except (for), apart from, save (*littér*), but (*seulement avec no one, nothing etc*). (*littér*) ~ **que** save that (*littér*).

b (*dans loc*) **mettre qn ~ la loi** to outlaw sb; **jeter** *ou* **mettre qn ~ de ses gonds** to make sb wild with rage; **St Paul ~ les murs** St Paul's without *ou* outside the walls; **théâtre ~ les murs** suburban theatre; **être présenté ~-concours** to be shown outside the competition (*because of outstanding merit*); **être mis ~-concours** to be declared ineligible to compete, be disqualified; (*fig*) **il est ~-concours** he's in a class of his own.

c (*espace, temps*) ~ **de** (*position*) outside, out of, away from; (*changement de lieu*) out of; **vivre ~ de la ville** to live out of town *ou* outside the town; **vivre ~ de son pays** to live away from *ou* outside one's own country; **le choc l'a projeté ~ de la pièce/de la voiture** the impact threw him out of the room/car; **il est plus agréable d'habiter ~ du centre** it is pleasanter to live away from *ou* outside the centre; ~ **de chez lui/son milieu, il est malheureux comme un poisson ~ de l'eau** he's like a fish out of water when he's away from (his) home/his familiar surroundings; **vivre ~ de son temps/la réalité** to live in a different age/ in a dream world; ~ **de saison** (*lit*) out of season; (*fig*, †: *inopportun*) untimely, out of place; ~ **d'ici!** get out of here!; (*Prov*) ~ **de l'Église, point de salut** without the Church there is no salvation.

d (*fig*) **il est ~ d'affaire** he is out of the wood (*Brit*) *ou* woods (*US*), he's over the worst; **un whisky ~ d'âge** a very old fine whisky; ~ **d'atteinte** (*lit*) out of reach; (*fig*) beyond reach; ~ **d'atteinte de** *projectiles* out of range *ou* reach of; **mettre ~ de combat** to put out of the fight *ou* contest (*Sport*); **être ~ de danger** to be out of danger, be safe; **il est ~ de doute qu'il a raison** he is undoubtedly right, it is beyond doubt that he is right; **mettre qn ~ d'état de nuire** to render sb harmless; ~ **d'haleine** out of breath; ~ **de mesure** *ou* **proportion** out of proportion (*avec* with); ~ **de portée** (*lit*) out of reach; (*fig*) beyond reach; **cette table est ~ de prix** the price of this table is exorbitant *ou* outrageous; **ce magasin est ~ de prix** the prices in this shop are exorbitant *ou* outrageous; ~ **de propos** untimely, inopportune; **c'est ~ de question** it is out of the question; **être ~ de soi** to be beside o.s. (with anger); **cette remarque l'a mise ~ d'elle** she was beside herself at this remark, this remark infuriated her; ~ **d'usage** out of service *ou* action; **mettre ~ d'usage** to put out of action.

2 comp ▸hors barème adj inv off the (salary) scale (*attrib*) **▸hors-bord nm inv** speedboat (*with outboard motor*) **▸hors cadre** (*Admin*) **adj inv** detached, seconded **▸hors champ** (*Ciné, TV*) **adj inv** off-camera (*attrib*) **▸hors circuit adj inv** *appareil* disconnected; *personne* out of the reckoning (*attrib*); **mettre hors circuit** *appareil* to disconnect; *personne* to push aside **▸hors classe adj inv** exceptional **▸hors commerce adj inv** for restricted sale only (*attrib*) **▸hors-cote** (*Bourse*) **adj inv** unlisted, not quoted on the Stock Exchange ◊ **nm** over-the-counter market, unofficial market, off-board market (*US*) **▸hors-d'œuvre nm inv** (*lit*) hors d'œuvre, starter* **▸hors jeu** (*Sport*) **adj inv** *joueur* offside; *ballon* out of play **▸hors-jeu nm inv** offside **▸hors-la-loi nm inv** outlaw **▸hors ligne adj inv, hors pair adj inv** outstanding, unparalleled, matchless **▸hors-piste** (*Ski*) **adj inv, adv** off-piste **▸hors série adj inv** *talent, don* incomparable, outstanding; **une table/machine hors série** a table/machine made to order, a custom-built table/machine **▸hors service adj inv** *appareil* out of order (*attrib*); (*) *personne* shattered*, done in* **▸hors sujet adj inv: votre dissertation est hors sujet** your essay is irrelevant; **faire du hors sujet** to go off the subject **▸hors-taxe adj inv, adv** *boutique, article* duty-free; (*sur facture*) exclusive of VAT; *prix* before tax (*attrib*) **▸hors-texte nm inv** plate **▸hors-tout adj inv: longueur/largeur hors-tout** overall length/width.

hortensia [ɔʀtɑ̃sja] **nm** hydrangea.

horticole [ɔʀtikɔl] **adj** horticultural.

horticulteur, -trice [ɔʀtikyltœʀ, tʀis] **nm,f** horticulturist.

horticulture [ɔʀtikyltyʀ] **nf** horticulture.

hosanna [oza(n)na] **nm** hosanna.

hospice [ɔspis] **nm a** (*hôpital*) home. ~ **de vieillards** old people's home; (*péj*) **mourir à l'~** to die in the poorhouse. **b** [*monastère*] hospice.

hospitalier, -ière [ɔspitalje, jɛʀ] **1 adj a** *services, personnel, médecine* hospital (*épith*). **établissement** ~ hospital. **b** (*accueillant*) hospitable. **2 nm,f a** (*religieux*) **(frère)** ~, **(sœur)** ~**ière** hospitaller. **b** (*infirmier*) nurse.

hospitalisation [ɔspitalizasjɔ̃] **nf** hospitalization. ~ **à domicile** home (medical) care.

hospitaliser [ɔspitalize] [1] **vt** to hospitalize, send to hospital. **malade hospitalisé** in-patient; **10% des malades hospitalisés** 10% of hospital patients *ou* cases.

hospitalisme [ɔspitalism] **nm** institutionalization.

hospitalité [ɔspitalite] **nf** hospitality. **donner l'~ à qn** to give *ou* offer sb hospitality.

hospitalo-universitaire, pl hospitalo-universitaires [ɔspitaloyniveʀsitɛʀ] **adj: centre** ~ teaching hospital.

hostellerie† [ɔstɛlʀi] **nf** hostelry†.

hostie [ɔsti] **nf** (*Rel*) host; (††: *victime*) sacrificial victim.

hostile [ɔstil] **adj** *foule, forces, accueil* hostile (*à* to, towards). ~ **à** *projet etc* opposed *ou* hostile to.

hostilement [ɔstilmɑ̃] **adv** hostilely.

hostilité [ɔstilite] **nf** hostility (*à, envers* to, towards). (*Mil*) **les ~s** hostilities; **ouvrir/reprendre les ~s** to open/re-open hostilities.

hosto* [ɔsto] **nm** hospital.

hot(-)dog, pl hot(-)dogs ['ɔtdɔg] **nm** hot dog.

hôte [ot] **1 nm** (*maître de maison*) host; (†: *aubergiste*) landlord, host; (*Bio*) host. (†, *littér: animal*) ~ **d'un bois/d'un marais** inhabitant of a wood/marsh; *voir* **chambre, table. 2 nmf** (*invité*) guest; (*client*) patron; (*locataire*) occupant. ~ **payant** paying guest.

hôtel [ɔtɛl] **1 nm** hotel. **vivre/coucher à l'~** to live/sleep in a hotel; **aller** *ou* **descendre à l'~** to put up at a hotel; *voir* **maître, rat. 2 comp ▸hôtel-Dieu nm (pl hôtels-Dieu)** general hospital **▸hôtel des impôts** tax office **▸hôtel-meublé nm (pl hôtels-meublés)** lodging house, residential hotel **▸l'hôtel de la Monnaie** ≃ the Mint (*Brit*) **▸hôtel (particulier)** (private) mansion **▸hôtel de passe** hotel used by prostitutes **▸hôtel-restaurant nm (pl hôtels-restaurant)** hotel (with public restaurant) **▸hôtel des ventes** saleroom, salesroom (*US*) **▸hôtel de ville** town hall.

hôtelier, -ière [ɔtəlje, jɛʀ] **1 adj** *industrie, profession* hotel (*épith*); *voir* **école. 2 nm,f** hotelier, hotel-keeper.

hôtellerie [ɔtɛlʀi] **nf** (*auberge*) inn, hostelry†; (*profession*) hotel business; (*matière enseignée*) hotel management. ~ **de plein air** camping and caravanning.

hôtesse [otɛs] **nf** (*maîtresse de maison*) hostess; (†: *aubergiste*) landlady. ~ **(de l'air)** air hostess (*Brit*), stewardess, flight attendant; ~ **(d'accueil)** [*hôtel, bureau*] receptionist; [*exposition, colloque*] hostess.

hotte ['ɔt] **nf** (*panier*) basket (*carried on the back*); [*cheminée*] hood. [*cuisine*] ~ **aspirante** cooker (*Brit*) *ou* range (*US*) hood; **la ~ du Père Noël** Father Christmas's sack.

hottentot, e ['ɔtɑ̃to, ɔt] **1 adj** Hottentot. **2 nm,f: H~(e)** Hottentot.

hou ['u] **excl** [*peur*] boo!; [*honte*] tut-tut!

houblon ['ublɔ̃] **nm** (*plante*) hop; (*comme ingrédient de la bière*) hops.

houblonnière ['ublɔnjɛʀ] **nf** hopfield.

houe ['u] **nf** hoe.

houille ['uj] **nf** coal. ~ **blanche** hydroelectric power; ~ **verte** marine power, wave energy; ~ **grasse/maigre** bituminous/lean coal.

houiller, -ère ['uje, ɛʀ] **1 adj** *bassin, industrie* coal (*épith*); *terrain* coal-bearing. **2 houillère nf** coalmine.

houle ['ul] **nf** swell. **une forte** ~ a heavy swell.

houlette ['ulɛt] **nf** [*pâtre, évêque*] crook; [*jardinier*] trowel, spud. (*fig*) **sous la ~ de** under the leadership of.

houleux, -euse ['ulø, øz] **adj** *mer* stormy; *séance* stormy, turbulent; *salle, foule* tumultuous, turbulent.

houp ['up] **excl = hop.**

houppe ['up] **nf** [*plumes, cheveux*] tuft; [*fils*] tassel. ~ **à poudrer** powder puff.

houppelande ['uplɑ̃d] **nf** (loose-fitting) greatcoat.

houppette ['upɛt] **nf** powder puff.

hourra ['uʀa] **excl** hurrah! **pousser des ~s** to cheer, shout hurrah; **salué par des ~s** greeted by cheers; *voir* **hip.**

houspiller ['uspije] [1] **vt** (*réprimander*) to scold, tell off, tick off* (*Brit*); (†: *malmener*) to hustle.

housse ['us] **nf** (*gén*) cover; [*meubles*] (*pour protéger temporairement*) dust cover; (*pour recouvrir à neuf*) loose cover; (*en tissu élastique*) stretch cover. ~ **de couette** quilt cover; [*habits*] ~ **(penderie)** hanging wardrobe.

houx ['u] **nm** holly.

hovercraft [ɔvœʀkʀaft] **nm** hovercraft.

hoverport [ɔvœʀpɔʀ] **nm** hoverport.

H.S.* [aʃɛs] **adj inv (abrév de hors service)** *appareil, véhicule* out of order (*attrib*), bust* (*attrib*) (*Brit*); *personne* beat* (*attrib*), shattered* (*attrib*) (*Brit*).

H.T, h.t. (abrév de **hors taxe**) *voir* **hors.**

huard*, huart ['ɥaʀ] nm (*Can: oiseau*) diver (*Brit*), loon (*US*).

hublot ['yblo] nm *[bateau]* porthole; *[avion, machine à laver]* window.

huche ['yʃ] nf (*coffre*) chest; (*pétrin*) dough *ou* kneading trough. ~ **à pain** bread bin.

hue ['y] excl gee up! (*fig*) **ils tirent tous à ~ et à dia** they are all pulling in the opposite direction.

huées ['ɥe] nfpl boos, hoots. **sous les ~ de la foule** to the boos of the crowd.

huer ['ɥe] [1] 1 vt to boo. 2 vi *[chouette]* to hoot.

hugolien, -ienne [ygɔljɛ̃, jɛn] adj of Victor Hugo.

huguenot, e ['yg(ə)no, ɔt] adj, nm,f Huguenot.

Hugues ['yg] nm Hugh.

huilage [ɥilaʒ] nm oiling, lubrication.

huile [ɥil] nf a (*liquide*) oil; (*Tech: pétrole*) petroleum, crude (oil). (*Culin*) **cuit à l'~** cooked in oil; ~ **vierge** unrefined olive oil; ~ **de ricin** castor oil; ~ **de table/de graissage/de bain/solaire** salad/lubricating/bath/sun(tan) oil; ~ **d'arachide** groundnut (*Brit*) *ou* peanut (*US*) oil; ~ **de maïs/d'olive/de tournesol** corn/olive/sunflower oil; ~ **de foie de morue** cod-liver oil; ~ **de lin** linseed oil; ~ **de paraffine** *ou* **de vaseline** liquid paraffin; ~ **de coude*** elbow grease*; ~ **pour friture** cooking *ou* frying oil; ~ **essentielle** essential oil; (*fig*) **jeter** *ou* **verser de l'~ sur le feu** to add fuel to the flames *ou* fire; (*fig*) **mettre de l'~ dans les rouages** to oil the wheels (*fig*); (*fig*) **une mer d'~** a glassy sea; *voir* **lampe, saint, tache.**
b (*: *notabilité*) bigwig*, big noise*, big shot*; (*Mil*) brass hat* (*Brit*), brass*. **les ~s** the top brass*, the big shots*.
c (*Peinture*) (*tableau*) oil painting; (*technique*) oil painting, oils. **peint à l'~** painted in oils; *voir* **peinture.**

huiler [ɥile] [1] vt *machine, serrure* to oil, lubricate. **papier huilé** oil-paper; **salade trop huilée** oily salad; (*fig*) **être bien huilé** to go *ou* run smoothly.

huilerie [ɥilʀi] nf (*usine*) oil-works; (*commerce*) oil-trade; (*moulin*) oil-mill.

huileux, -euse [ɥilø, øz] adj *liquide, matière* oily; *aspect, surface* oily, greasy.

huilier [ɥilje] nm (oil and vinegar) cruet, oil and vinegar bottle.

huis [ɥi] nm (††) door. (*Jur*) **à ~ clos** in camera; (*Jur*) **ordonner le ~ clos** to order proceedings to be held in camera; (*fig*) **les négociations se poursuivent à ~ clos** the talks are continuing behind closed doors.

huisserie [ɥisʀi] nf *[porte]* doorframe; *[fenêtre]* window frame; **les ~s** the woodwork.

huissier [ɥisje] nm a (*appariteur*) usher. b ~ **(de justice)** ≃ bailiff.

huit ['ɥi(t)] 1 adj inv eight; *pour loc voir* **six.** 2 nm inv (*chiffre, nombre, Cartes*) eight; (*figure*) figure of eight. **lundi/samedi en ~** a week on (*Brit*) *ou* from (*US*) Monday/Saturday, Monday/Saturday week* (*Brit*); *voir* **grand.** 3 comp ▸ **huit jours** nmpl (*une semaine*) a week; **dans huit jours** in a week; **donner ses huit jours à un domestique** to give a servant a week's notice ▸ **huit reflets** nm top hat.

huitain ['ɥitɛ̃] nm octet, octave.

huitaine ['ɥitɛn] nf eight or so, about eight. **dans une ~ (de jours)** in a week or so; (*Jur*) **son cas a été remis à ~** the hearing has been postponed for one week.

huitante ['ɥitɑ̃t] adj inv (*Suisse*) eighty.

huitième ['ɥitjɛm] 1 adj, nmf eighth. **la ~ merveille du monde** the eighth wonder of the world; *pour autres loc voir* **sixième.** 2 nf (*Scol*) class 8 (*penultimate class of primary school*), fifth grade (*US*). 3 nmpl (*Sport*) **~s de finale** second round in a five-round knock-out competition; **être en ~s de finale** to be in the last sixteen; **jouer les ~s de finale** to play the second round (*in a five-round knockout competition*).

huitièmement ['ɥitjɛmmɑ̃] adv eighthly.

huître [ɥitʀ] nf oyster. ~ **perlière** pearl oyster; (*fig*) **se (re)fermer comme une ~** to clam up.

huîtrier, -ière [ɥitʀije, ijɛʀ] 1 nm (*oiseau*) oyster catcher. 2 adj *industrie* oyster (*épith*).

hulotte ['ylɔt] nf tawny owl.

hululement ['ylylmɑ̃] nm hooting, screeching.

hululer ['ylyle] [1] vi to hoot, screech.

hum ['œm] excl hem!, h'm!

humain, e [ymɛ̃, ɛn] 1 adj (*gén*) human; (*compatissant, compréhensif*) humane. **justice/espèce/condition ~e** human justice/race/condition; **il n'avait plus figure ~e** he was disfigured beyond recognition; **se montrer ~** to show humanity, act humanely (*envers* towards); **il s'est sauvé — c'est ~** he ran away – it's only human; *voir* **être, géographie, nature, respect, science, voix** *etc.* 2 nm a (*Philos*) **l'~** the human element. b (*être humain*) human (being). **les ~s** humans, human beings.

humainement [ymɛnmɑ̃] adv (*avec bonté*) humanely; (*par l'homme*) humanly. **ce n'est pas ~ possible** it is not humanly possible; **~, on ne peut pas le renvoyer** we can't in all humanity dismiss him.

humanisation [ymanizasjɔ̃] nf humanization.

humaniser [ymanize] [1] 1 vt *doctrine* to humanize; *conditions* to make more humane, humanize. 2 **s'humaniser** vpr *[personne]* to become more human; *[architecture]* to become less forbidding *ou* impersonal.

humanisme [ymanism] nm humanism.

humaniste [ymanist] 1 adj humanist, humanistic. 2 nmf humanist.

humanitaire [ymanitɛʀ] adj humanitarian.

humanitarisme [ymanitaʀism] nm (*péj*) unrealistic humanitarianism.

humanitariste [ymanitaʀist] 1 adj (*péj*) unrealistically humanitarian. 2 nmf unrealistic humanitarian.

humanité [ymanite] nf a (*le genre humain*) **l'~** humanity, mankind. b (*bonté*) humaneness, humanity. **geste d'~** humane gesture. c (*Philos, Rel*) humanity. d (*Scol*) **les ~s** the classics, the humanities.

humanoïde [ymanɔid] nm humanoid.

humble [œ̃bl(ə)] adj (*modeste, pauvre*) humble; (*obscur*) humble, lowly. **d'~ naissance** of humble *ou* lowly birth *ou* origins; **à mon ~ avis** in my humble opinion.

humblement [œ̃bləmɑ̃] adv humbly.

humectage [ymɛktaʒ] nm (*voir* **humecter**) dampening; moistening.

humecter [ymɛkte] [1] vt *linge, herbe* to dampen; *front* to moisten, dampen. **s'~ le gosier*** to wet one's whistle*; **s'~ les lèvres** to moisten one's lips; **ses yeux s'humectèrent** his eyes filled with tears, tears welled in his eyes.

humer ['yme] [1] vt *plat* to smell; *air, parfum* to inhale, breathe in.

humérus [ymeʀys] nm humerus.

humeur [ymœʀ] nf a (*disposition momentanée*) mood, humour. **mettre/être de bonne ~** to put/be in a good mood *ou* humour, put/be in good spirits; **travailler dans la bonne ~** to work contentedly; **la bonne ~ régnait dans la maison** contentment reigned in the house; **être de mauvaise ~** to be in a bad mood; **se sentir d'~ à travailler** to feel in the mood for working *ou* for work *ou* in the mood to work; **il est d'~ massacrante, il est d'une ~ de dogue** *ou* **de chien** he's in a rotten* *ou* foul temper *ou* mood; ~ **noire** black mood; **roman/film plein de bonne ~** good-humoured novel/film, novel/film full of good humour; *voir* **saute.**
b (*tempérament*) temper, temperament. **être d'~** *ou* **avoir l'~ batailleuse** to be fiery-tempered; **être d'~ maussade** to be sullen, be a sullen type; **il est d'~ inégale/égale** he is moody/even-tempered; **il y a incompatibilité d'~ entre eux** they are temperamentally unsuited *ou* incompatible; **un enfant plein de bonne ~** a sunny-natured child, a child with a cheerful *ou* sunny nature.
c (*irritation*) bad temper, ill humour. **passer son ~ sur qn** to take out *ou* vent one's bad temper *ou* ill humour on sb; **accès** *ou* **mouvement d'~** fit of (bad) temper *ou* ill humour; **geste d'~** bad-tempered gesture; **agir par ~** to act in a fit of (bad) temper *ou* ill humour; **dire qch avec ~** to say sth ill-humouredly *ou* testily (*littér*); (*littér*) **cela lui donne de l'~** that makes him ill-humoured *ou* bad-tempered.
d (*Méd*) secretion. ~ **aqueuse/vitreuse** *ou* **vitrée de l'œil** aqueous/vitreous humour of the eye; **les ~s††** the humours††.

humide [ymid] adj *mains, front, terre* moist, damp; *torchon, habits, mur, poudre, herbe* damp; *local, climat, région, chaleur* humid; (*plutôt froid*) damp; *tunnel, cave* dank, damp; *saison, route* wet. **yeux ~s d'émotion** eyes moist with emotion; **elle lui lança un regard ~** she looked at him with moist eyes; **temps lourd et ~** muggy weather; **mains ~s et collantes** clammy hands.

humidificateur [ymidifikatœʀ] nm *air* humidifier.

humidification [ymidifikasjɔ̃] nf humidification.

humidifier [ymidifje] [7] vt *air* to humidify; *terre* to moisten; *linge* to moisten, dampen.

humidité [ymidite] nf *[air, climat]* humidity; (*plutôt froide*) dampness; *[sol, mur]* dampness; *[tunnel, cave]* dankness, dampness. ~ **(atmosphérique)** humidity (of the atmosphere); **air saturé d'~** air saturated with moisture; **dégâts causés par l'~** damage caused by (the) damp; **traces d'~ sur le mur** traces of moisture *ou* of damp on the wall; **taches d'~** damp patches, patches of damp; (*sur emballage*) **"craint l'~", "à protéger de l'~"** "to be kept dry", "keep in a dry place".

humiliant, e [ymiljɑ̃, jɑ̃t] adj humiliating.

humiliation [ymiljasjɔ̃] nf (*gén*) humiliation; (*Rel*) humbling (*NonC*).

humilier [ymilje] [7] vt (*rabaisser*) to humiliate; (††, *Rel: rendre humble*) to humble. **s'~ devant** to humble o.s. before.

humilité [ymilite] nf (*modestie*) humility, humbleness. **ton d'~** humble tone.

humoral, e, mpl **-aux** [ymɔʀal, o] adj humoral.

humoriste [ymɔʀist] nmf humorist.

humoristique [ymɔʀistik] adj humorous; *voir* **dessin.**

humour [ymuʀ] nm humour. ~ **noir** black humour; **manquer d'~** to have no sense of humour; **avoir beaucoup d'~** to have a good *ou* great sense of humour; **faire de l'~** to make jokes.

humus [ymys] nm humus.

Hun ['œ̃] nm (*Hist*) Hun.

hune ['yn] nf top. **mât de ~** topmast; **grande ~** maintop.

hunier ['ynje] nm topsail.

huppe ['yp] nf (*oiseau*) hoopoe; (*crête*) crest.

huppé, e ['ype] adj (*Orn*) crested; (*: *riche*) posh* (*Brit*), classy*.

hure ['yʀ] nf (*tête*) head. ~ **de sanglier** boar's head; (*Charcuterie*) **une tranche de ~** a slice of pork brawn.

hurlant, e ['yRlɑ̃, ɑ̃t] adj *foule* howling; *couleurs* clashing. **une confession ~e de vérité** a confession which has the ring of truth in every line.

hurlement ['yRləmɑ̃] nm (*voir* **hurler**) roaring (*NonC*), roar; yelling (*NonC*), yell; howling (*NonC*), howl; bellowing (*NonC*), bellow; squealing (*NonC*), squeal; wailing (*NonC*), wail.

hurler ['yRle] 1 **1** vi **a** *[personne]* (*de peur*) to shriek, scream; (*de douleur*) to scream, yell (out), howl; (*de colère*) to roar, bellow; *[foule]* to roar, yell (*de* with, in). **~ comme une bête qu'on égorge** to howl like a wounded animal. **b** *[chien]* to howl; *[vent]* to howl, roar; *[freins]* to squeal; *[sirène]* to wail; *[radio]* to blare. **faire ~ sa télé** to have one's TV going full blast*; **chien qui hurle à la lune** *ou* **à la mort** dog baying at the moon; **~ avec les loups** to follow the pack *ou* crowd (*fig*). **c** (*jurer*) *[couleurs]* to clash. **ce tableau bleu sur le mur vert, ça hurle!** that blue picture really clashes with the green wall. **2** vt to yell, roar, bellow.

hurleur ['yRlœR] adj m, nm: **(singe) ~** howler (monkey).

hurluberlu, e [yRlybɛRly] nm,f crank.

huron, -onne ['yRɔ̃, ɔn] adj, nm,f Huron. **le lac H~** Lake Huron.

hurrah ['uRa, huRa] excl = **hourra**.

husky, pl **huskies** ['œski] nm husky.

hussard ['ysaR] nm hussar.

hussarde ['ysaRd] nf: **à la ~** roughly.

hutte ['yt] nf hut.

hyacinthe [jasɛ̃t] nf (*pierre*) hyacinth, jacinth; (†: *fleur*) hyacinth.

hybridation [ibRidasjɔ̃] nf hybridization.

hybride [ibRid] adj, nm hybrid.

hybrider [ibRide] 1 vt to hybridize.

hybridisme [ibRidism] nm, **hybridité** [ibRidite] nf hybridism, hybridity.

hydracide [idRasid] nm hydracid.

hydratant, e [idRatɑ̃, ɑ̃t] **1** adj moisturizing. **2** nm moisturizer.

hydratation [idRatasjɔ̃] nf (*Chim, Méd*) hydration; *[peau]* moisturizing.

hydrate [idRat] nm hydrate. **~ de carbone** carbohydrate.

hydrater [idRate] 1 **1** vt (*gén*) to hydrate; *peau* to moisturize. **2** **s'hydrater** vpr to become hydrated.

hydraulique [idRolik] **1** adj hydraulic. **énergie ~** hydraulic energy; **station ~** waterworks (*sg*); (*Aut*) **circuit ~** hydraulic circuit; **freins ~s** hydraulic brakes. **2** nf hydraulics (*sg*).

hydravion [idRavjɔ̃] nm seaplane, hydroplane.

hydre [idR(ə)] nf hydra.

hydrocarbure [idRokaRbyR] nm hydrocarbon. **~s saturés/insaturés** saturated/unsaturated hydrocarbons.

hydrocéphale [idRɔsefal] **1** adj hydrocephalic, hydrocephalous. **2** nmf person suffering from hydrocephalus.

hydrocéphalie [idRɔsefali] nf hydrocephalus.

hydrocortisone [idRokɔRtizɔn] nf hydrocortisone.

hydrocution [idRɔkysjɔ̃] nf (*Méd*) immersion syncope.

hydrodynamique [idRodinamik] **1** adj hydrodynamic. **2** nf hydrodynamics (*sg*).

hydro(-)électricité [idRoelɛktRisite] nf hydroelectricity.

hydro(-)électrique [idRoelɛktRik] adj hydroelectric.

hydrofoil [idRofɔjl] nm hydrofoil (*boat*).

hydrofuge [idRɔfyʒ] adj *peinture* damp-proofing, anti-damp.

hydrogénation [idRɔʒenasjɔ̃] nf hydrogenation.

hydrogène [idRɔʒɛn] nm hydrogen. **~ lourd** heavy hydrogen; *voir* **bombe**.

hydrogéner [idRɔʒene] 6 vt to hydrogenate, hydrogenize.

hydroglisseur [idRoglisœR] nm hydroplane, jet-foil.

hydrographe [idRɔgRaf] nm hydrographer.

hydrographie [idRɔgRafi] nf hydrography.

hydrographique [idRɔgRafik] adj hydrographic(al).

hydrologie [idRɔlɔʒi] nf hydrology.

hydrologique [idRɔlɔʒik] adj hydrologic(al).

hydrologiste [idRɔlɔʒist] nmf, **hydrologue** [idRɔlɔg] nmf hydrologist.

hydrolyse [idRɔliz] nf hydrolysis.

hydrolyser [idRɔlize] 1 vt to hydrolyse.

hydromel [idRɔmɛl] nm mead.

hydromètre [idRɔmɛtR] nm (*Tech*) hydrometer.

hydrométrie [idRɔmetRi] nf hydrometry.

hydrométrique [idRɔmetRik] adj hydrometric(al).

hydrophile [idRɔfil] adj *lentilles cornéennes* hydrophilic; *voir* **coton**.

hydrophobe [idRɔfɔb] adj, nmf hydrophobic.

hydrophobie [idRɔfɔbi] nf hydrophobia.

hydropique [idRɔpik] **1** adj dropsical, hydropic(al). **2** nmf person suffering from dropsy.

hydropisie [idRɔpizi] nf dropsy.

hydroptère [idRɔptɛR] nm hydrofoil (*boat*).

hydrosphère [idRɔsfɛR] nf hydrosphere.

hydrostatique [idRɔstatik] **1** adj hydrostatic. **2** nf hydrostatics (*sg*).

hydrothérapie [idRoteRapi] nf (*traitement*) hydrotherapy; (*science*) hydrotherapeutics (*sg*).

hydrothérapique [idRoteRapik] adj (*voir* **hydrothérapie**) hydrotherapic; hydrotherapeutic.

hydroxyde [idRɔksid] nm hydroxide.

hyène [jɛn] nf hyena.

Hygiaphone [iʒjafɔn] nm ® Hygiaphone ®.

hygiène [iʒjɛn] nf hygiene; (*science*) hygienics (*sg*), hygiene; (*Scol*) health education. **ça manque d'~** it's unhygienic; **~ corporelle** personal hygiene; **~ mentale/publique** mental/public health; **~ du travail** industrial hygiene; **~ alimentaire** food hygiene; **pour une meilleure ~ de vie** for a healthier life; **avoir de l'~** to be fastidious about one's personal hygiene; **n'avoir aucune ~** to have no sense of hygiene.

hygiénique [iʒjenik] adj hygienic. **promenade ~** constitutional (walk); *voir* **papier, seau, serviette**.

hygiéniste [iʒjenist] nmf hygienist.

hygromètre [igRɔmɛtR] nm hygrometer.

hygrométrie [igRɔmetRi] nf hygrometry.

hygrométrique [igRɔmetRik] adj hygrometric.

hygroscope [igRɔskɔp] nm hygroscope.

hygrostat [igRɔsta] nm hygrostat.

hymen [imɛn] nm (*littér: mariage*) marriage; (*Anat*) hymen.

hyménée [imene] nm marriage.

hyménoptère [imenɔptɛR] nm: **~s** Hymenoptera.

hymne [imn] nm (*Littérat, Rel*) hymn. (*fig*) **son discours était un ~ à la liberté** his speech was a hymn to liberty; **~ national** national anthem.

hypallage [ipa(l)laʒ] nf hypallage.

hyper... [ipɛR] préf hyper... .

hyperacidité [ipɛRasidite] nf hyperacidity.

hyperbare [ipɛRbaR] adj hyperbaric.

hyperbole [ipɛRbɔl] nf (*Math*) hyperbola; (*Littérat*) hyperbole.

hyperbolique [ipɛRbɔlik] adj (*Math, Littérat*) hyperbolic.

hypercorrect, e [ipɛRkɔRɛkt] adj (*Ling*) hypercorrect.

hypercorrection [ipɛRkɔRɛksjɔ̃] nf (*Ling*) hypercorrection.

hyperémotivité [ipɛRemɔtivite] nf excess emotionality.

hyperesthésie [ipɛRɛstezi] nf hyperaesthesia.

hyperfocal, e, mpl **-aux** [ipɛRfɔkal, o] adj hyperfocal.

hyperglycémie [ipɛRglisemi] nf hyperglycaemia.

hyperkinétique [ipɛRkinetik] adj hyperkinetic.

hypermarché [ipɛRmaRʃe] nm hypermarket, superstore.

hypermétrope [ipɛRmetRɔp] adj long-sighted, hypermetropic (*SPÉC*).

hypermétropie [ipɛRmetRɔpi] nf long-sightedness, hypermetropia (*SPÉC*).

hypernerveux, -euse [ipɛRnɛRvø, øz] adj over-excitable.

hypernervosité [ipɛRnɛRvozite] nf over-excitability.

hyperonyme [ipeRɔnim] nm superordinate.

hyperréalisme [ipɛRRealism] nm hyperrealism.

hypersensibilité [ipɛRsɑ̃sibilite] nf hypersensitivity, hypersensitiveness.

hypersensible [ipɛRsɑ̃sibl] adj hypersensitive.

hypertendu, e [ipɛRtɑ̃dy] adj suffering from high blood pressure, suffering from hypertension (*SPÉC*).

hypertension [ipɛRtɑ̃sjɔ̃] nf high blood pressure, hypertension (*SPÉC*). **faire de l'~** to suffer from *ou* have high blood pressure.

hyperthyroïdie [ipɛRtiRɔidi] nf hyperthyroidism.

hypertrophie [ipɛRtRɔfi] nf hypertrophy.

hypertrophier vt, **s'hypertrophier** vpr [ipɛRtRɔfje] 7 to hypertrophy.

hypertrophique [ipɛRtRɔfik] adj hypertrophic.

hypervitaminose [ipɛRvitaminoz] nf hypervitaminosis.

hypnose [ipnoz] nf hypnosis. **sous ~, en état d'~** under hypnosis.

hypnotique [ipnɔtik] adj (*lit*) hypnotic; (*fig*) hypnotic, mesmeric, mesmerizing.

hypnotiser [ipnɔtize] 1 vt (*lit*) to hypnotize; (*fig*) to hypnotize, mesmerize.

hypnotiseur [ipnɔtizœR] nm hypnotist.

hypnotisme [ipnɔtism] nm hypnotism.

hypo... [ipɔ] préf hypo... .

hypoallergénique [ipoalɛRʒenik], **hypoallergique** [ipoalɛRʒik] adj hypoallergenic.

hypo-cagne, pl **hypo-cagnes** [ipɔkaɲ] nf *first year of two-year preparatory course for the arts section of the École normale supérieure*.

hypocalorique [ipokalɔRik] adj *aliment* low-calorie (*épith*).

hypocentre [iposɑ̃tR] nm hypocentre.

hypocondriaque [ipɔkɔ̃dRijak] **1** adj (*Méd*) hypochondriac; (*mélancolique*) gloomy. **2** nmf hypochondriac; gloomy type.

hypocondrie [ipɔkɔ̃dRi] nf hypochondria.

hypocrisie [ipɔkRizi] nf hypocrisy.

hypocrite [ipɔkRit] **1** adj hypocritical. **2** nmf hypocrite.

hypocritement [ipɔkRitmɑ̃] adv hypocritically.

hypodermique [ipɔdɛRmik] adj hypodermic.

hypogastre [ipɔgastR] nm hypogastrium.

hypoglosse [ipɔglɔs] adj hypoglossal.

hypoglycémie [ipoglisemi] nf hypoglycaemia.

hypo-khâgne, pl **hypo-khâgnes** [ipɔkaɲ] nf = **hypo-cagne**.

hyponyme [ipɔnim] nm hyponym.

hypophyse [ipɔfiz] nf pituitary gland, hypophysis (*SPÉC*).

hyposodé, e [iposɔde] adj low-salt (*épith*), low in salt (*attrib*).
hypostase [ipɔstɑz] nf (*Rel*) hypostasis.
hypo-taupe, pl **hypo-taupes** [ipotop] nf *first year of two-year preparatory course for the science section of the Grandes Écoles.*
hypotendu, e [ipotɑ̃dy] adj suffering from low blood pressure, suffering from hypotension (*SPÉC*)
hypotension [ipotɑ̃sjɔ̃] nf low blood pressure, hypotension (*SPÉC*).
hypoténuse [ipɔtenyz] nf hypotenuse.
hypothalamus [ipɔtalamys] nm hypothalamus.
hypothécable [ipɔtekabl] adj mortgageable.
hypothécaire [ipɔtekɛʀ] adj hypothecary. **garantie ~** mortgage security; **prêt ~** mortgage loan.
hypothèque [ipɔtɛk] nf mortgage.
hypothéquer [ipɔteke] 6 vt *maison* to mortgage; *créance* to secure (by mortgage); (*fig*) *avenir* to sign away.
hypothermie [ipɔtɛʀmi] nf hypothermia.
hypothèse [ipɔtɛz] nf hypothesis, surmise, assumption. **émettre l'~ que** ... to theorize that ..., make the assumption that ...; **l'~ du suicide n'a pas été écartée** the possibility of suicide has not been ruled out; **en toute ~** in any case, no matter what happens; **dans l'~ où** on the assumption that; **dans la meilleure des ~s** at an optimistic estimate; **~ de travail** working hypothesis; **je le pense mais ce n'est qu'une ~** I think so but it's only a hypothesis *ou* I'm just hypothesizing; **~ d'école** purely hypothetical case.
hypothétique [ipɔtetik] adj hypothetical. (*Jur*) **cas ~** moot case.
hypothétiquement [ipɔtetikmɑ̃] adv hypothetically.
hypovitaminose [ipovitaminoz] nf hypovitaminosis.
hysope [izɔp] nf hyssop.
hystérectomie [isteʀɛktɔmi] nf hysterectomy.
hystérie [isteʀi] nf hysteria. **~ collective** mass hysteria.
hystérique [isteʀik] 1 adj hysterical. 2 nmf (*Méd*) hysteric; (*péj*) hysterical sort.
hystérographie [isteʀɔgʀafi] nf hysterography.
Hz (**abrév de hertz**) Hz.

I

I, i [i] nm (*lettre*) I, i; *voir* **droit**[2], **point**[1].
iambe [jɑ̃b] nm (*Littérat*) (*pied*) iambus, iambic; (*vers, poème*) iambic.
iambique [jɑ̃bik] adj iambic.
IAO [iao] nf (abrév de **ingénierie assistée par ordinateur**) CAE.
ibère [ibɛʀ] 1 adj Iberian. 2 nmf: **I~** Iberian.
ibérique [ibeʀik] adj Iberian. **la péninsule I~** the Iberian Peninsula.
ibid. [ibid] adv, **ibidem** [ibidɛm] adv ibid., ibidem.
ibis [ibis] nm ibis.
Ibiza [ibiza] nf Ibiza.
Icare [ikaʀ] nm Icarus.
iceberg [ajsbɛʀg] nm iceberg; *voir* **partie**.
icelui [isəlɥi], **icelle** [isɛl], pl **iceux** [isø], **icelles** [isɛl] pron (††, *Jur, hum*) = **celui-ci, celle-ci, ceux-ci, celles-ci**.
ichtyologie [iktjɔlɔʒi] nf ichthyology.
ichtyologique [iktjɔlɔʒik] adj ichthyologic(al).
ichtyologiste [iktjɔlɔʒist] nmf ichthyologist.
ici [isi] adv a (*spatial*) here. **~!** (*à un chien*) here!; **loin/près d'~** far from/near here; **il y a 10 km d'~ à Paris** it's 10 km from here to Paris; **c'est à 10 minutes d'~** it's 10 minutes away (from here); **passez par ~** come this way; **par ~ s'il vous plaît** this way please; **~ même** on this very spot, in this very place; **c'est ~ que** this is the place where, it is (*ou* was) here that; **~ on est un peu isolé** we're a bit cut off (out) here; **le bus vient jusqu'~** *ou* **s'arrête ~** the bus comes as far as this *ou* this far.
b (*temporel*) **d'~ demain/la fin de la semaine** by tomorrow/the end of the week; **d'~ peu** before (very) long, shortly; **d'~ là** between now and then, before then, in the meantime; **jusqu'~** (up) until now; (*dans le passé*) (up) until then; **d'~ à ce qu'il se retrouve en prison, ça ne va pas être long** it won't be long before he lands up in jail (again); **d'~ à ce qu'il accepte, ça risque de faire long** it might be (quite) some time before he says yes; **le projet lui plaît, mais ~ à ce qu'il accepte!** he likes the plan, but there's a difference between just liking it and actually agreeing to it!; **d'~ à l'an 2000** by the year 2000.
c (*loc*) **ils sont d'~/ne sont pas d'~** they are/aren't local *ou* from around here *ou* from this area; **les gens d'~** the local people; **je vois ça d'~!*** I can just see that!; **tu vois d'~ la situation/sa tête!*** you can (just) imagine the situation/the look on his face!; **vous êtes ~ chez vous** please make yourself (quite) at home; **~ présent** here present; **"~ Alain Proviste"** (*au téléphone*) "Alain Proviste speaking *ou* here"; (*à la radio*) "this is Alain Proviste"; **"~ Radio Luxembourg"** "this is Radio Luxembourg"; **~ et là** here and there; (*Rel, hum*) **~-bas** here below; **les choses d'~-bas** things of this world *ou* of this life; **la vie d'~-bas** life here below; (*au marché*) **par ~, Mesdames, par ~ les belles laitues!** this way, ladies, lovely lettuces this way! *ou* over here!; **par ~ la sortie** this way out; (*dans le coin*) **par ~** around here.
icône [ikon] nf (*peinture, Ordin*) icon.
iconoclasme [ikɔnɔklasm] nm iconoclasm.
iconoclaste [ikɔnɔklast] 1 nmf iconoclast. 2 adj iconoclastic.
iconographe [ikɔnɔgʀaf] nmf iconographer.
iconographie [ikɔnɔgʀafi] nf (*étude*) iconography; (*images*) (collection of) illustrations.
iconographique [ikɔnɔgʀafik] adj iconographic(al).
ictère [iktɛʀ] nm icterus.
id. (abrév de **idem**) ditto, idem.
Idaho [idao] nm Idaho.
idéal, e, mpl **-als** *ou* **-aux** [ideal, o] 1 adj (*imaginaire*) ideal; (*rêvé, parfait*) *maison, vacances* ideal; *perfection* absolute. 2 nm a (*modèle, aspiration*) ideal; (*valeurs morales*) ideals. **il n'a pas d'~** he has no ideal in life, he hasn't any ideals. b (*le mieux*) **l'~ serait qu'elle l'épouse** the ideal thing *ou* solution would be for her to marry him, it would be ideal if she were to marry him *ou* if she married him; **dans l'~ c'est ce qu'il faudrait faire** ideally that's what we should do.
idéalement [idealmɑ̃] adv ideally.
idéalisation [idealizasjɔ̃] nf idealization.
idéaliser [idealize] 1 vt to idealize.
idéalisme [idealism] nm idealism.
idéaliste [idealist] 1 adj (*gén*) idealistic; (*Philos*) idealist. 2 nmf idealist.
idée [ide] 1 nf a (*concept*) idea. **l'~ de nombre/de beauté** the idea of number/of beauty; **l'~ que les enfants se font du monde** the idea *ou* concept children have of the world; **c'est lui qui a eu le premier l'~ d'un moteur à réaction** it was he who first thought of *ou* conceived the idea of the jet engine, he was the first to hit upon the idea of the jet engine.
b (*pensée*) idea. **il a eu l'~** *ou* **l'~ lui est venue de faire** he had the idea *ou* hit upon the idea of doing, the idea occurred to him to do; **l'~ ne lui viendrait jamais de nous aider** it would never occur to him to help us, he would never think of helping us; **ça m'a donné l'~ qu'il ne viendrait pas** that made me think that he wouldn't come; **à l'~ de faire qch/de qch** at the idea *ou* thought of doing sth/of sth; **tout est dans l'~ qu'on s'en fait** it's all in the mind; **avoir une ~ derrière la tête** to have something at the back of one's mind; *voir* **changer, haut, ordre**[1] *etc*.
c (*illusion*) idea. **tu te fais des ~s** you're imagining things; **ne te fais pas des ~s** don't get ideas into your head; **ça pourrait lui donner des ~s** it might give him ideas *ou* put ideas into his head; **quelle ~!** the (very) idea!, what an idea!; **il a de ces ~s!** the ideas he has!, the things he thinks up!; **on n'a pas ~ (de faire des choses pareilles)!*** it's incredible (doing things like that)!
d (*suggestion*) idea. **son ~ est meilleure** his idea is better; **quelques ~s pour votre jardin/vos menus** a few ideas *ou* suggestions for your garden/for meals to make; **de nouvelles ~s-vacances/~s-rangement** some new holiday/storage tips *ou* hints.
e (*vague notion*) idea. **donner à qn/se faire une ~ des difficultés** to give sb/get an *ou* some idea of the difficulties; **avez-vous une ~** *ou* **la moindre ~ de l'heure/de son âge?** have you got any idea of the time/of his age?; **je n'en ai pas la moindre ~** I haven't the faintest *ou* least *ou* slightest idea; **vous n'avez pas ~ de sa bêtise** you have no idea how stupid he is, you have no conception of his stupidity; **j'ai (comme une) ~ qu'il n'acceptera pas** I (somehow) have an idea *ou* a feeling *ou* I have a sort of feeling that he won't accept.
f (*opinion*) **~s** ideas, views; **~s politiques/religieuses** political/religious ideas *ou* views; **avoir des ~s avancées** to have progressive ideas; **ce n'est pas dans ses ~s** he doesn't hold with these views; **avoir des ~s larges/étroites** to be broad-minded/narrow-minded; (*péj*) **avoir les ~s courtes** to have limited ideas, not to think very deeply.
g (*goût, conception personnelle*) ideas. **juger selon** *ou* **à son ~** to judge in accordance with one's own ideas; **agir selon** *ou* **à son ~** to act *ou* do as one sees fit; **il n'en fait qu'à son ~** he does just as he likes; **pour être décorateur il faut de l'~** *ou* **un peu d'~** to be a decorator you have to have some imagination *ou* a few ideas; **il y a de l'~*** (*dessin, projet*) there's something in it; (*décoration intérieure*) it's got (a certain) something.
h (*esprit*) **avoir dans l'~ que** to have an idea that, have it in one's mind that; **il a dans l'~ de partir au Mexique** he's thinking of going to Mexico; **ça m'est sorti de l'~** it went clean* *ou* right out of my mind *ou* head; **cela ne lui viendrait jamais à l'~** it would never occur to him *ou* enter his head; **on ne m'ôtera pas de l'~ qu'il a menti** you won't get me to believe that he didn't lie; **il s'est mis dans l'~ de faire** he took *ou* got it into his head to do.
2 comp ►**idée fixe** idée fixe, obsession ►**idée-force** nf (pl **idées-forces**) strong point, key idea ►**idée de génie, idée lumineuse** brilliant idea, brainwave ►**idées noires** black *ou* gloomy thoughts ►**idée reçue** generally accepted idea.
idem [idɛm] adv ditto, idem. **il a mauvais caractère et son frère ~*** he's bad-tempered and so is his brother *ou* and his brother's the same; **une bière — ~ pour moi*** a beer – (the) same for me.
identifiable [idɑ̃tifjabl] adj identifiable.
identificateur [idɑ̃tifikatœʀ] nm (*Ling, Ordin*) identifier.
identification [idɑ̃tifikasjɔ̃] nf identification (*à, avec* with).

identifier [idɑ̃tifje] 7 1 vt (*reconnaître*) to identify. (*assimiler à*) ~ **qch/qn à** *ou* **avec** *ou* **et** to identify sth/sb with. 2 **s'identifier** vpr: **s'~ à** (*se mettre dans la peau de*) *personnage, héros* to identify with; (*être l'équivalent de*) to identify o.s. with, become identified with.

identique [idɑ̃tik] adj identical (*à* to). **elle reste toujours ~ à elle-même** she never changes, she's always the same.

identiquement [idɑ̃tikmɑ̃] adv identically.

identité [idɑ̃tite] nf a (*similarité*) identity, similarity; (*Math, Psych: égalité*) identity. **une ~ de goûts les rapprocha** (their) similar tastes brought them together. b (*Admin*) identity. **~ d'emprunt** assumed *ou* borrowed identity; **vérification/papiers d'~** identity check/papers; **l'I~ judiciaire** ≃ the Criminal Records Office; *voir* **carte, pièce.**

idéogramme [ideɔgʀam] nm ideogram.

idéographie [ideɔgʀafi] nf ideography.

idéographique [ideɔgʀafik] adj ideographic(al).

idéologie [ideɔlɔʒi] nf ideology.

idéologique [ideɔlɔʒik] adj ideological.

idéologue [ideɔlɔg] nmf ideologist.

ides [id] nfpl (*Antiq*) ides. **les ~ de mars** the ides of March.

idiolecte [idjɔlɛkt] nm idiolect.

idiomatique [idjɔmatik] adj idiomatic. **expression ~** idiom, idiomatic expression.

idiome [idjom] nm (*langage*) idiom.

idiosyncrasie [idjosɛ̃kʀazi] nf idiosyncrasy.

idiot, e [idjo, idjɔt] 1 adj *action, personne, histoire, erreur* idiotic, stupid; *accident* stupid; (†: *Méd*) idiotic. 2 nm,f (*gén*) idiot, fool; (†: *Méd*) idiot. **ne fais pas l'~*** (*n'agis pas bêtement*) don't be an idiot *ou* a fool; (*ne simule pas la bêtise*) stop acting stupid*; **l'~ du village** the village idiot; **dis-le moi, je ne veux pas mourir ~*** tell me, I don't want to go to my grave without knowing *ou* I don't want to die in ignorance; **bronzer/manger ~*** to do nothing but sunbathe/eat.

idiotement [idjɔtmɑ̃] adv idiotically, stupidly, foolishly.

idiotie [idjɔsi] nf a *[action, personne]* idiocy, stupidity; (*Méd*) idiocy. b (*action*) idiotic *ou* stupid *ou* foolish thing to do; (*parole*) idiotic *ou* stupid *ou* foolish thing to say; (*livre, film*) rubbish (*NonC*) (*Brit*), trash (*NonC*). **ne va pas voir cette ~** *ou* **de telles ~s** don't go and see such rubbish *ou* such an idiotic *ou* such a stupid film (*ou* play *etc*); **et ne dis/fais pas d'~s** and don't say/do anything stupid *ou* idiotic.

idiotisme [idjɔtism] nm idiom, idiomatic phrase.

idoine [idwan] adj (*Jur, hum: approprié*) appropriate, fitting.

idolâtre [idɔlɑtʀ] 1 adj (*Rel, fig*) idolatrous (*de* of). 2 nm (*Rel*) idolater. 3 nf (*Rel*) idolatress.

idolâtrer [idɔlɑtʀe] 1 vt to idolize.

idolâtrie [idɔlɑtʀi] nf (*Rel, fig*) idolatry.

idole [idɔl] nf (*Rel, fig*) idol.

IDS [ideɛs] nf (abrév de **initiative de défense stratégique**) SDI.

idylle [idil] nf (*poème*) idyll; (*amour*) romance, idyll.

idyllique [idilik] adj idyllic.

i.e. (abrév de **id est**) i.e.

if [if] nm (*arbre*) yew (tree); (*bois*) yew.

IFOP [ifɔp] nm (abrév de **Institut français d'opinion publique**) *French public opinion research institute,* ≃ MORI.

IGF [iʒeɛf] nm (abrév de **impôt sur les grandes fortunes**) *voir* **impôt.**

igloo, iglou [iglu] nm igloo.

IGN [iʒeɛn] nm (abrév de **Institut géographique national**) *voir* **institut.**

Ignace [iɲas] nm Ignatius. **saint ~ de Loyola** (St) Ignatius Loyola.

igname [iɲam] nf yam.

ignare [iɲaʀ] (*péj*) 1 adj ignorant. 2 nmf ignoramus.

ignifugation [iɲifygasjɔ̃] nf fireproofing.

ignifuge [iɲifyʒ] 1 adj *produit* fireproofing (*épith*). 2 nm fireproofing material *ou* substance.

ignifugé, e [iɲifyʒe] (ptp de **ignifuger**) adj fireproof(ed).

ignifugeant, e [iɲifyʒɑ̃, ɑ̃t] 1 adj fireproof. 2 nm fireproofing material *ou* substance.

ignifuger [iɲifyʒe] 3 vt to fireproof.

ignoble [iɲɔbl] adj (*abject*) ignoble, vile, base; (*sens affaibli: dégoûtant*) vile, revolting.

ignoblement [iɲɔbləmɑ̃] adv ignobly, vilely, basely.

ignominie [iɲɔmini] nf a (*caractère*) ignominy; (*acte*) ignominious *ou* disgraceful act; (*conduite*) ignominious *ou* disgraceful behaviour (*NonC*). b (*déshonneur*) ignominy, disgrace.

ignominieusement [iɲɔminjøzmɑ̃] adv ignominiously.

ignominieux, -ieuse [iɲɔminjø, jøz] adj ignominious.

ignorance [iɲɔʀɑ̃s] nf a (*inculture*) ignorance. (*méconnaissance*) **~ de** ignorance of; **tenir qn/être dans l'~ de qch** to keep sb/be in ignorance of sth *ou* in the dark about sth; **dans l'~ des résultats** ignorant of the results; **d'une ~ crasse*** pig ignorant‡. b (*manque*) **de graves ~s en anglais/en matière juridique** serious gaps in his knowledge of English/of legal matters; *voir* **pécher.**

ignorant, e [iɲɔʀɑ̃, ɑ̃t] 1 adj (*ne sachant rien*) ignorant (*en* about). (*ne connaissant pas*) **~ de** ignorant *ou* unaware of; **~ des usages, il ...** ignorant *ou* unaware of the customs, he ..., not knowing the customs, he ... . 2 nm,f ignoramus. **quel ~ tu fais!** what an ignoramus you are!; **ne fais pas l'~** stop pretending you don't know what I mean (*ou* what he said *etc*); **parler en ~** to speak from ignorance.

ignoré, e [iɲɔʀe] (ptp de **ignorer**) adj *travaux, chercheurs, événement* unknown. **~ de tous** (*inconnu*) unknown to anybody; (*boudé*) ignored by all; **vivre ~** to live in obscurity.

ignorer [iɲɔʀe] 1 1 vt a (*ne pas connaître*) *affaire, incident* to be unaware of, not to know about *ou* of; *fait, artiste, écrivain* not to know. **~ que** not to know that, be unaware that; **~ comment/si** not to know how/if; **vous n'ignorez certainement pas que/comment** you (will) doubtless know that/how; **j'ignore tout de cette affaire** I don't know anything *ou* I know nothing about this business; **je n'ignorais pas ces problèmes** I was (fully) aware of these problems, I was not unaware of these problems; **j'ignore avoir dit cela** I am not aware of having said that; *voir* **nul.**

b (*être indifférent à*) *personne, remarque, avertissement* to ignore.

c (*être sans expérience de*) *plaisir, guerre, souffrance* not to know, have had no experience of. (*hum*) **des gosses qui ignorent le savon** kids who have never seen (a cake of) soap *ou* who are unaware of the existence of soap; **des joues qui ignorent le rasoir** cheeks that never see a razor.

2 **s'ignorer** vpr (*se méconnaître*) **une tendresse qui s'ignore** an unconscious tenderness; **c'est un poète qui s'ignore** he's an unconscious poet.

IGPN [iʒepeɛn] nm (abrév de **Inspection générale de la police nationale**) *voir* **inspection.**

IGR [iʒeɛʀ] nm (abrév de **impôt général sur le revenu**) *voir* **impôt.**

IGS [iʒeɛs] nf (abrév de **Inspection générale des services**) *voir* **inspection.**

iguane [igwan] nm iguana.

iguanodon [igwanɔdɔ̃] nm iguanodon.

il [il] pron pers m a (*personne*) he; (*bébé, animal*) it, he; (*chose*) it; (*bateau, nation*) she, it. **~s** they; **~ était journaliste** he was a journalist; **prends ce fauteuil, ~ est plus confortable** have this chair – it's more comfortable; **je me méfie de son chien, ~ mord** I don't trust his dog – it bites; **l'insecte emmagasine la nourriture qu'~ trouve** the insect stores the food it finds; **le Japon/le Canada a décidé qu'~ n'accepterait pas** Japan/Canada decided she *ou* they wouldn't accept; *voir* **avoir, fumée, jeunesse.**

b (*impers*) it. **~ fait beau** it's a fine day; **~ y a un enfant/3 enfants** there is a child/are 3 children; **~ est vrai que** it is true that; **~ faut que j'y aille** I've got to go (there).

c (*interrog, emphatique,* *: *non traduit*) **Paul est-~ rentré?** is Paul back?; **le courrier est-~ arrivé?** has the mail come?; **les enfants sont-~s bien couverts?** are the children warmly wrapped up?; **~ est si beau cet enfant/cet arbre** this child/tree is so beautiful; **tu sais, ton oncle, ~ est arrivé*** your uncle has arrived you know.

île [il] 1 nf island, isle (*littér*). (*Antilles*) **les I~s** the (French) West Indies.

2 comp ►**les îles Anglo-Normandes** the Channel Islands ►**l'île de Beauté** Corsica ►**les îles Britanniques** the British Isles ►**les îles Caïmans** the Cayman Islands ►**l'Île de la Cité** the Île de la Cité ►**l'île du Diable** Devil's Island ►**les îles Féroé** the Faroe Islands ►**île flottante** (*Culin*) île flottante, floating island ►**l'Île-de-France** the Île-de-France ►**île de glace** (*Géog*) large ice floe ►**les îles Mariannes** the Mariana Islands ►**les îles Marshall** the Marshall Islands ►**l'île Maurice** Mauritius ►**l'île de Pâques** Easter Island ►**les îles Scilly** the Scilly Isles, the Scillies ►**les îles Shetland** the Shetland Islands, Shetland ►**les îles de la Sonde** the Sunda Islands ►**les îles Sorlingues** = **les îles Scilly** ►**l'île de la Tortue** Tortuga, La Tortue ►**les îles du Vent/Sous-le-Vent** the Windward/Leeward Islands ►**les îles Vierges** the Virgin Islands ►**l'île de Wight** the Isle of Wight.

iléon [ileɔ̃] nm ileum.

Iliade [iljad] nf: **l'~** the Iliad.

iliaque [iljak] adj iliac. **os ~** ilium.

îlien, îlienne [iljɛ̃, iljɛn] nm,f islander.

ilion [iljɔ̃] nm ilium.

illégal, e, mpl **-aux** [i(l)legal, o] adj illegal; (*Admin*) unlawful; *organisation, société* illegal, outlawed. **c'est ~** it's illegal, it's against the law.

illégalement [i(l)legalmɑ̃] adv illegally; (*Admin*) unlawfully.

illégalité [i(l)legalite] nf illegality; *[action]* illegality; (*Admin*) unlawfulness; (*acte illégal*) illegality. **vivre dans l'~** to live outside the law; **être/se mettre dans l'~** to break the law.

illégitime [i(l)leʒitim] adj a (*illégal*) *acte, enfant* illegitimate. b (*non fondé*) *optimisme, cruauté* unwarranted, unwarrantable, unfounded; *prétention, revendication* illegitimate.

illégitimement [i(l)leʒitimmɑ̃] adv (*voir* **illégitime**) illegitimately; unwarrantedly, unwarrantably.

illégitimité [i(l)leʒitimite] nf (*voir* **illégitime**) illegitimacy; unwarrantableness.

illettré, e [i(l)letʀe] adj, nm,f illiterate.

illettrisme [i(l)letʀism] nm illiteracy. **campagne contre l'~** literacy campaign.

illicite [i(l)lisit] adj illicit.

illicitement [i(l)lisitmɑ̃] adv illicitly.

illico* [i(l)liko] adv (*tout de suite*) ~ **(presto)** straightaway, right away, at once, pronto*.
illimité, e [i(l)limite] adj *moyen, domaine, ressource* unlimited, limitless; *confiance* boundless, unbounded, limitless; *congé, durée* indefinite, unlimited.
Illinois [ilinwa] nm Illinois.
illisibilité [i(l)lizibilite] nf illegibility.
illisible [i(l)lizibl] adj (*indéchiffrable*) illegible, unreadable; (*mauvais*) unreadable.
illisiblement [i(l)liziblәmɑ̃] adv illegibly.
illocutionnaire [i(l)lɔkysjɔnɛʀ] adj illocutionary.
illogique [i(l)lɔʒik] adj illogical.
illogiquement [i(l)lɔʒikmɑ̃] adv illogically.
illogisme [i(l)lɔʒism] nm illogicality.
illumination [i(l)lyminasjɔ̃] nf a (*action: voir* **illuminer**) lighting; illumination; floodlighting. b (*lumières*) ~s illuminations, lights; **les ~s de Noël** the Christmas lights *ou* illuminations. c (*inspiration*) flash of inspiration; (*Rel*) inspiration.
illuminé, e [i(l)lymine] (ptp de **illuminer**) 1 adj (*voir* **illuminer**) lit up (*attrib*); illuminated; floodlit. 2 nm,f (*péj: visionnaire*) visionary, crank (*péj*).
illuminer [i(l)lymine] [1] 1 vt a (*éclairer*) to light up, illuminate. ~ **au moyen de projecteurs** to floodlight. b (*fig*) *[joie, foi, colère]* to light up; (*Rel*) *prophète, âme* to enlighten, illuminate. **le bonheur illuminait son visage** his face shone *ou* was illuminated *ou* was aglow with happiness, happiness lit up his face; **un sourire illumina son visage** a smile lit up her face. 2 **s'illuminer** vpr *[visage, ciel]* to light up (*de* with); *[rue, vitrine]* to be lit up.
illusion [i(l)lyzjɔ̃] nf illusion. ~ **d'optique** optical illusion; **ne te fais aucune ~** don't be under any illusion, don't delude *ou* kid* yourself; **tu te fais des ~s** you're deluding *ou* kidding* yourself; **ça donne l'~ de grandeur** it gives an illusion of size; **ça lui donne l'~ de servir à quelque chose** *ou* **qu'il sert à quelque chose** it gives him the illusion *ou* it makes him feel that he's doing something useful; **cet imposteur/ce stratagème ne fera pas ~ longtemps** this impostor/tactic won't delude *ou* fool people for long; *voir* **bercer, jouet.**
illusionner [i(l)lyzjɔne] [1] 1 **s'illusionner** vpr to delude o.s. (*sur qch* about sth). **s'~ sur qn** to delude o.s. *ou* be mistaken about sb. 2 vt (*induire en erreur*) to delude.
illusionnisme [i(l)lyzjɔnism] nm conjuring.
illusionniste [i(l)lyzjɔnist] nmf conjurer, illusionist.
illusoire [i(l)lyzwaʀ] adj (*trompeur*) illusory, illusive.
illusoirement [i(l)lyzwaʀmɑ̃] adv deceptively, illusorily.
illustrateur, -trice [i(l)lystʀatœʀ, tʀis] nm,f illustrator.
illustratif, -ive [i(l)lystʀatif, iv] adj illustrative.
illustration [i(l)lystʀasjɔ̃] nf a (*gravure*) illustration; (*exemple*) illustration; (*iconographie*) illustrations. **à l'~ abondante** copiously illustrated. b (*action, technique*) illustration. **l'~ par l'exemple** illustration by example.
illustre [i(l)lystʀ] adj illustrious, renowned. (*frm, iro*) **l'~ M. X** the illustrious Mr X; (*hum*) **un ~ inconnu** a distinguished person of whom no one has (ever) heard (*hum*), a person of obscure repute (*hum*).
illustré, e [i(l)lystʀe] 1 adj illustrated. 2 nm (*journal*) comic.
illustrer [i(l)lystʀe] [1] 1 vt a (*avec images, notes*) to illustrate (*de* with). b (*littér: rendre fameux*) to bring fame to, render illustrious (*littér*). 2 **s'illustrer** vpr *[personne]* to win fame *ou* renown, become famous (*par, dans* through).
illustrissime [i(l)lystʀisim] adj (*hum ou* ††) most illustrious.
ILM [iɛlɛm] (abrév de **immeuble à loyer moyen** *ou* **modéré**) *voir* **immeuble.**
îlot [ilo] nm (*île*) small island, islet; (*bloc de maisons*) block; (*Comm*) gondola; (*fig: petite zone*) island. ~ **de fraîcheur/de verdure** oasis *ou* island of coolness/of greenery; ~ **de résistance** pocket of resistance.
îlotage [ilɔtaʒ] nm community policing.
ilote [ilɔt] nmf (*Hist*) Helot; (*fig*) slave, serf.
îlotier [ilɔtje] nm ≃ community policeman.
image [imaʒ] 1 nf a (*dessin*) picture. **les ~s d'un film** the frames of a film; (*Ciné, TV*) **l'~ est nette/floue** the picture is clear/fuzzy; **popularisé par l'~** popularized by the camera; **en ~s** on film, in pictures; (*TV*) **apparaître à l'~** to appear on screen; *voir* **chasseur, livre[1], sage.**
b ~ **de** (*représentation*) picture of; (*ressemblance*) image of; **une ~ fidèle de la France** an accurate picture of France; **ils présentent l'~ du bonheur** they are the picture of happiness; **fait à l'~ de** made in the image of; **Dieu créa l'homme à son ~** God created man in his own image.
c (*comparaison, métaphore*) image. **les ~s chez Blake** Blake's imagery; **s'exprimer par ~s** to express o.s. in images.
d (*reflet*) (*gén*) reflection, image; (*Phys*) image. **regarder son ~ dans l'eau** to gaze at one's reflection in the water; ~ **réelle/virtuelle** real/virtual image.
e (*vision mentale*) image, picture. ~ **visuelle/auditive** visual/auditory image; **se faire une ~ fausse/idéalisée de qch** to have a false/an idealized picture of sth.
2 comp ►**image d'Épinal** (*lit*) *popular 18th/19th century print depicting traditional scenes of French life;* (*fig*) **cette réunion familiale était une touchante image d'Épinal** the family reunion was a touching scene of traditional family life ►**image de marque** *[produit]* brand image; *[parti, firme, politicien]* public image ►**image pieuse** holy picture ►**image satellite** satellite picture ►**image de synthèse** computer-generated image *ou* picture ►**images de synthèse** (*domaine*) computer graphics; (*animées*) computer animation.
imagé, e [imaʒe] (ptp de **imager**) adj *poème, texte* full of imagery (*attrib*); (*euph*) *langage* colourful.
imager [imaʒe] [3] vt *style, langage* to embellish with images.
imagerie [imaʒʀi] nf (*Hist: commerce*) coloured-print trade; (*images, gravures*) prints; (*Littérat: images*) imagery. **l'~ médicale** medical scanning.
imagier [imaʒje] nm (*Hist*) (*peintre*) painter of popular pictures; (*sculpteur*) sculptor of figurines; (*imprimeur*) coloured-print maker; (*vendeur*) print seller.
imaginable [imaʒinabl] adj conceivable, imaginable. **difficilement ~** hard to imagine; **un tel comportement n'était pas ~ il y a 50 ans** such behaviour was inconceivable 50 years ago; *voir* **possible.**
imaginaire [imaʒinɛʀ] 1 adj (*fictif*) imaginary; *monde* make-believe, imaginary. **ces persécutés/incompris ~s** these people who (falsely) believe they are *ou* believe themselves persecuted/misunderstood; *voir* **malade, nombre.** 2 nm: **l'~** the imagination.
imaginairement [imaʒinɛʀmɑ̃] adv in (one's) imagination.
imaginatif, -ive [imaʒinatif, iv] adj imaginative.
imagination [imaʒinasjɔ̃] nf (*faculté*) imagination; (*chimère, rêve*) imagination (*NonC*), fancy. **tout ce qu'il avait vécu en ~** everything he had experienced in his imagination; **ce sont de pures ~s** that's sheer imagination, those are pure fancies; **monstres sortis tout droit de son ~** monsters straight out of his imagination; **en proie à ses ~s** a prey to his fancies *ou* imaginings; **avoir de l'~** to be imaginative, have a good imagination; **avoir trop d'~** to imagine things; **une ~ débordante** a lively *ou* wild imagination.
imaginer [imaʒine] [1] 1 vt a (*se représenter, supposer*) to imagine. ~ **que** to imagine that; **tu imagines la scène!** you can imagine *ou* picture the scene!; **on imagine mal leurs conditions de travail** their working conditions are hard to imagine; **je l'imaginais plus vieux** I imagined him to be older, I pictured him as being older; **qu'allez-vous ~ là?** what on earth are you thinking of?; (*ton de défi*) **et tu vas t'y opposer, j'imagine?** and I imagine *ou* suppose you're going to oppose it?
b (*inventer*) *système, plan* to devise, dream up. **qu'est-il encore allé ~?*** now what has he dreamed up? *ou* thought up?; **il a imaginé d'ouvrir un magasin** he has taken it into his head to open up a shop, he has dreamed up the idea of opening a shop.
2 **s'imaginer** vpr a (*se figurer*) to imagine. **imagine-toi une île paradisiaque** imagine *ou* picture an island paradise; **comme on peut se l'~ ...** as you can (well) imagine ... .
b (*se voir*) to imagine o.s., picture o.s. **s'~ à 60 ans/en vacances** to imagine *ou* picture o.s. at 60/on holiday.
c (*croire que*) **s'~ que** to imagine *ou* think that; **il s'imaginait pouvoir faire cela** he imagined *ou* thought he could do that; **si tu t'imagines que je vais te laisser faire!** don't think I'm going to let you get away with that!; **imagine-toi que je n'ai pas que ça à faire!** look, I have got other things to do!
imago [imago] nm ou nf (*Bio, Psych*) imago.
imam [imam] nm, **iman** [imɑ̃] nm ima(u)m.
imbattable [ɛ̃batabl] adj *prix, personne, record* unbeatable.
imbécile [ɛ̃besil] 1 adj (*stupide*) stupid, idiotic; (†: *Méd*) imbecilic (SPÉC), idiotic. 2 nmf a (*idiot*) idiot, imbecile. **faire l'~*** to act the fool; **ne fais pas l'~*** (*n'agis pas bêtement*) don't be an idiot* *ou* a fool; (*ne simule pas la bêtise*) stop acting stupid*; **le premier ~ venu te le dira** any fool will tell you; **c'est un ~ heureux** he's living in a fool's paradise; **les ~s heureux** the blissfully ignorant. b (†: *Méd*) imbecile, idiot.
imbécilement [ɛ̃besilmɑ̃] adv stupidly, idiotically.
imbécillité [ɛ̃besilite] nf a *[action, personne]* idiocy; (†: *Méd*) imbecility, idiocy. b (*action*) idiotic *ou* stupid *ou* imbecile thing to do; (*propos*) idiotic *ou* stupid *ou* imbecile thing to say; (*film, livre*) rubbish (*NonC*) (*Brit*), trash (*NonC*). **tu racontes des ~s** you're talking rot* *ou* rubbish (*Brit*); **ne va pas voir de telles ~s** don't go and see such rubbish (*Brit*) *ou* such an idiotic *ou* such a stupid film (*ou* play *etc*).
imberbe [ɛ̃bɛʀb] adj *personne* beardless, smooth-cheeked; *visage* beardless.
imbiber [ɛ̃bibe] [1] 1 vt (*imprégner*) ~ **un tampon/une compresse** *etc* **de** to soak *ou* moisten *ou* impregnate a pad/compress *etc* with; **imbibé d'eau** *chaussures, étoffe* saturated (with water), soaked; *terre* saturated, waterlogged; **gâteau imbibé de rhum** cake soaked in rum. 2 **s'imbiber** vpr: **s'~ de** to become saturated *ou* soaked with; (*fig*) **s'~ de vin*** to soak up wine; **être imbibé*** to be tipsy.
imbrication [ɛ̃bʀikasjɔ̃] nf *[problèmes, souvenirs, parcelles]* interweaving; *[plaques, tuiles]* overlapping.
imbriquer [ɛ̃bʀike] [1] 1 **s'imbriquer** vpr *[problèmes, affaires]* to be linked *ou* interwoven; *[plaques]* to overlap (each other). **ça s'imbrique l'un dans l'autre** *[cubes]* they fit into each other; *[problèmes]* they are

linked *ou* interwoven; **cette nouvelle question est venue s'~ dans une situation déjà compliquée** this new issue has arisen to complicate an already complex situation. 2 **vt** *cubes* to fit into each other; *plaques* to overlap.

imbroglio [ɛ̃bʀɔljo] **nm** imbroglio; (*Théât*) theatrical imbroglio.

imbu, e [ɛ̃by] **adj**: ~ **de lui-même** *ou* **de sa personne** pompous, full of himself, full of self-importance.

imbuvable [ɛ̃byvabl] **adj** (*lit*) undrinkable; (**: mauvais*) *personne* unbearable, insufferable; *film, livre* unbearably awful*.

imitable [imitabl] **adj** which can be imitated, imitable. **facilement** ~ easy to imitate, easily imitated.

imitateur, -trice [imitatœʀ, tʀis] 1 **adj** imitative. 2 **nm,f** imitator; (*Théât*) *[voix, personne]* impersonator; *[bruits etc]* imitator.

imitatif, -ive [imitatif, iv] **adj** imitative.

imitation [imitasjɔ̃] **nf** a (*action: voir* **imiter**) imitation; impersonation; mimicry; copying; forgery. **avoir le don d'~** to have a gift for imitating people *ou* for mimicry, be good at taking people off* (*Brit*). b (*pastiche*) imitation; (*sketch*) impression, imitation, impersonation; (*tableau, bijou, fourrure*) imitation. c (*loc*) **à l'~ de** in imitation of; **d'~, en ~** imitation (*épith*); **c'est en ~ cuir** it's imitation leather; **un portefeuille ~ cuir** an imitation leather wallet.

imiter [imite] 1 **vt** a *bruit* to imitate; *personnage célèbre* to imitate, impersonate, take off* (*Brit*); *voix, geste* to imitate, mimic; *modèle, héros, style* to imitate, copy; *document, signature* to forge. **il se leva et tout le monde l'imita** he got up and everybody did likewise *ou* followed suit. b (*avoir l'aspect de*) *[matière, revêtement]* to look like. **un lino qui imite le marbre** an imitation marble lino.

immaculé, e [imakyle] **adj** *linge, surface* spotless, immaculate; *blancheur* immaculate; *réputation* spotless, unsullied, immaculate; *honneur* unsullied. **d'un blanc ~** spotlessly white; (*Rel*) **l'I~e Conception** the Immaculate Conception.

immanence [imanɑ̃s] **nf** immanence.

immanent, e [imanɑ̃, ɑ̃t] **adj** immanent (*à* in); *voir* **justice**.

immangeable [ɛ̃mɑ̃ʒabl] **adj** uneatable, inedible.

immanquable [ɛ̃mɑ̃kabl] **adj** *cible, but* impossible to miss (*attrib*). **c'était ~!** it had to happen!, it was bound to happen!, it was inevitable!

immanquablement [ɛ̃mɑ̃kabləmɑ̃] **adv** inevitably, without fail.

immatérialité [i(m)mateʀjalite] **nf** immateriality.

immatériel, -elle [i(m)mateʀjɛl] **adj** *légèreté, minceur* ethereal; (*Philos*) immaterial.

immatriculation [imatʀikylasjɔ̃] **nf** registration; *voir* **carte, numéro, plaque**.

immatriculer [imatʀikyle] 1 **vt** *véhicule, personne* to register. **faire ~** *véhicule* to register; **se faire ~** to register (*à* with); **une voiture immatriculée dans le Vaucluse/CM 175** a car with a Vaucluse registration (number)/with (the) registration (*Brit*) *ou* license (*US*) number CM 175.

immature [imatyʀ] **adj** immature.

immaturité [imatyʀite] **nf** (*littér*) immaturity.

immédiat, e [imedja, jat] 1 **adj** (*Philos, gén*) immediate; *soulagement* immediate, instant (*épith*). **c'est en contact ~ avec le mur** it is in direct contact with the wall; **dans l'avenir ~** in the immediate future; **la mort fut ~e** death was instantaneous. 2 **nm**: **dans l'~** for the time being, for the moment.

immédiatement [imedjatmɑ̃] **adv** immediately, at once, directly. ~ **après** immediately after, straight after.

immédiateté [imedjatte] **nf** (*Philos*) immediacy.

immémorial, e, mpl -iaux [i(m)memɔʀjal, jo] **adj** age-old. (*littér*) **de temps ~** from time immemorial.

immense [i(m)mɑ̃s] **adj** (*gén*) immense; *mer, espace, horizon* boundless, vast, immense; *foule, fortune, pays* vast, immense, huge; *avenir* boundless; *influence, avantage, succès* immense, tremendous, huge. (*fig*) **un ~ acteur** a stupendous actor.

immensément [i(m)mɑ̃semɑ̃] **adv** immensely, tremendously; hugely.

immensité [i(m)mɑ̃site] **nf** (*voir* **immense**) immensity, immenseness; vastness; hugeness. (*littér*) **le regard perdu dans l'~** gazing into infinity.

immergé, e [imɛʀʒe] (**ptp de immerger**) **adj** *terres* submerged. ~ **par 100 mètres de fond** lying 100 metres down; **rochers ~s** submerged *ou* underwater rocks, rocks under water; **la partie ~e de la balise** the part of the buoy which is under water *ou* which is submerged; **économie ~e** black economy; *voir* **partie**.

immerger [imɛʀʒe] 3 1 **vt** *objet* to immerse, submerge; *fondations* to build under water; *déchets* to dump at sea, dispose of at sea; *câble* to lay under water; *corps* to bury at sea; (*Rel*) *catéchumène* to immerse. 2 **s'immerger vpr** *[sous-marin]* to dive, submerge.

immérité, e [imeʀite] **adj** undeserved, unmerited.

immersion [imɛʀsjɔ̃] **nf** (*voir* **immerger**) immersion; submersion; underwater building; dumping *ou* disposal at sea; underwater laying; burying at sea; diving.

immettable [ɛ̃metabl] **adj** *vêtement* unwearable.

immeuble [imœbl] 1 **nm** a (*bâtiment*) building; (*à usage d'habitation*) block of flats (*Brit*), apartment building (*US*); *voir* **gérant**. b (*Jur*) real estate (*NonC*). 2 **adj** (*Jur*) real, immovable. 3 **comp ▸immeuble de bureaux** office block (*Brit*) *ou* building (*US*) **▸immeuble à loyer moyen** *ou* **modéré** ≃ block of council flats (*Brit*) low-rent building (*US*) **▸immeuble de rapport** residential property (for renting), investment property **▸immeuble tour** tower block (*Brit*), tower (*US*) **▸immeuble à usage locatif** block of rented flats (*Brit*), rental apartment building (*US*).

immigrant, e [imigʀɑ̃, ɑ̃t] **adj, nm,f** immigrant.

immigration [imigʀasjɔ̃] **nf** immigration. **(les services de) l'~** the immigration department.

immigré, e [imigʀe] (**ptp de immigrer**) **adj, nm,f** immigrant. ~ **de la deuxième génération** second-generation immigrant.

immigrer [imigʀe] 1 **vi** to immigrate (*à, dans* into).

imminence [iminɑ̃s] **nf** imminence.

imminent, e [iminɑ̃, ɑ̃t] **adj** *danger, crise, départ* imminent, impending (*épith*).

immiscer (s') [imise] 3 **vpr**: **s'~ dans** to interfere in *ou* with.

immixtion [imiksjɔ̃] **nf**: ~ **dans** interference in *ou* with.

immobile [i(m)mɔbil] **adj** *personne, eau, air, arbre* motionless, still; *visage* immobile; *pièce de machine* fixed; (*littér, fig*) *dogme* immovable; *institutions* unchanging, permanent. **regard ~** fixed stare; **rester ~** to stay *ou* keep still.

immobilier, -ière [imɔbilje, jɛʀ] 1 **adj** (*Comm*) *vente, crise* property (*épith*); (*Jur*) *biens, succession* in real estate (*attrib*). **la situation ~ière est satisfaisante** the property situation is satisfactory, the state of the property market is satisfactory; *voir* **société, agence**. 2 **nm**: **l'~** (*Comm*) the property business, the real-estate business; (*Jur*) real estate immovables.

immobilisation [imɔbilizasjɔ̃] **nf** a *[membre blessé, circulation, capitaux]* immobilization. **cela a entraîné l'~ totale de la circulation/des affaires** that brought the traffic/brought business to a complete standstill, that brought about the complete immobilization of traffic/of business; **attendez l'~ totale du train/de l'avion** wait until the train is completely stationary/the aircraft has come to a complete standstill *ou* halt *ou* stop; **l'~ de la machine** (*elle s'immobilise*) the stopping of the machine; (*on la stoppe*) bringing the machine to a halt *ou* standstill, the stopping of the machine; (*on l'empêche de fonctionner*) the immobilization of the machine. b (*Jur*) *[bien]* conversion into an immovable. c (*Fin*) *[capitaux]* immobilization, tying up. **~s** fixed assets.

immobiliser [imɔbilize] 1 1 **vt** *troupes, membre blessé* to immobilize; *file, circulation, affaires* to bring to a standstill, immobilize; *machine, véhicule* (*stopper*) to stop, bring to a halt *ou* standstill; (*empêcher de fonctionner*) to immobilize; (*Jur*) *biens* to convert into immovables; (*Fin*) to immobilize, tie up. **ça l'immobilise à son domicile** it keeps him housebound; **avions immobilisés par la neige/le brouillard** aeroplanes grounded by snow/fog; **la peur l'immobilisait** he was paralyzed with fear, he was rooted to the spot with fear. 2 **s'immobiliser vpr** *[personne]* to stop, stand still; *[machine, véhicule, échanges commerciaux]* to come to a halt *ou* a standstill.

immobilisme [imɔbilism] **nm** *[gouvernement, firme]* opposition to progress *ou* change. **faire de/être partisan de l'~** to try to maintain/support the status quo.

immobiliste [imɔbilist] **adj** *politique* designed to maintain the status quo. **c'est un ~** he is a supporter of the status quo, he is opposed to progress.

immobilité [imɔbilite] 1 **nf** *[personne, foule, eau, arbre]* stillness, motionlessness; *[visage]* immobility; *[regard]* fixedness; *[institutions]* unchanging nature, permanence. **le médecin lui ordonna l'~ complète** the doctor ordered him not to move (at all). 2 **comp ▸immobilité forcée** forced immobility **▸immobilité politique** lack of political change, political inertia.

immodération [imɔdeʀasjɔ̃] **nf** immoderation.

immodéré, e [imɔdeʀe] **adj** immoderate, inordinate.

immodérément [imɔdeʀemɑ̃] **adv** immoderately, inordinately.

immodeste [imɔdɛst] **adj** immodest.

immodestement [imɔdɛstəmɑ̃] **adv** immodestly.

immodestie [imɔdɛsti] **nf** immodesty.

immolateur†† [imɔlatœʀ] **nm** immolator (*littér*).

immolation [imɔlasjɔ̃] **nf** (*voir* **immoler**) (*Hist, Rel*) immolation; sacrifice; sacrificing; self-sacrifice.

immoler [imɔle] 1 1 **vt** (*Hist, Rel*) to immolate (*littér*), sacrifice (*à* to); (*gén*) to sacrifice (*à* to); (*littér: massacrer*) to slay (*littér*). 2 **s'immoler vpr** to sacrifice o.s. (*à* to)

immonde [i(m)mɔ̃d] **adj** *taudis* squalid, foul; *langage, action, personne* base, vile; (*Rel*) unclean.

immondice [i(m)mɔ̃dis] **nf** a (*ordures*) **~s** refuse (*NonC*); (*littér*) **commettre/proférer des ~s** to do/say unspeakable things. b (*littér ou †: saleté*) filth (*NonC*).

immoral, e, mpl -aux [i(m)mɔʀal, o] **adj** immoral.

immoralement [i(m)mɔʀalmɑ̃] **adv** immorally.

immoralisme [i(m)mɔʀalism] **nm** immoralism.

immoraliste [i(m)mɔʀalist] **adj, nmf** immoralist.

immoralité [i(m)mɔʀalite] **nf** immorality.

immortaliser [imɔʀtalize] 1 1 **vt** to immortalize. 2 **s'immortaliser vpr** to win immortality, win eternal fame.

immortalité [imɔʀtalite] nf immortality.
immortel, -elle [imɔʀtɛl] 1 adj immortal. 2 nm: I~ *member of the Académie Française.* 3 **immortelle** nf (*fleur*) everlasting flower.
immotivé, e [i(m)mɔtive] adj *action, crime* unmotivated; *réclamation, crainte* groundless.
immuabilité [imɥabilite] nf = **immutabilité**.
immuable [imɥabl] adj *lois, passion* unchanging, immutable; *paysage, routine* unchanging; *sourire* unchanging, perpetual. **il est resté ~ dans ses convictions** he remained unchanged in his convictions; **vêtu de son ~ complet à carreaux** wearing that eternal checked suit of his.
immuablement [imɥabləmɑ̃] adv *fonctionner, se passer* immutably; *triste, grognon* perpetually.
immun, e [imœ̃, yn] adj immune. **complexe ~** immune complex, immunocomplex.
immunisation [imynizasjɔ̃] nf immunization.
immuniser [imynize] [1] vt (*Méd, fig*) to immunize (*contre* against). **immunisé contre** (*Méd*) immunized against, immune from *ou* to; (*fig*) immune from *ou* to; (*fig*) **être immunisé contre les tentations** to be immune to temptation; (*fig*) **ça l'immunisera contre le désir de recommencer** this'll stop him ever *ou* this'll cure him of ever wanting to do it again.
immunitaire [imynitɛʀ] adj immune. **défenses ~s** immunological defences; **réactions ~s** immune reactions.
immunité [imynite] nf (*Bio, Jur*) immunity. **~ diplomatique** diplomatic immunity; **~ parlementaire** ≃ parliamentary privilege; **~ fiscale** immunity from taxation, tax immunity.
immuno-déficitaire [imynodefisitɛʀ] adj immunodeficient; *voir* **syndrome**.
immuno-dépresseur [imynodepʀesœʀ] adj, nm immunodepressant.
immuno-dépressif, -ive [imynodepʀesif, iv] adj immunodepressant.
immuno-déprimé, e [imynodepʀime] adj immunocompromised.
immunogène [imynɔʒɛn] adj immunogenic.
immunoglob(ul)ine [imynoglɔb(yl)in] nf immunoglobulin.
immunologie [imynɔlɔʒi] nf immunology.
immunologique [imynɔlɔʒik] adj immunological.
immunologiste [imynɔlɔʒist] nmf immunologist.
immunosuppresseur [imynosypʀesœʀ] nm immunosuppressive, immunosuppressant.
immunothérapie [imynoteʀapi] nf immunotherapy.
immutabilité [i(m)mytabilite] nf immutability.
impact [ɛ̃pakt] nm (*lit, fig*) impact. **l'argument a de l'~** the argument has some impact; (*Admin, Écon*) **étude d'~** impact study; *voir* **point**[1].
impair, e [ɛ̃pɛʀ] 1 adj *nombre* odd, uneven; *jour* odd; *vers* irregular, *with uneven number of syllables; organe* unpaired. 2 nm a (*gaffe*) blunder, faux pas. **commettre un ~** to (make a) blunder, make a faux pas. b (*Casino*) **miser sur l'~** to put one's money on the odd numbers.
impala [impala] nm impala.
impalpable [ɛ̃palpabl] adj impalpable.
impaludation [ɛ̃palydasjɔ̃] nf infection with malaria.
impaludé, e [ɛ̃palyde] adj *malade* suffering from malaria; *région* malaria-infected.
imparable [ɛ̃paʀabl] adj *coup, tir* unstoppable. (*fig*) **une riposte ~** an unanswerable riposte.
impardonnable [ɛ̃paʀdɔnabl] adj *faute* unforgivable, unpardonable. **vous êtes ~ (d'avoir fait cela)** you cannot be forgiven (for doing that), it is unforgivable of you (to have done that).
imparfait, e [ɛ̃paʀfɛ, ɛt] 1 adj (*gén*) imperfect. 2 nm (*Ling*) imperfect tense. **à l'~** in the imperfect (tense).
imparfaitement [ɛ̃paʀfɛtmɑ̃] adv imperfectly. **connaître ~ qch** to have an imperfect knowledge of sth.
impartial, e, mpl **-iaux** [ɛ̃paʀsjal, jo] adj impartial, unbiased, unprejudiced.
impartialement [ɛ̃paʀsjalmɑ̃] adv impartially, without bias *ou* prejudice.
impartialité [ɛ̃paʀsjalite] nf impartiality. **en toute ~** from a completely impartial standpoint; **faire preuve d'~ dans ses jugements** to show impartiality in one's judgements.
impartir [ɛ̃paʀtiʀ] [2] vt (*littér: attribuer à*) **~ des devoirs à** to assign duties to; **~ des pouvoirs à** to invest powers in; **~ des dons à** to bestow gifts upon, impart gifts to; (*Jur: accorder à*) **~ un délai à** to grant an extension to; **dans les délais impartis** within the time allowed; (*Jeux*) **le temps qui vous était imparti est écoulé** your time is up; **les dons que Dieu nous a impartis** the gifts God has bestowed upon us *ou* has endowed us with *ou* has imparted to us.
impasse [ɛ̃pɑs] 1 nf a (*cul-de-sac*) dead end, cul-de-sac; (*sur panneau*) "no through road". b (*fig*) impasse. **être dans l'~** *[négociations]* to have reached an impasse, have reached deadlock; *[personne]* to be at a dead end; *[relation]* to have reached a dead end. c (*Scol, Univ*) **j'ai fait 3 ~s en géographie** I missed out (*Brit*) *ou* skipped over 3 topics in my geography revision. d (*Cartes*) finesse. **faire une ~** to (make a) finesse; **faire l'~ au roi** to finesse against the king. 2 comp ▸ **impasse budgétaire** (*Fin*) budget deficit.
impassibilité [ɛ̃pasibilite] nf impassiveness, impassivity.
impassible [ɛ̃pasibl] adj impassive.
impassiblement [ɛ̃pasibləmɑ̃] adv impassively.
impatiemment [ɛ̃pasjamɑ̃] adv impatiently.
impatience [ɛ̃pasjɑ̃s] nf impatience. **il était dans l'~ de la revoir** he was impatient to see her again, he couldn't wait to see her again; **il répliqua avec ~ que** he replied impatiently that; (*littér*) **se rappelant leurs ~s d'adolescents** remembering their impatient attitudes as teenagers *ou* the impatient moments of their adolescence; **avoir des ~s dans les jambes**† to have the fidgets*.
impatiens [ɛ̃pasjɑ̃s] = **impatiente**.
impatient, e [ɛ̃pasjɑ̃, jɑ̃t] 1 adj *personne, geste, attente* impatient. **~ de faire** impatient *ou* eager to do; **je suis si ~ de vous revoir** I am longing to see you again, I am so impatient to see you again, I just can't wait to see you again*; **quel ~!** what an impatient character! 2 **impatiente** nf (*Bot*) Busy Lizzie, impatiens (*SPÉC*).
impatientant, e [ɛ̃pasjɑ̃tɑ̃, ɑ̃t] adj irritating, annoying.
impatienter [ɛ̃pasjɑ̃te] [1] 1 vt to irritate, annoy. 2 **s'impatienter** vpr to grow *ou* get impatient, lose patience (*contre ou de qn* with sb; *contre ou de qch* at sth).
impavide [ɛ̃pavid] adj (*littér*) unruffled, impassive, cool. **~ devant le danger** cool *ou* unruffled in the face of danger.
impayable* [ɛ̃pɛjabl] adj (*drôle*) priceless*. **il est ~!** he's priceless!*, he's a scream!*
impayé, e [ɛ̃peje] 1 adj unpaid. 2 nm: **~s** outstanding payments.
impec* [ɛ̃pɛk] adj abrév de **impeccable**.
impeccable [ɛ̃pekabl] adj a (*parfait*) *travail, style* perfect, faultless, impeccable; *employé* perfect. **(c'est) ~!*** great!*, brilliant!* b (*propre*) *personne* impeccable, impeccably dressed; *appartement, voiture* spotless, spotlessly clean, impeccable.
impeccablement [ɛ̃pekabləmɑ̃] adv (*voir* **impeccable**) perfectly; faultlessly; impeccably; spotlessly.
impécunieux, -ieuse [ɛ̃pekynjø, jøz] adj (*littér*) impecunious.
impécuniosité [ɛ̃pekynjozite] nf (*littér*) impecuniousness.
impédance [ɛ̃pedɑ̃s] nf (*Élec*) impedance.
impedimenta [ɛ̃pedimɛ̃ta] nmpl (*Mil, fig*) impedimenta.
impénétrabilité [ɛ̃penetʀabilite] nf (*voir* **impénétrable**) impenetrability; unfathomableness; inscrutability.
impénétrable [ɛ̃penetʀabl] adj *forêt* impenetrable (*à* to, by); *mystère, desseins* unfathomable, impenetrable; *personnage, caractère* inscrutable, impenetrable, unfathomable; *visage* inscrutable, impenetrable.
impénitence [ɛ̃penitɑ̃s] nf unrepentance, impenitence.
impénitent, e [ɛ̃penitɑ̃, ɑ̃t] adj unrepentant, impenitent. **fumeur ~** unrepentant smoker.
impensable [ɛ̃pɑ̃sabl] adj *événement hypothétique* unthinkable; *événement arrivé* unbelievable.
imper* [ɛ̃pɛʀ] nm (abrév de **imperméable**) raincoat, mac* (*Brit*).
impératif, -ive [ɛ̃peʀatif, iv] 1 adj (*obligatoire, urgent*) *besoin, consigne* urgent, imperative; (*impérieux*) *geste, ton* imperative, imperious, commanding; (*Jur*) *loi* mandatory; *voir* **mandat**. 2 nm a (*Ling*) imperative mood. **à l'~** in the imperative (mood). b (*prescription*) *[fonction, charge]* requirement; *[mode]* demand; (*nécessité*) *[situation]* necessity; (*Mil*) imperative. **des ~s d'horaire nous obligent à ...** we are obliged by the demands *ou* constraints of our timetable to ... .
impérativement [ɛ̃peʀativmɑ̃] adv imperatively. **je le veux ~ pour demain** it is imperative that I have it for tomorrow, I absolutely must have it for tomorrow.
impératrice [ɛ̃peʀatʀis] nf empress.
imperceptibilité [ɛ̃pɛʀsɛptibilite] nf imperceptibility.
imperceptible [ɛ̃pɛʀsɛptibl] adj a (*non perceptible*) *son, détail, nuance* imperceptible (*à* to). b (*à peine perceptible*) *son, sourire* faint, imperceptible; *détail, changement, nuance* minute, imperceptible.
imperceptiblement [ɛ̃pɛʀsɛptibləmɑ̃] adv imperceptibly.
imperdable [ɛ̃pɛʀdabl] adj *partie, match* that cannot be lost.
imperfectible [ɛ̃pɛʀfɛktibl] adj which cannot be perfected, unperfectible.
imperfectif, -ive [ɛ̃pɛʀfɛktif, iv] 1 adj imperfective, continuous. 2 nm imperfective.
imperfection [ɛ̃pɛʀfɛksjɔ̃] nf (*caractère imparfait*) imperfection; (*défaut*) *[personne, caractère]* shortcoming, imperfection, defect; *[ouvrage, dispositif, mécanisme]* imperfection, defect, fault.
impérial, e, mpl **-iaux** [ɛ̃peʀjal, jo] 1 adj imperial. 2 **impériale** nf a *[autobus]* top *ou* upper deck. **autobus à ~e** ≃ double-decker (bus); **monter à l'~e** to go upstairs *ou* on top. b (*barbe*) imperial.
impérialement [ɛ̃peʀjalmɑ̃] adv imperially.
impérialisme [ɛ̃peʀjalism] nm imperialism.
impérialiste [ɛ̃peʀjalist] 1 adj imperialist(ic). 2 nmf imperialist.
impérieusement [ɛ̃peʀjøzmɑ̃] adv imperiously. **avoir ~ besoin de qch** to need sth urgently, have urgent need of sth.
impérieux, -ieuse [ɛ̃peʀjø, jøz] adj (*autoritaire*) *personne, ton, caractère* imperious; (*pressant*) *besoin, nécessité* urgent, pressing; *obligation* pressing.
impérissable [ɛ̃peʀisabl] adj *œuvre* imperishable; *souvenir, gloire* undying (*épith*), imperishable; *monument, valeur* undying (*épith*).
impéritie [ɛ̃peʀisi] nf (*littér: incompétence*) incompetence.
imperméabilisation [ɛ̃pɛʀmeabilizasjɔ̃] nf waterproofing.

imperméabiliser [ɛ̃pɛʀmeabilize] 1 vt to waterproof.
imperméabilité [ɛ̃pɛʀmeabilite] nf (*lit*) *[terrain]* impermeability; *[tissu]* waterproof qualities, impermeability. (*fig littér: insensibilité*) ~ **à** imperviousness to.
imperméable [ɛ̃pɛʀmeabl] 1 adj (*lit*) *terrain, roches* impermeable; *revêtement, tissu* waterproof. ~ **à l'eau** waterproof; ~ **à l'air** airtight; (*fig: insensible*) ~ **à** impervious to. 2 nm (*manteau*) raincoat, mackintosh (*Brit*).
impersonnalité [ɛ̃pɛʀsɔnalite] nf impersonality; (*Ling*) impersonal form.
impersonnel, -elle [ɛ̃pɛʀsɔnɛl] adj impersonal.
impersonnellement [ɛ̃pɛʀsɔnɛlmɑ̃] adv impersonally.
impertinemment [ɛ̃pɛʀtinamɑ̃] adv impertinently.
impertinence [ɛ̃pɛʀtinɑ̃s] nf (*caractère*) impertinence; (*propos*) impertinent remark, impertinence. **arrête tes ~s!** that's enough impertinence!, that's enough of your impertinent remarks!
impertinent, e [ɛ̃pɛʀtinɑ̃, ɑ̃t] adj impertinent. **c'est un petit ~!** he's an impertinent child!
imperturbabilité [ɛ̃pɛʀtyʀbabilite] nf imperturbability.
imperturbable [ɛ̃pɛʀtyʀbabl] adj *sang-froid, gaieté, sérieux* unshakeable; *personne, caractère* imperturbable. **rester ~** to remain unruffled.
imperturbablement [ɛ̃pɛʀtyʀbabləmɑ̃] adv imperturbably. **il écouta ~** he listened imperturbably *ou* unperturbed *ou* unruffled.
impétigo [ɛ̃petigo] nm impetigo.
impétrant, e [ɛ̃petʀɑ̃, ɑ̃t] nm,f (*Jur*) applicant.
impétueusement [ɛ̃petɥøzmɑ̃] adv (*littér*) impetuously.
impétueux, -euse [ɛ̃petɥø, øz] adj (*littér: fougueux*) *caractère, jeunesse* impetuous, hotheaded; *orateur* fiery; *rythme* impetuous; *torrent, vent* raging.
impétuosité [ɛ̃petɥozite] nf (*littér*) *[rythme, personne]* impetuousness, impetuosity. **il faut se méfier de l'~ des torrents de montagne** one must beware of raging mountain streams.
impie [ɛ̃pi] 1 adj *acte, parole* impious, ungodly, irreligious. 2 nmf ungodly *ou* irreligious person.
impiété [ɛ̃pjete] nf (*caractère*) impiety, ungodliness, irreligiousness; (*parole, acte*) impiety.
impitoyable [ɛ̃pitwajabl] adj (*gén*) merciless, pitiless, ruthless.
impitoyablement [ɛ̃pitwajabləmɑ̃] adv mercilessly, pitilessly, ruthlessly.
implacabilité [ɛ̃plakabilite] nf implacability.
implacable [ɛ̃plakabl] adj (*impitoyable*) implacable.
implacablement [ɛ̃plakabləmɑ̃] adv implacably.
implant [ɛ̃plɑ̃] nm (*Méd*) implant. **~ capillaire** hair graft; **~ dentaire** implant.
implantation [ɛ̃plɑ̃tasjɔ̃] nf (*voir* **implanter**) (*action*) introduction; settling; setting up; implanting; (*résultat*) introduction; settlement; establishment; implantation.
implanter [ɛ̃plɑ̃te] 1 1 vt (*introduire*) *usage, mode* to introduce; *immigrants* to introduce, settle; *usine, industrie* to set up, establish; *idée, préjugé* to implant; (*Méd*) to implant. **~ un produit sur le marché** to establish a product on the market. 2 **s'implanter** vpr *[établissements, usines]* to be set up *ou* established; *[immigrants]* to settle; *[idées]* to become implanted; *[parti politique]* to establish itself, become established. **il semble s'~ chez eux** he seems to be making himself quite at home with them; **des traditions solidement implantées** deeply-rooted *ou* deeply-entrenched traditions.
implémentation [ɛ̃plemɑ̃tasjɔ̃] nf (*Ordin*) implementation.
implémenter [ɛ̃plemɑ̃te] 1 vt (*Ordin*) to implement.
implication [ɛ̃plikasjɔ̃] nf a (*conséquences, répercussions*) **~s** implications. b (*relation logique*) implication. c **~ dans** (*mise en cause*) implication in; (*participation à*) implication *ou* involvement in.
implicite [ɛ̃plisit] adj *condition, foi, volonté* implicit. (*Ling*) **connaissance ~** tacit knowledge.
implicitement [ɛ̃plisitmɑ̃] adv implicitly.
impliquer [ɛ̃plike] 1 1 vt a (*supposer*) to imply (*que* that). b (*nécessiter*) to necessitate. c **~ qn dans** (*mettre en cause*) to implicate sb in; (*mêler à*) to implicate *ou* involve sb in. 2 **s'impliquer** vpr: **s'~ dans son travail/un projet** to get involved in one's work/a project; **s'~ beaucoup dans qch** to put a lot into sth, get heavily involved in sth.
implorant, e [ɛ̃plɔʀɑ̃, ɑ̃t] adj imploring, beseeching. **me regardant d'un air ~** looking at me imploringly *ou* beseechingly, giving me a beseeching *ou* an imploring look.
imploration [ɛ̃plɔʀasjɔ̃] nf entreaty.
implorer [ɛ̃plɔʀe] 1 vt (*supplier*) *personne, Dieu* to implore, beseech; (*demander*) *faveur, aide* to implore. **~ qn de faire** to implore *ou* beseech *ou* entreat sb to do.
imploser [ɛ̃ploze] 1 vi to implode.
implosif, -ive [ɛ̃plozif, iv] adj implosive.
implosion [ɛ̃plozjɔ̃] nf implosion.
impoli, e [ɛ̃pɔli] adj impolite, rude (*envers* to).
impoliment [ɛ̃pɔlimɑ̃] adv impolitely, rudely.
impolitesse [ɛ̃pɔlitɛs] nf (*attitude*) impoliteness, rudeness; (*remarque*) impolite *ou* rude remark; (*acte*) impolite thing to do, impolite action. **répondre avec ~** to answer impolitely *ou* rudely; **c'est une ~ de faire** it is impolite *ou* rude to do.
impolitique [ɛ̃pɔlitik] adj impolitic.
impondérabilité [ɛ̃pɔ̃deʀabilite] nf imponderability.
impondérable [ɛ̃pɔ̃deʀabl] adj, nm imponderable.
impopulaire [ɛ̃pɔpylɛʀ] adj unpopular (*auprès de* with).
impopularité [ɛ̃pɔpylaʀite] nf unpopularity.
import [ɛ̃pɔʀ] nm (abrév de **importation**) import. **faire de l'~-export** to be in the import-export business.
importable [ɛ̃pɔʀtabl] adj (*Écon*) importable; *vêtement* unwearable.
importance [ɛ̃pɔʀtɑ̃s] nf a *[problème, affaire, personne]* importance; *[événement, fait]* importance, significance. *[personne, question]* **avoir de l'~** to be important, be of importance; **ça a beaucoup d'~ pour moi** it is very important to me, it matters a great deal to me; **sans ~** *personne* unimportant; *problème, incident, détail* unimportant, insignificant; **c'est sans ~, ça n'a pas d'~** it doesn't matter, it's of no importance *ou* consequence; **d'une certaine ~** *problème, événement* fairly *ou* rather important; **de la plus haute ~, de la première ~** *problème, affaire* of paramount *ou* of the highest importance; *événement* momentous, of paramount *ou* of the highest importance.
b (*taille*) *[somme, effectifs, firme]* size; (*ampleur*) *[dégâts, désastre, retard]* extent. **d'une certaine ~** *firme* sizeable; *dégâts* considerable, extensive.
c (*loc*) **prendre de l'~** *[question]* to gain in importance, become more important; *[firme]* to increase in size; *[personne]* to become more important; (*péj*) **se donner de l'~, prendre des airs d'~** to act important *ou* in a self-important way; (*frm*) **l'affaire est d'~** this is no trivial matter, this is a matter of some seriousness; (*littér*) **tancer/rosser qn d'~** to give sb a thorough dressing-down/trouncing (*littér*).
important, e [ɛ̃pɔʀtɑ̃, ɑ̃t] a *personnage, question, rôle* important; *événement, fait* important, significant. **peu ~** of little *ou* of no great importance, of little significance; **rien d'~** nothing important *ou* of importance; **l'~ est de** the important thing is to. b (*quantitativement*) *somme* considerable, sizeable; *retard* considerable; *dégâts* extensive, considerable. **la présence d'un ~ service d'ordre** the presence of a considerable number *ou* a large contingent of police. c (*péj*) *airs* (self-)important; *personnage* self-important. **faire l'~** to act important *ou* in a self-important way.
importateur, -trice [ɛ̃pɔʀtatœʀ, tʀis] 1 adj importing. **pays ~ de blé** wheat-importing country. 2 nm,f importer.
importation [ɛ̃pɔʀtasjɔ̃] nf a (*Comm*) *[marchandises]* importing, importation. **articles d'~** imported articles. b *[animal, plante, maladie]* introduction. **le tabac est d'~ récente** tobacco is a recent import. c (*produit*) import.
importer¹ [ɛ̃pɔʀte] 1 vt *marchandises* to import; *coutumes, danses* to import, introduce (*de* from).
importer² [ɛ̃pɔʀte] 1 vi a (*être important*) to matter. **les conventions importent peu aux jeunes** conventions don't matter much *ou* aren't very important *ou* matter little to young people; **ce qui importe, c'est d'agir vite** the important thing is *ou* what matters is to act quickly; **que lui importe le malheur des autres?** what does he care about other people's unhappiness?, what does other people's unhappiness matter to him?; (*frm*) **il importe de faire** it is important to do; (*frm*) **il importe qu'elle connaisse les risques** it is important that she knows *ou* should know the risks.
b **peu importe** *ou* (*littér*) **qu'importe qu'il soit absent** what does it matter if he is absent?, it matters little that he is absent (*frm*); **peu importe le temps, nous sortirons** we'll go out whatever the weather *ou* no matter what the weather is like; **peu m'importe** (*je n'ai pas de préférence*) I don't mind; (*je m'en moque*) I don't care; **achetez des pêches ou des poires, peu importe** buy peaches or pears — it doesn't matter which; **quel fauteuil veux-tu? — oh, n'importe** which chair will you have? — it doesn't matter *ou* I don't mind *ou* any one will do; **il ne veut pas? qu'importe!** doesn't he want to? what does it matter? *ou* it doesn't matter!; **les maisons sont chères, n'importe, elles se vendent!** houses are expensive, but no matter *ou* but never mind, they still sell.
c **n'importe qui** anybody, anyone; **ce n'est pas n'importe qui** he is not just anybody; **n'importe quoi** anything; **il fait/dit n'importe quoi!*** he has no idea what he's doing!/saying!; **n'importe quoi!*** rubbish!, nonsense!; **n'importe comment** anyhow; **n'importe où** anywhere; **n'importe quand** anytime; **il a fait cela n'importe comment!** he did that anyhow *ou* any old how* (*Brit*); **n'importe comment, il part ce soir** he leaves tonight in any case *ou* anyhow; **n'importe lequel** *ou* **laquelle d'entre nous/vous** *etc* any (one) of us/you *etc;* **entrez dans n'importe quelle boutique** go into any shop; **n'importe quel docteur vous dira la même chose** any doctor will tell you the same thing; **venez à n'importe quelle heure** come (at) any time.
importun, e [ɛ̃pɔʀtœ̃, yn] 1 adj (*frm*) *curiosité, présence, pensée, plainte* troublesome, importunate (*frm*); *arrivée, visite* inopportune, ill-timed; *personne* importunate (*frm*), irksome. **je ne veux pas être ~** (*déranger*) I don't wish to disturb you *ou* to intrude; (*irriter*) I don't wish to be importunate (*frm*) *ou* irksome; **se rendre ~ par** to make o.s. objectionable by. 2 nm,f (*gêneur*) irksome individual; (*visiteur*) intruder.
importunément [ɛ̃pɔʀtynemɑ̃] adv (*frm*) (*de façon irritante*)

importunately (*frm*); (*à un mauvais moment*) inopportunely.

importuner [ɛ̃pɔʀtyne] 1 **vt** (*frm*) *[représentant, mendiant]* to importune (*frm*), bother; *[insecte, bruit]* to trouble, bother; *[interruptions, remarques]* to bother. **je ne veux pas vous ~** I don't wish to put you to any trouble *ou* to bother you.

importunité [ɛ̃pɔʀtynite] **nf** (*frm*) *[démarche, demande]* importunity (*frm*). (*sollicitations*) **~s** importunities.

imposable [ɛ̃pozabl] **adj** *personne, revenu* taxable; *voir* **matière**.

imposant, e [ɛ̃pozɑ̃, ɑ̃t] **adj** (*majestueux*) *personnage, stature* imposing; *allure* stately; (*considérable*) *majorité, mise en scène, foule* imposing, impressive. **~e paysanne** (*iro: gros*) peasant woman with an imposing figure; **la présence d'un ~ service d'ordre** the presence of an imposing number *ou* a large contingent of police.

imposé, e [ɛ̃poze] (**ptp de imposer**) **adj** (*Fin*) *personne, revenu* taxable; (*Sport*) *exercices, figures* compulsory. (*Comm*) **prix ~** set price; **tarif ~** set rate.

imposer [ɛ̃poze] 1 **1 vt a** (*prescrire*) *tâche, travail, date* to set; *règle, conditions* to impose, lay down; *punition, taxe* to impose (*à* on); *prix* to set, fix. **~ ses idées/sa présence à qn** to impose *ou* force one's ideas/one's company on sb; **~ des conditions à qch** to impose *ou* place conditions on sth; **~ un travail/une date à qn** to set sb a piece of work/a date; **~ un régime à qn** to put sb on a diet; **la décision leur a été imposée par les événements** the decision was forced *ou* imposed (up)on them by events; **il nous a imposé son candidat** he has imposed his candidate on us; **on lui a imposé le silence** silence has been imposed upon him.

b (*faire connaître*) **~ son nom** *[candidat]* to come to the fore; *[artiste]* to make o.s. known, compel recognition; *[firme]* to establish itself, become an established name; **il m'impose/sa conduite impose le respect** he commands/his behaviour compels respect.

c (*Fin: taxer*) *marchandise, revenu, salariés* to tax. **~ insuffisamment** to undertax.

d (*Typ*) to impose.

e (*Rel*) **~ les mains** to lay on hands.

f en ~ à qn to impress sb; **il en impose** he's an imposing individual; **sa présence/son intelligence en impose** his presence/his intelligence is imposing; **ne vous en laissez pas ~ par ses grands airs** don't let yourself be impressed by his haughty manner.

2 s'imposer vpr a (*être nécessaire*) *[décision, action]* to be essential *ou* vital *ou* imperative. **dans ce cas, le repos s'impose** in this case rest is essential *ou* vital *ou* imperative; **ces mesures ne s'imposaient pas** these measures were unnecessary; **quand on est à Paris une visite au Louvre s'impose** when in Paris, a visit to the Louvre is imperative *ou* is a must*.

b (*se contraindre à*) **s'~ une tâche** to set o.s. a task; **s'~ de faire** to make it a rule to do.

c (*montrer sa supériorité*) to assert o.s.; (*avoir une personnalité forte*) to be assertive; (*Sport*) to dominate. **s'~ par ses qualités** to stand out *ou* to compel recognition because of one's qualities; **il s'est imposé dans sa branche** he has made a name for himself in his branch; **il s'est imposé comme le seul susceptible d'avoir le prix** he emerged *ou* he established himself as the only one likely to get the prize.

d (*imposer sa présence à*) **s'~ à qn** to impose (o.s.) upon sb; **impose-toi!** go ahead!; **je ne voudrais pas m'~** I do not want to impose; **le soleil s'imposera peu à peu sur tout le pays** gradually sunshine will spread across the whole country.

imposition [ɛ̃pozisjɔ̃] **nf** (*Fin*) taxation; (*Typ*) imposition. (*Rel*) **l'~ des mains** the laying on of hands; (*Fin*) **double ~** double taxation.

impossibilité [ɛ̃pɔsibilite] **nf** impossibility. **l'~ de réaliser ce plan** the impossibility of carrying out this plan; **y a-t-il ~ à cela?** is that impossible?; **y a-t-il ~ à ce que je vienne?** is it impossible for me to come?; **être dans l'~ de faire qch** to be unable to do sth; **l'~ dans laquelle il se trouvait de ...** the fact that he was unable to ..., the fact that he found it impossible to ...; **se heurter à des ~s** to come up against insuperable obstacles.

impossible [ɛ̃pɔsibl] **1 adj a** (*irréalisable, improbable*) impossible. **~ à faire** impossible to do; **il est ~ de/que** it is impossible to/that; **il est ~ qu'il soit déjà arrivé** he cannot possibly have arrived yet; **il m'est ~ de le faire** it's impossible for me to do it, I can't possibly do it; **pouvez-vous venir lundi? — non, cela m'est ~** can you come on Monday? — no, I can't *ou* no, it's impossible; (*Prov*) **~ n'est pas français** there's no such word as "can't".

b (*pénible, difficile*) *enfant, situation* impossible. **rendre l'existence ~ à qn** to make sb's life impossible *ou* a misery; **elle a des horaires ~s** she has impossible *ou* terrible hours; **il mène une vie ~** he leads an incredible life.

c (*invraisemblable*) *nom, titre* ridiculous, impossible. **se lever à des heures ~s** to get up at an impossible *ou* a ridiculous time *ou* hour; **il lui arrive toujours des histoires ~s** impossible things are always happening to him.

2 nm a l'~ the impossible; **tenter l'~** to attempt the impossible; **je ferai l'~ (pour venir)** I'll do my utmost (to come).

b par ~ by some miracle, by some remote chance; **si par ~ je terminais premier ...** if by some miracle *ou* some remote chance I were to finish first ... .

imposte [ɛ̃pɔst] **nf** (*fenêtre*) fanlight (*Brit*), transom (window) (*US*).

imposteur [ɛ̃pɔstœʀ] **nm** impostor.

imposture [ɛ̃pɔstyʀ] **nf** imposture, deception.

impôt [ɛ̃po] **1 nm** (*taxe*) tax; (*taxes*) taxes, taxation; (*gén: contributions*) (income) tax. **les ~s** (*gén*) taxes; (*service local*) the tax office; (*service national*) the Inland Revenue (*Brit*), the Internal Revenue Service (*US*); **les ~s me réclament 10 000 F** the taxman* wants 10,000 francs from me; **payer des ~s** to pay tax; **je paye plus de 10 000 F d'~s** I pay more than 10,000 francs in tax *ou* 10,000 francs tax; **frapper d'un ~** to put a tax on; **~ direct/indirect/déguisé** direct/indirect/hidden tax; **~ retenu à la source** tax deducted at source; **bénéfices avant ~** pre-tax profits; **faire un bénéfice de 10 000 F avant ~** to make a profit *ou* profits of 10,000 francs; *voir* **assiette, déclaration, feuille** *etc.*

2 comp ▸impôt sur les bénéfices tax on profits, ≃ corporation tax **▸impôt sur le chiffre d'affaires** tax on turnover **▸impôt foncier** ≃ land tax **▸impôt (de solidarité) sur la fortune, impôt sur les grandes fortunes**† wealth tax **▸impôts locaux** rates, local taxes (*US*), ≃ council tax (*Brit*) **▸impôt sur les plus-values** ≃ capital gains tax **▸impôt sur le revenu (des personnes physiques)** income tax **▸impôt sur le transfert des capitaux** capital transfer tax **▸impôt de sang** (*littér*, †) blood tribute **▸impôt sur les sociétés** corporate tax.

impotence [ɛ̃pɔtɑ̃s] **nf** disability.

impotent, e [ɛ̃pɔtɑ̃, ɑ̃t] **1 adj** disabled, crippled. **l'accident l'a rendu ~** the accident has disabled *ou* crippled him. **2 nm,f** disabled person, cripple.

impraticable [ɛ̃pʀatikabl] **adj** *idée* impracticable, unworkable; *tâche* impracticable; (*Sport*) *terrain* unfit for play, unplayable; *route, piste* impassable. **~ pour les** *ou* **aux véhicules à moteur** unfit *ou* unsuitable for motor vehicles, impassable to motor vehicles.

imprécation [ɛ̃pʀekasjɔ̃] **nf** imprecation, curse.

imprécatoire [ɛ̃pʀekatwaʀ] **adj** (*littér*) imprecatory (*littér*).

imprécis, e [ɛ̃pʀesi, iz] **adj** (*gén*) imprecise; *tir* inaccurate.

imprécision [ɛ̃pʀesizjɔ̃] **nf** (*voir* **imprécis**) imprecision; inaccuracy.

imprégnation [ɛ̃pʀeɲasjɔ̃] **nf** (*voir* **imprégner**) (*gén*) impregnation; permeation; imbuing. **taux d'~ alcoolique** level of alcohol in the blood; **pour apprendre une langue, rien ne vaut une lente ~** to learn a language, there's nothing to beat slow immersion in it *ou* there's nothing to beat gradually immersing oneself in it.

imprégner [ɛ̃pʀeɲe] 6 **1 vt** *tissu, matière* (*de liquide*) to impregnate, soak (*de* with); (*d'une odeur, de fumée*) to impregnate (*de* with); *pièce, air* to permeate, fill (*de* with); *esprit* to imbue, impregnate (*de* with). **cette odeur imprégnait toute la rue** the smell filled *ou* pervaded the whole street; **l'amertume qui imprégnait ses paroles** the bitterness which pervaded his words; **maison imprégnée de lumière** house flooded with light; **imprégné des préjugés de sa caste** imbued with *ou* impregnated with the prejudices of his class.

2 s'imprégner vpr: s'~ de *[tissu, substance]* (*de liquide*) to become impregnated *ou* soaked with; (*d'une odeur, de fumée*) to become impregnated with; *[local, air]* to become permeated *ou* filled with; *[esprits, élèves]* to become imbued with, absorb; **séjourner à l'étranger pour s'~ de la langue étrangère** to live abroad to immerse o.s in *ou* to absorb the foreign language; (*fig*) **s'~ d'alcool** to soak up alcohol.

imprenable [ɛ̃pʀənabl] **adj** *forteresse* impregnable. **vue ~ sur la vallée** (*non bouchée*) unimpeded *ou* unrestricted outlook over the valley guaranteed; (*magnifique*) unbeatable *ou* breathtaking view of the valley.

impréparation [ɛ̃pʀepaʀasjɔ̃] **nf** lack of preparation.

imprésario [ɛ̃pʀesaʀjo] **nm** *[acteur, chanteur]* manager; *[troupes]* impresario, manager.

imprescriptibilité [ɛ̃pʀɛskʀiptibilite] **nf** (*Jur*) imprescriptibility.

imprescriptible [ɛ̃pʀɛskʀiptibl] **adj** (*Jur*) imprescriptible.

impression [ɛ̃pʀesjɔ̃] **nf a** (*sensation physique*) feeling, impression; (*sentiment, réaction*) impression. **ils échangèrent leurs ~s (de voyage)** they exchanged their impressions (of the journey); **l'~ que j'ai de lui** the impression I have of him, my impression of him; **ça m'a fait peu d'~/une grosse ~** that made little/a great impression upon me; **faire bonne/mauvaise ~** to make *ou* create a good/bad impression; **avoir l'~ que** to have a feeling that, get *ou* have the impression that; **créer/donner une ~ de** to create/give an impression of; **il ne me donne** *ou* **fait pas l'~ d'(être) un menteur** I don't get the impression that he is a liar, he doesn't give me the impression of being a liar; **faire ~** *[film, orateur]* to make an impression, have an impact.

b *[livre, tissu, motif]* printing. **~ en couleur** colour printing; **ce livre en est à sa 3e ~** this book is at its 3rd impression *ou* printing; **le livre est à l'~** the book is with the printers; **l'~ de ce livre est soignée** this book is beautifully printed; *voir* **faute**.

c (*motif*) pattern. **tissu à ~s florales** floral pattern(ed) fabric, fabric with a floral pattern.

d (*Phot*) *[image]* exposure. **temps d'~** exposure (time); **technique de double ~** technique of double exposure.

e (*Peinture*) **(couche d')~** undercoat.

f (†: *empreinte, pas*) imprint.

impressionnabilité [ɛ̃pʀesjɔnabilite] **nf** (*émotivité*) impressionability, impressionableness.

impressionnable [ɛ̃pʀesjɔnabl] **adj** *personne* impressionable.

impressionnant, e [ɛ̃pʀesjɔnɑ̃, ɑ̃t] **adj** (*imposant*) *somme, spectacle, monument* impressive; (*bouleversant*) *scène, accident* upsetting. **elle était ~e de calme** her calmness was impressive.

impressionner [ɛ̃pʀesjɔne] [1] **vt** a (*frapper*) to impress; (*bouleverser*) to upset. **ne te laisse pas ~** don't let yourself be overawed; **cela risque d'~ les enfants** this may upset children. b (*Opt, Phot*) *rétine* to show up on. **~ la pellicule** *[image, sujet]* to show up on; *[photographe]* to expose; **la pellicule n'a pas été impressionnée** the film hasn't been exposed.

impressionnisme [ɛ̃pʀesjɔnism] **nm** impressionism.

impressionniste [ɛ̃pʀesjɔnist] 1 **adj** impressionistic; (*Art, Mus*) impressionist. 2 **nmf** impressionist.

imprévisibilité [ɛ̃pʀevizibilite] **nf** unpredictability.

imprévisible [ɛ̃pʀevizibl] **adj** unforeseeable, unpredictable. **elle est assez ~ dans ses réactions** her reactions are quite unpredictable.

imprévoyance [ɛ̃pʀevwajɑ̃s] **nf** (*négligence*) lack of foresight; (*en matière d'argent*) improvidence.

imprévoyant, e [ɛ̃pʀevwajɑ̃, ɑ̃t] **adj** (*voir* **imprévoyance**) lacking (in) foresight; improvident.

imprévu, e [ɛ̃pʀevy] 1 **adj** *événement, succès, réaction* unforeseen, unexpected; *courage, geste* unexpected; *dépense(s)* unforeseen. **de manière ~e** unexpectedly.

2 **nm** a **l'~** the unexpected, the unforeseen; **j'aime l'~** I like the unexpected, I like not to foresee everything in advance, I like not knowing what's going to happen; **un peu d'~** an element of surprise *ou* of the unexpected *ou* of the unforeseen; **vacances pleines d'~** holidays full of surprises; **en cas d'~** if anything unexpected *ou* unforeseen crops up; **sauf ~** barring any unexpected *ou* unforeseen circumstances, unless anything unexpected *ou* unforeseen crops up.

b (*incident, ennui*) something unexpected *ou* unforeseen, unexpected *ou* unforeseen event. **il y a un ~** something unexpected *ou* unforeseen has cropped up; **tous ces ~s nous ont retardés** all these unexpected *ou* unforeseen events have delayed us.

imprimable [ɛ̃pʀimabl] **adj** printable.

imprimante [ɛ̃pʀimɑ̃t] **nf** printer. **~ matricielle/ligne par ligne/à jet d'encre/à marguerite/à laser** dot-matrix/line/ink-jet/daisy-wheel/laser printer.

imprimatur [ɛ̃pʀimatyʀ] **nm inv** imprimatur.

imprimé, e [ɛ̃pʀime] (**ptp de imprimer**) 1 **adj** *tissu, feuille* printed. 2 **nm** a (*formulaire*) printed form. (*Poste*) **"~s"** "printed matter"; **envoyer qch au tarif ~s** to send sth at the printed paper rate; **catalogue/section des ~s** catalogue/department of printed books. b (*tissu*) **l'~** printed material *ou* fabrics, prints; **~ à fleur** floral print (fabric *ou* material); **l'~ et l'uni** printed and plain fabrics *ou* material.

imprimer [ɛ̃pʀime] [1] **vt** a *livre, foulard, billets de banque, dessin* to print; (*Peinture*) *surface* to prime. b (*apposer*) *visa, cachet* to stamp (*dans* on, in). c (*marquer*) *rides, traces, marque* to imprint (*dans* in, on). **une scène imprimée dans sa mémoire** a scene imprinted on his memory. d (*publier*) *texte, ouvrage* to publish; *auteur* to publish the work of. **la joie de se voir imprimé** the joy of seeing o.s. *ou* one's work in print. e (*communiquer*) **~ un mouvement/une impulsion à** to impart *ou* transmit a movement/an impulse to; **~ une direction à** to give a direction to.

imprimerie [ɛ̃pʀimʀi] **nf** (*firme, usine*) printing works; (*atelier*) printing house; (*section*) printery; (*pour enfants*) printing outfit *ou* kit. (*technique*) **l'~** printing; **l'I~ nationale** ≃ the Government Printing Office; *voir* **caractère**.

imprimeur [ɛ̃pʀimœʀ] **nm** (*directeur*) printer. **(ouvrier) ~** printer; **~-éditeur** printer and publisher; **~-libraire** printer and bookseller.

improbabilité [ɛ̃pʀɔbabilite] **nf** unlikelihood, improbability.

improbable [ɛ̃pʀɔbabl] **adj** unlikely, improbable.

improbité [ɛ̃pʀɔbite] **nf** (*littér*) lack of integrity.

improductif, -ive [ɛ̃pʀɔdyktif, iv] **adj** unproductive.

improductivité [ɛ̃pʀɔdyktivite] **nf** unproductiveness, lack of productivity.

impromptu, e [ɛ̃pʀɔ̃pty] 1 **adj** (*improvisé*) *départ* sudden (*épith*); *visite* surprise (*épith*); *repas, exposé* impromptu (*épith*). **faire un discours ~ sur un sujet** to speak off the cuff *ou* make an impromptu speech on a subject, extemporize on a subject. 2 **nm** (*Littérat, Mus*) impromptu. 3 **adv** (*à l'improviste*) *arriver* impromptu; (*de chic*) *répondre* off the cuff, impromptu. **il arriva ~, un soir de juin** he arrived impromptu *ou* (quite) out of the blue one evening in June.

imprononçable [ɛ̃pʀɔnɔ̃sabl] **adj** unpronounceable.

impropre [ɛ̃pʀɔpʀ] **adj** a *terme* inappropriate. b **~ à** *outil, personne* unsuitable for, unsuited to; **eau ~ à la consommation** water unfit for (human) consumption.

improprement [ɛ̃pʀɔpʀəmɑ̃] **adv** *nommer* incorrectly, improperly. **s'exprimer ~** to express o.s. incorrectly, not to express o.s. properly.

impropriété [ɛ̃pʀɔpʀijete] **nf** *[forme]* incorrectness, inaccuracy. **~ (de langage)** (language) error, mistake.

improuvable [ɛ̃pʀuvabl] **adj** unprovable.

improvisateur, -trice [ɛ̃pʀɔvizatœʀ, tʀis] **nm,f** improviser.

improvisation [ɛ̃pʀɔvizasjɔ̃] **nf** improvisation. **faire une ~** to improvise; (*Jazz*) **~ collective** jam session.

improvisé, e [ɛ̃pʀɔvize] (**ptp de improviser**) **adj** (*de fortune*) *équipe* scratch (*épith*); *réforme, table* improvised, makeshift; *cuisinier, infirmier* acting, temporary; (*impromptu*) *pique-nique, discours, leçon* improvised. **avec des moyens ~s** with whatever means are available *ou* to hand.

improviser [ɛ̃pʀɔvize] [1] 1 **vt** a *discours, réunion, pique-nique* to improvise. **il a dû ~** *[organisateur]* he had to improvise; *[musicien]* he had to extemporize *ou* improvise; *[acteur, orateur]* he had to improvise *ou* extemporize *ou* ad-lib*. b **~ qn cuisinier/infirmier** to get sb to act as cook/nurse. 2 **s'improviser vpr** a *[secours, réunion]* to be improvised. b **s'~ cuisinier/infirmier** to act as cook/nurse; **on ne s'improvise pas menuisier** you don't just suddenly become a carpenter, you don't become a carpenter just like that.

improviste [ɛ̃pʀɔvist] **nm: à l'~** unexpectedly, without warning; **je lui ai fait une visite à l'~** I dropped in on him unexpectedly *ou* without warning; **prendre qn à l'~** to catch sb unawares.

imprudemment [ɛ̃pʀydamɑ̃] **adv** *circuler, naviguer* carelessly; *parler* unwisely, imprudently. **un inconnu qu'il avait ~ suivi** a stranger whom he had foolishly *ou* imprudently *ou* unwisely followed; **s'engager ~ sur la chaussée** to step out carelessly onto the road.

imprudence [ɛ̃pʀydɑ̃s] **nf** a (*caractère: voir* **imprudent**) carelessness; imprudence; foolishness; foolhardiness. **il a eu l'~ de mentionner ce projet** he was foolish *ou* unwise *ou* imprudent enough to mention the project; (*Jur*) **blessures par ~** injuries through negligence; *voir* **homicide**. b (*action imprudente*) **commettre une ~** to do something foolish *ou* imprudent; **ne faites pas d'~s** don't do anything foolish.

imprudent, e [ɛ̃pʀydɑ̃, ɑ̃t] 1 **adj** *conducteur, geste, action* careless; *alpiniste* careless, imprudent; *remarque* imprudent, unwise, foolish; *projet* foolish, foolhardy. **il est ~ de se baigner tout de suite après un repas** it's unwise *ou* not wise to swim immediately after a meal; **il se montra ~ en refusant de porter un gilet de sauvetage** he was unwise *ou* foolish to refuse to wear a life jacket. 2 **nm,f** imprudent *ou* careless person. **il faut punir ces ~s** (*conducteurs*) these careless drivers must be punished.

impubère [ɛ̃pybɛʀ] 1 **adj** below the age of puberty. 2 **nmf** (*Jur*) ≃ minor.

impubliable [ɛ̃pyblijabl] **adj** unpublishable.

impudemment [ɛ̃pydamɑ̃] **adv** (*frm: voir* **impudent**) impudently; brazenly, shamelessly.

impudence [ɛ̃pydɑ̃s] **nf** (*frm*) a (*caractère: voir* **impudent**) impudence; brazenness, shamelessness. **quelle ~!** what impudence! b (*acte*) impudent action; (*parole*) impudent remark. **je ne tolérerai pas ses ~s** I won't put up with *ou* tolerate his impudent behaviour *ou* his impudence.

impudent, e [ɛ̃pydɑ̃, ɑ̃t] **adj** (*frm*) (*insolent*) impudent; (*cynique*) brazen, shameless.

impudeur [ɛ̃pydœʀ] **nf** (*voir* **impudique**) immodesty; shamelessness.

impudicité [ɛ̃pydisite] **nf** (*voir* **impudique**) immodesty; shamelessness.

impudique [ɛ̃pydik] **adj** *personne* immodest, shameless; *regard, pose, décolleté* immodest; *propos* shameless.

impudiquement [ɛ̃pydikmɑ̃] **adv** (*voir* **impudique**) immodestly; shamelessly.

impuissance [ɛ̃pɥisɑ̃s] **nf** a (*faiblesse*) powerlessness, helplessness. **~ à faire** powerlessness *ou* incapacity to do; **réduire qn à l'~** to render sb powerless. b (*sexuelle*) impotence.

impuissant, e [ɛ̃pɥisɑ̃, ɑ̃t] 1 **adj** a *personne* powerless, helpless. **~ à faire** powerless to do, incapable of doing. b (*sexuellement*) impotent. 2 **nm** impotent man.

impulsif, -ive [ɛ̃pylsif, iv] **adj** impulsive.

impulsion [ɛ̃pylsjɔ̃] **nf** a (*mécanique, électrique*) impulse. b (*fig: élan*) impetus. **l'~ donnée à l'économie** the boost *ou* impetus given to the economy; **sous l'~ de leurs chefs/des circonstances** through the impetus given by their leaders/by circumstances; **sous l'~ de la vengeance/de la colère** driven *ou* impelled by a spirit of revenge/by anger, under the impulse of revenge/anger. c (*mouvement, instinct*) impulse. **cédant à des ~s morbides** yielding to morbid impulses; *voir* **achat**.

impulsivité [ɛ̃pylsivite] **nf** impulsiveness.

impunément [ɛ̃pynemɑ̃] **adv** with impunity. **on ne se moque pas ~ de lui** one can't make fun of him with impunity, you can't make fun of him and (expect to) get away with it.

impuni, e [ɛ̃pyni] **adj** unpunished.

impunité [ɛ̃pynite] **nf** impunity. **en toute ~** with complete impunity.

impur, e [ɛ̃pyʀ] **adj** a (*altéré*) *liquide, air* impure; *race* mixed; (*Rel*) *animal* unclean. b (*immoral*) *geste, pensée, personne* impure.

impureté [ɛ̃pyʀte] **nf** (*gén*) impurity. **vivre dans l'~** to live in a state of impurity; **~s** impurities.

imputabilité [ɛ̃pytabilite] **nf** (*Jur*) imputability.

imputable [ɛ̃pytabl] **adj** a **~ à** *faute, accident* imputable to, ascribable to, attributable to. b (*Fin*) **~ sur** chargeable to.

imputation [ɛ̃pytasjɔ̃] **nf** a (*accusation*) imputation (*frm*), charge. b (*Fin*) *[somme]* **~ à** charging to.

imputer [ɛ̃pyte] [1] **vt** a (*attribuer à*) ~ **à** to impute to, attribute to, ascribe to. b (*Fin*) ~ **à** *ou* **sur** to charge to.
imputrescibilité [ɛ̃pytʀesibilite] **nf** rotproof nature, imputrescibility (*SPÉC*).
imputrescible [ɛ̃pytʀesibl] **adj** rotproof, imputrescible (*SPÉC*).
in* [in] **adj** trendy*. **les bottes sont ~ cette année** boots are in* this year; **la boîte de nuit ~ en ce moment** the in* nightclub at the moment.
INA [ina] **nm** (**abrév de Institut national de l'audiovisuel**) *voir* **institut**.
inabordable [inabɔʀdabl] **adj** *personne* unapproachable; *lieu* inaccessible; *prix* prohibitive. **maintenant, le beurre est ~** butter is a prohibitive price these days.
inabrité, e [inabʀite] **adj** unsheltered, unprotected.
inabrogeable [inabʀɔʒabl] **adj** (*Jur*) unrepealable.
in absentia [inapsɑ̃sja] **adv** in absentia.
in abstracto [inapstʀakto] **adv** in the abstract.
inaccentué, e [inaksɑ̃tɥe] **adj** unstressed, unaccented, unaccentuated.
inacceptable [inaksɛptabl] **adj** (*non recevable*) *offre, plan* unacceptable; (*inadmissible*) *propos* unacceptable. **c'est ~** it's unacceptable.
inaccessibilité [inaksesibilite] **nf** inaccessibility.
inaccessible [inaksesibl] **adj** a *montagne, personne, but* inaccessible; *objet* inaccessible, out of reach (*attrib*). **une éducation ~ aux plus défavorisés** an education out of reach of the underprivileged. b *texte, littérature* (*obscur*) obscure; (*incompréhensible*) incomprehensible (*à* to). c ~ **à** (*insensible à*) impervious to.
inaccompli, e [inakɔ̃pli] **adj** (*littér*) *vœux* unfulfilled; *tâche* unaccomplished.
inaccomplissement [inakɔ̃plismɑ̃] **nm** (*littér*) */vœux/* non-fulfilment; */tâche/* non-execution.
inaccoutumé, e [inakutyme] **adj** unusual. (*littér*) ~ **à** unaccustomed to, unused to.
inachevé, e [inaʃ(ə)ve] **adj** unfinished, uncompleted. **une impression d'~** a feeling of incompleteness *ou* incompletion.
inachèvement [inaʃɛvmɑ̃] **nm** incompletion.
inactif, -ive [inaktif, iv] 1 **adj** a *vie, personne, capitaux, machine* inactive, idle; (*Bourse*) *marché* slack; *population* non-working; *volcan* inactive, dormant. b (*inefficace*) *remède* ineffective, ineffectual. 2 **nmpl: les ~s** the non-working population, those not in active employment.
inaction [inaksjɔ̃] **nf** (*oisiveté*) inactivity, idleness.
inactivité [inaktivite] **nf** (*non-activité*) inactivity. (*Admin, Mil*) **être en ~** to be out of active service.
inactuel, -elle [inaktɥɛl] **adj** irrelevant to the present day.
inadaptable [inadaptabl] **adj** *roman* impossible to adapt.
inadaptation [inadaptasjɔ̃] **nf** maladjustment. ~ **à** failure to adjust to *ou* adapt to; ~ **d'un enfant à la vie scolaire** a child's inability to cope with school life.
inadapté, e [inadapte] 1 **adj** *personne, enfance* maladjusted; *outil, moyens* unsuitable (*à* for). ~ **à** not adapted *ou* adjusted to; **un genre de vie complètement ~ à ses ressources** a way of life quite unsuited to his resources; **enfant ~ (à la vie scolaire)** maladjusted child, child with (school) behavioural problems. 2 **nm,f** (*péj: adulte*) misfit; (*Admin, Psych*) maladjusted person.
inadéquat, -quate [inadekwa(t), kwat] **adj** inadequate.
inadéquation [inadekwasjɔ̃] **nf** inadequacy.
inadmissibilité [inadmisibilite] **nf** (*Jur*) inadmissibility.
inadmissible [inadmisibl] **adj** a *conduite, négligence* inadmissible, intolerable. b (*Jur*) *témoignage, preuve* inadmissible.
inadvertance [inadvɛʀtɑ̃s] **nf** oversight. **par ~** inadvertently, by mistake.
inaliénabilité [inaljenabilite] **nf** inalienability.
inaliénable [inaljenabl] **adj** inalienable.
inaltérabilité [inalteʀabilite] **nf** (*voir* **inaltérable**) a stability; fastness; fade-resistance; permanence. ~ **à l'air** stability in air, ability to resist exposure to the atmosphere; ~ **à la chaleur** heat-resistance, ability to withstand heat; (*littér*) **l'~ du ciel** the unvarying blueness of the sky. b unchanging nature; unfailing nature; unshakeable nature; steadfastness. **l'~ de son calme** his unchanging *ou* unshakeable calmness.
inaltérable [inalteʀabl] **adj** a *métal, substance* stable; *couleur* (*au lavage*) fast; (*à la lumière*) fade-resistant; *vernis, encre* permanent; (*littér*) *ciel, cycle* unchanging. ~ **à l'air/à la chaleur** unaffected by air/heat. b *humeur, sentiments* unchanging, unfailing, unshakeable; *santé* unfailing; *principes, espoir* steadfast, unshakeable, unfailing. **leur amitié est restée ~** their friendship remained unaltered *ou* steadfast.
inaltéré, e [inalteʀe] **adj** unchanged, unaltered.
inamical, e, mpl -aux [inamikal, o] **adj** unfriendly.
inamovibilité [inamɔvibilite] **nf** (*Jur*) */fonction/* permanence; */juge, fonctionnaire/* irremovability.
inamovible [inamɔvibl] **adj** a (*Jur*) *juge, fonctionnaire* irremovable; *fonction, emploi* from which one is irremovable. b (*fixe*) *plaque, panneau, capuche* fixed. **cette partie est ~** this part is fixed *ou* cannot be removed. c (*hum*) *casquette, sourire* eternal. **il travaille toujours chez X? il est vraiment ~** is he still with X? – he's a permanent fixture *ou* he's built in with the bricks (*Brit hum*).
inanimé, e [inanime] **adj** *matière* inanimate; *personne, corps* (*évanoui*) unconscious, senseless; (*mort*) lifeless; (*Ling*) inanimate. **tomber ~** to fall senseless to the ground, fall to the ground unconscious.
inanité [inanite] **nf** */conversation/* inanity; */querelle, efforts/* futility, pointlessness; */espoirs/* vanity, futility. **dire des ~s** to talk trivialities.
inanition [inanisjɔ̃] **nf** exhaustion through lack of nourishment. **tomber/mourir d'~** to faint with/die of hunger.
inapaisable [inapɛzabl] **adj** *colère, chagrin, besoin* unappeasable; *soif* unquenchable.
inapaisé, e [inapeze] **adj** (*voir* **inapaisable**) unappeased; unquenched.
inaperçu, e [inapɛʀsy] **adj** unnoticed. **passer ~** to pass *ou* go unnoticed; **le geste ne passa pas ~** the gesture did not go unnoticed *ou* unremarked.
inappétence [inapetɑ̃s] **nf** (*manque d'appétit*) lack of appetite.
inapplicable [inaplikabl] **adj** *loi* unenforceable. **dans ce cas, la règle est ~** in this case, the rule cannot be applied *ou* is inapplicable (*à* to).
inapplication [inaplikasjɔ̃] **nf** a */élève/* lack of application. b */loi/* non-application, non-enforcement.
inappliqué, e [inaplike] **adj** a *écolier* lacking in application (*attrib*). **cet écolier est ~** this pupil lacks application, this pupil does not apply himself. b *méthode* not applied (*attrib*); *loi, règlement* not enforced (*attrib*).
inappréciable [inapʀesjabl] **adj** a (*précieux*) *aide, service* invaluable; *avantage, bonheur* inestimable. b (*difficilement décelable*) *nuance, différence* inappreciable, imperceptible.
inapproprié, e [inapʀɔpʀije] **adj** *terme, mesure, équipement* inappropriate.
inapte [inapt] **adj** (*incapable*) incapable. ~ **aux affaires/à certains travaux** unsuited to *ou* unfitted for business/certain kinds of work; **un accident l'a rendu ~ au travail** an accident has made him unfit for work; ~ **à faire** incapable of doing; (*Mil*) ~ **(au service)** unfit (for military service).
inaptitude [inaptityd] **nf** (*mentale*) inaptitude, incapacity; (*physique*) unfitness (*à qch* for sth, *à faire qch* for doing sth). (*Mil*) ~ **(au service)** unfitness (for military service).
inarrangeable [inaʀɑ̃ʒabl] **adj** *querelle* beyond reconciliation (*attrib*); *appareil, outil* beyond repair (*attrib*).
inarticulé, e [inaʀtikyle] **adj** *mots, cris* inarticulate.
inassimilable [inasimilabl] **adj** *notions, substance, immigrants* that cannot be assimilated.
inassimilé, e [inasimile] **adj** *notions, immigrants, substance* unassimilated.
inassouvi, e [inasuvi] **adj** *haine, colère, désir* unappeased; *faim* unsatisfied, unappeased; *soif* (*lit, fig*) unquenched; *personne* unfulfilled. **vengeance ~e** unappeased desire for revenge, unsated lust for revenge (*littér*); **soif ~e de puissance** unappeased *ou* unquenched lust for power.
inassouvissable [inasuvisabl] **adj** *faim* insatiable, unappeasable; *désir, soif* unquenchable, insatiable.
inassouvissement [inasuvismɑ̃] **nm: l'~ de sa faim/son désir** (*action*) the failure to appease his hunger/quench his desire; (*résultat*) his unappeased hunger/unquenched desire.
inattaquable [inatakabl] **adj** *poste, position* unassailable; *preuve* irrefutable; *argument* unassailable, irrefutable; *conduite, réputation* irreproachable, unimpeachable; *personne* (*par sa qualité*) beyond reproach (*attrib*); (*par sa position*) unassailable; *métal* corrosion-proof, rustproof.
inattendu, e [inatɑ̃dy] 1 **adj** *événement, réaction* unexpected, unforeseen; *visiteur, remarque* unexpected. 2 **nm: l'~** the unexpected, the unforeseen; **l'~ d'une remarque** the unexpectedness of a remark.
inattentif, -ive [inatɑ̃tif, iv] **adj** inattentive. ~ **à** (*ne prêtant pas attention à*) inattentive to; (*se souciant peu de*) *dangers, détails matériels* heedless of, unmindful of.
inattention [inatɑ̃sjɔ̃] **nf** a (*distraction*) lack of attention, inattention. b **(instant d')~** moment of inattention, moment's inattention; **(faute d')~** careless mistake. c (*littér: manque d'intérêt pour*) ~ **à** *convenances, détails matériels* lack of concern for.
inaudible [inodibl] **adj** (*non ou peu audible*) inaudible; (*péj: mauvais*) unbearable.
inaugural, e, mpl -aux [inogyʀal, o] **adj** *séance, cérémonie* inaugural; *vol, voyage* maiden (*épith*). **discours ~** */député/* maiden *ou* inaugural speech; (*lors d'une inauguration*) inaugural speech; (*lors d'un congrès*) opening *ou* inaugural speech.
inauguration [inogyʀasjɔ̃] **nf** (*voir* **inaugurer**) a (*action*) unveiling; inauguration; opening. **cérémonie/discours d'~** inaugural ceremony/lecture *ou* speech. b (*cérémonie*) opening ceremony; inauguration; unveiling ceremony.
inaugurer [inogyʀe] [1] **vt** a *monument, plaque* to unveil; *route, bâtiment* to inaugurate, open; *manifestation, exposition* to open. (*fig*) ~ **les chrysanthèmes*** to be a mere figurehead. b (*fig: commencer*) *politique, période* to inaugurate. **nous inaugurions une période de paix** we were entering a time of peace. c (*fig: utiliser pour la première fois*) *raquette, bureau, chapeau* to christen*; *procédé* to pioneer.
inauthenticité [inotɑ̃tisite] **nf** inauthenticity.
inauthentique [inotɑ̃tik] **adj** *document, fait* not authentic (*attrib*);

(*Philos*) *existence* unauthentic.

inavouable [inavwabl] adj *procédé, motifs, mœurs* shameful, too shameful to mention (*attrib*); *bénéfices* undisclosable.

inavoué, e [inavwe] adj *crime* unconfessed; *sentiments* unconfessed, unavowed.

INC [iɛnse] nm (abrév de **Institut national de la consommation**) ≃ CA (*Brit*), ≃ CPSC (*US*); *voir* **institut.**

inca [ɛ̃ka] 1 adj Inca. 2 nmf: **I~** Inca.

incalculable [ɛ̃kalkylabl] adj (*gén*) incalculable. **un nombre ~ de** countless numbers of, an incalculable number of.

incandescence [ɛ̃kɑ̃desɑ̃s] nf incandescence. **en ~** white-hot, incandescent; **porter qch à ~** to heat sth white-hot *ou* to incandescence; *voir* **lampe, manchon.**

incandescent, e [ɛ̃kɑ̃desɑ̃, ɑ̃t] adj *substance, filament* incandescent, white-hot; (*fig*) *imagination* burning.

incantation [ɛ̃kɑ̃tasjɔ̃] nf incantation.

incantatoire [ɛ̃kɑ̃tatwaʀ] adj incantatory; *voir* **formule.**

incapable [ɛ̃kapabl] 1 adj a (*inapte*) incapable, incompetent, useless*.

b **~ de faire** (*par incompétence, impossibilité morale*) incapable of doing; (*impossibilité physique, physiologique*) unable to do, incapable of doing; **j'étais ~ de bouger** I was unable to move, I was incapable of movement *ou* of moving; **elle est ~ de mentir** she's incapable of lying, she can't tell a lie.

c **~ d'amour** incapable of loving, unable to love; **~ de malhonnêteté** incapable of dishonesty *ou* of being dishonest; **~ du moindre effort** unable to make the least effort, incapable of making the least effort.

d (*Jur*) incapable.

2 nmf a (*incompétent*) incompetent. **c'est un ~** he's useless* *ou* incapable, he's an incompetent.

b (*Jur*) incapable person.

incapacitant, e [ɛ̃kapasitɑ̃, ɑ̃t] adj *gaz, grenade* stun (*épith*). **bombe ~e** stun-gas spray.

incapacité [ɛ̃kapasite] nf a (*incompétence*) incompetence, incapability. b (*impossibilité*) **~ de faire** incapacity *ou* inability to do; **être dans l'~ de faire** to be unable to do, be incapable of doing. c (*invalidité*) disablement, disability. **~ totale/partielle/permanente** total/partial/permanent disablement *ou* disability; **~ de travail** industrial disablement *ou* disability. d (*Jur*) incapacity. **~ de jouissance** incapacity (*by exclusion from a right*); **~ d'exercice** incapacity (*by restriction of a right*); **~ civile** civil incapacity.

incarcération [ɛ̃kaʀseʀasjɔ̃] nf incarceration, imprisonment.

incarcérer [ɛ̃kaʀseʀe] 6 vt to incarcerate, imprison.

incarnat, e [ɛ̃kaʀna, at] 1 adj *teint* rosy, pink; *teinture* crimson. 2 nm rosy hue, rosiness; crimson tint.

incarnation [ɛ̃kaʀnasjɔ̃] nf (*Myth, Rel*) incarnation. (*fig: image*) **être l'~ de** to be the incarnation *ou* embodiment of.

incarné, e [ɛ̃kaʀne] (ptp de **incarner**) adj a (*Rel*) incarnate; (*fig: personnifié*) incarnate, personified. **cette femme est la méchanceté ~e** this woman is wickedness incarnate *ou* personified, this woman is the embodiment of wickedness. b *ongle* ingrown.

incarner [ɛ̃kaʀne] 1 1 vt (*représenter*) *[personne]* to embody, personify, incarnate; *[œuvre]* to embody; (*Théât*) *[acteur]* to play; (*Rel*) to incarnate. 2 **s'incarner** vpr a (*être représenté par*) **s'~ dans** *ou* **en** to be embodied in; **tous nos espoirs s'incarnent en vous** you embody all our hopes, you are the embodiment of all our hopes. b (*Rel*) **s'~ dans** to become *ou* be incarnate in. c *[ongle]* to become ingrown.

incartade [ɛ̃kaʀtad] nf a (*écart de conduite*) prank, escapade. **ils étaient punis à la moindre ~** they were punished for the slightest prank; **faire une ~** to go on an escapade. b (*Équitation: écart*) swerve. **faire une ~** to shy.

incassable [ɛ̃kɑsabl] adj unbreakable.

incendiaire [ɛ̃sɑ̃djɛʀ] 1 nmf fire-raiser, arsonist. 2 adj *balle, bombe* incendiary; *discours, article* inflammatory, incendiary; *lettre d'amour, œillade* passionate; *voir* **blond.**

incendie [ɛ̃sɑ̃di] 1 nm a (*sinistre*) fire, blaze, conflagration (*littér*). **un ~ s'est déclaré dans ...** a fire broke out in ...; *voir* **assurance, foyer, pompe**[1]. b (*fig littér*) **l'~ du couchant** the blaze of the sunset, the fiery glow of the sunset; **l'~ de la révolte/de la passion** the fire of revolt/of passion. 2 comp ►**incendie criminel** arson (*NonC*), case of arson ►**incendie de forêt** forest fire.

incendié, e [ɛ̃sɑ̃dje] (ptp de **incendier**) adj: **les fermiers ~s ont tout perdu** the farmers who were the victims of the fire have lost everything.

incendier [ɛ̃sɑ̃dje] 7 vt a (*mettre le feu à*) to set fire to, set on fire, set alight; (*brûler complètement*) *bâtiment* to burn down; *voiture* to burn; *ville, récolte, forêt* to burn (to ashes).

b (*fig*) *désir, passion* to kindle, inflame; *imagination* to fire; *bouche, gorge* to burn, set on fire. **la fièvre lui incendiait le visage** (*sensation*) fever made his face burn; (*apparence*) his cheeks were burning *ou* glowing with fever; (*littér*) **le soleil incendie le couchant** the setting sun sets the sky ablaze.

c (**: réprimander*) **~ qn** to give sb a rocket* (*Brit*) *ou* a stiff telling-off*, tear a strip off sb*; **tu vas te faire ~** you'll catch it*, you'll get a rocket* (*Brit*); **elle l'a incendié du regard** she looked daggers at him, she shot him a baleful look.

incertain, e [ɛ̃sɛʀtɛ̃, ɛn] 1 adj a *personne* uncertain, unsure (*de qch* about *ou* as to sth). **~ de savoir la vérité, il ...** uncertain *ou* unsure as to whether he knew the truth, he ...; **encore ~ sur la conduite à suivre** still undecided *ou* uncertain about which course to follow. b *démarche* uncertain, hesitant. c *temps* uncertain, unsettled; *contour* indistinct, blurred; *allusion* vague; *lumière* dim, vague; **il est ~ pour le match de demain** he's doubtful for tomorrow's match. d *succès, entreprise, origine* uncertain, doubtful; *date, durée* uncertain, unspecified; *fait* uncertain, doubtful. 2 nm (*Fin*) **l'~** the exchange rate.

incertitude [ɛ̃sɛʀtityd] nf a (*NonC*) *[personne, résultat, fait]* uncertainty. **être dans l'~** to be in a state of uncertainty, feel uncertain; **être dans l'~ sur ce qu'on doit faire** to be uncertain as to the best course to follow. b **~s** (*hésitations*) doubts, uncertainties; (*impondérables*) *[avenir, entreprise]* uncertainties.

incessamment [ɛ̃sesamɑ̃] adv (*sans délai*) (very) shortly. **il doit arriver ~** he'll be here any minute now *ou* very shortly.

incessant, e [ɛ̃sesɑ̃, ɑ̃t] adj *pluie* incessant, unceasing; *efforts, activité* ceaseless, incessant, unremitting; *bruit, réclamations, coups de téléphone* incessant, unceasing, continual.

incessibilité [ɛ̃sesibilite] nf non-transferability.

incessible [ɛ̃sesibl] adj non-transferable.

inceste [ɛ̃sɛst] nm incest.

incestueusement [ɛ̃sɛstɥøzmɑ̃] adv incestuously.

incestueux, -euse [ɛ̃sɛstɥø, øz] 1 adj *relations, personne* incestuous; *enfant* born of incest. 2 nm,f (*Jur*) person guilty of incest.

inchangé, e [ɛ̃ʃɑ̃ʒe] adj unchanged, unaltered. **la situation/son expression reste ~e** the situation/his expression remains unchanged *ou* the same *ou* unaltered.

inchangeable [ɛ̃ʃɑ̃ʒabl] adj unchangeable.

inchantable [ɛ̃ʃɑ̃tabl] adj unsingable.

inchauffable [ɛ̃ʃofabl] adj impossible to heat (*attrib*).

inchavirable [ɛ̃ʃaviʀabl] adj uncapsizable, self-righting.

inchoatif, -ive [ɛ̃kɔatif, iv] adj inchoative, inceptive.

incidemment [ɛ̃sidamɑ̃] adv incidentally, in passing.

incidence [ɛ̃sidɑ̃s] nf (*conséquence*) effect; (*Écon, Phys*) incidence. **avoir une ~ sur** to affect, have an effect (up)on; *voir* **angle.**

incident, e [ɛ̃sidɑ̃, ɑ̃t] 1 adj (*frm, Jur: accessoire*) incidental; (*Phys*) incident. **puis-je vous demander, de manière toute ~e?** may I ask you, quite incidentally?; **je désirerais poser une question ~e** I'd like to ask a question in connection with this matter, I'd like to interpose a question.

2 nm (*gén*) incident; (*Jur*) point of law. **la vie n'est qu'une succession d'~s** life is just a series of minor incidents; **~ imprévu** unexpected incident, unforeseen event; **l'~ est clos** that's an end of the matter; **voyage sans ~(s)** uneventful journey; **se dérouler sans ~(s)** to go off without incident *ou* smoothly.

3 **incidente** nf (*Ling*) **(proposition) ~e** parenthesis, parenthetical clause.

4 comp ►**incident diplomatique** diplomatic incident ►**incident de frontière** border incident ►**incident de parcours** (*gén*) (minor *ou* slight) setback, hitch; (*santé*) (minor *ou* slight) setback ►**incident technique** (*lit, hum fig*) technical hitch.

incinérateur [ɛ̃sineʀatœʀ] nm incinerator. **~ à ordures** refuse incinerator.

incinération [ɛ̃sineʀasjɔ̃] nf (*voir* **incinérer**) incineration; cremation.

incinérer [ɛ̃sineʀe] 6 vt *ordures, cadavre* to incinerate; (*au crématorium*) to cremate. **se faire ~** to be cremated.

incipit [ɛ̃sipit] nm inv incipit.

incise [ɛ̃siz] nf (*Mus*) phrase. (*Ling*) **(proposition) ~** interpolated clause; **il m'a dit, en ~, que** he told me in passing *ou* in parenthesis that.

inciser [ɛ̃size] 1 vt *écorce, arbre* to incise, make an incision in; *peau* to incise; *abcès* to lance. **~ un arbre pour en extraire la résine** to tap a tree.

incisif, -ive [ɛ̃sizif, iv] 1 adj *ton, style, réponse* cutting, incisive; *regard* piercing. **il était très ~ dans ses questions** he was very incisive in his questioning, his questions were very incisive. 2 **incisive** nf (*dent*) incisor. **~ive supérieure/inférieure** upper/lower incisor.

incision [ɛ̃sizjɔ̃] nf a (*voir* **inciser**) incising; incision; lancing. b (*entaille*) incision. **faire une ~ dans** to make an incision in, incise.

incisive [ɛ̃siziv] *voir* **incisif.**

incitatif, -ive [ɛ̃sitatif, iv] adj: **mesure incitative** incentive; **aide incitative** incentive aid.

incitation [ɛ̃sitasjɔ̃] nf (*au meurtre, à la révolte*) incitement (*à* to); (*à l'effort, au travail*) incentive (*à* to; *à faire* to do).

inciter [ɛ̃site] 1 vt: **~ qn à faire** to incite *ou* urge sb to do; **cela m'incite à la méfiance** that prompts me to be on my guard, that puts me on my guard; **cela les incite à la violence/la révolte** that incites them to violence/revolt; **ça n'incite pas au travail** it doesn't (exactly) encourage one to work, it's no incentive to work; **ça vous incite à la paresse** it encourages laziness (in one), it encourages one to be lazy.

incivil, e [ɛ̃sivil] adj (*frm*) uncivil, rude.

incivilement [ɛ̃sivilmɑ̃] adv (*frm*) uncivilly, rudely.
incivilité [ɛ̃sivilite] nf (*frm*) *[attitude, ton]* incivility, rudeness; (*propos impoli*) uncivil *ou* rude remark. **ce serait commettre une ~ que de ...** it would be uncivil to ... .
inclassable [ɛ̃klɑsabl] adj which cannot be categorized, unclassifiable.
inclémence [ɛ̃klemɑ̃s] nf inclemency.
inclément, e [ɛ̃klemɑ̃, ɑ̃t] adj inclement.
inclinable [ɛ̃klinabl] adj *dossier de siège* reclining; *lampe* adjustable.
inclinaison [ɛ̃klinɛzɔ̃] 1 nf a (*déclivité*) *[plan, pente]* incline; *[route, voie ferrée]* incline, gradient; *[toit]* slope, slant, pitch; *[barre, tuyau]* slope, slant. **l'~ exceptionnelle de la route** the exceptionally steep gradient of the road, the exceptional steepness of the road; **toit à faible/forte ~** gently-sloping/steeply-sloping roof.
b (*aspect*) *[mur]* lean; *[mât, tour]* lean, tilt; *[chapeau]* slant, tilt; *[appareil, tête]* tilt; *[navire]* list. **l'~ comique de son chapeau sur l'oreille gauche** the comic way in which his hat was cocked *ou* tilted over his left ear; **accentuez l'~ de la tête** tilt your head further forward *ou* back *ou* sideways.
c (*Géom*) *[droite, surface]* angle; *voir* **angle**.
2 comp ► **inclinaison magnétique** (*Phys*) magnetic declination.
inclination [ɛ̃klinasjɔ̃] nf a (*penchant*) inclination. **suivre son ~** to follow one's (own) inclination; **son ~ naturelle au bonheur** his natural inclination *ou* tendency towards happiness; **~s altruistes** altruistic tendencies; **une certaine ~ à mentir** a certain inclination *ou* tendency *ou* propensity to tell lies; **avoir de l'~ pour la littérature** to have a strong liking *ou* a penchant for literature; **~ pour qn**† liking for sb. b **~ de (la) tête** (*acquiescement*) nod; (*salut*) inclination of the head; **~ (du buste)** bow.
incliné, e [ɛ̃kline] (ptp de **incliner**) adj a (*raide*) *toit* steep, sloping. b (*penché*) *tour, mur* leaning; *récipient* tilted; *voir* **plan**[1].
incliner [ɛ̃kline] [1] 1 vt a (*pencher*) *appareil, mât, bouteille* to tilt; (*littér: courber*) *arbre* to bend (over); *[architecte] toit, surface* to slope; *dossier de chaise* to tilt. **le vent incline le navire** the wind heels the boat over; **~ la tête *ou* le front** (*pour saluer*) to give a slight bow, incline one's head; (*pour acquiescer*) to nod (one's head), incline one's head; **~ la tête de côté** to tilt *ou* incline one's head on one side; **~ le buste *ou* le corps** (*saluer*) to bow, give a bow; **inclinez le corps plus en avant** lean *ou* bend forward more; *voir* **plan**[1].
b (*littér*) **~ qn à l'indulgence** to encourage sb to be indulgent; **ceci m'incline à penser que** that makes me inclined to think that, that leads me to believe that.
2 vi a **~ à** (*tendre à*) to tend towards; (*pencher pour*) to be *ou* feel inclined towards; **il incline à l'autoritarisme/à l'indulgence** he tends towards authoritarianism/indulgence, he tends to be authoritarian/indulgent; **dans ce cas, il inclinait à la clémence/sévérité** in this instance he felt inclined to be merciful/severe *ou* he inclined towards clemency/severity; **le ministre inclinait vers des mesures très sévères** the minister inclined towards (taking) strong measures; **~ à penser/croire que** to be inclined to think/believe that; **j'incline à accepter cette offre/rejeter cette solution** I'm inclined to accept this offer/reject this solution.
b (*littér*) *[mur]* to lean; *[arbre]* to bend. **la colline inclinait doucement vers la mer** the hill sloped gently (down) towards the sea.
c (*bifurquer*) **~ vers** to veer (over) towards *ou* to.
3 **s'incliner** vpr a (*se courber*) to bow (*devant* before). **s'~ jusqu'à terre** to bow to the ground.
b (*rendre hommage à*) **s'~ devant qn *ou* devant la supériorité de qn** to bow before sb's superiority; **devant tant de talent/de noblesse, je m'incline** I bow before such a wealth of talent/such nobleness; **devant un tel homme, on ne peut que s'~** one can only bow (down) before such a man; **il est venu s'~ devant la dépouille mortelle du président** he came to pay his last respects at the coffin of the president.
c (*céder*) **s'~ devant l'autorité de qn** to yield *ou* bow to sb's authority; **s'~ devant un ordre** to accept an order; **puisque vous me le commandez, je n'ai plus qu'à m'~ et obéir** since you order me to do it, I can only accept it and obey.
d (*s'avouer battu*) to admit defeat. **le boxeur s'inclina (devant son adversaire) à la 3e reprise** the boxer admitted defeat in the 3rd round; **il dut s'~ devant un adversaire plus fort que lui** faced with an opponent stronger than himself, he was forced to give in *ou* to admit defeat, he had to bow to his opponent who was stronger than him; (*Sport*) **Marseille s'est incliné devant Saint-Étienne (par) 2 buts à 3** Marseilles lost to Saint-Étienne by 2 goals to 3.
e *[arbre]* to bend over; *[mur]* to lean; *[navire]* to heel (over); *[chemin, colline]* to slope; *[toit]* to be sloping. **le soleil s'incline à l'horizon** the sun is sinking (down) towards the horizon.
inclure [ɛ̃klyʀ] [35] vt a (*insérer*) *clause* to insert (*dans* in); *nom* to include (*dans* in); (*joindre à un envoi*) *billet, chèque* to enclose (*dans* in).
b (*contenir*) to include. **ce récit en inclut un autre** this is a story within a story.
inclus, e [ɛ̃kly, yz] (ptp de **inclure**) adj a (*joint à un envoi*) enclosed. b (*compris*) *frais* included. **eux ~** including them; **jusqu'au 10 mars ~** until March 10th inclusive, up to and including March 10th; **jusqu'au 3e chapitre ~** up to and including the 3rd chapter; **les frais sont ~ dans la note** the bill is inclusive of expenses, expenses are included in the bill; *voir* **ci**. c (*Math*) (*ensemble*) **~ dans** included in; **A est ~ dans B** A is the subset of B.
inclusif, -ive [ɛ̃klyzif, iv] adj (*Gram, Logique*) inclusive.
inclusion [ɛ̃klyzjɔ̃] nf (*gén, Math*) inclusion (*dans* in).
inclusivement [ɛ̃klyzivmɑ̃] adv: **jusqu'au 16e siècle ~** up to and including the 16th century; **jusqu'au 1er janvier ~** until January 1st inclusive, up to and including January 1st.
incoercible [ɛ̃kɔɛʀsibl] adj *toux* uncontrollable; *besoin, désir, rire* uncontrollable, irrepressible.
incognito [ɛ̃kɔɲito] 1 adv incognito. 2 nm: **garder l'~, rester dans l'~** to remain incognito; **l'~ lui plaisait** he liked being incognito; **l'~ dont il s'entourait** the secrecy with which he surrounded himself.
incohérence [ɛ̃kɔeʀɑ̃s] nf a (*caractère: voir* **incohérent**) incoherency, incoherence; inconsistency. **l'~ entre les différentes parties du discours** the inconsistency of the different parts of the speech. b (*dans un texte etc*) inconsistency, discrepancy; (*propos, acte etc*) inconsistency. **les ~s de sa conduite** the inconsistency of his behaviour, the inconsistencies in his behaviour.
incohérent, e [ɛ̃kɔeʀɑ̃, ɑ̃t] adj *geste, langage, texte* incoherent; *comportement* inconsistent.
incollable [ɛ̃kɔlabl] adj a (*qui ne colle pas*) **riz ~** non-stick rice. b (**: imbattable*) unbeatable. **il est ~ (en histoire)** you can't catch him out* (on history) (*Brit*), he's got all the answers (on history).
incolore [ɛ̃kɔlɔʀ] adj *liquide, style* colourless; *verre, vernis* clear.
incomber [ɛ̃kɔ̃be] [1] **incomber à** vt indir (*frm*) *[devoirs, responsabilité]* to be incumbent (up)on; *[frais, réparations, travail]* to be sb's responsibility. **il m'incombe de faire** it falls to me to do, it is my responsibility to do, it is incumbent upon me to do, the onus is on me to do; **ces frais leur incombent entièrement** these costs are to be paid by them in full *ou* are entirely their responsibility.
incombustibilité [ɛ̃kɔ̃bystibilite] nf incombustibility.
incombustible [ɛ̃kɔ̃bystibl] adj incombustible.
incommensurabilité [ɛ̃kɔmɑ̃syʀabilite] nf incommensurability.
incommensurable [ɛ̃kɔmɑ̃syʀabl] adj a (*immense*) immeasurable. b (*sans commune mesure: Math, littér*) incommensurable (*avec* with).
incommensurablement [ɛ̃kɔmɑ̃syʀabləmɑ̃] adv (*voir* **incommensurable**) immeasurably; incommensurably.
incommodant, e [ɛ̃kɔmɔdɑ̃, ɑ̃t] adj *odeur* unpleasant, offensive; *bruit* annoying, unpleasant; *chaleur* uncomfortable.
incommode [ɛ̃kɔmɔd] adj a *pièce, appartement* inconvenient; *heure* awkward, inconvenient; *armoire, outil* impractical, awkward. b *siège* uncomfortable; (*fig*) *position, situation* awkward, uncomfortable.
incommodément [ɛ̃kɔmɔdemɑ̃] adv *installé, assis* awkwardly, uncomfortably; *logé* inconveniently; *situé* inconveniently, awkwardly.
incommoder [ɛ̃kɔmɔde] [1] vt: **~ qn** *[bruit]* to disturb *ou* bother sb; *[odeur, chaleur]* to bother sb; *[comportement]* to make sb feel ill at ease *ou* uncomfortable; **être incommodé par** to be bothered by; **se sentir incommodé** to feel indisposed *ou* unwell.
incommodité [ɛ̃kɔmɔdite] nf (*voir* **incommode**) inconvenience; awkwardness; impracticability; lack of comfort.
incommunicabilité [ɛ̃kɔmynikabilite] nf incommunicability.
incommunicable [ɛ̃kɔmynikabl] adj incommunicable.
incommutabilité [ɛ̃kɔmytabilite] nf inalienability.
incommutable [ɛ̃kɔmytabl] adj inalienable.
incomparable [ɛ̃kɔ̃paʀabl] adj (*remarquable*) incomparable, matchless; (*dissemblable*) not comparable. **est-ce plus confortable — c'est ~?** is it more comfortable?, there's no comparison!
incomparablement [ɛ̃kɔ̃paʀabləmɑ̃] adv: **~ plus/mieux** incomparably more/better.
incompatibilité [ɛ̃kɔ̃patibilite] nf (*gén, Sci*) incompatibility. (*Jur*) **~ d'humeur** (mutual) incompatibility; **il y a ~ d'humeur entre les membres de cette équipe** the members of this team are (temperamentally) incompatible; **~ de groupes sanguins** incompatibility of blood groups.
incompatible [ɛ̃kɔ̃patibl] adj incompatible (*avec* with).
incompétence [ɛ̃kɔ̃petɑ̃s] nf (*incapacité*) incompetence; (*ignorance*) lack of knowledge; (*Jur*) incompetence. **il reconnaît volontiers son ~ en musique** he freely admits to his lack of knowledge of music *ou* that he knows nothing about music.
incompétent, e [ɛ̃kɔ̃petɑ̃, ɑ̃t] adj (*incapable*) incompetent; (*ignorant*) ignorant, inexpert; (*Jur*) incompetent. **en ce qui concerne la musique/les maths je suis ~** as far as music goes/maths go I'm not competent *ou* I'm incompetent to judge.
incomplet, -ète [ɛ̃kɔ̃plɛ, ɛt] adj incomplete.
incomplètement [ɛ̃kɔ̃plɛtmɑ̃] adv *renseigné* incompletely; *rétabli, guéri* not completely.
incomplétude [ɛ̃kɔ̃pletyd] nf (*littér: insatisfaction*) non-fulfilment.
incompréhensibilité [ɛ̃kɔ̃pʀeɑ̃sibilite] nf incomprehensibility.
incompréhensible [ɛ̃kɔ̃pʀeɑ̃sibl] adj (*gén*) incomprehensible.
incompréhensif, -ive [ɛ̃kɔ̃pʀeɑ̃sif, iv] adj unsympathetic. **il s'est montré totalement ~** he (just) refused to understand, he was totally unsympathetic; **ses parents se montrent totalement ~s** his parents show a total lack of understanding.
incompréhension [ɛ̃kɔ̃pʀeɑ̃sjɔ̃] nf a (*voir* **incompréhensif**) lack of understanding (*envers* of); unwillingness to understand. b **l'~ d'un**

texte the failure to understand a text, the lack of understanding *ou* comprehension of a text.

incompressibilité [ɛ̃kɔ̃pʀesibilite] **nf** (*Phys*) incompressibility. **l'~ du budget** the irreducibility of the budget.

incompressible [ɛ̃kɔ̃pʀesibl] **adj** (*Phys*) incompressible. **nos dépenses sont ~s** our expenses cannot be reduced *ou* cut down.

incompris, e [ɛ̃kɔ̃pʀi, iz] **adj** misunderstood. **X fut un grand ~ à son époque** X was never understood by his contemporaries.

inconcevable [ɛ̃kɔ̃s(ə)vabl] **adj** (*gén*) inconceivable. **avec un toupet ~** with unbelievable *ou* incredible cheek (*Brit*) *ou* nerve.

inconcevablement [ɛ̃kɔ̃s(ə)vabləmɑ̃] **adv** inconceivably, incredibly.

inconciliabilité [ɛ̃kɔ̃siljabilite] **nf** irreconcilability.

inconciliable [ɛ̃kɔ̃siljabl] **adj** irreconcilable.

inconditionnalité [ɛ̃kɔ̃disjɔnalite] **nf** unreservedness, wholeheartedness. **l'~ de son soutien au gouvernement** his wholehearted *ou* unreserved support for the government.

inconditionnel, -elle [ɛ̃kɔ̃disjɔnɛl] **1 adj** *acceptation, ordre, soumission* unconditional; *appui* wholehearted, unconditional, unreserved; *partisan, foi* unquestioning. **2 nm,f** *[homme politique, doctrine]* unquestioning *ou* ardent supporter (*de* of); *[écrivain, chanteur]* ardent admirer (*de* of). **les ~s des sports d'hiver** winter sports enthusiasts *ou* fanatics; **c'est un ~ de l'informatique** he's a fanatic about computers.

inconditionnellement [ɛ̃kɔ̃disjɔnɛlmɑ̃] **adv** (*voir* **inconditionnel**) unconditionally; wholeheartedly; unreservedly; unquestioningly.

inconduite [ɛ̃kɔ̃dɥit] **nf** (*débauche*) wild *ou* loose *ou* shocking behaviour (*NonC*).

inconfort [ɛ̃kɔ̃fɔʀ] **nm** *[logement]* lack of comfort, discomfort; *[situation, position]* unpleasantness. **l'~ lui importait peu** discomfort didn't matter to him in the least; **vivre dans l'~** to live in uncomfortable surroundings.

inconfortable [ɛ̃kɔ̃fɔʀtabl] **adj** *maison, meuble* uncomfortable; (*lit, fig*) *position* uncomfortable, awkward.

inconfortablement [ɛ̃kɔ̃fɔʀtabləmɑ̃] **adv** (*voir* **inconfortable**) uncomfortably; awkwardly.

incongelable [ɛ̃kɔ̃ʒ(ə)labl] **adj** non-freezable, unsuitable for freezing.

incongru, e [ɛ̃kɔ̃gʀy] **adj** *attitude, bruit* unseemly; *remarque* incongruous, ill-placed, ill-chosen; (†, *littér*) *personne* uncouth.

incongruité [ɛ̃kɔ̃gʀyite] **nf** **a** (*caractère*) incongruity, unseemliness. **b** (*propos*) unseemly *ou* ill-chosen *ou* ill-placed remark; (*acte*) unseemly action, unseemly behaviour (*NonC*).

incongrûment [ɛ̃kɔ̃gʀymɑ̃] **adv** *agir, parler* in an unseemly way.

inconnaissable [ɛ̃kɔnɛsabl] **adj** unknowable.

inconnu, e [ɛ̃kɔny] **1 adj** *destination, fait* unknown; *odeur, sensation* new, unknown; *ville, personne* unknown, strange (*à, de* to). **son visage m'était ~** his face was new *ou* unknown to me, I didn't know his face; **une joie ~e l'envahit** he was seized with a strange joy *ou* a joy that was (quite) new to him; **on se sent très seul en pays ~** one feels very lonely in a strange country *ou* in a foreign country *ou* in strange surroundings; **s'en aller vers des contrées ~es** to set off in search of unknown *ou* unexplored *ou* uncharted lands; **~ à cette adresse** not known at this address; (*fig*) **il est ~ au bataillon*** no one's ever heard of him; *voir* **soldat**.

2 nm,f stranger, unknown person. **pour moi, ce peintre-là, c'est un ~** I don't know this painter, this painter is unknown to me; **le malfaiteur n'était pas un ~ pour la police** the culprit was known *ou* was not unknown *ou* was no stranger to the police; **ne parle pas à des ~s** don't talk to strangers; *voir* **illustre**.

3 nm (*ce qu'on ignore*) **l'~** the unknown.

4 inconnue nf (*élément inconnu*) unknown factor *ou* quantity; (*Math*) unknown. **dans cette entreprise, il y a beaucoup d'~es** there are lots of unknowns *ou* unknown factors in this venture.

inconsciemment [ɛ̃kɔ̃sjamɑ̃] **adv** (*involontairement*) unconsciously, unwittingly; (*à la légère*) thoughtlessly, recklessly, rashly.

inconscience [ɛ̃kɔ̃sjɑ̃s] **nf** **a** (*physique*) unconsciousness. **sombrer dans l'~** to lose consciousness, sink into unconsciousness. **b** (*morale*) thoughtlessness, recklessness, rashness. **mais c'est de l'~!** that's sheer madness! *ou* stupidity!

inconscient, e [ɛ̃kɔ̃sjɑ̃, jɑ̃t] **1 adj** (*évanoui*) unconscious; (*échappant à la conscience*) *sentiment* subconscious; (*machinal*) *mouvement* unconscious, automatic; (*irréfléchi*) *décision, action, personne* thoughtless, reckless, rash; (*: *fou*) mad*, crazy. **~ de** *événements extérieurs* unaware of, not aware of; *conséquence, danger* unaware of, not aware of, oblivious to; **c'est un ~*** he's completely reckless. **2 nm** (*Psych*) **l'~** the subconscious, the unconscious; **l'~ collectif** the collective unconscious.

inconséquence [ɛ̃kɔ̃sekɑ̃s] **nf** (*manque de logique*) inconsistency, inconsequence; (*légèreté*) thoughtlessness (*NonC*), fecklessness (*NonC*).

inconséquent, e [ɛ̃kɔ̃sekɑ̃, ɑ̃t] **adj** (*illogique*) *comportement, personne* inconsistent, inconsequent; (*irréfléchi*) *démarche, décision, personne* thoughtless.

inconsidéré, e [ɛ̃kɔ̃sideʀe] **adj** ill-considered, thoughtless, rash.

inconsidérément [ɛ̃kɔ̃sideʀemɑ̃] **adv** thoughtlessly, rashly, without thinking.

inconsistance [ɛ̃kɔ̃sistɑ̃s] **nf** (*voir* **inconsistant**) flimsiness; weakness; colourlessness; runniness; watery *ou* thin consistency.

inconsistant, e [ɛ̃kɔ̃sistɑ̃, ɑ̃t] **adj** **a** *preuve, idée, espoir* flimsy; *argumentation, intrigue de roman* flimsy, weak; *personne* colourless; *caractère* colourless, weak. **b** *crème* runny; *bouillie, soupe* watery, thin.

inconsolable [ɛ̃kɔ̃sɔlabl] **adj** *personne* disconsolate, inconsolable; *chagrin* inconsolable.

inconsolé, e [ɛ̃kɔ̃sɔle] **adj** *personne* disconsolate; *chagrin* unconsoled.

inconsommable [ɛ̃kɔ̃sɔmabl] **adj** unfit for consumption (*attrib*).

inconstance [ɛ̃kɔ̃stɑ̃s] **nf** *[conduite, temps, fortune]* fickleness; *[amour]* inconstancy, fickleness. (*littér*) **~s** (*dans le comportement*) inconsistencies; (*en amour*) infidelities, inconstancies.

inconstant, e [ɛ̃kɔ̃stɑ̃, ɑ̃t] **adj** (*voir* **inconstance**) fickle; inconstant.

inconstatable [ɛ̃kɔ̃statabl] **adj** impossible to ascertain (*attrib*), unascertainable.

inconstitutionnalité [ɛ̃kɔ̃stitysjɔnalite] **nf** unconstitutionality.

inconstitutionnel, -elle [ɛ̃kɔ̃stitysjɔnɛl] **adj** unconstitutional.

inconstitutionnellement [ɛ̃kɔ̃stitysjɔnɛlmɑ̃] **adv** unconstitutionally.

incontestabilité [ɛ̃kɔ̃tɛstabilite] **nf** incontestability.

incontestable [ɛ̃kɔ̃tɛstabl] **adj** (*indiscutable*) incontestable, unquestionable, indisputable. **il a réussi, c'est ~** he's succeeded, there is no doubt about that, it's undeniable that he has succeeded; **il est ~ qu'elle est la meilleure** she is incontestably *ou* indisputably *ou* unquestionably the best.

incontestablement [ɛ̃kɔ̃tɛstabləmɑ̃] **adv** incontestably, unquestionably, indisputably. **c'est prouvé? – ~** is it proved? – beyond any shadow of doubt.

incontesté, e [ɛ̃kɔ̃tɛste] **adj** *autorité, principe, fait* uncontested, undisputed. **le chef/maître ~** the undisputed chief/master; **le gagnant ~** the undisputed *ou* outright winner.

incontinence [ɛ̃kɔ̃tinɑ̃s] **1 nf** **a** (*Méd*) incontinence. **~ urinaire** incontinence, enuresis (*SPÉC*); **~ nocturne** bedwetting, enuresis (*SPÉC*). **b** (†, *littér: luxure*) incontinence. **2 comp ►incontinence de langage** lack of restraint in speech **►incontinence verbale** garrulousness, verbal diarrhoea*.

incontinent[1]**, e** [ɛ̃kɔ̃tinɑ̃, ɑ̃t] **adj** **a** (*Méd*) *personne* incontinent, enuretic (*SPÉC*); *vessie* weak. **b** (†, *littér: débauché*) incontinent (†, *littér*).

incontinent[2] [ɛ̃kɔ̃tinɑ̃] **adv** (†, *littér: sur-le-champ*) forthwith (†, *littér*).

incontournable [ɛ̃kɔ̃tuʀnabl] **adj** *réalité, fait* inescapable; *argument, problème, artiste* that can't be ignored.

incontrôlable [ɛ̃kɔ̃tʀolabl] **adj** (*non vérifiable*) unverifiable; (*irrépressible*) uncontrollable.

incontrôlé, e [ɛ̃kɔ̃tʀole] **adj** (*voir* **incontrôlable**) unverified; uncontrolled. **un groupe ~ de manifestants** an uncontrolled *ou* undisciplined group of demonstrators.

inconvenance [ɛ̃kɔ̃v(ə)nɑ̃s] **nf** **a** (*caractère*) impropriety, unseemliness. **b** (*acte*) impropriety, indecorous *ou* unseemly behaviour (*NonC*); (*remarque*) impropriety, indecorous *ou* unseemly language (*NonC*).

inconvenant, e [ɛ̃kɔ̃v(ə)nɑ̃, ɑ̃t] **adj** *comportement, parole* improper, indecorous, unseemly; *question* improper; *personne* ill-mannered.

inconvénient [ɛ̃kɔ̃venjɑ̃] **nm** **a** (*désavantage*) *[situation, plan]* disadvantage, drawback, inconvenience.

b (*conséquences fâcheuses*) **~s** (unpleasant) consequences, drawbacks; **il subit maintenant les ~s d'une situation qu'il a lui-même créée** he now has to put up with the consequences *ou* drawbacks of a situation which he himself created; **tu feras ce que tu voudras mais nous ne voulons pas en supporter les ~s** you can do what you like but we don't want to have to suffer the consequences.

c (*risque*) **n'y a-t-il pas d'~ à mettre ce plat en faïence au four?** isn't there a risk in putting this earthenware plate in the oven?; **peut-on sans ~ prendre ces deux médicaments ensemble?** can one safely take these two medicines together?, is there any danger in taking these two medicines together?; **on peut modifier sans ~ notre itinéraire** we can easily change our route, we can change our route without any difficulty *ou* inconvenience.

d (*obstacle, objection*) **l'~ c'est que je ne serai pas là** the snag *ou* the annoying thing *ou* the one drawback is that I won't be there; **pouvez-vous sans ~ vous libérer jeudi?** would it be convenient for you to get away on Thursday?, will you be able to get away on Thursday without any difficulty?; **voyez-vous un ~** *ou* **y a-t-il un ~ à ce que je parte ce soir?** have you *ou* is there any objection to my leaving this evening?; **si vous n'y voyez pas d'~ ...** if you have no objections ... .

inconvertibilité [ɛ̃kɔ̃vɛʀtibilite] **nf** inconvertibility.

inconvertible [ɛ̃kɔ̃vɛʀtibl] **adj** (*Fin*) inconvertible.

incoordination [ɛ̃kɔɔʀdinasjɔ̃] **nf** *[idées, opération]* lack of coordination; (*Méd*) incoordination, lack of coordination.

incorporable [ɛ̃kɔʀpɔʀabl] **adj** incorporable (*dans* in, into).

incorporalité [ɛ̃kɔʀpɔʀalite] **nf** incorporeality.

incorporation [ɛ̃kɔʀpɔʀasjɔ̃] **nf** **a** (*voir* **incorporer**) mixing; blending; incorporation; insertion; integration. **b** (*Mil*) (*appel*) enlistment (*à* into); (*affectation*) posting; *voir* **sursis**.

incorporéité [ɛ̃kɔʀpɔʀeite] = **incorporalité**.

incorporel, -elle [ɛ̃kɔʀpɔʀɛl] adj (*immatériel*) incorporeal; (*Fin*) intangible.
incorporer [ɛ̃kɔʀpɔʀe] 1 vt a *substance, aliment* to mix (*à, avec* with, into), blend (*à, avec* with). b *territoire* to incorporate (*dans, à* into); *chapitre* to incorporate (*dans* in, into), insert (*dans* in). c *personne* to incorporate, integrate (*dans, à* into). **il a très bien su s'~ à notre groupe** he was very easily incorporated into our group, he fitted very easily into our group. d (*Mil*) (*appeler*) to recruit. (*affecter*) **~ qn dans** to enrol *ou* enlist sb into; **on l'a incorporé dans l'infanterie** he was recruited *ou* drafted into the infantry.
incorrect, e [ɛ̃kɔʀɛkt] adj a (*fautif*) *réglage, interprétation* faulty; *solution* incorrect, wrong. b (*inconvenant*) *terme, langage* improper, impolite; *tenue* incorrect, indecent. c (*mal élevé*) *personne* discourteous, impolite. d (*déloyal*) *personne, procédé* underhand. **être ~ avec qn** to treat sb in an underhand way, behave in an underhand way towards sb.
incorrectement [ɛ̃kɔʀɛktəmɑ̃] adv (*voir* **incorrect**) faultily; incorrectly; wrongly; improperly; impolitely; indecently; discourteously; in an underhand way.
incorrection [ɛ̃kɔʀɛksjɔ̃] nf a (*NonC*) (*impropriété*) *[terme]* impropriety; (*inconvenance*) *[tenue, personne, langage]* impropriety, incorrectness; (*déloyauté*) *[procédés, concurrent]* dishonesty, underhand nature. b (*terme impropre*) impropriety; (*action inconvenante*) incorrect *ou* improper *ou* impolite behaviour (*NonC*); (*remarque inconvenante*) impolite *ou* improper remark.
incorrigible [ɛ̃kɔʀiʒibl] adj *enfant, distraction* incorrigible. **cet enfant est ~!** this child is incorrigible!, this child will never learn!; **être d'une ~ paresse** to be incorrigibly lazy.
incorruptibilité [ɛ̃kɔʀyptibilite] nf incorruptibility.
incorruptible [ɛ̃kɔʀyptibl] adj incorruptible.
incrédibilité [ɛ̃kʀedibilite] nf incredibility.
incrédule [ɛ̃kʀedyl] 1 adj (*sceptique*) incredulous; (*Rel*) unbelieving. 2 nmf (*Rel*) unbeliever, non-believer.
incrédulité [ɛ̃kʀedylite] nf (*voir* **incrédule**) incredulity; unbelief, lack of belief. **avec ~** incredulously, with incredulity.
incrément [ɛ̃kʀemɑ̃] nm (*Ordin*) increment.
incrémentation [ɛ̃kʀemɑ̃tasjɔ̃] nf (*Ordin*) incrementation.
incrémenter [ɛ̃kʀemɑ̃te] 1 vt (*Ordin*) to increment.
incrémentiel, -elle [ɛ̃kʀemɑ̃sjɛl] adj (*Ordin*) incremental.
increvable [ɛ̃kʀəvabl] adj *ballon* which cannot be burst, unburstable; *pneu* unpuncturable, puncture-proof; (*‡: infatigable*) *animal, travailleur* tireless; *moteur* which will never wear out *ou* pack in* (*Brit*).
incriminer [ɛ̃kʀimine] 1 vt (*mettre en cause*) *personne* to incriminate, accuse; *action, conduite* to bring under attack; (*mettre en doute*) *honnêteté, bonne foi* to call into question. **après avoir analysé la clause incriminée du contrat** ... after having analysed the offending clause *ou* the clause in question *ou* at issue in the contract ...; **il cherche à m'~ dans cette affaire** he's trying to incriminate *ou* implicate me in this business.
incrochetable [ɛ̃kʀɔʃ(ə)tabl] adj *serrure* burglar-proof, which cannot be picked.
incroyable [ɛ̃kʀwajabl] 1 adj (*invraisemblable*) incredible, unbelievable; (*inouï*) incredible, amazing. **~ mais vrai** incredible *ou* unbelievable but true; **il est ~ d'arrogance** he is incredibly *ou* unbelievably arrogant. 2 nmf (*Hist*) **les ~s** the Incroyables, *young dandies of the Directoire*.
incroyablement [ɛ̃kʀwajabləmɑ̃] adv (*étonnamment*) incredibly, unbelievably, amazingly.
incroyance [ɛ̃kʀwajɑ̃s] nf (*Rel*) unbelief. **être dans l'~** to be in a state of unbelief, be a non-believer.
incroyant, e [ɛ̃kʀwajɑ̃, ɑ̃t] 1 adj unbelieving. 2 nm,f unbeliever, non-believer.
incrustation [ɛ̃kʀystasjɔ̃] nf a (*Art*) (*technique*) inlaying; (*ornement*) inlay. **des ~s d'ivoire** inlaid ivory work, ivory inlays; **table à ~s d'ivoire** table inlaid with ivory; **~s de dentelle** lace panels. b (*TV*) superimposition. c (*croûte*) (*dans un récipient*) fur (*Brit*), residue (*US*); (*dans une chaudière*) scale; (*sur une roche*) incrustation. **pour empêcher l'~** to prevent furring (*Brit*), to prevent the formation of scale.
incruster [ɛ̃kʀyste] 1 1 vt a (*Art*) (*insérer*) **~ qch dans** to inlay sth into; (*décorer*) **~ qch de** to inlay sth with; **incrusté de** inlaid with.
b (*TV*) *nom, numéro* to superimpose.
c *chaudière* to coat with scale, scale up; *récipient* to fur up (*Brit*), become coated with residue (*US*).
2 **s'incruster** vpr a *[corps étranger, caillou]* **s'~ dans** to become embedded in; (*travail de marqueterie*) **l'ivoire s'incruste dans l'ébène** the ivory is inlaid in ebony.
b (*fig*) *[invité]* to take root (*fig*). **il va s'~ chez nous** he'll get himself settled down in our house and we'll never move him.
c *[radiateur, conduite]* to become incrusted (*de* with), fur up (*Brit*).
d (*TV*) *[nom, numéro]* to be superimposed.
incubateur, -trice [ɛ̃kybatœʀ, tʀis] 1 adj incubating. 2 nm incubator.
incubation [ɛ̃kybasjɔ̃] nf (*Méd*) incubation; *[œuf]* incubation; (*fig*) *[révolte]* incubation, hatching. **période d'~** incubation period; **~ artificielle** artificial incubation; **une ~ de 21 jours** 3 weeks' incubation, an incubation period of 3 weeks.
incube [ɛ̃kyb] nm incubus.
incuber [ɛ̃kybe] 1 vt to hatch, incubate.
inculcation [ɛ̃kylkasjɔ̃] nf inculcation, instilling.
inculpation [ɛ̃kylpasjɔ̃] nf (*chef d'accusation*) charge (*de* of); (*action*) charging. **sous l'~ de** on a charge of; **notifier à qn son ~** to inform sb of the charge against him; **la police a procédé à plusieurs ~s** the police have charged several people.
inculpé, e [ɛ̃kylpe] (ptp de **inculper**) nm,f: **l'~** ≃ the accused; **les deux ~s** the two accused, the two men accused.
inculper [ɛ̃kylpe] 1 vt to charge (*de* with), accuse (*de* of).
inculquer [ɛ̃kylke] 1 vt: **~ à qn** *principes, politesse, notions* to inculcate in sb, instil into sb.
inculte [ɛ̃kylt] adj *terre* uncultivated; *chevelure, barbe* unkempt; *esprit, personne* uneducated.
incultivable [ɛ̃kyltivabl] adj unfarmable, unworkable.
inculture [ɛ̃kyltyʀ] nf *[personne]* lack of education; *[terre]* lack of cultivation.
incunable [ɛ̃kynabl] nm early printed book, incunabulum.
incurabilité [ɛ̃kyʀabilite] nf incurability, incurableness.
incurable [ɛ̃kyʀabl] 1 adj (*Méd*) incurable; (*fig*) *bêtise, ignorance* incurable (*épith*), hopeless (*épith*). **les malades ~s** the incurably ill. 2 nmf (*Méd*) incurable.
incurablement [ɛ̃kyʀabləmɑ̃] adv incurably; (*fig*) hopelessly, incurably.
incurie [ɛ̃kyʀi] nf (*frm: négligence*) carelessness, negligence.
incursion [ɛ̃kyʀsjɔ̃] nf (*lit*) incursion, foray (*en, dans* into); (*fig: intrusion*) intrusion (*dans* into). **faire une ~ dans** (*lit*) to make an incursion *ou* a foray into.
incurvé, e [ɛ̃kyʀve] (ptp de **incurver**) adj curved.
incurver [ɛ̃kyʀve] 1 1 vt *pied de chaise, fer forgé* to form *ou* bend into a curve, curve. 2 **s'incurver** vpr a *[barre]* to bend, curve; *[poutre]* to sag. b *[ligne, profil, route]* to curve.
indatable [ɛ̃databl] adj undatable.
Inde [ɛ̃d] nf India. **les ~s** the Indies; (†† *Pol: Antilles*) **les ~s occidentales** the West Indies; (††*: Indonésie*) **les ~s orientales** the East Indies; *voir* **cochon**[1].
indéboulonnable* [ɛ̃debulɔnabl] adj *personne* unbudgeable*, impossible to budge. **il est complètement ~** they just can't get rid of him*.
indébrouillable [ɛ̃debʀujabl] adj *affaire* almost impossible *ou* difficult to sort out (*attrib*).
indécemment [ɛ̃desamɑ̃] adv indecently.
indécence [ɛ̃desɑ̃s] nf a (*caractère: voir* **indécent**) indecency; obscenity; impropriety. b (*action*) act of indecency, indecency; (*propos*) obscenity, indecency. **se livrer à des ~s** to indulge in indecent behaviour *ou* acts of indecency.
indécent, e [ɛ̃desɑ̃, ɑ̃t] adj (*impudique*) indecent; (*grivois*) *chanson* obscene, dirty*; (*déplacé*) improper, indecent; (*insolent*) *chance* disgusting. **il a une chance ~e** he's disgustingly lucky; **habille-toi, tu es ~!** get dressed, you're indecent! *ou* you're not decent!
indéchiffrable [ɛ̃deʃifʀabl] adj (*illisible*) *texte, partition* indecipherable; (*incompréhensible*) *traité, pensée* incomprehensible; (*impénétrable*) *personne, regard* inscrutable.
indéchirable [ɛ̃deʃiʀabl] adj tear-proof.
indécis, e [ɛ̃desi, iz] 1 adj a *personne* (*par nature*) indecisive; (*temporairement*) undecided. **~ sur** *ou* **devant** *ou* **quant à** undecided *ou* uncertain about. b (*douteux*) *temps, paix* unsettled; *bataille* indecisive; *problème* undecided, unsettled; *victoire* undecided. **le résultat est encore ~** the result is as yet undecided. c (*vague*) *réponse, sourire* vague; *pensée* undefined, vague; *forme, contour* indecisive, indistinct. 2 nm,f (*gén*) indecisive person; (*Sondages*) "don't know"; (*dans une élection*) floating voter.
indécision [ɛ̃desizjɔ̃] nf (*irrésolution chronique*) indecisiveness; (*temporaire*) indecision, uncertainty (*sur* about). **je suis dans l'~ quant à nos projets pour l'été** I'm uncertain *ou* undecided about our plans for the summer.
indéclinable [ɛ̃deklinabl] adj indeclinable.
indécollable [ɛ̃dekɔlabl] adj *objet* that won't come unstuck *ou* come off, that cannot be unstuck. **ces invités sont ~s*** you can't get rid of these guests.
indécomposable [ɛ̃dekɔ̃pozabl] adj (*gén*) that cannot be broken down (*en* into).
indécrochable [ɛ̃dekʀɔʃabl] adj (*lit*) that won't come unhooked *ou* come off; (** fig*) *diplôme* which it's impossible to get.
indécrottable* [ɛ̃dekʀɔtabl] adj (*borné*) hopelessly thick* (*Brit*), dumb*. (*incorrigible*) **c'est un paresseux ~** he's hopelessly lazy.
indéfectibilité [ɛ̃defɛktibilite] nf (*frm*) indestructibility.
indéfectible [ɛ̃defɛktibl] adj *foi, confiance* indestructible, unshakeable; *soutien, attachement* unfailing.
indéfectiblement [ɛ̃defɛktibləmɑ̃] adv unfailingly.
indéfendable [ɛ̃defɑ̃dabl] adj (*lit, fig*) indefensible.
indéfini, e [ɛ̃defini] adj (*vague*) *sentiment* undefined; (*indéterminé*)

quantité, durée indeterminate, indefinite; (*Ling*) indefinite.

indéfiniment [ɛ̃definimɑ̃] adv indefinitely.

indéfinissable [ɛ̃definisabl] adj *mot, charme, saveur* indefinable.

indéformable [ɛ̃defɔʀmabl] adj that will keep its shape.

indéfrisable† [ɛ̃defʀizabl] nf perm, permanent (*US*).

indélébile [ɛ̃delebil] adj (*lit, fig*) indelible.

indélébilité [ɛ̃delebilite] nf indelibility.

indélicat, e [ɛ̃delika, at] adj **a** (*mufle*) indelicate, tactless. **b** (*malhonnête*) *employé* dishonest; *procédé* dishonest, underhand.

indélicatement [ɛ̃delikatmɑ̃] adv (*voir* **indélicat**) indelicately, tactlessly; dishonestly.

indélicatesse [ɛ̃delikatɛs] nf **a** (*voir* **indélicat**) indelicacy, tactlessness (*NonC*); dishonesty (*NonC*). **b** (*acte malhonnête*) indiscretion. **commettre des ~s** to commit indiscretions.

indémaillable [ɛ̃demɑjabl] adj ladderproof (*Brit*), run-resistant, runproof. **en ~** *vêtement* in run-resistant *ou* run-proof material; *jersey, bas* run-resistant, run-proof.

indemne [ɛ̃dɛmn] adj (*sain et sauf*) unharmed, unhurt, unscathed. **il est sorti ~ de l'accident** he came out of the accident unharmed *ou* unscathed.

indemnisable [ɛ̃dɛmnizabl] adj *personne* entitled to compensation (*attrib*); *dommage* indemnifiable.

indemnisation [ɛ̃dɛmnizasjɔ̃] nf (*action*) indemnification; (*somme*) indemnity, compensation. **l'~ a été fixée à 10 F** the indemnity *ou* compensation was fixed at 10 francs; **10 F d'~** 10 francs compensation.

indemniser [ɛ̃dɛmnize] 1 vt (*dédommager*) to indemnify (*de* for); (*d'une perte*) to compensate (*de* for); (*de frais*) to indemnify, reimburse (*de* for). **se faire ~** to get indemnification *ou* compensation, get reimbursed; **~ qn en argent** to pay sb compensation in cash; **~ qn de ses frais** to reimburse sb for his expenses.

indemnité [ɛ̃dɛmnite] nf (*dédommagement*) *[perte]* compensation (*NonC*), indemnity; *[frais]* allowance. **~ de guerre** war indemnity; **~ journalière** daily allowance; **~ de logement/de transport/de résidence** housing/travel/weighting allowance; **~ de licenciement** redundancy payment *ou* money; **~ parlementaire** M.P.'s salary.

indémodable [ɛ̃demɔdabl] adj *vêtement, mobilier, livre* classic, that will never go out of fashion.

indémontable [ɛ̃demɔ̃tabl] adj which cannot be taken apart *ou* dismantled; (*fixé à une paroi etc*) which cannot be taken down; (*fig*) *argument* unanswerable, watertight.

indémontrable [ɛ̃demɔ̃tʀabl] adj indemonstrable, unprovable.

indéniable [ɛ̃denjabl] adj undeniable, indisputable, unquestionable. **vous avez grossi, c'est ~** there's no doubt that *ou* it's undeniable that you have put on weight.

indéniablement [ɛ̃denjabləmɑ̃] adv undeniably, indisputably, unquestionably.

indentation [ɛ̃dɑ̃tasjɔ̃] nf indentation.

indépassable [ɛ̃depɑsabl] adj *limite* impassable. **en plongée sous-marine, 800 mètres est la limite ~** in deep-sea diving 800 metres is the very deepest one can go; **au 100 mètres, 9 secondes est la limite ~** in the 100 metres race, 9 seconds cannot be bettered *ou* is unbeatable.

indépendamment [ɛ̃depɑ̃damɑ̃] adv **a** (*abstraction faite de*) **~ de** irrespective *ou* regardless of. **b** (*outre*) **~ de** apart from, over and above. **c** (*†: de façon indépendante*) independently.

indépendance [ɛ̃depɑ̃dɑ̃s] nf (*gén*) independence (*de, par rapport à* from). **~ d'esprit** independence of mind.

indépendant, e [ɛ̃depɑ̃dɑ̃, ɑ̃t] adj (*gén*) independent (*de* of). **pour des causes *ou* raisons ~es de notre volonté** for reasons beyond *ou* outside our control; **"à louer: chambre ~e"** "to let: self-contained bedsitter"; **maison ~e** detached house; **travailleur ~** (*non salarié*) freelance worker, freelancer; (*qui est son propre patron*) self-employed worker; **travailler en ~** to work freelance, be self-employed.

indépendantisme [ɛ̃depɑ̃dɑ̃tism] nm (*pression politique*) struggle for independence; (*sentiment*) desire for independence.

indépendantiste [ɛ̃depɑ̃dɑ̃tist] **1** adj: **mouvement ~** independence movement. **2** nmf member of an independence movement, freedom fighter. **les ~s (corses) ont revendiqué l'attentat** the (Corsican) independence movement claimed responsibility for the attack.

indéracinable [ɛ̃deʀasinabl] adj *préjugé* ineradicable.

indéréglable [ɛ̃deʀeglabl] adj foolproof, totally reliable.

Indes [ɛ̃d] *voir* **Inde.**

indescriptible [ɛ̃dɛskʀiptibl] adj *panique, désordre* indescribable.

indésirable [ɛ̃deziʀabl] adj, nmf undesirable.

indestructibilité [ɛ̃dɛstʀyktibilite] nf indestructibility.

indestructible [ɛ̃dɛstʀyktibl] adj *objet, sentiment, matériau* indestructible; (*fig*) *marque, impression* indelible.

indétectable [ɛ̃detɛktabl] adj *avion, erreur* undetectable.

indéterminable [ɛ̃detɛʀminabl] adj indeterminable.

indétermination [ɛ̃detɛʀminasjɔ̃] nf **a** (*imprécision*) vagueness. **b** (*irrésolution*) (*chronique*) indecisiveness; (*temporaire*) indecision, uncertainty.

indéterminé, e [ɛ̃detɛʀmine] adj **a** (*non précisé*) *date, cause, nature* unspecified; *forme, longueur, quantité* indeterminate. **pour des raisons ~es** for reasons which were not specified; **à une date encore ~e** at a date to be specified *ou* as yet unspecified *ou* as yet undecided. **b** (*imprécis*) *impression, sentiment* vague; *contours, goût* indeterminable, vague. **c** (*irrésolu*) **je suis encore ~ sur ce que je vais faire** I'm still undecided *ou* uncertain about what I'm going to do.

indétrônable [ɛ̃detʀonabl] adj (*Pol*) unassailable, impossible to topple; (*Sport*) *champion* invincible.

index [ɛ̃dɛks] nm **a** (*doigt*) forefinger, index finger; (*repère*) *[instrument]* pointer; (*aiguille*) *[cadran]* needle, pointer; (*liste alphabétique*) index; (*indice*) index. **b** (*Rel*) **l'I~** the Index; (*fig*) **mettre qn/qch à l'~** to blacklist sb/sth.

indexage [ɛ̃dɛksaʒ] nm, **indexation** [ɛ̃dɛksasjɔ̃] nf (*Écon*) indexing, indexation.

indexé, e [ɛ̃dɛkse] (ptp de **indexer**) adj *prix* indexed (*sur* to); *prêt* index-linked, index-tied. **salaire ~ sur l'inflation** salary index-linked to inflation.

indexer [ɛ̃dɛkse] 1 vt **a** (*Écon*) to index (*sur* to). **b** *document, mot* to index. **c** (*Ordin*) to index.

Indiana [ɛ̃djana] nm Indiana.

indic [ɛ̃dik] nm (*arg Police*) (abrév de **indicateur**) (copper's) nark (*arg Brit*), grass (*arg*), informer, fink‡ (*US*).

indicateur, -trice [ɛ̃dikatœʀ, tʀis] **1** adj *voir* **panneau, poteau.**

2 nm,f: **~ (de police)** (police) informer.

3 nm **a** (*guide*) guide; (*horaire*) timetable.

b (*Tech: compteur, cadran*) gauge, indicator.

c (*Chim: substance*) **~ (coloré)** indicator.

d (*Ling*) **~ (de sens)** (semantic) indicator.

4 comp ►**indicateur d'altitude** altimeter ►**indicateur des chemins de fer** railway timetable ►**indicateur de direction** (*Naut*) direction finder; *[voitures]* (direction) indicator ►**indicateur économique** *ou* **de conjoncture** (*Écon*) economic indicator ►**indicateur immobilier** property gazette ►**indicateur de niveau de carburant** fuel *ou* petrol (*Brit*) gauge ►**indicateur de niveau d'eau** water(-level) gauge ►**indicateur de pression** pressure gauge ►**indicateur des rues** street directory ►**indicateurs sociaux** social indicators ►**indicateur de tendance** (*Bourse*) economic indicator ►**indicateur de vitesse** (*Aut*) speedometer; (*Aviat*) airspeed indicator.

indicatif, -ive [ɛ̃dikatif, iv] **1** adj indicative (*de* of); (*Ling*) indicative; *voir* **titre.** **2** nm **a** (*Rad: mélodie*) theme *ou* signature tune. **b** *[Télex]* answer-back code. *[poste émetteur]* **~ (d'appel)** call sign; (*Téléc*) **~ téléphonique** (dialling) code; (*Téléc*) **~ départemental** area code. **c** (*Ling*) **l'~** the indicative; **à l'~** in the indicative.

indication [ɛ̃dikasjɔ̃] **1** nf **a** (*renseignement*) piece of information, information (*NonC*). **qui vous a donné cette ~?** who gave you that (piece of) information?, who told you that?

b (*mention*) **quelle ~ porte la pancarte?** what does the notice say?, what has the notice got on it?; **sans ~ de date/de prix** with no indication of the date/price, without a date stamp/price label; **les ~s du compteur** the reading on the meter.

c (*notification*) *[prix, danger, mode d'emploi]* indication. **l'~ du virage dangereux a permis d'éviter les accidents** signposting the dangerous bend has prevented accidents; **l'~ d'une date est impérative** a date stamp must be shown, the date must be indicated; **l'~ de l'heure vous sera fournie ultérieurement** you will be given the time *ou* informed of the time later; **rendre obligatoire l'~ des prix** to make it compulsory to mark *ou* show prices.

d (*indice*) indication (*de* of). **c'est une ~ suffisante de sa culpabilité** that's a good enough indication of his guilt.

e (*directive*) instruction, direction. **sauf ~ contraire** unless otherwise stated *ou* indicated; **sur son ~** on his instruction.

2 comp ►**indication d'origine** (*Comm*) place of origin ►**indications scéniques** (*Théât*) stage directions ►**indication (thérapeutique)** (*Méd*) *[remède, traitement]* indication.

indice [ɛ̃dis] nm **a** (*signe*) indication, sign. **être l'~ de** to be an indication *ou* a sign of; **il n'y avait pas le moindre ~ de leur passage** there was no sign *ou* evidence *ou* indication that they had been there.

b (*élément d'information*) clue; (*Jur: preuve*) piece of evidence. **rechercher des ~s du crime** to look for clues about the crime.

c (*Math*) suffix; (*degré de racine*) index; *[fonctionnaire]* rating, grading. (*Math*) **"a" ~ 2** a (suffix) two; **~ des prix/du coût de la vie** price/cost of living index; **l'~ de l'INSEE** ≃ the retail price index; (*TV, Rad*) **~ d'écoute** audience rating; (*TV, Rad*) **avoir un excellent ~ d'écoute** to have a high rating, get good ratings; (*Aut*) **~ d'octane** octane rating; (*Admin*) **~ de traitement** salary grading; (*Phot*) **~ de lumination/de pose** exposure value/index.

indiciaire [ɛ̃disjɛʀ] adj *traitement* grade-related. **classement ~ d'un fonctionnaire** grading of a civil servant.

indicible [ɛ̃disibl] adj *joie, peur* inexpressible; *souffrance* unspeakable; *beauté* indescribable.

indiciblement [ɛ̃disibləmɑ̃] adv inexpressibly, unspeakably.

indiciel, -elle [ɛ̃disjɛl] adj (*Écon*) indexed.

indien, -ienne [ɛ̃djɛ̃, jɛn] **1** adj Indian; *voir* **chanvre, file, océan.** **2** nm,f: **I~(ne)** *[Inde]* Indian; *[Amérique]* (Red *ou* American) Indian. **3** **indienne** nf **a** (*Hist: tissu*) printed calico. **b** overarm sidestroke.

nager *ou* faire l'~ne to swim sidestroke.

indifféremment [ɛ̃difeʀamɑ̃] adv a (*indistinctement*) indiscriminately, equally. **supporter ~ le froid et le chaud** to stand heat and cold equally well, stand either heat or cold; **fonctionner ~ au gaz ou à l'électricité** to run on either gas or electricity, run equally well on gas or electricity; **manger de tout ~** to eat indiscriminately, eat (just) anything; **il est impoli ~ avec ses chefs et ses subordonnés** he is equally impolite to those above him and to those below him. b (*littér: avec indifférence*) indifferently.

indifférence [ɛ̃difeʀɑ̃s] nf a (*désintérêt*) indifference (*à l'égard de, pour* to, towards), lack of concern (*à l'égard de* for). **avec ~** indifferently; **il les a regardés se battre en jouant l'~** he watched them fight with an air of indifference. b (*froideur*) indifference (*envers* to, towards).

indifférenciable [ɛ̃difeʀɑ̃sjabl] adj which cannot be differentiated.

indifférenciation [ɛ̃difeʀɑ̃sjasjɔ̃] nf lack of differentiation.

indifférencié, e [ɛ̃difeʀɑ̃sje] adj (*Bio, Sci*) undifferentiated.

indifférent, e [ɛ̃difeʀɑ̃, ɑ̃t] 1 adj a (*sans importance*) **il est ~ de faire ceci ou cela** it doesn't matter *ou* it's immaterial whether one does this or that; **elle m'est/ne m'est pas ~e** I am/am not indifferent to her; **son sort m'est ~** his fate is of no interest to me *ou* is a matter of indifference to me; **il m'est ~ de partir ou de rester** it is indifferent *ou* immaterial to me *ou* it doesn't matter to me whether I go or stay; **parler de choses ~es** to talk of this and that.

b (*peu intéressé*) *spectateur* indifferent (*à* to, towards), unconcerned (*à* about). **il était ~ à tout ce qui ne concernait pas sa spécialité** he was indifferent to *ou* unconcerned about everything outside his own speciality; **ça le laisse ~** it doesn't touch him in the least, he is quite unconcerned about it; **leur pauvreté/souffrance ne peut laisser personne ~** it's impossible to remain indifferent to their poverty/suffering; **son charme ne peut laisser personne ~** no-one is immune to his charm.

2 nm,f unconcerned person.

indifférer [ɛ̃difeʀe] 6 vt: **ceci/mon opinion l'indiffère totalement** he's quite indifferent to this/my opinion, he couldn't care less about this/my opinion.

indigence [ɛ̃diʒɑ̃s] nf (*misère*) poverty, destitution, indigence (*frm*); (*fig*) *[style]* poverty. **tomber/être dans l'~** to become/be destitute; **~ intellectuelle** intellectual penury, poverty of intellect; **~ d'idées** poverty *ou* paucity of ideas.

indigène [ɛ̃diʒɛn] 1 nmf (*aux colonies*) native; (*personne du pays*) local. 2 adj a (*des non-colons*) *coutume* native; *population* native, indigenous; (*Bot, Zool: non importé*) indigenous, native. **visitez la ville ~** visit the old town. b (*des gens du pays*) *main-d'œuvre, population* local.

indigent, e [ɛ̃diʒɑ̃, ɑ̃t] 1 adj *personne* destitute, poverty-stricken, indigent (*frm*); *imagination* poor; *végétation* poor, sparse. 2 nm,f pauper. **les ~s** the destitute, the poor, the indigent (*frm*).

indigeste [ɛ̃diʒɛst] adj (*lit, fig*) indigestible, difficult to digest (*attrib*).

indigestion [ɛ̃diʒɛstjɔ̃] nf attack of indigestion, indigestion (*NonC*). **il s'est donné une ~ de pâtisseries** (*lit*) he gave himself *ou* he got indigestion from eating too many cakes; (*fig: manger à satiété*) he sickened himself of cakes, he had a surfeit of cakes; (*fig*) **avoir/se donner une ~ de romans policiers** to be sick of/sicken o.s. of detective stories; **j'en ai une ~, de toutes ces histoires*** I'm sick (and tired) of all these complications*, I'm fed up with all these complications*.

indignation [ɛ̃diɲasjɔ̃] nf indignation. **avec ~** indignantly.

indigne [ɛ̃diɲ] adj a (*pas digne de*) **~ de** *amitié, confiance, personne* unworthy of, not worthy of; **il est ~ de ton amitié** he is unworthy of *ou* does not deserve your friendship; **il est ~ de vivre** he doesn't deserve to live, he's not fit to live; **ce livre est ~ de figurer dans ma bibliothèque** this book is not worthy of a place in my library; **c'est ~ de vous** (*travail, emploi*) it is beneath you; (*conduite, attitude*) it is unworthy of you. b (*abject*) *acte* shameful; (*lit, fig*) *personne* unworthy. **mère/époux ~** unworthy mother/husband; **c'est un père ~** he's not fit to be a father.

indigné, e [ɛ̃diɲe] (ptp de **indigner**) adj indignant (*par* at).

indignement [ɛ̃diɲmɑ̃] adv shamefully.

indigner [ɛ̃diɲe] 1 1 vt: **~ qn** to make sb indignant. 2 **s'indigner** vpr (*se fâcher*) to become *ou* get indignant *ou* annoyed (*de* about, at; *contre* with, about, at). (*être écœuré*) **s'~ que/de, être indigné que/de** to be indignant that/about *ou* at; **je l'écoutais s'~ contre les spéculateurs** I listened to him waxing indignant *ou* going on* *ou* sounding off* indignantly about speculators; **je m'indigne de penser/voir que** it makes me indignant *ou* it fills me with indignation *ou* it infuriates me to think/see that.

indignité [ɛ̃diɲite] nf a (*caractère*) *[personne]* unworthiness; *[conduite]* baseness, shamefulness. b (*acte*) shameful act. **c'est une ~!** it's a disgrace!, it's shameful!

indigo [ɛ̃digo] 1 nm (*matière, couleur*) indigo. 2 adj inv indigo (blue).

indigotier [ɛ̃digɔtje] nm (*Bot*) indigo-plant.

indiqué, e [ɛ̃dike] (ptp de **indiquer**) adj a (*conseillé*) advisable. **ce n'est pas très ~** it's not really advisable, it's really not the best thing to do.

b (*adéquat*) **prenons ça, c'est tout ~** let's take that – it's just the thing *ou* it's just what we need; **pour ce travail M. X est tout ~** Mr X is the obvious choice *ou* is just the man we need for that job; **c'est le moyen ~** it's the best *ou* right way to do it; **c'était un sujet tout ~** it was obviously an appropriate *ou* a suitable subject.

c (*prescrit*) *médicament, traitement* appropriate. **le traitement ~ dans ce cas est ...** the appropriate *ou* correct *ou* prescribed treatment in this case is ...; **ce remède est particulièrement ~ dans les cas graves** this drug is particularly appropriate *ou* suitable for serious cases.

indiquer [ɛ̃dike] 1 vt a (*désigner*) to point out, indicate. **~ qch/qn du doigt** to point sth/sb out (*à qn* to sb), point to sth/sb, indicate sth/sb; **~ qch de la main/tête** to indicate sth with one's hand/with a nod; **il m'indiqua du regard le coupable** his glance *ou* look directed me towards the culprit; **~ le chemin à qn** to give directions to sb, show sb the way; **~ la réception/les toilettes à qn** to direct sb to *ou* show sb the way to the reception desk/the toilets.

b (*montrer*) *[flèche, aiguille, voyant, écriteau]* to show, indicate. *[montre]* **~ l'heure** to give *ou* show *ou* tell the time; **la petite aiguille indique les heures** the small hand shows *ou* marks the hours; **l'horloge indiquait 2 heures** the clock said *ou* showed it was 2 o'clock; **qu'indique la pancarte?** what does the sign say?

c (*recommander*) **~ à qn** *livre, hôtel, médecin* to tell sb of, suggest to sb.

d (*dire*) *[personne] heure, solution* to tell; *dangers, désavantages* to point out, show. **il m'indiqua comment le réparer** he told me how to mend it; **il m'en indiqua le mode d'emploi** he told me how to use it.

e (*fixer*) *heure, date, rendez-vous* to give, name. **à l'heure indiquée, je ...** at the time indicated *ou* stated, I ...; at the agreed *ou* appointed time, I ...; **à la date indiquée** on the given *ou* agreed day; **au lieu indiqué** at the given *ou* agreed place.

f (*faire figurer*) *[étiquette, plan, cartographe]* to show; *[table, index]* to give, show. **est-ce indiqué sur la facture/dans l'annuaire?** is it given *ou* mentioned on the invoice/in the directory?; **il a sommairement indiqué les fenêtres sur le plan** he quickly marked *ou* drew in the windows on the plan; **quelques traits pour ~ les spectateurs/ombres** a few strokes to give an impression of spectators/shadows; **quelques rapides croquis pour ~ le jeu de scène** a few rapid sketches to give a rough idea of the action.

g (*dénoter*) to indicate, point to. **tout indique que les prix vont augmenter** everything indicates that prices are going to rise, everything points to a forthcoming rise in prices; **cela indique une certaine négligence/hésitation de sa part** that shows *ou* points to a certain carelessness/hesitation on his part.

indirect, e [ɛ̃diʀɛkt] adj (*gén*) indirect; (*Jur*) *ligne, héritier* collateral. **d'une manière ~e** in a roundabout *ou* an indirect way; **apprendre qch de manière ~e** to hear of sth in a roundabout way; *voir* **discours, éclairage, impôt**.

indirectement [ɛ̃diʀɛktəmɑ̃] adv (*gén*) indirectly; (*de façon détournée*) *faire savoir, apprendre* in a roundabout way.

indiscernable [ɛ̃disɛʀnabl] adj indiscernible, imperceptible.

indiscipline [ɛ̃disiplin] nf (*insubordination*) indiscipline, lack of discipline. **faire preuve d'~** to behave in an undisciplined *ou* unruly manner.

indiscipliné, e [ɛ̃disipline] adj *troupes, écolier* undisciplined; *cheveux* unmanageable, unruly.

indiscret, -ète [ɛ̃diskʀɛ, ɛt] adj a (*trop curieux*) *personne* inquisitive; *question, curiosité* indiscreet; *regard, yeux* inquisitive, prying. **à l'abri des regards ~s/des oreilles ~ètes** out of the reach of *ou* away from prying *ou* inquisitive eyes/of inquisitive eavesdroppers; **serait-ce ~ de vous demander?** would it be indiscreet to ask you?; **mettre des documents à l'abri des ~s** to put documents out of the reach of inquisitive people.

b (*qui divulgue*) *personne, bavardage* indiscreet. **secret révélé par des langues ~ètes** secret revealed by wagging tongues *ou* indiscreet prattlers; **ne confiez rien aux ~s** don't entrust anything to people who can't keep quiet.

indiscrètement [ɛ̃diskʀɛtmɑ̃] adv (*voir* **indiscret**) indiscreetly; inquisitively.

indiscrétion [ɛ̃diskʀesjɔ̃] nf a (*curiosité: voir* **indiscret**) indiscreetness, indiscretion; inquisitiveness. **excusez mon ~** forgive my indiscretion; (*suivi d'une question*) forgive me for asking; **elle pousse l'~ jusqu'à lire mon courrier** her inquisitiveness is such that she even reads my mail; **sans ~, peut-on savoir si ...** without wanting to be *ou* without being indiscreet, may we ask whether ... .

b (*tendance à divulguer*) indiscretion. **il est d'une telle ~!** he's so indiscreet!

c (*action ou parole indiscrète*) indiscreet word *ou* act, indiscretion. **son sort dépend d'une ~** it needs only one indiscreet remark to seal his fate; **la moindre ~ vous perdrait** the slightest indiscretion would finish you.

indiscutable [ɛ̃diskytabl] adj indisputable, unquestionable.

indiscutablement [ɛ̃diskytabləmɑ̃] adv indisputably, unquestionably.

indiscuté, e [ɛ̃diskyte] adj undisputed.

indispensable [ɛ̃dispɑ̃sabl] 1 adj essential. **ces outils/précautions sont ~s** these tools/precautions are essential; **ce collaborateur m'est ~** this collaborator is indispensable to me, I cannot do without this collaborator; **il est ~ que/de faire** it is essential *ou* absolutely necessary *ou* vital that/to do; **je crois qu'il est ~ qu'ils y aillent** I think it's vital *ou* essential that they (should) go; **emporter les vêtements ~s (pour le voyage)** to take the clothes which are essential *ou* indispensable (for the journey); **prendre les précautions ~s** to take the necessary precautions; **crédits/travaux ~s à la construction d'un bâtiment** funds/work essential *ou* vital for the construction of a building; **l'eau est un élément ~ à la vie** water is an indispensable *ou* essential element for life; **savoir se rendre ~** to make o.s. indispensable.

2 **nm: nous n'avions que l'~** we only had what was absolutely essential *ou* necessary *ou* indispensable; **faire l'~ d'abord** to do what is essential *ou* absolutely necessary first; **l'~ est de ...** it is absolutely necessary *ou* essential to ... .

indisponibilité [ɛ̃dispɔnibilite] **nf** unavailability.

indisponible [ɛ̃dispɔnibl] **adj** (*gén*) not available (*attrib*), unavailable; (*Jur*) unavailable.

indisposé, e [ɛ̃dispoze] (**ptp de indisposer**) **adj** (*fatigué, malade*) indisposed, unwell; (*euph*) *femme* indisposed.

indisposer [ɛ̃dispoze] [1] **vt** (*rendre malade*) *[aliment, chaleur]* to upset, indispose; (*mécontenter*) *[personne, remarque]* to antagonize. **il a des allures qui m'indisposent** his way of behaving irritates me *ou* puts me off him* (*Brit*); **~ qn contre soi** to antagonize sb, set sb against one, alienate sb; **tout l'indispose!** anything annoys him, he takes a dislike to everything!; **cette scène trop violente risque d'~ les spectateurs** this very violent scene is likely to alienate *ou* antagonize the audience.

indisposition [ɛ̃dispozisjɔ̃] **nf** (*malaise*) (slight) indisposition, upset; (*euph: règles*) period.

indissociable [ɛ̃disɔsjabl] **adj** *problèmes* indissociable.

indissolubilité [ɛ̃disɔlybilite] **nf** indissolubility.

indissoluble [ɛ̃disɔlybl] **adj** indissoluble.

indissolublement [ɛ̃disɔlybləmɑ̃] **adv** indissolubly. **~ liés** *problèmes* indissolubly linked (*à* to).

indistinct, e [ɛ̃distɛ̃(kt), ɛ̃kt] **adj** *forme, idée, souvenir* indistinct, vague; *rumeur, murmure* indistinct, confused; *couleurs* vague. **des voix ~es** a confused murmur of voices.

indistinctement [ɛ̃distɛ̃ktəmɑ̃] **adv** a (*confusément: voir* **indistinct**) indistinctly; vaguely. **des bruits qui me provenaient ~ du jardin** confused noises which reached my ears from the garden.

b (*ensemble*) indiscriminately. **confondus ~ dans la réprobation générale** indiscriminately included in the general criticism; **tuant ~ femmes et enfants** killing women and children indiscriminately *ou* without distinction.

c (*indifféremment*) **cette cuisinière marche ~ au gaz ou à l'électricité** this cooker runs either on gas or on electricity *ou* runs equally well on gas or on electricity; **sa haine se portait ~ sur les Blancs et les Noirs** his hatred was directed indiscriminately at *ou* was directed at Whites and Blacks alike.

indium [ɛ̃djɔm] **nm** indium.

individu [ɛ̃dividy] **nm** a (*gén, Bio: unité*) individual. b (*hum: anatomie*) **fort occupé de son ~** very taken up with himself, very preoccupied with his own little self; **dans la partie la plus charnue de son ~** in the fleshiest part of his anatomy. c (*péj: homme*) fellow, individual, character. **un ~ l'aborda** a fellow came up to him; **il aperçut un drôle d'~/un ~ chevelu** he noticed an odd-looking/a long-haired character *ou* individual.

individualisation [ɛ̃dividɥalizasjɔ̃] **nf** a (*voir* **individualiser**) individualization; personalization; tailoring to (suit) individual *ou* particular requirements. (*Jur*) **l'~ d'une peine** sentencing according to the characteristics of the offender. b (*voir* **s'individualiser**) individualization.

individualisé, e [ɛ̃dividɥalize] (**ptp de individualiser**) **adj** *caractères, groupe* distinctive; *objet personnel, voiture* personalized. **groupe fortement ~** highly distinctive group, group with a distinctive identity; **des solutions ~es selon les différents besoins** solutions which are tailored to suit individual *ou* particular requirements.

individualiser [ɛ̃dividɥalize] [1] 1 **vt** (*caractériser*) to individualize; (*personnaliser*) *objet personnel, voiture* to personalize; *solutions, horaire* to tailor to (suit) individual *ou* particular requirements; (*Jur*) *peine* to match with the characteristics of the offender. 2 **s'individualiser vpr** *[personne, groupe, région]* to acquire an identity of one's *ou* its own, become more individual.

individualisme [ɛ̃dividɥalism] **nm** individualism.

individualiste [ɛ̃dividɥalist] 1 **adj** individualistic. 2 **nmf** individualist.

individualité [ɛ̃dividɥalite] **nf** (*caractère individuel*) individuality; (*personne*) individual; (*personnalité*) personality.

individuel, -elle [ɛ̃dividɥɛl] **adj** a (*propre à l'individu*) (*gén*) individual; *responsabilité, défaut, contrôle, livret* personal, individual; *caractères* distinctive, individual. **propriété ~le** personal *ou* private property; **liberté ~le** personal freedom, freedom of the individual. b (*isolé*) *fait* individual, isolated; *sachet* individual. **les cas ~s seront examinés** individual cases *ou* each individual case will be examined. c (*Sport*) **épreuve ~le** individual event.

individuellement [ɛ̃dividɥɛlmɑ̃] **adv** individually.

indivis, e [ɛ̃divi, iz] **adj** (*Jur*) *propriété, succession* undivided, joint (*épith*); *propriétaires* joint (*épith*). **par ~** *posséder* jointly; *transmettre* to be held in common.

indivisaire [ɛ̃divizɛʀ] **nmf** (*Jur*) tenant in common.

indivisément [ɛ̃divizemɑ̃] **adv** (*Jur*) jointly. **posséder qch ~** to have joint ownership of sth, own sth jointly.

indivisibilité [ɛ̃divizibilite] **nf** indivisibility.

indivisible [ɛ̃divizibl] **adj** indivisible.

indivisiblement [ɛ̃divizibləmɑ̃] **adv** indivisibly.

indivision [ɛ̃divizjɔ̃] **nf** (*Jur*) joint possession *ou* ownership. **propriété en ~** jointly-held property.

Indochine [ɛ̃dɔʃin] **nf** Indo-China.

indochinois, e [ɛ̃dɔʃinwa, waz] 1 **adj** Indo-Chinese. 2 **nm,f: I~(e)** Indo-Chinese.

indocile [ɛ̃dɔsil] **adj** *enfant* unruly, recalcitrant, intractable; *mémoire* intractable.

indocilité [ɛ̃dɔsilite] **nf** (*voir* **indocile**) unruliness, recalcitrance; intractability.

indo-européen, -enne [ɛ̃doøʀɔpeɛ̃, ɛn] 1 **adj** Indo-European. 2 **nm** (*Ling*) Indo-European. 3 **nm,f: I~-E~(ne)** Indo-European.

indolemment [ɛ̃dɔlamɑ̃] **adv** indolently.

indolence [ɛ̃dɔlɑ̃s] **nf** *[élève]* idleness, indolence; *[pouvoirs publics]* apathy, lethargy; *[air, geste, regard]* indolence, languidness.

indolent, e [ɛ̃dɔlɑ̃, ɑ̃t] **adj** (*voir* **indolence**) idle; indolent; apathetic; lethargic; languid.

indolore [ɛ̃dɔlɔʀ] **adj** painless.

indomptable [ɛ̃dɔ̃(p)tabl] **adj** *animal, adversaire, peuple,* (*hum*) *personne* untameable, which (*ou* who) cannot be tamed; *cheval* untameable, which cannot be broken *ou* mastered; *enfant* unmanageable, uncontrollable; *caractère, courage, volonté* indomitable, invincible; *passion, haine* ungovernable, invincible, uncontrollable.

indompté, e [ɛ̃dɔ̃(p)te] **adj** *enfant, animal, peuple* untamed, wild; *cheval* unbroken, untamed; *courage* undaunted; *énergie* unharnessed, untamed; *passion* ungoverned, unsuppressed.

Indonésie [ɛ̃dɔnezi] **nf** Indonesia.

indonésien, -ienne [ɛ̃dɔnezjɛ̃, jɛn] 1 **adj** Indonesian. 2 **nm,f: I~(ne)** Indonesian.

indou, e [ɛ̃du] = **hindou**.

indu, e [ɛ̃dy] **adj** (*hum, littér: déplacé*) *joie* unseemly; *dépenses* unwarranted, unjustified. **sans optimisme ~** without undue optimism; *voir* **heure**.

indubitable [ɛ̃dybitabl] **adj** *preuve* indubitable, undoubted. **c'est ~** there is no doubt about it, it's beyond doubt, it's indubitable; **il est ~ qu'il a tort** he is undoubtedly wrong, there's no doubt (that) he's wrong.

indubitablement [ɛ̃dybitabləmɑ̃] **adv** (*assurément*) undoubtedly, indubitably. **vous vous êtes ~ trompé** you have undoubtedly made a mistake.

inductance [ɛ̃dyktɑ̃s] **nf** inductance.

inducteur, -trice [ɛ̃dyktœʀ, tʀis] 1 **adj** (*gén*) inductive. 2 **nm** (*aimant*) inductor.

inductif, -ive [ɛ̃dyktif, iv] **adj** (*gén*) inductive.

induction [ɛ̃dyksjɔ̃] **nf** (*gén*) induction. **raisonnement par ~** reasoning by induction.

induire [ɛ̃dɥiʀ] [38] **vt** a **~ qn en erreur** to mislead sb, lead sb astray. b (†: *inciter*) **~ qn à** *péché, gourmandise* to lead sb into; **~ qn à faire** to induce sb to do. c (*inférer*) to infer, induce (*de* from). **j'en induis que** I infer from it that. d (*occasionner*) to lead to, result in. e (*Élec*) to induce.

induit, e [ɛ̃dɥi, it] 1 **adj** (*Élec*) induced. 2 **nm** (*Élec*) armature.

indulgence [ɛ̃dylʒɑ̃s] **nf** a (*caractère: voir* **indulgent**) indulgence; leniency. **une erreur qui a rencontré l'~ du jury** a mistake for which the jury made allowances *ou* which the jury was prepared to overlook *ou* be lenient about; **il a demandé l'~ du jury pour son client** he asked the jury to make allowances for *ou* to show leniency towards his client; **avec ~** leniently, with leniency, indulgently; **sans ~** *juge, jugement* not at all lenient; *portrait, critique* brutally frank; *punir* without leniency; *critiquer* with brutal frankness; **regard plein d'~** indulgent look. b (*Rel*) indulgence.

indulgent, e [ɛ̃dylʒɑ̃, ɑ̃t] **adj** *parent* indulgent (*avec* with); *juge, examinateur* lenient (*envers* towards); *critique, commentaire* indulgent; *regard* indulgent. **15, c'est une note trop ~e** 15 is (far) too lenient *ou* kind a mark; **se montrer ~** *[juge]* to show leniency; *[examinateur]* to be lenient.

indûment [ɛ̃dymɑ̃] **adv** *protester* unduly; *détenir* without due cause *ou* reason, wrongfully. **s'ingérer ~ dans les affaires de qn** to interfere unnecessarily in sb's business.

induration [ɛ̃dyʀasjɔ̃] **nf** induration (*SPÉC*), hardening.

induré, e [ɛ̃dyʀe] (**ptp de indurer**) **adj** indurate (*SPÉC*), hardened.

indurer [ɛ̃dyʀe] [1] 1 **vt** to indurate (*SPÉC*), harden. 2 **s'indurer vpr** to indurate (*SPÉC*), become indurate (*SPÉC*), harden.

Indus [ɛ̃dys] **nm: l'~** the Indus.

industrialisation [ɛ̃dystʀijalizasjɔ̃] **nf** industrialization.

industrialiser [ɛ̃dystʀijalize] [1] 1 **vt** to industrialize. 2 **s'industrialiser vpr** to become industrialized.

industrialisme [ɛ̃dystʀijalism] **nm** industrialism.

industrialiste [ɛ̃dystʀijalist] **adj** *politique* which favours *ou* encourages industrialization.

industrie [ɛ̃dystʀi] 1 **nf** a (*activité, secteur, branche*) industry. ~ **légère/lourde** light/heavy industry; ~ **chimique/automobile** chemical/car *ou* automobile (*US*) industry; ~ **naissante** infant industry; **doter un pays d'une** ~ to provide a country with an industrial structure; *voir* **ministère, pointe.** b (*entreprise*) industry, industrial concern; *voir* **capitaine.** c (*littér,* †) (*ingéniosité*) ingenuity; (*ruse*) cunning. d (*activité*) **exerçant sa coupable** ~ practising his disreputable business *ou* trade; *voir* **chevalier.**
2 **comp** ▸ **industrie alimentaire** food (processing) industry ▸ **industries du livre** book-related industries ▸ **industrie de luxe** luxury goods industry ▸ **industrie de précision** precision tool industry ▸ **l'industrie du spectacle** the entertainment business, show business ▸ **industrie de transformation** processing industry.

industriel, -elle [ɛ̃dystʀijɛl] 1 **adj** industrial. **pain** ~ factory-baked bread; **équipement à usage** ~ heavy-duty equipment; **élevage** ~ (*système*) factory farming; (*ferme*) factory farm; *voir* **quantité, zone.** 2 **nm** (*chef d'industrie*) industrialist, manufacturer. **les ~s du textile/de l'automobile** textile/car *ou* automobile (*US*) manufacturers.

industriellement [ɛ̃dystʀijɛlmɑ̃] **adv** industrially. **géré** ~ run on *ou* along industrial lines.

industrieux, -ieuse [ɛ̃dystʀijø, ijøz] **adj** (*littér: besogneux*) industrious.

inébranlable [inebʀɑ̃labl] **adj** a *adversaire, interlocuteur* steadfast, unwavering; *personne, foi, résolution* unshakeable, steadfast, unwavering; *certitude* unshakeable, unwavering. **il était** ~ **dans sa conviction que ...** he was steadfast *ou* unshakeable *ou* unwavering in his belief that ... . b *objet massif, monumental* solid; *objet fixé ou encastré* immovable, solidly *ou* firmly fixed. **il avait si bien enfoncé le pieu qu'il était maintenant** ~ he had hammered the post in so hard that it was now as firm *ou* solid as a rock *ou* that it was now quite immovable.

inébranlablement [inebʀɑ̃labləmɑ̃] **adv** unshakeably.

inéchangeable [ineʃɑ̃ʒabl] **adj** (*Comm*) *article* not exchangeable (*attrib*).

inécoutable [inekutabl] **adj** *musique* unbearable, unbearable to listen to (*attrib*).

inécouté, e [inekute] **adj** *avis* unheeded; *prophète, expert* unlistened to (*attrib*), unheeded.

inédit, e [inedi, it] 1 **adj** a (*non publié*) *texte, auteur* (previously *ou* hitherto) unpublished. b (*nouveau*) *méthode, trouvaille* novel, new, original; *spectacle* new. **c'est de l'~** that's novel. 2 **nm** (*texte inédit*) (previously *ou* hitherto) unpublished material (*NonC*) *ou* work.

inéducable [inedykabl] **adj** ineducable.

ineffable [inefabl] **adj** ineffable.

ineffaçable [inefasabl] **adj** indelible, ineffaceable.

inefficace [inefikas] **adj** *remède, mesure* ineffective, ineffectual, inefficacious; *machine, employé* inefficient.

inefficacement [inefikasmɑ̃] **adv** (*voir* **inefficace**) ineffectively, ineffectually, inefficaciously; inefficiently.

inefficacité [inefikasite] **nf** (*voir* **inefficace**) ineffectiveness, ineffectualness, inefficacy; inefficiency.

inégal, e, **mpl -aux** [inegal, o] **adj** a (*différent*) unequal. **d'~e grosseur** of unequal size; **de force ~e** of unequal strength; **les hommes sont ~aux** men are not equal. b (*irrégulier*) *sol, pas, rythme, mouvement* uneven; *pouls* irregular, uneven; *artiste, sportif* erratic; *œuvre, jeu* uneven; *étalement, répartition* uneven; *humeur, caractère* uneven, changeable; *conduite* changeable. **d'intérêt** ~ of varying *ou* mixed interest; **de qualité ~e** of varying quality. c (*disproportionné*) *lutte, partage* unequal.

inégalable [inegalabl] **adj** incomparable, matchless.

inégalé, e [inegale] **adj** *record* unequalled, unbeaten; *charme, beauté* unrivalled.

inégalement [inegalmɑ̃] **adv** (*différemment, injustement*) unequally; (*irrégulièrement*) unevenly. **livre ~ apprécié** book which met (*ou* meets) with varying approval.

inégalité [inegalite] **nf** a (*différence*) *[hauteurs, volumes]* difference (*de* between); *[sommes, parts]* difference, disparity (*de* between). **l'~ de l'offre et de la demande** the difference *ou* disparity between supply and demand; **les ~s sociales** social inequalities. b (*Math*) inequality. c (*injustice*) inequality. d (*irrégularité*) *[sol, pas, rythme, répartition]* unevenness; *[humeur, caractère]* unevenness, changeability; *[conduite]* changeability. **dans ce livre il y a des ~s** there are weak parts in this book, the book is a bit patchy (*Brit*); **~s de terrain** unevenness of the ground, bumps in the ground; **~s d'humeur** unevenness of temper.

inélégamment [inelegamɑ̃] **adv** inelegantly.

inélégance [inelegɑ̃s] **nf** (*voir* **inélégant**) inelegance; ungainliness; discourtesy.

inélégant, e [inelegɑ̃, ɑ̃t] **adj** a (*sans grâce*) *geste, toilette, femme* inelegant; *allure* inelegant, ungainly. b (*indélicat*) *procédés* discourteous. **c'était très ~ de sa part d'agir ainsi** it was very poor taste on his part to behave like this.

inéligibilité [ineliʒibilite] **nf** (*Pol*) ineligibility.

inéligible [ineliʒibl] **adj** (*Pol*) ineligible.

inéluctabilité [inelyktabilite] **nf** inescapability, ineluctability (*frm*).

inéluctable [inelyktabl] **adj, nm** inescapable, ineluctable (*frm*).

inéluctablement [inelyktabləmɑ̃] **adv** inescapably, ineluctably (*frm*).

inemployable [inɑ̃plwajabl] **adj** *procédé* unusable.

inemployé, e [inɑ̃plwaje] **adj** (*sans utilisation présente*) *méthode, outil, argent, talent* unused; (*gâché*) *dévouement, énergie* unchannelled, unused.

inénarrable [inenaʀabl] **adj** a (*désopilant*) *incident, scène* hilarious, priceless*, too funny for words (*attrib*); *vêtement, démarche* incredibly funny, priceless*. **son ~ mari** her incredible husband*. b (*incroyable*) *péripéties, aventure* incredible.

inentamé, e [inɑ̃tame] **adj** *réserve d'essence, d'argent* intact (*attrib*); *victuailles* intact (*attrib*), untouched; *bouteille* unopened; *énergie, moral* (as yet) intact (*attrib*).

inenvisageable [inɑ̃vizaʒabl] **adj** which cannot be considered, unthinkable.

inéprouvé, e [inepʀuve] **adj** *méthode, vertu, procédé* untested, untried, not yet put to the test (*attrib*); *émotion* not yet experienced (*attrib*).

inepte [inɛpt] **adj** *personne* inept, useless*, hopeless*; *histoire, raisonnement* inept.

ineptie [inɛpsi] **nf** a (*caractère: gén*) ineptitude. b (*acte, propos*) ineptitude; (*idée, œuvre*) nonsense (*NonC*), rubbish (*Brit*) (*NonC*). **dire des ~s** to talk nonsense; **ce qu'il a fait est une ~** what he did was utterly stupid.

inépuisable [inepɥizabl] **adj** inexhaustible. **il est ~ sur ce sujet** he could talk for ever on that subject.

inéquation [inekwasjɔ̃] **nf** (*Math*) inequation.

inéquitable [inekitabl] **adj** inequitable.

inerte [inɛʀt] **adj** (*immobile*) *corps, membre* lifeless; *visage* expressionless; (*sans réaction*) *personne* passive, inert; *esprit, élève* apathetic; (*Sci*) inert. **réagis, ne reste pas ~ sur ta chaise, à ne rien faire** do something — don't just sit there passively as if you've got nothing to do.

inertie [inɛʀsi] **nf** *[personne]* inertia, passivity, apathy; *[service administratif]* apathy, inertia; *[élève]* apathy; (*Phys*) inertia; *voir* **force.**

inescompté, e [inɛskɔ̃te] **adj** unexpected, unhoped-for.

inespéré, e [inɛspeʀe] **adj** unexpected, unhoped-for.

inesthétique [inɛstetik] **adj** *pylône, usine, cicatrice* unsightly; *démarche, posture* ungainly.

inestimable [inɛstimabl] **adj** *aide* inestimable, invaluable; *valeur* priceless, incalculable, inestimable; *dommages* incalculable.

inévitable [inevitabl] **adj** *obstacle, accident* unavoidable; (*fatal*) *résultat* inevitable, inescapable; (*hum*) *chapeau, cigare* inevitable. **c'était ~!** it was inevitable!, it was bound to happen!, it had to happen!; **l'~** the inevitable.

inévitablement [inevitabləmɑ̃] **adv** inevitably.

inexact, e [inɛgza(kt), akt] **adj** a *renseignement, calcul, traduction, historien* inaccurate, inexact. **non, c'est ~** no, that's not correct *ou* that's wrong. b (*sans ponctualité*) unpunctual. **être ~ à un rendez-vous** to be late for an appointment.

inexactement [inɛgzaktəmɑ̃] **adv** *traduire, relater* inaccurately, incorrectly.

inexactitude [inɛgzaktityd] **nf** a (*manque de précision*) inaccuracy. b (*erreur*) inaccuracy. c (*manque de ponctualité*) unpunctuality (*NonC*).

inexaucé, e [inɛgzose] **adj** *prière* (as yet) unanswered; *vœu* (as yet) unfulfilled.

inexcusable [inɛkskyzabl] **adj** *faute, action* inexcusable, unforgivable. **vous êtes ~ (d'avoir fait cela)** you had no excuse (for doing that), it was inexcusable *ou* unforgivable of you (to have done that).

inexécutable [inɛgzekytabl] **adj** *projet* impractical, impracticable, unworkable, not feasible (*attrib*); *travail* which cannot be carried out, impractical, impracticable; *musique* unplayable; *ordre* which cannot be carried out *ou* executed.

inexécution [inɛgzekysjɔ̃] **nf** *[contrat, obligation]* non-fulfilment.

inexercé, e [inɛgzɛʀse] **adj** *soldats* inexperienced, untrained; *oreille* unpractised, untrained.

inexistant, e [inɛgzistɑ̃, ɑ̃t] **adj** (*absent*) *service d'ordre, réseau téléphonique, aide* non-existent; (*imaginaire*) *difficultés* imaginary, non-existent. (*péj*) **quant à son mari, il est ~** as for her husband, he's a (complete) nonentity *ou* cipher.

inexistence [inɛgzistɑ̃s] **nf** non-existence.

inexorabilité [inɛgzɔʀabilite] **nf** (*voir* **inexorable**) inexorability; inflexibility.

inexorable [inɛgzɔʀabl] **adj** *destin, vieillesse* inexorable; *juge* unyielding, inflexible, inexorable (*littér*). **il fut ~ à leurs prières** he was unmoved by their entreaties; **elle va échouer, c'est ~** she'll fail, it's inevitable.

inexorablement [inɛgzɔʀabləmɑ̃] **adv** inexorably.

inexpérience [inɛkspeʀjɑ̃s] **nf** inexperience, lack of experience.

inexpérimenté, e [inɛkspeʀimɑ̃te] **adj** *personne* inexperienced; *mouvements, gestes* inexpert; *arme, produit* untested.

inexpiable [inɛkspjabl] **adj** inexpiable.

inexpié, e [inɛkspje] adj unexpiated.
inexplicable [inɛksplikabl(ə)] adj inexplicable.
inexplicablement [inɛksplikabləmɑ̃] adv inexplicably.
inexpliqué, e [inɛksplike] adj unexplained.
inexploitable [inɛksplwatabl] adj unexploitable.
inexploité, e [inɛksplwate] adj unexploited; (*Fin*) *ressources* untapped.
inexplorable [inɛksplɔʀabl] adj unexplorable.
inexploré, e [inɛksplɔʀe] adj unexplored.
inexplosible [inɛksplozibl] adj non-explosive.
inexpressif, -ive [inɛkspʀesif, iv] adj *visage, regard* expressionless, inexpressive, blank; *style, mots* inexpressive.
inexpressivité [inɛkspʀesivite] nf inexpressiveness, expressionlessness.
inexprimable [inɛkspʀimabl] adj, nm inexpressible.
inexprimé, e [inɛkspʀime] adj *sentiment* unexpressed; *reproches, doutes* unspoken.
inexpugnable [inɛkspygnabl] adj *citadelle* impregnable, unassailable.
inextensible [inɛkstɑ̃sibl] adj *matériau* that does not stretch, unstretchable; *étoffe* non-stretch.
in extenso [inɛkstɛ̃so] 1 loc adv *écrire, publier, lire* in full. 2 loc adj *texte, discours* full (*épith*).
inextinguible [inɛkstɛ̃gibl] adj (*littér*) *passion* inextinguishable; *haine, besoin, soif* unquenchable; *rire* uncontrollable.
in extremis [inɛkstʀemis] 1 loc adv *sauver, arriver* at the last minute. 2 loc adj *sauvetage, succès* last-minute (*épith*). **faire un mariage/testament ~** to marry/to make a will on one's deathbed.
inextricable [inɛkstʀikabl] adj inextricable.
inextricablement [inɛkstʀikabləmɑ̃] adv inextricably.
infaillibilité [ɛ̃fajibilite] nf infallibility.
infaillible [ɛ̃fajibl] adj *méthode, remède, personne* infallible; *instinct* unerring, infallible.
infailliblement [ɛ̃fajibləmɑ̃] adv (*à coup sûr*) inevitably, without fail; (*sans erreur*) infallibly.
infaisable [ɛ̃fəzabl] adj impossible, impracticable, not feasible (*attrib*). **ce n'est pas ~** it's not impossible, it's (just about) feasible.
infalsifiable [ɛ̃falsifjabl] adj *passeport etc* impossible to forge.
infamant, e [ɛ̃famɑ̃, ɑ̃t] adj *acte* infamous, ignominious; *accusation* libellous; *propos* defamatory; *terme* derogatory; (*Jur*) *peine* infamous (*involving exile or deprivation of civil rights*).
infâme [ɛ̃fɑm] adj (*gen*) vile, loathsome; *métier, action, trahison* unspeakable, vile, loathsome; *traître* infamous, vile; *complaisance, servilité* shameful, vile; *entremetteur, spéculateur* despicable; *nourriture, odeur, taudis* revolting, vile, disgusting.
infamie [ɛ̃fami] nf a (*honte*) infamy. **couvert d'~** covered with infamy. b (*caractère infâme*) [*personne, acte*] infamy. c (*insulte*) vile abuse (*NonC*); (*action infâme*) infamous *ou* vile *ou* loathsome deed; (*ragot*) slanderous gossip (*NonC*). **c'est une ~** it's absolutely scandalous, it's an absolute scandal; **dire des ~s sur le compte de qn** to make slanderous remarks about sb.
infant [ɛ̃fɑ̃] nm infante.
infante [ɛ̃fɑ̃t] nf infanta.
infanterie [ɛ̃fɑ̃tʀi] nf infantry. **avec une ~ de 2 000 hommes** with 2,000 foot, with an infantry of 2,000 men; **~ légère** light infantry; **~ lourde** *ou* **de ligne** heavy infantry; **~ de marine** marines; **d'~** *bataillon etc* infantry (*épith*).
infanticide [ɛ̃fɑ̃tisid] 1 adj infanticidal. 2 nmf (*personne*) infanticide, child-killer. 3 nm (*acte*) infanticide.
infantile [ɛ̃fɑ̃til] adj (*Méd, Psych*) *maladie* infantile; *médecine, clinique* child (*épith*); (*puéril*) infantile, childish, babyish; *voir* **mortalité**.
infantilisant, e [ɛ̃fɑ̃tilizɑ̃, ɑ̃t] adj *émission, livre* infantile, childish.
infantiliser [ɛ̃fɑ̃tilize] 1 vt to make childish.
infantilisme [ɛ̃fɑ̃tilism] nm (*Méd, Psych*) infantilism; (*puérilité*) infantile *ou* childish *ou* babyish behaviour. **c'est de l'~!** how childish!
infarctus [ɛ̃faʀktys] nm (*Méd*) infarction (SPÉC), infarct (SPÉC). **~ du myocarde** coronary thrombosis, myocardial infarction (SPÉC); **il a eu** *ou* **fait trois ~** he has had three coronaries.
infatigable [ɛ̃fatigabl] adj indefatigable, tireless, untiring.
infatigablement [ɛ̃fatigabləmɑ̃] adv indefatigably, tirelessly, untiringly.
infatuation [ɛ̃fatɥasjɔ̃] nf (*frm: vanité*) self-conceit, self-importance.
infatué, e [ɛ̃fatɥe] (ptp de **s'infatuer**) adj *air, personne* conceited, vain. **être ~ de son importance** to be full of one's own importance; **être ~ de son physique** to be vain *ou* conceited about one's looks; **~ de sa personne** *ou* **de lui-même** full of himself *ou* of self-conceit, self-important.
infatuer (s') [ɛ̃fatɥe] 1 vpr a (*s'engouer de*) **s'~ de** *personne, choses* to become infatuated with. b (*tirer vanité de*) **s'~ de son importance** to become full of one's own importance; **s'~ de son physique** to become vain *ou* conceited about one's looks; **s'~ (de soi-même)** to become full of o.s. *ou* of self-conceit.
infécond, e [ɛ̃fekɔ̃, ɔ̃d] adj *terre, femme, animal* barren, sterile, infertile; *esprit* infertile, sterile.
infécondité [ɛ̃fekɔ̃dite] nf (*voir* **infécond**) barrenness; sterility; infertility.
infect, e [ɛ̃fɛkt] adj (*gén*) vile, loathsome; *goût, nourriture, vin, attitude,* revolting; *personne* obnoxious; *temps* filthy, foul; *taudis, chambre* revolting, disgusting; *livre, film* (*très mauvais*) rotten*, appalling; (*scandaleux*) revolting. **odeur ~e** stench, vile *ou* foul *ou* loathsome smell.
infecter [ɛ̃fɛkte] 1 1 vt (*gén*) *atmosphère, eau* to contaminate; (*Méd*) *personne, plaie* to infect; (*fig littér*) to poison, infect. 2 **s'infecter** vpr [*plaie*] to become infected, turn septic.
infectieux, -ieuse [ɛ̃fɛksjø, jøz] adj (*Méd*) infectious.
infection [ɛ̃fɛksjɔ̃] nf (*Méd*) infection; (*puanteur*) stench. **quelle ~!, c'est une ~!** what a stench!
inféodation [ɛ̃feɔdasjɔ̃] nf (*Pol*) allegiance (*à* to); (*Hist*) infeudation, enfeoffment.
inféoder [ɛ̃feɔde] 1 1 vt (*Hist*) to enfeoff. 2 **s'inféoder** vpr: **s'~ à** to give one's allegiance to, pledge allegiance *ou* o.s. to; **être inféodé à** to be pledged to.
inférence [ɛ̃feʀɑ̃s] nf inference.
inférer [ɛ̃feʀe] 6 vt to infer, gather (*de* from). **j'infère de ceci que ..., j'en infère que ...** I infer *ou* gather from this that ..., this leads me to conclude that ... .
inférieur, e [ɛ̃feʀjœʀ] 1 adj a (*dans l'espace*) (*gén*) lower; *mâchoire, lèvre* lower, bottom; *planètes* inferior. **la partie ~e de l'objet** the bottom part of the object; **le feu a pris dans les étages ~s** fire broke out on the lower floors; **descendez à l'étage ~** go down to the next floor *ou* the floor below, go to the next floor down; **le cours ~ d'un fleuve** the lower course *ou* stretches of a river.
b (*dans une hiérarchie*) *classes sociales, animaux, végétaux* lower. **à l'échelon ~** on the next rung down; **d'un rang ~** of a lower rank, lower in rank.
c *qualité* inferior, poorer; *vitesse* lower; *nombre* smaller, lower; *quantité* smaller; *intelligence, esprit* inferior. **forces ~es en nombre** forces inferior *ou* smaller in number(s).
d **~ à** *nombre* less *ou* lower *ou* smaller than, below; *somme* smaller *ou* less than; *production* inferior to, less *ou* lower than; **note ~e à 20** mark below 20 *ou* less than 20; **intelligence/qualité ~e à la moyenne** below average *ou* lower than average intelligence/quality; **travail d'un niveau ~ à ...** work of a lower standard than ... *ou* below the standard of ...; **roman/auteur ~ à un autre** novel/author inferior to another; **tu ne lui es ~ en rien** you're in no way inferior to him; **être hiérarchiquement ~ à qn** to be lower (down) than sb *ou* be below sb in the hierarchy; (*fig*) **il est ~ à sa tâche** he isn't equal to his task, he isn't up to his task.
2 nm,f inferior.
inférieurement [ɛ̃feʀjœʀmɑ̃] adv (*moins bien*) less well. **~ équipé** *armée, laboratoire, bateau* less well-equipped.
inférioriser [ɛ̃feʀjɔʀize] 1 vt (*sous-estimer*) to underestimate; (*complexer*) to make feel inferior.
infériorité [ɛ̃feʀjɔʀite] nf inferiority. **~ en nombre** numerical inferiority, inferiority in numbers; **en état** *ou* **position d'~** in an inferior position, in a position of inferiority; *voir* **comparatif, complexe**.
infermentescible [ɛ̃fɛʀmɑ̃tesibl] adj which cannot be fermented.
infernal, e, mpl **-aux** [ɛ̃fɛʀnal, o] adj a (*intolérable*) *bruit, allure, chaleur* infernal. **cet enfant est ~** this child is absolutely poisonous *ou* a little fiend. b (*satanique*) *caractère, personne, complot* diabolical, infernal, devilish. c (*effrayant*) *vision, supplice* diabolical; **pris dans ce cycle ~** caught in this vicious circle; *voir* **machine**³. d (*Myth*) *divinité* infernal.
infertile [ɛ̃fɛʀtil] adj (*lit, fig*) infertile.
infertilité [ɛ̃fɛʀtilite] nf (*littér: lit, fig*) infertility.
infestation [ɛ̃fɛstasjɔ̃] nf (*Méd*) infestation.
infester [ɛ̃fɛste] 1 vt (*gén*) to infest, overrun; (*Méd*) to infest. **infesté de moustiques** infested with mosquitos, mosquito-infested *ou* -ridden; **infesté de souris/pirates** infested with *ou* overrun with *ou* by mice/pirates.
infichu, e* [ɛ̃fiʃy] adj: **~ de faire qch** totally incapable of doing sth; **je suis ~ de me rappeler où je l'ai mis** I can't remember where the hell I put it*.
infidèle [ɛ̃fidɛl] 1 adj a *ami* unfaithful, disloyal (*à qn* to sb); *époux* unfaithful (*à qn* to sb). (*littér*) **être ~ à une promesse** to be untrue *ou* faithless (*littér*) to one's promise. b *récit, traduction, traducteur* unfaithful, inaccurate; *mémoire* unreliable. c (*Rel*) infidel. 2 nmf (*Rel*) infidel.
infidèlement [ɛ̃fidɛlmɑ̃] adv *traduire, raconter* unfaithfully, inaccurately.
infidélité [ɛ̃fidelite] nf a (*inconstance*) [*ami*] disloyalty, unfaithfulness; [*époux*] infidelity, unfaithfulness (*à* to). (*littér*) **~ à une promesse** faithlessness (*littér*) to a promise.
b (*acte déloyal*) [*époux*] **elle lui pardonna ses ~s** she forgave him his infidelities; **faire une ~ à qn** to be unfaithful to sb; **il a fait bien des ~s à sa femme** he has been unfaithful (to his wife) on many occasions, he has been guilty of infidelity (to his wife) on many occasions; (*hum*) **faire des ~s à son boucher/éditeur** to be unfaithful to *ou* forsake one's butcher/publisher (*hum*).
c (*manque d'exactitude*) [*description, historien*] inaccuracy;

[mémoire] unreliability.
d (*erreur*) *[description, traducteur]* inaccuracy. **on trouve beaucoup d'~s dans cette traduction** we find many inaccuracies in this translation.

infiltration [ɛ̃filtʀasjɔ̃] **nf** *[hommes, idées]* infiltration; *[liquide]* percolation, infiltration; (*Méd*) infiltration. **il y a une ~ *ou* des ~s dans la cave** there are leaks in the cellar, water is leaking into the cellar; (*Méd*) **se faire faire des ~s** to have injections.

infiltrer (s') [ɛ̃filtʀe] [1] **vpr** *[hommes, idées]* to infiltrate; *[liquide]* to percolate (through), seep in, infiltrate; *[lumière]* to filter through. **s'~ dans** *[personne]* to infiltrate; *[idées]* to filter into, infiltrate (into); *[liquide]* to percolate (through), seep through, infiltrate; *[lumière]* to filter into; **s'~ dans un groupe/chez l'ennemi** to infiltrate a group/the enemy.

infime [ɛ̃fim] **adj** (*minuscule*) tiny, minute, minuscule; (*inférieur*) lowly, inferior.

infini, e [ɛ̃fini] 1 **adj** a (*Math, Philos, Rel*) infinite.
b (*sans limites*) *espace* infinite, boundless; *patience, bonté* infinite, unlimited, boundless; *douleur* immense; *prudence, soin* infinite, immeasurable; *quantité* infinite, unlimited; *bêtise* infinite, immeasurable. **avec d'~es précautions** with infinite *ou* endless precautions.
c (*interminable*) *luttes, propos* interminable, never-ending. **un temps ~ me parut s'écouler** an eternity seemed to pass.
2 **nm: l'~** (*Philos*) the infinite; (*Math, Phot*) infinity; (*Phot*) **faire la mise au point à *ou* sur l'~** to focus to infinity; **l'~ des cieux** heaven's immensity, the infinity of heaven; **à l'~** *discourir* ad infinitum, endlessly; *multiplier* to infinity; *se diversifier, faire varier* infinitely; **les blés s'étendaient à l'~** the corn stretched away endlessly into the distance; **droite prolongée à l'~** straight line tending towards infinity.

infiniment [ɛ̃finimɑ̃] **adv** a (*immensément*) infinitely. b (*sens affaibli: beaucoup*) infinitely. **~ long/grand** immensely *ou* infinitely long/large; **je vous suis ~ reconnaissant** I am immensely *ou* extremely *ou* infinitely grateful (to you); **je regrette ~** I'm extremely sorry; **ça me plaît ~** I like it immensely; **~ meilleur/plus intelligent** infinitely better/more intelligent; **avec ~ de soin/de tendresse** with infinite care/tenderness. c **l'~ grand** the infinitely great; **l'~ petit** the infinitesimal.

infinité [ɛ̃finite] **nf** (*littér*) infinity. (*quantité infinie*) **une ~ de** an infinite number of.

infinitésimal, e, mpl -aux [ɛ̃finitezimal, o] **adj** (*Math, gén*) infinitesimal.

infinitif, -ive [ɛ̃finitif, iv] **adj, nm** infinitive. **~ de narration** historic infinitive; **à l'~** in the infinitive.

infirmatif, -ive [ɛ̃fiʀmatif, iv] **adj** (*Jur*) invalidating. **~ de** invalidating, annulling, quashing.

infirmation [ɛ̃fiʀmasjɔ̃] **nf** (*Jur*) invalidation, annulment, quashing.

infirme [ɛ̃fiʀm] 1 **adj** *personne* crippled, disabled; (*avec l'âge*) infirm. **l'accident l'avait rendu ~** the accident had left him crippled *ou* disabled; **il est ~ du bras droit** he's crippled in his right arm, he has a crippled *ou* disabled right arm; **être ~ de naissance** to be disabled from birth, be born disabled. 2 **nmf** cripple, disabled person. **les ~s** the crippled *ou* disabled; **~ mental/moteur** mentally/physically handicapped *ou* disabled person; **~ du travail** industrially disabled person; **~ de guerre** war cripple (*Brit*), handicapped veteran (*US*).

infirmer [ɛ̃fiʀme] [1] **vt** (*démentir*) to invalidate; (*Jur*) *décision, jugement* to invalidate, annul, quash.

infirmerie [ɛ̃fiʀməʀi] **nf** (*gén*) infirmary; *[école]* sickroom, sick bay, infirmary; (*Univ*) health centre (*Brit*), health service (*US*); *[navire]* sick bay.

infirmier [ɛ̃fiʀmje] **nm** (male) nurse. **~ en chef** charge nurse (*Brit*), head nurse (*US*).

infirmière [ɛ̃fiʀmjɛʀ] **nf** nurse; *[internat]* matron (*Brit*), nurse (*US*). **~ chef** sister (*Brit*), charge nurse (*Brit*), head nurse (*US*); **~ diplômée** registered nurse; **~ diplômée d'État** ≃ state registered nurse; **~-major** matron; **~ visiteuse** visiting nurse, ≃ district nurse (*Brit*); *voir* **élève**.

infirmité [ɛ̃fiʀmite] **nf** a (*invalidité*) disability. **~ motrice cérébrale** physical disability; **les ~s de la vieillesse** the infirmities of old age. b (*†: imperfection*) weakness, failing.

infixe [ɛ̃fiks] **nm** (*Ling*) infix.

inflammable [ɛ̃flamabl] **adj** inflammable, flammable.

inflammation [ɛ̃flamasjɔ̃] **nf** (*Méd*) inflammation.

inflammatoire [ɛ̃flamatwaʀ] **adj** (*Méd*) inflammatory.

inflation [ɛ̃flasjɔ̃] **nf** (*Écon*) inflation; (*fig*) (excessive) growth *ou* increase (*de* in).

inflationniste [ɛ̃flasjɔnist] 1 **adj** *tendance, danger* inflationary; *politique, économie* inflationist. 2 **nmf** inflationist.

infléchi, e [ɛ̃fleʃi] (**ptp de infléchir**) **adj** *voyelle* inflected.

infléchir [ɛ̃fleʃiʀ] [2] 1 **vt** (*lit*) *rayon* to inflect, bend; (*fig*) *politique* to reorientate, bend. 2 **s'infléchir vpr** *[route]* to bend, curve round; *[poutre]* to sag; (*fig*) *[politique]* to shift, move.

infléchissement [ɛ̃fleʃismɑ̃] **nm** (*voir* **infléchir**) (*fig*) reorientation; (*voir* **s'infléchir**) (*fig*) (slight) shift (*de* in).

inflexibilité [ɛ̃flɛksibilite] **nf** (*voir* **inflexible**) inflexibility; rigidity.

inflexible [ɛ̃flɛksibl] **adj** *caractère, personne* inflexible, rigid, unyielding; *volonté* inflexible; *règle* inflexible, rigid. **il demeura ~ dans sa résolution** he remained inflexible *ou* unyielding *ou* unbending in his resolution.

inflexiblement [ɛ̃flɛksibləmɑ̃] **adv** (*voir* **inflexible**) inflexibly; rigidly.

inflexion [ɛ̃flɛksjɔ̃] **nf** a (*inclinaison*) bend. **d'une légère ~ de la tête/du corps** with a slight nod/bow. b *[voix]* inflexion, modulation. c (*Ling*) **~ vocalique** vowel inflexion. d (*déviation*) *[route, direction]* bend, curve (*de* in); (*Phys*) *[rayon]* deflection; (*Math*) *[courbe]* inflexion. e (*fig*) *[politique]* reorientation (*de* of), shift (*de* in).

infliger [ɛ̃fliʒe] [3] **vt** *défaite, punition, tâche* to inflict (*à* on); *amende* to impose (*à* on); *affront* to deliver (*à* to). **~ de lourdes pertes à l'ennemi** to inflict heavy losses on the enemy; **~ sa présence à qn** to inflict one's presence *ou* o.s. on sb; (*Scol*) **~ un avertissement *ou* un blâme à qn** to give sb an order mark (*Brit*) *ou* a bad mark (*Brit*) *ou* a demerit point (*US*).

inflorescence [ɛ̃flɔʀesɑ̃s] **nf** inflorescence.

influençable [ɛ̃flyɑ̃sabl] **adj** easily influenced.

influence [ɛ̃flyɑ̃s] **nf** influence (*sur* on, upon). **c'est quelqu'un qui a de l'~** he's a person of influence, he's an influential person; **avoir une ~ bénéfique/néfaste sur** *[climat, médicament]* to have a beneficial/harmful effect on; **être sous l'~ de l'alcool** to be under the influence of alcohol; **être sous l'~ de la colère** to be in the grip of anger; **zone/sphère d'~** zone/sphere of influence; **ces fréquentations ont une mauvaise ~ sur ses enfants** these friends are a bad influence on her children; *voir* **trafic**.

influencer [ɛ̃flyɑ̃se] [3] **vt** (*gén*) to influence; (*agir sur*) to act upon. **il ne faut pas se laisser ~ par lui** you mustn't let yourself be influenced by him, you mustn't let him influence you.

influent, e [ɛ̃flyɑ̃, ɑ̃t] **adj** influential.

influenza [ɛ̃flyɑ̃za] **nf** influenza.

influer [ɛ̃flye] [1] **vi: ~ sur** to influence, have an influence on.

influx [ɛ̃fly] **nm** a (*Méd*) **~ nerveux** (nerve) impulse; **il manque d'~ nerveux** he lacks go *ou* drive. b (*fig: fluide*) influx††, inflow††.

info* [ɛ̃fo] **nf** (**abrév de information**) (*renseignement*) piece of information; (*Presse, TV*) news item, piece of news. (*Presse, TV*) **les ~s** the news.

infographie [ɛ̃fogʀafi] **nf** ® computer graphics.

infographiste [ɛ̃fogʀafist] **nmf** computer graphics artist.

in-folio, pl in-folio(s) [infɔljo] **nm, adj** folio.

informateur, -trice [ɛ̃fɔʀmatœʀ, tʀis] **nm,f** (*gén*) informant; (*Police*) informer.

informaticien, -ienne [ɛ̃fɔʀmatisjɛ̃, jɛn] **nm,f** computer scientist, computerist (*US*); (*pupitreur*) computer *ou* keyboard operator, keyboarder.

informatif, -ive [ɛ̃fɔʀmatif, iv] **adj** *brochure* informative. **campagne de publicité ~ive pour un produit/une chaîne d'hôtels** advertising campaign giving information on a product/a hotel chain.

information [ɛ̃fɔʀmasjɔ̃] **nf** a (*renseignement*) piece of information; (*Presse, TV: nouvelle*) piece of news, news (*sg*). **voilà une ~ intéressante** here's an interesting piece of information *ou* some interesting information; **recueillir des ~s sur** to gather information on; **voici nos ~s** here *ou* this is the news; **~s politiques** political news; **~s télévisées** television news; **écouter/regarder les ~s** to listen to/watch the news (bulletins); **c'était aux ~s de 10 heures** it was on the 10 o'clock news; **nous recevons une ~ de dernière minute** we've just received some last-minute *ou* late news; **aller aux ~s** to (go and) find out the news.
b (*diffusion de renseignements*) information. **pour votre ~, sachez que** for your (own) information you should know that; **pour l'~ des voyageurs** for the information of travellers; **assurer l'~ du public en matière d'impôts** to ensure that the public is informed *ou* has information on the subject of taxation; **l'opposition a la main sur l'~** the opposition has got hold of the information network; **journal/presse d'~** serious newspaper/press.
c (*Ordin, Sci*) **l'~** information; **traitement de l'~** data processing, processing of information; **théorie de l'~** information theory.
d (*Jur*) **~ officielle** (judicial) inquiry; **ouvrir une ~** to start an initial *ou* a preliminary investigation.

informatique [ɛ̃fɔʀmatik] 1 **nf** (*science*) computer science, computing; (*techniques*) data processing. **il est dans l'~** he's in computers; **l'ère de l'~** the age of the computer. 2 **adj** computer (*épith*).

informatiquement [ɛ̃fɔʀmatikmɑ̃] **adv: traiter qch ~** to use a computer to solve sth, process sth on a computer.

informatisation [ɛ̃fɔʀmatizasjɔ̃] **nf** computerization.

informatiser [ɛ̃fɔʀmatize] [1] **vt** to computerize.

informe [ɛ̃fɔʀm] **adj** *masse, tas* shapeless, formless; *vêtement* shapeless; *visage, être* misshapen, ill-shaped, ill-formed; *projet* rough, undefined.

informé [ɛ̃fɔʀme] *voir* **jusque**.

informel, -elle [ɛ̃fɔʀmɛl] **adj** (*gén, Art*) informal.

informer [ɛ̃fɔʀme] [1] 1 **vt** a (*d'un fait*) to inform, tell (*de* of, about); (*au sujet d'un problème*) to inform (*sur* about). **m'ayant informé de ce fait** having informed *ou* told me of this fact, having acquainted me with this fact; **nous vous informons que nos bureaux ouvrent à 8 heures** we are pleased to inform you that *ou* for your information our offices open at 8 a.m.; **informez-vous s'il est arrivé** find out *ou* ascertain whether he has arrived; **s'il vient, vous voudrez bien m'en ~**

if he comes, please let me know *ou* inform me *ou* tell me; **on vous a mal informé** (*faussement*) you've been misinformed *ou* wrongly informed; (*imparfaitement*) you've been badly informed *ou* ill-informed; **nous ne sommes pas assez informés** we don't have enough information; **journaux/milieux bien informés** well-informed *ou* authoritative newspapers/circles.

b (*Philos*) **les concepts informent la matière** concepts impart *ou* give form to matter.

2 **vi** (*Jur*) ~ **sur un crime** to inquire into *ou* investigate a crime; ~ **contre X** to start inquiries concerning X.

3 **s'informer vpr** (*d'un fait*) to inquire, find out, ask (*de* about); (*dans une matière*) to inform o.s. (*sur* about). **où puis-je m'~ de l'heure/à ce sujet/si?** where can I inquire *ou* find out *ou* ask about the time/about this matter/whether?; **s'~ de la santé de qn** to ask after *ou* inquire after *ou* about sb's health; **la nécessité pour l'homme moderne de s'~ (sur certains sujets)** the necessity for modern man to inform himself (about certain topics).

informulé, e [ɛ̃fɔʀmyle] **adj** unformulated.

infortune [ɛ̃fɔʀtyn] **nf** (*revers*) misfortune; (*adversité*) ill fortune, misfortune. **~s conjugales** marital misfortunes; **le récit de ses ~s** the tale of his woes *ou* misfortunes; *voir* **compagnon.**

infortuné, e [ɛ̃fɔʀtyne] 1 **adj** *personne* hapless (*épith*), ill-fated, luckless, wretched; *démarche, décision* ill-fated, wretched. 2 **nm,f** (poor) wretch.

infoutu, e** [ɛ̃futy] **adj**: ~ **de faire quoi que ce soit** totally bloody (*Brit*) *ou* damn incapable of doing anything**.

infra [ɛ̃fʀa] **adv**: **voir** ~ see below.

infraction [ɛ̃fʀaksjɔ̃] **nf** (*délit*) offence. (*Aut*) **être en** ~ to be committing an offence, be in breach of the law; ~ **à la loi** breach *ou* violation *ou* infraction of the law; ~ **au code de la route** offence against the Highway Code; ~ **à la coutume** breach *ou* violation of custom; **règle qui ne souffre aucune** ~ rule which suffers *ou* allows no infringement.

infranchissable [ɛ̃fʀɑ̃ʃisabl] **adj** (*lit*) impassable; (*fig*) insurmountable, insuperable.

infrangible [ɛ̃fʀɑ̃ʒibl] **adj** (*littér*) infrangible (*littér*).

infrarouge [ɛ̃fʀaʀuʒ] **adj, nm** infrared. **missile guidé par** ~ heat-seeking missile.

infrason [ɛ̃fʀasɔ̃] **nm** infrasonic vibration.

infrastructure [ɛ̃fʀastʀyktyʀ] **nf** (*Constr*) substructure, understructure; (*Écon, fig*) infrastructure; (*Aviat*) ground installations.

infréquentable [ɛ̃fʀekɑ̃tabl] **adj** not to be associated with. **ce sont des gens ~s** they're people you just don't associate with *ou* mix with.

infroissable [ɛ̃fʀwasabl] **adj** uncrushable, crease-resistant.

infructueux, -euse [ɛ̃fʀyktɥø, øz] **adj** fruitless, unfruitful, unsuccessful.

infumable [ɛ̃fymabl] **adj** unsmokable.

infus, e [ɛ̃fy, yz] **adj** (*littér*) innate, inborn (*à* in); *voir* **science.**

infuser [ɛ̃fyze] 1 **vt** a (*plus gén* **faire** ~) *tisane* to infuse; *thé* to brew, infuse. **laisser ~ le thé quelques minutes** leave the tea to brew *ou* infuse *ou* draw a few minutes; **le thé est-il assez infusé?** has the tea brewed *ou* infused (long) enough? b (*fig*) to infuse (*à* into). ~ **un sang nouveau à qch/à qn** to infuse *ou* inject *ou* instil new life into sth/sb.

Infusette [ɛ̃fyzɛt] **nf** ® (tea *ou* coffee *etc*) bag.

infusion [ɛ̃fyzjɔ̃] **nf** a (*tisane*) infusion, herb tea. ~ **de tilleul** lime tea; **boire une** ~ to drink some herb tea *ou* an infusion; **la verveine se boit en** ~ verbena is drunk as an infusion. b (*action*) infusion. **préparé par** ~ prepared by infusion.

ingambe [ɛ̃gɑ̃b] **adj** spry, nimble.

ingénier (s') [ɛ̃ʒenje] 7 **vpr**: **s'~ à faire** to strive (hard) to do, try hard to do; (*iro*) **chaque fois qu'on range ses affaires, il s'ingénie à les remettre en désordre** every time you tidy up his belongings, he goes out of his way *ou* he contrives to mess them up again.

ingénierie [ɛ̃ʒeniʀi] **nf** engineering. ~ **assistée par ordinateur** computer-assisted engineering.

ingénieur [ɛ̃ʒenjœʀ] **nm** engineer. ~ **chimiste/des mines/agronome** chemical/mining/agricultural engineer; ~ **électricien/en génie civil** electrical/civil engineer; ~ **système** system(s) engineer; **~-conseil** engineering consultant; ~ **du son** sound engineer; ~ **des eaux et forêts** forestry expert; ~ **des travaux publics** construction *ou* civil engineer.

ingénieusement [ɛ̃ʒenjøzmɑ̃] **adv** ingeniously, cleverly.

ingénieux, -ieuse [ɛ̃ʒenjø, jøz] **adj** ingenious, clever.

ingéniosité [ɛ̃ʒenjozite] **nf** ingenuity, cleverness.

ingénu, e [ɛ̃ʒeny] 1 **adj** ingenuous, artless, naïve. 2 **nm,f** ingenuous *ou* artless *ou* naïve person. 3 **ingénue nf** (*Théât*) ingénue. **jouer les ~es** to play ingénue roles.

ingénuité [ɛ̃ʒenɥite] **nf** ingenuousness, artlessness, naïvety.

ingénument [ɛ̃ʒenymɑ̃] **adv** ingenuously, artlessly, naïvely.

ingérence [ɛ̃ʒeʀɑ̃s] **nf** interference, interfering (*NonC*), meddling (*NonC*) (*dans* in).

ingérer [ɛ̃ʒeʀe] 6 1 **vt** to ingest. 2 **s'ingérer vpr**: **s'~ dans** to interfere in *ou* with, meddle in.

ingestion [ɛ̃ʒɛstjɔ̃] **nf** ingestion.

ingouvernable [ɛ̃guvɛʀnabl] **adj** (*Pol*) ungovernable.

ingrat, e [ɛ̃gʀa, at] **adj** *personne* ungrateful (*envers* to, towards); *tâche, métier, sujet* thankless (*épith*), unrewarding; *sol* stubborn, barren, sterile; *visage* unprepossessing, unattractive; *contrée* bleak, hostile; *mémoire* unreliable, treacherous. **tu es un** ~ you're an ungrateful person *ou* so-and-so*; *voir* **âge.**

ingratement [ɛ̃gʀatmɑ̃] **adv** (*littér*) ungratefully.

ingratitude [ɛ̃gʀatityd] **nf** ingratitude, ungratefulness (*envers* to, towards). **avec** ~ ungratefully.

ingrédient [ɛ̃gʀedjɑ̃] **nm** ingredient; (*fig*) ingredient, component.

inguérissable [ɛ̃geʀisabl] **adj** (*lit*) incurable; (*fig*) *habitude, paresse* incurable; *chagrin, amour* inconsolable.

inguinal, e, mpl -aux [ɛ̃gɥinal, o] **adj** inguinal.

ingurgitation [ɛ̃gyʀʒitasjɔ̃] **nf** ingurgitation.

ingurgiter [ɛ̃gyʀʒite] 1 **vt** *nourriture* to swallow, ingurgitate (*frm*); *vin* to gulp (down), swill (*péj*); (*fig*) to ingest, ingurgitate. **faire ~ de la nourriture/une boisson à qn** to make sb swallow food/a drink, force food/a drink down sb; **faire ~ des connaissances à qn** to force sb to take in facts, force *ou* stuff knowledge into sb; ~ **des connaissances pour un examen** to cram *ou* stuff one's head with facts for an exam.

inhabile [inabil] **adj** a *politicien, discours* inept; *manœuvre* inept, clumsy. **se montrer ~ dans la conduite des négociations** to mishandle the conduct of the negotiations, show a certain ineptitude in the handling of the negotiations. b (*manuellement*) *ouvrier* unskilful, clumsy; *gestes, mains, dessin, travail* clumsy. c (*Jur*) incapable. ~ **à tester** incapable of making a will.

inhabilement [inabilmɑ̃] **adv** ineptly.

inhabileté [inabilte] **nf** (*littér*: *voir* **inhabile**) ineptitude; clumsiness; unskilfulness.

inhabilité [inabilite] **nf** (*Jur*) incapacity (*à* to).

inhabitable [inabitabl] **adj** uninhabitable. **cette maison est** ~ it's impossible to live in this house, this house is uninhabitable.

inhabité, e [inabite] **adj** *région* uninhabited; *maison* uninhabited, unoccupied. **la maison a l'air ~e** the house looks uninhabited *ou* unoccupied *ou* unlived-in.

inhabituel, -elle [inabitɥɛl] **adj** unusual, unaccustomed.

inhalateur, -trice [inalatœʀ, tʀis] 1 **nm** inhaler. (*Aviat*) ~ **d'oxygène** oxygen mask. 2 **adj** inhaling.

inhalation [inalasjɔ̃] **nf** (*Méd*) inhalation. **faire** *ou* **prendre une** *ou* **des ~(s)** to have *ou* use an inhalation bath.

inhaler [inale] 1 **vt** (*Méd*) to inhale; (*littér*) to inhale, breathe (in).

inharmonieux, -ieuse [inaʀmɔnjø, jøz] **adj** (*littér*) inharmonious.

inhérence [ineʀɑ̃s] **nf** (*Philos*) inherence.

inhérent, e [ineʀɑ̃, ɑ̃t] **adj** inherent (*à* in, to).

inhiber [inibe] 1 **vt** (*Physiol, Psych*) to inhibit.

inhibiteur, -trice [inibitœʀ, tʀis] **adj** inhibitory, inhibitive.

inhibition [inibisjɔ̃] **nf** (*Physiol, Psych*) inhibition.

inhospitalier, -ière [inɔspitalje, jɛʀ] **adj** inhospitable.

inhumain, e [inymɛ̃, ɛn] **adj** inhuman.

inhumainement [inymɛnmɑ̃] **adv** (*littér*) inhumanly.

inhumanité [inymanite] **nf** (*littér*) inhumanity.

inhumation [inymasjɔ̃] **nf** burial, interment, inhumation (*frm*).

inhumer [inyme] 1 **vt** to bury, inter; *voir* **permis.**

inimaginable [inimaʒinabl] **adj** unimaginable, unbelievable.

inimitable [inimitabl] **adj** inimitable.

inimité, e [inimite] **adj**: **artiste qui est resté** ~ artist who has never been imitated.

inimitié [inimitje] **nf** enmity.

ininflammable [inɛ̃flamabl] **adj** non-flammable, non-inflammable.

inintelligemment [inɛ̃teliʒamɑ̃] **adv** unintelligently.

inintelligence [inɛ̃teliʒɑ̃s] **nf** [*personne, esprit*] lack of intelligence, unintelligence. (*incompréhension*) **l'~ du problème** the failure to understand the problem, the lack of understanding of the problem.

inintelligent, e [inɛ̃teliʒɑ̃, ɑ̃t] **adj** unintelligent.

inintelligibilité [inɛ̃teliʒibilite] **nf** unintelligibility.

inintelligible [inɛ̃teliʒibl] **adj** unintelligible.

inintelligiblement [inɛ̃teliʒibləmɑ̃] **adv** unintelligibly.

inintéressant, e [inɛ̃teʀesɑ̃, ɑ̃t] **adj** uninteresting.

ininterrompu, e [inɛ̃teʀɔ̃py] **adj** *suite, ligne* unbroken; *file de voitures* unbroken, steady (*épith*), uninterrupted; *flot, vacarme* steady (*épith*), uninterrupted, non-stop; *effort, travail* unremitting, continuous, steady (*épith*). **12 heures de sommeil** ~ 12 hours' uninterrupted *ou* unbroken sleep; **programme de musique ~e** programme of continuous music.

inique [inik] **adj** iniquitous.

iniquement [inikmɑ̃] **adv** iniquitously.

iniquité [inikite] **nf** (*gén, Rel*) iniquity.

initial, e, mpl -iaux [inisjal, jo] 1 **adj** initial. 2 **initiale nf** initial. **mettre ses ~es sur qch** to put one's initials on sth, initial sth; *voir* **vitesse.**

initialement [inisjalmɑ̃] **adv** initially.

initialisation [inisjalisasjɔ̃] **nf** (*Ordin*) initialization.

initialiser [inisjalize] 1 **vt** (*Ordin*) to initialize.

initiateur, -trice [inisjatœʀ, tʀis] 1 **adj** innovatory. 2 **nm,f** (*maître, précurseur*) initiator; [*mode, technique*] innovator, pioneer; [*idée*] initiator, originator.

initiation [inisjasjɔ̃] **nf** initiation (*à* into). (*titre d'ouvrage*) ~ **à la linguistique/philosophie** introduction to linguistics/philosophy.

initiatique [inisjatik] **adj** *rite* initiatory.
initiative [inisjativ] **nf** (*gén, Pol*) initiative. **prendre l'~ d'une action/de faire** to take the initiative for an action/in doing; **garder l'~** to keep the initiative; **avoir de l'~** to have *ou* show initiative *ou* enterprise; **à** *ou* **sur l'~ de qn** on sb's initiative; **de sa propre ~** on one's own initiative; **elle manque d'~** she lacks initiative *ou* enterprise; **~ de paix** peace initiative; **conférence à l'~ des USA** conference initiated by the USA; **~ de défense stratégique** Strategic Defense Initiative; **à l'~ de la France** ... following France's initiative ...; *voir* **droit³, syndicat.**
initié, e [inisje] (**ptp de initier**) **1 adj** initiated. **le lecteur ~/non ~** the initiated/uninitiated reader. **2 nm,f** initiated person, initiate (*frm*). **les ~s** the initiated *ou* initiates (*frm*); **les non-~s** the uninitiated; **art réservé aux ~s** art accessible only to the initiated.
initier [inisje] 7 **1 vt** to initiate (*à* into). **~ qn aux joies de la voile** to introduce sb to the joys of sailing. **2 s'initier vpr** to become initiated, initiate o.s. (*à* into).
injectable [ɛ̃ʒɛktabl] **adj** injectable.
injecté, e [ɛ̃ʒɛkte] (**ptp de injecter**) **adj** (*Méd, Tech*) injected (*de* with); *visage* congested. **yeux ~s de sang** bloodshot eyes.
injecter [ɛ̃ʒɛkte] 1 **vt** (*Méd, Tech*) to inject. **~ des fonds dans une entreprise** to pump money into a project.
injecteur, -trice [ɛ̃ʒɛktœʀ, tʀis] **1 adj** injection (*épith*). **2 nm** injector.
injection [ɛ̃ʒɛksjɔ̃] **nf** (*action, produit, piqûre*) injection; (*avec une poire etc*) douche; (*Géol, Tech*) injection. **à ~s** *seringue, tube* injection (*épith*); **à ~** *moteur, système* fuel injection (*épith*); **à ~ électronique** *moteur* electronic fuel injection (*épith*).
injoignable [ɛ̃ʒwaɲabl] **adj** impossible to contact; incommunicado (*frm, hum*).
injonction [ɛ̃ʒɔ̃ksjɔ̃] **nf** injunction, command, order. **sur son ~** on his orders *ou* command.
injouable [ɛ̃ʒwabl] **adj** *musique* unplayable; *pièce* unperformable.
injure [ɛ̃ʒyʀ] **nf a** (*insulte*) abuse (*NonC*), insult. **"espèce de salaud" est une ~** "bastard" is a swearword *ou* an insult; **bordée d'~s** string of abuse *ou* insults; (*Jur*) **l'~ et la diffamation** abuse and slander. **b** (*littér: affront*) **faire ~ à qn** to wrong sb, affront sb; **il m'a fait l'~ de ne pas venir** he insulted *ou* affronted me by not coming. **c** (*littér: dommage*) **l'~ des ans/du sort** the injury *ou* assault of years/of fate (*littér*).
injurier [ɛ̃ʒyʀje] 7 **vt** to abuse, insult, revile (*frm*).
injurieusement [ɛ̃ʒyʀjøzmɑ̃] **adv** (*voir* **injurieux**) abusively; offensively; insultingly.
injurieux, -ieuse [ɛ̃ʒyʀjø, jøz] **adj** *termes, propos* abusive, offensive; (*littér*) *attitude, article* insulting, offensive (*pour, à l'égard de* to).
injuste [ɛ̃ʒyst] **adj** (*contraire à la justice, manquant d'équité*) unjust; (*partial, tendancieux*) unfair (*avec, envers* to, towards).
injustement [ɛ̃ʒystəmɑ̃] **adv** (*voir* **injuste**) unjustly; unfairly.
injustice [ɛ̃ʒystis] **nf a** (*caractère: voir* **injuste**) injustice; unfairness. **b** (*acte*) injustice.
injustifiable [ɛ̃ʒystifjabl] **adj** unjustifiable.
injustifié, e [ɛ̃ʒystifje] **adj** unjustified, unwarranted.
inlassable [ɛ̃lɑsabl] **adj** *personne* tireless, untiring; *zèle* unflagging, tireless; *patience* inexhaustible.
inlassablement [ɛ̃lɑsabləmɑ̃] **adv** (*voir* **inlassable**) tirelessly; untiringly; unflaggingly.
inné, e [i(n)ne] **adj** innate, inborn. **idées ~es** innate ideas.
innervation [inɛʀvasjɔ̃] **nf** innervation.
innerver [inɛʀve] 1 **vt** to innervate.
innocemment [inɔsamɑ̃] **adv** innocently.
innocence [inɔsɑ̃s] **nf** (*gén*) innocence. **l'~ de ces farces** the innocence *ou* harmlessness of these pranks; **il l'a fait en toute ~** he did it in all innocence, he meant no harm (by it).
Innocent [inɔsɑ̃] **nm** Innocent.
innocent, e [inɔsɑ̃, ɑ̃t] **1 adj** (*Jur, Rel, gén*) innocent. **être ~ de qch** to be innocent of sth; **remarque/petite farce bien ~e** quite innocent *ou* harmless remark/little prank; **il est vraiment ~!** he is a real innocent!; **~ comme l'enfant** *ou* **l'agneau qui vient de naître** as innocent as a newborn babe.
2 nm,f a (*Jur*) innocent person.
b (*candide*) innocent (person); (*niais*) simpleton. **ne fais pas l'~** don't act *ou* play the innocent, don't come the innocent with me* (*Brit*), don't put on an air of innocence; **quel ~ tu fais!** how innocent can you be?*, how innocent you are!; **l'~ du village** the village simpleton *ou* idiot; (*Prov*) **aux ~s les mains pleines** fortune favours the innocent; *voir* **massacre.**
innocenter [inɔsɑ̃te] 1 **vt** (*Jur: disculper*) to clear, prove innocent (*de* of); (*fig: excuser*) to excuse, justify.
innocuité [inɔkɥite] **nf** (*frm*) innocuousness (*frm*), harmlessness.
innombrable [i(n)nɔ̃bʀabl] **adj** *détails, péripéties, variétés* innumerable, countless; *foule* vast.
innomé, e [i(n)nɔme] **adj** = **innommé.**
innommable [i(n)nɔmabl] **adj** *conduite, action* unspeakable, loathsome, unmentionable; *nourriture, ordures* foul, vile.
innommé, e [i(n)nɔme] **adj** (*non dénommé*) unnamed; (*obscur, vague*) nameless.
innovateur, -trice [inɔvatœʀ, tʀis] **1 adj** innovatory, innovative. **2 nm,f** innovator.
innovation [inɔvasjɔ̃] **nf** innovation.
innover [inɔve] 1 **vi** to innovate. **~ en matière de mode/d'art** *etc* to break new ground *ou* innovate in the field of fashion/art *etc;* **ce peintre innove par rapport à ses prédécesseurs** this painter is breaking new ground compared with his predecessors.
inobservable [inɔpsɛʀvabl] **adj** unobservable.
inobservance [inɔpsɛʀvɑ̃s] **nf** (*littér*) inobservance, non-observance.
inobservation [inɔpsɛʀvasjɔ̃] **nf** (*littér, Jur*) non-observance, inobservance.
inobservé, e [inɔpsɛʀve] **adj** (*littér, Jur*) unobserved.
inoccupation [inɔkypasjɔ̃] **nf** (*littér*) inoccupation (*littér*), inactivity.
inoccupé, e [inɔkype] **adj a** (*vide*) *appartement* unoccupied, empty; *siège, emplacement, poste* vacant, unoccupied, empty. **b** (*oisif*) unoccupied, idle.
in-octavo [inɔktavo] **adj, nm inv** octavo.
inoculable [inɔkylabl] **adj** inoculable.
inoculation [inɔkylasjɔ̃] **nf** (*Méd: volontaire*) inoculation; (*accidentelle*) infection. **l'~ (accidentelle) d'un virus/d'une maladie dans l'organisme par blessure** the (accidental) infection of the organism by a virus/by disease as a result of an injury.
inoculer [inɔkyle] 1 **vt a ~ un virus/une maladie à qn** (*Méd: volontairement*) to inoculate sb with a virus/a disease; (*accidentellement*) to infect sb with a virus/a disease; **~ un malade** to inoculate a patient (*contre* against). **b** (*fig: communiquer*) **~ une passion** *etc* **à qn** to infect *ou* imbue sb with a passion *etc;* **~ un vice/des opinions à qn** to inoculate sb with a vice/ideas.
inodore [inɔdɔʀ] **adj** *gaz* odourless; *fleur* scentless.
inoffensif, -ive [inɔfɑ̃sif, iv] **adj** *personne, plaisanterie* inoffensive, harmless, innocuous; *piqûre, animal, remède* harmless, innocuous.
inondable [inɔ̃dabl] **adj** liable to flooding.
inondation [inɔ̃dasjɔ̃] **nf a** (*voir* **inonder**) flooding; swamping; inundation. **b** (*lit*) flood; (*fig: afflux*) flood, deluge (*NonC*).
inonder [inɔ̃de] 1 **vt a** (*lit: d'eau*) to flood; (*fig: de produits*) to flood, swamp, inundate (*de* with). **les populations inondées** the flood victims; **tu as inondé toute la cuisine*** you've flooded the whole kitchen, you've literally swamped the kitchen; **nous sommes inondés de lettres** we have been inundated with letters, we have received a flood of letters; **inondé de soleil** bathed in sunlight; **inondé de lumière** suffused *ou* flooded with light; **la joie inonda son cœur** joy flooded into his heart.
b (*tremper*) to soak, drench. **se faire ~ (par la pluie)** to get soaked *ou* drenched (by the rain); **je suis inondé** I'm soaked (through) *ou* drenched *ou* saturated*; **~ ses cheveux de parfum** to saturate one's hair with scent; **la sueur inondait son visage** sweat was streaming down his face, his face was bathed in sweat; **inondé de larmes** *joues* streaming with tears; *yeux* full of tears.
inopérable [inɔpeʀabl] **adj** inoperable.
inopérant, e [inɔpeʀɑ̃, ɑ̃t] **adj** ineffectual, ineffective, inoperative.
inopiné, e [inɔpine] **adj** *rencontre* unexpected. **mort ~e** sudden death.
inopinément [inɔpinemɑ̃] **adv** unexpectedly.
inopportun, e [inɔpɔʀtœ̃, yn] **adj** *demande, remarque* ill-timed, inopportune, untimely. **le moment est ~** it is not the right *ou* best moment, it's not the most opportune moment.
inopportunément [inɔpɔʀtynemɑ̃] **adv** inopportunely.
inopportunité [inɔpɔʀtynite] **nf** (*littér*) inopportuneness, untimeliness.
inopposabilité [inɔpozabilite] **nf** (*Jur*) non-invocability.
inopposable [inɔpozabl] **adj** (*Jur*) non-invocable.
inorganique [inɔʀganik] **adj** inorganic.
inorganisé, e [inɔʀganize] **adj** *compagnie, industrie* unorganized; *personne* disorganized, unorganized; (*Sci*) unorganized.
inoubliable [inublijabl] **adj** unforgettable, never to be forgotten.
inouï, e [inwi] **adj** *événement, circonstances* unprecedented, unheard-of; *nouvelle* extraordinary, incredible; *vitesse, audace, force* incredible, unbelievable. **c'est/il est ~!*** it's/he's incredible! *ou* unbelievable!
inox [inɔks] **adj, nm** (**abrév de inoxydable**) stainless steel. **couteau/évier (en) ~** stainless steel knife/sink.
inoxydable [inɔksidabl] **1 adj** *acier, alliage* stainless; *couteau* stainless steel (*épith*). **2 nm** stainless steel.
inqualifiable [ɛ̃kalifjabl] **adj** *conduite, propos* unspeakable. **d'une ~ bassesse** unspeakably low.
in-quarto [inkwaʀto] **adj, nm inv** quarto.
inquiet, inquiète [ɛ̃kjɛ, ɛ̃kjɛt] **adj** *personne* (*momentanément*) worried, anxious; (*par nature*) anxious; *gestes* uneasy; *attente, regards* uneasy, anxious; *sommeil* uneasy, troubled; (*littér*) *curiosité, amour* restless. **je suis ~ de son absence** I'm worried at his absence, I'm worried *ou* anxious that he's not here; **je suis ~ de ne pas le voir** I'm worried *ou* anxious at not seeing him, I'm worried not to be able to see him; **je suis ~ qu'il ne m'ait pas téléphoné** I'm worried that he hasn't phoned me; **c'est un (éternel) ~** he's a (perpetual) worrier.
inquiétant, e [ɛ̃kjetɑ̃, ɑ̃t] **adj** (*gén*) disturbing, worrying, disquieting; *personne* disturbing.
inquiéter [ɛ̃kjete] 6 **1 vt a** (*alarmer*) to worry, disturb. **la santé de**

mon fils m'inquiète my son's health worries *ou* disturbs me, I'm worried *ou* bothered about my son's health; **le champion commence à ~ son adversaire** the champion is starting to get his opponent worried.

b (*harceler*) *ville, pays* to harass. **l'amant de la victime ne fut pas inquiété (par la police)** the victim's lover wasn't troubled *ou* bothered by the police.

2 **s'inquiéter** vpr a (*s'alarmer*) to worry. **ne t'inquiète pas** don't worry; **il n'y a pas de quoi s'~** there's nothing to worry about *ou* get worried about.

b (*s'enquérir*) **s'~ de** to inquire about; **s'~ de l'heure/de la santé de qn** to inquire what time it is/about sb's health.

c (*se soucier*) **s'~ de** to worry about, trouble (o.s.) about, bother about; **ne t'inquiète pas de ça, je m'en occupe** don't (you) trouble yourself *ou* worry *ou* bother about that – I'll see to it; **sans s'~ des circonstances/conséquences** without worrying *ou* bothering about the circumstances/consequences; **sans s'~ de savoir si ...** without troubling *ou* bothering to find out if ...; **je ne m'inquiète pas pour elle, elle se débrouille toujours** I'm not worried about her *ou* I'm not fretting about her, she always manages somehow.

inquiétude [ɛ̃kjetyd] nf anxiety; (*littér: agitation*) restlessness. **donner de l'~** *ou* **des ~s à qn** to worry sb, give sb cause for worry *ou* anxiety; **avoir** *ou* **éprouver des ~s au sujet de** to feel anxious *ou* worried about, feel some anxiety about; **soyez sans ~** have no fear; **fou d'~** mad with worry.

inquisiteur, -trice [ɛ̃kizitœʀ, tʀis] 1 adj inquisitive, prying. 2 nm inquisitor.

inquisition [ɛ̃kizisjɔ̃] nf a (*Hist*) **la (Sainte) I~** the Inquisition, the Holy Office. b (*péj: enquête*) inquisition.

inquisitoire [ɛ̃kizitwaʀ] adj (*Jur*): **procédure ~** proceeding presided over by an interrogating judge.

inquisitorial, e, mpl **-iaux** [ɛ̃kizitɔʀjal, jo] adj inquisitorial.

inracontable [ɛ̃ʀakɔ̃tabl] adj (*trop osé*) unrepeatable; (*trop compliqué*) unrecountable.

I.N.R.I. (abrév de **Iesus Nazarenus Rex Iudaeorum**) I.N.R.I.

insaisissabilité [ɛ̃sezisabilite] nf (*Jur*) non-seizability.

insaisissable [ɛ̃sezisabl] adj *fugitif, ennemi* elusive; *nuance, différence* imperceptible, indiscernible; (*Jur*) *biens* non-seizable.

insalissable [ɛ̃salisabl] adj dirt-proof.

insalubre [ɛ̃salybʀ] adj *climat* insalubrious, unhealthy; *bâtiment* insalubrious.

insalubrité [ɛ̃salybʀite] nf (*voir* **insalubre**) insalubrity; unhealthiness.

insanité [ɛ̃sanite] nf (*caractère*) insanity, madness; (*acte*) insane act; (*propos*) insane talk (*NonC*). **proférer des ~s** to talk insanely.

insatiabilité [ɛ̃sasjabilite] nf insatiability.

insatiable [ɛ̃sasjabl] adj insatiable.

insatiablement [ɛ̃sasjabləmɑ̃] adv insatiably.

insatisfaction [ɛ̃satisfaksjɔ̃] nf dissatisfaction.

insatisfait, e [ɛ̃satisfɛ, ɛt] adj *personne* (*non comblé*) unsatisfied; (*mécontent*) dissatisfied (*de* with); *désir, passion* unsatisfied. **c'est un éternel ~** he's never satisfied, he's perpetually dissatisfied.

insaturé, e [ɛ̃satyʀe] adj (*Chim*) unsaturated.

inscriptible [ɛ̃skʀiptibl] adj inscribable.

inscription [ɛ̃skʀipsjɔ̃] 1 nf a (*écrit*) (*gravée, imprimée, officielle*) inscription; (*manuscrite*) writing (*NonC*), inscription. **mur couvert d'~s** wall covered in writing *ou* inscriptions.

b (*action*) **l'~ du texte n'est pas comprise dans le prix** the inscription *ou* engraving of the text is not included in the price; **l'~ d'une question à l'ordre du jour** putting *ou* placing a question on the agenda; **cela a nécessité l'~ de nouvelles dépenses au budget** this necessitated adding further expenditure to the budget.

c (*immatriculation*) enrolment, registration, admission; (*à l'université*) matriculation (*Brit*), registration (*à* at); (*à un concours*) enrolment (*à* in), entering (*à* for). **l'~ à un parti/club** joining a party/club; **l'~ des enfants à l'école est obligatoire** it is compulsory to enrol *ou* register children for school; **il y a déjà 20 ~s pour la sortie de jeudi** 20 people have already signed on *ou* enrolled for Thursday's outing; **les ~s (en faculté) seront closes le 30 octobre** the closing date for enrolment *ou* matriculation (*Brit*) *ou* registration (at the university) is October 30th; **votre ~ sur la liste dépend de ...** the inclusion of your name on the list depends on ...; **faire son ~** *ou* **prendre ses ~s en faculté** to register (o.s.) *ou* enrol (o.s.) at the university; **les ~s sont en baisse de 5%** the intake is down by 5%; **droits d'~** enrolment fee.

2 comp ►**inscription de faux** (*Jur*) challenge (*to validity of document*) ►**inscription hypothécaire** (*Jur*) mortgage registration ►**inscription maritime** registration of sailors ►**l'Inscription maritime** (*service*) the Register of Sailors.

inscrire [ɛ̃skʀiʀ] 39 1 vt a (*marquer*) *nom, date* to note down, write down; (*Ftbl*) *but* to score, notch up. **~ des dépenses au budget** to list expenses in the budget; **~ une question à l'ordre du jour** to put *ou* place a question on the agenda; **ce n'est pas inscrit à l'ordre du jour** it isn't (down) on the agenda; **~ qch dans la pierre/le marbre** to inscribe *ou* engrave sth on stone/marble; (*fig*) **c'est demeuré inscrit dans ma mémoire** it has remained inscribed *ou* etched on my memory; (*fig*) **sa culpabilité est inscrite sur son visage** his guilt is written all over his face *ou* on his face; **greffier, inscrivez (sous ma dictée)** clerk, take *ou* note this down; **son nom est** *ou* **il est inscrit sur la liste des gagnants** his name is (written) on the list of winners.

b (*enrôler*) *client* to put down; *soldat* to enlist; *étudiant* to register, enrol. **~ qn sur une liste d'attente/pour un rendez-vous** to put sb down *ou* put sb's name down on a waiting list/for an appointment; **je ne peux pas vous ~ avant le 3 août, le docteur est en vacances** I can't put you down for an appointment *ou* I can't give you an appointment before August 3rd as the doctor is on holiday; **(faire) ~ un enfant à l'école** to put a child *ou* child's name down for school, enrol *ou* register a child for school; **(faire) ~ qn à la cantine/pour une vaccination** to register sb at the canteen/for a vaccination.

c (*Math*) to inscribe.

2 **s'inscrire** vpr a (*s'enrôler*) (*gén*) to join; (*sur la liste électorale*) to put one's name down (*sur* on); (*à l'université*) to register, enrol (*à* at); (*à un examen*) to register, enrol, enter (*à* for); (*à une épreuve sportive*) to put o.s. down, put one's name down, enter (*à* for). **s'~ à un parti/club** to join a party/club; **je me suis inscrit pour des cours du soir** I've enrolled in *ou* for some evening classes; **s'~ avant le 9 octobre** to enrol *ou* register before October 9th.

b (*s'insérer dans*) **ces réformes s'inscrivent dans le cadre de notre nouvelle politique** these reforms lie *ou* come within the scope *ou* framework of our new policy; **cette décision s'inscrit dans le cadre de la lutte contre le chômage** this decision fits in with *ou* is in line *ou* in keeping with the general struggle against unemployment.

c (*Math*) to be inscribed. (*fig*) **l'avion ennemi s'inscrivit dans le viseur** the enemy aircraft came up on the viewfinder; **la tour Eiffel s'inscrivait tout entière dans la fenêtre** the Eiffel Tower was framed in its entirety by the window.

d (*Jur*) **s'~ en faux** to lodge a challenge; **je m'inscris en faux contre de telles assertions** I strongly deny such assertions.

inscrit, e [ɛ̃skʀi, it] (ptp de **inscrire**) 1 adj a *étudiant* registered, enrolled; *candidat, électeur* registered; *voir* **non**. b (*Math*) inscribed. 2 nm,f (*membre d'un parti etc*) registered member; (*étudiant*) registered student; (*concurrent*) (registered) entrant; (*candidat*) registered candidate; (*électeur*) registered elector. **~ maritime** registered sailor.

insécable [ɛ̃sekabl] adj indivisible, undividable.

insecte [ɛ̃sɛkt] nm insect.

insecticide [ɛ̃sɛktisid] 1 nm insecticide. 2 adj insecticide (*épith*), insecticidal.

insectivore [ɛ̃sɛktivɔʀ] 1 nm insectivore. **~s** insectivores, Insectivora (*SPÉC*). 2 adj insectivorous.

insécurité [ɛ̃sekyʀite] nf insecurity.

INSEE [inse] nm (abrév de **Institut national de la statistique et des études économiques**) *French national institute of economic and statistical information.* **numéro d'~** INSEE number.

inséminateur [ɛ̃seminatœʀ] nm inseminator.

insémination [ɛ̃seminasjɔ̃] nf insemination. **~ artificielle** artificial insemination.

inséminer [ɛ̃semine] 1 vt to inseminate.

insensé, e [ɛ̃sɑ̃se] adj a (*fou*) *projet, action, espoir* insane; *personne, propos* insane, demented. **vouloir y aller seul, c'est ~!** it's insane *ou* crazy to want to go alone!; **c'est un ~!** he's demented! *ou* insane!, he's a madman!; **cela demande un travail ~!** it takes an incredible *ou* a ridiculous amount of work. b (*bizarre*) *architecture, arabesques* weird, extravagant.

insensibilisation [ɛ̃sɑ̃sibilizasjɔ̃] nf anaesthesia.

insensibiliser [ɛ̃sɑ̃sibilize] 1 vt to anaesthetize. (*fig*) **nous sommes insensibilisés aux atrocités de la guerre** we've become insensitive to the atrocities of war.

insensibilité [ɛ̃sɑ̃sibilite] nf (*morale*) insensitivity, insensibility; (*physique*) numbness. **~ au froid/à la douleur/aux reproches** insensitivity *ou* insensibility to cold/pain/blame.

insensible [ɛ̃sɑ̃sibl] adj a (*moralement*) insensible, insensitive (*à* to); (*physiquement*) numb. **~ au froid/à la douleur/à la poésie** insensible *ou* insensitive to cold/pain/poetry. b (*imperceptible*) imperceptible, insensible.

insensiblement [ɛ̃sɑ̃sibləmɑ̃] adv imperceptibly, insensibly.

inséparable [ɛ̃sepaʀabl] 1 adj inseparable (*de* from). **ils sont ~s** they are inseparable. 2 nm (*Zool*) **~s** lovebirds.

inséparablement [ɛ̃sepaʀabləmɑ̃] adv inseparably.

insérable [ɛ̃seʀabl] adj insertable (*dans* into).

insérer [ɛ̃seʀe] 6 1 vt *feuillet, clause* to insert (*dans* into); *annonce* to put, insert (*dans* in). 2 **s'insérer** vpr a (*faire partie de*) **s'~ dans** to fit into; **ces changements s'insèrent dans le cadre d'une restructuration de notre entreprise** these changes come within *ou* lie within *ou* fit into our overall plan for restructuring the firm. b (*s'introduire dans*) **s'~ dans** to filter into; **le rêve s'insère parfois dans la réalité** sometimes dreams invade reality. c (*s'attacher*) to be inserted *ou* attached.

INSERM [insɛʀm] nm (abrév de **Institut national de la santé et de la recherche médicale**) ≃ MRC (*Brit*), ≃ NIH (*US*); *voir* **institut.**

insert [ɛ̃sɛʀ] nm (*Ciné*) insert, cut-in.

insertion [ɛ̃sɛʀsjɔ̃] nf (*action*) insertion, inserting; (*résultat*) insertion. **~ sociale** social integration.

insidieusement [ɛ̃sidjøzmɑ̃] adv insidiously.

insidieux, -ieuse [ɛ̃sidjø, jøz] adj *maladie, question* insidious.

insigne¹ [ɛ̃siɲ] adj (*éminent*) *honneur* distinguished; *services* notable, distinguished; *faveur* signal (*épith*), notable; (*iro*) *maladresse, mauvais goût* remarkable.

insigne² [ɛ̃siɲ] nm (*cocarde*) badge. (*frm: emblème*) **l'~ de, les ~s de** the insignia of; **portant les ~s de sa fonction** wearing the insignia of his office.

insignifiance [ɛ̃siɲifjɑ̃s] nf (*voir* **insignifiant**) insignificance; triviality.

insignifiant, e [ɛ̃siɲifjɑ̃, jɑ̃t] adj *personne, visage, œuvre* insignificant; *affaire, somme* insignificant, trivial, trifling; *paroles* insignificant, trivial.

insinuant, e [ɛ̃sinɥɑ̃, ɑ̃t] adj *façons, ton, personne* ingratiating.

insinuation [ɛ̃sinɥasjɔ̃] nf insinuation, innuendo.

insinuer [ɛ̃sinɥe] [1] **1** vt to insinuate, imply. **que voulez-vous ~?** what are you insinuating? *ou* implying? *ou* suggesting? **2** **s'insinuer** vpr: **s'~ dans** *[personne]* to worm one's way into, insinuate o.s. into; *[eau, odeur]* to seep *ou* creep into; **l'humidité s'insinuait partout** the dampness was creeping in everywhere; **les idées qui s'insinuent dans mon esprit** the ideas that steal *ou* creep into my mind; **ces arrivistes s'insinuent partout** these opportunists worm their way in everywhere; **s'~ dans les bonnes grâces de qn** to worm one's way into *ou* insinuate o.s. into sb's favour.

insipide [ɛ̃sipid] adj *plat, boisson* insipid, tasteless; *conversation, style* insipid, wishy-washy, vapid; *écrivain, film, œuvre* insipid, wishy-washy.

insipidité [ɛ̃sipidite] nf (*voir* **insipide**) insipidness, insipidity; tastelessness; vapidity.

insistance [ɛ̃sistɑ̃s] nf insistence (*sur qch* on sth; *à faire* on doing). **avec ~** *répéter, regarder* insistently.

insistant, e [ɛ̃sistɑ̃, ɑ̃t] adj insistent.

insister [ɛ̃siste] [1] vi **a** **~ sur** *sujet, détail* to stress, lay stress on; *syllabe, note* to accentuate, emphasize, stress; **j'insiste beaucoup sur la ponctualité** I lay great stress upon punctuality; **frottez en insistant (bien) sur les taches** rub hard, paying particular attention to stains; **c'est une affaire louche, enfin n'insistons pas!** it's a shady business – however let us not dwell on it *ou* don't let us keep on about it*; **je préfère ne pas ~ là-dessus!** I'd rather not dwell on it, I'd rather let the matter drop; **j'ai compris, inutile d'~!** I understand, no need to dwell on it!

b (*s'obstiner*) to be insistent (*auprès de* with), insist. **il insiste pour vous parler** he is insistent about wanting to talk to you; **comme ça ne l'intéressait pas, je n'ai pas insisté** since it didn't interest him I didn't push the matter *ou* I didn't insist; **sonnez encore, insistez, elle est un peu sourde** ring again and keep (on) trying because she's a little deaf; **bon, je n'insiste pas, je m'en vais*** O.K., I won't insist – I'll go.

in situ [insity] adv in situ.

insociable [ɛ̃sɔsjabl] adj unsociable.

insolation [ɛ̃sɔlasjɔ̃] nf **a** (*malaise*) sunstroke (*NonC*). **j'ai eu une ~** I had a touch of sunstroke. **b** (*ensoleillement*) (period of) sunshine. **ces stations ont malheureusement une ~ très faible** unfortunately these resorts get very little sun(shine); **cette région reçoit habituellement une ~ de 1 000 heures par an** this region regularly has 1,000 hours of sunshine a year. **c** (*exposition au soleil*) *[personne]* exposure to the sun; *[pellicule]* exposure.

insolemment [ɛ̃sɔlamɑ̃] adv (*voir* **insolent**) insolently; arrogantly; unashamedly; blatantly; brazenly.

insolence [ɛ̃sɔlɑ̃s] nf (*caractère: impertinence*) insolence; (*littér: morgue*) arrogance; (*remarque*) insolent remark. **encore une ~ comme celle-ci et je te renvoie** one more insolent remark like that *ou* any more of your insolence and I'll send you out.

insolent, e [ɛ̃sɔlɑ̃, ɑ̃t] adj **a** (*impoli*) *personne, attitude, réponse* insolent; (*littér*) *parvenu, vainqueur* arrogant. **tu es un ~** you're an insolent fellow. **b** (*inouï*) *luxe, succès* unashamed; *joie* brazen, unashamed. **il a une chance ~e!** he has the luck of the devil!

insolite [ɛ̃sɔlit] adj unusual, strange.

insolubilité [ɛ̃sɔlybilite] nf (*voir* **insoluble**) insolubility; insolvability.

insoluble [ɛ̃sɔlybl] adj *problème* insoluble, insolvable. **~ (dans l'eau)** *substance* insoluble (in water).

insolvabilité [ɛ̃sɔlvabilite] nf insolvency.

insolvable [ɛ̃sɔlvabl] adj insolvent.

insomniaque [ɛ̃sɔmnjak] nmf insomniac. **c'est un ~, il est ~** he's an insomniac.

insomnie [ɛ̃sɔmni] nf insomnia (*NonC*). **ses nuits d'~** his sleepless nights; **ses ~s** his (periods of) insomnia.

insondable [ɛ̃sɔ̃dabl] adj *gouffre, mystère, douleur* unfathomable; *stupidité* immense, unimaginable.

insonore [ɛ̃sɔnɔʀ] adj soundproof.

insonorisation [ɛ̃sɔnɔʀizasjɔ̃] nf soundproofing.

insonoriser [ɛ̃sɔnɔʀize] [1] vt to soundproof. **immeuble mal insonorisé** badly soundproofed building.

insortable* [ɛ̃sɔʀtabl] adj: **tu es ~!** I (*ou* we *etc*) can't take you anywhere!*

insouciance [ɛ̃susjɑ̃s] nf (*nonchalance*) unconcern, lack of concern; (*manque de prévoyance*) heedless *ou* happy-go-lucky attitude. **vivre dans l'~** to live a carefree life.

insouciant, e [ɛ̃susjɑ̃, jɑ̃t] adj (*sans souci*) *personne, vie, humeur* carefree, happy-go-lucky; *rire, paroles* carefree; (*imprévoyant*) heedless, happy-go-lucky. **quel ~ (tu fais)!** what a heedless *ou* happy-go-lucky person you are!; **~ du danger** heedless of (the) danger.

insoucieux, -ieuse [ɛ̃susjø, jøz] adj carefree. **~ du lendemain** unconcerned about the future, not caring about what tomorrow may bring.

insoumis, e [ɛ̃sumi, iz] **1** adj *caractère, enfant* refractory, rebellious, insubordinate; *tribu, peuple, région* undefeated, unsubdued; (*Mil*) *soldat* absent without leave (*failing to report as instructed*). **2** nm (*Mil*) absentee.

insoumission [ɛ̃sumisjɔ̃] nf insubordination, rebelliousness; (*Mil*) absence without leave.

insoupçonnable [ɛ̃supsɔnabl] adj *personne* above *ou* beyond suspicion (*attrib*); *cachette* impossible to find; *desseins* unsuspected. **il a trouvé une cachette ~ pour les bijoux** no one will ever suspect where he has hidden the jewels.

insoupçonné, e [ɛ̃supsɔne] adj unsuspected, undreamt-of (*de* by).

insoutenable [ɛ̃sut(ə)nabl] adj *spectacle, douleur, chaleur* unbearable; *théorie* untenable. **d'une violence ~** unbearably violent.

inspecter [ɛ̃spɛkte] [1] vt (*contrôler*) to inspect; (*scruter*) to inspect, examine.

inspecteur, -trice [ɛ̃spɛktœʀ, tʀis] nm,f (*gén*) inspector. **~ des finances** *ou* **des impôts** ≃ tax inspector; **~ de police** police inspector, ≃ detective constable (*Brit*), detective sergeant (*Brit*), lieutenant (*US*); **~ de police principal** detective chief inspector (*Brit*), lieutenant (*US*); **~ de police judiciaire** police inspector from the criminal investigation department; **~ du travail** factory inspector; (*péj*) **~ des travaux finis*** (*qui critique le travail des autres*) expert (*iro*); (*qui ne travaille pas*) skiver* (*Brit*), layabout*; **~ primaire** primary school inspector; **~ d'Académie, ~ pédagogique régional** ≃ inspector of schools (*Brit*), accreditation officer (*US*); **~ général de l'instruction publique** ≃ chief inspector of schools.

inspection [ɛ̃spɛksjɔ̃] nf **a** (*examen*) inspection. **faire l'~ de** to inspect; **soumettre qch à une ~ en règle** to give sth a good *ou* thorough inspection *ou* going-over*. **b** (*inspectorat*) inspectorship; (*inspecteurs*) inspectorate. (*service*) **~ académique** school inspectorate, ≃ education authority (*Brit*); **~ du Travail/des Finances** ≃ factory/tax inspectorate; (*Police*) **l'I~ générale des services** the police monitoring service, ≃ the Police Complaints Board (*Brit*); **I~ générale de la police nationale** police disciplinary body, ≃ Complaints and Discipline Branch (*Brit*), ≃ Internal Affairs (*US*).

inspectorat [ɛ̃spɛktɔʀa] nm inspectorship.

inspirateur, -trice [ɛ̃spiʀatœʀ, tʀis] **1** adj *idée, force* inspiring; (*Anat*) inspiratory. **2** nm,f (*animateur*) inspirer; (*instigateur*) instigator. **le poète et son ~trice** the poet and the woman who inspires him.

inspiration [ɛ̃spiʀasjɔ̃] nf **a** (*divine, poétique etc*) inspiration. **avoir de l'~** to have inspiration, be inspired; **selon l'~ du moment** according to the mood of the moment, as the mood takes me (*ou* you *etc*); **Julie fut une source d'~ pour lui** Julie was an inspiration to him. **b** (*idée*) inspiration, brainwave*. **par une heureuse ~** thanks to a flash of inspiration; **j'eus la bonne/mauvaise ~ de refuser** I had the bright idea/bad idea of refusing. **c** (*instigation*) instigation; (*influence*) inspiration. **sous l'~ de qn** at sb's instigation, prompted by sb; **style/tableau d'~ romantique** style/picture of romantic inspiration. **d** (*respiration*) inspiration.

inspiré, e [ɛ̃spiʀe] (ptp de **inspirer**) adj **a** *poète, œuvre, air* inspired. (*iro*) **qu'est-ce que c'est que cet ~?** whoever's this cranky fellow? *ou* this weirdo?* (*péj*). **b** (*: *avisé*) **il serait bien ~ de partir** he'd be well advised *ou* he'd do well to leave; **j'ai été bien/mal ~ de refuser son chèque** *ou* **quand j'ai refusé son chèque** I was truly inspired/ill inspired when I refused his cheque. **c ~ de** inspired by; **une tragédie ~e des poèmes antiques** a tragedy inspired by the ancient poems; **une mode ~e des années cinquante** a style inspired by the Fifties.

inspirer [ɛ̃spiʀe] [1] **1** vt **a** *poète, prophète* to inspire. **sa passion lui a inspiré ce poème** his passion inspired him to write this poem; **cette idée ne m'inspire pas beaucoup*** I'm not very taken with that idea, I'm not all that keen on this idea* (*Brit*); **le sujet de dissertation ne m'a pas vraiment inspiré*** I didn't think the essay subject very inspiring*.

b (*susciter*) *acte, personne* to inspire. **~ un sentiment** to inspire sb with a feeling; **~ le respect à qn** to command sb's respect; **sa santé m'inspire des inquiétudes** his health gives me cause for concern; **il ne m'inspire pas confiance** he doesn't inspire confidence in me, he doesn't inspire me with confidence, I don't really trust him; **toute l'opération était inspirée par un seul homme** the whole operation was inspired by one man; **l'horreur qu'il m'inspire** the horror he fills me with.

c (*insuffler*) **~ de l'air dans qch** to breathe air into sth.

2 vi (*respirer*) to breathe in, inspire (*SPÉC*).

3 **s'inspirer** vpr: **s'~ d'un modèle** *[artiste]* to draw one's inspiration from a model, be inspired by a model; *[mode, tableau, loi]* to be inspired by a model.

instabilité [ɛ̃stabilite] nf (*voir* **instable**) instability; (emotional) instability; unsteadiness. **l'~ du temps** the unsettled (nature of the) weather; **l'~ d'une population nomade** the unsettled pattern of life of a nomadic population.

instable [ɛ̃stabl] **adj** (*Chim, Phys*) unstable; *opinions, situation, régime politique, prix* unstable; *personne, caractère* (emotionally) unstable; *temps* unsettled, unstable; *population nomade* unsettled; *meuble, échafaudage* unsteady; *voir* **équilibre**.

installateur [ɛ̃stalatœʀ] **nm** fitter. **~ en chauffage central** central heating installation engineer; **~ de cuisine** kitchen-fitter.

installation [ɛ̃stalasjɔ̃] **nf** a (*voir* **installer**) installation, installing; putting in; putting up; pitching; fitting out. **il lui fallait maintenant songer à l'~ de son fils** he now had to think about setting his son up; **l'~ du téléphone devrait être gratuite pour les retraités** the telephone should be put in *ou* installed free for pensioners; **ils s'occupent aussi de l'~ du mobilier** they also take care of moving the furniture in *ou* of installing the furniture.

b (*voir* **s'installer**) setting up, setting up shop; settling; settling in. **il voulait fêter son ~** he wanted to celebrate moving in; **leur ~ terminée** when they had finally settled in.

c (*appareils etc: gén pl*) fittings, installations; *[usine]* plant (*NonC*). **l'~ électrique est défectueuse** the wiring is faulty; **~(s) sanitaire(s)/électrique(s)** sanitary/electrical fittings *ou* installations; **les ~s industrielles d'une région** the industrial installations *ou* plant of a region; **~s nucléaires** nuclear plant; **~s portuaires** port installations; **le camping est doté de toutes les ~s nécessaires** the camping site is equipped with all the necessary facilities.

d (*ameublement etc*) living arrangements, setup*. **ils ont une ~ provisoire** they have temporary living arrangements *ou* a temporary setup*; **qu'est-ce que vous avez comme ~?** what kind of a setup* do you have?

e (*Art*) installation.

installé, e [ɛ̃stale] (**ptp de installer**) **adj** (*aménagé*) **bien/mal ~** *appartement* well/badly fitted out; *atelier, cuisine* well/badly equipped *ou* fitted out; **ils sont très bien ~s** they have a comfortable *ou* nice home; **c'est un homme ~†** he is well-established.

installer [ɛ̃stale] 1 1 **vt** a (*poser*) *électricité, chauffage central, téléphone, eau courante* to install, put in; *usine* to set up. **faire ~ le gaz/le téléphone** to have (the) gas/the telephone put in *ou* installed.

b (*accrocher*) *rideaux, étagère* to put up; (*placer, fixer*) *applique* to put in; *meuble* to put in, install; (*monter*) *tente* to put up, pitch. **où va-t-on ~ le lit?** where shall we put the bed?

c (*aménager*) *pièce, appartement* to fit out. **ils ont très bien installé leur petit appartement** they've got their flat well fitted out; **ils ont installé leur bureau dans le grenier, ils ont installé le grenier en bureau** they've turned the attic into a study, they've made a study in the attic; **comment la cuisine est-elle installée?** how is the kitchen laid out? *ou* fitted out?

d *malade, jeune couple etc* to get settled, settle. **ils installèrent leurs hôtes dans une aile du château** they installed their guests in a wing of the château, they put their guests in a wing of the château; **il a installé son fils dentiste/à son compte** he set his son up as a dentist/in his own business.

e (*Admin: nommer*) *fonctionnaire, évêque* to install. **il a été officiellement installé dans ses fonctions** he has been officially installed in his post.

2 **s'installer vpr** a *[artisan, commerçant, médecin]* to set o.s. up (*comme* as), set up shop (*comme* as). **s'~ à son compte** to set up on one's own, set up one's own business; **un dentiste s'est installé dans l'immeuble** a dentist has set himself up *ou* opened up in the building.

b (*se loger*) to settle; (*emménager*) to settle in. **laisse-leur le temps de s'~** give them time to settle in; **ils se sont installés à la campagne/à Lyon** they've settled *ou* set up house in the country/in Lyons; **pendant la guerre ils s'étaient installés chez des amis** during the war they moved in *ou* lived with friends; **s'~ dans une maison abandonnée** to set up home *ou* make one's home in an empty house; **ils sont bien installés dans leur nouvelle maison** they have made themselves very comfortable in their new house.

c (*sur un siège, à un emplacement*) to settle down. **s'~ commodément** to settle (down) comfortably; **s'~ par terre/dans un fauteuil** to settle down on the floor/in an armchair; **installe-toi comme il faut** (*confortablement*) make yourself comfortable; (*tiens-toi bien*) sit properly; **installons-nous près de cet arbre** let's sit down near this tree; **partout où il va il s'installe comme chez lui** wherever he goes he makes himself at home; **les forains se sont installés sur un terrain vague** the fairground people have set themselves up *ou* have parked on a piece of wasteland; **le fête s'est installée sur la place du marché** the fair has set up *ou* has been set up in the marketplace.

d (*fig*) *[grève, maladie]* to take a firm hold, become firmly established. *[personne]* **s'~ dans** *inertie* to sink into, be sunk in; *malhonnêteté* to entangle o.s. in, get entangled in; **s'~ dans la guerre** to settle into *ou* become accustomed to the state of war; **le doute s'installa dans mon esprit** my mind was gripped by doubt; **la peur s'était installée dans la ville** the town was gripped by fear.

instamment [ɛ̃stamɑ̃] **adv** insistently, earnestly.

instance [ɛ̃stɑ̃s] **nf** a (*autorité*) authority. **les ~s internationales** the international authorities; **les ~s communautaires** the EEC authorities; **le conflit devra être tranché par l'~ supérieure** the dispute will have to be resolved by a higher authority.

b (*Jur*) (legal) proceedings. **introduire une ~** to institute (legal) proceedings; **en seconde ~** on appeal; *voir* **juge, tribunal**.

c (*prière, insistance*) **demander qch avec ~** to ask for something with insistence *ou* earnestness; **~s** entreaties; **sur** *ou* **devant les ~s de ses parents** in the face of his parents' entreaties.

d (*en cours*) **l'affaire est en ~** the matter is pending; **être en ~ de divorce** to be waiting for a divorce; **le train est en ~ de départ** the train is on the point of departure *ou* about to leave; **courrier en ~** mail ready for posting *ou* due to be dispatched.

instant[1] [ɛ̃stɑ̃] **nm** a (*moment*) moment, instant. **des ~s de tendresse** tender moments, moments of tenderness; **j'ai cru (pendant) un ~ que** I thought for a moment *ou* a second *ou* one instant that; **(attendez) un ~!** wait *ou* just a moment!, wait one instant!

b (*le présent*) **il faut vivre dans l'~** you must live in the present (moment).

c (*loc*) **je l'ai vu à l'~** I've just this instant *ou* minute *ou* second seen him; **il faut le faire à l'~** we must do it this instant *ou* minute; **on me l'apprend à l'~** I've just been told *ou* I've just heard about it; **à l'~ (présent)** at this very instant *ou* moment *ou* minute; **à l'~ où je vous parle** as I'm speaking to you now; **à l'~ (même) où il sortit** just as he went out, (just) at the very moment *ou* instant he went out; **à chaque ~, à tout ~** (*d'un moment à l'autre*) at any moment *ou* minute; (*tout le temps*) all the time, every minute; **au même ~** at the (very) same moment *ou* instant; **d'~ en ~** from moment to moment, every moment; **dans l'~ (même)** the next instant, in (next to) no time (at all); **dans un ~** in a moment *ou* minute; **en un ~** in an instant, in no time (at all); **de tous les ~s** *surveillance* perpetual, constant; *dévouement, attention* constant; **par ~s** at times; **pour l'~** for the moment, for the time being; **je n'en doute pas un (seul) ~** I don't doubt it for a (single) moment; **dès l'~ où** *ou* **que vous êtes d'accord** (*puisque*) since you agree; **dès l'~ où je l'ai vu** (*dès que*) as soon as I saw him, from the moment I saw him.

instant[2]**, e** [ɛ̃stɑ̃, ɑ̃t] **adj** (*littér: pressant*) insistent, pressing, earnest.

instantané, e [ɛ̃stɑ̃tane] 1 **adj** *lait, café, soupe* instant; *mort, réponse, effet* instantaneous; (*littér: bref*) *vision* momentary. 2 **nm** (*Phot*) snapshot, snap*; (*fig*) snapshot.

instantanément [ɛ̃stɑ̃tanemɑ̃] **adv** instantaneously. **dissoudre dans de l'eau pour préparer ~ un bon café** dissolve in water to make good coffee instantly.

instar [ɛ̃staʀ] **nm: à l'~ de** following the example of, after the fashion of.

instauration [ɛ̃stɔʀasjɔ̃] **nf** institution.

instaurer [ɛ̃stɔʀe] 1 **vt** *usage, pratique* to institute; *méthode* to introduce; *couvre-feu* to impose. **la révolution a instauré la république** the revolution established the republic; **le doute s'est instauré dans les esprits** doubts began to creep into *ou* be raised in people's minds.

instigateur, -trice [ɛ̃stigatœʀ, tʀis] **nm,f** instigator.

instigation [ɛ̃stigasjɔ̃] **nf** instigation. **à l'~ de qn** at sb's instigation.

instillation [ɛ̃stilasjɔ̃] **nf** instillation.

instiller [ɛ̃stile] 1 **vt** (*Méd, littér*) to instil (*dans* in, into). **il m'a instillé la passion du jeu** he instilled the love of gambling in *ou* into me.

instinct [ɛ̃stɛ̃] **nm** (*gén*) instinct. **~ grégaire** gregarious *ou* herd instinct; **~ de conservation** instinct of self-preservation; **il a l'~ des affaires** he has an instinct for business; **faire qch d'~** *ou* **par ~** to do sth instinctively; **d'~, il comprit la situation** intuitively *ou* instinctively he understood the situation; **mon ~ me dit que** (my) instinct tells me that; **céder à ses (mauvais) ~s** to yield to one's (bad) instincts.

instinctif, -ive [ɛ̃stɛ̃ktif, iv] **adj** (*gén*) instinctive, instinctual. **c'est un ~** he (always) acts on instinct.

instinctivement [ɛ̃stɛ̃ktivmɑ̃] **adv** instinctively.

instit* [ɛ̃stit] **nmf abrév de instituteur, -trice.**

instituer [ɛ̃stitɥe] 1 1 **vt** *règle, pratique, organisation* to institute; *relations commerciales* to establish; *impôt* to introduce; (*Rel*) *évêque* to institute; (*Jur*) *héritier* to appoint, institute. 2 **s'instituer vpr** *[relations commerciales]* to start up, be (*ou* become) established.

institut [ɛ̃stity] 1 **nm** institute; (*Univ*) institute, school (*Brit*). **membre de l'I~** member of the Institut, ≃ Fellow of the Royal Society (*Brit*); **~ de beauté** beauty salon *ou* parlor (*US*); **I~ universitaire de technologie** ≃ polytechnic (*Brit*), ≃ technical school *ou* institute (*US*); **~ médico-légal** mortuary.

2 **comp** ►**l'Institut (de France)** the Institut de France (*the five French Academies*), ≃ the Royal Society (*Brit*) ►**institut géographique national** *French geographical institute,* ≃ Ordnance Survey (*Brit*), ≃ United States Geological Survey (*US*), ≃ USGS (*US*) ►**Institut national de l'audiovisuel** *library of radio and television archives* ►**Institut national de la consommation** *consumer research organization,* ≃ Consumers' Association (*Brit*), ≃ Consumer Product Safety Commission (*US*) ►**Institut national de la santé et de la recherche médicale** *national institute for health and medical research,* ≃ Medical Research Council (*Brit*), National Institute of

Health (*US*) ▸Institut de retraite complémentaire des agents non titulaires de l'Etat et des collectivités publiques *pension-awarding body for certain state employees* ▸Institut universitaire de formation des maîtres *teacher training college*.

instituteur, -trice [ɛ̃stitytœʀ, tʀis] 1 nm,f (primary school) teacher. ~ spécialisé teacher in special school (for the handicapped) (*Brit*), EMH teacher (*US*). 2 institutrice nf (*Hist: gouvernante*) governess.

institution [ɛ̃stitysjɔ̃] 1 nf (*gén*) institution; (*école*) private school. (*Pol*) nos ~s sont menacées our institutions are threatened. 2 comp ▸institution canonique (*Rel*) institution ▸institution d'héritier (*Jur*) appointment of an heir ▸institution religieuse (*pour filles*) convent school; (*pour garçons*) Catholic boys' school.

institutionnalisation [ɛ̃stitysjɔnalizasjɔ̃] nf institutionalization.

institutionnaliser [ɛ̃stitysjɔnalize] 1 1 vt to institutionalize. 2 s'institutionnaliser vpr to become institutionalized.

institutionnel, -elle [ɛ̃stitysjɔnɛl] adj institutional.

institutrice [ɛ̃stitytʀis] nf *voir* instituteur.

instructeur [ɛ̃stʀyktœʀ] 1 nm instructor. 2 adj (*Jur*) juge *ou* magistrat ~ examining magistrate; (*Mil*) capitaine/sergent ~ drill captain/sergeant.

instructif, -ive [ɛ̃stʀyktif, iv] adj instructive.

instruction [ɛ̃stʀyksjɔ̃] nf a (*enseignement*) education. l'~ que j'ai reçue the teaching *ou* education I received; niveau d'~ academic standard; ~ civique civics (*sg*); ~ militaire army training; ~ religieuse religious instruction, religious education *ou* studies; l'~ publique/privée/primaire/secondaire state/private/primary/secondary education.
b (*culture*) education. avoir de l'~ to be well educated; être sans ~ to have no education.
c (*Jur*) *pretrial investigation of a case*. ouvrir une ~ to initiate an investigation into a crime; *voir* juge.
d (*Admin: circulaire*) directive. ~ ministérielle/préfectorale ministerial/prefectural directive.
e (*ordres*) ~s instructions; (*mode d'emploi*) instructions, directions; (*étiquette*) ~s de lavage care label, washing instructions; (*Informatique*) instruction; suivre les ~s données sur le paquet to follow the instructions *ou* directions given on the packet; conformément/contrairement à vos ~s in accordance with/contrary to your instructions.

instruire [ɛ̃stʀɥiʀ] 38 1 vt a (*former*) (*gén*) to teach, educate; *recrue* to train. l'école où elle instruit ces enfants the school where she teaches those children; ~ qn dans l'art oratoire to educate *ou* instruct sb in the art of oratory; c'est la vie qui m'a instruit life has educated me, life has been my teacher; ~ qn par l'exemple to teach *ou* educate sb by example; instruit par son exemple having learnt from his example; ces émissions ne visent pas à ~ mais à divertir these broadcasts are not intended to teach *ou* educate *ou* instruct but to entertain.
b (*informer*) ~ qn de qch to inform *ou* advise sb of sth; on ne nous a pas instruits des décisions à prendre we haven't been informed *ou* advised of the decisions to be taken.
c (*Jur*) *affaire* to conduct the investigation for. ~ contre qn to conduct investigations concerning sb.
2 s'instruire vpr (*apprendre*) to educate o.s. (*hum*) c'est comme ça qu'on s'instruit! that's how you improve your knowledge!; s'~ de qch (*frm: se renseigner*) to obtain information about sth, find out about sth; s'~ auprès de qn des heures d'arrivée to obtain information *ou* find out from sb about the times of arrival.

instruit, e [ɛ̃stʀɥi, it] (ptp de instruire) adj educated. peu ~ uneducated.

instrument [ɛ̃stʀymɑ̃] nm (*lit, fig*) instrument. ~ de musique/de chirurgie/de mesure/à vent musical/surgical/measuring/wind instrument; ~s aratoires ploughing implements; ~ de travail tool; (*Aviat*) les ~s de bord the controls; naviguer aux ~s to fly on instruments; (*fig*) être l'~ de qn to be sb's tool; le président fut l'~ de/servit d'~ à la répression the president was the instrument *ou* tool of/served as an *ou* the instrument of repression; elle a été l'~ de sa vengeance she was *ou* served as the instrument of his revenge; elle a été l'~ de sa réussite she was instrumental in his success.

instrumental, e, mpl **-aux** [ɛ̃stʀymɑ̃tal, o] 1 adj (*Ling, Mus*) instrumental. 2 nm (*Ling*) instrumental.

instrumentation [ɛ̃stʀymɑ̃tasjɔ̃] nf instrumentation, orchestration.

instrumenter [ɛ̃stʀymɑ̃te] 1 1 vi (*Jur*) to draw up a formal document (*deed, contract etc*). 2 vt (*Mus*) to orchestrate.

instrumentiste [ɛ̃stʀymɑ̃tist] nmf instrumentalist.

insu [ɛ̃sy] nm a (*en cachette de*) à l'~ de qn without sb's knowledge, without sb's knowing. b (*inconsciemment*) à mon (*ou* ton *etc*) ~ without my *ou* me (*ou* your *ou* you *etc*) knowing it; je souriais à mon ~ I was smiling without knowing it.

insubmersible [ɛ̃sybmɛʀsibl] adj unsinkable.

insubordination [ɛ̃sybɔʀdinasjɔ̃] nf (*gén*) insubordination, rebelliousness; (*Mil*) insubordination.

insubordonné, e [ɛ̃sybɔʀdɔne] adj (*gén*) insubordinate, rebellious; (*Mil*) insubordinate.

insuccès [ɛ̃syksɛ] nm failure.

insuffisamment [ɛ̃syfizamɑ̃] adv (*voir* insuffisant) insufficiently; inadequately. tu dors ~ you're not getting adequate *ou* sufficient sleep.

insuffisance [ɛ̃syfizɑ̃s] nf a (*médiocrité*) inadequacy; (*manque*) insufficiency, inadequacy. l'~ de nos ressources the inadequacy of our resources, the shortfall in our resources, our inadequate *ou* insufficient resources; nous souffrons d'une (grande) ~ de moyens we are suffering from a (great) inadequacy *ou* insufficiency *ou* shortage of means; une ~ de personnel a shortage of staff. b (*faiblesses*) ~s inadequacies; avoir des ~s en maths to be weak in *ou* at maths; il y a des ~s dans son travail there are inadequacies in his work, his work has shortcomings. c (*Méd*) ~(s) cardiaque(s)/thyroïdienne(s) cardiac/thyroid insufficiency (*NonC*).

insuffisant, e [ɛ̃syfizɑ̃, ɑ̃t] adj (*en quantité*) insufficient; (*en qualité, intensité, degré*) inadequate; (*Scol*) (*sur une copie*) poor. ce qu'il nous donne est ~ what he gives us is insufficient *ou* inadequate *ou* not enough; il est ~ en maths he's weak in *ou* at maths, he's not up to standard in maths; nous travaillons avec un personnel ~ we're working with inadequate staffing *ou* with insufficient staff; nous sommes en nombre ~ we are insufficient in number; (*Méd*) les ~s cardiaques/respiratoires people with cardiac/respiratory insufficiency.

insufflateur [ɛ̃syflatœʀ] nm (*Méd*) insufflator.

insufflation [ɛ̃syflasjɔ̃] nf (*Méd*) insufflation.

insuffler [ɛ̃syfle] 1 vt a ~ le courage/le désir à qn to inspire sb with courage/desire, breathe courage/desire into sb; (*Rel*) ~ la vie à to breathe life into. b (*Méd*) *air* to blow, insufflate (*SPÉC*) (*dans* into).

insulaire [ɛ̃sylɛʀ] 1 adj *administration, population* island (*épith*); *conception, attitude* insular. 2 nmf islander.

insularité [ɛ̃sylaʀite] nf insularity.

insuline [ɛ̃sylin] nf insulin.

insulino-dépendance [ɛ̃sylinɔdepɑ̃dɑ̃s] nf insulin-dependent diabetes.

insulino-dépendant, e [ɛ̃sylinɔdepɑ̃dɑ̃, ɑ̃t] adj *diabète, diabétique* insulin-dependent.

insultant, e [ɛ̃syltɑ̃, ɑ̃t] adj insulting (*pour* to).

insulte [ɛ̃sylt] nf (*grossièreté*) abuse (*NonC*), insult; (*affront*) insult. (*frm*) c'est me faire ~ que de ne pas me croire you insult me by not believing me; (*fig*) c'est une ~ *ou* c'est faire ~ à son intelligence it's an insult *ou* affront to his intelligence.

insulté, e [ɛ̃sylte] (ptp de insulter) 1 adj insulted. 2 nm (*en duel*) injured party.

insulter [ɛ̃sylte] 1 vt (*faire affront à*) to insult; (*injurier*) to abuse, insult. (*fig littér*) ~ à to be an insult to.

insulteur [ɛ̃syltœʀ] nm insulter.

insupportable [ɛ̃sypɔʀtabl] adj *douleur, bruit, personne, spectacle* unbearable, intolerable, insufferable.

insupportablement [ɛ̃sypɔʀtabləmɑ̃] adv unbearably, intolerably, insufferably.

insupporter [ɛ̃sypɔʀte] 1 vt (*hum*) cela m'insupporte/l'insupporte I/he can't stand this.

insurgé, e [ɛ̃syʀʒe] (ptp de s'insurger) adj, nm,f rebel, insurgent.

insurger (s') [ɛ̃syʀʒe] 3 vpr (*lit, fig*) to rebel, rise up, revolt (*contre* against).

insurmontable [ɛ̃syʀmɔ̃tabl] adj *difficulté, obstacle* insurmountable, insuperable; *peur, dégoût* unconquerable.

insurmontablement [ɛ̃syʀmɔ̃tabləmɑ̃] adv (*voir* insurmontable) insurmountably, insuperably; unconquerably.

insurpassable [ɛ̃syʀpɑsabl] adj unsurpassable, unsurpassed.

insurrection [ɛ̃syʀɛksjɔ̃] nf (*lit*) insurrection, revolt, uprising; (*fig*) revolt. mouvement/foyer d'~ movement/nucleus of revolt.

insurrectionnel, -elle [ɛ̃syʀɛksjɔnɛl] adj *mouvement, gouvernement, force* insurrectionary.

intact, e [ɛ̃takt] adj *objet, réputation, argent* intact (*attrib*).

intangibilité [ɛ̃tɑ̃ʒibilite] nf inviolability.

intangible [ɛ̃tɑ̃ʒibl] adj (*impalpable*) intangible; (*sacré*) inviolable.

intarissable [ɛ̃taʀisabl] adj (*lit, fig*) inexhaustible. il est ~ he could talk for ever (*sur* about).

intarissablement [ɛ̃taʀisabləmɑ̃] adv inexhaustibly.

intégrable [ɛ̃tegʀabl] adj integrable.

intégral, e, mpl **-aux** [ɛ̃tegʀal, o] 1 adj complete. le remboursement ~ de qch the repayment in full of sth, the full *ou* complete repayment of sth; publier le texte ~ d'un discours to publish the text of a speech in full *ou* the complete text of a speech; (*Ciné*) version ~e uncut version; (*Presse*) texte ~ unabridged version; "texte ~" "unabridged"; le nu ~ complete *ou* total nudity; bronzage ~ all-over suntan; *voir* calcul. 2 intégrale nf (*Math*) integral; (*Mus*) (*série*) complete series; (*œuvre*) complete works. l'~e des symphonies de Sibelius the complete set of the symphonies of Sibelius.

intégralement [ɛ̃tegʀalmɑ̃] adv in full, fully. le concert sera retransmis ~ the concert will be broadcast in full.

intégralité [ɛ̃tegʀalite] nf whole. l'~ de la somme vous sera remboursée the whole of the sum will be repaid to you, the whole *ou* entire *ou* full sum *ou* amount will be repaid to you; la somme vous sera remboursée dans son ~ the sum will be repaid to you in its entirety *ou* in toto *ou* in full; le match sera retransmis dans son ~ the match will be broadcast in full; l'~ de mon salaire the whole of my salary, my whole *ou* entire salary; votre salaire vous sera versé en ~ en francs français you will be paid the whole of your salary *ou* your entire salary in French francs.

intégrant, e [ɛ̃tegʀɑ̃, ɑ̃t] adj *voir* **partie**[2].
intégrateur [ɛ̃tegʀatœʀ] nm integrator.
intégration [ɛ̃tegʀasjɔ̃] nf (*voir* **intégrer**) (*gén*) integration (*à, dans* into). (*arg Univ*) **après son ~ à Polytechnique** after getting into the École polytechnique; (*Ordin*) **~ à très grande échelle** very large-scale integration.
intègre [ɛ̃tɛgʀ] adj upright, honest.
intégré, e [ɛ̃tegʀe] (ptp de **intégrer**) adj *circuit, système* integrated. (*Ordin*) **traitement ~ (des données)** integrated data processing.
intégrer [ɛ̃tegʀe] 6 1 vt (*Math*) to integrate; (*incorporer*) *idées, personne* to integrate (*à, dans* into). **~ une entreprise/un club/une association** to join a company/a club/an association. 2 vi (*arg Univ*) **~ à Polytechnique** *etc* to get into the École polytechnique *etc.* 3 **s'intégrer** vpr to become integrated (*à, dans* into). **bien s'~ dans une société** to integrate well into a society; **cette maison s'intègre mal dans le paysage** this house doesn't really fit into the surrounding countryside.
intégrisme [ɛ̃tegʀism] nm fundamentalism.
intégriste [ɛ̃tegʀist] adj, nmf fundamentalist.
intégrité [ɛ̃tegʀite] nf (*totalité*) integrity; (*honnêteté*) integrity, honesty, uprightness.
intellect [ɛ̃telɛkt] nm intellect.
intellectualisation [ɛ̃telɛktɥalizasjɔ̃] nf intellectualization.
intellectualiser [ɛ̃telɛktɥalize] 1 vt to intellectualize.
intellectualisme [ɛ̃telɛktɥalism] nm intellectualism.
intellectualiste [ɛ̃telɛktɥalist] adj, nmf intellectualist.
intellectualité [ɛ̃telɛktɥalite] nf (*littér*) intellectuality.
intellectuel, -elle [ɛ̃telɛktɥɛl] 1 adj *facultés, effort, supériorité* mental, intellectual; *fatigue* mental; *personne, mouvement, œuvre, vie* intellectual; (*péj*) highbrow (*péj*), intellectual. **activité ~le** mental *ou* intellectual activity, brainwork*; **les travailleurs ~s** non-manual workers; *voir* **quotient.** 2 nm,f intellectual; (*péj*) highbrow (*péj*), intellectual.
intellectuellement [ɛ̃telɛktɥɛlmɑ̃] adv (*voir* **intellectuel**) mentally; intellectually.
intelligemment [ɛ̃teliʒamɑ̃] adv (*voir* **intelligent**) intelligently; cleverly.
intelligence [ɛ̃teliʒɑ̃s] nf a (*aptitude, ensemble des facultés mentales*) intelligence. **avoir l'~ vive** to have a sharp *ou* quick mind, be sharp *ou* quick; **faire preuve d'~** to show intelligence; **avoir l'~ de faire** to have the intelligence *ou* the wit to do, be intelligent enough to do; **travailler avec ~/sans ~** to work intelligently/unintelligently; **il met beaucoup d'~ dans ce qu'il fait** he applies great intelligence to what he does; **c'est une ~ exceptionnelle** he has a great intellect *ou* mind *ou* brain, he is a person of exceptional intelligence; **les grandes ~s** the great minds *ou* intellects; **~ artificielle** artificial intelligence.
b (*compréhension*) **~ de** understanding of; **pour l'~ du texte** for a clear understanding of the text, in order to understand the text; **avoir l'~ des affaires** to have a good grasp *ou* understanding of business matters, have a good head for business.
c (*complicité*) secret agreement. **agir d'~ avec qn** to act in (secret) agreement with sb; **signe/sourire d'~** sign/smile of complicity; **être d'~ avec qn** to have a (secret) understanding *ou* agreement with sb; **vivre en bonne/mauvaise ~ avec qn** to be on good/bad terms with sb.
d (*relations secrètes*) **~s** secret relations; **avoir des ~s dans la place** to have secret relations *ou* contacts in the place; **entretenir des ~s avec l'ennemi** to have secret dealings with the enemy.
intelligent, e [ɛ̃teliʒɑ̃, ɑ̃t] adj (*doué d'intellect*) intelligent; (*à l'esprit vif, perspicace*) intelligent, clever, bright. **peu ~** unintelligent; **ce chien est (très) ~** this dog is (very) clever; **son livre est ~** his book shows intelligence.
intelligentsia [ɛ̃teliʒɛnsja] nf: **l'~** the intelligentsia.
intelligibilité [ɛ̃teliʒibilite] nf intelligibility.
intelligible [ɛ̃teliʒibl] adj intelligible. **à haute et ~ voix** loudly and clearly; **s'exprimer de façon peu ~** to express o.s. unintelligibly *ou* in an unintelligible manner.
intelligiblement [ɛ̃teliʒibləmɑ̃] adv intelligibly.
intello* [ɛ̃telo] adj, nmf (*péj*) highbrow (*péj*), intellectual.
intempérance [ɛ̃tɑ̃peʀɑ̃s] nf (*voir* **intempérant**) intemperance; overindulgence. **~s** excesses; **une telle ~ de langage** such excessive language; **de telles ~s de langage** such excesses of language.
intempérant, e [ɛ̃tɑ̃peʀɑ̃, ɑ̃t] adj (*immodéré*) intemperate; (*sensuel*) overindulgent, intemperate.
intempéries [ɛ̃tɑ̃peʀi] nfpl bad weather. **nous allons affronter les ~** we're going to brave the (bad) weather.
intempestif, -ive [ɛ̃tɑ̃pɛstif, iv] adj untimely. **pas de zèle ~!** no misplaced *ou* excessive zeal!
intempestivement [ɛ̃tɑ̃pɛstivmɑ̃] adv at an untimely moment.
intemporalité [ɛ̃tɑ̃pɔʀalite] nf (*voir* **intemporel**) timelessness; immateriality.
intemporel, -elle [ɛ̃tɑ̃pɔʀɛl] adj (*littér*) (*sans durée*) timeless; (*immatériel*) immaterial.
intenable [ɛ̃t(ə)nabl] adj (*intolérable*) *chaleur, situation* intolerable, unbearable; *personne* unruly; (*indéfendable*) *position, théorie* untenable.
intendance [ɛ̃tɑ̃dɑ̃s] nf (*Mil*) (*service*) Supply Corps; (*bureau*) Supplies office; (*Scol*) (*métier*) school management, financial administration; (*bureau*) bursar's office; *[propriété]* (*métier*) estate management; (*bureau*) estate office; (*Hist: province*) intendancy. **les problèmes d'~** (*Mil*) the problems of supply; (*gén*) the day-to-day problems of running a school (*ou* a company *etc*).
intendant [ɛ̃tɑ̃dɑ̃] nm (*Mil*) quartermaster; (*Scol*) bursar; (*Hist*) intendant; (*régisseur*) steward.
intendante [ɛ̃tɑ̃dɑ̃t] nf a (*épouse*) intendant's wife. b (*Scol*) bursar; (*régisseur*) stewardess. c (*Rel*) Superior.
intense [ɛ̃tɑ̃s] adj *lumière, moment etc* intense; *froid, douleur* severe, intense; *circulation* dense, heavy.
intensément [ɛ̃tɑ̃semɑ̃] adv intensely.
intensif, -ive [ɛ̃tɑ̃sif, iv] 1 adj (*gén, Agr, Ling*) intensive; *voir* **cours, culture.** 2 nm (*Ling*) intensive.
intensification [ɛ̃tɑ̃sifikasjɔ̃] nf intensification.
intensifier vt, **s'intensifier** vpr [ɛ̃tɑ̃sifje] 7 to intensify.
intensité [ɛ̃tɑ̃site] nf a (*force: voir* **intense**) intensity; severity; density, heaviness. **l'~ de la lumière me força à fermer les yeux** the intensity of the light forced me to shut my eyes; **mesurer l'~ d'une source lumineuse** to measure the intensity of a light source; **moment d'une grande ~** moment of great intensity *ou* feeling. b (*Ling*) **accent d'~** stress accent.
intensivement [ɛ̃tɑ̃sivmɑ̃] adv intensively.
intenter [ɛ̃tɑ̃te] 1 vt: **~ un procès contre** *ou* **à qn** to start *ou* institute proceedings against sb; **~ une action contre** *ou* **à qn** to bring an action against sb.
intention [ɛ̃tɑ̃sjɔ̃] nf a intention. **agir dans une bonne ~** to act with good intentions; **elle l'a fait sans mauvaise ~** she didn't mean any harm; **c'est l'~ qui compte** it's the thought that counts; **il n'entre** *ou* **n'est pas dans ses ~s de démissionner** it's not his intention to resign, he has no intention of resigning; **à cette ~** with this intention, to this end; **avoir l'~ de faire** to intend *ou* mean to do, have the intention of doing; **je n'ai pas l'~ de le faire** I don't intend to do it, I have no intention of doing it; **avec** *ou* **dans l'~ de faire** with the intention of doing, with a view to doing; **avec** *ou* **dans l'~ de tuer** with intent to kill; *voir* **enfer, procès.**
b **à l'~ de qn** *collecte* for the benefit of sb, in aid of sb; *renseignement* for the benefit of sb, for the information of sb; *cadeau, prières, messe* for sb; *fête* in sb's honour; **livre/film à l'~ des enfants/du grand public** book/film aimed at children/the general public; **je l'ai acheté à votre ~** I bought it just *ou* specially for you.
intentionné, e [ɛ̃tɑ̃sjɔne] adj: **bien ~** well-meaning, well-intentioned; **mal ~** ill-intentioned.
intentionnel, -elle [ɛ̃tɑ̃sjɔnɛl] adj intentional, deliberate.
intentionnellement [ɛ̃tɑ̃sjɔnɛlmɑ̃] adv intentionally, deliberately.
inter [ɛ̃tɛʀ] nm (†: *Téléc*) = **interurbain.** (*Sport*) **~ gauche/droit** inside-left/-right.
inter... [ɛ̃tɛʀ] préf inter... .
interactif, -ive [ɛ̃tɛʀaktif, iv] adj interactive.
interaction [ɛ̃tɛʀaksjɔ̃] nf interaction (*entre* between).
interactivement [ɛ̃tɛʀaktivmɑ̃] adv (*gén, Ordin*) interactively.
interactivité [ɛ̃tɛʀaktivite] nf interactivity.
interallié, e [ɛ̃tɛʀalje] adj inter-Allied.
interarmes [ɛ̃tɛʀaʀm] adj inv *opération* combined arms (*épith*), interservice (*épith*).
interbancaire [ɛ̃tɛʀbɑ̃kɛʀ] adj *relations, marché* interbank.
intercalaire [ɛ̃tɛʀkalɛʀ] adj: **feuillet ~** inset, insert; **fiche ~** divider; **jour ~** intercalary day.
intercalation [ɛ̃tɛʀkalasjɔ̃] nf (*voir* **intercaler**) insertion; interpolation; intercalation.
intercaler [ɛ̃tɛʀkale] 1 1 vt *mot, exemple* to insert, interpolate; *feuillet* to inset, insert; *jour d'année bissextile* to intercalate. **~ quelques jours de repos dans un mois de stage** to fit a few days' rest into a month of training; **on a intercalé dans le stage des visites d'usines** the training course was interspersed with *ou* broken by visits to factories.
2 **s'intercaler** vpr: **s'~ entre** *[coureur, voiture, candidat]* to come in between.
intercéder [ɛ̃tɛʀsede] 6 vi to intercede (*en faveur de* on behalf of; *auprès de* with).
intercellulaire [ɛ̃tɛʀselylɛʀ] adj intercellular.
intercensitaire [ɛ̃tɛʀsɑ̃sitɛʀ] adj intercensal.
intercepter [ɛ̃tɛʀsɛpte] 1 vt *ballon, message, ennemi* to intercept; *lumière, chaleur* to cut *ou* block off.
intercepteur [ɛ̃tɛʀsɛptœʀ] nm interceptor (plane).
interception [ɛ̃tɛʀsɛpsjɔ̃] nf (*voir* **intercepter**) interception; cutting *ou* blocking off. (*Mil*) **avion** *ou* **chasseur d'~** interceptor(-plane).
intercesseur [ɛ̃tɛʀsesœʀ] nm (*Rel, littér*) intercessor.
intercession [ɛ̃tɛʀsesjɔ̃] nf (*Rel, littér*) intercession.
interchangeabilité [ɛ̃tɛʀʃɑ̃ʒabilite] nf interchangeability.
interchangeable [ɛ̃tɛʀʃɑ̃ʒabl] adj interchangeable.
interclasse [ɛ̃tɛʀklɑs] nm (*Scol*) break (*between classes*).
interclubs [ɛ̃tɛʀklœb] adj inv *tournoi, rencontre* interclub.
intercommunal, e, mpl **-aux** [ɛ̃tɛʀkɔmynal, o] adj *décision, stade* ≃ intervillage, ≃ intermunicipal (*shared by several French communes*).

intercommunication [ɛ̃tɛʀkɔmynikasjɔ̃] nf intercommunication.
interconnecter [ɛ̃tɛʀkɔnɛkte] [1] vt (*Élec*) to interconnect.
interconnexion [ɛ̃tɛʀkɔnɛksjɔ̃] nf interconnection.
intercontinental, e, mpl **-aux** [ɛ̃tɛʀkɔ̃tinɑ̃tal, o] adj intercontinental.
intercostal, e, mpl **-aux** [ɛ̃tɛʀkɔstal, o] 1 adj intercostal. 2 nmpl intercostal muscles, intercostals.
intercours [ɛ̃tɛʀkuʀ] nm (*Scol*) break (*between classes*).
interdépartemental, e, mpl **-aux** [ɛ̃tɛʀdepaʀtəmɑ̃tal, o] adj *shared by several French departments.*
interdépendance [ɛ̃tɛʀdepɑ̃dɑ̃s] nf interdependence.
interdépendant, e [ɛ̃tɛʀdepɑ̃dɑ̃, ɑ̃t] adj interdependent.
interdiction [ɛ̃tɛʀdiksjɔ̃] nf a ~ **de** banning of, ban on; **l'~ du col roulé/des cheveux longs dans cette profession** the ban on polo necks/long hair in this profession; **l'~ de coller des affiches/de servir de l'alcool** the ban on the posting of bills/the serving of alcohol, the ban on posting bills/serving alcohol; **"~ de coller des affiches"** "(stick *ou* post) no bills", "bill-sticking (*Brit*) *ou* bill-posting prohibited"; **"~ (formelle *ou* absolue) de fumer"** "(strictly) no smoking", "smoking (strictly) prohibited"; **"~ de tourner à droite"** "no right turn"; **~ d'en parler à quiconque/de modifier quoi que ce soit** it is (strictly) forbidden to talk to anyone/to alter anything; **malgré l'~ d'entrer** despite the fact that it was forbidden to enter *ou* that there was a "no entry" sign; **renouveler à qn l'~ de faire** to reimpose a ban on sb's doing; **~ lui a été faite de sortir** he has been forbidden to go out; **l'~ faite aux fonctionnaires de cumuler plusieurs emplois** the banning of civil servants from holding several positions.
b (*interdit*) ban. **enfreindre/lever une ~** to break/lift a ban; **écriteau portant une ~** notice prohibiting *ou* forbidding something; **un jardin public plein d'~s** a park full of notices *ou* signs forbidding this and that.
c (*suspension*) *[livre, film]* banning (*de* of), ban (*de* on); *[fonctionnaire]* banning from office; *[prêtre]* interdiction. (*Jur*) **~ légale** *suspension of a convict's civic rights;* **~ de séjour** *order denying former prisoner access to specified places.*
interdigital, e, mpl **-aux** [ɛ̃tɛʀdiʒital, o] adj interdigital.
interdire [ɛ̃tɛʀdiʀ] [37] 1 vt a (*prohiber*) to forbid; (*Admin*) *stationnement, circulation* to prohibit, ban. **~ l'alcool/le tabac à qn** to forbid sb alcohol/tobacco, forbid sb to drink/smoke; **~ à qn de faire qch** to tell sb not to do sth, forbid sb to do sth, prohibit (*frm*) sb from doing sth; **elle nous a interdit d'y aller seuls, elle a interdit que nous y allions seuls** she forbade us to go on our own; **on a interdit les camions dans le centre de la ville** lorries have been barred from *ou* banned from *ou* prohibited in the centre of the town.
b (*empêcher*) *[contretemps, difficulté]* to preclude, prevent; *[obstacle physique]* to block. **son état de santé lui interdit tout travail/effort** his state of health does not allow *ou* permit him to do any work/to make any effort; **sa maladie ne lui interdit pas le travail** his illness does not prevent him from working; **la gravité de la crise (nous) interdit tout espoir** the gravity of the crisis leaves us no hope, the gravity of the crisis precludes all hope; **leur attitude interdit toute négociation** their attitude precludes *ou* prevents any possibility of negotiation; **une porte blindée interdisait le passage** an armoured door blocked *ou* barred the way.
c (*frapper d'interdiction*) *fonctionnaire, prêtre* to ban from office; *film, réunion, journal* to ban. (*fig*) **on lui a interdit le club** he has been barred *ou* banned from the club; **~ sa porte aux intrus** to bar one's door to intruders.
2 **s'interdire** vpr: **s'~ toute remarque** to refrain *ou* abstain from making any remark; **nous nous sommes interdit d'intervenir** we have not allowed ourselves to intervene, we have refrained from intervening; **s'~ la boisson/les cigarettes** to abstain from drink *ou* drinking/smoking; **il s'interdit d'y penser** he doesn't let himself think about it *ou* allow himself to think about it; **il s'est interdit toute possibilité de revenir en arrière** he has (deliberately) denied himself *ou* not allowed himself any chance of going back on his decision.
interdisciplinaire [ɛ̃tɛʀdisiplinɛʀ] adj interdisciplinary.
interdisciplinarité [ɛ̃tɛʀdisiplinaʀite] nf interdisciplinarity.
interdit, e[1] [ɛ̃tɛʀdi, it] (ptp de **interdire**) 1 adj *film, livre* banned. **film ~ aux moins de dix-huit ans** ≃ X film†, ≃ 18 film (*Brit*); **film ~ aux moins de treize ans** ≃ A film†, ≃ PG film (*Brit*); **passage/stationnement ~** no entry/parking; **il est strictement ~ de faire** it is strictly forbidden *ou* prohibited to do; **(il est) ~ de fumer** no smoking, smoking (is) prohibited; **être ~ de chéquier** to have chequebook facilities withdrawn; (*Aviat*) **~ de vol** grounded; (*Comm*) **~ de vente** banned; *voir* **reproduction.** 2 nm,f adj: **~ de séjour** *person under interdiction de séjour.* 3 nm (*interdiction*) (*Rel*) interdict; (*social*) prohibition. (*fig*) **jeter l'~ sur *ou* contre qn** to bar sb.
interdit, e[2] [ɛ̃tɛʀdi, it] adj dumbfounded, taken aback (*attrib*), disconcerted. **la réponse le laissa ~** the answer took him aback, he was dumbfounded *ou* disconcerted by *ou* at the answer.
intéressant, e [ɛ̃teʀesɑ̃, ɑ̃t] adj a (*captivant*) *livre, détail, visage* interesting. **peu ~** (*ennuyeux*) *conférencier* uninteresting, dull; (*négligeable*) *personne* not worth bothering about (*attrib*); (*péj*) **un personnage peu ~** a worthless individual, an individual of little consequence; (*péj*) **il faut toujours qu'il cherche à se rendre ~ *ou* qu'il fasse son ~** he always has to be the centre of attraction *ou* focus of attention; *voir* **position.**
b (*avantageux*) *offre, affaire* attractive, worthwhile; *prix* favourable, attractive. **ce n'est pas très ~ pour nous** it's not really worth our while, it's not really worth it for us; **c'est une personne ~e à connaître** he's someone worth knowing.
intéressé, e [ɛ̃teʀese] (ptp de **intéresser**) adj a (*qui est en cause*) concerned, involved. **les ~s, les parties ~es** the interested parties, the parties involved *ou* concerned; **dans cette affaire, c'est lui le principal ~** in this matter, he is the person *ou* party principally involved *ou* concerned. b (*qui cherche son intérêt personnel*) *personne* self-seeking, self-interested; *motif* interested. **une visite ~e** a visit motivated by self-interest; **rendre un service ~** to do a good turn out of self-interest; **ce que je vous propose, c'est très ~** my suggestion to you is strongly motivated by self-interest.
intéressement [ɛ̃teʀɛsmɑ̃] nm (*Écon: système*) profit-sharing (scheme). **l'~ des travailleurs aux bénéfices de l'entreprise** (*action*) the workers' participation in *ou* sharing of the firm's profits.
intéresser [ɛ̃teʀese] [1] 1 vt a (*captiver*) to interest. **~ qn à qch** to interest sb in sth; **cela m'intéresserait de faire** I would be interested to do *ou* in doing, it would interest me to do; **ça ne m'intéresse pas** I'm not interested, it doesn't interest me; **rien ne l'intéresse** he is not interested *ou* takes no interest in anything; **le film l'a intéressé** he found the film interesting, the film interested him; **ça pourrait vous ~** this might interest you *ou* be of interest to you; **cette question n'intéresse pas (beaucoup) les jeunes** this matter is of no (great) interest to *ou* doesn't (greatly) interest young people; **il ne sait pas ~ son public** he doesn't know how to interest his audience; (*iro*) **continue, tu m'intéresses!** do go on – I find that very interesting *ou* I'm all ears!*
b (*concerner*) to affect, concern. **la nouvelle loi intéresse les petits commerçants** the new law affects *ou* concerns the small shopkeeper (*Brit*) *ou* merchant.
c (*Comm, Fin*) **~ le personnel de l'usine aux bénéfices** to give the factory employees a share *ou* an interest in the profits, operate a profit-sharing scheme in the factory; **être intéressé dans une affaire** to have a stake *ou* a financial interest in a business.
2 **s'intéresser** vpr: **s'~ à qch/qn** to be interested in sth/sb, take an interest in sth/sb; **il s'intéresse vivement/activement à cette affaire** he is taking a keen/an active interest in this matter; **il ne s'intéresse pas à nos activités** he is not interested in our activities, he doesn't concern himself with our activities; **il mérite qu'on s'intéresse à lui** he deserves one's *ou* people's interest; **il s'intéresse beaucoup à cette jeune fille** he is very interested in *ou* he is taking *ou* showing a great deal of interest in that girl.
intérêt [ɛ̃teʀɛ] nm a (*attention*) interest. **écouter avec ~/(un) grand ~** to listen with interest/with great interest; **prendre ~ à qch** to take an interest in sth; **il a perdu tout ~ à son travail** he has lost all interest in his work.
b (*bienveillance*) interest. **porter/témoigner de l'~ à qn** to take/show an interest in sb.
c (*originalité*) interest. **film dénué d'~ *ou* sans aucun ~** film devoid of interest; **tout l'~ réside dans le dénouement** the interest is all in the ending.
d (*importance*) significance, importance, relevance. **l'~ des recherches spatiales** the significance *ou* importance *ou* relevance of space research; **après quelques considérations sans ~** after a few unimportant *ou* minor considerations *ou* considerations of minor interest *ou* importance; **c'est sans ~ pour la suite de l'histoire** it's of no relevance *ou* consequence *ou* importance for the rest of the story; **une découverte du plus haut ~** a discovery of the greatest *ou* utmost importance *ou* significance *ou* relevance; **la nouvelle a perdu beaucoup de son ~** the news has lost much of its significance *ou* interest; **être déclaré d'~ public** to be officially recognized as of benefit to the country, be officially declared a national asset.
e (*avantage*) interest. **ce n'est pas (dans) leur ~ de le faire** it is not in their interest to do it; **agir dans/contre son ~** to act in/against one's own interests; **dans l'~ général** in the general interest; **il y trouve son ~** he finds it to his (own) advantage, he finds it worth his while; **il sait où est son ~** he knows where his interest lies, he knows which side his bread is buttered; **avoir tout ~ à faire qch** to be well advised to do sth; **il a (tout) ~ à accepter** it's in his interest to accept, he'd be well advised to accept, he'd do well to accept; **tu aurais plutôt ~ à te taire!*** you'd be well advised *ou* you'd do very well to keep quiet!; **y a-t-il (un) ~ quelconque à se réunir?** is there any point at all in getting together?
f (*Fin*) interest. **7% d'~** 7% interest; **prêt à ~ élevé** high-interest loan; **prêter à *ou* avec ~** to lend at *ou* with interest; **~s simples/composés** simple/compound interest; **~s courus** accrued interest; *voir* **taux.**
g (*recherche d'avantage personnel*) self-interest. **agir par ~** to act out of self-interest; *voir* **mariage.**
h **~s** interest(s); **la défense de nos ~s** the defence of our interests; (*Écon, Fin*) **il a des ~s dans l'affaire** he has a stake *ou* an interest *ou* a financial interest in the deal.
interface [ɛ̃tɛʀfas] nf interface. **~ utilisateur** user interface.

interfacer vt, **s'interfacer** vpr [ɛ̃tɛʀfase] 3 to interface (*avec* with).

interférence [ɛ̃tɛʀfeʀɑ̃s] nf (*Phys*) interference; (*fig*) (*conjonction*) conjunction; (*immixtion*) *[problème]* intrusion (*dans* into); *[personne, pays]* interference (*NonC*) (*dans* in). **l'~ des problèmes économiques et politiques** the conjunction of economic and political problems; **l'~ des problèmes économiques dans la vie politique** the intrusion of economic problems into political life; **il se produit des ~s entre les deux services gouvernementaux** there's interference between the two government services.

interférent, e [ɛ̃tɛʀfeʀɑ̃, ɑ̃t] adj (*Phys*) interfering.

interférer [ɛ̃tɛʀfeʀe] 6 vi to interfere (*avec* with; *dans* in). **les deux procédures interfèrent** the two procedures interfere with each other.

interféron [ɛ̃tɛʀfeʀɔ̃] nm interferon. **~ humain** human interferon.

interfluve [ɛ̃tɛʀflyv] nm interfluve.

intergalactique [ɛ̃tɛʀgalaktik] adj intergalactic.

intergouvernemental, e, mpl **-aux** [ɛ̃tɛʀguvɛʀnəmɑ̃tal, o] adj intergovernmental. (*Québec*) **Affaires ~es** Intergovernmental Affairs.

intérieur, e [ɛ̃teʀjœʀ] 1 adj *paroi, escalier* inner, interior, inside; *cour* inner; (*fig*) *vie, monde, voix* inner; *sentiment* inner, inward; (*Écon, Pol*) *politique, dette* domestic, internal; *marché* home (*épith*), domestic, internal; (*Transport*) *communication, réseau, navigation* inland; (*Aviat*) *vol* domestic. **le commerce ~** domestic trade; **mer ~e** inland sea; **la poche ~e de son manteau** the inside pocket of his coat; (*Géom*) **angle/point ~ à un cercle** angle/point interior to a circle; *voir* **conduite, for.**

2 nm a *[tiroir, piste, champ de course]* inside; *[maison]* inside, interior. **l'~ de la maison était lugubre** the house was gloomy inside, the inside *ou* the interior of the house was gloomy; **l'~ de la ville** the inner town; **écrin avec un ~ de satin** case with a satin lining; **fermé de l'~** locked from the inside; **à l'~** (*lit*) inside; (*fig*) within; **je vous attends à l'~** I'll wait for you inside; **à l'~ de la ville** inside the town; **à l'~ de l'entreprise** (*promotion, corruption*) within the company; *stage, formation* in-house; (*fig*) **à l'~ de lui-même, il pensait que** he thought inwardly *ou* within himself that; **rester à l'~** (*gén*) to stay inside; (*de la maison*) to stay inside *ou* indoors; **vêtement/veste d'~** indoor garment/jacket; **chaussures d'~** indoor *ou* house shoes; *voir* **femme.**

b *[pays]* interior. **l'~ (du pays) est montagneux** the interior (of the country) is mountainous, the inland part of the country is mountainous; **les villes de l'~** the inland cities *ou* towns, the cities *ou* towns of the interior; **la côte est riante mais l'~ est sauvage** the coast is pleasant, but it's wild further inland *ou* the hinterland is wild; **en allant vers l'~** going inland; **les ennemis de l'~** the enemies within (the country); (*Mil*) **le moral de l'~** the morale at home, the country's morale, the morale within the country; **à l'~ de nos frontières** within *ou* inside our frontiers; *voir* **ministère, ministre.**

c (*décor, mobilier*) interior. **un ~ bourgeois/douillet** a comfortable middle-class/cosy interior.

d (*Ftbl*) **~ gauche/droit** inside-left/-right.

intérieurement [ɛ̃teʀjœʀmɑ̃] adv inwardly. **rire ~** to laugh inwardly *ou* to o.s.

intérim [ɛ̃teʀim] nm a (*période*) interim period. **il prendra toutes les décisions dans** *ou* **pendant l'~** he will make all the decisions in the interim; **il assure l'~ en l'absence du directeur** he deputizes for the manager in his absence *ou* in the interim; **diriger une firme par ~** to run a firm temporarily *ou* in a temporary capacity; **président/ministre par ~** acting *ou* interim president *ou* chairman/minister. b (*travail à temps partiel*) temporary work, temping. **société d'~** temping agency, temporary employment office (*US*); **faire de l'~** to temp.

intérimaire [ɛ̃teʀimɛʀ] 1 adj *directeur, ministre* acting (*épith*), interim (*épith*); *secrétaire, personnel, fonctions* temporary; *mesure, solution* interim (*épith*), temporary; (*Pol*) *gouvernement, chef de parti* caretaker (*épith*). 2 nmf (*secrétaire*) temporary secretary, temp (*Brit*), Kelly girl (*US*); (*fonctionnaire*) deputy; (*médecin, prêtre*) locum (tenens). **travailler comme ~** to temp.

interindividuel, -elle [ɛ̃tɛʀɛ̃dividɥɛl] adj interpersonal. **psychologie ~le** psychology of interpersonal relationships.

intériorisation [ɛ̃teʀjɔʀizasjɔ̃] nf (*voir* **intérioriser**) internalization; interiorization.

intérioriser [ɛ̃teʀjɔʀize] 1 vt *conflit, émotion* to internalize, interiorize; (*Ling*) *règles* to internalize.

intériorité [ɛ̃teʀjɔʀite] nf interiority.

interjectif, -ive [ɛ̃tɛʀʒɛktif, iv] adj interjectional.

interjection [ɛ̃tɛʀʒɛksjɔ̃] nf (*Ling*) interjection; (*Jur*) lodging of an appeal.

interjeter [ɛ̃tɛʀʒəte] 4 vt (*Jur*) **~ appel** to lodge an appeal.

interlignage [ɛ̃tɛʀliɲaʒ] nm (*Typ*) interline spacing.

interligne [ɛ̃tɛʀliɲ] 1 nm (*espace*) space between the lines; (*annotation*) insertion between the lines. **double ~** double spacing; **écrire qch dans l'~** to write *ou* insert sth between the lines *ou* in the space between the lines; **taper un texte en double ~** to type a text in double spacing. 2 nf (*Typ*) lead.

interligner [ɛ̃tɛʀliɲe] 1 vt (*espacer*) to space; (*inscrire*) to write between the lines.

interlocuteur, -trice [ɛ̃tɛʀlɔkytœʀ, tʀis] nm,f speaker, interlocutor (*frm*). **son/mon ~** the person he/I was speaking to; (*Pol*) **~ valable** valid negotiator *ou* representative; **les syndicats sont les ~s privilégiés d'un gouvernement de gauche** the unions have a privileged relationship with *ou* tend to have the ear of a left-wing government.

interlope [ɛ̃tɛʀlɔp] adj a (*équivoque*) shady. b (*illégal*) illicit, unlawful. **navire ~** *ship carrying illicit merchandise.*

interloquer [ɛ̃tɛʀlɔke] 1 vt to take aback.

interlude [ɛ̃tɛʀlyd] nm (*Mus, TV*) interlude.

intermariage [ɛ̃tɛʀmaʀjaʒ] nm intermarriage.

intermède [ɛ̃tɛʀmɛd] nm (*Théât, interruption*) interlude.

intermédiaire [ɛ̃tɛʀmedjɛʀ] 1 adj *niveau, choix, position* intermediate, middle (*épith*), intermediary. **une solution/couleur ~ entre** a solution/colour halfway between; **une date ~ entre le 25 juillet et le 3 août** a date midway between 25th July and 3rd August. 2 nm: **sans ~** *vendre, négocier* directly; **par l'~ de qn** through (the intermediary *ou* agency of) sb; **par l'~ de la presse** through the medium of the press. 3 nmf (*médiateur*) intermediary, mediator, go-between; (*Comm, Écon*) middleman.

intermezzo [ɛ̃tɛʀmɛdzo] nm intermezzo.

interminable [ɛ̃tɛʀminabl] adj *conversation, série* endless, interminable, never-ending; (*hum*) *jambes, mains* extremely long.

interminablement [ɛ̃tɛʀminabləmɑ̃] adv endlessly, interminably.

interministériel, -elle [ɛ̃tɛʀministeʀjɛl] adj interdepartmental.

intermission [ɛ̃tɛʀmisjɔ̃] nf (*Méd*) intermission.

intermittence [ɛ̃tɛʀmitɑ̃s] nf a **par ~** *travailler* in fits and starts, sporadically, intermittently; *pleuvoir* on and off, sporadically, intermittently; **le bruit nous parvenait par ~** the noise reached our ears at (sporadic) intervals. b (*Méd*) (*entre deux accès*) remission; *[pouls, cœur]* irregularity. c (*littér*) intermittence, intermittency.

intermittent, e [ɛ̃tɛʀmitɑ̃, ɑ̃t] adj *fièvre, lumière* intermittent; *douleur* sporadic, intermittent; *travail, bruit* sporadic, periodic; *pouls* irregular, intermittent. **pluies ~es sur le nord** scattered showers in the north.

intermoléculaire [ɛ̃tɛʀmɔlekylɛʀ] adj intermolecular.

intermusculaire [ɛ̃tɛʀmyskylɛʀ] adj intermuscular.

internat [ɛ̃tɛʀna] nm a (*Scol*) (*établissement*) boarding school; (*système*) boarding; (*élèves*) boarders; *voir* **maître.** b (*Méd*) (*concours*) entrance examination (for hospital work); (*stage*) hospital training (*as a doctor*), period *or* time as a houseman (*Brit*) *or* an intern (*US*), internship (*US*).

international, e, mpl **-aux** [ɛ̃tɛʀnasjɔnal, o] 1 adj international. 2 nm,f (*Ftbl, Tennis etc*) international player; (*Athlétisme*) international athlete. 3 **Internationale** nf (*association*) International; (*hymne*) Internationale.

internationalement [ɛ̃tɛʀnasjɔnalmɑ̃] adv internationally.

internationalisation [ɛ̃tɛʀnasjɔnalizasjɔ̃] nf internationalization.

internationaliser [ɛ̃tɛʀnasjɔnalize] 1 vt to internationalize.

internationalisme [ɛ̃tɛʀnasjɔnalism] nm internationalism.

internationaliste [ɛ̃tɛʀnasjɔnalist] nmf internationalist.

internationalité [ɛ̃tɛʀnasjɔnalite] nf internationality.

interne [ɛ̃tɛʀn] 1 adj *partie, politique, organe, hémorragie* internal; *oreille* inner; *angle* interior. **médecine ~** internal medicine. 2 nmf a (*Scol*) boarder. **être ~** to be at boarding school. b (*Méd*) **~ (des hôpitaux)** house doctor (*Brit*), houseman (*Brit*), intern (*US*); **~ en médecine/chirurgie** house physician/surgeon. c **en ~: travail réalisé en ~** work carried out in-house.

interné, e [ɛ̃tɛʀne] (ptp de **interner**) nm,f (*Pol*) internee; (*Méd*) inmate (of a mental hospital).

internement [ɛ̃tɛʀnəmɑ̃] nm (*Pol*) internment; (*Méd*) confinement (to a mental hospital).

interner [ɛ̃tɛʀne] 1 vt (*Pol*) to intern. (*Méd*) **~ qn (dans un hôpital psychiatrique)** to confine sb to a mental hospital, institutionalize sb (*US*); **on devrait l'~** he ought to be locked up *or* certified* (*Brit*), he should be put away* (*Brit*).

interocéanique [ɛ̃tɛʀɔseanik] adj interoceanic.

interosseux, -euse [ɛ̃tɛʀɔsø, øz] adj interosseous.

interparlementaire [ɛ̃tɛʀpaʀləmɑ̃tɛʀ] adj interparliamentary.

interpellateur, -trice [ɛ̃tɛʀpelatœʀ, tʀis] nm,f (*voir* **interpeller**) interpellator; questioner; heckler.

interpellation [ɛ̃tɛʀpelasjɔ̃] nf (*voir* **interpeller**) hailing (*NonC*); interpellation; questioning (*NonC*); heckling (*NonC*). (*Police*) **il y a eu une dizaine d'~s** about ten people were detained *or* taken in for questioning.

interpeller [ɛ̃tɛʀpəle] 1 vt a (*appeler*) to call out to, shout out to, hail; (*apostropher*) to shout at; (*à la Chambre*) to interpellate, question; (*dans une réunion*) to question; (*avec insistance*) to heckle; (*Police*) to question. **les automobilistes se sont interpellés grossièrement** the motorists shouted insults at each other. b (**: concerner*) *[problème, situation]* to concern, be of concern to. c (**: plaire à*) *[chose, idée]* to appeal to.

interpénétration [ɛ̃tɛʀpenetʀasjɔ̃] nf interpenetration.

interpénétrer (s') [ɛ̃tɛʀpenetʀe] 6 vpr to interpenetrate.

interphone [ɛ̃tɛʀfɔn] nm intercom, interphone; *[immeuble]* entry phone.

interplanétaire [ɛ̃tɛʀplanetɛʀ] adj interplanetary.

Interpol [ɛ̃tɛʀpɔl] nm (abrév de **International Criminal Police Organization**) Interpol.

interpolation [ɛ̃tɛʀpɔlasjɔ̃] **nf** interpolation.

interpoler [ɛ̃tɛʀpɔle] [1] **vt** to interpolate.

interposé, e [ɛ̃tɛʀpoze] (**ptp de interposer**) **adj: par personne ~e** through an intermediary *or* a third party; **par service ~** through another department.

interposer [ɛ̃tɛʀpoze] [1] **1 vt** (*lit, fig*) to interpose (*entre* between). **2 s'interposer vpr** to intervene, interpose o.s. (*frm*) (*dans* in). **elle s'interposa entre le père et le fils** she intervened *or* came between *ou* interposed herself (*frm*) between father and son.

interposition [ɛ̃tɛʀpozisjɔ̃] **nf** (*voir* **interposer**) interposition; intervention; (*Jur*) fraudulent representation of one's identity (*by use of a third party's identity*).

interprétable [ɛ̃tɛʀpʀetabl] **adj** interpretable.

interprétariat [ɛ̃tɛʀpʀetaʀja] **nm** interpreting. **école d'~** interpreting school.

interprétation [ɛ̃tɛʀpʀetasjɔ̃] **nf** (*voir* **interpréter**) rendering, interpretation. **donner de qch une ~ fausse** to give a false interpretation of sth, misinterpret sth; **l'~ des rêves** the interpretation of dreams; **c'est une erreur d'~** it's a mistake in interpretation; **~ simultanée** simultaneous translation; *voir* **prix**.

interprète [ɛ̃tɛʀpʀɛt] **nmf a** (*Mus, Théât*) performer, interpreter; (*gén*) player (*ou* singer *etc*). (*Théât*) **les ~s par ordre d'entrée en scène ...** the cast in order of appearance ...; **un ~ de Molière/Bach** a performer *ou* an interpreter of Molière/Bach; **un ~ de Macbeth** a performer *ou* an interpreter of Macbeth, a Macbeth; **Paul était l'~ de cette sonate** Paul played this sonata; **Paul était l'~ de cette chanson** Paul was the singer of *ou* sang this song.
b (*traducteur*) interpreter. **~ de conférence** conference interpreter; **faire l'~, servir d'~** to act as an interpreter.
c (*porte-parole*) **servir d'~ à qn/aux idées de qn** to act *ou* serve as a spokesman for sb/for sb's ideas; **je me ferai votre ~ auprès du ministre** I'll speak to the minister on your behalf; (*fig*) **les gestes et les yeux sont les ~s de la pensée** gestures and the look in one's eyes express *ou* interpret one's thoughts.
d (*exégète*) *[texte]* interpreter, exponent; *[rêves, signes]* interpreter.

interpréter [ɛ̃tɛʀpʀete] [6] **vt a** (*Mus, Théât*) to perform, interpret. **il va (vous) ~ Hamlet/une sonate** he's going to play Hamlet/a sonata (for you); **il va (vous) ~ une chanson** he's going to sing (you) a song. **b** (*comprendre*) to interpret. **comment ~ son silence?** what does his silence mean?; **il a mal interprété mes paroles** he misinterpreted my words; **~ qch en bien/mal** to take sth the right/wrong way; **son attitude peut s'~ de plusieurs façons** there are several ways of interpreting his attitude.

interpréteur [ɛ̃tɛʀpʀetœʀ] **nm** (*Ordin*) interpreter.

interprofessionnel, -elle [ɛ̃tɛʀpʀɔfesjɔnɛl] **adj** *réunion* interprofessional; *voir* **salaire**.

interrègne [ɛ̃tɛʀʀɛɲ] **nm** interregnum.

interrogateur, -trice [ɛ̃teʀɔgatœʀ, tʀis] **1 adj** *air, regard, ton* questioning (*épith*), inquiring (*épith*). **d'un air** *ou* **ton ~** questioningly, inquiringly. **2 nm,f** (oral) examiner. **3 nm** (*Téléc*) **~ à distance** remote control, remote interrogator.

interrogatif, -ive [ɛ̃teʀɔgatif, iv] **1 adj** *air, regard* questioning (*épith*), inquiring (*épith*); (*Ling*) interrogative. **2 nm** interrogative (word). **mettre à l'~** to put into the interrogative. **3 interrogative nf** interrogative clause.

interrogation [ɛ̃teʀɔgasjɔ̃] **nf a** (*voir* **interroger**) questioning; interrogation; examination; consultation; testing. (*Ordin, Téléc*) **système d'~ à distance** remote control system.
b (*question*) question. (*Scol*) **~ (écrite)** short (written) test (*Brit*), quiz (*US*); (*Scol*) **il y a 15 minutes d'~ (orale)** there's a 15-minute oral (test); (*Gram*) **~ directe/indirecte** direct/indirect question; **les sourcils levés, en signe d'~** his eyebrows raised questioningly *ou* inquiringly; **les yeux pleins d'une ~ muette** his eyes silently questioning; *voir* **point¹**.
c (*réflexions*) **~s** questioning; **ces ~s continuelles sur la destinée humaine** this continual questioning about human destiny.

interrogatoire [ɛ̃teʀɔgatwaʀ] **nm** (*Police*) questioning; (*au tribunal*) cross-examination, cross-questioning (*NonC*); (*compte rendu*) statement; (*fig: série de questions*) cross-examination, interrogation. **subir un ~ en règle** to undergo a thorough *ou* detailed interrogation.

interroger [ɛ̃teʀɔʒe] [3] **1 vt** (*gén*) to question; (*pour obtenir un renseignement*) to ask; (*Police*) to interview, question; (*de manière serrée, prolongée*) to interrogate (*sur* about); *ciel, conscience* to examine; *mémoire* to search; (*sondage*) to poll; (*Ordin*) *données* to interrogate. **~ un élève** to test *ou* examine a pupil (orally); **~ par écrit les élèves** to give a written test to the pupils; **~ qn du regard** to give sb a questioning *ou* an inquiring look, look questioningly *ou* inquiringly at sb; **elle a été interrogée sur un sujet difficile** she was examined *ou* questioned on a difficult subject; (*sondage*) **personne interrogée** respondent.
2 s'interroger vpr (*sur un problème*) to question o.s., wonder (*sur* about). **s'~ sur la conduite à tenir** to ponder over *ou* ask o.s. (about) *ou* wonder what course to follow.

interrompre [ɛ̃teʀɔ̃pʀ] [41] **1 vt a** (*arrêter*) *voyage, circuit électrique* to break, interrupt; *conversation* (*gén*) to interrupt, break off; (*pour s'interposer*) to break into, cut into; *études* to break off, interrupt; *émission* to interrupt; *négociations* to break off. **il a interrompu la conversation pour téléphoner** he broke off *ou* interrupted his conversation to telephone; **le match a été interrompu par la pluie** the match was stopped by rain; **sans ~ sa lecture** without looking up (from his *ou* her book *etc*); (*Méd*) **~ une grossesse** to terminate a pregnancy.
b (*couper la parole à, déranger*) **~ qn** to interrupt sb; **je ne veux pas qu'on m'interrompe (dans mon travail)** I don't want to be interrupted (in my work); **je ne veux pas ~ mais ...** I don't want to cut in *ou* interrupt but ... .
2 s'interrompre vpr *[personne, conversation]* to break off. (*TV*) **nos émissions s'interrompront à 23 h 50** we will be closing down (*Brit*) *ou* we will close our broadcasting day (*US*) at 11.50 pm.

interrupteur, -trice [ɛ̃teʀyptœʀ, tʀis] **1 nm** (*Élec*) switch. **2 nm,f** interrupter.

interruption [ɛ̃teʀypsjɔ̃] **nf** (*action*) interruption (*de* of); (*état*) break (*de* in), interruption (*de* of, in); (*Jur*) interruption of prescription. **une ~ de deux heures/trois mois** a break *ou* an interruption of two hours/three months; **~ (volontaire) de grossesse** termination (of pregnancy); **il y a eu une ~ de courant** there has been a power cut; **après l'~ des hostilités** after hostilities had ceased; **sans ~** *parler* without a break *ou* an interruption, uninterruptedly, continuously; *pleuvoir* without stopping, without a break, continuously; **un moment d'~** a moment's break.

intersaison [ɛ̃tɛʀsɛzɔ̃] **nf** (*Sport*) close season; (*Tourisme*) low season. **à** *ou* **pendant l'~** (*Sport*) during the close season; (*Tourisme*) out of season.

interscolaire [ɛ̃tɛʀskɔlɛʀ] **adj** inter-schools.

intersection [ɛ̃tɛʀsɛksjɔ̃] **nf** *[lignes]* intersection; *[routes]* intersection, junction; *voir* **point¹**.

intersession [ɛ̃tɛʀsesjɔ̃] **nf** (*Pol*) recess.

intersexualité [ɛ̃tɛʀsɛksɥalite] **nf** intersexuality.

intersexuel, -elle [ɛ̃tɛʀsɛksɥɛl] **adj** intersexual.

intersidéral, e, mpl -aux [ɛ̃tɛʀsideʀal, o] **adj** intersidereal.

interstellaire [ɛ̃tɛʀstelɛʀ] **adj** interstellar.

interstice [ɛ̃tɛʀstis] **nm** (*gén*) crack, chink, interstice; *[volet, cageot]* slit. **à travers les ~s des rideaux** through the chinks in the curtains.

intersubjectif, -ive [ɛ̃tɛʀsybʒɛktif, iv] **adj** intersubjective.

intersubjectivité [ɛ̃tɛʀsybʒɛktivite] **nf** intersubjectivity.

intersyndical, e, mpl -aux [ɛ̃tɛʀsɛ̃dikal, o] **adj** interunion.

intertitre [ɛ̃tɛʀtitʀ] **nm** (*Presse*) subheading; (*Ciné*) subtitle, title.

intertropical, e, mpl -aux [ɛ̃tɛʀtʀɔpikal, o] **adj** intertropical.

interurbain, e [ɛ̃teʀyʀbɛ̃, ɛn] **1 adj a** *relations* interurban. **b** (*Téléc*) *communication* trunk (*Brit, épith*), long-distance; *téléphone* long-distance (*épith*). **2 nm: l'~** the trunk call service (*Brit*), the long-distance telephone service.

intervalle [ɛ̃tɛʀval] **nm a** (*espace*) space, distance; (*entre 2 mots, 2 lignes*) space; (*temps*) interval; (*Mus*) interval. **b** (*loc*) **c'est arrivé à 2 jours/mois d'~** it happened after a space *ou* an interval of two days/months; **ils sont nés à 3 mois d'~** they were born 3 months apart; **à ~s réguliers/rapprochés** at regular/close intervals; **à ~s de 5 mètres** 5 metres apart; **par ~s** at intervals; **dans l'~** (*temporel*) in the meantime, meanwhile; (*spatial*) in between.

intervenant, e [ɛ̃tɛʀvənɑ̃, ɑ̃t] **nm,f** (*Jur*) intervener; (*conférencier*) contributor; (*Écon*) participant. **inviter un ~ extérieur** to invite an outside contributor.

intervenir [ɛ̃tɛʀvəniʀ] [22] **vi a** (*entrer en action*) to intervene; (*contribuer*) to play a part. (*dans une discussion*) **puis-je ~?** may I interrupt?, can I say something (here)?*; **il est intervenu en notre faveur** he interceded *ou* intervened on our behalf; **~ militairement dans un pays** to intervene militarily in the affairs of a country; **on a dû faire ~ l'armée** the army had to be brought in *ou* called in; **les pompiers n'ont pas pu ~** the firemen were unable to help.
b (*Méd*) to operate.
c (*survenir*) *[fait, événement]* to take place, occur; *[accord]* to be reached, be entered into; *[décision, mesure]* to be taken; *[élément nouveau]* to arise, come up. **cette mesure intervient au moment où ...** this measure is being taken *ou* comes at a time when ... .
d (*Jur*) to intervene.

intervention [ɛ̃tɛʀvɑ̃sjɔ̃] **nf** (*gén, Jur*) intervention; (*Méd*) operation; (*discours*) speech. **cela a nécessité l'~ de la police** the police had to be brought in, the police had to intervene; **son ~ en notre faveur** his intercession *ou* intervention on our behalf; **~ chirurgicale** surgical operation; **~ armée** armed intervention; **~ de l'État** state intervention; (*Écon*) **prix d'~** intervention price; **beurre d'~** (EEC) subsidized butter; *voir* **force**.

interventionnisme [ɛ̃tɛʀvɑ̃sjɔnism] **nm** interventionism.

interventionniste [ɛ̃tɛʀvɑ̃sjɔnist] **adj, nmf** interventionist.

interversion [ɛ̃tɛʀvɛʀsjɔ̃] **nf** inversion. **~ des rôles** reversal *ou* inversion of roles.

intervertir [ɛ̃tɛʀvɛʀtiʀ] [2] **vt** to invert *ou* reverse the order of, invert. **~ les rôles** to reverse *ou* invert roles.

interview [ɛ̃tɛʀvju] **nf** (*Presse, TV*) interview.

interviewé, e [ɛ̃tɛʀvjuve] (**ptp de interviewer**) **nm,f** (*Presse, TV*) interviewee.

interviewer¹ [ɛ̃tɛʀvjuve] [1] **vt** (*Presse, TV*) to interview.

interviewer² [ɛ̃tɛʀvjuvœʀ] **nmf** (*journaliste*) interviewer.

intervocalique [ɛ̃tɛʀvɔkalik] adj intervocalic.

intestat [ɛ̃tɛsta] 1 adj (*Jur*) **mourir ~** to die intestate. 2 nmpl intestates.

intestin[1] [ɛ̃tɛstɛ̃] nm intestine. **~s** intestines, bowels; **~ grêle** small intestine; **gros ~** large intestine.

intestin[2], **e** [ɛ̃tɛstɛ̃, in] adj (*fig*) *querelle, guerre* internal.

intestinal, e, mpl **-aux** [ɛ̃tɛstinal, o] adj intestinal; *voir* **grippe**.

intimation [ɛ̃timasjɔ̃] nf (*Jur*) (*assignation*) summons (*sg*) (*before an appeal court*); (*signification*) notification.

intime [ɛ̃tim] 1 adj a (*privé*) *hygiène* personal, intimate; *vie* private; *chagrin, confidences* intimate; *secret* close, intimate; *cérémonie, mariage* quiet; *salon, atmosphère* intimate, cosy. **carnet** *ou* **journal ~** intimate *ou* private diary; **un dîner ~** (*entre amis*) a dinner with (old) friends; (*entre amoureux*) a romantic dinner.

b (*étroit*) *mélange, relation, rapport* intimate; *union* close; *ami* close, intimate, bosom (*épith*). **être ~ avec qn** to be intimate with *ou* close to sb; **avoir des relations** *ou* **rapports ~s avec qn** to be on intimate terms with sb, have close relations with sb.

c (*profond*) *nature, structure* intimate, innermost; *sens, sentiment, conviction* inner(most), inmost, intimate.

2 nmf close friend. **seuls les ~s sont restés dîner** only those who were close friends stayed to dinner; (*hum*) **Jo pour les ~s*** Jo to his friends *ou* buddies* (*hum*).

intimé, e [ɛ̃time] (ptp de **intimer**) nm,f (*Jur*) respondent, appellee.

intimement [ɛ̃timmɑ̃] adv intimately. **~ persuadé** deeply *ou* firmly convinced.

intimer [ɛ̃time] [1] vt a **~ à qn (l'ordre) de faire** to order sb to do. b (*Jur*) (*assigner*) to summon (*before an appeal court*); (*signifier*) to notify.

intimidable [ɛ̃timidabl] adj easily intimidated.

intimidant, e [ɛ̃timidɑ̃, ɑ̃t] adj intimidating.

intimidateur, -trice [ɛ̃timidatœʀ, tʀis] adj intimidating.

intimidation [ɛ̃timidasjɔ̃] nf intimidation. **manœuvre/moyens d'~** device/means of intimidation; **on l'a fait parler en usant d'~** they scared *ou* frightened him into talking.

intimider [ɛ̃timide] [1] vt to intimidate. **ne te laisse pas ~ par lui** don't let him intimidate you, don't let yourself be intimidated by him.

intimisme [ɛ̃timism] nm (*Art, Littérat*) intimism.

intimiste [ɛ̃timist] adj, nmf (*Art, Littérat*) intimist.

intimité [ɛ̃timite] nf a (*vie privée*) privacy. **dans l'~ c'est un homme très simple** in private life, he's a man of simple tastes; **nous serons dans l'~** there will only be a few of us *ou* a few close friends or relatives; **se marier dans l'~** to have a quiet wedding; **la cérémonie a eu lieu dans la plus stricte ~** the ceremony took place in the strictest privacy; **pénétrer dans l'~ de qn** to be admitted into sb's private life; **vivre dans l'~ de qn** to share sb's private life.

b (*familiarité*) intimacy. **dans l'~ conjugale** in the intimacy of one's married life; **vivre dans la plus grande ~ avec qn** to live on very intimate terms with sb.

c (*confort*) *[atmosphère, salon]* cosiness, intimacy.

d (*littér: profondeur*) depths. **dans l'~ de sa conscience** in the depths of *ou* innermost recesses of one's conscience.

intitulé [ɛ̃tityle] nm *[livre, loi, jugement]* title; *[chapitre]* heading, title; *[sujet de dissertation]* wording; *[compte en banque]* (*type de compte*) type; (*coordonnées du titulaire*) name, address and account number.

intituler [ɛ̃tityle] [1] 1 vt to entitle, call. 2 **s'intituler** vpr *[livre, chapitre]* to be entitled *ou* called; *[personne]* to call o.s., give o.s. the title of.

intolérable [ɛ̃tɔleʀabl] adj intolerable.

intolérablement [ɛ̃tɔleʀabləmɑ̃] adv intolerably.

intolérance [ɛ̃tɔleʀɑ̃s] nf intolerance. **~ à un médicament, ~ médicamenteuse** inability to tolerate a drug.

intolérant, e [ɛ̃tɔleʀɑ̃, ɑ̃t] adj intolerant.

intonation [ɛ̃tɔnasjɔ̃] nf (*Ling, Mus*) intonation. **voix aux ~s douces** soft-toned voice.

intouchable [ɛ̃tuʃabl] adj, nmf untouchable.

intox(e)* [ɛ̃tɔks] nf (*Pol*) (abrév de **intoxication**) brainwashing. **il nous fait de l'~ pour avoir un magnétoscope** he's trying to brainwash us into getting (him) a video recorder.

intoxication [ɛ̃tɔksikasjɔ̃] nf (*voir* **intoxiquer**) poisoning (*NonC*); brainwashing, indoctrination. **~ alimentaire** food poisoning (*NonC*).

intoxiqué, e [ɛ̃tɔksike] (ptp de **intoxiquer**) nm,f (*par la drogue*) drug addict; (*par l'alcool*) alcoholic.

intoxiquer [ɛ̃tɔksike] [1] 1 vt (*lit*) to poison; (*fig*) (*Pol*) to brainwash, indoctrinate; (*corrompre*) to poison the mind of. **être intoxiqué par le tabac/l'alcool/la drogue** to be poisoned by the effects of tobacco/alcohol/drugs; **intoxiqué par la publicité** brainwashed by publicity. 2 **s'intoxiquer** vpr to poison o.s.

intracellulaire [ɛ̃tʀaselylɛʀ] adj intracellular.

intradermique [ɛ̃tʀadɛʀmik] adj intradermal, intradermic, intracutaneous.

intradermo(-)réaction [ɛ̃tʀadɛʀmoʀeaksjɔ̃] nf inv skin test.

intraduisible [ɛ̃tʀadɥizibl] adj *texte* untranslatable; *sentiment, idée* inexpressible. **il eut une intonation ~** his intonation was impossible to reproduce.

intraitable [ɛ̃tʀɛtabl] adj uncompromising, inflexible. **il est ~ sur la discipline** he's a stickler for discipline, he's uncompromising *ou* inflexible about discipline.

intra-muros [ɛ̃tʀamyʀos] adv: **habiter ~** to live inside the town (*ou* city *etc*); **Paris ~ comprend environ 2 millions d'habitants** the inner-city area of Paris has about 2 million inhabitants.

intramusculaire [ɛ̃tʀamyskylɛʀ] adj intramuscular.

intransigeance [ɛ̃tʀɑ̃ziʒɑ̃s] nf intransigence.

intransigeant, e [ɛ̃tʀɑ̃ziʒɑ̃, ɑ̃t] adj *personne* uncompromising, intransigent, hard-nosed*; *morale* uncompromising. **se montrer ~** *ou* **adopter une ligne (de conduite) ~e envers qn** to take a hard line with sb; **les ~s** the intransigents.

intransitif, -ive [ɛ̃tʀɑ̃zitif, iv] adj, nm intransitive.

intransitivement [ɛ̃tʀɑ̃zitivmɑ̃] adv intransitively.

intransitivité [ɛ̃tʀɑ̃zitivite] nf intransitivity, intransitiveness.

intransmissibilité [ɛ̃tʀɑ̃smisibilite] nf intransmissibility; (*Jur*) untransferability, non-transferability.

intransmissible [ɛ̃tʀɑ̃smisibl] adj intransmissible; (*Jur*) untransferable, non-transferable.

intransportable [ɛ̃tʀɑ̃spɔʀtabl] adj *objet* untransportable; *malade* who is unfit *ou* unable to travel.

intra-utérin, e [ɛ̃tʀayteʀɛ̃, in] adj intra-uterine.

intraveineux, -euse [ɛ̃tʀavɛnø, øz] 1 adj intravenous. 2 **intraveineuse** nf intravenous injection.

intrépide [ɛ̃tʀepid] adj (*courageux*) intrepid, dauntless, bold; (*résolu*) dauntless; *bavard* unashamed; *menteur* barefaced (*épith*), unashamed.

intrépidement [ɛ̃tʀepidmɑ̃] adv intrepidly, dauntlessly, boldly.

intrépidité [ɛ̃tʀepidite] nf intrepidity, dauntlessness, boldness. **avec ~** intrepidly, dauntlessly, boldly.

intrigant, e [ɛ̃tʀigɑ̃, ɑ̃t] 1 adj scheming. 2 nm,f schemer, intriguer.

intrigue [ɛ̃tʀig] nf (*manœuvre*) intrigue, scheme; (*liaison*) (love) affair, intrigue; (*Ciné, Littérat, Théât*) plot.

intriguer [ɛ̃tʀige] [1] 1 vt to intrigue, puzzle. 2 vi to scheme, intrigue.

intrinsèque [ɛ̃tʀɛ̃sɛk] adj intrinsic.

intrinsèquement [ɛ̃tʀɛ̃sɛkmɑ̃] adv intrinsically.

introducteur, -trice [ɛ̃tʀɔdyktœʀ, tʀis] nm,f (*initiateur*) initiator (*à* to).

introduction [ɛ̃tʀɔdyksjɔ̃] nf a introduction (*à, auprès de* to). **paroles/chapitre d'~** introductory words/chapter; **lettre/mot d'~** letter/note of introduction. b (*voir* **introduire**) insertion; introduction; launching; smuggling; institution. c (*voir* **s'introduire**) admission, introduction. d (*Rugby*) put-in.

introduire [ɛ̃tʀɔdɥiʀ] [38] 1 vt a (*faire entrer*) *objet* to place (*dans* in), insert, introduce (*dans* into); *liquide* to introduce (*dans* into); *visiteur* to show in; *mode* to launch, introduce; *idées nouvelles* to bring in, introduce; (*Ling*) *mot* to introduce (*dans* into). **il introduisit sa clef dans la serrure** he placed his key in the lock, he introduced *ou* inserted his key into the lock; **on m'introduisit dans le salon/auprès de la maîtresse de maison** I was shown into *ou* ushered into the lounge/shown in *ou* ushered in to see the mistress of the house; **~ des marchandises en contrebande** to smuggle in goods; (*Rugby*) **~ la balle en mêlée** to put the ball into the scrum.

b (*présenter*) *ami, protégé* to introduce. **il m'introduisit auprès du directeur/dans le groupe** he put me in contact with *ou* introduced me to the manager/the group.

c (*Jur*) *instance* to institute.

2 **s'introduire** vpr a (*lit*) **s'~ dans un groupe** to work one's way into a group, be *ou* get o.s. admitted *ou* accepted into a group; **s'~ chez qn par effraction** to break into sb's home; **s'~ dans une pièce** to get into *ou* enter a room; **les prisonniers s'introduisaient un à un dans le tunnel** one by one the prisoners worked *ou* wriggled their way into the tunnel; **l'eau/la fumée s'introduisait partout** the water/smoke was getting in *ou* penetrating everywhere.

b (*fig*) *[usage, mode, idée]* to be introduced (*dans* into).

introduit, e [ɛ̃tʀɔdɥi, it] (ptp de **introduire**) adj (*frm*) **être bien ~ dans un milieu** to be well received in a certain milieu.

intromission [ɛ̃tʀɔmisjɔ̃] nf intromission.

intronisation [ɛ̃tʀɔnizasjɔ̃] nf (*voir* **introniser**) enthronement; establishment.

introniser [ɛ̃tʀɔnize] [1] vt *roi, pape* to enthrone; (*fig*) to establish.

introspectif, -ive [ɛ̃tʀɔspɛktif, iv] adj introspective.

introspection [ɛ̃tʀɔspɛksjɔ̃] nf introspection.

introuvable [ɛ̃tʀuvabl] adj which (*ou* who) cannot be found. **ma clef est ~** I can't find my key anywhere, my key is nowhere to be found; **l'évadé demeure toujours ~** the escaped prisoner has still not been found *ou* discovered, the whereabouts of the escaped prisoner remain unknown; **ces meubles sont ~s aujourd'hui** furniture like this is unobtainable *ou* just cannot be found these days; **l'accord reste ~ entre les deux pays** the two countries are still unable to reach an agreement.

introversion [ɛ̃tʀɔvɛʀsjɔ̃] nf introversion.

introverti, e [ɛ̃tʀɔvɛʀti] 1 adj introverted. 2 nm,f introvert.

intrus, e [ɛ̃tʀy, yz] 1 adj intruding, intrusive. 2 nm,f intruder. (*jeu*) **cherchez l'~** find the odd one out.

intrusion [ɛ̃tʀyzjɔ̃] nf (*gén, Géol*) intrusion. **~ dans les affaires de qn**

interference *ou* intrusion in sb's affairs; (*Géol*) **roches d'~** intrusive rocks.
intubation [ɛ̃tybasjɔ̃] **nf** (*Méd*) intubation.
intuber [ɛ̃tybe] [1] **vt** (*Méd*) to intubate.
intuitif, -ive [ɛ̃tɥitif, iv] **adj** intuitive.
intuition [ɛ̃tɥisjɔ̃] **nf** intuition. **avoir de l'~** to have intuition; **l'~ féminine** feminine intuition; **elle eut l'~ que/de** she had an intuition that/of; **mon ~ me dit que** instinct *ou* my intuition tells me that.
intuitivement [ɛ̃tɥitivmɑ̃] **adv** intuitively.
intumescence [ɛ̃tymesɑ̃s] **nf** (*Anat*) intumescence.
intumescent, e [ɛ̃tymesɑ̃, ɑ̃t] **adj** intumescent.
inuit, e [inɥit] **adj, nmf** Inuit.
inusable [inyzabl] **adj** *vêtement* hard-wearing.
inusité, e [inyzite] **adj** *mot* uncommon, not in (common) use (*attrib*). **ce mot est pratiquement ~** this word is practically never used.
inusuel, -elle [inyzɥɛl] **adj** (*littér*) unusual.
in utero [inyteʀo] **adj, adv** in utero.
inutile [inytil] **adj** **a** (*qui ne sert pas*) *objet* useless; *effort, parole* pointless. **amasser des connaissances ~s** to gather a lot of useless knowledge; **sa voiture lui est ~ maintenant** his car is (of) no use *ou* is no good *ou* is useless to him now; **c'est ~ (d'insister)!** it's useless *ou* no use *ou* no good (insisting)!, there's no point *ou* it's pointless (insisting)!; **c'est un ~** he's a useless character, he's useless *ou* no use. **b** (*superflu*) *paroles, crainte, travail, effort* needless, unnecessary. **~ de vous dire que je ne suis pas resté** needless to say I didn't stay, I hardly need tell you I didn't stay; *voir* **bouche.**
inutilement [inytilmɑ̃] **adv** needlessly, unnecessarily.
inutilisable [inytilizabl] **adj** unusable.
inutilisé, e [inytilize] **adj** unused.
inutilité [inytilite] **nf** (*voir* **inutile**) uselessness; pointlessness; needlessness.
invaincu, e [ɛ̃vɛ̃ky] **adj** unconquered, unvanquished; (*Sport*) unbeaten.
invalidant, e [ɛ̃validɑ̃, ɑ̃t] **adj** *maladie* incapacitating, disabling.
invalidation [ɛ̃validasjɔ̃] **nf** *[contrat, élection]* invalidation; *[député]* removal (from office).
invalide [ɛ̃valid] **1** **nmf** disabled person. **~ de guerre** disabled ex-serviceman, invalid soldier; **~ du travail** industrially disabled person. **2** **adj** (*Méd*) disabled; (*Jur*) invalid.
invalider [ɛ̃valide] [1] **vt** (*Jur*) to invalidate; (*Pol*) *député* to remove from office; *élection* to invalidate.
invalidité [ɛ̃validite] **nf** disablement, disability; *voir* **assurance.**
invariabilité [ɛ̃vaʀjabilite] **nf** invariability.
invariable [ɛ̃vaʀjabl] **adj** (*gén, Ling*) invariable; (*littér*) unvarying.
invariablement [ɛ̃vaʀjabləmɑ̃] **adv** invariably.
invariant, e [ɛ̃vaʀjɑ̃, jɑ̃t] **adj, nm** invariant.
invasion [ɛ̃vazjɔ̃] **nf** invasion. **c'est l'~!** it's an invasion!
invective [ɛ̃vɛktiv] **nf** invective. **~s** abuse, invectives.
invectiver [ɛ̃vɛktive] [1] **1** **vt** to hurl *ou* shout abuse at. **ils se sont violemment invectivés** they hurled *ou* shouted violent abuse at each other. **2** **vi** to inveigh, rail (*contre* against).
invendable [ɛ̃vɑ̃dabl] **adj** (*gén*) unsaleable; (*Comm*) unmarketable.
invendu, e [ɛ̃vɑ̃dy] **1** **adj** unsold. **2** **nm** unsold article. **retourner les ~s** (*magazines etc*) to return (the) unsold copies.
inventaire [ɛ̃vɑ̃tɛʀ] **nm** (*gén, Jur*) inventory; (*Comm*) (*liste*) stocklist; (*opération*) stocktaking; (*fig: recensement*) *[monuments, souvenirs]* survey. (*gén, Jur*) **faire un ~** to make an inventory; (*Comm*) to take stock, do the stocktaking; **"fermé pour cause d'~"** "closed for stocktaking"; (*fig*) **faire l'~ de** to assess, make an assessment of, take stock of; *voir* **bénéfice.**
inventer [ɛ̃vɑ̃te] [1] **vt** **a** (*créer, découvrir*) (*gén*) to invent; *moyen, procédé* to devise; *mot* to coin. **il n'a pas inventé la poudre** *ou* **le fil à couper le beurre** *ou* **l'eau chaude** he'll never set the Thames on fire, he's no bright spark.
b (*imaginer, trouver*) *jeu* to think up, make up; *mot* to make up; *excuse, histoire fausse* to invent, make *ou* think up. **il ne sait plus quoi ~ pour échapper à l'école** he doesn't know what to think up *ou* dream up next to get out of school; **ils avaient inventé de faire entrer les lapins dans le salon** they hit upon the idea *ou* they had the bright idea of bringing the rabbits into the drawing room; **je n'invente rien** I'm not making anything up, I'm not inventing a thing; **ce sont des choses qui ne s'inventent pas** those are things people just don't make up; *voir* **pièce.**
c (*Jur*) *trésor* to find.
inventeur, -trice [ɛ̃vɑ̃tœʀ, tʀis] **nm,f** inventor; (*Jur*) finder.
inventif, -ive [ɛ̃vɑ̃tif, iv] **adj** *esprit* inventive; *personne* resourceful, inventive.
invention [ɛ̃vɑ̃sjɔ̃] **nf** (*gén, péj*) invention; (*ingéniosité*) inventiveness, spirit of invention; (*Jur*) *[trésor]* finding. **cette excuse est une pure** *ou* **de la pure ~** that excuse is a pure invention *ou* fabrication; **l'histoire est de son ~** the story was made up *ou* invented by him *ou* was his own invention; **un cocktail de mon ~** a cocktail of my own creation; *voir* **brevet.**
inventivité [ɛ̃vɑ̃tivite] **nf** (*voir* **inventif**) inventiveness; resourcefulness.
inventorier [ɛ̃vɑ̃tɔʀje] [7] **vt** (*gén, Jur*) to make an inventory of; (*Comm*) to make a stocklist of.
invérifiable [ɛ̃veʀifjabl] **adj** unverifiable.
inverse [ɛ̃vɛʀs] **1** **adj** (*gén*) opposite; (*Logique, Math*) inverse. **arriver en sens ~** to arrive from the opposite direction; **l'image apparaît en sens ~ dans le miroir** the image is reversed in the mirror; **dans l'ordre ~** in (the) reverse order; **dans le sens ~ des aiguilles d'une montre** anticlockwise, counterclockwise.
2 **nm: l'~** (*gén*) the opposite, the reverse; (*Philos*) the converse; **tu as fait l'~ de ce que je t'ai dit** you did the opposite to *ou* of what I told you; **t'a-t-il attaqué ou l'~?** did he attack you or vice versa?, did he attack you or was it the other way round?; **à l'~** conversely; **cela va à l'~ de nos prévisions** that goes contrary to our plans.
inversé, e [ɛ̃vɛʀse] (**ptp de inverser**) **adj** *image* reversed; *relief* inverted.
inversement [ɛ̃vɛʀsəmɑ̃] **adv** (*gén*) conversely; (*Math*) inversely. **... et/ou ~** ... and/or vice versa.
inverser [ɛ̃vɛʀse] [1] **vt** *ordre* to reverse, invert; *courant électrique* to reverse.
inverseur [ɛ̃vɛʀsœʀ] **nm** (*Élec, Tech*) reverser.
inversion [ɛ̃vɛʀsjɔ̃] **nf** (*gén, Anat, Ling, Psych*) inversion; (*Élec*) reversal. (*Mét*) **~ thermique** temperature inversion.
invertase [ɛ̃vɛʀtɑz] **nf** sucrase.
invertébré, e [ɛ̃vɛʀtebʀe] **adj, nm** invertebrate. **~s** invertebrates, Invertebrata (*SPÉC*).
inverti, e [ɛ̃vɛʀti] (**ptp de invertir**) **nm,f** homosexual, invert (*SPÉC*).
invertir† [ɛ̃vɛʀtiʀ] [2] **vt** to invert.
investigateur, -trice [ɛ̃vɛstigatœʀ, tʀis] **1** **adj** *technique* investigative; *esprit* inquiring (*épith*); *regard* searching (*épith*), scrutinizing (*épith*). **2** **nm,f** investigator.
investigation [ɛ̃vɛstigasjɔ̃] **nf** investigation. **~s** investigations; **après une minutieuse ~** *ou* **de minutieuses ~s le médecin diagnostiqua du diabète** after a thorough examination the doctor diagnosed diabetes; **au cours de ses ~s le savant découvrit que ...** in the course of his research *ou* investigations the scientist discovered that ... .
investir [ɛ̃vɛstiʀ] [2] **1** **vt** **a** (*Fin*) *capital* to invest. **b** *fonctionnaire* to induct; *évêque* to invest. **~ qn de pouvoirs/droits** to invest *ou* vest sb with powers/rights, vest powers/rights in sb; **~ qn de sa confiance** to place one's trust in sb. **c** (*Mil*) *ville, forteresse* to surround, besiege; (*Police*) to surround, encircle. **2** **s'investir** **vpr: s'~ dans son travail/une relation** to put a lot into one's work/a relationship; **s'~ beaucoup pour faire qch** to put a lot of effort into doing sth.
investissement [ɛ̃vɛstismɑ̃] **nm** (*Écon, Méd, Psych*) investment; (*Mil*) investing; (*efforts*) contribution.
investisseur [ɛ̃vɛstisœʀ] **nm** investor.
investiture [ɛ̃vɛstityʀ] **nf** *[candidat]* nomination; *[président du Conseil]* appointment; *[évêché]* investiture.
invétéré, e [ɛ̃veteʀe] **adj** *fumeur, joueur, menteur* inveterate, confirmed; *habitude* inveterate, deep-rooted.
invincibilité [ɛ̃vɛ̃sibilite] **nf** *[adversaire, nation]* invincibility.
invincible [ɛ̃vɛ̃sibl] **adj** *adversaire, nation* invincible, unconquerable; *courage* invincible, indomitable; *charme* irresistible; *difficultés* insurmountable, insuperable; *argument* invincible, unassailable.
invinciblement [ɛ̃vɛ̃sibləmɑ̃] **adv** invincibly.
inviolabilité [ɛ̃vjɔlabilite] **nf** *[droit]* inviolability; *[serrure]* impregnability; *[parlementaire, diplomate]* immunity.
inviolable [ɛ̃vjɔlabl] **adj** *droit* inviolable; *serrure* impregnable, burglar-proof; *parlementaire, diplomate* immune (*épith*).
inviolablement [ɛ̃vjɔlabləmɑ̃] **adv** inviolably.
inviolé, e [ɛ̃vjɔle] **adj** inviolate, unviolated.
invisibilité [ɛ̃vizibilite] **nf** invisibility.
invisible [ɛ̃vizibl] **1** **adj** (*impossible à voir*) invisible; (*minuscule*) barely visible (*à* to); (*Écon*) invisible. **la maison était ~ derrière les arbres** the house was invisible *ou* couldn't be seen behind the trees; **danger ~** unseen *ou* hidden danger; **il est ~ pour l'instant** he can't be seen *ou* he's unavailable at the moment; **il est ~ depuis 2 mois** he hasn't been seen (around) for 2 months. **2** **nm: l'~** the invisible.
invisiblement [ɛ̃viziblǝmɑ̃] **adv** invisibly.
invitation [ɛ̃vitasjɔ̃] **nf** invitation, invite* (*à* to). **carte** *ou* **carton d'~** invitation card; **lettre d'~** letter of invitation; **~ à dîner** invitation to dinner; **faire une ~ à qn** to invite sb, extend an invitation to sb; **venir sans ~** to come uninvited *ou* without (an) invitation; **à** *ou* **sur son ~** at his invitation; (*fig*) **une ~ à déserter** *etc* an (open) invitation to desert *etc*.
invite [ɛ̃vit] **nf** (*littér*) invitation. **à son ~** at his invitation.
invité, e [ɛ̃vite] (**ptp de inviter**) **nm,f** guest.
inviter [ɛ̃vite] [1] **vt** **a** (*convier*) to invite, ask (*à* to). **~ qn chez soi/à dîner** to invite *ou* ask sb to one's house/to *ou* for dinner; **elle ne l'a pas invité à entrer/monter** she didn't invite *ou* ask him (to come) in/up; **il s'est invité** he invited himself. **b** (*engager*) **~ à** to invite to; **~ qn à démissionner** to invite sb to resign; **il l'invita de la main à s'approcher** he beckoned *ou* motioned (to) her to come nearer; **ceci invite à croire que ...** this induces *ou* leads us to believe that ..., this suggests that ...; **la chaleur invitait au repos** the heat tempted one to rest.
in vitro [invitʀo] **adj, adv** in vitro.
invivable [ɛ̃vivabl] **adj** unbearable.

in vivo [invivo] adj, adv in vivo.
invocation [ɛ̃vɔkasjɔ̃] nf invocation (*à* to).
invocatoire [ɛ̃vɔkatwaʀ] adj (*littér*) invocatory (*littér*).
involontaire [ɛ̃vɔlɔ̃tɛʀ] adj *sourire, mouvement* involuntary; *peine, insulte* unintentional, unwitting; *témoin, complice* unwitting.
involontairement [ɛ̃vɔlɔ̃tɛʀmɑ̃] adv *sourire* involuntarily; *bousculer qn* unintentionally, unwittingly. **l'accident dont je fus (bien) ~ le témoin** the accident to *ou* of which I was an *ou* the unwitting witness.
involutif, -ive [ɛ̃vɔlytif, iv] adj (*Bio, Math*) involute. (*Méd*) **(processus) ~** involution.
involution [ɛ̃vɔlysjɔ̃] nf (*Bio, Méd, Math*) involution.
invoquer [ɛ̃vɔke] [1] vt a (*alléguer*) *argument* to put forward; *témoignage* to call upon; *excuse, jeunesse, ignorance* to plead; *loi, texte* to cite, refer to. (*Jur*) **~ les règles de compétence** to avail o.s. of the rules of jurisdiction; **les arguments de fait et de droit invoqués** the points of fact and law relied on. b (*appeler à l'aide*) *Dieu* to invoke, call upon. **~ le secours de qn** to call upon sb for help; **~ la clémence de qn** to beg sb *ou* appeal to sb for clemency.
invraisemblable [ɛ̃vʀɛsɑ̃blabl] adj (*improbable*) *fait, nouvelle* unlikely, improbable; *argument* implausible; (*extravagant*) *insolence, habit* incredible.
invraisemblablement [ɛ̃vʀɛsɑ̃blabləmɑ̃] adv (*voir* **invraisemblable**) improbably; implausibly; incredibly.
invraisemblance [ɛ̃vʀɛsɑ̃blɑ̃s] nf (*voir* **invraisemblable**) unlikelihood (*NonC*), unlikeliness (*NonC*), improbability; implausibility. **plein d'~s** full of improbabilities *ou* implausibilities.
invulnérabilité [ɛ̃vylneʀabilite] nf invulnerability.
invulnérable [ɛ̃vylneʀabl] adj (*lit*) invulnerable. (*fig*) **~ à** not vulnerable to, immune to.
iode [jɔd] nm iodine; *voir* **phare, teinture**.
ioder [jɔde] [1] vt to iodize.
iodler [jɔdle] [1] vt = **jodler**.
iodoforme [jɔdɔfɔʀm] nm iodoform.
ion [jɔ̃] nm ion.
ionien, -ienne [jɔnjɛ̃, jɛn] 1 adj Ionian. 2 nm (*Ling*) Ionic.
ionique [jɔnik] 1 adj (*Archit*) Ionic; (*Sci*) ionic. 2 nm (*Archit*) **l'~** the Ionic.
ionisant, e [jɔnizɑ̃, ɑ̃t] adj ionizing.
ionisation [jɔnizasjɔ̃] nf ionization.
ioniser [jɔnize] [1] vt to ionize.
ionosphère [jɔnɔsfɛʀ] nf ionosphere.
iota [jɔta] nm iota. **je n'y ai pas changé un ~** I didn't change it one iota, I didn't change one *ou* an iota of it.
iourte [juʀt] = **yourte**.
Iowa [ajɔwa] nm Iowa.
ipéca [ipeka] nm ipecacuanha, ipecac (*US*).
IPR [ipeɛʀ] nm (abrév de **inspecteur pédagogique régional**) *voir* **inspecteur**.
ipso facto [ipsofakto] adv ipso facto.
IRA [iʀa] nf (abrév de **Irish Republican Army**) IRA.
Irak [iʀak] nm Iraq, Irak.
irakien, -ienne [iʀakjɛ̃, jɛn] 1 adj Iraqi. 2 nm (*Ling*) Iraqi. 3 nm,f: **I~(ne)** Iraqi.
Iran [iʀɑ̃] nm Iran.
iranien, -ienne [iʀanjɛ̃, jɛn] 1 adj Iranian. 2 nm (*Ling*) Iranian. 3 nm,f: **I~(ne)** Iranian.
Iraq [iʀak] nm = **Irak**.
iraquien, -ienne [iʀakjɛ̃, jɛn] = **irakien**.
irascibilité [iʀasibilite] nf short- *ou* quick-temperedness, irascibility.
irascible [iʀasibl] adj: **(d'humeur) ~** short- *ou* quick-tempered, irascible.
IRCANTEC [iʀkɑ̃tɛk] nm (abrév de **Institut de retraite complémentaire des agents non titulaires de l'État et des collectivités publiques**) *voir* **institut**.
ire [iʀ] nf (*littér*) ire (*littér*).
iridié, e [iʀidje] adj *voir* **platine**.
iridium [iʀidjɔm] nm iridium.
iris [iʀis] nm (*Anat, Phot*) iris; (*Bot*) iris, flag.
irisation [iʀizasjɔ̃] nf iridescence, irisation.
irisé, e [iʀize] (ptp de **iriser**) adj iridescent.
iriser [iʀize] [1] 1 vt to make iridescent. 2 **s'iriser** vpr to become iridescent.
irlandais, e [iʀlɑ̃dɛ, ɛz] 1 adj Irish. 2 nm a (*Ling*) Irish. b **I~** Irishman; **les I~** the Irish; **les I~ du Nord** the Northern Irish. 3 **Irlandaise** nf Irishwoman.
Irlande [iʀlɑ̃d] nf (*pays*) Ireland; (*État*) Irish Republic, Republic of Ireland, Eire. **l'~ du Nord** Northern Ireland, Ulster; **de l'~ du Nord** Northern Irish.
ironie [iʀɔni] nf (*lit, fig*) irony. **par une curieuse ~ du sort** by a strange irony of fate.
ironique [iʀɔnik] adj ironic(al).
ironiquement [iʀɔnikmɑ̃] adv ironically.
ironiser [iʀɔnize] [1] vi to be ironic(al) (*sur* about). **ce n'est pas la peine d'~** there's no need to be ironic(al) (about it).
ironiste [iʀɔnist] nmf ironist.
iroquois, e [iʀɔkwa, waz] 1 adj *peuplade* Iroquoian; (*Hist*) Iroquois. 2 nm (*Ling*) Iroquoian. 3 nm,f: **I~(e)** Iroquoian; Iroquois.

IRPP [iɛʀpepe] nm (abrév de **impôt sur le revenu des personnes physiques**) *voir* **impôt**.
irradiant, e [iʀadjɑ̃, jɑ̃t] adj radiant; irradiant (*littér*).
irradiation [iʀadjasjɔ̃] nf (*action*) irradiation; (*halo*) irradiation; (*rayons*) radiation, irradiation; (*Méd*) radiation.
irradier [iʀadje] [7] 1 vt to irradiate. **les personnes irradiées** the people who were irradiated *ou* exposed to radiation. 2 vi *[lumière etc]* to radiate, irradiate; *[douleur]* to radiate; (*fig*) to radiate.
irraisonné, e [iʀɛzɔne] adj *mouvement* irrational; *crainte* irrational, unreasoning.
irrationalisme [iʀasjɔnalism] nm irrationalism.
irrationalité [iʀasjɔnalite] nf irrationality.
irrationnel, -elle [iʀasjɔnɛl] adj (*gén, Math*) irrational.
irrationnellement [iʀasjɔnɛlmɑ̃] adv irrationally.
irrattrapable [iʀatʀapabl] adj *bévue* irretrievable.
irréalisable [iʀealizabl] adj (*gén*) unrealizable, unachievable; *projet* impracticable, unworkable. **c'est ~** it's unfeasible *ou* unworkable.
irréalisé, e [iʀealize] adj (*littér*) unrealized, unachieved.
irréalisme [iʀealism] nm lack of realism, unrealism.
irréaliste [iʀealist] adj unrealistic.
irréalité [iʀealite] nf unreality.
irrecevabilité [iʀəs(ə)vabilite] nf (*voir* **irrecevable**) inadmissibility; unacceptability.
irrecevable [iʀəs(ə)vabl] adj (*Jur*) inadmissible. **témoignage ~** inadmissible evidence.
irréconciliable [iʀekɔ̃siljabl] adj irreconcilable, unreconcilable (*avec* with).
irréconciliablement [iʀekɔ̃siljabləmɑ̃] adv irreconcilably, unreconcilably.
irrécouvrable [iʀekuvʀabl] adj irrecoverable.
irrécupérable [iʀekypeʀabl] adj (*gén*) irretrievable; *ferraille, meubles* unreclaimable; *voiture* beyond repair (*attrib*). **il est ~** he's beyond redemption.
irrécusable [iʀekyzabl] adj *témoin, juge* unimpeachable; *témoignage, preuve* incontestable, indisputable.
irréductibilité [iʀedyktibilite] nf (*voir* **irréductible**) irreducibility; insurmountability, invincibility; indomitability; implacability.
irréductible [iʀedyktibl] adj *fait, élément* irreducible; (*Chim, Math, Méd*) irreducible; (*invincible*) *obstacle* insurmountable, invincible; *volonté* indomitable, invincible; (*farouche*) *opposition, ennemi* out-and-out (*épith*), implacable. **les ~s du parti** the hard core of the party.
irréductiblement [iʀedyktibləmɑ̃] adv implacably. **être ~ opposé à une politique** *etc* to be in out-and-out opposition to *ou* implacably opposed to a policy *etc*.
irréel, -elle [iʀeɛl] adj unreal. (*Ling*) **(mode) ~** *mood expressing unreal condition*.
irréfléchi, e [iʀefleʃi] adj *geste, paroles, action* thoughtless, unconsidered; *personne* unthinking, hasty; *enfant* impulsive, hasty; *courage, audace* reckless, impetuous.
irréflexion [iʀeflɛksjɔ̃] nf thoughtlessness.
irréfutabilité [iʀefytabilite] nf irrefutability.
irréfutable [iʀefytabl] adj irrefutable.
irréfutablement [iʀefytabləmɑ̃] adv irrefutably.
irréfuté, e [iʀefyte] adj unrefuted.
irrégularité [iʀegylaʀite] nf a (*voir* **irrégulier**) irregularity; unevenness; variation; fitfulness; erratic performance; dubiousness. b (*action, caractéristique: gén pl*) irregularity. **les ~s du terrain/de ses traits** the irregularities of the land/in his features; **des ~s ont été commises lors du scrutin** irregularities occurred during the ballot.
irrégulier, -ière [iʀegylje, jɛʀ] 1 adj a (*non symétrique etc*) *polygone, façade, traits* irregular; *écriture, terrain* irregular, uneven.
b (*non constant*) *développement, accélération* irregular; *rythme, courant, vitesse* irregular, varying (*épith*); *sommeil, pouls, respiration* irregular, fitful; *vent* fitful; *travail, effort, qualité* uneven; *élève, athlète* erratic.
c (*en fréquence*) *horaire, service, visites, intervalles* irregular.
d (*peu honnête ou légal*) *tribunal, troupes, opération, situation* irregular; *vie* unorthodox, irregular; *agent, homme d'affaires* dubious. (*Jur*) **absence ~** unauthorized absence.
e (*Ling*) *verbe, construction* irregular.
2 nm (*Mil: gén pl*) irregular.
irrégulièrement [iʀegyljɛʀmɑ̃] adv (*voir* **irrégulier**) irregularly; unevenly; fitfully; erratically; dubiously.
irréligieusement [iʀeliʒjøzmɑ̃] adv irreligiously.
irréligieux, -ieuse [iʀeliʒjø, jøz] adj irreligious.
irréligion [iʀeliʒjɔ̃] nf irreligiousness, irreligion.
irrémédiable [iʀemedjabl] adj *dommage, perte* irreparable; *mal, vice* incurable, irremediable, beyond remedy (*attrib*). **essayer d'éviter l'~** to try to avoid reaching the point of no return.
irrémédiablement [iʀemedjabləmɑ̃] adv (*voir* **irrémédiable**) irreparably; incurably, irremediably.
irrémissible [iʀemisibl] adj (*littér*) irremissible.
irrémissiblement [iʀemisibləmɑ̃] adv (*littér*) irremissibly.

irremplaçable [iʀɑ̃plasabl] **adj** irreplaceable.

irréparable [iʀepaʀabl] **adj** *objet* irreparable, unmendable, beyond repair (*attrib*); *dommage, perte, gaffe* irreparable; *désastre* irretrievable. **la voiture est ~** the car is beyond repair *ou* is a write-off.

irréparablement [iʀepaʀabləmɑ̃] **adv** (*voir* **irréparable**) irreparably; irretrievably.

irrépréhensible [iʀepʀeɑ̃sibl] **adj** (*littér*) irreprehensible.

irrépressible [iʀepʀesibl] **adj** irrepressible.

irrépressiblement [iʀepʀesibləmɑ̃] **adv** irrepressibly.

irréprochable [iʀepʀɔʃabl] **adj** *personne, conduite, vie* irreproachable, beyond reproach (*attrib*); *tenue* impeccable, faultless.

irréprochablement [iʀepʀɔʃabləmɑ̃] **adv** (*voir* **irréprochable**) (*littér*) irreproachably; impeccably, faultlessly.

irrésistible [iʀezistibl] **adj** *femme, charme, plaisir, force* irresistible; *besoin, désir, preuve, logique* compelling. **il est ~!** (*amusant*) he's hilarious!

irrésistiblement [iʀezistibləmɑ̃] **adv** irresistibly.

irrésolu, e [iʀezɔly] **adj** *personne* irresolute, indecisive; *problème* unresolved, unsolved.

irrésolution [iʀezɔlysjɔ̃] **nf** irresolution, irresoluteness, indecisiveness.

irrespect [iʀɛspɛ] **nm** disrespect.

irrespectueusement [iʀɛspɛktɥøzmɑ̃] **adv** disrespectfully.

irrespectueux, -euse [iʀɛspɛktɥø, øz] **adj** disrespectful (*envers* to, towards).

irrespirable [iʀɛspiʀabl] **adj** *air* unbreathable; (*fig: étouffant*) oppressive, stifling; (*dangereux*) unsafe, unhealthy. (*fig*) **c'était ~, l'air** *ou* **l'atmosphère était ~** you could have cut the atmosphere with a knife*, the atmosphere was oppressive *ou* stifling.

irresponsabilité [iʀɛspɔ̃sabilite] **nf** irresponsibility.

irresponsable [iʀɛspɔ̃sabl] **adj** irresponsible (*de* for). **c'est un ~!** he's (totally) irresponsible!; **notre pays est entre les mains d'~s** this country is in irresponsible hands.

irrétrécissable [iʀetʀesisabl] **adj** (*sur étiquette, publicité*) unshrinkable, non-shrink.

irrévérence [iʀeveʀɑ̃s] **nf** (*caractère*) irreverence; (*propos*) irreverent word; (*acte*) irreverent act.

irrévérencieusement [iʀeveʀɑ̃sjøzmɑ̃] **adv** irreverently.

irrévérencieux, -ieuse [iʀeveʀɑ̃sjø, jøz] **adj** irreverent.

irréversibilité [iʀevɛʀsibilite] **nf** irreversibility.

irréversible [iʀevɛʀsibl] **adj** irreversible.

irrévocabilité [iʀevɔkabilite] **nf** (*Jur, littér*) irrevocability.

irrévocable [iʀevɔkabl] **adj** (*gén*) irrevocable; *temps, passé* beyond *ou* past recall (*attrib*), irrevocable. **l'~** the irrevocable.

irrévocablement [iʀevɔkabləmɑ̃] **adv** irrevocably.

irrigable [iʀigabl] **adj** irrigable.

irrigateur [iʀigatœʀ] **nm** (*Agr, Méd*) irrigator (*machine*).

irrigation [iʀigasjɔ̃] **nf** (*Agr, Méd*) irrigation.

irriguer [iʀige] [1] **vt** (*Agr, Méd*) to irrigate.

irritabilité [iʀitabilite] **nf** irritability.

irritable [iʀitabl] **adj** irritable.

irritant, e [iʀitɑ̃, ɑ̃t] **1 adj** irritating, annoying, irksome; (*Méd*) irritant. **2 nm** irritant.

irritation [iʀitasjɔ̃] **nf** (*colère*) irritation, annoyance; (*Méd*) irritation.

irrité, e [iʀite] (**ptp de irriter**) **adj** *gorge* irritated, inflamed; *geste, regard* irritated, annoyed, angry. **être ~ contre qn** to be annoyed *ou* angry with sb.

irriter [iʀite] [1] **1 vt a** (*agacer*) to irritate, annoy, irk. **b** (*enflammer*) *œil, peau, blessure* to make inflamed, irritate. **il avait la gorge irritée par la fumée** the smoke irritated his throat. **c** (*littér: aviver*) *intérêt, curiosité* to arouse. **2 s'irriter vpr a** (*s'agacer*) **s'~ de qch/contre qn** to get annoyed *ou* angry at sth/with sb, feel irritated at sth/with sb. **b** *[œil, peau, blessure]* to become inflamed *ou* irritated.

irruption [iʀypsjɔ̃] **nf** (*entrée subite ou hostile*) irruption (*NonC*). **faire ~ (chez qn)** to burst in (on sb); **les eaux firent ~ dans les bas quartiers** the waters swept into *ou* flooded the low-lying parts of the town.

Isaac [izak] **nm** Isaac.

Isabelle [izabɛl] **nf** Isabel.

isabelle [izabɛl] **1 adj** light-tan. **2 nm** light-tan horse.

Isaïe [isai] **nm** Isaiah. **(le livre d')~** (the Book of) Isaiah.

isard [izaʀ] **nm** izard.

isba [izba] **nf** isba.

ISBN [iɛsbeɛn] **adj, nm** (**abrév de International Standard Book Number**) ISBN.

ischémie [iskemi] **nf** ischeamia, ischemia (*US*).

ischion [iskjɔ̃] **nm** ischium.

Iseu(l)t [isø] **nf** Isolde.

ISF [iɛsɛf] **nm** (**abrév de impôt de solidarité sur la fortune**) *voir* **impôt**.

Isis [izis] **nf** Isis.

Islam [islam] **nm: l'~** Islam.

Islamabad [islamabad] **n** Islamabad.

islamique [islamik] **adj** Islamic. **la République ~ de ...** the Islamic Republic of ... .

islamisation [islamizasjɔ̃] **nf** Islamization.

islamiser [islamize] [1] **vt** to Islamize.

islamisme [islamism] **nm** Islamism.

islandais, e [islɑ̃dɛ, ɛz] **1 adj** Icelandic. **2 nm** (*Ling*) Icelandic. **3 nm,f: I~(e)** Icelander.

Islande [islɑ̃d] **nf** Iceland.

isobare [izobaʀ] **1 adj** isobaric. **2 nf** isobar.

isocèle [izɔsɛl] **adj** isoceles.

isochrone [izɔkʀɔn] **adj** isochronal, isochronous.

isoglosse [izɔglɔs] **nf** isogloss.

isolable [izɔlabl] **adj** isolable.

isolant, e [izɔlɑ̃, ɑ̃t] **1 adj** (*Constr, Élec*) insulating; (*insonorisant*) soundproofing, sound-insulating; (*Ling*) isolating. **2 nm** insulator, insulating material. **~ thermique/électrique** heat/electrical insulator.

isolateur [izɔlatœʀ] **nm** (*support*) insulator.

isolation [izɔlasjɔ̃] **nf** (*Élec*) insulation. **~ phonique** *ou* **acoustique** soundproofing, sound insulation; **~ thermique** thermal *ou* heat insulation.

isolationnisme [izɔlasjɔnism] **nm** isolationism.

isolationniste [izɔlasjɔnist] **adj, nmf** isolationist.

isolé, e [izɔle] (**ptp de isoler**) **1 adj** *cas, personne, protestation* isolated; *lieu* isolated, lonely, remote; *philosophe, tireur, anarchiste* lone (*épith*); (*Élec*) insulated. **se sentir ~** to feel isolated; **vivre ~** to live in isolation. **2 nm,f** (*théoricien*) loner; (*personne délaissée*) lonely person. **le problème des ~s** the problem of the lonely *ou* isolated; **on a rencontré quelques ~s** we met a few isolated people.

isolement [izɔlmɑ̃] **nm** *[personne délaissée, maison]* loneliness, isolation; *[théoricien, prisonnier, malade]* isolation; (*Pol*) *[pays]* isolation; (*Élec*) *[câble]* insulation. **sortir de son ~** to come out of one's isolation.

isolément [izɔlemɑ̃] **adv** in isolation, individually. **chaque élément pris ~** each element considered separately *ou* individually *ou* in isolation.

isoler [izɔle] [1] **1 vt a** *prisonnier* to place in solitary confinement; *malade, citation, fait, mot* to isolate; *ville* to cut off, isolate. **ville isolée du reste du monde** town cut off from the rest of the world; **ses opinions l'isolent** his opinions isolate him *ou* set him apart. **b** (*contre le froid, Élec*) to insulate; (*contre le bruit*) to soundproof, insulate; (*Bio, Chim*) to isolate. **2 s'isoler vpr** (*dans un coin, pour travailler*) to isolate o.s. **s'~ du reste du monde** to cut o.s. off *ou* isolate o.s. from the rest of the world; **ils s'isolèrent quelques instants** they stood aside for a few seconds.

isoloir [izɔlwaʀ] **nm** polling booth.

isomère [izɔmɛʀ] **1 adj** isomeric. **2 nm** isomer.

isométrique [izɔmetʀik] **adj** (*Math, Sci*) isometric.

isomorphe [izɔmɔʀf] **adj** (*Chim*) isomorphic, isomorphous; (*Math, Ling*) isomorphic.

isomorphisme [izɔmɔʀfism] **nm** isomorphism.

isorel [izɔʀɛl] **nm** ® hardboard.

isotherme [izɔtɛʀm] **1 adj** isothermal. **camion ~** refrigerated lorry (*Brit*) *ou* truck (*US*). **2 nf** isotherm.

isotope [izɔtɔp] **1 adj** isotopic. **2 nm** isotope.

Israël [isʀaɛl] **nm** Israel. **en ~** in Israel; **l'État d'~** the state of Israel.

israélien, -ienne [isʀaeljɛ̃, jɛn] **1 adj** Israeli. **2 nm,f: I~(ne)** Israeli.

israélite [isʀaelit] **1 adj** Jewish. **2 nm** (*gén*) Jew; (*Hist*) Israelite. **3 nf** Jewess; Israelite.

ISSN [iɛsɛsɛn] **adj, nm** (**abrév de International Standard Serial Number**) ISSN.

issu, e[1] [isy] **adj: ~ de** (*résultant de*) stemming from; (*né de*) descended from, born of; **être ~ de** (*résulter de*) to stem from; (*être né de*) to be descended from *ou* born of.

issue[2] [isy] **nf a** (*sortie*) exit; *[eau, vapeur]* outlet. **voie sans ~** (*lit, fig*) dead end; (*panneau*) "no through road"; **~ de secours** emergency exit; (*fig*) **il a su se ménager une ~** he has managed to leave himself a way out. **b** (*solution*) way out, solution. **la situation est sans ~** there is no way out of *ou* no solution to the situation; **un avenir sans ~** a future which has no prospect *ou* which leads nowhere *ou* without prospects. **c** (*fin*) outcome. **heureuse ~** happy outcome *ou* issue; **~ fatale** fatal outcome; **à l'~ de** at the conclusion *ou* close of.

Istanbul [istɑ̃bul] **n** Istanbul.

isthme [ism] **nm** (*Anat, Géog*) isthmus.

isthmique [ismik] **adj** isthmian.

Istrie [istʀi] **nf** Istria.

italianisant, e [italjanizɑ̃, ɑ̃t] **nm,f** (*Univ*) italianist; (*artiste*) italianizer.

italianisme [italjanism] **nm** (*Ling*) italianism.

Italie [itali] **nf** Italy.

italien, -ienne [italjɛ̃, jɛn] **1 adj** Italian. **2 nm** (*Ling*) Italian. **3 nm,f: I~(ne)** Italian.

italique [italik] **1 nm a** (*Typ*) italics. **mettre un mot en ~(s)** to put a word in italics, italicize a word. **b** (*Hist, Ling*) Italic. **2 adj** (*Typ*) italic; (*Hist, Ling*) Italic.

item [itɛm] **1 adv** (*Comm*) ditto. **2 nm** (*Ling, Psych*) item.

itératif, -ive [iteʀatif, iv] **adj** (*gén, Gram*) iterative; (*Jur*) reiterated, repeated.

itération [iteʀasjɔ̃] **nf** iteration.

Ithaque [itak] **nf** Ithaca.

itinéraire [itineʀɛʀ] **nm** (*chemin*) route, itinerary; (*Alpinisme*) route.

(*fig*) **son ~ philosophique/religieux** his philosophical/religious path; **~ bis** diversion; **faire** *ou* **tracer un ~** to map out a route *ou* an itinerary.
itinérant, e [itineʀɑ̃, ɑ̃t] **adj** itinerant, travelling. **ambassadeur ~** roving ambassador; **troupe ~e** (band of) strolling players.
itou*† [itu] **adv** likewise. **et moi ~!** (and) me too!*
IUFM [iyɛfɛm] **nm** (**abrév de Institut universitaire de formation des maîtres**) *voir* **institut.**
IUT [iyte] **nm** (**abrév de Institut universitaire de technologie**) polytechnic (*Brit*), technical institute (*US*).
Ivan [ivɑ̃] **nm** Ivan. **~ le Terrible** Ivan the Terrible.
IVG [iveʒe] **nf** (**abrév de interruption volontaire de grossesse**) *voir* **interruption.**
ivoire [ivwaʀ] **nm** ivory. **en** *ou* **d'~** ivory (*épith*); *voir* **côte, tour**[1].
ivoirien, -ienne [ivwaʀjɛ̃, jɛn] **1 adj** of *ou* from the Ivory Coast. **2 nm,f: I~(ne)** inhabitant *ou* native of the Ivory Coast.
ivraie [ivʀɛ] **nf** (*Bot*) rye grass; *voir* **séparer.**
ivre [ivʀ] **adj** drunk, intoxicated. **~ de colère/de vengeance/d'espoir** wild with anger/vengeance/hope; **~ de joie** wild with joy, beside o.s. with joy; **~ mort** dead *ou* blind drunk; **légèrement ~** slightly drunk, tipsy.
ivresse [ivʀɛs] **nf** (*ébriété*) drunkenness, intoxication. **dans l'~ du combat/de la victoire** in the exhilaration of the fight/of victory; **l'~ du plaisir** the (wild) ecstasy of pleasure; **avec ~** rapturously, ecstatically; **instants/heures d'~** moments/hours of rapture *ou* (wild) ecstasy; **~ chimique** drug dependence; *voir* **état.**
ivrogne [ivʀɔɲ] **1 nmf** drunkard; *voir* **serment. 2 adj** drunken (*épith*).
ivrognerie [ivʀɔɲʀi] **nf** drunkenness.

J

J¹, j [ʒi] nm (*lettre*) J, j; *voir* **jour**.
J² (abrév de **Joule**) J.
j' [ʒ] *voir* **je**.
jabot [ʒabo] nm **a** *[oiseau]* crop. **b** (*Habillement*) jabot.
jacasse [ʒakas] nf (*Zool*) magpie.
jacassement [ʒakasmɑ̃] nm *[pie]* chatter (*NonC*); (*péj*) *[personnes]* jabber(ing) (*NonC*), chatter(ing) (*NonC*).
jacasser [ʒakase] 1 vi *[pie]* to chatter; (*péj*) *[personne]* to jabber, chatter.
jacasserie [ʒakasʀi] nf = **jacassement**.
jacasseur, -euse [ʒakasœʀ, øz] **1** adj jabbering, prattling. **2** nm,f chatterbox, prattler.
jachère [ʒaʃɛʀ] nf fallow; (*procédé*) practice of fallowing land. **laisser une terre en ~** to leave a piece of land fallow, let a piece of land lie fallow; **rester en ~** to lie fallow.
jacinthe [ʒasɛ̃t] nf hyacinth. **~ sauvage** *ou* **des bois** bluebell.
jack [(d)ʒak] nm (*Téléc, Tex*) jack.
Jacob [ʒakɔb] nm Jacob. **l'échelle de ~** Jacob's ladder.
jacobin, e [ʒakɔbɛ̃, in] **1** adj Jacobinic(al). **2** nm (*Hist*) **J~** Jacobin.
jacobinisme [ʒakɔbinism] nm Jacobinism.
jacobite [ʒakɔbit] nm Jacobite.
Jacot [ʒako] nm = **Jacquot**.
jacquard [ʒakaʀ] **1** adj *pull* Fair Isle. **2** nm (*métier*) Jacquard loom; (*tissu*) Jacquard (weave).
Jacqueline [ʒaklin] nf Jacqueline.
jacquerie [ʒakʀi] nf jacquerie. (*Hist*) **J~** Jacquerie.
Jacques [ʒak] nm James. **faire le ~*** to play *ou* act the fool, fool about.
jacquet [ʒakɛ] nm backgammon.
Jacquot [ʒako] nm (*personne*) Jimmy; (*perroquet*) Polly.
jactance [ʒaktɑ̃s] nf **a** (‡: *bavardage*) chat. **il a de la ~!** he's got the gift of the gab!* **b** (*littér: vanité*) conceit.
jacter‡ [ʒakte] 1 vi to jabber, gas*; (*arg Police*) to talk, come clean‡.
jacuzzi [ʒakyzi] nm ® Jacuzzi ®.
jade [ʒad] nm (*pierre*) jade; (*objet*) jade object *ou* ornament. **de ~** jade.
jadis [ʒadis] **1** adv in times past, formerly, long ago. **mes amis de ~** my friends of long ago *ou* of old; **~ on se promenait dans ces jardins** in olden days *ou* long ago they used to walk in these gardens. **2** adj: **dans le temps ~, au temps ~** in days of old, in days gone by, once upon a time; **du temps ~** of times gone by, of olden days.
jaguar [ʒagwaʀ] **1** nm (*animal*) jaguar. **2** nf (*voiture:* ®) **J~** Jaguar ®.
jaillir [ʒajiʀ] 2 vi **a** *[liquide, sang]* to spurt out, gush forth; *[larmes]* to flow; *[geyser]* to spout up, gush forth; *[vapeur, source]* to gush forth; *[flammes]* to shoot up, spurt out; *[étincelles]* to fly out; *[lumière]* to flash on (*de* from, out of). **faire ~ des étincelles** to make sparks fly; **un éclair jaillit dans l'obscurité** a flash of lightning split the darkness, lightning flashed in the darkness.
b (*apparaître*) **des soldats jaillirent de tous côtés** soldiers sprang out *ou* leapt out from all directions; **le train jaillit du tunnel** the train shot *ou* burst out of the tunnel; **des montagnes jaillissaient au-dessus de la plaine** mountains reared up over the plain *ou* towered above the plain; **des immeubles-tours qui jaillissent de terre** tower blocks which soar up (from ground level); **des monstres jaillis de son imagination** monsters sprung from his imagination.
c *[cris, rires, réponses]* to burst forth *ou* out.
d *[idée]* to spring up; *[vérité, solution]* to spring (*de* from).
jaillissement [ʒajismɑ̃] nm *[liquide, vapeur]* spurt, gush; *[idées]* springing up, outpouring.
jais [ʒɛ] nm (*Minér*) jet. **perles de ~** jet beads; **bijoux en ~** jet jewellery; **des cheveux de ~** jet-black hair; *voir* **noir**.
Jakarta [dʒakaʀta] n Jakarta.
jalon [ʒalɔ̃] nm (*lit*) ranging-pole; *[arpenteur]* (surveyor's) staff; (*fig*) landmark, milestone. (*fig*) **planter** *ou* **poser les premiers ~s de qch** to prepare the ground for sth, pave the way for sth; **il commence à poser des ~s** he's beginning to prepare the ground.
jalonnement [ʒalɔnmɑ̃] nm *[route]* marking out.
jalonner [ʒalɔne] 1 vt **a** (*déterminer un tracé*) *route, chemin de fer* to mark out *ou* off. **il faut d'abord ~** first the ground must be marked out. **b** (*border, s'espacer sur*) to line, stretch along. **des champs de fleurs jalonnent la route** fields of flowers line the road; (*fig*) **carrière jalonnée de succès/d'obstacles** career punctuated with successes/obstacles.
jalousement [ʒaluzmɑ̃] adv jealously.
jalouser [ʒaluze] 1 vt to be jealous of.
jalousie [ʒaluzi] nf **a** (*entre amants*) jealousy; (*envie*) jealousy, envy. **des petites ~s mesquines entres femmes** petty jealousies between women; **être malade de ~, crever de ~*** to be green with envy. **b** (*persienne*) slatted blind, jalousie.
jaloux, -ouse [ʒalu, uz] adj **a** (*en amour*) jealous; (*envieux*) jealous, envious. **~ de qn/de la réussite de qn** jealous of sb/of sb's success; **~ de son autorité** jealous of his authority; **~ comme un tigre** madly jealous; **observer qn d'un œil ~** to keep a jealous eye on sb, watch sb jealously; **faire des ~** to make people jealous. **b** (*littér: désireux*) **~ de** intent upon, eager for; **~ de perfection** eager for perfection.
jamaïquain, e [ʒamaikɛ̃, ɛn] **1** adj Jamaican. **2** nm,f: **J~(e)** Jamaican.
Jamaïque [ʒamaik] nf Jamaica.
jamais [ʒamɛ] adv **a** (*avec ou sans ne: négatif*) never, not ever. **il n'a ~ avoué** he never confessed; **n'a-t-il ~ avoué?** did he never confess?, didn't he ever confess?; **il travaille comme ~ il n'a travaillé** he's working as he's never worked before; **il n'a ~ autant travaillé** he has never worked as hard (before), he has never done so much work (before); **~ je n'ai vu un homme si égoïste** I have never met *ou* seen such a selfish man (before), never (before) have I met *ou* seen such a selfish man; **~ mère ne fut plus heureuse** there was never a happier mother; **il n'est ~ trop tard** it's never too late; **il ne lui a ~ plus écrit** he never wrote to her again, he has never *ou* he hasn't ever written to her since; **on ne l'a ~ encore entendu se plaindre** he's never yet been heard to complain; **ne dites ~ plus cela!** never say that again!, don't you ever say that again!; **il partit pour ne ~ plus revenir** he departed never (more) to return; **~ plus** *ou* **~ au grand ~ on ne me prendra à le faire** you'll never *ou* you won't ever catch me doing it again; **nous sommes restés 2 ans sans ~ recevoir de nouvelles** we were *ou* went 2 years without ever hearing any news, for 2 years we never (once) heard any news; **elle sort souvent mais ~ sans son chien** she often goes out but never without her dog; **il n'a ~ fait que critiquer (les autres)** he's never done anything but criticize (others); **ça ne fait ~ que deux heures qu'il est parti** it's no more than 2 hours since he left; **ce n'est ~ qu'un enfant** he is only a child (after all); **je n'ai ~ de ma vie vu un chien aussi laid** never in my life have I *ou* I have never in my life seen such an ugly dog; **accepterez-vous? — ~ de la vie!** will you accept? — never! *ou* not on your life!*; **le ferez-vous encore? — ~ plus!** *ou* **plus ~!** will you do it again? — never (again)!; **c'est ce que vous avez dit — ~!** that's what you said — never! *ou* I never did!* *ou* I never said that!; **presque ~** hardly *ou* scarcely ever, practically never; **c'est maintenant ou ~, c'est le moment ou ~** it's now or never; **c'est le moment ou ~ d'acheter** now is the time to buy, if ever there was a time to buy it's now; **une symphonie ~ jouée/terminée** an unplayed/unfinished symphony; **~ deux sans trois!** (*gén*) there's always a third time!; (*malheur*) it never rains but it pours!; (*iro*) **alors, ~ on ne dit "merci"?*** did nobody ever teach you to say "thank you"? (*iro*); *voir* **mieux, savoir**.
b (*sans ne: temps indéfini*) ever. **a-t-il ~ avoué?** did he ever confess?; **si ~ vous passez par Londres venez nous voir** if ever you're passing *ou* if ever you should pass *ou* should you ever pass through London come and see us; **si ~ j'avais un poste pour vous je vous préviendrais** if ever I had *ou* if I ever had a job for you I'd let you know; **si ~ tu rates le train, reviens** if by (any) chance you miss *ou* if you (should) happen to miss the train, come back; **si ~ tu recommences, gare!** watch out if you ever start that again!; **les œufs sont plus chers que ~** eggs are

more expensive than ever (before); **c'est pire que ~** it's worse than ever; **avez-vous ~ vu ça?** have you ever seen *ou* did you ever see such a thing?; **c'est le plus grand que j'aie ~ vu** it's the biggest I've ever seen; **il désespère d'avoir ~ de l'avancement** he despairs of ever getting promotion *ou* of ever being promoted; **à ~** for good, for ever; **à tout ~, pour ~** for ever (and ever), for good and all*, for evermore (*littér*); **je renonce à tout ~ à le lui faire comprendre** I've given up ever trying to make him understand it; **leur amitié est à ~ compromise** their friendship will never be the same again.

jambage [ʒɑ̃baʒ] **nm** **a** *[lettre]* downstroke. **b** (*Archit*) jamb.

jambe [ʒɑ̃b] **nf** **a** (*Anat, Habillement, Zool*) leg. **fille aux longues ~s** *ou* **toute en ~s** girl with long legs, long-legged *ou* leggy* girl; **remonte ta ~ (de pantalon)** roll up your trouser leg; (*Méd*) **~ de bois/artificielle/articulée** wooden/artificial/articulated leg; *voir* **mi-**.
b (*loc*) **avoir les ~s comme du coton** *ou* **en coton** to have legs like *ou* of jelly *ou* cotton wool; **avoir les ~s brisées, n'avoir plus de ~s, en avoir plein les ~s*** to be worn out *ou* on one's last legs* *ou* on one's knees*; **avoir 20 km dans les ~s** to have walked 20 km; **je n'ai plus mes ~s de 20 ans!** I'm not as quick on my feet as I used to be!; **la peur/l'impatience lui donnait des ~s** fear/impatience lent new strength to his legs *ou* lent him speed; (*Sport*) **se mettre en ~s** to warm up, limber up; **tirer** *ou* **traîner la ~** (*par fatigue*) to drag one's steps; (*boiter*) to limp along; **elle ne peut plus (se) tenir sur ses ~s** her legs are giving way under her, she can hardly stand; **prendre ses ~s à son cou** to take to one's heels; **traiter qn par-dessous** *ou* **par-dessus la ~*** to treat sb offhandedly; **faire qch par-dessous** *ou* **par-dessus la ~*** to do sth carelessly *ou* in a slipshod way; **il m'a tenu la ~ pendant des heures*** he kept me hanging about talking for hours*; **tirer dans les ~s de qn*** to make life difficult for sb; **il s'est jeté dans nos ~s*** he got under our feet; **elle est toujours dans mes ~s*** she's always getting in my way *ou* under my feet; **j'en ai eu les ~s coupées!** it knocked me sideways!*, it knocked me for six!* (*Brit*); *voir* **beau, dégourdir, partie**[2] *etc.*
c (*Tech*) *[compas]* leg; (*étai*) prop, stay. **~ de force** (*Constr*) strut; (*Aut*) torque rod.

jambier, -ière[1] [ʒɑ̃bje, jɛʀ] **adj, nm: (muscle) ~** leg muscle.

jambière[2] [ʒɑ̃bjɛʀ] **nf** (*gén*) legging, gaiter; (*Sport*) pad; (*armure*) greave. (*en laine*) **~s** leg-warmers.

jambon [ʒɑ̃bɔ̃] **nm** **a** (*Culin*) ham. **~ cru salé/fumé** salted/smoked (raw) ham; **~ blanc** *ou* **de Paris** boiled *ou* cooked ham; **~ de pays = ~ cru; ~ de Parme** Parma ham; **~ à l'os** ham on the bone; **~ au torchon** top quality cooked ham. **b** (‡: *cuisse*) thigh.

jambonneau, pl ~x [ʒɑ̃bɔno] **nm** knuckle of ham.

jamboree [ʒɑ̃bɔʀe] **nm** (*Scoutisme*) jamboree.

janissaire [ʒanisɛʀ] **nm** janissary.

jansénisme [ʒɑ̃senism] **nm** Jansenism; (*fig*) austere code of morals.

janséniste [ʒɑ̃senist] **1 adj** Jansenist. **2 nmf: J~** Jansenist.

jante [ʒɑ̃t] **nf** *[bicyclette, voiture]* rim. (*Aut*) **~s alu** alloy wheels.

Janus [ʒanys] **nm** Janus.

janvier [ʒɑ̃vje] **nm** January; *pour loc voir* **septembre**.

Japon [ʒapɔ̃] **nm** Japan.

japonais, e [ʒapɔnɛ, ɛz] **1 adj** Japanese. **2 nm** (*Ling*) Japanese. **3 nm,f: J~(e)** Japanese.

japonaiserie [ʒapɔnɛzʀi] **nf, japonerie** [ʒapɔnʀi] **nf** Japanese curio.

japonisant, e [ʒapɔnizɑ̃, ɑ̃t] **nm,f** expert on Japan.

jappement [ʒapmɑ̃] **nm** yap, yelp.

japper [ʒape] [1] **vi** to yap, yelp.

jaquette [ʒakɛt] **nf** *[homme]* morning coat; *[femme]* jacket; *[livre]* (dust) jacket, (dust) cover; *[cassette vidéo]* (plastic) cover; *[dent]* crown.

jardin [ʒaʀdɛ̃] **nm** garden, yard (*US*). **rester au** *ou* **dans le ~** to stay in the garden; **siège/table de ~** garden seat/table; **~ d'acclimatation** zoological garden(s); **~ d'agrément** pleasure garden; **~ anglais** *ou* **à l'anglaise** landscape garden; **~ botanique** botanical garden(s); **~ d'enfants** kindergarten, ≃ playschool (*Brit*); **~ à la française** formal garden; **~ d'hiver** winter garden; **~ japonais** Japanese garden; (*Bible*) **le ~ des Oliviers** the Garden of Gethsemane; **~ potager** vegetable *ou* kitchen garden; **~ public** (public) park, public gardens; **~ de rapport** market garden; **~s suspendus** terraced gardens, hanging gardens; **~ zoologique = ~ d'acclimatation;** *voir* **côté, cultiver, pierre**.

jardinage [ʒaʀdinaʒ] **nm** gardening.

jardiner [ʒaʀdine] [1] **vi** to garden, do some gardening.

jardinerie [ʒaʀdinʀi] **nf** garden centre.

jardinet [ʒaʀdinɛ] **nm** small garden. **les ~s des pavillons de banlieue** the small gardens *ou* the little patches of garden round suburban houses.

jardinier, -ière [ʒaʀdinje, jɛʀ] **1 adj** garden (*épith*). **culture ~ière** horticulture; **plantes ~ières** garden plants. **2 nm,f** gardener. **3 jardinière nf** **a** (*caisse à fleurs*) window box; (*d'intérieur*) jardiniere. **b** (*Culin*) **~ière (de légumes)** mixed vegetables, jardiniere. **c** (*Scol*) **~ière d'enfants** kindergarten teacher, ≃ playschool supervisor (*Brit*).

jargon [ʒaʀgɔ̃] **nm** **a** (*baragouin*) gibberish (*NonC*), double Dutch* (*NonC*) (*Brit*). **b** (*langue professionnelle*) jargon (*NonC*), lingo*† (*NonC*). **il ne connaît pas encore le ~** he doesn't know the jargon yet; **~ administratif** officialese (*NonC*), official jargon; **~ informatique** computerese* (*NonC*); **~ journalistique** journalese (*NonC*); **~ de la médecine** medical jargon; **~ de métier** trade jargon *ou* slang; (*Jur*) **~ du palais** legal jargon, legalese (*NonC*).

jargonner [ʒaʀgɔne] [1] **vi** to jabber; (*utiliser un jargon*) to talk (professional *etc*) jargon.

Jarnac [ʒaʀnak] **n: coup de ~** stab in the back.

jarre [ʒaʀ] **nf** (earthenware) jar.

jarret [ʒaʀɛ] **nm** **a** (*Anat*) *[homme]* back of the knee, ham; *[animal]* hock. **avoir des ~s d'acier** to have strong legs. **b** (*Culin*) **~ de veau** knuckle *ou* shin of veal, veal shank (*US*).

jarretelle [ʒaʀtɛl] **nf** suspender (*Brit*), garter (*US*).

jarretière [ʒaʀtjɛʀ] **nf** garter; *voir* **ordre**[1].

jars [ʒaʀ] **nm** (*animal*) gander.

jaser [ʒɑze] [1] **vi** **a** *[enfant]* to chatter, prattle; *[personne]* to chat away, chat on*; *[oiseau]* to twitter; *[jet d'eau, ruisseau]* to babble, sing. **on entend ~ la pie/le geai** you can hear the magpie/jay chattering. **b** (*arg Police*) to talk, give the game away*. **essayer de faire ~ qn** to try to make sb talk. **c** (*médire*) to gossip. **cela va faire ~ les gens** that'll set tongues wagging, that'll set people talking *ou* gossiping.

jaseur, -euse [ʒɑzœʀ, øz] **1 adj** *enfant* chattering (*épith*), prattling (*épith*); *oiseau* chattering (*épith*), twittering (*épith*); *ruisseau, jet d'eau* singing (*épith*), babbling (*épith*); *personne* (*médisant*) tittle-tattling (*épith*), gossipy. **2 nm** (*bavard*) gasbag*, chatterbox; (*médisant*) gossip, tittle-tattle; (*Zool*) waxwing.

jasmin [ʒasmɛ̃] **nm** (*arbuste*) jasmine. (*parfum*) **(essence de) ~** jasmine (perfume).

Jason [ʒazɔ̃] **nm** Jason.

jaspe [ʒasp] **nm** (*matière*) jasper; (*objet*) jasper ornament. **~ sanguin** bloodstone.

jaspé, e [ʒaspe] **adj** mottled, marbled.

jaspiner‡ [ʒaspine] [1] **vi** to natter* (*Brit*), chatter.

jatte [ʒat] **nf** (shallow) bowl, basin.

jauge [ʒoʒ] **nf** **a** (*instrument*) gauge. **~ d'essence** petrol gauge; **~ (de niveau) d'huile** (oil) dipstick. **b** (*capacité*) *[réservoir]* capacity; *[navire]* tonnage, burden; (*Tex*) tension.

jaugeage [ʒoʒaʒ] **nm** *[navire, réservoir]* gauging.

jauger [ʒoʒe] [3] **1 vt** **a** (*lit*) *réservoir* to gauge the capacity of; *navire* to measure the tonnage of.
b (*fig*) *personne* to size up. **il le jaugea du regard** he gave him an appraising look; **~ qn d'un coup d'œil** to size sb up at a glance.
2 vi to have a capacity of. **navire qui jauge 500 tonneaux** ship with a tonnage of 500, ship of 500 tonnes *ou* tons burden.

jaunâtre [ʒonɑtʀ] **adj** *lumière couleur* yellowish; *teint* sallow, yellowish.

jaune [ʒon] **1 adj** *couleur, race* yellow; (*littér*) *blés* golden. **il a le teint ~** (*mauvaise mine*) he looks yellow *ou* sallow; (*basané*) he has a sallow complexion; **dents ~s** yellow teeth; **~ citron** lemon, lemon yellow; **~ d'or** golden yellow; **~ paille** straw coloured; **~ serin** *ou* **canari** canary yellow; **~ comme un citron** *ou* **un coing** as yellow as a lemon; *voir* **corps, fièvre, nain** *etc.* **2 nm** **a** (*péj,* ‡) **J~** Asian (man); (*Chinois*) Chink‡; (*Japonais*) Jap‡, Nip‡; **les J~s** the yellow races; *voir* **péril**. **b** (*couleur*) yellow. **c ~ (d'œuf)** (egg) yolk. **d** (*péj: non-gréviste*) blackleg (*Brit*), scab‡. **3 nf** **a** (*péj,* ‡) **J~** Asian woman; (*Chinoise*) Chink‡; (*Japonaise*) Jap‡, Nip‡. **b** (*péj: non-gréviste*) blackleg (*Brit*), scab‡.

jaunet, -ette [ʒonɛ, ɛt] **1 adj** slightly yellow, yellowish. **2 nm** (††) gold coin.

jaunir [ʒoniʀ] [2] **1 vt** *feuillage, vêtements* to turn yellow. **doigts jaunis par la nicotine** fingers yellowed *ou* discoloured with nicotine. **2 vi** to yellow, turn *ou* become yellow.

jaunissant, e [ʒonisɑ̃, ɑ̃t] **adj** (*littér*) *papier, feuillage* yellowing; *blé* ripening, yellowing (*littér*).

jaunisse [ʒonis] **nf** (*Méd*) jaundice. **en faire une ~*** (*de dépit*) to have one's nose put out of joint, be pretty miffed*; (*de jalousie*) to be *ou* turn green with envy.

jaunissement [ʒonismɑ̃] **nm** yellowing.

Java [ʒava] **nf** Java.

java [ʒava] **nf** (*danse*) popular waltz. (*fig*) **faire la ~‡** to live it up*, have a rave-up‡ (*Brit*); **ils ont fait une de ces ~s** they had a really wild time* *ou* a real rave-up‡.

javanais, e [ʒavanɛ, ɛz] **1 adj** Javanese. **2 nm** (*Ling*) Javanese; (*argot*) "av" slang; (*charabia*) double Dutch* (*Brit*), gibberish. **3 nm,f: J~(e)** Javanese; **les J~** the Javanese.

Javel [ʒavɛl] **nf: (eau de) ~** bleach.

javeline [ʒavlin] **nf** javelin.

javelle [ʒavɛl] **nf** *[céréales]* swath. **mettre en ~s** to lay in swathes.

javellisation [ʒavelizasjɔ̃] **nf** chlorination.

javelliser [ʒavelize] [1] **vt** to chlorinate. **cette eau est trop javellisée** there's too much chlorine in this water; **eau très javellisée** heavily chlorinated water.

javelot [ʒavlo] **nm** (*Mil, Sport*) javelin; *voir* **lancement**.

jazz [dʒɑz] **nm** jazz. **la musique (de) ~** jazz (music).

jazzman [dʒɑzman], **pl jazzmen** [dʒɑzmɛn] **nm** jazzman, jazz player.

J.-C. **abrév de Jésus-Christ**.

je, j' [ʒ(ə)] **1 pron pers** I. **2 nm: le ~** (*Ling*) the I-form, the 1st person; (*Philos*) the I. **3 comp ►je-m'en-fichisme* nm** (I-)couldn't-care-less attitude* ▸**je-m'en-fichiste*** adj (I-)couldn't-care-less* (*épith*) ◊ nmf couldn't-care-less type* ▸**je-m'en-foutisme‡** nm (I-)couldn't-give-a-damn attitude‡ ▸**je-m'en-foutiste‡** adj (I-)couldn't-give-a-damn‡ (*épith*) ◊ nmf couldn't-give-a-damn type‡ ▸**je-ne-sais-quoi** nm inv (certain) something; **elle a un je-ne-sais-quoi qui attire** there's (a certain) something about her that is very attractive.

Jean [ʒɑ̃] nm John. **(saint) ~-Baptiste** (St) John the Baptist; **(saint) ~ de la Croix** St John of the Cross; (*Hist*) **~ sans Terre** John Lackland.

jean [dʒin] nm (*tissu*) denim; (*vêtement*) (pair of) jeans, (pair of) denims. **~ (de ou en) velours** cord(uroy) jeans; **blouson en ~ vert** green denim jacket.

jean-foutre [ʒɑ̃futʀ] nm inv (*péj*) jackass (*péj*).

Jeanne [ʒan] nf Jane, Joan, Jean. **~ d'Arc** Joan of Arc; **coiffure à la ~ d'Arc** bobbed hair with a fringe (*Brit*) *ou* with bangs (*US*).

jeannette [ʒanɛt] nf a **(croix à la) ~** gold cross (*worn around neck*). b (*planche à repasser*) sleeve-board. c (*prénom*) **J~** Janet, Jenny. d (*Scoutisme*) Brownie (Guide).

Jeannot [ʒano] nm Johnny. **~ lapin** bunny (rabbit), Mr Rabbit.

jeans [dʒins] nm, pl inv = **jean**.

Jeep [(d)ʒip] nf ® Jeep ®.

Jéhovah [ʒeova] nm Jehovah; *voir* **témoin**.

jéjunum [ʒeʒynɔm] nm jejunum.

jennérien, -ienne [ʒeneʀjɛ̃, jɛn] adj Jennerian.

jenny [ʒeni] nf spinning jenny.

jérémiades* [ʒeʀemjad] nfpl moaning, whining.

Jérémie [ʒeʀemi] nm Jeremy; (*prophète*) Jeremiah.

Jéricho [ʒeʀiko] n Jericho.

Jéroboam [ʒeʀɔbɔam] nm Jeroboam. **j~** (*bouteille*) jeroboam (*bottle containing 3 litres*).

Jérôme [ʒeʀom] nm Jerome.

jerrican(e) nm, **jerrycan** [(d)ʒeʀikan] nm jerry can.

Jersey [ʒɛʀzɛ] nf Jersey.

jersey [ʒɛʀzɛ] nm a (*vêtement*) jersey top (*ou* garment *etc*), jumper (*Brit*), sweater. b (*tissu*) jersey (cloth). **~ de laine/de soie** jersey wool/silk; **point de ~** stocking stitch; **tricoter un pull en ~** to knit a jumper in stocking stitch.

jersiais, e [ʒɛʀzjɛ, jɛz] 1 adj Jersey (*épith*), of *ou* from Jersey. (*Agr*) **race ~e** Jersey breed; **(vache) ~e** Jersey, Jersey cow. 2 nm,f: **J~(e)** inhabitant *ou* native of Jersey.

Jérusalem [ʒeʀyzalɛm] n Jerusalem. **la ~ nouvelle/céleste** the New/Heavenly Jerusalem.

jésuite [ʒezɥit] 1 nm (*Rel*) Jesuit. 2 adj *air, parti* Jesuit.

jésuitique [ʒezɥitik] adj Jesuitical.

jésuitiquement [ʒezɥitikmɑ̃] adv Jesuitically.

jésuitisme [ʒezɥitism] nm Jesuitism, Jesuitry.

jésus [ʒezy] nm a **J~** Jesus; **J~-Christ** Jesus Christ; **en 300 avant/après J~-Christ** in 300 B.C./A.D. b **(papier) ~** super royal (printing paper); **(papier) petit ~** super royal (writing paper). c (*statue*) statue of the infant Jesus. d (*terme d'affection*) **mon ~** (my) darling. e (*saucisson*) *kind of pork sausage*.

jet¹ [ʒɛ] 1 nm a (*jaillissement*) *[eau, gaz, flamme]* jet; *[sang]* spurt, gush; *[salive]* stream; *[pompe]* flow. **~ de lumière** beam of light.
b *[pierre, grenade]* (*action*) throwing; (*résultat*) throw. **à un ~ de pierre** at a stone's throw, a stone's throw away; **un ~ de 60 mètres au disque** a 60-metre discus throw; (*Boxe*) **il a gagné par ~ de l'éponge au 3ᵉ round** he won because his opponent's corner threw in the towel in the third round; *voir* **arme**.
c (*loc*) **premier ~** first sketch, rough outline; **du premier ~** at the first attempt *ou* shot *ou* go; **écrire d'un (seul) ~** to write in one go; **à ~ continu** in a continuous *ou* an endless stream.
d (*Tech*) (*coulage*) casting; (*masselotte*) head. **couler une pièce d'un seul ~** to produce a piece in a single casting.
e (*Bot*) (*pousse*) main shoot; (*rameau*) branch.
2 comp ▸**jet d'eau** (*fontaine*) fountain; (*gerbe*) spray; (*au bout d'un tuyau*) nozzle; (*Archit*) weathering ▸**jet à la mer** (*Naut*) jettison(ing).

jet² [dʒɛt] nm (*Aviat*) jet.

jetable [ʒ(ə)tabl] adj *briquet, mouchoir, rasoir* disposable.

jeté, e¹ [ʒ(ə)te] 1 adj (‡: *fou*) mad*, crazy*. 2 nm a (*Danse*) **~ (simple)** jeté; **~ battu** grand jeté. b (*Sport*) snatch; *voir* **épaulé**. c (*Tricot*) **~ (simple)** make one; **faire un ~** to drop a stitch. 3 comp ▸**jeté de lit** bedspread ▸**jeté de table** table runner.

jetée² [ʒ(ə)te] nf jetty; (*grande*) pier. **~ flottante** floating bridge.

jeter [ʒ(ə)te] [4] 1 vt a (*lancer*) to throw; (*avec force*) to fling, hurl, sling; *dés* to throw. **~ qch à qn** (*pour qu'il l'attrape*) to throw sth to sb; (*agressivement*) to throw *ou* fling *ou* hurl sth at sb; **~ qch par terre/par la fenêtre** to throw sth on the ground *ou* down/out of the window; **~ dehors** *ou* **à la porte** *visiteur* to throw out, chuck out‡ (*Brit*); *employé* to fire, sack (*Brit*), give the push to* (*Brit*); **~ qn en prison** to throw *ou* sling* (*Brit*) sb into prison; **il a jeté son agresseur à terre** he threw his attacker to the ground; **~ bas qch** to throw sth down; *[cheval]* **~ qn à terre** *ou* **à bas** to throw sb; **elle lui a jeté son cadeau à la tête** she threw *ou* hurled his present at him; (*Naut*) **~ à la mer** *personne* to throw overboard; *objet* to throw overboard, jettison; (*Naut*) **le navire a été jeté à la côte** the ship was driven towards the coast; *voir* **ancre**.
b (*mettre au rebut*) *papiers, objets* to throw away *ou* out; (*Cartes*) to discard. **~ qch au panier/à la poubelle/au feu** to throw sth into the wastepaper basket/in the dustbin/in *ou* on the fire; **jette l'eau sale dans l'évier** pour *ou* tip (away) the dirty water down the sink; **se faire ~‡** (*d'une réunion*) to get chucked‡ out (*Brit*), get thrown out; (*lors d'une requête, déclaration d'amour*) to be sent packing*; *voir* **bon¹**.
c (*construire*) *pont* to throw (*sur* over, across); *fondations* to lay. **~ un pont sur une rivière** to bridge a river, throw a bridge over a river; (*fig*) **~ les bases d'une nouvelle Europe** to lay the foundations of a new Europe; (*Naut*) **jetez la passerelle!** set up the gangway!
d (*émettre*) *lueur* to give, give out, cast, shed; *son* to let out, give out. **le diamant jette mille feux** the diamond flashes *ou* sparkles brilliantly; **ce nouveau tapis dans le salon, ça jette (du jus)‡** this new carpet really does something for the sitting room*, the new carpet in the sitting room is really quite something*; **elle (en) jette, cette voiture!*** that's a really smart car!, that's some car!*.
e (*: *mettre rapidement*) **~ des vêtements dans un sac** to sling *ou* throw some clothes into a bag; **va ~ cette carte à la boîte** go and slip *ou* pop* this card into the postbox; **~ une veste sur ses épaules** to slip a jacket over *ou* round one's shoulders; **~ une idée sur le papier** to jot down an idea.
f (*fig: mettre, plonger*) to plunge, throw. **~ qn dans le désespoir** to plunge sb into despair; **~ qn dans les frais** to plunge sb into *ou* involve sb in a lot of expense; **~ qn dans l'embarras** to throw sb into confusion.
g (*répandre*) to cast. **~ l'effroi chez/parmi** to sow alarm and confusion in/among; **~ le trouble chez qn** to disturb *ou* trouble sb; **~ le discrédit sur qn/qch** to cast discredit on sb/sth; **~ un sort à qn** to cast a spell on sb; **sa remarque a jeté un froid** his remark cast a chill.
h (*dire*) to say (*à* to). **il me jeta en passant que c'était commencé** he said to me as he went by that it had begun; **~ des remarques dans la conversation** to throw in *ou* toss in remarks; **~ un cri** to let out *ou* give *ou* utter a cry; **~ des cris** to cry out, scream; **~ des insultes/menaces** to hurl insults/threats; **je lui ai jeté la vérité/l'accusation à la figure** *ou* **à la tête** I hurled *ou* flung the truth/accusation at him; **il lui jeta à la tête qu'il n'était qu'un imbécile** he burst out at him that he was nothing but a fool; **ils se jetèrent des injures à la tête** they hurled insults at each other.
i (*prendre une attitude*) **~ les épaules/la tête en avant** to throw *ou* thrust one's shoulders/head forward; **~ les bras autour du cou de qn** to throw *ou* fling one's arms round sb's neck; **elle lui jeta un regard plein de mépris** she cast a withering look at him, she looked *ou* glanced witheringly at him; **elle lui jeta un coup d'œil ironique** she flashed *ou* threw him an ironical glance, she glanced at him ironically.
j (*loc*) **~ les yeux sur qn** (*frm: regarder*) to cast a glance at sb; (*fig: vouloir épouser*) to have one's eye on sb; **~ un coup d'œil sur un livre** to glance at a book, take a quick look at a book; **~ un coup d'œil sur les enfants** to take a look at *ou* check up on the children; **~ un œil (sur qch)*** to take a look (at sth); **~ son bonnet par-dessus les moulins** to kick over the traces, have one's fling; **~ la première pierre** to cast the first stone; **je ne veux pas lui ~ la pierre** I don't want to be too hard on him; **~ son dévolu sur qch/qn** to set one's heart on sth/sb; (*boisson*) **on va s'en ~ un (derrière la cravate)‡** we'll have a quick one*; **n'en jetez plus (la cour est pleine)!*** (*après compliments*) don't! *ou* stop it! you're embarrassing me; (*après injures etc*) cut it out!*, pack it in!* (*Brit*); **~ l'argent par les fenêtres** to spend money like water, throw money down the drain; **~ la soutane** *ou* **le froc aux orties** to unfrock o.s., leave the priesthood; **~ sa gourme** to sow one's wild oats; **~ le manche après la cognée** to throw in one's hand; **~ de la poudre aux yeux de qn** to impress sb; (*Boxe, fig*) **~ l'éponge** to throw in the sponge *ou* towel; *voir* **huile, lest, masque**.
2 **se jeter** vpr a (*s'élancer*) **se ~ par la fenêtre** to throw o.s. out of the window; **se ~ dans les bras/aux pieds de qn** to throw o.s. into sb's arms/at sb's feet; **se ~ à la tête de qn** to throw o.s. at sb; **se ~ du douzième étage** to throw o.s. off the twelfth floor; **se ~ à genoux** to throw o.s. down on one's knees; **se ~ sur qn** to launch o.s. at sb, rush at sb; **se ~ sur sa proie** to swoop down *ou* pounce on one's prey; **il se jette sur la nourriture comme un affamé** he falls (up)on *ou* goes at the food like a starving man; **un chien s'est jeté sous les roues de notre voiture** a dog rushed out under the wheels of our car; **sa voiture s'est jetée contre un arbre** his car crashed into a tree; **se ~ à l'eau** (*lit*) to launch o.s. *ou* plunge into the water; (*fig*) to take the plunge; (*fig*) **se ~ à corps perdu dans une entreprise/dans la mêlée** to throw o.s. wholeheartedly into an enterprise/into the fray; (*fig*) **se ~ dans la politique/les affaires** to launch out into politics/business.
b *[rivière]* to flow (*dans* into). **le Rhône se jette dans la Méditerranée** the Rhone flows into the Mediterranean.

jeteur [ʒ(ə)tœʀ] nm: **~ de sort** wizard.

jeteuse [ʒ(ə)tøz] nf: **~ de sort** witch.

jeton [ʒ(ə)tɔ̃] nm a (*pièce*) (*gén*) token; (*Jeux*) counter; (*Roulette*) chip. **~ de téléphone** telephone token; **~ (de présence)** (*argent*) director's fees; (*objet*) token; (*somme*) **toucher ses ~s** to draw one's fees; *voir* **faux²**. b (‡) (*coup*) bang; (*marque*) dent. **recevoir un ~** to get a bang; **avoir les ~s** to have the jitters* *ou* the willies‡; **ça lui a**

fichu les ~s he got the wind up* (*Brit*), it gave him the jitters* *ou* the willies‡.

jeu, pl **~x** [ʒø] 1 **nm** a (*amusement, divertissement*) **le ~** play; **le ~ fait partie de l'éducation du jeune enfant** play forms part of the young child's education; **elle ne prend jamais part au ~ de ses camarades** she never joins in her friends' play; (*fig*) **le ~ du soleil sur l'eau** the play of the sun on the water.

b (*gén avec règles*) game. **~ d'intérieur/de plein air** indoor/outdoor game; **~ d'adresse** game of skill; **~ de cartes** card game; **le ~ d'échecs/de boules/de quilles** the game of chess/bowls/skittles; *voir* **règle.**

c (*Sport: partie*) game. (*Tennis*) **il mène (par) 5 ~x à 2** he leads (by) 5 games to 2; **~ blanc** love game; **"~, set, et match"** "game, set and match"; **la pluie a ralenti le ~** the rain slowed down play (in the game); (*Rugby*) **jouer un ~ ouvert** to keep the game open.

d (*Sport: limites du terrain*) **en ~** in play; **hors ~** (*Tennis*) out (of play); (*Rugby, Ftbl*) offside; **la balle est sortie du ~** the ball has gone out of play; **mettre** *ou* **remettre en ~** to throw in; **remise en ~** throw-in; (*Rugby, Ftbl*) **mettre qn hors ~** to put sb offside.

e (*Casino*) gambling. **il a perdu toute sa fortune au ~** he has gambled away his entire fortune, he lost his fortune (at) gambling; *voir* **heureux, jouer.**

f (*ensemble des pions, boîte*) game, set. **~ d'échecs/de boules/de quilles** chess/bowls/skittle set; **~ de 52 cartes** pack *ou* deck (*US*) of 52 cards.

g (*lieu*) **~ de boules** bowling green; **~ de quilles** skittle alley.

h (*série complète*) *[clefs, aiguilles]* set. **~ d'orgue(s)** organ stop.

i (*Cartes*) hand. **il laisse voir son ~** he shows his hand; **je n'ai jamais de ~** I never have a good hand; (*fig*) **cacher/dévoiler son ~** to conceal/show one's hand.

j (*façon de jouer*) (*Sport*) game; (*Mus*) technique, (manner of) playing; (*Ciné, Théât*) acting. (*Sport*) **il a un ~ rapide/lent/efficace** he plays a fast/a slow/an effective game; (*Mus*) **elle a un ~ saccadé/dur** she plays jerkily/harshly, her playing is jerky/harsh.

k (*Admin, Pol etc: fonctionnement*) working, interaction, interplay. **le ~ des alliances/des institutions** the interplay of alliances/of institutions; *voir* **mise.**

l (*manège*) **j'observais le ~ de l'enfant** I watched the child's little game; **j'ai compris son petit ~!** I know his little game *ou* what he's up to!; **à quel ~ joues-tu?** what ARE you playing at?; **c'est un ~ de dupes** it's a fool's *ou* mug's* (*Brit*) game; **le ~ muet de deux complices** the silent exchanges of two accomplices.

m (*Tech*) play. **le ~ des pistons** the play of the pistons; **donner du ~ à qch** to loosen sth up a bit; **la vis a pris du ~** the screw has worked loose; **la porte ne ferme pas bien – il y a du ~** the door doesn't shut tight – there's a bit of play.

n (*loc*) **le ~ n'en vaut pas la chandelle** the game is not worth the candle; **il a beau ~ de protester maintenant** it's easy for him to complain now; **les forces en ~** the forces at work; **être en ~** to be at stake; **entrer/mettre en ~** to come/bring into play; **entrer dans le ~ de qn** to play sb's game, join in sb's game; **faire** *ou* **jouer le ~ de qn** to play into sb's hands; **faire ~ égal avec qn** to be evenly matched; **il s'est fait un ~ de résoudre la difficulté** he made light work *ou* easy work of the problem; **c'est le ~** it's fair (play); **ce n'est pas de ~*** that's not (playing) fair; **c'est un ~ d'enfant** it's child's play, it's a snap* (*US*); **ce n'est qu'un ~** it's just a game; **par ~** for fun; **se piquer/se prendre au ~** to get excited over/get caught up in *ou* involved in the game; **être pris à son propre ~** to be caught out at one's own game, be hoist with one's own petard; **il mettra tout en ~ pour nous aider** he'll risk everything to help us; **~x de main, ~x de vilain!** stop fooling around or it will end in tears!; (*Casino*) **"faites vos ~x"** "place your bets"; **les ~x sont faits** (*Casino*) "les jeux sont faits"; (*fig*) the die is cast; *voir* **beau, double, entrée** *etc.*

2 **comp** ▸**jeu d'arcade** video game ▸**jeux du cirque** (*Hist*) circus games ▸**jeu-concours** (*Presse, Rad, TV*) **nm (pl jeux-concours)** competition; (*avec questions*) quiz, competition ▸**jeu de construction** building *ou* construction set ▸**jeux d'eau** fountains ▸**jeu d'écritures** (*Comm*) dummy entry ▸**jeu d'essai** (*Ordin*) benchmark ▸**jeu de hasard** game of chance ▸**jeu de jambes** (*Sport*) footwork, leg movement ▸**jeux de lumière** (*artificiels*) lighting effects; (*naturels*) play of light (*NonC*) ▸**jeu de mains** *[pianiste]* playing, technique ▸**jeu de massacre** (*à la foire*) Aunt Sally; (*fig*) wholesale massacre *ou* slaughter ▸**jeu de mots** play on words (*NonC*), pun ▸**jeu de l'oie** ≃ snakes and ladders ▸**Jeux olympiques** Olympic games; **Jeux olympiques d'hiver** Winter Olympics; **Jeux olympiques pour handicapés** Paralympics ▸**jeu de patience** puzzle ▸**jeux de physionomie** facial expressions ▸**jeu de piste** treasure hunt ▸**jeu radiophonique** radio game ▸**jeu de rôles** role play ▸**jeu de scène** (*Théât*) stage business (*NonC*) ▸**jeu de société** parlour game ▸**jeux du stade** (*Hist*) (ancient) Olympic games ▸**jeu de stratégie** game of strategy ▸**jeu télévisé** television game; (*avec questions*) (television) quiz ▸**jeu vidéo** video game.

jeudi [ʒødi] **nm** Thursday. **le ~ de l'Ascension** Ascension Day; **le ~ saint** Maundy Thursday; *pour autres loc voir* **samedi.**

jeun [ʒœ̃] **adv: à ~** with *ou* on an empty stomach; **être à ~** (*n'avoir rien mangé/bu*) to have eaten/drunk nothing, have let nothing pass one's lips; (*ne pas être ivre*) to be sober; **rester à ~** to remain without eating anything, not to eat anything; **boire à ~** to drink on an empty stomach; (*Méd*) **à prendre à ~** to be taken on an empty stomach.

jeune [ʒœn] 1 **adj** a (*âge*) young. **c'est un homme ~** he's a young man; **mes ~s années** my youth, the years of my youth; **dans mon ~ âge** *ou* **temps** in my younger days, when I was younger; **vu son ~ âge** in view of his youth; **il n'est plus tout** *ou* **très ~** he's not as young as he was, he's not the young man he was, he's not in his first youth; **il est plus ~ que moi de 5 ans** he's 5 years younger than me, he's 5 years my junior; **~ chien** puppy, pup.

b (*qualité*) (*après n*) new, young; *industrie* new; (*dynamique*) forward-looking; *vin* young; *apparence, visage* youthful; *couleur, vêtement* young, which makes one look young. **soyez/restez ~s!** be/stay young! *ou* youthful!

c **être ~ d'allure** to be young-looking, be youthful in appearance, have a youthful look about one; **être ~ de caractère** *ou* **d'esprit** (*puéril*) to have a childish outlook, be immature; (*dynamique*) to have a youthful *ou* fresh outlook; **être ~ de cœur** to be young at heart; **être ~ de corps** to have a youthful figure.

d (*avoir l'air ~*) **ils font ~(s)** they look young; **il fait plus ~ que son âge** he looks younger than his age, he doesn't look his age; **qu'est-ce que ça le fait paraître ~, ce costume!** how youthful *ou* young that suit makes him look!

e (*inexpérimenté*) raw, inexperienced, green*. **il est encore bien ~** he's still very inexperienced; **être ~ dans le métier** to be new *ou* a newcomer to the trade.

f (*cadet*) junior. **mon ~ frère** my younger brother; **mon plus ~ frère** my youngest brother; **Durand ~** Durand junior.

g (*: *insuffisant*) short, skimpy. **ça fait ~, c'est un peu ~** *[temps]* it's cutting it a bit short *ou* fine; *[argent]* that's not much; *[tissu]* it's not (going to be) enough; *[boisson, nourriture]* that's not much *ou* enough to go round.

2 **nm** a (*personne*) youngster, youth, young man. **~ (homme)** young man; **les ~s de maintenant** young people *ou* the young *ou* the youth of today; **club** *ou* **maison de ~s** youth club.

b (*animal*) young.

3 **nf** girl.

4 **adv: s'habiller ~** to dress young for one's age *ou* younger than one's years; **se coiffer ~** to have a young *ou* modern hairstyle.

5 **comp** ▸**jeune femme** young woman ▸**jeune fille** girl ▸**jeune garçon** boy, young lad *ou* fellow ▸**jeune génération** younger generation ▸**jeunes gens** (*gén*) young people; (*garçons*) boys ▸**jeune homme** young man ▸**jeune loup** (*fig*) young Turk ▸**jeune marié** bridegroom; **les jeunes mariés** the newly-weds; **ils sont jeunes mariés** they are young marrieds *ou* newly-weds; **un couple de jeunes mariés** a couple of newly-weds ▸**jeune mariée** bride ▸**jeune premier** (*Ciné, Théât*) leading man ▸**jeune première** leading lady.

jeûne [ʒøn] **nm** fast. **rompre le ~** to break one's fast; **jour de ~** fast day.

jeûner [ʒøne] 1 **vi** (*gén*) to go without food; (*Rel*) to fast. **faire ~ un malade** to make a sick person go without food; **laisser ~ ses enfants** to let one's children go hungry.

jeunesse [ʒœnɛs] **nf** a (*période*) youth. (*littér*) **la ~ du monde** the dawn of the world; **en pleine ~** in the prime of youth; **dans ma ~** in my youth, in my younger days; **folie/erreur/péché de ~** youthful prank/mistake/indiscretion; **je n'ai pas eu de ~** I didn't have much of a childhood; **en raison de son extrême ~** owing to his extreme youth; (*Prov*) **il faut que ~ se passe** youth must have its fling; *voir* **fou, œuvre, premier** *etc.*

b (*qualité*) youth, youthfulness. **~ de cœur** youthfulness of heart; **la ~ de son visage/de son corps peut vous tromper** his youthful face/figure may mislead you; **étant donné la ~ de ce vin** because this wine is so young, because of the immaturity of this wine; **avoir un air de ~** to have a youthful look (about one); **sa ~ d'esprit** his youthfulness of mind.

c (*personnes jeunes*) youth, young people. **la ~ dorée** the young jet set; **la ~ ouvrière** (the) young workers; **la ~ étudiante/des écoles** young people at university/at school; **livres pour la ~** books for the young *ou* for young people; **la ~ est partie devant** the young ones *ou* the young people have gone on ahead; (*Prov*) **si ~ savait, si vieillesse pouvait** if youth but knew, if old age but could; *voir* **auberge, voyage.**

d (*†: *jeune fille*) (young) girl.

e (*gén pl: groupe*) youth. **les ~s communistes** the Communist Youth Movement.

jeunet, -ette* [ʒœnɛ, ɛt] **adj** (*péj*) rather young. **il est un peu ~ pour lire ce roman** he's rather young *ou* he's a bit on the young side to be reading this novel.

jeûneur, -euse [ʒønœʀ, øz] **nm,f** person who fasts *ou* is fasting.

jeunot, -otte* [ʒœno, ɔt] 1 **adj** = **jeunet***. 2 **nm** (*péj*) young fellow*.

Jézabel [ʒezabɛl] **nf** Jezabel.

jf (**abrév de jeune fille, jeune femme**) *voir* **jeune.**

jh (**abrév de jeune homme**) *voir* **jeune.**

jiu-jitsu [ʒjyʒitsy] **nm** jujitsu.

JO [ʒio] 1 **nmpl** (**abrév de Jeux olympiques**) Olympics. 2 **nm** (**abrév de Journal officiel**) *voir* **journal**.

joaillerie [ʒoajʀi] **nf** a (*travail*) jewelling; (*commerce*) jewel trade. **travailler dans la ~** to work in jewellery *ou* in the jewel trade. b (*marchandise*) jewellery. c (*magasin*) jeweller's (shop).

joaillier, -ière [ʒoaje, jɛʀ] **nm,f** jeweller.

Job [ʒɔb] **nm** (*Rel*) Job; *voir* **pauvre**.

job [dʒɔb] 1 **nm** (**: travail*) (temporary) job. 2 **nf** (*Can*) job.

jobard, e* [ʒɔbaʀ, aʀd] 1 **adj** gullible. 2 **nm,f** (*dupe*) sucker*, mug* (*Brit*), wally*.

jobarderie* [ʒɔbaʀd(ə)ʀi] **nf**, **jobardise*** [ʒɔbaʀdiz] **nf** gullibility.

jockey [ʒɔkɛ] **nm** jockey.

Joconde [ʒɔkɔ̃d] **nf**: **la ~** the Mona Lisa.

jocrisse† [ʒɔkʀis] **nm** (*niais*) simpleton.

jodhpurs [dʒɔdpyʀ] **nmpl** jodhpurs.

jodler [jɔdle] [1] **vt** to yodel.

Joël [ʒɔɛl] **nm** Joel.

Joëlle [ʒɔɛl] **nf** Joelle.

joggeur, -euse [dʒɔgœʀ, øz] **nm,f** jogger.

jogging [dʒɔgiŋ] **nm** (*sport*) jogging; (*survêtement*) jogging *ou* sweat (*esp US*) suit. **faire du ~** to go jogging.

Johannesburg [ʒɔanɛsbuʀ] **n** Johannesburg.

joie [ʒwa] **nf** a (*sentiment*) joy; (*sens diminué*) pleasure. **à ma grande ~** to my great joy *ou* delight; **fou** *ou* **ivre de ~** wild with joy *ou* delight; **la nouvelle le mit au comble de la ~** he was overjoyed at hearing the news *ou* to hear the news; **accueillir une nouvelle avec une ~ bruyante** to greet the news with great shouts of joy; **ses enfants sont sa plus grande ~** his children are his greatest delight *ou* joy; **c'était une ~ de le regarder** it was a joy *ou* delight to look at him, he was a joy to look at; **quand aurons-nous la ~ de vous revoir?** when shall we have the pleasure of seeing you again?; **il accepta avec ~** he accepted with delight; **sauter** *ou* **bondir de ~** to jump for joy; *voir* **cœur, feu**[1], **fille**.
b **les ~s de la vie** the joys of life; (*Rel*) **les ~s du monde** *ou* **de la terre** worldly *ou* earthly pleasures *ou* joys; **les ~s du mariage** the joys of marriage; (*iro*) **encore une panne, ce sont les ~s de la voiture** another breakdown, that's one of the joys *ou* delights of motoring (*iro*).
c (*loc*) **~ de vivre** joy in life, joie de vivre; **être plein de ~ de vivre** to be full of joie de vivre *ou* the joys of life; **cela le mit en ~** he was overjoyed at this; **ce livre a fait la ~ de tous** this book has delighted *ou* has given great pleasure to everyone; **le clown tomba pour la plus grande ~ des enfants** the clown fell over to the (great) delight of the children; **il se faisait une telle ~ d'y aller** he was so looking forward to going; **je me ferai une ~ de le faire** I shall be delighted *ou* only too pleased to do it; **c'est pas la ~!*** it's no fun, I'm (*ou* we're *ou* they're *etc*) not exactly ecstatic (about it)*, I'm (*ou* we're *ou* they're *etc*) feeling pretty down*.

joignable [ʒwaɲabl] **adj**: **être difficilement ~** to be difficult to reach *ou* contact.

joindre [ʒwɛ̃dʀ] [49] 1 **vt** a (*mettre ensemble*) to join, put together. **~ 2 tables/planches** to put 2 tables/planks together; **~ 2 bouts de ficelle** to join 2 pieces of string; **~ un bout de ficelle à un autre** to join one piece of string to another; **~ les mains** to put *ou* bring one's hands together, clasp one's hands; **~ les talons/les pieds** to put one's heels/feet together; **il se tenait debout les talons joints** he was standing with his heels together.
b (*relier*) to join, link. **une digue/un câble joint l'île au continent** a dyke/a cable links the island with the mainland.
c (*unir*) *efforts etc* to combine, join; *personnes* (*en mariage*) to join. **~ l'utile à l'agréable** to combine business with pleasure; **elle joint l'intelligence à la beauté** she combines intelligence and beauty; **~ le geste à la parole** to suit the action to the word; (*fig*) **~ les deux bouts*** to make (both) ends meet.
d (*ajouter*) to add, attach (*à* to); (*inclure*) *timbre, chèque etc* to enclose (*à* with). **les avantages joints à ce poste** the advantages attached to this post, the fringe benefits of this post; **carte jointe à un bouquet/cadeau** card attached to a bouquet/a gift; *[lettre]* **pièces jointes** enclosures; *voir* **ci**.
e (*communiquer avec*) *personne* to get in touch with, contact. **essayez de le ~ par téléphone** try to get in touch with *ou* try to get hold of *ou* try to contact him by telephone.
2 **vi** *[fenêtre, porte]* to shut, close. **ces fenêtres joignent mal** these windows don't shut *ou* close properly; *[planches etc]* **est-ce que ça joint bien?** does it make a good join?, does it join well?
3 **se joindre vpr** a (*s'unir à*) **se ~ à** to join; **se ~ à la procession** to join the procession; **se ~ à la foule** to mingle *ou* mix with the crowd; **voulez-vous vous ~ à nous?** would you like to join us?; **se ~ à la discussion** to join in the discussion; **mon mari se joint à moi pour vous exprimer notre sympathie** my husband and I wish to express our sympathy, my husband joins me in offering our sympathy (*frm*).
b *[mains]* to join.

joint [ʒwɛ̃] **nm** a (*Anat, Géol, Tech: assemblage, articulation*) joint; (*ligne de jonction*) join; (*en ciment, mastic*) pointing. **~ de robinet** washer; **~ de cardan** cardan joint; **~ de culasse** cylinder head gasket; **~ d'étanchéité** seal. b (*arg Drogue*) joint (*arg*). c (*loc*) **faire le ~*** *[provisions]* to last *ou* hold out; *[argent]* to bridge the gap (*jusqu'à* until); **chercher/trouver le ~*** to look (around) for/come up with the solution.

jointé, e [ʒwɛ̃te] **adj**: **cheval court-~/long-~** short-/long-pasterned horse, horse with short/long pasterns.

jointif, -ive [ʒwɛ̃tif, iv] **adj** joined, contiguous; *planches* butt-jointed. **(cloison) ~ive** butt-jointed partition.

jointure [ʒwɛ̃tyʀ] **nf** a (*Anat*) joint. **~ du genou** knee joint; **à la ~ du poignet** at the wrist (joint); **faire craquer ses ~s** to crack one's knuckles; **à la ~ de 2 os** at the joint between 2 bones; **les ~s du cheval** fetlock-joints, pastern-joints. b (*Tech*) (*assemblage*) joint; (*ligne de jonction*) join.

jojo* [ʒoʒo] 1 **adj**: **il n'est/ce n'est pas ~** he is/it is not much to look at*. 2 **nm**: **c'est un affreux ~** (*enfant*) he's a cheeky little rascal *ou* beggar (*Brit*); (*adulte*) he's a nasty piece of work* (*Brit*), he's a bad one.

joker [(d)ʒɔkɛʀ] **nm** (*Cartes*) joker. **jouer** *ou* **sortir son ~** (*lit*) to play one's joker; (*fig*) to play one's trump card.

joli, e [ʒɔli] **adj** a *enfant, femme* pretty, attractive; *chanson, objet* pretty, nice; *pensée, promenade, appartement* nice. **d'ici la vue est très ~e** you get a very nice *ou* attractive view from here; **~ comme un cœur** pretty as a picture; **il est ~ garçon** he is (quite) good-looking; **le ~ et le beau sont deux choses bien différentes** prettiness and beauty are two very different things.
b (**: non négligeable*) *revenu, profit* nice (*épith*), good, handsome (*épith*); *résultat* nice (*épith*), good. **ça fait une ~e somme** it's quite a tidy sum of money, it's a handsome sum of money, it's a good bit of money; **il a une ~e situation** he has a good position.
c (*iro: déplaisant*) nasty, unpleasant, fine (*iro*), nice (*iro*). **embarquez tout ce ~ monde!** take the whole nasty bunch *ou* crew* away!; **un ~ gâchis** a fine mess (*iro*); **un ~ coco*** *ou* **monsieur** a nasty character, a nasty piece of work* (*Brit*); **être dans un ~ pétrin** *ou* **de ~s draps** to be in a fine mess (*iro*).
d (*loc*) **tout ça c'est bien ~ mais** that's all very well but; **le plus ~ (de l'histoire) c'est que** the best bit of it all *ou* about it all is that; **vous avez fait du ~!** you've made a fine mess of things!; **tu as encore menti — c'est du ~!** you've lied again — that's great!* *ou* that's a great help!; **faire le ~ cœur** to play the ladykiller; **ce n'est pas ~ de mentir** it's not nice to tell lies; **ce n'était pas ~ à voir** it wasn't a pleasant *ou* pretty sight; (*iro*) **elle est ~e, votre idée!** that's a nice *ou* great* idea! (*iro*); (*iro*) **c'est ~ de dire du mal des gens!** that's nice spreading nasty gossip about people!; **c'est pas ~-~!*** (*laid*) it's not a pretty sight*; (*méchant*) that was a mean thing to do*.

joliesse [ʒɔljɛs] **nf** (*littér*) *[personne]* prettiness; *[gestes]* grace.

joliment [ʒɔlimɑ̃] **adv** a (*d'une manière jolie*) nicely. **pièce ~ décorée** attractively *ou* nicely decorated room; **enfant ~ habillé** prettily *ou* attractively dressed child; (*iro*) **il l'a ~ arrangé** he sorted him out nicely *ou* good and proper*. b (**: très, beaucoup*) pretty*, jolly* (*Brit*). **il a ~ raison** he's quite right, he's dead right* (*Brit*); **il était ~ content/en retard** he was pretty* *ou* jolly* (*Brit*) glad/late.

Jonas [ʒɔnas] **nm** Jonah, Jonas.

Jonathan [ʒɔnatɑ̃] **nm** Jonathan.

jonc [ʒɔ̃] **nm** a (*plante*) rush, bulrush; (*canne*) cane, rattan. **corbeille** *ou* **panier de ~** rush basket. b (*Aut*) trim. c (*bijou*) **~ (d'or)** (plain gold) bangle *ou* ring.

jonché, e [ʒɔ̃ʃe] (**ptp de joncher**) 1 **adj**: **~ de** littered *ou* strewn with. 2 **jonchée nf** spray *ou* swath of flowers *ou* leafy branches (*for strewing*). **des ~es de feuilles mortes couvraient la pelouse** dead leaves lay in drifts on *ou* lay scattered *ou* strewn over the lawn.

joncher [ʒɔ̃ʃe] [1] **vt**: **~ qch de** to strew sth with.

jonchets [ʒɔ̃ʃɛ] **nmpl** jackstraws, spillikins.

jonction [ʒɔ̃ksjɔ̃] **nf** (*action*) joining, junction; (*état*) junction. **à la ~ des 2 routes** at the junction of the 2 roads, where the 2 roads meet; (*Mil*) **opérer une ~** to effect a junction, link up; **point de ~** junction, meeting point; (*Jur*) **~ d'instance** joinder.

joncture [ʒɔ̃ktyʀ] **nf** (*Ling*) juncture.

jongler [ʒɔ̃gle] [1] **vi** (*lit*) to juggle (*avec* with). (*fig*) **~ avec** *chiffres* to juggle with, play with; *difficultés* to juggle with.

jonglerie [ʒɔ̃gləʀi] **nf** jugglery, juggling.

jongleur, -euse [ʒɔ̃glœʀ, øz] **nm,f** a (*gén*) juggler. b (*Hist*) (wandering) minstrel, jongleur.

jonque [ʒɔ̃k] **nf** (*Naut*) junk.

jonquille [ʒɔ̃kij] 1 **nf** daffodil, jonquil. 2 **adj inv** (bright) yellow.

Jordanie [ʒɔʀdani] **nf** Jordan.

jordanien, -ienne [ʒɔʀdanjɛ̃, jɛn] 1 **adj** Jordanian. 2 **nm,f**: **J~(ne)** Jordanian.

Joseph [ʒozɛf] **nm** Joseph.

Joséphine [ʒozefin] **nf** Josephine.

Josué [ʒozɥe] **nm** Joshua.

jouable [ʒwabl] **adj** playable.

joual [ʒwal] **nm** (*Can*) joual (*Can*).

joue [ʒu] **nf** a (*Anat*) cheek. **~ contre ~** cheek to cheek; **tendre la ~** to offer one's cheek; **présenter** *ou* **tendre l'autre ~** to turn the other cheek. b (*Mil*) **en ~!** take aim!; **coucher** *ou* **mettre une cible/une personne en**

~ to aim at *ou* take aim at a target/a person; **coucher** *ou* **mettre en ~ un fusil** to take aim with a rifle, aim a rifle. c (*Naut*) **~s d'un navire** bows of a ship.

jouer [ʒwe] [1] 1 **vi** a (*s'amuser*) to play (*avec* with). **arrête, je ne joue plus** stop it, I'm not playing any more; **elle jouait avec son crayon/son collier** she was toying *ou* fiddling with her pencil/necklace; (*fig*) **~ avec les sentiments de qn** to play *ou* trifle with sb's feelings; (*fig*) **~ avec sa vie/sa santé** to gamble with one's life/health; (*fig*) **on ne joue pas avec ces choses-là** matters like these are not to be treated lightly.

b **~ à la poupée** to play with one's dolls; **~ aux soldats/aux cowboys et aux Indiens** to play (at) soldiers/(at) cowboys and Indians; **~ au docteur (et au malade)** to play (at) doctors and nurses; **~ à qui sautera le plus loin** to play at seeing who can jump the furthest; **~ à faire des bulles de savon** to play at making *ou* blowing soap bubbles; **~ aux cartes/aux échecs** to play cards/chess; **~ au chat et à la souris (avec qn)** to play cat and mouse with sb; **il joue bien (au tennis)** he is a good (tennis) player, he plays (tennis) well, he plays a good game (of tennis); **il a demandé à ~ avec** *ou* **contre X aux échecs** he asked to play X at chess; (*fig*) **~ au héros/à l'aristocrate** to play the hero/the aristocrat; *voir* **bille** *etc*.

c (*Mus*) to play. **~ du piano/de la guitare** to play the piano/the guitar; **l'orchestre joue ce soir à l'opéra** the orchestra is playing at the opera this evening; **ce pianiste joue bien/mal** this pianist plays well/badly.

d (*Casino*) to gamble. **~ à la Bourse** to speculate *ou* gamble on the Stock Exchange; **~ sur les valeurs minières** to speculate in mining stock; **~ sur la hausse/la baisse d'une matière première** to gamble on the rise/the fall of a commodity; **~ à la roulette** to play roulette; **~ pair/impair** to play (on) the even/odd numbers; **~ aux courses** to bet on the horses; **ils ont joué sur la faiblesse/la pauvreté des paysans** they reckoned on *ou* were banking *ou* relying on the peasants' weakness/poverty.

e (*Ciné, Théât, TV*) to act. **il joue dans "Hamlet"** he is acting *ou* he is in "Hamlet"; **il joue au théâtre X** he is playing *ou* acting at the X theatre; **elle joue très bien** she is a very good actress, she acts very well; **on joue à guichets fermés** the performance is fully booked *ou* is booked out (*Brit*).

f (*fonctionner*) to work. **la clef joue mal dans la serrure** the key doesn't fit (in) the lock very well; **faire ~ un ressort** to activate *ou* trigger a spring; **la barque jouait sur son ancre** the boat bobbed about at anchor.

g (*joindre mal*) to fit loosely, be loose; *[bois]* (*travailler*) to warp. **la clef joue dans la serrure** the key fits loosely in the lock.

h *[soleil, lumière etc]* to play. **la lumière jouait au plafond** the light played *ou* danced on the ceiling.

i (*intervenir, s'appliquer*) to apply (*pour* to). **l'âge ne joue pas** age doesn't come into it *ou* is of no consequence; **cet argument joue à plein** this argument is entirely applicable; **cette augmentation joue pour tout le monde** this rise applies to *ou* covers everybody; **l'augmentation joue depuis le début de l'année** the rise has been operative from *ou* since the beginning of the year; **les préférences des uns et des autres jouent finalement** different people's preferences are what matter *ou* what count in the end; **cet élément a joué en ma faveur** this factor worked in my favour; **il a fait ~ ses appuis politiques pour obtenir ce poste** he made use of his political connections to get this post; **le temps joue contre lui** time is against him *ou* is not on his side.

j (*loc*) **~ sur les mots** to play with words; (*fig*) **à quoi joues-tu?** what are you playing at?; **faire qch pour ~** to do sth for fun; **~ serré** to play (it) tight, play a close game; **~ perdant/gagnant** to play a losing/winning game; (*Tennis*) **~ petit bras** to play underarm; **~ au plus fin** *ou* **malin** to try to outsmart sb, see who can be the smartest; **~ à qui perd gagne** to play so that the winner is the one who loses; **~ au petit soldat** to throw one's weight around (*Brit*); **faire ~ la corde sensible** to appeal to the emotions; **~ de malheur** *ou* **de malchance** to be dogged by ill luck; (*lit, fig*) **à vous (***ou* **moi** *etc***) de ~!** your (*ou* my *etc*) go! *ou* turn!; (*Échecs*) your (*ou my etc*) move!; **bien joué!** (*lit*) well played!; (*lit, fig*) well done!; **~ avec le feu** to play with fire; (*fig*) **~ dans la cour des grands** to play with the big boys (*fig*) *ou* in the major league (*fig*).

2 **vt** a (*Ciné, Théât*) *rôle* to play, act; (*représenter*) *pièce, film* to put on, show. **on joue "Macbeth" ce soir** "Macbeth" is on *ou* is being played this evening; **elle joue toujours les soubrettes** she always has the maid's part; (*fig*) *[personne]* **~ un rôle** to play a part (*dans* in), put on an act; *[fait, circonstance]* to play a part (*dans* in); (*fig*) **~ la comédie** to put on an act, put it on*; **il a joué un rôle ridicule dans cette affaire** he acted like a fool *ou* he made himself look ridiculous in that business; **la pièce se joue au théâtre X** the play is on at the X theatre; (*fig*) **le drame s'est joué très rapidement** the tragedy happened very quickly.

b (*simuler*) **~ les héros/les victimes** to play the hero/the victim; **~ la surprise/le désespoir** to affect *ou* feign surprise/despair.

c (*Mus*) *concerto, valse* to play. **il va ~ du Bach** he is going to play (some) Bach; **il joue très mal Chopin** he plays Chopin very badly.

d (*Jeux, Sport*) *partie d'échecs, de tennis* to play; *carte* to play; *pion* to play, move. (*Ftbl*) **il est interdit de ~ le ballon à la main** it is forbidden to handle the ball; (*Rugby*) **préférer ~ le ballon à la main** to prefer to throw the ball; **jouez le ballon plutôt que l'adversaire** play the ball, not your opponent; **~ atout** to play trumps; **~ un coup facile/difficile** (*Sport*) to play an easy/a difficult shot; (*Échecs*) to make an easy/a difficult move; (*fig*) **la partie est/n'est pas jouée** it (*ou* things *etc*) has/hasn't been decided; (*fig*) **~ la montre** to play for time, kill the clock (*US*).

e (*Casino*) *argent* to stake, wager; (*Courses*) *argent* to bet, stake (*sur* on); *cheval* to back, bet on; (*fig*) *fortune, possessions, réputation* to wager. **~ gros jeu** *ou* **un jeu d'enfer** to play for high stakes; **il ne joue que des petites sommes** he only places small bets *ou* plays for small stakes; **il a joué et perdu une fortune** he gambled away a fortune; **~ sa réputation sur qch** to stake *ou* wager one's reputation on sth; (*Pol*) **~ son mandat/ministère sur qch** to stake one's re-election prospects/one's ministerial position on sth; (*fig: décidé*) **rien n'est encore joué** nothing is settled *ou* decided yet; **tout va se ~ demain** everything will be settled *ou* decided tomorrow.

f (*frm: tromper*) *personne* to deceive, dupe.

g (*opter pour*) **~ la prudence/la sécurité** to be cautious/play safe; (*Pol*) **~ la carte de la solidarité/de l'alliance** to play the solidarity/alliance card.

h (*loc*) **il faut ~ le jeu** you've got to play the game; **~ franc jeu** to play fair; **~ un double jeu** to play a double game; **~ son va-tout** *ou* **le tout pour le tout** to stake one's all; **~ un (mauvais) tour/une farce à qn** to play a (dirty) trick/a joke on sb; **cela te jouera un mauvais** *ou* **vilain tour** you'll get your comeuppance*, you'll be sorry for it; **~ sa dernière carte** to play one's last card; **~ la fille de l'air** to vanish into thin air; *voir* **gros**.

3 **jouer de vt indir** a (*manier*) to make use of, use. **ils durent ~ du couteau/du revolver pour s'enfuir** they had to use knives/revolvers to get away; **ils jouent trop facilement du couteau** they are too quick with their knives, they use knives *ou* the knife too readily; (*hum*) **~ de la fourchette** to tuck in* (*Brit*), dig in*; **~ des jambes*** *ou* **des flûtes‡** to run away, take to one's heels; (*hum*) **~ de l'œil** *ou* **de la prunelle** to wink; **~ des coudes pour parvenir au bar/pour entrer** to elbow one's way to the bar/one's way in.

b (*utiliser*) to make use of. **il joue de sa maladie pour ne rien faire** he plays on his illness to get out of doing anything; **~ de son influence pour obtenir qch** to use *ou* make use of one's influence to get sth.

4 **se jouer vpr** (*frm*) **se ~ de:** (*tromper*) **se ~ de qn** to deceive sb, dupe sb; (*moquer*) **se ~ des lois/de la justice** to scoff at the law/at justice; (*triompher facilement de*) **se ~ des difficultés** to make light of the difficulties; **il fait tout cela en se jouant** he does it all without trying.

jouet [ʒwɛ] **nm** a (*lit*) toy, plaything. b (*fig*) **navire qui est le ~ des vagues** ship which is the plaything of the waves; **être le ~ d'une illusion/hallucination** to be the victim of an illusion/a hallucination; **être/devenir le ~ du hasard** to be/become a hostage to fortune.

joueur, -euse [ʒwœʀ, øz] **nm,f** (*Échecs, Mus, Sport*) player; (*Jeux*) gambler. **~ de golf** golfer; **~ de cornemuse** (bag)piper; **~ de cartes** card player; **être beau/mauvais ~** to be a good/bad loser; **sois beau ~!** be a good sport!, be gracious in defeat!; **il a un tempérament ~, il est très ~** *[enfant, animal]* he loves to play, he's very playful; *[parieur]* he's very keen on gambling (*Brit*), he's a keen gambler.

joufflu, e [ʒufly] **adj** *personne* chubby-cheeked, round-faced; *visage* chubby.

joug [ʒu] **nm** a (*Agr, fig*) yoke. **tomber sous le ~ de** to come under the yoke of; **mettre sous le ~** to yoke, put under the yoke. b *[balance]* beam. c (*Antiq*) yoke.

jouir [ʒwiʀ] [2] 1 **jouir de vt indir** (*frm: savourer, posséder*) to enjoy. **il jouissait de leur embarras évident** he delighted at *ou* enjoyed their evident embarrassment; **~ de toutes ses facultés** to be in full possession of one's faculties; **cette pièce jouit d'une vue sur le jardin** this room commands a view of the garden; **le Midi jouit d'un bon climat** the South of France has a good climate. 2 **vi** (‡) (*plaisir sexuel*) to come**; (*douleur*) to suffer agonies. **on va ~!** we're going to have a hell of a time!‡, we aren't half going to have fun!*; **ça me fait ~ de les voir s'empoigner** I get a great kick out of seeing them at each other's throats‡.

jouissance [ʒwisɑ̃s] **nf** a (*volupté*) pleasure, enjoyment, delight; (*sensuelle*) sensual pleasure; (**: orgasme*) climax. (*frm*) **cela lui a procuré une vive ~** this afforded him intense pleasure. b (*Jur: usage*) use, possession; *[propriété, bien]* use, enjoyment. **avoir la ~ de certains droits** to enjoy certain rights.

jouisseur, -euse [ʒwisœʀ, øz] 1 **adj** sensual. 2 **nm,f** sensualist.

jouissif, -ive‡ [ʒwisif, iv] **adj** great*, brilliant*.

joujou, pl **~x** [ʒuʒu] **nm** (*langage enfantin*) toy; (**: revolver*) gun. **faire ~ avec une poupée** to play with a doll; **elle ne l'aime pas, elle fait ~ avec lui** she's not in love with him, she's just playing with him; **cette voiture est son nouveau ~** this car is his new toy.

joule [ʒul] **nm** joule.

jour [ʒuʀ] 1 **nm** a (*lumière*) day(light); (*période*) day(time). **il fait ~** it is daylight; **je fais ça le ~** I do it during the day *ou* in the daytime; **voyager de ~** to travel by day; **service de ~** day service; (*Mil*) **être de ~** to be on day duty; **~ et nuit** day and night; **se lever avant le ~** to get up *ou* rise before dawn *ou* daybreak; **un faible ~ filtrait à travers les**

volets a faint light filtered through the shutters; le ~ entra à flots daylight streamed ou flooded in; le ~ tombe it's getting dark; avoir le ~ dans les yeux to have the light in one's eyes; (fig) ces enfants sont le ~ et la nuit these children are as different as chalk and cheese (Brit) ou night and day; (fig) ça va mieux avec le nouveau produit? — c'est le ~ et la nuit! is it better with this new product? — there's absolutely no comparison!; voir demain, grand, lumière etc.

b (espace de temps) day. quinze ~s a fortnight (Brit), two weeks; dans huit ~s in a week, in a week's time; tous les ~s every day; tous les deux ~s every other day, every two days; tous les ~s que (le bon) Dieu fait every blessed day, day in day out; c'était il y a 2 ~s it was 2 days ago; des poussins d'un ~ day-old chicks; (fig) d'un ~ célébrité, joie short-lived, fleeting; c'est à 2 ~s de marche/de voiture de ... it is a 2 days' walk/drive from ...; faire 30 ~s (de prison) to do 30 days (in jail ou inside*); dans 2 ~s in 2 days' time, in 2 days; (Prov) les ~s se suivent et ne se ressemblent pas time goes by and every day is different, the days go by and each is different from the last.

c (époque précise) day. un ~ viendra où ... a day will come when ...; le ~ n'est pas loin où ... the day is not far off when ...; un de ces ~s one of these (fine) days; à un de ces ~s! see you again sometime!, be seeing you!*; un ~ il lui écrivit one day he wrote to her; par un ~ de pluie/de vent on a rainy/windy day; le ~ d'avant the day before, the previous day; le ~ d'après the day after, the next day, the following day; le ~ de Noël/de Pâques Christmas/Easter Day; le ~ du marché market day; il m'a téléphoné l'autre ~ he phoned me the other day; prendre ~ avec qn to fix a day with sb, make a date with sb; (iro) décidément c'est mon ~! I'm having a real day of it today! (iro), really it's just not my day today!; ce n'est vraiment pas le ~! you (ou we etc) have picked the wrong day! (de ou pour faire to do); le goût/la mode du ~ the style/the fashion of the day; l'homme du ~ the man of the moment; nouvelles du ~ news of the day, the day's news; un œuf du ~ a new-laid egg, a freshly-laid egg; dès le premier ~ from day one, from the outset ou beginning; voir cours, grand, plat[2].

d (époque indéterminée, vie) ~s time, days, life. la fuite des ~s the swift passage of time; finir ses ~s à l'hôpital to end one's days in hospital; attenter à/mettre fin à ses ~s to make an attempt on/put an end to one's life; nous gardons cela pour nos vieux ~s/pour les mauvais ~s we're keeping that for our old age/for a rainy day ou for hard times; il faut attendre des ~s meilleurs we must wait for better times ou days; nous connaissons des ~s bien anxieux this is an anxious time for us, we're going through an anxious time; être dans un bon/mauvais ~ to be in a good/bad mood; il est dans (un de) ses bons ~s/ses mauvais ~s he's having a good spell/a bad spell, it's one of his good/bad days; voir beau, couler.

e (éclairage: lit, fig) light. le tableau est dans un mauvais ~ the picture is in a bad light; montrer/présenter/voir qch sous un ~ favorable/flatteur to show/present/see sth in a favourable/flattering light; jeter un ~ nouveau sur to throw (a) new light on; se présenter sous un ~ favorable [projet] to look promising ou hopeful; [personne] to show o.s. to advantage ou in a favourable light; nous le voyons maintenant sous son véritable ~ now we see him in his true colours ou see what he is really like; voir faux.

f (ouverture) [mur] gap, chink; [haie] gap. clôture à ~ openwork fence.

g (Couture) ~ simple openwork, drawn-threadwork; drap à ~ sheet with an openwork border; faire des ~s dans un drap/dans un mouchoir to hemstitch a sheet/handkerchief.

h (loc) donner le ~ à to give birth to, bring into the world; voir le ~ [enfant] to be born, come into the world; [projet] to be born, come into being; [enfant] venir au ~ to be born, come into the world; (révéler) mettre au ~ to bring to light; se faire ~ to become clear, come out*; il se fit ~ dans mon esprit it all became clear to me, the light dawned on me; vivre au ~ le ~ (sans soucis) to live from day to day; (pauvrement) to live from hand to mouth; (être/mettre/tenir) à ~ (to be/bring/keep) up to date; mise à ~ (action) updating; (résultat) update; la mise à ~ d'un compte/dossier the updating of an account/a file; la mise à ~ d'un dictionnaire the revision ou updating of a dictionary; de ~ en ~ day by day, from day to day; on l'attend d'un ~ à l'autre he is expected any day (now); ~ après ~ day after day; (il change d'avis) d'un ~ à l'autre (he changes his mind) from one day to the next; un ~ ou l'autre sometime or other, sooner or later; du ~ au lendemain overnight; cela arrive tous les ~s it happens every day, it's an everyday occurrence; de tous les ~s everyday (épith), ordinary; de nos ~s these days, nowadays, in this day and age; à ce ~ nous n'avons rien reçu to date we have received nothing; (†, hum) au ~ d'aujourd'hui in this day and age; (à prendre) 3 fois par ~ (to be taken) 3 times a day; il y a 2 ans ~ pour ~ 2 years ago to the day.

2 comp ▸jour d'action de grâce(s) Thanksgiving Day ▸le jour de l'An New Year's Day ▸jour d'arrêt (Mil) day of detention; donner 8 jours d'arrêt to give a week's detention ▸jour de congé day off, holiday ▸jour de deuil day of mourning ▸jour férié public ou Bank holiday ▸jour de fête feastday, holiday ▸le jour du Grand Pardon the Day of Atonement ▸le jour J D-day ▸jour mobile discretionary holiday (granted by company, boss etc) ▸le jour des Morts All Souls' Day ▸jour ouvrable weekday, working day ▸jour ouvré working day ▸le jour de la Pentecôte Whitsunday ▸jour des prix (Scol) prize (giving) day ▸jour de réception (Admin) day of opening (to the public); [dame du monde] "at home" day; le jour de réception du directeur est le lundi the director is available to see people on Mondays ▸jour de repos [ouvrier] day off ▸le jour des Rois Epiphany, Twelfth Night ▸le jour du Seigneur Sunday, the Sabbath† ▸jour de sortie [domestique] day off, day out; [élève] day out ▸jour de travail working day.

Jourdain [ʒuʀdɛ̃] nm (fleuve) (river) Jordan.

journal, pl -aux [ʒuʀnal, o] 1 nm a (Presse) (news)paper; (magazine) magazine; (bulletin) journal. (bureaux) je suis passé au ~ I dropped by at the office ou paper; dans ou sur le ~ in the (news)paper; elle travaille pour le ~ local she works on ou for the local paper; un grand ~ a big ou national (Brit) paper ou daily*; ~ du matin/du soir morning/evening paper; voir papier.

b (TV, Rad) news (bulletin). c'était au ~ de 20 h it was on the 8-o'clock news (in the evening).

c (intime) diary, journal. tenir son ~ intime to keep a private ou personal diary.

2 comp ▸journal de bord (Naut) (ship's) log; (Aviat) flight log ▸journal électronique = journal lumineux ▸journal d'enfants ou pour enfants children's comic ou paper ▸journal interne d'entreprise in-house newsletter ▸journal littéraire literary journal ▸journal lumineux electronic bulletin board ▸journal de mode fashion magazine ▸le Journal officiel (de la République française) bulletin issued by the French Republic giving details of laws and official announcements, ≃ the gazette (Brit) ▸journal parlé (Rad) radio news ▸journal sportif sporting magazine ▸journal télévisé (TV) television news.

journalier, -ière [ʒuʀnalje, jɛʀ] 1 adj (de chaque jour) travail, trajet daily (épith); (banal) existence everyday (épith), humdrum (épith). c'est ~ it happens every day. 2 nm (Agr) day labourer.

journalisme [ʒuʀnalism] nm (métier, style) journalism. faire du ~ to be in journalism, be a journalist.

journaliste [ʒuʀnalist] nmf journalist. ~ sportif/parlementaire sports/parliamentary correspondent; ~ de radio/de télévision radio/television reporter ou journalist; ~ de (la) presse écrite newspaper ou print (US) journalist; il est ~ à la radio he's a reporter on the radio, he's a radio reporter.

journalistique [ʒuʀnalistik] adj journalistic. style ~ journalistic style; (péj) journalese (NonC).

journée [ʒuʀne] nf a (jour) day. dans ou pendant la ~ during the day, in the daytime; dans la ~ d'hier yesterday, in the course of yesterday; passer sa ~/toute sa ~ à faire qch to spend the day/one's entire day doing sth; passer des ~s entières à rêver to daydream for whole days on end; (grève) ~ d'action day of action; ~ portes ouvertes open day.

b [ouvrier] ~ (de travail) day's work; ~ (de salaire) day's wages ou pay; faire de dures ~s to put in a heavy day's work; faire des ~s ou aller en ~ chez les autres to work as a domestic help ou daily help; il se fait de bonnes ~s he gets a good daily wage, he makes good money (every day); travailler/être payé à la ~ to work/be paid by the day; faire la ~ continue [bureau, magasin] to remain open over lunch ou all day; [personne] to work over lunch; la ~ de 8 heures the 8-hour day; ~ de repos day off, rest day.

c (événement) day. ~s historiques historic days; ~s d'émeute days of rioting; (Mil) la ~ a été chaude, ce fut une chaude ~ it was a hard struggle ou a stiff fight; ~s d'études seminar.

d (distance) à 3 ~s de voyage/de marche 3 days' journey/walk away; voyager à petites ~s† to travel in short ou easy stages.

journellement [ʒuʀnɛlmɑ̃] adv (quotidiennement) daily; (souvent) every day.

joute [ʒut] nf a (Hist, Naut) joust, tilt. b (fig) duel, joust, tilt. ~s oratoires verbal sparring match; ~s d'esprit battle of wits; ~s nautiques water tournament.

jouter [ʒute] 1 vi (Hist) to joust, tilt; (fig) to joust (contre against), spar (contre with).

jouteur [ʒutœʀ] nm jouster, tilter.

jouvence [ʒuvɑ̃s] nf: Fontaine de J~ Fountain of Youth; eau de ~ waters of youth; voir bain.

jouvenceau, pl ~x [ʒuvɑ̃so] nm (††, hum) stripling††, youth.

jouvencelle [ʒuvɑ̃sɛl] nf (††, hum) damsel (††, hum).

jouxter [ʒukste] 1 vt to adjoin, be next to, abut on.

jovial, e, mpl -iaux ou ~s [ʒɔvjal, jo] adj jovial, jolly. d'humeur ~e in a jovial mood; avoir la mine ~e to look jolly ou jovial.

jovialement [ʒɔvjalmɑ̃] adv jovially.

jovialité [ʒɔvjalite] nf joviality, jollity.

joyau, pl ~x [ʒwajo] nm (lit, fig) gem, jewel. les ~x de la couronne the crown jewels; c'est un ~ de l'art gothique it's a jewel of gothic art.

joyeusement [ʒwajøzmɑ̃] adv célébrer merrily, joyfully; accepter gladly, gaily.

joyeux, -euse [ʒwajø, øz] adj a personne, groupe merry, joyful, joyous; repas cheerful; cris joyful, merry; musique joyful, joyous; visage joyful. c'est un ~ luron ou drille he's a great one for laughs*, he is a jolly fellow; **être en ~euse compagnie** to be in merry company *ou* with a merry group; **mener ~euse vie** to lead a merry life; **être d'humeur ~euse** to be in a joyful mood; **ils étaient partis ~** they had set out merrily *ou* in a merry group; **il était tout ~ à l'idée de partir** he was overjoyed *ou* (quite) delighted at the idea of going; (*iro*) **c'est ~!*** fantastic!* (*iro*), brilliant!* (*iro*); **ce n'est pas ~!*** (*film etc*) it's not a bundle of laughs (*Brit*), it's not very funny; *[histoire triste etc]* it's no joke!

b *nouvelle* joyful. ~ **Noël!** merry *ou* happy Christmas!; **~euse fête!** many happy returns!

JT [ʒite] **nm** (**abrév de journal télévisé**) *voir* **journal**.

jubé [ʒybe] **nm** (*clôture*) jube; rood-screen; (*galerie*) jube, rood-loft.

jubilaire [ʒybilɛʀ] **adj** (*Rel*) jubilee (*épith*).

jubilation [ʒybilasjɔ̃] **nf** jubilation, exultation.

jubilé [ʒybile] **nm** jubilee.

jubiler* [ʒybile] 1 **vi** to be jubilant, exult, gloat (*péj*).

jucher vt, se jucher vpr [ʒyʃe] 1 to perch (*sur* on, upon).

Juda [ʒyda] **nm** Judah.

judaïque [ʒydaik] **adj** (*loi*) Judaic; (*religion*) Jewish.

judaïsme [ʒydaism] **nm** Judaism.

judas [ʒyda] **nm** (*fourbe*) Judas; (*Archit*) judas hole. (*Bible*) **J~** Judas; **le baiser de J~** the kiss of Judas.

Jude [ʒyd] **nm** Jude.

Judée [ʒyde] **nf** Judaea *ou* Judea.

judéo- [ʒydeɔ] **préf: judéo-allemand, e** Yiddish; **judéo-chrétien, -ienne** Judeo-Christian; **judéo-christianisme** Judeo-Christianity; **judéo-espagnol, e** Judeo-Spanish.

judiciaire [ʒydisjɛʀ] 1 **adj** judicial. **pouvoir ~** judicial power; **poursuites ~s** judicial *ou* legal proceedings; **vente ~** sale by order of the court; **enquête ~** judicial inquiry, legal examination; **actes ~s et extra-~s** judicial and extrajudicial documents; *voir* **casier, erreur.** 2 **nm: le ~** the judiciary.

judiciairement [ʒydisjɛʀmɑ̃] **adv** judicially.

judicieusement [ʒydisjøzmɑ̃] **adv** judiciously.

judicieux, -ieuse [ʒydisjø, jøz] **adj** judicious. **faire un emploi ~ de son temps** to use one's time judiciously, make judicious use of one's time.

Judith [ʒydit] **nf** Judith.

judo [ʒydo] **nm** judo.

judoka [ʒydɔka] **nmf** judoka.

juge [ʒyʒ] 1 **nm** (*Jur, Rel, Sport, fig*) judge. **oui, Monsieur le J~** yes, your Honour; **(madame)/(monsieur) le ~ X** Mrs/Mr Justice X; **prendre qn pour ~** to appeal to sb's judgment, ask sb to be (the) judge; **être bon/mauvais ~** to be a good/bad judge (*en matière de* of); **être à la fois ~ et partie** to be both judge and judged; **je vous fais ~ (de tout ceci)** I'll let you be the judge (of it all); **se faire ~ de ses propres actes/de qch** to be the judge of one's own actions/of sth; **il est seul ~ en la matière** he is the only one who can judge; **aller devant le ~** to go before the judge; (*Bible*) **le livre des J~s** the Book of Judges.

2 **comp ▸juge de l'application des peines** *judge responsible for overseeing the terms and conditions of a prisoner's sentence* **▸juge-arbitre** (*Boxe, Tennis*) **nm** (**pl juges-arbitres**) referee **▸juge d'arrivée** (*Sport*) finishing judge **▸juge aux affaires matrimoniales** divorce court judge **▸juge consulaire** *judge in a commercial court* **▸juge de fond** (*Tennis*) foot-fault judge **▸juge des *ou* pour enfants** children's judge, ≃ juvenile magistrate (*Brit*) **▸juge de filet** (*Tennis*) net-call judge **▸juge d'instance** justice of the peace, magistrate **▸juge d'instruction** examining judge *ou* magistrate (*Brit*), committing magistrate (*US*) **▸juge de ligne** (*Tennis*) line judge, linesman **▸juge de paix†** = **juge d'instance;** (*fig*) **cette épreuve sera le juge de paix** this test will be the determining factor *ou* will determine the outcome **▸juge de touche** (*Rugby*) touch judge, linesman; (*Ftbl*) linesman.

jugé [ʒyʒe] **nm: au ~** (*lit, fig*) by guesswork; **tirer au ~** to fire blind; **faire qch au ~** to do sth by guesswork.

jugeable [ʒyʒabl] **adj** (*Jur*) subject to judgment in court. (*évaluable*) **difficilement ~** difficult to judge.

jugement [ʒyʒmɑ̃] **nm** a (*Jur: décision, verdict*) *[affaire criminelle]* sentence; *[affaire civile]* decision, award. **prononcer *ou* rendre un ~** to pass sentence; **passer en ~** to be brought for *ou* stand trial; **faire passer qn en ~** to put sb on trial; **poursuivre qn en ~** to sue sb, take legal proceedings against sb; **on attend le ~ du procès** we (*ou* they) are awaiting the verdict; **~ par défaut** judgment by default; **~ déclaratoire** declaratory judgment; **détention sans ~** detention without trial.

b (*opinion*) judgment, opinion. **~ de valeur** value judgment; **exprimer/formuler un ~** to express/formulate an opinion; **porter un ~ (sur)** to pass judgment (on); **s'en remettre au ~ de qn** to defer to sb's judgment; **~ préconçu** prejudgment, preconception.

c (*discernement*) judgment. **avoir du/manquer de ~** to have/lack (good) judgment; **on peut faire confiance à son ~** you can trust his judgment; **il a une grande sûreté de ~** he has very sound judgment.

d (*Rel*) judgment. **le ~ de Dieu** the will of the Lord; (*Hist*) the Ordeal; **le J~ dernier** the Last Judgment, Doomsday.

jugeote* [ʒyʒɔt] **nf** commonsense, gumption* (*Brit*). **ne pas avoir deux sous de ~** to have not an ounce of commonsense, have no gumption* (*Brit*); **(aie) un peu de ~!** use your head! *ou* loaf!*, wise up!‡ (*surtout US*).

juger [ʒyʒe] 3 1 **vt** a (*Jur*) *affaire* to judge, try; *accusé* to try. **le tribunal jugera** the court will decide; **être jugé pour meurtre** to be tried for murder; **le jury a jugé qu'il n'était pas coupable** the jury found him not guilty; **l'affaire doit se ~ à l'automne** the case is to come before the court *ou* is to be heard in the autumn.

b (*décider, statuer*) to judge, decide. **à vous de ~ (ce qu'il faut faire/si c'est nécessaire)** it's up to you to decide *ou* to judge (what must be done/whether *ou* if it is necessary); **~ un différend** to arbitrate in a dispute.

c (*apprécier*) *livre, film, personne, situation* to judge. **~ qn sur la mine/d'après les résultats** to judge sb by his appearance/by *ou* on his results; **il ne faut pas ~ d'après les apparences** you must not judge from *ou* go by appearances; **~ qch/qn à sa juste valeur** to judge sth/sb at its/his real value; **~ bien/mal les gens** to be a good/bad judge of character; **jugez combien j'étais surpris *ou* si ma surprise était grande** imagine how surprised I was *ou* what a surprise I got.

d (*estimer*) **~ qch/qn ridicule** to consider *ou* find *ou* think sth/sb ridiculous; **~ que** to think *ou* consider that; **nous la jugeons stupide** we consider her stupid, we think she's stupid; **pourquoi est-ce que vous me jugez mal?** why do you think badly of me?, why do you have a low opinion of me?; **si vous le jugez bon** if you think it's a good idea *ou* it's advisable; **~ bon/malhonnête de faire** to consider it a good thing *ou* advisable/dishonest to do; **il se jugea perdu** he thought *ou* considered himself lost; **il se juge capable de le faire** he thinks *ou* reckons he is capable of doing it; **je n'ai pas jugé utile de la prévenir** I didn't think it was worth telling her (about it).

2 **juger de vt indir** to appreciate, judge. **si j'en juge par mon expérience/mes sentiments** judging by *ou* if I (can) judge by my experience/my feelings; **à en ~ par** judging by, to judge by; **à en ~ par ce résultat, il ...** if this result is any indication, he ...; **lui seul peut ~ de l'urgence** only he can appreciate the urgency, only he can tell how urgent it is; **autant que je puisse en ~** as far as I can judge; **jugez de ma surprise!** imagine my surprise!

3 **nm: au ~ = au jugé;** *voir* **jugé.**

jugulaire [ʒygylɛʀ] 1 **adj** *veines, glandes* jugular. (*hum*) **il est ~ ~*** he's a stickler for the rules. 2 **nf** a (*Mil*) chin strap. b (*Anat*) jugular vein.

juguler [ʒygyle] 1 **vt** *maladie* to arrest, halt; *envie, désirs* to suppress, repress; *inflation* to curb, stamp out; *révolte* to put down, quell, repress; *personne* to stifle, sit upon*.

juif, juive [ʒɥif, ʒɥiv] 1 **adj** Jewish. 2 **nm: J~** Jew; **le J~ errant** the Wandering Jew. 3 **Juive nf** Jew, Jewess, Jewish woman.

juillet [ʒɥijɛ] **nm** July. **la révolution/monarchie de J~** the July revolution/monarchy; *pour autres loc voir* **septembre** *et* **quatorze.**

juilletiste [ʒɥijɛtist] **nmf** July holiday-maker (*Brit*) *ou* vacationer (*US*).

juin [ʒɥɛ̃] **nm** June; *pour loc voir* **septembre.**

juive [ʒɥiv] *voir* **juif.**

juiverie [ʒɥivʀi] **nf** (*péj*) **la ~** the Jews, the Jewish people.

jujube [ʒyʒyb] **nm** (*fruit, pâte*) jujube.

juke-box, pl juke-boxes [ʒykbɔks] **nm** jukebox.

julep [ʒylɛp] **nm** julep.

jules [ʒyl] **nm** a (*nom*) **J~** Julius; (*: *amoureux*) man, bloke* (*Brit*), guy*; (‡: *proxénète*) pimp, ponce‡; **J~ César** Julius Caesar. b (*: *vase de nuit*) chamberpot, jerry‡ (*Brit*).

julien, -ienne [ʒyljɛ̃, jɛn] 1 **adj** (*Astron*) Julian. 2 **nm: J~** Julian. 3 **julienne nf** a **J~ne** Juliana, Gillian. b (*Culin*) (*légumes*) julienne; (*poisson*) ling. c (*Bot*) rocket.

Juliette [ʒyljɛt] **nf** Juliet.

jumeau, -elle, mpl ~x [ʒymo, ɛl] 1 **adj** *lit, frère, sœur* twin. **c'est mon frère ~** he is my twin (brother); **fruits ~x** double fruits; **maisons ~elles** semidetached houses; **muscles ~x** gastrocnemius (*sg*). 2 **nm,f** a (*personne*) twin. **vrais/faux ~x, vraies/fausses ~elles** identical/fraternal twins. b (*sosie*) double. **c'est mon ~/ma ~elle** he's/she's my double; **j'aimerais trouver le ~ de ce vase ancien** I'd like to find the partner to this antique vase. 3 **nm** (*Culin*) clod of beef. 4 **jumelle nf** a (*Optique*) binoculars. **~elles de spectacle *ou* théâtre/de campagne** opera/field glasses; **~elle marine** binoculars. b *[mât]* fish. (*Aut*) **~elle de ressort** shackle.

jumelage [ʒym(ə)laʒ] **nm** twinning.

jumelé, e [ʒym(ə)le] (**ptp de jumeler**) **adj: colonnes ~es** twin pillars; **roues ~es** double wheels; (*loterie*) **billets ~s** double series ticket; **vergue ~e** twin yard; **mât ~** twin mast; **villes ~es** twin towns; *[deux villes]* **être ~** to be twin towns; **cette ville est ~e avec ...** this town is twinned with ...; (*Course*) **pari ~** dual forecast (*for first and second place in the same race*).

jumeler [ʒym(ə)le] 4 **vt** *villes* to twin; *efforts* to join; *mâts, poutres* to double up, fish (*SPÉC*).

jumelle [ʒymɛl] *voir* **jumeau.**

jument [ʒymɑ̃] **nf** mare.

jumping [dʒœmpiŋ] **nm** (*gén*) jumping; (*concours équestre*) show jumping.

jungle [ʒœ̃gl] **nf** (*lit, fig*) jungle. **la ~ des affaires** the jungle of the business world, the rat race of business; *voir* **loi.**

junior [ʒynjɔʀ] 1 adj (*Comm, Sport, hum*) junior. **Dupont ~** Dupont junior; **équipe ~** junior team; **mode ~** young *ou* junior fashion. 2 nmf (*Sport*) junior.

Junon [ʒynɔ̃] nf Juno.

junte [ʒœ̃t] nf junta.

jupe [ʒyp] 1 nf (*Habillement, Tech*) skirt. **~ plissée/droite** pleated/straight skirt; **~s** skirts; (*fig*) **être toujours dans les ~s de sa mère** to cling to one's mother's apron strings; **il est toujours dans mes ~s** he's always under my feet. 2 comp ▸**jupe-culotte** nf (pl **jupes-culottes**) culotte, culottes, divided skirt ▸**jupe portefeuille** wrap-around skirt.

jupette [ʒypɛt] nf (short) skirt.

Jupiter [ʒypitɛʀ] nm (*Astron*) Jupiter; (*Myth*) Jove, Jupiter; *voir* **cuisse.**

jupon [ʒypɔ̃] nm a (*Habillement*) waist petticoat *ou* slip, underskirt. b (*fig †: femme*) bit of skirt*. **aimer le ~** to love anything in a skirt; *voir* **courir.**

juponné, e [ʒypɔne] adj: **robe ~e** *dress worn with a full petticoat.*

Jura [ʒyʀɑ] nm: **le ~** the Jura (Mountains).

jurassien, -ienne [ʒyʀasjɛ̃, jɛn] 1 adj of the Jura Mountains, Jura (*épith*). 2 nm,f: **J~(ne)** inhabitant *ou* native of the Jura Mountains.

jurassique [ʒyʀasik] adj, nm Jurassic.

juré, e [ʒyʀe] (ptp de **jurer**) 1 adj (*qui a prêté serment*) sworn. (*fig*) **ennemi ~** sworn enemy. 2 nm juror, juryman. **Messieurs les ~s apprécieront** the members of the jury will bear that in mind; **être convoqué comme ~** to have to report for jury duty. 3 **jurée** nf juror, jurywoman.

jurer [ʒyʀe] [1] 1 vt a (*promettre, prêter serment*) to swear, vow. **~ fidélité/obéissance/amitié à qn** to swear *ou* pledge loyalty/obedience/friendship to sb; **~ la perte de qn** to swear to ruin sb *ou* bring about sb's downfall; **je jure que je me vengerai** I swear *ou* vow I'll get *ou* have my revenge; **faire ~ à qn de garder le secret** to swear *ou* pledge sb to secrecy; **jure-moi que tu reviendras** swear (to me) you'll come back; **"levez la main droite et dites je le jure"** "raise your right hand and say I swear"; **~ sur la Bible/sur la croix/(devant) Dieu** to swear on the Bible/on the cross/to God; **~ sur la tête de ses enfants** *ou* **de sa mère** to swear by all that one holds dearest *ou* with one's hand on one's heart; **il jurait ses grands dieux qu'il n'avait rien fait** he swore blind* *ou* by all the gods† *ou* to heaven that he hadn't done anything; **je vous jure que ce n'est pas facile** I can tell you *ou* assure you that it isn't easy; **ah! je vous jure!** honestly!; **il faut de la patience, je vous jure, pour la supporter!** it takes *ou* you need patience, I can assure you, to put up with her.

b (*admiration*) **on ne jure plus que par lui** everyone swears by him; **on ne jure plus que par ce nouveau remède** everyone swears by this new medicine.

2 **jurer de** vt indir to swear to. **j'en jurerais** I could swear to it, I'd swear to it; **je suis prêt à ~ de son innocence** I'm willing to swear to his innocence; (*Prov*) **il ne faut ~ de rien** you never can tell.

3 vi a (*pester*) to swear, curse. **~ après** *ou* **contre qch/qn** to swear *ou* curse at sth/sb; **~ comme un charretier** to swear like a trooper.

b *[couleurs]* to clash, jar; *[propos]* to jar.

4 **se jurer** vpr a (*à soi-même*) to vow to o.s., promise o.s. **il se jura bien que c'était la dernière fois** he vowed it was the last time.

b (*réciproquement*) to pledge (to) each other, swear, vow. **ils se sont juré un amour éternel** they pledged *ou* vowed *ou* swore (each other) eternal love.

juridiction [ʒyʀidiksjɔ̃] nf a (*compétence*) jurisdiction. **hors de/sous sa ~** beyond/within his jurisdiction; **exercer sa ~** to exercise one's jurisdiction; **tombant sous la ~ de** falling *ou* coming within the jurisdiction of. b (*tribunal*) court(s) of law.

juridique [ʒyʀidik] adj legal, juridical. **études ~s** law *ou* legal studies.

juridiquement [ʒyʀidikmɑ̃] adv juridically, legally.

jurisconsulte [ʒyʀiskɔ̃sylt] nm jurisconsult.

jurisprudence [ʒyʀispʀydɑ̃s] nf: **la ~** (*source de droit*) ≃ case law, jurisprudence; (*décisions*) precedents, judicial precedent; **faire ~** to set a precedent; **cas qui fait ~** test case.

juriste [ʒyʀist] nm *[compagnie]* lawyer; (*auteur, légiste*) jurist. **un esprit de ~** a legal turn of mind.

juron [ʒyʀɔ̃] nm oath, curse, swearword. **dire des ~s** to swear, curse.

jury [ʒyʀi] nm (*Jur*) jury; (*Art, Sport*) panel of judges; (*Scol*) board of examiners, jury. (*Jur*) **président du ~** foreman of the jury; (*Jur*) **membre du ~** member of the jury, juror; (*Univ*) **~ de thèse** Ph.D. examining board.

jus [ʒy] nm a (*liquide*) juice. **~ de fruit** fruit juice; **~ de raisin** grape juice; **~ de viande** juice(s) from the meat, ≃ gravy; **plein de ~** juicy; **~ de la treille*** juice of the vine (*hum*), wine; *voir* **cuire, jeter, mijoter** *etc.*

b (*) (*café*) coffee; (*courant*) juice*; (*discours, article*) talk. **c'est un ~ infâme** it's a foul brew*; **au ~!** coffee's ready!, coffee's up!*; (*péj*) **~ de chaussette** dishwater (*NonC*).

c (**loc*) **jeter/tomber au ~** *ou* **dans le ~** to throw/fall into the water *ou* drink*; **au ~!** (*en poussant qn*) into the water with him!, in he goes!; (*en y allant*) here I come!

d (*arg Mil*) **soldat de 1er ~** ≃ lance corporal (*Brit*); **soldat de 2e ~** ≃ private; **c'est du 8 au ~** only a week to go (to the end of military service).

jusant [ʒyzɑ̃] nm ebb tide.

jusque [ʒysk(ə)] 1 prép a (*lieu*) **jusqu'à la, jusqu'au** to, as far as, (right) up to, all the way to; **j'ai couru jusqu'à la maison/l'école** I ran all the *ou* right the way home/to school; **j'ai marché jusqu'au village puis j'ai pris le car** I walked to *ou* as far as the village then I took the bus; **ils sont montés jusqu'à 2 000 mètres** they climbed up to 2,000 metres; **il s'est avancé jusqu'au bord du précipice** he walked (right) up to the edge of the precipice; **il a rampé jusqu'à nous** he crawled up to us; **il avait de la neige jusqu'aux genoux** he had snow up to his knees, he was knee-deep in snow; **la nouvelle est venue jusqu'à moi** the news has reached me; (*fig*) **il menace d'aller jusqu'au ministre** he's threatening to go right to the minister.

b (*temps*) **jusqu'à, jusqu'en** until, till, up to; **jusqu'en mai** until May; **jusqu'à samedi** until Saturday; **du matin jusqu'au soir** from morning till night; **jusqu'à 5 ans il vécut à la campagne** he lived in the country until *ou* up to the age of 5; **les enfants restent dans cette école jusqu'à (l'âge de) 10 ans** (the) children stay at this school until they are 10 *ou* until the age of 10; **marchez jusqu'à ce que vous arriviez à la mairie** walk until you reach the town hall, walk as far as the town hall; **rester jusqu'au bout** *ou* **à la fin** to stay till *ou* to the end; **de la Révolution jusqu'à nos jours** from the Revolution (up) to the present day.

c (*limite*) **jusqu'à 20 kg** up to 20 kg, not exceeding 20 kg; **véhicule transportant jusqu'à 15 personnes** vehicle which can carry up to *ou* as many as 15 people; **pousser l'indulgence jusqu'à la faiblesse** to carry indulgence to the point of weakness; **aller jusqu'à dire/faire** to go so far as to say/do; **j'irai bien jusqu'à lui prêter 50 F** I am prepared to lend him *ou* I'll go as far as to lend him 50 francs; **j'irai jusqu'à 100** I'll go as far as *ou* up to 100; **je n'irais pas jusqu'à faire ça** I wouldn't go so far as to do that.

d (*y compris*) even. **il a mangé jusqu'aux arêtes** he ate everything including *ou* even the bones, he ate the lot – bones and all; **ils ont regardé ~ sous le lit** they even looked under the bed; **tous jusqu'au dernier l'ont critiqué** they all criticized him to a man, every single *ou* last one of them criticized him.

e (*avec prép ou adv*) **accompagner qn ~ chez lui** to take *ou* accompany sb (right) home; **veux-tu aller ~ chez le boucher pour moi?** would you go (along) to the butcher's for me?; **jusqu'où?** how far?; **jusqu'à quand?** until when?, how long?; **jusqu'à quand restez-vous?** how long *ou* till when are you staying?; **jusqu'ici** (*temps présent*) so far, until now; (*au passé*) until then; (*lieu*) up to *ou* as far as here; **~-là** (*temps*) until then; (*lieu*) up to there; **jusqu'alors, ~s alors** until then; **en avoir ~-là*** to be sick and tired (*de* of), be fed up to the (back) teeth* (*de* with) (*Brit*); **j'en ai ~-là!** I'm sick and tired of it!, I've had about as much as I can take!; **s'en mettre ~-là*** to stuff o.s. to the gills*; **jusqu'à maintenant, jusqu'à présent** until now, so far; **~ (très) tard** until (very) late; **~ vers 9 heures** until about 9 o'clock.

f (*loc*) **jusqu'au bout** to the (very) end; **jusqu'à concurrence de 100 F** to the amount of 100 francs; **vrai jusqu'à un certain point** true up to a certain point; **jusqu'au fond** to the (very) bottom; **elle a été touchée jusqu'au fond du cœur** she was most deeply touched; **rougir jusqu'aux oreilles** to blush to the roots of one's hair; **il avait un sourire jusqu'aux oreilles** he was grinning *ou* beaming from ear to ear; (*Admin*) **jusqu'à nouvel ordre** until further notice; **jusqu'à plus ample informé** until further information is available, pending further information; **tu vois jusqu'à quel point tu t'es trompé** you see how wrong you were; **jusqu'au moment où** until, till; **faire qch jusqu'à plus soif*** to do sth until one has had more than enough; **jusqu'à la gauche*** to the (bitter) end.

2 adv: **~(s) et y compris** up to and including; **jusqu'à** (*même*) even; **j'ai vu jusqu'à des enfants tirer sur des soldats** I even saw children shooting at soldiers; **il n'est pas jusqu'au paysage qui n'ait changé** the very landscape *ou* even the landscape has changed.

3 conj: **jusqu'à ce que, jusqu'à tant que** until; **sonnez jusqu'à ce que l'on vienne ouvrir** ring until someone answers the door; **il faudra le lui répéter jusqu'à ce** *ou* **jusqu'à tant qu'il ait compris** you'll have to keep on telling him until he has understood.

4 comp ▸**jusqu'au-boutisme** nm (*politique*) hard-line policy; (*attitude*) extremist attitude ▸**jusqu'au-boutiste** nmf (pl **jusqu'au-boutistes**) extremist, hard-liner; **c'est un jusqu'au-boutiste** he takes things to the bitter end, he always goes the whole hog*.

jusques [ʒysk(ə)] (†, *littér*) = **jusque.**

justaucorps [ʒystokɔʀ] nm (*Hist*) jerkin; *[gymnaste]* leotard.

juste [ʒyst] 1 adj a (*équitable*) *personne, notation* just, fair; *sentence, guerre, cause* just. **être ~ pour** *ou* **envers** *ou* **à l'égard de qn** to be fair to sb; **c'est un homme ~** he is a just man; **il faut être ~** one must be fair; **pour être ~ envers lui** in fairness to him, to be fair to him; **il n'est pas ~ de l'accuser** it is unfair to accuse him; **par un ~ retour des choses** by a fair *ou* just twist of fate.

b (*légitime*) *revendication, vengeance, fierté* just; *colère* righteous, justifiable. **à ~ titre** justly, rightly; **il en est fier, et à ~ titre** he's proud of it and rightly *ou* understandably so; **la ~ récompense de son travail** the just reward for his work.

c (*exact*) *addition, réponse, heure* right, exact. **à l'heure** ~ right on time, dead on time* (*Brit*); **à 6 heures ~s** on the stroke of 6, dead on 6 o'clock*; **apprécier qch à son ~ prix/sa ~ valeur** to appreciate the true price/the true worth of sth; **le ~ milieu** the happy medium, the golden mean; (*Pol*) the middle course *ou* way.

d (*pertinent, vrai*) *idée, raisonnement* sound; *remarque, expression* apt. **il a dit des choses très ~s** he made some pertinent points, he said some very sound things; **très ~!** good point!, quite right!; **c'est ~** that's right, that's a fair point.

e (*qui apprécie avec exactitude*) *appareil, montre* accurate, right (*attrib*); *esprit* sound; *balance* accurate, true; *coup d'œil* appraising; *oreille* good.

f (*Mus*) *note* right, true; *voix* true; *instrument* in tune (*attrib*), well-tuned. **il a une voix ~** he has a true voice, he sings in tune; **quinte ~** perfect fifth.

g (*trop court, étroit*) *vêtement, chaussure* tight; (*longueur, hauteur*) on the short side. (*quantité*) **1 kg pour 6 — c'est un peu ~** 1 kg for 6 people — it's barely enough *ou* it's a bit on the short *ou* skimpy side; **3 heures pour faire cette traduction — c'est ~** 3 hours to do that translation — it's barely (allowing) enough; **elle n'a pas raté son train mais c'était ~** she didn't miss her train but it was a close thing.

h (*excl*) **~ ciel!†** heavens (above)!; **~ Dieu!†** almighty God!, ye Gods!

2 adv a (*avec exactitude*) *compter, viser* accurately; *raisonner* soundly; *deviner* rightly, correctly; *chanter* in tune. **tomber ~** (*deviner*) to say just the right thing, hit the nail on the head; **division qui tombe ~** division which works out exactly; **la pendule va ~** the clock is keeping good time.

b (*exactement*) just, exactly. **~ au-dessus** just above; **~ au coin** just on *ou* round the corner; **il a dit ~ ce qu'il fallait** he said exactly *ou* just what was needed; **c'est ~ le contraire** it's exactly *ou* just the opposite; **~ au moment où j'entrais, il sortait** (just) at the very moment when I was coming in, he was going out; **je suis arrivé ~ quand/comme il sortait** I arrived just when/as he was leaving; **j'ai ~ assez** I have just enough; **3 kg ~** 3 kg exactly.

c (*seulement*) only, just. **j'ai ~ à passer un coup de téléphone** I only *ou* just have to make a telephone call; **il est parti il y a ~ un moment** he left just *ou* only a moment ago.

d (**un peu**) **~** *compter, prévoir* not quite enough, too little; **il est arrivé un peu ~ ou bien ~** he cut it a bit too fine* (*Brit*) *ou* close, he arrived at the last minute; **il a mesuré trop ~** he didn't allow quite enough, he cut it a bit too fine* (*Brit*).

e (*loc*) **que veut-il au ~?** what exactly does he want? *ou* is he after?*, what does he actually want?; **au plus ~ prix** at the lowest *ou* minimum price; **calculer au plus ~** to work things out to the minimum; **comme de ~*** as usual, of course, naturally; **comme de ~ il pleuvait!** and of course *ou* inevitably it was raining!; **tout ~** (*seulement*) only just; (*à peine*) hardly, barely; (*exactement*) exactly; **c'est tout ~ s'il ne m'a pas frappé** he almost hit me; **son livre vaut tout ~ la peine qu'on le lise** his book is barely worth reading; **c'est tout ~ passable** it's just *ou* barely passable; **avoir la conscience du ~** to have a clear *ou* an untroubled conscience.

3 nm (*Rel*) just man. **les ~s** (*gén*) the just; (*Rel*) the righteous; *voir* **dormir**.

justement [ʒystəmɑ̃] adv a (*précisément*) exactly, just, precisely. **il ne sera pas long, ~, il arrive** he won't be long, in fact he's just coming; **on parlait ~ de vous** we were just talking about you. b (*à plus forte raison*) **puisque vous me l'interdisez ... eh bien, ~ je le lui dirai** since you forbid me to ... just for that I'll tell him. c (*avec justesse, justice*) *raisonner, remarquer* rightly, justly, soundly. **~ puni** justly punished; **~ inquiet/fier** justifiably anxious/proud; **comme l'a rappelé fort ~ l'orateur précédent** as the previous speaker has quite rightly pointed out.

justesse [ʒystɛs] nf a (*exactitude*) *[appareil, montre, balance, tir]* accuracy, precision; *[calcul]* accuracy, correctness; *[réponse, comparaison, observation]* exactness; *[coup d'œil, oreille]* accuracy.

b *[note, voix, instrument]* accuracy.

c (*pertinence*) *[idée, raisonnement]* soundness; *[remarque, expression]* aptness, appropriateness. **on est frappé par la ~ de son esprit** one is struck by the soundness of his judgment *ou* by how sound his judgment is.

d (*loc*) **de ~** just, barely; **gagner de ~** to win by a narrow margin; **j'ai évité l'accident de ~** I barely *ou* only just escaped an accident, I avoided the accident by a hair's breadth, I had a narrow escape; **il s'en est tiré de ~** he got out of it by the skin of his teeth; **il a eu son examen de ~** he only just passed his exam, he scraped through his exam.

justice [ʒystis] nf a (*équité*) fairness, justice. **en bonne ou toute ~** in all fairness; **on lui doit cette ~ que ...** it must be said in fairness to him that ...; **ce n'est que ~ qu'il soit récompensé** it's only fair *ou* just that he should have his reward; **il a la ~ pour lui** justice is on his side; **traiter qn avec ~** to treat sb justly *ou* fairly.

b (*fait de juger*) justice. **exercer la ~** to exercise justice; **passer en ~** to stand trial; **les décisions de la ~** judicial *ou* juridical decisions; **aller en ~** to take a case to court; **demander/obtenir ~** to demand/obtain justice; **être traduit en ~** to be brought before the court(s); **~ de paix†** court of first instance; (*Rel, Philos*) **~ immanente** immanent justice; (*fig*) **sans le vouloir, il s'est puni lui-même, il y a une sorte de ~ immanente** there's a sort of poetic justice in the fact that, without meaning to, he punished himself; *voir* **déni, palais, repris** *etc*.

c (*loi*) **la ~** the law; **la ~ le recherche** he is wanted by the law; **il a eu des démêlés avec la ~** he's had a brush *ou* he's had dealings with the law; **la ~ de notre pays** the law of our country; **c'est du ressort de la ~ militaire** it comes under military law.

d **rendre ~ à qn** to do sb justice; **rendre la ~** to dispense justice; **faire ~ de qch** (*récuser*) to refute sth; (*réfuter*) to disprove sth; **il a pu faire ~ des accusations** he was able to refute the accusations; **se faire ~** (*se venger*) to take the law into one's own hands, take (one's) revenge; (*se suicider*) to take one's life; **il faut lui rendre cette ~ qu'il n'a jamais cherché à nier** we must do him justice in one respect and that is that he's never tried to deny it, in fairness to him it must be said that he's never tried to deny it; **on n'a jamais rendu ~ à son talent** his talent has never had fair *ou* due recognition.

justiciable [ʒystisjabl] 1 adj: **criminel ~ de la cour d'assises** criminal subject to the criminal court *ou* to trial in the assizes; (*fig*) **l'homme politique est ~ de l'opinion publique** politicians are answerable to public opinion; (*fig*) **situation ~ de mesures énergiques** situation where strong measures are indicated *ou* required, situation requiring strong measures. 2 nmf (*Jur*) *person subject to trial.* **les ~s** those to be tried.

justicier, -ière [ʒystisje, jɛʀ] nm,f a (*gén*) upholder of the law, dispenser of justice. b (*Jur* ††) dispenser of justice.

justifiable [ʒystifjabl] adj justifiable. **cela n'est pas ~** that is unjustifiable, that can't be justified.

justificateur, -trice [ʒystifikatœʀ, tʀis] adj *raison, action* justificatory, justifying.

justificatif, -ive [ʒystifikatif, iv] 1 adj *démarche, document* supporting, justificatory. **pièce ~ive** written proof *ou* evidence. 2 nm (*preuve*) written proof, documentary evidence.

justification [ʒystifikasjɔ̃] nf a (*explication*) justification. **~ de la guerre** justification of war; **fournir des ~s** to give some justification. b (*preuve*) proof. c (*Typ*) justification.

justifier [ʒystifje] 7 1 vt a (*légitimer*) *personne, attitude, action* to justify. **rien ne justifie cette colère** such anger is quite unjustified.

b (*donner raison*) *opinion* to justify, bear out, vindicate; *espoir* to justify. **ça justifie mon point de vue** it bears out *ou* vindicates my opinion; **~ qn d'une erreur** to clear sb of having made a mistake; **les faits ont justifié son inquiétude** events justified his anxiety; **des craintes parfaitement justifiées** perfectly *ou* quite justified fears.

c (*prouver*) to prove, justify. **pouvez-vous ~ ce que vous affirmez?** can you justify *ou* prove your assertions?; **cette quittance justifie du paiement** this invoice is evidence *ou* proof of payment.

d (*Typ*) to justify. **~ à droite/gauche** to justify right/left, right(-)/left(-)justify.

2 **justifier de** vt indir to prove. **~ de son identité** to prove one's identity; **~ de sa domiciliation** to show proof of one's address.

3 **se justifier** vpr to justify o.s. **se ~ d'une accusation** to clear o.s. of an accusation.

jute [ʒyt] nm jute; *voir* **toile**.

juter [ʒyte] 1 vi a *[fruit]* to be juicy, drip with juice. **pipe qui jute*** dribbling pipe. b (*: *faire un discours etc*) to spout*, hold forth.

juteux, -euse [ʒytø, øz] 1 adj *fruit* juicy; (*) *affaire* lucrative. 2 nm (*arg Mil: adjudant*) adjutant.

Juvénal [ʒyvenal] nm Juvenal.

juvénile [ʒyvenil] adj *allure* young, youthful. **plein de fougue ~** full of youthful enthusiasm.

juvénilité [ʒyvenilite] nf (*littér*) youthfulness.

juxtalinéaire [ʒykstalineɛʀ] adj (*littér*) **traduction ~** line by line translation.

juxtaposer [ʒykstapoze] 1 vt to juxtapose, place side by side. **propositions juxtaposées** juxtaposed clauses; **son français se réduit à des mots juxtaposés** his French is little more than a string of unconnected words.

juxtaposition [ʒykstapozisjɔ̃] nf juxtaposition.

K

K, k [kɑ] **nm** (*lettre*) K, k; (*Ordin*) K. *[magnétophone, vidéo]* **K 7** cassette.
kabbale [kabal] **nf = cabale.**
kabbaliste [kabalist] **nmf = cabaliste.**
Kaboul, Kabul [kabul] **n** Kabul.
kabyle [kabil] **1** **adj** Kabyle. **2** **nm** (*Ling*) Kabyle. **3** **nmf: K~** Kabyle.
Kabylie [kabili] **nf** Kabylia.
kafkaïen, -ïenne [kafkajɛ̃, jɛn] **adj** (*digne de Kafka*) Kafkaesque; (*de Kafka*) **l'œuvre ~ne** Kafka's work.
kakatoès [kakatɔɛs] **nm = cacatoès.**
kaki [kaki] **1** **adj** khaki, olive drab (*US*). **2** **nm** **a** (*couleur*) khaki, olive drab (*US*). **b** (*Agr*) persimmon, sharon fruit.
Kalahari [kalaaʀi] **n: désert du ~** Kalahari Desert.
kaléidoscope [kaleidɔskɔp] **nm** kaleidoscope.
kaléidoscopique [kaleidɔskɔpik] **adj** kaleidoscopic.
kamikaze [kamikaz] **nm** kamikaze. (*fig*) **être ~*** *[personne]* to have a death wish, be suicidal; *[projet]* to be kamikaze *ou* suicidal.
Kampala [kɑ̃pala] **n** Kampala.
Kampuchéa [kɑ̃putʃea] **nm: ~ (démocratique)** Democratic Kampuchea.
kampuchéen, -enne [kɑ̃putʃeɛ̃, ɛn] **1** **adj** Kampuchean. **2** **nm,f: K~(ne)** Kampuchean.
kanak, e [kanak] **adj, nm,f = canaque.**
kangourou [kɑ̃guʀu] **nm** kangaroo. **sac** *ou* **poche ~** baby carrier.
Kansas [kɑ̃sas] **nm** Kansas.
kantien, -ienne [kɑ̃sjɛ̃, jɛn] **adj** Kantian.
kantisme [kɑ̃tism] **nm** Kantianism.
kaolin [kaɔlɛ̃] **nm** kaolin.
kapok [kapɔk] **nm** kapok.
kaput* [kaput] **adj** *personne* shattered*, bushed*, dead(-beat)*; *machine* kaput*.
karaté [kaʀate] **nm** karate.
karateka, karatéka [kaʀateka] **nm** karateka.
karité [kaʀite] **nm** shea(-tree). **beurre de ~** shea butter.
karma [kaʀma] **nm** karma.
karstique [kaʀstik] **adj** karstic.
kart [kaʀt] **nm** go-cart, kart.
karting [kaʀtiŋ] **nm** go-carting, karting. **faire du ~** to go-cart, go karting.
kasbah [kazba] **nf = casbah.**
kascher [kaʃɛʀ] **adj** kosher.
Katmandou [katmɑ̃du] **n** Katmandu.
kawa* [kawa] **nm** (*café*) (cup of) coffee.
kayak [kajak] **nm** *[esquimau]* kayak; (*Sport*) canoe, kayak. **faire du ~** to go canoeing.
kazakh [kaʒak] **1** **adj** kazakh. **2** **nm** (*langue*) Kazakh. **3** **K~ nmf** Kazakh.
Kazakhstan [kaʒakstɑ̃] **n** Kazakhstan.
Kentucky [kɛntyki] **nm** Kentucky.
Kenya [kenja] **nm** Kenya. **le mont ~** Mount Kenya.
kényan, -ane [kenjɑ̃, an] **1** **adj** Kenyan. **2** **nm,f: K~(e)** Kenyan.
képi [kepi] **nm** kepi.
kératine [keʀatin] **nf** keratin.
kératose [keʀatoz] **nf** keratosis.
kermesse [kɛʀmɛs] **nf** (*fête populaire*) fair; (*fête de charité*) bazaar, charity fête. **~ paroissiale** church fête *ou* bazaar.
kérosène [keʀozɛn] **nm** *[avion]* aviation fuel, kerosene (*US*); *[jet]* (jet) fuel; *[fusée]* (rocket) fuel.
keuf‡ [kœf] **nm** cop*, pig‡.
kF [kaɛf] (**abrév de kilofranc**) ≃ K. (*salaires*) **240 kF** ≃ £24 K, ≃ $48K.
kg (**abrév de kilogramme**) kg.
KGB [kaʒebe] **nm** (**abrév de Komitet Gosudarstvennoy Bezopasnosti**) (*comité pour la sécurité de l'État*) KGB.
khâgne [kaɲ] **nf = cagne.**
khâgneux, -euse [kaɲø, øz] **nm,f = cagneux[2].**
khalife [kalif] **nm = calife.**
khan [kɑ̃] **nm** khan.
Khartoum [kaʀtum] **n** Khartoum.
khédive [kediv] **nm** khedive.
khmer, -ère [kmɛʀ] **1** **adj** Khmer. **République ~ère** Khmer Republic. **2** **nmpl: les K~s** the Khmers; **K~ rouge** Khmer Rouge.
khôl [kol] **nm** kohl.
kibboutz [kibuts] **nm inv** kibbutz.
Kichinev [kitʃinɛv] **n** Kichinev.
kidnappage [kidnapaʒ] **nm = kidnapping.**
kidnapper [kidnape] [1] **vt** to kidnap, abduct.
kidnappeur, -euse [kidnapœʀ, øz] **nm,f** kidnapper, abductor.
kidnapping [kidnapiŋ] **nm** (*rare*) kidnapping, abduction.
kief [kjɛf] **nm, kif[1]** [kif] **nm** kif, kef.
Kiev [kjev] **n** Kiev.
kif[2]* [kif] **nm: c'est du ~** it's all the same, it's all one, it makes no odds* (*Brit*).
kif-kif* [kifkif] **adj inv: c'est ~** it's all the same, it's all one, it makes no odds* (*Brit*).
Kigali [kigali] **n** Kigali.
kiki* [kiki] **nm: serrer le ~ à qn** *[personne]* to throttle sb, grab sb by the throat; *[cravate, encolure]* to choke sb; *voir* **partir.**
kil‡ [kil] **nm: ~ de rouge** bottle of plonk* (*Brit*) *ou* cheap (red) wine.
Kilimandjaro [kilimɑ̃dʒaʀo] **nm: le ~** Mount Kilimanjaro.
kilo [kilo] **nm** kilo.
kilo... [kilo] **préf** kilo... .
kilobar [kilɔbaʀ] **nm** kilobar.
kilocalorie [kilokalɔʀi] **nf** kilocalorie.
kilocycle [kilosikl] **nm** kilocycle.
kilofranc [kilofʀɑ̃] **nm** thousand francs. **10 ~s** 10,000 francs.
kilogramme [kilɔgʀam] **nm** kilogramme.
kilohertz [kiloɛʀts] **nm** kilohertz.
kilométrage [kilɔmetʀaʒ] **nm** *[voiture, distance]* ≃ mileage; *[route]* ≃ marking with milestones. *[voiture]* **peu/beaucoup de ~** ≃ low/high mileage.
kilomètre [kilɔmɛtʀ] **nm** kilometre. **manger** *ou* **bouffer du ~*** ≃ to eat up the miles*; **~-passager** passenger kilometre, ≃ passenger mile; **d'ici à ce qu'il ne vienne pas du tout il n'y a pas des ~s*** I wouldn't be surprised if he didn't turn up at all.
kilométrer [kilɔmetʀe] [6] **vt** *route* ≃ to mark with milestones.
kilométrique [kilɔmetʀik] **adj: distance ~** distance in kilometres; **borne ~** ≃ milestone; **indemnité ~** mileage allowance.
kilo-octet [kiloɔktɛ] **nm** kilobyte.
kilotonne [kilotɔn] **nf** kiloton.
kilowatt [kilowat] **nm** kilowatt.
kilowatt-heure, pl kilowatts-heures [kilowatœʀ] **nm** kilowatt-hour.
kilt [kilt] **nm** kilt; (*pour femme*) pleated *ou* kilted skirt.
kimono [kimɔno] **nm** kimono. *voir* **manche[1].**
kinase [kinɑz] **nf** kinase.
kiné(si)* [kine(zi)] **nmf** (**abrév de kinésithérapeute**) physio*.
kinésithérapeute [kineziteʀapøt] **nmf** physiotherapist (*Brit*), physical therapist (*US*).
kinésithérapie [kineziteʀapi] **nf** physiotherapy (*Brit*), physical therapy (*US*).
kinesthésique [kinɛstezik] **adj** kinaesthetic.
Kingston [kiŋstɔn] **n** Kingston.
Kingstown [kiŋstaun] **n** Kingstown.
Kinshasa [kinʃasa] **n** Kinshasa.
kiosque [kjɔsk] **nm** *[fleurs etc]* kiosk, stall; *[jardin]* pavilion, summerhouse; *[sous-marin]* conning tower; *[bateau]* wheelhouse. **~ à musique** bandstand; **~ à journaux** newsstand, newspaper kiosk; **~ télématique** ® *information service provided by Minitel;* **en vente en ~** on sale at newsstands.
kiosquier, -ière [kjɔskje, jɛʀ] **nm,f** newspaper seller (*at kiosk*).

kippa [kipa] nf kippa.
kir [kiʀ] nm kir (*white wine with blackcurrant liqueur*). ~ **royal** kir royal (*champagne with blackcurrant liqueur*).
kirghiz [kiʀgiz] 1 adj Kirghiz. 2 nm (*langue*) Kirghiz. 3 **K~** nmf Kirghiz.
Kirghizstan [kiʀgistɑ̃] nm Kirghiszia.
kirsch [kiʀʃ] nm kirsch.
kit [kit] nm kit. **en ~** in kit form.
kitchenette [kitʃ(ə)nɛt] nf kitchenette.
kit(s)ch [kitʃ] adj inv, nm kitsch.
kiwi [kiwi] nm a (*oiseau*) kiwi. b (*arbre*) kiwi tree; (*fruit*) kiwi (fruit), Chinese gooseberry.
klaxon, Klaxon [klaksɔn] nm ® (*Aut*) horn.
klaxonner [klaksɔne] 1 vt (*fort*) to hoot (one's horn), sound one's horn, (*doucement*) to toot (the horn). **klaxonne, il ne t'a pas vu** give a hoot *ou* toot on your horn *ou* give him a toot*, he hasn't seen you.
kleb(s)* [klɛp(s)] nm = **clebs***.
Kleenex [klinɛks] nm ® tissue, paper hanky, Kleenex ®.
kleptomane [klɛptɔman] adj, nmf kleptomaniac.
kleptomanie [klɛptɔmani] nf kleptomania.
km (abrév de **kilomètre(s)**) km.
km/h (abrév de **kilomètres/heure**) km/h, kph, ≃ mph.
knock-out [nɔkaut] (*Boxe*, ‡) 1 adj knocked out, out for the count*. **mettre qn ~** to knock sb out; **il est complètement ~** he's out cold*. 2 nm knockout.
knout [knut] nm knout.
K.-O. [kao] (abrév de **knock out**) 1 nm (*Boxe*) K.O. **perdre par ~** to be knocked out; **gagner par ~** to win by a knockout. 2 adj (*: *fatigué*) shattered*, knackered‡.
Ko (abrév de **kilo-octet**) kb.
koala [kɔala] nm koala (bear).
kola [kɔla] nm = **cola**.
kolkhoze [kɔlkoz] nm kolkhoz, Russian collective farm.
kolkhozien, -ienne [kɔlkozjɛ̃, jɛn] adj, nm,f kolkhozian.
kopeck [kɔpɛk] nm kopeck. **je n'ai plus un ~*** I haven't got a sou.
koran [kɔʀɑ̃] nm = **coran**.
kouglof [kuglɔf] nm kugelhopf, *kind of bun*.
Koweit [kɔwɛt] nm Kuwait.
koweitien,-ienne [kɔwɛtjɛ̃, jɛn] 1 adj Kuwaiti. 2 nm,f: **K~(ne)** Kuwaiti.
krach [kʀak] nm (*Bourse*) crash. **~ boursier** stock market crash.
kraft [kʀaft] nm *voir* **papier**.
Kremlin [kʀɛmlɛ̃] nm: **le ~** the Kremlin.
krypton [kʀiptɔ̃] nm krypton.
Kuala Lumpur [kwalalumpuʀ] n Kuala Lumpur.
Ku Klux Klan [ky klyks klɑ̃] nm Ku Klux Klan.
kummel [kymɛl] nm kümmel.
kumquat [kɔmkwat] nm kumquat.
kurde [kyʀd] 1 adj Kurdish. 2 nm (*Ling*) Kurdish. 3 nmf: **K~** Kurd.
Kurdistan [kyʀdistɑ̃] nm Kurdistan.
kW (abrév de **kilowatt**) kW.
K-way [kawɛ] nm ® (lightweight nylon) cagoule.
kWh (abrév de **kilowatt heure**) kWh.
kyrie [kiʀje] , **kyrie eleison** [kiʀjeeleisɔn] nm, inv (*Rel, Mus*) Kyrie (eleison).
kyrielle [kiʀjɛl] nf *[injures, réclamations]* string, stream; *[personnes]* crowd, stream; *[objets]* pile.
kyste [kist] nm cyst.
kystique [kistik] adj cystic.

L

L, l [ɛl] **nm ou nf** (*lettre*) L, l.
l **abrév de litre(s).**
l' [l] *voir* **le**[1], **le**[2].
la[1] [la] *voir* **le**[1], **le**[2].
la[2] [la] **nm inv** (*Mus*) A; (*en chantant la gamme*) lah. **donner le ~** (*lit*) to give an A; (*fig*) to set the tone *ou* the fashion.
là [la] 1 **adv** a (*par opposition à ici*) there; (*là-bas*) over there. **~, on s'occupera bien de vous** you will be well looked after there; **je le vois ~, sur la table** I can see it (over) there, on the table; **c'est ~ où** *ou* **que je suis né** that's where I was born; **il est allé à Paris, et de ~ à Londres** he went to Paris, and from there to London *ou* and then (from there) on to London; **c'est à 3 km de ~** it's 3 km away (from there); **quelque part par ~** somewhere around there *ou* near there; **passez par ~** go that way; *voir* **çà**.

b (*ici*) here, there. **ne restez pas ~ au froid** don't stand here *ou* there in the cold; **M. X n'est pas ~** Mr X isn't here *ou* in; **c'est ~ qu'il est tombé** that's *ou* this is where he fell; **déjà ~!** (are) you here already?; **qu'est-ce que tu fais ~?** (*lit*) what are you doing here?; (*fig: manigancer*) what are you up to?; **les faits sont ~** there's no getting away from the facts, those are the facts.

c (*dans le temps*) then, (at) this *ou* that moment. **c'est ~ qu'il comprit qu'il était en danger** that was when he realized *ou* it was then that he realized he was in danger; **à partir de ~** from then on, after that; **jusque-~** until then, until that moment *ou* time; **à quelques jours de ~** a few days later *ou* after(wards); *voir* **ici**.

d (*dans cette situation*) **tout cela pour en arriver** *ou* **en venir ~!** all that effort just for this!; **il faut s'en tenir** *ou* **en rester ~** we'll have to leave it at that *ou* stop there; **la situation en est ~** that's how the situation stands at the moment, that's the state of play at present; **ils en sont ~** (*lit*) that's how far they've got up to, that's the stage they've reached; (*péj*) that's how low they've sunk; **j'en étais ~ de mes réflexions lorsqu'il est entré** such was my state of mind when he walked in; **ils n'en sont pas encore ~** they haven't got that far yet *ou* reached that stage yet; (*péj*) they haven't reached that stage yet *ou* come to that yet; **~ est la difficulté, c'est ~ qu'est la difficulté** that's where the difficulty lies; **il a bien fallu en passer par ~** it had to come (to that) in the end; **c'est bien ~ qu'on voit les paresseux!** that's where *ou* when you see who the lazy ones are!; **c'est ~ où** *ou* **que nous ne sommes plus d'accord** that's where I take issue *ou* start to disagree with you.

e (*intensif*) that. **ce jour-~** that day; **en ce temps-~** in those days; **cet homme-~ est détesté par tout le monde** everybody hates that man; **je veux celui-~** I want that one; **celui-/celle-~ alors!** (*irritation*) oh, that one!, oh him/her!; (*surprise*) how does he/she manage!, he/she is a wonder!; **c'est à ce point-~?** it's as bad as that, is it?; **ce qu'il dit ~ n'est pas bête** what he has just said isn't a bad idea; **la question n'est pas ~** that's not the point; **ne croyez pas ~ qu'on ne veuille pas de vous** don't get the idea that you're not wanted; **il y a ~ une contradiction** there's a contradiction in that; **il est entré dans une rage, mais ~, une de ces rages!** he flew into a rage, and what a rage!

f (*loc*) **de ~ son désespoir** hence his despair; **de ~ vient que nous ne le voyons plus** that's why we no longer see him; **de ~ à croire qu'il ment, il n'y a qu'un pas** there isn't much difference between saying that and thinking he's lying, that's tantamount to saying he's a liar; **de ~ à prétendre qu'il a tout fait seul, il y a loin** there's a big difference between saying that and claiming that he did it all himself; **il n'a pas travaillé, de ~ son échec** he didn't work, hence his failure *ou* which explains his failure; **qu'entendez-vous par ~?** what do you mean by that?; **loin de ~** far from it; **tout est ~** that's the whole question; **il est (~ et) un peu ~*** you can't miss him, he makes his presence felt; **comme menteur, il se pose ~ et un peu ~** he's an absolutely shameless liar, he's some liar*, he isn't half a liar* (*Brit*); **fiche-moi la paix ~!*** leave me in peace, will you!*; **oh ~** *ou* **alors ~, ça ne me surprend pas** (oh) now, that doesn't surprise me; **hé ~!** (*appel*) hey!; (*surprise*) good grief!; **~ ~ du calme!** now now calm down!, there there calm down!; **oh ~ ~ (~ ~)** oh dear! oh dear!, dear *ou* dearie me!

2 **comp ►là-bas** (over) there, yonder (†, *littér*); **là-bas aux USA** over in the USA; **là-bas dans le nord** up (there) in the north **►là-dedans** (*lit*) inside, in there; **je ne comprends rien là-dedans** I don't understand a thing about it; **il n'a rien à voir là-dedans** it's nothing to do with him; **il a voulu mettre de l'argent là-dedans** he wanted to put some money into it; **quand il s'est embarqué là-dedans** when he got involved in that *ou* in it **►là-dessous** underneath, under there, under that; (*fig*) **il y a quelque chose là-dessous** there's something odd about it *ou* that, there's more to it than meets the eye **►là-dessus** (*lieu*) on that, on there; (*sur ces mots*) at that point, thereupon (*frm*); (*à ce sujet*) about that, on that point; **vous pouvez compter là-dessus** you can count on that **►là-haut** up there; (*dessus*) up on top; (*à l'étage*) upstairs; (*fig: au ciel*) on high, in heaven above.
labbe [lab] **nm** skua. **~ parasite** Arctic skua.
label [labɛl] **nm** (*Comm*) stamp, seal; (*Ordin*) label. **~ d'origine/de qualité** stamp *ou* seal of origin/quality; (*fig*) **c'est un ~ de qualité** it is a guarantee of quality; (*fig*) **~ politique** political label.
labelliser [labelize] 1 **vt** to label, put a label on.
labeur [labœʀ] **nm** (*littér*) labour, toil (*NonC*). **c'est un dur ~** it's hard work.
labial, e, mpl -iaux [labjal, jo] 1 **adj** *consonne* labial; *muscle* lip (*épith*), labial (*SPÉC*). 2 **labiale nf** labial.
labialisation [labjalizasjɔ̃] **nf** (*voir* **labialiser**) labialization; rounding.
labialiser [labjalize] 1 **vt** *consonne* to labialize; *voyelle* to labialize, round.
labié, e [labje] **adj** (*Bot*) labiate.
labiodental, e, mpl -aux [labjodɑ̃tal, o] **adj, nf** labiodental.
labo* [labo] **nm** (**abrév de laboratoire**) lab*.
laborantin, e [labɔʀɑ̃tɛ̃, in] **nm,f** laboratory *ou* lab* assistant.
laboratoire [labɔʀatwaʀ] **nm** laboratory. **~ de langues/de recherches** language/research laboratory; **~ d'analyses (médicales)** (medical) analysis laboratory.
laborieusement [labɔʀjøzmɑ̃] **adv** laboriously, with much effort. **gagner ~ sa vie** to earn a *ou* one's living by the sweat of one's brow.
laborieux, -ieuse [labɔʀjø, jøz] **adj** a (*pénible*) laborious, painstaking; *entreprise, recherches* laborious; *style, récit* laboured, laborious; *digestion* heavy. **il a enfin fini, ça a été ~!*** he has finished at long last, it has been heavy going *ou* he made heavy weather of it. b (*travailleur*) hard-working, industrious. **les classes ~euses** the working *ou* labouring classes; **les masses ~euses** the toiling masses; **une vie ~euse** a life of toil *ou* hard work.
labour [labuʀ] **nm** (*avec une charrue*) ploughing (*Brit*), plowing (*US*); (*avec une bêche*) digging (over). **cheval de ~** plough-horse, cart-horse; **bœuf de ~** ox; **champ en ~** ploughed field; **terre de ~** ploughland; **marcher dans les ~s** to walk in the ploughed fields.
labourable [labuʀabl] **adj** (*voir* **labour**) ploughable (*Brit*), plowable (*US*), which can be ploughed; which can be dug.
labourage [labuʀaʒ] **nm** (*voir* **labour**) ploughing (*Brit*), plowing (*US*); digging.
labourer [labuʀe] 1 **vt** a (*avec une charrue*) to plough (*Brit*), plow (*US*); (*avec une bêche*) to dig (over). **terre qui se laboure bien** land which ploughs well *ou* is easy to plough; (*Naut*) **~ le fond** *[navire]* to scrape *ou* graze the bottom; *[ancre]* to drag; **terrain labouré par les sabots des chevaux** ground churned *ou* ploughed up by the horses' hooves.

b *visage* to make deep gashes in, rip *ou* slash into. **la balle lui avait labouré la jambe** the bullet had ripped into *ou* gashed his leg; **labouré de rides** lined *ou* furrowed with wrinkles; **ce corset me laboure les côtes** this corset is digging into my sides; **se ~ le visage/les mains** to gash *ou* lacerate one's face/hands.
laboureur [labuʀœʀ] **nm** ploughman (*Brit*), plowman (*US*); (*Hist*) husbandman.
Labrador [labʀadɔʀ] **nm** (*Géog, chien*) Labrador.

labyrinthe [labiʀɛ̃t] **nm** (*lit, fig*) maze, labyrinth; (*Anat*) labyrinth.
labyrinthique [labiʀɛ̃tik] **adj** labyrinthine.
lac [lak] **nm** lake. **le ~ Léman** *ou* **de Genève** Lake Geneva; **le ~ Majeur** Lake Maggiore; **les ~s écossais** the Scottish lochs; **le L~ des Cygnes** Swan Lake; (*fig*) **être (tombé) dans le ~*** to have fallen through, have come to nothing.
laçage [lasaʒ] **nm** lacing(-up).
Lacédémone [lasedemɔn] **n** Lacedaemonia.
lacédémonien, -ienne [lasedemɔnjɛ̃, jɛn] **adj, nm,f** Lacedaemonian.
lacement [lasmɑ̃] **nm** = **laçage**.
lacer [lase] 3 **vt** *chaussure* to tie (up); *corset* to lace up; (*Naut*) *voile* to lace. **lace tes chaussures** *ou* **tes lacets** do up *ou* tie your shoelaces; **ça se lace (par) devant** it laces up at the front.
lacération [laseʀasjɔ̃] **nf** (*voir* **lacérer**) ripping up, tearing up; ripping *ou* tearing to shreds; laceration; shredding. **détruire des documents par ~** to put documents through the shredder, shred documents.
lacérer [laseʀe] 6 **vt** *vêtement* to tear *ou* rip up, tear to shreds; *corps, visage* to lacerate; *papier* to tear up, shred.
lacet [lasɛ] **nm** a *[chaussure]* (shoe) lace; *[corset]* lace. **chaussures à ~s** lace-up shoes, shoes with laces. b *[route]* (sharp) bend, twist. **en ~** winding, twisty; **la route fait des ~s** *ou* **monte en ~s** the road twists *ou* winds steeply up(wards). c (*piège*) snare. **prendre des lièvres au ~** to trap *ou* snare hares. d (*Couture*) braid.
lâchage* [lɑʃaʒ] **nm** (*abandon*) desertion. **écœuré par le ~ de ses amis** disgusted at the way his friends had deserted him *ou* run out on him.
lâche [lɑʃ] 1 **adj** a (*détendu*) *corde, ressort* slack; *nœud* loose; *vêtement* loose(-fitting); *tissu* loosely-woven, open-weave (*épith*); *discipline, morale* lax; *règlement, canevas* loose; *style, expression* loose, woolly. **dans ce roman, l'intrigue est ~** the plot is loose *ou* rather diffuse in this novel. b (*couard*) *personne, fuite, attitude* cowardly, craven (*littér*). **se montrer ~** to show o.s. a coward; **c'est assez ~ de sa part d'avoir fait ça** it was pretty cowardly of him to do that. c (*bas, vil*) *attentat* vile, despicable; *procédés* low. d (*littér: faible*) weak, feeble. 2 **nmf** coward.
lâchement [lɑʃmɑ̃] **adv** (*voir* **lâche**) loosely; in a cowardly way. **il a ~ refusé** like a coward, he refused.
lâcher [lɑʃe] 1 1 **vt** a *ceinture* to loosen, let out, slacken. **~ la taille d'une jupe** to let a skirt out at the waist; (*Pêche*) **~ du fil** to let out some line.
b *main, proie* to let go of; *bombes* to drop, release; *pigeon, ballon* to release; *chien de garde* to unleash, set loose; *frein* to release, let out; (*Naut*) *amarres* to cast off; (*Chasse*) *chien, faucon* to slip. **lâche-moi!** let *ou* leave go (of me)!; **attention! tu vas ~ le verre** careful, you're going to drop the glass; **le professeur nous a lâchés à 4 heures*** the teacher let us go *ou* out at 4; **~ un chien sur qn** to set a dog on sb; **s'il veut acheter ce tableau, il va falloir qu'il les lâche*** *ou* **qu'il lâche ses sous*** if he wants this picture, he'll have to part with the cash*; **il les lâche difficilement*** he hates to part with his money.
c *bêtise, juron* to come out with; *pet* to let out; (†) *coup de fusil* to fire. **voilà le grand mot lâché!** there's the fatal word!; **~ un coup de poing/pied à qn**† to deal *ou* fetch (*Brit*) sb a blow with one's fist/foot, let fly at sb with one's fist/foot.
d (*: *abandonner*) *époux* to leave, walk out on; *amant* to throw over*, jilt, drop*, chuck‡ (*Brit*); *copain* to throw over*, drop*; *études, métier* to give up, throw up*, pack in* (*Brit*), chuck in‡ (*Brit*); *avantage* to give up. (*Sport*) **~ le peloton** to leave the rest of the field behind, build up a good lead (over the rest of the pack); **ne pas ~ qn** *[poursuivant, créancier]* to stick to sb; *[importun, représentant]* not to leave sb alone; *[mal de tête]* not to let up on* *ou* leave sb; **il nous a lâchés en plein milieu du travail** he walked out on us right in the middle of the work; **il ne m'a pas lâché d'une semelle** he stuck close all the time, he stuck (to me) like a leech; **une bonne occasion, ça ne se lâche pas** *ou* **il ne faut pas la ~** you don't miss *ou* pass up* an opportunity like that.
e (*loc*) **~ prise** (*lit*) to let go; (*fig*) to loosen one's grip; **~ pied** to fall back, give way; **~ la proie pour l'ombre** to chase shadows, give up what one has (already) for some uncertain *ou* fanciful alternative; **~ le morceau*** *ou* **le paquet*** to come clean*, sing‡; **~ la bride** *ou* **les rênes à un cheval** to give a horse its head; (*fig*) **~ la bride à qn** to give *ou* let sb have his head; **lâche-moi les baskets*** *ou* **la grappe*‡** get off my back*; **il les lâche avec des élastiques‡** he's as stingy as hell‡, he's a tight-fisted so-and-so*; *voir* **lest**.
2 **vi** *[corde]* to break, give way; *[frein]* to fail. (*fig*) **ses nerfs ont lâché** he broke down, he couldn't take the strain.
3 **nm**: **~ de ballons** release of balloons; **~ de pigeons** release of pigeons.
lâcheté [lɑʃte] **nf** a (*couardise*) cowardice, cowardliness; (*bassesse*) lowness. **par ~** through *ou* out of cowardice. b (*acte*) cowardly act, act of cowardice; low deed. c (*littér: faiblesse*) weakness, feebleness.
lâcheur, -euse* [lɑʃœʀ, øz] **nm,f** unreliable *ou* fickle so-and-so*. **alors, tu n'es pas venu, ~!** so you didn't come then – you're a dead loss!*, so you deserted us *ou* you let us down, you old so-and-so!*; **c'est une ~euse, ta sœur** your sister's a right one (*Brit*) for letting people down*, your sister's a so-and-so the way she lets people down*.
lacis [lasi] **nm** *[ruelles]* maze; *[veines]* network; *[scie]* web.
laconique [lakɔnik] **adj** *personne, réponse, style* laconic, terse.
laconiquement [lakɔnikmɑ̃] **adv** laconically, tersely.
laconisme [lakɔnism] **nm** terseness.
lacrymal, e, **mpl -aux** [lakʀimal, o] **adj** lachrymal (*SPÉC*), tear (*épith*).
lacrymogène [lakʀimɔʒɛn] **adj** *voir* **gaz, grenade**.
lacs [lɑ] **nmpl** (††, *littér*) snare. **~ d'amour** lover's *ou* love knot.
lactaire [laktɛʀ] 1 **adj** (*Anat*) lacteal. 2 **nm** (*Bot*) (lacteous) mushroom.
lactalbumine [laktalbymin] **nf** lactalbumin.
lactase [laktɑz] **nf** lactase.
lactation [laktasjɔ̃] **nf** lactation.
lacté, e [lakte] **adj** *sécrétion* milky, lacteal (*SPÉC*); *couleur, suc* milky; *régime* milk (*épith*); *voir* **voie**.
lactifère [laktifɛʀ] **adj** lactiferous.
lactique [laktik] **adj** lactic.
lactogène [laktɔʒɛn] **adj** lactogenic.
lactose [laktoz] **nm** lactose.
lacunaire [lakynɛʀ] **adj** (*Bio*) *tissu* lacunary, lacunal; *documentation* incomplete, deficient.
lacune [lakyn] **nf** a *[texte, mémoire]* gap, blank; *[manuscrit]* lacuna; *[connaissances]* gap, deficiency. **il y a de sérieuses ~s dans ce livre** this book has some serious deficiencies *ou* leaves out *ou* overlooks some serious points. b (*Anat, Bot*) lacuna.
lacuneux, -euse [lakynø, øz] **adj** = **lacunaire**.
lacustre [lakystʀ] **adj** lake (*épith*), lakeside (*épith*). **cité ~** lakeside village (on piles).
lad [lad] **nm** (*Équitation*) stable-lad.
ladite [ladit] **adj** *voir* **ledit**.
ladre [lɑdʀ] 1 **adj** (*littér: avare*) mean, miserly. 2 **nmf** (*littér*) miser.
ladrerie [lɑdʀəʀi] **nf** a (*littér: avarice*) meanness, miserliness. b (*Hist: hôpital*) leper-house.
lagon [lagɔ̃] **nm** lagoon.
lagopède [lagɔpɛd] **nm**: **~ d'Écosse** (red) grouse; **~ des Alpes** ptarmigan.
lagunaire [lagynɛʀ] **adj** lagoon (*épith*), of a lagoon.
lagune [lagyn] **nf** lagoon.
lai¹ [lɛ] **nm** (*Poésie*) lay.
lai², e [lɛ] **adj** (*Rel*) lay. **frère ~** lay brother.
laïc [laik] **adj, nm** = **laïque**.
laîche [lɛʃ] **nf** sedge.
laïcisation [laisizasjɔ̃] **nf** secularization.
laïciser [laisize] **vt** *institutions* to secularize. **l'enseignement est aujourd'hui laïcisé** education is now under secular control.
laïcisme [laisism] **nm** secularism.
laïcité [laisite] **nf** (*caractère*) secularity; (*Pol: système*) secularism. **préserver la ~ de l'enseignement** to maintain the non-religious nature of the education system, keep religion out of education.
laid, e [lɛ, lɛd] **adj** a (*physiquement*) *personne, visage, animal* ugly(-looking); *ville, région* ugly, unattractive; *bâtiment, meubles, dessin* ugly, unattractive, unsightly, awful*. **~ comme un singe** *ou* **un pou** *ou* **les sept péchés capitaux** *ou* **à faire peur** ugly as sin; **il est très ~ de visage** he's got a terribly ugly face. b (*frm: moralement*) *action* despicable, disgusting, wretched, low, mean; *vice* ugly, loathsome. **c'est ~ de montrer du doigt** it's rude *ou* not nice to point; **c'est ~, ce que tu as fait** that was a nasty *ou* disgusting thing to do.
laidement [lɛdmɑ̃] **adv** (*sans beauté*) in an ugly way; (*littér: bassement*) despicably, disgustingly, wretchedly, meanly.
laideron [lɛdʀɔ̃] **nm** ugly girl *ou* woman. **c'est un vrai ~** she's a real ugly duckling.
laideur [lɛdœʀ] **nf** (*voir* **laid**) a (*caractère*) ugliness; unattractiveness; unsightliness; wretchedness, lowness, meanness. **la guerre/l'égoïsme dans toute sa ~** the full horror of war/selfishness, war/selfishness in all its ugliness. b **les ~s de la vie** the ugly side of life, the ugly things in life; **les ~s de la guerre** the ugliness of war.
laie¹ [lɛ] **adj f** *voir* **lai²**.
laie² [lɛ] **nf** (*Zool*) wild sow.
laie³ [lɛ] **nf** (*sentier*) forest track *ou* path.
lainage [lɛnaʒ] **nm** a (*vêtement*) woollen (garment), woolly*. **la production des ~s** the manufacture of woollens *ou* of woollen goods. b (*étoffe*) woollen material *ou* fabric. **un beau ~** fine quality woollen material.
laine [lɛn] 1 **nf** (*matière*) wool. **de ~** *vêtement, moquette* wool, woollen; **tapis de haute ~** deep *ou* thick pile wool carpet; (*vêtement*) **il faut mettre une petite ~** you'll need a woolly* *ou* a cardigan; *voir* **bas²**. 2 **comp** ▸**laine à matelas** flock ▸**laine peignée** *[pantalon, veston]* worsted wool; *[pull]* combed wool ▸**laine à tricoter** knitting wool ▸**laine de verre** glass wool ▸**laine vierge** new wool.
laineux, -euse [lɛnø, øz] **adj** *tissu, plante* woolly.
lainier, -ière [lɛnje, jɛʀ] 1 **adj** *industrie* woollen (*épith*); *région* wool-producing. 2 **nm,f** (*marchand*) wool merchant; (*ouvrier*) wool worker.
laïque [laik] 1 **adj** *tribunal* lay, civil; *vie* secular; *habit* ordinary; *collège* non-religious. **l'enseignement** *ou* **l'école ~** state education (*in France*). 2 **nm** layman. **les ~s** laymen, the laity. 3 **nf** laywoman.

laisse [lɛs] **nf** a (*attache*) leash, lead. **tenir en ~** *chien* to keep on a leash *ou* lead; (*fig*) *personne* to keep on a lead *ou* in check. b (*Géog*) foreshore. **~ de haute/basse mer** high-/low-water mark. c (*Poésie*) laisse.

laissé-pour-compte, *f* **laissée-pour-compte,** **pl laissés-pour-compte** [lesepuʀkɔ̃t] 1 **adj** a (*Comm*) (*refusé*) rejected, returned; (*invendu*) unsold, left over.

b (*fig*) *personne* rejected; *chose* rejected, discarded.

2 **nm** (*Comm*) (*refusé*) reject; (*invendu*) unsold article. **vendre à bas prix les laissés-pour-compte** to sell off old *ou* leftover stock cheaply; (*fig*) **les laissés-pour-compte de la société** society's rejects; (*fig*) **les ouvriers ne veulent pas être des laissés-pour-compte maintenant que la mécanisation supprime de la main-d'œuvre** workers don't want to find themselves left on the scrap heap *ou* cast to one side now that mechanization is replacing manual labour; (*fig*) **ce sont les laissés-pour-compte du progrès** these people are the casualties of progress, progress has left these people out in the cold *ou* on the scrap heap.

laisser [lese] [1] 1 **vt** a (*abandonner*) *place, fortune, femme, objet* to leave. **~ sa clef au voisin** to leave one's key with the neighbour, leave the neighbour one's key; **laisse-lui du gâteau** leave *ou* save him some cake, leave *ou* save some cake for him; **il m'a laissé ce vase pour 10 F** he let me have this vase for 10 francs; **laisse-moi le soin de le lui dire** leave it to me to tell him; **laissez, je vais le faire/c'est moi qui paie** leave that, I'll do it/I'm paying; **laisse-moi le temps d'y réfléchir** give me time to think about it; **laisse-moi devant la banque** drop *ou* leave me at the bank; **il a laissé un bras/la vue dans l'accident** he lost an arm/his sight in the accident; **l'expédition était dangereuse: il y a laissé sa vie** it was a dangerous expedition and it cost him his life; **elle l'a laissé de meilleure humeur** she left him in a better mood; **au revoir, je vous laisse** bye-bye, I must leave you; **je l'ai laissé à son travail** I left him to get on with his work.

b (*faire demeurer*) *trace, regrets, goût* to leave. **~ qn indifférent/dans le doute** to leave sb unmoved/in doubt; **~ qn debout** to keep sb standing (up); **on lui a laissé ses illusions, on l'a laissé à ses illusions** we didn't disillusion him; **elle m'a laissé une bonne impression** she left *ou* made a good impression on me; **on l'a laissé dans l'erreur** we didn't tell him that he was mistaken; **il vaut mieux le ~ dans l'ignorance de nos projets** it is best to leave him in the dark *ou* not to tell him about our plans; **~ un enfant à ses parents** (*gén*) to leave a child with his parents; (*Jur*) to leave a child in the custody of his parents; **vous laissez le village sur votre droite** you go past the village on your right; **~ la vie à qn** to spare sb's life; **~ qn en liberté** to allow sb to stay free; **cette opération ne doit pas laisser de séquelles** this operation should leave *ou* have no aftereffects.

c (*loc*) **~ la porte ouverte** (*lit, fig*) to leave the door open; **il ne laisse jamais rien au hasard** he never leaves anything to chance; **c'était à prendre ou à ~** it was a case of take it or leave it; **avec lui il faut en prendre et en ~** you can only believe half of what he says, you must take what he tells you with a pinch of salt; **on l'a laissé pour mort** he was left for dead; **il laisse tout le monde derrière lui pour le** *ou* **par son talent/courage** he puts everyone else in the shade with his talent/courage; **il laisse tout le monde derrière en math** he is head and shoulders above *ou* streets* (*Brit*) *ou* miles ahead of the others in maths; **~ le meilleur pour la fin** to leave the best till last; (*littér*) **il n'a pas laissé de me le dire** he didn't fail to tell me, he could not refrain from telling me; (*littér*) **cela n'a pas laissé de me surprendre** I couldn't fail to be surprised by *ou* at that; (*littér*) **cela ne laisse pas d'être vrai** it is true nonetheless; **je le laisse à penser combien il était content** you can imagine *ou* I don't need to tell you how pleased he was; *voir* **champ, désirer, plan[1]**.

2 **vb aux: ~ (qn) faire qch** to let sb do sth; **laisse-le entrer/partir** let him in/go; **laisse-le monter/descendre** let him come *ou* go up/down; **laissez-moi rire** don't make me laugh; **~ voir ses sentiments** to let one's feelings show; **il n'en a rien laissé voir** he showed no sign of it, he gave no inkling of it; **laisse-le faire** (*sans l'aider*) let him alone, let him do it himself; (*à sa manière*) let him do it his own way; (*ce qui lui plaît*) let him do (it) as he likes *ou* wants; **il faut ~ faire le temps** we must let things take their course; **laisse faire!** oh, never mind!, don't bother!; **j'ai été attaqué dans la rue et les gens ont laissé faire** I was attacked in the street and people did nothing *ou* people just stood by; *voir* **courir, penser, tomber.**

3 **se laisser vpr: se ~ persuader/exploiter/duper** to let o.s. be persuaded/exploited/fooled; **il s'est laissé attendrir par leur pauvreté** he was moved by their poverty; **il ne faut pas se ~ décourager/abattre** you mustn't let yourself become *ou* allow yourself to become discouraged/downhearted; **je me suis laissé surprendre par la pluie** I got caught in the rain; **il se laisse mener par le bout du nez** he lets himself be led by the nose *ou* be pushed around; **ce petit vin se laisse boire*** this wine goes down well *ou* nicely; **se ~ aller** to let o.s. go; **se ~ aller à mentir** to stoop to telling lies; **je me suis laissé faire*** I let myself be persuaded, I let myself be talked into it; **je n'ai pas l'intention de me ~ faire** I'm not going to let myself be pushed around; **laisse-toi faire!** (*à qn que l'on soigne, habille etc*) oh come on, it won't hurt (you)! *ou* let me do it!; (*en offrant une liqueur etc*) oh come on, be a devil!* *ou* it won't do you any harm!; **laisse-toi faire, je vais te peigner** just let me comb your hair, keep still while I comb your hair; *voir* **conter, dire, vivre.**

4 **comp** ►**laisser-aller nm inv** (*gén*) casualness, carelessness; *[travail, langage, vêtements]* slovenliness, carelessness ►**laisser-faire nm** (*Écon*) laissez-faire policy ►**laissez-passer nm inv** (*gén*) pass; (*Douane*) transire.

lait [lɛ] 1 **nm** milk. **~ de vache/de chèvre/d'ânesse** cow's/goat's/ass's milk; **~ concentré/condensé non sucré/entier/écrémé** condensed/(unsweetened) evaporated/unskimmed/skimmed milk; **~ cru** milk straight from the cow; **mettre qn au ~** to put sb on a milk diet; (*fig*) **boire du (petit) ~** to lap it up (*fig*); **cela se boit comme du petit ~** you don't notice you're drinking it; **frère/sœur de ~** foster brother/sister; **chocolat au ~** milk chocolate; *voir* **café, cochon[1], dent.**

2 **comp** ►**lait d'amande** almond oil ►**lait de beauté** beauty lotion ►**lait caillé** curds ►**lait de chaux** lime water ►**lait de coco** coconut milk ►**lait démaquillant** cleansing milk ►**lait longue conservation** UHT milk ►**lait maternel** mother's milk, breast milk ►**lait maternisé** baby milk (*Brit*), formula (*US*) ►**lait en poudre** dried *ou* powdered milk ►**lait de poule** (*Culin*) eggflip ►**lait solaire** sun cream ►**lait végétal** latex.

laitage [lɛtaʒ] **nm** (*lait*) milk; (*produit laitier*) dairy product.

laitance [lɛtɑ̃s] **nf** soft roe.

laiterie [lɛtʀi] **nf** (*usine, magasin*) dairy; (*industrie*) dairy industry.

laiteux, -euse [lɛtø, øz] **adj** *couleur, liquide, teint* milky; *chair* creamy.

laitier, -ière [letje, jɛʀ] 1 **adj** *industrie, produit* dairy (*épith*); *production, vache* milk (*épith*), dairy (*épith*). 2 **nm** a (*livreur*) milkman; (*vendeur*) dairyman. b (*Ind*) slag. 3 **laitière nf** (*vendeuse*) dairywoman. (*vache*) **une (bonne) ~ière** a (good) milker.

laiton [lɛtɔ̃] **nm** (*alliage*) brass; (*fil*) brass wire.

laitue [lety] **nf** lettuce. **~ romaine** cos lettuce (*Brit*), romaine lettuce (*US*).

laïus* [lajys] **nm inv** (*discours*) long-winded speech; (*verbiage*) verbiage (*NonC*), padding (*NonC*). **faire un ~** to hold forth at great length, give a long-winded speech.

laïusser* [lajyse] [1] **vi** to expatiate, hold forth, spout* (*sur* on).

lama [lama] **nm** (*Zool*) llama; (*Rel*) lama.

lamaïsme [lamaism] **nm** Lamaism.

lamaïste [lamaist] **adj, nm,f** Lamaist.

lamantin [lamɑ̃tɛ̃] **nm** manatee.

lamaserie [lamazʀi] **nf** lamasery.

lambada [lɑ̃bada] **nf** lambada.

lambda [lɑ̃bda] **nm** lambda. **le citoyen ~** the uninformed citizen.

lambeau, pl ~x [lɑ̃bo] **nm** scrap. **en ~x** *vêtements* in tatters *ou* rags, tattered; *affiche* in tatters, tattered; **mettre en ~x** to tear to shreds *ou* bits; **tomber** *ou* **partir en ~x** to fall to pieces *ou* bits; (*fig*) **~x de conversation** scraps of conversation; **~x du passé** fragments *ou* remnants of the past.

lambic(k) [lɑ̃bik] **nm** *kind of strong Belgian beer*; *voir* **gueuse.**

lambin, e* [lɑ̃bɛ̃, in] 1 **adj** slow. **que tu es ~** what a dawdler *ou* slowcoach* (*Brit*) *ou* slowpoke* (*US*) you are. 2 **nm,f** dawdler*, slowcoach* (*Brit*), slowpoke* (*US*).

lambiner* [lɑ̃bine] [1] **vi** to dawdle, dillydally*.

lambourde [lɑ̃buʀd] **nf** (*pour parquet*) backing strip (*on joists*); (*pour solive*) wall-plate.

lambrequin [lɑ̃bʀəkɛ̃] **nm** *[fenêtre]* pelmet.

lambris [lɑ̃bʀi] **nm** (*gén*) panelling (*NonC*); (*bois*) panelling (*NonC*), wainscoting (*NonC*).

lambrisser [lɑ̃bʀise] [1] **vt** (*voir* **lambris**) to panel; to wainscot.

lame [lam] 1 **nf** a *[métal, verre]* strip; *[bois]* strip, lath; (*Aut*) *[ressort]* leaf; *[store]* slat; (*pour microscope*) slide. b *[poignard, tondeuse, scie]* blade. (*fig*) **visage en ~ de couteau** hatchet face. c (*fig*) (*épée*) sword; (*escrimeur*) swordsman (*ou* swordswoman). **bonne** *ou* **fine ~** a good swordsman (*ou* swordswoman). d (*vague*) wave. e (*partie de la langue*) blade. 2 **comp** ►**lame de fond** ground swell (*NonC*) ►**lame de parquet** floorboard, strip of parquet flooring ►**lame de rasoir** razor blade.

lamé, e [lame] 1 **adj** lamé (*épith*). **robe ~e (d')or** gold lamé dress. 2 **nm** lamé.

lamelle [lamɛl] **nf** (*gén: de métal, plastique*) (small) strip; *[persiennes]* slat; *[champignon]* gill; (*pour microscope*) coverglass. **~ de mica** mica flake; **couper en ~s** *légumes* to cut into thin strips *ou* slices.

lamellibranches [lamelibʀɑ̃ʃ] **nmpl** lamellibranchia.

lamentable [lamɑ̃tabl] **adj** *résultat, état* lamentable, appalling, awful; *concurrent* appalling, awful; *sort, spectacle* miserable, pitiful; *cri* pitiful, woeful; *histoire* dreadful, appalling.

lamentablement [lamɑ̃tabləmɑ̃] **adv** *échouer* miserably, lamentably.

lamentation [lamɑ̃tasjɔ̃] **nf** (*cri de désolation*) lamentation, wailing (*NonC*); (*péj: jérémiade*) moaning (*NonC*). (*Bible*) **le livre des L~s** (the Book of) Lamentations; *voir* **mur.**

lamenter (se) [lamɑ̃te] [1] **vpr** to moan, lament. **se ~ sur qch** to moan over sth, bemoan sth; **se ~ sur son sort** to bemoan *ou* bewail *ou* lament one's fate; **arrête de te ~ sur ton propre sort** stop feeling sorry for yourself; **il se lamente d'avoir échoué** he is moaning over his failure.

lamento [lamɛnto] **nm** lament.

laminage [laminaʒ] nm lamination.

laminer [lamine] 1 vt *métal* to laminate. (*fig*) **ses marges bénéficiaires ont été laminées par les hausses** his profit margins have been eaten away *ou* eroded by price rises; (*fig*) **les petites formations politiques ont été laminées aux dernières élections** the small political groupings were wiped out *ou* obliterated at the last election.

lamineur [laminœʀ] 1 adj m: **cylindre** ~ roller. 2 nm rolling mill operator.

laminoir [laminwaʀ] nm rolling mill. (*fig*) **passer/mettre qn au** ~ to go/put sb through the mill *ou* through it*.

lampadaire [lɑ̃padɛʀ] nm *[intérieur]* standard lamp; *[rue]* street lamp. **(pied du)** ~ *[intérieur]* lamp standard; *[rue]* lamppost.

lampant [lɑ̃pɑ̃] adj m *voir* **pétrole**.

lamparo [lɑ̃paʀo] nm lamp. **pêche au** ~ fishing by lamplight (*in the Mediterranean*).

lampe [lɑ̃p] 1 nf lamp, light; (*ampoule*) bulb; (*Rad*) valve. **éclairé par une** ~ lit by lamplight *ou* by the light of a lamp; *voir* **mettre**.

2 comp ▸**lampe à acétylène** acetylene lamp (*Brit*) *ou* torch (*US*) ▸**lampe à alcool** spirit lamp ▸**lampe à arc** arc light *ou* lamp ▸**lampe d'architecte** Anglepoise lamp ® ▸**lampe à bronzer** sun lamp ▸**lampe de bureau** desk lamp *ou* light ▸**lampe à carbure** carbide lamp ▸**lampe de chevet** bedside lamp *ou* light ▸**lampe-éclair** nf (pl **lampes-éclair**) **lampe-flash**, nf (pl **lampes-flash**) flashlight ▸**lampe électrique** torch (*Brit*), flashlight ▸**lampe à huile** oil lamp ▸**lampe à incandescence** incandescent lamp ▸**lampe halogène** *ou* **à iode** halogen lamp ▸**lampe de lecture** reading lamp ▸**lampe de mineur** (miner's) safety lamp ▸**lampe au néon** neon light ▸**lampe à pétrole** paraffin (*Brit*) *ou* kerosene (*US*) *ou* oil lamp ▸**lampe de poche** torch (*Brit*), flashlight ▸**lampe solaire** sun lamp ▸**lampe à souder** (*lit*) blowlamp (*Brit*), blow-torch; (*arg Mil*) machine gun ▸**lampe-témoin** nf (pl **lampes-témoin**) (*gén*) warning light; *[magnétoscope etc]* light (*showing power is on*) ▸**lampe-tempête** nf (pl **lampes-tempête**) storm lantern, hurricane lamp.

lampée* [lɑ̃pe] nf gulp, swig*. **boire qch à grandes ~s** to gulp *ou* swig* sth down.

lamper*† [lɑ̃pe] 1 vt to gulp down, swig (down)*.

lampion [lɑ̃pjɔ̃] nm Chinese lantern; *voir* **air³**.

lampiste [lɑ̃pist] nm (*lit*) light (maintenance) man; (* *hum: subalterne*) underling, dogsbody* (*Brit*), toady* (*US*). **c'est toujours la faute du ~*** it's always the underling who gets the blame.

lamproie [lɑ̃pʀwa] nf lamprey. ~ **de mer** lamprey; ~ **de rivière** river lamprey, lampern.

Lancastre [lɑ̃kastʀ(ə)] n Lancaster.

lance [lɑ̃s] nf a (*arme*) spear; *[tournoi]* lance. **donner un coup de ~ à qn, frapper qn d'un coup de** ~ to hit sb with one's lance; *voir* **fer, rompre**. b (*tuyau*) hose. ~ **à eau** water hose; ~ **d'arrosage** garden hose; ~ **d'incendie** fire hose.

lance- [lɑ̃s] préf *voir* **lancer**.

lancée [lɑ̃se] nf: **être sur sa** ~ to be *ou* have got under way; **continuer sur sa** ~ to keep going, forge ahead; **il a encore travaillé 3 heures sur sa** ~ once he was under way *ou* he'd got going he worked for another 3 hours; **je peux encore courir 2 km sur ma** ~ now I'm in my stride I can run another 2 km; **je ne voulais pas t'interrompre sur ta** ~ I didn't want to interrupt you in full flow.

lancement [lɑ̃smɑ̃] nm a (*voir* **lancer 1d** *et* **e**) launching; sending up; starting up; issuing; floating. b (*Sport*) throwing. ~ **du disque/du javelot/du marteau** throwing the discus/javelin/hammer, discus/javelin/hammer throwing; ~ **du poids** putting the shot, shot put; (*Espace*) **fenêtre** *ou* **créneau de** ~ launch window.

lancer [lɑ̃se] 3 1 vt a (*jeter*) (*gén*) to throw (*à* to); *bombes* to drop (*sur* on); (*Sport*) *disque, marteau, javelot* to throw. ~ **une balle/son chapeau en l'air** to throw *ou* toss a ball/one's hat into the air *ou* up in the air; **lance-moi mes clefs** throw me my keys; (*Pêche*) ~ **sa ligne** to cast one's line; (*agressivement*) ~ **une pierre à qn** to hurl *ou* fling a stone at sb; **il lança sa voiture dans la foule** he smashed his car into the crowd, he drove his car straight at the crowd; ~ **son chien contre qn** to set one's dog on sb; (*Mil*) ~ **ses hommes contre l'ennemi/à l'assaut** to launch one's men against the enemy/into the assault; ~ **les jambes en avant** to fling one's legs forward; ~ **son poing dans la figure de qn** to thump sb in the face; ~ **un coup de poing** to lash out with one's fist, throw a punch; ~ **un coup de pied** to kick out, lash out with one's foot; (*Sport*) ~ **le poids** to put the shot; **il lance à 15 mètres** he can throw 15 metres; (*fig*) ~ **un pont sur une rivière** to throw a bridge across a river; **la tour lance ses flèches de béton vers le ciel** the concrete spires of the tower thrust up into the sky.

b (*projeter*) *fumée* to send up *ou* out; *flammes, lave* to throw out. *[yeux, bijoux]* ~ **des éclairs** to sparkle.

c (*émettre*) *accusations* to level; *menaces, injures* to hurl, fling; *avertissement, proclamation, mandat d'arrêt* to issue, put out; *théorie* to put forward, advance; *S.O.S.* to send out; *fausse nouvelle* to put out; *hurlement* to give out. ~ **un cri** to cry out; ~ **une plaisanterie** to crack a joke; **elle lui lança un coup d'œil furieux** she flashed *ou* darted a furious glance at him; **"je refuse" lança-t-il fièrement** "I refuse" he retorted proudly; **"salut" me lança-t-il du fond de la salle** "hello" he called out to me from the far end of the room.

d (*faire démarrer*) *fusée* to launch, send up; *obus* to launch; *torpille* to fire, launch; *navire, attaque, campagne électorale* to launch; *souscription, idée* to launch, float; *affaire, entreprise* to launch, start up; *emprunt* to issue, float. ~ **une idée en l'air** to toss out an idea; **il a lancé son parti dans une aventure dangereuse** he has launched his party into *ou* set his party off on a dangerous venture; **ne le lancez pas sur son sujet favori*** don't set him off on *ou* don't let him get launched on his pet subject; **une fois lancé*, on ne peut plus l'arrêter!** once he gets the bit between his teeth *ou* once he gets warmed up *ou* launched there's no stopping him!

e (*mettre en renom*) *vedette* to launch; *produit* to launch, bring out. ~ **une nouvelle mode** to launch *ou* start a new fashion; ~ **qn dans la politique/les affaires/le monde** to launch sb into politics/in business/in society; **ce chanteur est lancé maintenant** this singer has made a name for himself *ou* has made his mark now.

f (*donner de l'élan*) *moteur* to open up; *voiture* to get up to full speed; *balançoire* to set going. ~ **un cheval** to give a horse its head; **lance le balancier de l'horloge** set the pendulum in the clock going; **la voiture lancée à fond dévala la pente** the car roared away at top speed and hurtled down the slope; **la voiture une fois lancée** once the car gets up speed *ou* builds up speed.

g (*faire mal à*) **ça me lance (dans le bras** *etc*) I've got shooting pains (in my arm *etc*).

2 **se lancer** vpr a (*prendre de l'élan*) to build up *ou* get up momentum *ou* speed. **il recula pour se** ~ he moved back to get up speed *ou* momentum; **pour faire de la balançoire, il faut bien se** ~ to get a swing going you have to give yourself a good push forward.

b (*sauter*) to leap, jump; (*se précipiter*) to dash, rush. **se ~ dans le vide** to leap *ou* jump into space; **se ~ contre un obstacle** to dash *ou* rush at an obstacle; **se ~ en avant** to dash *ou* rush *ou* run forward; **se ~ à l'assaut d'une forteresse** to launch an assault on a fortress; **se ~ à l'assaut** to leap to the attack; **se ~ dans la bagarre** to pitch into the fight; **n'hésite pas, lance-toi** don't hesitate, off you go *ou* let yourself go.

c (*s'engager*) **se ~ dans** *discussion* to launch (forth) into, embark on; *aventure* to embark on, set off on; *dépenses* to embark on, take on; *passe-temps* to take up; **se ~ dans la politique/les affaires** (*essayer*) to launch out into politics/business; (*comme métier*) to take up politics/business; **se ~ dans la lecture d'un roman** to set about *ou* begin reading a novel; **il construit un bateau — il se lance*** he's building a boat — he's aiming high! *ou* he's thinking big!*; **lance-toi!*** on you go!*, go for it!*

d (*: *se faire une réputation*) **il cherche à se** ~ he's trying to make a name for himself.

3 nm a (*Sport*) (*gén*) throw. **il a droit à 3 ~s** he is allowed 3 attempts *ou* throws; ~ **annulé** no throw; (*Basket-ball*) ~ **franc** free throw, charity toss (*US*); (*Alpinisme*) ~ **de corde** lassoing (*NonC*), lasso; **le ~ du poids** *etc voir* **lancement**.

b (*Pêche*) (*attirail*) rod and reel. **(pêche au)** ~ rod and reel fishing.

4 comp ▸**lance-bombes** nm inv bomb launcher ▸**lance-flammes** nm inv flamethrower ▸**lance-fusées** nm inv rocket launcher ▸**lance-grenades** nm inv grenade launcher ▸**lance-missiles** nm inv missile launcher ▸**lance-pierre(s)** nm inv catapult; (*fig*) **manger avec un lance-pierres*** to grab a quick bite (to eat)* ▸**lance-roquettes** nm inv rocket launcher ▸**lance-satellites** nm inv satellite launcher ▸**lance-torpilles** nm inv torpedo tube.

lancette [lɑ̃sɛt] nf (*Archit, Méd*) lancet.

lanceur, -euse [lɑ̃sœʀ, øz] 1 nm,f a *[javelot etc]* thrower; (*Cricket*) bowler; (*Base-ball*) pitcher. b *[entreprise, actrice]* promoter. 2 nm (*Espace, sous-marin*) launcher. ~ **de satellites** satellite launcher.

lancier [lɑ̃sje] nm (*Mil*) lancer. (*danse*) **les ~s** the lancers.

lancinant, e [lɑ̃sinɑ̃, ɑ̃t] adj a *douleur* shooting (*épith*), piercing (*épith*). b (*obsédant*) *souvenir* haunting; *musique* insistent, monotonous. **ce que tu peux être ~ à toujours réclamer*** you are a real pain* *ou* you get on my nerves the way you're always asking for things.

lanciner [lɑ̃sine] 1 1 vi to throb. 2 vt *[pensée]* to obsess, trouble, haunt, plague; (*) *[enfant]* to torment, plague. **il nous a lancinés pendant 3 jours pour aller au cirque** he tormented *ou* plagued us *ou* he went on at us* for 3 days about going to the circus.

lançon [lɑ̃sɔ̃] nm sand-eel.

landais, e [lɑ̃dɛ, ɛz] adj from the Landes (region) (*south-west France*).

landau [lɑ̃do] nm (*voiture d'enfant*) pram, baby carriage (*US*); (*carrosse*) landau.

lande [lɑ̃d] nf moor. **les L~s** (*Géog*) the Landes (region) (*south-west France*); (*Admin*) the Landes department.

landgrave [lɑ̃dgʀav] nm (*Hist*) landgrave.

langage [lɑ̃gaʒ] 1 nm (*Ling, style*) language. **le ~ de l'amour/des fleurs** the language of love/of flowers; **en ~ administratif/technique** in administrative/technical jargon *ou* language; **quel ~!** what language!; **son ~ est incompréhensible** what he says *ou* the language he uses is incomprehensible; **je n'aime pas que l'on me tienne ce** ~ I don't like being spoken to like that; **il m'a tenu un drôle de** ~ he said some odd things to me; **quel ~ me tenez-vous là?** what do you mean by saying that?; **changer de** ~ to change one's tune.

2 comp ►**le langage des animaux** animal language ►**langage argotique** slang ►**langage chiffré** cipher, code (language) ►**langage de contrôle de travaux** (*Ordin*) job control language ►**langage enfantin** childish *ou* children's language, *[bébé]* baby talk ►**langage évolué** (*Ordin*) high-level language ►**langage de haut/bas niveau** (*Ordin*) high-/low-level language ►**langage intérieur** (*Philos*) inner language ►**langage machine** (*Ordin*) machine language ►**langage naturel** (*Ordin*) natural language ►**langage parlé** spoken language, speech ►**langage populaire** popular speech ►**langage de programmation** (*Ordin*) programming language.

langagier, -ière [lɑ̃gaʒje, jɛʀ] adj linguistic, of language (*épith*). **tic** ~ verbal tic.

lange [lɑ̃ʒ] nm (baby's) small flannel blanket. ~**s**†† swaddling clothes††; (*fig*) **dans les** ~**s** in (its) infancy.

langer [lɑ̃ʒe] 3 vt *bébé* to change (the nappy (*Brit*) *ou* diaper (*US*) of); (††) to wrap an extra blanket round. **table/matelas à** ~ changing table/mat.

langoureusement [lɑ̃guʀøzmɑ̃] adv languorously, languishingly.

langoureux, -euse [lɑ̃guʀø, øz] adj languorous.

langouste [lɑ̃gust] nf crayfish (*Brit*), spiny *ou* rock lobster.

langoustier [lɑ̃gustje] nm (*filet*) crayfish net; (*bateau*) fishing boat (*for crayfish*).

langoustine [lɑ̃gustin] nf Dublin bay prawn. (*Culin*) ~**s (frites)** (fried) scampi.

langue [lɑ̃g] 1 nf a (*Anat*) tongue. ~ **de bœuf/veau** ox/veal tongue; **avoir la** ~ **blanche** *ou* **chargée** *ou* **pâteuse** to have a coated *ou* furred tongue; **tirer la** ~ (*au médecin*) to stick out *ou* put out one's tongue (*à qn* for sb); (*par impolitesse*) to stick out *ou* put out one's tongue (*à qn* at sb); (**: être dans le besoin*) to have a rough time of it*; (**: être frustré*) to be green with envy; (**: avoir soif*) **il tirait la** ~ his tongue was hanging out*, he was dying of thirst*; **coup de** ~ lick; **le chien lui a donné un coup de** ~ the dog licked him.

b (*organe de la parole*) tongue. **avoir la** ~ **déliée** *ou* **bien pendue** to have a ready tongue; **avoir la** ~ **bien affilée** to have a quick *ou* sharp tongue; (*hum*) **avoir la** ~ **fourchue** to speak with a forked tongue; **il a la** ~ **trop longue** he talks too much, he doesn't know how to keep his mouth shut; **il ne sait pas tenir sa** ~ he can't hold his tongue, he doesn't know when to hold his tongue; **mettre sa** ~ **dans sa poche** to bite one's tongue; **il n'a pas la** ~ **dans sa poche** he's never at a loss for words; **perdre/retrouver sa** ~ to lose/find one's tongue; **délier** *ou* **dénouer la** ~ **à qn** to loosen sb's tongue; **donner sa** ~ **au chat** to give in *ou* up; **j'ai le mot sur (le bout de) la** ~ the word is on the tip of my tongue; **prendre** ~ **avec qn**† to make contact with sb; (*hum*) **les** ~**s vont aller bon train** tongues will start wagging *ou* will wag.

c (*personne*) **mauvaise** *ou* **méchante** ~ spiteful *ou* malicious gossip; (*iro*) **les bonnes** ~**s diront que ...** worthy *ou* upright folk will remark earnestly that ... .

d (*Ling*) language, tongue (*frm*). **la** ~ **française/anglaise** the French/English language; **les gens de** ~ **anglaise/française** English-speaking/French-speaking people; ~ **maternelle** mother tongue; ~ **mère** parent language; **une** ~ **vivante/morte/étrangère** a living/dead/foreign language; **la** ~ **écrite/parlée** the written/spoken language; (*Ling: en traduction*) ~ **source** *ou* **de départ/cible** *ou* **d'arrivée** source *ou* departure/target language; ~ **vernaculaire** vernacular language; **la** ~ **de Blake** the language of Blake; **il parle une** ~ **très pure** his use of the language is very pure, his spoken language is very pure; (*lit, fig*) **nous ne parlons pas la même** ~ we don't speak the same language.

2 comp ►**la langue du barreau** legal parlance, the language of the courts ►**langue-de-bœuf** (*Bot*) nf (pl **langues-de-bœuf**) beef-steak mushroom ►**langue de bois** (*péj*) set language, stereotyped formal language ►**langue-de-chat** nf (pl **langues-de-chat**) (flat) finger biscuit, langue de chat ►**la langue diplomatique** the language of diplomacy ►**langue de feu** tongue of fire ►**la langue journalistique** journalistic language, journalese (*péj*) ►**langue d'oc** langue d'oc, southern French ►**langue d'oïl** langue d'oïl, northern French ►**langue populaire** (*idiome*) popular language; (*usage*) popular speech ►**langue de spécialité** specialist language ►**langue de terre** strip *ou* spit of land ►**langue de travail** working language ►**langue verte** slang ►**langue de vipère** spiteful gossip.

Languedoc [lɑ̃gdɔk] nm: **le** ~ (the) Languedoc.

languedocien, -ienne [lɑ̃gdɔsjɛ̃, jɛn] 1 adj of *ou* from (the) Languedoc. 2 nm,f: **L~(ne)** inhabitant *ou* native of (the) Languedoc.

languette [lɑ̃gɛt] nf *[bois, cuir]* tongue; *[papier]* (narrow) strip.

langueur [lɑ̃gœʀ] nf languidness, languor; (*fig*) *[style]* languidness. **regard plein de** ~ languid *ou* languishing look; *voir* **maladie.**

languide [lɑ̃gid] adj (*littér*) languid, languishing.

languir [lɑ̃giʀ] 2 vi a (*dépérir*) to languish. ~ **dans l'oisiveté/d'ennui** to languish in idleness/in boredom; **(se)** ~ **d'amour pour qn** to be languishing with love for sb. b (*fig*) *[conversation, affaires, intrigue]* to flag. c (*littér: désirer*) ~ **après qn/qch** to languish for *ou* pine for *ou* long for sb/sth. d (**: attendre*) to wait, hang around*. **je ne languirai pas longtemps ici** I'm not going to hang around here for long*; **faire** ~ **qn** to keep sb waiting; **ne nous fais pas** ~**, raconte!** don't keep us in suspense, tell us about it!

languissamment [lɑ̃gisamɑ̃] adv (*littér*) languidly.

languissant, e [lɑ̃gisɑ̃, ɑ̃t] adj *personne* languid, listless; *regard* languishing (*épith*); *conversation, industrie* flagging (*épith*); *récit, action* dull; *affaires* slack, flat.

lanière [lanjɛʀ] nf *[cuir]* thong, strap; *[étoffe]* strip; *[fouet]* lash; *[appareil photo]* strap.

lanoline [lanɔlin] nf lanolin.

lansquenet [lɑ̃skənɛ] nm (*Cartes, Hist*) lansquenet.

lanterne [lɑ̃tɛʀn] 1 nf lantern; (*électrique*) lamp, light; (*Hist: réverbère*) street lamp; (*Archit*) lantern. (*Aut*) **se mettre en** ~**s, allumer ses** ~**s** to switch on one's (side)lights; **éclairer la** ~ **de qn** to enlighten sb; **les aristocrates à la** ~! string up the aristocracy!; *voir* **vessie.** 2 comp ►**lanterne arrière** (*Aut*) rear light ►**lanterne de bicyclette** bicycle lamp ►**lanterne magique** magic lantern ►**lanterne de projection** slide projector ►**lanterne rouge** *[convoi]* rear *ou* tail light; *[maison close]* red light; (*fig: dernier*) tail-ender ►**lanterne sourde** dark lantern ►**lanterne vénitienne** Chinese lantern.

lanterneau, pl ~**x** [lɑ̃tɛʀno] nm *[coupole]* lantern; *[escalier, atelier]* skylight.

lanterner [lɑ̃tɛʀne] 1 vi (*traîner*) to dawdle. **sans** ~! be quick about it!; **(faire)** ~ **qn** to let sb cool his heels, keep sb hanging about (*Brit*) *ou* waiting around.

lanthane [lɑ̃tan] nm lanthanum.

Laos [laɔs] nm Laos.

laotien, -ienne [laɔsjɛ̃, jɛn] 1 adj Laotian. 2 nm (*Ling*) Laotian. 3 nm,f: **L~(ne)** Laotian.

Lao-Tseu [laɔtsø] nm Lao-tze.

lapalissade [lapalisad] nf statement of the obvious. **c'est une** ~ **de dire que ...** it's stating the obvious to say that ... .

laparoscopie [lapaʀɔskɔpi] nf laparoscopy.

laparotomie [lapaʀɔtɔmi] nf laparotomy.

La Paz [lapaz] n La Paz.

lapement [lapmɑ̃] nm lapping (*NonC*); (*gorgée*) lap.

laper [lape] 1 1 vt to lap up. 2 vi to lap.

lapereau, pl ~**x** [lapʀo] nm young rabbit.

lapidaire [lapidɛʀ] 1 adj (*lit*) lapidary; (*fig: concis*) *style, formule* succinct, terse. 2 nm (*artisan*) lapidary.

lapidation [lapidasjɔ̃] nf stoning.

lapider [lapide] 1 vt (*tuer*) to stone (to death); (*attaquer*) to stone, throw *ou* hurl stones at.

lapin [lapɛ̃] nm (*animal*) (buck) rabbit, cony (*US*); (*fourrure*) rabbit(skin), cony(skin) (*US*). **manteau en** ~ rabbitskin coat; ~ **domestique/de garenne** domestic/wild rabbit; **c'est un fameux** ~* he's quite a lad*; (*terme d'affection*) **mon petit** ~ my lamb, my sweetheart; **coup du** ~* rabbit punch; (*dans un accident de voiture*) whiplash; **faire le coup du** ~ **à qn*** to give sb a rabbit punch; *voir* **chaud, courir, poser.**

lapine [lapin] nf (doe) rabbit. (*péj*) **c'est une vraie** ~ she's a real baby-machine (*péj*).

lapiner [lapine] 1 vi to litter, give birth. (*péj*) *[femme]* **elle n'arrête pas de** ~ she churns out babies one after another (*péj*).

lapinière [lapinjɛʀ] nf rabbit hutch.

lapis(-lazuli) [lapis(lazyli)] nm inv lapis lazuli.

lapon, e [lapɔ̃, ɔn] 1 adj Lapp, Lappish. 2 nm (*Ling*) Lapp, Lappish. 3 nm,f: **L~(e)** Lapp, Laplander.

Laponie [lapɔni] nf Lapland.

laps [laps] nm: ~ **de temps** lapse of time.

lapsus [lapsys] nm (*parlé*) slip of the tongue; (*écrit*) slip of the pen. ~ **révélateur** Freudian slip; **faire un** ~ to make a slip of the tongue (*ou* of the pen).

laquage [lakaʒ] nm lacquering.

laquais [lakɛ] nm lackey, footman; (*fig, péj*) lackey (*péj*), flunkey (*péj*).

laque [lak] 1 nf (*produit brut*) lac, shellac; (*vernis*) lacquer; (*pour les cheveux*) (hair) lacquer, hair spray. (*peinture*) ~ **(brillante)** gloss paint. 2 nm ou f (*de Chine*) lacquer. 3 nm (*objet d'art*) piece of lacquer ware.

laqué, e [lake] (ptp de **laquer**) adj lacquered. **meuble (en)** ~ **blanc** piece of furniture with a white gloss finish; **murs** ~**s blanc** walls painted in white gloss; (*Culin*) **canard** ~ Peking duck.

laquelle [lakɛl] *voir* **lequel.**

laquer [lake] 1 vt to lacquer.

larbin* [laʀbɛ̃] nm (*péj*) servant, flunkey (*péj*).

larcin [laʀsɛ̃] nm (*littér*) (*vol*) theft; (*butin*) spoils (*pl*), booty. **dissimuler son** ~ to hide one's spoils *ou* what one has stolen.

lard [laʀ] nm (*gras*) fat (*of pig*); (*viande*) bacon. ~ **fumé** ≃ smoked bacon; ~ **maigre, petit** ~ ≃ streaky bacon (*usually diced or in strips*); (*fig*) **(se) faire du** ~⁑ to lie back *ou* sit around and grow fat; (*fig*) **un gros** ~⁑ a fat lump⁑ (*Brit*), a clod⁑ (*US*); **on ne sait jamais avec lui si c'est du** ~ **ou du cochon*** you never know where you are with him* *ou* whether or not he's being serious; *voir* **rentrer, tête.**

larder [laʀde] 1 vt (*Culin*) *viande* to lard. (*fig*) ~ **qn de coups de couteau** to hack at sb with a knife; (*fig*) **texte lardé de citations** text larded *ou* loaded with quotations.

lardoire [laʀdwaʀ] nm (*Culin*) larding-needle, larding-pin; (**: épée*) sword, steel.

lardon [laʀdɔ̃] nm (*Culin*) (*pour larder*) lardon *ou* lardoon; (**: enfant*) kid*.

lares [laʀ] nmpl, adj pl: **(dieux)** ~ lares.

largable [laʀgabl] adj releasable.

largage [laʀgaʒ] nm *[amarres]* casting off; *[étage de fusée]* staging; *[parachutiste, bombe, travailleurs]* dropping.

large [laʀʒ] 1 adj a (*gén, dans la mensuration*) wide; (*impression visuelle d'étendue*) broad; *pantalon, meuble* wide; *dos, lame* broad, wide; *visage, main* broad. **à cet endroit, le fleuve est le plus** ~ at this point the river is at its widest; **le** ~ **ruban d'argent du Rhône** the broad silver ribbon of the Rhône; **trop** ~ **de 3 mètres** 3 metres too wide; **chapeau à** ~**s bords** broad-brimmed *ou* wide-brimmed hat; **décrire un** ~ **cercle** to describe a big *ou* wide circle; **ouvrir une** ~ **bouche** to open one's mouth wide; **d'un geste** ~ with a broad *ou* sweeping gesture; **avec un** ~ **sourire** with a broad smile, smiling broadly; **ce veston est trop** ~ this jacket is too big *ou* wide; **cette robe est trop juste, avez-vous quelque chose d'un peu plus** ~? this dress is too tight, do you have anything slightly looser? *ou* fuller?; **pantalon** ~ baggy trousers (*Brit*) *ou* pants (*US*); **être** ~ **d'épaules** *[personne]* to be broad-shouldered; *[vêtements]* to be wide *ou* broad at the shoulders; **être** ~ **de dos/de hanches** *[personne]* to have a broad back/wide hips; *[vêtement]* to be wide at the back/the hips.

b (*important*) *concession, amnistie* broad, wide; *pouvoirs, diffusion* wide, extensive. **retransmettre de** ~**s extraits d'un match** to show extensive (recorded) extracts of a match; **faire une** ~ **part à qch** to give great weight to sth; **dans une** ~ **mesure** to a great *ou* large extent; **il a une** ~ **part de responsabilité dans l'affaire** he must take a large share of the responsibility *ou* blame in this matter.

c (*généreux*) *personne* generous. **1 kg de viande pour 4, c'est** ~ 1 kg of meat for 4 is ample *ou* plenty; **une vie** ~ a life of ease.

d (*non borné*) *opinion, esprit* broad (*épith*); *conscience* accommodating. ~**s vues** liberal views; **il est** ~ **d'idées** he is broad-minded; **dans son acception** *ou* **sens** ~ in the broad sense of the term.

2 adv: **voir** ~ to think big; **prends un peu plus d'argent, il vaut mieux prévoir** ~ take a bit more money, it's better to be on the generous side *ou* to allow a bit extra *ou* too much (than too little); **calculer/mesurer** ~ to be generous *ou* allow a bit extra in one's calculations/measurements; (*Aut*) **prendre un virage** ~ to take a bend wide; **cette marque taille** *ou* **habille** ~ the sizes in this brand tend to be on the large side.

3 nm a (*largeur*) width. **une avenue de 8 mètres de** ~ an avenue 8 metres wide *ou* 8 metres in width; **être au** ~ (*avoir de la place*) to have plenty of room *ou* space; (*avoir de l'argent*) to be well-provided for, have plenty of money; **acheter une moquette en 2 mètres de** ~ to buy a carpet 2 metres wide; **cela se fait en 2 mètres et 4 mètres de** ~ that comes in 2-metre and 4-metre widths; *voir* **long, mener**.

b (*Naut*) **le** ~ the open sea; **se diriger vers le/gagner le** ~ to head for/reach the open sea; **au** ~ **de Calais** off Calais; **l'appel du** ~ the call of the sea; (*fig*) **prendre le** ~* to clear off*, hop it* (*Brit*), make o.s. scarce; **ils ont pris le** ~ **avec les bijoux** they made off with the jewels.

largement [laʀʒəmɑ̃] adv a (*lit*) *écarter* widely. ~ **espacés** *arbres, maisons* widely spaced, wide apart; **fenêtre** ~ **ouverte** wide open window; **robe** ~ **décolletée** dress with a very open *ou* very scooped neckline.

b (*sur une grande échelle*) *répandre, diffuser* widely. **amnistie** ~ **accordée** wide *ou* widely-extended amnesty; **idée** ~ **répandue** widespread *ou* widely held view; **bénéficier de pouvoirs** ~ **étendus** to hold greatly increased powers.

c (*de loin*) considerably, greatly. **succès qui dépasse** ~ **nos prévisions** success which greatly exceeds our expectations *ou* is far beyond our expectations; **ce problème dépasse** ~ **ses compétences** this problem is altogether beyond *ou* is way beyond* his capabilities; **vous débordez** ~ **le sujet** you are greatly overstepping the subject, you are going well beyond the limits of the subject; **elle vaut** ~ **son frère** she's every bit as *ou* at least as good (*ou* as bad) as her brother.

d (*amplement*) **vous avez** ~ **le temps** you have ample time *ou* plenty of time; **il y en a** ~ **(assez)** there's more than enough; **c'est** ~ **suffisant** that's plenty, that's more than enough; **cela me suffit** ~ that's plenty *ou* ample *ou* more than enough for me; **il est** ~ **temps de commencer** it's high time we started; **j'ai été** ~ **récompensé de ma patience** my patience has been amply rewarded; **ça vaut** ~ **la peine/la visite** it's well worth the trouble/the visit.

e (*généreusement*) *payer, donner* generously. **ils nous ont servis/indemnisés** ~ they gave us generous *ou* ample helpings/compensation; **vivre** ~ to live handsomely.

f (*au moins*) easily, at least. **il gagne** ~ **15 000 F par mois** he earns easily *ou* at least 15,000 francs a month; **il est** ~ **2 heures** it's well past 2 o'clock; **il a** ~ **50 ans** he is well past 50, he is well into his fifties; **c'est à 5 minutes/5 km d'ici,** ~ it's easily *ou* a good 5 minutes/5 km from here.

largesse [laʀʒɛs] nf a (*caractère*) generosity. **avec** ~ generously. b (*dons*) ~**s** liberalities. **faire des** ~**s** to make generous gifts.

largeur [laʀʒœʀ] nf a (*gén: voir* **large**) width; breadth; *[voie ferrée]* gauge. **sur toute la** ~ right across, all the way across; **dans le sens de la** ~ widthways, widthwise; **quelle est la** ~ **de la fenêtre?** what is the width of the window?, how wide is the window?; **tissu en grande/petite** ~ double width/single width material.

b *[idées]* broadness. ~ **d'esprit** broad-mindedness; ~ **de vues** broadness of outlook.

c (** loc*) **dans les grandes** ~**s** with a vengeance, well and truly; **il s'est trompé dans les grandes** ~**s** he has slipped up with a vengeance, he has boobed this time, and how!‡; **cette fois on les a eus dans les grandes** ~**s** we didn't half put one over on them this time‡ (*Brit*), we had them well and truly this time*.

largo [laʀgo] adv, nm largo.

largué, e [laʀge] (ptp de **larguer**) adj: **être** ~* to be all at sea.

larguer [laʀge] 1 vt a (*Naut*) *cordage* to loose, release; *voile* to let out, unfurl; *amarres* to cast off, slip. b *parachutiste, bombe* to drop; *cabine spatiale* to release. c (**: se débarrasser de*) *ami, emploi* to throw over*, chuck‡; *amant* to ditch*, chuck‡; *collaborateur* to drop, get rid of, dump*; *objet* to chuck out‡, get rid of; *principes* to jettison, chuck (out)‡.

larigot [laʀigo] nm *voir* **tirer**.

larme [laʀm] 1 nf a tear. **en** ~**s** in tears; **au bord des** ~**s** on the verge of tears; ~**s de joie/de colère** tears of joy/rage; **verser toutes les** ~**s de son corps** to cry one's eyes out; **avec des** ~**s dans la voix** with tears in his voice, with a tearful voice; **avoir les** ~**s aux yeux** to have tears in one's eyes; **ça lui a fait venir les** ~**s aux yeux** it brought tears to his eyes; **elle a la** ~ **facile** she is easily moved to tears, tears come easily to her; **y aller de sa** ~* to have a good cry; **avoir toujours la** ~ **à l'œil** to be a real cry-baby *ou* weeper; *voir* **fondre, rire, vallée** *etc.*

b (**: goutte*) *[vin]* drop.

2 comp ▶**larmes de crocodile** crocodile tears ▶**larmes de sang** tears of blood.

larmier [laʀmje] nm (*Archit*) dripstone.

larmoiement [laʀmwamɑ̃] nm (*voir* **larmoyer**) watering (of the eyes); whimpering (*NonC*), snivelling (*NonC*).

larmoyant, e [laʀmwajɑ̃, ɑ̃t] adj *yeux* tearful, watery; *personne* tearful; *ton* snivelling, whining; *voix* tearful, whimpering; *récit* maudlin.

larmoyer [laʀmwaje] 8 vi a (*involontairement*) *[yeux]* to water, run. b (*pleurnicher*) to whimper, snivel.

larron [laʀɔ̃] nm (†, *Bible*) thief. **s'entendre comme** ~**s en foire** to be as thick as thieves; *voir* **occasion, troisième**.

larvaire [laʀvɛʀ] adj (*Zool*) larval; (*fig*) embryonic.

larve [laʀv] nf (*Zool*) larva; (*asticot*) grub. (*péj*) ~ **(humaine)** worm (*péj*), creature.

larvé, e [laʀve] adj *guerre, dictature* latent, (lurking) below the surface (*attrib*); (*Méd*) *fièvre, maladie* larvate (SPÉC). **inflation** ~**e** creeping inflation.

laryngé, e [laʀɛ̃ʒe] adj, **laryngien, -ienne** [laʀɛ̃ʒjɛ̃, jɛn] adj laryngeal.

laryngectomie [laʀɛ̃ʒɛktɔmi] nf laryngectomy.

laryngite [laʀɛ̃ʒit] nf laryngitis.

laryngologie [laʀɛ̃gɔlɔʒi] nf laryngology.

laryngologiste [laʀɛ̃gɔlɔʒist] nmf, **laryngologue** [laʀɛ̃gɔlɔg] nmf throat specialist, laryngologist.

laryngoscope [laʀɛ̃gɔskɔp] nm laryngoscope.

laryngoscopie [laʀɛ̃gɔskɔpi] nf laryngoscopy.

laryngotomie [laʀɛ̃gɔtɔmi] nf laryngotomy.

larynx [laʀɛ̃ks] nm larynx, voice-box*.

las[1], lasse [lɑ, lɑs] adj (*frm*) weary, tired. ~ **de qn/de faire qch/de vivre** tired *ou* weary of sb/of doing sth/of life; *voir* **guerre**.

las[2]†† [lɑs] excl alas!

lasagne [lazaɲ] nf lasagne.

lascar†* [laskaʀ] nm (*type louche*) character; (*malin*) rogue; (*hum: enfant*) terror. **drôle de** ~ (*louche*) shady character*; (*malin*) real rogue, smart customer*; **je vous aurai, mes** ~**s!** (*à des adultes*) I'll have you yet, you old rogues!*; (*à des enfants*) I'll have you yet, you little *ou* young rascals!*

lascif, -ive [lasif, iv] adj lascivious, lustful.

lascivement [lasivmɑ̃] adv lasciviously, lustfully.

lascivité [lasivite] nf lasciviousness, lustfulness.

laser [lazɛʀ] nm laser. **disque/rayon** ~ laser disc/beam.

lassant, e [lɑsɑ̃, ɑ̃t] adj (*frm*) wearisome, tiresome.

lasser [lɑse] 1 1 vt (*frm*) *auditeur, lecteur* to weary, tire. ~ **la patience/bonté de qn** to try *ou* tax sb's patience/goodness; **sourire lassé** weary smile; **lassé de tout** weary of everything. 2 **se lasser** vpr: **se** ~ **de qch/de faire qch** to (grow) weary of sth/of doing sth, tire *ou* grow tired of sth/of doing sth; **parler sans se** ~ to speak without tiring *ou* flagging.

lassitude [lɑsityd] nf (*frm*) weariness (*NonC*), lassitude (*NonC*). **avec** ~ wearily.

lasso [laso] nm lasso. **prendre au** ~ to lasso.

latence [latɑ̃s] nf latency. **temps de** ~ latent period; **période de** ~ latency period.

latent, e [latɑ̃, ɑ̃t] adj (*gén*) latent. **à l'état** ~ latent, in the latent state.

latéral, e, mpl **-aux** [lateʀal, o] 1 adj side (*épith*), lateral (*frm*). 2 **latérale** nf lateral (consonant).

latéralement [lateʀalmɑ̃] adv (*gén*) laterally; *être situé* on the side; *arriver, souffler* from the side; *diviser* sideways.

latérite [lateʀit] nf laterite.

latéritique [lateʀitik] adj lateritic.

latex [latɛks] nm inv latex.

latin, e [latɛ̃, in] 1 adj (*gén*) Latin; (*Rel*) *croix, église, rite* Latin. (*Ling*) **les langues ~es** the romance *ou* latin languages; *voir* **Amérique, quartier, voile¹**.
2 nm (*Ling*) Latin. **~ vulgaire** vulgar Latin; (*péj*) **~ de cuisine** dog Latin; *voir* **bas¹, perdre.**
3 nm,f: **L~(e)** Latin; **les L~s** the Latin people, the Latins.

latinisation [latinizasjɔ̃] nf latinization.

latiniser [latinize] [1] vti to latinize.

latinisme [latinism] nm latinism.

latiniste [latinist] nmf (*spécialiste*) latinist, Latin scholar; (*enseignant*) Latin teacher; (*étudiant*) Latin student.

latinité [latinite] nf (*Ling: caractère*) latinity; (*civilisation*) Latin world.

latino-américain, e [latinoameʀikɛ̃, ɛn] 1 adj Latin-American, Hispanic. 2 nm,f: **L~-A~(e)** Latin-American, Hispanic.

latitude [latityd] nf a (*Astron, Géog*) latitude. **Paris est à 48° de ~ Nord** Paris is situated at latitude 48° north.
b (*région: gén pl*) latitude. **sous toutes les ~s** in all latitudes, in all parts of the world.
c (*fig*) latitude, scope. **avoir toute ~ de faire qch** to be quite free *ou* at liberty to do sth; **laisser/donner toute ~ à qn** to allow/give sb full scope; **on a une certaine ~** we have some latitude *ou* some freedom of movement.

latitudinaire [latitydinɛʀ] adj, nmf (*littér*) latitudinarian.

latrines [latʀin] nfpl latrines.

lattage [lataʒ] nm lathing.

latte [lat] nf (*gén*) lath; *[plancher]* board. (*Ski*) **~s*** boards*.

latter [late] [1] vt to lath.

lattis [lati] nm lathing (*NonC*), lathwork (*NonC*).

laudanum [lodanɔm] nm laudanum.

laudateur, -trice [lodatœʀ, tʀis] nm,f (*littér*) adulator, laudator (*frm*).

laudatif, -ive [lodatif, iv] adj laudatory. **parler de qn en termes ~s** to speak highly *ou* in laudatory terms of sb, be full of praise for sb.

Laure [lɔʀ] nf Laura.

lauréat, e [lɔʀea, at] 1 adj (prize) winning. 2 nm,f (prize) winner, award winner. **les ~s du prix Nobel** the Nobel prizewinners.

Laurence [lɔʀɑ̃s] nf Laurence.

Laurent [lɔʀɑ̃] nm Lawrence, Laurence. **~ le Magnifique** Lorenzo the Magnificent.

laurier [lɔʀje] 1 nm bay-tree, (sweet) bay. (*Culin*) **feuille de ~** bay leaf; (*Culin*) **mettre du ~** to put in some bay leaves; (*fig*) **~s** laurels; **s'endormir** *ou* **se reposer sur ses ~s** to rest on one's laurels; **être couvert de ~s** to be showered with praise. 2 comp ►**laurier-cerise** nm (pl **lauriers-cerises**) cherry laurel ►**laurier commun** = **laurier-sauce** ►**laurier-rose** nm (pl **lauriers-roses**) oleander ►**laurier-sauce** nm (pl **lauriers-sauce**) (sweet) bay, bay-tree.

lavable [lavabl] adj washable. **vêtement ~ en machine** machine-washable garment; **papier peint ~ (et lessivable)** washable wallpaper.

lavabo [lavabo] nm washbasin. (*euph*) **~s** toilets, loo* (*Brit*).

lavage [lavaʒ] 1 nm a *[plaie]* bathing; *[corps, cheveux]* washing. (*Méd*) **~ d'intestin** intestinal wash; **on lui a fait un ~ d'estomac** he had his stomach pumped out.
b *[mur, vêtement, voiture]* washing (*NonC*); *[tache]* washing off *ou* out (*NonC*). **après le ~ vient le rinçage** after the wash comes the rinse; **pour un meilleur ~, utilisez ...** for a better wash, use ...; **le ~ des sols à la brosse/à l'éponge** scrubbing/sponging (down) floors; **on a dû faire 3 ~s: c'était si sale!** it had to be washed 3 times *ou* it had to have 3 washes it was so dirty!; **le ~ de la vaisselle** dish-washing, washing-up (*Brit*).
c (*Tech*) *[gaz, charbon, laine]* washing.
2 comp ►**lavage de cerveau** brainwashing; **on lui a fait subir un lavage de cerveau** he was brainwashed ►**lavage de tête*** telling-off*, dressing down*.

La Valette [lavalɛt] n Valletta.

lavallière [lavaljɛʀ] nf: **(cravate) ~** lavallière.

lavande [lavɑ̃d] nf lavender. **(eau de) ~** lavender water; **(bleu) ~** lavender (blue).

lavandière [lavɑ̃djɛʀ] nf (*laveuse*) washerwoman; (*oiseau*) wagtail.

lavaret [lavaʀɛ] nm (*poisson*) pollan.

lavasse* [lavas] nf dishwater* (*fig*). **ce café, c'est de la ~** *ou* **une vraie ~** this coffee tastes like dishwater*.

lave [lav] nf lava (*NonC*); *voir* **coulée.**

lave- [lav] préf *voir* **laver.**

lavé, e [lave] (ptp de **laver**) adj *couleur* watery, washy, washed-out; (*Art*) wash (*épith*); (*fig*) *ciel, yeux* pale, colourless.

lavement [lavmɑ̃] nm (*Méd*) enema, rectal injection.

laver [lave] [1] 1 vt a (*gén*) to wash; *mur* to wash (down); *plaie* to bathe, cleanse; *tache* to wash out *ou* off; (*Méd*) *intestin* to wash out. **~ avec une brosse** to scrub (down); **~ avec une éponge** to wash with a sponge; **~ à grande eau** *sol* to swill down, sluice down; *légume* to wash thoroughly; **~ la vaisselle** to wash the dishes, wash up (*Brit*), do the washing-up (*Brit*); (*fig*) **il faut ~ son linge sale en famille** it doesn't do to wash one's dirty linen in public; (*fig*) **~ la tête à qn** to haul sb over the coals, give sb a dressing down*; *voir* **machine³.**
b (*emploi absolu*) *[personne]* to do the washing. **ce savon lave bien** this soap washes well.
c (*fig*) *affront, injure* to avenge; *péchés, honte* to cleanse, wash away. **~ qn d'une accusation/d'un soupçon** to clear sb of an accusation/of suspicion.
d (*Art*) *couleur* to dilute; *dessin* to wash.
2 **se laver** vpr a to wash, have a wash. **se ~ la figure/les mains** to wash one's face/hands; **se ~ les dents** to clean *ou* brush one's teeth; **se ~ dans un lavabo/une baignoire** to have a stand-up wash/a bath, wash (o.s.) at the basin/in the bath; **ce tissu se lave bien** this material washes well; **le cuir ne se lave pas** leather isn't washable *ou* won't wash.
b **se ~ de** *accusation* to clear o.s. of; *affront* to avenge o.s. of; (*fig*) **je m'en lave les mains** I wash my hands of the matter.
3 comp ►**lave-auto** nm (pl **lave-autos**) (*Can*) car wash ►**lave-glace** nm (pl **lave-glaces**) windscreen (*Brit*) *ou* windshield (*US*) washer, screen wash(er) (*Brit*) ►**lave-linge** nm inv washing machine ►**lave-mains** nm inv wash-stand ►**lave-vaisselle** nm inv dishwasher.

laverie [lavʀi] nf a laundry. **~ (automatique)** Launderette ® (*Brit*), Laundromat ® (*US*). b (*Ind*) washing *ou* preparation plant.

lavette [lavɛt] nf (*chiffon*) dish cloth; (*brosse*) dish mop; (*Suisse: gant de toilette*) (face) flannel; (*fig, péj: homme*) wimp*, weak-kneed individual, drip*.

laveur [lavœʀ] nm washer. **~ de carreaux** *ou* **de vitres** window cleaner; *voir* **raton.**

laveuse [lavøz] nf washerwoman.

lavis [lavi] nm (*procédé*) washing. **(dessin au) ~** wash drawing; **colorier au ~** to wash-paint.

lavoir [lavwaʀ] nm (*dehors*) washing-place; (*édifice*) wash house; (*bac*) washtub; (*Tech*) (*machine*) washer; (*atelier*) washing plant; *voir* **bateau.**

lavure [lavyʀ] nf a (*lit, fig*) **~ (de vaisselle)** dishwater. b (*Min*) *[minerai]* washing. **~s** washings.

lawrencium [lɔʀɑ̃sjɔm] nm lawrencium.

laxatif, -ive [laksatif, iv] adj, nm laxative.

laxisme [laksism] nm (*Rel*) latitudinarianism; (*indulgence*) laxness. **le gouvernement est accusé de ~ à l'égard des syndicats** the government is accused of being too soft *ou* lax with *ou* too easy on the trade unions.

laxiste [laksist] 1 adj (*Rel*) latitudinarian; (*indulgent*) lax, overliberal.
2 nmf (*Rel*) latitudinarian; (*indulgent*) lax person.

layette [lɛjɛt] nf baby clothes (*pl*), layette. **rayon ~ d'un grand magasin** babywear department in a large store; **couleurs ~** baby *ou* pastel colours; **bleu/rose ~** baby blue/pink.

layon [lɛjɔ̃] nm (forest) track *ou* trail.

Lazare [lazaʀ] nm Lazarus.

lazaret [lazaʀɛ] nm lazaret.

lazulite [lazylit] nf lazulite.

lazzi [la(d)zi] nm gibe. **être l'objet des ~(s) des spectateurs** to be gibed at by the onlookers.

le¹ [l(ə)] **, la** [la] **, les** [le] art déf (*contraction avec à, de* **au, aux, du, des**) a (*détermination*) the; (*devant nom propre: sg*) *non traduit*; (*pl*) the. **~ propriétaire de l'auto bleue** the owner of the blue car; **la femme de l'épicier** the grocer's wife; **les commerçants de la ville sont en grève** the town's tradesmen are on strike; **je suis inquiète, les enfants sont en retard** I'm worried because the children are late; **~ thé/~ café que je viens d'acheter** the tea/coffee I have just bought; **allons à la gare/à l'église ensemble** let's go to the station/to the church together; **il n'a pas ~ droit/l'intention de le faire** he has no right to do it/no intention of doing it; **il n'a pas eu la patience/l'intelligence d'attendre** he didn't have the patience/the sense to wait; **il a choisi ~ tableau ~ plus original de l'exposition** he chose the most original picture in the exhibition; **~ plus petit des deux frères est ~ plus solide** the smaller of the two brothers is the more robust *ou* the stronger; **l'Italie de Mussolini** Mussolini's Italy; **l'Angleterre que j'ai connue** the England (that) I knew.
b (*détermination: temps*) the (*souvent omis*). **~ dimanche de Pâques** Easter Sunday; **venez ~ dimanche de Pâques** come on Easter Sunday; **ne venez pas ~ jour de la lessive** don't come on wash(ing) day; **l'hiver dernier/prochain** last/next winter; **l'hiver 1973** the winter of 1973; **~ premier/dernier lundi du mois** the first/last Monday of *ou* in the month; **il ne travaille pas ~ samedi** he doesn't work on Saturdays *ou* on a Saturday; **il ne sort jamais ~ matin** he never goes out in the morning; **elle travaille ~ matin** she works mornings *ou* in the morning; **vers les 5 heures** at about 5 o'clock; **il est parti ~ 5 mai** he left on the 5th of May *ou* on May the 5th (*style parlé*); he left on May 5th (*style écrit*); **il n'a pas dormi de la nuit** he didn't sleep (a wink) all night.
c (*distribution*) a, an. **20 F ~ mètre/~ kg/~ litre/la pièce** 20 francs a metre/a kg/a litre/each *ou* a piece; **60 km à l'heure** 60 km an *ou* per hour; **deux fois la semaine/l'an** twice a week/year.

d (*fraction*) a, an. ~ **tiers/quart** a third/quarter; **j'en ai fait à peine la moitié/~ dixième** I have barely done (a) half/a tenth of it.

e (*généralisation, abstraction*) *gén non traduit.* ~ **hibou vole surtout la nuit** owls fly *ou* the owl flies mainly at night; **l'homme est un roseau pensant** man is a thinking reed; **les femmes détestent la violence** women hate violence; **les enfants sont méchants avec les animaux** children are cruel to animals; **l'enfant** *ou* **les enfants n'aime(nt) pas l'obscurité** children don't like the dark; **la tuberculose** tuberculosis; **la grippe** flu; **la jeunesse est toujours pressée** youth is *ou* the young are always in a hurry; **les prix montent en flèche** prices are rocketing; ~ **thé et ~ café sont chers** tea and coffee are expensive; **il apprend l'histoire et l'anglais** he is learning history and English; **j'aime la musique/la poésie/la danse** I like music/poetry/dancing; ~ **beau/~ grotesque** the beautiful/grotesque; **les riches** the rich; **il aime la bagarre*** he loves a fight; **aller au concert/au restaurant** to go to a concert/out for a meal.

f (*possession*) *gén adj poss, parfois art indéf.* **elle ouvrit les yeux/la bouche** she opened her eyes/mouth; **elle est sortie ~ manteau sur ~ bras** she went out, with her coat over her arm; **la tête baissée, elle pleurait** she hung her head and wept; **assis, (les) jambes pendantes** sitting with one's legs dangling; **j'ai mal à la main droite/au pied** I've a pain in my right hand/in my foot, my right hand/my foot hurts; **il a la jambe cassée** he has got a broken leg; **avoir mal à la tête/à la gorge** to have a headache/a sore throat; **croisez les bras** cross your arms; **levez tous la main** all put your hands up, hands up everyone; **il a ~ visage fatigué/~ regard malin** he has a tired look/a mischievous look; **il a les cheveux noirs/~ cœur brisé** he has black hair/a broken heart; **il n'a pas la conscience tranquille** he has a guilty conscience; **il a l'air hypocrite** he looks a hypocrite.

g (*valeur démonstrative*) **il ne faut pas agir de la sorte** you must not do that kind of thing *ou* things like that; **que pensez-vous de la pièce/de l'incident?** what do you think of the play/incident?; **faites attention, les enfants!** be careful children!; **oh ~ beau chien!** what a lovely dog!, (just) look at that lovely dog!

le[2] [l(ə)] , **la** [la] , **les** [le] **pron m,f,pl** a (*homme*) him; (*femme, nation, bateau*) her; (*animal, bébé*) it, him, her; (*chose*) it. **les** them; **je ne ~/la/les connais pas** I don't know him/her/them; **regarde-~/-la/-les** look at him *ou* it/her *ou* it/them; **ce sac/cette écharpe est à vous, je l'ai trouvé(e) par terre** this bag/scarf is yours, I found it on the floor; **voulez-vous ces fraises? je les ai apportées pour vous** would you like these strawberries? I brought them for you; **le Canada demande aux USA de ~ soutenir** Canada is asking the USA to give them their support.

b (*emphatique*) **il faut ~ féliciter ce garçon!** you must congratulate this boy!; **cette femme-là, je la déteste** I can't bear that woman; **cela vous ~ savez aussi bien que moi** you know that as well as I; **vous l'êtes, beau** you really do look smart; *voir* **copier, voici, voilà.**

c (*neutre: souvent non traduit*) **vous savez qu'il est malade? — je l'ai entendu dire** did you know he's ill? — I have heard it said *ou* I had heard; **elle n'est pas heureuse, mais elle ne l'a jamais été et elle ne ~ sera jamais** she is not happy but she never has been and never will be; **pourquoi il n'est pas venu? — demande-~-lui/je me ~ demande** why hasn't he come? — ask him/I wonder; **il était ministre, il ne l'est plus** he was a minister but he isn't (one) any longer; **elle sera punie comme elle ~ mérite** she'll be punished as she deserves, she'll get her just deserts.

lé [le] **nm** *[étoffe]* width; *[papier peint]* length, strip.

LEA [ɛləa] **nm** (**abrév de (département de) langues étrangères appliquées**) department of modern languages.

leader [lidœʀ] **nm** (*Pol, Presse, Sport*) leader.

leasing [liziŋ] **nm** leasing. **acheter qch en ~** to buy sth leasehold.

léchage [leʃaʒ] **nm** (*gén*) licking. ~ **(de bottes)*** bootlicking*, toadying.

lèche** [lɛʃ] **nf** bootlicking*, toadying. **faire de la ~** to be a bootlicker*; **faire de la ~ à qn** to suck up to sb**, lick sb's boots*.

lèche- [lɛʃ] **préf** *voir* **lécher.**

lèchefrite [lɛʃfʀit] **nf** dripping-pan.

lécher [leʃe] 6 1 **vt** a (*gén*) to lick; *assiette* to lick clean. **se ~ les doigts** to lick one's fingers; ~ **la confiture d'une tartine** to lick the jam off a slice of bread; *voir* **ours.**

b *[flammes]* to lick; *[vagues]* to wash against, lap against.

c (*: *fignoler*) to polish up. **trop léché** overdone (*attrib*), overpolished.

d (*loc*) ~ **les bottes de qn*** to suck up to sb**, lick sb's boots*; ~ **le cul à** *ou* **de qn***** to lick sb's arse*** (*Brit*), kiss sb's ass*** (*US*); ~ **les vitrines*** to go window-shopping; **s'en ~ les doigts/babines** to lick one's lips/chops over it.

2 **comp** ► **lèche-bottes*** **nmf inv** bootlicker*, toady ► **lèche-cul** **nm inv** arse-licker*** (*Brit*), ass-kisser*** (*US*), brown nose** (*US*) ► **lèche-vitrines*** **nm inv: faire du lèche-vitrines** to go window-shopping.

lécheur, -euse* [leʃœʀ, øz] **nm,f** bootlicker*, toady. **il est du genre ~** he's the bootlicking type*, he's always sucking up to someone**.

leçon [l(ə)sɔ̃] **nf** a (*Scol*) (*cours*) lesson, class; (*à apprendre*) lesson, homework (*NonC*). ~ **de danse/de français/de piano** dancing/French/piano lesson; **~s particulières** private lessons *ou* tuition (*Brit*); **~s de choses** general science; **faire la ~** to teach; **réciter sa ~** (*lit*) to recite one's lesson; (*fig*) to repeat something parrot fashion, rattle something off; **elle a bien appris sa ~** (*lit*) she's learnt her subject well; (*fig hum*) she's learnt her script *ou* lines well; (*fig*) **il peut vous donner des ~s** he could teach you a thing or two.

b (*conseil*) advice, teaching. **suivre les ~s de qn** to heed sb's advice, take a lesson from sb; **je n'ai pas de ~ à recevoir de toi** I don't need your advice; **faire la ~ à qn** (*endoctriner*) to tell sb what he must do, give sb instructions; (*réprimander*) to give sb a lecture; **faire des ~s de morale à qn** to sit in judgment on sb; **je n'ai pas besoin de tes ~s de morale**I don't need your moralizing.

c (*enseignement*) *[fable, parabole]* lesson. **les ~s de l'expérience** the lessons of experience *ou* that experience teaches; **que cela te serve de ~** let that be a lesson to you, that will teach you a lesson; **cela m'a servi de ~** that taught me a lesson; **nous avons tiré la ~ de notre échec** we learnt a lesson from our failure; **maintenant que notre plan a échoué, il faut en tirer la ~** now that our plan has failed we should draw a lesson from it; **cela lui donnera une ~** that'll teach him a lesson.

d *[manuscrit, texte]* reading.

lecteur, -trice [lɛktœʀ, tʀis] 1 **nm,f** a (*gén*) reader. **c'est un grand ~ de poésie** he's a great poetry-reader; **"avis au ~"** foreword, "to the reader"; **le nombre de ~s de ce journal a doublé** the readership of this paper has doubled.

b (*Univ*) university assistant (*Brit*), lector (*Brit*), (foreign language) assistant, (foreign) teaching assistant (*US*).

2 **comp** ► **lecteur de cartes** (*Aut*) map-light ► **lecteur de cartes perforées** (*Ordin*) card reader ► **lecteur de cassettes** cassette player ► **lecteur de disques compacts** CD player, compact disc player ► **lecteur de disquettes** (*Ordin*) disk drive ► **lecteur de document** (*Ordin*) document reader ► **lecteur optique** (*Ordin*) optical character reader ► **lecteur de son** (reading) head.

lectorat [lɛktɔʀa] **nm** a (*Univ*) assistantship. b *[magazine]* readership.

lecture [lɛktyʀ] **nf** a *[carte, texte]* reading; (*interprétation*) reading, interpretation. **la ~ de Proust est difficile** reading Proust is difficult, Proust is difficult to read; **aimer la ~** to like reading; **d'une ~ facile** easy to read, very readable; **livre d'une ~ agréable** book that makes pleasant reading; ~ **à haute voix** reading aloud; **faire la ~ à qn** to read to sb; (*frm*) **donner** *ou* **faire ~ de qch** to read sth out (*à qn* to sb); (*Mus*) ~ **à vue** sight-reading; **méthode de ~** method of teaching reading; ~ **rapide** speed reading; **nous n'avons pas la même ~ des événements** we have a different interpretation of the events; *voir* **cabinet, livre**[1].

b (*livre*) reading (*NonC*), book. **c'est une ~ à recommander** it is recommended reading *ou* it's a book to be recommended (*à* for); **apportez-moi de la ~** bring me something to read *ou* some reading matter; **~s pour la jeunesse** books for children; **quelles sont vos ~s favorites?** what do you like reading best?; **enrichi par ses ~s** enriched by his reading *ou* by what he has read; **elle a de mauvaises ~s** she reads the wrong things.

c *[projet de loi]* reading. **examiner un projet en première ~** to give a bill its first reading; **le projet a été accepté en seconde ~** the bill passed its second reading.

d (*Tech*) *[disque]* reading. (*Ordin*) ~ **optique** optical character reading; (*Ordin*) **procédé de ~-écriture** read-write cycle; *voir* **tête.**

Léda [leda] **nf** (*Myth*) Leda.

ledit [lədi] , **ladite** [ladit] , **mfpl lesdit(e)s** [ledi(t)] **adj** (*frm*) the aforementioned (*frm*), the aforesaid (*frm*), the said (*frm*).

légal, e, **mpl -aux** [legal, o] **adj** *âge, dispositions, formalité* legal; *armes, moyens* legal, lawful; *adresse* registered, official. **cours ~ d'une monnaie** official rate of exchange of a currency; **monnaie ~e** legal tender, official currency; **recourir aux moyens ~aux contre qn** to take legal action against sb; *voir* **fête, heure, médecine.**

légalement [legalmɑ̃] **adv** legally, lawfully.

légalisation [legalizasjɔ̃] **nf** (*voir* **légaliser**) legalization; authentication.

légaliser [legalize] 1 **vt** (*rendre légal*) to legalize; (*certifier*) to authenticate.

légalisme [legalism] **nm** legalism.

légaliste [legalist] 1 **adj** legalist(ic). 2 **nmf** legalist.

légalité [legalite] **nf** *[régime, acte]* legality, lawfulness. (*loi*) **la ~** the law; **rester dans/sortir de la ~** to keep within/step outside the law.

légat [lega] **nm:** ~ **(du Pape)** (papal) legate.

légataire [legatɛʀ] **nmf** legatee, devisee. ~ **universel** sole legatee.

légation [legasjɔ̃] **nf** (*Diplomatie*) legation.

légendaire [leʒɑ̃dɛʀ] **adj** (*gén*) legendary.

légende [leʒɑ̃d] **nf** a (*histoire, mythe*) legend. **entrer dans la ~** to go down in legend, become legendary; **entrer vivant dans la ~** to become a legend in one's own lifetime. b (*inscription*) *[médaille]* legend; *[dessin]* caption; *[liste, carte]* key. c (*péj: mensonge*) fairy tale.

léger, -ère [leʒe, ɛʀ] **adj** a (*lit*) *objet, poids, repas, gaz* light; (*délicat*) *parfum, mousseline, style* light. **arme/industrie ~ère** light weapon/industry; **construction ~ère** light *ou* flimsy (*péj*) building; **cuisine ~ère** light cooking; ~ **comme une plume** as light as a feather; **se sentir plus ~** (*fig: être soulagé*) to feel a great weight off one's mind; (*hum*) **je**

me sens plus ~ de 100 F I feel 100 francs lighter; (*fig*) **faire qch d'un cœur ~** to do sth with a light heart; **manger ~** (*non gras*) to eat low-fat foods, avoid fatty foods; (*peu*) to eat lightly; *voir* **poids, sommeil.**

b (*agile, souple*) *personne, geste, allure* light, nimble. **se sentir ~ (comme un oiseau)** to feel as light as a bird; **il partit d'un pas ~** he walked away with a light *ou* springy step; **avec une grâce ~ère** with an airy gracefulness; *voir* **main.**

c (*faible*) (*gén*) slight; *brise* gentle, slight; *bruit* slight, faint; *couche* thin, light; *thé* weak; *vin* light; *alcool* not very strong; *tabac* mild; *coup* light; *maladie, châtiment* mild, slight. **une ~ère pointe de sel/d'ironie** a (light) touch of salt/irony; **un blessé ~** a slightly injured person; **il y a un ~ mieux** there's a slight improvement; (*Mus*) **soprano/tenor ~** light soprano/tenor; **il a été condamné à une peine ~ère** he was given a mild *ou* light (prison) sentence.

d (*superficiel*) *personne* light-minded, thoughtless; *preuve, argument* lightweight, flimsy; *jugement, propos* thoughtless, flippant, careless. **se montrer ~ dans ses actions** to act without proper thought; **pour une thèse, c'est un peu ~** it's rather lightweight *ou* a bit on the flimsy side for a thesis; **parler/agir à la ~ère** to speak/act rashly *ou* thoughtlessly *ou* without giving the matter proper consideration; **il prend toujours tout à la ~ère** he never takes anything seriously.

e (*frivole*) *personne, caractère, humeur* fickle; *propos, plaisanterie* ribald, broad. **femme ~ère** *ou* **de mœurs ~ères** loose woman, woman of easy virtue; **avoir la cuisse ~ère** to be free with one's favours; *voir* **musique.**

légèrement [leʒɛʀmɑ̃] **adv** a *habillé, armé, poser* lightly. **il a mangé ~** he ate a light meal, he didn't eat much. b *courir* lightly, nimbly. c *blesser, bouger, surprendre* slightly. **~ plus grand** slightly bigger. d *agir* thoughtlessly, rashly, without thinking (properly). **parler ~ de la mort de qn** to speak flippantly *ou* lightly of sb's death, speak of sb's death in an offhand way *ou* a flippant way.

légèreté [leʒɛʀte] **nf** a *[objet, tissu, style, repas]* lightness.

b *[démarche]* lightness, nimbleness. **~ de main** light-handedness; **avec une ~ d'oiseau** with the lightness of a bird; **marcher/danser avec ~** to walk/dance lightly *ou* with a light step.

c *[punition, coup]* lightness, mildness; *[tabac]* mildness; *[thé]* weakness; *[vin]* lightness.

d (*superficialité*) *[conduite, personne, propos]* thoughtlessness; *[preuves, argument]* flimsiness. **faire preuve de ~** to speak (*ou* behave) rashly *ou* irresponsibly *ou* without due thought.

e (*frivolité*) *[personne]* fickleness, flightiness; *[propos]* flippancy; *[plaisanterie]* ribaldry. **sa ~ est bien connue** she is well-known for her free-and-easy morals.

légiférer [leʒifeʀe] [6] **vi** (*lit*) to legislate, make legislation; (*fig*) to lay down the law.

légion [leʒjɔ̃] **nf** (*Hist, fig*) legion. **~ de gendarmerie** corps of gendarmes; **la L~ (étrangère)** the Foreign Legion; **L~ d'honneur** Legion of Honour; **ils sont ~** they are legion, there are any number of them.

légionnaire [leʒjɔnɛʀ] 1 **nm** (*Hist*) legionary; *[Légion étrangère]* legionnaire; *voir* **maladie.** 2 **nmf** *[Légion d'honneur]* holder of the Legion of Honour.

législateur, -trice [leʒislatœʀ, tʀis] **nm,f** legislator, lawmaker. (*la loi*) **le ~ a prévu ce cas** the law has allowed for *ou* foreseen this case.

législatif, -ive [leʒislatif, iv] 1 **adj** legislative. **élections ~ives** elections to the legislature, ≃ general election (*Brit*). 2 **nm** legislature.

législation [leʒislasjɔ̃] **nf** legislation. **~ fiscale** fiscal *ou* tax legislation, tax laws; **~ du travail** labour laws, industrial *ou* job legislation.

législature [leʒislatyʀ] **nf** (*Parl*) (*durée*) term (of office); (*corps*) legislature.

légiste [leʒist] **nm** legist, jurist; *voir* **médecin.**

légitimation [leʒitimasjɔ̃] **nf** *[enfant]* legitimization; *[pouvoir]* recognition; (*littér*) *[action, conduite]* legitimization, legitimatization, justification.

légitime [leʒitim] 1 **adj** a (*légal*) *droits* legitimate, lawful; *union, femme* lawful; *enfant* legitimate. **j'étais en état de ~ défense** I was acting in self-defence. b (*juste*) *excuse* legitimate; *colère* justifiable, justified; *revendication* legitimate, rightful; *récompense* just, legitimate. **rien de plus ~ que ...** nothing could be more justified than .... 2 **nf** (†*) missus*. **ma ~** the missus*, the wife*.

légitimement [leʒitimmɑ̃] **adv** (*gén*) rightfully; (*Jur*) legitimately.

légitimer [leʒitime] [1] **vt** *enfant* to legitimate, legitimize; *conduite, action* to legitimate, legitimize, justify; *titre, pouvoir* to recognize.

légitimisme [leʒitimism] **nm** (*Hist*) legitimism.

légitimiste [leʒitimist] (*Hist*) **nmf, adj** legitimist.

légitimité [leʒitimite] **nf** (*gén*) legitimacy.

Lego [lego] **nm** ® Lego ®. **en ~** Lego (*épith*).

Le Greco [ləgʀekɔ] **nm** El Greco.

legs [lɛg] **nm** (*Jur*) legacy, bequest; (*fig: héritage*) legacy, heritage. **faire un ~ à qn** to leave sb a legacy; **~ (de biens immobiliers)** devise; **~ (de biens mobiliers)** legacy.

léguer [lege] [6] **vt** (*Jur*) to bequeath; *tradition, vertu, tare* to hand down *ou* on, pass on. **~ qch à qn par testament** to bequeath sth to sb (in one's will); (*fig*) **la mauvaise gestion qu'on nous a léguée** the bad management which we inherited.

légume [legym] 1 **nm** vegetable. **~s secs** pulses; **~s verts** green vegetables, greens*; *voir* **bouillon.** 2 **nf**: **une grosse ~*** a bigwig*.

légumier, -ière [legymje, jɛʀ] 1 **adj** vegetable (*épith*). 2 **nm** (*plat*) vegetable dish; (*Belgique: commerçant*) greengrocer.

légumineuse [legyminøz] **nf** legume, leguminous plant.

Le Havre [ləɑvʀ] **n** Le Havre.

leibnizien, -ienne [lajbnitsjɛ̃, jɛn] **adj, nm,f** Leibnitzian.

leitmotiv [lɛjtmɔtiv] **nm** (*lit, fig*) leitmotiv, leitmotif.

Léman [lemɑ̃] **nm** *voir* **lac.**

lemmatisation [lematizasjɔ̃] **nf** lemmatization.

lemmatiser [lematize] [1] **vt** to lemmatize.

lemme [lɛm] **nm** lemma.

lemming [lemiŋ] **nm** lemming.

lémurien [lemyʀjɛ̃] **nm** lemur.

lendemain [lɑ̃dmɛ̃] **nm** a (*jour suivant*) **le ~** the next *ou* following day, the day after; **le ~ de son arrivée/du mariage** the day after he arrived/after the marriage, the day following his arrival/the marriage; **le ~ matin/soir** the next *ou* following morning/evening; **~ de fête** day after a holiday; **au ~ d'un si beau jour** on the morrow of such a glorious day (*littér*); **au ~ de la défaite/de son mariage** soon after *ou* in the days following the defeat/his marriage; *voir* **jour, remettre.**

b (*avenir*) **le ~** tomorrow, the future; **penser au ~** to think of tomorrow *ou* the future, take thought for the morrow (*littér*); **bonheur/succès sans ~** short-lived happiness/success.

c **~s** (*conséquences*) consequences, repercussions; (*perspectives*) prospects, future; **cette affaire a eu de fâcheux ~s** this business had unfortunate consequences *ou* repercussions; **des ~s qui chantent** a brighter *ou* better future; **ça nous promet de beaux ~s** the future looks very promising for us.

lénifiant, e [lenifjɑ̃, jɑ̃t] **adj** (*apaisant*) *médicament, propos* soothing; (*péj: amollissant*) *atmosphère* languid, enervating; *discours* enervating, dull; *climat* enervating, draining (*attrib*).

lénifier [lenifje] [7] **vt** (*apaiser*) to soothe; (*péj: amollir*) to smooth away.

Lénine [lenin] **nm** Lenin.

Leningrad [leningʀad] **n** Leningrad.

léninisme [leninism] **nm** Leninism.

léniniste [leninist] **adj, nmf** Leninist.

lénitif, -ive [lenitif, iv] **adj, nm** lenitive.

lent, e[1] [lɑ̃, lɑ̃t] **adj** (*gén*) slow; *poison* slow, slow-acting; *mort* slow, lingering; (*Fin*) *croissance* sluggish, slow. **à l'esprit ~** slow-witted, dim-witted; **il est ~ à comprendre** he is slow to understand *ou* slow on the uptake*; **elle est ~e à manger** she's a slow eater, she eats slowly; **marcher d'un pas ~** to walk at a slow pace *ou* slowly.

lente[2] [lɑ̃t] **nf** (*Zool*) nit.

lentement [lɑ̃tmɑ̃] **adv** slowly. **progresser ~** to make slow progress; **~ mais sûrement** slowly but surely.

lenteur [lɑ̃tœʀ] **nf** slowness. **avec ~** slowly; **~ d'esprit** slow-wittedness; **la ~ de la construction** the slow progress of the building; **les ~s du procès** the slowness of the trial.

lentigo [lɑ̃tigo] **nm** lentigo.

lentille [lɑ̃tij] **nf** (*Bot, Culin*) lentil; (*Opt*) lens. **gros comme une ~** as big as a small pea; **~s (cornéennes** *ou* **de contact)** contact lenses; **~s (cornéennes** *ou* **de contact) dures/souples** hard/soft contact lenses; **~ micro-cornéenne** microcorneal lens; **~s d'eau** duckweed.

Léon [leɔ̃] **nm** Leo.

Léonard [leɔnaʀ] **nm** Leonard. **~ de Vinci** Leonardo da Vinci.

Léonie [leɔni] **nf** Leonie.

léonin, e [leɔnɛ̃, in] **adj** *mœurs, aspect, rime* leonine; (*fig*) *contrat, partage* one-sided.

Léonore [leɔnɔʀ] **nf** Leonora.

léopard [leɔpaʀ] **nm** leopard. **manteau de ~** leopard-skin coat; (*Mil*) **tenue ~** camouflage (uniform).

Léopold [leɔpɔl(d)] **nm** Leopold.

LEP [lɛp] **nm** (**abrév de livret d'épargne populaire**) *voir* **livret.**

lépidoptère [lepidɔptɛʀ] 1 **adj** lepidopterous. 2 **nm** lepidopteran, lepidopterous insect. **les ~s** the Lepidoptera.

lèpre [lɛpʀ] **nf** (*Méd*) leprosy; (*fig: mal*) plague. **mur rongé de ~** flaking *ou* scaling *ou* peeling wall.

lépreux, -euse [lepʀø, øz] 1 **adj** (*lit*) leprous, suffering from leprosy; *mur* flaking, scaling, peeling; *quartier* rundown. 2 **nm,f** (*lit, fig*) leper.

léproserie [lepʀozʀi] **nf** leper-house.

lequel [ləkɛl] **, laquelle** [lakɛl] **, mfpl lesquel(le)s** [lekɛl] (*contraction avec à, de* **auquel, auxquels, auxquelles, duquel, desquels, desquelles**) 1 **pron** a (*relatif*) (*personne: sujet*) who; (*personne: objet*) whom; (*chose*) which. **j'ai écrit au directeur de la banque, ~ n'a jamais répondu** I wrote to the bank manager, who has never answered; **la patience avec laquelle il écoute** the patience with which he listens; **le règlement d'après ~ ...** the ruling whereby ...; **la découverte sur laquelle on a tant parlé** the discovery which has been so much talked about *ou* about which there has been so much talk; **la femme à laquelle j'ai acheté mon chien** the woman from whom I bought my dog; **c'est un problème auquel je n'avais pas pensé** that's a problem I hadn't thought of *ou* which hadn't occurred to me; **le pont sur ~ vous êtes passé** the bridge you came over *ou* over which you came; **le docteur/le traitement sans ~ elle serait morte** the doctor without whom/the treatment without which she would have died; **cette société sur le compte de laquelle on dit tant de mal** this society about which so much ill is spoken; **la plupart desquels** (*personnes*) most of whom; (*choses*) most of which; **les gens chez lesquels j'ai logé** the people at whose house I stayed; *voir* **importer[2]**.

b (*interrogatif*) which. ~ **des 2 acteurs préférez-vous?** which of the 2 actors do you prefer?; **dans ~ de ces hôtels avez-vous logé?** in which of these hotels did you stay?; **laquelle des sonates de Mozart avez-vous entendue?** which of Mozart's sonatas *ou* which Mozart sonata did you hear?; **laquelle des chambres est la sienne?** which is his room?, which of the rooms is his?; **je ne sais à laquelle des vendeuses m'adresser** I don't know which saleswoman I should speak to *ou* which saleswoman to speak to; **devinez lesquels de ces tableaux elle aimerait avoir** guess which of these pictures she would like to have; **donnez-moi 1 melon/2 melons — ~?/lesquels?** give me 1 melon/2 melons — which one?/which ones? *ou* which (2)?; **va voir ma sœur — laquelle?** go and see my sister — which one?

2 adj: **son état pourrait empirer, auquel cas je reviendrais** his condition could worsen, in which case I would come back; (*littér, iro*) **il écrivit au ministre, ~ ministre ne répondit jamais** he wrote to the minister but the said (*littér, iro*) minister never replied.

lerch(e)* [lɛʀʃ] adv: **pas ~** not much; **il n'y en a pas ~** there's not much of it; **c'est pas ~** that's not much.

lérot [leʀo] nm lerot, garden dormouse.

les [le] *voir* **le[1]**, **le[2]**.

lesbianisme [lɛsbjanism] nm lesbianism.

lesbienne [lɛsbjɛn] nf lesbian.

lèse-majesté [lɛzmaʒɛste] nf lese-majesty; *voir* **crime**.

léser [leze] [6] vt a (*Jur: frustrer*) *personne* to wrong; *intérêts* to damage. **la partie lésée** the injured party; **~ les droits de qn** to infringe on sb's rights. b (*Méd: blesser*) *organe* to injure.

lésiner [lezine] [1] vi to skimp (*sur qch* on sth). **ne pas ~ sur les moyens** (*gén*) to use all the means at one's disposal; (*pour mariage, repas etc*) to push the boat out*, pull out all the stops*.

lésinerie [lezinʀi] nf (*avarice*) stinginess; (*action avare*) stingy act.

lésion [lezjɔ̃] nf (*Jur, Méd*) lesion. (*Méd*) **~s internes** internal injuries.

lésionnel, -elle [lezjɔnɛl] adj *trouble* caused by a lesion; *syndrome* of a lesion.

Lesotho [lezɔto] nm: **le royaume du ~** the kingdom of Lesotho.

lessivable [lesivabl] adj *papier peint* washable.

lessivage [lesivaʒ] nm (*gén*) washing; (*Chim, Géol*) leaching.

lessive [lesiv] nf a (*produit*) (*gén*) washing powder; (*Tech: soude*) lye. b (*lavage*) washing, wash. **mon jour de ~** my wash *ou* washing day; **faire la ~** to do the washing; **faire 4 ~s par semaine** to do 4 washes a week. c (*linge*) washing (*NonC*). **porter sa ~ à la blanchisserie** to take one's washing to the laundry.

lessiver [lesive] [1] vt a (*lit*) *mur, plancher, linge* to wash. b (*Chim, Géol*) to leach. c (*‡: battre*) (*au jeu*) to clean out*; *adversaire* to lick‡. d (*: fatiguer*) to tire out, exhaust. **être lessivé** to be dead-beat* *ou* all-in* *ou* tired out.

lessiveuse [lesivøz] nf boiler (*for washing laundry*).

lessiviel [lesivjɛl] adj m: **produit ~** detergent product.

lest [lɛst] nm ballast. (*Naut*) **sur son ~** in ballast; **garnir un bateau de ~** to ballast a ship; **jeter** *ou* **lâcher du ~** (*lit*) to dump ballast; (*fig*) to make concessions.

lestage [lɛstaʒ] nm ballasting.

leste [lɛst] adj a *animal* nimble, agile; *personne* sprightly, agile; *démarche* sprightly, light, nimble; *voir* **main**. b (*grivois*) *plaisanterie* risqué; (*cavalier*) *ton, réponse* offhand.

lestement [lɛstəmɑ̃] adv (*voir* **leste**) nimbly, agilely; in a sprightly manner; lightly; offhandedly. **plaisanter ~** to make (rather) risqué jokes; **mener ~ une affaire** to conduct a piece of business briskly.

lester [lɛste] [1] vt a (*garnir de lest*) to ballast. b (*: remplir*) *portefeuille, poches* to fill, cram. **~ son estomac, se ~ (l'estomac)** to fill one's stomach; **lesté d'un repas copieux** weighed down with a heavy meal.

let [lɛt] nm (*Tennis*) let. **faire un ~** to play a let.

létal, e, mpl **-aux** [letal, o] adj *dose, gène* lethal.

letchi [lɛtʃi] nm = **litchi**.

léthargie [letaʀʒi] nf (*apathie, Méd*) lethargy. **tomber en ~** to fall into a state of lethargy.

léthargique [letaʀʒik] adj lethargic. **état ~** lethargic state, state of lethargy.

lette [lɛt] 1 adj Latvian. 2 nm (*Ling*) Latvian. 3 nmf: **L~** Latvian.

letton, -onne [lɛtɔ̃, ɔn] 1 adj Latvian, Lett, Lettish. 2 nm (*Ling*) Latvian, Lett, Lettish. 3 nm,f: **L~(ne)** Latvian, Lett.

Lettonie [lɛtɔni] nf Latvia.

lettrage [lɛtʀaʒ] nm lettering.

lettre [lɛtʀ] 1 nf a (*caractère*) letter. **~ majuscule/minuscule** capital/small letter; **c'est en toutes ~s dans les journaux** it's there in black and white *ou* it's there for all to read in the newspapers; **c'est en grosses ~s dans les journaux** it's splashed across the newspapers, it has made headlines in the papers; **écrire un nom en toutes ~s** to write (out) a name in full; **écrivez la somme en (toutes) ~s** write out the sum in words; **un mot de 6 ~s** a 6-letter word, a word of 6 letters; **c'est écrit en toutes ~s sur sa figure** it's written all over his face; **c'est à écrire en ~s d'or** it is a momentous event, it is something to celebrate; **inscrit** *ou* **gravé en ~s de feu** written in letters of fire; **cette lutte est écrite en ~s de sang** this gory struggle will remain engraved on people's minds; *voir* **cinq**.

b (*missive*) letter. **~s** (*courrier*) letters, mail; **jeter** *ou* **mettre une ~ à la boîte** *ou* **à la poste** to post *ou* mail (*US*) a letter; **est-ce qu'il y avait des ~s aujourd'hui?** were there any letters today?, was there any mail today?; **écris-lui donc une petite ~** write him a note, drop him a line*; **il a reçu une ~ d'injures** he got a rude letter *ou* an abusive letter; **~ de condoléances/de félicitations/de réclamation** letter of condolence/of congratulations/of complaint; **~ d'amour/d'affaires** love/business letter.

c (*sens strict*) **prendre qch au pied de la ~** to take sth literally; **suivre la ~ de la loi** to follow the letter of the law; **exécuter des ordres à la ~** to carry out orders to the letter.

d **les ~s, les belles ~s** (*culture littéraire*) literature; **femme/homme/gens de ~s** woman/man/men of letters; **le monde des ~s** the literary world; **avoir des ~s** to be well-read.

e (*Scol, Univ*) arts (subjects). **il est très fort en ~s** he's very good at arts subjects; **il fait des ~s** he's doing an arts degree; **professeur de ~s** teacher of French, French teacher (*in France*); **~s classiques** classics (*sg*); *voir* **faculté, licence**.

f (*loc*) **rester ~ morte** *[remarque, avis, protestation]* to go unheeded; **devenir ~ morte** *[loi, traité]* to become a dead letter; **c'est passé comme une ~ à la poste*** it went off smoothly *ou* without a hitch; *voir* **avant**.

2 comp ▸**lettre de cachet** (*Hist*) lettre de cachet ▸**lettre de change** (*Comm*) bill of exchange ▸**lettre circulaire** (*Admin*) circular ▸**lettres de créance** credentials ▸**lettre de crédit** (*Fin*) letter of credit ▸**lettre exprès** express letter ▸**lettre de faire-part (de mariage)** formal announcement of a wedding, ≃ wedding invitation ▸**lettre d'intention** (*Fin*) letter of intent ▸**lettre missive** (*Admin*) letter(s) missive ▸**lettres modernes: section de lettres modernes** (*Univ*) French department, department of French (language and literature) ▸**lettres de noblesse** (*lit*) letters patent of nobility; (*fig*) **gagner ses lettres de noblesse** to win acclaim, establish one's pedigree ▸**lettre ouverte** (*Presse*) open letter ▸**lettres patentes** letters (of) patent ▸**lettre de recommandation** letter of recommendation, reference ▸**lettre recommandée** (*attestant sa remise*) recorded delivery letter; (*assurant sa valeur*) registered letter ▸**lettre de service** notification of command ▸**lettres supérieures** (*Scol*) *preparatory class (after the baccalauréat) leading to the École Normale Supérieure* ▸**lettre de voiture** (*Comm*) consignment note, waybill.

lettré, e [letʀe] adj well-read.

lettrine [letʀin] nf a *[dictionnaire]* headline. b *[chapitre]* dropped initial.

leu [lø] nm *voir* **queue**.

leucémie [løsemi] nf leukaemia.

leucémique [løsemik] 1 adj leukaemic. 2 nmf person suffering from leukaemia.

leucocyte [løkɔsit] nm leucocyte. **~ mononucléaire** monocyte; **~ polynucléaire** polymorphonuclear leucocyte.

leucorrhée [løkɔʀe] nf leucorrhoea.

leucotomie [løkɔtɔmi] nf leucotomy.

leur [lœʀ] 1 pron pers mf them. **je le ~ ai dit** I told them; **il ~ est facile de le faire** it is easy for them to do it; **elle ~ serra la main** she shook their hand, she shook them by the hand; **je ~ en ai donné** I gave them some, I gave some to them.

2 adj poss a their. **~ jardin à eux est une vraie forêt vierge** their own garden is a real jungle; **à ~ vue** at the sight of them, on seeing them; **~ maladroite de sœur** that clumsy sister of theirs; **ils ont passé tout ~ dimanche à travailler** they spent the whole of *ou* all Sunday working; **ils ont ~s petites manies** they have their little fads.

b (*littér*) theirs, their own. **un ~ cousin** a cousin of theirs; **ils ont fait ~s ces idées** they made theirs these ideas, they made these ideas their own; **ces terres qui étaient ~s** these estates of theirs *ou* which were theirs.

3 pron poss: **le ~, la ~, les ~s** theirs, their own; **ces sacs sont les ~s** these bags are theirs, these are their bags; **ils sont partis dans une voiture qui n'était pas la ~** they left in a car which wasn't theirs *ou* their own; **à la (bonne) ~!** their good health!, here's to them!; *pour autres exemples voir* **sien**.

4 nm a **ils ont mis du ~** they pulled their weight, they did their bit*; *voir aussi* **sien**.

b **les ~s** (*famille*) their family, their (own) folks*; (*partisans*) their own people; **ils ont encore fait des ~s*** they've (gone and) done it again*, they've been at it again*; **nous étions des ~s** we were with them.

leurre [lœʀ] nm (*illusion*) delusion, illusion; (*duperie*) deception; (*piège*) trap, snare; (*Fauconnerie, Pêche: appât*) lure; (*Chasse, Mil*) decoy, lure.

leurrer [lœʀe] 1 vt (*gén*) to deceive, delude; (*Fauconnerie, Pêche*) to lure. **ils nous ont leurrés par des promesses fallacieuses** they deluded us with false promises; **ils se sont laissé ~** they let themselves be taken in *ou* deceived; **ne vous leurrez pas** don't delude yourself; **ne nous leurrons pas sur leurs intentions** we should not delude ourselves about their intentions.

levage [ləvaʒ] nm (*Tech*) lifting; (*Culin*) rising, raising; *voir* **appareil**.

levain [ləvɛ̃] nm leaven. **sans ~** unleavened; **pain au ~** leavened bread; (*fig*) **~ de haine/de vengeance** seed of hate/of vengeance.

levant [ləvɑ̃] 1 adj: **soleil ~** rising sun; **au soleil ~** at sunrise. 2 nm: **du ~ au couchant** from the rising to the setting sun; **les chambres sont au ~** the bedrooms are on the east side; **le L~** the Levant.

levantin, -ine [ləvɑ̃tɛ̃, in] 1 adj Levantine. 2 nm,f: **L~(e)** Levantine.

levé[1] [l(ə)ve] nm (*plan*) survey. **un ~ de terrain** a land survey; **faire un ~ de terrain** to survey a piece of land.

levé[2]**, e**[1] [l(ə)ve] (ptp de **lever**) 1 adj: **être ~** to be up; **sitôt ~** as soon as he is (*ou* was *etc*) up; **il n'est pas encore ~** he is not up yet; **toujours le premier ~** always the first up; *voir* **pierre**. 2 nm (*Mus*) up-beat.

lève- [lɛv] préf *voir* **lever**.

levée[2] [l(ə)ve] 1 nf a *[blocus, siège]* raising; *[séance]* closing; *[interdiction, punition]* lifting.

b (*Poste*) collection. **la ~ du matin est faite** the morning collection has been made, the morning post has gone (*Brit*); **dernière ~ à 19 heures** last collection (at) 7 p.m.

c (*Cartes*) trick. **faire une ~** to take a trick.

d *[impôts]* levying; *[armée]* raising, levying.

e (*remblai*) levee.

2 comp ▸**levée de boucliers** (*fig*) general outcry, hue and cry ▸**levée du corps: la levée du corps aura lieu à 10 heures** the funeral will start from the house at 10 o'clock ▸**levée d'écrou** (*Jur*) release (from prison) ▸**levée de jugement** (*Jur*) transcript (of a verdict) ▸**levée en masse** (*Mil*) levy en masse ▸**levée des scellés** (*Jur*) removal of the seals ▸**levée de terre** levee.

lever [l(ə)ve] 5 1 vt a (*soulever, hausser*) *poids, objet* to lift; *vitre* to put up, raise; *tête* to raise, lift up; *main, bras* (*pour prendre qch, saluer, voter, prêter serment*) to raise; (*en classe*) to put up. **lève ton coude, je veux prendre le papier** lift *ou* raise your elbow, I want to take the paper away; **~ les yeux** to lift up *ou* raise one's eyes, look up (*de* from); **~ les yeux sur qn** (*lit: regarder*) to look at sb; (*fig: vouloir épouser*) to set one's heart on marrying sb; **~ le visage vers qn** to look up at sb; **~ un regard suppliant/éploré vers qn** to look up imploringly/tearfully at sb; (*en classe*) **levez le doigt pour répondre** put up your hand to answer.

b (*faire cesser, supprimer*) *blocus* to raise; *séance, audience* to close; *obstacle, difficulté* to remove; *interdiction, punition* to lift; *ambiguïté* to clear up; (*Comm, Jur*) *option* to exercise, take up. **~ les scellés** to remove the seals; **cela a levé tous ses scrupules** that has removed all his scruples; **on lève la séance?*** shall we break up?, shall we call it a day?

c (*ramasser*) *impôts* to levy; *armée* to raise, levy; (*Cartes*) *pli* to take; *[facteur] lettres* to collect.

d (*Chasse*) *lièvre* to start; *perdrix* to flush; (*‡ fig*) *femme* to pick up*, pull‡ (*US*). (*fig*) **~ un lièvre** to uncover sth by chance.

e (*établir*) *plan* to draw (up); *carte* to draw.

f (*†: prélever*) to cut off.

g (*sortir du lit*) *enfant, malade* to get up. **le matin, pour le faire ~, il faut se fâcher** in the morning, you have to get angry before he'll get up *ou* to get him out of bed.

h (*prélever*) *morceau de viande etc* to take off, remove.

i (*loc*) **~ l'ancre** (*Naut*) to weigh anchor; (*fig*) to make tracks*; **~ les bras au ciel** to throw one's arms up in the air; **~ les yeux au ciel** to raise one's eyes heavenwards; **~ le camp** (*lit*) to strike *ou* break camp; (*fig: partir*) to clear off*; **~ le siège** (*lit*) to lift *ou* raise the siege; (*fig: partir*) to clear off*; **il lève bien le coude*** he enjoys a drink, he drinks a fair bit*; **il n'a pas levé le petit doigt pour m'aider** he didn't lift a finger to help me; **~ l'étendard de la révolte** to raise the standard of revolt; **il ne lève jamais le nez de ses livres** he never takes his nose out of his books; **il ne lève jamais le nez de son travail/son pupitre** he never lifts his nose from his work/his desk; *[chien]* **~ la patte** (*pour pisser*) to cock *ou* lift its leg; (*pour dire bonjour*) to give a paw; **~ le pied** (*disparaître*) to vanish; (*Aut: ralentir*) to slow down; **~ le poing** to raise one's fist; **~ la main sur qn** to raise one's hand to sb; (*Théât*) **~ le rideau** to raise the curtain; **~ le voile** to reveal the truth (*sur* about); **~ le masque** to unmask o.s.; **~ son verre à la santé de qn** to raise one's glass to sb, drink to sb's health; *voir* **main, pied**.

2 vi a *[plante, blé]* to come up.

b (*Culin*) to rise. **faire ~ la pâte** to make the dough rise, leave the dough to rise.

3 **se lever** vpr a *[rideau, main]* to go up. **toutes les mains se levèrent** every hand went up.

b (*se mettre debout*) to get up. **se ~ de table/de sa chaise** to get up from the table/from one's chair; **le maître les fit se lever** the teacher made them stand up *ou* get up *ou* get to their feet.

c (*sortir du lit*) to get up. **se ~ tôt** to get up early, rise early; **le convalescent commence à se ~** the convalescent is starting to get up (and about); **ce matin, il s'est levé du pied gauche** this morning he got out of bed on the wrong side; **se ~ sur son séant** to sit up.

d *[Soleil, Lune]* to rise; *[jour]* to break. **le soleil n'était pas encore levé** the sun had not yet risen *ou* was not yet up.

e (*Mét*) *[vent, orage]* to get up, rise; *[brume]* to lift, clear; *[mer]* to swell. **le temps se lève, cela se lève** the weather *ou* it is clearing.

f (*se révolter*) to rise up.

4 nm a **~ de soleil** sunrise, sunup*; **~ du jour** daybreak, dawn.

b (*au réveil*) **prenez 3 comprimés au ~** take 3 tablets when you get up *ou* on rising; **au ~, à son ~** (*présent*) when he gets up; (*passé*) when he got up; **le ~ du roi** the levee of the king.

c (*Théât*) **le ~ du rideau** (*commencement d'une pièce*) curtain up; (*action de lever le rideau*) the raising of the curtain; (*pièce, match*) **un ~ de rideau** a curtain-raiser; **en ~ de rideau, nous avons ...** as a curtain-raiser *ou* to start with, we have ... .

d = **levé**[1].

5 comp ▸**lève-glace** nm inv, **lève-vitre** nm inv (window) winder ▸**lève-tôt** nm inv early riser ▸**lève-tard** nm inv late riser.

levier [ləvje] nm lever. **~ de commande/de changement de vitesse** control/gear lever; **~ de frein** handbrake (lever); **faire ~ sur qch** to lever sth up (*ou* off *etc*); (*fig*) **être aux ~s de commande** to be in control *ou* command; (*fig*) **l'argent est un puissant ~** money is a powerful lever.

lévitation [levitasjɔ̃] nf levitation.

lévite [levit] nm Levite.

Lévitique [levitik] nm Leviticus.

levraut [ləvʀo] nm leveret.

lèvre [lɛvʀ] nf (*gén*) lip; *[plaie]* edge; *[vulve]* lip, labium (*SPÉC*); (*Géog*) *[faille]* side. (*Géog*) **~ soulevée/abaissée** upthrow/downthrow side; **le sourire aux ~s** with a smile on one's lips; **la cigarette aux ~s** with a cigarette between one's lips; **son nom est sur toutes les ~s** his name is on everyone's lips; (*fig*) **j'ai les ~s scellées** my lips are sealed; **petites/grandes ~s** labia minora/majora (*SPÉC*); *voir* **bout, pincer, rouge** *etc*.

levrette [ləvʀɛt] nf (*femelle*) greyhound bitch; (*variété de lévrier*) Italian greyhound.

lévrier [levʀije] nm greyhound. **courses de ~s** greyhound racing; **~ afghan** Afghan (hound).

levure [l(ə)vyʀ] nf (*ferment*) yeast. **~ de bière** brewers' yeast; **~ chimique** brewers' yeast, dried yeast.

lexème [lɛksɛm] nm lexeme.

lexical, e, mpl **-aux** [lɛksikal, o] adj lexical.

lexicalisation [lɛksikalizasjɔ̃] nf lexicalization.

lexicaliser [lɛksikalize] 1 vt to lexicalize.

lexicographe [lɛksikɔgʀaf] nmf lexicographer.

lexicographie [lɛksikɔgʀafi] nf lexicography.

lexicographique [lɛksikɔgʀafik] adj lexicographical.

lexicologie [lɛksikɔlɔʒi] nf lexicology.

lexicologique [lɛksikɔlɔʒik] adj lexicological.

lexicologue [lɛksikɔlɔg] nmf lexicologist.

lexie [lɛksi] nf lexical item.

lexique [lɛksik] nm vocabulary, lexis; (*glossaire*) lexicon.

lézard [lezaʀ] nm (*animal*) lizard; (*peau*) lizardskin. **~ vert** green lizard; **sac/gants en ~** lizardskin bag/gloves; **faire le ~ (au soleil)*** to bask in the sun; **il n'y a pas de ~*!** no problem*! *ou* no probs‡! (*Brit*).

lézarde [lezaʀd] nf (*fissure*) crack.

lézarder[1] [lezaʀde] 1 vi to bask in the sun.

lézarder[2] vt, **se lézarder** vpr [lezaʀde] 1 to crack.

Lhassa [lasa] n Lhasa, Lassa.

liaison [ljɛzɔ̃] nf a (*fréquentation*) **~ (amoureuse)** (love) affair, liaison; **~ (d'affaires)** business relationship *ou* connection; **avoir/rompre une ~** to have/break off an affair *ou* a love affair; **avoir une** *ou* **être en ~ d'affaires avec qn** to have business relations with sb.

b (*contact*) **entrer/être en ~ étroite avec qn** to get/be in close contact with sb; **travailler en ~ étroite avec qn** to work closely with *ou* in close collaboration with sb; **en ~ (étroite) avec nos partenaires, nous avons décidé de ...** in (close) collaboration with *ou* after close consultation with our partners, we have decided to ...; **établir une ~ radio avec un pilote** to establish radio contact with a pilot; **les ~s téléphoniques avec le Japon** telephone links with Japan; (*péj*) **avoir des ~s avec** to have links *ou* dealings with; (*Mil*) **se tenir en ~ avec l'état-major** to keep in contact with headquarters, liaise with headquarters; (*Mil*) **officier** *ou* **agent de ~** liaison officer; **j'espère que nous allons rester en ~** I hope that we shall remain in contact.

c (*rapport, enchaînement*) connection. **manque de ~ entre 2 idées** lack of connection between 2 ideas; **il n'y a aucune ~ entre les 2 idées/événements** there is no connection *ou* link between the 2 ideas/events; **la ~ des idées n'est pas évidente** the connection of ideas isn't obvious.

d (*Phonétique*) liaison. **consonne de ~** linking consonant; (*Gram*) **mot** *ou* **terme de ~** link-word; (*Phonétique*) **en français il ne faut pas faire la ~ devant un h aspiré** in French one mustn't make a liaison before an aspirate h.

e (*Transport*) link. **~ aérienne/routière/ferroviaire/maritime** air/road/rail/sea link.

f (*Culin*) liaison.
g (*Ordin*) ~ **de transmission** data link.
h (*Mus*) (*même hauteur*) tie; (*hauteurs différentes*) slur.
i (*Chim*) bond.

liane [ljan] nf creeper, liana.

liant, liante [ljɑ̃, ljɑ̃t] 1 adj sociable. 2 nm a (*littér: affabilité*) sociable disposition. **il a du** ~ he has a sociable disposition *ou* nature, he is sociable. b (*Métal: souplesse*) flexibility. c (*substance*) binder.

liard [ljaʀ] nm (*Hist*) farthing. (*fig*) **je n'ai pas un** ~ I haven't (got) a farthing.

lias [ljɑs] nm (*Géol*) Lias.

liasique [ljɑzik] adj (*Geol*) Liassic.

liasse [ljas] nf *[billets, papiers]* bundle, wad.

Liban [libɑ̃] nm: **(le)** ~ (the) Lebanon.

libanais, e [libanɛ, ɛz] 1 adj Lebanese. 2 nm,f: **L~(e)** Lebanese.

libations [libasjɔ̃] nfpl (*Antiq*) libations. (*fig*) **faire de copieuses** ~ to indulge in great libations (*hum*).

libelle [libɛl] nm (*satire*) lampoon. **faire des ~s contre qn** to lampoon sb.

libellé [libele] nm wording.

libeller [libele] 1 vt *acte* to draw up; *chèque* to make out (*au nom de* to); *lettre, demande, réclamation* to word. **sa lettre était ainsi libellée** so went his letter, his letter was worded thus.

libelliste [libelist] nm (*littér*) lampoonist.

libellule [libelyl] nf dragonfly.

liber [libɛʀ] nm (*Bot*) phloem.

libérable [libeʀabl] adj *militaire* dischargeable. **permission** ~ leave in hand (*allowing early discharge*).

libéral, e, mpl **-aux** [libeʀal, o] adj, nm,f (*gén*) liberal; (*Pol*) Liberal; *voir* **profession.**

libéralement [libeʀalmɑ̃] adv liberally.

libéralisation [libeʀalizasjɔ̃] nf *[lois, régime]* liberalization. **la** ~ **du commerce** the easing of restrictions on trade.

libéraliser [libeʀalize] 1 vt (*voir* **libéralisation**) to liberalize.

libéralisme [libeʀalism] nm (*tous sens*) liberalism. **être partisan du** ~ **économique** to be a supporter of economic liberalism *ou* of free enterprise.

libéralité [libeʀalite] nf (*littér*) (*générosité*) liberality; (*gén pl: don*) generous *ou* liberal gift, liberality. **vivre des ~s d'un ami** to live off a friend's generosity.

libérateur, -trice [libeʀatœʀ, tʀis] 1 adj (*Pol*) **guerre/croisade ~trice** war/crusade of liberation; (*Psych*) **rire** ~ liberating laugh; **expérience ~trice** liberating experience. 2 nm,f liberator.

libération [libeʀasjɔ̃] nf (*voir* **libérer**) discharge; release; freeing; liberation; decontrolling. ~ **anticipée** early release; ~ **conditionnelle** release on parole; ~ **de la femme** Women's Liberation; (*Hist*) **la L~** the Liberation; *voir* **vitesse.**

libératoire [libeʀatwaʀ] adj (*Fin*) **paiement** ~ payment in full discharge; **prélèvement** ~ levy at source (*on share dividends*).

libéré, e [libeʀe] (ptp de **libérer**) adj liberated.

libérer [libeʀe] 6 1 vt a (*relâcher*) *prisonnier* to discharge, release (*de* from); *soldat* to discharge (*de* from). (*Jur*) **être libéré sous caution/sur parole** to be released on bail/on parole.
b (*délivrer*) *pays, peuple* to free, liberate; (*fig*) *esprit, personne* (*de soucis etc*) to free (*de* from); (*d'inhibitions etc*) to liberate (*de* from). ~ **qn de** *liens* to release *ou* free sb from; *promesse* to release sb from; *dette* to free sb from.
c (*Tech*) *levier, cran d'arrêt* to release; (*Écon*) *échanges commerciaux* to ease restrictions on; *prix* to decontrol; (*Méd*) *intestin* to unblock. (*fig*) ~ **le passage** to free *ou* unblock the way.
d (*soulager*) ~ **son cœur/sa conscience** to unburden one's heart/conscience; ~ **ses instincts** to give free rein to one's instincts.
e (*Sci*) *énergie, électrons* to release; *gaz* to release, give off.
2 **se libérer** vpr (*de ses liens*) to free o.s. (*de* from); (*d'une promesse*) to release o.s. (*de* from); (*d'une dette*) to clear o.s. (*de* of). **se** ~ **d'un rendez-vous** to get out of a meeting; **désolé, jeudi je ne peux pas me** ~ I'm sorry I can't be free *ou* I'm not free on Thursday; **se** ~ **du joug de l'oppresseur** to free o.s. from the yoke of one's oppressor.

Libéria [libeʀja] nm Liberia.

libérien, -ienne [libeʀjɛ̃, jɛn] 1 adj Liberian. 2 nm,f: **L~(ne)** Liberian.

libériste [libeʀist] 1 nmf hang-glider. 2 adj hang-gliding.

libéro [libeʀo] nm (*Ftbl*) libero (*SPÉC*), ≃ sweeper.

libertaire [libɛʀtɛʀ] adj, nmf libertarian.

liberté [libɛʀte] 1 nf a (*gén, Jur*) freedom, liberty. **mettre en** ~ to free, release, set free; *[prisonnier]* **mise en** ~ discharge, release; **être en** ~ to be free; **animaux en** ~ animals in the wild *ou* natural state; **les animaux sont en** ~ **dans le parc** the animals roam free in the park; **le voleur est encore en** ~ the thief is still at large; **rendre la** ~ **à un prisonnier** to free *ou* release a prisoner, set a prisoner free; **remettre un animal en** ~ to set an animal free (again); **elle a quitté son mari et repris sa** ~ she has left her husband and regained her freedom *ou* her independence; **agir en toute** *ou* **pleine** ~ to act with complete freedom, act quite freely; **sans la** ~ **de critiquer/de choisir aucune opinion n'a de valeur** without the freedom to criticize/to choose any opinion is valueless; **avoir toute** ~ **pour agir** to have full liberty *ou* freedom to act; **donner à qn toute** ~ **d'action** to give sb complete freedom of action, give sb a free hand to act, give sb carte blanche.
b (*gén, Pol: indépendance*) freedom. ~ **de la presse/d'opinion/de conscience** *etc* freedom of the press/of thought/of conscience *etc;* ~ **du culte/d'expression** freedom of worship/of expression; ~ **individuelle** personal freedom; ~ **d'information** freedom of information; ~ **religieuse** religious freedom, freedom of worship; **vive la** ~! long live freedom!; ~**, égalité, fraternité** liberty, equality, fraternity.
c (*loisir*) **heures/moments de** ~ free hours/moments; **ils ont droit à 2 jours de** ~ **par semaine** they are allowed 2 free days a week *ou* 2 days off each week; **son travail ne lui laisse pas beaucoup de** ~ his work doesn't leave him much free time.
d (*absence de retenue, de contrainte*) liberty. ~ **d'esprit/de jugement** independence of mind/judgment; ~ **de langage/de mœurs** freedom of language/morals; **s'exprimer avec (grande)** ~ to express o.s. very freely; (*formule*) **prendre la** ~ **de faire** to take the liberty of doing; **prendre** *ou* **se permettre des ~s avec** *personne, texte, grammaire, règlement*to take liberties with.
e (*droit*) **la** ~ **du travail** the right *ou* freedom to work; ~ **d'association/de réunion** right of association/to meet *ou* hold meetings; **les ~s syndicales** union rights; (*Hist*) **~s des villes** borough franchises.
2 comp ▸ **liberté sous caution** (*Jur*) release on bail; **mise en liberté sous caution** release on bail ▸ **liberté conditionnelle** (*Jur*) parole; **mettre en liberté conditionnelle** to release on parole; **être mis en liberté conditionnelle** to be granted parole, be released on parole; **mise en liberté conditionnelle** release on parole ▸ **liberté provisoire** (*Jur*) bail; **être mis en liberté provisoire** to be granted bail, be released on bail ▸ **liberté surveillée** (*Jur*) release on probation; **être mis en liberté surveillée** to be put on probation.

libertin, e [libɛʀtɛ̃, in] 1 adj (*littér*) (*dissolu*) *personne* libertine, dissolute; (*grivois*) *roman* licentious; (*Hist: irréligieux*) *philosophe* libertine. 2 nm,f (*littér: dévergondé*) libertine. 3 nm (*Hist: libre-penseur*) libertine, freethinker.

libertinage [libɛʀtinaʒ] nm (*littér*) (*débauche*) *[personne]* debauchery, dissoluteness; (*grivoiserie*) *[roman]* licentiousness; (*Hist: impiété*) *[philosophe]* libertine outlook *ou* philosophy.

libidineux, -euse [libidinø, øz] adj (*littér, hum*) libidinous, lustful.

libido [libido] nf libido.

libraire [libʀɛʀ] nmf bookseller. **~-éditeur** publisher and bookseller.

librairie [libʀeʀi] nf a (*magasin*) bookshop. ~ **d'art** art bookshop; **~-papeterie** bookseller's and stationer's; **ça ne se vend plus en** ~ it's no longer in the bookshops, the bookshops no longer sell it; **ce livre va bientôt paraître en** ~ this book will soon be on sale (in the shops) *ou* will soon be published *ou* out*. b **la** ~ (*activité*) bookselling (*NonC*); (*corporation*) the book trade.

libre [libʀ] 1 adj a (*gén, Pol: sans contrainte*) *personne, presse, commerce, prix* free; *vente* unrestricted. **médicament en vente** ~ medicine on open sale *ou* on unrestricted sale *ou* on sale without prescription, over-the-counter medicine; **il est difficile de garder l'esprit** *ou* **la tête** ~ **quand on a des ennuis** it's difficult to keep one's mind free of worries *ou* to keep a clear mind when one is in trouble; **être** ~ **comme l'air** to be as free as a bird; **être/rester** ~ (*non marié*) to be/remain unattached; **je ne suis pas** ~ I'm not free *ou* available; **il n'est plus** ~ **(de lui-même)** he is no longer a free agent; **être** ~ **de ses mouvements** to be free to do what one pleases; (*Jur*) **avoir la** ~ **disposition de ses biens** to have free disposal of one's goods; **un partisan de la** ~ **entreprise** *ou* **concurrence** a supporter of the free-market economy *ou* of free enterprise; (*Pol*) **le monde** ~ the free world.
b ~ **de** free from; ~ **de tout engagement/préjugé** free from any commitment/all prejudice; ~ **de faire** free to do; ~ **à vous de poser vos conditions** you are free to *ou* it's (entirely) up to you to state your conditions; **vous êtes parfaitement** ~ **de refuser l'invitation** you're quite free *ou* at liberty to refuse the invitation.
c (*non occupé*) *passage, voie* clear; *taxi* empty; *personne, place* free; *salle* free, available. **appartement** ~ **à la vente** flat for sale with vacant possession *ou* immediate entry; (*Téléc*) **la ligne n'est pas** ~ the line *ou* number is engaged (*Brit*) *ou* busy; (*Téléc*) **ça ne sonne pas** ~ the engaged tone (*Brit*) *ou* busy signal (*US*) is ringing, it's giving *ou* I'm getting the engaged tone (*Brit*) *ou* busy signal (*US*); **est-ce que cette place est** ~**?** is this seat free? *ou* empty? *ou* vacant?; **avoir du temps (de)** ~ to have some spare *ou* free time; **avoir des journées ~s** to have some free days; **êtes-vous** ~ **ce soir?** are you free this evening?; **vous ne pouvez pas voir M. X, il n'est pas** ~ **aujourd'hui** you can't see Mr X, he is not free *ou* available today; **le jeudi est son jour** ~ Thursday is his free day *ou* his day off; **je vais essayer de me rendre** ~ **pour demain** I'm going to try to make myself free tomorrow *ou* to keep tomorrow free; *voir* **air**[1]**, champ.**
d (*Scol: non étatisé*) *enseignement* private and Roman Catholic. **école** ~ private *ou* independent Roman Catholic school.
e (*autorisé, non payant*) *entrée, accès* free. **"entrée ~"** (*exposition etc*) "entrance free"; (*galerie d'artisanat, magasin d'exposition-vente etc*) "please walk round", "please come in and look around"; (*Univ*)

auditeur ~ non-registered student (*US*).

f (*lit, fig: non entravé*) *mouvement, respiration* free; *traduction, improvisation, adaptation* free; (*Tech*) *pignon, engrenage* disengaged. **robe qui laisse le cou ~** dress which leaves the neck bare *ou* which shows the neck; **robe qui laisse la taille ~** dress which is not tight-fitting round the waist *ou* which fits loosely at the waist; **avoir les cheveux ~s** to have one's hair loose; **de nos jours on laisse les jambes ~s aux bébés** nowadays we leave babies' legs free; **le sujet de la dissertation est ~** the subject of this essay is left open; *voir* **main, roue, vers**[2].

g (*sans retenue*) *personne* free *ou* open in one's behaviour; *plaisanteries* broad. **tenir des propos assez ~s sur la politique du gouvernement** to be fairly plain-spoken *ou* make fairly candid remarks about the policies of the government; **être très ~ avec qn** to be very free with sb; **donner ~ cours à sa colère/son indignation** to give free rein *ou* vent to one's anger/indignation.

2 **comp** ►**libre arbitre** free will ►**libre-échange nm** free trade ►**libre-échangiste (pl libre-échangistes) nm** free-trader ◊ **adj** free-market (*épith*), free-trade (*épith*) ►**libre entreprise** free enterprise ►**libre pensée** freethinking ►**libre penseur, -euse** freethinker ►**libre-service nm (pl libres-services)** (*restaurant*) self-service restaurant; (*magasin*) self-service store.

librement [libʀəmɑ̃] **adv** freely.

librettiste [libʀetist] **nmf** librettist.

libretto† [libʀeto], **pl ~s** *ou* **libretti** [libʀeti] **nm** libretto.

Libreville [libʀəvil] **n** Libreville.

Libye [libi] **nf** Libya.

libyen, -enne [libjɛ̃, ɛn] 1 **adj** Libyan. 2 **nm,f: L~(ne)** Libyan.

lice [lis] **nf** (*Hist*) lists (*pl*). (*fig*) **entrer en ~** to enter the lists; **les candidats encore en ~** candidates still in contention.

licence [lisɑ̃s] **nf** a (*Univ*) degree, ≃ bachelor's degree. **~ ès lettres** Arts degree, ≃ B.A.; **~ ès sciences** Science degree, ≃ B.Sc.; **faire une ~ d'anglais** to do a degree course in English.

b (*autorisation*) permit; (*Comm, Jur*) licence (*Brit*), license (*US*); (*Sport*) permit (*showing membership of a federation and giving the right of entry into competitions*). **produit sous ~** licensed product; **fabriqué sous ~ française** manufactured under French licence (*Brit*) *ou* license (*US*).

c (*littér: liberté*) **~ (des mœurs)** licentiousness (*NonC*); **prendre des ~s avec qn** to take liberties with sb; (*Littérat*) **~ poétique** poetic licence; **encor écrit au lieu de encore est une ~ orthographique!** writing encor instead of encore is an example of the liberties one can take with spelling.

licencié, e [lisɑ̃sje] 1 **adj: professeur ~** graduate teacher; **elle est ~e** she is a graduate (*Brit*) *ou* a college graduate. 2 **nm,f** a (*Univ*) **~ ès lettres/ès sciences/en droit** Bachelor of Arts/of Science/of Law, arts/science/law graduate. b (*Sport*) permit-holder. c (*Jur*) licensee.

licenciement [lisɑ̃simɑ̃] **nm** (*voir* **licencier**) making redundant (*Brit*), redundancy (*Brit*), lay-off; dismissal. **il y a eu des centaines de ~s** hundreds of people were made redundant (*Brit*) *ou* were laid off, there were hundreds of redundancies; **~ abusif** unfair dismissal; **~ collectif** mass redundancy *ou* redundancies (*Brit*) *ou* lay-offs*; **~ (pour raison) économique** lay-off, redundancy (*Brit*); **lettre de ~** letter of dismissal, pink slip (*US*).

licencier [lisɑ̃sje] 7 **vt** (*débaucher*) to make redundant (*Brit*), lay off*; (*renvoyer*) to dismiss.

licencieusement [lisɑ̃sjøzmɑ̃] **adv** licentiously.

licencieux, -ieuse [lisɑ̃sjø, jøz] **adj** (*littér*) licentious.

lichen [likɛn] **nm** (*Bot, Méd*) lichen.

licher* [liʃe] 1 **vt** (*boire*) to drink; (*lécher*) to lick.

lichette* [liʃɛt] **nf: ~ de pain/de fromage** nibble of bread/cheese; **tu en veux une ~?** do you want a nibble?; **il n'en restait qu'une ~** there was only a (tiny) taste left.

licite [lisit] **adj** lawful, licit.

licitement [lisitmɑ̃] **adv** lawfully, licitly.

licol† [likɔl] **nm** halter.

licorne [likɔʀn] **nf** unicorn. **~ de mer** narwhal, sea unicorn.

licou [liku] **nm** halter.

licteur [liktœʀ] **nm** lictor.

lie [li] 1 **nf** [*vin*] dregs, sediment. (*fig*) **la ~ (de la société)** the dregs of society; *voir* **boire**. 2 **comp** ►**lie de vin adj** wine(-coloured).

lié, e [lje] (**ptp de lier**) **adj: être très ~ avec qn** to be very friendly with sb; **ils sont très ~s** they're very close *ou* friendly, they're very close friends; (*Mus*) **note ~e** tied note; (*Ling*) **morphème ~** bound morpheme.

Liechtenstein [liʃtɛnʃtajn] **nm** Liechtenstein.

liechtensteinois, e [liʃtɛnʃtajnwa, waz] 1 **adj** of Liechtenstein. 2 **nm,f: L~(e)** inhabitant *ou* native of Liechtenstein.

lied [lid], **pl lieder** [lidœʀ] *ou* **lieds nm** Lied.

liège [ljɛʒ] **nm** cork. **semelle** *etc* **de ~** cork sole *etc*; *voir* **bout**.

liégeois, e [ljeʒwa, waz] 1 **adj** of *ou* from Liège. **café/chocolat ~** coffee/chocolate ice cream with crème Chantilly *ou* whipped cream. 2 **nm,f: L~(e)** inhabitant *ou* native of Liège.

lien [ljɛ̃] **nm** a (*lit, fig: attache*) bond. **le prisonnier se libéra de ses ~s** the prisoner freed himself from his bonds; **de solides ~s de cuir** strong leather straps; (*fig*) **les ~s du serment** the bonds of an oath; **un ~ très fort l'attache à son pays** he has a very strong bond with his home country.

b (*corrélation*) link, connection. **il y a un ~ entre les 2 événements** there's a link *ou* connection between the 2 events; **servir de ~ entre 2 personnes** to act as a link between 2 people; **idées sans ~** unconnected *ou* unrelated ideas.

c (*relation*) tie. **~s affectifs** emotional ties *ou* bonds; **~s de parenté/de sang** family/blood ties; **avoir un ~ de parenté avec qn** to be related to sb; **~s d'amitié** bonds of friendship; **~ qui unit 2 personnes** bond which unites 2 people; **~s du mariage** marriage bonds *ou* ties.

lier [lje] 7 1 **vt** a (*attacher*) *mains, pieds* to bind, tie up; *fleurs, bottes de paille* to tie up. **elle lui a lié les pieds et les mains** she bound him hand and foot; **~ la paille en bottes** to bind *ou* tie the straw into bales; **~ qn à un arbre/une chaise** to tie sb to a tree/chair; **~ avec une ficelle** to tie with a piece of string; *voir* **fou, partie**[2], **pied**.

b (*relier*) *mots, phrases* to link up, join up. **~ la cause à l'effet** to link cause to effect; **tous ces événements sont étroitement liés** all these events are closely linked *ou* connected; **cette maison est liée à tout un passé** this house has a whole history; **tout est lié** everything links up *ou* ties up; (*Mus*) **~ les notes** to slur the notes.

c (*unir*) *personnes* to bind, unite. **l'amitié qui nous lie à lui** the friendship which binds us to him; **l'amitié qui les lie** the friendship which unites them; **un goût/un mépris commun pour le théâtre les liait** they were united by a common liking/scorn for the theatre.

d [*contrat*] to bind. **~ qn par un serment/une promesse** to bind sb with an oath/a promise.

e (*Culin*) *sauce* to thicken. (*Constr*) **~ des pierres avec du mortier** to bind stones with mortar.

f (*loc*) **~ amitié/conversation** to strike up a friendship/conversation; **~ la langue à qn** to make sb tongue-tied.

2 **se lier vpr** to make friends (*avec qn* with sb). **se ~ d'amitié avec qn** to strike up a friendship with sb; **il ne se lie pas facilement** he doesn't make friends easily; **se ~ par un serment** to bind o.s. by an oath.

lierre [ljɛʀ] **nm** ivy. **~ terrestre** ground ivy.

liesse [ljɛs] **nf** (*littér: joie*) jubilation. **en ~** jubilant.

lieu[1], **pl ~x** [ljø] 1 **nm** a (*gén: endroit*) place; [*événement*] scene. (*Gram*) **adverbe de ~** adverb of place; **~ de pèlerinage/résidence/retraite/travail** place of pilgrimage/residence/retreat/work; **en quelque ~ qu'il soit** wherever he (may) be, wherever he is; **en tous ~x** everywhere; **en aucun ~ (du monde)** nowhere (in the world); **cela varie avec le ~** it varies from place to place; **en ~ sûr** in a safe place; *voir* **haut, nom**.

b **sur les ~x: se rendre sur les ~x du crime** to go to the scene of the crime; **être sur les ~x de l'accident** to be at *ou* on the scene of the accident; **notre envoyé est sur les ~x** our special correspondent is on the spot *ou* at the scene.

c (*locaux*) **les ~x** the premises; **quitter** *ou* **vider les ~x** (*gén*) to get out, leave; (*Admin*) to vacate the premises; *voir* **état**.

d (*avec notion temporelle*) **en premier/second ~** in the first/second place, firstly/secondly; **en dernier ~** lastly; **ce n'est pas le ~ d'en parler** this isn't the place to speak about it; **en son ~** in due course; *voir* **temps**[1].

e **au ~ de qch** instead of sth, in place of sth; **tu devrais téléphoner au ~ d'écrire** you should telephone instead of writing; **il devrait se réjouir, au ~ de cela, il se plaint** he should be glad, instead of which he complains *ou* (but) instead he complains; **signer en ~ et place de qn** to sign for and on behalf of sb; **au ~ que nous partions** instead of us leaving.

f (*loc*) **avoir ~** (*se produire*) to take place; **avoir ~ d'être inquiet/de se plaindre** to have (good) grounds for being worried/for complaining, have (good) reason to be worried/to complain; **il y a ~ d'être inquiet** there is cause *ou* good reason for anxiety; **vous appellerez le docteur, s'il y a ~** you must send for the doctor if necessary; **donner ~ à des critiques/désagréments** to give rise to criticism/trouble; **ça donne ~ de craindre le pire** that tends to make one fear *ou* leads one to fear the worst; **tenir ~ de** to take the place of; **elle lui a tenu ~ de mère** she took the place of his mother; **ce vieux manteau tient ~ de couverture** this old overcoat serves as a blanket *ou* does instead of a blanket.

2 **comp** ►**lieux d'aisances**† lavatory ►**lieu commun** commonplace ►**lieu de débauche** († *ou hum*) den of iniquity ►**lieu-dit, lieudit (pl lieux-dits, lieuxdits)** locality ►**lieu géométrique** (*Math*) locus ►**lieu de naissance** (*gén*) birthplace; (*Admin*) place of birth ►**lieu de passage** (*entre régions*) crossing point; (*entre villes*) stopping-off place; (*dans un bâtiment*) place where people are constantly coming and going ►**lieu de perdition** den of iniquity ►**lieu de promenade** place *ou* spot for walking ►**lieu public** public place ►**les Lieux saints** the Holy Places ►**lieu de vacances** (*gén*) place *ou* spot for (one's) holidays (*Brit*) *ou* vacation (*US*); (*ville*) holiday (*Brit*) *ou* vacation (*US*) resort.

lieu[2] [ljø] **nm** (*poisson*) **~ jaune** pollack, pollock; **~ noir** saithe, coley, coalfish.

lieue [ljø] **nf** league. **j'étais à mille ~s de penser à vous** I was far from thinking of you, you were far from my mind; **j'étais à mille ~s de penser qu'il viendrait** it never occurred to me *ou* I never dreamt for a moment that he'd come; **j'étais à cent ~s de supposer cela** that never occurred to me; **il sent son marin d'une ~** you can tell he's a sailor a mile off*, the fact that he's a sailor sticks out a mile; **à 20 ~s à la ronde** for 20 leagues round about.

lieuse [ljøz] **nf** (*Agr*) binder; *voir* **moissonneur.**

lieutenant [ljøt(ə)nɑ̃] 1 **nm** (*armée de terre*) lieutenant (*Brit*), first lieutenant (*US*); (*armée de l'air*) flying officer (*Brit*), first lieutenant (*US*); (*marine marchande*) mate; (*gén: second*) lieutenant, second in command. 2 **comp ▸lieutenant-colonel nm (pl lieutenants-colonels)** (*armée de terre*) lieutenant colonel; (*armée de l'air*) wing commander (*Brit*), lieutenant colonel (*US*) **▸lieutenant de vaisseau** (*marine nationale*) lieutenant.

lièvre [ljɛvʀ] **nm** (*Zool*) hare; (*Sport*) pacemaker. (*fig*) **courir** *ou* **chasser deux ~s à la fois** to try to keep two pots on the boil; (*fig*) **lever** *ou* **soulever un ~** to stumble (up)on sth important.

lift [lift] **nm** topspin.

lifter [lifte] [1] 1 **vt** to put topspin on. **balle liftée** ball with topspin; **elle a un jeu très lifté** she uses a lot of topspin. 2 **vi** to put topspin on the ball.

liftier [liftje] **nm** lift (*Brit*) *ou* elevator (*US*) attendant.

lifting [liftiŋ] **nm** (*lit, fig*) face lift. **se faire faire un ~** to have a face lift.

ligament [ligamɑ̃] **nm** ligament.

ligamenteux, -euse [ligamɑ̃tø, øz] **adj** ligamentous, ligamentary.

ligature [ligatyʀ] **nf** a (*Méd: opération, lien*) ligature. **~ des trompes** tying of the Fallopian tubes. b (*Agr*) (*opération*) tying up; (*lien*) tie. c (*Typ*) ligature. d (*Mus*) ligature, tie.

ligaturer [ligatyʀe] [1] **vt** (*Méd*) to ligature, tie up; (*Agr*) to tie up. (*Méd*) **se faire ~ les trompes** to have one's Fallopian tubes tied.

lige [liʒ] **adj** liege. **homme ~** (*Hist*) liegeman; (*fig*) **être l'homme ~ de qn** to be sb's faithful henchman.

light [lajt] **adj inv** light, diet (*épith*), low-calorie.

lignage [liɲaʒ] **nm** a lineage. **de haut ~** of noble lineage. b (*Typ*) number of printed lines.

ligne[1] [liɲ] 1 **nf** a (*trait, limite*) line; (*Mil*) line. **~ droite/brisée** straight/broken line; **~ discontinue** *ou* **pointillée** dotted line; **~ de départ/d'arrivée/de partage** starting/finishing/dividing line; (*Rugby*) **la ~ des 10/22 mètres** the 10/22 metre line; **~ de fortifications** line of fortifications; **~ de tranchées** trench line; **les ~s de la main** the lines of the hand; **~ de vie/de cœur** life/love line; **la ~ des collines dans le lointain** the line of hills in the distance; (*Math*) **la ~ des x/des y** the X/Y axis; (*Math*) **la ~ des abscisses** the abscissa; (*Math*) **la ~ des ordonnées** the ordinate axis; (*Mus*) **~ supplémentaire** ledger line; **passer la ~ (de l'équateur)** to cross the line; **courir en ~ droite** to run in a straight line; **en ~ droite, la ville est à 10 km** the town is 10 km from here as the crow flies; (*Aut*) **~ droite** stretch of straight road; (*lit, fig*) **la dernière ~ droite avant l'arrivée** the final *ou* home straight.

b (*contour*) *[meuble, voiture]* line(s); (*silhouette*) *[femme]* figure. **avoir la ~** to have a slim figure; **garder/perdre la ~** to keep/lose one's figure; **elle mange peu pour (garder) la ~** she doesn't eat much because she's watching her figure; **la ~ lancée par la dernière mode** the look launched by the most recent collections; **voiture aux ~s aérodynamiques** streamlined car, car built on aerodynamic lines.

c (*règle*) line. **~ de conduite/d'action** line of conduct/of action; **~ politique** political line; **la ~ du devoir** the path of duty; **la ~ du parti** the party line; **ne pas dévier de la ~ droite** to keep to the straight and narrow; **les grandes ~s d'un programme** the broad lines *ou* outline of a programme.

d (*suite de personnes, de choses, Mil*) line; (*rangée*) row; *[cocaïne]* line. (*Sport*) **la ~ d'avants** *ou* **des avants/d'arrières** *ou* **des arrières** (*Rugby*) the front/back row; (*Ftbl*) the forwards/backs; (*Rugby*) **la première/deuxième/troisième ~ (de mêlée)** the front/second/back row (of the scrum); **un premier ~** a man in the front row; **enfants placés en ~** children in a line *ou* lined up; **coureurs en ~ pour le départ** runners lined up for the start *ou* on the starting line; **une ~ d'arbres le long de l'horizon** a line *ou* row of trees on the horizon; **mettre des personnes en ~** to line people up, get people lined up; **se mettre en ~** to line up, get lined up, get into line; (*Mil*) **monter en ~** to go off to war *ou* to fight; (*Ordin*) **en ~** on line; (*Mil, fig*) **en première ~** on the front line.

e (*Rail*) line. (*Aut*) **~ d'autobus** (*service*) bus service; (*parcours*) bus route; (*Aviat, Naut*) **~ d'aviation** *ou* **aérienne/de navigation** (*compagnie*) air/shipping line; (*service*) (air/shipping) service; (*trajet*) (air/shipping) route; **~ de chemin de fer/de métro** railway/underground *ou* subway line; **la ~ d'autobus passe dans notre rue** the bus (route) goes along our street; **quelle ~ faut-il prendre?** which train (*ou* bus) should I take?; **il faut prendre la ~ (d'autobus) numéro 12 pour y aller** you have to take the number 12 bus to go there; **~ secondaire** branch line; **~ de banlieue** suburban line; *voir* **avion, grand, pilote.**

f (*Élec, Téléc*) (*gén*) line; (*câbles*) wires; (*TV: définition*) line. **la ~ est occupée** the line is engaged (*Brit*) *ou* busy (*US*); **être en ~** to be connected; **vous êtes en ~** you're connected *ou* through now, I am connecting you now; **je suis encore en ~** I'm still holding; **M. X est en ~** (*il est occupé*) Mr X's line is engaged (*Brit*) *ou* busy (*US*); (*il veut vous parler*) I have Mr X on the line for you; **la ~ passe dans notre jardin** the wires go through our garden.

g *[texte écrit]* line. (*dictée*) **"à la ~"** "new paragraph", "new line"; **aller à la ~** to start on the next line, begin a new paragraph; **écrire quelques ~s** to write a few lines; **donner 100 ~s à faire à un élève** to give a pupil 100 lines to do; (*Presse*) **tirer à la ~** to pad out an article; **je vous envoie ces quelques ~s** I'm sending you these few lines *ou* this short note; *voir* **lire.**

h (*Comm*) **~ de produits** (product) line.

i (*Pêche*) fishing line; *voir* **pêche**[2].

j (*série de générations*) **~ directe/collatérale** direct/collateral line; **descendre en ~ directe de ...** to be a direct descendant of ... .

k (*Fin*) **~ de crédit** credit line, line of credit.

l (*loc*) **mettre sur la même ~** to put on the same level; **entrer en ~ de compte** to be taken into account *ou* consideration; **mettre** *ou* **faire entrer en ~ de compte** to take into account *ou* consideration; **votre vie privée n'entre pas en ~ de compte** your private life doesn't come *ou* enter into it; **sur toute la ~** from start to finish.

2 **comp ▸ligne de ballon mort** (*Rugby*) dead-ball line **▸ligne blanche** (*Aut*) white line (*in the centre of the road*) **▸ligne blanche continue/discontinue** solid/broken *ou* dotted white line **▸ligne de but** goal line **▸lignes de côté** (*Tennis*) tramlines **▸ligne de crédit** (*Fin*) *voir* **1k ▸ligne de crête = ligne de faîte ▸ligne de démarcation** (*gén*) boundary; (*Mil*) line of demarcation, demarcation line **▸ligne directrice** (*Géom*) directrix; (*fig*) guiding line **▸ligne de faille** fault line **▸ligne de faîte** watershed **▸ligne de feu** line of fire **▸ligne de flottaison** water line **▸ligne de flottaison en charge** load line, Plimsoll line **▸ligne de fond** (*Pêche*) ledger line; (*Basketball*) end line; (*Tennis*) baseline **▸lignes de force** (*Phys*) lines of force; (*fig*) *[discours, politique]* main themes **▸ligne à haute tension** high-tension line **▸ligne d'horizon** skyline **▸ligne jaune** (*Aut*) **= ligne blanche ▸ligne médiane** (*Ftbl, Rugby etc*) halfway line; (*Tennis*) centre line **▸ligne de mire** line of sight **▸ligne de partage des eaux** watershed **▸ligne de service** (*Tennis*) service line **▸ligne de tir = ligne de feu ▸ligne de touche** (*Ftbl, Rugby etc*) touchline; (*Basket-ball*) boundary line **▸ligne de visée = ligne de mire.**

ligne[2] [liɲ] **nf** (*Can*) line (*3,175 mm*).

lignée [liɲe] **nf** (*postérité*) descendants (*pl*); (*race, famille*) line, lineage. **laisser une nombreuse ~** to leave a lot of descendants; **le dernier d'une longue ~** the last (one) of a long line; **de bonne ~ irlandaise** of good Irish stock *ou* lineage; (*fig*) **la ~ des grands romanciers** the tradition of the great novelists.

ligneux, -euse [liɲø, øz] **adj** woody, ligneous (*SPÉC*).

lignifier (se) [liɲifje] [7] **vpr** to lignify.

lignite [liɲit] **nm** lignite, brown coal.

ligoter [ligɔte] [1] **vt** *personne* to bind hand and foot. **~ à un arbre** to tie to a tree.

ligue [lig] **nf** league. **la L~ des droits de l'homme** the League of Human Rights.

liguer [lige] [1] 1 **vt** to unite (*contre* against). **être ligué avec** to be in league with. 2 **se liguer vpr** to league, form a league (*contre* against). **tout se ligue contre moi** everything is in league *ou* is conspiring against me.

ligueur, -euse [ligœʀ, øz] **nm,f** member of a league.

Ligurie [ligyʀi] **nf** Liguria.

lilas [lilɑ] **nm, adj inv** lilac.

lilliputien, -ienne [lilipysjɛ̃, jɛn] 1 **adj** Lilliputian. 2 **nm,f: L~(ne)** Lilliputian.

lillois, e [lilwa, waz] 1 **adj** of *ou* from Lille. 2 **nm,f: L~(e)** inhabitant *ou* native of Lille.

Lilongwe [lilɔ̃gwe] **n** Lilongwe.

Lima [lima] **n** Lima.

limace [limas] **nf** (*Zool*) slug; (*‡: chemise*) shirt. (*fig*) **quelle ~!** (*personne*) what a sluggard! *ou* slowcoach! (*Brit*); (*train etc*) this train is just crawling along!, what a dreadfully slow train!

limaçon [limasɔ̃] **nm** (*††*) snail; (*Anat*) cochlea.

limage [limaʒ] **nm** (*voir* **limer**) filing down; filing off.

limaille [limɑj] **nf** filings (*pl*). **~ de fer** iron filings.

limande [limɑ̃d] **nf** (*poisson*) dab. **~-sole** lemon sole; **fausse ~** flatfish; *voir* **plat**[1].

limbe [lɛ̃b] **nm** a (*Astron, Bot, Math*) limb. b (*Rel*) **les ~s** limbo; **dans les ~s** (*Rel*) in limbo; (*fig*) *[projet, science]* **c'est encore dans les ~s** it is still in the air.

lime [lim] **nf** a (*Tech*) file. **~ douce** smooth file; **~ à ongles** nail file (*Brit*), fingernail file (*US*). b (*Zool*) lima. c (*Bot*) (*fruit*) lime; (*arbre*) lime (tree).

limer [lime] [1] **vt** *ongles* to file; *métal* to file (down); *aspérité* to file off. **le prisonnier avait limé un barreau pour s'échapper** the prisoner had filed through a bar to escape.

limier [limje] **nm** (*Zool*) bloodhound; (*fig*) sleuth, detective. **c'est un fin ~** he's a really good sleuth.

liminaire [liminɛʀ] **adj** *discours, note* introductory.

limitable [limitabl] **adj** capable of being limited (*attrib*).

limitatif, -ive [limitatif, iv] **adj** restrictive. **liste ~ive/non ~ive** open/

closed list.

limitation [limitasjɔ̃] nf limitation, restriction. **~ des prix/des naissances** price/birth control; **un accord sur la ~ des armements** an agreement on arms limitation *ou* control; **sans ~ de temps** without a *ou* with no time limit; (*Aut*) **une ~ de vitesse (à 60 km/h)** a (60 km/h) speed limit; **l'introduction de ~s de vitesse** the introduction of speed restrictions *ou* limits.

limite [limit] 1 nf a *[pays, jardin]* boundary; *[pouvoir, période]* limit. **~ d'âge/de poids** age/weight limit; **~ des arbres** tree line; **~ des neiges** snow line; **sans ~** boundless, limitless; **homme qui connaît ses ~s** man who knows his limits; **ma patience a des ~s!** there's a limit to my patience!; **la bêtise a des ~s!** foolishness has its limits!; **sa joie ne connaissait pas de ~s** his joy knew no bounds; **sa colère ne connaît pas de ~s** his anger knows no limits; **ce crime atteint les ~s de l'horreur** this crime is too horrible to imagine; **il franchit *ou* dépasse les ~s!** he's going a bit too far!

b (*Math*) limit.

c (*loc*) **à la ~ on croirait qu'il le fait exprès** you'd almost think he is doing it on purpose; **à la ~, j'accepterais ces conditions, mais pas plus** if pushed *ou* if absolutely necessary, I'd accept those conditions, but no more; **à la ~ tout roman est réaliste** ultimately *ou* at a pinch you could say any novel is realistic; **dans une certaine ~** up to a point, to a certain extent *ou* degree; **dans les ~s du possible/du sujet** within the limits of what is possible/of the subject; **dans les ~s de mes moyens** (*aptitude*) within (the limits of) my capabilities; (*argent*) within my means; **jusqu'à la dernière ~** *rester, résister* to the bitter end, till the end; *se battre* to the death; **jusqu'à la ~ de ses forces** to the point of exhaustion, until his strength is (*ou* was *etc*) exhausted; (*Boxe*) **avant la ~** inside *ou* within the distance; (*Boxe*) **aller *ou* tenir jusqu'à la ~** to go the distance.

2 adj: **cas ~** borderline case; **prix ~** upper price limit; (*Bourse*) **cours ~** limit price; **valeur ~** limiting value; **vitesse/âge ~** maximum speed/age; **date ~** (*pour s'inscrire*) deadline, closing date; (*pour finir*) deadline; **hauteur/longueur/charge ~** maximum height/length/load; **elle a réussi son examen/à attraper la balle, mais c'était ~*** she passed her exam/managed to catch the ball – but only just; **ils ne se sont pas battus/injuriés, mais c'était ~*** they didn't come to blows/insult each other – but they very nearly did.

3 comp ▸**limite d'élasticité** elastic limit ▸**limite de rupture** breaking point.

limité, e [limite] (ptp de **limiter**) adj *durée, choix, portée* limited; *nombre* limited, restricted. **je n'ai qu'une confiance ~e en ce remède** I've got limited confidence in this cure; (*intellectuellement*) **il est un peu ~*** he's not very bright; **comme romancier, il est un peu ~** as a novelist, he's a bit limited; *voir* **société, tirage**.

limiter [limite] [1] 1 vt a (*restreindre*) *dépenses, pouvoirs, temps* to limit, restrict. **ils en étaient à s'arracher les cheveux quand je suis intervenu pour ~ les dégâts*** they were practically tearing each other's hair out when I intervened before things got even worse *ou* to stop things getting any worse; **ils ont dû liquider leur affaire pour ~ les dégâts** they had to sell up the business to cut *ou* minimize their losses; **l'équipe du Brésil menait par 5 à 0, heureusement on a réussi à ~ les dégâts en marquant 3 buts à la fin du match** the Brazilian team was leading by 5 to nil but fortunately we managed to limit the damage *ou* avert disaster by scoring 3 goals at the end of the match; **nous limiterons notre étude à quelques cas généraux** we'll limit *ou* restrict our study to a few general cases.

b (*délimiter*) *[frontière, montagnes]* to border. **les collines qui limitent l'horizon** the hills which bound the horizon.

2 **se limiter** vpr *[personne]* **se ~ (à qch/à faire)** to limit *ou* confine o.s. (to sth/to doing); **il faut savoir se ~** you have to know when to stop; *[chose]* **se ~ à** to be limited to.

limitrophe [limitʀɔf] adj *département, population* border (*épith*). **provinces ~s de la France** (*françaises*) border provinces of France; (*étrangères*) provinces bordering on France.

limogeage [limɔʒaʒ] nm dismissal.

limoger [limɔʒe] [3] vt (*destituer*) to dismiss, fire*.

limon [limɔ̃] nm a (*Géog*) alluvium; (*gén*) silt. b *[attelage]* shaft; (*Constr*) string-board.

limonade [limɔnad] nf a (*gazeuse*) (fizzy) lemonade (*Brit*), Seven-Up ® (*US*). b (†: *citronnade*) (home-made) lemonade *ou* lemon drink.

limonadier, -ière [limɔnadje, jɛʀ] nm,f a (*fabricant*) soft drinks manufacturer. b (*commerçant*) café owner.

limoneux, -euse [limɔnø, øz] adj silt-laden, muddy.

limousin, e[1] [limuzɛ̃, in] 1 adj of *ou* from Limousin. 2 nm a (*Ling*) Limousin dialect. b (*région*) Limousin. 3 nm,f: **L~(e)** inhabitant *ou* native of Limousin.

limousine[2] [limuzin] nf (*pèlerine*) cloak; (*voiture*) limousine.

limpide [lɛ̃pid] adj *eau, air, ciel, regard* limpid; *explication* lucid; *style* lucid, limpid; *affaire* clear, straightforward.

limpidité [lɛ̃pidite] nf *[eau, air, ciel]* clearness; *[regard]* limpidity; *[explication]* clarity, lucidity; *[style]* lucidity, limpidity; *[affaire]* clarity, straightforwardness.

lin [lɛ̃] nm (*plante, fibre*) flax; (*tissu*) linen; *voir* **huile, toile**.

linceul [lɛ̃sœl] nm (*lit, fig*) shroud.

linéaire [lineɛʀ] 1 adj linear. 2 nm (*Comm*) shelf space.

linéament [lineamɑ̃] nm (*littér, gén pl*) a (*ligne*) *[visage]* lineament, feature; *[forme]* line, outline. b (*ébauche*) outline.

linge [lɛ̃ʒ] 1 nm a **le ~, du ~** (*draps, serviettes*) linen; (*sous-vêtements*) underwear; **le gros ~** the household linen, the main items of linen; **le petit ~** the small *ou* light items for washing, the small items of linen. b (*lessive*) **le ~** the washing; **laver/tendre le *ou* son ~** to wash/hang out the *ou* one's washing; *voir* **laver**. c (*morceau de tissu*) cloth. **essuyer avec un ~** to wipe with a cloth; **blanc *ou* pâle comme un ~** as white as a sheet. 2 comp ▸**linges d'autel** (*Rel*) altar cloths ▸**linge de corps** body linen ▸**linge de maison** household linen ▸**linge de table** table linen ▸**linge de toilette** bathroom linen.

lingère [lɛ̃ʒɛʀ] nf (*personne*) linen maid; (*meuble*) linen cupboard.

lingerie [lɛ̃ʒʀi] nf a (*local*) linen room. b (*sous-vêtements féminins*) lingerie, (women's) underwear. **~ fine** fine lingerie; **rayon ~** lingerie department.

lingot [lɛ̃go] nm ingot. **~ d'or** gold ingot.

lingual, e, pl **-aux** [lɛ̃gwal, o] adj lingual.

lingue [lɛ̃g] nf (*poisson*) ling.

linguiste [lɛ̃gɥist] nmf linguist, specialist in linguistics.

linguistique [lɛ̃gɥistik] 1 nf linguistics (*sg*). 2 adj linguistic. **communauté ~** speech community.

linguistiquement [lɛ̃gɥistikmɑ̃] adv linguistically.

liniment [linimɑ̃] nm liniment.

lino [lino] nm (abrév de **linoléum**) lino.

linoléum [linɔleɔm] nm linoleum.

linon [linɔ̃] nm (*tissu*) lawn.

linotte [linɔt] nf linnet; *voir* **tête**.

Linotype [linɔtip] nf ® Linotype ®.

linteau, pl **~x** [lɛ̃to] nm lintel.

lion [ljɔ̃] nm (*Zool, fig*) lion. (*Astron*) **le L~** Leo, the Lion; **être (du) L~** to be (a) Leo; **~ de mer** sea lion; (*fig*) **tu as mangé *ou* bouffé* du ~!** YOU'RE lively!; *voir* **fosse, part**.

lionceau, pl **~x** [ljɔ̃so] nm lion cub.

lionne [ljɔn] nf lioness.

lipase [lipɑz] nf lipase.

lipide [lipid] nm lipid.

lipo-aspiration [lipoaspiʀasjɔ̃] nf liposuction.

liposome [lipozom] nm liposome.

lippe [lip] nf (*littér*) (fleshy) lower lip. **faire la ~** (*bouder*) to sulk; (*faire la moue*) to pout; (*faire la grimace*) to make *ou* pull a face.

lippu, e [lipy] adj thick-lipped.

liquéfaction [likefaksjɔ̃] nf liquefaction.

liquéfiable [likefjabl] adj liquefiable.

liquéfiant, e [likefjɑ̃, jɑ̃t] adj (*Chim*) liquefying; *atmosphère, chaleur* draining (*attrib*), exhausting.

liquéfier [likefje] [7] 1 vt (*Chim*) to liquefy; (*: *amollir*) to drain, exhaust. **je suis liquéfié*** I'm dead beat* *ou* dog-tired*. 2 **se liquéfier** vpr (*lit*) to liquefy; (*fig*) (*: *avoir peur*) to turn to jelly.

liquette* [likɛt] nf shirt.

liqueur [likœʀ] nf (*boisson*) liqueur; (††: *liquide*) liquid. (*Pharm*) **~ titrée/de Fehling** standard/Fehling's solution.

liquidateur, -trice [likidatœʀ, tʀis] nm,f (*Jur*) ≃ liquidator, receiver. **~ judiciaire *ou* de faillite** ≃ official liquidator; **placer une entreprise entre les mains d'un ~** to put a company into the hands of a receiver *ou* into receivership.

liquidatif, -ive [likidatif, iv] adj: **valeur ~ive** market price *ou* value.

liquidation [likidasjɔ̃] nf a (*règlement légal*) *[dettes, compte]* settlement, payment; *[société]* liquidation; *[biens, stock]* selling off, liquidation; *[succession]* settlement; (*fig*) *[problème]* elimination; (*fig*) *[compte]* settling. **~ judiciaire** compulsory liquidation; **mettre une compagnie en ~** to put a company into liquidation *ou* receivership, liquidate a company; **la ~ de vos impôts doit se faire avant la fin de l'année** your taxes must be paid before the end of the year; **afin de procéder à la ~ de votre retraite** in order to commence payment of your pension; *voir* **bilan**.

b (*vente*) selling (off), sale.

c (*: *meurtre*) liquidation, elimination.

d (*Bourse*) **~ de fin de mois** (monthly) settlement.

liquide [likid] 1 adj *corps, son* liquid. **sauce trop ~** sauce which is too runny *ou* too thin; **argent ~** cash. 2 nm a (*substance*) liquid. **~ de frein** brake fluid; **~ correcteur** correction fluid. b (*argent*) **du ~** cash; **je n'ai pas beaucoup de ~** I haven't much ready money *ou* ready cash; **payer *ou* régler en ~** to pay (in) cash. 3 nf (*Ling*) liquid.

liquider [likide] [1] vt a (*Jur: régler légalement*) *succession, dettes, compte* to settle, pay; *société* to liquidate; *biens, stock* to liquidate, sell off; (*fig*) *problème* to eliminate; (*fig*) *compte* to settle. b (*vendre*) to sell (off). c (*) (*tuer*) to liquidate, eliminate; (*se débarrasser de*) to get rid of; (*finir*) to finish off. **c'est liquidé maintenant** it is all finished *ou* over now.

liquidité [likidite] nf (*Chim, Jur*) liquidity. **~s** liquid assets.

liquoreux, -euse [likɔʀø, øz] adj *vin* syrupy, sweet and cloying.

lire[1] [liʀ] [43] vt a *roman, journal, partition, carte géographique* to read. **à**

5 ans, il ne lit pas encore *ou* **il ne sait pas encore** ~ he's 5 and he still can't read; ~ **sur les lèvres** to lip-read; ~ **ses notes avant un cours** to read over *ou* read through *ou* go over one's notes before a lecture; ~ **un discours/un rapport devant une assemblée** to read (out) a speech/a report at a meeting; **il l'a lu dans le journal** he read (about) it in the paper; **chaque soir, elle lit des histoires à ses enfants** every night she reads stories to her children; **à le ~, on croirait que ...** from what he writes *ou* from reading what he writes one would think that ...; (*erratum*) **là où il y a 634,** ~ *ou* **lisez 643** for 634 read 643; **ce roman se lit bien** *ou* **se laisse** ~ this novel is very readable; **ce roman se lit facilement/très vite** this novel makes easy/quick reading; **ce roman mérite d'être lu** *ou* **est à** ~ this novel is worth reading; **elle a continué à ~ malgré le bruit** she continued to read *ou* she went on reading despite the noise; (*fig*) ~ **entre les lignes** to read between the lines; *voir* **lu**.

b (*fig: deviner*) to read. ~ **dans le cœur de qn** to see into sb's heart; **la peur se lisait** *ou* **on lisait la peur sur son visage/dans ses yeux** you could see *ou* read fear in her face/eyes, fear showed on her face/in her eyes; ~ **l'avenir dans les lignes de la main de qn** to read the future in sb's hand; ~ **l'avenir dans le marc de café** ≃ to read (the future in) tea leaves; (*lit*) ~ **dans une boule de cristal** to read a crystal ball; (*fig*) **je ne lis pas dans les boules de cristal!** I don't have a crystal ball!; **elle m'a lu les lignes de la main** she read my hand; ~ **dans le jeu de qn** to see sb's (little) game, see what sb is up to.

c (*formule de lettre*) **nous espérons vous ~ bientôt** we hope to hear from you soon; **à bientôt de vous ~** hoping to hear from you soon.

d (*interpréter*) *statistiques, événement* to read, interpret.

lire[2] [liʀ] **nf** lira.

lis [lis] **nm** lily; *voir* **fleur.**

Lisbonne [lisbɔn] **n** Lisbon.

liseré [liz(ə)ʀe] **nm, liséré** [lizeʀe] **nm** (*bordure*) border, edging. **un ~ de ciel bleu** a strip of blue sky.

lisérer [lizeʀe] [6] **vt** to edge with ribbon.

liseron [lizʀɔ̃] **nm** bindweed, convolvulus.

liseur, -euse [lizœʀ, øz] 1 **nm,f** reader. 2 **liseuse nf** (*couvre-livre*) binder, folder, book-cover; (*vêtement*) bed jacket; (*lampe*) reading light; (*signet*) paper knife(-cum-bookmark).

lisibilité [lizibilite] **nf** (*voir* **lisible**) legibility; readability.

lisible [lizibl] **adj** *écriture* legible; *livre* (*facile*) which reads easily, readable; (*intéressant*) worth reading.

lisiblement [lizibləmɑ̃] **adv** legibly.

lisière [lizjɛʀ] **nf** (*Tex*) selvage; *[bois, village]* edge.

lissage [lisaʒ] **nm** smoothing.

lisse[1] [lis] **adj** *peau, surface* smooth; *cheveux* sleek, smooth.

lisse[2] [lis] **nf** (*Naut*) (*rambarde*) handrail; (*de la coque*) ribband.

lisser [lise] [1] **vt** *cheveux* to smooth (down); *moustache* to smooth, stroke; *papier, drap froissé* to smooth out; *vêtement* to smooth (out). **l'oiseau lisse ses plumes** *ou* **se lisse les plumes** the bird is preening itself *ou* its feathers; **fromage blanc lissé** creamy fromage blanc.

listage [listaʒ] **nm** (*action*) listing; (*liste*) list; (*Ordin*) print-out.

liste[1] [list] 1 **nf** list. **en tête/en fin de** ~ at the top *ou* head/at the bottom *ou* foot of the list; **faire la ~ de** to make out a list of, list; **s'il fallait faire la ~ de tous ses défauts!** if one had to list *ou* make out a list of all his faults!; **faites-moi la ~ des absents** make me out a list of those absent; ~ **nominative des élèves** class roll *ou* list; *voir* **scrutin.**

2 **comp ▸ liste d'attente** waiting list **▸ liste civile** civil list **▸ liste de contrôle = liste de vérification ▸ liste électorale** electoral roll **▸ liste d'envoi** mailing list **▸ liste de mariage** wedding list **▸ liste noire** blacklist; (*pour élimination*) hit list **▸ liste rouge: demander à être sur la liste rouge** (*Téléc*) (to ask) to go ex-directory (*Brit*) *ou* unlisted (*US*) **▸ liste de vérification** check list.

liste[2] [list] **nf** *[cheval]* list.

listel, pl ~s *ou* **-eaux** [listɛl, o] **nm** (*Archit*) listel, fillet; *[monnaie]* rim.

lister [liste] [1] **vt** to list.

listing [listiŋ] **nm = listage.**

lit [li] 1 **nm** a *[personne, rivière]* bed. ~ **d'une/de deux personne(s)** single/double bed; ~ **de fer/de bois** iron/wooden bedstead; ~ **d'hôpital/d'hôtel** hospital/hotel bed; **aller** *ou* **se mettre au** ~ to go to bed; **prendre le** ~ to take to one's bed; **être/lire au** ~ to be/read in bed; **faire le** ~ to make the bed; (*fig*) **faire le ~ de** (*renforcer*) to bolster; (*préparer le terrain pour*) to pave the way for; **faire ~ à part** to sleep in separate beds; **le ~ n'avait pas été défait** the bed had not been slept in, the bedclothes hadn't been disturbed; **au ~ les enfants!** bedtime *ou* off to bed children!; **arracher** *ou* **sortir** *ou* **tirer qn du** ~ to drag *ou* haul sb out of bed; (*littér,* †) **sur son ~ de misère** in childbed††; **les pluies ont fait sortir le fleuve de son** ~ the river has burst *ou* overflowed its banks because of the rains; *voir* **comme, jumeau, saut** *etc.*

b (*couche, épaisseur*) bed, layer. ~ **d'argile** bed *ou* layer of clay; ~ **de cendres** *ou* **de braises** bed of hot ashes; (*Culin*) ~ **de salade** bed of lettuce.

c (*Jur: mariage*) **enfants du premier/deuxième** ~ children of the first/second marriage; **enfants d'un autre** ~ children of a previous marriage.

2 **comp ▸ lit à baldaquin** canopied fourposter bed **▸ lit-cage nm (pl lits-cages)** (folding metal) cot **▸ lit de camp** campbed **▸ lit-clos nm (pl lits-clos)** box bed **▸ lit de coin** bed (standing) against the wall **▸ lit à colonnes** fourposter bed **▸ lit conjugal** marriage bed **▸ lit de douleur** bed of pain **▸ lit d'enfant** cot **▸ lit gigogne** pullout *ou* stowaway bed **▸ lits jumeaux** twin beds **▸ lit de milieu** bed (standing) away from the wall *ou* in the middle of a room **▸ lit de mort** deathbed **▸ lit nuptial** wedding-bed **▸ lit-pliant nm (pl lits-pliants)** folding bed **▸ lit en portefeuille** apple pie bed **▸ lit de repos** couch **▸ lit de sangle** trestle bed **▸ lits superposés** bunk beds **▸ le lit du vent** (*Naut*) the set of the wind.

litanie [litani] **nf** (*Rel, fig péj*) litany.

litchi [litʃi] **nm** litchi.

liteau [lito] **nm** (*pour toiture*) batten; (*pour tablette*) bracket; (*dans tissu*) stripe.

litée [lite] **nf** (*jeunes animaux*) litter.

literie [litʀi] **nf** bedding.

lithiase [litjɑz] **nf** lithiasis.

lithiné, e [litine] 1 **adj: eau ~e** lithia water. 2 **nmpl: ~s** lithium salts.

lithium [litjɔm] **nm** lithium.

litho [lito] **nf** (**abrév de lithographie**) litho.

lithographe [litɔgʀaf] **nmf** lithographer.

lithographie [litɔgʀafi] **nf** (*technique*) lithography; (*image*) lithograph.

lithographier [litɔgʀafje] [7] **vt** to lithograph.

lithographique [litɔgʀafik] **adj** lithographic.

lithosphère [litɔsfɛʀ] **nf** lithosphere.

lithotritie [litɔtʀisi] **nf** lithotrity.

litière [litjɛʀ] **nf** (*couche de paille*) litter (*NonC*); (*Hist: palanquin*) litter. **il s'était fait une ~ avec de la paille** he had made himself a bed of sorts in some straw; ~ **pour chats** cat litter (*Brit*), Kitty Litter ® (*US*).

litige [litiʒ] **nm** (*gén*) dispute; (*Jur*) lawsuit. **être en** ~ (*gén*) to be in dispute; (*Jur*) to be at law *ou* in litigation; (*Jur*) **les parties en** ~ the litigants, the disputants (*US*); **point/objet de** ~ point/object of contention.

litigieux, -ieuse [litiʒjø, jøz] **adj** litigious, contentious.

litorne [litɔʀn] **nf** fieldfare.

litote [litɔt] **nf** (*Littérat*) litotes, understatement. (*hum*) **quand je dis pas très belle, c'est une** ~ when I say it's not very beautiful, I'm not exaggerating *ou* that's putting it mildly *ou* that's an understatement.

litre [litʀ] **nm** (*mesure*) litre; (*récipient*) litre bottle.

litron‡ [litʀɔ̃] **nm: ~ (de vin)** litre of wine.

littéraire [liteʀɛʀ] 1 **adj** (*gén*) literary; *personne, esprit* with a literary bent; *souffrance, passion* affected. 2 **nmf** (*par don, goût*) literary *ou* arts person; (*étudiant*) arts student; (*enseignant*) arts teacher, teacher of arts subjects.

littérairement [liteʀɛʀmɑ̃] **adv** in literary terms.

littéral, e, mpl -aux [liteʀal, o] **adj** (*littér, Math*) literal. **arabe ~** written Arabic.

littéralement [liteʀalmɑ̃] **adv** (*lit, fig*) literally.

littérateur [liteʀatœʀ] **nm** (*péj: écrivain*) literary hack.

littérature [liteʀatyʀ] **nf** a **la** ~ (*art*) literature; (*profession*) writing; **faire de la** ~ to go in for writing, write; (*péj*) **tout cela, c'est de la** ~ it's of trifling importance; **écrire de la ~ alimentaire** to write potboilers; ~ **de colportage** chapbooks. b (*manuel*) history of literature; (*ensemble d'ouvrages*) literature; (*bibliographie*) literature. **il existe une abondante ~ sur ce sujet** there's a wealth of literature *ou* material on this subject.

littoral, e, mpl -aux [litɔʀal, o] 1 **adj** coastal, littoral (*SPÉC*); *voir* **cordon.** 2 **nm** coast, littoral (*SPÉC*).

Lituanie [litɥani] **nf** Lithuania.

lituanien, -ienne [litɥanjɛ̃, jɛn] 1 **adj** Lithuanian. 2 **nm** (*Ling*) Lithuanian. 3 **nm,f: L~(ne)** Lithuanian.

liturgie [lityʀʒi] **nf** liturgy.

liturgique [lityʀʒik] **adj** liturgical.

livarde [livaʀd] **nf** sprit.

livide [livid] **adj** (*pâle*) pallid; (*littér: bleuâtre*) livid.

lividité [lividite] **nf** lividness.

living [liviŋ] **nm, living-room, pl living-rooms** [liviŋʀum] **nm** (*pièce*) living room; (*meuble*) living room unit.

Livourne [livuʀn] **n** Leghorn, Livorno.

livrable [livʀabl] **adj** which can be delivered. **cet article est ~ dans les 10 jours/à domicile** this article will be delivered within 10 days/can be delivered to your home.

livraison [livʀɛzɔ̃] **nf** a *[marchandise]* delivery. (*avis*) "**~ à domicile**" "we deliver", "deliveries carried out"; **payable à la** ~ payable on delivery; **la ~ à domicile est comprise dans le prix** the price includes (the cost of) delivery; **faire une** ~ to make a delivery; **faire la ~ de qch** to deliver sth; **prendre ~ de qch** to take delivery of sth. b *[revue]* part, number, issue, fascicule.

livre[1] [livʀ] 1 **nm** a (*ouvrage*) book. (*commerce*) **le** ~ the book trade (*Brit*), the book industry; ~ **de géographie** geography book; (*Scol*) ~ **du maître/de l'élève** teacher's/pupil's text book; **il a toujours le nez dans les ~s, il vit dans les ~s** he's always got his nose in a book; **je ne connais l'Australie que par les ~s** I only know Australia through *ou* from books; **écrire/faire un ~ sur** to write/do a book on; **traduire l'anglais à ~**

ouvert to translate English off the cuff *ou* at sight; *voir* **grand, parler.**

b (*partie: volume*) book. **le ~ 2** *ou* **le second ~ de la Genèse** book 2 of Genesis, the second book of Genesis.

2 **comp** ▸**livre blanc** official report (*published by independent organization, following war, famine etc*) ▸**livre de bord** (*Naut*) log-book ▸**livre de caisse** (*Comm*) cashbook ▸**livre-cassette nm** (**pl livres-cassettes**) talking book ▸**livre de chevet** bedside book ▸**livre de classe** schoolbook ▸**livres de commerce** (*Comm*) the books ▸**livre de comptes** account(s) book ▸**livre de cuisine** cookery book (*Brit*), cookbook ▸**livre d'enfant** children's book ▸**livre d'heures** book of hours ▸**livre d'images** picture book ▸**livre-jeu nm** (**pl livres-jeux**) book-game ▸**livre journal** (*Comm*) daybook ▸**livre de lecture** reader, reading book ▸**livre de messe** mass book, missal, prayer book ▸**livre d'or** visitors' book ▸**livre de poche** paperback ▸**livre de prières** prayer book ▸**livre scolaire** schoolbook, textbook ▸**livre à succès** bestseller.

livre[2] [livʀ] **nf** a (*poids*) ≃ pound, half a kilo; (*Can*) pound (*0,453 kg*). b (*monnaie*) pound; (*Hist française*) livre. **~ sterling** pound sterling; **~ égyptienne** Egyptian pound; **ce chapeau coûte 6 ~s** this hat costs £6.

livrée [livʀe] **nf** a (*uniforme*) livery. **en ~** in livery (*attrib*), liveried. b *[animal, oiseau]* markings *pl*.

livrer [livʀe] [1] 1 **vt** a (*Comm*) *commande, marchandises* to deliver. **~ un paquet à domicile** to deliver a packet to the home.

b (*abandonner*) (*à la police, à l'ennemi*) to hand over (*à* to). **~ qn à la mort** to send sb to his death; **~ qn au bourreau** to deliver sb up *ou* hand sb over to the executioner; **ce pays a été livré au pillage/à l'anarchie** this country was given over to pillage/to anarchy; **~ son âme au diable** to give one's soul to the devil; **être livré à soi-même** to be left to o.s. *ou* to one's own devices.

c (*confier*) **~ les secrets de son cœur** to give away the secrets of one's heart; **il m'a livré un peu de lui-même** he revealed a bit of himself to me.

d (*loc*) **~ bataille** to do *ou* join battle (*à* with); **~ passage à qn** to let sb pass.

2 **se livrer vpr** a (*se laisser aller à*) **se ~ à** *destin* to abandon o.s. to; *plaisir, excès, douleur* to give o.s. over to; **se ~ à des pratiques répréhensibles** to indulge in undesirable practices; **se ~ à la police** to give o.s. up to the police; **elle s'est livrée à son amant** she gave herself to her lover; **se ~ à un ami** to bare one's heart to a friend; **il ne se livre pas facilement** he doesn't unburden himself easily *ou* open up easily.

b (*se consacrer à*) **se ~ à** *sport* to practise; *occupation* to be engaged in; *recherches* to do, engage in; *enquête* to hold, set up; **se ~ à l'étude** to study, devote o.s. to study.

livresque [livʀɛsk] **adj** (*gén péj*) bookish.

livret [livʀɛ] 1 **nm** a (*Mus*) libretto. b (†: *petit livre*) booklet; (*catalogue*) catalogue. **~ d'épargne populaire** (*carnet*) ≃ National Savings Bank passbook (*Brit*); (*compte*) ≃ National Savings Bank account (*Brit*); **~ de caisse d'épargne** (*carnet*) (savings) bankbook; (*compte*) savings account; **~ de famille** (official) family record book (*containing registration of births and deaths in a family*); **~ militaire** military record; **~ scolaire** (school) report book, (school) report. 2 **comp** ▸**livret matricule** (*Mil*) army file.

livreur [livʀœʀ] **nm** delivery man (*ou* boy).

livreuse [livʀøz] **nf** delivery girl (*ou* woman).

lob [lɔb] **nm** (*Tennis*) lob. **faire un ~** to hit a lob.

lobby, pl lobbies [lɔbi] **nm** lobby.

lobbying [lɔbiiŋ] **nm, lobbyisme** [lɔbiism] **nm** lobbying.

lobbyiste [lɔbiist] **nmf** lobbyist.

lobe [lɔb] **nm** a (*Anat, Bot*) lobe. **~ de l'oreille** ear lobe. b (*Archit*) foil.

lobé, e [lɔbe] 1 **ptp de lober.** 2 **adj** (*Bot*) lobed; (*Archit*) foiled.

lobectomie [lɔbɛktɔmi] **nf** lobectomy.

lobélie [lɔbeli] **nf** lobelia.

lober [lɔbe] [1] 1 **vi** (*Tennis*) to lob. 2 **vt** (*Ftbl, Tennis*) to lob (over).

lobotomie [lɔbɔtɔmi] **nf** lobotomy.

lobule [lɔbyl] **nm** lobule.

local, e, mpl -aux [lɔkal, o] 1 **adj** local. **éclaircies ~es** bright spells in places; **averses ~es** scattered *ou* local showers, rain in places; **anesthésie ~e** local anaesthetic; *voir* **couleur, impôt.**

2 **nm** a (*salle*) premises. **~ à usage commercial** shop *ou* commercial premises; **~ d'habitation** domestic premises, private (dwelling) house; **le club cherche un ~** the club is looking for premises, the club is looking for a place in which to meet; **il a un ~ au fond de la cour qui lui sert d'atelier** he has got a place *ou* room at the far end of the yard which he uses as a workshop.

b (*bureaux*) **~aux** offices, premises; **dans les ~aux de la police** on police premises; **les ~aux de la compagnie sont au deuxième étage** the company's offices *ou* premises are on the second floor.

localement [lɔkalmɑ̃] **adv** (*ici*) locally; (*par endroits*) in places.

localisable [lɔkalizabl] **adj** localizable.

localisation [lɔkalizasjɔ̃] **nf** localization. **~s graisseuses** fatty patches *ou* areas.

localiser [lɔkalize] [1] **vt** a (*circonscrire*) (*gén*) to localize; *épidémie, incendie* to confine. **l'épidémie s'est localisée dans cette région** the epidemic was confined to this district; **conflit localisé** localized conflict; **douleur localisée** localized pain. b (*repérer*) to locate.

localité [lɔkalite] **nf** (*ville*) town; (*village*) village.

locataire [lɔkatɛʀ] **nmf** (*gen*) tenant; (*habitant avec le propriétaire*) lodger, roomer (*US*). **les ~s de mon terrain** the people who rent land from me, the tenants of my land; **avoir/prendre des ~s** to have/take in tenants; **~ principal** leaseholder (*who sublets a property to somebody else*).

locatif, -ive [lɔkatif, iv] 1 **adj** a **local à usage ~** premises for letting (*Brit*) *ou* renting (*US*); **risques ~s** tenant's risks; **réparations ~ives** repairs incumbent upon the tenant; **valeur ~ive** rental value; *voir* **charges.** b (*Gram*) **préposition ~ive** preposition of place. 2 **nm** (*Gram*) locative (case).

location [lɔkasjɔ̃] 1 **nf** a (*par le locataire*) *[maison, terrain]* renting; *[voiture]* hiring (*Brit*), renting (*US*). **prendre en ~** *maison* to rent; *bateau* to hire (*Brit*), rent (*US*); **c'est pour un achat ou pour une ~?** is it to buy or to rent?

b (*par le propriétaire*) *[maison, terrain]* renting (out), letting (*Brit*); *[voiture]* hiring (out) (*Brit*), renting (*US*). **donner en ~** *maison* to rent out, let (*Brit*); *véhicule* to hire out (*Brit*), rent (*US*); **~ de voitures** (*écriteau*) "cars for hire", "car-hire" (*Brit*), "car rental" (*US*); (*métier*) car rental, car hiring (*Brit*); **"~ de voitures sans chauffeur"** "self-drive car hire (*Brit*) *ou* rental" (*US*); **c'est pour une vente ou pour une ~?** is it to sell or to let? (*Brit*) *ou* to rent? (*US*).

c (*bail*) lease. **contrat de ~** lease.

d (*maison*) **il a 3 ~s dans la région** he has got 3 properties (for letting) in the nearby region; **il a pris une ~ pour un mois au bord de la mer** he has taken *ou* rented a house by the sea for a month; **habiter en ~** to live in rented accommodation.

e (*réservation*) **bureau de ~** (advance) booking office; (*Théât*) box office, booking office.

f **~ d'utérus** womb-leasing.

2 **comp** ▸**location-gérance nf** (**pl locations-gérances**): **être en location-gérance** to be run by a manager ▸**location avec option d'achat** leasing, lease-option agreement ▸**location saisonnière** holiday let (*Brit*), vacation rental (*US*), summer rental (*US*) ▸**location-vente nf** (**pl locations-ventes**) hire purchase (*Brit*), installment plan (*US*); **acheter un appartement en location-vente** to buy a flat on instalments.

loch [lɔk] **nm** (*Naut*) log; (*lac*) loch.

loche [lɔʃ] **nf** a (*poisson*) **~ (de rivière)** loach; **~ de mer** rockling. b (*limace*) grey slug.

loci [lɔki] **nmpl de locus.**

lock-out [lɔkaut] **nm inv** lockout.

lock-outer [lɔkaute] [1] **vt** to lock out.

loco* [lɔko] **nf abrév de locomotive.**

locomoteur, -trice[1] [lɔkɔmɔtœʀ, tʀis] **adj** locomotive. **ataxie ~trice** locomotor ataxia.

locomotion [lɔkɔmosjɔ̃] **nf** locomotion; *voir* **moyen.**

locomotive [lɔkɔmɔtiv] **nf** (*Rail*) locomotive, engine; (*fig*) (*personnalité mondaine*) pace-setter; (*leader, groupe ou région de pointe*) dynamo, pacemaker, powerhouse; (*coureur*) pacer. (*Rail*) **~ haut le pied** light engine (*Brit*), wildcat (*US*).

locomotrice[2] [lɔkɔmɔtʀis] **nf** motive *ou* motor unit.

locus [lɔkys] **nm, pl ~** *ou* **loci** (*Bio*) locus.

locuste [lɔkyst] **nf** locust.

locuteur, -trice [lɔkytœʀ, tʀis] **nm,f** (*Ling*) speaker. **~ natif** native speaker.

locution [lɔkysjɔ̃] **nf** phrase, locution, idiom. **~ figée** set phrase; **~ verbale/adverbiale** verbal/adverbial phrase.

loden [lɔdɛn] **nm** (*tissu*) loden; (*manteau*) loden coat.

lœss [løs] **nm** loess.

lof [lɔf] **nm** (*Naut*) windward side. **aller** *ou* **venir au ~** to luff; **virer ~ pour ~** to wear (ship).

lofer [lɔfe] [1] **vi** (*Naut*) to luff.

loft [lɔft] **nm** warehouse (*ou* studio *etc*) conversion, loft (*US*).

log [lɔg] **nm** (**abrév de logarithme**) log.

logarithme [lɔgaʀitm] **nm** logarithm.

logarithmique [lɔgaʀitmik] **adj** logarithmic.

loge [lɔʒ] **nf** a *[concierge, francs-maçons]* lodge; (†) *[bûcheron]* hut. b (*Théât*) *[artiste]* dressing room; (*spectateur*) box. **secondes ~s** boxes in the upper circle; **premières ~s** boxes in the grand (*Brit*) *ou* dress circle; (*fig*) **être aux premières ~s** to have a ringside seat (*fig*). c (*Scol: salle de préparation*) (individual) exam room (*for Prix de Rome*). d (*Archit*) loggia.

logé, e [lɔʒe] (**ptp de loger**) **adj**: **être ~ rue X** to live in X street; **être ~, nourri, blanchi** to have board and lodging and one's laundry done; **être bien/mal ~** (*appartement etc*) to have good *ou* comfortable/poor lodgings *ou* accommodation; (*maison*) to be well *ou* comfortably/badly housed; (*fig*) **être ~ à la même enseigne** to be in the same boat (*fig*).

logeable [lɔʒabl] **adj** (*habitable*) habitable, fit to live in (*attrib*); (*spacieux, bien conçu*) roomy.

logement [lɔʒmɑ̃] **nm** a (*hébergement*) housing. **le ~ était un gros problème en 1950** housing was a great problem in 1950; **trouver un ~**

provisoire chez des amis to find temporary accommodation *ou* lodging with friends.

b (*appartement*) flat (*Brit*), apartment (*US*), accommodation (*NonC*), lodgings. **construire des ~s ouvriers** to build flats (*Brit*) *ou* apartments (*US*) *ou* accommodation for workers; **~ de fonction** free (*ou* subsidized) accommodation (*NonC*); **avoir un ~ de fonction** to have free (*ou* subsidized) accommodation with one's job; **~s sociaux** ≃ council houses (*ou* flats) (*Brit*), local authority housing (*NonC*) (*Brit*), housing project (*US*); **il a réussi à trouver un ~** he managed to find lodgings.

c (*Mil*) *[troupes]* (*à la caserne*) quartering; (*chez l'habitant*) billeting. **~s** (*à la caserne*) quarters; (*chez l'habitant*) billet.

d (*Tech*) housing, case.

loger [lɔʒe] 3 **1 vi a** *[personne]* to live (*dans* in; *chez* with, at). **~ à l'hôtel/rue X** to live in a hotel/in X street; (*Mil*) **~ chez l'habitant** to be billeted on the local inhabitants.

b *[meuble, objet]* to belong, go.

2 vt a *amis* to put up; *clients, élèves* to accommodate; *objet* to put; *soldats* (*chez l'habitant*) to billet. **~ les malles dans le grenier** to put *ou* store the trunks in the loft.

b (*contenir*) to accommodate. **hôtel qui peut ~ 500 personnes** hotel which can accommodate *ou* take (in) 500 people; **salle qui loge beaucoup de monde** room which can hold *ou* accommodate a lot of people.

c (*envoyer*) **~ une balle/une bille dans** to lodge a bullet/a marble in; **il s'est logé une balle dans la tête** he shot himself in the head, he put a bullet through his head.

3 se loger vpr **a** (*habiter*) *[jeunes mariés]* to find a house (*ou* flat *etc*), find somewhere to live; *[touristes]* to find accommodation; *[étudiant, saisonnier]* to find lodgings *ou* accommodation. **il n'a pas trouvé à se ~** he hasn't found anywhere to live *ou* any accommodation; **il a trouvé à se ~ chez un ami** he found accommodation with a friend, he was put up by a friend; **il a trouvé à se ~ dans un vieil immeuble** he found lodgings *ou* accommodation in an old block of flats; (*fig*) **la haine se logea dans son cœur** hatred filled his heart.

b (*tenir*) **crois-tu qu'on va tous pouvoir se ~ dans la voiture?** do you think that we'll all be able to fit into the car?

c (*se ficher ou coincer dans*) *[balle, ballon]* **se ~ dans/entre** to lodge itself in/between; **le ballon alla se ~ entre les barreaux de la fenêtre** the ball went and lodged itself *ou* got stuck between the bars of the window; **le chat est allé se ~ sur l'armoire** the cat sought refuge on top of the cupboard; *[objet tombé]* **où est-il allé se ~?** where has it gone and hidden itself?, where has it got to?

logeur [lɔʒœʀ] nm landlord (*who lets furnished rooms*).

logeuse [lɔʒøz] nf landlady.

loggia [lɔdʒja] nf loggia.

logiciel [lɔʒisjɛl] nm software (*NonC*), application program *ou* package. **acheter un ~** to buy software *ou* an application program; **~ intégré** integrated software.

logicien, -ienne [lɔʒisjɛ̃, jɛn] nm,f logician.

logique [lɔʒik] **1 nf a** (*rationalité*) logic. **cela manque un peu de ~** that's not very logical; **cela est dans la ~ des choses** it's in the nature of things. **b** (*façon de raisonner*) logic. **~ déductive** deductive reasoning. **c** (*science*) **la ~** logic. **2 adj** logical. **sois ~ avec toi-même** don't contradict yourself; *voir* **analyse. 3 comp ►logique formelle** formal logic **►logique moderne** (*Math*) modern logic **►logique pure** = **logique formelle.**

logiquement [lɔʒikmɑ̃] adv logically.

logis [lɔʒi] nm (*littér*) dwelling, abode (*littér*). **rentrer au ~** to return to one's abode (*littér*); **quitter le ~ paternel** to leave the paternal home; *voir* **corps, fée, fou, maréchal.**

logisticien, -ienne [lɔʒistisjɛ̃, jɛn] nm,f logistician.

logistique [lɔʒistik] **1 adj** logistic. **2 nf** logistics (*sg*).

logithèque [lɔʒitɛk] nf software library.

logo [lɔgo] nm logo.

logomachie [lɔgɔmaʃi] nf (*verbiage*) overweening verbosity.

logomachique [lɔgɔmaʃik] adj verbose.

logorrhée [lɔgɔʀe] nf logorrhoea (*Brit*), logorrhea (*US*).

logotype [lɔgɔtip] nm = **logo.**

loi [lwa] **1 nf a la ~** the law; **la ~ du plus fort** the law of the strongest; **c'est la ~ de la jungle** it's the law of the jungle; **la ~ naturelle** *ou* **de la nature** natural law; (*frm*) **subir la ~ de qn** to be ruled by sb; (*frm*) **se faire une ~ de faire** to make a point *ou* rule of doing, make it a rule to do; **avoir la ~ pour soi** to have the law on one's side; **il n'a pas la ~ chez lui!*** he's not the boss in his own house!*; **tu ne feras pas la ~ ici!*** you're not going to lay down the law here!; **ce qu'il dit fait ~** his word is law, what he says goes*; (*fig*) **c'est la ~ et les prophètes** it's taken as gospel; *[activité, acte]* **tomber sous le coup de la ~** to be an offence *ou* a criminal offence; *voir* **force, nom** *etc.*

b (*décret*) law, act. **voter une ~** to pass a law *ou* an act; **les ~s de la République** the laws of the Republic.

c (*vérité d'expérience*) law. **la ~ de la chute des corps** the law of gravity; **la ~ de Faraday** Faraday's law.

d (*fig: code humain*) **les ~s de la mode** the dictates of fashion; **les ~s de l'honneur** the code of honour; **les ~s de l'hospitalité** the laws of hospitality; **la ~ du milieu** the law of the underworld; **la ~ du silence** the law of silence; **les ~s de l'étiquette** the rules of etiquette; (*Comm*) **la ~ de l'offre et de la demande** the law of supply and demand.

2 comp ►loi-cadre nf (pl **lois-cadres**) outline *ou* blueprint law **►loi d'engagement** = **loi-programme ►loi de finances** finance law **►loi informatique et liberté** ≃ data protection act (*Brit*) **►loi martiale** martial law **►loi d'orientation** *the law governing higher education* **►loi-programme** nf (pl **lois-programmes**) *act providing framework for government programme (financial, social etc)* **►loi salique** salic law **►loi du talion** (*Hist*) lex talionis; (*fig*) **appliquer la loi du talion** to demand an eye for an eye.

loin [lwɛ̃] adv **a** (*distance*) far, a long way. **est-ce ~?** is it far?; **ce n'est pas très ~** it's not very far; **c'est assez ~ d'ici** it's quite a long way from here; **plus ~** further, farther; **moins ~** not so far; **la gare n'est pas ~ du tout** the station is no distance at all *ou* isn't far at all; **vous nous gênez, mettez-vous plus ~** you're in our way, go further away *ou* move away; **il est ~ derrière/devant** he's a long way behind/in front, he's far behind/ahead; **aussi ~ que vous alliez, vous ne trouverez pas d'aussi beaux jardins** however far you go *ou* wherever you go, you won't find such lovely gardens; **au ~** in the distance, far off; **partir au ~** to leave for distant parts *ou* places; **de ~** from a distance; **de très ~** from a great distance, from afar (*littér*); **il voit mal de ~** he can't see distant objects very easily; **d'aussi ~** *ou* **de plus ~ qu'elle le vit, elle courut vers lui** seeing him from afar *ou* seeing him a long way off *ou* seeing him a long way in the distance she ran towards him; **de ~ en ~ brillaient quelques lumières** a few lights shone at distant intervals *ou* here and there; **nous n'avons pas ~ à aller** we don't have far to go, we have no distance to go; **il ne doit pas y avoir ~ de 5 km d'ici à la gare** there can't be much less than 5-km *ou* it can't be far off 5 km *ou* far short of 5 km from here to the station; *voir* **aller, pousser.**

b (*temps*) **le temps est ~ où cette banlieue était un village** it's a long time since this suburb was a village; **c'est ~ tout cela!, comme c'est ~!** (*passé*) that was a long time ago!, what a long time ago that was!; (*futur*) that's a long way in the future!, that's (still) a long way off!; **l'été n'est plus ~ maintenant** summer's not far off now, summer's just around the corner; **Noël est encore ~** Christmas is still a long way off; **en remontant plus ~ encore dans le passé** (by) looking even further back into the past; **~ dans le passé** in the remote past, in far-off times, a long time ago; **voir** *ou* **prévoir ~** to see a long way *ou* far ahead, see far *ou* a long way into the future; **d'aussi ~ que je me rappelle** for as long as I can remember; **en remontant ~ dans le temps** if you go back a long way in time; **de ~ en ~** every now and then, every now and again, at scattered intervals; **il n'est pas ~ de 10 heures** it's not far off 10 o'clock, it's getting on for 10 o'clock; **il n'y a pas ~ de 5 ans qu'ils sont partis** it's not far off 5 years since they left.

c (*fig*) far. **il faudrait aller** *ou* **chercher (très) ~ pour trouver un si bon secrétaire** you'd have to look far and wide *ou* far afield to find such a good secretary; **j'irais même plus ~** I would go even further; **une histoire** *ou* **une affaire qui peut mener (très) ~** a matter that could lead us (*ou* them *etc*) a long way *ou* which could have unforeseen repercussions; **il est de (très) ~ le meilleur** he is by far the best, he is far and away the best; **le directeur voit ces problèmes pratiques de très ~** the manager sees these practical problems from a great distance *ou* from afar; **suivre de ~ les événements** to follow events from a distance; **d'ici à l'accuser de vol il n'y a pas ~** it's tantamount to an accusation of theft, it's practically an accusation of theft; **il leur doit pas ~ de 1 000 F** he owes them little short of *ou* not far off 1,000 francs.

d **~ de** far from, a long way from, far away from; **~ de là** (*lieu*) far from there; (*fig*) far from it; **non ~ de là** not far from there; **il n'est pas ~ de minuit** it isn't far off *ou* far from midnight; **leur maison est ~ de toute civilisation** their house is far *ou* remote from all civilization; **on est encore ~ de la vérité/d'un accord** we're still a long way from the truth/from reaching an agreement; (*fig*) **on est ~ du compte** it falls far short of the target *ou* of what is needed; **être très ~ du sujet** to be way off the subject; **~ de moi/de lui la pensée de vous blâmer!** far be it from me/him to blame you!; (*littér, hum*) **~ de moi/de nous!** begone from me/us! (*littér, hum*); **elle est ~ d'être certaine de réussir** she is far from being certain of success, she is by no means assured of success; **ils ne sont pas ~ de le croire coupable** they almost believe him to be guilty; **ceci est ~ de lui plaire** he's far from pleased with this; **c'est très ~ de ce que nous attendions de lui** this is a far cry from what we expected of him.

e (*Prov*) **~ des yeux, ~ du cœur** out of sight, out of mind (*Prov*); (*Prov*) **il y a ~ de la coupe aux lèvres** there's many a slip 'twixt (the) cup and (the) lip (*Prov*).

lointain, e [lwɛ̃tɛ̃, ɛn] **1 adj a** (*espace*) *région* faraway, distant, remote; *musique* faraway, distant; *horizons, exil* distant. **b** (*temps*) *passé* distant, remote; *avenir* distant. **les jours ~s** far-off days. **c** (*vague*) *parent* remote, distant; *regard* faraway; *cause* indirect, distant; *rapport* distant, remote; *ressemblance* remote. **2 nm a au ~, dans le ~** in the distance. **b** (*Peinture*) background.

loir [lwaʀ] nm dormouse; *voir* **dormir.**

Loire [lwaʀ] nf: **la ~** (*fleuve, département*) the Loire.

loisible [lwazibl] adj (*frm*) **s'il vous est ~ de vous libérer quelques instants** if you could spare a few moments; **il vous est tout à fait ~ de refuser** you are perfectly at liberty to refuse.

loisir [lwaziʀ] nm a (*gén pl: temps libre*) leisure (*NonC*), spare time (*NonC*). **pendant mes heures de ~** in my spare *ou* free time, in my leisure hours *ou* time; **que faites-vous pendant vos ~s?** what do you do in your spare *ou* free time?
b (*activités*) **~s** leisure *ou* spare-time activities; **quels sont vos ~s préférés?** what are your favourite leisure(-time) activities?, what do you like doing best in your spare *ou* free time?; **~s dirigés** (organized) leisure activities.
c (*loc frm*) **avoir (tout) le ~ de faire** to have leisure (*frm*) *ou* time to do; **je n'ai pas eu le ~ de vous écrire** I have not had the leisure *ou* time to write to you; **(tout) à ~** (*en prenant son temps*) at leisure; (*autant que l'on veut*) at will, at one's pleasure (*frm*), as much as one likes; **donner** *ou* **laisser à qn le ~ de faire** to allow sb (the opportunity) to do.

lolo [lolo] nm a (*langage enfantin*) milk. b (*‡: sein*) tit‡, boob‡.

lombago [lɔ̃bago] nm = **lumbago.**

lombaire [lɔ̃bɛʀ] 1 adj lumbar; *voir* **ponction.** 2 nf lumbar vertebra.

lombalgie [lɔ̃balʒi] nf lumbago.

lombard, e [lɔ̃baʀ, aʀd] 1 adj Lombard. 2 nm (*Ling*) Lombard dialect. 3 nm,f: **L~(e)** Lombard.

Lombardie [lɔ̃baʀdi] nf Lombardy.

lombes [lɔ̃b] nmpl loins.

lombric [lɔ̃bʀik] nm earthworm.

Lomé [lɔme] n Lomé.

lompe [lɔ̃p] nm lumpfish, lumpsucker.

londonien, -ienne [lɔ̃dɔnjɛ̃, jɛn] 1 adj London (*épith*), of London. 2 nm,f: **L~(ne)** Londoner.

Londres [lɔ̃dʀ] n London.

long, longue [lɔ̃, lɔ̃g] 1 adj a (*dans l'espace*) *cheveux, liste, robe* long. **un pont ~ de 30 mètres** a 30-metre bridge, a bridge 30 metres long; **2 cm plus ~/trop ~** 2 cm longer/too long; **plus ~/trop ~ de 2 cm** longer/too long by 2 cm; **elle avait de longues jambes maigres** she had long skinny legs; **la mode est aux jupes longues** long skirts are the fashion *ou* in fashion; *voir* **chaise, culotte.**
b (*dans le temps*) *voyage etc* long, lengthy; *amitié, habitude* long-standing. **il écouta (pendant) un ~ moment le bruit** he listened to the noise for a long while; **l'attente fut longue** there was a long *ou* lengthy wait, I (*ou* they *etc*) waited a long time; **la conférence lui parut longue** he found the lecture long; **les heures lui paraissaient longues** the hours seemed long to him *ou* seemed to drag by; **faire de longues phrases** to produce long-winded sentences; **avoir une longue habitude de qch/de faire** to be long accustomed to sth/to doing; **ce travail est ~ à faire** this work takes a long time; **il fut ~ à se mettre en route/à s'habiller** he took a long time *ou* it took him a long time to get started/to get dressed; **il/la réponse était ~/longue à venir** he/the reply was a long time coming; **5 heures, c'est ~** 5 hours is a long time; **ne sois pas trop ~** don't be too long; **nous pouvons vous avoir ce livre, mais ce sera ~** we can get you the book, but it will take some time *ou* a long time.
c (*Culin*) *sauce* thin. **vin ~ en bouche** wine which lingers long on the palate.
d (*loc*) **au ~ cours** *voyage* ocean (*épith*); *navigation* deep-sea (*épith*), ocean (*épith*); *capitaine* seagoing (*épith*), ocean-going (*épith*); **ils se connaissent de longue date** they have known each other for a very long time; **un ami de longue date** a long-standing friend; **à longue échéance, à ~ terme** *prévoir* in the long term *ou* run; *projet, emprunt* long-term; **à plus ou moins longue échéance, à plus ou moins ~ terme** sooner or later; **faire ~ feu** *[projet]* to fall through; **ce pot de confiture n'a pas fait ~ feu** that jar of jam didn't last long; **de longue haleine** *travail* longterm; **préparé de longue main** prepared well beforehand *ou* in advance; **les chômeurs de longue durée** the long-term unemployed; **à longue portée** *canon* long-range; **boire qch à ~s traits** to drink sth in long draughts *ou* big gulps; **respirer l'air à ~s traits** to breathe the air in deeply; **il est ~ comme un jour sans pain** he's like a beanpole.
2 adv: **s'habiller ~** to wear long clothes; **s'habiller trop ~** to wear one's clothes too long; **en savoir ~/trop ~/plus ~** to know a lot/too much/more (*sur* about); *[attitude etc]* **en dire ~** to speak volumes; **regard qui en dit ~** meaningful *ou* eloquent look, look that speaks volumes; **cela en dit ~ sur ses intentions** that tells you a good deal *ou* speaks volumes about his intentions.
3 nm a **un bateau de 7 mètres de ~** a boat 7 metres long; **en ~** lengthways, lengthwise; **ils sont venus par le plus ~** they came the longest *ou* long way, they took the longest route.
b (*vêtements*) long clothes.
c (*loc*) **tomber de tout son ~** to measure one's length, go full length; **étendu de tout son ~** spread out at full length; **(tout) le ~ du fleuve/de la route** (all) along the river/the road; **tout le ~ du jour/de la nuit** all *ou* the whole day/night long; **tout au ~ de sa carrière/son récit** throughout his career/his story; **l'eau coule le ~ de la gouttière** the water flows down *ou* along the gutter; **grimper le ~ d'un mât** to climb up a mast; **tirer un trait tout du ~ (de la page)** to draw a line right along the page; **tout du ~** throughout the whole time, all along; **tout au ~ du parcours** all along the route, the whole way along the route; **de ~ en large** back and forth, to and fro, up and down; **en ~ et en large** in great detail, at great length.
4 **longue** nf (*Ling: voyelle*) long vowel; (*Poésie: syllabe*) long syllable; (*Mus: note*) long note. (*Cartes*) **avoir une longue à carreaux** to have a long suit of diamonds; **à la longue: à la longue il s'est calmé** at long last *ou* in the end he calmed down; **à la longue, ça a fini par coûter cher** in the long run *ou* in the end it turned out very expensive; **à la longue ça s'arrangera/ça s'usera** it will sort itself out/wear out in time *ou* eventually.
5 comp ▸**long-courrier** (pl **long-courriers**) adj (*Naut*) ocean-going (*épith*); (*Aviat*) long-haul (*épith*), long-distance (*épith*) ◊ nm (*Naut*) ocean liner, ocean-going ship; (*Aviat*) long-haul *ou* long-distance aircraft ▸**long métrage** full-length film ▸**longue-vue** nf (pl **longues-vues**) telescope.

longanimité [lɔ̃ganimite] nf (*littér*) long suffering, forbearance.

longe [lɔ̃ʒ] nf a (*pour attacher*) tether; (*pour mener*) lead. b (*Boucherie*) loin.

longer [lɔ̃ʒe] 3 vt *[mur, bois]* to border; *[sentier, voie ferrée]* to border, run along(side); *[personne]* to go along, walk along *ou* alongside; *[voiture, train]* to go *ou* pass along *ou* alongside. **le bois longe la voie ferrée** the wood borders the railway line; **la voie ferrée longe la nationale** the railway line runs along(side) the main road; **naviguer en longeant la côte** to sail along *ou* hug the coast; **~ les murs pour ne pas se faire voir** to keep close to the walls to stay out of sight.

longeron [lɔ̃ʒʀɔ̃] nm a *[pont]* (central) girder. b *[châssis]* side frame; *[fuselage]* longeron; *[aile]* spar.

longévité [lɔ̃ʒevite] nf longevity. **il attribue sa ~ à la pratique de la bicyclette** he attributes his long life *ou* longevity to cycling; **étudier la ~ de certaines espèces/races** to study the longevity of certain species/races; **tables de ~** life-expectancy tables.

longiligne [lɔ̃ʒiliɲ] adj *forme, silhouette* rangy.

longitude [lɔ̃ʒityd] nf longitude. **à** *ou* **par 50° de ~ ouest/est** at 50° longitude west/east.

longitudinal, e, mpl **-aux** [lɔ̃ʒitydinal, o] adj *section, coupe* longitudinal; *vallée, poutre, rainure* running lengthways. **moteur ~** front-to-back engine.

longitudinalement [lɔ̃ʒitydinalmɑ̃] adv (*voir* **longitudinal**) longitudinally; lengthways.

longtemps [lɔ̃tɑ̃] adv a *parler, attendre etc* (for) a long time; (*dans phrase nég ou interrog*) (for) long. **pendant ~** (for) a long time; (for) long; **absent pendant ~** absent (for) a long time; **pendant ~ ils ne sont pas sortis** for a long time *ou* while they didn't go out; **avant ~** (*sous peu*) before long; (*dans phrase nég*) **pas avant ~** not for a long time; **~ avant/après** long before/after; **on ne le verra pas de ~** we won't see him for a long time *ou* for ages; **il ne reviendra pas d'ici ~** he won't be back for a long time *ou* for ages yet; **il vivra encore ~** he'll live (for) a long time yet; **il n'en a plus pour ~** (*pour finir*) he hasn't much longer to go *ou* he won't take much longer now; (*avant de mourir*) he can't hold out *ou* last much longer now; **y a-t-il ~ à attendre?** is there long to wait?, is there a long wait?, will it be long?; **je n'en ai pas pour ~** I won't be long, it won't take me long; **il a mis** *ou* **été ~, ça lui a pris ~** it took him a long time, he was a long time over it *ou* doing it; **il arrivera dans ~?** will it be long before he gets here?; **rester assez ~ quelque part** (*trop*) to stay somewhere (for) quite *ou* rather a long time *ou* (for) quite a while; (*suffisamment*) to stay somewhere long enough; **tu es resté si ~!** you've stayed so long! *ou* (for) such a long time!
b (*avec depuis, il y a etc*) (*indiquant une durée*) (for) a long time; (for) long; (*indiquant une action terminée*) a long time ago, long ago. **il habite ici depuis ~, il y a** *ou* **cela fait** *ou* **voilà ~ qu'il habite ici** he has been living here (for) a long time; **il n'était pas là depuis ~ quand je suis arrivé** he hadn't been here (for) long when I arrived; **c'était il y a ~/il n'y a pas ~** that was a long time ago/not long ago; **j'ai fini depuis ~** I finished a long time ago; **il y a** *ou* **cela fait** *ou* **voilà ~ que j'ai fini** I have been finished for a long time *ou* for ages now; **ça fait ~ qu'il n'est plus venu** it's (been) a long time now since he came, he hasn't been coming for a long time *ou* for ages now; **je n'y mangeais plus depuis ~** I had given up eating there long before then *ou* ages ago.

longue [lɔ̃g] *voir* **long.**

longuement [lɔ̃gmɑ̃] adv (*longtemps*) *regarder, parler* for a long time; (*en détail*) *expliquer, étudier, raconter* at length. **plus ~** for longer; (*en plus grand détail*) at greater length; **plan ~ médité** long-considered plan, plan pondered over at length.

longuet, -ette* [lɔ̃gɛ, ɛt] adj *film, discours* a bit long (*attrib*), a bit on the long side* (*attrib*). **tu as été ~!** you took your time!; **il est ~ à manger** he's a bit of a slow eater.

longueur [lɔ̃gœʀ] nf a (*espace*) length. **mesures/unités de ~** measures/units of length, linear measures/units; **la pièce fait 3 mètres de** *ou* **en ~** the room is 3 metres in length *ou* 3 metres long; **la plage s'étend sur une ~ de 7 km** the beach stretches for 7 km; **dans le sens de la ~** lengthways, lengthwise; **s'étirer en ~** to stretch out lengthways; **pièce tout en ~** long narrow room; (*lit, fig*) **~ d'onde** wavelength.
b (*durée*) length. **à ~ de journée/de semaine/d'année** all day/week/year long; **à ~ de temps** all the time; **traîner** *ou* **tirer en ~** to drag on; **tirer les choses en ~** to drag things out; **attente qui tire** *ou* **traîne en ~**

long-drawn-out wait; **les ~s de la justice** the slowness of the judicial process.

c (*courses, natation*) length. **saut en ~** long jump; **l'emporter de plusieurs ~s** to win by several lengths; **prendre 2 ~s d'avance** to go into a 2-length lead; (*Alpinisme*) **~ de corde** (*passage*) pitch; (*distance*) rope-length.

d (*remplissage*) **~s** boringly long moments *ou* passages, overlong passages; **ce film/livre a des ~s** there are some episodes which are overlong *ou* which are too dragged out in this film/book.

look* [luk] **nm** (*style, allure*) *[personne]* look, image; *[chose]* look, style. **soigner son ~** to pay great attention to one's look *ou* one's image.

looping [lupiŋ] **nm** (*Aviat*) looping the loop. **faire des ~s** to loop the loop.

lope‡ [lɔp] **nf**, **lopette** [lɔpɛt] **nf** queer‡ (*péj*), fag‡ (*péj, surtout US*).

lopin [lɔpɛ̃] **nm**: **~ (de terre)** patch of land, plot (of land).

loquace [lɔkas] **adj** talkative, loquacious (*frm*).

loquacité [lɔkasite] **nf** talkativeness, loquacity (*frm*).

loque [lɔk] **nf** **a** (*vêtements*) **~s** rags, rags and tatters; **être en ~s** to be in rags; **vêtu de ~s** dressed in rags; **tomber en ~s** to be in tatters *ou* all tattered. **b** (*fig péj*) **une ~ (humaine)** a (human) wreck; **je suis une vraie ~ ce matin** I feel a wreck *ou* like a wet rag this morning.

loquet [lɔkɛ] **nm** latch.

loqueteau, pl ~x [lɔk(ə)to] **nm** (small) latch, catch.

loqueteux, -euse [lɔk(ə)tø, øz] **adj** *personne* ragged, (dressed) in rags *ou* in tatters (*attrib*); *vêtement, livre* tattered, ragged.

lordose [lɔʀdoz] **nf** hollow-back (*NonC*), lordosis (*SPÉC*).

lorgner* [lɔʀɲe] [1] **1 vt** *objet* to peer at, eye; *femme* to ogle, eye up* (*Brit*); *poste, décoration, héritage* to have one's eye on. **~ qch du coin de l'œil** to look *ou* peer at sth out of the corner of one's eye, cast sidelong glances at sth. **2 vi**: **~ sur** *journal, copie* to sneak a look at; *personne* to ogle, eye up* (*Brit*).

lorgnette [lɔʀɲɛt] **nf** opera glasses. (*fig*) **regarder les choses par le petit bout de la ~** to take a very limited *ou* narrow view of things.

lorgnon [lɔʀɲɔ̃] **nm** (*face-à-main*) lorgnette; (*pince-nez*) pince-nez.

lori [lɔʀi] **nm** (*oiseau*) lory.

loriot [lɔʀjo] **nm**: **~ jaune** golden oriole.

lorrain, e [lɔʀɛ̃, ɛn] **1 adj** of *ou* from Lorraine; *voir* **quiche**. **2 nm** (*Ling*) Lorraine dialect. **3 nm,f**: **L~(e)** inhabitant *ou* native of Lorraine. **4 Lorraine nf** (*région*) Lorraine.

lors [lɔʀ] **adv**: **~ de** at the time of; **~ de sa mort** at the time of his death; **~ même que** even though *ou* if; **~ même que la terre croulerait** even though *ou* if the earth should crumble; *voir* **dès**.

lorsque [lɔʀsk(ə)] **conj** when. **lorsqu'il entra/entrera** when *ou* as he came/comes in.

losange [lɔzɑ̃ʒ] **nm** diamond, lozenge. **en forme de ~** diamond-shaped; **dallage en ~s** diamond tiling.

losangé, e [lɔzɑ̃ʒe] **adj** *morceau* diamond-shaped; *dessin, tissu* with a diamond pattern.

Los Angeles [lɔsɑ̃ʒəlɛs] **n** Los Angeles.

lot [lo] **nm** **a** (*Loterie*) prize. **le gros ~** the first prize, the jackpot; **~ de consolation** consolation prize. **b** (*portion*) share. **~ (de terre)** plot (of land). **c** (*assortiment*) *[livres, chiffons]* batch; *[draps, vaisselle]* set; (*aux enchères*) lot. **~ de 10 chemises** set of 10 shirts; **dans le ~, il n'y avait que 2 candidats valables** in the whole batch there were only 2 worthwhile applicants. **d** (*fig littér: destin*) lot (*littér*), fate.

loterie [lɔtʀi] **nf** (*lit, fig*) lottery; (*avec billets*) raffle, tombola, lottery. **mettre qch en ~** to put sth up to be raffled; **la L~ nationale** the French national lottery *ou* sweepstake; **jouer à la ~** to buy tickets for the raffle *ou* lottery *ou* tombola; **gagner à la ~** to win on the raffle *ou* lottery *ou* tombola; (*fig*) **c'est une vraie ~** it's (all) the luck of the draw; **la vie est une ~** life is a game of chance, life is a lottery.

Loth [lɔt] **nm** Lot.

loti, e [lɔti] (**ptp de lotir**) **adj**: **être bien/mal ~** to be well-/badly off; (*iro*) **on est bien ~ avec une secrétaire comme ça!** with a secretary like her who could ask for more? (*iro*).

lotion [losjɔ̃] **nf** lotion. **~ capillaire** hair lotion; **~ après rasage** aftershave lotion; **~ avant rasage** preshave lotion.

lotionner [losjɔne] [1] **vt** to apply (a) lotion to.

lotir [lɔtiʀ] [2] **vt** *terrain* (*diviser*) to divide into plots; (*vendre*) to sell by lots; (*Jur*) *succession* to divide up, share out. **~ qn de qch** to allot sth to sb, provide sb with sth.

lotissement [lɔtismɑ̃] **nm** **a** (*terrains à bâtir*) housing estate *ou* site; (*terrains bâtis*) (housing) development *ou* estate; (*parcelle*) plot, lot. **b** (*action: voir* **lotir**) division; sale (by lots); sharing out.

loto [lɔto] **nm** (*jeu traditionnel*) lotto; (*matériel pour ce jeu*) lotto set; (*loterie à numéros*) national bingo game. **le ~ sportif** ≃ the pools.

lotte [lɔt] **nf** (*de rivière*) burbot; (*de mer*) angler (fish), devilfish, monkfish.

lotus [lɔtys] **nm** lotus.

louable [lwabl] **adj** **a** praiseworthy, commendable, laudable. **b** *maison* rentable. **appartement difficilement ~ à cause de sa situation** flat that is hard to let (*Brit*) *ou* rent (*US*) because of its situation.

louablement [lwabləmɑ̃] **adv** commendably.

louage [lwaʒ] **nm** hiring. **(contrat de) ~** rental contract; **~ de services** work contract.

louange [lwɑ̃ʒ] **nf** praise. **il méprise les ~s** he despises praise; **chanter les ~s de qn** to sing sb's praises; **faire un discours à la ~ de qn** to make a speech in praise of sb; **je dois dire, à sa ~, que ...** I must say, to his credit *ou* in his praise, that ... .

louangeur, -euse [lwɑ̃ʒœʀ, øz] **adj** (*littér*) laudatory (*frm*), laudative (*frm*).

loubar(d) [lubaʀ] **nm** hooligan, thug.

louche[1] [luʃ] **adj** **a** *affaire, manœuvre, milieu, passé* shady; *individu* shifty, shady, dubious; *histoire* dubious, fishy*; *conduite, acte, établissement* dubious, suspicious, shady; *réaction, attitude* dubious, suspicious. **j'ai entendu du bruit, c'est ~** I heard a noise, that's funny *ou* odd; **il y a du ~ dans cette affaire** this business is a bit shady *ou* fishy* *ou* isn't quite above board. **b** (†) *liquide* cloudy; *couleur, éclairage* murky. **c** *œil, personne* squinting (*épith*).

louche[2] [luʃ] **nf** ladle. **serrer la ~ à qn**‡ to shake hands with sb, shake sb's hand.

loucher [luʃe] [1] **vi** (*lit*) to squint, have a squint. (*fig*) **~ sur*** *objet* to eye; *personne* to ogle, eye up* (*Brit*); *poste, héritage* to have one's eye on.

louer[1] [lwe] [1] **1 vt** to praise. **~ qn de** *ou* **pour qch** to praise sb for sth; **on ne peut que le ~ d'avoir agi ainsi** he deserves only praise *ou* one can only praise him for acting in that way; (*Rel*) **louons le Seigneur!** (let us) praise the Lord!; (*fig*) **Dieu soit loué!** thank God!

2 se louer vpr: **se ~ de** *employé, appareil* to be very happy *ou* pleased with; *action, mesure* to congratulate o.s. on; **se ~ d'avoir fait qch** to congratulate o.s. on *ou* for having done sth; **n'avoir qu'à se ~ de** *employé, appareil* to have every cause for satisfaction with, be completely satisfied with, have nothing but praise for; **nous n'avons qu'à nous ~ de ses services** we have nothing but praise for the service he gives, we have every cause for satisfaction with his services.

louer[2] [lwe] [1] **vt** **a** *[propriétaire] maison, chambre* to let (out) (*Brit*), rent out; *voiture, tente, téléviseur* to hire out (*Brit*), rent (out). **~ une maison au mois** to let (*Brit*) *ou* to rent out a house by the month; **~ ses services** *ou* **se ~ à un fermier** to hire o.s. (out) to a farmer. **b** *[locataire] maison, chambre* to rent; *voiture, tente* to hire (*Brit*), rent; *place* to book. **ils ont loué une maison au bord de la mer** they took *ou* rented a house by the sea; **à ~** *chambre etc* to let (*Brit*), to rent (*US*); *voiture etc* for hire (*Brit*), for rent (*US*); **cet appartement doit se ~ cher** that flat must be expensive to rent.

loueur, -euse [lwœʀ, øz] **nm,f** (*propriétaire*) hirer out (*Brit*), renter out. **c'est un ~ de chevaux** he hires out (*Brit*) *ou* rents out horses.

loufiat‡ [lufja] **nm** waiter.

loufoque* [lufɔk] **adj** wild, crazy, barmy*.

loufoquerie [lufɔkʀi] **nf** **a** (*caractère*) craziness, barminess*. **b** (*acte*) bit of daftness*, crazy goings-on (*pl*).

Louis [lwi] **nm** Lewis; (*Hist française*) Louis.

louis [lwi] **nm**: **~ (d'or)** (gold) louis.

louise-bonne, pl louises-bonnes [lwizbɔn] **nf** louise-bonne pear.

Louisiane [lwizjan] **nf** Louisiana.

louis-philippard, e [lwifilipaʀ, aʀd] **adj** (*péj*) of *ou* relating to the reign of Louis Philippe.

loukoum [lukum] **nm** Turkish delight (*NonC*). **manger 3 ~s** to eat 3 pieces of Turkish delight.

loulou[1] [lulu] **nm** (*chien*) spitz. **~ de Poméranie** Pomeranian dog, Pom.

loulou[2]* [lulu] **nm**, **louloutte*** [lulut] **nf** **a** (*terme affectueux*) darling; (*péj*) fishy customer*, oddball*, nasty bit of work (*Brit*). **b** = **loubar(d)**.

loup [lu] **1 nm** **a** (*carnassier*) wolf; (*poisson*) bass; (*masque*) (eye) mask. **mon (gros** *ou* **petit) ~*** (my) pet* *ou* love; (*Prov*) **les ~s ne se mangent pas** *ou* **ne se dévorent pas entre eux** dog does not eat dog, there is honour among thieves (*Prov*); **l'homme est un ~ pour l'homme** brother will turn on brother; **enfermer** *ou* **mettre le ~ dans la bergerie** to set the fox to mind the geese; *voir* **gueule, hurler, jeune** *etc.* **b** (*malfaçon*) flaw. **2 comp ▸loup-cervier nm (pl loups-cerviers)** lynx **▸loup-garou (pl loups-garous) nm** (*Hist*) werewolf; **le loup-garou va te manger!** the Bogeyman will get you! **▸loup de mer** (**: marin*) old salt*, old seadog*; (*vêtement*) (short-sleeved) jersey.

loupage* [lupaʒ] **nm** (*voir* **louper**) missing; messing up*; flunking*; spoiling. **après plusieurs ~s** after several failures.

loupe [lup] **nf** (*Opt*) magnifying glass; (*Méd*) wen; (*sur un arbre*) burr. **regarder qch à la ~** (*lit*) to look at sth with a magnifying glass; (*fig*) to put sth under a microscope; **table en ~ de noyer** table in burr walnut.

loupé* [lupe] (**ptp de louper**) **nm** (*échec*) failure; (*défaut*) defect, flaw.

louper* [lupe] [1] **1 vt** (*rater*) *occasion, train, personne* to miss; *travail, gâteau* to mess up*, make a mess of; *examen* to flunk*. **ma sauce est loupée** my sauce hasn't come off, I spoilt my sauce; **ma soirée est loupée** my party is spoilt *ou* is a flop*; **loupé!** missed!; (*iro*) **il n'en loupe pas une!** he's forever putting his big foot in it!*; **la prochaine fois je ne te louperai pas** I'll get you next time; **~ son entrée** to fluff* *ou* bungle one's entrance; **il a loupé son coup/suicide** he bungled *ou* botched* it/his suicide bid.

2 vi: **je t'ai dit qu'il ferait une erreur; ça n'a pas loupé!** I told you that he'd make a mistake and sure enough he did!; **ça va tout faire ~** that'll put everything up the spout* (*Brit*), that'll muck everything up*.

3 **se louper*** vpr (*rater son suicide*) to bungle one's suicide attempt. (*accident*) **elle ne s'est pas loupée!** she made a good job of it!*

loupiot, -iotte* [lupjo, jɔt] nm,f kid*.

loupiote* [lupjɔt] nf (*lampe*) (small) light.

lourd, e[1] [luʀ, luʀd] adj a (*lit, fig: pesant*) *objet, poids, vêtement* heavy; *silence, sommeil* heavy, deep; *chagrin* deep; *ciel, nuage* heavy; *temps, chaleur* sultry, close; *parfum, odeur* heavy, strong; *aliment, vin* heavy; *repas* heavy, big; *paupières* heavy; (*Bourse*) *marché* slack, sluggish; *chirurgie* extensive; *artillerie, industrie* heavy (*épith*); *infrastructure* cumbersome; *dispositif* unwieldy. **terrain ~** heavy *ou* soft ground; **marcher d'un pas ~** to tread heavily, walk with a heavy step; **yeux ~s de sommeil/de fatigue** eyes heavy with sleep/tiredness; **c'est ~ (à digérer)** it's heavy (on the stomach *ou* the digestion); **se sentir ~, avoir l'estomac ~** to feel bloated; **j'ai** *ou* **je me sens les jambes ~es** my legs feel heavy; **j'ai** *ou* **je me sens la tête ~e** my head feels fuzzy, I feel a bit headachy; **3 enfants à élever, c'est ~/trop ~ (pour elle)** bringing up 3 children is a lot/too much (for her) *ou* is a big responsibility/is too heavy a responsibility (for her); *voir* **eau, franc**[2], **hérédité**.

b (*important*) *dettes, impôts, tâche* heavy, weighty; *pertes* heavy, severe, serious; *faute* serious, grave; *responsabilité, charge* heavy, weighty. **de ~es présomptions pèsent sur lui** suspicion falls heavily on him.

c (*massif, gauche*) *construction* ponderous (*frm*), inelegant, monolithic; *silhouette* heavy; *démarche* heavy, cumbersome; *mouvement, style* heavy, ponderous; *plaisanterie* predictable; *compliment* clumsy. **oiseau au vol ~** bird with a heavy *ou* clumsy flight; **avoir l'esprit ~** to be slow-witted *ou* dull-witted; (*à un plaisantin*) **tu es un peu ~*** you're just not funny.

d (*loc*) **le silence était ~ de menaces** the silence was heavy with threat, there was a threatening *ou* an ominous silence; **le silence était ~ de sous-entendus** the silence was heavy with insinuations; **décision ~e de conséquences** decision charged *ou* fraught with consequences; **en avoir ~ sur la conscience** to have a heavy conscience (about sth); **il n'y a pas ~ de pain*** there isn't much bread; **du bon sens, il n'en a pas ~!*** he hasn't got much common sense, he isn't overendowed with common sense; **il n'en sait/ne fait pas ~** he doesn't know/do much; (*Mét*) **il fait ~** the weather is close, it's sultry; *voir* **main, peser**.

lourdaud, e* [luʀdo, od] 1 adj oafish, clumsy. 2 nm,f oaf.

lourde[2]**‡** [luʀd] nf (*porte*) door.

lourdement [luʀdəmɑ̃] adv (*gén*) heavily. **marcher ~** to walk with a heavy tread; **se tromper ~** to be sadly mistaken, commit a gross error (*frm*), make a big mistake; **insister ~ sur qch/pour faire** to insist strenuously on sth/on doing.

lourder‡ [luʀde] [1] vt to kick out*, boot out‡. **se faire ~** to get kicked out* *ou* booted out‡.

lourdeur [luʀdœʀ] nf a (*pesanteur*) *[objet, fardeau]* heaviness, weight; *[bureaucratie, infrastructure]* cumbersomeness; *[tâche, responsabilité]* weight; (*Bourse*) *[marché]* slackness, sluggishness. b *[édifice]* heaviness, massiveness; *[démarche]* heaviness; *[style, forme]* heaviness, ponderousness. **~ d'esprit** dull-wittedness, slow-wittedness; **s'exprimer avec ~** to express o.s. clumsily *ou* ponderously; **avoir des ~s de tête** to have a fuzzy head, feel headachy; **avoir des ~s d'estomac** to have indigestion, feel a bit bloated. c *[temps]* sultriness, closeness.

lourdingue* [luʀdɛ̃g] adj *plaisanterie* predictable; *personne* oafish, clumsy; *construction* hefty-looking*; *phrase* laboured (*Brit*), labored (*US*), clumsy.

loustic* [lustik] nm (*enfant*) kid*; (*taquin*) villain* (*hum*); (*type*) (funny) chap* (*Brit*) *ou* fellow* *ou* guy*, oddbod* (*Brit*). **faire le ~** to act the goat*, play the fool; **un drôle de ~** (*type*) an oddball*, an oddbod* (*Brit*); (*enfant*) a little villain* (*hum*) *ou* rascal.

loutre [lutʀ] nf (*animal*) otter; (*fourrure*) otter-skin. **~ de mer** sea otter.

louve [luv] nf she-wolf.

louveteau, pl **~x** [luv(ə)to] nm (*Zool*) (wolf) cub; (*scout*) cub scout, cub.

louvoiement [luvwamɑ̃] nm (*Naut*) tacking (*NonC*); (*fig*) hedging (*NonC*), evasion. **assez de ~s** stop hedging, stop beating about the bush.

louvoyer [luvwaje] [8] vi (*Naut*) to tack; (*fig*) to hedge, evade the issue, beat about the bush.

Louxor [luksɔʀ] n Luxor.

lover [lɔve] [1] 1 vt to coil. 2 **se lover** vpr *[serpent]* to coil up.

loyal, e, mpl **-aux** [lwajal, o] adj a (*fidèle*) *sujet, ami* loyal, faithful, trusty. **après 50 ans de bons et ~aux services** after 50 years of good and faithful service. b (*honnête*) *personne, procédé* fair, honest; *conduite* upright, fair; *jeu* fair, straight*. **se battre à la ~e*** to fight cleanly.

loyalement [lwajalmɑ̃] adv *agir* fairly, honestly; *servir* loyally, faithfully; *se battre* cleanly. **accepter ~ une défaite** to take a defeat sportingly *ou* in good part *ou* like a gentleman.

loyalisme [lwajalism] nm loyalty.

loyaliste [lwajalist] 1 adj loyal. 2 nmf loyal supporter.

loyauté [lwajote] nf a (*fidélité*) loyalty, faithfulness. b (*honnêteté*) honesty, fairness; *[conduite]* fairness, uprightness. **avec ~** fairly.

loyer [lwaje] nm rent. (*Fin*) **~ de l'argent** rate of interest, interest rate; **~ matriciel** ≃ rateable value.

LP [ɛlpe] nm (abrév de **lycée professionnel**) *voir* **lycée**.

L.S.D. [ɛlɛsde] nm (abrév de **Lysergsäure Diethylamid**) (*acide lysergique diéthylamide*) LSD.

lu, e [ly] (ptp de **lire**) adj: **~ et approuvé** read and approved; **elle est très ~e en Europe** she is widely read in Europe.

Luanda [luɑ̃nda] n Luanda.

lubie [lybi] nf whim, craze, fad. **avoir des ~s** to have *ou* get whims *ou* crazes *ou* fads; **il lui a pris la ~ de ne plus manger de pain** he has taken it into his head not to eat bread any more, he has got the mad idea of not eating bread any more; **c'est sa dernière ~** it's his latest craze.

lubricité [lybʀisite] nf *[personne]* lustfulness, lechery; *[propos, conduite]* lewdness.

lubrifiant, e [lybʀifjɑ̃, jɑ̃t] 1 adj lubricating. 2 nm lubricant.

lubrification [lybʀifikasjɔ̃] nf lubrication.

lubrifier [lybʀifje] [7] vt to lubricate.

lubrique [lybʀik] adj *personne* lustful, lecherous; *propos* lewd, libidinous; *danse* lewd; *amour* lustful, carnal. **regarder qch d'un œil ~** to gaze at sth with a lustful eye.

lubriquement [lybʀikmɑ̃] adv (*voir* **lubrique**) lustfully; lecherously; lewdly; libidinously.

Luc [lyk] nm Luke.

lucarne [lykaʀn] nf *[toit]* skylight; (*en saillie*) dormer window. (*Ftbl*) **envoyer la balle dans la ~** to send the ball into the top corner of the net.

lucide [lysid] adj a (*conscient*) *malade, vieillard* lucid; *accidenté* conscious. b (*perspicace*) *personne* lucid, clear-minded, clear-headed; *esprit, analyse, raisonnement* lucid, clear. **le témoin le plus ~ de son temps** the most clear-sighted *ou* perceptive observer of the times he lived in; **juger qch d'un œil ~** to judge sth with a lucid *ou* clear eye.

lucidement [lysidmɑ̃] adv lucidly, clearly.

lucidité [lysidite] nf (*voir* **lucide**) lucidity; consciousness; clear-mindedness, clear-headedness; clearness. **un vieillard qui a gardé sa ~** an old man who has retained (the use of) his faculties *ou* has remained quite clear-thinking.

Lucie [lysi] nf Lucy.

Lucien [lysjɛ̃] nm Lucian.

Lucifer [lysifɛʀ] nm Lucifer.

luciole [lysjɔl] nf firefly.

lucratif, -ive [lykʀatif, iv] adj *entreprise* lucrative, profitable; *emploi* lucrative, well-paid. **association créée dans un but ~/non ~** profit-making/non-profit-making organization.

lucrativement [lykʀativmɑ̃] adv lucratively.

lucre [lykʀ] nm (*péj*) lucre (*péj*).

Lucrèce [lykʀɛs] 1 nm Lucretius. 2 nf Lucretia.

ludiciel [lydisjɛl] nm computer game. **~s** computer games, game software (*NonC*).

ludion [lydjɔ̃] nm Cartesian diver.

ludique [lydik] adj (*Psych*) play (*épith*). **activité ~** play activity.

ludothèque [lydɔtɛk] nf games library.

luette [lɥɛt] nf uvula.

lueur [lɥœʀ] nf a *[flamme]* glimmer (*NonC*); *[étoile, lune, lampe]* (faint) light; *[braises]* glow (*NonC*). **à la ~ d'une bougie** by candlelight *ou* candle-glow; **les ~s de la ville** the city lights, the glow of the city; **les premières ~s de l'aube/du jour** the first light of dawn/of day; **les ~s du couchant** the glow of sunset, the sunset glow. b (*fig*) *[désir, colère]* gleam; *[raison, intelligence]* glimmer. **une ~ malicieuse dans le regard** a malicious gleam in one's eyes; **pas la moindre ~ d'espoir** not the faintest glimmer of hope.

luge [lyʒ] nf sledge (*Brit*), sled (*US*), toboggan. **faire de la ~** to sledge (*Brit*), sled (*US*), toboggan.

luger [lyʒe] [3] vi to sledge (*Brit*), sled (*US*), toboggan.

lugeur, -euse [lyʒœʀ, øz] nm,f tobogganist.

lugubre [lygybʀ] adj *personne, pensée, ambiance, récit* lugubrious, gloomy, dismal; *prison, paysage* gloomy, dismal.

lugubrement [lygybʀəmɑ̃] adv lugubriously, gloomily, dismally.

lui [lɥi] 1 pron pers mf (*objet indirect*) (*homme*) him; (*femme*) her; (*animal, bébé*) it, him, her; (*bateau, nation*) her, it; (*insecte, chose*) it. **je le ~ ai dit** (*à un homme*) I told him; (*à une femme*) I told her; **tu ~ as donné de l'eau?** (*à un animal*) have you given it *ou* him *ou* her some water?; (*à une plante*) have you watered it?; **je ne le ~ ai jamais caché** I have never kept it from him *ou* her; **il ~ est facile de le faire** it's easy for him *ou* her to do it; **elle ~ serra la main** she shook his *ou* her hand, she shook him *ou* her by the hand; **je ne ~ connais pas de défauts** I know of no faults in him *ou* her; **je ~ ai entendu dire que** I heard him *ou* her say that; **la tête ~ a tourné et elle est tombée** her head spun and she fell; **le bateau est plus propre depuis qu'on ~ a donné un coup de peinture** the boat is cleaner now they've given her *ou* it a coat of paint.

2 pron m a (*fonction objet*) (*personne*) him; (*animal*) him, her, it; (*chose*) it; (*pays, bateau*) her, it. **elle n'admire que ~** she only admires him; **à ~ elle n'a pas dit un mot** she never said a word to him; **~ le revoir? jamais!** see him again? never!; **c'est ~, je le reconnais** it's him, I recognize him; **je l'ai bien vu ~!** I saw him all right!, I definitely saw him!; **si j'étais ~ j'accepterais** if I were him *ou* he (*frm*) I would

accept; *voir aussi* **même, non, seul.**

b (*sujet, gén emphatique*) (*personne*) he; (*chose*) it; (*animal*) it, he, she. **elle est vendeuse, ~ est maçon** she's a saleswoman and he's a mason; **~, furieux, a refusé** furious, he refused; **le Japon, ~, serait d'accord** Japan, for its *ou* her part, would agree; **l'enfant, ~, avait bien vu les bonbons** the child had seen the sweets all right; **qu'est-ce qu'ils ont dit? — ~ rien** what did they say? — he said nothing; **elle est venue mais pas ~** she came but not him *ou* but he didn't; **mon frère et ~ sont partis ensemble** my brother and he went off together; **~ parti, j'ai pu travailler** with him gone *ou* after he had gone I was able to work; **~ (il) n'aurait jamais fait ça, il n'aurait jamais fait ça ~** he would never have done that; **est-ce qu'il le sait ~?, est-ce que ~ (il) le sait?** does he know about it?; **~ se marier?, pas si bête!** him get married?, not likely!

c (*emphatique avec qui, que*) **c'est ~ que nous avions invité** it's *ou* it was him we had invited; **c'est à ~ que je veux parler** it's him I want to speak to, I want to speak to him; **il y a un hibou dans le bois, c'est ~ que j'ai entendu** there is an owl in the wood — that's what I heard; **c'est ~ qui me l'a dit** he told me himself, it's he who told me; (*iro*) **c'est ~ qui le dit!** that's his story!, that's what he says!; (*frm*) **ce fut ~ qui le premier découvrit ...** it was he *ou* he it was (*frm*) who first discovered ...; **chasse le chien, c'est ~ qui m'a mordu** chase that dog away — it's the one that bit me; **de tous les arbres c'est ~ qui a le bois le plus dur** of all the trees it's this one that has the hardest wood; **ils ont 3 chats et ~ qui ne voulait pas d'animaux!** they have 3 cats and to think that he didn't want any animals!

d (*avec prép*) (*personne*) him; (*animal*) him, it; (*chose*) it. **ce livre est à ~** this book belongs to him *ou* is his; **il a un appartement à ~** he has a flat of his own; **c'est gentil à ~ d'avoir écrit** it was kind of him to write; **un ami à ~** a friend of his, one of his friends; **il ne pense qu'à ~** he only thinks of himself; **qu'est-ce qu'elle ferait sans ~!** what would she do without him!; **ce poème n'est pas de ~** this poem is not one of his *ou* not one he wrote; **elle veut une photo de ~** she wants a photo of him; **vous pouvez avoir toute confiance en ~** (*homme*) he is thoroughly reliable, you can have complete confidence in him; (*machine etc*) it is thoroughly reliable.

e (*dans comparaisons*) (*sujet*) he, him*; (*objet*) him. **elle est plus mince que ~** she is slimmer than he is *ou* than him*; **j'ai mangé plus/moins que ~** I ate more/less than he did *ou* than him*; **ne fais pas comme ~** don't do as he does *ou* did, don't do like him* *ou* the same as he did; **je ne la connais pas aussi bien que ~** (*que je le connais*) I don't know her as well as (I know) him; (*qu'il la connaît*) I don't know her as well as he does *ou* as him*.

luire [lɥiʀ] 38 **vi** (*gén*) to shine, gleam; *[surface mouillée]* to glisten; *[reflet intermittent]* to glint; (*en scintillant*) to glimmer, shimmer; (*en rougeoyant*) to glow. **l'herbe couverte de rosée/l'étang luisait au soleil du matin** the dew-covered grass/the pond glistened in the morning sunlight; **yeux qui luisent de colère/d'envie** eyes which gleam with anger/desire; **le lac luisait sous la lune** the lake shimmered *ou* glimmered *ou* gleamed in the moonlight; **l'espoir luit encore** there is still a gleam *ou* glimmer of hope.

luisant, e [lɥizɑ̃, ɑ̃t] 1 **adj** (*voir* **luire**) gleaming; shining; glowing. **front ~ de sueur** forehead gleaming *ou* glistening with sweat; **vêtements ~s d'usure** clothes shiny with wear; **yeux ~s de fièvre** eyes bright with fever; *voir* **ver.** 2 **nm** *[étoffe]* sheen; *[poil d'animal]* gloss.

lumbago [lɔ̃bago] **nm** lumbago.

lumière [lymjɛʀ] 1 **nf** a (*Phys, gén*) light. **la ~ du jour** daylight; **la ~ du soleil l'éblouit** he was dazzled by the sunlight; **à la ~ des étoiles** by the light of the stars, by starlight; **à la ~ artificielle/électrique** by artificial/electric light; **la ~ entrait à flots dans la pièce** daylight streamed into the room; **il n'y a pas beaucoup/ça ne donne guère de ~** there isn't/it doesn't give much light; **donne-nous de la ~** switch *ou* put the light on, will you?; **il y a de la ~ dans sa chambre** there's a light on in his room; **les ~s de la ville** the lights of the town; *voir* **effet, habit.**

b (*fig*) light. (*littér*) **avoir/acquérir quelque ~ sur qch** to have/gain some knowledge of sth, have/gain some insight into sth; **avoir des ~s sur une question** to have some ideas *ou* some knowledge on a question, know something about a question; **aidez-nous de vos ~s** give us the benefit of your wisdom *ou* insight; **mettre qch en ~** to bring sth to light, bring sth out; **jeter une nouvelle ~ sur qch** to throw *ou* shed new light on sth; **à la ~ des récents événements** in the light of recent events; **faire (toute) la ~ sur qch** to get right to the bottom of sth; **la ~ de la foi/de la raison** the light of faith/reason; **entrevoir la ~ au bout du tunnel** to see the light at the end of the tunnel; *voir* **siècle[1].**

c (*personne*) light. **il fut une des ~s de son siècle** he was one of the (shining) lights of his age; **le pauvre garçon, ce n'est pas une ~** the poor boy, he's no bright spark*.

d (*Tech*) *[machine à vapeur]* port; *[canon]* sight. (*Aut*) **~ d'admission/d'échappement** inlet/exhaust port *ou* valve.

2 **comp** ▸**lumière blanche** (*Phys*) white light ▸**lumière cendrée** (*Astron*) earth-light, earthshine ▸**lumière noire** (*Phys*) black light ▸**lumière stroboscopique** strobe lighting ▸**lumière de Wood** (*Phys*) = **lumière noire.**

lumignon [lymiɲɔ̃] **nm** (*lampe*) (small) light; (*bougie*) candle-end.

luminaire [luminɛʀ] **nm** (*gén*) light, lamp; (*cierge*) candle. **magasin de ~s** lighting shop, shop selling lighting fitments.

lumination [lyminasjɔ̃] **nf** (*Phot*) **indice de ~** exposure value.

luminescence [lyminesɑ̃s] **nf** luminescence.

luminescent, e [lyminesɑ̃, ɑ̃t] **adj** luminescent.

lumineusement [lyminøzmɑ̃] **adv** *expliquer* lucidly, clearly.

lumineux, -euse [lyminø, øz] **adj** a *corps, intensité* luminous; *fontaine, enseigne* illuminated; *rayon, faisceau, source* of light; *cadran, aiguille* luminous. **onde/source ~euse** light wave/source; **intensité ~euse** luminous intensity; *voir* **flèche[1].** b *teint, regard* radiant; *ciel, couleur* luminous. c (*littér: pur, transparent*) luminous (*littér*), lucid; (*iro*) *exposé* limpid, brilliant. **j'ai compris, c'est ~** I understand, it's as clear as daylight *ou* it's crystal clear; *voir* **idée.**

luminosité [lyminozite] **nf** a *[teint, regard]* radiance; *[ciel, couleur]* luminosity. **il y a beaucoup de ~** the light is very bright. b (*Phot, Sci*) luminosity.

lump [lœ̃p] **nm** lumpfish, lump-sucker; *voir* **œuf.**

lunaire[1] [lynɛʀ] **adj** (*Astron*) *paysage* lunar; *roche* moon (*épith*); (*fig*) *visage* moonlike.

lunaire[2] [lynɛʀ] **nf** (*Bot*) honesty.

lunaison [lynɛzɔ̃] **nf** lunar month.

lunapark [lynapaʀk] **nm** (fun)fair.

lunatique [lynatik] **adj** quirky, whimsical, temperamental.

lunch [lœntʃ] **nm** buffet.

lundi [lœ̃di] **nm** Monday. **le ~ de Pâques/de Pentecôte** Easter/Whit Monday; *pour autres loc voir* **samedi.**

lune [lyn] **nf** a (*lit*) moon. **pleine/nouvelle ~** full/new moon; **nuit sans ~** moonless night; **~ rousse** April moon; **croissant/quartier de ~** crescent/quarter moon; *voir* **clair[1].** b (**: derrière*) bottom*, backside*.

c (*loc*) **~ de miel** honeymoon; **être dans la ~** to have one's head in the clouds, be in a dream; **demander** *ou* **vouloir la ~** to ask *ou* cry for the moon; **promettre la ~** to promise the moon *ou* the earth; **elle veut lui faire voir la ~ en plein midi** she's trying to pull the wool over his eyes; **il y a (bien) des ~s†** many moons ago; **vieilles ~s** outdated notions; *voir* **face.**

luné, e* [lyne] **adj: être bien/mal ~** to be in a good/bad mood; **comment est-elle ~e ce matin?** what sort of (a) mood is she in this morning?

lunetier, -ière [lyn(ə)tje, jɛʀ] 1 **adj** spectacle manufacturing. 2 **nm,f** optician, spectacle manufacturer.

lunette [lynɛt] 1 **nf** a **~s** (*correctives*) glasses, specs*, spectacles†; (*de protection*) goggles, glasses; (*fig*) **mets tes ~s!** put your specs* on!

b (*Astron: télescope*) telescope; *[fusil]* sight(s). **fusil à ~** rifle equipped with sights.

c (*Archit*) lunette.

2 **comp** ▸**lunette d'approche** telescope ▸**lunette arrière** (*Aut*) rear window ▸**lunette astronomique** astronomical telescope ▸**lunette des cabinets** (*cuvette*) toilet bowl; (*siège*) toilet rim ▸**lunettes d'écaille** horn-rimmed spectacles ▸**lunette méridienne** meridian circle ▸**lunettes noires** dark glasses ▸**lunettes de plongée** swimming *ou* diving goggles ▸**lunettes de soleil** sunglasses, shades* ▸**lunettes de vue** prescription *ou* corrective glasses.

lunetterie [lynɛtʀi] **nf** spectacle trade.

lunule [lynyl] **nf** *[ongle]* half-moon, lunula (*SPÉC*); (*Math*) lune.

lupanar [lypanaʀ] **nm** (*littér*) brothel.

lupin [lypɛ̃] **nm** lupin.

lupus [lypys] **nm** lupus.

lurette [lyʀɛt] **nf** *voir* **beau.**

lurex [lyʀɛks] **nm** lurex.

luron* [lyʀɔ̃] **nm: (joyeux** *ou* **gai) ~** gay dog; **c'est un (sacré) ~†** he's quite a lad*.

luronne* [lyʀɔn] **nf: (gaie) ~** (lively) lass; **c'est une (sacrée) ~†** she's quite a lass*.

Lusaka [lusaka] **n** Lusaka.

lusitanien, -ienne [lyzitanjɛ̃, jɛn] 1 **adj** Lusitanian. 2 **nm,f: L~(ne)** Lusitanian.

lustrage [lystʀaʒ] **nm** (*Tech*) *[étoffe, peaux, fourrures]* lustring; *[glace]* shining.

lustral, e, mpl -aux [lystʀal, o] **adj** (*littér*) lustral (*littér*).

lustre [lystʀ] **nm** a *[objet, peaux, vernis]* lustre, shine; (*fig*) *[personne, cérémonie]* lustre. **redonner du ~ à une institution** to give new lustre to an institution. b (*luminaire*) centre light (*with several bulbs*). c (*littér: 5 ans*) lustrum (*littér*). (*fig*) **depuis des ~s** for ages, for aeons.

lustré, e [lystʀe] (**ptp de lustrer**) **adj** *cheveux, fourrure, poil* glossy; *manche usée* shiny.

lustrer [lystʀe] 1 **vt** (*Tech*) *étoffe, peaux, fourrures* to lustre; *glace* to shine; (*gén: faire briller*) to shine, put a shine on; (*par l'usure*) to make shiny. **le chat lustre son poil** the cat is licking its fur; **la pluie lustrait le feuillage** the rain put a sheen on the leaves; **tissu qui se lustre facilement** fabric that soon becomes shiny.

lustrerie [lystʀəʀi] **nf** lighting (appliance) trade.

lustrine [lystʀin] **nf** (*Tex*) lustre.

Lutèce [lytɛs] **nf** Lutetia.

lutécien, -ienne [lytesjɛ̃, jɛn] 1 **adj** Lutetian. 2 **nm,f: L~(ne)** Lutetian.

lutétium [lytesjɔm] **nm** lutetium.

luth [lyt] nm lute.
Luther [lytɛʀ] nm Luther.
luthéranisme [lyteʀanism] nm Lutheranism.
luthérien, -ienne [lyteʀjɛ̃, jɛn] 1 adj Lutheran. 2 nm,f: **L~(ne)** Lutheran.
luthier [lytje] nm (stringed-)instrument maker.
luthiste [lytist] nm lutanist.
lutin, e [lytɛ̃, in] 1 adj impish, mischievous. 2 nm (*esprit*) imp, sprite, goblin. (*fig*) **(petit) ~** (little) imp.
lutiner [lytine] [1] vt *femme* to fondle, tickle. **il aimait ~ les servantes** he enjoyed a bit of slap and tickle (*Brit*) *ou* fooling around with the serving girls.
lutrin [lytʀɛ̃] nm lectern.
lutte [lyt] 1 nf a (*gén: combat*) struggle, fight (*contre* against). **les ~s politiques qui ont déchiré le pays** the political struggles which have torn the country apart; **~ antipollution** fight against pollution; **~ contre l'alcoolisme** struggle *ou* fight against alcoholism; **~ contre le crime** crime prevention; **~ antidrogue** battle *ou* fight against drugs; **~ pour la vie** (*Bio, fig*) struggle for existence, struggle *ou* fight for survival; **aimer la ~** to enjoy a struggle; **entrer/être en ~ (contre qn)** to enter into/be in conflict (with sb); **en ~ ouverte contre sa famille** in open conflict with his family; **travailleurs en ~** (*en grève*) striking workers; **engager/abandonner la ~** to take up/give up the struggle *ou* fight; **nous soutenons une ~ inégale** we're fighting an uneven battle, it's an unequal struggle; **après plusieurs années de ~** after several years of struggling; (*Mil*) **le pays en ~** the country at war; (*Pol*) **les partis en ~** the opposing parties; **gagner *ou* conquérir qch de haute ~** to win sth by a hard-fought struggle *ou* after a brave fight *ou* struggle; **~ entre le bien et le mal** conflict *ou* struggle between good and evil; **~ de l'honneur et de l'intérêt** conflict between honour and self-interest.
b (*Sport*) wrestling. **~ libre/gréco-romaine** all-in/Graeco-Roman wrestling.
2 comp ►**lutte armée** armed struggle; **en lutte armée** in armed conflict ►**lutte des classes** class struggle *ou* war ►**lutte d'intérêts** conflict *ou* clash of interests.
lutter [lyte] [1] vi a (*se battre*) to struggle, fight. **~ contre un adversaire** to struggle *ou* fight against an opponent; **~ contre le vent** to fight against *ou* battle with the wind; **~ contre l'ignorance/un incendie** to fight ignorance/a fire; **~ contre l'adversité/le sommeil** to fight off adversity/sleep; **~ contre la mort** to fight *ou* struggle for one's life; **~ avec sa conscience** to struggle *ou* wrestle with one's conscience; **les deux navires luttaient de vitesse** the two ships were racing each other.
b (*Sport*) to wrestle.
lutteur, -euse [lytœʀ, øz] nm,f (*Sport*) wrestler; (*fig*) fighter.
lux [lyks] nm lux.
luxation [lyksasjɔ̃] nf dislocation, luxation (*SPÉC*).
luxe [lyks] nm a (*richesse*) wealth, luxury; *[maison, objet]* luxuriousness, sumptuousness. **vivre dans le ~** to live in (the lap of) luxury; **de ~** *voiture, appartement* luxury (*épith*); (*Aut*) **modèle (de) grand ~** de luxe model; (*Comm*) *produits* de luxe; **boutique de ~** shop selling luxury goods; **2 salles de bain dans un appartement, c'est du ~!** 2 bathrooms in a flat, it's the height of luxury! *ou* what luxury!; **je me suis acheté un nouveau manteau, ce n'était pas du ~** I bought myself a new coat — I had to have one *ou* I really needed one *ou* it was a basic necessity; **j'ai lavé la cuisine, ce n'était pas du ~!** I washed the kitchen floor, it had to be done.
b (*plaisir coûteux*) luxury. **il s'est offert *ou* payé le ~ d'aller au casino** he allowed himself the indulgence *ou* luxury of a trip to the casino; **je ne peux pas me payer le ~ d'être malade/d'aller au restaurant** I can't afford the luxury of being ill/eating out.
c (*fig: profusion*) wealth, host. **un ~ de détails/précautions** a host *ou* wealth of details/precautions.
Luxembourg [lyksɑ̃buʀ] nm: **(le grand-duché de) ~** (the Grand Duchy of) Luxembourg; (*Pol*) **le palais du ~** *the seat of the French Senate.*
luxembourgeois, e [lyksɑ̃buʀʒwa, waz] 1 adj of *ou* from Luxembourg. 2 nm,f: **L~(e)** inhabitant *ou* native of Luxembourg.
luxer [lykse] [1] vt to dislocate, luxate (*SPÉC*). **se ~ un membre** to dislocate a limb; **avoir l'épaule luxée** to have a dislocated shoulder.
luxueusement [lyksɥøzmɑ̃] adv luxuriously.
luxueux, -euse [lyksɥø, øz] adj luxurious.
luxure [lyksyʀ] nf lust.
luxuriance [lyksyʀjɑ̃s] nf luxuriance.
luxuriant, e [lyksyʀjɑ̃, jɑ̃t] adj *végétation* luxuriant, lush; (*fig*) *imagination* fertile, luxuriant (*littér*).
luxurieux, -ieuse [lyksyʀjø, jøz] adj lustful, lascivious, sensual.
luzerne [lyzɛʀn] nf lucerne, alfalfa.
LV [ɛlve] nf (abrév de **langue vivante**) modern language.
lycanthropie [likɑ̃tʀɔpi] nf lycanthropy.
lycée [lise] nm lycée, ≃ secondary school (*Brit*), high school (*US*). **~ technique, ~ professionnel** *secondary school for vocational training.*
lycéen [liseɛ̃] nm secondary school (*Brit*) *ou* high-school (*US*) boy *ou* pupil. **lorsque j'étais ~** when I was at secondary school; **quelques ~s étaient attablés à la terrasse** some boys from the secondary school were sitting at a table outside the café; **les ~s sont en grève** pupils at secondary schools are on strike.
lycéenne [liseɛn] nf secondary school (*Brit*) *ou* high-school (*US*) girl *ou* pupil.
lychee [litʃi] nm = **litchi**.
Lycra [likʀa] nm ® Lycra ®. **en ~** Lycra (*épith*).
lymphatique [lɛ̃fatik] adj (*Bio*) lymphatic; (*fig*) lethargic, sluggish, lymphatic (*frm*).
lymphe [lɛ̃f] nf lymph.
lymphocyte [lɛ̃fɔsit] nm lymphocyte.
lymphoïde [lɛ̃fɔid] adj lymphoid.
lynchage [lɛ̃ʃaʒ] nm lynching.
lyncher [lɛ̃ʃe] [1] vt to lynch.
lynx [lɛ̃ks] nm lynx; *voir* **œil**.
Lyon [ljɔ̃] n Lyons.
lyonnais, e [ljɔnɛ, ɛz] 1 adj of *ou* from Lyons; (*Culin*) Lyonnaise. 2 nm,f: **L~(e)** inhabitant *ou* native of Lyons.
lyophile [ljɔfil] adj lyophilic.
lyophiliser [ljɔfilize] [1] vt to freeze-dry, lyophilize (*SPÉC*). **café lyophilisé** freeze-dried coffee.
lyre [liʀ] nf (*Mus*) lyre; *voir* **oiseau**.
lyrique [liʀik] adj a (*Poésie*) lyric. b (*Mus, Théât*) **art ~** opera; **artiste/théâtre ~** opera singer/house; **ténor/soprano ~** lyric tenor/soprano; **drame ~** lyric drama, opera; **comédie ~** comic opera. c (*enthousiaste*) lyrical.
lyrisme [liʀism] nm lyricism. **s'exprimer avec ~ sur** to wax lyrical about, enthuse over.
lys [lis] nm = **lis**.

M

M, m [ɛm] **nm** a (*lettre*) M, m. b **M.** (**abrév de Monsieur**) Mr; **M. Martin** Mr Martin. c **m** (**abrév de mètre**) m.
m' [m] *voir* **me.**
ma [ma] **adj poss** *voir* **mon.**
MA [ɛma] **nmf** (**abrév de maître auxiliaire**) *voir* **maître.**
maboul, e*† [mabul] **adj, nm,f** (*fou*) loony*, crackpot*.
mac‡ [mak] **nm** (*souteneur*) pimp, ponce‡.
macabre [makɑbʀ] **adj** *histoire, découverte* macabre, gruesome; *goûts, humour* macabre, ghoulish.
macache‡† [makaʃ] **adv:** ~! **tu ne l'auras pas** not flipping likely!‡ (*Brit*) *ou* nothing doing!* you're not getting it; ~ **(bono)! il n'a pas voulu** nothing doing!* *ou* not a chance!* he wouldn't have it.
macadam [makadam] **nm** a (*substance*) *[pierres]* macadam; *[goudron]* Tarmac(adam) ®. ~ **goudronné** Tarmac(adam) ®. b (*fig: rue, route*) road.
macadamisage [makadamizaʒ] **nm, macadamisation** [makadamizasjɔ̃] **nf** (*voir* **macadamiser**) macadamization, macadamizing; tarmacking.
macadamiser [makadamize] 1 **vt** (*empierrer*) to macadamize; (*goudronner*) to tarmac. **chaussée** *ou* **route macadamisée** macadamized road; tarmac road.
Macao [makao] **n** Macao.
macaque [makak] **nm** (*Zool*) macaque. ~ **rhésus** rhesus monkey; (*fig*) **qui est ce (vieux)** ~?* who's that ugly (old) ape?‡
macareux [makaʀø] **nm** puffin.
macaron [makaʀɔ̃] **nm** a (*Culin*) macaroon. b (*insigne*) (round) badge; (*autocollant*) (round) sticker; (*: *décoration*) medal, gong*. ~ **publicitaire** publicity badge; (*sur voiture*) advertising sticker. c (*Coiffure*) ~**s** coils, earphones*. d (‡: *coup*) blow, cuff, clout* (*Brit*).
macaroni [makaʀɔni] **nm** a (*Culin*) piece of macaroni. **manger des** ~**s** to eat macaroni; ~**(s) au gratin** macaroni cheese (*Brit*), macaroni and cheese (*US*). b (*péj: Italien*) **(mangeur de)** ~**‡** Eyeti(e)‡ (*péj*), wop‡ (*péj*).
macaronique [makaʀɔnik] **adj** *vers etc* macaronic.
macchabée‡ [makabe] **nm** stiff‡ (*corpse*).
macédoine [masedwan] **nf** a (*Culin*) ~ **de légumes** mixed vegetables, macedoine (of vegetables); ~ **de fruits** (*gén*) fruit salad; (*en boîte*) fruit cocktail. b (* *fig: mélange*) jumble, hotchpotch. c (*Géog*) **M**~ Macedonia.
macédonien, -ienne [masedɔnjɛ̃, jɛn] 1 **adj** Macedonian. 2 **nm,f: M**~**(ne)** Macedonian.
macération [maseʀasjɔ̃] **nf** (*voir* **macérer**) a (*procédé*) maceration, steeping, soaking. **pendant leur** ~ **dans le vinaigre** while they are soaking in vinegar. b (*Rel: mortification*) mortification, scourging (of the flesh). **s'infliger des** ~**s** to scourge one's body *ou* flesh.
macérer [maseʀe] 6 1 **vt** a (*aussi* **faire** *ou* **laisser** ~) to macerate, steep, soak. b (*Rel: mortifier*) ~ **sa chair** to mortify one's *ou* the flesh. 2 **vi** a *[aliment]* to macerate, steep, soak. b (*fig péj*) ~ **dans son ignorance** to wallow in one's ignorance; (*faire attendre*) **laisser** ~ **qn (dans son jus)*** to keep sb hanging about*, keep sb waiting.
macfarlane [makfaʀlan] **nm** (*manteau*) Inverness cape.
Mach [mak] **nm** mach. **voler à** ~ **2** to fly at mach 2; **nombre de** ~ mach (number).
mâche [mɑʃ] **nf** corn salad, lambs' lettuce.
mâchefer [mɑʃfɛʀ] **nm** clinker (*NonC*), cinders.
mâcher [mɑʃe] 1 **vt** *[personne]* to chew; (*avec bruit*) to munch; *[animal]* to chomp; (*Tech*) to chew up. **il faut lui** ~ **tout le travail** you have to do half his work for him *ou* to spoon-feed him*; **il ne mâche pas ses mots** he doesn't mince his words; *voir* **papier.**
machette [maʃɛt] **nf** machete.
Machiavel [makjavɛl] **nm** Machiavelli.
machiavélique [makjavelik] **adj** Machiavellian.
machiavélisme [makjavelism] **nm** Machiavell(ian)ism.
mâchicoulis [mɑʃikuli] **nm** machicolation. **à** ~ machicolated.

machin* [maʃɛ̃] **nm** a (*chose, truc*) (*dont le nom échappe*) thingummyjig* (*Brit*), thingamajig (*US*), whatsit*, what-d'you-call-it*; (*qu'on n'a jamais vu avant*) thing, contraption; (*tableau, statue etc*) thing. **passe-moi ton** ~ give me your whatsit*; **les antibiotiques! il faut te méfier de ces** ~**s-là** antibiotics! you should beware of those things; **espèce de vieux** ~! you doddering old fool!* b (*personne*) **M**~ **(chouette), M**~ **(chose)** what's-his-name*, what-d'you-call-him*, thingumabob‡; **hé! M**~! hey (you), what's-your-name!*; **le père/la mère M**~ Mr/Mrs what's-his-/her-name*; *voir aussi* **Machine.**
machinal, e, **mpl -aux** [maʃinal, o] **adj** (*automatique*) mechanical, automatic; (*involontaire*) automatic, unconscious.
machinalement [maʃinalmɑ̃] **adv** (*voir* **machinal**) mechanically; automatically; unconsciously. **j'ai fait ça** ~ I did it automatically *ou* without thinking.
machination [maʃinasjɔ̃] **nf** (*frm: complot*) plot, machination; (*coup monté*) put-up job*, frame-up. **être l'objet d'odieuses** ~**s** to be the victim of foul machinations *ou* schemings.
Machine* [maʃin] **nf** (*personne*) what's-her-name*, what-d'you-call-her*. **hé!** ~! hey! (you) what's-your-name!*; *voir aussi* **machin.**
machine [maʃin] 1 **nf** a (*Tech*) machine; (*locomotive*) engine, locomotive; (*avion*) plane, machine; (*: *bicyclette, moto*) bike*, machine. (*fig*) **il n'est qu'une** ~ **à penser** he's nothing more than a sort of thinking machine; (* *fig: corps*) **la** ~ **est usée/fatiguée** the old body is wearing out/getting tired; **le siècle de la** ~ the century of the machine; *voir* **salle.**

b (*structure*) machine; (*processus*) machinery. **la** ~ **politique/parlementaire** the political/parliamentary machine; **la** ~ **de l'État** the machinery of state; **la** ~ **humaine** the human body; **la** ~ **administrative** the bureaucratic machine *ou* machinery.

c **faire qch à la** ~ to machine sth, do sth on a machine; **fait à la** ~ machine-made, done *ou* made on a machine; **cousu/tricoté à la** ~ machine-sewn/-knitted; *voir* **taper.**

d (*Naut*) engine. **faire** ~ **arrière** (*lit*) to go astern; (*fig*) to backpedal, draw back, retreat; **le gouvernement a dû faire** ~ **arrière** the government was forced to retreat; *voir* **salle.**

2 **comp** ►**machine à affranchir** franking machine ►**machine agricole** agricultural machine ►**machine de bureau** business *ou* office machine ►**machine à café** coffee machine ►**machine à calculer** calculating machine ►**machine comptable** adding machine, calculating machine ►**machine à coudre** sewing machine ►**machine à écrire** typewriter ►**machine de guerre** (*gén*) machine of war, instrument of warfare ►**machine infernale†** time bomb, (explosive) device ►**machine à laver** washing machine ►**machine à laver la vaisselle** dishwasher ►**machine-outil** **nf** (**pl machines-outils**) machine tool ►**machine simple** simple machine ►**machine à sous** (*pour parier de l'argent*) one-armed bandit, fruit machine (*Brit*); (*distributeur automatique*) slot machine ►**machine à timbrer** = **machine à affranchir** ►**machine à tisser** power loom ►**machine à traitement de texte (dédiée)** (dedicated) word processor ►**machine à tricoter** knitting machine ►**machine à vapeur** steam engine; **machine à vapeur à simple effet** simple steam engine; **machine à vapeur à double effet** double-acting engine.
machiner [maʃine] 1 **vt** *trahison* to plot; *complot* to hatch. **tout était machiné d'avance** the whole thing was fixed beforehand *ou* was prearranged, it was all a put-up job*; **c'est lui qui a tout machiné** he engineered the whole thing; **qu'est-ce qu'il est en train de** ~? what is he hatching?*
machinerie [maʃinʀi] **nf** a (*équipement*) machinery, plant (*NonC*). b (*salle*) (*Naut*) engine room; (*atelier*) machine room.
machinisme [maʃinism] **nm** mechanization.
machiniste [maʃinist] **nm** (*Théât*) scene shifter, stagehand; (*Ciné*) (special) effects man; (*Transport*) driver (*of bus, underground train etc*). **"faire signe au** ~**"** ≃ "request stop".
machisme [ma(t)ʃism] **nm** a (*phallocratie*) male chauvinism. b

(*virilité*) machismo.
machiste [ma(t)ʃist] **adj** (male) chauvinist.
macho* [matʃo] **nm** a (*phallocrate*) male chauvinist (pig)*. **il est ~, c'est un ~** he's a male chauvinist pig*. b (*viril*) macho.
mâchoire [mɑʃwaʀ] **nf** (*Anat, Tech, Zool*) jaw. (*Aut*) **~s de frein** brake shoes; *voir* **bâiller**.
mâchonnement [mɑʃɔnmɑ̃] **nm** chewing; (*Méd*) bruxism (*SPÉC*).
mâchonner [mɑʃɔne] 1 **vt** a (*) *[personne]* to chew (at); *[cheval]* to munch. **~ son crayon** to chew *ou* bite one's pencil. b (*fig: marmonner*) to mumble, mutter.
mâchouiller* [mɑʃuje] 1 **vt** to chew (away) at *ou* on.
mâchure [mɑʃyʀ] **nf** *[drap, velours]* flaw.
mâchurer [mɑʃyʀe] 1 **vt** a (*salir*) *papier, habit* to stain (black); *visage* to blacken; (*Typ*) to mackle, blur. b (*Tech: écraser*) to dent. c (*mâcher*) to chew.
macle[1] [makl] **nf** water chestnut.
macle[2] [makl] **nf** (*cristal*) twin, macle; (*Hér*) mascle.
maclé, e [makle] **adj** *cristal* twinned, hemitrope.
mâcon [mɑkɔ̃] **nm** Mâcon (wine).
maçon [masɔ̃] **nm** a (*gén*) builder; (*qui travaille la pierre*) (stone) mason; (*qui pose les briques*) bricklayer. **ouvrier** *ou* **compagnon ~** bricklayer's mate. b = **franc-maçon**; *voir* **franc**[1].
maçonnage [masɔnaʒ] **nm** (*travail*) building; (*en briques*) bricklaying; (*ouvrage*) masonry, stonework; brickwork; (*revêtement*) facing.
maçonne [masɔn] **adjf** *voir* **abeille, fourmi**.
maçonner [masɔne] 1 **vt** (*construire*) to build; (*consolider*) to build up; (*revêtir*) to face; (*boucher*) (*avec briques*) to brick up; (*avec pierres*) to block up (with stone).
maçonnerie [masɔnʀi] **nf** a *[pierres]* masonry, stonework; *[briques]* brickwork. **~ de béton** concrete; **~ en blocage** *ou* **de moellons** rubble work. b (*travail*) building; (*avec briques*) bricklaying. **entrepreneur/entreprise de ~** building contractor/firm; **grosse ~** erection of the superstructure; **petite ~** finishing and interior building. c = **franc-maçonnerie**; *voir* **franc**[1].
maçonnique [masɔnik] **adj** masonic, Masonic.
macramé [makʀame] **nm** macramé. **en ~** macramé (*épith*).
macre [makʀ] **nf** = **macle**[1].
macreuse [makʀøz] **nf** (*Culin*) shoulder of beef; (*Orn*) scoter.
macro... [makʀɔ] **préf** macro... .
macrobiotique [makʀɔbjɔtik] 1 **adj** macrobiotic. 2 **nf** macrobiotics (*sg*).
macrocéphale [makʀosefal] **adj** macrocephalic.
macrocosme [makʀɔkɔsm] **nm** macrocosm.
macro-économie [makʀoekɔnɔmi] **nf** macroeconomics (*sg*).
macro-économique [makʀoekɔnɔmik] **adj** macroeconomic.
macrographie [makʀɔgʀafi] **nf** macrography.
macromolécule [makʀomɔlekyl] **nf** macromolecule.
macrophage [makʀɔfaʒ] 1 **adj** macrophagic. 2 **nm** macrophage.
macrophotographie [makʀofɔtɔgʀafi] **nf** macrophotography.
macroscopique [makʀɔskɔpik] **adj** macroscopic.
macrostructure [makʀostʀyktyʀ] **nf** macrostructure.
maculage [makylaʒ] **nm, maculation** [makylasjɔ̃] **nf** a (*gén*) maculation. b (*Typ*) (*action*) offsetting; (*tache*) offset, set-off.
maculature [makylatyʀ] **nf** (*Typ*) spoil (sheets), waste (sheets); (*feuille intercalaire*) interleaf.
macule [makyl] **nf** *[encre]* mackle, smudge; (*Astron, Méd*) macula; (*Typ*) smudge, set-off, blot, mackle; (*papier*) rough brown (wrapping) paper.
maculer [makyle] 1 **vt** to stain (*de* with); (*Typ*) to mackle, blur. **une chemise maculée de boue** a shirt spattered *ou* covered with mud.
Madagascar [madagaskaʀ] **nf** Madagascar. **République démocratique de ~** Malagasy Republic.
Madame [madam], **pl Mesdames** [medam] **nf** a (*s'adressant à qn*) **bonjour ~** (*courant*) good morning; (*nom connu*) good morning, Mrs X; (*frm*) good morning, Madam; **bonjour Mesdames** good morning (ladies); **~, vous avez oublié quelque chose** excuse me *ou* Madam (*frm*) you've forgotten something; (*devant un auditoire*) **Mesdames** ladies; **Mesdames, Mesdemoiselles, Messieurs** ladies and gentlemen; **~ la Présidente** *[société, assemblée]* Madam Chairman; *[gouvernement]* Madam President; **oui ~ la Générale/la Marquise** yes Mrs X/Madam; (*Scol*) **~!** please Mrs X!, please Miss!; (*au restaurant*) **et pour (vous) ~?** and for (you) madam?; (*frm*) **~ est servie** dinner is served (Madam); (*iro*) **~ n'est pas contente!** her ladyship *ou* Madam isn't pleased! (*iro*).
b (*parlant de qn*) **~ X est malade** Mrs X is ill; **~ votre mère†** your dear *ou* good mother; (*frm*) **~ est sortie** Madam *ou* the mistress is not at home; **je vais le dire à ~** (*parlant à un visiteur*) I will inform Madam (*frm*) *ou* Mrs X; (*parlant à un autre domestique*) I'll tell Mrs X *ou* the missus*†; **~ dit que c'est à elle** the lady says it belongs to her; **~ la Présidente** the chairperson, the chairman; **veuillez vous occuper de ~** please attend to this lady('s requirements).
c (*sur une enveloppe*) **~ X** Mrs X; (*Admin*) **~ veuve X** Mrs X, widow of the late John *etc* X; **Mesdames X** the Mrs X; **Mesdames X et Y** Mrs X and Mrs Y; **Monsieur X et ~** Mr and Mrs X; **~ la Maréchale X** Mrs X; **~ la Marquise de X** the Marchioness of X; **Mesdames les employées du service de comptabilité** (the ladies on) the staff of the accounts department.
d (*en-tête de lettre*) Dear Madam. **Chère ~** Dear Mrs X; (*Admin*) **~, Mademoiselle, Monsieur** Dear Sir or Madam; **~ la Maréchale/Présidente/Duchesse** Dear Madam.
e (*Hist: parente du roi*) Madame.
f (*sans majuscule, pl madames*) (* *ou péj*) lady. **jouer à la m~** to play the fine lady, put on airs and graces; **toutes ces (belles) madames** all these fine ladies; **c'est une petite m~ maintenant** she's quite a (grown-up) young lady now.
madeleine [madlɛn] **nf** a (*Culin*) madeleine. b **M~** Magdalen(e), Madel(e)ine; *voir* **pleurer**.
Madelinot, e [madlino, ɔt] **nm,f** inhabitant *ou* native of the Magdalen Islands.
Madelon [madlɔ̃] **nf** (**dim de Madeleine**).
Mademoiselle [madmwazɛl], **pl Mesdemoiselles** [medmwazɛl] **nf** a (*s'adressant à qn*) **bonjour ~** (*courant*) good morning; (*nom connu: frm*) good morning, Miss X; **bonjour Mesdemoiselles** good morning ladies; (*jeunes filles*) good morning young ladies; **~, vous avez oublié quelque chose** excuse me miss, you've forgotten something; (*au restaurant*) **et pour vous ~?** and for the young lady?, and for you, miss?; (*devant un auditoire*) **Mesdemoiselles** ladies; (*iro*) **~ n'est pas contente!** her ladyship isn't pleased!
b (*parlant de qn*) **~ X est malade** Miss X is ill; **~ votre sœur†** your dear sister; (*frm*) **~ est sortie** the young lady (of the house) is out; **je vais le dire à ~** I shall tell Miss X; **~ dit que c'est à elle** the young lady says it's hers.
c (*sur une enveloppe*) **~ X** Miss X; **Mesdemoiselles X** the Misses X; **Mesdemoiselles X et Y** Miss X and Miss Y.
d (*en-tête de lettre*) Dear Madam. **Chère ~** Dear Miss X.
e (*Hist: parente du roi*) Mademoiselle.
Madère [madɛʀ] **nf: (l'île de) ~** Madeira.
madère [madɛʀ] **nm** Madeira (wine); *voir* **sauce**.
madériser (se) [madeʀize] 1 **vpr** *[eau-de-vie, vin]* to oxidize.
Madone [madɔn] **nf** a (*Art, Rel*) Madonna. b (*fig*) **m~** beautiful woman, madonna-like woman; **elle a un visage de m~** she has the face of a madonna.
madras [madʀɑs] 1 **nm** (*étoffe*) madras (cotton); (*foulard*) (madras) scarf. 2 **n: M~** Madras.
madré, e [mɑdʀe] **adj** a *paysan* crafty, wily, sly. (*hum*) **c'est une petite ~e!** she is a crafty *ou* fly* (*Brit*) one! (*hum*). b *bois* whorled.
madrépore [madʀepɔʀ] **nm** madrepore. **~s** Madrepora.
Madrid [madʀid] **n** Madrid.
madrier [madʀije] **nm** beam.
madrigal, pl -aux [madʀigal, o] **nm** (*Littérat, Mus*) madrigal; (†*: propos galant*) compliment.
madrilène [madʀilɛn] 1 **adj** of *ou* from Madrid. 2 **nmf: M~** inhabitant *ou* native of Madrid.
maelstrom [malstʀɔm] **nm** (*lit, fig*) maelstrom.
maestria [maɛstʀija] **nf** (masterly) skill, mastery (*à faire qch* in doing sth). **avec ~** brilliantly, in a masterly fashion, with consummate skill.
maestro [maɛstʀo] **nm** (*Mus*) maestro.
maf(f)ia [mafja] **nf** a **la M~** the Maf(f)ia. b (*fig*) *[bandits, trafiquants]* gang, ring. **~ d'anciens élèves** old boys' network; **c'est une vraie ~!** what a bunch* *ou* shower‡ (*Brit*) of crooks!
maf(f)ieux, -ieuse [mafjø, jøz] 1 **adj** Mafia (*épith*). 2 **nm,f** maf(f)ioso.
maf(f)ioso [mafjozo], **pl maf(f)iosi** [mafjozi] **nm** maf(f)ioso.
mafflu, e [mafly] **adj** (*littér*) *visage, joues* round, full.
magasin [magazɛ̃] 1 **nm** a (*boutique*) shop, store; (*entrepôt*) warehouse. **faire** *ou* **courir les ~s** to go shopping, go (a)round *ou* do the shops; **nous ne l'avons pas en ~** we haven't got it in stock; *voir* **chaîne, grand**.
b (*Tech*) *[fusil, appareil-photo]* magazine.
2 **comp ▸ magasin des accessoires** (*Théât*) prop room **▸ magasin d'alimentation** grocery store **▸ magasin d'armes** (*Mil*) armoury **▸ magasin de confection** (ready-to-wear) dress shop *ou* tailor's (*Brit*), clothing store (*US*) **▸ magasin des décors** (*Théât*) scene dock **▸ magasins généraux** (*Comm, Jur*) bonded warehouse **▸ magasin à grande surface** hypermarket (*Brit*), supermarket **▸ magasin d'habillement** (*Mil*) quartermaster's stores **▸ magasin (à) libre service** self-service store **▸ magasin à prix unique** one-price store, dime store (*US*), ten-cent store (*US*) **▸ magasin à succursales (multiples)** chain store **▸ magasin d'usine** factory shop **▸ magasin de vivres** (*Mil*) quartermaster's stores.
magasinage [magazinaʒ] **nm** a (*Comm*) warehousing. **frais de ~** storage costs. b (*Can*) shopping. **faire son ~** to do one's shopping.
magasiner [magazine] 1 **vi** (*Can*) to go shopping.
magasinier [magazinje] **nm** *[usine]* storekeeper, storeman; *[entrepôt]* warehouseman.
magazine [magazin] **nm** (*Presse*) magazine. (*Rad, TV*) **~ féminin/pour les jeunes** woman's/children's hour; **~ d'actualités** news magazine; **~ hebdomadaire/mensuel** weekly/monthly (magazine); **~ de luxe** glossy*

(magazine).

mage [maʒ] nm (*Antiq, fig*) magus; (*devin, astrologue*) witch. (*Rel*) **les (trois) Rois ~s** the Magi, the (Three) Wise Men.

magenta [maʒɛ̃ta] adj inv, nm magenta.

Maghreb [magʀɛb] nm: **le ~** the Maghreb, North Africa.

maghrébin, e [magʀebɛ̃, in] 1 adj of *ou* from the Maghreb *ou* North Africa. 2 nm,f: **M~(e)** North African.

magicien, -ienne [maʒisjɛ̃, jɛn] nm,f (*sorcier, illusionniste*) magician; (*fig*) wizard, magician.

magie [maʒi] nf magic. **~ blanche/noire** white/black magic; **la ~ du verbe** the magic of words; **comme par ~** like magic, (as if) by magic; **c'est de la ~** it's (like) magic; *[prestidigitateur]* **faire de la ~** to perform *ou* do magic tricks.

magique [maʒik] adj *mot, baguette, pouvoir* magic; (*enchanteur*) *spectacle* magical; *voir* **lanterne**.

magiquement [maʒikmɑ̃] adv magically.

magister† [maʒistɛʀ] nm (village) schoolmaster; (*péj*) pedant.

magistère [maʒistɛʀ] nm a (*Univ*) *diploma taken over 3 years after completing 2 years at university, usually in vocational subjects,* ≃ master's degree. b (*Rel*) magisterium. c (*Alchimie*) magistery.

magistral, e, mpl **-aux** [maʒistʀal, o] adj a (*éminent*) *œuvre* masterly, brilliant; *réussite* brilliant, magnificent; *adresse* masterly. b (*hum: gigantesque*) *claque, râclée* thorough, colossal, sound. c (*doctoral*) *ton* authoritative, masterful; (*Univ*) **cours ~** lecture; **enseignement ~** lecturing. d (*Pharm*) magistral. e (*Tech*) **ligne ~e** magistral line.

magistralement [maʒistʀalmɑ̃] adv (*voir* **magistral**) in a masterly manner; brilliantly; magnificently.

magistrat [maʒistʀa] nm magistrate.

magistrature [maʒistʀatyʀ] nf a (*Jur*) magistracy, magistrature. **la ~ assise** *ou* **du siège** the judges, the bench; **la ~ debout** the state prosecutors. b (*Admin, Pol*) public office. **la ~ suprême** the supreme *ou* highest office.

magma [magma] nm (*Chim, Géol*) magma; (*fig: mélange*) jumble, muddle.

magmatique [magmatik] adj magmatic.

magnanime [maɲanim] adj magnanimous. **se montrer ~** to show magnanimity.

magnanimement [maɲanimmɑ̃] adv magnanimously.

magnanimité [maɲanimite] nf magnanimity.

magnat [magna] nm tycoon, magnate. **~ de la presse/du textile** press/textile baron *ou* lord *ou* tycoon; **~ du pétrole** oil tycoon.

magner (se)* [maɲe] 1 vpr to get a move on*, hurry up. **magne-toi (le train** *ou* **le popotin)!** get a move on!*, get moving!*, hurry up!

magnésie [maɲezi] nf magnesia.

magnésium [maɲezjɔm] nm magnesium; *voir* **éclair**.

magnétique [maɲetik] adj (*Phys, fig*) magnetic. **champ/pôle ~** magnetic field/pole; *voir* **bande¹**.

magnétisable [maɲetizabl] adj (*voir* **magnétiser**) magnetizable; hypnotizable.

magnétisation [maɲetizasjɔ̃] nf (*voir* **magnétiser**) magnetization; mesmerization, hypnotization.

magnétiser [maɲetize] 1 vt a (*Phys, fig*) to magnetize. b (*hypnotiser*) to mesmerize, hypnotize.

magnétiseur, -euse [maɲetizœʀ, øz] nm,f hypnotizer.

magnétisme [maɲetism] nm (*Phys, charme*) magnetism; (*hypnotisme*) hypnotism, mesmerism. **~ terrestre** terrestrial magnetism; **le ~ d'un grand homme** the magnetism *ou* charisma of a great man.

magnétite [maɲetit] nf lodestone, magnetite.

magnéto¹ [maɲeto] nm abrév de **magnétophone**.

magnéto² [maɲeto] nf (*Élec*) magneto.

magnéto-cassette, pl **magnéto-cassettes** [maɲetokasɛt] nm cassette player *ou* recorder.

magnéto-électrique [maɲetoelɛktʀik] adj magnetoelectric.

magnétophone [maɲetɔfɔn] nm tape recorder. **~ à cassette(s)** cassette recorder; **enregistré au ~** (tape-)recorded, taped.

magnétoscope [maɲetɔskɔp] nm (*appareil*) video (tape *ou* cassette) recorder; (*bande*) video-tape. **enregistrer au ~** to video, video-tape, take a video (recording) of.

magnétoscoper [maɲetɔskɔpe] 1 vt to video, video-tape, take a video (recording) of.

magnétoscopique [maɲetɔskɔpik] adj: **enregistrement ~** video (tape *ou* cassette) recording.

magnificat [maɲifikat] nm inv magnificat.

magnificence [maɲifisɑ̃s] nf (*littér*) a (*faste*) magnificence, splendour. b (*prodigalité*) munificence (*littér*), lavishness.

magnifier [maɲifje] 7 vt (*littér: louer*) to magnify (*littér*), glorify; (*idéaliser*) to idealize.

magnifique [maɲifik] adj a (*somptueux*) *appartement, repas* magnificent, sumptuous; *cortège* splendid, magnificent; *cadeau, réception* magnificent, lavish. b (*splendide*) *femme, fleur* gorgeous, superb; *paysage, temps* magnificent, glorious, gorgeous; *projet, situation* magnificent, marvellous. **~!*** fantastic!*, great!*; **il a été ~ hier soir!** he was magnificent *ou* fantastic* *ou* great* last night! c **Soliman le M~** Soliman the Magnificent.

magnifiquement [maɲifikmɑ̃] adv (*voir* **magnifique**) magnificently; sumptuously; lavishly; gorgeously; superbly; marvellously.

magnitude [maɲityd] nf (*Astron, Géol*) magnitude. **séisme de ~ 7 sur l'échelle de Richter** earthquake measuring 7 *ou* of magnitude 7 on the Richter scale.

magnolia [maɲɔlja] nm, **magnolier** [maɲɔlje] nm magnolia.

magnum [magnɔm] nm magnum.

magot [mago] nm a (*Zool*) Barbary ape, magot. b (*Sculp*) magot. c (*) (*somme d'argent*) pile (of money)*, packet*; (*économies*) savings, nest egg. **ils ont amassé un joli ~** they've made a nice little pile* *ou* packet*, they've got a tidy sum put by *ou* a nice little nest egg.

magouillage* [magujaʒ] nm, **magouille*** [maguj] nf (*péj*) scheming (*péj*), fiddle*. **c'est le roi de la magouille** he's a born schemer; **magouillage électoral** pre-election scheming; **sombre magouille** dirty bit of business.

magouiller* [maguje] 1 vi (*péj*) to scheme (*péj*).

magouilleur, -euse* [magujœʀ, øz] 1 adj (*péj*) fly*, crafty*. 2 nm,f (*péj*) schemer (*péj*), crafty operator* (*Brit*).

magret [magʀɛ] nm: **~ (de canard)** steaklet of duck, duck cutlet.

magyar, e [magjaʀ] 1 adj Magyar. 2 nm,f: **M~(e)** Magyar.

mahara(d)jah [maaʀa(d)ʒa] nm Maharajah.

maharani [ma(a)ʀani] nf, **maharané** [maaʀane] nf Maharanee.

mahatma [maatma] nm mahatma.

mah-jong [maʒɔ̃g] nm mah-jong(g).

Mahomet [maɔmɛt] nm Mahomet, Mohammed.

mahométan, -ane† [maɔmetɑ̃, an] adj Mahometan, Mohammedan.

mahométisme† [maɔmetism] nm Mohammedanism.

mahous* [maus] adj = **maous***.

mai [mɛ] nm May; *pour loc voir* **septembre** *et* **premier**.

maie [mɛ] nf (*huche*) bread box; (*pour pétrir*) dough trough.

maïeutique [majøtik] nf maieutics (*sg*).

maigre [mɛgʀ] 1 adj a *personne* thin, skinny (*péj*); *animal* thin, scraggy; *visage, joue* thin, lean; *membres* thin, scrawny (*péj*), skinny. **~ comme un clou** *ou* **un chat de gouttière*** as thin as a rake *ou* a lath (*Brit*) *ou* a rail (*US*).

b (*Culin: après n*) *bouillon* clear; *viande* lean; *fromage* low-fat.

c (*Rel*) **repas ~** meal without meat; **faire ~ (le vendredi)** (*gén*) to abstain from meat (on Fridays); (*manger du poisson*) to eat fish (on Fridays); **le vendredi est un jour ~** people don't eat meat on Fridays.

d (*peu important*) *profit, revenu* meagre, small, slim, scanty; *ration, salaire* meagre, poor; *résultat* poor; *exposé, conclusion* sketchy, skimpy, slight; *espoir, chance* slim, slight. **comme dîner, c'est un peu ~** it's a bit of a skimpy *ou* meagre dinner, it's not much of a dinner.

e (*peu épais*) *végétation* thin, sparse; *récolte, terre* poor. **un ~ filet d'eau** a thin trickle of water; **~ eau** shallow water; (*hum*) **avoir le cheveu ~** to be a bit thin on top.

f (*Typ*) **caractère ~** light-faced letter.

2 nmf: **grand/petit ~** tall/small thin person; **les gros et les ~s** fat people and thin people; **c'est une fausse ~** she looks deceptively thin.

3 nm a (*Culin*) (*viande*) lean meat; (*jus*) thin gravy.

b (*Géog*) *[fleuve]* **~s** shallows.

c (*Typ*) light face.

d (*poisson*) meagre.

maigrelet, -ette [mɛgʀəlɛ, ɛt] adj thin, scrawny, skinny. **un gamin ~** a skinny little kid*; **un petit ~** a skinny little chap *ou* fellow *ou* man.

maigrement [mɛgʀəmɑ̃] adv poorly, meagrely. **être ~ payé** to be badly *ou* poorly paid.

maigreur [mɛgʀœʀ] nf *[personne]* thinness, leanness; *[animal]* thinness, scrawniness, scragginess; *[membre]* thinness, scrawniness, skinniness; *[végétation]* thinness, sparseness; *[sol]* poverty; *[profit]* meagreness, smallness, scantiness; *[salaire]* meagreness, poorness; *[réponse, exposé]* sketchiness, poverty; *[preuve, sujet, auditoire]* thinness; *[style]* thinness, baldness. **il est d'une ~!** he's so thin! *ou* skinny!

maigrichon, -onne* [mɛgʀiʃɔ̃, ɔn] adj, **maigriot, -iotte*** [mɛgʀijo, ijɔt] adj = **maigrelet**.

maigrir [mɛgʀiʀ] 2 1 vi to grow *ou* get thinner, lose weight. **je l'ai trouvé maigri** I thought he had got thinner *ou* he was thinner *ou* he had lost weight; **il a maigri de visage** his face has got thinner; **il a maigri de 5 kg** he has lost 5 kg; **régime/pastilles pour ~** slimming (*Brit*) *ou* reducing (*US*) diet/tablets; **se faire ~** to slim (*Brit*), diet (to lose weight). 2 vt: **~ qn** *[vêtement]* to make sb look slim(mer); **(faire) ~ qn** *[maladie, régime]* to make sb lose weight; **faire ~ qn** *[médecin]* to make sb take off *ou* lose weight.

mail [maj] nm a (*promenade*) mall†, (riverside) tree-lined walk. b (††) (*jeu, terrain*) (pall-)mall; (*maillet*) mall.

mailing [meliŋ] nm mailing. **faire un ~** to do a mailing *ou* a mailshot.

maille [maj] nf a (*Couture*) stitch. *[tissu, tricot]* **~ qui a filé** stitch which has run; *[bas]* **~ filée** ladder (*Brit*), run; **~ (à l')endroit** plain (stitch); **~ (à l')envers** purl (stitch); **une ~ à l'endroit, une ~ à l'envers** knit one, purl one; **tissu à fines ~s** fine-knit material; **la ~** (*tissu*) tricot; (*secteur économique*) the knitwear industry. b *[filet]* mesh. (*lit, fig*) **passer entre** *ou* **à travers les ~s (du filet)** to slip through the net; **à**

larges/fines ~s wide/fine mesh (*épith*). c *[armure, grillage]* link; *voir* **cotte.** d **avoir ~ à partir avec qn** to get into trouble with sb, have a brush with sb.

maillechort [majʃɔʀ] **nm** nickel silver.

maillet [majɛ] **nm** mallet.

mailloche [majɔʃ] **nf** (*Tech*) beetle, maul; (*Mus*) bass drumstick.

maillon [mɑjɔ̃] **nm** a (*anneau*) link. (*fig*) **il n'est qu'un ~ de la chaîne** he's just one link in the chain. b (*petite maille*) small stitch.

maillot [majo] 1 **nm** a (*gén*) vest; (*Danse*) leotard; *[footballeur]* (football) shirt *ou* jersey; *[coureur]* vest, singlet. (*Sport*) **porter le ~ jaune, être ~ jaune** to wear the yellow jersey, be leader of the Tour (de France *etc*). b *[bébé]* swaddling clothes (*Hist*), baby's wrap. **enfant** *ou* **bébé au ~** babe in arms. 2 **comp ▸ maillot de bain** *[homme]* swimming *ou* bathing trunks, bathing suit†; *[femme]* swimming *ou* bathing costume, swimsuit; **maillot de bain une pièce/deux pièces** one-piece/two-piece swimsuit **▸ maillot de corps** vest (*Brit*), undershirt (*US*).

main [mɛ̃] 1 **nf** a hand. **serrer la ~ à** *ou* **de qn** to shake hands with sb; **se donner** *ou* **se serrer la ~** to shake hands; **tendre la ~ à qn** to hold out one's hand to sb; **donner la ~ à qn, tenir la ~ à** *ou* **de qn** to hold sb's hand; **donne-moi la ~ pour traverser** give me your hand *ou* let me hold your hand to cross the street; **ils se tenaient (par) la ~** *ou* **se donnaient la ~** they were holding hands; **il me salua de la ~** he waved to me; **il me fit adieu de la ~** he waved goodbye to me; **il entra le chapeau à la ~** he came in with his hat in his hand; **être adroit/maladroit de ses ~s** to be clever/clumsy with one's hands; **d'une ~ experte** with an expert hand; **à ~s nues** *boxer* without gloves, with bare fists *ou* hands; **les ~s nues** (*sans gants*) with bare hands; **prendre des deux ~s/de la ~ gauche** to take with both hands/with one's left hand; (*Ftbl*) **il y a ~!** hands!, hand ball!; **de ~ en ~** from hand to hand; **la ~ dans la ~** *[promeneurs]* hand in hand; *[escrocs]* hand in glove; **regarde, sans les ~s!** look, no hands!; **les ~s en l'air!** hands up!, stick 'em up!

b (*symbole d'autorité, de possession, d'aide*) hand. **la ~ de Dieu/de la fatalité** the hand of God/of fate; **trouver une ~ secourable** to find a helping hand; (*aider*) **donner la ~ à qn** to give sb a hand; (*s'aider*) **se donner la ~** to give one another a helping hand; **tu es aussi maladroit que moi, on peut se donner la ~** you're as clumsy as me, we're two of a kind; **il lui faut une ~ ferme** he needs a firm hand; **une ~ de fer dans un gant de velours** an iron hand in a velvet glove; **dans des ~s indignes** in unworthy hands; *[affaire, dossier]* **être entre les ~s de qn** to be in sb's hands; **ma vie est entre vos ~s** my life is in your hands; **tomber aux** *ou* **dans les ~s de l'ennemi** to fall into the hands of the enemy; **obtenir la ~ d'une jeune fille (en mariage)** to win a girl's hand (in marriage); **accorder la ~ de sa fille à qn** to give sb one's daughter's hand in marriage; *voir* **haut.**

c (*manière, habileté*) **de la ~ de Cézanne** by Cézanne; **reconnaître la ~ de l'artiste/de l'auteur** to recognize the artist's/writer's stamp; **de ~ de maître** with a master's hand; **perdre la ~** to lose one's touch; **garder la ~** to keep one's hand in; **se faire la ~** to get one's hand in.

d (*Cartes*) **avoir/perdre la ~** to have/lose the lead; *voir aussi* **j.**

e (*écriture*) hand(writing). **c'était (écrit) de sa ~** it was in his hand(writing).

f (*couturière*) **petite ~** apprentice seamstress.

g (*Comm*) *[papier]* ≃ quire (*25 sheets*).

h (*Afrique*) *[bananes]* hand, bunch.

i (*loc*) **à ~ droite/gauche** on the right-/left-hand side; **ce livre est en ~** this book is in use *ou* is out; **l'affaire est en ~** the matter is being dealt with *ou* attended to; **en ~s sûres** in(to) safe hands; (*Fin*) **en ~ tierce** in escrow; **avoir une voiture bien en ~** to have the feel of a car; **avoir la situation bien en ~** to have the situation well in hand *ou* well under control; **de la ~ à la ~** directly (*without receipt*); **préparé de longue ~** prepared long beforehand; **de première/seconde ~** *information, ouvrage* firsthand/secondhand; (*Comm*) **de première ~** secondhand (*only one previous owner*); **fait (à la) ~** handmade, done *ou* made by hand; **cousu (à la) ~** hand-sewn; **vol/attaque à ~ armée** armed robbery/attack; **(pris) la ~ dans le sac** caught red-handed, caught in the act; **(en) sous ~** *négocier, agir* secretly; **les ~s vides** empty-handed; (*fig: sans rien préparer*) **les ~s dans les poches** unprepared; **avoir tout sous la ~** to have everything to hand *ou* at hand *ou* handy; **on prend ce qui tombe sous la ~** we take whatever comes to hand; **ce papier m'est tombé sous la ~** I came across this paper; **à ~ levée** *vote* on *ou* by a show of hands; *dessin* freehand; **un coup de ~*** (*aide*) a (helping) hand, help; (*raid*) a raid; **donne-moi un coup de ~*** give me a hand.

j (*loc verbales*) **il a eu la ~ heureuse: il a choisi le numéro gagnant** it was a lucky shot his picking the winning number; **en engageant cet assistant on a vraiment eu la ~ heureuse** when we took on that assistant we really picked a winner; **avoir la ~ malheureuse** to be heavy-handed *ou* clumsy; **avoir la ~ lourde** *[commerçant]* to be heavy-handed *ou* over-generous; *[juge]* to mete out justice with a heavy hand; **ce boucher a toujours la ~ lourde** this butcher always gives *ou* cuts you more than you ask for; **le juge a eu la ~ lourde** the judge gave him a stiff sentence; **avoir la ~ légère** to rule with a light hand; **avoir la ~ leste** to be free *ou* quick with one's hands; (*fig*) **avoir les ~s liées** to have one's hands tied; **il faudrait être à sa ~ pour réparer ce robinet** you'd have to be able to get at this tap properly to mend it; **je ne suis pas à ma ~** I can't get a proper hold *ou* grip, I'm not in the right position; **faire ~ basse sur qch*** to run off *ou* make off with sth, help o.s. to sth; **ils font ~ basse sur nos plus beaux hôtels** they're buying up all our best hotels; **laisser les ~s libres à qn** to give sb a free hand *ou* rein; **mettre la ~ au collet de qn** to arrest sb, collar* sb; **en venir aux ~s** to come to blows; **mettre la ~ sur** *objet, livre* to lay (one's) hands on; *coupable* to arrest, lay hands on, collar*; **je ne peux pas mettre la ~ sur mon passeport** I can't lay hands on my passport; **mettre la ~ à la pâte** to lend a hand, muck in*; **mettre la dernière ~ à** to put the finishing *ou* crowning touches to; **passer la ~** to stand down, make way for someone else; **passer la ~ dans le dos à qn** to rub sb up the right way; **se passer la ~ dans le dos** to pat one another on the back; **tu n'as qu'à te prendre par la ~** you (will) just have to go for it; **prendre qch/qn en ~** to take sth/sb in hand; **il me l'a remis en ~s propres** he handed *ou* gave it to me personally; **prendre qn/qch en ~** to take sb/sth in hand; **il n'y va pas de ~ morte** (*exagérer*) he doesn't do things by halves; (*frapper*) he doesn't pull his punches; **j'en mettrais ma ~ au feu** *ou* **à couper** I'd stake my life on it; *voir* **lever, salir.**

2 **comp ▸ la main chaude** (*Jeux*) hot cockles **▸ main courante** (*câble*) handrail; (*Comm*) rough book, daybook; **faire établir une main courante** (*Police*) to notify the police of a complaint **▸ main de Fatma** hand of Fatima **▸ main-forte: prêter** *ou* **donner main-forte à qn** to come to sb's assistance, come to help sb **▸ main-d'œuvre nf** labour, manpower, labour force, workforce; **main-d'œuvre qualifiée** skilled labour; **il m'a compté 2 heures de main-d'œuvre** he charged me 2 hours' labour **▸ main de ressort** (*Aut*) dumb iron.

mainate [mɛnat] **nm** myna(h) bird.

Maine [mɛn] **nm** Maine.

mainlevée [mɛ̃l(ə)ve] **nf** (*Jur*) withdrawal. (*Fin*) **~ d'hypothèque** release of mortgage.

mainmise [mɛ̃miz] **nf** (*Jur*) seizure; (*Pol*) takeover. **la ~ de l'État sur cette entreprise** the seizure of this company by the state.

maint, mainte [mɛ̃, mɛ̃t] **adj** (*littér*) (a great *ou* good) many (+ *npl*), many a (+ *n sg*). **~ étranger** many a foreigner; **~s étrangers** many foreigners; **à ~es reprises, (~es et) ~es fois** time and (time) again, many a time.

maintenance [mɛ̃t(ə)nɑ̃s] **nf** maintenance, servicing.

maintenant [mɛ̃t(ə)nɑ̃] **adv** a (*en ce moment*) now. **que fait-il ~?** what's he doing now?; **il doit être arrivé ~** he must have arrived by now; **~ qu'il est grand** now that he's bigger; *voir* **dès, jusque, partir**[1].

b (*à ce moment*) now, by now. **ils devaient ~ chercher à se nourrir** they had now to try and find something to eat; **ils étaient ~ très fatigués** by now they were very tired; **ils marchaient ~ depuis 2 heures** they had (by) now been walking for 2 hours.

c (*actuellement*) today, nowadays. **les jeunes de ~** young people nowadays *ou* today.

d (*ceci dit*) now (then). **~ ce que j'en dis c'est pour ton bien** now (then) what I say is for your own good; **il y a un cadavre, certes: ~, y a-t-il un crime?** we're agreed there's a corpse, now the question is, is there a crime?

maintenir [mɛ̃t(ə)niʀ] [22] 1 **vt** a (*soutenir, contenir*) *édifice* to hold *ou* keep up, support; *cheville, os* to give support to, support; *cheval* to hold in. **~ qch fixe/en équilibre** to keep *ou* hold sth in position/balanced; **les oreillers le maintiennent assis** the pillows keep him in a sitting position *ou* keep him sitting up; **~ la tête hors de l'eau** to keep one's head above water; **~ la foule** to keep *ou* hold the crowd back *ou* in check; **~ les prix** to keep prices steady *ou* in check.

b (*garder*) (*gén*) to keep; *statu quo, tradition* to maintain, preserve, uphold; *régime* to uphold, support; *décision* to maintain, stand by, uphold; *candidature* to maintain. **~ qn en vie** to keep sb alive; **~ des troupes en Europe** to keep troops in Europe; **~ l'ordre/la paix** to keep *ou* maintain law and order/the peace; **~ qn en poste** to keep sb on, keep sb at *ou* in his job.

c (*affirmer*) to maintain. **je l'ai dit et je le maintiens!** I've said it and I'm sticking to it! *ou* I'm standing by it!; **~ que** to maintain *ou* hold that.

2 **se maintenir vpr** *[temps]* to stay fair; *[amélioration]* to persist; *[préjugé]* to live on, persist, remain; *[malade]* to hold one's own. **se ~ en bonne santé** to keep in good health, manage to keep well; **les prix se maintiennent** prices are keeping *ou* holding steady; **cet élève devrait se ~ dans la moyenne** this pupil should be able to keep up with the middle of the class; **comment ça va? — ça se maintient*** how are you getting on? — bearing up* *ou* so-so* *ou* not too badly; **se ~ en équilibre sur un pied/sur une poutre** to balance on one foot/on a beam; **se ~ sur l'eau pendant plusieurs minutes sans bouée** to stay afloat for several minutes without a lifebelt.

maintien [mɛ̃tjɛ̃] **nm** a (*sauvegarde*) *[tradition]* preservation, upholding, maintenance; *[régime]* upholding. **assurer le ~ de** *tradition* to maintain, preserve, uphold; *régime* to uphold, support; **le ~ des prix/de troupes/de l'ordre** the maintenance of prices/of troops/of law and order; **qu'est-ce qui a pu justifier le ~ de sa décision/candidature?** what(ever) were his reasons for standing by his decision/for maintaining his candidature? b (*posture*) bearing, deportment. **leçon de ~** lesson in deportment; **professeur de ~** teacher of deportment.

maire [mɛʀ] **nm** mayor. (*hum*) **passer devant (monsieur) le ~** to get hitched*, get married; *voir* **adjoint, écharpe.**

mairesse† [mɛʀɛs] **nf** mayoress.

mairie [meʀi] **nf** (*bâtiment*) town hall, city hall; (*administration*) town council, municipal corporation; (*charge*) mayoralty, office of mayor. **la ~ a décidé que ...** the (town) council has decided that ...; *voir* **secrétaire.**

mais¹ [mɛ] 1 **conj** a (*objection, restriction, opposition*) but. **ce n'est pas bleu ~ (bien) mauve** it isn't blue, it's (definitely) mauve; **non seulement il boit ~ (encore *ou* en outre) il bat sa femme** not only does he drink but on top of that *ou* even worse he beats his wife; **il est peut-être le patron ~ tu as quand même des droits** he may be the boss but you've still got your rights; **il est parti? ~ tu m'avais promis qu'il m'attendrait!** he has left? but you promised he'd wait for me!

b (*renforcement*) **je n'ai rien mangé hier, ~ vraiment rien** I ate nothing at all yesterday, absolutely nothing; **tu me crois? — ~ oui *ou* bien sûr *ou* certainement** do you believe me? — (but) of course *ou* of course I do; **~ je te jure que c'est vrai!** but I swear it's true!; **~ si je veux bien!** but of course I agree!, sure, I agree!; **~ ne te fais pas de soucis!** don't you worry!

c (*transition, surprise*) **~ qu'arriva-t-il?** but what happened (then)?; **~ alors qu'est-ce qui est arrivé?** well then *ou* for goodness' sake what happened?; **~ dites-moi, c'est intéressant tout ça!** well, well *ou* well now that's all very interesting!; **~ j'y pense, vous n'avez pas déjeuné** by the way I've just thought, you haven't had any lunch; **~, vous pleurez** good Lord *ou* gracious, you're crying; **~ enfin, tant pis!** well, too bad!

d (*protestation, indignation*) **ah ~! il verra de quel bois je me chauffe** I can tell you he'll soon see what I have to say about it; **non ~ (des fois)! *ou* (alors)!*** hey look here!*, for goodness sake!*; **non ~ (des fois)* tu me prends pour un imbécile?** I ask you* *ou* come off it*, do you think I'm a complete idiot?; **~ enfin tu vas te taire?*** look here, are you going to *ou* will you shut up?*

2 **nm** (*sg*) objection, snag; (*pl*) buts. **je ne veux pas de ~** I don't want any buts; **il n'y a pas de ~ qui tienne** there's no but about it; **il y a un ~** there's one snag *ou* objection; **il va y avoir des si et des ~** there are sure to be some ifs and buts.

mais² [mɛ] **adv** (*littér*, †) **il n'en pouvait ~** (*impuissant*) he could do nothing about it; (*épuisé*) he was exhausted *ou* worn out.

maïs [mais] **nm** maize (*Brit*), Indian corn (*Brit*), corn (*US*); *voir* **farine.**

maison [mɛzɔ̃] 1 **nf** a (*bâtiment*) house; (*immeuble*) building; (*locatif*) block of flats (*Brit*), apartment building (*US*). **~ (d'habitation)** dwelling house, private house; **une ~ de 5 pièces** a 5-roomed house; **~ individuelle** house (*as opposed to apartment*); (*secteur*) **la ~ individuelle** private housing; **ils ont une petite ~ à la campagne** they have a cottage in the country; *voir* **pâté.**

b (*logement, foyer*) home. **être/rester à la ~** to be/stay at home *ou* in; **rentrer à la ~** to go (back) home; **quitter la ~** to leave home; **tenir la ~ de qn** to keep house for sb; **les dépenses de la ~** household expenses; **fait à la ~** home-made; **c'est la ~ du bon Dieu, c'est une ~ accueillante** they keep open house, their door is always open; *voir* **linge, maître, train.**

c (*famille, maisonnée*) family. **quelqu'un de la ~ m'a dit** someone in the family told me; **un ami de la ~** a friend of the family; **il n'est pas heureux à la ~** he doesn't have a happy home life *ou* family life; **nous sommes 7 à la ~** there are 7 of us at home.

d (*entreprise commerciale*) firm, company; (*magasin de vente*) (*grand*) store, (*petit*) shop. **il est dans la ~ depuis 15 ans, il a 15 ans de ~** he's been *ou* he has worked with the firm for 15 years; **la ~ n'est pas responsable de ...** the company *ou* management accepts no responsibility for ...; **c'est offert par la ~** it's on the house; **la ~ ne fait pas crédit** no credit (given); **la M~ du Disque/du Café** the Record/Coffee Shop; *voir* **confiance.**

e (*famille royale*) House. **la ~ des Hanovre/des Bourbon** the House of Hanover/of Bourbon.

f (*place de domestiques, domesticité*) household. **la ~ du Roi/du président de la République** the Royal/Presidential Household; **~ civile/militaire** civil/military household; **gens† *ou* employés de ~** servants, domestic staff.

g (*Astrol*) house, mansion; (*Rel*) house.

2 **adj inv** a (*fait à la maison*) *gâteau* home-made; (**: formé sur place*) *ingénieur* trained by the firm. (*Comm: spécialité*) **pâté ~** pâté maison, chef's own pâté.

b (**: intensif*) first-rate. **il y a eu une bagarre ~ *ou* une bagarre quelque chose de ~** there was an almighty* *ou* a stand-up row.

3 **comp** ▸**maison d'arrêt** prison ▸**la Maison Blanche** the White House ▸**maison bourgeoise** large impressive house ▸**maison de campagne** (*grande*) house in the country; (*petite*) (country) cottage ▸**maison centrale** prison, (state) penitentiary (*US*) ▸**maison close** brothel ▸**maison de commerce** (commercial) firm ▸**maison de correction†** (*Jur*) reformatory† (*Brit*), industrial training school† ▸**maison de couture** couture house ▸**maison de la culture** (community) arts centre ▸**la Maison de Dieu** = **la Maison du Seigneur** ▸**maison d'édition** publishing house ▸**maison d'éducation surveillée** ≃ approved school (*Brit*), reformatory (*US*) ▸**maison de fous*** (*lit, fig*) ≃ madhouse ▸**maison de gros** wholesaler's ▸**maison de jeu** gambling *ou* gaming club ▸**maison des jeunes et de la culture** ≃ community arts centre, youth club and arts centre ▸**maison jumelle** semi-detached (house) (*Brit*), duplex (*US*) ▸**maison de maître** family mansion ▸**maison mère** (*Comm*) parent company; (*Rel*) mother house ▸**maison de passe** *hotel used as a brothel* ▸**maison de poupée** doll's house ▸**maison de la presse** ≃ newsagent's (*Brit*), ≃ newsdealer (*US*) ▸**maison de rapport** block of flats for letting (*Brit*), rental apartment building (*US*) ▸**maison de redressement†** reformatory† (*Brit*), industrial training school† ▸**maison religieuse** convent ▸**maison de rendez-vous** *house used by lovers as a discreet meeting-place* ▸**maison de repos** convalescent home ▸**maison de retraite** old people's home ▸**maison de santé** (*clinique*) nursing home; (*asile*) mental home ▸**la Maison du Seigneur** the House of God ▸**maison de tolérance** = **maison close.**

maisonnée [mɛzɔne] **nf** household, family.

maisonnette [mɛzɔnɛt] **nf** small house, maisonette; (*rustique*) cottage.

maistrance [mɛstʀɑ̃s] **nf** petty officers.

maître, maîtresse [mɛtʀ, mɛtʀɛs] 1 **adj** a (*principal*) *branche* main; *pièce, œuvre* main, major; *qualité* chief, main, major; (*Cartes*) *atout, carte* master (*épith*). **c'est une œuvre maîtresse** it's a major work; **c'est la pièce maîtresse de la collection** it's the major *ou* main *ou* principal piece in the collection; **poutre maîtresse** main beam; **position maîtresse** major *ou* key position; **idée maîtresse** principal *ou* governing idea.

b (*avant n: intensif*) **un ~ filou *ou* fripon** an arrant *ou* out-and-out rascal; **une maîtresse femme** a managing woman.

2 **nm** a (*gén*) master; (*Art*) master; (*Pol: dirigeant*) ruler. **parler/agir en ~** to speak/act authoritatively; **ils se sont installés en ~s dans ce pays** they have set themselves up as the ruling power in the country, they have taken command of the country; **d'un ton de ~** in an authoritative *ou* a masterful tone; **je vais t'apprendre qui est le ~ ici!** I'll teach you who is the boss* round here! *ou* who's in charge round here!; **la main/l'œil du ~** the hand/eye of a master; (*fig*) **le grand ~ des études celtiques** the greatest authority on Celtic studies; **le ~ de céans** the master of the house; (*Naut*) **seul ~ à bord après Dieu** sole master on board under God; *voir* **chauffeur, toile.**

b (*Scol*) **~ (d'école)** teacher, (school)master; **~ de piano/d'anglais** piano/English teacher.

c (*artisan*) **~ charpentier/maçon** master carpenter/mason *ou* builder.

d (*titre*) **M~** *term of address given to lawyers, artists, professors etc;* (*dans la marine*) petty officer; **mon cher M~** Dear Mr *ou* Professor *etc* X; (*Art*) maestro; (*Jur*) **M~ X** Mr X.

e (*loc*) **coup de ~** masterstroke; (*Cartes*) **être ~ à cœur** to have *ou* hold the master *ou* best heart; **le roi de cœur est ~** the king of hearts is master, the king is the master *ou* best heart; **être ~ chez soi** to be master in one's own home; **être son (propre) ~** to be one's own master; **être ~ de refuser/de faire** to be free to refuse/do; **rester ~ de soi** to retain *ou* keep one's self-control; **être ~ de soi** to be in control *ou* have control of o.s.; **être/rester ~ de la situation** to be/remain in control of the situation, have/keep the situation under control; **être/rester ~ de sa voiture** to be/remain in control of one's car; **être ~ de sa destinée** to be the master of one's fate; **être/rester ~ du pays** to be/remain in control *ou* command of the country; **être ~ d'un secret** to be in possession of a secret; **être ~ de son sujet** to have a mastery of one's subject; **se rendre ~ de** *ville, pays* to gain control *ou* possession of; *personne, animal, incendie, situation* to bring *ou* get under control; **il est passé ~ dans l'art de mentir** he's a past master in the art of lying.

3 **maîtresse nf** a (*gén*) mistress; (*amante, petite amie*) mistress.

b (*Scol*) **maîtresse (d'école)** teacher, (school)mistress; **maîtresse!** (please) Miss!

c (*loc*) **être/rester/se rendre/passer maîtresse (de)** *voir* **2 e.**

4 **comp** ▸**maître d'armes** (*Sport*) fencing master ▸**maître assistant** (*Univ*) ≃ (senior) lecturer (*Brit*), assistant professor (*US*) ▸**maître-autel nm, (pl maîtres-autels)** (*Rel*) high altar ▸**maître auxiliaire** (*Scol*) supply teacher (*Brit*), substitute teacher (*US*) ▸**maître/maîtresse de ballet** (*Danse*) ballet master/mistress ▸**maître des cérémonies** master of ceremonies ▸**maître chanteur** blackmailer; (*Mus*) Meistersinger, mastersinger ▸**maître de chapelle** (*Mus*) choirmaster, precentor ▸**maître-chien nm, (pl maîtres-chiens)** dog handler ▸**maître de conférences mf** (*Univ*) ≃ (senior) lecturer (*Brit*), assistant professor (*US*) ▸**maître d'équipage** boatswain ▸**maître/maîtresse d'études** (*Scol*) master/mistress in charge of homework preparation ▸**maître de forges†** ironmaster ▸**maître d'hôtel** *[maison]* butler; *[hôtel, restaurant]* head waiter; (*Naut*) chief steward; (*Culin*) **pommes de terre maître d'hôtel** maître d'hôtel potatoes ▸**maître/maîtresse d'internat** house master/mistress ▸**maître Jacques** jack-of-all-trades ▸**maître de maison** host ▸**maîtresse de maison** housewife; (*hôtesse*) hostess ▸**maître nageur** swimming teacher *ou* instructor ▸**maître d'œuvre** (*Constr*) project manager; **la mairie est maître d'œuvre de ce projet** the town council is in charge of the project ▸**maître d'ouvrage** (*Constr*) owner ▸**maître à penser** intellectual guide *ou* leader ▸**maître queux** (*Culin*) chef ▸**maître des requêtes** (*Admin*) **mf** counsel of the Conseil d'État

▸ **maître titulaire** permanent teacher (*in primary school*).
maîtrisable [metʀizabl] adj (*gén nég*) controllable. **difficilement** *ou* **guère** ~ almost uncontrollable, scarcely controllable.
maîtrise [metʀiz] nf a (*sang-froid*) ~ **(de soi)** self-control, self-command, self-possession.
b (*contrôle*) mastery, command, control. (*Mil*) **avoir la ~ de la mer** to have control *ou* mastery of the sea, control the sea; (*Comm*) **avoir la ~ d'un marché** to control *ou* have control of a market; **sa ~ du français** his mastery *ou* command of the French language; **avoir la ~ de l'atome** to have mastered the atom.
c (*habileté*) skill, mastery, expertise. **faire** *ou* **exécuter qch avec ~** to do sth with skill *ou* skilfully.
d (*Ind*) supervisory staff; *voir* **agent**.
e (*Rel*) (*école*) choir school; (*groupe*) choir.
f (*Univ*) *research degree*, ≃ master's degree. **~ de conférences** ≃ senior lectureship.
maîtriser [metʀize] 1 1 vt a (*soumettre*) *cheval, feu, foule, forcené* to control, bring under control; *adversaire* to overcome, overpower; *émeute, révolte* to suppress, bring under control; *problème, difficulté* to master, overcome; *inflation* to curb; *langue, technique* to master. b (*contenir*) *émotion, geste, passion* to control, master, restrain; *larmes, rire* to force back, restrain, control. **il ne peut plus ~ ses nerfs** he can no longer control *ou* contain his temper. 2 **se maîtriser** vpr to control o.s. **elle ne sait pas se ~** she has no self-control.
maïzena [maizena] nf ® cornflour (*Brit*), cornstarch (*US*).
majesté [maʒɛste] nf a (*dignité*) majesty; (*splendeur*) majesty, grandeur. **la ~ divine** divine majesty; (*Art*) **de** *ou* **en ~** in majesty, enthroned. b **Votre M~** Your Majesty; **Sa M~** (*roi*) His Majesty; (*reine*) Her Majesty; *voir* **lèse-majesté, pluriel**.
majestueusement [maʒɛstɥøzmɑ̃] adv majestically, in a stately way.
majestueux, -euse [maʒɛstɥø, øz] adj (*solennel*) *personne, démarche* majestic, stately; (*imposant*) *taille* imposing, impressive; (*beau*) *fleuve, paysage* majestic, magnificent.
majeur, e [maʒœʀ] 1 adj a *ennui, empêchement* (*très important*) major; (*le plus important*) main, major, greatest. **ils ont rencontré une difficulté ~e** they came up against a major *ou* serious difficulty; **sa préoccupation ~e** his major *ou* main *ou* greatest concern; **pour des raisons ~es** for reasons of the greatest importance; **en ~e partie** for the most part; **la ~e partie de** the greater *ou* major part of, the bulk of; **la ~e partie des gens sont restés** most of *ou* the majority of the people have stayed on; *voir* **cas**.
b (*Jur*) of age (*attrib*). **il sera ~ en l'an 2000** he will come of age in the year 2000; **il n'est pas encore ~** he's not 18 yet, he's under 18; (*hum*) **il est ~ et vacciné** he's old enough to look after himself; (*fig*) **peuple ~** responsible *ou* adult nation; (*fig*) **électorat ~** adult electorate.
c (*Mus*) *intervalle, mode* major. **en sol ~** in G major.
d (*Logique*) *terme, prémisse* major.
e (*Rel*) **ordres ~s** major orders; **causes ~es** causae majores.
f (*Cartes*) **tierce/quarte ~e** tierce/quart major.
2 nm,f person who has come of *ou* who is of age, person who has attained his (*ou* her) majority, major (*SPÉC*).
3 nm middle finger.
4 **majeure** nf a (*Logique*) major premise.
b (*Univ: matière*) main subject (*Brit*), major (*US*).
major [maʒɔʀ] 1 nm a (*Mil*) ≃ adjutant. (*Mil*) **(médecin) ~** medical officer, M.O.; **~ général** (*Mil*) ≃ deputy chief of staff (*Brit*), major general (*US*); (*Naut*) ≃ rear admiral. b (*Univ etc*) **être ~ de promotion** ≃ to be *ou* come first in one's year. 2 adj inv *voir* **état-major, infirmière, sergent[1], tambour**.
majoration [maʒɔʀasjɔ̃] nf (*hausse*) rise, increase (*de* in); (*supplément*) surcharge, additional charge; (*surestimation*) overvaluation, overestimation. **~ sur une facture** surcharge on a bill; **~ pour retard de paiement** surcharge *ou* additional charge for late payment.
majordome [maʒɔʀdɔm] nm majordomo.
majorer [maʒɔʀe] 1 vt *impôt, prix* to increase, raise, put up (*de* by); *facture* to increase, put a surcharge on.
majorette [maʒɔʀɛt] nf (drum) majorette.
majoritaire [maʒɔʀitɛʀ] 1 adj *actionnaire, groupe, motion* majority (*épith*). **vote ~** majority vote; **les femmes sont ~s dans cette profession** women are in the majority in this profession; **les socialistes sont ~s dans le pays** the socialists are the majority *ou* largest party in the country; **ils sont ~s à l'assemblée** they are the majority party *ou* in the majority in Parliament; **dans ce vote, nous serons sûrement ~s** we shall certainly have a majority on this vote; *voir* **scrutin**. 2 nmf (*Pol*) member of the majority party.
majorité [maʒɔʀite] nf a (*électorale*) majority. **~ absolue/relative/simple** absolute/relative/simple majority; **~ qualifiée** *ou* **renforcée** qualified majority; **élu à une ~ de** elected by a majority of; **avoir la ~** to have the majority.
b (*parti majoritaire*) government, party in power. **député de la ~** member of the governing party *ou* of the party in power, ≃ government backbencher (*Brit*), majority party Representative (*US*); **la ~ et l'opposition** the government (*Brit*) *ou* the majority party and the opposition.
c (*majeure partie*) majority. **la ~ silencieuse** the silent majority; **être en ~** to be in (the) majority; **la ~ est d'accord** the majority agree; **les hommes dans leur grande ~** the great majority of mankind; **dans la ~ des cas** in the majority of cases, in most cases; **groupe composé en ~ de** group mainly *ou* mostly composed of.
d (*Jur*) **atteindre sa ~** to come of age, reach one's majority; **jusqu'à sa ~** until he comes of age *ou* reaches his majority.
Majorque [maʒɔʀk] nf Majorca.
majorquin, e [maʒɔʀkɛ̃, in] 1 adj Majorcan. 2 nm,f: **M~(e)** Majorcan.
Majuro [maʒyʀo] n Majuro.
majuscule [maʒyskyl] 1 adj capital; (*Typ*) upper case. **A ~** capital A. 2 nf: **(lettre) ~** capital letter; (*Typ*) upper case letter; **en ~s d'imprimerie** in block *ou* capital letters; **écrivez votre nom en ~s (d'imprimerie)** please print your name in block letters; **mettre une ~ à qch** (*gén*) to write sth with a capital; (*Typ*) to capitalize sth.
makaire [makɛʀ] nm (*poisson*) marlin.
mal [mal] 1 adv a (*de façon défectueuse*) *jouer, dormir* badly; *fonctionner* not properly, badly. **cette porte ferme ~** this door shuts badly *ou* doesn't shut properly; **il parle ~ l'anglais** he speaks English badly; **elle est ~ coiffée aujourd'hui** her hair's a mess today, her hair is not well *ou* nicely done today; **ce travail est ~ fait** this work is badly done; **c'est du travail ~ fait** this is poor *ou* shoddy work; **nous sommes ~ nourris/logés à l'hôtel** the food/accommodation is poor *ou* bad at the hotel, we don't find the food good at the hotel/the hotel comfortable; **ils vivent très ~ avec une seule paye** they live very meagrely on *ou* off just one wage; **redresse-toi, tu te tiens ~** stand up straight, you're not holding yourself properly; **il a ~ pris ce que je lui ai dit** he took exception *ou* did not take kindly to what I said to him; **il s'y est ~ pris (pour le faire)** he set about (doing) it *ou* he went about it the wrong way; **tu le connais ~** you don't know him; **de ~ en pis** from bad to worse.
b **~ choisi/informé/inspiré** *etc* ill-chosen/-informed/-advised *etc*; **~ acquis** ill-gotten; **~ à l'aise** ill-at-ease; **~ avisé** ill-advised; **~ embouché** coarse, ill-spoken; **~ famé** of ill fame, disreputable; **~ pensant** heretical, unorthodox; **~ en point** in a bad *ou* sorry state, in a poor condition; **~ à propos** at the wrong moment; **avoir l'esprit ~ tourné** to have a low *ou* dirty mind *ou* that sort of mind; **il est ~ venu de se plaindre** he is scarcely in a position to complain, he should be the last (one) to complain; *voir* **ours, vu[2]**.
c **~ comprendre** to misunderstand; **~ interpréter** to misinterpret; **~ renseigner** to misinform; **il comprend ~ ce qu'on lui dit** he doesn't understand properly what he is told; **il a ~ compris ce qu'ils lui ont dit** he didn't understand properly *ou* he misunderstood what they told him; **j'ai été ~ renseigné** I was misinformed *ou* given (the) wrong information; **phrase ~ formée** ill-formed sentence; *voir* **juger** *etc*.
d (*avec difficulté*) with difficulty. **il respire ~** he has difficulty in breathing, he can't breathe properly; **on s'explique** *ou* **comprend ~ pourquoi** it is not easy *ou* it is difficult to understand why; **nous voyons très ~ comment** ... we fail to see how ... .
e (*de façon répréhensible*) *se conduire* badly, wrongly. **il ne pensait pas ~ faire** he didn't think he was doing the wrong thing *ou* doing wrong; **il ne pense qu'à ~ faire** he's always looking for trouble, he's always thinking up some nasty trick; **se tenir ~ à table** to have bad table manners, behave badly at table; **trouves-tu ~ qu'il y soit allé?** do you think it was wrong of him to go?; **ça lui va ~ d'accuser les autres** who is he to accuse others?, it ill becomes him to accuse others (*littér*).
f (*malade*) **se sentir ~** to feel ill *ou* unwell *ou* sick, not to feel very well; **aller** *ou* **se porter ~, être ~ portant** to be in poor health; **elle s'est trouvée ~ à cause de la chaleur/en entendant la nouvelle** she fainted *ou* passed out in the heat/on hearing the news.
g **pas ~** (*assez bien*) not badly, rather well; **c'est pas ~*** it's quite good, it's not bad*; **on n'est pas ~ (assis) dans ces fauteuils** these armchairs are quite comfortable; **il n'a pas ~ travaillé ce trimestre** he's worked quite well this term; **vous (ne) vous en êtes pas ~ tirés** you haven't done *ou* come off badly, you've done rather well; **vous (ne) feriez pas ~ de le surveiller** you would be well-advised to keep *ou* it wouldn't be a bad thing if you kept an eye on him; **ça va? — pas ~** how are you? — not (too) bad* *ou* pretty good* *ou* pretty well*.
h **pas ~ (de)*** (*beaucoup*) quite a lot (of); **il y a pas ~ de temps qu'il est parti** it's quite a time since he left, he's been away for quite a time; **on a pas ~ travaillé aujourd'hui** we've done quite a lot of work today, we've worked pretty hard today*; **il est pas ~ fatigué** he is rather *ou* pretty* tired; **je m'en fiche pas ~!** I couldn't care less!, I don't give a damn!‡
2 adj inv a (*contraire à la morale*) wrong, bad. **il est** *ou* **c'est ~ de mentir/de voler** it is bad *ou* wrong to lie/to steal; (*iro*) **(pour elle) il ne peut rien faire de ~** (in her eyes) he can do no wrong; **c'est ~ à lui de dire cela** it's bad *ou* wrong of him to say this.
b (*malade*) ill. **il va** *ou* **est (très) ~ ce soir** he is (very) ill tonight; **il est au plus ~** he is very close to death, he's on the point of death.
c (*mal à l'aise*) uncomfortable. **vous devez être ~ sur ce banc** you must be uncomfortable on that seat, that seat can't be comfortable (for you); **je marche beaucoup, je ne m'en suis jamais trouvé ~** I walk a lot

and I'm none the worse for it *ou* and it's never done me any harm; **il est ~ dans sa peau** he's at odds with himself.

d **être ~ avec qn** to be on bad terms with sb, be in sb's bad books*; **se mettre ~ avec qn** to get on the wrong side of sb, get into sb's bad books*; **il sont au plus ~** they are at daggers drawn.

e **pas ~** (*bien*) not bad, quite *ou* rather good; (*assez beau*) quite attractive; (*compétent*) quite competent; **vous n'êtes pas ~ sur cette photo** this photo is not bad of you *ou* is rather good of you; *voir* **bon¹**.

3 **nm, pl maux** [mo] a (*ce qui est contraire à la morale*) **le ~** evil; **le bien et le ~** good and evil, right and wrong; **faire le ~ pour le ~** to do *ou* commit evil for its own sake *ou* for evil's sake.

b (*souffrance morale*) sorrow, pain. **le ~ du siècle** (*fléau*) the scourge of the age; (*littér*) world-weariness; **~ du pays** homesickness; **des paroles qui font du ~** words that hurt, hurtful words; (*fig*) **journaliste en ~ de copie** journalist short of copy; **en ~ d'argent** short of money; **être en ~ de tendresse** to yearn for a little tenderness; **être en ~ d'inspiration**to be lacking in inspiration, have no inspiration.

c (*travail pénible, difficulté*) difficulty, trouble. **ce travail/cet enfant m'a donné du ~** this work/child gave me some trouble; **se donner du ~ à faire qch** to take trouble *ou* pains over sth, go to great pains to do sth; **se donner un ~ de chien à faire qch*** to bend over backwards *ou* go to great lengths to do sth; **avoir du ~ à faire qch** to have trouble *ou* difficulty doing sth; **ne vous donnez pas le ~ de faire ça** don't bother to do that; **on n'a rien sans ~** you get nothing without (some) effort; **faire qch sans trop de ~/non sans ~** to do sth without undue difficulty/not without difficulty; **il a dû prendre son ~ en patience** (*attendre*) he had to put up with the delay; (*supporter*) he had to grin and bear it.

d (*ce qui cause un dommage, de la peine*) harm. **mettre qn à ~** to harm sb; **faire du ~ à** to harm, hurt; **il ne ferait pas de ~ à une mouche** he wouldn't hurt *ou* harm a fly; **excusez-moi — il n'y a pas de ~** I'm sorry — no harm done; **il n'y a pas de ~ à cela** there's no harm in that; **~ lui en a pris!** he's had cause to rue it!; **~ m'en a pris de sortir** going out was a grave mistake (on my part); **ça va faire ~!*** (*match*) it's going to be a real ding-dong match* (*Brit*) *ou* a real cracker* (*Brit*); (*produit*) it's going to be a big hit!; **ça me ferait ~!** it would make me sick!, it would madden me!; *voir* **vouloir**.

e (*ce qui est mauvais*) evil, ill. **les maux dont souffre notre société** the ills *ou* evils afflicting our society; **c'est un ~ nécessaire** it's a necessary evil; **de deux maux, il faut choisir le moindre** one must choose the lesser of two evils; **penser/dire du ~ de qn/qch** to think/speak ill of sb/sth; **sans penser** *ou* **songer à ~** without meaning any harm; *voir* **peur**.

f (*douleur physique*) pain, ache; (*maladie*) illness, disease, sickness. **prendre ~**† to be taken ill, feel unwell; **avoir ~ partout** to be aching all over; **où avez-vous ~?** where does it hurt?, where is the pain?; **le ~ s'aggrave** (*lit*) the disease is getting worse, he (*ou* she *etc*) is getting worse; (*fig*) the situation is deteriorating, things are getting worse; **j'ai ~ dans le dos/à l'estomac** I've got a pain in my back/in my stomach, my back/stomach hurts *ou* aches; **avoir un ~ de tête, avoir ~ à la tête** to have a headache *ou* a bad head*; **avoir ~ à la gorge** to have a sore throat; **avoir ~ aux dents/aux oreilles** to have toothache/earache; **avoir ~ au pied** to have a sore foot; **des maux d'estomac** stomach pains, an upset stomach; **un ~ blanc** a whitlow; **il s'est fait (du) ~ en tombant** he hurt himself in falling *ou* when he fell; **se faire ~ au genou** to hurt one's knee; **ces chaussures me font ~ (au pied)** these shoes hurt *ou* pinch (my feet); **avoir le ~ de mer/de l'air/de la route** to be seasick/airsick/carsick; **contre le ~ de mer/de l'air/de la route** against seasickness/airsickness/carsickness; **~ des montagnes/de l'espace** mountain/space sickness; **~ des transports** travel *ou* motion (*US*) sickness; **pilule contre le ~ des transports** travel-sickness pill, anti-motion-sickness pill (*US*); **~ des grands ensembles** depression resulting from life in a high-rise flat; (*hum*) **le ~ joli** the pains of (giving) birth; *voir* **cœur, ventre**.

Malabar [malabaʀ] **nm: le ~, la côte de ~** the Malabar (Coast).

malabar* [malabaʀ] **nm** muscle man*, hefty fellow*.

Malabo [malabo] **n** Malabo.

Malachie [malaʃi] **nm** Malachi.

malachite [malaʃit] **nf** malachite.

malade [malad] 1 **adj** a (*atteint*) *homme* ill, sick, unwell (*attrib*); *organe* diseased; *plante* diseased; *dent, poitrine* bad; *jambe, bras* bad, game* (*épith*), gammy* (*Brit*) (*épith*). **être bien/gravement/sérieusement ~** to be really/gravely/seriously ill; **être ~ du cœur, avoir le cœur ~** to have heart trouble *ou* a bad heart *ou* a heart condition; **être ~ des reins** to have kidney trouble; **tomber ~** to fall ill *ou* sick; **se faire porter ~** to report *ou* go sick; **je me sens (un peu) ~** I feel (a bit) peculiar* *ou* sick, I don't feel very well; **être ~ comme un chien** *ou* **une bête** (*gén*) to be dreadfully ill; (*euph: vomir*) to be as sick as a dog; **être ~ à crever‡** to be dreadfully ill, feel ghastly* *ou* like death (warmed up (*Brit*) *ou* warmed over (*US*))*; **j'ai été ~ après avoir mangé des huîtres** I was ill after eating oysters.

b (*fou*) mad. **tu n'es pas (un peu) ~?‡** are you quite right in the head?*, are you out of your mind?; **être ~ d'inquiétude** to be sick *ou* ill with worry; **être ~ de jalousie** to be mad *ou* sick with jealousy; **rien que d'y penser j'en suis ~, ça me rend ~ rien que d'y penser*** the very thought of it makes me sick *ou* ill, I'm sick at the very thought of it.

c (*en mauvais état*) *objet* in a sorry state. **l'entreprise étant ~ ils durent licencier** the business was failing *ou* was in a dicky* (*Brit*) *ou* shaky state and they had to pay people off; **le gouvernement est trop ~ pour durer jusqu'aux élections** the government is too shaky to last till the elections.

2 **nmf** a (*Méd*) (*gén*) invalid, sick person; (*d'un médecin*) patient. **grand ~** seriously ill person; **~ imaginaire** hypochondriac; **~ mental** mentally sick *ou* ill person; **les ~s** the sick; **les grands ~s** the seriously *ou* critically ill; **le médecin et ses ~s** the doctor and his patients.

b (**: fanatique*) **un ~ de la moto** a (motor)bike freak‡; **un ~ de la vitesse** a speed merchant*.

c (**: fou*) maniac*, madman*. **il conduit comme un ~** he drives like a maniac* *ou* madman*; **frapper comme un ~** to knock like mad* *ou* like a madman*.

maladie [maladi] 1 **nf** a (*Méd*) illness, disease; *[plante, vin]* disease. **~ bénigne** minor *ou* slight illness, minor complaint; **~ grave** serious illness; **~ de cœur/foie** heart/liver complaint *ou* disease; **ces enfants ont eu une ~ après l'autre** these children have had one sickness *ou* illness after another; **le cancer est la ~ du siècle** cancer is the disease of this century; **il a fait une petite ~*** he's been slightly ill, he's had a minor illness; **elle est en ~*** she's off sick*; **en longue ~** (off) on extended sick leave; (** fig*) **il en a fait une ~** he got into a terrible state about it, he had a fit*; (** fig*) **tu ne vas pas en faire une ~!** don't you get in (such) a state over it!, don't make a song and dance about it!*; **mes rosiers ont la ~***my rose bushes are in a bad way*.

b **la ~** sickness, illness, ill health, disease; *voir* **assurance**.

c (*Vét*) **la ~** distemper.

d (**: obsession*) mania. **avoir la ~ de la vitesse** to be a speed maniac; **quelle ~ as-tu de toujours intervenir!** what a mania you have for interfering!; **c'est une ~ chez lui** it's a mania with him.

2 **comp** ►**la maladie bleue** the blue disease ►**maladie de Carré** distemper ►**maladie contagieuse** contagious illness *ou* disease ►**maladie honteuse**† = **maladie vénérienne** ►**maladie infantile** *ou* **d'enfant** childhood *ou* infantile disease *ou* complaint ►**maladie infectieuse** infectious disease ►**maladie de langueur** wasting disease ►**maladie du légionnaire** legionnaires' disease ►**maladie mentale** mental illness ►**maladie mortelle** fatal illness *ou* disease ►**maladie de Parkinson** Parkinson's disease ►**maladie de peau** skin disease *ou* complaint ►**maladie sexuellement transmissible** sexually transmitted disease, STD ►**la maladie du sommeil** sleeping sickness ►**maladies du travail** occupational diseases ►**maladie tropicale** tropical disease ►**maladie vénérienne** venereal disease, VD.

maladif, -ive [maladif, iv] **adj** *personne* sickly, weak; *air, pâleur* sickly, unhealthy; *obsession, peur* pathological (*fig*). **il faut qu'il mente, c'est ~ chez lui** he has to lie, it's compulsive with him, he has a pathological need to lie.

maladivement [maladivmɑ̃] **adv** (*voir* **maladif**) unhealthily; pathologically.

maladrerie† [maladʀəʀi] **nf** lazaret†, lazar house†.

maladresse [maladʀɛs] **nf** a (*caractère: voir* **maladroit**) clumsiness; awkwardness; tactlessness. b (*gaffe*) blunder, gaffe. **~s de style** awkward *ou* clumsy turns of phrase.

maladroit, e [maladʀwa, wat] 1 **adj** a (*inhabile*) *personne, geste, expression* clumsy, ankward; *ouvrage, style* clumsy; *intervention, initiative* clumsy. **il est vraiment ~ de ses mains** he's really useless with his hands. b (*indélicat*) *personne, remarque* clumsy, tactless. **ce serait ~ de lui en parler** it would be tactless *ou* ill-considered to mention it to him. 2 **nm,f** (*inhabile*) clumsy person *ou* oaf*; (*qui fait tout tomber*) butterfingers; (*indélicat*) tactless person *ou* blunderer*.

maladroitement [maladʀwatmɑ̃] **adv** *marcher, dessiner* clumsily, awkwardly; *agir* clumsily, tactlessly.

malaga [malaga] **nm** (*vin*) Malaga (wine); (*raisin*) Malaga grape.

malais, e¹ [malɛ, ɛz] 1 **adj** Malay(an). 2 **nm** (*Ling*) Malay. 3 **nm,f: M~(e)** Malay(an).

malaise² [malɛz] **nm** a (*Méd*) feeling of sickness *ou* faintness; (*gén*) feeling of general discomfort *ou* ill-being. **être pris d'un ~, avoir un ~** to feel faint *ou* dizzy, come over faint *ou* dizzy. b (*fig: trouble*) uneasiness, disquiet. **éprouver un ~** to feel uneasy, feel a sense of disquiet; **le ~ étudiant/politique** student/political discontent *ou* unrest.

malaisé, e [maleze] **adj** difficult.

malaisément [malezemɑ̃] **adv** with difficulty.

Malaisie [malɛzi] **nf** Malaysia.

malaisien, -ienne [malɛzjɛ̃, jɛn] 1 **adj** Malaysian. 2 **nm,f: M~(ne)** Malaysian.

malandrin [malɑ̃dʀɛ̃] **nm** (†: *littér*) brigand (*littér*), bandit.

malappris, e [malapʀi, iz] 1 **adj** ill-mannered, boorish. 2 **nm** ill-mannered lout, boor, yob‡ (*Brit*).

malard [malaʀ] **nm** drake; (*sauvage*) mallard.

malaria [malaʀja] **nf** malaria (*NonC*).

malavisé, e [malavize] **adj** *personne, remarque* ill-advised, injudicious, unwise.

Malawi [malawi] **nm** Malawi.

malawien, -ienne [malawjɛ̃, jɛn] 1 adj Malawian. 2 nm,f: **M~(ne)** Malawian.

malaxage [malaksaʒ] nm (*voir* **malaxer**) kneading; massaging; creaming; blending; mixing.

malaxer [malakse] 1 vt a (*triturer*) *argile, pâte* to knead; *muscle* to massage. ~ **du beurre** to cream butter. b (*mélanger*) *plusieurs substances* to blend, mix; *ciment, plâtre* to mix.

malaxeur [malaksœʀ] 1 adj m mixing. 2 nm mixer.

malchance [malʃɑ̃s] nf (*déveine*) bad *ou* ill luck, misfortune; (*mésaventure*) misfortune, mishap. **il a eu beaucoup de** ~ he's had a lot of bad luck; **j'ai eu la** ~ **de** I had the misfortune to, I was unlucky enough to; **par** ~ unfortunately, as ill luck would have it; *voir* **jouer**.

malchanceux, -euse [malʃɑ̃sø, øz] adj unlucky.

malcommode [malkɔmɔd] adj *objet, vêtement* impractical, unsuitable; *horaire* awkward, inconvenient; *outil, meuble* inconvenient, impractical. **ça m'est vraiment très** ~ it's really most inconvenient for me, it really doesn't suit me at all.

Maldives [maldiv] nfpl: **les** ~ the Maldives.

maldonne [maldɔn] nf (*Cartes*) misdeal. **faire (une)** ~ to misdeal, deal the cards wrongly; **il y a** ~ (*lit*) there's been a misdeal, the cards have been dealt wrongly; (*fig*) there's been a misunderstanding *ou* a mistake somewhere.

Malé [male] n Malé.

mâle [mɑl] 1 adj a (*Bio, Tech*) male. b (*viril*) *voix, courage* manly; *style, peinture* virile, strong, forceful. 2 nm male. **c'est un** ~ **ou une femelle?** is it a he or a she?*, is it a male or a female?; **c'est un beau** ~* he's a real he-man* (*hum*); **(éléphant)** ~ bull (elephant); **(lapin)** ~ buck (rabbit); **(moineau)** ~ cock (sparrow); **(ours)** ~ he-bear; **souris** ~ male mouse.

malédiction [malediksjɔ̃] 1 nf (*Rel: imprécation, adversité*) curse, malediction (*littér*). **la** ~ **divine** the curse of God; **n'écoute pas les** ~**s de cette vieille folle** don't listen to the curses of that old fool; **la** ~ **pèse sur nous** a curse hangs over us; **donner sa** ~ **à qn, appeler la** ~ **sur qn** to call down curses upon sb. 2 excl (††, *hum*) curse it!*, damn!* ~! **j'ai perdu la clef** curse it!* I've lost the key.

maléfice [malefis] nm evil spell.

maléfique [malefik] adj *étoile* malefic (*littér*), unlucky; *pouvoir* evil, baleful.

malemort [malmɔʀ] nf (††, *littér*) cruel death. **mourir de** ~ to die a cruel *ou* violent death.

malencontreusement [malɑ̃kɔ̃tʀøzmɑ̃] adv *arriver* at the wrong moment, inopportunely, inconveniently; *faire tomber* inadvertently. **faire** ~ **remarquer que** to make the unfortunate *ou* untoward remark that.

malencontreux, -euse [malɑ̃kɔ̃tʀø, øz] adj unfortunate, awkward, untoward.

malentendant, e [malɑ̃tɑ̃dɑ̃, ɑ̃t] nm,f person who is hard of hearing. **les** ~**s** the hard of hearing.

malentendu [malɑ̃tɑ̃dy] nm misunderstanding. **il y a un** ~ **entre nous** we are at cross purposes.

malfaçon [malfasɔ̃] nf fault, defect (*due to bad workmanship*).

malfaisant, e [malfəzɑ̃, ɑ̃t] adj *personne* evil, wicked, harmful; *influence* evil, harmful, baleful; *animal, théories* harmful.

malfaiteur [malfɛtœʀ] nm (*gén*) criminal; (*gangster*) gangster; (*voleur*) burglar, thief. **dangereux** ~ dangerous criminal.

malformation [malfɔʀmasjɔ̃] nf malformation.

malfrat [malfʀa] nm (*escroc*) crook; (*bandit*) thug, gangster.

malgache [malgaʃ] 1 adj Malagasy, Madagascan. 2 nm (*Ling*) Malagasy. 3 nmf: **M~** Malagasy, Madagascan.

malgracieux, -ieuse [malgʀasjø, jøz] adj (*littér*) *silhouette* ungainly, clumsy; (†) *caractère* loutish, churlish, boorish.

malgré [malgʀe] 1 prép a (*en dépit de*) in spite of, despite. ~ **son père/l'opposition de son père, il devint avocat** despite his *ou* in spite of his father/his father's objections he became a barrister; ~ **son intelligence, il n'a pas réussi** in spite of *ou* for all *ou* notwithstanding (*frm*) his undoubted intelligence he hasn't succeeded; **j'ai signé ce contrat** ~ **moi** (*en hésitant*) I signed the contract reluctantly *ou* against my better judgment; (*contraint et forcé*) I signed the contract against my will; **j'ai fait cela presque** ~ **moi** I did it almost in spite of myself.

b (*loc*) ~ **tout** (*en dépit de tout*) in spite of everything, despite everything; (*concession: quand même*) all the same, even so, after all; ~ **tout, c'est dangereux** all the same *ou* after all it's dangerous; **il a continué** ~ **tout** he went on in spite of *ou* despite everything; **je le ferai** ~ **tout** I'll do it all the same *ou* come what may.

2 conj: ~ **que*** in spite of the fact that, despite the fact that, although; (*littér*) ~ **qu'il en ait** whether he likes it or not.

malhabile [malabil] adj clumsy, awkward. ~ **à (faire) qch** unskilful *ou* bad at (doing) sth.

malhabilement [malabilmɑ̃] adv clumsily, awkwardly, unskilfully.

malheur [malœʀ] nm a (*événement pénible*) misfortune; (*très grave*) calamity; (*épreuve*) ordeal, hardship; (*accident*) accident, mishap. **il a supporté ses** ~**s sans se plaindre** he suffered his misfortunes *ou* his hardships without complaint; **cette famille a eu beaucoup de** ~**s** this family has had a lot of misfortune *ou* hardship; **un** ~ **est si vite arrivé** accidents *ou* mishaps happen so easily; (*Prov*) **un** ~ **ne vient jamais seul** troubles never come singly, it never rains but it pours (*Prov*); **cela a été le grand** ~ **de sa vie** it was the great tragedy of his life; **ce n'est pas un gros** ~**!, c'est un petit** ~! it's not such a calamity! *ou* tragedy! *ou* disaster!

b **le** ~ (*adversité*) adversity; (*malchance*) ill luck, misfortune; **ils ont eu le** ~ **de perdre leur mère** they had the misfortune to lose their mother; **une famille qui est dans le** ~ a family in misfortune *ou* faced with adversity; **le** ~ **des uns fait le bonheur des autres** one man's joy is another man's sorrow; **c'est dans le** ~ **qu'on connaît ses amis** a friend in need is a friend indeed (*Prov*); **le** ~ **a voulu qu'un agent le voie** as ill luck would have it a policeman saw him; *voir* **arriver**.

c **de** ~* (*maudit*) wretched; **cette pluie de** ~ **a tout gâché** this wretched rain has spoilt everything; *voir* **oiseau**.

d (*loc*) ~! oh, lord!*, hell!**; ~ **à (celui) qui**† woe betide him who; ~ **à toi si tu y touches!** woe betide you if you touch it!; **par** ~ unfortunately, as ill luck would have it; **le** ~ **c'est que ..., il n'y a qu'un** ~, **c'est que ...** the trouble *ou* snag is that ...; **son** ~ **c'est qu'il boit** his trouble is that he drinks; **faire le** ~ **de ses parents** to bring sorrow to one's parents, cause one's parents nothing but unhappiness; **faire un** ~ (*avoir un gros succès*) *[spectacle]* to be a big hit; *[artiste, joueur]* to make a great hit, be a sensation; **s'il continue à m'ennuyer je fais un** ~* if he carries on annoying me I'll do something violent *ou* I shall go wild; **quel** ~ **qu'il ne soit pas venu** what a shame *ou* pity he didn't come; **il a eu le** ~ **de dire que cela ne lui plaisait pas** he made the big mistake of saying he didn't like it, he was unlucky enough to say he didn't like it; **pour son** ~ for his sins; *voir* **comble, jouer**.

malheureusement [maløʀøzmɑ̃] adv unfortunately.

malheureux, -euse [maløʀø, øz] 1 adj a (*infortuné*) unfortunate. **les** ~**euses victimes des bombardements** the unfortunate *ou* unhappy victims of the bombings.

b (*regrettable, fâcheux*) *résultat, jour, geste* unfortunate. **pour un mot** ~ because of an unfortunate remark; **c'est bien** ~ **qu'il ne puisse pas venir** it's very unfortunate *ou* it's a great shame *ou* it's a great pity that he can't come; **si c'est pas** ~ **d'entendre ça!*** it makes you sick to hear that!*; **ah te voilà enfin, c'est pas** ~**!*** oh there you are at last and about time too!*

c (*triste, qui souffre*) *enfant, vie* unhappy, miserable. **on a été très** ~ **pendant la guerre** we had a miserable life during the war; **il était très** ~ **de ne pouvoir nous aider** he was most distressed *ou* upset at not being able to help us; **prendre un air** ~ to look unhappy *ou* distressed; **rendre qn** ~ to make sb unhappy; **être** ~ **comme les pierres** to be wretchedly unhappy *ou* utterly wretched.

d (*après n*) (*malchanceux*) *candidat* unsuccessful, unlucky; *tentative* unsuccessful. **il prit une initiative** ~**euse** he took an unfortunate step; **X a été félicité par ses adversaires** ~ X was congratulated by his defeated opponents; **être** ~ **au jeu/en amour** to be unlucky at gambling/in love; **amour** ~ unhappy love affair; *voir* **heureux, main**.

e (*: *avant n: insignifiant*) wretched, miserable. **toute une histoire pour un** ~ **billet de 100 F/pour une** ~**euse erreur** such a to-do for a wretched *ou* mouldy* (*Brit*) *ou* measly* 100-franc note/for a miserable mistake; **il y avait 2 ou 3** ~ **spectateurs** there was a miserable handful of spectators; **sans même un** ~ **coup de fil** without so much as a phone call.

2 nm,f (*infortuné*) poor wretch *ou* soul *ou* devil*; (*indigent*) needy person. **il a tout perdu? le** ~! did he lose everything? the poor man!; **un** ~ **de plus** another poor devil*; **ne fais pas cela,** ~! don't do that, you fool!; **aider les** ~ (*indigents*) to help the needy *ou* those who are badly off; **la** ~**euse a agonisé pendant des heures** the poor woman suffered for hours before she died.

malhonnête [malɔnɛt] adj a (*déloyal, voleur*) *personne, procédé* dishonest, crooked. b (*impoli*) rude; *voir* **proposition**.

malhonnêtement [malɔnɛtmɑ̃] adv (*voir* **malhonnête**) dishonestly, crookedly; rudely.

malhonnêteté [malɔnɛtte] nf a (*improbité*) dishonesty, crookedness. **faire des** ~**s** to carry on dishonest *ou* crooked dealings. b (*manque de politesse*) rudeness. **dire des** ~**s** to make rude remarks, say rude things.

Mali [mali] nm Mali.

malice [malis] nf a (*espièglerie*) mischief, mischievousness; roguishness (*littér*). **dit-il non sans** ~ he said somewhat mischievously; **petites** ~**s**† mischievous little ways; **boîte** *ou* **sac à** ~ box *ou* bag of tricks. b (*méchanceté*) malice, spite. **par** ~ out of malice *ou* spite; **il est sans** ~ he is quite guileless; **il n'y voit** *ou* **entend pas** ~ he means no harm by it.

malicieusement [malisjøzmɑ̃] adv mischievously, roguishly.

malicieux, -ieuse [malisjø, jøz] adj *personne, remarque* mischievous, roguish; *sourire* mischievous, impish, roguish. **notre oncle est très** ~ our uncle is a great tease; **petit** ~! little imp *ou* monkey!

malien, -enne [maljɛ̃, ɛn] 1 adj of *ou* from Mali, Malian. 2 nm,f: **M~(ne)** Malian, inhabitant *ou* native of Mali.

maligne [maliɲ] *voir* **malin**.

malignement [maliɲmɑ̃] adv (*rare*) maliciously, spitefully.

malignité [maliɲite] nf a (*malveillance*) malice, spite. b (*Méd*) malignancy.

malin, maligne [malɛ̃, maliɲ] *ou* **maline*** [malin] 1 adj a (*intelligent*) *personne, air* smart, shrewd, cunning. **sourire ~** cunning *ou* knowing *ou* crafty smile; **il est ~ comme un singe** (*gén*) he is as artful as a cartload of monkeys; *[enfant]* he is an artful little monkey; **bien ~ qui le dira** it'll take a clever man to say that; **il n'est pas bien ~** he isn't very bright; (*iro*) **c'est ~!** that's clever *ou* bright, isn't it? (*iro*); **si tu te crois ~ de faire ça!** do you think it's *ou* you're clever to do that?; *voir* **jouer.**

b (**: difficile*) **ce n'est pourtant pas bien ~** but it isn't so difficult *ou* tricky; **ce n'est pas plus ~ que ça** it's as easy *ou* simple as that, it's as easy as pie*, that's all there is to it.

c (*mauvais*) *influence* malignant, baleful, malicious. **prendre un ~ plaisir à** to take a malicious pleasure in; **l'esprit ~** the devil.

d (*Méd*) malignant.

2 nm,f: **c'est un (petit) ~** he's a crafty one, he knows a thing or two, there are no flies on him (*Brit*); (*iro*) **gros ~!** you're a bright one! (*iro*); **ne fais pas ton** *ou* **le ~*** don't try to show off; **à ~, ~ et demi** there's always someone cleverer than you; **le M~** the Devil.

malingre [malɛ̃gʀ] adj *personne* sickly, puny; *corps* puny.

malinois [malinwa] nm police dog, ≃ Alsatian (*Brit*), German shepherd.

malintentionné, e [malɛ̃tɑ̃sjɔne] adj ill-intentioned, malicious, spiteful (*envers* towards).

malle [mal] 1 nf a (*valise*) trunk. **faire sa** *ou* **ses ~(s)** to pack one's trunk; **ils se sont fait la ~‡** they've hightailed it*, they've scarpered‡ (*Brit*), they've done a bunk‡ (*Brit*); **on a intérêt à se faire la ~‡** we'd better scarper‡ (*Brit*) *ou* make ourselves scarce*; **il a quitté sa famille avec sa ~ à quatre nœuds** he left home with all his worldly possessions tied up in a bundle. b (*Aut*) **~ (arrière)** boot (*Brit*), trunk (*US*). 2 comp ▸**malle-poste** (pl **malles-poste**) nf (*Hist*) (*diligence*) mail coach; (*bateau*) packet.

malléabilité [maleabilite] nf *[métal]* malleability; *[caractère]* malleability, pliability, flexibility.

malléable [maleabl] adj *métal* malleable; *caractère* malleable, pliable, flexible.

mallette [malɛt] nf (*valise*) (small) suitcase; (*porte-documents*) briefcase, attaché case. **~ de voyage** overnight case, grip.

malmener [malməne] 5 vt (*brutaliser*) *personne* to manhandle, handle roughly; (*Mil, Sport*) *adversaire* to give a rough time *ou* handling to. (*fig*) **être malmené par la critique** to be given a rough ride *ou* handling by the critics.

malnutrition [malnytʀisjɔ̃] nf malnutrition.

malodorant, e [malɔdɔʀɑ̃, ɑ̃t] adj *personne, pièce* foul- *ou* ill-smelling, malodorous (*frm*), smelly; *haleine* foul (*Brit*), bad.

malotru, e [malɔtʀy] nm,f lout, boor, yob‡ (*Brit*).

malouin, e [malwɛ̃, in] 1 adj of *ou* from Saint-Malo. 2 nm,f: **M~(e)** inhabitant *ou* native of Saint-Malo. 3 nfpl: **les (îles) M~es** the Falkland Islands, the Falklands.

malpoli, e [malpɔli] adj impolite, discourteous.

malpropre [malpʀɔpʀ] 1 adj a (*sale*) *personne, objet* dirty, grubby, grimy; *travail* shoddy, slovenly, sloppy. b (*indécent*) *allusion, histoire* smutty, dirty, unsavoury. c (*indélicat*) *conduite, personne, action* unsavoury, dishonest, despicable. 2 nmf (*hum*) swine (*pl inv*). **se faire chasser comme un ~*** to be thrown *ou* kicked* out, be sent packing.

malproprement [malpʀɔpʀəmɑ̃] adv in a dirty way. **manger ~** to be a messy eater.

malpropreté [malpʀɔpʀəte] nf a **la ~** dirtiness, grubbiness, griminess. b (*acte*) low *ou* shady *ou* despicable trick; (*parole*) low *ou* unsavoury remark. **raconter** *ou* **dire des ~s** to talk smut, tell dirty stories.

malsain, e [malsɛ̃, ɛn] adj *logement* unhealthy; *influence, littérature, curiosité* unhealthy, unwholesome; *esprit, mentalité* nasty, unhealthy. (* *fig*) **sauvons-nous, ça devient ~** let's get out of here, things are turning nasty *ou* things aren't looking too healthy*.

malséant, e [malseɑ̃, ɑ̃t] adj (*littér*) unseemly, unbecoming, improper.

malsonnant, e [malsɔnɑ̃, ɑ̃t] adj (*littér*) *propos* offensive.

malt [malt] nm malt. **whisky pur ~** malt (whisky).

maltage [maltaʒ] nm malting.

maltais, e [maltɛ, ɛz] 1 adj Maltese. 2 nm (*Ling*) Maltese. 3 nm,f: **M~(e)** Maltese.

maltase [maltɑz] nf maltase.

Malte [malt] nf Malta.

malter [malte] 1 vt to malt.

malthusianisme [maltyzjanism] nm (*Sociol*) Malthusianism. **~ économique** Malthusian economics (*sg*).

malthusien, -ienne [maltyzjɛ̃, jɛn] 1 adj (*Écon, Sociol*) Malthusian. 2 nm,f Malthusian.

maltose [maltoz] nm maltose, malt sugar.

maltraiter [maltʀete] 1 vt a (*brutaliser*) to manhandle, handle roughly, ill-treat; *enfant* to abuse. b (*mal user de*) *langue, grammaire* to misuse. c (*critiquer*) *œuvre, auteur* to slate* (*Brit*), pan, run down*.

malus [malys] nm (car insurance) surcharge.

malveillance [malvɛjɑ̃s] nf (*méchanceté*) spite, malevolence; (*désobligeance*) ill will (*pour, envers* towards). (*Jur*) **avoir agi sans ~** to have acted without malicious intent; **propos dus à la ~ publique** spiteful *ou* malicious public rumour; **regarder qn avec ~** to look at sb malevolently; **je dis cela sans ~ à son égard** I say that without wishing to be spiteful to him; **c'est par pure ~ qu'il a agi ainsi** he did that out of sheer spite *ou* malevolence.

malveillant, e [malvɛjɑ̃, ɑ̃t] adj *personne, regard, remarque* malevolent, malicious, spiteful.

malvenu, e [malvəny] adj (*déplacé*) out of place (*attrib*), out-of-place (*épith*); (*mal développé*) malformed; *voir aussi* **mal 1b.**

malversation [malvɛʀsasjɔ̃] nf (*gén pl*) embezzlement, misappropriation of funds.

malvoisie [malvwazi] nm malmsey (wine).

malvoyant, e [malvwajɑ̃, ɑ̃t] nm,f person who is partially sighted. **les ~s** the partially sighted.

maman [mamɑ̃] nf mummy, mother, mum* (*Brit*), mom* (*US*). **"~", "M~"** "mummy", mum* (*Brit*), mom* (*US*); **les ~s attendaient devant l'école** the mothers *ou* mums* (*Brit*) were waiting outside the school; *voir* **futur.**

mambo [mɑ̃(m)bo] nm mambo.

mamelle [mamɛl] nf a (*Zool*) teat; (*pis*) udder, dug. b (†) *[femme]* breast; (*péj*) tit‡; *[homme]* breast. **à la ~** at the breast; (*fig*) **dès la ~** from infancy; (*fig*) **les deux ~s de** the lifeblood of.

mamelon [mam(ə)lɔ̃] nm a (*Anat*) nipple. b (*Géog*) knoll, hillock.

mamelonné, e [mam(ə)lɔne] adj hillocky.

mamel(o)uk [mamluk] nm Mameluke.

mamie[1] [mami] nf (*grand-mère*) granny*, gran*.

mamie[2], **m'amie** [mami] nf (††) = **ma mie**; *voir* **mie**[2].

mammaire [mamɛʀ] adj mammary.

mammectomie [mamɛktɔmi] nf mastectomy.

mammifère [mamifɛʀ] 1 nm mammal. **les ~s** mammals. 2 adj mammalian.

mammographie [mamɔgʀafi] nf mammography.

Mammon [mamɔ̃] nm Mammon.

mammouth [mamut] nm mammoth.

mamours* [mamuʀ] nmpl (*hum*) **faire des ~ à qn** to caress *ou* fondle sb; **se faire des ~** to bill and coo.

mam'selle*, mam'zelle* [mamzɛl] nf abrév de **mademoiselle.**

mammy [mami] nf = **mamie**[1].

manade [manad] nf (*en Provence*) *[taureaux]* herd of bulls; *[chevaux]* herd of horses.

management [manaʒmɛnt] nm management.

manager[1] [manadʒɛʀ] nm (*Écon, Sport*) manager; (*Théât*) agent.

manager[2] [mana(d)ʒe] 3 vt to manage.

Managua [managwa] n Managua.

Manama [manama] n Manama.

manant [manɑ̃] nm a (†, *littér*) churl††. b (*Hist: villageois*) yokel; (*vilain*) villein.

manceau, -elle, mpl **~x** [mɑ̃so, ɛl] 1 adj of *ou* from Le Mans. 2 nm,f: **M~(-elle)** inhabitant *ou* native of Le Mans.

manche[1] [mɑ̃ʃ] 1 nf a (*Habillement*) sleeve. **à ~s courtes/longues** short-/long-sleeved; **sans ~s** sleeveless; (*fig*) **avoir qn dans sa ~** to be well in with sb*, have sb in one's pocket; (*fig*) **relever** *ou* **retrousser ses ~s** to roll up one's sleeves (*fig*); **faire la ~‡** to pass the hat round; *voir* **autre, chemise, effet.**

b (*partie*) (*gén, Pol, Sport*) round (*fig*); (*Bridge*) game; (*Tennis*) set. (*fig*) **pour obtenir ce contrat on a gagné la première ~** we've won the first round in the battle for this contract.

c (*Aviat*) *[ballon]* neck.

d (*Géog*) **la M~** the English Channel.

2 comp ▸**manche à air** (*Aviat*) wind sock; (*Naut*) airshaft ▸**manche ballon** puff sleeve ▸**manche à crevés** slashed sleeve ▸**manche gigot** leg-of-mutton sleeve ▸**manche kimono** kimono *ou* loose sleeve ▸**manche montée** set-in sleeve ▸**manche raglan** raglan sleeve ▸**manche trois-quarts** three-quarter sleeve ▸**manche à vent** airshaft.

manche[2] [mɑ̃ʃ] 1 nm a (*gén*) handle; (*long*) shaft; (*Mus*) neck. (*fig*) **être du côté du ~** to have the whip hand; *voir* **branler, jeter.** b (**: incapable*) clumsy fool *ou* oaf, clot (*Brit*). **conduire comme un ~** to be a hopeless *ou* rotten* driver; **s'y prendre comme un ~ pour faire qch** to set about (doing) sth in a ham-fisted* *ou* ham-handed* way. 2 comp ▸**manche à balai** (*gén*) broomstick, broomshaft (*Brit*); (*Aviat*) joystick ▸**manche à gigot** leg-of-mutton holder ▸**manche de gigot** knuckle (of a leg-of-mutton).

manchette [mɑ̃ʃɛt] nf a *[chemise]* cuff; (*protectrice*) oversleeve. b (*Presse*) (*titre*) headline. **mettre en ~** to headline, put in headlines. c (*note*) marginal note. **en ~** in the margin. d (*coup*) forearm blow.

manchon [mɑ̃ʃɔ̃] nm a *[fourrure]* muff; *voir* **chien.** b **~ à incandescence** incandescent (gas) mantle.

manchot, e [mɑ̃ʃo, ɔt] 1 adj (*d'un bras*) one-armed; (*des deux bras*) armless; (*d'une main*) one-handed; (*des deux mains*) with no hands, handless. **être ~ du bras droit/gauche** to have the use of only one's left/right arm; (*fig*) **il n'est pas ~!*** (*adroit*) he's clever *ou* he's no fool with his hands! 2 nm,f (*d'un bras*) one-armed person; (*des deux bras*) person with no arms. 3 nm (*Orn*) penguin. **~ royal/empereur** king/emperor penguin.

manchou, e [mɑ̃dʃu] adj, nm,f = **mandchou.**
mandala [mɑ̃dala] nm mandala.
mandale‡ [mɑ̃dal] nf biff*, clout (*Brit*), cuff.
mandant, e [mɑ̃dɑ̃, ɑ̃t] nm,f (*Jur*) principal. (*Pol frm*) **je parle au nom de mes ~s** I speak on behalf of those who have given me a mandate *ou* of my electors *ou* of my constituents.
mandarin [mɑ̃daʀɛ̃] nm (*Hist, péj*) mandarin; (*Ling*) Mandarin (Chinese); (*Orn*) mandarin duck.
mandarinal, e, mpl **-aux** [mɑ̃daʀinal, o] adj mandarin.
mandarinat [mɑ̃daʀina] nm (*Hist*) mandarinate; (*péj*) academic Establishment (*péj*).
mandarine [mɑ̃daʀin] 1 nf mandarin (orange), tangerine. 2 adj inv tangerine.
mandarinier [mɑ̃daʀinje] nm mandarin (orange) tree.
mandat [mɑ̃da] 1 nm a (*gén, Pol*) mandate. **donner à qn ~ de faire** to mandate sb to do, give sb a mandate to do; **obtenir le renouvellement de son ~** to be re-elected, have one's mandate renewed; **territoires sous ~** mandated territories, territories under mandate.
b (*Comm: aussi* **~-poste**) postal order (*Brit*), money order.
c (*Jur: procuration*) power of attorney, proxy; (*Police etc*) warrant.
2 comp ▸**mandat d'amener** (*Jur*) ≃ summons ▸**mandat d'arrêt** ≃ warrant for arrest ▸**mandat-carte** (pl **mandats-cartes**) nm (*Comm*) money order (*in postcard form*) ▸**mandat de comparution** (*Jur*) ≃ summons (to appear), subpoena ▸**mandat de dépôt** (*Jur*) ≃ committal order; **placer qn sous mandat de dépôt** ≃ to place sb under a committal order ▸**mandat d'expulsion** eviction order ▸**mandat international** (*Fin*) international money order ▸**mandat-lettre** (pl **mandats-lettres**) nm (*Comm*) money order (*with space for correspondence*) ▸**mandat de perquisition** (*Jur*) search warrant.
mandataire [mɑ̃datɛʀ] nmf (*Jur*) proxy, attorney; (*représentant*) representative. **je ne suis que son ~** I'm only acting as a proxy for him; **~ aux Halles** (sales) agent (at the Halles).
mandatement [mɑ̃datmɑ̃] nm [*somme*] payment (by money order).
mandater [mɑ̃date] [1] vt a (*donner pouvoir à*) *personne* to appoint, commission; (*Pol*) *député* to give a mandate to, elect. b (*Fin*) **~ une somme** (*écrire*) to write out a money order for a sum; (*payer*) to pay a sum by money order.
mandchou, e [mɑ̃tʃu] 1 adj Manchu(rian). 2 nm (*Ling*) Manchu. 3 nm,f: **M~(e)** Manchu.
Mandchourie [mɑ̃tʃuʀi] nf Manchuria.
mandement [mɑ̃dmɑ̃] nm a (*Rel*) pastoral. b (††) (*ordre*) mandate, command; (*Jur: convocation*) subpoena.
mander [mɑ̃de] [1] vt a (††) (*ordonner*) to command; (*convoquer*) to summon. b (*littér: dire par lettre*) **~ qch à qn** to send *ou* convey the news of sth to sb, inform sb of sth.
mandibule [mɑ̃dibyl] nf mandible. (*fig*) **jouer des ~s*** to nosh* (*Brit*), chow down* (*US*).
mandoline [mɑ̃dɔlin] nf mandolin(e).
mandragore [mɑ̃dʀagɔʀ] nf mandrake.
mandrill [mɑ̃dʀil] nm mandrill.
mandrin [mɑ̃dʀɛ̃] nm (*pour serrer*) chuck; (*pour percer, emboutir*) punch; (*pour élargir, égaliser des trous*) drift.
manducation [mɑ̃dykasjɔ̃] nf manducation.
manécanterie [manekɑ̃tʀi] nf (parish) choir school.
manège [manɛʒ] nm a **~ (de chevaux de bois)** roundabout (*Brit*), merry-go-round, carousel (*US*); *voir* **tour²**. b (*Équitation*) (*piste, salle*) ring, school. **~ couvert** indoor school; **faire du ~** to do exercises in the indoor school. c (*fig: agissements*) game, ploy. **j'ai deviné son petit ~** I guessed what he was up to, I saw through his little game.
mânes [mɑn] nmpl (*Antiq Rel*) manes. (*littér, fig*) **les ~ de ses ancêtres** the shades of his ancestors (*littér*), the spirits of the dead.
maneton [man(ə)tɔ̃] nm (*Aut*) clankpin.
manette [manɛt] nf lever, tap. (*Aut*) **~ des gaz** throttle lever; (*Ordin*) **~ de jeux** joystick.
manganate [mɑ̃ganat] nm manganate.
manganèse [mɑ̃ganɛz] nm manganese.
mangeable [mɑ̃ʒabl] adj (*lit, fig*) edible, eatable.
mangeaille [mɑ̃ʒɑj] nf (*péj*) (*nourriture mauvaise*) pigswill, disgusting food; (*grande quantité de nourriture*) mounds of food. **il nous venait des odeurs de ~** we were met by an unappetizing smell of food (cooking).
mange-disques [mɑ̃ʒdisk] nm inv slot-in record player (*for singles*).
mangeoire [mɑ̃ʒwaʀ] nf (*gén*) trough, manger; [*oiseaux*] feeding dish.
mangeotter* [mɑ̃ʒɔte] [1] vt to nibble.
manger [mɑ̃ʒe] [3] 1 vt a to eat; *soupe* to drink, eat. **~ dans une assiette/dans un bol** to eat off *ou* from a plate/out of a bowl; **il mange peu** he doesn't eat much; **il ne mange pas** *ou* **rien en ce moment** he's off his food at present, he is not eating at all at present; **ils ont mangé tout ce qu'elle avait (à la maison)** they ate her out of house and home; **vous mangerez bien un morceau avec nous?*** won't you have a bite (to eat) with us?; **il a mangé tout ce qui restait** he has eaten (up) all that was left; **cela se mange?** can you eat it?, is it edible?; **ce plat se mange très chaud** this dish should be eaten piping hot; **ils leur ont fait** *ou* **donné à ~ un excellent poisson** they served *ou* gave them some excellent fish (to eat); **faire ~ qn** to feed sb; **faire ~ qch à qn** to give sb sth to eat, make sb eat sth; **donner à ~ à un bébé/un animal** to feed a baby/an animal; **~ goulûment** to wolf down one's food, eat greedily; **~ salement** to be a messy eater; **~ comme un cochon*** to eat like a pig*; **finis de ~!, mange!** eat up!; **on mange bien/mal à cet hôtel** the food is good/bad at this hotel; **les enfants ne mangent pas à leur faim à l'école** the children don't get *ou* are not given enough to eat at school.
b (*emploi absolu: faire un repas*) **~ dehors** *ou* **au restaurant** to eat out, have a meal out; **c'est l'heure de ~** (*midi*) it's lunchtime; (*soir*) it's dinnertime; **inviter qn à ~** to invite sb for a meal; **boire en mangeant** to drink with a meal; **~ sur le pouce** to have a (quick) snack, snatch a bite (to eat); *voir* **carte.**
c (*fig: dévorer*) **~ qn des yeux** to gaze hungrily at sb, devour sb with one's eyes; **~ qn de baisers** to smother sb with kisses; **allez le voir, il ne vous mangera pas** go and see him, he won't eat you; **il va te ~ tout cru** he'll make mincemeat of you, he'll swallow you whole; **se faire ~ par les moustiques** to get eaten alive *ou* bitten to death by mosquitoes; (*iro*) **~ du curé/du communiste** to be violently anti-clerical/anti-communist.
d (*ronger*) to eat (away). **mangé par les mites** *ou* **aux mites** moth-eaten; **la grille (de fer) a été mangée par la rouille** the (iron) railing is eaten away with *ou* by rust; **le soleil a mangé la couleur** the sun has taken out *ou* faded the colour.
e (*faire disparaître, consommer*) **ce poêle mange beaucoup de charbon** this stove gets through *ou* uses a lot of coal *ou* is heavy on coal; **toutes ces activités lui mangent son temps** all these activities take up his time; (*avaler*) **~ ses mots** to swallow one's words; **de nos jours les grosses entreprises mangent les petites** nowadays the big firms swallow up the smaller ones; **une barbe touffue lui mangeait le visage** his face was half hidden under a bushy beard; **des yeux énormes lui mangeaient le visage** his face seemed to be just two great eyes.
f (*dilapider*) *fortune, capital, économies* to go through, squander. **l'entreprise mange de l'argent** the business is eating money; **dans cette affaire il mange de l'argent** he's spending more than he earns *ou* his outgoings are more than his income in this business.
g (*loc*) **~ la consigne** *ou* **la commission** to forget one's errand; **~ comme quatre/comme un oiseau** to eat like a horse/like a bird; **~ du bout des dents** to pick *ou* nibble at one's food; (*fig*) **~ le morceau**‡ to spill the beans‡, talk, come clean*; **~ son pain blanc le premier** to have it easy at the start; **je ne mange pas de ce pain-là!** I'm having nothing to do with that!, I'm not stooping to anything like that!; **ça ne mange pas de pain!** it doesn't cost much!, you won't have to do much!; **~ de la vache enragée** to have a very lean time of it; **~ son blé en herbe** to spend one's money in advance *ou* before one gets it; **~ à tous les rateliers** to cash in* on all sides; **se laisser** *ou* **se faire ~ la laine sur le dos*** to let oneself get walked all over*; *voir* **sang.**
2 nm food. **préparer le ~ des enfants*** to get the children's food *ou* meal ready; **"ici on peut apporter son ~"*** "customers may consume their own food on the premises"; **à prendre après ~** to be taken after meals; **je rentrerai avant ~** I'll be back before lunch (*ou* dinner); *voir* **perdre.**
mange-tout [mɑ̃ʒtu] nm inv: **pois ~** mange-tout peas; **haricots ~** runner beans, string beans.
mangeur, -euse [mɑ̃ʒœʀ, øz] nm,f eater. **être gros** *ou* **grand/petit ~** to be a big/small eater; **c'est un gros ~ de pain** he eats a lot of bread, he's a big bread-eater*; **~ d'hommes** man-eater.
manglier [mɑ̃glije] nm mangrove tree.
mangoustan [mɑ̃gustɑ̃] nm mangosteen.
mangouste [mɑ̃gust] nf (*animal*) mongoose; (*fruit*) mangosteen.
mangrove [mɑ̃gʀɔv] nf mangrove swamp.
mangue [mɑ̃g] nf mango (*fruit*).
manguier [mɑ̃gje] nm mango (*tree*).
maniabilité [manjabilite] nf [*objet*] handiness, manageability; [*voiture*] driveability; [*avion*] manoeuvrability. **appareil d'une grande ~** implement which is very easy to handle, very handy implement; **c'est un véhicule d'une étonnante ~** this vehicle is incredibly easy to handle *ou* drive.
maniable [manjabl] adj a *objet, taille* handy, manageable, easy to handle (*attrib*); *véhicule* easy to handle *ou* drive (*attrib*); *avion* easy to manoeuvre (*attrib*). b (*influençable*) *électeur* easily swayed *ou* influenced (*attrib*). c (*accommodant*) *homme, caractère* accommodating, amenable.
maniaco-dépressif, -ive [manjakodepʀesif, iv] adj manic-depressive.
maniaque [manjak] 1 adj *personne* finicky, fussy, pernickety. **faire qch avec un soin ~** to do sth with almost fanatical care. 2 nmf a (†: *Admin, Presse: fou*) maniac, lunatic. **~ sexuel** sex maniac. b (*méticuleux*) fusspot; (*fanatique*) fanatic, enthusiast. **c'est un ~ de la propreté** he's fanatical about cleanliness, cleanliness is an obsession with him; **c'est un ~ de l'exactitude** he is fanatical about punctuality, he's a stickler for punctuality; **c'est un ~ de la voile** he's sailing mad *ou* a sailing fanatic.
maniaquerie [manjakʀi] nf fussiness, pernicketiness.
manichéen, -enne [manikeɛ̃, ɛn] adj, nm,f Manich(a)ean.

manichéisme [manikeism] **nm** (*Philos*) Maniche(an)ism; (*péj*) oversimplification. (*fig*) **il fait du ~** he sees everything in black and white, everything is either good or bad to him.

manie [mani] **nf** a (*habitude*) odd *ou* queer habit. **elle est pleine de (petites) ~s** she's got all sorts of funny little ways *ou* habits; **mais quelle ~ tu as de te manger les ongles!** you've got a terrible habit of biting your nails!; **elle a la ~ de tout nettoyer** she's a compulsive *ou* obsessive cleaner. b (*obsession*) mania. (*Méd*) **~ de la persécution** persecution mania.

maniement [manimɑ̃] **nm** a handling. **d'un ~ difficile** difficult to handle; **le ~ de cet objet est pénible** this object is difficult to handle; **il possède à fond le ~ de la langue** he has a thorough understanding of how to use *ou* handle the language. b (*Mil*) **~ d'armes** arms drill (*Brit*), manual of arms (*US*).

manier [manje] 7 1 **vt** *objet, langue, foule* to handle; *épée, outil* to wield, handle; *personne* to handle; (*péj*) to manipulate. **~ l'aviron** to pull *ou* ply (*littér*) the oars; **~ de grosses sommes d'argent** to handle large sums of money; **cheval/voiture facile à ~** horse/car which is easy to handle; **il sait ~ le pinceau, il manie le pinceau avec adresse** he knows how to handle a brush, he's a painter of some skill; **savoir ~ la plume** to be a good writer; **savoir ~ l'ironie** to handle irony skilfully. 2 **se manier vpr** = **se magner**.

manière [manjɛʀ] **nf** a (*façon*) way. **sa ~ d'agir/de parler** the way he behaves/speaks; **il le fera à sa ~** he'll do it (in) his own way; **~ de vivre** way of life; **~ de voir (les choses)** outlook (on things); **c'est sa ~ d'être habituelle** that's just the way he is, that's just how he usually is; **ce n'est pas la bonne ~ de s'y prendre** this is not the right *ou* best way to go about it; **d'une ~ efficace** in an efficient way; **de quelle ~ as-tu fait cela?** how did you do that?; **à la ~ d'un singe** like a monkey, as a monkey would do.

b (*Art: style*) **c'est un Matisse dernière ~** it's a late Matisse *ou* an example of Matisse's later work; **dans la ~ classique** in the classical style; **à la ~ de Racine** in the style of Racine.

c (*Gram*) **adverbe/complément de ~** adverb/adjunct of manner.

d (*loc*) **employer la ~ forte** to use strong measures *ou* strong-arm tactics, take a tough line*; **il l'a giflé de belle ~!** he gave him a sound *ou* good slap; **en ~ d'excuse** by way of (an) excuse; **d'une certaine ~, il a raison** in a way *ou* in some ways he is right; **d'une ~ générale** generally speaking, as a general rule; **de toute(s) ~(s)** in any case, at any rate, anyway; **de cette ~** (in) this way; **de telle ~ que** in such a way that; **d'une ~ ou d'une autre** somehow or other; **en aucune ~** in no way, under no circumstances; **je n'accepterai en aucune ~** I shall not agree on any account; **de ~ à faire** so as to do; **de ~ (à ce) que nous arrivions à l'heure, de ~ à arriver à l'heure** so that we get there on time.

e **~s: avoir de bonnes/mauvaises ~s** to have good/bad manners; **apprendre les belles ~s** to learn good manners; **il n'a pas de ~s, il est sans ~s** he has no manners; **ce ne sont pas des ~s!** that's no way to behave!; **en voilà des ~s!** what a way to behave!; **je n'aime pas ces ~s!** I don't like this kind of behaviour!; **faire des ~s** (*minauderies*) to be affected, put on airs; (*chichis*) to make a fuss.

f (†: *genre*) **une ~ de pastiche** a kind of pastiche; **quelle ~ d'homme est-ce?** what kind *ou* sort of a man is he?, what manner of man is he?†

maniéré, e [manjeʀe] **adj** a (*péj: affecté*) *personne, style, voix* affected. b (*Art*) *genre* mannered. **les tableaux très ~s de ce peintre** the mannered style of this painter.

maniérisme [manjeʀism] **nm** (*Art*) mannerism.

manieur, -ieuse [manjœʀ, jøz] **nm,f**: **~ d'argent** *ou* **de fonds** big businessman.

manif* [manif] **nf** (**abrév de manifestation**) demo*.

manifestant, e [manifɛstɑ̃, ɑ̃t] **nm,f** demonstrator, protester.

manifestation [manifɛstasjɔ̃] **nf** a (*Pol*) demonstration. b (*expression*) *[opinion, sentiment]* expression; *[maladie]* (*apparition*) appearance; (*symptômes*) outward sign *ou* symptom. **~ de mauvaise humeur** show of bad temper; **~ de joie** demonstration *ou* expression of joy; **accueillir qn avec de grandes ~s d'amitié** to greet sb with great demonstrations of friendship. c *[Dieu, vérité]* revelation. d (*réunion, fête*) event. **~ artistique/culturelle/sportive** artistic/cultural/sporting event; **le maire assistait à cette sympathique ~** the mayor was present at this happy gathering *ou* on this happy occasion.

manifeste [manifɛst] 1 **adj** *vérité* manifest, obvious, evident; *sentiment, différence* obvious, evident. **erreur ~** glaring error; **il est ~ que vous n'y avez pas réfléchi** obviously you haven't *ou* it is quite obvious *ou* evident that you haven't given it much thought. 2 **nm** (*Littérat, Pol*) manifesto; (*Aviat, Naut*) manifest.

manifestement [manifɛstəmɑ̃] **adv** (*voir* **manifeste**) manifestly; obviously, evidently.

manifester [manifɛste] 1 1 **vt** *opinion, intention, sentiment* to show, indicate; *courage* to show, demonstrate. **il m'a manifesté son désir de** he indicated to me his wish to, he signified his wish to; (*frm*) **par ce geste la France tient à nous ~ son amitié** France intends this gesture as a demonstration *ou* an indication of her friendship towards us.

2 **vi** (*Pol*) to demonstrate, hold a demonstration.

3 **se manifester vpr** a (*se révéler*) *[émotion]* to show itself, express itself; *[difficultés]* to emerge, arise. **en fin de journée une certaine détente se manifesta** at the end of the day there was evidence of *ou* there were indications of a certain thaw in the atmosphere, at the end of the day a more relaxed atmosphere could be felt; **la crise se manifeste par des troubles sociaux** the crisis shows itself in social unrest; (*Rel*) **Dieu s'est manifesté aux hommes** God revealed himself to mankind.

b (*se présenter*) *[personne]* to appear, turn up; (*par téléphone*) to get in touch *ou* contact; *[candidat, témoin]* to come forward. **depuis son échec il n'ose pas se ~ ici** since his defeat he dare not show his face here.

c (*se faire remarquer*) *[personne]* to make o.s. known, come to the fore. **cette situation difficile lui a permis de se ~** this difficult situation gave him the chance to make himself known *ou* to come to the fore *ou* to make his mark; **il n'a pas eu l'occasion de se ~ dans le débat** he didn't get a chance to assert himself *ou* to make himself heard in the discussion; **il s'est manifesté par une déclaration fracassante** he came to public notice *ou* he attracted attention with a sensational statement.

manifold [manifɔld] **nm** (*carnet*) duplicate book; (*tuyaux*) manifold.

manigance [manigɑ̃s] **nf** (*gén pl*) scheme, trick, ploy. **encore une de ses ~s** another of his little schemes *ou* tricks *ou* ploys.

manigancer [manigɑ̃se] 3 **vt** to plot, devise. **qu'est-ce qu'il manigance maintenant?** what's he up to now?, what's his latest little scheme?; **c'est lui qui a tout manigancé** he set the whole thing up*, he engineered it all.

manille¹ [manij] 1 **nm** Manila cigar. 2 **n: M~** Manila.

manille² [manij] **nf** a (*Cartes*) (*jeu*) manille; (*dix*) ten. b (*Tech*) shackle.

manillon [manijɔ̃] **nm** ace (*in game of manille*).

manioc [manjɔk] **nm** manioc, cassava.

manip* [manip] **nf abrév de manipulation**.

manipulateur, -trice [manipylatœʀ, tʀis] 1 **nm,f** a (*technicien*) technician. **~ de laboratoire** laboratory technician. b (*péj*) manipulator. c (*prestidigitateur*) conjurer. 2 **nm** (*Téléc*) key.

manipulation [manipylasjɔ̃] **nf** a (*maniement*) handling. **ces produits chimiques sont d'une ~ délicate** these chemicals should be handled with great care, great care should be taken in handling these chemicals. b (*Scol: Chim, Phys*) experiment. c (*Pol: fig, péj*) manipulation (*NonC*). **il y a eu des ~s électorales** there was rigging of the elections, some elections were rigged. d (*prestidigitation*) sleight of hand. e (*Méd: gén pl*) manipulation (*NonC*). **obtenu par ~ génétique** genetically engineered; **les ~s génétiques posent des problèmes éthiques** genetic engineering poses ethical problems.

manipule [manipyl] **nm** (*Antiq, Rel*) maniple.

manipuler [manipyle] 1 **vt** a *objet, produit* to handle. b (*fig, péj*) *électeurs* to manipulate. **~ une élection** to rig an election; **~ les écritures** to rig *ou* fiddle* (*Brit*) the accounts, cook the books* (*Brit*).

Manitoba [manitɔba] **nm** Manitoba.

manitobain, e [manitɔbɛ̃, ɛn] 1 **adj** Manitoban. 2 **nm,f: M~(e)** Manitoban.

manitou [manitu] **nm** a **grand ~*** big shot*, big noise* (*Brit*). **le grand ~ de la firme** the big shot* in the firm. b (*Rel*) manitou.

manivelle [manivɛl] **nf** (*gén*) crank; (*pour changer une roue*) wheel crank; (*pour démarrer*) crank, starting handle. **faire partir à la ~** to crank, give a crankstart to; *voir* **retour**.

manne [man] **nf** a (*Rel*) **la ~** manna; **recevoir la ~ (céleste)** (*la bonne parole*) to receive the word from on high. b (*fig*) (*aubaine*) godsend, manna. **ça a été pour nous une ~ (providentielle** *ou* **céleste)** that was a godsend for us, it was heaven-sent. c (*Bot*) manna. d (*panier*) large wicker basket.

mannequin [mankɛ̃] **nm** a (*personne*) model, mannequin†; *voir* **défilé, taille¹**. b (*objet*) *[couturière]* dummy; *[vitrine]* model, dummy; *[peintre]* model; (*fig: pantin*) stuffed dummy. c (*panier*) small (gardener's) basket.

manœuvrabilité [manœvʀabilite] **nf** (*gén*) manoeuvrability; (*Aut*) driveability.

manœuvrable [manœvʀabl] **adj** (*gén*) manoeuvrable, easy to handle; *voiture* easy to handle *ou* drive.

manœuvre [manœvʀ] 1 **nf** a (*opération*) manoeuvre, operation; (*Rail*) shunting. **diriger/surveiller la ~** to control/supervise the manoeuvre *ou* operation; **la ~ d'un bateau n'est pas chose facile** manoeuvring a boat is no easy thing to do, it's not easy to manoeuvre a boat; (*Aut, Naut*) **faire une ~** to do a manoeuvre; **il a manqué sa ~** he mishandled *ou* muffed* the manoeuvre; **il a réussi sa ~** he carried off the manoeuvre successfully; **fausse ~** mistake; (*Rail*) **faire la ~** to shunt.

b (*Mil*) manoeuvre. **champ** *ou* **terrain de ~s** parade ground; **~ d'encerclement** encircling movement; **les grandes ~s de printemps** spring army manoeuvres *ou* exercises; **être en ~s, faire des ~s** to be on manoeuvres.

c (*agissement, combinaison*) manoeuvre; (*machination, intrigue*) manoeuvring, ploy. **il a toute liberté de ~** he has complete freedom to manoeuvre; **~s électorales** vote-catching manoeuvres *ou* ploys; **~s frauduleuses** fraudulent schemes *ou* devices; **~ d'obstruction** obstructive move; ~ **boursière** stockmarket manipulation; **il a été victime d'une ~ de l'adversaire** he was caught out by a clever move *ou* trick on the part of his opponents.

d (*Naut*) ~**s dormantes/courantes** standing/running rigging.

2 nm (*gén*) labourer; (*en usine*) unskilled worker. **c'est un travail de ~** it's unskilled labour *ou* work; ~ **agricole** farm labourer *ou* hand.

manœuvrer [manœvʀe] [1] 1 vt *véhicule* to manoeuvre; *machine* to operate, work; (*fig: manipuler*) *personne* to manipulate. **se laisser ~ par sa femme** to allow o.s. to be manipulated by one's wife. 2 vi (*gén*) to manoeuvre. (*fig*) **il a manœuvré habilement** he moved *ou* manoeuvred skilfully.

manœuvrier, -ière [manœvʀije, ijɛʀ] 1 adj manoeuvring. 2 nm,f (*Mil*) tactician; (*Pol*) manoeuvrer.

manoir [manwaʀ] nm manor *ou* country house.

manomètre [manɔmɛtʀ] nm gauge, manometer.

manométrique [manɔmetʀik] adj manometric.

manouche* [manuʃ] nmf (*péj*) gipsy, gippo**.

manouvrier, -ière† [manuvʀije, ijɛʀ] nm,f (casual) labourer.

manquant, e [mɑ̃kɑ̃, ɑ̃t] adj missing.

manque [mɑ̃k] nm a ~ **de** (*pénurie*) lack of, shortage of, want of; (*faiblesse*) lack of, want of; ~ **de nourriture/d'argent** lack *ou* shortage *ou* want of food/money; ~ **d'intelligence/de goût** lack *ou* want of intelligence/taste; **son ~ de sérieux** his lack of seriousness, his flippancy; **par ~ de** through lack *ou* shortage of, for want of; **quel ~ de chance!** *ou* **de pot!**‡ what bad *ou* hard luck!; ~ **à gagner** loss of profit *ou* earnings; **cela représente un sérieux ~ à gagner pour les cultivateurs** that means a serious loss of income *ou* a serious drop in earnings *ou* income for the farmers.

b ~**s** (*défauts*) *[roman]* faults; *[personne]* failings, shortcomings; *[mémoire, connaissances]* gaps.

c (*vide*) gap, emptiness; (*Drogue*) withdrawal. **je ressens comme un grand ~** it's as if there were a great emptiness inside me; **un ~ que rien ne saurait combler** a gap which nothing could fill; **symptômes de ~** withdrawal symptoms; **être en état de ~** to be experiencing withdrawal symptoms.

d (*Tex*) flaw. **il faut faire un raccord (de peinture), il y a des ~s** we'll have to touch up the paintwork, there are bare patches.

e (*Roulette*) manque.

f (‡) **à la ~: un chanteur à la ~** a crummy‡ *ou* second-rate singer; **lui et ses idées à la ~** him and his half-baked* *ou* crummy‡ ideas.

manqué, e [mɑ̃ke] (ptp de **manquer**) adj *essai* failed, abortive; *rendez-vous* missed; *photo* spoilt; *vie* wasted; (*Tech*) *pièce* faulty. **occasion ~e** lost *ou* wasted opportunity; **un roman ~** a novel which doesn't quite succeed *ou* come off*; **c'est un écrivain ~** (*mauvais écrivain*) he is a failure as a writer; (*il aurait dû être écrivain*) he should have been a writer; (*Culin*) **(gâteau) ~** ≃ sponge cake; *voir* **garçon**.

manquement [mɑ̃kmɑ̃] nm (*frm*) ~ **à** *discipline, règle* breach of; ~ **au devoir** dereliction of duty; **au moindre ~** at the slightest lapse; (*Jur*) ~ **(à des obligations contractuelles)** default.

manquer [mɑ̃ke] [1] 1 vt a (*ne pas atteindre ou saisir*) *but, occasion, train* to miss; (*ne pas tuer; ne pas atteindre ou rencontrer*) *personne* to miss. ~ **une marche** to miss a step; ~ **qn de peu** (*en lui tirant dessus*) to miss sb by a fraction, just to miss sb; (*à un rendez-vous*) just to miss sb; **je l'ai manqué de 5 minutes** I missed him by 5 minutes; **c'est un film/une pièce à ne pas ~** this film/play is a must*, it's a film/play that shouldn't be missed; (*iro*) **il n'en manque jamais une*!** he blunders *ou* boobs‡ every time!, he puts his foot in it every time!*; **vous n'avez rien manqué (en ne venant pas)** you didn't miss anything (by not coming); **je ne le manquerai pas** (*je vais lui donner une leçon*) I won't let him get away with it; *voir* **coche**.

b (*ne pas réussir*) *photo, gâteau* to spoil, make a mess of*, botch*; *examen* to fail. **il a manqué sa vie** he has wasted his life; **ils ont (complètement) manqué leur coup** their attempt failed completely, they completely botched* the attempt *ou* the job*.

c (*être absent de*) to be absent from, miss. ~ **l'école** to be absent from *ou* miss school; **il a manqué deux réunions** he missed two meetings.

2 vi a (*faire défaut*) to be lacking. **l'argent/la nourriture vint à ~** money/food ran out *ou* ran short; **rien ne manque** nothing is lacking; **les occasions ne manquent pas (de faire)** there is no lack of *ou* there are endless opportunities (to do).

b (*être absent*) to be absent; (*avoir disparu*) to be missing. **il ne manque jamais** he's never absent, he never misses; **rien ne manque** nothing is missing.

c (*échouer*) *[expérience etc]* to fail.

d ~ **à** (*faire défaut à*): **ce qui lui manque, c'est l'argent** what he lacks *ou* what he hasn't got is (the) money; **les mots me manquent pour exprimer** I can't find the words to express, I am at a loss for words to express; **le temps me manque pour m'étendre sur ce sujet** there's no time for me to enlarge on this theme; **ce n'est pas l'envie** *ou* **le désir qui me manque d'y aller** it's not that I don't want to go, it's not that I am unwilling to go; **le pied lui manqua** his foot slipped, he missed his footing; **la voix lui manqua** words failed him, he stood speechless; **un carreau manquait à la fenêtre** there was a pane missing in *ou* from the window; (*hum*) **qu'est-ce qui manque à ton bonheur?** is there something not to your liking?, what are you unhappy about?

3 **manquer à** vt indir a (*ne pas respecter*) ~ **à son honneur/son devoir** to fail in one's honour/duty; ~ **à ses promesses** to renege on one's promises, fail to keep one's word; ~ **à tous les usages** to flout every convention; **il manque à tous ses devoirs** he neglects all his duties; **sa femme lui a manqué, il l'a battue**† his wife wronged him so he beat her; ~ **à qn**† (*être impoli envers qn*) to be disrespectful to sb.

b (*être absent de*) *réunion* to be absent from, miss. ~ **à l'appel** (*lit*) to be absent from roll call; (*fig*) to be missing.

c (*être regretté*) ~ **à qn: il nous manque, sa présence nous manque** we miss him; **la campagne nous manque** we miss the country.

4 **manquer de** vt indir a (*être dépourvu de*) *intelligence, générosité* to lack; *argent, main-d'œuvre* to be short of, lack. **ils ne manquent de rien** they want for nothing, they lack nothing; **le pays ne manque pas d'un certain charme** the country is not without a certain charm; **on manque d'air ici** there's no air in here; (*fig*) **tu ne manques pas d'audace** *ou* **d'air*** *ou* **de culot*!** you've got a *ou* some nerve!*; **nous manquons de personnel** we're short-staffed, we're short of staff, we lack staff.

b (*faillir*) **elle a manqué (de) se faire écraser** she nearly got run over; **il a manqué mourir** he nearly *ou* almost died.

c (*formules nég*) **ne manquez pas de le remercier pour moi** don't forget to thank him for me, be sure to thank him for me; **je ne manquerai pas de le lui dire** I'll be sure to tell him; **nous ne manquerons pas de vous en informer** we shall inform you without fail; **il n'a pas manqué de le lui dire** he made sure he told him; **remerciez-la — je n'y manquerai pas** thank her — I won't forget; **on ne peut ~ d'être frappé par** one cannot fail to marvel at, one cannot help but be struck by; **ça ne va pas ~ (d'arriver)*** it's bound to happen; **ça n'a pas manqué (d'arriver)*!** sure enough it was bound to happen!

5 vb impers: **il manque un pied à la chaise** there's a leg missing from the chair; **il (nous) manque 10 personnes/2 chaises** (*elles ont disparu*) there are 10 people/2 chairs missing; (*on en a besoin*) we are 10 people/2 chairs short, we are short of 10 people/2 chairs; **il ne manquera pas de gens pour dire** there'll be no shortage *ou* lack of people to say; **il ne lui manque que d'être intelligent** the only thing he's lacking in is intelligence; **il ne manquait plus que ça** that's all we needed, that beats all*, that's the last straw*; **il ne manquerait plus qu'il parte sans elle!** it would be the last straw if he went off without her!*

6 **se manquer** vpr (*rater son suicide*) to fail (in one's attempt to commit suicide).

mansarde [mɑ̃saʀd] nf (*pièce*) attic, garret.

mansardé, e [mɑ̃saʀde] adj *chambre, étage* attic (*épith*). **la chambre est ~e** the room has a sloping ceiling, it is an attic room.

mansuétude [mɑ̃sɥetyd] nf leniency, indulgence.

mante [mɑ̃t] nf a (*Zool*) mantis. ~ **religieuse** (*lit*) praying mantis; (*fig*) man-eater (*fig hum*). b (†: *manteau*) (woman's) mantle, cloak.

manteau, pl ~**x** [mɑ̃to] 1 nm a (*Habillement*) coat. ~ **de pluie** raincoat; ~ **trois-quarts** three-quarter length coat; (*loc*) **sous le ~** clandestinely, on the sly. b (*fig littér*) *[neige]* mantle, blanket; *[ombre, hypocrisie]* cloak. **sous le ~ de la nuit** under cover of night, under the cloak of darkness. c (*Zool*) *[mollusque]* mantle. d (*Hér*) mantle, mantling. e (*Géol*) mantle. 2 comp ►**manteau d'Arlequin** proscenium arch ►**manteau de cheminée** mantelpiece.

mantelet [mɑ̃t(ə)lɛ] nm (*Habillement*) short cape, mantelet; (*Naut*) deadlight.

mantille [mɑ̃tij] nf mantilla.

mantisse [mɑ̃tis] nf mantissa.

Mantoue [mɑ̃tu] n Mantua.

mantra [mɑ̃tʀa] nm mantra.

manucure [manykyʀ] nmf manicurist.

manucurer [manykyʀe] [1] vt to manicure.

manuel, -elle [manɥɛl] 1 adj manual. 2 nm,f (*travailleur manuel*) manual worker; (*qui a du sens pratique*) practical man (*ou* woman). 3 nm (*livre*) manual, handbook. ~ **de lecture** reader; ~ **scolaire** textbook; ~ **d'entretien** service manual.

manuellement [manɥɛlmɑ̃] adv *fabriquer* by hand, manually; *fonctionner* manually. **être bon ~** to be good with one's hands.

manufacturable [manyfaktyʀabl] adj manufacturable.

manufacture [manyfaktyʀ] nf a (*usine*) factory. ~ **d'armes/de porcelaine/de tabac** munitions/porcelain/tobacco factory; ~ **de tapisserie** tapestry workshop. b (*fabrication*) manufacture.

manufacturer [manyfaktyʀe] [1] vt to manufacture; *voir* **produit**.

manufacturier, -ière [manyfaktyʀje, jɛʀ] 1 adj manufacturing (*épith*). 2 nm (†) factory owner.

manu militari [manymilitaʀi] adv by (main) force.

manuscrit, e [manyskʀi, it] 1 adj (*écrit à la main*) handwritten. **pages ~es** manuscript pages. 2 nm manuscript; (*dactylographié*) manuscript, typescript. **les ~s de la mer Morte** the Dead Sea Scrolls.

manutention [manytɑ̃sjɔ̃] nf (*opération*) handling; (*local*) storehouse. (*Comm*) **frais de ~** handling charges.

manutentionnaire [manytɑ̃sjɔnɛʀ] nmf packer.

manutentionner [manytɑ̃sjɔne] [1] vt to handle, pack.

maoïsme [maɔism] nm Maoism.
maoïste [maɔist] adj, nmf Maoist.
Mao (Tsê-Tung) [mao(tsetuŋ)] nm Mao (Tse Tung).
maous, -ousse* [maus] adj *personne* hefty; *animal, objet* whacking great‡ (*Brit, épith*), colossal.
mappemonde [mapmɔ̃d] nf (*carte*) map of the world (in two hemispheres); (*sphère*) globe.
Maputo [maputo] n Maputo.
maquer (se)‡ [make] 1 vpr: **se ~ avec qn** to (go and) live with sb, be shacked up with sb‡ (*péj*); **elle est maquée avec lui** she's living with him, she's shacked up with him‡ (*péj*).
maquereau¹, pl **~x** [makʀo] nm (*poisson*) mackerel; *voir* **groseille**.
maquereau²‡, pl **~x** [makʀo] nm (*proxénète*) pimp, ponce‡ (*Brit*).
maquerelle‡ [makʀɛl] nf madam*.
maquette [makɛt] nf a (*à échelle réduite*) (*Archit, Ind*) (scale) model; (*Art, Théât*) model. b (*grandeur nature*) (*Ind*) mock-up, model; (*livre*) dummy. c (*Peinture: carton*) sketch. d (*Typ*) (*mise en pages*) paste-up; (*couverture*) artwork.
maquettiste [maketist] nmf model maker.
maquignon [makiɲɔ̃] nm (*lit*) horse dealer; (*péj*) shady *ou* crooked dealer.
maquignonnage [makiɲɔnaʒ] nm (*lit*) horse dealing; (*fig, péj*) sharp practice, underhand dealings.
maquignonner [makiɲɔne] 1 vt (*péj*) *animal* to sell by shady methods; *affaire* to rig, fiddle.
maquillage [makijaʒ] nm a (*résultat*) make-up. **passer du temps à son ~** to spend a long time putting on one's make-up *ou* making up. b (*péj*) [*voiture*] disguising, doing over*; [*document, vérité, faits*] faking, doctoring.
maquiller [makije] 1 1 vt a *visage, personne* to make up. **très maquillé** heavily made-up. b (*fig*) *document, vérité, faits* to fake, doctor; *résultats, chiffres* to juggle (with), fiddle* (*Brit*); *voiture* to do over*, disguise. **meurtre maquillé en accident** murder faked up to look like an accident. 2 **se maquiller** vpr to make up, put on one's make-up. **elle est trop jeune pour se ~** she is too young to use make-up.
maquilleur [makijœʀ] nm make-up artist, make-up man.
maquilleuse [makijøz] nf make-up artist, make-up girl.
maquis [maki] nm a (*Géog*) scrub, bush. **le ~ corse** the Corsican scrub; **prendre le ~** to take to the bush. b (*fig: labyrinthe*) tangle, maze. **le ~ de la procédure** the minefield *ou* jungle of legal procedure. c (*Hist: 2e Guerre mondiale*) maquis. **prendre le ~** to take to the maquis, go underground.
maquisard [makizaʀ] nm maquis, member of the Resistance.
marabout [maʀabu] nm (*Orn*) marabou(t); (*Rel*) marabout.
maraca [maʀaka] nf maraca.
maraîchage [maʀɛʃaʒ] nm market gardening (*Brit*), truck farming (*US*). **~ sous verre** glasshouse cultivation.
maraîcher, -ère [maʀeʃe, ɛʀ] 1 nm,f market gardener (*Brit*), truck farmer (*US*). 2 adj: **culture ~ère** market gardening (*NonC*) (*Brit*), truck farming (*NonC*) (*US*); **produit ~** market garden produce (*NonC*) (*Brit*), truck (*NonC*) (*US*); **jardin ~** market garden (*Brit*), truck farm (*US*).
marais [maʀɛ] nm a marsh, swamp. **~ salant** saltern; *voir* **gaz**. b **le M~** the Marais (*district of Paris*).
marasme [maʀasm] nm a (*Écon, Pol*) stagnation, slump, paralysis. **les affaires sont en plein ~** business is completely stagnant, there is a complete slump in business. b (*accablement*) dejection, depression. c (*Méd*) marasmus.
marasquin [maʀaskɛ̃] nm maraschino.
marathon [maʀatɔ̃] nm (*Sport, fig*) marathon. (*ville*) **M~** Marathon; **~ de danse** dance marathon; **visite-/négociations-~** marathon visit/talks.
marathonien, -ienne [maʀatɔnjɛ̃, jɛn] nm,f marathon runner.
marâtre [maʀɑtʀ] nf (*mauvaise mère*) cruel *ou* unnatural mother; (*††: belle-mère*) stepmother.
maraud, e¹†† [maʀo, od] nm,f rascal, rogue, scoundrel.
maraudage [maʀodaʒ] nm pilfering, thieving (*of poultry, crops etc*).
maraude² [maʀod] nf a (*vol*) thieving, pilfering (*of poultry, crops etc*); pillaging (*from farms, orchards*). b **taxi en ~** *ou* **qui fait la ~** cruising *ou* prowling taxi, taxi cruising *ou* prowling for fares; **vagabond en ~** tramp on the prowl.
marauder [maʀode] 1 vi [*personne*] to thieve, pilfer; [*taxi*] to cruise *ou* prowl for fares.
maraudeur, -euse [maʀodœʀ, øz] nm,f (*voleur*) prowler; (*soldat*) marauder. **oiseau ~** thieving bird; **taxi ~** cruising *ou* prowling taxi.
marbre [maʀbʀ] nm a (*Géol*) marble. **de** *ou* **en ~** marble; **~ de Carrare** Carrara marble; (*fig*) **rester de ~, garder un visage de ~** to remain stonily indifferent; **avoir un cœur de ~** to have a heart of stone; (*Aut*) **passer une voiture au ~** to check a car for structural damage; *voir* **froid**. b (*surface*) marble top; (*statue*) marble (statue). c (*Typ*) stone, bed. **être sur le ~** [*journal*] to be put to bed, be on the stone; [*livre*] to be on the press; **rester sur le ~** to be excess copy.
marbrer [maʀbʀe] 1 vt a (*Tech*) *papier, cuir* to marble. b *peau* [*froid*] to blotch, mottle; [*coup*] to mark, leave marks on; [*coup violent*] to mottle. **peau naturellement marbrée** naturally mottled skin; **visage marbré par le froid** face blotchy *ou* mottled with cold. c (*gén: veiner*) *bois, surface* to vein, mottle. (**gâteau**) **marbré** marble cake.
marbrerie [maʀbʀəʀi] nf (*atelier*) marble mason's workshop *ou* yard; (*industrie*) marble industry. **travailler dans la ~** to be a marble mason; (*funéraire*) to be a monumental mason.
marbrier, -ière [maʀbʀije, ijɛʀ] 1 adj *industrie* marble (*épith*). 2 nm (*funéraire*) monumental mason. 3 **marbrière** nf marble quarry.
marbrure [maʀbʀyʀ] nf (*gén pl*) (*voir* **marbrer**) marbling; blotch; mottling; mark; vein.
Marc [maʀk] nm Mark. **~ Aurèle** Marcus Aurelius; **~-Antoine** Mark Antony.
marc¹ [maʀ] nm (*poids, monnaie*) mark. (*Jur*) **au ~ le franc** pro rata, proportionally.
marc² [maʀ] nm [*raisin, pomme*] marc. **~ (de café)** (coffee) grounds *ou* dregs; (**eau de vie de**) **~** marc brandy.
marcassin [maʀkasɛ̃] nm young wild boar.
marchand, e [maʀʃɑ̃, ɑ̃d] 1 adj *valeur* market (*épith*); *prix* trade (*épith*). **navire ~** merchant ship; *voir* **galerie, marine²**.
2 nm,f (*boutiquier*) shopkeeper, tradesman (*ou* tradeswoman); (*sur un marché*) stallholder; [*vins, fruits, charbon, grains*] merchant; [*meubles, bestiaux, cycles*] dealer. **~ au détail** retailer; **~ en gros** wholesaler; **la ~e de chaussures me l'a dit** the woman in the shoeshop *ou* the shoe-shop owner told me; **rapporte-le chez le ~/chez le ~ de fromages** take it back to the shop *ou* shopkeeper/to the cheese merchant's; (*hum, péj*) **c'est un ~ de vacances** he is in the holiday business *ou* racket (*péj*).
3 comp ▸**marchand ambulant** hawker, pedlar (*Brit*), peddler (*US*), door-to-door salesman ▸**marchande d'amour** (*hum*) lady of pleasure (*hum*) ▸**marchand de biens** estate agent (*Brit*), realtor (*US*) ▸**marchand de canons** (*péj*) arms dealer ▸**marchand de couleurs** ironmonger (*Brit*), hardware dealer ▸**marchand de fromages** cheesemonger (*Brit*), cheese merchant ▸**marchand de fruits** fruiterer (*Brit*), fruit merchant ▸**marchand d'illusions** purveyor of illusions, illusionmonger ▸**marchand de journaux** newsagent ▸**marchand de légumes** greengrocer, produce dealer (*US*) ▸**marchand de marée** fish merchant ▸**marchand de marrons** chestnut seller ▸**marchand de poissons** fishmonger (*Brit*), fish merchant ▸**marchand de quatre saisons** costermonger (*Brit*), street merchant (selling fresh fruit and vegetables) ▸**marchand de rêves** dream-merchant ▸**marchand de sable** (*fig*) sandman ▸**marchand de sommeil** (*péj*) slum landlord, slumlord (*US*) ▸**marchand de soupe** (*péj*) (*restaurateur*) low-grade restaurateur, profiteering café owner; (*Scol*) money-grubbing *ou* profit-minded headmaster (of a private school) ▸**marchand de tableaux** art dealer ▸**marchand de tapis** carpet dealer; (*péj*) **c'est un vrai marchand de tapis** he drives a really hard bargain, he haggles over everything; **des discussions de marchand de tapis** fierce bargaining, endless haggling ▸**marchand de voyages** tour operator.
marchandage [maʀʃɑ̃daʒ] nm a (*au marché*) bargaining, haggling; (*péj: aux élections*) bargaining. **se livrer à de sordides ~s** to get down to some sordid bargaining. b (*Jur*) **le ~** ≃ the lump, *illegal subcontracting of labour*.
marchander [maʀʃɑ̃de] 1 vt a *objet* to haggle over, bargain over. **il a l'habitude de ~** he is used to haggling *ou* bargaining. b (*fig*) **il ne marchande pas sa peine** he spares no pains, he grudges no effort; **il ne m'a pas marchandé ses compliments** he wasn't sparing of his compliments. c (*Jur*) to subcontract.
marchandeur, -euse [maʀʃɑ̃dœʀ, øz] nm,f a haggler. b (*Jur*) subcontractor (of labour).
marchandisage [maʀʃɑ̃dizaʒ] nm marketing.
marchandise [maʀʃɑ̃diz] nf a (*article, unité*) commodity. **~s** goods, merchandise (*NonC*), wares†; **train/gare de ~s** goods train/station; **~s en gros/au détail** wholesale/retail goods; **il a de la bonne ~** he has *ou* sells good stuff. b (*cargaison, stock*) **la ~** the goods, the merchandise; **la ~ est dans l'entrepôt** the goods are *ou* the merchandise is in the warehouse; **faire valoir** *ou* **vanter la ~*** to show o.s. off *ou* to show off one's wares to advantage, make the most of o.s. *ou* one's wares; **tromper** *ou* **rouler qn sur la ~*** to sell sb a pup* (*Brit*) *ou* a dud*; **elle étale la ~‡** she displays her charms (*hum*), she shows you all she's got*.
marchante [maʀʃɑ̃t] adj f *voir* **aile**.
marche¹ [maʀʃ] 1 nf a (*action, Sport*) walking. **il fait de la ~** he goes in for walking, he does quite a bit of walking; **poursuivre sa ~** to walk on; **chaussures de ~** walking shoes.
b (*allure, démarche*) walk, step, gait; (*allure, rythme*) pace, step. **une ~ pesante** a heavy step *ou* gait; **régler sa ~ sur celle de qn** to adjust one's pace *ou* step to sb else's.
c (*trajet*) walk. **faire une longue ~** to go for a long walk; **le village est à 2 heures/à 10 km de ~ d'ici** the village is a 2-hour walk/a 10-km walk from here; **une ~ de 10 km** a 10-km walk.
d (*mouvement d'un groupe, Mil, Pol*) march. **air/chanson de ~** marching tune/song; **fermer la ~** to bring up the rear; **ouvrir la ~** to lead the way; **faire ~ sur** to march upon; **~ victorieuse sur la ville** victorious march on the town; **en avant, ~!** quick march!, forward march!; *voir* **ordre¹**.

e (*mouvement, déplacement d'un objet*) (*Aut, Rail*) *[véhicule]* running; (*Tech*) *[machine]* running, working; (*Naut*) *[navire]* sailing; (*Astron*) *[étoile]* course; *[horloge]* working; (*Admin*) *[usine, établissement]* running, working, functioning. **dans le sens de la ~** facing the engine; **dans le sens contraire de la ~** with one's back to the engine; **ne montez pas dans un véhicule en ~** do not board a moving vehicle; **j'ai pris le bus en ~** I jumped onto the bus while it was moving; **en (bon) état de ~** in (good) working order; **régler la ~ d'une horloge** to adjust the workings *ou* movement of a clock; **assurer la bonne ~ d'un service** to ensure the smooth running of a service; (*Tech*) **~ — arrêt** on — off.

f (*développement*) *[maladie]* progress; *[affaire, événements, opérations]* course; *[histoire, temps, progrès]* march. **la ~ de l'intrigue** the unfolding *ou* development of the plot.

g (*loc*) **être en ~** *[personnes, armées]* to be on the move; *[moteur]* to be running; *[machine]* to be (turned) on; **se mettre en ~** *[personne]* to make a move, get moving; *[machine]* to start; **mettre en ~** *moteur, voiture* to start (up); *machine* to put on, turn on, set going; *pendule* to start going; *voir* **train**.

h (*Mus*) march. **~ funèbre/militaire/nuptiale** funeral/military/wedding march.

2 comp ▸**marche arrière** (*Aut*) reverse; **entrer/sortir en marche arrière** to reverse in/out, back in/out; **faire marche arrière** (*Aut*) to reverse; (*fig*) to back-pedal, to backtrack ▸**marche forcée** (*Mil*) forced march; **se rendre vers un lieu à marche(s) forcée(s)** to get to a place by forced marches ▸**marche à suivre** (correct) procedure (*pour* for); (*mode d'emploi*) directions (for use).

marche² [maʀʃ] nf *[véhicule]* step; *[escalier]* step, stair. **manquer une ~** to miss a step; **attention à la ~** mind the step; **sur les ~s** (*de l'escalier*) on the stairs; (*de l'escalier extérieur, de l'escabeau*) on the steps; (*lit, fig*) **monter sur la plus haute ~ du podium** to get first prize; **~ palière** last step before the landing, ≃ top step.

marche³ [maʀʃ] nf (*gén pl*) (*Géog, Hist*) march. **les ~s** the Marches.

marché [maʀʃe] 1 nm a (*lieu*) market; (*ville*) trading centre. **~ aux bestiaux/aux fleurs/aux poissons** cattle/flower/fish market; **~ couvert/en plein air** covered/open-air market; **aller au ~, aller faire le ~** to go to (the) market; **aller faire son ~** to go to the market; (*plus gén*) to go shopping; *[marchand, acheteur]* **faire les ~s** to go round *ou* do the markets; **vendre/acheter au ~** *ou* **sur les ~s** to buy/sell at the market; **Lyon, le grand ~ des soieries** Lyons, the great trading centre for silk goods.

b (*Comm, Écon: débouchés, opérations*) market. **~ monétaire** money market; **~ libre/des valeurs** open/securities market; **le ~ unique européen** the single European market; (*Pétrole*) **le ~ libre de Rotterdam** the Rotterdam spot market; **acquérir** *ou* **trouver de nouveaux ~s (pour)** to find new markets (for); **lancer/offrir qch sur le ~** to launch/put sth on the market; **analyse/étude de ~** market analysis/research; **le ~ du travail** the labour market; **il n'y a pas de ~ pour ces produits** there is no market for these goods.

c (*transaction, contrat*) bargain, transaction, deal. **faire un ~ avantageux** to make *ou* strike a good bargain; **un ~ de dupes** a fool's bargain *ou* deal; **conclure** *ou* **passer un ~ avec qn** to make a deal with sb; **~ conclu!** it's a deal!; **~ ferme** firm deal; **~ de gré à gré** mutual agreement, private contract; **~ public** procurement contract; (*fig*) **mettre le ~ en main à qn** to give sb an ultimatum; *voir* **bon¹**.

d (*Bourse*) market. **le ~ est animé** the market is lively; **le ~ des valeurs** the stock market; **le ~ des changes** *ou* **des devises** the foreign exchange market; **~ financier** financial market; **~ obligataire** bond market; **~ à prime** option (bargain); **~ au comptant/à terme** *ou* **à règlement mensuel** spot *ou* cash/forward market; **~ à terme d'instruments financiers, ~ à terme international de France** *French financial futures market*, ≃ LIFFE (*Brit*).

2 comp ▸**Marché commun** Common Market ▸**marché-gare** nm (pl **marchés-gares**) wholesale food market ▸**marché international du disque et de l'édition musicale** *music industry trade fair* ▸**marché d'intérêt national** *wholesale market for fruit, vegetables and agricultural products* ▸**marché noir** black market; **faire du marché noir** to buy and sell on the black market ▸**marché aux puces** flea market.

marchepied [maʀʃəpje] nm (*Rail*) step; (*Aut*) running board; (*fig*) stepping stone.

marcher [maʀʃe] 1 vi a to walk; *[soldats]* to march. **~ à grandes enjambées** *ou* **à grands pas** to stride (along); **il marche en boitant** he walks with a limp; **~ en canard** to walk like a duck; **venez, on va ~ un peu** come on, let's have a walk *ou* let's go for a walk; **il marchait lentement par les rues** he strolled *ou* wandered along the streets; **il marchait sans but** he walked (along) aimlessly; (*fig*) **~ sur des œufs** to act with caution; **faire ~ un bébé** to get a baby to walk, help a baby walk; **c'est marche ou crève!‡** it's sink or swim!; *voir* **pas¹**.

b (*mettre le pied sur, dans*) **~ dans une flaque d'eau** to step in a puddle; **défense de ~ sur les pelouses** keep off the grass; (*lit*) **~ sur les pieds de qn/sur sa robe** to stand *ou* tread on sb's toes/on one's dress; (*fig*) **ne te laisse pas ~ sur les pieds** don't let anyone tread on your toes (*fig*) *ou* take advantage of you; (*fig*) **~ sur qn** to walk all over sb; (*fig*) **~ sur les plates-bandes** *ou* **les brisées de qn*** to poach *ou* intrude on sb's preserves; **~ sur les pas** *ou* **les traces** *ou* **dans le sillage de qn** to follow in sb's footsteps; *voir* **côté**.

c (*fig: progresser*) **~ à la conquête de la gloire/vers le succès** to be on the road to fame/success, step out *ou* stride towards fame/success; **~ au supplice** to walk to one's death *ou* to the stake; **~ au combat** to march into battle; (*Mil*) **~ sur une ville/sur un adversaire** to advance on *ou* march against a town/an enemy.

d (*fig: obéir*) to toe the line; (**: consentir*) to agree, play*. (**: croire naïvement*) **il marche à tous les coups** he is taken in *ou* falls for it* every time; **on lui raconte n'importe quoi et il marche** you can tell him anything and he'll swallow it*; **il n'a pas voulu ~ dans la combine** he did not want to be involved in the affair; **faire ~ qn** (*taquiner*) to pull sb's leg; (*tromper*) to take sb for a ride*, lead sb up the garden path*; **il sait faire ~ sa grand-mère** he knows how to get round his grandmother; **son père saura le faire ~ (droit)** his father will soon have him toeing the line.

e (*avec véhicule*) **le train a/nous avons bien marché jusqu'à Lyon** the train/we made good time as far as Lyons; **nous marchions à 100 à l'heure** we were doing a hundred.

f (*fonctionner*) *[appareil]* to work; *[ruse]* to work, come off; *[usine]* to work (well); *[affaires, études]* to go (well). **faire ~** *appareil* to work, operate; *entreprise* to run; **ça fait ~ les affaires** it's good for business; **ça marche à l'électricité** it works by *ou* on electricity; **est-ce que le métro marche aujourd'hui?** is the underground running today?; **ces deux opérations marchent ensemble** these two procedures go *ou* work together; **les affaires marchent mal** things are going badly, business is bad; **les études, ça marche?*** how's studying going?; **rien ne marche** nothing's going right, nothing's working; **"ça marche!"** (*dans un restaurant*) "coming up!"; (*c'est d'accord*) great!‡, OK!*; **ça marche pour 20 h/lundi** 8 o'clock/Monday is fine; *voir* **roulette**.

marcheur, -euse [maʀʃœʀ, øz] nm,f (*gén*) walker; (*Pol etc*) marcher.

Marco Polo [maʀkopolo] nm Marco Polo.

marcottage [maʀkɔtaʒ] nm (*Bot*) layering.

marcotte [maʀkɔt] nf (*Bot*) layer, runner.

marcotter [maʀkɔte] 1 vt (*Bot*) to layer.

mardi [maʀdi] nm Tuesday. **M~ gras** Shrove *ou* Pancake (*Brit*) Tuesday; (*hum*) **elle se croit à ~ gras!** she's dressed up like a dog's dinner!; *pour autres loc voir* **samedi**.

mare [maʀ] nf a (*étang*) pond. **~ aux canards** duck pond; *voir* **pavé**. b (*flaque*) pool. **~ de sang/d'huile** pool of blood/oil.

marécage [maʀekaʒ] nm marsh, swamp, bog.

marécageux, -euse [maʀekaʒø, øz] adj *terrain* marshy, swampy, boggy; *plante* marsh (*épith*).

maréchal, pl **-aux** [maʀeʃal, o] nm (*armée française*) marshal (of France); (*armée britannique*) field marshal. (*Hist*) **~ de camp** brigadier; **~-ferrant** blacksmith, farrier; **M~ de France** Marshal of France; **~ des logis** sergeant (*artillery, cavalry etc*); **~ des logis-chef** battery *ou* squadron sergeant-major; *voir* **bâton**.

maréchalat [maʀeʃala] nm rank of marshal, marshalcy.

maréchale [maʀeʃal] nf marshal's wife; *voir* **Madame**.

maréchalerie [maʀeʃalʀi] nf (*atelier*) smithy, blacksmith's (shop); (*métier*) blacksmith's trade.

maréchaussée [maʀeʃose] nf (*hum*) constabulary, police (force); (*Hist*) mounted constabulary.

marée [maʀe] nf a tide. **~ montante/descendante** flood *ou* rising/ebb tide; **à la ~ montante/descendante** when the tide goes in/out, when the tide is rising/ebbing *ou* falling; **(à) ~ haute** (at) high tide *ou* water; **(à) ~ basse** (at) low tide *ou* water; **grande ~** spring tide; **faible** *ou* **petite ~** neap tide; **~ noire** oil slick, black tide. b (*fig*) *[bonheur, colère]* surge, wave; *[nouveaux immeubles, supermarchés]* flood. **~ humaine** great flood *ou* surge *ou* influx of people. c (*Comm: poissons de mer*) **la ~** fresh catch, fresh (sea) fish; *voir* **marchand**.

marelle [maʀɛl] nf (*jeu*) hopscotch; (*dessin*) (drawing of a) hopscotch game.

marémoteur, -trice [maʀemɔtœʀ, tʀis] adj (*Élec*) *énergie* tidal. **usine ~trice** tidal power station.

marengo [maʀɛ̃go] 1 adj inv (*Culin*) **poulet/veau (à la) ~** chicken/veal marengo. 2 nm *black flecked cloth*.

marennes [maʀɛn] nf Marennes oyster.

mareyeur, -euse [maʀɛjœʀ, øz] nm,f wholesale fish merchant.

margarine [maʀgaʀin] nf margarine, marge* (*Brit*). **~ de régime** low-fat margarine.

marge [maʀʒ] 1 nf (*gén*) margin. **faire des annotations en ~** to make notes in the margin; **donner de la ~ à qn** (*temps*) to give sb a reasonable margin of time; (*latitude*) to give sb some leeway *ou* latitude *ou* scope; **je ne suis pas pressé, j'ai encore de la ~** I'm not in a hurry, I still have time to spare; **en ~ (de la société)** on the fringe (of society); **il a décidé de vivre en ~ de la société** he has opted out (of society); **vivre en ~ du monde/des affaires** to live cut off from the world/from business; **activités en ~ du festival** fringe activities; **en ~ de cette affaire, on peut aussi signaler que** with the *ou* this subject, one might also point out that.

2 comp ▸**marge (bénéficiaire)** (profit) margin, mark-up ▸**marge**

brute d'autofinancement cash flow ▸**marge d'erreur** margin of error ▸**marge de garantie** (*Fin*) margin ▸**marge de manœuvre** room to manoeuvre; **leur attitude ne nous laisse pas une grande marge de manœuvre** their attitude doesn't leave us much room for manoeuvre ▸**marge de sécurité** safety margin ▸**marge de tolérance** tolerance.

margelle [marʒɛl] nf: ~ (**de puits**) coping (of a well).

marger [marʒe] 3 vt *machine à écrire, feuille* to set the margins on; (*Typ*) to feed (in).

margeur [marʒœr] nm *[machine à écrire]* margin stop.

marginal, e, mpl **-aux** [marʒinal, o] 1 adj (*gén, Écon*) marginal; *coût* incremental. **groupe** ~ fringe group; **récifs** ~**aux** fringing reefs; **notes** ~**es** marginal notes, marginalia (*pl*). 2 nm (*excentrique*) freak*, eccentric; (*artiste, homme politique*) independent; (*déshérité*) dropout. (*contestataires*) **les** ~**aux** the dissident minority *ou* fringe.

marginalisation [marʒinalizasjɔ̃] nf marginalization.

marginaliser [marʒinalize] 1 1 vt to marginalize, edge out*. 2 **se marginaliser** vpr to put o.s. on the fringe.

marginalité [marʒinalite] nf marginality.

margis [marʒi] nm (*arg Mil*) (abrév de **maréchal des logis**) sarge (*arg*).

Margot [margo] nf (dim de **Marguerite**) Maggie.

margoulette‡ [margulɛt] nf (*mâchoires, visage*) face, mug‡.

margoulin [margulɛ̃] nm (*péj*) swindler, shark (*fig*).

margrave [margrav] nm (*Hist*) margrave.

marguerite [margərit] nf a (*Bot*) marguerite, (oxeye) daisy; *voir* **effeuiller, reine**. b **M**~ Margaret. c (*Typ*) daisywheel. **imprimante à** ~ daisywheel printer.

marguillier [margije] nm (*Hist*) churchwarden.

mari [mari] nm husband. **son petit** ~ her hubby*.

mariable [marjabl] adj marriageable.

mariage [marjaʒ] 1 nm a (*institution, union*) marriage; (*Rel*) matrimony. **50 ans de** ~ 50 years of married life *ou* of marriage; **ils ont fêté leurs 20 ans de** ~ they celebrated their 20th (wedding) anniversary; **au début de leur** ~ when they were first married, at the beginning of their marriage; **son** ~ **avec son cousin** her marriage to her cousin; **on parle de** ~ **entre eux** there is talk of their getting married; **il avait un enfant d'un premier** ~ he had a child from his first marriage; **né hors du** ~ born out of wedlock; **promettre/donner qn en** ~ **à** to promise/give sb in marriage to; **elle lui a apporté beaucoup d'argent en** ~ she brought him a lot of money when she married him; **faire un riche** ~ to marry into money; *voir* **acte, demande**.

b (*cérémonie*) wedding. **grand** ~ society wedding; **cadeau/faire-part/messe de** ~ wedding present/invitation/service; *voir* **corbeille, liste**.

c (*fig*) *[couleurs, parfums, matières]* marriage, blend; *[entreprises]* merger, amalgamation. **c'est le** ~ **de la carpe et du lapin** they are strange *ou* unlikely bedfellows.

d (*Cartes*) **avoir le** ~ **à cœur** to have *ou* hold (the) king and queen *ou* king/queen of hearts; **faire des** ~**s** to collect kings and queens.

2 comp ▸**mariage d'amour** love match; **faire un mariage d'amour** to marry for love, make a love match ▸**mariage d'argent** marriage for money, money match ▸**mariage blanc** unconsummated marriage ▸**mariage en blanc** white wedding ▸**mariage civil** civil wedding ▸**mariage de convenance** marriage of convenience ▸**mariage à l'essai** trial marriage ▸**mariage d'intérêt** money *ou* social match; **faire un mariage d'intérêt** to marry for money ▸**mariage mixte** mixed marriage ▸**mariage politique** political alliance ▸**mariage de raison** marriage of convenience ▸**mariage religieux** church wedding.

marial, e, mpl ~**s** [marjal] adj (*Rel*) *culte* Marian.

Marianne [marjan] nf (*prénom*) Marion; (*Pol*) Marianne, *symbol of the French Republic*.

marie [mari] 1 nf: **M**~ Mary; ~**-Madeleine** Mary Magdalene; ~ **Stuart** Mary Queen of Scots, Mary Stuart. 2 comp ▸**marie-couche-toi-là**‡† nf inv (*prostituée*) harlot†, strumpet† ▸**marie-jeanne** (*marijuana*) Mary Jane (*arg*), pot (*arg*) ▸**marie-salope** nf (pl **maries-salopes**) (*bateau*) mud dredger; (‡: *souillon*) slut.

marié, e [marje] (ptp de **marier**) 1 adj married. **non** ~ unmarried, single. 2 nm (bride) groom. **les** ~**s** (*jour du mariage*) the bride and (bride)groom; (*après le mariage*) the newly-weds; *voir* **jeune, nouveau**. 3 **mariée** nf bride. **trouver** *ou* **se plaindre que la** ~**e est trop belle** to object that everything's too good to be true; **couronne/robe/voile** *etc* **de** ~**e** wedding headdress/dress/veil *etc; voir* **jeune**.

marier [marje] 7 1 vt a *[maire, prêtre]* to marry. **il a marié sa fille à un homme d'affaires** he married his daughter to a businessman; **il a fini par** ~ **sa fille** he finally got his daughter married, he finally married off his daughter; (*hum*) **demain, je marie mon frère** tomorrow I see my brother (get) married; **nous sommes mariés depuis 15 ans** we have been married for 15 years; **il a encore 2 filles à** ~ he still has 2 unmarried daughters, he still has 2 daughters to marry off; **fille à** ~ daughter of marriageable age, marriageable daughter; (*fig*) **on n'est pas mariés avec lui!*** we don't have to suit him all the time!, we're not obliged to do as he says!

b *couleurs, goûts, parfums, styles* to blend, harmonize; *entreprises* to merge, amalgamate.

2 **se marier** vpr a *[personne]* to get married. **se** ~ **à** *ou* **avec qn** to marry sb, get married to sb; **se** ~ **à la mairie/l'église** to get married at a registry office/in church; **se** ~ **de la main gauche** to live as man and wife.

b *[couleurs, goûts, parfums, styles]* to blend, harmonize.

marieur, -ieuse [marjœr, jøz] nm,f matchmaker.

marigot [marigo] nm backwater, cutoff, oxbow lake.

marihuana [marirɥana] nf, **marijuana** [marirwana] nf marijuana.

marin, e[1] [marɛ̃, in] 1 adj *air* sea (*épith*); *carte* maritime (*épith*), navigational (*épith*); *faune, flore* marine (*épith*), sea (*épith*). **bateau (très)** ~ seaworthy ship; **missile** ~ sea-based missile; **sciences** ~**es** marine science; **costume** ~ sailor suit; *voir* **mille**[2], **pied** *etc*. 2 nm sailor. (*grade*) (**simple**) ~ ordinary seaman; ~ **d'eau douce** landlubber; **un peuple de** ~**s** a seafaring nation, a nation of seafarers; **béret/tricot de** ~ sailor's hat/jersey; *voir* **fusilier**.

marina [marina] nf marina.

marinade [marinad] nf a marinade. ~ **de viande** meat in (a) marinade, marinaded meat. b (*Can*) ~**s** pickles.

marine[2] [marin] 1 nf a (*flotte, administration*) navy. **terme de** ~ nautical term; **au temps de la** ~ **à voiles** in the days of sailing ships; ~ (**de guerre**) navy; ~ **marchande** merchant navy; *voir* **lieutenant, officier**[1]. b (*tableau*) seascape. 2 nm (*soldat*) (*US*) marine. 3 adj inv (*couleur*) navy (blue); *voir* **bleu**.

mariner [marine] 1 1 vt (*Culin: aussi* **faire** ~) to marinade, marinate. 2 vi a (*Culin*) to marinade, marinate. **harengs marinés** soused (*Brit*) *ou* pickled herrings. b (*: *attendre*) to hang about*. ~ **en prison** to stew* in prison; **faire** *ou* **laisser** ~ **qn** (*à un rendez-vous*) to keep sb hanging about* *ou* kicking his heels (*Brit*); (*pour une décision*) to let sb stew* for a bit.

maringouin [marɛ̃gwɛ̃] nm (*Can*) mosquito.

marinier [marinje] nm bargee (*Brit*), bargeman (*US*); *voir* **officier**.

marinière [marinjɛr] nf (*Habillement*) overblouse, smock; (*Nage*) sidestroke; *voir* **moule**[2].

mariol(le)* [marjɔl] nm: **c'est un** ~ (*malin*) he is a crafty *ou* sly one; (*peu sérieux*) he's a bit of a joker *ou* a waster*; (*incompétent*) he's a bungling idiot*; (**ne**) **fais pas le** ~ stop trying to be clever *ou* smart*, stop showing off.

marionnette [marjɔnɛt] nf (*lit, fig: pantin*) puppet. (*spectacle*) ~**s** puppet show; ~ **à fils** marionette; ~ **à gaine** glove puppet; *voir* **montreur, théâtre**.

marionnettiste [marjɔnetist] nmf puppeteer, puppet-master (*ou* -mistress).

mariste [marist] nmf Marist. **frère/sœur** ~ Marist brother/sister.

marital, e, mpl **-aux** [marital, o] adj (*Jur*) **autorisation** ~**e** husband's permission *ou* authorization.

maritalement [maritalmɑ̃] adv: **vivre** ~ to live as husband and wife, cohabit.

maritime [maritim] adj a *localisation* maritime; *ville* seaboard, coastal, seaside; *province* seaboard, coastal, maritime; *voir* **gare**[1], **pin, port**[1]. b *navigation* maritime; *commerce, agence* shipping; *droit* shipping, maritime. **affecté à la navigation** ~ sea-going; *voir* **arsenal**.

maritorne† [maritɔrn] nf (*souillon*) slut, slattern.

marivaudage [marivodaʒ] nm (*littér: badinage*) light-hearted gallantries; (*Littérat*) sophisticated banter in the style of Marivaux.

marivauder [marivode] 1 vi (*littér*) to engage in lively sophisticated banter; (†: *Littérat*) to write in the style of Marivaux.

marjolaine [marʒɔlɛn] nf marjoram.

mark [mark] nm (*Fin*) mark.

marketing [markətiŋ] nm marketing.

marlin [marlɛ̃] nm marlin.

marlou‡ [marlu] nm (*souteneur*) pimp; (*voyou*) wide boy‡ (*Brit*), punk‡ (*US*).

marmaille* [marmɑj] nf gang *ou* horde of kids* *ou* brats* (*péj*). **toute la** ~ **était là** the whole brood was there.

marmelade [marməlad] nf a (*Culin*) stewed fruit, compote. ~ **de pommes/poires** stewed apples/pears, compote of apples/pears; ~ **d'oranges** (orange) marmalade. b (*) **en** ~ *légumes, fruits* (*cuits*) cooked to a mush; (*crus*) reduced to a pulp; **avoir le nez en** ~ to have one's nose reduced to a pulp; **réduire qn en** ~ to smash sb to pulp, reduce sb to a pulp. c (*fig: gâchis*) mess.

marmite [marmit] 1 nf (*Culin*) (cooking-)pot; (*arg Mil*) heavy shell. **une** ~ **de soupe** a pot of soup; *voir* **bouillir, nez**. 2 comp ▸**marmite** (**de géants**) (*Géog*) pothole ▸**marmite norvégienne** ≃ haybox.

marmiton [marmitɔ̃] nm kitchen boy.

marmonnement [marmɔnmɑ̃] nm mumbling, muttering.

marmonner [marmɔne] 1 vti to mumble, mutter. ~ **dans sa barbe** to mutter into one's beard, mutter to o.s.

marmoréen, -éenne [marmɔreɛ̃, ɛn] adj (*littér*) marble (*épith*), marmoreal (*littér*).

marmot* [marmo] nm kid*, brat* (*péj*); *voir* **croquer**.

marmotte [marmɔt] nf (*Zool*) marmot; (*fig*) sleepyhead, dormouse; *voir* **dormir**.

marmottement [marmɔtmɑ̃] nm mumbling, muttering.

marmotter [marmɔte] 1 vti to mumble, mutter. **qu'est-ce que tu as à** ~**?*** what are you mumbling (on) about? *ou* muttering about?

marmouset [marmuzɛ] **nm** (*Sculp*) quaint *ou* grotesque figure; (*†: *enfant*) pipsqueak*.
marnage¹ [marnaʒ] **nm** (*Agr*) marling.
marnage² [marnaʒ] **nm** (*Naut*) tidal range.
marne [marn] **nf** (*Géol*) marl, calcareous clay.
marner [marne] 1 1 **vt** (*Agr*) to marl. 2 **vi** (*: *travailler dur*) to slog*. **faire ~ qn** to make sb slog*.
marneux, -euse [marnø, øz] **adj** marly.
marnière [marnjɛr] **nf** marlpit.
Maroc [marɔk] **nm** Morocco.
marocain, e [marɔkɛ̃, ɛn] 1 **adj** Moroccan. 2 **nm,f: M~(e)** Moroccan.
maronite [marɔnit] 1 **adj** Maronite. 2 **nmf: M~** Maronite.
maronner* [marɔne] 1 **vi** to grouse*, moan*.
maroquin [marɔkɛ̃] **nm** a (*cuir*) morocco (leather). **relié en ~** morocco-bound. b (*fig: portefeuille*) (minister's) portfolio. **obtenir un ~** to be made a minister.
maroquinerie [marɔkinri] **nf** (*boutique*) shop selling fancy *ou* fine leather goods; (*atelier*) tannery; (*Ind*) fine leather craft; (*préparation*) tanning. **(articles de)** ~ fancy *ou* fine leather goods; **il travaille dans la ~** (*artisan*) he does fine leatherwork; (*commerçant*) he is in the (fine) leather trade.
maroquinier [marɔkinje] **nm** (*marchand*) dealer in fine leather goods; (*fabricant*) leather worker *ou* craftsman.
marotte [marɔt] **nf** a (*dada*) hobby, craze. **c'est sa ~!** it's his pet craze!; **il a la ~ des jeux de patience** he has a craze for jigsaw puzzles; **le voilà lancé sur sa ~!** there he goes on his pet hobby-horse! b (*Hist: poupée*) fool's bauble; (*Coiffure, Habillement: tête*) (milliner's, hairdresser's) dummy head, (milliner's, hairdresser's) model.
marquage [markaʒ] **nm** a *[linge, marchandises]* marking; *[animal]* branding; *[arbre]* blazing; (*Sport*) *[joueur]* marking. b (*Aut: sur la chaussée*) road-marking.
marquant, e [markɑ̃, ɑ̃t] **adj** *personnage, événement* outstanding; *souvenir* vivid. **je n'ai rien vu de très ~** I saw nothing very striking *ou* nothing worth talking about; **le fait le plus ~** the most significant *ou* striking fact.
marque [mark] **nf** a (*repère, trace*) mark; (*signe*) (*lit, fig*) mark, sign; (*fig*) token; *[livre]* bookmark; *[linge]* name tab. **~s de doigts** fingermarks, fingerprints; **~s de pas** footmarks, footprints; **~s d'une blessure/de coups/de fatigue** marks of a wound/of blows/of fatigue; **il porte encore les ~s de son accident** he still bears the scars from his accident; **faites une ~ au crayon devant chaque nom** put a pencil mark beside each name; (*fig*) **~ de confiance/de respect** sign *ou* token *ou* mark of confidence/respect; **porter la ~ du pluriel** to be in the plural (form).
b (*estampille*) *[or, argent]* hallmark; *[meubles, œuvre d'art]* mark; *[viande, œufs]* stamp. (*fig*) **la ~ du génie** the hallmark *ou* stamp of genius.
c (*Comm*) *[nourriture, produits chimiques]* brand; *[automobiles, produits manufacturés]* make. **~ de fabrique** *ou* **de fabrication** *ou* **du fabricant** trademark, trade name, brand name; **~ d'origine** maker's mark; **~ déposée** registered trademark *ou* trade name *ou* brand name; **une grande ~ de vin/de voiture** a well-known brand of wine/make of car; **produits de ~** high-class products; (*fig*) **un personnage de ~** a distinguished person, a VIP; **visiteur de ~** important *ou* distinguished visitor; *voir* **image**.
d (*insigne*) *[fonction, grade]* badge. (*frm*) **les ~s de sa fonction** the insignia *ou* regalia of his office.
e (*décompte de points*) **la ~** the score; **tenir la ~** to keep (the) score; **mener à la ~** to lead on the scoresheet, be ahead on goals, be in the lead; **ouvrir la ~** to open the scoring.
f (*Sport: empreinte*) marker. **à vos ~s! prêts! partez!** (*athlètes*) on your marks!, get set!, go!; (*enfants*) ready, steady, go!; **prendre ses ~s** to place one's marker (*for one's run-up*); (*Rugby*) ~! mark!
marqué, e [marke] (**ptp de marquer**) **adj** a (*accentué*) marked, pronounced; (*Ling*) marked. b (*signalé*) **le prix ~** the price on the label; **au prix ~** at the labelled price, at the price shown on the label; (*fig*) **c'est un homme ~** he's a marked man; **il est ~ par la vie** life has left its mark on him.
marquer [marke] 1 1 **vt** a (*par un signe distinctif*) *objet personnel* to mark (*au nom de qn* with sb's name); *animal, criminel* to brand; *arbre* to blaze; *marchandise* to label, stamp.
b (*indiquer*) *limite, position* to mark; (*sur une carte*) *village, accident de terrain* to mark, show, indicate; *[horloge]* to show; *[thermomètre]* to show, register; *[balance]* to register. **marquez la longueur voulue d'un trait de crayon** mark off the length required with a pencil; **j'ai marqué ce jour-là d'une pierre blanche/noire** I'll remember it as a red-letter day/black day; **marquez d'une croix l'emplacement du véhicule** mark the position of the vehicle with a cross; **la pendule marque 6 heures** the clock points to *ou* shows *ou* says 6 o'clock; (*Couture*) **des pinces marquent/une ceinture marque la taille** darts emphasize/a belt emphasizes the waist(line); **une robe qui marque la taille** a dress which shows off the waistline; **cela marque (bien) que le pays veut la paix** that definitely indicates *ou* shows that the country wants peace, that's a clear sign that the country wants peace.
c *événement* to mark. **un bombardement a marqué la reprise des hostilités** a bomb attack marked the renewal *ou* resumption of hostilities; **des réjouissances populaires ont marqué la prise de pouvoir par la junte** the junta's takeover was marked by public celebrations; **pour ~ cette journée on a distribué ...** to mark *ou* commemorate this day they distributed ... .
d (*écrire*) *nom, rendez-vous, renseignement* to write down, note down, make a note of. **~ les points** *ou* **les résultats** to keep *ou* note the score; **on l'a marqué absent** he was marked absent; **j'ai marqué 3 heures sur mon agenda** I've got 3 o'clock (noted) down in my diary; **il a marqué qu'il fallait prévenir les élèves** he noted down that the pupils should be told, he made a note to tell the pupils; **qu'y a-t-il de marqué?** what does it say?, what's written (on it)?
e (*endommager*) *glace, bois* to mark; (*fig: affecter*) *personne* to mark. (*influencer*) **~ son époque** to put one's mark *ou* stamp on one's time; **la souffrance l'a marqué** suffering has left its mark on him; **visage marqué par la maladie** face marked by illness; **visage marqué par la petite vérole** face pitted *ou* scarred with smallpox; **la déception se marquait sur son visage** disappointment showed in his face *ou* was written all over his face.
f (*manifester, montrer*) *désapprobation, fidélité, intérêt* to show.
g (*Sport*) *joueur* to mark; *but, essai* to score. **~ qn de très près** to mark sb very closely *ou* tightly.
h (*loc*) **~ le coup*** (*fêter un événement etc*) to mark the occasion; (*accuser le coup*) to react; **j'ai risqué une allusion, mais il n'a pas marqué le coup*** I made an allusion to it, but he showed no reaction; **~ un point/des points (sur qn)** to score a point/several points (against sb); **~ la mesure** to keep the beat; **~ le pas** (*lit*) to beat *ou* mark time; (*fig*) to mark time; **~ une pause** *ou* **un temps d'arrêt** to pause momentarily.
2 **vi** a *[événement, personnalité]* to stand out, be outstanding; *[coup]* to reach home, tell. **cet incident a marqué dans sa vie** that particular incident stood out in *ou* had a great impact on his life.
b *[crayon]* to write; *[tampon]* to stamp. **ne pose pas le verre sur ce meuble, ça marque** don't put the glass down on that piece of furniture, it will leave a mark.
marqueté, e [markəte] **adj** *bois* inlaid.
marqueterie [markɛtri] **nf** (*Art*) marquetry, inlaid work; (*fig*) mosaic. **table en ~** inlaid table.
marqueur, -euse [markœr, øz] 1 **nm,f** *[bétail]* brander; (*Sport, Jeux*) *[points]* score-keeper, scorer; (*buteur*) scorer. 2 **nm** a (*stylo*) felt-tip pen; (*indélébile*) marker pen; (*Méd*) tracer. b (*Ling*) marker. (*Ling*) **~ syntagmatique** phrase marker. 3 **marqueuse nf** (*Comm: appareil*) (price) labeller.
marquis [marki] **nm** marquis, marquess.
marquisat [markiza] **nm** marquisate.
marquise [markiz] **nf** a (*noble*) marchioness; *voir* **Madame**. b (*auvent*) glass canopy *ou* awning. c **les (îles) M~s** the Marquesas Islands. d (*Culin*) **~ au chocolat** *type of chocolate ice-cream.*
marraine [marɛn] **nf** *[enfant]* godmother; *[navire]* christener, namer; (*dans un club*) sponsor, proposer. **~ de guerre** *(woman) penfriend to soldier etc on active service.*
marrant, e* [marɑ̃, ɑ̃t] **adj** a (*amusant*) funny, killing*. **c'est un ~, il est ~** he's a scream* *ou* a great laugh*; **ce n'est pas ~** it's not funny, it's no joke; **il n'est pas ~** (*ennuyeux, triste*) he's pretty dreary*, he's not much fun; (*sévère*) he's pretty grim*; (*empoisonnant*) he's a pain in the neck*. b (*étrange*) funny, odd.
marre‡ [mar] **adv: en avoir ~** to be fed up* *ou* cheesed off‡ (*Brit*) (*de* with), be sick* (*de* of); **j'en ai ~ de toi** I've just about had enough of you*, I am fed up with you*; **c'est ~!, il y en a ~!** that'll be enough, that'll do!
marrer (se)‡ [mare] 1 **vpr** to laugh, have a good laugh*. **il se marrait comme un fou** he was in fits* *ou* kinks‡ (*Brit*); **on ne se marre pas tous les jours au boulot!** work isn't always fun and games* *ou* a laugh a minute; **tu me fais ~ avec ta démocratie!** you make me laugh with all your talk about democracy!
marri, e [mari] **adj** (*littér*, †) (*triste*) sad, doleful; (*désolé*) sorry, grieved†.
marron¹ [marɔ̃] 1 **nm** a (*Bot, Culin*) chestnut. **~ d'Inde** horse chestnut; **~s chauds** roast chestnuts; **~ glacé** marron glacé; **tirer les ~s du feu** (*être le bénéficiaire*) to reap the benefits; (*être la victime*) to be sb's cat's paw; *voir* **purée**. b (*couleur*) brown. c (‡: *coup*) blow, thump, cuff, clout (*Brit*). **tu veux un ~?** do you want a thick ear?* (*Brit*) *ou* a cuff? 2 **adj inv** a (*couleur*) brown. b (‡) **être ~** (*être trompé*) to be the sucker‡, be had*.
marron², -onne [marɔ̃, ɔn] **adj:** (*sans titres*) **médecin ~** quack, unqualified doctor; (*sans scrupules*) **notaire/avocat ~** crooked notary/lawyer; (*Hist*) **esclave ~** runaway *ou* fugitive slave.
marronnier [marɔnje] **nm** a (*Bot*) chestnut tree. **~ (d'Inde)** horse chestnut tree. b (*arg Presse*) chestnut (*arg*).
Mars [mars] 1 **nm** (*Myth*) Mars; *voir* **champ**. 2 **nf** (*planète*) Mars.
mars [mars] **nm** (*mois*) March. **arriver** *ou* **venir** *ou* **tomber comme ~ en carême** to come *ou* happen as sure as night follows day; *pour loc voir* **septembre**.
marseillais, e [marsɛjɛ, ɛz] 1 **adj** of *ou* from Marseilles; *voir* **histoire**.

2 nm,f: **M~(e)** inhabitant *ou* native of Marseilles. 3 nf: **la M~e** the Marseillaise, *French national anthem.*

Marseille [marsɛj] n Marseilles.

marsouin [marswɛ̃] nm (*Zool*) porpoise; (*Mil* †) marine.

marsupial, e, mpl **-iaux** [marsypjal, jo] adj, nm marsupial. **poche ~e** marsupium.

marte [mart] nf = **martre.**

marteau, pl **~x** [marto] 1 nm (*Anat, Menuiserie, Mus, Sport*) hammer; *[enchères, médecin]* hammer; *[président, juge]* gavel; *[horloge]* striker; *[porte]* knocker; *[forgeron]* (sledge) hammer. (*fig*) **entre le ~ et l'enclume** between the devil and the deep blue sea; (* *fig*) **être ~** to be nuts* *ou* bats* *ou* cracked*; **passer sous le ~ du commissaire-priseur** to be put up for auction, go under the (auctioneer's) hammer; *voir* **coup, faucille, requin.**

2 comp ►**marteau-perforateur** nm (pl **marteaux-perforateurs**) hammer drill ►**marteau-pilon** nm (pl **marteaux-pilons**) power hammer ►**marteau-piolet** nm (pl **marteaux-piolets**) ice-hammer, north-wall hammer ►**marteau-piqueur** nm (pl **marteaux-piqueurs**), **marteau pneumatique** pneumatic drill.

martel [martɛl] nm: **se mettre ~ en tête** to worry o.s. sick, get worked up*.

martelage [martəlaʒ] nm (*Métal*) hammering, planishing.

martelé, e [martəle] (ptp de **marteler**) adj: **cuivre ~** planished *ou* beaten copper; (*Mus*) **notes ~es** martelé notes.

martèlement [martɛlmɑ̃] nm *[bruit, obus]* hammering, pounding; *[pas]* pounding, clanking; *[mots]* hammering out, rapping out.

marteler [martəle] 5 vt *[marteau, obus, coups de poings]* to hammer, pound; *objet d'art* to planish, beat. **~ ses mots** to hammer out *ou* rap out one's words; **ce bruit qui me martèle la tête** that noise hammering *ou* pounding through my head; **ses pas martelaient le sol gelé** his footsteps were pounding on the frozen ground.

martellement [martɛlmɑ̃] nm = **martèlement.**

Marthe [mart] nf Martha.

martial, e, mpl **-iaux** [marsjal, jo] adj (*hum, littér*) *peuple, discours* martial, warlike, soldier-like; *allure* soldierly, martial. **arts ~aux** martial arts; *voir* **cour, loi.**

martialement [marsjalmɑ̃] adv (*hum, littér*) martially, in a soldierly manner.

martien, -ienne [marsjɛ̃, jɛn] adj, nm,f Martian.

Martin [martɛ̃] nm Martin; (*âne*) Neddy.

martinet [martinɛ] nm a small whip (*used on children*), strap. b (*Orn*) swift. c (*Tech*) tilt hammer.

martingale [martɛ̃gal] nf (*Habillement*) half belt; (*Équitation*) martingale; (*Roulette*) (*combinaison*) winning formula; (*mise double*) doubling-up.

martiniquais, e [martinikɛ, ɛz] 1 adj of *ou* from Martinique. 2 nm,f: **M~(e)** inhabitant *ou* native of Martinique.

Martinique [martinik] nf Martinique.

martin-pêcheur, pl **martins-pêcheurs** [martɛ̃pɛʃœr] nm kingfisher.

martre [martr] nf marten. **~ zibeline** sable.

martyr, e¹ [martir] 1 adj *soldats, peuple* martyred. **mère ~e** stricken mother; **enfant ~** battered child. 2 nm,f martyr (*d'une cause* in *ou* to a cause). **ne prends pas ces airs de ~!** stop acting the martyr, it's no use putting on your martyred look; **c'est le ~ de la classe** he's always being bullied *ou* baited by the class.

martyre² [martir] nm (*Rel*) martyrdom; (*fig: souffrance*) martyrdom, agony. **le ~ de ce peuple** the martyrdom *ou* suffering of this people; **sa vie fut un long ~** his life was one long agony; **cette longue attente est un ~** it's agony waiting so long; **mettre au ~** to martyrize, torture; **souffrir le ~** to suffer agonies, go through torture.

martyriser [martirize] 1 vt a (*faire souffrir*) *personne, animal* to torture, martyrize; *élève* to bully, bait; *enfant, bébé* to batter. b (*Rel*) to martyr.

martyrologe [martirɔlɔʒ] nm martyrology.

marxien, -ienne [marksjɛ̃, jɛn] adj Marxian.

marxisant, e [marksizɑ̃, ɑ̃t] adj leaning towards Marxism.

marxisme [marksism] nm Marxism. **~-léninisme** *nm* Marxism-Leninism.

marxiste [marksist] adj, nmf Marxist. **~-léniniste** Marxist-Leninist.

maryland [marilɑ̃(d)] nm *type of Virginia tobacco,* ≃ virginia. (*État*) **le M~** Maryland.

mas [mɑ(s)] nm mas, *house or farm in South of France.*

mascabina [maskabina] nm (*Can*) service tree.

mascara [maskara] nm mascara.

mascarade [maskarad] nf a (*péj: tromperie*) farce, masquerade. **ce procès est une ~** this trial is a farce. b (*réjouissance, déguisement*) masquerade.

mascaret [maskarɛ] nm (tidal) bore.

mascotte [maskɔt] nf mascot.

masculin, e [maskylɛ̃, in] 1 adj *mode, hormone, population, sexe* male; *force, courage* manly; (*péj: hommasse*) *femme, silhouette* mannish, masculine; (*Gram*) masculine. **voix ~e** *[homme]* male voice; *[femme]* masculine *ou* gruff voice; (*virile*) manly voice; *voir* **rime.** 2 nm (*Gram*) masculine. **"fer" est (du) ~** "fer" is masculine.

masculiniser [maskylinize] 1 vt a **~ qn** to make sb look mannish *ou* masculine. b (*Bio*) to make masculine.

masculinité [maskylinite] nf masculinity; (*virilité*) manliness.

Maseru [mazeru] n Maseru.

maskinongé [maskinɔ̃ʒe] nm (*Can: brochet*) muskellunge, muskie (*Can* *), maskinonge.

maso* [mazo] abrév de **masochiste.**

masochisme [mazɔʃism] nm masochism.

masochiste [mazɔʃist] 1 adj masochistic. 2 nmf masochist.

masquage [maskaʒ] nm masking.

masque [mask] 1 nm a (*objet, Méd, Ordin*) mask. **~ de saisie** data entry form.

b (*faciès*) mask-like features, mask; (*expression*) mask-like expression.

c (*fig: apparence*) mask, façade, front. **ce n'est qu'un ~** it's just a mask *ou* front *ou* façade; **présenter un ~ d'indifférence** to put on an air *ou* appearance of indifference; **sous le ~ de la respectabilité** beneath the façade of respectability; **lever** *ou* **jeter le ~** to unmask o.s., reveal o.s. in one's true colours; **arracher son ~ à qn** to unmask sb.

d (*Hist: personne déguisée*) mask, masker.

2 comp ►**masque antirides, masque de beauté** face pack ►**masque de carnaval** mask ►**masque funéraire** funeral mask ►**masque à gaz** gas mask ►**masque mortuaire** death mask ►**masque à oxygène** oxygen mask ►**masque de plongée** diving mask.

masqué, e [maske] (ptp de **masquer**) adj *bandit* masked; *enfant* wearing *ou* in a mask. (*Aut*) **sortie ~e** concealed exit; (*Aut*) **virage ~** blind corner *ou* bend; (*Naut*) **tous feux ~s** with all lights obscured; *voir* **bal.**

masquer [maske] 1 1 vt (*lit, fig: cacher*) to hide, mask, conceal (*à qn* from sb). **~ un goût** (*exprès*) to hide *ou* disguise *ou* mask a taste; (*involontairement*) to obscure a flavour; **~ la lumière** to screen *ou* shade the light; **~ la vue** to block (out) the view; (*Mil*) **~ des troupes** to screen *ou* mask troops; **ces questions secondaires ont masqué l'essentiel** these questions of secondary importance masked *ou* obscured the essential point; **avec un mépris à peine masqué** with barely concealed contempt. 2 **se masquer** vpr a (*mettre un masque*) to put on a mask. b (*se cacher*) *[sentiment]* to be hidden; *[personne]* to hide, conceal o.s. (*derrière* behind)

Massachusetts [masaʃysɛts] nm Massachusetts.

massacrante [masakrɑ̃t] adj f *voir* **humeur.**

massacre [masakr] nm a (*tuerie*) *[personnes]* slaughter (*NonC*), massacre; *[animaux]* slaughter (*NonC*). **c'est un véritable ~** *[prisonniers]* it is an absolute massacre; *[gibier]* **c'est du ~** it is sheer butchery; **échapper au ~** to escape the massacre *ou* slaughter; (*Bible*) **le ~ des innocents** the massacre of the innocents; *voir* **jeu.** b (**: sabotage*) **quel ~!, c'est un vrai ~!*** it's a complete botch-up!*; it's a real mess!; (*Sport*) what a massacre!* c (*Chasse*) stag's head, stag's antlers. d (*Hér*) attire.

massacrer [masakre] 1 vt a (*tuer*) *personnes* to slaughter, massacre; *animaux* to slaughter, butcher. **se ~** to massacre *ou* slaughter one another. b (**: saboter*) *opéra, pièce* to murder, botch up; *travail* to make a mess *ou* hash* of; (*mal découper, scier*) *viande, planche* to hack to bits, make a mess of; *candidat* to make mincemeat* of; *adversaire* to massacre, slaughter, make mincemeat* of. **il s'est fait ~ par son adversaire** he was massacred by his opponent, his opponent made mincemeat* of him.

massacreur, -euse [masakrœr, øz] nm,f (**: saboteur*) bungler, botcher; (*tueur*) slaughterer, butcher.

massage [masaʒ] nm massage. **faire un ~ cardiaque à qn** to give sb cardiac massage.

masse [mas] nf a (*volume, Phys*) mass; (*forme*) massive shape *ou* bulk. **~ d'eau** *[lac]* body *ou* expanse of water; *[chute]* mass of water; **~ de nuages** bank of clouds; (*Mét*) **~ d'air** air mass; **la ~ de l'édifice** the massive structure of the building; **pris** *ou* **taillé dans la ~** carved from the block; **la ~ instrumentale/vocale** the massed instruments/voices; **s'écrouler** *ou* **tomber comme une ~** to slump down *ou* fall in a heap.

b (*foule*) **les ~s (laborieuses)** the (working) masses; **les ~s populaires** the masses; **les ~s paysannes** the agricultural work force; (†) the peasantry; **la (grande) ~ des lecteurs** the (great) majority of readers; (*péj*) **c'est ce qui plaît à la ~** *ou* **aux ~s** that's the kind of thing that appeals to the masses; **éducation/psychologie des ~s** education/psychology of the masses; **culture/manifestation** *etc* **de ~** mass culture/demonstration *etc.*

c **une ~ de*, des ~s* de** masses of, loads of*; **des ~s de touristes*** crowds *ou* masses of tourists; **des gens comme lui, je n'en connais pas des ~s*** I don't know many people like him, you don't meet his sort every day; **tu as aimé ce film? — pas des ~s!‡** did you like that film? — not desperately!* *ou* not all that much!; **il n'y en a pas des ~s*** *[eau, argent]* there isn't much; *[chaises, spectateurs]* there aren't many.

d (*Élec*) earth (*Brit*), ground (*US*). **mettre à la ~** to earth (*Brit*), ground (*US*); **faire ~** to act as an earth (*Brit*) *ou* a ground (*US*); (*fig*) **être à la ~*** to be nuts‡ *ou* crazy*.

e (*Fin*) (*caisse commune*) kitty; (*Mil*) fund; (*Prison*) prisoner's earnings. (*Fin*) **~ monétaire** money supply; (*Comm*) **~ salariale** wage bill; (*Jur*) ~ **active** assets; ~ **passive** liabilities.

f (*maillet*) sledgehammer, beetle; *[huissier]* mace. (*Hist*) ~ **d'armes** mace.

g **en** ~: **exécutions/production** *etc* **en** ~ mass executions/production *etc;* **fabriquer** *ou* **produire en** ~ to mass-produce; **acheter/vendre en** ~ to buy/sell in bulk; **manifester/protester en** ~ to hold a mass demonstration/protest; **venir en** ~ to come in a large body, come en masse; **il en a en** ~ he has masses *ou* lots *ou* loads* (of them).

massé [mase] **nm** (*Billard*) massé (shot). **faire un** ~ to play a massé shot.

masselotte [mas(ə)lɔt] **nf** (*Aut*) lead (for wheel balancing).

massepain [maspɛ̃] **nm** marzipan.

masser¹ [mase] [1] **1 vt a** (*grouper*) *gens* to assemble, bring *ou* gather together; *choses* to put *ou* gather together; *troupes* to mass. **les cheveux massés en (un) chignon/derrière la tête** hair gathered in a chignon/at the back of the head. **b** (*Art*) to group. **2 se masser vpr** *[foule]* to mass, gather, assemble.

masser² [mase] [1] **vt a** (*frotter*) *personne* to massage. **se faire** ~ to have a massage, be massaged; **masse-moi le dos!** massage *ou* rub my back! **b** (*Billard*) ~ **la bille** to play a massé shot.

massette [masɛt] **nf a** (*Tech*) sledgehammer. **b** (*Bot*) bulrush, reed mace.

masseur [masœʀ] **nm** (*personne*) masseur; (*machine*) vibrator. ~ **kinésithérapeute** physiotherapist.

masseuse [masøz] **nf** masseuse.

massicot [masiko] **nm** (*Typ*) guillotine; (*Chim*) massicot.

massicoter [masikɔte] [1] **vt** *papier* to guillotine.

massif, -ive [masif, iv] **1 adj a** (*d'aspect*) *meuble, bâtiment, porte* massive, solid, heavy; *personne* sturdily built; *visage* large, heavy. **front** ~ massive forehead; **homme de carrure** ~**ive** big strong man. **b** (*pur*) **or/argent/chêne** ~ solid gold/silver/oak. **c** (*intensif*) *bombardements, dose, vote* massive, heavy; *refus* massive. **manifestation** ~**ive** mass demonstration; **départs** ~**s** mass exodus (*sg*). **2 nm** (*Géog*) massif; (*Bot*) *[fleurs]* clump, bank; *[arbres]* clump. **le M**~ **central** the Massif Central.

massique [masik] **adj: puissance** ~ power-weight ratio; **volume** ~ mass volume.

massivement [masivmɑ̃] **adv** *démissionner, partir, répondre* en masse; *injecter, administrer* in massive doses. **ils ont** ~ **approuvé le projet** the overwhelming *ou* massive majority was in favour of the project.

mass(-)media [masmedja] **nmpl** mass media.

massue [masy] **nf** club, bludgeon. ~ **de gymnastique** (Indian) club; **coup de** ~ (*lit*) blow with a club (*ou* bludgeon); **ça a été le coup de** ~* (*très cher*) it cost a bomb*; (*inattendu*) it was a bolt from the blue*; *voir* **argument**.

mastaba [mastaba] **nm** mastaba(h).

mastectomie [mastɛktɔmi] **nf** = **mammectomie**.

mastic [mastik] **1 nm a** *[vitrier]* putty; *[menuisier]* filler, mastic. **b** (*Bot*) mastic. **c** (*Typ*) *[caractères, pages]* (faulty) transposition. **2 adj** putty-coloured. **imperméable (couleur)** ~ light-coloured *ou* off-white raincoat.

masticage [mastikaʒ] **nm** *[vitre]* puttying; *[fissure]* filling.

masticateur, -trice [mastikatœʀ, tʀis] **adj** chewing (*épith*), masticatory.

mastication [mastikasjɔ̃] **nf** chewing, mastication.

masticatoire [mastikatwaʀ] **1 adj** chewing, masticatory. **2 nm** masticatory.

mastiquer¹ [mastike] [1] **vt** (*mâcher*) to chew, masticate.

mastiquer² [mastike] [1] **vt** (*Tech*) *vitre* to putty, apply putty to; *fissure* to fill, apply filler to.

mastoc* [mastɔk] **adj inv** *personne* hefty*, strapping (*épith*); *chose* large and cumbersome. **c'est un (type)** ~ he's a big hefty bloke‡ (*Brit*), he's a great strapping fellow*; **une statue** ~ a great hulking statue.

mastodonte [mastɔdɔ̃t] **nm** (*Zool*) mastodon; (*fig hum*) (*personne, animal*) colossus, mountain of a man (*ou* of an animal); (*véhicule*) great bus (*hum*) *ou* tank (*hum*); (*camion*) huge vehicle, juggernaut (*Brit*).

mastoïde [mastɔid] **nf** (*os*) mastoid.

mastroquet*† [mastʀɔkɛ] **nm** (*bar*) pub, bar; (*tenancier*) publican.

masturbation [mastyʀbasjɔ̃] **nf** masturbation. (*péj*) **c'est de la** ~ **intellectuelle** it's mental masturbation.

masturber vt, se masturber vpr [mastyʀbe] [1] to masturbate.

m'as-tu-vu, e* [matyvy] **nm,f (pl inv)** show-off*, swank*. **il est du genre** ~ he's a real show-off*.

masure [mɑzyʀ] **nf** tumbledown *ou* dilapidated cottage *ou* house, hovel.

mat¹ [mat] **1 adj inv** (*Échecs*) checkmated. **être** ~ to be checkmate; **faire** ~ to checkmate; **(tu es)** ~! (you're) checkmate!; **tu m'as fait** ~ **en 10 coups** you've (check)mated me in 10 moves. **2 nm** checkmate; *voir* **échec²**.

mat², e [mat] **adj** (*sans éclat*) *métal* mat(t), unpolished, dull; *couleur* mat(t), dull, flat; *peinture, papier* mat(t). **bruit** ~ dull noise, thud; **teint** ~ mat complexion.

mat'* [mat] **nm** (**abrév de matin**) morning. **à 2/6 heures du** ~ at 2/6 in the morning.

mât [mɑ] **1 nm** (*Naut*) mast; (*pylône, poteau*) pole, post; (*hampe*) flagpole; (*Sport*) climbing pole; *voir* **grand, trois**. **2 comp** ►**mât d'artimon** mizzenmast ►**mât de charge** derrick ►**mât de cocagne** greasy pole ►**mât de misaine** foremast.

matador [matadɔʀ] **nm** matador, bullfighter.

mataf [mataf] **nm** (*arg Marine*) sailor.

matage [mataʒ] **nm** *[dorure, verre]* matting; *[soudure]* caulking.

matamore [matamɔʀ] **nm** (*fanfaron*) bully boy. **faire le** ~ to throw one's weight around.

Mata Utu [matautu] **n** Mata-Utu.

match [matʃ] **nm** (*Sport*) match (*surtout Brit*), game (*US*). ~ **aller** first leg; ~ **retour** return match, second leg; ~ **amical** friendly (match); ~ **nul** draw, tie (*US*); ~ **sur terrain adverse** *ou* **à l'extérieur** away match; ~ **sur son propre terrain** *ou* **à domicile** home match; **faire un** ~ **de tennis/volley-ball** to play a tennis/volleyball match; **ils ont fait** ~ **nul** they drew (*Brit*), they tied (*US*); *voir* **disputer**.

maté [mate] **nm** maté.

matelas [mat(ə)lɑ] **nm** mattress. ~ **de laine/à ressorts** wool/(interior-)spring mattress; (*Constr*) ~ **d'air** air space *ou* cavity; ~ **(de billets)*** wad of notes; **il a un joli petit** ~* he's got a cosy sum put by*; **dormir sur un** ~ **de feuilles mortes** to sleep on a carpet of dead leaves; ~ **pneumatique** air mattress *ou* bed, Lilo ®; *voir* **toile**.

matelasser [mat(ə)lase] [1] **vt** *meuble, porte* to pad, upholster; *tissu* to quilt; *vêtement* (*rembourrer*) to pad; (*doubler*) to line; (*avec tissu matelassé*) to quilt. **veste matelassée** quilted *ou* padded jacket.

matelassier, -ière [mat(ə)lasje, jɛʀ] **nm,f** mattress maker.

matelassure [mat(ə)lasyʀ] **nf** (*rembourrage*) padding; (*doublure*) quilting, lining.

matelot [mat(ə)lo] **nm a** (*gén: marin*) sailor, seaman; (*dans la Marine de guerre*) ordinary rating (*Brit*), seaman recruit (*US*). ~ **de première/deuxième/troisième classe** leading/able/ordinary seaman; ~ **breveté** able rating (*Brit*), seaman apprentice (*US*). **b** (*navire*) ~ **d'avant/d'arrière** (next) ship ahead/astern.

matelote [mat(ə)lɔt] **nf a** (*plat*) matelote; (*sauce*) matelote sauce (*made with wine*). ~ **d'anguille** eels stewed in wine sauce. **b** (*danse*) hornpipe.

mater¹ [mate] [1] **vt a** *rebelles* to bring to heel, subdue; *terroristes* to bring *ou* get under control; *enfant* to take in hand, curb; *révolution* to put down, quell, suppress; *incendie* to bring under control, check. **b** (*Échecs*) to checkmate, mate.

mater²‡ [mate] [1] **vt** (*regarder*) to eye up*, ogle*; (*épier*) to spy on. **mate si le prof arrive!** keep an eye out for the teacher coming!

mater³ [mate] [1] **vt a** (*marteler*) to caulk (*riveted joint*). **b** = **matir**.

mater⁴‡ [matɛʀ] **nf** mum* (*Brit*), mom* (*US*). **ma** ~ my old woman *ou* mum‡ (*Brit*) *ou* mom* (*US*).

mâter [mɑte] [1] **vt** (*Naut*) to mast.

matérialisation [mateʀjalizasjɔ̃] **nf** *[projet, promesse, doute]* materialization; (*Phys*) mass energy conversion; (*Spiritisme*) materialization.

matérialiser [mateʀjalize] [1] **1 vt** (*concrétiser*) *projet, promesse, doute* to make materialize; (*symboliser*) *vertu, vice* to embody; (*Philos*) to materialize. **2 se matérialiser vpr** to materialize.

matérialisme [mateʀjalism] **nm** materialism. ~ **dialectique** dialectic materialism.

matérialiste [mateʀjalist] **1 adj** materialistic. **2 nmf** materialist.

matérialité [mateʀjalite] **nf** materiality.

matériau [mateʀjo] **nm inv** (*Constr*) material. **un** ~ **moderne** a modern (building) material.

matériaux [mateʀjo] **nmpl a** (*Constr*) material(s). ~ **de construction** building material; *voir* **résistance**. **b** (*documents*) material (*NonC*).

matériel, -elle [mateʀjɛl] **1 adj a** (*gén, Philos: effectif*) *monde, preuve* material. **être** ~ material *ou* physical being; **dégâts** ~**s** material damage; **j'ai la preuve** ~**le de son crime** I have tangible *ou* material proof of his crime; **je suis dans l'impossibilité** ~**le de le faire** it's materially impossible for me to do it; **je n'ai pas le temps** ~ **de le faire** I simply have not the time to do it.

b *bien-être, confort* material; (*du monde*) *plaisirs, biens, préoccupations* material; (*terre à terre*) *esprit* material, down-to-earth. **sa vie** ~**le est assurée** she is provided for materially, her material needs are provided for.

c (*financier*) *gêne, problèmes* financial; (*pratique*) *organisation, obstacles* practical. **aide** ~**le** material aid; **de nombreux avantages** ~**s** a number of material advantages.

2 nm (*Agr, Mil*) equipment (*NonC*), materials; (*Tech*) equipment (*NonC*), plant (*NonC*); (*attirail*) gear (*NonC*), kit (*NonC*); (*fig: corpus, donnée*) material (*NonC*). (*Ordin*) **le** ~ the hardware; ~ **de bureau/d'imprimerie** *etc* office/printing *etc* equipment; **tout son** ~ **d'artiste** all his artist's materials *ou* gear*.

3 comp ►**matériel d'enregistrement** recording equipment ►**matériel d'exploitation** plant (*NonC*) ►**matériel de guerre** weaponry (*NonC*) ►**matériel humain** human material, labour force ►**matériel de pêche** fishing tackle ►**matériel pédagogique** teaching equipment *ou* aids ►**matériel roulant** (*Rail*) rolling stock ►**matériel scolaire** (*livres, cahiers*) school (reading *ou* writing)

materials; (*pupitres, projecteurs*) school equipment.
matériellement [mateʀjɛlmɑ̃] **adv** (*voir* **matériel**) materially; financially; practically. **c'est ~ impossible** it's materially impossible.
maternage [matɛʀnaʒ] **nm** (*voir* **materner**) mothering, babying*, cosseting; spoonfeeding.
maternel, -elle [matɛʀnɛl] **adj** **a** (*d'une mère*) *instinct, amour* maternal, motherly; (*comme d'une mère*) *geste, soin* motherly. **b** (*de la mère*) of the mother, maternal. (*Généalogie*) **du côté ~** on the maternal side; **grand-père ~** maternal grandfather; **il avait gardé les habitudes ~les** he had retained his mother's habits; **écoute les conseils ~s!** listen to your mother's advice!; (*Admin*) **la protection ~le et infantile** ≃ mother and infant welfare; *voir* **allaitement, lait, langue.** **c** **(école) ~le** (state) nursery school.
maternellement [matɛʀnɛlmɑ̃] **adv** maternally, like a mother.
materner [matɛʀne] [1] **vt** to mother, baby*, cosset; (*mâcher le travail*) to spoonfeed. **se faire ~** to be babied*; to be spoonfed.
maternité [matɛʀnite] **nf** **a** (*bâtiment*) maternity hospital *ou* home. **b** (*Bio*) pregnancy. **fatiguée par plusieurs ~s** tired after several pregnancies *ou* after having had several babies. **c** (*état de mère*) motherhood, maternity. **la ~ l'a mûrie** motherhood *ou* being a mother has made her more mature; *voir* **allocation.** **d** (*Art*) *painting of mother and child or children.*
math* [mat] **nfpl** (**abrév de mathématiques**) maths* (*Brit*), math* (*US*). **être en ~ sup/spé** *to be in the first/second year advanced maths class preparing for the Grandes Écoles.*
mathématicien, -ienne [matematisjɛ̃, jɛn] **nm,f** mathematician.
mathématique [matematik] [1] **adj** *problème, méthode,* (*fig*) *précision, rigueur* mathematical. **c'est ~!*** it's bound to happen!, it's logical!, it's a dead cert!‡ (*Brit*). [2] **nfpl: les ~s** mathematics; **~s appliquées** applied maths (*Brit*) *ou* math (*US*); **~s supérieures** *first year advanced maths class preparing for the Grandes Écoles;* **~s spéciales** *second year advanced maths class preparing for the Grandes Écoles.*
mathématiquement [matematikmɑ̃] **adv** (*Math, fig*) mathematically. **~, il n'a aucune chance** logically he hasn't a hope.
matheux, -euse* [matø, øz] **nm,f** mathematician, maths (*Brit*) *ou* math (*US*) specialist; (*arg Scol*) maths (*Brit*) *ou* math (*US*) student. **leur fille, c'est la ~euse de la famille** their daughter is the mathematician *ou* maths expert in the family.
Mathieu [matjø] **nm** Matthew; *voir* **fesse.**
Mathilde [matild] **nf** Matilda.
maths* [mat] **nfpl** = **math***.
Mathusalem [matyzalɛm] **nm** Mathuselah. **ça date de ~*** *[situation]* it goes back a long way; *[objet]* it's as old as the hills.
matière [matjɛʀ] [1] **nf** **a** (*Philos, Phys*) **la ~** matter; **la ~ vivante** living matter.
b (*substance(s)*) matter (*NonC*), material. **~ combustible/inflammable** combustible/inflammable material; **~ organique** organic matter; **~s colorantes** *[aliments]* colouring (matter); *[tissus]* dye stuff; **~ précieuse** precious substance; (*Méd*) **~s (fécales)** faeces.
c (*fond, sujet*) material, matter, subject matter; (*Scol*) subject. **cela lui a fourni la ~ de son dernier livre** that gave him the material *ou* the subject matter for his latest book; (*Scol*) **il est bon dans toutes les ~s** he is good at all subjects; **il est très ignorant en la ~** he is completely ignorant on the subject, it's a matter *ou* subject he knows nothing about; (*Univ*) **~ principale** main subject (*Brit*), major (*US*); **~ secondaire** subsidiary (*Brit*), second subject (*Brit*), minor (*US*); *voir* **entrée, option, table.**
d (*loc*) **en ~ poétique/commerciale** where *ou* as far as poetry/commerce is concerned, in the matter of poetry/commerce (*frm*); **en ~ d'art/de jardinage** as regards art/gardening; **donner ~ à plaisanter** to give cause for laughter; **il y a là ~ à réflexion** this is a matter for serious thought; **ça lui a donné ~ à réflexion** it gave him food for thought; **il n'y a pas là ~ à rire** this is no laughing matter; **il n'y a pas là ~ à se réjouir** this is no matter for rejoicing.
[2] **comp ▸matière(s) grasse(s)** fat content, fat **▸matière grise** (*lit, fig*) grey matter; **faire travailler sa matière grise** to use one's grey matter **▸matière plastique** plastic **▸matière première** raw material.
MATIF [matif] **nm** **a** (**abrév de marché à terme d'instruments financiers**) *voir* **marché.** **b** (**abrév de marché à terme international de France**) *voir* **marché.**
Matignon [matiɲɔ̃] **nm: (l'hôtel) ~** the Hotel Matignon, *the offices of the Prime Minister of the French Republic.*
matin [matɛ̃] [1] **nm** **a** morning. **par un ~ de juin** on a June morning, one June morning; **le 10 au ~, le ~ du 10** on the morning of the 10th; **2h du ~** 2 a.m., 2 in the morning; **du ~ au soir** from morning till night, morning noon and night; **je ne travaille que le ~** I only work mornings* *ou* in the morning; (*Méd*) **à prendre ~ midi et soir** to be taken three times a day; **jusqu'au ~** until morning; **de bon** *ou* **de grand ~** early in the morning; **au petit ~** at dawn *ou* daybreak; **être du ~** to be an early riser, be *ou* get up early; *voir* **quatre.** **b** (*littér*) **au ~ de sa vie** in the morning of one's life. [2] **adv: partir/se lever ~** to leave/get up very early *ou* at daybreak.
mâtin, e [mɑtɛ̃, in] [1] **nm,f** (†: *coquin*) cunning devil‡, sly dog*. (*hum*) **~e** hussy, minx. [2] **nm** (*chien*) (*de garde*) (big) watchdog; (*de chasse*) hound. [3] **excl** † by Jove!, my word!
matinal, e, **mpl -aux** [matinal, o] **adj** *tâches, toilette* morning (*épith*). **gelée ~e** early morning frost; **heure ~e** early hour; **être ~** to be an early riser, get up early; **il est bien ~ aujourd'hui** he's up early today.
matinalement [matinalmɑ̃] **adv** (*littér*) early (in the morning), betimes (*littér*).
mâtiné, e [mɑtine] (**ptp de mâtiner**) **adj** *animal* crossbred. **chien ~** mongrel (dog); **~ de** (*Zool*) crossed with; (*fig*) mixed with; **il parle un français ~ d'espagnol** he speaks a mixture of French and Spanish; (*péj*) **il est ~ cochon d'Inde*** he's a bit of a half-breed (*péj*).
matinée [matine] **nf** **a** (*matin*) morning. **je le verrai demain dans la ~** I'll see him sometime (in the course of) tomorrow morning; **en début/en fin de ~** at the beginning/at the end of the morning; **après une ~ de chasse** after a morning's hunting; *voir* **gras.** **b** (*Ciné, Théât*) matinée, afternoon performance. **j'irai en ~** I'll go to the matinée; **une ~ dansante** an afternoon dance; **~ enfantine** children's matinée.
mâtiner [mɑtine] [1] **vt** *chien* to cross.
matines [matin] **nfpl** matins.
matir [matiʀ] [2] **vt** *verre, argent* to mat(t), dull.
matois, e [matwa, waz] **adj** (*littér: rusé*) wily, sly, crafty. **c'est un(e) ~(e)** he's (she's) a sly character *ou* a crafty one *ou* a sly one.
maton, -onne [matɔ̃, ɔn] **nm,f** (*arg Prison*) screw (*arg*).
matos* [matos] **nm** equipment (*NonC*).
matou [matu] **nm** tomcat, tom.
matraquage [matʀakaʒ] **nm** **a** (*par la police*) beating (up) (*with a truncheon*). **b** (*Presse, Rad*) plugging. **le ~ publicitaire** media hype* *ou* overkill; **mettre fin au ~ du public par la chanson** to stop bombarding the public with songs.
matraque [matʀak] **nf** *[police]* truncheon (*Brit*), billy (*US*), night stick (*US*); *[malfaiteur]* cosh (*Brit*), club. **coup de ~** blow from *ou* with a truncheon *ou* cosh (*Brit*) *ou* club.
matraquer [matʀake] [1] **vt** **a** *[police]* to beat up (*with a truncheon*); *[malfaiteur]* to cosh (*Brit*), club. (***:** *fig*) **~ le client** to soak‡ (*US*) *ou* overcharge customers; (***:** *fig*) **se faire ~** to get ripped off* *ou* fleeced* *ou* done*. **b** (*Presse, Rad*) *chanson, publicité* to plug, hype*; *public* to bombard (*de* with).
matraqueur [matʀakœʀ] **nm** (*arg Sport*) dirty player, hatchet-man*; (*policier, malfaiteur*) dirty worker‡.
matriarcal, e, **mpl -aux** [matʀijaʀkal, o] **adj** matriarchal.
matriarcat [matʀijaʀka] **nm** matriarchy.
matrice [matʀis] **nf** **a** (*utérus*) womb. **b** (*Tech*) mould, die; (*Typ*) matrix. **c** (*Ling, Math*) matrix. **~ réelle/complexe** matrix of real/complex numbers. **d** (*Admin*) register. **~ cadastrale** cadastre; **~ du rôle des contributions** ≃ original of register of taxes.
matricide [matʀisid] [1] **adj** matricidal. [2] **nmf** matricide. [3] **nm** (*crime*) matricide.
matriciel, -ielle [matʀisjɛl] **adj** (*Math*) matrix (*épith*), done with a matrix; (*Admin*) pertaining to assessment of taxes. **loyer ~** rent assessment (*to serve as basis for calculation of rates* (*Brit*) *ou taxes* (*US*)) **imprimante ~le** dot-matrix printer.
matricule [matʀikyl] [1] **nm** (*Mil*) regimental number; (*Admin*) administrative *ou* official *ou* reference number. **dépêche-toi sinon ça va barder pour ton ~!‡** hurry up or your number'll be up!* *ou* you'll really get yourself bawled out!‡ [2] **nf** roll, register. [3] **adj: numéro ~** = **matricule 1; registre ~** = **matricule 2;** *voir* **livret.**
matrimonial, e, **mpl -iaux** [matʀimɔnjal, jo] **adj** matrimonial, marriage (*épith*); *voir* **agence, régime**[1].
matrone [matʀɔn] **nf** (*péj*) (*mère de famille*) matronly woman; (*grosse femme*) stout woman.
Matthieu [matjø] **nm** Matthew.
maturation [matyʀasjɔ̃] **nf** (*Bot, Méd*) maturation; (*Tech*) *[fromage]* maturing, ripening.
mature [matyʀ] **adj** (*mûr*) mature.
mâture [mɑtyʀ] **nf** masts. **dans la ~** aloft.
maturité [matyʀite] **nf** **a** (*Bio, Bot, fig*) maturity. *[fruit, idée]* **venir à ~** to come to maturity; **manquer de ~** to be immature; **un homme en pleine ~** a man in his prime *ou* at the height of his powers; **~ d'esprit** maturity of mind; **enfant d'une grande ~** very mature child. **b** (*en Suisse = baccalauréat*) *secondary school examination giving university entrance qualification,* ≃ A-levels (*Brit*), ≃ high school diploma (*US*).
maudire [modiʀ] [2] **vt** to curse.
maudit, e [modi, it] (**ptp de maudire**) [1] **adj** **a** (*****) (*avant n*) blasted*, beastly* (*Brit*), confounded*. **b** (*littér: réprouvé*) (*après n*) (ac)cursed (*by God, society*). (*Littérat*) **poète/écrivain ~** accursed poet/writer. **c** (*littér*) **~e soit la guerre!, la guerre soit ~e!** cursed be the war!; **~ soit le jour où ...** cursed be the day on which ..., a curse *ou* a plague on the day on which ... ; **soyez ~!** curse you!, a plague on you! [2] **nm,f** damned soul. **les ~s** the damned. [3] **nm: le M~** the Devil.
maugréer [mogʀee] [1] **vi** to grouse, grumble (*contre* about, at).
maul [mol] **nm** (*Rugby*) loose scrum, maul, ruck. **faire un ~** to make *ou* form a loose scrum.
maure, mauresque [mɔʀ, mɔʀɛsk] [1] **adj** Moorish. [2] **nm: M~** Moor. [3] **Mauresque** **nf** Moorish woman.

Maurice [mɔʀis] nm Maurice, Morris; *voir* **île.**

mauricien, -ienne [mɔʀisjɛ̃, jɛn] 1 adj Mauritian. 2 nm,f: **M~(ne)** Mauritian.

Mauritanie [mɔʀitani] nf Mauritania.

mauritanien, -ienne [mɔʀitanjɛ̃, jɛn] 1 adj Mauritanian. 2 nm,f: **M~(ne)** Mauritanian.

mausolée [mozɔle] nm mausoleum.

maussade [mosad] adj *personne* sullen, glum, morose; *ciel, temps, paysage* gloomy, sullen.

maussadement [mosadmɑ̃] adv sullenly, glumly, morosely.

maussaderie [mosadʀi] nf sullenness, glumness, moroseness.

mauvais, e [mɔvɛ, ɛz] 1 adj a (*défectueux*) *appareil, instrument* bad, faulty; *marchandise* inferior, shoddy, bad; *route* bad, in bad repair; *santé, vue, digestion, mémoire* poor, bad; *roman, film* poor, bad, feeble. **elle a de ~ yeux** her eyes are *ou* her eyesight is bad, she has bad eyes; **~e excuse** poor *ou* bad *ou* lame excuse; (*Élec*) **un ~ contact** a faulty contact; (*Tennis*) **la balle est ~e** the ball is out; **son français est bien ~** his French is very bad *ou* poor.

b (*inefficace, incapable*) *père, élève, acteur, ouvrier* poor, bad. **il est ~ en géographie** he's bad *ou* weak at geography; (*Prov*) **les ~ ouvriers ont toujours de ~ outils** a bad workman always blames his tools (*Prov*).

c (*erroné*) *méthode, moyens, direction, date* wrong. **le ~ numéro/cheval** the wrong number/horse; **il roulait sur le ~ côté de la route** he was driving on the wrong side of the road; **c'est un ~ calcul de sa part** he's badly misjudged it *ou* things; **il ne serait pas ~ de se renseigner** *ou* **que nous nous renseignions** it wouldn't be a bad idea *ou* it would be no bad thing if we found out more about this.

d (*inapproprié*) *jour, heure* awkward, bad, inconvenient. **il a choisi un ~ moment** he picked an awkward *ou* a bad time; **il a choisi le ~ moment** he picked the wrong time.

e (*dangereux, nuisible*) *maladie, blessure* nasty, bad. **il a fait une ~e grippe/rougeole** he's had a bad *ou* nasty *ou* severe attack *ou* bout of flu/measles; **la mer est ~e** the sea is rough; **c'est ~ pour la santé** it's bad for one's *ou* the health; **il est ~ de se baigner en eau froide** it's bad *ou* it's a bad idea to bathe in cold water; **vous jugez ~ qu'il sorte le soir?** do you think it's a bad thing his going out at night?; **être en ~e posture** to be in a dangerous *ou* tricky *ou* nasty position.

f (*défavorable*) *rapport, critique* unfavourable, bad; (*Scol*) *bulletin, note* bad.

g (*désagréable*) *temps* bad, unpleasant, nasty; *nourriture, repas* bad, poor; *odeur* bad, unpleasant, offensive; (*pénible*) *nouvelle, rêve* bad. **la soupe a un ~ goût** the soup has an unpleasant *ou* a nasty taste, the soup tastes nasty; **ce n'est qu'un ~ moment à passer** it's just a bad spell *ou* patch you've got to get through; *voir* **caractère, gré, volonté.**

h (*immoral, nuisible*) *instincts, action, fréquentations, livre, film* bad. **il n'a pas un ~ fond** he's not bad at heart; *voir* **génie.**

i (*méchant*) *sourire, regard etc* nasty, malicious, spiteful; *personne, joie* malicious, spiteful. **être ~ comme la gale*** to be perfectly poisonous (*fig*); **ce n'est pas un ~ garçon** he's not a bad boy.

j (*loc*) **ce n'est pas ~!** it's not bad!, it's quite good!; **quand on l'a renvoyé, il l'a trouvée** *ou* **eue ~e*** when he was dismissed he didn't appreciate it one little bit *ou* he was very put out about it *ou* he took it very badly; **aujourd'hui il fait ~** today the weather is bad; **il fait ~ le contredire** it is not advisable to contradict him; **prendre qch en ~e part** to take sth in bad part, take sth amiss; **faire contre ~e fortune bon cœur** to make the best of it; **se faire du ~ sang** to worry, get in a state.

2 nm a **enlève le ~ et mange le reste** cut out the bad part and eat the rest; **la presse ne montre que le ~** the press only shows the bad side (of things).

b (*personnes*) **les ~** the wicked; *voir* **bon[1]**.

3 comp ►**mauvais coucheur** awkward customer ►**mauvais coup**: **recevoir un mauvais coup** to get a nasty blow; **un mauvais coup porté à nos institutions** a blow to *ou* an attack on our institutions; **faire un mauvais coup** to play a mean *ou* dirty trick (*à qn* on sb) ►**mauvais esprit** troublemaker; **faire du mauvais esprit** to make snide remarks ►**mauvais garçon** tough ►**mauvaise graine**: **c'est de la mauvaise graine** he's (*ou* she's *ou* they're) a bad lot ►**mauvaise herbe** weed; **enlever** *ou* **arracher les mauvaises herbes du jardin** to weed the garden; (*hum*) **la mauvaise herbe, ça pousse!** kids grow like weeds! (*hum*) ►**mauvaise langue** gossip, scandalmonger; **je ne voudrais pas être mauvaise langue mais ...** I don't want to tittle-tattle *ou* to spread scandal but ... ►**mauvais lieu** place of ill repute ►**mauvais œil**: **avoir le mauvais œil** to have the evil eye ►**mauvais pas**: **tirer qn d'un mauvais pas** to get sb out of a tight spot *ou* corner ►**mauvais plaisant** hoaxer ►**mauvaise plaisanterie** rotten trick ►**mauvais rêve** bad dream, nightmare ►**mauvaise saison** rainy season ►**mauvais sort** misfortune, ill fate ►**mauvais sujet** bad lot ►**mauvaise tête**: **c'est une mauvaise tête** he's headstrong; **faire la** *ou* **sa mauvaise tête** to sulk ►**mauvais traitement** ill treatment; **subir de mauvais traitements** to be ill-treated; **mauvais traitements à enfants** child abuse, child battering; **faire subir de mauvais traitements à** to ill-treat; *voir* **passe[1]**.

mauve [mov] 1 adj, nm (*couleur*) mauve. 2 nf (*Bot*) mallow.

mauviette [movjɛt] nf (*péj*) wimp*, weakling.

mauvis [movi] nm redwing.

max‡ [maks] adj, nm (abrév de **maximum**) max*. *coûter, dépenser* **un ~**‡ a hell of a lot‡; **ça craint un ~**‡ it scares me (*ou* him *etc*) stiff*; **il m'agace un ~**‡ he really drives me up the wall*, he bugs me no end‡.

maxi [maksi] 1 préf: **maxi ...** maxi ...; **~-jupe** *nf* maxi; **~-bouteille/paquet** giant-size bottle/packet. 2 adj inv a (*: *maximum*) maximum. b **la mode ~** the maxi-length fashion. 3 nf (*robe*) maxi. 4 nm (*mode*) maxi. **elle s'habille en ~** she wears maxis; **la mode est au ~** maxis are in (fashion).

maxillaire [maksilɛʀ] 1 adj maxillary. **os ~** jawbone. 2 nm jaw, maxilla (*SPÉC*). **~ supérieur/inférieur** upper/lower maxilla (*SPÉC*) *ou* jawbone.

maxima [maksima] *voir* **appel, maximum.**

maximal, e, mpl **-aux** [maksimal, o] adj maximal.

maximaliste [maksimalist] adj, nmf radical, extremist.

Maxime [maksim] nm Maximus.

maxime [maksim] nf maxim.

maximiser [maksimize] [1] vt to maximize.

maximum [maksimɔm], *f* **~** *ou* **maxima** [maksima], pl **maximum(s)** *ou* **maxima** 1 adj maximum. **la température ~** the maximum *ou* highest temperature; **j'attends de vous une aide ~** I expect a maximum of help *ou* maximum help from you; **j'en ai pour 2 heures ~** I'll be 2 hours maximum.

2 nm a (*gén, Math*) maximum; (*Jur*) maximum sentence. **faire le** *ou* **son ~** to do one's level best (*pour* to); **avec le ~ de profit** with the maximum (of) profit, with the highest profit, with the greatest possible profit; **il faut travailler au ~** one must work to the utmost of one's ability; **être au ~ de ses possibilités** to be stretched to one's limits; **sa radio était au ~** his radio was on full; **atteindre son ~** *[production]* to reach its maximum, reach an all-time high*; *[valeur]* to reach its highest *ou* maximum point; **il y a un ~ de frais sur un bateau*** boats cost a fortune to run*; **il m'a fait payer un ~*** he charged me a fortune*; **ça consomme un ~ ces voitures*** these cars are really heavy on petrol; *voir* **thermomètre.**

b (*loc*) **au (grand) ~** at the (very) maximum, at the (very) most; **il faut rester au** *ou* **le ~ à l'ombre** one must stay as much as possible in the shade.

mayday [mɛdɛ] nm (*Naut*) Mayday.

Mayence [majɑ̃s] n Mainz.

mayonnaise [majɔnɛz] nf mayonnaise. **poisson/œufs (à la) ~** fish/eggs (with *ou* in) mayonnaise; (*fig*) **la ~ n'a pas pris*** the mix was all wrong.

mazagran [mazagʀɑ̃] nm pottery goblet (*for coffee*).

mazette† [mazɛt] 1 excl (*admiration, étonnement*) my!, my goodness! 2 nf (*incapable*) weakling.

mazout [mazut] nm heating oil. **chaudière/poêle à ~** oil-fired boiler/stove; **chauffage central au ~** oil-fired central heating.

mazouté, e [maʒute] adj *mer, plage* oil-polluted (*épith*), polluted with oil (*attrib*); *oiseaux* oil-covered (*épith*), covered in oil (*attrib*).

Mbabane [mbaban] n Mbabane.

Me (abrév de **Maître**) *barrister's title.* **~ Martin** ≃ Mr (*ou* Mrs) Martin Q.C. (*Brit*).

me, m' [m(ə)] pron pers (*objet direct ou indirect*) me; (*réfléchi*) myself. **~ voyez-vous?** can you see me?; **elle m'attend** she is waiting for me; **il ~ l'a dit** he told me (it), he told me about it; **il m'en a parlé** he spoke to me about it; **il ~ l'a donné** he gave it to me, he gave it me; **je ne ~ vois pas dans ce rôle-là** I can't see myself in that part.

mea-culpa* [meakylpa] excl my fault!, my mistake! **faire son ~** (*lit*) to say one's mea culpa; (*fig*) to blame oneself.

méandre [meɑ̃dʀ] nm (*Art, Géog*) meander; (*fig*) *[politique]* twists and turns. **les ~s de sa pensée** the twists and turns *ou* ins and outs *ou* complexities of his thought.

méat [mea] nm (*Anat*) meatus; (*Bot*) lacuna.

mec‡ [mɛk] nm guy*, bloke* (*Brit*). **son ~** her man*.

mécanicien, -ienne [mekanisjɛ̃, jɛn] 1 adj *civilisation* mechanistic. 2 nm,f a (*Aut*) (garage *ou* motor) mechanic. **ouvrier ~** garage hand; **c'est un bon ~** he is a good mechanic, he is good with cars *ou* with machines. b (*Naut, Aviat*) engineer. (*Aviat*) **~ navigant, ~ de bord** flight engineer. c (*Rail*) train *ou* engine driver (*Brit*), engineer (*US*). d (†: *Méd*) **~-dentiste** dental technician *ou* mechanic.

mécanique [mekanik] 1 adj a (*Tech, gén*) mechanical; *dentelle, tapis* machine-made; *jouet* clockwork (*épith*). **les industries ~s** mechanical engineering industries; (*Aut, Aviat*) **avoir des ennuis ~s** to have engine trouble; *voir* **escalier, piano, rasoir.**

b (*machinal*) *geste, réflexe* mechanical.

c (*Philos, Sci*) mechanical. **énergie ~** mechanical energy; **lois ~s** laws of mechanics.

2 nf a (*Sci*) (mechanical) engineering; (*Aut, Tech*) mechanics (*sg*). **la ~, ça le connaît*** he knows what he's doing in mechanics; **~ céleste/ondulatoire** celestial/wave mechanics; **~ hydraulique** hydraulics (*sg*).

b (*mécanisme*) **la ~ d'une horloge** the mechanism of a clock; **cette voiture, c'est de la belle ~** this car is a fine piece of engineering.

mécaniquement [mekanikmɑ̃] adv mechanically. **objet fait ~**

machine-made object.

mécanisation [mekanizasjɔ̃] nf mechanization.

mécaniser [mekanize] 1 vt to mechanize.

mécanisme [mekanism] nm (*Bio, Philos, Psych, Tech*) mechanism. **les ~s psychologiques/biologiques** psychological/biological workings *ou* mechanisms; **le ~ administratif** the administrative mechanism; **~(s) politique(s)** political machinery, mechanism of politics; **le ~ d'une action** the mechanics of an action.

mécaniste [mekanist] adj mechanistic.

mécano* [mekano] nm (abrév de **mécanicien**) mechanic, grease monkey‡ (*US*).

mécanographe [mekanɔgʀaf] nmf comptometer operator, punch card operator.

mécanographie [mekanɔgʀafi] nf (*procédé*) (mechanical) data processing; (*service*) comptometer department.

mécanographique [mekanɔgʀafik] adj *classement* mechanized, automatic. **service ~** comptometer department, (mechanical) data processing department; **machine ~** calculator.

Meccano [mekano] nm ® Meccano ®.

mécénat [mesena] nm (*Art*) patronage. **~ d'entreprise** corporate philanthropy *ou* sponsorship.

mécène [mesɛn] nm (*Art*) patron. (*Antiq*) **M~** Maecenas.

méchamment [meʃamɑ̃] adv a (*cruellement*) *rire, agir* spitefully, nastily, wickedly. b (*: *très*) fantastically*, terrifically*. **c'est ~ bon** it's fantastically* *ou* bloody*‡ (*Brit*) good; **c'est ~ abîmé** it's really badly damaged; **ça fait ~ mal** it's terribly painful, it hurts like mad*; **il a été ~ surpris** he got one hell *ou* heck of a surprise*.

méchanceté [meʃɑ̃ste] nf a (*caractère*) *[personne, action]* nastiness, spitefulness, wickedness. **faire qch par ~** to do sth out of spite. b (*action, parole*) mean *ou* spiteful *ou* nasty *ou* wicked action *ou* remark. **~ gratuite** unwarranted piece of unkindness *ou* spitefulness; **dire des ~s à qn** to say spiteful things to sb.

méchant, e [meʃɑ̃, ɑ̃t] 1 adj a (*malveillant*) *personne, intention* spiteful, nasty, wicked; *enfant* naughty. **devenir ~** to turn *ou* get nasty; **la mer est ~e** the sea is rough; **arrête, tu es ~** stop it, you're wicked *ou* you're (being) horrid *ou* nasty; **ce n'est pas un ~ homme** he's not such a bad fellow; *voir* **chien**.

b (*dangereux, désagréable*) **ce n'est pas bien ~*** *[blessure, difficulté, dispute]* it's nothing to worry about; *[examen]* it's not too difficult *ou* stiff*; **s'attirer une ~e affaire** (*dangereuse*) to get mixed up in a nasty business; (*désagréable*) to get mixed up in an unpleasant *ou* unsavoury (bit of) business; **de ~e humeur** in a foul *ou* rotten mood.

c (†: *médiocre, insignifiant*) (*avant n*) miserable, pathetic*, mediocre, sorry-looking. **~ vers/poète** poor *ou* second-rate verse/poet; **un ~ morceau de fromage** one miserable *ou* sorry-looking bit of cheese; **que de bruit pour une ~e clef perdue** what a fuss over one wretched lost key.

d (‡: *sensationnel*) (*avant n*) **il avait (une) ~e allure** he looked terrific*; **il a une ~e moto** he's got a fantastic* *ou* bloody marvellous*‡ (*Brit*) bike; **une ~e cicatrice** a hell of a scar‡; **un ~ cigare** a bloody great (big) cigar‡ (*Brit*), a hell of a big cigar‡.

2 nm,f: **tais-toi, ~!** be quiet you naughty boy!; **les ~s** the wicked; (*dans un western*) the baddies*, the bad guys* (*US*); **faire le ~*** to be difficult, be nasty.

mèche [mɛʃ] nf a (*inflammable*) *[bougie, briquet, lampe]* wick; *[bombe, mine]* fuse. **~ fusante** safety fuse; *voir* **vendre**. b *[cheveux]* tuft of hair, lock; (*sur le front*) forelock, lock of hair. **~ postiche, fausse ~** hairpiece; **~s folles** straggling locks *ou* wisps of hair; **~ rebelle** cowlick; **se faire faire des ~s** to have highlights put in, have one's hair streaked (blond). c (*Méd*) pack, dressing; *[fouet]* lash; *[perceuse]* bit. d (**loc*) **être de ~ avec qn*** to be hand in glove with sb*, be in collusion *ou* league with sb; **y a pas ~‡** nothing doing*, it's no go*, you're not on‡.

mécher [meʃe] 6 vt (*Tech*) to sulphurize; (*Méd*) to pack with gauze.

méchoui [meʃwi] nm (*repas*) barbecue of a whole roast sheep.

mécompte [mekɔ̃t] nm (*frm*) a (*désillusion*) (*gén pl*) disappointment. b (*erreur de calcul*) miscalculation, miscount.

méconnaissable [mekɔnɛsabl] adj (*impossible à reconnaître*) unrecognizable; (*difficile à reconnaître*) hardly recognizable.

méconnaissance [mekɔnɛsɑ̃s] nf (*ignorance*) lack of knowledge (*de* about), ignorance (*de* of); (*littér: mauvais jugement*) lack of comprehension, misappreciation (*de* of); (*refus de reconnaître*) refusal to take into consideration.

méconnaître [mekɔnɛtʀ] 57 vt (*frm*) a (*ignorer*) *faits* to be unaware of, not to know. **je ne méconnais pas que** I am fully *ou* quite aware that, I am alive to the fact that. b (*mésestimer*) *situation, problème* to misjudge; *mérites, personne* to underrate. c (*ne pas tenir compte de*) *lois, devoirs* to ignore.

méconnu, e [mekɔny] (ptp de **méconnaître**) adj *talent, génie* unrecognized; *musicien, écrivain* underrated. **il se prend pour un ~** he sees himself as a misunderstood man.

mécontent, e [mekɔ̃tɑ̃, ɑ̃t] 1 adj (*insatisfait*) discontented, displeased, dissatisfied (*de* with); (*contrarié*) annoyed (*de* with, at). **il a l'air très ~** he looks very annoyed *ou* displeased; **il n'est pas ~ de** he is not altogether dissatisfied *ou* displeased with. 2 nm,f grumbler*; (*Pol*) malcontent.

mécontentement [mekɔ̃tɑ̃tmɑ̃] nm (*Pol*) discontent; (*déplaisir*) dissatisfaction, displeasure; (*irritation*) annoyance.

mécontenter [mekɔ̃tɑ̃te] 1 vt to displease, annoy.

Mecque [mɛk] nf: **la ~** (*lit*) Mecca; (*fig*) the Mecca.

mécréant, e [mekʀeɑ̃, ɑ̃t] adj, nm,f a (†, *hum: non-croyant*) infidel, non-believer. b († *péj: bandit*) scoundrel, miscreant†.

médaille [medaj] nf a (*pièce, décoration*) medal; (*: *tache*) stain, mark. **~ militaire** military decoration; **~ pieuse** medal (*of a saint etc*); **~ du travail** long-service medal (*in industry etc*); *voir* **revers**. b (*insigne d'identité*) *[employé]* badge; *[chien]* identification disc, name tag; *[volaille]* guarantee tag.

médaillé, e [medaje] (ptp de **médailler**) 1 adj (*Admin, Mil*) decorated (*with a medal*); (*Sport*) holding a medal. 2 nm,f medal-holder. **il est *ou* c'est un ~ olympique** he is an Olympic medallist, he is the holder of an Olympic medal.

médailler [medaje] 1 vt (*Admin, Sport etc*) to award a medal to; (*Mil*) to decorate, award a medal to. (*se tacher*) **se ~*** to get a stain *ou* mark on one's clothing.

médaillon [medajɔ̃] nm (*Art*) medallion; (*bijou*) locket; (*Culin*) médaillon, *thin, round slice of meat etc.*

mède [mɛd] 1 adj of Media. 2 nmf: **M~** Mede.

médecin [med(ə)sɛ̃] nm doctor, physician (*frm*). (*fig*) **~ de l'âme** confessor; (*Naut*) **~ de bord** ship's doctor; **~-chef** head doctor; **~-conseil** medical adviser; **~ de famille** family practitioner *ou* doctor; **~ d'hôpital *ou* des hôpitaux** ≃ consultant, doctor *ou* physician with a hospital appointment; **~ légiste** forensic scientist, expert in forensic medicine, medical examiner (*US*); **~ généraliste *ou* de médecine générale** general practitioner, G.P.; **~ militaire** army medical officer; **~ scolaire** school doctor, schools medical officer (*Brit Admin*); **~ traitant** attending physician; **votre ~ traitant** your (usual *ou* family) doctor; **~ du travail** company doctor; **~ de ville** doctor (*working in a town*).

médecine [med(ə)sin] nf a (*Sci*) medicine. **~ alternative *ou* douce *ou* naturelle** alternative medicine; **~ curative** remedial medicine; **~ générale** general medicine; **~ infantile** paediatrics (*sg*); **~ légale** forensic medicine *ou* science; **~ opératoire** surgery; **~ parallèle** complementary medicine; **~ préventive** preventive medicine; **~ du travail** occupational *ou* industrial medicine; **~ spécialisée** specialized branches of medicine; **~ de ville** general medicine (*as practised in towns*); **~ d'urgence** (*soins*) emergency treatment; (*service*) casualty (department); **faire des études de ~, faire sa ~** to study *ou* do medicine; **pratiquer une ~ révolutionnaire** to practise a revolutionary type of medicine; **il exerçait la ~ dans un petit village** he had a (medical) practice *ou* he was a doctor in a small village; *voir* **docteur, étudiant, faculté**.

b (†: *médicament*) medicine.

medecine-ball, pl **medecine-balls** [medsinbol] nm medicine ball.

Médée [mede] nf Medea.

media [medja] nm: **les ~s** the media; **dans les ~s** in the media.

médial, e, mpl **-aux** [medjal, o] adj medial.

médian, e [medjɑ̃, jan] 1 adj (*Math, Statistique*) median; (*Ling*) medial. 2 **médiane** nf (*Math, Statistique*) median; (*Ling*) medial sound, mid vowel; *voir* **ligne[1]**.

médiante [medjɑ̃t] nf (*Mus*) mediant.

médiat, e [medja, jat] adj mediate.

médiateur, -trice [medjatœʀ, tʀis] 1 adj (*gén, Pol*) mediatory, mediating; (*Ind*) arbitrating. 2 nm,f (*gén*) mediator; (*Ind*) arbitrator; (*Pol*) ≃ Parliamentary Commissioner (*Brit*), Ombudsman. (*Méd*) **~ chimique** transmitter substance. 3 **médiatrice** nf (*Géom*) median.

médiathèque [medjatɛk] nf reference library (*with multi-media collections and facilities*).

médiation [medjasjɔ̃] nf a (*gén, Philos, Pol*) mediation; (*Ind*) arbitration. **offrir sa ~ dans un conflit** (*Pol*) to offer to mediate in a conflict; (*Ind*) to offer to arbitrate *ou* intervene in a dispute. b (*Logique*) mediate inference.

médiatique [medjatik] adj *personnalité, événement* media (*épith*); *sport* popularized through the media (*attrib*).

médiatisation [medjatizasjɔ̃] nf (*voir* **médiatiser**) mediatization; promotion through the media.

médiatiser [medjatize] 1 vt (*Hist, Philos*) to mediatize; (*à la TV*) to give *ou* devote media coverage to.

médiator [medjatɔʀ] nm plectrum.

médiatrice [medjatʀis] *voir* **médiateur**.

médical, e, mpl **-aux** [medikal, o] adj medical; *voir* **examen, visite**.

médicalement [medikalmɑ̃] adv medically.

médicalisation [medikalizasjɔ̃] nf (*voir* **médicaliser**) medicalization; bringing medical care to. **la ~ des populations touchées par la faim** the provision of medical care for the famine victims.

médicaliser [medikalize] 1 vt *région, population* to provide with medical care. **~ la maternité** to medicalize childbirth; **~ la population rurale** to provide the rural population with medical care; **résidence médicalisée** nursing home.

médicament [medikamɑ̃] nm medicine, drug. **~ de confort** palliative.

médicamenteux, -euse [medikamɑ̃tø, øz] adj *plante, substance* medicinal.
médicastre [medikastʀ] nm (†, *hum*) medical charlatan, quack.
médication [medikasjɔ̃] nf (medical) treatment, medication.
médicinal, e, mpl **-aux** [medisinal, o] adj *plante, substance* medicinal.
medicine-ball, pl **medicine-balls** [medisinbol] nm medicine ball.
Médicis [medisis] nmf Medici. **les ~** the Medicis.
médico- [medikɔ] préf: **~légal** medico-legal, forensic; **~social** medico-social; **branche ~sportive** branch of medicine concerned with sports injuries; *voir* **institut**.
Médie [medi] nf Media.
médiéval, e, mpl **-aux** [medjeval, o] adj medieval.
médiéviste [medjevist] nmf medievalist.
médina [medina] nf medina.
Médine [medin] n Medina.
médiocre [medjɔkʀ] 1 adj *travail, roman, élève* mediocre, indifferent, second-rate; (*sur copie d'élève*) poor; *intelligence, qualité* poor, mediocre, inferior; *revenu, salaire* meagre, poor; *vie, existence* mediocre, narrow. **il occupe une situation ~** he holds some second-rate position; **gagner un salaire ~** to earn a mere pittance *ou* a poor *ou* meagre wage; **il a montré un intérêt ~ pour ce projet** he showed little or no interest in the project; **génie incompris par les esprits ~s** genius misunderstood by the petty-minded *ou* those with small minds. 2 nmf nonentity, second-rater*.
médiocrement [medjɔkʀəmɑ̃] adv: **gagner ~ sa vie** to earn a poor living; **être ~ intéressé par** not to be particularly interested in; **~ intelligent** not very *ou* not particularly intelligent; **~ satisfait** barely satisfied, not very well satisfied; **il joue ~ du piano** he plays the piano indifferently, he's not very good at (playing) the piano.
médiocrité [medjɔkʀite] nf *[travail]* poor quality, mediocrity; *[élève, homme politique]* mediocrity; *[copie d'élève]* poor standard; *[revenu, salaire]* meagreness, poorness; *[intelligence]* mediocrity, inferiority; *[vie]* narrowness, mediocrity. **les politiciens de maintenant, quelle ~!** what mediocrity *ou* poor quality in present-day politicians!; **étant donné la ~ de ses revenus** given the slimness of his resources, seeing how slight *ou* slim his resources are *ou* were; **cet homme, c'est une (vraie) ~** this man is a complete mediocrity *ou* second-rater.
médique [medik] adj (*Antiq*) Median.
médire [mediʀ] 37 vi: **~ de qn** to speak ill of sb; (*à tort*) to malign sb; **elle est toujours en train de ~** she's always running people down; **je ne voudrais pas ~ mais ...** I don't want to tittle-tattle *ou* to spread scandal, but ... .
médisance [medizɑ̃s] nf a (*diffamation*) scandalmongering. **être en butte à la ~** to be made a target for scandalmongering *ou* for malicious gossip. b (*propos*) piece of scandal. **~s** scandal (*NonC*), gossip (*NonC*); **ce sont des ~s!** that's just scandal! *ou* malicious gossip!; **arrête de dire des ~s** stop spreading scandal *ou* gossip.
médisant, e [medizɑ̃, ɑ̃t] 1 adj *paroles* slanderous. **les gens sont ~s** people say nasty things *ou* spread scandal. 2 nm,f scandalmonger, slanderer.
méditatif, -ive [meditatif, iv] adj *caractère* meditative, thoughtful; *air* musing, thoughtful.
méditation [meditasjɔ̃] nf (*pensée*) meditation; (*recueillement*) meditation (*NonC*). **après de longues ~s sur le sujet** after giving the subject much *ou* deep thought, after lengthy meditation on the subject; **il était plongé dans la ~** *ou* **une profonde ~** he was sunk in deep thought, he was deep in thought.
méditer [medite] 1 1 vt *pensée* to meditate on, ponder (over); *livre, projet, vengeance* to meditate. **~ de faire qch** to contemplate doing sth, plan to do sth. 2 vi to meditate. **~ sur qch** to ponder *ou* muse over sth.
Méditerranée [mediteʀane] nf: **la mer ~, la ~** the Mediterranean (Sea).
méditerranéen, -enne [mediteʀaneɛ̃, ɛn] 1 adj Mediterranean. 2 nm,f: **M~(ne)** (*gén*) inhabitant *ou* native of a Mediterranean country; (*en France*) (French) Southerner.
médium [medjɔm] nm (*Spiritisme*) medium; (*Mus*) middle register; (*Logique*) middle term.
médiumnique [medjɔmnik] adj *dons, pouvoir* of a medium.
médius [medjys] nm middle finger.
médoc [medɔk] nm Médoc (wine). (*région*) **le M~** the Médoc.
médullaire [medylɛʀ] adj medullary.
méduse [medyz] nf jellyfish. (*Myth*) **M~** Medusa.
méduser [medyze] 1 vt (*gén pass*) to dumbfound, paralyze. **je suis resté médusé par ce spectacle** I was rooted to the spot *ou* dumbfounded by this sight.
meeting [mitiŋ] nm (*Pol, Sport*) meeting. **~ aérien** *ou* **d'aviation** air show *ou* display; **~ d'athlétisme** athletics meeting.
méfait [mefɛ] nm a (*ravage*) (*gén pl*) *[temps, drogue]* damage (*NonC*), ravages; *[passion, épidémie]* ravages, damaging effect. **l'un des nombreux ~s de l'alcoolisme** one of the numerous damaging *ou* ill effects of alcoholism. b (*acte*) wrongdoing; (*hum*) misdeed.
méfiance [mefjɑ̃s] nf distrust, mistrust, suspicion. **avoir de la ~ envers qn** to mistrust *ou* distrust sb; **apaiser/éveiller la ~ de qn** to allay/arouse sb's suspicion(s); **être sans ~** (*avoir toute confiance*) to be completely trusting; (*ne rien soupçonner*) to be quite unsuspecting.
méfiant, e [mefjɑ̃, jɑ̃t] adj *personne* distrustful, mistrustful, suspicious. **air** *ou* **regard ~** distrustful *ou* mistrustful *ou* suspicious look, look of distrust *ou* mistrust *ou* suspicion.
méfier (se) [mefje] 7 vpr a **se ~ de qn/des conseils de qn** to mistrust *ou* distrust sb/sb's advice; **je me méfie de lui** I mistrust him, I do not trust him, I'm suspicious of him; **méfiez-vous de lui, il faut vous ~ de lui** do not trust him, beware of him, be on your guard against him; **je ne me méfie pas assez de mes réactions** I should be more wary of my reactions. b (*faire attention*) **se ~ de qch** to be careful about sth; **il faut vous ~** you must be careful, you've got to be on your guard; **méfie-toi de cette marche** mind (*Brit*) *ou* watch the step, look out for that step*; **méfie-toi, tu vas tomber** look out* *ou* be careful or you'll fall.
méforme [mefɔʀm] nf (*Sport*) lack of fitness, unfitness. **traverser une période de ~** to be (temporarily) off form.
méga [mega] préf mega. (*) **~-dissertation** essay and a half*; **un ~-cigare à la bouche** a whopping great cigar in his mouth‡; **recevoir une ~-dérouillée** to get a hell of a thrashing‡, get a thrashing and a half*; **~-entreprise** huge *ou* enormous company; **~-institution** huge *ou* enormous institution.
mégacycle [megasikl] nm megacycle.
mégahertz [megaɛʀts] nm megahertz.
mégalithe [megalit] nm megalith.
mégalithique [megalitik] adj megalithic.
mégalo* [megalo] adj, nmf abrév de **mégalomane**.
mégalomane [megalɔman] adj, nmf megalomaniac.
mégalomanie [megalɔmani] nf megalomania.
mégalopole [megalɔpɔl] nf megalopolis.
mégaoctet [megaɔktɛ] nm megabyte.
mégaphone† [megafɔn] nm (*porte-voix*) megaphone.
mégarde [megaʀd] nf: **par ~** (*accidentellement*) accidentally, by accident; (*par erreur*) by mistake, inadvertently; (*par négligence*) accidentally; **un livre que j'avais emporté par ~** a book which I had accidentally *ou* inadvertently taken away with me.
mégatonne [megatɔn] nf megaton.
mégère [meʒɛʀ] nf (*péj: femme*) shrew. (*Théât*) **la M~ apprivoisée** the Taming of the Shrew.
mégot* [mego] nm *[cigarette]* cigarette butt *ou* end, fag end‡ (*Brit*); *[cigare]* stub, butt.
mégotage* [megɔtaʒ] nm cheeseparing *ou* miserly attitude.
mégoter* [megɔte] 1 vi to skimp. **le patron mégote sur des détails et dépense des fortunes en repas d'affaires** the boss is cheeseparing over *ou* skimps over small items and spends a fortune on business lunches; **pour marier leur fille ils n'ont pas mégoté** they really went to town* for *ou* they spent a small fortune on their daughter's wedding.
méhari [meaʀi] nm fast dromedary, mehari.
méhariste [meaʀist] nm meharist, *rider of mehari or soldier of French Camel corps.*
meilleur, e [mɛjœʀ] 1 adj (*compar, superl de* **bon**) better. **le ~ des deux** the better of the two; **le ~ de tous, la ~e de toutes** the best of the lot; **c'est le ~ des hommes, c'est le ~ homme du monde** he is the best of men, he's the best man in the world; (*plus charitable*) **il est ~ que moi** he's a better person than I am; (*plus doué*) **il est ~ que moi (en)** he's better than I am (at); *[aliment]* **avoir ~ goût** to taste better; **ce gâteau est (bien) ~ avec du rhum** this cake tastes *ou* is (much) better with rum; **il est ~ chanteur que compositeur** he makes a better singer than (a) composer, he is better at singing than (at) composing; **de ~e qualité** of better *ou* higher quality; **tissu de la ~e qualité** best quality material; **les ~s spécialistes** the best *ou* top specialists; **son ~ ami** his best *ou* closest friend; **servir les ~s mets/vins** to serve the best *ou* finest dishes/wines; **information tirée des ~es sources** information from the most reliable sources; **~ marché** cheaper; **le ~ marché** the cheapest; (*Comm*) **acheter au ~ prix** to buy at the lowest price; **être en ~e santé** to be better, be in better health; (*Sport*) **faire un ~ temps au deuxième tour** to put up *ou* do a better time on the second lap; **partir de ~e heure** to leave earlier; **prendre (une) ~e tournure** to take a turn for the better; **~s vœux** best wishes; **ce sera pour des jours/des temps ~s** that will be for better days/happier times; **il n'y a rien de ~** there is nothing better, there's nothing to beat it.

2 adv: **il fait ~ qu'hier** it's better *ou* nicer (weather) than yesterday; **sentir ~** to smell better *ou* nicer.

3 nm,f (*celui qui est meilleur*) **le ~, la ~e** the best one; **ce ne sont pas toujours les ~s qui sont récompensés** it is not always the best (people) who win *ou* who reap the rewards; **que le ~ gagne** may the best man win; **j'en passe et des ~es** and that's not all – I could go on, and that's the least of them; **tu connais la ~e? il n'est même pas venu!** haven't you heard the best (bit) though? he didn't even come!; *voir* **raison**.

4 nm (*ce qui est meilleur*) **le ~** the best; **il a choisi le ~** he took the best (one); **pour le ~ et pour le pire** for better or for worse; **donner le ~ de soi-même** to give of one's best; **passer le ~ de sa vie à faire** to spend the best days *ou* years of one's life doing; **le ~ de notre pays fut tué pendant la guerre** the finest *ou* best men of our country were killed

during the war; (*Sport*) **prendre le ~ sur qn** to get the better of sb; **garder** *ou* **réserver le ~ pour la fin** to keep the best (bit *ou* part) till *ou* for the end; **et le ~ dans tout ça, c'est qu'il avait raison!** and the best bit about it all was that he was right!

méiose [mejoz] **nf** meiosis.

meistre [mɛstʀ] **nm** = **mestre**.

méjuger [meʒyʒe] ③ (*littér*) **1 vt** to misjudge. **2 vi: ~ de** to underrate, underestimate. **3 se méjuger vpr** to underestimate o.s.

Mékong [mekɔ̃g] **nm** Mekong.

mélamine [melamin] **nf** melamine.

mélaminé, e [melamine] **adj** melamine-coated.

mélancolie [melɑ̃kɔli] **nf** melancholy, gloom; (*Méd*) melancholia; *voir* **engendrer**.

mélancolique [melɑ̃kɔlik] **adj** *personne, paysage, musique* melancholy; (*Méd*) melancholic.

mélancoliquement [melɑ̃kɔlikmɑ̃] **adv** with a melancholy air, melancholically.

Mélanésie [melanezi] **nf** Melanesia.

mélanésien, -ienne [melanezjɛ̃, jɛn] **1 adj** Melanesian. **2 nm** (*Ling*) Melanesian. **3 nm,f: M~(ne)** Melanesian.

mélange [melɑ̃ʒ] **nm a** (*opération*) *[produits]* mixing; *[vins, tabacs]* blending. **faire un ~ de** *substances* to make a mixture of; *idées* to mix up; **quand on boit il ne faut pas faire de ~s** you shouldn't mix your drinks. **b** (*résultat*) (*gén, Chim, fig*) mixture; (*vins, tabacs, cafés*) blend. **~ détonant** explosive mixture; **~ réfrigérant** freezing mixture; (*Aut etc*) **~ pauvre/riche** weak/rich mixture; **joie sans ~** unalloyed *ou* unadulterated joy; (*littér*) **sans ~ de** free from, unadulterated by; (*Littérat*) **~s** miscellanies, miscellany.

mélanger [melɑ̃ʒe] ③ **1 vt** (*gén, Chim, Culin*) to mix; *couleurs, vins, parfums, tabacs* to blend; *dates, idées* to mix (up), muddle up, confuse; *documents* to mix up, muddle up. **~ du beurre et de la farine** to rub butter in with flour, mix butter and flour together; **tu mélanges tout!** you're getting it all mixed up! *ou* muddled up!; **un public très mélangé** a very varied *ou* mixed public; (*fig*) **il ne faut pas ~ les torchons et les serviettes** we (*ou* you *etc*) must divide *ou* separate the sheep from the goats.

2 se mélanger vpr *[produits]* to mix; *[vins]* to mix, blend. **les dates se mélangent dans ma tête** I'm confused about the dates, I've got the dates mixed up *ou* in a muddle; **se ~ les pieds*** *ou* **les pédales*** *ou* **les pinceaux*** *ou* **les crayons*** to get into a muddle.

mélangeur [melɑ̃ʒœʀ] **nm** (*appareil*) mixer; (*Plomberie*) mixer tap (*Brit*), mixing faucet (*US*); (*Ciné, Rad*) mixer.

mélanine [melanin] **nf** melanin.

mélanome [melanom] **nm** melanoma.

mélasse [melas] **nf** (*Culin*) treacle (*Brit*), molasses (*US*); (*péj: boue*) muck; (*brouillard*) murk. (*fig*) **quelle ~!** what a mess!; **être dans la ~*** (*avoir des ennuis*) to be in the soup*, be in a sticky situation*; (*être dans la misère*) to be down and out, be on one's beam ends* (*Brit*).

Melba [mɛlba] **adj inv** Melba. **pêche/ananas ~** peach/pineapple Melba.

Melbourne [mɛlbuʀn] **n** Melbourne.

mêlé, e [mele] (**ptp de mêler**) **1 adj a** *sentiments* mixed, mingled; *couleurs, tons* mingled, blending; *monde, société* mixed; *voir* **sang**.

b ~ de mingled with; **joie ~e de remords** pleasure mixed with *ou* tinged with remorse; **vin ~ d'eau** wine mixed with water.

2 mêlée nf a (*bataille*) mêlée; (*fig hum*) fray, kerfuffle* (*Brit*). **~e générale** free-for-all; **la ~e devint générale** it developed into a free-for-all, scuffles broke out all round *ou* on all sides; (*lit, fig*) **se jeter dans la ~e** to plunge into the fray; (*fig*) **rester au-dessus de** *ou* **à l'écart de la ~e** to stay *ou* keep aloof, keep out of the fray.

b (*Rugby*) scrum, scrummage. **~e ordonnée** set scrum; **~e ouverte** *ou* **spontanée** ruck, loose scrum; **dans la ~e ouverte** in the loose.

mêlé-cassе† [melekas] **nm** blackcurrant and brandy cocktail.

mêlée [mele] *voir* **mêlé**.

mêler [mele] ① **1 vt a** (*unir, mettre ensemble*) *substances* to mingle, mix together; *races* to mix; (*Vét*) to cross; (*Culin: amalgamer, mélanger*) to mix, blend; (*joindre, allier*) *traits de caractère* to combine, mingle. **les deux fleuves mêlent leurs eaux** the two rivers mingle their waters; **elles mêlèrent leurs larmes/leurs soupirs** their tears/their sighs mingled.

b (*mettre en désordre, embrouiller*) *papiers, dossiers* to muddle (up), mix up; (*battre*) *cartes* to shuffle. **~ la réalité et le rêve** to confuse reality and dream.

c ~ à *ou* **avec** (*ajouter*) to mix *ou* mingle with; **~ la douceur à la fermeté** to combine gentleness with firmness; **~ du feuillage à un bouquet** to put some greenery in with a bouquet; **un récit mêlé de détails comiques** a story interspersed with comic(al) details.

d (*impliquer*) **~ à** to involve in; (*fig*) **~ qn à une affaire** to involve sb in some business, get sb mixed up *ou* involved in an affair; **j'y ai été mêlé contre mon gré** I was dragged into it against my wishes, I got mixed up *ou* involved in it against my will; **~ qn à la conversation** to bring *ou* draw sb into the conversation.

2 se mêler vpr a to mix, mingle, combine. **ces deux races ne se mêlent jamais** these two races never mix.

b se ~ à (*se joindre à*) to join; (*s'associer à*) to mix with; *[cris, sentiments]* to mingle with; **il se mêla à la foule** he joined the crowd, he mingled with the crowd; **il ne se mêle jamais aux autres enfants** he never mixes with other children; **se ~ à une querelle** to get mixed up *ou* involved in a quarrel; **il se mêlait à toutes les manifestations** he got involved *ou* took part in all the demonstrations; **des rires se mêlaient aux applaudissements** there was laughter mingled with the applause; **se ~ à la conversation** to join in *ou* come in on* the conversation.

c se ~ à *ou* **de** (*s'occuper de*) to meddle with, get mixed up in; **se ~ des affaires des autres** to meddle *ou* interfere in other people's business *ou* affairs; **ne vous mêlez pas d'intervenir!** don't you take it into your head to interfere!, just you keep out of it!; **mêle-toi de ce qui te regarde!** *ou* **de tes affaires!** *ou* **de tes oignons!*** mind your own business!; (*iro*) **de quoi je me mêle!*** what business is it of yours?, what's it got to do with you?; **se ~ de faire qch** to take it upon o.s. to do sth, make it one's business to do sth; **voilà qu'il se mêle de nous donner des conseils!** who is he to give us advice!, look at him butting in with his advice!

mélèze [melɛz] **nm** larch.

méli-mélo*, **pl mélis-mélos** [melimelo] **nm** *[situation]* muddle; *[objets]* jumble. **cette affaire est un véritable ~!** what a terrible muddle this business is!

mélisse [melis] **nf** (*Bot*) balm.

mélo* [melo] **1 adj** *film, roman* (**abrév de mélodramatique**) soppy*, sentimental. **feuilleton ~** (*gén*) sentimental serial; (*TV*) soap (opera). **2 nm abrév de mélodrame**.

mélodie [melɔdi] **nf a** (*motif, chanson*) melody, tune. **les ~s de Debussy** Debussy's melodies *ou* songs; **une petite ~ entendue à la radio** a little tune heard on the radio. **b** (*qualité*) melodiousness.

mélodieusement [melɔdjøzmɑ̃] **adv** melodiously, tunefully.

mélodieux, -ieuse [melɔdjø, jøz] **adj** melodious, tuneful.

mélodique [melɔdik] **adj** melodic.

mélodramatique [melɔdʀamatik] **adj** (*Littérat, péj*) melodramatic.

mélodrame [melɔdʀam] **nm** (*Littérat, péj*) melodrama.

mélomane [melɔman] **1 adj** music-loving (*épith*), keen on music (*attrib*). **2 nmf** music lover.

melon [m(ə)lɔ̃] **nm a** (*Bot*) melon. **~ d'Espagne** ≈ honeydew melon; **~ (cantaloup)** cantaloupe melon; **~ d'eau** watermelon. **b** (*Habillement*) **(chapeau) ~** bowler (hat).

mélopée [melɔpe] **nf a** (*gén: chant monotone*) monotonous chant, threnody (*littér*). **b** (*Hist Mus*) recitative.

membrane [mɑ̃bʀan] **nf** membrane.

membraneux, -euse [mɑ̃bʀanø, øz] **adj** membran(e)ous.

membre [mɑ̃bʀ] **nm a** (*Anat, Zool*) limb. **~ inférieur/supérieur/antérieur/postérieur** lower/upper/fore/rear limb; **~ (viril)** male member *ou* organ.

b *[famille, groupe, société savante]* member; *[académie]* fellow. **~ fondateur** founder member; **~ perpétuel** life member; **~ actif/associé** active/associate member; **un ~ de la société/du public** a member of society/of the public; **être ~ de** to be a member of; **devenir ~ d'un club** to become a member of a club, join a club; **ce club a 300 ~s** this club has a membership of 300 *ou* has 300 members; **pays/États ~s (de la Communauté)** member countries/states (of the Community).

c (*Math*) member. **premier/second ~** left-hand/right-hand member.

d (*Ling*) **~ de phrase** (sentence) member.

e (*Archit*) member.

f (*Naut*) timber, rib.

membré, e [mɑ̃bʀe] **adj** limbed. **bien/mal ~** strong-/weak-limbed.

membru, e [mɑ̃bʀy] **adj** (*littér*) strong-limbed.

membrure [mɑ̃bʀyʀ] **nf** (*Anat*) limbs, build; (*Naut*) rib; (*collectif*) frame. **homme à la ~ puissante** strong-limbed *ou* powerfully built man.

même [mɛm] **1 adj a** (*identique, semblable: avant n*) same, identical. **des bijoux de ~ valeur** jewels of equal *ou* of the same value; **ils ont la ~ taille/la ~ couleur, ils sont de ~ taille/de ~ couleur** they are the same size/the same colour; **j'ai exactement la ~ robe qu'hier** I am wearing the very same dress I wore yesterday *ou* exactly the same dress as yesterday; **nous sommes du ~ avis** we are of the same mind *ou* opinion, we agree; **ils ont la ~ voiture que nous** they have the same car as we have *ou* as us*; **que vous veniez ou non c'est la ~ chose** whether you come or not it's all one, it makes no odds whether you come or not; **c'est toujours la ~ chose!** it's always the same (old story)!; (*c'est équivalent*) **c'est la ~ chose** it's six of one and half a dozen of the other*; **arriver en ~ temps (que)** to arrive at the same time (as); **en ~ temps qu'il le faisait l'autre s'approchait** as *ou* while he was doing it the other drew nearer.

b (*après n ou pron*) very, actual. **ce sont ses paroles ~s** those are his very *ou* actual words; **il est la générosité/gentillesse ~** he is generosity/kindness itself, he is the (very) soul of generosity/kindness; **il est la méchanceté/bêtise ~** he's wickedness/stupidity itself; **la grande maison, celle-là ~ que vous avez visitée** the big house, the very one you visited *ou* precisely the one you visited.

c moi-~ myself; **toi-~** yourself; **lui-~** himself; **elle-~** herself; **nous-~s** ourselves; **vous-~** yourself; **vous-~s** yourselves; **eux-** *ou* **elles-~s** themselves; **on est soi-~ conscient de ses propres erreurs** one is aware (oneself) of one's own mistakes; **nous devons y aller nous-~s** we must go ourselves; **s'apitoyer sur soi-~** to feel sorry for oneself; **tu n'as aucune confiance en toi-~** you have no confidence in yourself; **c'est lui-~ qui l'a dit, il l'a dit lui-~** he said it himself, he himself said it; **au plus profond d'eux-~s/de nous-~s** in their/our heart of hearts; **elle fait ses habits elle-~** she makes her own clothes, she makes her clothes herself; **c'est ce que je me dis en** *ou* **à moi-~** that's what I tell myself (inwardly), that's what I think to myself; **elle se disait en elle-~ que ...** she thought to herself that ..., she thought privately *ou* inwardly that ...; **faire qch de soi-~** to do sth on one's own initiative *ou* off one's own bat* (*Brit*); **faire qch (par) soi-~** to do sth (by) oneself.

2 **pron indéf** (*avec le, la, les*) **ce n'est pas le ~** it's not the same (one); **la réaction n'a pas été la ~ qu'à Paris** the reaction was not the same as in Paris; **elle est bien toujours la ~!** she's just the same as ever!; (*fig*) **ce sont toujours les ~s qui se font prendre** it's always the same ones who catch it*; *voir* **pareil, revenir.**

3 **adv** a even. **ils sont tous sortis, ~ les enfants** they are all out, even the children; **il n'a ~ pas de quoi écrire** *ou* **pas ~ de quoi écrire** he hasn't even got anything to write with; **il est intéressant et ~ amusant** he is interesting and amusing too *ou* besides; **elle ne me parle ~ plus** she no longer even speaks to me, she doesn't even speak to me anymore; **~ lui ne sait pas** even he doesn't know; **personne ne sait, ~ pas lui** nobody knows, not even him; **~ si** even if, even though; **c'est vrai, ~ que je peux le prouver!*** it's true, and what's more I can prove it!

b (*précisément*) **aujourd'hui ~** this very day; **ici ~** in this very place, on this very spot; **c'est celui-là ~ qui** he's the very one who; **c'est cela ~** that's just *ou* exactly it.

c (*loc*) **boire à ~ la bouteille** to drink (straight) from the bottle; **coucher à ~ le sol** to lie on the bare ground; **à ~ la peau** next to the skin; **mettre qn à ~ de faire** to enable sb to do; **être à ~ de faire** to be able *ou* to be in a position to do; **je ne suis pas à ~ de juger** I am in no position to judge; **il fera de ~** he'll do the same, he'll do likewise, he'll follow suit; **vous le détestez? moi de ~** you hate him? so do I *ou* I do too *ou* me too* *ou* same here*; **de ~ qu'il nous a dit que ...** just as he told us that ...; **il en est** *ou* **il en va de ~ pour moi** it's the same for me, same here*; **quand ~, tout de ~** all the same, for all that, even so; **tout de ~** *ou* **quand ~, il aurait pu nous prévenir** all the same *ou* even so he might have warned us; **il exagère tout de ~!** well really he's going too far!; **il a tout de ~ réussi à s'échapper** he managed to escape nevertheless *ou* all the same.

mémé* [meme] **nf** (*langage enfantin: grand-mère*) gran(ny)*, grandma; (*péj: vieille dame*) old girl*, old dear*.

mêmement [mɛmmɑ̃] **adv** (*frm*) likewise.

mémento [memɛ̃to] **nm** (*agenda*) appointments diary *ou* book, engagement diary; (*Scol: aide-mémoire*) summary. (*Rel*) **~ des vivants/des morts** prayers for the living/the dead; **le ~ de l'homme d'affaires/de l'étudiant** the businessman's/student's handbook *ou* guide.

mémère* [memɛʀ] **nf** (*langage enfantin*) granny*, grandma; (*péj: vieille dame*) old girl* *ou* dear*. (*hum*) **le petit chien à sa ~** mummy's little doggy (*hum*); **elle fait ~ avec ce chapeau** she looks ancient in that hat*.

mémo* [memo] **nm** (**abrév de mémorandum**) memo.

mémoire[1] [memwaʀ] **nf** a (*Psych*) memory. **citer de ~** to quote from memory; **de ~ d'homme** in living memory; **de ~ de Parisien, on n'avait jamais vu ça!** no one could remember such a thing happening in Paris before; **pour ~** (*gén*) as a matter of interest; (*Comm*) for the record; **~ associative** associative memory; **~ auditive/visuelle/olfactive** aural/visual/olfactory memory; *voir* **effort, rafraîchir, trou.**

b (*loc*) **avoir la ~ des noms** to have a good memory for names; **je n'ai pas la ~ des dates** I have no memory for dates, I can never remember dates; **si j'ai bonne ~** if I remember rightly, if my memory serves me right; **avoir la ~ courte** to have a short memory; **avoir une ~ d'éléphant** to have a memory like an elephant('s); **j'ai gardé (la) ~ de cette conversation** I remember *ou* recall this conversation, this conversation remains in my memory; **perdre la ~** to lose one's memory; **chercher un nom dans sa ~** to try to recall a name, rack one's brains to remember a name; **ça me revient en ~** it comes back to me; **il me l'a remis en ~** he reminded me of it, he brought it back to me; **son nom restera (gravé) dans notre ~** his name will remain (engraved) in our memories.

c (*réputation*) memory, good name; (*renommée*) memory, fame, renown. **soldat de glorieuse ~** soldier of blessed memory; **de sinistre ~** of evil memory, remembered with fear *ou* horror; (*hum*) fearful, ghastly; **salir la ~ de qn** to sully the memory of sb; **à la ~ de** in memory of, to the memory of.

d (*Ordin*) memory, store, storage. **~ externe** external storage; **~ vive** RAM, random access memory; **~ morte** ROM, read only memory; **~ volatile** volatile memory; **~ de masse, ~ auxiliaire** mass memory; **~ centrale** *ou* **principale** main memory; **avoir 512 K de ~ centrale** to have 512 K of main memory; **~-tampon** buffer memory; **capacité de ~** storage capacity, memory size; **machine à écrire à ~** memory typewriter.

mémoire[2] [memwaʀ] **nm** (*requête*) memorandum; (*rapport*) report; (*exposé*) dissertation, paper; (*facture*) bill; (*Jur*) statement of case. (*souvenirs*) **~s** memoirs; (*hum*) **tu écris tes ~s?** are you writing your life story? (*hum*); (*Univ*) **~ de maîtrise** dissertation (*Brit*), master's paper *ou* essay *ou* thesis (*US*).

mémorable [memɔʀabl] **adj** memorable, unforgettable.

mémorablement [memɔʀabləmɑ̃] **adv** memorably.

mémorandum [memɔʀɑ̃dɔm] **nm** (*Pol*) memorandum; (*Comm*) order sheet, memorandum; (*carnet*) notebook, memo book.

mémorial, pl -iaux [memɔʀjal, jo] **nm** (*Archit*) memorial. (*Littérat*) **M~** Chronicles.

mémorialiste [memɔʀjalist] **nmf** memorialist, writer of memoirs.

mémorisation [memɔʀizasjɔ̃] **nf** memorization, memorizing; (*Ordin*) storage.

mémoriser [memɔʀize] [1] **vt** to memorize, commit to memory; (*Ordin*) to store.

menaçant, e [mənasɑ̃, ɑ̃t] **adj** *geste, paroles, foule, orage* threatening, menacing; *regard, ciel* lowering (*épith*), threatening, menacing.

menace [mənas] **nf** a (*intimidation*) threat. **il eut un geste de ~** he made a threatening gesture; **il eut des paroles de ~** he said some threatening words; **par/sous la ~** by/under threat; **~ en l'air** idle threat; **il y a des ~s de grève** there's a threat of strike action. b (*danger*) imminent *ou* impending danger *ou* threat. **~ d'épidémie** impending epidemic, threat of an epidemic. c (*Jur*) **~s** intimidation, threats; **recevoir des ~s de mort** to receive death threats *ou* threats on one's life.

menacer [mənase] [3] **vt** a to threaten, menace (*gén pass*). **~ qn de mort/d'un revolver** to threaten sb with death/with a gun; **~ qn du poing/de sa canne** to shake one's fist/stick at sb; **~ de faire qch** to threaten to do sth; **ses jours sont menacés** his life is threatened *ou* in danger; **la guerre menaçait le pays** the country was threatened *ou* menaced by *ou* with war; **espèces menacées** threatened *ou* endangered species; **la paix est menacée** peace is endangered.

b (*fig*) **orage qui menace d'éclater** storm which is about to break *ou* is threatening to break; **la pluie menace** it looks like rain, it is threatening rain; **le temps menace** the weather looks threatening; **chaise qui menace de se casser** chair which is showing signs of *ou* looks like breaking (*Brit*) *ou* looks like it will break; **pluie/discours qui menace de durer** rain/speech which threatens to last some time; **la maison menace ruine** the house is in danger of falling down.

ménage [menaʒ] **nm** a (*entretien d'une maison*) housekeeping; (*nettoyage*) housework. **les soins du ~** the housework, the household duties; **s'occuper de son ~, tenir son ~** to look after one's house, keep house; **faire du ~** to do some housework *ou* cleaning; **faire le ~** (*lit: nettoyer*) to do the housework; (*fig: licencier*) to get rid of the deadwood; (*fig: Pol*) to get rid of the lame ducks; (*fig: Sport*) to sort out the opposition; **faire le ~ à fond** to clean the house from top to bottom, do the housework thoroughly; **faire des ~s** to go out charring (*Brit*), work as a cleaning woman; (*Can*) **le grand ~** the spring-cleaning; *voir* **femme, monter[2].**

b (*couple, communauté familiale*) married couple, household; (*Écon*) household. **~ sans enfant** childless couple; **~ à trois** ménage à trois; **jeune/vieux ~** young/old couple; **ils font un gentil petit ~** they make a nice (young) couple; **cela ne va pas dans le ~** they don't get on* in that household, their marriage is a bit shaky *ou* isn't really working; **être heureux/malheureux en ~** to have a happy/an unhappy married life; **se mettre en ~ avec qn** to set up house with sb, move in with sb*; **querelles/scènes de ~** domestic quarrels/rows; **il lui a fait une scène de ~** he had a row* with her; (*fig*) **faire bon/mauvais ~ avec qn** to get on well/badly with sb, hit it off/not hit it off with sb*; **notre chat et la perruche font très bon ~** our cat and the budgie get on famously *ou* like a house on fire*; *voir* **paix.**

c (*†: ordinaire*) **de ~** *chocolat* for ordinary *ou* everyday consumption; *pain* homemade.

ménagement [menaʒmɑ̃] **nm** a (*douceur*) care; (*attention*) attention. **traiter qn avec ~** to treat sb considerately *ou* tactfully; (*brutaliser*) **traiter qn sans ~** to manhandle sb; **il les a congédiés sans ~** he dismissed them without further ado *ou* with scant ceremony; **annoncer qch sans ~ à qn** to break the news of sth bluntly to sb, tell sb sth bluntly; **il lui annonça la nouvelle avec ~** he broke the news to her gently *ou* cautiously; **elle a besoin de ~ car elle est encore très faible** being still very weak she needs care and attention. b (*égards*) **~s** (respectful) consideration (*NonC*) *ou* attention.

ménager[1], -ère [menaʒe, ɛʀ] 1 **adj** *ustensiles, appareils* household (*épith*), domestic (*épith*). **travaux ~s** housework, domestic chores; **école/collège d'enseignement ~** school/college of domestic science; *voir* **art, eau, ordure.** 2 **ménagère nf** a (*femme d'intérieur*) housewife. b (*couverts*) canteen of cutlery.

ménager[2] [menaʒe] [3] **vt** a (*traiter avec prudence*) *personne puissante, adversaire* to handle carefully, treat tactfully *ou* considerately, humour; *sentiments, susceptibilité* to spare, show consideration for. **elle est très sensible, il faut la ~** she is very sensitive, you must treat her gently; **~ les deux partis** to humour both parties; (*fig*) **~ la chèvre et le chou** (*rester neutre*) to sit on the fence; (*être conciliant*) to keep both parties sweet*.

b (*utiliser avec économie ou modération*) *réserves* to use carefully *ou* sparingly; *vêtement* to use carefully, treat with care; *argent, temps* to be sparing in the use of, use carefully, economize; *expressions* to moderate, tone down. **c'est un homme qui ménage ses paroles** he is a man of few words; ~ **ses forces** to conserve one's strength; ~ **sa santé** to take great care of one's health, look after o.s.; **il faut** *ou* **vous devriez vous ~ un peu** you should take things easy, you should try not to overtax yourself; **l'athlète se ménage pour la finale** the athlete is conserving his energy *ou* is saving himself for the final; **il n'a pas ménagé ses efforts** he spared no effort; **nous n'avons rien ménagé pour vous plaire** we have spared no pains to please you; **il ne lui a pas ménagé les reproches** he didn't spare him his complaints.

c (*préparer*) *entretien, rencontre* to arrange, organize, bring about; *transition* to contrive, bring about. ~ **l'avenir** to prepare for the future; **il nous ménage une surprise** he has a surprise in store for us; **se ~ une revanche** to plan one's revenge.

d (*disposer, pratiquer*) *porte, fenêtre* to put in; *chemin* to cut. ~ **un espace entre** to make a space between; ~ **une place pour** to make room for; (*fig*) **se ~ une porte de sortie** to leave o.s. a way out *ou* a loophole.

ménagère [menaʒɛʀ] *voir* **ménager**[1].

ménagerie [menaʒʀi] **nf** (*lit*) menagerie; (* *fig*) zoo.

mendélévium [mɛ̃delevjɔm] **nm** mendelevium.

mendiant, e [mɑ̃djɑ̃, jɑ̃t] **nm,f** beggar, mendicant (†, *littér*). (*Culin*) ~, **(quatre) ~s** mixed dried fruit(s) and nuts (*raisins, hazelnuts, figs, almonds*); *voir* **frère, ordre**[1].

mendicité [mɑ̃disite] **nf** begging. **arrêter qn pour ~** to arrest sb for begging; **être réduit à la ~** to be reduced to beggary *ou* begging; **la ~ est interdite** it is forbidden to beg, no begging allowed.

mendier [mɑ̃dje] 7 1 **vt** *argent, nourriture, caresse* to beg (for); (*Pol*) *voix* to solicit, canvass. ~ **qch à qn** to beg sb for sth, beg sth from sb; ~ **des compliments** to fish for compliments. 2 **vi** to beg (for alms).

mendigot, e* [mɑ̃digo, ɔt] **nm,f** (*péj*) beggar.

mendigoter* [mɑ̃digɔte] 1 **vti** to beg. **toujours à ~ (quelque chose)** always begging (for something).

meneau, **pl ~x** [məno] **nm** (*horizontal*) transom; (*vertical*) mullion; *voir* **fenêtre.**

menées [məne] **nfpl** (*machinations*) intrigues, manoeuvres, machinations. **déjouer les ~ de qn** to foil sb's manoeuvres *ou* little game*; ~ **subversives** subversive activities.

Ménélas [menelas] **nm** Menelaus.

mener [m(ə)ne] 5 **vt** a (*conduire*) *personne* to take, lead; (*en voiture*) to drive, take (*à* to, *dans* into). ~ **un enfant à l'école/chez le médecin** to take a child to school/to the doctor; ~ **la voiture au garage** to take the car to the garage; **mène ton ami à sa chambre** show *ou* take *ou* see your friend to his room; ~ **promener le chien** to take the dog for a walk; (*fig*) ~ **qn en bateau*** to take sb for a ride*, lead sb up the garden path*, have sb on*.

b *[véhicule] personne* to take; *[route etc]* to lead, go, take; *[profession, action etc]* to lead, get (*à* to, *dans* into). **c'est le chemin qui mène à la mer** this is the path (leading) to the sea; **le car vous mène à Chartres en 2 heures** the bus will take *ou* get you to Chartres in 2 hours; **cette route vous mène à Chartres** this road will take you to Chartres, you'll get to Chartres on this road; **où tout cela va-t-il nous ~?** where's all this going to get us?, where does all this lead us?; **cela ne (nous) mène à rien** this won't get us anywhere, this will get us nowhere; **ces études les mènent à de beaux postes** this training will get them good jobs; **le journalisme mène à tout** all roads are open to you in journalism; **de telles infractions pourraient le ~ loin** offences such as these could get him into trouble *ou* into deep water; ~ **qn à faire ...** to lead sb to do ...; *voir* **tout.**

c (*commander*) *personne, cortège* to lead; *pays* to run, rule; *entreprise* to manage, run; *navire* to command. **il sait ~ les hommes** he knows how to lead men, he is a good leader; ~ **qn par le bout du nez** to lead sb by the nose; **il est mené par le bout du nez par sa femme** his wife has got him on a string; ~ **qn à la baguette** *ou* **au doigt et à l'œil** to have sb under one's thumb; **elle se laisse ~ par son frère** she lets herself be led *ou* (*péj*) bossed about* by her brother; **l'argent mène le monde** money rules the world, money makes the world go round; ~ **le jeu** *ou* **la danse** to call the tune, say what goes*; ~ **les débats** to chair the discussion.

d (*Sport, gén: être en tête*) to lead; (*emploi absolu*) to lead, be in the lead. **il mène par 3 jeux à 1** he is leading by 3 games to 1; **la France mène (l'Écosse par 2 buts à 1)** France is in the lead (by 2 goals to 1 against Scotland), France is leading (Scotland by 2 goals to 1).

e (*orienter*) *vie* to lead, live; *négociations, lutte, conversation* to carry on; *enquête* to carry out, conduct; *affaires* to manage, run; *carrière* to handle, manage. ~ **les choses rondement** to manage things efficiently, make short work of things; ~ **qch à bien** *ou* **à bonne fin** *ou* **à terme** to see sth through, carry sth through to a successful conclusion; (*fig*) **il mène bien sa barque** he manages his affairs efficiently; **il mène 2 affaires de front** he runs *ou* manages 2 businesses at once; ~ **la vie dure à qn** to rule sb with an iron hand, keep a firm hand on sb; **il n'en menait pas large** his heart was in his boots; ~ **grand bruit** *ou* **tapage autour d'une affaire** to give an affair a lot of publicity, make a great hue and cry about an affair.

f (*Math*) ~ **une parallèle à une droite** to draw a line parallel to a straight line.

ménestrel [menɛstʀɛl] **nm** minstrel.

ménétrier† [menetʀije] **nm** (strolling) fiddler.

meneur, -euse [mənœʀ, øz] **nm,f** (*chef*) (ring) leader; (*agitateur*) agitator. ~ **d'hommes** born leader, popular leader; ~ **de jeu** *[spectacles, variétés]* compère (*Brit*), master of ceremonies; *[jeux-concours]* quizmaster; (*Sport*) team leader; (*Music-hall*) **~euse de revue** captain (*of chorus girls*).

menhir [meniʀ] **nm** menhir, standing stone.

méninge [menɛ̃ʒ] **nf** a (*) **~s** brain; **se creuser les ~s** to rack one's brains; **tu ne t'es pas fatigué les ~s!** you didn't strain yourself!*, you didn't overtax your brain! b (*Méd*) meninx. **~s** meninges.

méningé, e [menɛ̃ʒe] **adj** meningeal.

méningite [menɛ̃ʒit] **nf** meningitis. **faire une ~** to have meningitis; **ce n'est pas lui qui attrapera une ~*!** he's not one to strain himself!* (*iro*), there's no fear of his getting brain fever!

ménisque [menisk] **nm** (*Anat, Opt, Phys*) meniscus; (*Bijouterie*) *crescent-shaped jewel.*

ménopause [menopoz] **nf** menopause.

ménopausée [menopoze] 1 **adj f** post-menopausal. 2 **nf** post-menopausal woman, woman past the menopause.

ménopausique [menɔpozik] **adj** *troubles* menopausal.

menotte [mənɔt] **nf** a **~s** handcuffs; **mettre** *ou* **passer les ~s à qn** to handcuff sb. b (*langage enfantin*) little *ou* tiny hand, handy (*langage enfantin*).

mensonge [mɑ̃sɔ̃ʒ] **nm** a (*contre-vérité*) lie, fib*, falsehood (*frm*), untruth. **faire** *ou* **dire un ~** to tell a lie; **pieux ~** white lie; (*hum*) **c'est vrai, ce ~?** sure you're telling the truth?; **tout ça, c'est des ~s*** it's all a pack of lies; *voir* **détecteur.** b **le ~** lying, untruthfulness; **je hais le ~** I hate untruthfulness *ou* lies; **il vit dans le ~** his whole life is a lie. c (*littér: illusion*) illusion.

mensonger, -ère [mɑ̃sɔ̃ʒe, ɛʀ] **adj** (*faux*) *rapport, nouvelle* untrue, false; *promesse* deceitful, false; (*littér: trompeur*) *bonheur* illusory, delusive, deceptive.

mensongèrement [mɑ̃sɔ̃ʒɛʀmɑ̃] **adv** untruthfully, falsely, deceitfully.

menstruation [mɑ̃stʀyasjɔ̃] **nf** menstruation.

menstruel, -elle [mɑ̃stʀyɛl] **adj** menstrual.

menstrues [mɑ̃stʀy] **nfpl** menses.

mensualisation [mɑ̃sɥalizasjɔ̃] **nf** *[salaires, impôts, factures]* monthly payment. **effectuer la ~ des salaires** to put workers on monthly salaries, pay salaries monthly; **la ~ de l'impôt** the monthly payment of tax.

mensualiser [mɑ̃sɥalize] 1 **vt** *salaires, employés, impôts, factures* to pay on a monthly basis. **être mensualisé** *[salaire, employé]* to be paid monthly *ou* on a monthly basis; *[employé]* to be on a monthly salary; *[contribuable]* to pay income tax monthly, ≃ be on P.A.Y.E. (*Brit*).

mensualité [mɑ̃sɥalite] **nf** (*traite*) monthly payment *ou* instalment; (*salaire*) monthly salary.

mensuel, -elle [mɑ̃sɥɛl] 1 **adj** monthly. 2 **nm,f** employee paid by the month. 3 **nm** (*Presse*) monthly (magazine).

mensuellement [mɑ̃sɥɛlmɑ̃] **adv** *payer* monthly, every month. **être payé ~** to be paid monthly *ou* every month.

mensuration [mɑ̃syʀasjɔ̃] **nf** (*mesure, calcul*) mensuration. (*mesures*) **~s** measurements.

mental, e, **mpl -aux** [mɑ̃tal, o] **adj** *maladie, âge, processus* mental; *voir* **calcul, malade.**

mentalement [mɑ̃talmɑ̃] **adv** mentally.

mentalité [mɑ̃talite] **nf** mentality. (*iro*) **quelle ~!, jolie ~!** what an attitude of mind!, nice mind you've (*ou* he's *etc*) got!* (*iro*); **avoir une sale ~*** to be a nasty piece of work*, be evil-minded; **avoir une ~ de fonctionnaire** to think like a civil servant, have the mind *ou* mentality of a civil servant.

menterie [mɑ̃tʀi] **nf** (†: *mensonge*) untruth, falsehood. (*hum*) **ce sont des ~s** it's all a pack of lies.

menteur, -euse [mɑ̃tœʀ, øz] 1 **adj** *proverbe* fallacious, false; *rêve, espoir* delusive, illusory, false; *enfant* untruthful, lying. **il est très ~** he is a great liar. 2 **nm,f** liar, fibber*. 3 **nm** (*Cartes*) cheat.

menthe [mɑ̃t] **nf** a (*Bot*) mint. ~ **poivrée** peppermint; ~ **verte** spearmint, garden mint; **de ~, à la ~** mint (*épith*); *voir* **alcool, pastille, thé.** b (*boisson*) peppermint cordial. **une ~ à l'eau** a glass of peppermint cordial; *voir* **diabolo.**

menthol [mɑ̃tɔl] **nm** menthol.

mentholé, e [mɑ̃tɔle] **adj** mentholated, menthol (*épith*).

mention [mɑ̃sjɔ̃] **nf** a (*note brève*) mention. **faire ~ de** to mention, make mention of; **il n'y a pas ~ de son nom dans la liste** there's no reference to his name on the list, he isn't mentioned on the list; **faire l'objet d'une ~** to be mentioned.

b (*annotation*) note, comment. **le paquet est revenu avec la ~ "adresse inconnue"** the parcel was returned marked "address unknown"; (*Admin*) **"rayer la ~ inutile"** "delete as appropriate".

c (*Scol*) ~ **passable/assez bien/bien/très bien** ≃ grade D/C/B/A pass; (*Univ: licence, maîtrise*) 3rd class/lower 2nd class/upper 2nd class/1st class Honours; (*doctorat*) ~ **très honorable** (with) distinction; (*Scol*) **être reçu avec ~ bien/très bien** ≃ to get a B/an A.

mentionner [mɑ̃sjɔne] 1 **vt** to mention. **la personne mentionnée ci-dessus** the above-mentioned person.

mentir [mɑ̃tiʀ] 16 1 vi a *[personne]* to lie (*à qn* to sb, *sur* about); *[photo, apparences]* to be deceptive. **tu mens!** you're a liar!, you're lying!; ~ **effrontément** to lie boldly, be a barefaced liar; **je t'ai menti** I lied to you, I told you a lie; **sans** ~ (quite) honestly; **il ment comme il respire** *ou* **comme un arracheur de dents** he's a compulsive liar, he lies in *ou* through his teeth*; (*Prov*) **a beau** ~ **qui vient de loin** long ways long lies (*Prov*).

b **faire** ~: **ne me fais pas** ~! don't prove me wrong!; **faire** ~ **le proverbe** to give the lie to the proverb, disprove the proverb; *voir* **bon**[1].

c (*littér*) ~ **à** (*manquer à*) to betray; (*démentir*) to belie; **il ment à sa réputation** he belies *ou* does not live up to his reputation; (†, *hum*) **vous en avez menti** you told an untruth.

2 **se mentir** vpr: **se** ~ **à soi-même** to fool o.s.; **il se ment à lui-même** he's not being honest with himself, he's fooling himself.

menton [mɑ̃tɔ̃] nm chin. ~ **en galoche** protruding *ou* jutting chin; ~ **fuyant** receding chin, weak chin; **double/triple** ~ double/treble chin.

mentonnière [mɑ̃tɔnjɛʀ] nf *[coiffure]* (chin) strap; (*Hist*) *[casque]* chin piece; (*Mus*) chin rest; (*Méd*) chin bandage.

mentor [mɛ̃tɔʀ] nm (*littér*) mentor.

menu[1] [məny] nm a (*repas*) meal; (*carte*) menu. **faites votre** ~ **à l'avance** plan your meal in advance; **quel est le** *ou* **qu'y a-t-il au** ~? what's on the menu?; **vous prenez le** ~ **(à prix fixe) ou la carte?** are you having the set menu or the (menu) à la carte?; ~ **du jour** today's menu; ~ **touristique** economy(-price) *ou* standard menu; ~ **gastronomique** gourmet's menu. b (*Ordin*) menu.

menu[2], **e** [məny] 1 adj a (*fin*) *doigt, tige, taille* slender, slim; *personne* slim, slight; *herbe* fine; *écriture, pas* small, tiny; *voix* thin. **en** ~**s morceaux** in tiny pieces.

b (*peu important*) *difficultés, incidents, préoccupations* minor, petty, trifling. **dire/raconter dans les** ~**s détails** to tell/relate in minute detail; ~**s frais** incidental *ou* minor expenses; (*lit, fig*) ~ **fretin** small fry; ~ **gibier** small game; ~**e monnaie** small *ou* loose change; ~ **peuple** humble folk; (*Hist*) **M**~**s Plaisirs** (royal) entertainment (*NonC*); **se réserver de l'argent pour ses** ~**s plaisirs** to keep some money by for (one's) amusements; ~**s propos** small talk (*NonC*).

c (*loc*) **par le** ~ in detail; **raconter qch par le** ~ to relate sth in great detail; **on fit par le** ~ **la liste des fournitures** they made a detailed list of the supplies.

2 adv *couper, hacher, piler* fine. **écrire** ~ to write small.

menuet [mənɥɛ] nm minuet.

menuiserie [mənɥizʀi] nf a (*métier*) joinery, carpentry. ~ **d'art** cabinetwork; **spécialiste en** ~ **métallique** specialist in metal (door and window *etc*) fittings; (*passe-temps*) **faire de la** ~ to do woodwork *ou* carpentry *ou* joinery. b (*atelier*) joiner's workshop. c (*ouvrage*) (piece of) woodwork (*NonC*) *ou* joinery (*NonC*) *ou* carpentry (*NonC*).

menuisier [mənɥizje] nm *[meubles]* joiner; *[bâtiment]* carpenter. ~ **d'art** cabinet-maker.

Méphistophélès [mefistɔfelɛs] nm Mephistopheles.

méphistophélique [mefistɔfelik] adj Mephistophelean.

méphitique [mefitik] adj noxious, noisome†, mephitic.

méphitisme [mefitism] nm sulphurous (air) pollution.

méplat [mepla] nm (*Anat, Archit*) plane.

méprendre (se) [mepʀɑ̃dʀ] 58 vpr (*littér*) to make a mistake, be mistaken (*sur* about). **se** ~ **sur qn** to misjudge sb, be mistaken about sb; **se** ~ **sur qch** to make a mistake about sth, misunderstand sth; **ils se ressemblent tellement que c'est à s'y** ~ *ou* **qu'on pourrait s'y** ~ they are so alike that you can't tell them apart *ou* that it's difficult to tell which is which.

mépris [mepʀi] nm a (*mésestime*) contempt, scorn. **avoir** *ou* **éprouver du** ~ **pour qn** to despise sb, feel contempt for sb; **sourire/regard de** ~ scornful *ou* contemptuous smile/look; **avec** ~ contemptuously, scornfully, with contempt, with scorn. b (*indifférence*) ~ **de** contempt for, disregard for; **avoir le** ~ **des convenances/traditions** to have no regard for conventions/traditions; **au** ~ **du danger/des lois** regardless *ou* in defiance of danger/the law.

méprisable [mepʀizabl] adj contemptible, despicable.

méprisant, e [mepʀizɑ̃, ɑ̃t] adj contemptuous, scornful; (*hautain*) disdainful.

méprise [mepʀiz] nf (*erreur de sens*) mistake, error; (*malentendu*) misunderstanding. **par** ~ by mistake.

mépriser [mepʀize] 1 vt *personne* to scorn, despise (*Brit*), look down on; *danger, conseil, offre* to scorn, spurn; *vice, faiblesse* to scorn, despise (*Brit*). ~ **les conventions** to scorn *ou* spurn convention.

mer [mɛʀ] 1 nf a (*océan, aussi fig*) sea. ~ **fermée** *ou* **intérieure** inland *ou* landlocked sea; ~ **de glace** glacier; ~ **de sable** sea of sand; **naviguer sur une** ~ **d'huile** to sail on a glassy sea *ou* on a sea as calm as a millpond; **aller en vacances à la** ~ to go to the seaside for one's holidays; **il a navigué sur toutes les mers** he has sailed the seven seas; **vent/port** *etc* **de** ~ sea breeze/harbour *etc*; **gens de** ~ sailors, seafarers, seafaring men; **coup de** ~ heavy swell; *voir* **bras, mal** *etc*.

b (*marée*) tide. **la** ~ **est haute** *ou* **pleine/basse** the tide is high *ou* in/low *ou* out; **c'est la haute** *ou* **pleine/basse** ~ it is high/low tide.

c (*loc*) **en** ~ at sea; **les pêcheurs sont en** ~ **aujourd'hui** the fishermen are out today *ou* at sea today; **en haute** *ou* **pleine** ~ out at sea, on the open sea; **prendre la** ~ to put out to sea; **mettre (une embarcation) à la** ~ to bring *ou* get out a boat; **bateau qui tient bien la** ~ good seagoing boat; **aller/voyager par** ~ to go/travel by sea; (*fig*) **ce n'est pas la** ~ **à boire!** it's no great hardship!, it's not asking the impossible!

2 comp ►**la mer des Antilles** *ou* **des Caraïbes** the Caribbean (Sea) ►**la mer Adriatique** the Adriatic Sea ►**la mer Baltique** the Baltic Sea ►**la mer Caspienne** the Caspian Sea ►**la mer de Chine** the China Sea ►**la mer Égée** the Aegean Sea ►**la mer d'Irlande** the Irish Sea ►**la mer d'Iroise** *part of the Atlantic Ocean off the coast of Brittany* ►**la mer de Marmara** the Marmara Sea ►**la mer Morte** the Dead Sea ►**la mer Noire** the Black Sea ►**la mer du Nord** the North Sea ►**la mer Rouge** the Red Sea ►**la mer des Sargasses** the Sargasso Sea ►**les mers du Sud** the South Seas ►**la mer Tyrrhénienne** the Tyrrhenian Sea.

mercanti [mɛʀkɑ̃ti] nm (*péj*) profiteer, swindler, shark*; (*marchand oriental ou africain*) bazaar merchant.

mercantile [mɛʀkɑ̃til] adj (*péj*) mercenary, venal.

mercantilisme [mɛʀkɑ̃tilism] nm (*péj*) mercenary *ou* venal attitude; (*Écon, Hist*) mercantile system, mercantilism.

mercatique [mɛʀkatik] nf marketing.

mercenaire [mɛʀsənɛʀ] 1 adj (*péj*) *attitude* mercenary; *soldat* hired. 2 nm (*Mil*) mercenary; (*fig péj: salarié*) hireling.

mercerie [mɛʀsəʀi] nf (*boutique*) haberdasher's shop (*Brit*), notions store (*US*); (*articles*) haberdashery (*Brit*), notions (*US*), dry goods (*US*); (*profession*) **la** ~ the haberdashery (*Brit*) *ou* notions (*US*) (trade).

merceriser [mɛʀsəʀize] 1 vt to mercerize. **coton mercerisé** mercerized cotton.

merci [mɛʀsi] 1 excl a (*pour remercier*) thank you. ~ **bien** thank you, many thanks; ~ **beaucoup** thank you very much, thanks a lot*; ~ **mille fois** thank you (ever) so much; ~ **de** *ou* **pour votre carte** thank you for your card; ~ **d'avoir répondu** thank you for replying; **sans même me dire** ~ without even thanking me, without even saying thank you; (*iro*) ~ **du compliment!** thanks for the compliment!; ~ **mon chien!*** thank you too! (*iro*), there's no need to thank! (*iro*); *voir* **dieu**.

b (*pour refuser*) **Cognac? — (non,)** ~ Cognac? — no thank you; **y retourner?** ~ **(bien), pour me faire traiter comme un chien!** go back there? what, and be treated like a dog?, no thank you!

2 nm thank-you. **je n'ai pas eu un** ~ I didn't get *ou* hear a word of thanks; **nous vous devons/nous devons vous dire un grand** ~ **pour** we owe you/we must say a big thank-you for; **et encore un grand** ~ **pour votre cadeau** and once again thank you so much *ou* many thanks for your present; **mille** ~**s** (very) many thanks.

3 nf a (*pitié*) mercy. **crier/implorer** ~ to cry/beg for mercy; **sans** ~ *combat etc* merciless, ruthless.

b (*risque, éventualité, pouvoir*) **à la** ~ **de qn** at the mercy of sb, in sb's hands; **tout le monde est à la** ~ **d'une erreur** anyone can make a mistake; **chaque fois que nous prenons la route nous sommes à la** ~ **d'un accident** every time we go on the road we expose ourselves *ou* lay ourselves open to accidents *ou* we run the risk of an accident; **exploitable à** ~ liable to be ruthlessly exploited, open to ruthless exploitation; *voir* **taillable**.

mercier, -ière [mɛʀsje, jɛʀ] nm,f haberdasher (*Brit*), notions dealer (*US*).

mercredi [mɛʀkʀədi] nm Wednesday. ~ **des Cendres** Ash Wednesday; *pour autres loc voir* **samedi**.

mercure [mɛʀkyʀ] 1 nm a (*Chim*) mercury. b (*Myth*) **M**~ Mercury. 2 nf (*Astron*) **M**~ Mercury.

mercuriale[1] [mɛʀkyʀjal] nf (*littér: reproche*) reprimand, rebuke.

mercuriale[2] [mɛʀkyʀjal] nf (*Bot*) mercury.

mercuriale[3] [mɛʀkyʀjal] nf (*Comm*) market price list.

Mercurochrome [mɛʀkyʀokʀom] nm ® mercurochrome (*NonC*).

merde [mɛʀd] 1 nf (**) (*excrément*) shit**; (*étron*) turd**; (*livre, film*) crap**. **il y a une** ~ **(de chien) devant la porte** there's some dog('s) shit** *ou* a dog turd** in front of the door; **son dernier bouquin est de la vraie** *ou* **une vraie** ~ his most recent book is a load of crap**; **quelle voiture de** ~! what a fucking awful car!**; (*fig*) **il ne se prend pas pour de la** *ou* **une** ~ he thinks the sun shines out of his arse!**, he thinks he's one hell of a big nob* (*Brit*); (*fig*) **on est dans la** ~ we're in a bloody mess** (*Brit*) *ou* one hell of a mess*.

2 excl (*) (*impatience, contrariété*) hell!*, shit!**; (*indignation, surprise*) bloody hell!** (*Brit*), shit!**. ~ **alors!** hell's bells*!; ~ **pour X!** to hell with X!*

merder** [mɛʀde] 1 vti to cock up**, fuck up**.

merdeux, -euse** [mɛʀdø, øz] 1 adj shitty**, filthy. 2 nm,f squirt*, twerp*.

merdier** [mɛʀdje] nm muck-up*, shambles (*sg*). **être dans un beau** ~ to be in a fine bloody mess** (*Brit*) *ou* one hell of a mess*.

merdique* [mɛʀdik] adj *film, discours, idée* pathetic, moronic, crappy**. **c'était** ~, **cette soirée** that party was the pits* *ou* was bloody awful** (*Brit*).

merdoyer** [mɛʀdwaje] 8 vi to be *ou* get in a hell of a mess*, be *ou* get all tied up.

mère [mɛʀ] 1 nf a (*génitrice*) mother. **elle est** ~ **de 4 enfants** she is a *ou* the mother of 4 (children); (*fig hum*) **tu es une ~ pour moi** you are like a mother to me; (*littér*) **la France, ~ des arts** France, mother of the arts; **frères par la ~** half-brothers (on the mother's side); **devenir ~** to become a mother; *voir* **fille, Madame, reine** *etc.*

b (*fig: femme*) (*péj*) **la ~ X*** old mother X, old Ma X (*péj*); **allons la petite ~, dépêchez-vous*!** come on missis, hurry up!*; (*affectueux: à une enfant, un animal*) **ma petite ~** my little pet *ou* love; (*dial*) **bonjour, ~ Martin** good day to you, Mrs Martin.

c (*Rel*) mother. **(la) M~ Catherine** Mother Catherine; **oui, ma ~** yes, Mother.

d (*Tech: moule*) mould.

e (*apposition: après n*) *cellule, compagnie* parent. (*Comm*) **maison ~** parent company, head office; (*Ordin*) **disquette ~** master disk; (*Ling*) **langue ~** mother tongue *ou* language.

2 comp ►**Mère abbesse** (*Rel*) mother abbess ►**mère d'accueil** = **mère porteuse** ►**mère biologique** natural *ou* biological mother ►**mère célibataire** (*Admin*) unmarried mother ►**mère de famille** mother, housewife ►**mère génétique** = **mère biologique** ►**mère-grand†** nf (pl **mères-grand**) grandmama† ►**mère patrie** motherland ►**mère porteuse** surrogate mother ►**mère poule*** motherly mum* (*Brit*) *ou* mom* (*US*); **c'est une vraie mère poule*, elle est très mère poule*** she's a real mother hen, she's a very motherly type ►**mère de remplacement** *ou* **de substitution** = **mère porteuse** ►**Mère supérieure** (*Rel*) Mother Superior ►**mère de vinaigre** (*Chim*) mother of vinegar.

merguez [mɛʀgɛz] nf merguez sausage, *type of spicy sausage from N Africa.*

mergule [mɛʀgyl] nm: **~ (nain)** little auk.

méridien, -ienne [meʀidjɛ̃, jɛn] 1 adj (*Sci*) meridian; (*littér*) meridian (*littér*), midday (*épith*). 2 nm (*Astron, Géog*) meridian. **~ d'origine** prime meridian. 3 **méridienne** nf (*Astron*) meridian line; (*Géodésie*) line of triangulation points.

méridional, e, mpl **-aux** [meʀidjɔnal, o] 1 adj (*du Sud*) southern; (*du sud de la France*) Southern (French). 2 nm,f: **M~(e)** (*du Sud*) Southerner; (*du sud de la France*) Southern Frenchman *ou* Frenchwoman, Southerner.

meringue [məʀɛ̃g] nf meringue. **un dessert avec de la ~/des petites ~s** a dessert with meringue/little meringues.

meringuer [məʀɛ̃ge] 1 vt (*gén ptp*) to coat *ou* cover with meringue.

mérinos [meʀinos] nm merino; *voir* **pisser.**

merise [məʀiz] nf wild cherry.

merisier [məʀizje] nm (*arbre*) wild cherry (tree); (*bois*) cherry.

méritant, e [meʀitɑ̃, ɑ̃t] adj deserving.

mérite [meʀit] nm a (*vertu intrinsèque*) merit; (*respect accordé*) credit. **le ~ de cet homme est grand** that man has great merit, he is a man of great merit; **il n'en a que plus de ~** he deserves all the more credit, it's all the more to his credit; **il n'y a aucun ~ à cela** there's no merit in that, one deserves no credit for that; **tout le ~ lui revient** all the credit is due to him, he deserves all the credit; **il a le grand ~ d'avoir réussi** it's greatly to his credit that *ou* his great merit is that he succeeded; **il a au moins le ~ d'être franc** there's one thing to his credit *ou* in his favour that at least he's frank.

b (*valeur*) merit, worth; (*qualité*) quality. **de grand ~** of great worth *ou* merit; **ce n'est pas sans ~** it's not without merit; **si nombreux que soient ses ~s** however many qualities he may have; **son intervention n'a eu d'autre ~ que de faire suspendre la séance** the only good point about *ou* merit in his intervention was that the sitting was adjourned.

c (*décoration*) **l'ordre national du M~** the national order of merit, *French decoration.*

d (*Rel*) **~(s) du Christ** merits of Christ.

mériter [meʀite] 1 vt a *louange, châtiment* to deserve, merit. **tu mériterais qu'on t'en fasse autant** you deserve (to get) the same treatment; **cette action mérite des louanges/une punition** this action deserves *ou* merits *ou* warrants praise/punishment; **~ l'estime de qn** to be worthy of *ou* deserve *ou* merit sb's esteem; **tu n'as que ce que tu mérites** you've got (just) what you deserved, it serves you right; **il mérite la prison/la corde** he deserves to go to prison/to be hanged; **repos/blâme bien mérité** well-deserved rest/reprimand.

b (*valoir*) to merit, deserve, be worth; (*exiger*) to call for, require. **le fait mérite d'être noté** the fact is worth noting, the fact is worthy of note; **ceci mérite réflexion** *ou* **qu'on y réfléchisse** (*exiger*) this calls for *ou* requires careful thought; (*valoir*) this merits *ou* deserves careful thought; **ça lui a mérité le respect de tous** this earned him everyone's respect.

c **il a bien mérité de la patrie** (*frm*) he deserves well of his country; (*hum*) he deserves a medal for that (*iro*).

méritocratie [meʀitɔkʀasi] nf meritocracy.

méritoire [meʀitwaʀ] adj meritorious, praiseworthy, commendable.

merlan [mɛʀlɑ̃] nm a (*Zool*) whiting. b (†*: *coiffeur*) barber, hairdresser.

merle [mɛʀl] nm a (*Orn*) blackbird. **~ à plastron** ring ouzel; **elle cherche le ~ blanc** (*gén*) she's asking for the impossible; (*mari*) she's looking for her Prince Charming. b (*péj*) **vilain** *ou* (*iro*) **beau ~** nasty customer. c (*Can Orn*) (American) robin.

merlette [mɛʀlɛt] nf female blackbird, she-blackbird.

merlin [mɛʀlɛ̃] nm a *[bûcheron]* axe; (*Boucherie*) cleaver. b (*Naut*) marline.

merlu [mɛʀly] nm hake.

merluche [mɛʀlyʃ] nf a (*Culin*) dried cod, stockfish. b = **merlu.**

merluchon [mɛʀlyʃɔ̃] nm small hake.

mérou [meʀu] nm grouper.

mérovingien, -ienne [meʀɔvɛ̃ʒjɛ̃, jɛn] 1 adj Merovingian. 2 nm,f: **M~(ne)** Merovingian.

merveille [mɛʀvɛj] nf a marvel, wonder. **les ~s de la technique moderne** the wonders *ou* marvels of modern technology; **cette montre est une ~ de précision** this watch is a marvel of precision; **les ~s de la nature** the wonders of nature; **cette machine est une (petite) ~** this machine is a (little) marvel.

b (*loc*) **à ~** perfectly, wonderfully, marvellously; **cela te va à ~** it suits you perfectly *ou* to perfection; **se porter à ~** to be in excellent health, be in the best of health; **ça s'est passé à ~** it went off like a dream *ou* without a single hitch; **ça tombe à ~** this comes at an ideal moment *ou* just at the right time; **faire ~** *ou* **des ~s** to work wonders; **c'est ~ que vous soyez vivant** it's a wonder *ou* a marvel that you are alive; **on en dit ~** *ou* **des ~s** it's praised to the skies *ou* said to be marvellous; *voir* **huitième, sept.**

merveilleusement [mɛʀvɛjøzmɑ̃] adv marvellously, wonderfully.

merveilleux, -euse [mɛʀvɛjø, øz] 1 adj (*magnifique*) *paysage, bijoux etc* wonderful; (*sensationnel*) *nouvelle, événement heureux* wonderful, fantastic; (*après n: surnaturel*) magic. 2 nm a **le ~** the supernatural; (*Art, Littérat*) the fantastic element. b (*Hist*) coxcomb††, fop†. 3 **merveilleuse** nf (*Hist*) fine lady, belle.

mes [me] adj poss *voir* **mon.**

mésalliance [mezaljɑ̃s] nf misalliance, marriage beneath one's station†. **faire une ~** to marry beneath o.s. *ou* one's station†.

mésallier (se) [mezalje] 7 vpr to marry beneath o.s. *ou* one's station†.

mésange [mezɑ̃ʒ] nf tit(mouse). **~ bleue** blue tit; **~ charbonnière** great tit; **~ huppée** crested tit; **~ à longue queue** long-tailed tit; **~ noire** coal tit.

mésaventure [mezavɑ̃tyʀ] nf misadventure, misfortune.

mescaline [mɛskalin] nf mescaline.

Mesdames [medam] nfpl *voir* **Madame.**

Mesdemoiselles [medmwazɛl] nfpl *voir* **Mademoiselle.**

mésencéphale [mezɑ̃sefal] nm midbrain, mesencephalon (*SPÉC*).

mésentente [mezɑ̃tɑ̃t] nf dissension, disagreement. **la ~ règne dans leur famille** there is constant disagreement in their family, they are always at loggerheads (with each other) in that family.

mésentère [mezɑ̃tɛʀ] nm mesentery.

mésentérique [mezɑ̃teʀik] adj mesenteric.

mésestimation [mezɛstimasjɔ̃] nf (*littér*) *[chose]* underestimation.

mésestime [mezɛstim] nf (*littér*) *[personne]* low regard, low esteem. **tenir qn en ~** to have little regard for sb.

mésestimer [mezɛstime] 1 vt (*littér: sous-estimer*) *difficulté, adversaire* to underestimate, underrate; *opinion* to set little store by, have little regard for; *personne* to have little regard for.

mésintelligence [mezɛ̃teliʒɑ̃s] nf disagreement (*entre* between), dissension, discord.

mesmérisme [mɛsmeʀism] nm mesmerism.

Mésopotamie [mezɔpɔtami] nf Mesopotamia.

mésopotamien, -ienne [mezɔpɔtamjɛ̃, jɛn] 1 adj Mesopotamian. 2 nm,f: **M~(ne)** Mesopotamian.

mesquin, e [mɛskɛ̃, in] adj (*avare*) mean, stingy; (*vil*) mean, petty. **c'est un esprit ~** he is a mean-minded *ou* small-minded *ou* petty person; **le repas faisait un peu ~** the meal was a bit stingy.

mesquinement [mɛskinmɑ̃] adv *agir* meanly, pettily; *distribuer* stingily.

mesquinerie [mɛskinʀi] nf *[personne, procédé]* (*étroitesse*) meanness, pettiness; (*avarice*) stinginess, meanness; (*procédé*) mean *ou* petty trick.

mess [mɛs] nm (*Mil*) mess.

message [mesaʒ] nm (*gén, Jur, Littérat, Tech*) message. **~ chiffré** coded message, message in code *ou* cipher; **~ publicitaire** *ou* **commercial** commercial, advertisement; **~ téléphoné** telegram (*dictated by telephone*).

messager, -ère [mesaʒe, ɛʀ] nm,f messenger. (*littér*) **~ de bonheur/du printemps** harbinger of glad tidings/of spring (*littér*); **~ de malheur** bearer of bad tidings.

messageries [mesaʒʀi] nfpl: **(service de) ~** parcels service; (*Hist*) mail-coach service; **~ aériennes/maritimes** air freight/shipping company; **~ de presse** press distributing service; (*Ordin*) **~ électroniques** electronic bulletin board.

messe [mɛs] 1 nf (*Mus, Rel*) mass. **aller à la ~** to go to mass; **célébrer la ~** to celebrate mass; *voir* **entendre, livre**[1] *etc.* 2 comp ►**messe basse** (*Rel*) low mass; (*fig péj*) **messes basses** muttering, muttered conversation *ou* talk; **finissez vos messes basses** stop muttering *ou* whispering together ►**messe chantée** sung mass ►**messe de minuit** midnight mass ►**messe des morts** mass for the dead ►**messe noire**

(*Spiritisme*) black mass.

Messeigneurs [mesɛɲœʀ] **nmpl** *voir* **Monseigneur.**

messeoir [meswaʀ] 26 **vi** (††, *littér*) (*moralement*) to be unseemly (*à* for) (*littér*), ill befit (*littér*); (*pour l'allure*) to ill become (*littér*), be unbecoming (*à* to) (*littér*). **avec un air qui ne lui messied pas** with a look that does not ill become him *ou* that is not unbecoming to him; **il vous messiérait de le faire** it would be unseemly for you to do it.

messianique [mesjanik] **adj** messianic.

messianisme [mesjanism] **nm** (*Rel*) messianism. (*fig*) **la tendance au ~ de certains révolutionnaires** the messianic tendencies of certain revolutionaries.

messidor [mesidɔʀ] **nm** Messidor, *tenth month in the French Republican Calendar.*

messie [mesi] **nm** messiah. **le M~** the Messiah.

Messieurs [mesjø] **nmpl** *voir* **Monsieur.**

messin, e [mesɛ̃, in] 1 **adj** of *ou* from Metz. 2 **nm,f: M~(e)** inhabitant *ou* native of Metz.

messire†† [mesiʀ] **nm** (*noblesse*) my lord; (*bourgeoisie*) Master. **oui ~** yes my lord, yes sir; **~ Jean** my lord John, master John.

mestrance [mɛstʀɑ̃s] **nf** = **maistrance.**

mestre [mɛstʀ] **nm** (*Naut*) mainmast.

mesurable [məzyʀabl] **adj** *grandeur* measurable; *quantité* measurable. **c'est difficilement ~** it is hard to measure.

mesurage [məzyʀaʒ] **nm** measuring, measurement.

mesure [m(ə)zyʀ] **nf** a (*évaluation, dimension*) measurement. **appareil de ~** gauge; **système de ~** system of measurement; **prendre les ~s de qch** to take the measurements of sth; *voir* **poids.**

b (*fig: taille*) **la ~ de ses forces/sentiments** the measure of his strength/feelings; **monde/ville à la ~ de l'homme** world/town on a human scale; **il est à ma ~** *[travail]* it's within my capabilities, I am able to do it; *[adversaire]* he's a match for me; **prendre la (juste) ~ de qn/qch** to size sb/sth up (exactly), get the measure of sb/sth; **donner (toute) sa ~** to show one's worth, show what one is capable of *ou* made of.

c (*unité, récipient, quantité*) measure. **~ de capacité** (*pour liquides*) liquid measure; (*pour poudre, grains*) dry measure; **~ de superficie/volume** square/cubic measure; **~ de longueur** measure of length; **~ à grains/à lait** corn/milk measure; **~ graduée** measuring jug; **~ d'un demi-litre** half-litre measure; **donne-lui 2 ~s d'avoine** give him 2 measures of oats; **faire bonne ~** to give good measure; (*fig*) **pour faire bonne ~** for good measure.

d (*quantité souhaitable*) **la juste** *ou* **bonne ~** the happy medium; **la ~ est comble** that's the limit; **dépasser** *ou* **excéder** *ou* **passer la ~** to overstep the mark, go too far; **boire outre ~** to drink immoderately *ou* to excess; **cela ne me gêne pas outre ~** that doesn't bother me overmuch, I'm not too bothered.

e (*modération*) moderation. **le sens de la ~** a sense of moderation; **il n'a pas le sens de la ~** he has no sense of moderation, he knows no measure; **avec ~** with *ou* in moderation; **il a beaucoup de ~** he's very moderate; **orgueil sans ~** immoderate *ou* measureless pride, pride beyond measure; **se dépenser sans ~** (*se dévouer*) to give one's all; (*se fatiguer*) to overtax one's strength *ou* o.s.

f (*disposition, moyen*) measure, step. **prendre des ~s d'urgence** to take emergency action *ou* measures; **~s d'ordre social** social measures; **~s de soutien à l'économie** measures to bolster the economy; **~s de rétorsion** reprisals, retaliatory measures; **j'ai pris mes ~s pour qu'il vienne** I have made arrangements for him to come, I have taken steps to ensure that he comes; **par ~ de restriction** as a restrictive measure; *voir* **contre, demi²**.

g (*Mus*) (*cadence*) time, tempo; (*division*) bar; (*Poésie*) metre. **en ~** in time *ou* tempo; **~ composée/simple/à deux temps/à quatre temps** compound/simple/duple/common *ou* four-four time; **être/ne pas être en ~** to be in/out of time; **jouer quelques ~s** to play a few bars; **2 ~s pour rien** 2 bars for nothing; *voir* **battre.**

h (*Habillement*) measure, measurement. **prendre les ~s de qn** to take sb's measurements; **est-ce que ce costume est bien à ma ~?** *ou* **à mes ~s?** is this suit my size?, will this suit fit me?; **acheter** *ou* **s'habiller sur ~** to have one's clothes made to measure; **costume fait à la ~** *ou* **sur ~** made-to-measure suit; **tailleur à la ~** bespoke tailor; (*fig*) **j'ai un emploi du temps/un patron sur ~** my schedule/boss suits me down to the ground; (*fig*) **c'est un rôle/emploi (fait) sur ~** it's a role/job that was tailor-made for me (*ou* him *etc*).

i (*loc*) **dans la ~ de ses forces** *ou* **capacités** as far as *ou* insofar as one is able, to the best of one's ability; **dans la ~ de ses moyens** as far as one's circumstances permit, as far as one is able; **dans la ~ du possible** as far as possible; **dans la ~ où** inasmuch as, insofar as; **dans une certaine ~** to some *ou* a certain extent; **dans une large ~** to a large extent, to a great extent; **être en ~ de faire qch** to be in a position to do sth; **(au fur et) à ~ que** as; **il les pliait et me les passait (au fur et) à ~** he folded them and handed them to me one by one *ou* as he went along; *voir* **commun.**

mesuré, e [məzyʀe] (**ptp de mesurer**) **adj** *ton* steady; *pas* measured; *personne* moderate. **il est ~ dans ses paroles/ses actions** he is moderate *ou* temperate in his language/actions.

mesurément [məzyʀemɑ̃] **adv** with *ou* in moderation.

mesurer [məzyʀe] 1 1 **vt** a *chose* to measure; *personne* to take the measurements of, measure (up); (*par le calcul*) *distance, pression, volume* to calculate; *longueur à couper* to measure off *ou* out. **il mesura 3 cl d'acide** he measured out 3 cl of acid; **il me mesura 3 mètres de tissu** he measured me off *ou* out 3 metres of fabric.

b (*évaluer, juger*) *risque, efficacité* to assess, weigh up; *valeur d'une personne* to assess, rate. **vous n'avez pas mesuré la portée de vos actes!** you did not weigh up *ou* consider the consequences of your actions!; **on n'a pas encore mesuré l'étendue des dégâts** the extent of the damage has not yet been assessed; **~ les efforts aux** *ou* **d'après les résultats (obtenus)** to gauge *ou* assess the effort expended by *ou* according to the results (obtained); **~ ses forces avec qn** to pit oneself against sb, measure one's strength with sb; **~ qn du regard** to look sb up and down; **se ~ des yeux** to weigh *ou* size each other up.

c (*avoir pour mesure*) to measure. **cette pièce mesure 3 mètres sur 10** this room measures 3 metres by 10; **il mesure 1 mètre 80** *[personne]* he's 1 metre 80 tall; *[objet]* it's 1 metre 80 long *ou* high, it measures 1 metre 80.

d (*avec parcimonie*) to limit. **elle leur mesure la nourriture** she rations them on food, she limits their food; **le temps nous est mesuré** our time is limited, we have only a limited amount of time; **ne pas ~ sa peine**to spare no effort.

e (*avec modération*) **~ ses paroles** (*savoir rester poli*) to moderate one's language; (*être prudent*) to weigh one's words.

f (*proportionner*) to match (*à, sur* to), gear (*à, sur* to). **~ le travail aux forces de qn** to match *ou* gear the work to sb's strength; **~ le châtiment à l'offense** to make the punishment fit the crime, match the punishment to the crime; *voir* **brebis.**

2 **se mesurer vpr: se ~ avec** *personne* to have a confrontation with, pit o.s. against; *difficulté* to confront, tackle.

mesureur [məzyʀœʀ] **nm** (*personne*) measurer; (*appareil*) gauge, measure.

mésuser [mezyze] 1 **mésuser de vt indir** (*littér*) (*gén*) to misuse. **~ de son pouvoir** to abuse one's power.

métabolique [metabɔlik] **adj** metabolic.

métabolisme [metabɔlism] **nm** metabolism.

métacarpe [metakaʀp] **nm** metacarpus.

métacarpien, -ienne [metakaʀpjɛ̃, jɛn] 1 **adj** metacarpal. 2 **nmpl: ~s** metacarpals, metacarpal bones.

métairie [meteʀi] **nf** smallholding, farm (*held on a métayage agreement*); *voir* **métayage.**

métal, pl **-aux** [metal, o] **nm** a (*gén, Chim, Fin, Min*) metal. (*Fin*) **le ~ jaune** gold; **les ~aux précieux comme l'or et l'argent** precious metals such as gold and silver; *couverts* **en ~ argenté/doré** silver-/gold-plated.

b (*littér*) metal (*littér*), stuff.

métalangue [metalɑ̃g] **nf, métalangage** [metalɑ̃gaʒ] **nm** metalanguage.

métalinguistique [metalɛ̃gɥistik] 1 **adj** metalinguistic. 2 **nf** metalinguistics (*sg*).

métallifère [metalifɛʀ] **adj** metalliferous (*SPÉC*), metal-bearing.

métallique [metalik] **adj** a (*gén, Chim*) metallic; *voix, couleur* metallic; *objet* (*en métal*) metal (*épith*); (*qui ressemble au métal*) metallic. **bruit** *ou* **son ~** *[clefs]* jangle, clank; *[épée]* clash. b (*Fin*) *voir* **encaisse, monnaie.**

métallisation [metalizasjɔ̃] **nf** *[métal]* plating; *[miroir]* silvering.

métallisé, e [metalize] (**ptp de métalliser**) **adj** *bleu, gris* metallic; *peinture, couleur* metallic, with a metallic finish; *miroir* silvered.

métalliser [metalize] 1 **vt** *surface* to plate; *miroir* to silver.

métallo* [metalo] **nm** (**abrév de métallurgiste**) steelworker, metalworker.

métallographie [metalɔgʀafi] **nf** metallography.

métallographique [metalɔgʀafik] **adj** metallographic.

métalloïde [metalɔid] **nm** metalloid.

métalloplastique [metaloplastik] **adj** copper asbestos (*épith*).

métallurgie [metalyʀʒi] **nf** (*industrie*) metallurgical industry; (*technique, travail*) metallurgy.

métallurgique [metalyʀʒik] **adj** metallurgic.

métallurgiste [metalyʀʒist] **nm** a **(ouvrier) ~** steelworker, metalworker. b **(industriel) ~** metallurgist.

métamorphique [metamɔʀfik] **adj** metamorphic, metamorphous.

métamorphiser [metamɔʀfize] 1 **vt** (*Géol*) to metamorphose.

métamorphisme [metamɔʀfism] **nm** metamorphism.

métamorphosable [metamɔʀfozabl] **adj** that can be transformed (*en* into).

métamorphose [metamɔʀfoz] **nf** (*Bio, Myth*) metamorphosis; (*fig*) transformation, metamorphosis.

métamorphoser [metamɔʀfoze] 1 1 **vt** (*Myth, fig*) to transform, metamorphose (*gén pass*) (*en* into). **son succès l'a métamorphosé** his success has transformed him *ou* made a new man of him. 2 **se métamorphoser vpr** (*Bio*) to be metamorphosed; (*Myth, fig*) to be transformed (*en* into).

métaphore [metafɔʀ] **nf** metaphor.

métaphorique [metafɔʀik] **adj** *expression, emploi, valeur* metaphorical, figurative; *style* metaphorical.

métaphoriquement [metafɔʀikmɑ̃] adv metaphorically, figuratively.
métaphysicien, -ienne [metafizisjɛ̃, jɛn] 1 adj metaphysical. 2 nm,f metaphysician, metaphysicist.
métaphysique [metafizik] 1 adj (*Philos*) metaphysical; *amour* spiritual; (*péj*) *argument* abstruse, obscure. 2 nf (*Philos*) metaphysics (*sg*).
métaphysiquement [metafizikmɑ̃] adv metaphysically.
métapsychique [metapsiʃik] adj psychic. **recherches ~s** psychic(al) research.
métapsychologie [metapsikɔlɔʒi] nf parapsychology, metapsychology.
métastase [metastɑz] nf metastasis. **~s** metastases.
métastaser [metastaze] 1 vi to metastasize.
métatarse [metataʀs] nm metatarsus.
métatarsien, -ienne [metataʀsjɛ̃, jɛn] 1 adj metatarsal. 2 nmpl: **~s** metatarsals, metatarsal bones.
métathèse [metatɛz] nf (*Ling*) metathesis.
métayage [metejaʒ] nm métayage system (*farmer pays rent in kind*), sharecropping (*US*).
métayer [meteje] nm (tenant) farmer (*paying rent in kind*), sharecropper (tenant) (*US*).
métayère [metejɛʀ] nf (*épouse*) farmer's *ou* sharecropper's (*US*) wife; (*paysanne*) (woman) farmer *ou* sharecropper (*US*).
métazoaire [metazɔɛʀ] nm metazoan. **~s** Metazoa.
méteil [metɛj] nm *mixed crop of wheat and rye.*
métempsycose [metɑ̃psikoz] nf metempsychosis.
météo [meteo] 1 adj abrév de **météorologique.** 2 nf a (*Sci, services*) = **météorologie.** b (*bulletin*) (weather) forecast, weather report. **la ~ est bonne/mauvaise** the weather forecast is good/bad.
météore [meteɔʀ] nm (*lit*) meteor. (*fig*) **passer comme un ~** to have a brief but brilliant career.
météorique [meteɔʀik] adj (*Astron*) meteoric.
météorisme [meteɔʀism] nm (*Méd*) meteorism.
météorite [meteɔʀit] nm ou f meteorite.
météorologie [meteɔʀɔlɔʒi] nf (*Sci*) meteorology. (*services*) **la ~ nationale** the Meteorological Office, the Met Office*.
météorologique [meteɔʀɔlɔʒik] adj *phénomène, observation* meteorological; *carte, prévisions, station* weather (*épith*); *voir* **bulletin.**
météorologiste [meteɔʀɔlɔʒist] nmf, **météorologue** [meteɔʀɔlɔg] nmf meteorologist.
métèque [metɛk] nmf a (*péj*) wog** (*Brit péj*), wop** (*péj*). b (*Hist*) metic.
méthane [metan] nm methane.
méthanier [metanje] nm (liquefied) gas carrier *ou* tanker.
méthanol [metanɔl] nm methanol.
méthode [metɔd] nf a (*moyen*) method. **de nouvelles ~s d'enseignement du français** new methods of *ou* for teaching French, new teaching methods for French; **avoir une bonne ~ de travail** to have a good way *ou* method of working; **avoir sa ~ pour faire qch** to have one's own way of *ou* method for *ou* of doing sth. b (*ordre*) **il a beaucoup de ~** he's very methodical, he's a man of method; **il n'a aucune ~** he's not in the least methodical, he has no (idea of) method; **faire qch avec/sans ~** to do sth methodically *ou* in a methodical way/unmethodically. c (*livre*) manual, tutor. **~ de piano** piano manual *ou* tutor; **~ de latin** latin primer.
méthodique [metɔdik] adj methodical.
méthodiquement [metɔdikmɑ̃] adv methodically.
méthodisme [metɔdism] nm Methodism.
méthodiste [metɔdist] adj, nmf Methodist.
méthodologie [metɔdɔlɔʒi] nf methodology.
méthodologique [metɔdɔlɔʒik] adj methodological.
méthyle [metil] nm methyl.
méthylène [metilɛn] nm (*Comm*) methyl alcohol; (*Chim*) methylene; *voir* **bleu.**
méthylique [metilik] adj methyl.
méticuleusement [metikyløzmɑ̃] adv meticulously.
méticuleux, -euse [metikylø, øz] adj *soin, propreté* meticulous, scrupulous; *personne* meticulous.
méticulosité [metikylozite] nf meticulousness.
métier [metje] nm a (*gén: travail*) job; (*Admin*) occupation; (*commercial*) trade; (*artisanal*) craft; (*intellectuel*) profession. **les ~s manuels** (the) manual occupations; **donner un ~ à son fils** to have one's son learn a job (*ou* trade *ou* craft *ou* profession); **enseigner son ~ à son fils** to teach one's son one's trade; **il a fait tous les ~s** he has tried his hand at everything, he has been everything; **après tout ils font leur ~** they are (only) doing their job after all; **les ~s du livre/de la communication** the publishing/communications industry; **prendre le ~ des armes** to become a soldier, join the army; **apprendre son ~ de roi** to learn one's job as king; *voir* **corps, gâcher** *etc*.
b (*technique, expérience*) (acquired) skill, (acquired) technique, experience. **avoir du ~** to have practical experience; **manquer de ~** to be lacking in expertise *ou* in practical technique; **avoir 2 ans de ~** to have been 2 years in the job (*ou* trade *ou* profession).
c (*loc*) **homme de ~** expert, professional, specialist; **il est plombier de son ~** he is a plumber by *ou* to trade; (*euph*) **le plus vieux ~ du monde** the oldest profession; **il est du ~** he is in the trade *ou* profession *ou* business; **il connaît son ~** he knows his job (all right)*; **je connais mon ~!, tu ne vas pas m'apprendre mon ~!** I know what I'm doing!, you're not going to teach me my job!; **ce n'est pas mon ~** it's not my job *ou* line; **quel ~!*** what a job!; (*hum*) **c'est le ~ qui rentre*** it's just learning the hard way.
d (*Tech: machine*) loom. **~ à tisser** (weaving) loom; **~ à filer** spinning frame; **~ (à broder)** embroidery frame; (*fig, littér*) **remettre qch sur le ~** to make some improvements to sth.
métis, -isse [metis] 1 adj *personne* half-caste, half-breed; *animal* crossbreed, mongrel; *plante* hybrid; *tissu, toile* made of cotton and linen. 2 nm,f (*personne*) half-caste, half-breed; (*animal, plante*) mongrel. 3 nm (*Tex*) **(toile/drap de) ~** fabric/sheet made of cotton and linen mixture.
métissage [metisaʒ] nm *[gens]* interbreeding; *[animaux]* crossbreeding, crossing; *[plantes]* crossing.
métisser [metise] 1 vt to crossbreed, cross.
métonymie [metɔnimi] nf metonymy.
métonymique [metɔnimik] adj metonymical.
métrage [metʀaʒ] nm a (*Couture*) length, yardage. **grand ~** long length; **petit ~** short length; **quel ~ vous faut-il, Madame?** what yardage do you need, madam? b (*mesure*) measurement, measuring (in metres). **procéder au ~ de qch** to measure sth out. c (*Ciné*) footage, length; *voir* **court¹, long, moyen.**
mètre [mɛtʀ] nm a (*Math*) metre. **~ carré/cube** square/cubic metre; **vendre qch au ~ linéaire** to sell sth by the metre. b (*instrument*) (metre) rule. **~ étalon** standard metre; **~ pliant** folding rule; **~ à ruban** tape measure, measuring tape. c (*Athlétisme*) **un 100 ~s** a 100-metre race; **le 100/400 ~s** the 100/400 metres, the 100-/400-metre race. d (*Ftbl, Rugby*) **les 22/50** *etc* **~s** the 22 metre/halfway *etc* line. e (*Littérat*) metre.
métré [metʀe] nm (*métier*) quantity surveying; (*mesure*) measurement; (*devis*) estimate of cost.
métrer [metʀe] 6 vt (*Tech*) to measure (in metres); *[vérificateur]* to survey.
métreur, -euse [metʀœʀ, øz] nm,f: **~ (vérificateur (*f* -trice))** quantity surveyor.
métrique [metʀik] 1 adj (*Littérat*) metrical, metric; (*Mus*) metrical; (*Math*) *système, tonne* metric. **géométrie ~** metrical geometry. 2 nf (*Littérat*) metrics; (*Math*) metric theory.
métro [metʀo] 1 nm underground, subway (*US*). **~ aérien** elevated railway; **le ~ de Paris** the Paris metro *ou* underground; **le ~ de Londres** the London tube *ou* underground; **j'irai en ~** I'll go by underground *ou* tube; **c'est ~, boulot, dodo*** it's the same old routine day in day out, it's work work work; **il a pris le rythme ~, boulot, dodo** he's got used to having the same old routine day in day out, he's got used to a life of work work work. 2 nmf (*: *de la métrople*) person from metropolitan France.
métrologie [metʀɔlɔʒi] nf (*Sci*) metrology; (*traité*) metrological treatise, treatise on metrology.
métrologique [metʀɔlɔʒik] adj metrological.
métrologiste [metʀɔlɔʒist] nmf metrologist.
métronome [metʀɔnɔm] nm metronome. (*fig*) **avec la régularité d'un ~** with clockwork regularity, like clockwork.
métropole [metʀɔpɔl] nf a (*ville*) metropolis. **la M~** (metropolitan) France; **quand est prévu votre retour en ~?** when do you go back home? *ou* back to the home country?; **en ~ comme à l'étranger** at home and abroad. b (*Rel*) metropolis.
métropolitain, e [metʀɔpɔlitɛ̃, ɛn] 1 adj (*Admin, Rel*) metropolitan. **la France ~e** metropolitan France; **troupes ~es** home troops. 2 nm a (*Rel*) metropolitan. b (†: *métro*) underground, subway (*US*).
mets [mɛ] nm dish (*Culin*).
mettable [metabl] adj (*gén nég*) wearable, decent. **ça n'est pas ~** this is not fit to wear *ou* to be worn; **je n'ai rien de ~** I've got nothing (decent) to wear *ou* nothing that's wearable; **ce costume est encore ~** you can still wear that suit, that suit is still decent *ou* wearable.
metteur [metœʀ] nm (*Bijouterie*) **~ en œuvre** mounter; (*Rad*) **~ en ondes** producer; (*Typ*) **~ en pages** compositor (responsible for upmaking); (*Tech*) **~ au point** adjuster; **~ en scène** (*Théât, Ciné*) director.
mettre [mɛtʀ] 56 1 vt a (*placer*) to put (*dans* in, into, *sur* on); (*fig: classer*) to rank, rate. **~ une assiette/une carte sur une autre** to put one *ou* a plate/card on top of another; **où mets-tu tes verres?** where do you keep your glasses?, where are your glasses kept?; **elle lui mit la main sur l'épaule** she put *ou* laid her hand on his shoulder; **elle met son travail avant sa famille** she puts her work before her family; **je mets Molière parmi les plus grands écrivains** I rank *ou* rate Molière among the greatest writers; **~ qch debout** to stand sth up; **~ qn sur son séant/sur ses pieds** to sit/stand sb up; **~ qch à** *ou* **par terre** to put sth down (on the ground); **~ qch à l'ombre/au frais** to put sth in the shade/ in a cool place; **~ qch à plat** to lay sth down (flat); **~ qch droit** to put *ou* set sth straight *ou* to rights, straighten sth out *ou* up; **~ qn au** *ou* **dans le train** to put sb on the train; **mettez-moi à la gare*, s'il vous plaît** take me to *ou* drop me at the station please; **elle a mis la tête à la fenê-**

tre she put *ou* stuck her head out of the window; **mettez les mains en l'air** put your hands up, put your hands in the air; **mets le chat dehors** *ou* **à la porte** put the cat out.

b (*ajouter*) ~ **du sucre dans son thé** to put sugar in one's tea; ~ **une pièce à un drap** to put a patch in *ou* on a sheet, patch a sheet; ~ **une idée dans la tête de qn** to put an idea into sb's head; **ne mets pas d'encre sur la nappe** don't get ink on the tablecloth.

c (*placer dans une situation*) ~ **un enfant à l'école** to send a child to school; ~ **qn au régime** to put sb on a diet; ~ **qn dans la nécessité** *ou* **l'obligation de faire** to oblige *ou* compel sb to do; ~ **au désespoir** to throw into despair; **cela m'a mis dans une situation difficile** that has put me in *ou* got me into a difficult position; **on l'a mis* à la manutention/aux réclamations** he was put in the handling/complaints department; ~ **qn au pas** to bring sb into line, make sb toe the line; (*Gram*) ~ **à l'infinitif/au futur** to put in(to) the infinitive/the future tense; *voir* **aise, contact, présence** *etc.*

d (*revêtir*) *vêtements, lunettes* to put on. ~ **une robe/du maquillage** to put on a dress/some make-up; **depuis qu'il fait chaud je ne mets plus mon gilet** since it has got warmer I've stopped wearing *ou* I've left off my cardigan; **elle n'a plus rien à ~ sur elle** she's got nothing (left) to wear; **mets-lui son chapeau et on sort** put his hat on (for him) and we'll go; **il avait mis un manteau** he was wearing a coat, he had a coat on; **elle avait mis du bleu** she was wearing blue, she was dressed in blue.

e (*consacrer*) **j'ai mis 2 heures à le faire** I took 2 hours to do it *ou* 2 hours over it, I spent 2 hours on *ou* over it *ou* 2 hours doing it; **le train met 3 heures** it takes 3 hours by train, the train takes 3 hours; ~ **toute son énergie à faire** to put all one's effort *ou* energy into doing; ~ **tous ses espoirs dans** to pin all one's hopes on; ~ **beaucoup de soin à faire** to take great care in doing, take great pains to do; ~ **de l'ardeur à faire qch** to do sth eagerly *ou* with great eagerness; **il y a mis le temps!** he's taken his time (about it)!, he's taken an age *ou* long enough!; *voir* **cœur**.

f (*faire fonctionner*) ~ **la radio/le chauffage** to put *ou* switch *ou* turn the radio/heating on; ~ **les informations** to put *ou* turn the news on; ~ **le réveil (à 7 heures)** to set the alarm (for 7 o'clock); ~ **le réveil à l'heure** to put the alarm clock right; ~ **le verrou** to bolt (*Brit*) *ou* lock the door; **mets France Inter/la 2e chaîne** put on France Inter/the 2nd channel; ~ **une machine en route** to start up a machine.

g (*installer*) *eau* to lay on; *placards* to put in, build, install; *étagères* to put up *ou* in, build; *moquette* to fit, lay; *rideaux* to put up. ~ **du papier peint** to hang some wallpaper; ~ **de la peinture** to put on a coat of paint.

h (*avec à + infin*) ~ **qch à cuire/à chauffer** to put sth on to cook/heat; ~ **du linge à sécher** (*à l'intérieur*) to put *ou* hang washing up to dry; (*à l'extérieur*) to put *ou* hang washing out to dry.

i (*écrire*) ~ **en anglais/au pluriel** to put into English/the plural; ~ **des vers en musique** to set verse to music; ~ **sa signature (à)** to put *ou* append one's signature (to); ~ **un mot à qn*** to drop a line to sb; **mets 100 F, ils ne vérifieront pas** put (down) 100 francs, they'll never check up; **mettez bien clairement que** put (down) quite clearly that; **il met qu'il est bien arrivé** he says in his letter *ou* writes that he arrived safely.

j (*dépenser*) ~ **de l'argent sur un cheval** to lay money (down) *ou* put money on a horse; ~ **de l'argent dans une affaire** to put money into a business; **combien avez-vous mis pour cette table?** how much did you give for that table?; ~ **de l'argent sur son compte** to put money into one's account; **je suis prêt à ~ 500 F** I'm willing to give *ou* I don't mind giving 500 francs; **si on veut du beau il faut y ~ le prix** if you want something nice you have to pay the price *ou* pay for it; *voir* **caisse**.

k (*lancer*) ~ **la balle dans le filet** to put the ball into the net; ~ **une balle dans la peau de qn‡** to put a bullet through sb *ou* in sb's hide*; ~ **son poing dans** *ou* **sur la figure de qn** to punch sb in the face, give sb a punch in the face.

l (*supposer*) **mettons que je me suis** *ou* **sois trompé** let's say *ou* (just) suppose *ou* assume I've got it wrong; **nous arriverons vers 10 heures, mettons, et après?** say we arrive about 10 o'clock then what?, we'll arrive about 10 o'clock, say, then what?

m (‡*loc*) ~ **les bouts** *ou* **les voiles, les ~** to clear off‡, beat it‡, scarper‡ (*Brit*); **qu'est-ce qu'ils nous ont mis!** what a licking* *ou* hiding* they gave us!; **va te faire ~!** get lost‡, take a hike‡! (*US*).

2 **se mettre** vpr a (*se placer*) *[personne]* to put o.s. *[objet]* to go. **mets-toi là** (*debout*) (go and) stand there; (*assis*) (go and) sit there; **se ~ au piano/dans un fauteuil** to sit down at the piano/in an armchair; **se ~ au chaud/à l'ombre** to come *ou* go into the warmth/into the shade; (*fig*) **elle ne savait plus où se ~** she didn't know where to hide herself *ou* what to do with herself; **il s'est mis dans une situation délicate** he's put himself in *ou* got himself into an awkward situation; **se ~ une idée dans la tête** to get an idea into one's head; **il s'est mis de l'encre sur les doigts** he's got ink on his fingers; **il s'en est mis partout*** he's covered in it, he's got it all over him; **se ~ autour (de)** to gather round; **ces verres se mettent dans le placard** these glasses go in the cupboard; **l'infection s'y est mise** it has become infected; **les vers s'y sont mis** the maggots have got at it; **il y a un bout de métal qui s'est mis dans l'engrenage** a piece of metal has got caught in the works; **se ~ au vert** to lie low for a while; *voir* **poil, rang, table**.

b *[temps]* **se ~ au froid/au chaud/à la pluie** to turn cold/warm/wet; **on dirait que ça se met à la pluie** it looks like rain, it looks as though it's turning to rain.

c (*s'habiller*) **se ~ en robe/en short, se ~ une robe/un short** to put on a dress/a pair of shorts; **se ~ en bras de chemise** to take off one's jacket; **se ~ nu** to strip (off *ou* naked), take (all) one's clothes off; **comment je me mets?** what (sort of thing) should I wear?; **elle s'était mise très simplement** she was dressed very simply; **elle s'était mise en robe du soir** she was wearing *ou* she had on an evening dress; **se ~ une veste/du maquillage** to put on a jacket/some make-up; **elle n'a plus rien à se ~** she's got nothing (left) to wear.

d **se ~ à: se ~ à rire/à manger** to start laughing/eating, start *ou* begin to laugh/eat; **se ~ au régime** to go on a diet; **se ~ au travail** to set to work, get down to work, set about one's work; **se ~ à une traduction** to start *ou* set about (doing) a translation; **se ~ à traduire** to start to translate, start translating, set about translating; **il est temps de s'y ~** it's (high) time we got down to it *ou* got on with it; **se ~ à boire** to take to drink *ou* the bottle*; **se ~ à la peinture** *ou* **à peindre** to take up painting, take to painting; **se ~ au latin** to take up Latin; **il s'est bien mis à l'anglais** he's really taken to English; **voilà qu'il se met à pleuvoir!** and now it's coming on to (*Brit*) *ou* beginning *ou* starting to rain!; **qu'est-ce que tu es énervant quand tu t'y mets!***you can be a real pain when you get going* *ou* once you get started!*

e (*se grouper*) **ils se sont mis à plusieurs/2 pour pousser la voiture** several of them/the 2 of them joined forces to push the car; **se ~ avec qn** (*faire équipe*) to team up with sb; (*prendre parti*) to side with sb; (*: *en ménage*) to move in with sb*, shack up‡ (*péj*) with sb; **se ~ bien/mal avec qn** to get on the right/wrong side of sb; **se ~ d'un parti/d'une société** to join a party/a society; *voir* **partie²**.

f (*loc*) **on s'en est mis jusque-là** *ou* **plein la lampe*** we had a real blow-out‡; **qu'est-ce qu'ils se sont mis!*** they didn't half (*Brit*) lay into each other!* *ou* have a go at each other!*, they really laid into each other!* *ou* had a go at each other!*; *voir* **dent**.

meublant, e [mœblɑ̃, ɑ̃t] adj *papier, étoffe* decorative, effective. **ce papier est très ~** this paper finishes off the room nicely, this paper really makes* the room; *voir* **meuble**.

meuble [mœbl] 1 nm a (*objet*) piece of furniture. **(les) ~s** (the) furniture; **se cogner à** *ou* **dans un ~** to bump into a *ou* some piece of furniture; ~ **de rangement** cupboard, storage unit; **faire la liste des ~s** to make a list *ou* an inventory of the furniture, list each item of furniture; **nous sommes dans nos ~s** we have our own home. b (*ameublement*) **le ~** furniture; **le ~ de jardin** garden furniture. c (*Jur*) movable. **~s meublants** furniture, movables. d (*Hér*) charge. 2 adj a *terre, sol* loose, soft; *roche* soft, crumbly. b (*Jur*) **biens ~s** movables, personal estate, personalty.

meublé, e [mœble] (ptp de **meubler**) 1 adj furnished. **non ~** unfurnished. 2 nm (*pièce*) furnished room; (*appartement*) furnished flat. **être** *ou* **habiter en ~** to be *ou* live in furnished accommodation *ou* rooms.

meubler [mœble] [1] 1 vt *pièce, appartement* to furnish (*de* with); *pensée, mémoire, loisirs* to fill (*de* with); *dissertation* to fill out, pad out (*de* with). ~ **la conversation** to keep the conversation going; **une table et une chaise meublaient la pièce** the room was furnished with a table and a chair; **étoffe/papier qui meuble bien** decorative *ou* effective material/paper. 2 **se meubler** vpr to buy *ou* get (some) furniture, furnish one's home. **ils se sont meublés dans ce magasin/pour pas cher** they got *ou* bought their furniture from this shop/for a very reasonable price.

meuf‡ [mœf] nf bird‡ (*esp Brit*), chick‡.

meuglement [møgləmɑ̃] nm mooing (*NonC*), lowing† (*NonC*).

meugler [møgle] [1] vi to moo, low†.

meulage [mølaʒ] nm grinding.

meule¹ [møl] nf a (*à moudre*) millstone; (*à polir*) buff wheel. ~ **(à aiguiser)** grindstone; ~ **courante** *ou* **traînante** upper (mill)stone; (*Culin*) ~ **(de gruyère)** round of gruyère. b (‡ *motocyclette*) bike*, hog‡.

meule² [møl] nf (*Agr*) stack, rick. ~ **de foin** haystack, hayrick; ~ **de paille** stack of straw; **mettre en ~s** to stack, rick.

meuler [møle] [1] vt (*Tech*) to grind down.

meulière [møljɛʀ] nf: **(pierre) ~** millstone, buhrstone.

meunerie [mønʀi] nf (*industrie*) flour trade; (*métier*) milling. **opérations de ~** milling operations.

meunier, -ière [mønje, jɛʀ] 1 adj milling. **sole/truite ~ière** sole/trout meunière. 2 nm miller. 3 **meunière** nf miller's wife.

meurt-de-faim [mœʀdəfɛ̃] nmf inv pauper.

meurtre [mœʀtʀ] nm murder. **au ~!** murder!

meurtrier, -ière [mœʀtʀije, ijɛʀ] 1 adj *intention, fureur* murderous; *arme* deadly, lethal, murderous; *combat* bloody, deadly; *épidémie* fatal; (†) *personne* murderous. **week-end ~** weekend of carnage on the roads; **cette route est ~ière** this road is lethal *ou* a deathtrap. 2 nm murderer. 3 **meurtrière** nf a (*criminelle*) murderess. b (*Archit*) loophole.

meurtrir [mœʀtʀiʀ] [2] vt a (*lit*) *chair, fruit* to bruise. **être tout meurtri**

to be covered in bruises, be black and blue all over. b (*fig littér*) *personne, âme* to wound, bruise (*littér*).

meurtrissure [mœʀtʀisyʀ] **nf** a (*lit*) *[chair, fruit]* bruise. b (*fig littér*) *[âme]* scar, bruise. **les ~s laissées par la vie/le chagrin** the scars *ou* bruises left by life/sorrow.

Meuse [mœz] **nf: la ~** the Meuse, the Maas.

meute [møt] **nf** (*Chasse, fig*) pack.

mévente [mevɑ̃t] **nf** a slump. **une période de ~** a period of poor sales; **à cause de la ~** because of the slump in sales. b (†: *vente à perte*) sale *ou* selling at a loss.

mexicain, e [mɛksikɛ̃, ɛn] 1 **adj** Mexican. 2 **nm,f: M~(e)** Mexican.

Mexico [mɛksiko] **n** Mexico City.

Mexique [mɛksik] **nm** Mexico.

mézigue‡ [mezig] **pron pers** me, yours truly*, number one*. **c'est pour ~** it's for yours truly*.

mezzanine [mɛdzanin] **nf** (*Archit*) (*étage*) mezzanine (floor); (*fenêtre*) mezzanine window; (*Théât*) mezzanine.

mezza-voce [mɛdzavɔtʃe] **adv** (*littér*) in an undertone.

mezzo [mɛdzo] 1 **nm** mezzo (voice). 2 **nf** mezzo.

mezzo-soprano, **pl mezzo-sopranos** [mɛdzosɔpʀano] 1 **nm** mezzo-soprano (voice). 2 **nf** mezzo-soprano.

mezzo-tinto [mɛdzotinto] **nm inv** mezzotint.

MF a (**abrév de modulation de fréquence**) FM b **abrév de millions de francs.**

mg (**abrév de milligramme**) mg.

Mgr (**abrév de Monseigneur**) *title given to French bishops.*

mi [mi] **nm** (*Mus*) E; (*en chantant la gamme*) mi, me.

mi- [mi] 1 **préf** half, mid-. **la mi-janvier** *etc* the middle of January *etc*, mid-January *etc;* **pièce mi-salle à manger mi-salon** room which is half dining room half lounge, dining room cum living room, lounge-diner* (*Brit*); **mi-riant mi-pleurant** half-laughing half-crying, halfway between laughing and crying.

2 **comp** ►**mi-bas nm inv** knee *ou* long socks ►**la mi-carême** *the third Thursday in Lent* ►**mi-chemin: je l'ai rencontré à mi-chemin** I met him halfway there; **la poste est à mi-chemin** the post office is halfway there *ou* is halfway *ou* midway between the two; **à mi-chemin entre** (*lit, fig*) halfway *ou* midway between ►**mi-clos, e adj** half-closed; **les yeux mi-clos** with half-closed eyes, with one's eyes half-closed ►**mi-combat: à mi-combat** halfway through the match ►**mi-corps: à mi-corps** up to *ou* down to the waist; **portrait à mi-corps** half-length portrait ►**mi-côte: à mi-côte** halfway up *ou* down the hill ►**mi-course: à mi-course** halfway through the race, at the halfway mark ►**mi-cuisses: les bottes qui lui venaient à mi-cuisses** boots that came up to his thighs *ou* over his knees; **ils avaient de l'eau (jusqu')à mi-cuisses** they were thigh-deep in water, they were up to their thighs in water ►**à mi-distance** halfway (along), midway ►**mi-figue mi-raisin adj inv** *sourire* wry; *remarque* half-humorous, wry; **on leur fit un accueil mi-figue mi-raisin** they received a mixed reception ►**mi-fil, mi-coton** 50% linen 50% cotton, half-linen half-cotton ►**mi-fin adj** medium ►**mi-hauteur: à mi-hauteur** halfway up (*ou* down) ►**mi-jambes: à mi-jambes** (up *ou* down) to the knees ►**mi-long, mi-longue adj** *bas* knee-length; *manteau, jupe* calf-length; *manche* elbow-length ►**mi-lourd** (*Boxe*) **nm, adj** light heavyweight ►**mi-moyen** (*Boxe*) **nm, adj** welterweight ►**mi-pente: à mi-pente** = **à mi-côte** ►**mi-souriant** with a half-smile, half-smiling ►**mi-temps** *voir* **mi-temps** ►**mi-vitesse: à mi-vitesse** at half speed ►**mi-voix: à mi-voix** in a low *ou* hushed voice, in an undertone.

MIAGE [mjaʒ] **nf** (**abrév de maîtrise d'informatique appliquée à la gestion des entreprises**) *master's degree in business data processing.*

miam-miam* [mjammjam] **excl** yum-yum*.

miaou [mjau] **nm** miaow. **faire ~** to miaow.

miasmatique [mjasmatik] **adj** (*littér*) miasmic, miasmatic.

miasme [mjasm] **nm** (*gén pl*) miasma. **~s** putrid fumes, miasmas.

miaulement [mjolmɑ̃] **nm** (*voir* **miauler**) mewing; caterwaul(ing).

miauler [mjole] 1 **vi** to mew; (*fortement*) to caterwaul.

mica [mika] **nm** (*roche*) mica; (*vitre*) Muscovy glass.

micacé, e [mikase] **adj** *couleur* mica-tinted; *substance* mica-bearing.

micaschiste [mikaʃist] **nm** mica schist.

miche [miʃ] **nf** round loaf, cob loaf (*Brit*). (‡) **~s** (*fesses*) bum‡ (*Brit*), butt‡; (*seins*) boobs‡.

Michel [miʃɛl] **nm** Michael.

Michel-Ange [mikɛlɑ̃ʒ] **nm** Michelangelo.

Michèle [miʃɛl] **nf** Michel(l)e.

micheline [miʃlin] **nf** railcar.

Michelle [miʃɛl] **nf** = **Michèle**.

Michigan [miʃigɑ̃] **nm** Michigan. **le lac ~** Lake Michigan.

micmac* [mikmak] **nm** (*péj*) (*intrigue*) (little) game* (*péj*), funny business* (*péj*); (*complications*) fuss*, carry-on‡ (*Brit péj*). **je devine leur petit ~** I can guess their little game* *ou* what they're playing at*; **tu parles d'un ~!** what a carry-on!‡ (*Brit péj*) *ou* fuss!* *ou* mix-up!

micro [mikʀo] 1 **nm** a (**abrév de microphone**) microphone, mike*. (*Rad, TV*) **dites-le au ~** *ou* **devant le ~** say it in front of the mike*. b = **micro-ordinateur.** 2 **nf** = **micro-informatique.** 3 **comp** ►**micro-cravate nm (pl micros-cravates)** clip-on microphone, clip-on mike* ►**micro-trottoir nm (pl micros-trottoirs):faire un micro-trottoir** to interview people in the street.

micro... [mikʀo] **préf** micro... .

micro-ampère, pl micro-ampères [mikʀoɑ̃pɛʀ] **nm** microamp.

microbalance [mikʀobalɑ̃s] **nf** microbalance.

microbe [mikʀɔb] **nm** a (*Méd*) germ, microbe (*SPÉC*). b (*: *enfant*) tiddler*, tich‡ (*Brit*); (*péj: nabot*) little runt‡ (*péj*).

microbicide [mikʀɔbisid] 1 **adj** germ-killing. 2 **nm** germ-killer, microbicide (*SPÉC*).

microbien, -ienne [mikʀɔbjɛ̃, jɛn] **adj** *culture* microbial, microbic; *infection* bacterial. **maladie ~ne** bacterial disease.

microbiologie [mikʀobjɔlɔʒi] **nf** microbiology.

microbiologique [mikʀobjɔlɔʒik] **adj** microbiological.

microbiologiste [mikʀobjɔlɔʒist] **nmf** microbiologist.

microcéphale [mikʀosefal] **adj, nmf** microcephalic.

microchirurgie [mikʀoʃiʀyʀʒi] **nf** microsurgery.

microcircuit [mikʀosiʀkɥi] **nm** microchip.

microclimat [mikʀoklima] **nm** microclimate.

microcoque [mikʀɔkɔk] **nm** micrococcus.

microcosme [mikʀɔkɔsm] **nm** microcosm. **en ~** in microcosm.

microcosmique [mikʀɔkɔsmik] **adj** microcosmic.

microcoupure [mikʀokupyʀ] **nf** (*Ordin*) power dip.

microculture [mikʀokyltyʀ] **nf** (*Bio*) microculture.

micro-économie [mikʀoekɔnɔmi] **nf** microeconomics (*sg*).

micro-économique [mikʀoekɔnɔmik] **adj** microeconomic.

micro-édition [mikʀoedisjɔ̃] **nf** desktop publishing, DTP.

micro-électronique [mikʀoelɛktʀɔnik] **nf** microelectronics (*sg*).

microfiche [mikʀofiʃ] **nf** microfiche.

microfilm [mikʀofilm] **nm** microfilm.

micrographie [mikʀɔgʀafi] **nf** micrography.

micrographique [mikʀɔgʀafik] **adj** micrographic.

micro-informatique [mikʀoɛ̃fɔʀmatik] **nf** microcomputing.

micromètre [mikʀɔmɛtʀ] **nm** micrometer.

micrométrie [mikʀɔmetʀi] **nf** micrometry.

micrométrique [mikʀɔmetʀik] **adj** micrometric(al).

micron [mikʀɔ̃] **nm** micron.

Micronésie [mikʀonezi] **nf** Micronesia.

micro-onde, pl micro-ondes [mikʀoɔ̃d] **nf** microwave; *voir* **four**.

micro-ordinateur, pl micro-ordinateurs [mikʀoɔʀdinatœʀ] **nm** microcomputer.

micro-organisme, pl micro-organismes [mikʀoɔʀganism] **nm** micro-organism.

microphone [mikʀɔfɔn] **nm** microphone.

microphotographie [mikʀofɔtɔgʀafi] **nf** (*procédé*) photomicrography; (*image*) photomicrograph.

microphysique [mikʀofizik] **nf** microphysics (*sg*).

microplaquette [mikʀoplakɛt] **nf** (*Ordin*) microchip.

microprisme [mikʀopʀism] **nm** microprism.

microprocesseur [mikʀopʀɔsesœʀ] **nm** microprocessor.

microscope [mikʀɔskɔp] **nm** microscope. **examiner au ~** (*lit*) to study under *ou* through a microscope; (*fig*) to study in microscopic detail, subject to a microscopic examination; **~ électronique** electron microscope; **~ (électronique) à balayage (par transmission)** scanning electron microscope.

microscopique [mikʀɔskɔpik] **adj** microscopic.

microseconde [mikʀos(ə)gɔ̃d] **nf** microsecond.

microsillon [mikʀosijɔ̃] **nm** (*sillon*) microgroove. **(disque) ~** record.

microsonde [mikʀosɔ̃d] **nf** microprobe.

microstructure [mikʀostʀyktyʀ] **nf** microstructure.

miction [miksjɔ̃] **nf** micturition.

MIDEM [midɛm] **nm** (**abrév de marché international du disque et de l'édition musicale**) *voir* **marché**.

midi [midi] **nm** a (*heure*) midday, 12 (o'clock), noon. **~ dix** 10 past 12; **de ~ à 2 heures** from 12 *ou* (12) noon to 2; **entre ~ et 2 heures** between 12 *ou* (12) noon and 2; **hier à ~** yesterday at 12 o'clock *ou* at noon *ou* at midday; **pour le ravoir, c'est ~ (sonné)*** there isn't a hope in hell‡ of getting it back, as for getting it back not a hope* *ou* you've had it*; *voir* **chacun, chercher, coup.**

b (*période du déjeuner*) lunchtime, lunch hour; (*période de la plus grande chaleur*) midday, middle of the day. **à/pendant ~** at/during lunchtime, at/during the lunch hour; **demain ~** tomorrow lunchtime; **tous les ~s** every lunchtime *ou* lunch hour; **que faire ce ~?** what shall we do at lunchtime? *ou* midday?, what shall we do this lunch hour?; **le repas de ~** the midday meal, lunch; **qu'est-ce que tu as eu à ~?** what did you have for lunch?; **à ~ on va au café Duval** we're going to the Café Duval for lunch (today); **ça s'est passé en plein ~** it happened right in the middle of the day; **en plein ~ on étouffe de chaleur** at midday *ou* in the middle of the day it's stiflingly hot; *voir* **démon.**

c (*Géog: sud*) south. **exposé au** *ou* **en plein ~** facing south; **le ~ de la France, le M~** the South of France, the Midi; *voir* **accent.**

midinette [midinɛt] **nf** (†: *vendeuse*) shopgirl (*in the dress industry*); (†: *ouvrière*) dressmaker's apprentice. (*péj*) **elle a des goûts de ~** she has the tastes of a sixteen-year-old office girl.

mie[1] [mi] **nf** soft part of the bread, crumb (of the loaf); (*Culin*) bread with crusts removed. **il a mangé la croûte et laissé la ~** he's eaten the crust and left the soft part *ou* the inside (of the bread); **faire une farce avec de la ~ de pain** to make stuffing with breadcrumbs; *voir* **pain.**

mie[2] [mi] **nf** (††, *littér: bien-aimée*) lady-love†, beloved (*littér*).

mie[3]†† [mi] **adv** not. **ne le croyez ~** believe it not††.

miel [mjɛl] 1 **nm** honey. **bonbon/boisson au ~** honey sweet (*Brit*) *ou* candy (*US*)/drink; *[personne]* **être tout ~ (et tout sucre)** to be syrupy, have a rather unctuous manner; **~ rosat** rose honey; (*fig*) **faire son ~ de qch** to have a field day with sth; *voir* **gâteau, lune.** 2 **excl** (*euph* *) sugar!*

miellé, e [mjele] **adj** (*littér*) honeyed.

mielleusement [mjɛløzmɑ̃] **adv** (*péj*) unctuously.

mielleux, -euse [mjelø, øz] **adj** (*péj*) *personne* unctuous, syrupy, smooth-faced, smooth-tongued; *paroles* honeyed, smooth; *ton* honeyed, sugary; *sourire* sugary, sickly sweet; *saveur* sickly sweet.

mien, mienne [mjɛ̃, mjɛn] 1 **pron poss: le ~, la mienne, les ~s, les miennes** mine, my own; **ce sac n'est pas le ~** this bag is not mine, this is not my bag; **vos fils/filles sont sages comparé(e)s aux ~s/miennes** your sons/daughters are well-behaved compared to mine *ou* my own.
2 **nm** a **il n'y a pas à distinguer le ~ du tien** what's mine is yours; *pour autres exemples voir* **sien.** b **les ~s** my family, my (own) folks*.
3 **adj poss** (*littér*) **un ~ cousin** a cousin of mine; **je fais miennes vos observations** I agree wholeheartedly (with you); *voir* **sien.**

miette [mjɛt] **nf** *[pain, gâteau]* crumb. **en ~s** *verre* in bits *ou* pieces; *gâteau* in crumbs *ou* pieces; (*fig*) *bonheur* in pieces *ou* shreds; (*fig*) **les ~s de sa fortune** the (tattered) remnants of his fortune; **je n'en prendrai qu'une ~** I'll just have a tiny bit *ou* a sliver; **il n'en a pas laissé une ~** (*repas*) he didn't leave a scrap; (*fortune*) he didn't leave a ha'penny (*Brit*) *ou* cent (*US*); **mettre** *ou* **réduire en ~s** to break *ou* smash to bits *ou* to smithereens; **il ne s'en fait pas une ~**† he doesn't care a jot; **il ne perdait pas une ~ de la conversation/du spectacle** he didn't miss a scrap of the conversation/the show.

mieux [mjø] (*compar, superl de* **bien**) 1 **adv** a better. **aller** *ou* **se porter ~** to be better; **il ne s'est jamais ~ porté** he's never been in such fine form, he's never been *ou* felt better in his life; **plus il s'entraîne ~ il joue** the more he practises the better he plays; **elle joue ~ que lui** she plays better than he does; **c'est (un peu/beaucoup) ~ expliqué** it's (slightly/much) better explained; **il n'écrit pas ~ qu'il ne parle** he writes no better than he speaks; **s'attendre à ~** to expect better; **espérer ~** to hope for better (things); **il peut faire ~** he can do *ou* is capable of better; *voir* **reculer, tant, valoir** *etc.*
b **le ~, la ~, les ~** (the) best; (*de deux*) (the) better; **c'est à Paris que les rues sont le ~ éclairées** it is Paris that has the best street lighting, it is in Paris that the streets are (the) best lit; **en rentrant je choisis les rues les ~ éclairées** when I come home I choose the better *ou* best lit streets; **c'est ici qu'il dort le ~** he sleeps best here, this is where he sleeps best; **tout va le ~ du monde** everything's going beautifully; **un lycée des ~ conçus/aménagés** one of the best planned/best equipped schools; **un dîner des ~ réussis** a most *ou* highly successful dinner; **j'ai fait le ~** *ou* **du ~ que j'ai pu** I did my best *ou* the best I could; **des deux, elle est la ~ habillée** of the two, she is the better dressed.
c (*loc*) **~ que jamais** better than ever; (*Prov*) **~ vaut tard que jamais** better late than never (*Prov*); (*Prov*) **~ vaut prévenir que guérir** prevention is better than cure (*Prov*); (*Prov*) **~ vaut plier que rompre** adapt and survive!; **il va de ~ en ~** he's getting better and better, he goes from strength to strength; (*iro*) **de ~ en ~! maintenant il s'est mis à boire** that's great *ou* terrific (*iro*), now he has even taken to the bottle*; **il nous a écrit, ~ il est venu nous voir** he wrote to us, and better still he came to see us; **ils criaient à qui ~ ~** they vied with each other in shouting, each tried to outdo the other in shouting; **c'est on ne peut ~** it's (just) perfect.
2 **adj inv** a (*plus satisfaisant*) better. **le ~, la ~, les ~** (*de plusieurs*) (the) best; (*de deux*) (the) better; **c'est la ~ de nos secrétaires*** (*de toutes*) she is the best of our secretaries, she's our best secretary; (*de deux*) she's the better of our secretaries; **il est ~ qu'à son arrivée** he's improved since he (first) came, he's better than when he (first) came *ou* arrived; **c'est beaucoup ~ ainsi** it's (much) better this way; **le ~ serait de** the best (thing *ou* plan) would be to; **c'est ce qu'il pourrait faire de ~** it's the best thing he could do.
b (*en meilleure santé*) better; (*plus à l'aise*) better, more comfortable. **le ~, la ~, les ~** (the) best, (the) most comfortable; **être ~/le ~ du monde** to be better/in perfect health *ou* excellent form; **je le trouve ~ aujourd'hui** I think he is looking better *ou* he seems better today; **ils seraient ~ à la campagne qu'à la ville** they would be better (off) in the country than in (the) town; **c'est à l'ombre qu'elle sera le ~** she'll be best *ou* most comfortable in the shade; *voir* **sentir.**
c (*plus beau*) better looking, more attractive. **le ~, la ~, les ~** (*de plusieurs*) (the) best looking, (the) most attractive; (*de deux*) (the) better looking, (the) more attractive; **elle est ~ les cheveux longs** she looks better with her hair long *ou* with long hair, long hair suits her better; **c'est avec les cheveux courts qu'elle est le ~** she looks best with her hair short *ou* with short hair, short hair suits her best; **il est ~ que son frère** he's better looking than his brother.
d (*loc*) **au ~** (*gén*) at best; (*pour le mieux*) for the best; **en mettant les choses au ~** at (the very) best; **faites pour le ~** *ou* **au ~** do what you think best *ou* whatever is best; (*Fin*) **acheter/vendre au ~** to buy/sell at the best price; **être le ~ du monde** *ou* **au ~ avec qn** to be on the best of terms with sb; **c'est ce qui se fait de ~** it's the best there is *ou* one can get; **tu n'as rien de ~ à faire que (de) traîner dans les rues?** haven't you got anything better to do than hang around the streets?; **partez tout de suite, c'est le ~** it's best (that) you leave immediately, the best thing would be for you to leave immediately; **c'est son frère, en ~** he's (just) like his brother only better looking; **ce n'est pas mal, mais il y a ~** it's not bad, but I've seen better; **qui ~ est** even better, better still; **au ~ de sa forme** in peak condition; **au ~ de nos intérêts** in our best interests.
3 **nm** a best. (*Prov*) **le ~ est l'ennemi du bien** (it's better to) let well alone; (*loc*) **faire de son ~** to do one's best *ou* the best one can; **aider qn de son ~** to do one's best to help sb, help sb the best one can *ou* to the best of one's ability; *voir* **changer, faute.**
b (*amélioration, progrès*) improvement. **il y a un ~** *ou* **du ~** there's (been) some improvement.
4 **comp** ►**mieux-être nm** greater welfare; (*matériel*) improved standard of living ►**mieux-vivre nm** improved standard of living.

mièvre [mjɛvʀ] **adj** *roman, genre* precious, sickly sentimental; *tableau* pretty-pretty; *sourire* mawkish; *charme* vapid. **elle est un peu ~** she's a bit colourless *ou* insipid.

mièvrerie [mjɛvʀəʀi] **nf** a (*caractère: voir* **mièvre**) preciousness, sickly sentimentality; pretty-prettiness; mawkishness; vapidity; colourlessness, insipidness. b (*œuvre d'art*) insipid creation; (*comportement*) childish *ou* silly behaviour (*NonC*); (*propos*) insipid *ou* sentimental talk (*NonC*).

mignard, e [miɲaʀ, aʀd] **adj** *style* mannered, precious; *décor* pretty-pretty, over-ornate; *musique* pretty-pretty, over-delicate; *manières* precious, dainty, simpering (*péj*).

mignardise [miɲaʀdiz] **nf** a *[tableau, poème, style]* preciousness; *[décor]* ornateness; *[manières]* preciousness (*péj*), daintiness, affectation (*péj*). b (*fleur*) **de la ~, des œillets ~** pinks.

mignon, -onne [miɲɔ̃, ɔn] 1 **adj** (*joli*) *enfant, objet* sweet, cute*; *bras, pied, geste* dainty; *femme* sweet, pretty; (*gentil, aimable*) nice, sweet. **donne-le-moi, tu seras ~ne*** give it to me there's a dear* *ou* love* (*Brit*), be a dear* and give it to me; **c'est ~ chez vous** you've got an adorable little place; *voir* **péché.** 2 **nm,f** (little) darling, cutie* (*US*), poppet*. **mon ~, ma ~ne** sweetheart, pet*, lovie* (*Brit*). 3 **nm** (††: *favori*) minion; *voir* **filet.**

mignonnement† [miɲɔnmɑ̃] **adv** prettily.

mignonnet, -ette [miɲɔnɛ, ɛt] 1 **adj** *enfant, objet* sweet, cute*. **c'est ~ chez eux** they've got a cute little place*. 2 **mignonnette nf** a (*bouteille*) miniature. b (*Bot*) reseda.

migraine [migʀɛn] **nf** (*gén*) headache; (*Méd*) migraine, sick headache. **j'ai la ~** I've got a bad headache, my head aches.

migrant, e [migʀɑ̃, ɑ̃t] **adj, nm,f** migrant.

migrateur, -trice [migʀatœʀ, tʀis] 1 **adj** migratory. 2 **nm** migrant, migratory bird.

migration [migʀasjɔ̃] **nf** (*gén*) migration; (*Rel*) transmigration. **oiseau en ~** migrating bird.

migratoire [migʀatwaʀ] **adj** migratory.

migrer [migʀe] 1 **vi** to migrate (*vers* to).

mijaurée [miʒɔʀe] **nf** pretentious *ou* affected woman *ou* girl. **faire la ~** to give oneself airs (and graces); **regarde-moi cette ~!** just look at her with her airs and graces!; **petite ~!** little madam!

mijoter [miʒɔte] 1 1 **vt** a (*Culin: cuire*) *plat, soupe* to simmer; (*préparer avec soin*) to cook *ou* prepare lovingly. **un plat mijoté** a dish which has been slow-cooked *ou* simmered; **(faire) ~ un plat** to simmer a dish, allow a dish to simmer; **elle lui mijote des petits plats** she cooks (up) *ou* concocts tempting *ou* tasty dishes (for him).
b (* *fig: tramer*) to plot, scheme, cook up*. **~ un complot** to hatch a plot; **il mijote un mauvais coup** he's cooking up* *ou* plotting some mischief; **qu'est-ce qu'il peut bien ~?** what's he up to?*, what's he cooking up?*; **il se mijote quelque chose** something's brewing *ou* cooking*.
c **laisser qn ~ (dans son jus)*** to leave sb to stew*, let sb stew in his own juice.
2 **vi** *[plat, soupe]* to simmer; *[complot]* to be brewing.

mijoteuse [miʒɔtøz] **nf** ® slow cooker.

mikado [mikado] **nm** (*jeu*) jackstraws, spillikins.

mil[1] [mil] **nm** (*dans une date*) a *ou* one thousand.

mil[2] [mij, mil] **nm** = **millet.**

milady [miledi] **nf** (titled English) lady. **oui ~** yes my lady.

Milan [milɑ̃] **n** Milan.

milan [milɑ̃] **nm** (*Orn*) kite.

milanais, e [milanɛ, ɛz] 1 **adj** Milanese. (*Culin*) **escalope** *etc* **(à la) ~e** escalope *etc* milanaise. 2 **nm,f: M~(e)** Milanese.

mildiou [mildju] **nm** (*Agr*) mildew.

mildiousé, e [mildjuze] **adj** (*Agr*) mildewed.

mile [majl] **nm** mile (*1 609 m*).

milice [milis] **nf** militia.

milicien [milisjɛ̃] **nm** militiaman.

milicienne [milisjɛn] **nf** woman serving in the militia.

milieu, pl ~x [miljø] **nm** a (*centre*) middle. **casser/couper/scier qch en**

son ~ *ou* **par le ~** to break/cut/saw sth down *ou* through the middle; **le bouton/la porte du ~** the middle *ou* centre knob/door; **je prends celui du ~** I'll take the one in the middle *ou* the middle one; **tenir le ~ de la chaussée** to keep to the middle of the road; (*Ftbl*) **~ de terrain** midfield player; (*Ftbl*) **le ~ du terrain** the midfield; **il est venu vers le ~ de l'après-midi/la matinée** he came towards the middle of the afternoon/morning, he came about mid-afternoon/mid-morning; **vers/depuis le ~ du 15e siècle** towards/since the mid-15th century, towards/since the mid-1400s.

b **au ~ de** (*au centre de*) in the middle of; (*parmi*) amid, among, in the midst of, amidst (*littér*); **il est là au ~ de ce groupe** he's over there in the middle of that group; **au beau ~ (de), en plein ~ (de)** right *ou* slap bang* in the middle (of), in the very middle (of); **au ~ de toutes ces difficultés/aventures** in the middle *ou* midst of *ou* amidst all these difficulties/adventures; **au ~ de son affolement** in the middle *ou* midst of his panic; **elle n'est heureuse qu'au ~ de sa famille/de ses enfants** she's only happy when she's among *ou* surrounded by her family/children *ou* with her family/children around her; **au ~ de la journée** in the middle of the day; **au ~ de la nuit** in the middle of the night, at dead of night; **comment travailler au ~ de ce vacarme?** how can anyone work in *ou* surrounded by this din?; **au ~ de la descente** halfway down (the hill); **au ~ de la page** in the middle of the page, halfway down the page; **au ~/en plein ~ de l'hiver** in mid-winter/the depth of winter; **au ~ de l'été** in mid-summer, at the height of summer; **il est parti au beau ~ de la réception** he left when the party was in full swing, he left right in the middle of the party.

c (*état intermédiaire*) middle course *ou* way. **il n'y a pas de ~ (entre)** there is no middle course *ou* way (between); **c'est tout noir ou tout blanc, il ne connaît pas de ~** he sees everything as either black or white, he knows no mean (*frm*) *ou* there's no happy medium (for him); **le juste ~** the happy medium, the golden mean; **un juste ~** a happy medium; **il est innocent ou coupable, il n'y a pas de ~** he is either innocent or guilty, he can't be both; **tenir le ~** to steer a middle course.

d (*Bio, Géog*) environment. (*Phys*) **~ réfringent** refractive medium; **~ physique/géographique/humain** physical/geographical/human environment; **les animaux dans leur ~ naturel** animals in their natural surroundings *ou* environment *ou* habitat.

e (*entourage social, moral*) milieu, environment; (*groupe restreint*) set, circle; (*provenance*) background. **le ~ familial** the family circle; (*Sociol*) the home *ou* family background, the home environment; **s'adapter à un nouveau ~** to adapt to a different milieu *ou* environment; **il ne se sent pas dans son ~** he feels out of place, he doesn't feel at home; **elle se sent** *ou* **est dans son ~ chez nous** she feels (quite) at home with us; **de quel ~ sort-il?** what is his (social) background?; **les ~x littéraires/financiers** literary/financial circles; **de ~x autorisés/bien informés** from official/well-informed sources; **c'est un ~ très fermé** it is a very closed circle *ou* exclusive set.

f (*Crime*) **le ~** the underworld; **les gens du ~** (people of) the underworld; **membre du ~** gangster, mobster.

militaire [militɛʀ] 1 adj military, army (*épith*). **la vie ~** military *ou* army life; **camion ~** army lorry (*Brit*) *ou* truck (*US*); *voir* **attaché, service.** 2 nm serviceman. **il est ~** he is in the forces *ou* services; **~ de carrière** (*terre*) regular (soldier); (*air*) (serving) airman.

militairement [militɛʀmɑ̃] adv *mener une affaire, saluer* in military fashion *ou* style. **la ville a été occupée ~** the town was occupied by the army; **occuper ~ une ville** to (send in the army to) occupy a town.

militant, e [militɑ̃, ɑ̃t] adj, nm,f militant. **~ de base** rank and file *ou* grassroots militant.

militantisme [militɑ̃tism] nm militancy.

militarisation [militaʀizasjɔ̃] nf militarization.

militariser [militaʀize] 1 vt to militarize.

militarisme [militaʀism] nm militarism.

militariste [militaʀist] 1 adj militaristic. 2 nmf militarist.

militer [milite] 1 vi a [*personne*] to be a militant. **il milite au parti communiste** he is a communist party militant, he is a militant in the communist party; **~ pour les droits de l'homme** to campaign for human rights. b [*arguments, raisons*] **~ en faveur de** *ou* **pour** to militate in favour of, argue for; **~ contre** to militate *ou* tell against.

millage [milaʒ] nm (*Can*) mileage.

mille[1] [mil] 1 adj inv a a *ou* one thousand. **~ un** a *ou* one thousand and one; **trois ~** three thousand; **deux ~ neuf cents** two thousand nine hundred; **page ~** page a *ou* one thousand; (*dans les dates: aussi* **mil**) **l'an ~** the year one thousand; **un billet de ~*** a thousand-franc note; *voir* **donner.**

b (*nombreux*) **~ regrets** I'm *ou* we're terribly *ou* extremely sorry; **~ baisers** fondest love; **je lui ai dit ~ fois** I've told him a thousand times; **c'est ~ fois trop grand** it's far too big.

c (*loc*) **~ et un problèmes/exemples** a thousand and one problems/examples; **"les M~ et Une Nuits"** "the Thousand and One Nights", "the Arabian Nights"; **les contes des M~ et Une Nuits** tales from the Arabian Nights; **je vous le donne en ~*** you'll never guess.

2 nm inv a (*Comm, Math*) a *ou* one thousand. **5 pour ~ d'alcool** 5 parts of alcohol to a thousand; **5 enfants sur ~** 5 children out of *ou* in every thousand; **vendre qch au ~** to sell sth by the thousand; (*Comm*) **2 ~ de boulons** 2 thousand bolts; **ouvrage qui en est à son centième ~** book which has sold 100,000 copies; *voir* **gagner.**

b (*Sport*) [*cible*] bull (*Brit*), bull's-eye. **mettre** *ou* **taper (en plein) dans le ~** (*lit*) to hit the bull (*Brit*) *ou* bull's-eye, hit the spot*; (*fig*) to score a bull's-eye, be bang on target*; **tu as mis dans le ~ en lui faisant ce cadeau** you were bang on target with the present you gave him*.

3 comp ►**mille-feuille** (*Culin*) nm (pl **mille-feuilles**) mille feuilles, cream *ou* vanilla slice (*Brit*) ►**mille-pattes** nm inv centipede ►**mille-raies** nm inv (*tissu*) finely-striped material; **velours mille-raies** needlecord.

mille[2] [mil] nm a **~ (marin)** nautical mile. b (*Can*) mile (*1 609 m*).

millénaire [milenɛʀ] 1 nm (*période*) millennium, a thousand years; (*anniversaire*) thousandth anniversary, millennium. **c'est le deuxième ~** *ou* **le bi-~ de** it is the two-thousandth anniversary of. 2 adj (*lit*) thousand-year-old (*épith*), millenial; (*fig: très vieux*) ancient, very old. **des rites plusieurs fois ~s** rites several thousand years old, age-old rites; **ce monument ~** this thousand-year-old monument.

millénarisme [milenaʀism] nm millenarianism.

millénariste [milenaʀist] adj, nmf millenarian.

millénium [milenjɔm] nm millennium.

mille(-)pertuis [milpɛʀtɥi] nm St.-John's-wort.

millésime [milezim] nm (*Admin, Fin: date*) year, date; [*vin*] year, vintage. **vin d'un bon ~** vintage wine; **quel est le ~ de ce vin?** what is the vintage *ou* year of this wine?

millésimé, e [milezime] adj vintage. **bouteille ~e** bottle of vintage wine; **un bordeaux ~** a vintage Bordeaux.

millet [mijɛ] nm (*Agr*) millet. **donner des grains de ~ aux oiseaux** to give the birds some millet *ou* (bird)seed.

milli... [mili] préf milli... .

milliaire [miljɛʀ] adj (*Antiq*) milliary. **borne ~** milliary column.

milliampère [miliɑ̃pɛʀ] nm milliamp.

milliard [miljaʀ] nm thousand million, milliard (*Brit*), billion (*US*). **un ~ de gens** a thousand million *ou* a billion (*US*) people; **10 ~s de francs** 10 thousand million francs, 10 billion francs (*US*); **des ~s de** thousands of millions of, billions of.

milliardaire [miljaʀdɛʀ] nmf multimillionaire (*Brit*), billionaire (*US*). **il est ~** he's a multimillionaire (*Brit*), he's worth millions; **une société plusieurs fois ~ en dollars** a company worth (many) millions of dollars.

milliardième [miljaʀdjɛm] adj, nm thousand millionth, billionth (*US*).

millibar [milibaʀ] nm millibar.

millième [miljɛm] adj, nm thousandth.

millier [milje] nm thousand. **un ~ de têtes** a thousand (or so) heads, (about) a thousand heads; **par ~s** in (their) thousands, by the thousand; **il y en a des ~s** there are thousands (of them).

milligramme [miligʀam] nm milligram(me).

millilitre [mililitʀ] nm millilitre.

millimètre [milimɛtʀ] nm millimetre.

millimétré, e [milimetʀe] adj graduated (*in millimetres*).

millimétrique [milimetʀik] adj millimetric.

million [miljɔ̃] nm million. **2 ~s de francs** 2 million francs; **être riche à ~s** to be a millionaire, have millions, be worth millions.

millionième [miljɔnjɛm] adj, nmf millionth.

millionnaire [miljɔnɛʀ] nmf millionaire. **la société est ~** the company is worth millions *ou* worth a fortune; **il est plusieurs fois ~** he's a millionaire several times over; **un ~ en dollars** a dollar millionaire.

millivolt [milivɔlt] nm millivolt.

milord†* [milɔʀ] nm (*noble anglais*) lord, nobleman; (*riche étranger*) immensely rich foreigner. **oui ~!** yes my lord!

mime [mim] nm a (*personne*) (*Théât: professionnel*) mimer, mime; (*gén: imitateur*) mimic. b (*Théât: art*) (*action*) mime, miming; (*pièce*) mime. **le ~ est un art difficile** miming is a difficult art; **il fait du ~** he is a mime; **aller voir un spectacle de ~** to go to watch *ou* see a mime.

mimer [mime] 1 vt (*Théât*) to mime; (*singer*) to mimic, imitate; (*pour ridiculiser*) to take off.

mimétique [mimetik] adj mimetic.

mimétisme [mimetism] nm (*Bio*) (protective) mimicry; (*fig*) unconscious mimicry, mimetism. **par un ~ étrange, il en était venu à ressembler à son chien** through some strange process of imitation he had grown to look just like his dog; **le ~ qui finit par faire se ressembler l'élève et le maître** the unconscious imitation through which the pupil grows like his master.

mimi* [mimi] nm (*langage enfantin*) (*chat*) pussy(cat), puss*; (*baiser*) little kiss.

mimique [mimik] nf a (*grimace comique*) comical expression, funny face. **ce singe a de drôles de ~s!** this monkey makes such funny faces! b (*signes, gestes*) gesticulations (*pl*), sign language (*NonC*). **il eut une ~ expressive pour dire qu'il avait faim** his gestures *ou* gesticulations made it quite clear that he was hungry.

mimodrame [mimɔdʀam] nm (*Théât*) mimodrama.

mimolette [mimɔlɛt] nf *type of Dutch cheese.*

mimosa [mimoza] nm mimosa; *voir* **œuf.**

MIN [min] nm (abrév de **marché d'intérêt national**) *voir* **marché.**

min (abrév de **minimum**) min.

minable [minabl] 1 adj (*décrépit*) *lieu, aspect, personne* shabby(-looking), seedy(-looking); (*médiocre*) *devoir, film, personne* hopeless*, useless*, pathetic*; *salaire, vie* miserable, wretched. **l'histoire ~ de cette veuve avec 15 enfants à nourrir** the sorry *ou* dismal tale of that widow with 15 children to feed; **habillé de façon ~** seedily dressed. 2 nmf (*péj*) dead loss*, second-rater*, washout*. **c'est un ~** he's a dead loss*, he's (just) hopeless* *ou* pathetic*; **une bande de ~s** a pathetic *ou* useless bunch*.

minage [minaʒ] nm *[pont, tranchée]* mining.

minaret [minaʀɛ] nm minaret.

minauder [minode] 1 vi to simper, put on simpering airs. **oh oui, dit-elle en minaudant** oh yes, she simpered; **je n'aime pas sa façon de ~** I don't like her (silly) simpering ways.

minauderie [minodʀi] nf: **~s** simpering (airs); **faire des ~s** to put on simpering airs, simper.

minaudier, -ière [minodje, jɛʀ] adj affected, simpering (*épith*).

mince [mɛ̃s] 1 adj a (*peu épais*) thin; (*svelte, élancé*) slim, slender. **tranche ~** *[pain]* thin slice; *[saucisson, jambon]* sliver, thin slice; **~ comme une feuille de papier à cigarette** *ou* **comme une pelure d'oignon** paper-thin, wafer-thin; **avoir la taille ~** to be slim *ou* slender.

b (*fig: faible, insignifiant*) *profit* slender; *salaire* meagre, small; *prétexte* lame, weak, slight; *preuve, chances* slim, slender, slight; *connaissances, rôle, mérite* slight, small. **l'intérêt du film est bien ~** the film is decidedly lacking in interest *ou* is of very little interest; **le prétexte est bien ~** it's a very weak *ou* lame pretext; **ce n'est pas une ~ affaire que de faire** it's quite a job *ou* business doing, it's no easy task to do; **c'est un peu ~ comme réponse** that's a rather lame *ou* feeble reply, that's not much of an answer.

2 adv *couper* thinly, in thin slices.

3 excl (*) **~ (alors)!** (*contrariété*) drat (it)!*, blow (it)!* (*Brit*); (*surprise*) you don't say!; (*admiration*) wow!*

minceur [mɛ̃sœʀ] nf (*voir* **mince**) thinness; slimness, slenderness. **la ~ des preuves** the slimness *ou* the insufficiency of the evidence; **cuisine ~** cuisine minceur.

mincir [mɛ̃siʀ] 2 1 vi to get slimmer, get thinner. 2 vt: **cette robe te mincit** this dress makes you look slimmer.

mine[1] [min] nf a (*physionomie*) expression, look. **dit-il, la ~ réjouie** he said with a cheerful *ou* delighted expression; **ne fais pas cette ~-là** stop making *ou* pulling that face; **elle avait la ~ longue** she was pulling a long face; **avoir** *ou* **faire triste ~, avoir** *ou* **faire piètre ~** to cut a sorry figure, look a sorry sight; **faire triste ~ à qn** to give sb a cool reception, greet sb unenthusiastically; *voir* **gris**.

b **~s** *[femme]* simpering airs; *[bébé]* expressions; **faire des ~s** to put on simpering airs, simper; *[bébé]* **il fait ses petites ~s** he makes (funny) little faces, he gives you these funny looks.

c (*allure*) exterior, appearance. **ne vous fiez pas à sa ~ affairée/tranquille** don't be taken in by his busy/calm exterior *ou* appearance; **tu as la ~ de quelqu'un qui n'a rien compris** you look as if you haven't understood a single thing; **il cachait sous sa ~ modeste un orgueil sans pareil** his appearance of modesty *ou* his modest exterior concealed an overweening pride; **votre poulet/rôti a bonne ~** your chicken/roast looks good *ou* lovely *ou* inviting; (*iro*) **tu as bonne ~ maintenant!** now you look an utter *ou* a right* idiot! (*Brit*) *ou* a fine fool!; *voir* **juger, payer**.

d (*teint*) **avoir bonne ~** to look well; **il a mauvaise ~** he doesn't look well, he looks unwell *ou* poorly; **avoir une sale ~** to look awful* *ou* dreadful; **avoir une ~ de papier mâché/de déterré** to look washed out/like death warmed up* (*Brit*) *ou* warmed over* (*US*); **il a meilleure ~ qu'hier** he looks better than (he did) yesterday.

e (*loc*) **faire ~ de faire** to make a show *ou* pretence of doing, go through the motions of doing; **j'ai fait ~ de le croire** I acted as if I believed it, I made a show *ou* pretence of believing it; **j'ai fait ~ de lui donner une gifle** I made as if to slap him; **il n'a même pas fait ~ de résister** he didn't even put up a token resistance, he didn't offer even a show of resistance; **il est venu nous demander comment ça marchait, ~ de rien*** he came and asked us with a casual air *ou* all casually* *ou* all casual like* how things were going; **~ de rien, tu sais qu'il n'est pas bête*** though you wouldn't think it to look at him, he's not daft* *ou* he's no dummy* you know.

mine[2] [min] nf a (*gisement*) deposit, mine; (*exploité*) mine. (*lit, fig*) **~ d'or** gold mine; **région de ~s** mining area *ou* district; **~ à ciel ouvert** opencast mine; **la nationalisation des ~s** (*gén*) the nationalization of the mining industry; (*charbon*) the nationalization of coal *ou* of the coalmining industry; **~ de charbon** (*gén*) coalmine; (*puits*) pit, mine; (*entreprise*) colliery; **descendre dans la ~** to go down the mine *ou* pit; *voir* **carreau, galerie, puits**.

b (*Admin*) **les M~s** ≃ the (National) Mining and Geological service; **École des M~s** ≃ (National) School of Mining Engineering; **ingénieur des M~s** (state qualified) mining engineer; **le service des M~s** ≃ MOT (*Brit*), *the French government vehicle testing service*.

c (*fig: source*) mine, source, fund (*de* of). **~ de renseignements** mine of information; **une ~ inépuisable de documents** an inexhaustible source of documents.

d **~ (de crayon)** lead (of pencil); **crayon à ~ dure/douce** hard/soft pencil, pencil with a hard/soft lead; **~ de plomb** black lead, graphite; *voir* **porter**.

e (*Mil*) (*galerie*) gallery, sap, mine; (*explosif*) mine. **~ dormante** unexploded mine; **~ terrestre** landmine; *voir* **champ, détecteur**.

miner [mine] 1 vt a (*garnir d'explosifs*) to mine. **ce pont est miné** this bridge has been mined. b (*ronger*) *falaise, fondations* to undermine, erode, eat away; (*fig*) *société, autorité, santé* to undermine, erode; *force, énergie* to sap, drain, undermine. **la maladie l'a miné** his illness has left him drained (of energy) *ou* has sapped his strength; **être miné par le chagrin/l'inquiétude** to be worn down by grief/anxiety; **miné par la jalousie** wasting away *ou* consumed with jealousy; **ses cours sont vraiment minants*** his classes are a real bore *ou* are really deadly*.

minerai [minʀɛ] nm ore. **~ de fer/cuivre** iron/copper ore.

minéral, e, mpl **-aux** [mineʀal, o] 1 adj *huile, sel* mineral; (*Chim*) inorganic; *voir* **chimie, eau**. 2 nm mineral.

minéralier [mineʀalje] nm ore tanker.

minéralisation [mineʀalizasjɔ̃] nf mineralization.

minéraliser [mineʀalize] 1 vt to mineralize.

minéralogie [mineʀalɔʒi] nf mineralogy.

minéralogique [mineʀalɔʒik] adj (*Géol*) mineralogical. (*Aut*) **numéro ~** registration (*Brit*) *ou* license (*US*) number; (*Aut*) **plaque ~** number (*Brit*) *ou* license (*US*) plate.

minéralogiste [mineʀalɔʒist] nmf mineralogist.

minerve [minɛʀv] nf (*Méd*) (surgical) collar; (*Typ*) platen machine. (*Myth*) **M~** Minerva.

minet, -ette [minɛ, ɛt] 1 nm,f (*langage enfantin: chat*) puss*, pussy(-cat) (*langage enfantin*). (*terme affectif*) **mon ~, ma ~te** (my) pet*, sweetie(-pie)*. 2 nm (*péj: jeune élégant*) young dandy *ou* trendy* (*Brit*). 3 **minette** nf (*: *jeune fille*) dollybird* (*Brit*), (cute) chick* (*US*).

mineur[1]**, e** [minœʀ] 1 adj a (*Jur*) minor. **enfant ~** minor; **être ~** to be under age, be a minor. b (*peu important*) *soucis, œuvre, artiste* minor; *voir* **Asie**. c (*Mus*) *gamme, intervalle* minor. **en do ~** in C minor. d (*Logique*) minor. **terme ~** minor term; **proposition ~e** minor premise. 2 nm,f (*Jur*) minor, young person under 18 (years of age). **établissement interdit aux ~s** no person under 18 allowed on the premises; *voir* **détournement**. 3 nm (*Mus*) minor. **en ~** in a minor key. 4 **mineure** nf a (*Logique*) minor premise. b (*Univ: matière*) subsidiary (*Brit*), second subject (*Brit*), minor (*US*).

mineur[2] [minœʀ] nm a (*Ind*) miner; *[houille]* (coal) miner. **~ de fond** pitface *ou* underground worker, miner at the pitface; **village de ~s** mining village. b (*Mil*) sapper (*who lays mines*).

mini [mini] 1 préf: **mini... mini...; on va faire un ~ repas** we'll have a snack lunch. 2 adj inv: **la mode ~** the mini-length fashion; **c'est ~ chez eux*** they've got a minute *ou* tiny (little) place; **partir en vacances avec un ~ budget** *ou* **un budget ~** to go off on holiday on a tiny budget. 3 nf = **mini-informatique**. 4 nm inv a (*Mode*) **elle s'habille (en) ~** she wears minis; **la mode est au ~** minis are in (fashion). b = **mini-ordinateur**.

miniature [minjatyʀ] 1 nf a (*gén*) miniature. **en ~** in miniature; **cette province, c'est la France en ~** this province is a miniature France *ou* France in miniature. b (*Art*) miniature; (*lettre*) miniature. c (*: *nabot*) (little) shrimp* *ou* tich* (*Brit*), tiddler*. **tu as vu cette ~?** did you see that little shrimp?* 2 adj miniature. **train/lampes ~(s)** miniature train/lights.

miniaturisation [minjatyʀizasjɔ̃] nf miniaturization.

miniaturiser [minjatyʀize] 1 vt to miniaturize. **transistor miniaturisé** miniaturized transistor.

miniaturiste [minjatyʀist] nmf miniaturist.

mini-boom, pl **mini-booms** [minibum] nm mini boom.

minibus [minibys] nm minibus.

minicassette [minikasɛt] nf ® minicassette.

minichaîne [miniʃɛn] nf mini system.

minier, -ière [minje, jɛʀ] adj mining.

mini-golf, pl **mini-golfs** [minigɔlf] nm crazy golf.

mini-informatique [miniɛ̃fɔʀmatik] nf minicomputing.

mini-jupe, pl **mini-jupes** [miniʒyp] nf miniskirt.

minima [minima] *voir* **minimum**.

minimal, e, mpl **-aux** [minimal, o] adj *température, pension* minimal, minimum. (*Phon*) **paire ~e** minimal pair; (*Art*) **art ~** minimal art.

minimalisme [minimalism] nm (*Art*) minimalism.

minimaliste [minimalist] adj, nmf minimalist.

minime [minim] 1 adj *dégât, rôle, différence* minor, minimal; *fait* trifling, trivial; *salaire, somme* paltry. 2 nmf a (*Sport*) junior (*13-15 years*). b (*Rel*) Minim.

minimisation [minimizasjɔ̃] nf minimization.

minimiser [minimize] 1 vt *risque, rôle* to minimize; *incident* to play down.

minimum [minimɔm], *f* **~** *ou* **minima** [minima], pl **~(s)** *ou* **minima** 1 adj minimum. **vitesse/âge ~** minimum speed/age; *voir* **salaire**.

2 nm (*gén, Math*) minimum; (*Jur*) minimum sentence. **dans le ~ de temps** in the shortest time possible; **il faut un ~ de temps/d'intelligence pour le faire** you need a minimum amount of time/a modicum of intelligence to be able to do it; **il faut quand même travailler un ~** you still have to do a minimum (amount) of work; **avec un ~ d'efforts il**

aurait réussi with a minimum of effort he would have succeeded; **il n'a pris que le ~ de précautions** he took only minimum *ou* minimal precautions; **la production/la valeur des marchandises a atteint son ~** the production/the value of the goods has sunk to its lowest level (yet) *ou* an all-time low; **dépenses réduites au/à un ~** expenditure cut (down) to the/a minimum; **avoir tout juste le ~ vital** (*salaire*) to earn barely a living wage; (*subsistance*) to be *ou* live at subsistence level, be on the bread line*; **ça coûte au ~ 100 F** it costs at least 100 francs *ou* a minimum of 100 francs; **au grand ~** at the very least; **il faut rester le ~ (de temps) au soleil** you must stay in the sun as little as possible; (*Jur*) **~ vieillesse** basic old age pension.

mini-ordinateur, pl **mini-ordinateurs** [miniɔʀdinatœʀ] **nm** minicomputer.

minipilule [minipilyl] **nf** minipill.

ministère [ministɛʀ] 1 **nm** a (*département*) ministry (*Brit*), department (*surtout US*). **employé de ~** government *ou* Crown (*Brit*) employee; **~ de l'Agriculture/de l'Éducation (nationale)** *etc* ministry (*Brit*) *ou* department (*US*) of Agriculture/Education *etc; voir aussi* **2**.

b (*cabinet*) government, cabinet. **sous le ~ (de) Pompidou** under the premiership of Pompidou, under Pompidou's government; **le premier ~ Poincaré** Poincaré's first government *ou* cabinet; **former un ~** to form a government *ou* a cabinet; **~ de coalition** coalition government.

c (*Jur*) **le ~ public** (*partie*) the Prosecution; (*service*) *the public prosecutor's office;* **par ~ d'huissier** served by a bailiff.

d (*Rel*) ministry. **exercer son ~ à la campagne** to have a country parish.

e (*littér: entremise*) agency. **proposer son ~ à qn** to offer to act for sb.

2 **comp ►ministère des Affaires étrangères** Ministry of Foreign Affairs, Foreign Office (*Brit*), Department of State (*US*), State Department (*US*) **►ministère des Affaires européennes** Ministry of European Affairs **►ministère des Affaires sociales** Social Services Ministry **►ministère des Anciens Combattants** *Ministry responsible for ex-servicemen,* ≃ Veterans Administration (*US*) **►ministère du Commerce** Ministry of Trade, Department of Trade and Industry (*Brit*), Department of Commerce (*US*) **►ministère du Commerce extérieur** Ministry of Foreign Trade, Board of Trade (*Brit*) **►ministère de la Culture et de la Communication** Ministry for the Arts **►ministère de la Défense nationale** Ministry of Defence (*Brit*), Department of Defense (*US*) **►ministère des Départements et Territoires d'outre-mer** *Ministry for French overseas territories* **►ministère de l'Économie et des Finances** Ministry of Finance, Treasury (*Brit*), Treasury Department (*US*) **►ministère de l'Environnement** Ministry of the Environment, Department of the Environment (*Brit*), Environmental Protection Agency (*US*) **►ministère de l'Industrie** ≃ Department of Trade and Industry (*Brit*), ≃ Department of Commerce (*US*) **►ministère de l'Intérieur** Ministry of the Interior, Home Office (*Brit*) **►ministère de la Jeunesse et des Sports** Ministry of Sport **►ministère de la Justice** Ministry of Justice, Lord Chancellor's Office (*Brit*), Department of Justice (*US*) **►ministère de la Santé (et de la Sécurité sociale)** Ministry of Health, Department of Health and Social Security (*Brit*), Department of Health and Human Services (*US*) **►ministère des Transports** Ministry of Transport (*Brit*), Department of Transportation (*US*) **►ministère du Travail** Ministry of Employment (*Brit*), Department of Labor (*US*).

ministériel, -elle [ministeʀjɛl] **adj** *fonction, circulaire* ministerial; *crise, remaniement* cabinet (*épith*). **solidarité ~le** ministerial solidarity; **département ~** ministry (*Brit*), department (*surtout US*); **journal ~** pro-government newspaper, newspaper which backs *ou* supports the government; *voir* **arrêté, officier**[1].

ministrable [ministʀabl] **adj: il est ~, c'est un ~** he's a potential minister *ou* likely to be appointed minister, he's in line for a ministerial post.

ministre [ministʀ] 1 **nm** a *[gouvernement]* minister (*Brit*), secretary (*surtout US*). **pourriez-vous nous dire Monsieur (*ou* Madame) le ~ ...** could you tell us Minister (*Brit*), could you tell us Mr (*ou* Madam) Secretary (*US*) ...; **les ~s** the members of the cabinet; **~ de l'Agriculture/de l'Éducation (nationale)** *etc* minister (*Brit*) *ou* secretary (*surtout US*) of Agriculture/Education *etc*, Agriculture/Education *etc* minister (*Brit*) *ou* secretary (*surtout US*); **~ délégué** minister of state (*auprès de* to); **~ d'État** (*sans portefeuille*) minister without portfolio; (*de haut rang*) senior minister; **~ sans portefeuille** minister without portfolio; *voir aussi* **2** *et* **bureau, conseil, papier, premier.**

b (*envoyé, ambassadeur*) envoy. **~ plénipotentiaire** (minister) plenipotentiary (*Brit*), ambassador plenipotentiary (*US*).

c (*Rel*) (*protestant*) minister, clergyman; (*catholique*) priest. **~ du culte** minister of religion; **~ de Dieu** minister of God.

d (*littér: représentant*) agent.

2 **comp ►ministre des Affaires étrangères** *ou* **des Relations extérieures** Minister of Foreign Affairs, Foreign Secretary (*Brit*), Secretary of State (*US*), State Secretary (*US*) **►ministre des Affaires européennes** Minister of European Affairs **►ministre des Affaires sociales** Social Services Minister **►ministre du Commerce** Minister of Trade (*Brit*), Secretary of Commerce (*US*) **►ministre de la Culture et de la Communication** ≃ Minister for Arts **►ministre de la Défense nationale** Defence Minister (*Brit*), Defense Secretary (*US*) **►ministre des Départements et Territoires d'outre-mer** *Minister for French overseas territories* **►ministre de l'Économie et des Finances** Finance Minister *ou* Secretary, Chancellor of the Exchequer (*Brit*), Secretary of the Treasury (*US*) **►ministre de l'Environnement** Minister of the Environment (*Brit*), Director of the Environmental Protection Agency (*US*) **►ministre de l'Industrie** Secretary of State for Trade and Industry (*Brit*), Secretary of Commerce (*US*) **►ministre de l'Intérieur** Minister of the Interior, Home Secretary (*Brit*) **►ministre de la Jeunesse et des Sports** Sports Minister **►ministre de la Justice** Minister of Justice, Lord Chancellor (*Brit*), Attorney General (*US*) **►ministre de la Santé (et de la Sécurité sociale)** Minister of Health and Social Security (*Brit*), Secretary of Health and Human Services (*US*) **►ministre des Transports** Minister of Transport (*Brit*), Transportation Secretary (*US*) **►ministre du Travail** Minister of Employment (*Brit*), Labor Secretary (*US*).

ministresse [ministʀɛs] **nf** (*femme de ministre*) minister's wife (*Brit*), secretary's wife (*surtout US*); (*ministre femme*) woman minister (*Brit*), woman secretary (*surtout US*).

minitel [minitɛl] **nm** ® *home terminal of the French telecommunications system.* **obtenir un renseignement par (le) ~** to get information on minitel ®; **~ rose** ≃ sex chatline.

miniteliste [minitelist] **nmf** minitel user.

minium [minjɔm] **nm** (*Chim*) red lead, minium; (*Peinture*) red lead paint.

minivague [minivag] **nf** soft perm. **se faire faire une ~** to have a soft perm.

Minnesota [minezɔta] **nm** Minnesota.

minois [minwa] **nm** (*visage*) little face. **son joli ~** her pretty little face.

minoration [minɔʀasjɔ̃] **nf** cut, reduction (*de* in).

minorer [minɔʀe] 1 **vt** *taux, impôts* to cut, reduce (*de* by).

minoritaire [minɔʀitɛʀ] 1 **adj** minority (*épith*). **groupe ~** minority group; **ils sont ~s** they are a minority *ou* in the minority. 2 **nmf** member of a minority party (*ou* group *etc*). **les ~s** the minority (party).

minorité [minɔʀite] **nf** a (*âge*) (*gén*) minority; (*Jur*) minority, (legal) infancy, nonage. **pendant sa ~** while he is *ou* was under age, during his minority *ou* infancy (*Jur*); (*Jur*) **~ pénale** ≃ legal infancy.

b (*groupe*) minority, minority group. **~ ethnique/nationale** racial *ou* ethnic/national minority; **~ opprimée** oppressed minority; **~ agissante** active minority; (*Écon*) **~ de blocage** minority vote sufficient to block a motion.

c **~ de** minority of; **dans la ~ des cas** in the minority of cases; **je m'adresse à une ~ d'auditeurs** I'm addressing a minority of listeners.

d **être en ~** to be in the minority, be a minority; **le gouvernement a été mis en ~ sur la question du budget** the government was defeated on the budget.

Minorque [minɔʀk] **nf** Minorca.

minorquin, e [minɔʀkɛ̃, in] 1 **adj** Minorcan. 2 **nm,f: M~(e)** Minorcan.

Minos [minɔs] **nm** Minos.

Minotaure [minɔtɔʀ] **nm** Minotaur.

minoterie [minɔtʀi] **nf** (*industrie*) flour-milling (industry); (*usine*) (flour-)mill.

minotier [minɔtje] **nm** miller.

minou [minu] **nm** (*langage enfantin*) pussy(cat), puss*. (*terme d'affection*) **oui mon ~** yes sweetie(-pie)* *ou* (my) pet*.

Minsk [minsk] **n** Minsk.

minuit [minɥi] **nm** midnight, twelve (o'clock) (at night), twelve midnight. **~ vingt** twenty past twelve *ou* midnight; *voir* **messe**.

minus [minys] **nmf** (*péj*) dead loss*, second-rater*, washout*. **~ habens** moron; **leur fils est un ~** their son is a useless specimen* *ou* a waster.

minuscule [minyskyl] 1 **adj** a (*très petit*) minute, tiny, minuscule. b (*Écriture*) small; (*Typ*) lower case. **h ~** small h. 2 **nf: (lettre) ~** small letter; (*Typ*) lower case letter.

minutage [minytaʒ] **nm** minute by minute timing, (strict *ou* precise) timing.

minute [minyt] **nf** a (*division de l'heure, d'un degré*) minute; (*moment*) minute, moment. **je n'ai pas une ~ à moi/à perdre** I don't have a minute *ou* moment to myself/to lose; **une ~ d'inattention a suffi** a moment's inattention was enough; **~ (papillon)!*** not so fast!, hey, just a minute!*, hold *ou* hang on (a minute)!*; **une ~ de silence** a minute's silence, a minute of silence; **la ~ de vérité** the moment of truth; **steak** *ou* **entrecôte ~** minute steak; **"talons ~"** heel bar, on-the-spot shoe repairs, "shoes repaired while you wait"; *voir* **cocotte**.

b **à la ~: on me l'a apporté à la ~** it has just this instant *ou* moment been brought to me; **avec toi il faut toujours tout faire à la ~** you always have to have things done there and then *ou* on the spot; **réparations à la ~** on the spot repairs, repairs while you wait; **elle arrive toujours à la ~ (près)** she's always there on the dot*, she always arrives to the minute *ou* right on time*.

c (*Jur*) minute. **les ~s de la réunion** the minutes of the meeting; **rédiger les ~s de qch** to minute sth.

minuter [minyte] 1 **vt** a (*organiser*) to time (carefully *ou* to the last minute); (*chronométrer, limiter*) to time. **dans son emploi du temps tout est minuté** everything's worked out *ou* timed down to the last second in his timetable; **emploi du temps minuté** strict schedule *ou* timetable. b (*Jur*) to draw up, draft.

minuterie [minytʀi] **nf** *[lumière]* time switch; *[horloge]* regulator; *[four]* timer. **allumer la ~** to switch on the (automatic) light (*on stairs, in passage etc*).

minuteur [minytœʀ] **nm** *[horloge, four]* timer.

minutie [minysi] **nf** a *[personne, travail]* meticulousness; *[ouvrage, inspection]* minute detail. **j'ai été frappé par la ~ de son inspection** I was amazed by the detail of his inspection, I was amazed how detailed his inspection was; **l'horlogerie demande beaucoup de ~** clock-making requires a great deal of precision; **avec ~** (*avec soin*) meticulously; (*dans le détail*) in minute detail. b (*détails: péj*) **~s** trifles, trifling details, minutiae.

minutieusement [minysjøzmɑ̃] **adv** (*avec soin*) meticulously; (*dans le détail*) in minute detail.

minutieux, -ieuse [minysjø, jøz] **adj** *personne, soin* meticulous; *ouvrage, dessin* minutely detailed; *description, inspection* minute. **il s'agit d'un travail ~** it's a job that demands painstaking attention to detail; **c'est une opération ~ieuse** it's an operation demanding great care, it's an extremely delicate *ou* finicky operation; **il est très ~** he is very meticulous *ou* careful of detail.

miocène [mjɔsɛn] **adj, nm** Miocene.

mioche [mjɔʃ] **nmf** (*: *gosse*) kid*, nipper* (*Brit*); (*péj*) brat*. **sale ~!** dirty *ou* horrible little brat!*

mirabelle [miʀabɛl] **nf** (*prune*) (cherry) plum; (*alcool*) plum brandy.

mirabellier [miʀabelje] **nm** cherry-plum tree.

miracle [miʀakl] 1 **nm** a (*lit*) miracle; (*fig*) miracle, marvel. **~ économique** economic miracle; **son œuvre est un ~ d'équilibre** his work is a miracle *ou* marvel of balance; **cela tient du ~** it's a miracle; **faire** *ou* **accomplir des ~s** (*lit*) to work *ou* do *ou* accomplish miracles; (*fig*) to work wonders *ou* miracles; **c'est ~ qu'il résiste dans ces conditions** it's a wonder *ou* a miracle he manages to cope in these conditions; **par ~** miraculously, by a *ou* by some miracle; (*iro*) **comme par ~** by some miracle; *voir* **crier.** b (*Hist, Littérat*) miracle (play). 2 **adj inv: le remède/la solution** *etc* **~** the miracle cure/solution *etc.*

miraculé, e [miʀakyle] **adj, nm,f: (malade) ~** (person) who has been miraculously cured *ou* who has been cured by a miracle; **les 3 ~s de la route** the 3 (people) who miraculously *ou* who by some miracle survived the accident; (*hum*) **voilà le ~!** here comes the miraculous recovery!

miraculeusement [miʀakyløzmɑ̃] **adv** miraculously, (as if) by a miracle.

miraculeux, -euse [miʀakylø, øz] **adj** *guérison* miraculous; *progrès, réussite* wonderful. **traitement** *ou* **remède ~** miracle cure; **ça n'a rien de ~** there's nothing so miraculous *ou* extraordinary about that.

mirador [miʀadɔʀ] **nm** (*Mil*) watchtower, mirador; (*Archit*) mirador.

mirage [miʀaʒ] **nm** a (*lit, fig*) mirage. **tu rêves! c'est un ~*** you're dreaming! you're seeing things! b *[œufs]* candling.

miraud, e* [miʀo, od] **adj** (*myope*) short-sighted. **tu es ~!** you need glasses!

mire [miʀ] **nf** (*TV*) test card; (*Arpentage*) surveyor's rod. (*viser*) **prendre sa ~** to take aim; *voir* **cran, ligne**[1], **point**[1].

mire-œufs [miʀø] **nm inv** light (*for testing eggs*).

mirer [miʀe] 1 1 **vt** a *œufs* to candle. b (*littér*) to mirror. 2 **se mirer vpr** (*littér*) *[personne]* to gaze at o.s. (*in the mirror, water etc*); *[chose]* to be mirrored *ou* reflected (*in the water etc*). to be mirrored *or* reflected (*in the water etc*).

mirettes* [miʀɛt] **nfpl** eyes, peepers* (*hum*).

mirifique [miʀifik] **adj** (*hum*) wonderful, fantabulous*, fantastic.

mirliflore†† [miʀliflɔʀ] **nm** fop†, coxcomb††. (*péj*) **faire le ~** to put on foppish airs†, play the fine fellow.

mirliton [miʀlitɔ̃] **nm** (*Mus*) reed pipe, mirliton; *[carnaval]* novelty whistle, kazoo.

mirmidon [miʀmidɔ̃] **nm** = **myrmidon.**

mirobolant, e* [miʀɔbɔlɑ̃, ɑ̃t] **adj** (*hum*) fabulous, fantastic.

miroir [miʀwaʀ] **nm** (*lit*) mirror; (*fig*) mirror, reflection. (*littér*) **le ~ des eaux** the glassy waters; **ce roman est-il bien le ~ de la réalité?** is this novel a true reflection of reality?, does this novel really mirror reality?; **~ déformant** distorting mirror; **~ grossissant** magnifying mirror; **~ aux alouettes** (*lit*) decoy; (*fig*) lure; (*Aut*) **~ de courtoisie** vanity mirror; **écriture/image en ~** mirror writing/image.

miroitement [miʀwatmɑ̃] **nm** (*voir* **miroiter**) sparkling (*NonC*), gleaming (*NonC*); shimmering (*NonC*).

miroiter [miʀwate] 1 **vi** (*étinceler*) to sparkle, gleam; (*chatoyer*) to shimmer. (*fig*) **il lui fit ~ les avantages qu'il aurait à accepter ce poste** he painted in glowing colours the advantages *ou* he painted an enticing picture of the advantages he would gain from taking the job.

miroiterie [miʀwatʀi] **nf** a (*Comm*) mirror trade; (*Ind*) mirror industry. b (*usine*) mirror factory.

miroitier, -ière [miʀwatje, jɛʀ] **nm,f** (*vendeur*) mirror dealer; (*fabricant*) mirror manufacturer; (*artisan*) mirror cutter, silverer.

miroton [miʀɔtɔ̃] **nm**, **mironton*** [miʀɔ̃tɔ̃] **nm: (bœuf) ~** boiled beef in onion sauce.

mis, e[1] [mi, miz] (**ptp de mettre**) **adj** (†: *vêtu*) attired†, clad. **bien ~** nicely turned out.

misaine [mizɛn] **nf: (voile de) ~** foresail; *voir* **mât.**

misanthrope [mizɑ̃tʀɔp] **nmf** misanthropist, misanthrope. **il est devenu très ~** he's come to dislike everyone *ou* to hate society, he's turned into a real misanthropist; **une attitude (de) ~** a misanthropic attitude.

misanthropie [mizɑ̃tʀɔpi] **nf** misanthropy.

misanthropique [mizɑ̃tʀɔpik] **adj** (*littér*) misanthropic, misanthropical.

miscible [misibl] **adj** miscible.

mise[2] [miz] 1 **nf** a (*action de mettre*) putting, setting. **~ en bouteilles** bottling; **~ en sacs** packing; **~ en gage** pawning; **la ~ en service des nouveaux autobus est prévue pour le mois prochain** the new buses are due to be put into service next month; **la ~ en pratique ne sera pas aisée** putting it into practice won't be easy, it won't be easy to put it into practice *ou* to carry it out in practice; **la ~ à jour de leurs registres sera longue** it will be a lengthy business updating their registers, the updating of their registers will take a long time; **lire les instructions avant la ~ en marche de l'appareil** read the instructions before starting the machine; *voir aussi* **2** *et* **accusation, bière**[2], **condition** *etc.*

b (*enjeu*) stake, ante; (*Comm*) outlay. **récupérer sa ~** to recoup one's outlay; **gagner 1000 F pour une ~ de 100 F** to make 1 000 francs on an outlay of 100 francs; *voir* **sauver.**

c (*habillement*) attire, clothing, garb (*hum*). **avoir une ~ débraillée** to be untidily dressed, have an untidy appearance; **juger qn sur** *ou* **à sa ~** to judge sb by his clothes *ou* by what he wears; **soigner sa ~** to take pride in one's appearance.

d **être de ~** (†† *Fin*) to be in circulation, be legal currency; (*fig*) to be acceptable, be in place *ou* season (*fig*); **ces propos ne sont pas de ~** those remarks are out of place.

2 **comp** ▸**mise-bas** (*Vét*) dropping, birth ▸**mise en boîte** (*lit*) canning; (*fig*) **la mise en boîte* du gouvernement par les journaux satiriques** the ridiculing of the government by the satirical press; **il ne supporte pas la mise en boîte*** he can't stand having his leg pulled, he can't stand being made a joke of ▸**mise en demeure** formal demand, notice ▸**mise à exécution** *[projet, idée]* implementation, implementing, execution; *[loi]* implementation, enforcement ▸**mise à feu** (*Espace*) firing ▸**mise de fonds** (*Fin*) capital outlay; (*Fin*) **mise de fonds initiale** seed money, venture capital; **faire une mise de fonds** to lay out capital ▸**mise en forme** (*Typ*) imposition; (*Sport*) warm-up *ou* limbering-up exercises ▸**mise en jeu** involvement, bringing into play ▸**mise en ligne** (*Mil*) alignment ▸**mise au monde** birth ▸**mise à mort** kill ▸**mise en ondes** (*Rad*) production ▸**mise en page** (*Typ*) make-up, making up, up-making ▸**mise à pied** (*Ind*) dismissal ▸**mise sur pied** setting up ▸**mise en plis** (*Coiffure*) set; **se faire faire une mise en plis** to have a set, have one's hair set ▸**mise au point** (*Aut*) tuning; (*Phot*) focusing; (*Tech*) adjustment; (*Ordin*) debugging; *[affaire]* finalizing, settling; *[procédé technique]* perfecting; (*fig: explication, correction*) clarification; **publier une mise au point** to issue a statement (setting the record straight *ou* clarifying a point) ▸**mise à prix** (*enchères*) reserve price (*Brit*), upset price (*US*) (*voir aussi* **prix**) ▸**mise en scène** (*Ciné, Théât*) production; (*fig*) **son indignation n'est qu'une mise en scène** his indignation is just for show *ou* is just put on; (*fig*) **toute cette mise en scène pour nous faire croire que ...** this great build-up *ou* performance just to make us believe that ... ▸**mise en valeur** *[terre]* development; *[maison]* improvement; *[meuble, tableau]* setting-off ▸**mise en vigueur** enforcement.

miser [mize] 1 **vt** a *argent* to stake, bet (*sur* on). **~ sur un cheval** to bet on a horse, put money on a horse; **~ à 8 contre 1** to bet at *ou* accept odds of 8 to 1, take 8 to 1; (*fig*) **il a misé sur le mauvais cheval** he backed the wrong horse (*fig*); *voir* **tableau.** b (*: *compter sur*) **~ sur** to bank on, count on.

misérabilisme [mizeʀabilism] **nm** (*Littérat*) preoccupation with the sordid aspects of life.

misérabiliste [mizeʀabilist] **adj** (*Littérat*) who *ou* which concentrates on the sordid aspects of life.

misérable [mizeʀabl] 1 **adj** a (*pauvre*) *famille, personne* destitute, poverty-stricken; *région* impoverished, poverty-stricken; *logement* seedy, mean, shabby, dingy; *vêtements* shabby. **d'aspect ~** of mean appearance, seedy-looking.

b (*pitoyable*) *existence, conditions* miserable, wretched, pitiful; *personne, famille* pitiful, wretched.

c (*sans valeur, minable*) *somme d'argent* paltry, miserable. **un salaire ~** a pittance, a miserable salary; **ne te mets pas en colère pour un ~ billet de 20 F** don't get angry about a measly* *ou* mouldy* 20-franc note.

d (††, *littér: méprisable*) vile†, base†, contemptible.

2 **nmf** (†, *littér: méchant*) wretch, scoundrel; (*pauvre*) poor wretch. **petit ~!** you (little) rascal! *ou* wretch!

misérablement [mizeʀabləmɑ̃] **adv** (*pitoyablement*) miserably, wretchedly; (*pauvrement*) in great *ou* wretched poverty.

misère [mizɛʀ] **nf** a (*pauvreté*) (extreme) poverty, destitution (*frm*). **la ~ en gants blancs** *ou* **en faux-col** genteel poverty; **être dans la ~** to be destitute *ou* poverty-stricken; **vivre dans la ~** to live in poverty; **tomber dans la ~** to fall on hard *ou* bad times, become impoverished *ou* destitute; **crier** *ou* **pleurer ~** to bewail *ou* bemoan one's poverty; **traitement** *ou* **salaire de ~** starvation wage; **~ dorée** splendid poverty; **~ noire** utter destitution; **réduire qn à la ~** to make sb destitute, reduce sb to a state of (dire) poverty.
b (*malheur*) **~s** woes, miseries, misfortunes; (**: ennuis*) **petites ~s** little troubles *ou* adversities, mild irritations; **faire des ~s à qn*** to be nasty to sb; **les ~s de la guerre** the miseries of war; **c'est une ~ de la voir s'anémier** it's pitiful *ou* wretched to see her growing weaker; **quelle ~!** what a wretched shame!; (†, *hum*) **~!**, **~ de nous!** woe is me! (†, *hum*), misery me! (†, *hum*); (*Rel*) **la ~ de l'homme** man's wretchedness; *voir* **collier, lit.**
c (*somme négligeable*) **il l'a eu pour une ~** he got it for a song *ou* for next to nothing; **c'est une ~ pour eux** that's nothing *ou* a trifle to them.
d (*plante*) wandering sailor.

miserere, miséréré [mizeʀeʀe] **nm** (*psaume, chant*) Miserere.

miséreux, -euse [mizeʀø, øz] 1 **adj** poverty-stricken. 2 **nm,f**: **un ~** a down-and-out, a poverty-stricken man; **les ~** the down-and-out(s), the poverty-stricken.

miséricorde [mizeʀikɔʀd] 1 **nf** a (*pitié*) mercy, forgiveness. **la ~ divine** divine mercy; *voir* **péché.** b (*Constr*) misericord. 2 **excl** (†) mercy me!†, mercy on us!†

miséricordieusement [mizeʀikɔʀdjøzmɑ̃] **adv** mercifully.

miséricordieux, -ieuse [mizeʀikɔʀdjø, jøz] **adj** merciful, forgiving.

misogyne [mizɔʒin] 1 **adj** misogynous. 2 **nmf** misogynist, woman-hater.

misogynie [mizɔʒini] **nf** misogyny.

miss [mis] **nf** a [*concours de beauté*] beauty queen. **M~ France** Miss France. b (*nurse*) English *ou* American governess. **2 enfants et leur ~** 2 children and their (English) governess. c (*vieille demoiselle*) **~ anglaise** old English spinster.

missel [misɛl] **nm** missal.

missile [misil] **nm** (*Aviat*) missile. **~ antimissile** antimissile missile; **~ autoguidé/balistique** self-guiding/ballistic missile; **~ sol-sol/sol-air** *etc* ground-to-ground/ground-to-air *etc* missile; **~ de moyenne portée** intermediate-range weapon *ou* missile; **~ de croisière** cruise missile.

mission [misjɔ̃] **nf** a (*charge, tâche*) (*gén, Rel*) mission; (*Pol*) mission, assignment; [*intérimaire*] brief, assignment. **~ lui fut donnée de** he was commissioned to; **partir/être en ~** (*Admin, Mil*) to go/be on an assignment; [*prêtre*] to go/be on a mission; **~ accomplie** mission accomplished; (*Mil*) **~ de reconnaissance** reconnaissance (mission), recce*; *voir* **chargé, ordre²**. b (*but, vocation*) task, mission. **la ~ de la littérature** the task of literature; **il s'est donné pour ~ de faire** he set himself the task of doing, he has made it his mission (in life) to do. c (*Rel*) (*bâtiment*) mission (station); (*groupe*) mission.

missionnaire [misjɔnɛʀ] **adj, nmf** missionary.

Mississippi [misisipi] **nm** Mississippi.

missive [misiv] **adj, nf** missive.

Missouri [misuʀi] **nm** Missouri.

mistoufle†* [mistufl] **nf**: **être dans la ~** to be on one's beam ends* (*Brit*), have hit hard *ou* bad times, be on one's uppers* (*Brit*); **faire des ~s à qn** to play (nasty) tricks on sb.

mistral [mistʀal] **nm** mistral.

mitaine [mitɛn] **nf** (fingerless) mitten *ou* mitt.

mitan [mitɑ̃] **nm** (†† *ou dial*) middle, centre. **dans le ~ de** in the middle of.

mitard [mitaʀ] **nm** (*arg Crime*) solitary*. **il a fait 15 jours de ~** he did 2 weeks (in) solitary*.

mite [mit] **nf** clothes moth. **mangé aux ~s** moth-eaten; **~ du fromage** cheese-mite; **avoir la ~ à l'œil**†* to have sleep in one's eyes (*fig*).

mité, e [mite] **adj** moth-eaten.

mi-temps [mitɑ̃] **nf inv** a (*Sport*) (*période*) half; (*repos*) half-time. **à la ~** at half-time; **première/seconde ~** first/second half; **l'arbitre a sifflé la ~** the referee blew (the whistle) for half-time. b **à ~** part-time; **le travail à ~** part-time work; **travailler à ~** to work part-time, do part-time work; **elle est dactylo à ~** she's a part-time typist.

miter (se) [mite] 1 **vpr** to be *ou* become moth-eaten. **pour éviter que les vêtements se mitent** to stop the moths getting at the clothes.

miteux, -euse [mitø, øz] **adj** *lieu* seedy, dingy, grotty‡ (*Brit*); *vêtement* shabby, tatty*, grotty‡ (*Brit*); *personne* shabby(-looking), seedy(-looking). **un ~*** a seedy(-looking) character.

Mithridate [mitʀidat] **nm** Mithridates.

mithridatiser [mitʀidatize] 1 **vt** to mithridatize.

mitigation [mitigasjɔ̃] **nf** (*Jur*) mitigation.

mitigé, e [mitiʒe] (**ptp de mitiger**) **adj** *ardeur* mitigated; *convictions* lukewarm, reserved. **sentiments ~s** mixed feelings; **joie ~e de regrets** joy mixed *ou* mingled with regret.

mitiger† [mitiʒe] 3 **vt** to mitigate.

mitigeur [mitiʒœʀ] **nm** mixer tap (*Brit*) *ou* faucet (*US*). **~ thermostatique** temperature control.

mitonner [mitɔne] 1 1 **vt** a (*Culin*) (*à feu doux*) to simmer, cook slowly; (*avec soin*) to prepare *ou* cook with loving care. **elle (lui) mitonne des petits plats** she cooks (up) *ou* concocts tempting *ou* tasty dishes (for him). b (*) *affaire* to cook up quietly*; *personne* to cosset. 2 **vi** to simmer, cook slowly.

mitose [mitoz] **nf** mitosis. **se reproduire par ~** to replicate; **reproduction par ~** replication.

mitoyen, -yenne [mitwajɛ̃, jɛn] **adj**: **mur ~** party *ou* common wall; **le mur est ~** it is a party wall; **cloison ~ne** partition wall; **maisons ~nes** (*deux*) semi-detached houses (*Brit*), duplex houses (*US*); (*plus de deux*) terraced houses (*Brit*), town houses (*US*); **notre jardin est ~ avec le leur** our garden adjoins theirs.

mitoyenneté [mitwajɛnte] **nf** [*mur*] common ownership. **la ~ des maisons** the (existence of a) party wall between the houses.

mitraillade [mitʀɑjad] **nf** a (*coups de feu*) (volley of) shots; (*échauffourée*) exchange of shots. b = **mitraillage.**

mitraillage [mitʀɑjaʒ] **nm** machine-gunning; (*Scol etc*) quick-fire questioning. **~ au sol** strafing.

mitraille [mitʀɑj] **nf** a (*Mil*) (†: *projectiles*) grapeshot; (*décharge*) volley of shots, hail of bullets. **fuir sous la ~** to flee under a hail of bullets. b (*: *petite monnaie*) loose *ou* small change.

mitrailler [mitʀɑje] 1 **vt** a (*Mil*) to machine-gun. **~ au sol** to strafe; **~ qn avec des élastiques*** to pelt sb with rubber bands. b (*: *Phot*) *monument* to take shot after shot of. **les touristes mitraillaient la cathédrale** the tourists' cameras were clicking away madly at the cathedral; **être mitraillé par les photographes** to be bombarded by the photographers. c (*fig*) **~ qn de questions** to bombard sb with questions, fire questions at sb.

mitraillette [mitʀɑjɛt] **nf** submachine gun, tommy gun*.

mitrailleur [mitʀɑjœʀ] **nm** (*Mil*) machine gunner; (*Aviat*) air gunner; *voir* **fusil, pistolet.**

mitrailleuse [mitʀɑjøz] **nf** machine gun. **~ légère/lourde** light/heavy machine gun.

mitral, e, mpl -aux [mitʀal, o] **adj** (*Anat*) mitral. **valvule ~** mitral valve.

mitre [mitʀ] **nf** a (*Rel*) mitre. **recevoir** *ou* **coiffer la ~** to be appointed bishop, be mitred. b (*Tech*) [*cheminée*] cowl.

mitré, e [mitʀe] **adj** mitred; *voir* **abbé.**

mitron [mitʀɔ̃] **nm** (*boulanger*) baker's boy; (*pâtissier*) pastrycook's boy.

mixage [miksaʒ] **nm** (*Ciné, Rad*) (sound) mixing.

mixer¹ [mikse] 1 **vt** (*Ciné, Rad*) to mix; (*Culin*) to blend.

mixer², mixeur [miksœʀ] **nm** (*Culin*) mixer, liquidizer, blender, juicer (*US*).

mixité [miksite] **nf** (*Scol*) coeducation, coeducational system; [*équipe, groupe*] mix.

mixte [mikst] **adj** a (*deux sexes*) *équipe* mixed; *classe, école, enseignement* mixed, coeducational, coed*; *voir* **double.** b (*comportant éléments divers*) *mariage, train* mixed (*épith*); *équipe* combined (*épith*); *tribunal, commission* joint; *rôle* dual (*épith*); *appareil électrique* dual voltage; *radio, électrophone* battery-mains (operated) (*Brit*), electrically-operated (*US*); (*Chim, Géog*) *roche, végétation* mixed. **outil à usage ~** dual-purpose tool; **peaux ~s** combination skin; **navire** *ou* **cargo ~** cargo-passenger ship *ou* vessel; **cuisinière ~** combined gas and electric cooker (*Brit*) *ou* stove; **l'opéra-bouffe est un genre ~** comic opera is a mixture of genres.

mixtion [mikstjɔ̃] **nf** (*Chim, Pharm*) (*action*) blending, compounding; (*médicament*) mixture.

mixture [mikstyʀ] **nf** (*Chim, Pharm*) mixture; (*Culin*) mixture, concoction; (*péj, fig*) concoction.

MJC [ɛmʒise] **nf** (**abrév de maison des jeunes et de la culture**) *voir* **maison.**

ml (**abrév de millilitre**) ml.

MLF [ɛmɛlɛf] **nm** (**abrév de Mouvement de libération de la femme**) Women's Liberation Movement, Women's Lib*.

Mlle (**abrév de Mademoiselle**) **~ Martin** Miss Martin.

Mlles **abrév de Mesdemoiselles.**

MM (**abrév de Messieurs**) Messrs.

mm (**abrév de millimètre**) mm.

Mme (**abrév de Madame**) **~ Martin** Mrs Martin.

Mmes **abrév de Mesdames.**

mn (**abrév de minute**) min.

mnémonique [mnemɔnik] **adj** mnemonic.

mnémotechnique [mnemotɛknik] 1 **adj** mnemonic. 2 **nf** mnemonics (*sg*), mnemotechnics (*sg*).

Mo (**abrév de mégaoctet**) Mb, MB.

mob* [mɔb] **nf abrév de mobylette** ®.

mobile [mɔbil] 1 **adj** a *pièce de moteur* moving; *élément de meuble, casier, panneau* movable; *feuillets* (*de cahier, calendrier*) loose; *voir* **échelle, fête.**
b *main-d'œuvre, population* mobile.
c *reflet* changing; *traits* mobile, animated; *regard, yeux* mobile, darting (*épith*); *esprit* nimble, agile.
d *troupes* mobile. **boxeur très ~** boxer who is very quick on his feet, nimble-footed boxer; **avec la voiture on est très ~** you can really get

around *ou* about with a car, having a car makes you very mobile; *voir* **garde[1], garde[2].**

2 **nm** a (*impulsion*) motive (*de* for). **quel était le ~ de son action?** what was the motive for *ou* what prompted his action?; **chercher le ~ du crime** to look for the motive for the crime.

b (*Art*) mobile.

c (*Phys*) moving object *ou* body.

mobilier, -ière [mɔbilje, jɛʀ] 1 **adj** (*Jur*) *propriété, bien* movable, personal; *valeurs* transferable. **saisie/vente ~ière** seizure/sale of personal *ou* movable property; **contribution** *ou* **cote ~ière†** property tax. 2 **nm** a (*ameublement*) furniture. **le ~ du salon** the lounge furniture; **nous avons un ~ Louis XV** our furniture is Louis XV, our house is furnished in Louis XV (style); (*fig hum*) **il fait partie du ~** he's part of the furniture (*hum*); **le M~ national** State-owned furniture (*used to furnish buildings of the State*); **~ urbain** street furniture. b (*Jur*) personal *ou* movable property.

mobilisable [mɔbilizabl] **adj** *soldat* who can be called up *ou* mobilized; *énergie, ressources* that can be mobilized, that can be summoned up, summonable; *capitaux* mobilizable. (*Mil*) **il n'est pas ~** he cannot be called up.

mobilisateur, -trice [mɔbilizatœʀ, tʀis] **adj**: **slogan ~** rallying call *ou* cry, slogan which will stir people into action; **projet ~** plan which will stir people into action; **politique peu ~trice** policies which do not attract much support.

mobilisation [mɔbilizasjɔ̃] **nf** *[citoyens]* mobilization, calling up; *[troupes, ressources]* mobilization. **~ générale/partielle** general/partial mobilization; **la ~ de la gauche contre le racisme** the mobilization *ou* rallying of the left against racism.

mobiliser [mɔbilize] 1 **vt** *citoyens* to call up, mobilize; *troupes, ressources, adhérents* to mobilize; *fonds* to raise, mobilize. **~ les enthousiasmes** to summon up *ou* mobilize people's enthusiasm; **~ les esprits (en faveur d'une cause)** to rally people's interest (in a cause); **les (soldats) mobilisés** the mobilized troops; (*fig*) **tout le monde était mobilisé pour la servir** everyone was put to work attending to her needs, everyone had to jump to (it) and attend to her needs; **il faut se ~ contre le chômage** we must take action *ou* mobilize to fight unemployment.

mobilité [mɔbilite] **nf** (*gén*) mobility. **~ professionnelle** professional mobility; **~ sociale** social mobility; **~ sociale ascendante** upward (social) mobility; **la ~ de son regard** his darting eyes; **la voiture nous permet une plus grande ~** having the car means we can get around more easily *ou* makes us more mobile *ou* gives us greater mobility.

Mobylette [mɔbilɛt] **nf** ® Mobylette ®, moped (*Brit*).

mocassin [mɔkasɛ̃] **nm** moccasin.

moche* [mɔʃ] **adj** a (*laid*) ugly, awful, ghastly*. **elle est ~ comme un pou** she's got a face like the back of a bus* (*Brit*), she's as ugly as sin. b (*mauvais*) rotten*, lousy‡; (*méchant*) rotten*, nasty. **tu es ~ avec elle** you're rotten* to her; **il a la grippe, c'est ~ pour lui** he's got flu, that's hard on him *ou* that's rotten for him*.

mocheté* [mɔʃte] **nf** a (*laideur*) ugliness. b (*personne*) fright; (*objet*) eyesore. **c'est une vraie ~!** she's an absolute fright! *ou* as ugly as sin!

modal, e, **mpl -aux** [mɔdal, o] 1 **adj** modal. 2 **nm** (*verbe*) modal (verb).

modalité [mɔdalite] **nf** a (*forme*) form, mode. **~ d'application de la loi** mode of enforcement of the law; **~s de paiement** methods *ou* modes of payment; (*Jur*) **~s de mise en œuvre** details of implementation; (*Scol*) **~s de contrôle** methods of assessment. b (*Ling, Mus, Philos*) modality. **adverbe de ~** modal adverb. c (*Jur: condition*) clause.

mode[1] [mɔd] 1 **nf** a fashion. **suivre la ~** to keep in fashion, keep up with the fashions; (*péj*) **une de ces nouvelles ~s** one of these new fads *ou* crazes; **à la ~** fashionable, in fashion; **une femme très à la ~** a very fashionable woman; **c'est la ~ des boucles d'oreilles, les boucles d'oreilles sont à la ~** earrings are in fashion *ou* are in* *ou* are all the rage*; **être habillé très à la ~** (*gén*) to be very fashionably dressed; *[jeunes]* to be very trendily* (*Brit*) dressed; **habillé à la dernière ~** dressed in the latest fashion *ou* style; **mettre qch à la ~** to make sth fashionable, bring sth into fashion; **revenir à la ~** to come back into fashion *ou* vogue, to come back (in)*; **passer de ~** to go out of fashion; **marchande de ~s††** milliner.

b (*Comm, Ind: Habillement*) fashion industry *ou* business. **travailler dans la ~** to work *ou* be in the fashion world *ou* industry *ou* business; **journal/présentation de ~** fashion magazine/show; *voir* **gravure.**

c (†: *mœurs*) custom; (*goût, style*) style, fashion. **selon la ~ de l'époque** according to the custom of the day; **(habillé) à l'ancienne ~** (dressed) in the old style; (*hum*) **cousin à la ~ de Bretagne** distant cousin, cousin six times removed (*hum*); (*Jur, hum*) **oncle** *ou* **neveu à la ~ de Bretagne** first cousin once removed; **à la ~ du 18e siècle** in the style of *ou* after the fashion of the 18th century, in 18th century style; *voir* **bœuf, tripe.**

2 **adj inv**: **tissu ~** fashion fabric; **coloris ~** fashion *ou* fashionable colours.

mode[2] [mɔd] **nm** a (*méthode*) form, mode, method; (*genre*) way. **quel est le ~ d'action de ce médicament?** how does this medicine work?; **~ de gouvernement/de transport** form *ou* mode of government/of transport; **~ de pensée/de vie** way of thinking/of life; **~ de paiement** method *ou* mode of payment; **~ d'emploi** directions for use. b (*Gram, Ling*) mood; (*Ordin, Mus, Philos*) mode. **au ~ subjonctif** in the subjunctive mood; (*Ordin*) **~ synchrone/asynchrone/interactif** synchronous/asynchronous/interactive mode; (*Ordin*) **fonctionner en ~ local** to operate in local mode.

modelage [mɔd(ə)laʒ] **nm** (*activité*) modelling; (*ouvrage*) (piece of) sculpture; piece of pottery.

modèle [mɔdɛl] 1 **nm** a (*chose*) (*gén, Écon*) model; (*Tech*) pattern; (*type*) type; (*Habillement*) design, style; (*exemple*) example, model; (*Ling*) model, pattern; (*Scol: corrigé*) fair copy. **nous avons tous nos ~s en vitrine** our full range is *ou* all our models are in the window; **petit/grand ~** small/large version *ou* model; (*boîte*) **voulez-vous le petit ou le grand ~?** do you want the small or the big size (box)?; (*voiture*) **il a le ~ 5 portes** he has the 5-door hatchback model *ou* version; (*Mode*) **X présente ses ~s d'automne** X presents his autumn models *ou* styles; **fabriquer qch d'après le ~** to make sth from the model *ou* pattern; **faire qch sur le ~ de** to model sth on, make sth on the pattern *ou* model of; (*Gram*) **~ de conjugaison/déclinaison** conjugation/declension pattern; **son courage devrait nous servir de ~** his courage should be a model *ou* an example to us.

b (*personne*) (*gén*) model, example; (*Art*) model. **~ de vertu** paragon of virtue; **X est le ~ du bon élève/ouvrier** X is a model pupil/workman, X is the epitome of the good pupil/workman; **elle est un ~ de loyauté** she is a model of *ou* the very model of loyalty; **il restera pour nous un ~** he will remain an example to us; **prendre qn pour ~** to model *ou* pattern o.s. upon sb.

2 **adj** (*parfait*) *conduite, ouvrier, usine* model (*épith*); (*de référence*) *appartement* show (*épith*).

3 **comp** ►**modèle courant** *ou* **de série** standard *ou* production model ►**modèle déposé** registered design ►**modèle de fabrique** factory model ►**modèle réduit** small-scale model; **modèle réduit au 1/100** model on the scale (of) 1 to 100; **modèle réduit d'avion, avion modèle réduit** scale model of an aeroplane; **il aime monter des modèles réduits d'avions/de bateaux** he likes to build model aircraft/ships.

modelé [mɔd(ə)le] **nm** *[peinture]* relief; *[sculpture, corps]* contours; (*Géog*) relief.

modeler [mɔd(ə)le] 5 **vt** a (*façonner*) *statue, poterie, glaise* to model, fashion, mould; *intelligence, caractère* to shape, mould. **l'exercice physique peut ~ les corps jeunes** exercise can shape young bodies; (*Géol*) **le relief a été modelé par la glaciation** the ground *ou* the terrain was moulded *ou* shaped by glaciation; **cuisse bien modelée** shapely *ou* well-shaped *ou* nicely shaped thigh; *voir* **pâte.** b (*conformer*) **~ ses attitudes/réactions sur** to model one's attitudes/reactions on; **se ~ sur qn/qch** to model *ou* pattern o.s. (up)on sb/sth.

modeleur, -euse [mɔd(ə)lœʀ, øz] **nm,f** (*Art*) modeller; (*Tech*) pattern maker.

modélisme [mɔdelism] **nm** model building.

modéliste [mɔdelist] **nmf** a *[mode]* (dress) designer. **ouvrière ~** dress designer's assistant. b *[maquette]* model builder.

modem [mɔdɛm] **nm** (**abrév de modulateur-démodulateur**) modem.

Modène [mɔdɛn] **n** Modena.

modérantisme [mɔdeʀɑ̃tism] **nm** (*Hist*) moderantism.

modérantiste [mɔdeʀɑ̃tist] **adj, nmf** (*Hist*) moderantist.

modérateur, -trice [mɔdeʀatœʀ, tʀis] 1 **adj** *action, influence* moderating (*épith*), restraining (*épith*). 2 **nm** (*Tech*) regulator. **~ de pile atomique** moderator (of nuclear reactor); *voir* **ticket.**

modération [mɔdeʀasjɔ̃] **nf** a (*retenue*) moderation, restraint. **avec ~** in moderation. b (*gén, Sci: diminution*) reduction, diminution, lessening. c (*Jur: diminution*) *[peine]* mitigation; *[impôt]* reduction.

modéré, e [mɔdeʀe] (**ptp de modérer**) **adj** *personne* (*dans ses opinions, idées*) moderate; (*dans ses sentiments, désirs*) moderate, restrained; (*Pol*) moderate (*dans* in); *prix* reasonable, moderate; *chaleur, vent* moderate. (*Pol*) **les ~s** the moderates; **il a tenu des propos très ~s** he took a very moderate line in the discussion, he was very restrained in what he said; *voir* **habitation.**

modérément [mɔdeʀemɑ̃] **adv** *boire, manger* in moderation, a moderate amount. **être ~ satisfait** to be moderately *ou* fairly satisfied.

modérer [mɔdeʀe] 6 1 **vt** *colère, passion* to restrain; *ambitions, exigences* to moderate; *dépenses, désir, appétit* to curb; *vitesse* to reduce; *impact négatif* to reduce, limit. **modérez vos expressions!** moderate *ou* mind your language! 2 **se modérer** **vpr** (*s'apaiser*) to calm down, control o.s.; (*montrer de la mesure*) to restrain o.s.

moderne [mɔdɛʀn] 1 **adj** (*gén*) modern; *cuisine, équipement* up-to-date, modern; *méthode, idées* progressive, modern; (*opposé à classique*) *études* modern. **le héros ~** the modern-day hero; **la jeune fille ~ se libère** the young woman of today *ou* today's young woman is becoming more liberated; **à l'époque ~** in modern times; *voir* **confort, lettre.** 2 **nm** (*style*) modern style; (*meubles*) modern furniture. **aimer le ~** to like modern (style) furniture *ou* the contemporary style of furniture; **meublé en ~** with modern furniture, furnished in contemporary style; **ce peintre/romancier est un ~** he is a modern painter/novelist; *voir* **ancien.**

modernisateur, -trice [mɔdɛʀnizatœʀ, tʀis] 1 adj modernizing. 2 nm,f modernizer.
modernisation [mɔdɛʀnizasjɔ̃] nf modernization.
moderniser [mɔdɛʀnize] [1] vt to modernize, bring up to date.
modernisme [mɔdɛʀnism] nm modernism.
moderniste [mɔdɛʀnist] 1 nmf modernist. 2 adj modernistic.
modernité [mɔdɛʀnite] nf modernity.
modern style [mɔdɛʀnstil] nm ≃ Art Nouveau.
modeste [mɔdɛst] adj a (*simple*) *vie, appartement, salaire, tenue* modest. **c'est un cadeau bien** ~ it's a very modest gift *ou* thing, it's not much of a present; **un train de vie** ~ an unpretentious *ou* a modest way of life; **je ne suis qu'un** ~ **ouvrier** I'm only a simple *ou* modest working man; **être d'un milieu** *ou* **d'origine** ~ to have *ou* come from a modest *ou* humble background; **il est** ~ **dans ses ambitions** his ambitions are modest, he has modest ambitions.
b (*sans vanité*) *héros, attitude* modest. **faire le** ~ to put on *ou* make a show of modesty; **tu fais le** ~ you're just being modest; **avoir le triomphe** ~ to be a modest winner, be modest about one's triumphs *ou* successes.
c (*réservé, effacé*) *personne, air*modest, unassuming, self-effacing.
d († *ou littér: pudique*) modest.
modestement [mɔdɛstəmɑ̃] adv (*voir* **modeste**) modestly; unassumingly, self-effacingly.
modestie [mɔdɛsti] nf (*absence de vanité*) modesty; (*réserve, effacement*) self-effacement; (*littér: pudeur*) modesty. **fausse** ~ false modesty.
modicité [mɔdisite] nf *[prix]* lowness; *[salaire]* lowness, smallness.
modifiable [mɔdifjabl] adj modifiable.
modifiant, e [mɔdifjɑ̃, ɑ̃t] adj modifying.
modificateur, -trice [mɔdifikatœʀ, tʀis] 1 adj modifying, modificatory. 2 nm modifier.
modificatif, -ive [mɔdifikatif, iv] adj modifying.
modification [mɔdifikasjɔ̃] nf modification, alteration. (*Psych*) ~ **du comportement** behaviour modification.
modifier [mɔdifje] [7] 1 vt (*gén, Gram*) to modify, alter. 2 **se modifier** vpr to alter, be modified.
modique [mɔdik] adj *salaire, prix* modest. **pour la** ~ **somme de** for the modest sum of; **il ne recevait qu'une pension** ~ he received only a modest *ou* meagre pension.
modiquement [mɔdikmɑ̃] adv poorly, meagrely.
modiste [mɔdist] nf milliner.
modulaire [mɔdylɛʀ] adj modular.
modulateur, -trice [mɔdylatœʀ, tʀis] nm,f (*Rad, Élec*) modulator.
modulation [mɔdylasjɔ̃] nf (*Ling, Mus, Rad*) modulation; *[tarif, mesure]* adjustment. ~ **d'amplitude** amplitude modulation; ~ **de fréquence** frequency modulation; **poste à** ~ **de fréquence** VHF *ou* FM radio; **écouter une émission sur** *ou* **en** ~ **de fréquence** to listen to a programme on VHF *ou* on FM.
module [mɔdyl] nm (*Archit, Espace, étalon*) module; (*Math, Phys*) modulus; (*Univ*) module, unit; (*éléments d'un ensemble*) unit. ~ **lunaire** lunar module, mooncraft; **acheter une cuisine par** ~**s** to buy a kitchen in separate units.
moduler [mɔdyle] [1] 1 vt *voix* to modulate, inflect; *air* to warble; *son* to modulate; *tarif, mesure* to adjust; (*Mus, Rad*) to modulate. **les cris modulés des marchands** the singsong cries of the tradesmen; ~ **les peines en fonction des délits** to make the punishment to fit the crime. 2 vi (*Mus*) to modulate.
modus vivendi [mɔdysvivɛ̃di] nm inv modus vivendi, working arrangement.
moelle [mwal] nf (*Anat*) marrow, medulla (SPÉC); (*Bot*) pith; (*fig*) pith, core. (*fig*) **être transi jusqu'à la** ~ **(des os)** to be frozen to the marrow; **frissonner jusqu'à la** ~ to tremble to the very depths of one's being; ~ **épinière** spinal cord; (*Culin*) ~ **(de bœuf)** beef marrow; *voir* **os, substantifique.**
moelleusement [mwaløzmɑ̃] adv *étendu* luxuriously.
moelleux, -euse [mwalø, øz] 1 adj *forme, tapis, lit* soft; *couleur* mellow; *aliment* creamy, smooth; *son, vin* mellow. 2 nm *[lit, tapis]* softness; *[vin]* mellowness; *[aliment]* smoothness.
moellon [mwalɔ̃] nm (*Constr*) rubble stone.
mœurs [mœʀ(s)] nfpl a (*morale*) morals. **avoir des** ~ **sévères** to have high morals *ou* strict moral standards; **soupçonner les** ~ **de qn** to have doubts about sb's morals *ou* standards of behaviour; (*euph*) **il a des** ~ **particulières** he has certain tendencies (*euph*); **contraire aux bonnes** ~ contrary to accepted standards of (good) behaviour; **femme de** ~ **légères** *ou* **faciles** woman of easy virtue; **femme de mauvaises** ~ loose woman; (*Jur, Presse*) **affaire** *ou* **histoire de** ~ sex case; **la police des** ~, **les M**~* ≃ the vice squad; *voir* **attentat, certificat, outrage.**
b (*coutumes, habitudes*) *[peuple, époque]* customs, habits; *[abeilles, fourmis]* habits. **c'est (entré) dans les** ~ it's (become) normal practice, it's (become) a standard *ou* an everyday feature of life; **il faut vivre avec les** ~ **de son temps** one must keep up with present-day customs *ou* habits; **les** ~ **politiques/littéraires de notre siècle** the political/literary practices *ou* usages of our century; **avoir des** ~ **simples/aristocratiques** to lead a simple/an aristocratic life, have a simple/an aristocratic life style; *voir* **autre.**
c (*manières*) manners, ways; (*Littérat*) manners. **ils ont de drôles de** ~ they have some peculiar ways *ou* manners; **quelles** ~!, **drôles de** ~! what a way to behave! *ou* carry on!, what manners!; **peinture/comédie de** ~ portrayal/comedy of manners.
Mogadiscio [mogadiʃjo] n Mogadishu.
mohair [mɔɛʀ] nm mohair.
Mohammed [mɔamɛd] nm Mohammed.
moi [mwa] 1 pron pers a (*objet direct ou indirect*) me. **aide-**~ help me, give me a hand; **donne-**~ **ton livre** give me your book, give your book to me; **donne-le-**~ give it to me, give me it*, give it me*; **si vous étiez** ~ **que feriez vous?** if you were me *ou* in my shoes what would you do?; **il nous a regardés ma femme et** ~ he looked at my wife and me; **écoute-**~ **ça!*** just listen to that!; **elle me connaît bien,** ~ she knows me all right!; **il n'obéit qu'à** ~ he only obeys me, I'm the only one he obeys; ~, **elle me déteste** she hates me; *voir aussi* **même, non, seul.**
b (*sujet*) I (*emphatique*), I myself (*emphatique*), me*. **qui a fait cela? — (c'est)** ~**/(ce n'est) pas** ~ who did this? — I did/I didn't *ou* me*/not me*; ~, **le saluer?, jamais!** me, greet him?, never!; **mon mari et** ~ **(nous) refusons** my husband and I refuse; ~ **parti/malade que ferez-vous?** when I'm gone/ill what will you do?, what will you do with me away/ill?; **et** ~ **de rire de plus belle!** and so I (just) laughed all the more!; **je ne l'ai pas vu,** ~ I didn't see him myself, I myself didn't see him; ~, **je ne suis pas d'accord** (for my part) I don't agree; **alors** ~, **je ne compte pas?** hey, what about me? *ou* where do I come in?*
c (*emphatique avec qui, que*) **c'est** ~ **qui vous le dis!** you can take it from me!, I'm telling you!; **merci — c'est** ~ **(qui vous remercie)** thank you — thank YOU; **et** ~ **qui n'avais pas le sou!** there was me without a penny!*, and to think I didn't have a penny!; ~ **qui vous parle, je l'ai vu** I saw him personally; **c'est** ~ **qu'elle veut voir** it's me she wants to see; **il me dit cela à** ~ **qui l'ai tant aidé** he says that to me after I've helped him so much; **et** ~ **qui avais espéré gagner!** and to think that I had hoped to win!; ~ **que le théâtre passionne, je n'ai jamais vu cette pièce** even I, with all my great love for the theatre, have never seen this play.
d (*avec prép*) **à** ~**!** (*au secours*) help (me)!; (*passe au rugby etc*) over here!; **à** ~ **il le dira** he'll tell me (all right); **avec/sans** ~ with/without me; **sans** ~ **il ne les aurait jamais retrouvés** but for me *ou* had it not been for me, he would never have found them; **venez chez** ~ come to my place; **le poème n'est pas de** ~ the poem isn't one I wrote *ou* isn't one of mine; **un élève à** ~ a pupil of mine; **j'ai un appartement à** ~ I have a flat of my own; **ce livre est à** ~ this book belongs to me *ou* is mine; **mes livres à** ~ **sont bien rangés** my books are arranged tidily; **elle l'a appris par** ~ she heard about it from me *ou* through me; **cette lettre ne vient pas de** ~ this letter isn't from me *ou* isn't one I wrote; **il veut une photo de** ~ he wants a photo of me; **c'est à** ~ **de décider** it's up to me to decide.
e (*dans comparaisons*) I, me. **il est plus grand que** ~ he is taller than I (am) *ou* than me; **il mange plus/moins que** ~ he eats more/less than I (do) *ou* than me; **fais comme** ~ do as I do, do like me*, do the same as me; **il l'aime plus que** ~ (*plus qu'il ne m'aime*) he loves her more than (he loves) me; (*plus que je ne l'aime*) he loves her more than I do.
2 nm: **le** ~ the self, the ego; **le** ~ **est haïssable** the ego *ou* the self is detestable; **notre vrai** ~ our true self.
moignon [mwaɲɔ̃] nm stump. **il n'avait plus qu'un** ~ **de bras** he had just the *ou* a stump of an arm left.
moi-même [mwamɛm] pron *voir* **autre, même.**
moindre [mwɛ̃dʀ] adj a (*compar*) (*moins grand*) less, lesser; (*inférieur*) lower, poorer. **les dégâts sont bien** *ou* **beaucoup** ~**s** the damage is much less; **à un** ~ **degré, à un degré** ~ to a lesser degree *ou* extent; **à** ~ **prix** at a lower price; **de** ~ **qualité, de qualité** ~ of lower *ou* poorer quality; **enfant de** ~ **intelligence** child of lower intelligence; **une épidémie de** ~ **étendue** a less widespread epidemic; **c'est un inconvénient** ~ it's less of a drawback, it's a lesser drawback; *voir* **mal.**
b (*superl*) **le** ~, **la** ~, **les** ~**s** the least, the slightest; (*de deux*) the lesser; **le** ~ **bruit** the slightest noise; **la** ~ **chance/idée** the slightest *ou* remotest chance/idea; **jusqu'au** ~ **détail** down to the smallest detail; **le** ~ **de deux maux** the lesser of two evils; **sans se faire le** ~ **souci** without worrying in the slightest; **c'est la** ~ **de mes difficultés** that's the least of my difficulties; **merci — c'est la** ~ **des choses!** thank you — it's a pleasure! *ou* you're welcome! *ou* not at all!; **remerciez-le de m'avoir aidé — c'était la** ~ **des choses** thank him for helping me — it was the least he could do; **certains spécialistes et non des** ~**s disent que** some specialists and important ones at that say that; **la** ~ **des politesses veut que** ... common politeness demands that ...; **il n'a pas fait le** ~ **commentaire** he didn't make a single comment; **la loi du** ~ **effort** the line of least resistance *ou* effort, the law of least effort; **c'est un des problèmes et non le** ~ it is by no means the least of our problems.
moindrement [mwɛ̃dʀəmɑ̃] adv (*littér*) (*avec nég*) **il n'était pas le** ~ **surpris** he was not in the least surprised, he was not surprised in the slightest; **sans l'avoir le** ~ **voulu** without having in any way wanted this.
moine [mwan] nm a (*Rel*) monk, friar. ~ **bouddhiste** buddhist monk;

voir **habit.** b (*Zool*) monk seal; (*Orn*) black vulture. c (*Hist: chauffe-lit*) bedwarmer.

moineau, pl ~x [mwano] nm (*Orn*) sparrow. ~ **domestique** house sparrow; (*péj*) **sale** *ou* **vilain** ~ dirty dog (*péj*).

moinillon [mwanijɔ̃] nm (*hum*) little monk (*hum*).

moins [mwɛ̃] 1 adv *emploi comparatif* a (*avec adj ou adv*) less. ~ **que ...** less ... than, not so ... as; **beaucoup/un peu** ~ much/a little less; **tellement** ~ so much less; **encore** ~ even less; **3 fois** ~ 3 times less; **il est** ~ **grand/intelligent que son frère/que nous/que je ne pensais** he is not as *ou* so tall/intelligent as his brother/as us *ou* as we are/as I thought, he is less tall/intelligent than his brother/than us *ou* than we are/than I thought; **rien n'est** ~ **sûr, il n'y a rien de** ~ **sûr** nothing is less certain; **c'est tellement** ~ **cher** it's so much cheaper *ou* less expensive; **il ressemble à son père, en** ~ **grand** he looks like his father only he's not so tall, he looks like a smaller version of his father; **c'est le même genre de livre, en** ~ **bien** it's the same kind of book, only (it's) not so good *ou* but not so good.

b (*avec vb*) less. **exiger/donner** ~ to demand/give less; **je gagne (un peu)** ~ **que lui** I earn (a little) less than him *ou* than he does; **cela m'a coûté** ~ **que rien** it cost me next to nothing; **vous ne l'obtiendrez pas à** ~ you won't get it for less; **cela coûtait trois fois** ~ it was one-third as expensive; **il travaille** ~**/**~ **vite que vous** he works less/less quickly than you (do), he does not work as hard/as quickly as you do; **il a fait encore** ~ **beau en août qu'en juillet** the weather was even worse in August than in July; **sortez** ~ **(souvent)** go out less often, don't go out so often *ou* so much; **j'aime** ~ **la campagne en hiver (qu'en été)** I don't like the country as *ou* so much in winter (as in summer), I like the country less in winter (than in summer).

c ~ **de** (*quantité*) less, not so much; (*nombre*) fewer, not so many; (*heure*) before, not yet; (*durée, âge, distance*) less than, under; **mange** ~ **de bonbons et de chocolat** eat fewer sweets and less chocolate; **il y a** ~ **de 2 ans qu'il vit ici** he has been living here (for) less than 2 years; **les enfants de** ~ **de 4 ans voyagent gratuitement** children under 4 *ou* of less than 4 years of age travel free; **il est** ~ **de minuit** it is not yet midnight; **il était un peu** ~ **de 6 heures** it was a little before 6 o'clock; **vous ne pouvez pas lui donner** ~ **de 100 F** you can't give him less than 100 francs; **vous ne trouverez rien à** ~ **de 100 F** you won't find anything under 100 francs *ou* for less than 100 francs; **il a eu** ~ **de mal que nous à trouver une place** he had less trouble than we had *ou* than us (in) finding a seat; **ils ont** ~ **de livres que de jouets** they have fewer books than toys; **nous l'avons fait en** ~ **de 5 minutes** we did it in less than *ou* in under 5 minutes; **en** ~ **de deux*** in a flash *ou* a trice, in the twinkling of an eye; **il y aura** ~ **de monde demain** there will be fewer people tomorrow, there will not be so many people tomorrow; **il devrait y avoir** ~ **de 100 personnes** there should be under 100 people *ou* less than 100 people; **en** ~ **de rien** in less than no time.

d **de** ~**, en** ~**: il gagne 500 F de** ~ **qu'elle** he earns 500 francs less than she does; **vous avez 5 ans de** ~ **qu'elle** you are 5 years younger than her *ou* than she is; **il y a 3 verres en** ~ (*qui manquent*) there are 3 glasses missing; (*trop peu*) we are 3 glasses short; **c'est le même climat, le brouillard en** ~ it's the same climate except for the fog *ou* minus the fog.

e ~ **...** ~ the less ... the less; ~ **... plus** the less ... the more; ~ **je mange,** ~ **j'ai d'appétit** the less I eat the less hungry I feel; ~ **je fume, plus je mange** the less I smoke the more I eat.

f (*loc*) **à** ~ **qu'il ne vienne** unless he comes; **à** ~ **de faire une bêtise il devrait gagner** unless he does something silly he should win; **à** ~ **d'un accident ça devrait marcher** barring accidents *ou* accidents apart it should work; **c'est de** ~ **en** ~ **bon** it's less and less good; *voir* **autant, plus.**

2 adv *emploi superlatif* a (*avec adj ou adv*) **le** ~**, la** ~ (*de plusieurs*) the least; (*de deux*) the less; **c'est la** ~ **douée de mes élèves** she's the least gifted of my pupils; **c'est le** ~ **doué des deux** he's the less gifted of the two; **la température la** ~ **haute de l'été** the lowest temperature of the summer; **ce sont les fleurs les** ~ **chères** they are the least expensive *ou* the cheapest flowers.

b (*avec vb*) **le** ~ (the) least; **c'est celui que j'aime le** ~ it's the one I like (the) least; **l'émission que je regarde le** ~ **souvent** the programme I watch (the) least often; **de nous tous c'est lui qui a bu le** ~ **(d'alcool)** he's the one who drank the least (alcohol) of us all, of all of us he drank the least (alcohol).

c (*loc*) **c'est bien le** ~ **que l'on puisse faire** it's the least one can do; **c'est le** ~ **que l'on puisse dire!** that's the least one can say!; **si vous êtes le** ~ **du monde soucieux** if you are in the slightest bit *ou* in the least bit *ou* in the least worried; **au** ~ at (the) least; **elle a payé cette robe au** ~ **3 000 F** she paid at least 3,000 francs for this dress; **600 au** ~ at least 600, fully 600; **la moitié au** ~ at least half, fully half; **cela fait au** ~ **10 jours qu'il est parti** it is at least 10 days since he left; **vous avez (tout) au** ~ **appris la nouvelle** you must at least have heard the news; **à tout le** ~**, pour le** ~ to say the least, at the very least; **sa décision est pour le** ~ **bizarre** his decision is odd to say the least; **du** ~ (*restriction*) at least; **il ne pleuvra pas, du** ~ **c'est ce qu'annonce la radio** it's not going to rain, at least that's what it says on the radio *ou* at least so the radio says; **si du** ~ that is if; **laissez-le sortir, si du** ~ **il ne fait pas froid** let him go out, that is (only) if it is not cold.

3 prép a (*soustraction*) **6** ~ **2 font 4** 6 minus 2 equals 4, 2 from 6 makes 4; **j'ai retrouvé mon sac,** ~ **le portefeuille** I found my bag, minus the wallet.

b (*heure*) to. **il est 4 heures** ~ **5 (minutes)** it is 5 (minutes) to 4; **nous avons le temps, il n'est que** ~ **10*** we have plenty of time, it's only 10 to*; (*fig*) **il s'en est tiré, mais il était** ~ **cinq*** *ou* ~ **une*** he got out of it but it was a close shave* *ou* a near thing*.

c (*température*) below. **il fait** ~ **5°** it is 5° below freezing *ou* minus 5°.

4 nm (*Math*) **(le signe)** ~ the minus sign.

5 comp ►**moins-perçu** nm amount not drawn, short payment ►**moins que rien*** nmf (*péj : minable*) dead loss*, second-rater*, washout*, schlemiel‡ (*US*) ►**moins-value** (*Comm*) nf depreciation.

moirage [mwaʀaʒ] nm (*procédé*) watering; (*reflet*) watered effect.

moire [mwaʀ] nf (*tissu*) moiré, watered fabric; (*procédé*) watering. **on voit la** ~ **du papier** you can see the mottled effect in the paper.

moiré, e [mwaʀe] (ptp de **moirer**) 1 adj (*Tech*) watered, moiré; (*fig*) shimmering. 2 nm (*Tech*) moiré, water; (*littér*) shimmering ripples.

moirer [mwaʀe] [1] vt (*Tech*) to water. (*littér*) **la lune moirait l'étang de reflets argentés** the moon cast a shimmering silvery light over the pool.

moirure [mwaʀyʀ] nf (*Tech*) moiré; (*littér*) shimmering ripples.

mois [mwa] nm a (*période*) month. (*Rel*) **le** ~ **de Marie** the month of Mary; (*Culin*) **les** ~ **en R** when there is an R in the month; **au** ~ **de janvier** in (the month of) January; **dans un** ~ in a month('s time); (*Comm*) **le 10 de ce** ~ the 10th inst(ant) (*Brit*), the 10th of this month; **être payé au** ~ to be paid monthly; **louer au** ~ to rent by the month; **30 F par** ~ 30 francs a *ou* per month; (*Comm*) **billet à 3** ~ bill at 3 months; **un bébé de 6** ~ a 6-month(-old) baby; **tous les 4** ~ every 4 months; **devoir 3** ~ **de loyer** to owe 3 months' rent; **devoir 3** ~ **de factures** to be 3 months behind with one's bills; *voir* **enceinte[1], tout.**

b (*salaire*) monthly pay, monthly salary. **toucher son** ~***** to draw one's pay *ou* salary for the month *ou* one's month's pay *ou* salary; ~ **double** extra month's pay (*as end-of-year bonus*); **treizième/quatorzième** ~ one month's/two months' extra pay; *voir* **fin[2].**

Moïse [mɔiz] nm a (*Bible*) Moses. b (*berceau*) **m**~ Moses basket.

moisi, e [mwazi] (ptp de **moisir**) 1 adj mouldy, mildewed. 2 nm mould (*NonC*), mildew (*NonC*). **odeur de** ~ musty *ou* fusty smell; **goût de** ~ musty taste; **ça sent le** ~ it smells musty *ou* fusty.

moisir [mwaziʀ] [2] 1 vt to make mouldy. 2 vi a to go mouldy, mould. b (*fig*) ~ **en province** to stagnate in the country; ~ **dans un cachot** to rot in a dungeon; **on ne va pas** ~ **ici jusqu'à la nuit!*** we're not going to hang around here till night-time!*

moisissure [mwazisyʀ] nf (*gén*) mould (*NonC*); (*par l'humidité*) mould (*NonC*), mildew (*NonC*). **enlever les** ~**s sur un fromage** to scrape the mould off a piece of cheese.

moisson [mwasɔ̃] nf (*saison, travail*) harvest; (*récolte*) harvest; (*fig*) wealth, crop. **à l'époque de la** ~ at harvest time; **la** ~ **est en avance/en retard** the harvest is early/late; **rentrer la** ~ to bring in the harvest; **faire la** ~ to harvest, reap; (*fig*) **faire (une) ample** ~ **de renseignements/souvenirs** to gather *ou* amass a wealth *ou* a good crop of information/memories; (*fig*) **faire une ample** ~ **de lauriers** to carry off a fine crop of prizes.

moissonner [mwasɔne] [1] vt (*Agr*) *céréale* to harvest, reap, gather in; *champ* to reap; († *ou littér*) *récompenses* to collect, carry off; *renseignements, souvenirs* to gather, collect. (*littér*) **cette génération moissonnée par la guerre** this generation cut down by the war.

moissonneur, -euse [mwasɔnœʀ, øz] 1 nm,f harvester, reaper († *ou littér*). 2 **moissonneuse** nf (*machine*) harvester. 3 comp ►**moissonneuse-batteuse(-lieuse)** nf (pl **moissonneuses-batteuses(-lieuses)**) combine harvester ►**moissonneuse-lieuse** nf (pl **moissonneuses-lieuses**) self-binder.

moite [mwat] adj *peau, mains* sweaty, sticky; *atmosphère* sticky, muggy; *chaleur* sticky.

moiteur [mwatœʀ] nf (*voir* **moite**) sweatiness; stickiness; mugginess. **essuyer la** ~ **de ses paumes** to wipe the sweatiness *ou* stickiness from one's hands.

moitié [mwatje] nf a (*partie*) half. **partager qch en deux** ~**s** to halve sth, divide sth in half *ou* into (two) halves; **quelle est la** ~ **de 40?** what is half of 40?; **donne-m'en la** ~ give me half (of it); **faire la** ~ **du chemin avec qn** to go halfway *ou* half of the way with sb; **la** ~ **des habitants a été sauvée** *ou* **ont été sauvés** half (of) the inhabitants were rescued; **la** ~ **du temps** half the time; **il en faut** ~ **plus/moins** you need half as much again/half (of) that; ~ **anglais,** ~ **français** half English, half French.

b (*milieu*) halfway mark, half. **parvenu à la** ~ **du trajet** having completed half the journey, having reached halfway *ou* the halfway mark; **parvenu à la** ~ **de la vie** when one reaches the middle of one's life, when one has completed half one's lifespan; **arrivé à la** ~ **du travail** having done half the work *ou* got halfway through the work, having reached the halfway point *ou* mark in the work.

c (*hum: épouse*) **ma/sa** ~ my/his better half* (*hum*); **ma tendre** ~ my ever-loving wife (*hum*).

d **à** ~ half; **il a fait le travail à** ~ he has (only) half done the work;

il a mis la table à ~ he has half set the table; **il ne fait jamais rien à** ~ he never does things by halves; **à** ~ **plein/mûr** half-full/-ripe; **à** ~ **chemin** (at) halfway, at the halfway mark; **à** ~ **prix** (at) half-price.

e (*loc*) **de** ~ by half; **réduire de** ~ *trajet, production, coût* to cut *ou* reduce by half, halve; **plus grand de** ~ half as big again, bigger by half; **être/se mettre de** ~ **dans une entreprise** to have half shares/go halves in a business; **par** ~ in two, in half; **diviser qch par** ~ to divide sth in two *ou* in half; **il est pour** ~ **dans cette faillite** he is half responsible *ou* half to blame for this bankruptcy; **on a partagé le pain** ~ ~ we halved the bread between us, we shared the bread half-and-half *ou* fifty-fifty*; **ils ont partagé** *ou* **fait** ~ ~ they went halves; **ça a marché?** — ~ ~* how did it go? — so-so*.

moka [mɔka] **nm** (*gâteau à la crème*) cream gâteau; (*gâteau au café*) mocha (*Brit*) *ou* coffee gâteau; (*café*) mocha coffee.

mol [mɔl] **adj m** *voir* **mou[1]**.

molaire[1] [mɔlɛʀ] **nf** (*dent*) molar.

molaire[2] [mɔlɛʀ] **adj** (*Chim*) molar.

molasse [mɔlas] **nf** = **mollasse[2]**.

moldave [mɔldav] **1** **adj** Moldavian. **2** **nmf**: **M**~ Moldavian.

Moldavie [mɔldavi] **nf** Moldavia.

mole [mɔl] **nf** (*Chim*) mole, mol.

môle [mol] **nm** (*digue*) breakwater, mole, jetty; (*quai*) pier, jetty.

moléculaire [mɔlekylɛʀ] **adj** molecular.

molécule [mɔlekyl] **nf** molecule. ~**-gramme** gram molecule.

moleskine [mɔlɛskin] **nf** imitation leather. **il avait usé ses pantalons sur la** ~ **des cafés** he had spent half his life sitting around in cafés.

molester [mɔlɛste] 1 **vt** to manhandle, maul (about). **molesté par la foule** mauled by the crowd.

moleté, e [mɔlte] **adj** *roue, vis* milled, knurled.

molette [mɔlɛt] **nf** **a** (*Tech*) toothed wheel, cutting wheel; *voir* **clef**. **b** *[briquet, clef]* knurl; *[éperon]* rowel.

moliéresque [mɔljeʀɛsk] **adj** Molieresque.

mollah [mɔ(l)la] **nm** mulla(h).

mollard‡ [mɔlaʀ] **nm** (*crachat*) gob of spit‡.

mollasse[1]* [mɔlas] **1** **adj** (*péj*) (*léthargique*) sluggish, lethargic; (*flasque*) flabby, flaccid. **une grande fille** ~ a great lump* (*Brit*) *ou* pudding* of a girl. **2** **nmf** lazy lump* (*Brit*), lazybones.

mollasse[2] [mɔlas] **nf** (*Géol*) molasse.

mollasserie [mɔlasʀi] **nf** sluggishness, lethargy.

mollasson, -onne* [mɔlasɔ̃, ɔn] (*péj*) **1** **adj** sluggish, lethargic. **2** **nm,f** lazy lump* (*Brit*), lazybones.

molle [mɔl] **adj f** *voir* **mou[1]**.

mollement [mɔlmɑ̃] **adv** (*doucement*) *tomber* softly; *couler* gently, sluggishly; (*paresseusement*) *travailler* half-heartedly, lethargically, unenthusiastically, languidly; (*faiblement*) *réagir, protester* feebly, weakly. **les jours s'écoulaient** ~ the days slipped gently by.

mollesse [mɔlɛs] **nf** **a** (*au toucher*) *[substance, oreiller]* softness; *[poignée de main]* limpness, flabbiness.

b (*à la vue*) *[contours, lignes]* softness; *[relief]* softness, gentleness; *[traits du visage]* flabbiness, sagginess; (*Peinture*) *[dessin, traits]* lifelessness, weakness.

c (*manque d'énergie*) *[geste]* lifelessness, feebleness; *[protestations, opposition]* weakness, feebleness; (†) *[vie]* indolence, softness; *[style]* woolliness; (*Mus*) *[exécution]* lifelessness, dullness; *[personne]* (*indolence*) sluggishness, lethargy; (*manque d'autorité*) spinelessness; (*grande indulgence*) laxness. **vivre dans la** ~ to live the soft life; **la** ~ **de la police face aux manifestants** the feebleness of the police's response to the demonstrators.

mollet[1], -ette [mɔlɛ, ɛt] **adj** *voir* **œuf**.

mollet[2] [mɔlɛ] **nm** (*Anat*) calf. (*fig*) ~**s de coq** wiry legs.

molletière [mɔltjɛʀ] **nf**: **(bande)** ~ puttee.

molleton [mɔltɔ̃] **nm** (*tissu*) flannelette; (*pour table etc*) felting.

molletonner [mɔltɔne] 1 **vt** to line with flannelette, put a warm lining in. **gants molletonnés** fleece-lined gloves; **anorak molletonné** quilted anorak, anorak with a warm lining.

molletonneux, -euse [mɔltɔnø, øz] **adj** fleecy.

mollir [mɔliʀ] 2 **vi** **a** (*fléchir*) *[sol]* to give (way), yield; *[ennemi]* to yield, give way, give ground; *[père, créancier]* to come round, relent; *[courage, personne]* to flag. **nos prières l'ont fait** ~ our pleas softened his attitude *ou* made him relent; **ce n'est pas le moment de** ~ you (*ou* we *etc*) can't give in now!; (*fig*) **il a senti ses jambes/genoux** ~ **sous lui** he felt his legs/knees give way beneath him. **b** *[substance]* to soften, go soft. **c** *[vent]* to abate, die down.

mollo‡ [mɔlo] **adv**: **(vas-y)** ~**!*** take it easy!*, (go) easy*!, easy does it!

mollusque [mɔlysk] **nm** (*Zool*) mollusc; (* *péj*) lazy lump* (*Brit*), lazybones.

molosse [mɔlɔs] **nm** (*littér*) big (ferocious) dog, huge hound (*hum*).

Molotov [mɔlɔtɔf] **nm** *voir* **cocktail**.

molybdène [mɔlibdɛn] **nm** molybdenum.

môme [mom] **nmf** (*: *enfant*) kid*; (*péj*) brat*; (‡: *fille*) bird‡ (*Brit*), chick‡ (*US*). **belle** ~‡ nice-looking piece‡ (*Brit*) *ou* chick‡ (*US*).

moment [mɔmɑ̃] **nm** **a** (*long instant*) while, moment. **pendant un court** ~ **elle le crut** for a moment *ou* a few moments she believed him; **je ne l'ai pas vu depuis un (bon)** ~ I haven't seen him for a (good) while *ou* for quite a time *ou* while; **cette réparation va prendre un** ~ this repair job will take some time *ou* a good while; **elle en a pour un petit** ~ (*lit*) she won't be long *ou* a moment, it'll only take her a moment; (*iro*) she'll be some *ou* a little while.

b (*court instant*) moment. **il réfléchit un** ~ he thought for a moment; **c'est l'affaire d'un** ~ it won't take a minute *ou* moment, it will only take a minute, it'll be done in a jiffy*; **ça ne dure qu'un** ~ it doesn't last long, it (only) lasts a minute; **un** ~ **de silence** a moment of silence, a moment's silence; **j'ai eu un** ~ **de panique** I had a moment's panic, for a moment I panicked; **en un** ~ in a matter of minutes; **dans un** ~ **de colère** in a moment of anger, in a momentary fit of anger; **dans un** ~ in a little while, in a moment; **un** ~**, il arrive!** just a moment *ou* a minute *ou* a mo'* (*Brit*), he's coming!

c (*période*) time. **à quel** ~ **est-ce arrivé?** at what point in time *ou* when exactly did this occur?; **connaître/passer de bons** ~**s** to have/spend (some) happy times; **les** ~**s que nous avons passés ensemble** the times we spent together; **il a passé un mauvais** *ou* **sale** ~* he went through *ou* had a difficult time, he had a rough time *ou* passage; **je n'ai pas un** ~ **à moi** I haven't a moment to myself; **le** ~ **présent** the present time; **à ses** ~**s perdus** in his spare time; **les grands** ~**s de l'histoire** the great moments of history; **il a ses bons et ses mauvais** ~**s** he has his good times and his bad (times); **il est dans un de ses mauvais** ~**s** it's one of his off *ou* bad spells, he's having one of his off *ou* bad spells; **la célébrité/le succès du** ~ the celebrity/success of the moment *ou* day.

d (*occasion*) **il faut profiter du** ~ you must take advantage of *ou* seize the opportunity; **ce n'est pas le** ~ **(de protester)** this is no time *ou* not the time (to protest *ou* for protesting), this is not the (right) moment (to protest); **tu arrives au bon** ~ you've come just at the right time; **c'était le** ~ **de réagir** it was time to react, a reaction was called for; **le** ~ **psychologique** the psychological moment; *voir* **jamais**.

e (*Tech*) moment; (*Phys*) momentum.

f (*loc*) **en ce** ~ at the moment, at present, just now; **au** ~ **de l'accident** at the time of the accident, when the accident happened; **au** ~ **de partir** just as I (*ou* he *etc*) was about to leave, just as I (*ou* he *etc*) was on the point of leaving; **au** ~ **où elle entrait, lui sortait** as she was going in he was coming out; **au** ~ **où il s'y attendait le moins** (at a time) when he was least expecting it; **à un** ~ **donné il cesse d'écouter** at a certain point he stops listening; **il se prépare afin de savoir quoi dire le** ~ **venu** he's getting ready so that he'll know what to say when the time comes; **le** ~ **venu ils s'élancèrent** when the time came they hurled themselves forward; **des voitures arrivaient à tout** ~ *ou* **à tous** ~**s** cars were constantly *ou* continually arriving, cars kept on arriving; **il peut arriver à tout** ~ he may arrive (at) any time (now) *ou* any moment (now); **à ce** ~**-là** (*temps*) at that point *ou* time; (*circonstance*) in that case, if that's the case, if that's so; **à aucun** ~ **je n'ai dit que** I never at any time said that, at no point did I say that; **on l'attend d'un** ~ **à l'autre** he is expected any moment now *ou* (at) any time now; **du** ~ **où** *ou* **que** since, seeing that; **dès le** ~ **que** *ou* **où** as soon as, from the moment *ou* time when; **par** ~**s** now and then, at times, every now and again; **pour le** ~ for the time being *ou* the moment, at present; **sur le** ~ at the time.

momentané, e [mɔmɑ̃tane] **adj** *gêne, crise, arrêt* momentary (*épith*); *espoir, effort* short-lived, brief. **cette crise n'est que** ~**e** this is only a momentary crisis.

momentanément [mɔmɑ̃tanemɑ̃] **adv** (*en ce moment*) at *ou* for the moment, at present; (*un court instant*) for a short while, momentarily.

momeries [mɔmʀi] **nfpl** (*littér*) mumbo jumbo.

mômeries* [momʀi] **nfpl** childish behaviour. **arrête tes** ~**!** stop your silly nonsense!*, stop acting like a big baby!*

momie [mɔmi] **nf** mummy. (* *fig*) **ne reste pas là comme une** ~ don't stand there like a stuffed dummy*.

momification [mɔmifikasjɔ̃] **nf** mummification.

momifier [mɔmifje] 7 **1** **vt** to mummify. **2** **se momifier** **vpr** (*fig*) to atrophy, fossilize.

mon [mɔ̃], **ma** [ma], **mes** [me] **adj poss** **a** (*possession, relation*) my, my own (*emphatique*). ~ **fils et ma fille** my son and (my) daughter; **j'ai** ~ **idée là-dessus** I have my own ideas *ou* views about that; *pour autres exemples voir* **son[1]**.

b (*valeur affective, ironique, intensive*) **alors voilà** ~ **type/**~ **François qui se met à m'injurier*** and then the fellow/our François starts bawling insults at me; **voilà** ~ **mal de tête qui me reprend** that's my headache back again; **on a changé** ~ **Paris** they've changed the Paris I knew *ou* what I think of as Paris; **j'ai** ~ **samedi cette année*** I've got Saturday(s) off this year, I have my Saturdays free this year; *voir* **son[1]**.

c (*dans termes d'adresse*) my. **viens** ~ **petit/ma chérie** come along lovie*/(my) darling; ~ **cher ami** my dear friend; ~ **cher Monsieur** my dear sir; ~ **vieux** my dear fellow; **ma vieille** my dear girl; **eh bien** ~ **vieux, si j'avais su!*** well I can tell you old chap* (*Brit*) *ou* fellow*, if I'd known!; (*Rel*) **oui** ~ **père/ma sœur/ma mère** yes Father/Sister/Mother; (*Rel*) **mes (bien chers) frères** my (dear) brethren; (*Rel*) ~ **Dieu, ayez pitié de nous** dear Lord *ou* O God, have mercy upon us; (*Mil*) **oui** ~ **lieutenant/général** yes sir/sir *ou* general; **eh bien** ~ **salaud** *ou* **cochon, tu as du toupet!‡** you so-and-so *ou* you old devil, you've got some nerve!*; ~ **Dieu, j'ai oublié mon portefeuille** oh dear, *ou* heavens, I've forgotten my wallet.

monacal, e, mpl **-aux** [mɔnakal, o] **adj** (*lit, fig*) monastic.

Monaco [mɔnako] **nm: (la principauté de) ~** (the principality of) Monaco.

monade [mɔnad] **nf** monad.

monarchie [mɔnaʀʃi] **nf** monarchy. **~ absolue/constitutionnelle/élective** absolute/constitutional/elective monarchy.

monarchique [mɔnaʀʃik] **adj** monarchistic, monarchial.

monarchisme [mɔnaʀʃism] **nm** monarchism.

monarchiste [mɔnaʀʃist] **adj, nmf** monarchist.

monarque [mɔnaʀk] **nm** monarch. **~ absolu** absolute monarch; **~ de droit divin** monarch *ou* king by divine right.

monastère [mɔnastɛʀ] **nm** monastery.

monastique [mɔnastik] **adj** monastic.

monaural, e, mpl **-aux** [mɔnɔʀal, o] **adj** monophonic, monaural.

monceau, pl **~x** [mɔ̃so] **nm: un ~ de** (*amoncellement*) a heap *ou* pile of; (*accumulation*) a heap *ou* load* of; **des ~x de** heaps *ou* piles of; heaps *ou* loads* *ou* stacks* of.

mondain, e [mɔ̃dɛ̃, ɛn] 1 **adj** a *réunion, vie* society (*épith*); *public* fashionable. **plaisirs ~s** pleasures of society; **mener une vie ~e** to lead a busy social life, be in the social round, move in fashionable circles; **goût pour la vie ~e** taste for society life *ou* living; **carnet/romancier ~** society column/novelist; **soirée ~e** evening reception (*with people from high society*); **chronique ~e** society gossip column; **leurs obligations ~es** their social obligations; **ils sont très ~s** they are great society people *ou* great socialites, they like moving in fashionable society *ou* circles.

b *politesse, ton* refined, urbane, sophisticated. **il a été très ~ avec moi** he treated me with studied politeness *ou* courtesy.

c (*Philos*) mundane; (*Rel*) worldly, earthly.

d **la police** *ou* **brigade ~e, la M~e*** ≃ the vice squad.

2 **nm,f** society man (*ou* woman), socialite.

mondanité [mɔ̃danite] **nf** a **~s** (*divertissements, soirées*) society life; (*politesses, propos*) society *ou* polite small talk; (*Presse: chronique*) society gossip column; **toutes ces ~s sont fatigantes** we are exhausted by this social whirl *ou* round. b (*goût*) taste for society life, love of society life; (*habitude, connaissance des usages*) savoir-faire. c (*Rel*) worldliness.

monde [mɔ̃d] **nm** a (*univers, terre*) world. **dans le ~ entier,** (*littér*) **de par le ~** all over the world, the world over, throughout the world; **le ~ entier s'indigna** the whole world was outraged; **le ~ des vivants** the land of the living; **il se moque** *ou* **se fiche*** *ou* **se fout*** **du ~** he's got a nerve* *ou* cheek* (*Brit*), he's got a damn* *ou* bloody** (*Brit*) nerve; **venir au ~** to come into the world; **mettre un enfant au ~** to bring a child into the world; **si je suis encore de ce ~** if I'm still here *ou* in the land of the living; **depuis qu'il est de ce ~** since he was born; **elle n'est plus de ce ~** she is no longer with us, she has departed this life; **rêver à un ~ meilleur** to dream of a better world; **où va le ~?** whatever is the world coming to?; **dans ce (bas) ~** here below, in this world; **l'Ancien/le Nouveau M~** the Old/New World; **le Tiers-/Quart-~** the Third/Fourth World; *voir* **depuis, unique.**

b (*ensemble, groupement spécifique*) world. **le ~ végétal/animal** the vegetable/animal world; **le ~ des affaires/du théâtre** the world of business/(the) theatre, the business/theatre world; **le ~ chrétien/communiste/capitaliste** the Christian/communist/capitalist world.

c (*domaine*) world, realm. **le ~ de l'illusion/du rêve** the realm of illusion/dreams; **le ~ de la folie** the world *ou* realm of madness.

d (*intensif*) **du ~, au ~** in the world, on earth; **produit parmi les meilleurs au** *ou* **du ~** product which is among the best in the world *ou* among the world's best; (*littér*) **au demeurant, le meilleur homme du** *ou* **au ~** otherwise, the finest man alive; **tout s'est passé le mieux du ~** everything went (off) perfectly *ou* like a dream*; **il n'était pas le moins du ~ anxieux** he was not the slightest *ou* least bit worried, he wasn't worried in the slightest *ou* least; **je ne m'en séparerais pour rien au ~, je ne m'en séparerais pas pour tout l'or du ~** I wouldn't part with it for anything (in the world) *ou* for all the world *ou* for all the tea in China; **nul au ~ ne peut ...** nobody in the world can ...; **j'en pense tout le bien du ~** I have the highest opinion of him *ou* her *ou* it.

e (*loc*) **c'est le ~ à l'envers** *ou* **renversé** the world's gone crazy; **comme le ~ est petit!** it's a small world!; **se faire (tout) un ~ de qch** to make a (great deal of) fuss about *ou* a (great) song and dance about sth; **se faire un ~ de rien** to make a mountain out of a molehill, make a fuss over nothing; **se faire un ~ de tout** to make a fuss over everything, make everything into a great issue; **c'est un ~!*** it's (just) not on!*; **il y a un ~ entre ces deux personnes/conceptions** these two people/concepts are worlds apart, there is a world of difference between these two people/concepts.

f (*gens*) **j'entends du ~ à côté** I can hear people in the next room; **est-ce qu'il y a du ~?** (*qn est-il présent?*) is there anybody there?; (*y a-t-il foule?*) are there many there?, are there a lot of people there?; **il y a du ~** (*ce n'est pas vide*) there are some people there; (*il y a foule*) there's quite a crowd; **il y a beaucoup de ~** there's a real crowd, there are a lot of people; **il y avait un ~!** *ou* **un ~ fou!*** there were crowds!, the place was packed!; **ils voient beaucoup de ~** they have a busy social life; **ils reçoivent beaucoup de ~** they entertain a lot, they do a lot of entertaining; **ce week-end nous avons du ~** we have people coming *ou* visitors *ou* company this weekend; (*fig*) **il y a du ~ au balcon!*** what a pair!*, what a frontage* she's got! (*Brit*); **elle promène tout son petit ~** she's out with all her brood; **tout ce petit ~ s'est bien amusé?** and did everyone have a nice time?, did we all enjoy ourselves?; **il connaît son ~** he knows the people he deals with; **je n'ai pas encore tout mon ~** my set *ou* group *ou* lot* (*Brit*) isn't all here yet; *voir* **Monsieur, tout.**

g (*Rel*) **le ~** the world; **les plaisirs du ~** worldly pleasures, the pleasures of the world.

h (*milieu social*) set, circle. (*la bonne société*) **le (grand** *ou* **beau) ~** (high) society; **aller dans le ~** to mix with high society; **appartenir au meilleur ~** to move in the best circles; **il n'est pas de notre ~** he is from a different set, he's not one of our set *ou* crowd*; **nous ne sommes pas du même ~** we don't move in *ou* belong to the same circles (of society); **cela ne se fait pas dans le ~** that isn't done in the best of circles *ou* in polite society; **homme/femme/gens du ~** society man/woman/people; *voir* **beau, grand.**

monder [mɔ̃de] [1] **vt** *orge* to hull; *amandes* to blanch.

mondial, e, mpl **-iaux** [mɔ̃djal, jo] **adj** world (*épith*), world-wide. **guerre/population/production ~e** world war/population/production; **influence/crise ~e** world-wide influence/crisis; **à l'échelle ~e** on a world-wide scale, world-wide; **une célébrité ~e** a world-famous personality *ou* celebrity.

mondialement [mɔ̃djalmɑ̃] **adv** throughout the world, the (whole) world over. **il est ~ connu** he is known the (whole) world over *ou* throughout the world, he is world-famous.

mondialisation [mɔ̃djalizasjɔ̃] **nf** *[technique]* internationalization. **redoutant la ~ du conflit** fearing that the conflict will (*ou* would) spread throughout the world, fearing the spread of the conflict worldwide *ou* throughout the world.

mondialisme [mɔ̃djalism] **nm** internationalism.

mondialiste [mɔ̃djalist] **adj, nmf** internationalist.

mond(i)ovision [mɔ̃d(j)ɔvizjɔ̃] **nf** worldwide (satellite) television broadcast. **retransmis en ~** broadcast (by satellite) worldwide.

monégasque [mɔnegask] 1 **adj** Monegasque, Monacan. 2 **nmf: M~** Monegasque, Monacan.

monème [mɔnɛm] **nm** moneme.

monétaire [mɔnetɛʀ] **adj** *valeur, unité, système* monetary. **la circulation ~** the circulation of currency; *voir* **masse.**

monétarisme [mɔnetaʀism] **nm** monetarism.

monétariste [mɔnetaʀist] **adj, nmf** monetarist.

monétique [mɔnetik] **nf** use of plastic money.

monétiser [mɔnetize] [1] **vt** to monetize.

mongol, e [mɔ̃gɔl] 1 **adj** Mongol, Mongolian. **République populaire ~e** Mongolian People's Republic. 2 **nm** (*Ling*) Mongolian. 3 **nm,f** (*Géog*) **M~(e)** (*gén*) Mongol, Mongoloid; (*habitant ou originaire de la Mongolie*) Mongolian.

Mongolie [mɔ̃gɔli] **nf** Mongolia. **République populaire de ~** Mongolian People's Republic, People's Republic of Mongolia; **~-Extérieure** Outer Mongolia; **~-Intérieure** Inner Mongolia.

mongolien, -ienne [mɔ̃gɔljɛ̃, jɛn] (*Méd*) 1 **adj** mongol†, with Down's syndrome (*attrib*), Down's syndrome (*épith*). 2 **nm,f** (*bébé, enfant*) mongol†, Down's syndrome baby (*ou* boy *ou* girl); (*adulte*) mongol†, person with Down's syndrome.

mongolique [mɔ̃gɔlik] **adj** (*Géog*) Mongol(ic), Mongolian.

mongolisme [mɔ̃gɔlism] **nm** mongolism†, Down's syndrome.

Monique [mɔnik] **nf** Monica.

monisme [mɔnism] **nm** monism.

moniste [mɔnist] 1 **adj** monistic. 2 **nmf** monist.

moniteur [mɔnitœʀ] **nm** a (*Sport*) instructor, coach; *[colonie de vacances]* supervisor (*Brit*), (camp) counsellor (*US*). **~ de ski** skiing instructor; **~ d'auto-école** driving instructor. b (*Tech, Ordin: appareil*) monitor. **~ cardiaque** heart-rate monitor. c (*Univ*) graduate assistant.

monitorage [mɔnitɔʀaʒ] **nm = monitoring.**

monitorat [mɔnitɔʀa] **nm** (*formation*) training to be an instructor; (*fonction*) instructorship.

monitoring [mɔnitɔʀiŋ] **nm** (*Méd*) monitoring.

monitrice [mɔnitʀis] **nf** (*Sport*) instructress; *[colonie de vacances]* supervisor (*Brit*), (camp) counsellor (*US*); (*Univ*) graduate assistant.

monnaie [mɔnɛ] 1 **nf** a (*Écon, Fin: espèces, devises*) currency. **une ~ forte** a strong currency; **~ d'or/d'argent** gold/silver currency; **~ décimale** decimal coinage *ou* currency; (*Bourse*) **la ~ américaine** the American dollar; *voir* **battre, faux[2].**

b (*pièce, médaille*) coin. **une ~ d'or** a gold coin; **émettre/retirer une ~** to issue/withdraw a coin.

c (*pièces inférieures à l'unité, appoint*) change; (*petites pièces*) (loose) change. **petite** *ou* **menue ~** small change; **vous n'avez pas de ~?** (*pour payer*) haven't you got (the) change? *ou* any change?; **auriez-vous de la ~?, pourriez-vous me faire de la ~?** could you give me some change?; **faire de la ~** to get (some) change; **faire la ~ de 100 F** to get change for *ou* to change a 100-franc note *ou* 100 francs; **faire** *ou* **donner**

à qn la ~ de 50 F to change 50 francs for sb, give sb change for 50 francs; **elle m'a rendu la ~ sur 50 F** she gave me the change out of *ou* from 50 francs; **passez la ~!*** let's have the money!, cough up* everyone!

d (*bâtiment*) **la M~, l'hôtel des ~s** the mint, the Mint (*Brit*).

e (*loc*) **c'est ~ courante** *[faits, événements]* it's common *ou* widespread, it's a common occurrence; *[actions, pratiques]* it's common practice; (*fig*) **donner** *ou* **rendre à qn la ~ de sa pièce** to pay sb back in the same *ou* in his own coin, repay sb in kind; **à l'école les billes servent de ~ d'échange** at school marbles are used as money *ou* as a currency; **ôtages qui servent de ~ d'échange** hostages who are used as bargaining counters; **payer qn en ~ de singe** to fob sb off with empty promises.

2 comp ▸monnaie de banque = **monnaie scripturale ▸monnaie divisionnaire** fractional currency **▸monnaie électronique** plastic money **▸monnaie fiduciaire** fiduciary currency, paper money **▸monnaie légale** legal tender **▸monnaie locale** local currency **▸monnaie métallique** coin (*NonC*) **▸monnaie-du-pape nf (pl monnaies-du-pape)** honesty **▸monnaie de papier** paper money **▸monnaie plastique** plastic money **▸monnaie scripturale** representative *ou* bank money **▸monnaie verte** green currency.

monnayable [mɔnɛjabl] **adj** (*voir* **monnayer**) convertible into cash.

monnayer [mɔneje] [8] **vt** *terres, titres* to convert into cash. (*fig*) **~ son talent/ses capacités** to make money from one's talents/abilities.

monnayeur [mɔnɛjœʀ] **nm** *voir* **faux²**.

mono [mɔno] **1 nm** (*arg Scol*) **abrév de moniteur. 2 nf** (**abrév de monophonie**) **en ~** in mono. **3 adj** *disque, électrophone* mono.

mono... [mɔnɔ] **préf** mono... .

monoacide [mɔnoasid] **adj** mon(o)acid.

monobasique [mɔnobɑzik] **adj** monobasic.

monobloc [mɔnoblɔk] **adj** cast in one piece.

monocaméral, pl -aux [mɔnokameʀal, o] **adj m** unicameral.

monocamérisme [mɔnokameʀism] **nm** unicameralism.

monochrome [mɔnokʀom] **adj** monochrome, monochromatic.

monocle [mɔnɔkl] **nm** monocle, eyeglass.

monocoque [mɔnɔkɔk] **1 adj** *voiture, avion* monocoque. **voilier ~** monohull *ou* single-hull sailing dinghy. **2 nm** (*voilier*) monohull.

monocorde [mɔnɔkɔʀd] **1 adj** *instrument* with a single chord; *voix, timbre, discours* monotonous. **2 nm** monochord.

monocratie [mɔnɔkʀasi] **nf** monocracy.

monoculture [mɔnɔkyltyʀ] **nf** single-crop farming, monoculture.

monocycle [mɔnosikl] **nm** unicycle.

monocyte [mɔnɔsit] **nm** monocyte.

monodie [mɔnɔdi] **nf** monody.

monogame [mɔnɔgam] **adj** monogamous. (*Zool*) **union ~** pair-bonding.

monogamie [mɔnɔgami] **nf** monogamy.

monogamique [mɔnɔgamik] **adj** monogamistic.

monogramme [mɔnɔgʀam] **nm** monogram.

monographie [mɔnɔgʀafi] **nf** monograph.

monoï [mɔnɔj] **nm inv** perfumed oil (*made from coconut and Tahitian flowers*).

monokini [mɔnɔkini] **nm** topless swimsuit, monokini.

monolingue [mɔnɔlɛ̃g] **adj** monolingual.

monolinguisme [mɔnɔlɛ̃gɥism] **nm** monolingualism.

monolithe [mɔnɔlit] **1 nm** monolith. **2 adj** monolithic.

monolithique [mɔnɔlitik] **adj** (*lit, fig*) monolithic.

monolithisme [mɔnɔlitism] **nm** (*Archit, Constr*) monolithism.

monologue [mɔnɔlɔg] **nm** monologue, soliloquy. (*Littérat*) **~ intérieur** stream of consciousness.

monologuer [mɔnɔlɔge] [1] **vi** to soliloquize. (*péj*) **il monologue pendant des heures** he talks away *ou* holds forth for hours.

monomane [mɔnɔman] **nmf, monomaniaque** [mɔnɔmanjak] **nmf** monomaniac.

monomanie [mɔnɔmani] **nf** monomania.

monôme [mɔnom] **nm** (*Math*) monomial; (*arg Scol*) students' rag procession (*in single file through the streets*).

monométallisme [mɔnometalism] **nm** (*Écon*) monometallism.

monomoteur, -trice [mɔnomɔtœʀ, tʀis] **1 adj** single-engined. **2 nm** single-engined aircraft.

mononucléaire [mɔnonykleɛʀ] **1 adj** (*Bio*) mononuclear. **2 nm** mononuclear (cell), mononucleate.

mononucléose [mɔnonykleoz] **nf** mononucleosis (*SPÉC*). **~ infectieuse** glandular fever, infectious mononucleosis (*SPÉC*).

monoparental, e, mpl -aux [mɔnopaʀɑ̃tal, o] **adj: familles ~es** single-parent *ou* one-parent families.

monophasé, e [mɔnɔfɑze] **1 adj** single-phase (*épith*). **2 nm** single-phase current.

monophonie [mɔnɔfɔni] **nf** monaural reproduction.

monophonique [mɔnɔfɔnik] **adj** monaural, monophonic.

monophtongue [mɔnɔftɔ̃g] **nf** monophthong.

monoplace [mɔnoplas] **nmf** (*Aut, Aviat*) single-seater, one-seater.

monoplan [mɔnoplɑ̃] **nm** monoplane.

monoplégie [mɔnɔpleʒi] **nf** monoplegia.

monopole [mɔnɔpɔl] **nm** (*Écon, fig*) monopoly. **avoir le ~ de** to have the monopoly of; **avoir un ~ sur** to have a monopoly in; **~ d'achat** monopsony; **~ d'État** state *ou* public monopoly; **~ fiscal** tax monopoly.

monopolisateur, -trice [mɔnɔpɔlizatœʀ, tʀis] **nm,f** monopolizer.

monopolisation [mɔnɔpɔlizasjɔ̃] **nf** monopolization.

monopoliser [mɔnɔpɔlize] [1] **vt** (*lit, fig*) to monopolize.

monopoliste [mɔnɔpɔlist] **adj, monopolistique** [mɔnɔpɔlistik] **adj** monopolistic.

monoprix [mɔnɔpʀi] **nm** ® department store (*for inexpensive goods*), ≃ five and ten (*US*), ≃ Woolworth's ® (*Brit*).

monorail [mɔnoʀɑj] **nm** (*voie*) monorail; (*voiture*) monorail coach.

monoski [mɔnoski] **nm** monoski. **faire du ~** to go monoskiing.

monosyllabe [mɔnosi(l)lab] **nm** (*lit, fig*) monosyllable.

monosyllabique [mɔnosi(l)labik] **adj** (*lit, fig*) monosyllabic.

monosyllabisme [mɔnosil(l)abism] **nm** monosyllabism.

monothéique [mɔnɔteik] **adj** monotheistic.

monothéisme [mɔnɔteism] **nm** monotheism.

monothéiste [mɔnɔteist] **1 adj** monotheistic. **2 nmf** monotheist.

monotone [mɔnɔtɔn] **adj** *son, voix* monotonous; *spectacle, style, discours* monotonous, dull, dreary, drab; *existence, vie* monotonous, humdrum, dull, dreary, drab.

monotonie [mɔnɔtɔni] **nf** *[son, voix]* monotony; *[discours, spectacle, vie]* monotony, dullness, dreariness, drabness.

monotype [mɔnɔtip] **nm** monotype.

monovalent, e [mɔnovalɑ̃, ɑ̃t] **adj** (*Chim*) monovalent, univalent.

monozygote [mɔnɔzigɔt] **adj** monozygotic.

Monrovia [mɔ̃ʀɔvja] **n** Monrovia.

Monseigneur [mɔ̃sɛɲœʀ], **pl Messeigneurs** [mesɛɲœʀ] **nm** **a** (*formule d'adresse*) (*à archevêque, duc*) Your Grace; (*à cardinal*) Your Eminence; (*à évêque*) Your Grace, Your Lordship, My Lord (Bishop); (*à prince*) Your (Royal) Highness. **b** (*à la troisième personne*) His Grace; His Eminence; His Lordship; His (Royal) Highness. **c** *voir* **pince**.

Monsieur [məsjø], **pl Messieurs** [mesjø] **nm** **a** (*s'adressant à qn*) **bonjour ~** (*courant*) good morning; (*nom connu*) good morning Mr X; (*nom inconnu*) good morning, good morning sir (*frm*); **bonjour Messieurs** good morning (gentlemen); (*hum*) **(bonjour) Messieurs Dames*** morning all *ou* everyone*; **~, vous avez oublié quelque chose** excuse me, you've forgotten something; (*au restaurant*) **et pour (vous) ~/Messieurs?** and for you, sir/gentlemen?; (*devant un auditoire*) **Messieurs** gentlemen; **Messieurs et chers collègues** gentlemen; **~ le Président** *[gouvernement]* Mr President; *[compagnie]* Mr Chairman; **oui, ~ le juge** ≃ yes, Your Honour *ou* My Lord *ou* Your Worship; **~ l'abbé** Father; **~ le curé** Father; **~ le ministre** Minister; **~ le duc** Your Grace; **~ le comte** *etc* Your Lordship, my Lord; (*frm*) **~ devrait prendre son parapluie** I suggest you take your umbrella, sir (*frm*); (*frm*) **~ est servi** dinner is served, sir (*frm*); (*iro*) **~ n'est pas content?** is something not to Your Honour's (*iro*) *ou* Your Lordship's (*iro*) liking?; **mon bon** *ou* **pauvre ~*** my dear sir; *voir* **Madame**.

b (*parlant de qn*) **~ X est malade** Mr X is ill; († *ou iro*) **~ votre fils** your dear son; (*frm*) **~ est sorti** Mr X *ou* the Master (of the house) is not at home; **~ dit que c'est à lui** the gentleman says it's his; **~ le Président** the President; the Chairman; **~ le juge X** ≃ (His Honour) Judge X; **~ le duc de X** (His Grace) the Duke of X; **~ l'abbé (X)** Father X; **~ le curé** the parish priest; **~ le curé X** Father X; **~ tout le monde** the average man.

c (*sur une enveloppe*) **~ John X** Mr John X, John X Esq.; (*à un enfant*) Master John X; **Messieurs Dupont** Messrs Dupont and Dupont; **Messieurs J. et P. Dupont** Messrs J and P Dupont; (*Comm*) **MM. Dupont et fils** Messrs Dupont and Son; **Messieurs X et Y** Messrs X and Y; *voir* **Madame**.

d (*en-tête de lettre*) **~** (*gén*) Dear Sir; (*personne connue*) Dear Mr X; **cher ~** Dear Mr X; **~ et cher collègue** My dear Sir, Dear Mr X; **~ le Président** Dear Mr President; Dear Mr Chairman.

e (*Hist: parent du roi*) Monsieur.

f (*sans majuscule*) gentleman; (*personnage important*) great man. **ces messieurs désirent?** what would you like, gentlemen?, what is it for you, gentlemen?; **maintenant il se prend pour un m~** he thinks he's quite the gentleman now, he fancies himself as a (proper) gentleman now (*Brit*); **c'est un grand m~** he is a great man, he's quite someone; (*langage enfantin*) **un méchant m~** a nasty man.

monstre [mɔ̃stʀ] **1 nm** **a** (*Bio, Zool*) (*par la difformité*) freak (of nature), monster; (*par la taille*) monster.

b (*Myth*) monster.

c (*fig péj*) monster, brute. **c'est un ~ de laideur** he is monstrously *ou* hideously ugly, he is a hideous brute; **c'est un ~ (de méchanceté)** he is a wicked *ou* an absolute monster; **quel ~ d'égoïsme/d'orgueil!** what fiendish *ou* monstrous egoism/pride!

d (**: affectueux*) **viens ici, petit ~!** come here, you little monster* *ou* horror!*

e (*Ciné, Théât*) **~ sacré** superstar, public idol.

2 adj (***) monstrous, colossal, mammoth. **rabais ~s** gigantic *ou* colossal *ou* mammoth reductions; **succès ~** runaway *ou* raving* success; **manifestation ~** massive demonstration; **elle a un culot ~** she's got fantastic cheek*; **faire une publicité ~ à qch** to launch a massive publicity campaign for sth; j'ai un travail ~ I've got loads* of work to do ou a monstrous amount of work to do; un dîner ~ a whacking* great dinner (Brit), a colossal dinner.

monstrueusement [mɔ̃stʀyøzmɑ̃] adv laid monstrously, hideously; intelligent prodigiously, stupendously; riche enormously.

monstrueux, -euse [mɔ̃stʀyø, øz] adj (difforme) monstrous, freakish, freak (épith); (abominable) monstrous, outrageous; (*: gigantesque) monstrous.

monstruosité [mɔ̃stʀyozite] nf a (caractère criminel) monstrousness, monstrosity. b (acte) outrageous ou monstrous act, monstrosity; (propos) monstrous ou horrifying remark. dire des ~s to say monstrous ou horrifying things, make monstrous ou horrifying remarks. c (Méd) deformity.

mont [mɔ̃] 1 nm a (montagne: littér) mountain. (avec un nom propre) le ~ X Mount X; (littér) par ~s et par vaux up hill and down dale; être toujours par ~s et par vaux* to be always on the move*; voir promettre.
b (Voyance) [main] mount.
2 comp ▸ les monts d'Auvergne the mountains of Auvergne, the Auvergne mountains ▸ le mont Blanc Mont Blanc ▸ mont-blanc (pl monts-blancs) nm (Culin) chestnut cream dessert (topped with cream) ▸ le mont Carmel Mount Carmel ▸ le mont Everest Mount Everest ▸ le mont des Oliviers the Mount of Olives ▸ mont-de-piété nm (pl monts-de-piété) (state-owned) pawnshop ou pawnbroker's; mettre qch au mont-de-piété to pawn sth ▸ mont de Vénus (Anat) mons veneris.

montage [mɔ̃taʒ] nm a (assemblage) [appareil, montre] assembly; [bijou] mounting, setting; [manche] setting in; [tente] pitching, putting up. le ~ d'une opération publicitaire the mounting ou organization of an advertising campaign; trouver un ~ financier pour développer un produit en commun to set up a financial deal ou arrangement to enable (the) joint development of a product; voir chaîne.
b (Ciné) (opération) editing. ce film est un bon ~ this film has been well edited ou is a good piece of editing; ~ réalisé par edited by, editing by; ~ de photographies photomontage.
c (Élec) wiring (up); (Rad etc) assembly. ~ en parallèle/en série connection in parallel/series.
d (Typ) page make-up.

montagnard, e [mɔ̃taɲaʀ, aʀd] 1 adj mountain (épith), highland (épith); (Hist) Mountain (épith). 2 nm,f a mountain dweller. ~s mountain people ou dwellers. b (Hist) M~(e) Montagnard.

montagne [mɔ̃taɲ] 1 nf a (sommet) mountain. (région montagneuse) la ~ the mountains; vivre à ou habiter la ~ to live in the mountains; haute/moyenne/basse ~ high/medium/low mountains; plantes des ~s mountain plants; voir chaîne, guide.
b (fig) une ~ de a mountain of, masses* ou mountains of; une ~ de travail l'attendait a mountain of work was waiting for him, there was masses* of work waiting for him; recevoir une ~ de lettres/cadeaux to receive a whole stack of ou a (great) mountain of letters/presents.
c (loc) se faire une ~ de rien to make a mountain out of a molehill; il se fait une ~ de cet examen he's making a great song and dance ou a great fuss over this exam; (Prov) il n'y a que les ~s qui ne se rencontrent pas there are none so distant that fate cannot bring them together; c'est la ~ qui accouche d'une souris after all that it's (a bit of) an anticlimax, what a great to-do with precious little to show for it.
d (Hist) la M~ the Mountain.
2 comp ▸ les montagnes Rocheuses the Rocky Mountains, the Rockies ▸ montagnes russes roller-coaster, big dipper ▸ montagne à vaches: nous ne faisons que de la montagne à vaches*, mais pas d'escalade (hum) we only go hill walking, not rock climbing.

montagneux, -euse [mɔ̃taɲø, øz] adj (gén, Géog) mountainous; (basse montagne: accidenté) hilly.

Montana [mɔ̃tana] nm Montana.

montant, e [mɔ̃tɑ̃, ɑ̃t] 1 adj mouvement upward, rising; bateau (travelling) upstream; col high; robe, corsage high-necked; chemin uphill. chaussures ~es boots; train/voie ~(e) up train/line; voir colonne, garde¹.
2 nm a (portant) [échelle] upright; [lit] post. les ~s de la fenêtre the uprights of the window frame; (Ftbl) ~ (de but) (goal) post.
b (somme) (sum) total, total amount. le ~ s'élevait à the total added up to, the total (amount) came to ou was; (Marché Commun) ~ compensatoire subsidy; supprimer les ~s compensatoires en matière agricole to eliminate farming subsidies; (Fin, Jur) ~ dû/forfaitaire outstanding/flat-rate amount; (Fin, Jur) ~ nominal par value; (Jur) ~ net d'une succession residuary estate.
c (Équitation) cheek-strap.

monte [mɔ̃t] nf a (Équitation) horsemanship. b (Vét) station/service de ~ stud farm/service; mener une jument à la ~ to take a mare to be covered.

monte- [mɔ̃t] voir monter¹.

montée [mɔ̃te] nf a (escalade) climb, climbing. la ~ de la côte the ascent of the hill, the climb up the hill, climbing ou going up the hill; la ~ de l'escalier climbing the stairs; c'est une ~ difficile it's a hard ou difficult climb; en escalade, la ~ est plus facile que la descente when you're climbing, going up is easier than coming down; la côte était si raide qu'on a fait la ~ à pied the hill was so steep that we walked up ou we went up on foot.
b (ascension) [ballon, avion] ascent. pendant la ~ de l'ascenseur while the lift is (ou was) going up.
c (mouvement ascendant) [eaux] rise, rising; [lait] inflow; [sève, homme politique, colère, hostilités] rise. la soudaine ~ des prix/de la température the sudden rise in prices/(the) temperature; la ~ du mécontentement populaire the rise of ou growth in popular discontent; la ~ des périls en Europe the rising ou growing danger in Europe, the rising threat of war in Europe; ~ en puissanceincrease in popularity.
d (côte, pente) hill, uphill slope. la maison était en haut de la ~ the house stood at the top of the hill ou rise; une petite ~ mène à leur maison there is a little slope leading up to their house.

monter¹ [mɔ̃te] 1 1 vi (avec auxiliaire être) a (gén) to go up (à to, dans into); [oiseau] to fly up; [avion] to climb. ~ à pied/à bicyclette/en voiture to walk/cycle/drive up; ~ en courant/en titubant to run/stagger up; ~ en train/par l'ascenseur to go up by train/in the lift; ~ dans ou à sa chambre to go up(stairs) to one's room; ~ sur la colline to go up ou climb up ou walk up the hill; j'ai dû ~ en courant de la cave au grenier I had to run upstairs from the cellar (up) to the attic; monte me voir come up and see me; monte le prévenir go up and tell him; ~ à Paris (en voyage) to go up to Paris; (pour travailler) to go to work in Paris.
b ~ sur table, rocher, toit to climb (up) on ou onto; monté sur une chaise, il accrochait un tableau he was standing on a chair hanging a picture; ~ sur une échelle to climb up a ladder; monté sur un cheval gris riding ou on a grey horse.
c (moyen de transport) ~ en voiture to get into a car; ~ dans un train/un avion to get on ou into a train/an aircraft, board a train/an aircraft; beaucoup de voyageurs sont montés à Lyon a lot of people got on at Lyons; (Naut) ~ à bord (d'un navire) to go on board ou aboard (a ship); ~ à cheval (se mettre en selle) to get on ou mount a horse; (faire du cheval) to ride, go riding; ~ à bicyclette to get on a bicycle; to ride a bicycle; je n'ai jamais monté I've never been on a horse; elle monte bienshe's a good horsewoman, she rides well.
d (progresser) [vedette] to be on the way up; [réputation] to rise, go up. ~ en grade to be promoted; artiste qui monte up-and-coming artist; les générations montantes the rising generations.
e [eau, vêtements] ~ à ou jusqu'à to come up to; robe qui monte jusqu'au cou high-necked dress; la vase lui montait jusqu'aux genoux the mud came right up to his knees, he was knee-deep in the mud.
f (s'élever) [colline, route] to go up, rise; [soleil, flamme, brouillard] to rise. ~ en pente douce to slope gently upwards, rise gently; le chemin monte en lacets the path winds ou twists upwards; de nouveaux gratte-ciel montent chaque jour new skyscrapers are going ou springing up every day; notre maison monte très lentement building is progressing very slowly on our house, our house is going up very slowly; un bruit/une odeur montait de la cave there was a noise/a smell coming from (down) in the cellar, noise was drifting up/a smell was wafting up from the cellar.
g (hausser de niveau) [mer, marée] to come in; [fleuve] to rise; [prix, température, baromètre] to rise, go up; (Mus) [voix, note] to go up. le lait monte (sur le feu) the milk is on the boil; (dans le sein) the milk is coming in; ~ dans l'estime de qn to go up ou rise in sb's estimation; les prix montent en flèche prices are rocketing (up) ou soaring; ça a fait ~ les prix it sent ou put ou pushed prices up; la colère monte tempers are rising; le ton monte (colère) the discussion is getting heated, voices are beginning to be raised; (animation) voices are rising, the conversation is getting noisier; le tricot monte vite avec cette laine* this wool knits up quickly, the knitting grows quickly with this wool; (Culin) les blancs montent/n'arrivent pas à ~ the egg whites are whipping up/won't whip up ou are going stiff/won't go stiff.
h (exprimant des émotions) le sang ou le rouge lui monta au visage the blood rushed to his face; elle sentait la colère/la peur ~ en elle she could feel (the) anger/fear well up inside her; les larmes lui montent aux yeux tears are welling up in her eyes, tears come into her eyes; le succès/le vin lui monte à la tête success/wine goes to his head; un cri lui monta à la gorge a cry rose (up) in his throat; ça lui a fait ~ le rouge aux joues it made him blush; ça lui a fait ~ les larmes aux yeux it brought tears to his eyes; voir moutarde.
i (Agr) [plante] to bolt, go to seed. salade qui monte en graine lettuce which bolts ou goes to seed; la salade est (toute) montée the lettuce has (all) bolted.
j (loc) (Mil) ~ à l'assaut ou à l'attaque to go into the attack; ~ à l'assaut de la forteresse to launch an attack on the fortress; ~ en chaire to go up into ou ascend the pulpit; ~ au créneau pour défendre sa politique to leap to the defence of one's policies; ~ à l'échafaud to climb the scaffold; (fig) faire ~ qn à l'échelle* to have sb on*, pull sb's leg*; (Tennis) ~ au filet to go up to the net; (Mil) ~ au front, ~ en ligne to go to the front (line); ~ sur ses grands chevaux to get on one's high horse; (Théât) ~ sur les planches to go on the stage; (Parl etc) ~ à la tribune to come forward to speak, ≃ take the floor; ~ sur le trône to come to ou ascend the throne.
2 vt (avec auxiliaire avoir) a to go up. ~ l'escalier ou les marches précipitamment to rush upstairs ou up the steps; ~ l'escalier ou les mar-

ches quatre à quatre to go upstairs *ou* up the steps four at a time; ~ **la rue** to walk *ou* go *ou* come up the street; (*en courant*) to run up the street; (*Mus*) ~ **la gamme** to go up the scale.

b (*porter*) *valise, meuble* to take *ou* carry *ou* bring up. **montez-lui son petit déjeuner** take his breakfast up to him; **faire** ~ **ses valises** to have one's luggage brought *ou* taken *ou* sent up.

c ~ **un cheval** to ride a horse; **ce cheval n'a jamais été monté** this horse has never been ridden.

d (*exciter*) ~ **qn contre qn** to set sb against sb; **être monté contre qn** to be dead set against sb; **quelqu'un lui a monté la tête** someone has put the wrong idea into his head; **il se monte la tête pour un rien** he gets het up* *ou* worked up over nothing.

e (*organiser*) *opération, campagne publicitaire* to mount, organize, set up. **c'est lui qui a tout monté** he organized *ou* set up the whole thing.

f (*Vét: couvrir*) to cover, serve.

g ~ **la garde** (*Mil*) to mount guard, go on guard; *[chien]* to be on guard.

h (*Culin*) **(faire)** ~ **les blancs en neige** to whip *ou* beat *ou* whisk (up) the egg whites (until they are stiff).

3 **se monter** vpr a *[prix, frais]* **se** ~ **à** to come to, amount to; **ça va se** ~ **à 2 000 F** it will come to *ou* amount to *ou* add up to 2,000 francs.

b **se** ~ **la tête** *ou* **le bourrichon*** to get (all) worked up *ou* het up*.

4 comp ►**monte-charge** nm inv goods lift (*Brit*), hoist, service elevator (*US*) ►**monte-en-l'air** (*: *voleur*) nm inv cat burglar ►**monte-plats** nm inv service lift (*Brit*), dumbwaiter.

monter² [mɔ̃te] 1 vt (*avec auxiliaire avoir*) a (*assembler*) *machine* to assemble; *tente* to pitch, put up; *film* to edit, cut; *robe* to assemble, sew together. ~ **des mailles** to cast on stitches; (*Élec, Rad*) ~ **en parallèle/en série** to connect in parallel/in series.

b (*organiser*) *pièce de théâtre* to put on, produce, stage; *affaire* to set up; *farce, canular* to play. ~ **un coup** to plan a job; ~ **le coup à qn**‡ to take sb for a ride‡; ~ **un bateau (à qn)** to play a practical joke (on sb); **coup monté** put-up job*, frame-up*; ~ **un complot** to hatch a plot; ~ **une histoire pour déshonorer qn** to cook up* *ou* fix* a scandal to ruin sb's good name.

c (*pourvoir, équiper*) to equip. ~ **son ménage** *ou* **sa maison** to set up house; **être bien/mal monté en qch** to be well-/ill-equipped with sth; **tu es bien montée, avec deux garnements pareils*** you're well set up with that pair of rascals!*; **se** ~ **en linge** to equip o.s. with linen; **se** ~ to get o.s. (well) set up.

d (*fixer*) *diamant, perle* to set, mount; *pneu* to put on. (*fig*) ~ **qch en épingle** to blow sth up out of all proportion, make a thing of sth*.

monteur, -euse [mɔ̃tœr, øz] nm,f a (*Tech*) fitter. b (*Ciné*) (film) editor. c (*Typ*) paste-up artist.

Montevideo [mɔ̃tevideo] n Montevideo.

montgolfière [mɔ̃gɔlfjɛr] nf montgolfier, hot air balloon.

monticule [mɔ̃tikyl] nm (*colline*) hillock, mound; (*tas*) mound, heap.

montmartrois, e [mɔ̃martrwa, waz] 1 adj of *ou* from Montmartre. 2 nm,f: **M~(e)** inhabitant *ou* native of Montmartre.

montmorency [mɔ̃mɔrɑ̃si] nf inv morello cherry.

montrable [mɔ̃trabl] adj fit to be seen (*attrib*).

montre¹ [mɔ̃tr] nf a watch. ~ **analogique** analogue watch; **~-bracelet** wrist watch; ~ **digitale** *ou* **à affichage numérique** digital watch; ~ **de gousset** fob watch; ~ **de plongée** diver's watch; ~ **de précision** precision watch; ~ **à quartz** quartz watch; ~ **à remontoir** stem-winder, stem-winding watch; ~ **à répétition** repeating *ou* repeater watch. b (*loc*) **il est 2 heures à ma** ~ it is 2 o'clock by my watch; (*fig*) **j'ai mis 2 heures** ~ **en main** it took me exactly *ou* precisely 2 hours, it took me 2 hours exactly by the clock; *voir* **chaîne, course, sens.**

montre² [mɔ̃tr] nf a **faire** ~ **de** *courage, ingéniosité* to show, display. b (*littér: ostentation*) **pour la** ~ for show, for the sake of appearances. c (*Comm* †: *en vitrine*) display, show. **publication interdite à la** ~ publication banned from public display; **un ouvrage qu'il avait en** ~ a work that he had on display *ou* show.

Montréal [mɔ̃real] n Montreal.

montréalais, e [mɔ̃realɛ, ɛz] 1 adj of *ou* from Montreal. 2 nm,f: **M~(e)** Montrealer.

montrer [mɔ̃tre] 1 1 vt a (*gén*) to show (*à* to); (*par un geste*) to point to; (*faire remarquer*) *détail, personne, faute* to point out (*à* to); (*avec ostentation*) to show off, display (*à* to). (*faire visiter*) **je vais vous** ~ **le jardin** I'll show you (round) the garden; ~ **un enfant au docteur** to let the doctor see a child; **l'aiguille montre le nord** the needle points north.

b (*laisser voir*) to show. **jupe qui montre le genou** skirt which leaves the knee uncovered *ou* bare; **elle montrait ses jambes en s'asseyant** she showed her legs as she sat down; (*hum*) **elle montre ses charmes** she's showing off *ou* displaying her charms (*hum*).

c (*mettre en évidence*) to show, prove. **il a montré que l'histoire était fausse** he has shown *ou* proved the story to be false *ou* that the story was false; **l'avenir montrera qui avait raison** the future will show *ou* prove who was right; ~ **la complexité d'un problème** to show how complex a problem is, demonstrate the complexity of a problem; **l'auteur montre un pays en décadence** the author shows *ou* depicts a country in decline; **ce qui montre bien que j'avais raison** which just goes to show that I was right.

d (*manifester*) *humeur, surprise, courage* to show, display. **son visage montra de l'étonnement** his face registered (his) surprise.

e (*apprendre*) ~ **à qn à faire qch**, ~ **à qn la manière de faire qch** to show sb how *ou* the way to do sth.

f (*loc*) **c'est l'avocat/le maître d'école qui montre le bout de l'oreille** it's the lawyer/the schoolteacher coming out in him, it's the lawyer/the schoolteacher in him showing through; **je lui montrerai de quel bois je me chauffe** I'll show him (what I'm made of), I'll give him something to think about; (*lit, fig*) ~ **les dents** to bare one's teeth; ~ **qn du doigt** (*lit*) to point sb out; (*fig*) to point the finger at sb; ~ **le bon exemple** to set a good example; (*lit, fig*) ~ **le chemin** to show the way; ~ **le** *ou* **son nez**, ~ **le bout du nez** to put in an appearance, show one's face; ~ **patte blanche** to show one's credentials; ~ **le poing** to shake one's fist; ~ **la porte à qn** to show sb the door.

2 **se montrer** vpr a *[personne]* to appear, show o.s. *[chose]* to appear. **se** ~ **à son avantage** to show o.s. (off) to advantage; (*fig*) **ton père devrait se** ~ **davantage** your father should assert himself more *ou* show his authority more; **sa lâcheté s'est montrée au grand jour** his cowardice was plain for all to see.

b (*s'avérer*) *[personne]* to show o.s. (to be), prove (o.s.) (to be); *[chose]* to prove (to be). **se** ~ **digne de sa famille** to show o.s. (to be) *ou* prove o.s. worthy of one's family; **il s'est montré très désagréable** he was very unpleasant, he behaved very unpleasantly; **il s'est montré intraitable avec les fautifs** he was *ou* he showed himself quite unrelenting with the culprits; **le traitement s'est montré efficace** the treatment proved (to be) effective; **se** ~ **d'une lâcheté révoltante** to show *ou* display despicable cowardice; **si les circonstances se montrent favorables** if conditions prove (to be) *ou* turn out to be favourable; **il faut se** ~ **ferme** you must appear firm, you must show firmness.

montreur, -euse [mɔ̃trœr, øz] nm,f: ~ **de marionnettes** puppet master (*ou* mistress), puppeteer; ~ **d'ours** bear leader.

montueux, -euse [mɔ̃tɥø, øz] adj (*littér*) (very) hilly.

monture [mɔ̃tyr] nf a (*cheval*) mount; *voir* **qui.** b (*Tech*) mounting; *[lunettes]* frame; *[bijou, bague]* setting.

monument [mɔnymɑ̃] nm a (*statue, ouvrage commémoratif*) monument, memorial. ~ **élevé à la gloire d'un grand homme** monument *ou* memorial erected in remembrance of a great man; ~ **(funéraire)** monument; ~ **aux morts** war memorial.

b (*bâtiment, château*) monument, building. ~ **historique** ancient monument, historic building; ~ **public** public building; **visiter les ~s de Paris** to go sight-seeing in Paris, see the sights of Paris.

c (*fig*) (*roman, traité scientifique*) monument. **la "Comédie humaine" est un** ~ **de la littérature française** the "Comédie Humaine" is one of the monuments of French literature; **ce buffet est un** ~**, on ne peut pas le soulever** this sideboard is colossal, we can't shift it*; **c'est un** ~ **de bêtise!*** what colossal *ou* monumental stupidity!

monumental, e, mpl **-aux** [mɔnymɑ̃tal, o] adj a *taille, erreur* monumental, colossal; *œuvre* monumental. **être d'une bêtise ~e** to be incredibly *ou* monumentally *ou* unbelievably stupid. b (*Archit*) monumental.

moquer [mɔke] 1 1 vt († *ou littér*) to mock. **j'ai été moqué** I was laughed at *ou* mocked.

2 **se moquer** vpr: **se** ~ **de** a (*ridiculiser*) to make fun of, laugh at, poke fun at. **tu vas te faire** ~ **de toi, on va se** ~ **de toi** people will laugh at you *ou* make fun of you, you'll make yourself a laughing stock; († *ou frm*) **vous vous moquez, j'espère** I trust that you are not in earnest (*frm*).

b (*tromper*) **non mais, vous vous moquez du monde!** really you've got an absolute nerve! *ou* a damn‡ cheek! (*Brit*) *ou* nerve!; **je n'aime pas qu'on se moque de moi!** I don't like being made a fool of; **il ne s'est pas moqué de toi, c'est superbe!**he obviously thinks a lot of you, it's lovely!

c (*mépriser*) **il se moque bien de nous maintenant qu'il est riche** he looks down on us *ou* looks down his nose at us now that he's rich; **je m'en moque (pas mal)*** I couldn't care less*; **je m'en moque comme de l'an quarante** *ou* **comme de ma première chemise*** I don't care twopence (*Brit*) *ou* a damn‡ *ou* a hoot*; **il se moque du tiers comme du quart*** he doesn't care about anything or anybody; **je me moque d'y aller*** I'm darned* if I'll go; **elle se moque du qu'en-dira-t-on** she doesn't care what people say (about her).

moquerie [mɔkri] nf a (*caractère*) mockery, mocking. b (*quolibet, sarcasme*) mockery (*NonC*), barracking (*NonC*). **en butte aux ~s continuelles de sa sœur** the target of constant mockery from his sister *ou* of his sister's constant mockery.

moquette [mɔkɛt] nf (*tapis*) fitted carpet (*Brit*), wall-to-wall carpeting (*NonC*); (*Tex*) moquette. **faire poser une** ~ *ou* **de la** ~ to have a fitted (*Brit*) *ou* a wall-to-wall carpet laid; ~ **murale** (heavy) fabric wall covering.

moquetter [mɔkete] 1 vt to carpet (with a fitted (*Brit*) *ou* wall-to-wall carpet). **chambre moquettée** bedroom with (a) fitted carpet *ou* a wall-to-wall carpet.

moqueur, -euse [mɔkœr, øz] adj *remarque, sourire* mocking. **il est**

très ~, c'est un ~ he's always making fun of people.

moqueusement [mɔkøzmɑ̃] adv mockingly.

moraine [mɔʀɛn] nf moraine.

morainique [mɔʀenik] adj morainic, morainal.

moral, e, mpl **-aux** [mɔʀal, o] 1 adj a (*éthique*) *valeurs, problème* moral. **j'ai pris l'engagement ~ de le faire** I'm morally committed to doing it; **avoir l'obligation ~e de faire** to be under a moral obligation *ou* be morally obliged to do; **sens/conscience ~(e)** moral sense/conscience; **conduite ~e** moral *ou* ethical behaviour.

b (*mental, psychologique*) *courage, support, victoire* moral. **il a fait preuve d'une grande force ~e** he showed great moral fibre; **j'ai la certitude ~e que** I am morally certain that, I feel deep down that; **les douleurs ~es et physiques** mental and physical pain.

2 nm a **au ~ comme au physique** mentally as well as physically; **au ~ il est irréprochable** morally he is beyond reproach.

b (*état d'esprit*) morale. **avoir un ~ d'acier** to have a fighting spirit; **les troupes ont bon/mauvais ~** the morale of the troops is high/low; **avoir le ~*, avoir (un) bon ~*** to be in good spirits; **le malade a mauvais ~** the patient is in low *ou* poor spirits; **avoir le ~ à zéro*** to be (feeling) down in the dumps*; **le ~ est atteint** it has shaken *ou* undermined his morale *ou* his confidence; **garder le ~** to keep one's spirits up; *voir* **remonter.**

3 **morale** nf a (*doctrine*) moral doctrine *ou* code, ethic (*Philos*); (*mœurs*) morals; (*valeurs traditionnelles*) morality, moral standards, ethic (*Philos*). (*Philos*) **la ~e** moral philosophy, ethics; **action conforme à la ~e** act in keeping with morality *ou* moral standards; **faire la ~e à qn** to lecture sb, preach at sb; **avoir une ~e relâchée** to have loose morals; **~e protestante** Protestant ethic.

b *[fable]* moral. **la ~e de cette histoire** the moral of this story.

moralement [mɔʀalmɑ̃] adv *agir, se conduire* morally. **une action ~ bonne** a morally *ou* an ethically sound act; **il était ~ vainqueur** he scored a moral victory.

moralisant, e [mɔʀalizɑ̃, ɑ̃t] adj moralizing.

moralisateur, -trice [mɔʀalizatœʀ, tʀis] 1 adj *discours, ton* moralizing, sententious, sanctimonious; *histoire* edifying, elevating. 2 nm,f moralizer.

moralisation [mɔʀalizasjɔ̃] nf raising of moral standards.

moraliser [mɔʀalize] 1 1 vi to moralize, sermonize (*péj*). 2 vt (†: *sermonner*) **~ qn** to preach at sb, lecture sb.

moralisme [mɔʀalism] nm moralism.

moraliste [mɔʀalist] 1 adj moralistic. 2 nmf moralist.

moralité [mɔʀalite] nf a (*mœurs*) morals, morality, moral standards. **d'une ~ douteuse** *personne* of doubtful morals; *film* of dubious morality; **d'une haute ~** *personne* of high moral standards; *discours* of a high moral tone; **la ~ publique** public morality; *voir* **témoin.** b (*valeur*) *[attitude, action]* morality. c (*enseignement*) *[fable]* moral. **~: il ne faut jamais mentir!** the moral is: never tell lies!; **~, j'ai eu une indigestion*** the result was (that) I had indigestion. d (*Littérat*) morality play.

morasse [mɔʀas] nf (*Typ*) final *ou* foundry proof.

moratoire[1] [mɔʀatwaʀ] adj moratory. **intérêts ~s** interest on arrears.

moratoire[2] [mɔʀatwaʀ] nm, **moratorium** [mɔʀatɔʀjɔm] nm (*Jur*) moratorium.

morave [mɔʀav] 1 adj Moravian. 2 nmf: **M~** Moravian.

Moravie [mɔʀavi] nf Moravia.

morbide [mɔʀbid] adj *curiosité, goût, imagination* morbid, unhealthy; *littérature, personne* morbid; (*Méd*) morbid.

morbidement [mɔʀbidmɑ̃] adv morbidly.

morbidité [mɔʀbidite] nf morbidity.

morbleu†† [mɔʀblø] excl zounds!††, gadzooks!††

morceau, pl **~x** [mɔʀso] nm a (*comestible*) *[pain]* piece, bit; *[sucre]* lump; *[viande]* (*à table*) piece, bit; (*chez le boucher*) piece, cut. **~ de choix** choice cut *ou* piece; **c'était un ~ de roi** *ou* **de prince** it was fit for a king; **manger** *ou* **prendre un ~** to have a bite (to eat) *ou* a snack; (*fig*) **manger** *ou* **lâcher** *ou* **cracher le ~‡** to spill the beans*, come clean*, talk*; (*fig: gagner*) **il a emporté le ~*** he carried it off; *voir* **bas**[1]**, sucre.**

b (*gén*) piece; *[bois]* piece, lump; *[fer]* lump; *[ficelle]* bit, piece; *[terre]* piece, patch, plot; *[tissu]* piece, length. **en ~x** in pieces; **couper en ~x** to cut into pieces; **mettre qch en ~x** to pull sth to bits *ou* pieces; **essayant d'assembler les ~x du vase** trying to piece together the bits of the vase *ou* the broken vase.

c (*Littérat*) passage, extract, excerpt; (*Art, Mus*) piece, item, passage; (*poème*) piece. **(recueil de) ~x choisis** (collection of) selected extracts *ou* passages; **un beau ~ d'éloquence** a fine piece of eloquence; **c'est un véritable ~ d'anthologie** it's destined to become a classic; **~ de bravoure** purple passage; **~ de concours** competition piece; **~ pour piano/violon** piece for piano/violin.

d (* *loc*) **beau ~** (*femme*) nice bit of stuff‡ (*Brit*), nice chick‡ (*US*); **c'est un sacré ~** he (*ou* it *etc*) is a hell of a size*.

morceler [mɔʀsəle] 4 vt *domaine, terrain* to parcel out, break up, divide up; *héritage* to divide up; *troupes, territoire* to divide up, split up.

morcellement [mɔʀsɛlmɑ̃] nm (*voir* **morceler**) (*action*) parcelling (out); division; dividing (up); splitting (up); (*état*) division.

mordant, e [mɔʀdɑ̃, ɑ̃t] 1 adj a (*caustique*) *ton, réplique* cutting, scathing, mordant, caustic; *pamphlet* scathing, cutting; *polémiste, critique* scathing. **avec une ironie ~e** with caustic *ou* biting *ou* mordant irony. b *froid* biting (*épith*). 2 nm a (*dynamisme, punch*) *[personne]* spirit, drive; *[troupe, équipe]* spirit, keenness; *[style, écrit]* bite, punch. **discours plein de ~** speech full of bite *ou* punch. b *[scie]* bite. c (*Tech*) mordant. d (*Mus*) mordent.

mordicus* [mɔʀdikys] adv *soutenir, affirmer* obstinately, stubbornly.

mordieu†† [mɔʀdjø] excl 'sdeath!††

mordillage [mɔʀdijaʒ] nm, **mordillement** [mɔʀdijmɑ̃] nm nibble, nibbling (*NonC*).

mordiller [mɔʀdije] 1 vt to chew at, nibble at.

mordoré, e [mɔʀdɔʀe] adj, nm (lustrous) bronze. **les tons ~s de l'automne** the glowing bronze tones *ou* the browns and golds of autumn.

mordorer [mɔʀdɔʀe] 1 vt (*littér*) to bronze.

mordorure [mɔʀdɔʀyʀ] nf (*littér*) bronze. **les ~s de l'étoffe** the bronze lustre of the cloth.

mordre [mɔʀdʀ] 41 1 vt a *[animal, insecte, personne]* to bite; *[oiseau]* to peck. **~ qn à la main** to bite sb's hand; **un chien l'a mordu à la jambe, il s'est fait ~ à la jambe par un chien** a dog bit him on the leg, he was bitten on the leg by a dog; **~ une pomme (à belles dents)** to bite (deeply) into an apple; **~ un petit bout de qch** to bite off a small piece of sth, take a small bite (out) of sth; **le chien l'a mordu (jusqu')au sang** the dog bit him and drew blood; **approche, il ne mord pas** come closer, he doesn't *ou* won't bite; (*fig*) **~ la poussière** to bite the dust; **faire ~ la poussière à qn** to make sb bite the dust.

b *[lime, vis]* to bite into; *[acide]* to bite (into), eat into; *[froid]* to bite, nip. **les crampons mordaient la glace** the crampons gripped the ice *ou* bit into the ice; **l'inquiétude/la jalousie lui mordait le cœur** worry/ jealousy was eating at *ou* gnawing at his heart.

c (*empiéter sur*) **la balle a mordu la ligne** the ball (just) touched the line; **~ la ligne de départ** to be touching the starting line; **~ la ligne continue** to stray onto the (solid) white line.

2 **mordre sur** vt indir (*empiéter sur*) to cut into, go over into, overlap into; (*corroder*) to bite into. **ça va ~ sur l'autre semaine** that will go over into *ou* overlap into *ou* cut into the following week; **~ sur la marge** to go over into the margin; **ils mordent sur notre clientèle** they're eating into our customer base.

3 vi a **~ dans une pomme** to bite into an apple; (*Naut*) *[ancre]* **~ dans le sable** to grip *ou* hold the sand.

b (*Pêche, fig*) to bite. (*lit, fig*) **~ (à l'hameçon** *ou* **à l'appât)** to bite, rise (to the bait); (*Pêche*) **ça mord aujourd'hui?** are the fish biting *ou* rising today?; (*fig*) **il a mordu au latin/aux maths*** he's taken to Latin/ maths.

c (*Gravure*) to bite; (*Tex*) *[étoffe]* to take the dye; *[teinture]* to take.

d (*Tech*) **l'engrenage ne mord plus** the gear won't mesh any more.

4 **se mordre** vpr: **se ~ la langue** (*lit*) to bite one's tongue; (*fig*) (*se retenir*) to hold one's tongue; (*se repentir*) to bite one's tongue; (*fig*) **se ~** *ou* **s'en ~ les doigts** to kick o.s.* (*fig*); **maintenant il s'en mord les doigts** he could kick himself now*; **tu t'en mordras les doigts** you'll live to regret it, you'll rue the day.

mordu, e [mɔʀdy] (ptp de **mordre**) 1 adj a (*: *amoureux*) madly in love (*de* with). **il en est bien ~** he is mad* *ou* wild* about her, he is crazy* over *ou* about her. b (*: *fanatique*) **~ de football/jazz** crazy* *ou* mad* about *ou* mad keen* on football/jazz. 2 nm,f (*: *fanatique*) enthusiast, buff*, fan. **un ~ de la voile** a sailing enthusiast; **un ~ de la musique** a great music lover; **un ~ de l'ordinateur** a computer buff* *ou* freak*; **il aime le sport, c'est un ~** he loves sport, he's an enthusiast; **c'est un ~ du football** he is a great one for football, he is a great football fan *ou* buff*.

more, moresque [mɔʀ, mɔʀɛsk] = **maure.**

morfal, e, mpl **~s‡** [mɔʀfal] nm,f greedy guts‡, pig‡.

morfondre (se) [mɔʀfɔ̃dʀ] 42 vpr (*après une déception*) to mope, fret; (*dans l'attente de qch*) to fret. **il se morfondait en attendant le résultat des examens** he fretted as he waited for the exam results.

morfondu, e [mɔʀfɔ̃dy] (ptp de **morfondre**) adj dejected, crestfallen.

morganatique [mɔʀganatik] adj morganatic.

morgue[1] [mɔʀg] nf (*littér: orgueil*) pride, haughtiness. **il me répondit plein de ~ que** he answered me haughtily that.

morgue[2] [mɔʀg] nf (*Police*) morgue; *[hôpital]* mortuary.

moribond, e [mɔʀibɔ̃, ɔ̃d] 1 adj (*lit, fig*) dying, moribund. 2 nm,f: **un ~** a dying man; **les ~s** the dying.

moricaud, e** [mɔʀiko, od] 1 adj dark(-skinned). 2 nm,f darkie**, wog**.

morigéner [mɔʀiʒene] 6 vt (*littér*) to take to task, reprimand, sermonize. **il faut le ~** he will have to be taken to task (over it) *ou* reprimanded (for it).

morille [mɔʀij] nf morel.

morillon [mɔʀijɔ̃] nm (*Zool*) tufted duck.

mormon, e [mɔʀmɔ̃, ɔn] adj, nm,f Mormon. **la secte ~e** the Mormon sect.

mormonisme [mɔʀmɔnism] nm Mormonism.

morne [mɔʀn] adj *personne, visage* doleful, glum, gloomy; *ton, temps* gloomy, dismal; *silence* mournful, gloomy, dismal; *conversation, vie, paysage, ville* dismal, dreary. **passer un après-midi ~** to spend a dreary *ou* dismal afternoon.

mornifle* [mɔʀnifl] **nf** clout*, clip* on the ear. **donner** *ou* **filer une ~ à qn** to give sb a clip round the ear, clip sb round the ear.

Moroni [mɔʀɔni] **n** Moroni.

morose [mɔʀoz] **adj** *humeur, personne, ton* sullen, morose.

morosité [mɔʀozite] **nf** sullenness, moroseness. **climat de ~ économique/sociale** gloomy *ou* depressed economic/social climate.

morphe [mɔʀf] **nm** morph.

Morphée [mɔʀfe] **nm** Morpheus.

morphème [mɔʀfɛm] **nm** morpheme. **~ libre/lié** free/bound morpheme.

morphémique [mɔʀfemik] **nf**, **morphématique** [mɔʀfematik] **nf** morphemics *(sg)*.

morphine [mɔʀfin] **nf** morphine. **~-base** base-morphium.

morphinisme [mɔʀfinism] **nm** morphinism.

morphinomane [mɔʀfinɔman] 1 **adj** addicted to morphine. 2 **nmf** morphine addict.

morphinomanie [mɔʀfinɔmani] **nf** morphine addiction, morphinomania.

morphologie [mɔʀfɔlɔʒi] **nf** morphology.

morphologique [mɔʀfɔlɔʒik] **adj** morphological.

morphologiquement [mɔʀfɔlɔʒikmɑ̃] **adv** morphologically.

morphophonémique [mɔʀfɔfɔnemik] **nf** morphophonemics *(sg)*.

morphophonologie [mɔʀfɔfɔnɔlɔʒi] **nf** morphophonology.

morphosyntaxe [mɔʀfosɛ̃taks] **nf** morphosyntax.

morphosyntaxique [mɔʀfɔsɛ̃taksik] **adj** morphosyntactical.

morpion [mɔʀpjɔ̃] **nm** *(Jeux)* ≃ noughts and crosses *(Brit)*, tic tac toe *(US)*; (**: pou du pubis*) crab*; (* *péj: gamin*) brat*.

mors [mɔʀ] **nm** a *(Équitation)* bit. **prendre le ~ aux dents** *[cheval]* to take the bit between its teeth; *(fig) (agir)* to take action; *(s'emporter)* to fly off the handle*, blow one's top* *(Brit)* *ou* stack* *(US)*; *(prendre l'initiative)* to take the matter into one's own hands. b *(Tech)* jaw; *(Reliure)* joint.

morse[1] [mɔʀs] **nm** *(Zool)* walrus.

morse[2] [mɔʀs] **nm** *(code)* Morse (code). **en ~** Morse (code) *(épith)*.

morsure [mɔʀsyʀ] **nf** bite.

mort[1] [mɔʀ] 1 **nf** a death. **~ relative, ~ cérébrale** *ou* **clinique** brain death; **~ absolue, ~ définitive** clinical death; **~ apparente** apparent death; **~ naturelle** natural death; **trouver la ~ dans un accident** to die *ou* be killed in an accident; **souhaiter la ~** to long for death, long to die; **souhaiter la ~ de qn** to wish death upon sb *(littér)*, wish sb (were) dead; **donner la ~ (à qn)** to kill (sb); **se donner la ~** to take one's own life, kill o.s.; **il est en danger** *ou* **en péril de ~** he is in danger of dying *ou* of his life; **périr** *ou* **mourir de ~ violente/accidentelle** to die a violent/accidental death; **~ volontaire** suicide; **mourir dans son sommeil, c'est une belle ~** dying in one's sleep is a good way to go; **à la ~ de sa mère** on the death of his mother, when his mother died; **il a vu la ~ de près** he has been face to face with death; **il n'y a pas eu ~ d'homme** no one was killed, there was no loss of life; **être à la ~** to be at death's door; *(littér)* **la petite ~** orgasm, petite mort *(littér)*; **ce n'est pas la ~!*** it won't kill you *(ou* me *etc)*!*; *voir* **hurler, pâle** *etc*.

b **de ~: silence de ~** deathly *ou* deathlike hush; **d'une pâleur de ~** deathly *ou* deadly pale; **engin de ~** lethal *ou* deadly weapon; **arrêt/peine de ~** death warrant/penalty; *(fig)* **il avait signé son arrêt de ~** he had signed his own death warrant; **menaces de ~** threats of death; **proférer des menaces de ~ (contre qn)** to threaten (sb with) death.

c **à ~: lutte à ~** fight to the death; **détester qn à ~** to hate sb like poison; **blessé à ~** *(dans un combat)* mortally wounded; *(dans un accident)* fatally injured; **condamnation à ~** death sentence; **frapper qn à ~** to strike sb dead; **mettre à ~** *personne* to deliver the death blow to; *taureau* to put to death; *(fig)* **nous sommes fâchés à ~** we're at daggers drawn (with each other); *(fig)* **en vouloir à qn à ~** to be bitterly resentful of sb; **il m'en veut à ~** he hates me *ou* my guts* (for it); *(fig)* **défendre qch à ~** to defend sth to the bitter end; **freiner à ~*** to jam on the brakes *ou* the anchors* *(Brit)*; **s'ennuyer à ~** to be bored to death; **visser qch à ~*** to screw sth right home, screw sth tight; *voir* **mise**[2].

d *(destruction, fin)* death, end. **c'est la ~ de ses espoirs** that puts paid to his hopes *(Brit)*, that puts an end to *ou* is the end of his hopes; **le supermarché sera la ~ du petit commerce** supermarkets will mean the end of *ou* the death of *ou* will put an end to small businesses; **notre secrétaire est la ~ des machines à écrire*** our secretary is lethal to *ou* the ruin of typewriters; **cet enfant sera ma ~!*** this child will be the death of me!*

e *(douleur)* **souffrir mille ~s** to suffer agonies, be in agony; **la ~ dans l'âme** with an aching *ou* a heavy heart, grieving inwardly; **il avait la ~ dans l'âme** his heart ached.

f **~ au tyran!, à ~ le tyran!** down with the tyrant!, death to the tyrant!; **~ aux vaches!*** down with the cops!* *ou* pigs!*; *voir* **mort**[2].

2 **comp ▸ mort-aux-rats nf** rat poison.

mort[2], **e** [mɔʀ, mɔʀt] **(ptp de mourir)** 1 **adj** a *être animé, arbre, feuille* dead. **il est ~ depuis 2 ans** he's been dead (for) 2 years, he died 2 years ago; **laissé pour ~** left for dead; **il est ~ et bien ~, il est ~ et enterré** he's dead and gone, he's dead and buried; **ramenez-les ~s ou vifs** bring them back dead or alive; *(Mil)* **~ au champ d'honneur** killed in action; **il était comme ~** he looked (as though he were) dead; **tu es un homme ~!*** you're a dead man!*

b *(fig)* **je suis ~ (de fatigue)!** I'm dead (tired)! *ou* dead beat!*, I'm all in!*; **il était ~ de peur** *ou* **plus ~ que vif** he was frightened to death *ou* scared stiff*; *voir* **ivre**.

c *(inerte, sans vie) chair, peau* dead; *pied, doigt etc* dead, numb; *(yeux)* lifeless, dull; *(Fin) marché* dead. **la ville est ~e le dimanche** the town is dead on a Sunday; *voir* **poids, point**[1], **temps**[1] *etc*.

d *(qui n'existe plus) civilisation* extinct, dead; *langue* dead. **leur vieille amitié est ~e** their old friendship is dead; **le passé est bien ~** the past is over and done with *ou* is dead and gone.

e (**: usé, fini*) *pile, radio, moteur* dead.

2 **nm** a dead man. **les ~s** the dead; **les ~s de la guerre** those *ou* the men killed in the war, the war dead; **il y a eu un ~** one person was killed; **il y a eu de nombreux ~s** many (people) were killed, there were many killed; **l'accident a fait 5 ~s** 5 (people) were killed in the accident; **jour** *ou* **fête des ~s** All Souls' Day; *(Rel)* **office/messe/prière des ~s** office/mass/prayer for the dead; **cet homme est un ~ vivant/un ~ en sursis** this man is more dead than alive/is living on borrowed time; **faire le ~** *(lit)* to pretend to be dead, sham death; *(fig: ne pas se manifester)* to lie low; *(Aut)* **la place du ~** the (front) seat next to the driver; *voir* **monument, tête**.

b *(Cartes)* dummy. **être le ~** to be dummy.

3 **morte nf** dead woman.

4 **comp ▸ morte-eau nf (pl mortes-eaux)** neap tide **▸ mort-né, mort-née (mpl mort-nés) adj** *enfant* stillborn; *projet* abortive, stillborn **▸ morte-saison nf (pl mortes-saisons)** slack *ou* off season.

mortadelle [mɔʀtadɛl] **nf** mortadella.

mortaise [mɔʀtɛz] **nf** *(Menuiserie)* mortise.

mortaiser [mɔʀteze] [1] **vt** to mortise.

mortalité [mɔʀtalite] **nf** mortality, death rate. **taux de ~** death rate, mortality (rate); **~ infantile** infant mortality; **régression de la ~** fall in the death rate.

mortel, -elle [mɔʀtɛl] 1 **adj** a *(sujet à la mort)* mortal; *voir* **dépouille**.

b *(entraînant la mort) chute* fatal; *blessure, plaie* fatal, mortal, lethal; *poison* deadly, lethal. **danger ~** mortal danger; **coup ~** lethal *ou* fatal *ou* mortal blow, death-blow; **cette révélation lui serait ~le** such a discovery would kill him *ou* would be fatal to him.

c *(intense) frayeur, jalousie* mortal; *pâleur, silence* deadly, deathly; *ennemi, haine* mortal, deadly. **il fait un froid ~** it is deathly cold, it is as cold as death; **cette attente ~le se prolongeait** this deadly wait dragged on; **allons, ce n'est pas ~!*** come on, it's not all that bad! *ou* it's not the end of everything!*

d (**: ennuyeux*) *livre, soirée* deadly*, deadly boring *ou* dull. **il est ~** he's a deadly* *ou* crashing* bore.

2 **nm,f** *(littér, hum)* mortal. **heureux ~!*** lucky chap!* *(Brit)* *ou* fellow!*; *voir* **commun**.

mortellement [mɔʀtɛlmɑ̃] **adv** *blesser* fatally, mortally; *(fig) offenser, vexer* mortally, deeply. **~ pâle** deadly *ou* deathly pale; *(fig)* **c'est ~ ennuyeux** it's deadly boring *ou* dull.

mortier [mɔʀtje] **nm** *(Constr, Culin, Mil, Pharm)* mortar; *(toque)* cap *(worn by certain French judges)*.

mortification [mɔʀtifikasjɔ̃] **nf** mortification.

mortifier [mɔʀtifje] [7] **vt** *(Méd, Rel, aussi vexer)* to mortify.

mortinatalité [mɔʀtinatalite] **nf** rate of stillbirths.

mortuaire [mɔʀtɥɛʀ] **adj** *chapelle* mortuary *(épith)*; *rites* mortuary *(épith)*, funeral *(épith)*; *cérémonie* funeral *(épith)*. **acte/avis ~** death certificate/announcement; **drap ~** pall; *(Can)* **salon ~** funeral home *ou* parlor *(US, Can)*; **la chambre ~** the death chamber; **la maison ~** the house of the departed *ou* deceased; *voir* **couronne**.

morue [mɔʀy] **nf** a *(Zool)* cod. **~ fraîche/séchée/salée** fresh/dried/salted cod; *voir* **brandade, huile**. b (**: prostituée*) tart*, whore.

morutier, -ière [mɔʀytje, jɛʀ] 1 **adj** cod-fishing. 2 **nm** *(pêcheur)* cod-fisherman; *(bateau)* cod-fishing boat.

morvandeau, -elle, mpl ~x [mɔʀvɑ̃do, ɛl] 1 **adj** of *ou* from the Morvan region. 2 **nm,f: M~(-elle)** inhabitant *ou* native of the Morvan region.

morve [mɔʀv] **nf** snot*, (nasal) mucus; *(Zool)* glanders *(sg)*.

morveux, -euse [mɔʀvø, øz] 1 **adj** a *enfant* snotty(-nosed)*; *voir* **qui**. b *(Zool)* glandered. 2 **nm,f** (**: personne*) (little) jerk*.

mosaïque[1] [mɔzaik] **nf** *(Art, Bot)* mosaic; *[États, champs]* chequered pattern, patchwork; *[idées, peuples]* medley. **de** *ou* **en ~** mosaic *(épith)*.

mosaïque[2] [mɔzaik] **adj** *(Bible)* Mosaic(al), of Moses.

Moscou [mɔsku] **n** Moscow.

moscovite [mɔskɔvit] 1 **adj** of *ou* from Moscow, Moscow *(épith)*, Muscovite. 2 **nmf: M~** Muscovite.

Moselle [mɔzɛl] **nf** Moselle.

mosquée [mɔske] **nf** mosque.

mot [mo] 1 **nm** a *(gén)* word. **le ~ (d')orange** the word "orange"; **les ~s me manquent pour exprimer** words fail me when I try to express, I can't find the words to express; **ce ne sont que des ~s** it's just (so many) empty words; **je n'en crois pas un (traître) ~** I don't believe a (single) word of it; **qu'il soit paresseux, c'est bien le ~!** lazybones is the right word to describe him!; **ça alors, c'est bien le ~!** you've said it!, you never spoke *ou* said a truer word!; **à/sur ces ~s** at/with these words; **à ~s couverts** in veiled terms; **en d'autres ~s** in other words; **en un ~** in a word; **en un ~ comme en cent** in a nutshell, in brief; **faire du ~ à ~, traduire ~ à ~** to translate word for word; **c'est du ~ à ~** it's a word for word rendering *ou* translation; **rapporter une conversation ~ pour ~** to give a word for word *ou* a verbatim report of a conversation; (*Ling*) **~ apparenté** cognate.

b (*message*) word; (*courte lettre*) note, line. (*Scol*) **~ d'excuse** excuse note; **en dire *ou* en toucher un ~ à qn** to have a word with sb about it; **glisser un ~ à qn** to have a word in sb's ear; **se donner *ou* se passer le ~** to send *ou* pass the word round, pass the word on; **mettez-lui un petit ~** drop him a line *ou* note, write him a note.

c (*expression frappante*) saying. **~s célèbres/historiques** famous/historic sayings; **bon ~** witticism, witty remark.

d (*Ordin*) word. **~ machine** machine word.

e (*loc*) **avoir des ~s avec qn** to have words with sb; **avoir toujours le ~ pour rire** to be a born joker; **avoir *ou* tenir le ~ de l'énigme** to have *ou* hold the key to the mystery; **avoir le ~ de la fin** to have the last word; **sans ~ dire** without saying a *ou* one word; **vous n'avez qu'un ~ à dire et je le ferai** (you have only to) say the word and I'll do it; **j'estime avoir mon ~ à dire dans cette affaire** I think I'm entitled to have my say in this matter; **je vais lui dire deux ~s** I'll give him a piece of my mind; **prendre qn au ~** to take sb at his word; **il ne sait pas le premier ~ de sa leçon** he doesn't know a word of his lesson; **il ne sait pas un (traître) ~ d'allemand** he doesn't know a (single) word of German; **je n'ai pas pu lui tirer un ~** I couldn't get a word out of him; **il lui a dit le ~ de Cambronne** ≃ he said a four-letter word to him; *voir* **dernier**.

2 **comp** ▸**mot d'auteur** revealing *ou* witty remark from the author; **c'est un mot d'auteur** it's the author having his say ▸**mot-clé** **nm (pl mots-clés)** keyword; **c'est ça le mot-clé** that's the operative *ou* key word ▸**mot composé** compound ▸**mots croisés** crossword (puzzle); **faire les mots croisés** (*gén*) to do crosswords; *[journal particulier]* to do the crossword (puzzle) ▸**mot d'emprunt** loanword ▸**mot d'enfant** child's (funny) remark *ou* saying ▸**mot d'esprit** witticism, witty remark ▸**mot d'excuse** (*Scol*) (absence) note ▸**mot d'ordre** watchword, slogan ▸**mot-outil** **nm (pl mots-outils)** grammatical word ▸**mot de passe** password ▸**mot souche** root-word ▸**mot-valise** **nm (pl mots-valises)** portmanteau word.

motard, -arde [mɔtaʀ, aʀd] 1 **nm,f** motorcyclist, biker*. 2 **nm** (*Police*) motorcycle policeman *ou* cop*; (*Mil: dans l'armée*) motorcyclist. **les ~s de l'escorte** the motorcycle escort.

motel [mɔtɛl] **nm** motel.

motet [mɔtɛ] **nm** motet, anthem.

moteur¹ [mɔtœʀ] **nm** a (*gén*) engine; (*électrique*) motor. **~ atmosphérique** atmospheric engine; **~ à combustion interne, ~ à explosion** internal combustion engine; **~ diesel** diesel engine; **~ électrique** electric motor; **~ à injection** fuel injection engine; **~ à réaction** jet engine; **~ turbo** turbo(-charged) engine; **~ à 2/4 temps** 2-/4-stroke engine; **à ~** power-driven, motor (*épith*); *voir* **bloc, frein**. b (*fig*) mover, mainspring. (*littér*) **le grand ~ de l'univers** the prime mover of the universe; **être le ~ de qch** to be the mainspring of sth, be the driving force behind sth.

moteur², -trice¹ [mɔtœʀ, tʀis] **adj** a (*Anat*) *muscle, nerf, troubles* motor (*épith*). b (*Tech*), *force* (*lit, fig*) driving. **arbre ~** driving shaft; **voiture à roues ~trices avant/arrière** front-/rear-wheel drive car.

motif [mɔtif] **nm** a (*raison*) motive (*de* for), grounds (*de* for); (*but*) purpose (*de* of). **quel est le ~ de votre visite?** what is the motive for *ou* the purpose of your visit?; **quel ~ as-tu de te plaindre?** what grounds have you got for complaining?; **il a de bons ~s pour le faire** he has good grounds for doing it; († *ou hum*) **fréquenter une jeune fille pour le bon ~** to court a girl with honourable intentions; **faire qch sans ~** to have no motive for doing sth; **colère sans ~** groundless *ou* irrational anger.

b (*ornement*) motif, design, pattern; (*Peinture, Mus*) motif. **papier peint à ~ de fleurs** floral wallpaper, wallpaper with a floral design.

c (*Jur*) *[jugement]* grounds (*de* for).

motion [mosjɔ̃] **nf** motion. **déposer une ~ de censure** to table a censure motion *ou* a motion of censure; **voter la ~ de censure** to pass a vote of no confidence *ou* of censure.

motivant, e [mɔtivɑ̃, ɑ̃t] **adj** rewarding, satisfying. **rémunération ~e** attractive salary.

motivation [mɔtivasjɔ̃] **nf** (*justification*) motivation (*de* for); (*dynamisme*) motivation. (*raisons personnelles*) **quelles sont ses ~s?** what are his motives? (*pour* for); **études *ou* recherche de ~** motivational research; **lettre de ~** letter in support of one's application.

motivé, e [mɔtive] (**ptp de motiver**) **adj** a *action* (*dont on donne les motifs*) reasoned, justified; (*qui a des motifs*) well-founded, motivated. **non ~** unexplained, unjustified; (*Scol*) **absence ~e** legitimate *ou* genuine absence; **refus ~** justified refusal. b *personne* (well-)motivated. **non ~** unmotivated.

motiver [mɔtive] 1 **vt** a (*justifier, expliquer*) *action, attitude, réclamation* to justify, account for. **il a motivé sa conduite en disant que** he justified his behaviour by saying that; **rien ne peut ~ une telle conduite** nothing can justify *ou* warrant such behaviour. b (*fournir un motif à*) *refus, intervention, jugement* to motivate, found; (*Psych*) to motivate. c (*pousser à agir*) *[personne, salaire]* to motivate.

moto [moto] (**abrév de motocyclette**) **nf** a (*véhicule*) (motor)bike, bike*. **je viendrai à *ou* en ~** I'll come by bike* *ou* on my bike*; **~ de trial** trail bike (*Brit*), dirt bike (*US*). b (*activité*) motorcycling, biking*. **~ verte** scrambling.

moto-cross [motokʀɔs] **nm inv** motocross, scrambling (*Brit*).

motoculteur [mɔtɔkyltœʀ] **nm** (motorized) cultivator.

motocycle [mɔtɔsikl] **nm** (*Admin*) motor bicycle.

motocyclette [mɔtɔsiklɛt] **nf** motorcycle.

motocyclisme [mɔtɔsiklism] **nm** motorcycle racing.

motocycliste [mɔtɔsiklist] 1 **nmf** motorcyclist. 2 **adj** *course* motorcycle (*épith*). **le sport ~** motorcycle racing.

motonautique [motonotik] **adj: sport ~** speedboat *ou* motorboat racing.

motonautisme [motonotism] **nm** speedboat *ou* motorboat racing.

motoneige [motonɛʒ] **nf** snow-bike, skidoo (*Can*).

motoneigiste [motonɛʒist] **nmf** snow-bike *ou* skidoo (*Can*) rider.

motopompe [motopɔ̃p] **nf** motor-pump, power-driven pump.

motopropulseur [motopʀɔpylsœʀ] **adj m: groupe ~** power unit.

motorisation [mɔtɔʀizasjɔ̃] **nf** motorization.

motoriser [mɔtɔʀize] 1 **vt** (*Mil, Tech*) to motorize. **être motorisé*** to have transport, have one's *ou* a car, be car-borne*.

motrice¹ [mɔtʀis] **adj** *voir* **moteur²**.

motrice² [mɔtʀis] **nf** power unit.

motricité [mɔtʀisite] **nf** motivity.

motte [mɔt] **nf** a (*Agr*) **~ (de terre)** lump of earth, clod (of earth); **~ de gazon** turf, sod. b (*Culin*) **~ de beurre** lump *ou* block of butter; **acheter du beurre en *ou* à la ~** to buy a slab of butter (*from a large block, not prewrapped*).

motus* [mɔtys] **excl: ~ (et bouche cousue)!** mum's the word!*, keep it under your hat!, don't breathe a word!

mou¹, molle [mu, mɔl] (*masculin:* **mol** [mɔl] *devant voyelle ou h muet*) 1 **adj** a (*au toucher*) *substance, oreiller* soft; *tige, tissu* limp; *chair, visage* flabby. **ce melon est tout ~** this melon has gone all soft *ou* mushy; *voir* **chapeau**.

b (*à la vue*) *contours, lignes, relief, collines* soft, gentle; *traits du visage*, (*Art*) *dessin, trait* weak, slack.

c (*à l'oreille*) **bruit ~** muffled noise, soft thud; **voix aux molles inflexions** gently lilting voice.

d (*sans énergie*) *geste, poignée de main* limp, lifeless; *protestations, opposition* weak, feeble; (†) *vie* soft, indolent; (*Littérat*) *style* feeble, dull, woolly; (*Mus*) *exécution* dull, lifeless. **personne molle** (*apathique*) indolent *ou* lethargic *ou* sluggish person; (*sans autorité*) spineless character; (*trop indulgent*) lax *ou* soft person; **il est ~ comme une chiffe *ou* chique, c'est un ~** he is spineless *ou* a spineless character.

e *temps* muggy; *tiédeur* languid.

2 **adv: jouer/dessiner ~** to play/draw without energy, play/draw languidly; (‡) **vas-y ~** go easy*, take it easy*.

3 **nm** a (*qualité*) softness.

b *[corde]* **avoir du ~** to be slack *ou* loose; **donner du ~** to slacken, loosen; (*Aut*) **il y a du ~ dans la pédale de frein** the brakes are soft *ou* spongy; **donne un peu de ~ pour que je puisse faire un nœud** let the rope out a bit *ou* give a bit of play on the rope so that I can make a knot.

mou² [mu] **nm** a (*Boucherie*) lights, lungs; *voir* **rentrer**. b (‡*loc*) **bourrer le ~ à qn** to have sb on* (*Brit*), take sb in.

mouchard, e [muʃaʀ, aʀd] 1 **nm,f** (*) (*Scol*) sneak*. 2 **nm** a (*arg Police*) grass (*arg Brit*), fink (*US arg*), informer. b (*Tech*) *[avion, train]* black box; *[veilleur de nuit]* control clock; (*Mil*) spy plane.

mouchardage* [muʃaʀdaʒ] **nm** (*voir* **moucharder**) sneaking*; grassing (*Brit arg*), informing.

moucharder* [muʃaʀde] 1 **vt** (*Scol*) to split on*, sneak on*; (*arg Police*) to grass on (*Brit arg*), inform on. **arrête de ~!** stop sneaking!*

mouche [muʃ] 1 **nf** a (*Zool*) fly. **quelle ~ t'a piqué?** what has bitten you?*, what has got into you?; **il faut toujours qu'il fasse la ~ du coche** he's always fussing around as if he's indispensable; **mourir/tomber comme des ~s** to die (off)/fall like flies; **prendre la ~** to get into *ou* go into a huff* (*Brit*), get huffy* (*Brit*), get the sulks; (*Prov*) **on ne prend pas les ~s avec du vinaigre** you won't get him (*ou* me *etc*) to swallow that bait; *voir* **entendre, fin¹, mal**.

b (*Sport*) (*Escrime*) button; (*Pêche*) fly. **faire ~** (*Tir*) to score a *ou* hit the bull's-eye; (*fig*) to score, hit home; *voir* **poids**.

c (*en taffetas*) patch, beauty spot; (*touffe de poils sous la lèvre*) short goatee.

d (*Opt*) **~s** specks, spots.

2 **comp** ▸**mouche bleue** = **mouche de la viande** ▸**mouche d'escadre** (*Naut*) advice boat ▸**mouche à feu** (*Can*) firefly ▸**mouche à miel** honey bee ▸**mouche tsé-tsé** tsetse fly ▸**mouche à vers** blowfly ▸**mouche de la viande** bluebottle ▸**mouche du vinaigre** fruit fly.

moucher [muʃe] [1] 1 vt a ~ **(le nez de) qn** to blow sb's nose; **mouche ton nez** blow your nose; **il mouche du sang** there are traces of blood (in his handkerchief) when he blows his nose. b (* *fig: remettre à sa place*) ~ **qn** to put sb in his place; **se faire** ~ to get put in one's place. c *chandelle* to snuff (out). 2 **se moucher** vpr to blow one's nose. **mouche-toi** blow your nose; (*loc*) **il ne se mouche pas du coude*** *ou* **du pied*** (*il est prétentieux*) he thinks he's it* *ou* the cat's whiskers*, he thinks himself no small beer; (*il ne se refuse rien*) he doesn't deny himself anything; *voir* **morveux**.

moucheron [muʃʀɔ̃] nm (*Zool*) midge, gnat; (*: *enfant*) kid*, nipper* (*Brit*).

moucheté, e [muʃ(ə)te] (ptp de **moucheter**) adj *œuf* speckled; *poisson* spotted; *laine* flecked; *fleuret* buttoned.

moucheter [muʃ(ə)te] [4] vt (*tacheter: voir* **moucheté**) to speckle; to spot; to fleck (*de* with); to button.

mouchetis [muʃ(ə)ti] nm (*Constr*) roughcast.

mouchettes [muʃɛt] nfpl (*Hist*) snuffers.

moucheture [muʃ(ə)tyʀ] nf (*sur les habits*) speck, spot, fleck; (*sur un animal*) spot, patch. (*Hér*) ~**s d'hermine** ermine tips.

mouchoir [muʃwaʀ] nm (*dans la poche*) handkerchief; (†: *autour du cou*) neckerchief. ~ **en papier** tissue, paper hanky; **jardin grand comme un** ~ **de poche** garden as big as *ou* the size of *ou* no bigger than a pocket handkerchief; **cette pièce est grande comme un** ~ **de poche** there's no room to swing a cat in this room; (*fig*) **ils sont arrivés dans un** ~ it was a close finish; *voir* **nœud**.

moudjahiddin [mudʒa(j)idin] nmpl mujaheddin, muja-hedeen.

moudre [mudʀ] [47] vt *blé* to mill, grind; *café, poivre* to grind; (†: *Mus*) *air* to grind out. ~ **qn de coups**† to thrash sb, give sb a drubbing; *voir* **moulu**.

moue [mu] nf pout. **faire la** ~ (*gén: tiquer*) to pull a face; *[enfant gâté]* to pout; **faire une** ~ **de dédain/de dégoût** to give a disdainful pout/a pout of disgust.

mouette [mwɛt] nf (sea) gull. ~ **rieuse** black-headed gull; ~ **tridactyle** kittiwake.

mouf(e)ter‡ [mufte] [1] *ou* [4] vi to blink. **il n'a pas moufté** he didn't bat an eyelid.

mou(f)fette [mufɛt] nf skunk.

moufle [mufl] 1 nf mitt, mitten. 2 nm ou f (*Tech*) pulley block.

mouflet, -ette* [muflɛ, ɛt] nm,f brat* (*péj*), kid*.

mouflon [muflɔ̃] nm mouf(f)lon.

mouillage [mujaʒ] nm a (*Naut: action*) *[navire]* anchoring, mooring; *[ancre]* casting; *[mine]* laying. b (*Naut: abri, rade*) anchorage, moorage. c (*Tech*) *[cuir, linge]* moistening, damping; *[vin, lait]* watering(-down).

mouillé, e [muje] (ptp de **mouiller**) adj a *herbe, vêtement, personne* wet. **tout** ~, ~ **comme une soupe** *ou* **jusqu'aux os** soaked through (and through), soaked *ou* drenched to the skin; (*hum*) **il pèse 50 kilos tout** ~ he weighs 50 kilos with his socks on (*hum*); **tu sens le chien** ~ you smell like a wet dog; **ne marche pas dans le** ~ don't walk in the wet; *voir* **poule**[1]. b (*Ling*) **l** ~ palatalized l, palatal l.

mouillement [mujmɑ̃] nm (*Ling*) palatalization.

mouiller [muje] [1] 1 vt a (*gén*) to wet. ~ **son doigt pour tourner la page** to moisten one's finger to turn the page; (*fig*) ~ **sa chemise** *ou* **son maillot*** to put in some hard graft* (*Brit*) *ou* work.

b *[pluie] route* to wet; *personne* to wet; (*complètement*) to drench, soak. **se faire** ~ to get wet *ou* drenched *ou* soaked; **un sale brouillard qui mouille** a horrible wetting (*Brit*) *ou* wet fog.

c (*Culin*) *vin, lait* to water (down); *viande* to cover with stock *ou* wine *etc*, add stock *ou* wine *etc* to.

d (*Naut*) *mine* to lay; *sonde* to heave. ~ **l'ancre** to cast *ou* drop anchor.

e (‡: *compromettre*) *personne* to drag (*dans* into), mix up (*dans* in).

f (*Ling*) to palatalize.

2 vi a (*Naut*) to lie *ou* be at anchor. **ils mouillèrent 3 jours à Papeete** they anchored *ou* they lay at anchor at Papeete for 3 days.

b (**: *avoir peur*) to be scared out of one's mind, be shit-scared **.

3 **se mouiller** vpr a (*au bord de la mer: se tremper*) (*accidentellement*) to get o.s. wet; (*pour un bain rapide*) to have a quick dip. **se** ~ **les pieds** (*sans faire exprès*) to get one's feet wet; (*exprès*) to dabble one's feet in the water, have a little paddle.

b *[yeux]* to fill *ou* brim with tears.

c (‡ *fig*) (*prendre des risques*) to get one's feet wet, commit o.s.; (*se compromettre*) to get mixed up *ou* involved (*dans* in).

mouillette [mujɛt] nf finger of bread, sippet†, soldier* (*Brit*).

mouilleur [mujœʀ] nm a *[timbres]* (stamp) sponge. b (*Naut*) *[ancre]* tumbler. ~ **de mines** minelayer.

mouillure [mujyʀ] nf a (*trace*) wet mark. b (*Ling*) palatalization.

mouise‡ [mwiz] nf: **être dans la** ~ (*misère*) to be flat broke*, be on one's beam-ends* (*Brit*); (*ennuis*) to be in a (bit of a) fix; **c'est la** ~ **chez eux** they've hit hard times.

moujik [muʒik] nm mujik, muzhik.

moujingue‡ [muʒɛ̃g] nmf brat* (*péj*), kid*.

moukère [mukɛʀ] nf Arab woman; (†‡) woman, female.

moulage[1] [mulaʒ] nm a (*voir* **mouler**) moulding; casting. **le** ~ **d'un bas-relief** making *ou* taking a cast of a bas-relief. b (*objet*) cast. **sur la cheminée il y avait le** ~ **en plâtre d'une statue** there was a plaster (of Paris) figure on the mantelpiece; **prendre un** ~ **de** to take a cast of; (*Art*) **ce n'est qu'un** ~ it is only a copy.

moulage[2] [mulaʒ] nm *[grain]* milling, grinding.

moulant, e [mulɑ̃, ɑ̃t] adj *robe* figure-hugging; *pantalons* tight(-fitting).

moule[1] [mul] 1 nm (*lit, fig*) mould; (*Typ*) matrix. **il n'a jamais pu sortir du** ~ **étroit de son éducation** he has never been able to free himself from the straitjacket of his education; (*lit, fig*) **fait sur** *ou* **coulé dans le même** ~ cast in the same mould; (*être beau*) **être fait au** ~ to be shapely. 2 comp ▸**moule à briques** brick mould ▸**moule à beurre** butter print ▸**moule à gâteaux** cake tin (*for baking*) (*Brit*), cake pan (*US*) ▸**moule à gaufre** waffle-iron ▸**moule à manqué** (deep) sandwich tin (*Brit*), deep cake pan (*US*) ▸**moule à pisé** clay mould ▸**moule à tarte** pie plate, flan dish.

moule[2] [mul] nf a (*Zool*) mussel. ~**s marinières** moules marinières, *mussels cooked in their own juice with onions.* b (*: *idiot*) idiot, twit*.

mouler [mule] [1] vt a (*faire*) *briques* to mould; *caractères d'imprimerie* to cast; *statue, buste* to cast. ~ **un buste en plâtre** to cast a bust in plaster.

b (*reproduire*) *bas-relief, buste* to make *ou* take a cast of. ~ **en plâtre** *visage, buste* to make a plaster cast of.

c (*écrire avec soin*) *lettre, mot* to shape *ou* form with care.

d (*conformer à*) ~ **son style/sa conduite sur** to model one's style/conduct on.

e (*coller à*) *cuisses, hanches* to hug, fit closely round. **une robe qui moule** a figure-hugging dress; **des pantalons qui moulent** tight(-fitting) trousers; **une robe qui lui moulait les hanches** a dress which clung to *ou* around her hips, a dress which fitted closely round her hips; **son corps se moulait au sien** her body pressed closely against his.

mouleur [mulœʀ] nm caster, moulder.

moulin [mulɛ̃] nm a (*instrument, bâtiment*) mill. ~ **à eau** water mill; ~ **à vent** windmill; ~ **à café/poivre** coffee/pepper mill; ~ **à légumes** vegetable mill; (*fig*) ~ **à paroles** chatterbox; ~ **à prières** prayer wheel; *voir* **entrer**. b (*: *moteur*) engine.

mouliner [muline] [1] vt (*Culin*) to put through a vegetable mill; (*Pêche*) to reel in; (*Ordin*) to process.

moulinet [mulinɛ] nm (*Pêche*) reel; (*Tech*) winch; (*Escrime*) flourish. **faire des** ~**s avec une canne** to twirl *ou* whirl a walking stick; **faire des** ~**s avec les bras** to whirl one's arms about *ou* round.

moulinette [mulinɛt] nf ® vegetable mill. **passer qch à la** ~ (*Culin*) to put sth through the vegetable mill; (*Ordin*) to process sth.

moult [mult] adv (†† *ou hum*) (*beaucoup*) many; (*très*) very. ~ **(de) gens** many people, many a person; ~ **fois** oft(en)times (*hum*), many a time.

moulu, e [muly] (ptp de **moudre**) adj a *café, poivre* ground (*épith*). b (†: *meurtri*) bruised, black and blue. ~ **(de fatigue)*** dead-beat*, worn-out, all-in*.

moulure [mulyʀ] nf moulding.

moulurer [mulyʀe] [1] vt to decorate with mouldings. **machine à** ~ moulding machine; **panneau mouluré** moulded panel.

moumoute* [mumut] nf a (*hum*) (*perruque*) wig; (*postiche*) (*pour hommes*) hairpiece, toupee; (*pour femmes*) hairpiece. b (*veste*) fleece-lined *ou* fleecy jacket.

mouquère [mukɛʀ] nf = **moukère**.

mourant, e [muʀɑ̃, ɑ̃t] 1 adj a *personne* dying; *voix* faint; *regard* languishing; *feu, jour* dying. b (*: *lent, ennuyeux*) *rythme, allure, soirée* deadly* (dull). 2 nm,f: **un** ~ a dying man; **les** ~**s** the dying.

mourir [muʀiʀ] [19] vi a *[être animé, plante]* to die. ~ **dans son lit** to die in one's bed; ~ **de sa belle mort** to die a natural death; ~ **avant l'âge** to die young *ou* before one's time; ~ **à la peine** *ou* **à la tâche** to die in harness (*fig*); ~ **assassiné** to be murdered; ~ **empoisonné** (*crime*) to be poisoned (and die); (*accident*) to die of poisoning; ~ **en héros** to die a hero's death; **il est mort très jeune** he died very young, he was very young when he died; **faire** ~ **qn** to kill sb; (*fig*) **cet enfant me fera** ~ this child will be the death of me; **une simple piqûre, tu n'en mourras pas!** it's only a little injection, it won't kill you!; **je l'aime à (en)** ~ I love him more than life itself; **s'ennuyer à** ~ to be bored to death *ou* to tears; **ennuyeux à** ~ deadly boring; **il attend que le patron meure pour prendre sa place** he is waiting to step into his dead boss's shoes; (*Prov*) **on ne meurt qu'une fois** you only die once (*Prov*); (*littér*) **se** ~ to be dying.

b *[civilisation, empire, coutume]* to die out; *[bruit]* to die away; *[jour]* to fade, die; *[feu]* to die out, die down. **la vague vint** ~ **à ses pieds** the wave died away at his feet; **le ballon vint** ~ **à ses pieds** the ball came to rest at his feet.

c ~ **de qch:** ~ **de vieillesse/chagrin** *etc* to die of old age/grief *etc;* ~ **d'une maladie/d'une blessure** to die of a disease/from a wound; ~ **de froid** (*lit*) to die of exposure; (*fig*) **on meurt de froid ici** it's freezing *ou* perishing (*Brit*) cold in here; ~ **de faim** (*lit*) to starve to death, die of hunger; (*fig: avoir faim*) to be starving *ou* famished *ou* ravenous; **faire** ~ **qn de faim** to starve sb to death; ~ **de soif** (*lit*) to die of thirst; (*fig:*

avoir soif) to be parched; (*fig*) ~ **de tristesse** to be weighed down with sadness; ~ **d'inquiétude** to be worried to death; **il me fera** ~ **d'inquiétude** he'll drive me to my death with worry; ~ *ou* **être mort de peur** to be scared to death, be dying of fright; **il me fera** ~ **de peur** he'll frighten the life out of me; ~ **d'ennui** to be bored to death *ou* to tears; **il meurt d'envie de le faire** he's dying to do it; **faire** ~ **qn d'impatience** to keep sb on tenterhooks; **c'est à** ~ **de rire** it would make you die laughing, it's hilarious; **faire** ~ **qn à petit feu** (*lit*) to kill sb slowly *ou* by inches; (*fig*) to torment the life out of sb; (*littér*) **(se)** ~ **d'amour pour qn** to pine for sb.

mouroir [muʀwaʀ] **nm** (*péj*) old people's home.

mouron [muʀɔ̃] **nm** pimpernel. ~ **rouge** scarlet pimpernel; ~ **blanc** *ou* **des oiseaux** chickweed; (*fig*) **se faire du** ~* to worry o.s. sick*.

mouscaille* [muskɑj] **nf: être dans la** ~ (*misère*) to be down and out, be stony broke*, be on one's beam-ends* (*Brit*); (*ennuis*) to be up the creek‡.

mousquet [muskɛ] **nm** musket.

mousquetaire [muskətɛʀ] **nm** musketeer.

mousqueton [muskətɔ̃] **nm** (*boucle*) snap hook, clasp; (*fusil*) carbine; (*Alpinisme*) crab, karabiner. **coup de** ~ musket shot.

moussaillon* [musajɔ̃] **nm** ship's boy. **par ici** ~! over here, (my) boy!

moussaka [musaka] **nf** moussaka.

moussant, e [musɑ̃, ɑ̃t] **adj** *savon, crème à raser* foaming, lathering. **bain** ~ bubble bath.

mousse¹ [mus] 1 **nf** a (*Bot*) moss; *voir* **pierre, vert.** b (*écume*) *[bière, eau]* froth, foam; *[savon]* lather; *[champagne]* bubbles. **la** ~ **sur le verre de bière** the head on the beer. c (*: *bière*) pint*. d (*Culin*) mousse. ~ **au chocolat** chocolate mousse. e (*caoutchouc*) **balle (en)** ~ rubber ball; (*nylon*) **collant/bas** ~ stretch tights (*Brit*) *ou* pantyhose (*US*)/stockings; ~ **de caoutchouc** foam rubber. f **se faire de la** ~* to worry o.s. sick*, get all het up*. 2 **comp ▸ mousse carbonique** (fire-fighting) foam **▸ mousse de nylon** (*tissu*) stretch nylon; (*pour rembourrer*) foam **▸ mousse de platine** platinum sponge; *voir* **point²**.

mousse² [mus] **nm** ship's boy.

mousseline [muslin] **nf** (*Tex*) (*coton*) muslin; (*soie, tergal*) chiffon; *voir* **pomme, sauce.**

mousser [muse] 1 **vi** a *[bière, eau]* to froth, foam; *[champagne]* to bubble, sparkle; *[détergent]* to foam, lather; *[savon]* to lather. **faire** ~ *savon, détergent* to lather up. b **faire** ~ **qn**‡ (*vanter*) to boost sb*, puff sb up* (*US*); (*mettre en colère*) to make sb mad* *ou* wild*; **se faire** ~‡ (*gén*) to blow one's own trumpet, sing one's own praises (*auprès* to); (*auprès d'un supérieur*) to sell o.s. hard* (*auprès de* to).

mousseron [musʀɔ̃] **nm** meadow mushroom.

mousseux, -euse [musø, øz] 1 **adj** *vin* sparkling (*épith*); *bière, chocolat* frothy. **eau** ~**euse** soapy water. 2 **nm** sparkling wine.

mousson [musɔ̃] **nf** monsoon.

Moussorgski [musɔʀgski] **nm** Mussorgsky.

moussu, e [musy] **adj** *sol, arbre* mossy; *banc* moss-covered.

moustache [mustaʃ] **nf** *[homme]* moustache, mustache (*US*). *[animal]* ~**s** whiskers; **porter la** ~ *ou* **des** ~**s** to have *ou* wear a moustache; *[femme]* **avoir de la** ~ to have a moustache, have hair on one's upper lip; ~ **en brosse** toothbrush moustache; ~ **en croc** *ou* **en guidon de vélo** handlebar moustache; ~ **(à la) gauloise** walrus moustache.

moustachu, e [mustaʃy] **adj** with a moustache. **c'est un** ~ he has a moustache.

moustiquaire [mustikɛʀ] **nf** (*rideau*) mosquito net; *[fenêtre, porte]* screen; (*Can*) (window *ou* door) screen.

moustique [mustik] **nm** (*Zool*) mosquito; (*: *enfant*) tich* (*Brit*), (little) kid*, nipper* (*Brit*).

moût [mu] **nm** *[raisin etc]* must; *[bière]* wort.

moutard* [mutaʀ] **nm** brat* (*péj*), kid*.

moutarde [mutaʀd] 1 **nf** mustard. ~ **(extra-)forte** English mustard; ~ **à l'estragon** *ou* **aux aromates** French mustard; (*fig*) **la** ~ **me monta au nez!** I flared up!, I lost my temper! 2 **adj inv** mustard(-coloured); *voir* **gaz, sauce.**

moutardier [mutaʀdje] **nm** (*pot*) mustard pot; (*fabricant*) mustard maker *ou* manufacturer.

mouton¹ [mutɔ̃] 1 **nm** a (*animal*) sheep; (*peau*) sheepskin. **doublé de** ~ lined with sheepskin; **relié en** ~ bound in sheepskin, sheepskin-bound; (*fig*) **mais revenons** *ou* **retournons à nos** ~**s** but let's get back to the subject, but to get back to the subject; *voir* **compter, sauter.**

b (*viande*) mutton. **côte de** ~ mutton chop.

c (*: *personne*) (*grégaire, crédule*) sheep; (*doux, passif*) sheep, lamb. **c'est un** ~ (*grégaire*) he is easily led, he goes with the crowd; (*doux*) he is as mild *ou* gentle as a lamb; **il m'a suivi comme un** ~ he followed me like a lamb; **se conduire en** ~**s de Panurge** to behave like a lot of sheep, follow one another (around) like sheep.

d (*arg Police: dans une prison*) stool pigeon (*arg*), grass (*Brit arg*).

e ~**s** (*sur la mer*) white horses (*Brit*), caps (*US*); (*sur le plancher*) (bits of) fluff; (*dans le ciel*) fluffy *ou* fleecy clouds.

f (*Constr*) ram, monkey.

2 **comp ▸ mouton à cinq pattes** rara avis (*littér*), world's wonder **▸ mouton à laine** sheep reared for wool **▸ mouton à viande** sheep reared for meat.

mouton², -onne [mutɔ̃, ɔn] **adj** sheeplike.

moutonnant, e [mutɔnɑ̃, ɑ̃t] **adj** *mer* flecked with white horses (*Brit*) *ou* with caps (*US*); (*littér*) *collines* rolling (*épith*).

moutonné, e [mutɔne] (**ptp de moutonner**) **adj** *ciel* flecked with fleecy *ou* fluffy clouds.

moutonnement [mutɔnmɑ̃] **nm** *[mer]* breaking into *ou* becoming flecked with white horses (*Brit*) *ou* with caps (*US*) *ou* foam. (*littér*) **le** ~ **des collines** the rolling hills.

moutonner [mutɔne] 1 1 **vi** *[mer]* to be covered in white horses (*Brit*) *ou* in caps (*US*), be flecked with foam; (*littér*) *[collines]* to roll. 2 **se moutonner vpr** *[ciel]* to be flecked with fleecy *ou* fluffy clouds.

moutonneux, -euse [mutɔnø, øz] **adj** *mer* flecked with white horses (*Brit*) *ou* with caps (*US*); *ciel* flecked with fleecy *ou* fluffy clouds.

moutonnier, -ière [mutɔnje, jɛʀ] **adj** (*fig*) sheeplike.

mouture [mutyʀ] **nf** a (*action*) *[blé]* milling, grinding; *[café]* grinding. b (*résultat*) *[café]* **une** ~ **fine** finely ground coffee; *[article, rapport]* **c'est la première** ~ it's the first draft; (*fig péj*) **c'est la 3e** ~ **du même livre** it's the 3rd rehash of the same book.

mouvance [muvɑ̃s] **nf** a (*Hist*) tenure; (*Philos*) mobility; (*fig littér*) (*domaine d'influence*) sphere of influence. **entraîner qn dans sa** ~ to draw sb into one's sphere of influence. b (*péj*) *[pensée, situation]* ever-changing nature. **la** ~ **politique/sociale** the ever-changing political/social scene.

mouvant, e [muvɑ̃, ɑ̃t] **adj** *situation* unsettled, fluid; *ombre, flamme* moving, changing; *pensée, univers* changing; *terrain* unsteady, shifting. (*fig*) **être en terrain** ~ to be on shaky *ou* uncertain ground; *voir* **sable¹**.

mouvement [muvmɑ̃] **nm** a (*geste*) movement, motion. ~**s de gymnastique** (physical) exercises; **il a des** ~**s très lents** he is very slow in his movements; **il approuva d'un** ~ **de tête** he nodded his approval, he gave a nod of approval; **elle refusa d'un** ~ **de tête** she shook her head in refusal, she refused with a shake of her head; **elle eut un** ~ **de recul** she started back; **un** ~ **de dégoût** *etc* a movement of disgust *etc;* **le** ~ **des lèvres** the movement of the lips; *voir* **temps¹**.

b (*impulsion, réaction*) impulse, reaction. **avoir un bon** ~ to make a nice *ou* kind gesture; **dans un bon** ~ on a kindly impulse; **dans un** ~ **de colère/d'indignation** in a fit *ou* a burst *ou* an upsurge of anger/indignation; **les** ~**s de l'âme** the impulses of the soul; **des** ~**s dans l'auditoire** a stir in the audience; **discours accueilli avec des** ~**s divers** speech which got a mixed reception; **son premier** ~ **fut de refuser** his first impulse was to refuse; **agir de son propre** ~ to act of one's own accord.

c (*activité*) *[ville, entreprise]* activity, bustle. **une rue pleine de** ~ a busy *ou* lively street; **il aime le** ~ he likes to be on the go.

d (*déplacement*) (*Astron, Aviat, Naut, Mil*) movement. **être sans cesse en** ~ to be constantly on the move *ou* on the go; **mettre qch en** ~ to set sth in motion, set sth going; **se mettre en** ~ to set off, get going; **suivre le** ~ to go along with the majority; **le** ~ **perpétuel** perpetual motion; ~ **de foule** movement *ou* sway in the crowd; (*Sociol*) ~**s de population** shifts in population; **d'importants** ~**s de troupes à la frontière** large-scale troop movements at *ou* along the frontier; (*Mil*) ~ **de repli** withdrawal; ~ **tournant** (out)flanking movement; (*Écon*) ~ **de marchandises/de capitaux** *ou* **de fonds** movement of goods/capital; (*Admin*) ~ **de personnel** changes in staff *ou* personnel; *voir* **guerre.**

e (*Philos, Pol etc: évolution*) **le** ~ **des idées** the evolution of ideas; **le parti du** ~ the party in favour of change, the party of progress; **être dans le** ~ to keep up-to-date; **un** ~ **d'opinion se dessine en faveur de** one can detect a trend of opinion in favour of; (*Fin*) **le** ~ **des prix** the trend of prices; (*Fin*) ~ **de baisse/de hausse (sur les ventes)** downward/upward movement *ou* trend (in sales); ~**(s) de grève** strike action (*NonC*).

f (*rythme*) *[phrase]* rhythm; *[tragédie]* movement, action; *[mélodie]* tempo.

g (*Pol, Sociol: groupe*) movement. ~ **politique/de jeunesse** political/youth movement; **le** ~ **ouvrier** the labour movement; **M**~ **de libération de la femme** Women's Liberation Movement, Women's Lib*; **le** ~ **syndical** the trade-union *ou* labor-union (*US*) movement.

h (*Mus*) *[symphonie etc]* (*section*) movement; (*style*) movement, motion.

i (*Tech: mécanisme*) movement. **par un** ~ **d'horlogerie** by clockwork; **fermeture à** ~ **d'horlogerie** time lock.

j (*ligne, courbe*) *[sculpture]* contours; *[draperie, étoffe]* drape; *[collines]* undulations, rise and fall (*NonC*).

mouvementé, e [muvmɑ̃te] **adj** *vie, poursuite, récit* eventful; *séance* turbulent, stormy; *terrain* rough.

mouvoir [muvwaʀ] 27 1 **vt** (*gén ptp*) a *machine* to drive, power; *bras, levier* to move. **faire** ~ to drive, power; to move; **il se leva comme mû par un ressort** he sprang up as if propelled by a spring *ou* like a Jack-in-the-box. b *[motif, sentiment]* to drive, prompt. 2 **se mouvoir vpr** to move.

moyen, -yenne [mwajɛ̃, jɛn] 1 **adj** a (*qui tient le milieu*) *taille* medium (*épith*), average; *prix* moderate, medium (*épith*). **de taille** ~**ne** of medium height; **une maison de dimensions** ~**nes** a medium-sized *ou* moderate-sized house; (*Comm*) **il ne reste plus de tailles** ~**nes** there are no medium sizes left; **les régions de la Loire** ~**ne** the middle regions of the Loire, the mid-Loire regions; **la solution ~ne** the middle-of-the-road solution; **une ~ne entreprise** a medium-sized company; *voir* **cours, onde, poids.**

b (*du type courant*) average. **le Français/le lecteur ~** the average Frenchman/reader.

c (*ni bon ni mauvais*) *résultats, intelligence* average; (*Scol*) (*sur copie d'élève*) fair, average. **nous avons eu un temps ~** we had mixed weather, the weather was so-so*; **un élève qui est ~ en géographie** a pupil who is average at geography; **bien ~** mediocre; **très ~** pretty poor*.

d (*d'après des calculs*) *température* average, mean (*épith*); *âge, prix etc* average.

e (*Ling*) **voyelle ~ne** mid *ou* central vowel.

2 **nm** a (*possibilité, manière*) means, way. **il y a toujours un ~** there's always a way, there are ways and means; **par quel ~ allez-vous le convaincre?** how will you manage to convince him?; **connaissez-vous un bon ~ pour ...?** do you know a good way to ...?; (*péj*) **par tous les ~s** by fair means or foul, by hook or by crook; **j'ai essayé par tous les ~s de le convaincre** I've done everything to try and convince him; **tous les ~s lui sont bons** he'll stop at nothing *ou* he'll do anything to get what he wants; **tous les ~s seront mis en œuvre pour réussir** we shall use all possible means to succeed; **c'est l'unique ~ de s'en sortir** it's the only way out, it's the only way we can get out of it; **employer les grands ~s** to have to resort to drastic means *ou* measures; **se débrouiller avec les ~s du bord** to get by as best one can, make do and mend; **au ~ de, par le ~ de** by means of, with the help of; *voir* **fin²**.

b **est-ce qu'il y a ~ de lui parler?** is it possible to speak to him?; **il n'y a pas ~ de sortir par ce temps** you can't get out in this weather; (*Téléc*) **pas ~ d'obtenir la communication** I can't get through, the number is unobtainable; **le ~ de dire autre chose!** what else could I say!; **le ~ de lui refuser!** how could I possibly refuse!; **non, il n'y a pas ~!** no, nothing doing!*; **il n'y a jamais ~ qu'il fasse attention** you will never get him to take care, he'll never take care; *voir* **trouver.**

c (*capacités intellectuelles, physiques*) **il a de grands ~s (intellectuels)** he has great powers of intellect *ou* intellectual powers; **ça lui a enlevé** *ou* **fait perdre tous ses ~s** it left him completely at a loss, it completely threw him*; **il était en (pleine) possession de tous ses ~s** his powers were at their peak; **c'est au-dessus de ses ~s** it's beyond him; **par ses propres ~s** all by himself, on his own; **ils ont dû rentrer par leurs propres ~s** they had to go home under their own steam*, they had to make their own way home; *voir* **perdre.**

d (*ressources financières*) **~s** means; **il n'a pas les ~s de s'acheter une voiture** he can't afford to buy a car; **c'est au-dessus de ses ~s** he can't afford it, it's beyond his means; **il a les ~s** he's got the means, he can afford it; **avoir de gros/petits ~s** to have a large/small income, be well/badly off; **il vit au-dessus de ses ~s** he lives beyond his means *ou* income.

3 **adv** (*) so-so*, fair to middling*.

4 **moyenne nf** a (*gén*) average; (*Aut*) average speed. **au-dessus/au-dessous de la ~ne** above/below average; **faites-moi la ~ne de ces chiffres** work out the average of these figures; **la ~ne d'âge** the average age; **la ~ne des températures** the mean *ou* average temperature; **la ~ne des gens pensent que** most people think that, the broad mass of people think that; **faire du 100 de ~ne** to average 100 km/h, drive at an average speed of 100 km/h, do 100 km/h on average; (*Math*) **~ne géométrique/arithmétique** geometric/arithmetic mean; **en ~ne** on (an) average.

b (*Scol*) **avoir la ~ne** (*devoir*) to get fifty per cent, get half marks (*Brit*); (*examen*) to get a pass *ou* a passmark (*Brit*); **~ne générale (de l'année)** average (for the year); **cet élève est dans la ~ne/la bonne ~ne** this pupil is about/above average.

5 **comp** ►**moyen d'action** measures, means of action ►**le Moyen Âge** the Middle Ages (*voir* **haut**) ►**moyenâgeux, -euse** *ville, costumes* medieval, historic; (*péj*) *attitudes, théories* antiquated, outdated, old-fashioned ►**moyen anglais** Middle English ►**moyens audiovisuels** audiovisual aids ►**moyen-courrier (pl moyens-courriers) nm** (*Aviat*) medium-haul (aeroplane) ►**moyen de défense** means of defence ►**moyen d'existence** means of existence ►**moyen d'expression** means of expression ►**moyen de fortune** makeshift device *ou* means ►**moyen de locomotion** means of transport ►**moyen métrage** (*Ciné*) medium-length film ►**le Moyen-Orient** the Middle East ►**moyen de pression** means of applying pressure; **nous n'avons aucun moyen de pression sur lui** we have no means of applying pressure on him *ou* no hold on him ►**moyen de production** means of production ►**moyen terme** (*gén*) middle course; (*Logique*) middle term ►**moyen de transport** means of transport ►**moyens de trésorerie** *means of raising revenue.*

moyennant [mwajɛnɑ̃] **prép** *argent* for; *service* in return for; *travail, effort* with. **~ finance** for a fee *ou* a consideration; **~ quoi** in return for which, in consideration of which.

moyenne [mwajɛn] *voir* **moyen.**

moyennement [mwajɛnmɑ̃] **adv** *bon, satisfaisant* fairly, moderately; *s'entendre, travailler* fairly well, moderately well. **ça va? – ~*** how are things? – so-so* *ou* not too bad* *ou* average.

moyeu, pl ~x [mwajø] **nm** *[roue]* hub; *[hélice]* boss.

mozambicain,e [mɔzɑ̃bikɛ̃,ɛn] 1 **adj** Mozambican. 2 **nm,f: M~(e)** Mozambican.

Mozambique [mɔzɑ̃bik] **nm** Mozambique.

Mozart [mɔzaʀ] **nm** Mozart.

mozartien, -ienne [mɔzaʀtjɛ̃, jɛn] **adj** Mozartian, of Mozart.

MRAP [mʀap] **nm** (**abrév de mouvement contre le racisme, l'antisémitisme et pour la paix**) *French anti-racist and peace movement.*

MRG [ɛmɛʀʒe] **nm** (**abrév de Mouvement des radicaux de gauche**) *French political party.*

ms (**abrév de manuscrit**) MS.

MST [ɛmɛste] **nf** a (**abrév de maladie sexuellement transmissible**) STD. b (**abrév de maîtrise de sciences et techniques**) *master's degree in science and technology.*

mû, mue¹ [my] **ptp de mouvoir.**

mucosité [mykozite] **nf** (*gén pl*) mucus (*NonC*).

mucoviscidose [mykovisidoz] **nf** mucoviscidosis.

mucus [mykys] **nm** mucus (*NonC*).

mue² [my] **nf** a (*transformation*) *[oiseau]* moulting; *[serpent]* sloughing; *[mammifère]* shedding, moulting; *[cerf]* casting; *[voix]* breaking (*Brit*), changing (*US*). **la ~ (de la voix) intervient vers 14 ans** the voice breaks (*Brit*) *ou* changes (*US*) at round about 14 years of age. b (*époque*) moulting *etc* season. c (*peau, plumes*) *[serpent]* slough; *[oiseau, mammifère]* moulted *ou* shed hair, feathers *etc.* d (*Agr: cage*) coop.

muer [mɥe] 1 1 **vi** *[oiseau]* to moult; *[serpent]* to slough, shed its skin; *[mammifère]* to moult, shed hair *ou* skin *etc.* **sa voix mue, il mue** his voice is breaking (*Brit*) *ou* changing (*US*). 2 **vt** (*littér*) **~ qch en** to transform *ou* change *ou* turn sth into. 3 **se muer vpr** (*littér*) **se ~ en** to transform *ou* change *ou* turn into.

müesli [myysli] **nm** muesli.

muet, muette [mɥɛ, mɥɛt] 1 **adj** a (*infirme*) dumb; *voir* **sourd.**

b (*silencieux*) *colère, prière, personne* silent, mute; (*littér*) *forêt* silent. **~ de colère/surprise** speechless with anger/surprise; **~ de peur** dumb with fear; **le code est ~ à ce sujet** the law is silent on this matter; **en rester ~ (d'étonnement)** to stand speechless, be struck dumb (with astonishment); **~ comme une tombe** (as) silent as the grave; **il est resté ~ comme une carpe** he never opened his mouth.

c (*Ciné, Théât*) *film, cinéma* silent; *rôle* non-speaking (*épith*); *scène* with no dialogue. (*au restaurant*) **carte ~te** menu without prices (*given to guests*); *voir* **jeu, rôle.**

d (*Ling*) mute, silent.

e (*Scol*) (*Géog*) *carte, clavier de machine à écrire* blank. (*Mus*) **clavier ~** dummy keyboard.

2 **nm** a (*infirme*) mute, dumb man.

b (*Ciné*) **le ~** the silent cinema.

3 **muette nf** mute, dumb woman; *voir* **grand.**

muezzin [mɥɛdzin] **nm** muezzin.

mufle [myfl] **nm** a (*Zool: museau*) *[bovin]* muffle; *[chien, lion]* muzzle. b (*‡: goujat*) boor, lout, yob‡ (*Brit*). **ce qu'il est ~ alors!‡** what a yob‡ (*Brit*) *ou* lout he is!, what a boorish fellow he is!

muflerie [myfləʀi] **nf** boorishness (*NonC*), loutishness (*NonC*).

muflier [myflije] **nm** antirrhinum, snapdragon.

mufti [myfti] **nm** (*Rel*) mufti.

muge [myʒ] **nm** grey mullet.

mugir [myʒiʀ] 2 **vi** a *[vache]* to low, moo; *[bœuf]* to bellow. b (*littér*) *[vent]* to howl, roar, bellow; *[mer]* to howl, roar, boom; *[sirène]* to howl.

mugissement [myʒismɑ̃] **nm** (*voir* **mugir**) lowing, mooing; bellowing; howling; roaring; booming.

muguet [mygɛ] **nm** (*Bot*) lily of the valley; (*Méd*) thrush; (*†: élégant*) fop, coxcomb††, popinjay††.

muid [mɥi] **nm** (*†: tonneau*) hogshead.

mulâtre, mulâtresse [mylɑtʀ, mylɑtʀɛs] **nm,f, mulâtre adj inv** mulatto.

mule [myl] **nf** a (*Zool*) (she-)mule; *voir* **tête, têtu.** b (*pantoufle*) mule. c (*arg Drogue*) small-time dealer.

mulet [mylɛ] **nm** a (*Zool*) (he-)mule; (*poisson*) mullet. b (*arg Aut*) spare *ou* replacement car.

muletier, -ière [myl(ə)tje, jɛʀ] 1 **adj: sentier** *ou* **chemin ~** mule track. 2 **nm,f** mule-driver, muleteer.

mullah [myla] **nm = mollah.**

mulot [mylo] **nm** field mouse.

multi... [mylti] **préf** multi... .

multicarte [myltikaʀt] **adj** *voir* **représentant.**

multicellulaire [myltiselylɛʀ] **adj** multicellular.

multicolore [myltikɔlɔʀ] **adj** multicoloured, many-coloured.

multicoque [myltikɔk] **adj, nm: (voilier) ~** multihull.

multicouche [myltikuʃ] **adj: objectif ~** lens with multiple coatings.

multiculturalisme [myltikyltyʀalism] **nm** multiculturalism.

multiculturel, -elle [myltikyltyʀɛl] **adj** multicultural.

multidimensionnel, -elle [myltidimɑ̃sjɔnɛl] **adj** multidimensional.

multidisciplinaire [myltidisiplinɛʀ] **adj** multidisciplinary.

multifenêtre [myltifənɛtʀ] **adj** (*Ordin*) multi-window (*épith*).

multiflore [myltiflɔʀ] **adj** multiflora.

multifonctions [myltifɔ̃ksjɔ̃] adj (*Ordin*) multiprocessing (*épith*), multitasking (*épith*).
multiforme [myltifɔʀm] adj *apparence* multiform; *problème* many-sided.
multigrade [myltigʀad] adj: **huile ~** multigrade oil.
multilatéral, e, mpl **-aux** [myltilateʀal, o] adj multilateral.
multilingue [myltilɛ̃g] adj multilingual.
multilinguisme [myltilɛ̃gɥism] nm multilingualism.
multimédia [myltimedja] adj multimedia. **campagne de publicité ~** multimedia advertising campaign.
multimilliardaire [myltimiljaʀdɛʀ] adj, nmf, **multimillionnaire** [myltimiljɔnɛʀ] adj, nmf multimillionaire.
multinational, e, mpl **-aux** [myltinasjɔnal, o] 1 adj multinational. 2 **multinationale** nf multinational (company).
multiniveaux [myltinivo] adj multilevel.
multipare [myltipaʀ] 1 adj multiparous. 2 nf (*femme*) multipara; (*animal*) multiparous animal.
multipartisme [myltipaʀtism] nm (*Pol*) multiparty system.
multiplace [myltiplas] adj, nm: **cet avion est (un) ~** it's a passenger aircraft.
multiple [myltipl] 1 adj a (*nombreux*) numerous, multiple, many; (*Méd*) *fracture, blessures* multiple. **dans de ~s cas** in numerous *ou* many instances; **en de ~s occasions** on numerous *ou* many multiple occasions; **pour des raisons ~s** *ou* **de ~s raisons** for multiple reasons; **à de ~s reprises** time and again, repeatedly; **à têtes ~s** *missile* multiple-warhead; *outil* with (a range of) attachments; **outil à usages ~s** multi-purpose tool; **choix ~** multiple choice; *voir* **magasin, pris.**
b (*variés*) *activités, aspects* many, multifarious, manifold.
c (*complexe*) *pensée, problème, homme* many-sided, multifaceted; *monde* complex, mixed.
d (*Math*) **100 est ~ de 10** 100 is a multiple of 10.
2 nm multiple. **plus petit commun ~** lowest common multiple.
multiplex [myltiplɛks] adj, nm (*Téléc*) multiplex.
multiplexage [myltiplɛksaʒ] nm (*Téléc*) multiplexing.
multiplexeur [myltiplɛksœʀ] nm (*Téléc*) multiplexer.
multipliable [myltiplijabl] adj multipli(c)able.
multiplicande [myltiplikɑ̃d] nm multiplicand.
multiplicateur, -trice [myltiplikatœʀ, tʀis] 1 adj multiplying. **effet ~** multiplier effect. 2 nm multiplier.
multiplicatif, -ive [myltiplikatif, iv] adj (*Math*) multiplying; (*Gram*) multiplicative.
multiplication [myltiplikasjɔ̃] nf a (*prolifération*) increase in the number of. (*Bible*) **la ~ des pains** the miracle of the loaves and fishes. b (*Bot, Math*) multiplication. (*Math*) **faire une ~** to do a multiplication. c (*Tech*) gear ratio.
multiplicité [myltiplisite] nf multiplicity.
multiplier [myltiplije] 7 1 vt (*Math*) to multiply (*par* by); *attaques, difficultés, avertissements* to multiply, increase. **malgré nos efforts multipliés** in spite of our increased efforts. 2 **se multiplier** vpr a *[incidents, attaques, difficultés]* to multiply, increase, grow in number. b (*se reproduire*) *[animaux]* to multiply; *voir* **croître.** c (*fig: se donner à fond*) *[infirmier, soldat]* to do one's utmost, give of one's best (*pour faire* in order to do).
multipolaire [myltipɔlɛʀ] adj multipolar.
multiposte [myltipɔst] adj *voir* **configuration.**
multiprise [myltipʀiz] nf adaptor.
multiprocesseur [myltipʀɔsesœʀ] nm (*Ordin*) multiprocessor.
multiprogrammation [myltipʀɔgʀamasjɔ̃] nf (*Ordin*) multiprogramming.
multipropriété [myltipʀɔpʀijete] nf timesharing. **acheter un studio en ~** to buy a timeshare in a flatlet.
multiracial, e, mpl **-iaux** [myltiʀasjal, jo] adj multiracial.
multirisque [myltiʀisk] adj multiple-risk (*épith*).
multisalles [myltisal] adj: **(cinéma** *ou* **complexe) ~** film centre, cinema complex.
multistandard [myltistɑ̃daʀ] adj: **(téléviseur) ~** multistandard television.
multitâche [myltitaʃ] adj (*Ordin*) multitask(ing) (*épith*).
multitraitement [myltitʀɛtmɑ̃] nm (*Ordin*) multiprocessing.
multitude [myltityd] nf a (*grand nombre*) **(toute) une ~ de** *personnes* a multitude of, a vast number of; *objets, idées* a vast number of; **la ~ des gens** the (vast) majority of people. b (*ensemble, masse*) mass. **on pouvait voir d'en haut la ~ des champs** from the air you could see the mass of fields. c († *ou littér: foule de gens*) multitude, throng.
mumuse* [mymyz] nf: **faire ~** to play (*avec* with).
Munich [mynik] n Munich.
munichois, e [mynikwa, waz] 1 adj of *ou* from Munich, Munich (*épith*). **bière ~e** Munich beer. 2 nm,f: **M~(e)** inhabitant *ou* native of Munich; (*Pol*) **les ~** the men of Munich.
municipal, e, mpl **-aux** [mynisipal, o] adj *élection, taxe, théâtre, stade* municipal; *conseil, conseiller* local, town (*épith*), borough (*épith*). **règlement/arrêté ~** local by-law; **piscine/bibliothèque ~e** public swimming pool/library.
municipalité [mynisipalite] nf a (*ville*) town, municipality. b (*conseil*) town council, corporation.
munificence [mynifisɑ̃s] nf (*littér*) munificence.
munificent, e [mynifisɑ̃, ɑ̃t] adj (*littér*) munificent.
munir [myniʀ] 2 1 vt: **~ de: ~ un objet de** to provide *ou* fit an object with; **~ une machine de** to equip *ou* fit a machine with; **~ un bâtiment de** to equip *ou* fit up *ou* fit out a building with; **~ qn de** to provide *ou* supply *ou* equip sb with; **canne munie d'un bout ferré** walking stick with an iron tip; **muni de ces conseils** armed with this advice; **muni d'un bon dictionnaire** equipped with a good dictionary; (*Rel*) **muni des sacrements de l'Église** fortified with the rites of the Church.
2 **se munir** vpr: **se ~ de** *papiers, imperméable* to arm o.s. with; *argent, nourriture* to take a supply of; **se ~ de patience** to arm o.s. with patience; **se ~ de courage** to pluck up one's courage; **munissez-vous de votre passeport** take your passport (with you).
munitions [mynisjɔ̃] nfpl a ammunition (*NonC*), munitions. **dépôt de ~** munitions *ou* ammunition dump. b (†: *ressources*) supplies.
munster [mœ̃stɛʀ] nm Munster (cheese).
muphti [myfti] nm = **mufti.**
muqueux, -euse [mykø, øz] 1 adj mucous. 2 **muqueuse** nf mucous membrane.
mur [myʀ] 1 nm a (*gén*) wall. **leur jardin est entouré d'un ~** their garden is walled *ou* is surrounded by a wall; **une maison aux ~s de brique** a brick house; **~ d'appui** parapet; **mettre/pendre qch au ~** to put/hang sth on the wall; **sauter** *ou* **faire le ~*** to leap over *ou* jump the wall; (*Sport*) **faire le ~** to make a wall; **ils n'ont laissé que les (quatre) ~s** they left nothing but the bare walls; **rester entre quatre ~s** *[prisonnier]* to stay within the confines of one's cell; (*chez soi*) to stay indoors *ou* inside; **ils l'ont collé au ~** they stuck him up against a wall and put a bullet in him; **l'ennemi est dans nos ~s** the enemy is within our gates; **M. X est dans nos ~s aujourd'hui** we have Mr X with us today; **maintenant que nous sommes dans nos ~s** now (that) we're in our new house (*ou* flat *etc*), now we have our own four walls; (*Jur*) **être propriétaire des ~s** to own the premises; (*fig*) **les ~s ont des oreilles** walls have ears; (*Mil, Pol*) **le ~ de Berlin/de l'Atlantique** the Berlin/the Atlantic Wall; **le ~ d'Hadrien** Hadrian's Wall.
b (*obstacle*) (*Ski*) wall; *[feu, pluie]* wall; *[silence, hostilité]* barrier, wall. **il y a un ~ entre nous** there is a barrier between us; **se heurter à** *ou* **se trouver devant un ~** to come up against a stone *ou* a brick wall; **être** *ou* **avoir le dos au ~** to have one's back to the wall; **on parle à un ~** it's like talking to a brick wall; *voir* **pied.**
c (*Aviat*) **~ du son/de la chaleur** sound/heat barrier; **passer** *ou* **franchir le ~ du son** to break the sound barrier.
2 comp ►**mur artificiel** = mur d'escalade ►**mur de clôture** enclosing wall ►**mur d'enceinte** outer wall(s) ►**mur d'escalade** climbing wall ►**le Mur des Lamentations** the Wailing Wall ►**mur mitoyen** party wall ►**mur de pierres sèches** dry-stone wall ►**mur portant** load-bearing wall ►**mur de refend** supporting (partition) wall ►**mur de séparation** dividing wall ►**mur de soutènement** retaining *ou* breast wall.
mûr, e[1] [myʀ] adj a *fruit, projet* ripe; *toile, tissu* worn. **fruit pas ~ /trop ~** unripe/overripe fruit. b *personne* (*sensé*) mature; (*âgé*) middle-aged. **il est ~ pour le mariage** he is ready for marriage; **il n'est pas encore assez ~** he's not yet mature enough, he's still rather immature; **une femme assez ~e** a woman of mature years. c (‡: *ivre*) tight*, plastered‡. d **après ~e réflexion** after mature reflection, after (giving the subject) much thought, after careful consideration (of the subject).
murage [myʀaʒ] nm *[ouverture]* walling up, bricking up, blocking up.
muraille [myʀɑj] nf (high) wall. **la Grande M~ de Chine** the Great Wall of China; **~ de glace/roche** wall of ice/rock, ice/rock barrier; **couleur (de) ~** (stone) grey.
mural, e, mpl **-aux** [myʀal, o] adj wall (*épith*); (*Art*) mural.
mûre[2] [myʀ] nf *[ronce]* blackberry, bramble; *[mûrier]* mulberry.
mûrement [myʀmɑ̃] adv: **ayant ~ réfléchi** *ou* **délibéré** after giving it much thought, after mature reflection *ou* lengthy deliberation.
murène [myʀɛn] nf moray (eel), mur(a)ena.
murer [myʀe] 1 1 vt a *ouverture* to wall up, brick up, block up; *lieu, ville* to wall (in). b *personne* (*lit*) to wall in, wall up; (*fig*) to isolate. 2 **se murer** vpr (*chez soi*) to shut o.s. away. **se ~ dans sa douleur/son silence** to immure o.s. in one's grief/in silence.
muret [myʀɛ] nm, **murette** [myʀɛt] nf low wall.
murex [myʀɛks] nm murex.
mûrier [myʀje] nm (*arbre*) mulberry tree; (*ronce*) blackberry bush, bramble bush.
mûrir [myʀiʀ] 2 1 vi *[fruit]* to ripen; *[idée]* to mature, develop; *[personne]* to mature; *[abcès, bouton]* to come to a head. 2 vt *fruit* to ripen; *idée, projet* to nurture; *personne* to (make) mature. **faire ~** *fruit* to ripen.
mûrissage [myʀisaʒ] nm *[fruits]* ripening.
mûrissant, e [myʀisɑ̃, ɑ̃t] adj *fruit* ripening; *personne* of mature years.
mûrissement [myʀismɑ̃] nm *[fruit]* ripening; *[idée]* maturing, development; *[projet]* nurturing.
mûrisserie [myʀisʀi] nf *[bananes]* ripening room.
murmure [myʀmyʀ] nm a (*chuchotement*) *[personne]* murmur; *[ruisseau]* murmur(ing), babble; *[vent]* murmur(ing); *[oiseaux]*

twitter(ing). b (*commentaire*) murmur. ~ **d'approbation/de protestation** murmur of approval/of protest; **obéir sans** ~ to obey without a murmur; ~**s** (*protestations*) murmurings, mutterings, grumblings; (*objections*) objections.

murmurer [myʀmyʀe] 1 1 **vt** to murmur. **on murmure que** ... it's whispered that ..., rumour has it that ... . 2 **vi** a (*chuchoter*) *[personne, vent]* to murmur; *[ruisseau]* to murmur, babble; *[oiseaux]* to twitter. b (*protester*) to mutter, complain, grumble (*contre* about). **il a consenti sans** ~ he agreed without a murmur (of protest).

musaraigne [myzaʀɛɲ] **nf** (*Zool*) shrew.

musarder [myzaʀde] 1 **vi** (*littér*) (*en se promenant*) to dawdle (along); (*en perdant son temps*) to idle (about).

musc [mysk] **nm** musk.

muscade [myskad] **nf** a (*Culin*) nutmeg; *voir* **noix**. b (conjurer's) ball. **passez** ~! (*lit*) *[jongleur]* hey presto!; (*fig*) quick as a flash!

muscadet [myskadɛ] **nm** muscadet (wine).

muscadier [myskadje] **nm** nutmeg (tree).

muscadin [myskadɛ̃] **nm** (*Hist* ††: *élégant*) fop, coxcomb††, popinjay††.

muscari [myskaʀi] **nm** grape hyacinth.

muscat [myska] **nm** (*raisin*) muscat grape; (*vin*) muscatel (wine).

muscle [myskl] **nm** muscle. (*Anat*) ~**s lisses/striés** smooth/striated muscles; **il est tout en** ~ he's all muscle; **il a des** ~**s** *ou* **du** ~* he is brawny, he's got plenty of beef*.

musclé, e [myskle] (**ptp de muscler**) **adj** *corps, membre* muscular; *homme* brawny; (*fig*) *style* sinewy; *pièce de théâtre* powerful; *régime, appariteur* strong-arm (*épith*). (*arg Scol*) **un problème** ~ a stinker‡ of a problem, a stiff problem.

muscler [myskle] 1 **vt** to develop the muscle of.

muscu* [mysky] **nf abrév de musculation.**

musculaire [myskylɛʀ] **adj** *force* muscular. **fibre** ~ muscle fibre.

musculation [myskylasjɔ̃] **nf** body building. **exercices de** ~ muscle-development exercises; **faire de la** ~ to do body building.

musculature [myskylatyʀ] **nf** muscle structure, musculature (SPÉC). **il a une** ~ **imposante** he has an impressive set of muscles.

musculeux, -euse [myskylø, øz] **adj** *corps, membre* muscular; *homme* muscular, brawny.

muse [myz] **nf** (*Littérat, Myth*) Muse. **les (neuf)** ~**s** the Muses; (*hum*) **cultiver** *ou* **taquiner la** ~ to court the Muse (*hum*).

museau, pl ~**x** [myzo] **nm** a *[chien, bovin]* muzzle; *[porc]* snout. b (*Culin*) brawn (*Brit*), headcheese (*US*). c (*: *visage*) face, snout*.

musée [myze] **nm** (*art, peinture*) art gallery; (*technique, scientifique*) museum. ~ **de cire** waxworks (*sg*); **Nîmes est une ville-**~ Nîmes is a historical town, Nîmes is a town of great historical interest; (*hum*) ~ **des horreurs** junkshop (*hum*); **elle ferait bien dans un** ~ **des horreurs** she should be in a chamber of horrors; (*lit, fig*) **objet** *ou* **pièce de** ~ museum piece.

museler [myz(ə)le] 4 **vt** (*lit*) *animal* to muzzle; (*fig*) *personne, liberté, presse* to muzzle, gag, silence.

muselière [myzəljɛʀ] **nf** muzzle. **mettre une** ~ **à** to muzzle.

musellement [myzɛlmɑ̃] **nm** (*lit*) *[animal]* muzzling; (*fig*) *[personne, liberté, presse]* muzzling, gagging, silencing.

muséobus [myzeobys] **nm** mobile museum.

muser [myze] 1 **vi** († *ou littér*) (*en se promenant*) to dawdle (along); (*en perdant son temps*) to idle (about).

musette [myzɛt] 1 **nf** a (*sac*) *[ouvrier]* lunchbag; (††) *[écolier]* satchel; *[soldat]* haversack. b (*Mus: instrument, air*) musette. c (*Zool*) common shrew. 2 **nm** (*bal*) popular dance (*to the accordion*). (*genre*) **le** ~ accordion music. 3 **adj inv** *genre, style* musette; *orchestre* accordion (*épith*); *voir* **bal.**

muséum [myzeɔm] **nm**: ~ **(d'histoire naturelle)** (natural history) museum.

musical, e, mpl -aux [myzikal, o] **adj** musical. **avoir l'oreille** ~**e** to have a good ear for music; *voir* **comédie.**

musicalement [myzikalmɑ̃] **adv** musically.

musicalité [myzikalite] **nf** musicality, musical quality.

music-hall, pl music-halls [myzikol] **nm** (*salle*) variety theatre, music hall. **faire du** ~ to be in *ou* do variety; **spectacle/numéro de** ~ variety show/turn *ou* act *ou* number.

musicien, -ienne [myzisjɛ̃, jɛn] 1 **adj** musical. 2 **nm,f** musician.

musicographe [myzikɔgʀaf] **nmf** musicographer.

musicographie [myzikɔgʀafi] **nf** musicography.

musicologie [myzikɔlɔʒi] **nf** musicology.

musicologue [myzikɔlɔg] **nmf** musicologist.

musique [myzik] 1 **nf** a (*art, harmonie, notations*) music. ~ **militaire/sacrée** military/sacred music; ~ **pour piano** piano music; (*Rad*) **programme de** ~ **variée** programme of selected music; **la** ~ **adoucit les mœurs** music has a civilizing influence; **elle fait de la** ~ she does music, she plays an instrument; **si on faisait de la** ~ let's make some music; **mettre un poème en** ~ to set a poem to music; **déjeuner en** ~ to lunch against a background of music; **travailler en** ~ to work to music; **je n'aime pas travailler en** ~ I don't like working against music *ou* with music playing; (*fig*) **c'est toujours la même** ~* it's always the same old refrain *ou* song; *voir* **boîte, connaître, papier.**

b (*orchestre, fanfare*) band. ~ **militaire** military band; (*Mil*) **marcher** *ou* **aller** ~ **en tête** to march with the band leading; *voir* **chef**[1].

2 **comp** ▸**musique d'ambiance** background music ▸**musique de ballet** ballet music ▸**musique de chambre** chamber music ▸**musique classique** classical music ▸**musique concrète** concrete music, musique concrète ▸**musique douce** soft music ▸**musique folklorique** folk music ▸**musique de fond** background music ▸**musique légère** light music ▸**musique noire** negro music ▸**musique pop** pop music ▸**musique de scène** incidental music.

musiquette [myzikɛt] **nf** muzak.

musli [mysli] **nm** = **müesli.**

musoir [myzwaʀ] **nm** (*Naut*) pierhead.

musqué, e [myske] **adj** *odeur, goût* musky. **rat** ~ muskrat; **bœuf** ~ musk ox; **rose** ~**e** musk rose.

must* [mœst] **nm** (*film, livre etc*) **c'est un** ~ it's a must*.

musulman, e [myzylmɑ̃, an] **adj, nm,f** Moslem, Muslim.

mutabilité [mytabilite] **nf** (*Bio, Jur etc*) mutability.

mutagène [mytaʒɛn] **adj** mutagenic.

mutant, e [mytɑ̃, ɑ̃t] **adj, nm,f** mutant.

mutation [mytasjɔ̃] **nf** a (*transfert*) *[employé]* transfer. b (*changement*) (*gén*) transformation; (*Bio*) mutation. **société en** ~ changing society; **entreprise en pleine** ~ company undergoing massive changes. c (*Jur*) transfer; (*Mus*) mutation. (*Ling*) ~ **consonantique/vocalique/phonétique** consonant/vowel/sound shift.

muter [myte] 1 **vt** (*Admin*) to transfer, move.

mutilant, e [mytilɑ̃, ɑ̃t] **adj** *opération* mutilating, mutilative.

mutilateur, -trice [mytilatœʀ, tʀis] (*littér*) 1 **adj** mutilating, mutilative. 2 **nm,f** mutilator.

mutilation [mytilasjɔ̃] **nf** *[corps]* mutilation, maiming; *[texte, statue, arbre]* mutilation. ~ **volontaire** self-inflicted injury.

mutilé, e [mytile] (**ptp de mutiler**) **nm,f** (*infirme*) cripple, disabled person. **les (grands)** ~**s** the (badly *ou* severely) disabled; ~ **de la face** disfigured person; ~ **de guerre** disabled ex-serviceman; ~ **du travail** disabled worker.

mutiler [mytile] 1 **vt** *personne* to mutilate, maim; *tableau, statue, paysage, arbre* to mutilate, deface; *texte* to mutilate. **gravement mutilé** badly disabled; **être mutilé des deux jambes** to have lost both legs; **se** ~ **(volontairement)** to injure o.s. (on purpose), inflict an injury on o.s.

mutin, e [mytɛ̃, in] 1 **adj** (*espiègle*) mischievous, impish. 2 **nm** (*Mil, Naut*) mutineer; (*gén: révolté*) rebel.

mutiné, e [mytine] (**ptp de se mutiner**) 1 **adj** *marin, soldat* mutinous. 2 **nm** (*Mil, Naut*) mutineer; (*gén*) rebel.

mutiner (se) [mytine] 1 **vpr** (*Mil, Naut*) to mutiny; (*gén*) to rebel, revolt.

mutinerie [mytinʀi] **nf** (*Mil, Naut*) mutiny; (*gén*) rebellion, revolt.

mutisme [mytism] **nm** a silence. **la presse observe un** ~ **total** the press is maintaining a complete silence *ou* blackout on the subject. b (*Méd*) dumbness, muteness; (*Psych*) mutism.

mutité [mytite] **nf** (*Méd*) muteness.

mutualisme [mytɥalism] **nm** mutual (benefit) insurance system.

mutualiste [mytɥalist] 1 **adj** mutualistic. 2 **nmf** mutualist.

mutualité [mytɥalite] **nf** a (*système d'entraide*) mutual (benefit) insurance system. b (*réciprocité*) mutuality.

mutuel, -elle [mytɥɛl] 1 **adj** (*réciproque*) mutual; *voir* **pari.** 2 **mutuelle nf** mutual benefit society, mutual (benefit) insurance company, ≃ Friendly Society (*Brit*). **payer sa cotisation à la** ~**le** ≃ to pay one's insurance premium (*for back-up health cover*).

mutuellement [mytɥɛlmɑ̃] **adv** one another, each other. ~ **ressenti** mutually felt; **s'aider** ~ to give each other mutual help, help one another.

mycélium [miseljɔm] **nm** mycelium.

mycénien, -ienne [misenjɛ̃, jɛn] 1 **adj** Mycenaean. 2 **nm,f: M**~**(ne)** Mycenaean.

mycologie [mikɔlɔʒi] **nf** mycology.

mycologique [mikɔlɔʒik] **adj** mycologic(al).

mycologue [mikɔlɔg] **nmf** mycologist.

mycose [mikoz] **nf** mycosis. **la** ~ **du pied** athlete's foot.

myéline [mjelin] **nf** myelin.

myélite [mjelit] **nf** myelitis.

mygale [migal] **nf** trap-door spider.

myocarde [mjɔkaʀd] **nm** myocardium; *voir* **infarctus.**

myopathe [mjɔpat] **nmf** myopathic.

myopathie [mjɔpati] **nf** myopathy.

myope [mjɔp] **adj** short-sighted, near-sighted, myopic (SPÉC). ~ **comme une taupe*** (as) blind as a bat*.

myopie [mjɔpi] **nf** short-sightedness, near-sightedness, myopia (SPÉC).

myosotis [mjɔzɔtis] **nm** forget-me-not.

myriade [miʀjad] **nf** myriad.

myriapode [miʀjapɔd] **nm** myriapod. ~**s** Myriapoda.

myrmidon [miʀmidɔ̃] **nm** († *péj: nabot*) pipsqueak*.

myrrhe [miʀ] **nf** myrrh.

myrte [miʀt] **nm** myrtle.

myrtille [miʀtij] **nf** bilberry (*Brit*), blueberry (*US*), whortleberry.

mystère [mistɛʀ] **nm** a (*énigme, dissimulation*) mystery. **pas tant de** ~**(s)!** don't be so mysterious! *ou* secretive!; **faire (un)** ~ **de** to make a mystery out of; **elle en fait grand ~** she makes a big mystery of it; **il restera un ~ pour moi** he'll always be a mystery *ou* a closed book to me; **~ (et boule de gomme*)!** who knows!, search me!* **b** (*Littérat, Rel*) mystery, mystery play. **les ~s du Moyen Âge** the mediaeval mystery plays; **le ~ de la passion** the Mystery of the Passion. **c** (*glace*) ® *ice-cream with a meringue centre, decorated with chopped hazelnuts.*

mystérieusement [misteʀjøzmɑ̃] adv mysteriously.

mystérieux, -ieuse [misteʀjø, jøz] adj (*secret, bizarre*) mysterious; (*cachottier*) secretive.

mysticisme [mistisism] nm mysticism.

mystificateur, -trice [mistifikatœʀ, tʀis] **1** adj: **j'ai reçu un coup de fil ~** I had a phone call which was a hoax; **tenir des propos ~s à qn** to say things to trick sb. **2** nm,f (*farceur*) hoaxer, practical joker.

mystification [mistifikasjɔ̃] nf (*farce*) hoax, practical joke; (*péj: mythe*) myth.

mystifier [mistifje] **7** vt to fool, take in, bamboozle*.

mystique [mistik] **1** adj mystic(al). **2** nmf (*personne*) mystic. **3** nf (*science, pratiques*) mysticism; (*péj: vénération*) blind belief (*de* in). **avoir la ~ du travail** to have a blind belief in work.

mystiquement [mistikmɑ̃] adv mystically.

mythe [mit] nm (*gén*) myth.

mythique [mitik] adj mythical.

mythologie [mitɔlɔʒi] nf mythology.

mythologique [mitɔlɔʒik] adj mythological.

mythomane [mitɔman] adj, nmf mythomaniac.

mythomanie [mitɔmani] nf mythomania.

myxomatose [miksomatoz] nf myxomatosis.

N

N¹, n [ɛn] **nm** (*lettre*) N, n; (*Math*) n.
N² (**abrév de Nord**) N.
n' [n] *voir* **ne.**
na [na] **excl** (*langage enfantin*) so there! **je n'en veux pas, ~!** I don't want any, so there!
nabab [nabab] **nm** (*Hist ou † ou littér*) nabob.
nabot, e [nabo, ɔt] 1 **adj** dwarfish, tiny. 2 **nm,f** (*péj*) dwarf, midget.
nabuchodonosor [nabykɔdɔnɔzɔʀ] **nm** (*bouteille*) nebuchadnezzar. **N~** Nebuchadnezzar.
nacelle [nasɛl] **nf** *[ballon]* nacelle; *[landau]* carriage; *[engin spatial]* pod; (*littér: bateau*) skiff.
nacre [nakʀ] **nf** mother-of-pearl.
nacré, e [nakʀe] (**ptp de nacrer**) **adj** iridescent, nacreous (*littér*); *vernis à ongles* pearlized.
nacrer [nakʀe] [1] **vt** (*iriser*) to cast a pearly sheen over; (*Tech*) to give a pearly gloss to.
nadir [nadiʀ] **nm** nadir.
nævus [nevys], **pl nævi** [nevi] **nm** naevus.
Nagasaki [nagazaki] **n** Nagasaki.
nage [naʒ] **nf** a (*activité*) swimming; (*manière*) stroke, style of swimming. **~ sur le dos** backstroke; **~ indienne** sidestroke; **~ libre** freestyle; **faire un 100 m ~ libre** to swim a 100 m (in) freestyle; **~ sous-marine** underwater swimming, skin diving; **~ de vitesse** speed stroke; **~ synchronisée** synchronized swimming.

b **à la ~: se sauver à la ~** to swim away *ou* off; **gagner la rive/traverser une rivière à la ~** to swim to the bank/across a river; **faire traverser son chien à la ~** to get one's dog to swim across; (*Culin*) **homard/écrevisses** *etc* **à la ~** lobster/crayfish *etc* (cooked) in a court-bouillon.

c **il était tout en ~** he was pouring with sweat *ou* bathed in sweat; **cela m'a mis en ~** that made me sweat; **ne te mets pas en ~** don't get yourself in a lather.

d (*Naut*) **~ à couple/en pointe** rowing two abreast/in staggered pairs; *voir* **chef.**

nageoire [naʒwaʀ] **nf** *[poisson]* fin; *[phoque etc]* flipper. **~ anale/dorsale/ventrale** anal/dorsal/ventral fin; **~ caudale** *[poisson]* caudal fin; *[baleine]* tail flukes.
nager [naʒe] [3] 1 **vi** a *[personne, poisson]* to swim; *[objet]* to float. **elle nage bien** she's a good swimmer; **~ comme un fer à repasser*/comme un poisson** to swim like a brick/like a fish; (*fig*) **~ entre deux eaux** to sit on the fence; **la viande nage dans la graisse** the meat is swimming in fat; **attention, tes manches nagent dans la soupe** look out, your sleeves are dipping *ou* getting in the soup; **on nageait dans le sang** the place was swimming in *ou* with blood, the place was awash with blood; *voir* **apprendre, savoir.**

b (*fig*) **il nage dans la joie** he is overjoyed, his joy knows no bounds; **~ dans l'opulence** to be rolling in money*; **il nage dans ses vêtements** his clothes drown him; **on nage dans l'absurdité/le grotesque dans ce film** this film is totally ridiculous/grotesque; **en allemand, je nage complètement*** I'm completely at sea* *ou* lost in German.

c (*Naut*) to row. **~ à couple** to row two abreast; **~ en pointe** to row in staggered pairs.

2 **vt** to swim. **~ la brasse/le 100 mètres** to swim breast-stroke/the 100 metres.

nageur, -euse [naʒœʀ, øz] **nm,f** swimmer; (*rameur*) rower. (*Mil*) **~ de combat** naval frogman.
naguère [nagɛʀ] **adv** (*frm*) (*il y a peu de temps*) not long ago, a short while ago, of late; (*autrefois*) formerly.
naïade [najad] **nf** (*Bot, Myth*) naïad; (*hum, littér*) nymph.
naïf, naïve [naif, naiv] 1 **adj** *personne* (*ingénu*) innocent, naïve; (*crédule*) naïve, gullible; *réponse, foi, gaieté* naïve. (*Art*) **peintre/art ~** naïve painter/art. 2 **nm,f** gullible fool, innocent. **vous me prenez pour un ~** you must think I'm a gullible fool *ou* a complete innocent.
nain, e [nɛ̃, nɛn] 1 **adj** dwarfish, dwarf (*épith*). **chêne/haricot ~** dwarf oak/runner bean; (*Astron*) **étoile ~e** dwarf star. 2 **nm,f** dwarf. (*Cartes*) **le ~ jaune** pope Joan.
Nairobi [neʀobi] **n** Nairobi.
naissain [nɛsɛ̃] **nm** spat.
naissance [nɛsɑ̃s] **nf** a *[personne, animal]* birth. **à la ~** at birth; **il est aveugle/muet/sourd de ~** he has been blind/dumb/deaf from birth, he was born blind/dumb/deaf; **français de ~** French by birth; **chez lui, c'est de ~*** he was born like that; **nouvelle ~** new arrival *ou* baby; **~ double** birth of twins; **~ multiple** multiple birth; *voir* **contrôle, extrait, limitation** *etc.*

b (*frm: origine, source*) **de ~ obscure/illustre** of obscure/illustrious birth; **de haute** *ou* **bonne ~** of high birth; **peu importe sa ~** no matter what his birth *ou* parentage (is).

c (*point de départ*) *[rivière]* source; *[langue, ongles]* root; *[cou, colonne]* base. **à la ~ des cheveux** at the roots of the hair.

d (*littér: commencement*) *[printemps, monde, idée, amour]* dawn, birth. **la ~ du jour** daybreak.

e (*loc*) **prendre ~** *[projet, idée]* to originate, take form; *[rivière]* to rise, originate; *[soupçon, sentiment]* to arise, take form; **donner ~ à** *enfant* to give birth to; *rumeurs, sentiment* to give rise to.

naissant, e [nɛsɑ̃, ɑ̃t] **adj** (*littér, Chim*) nascent.
naître [nɛtʀ] [59] 1 **vi** a *[personne, animal]* to be born. **quand l'enfant doit-il ~?** when is the child to be born? when is the child due?; **il vient tout juste de ~** he has only just been born, he is just newly born; **X est né** *ou* **X naquit** (*frm*) **le 4 mars** X was born on March 4; **l'homme naît libre** man is born free; **il est né poète** he is a born *ou* natural poet; **l'enfant qui naît aveugle/infirme** the child who is born blind/disabled *ou* a cripple; **l'enfant qui va ~, l'enfant à ~** the unborn child; **l'enfant qui vient de ~** the newborn child; **en naissant** at birth; **prématuré né à 7 mois** baby born prematurely at 7 months, premature baby born at 7 months; **né sous le signe du Verseau** born under (the sign of) Aquarius; **enfant né de père inconnu** child of an unknown father; **Mme Durand, née Dupont** Mme Durand, née Dupont; **être né de parents français** to be of French parentage, be born of French parents; **être né d'une mère anglaise** to be born of an English mother; (*Bible*) **un sauveur nous est né** a saviour is born to us; (*Méd*) **être né coiffé** to be born with a caul; (*fig*) **être né coiffé** *ou* **sous une bonne étoile** to be born lucky *ou* under a lucky star; (*fig*) **il n'est pas né d'hier** *ou* **de la dernière pluie** *ou* **de la dernière couvée** he wasn't born yesterday, he is not as green as he looks; *voir* **terme.**

b (*fig*) *[sentiment, craintes]* to arise, be born; *[idée, projet]* to be born; *[ville, industrie]* to spring up; *[jour]* to break; *[difficultés]* to arise; *[fleur, plante]* to burst forth. **la rivière naît au pied de ces collines** the river has its source *ou* rises at the foot of these hills; **je vis ~ un sourire sur son visage** I saw the beginnings of a smile on his face, I saw a smile creep over *ou* dawn on his face; **faire ~ une industrie/des difficultés** to create an industry/difficulties; **faire ~ des soupçons/le désir** to arouse suspicions/desire.

c **~ de** (*résulter de*) to spring from, arise from; **la haine née de ces querelles** the hatred arising from *ou* which sprang from these quarrels; **de cette rencontre naquit le mouvement qui ...** from this meeting sprang the movement which ... .

d (*être destiné à*) **il était né pour commander/pour la magistrature** he was born to command/to be a magistrate; **ils sont nés l'un pour l'autre** they were made for each other.

e (*littér: s'éveiller à*) **~ à l'amour/la poésie** to awaken to love/poetry.

2 **vb impers: il naît plus de filles que de garçons** there are more girls born than boys, more girls are born than boys; (*littér*) **il vous est né un fils** a son has been born to you (*littér*); *voir aussi* **né.**

naïvement [naivmɑ̃] **adv** (*voir* **naïf**) innocently; naïvely.
naïveté [naivte] **nf** (*voir* **naïf**) innocence; naïvety, gullibility. **il a eu la ~ de le croire** he was naïve enough to believe him (*ou* it).
naja [naʒa] **nm** cobra.
Namibie [namibi] **nf** Namibia.

namibien, -ienne [namibjɛ̃, jɛn] 1 adj Namibian. 2 nm,f: **N~(ne)** Namibian.
nana* [nana] nf *(femme)* bird‡ *(Brit)*, chick‡.
nanan* [nanɑ̃] nm: **c'est du ~** *(agréable)* it's a bit of all right*; *(facile)* it's a walkover* *ou* a doddle* *(Brit)*; *(succulent)* it's scrumptious*.
nanar* [nanaʀ] nm *(péj)* *(objet invendable)* piece of junk. *(film démodé)* **~ des années 30** second-rate film from the 1930s.
nanisme [nanism] nm dwarfism, nanism *(SPÉC)*.
Nankin [nɑ̃kɛ̃] n *(ville)* Nanking.
nankin [nɑ̃kɛ̃] nm *(tissu)* nankeen.
nano... [nano] préf nano... .
nanoseconde [nanos(ə)gɔ̃d] nf nanosecond.
nantais, e [nɑ̃tɛ, ɛz] 1 adj of *ou* from Nantes. 2 nm,f: **N~(e)** inhabitant *ou* native of Nantes.
nanti, e [nɑ̃ti] (ptp de **nantir**) adj rich, affluent, well-to-do. **les ~s** the rich, the affluent, the well-to-do.
nantir [nɑ̃tiʀ] [2] 1 vt († *Jur*) *créancier* to secure. *(fig, littér: munir)* **~ qn de** to provide sb with. 2 **se nantir** vpr († *Jur*) to secure o.s. *(fig, littér)* **se ~ de** to provide o.s. with, equip o.s. with.
nantissement [nɑ̃tismɑ̃] nm *(Jur)* security.
napalm [napalm] nm napalm.
naphtaline [naftalin] nf *(antimite)* mothballs *(pl)*.
naphte [naft] nm naphtha.
Naples [napl] n Naples.
Napoléon [napɔleɔ̃] nm Napoleon.
napoléon [napɔleɔ̃] nm *(Fin)* napoleon.
napoléonien, -ienne [napɔleɔnjɛ̃, jɛn] adj Napoleonic.
napolitain, e [napɔlitɛ̃, ɛn] 1 adj Neapolitan. 2 nm,f: **N~(e)** Neapolitan.
nappage [napaʒ] nm *(Culin)* topping.
nappe [nap] 1 nf *[table]* tablecloth. **~ de gaz/de pétrole** *etc* layer of gas/oil *etc*; **~ d'eau** sheet *ou* expanse of water; **mettre la ~** to put the tablecloth on. 2 comp ▸**nappe d'autel** altar cloth ▸**nappe de brouillard** blanket *ou* layer of fog; **des nappes de brouillard** fog patches ▸**nappe de charriage** nappe ▸**nappe de feu** sheet of flame ▸**nappe de mazout** oil slick ▸**nappe phréatique** ground water.
napper [nape] [1] vt *(Culin)* to top *(de* with). **nappé de chocolat** topped with chocolate, with a chocolate topping.
napperon [napʀɔ̃] nm doily, tablemat; *(pour vase, lampe etc)* mat.
narcisse [naʀsis] nm *(Bot)* narcissus; *(péj: égocentrique)* narcissus, narcissistic individual. *(Myth)* **N~** Narcissus.
narcissique [naʀsisik] 1 adj narcissistic. 2 nmf narcissist.
narcissisme [naʀsisism] nm narcissism.
narcodollars [naʀkodɔlaʀ] nmpl drug money *(usually in dollars)*. **3 000 000 de ~** 3,000,000 dollars' worth of drug money.
narcose [naʀkoz] nf narcosis.
narcotique [naʀkɔtik] adj, nm narcotic.
narcotrafic [naʀkotʀafik] nm drug trafficking.
narcotrafiquant, e [naʀkotʀafikɑ̃, ɑ̃t] nm,f drug trafficker.
narghileh [naʀgilɛ] nm hookah, nargileh, narghile.
narguer [naʀge] [1] vt *danger, traditions* to flout, thumb one's nose at; *personne* to deride, scoff at.
narguilé [naʀgile] nm = **narghileh**.
narine [naʀin] nf nostril.
narquois, e [naʀkwa, waz] adj *(railleur)* derisive, sardonic, mocking.
narquoisement [naʀkwazmɑ̃] adv derisively, sardonically, mockingly.
narrateur, -trice [naʀatœʀ, tʀis] nm,f narrator.
narratif, -ive [naʀatif, iv] adj narrative.
narration [naʀasjɔ̃] nf a *(NonC)* narration; *voir* **infinitif, présent**[1]. b *(récit)* narration, narrative, account; *(Scol: rédaction)* essay, composition; *(Rhétorique)* narration.
narrer [naʀe] [1] vt *(frm)* to narrate, relate.
narthex [naʀtɛks] nm narthex.
narval [naʀval] nm narwhal.
NASA [naza] nf (abrév de **National Aeronautics and Space Administration**) NASA.
nasal, e, mpl **-aux** [nazal, o] 1 adj nasal. 2 **nasale** nf nasal; *voir* **fosse**.
nasalisation [nazalizasjɔ̃] nf nasalization.
nasaliser [nazalize] [1] vt to nasalize.
nasalité [nazalite] nf nasality.
nase‡ [nɑz] adj a *(hors d'usage)* bust* *(attrib)*, kaput* *(attrib)*. **ma télé est ~** my TV has conked out‡ *ou* is bust*; **je suis ~** I'm knackered‡ *ou* shattered*. b *(fou)* cracked* *(attrib)*, touched* *(attrib)*.
naseau, pl **~x** [nazo] nm *[cheval, bœuf]* nostril.
nasillard, e [nazijaʀ, aʀd] adj *voix, instrument* nasal; *gramophone* whiny.
nasillement [nazijmɑ̃] nm *[voix]* (nasal) twang; *[microphone, gramophone]* whine; *[instrument]* nasal sound; *[canard]* quack.
nasiller [nazije] [1] 1 vt to say *(ou* sing *ou* intone) with a (nasal) twang. 2 vi *[personne]* to have a (nasal) twang, speak with *ou* in a nasal voice; *[instrument]* to give a whiny *ou* twangy sound; *[microphone, gramophone]* to whine; *[canard]* to quack.
Nassau [naso] n Nassau.
nasse [nɑs] nf hoop net.
Natal [natal] nm Natal.
natal, e, mpl **~s** [natal] adj native. **ma maison ~e** the house where I was born; **ma terre ~e** my native soil.
nataliste [natalist] adj *politique* which supports a rising birth rate.
natalité [natalite] nf: **(taux de) ~** birth rate.
natation [natasjɔ̃] nf swimming. **~ artistique** *ou* **synchronisée** synchronized swimming.
natatoire [natatwaʀ] adj swimming *(épith)*; *voir* **vessie**.
natif, -ive [natif, iv] adj, nm,f *(gén)* native. **~ de Nice** native of Nice; **locuteur ~** native speaker.
nation [nasjɔ̃] nf *(pays, peuple)* nation. **les N~s Unies** the United Nations; *voir* **société**.
national, e, mpl **-aux** [nasjɔnal, o] 1 adj *(gén)* national; *économie, monnaie* domestic. **au plan ~ et international** at home and abroad, at the national and international level; *(Écon)* **entreprise ~e** state-owned company; **grève ~e** nationwide *ou* national strike; **obsèques ~es** state funeral; **(route) ~e** ≃ "A" *ou* trunk road *(Brit)*, state highway *(US)*; *voir* **assemblée, éducation, fête.** 2 **nationaux** nmpl *(citoyens)* nationals. 3 comp ▸**national-socialisme** nm national socialism ▸**national(e)-socialiste** adj, nm,f (mpl **nationaux-socialistes**) national socialist.
nationalement [nasjɔnalmɑ̃] adv nationally.
nationalisable [nasjɔnalizabl] adj targetted for nationalization.
nationalisation [nasjɔnalizasjɔ̃] nf nationalization.
nationaliser [nasjɔnalize] [1] vt to nationalize. **les (entreprises) nationalisées** the nationalized companies.
nationalisme [nasjɔnalism] nm nationalism.
nationaliste [nasjɔnalist] adj, nmf nationalist.
nationalité [nasjɔnalite] nf nationality. **les personnes de ~ française** French citizens.
nativisme [nativism] nm *(Philos)* nativism.
nativiste [nativist] adj *(Philos)* nativistic.
nativité [nativite] nf nativity; *(Art)* (painting of the) nativity, nativity scene.
natte [nat] nf *(tresse)* plait, braid; *(paillasse)* mat, matting *(NonC)*. **se faire des ~s** to plait *ou* braid one's hair, put one's hair in plaits *ou* braids.
natter [nate] [1] vt *cheveux* to plait, braid; *laine etc* to weave.
naturalisation [natyʀalizasjɔ̃] nf *(Bot, Ling, Pol)* naturalization; *[animaux morts]* stuffing; *[plantes séchées]* pressing, drying.
naturalisé, e [natyʀalize] (ptp de **naturaliser**) 1 adj: **Français ~** naturalized Frenchman; **il est ~ (français)** he's a naturalized Frenchman. 2 nm,f naturalized person.
naturaliser [natyʀalize] [1] vt *(Bot, Ling, Pol)* to naturalize; *animal mort* to stuff; *plante coupée* to preserve *(with glycerine)*. **se faire ~ français** to become a naturalized Frenchman.
naturalisme [natyʀalism] nm naturalism.
naturaliste [natyʀalist] 1 adj naturalistic. 2 nmf *(Littérat, Sci)* naturalist; *(empailleur)* taxidermist; *(pour les plantes)* flower-preserver.
nature [natyʀ] 1 nf a *(caractère)* *[personne, substance, sentiment]* nature. **la ~ humaine** human nature; **c'est une** *ou* **il est de** *ou* **d'une ~ arrogante** he has an *ou* he is of an arrogant nature; **il est arrogant de** *ou* **par ~** he is naturally arrogant *ou* arrogant by nature; **ce n'est pas dans sa ~** it is not (in) his nature *(d'être* to be); **c'est/ce n'est pas de ~ à arranger les choses** it's liable to/not likely to make things easier; **il n'est pas de ~ à accepter** he's not the sort of person who would agree; **avoir une heureuse ~** to have a happy nature, be of a happy disposition; **c'est dans la ~ des choses** it's in the nature of things; *voir* **habitude, second.**
b *(monde physique, principe fondamental)* **la ~** nature; **vivre (perdu) dans la ~** to live (out) in the country *ou* in the wilds *ou* at the back of beyond *(Brit)* *ou* in the boondocks *(US)*; **en pleine ~** in the middle of nowhere; **la ~ a horreur du vide** nature abhors a vacuum; **laisser agir la ~** to leave it to nature, let nature take its course; **lâcher qn dans la ~*** *(sans indication)* to send sb off without any directions; *(pour commettre un crime)* to let sb loose; **disparaître dans la ~*** *[personne]* to vanish into thin air; *[ballon]* to disappear into the undergrowth *ou* bushes; **actions/crimes/vices/goûts contre ~** unnatural acts/crimes/vices/tastes, acts/crimes/vices/tastes which go against nature *ou* which are contrary to nature; *voir* **force, retour.**
c *(sorte)* nature, kind, sort. **de toute(s) ~(s)** of all kinds, of every kind.
d *(Art)* **peindre d'après ~** to paint from life; **plus grand que ~** more than life-size, larger than life; **~ morte** still life; *voir* **grandeur.**
e *(Fin)* **en ~** *payer, don* in kind.
2 adj inv a **café ~** black coffee; **eau ~** plain water; **thé ~** tea without milk, plain tea; **omelette/crêpe ~** plain omelette/pancake; **yaourt ~** natural yoghurt; **riz ~** (plain) boiled rice; **boire le whisky ~** to drink whisky neat *ou* straight; **manger les fraises** *etc* **~** to eat strawberries *etc* without anything on them.
b **il est ~!*** he is so natural!, he is completely uninhibited!
naturel, -elle [natyʀɛl] 1 adj a *caractère, frontière, produit, phénomène* natural; *besoins, fonction* bodily *(épith)*; *soie, laine* pure. **aliments/produits ~s** natural *ou* organic foods/products.
b *(inné)* natural. **son intelligence ~le** his natural intelligence, his native wit; **elle a un talent ~ pour le piano** playing the piano comes

naturally to her, she has a natural talent for the piano.

c (*normal, habituel*) natural. **avec sa voix ~le** in his normal voice; **c'est un geste ~ chez lui** it's a natural gesture *ou* quite a normal gesture for him, this gesture comes (quite) naturally to him; **votre indignation est bien ~le** your indignation is quite *ou* very natural *ou* understandable; **je vous remercie! – c'est (tout) ~** thank you! – don't mention it *ou* you're welcome; **ne me remerciez pas, c'est bien *ou* tout ~** don't thank me, anybody would have done the same *ou* it was the obvious thing to do; **il est bien ~ qu'on en vienne à cette décision** it's only natural that this decision should have been reached; **il trouve ça tout ~** he finds it the most natural thing in the world *ou* perfectly normal.

d (*simple, spontané*) *voix, style, personne* natural, unaffected. **elle sait rester très ~le** she manages to stay very natural; **être ~ sur les photos** to be very natural in photos, take a good photo.

e (*Mus*) natural.

2 **nm** a (*caractère*) nature, disposition. **être d'un *ou* avoir un bon ~** to have a good *ou* happy nature *ou* disposition; *voir* **chasser.**

b (*absence d'affectation*) naturalness. **avec (beaucoup de) ~** (completely) naturally; **il manque de ~** he's not very natural, he has a rather self-conscious manner.

c (*indigène*) native.

d (*loc*) **au ~** (*Culin: sans assaisonnement*) water-packed; (*en réalité*) **elle est mieux en photo qu'au ~** she's better in photos than in real life.

naturellement [natyʀɛlmɑ̃] **adv** a (*sans artifice, normalement*) naturally; (*avec aisance*) naturally, unaffectedly. b (*bien sûr*) naturally, of course.

naturisme [natyʀism] **nm** (*nudisme*) naturism; (*Philos*) naturism; (*Méd*) naturopathy.

naturiste [natyʀist] **adj, nmf** (*nudiste*) naturist; (*Philos*) naturist; (*Méd*) naturopath.

naufrage [nofʀaʒ] **nm** a *[bateau]* wreck. **le ~ de ce navire** the wreck of this ship; **un ~** a shipwreck; **faire ~** *[bateau]* to be wrecked; *[marin etc]* to be shipwrecked. b (*fig: déchéance*) *[ambitions, réputation]* ruin, ruination; *[projet, pays]* foundering, ruination. **sauver du ~** *personne* to save from disaster; *argent, biens* to salvage (from the wreckage).

naufragé, e [nofʀaʒe] 1 **adj** *marin* shipwrecked; *bateau* wrecked. 2 **nm,f** shipwrecked person; (*sur une île*) castaway. (*fig*) **les ~s de la croissance économique** the casualties of economic growth.

naufrageur, -euse [nofʀaʒœʀ, øz] **nm,f** (*lit, fig*) wrecker.

nauséabond, e [nozeabɔ̃, ɔ̃d] **adj** (*lit*) putrid, evil-smelling, foul-smelling, nauseating, sickening; (*fig*) nauseating, sickening.

nausée [noze] **nf** (*sensation*) nausea (*NonC*); (*haut-le-cœur*) bout of nausea. **avoir la ~** to feel sick; **avoir des ~s** to have bouts of nausea; (*lit, fig*) **ça me donne la ~** it makes me (feel) sick.

nauséeux, -euse [nozeø, øz] **adj** nauseous.

nautile [notil] **nm** (*Zool*) nautilus.

nautique [notik] **adj** *science* nautical. **sports ~s** water sports; **fête ~** water festival; **ballet ~** synchronized swimming; **club ~** water-sports club; *voir* **ski.**

nautisme [notism] **nm** water sport(s).

naval, e, **mpl ~s** [naval] **adj** *combat, base* naval; *industrie* shipbuilding. **école ~e** naval college; *voir* **chantier, construction, force.**

navarin [navaʀɛ̃] **nm** navarin lamb, ≃ mutton stew (*Brit*).

navarrais, e [navaʀɛ, ɛz] 1 **adj** Navarrian. 2 **nm,f: N~(e)** Navarrian.

Navarre [navaʀ] **nf** Navarre.

navet [navɛ] **nm** a (*légume*) turnip; *voir* **sang.** b (*péj*) (*film*) rubbishy *ou* third-rate film; (*roman*) rubbishy *ou* third-rate novel; (*tableau*) daub. **c'est un ~** it's (a piece of) rubbish, it's tripe, it's a turkey* (*US*).

navette[1] [navɛt] **nf** a (*Tex*) shuttle. b (*service de transport*) shuttle (service). **~ diplomatique** diplomatic shuttle; **faire la ~ entre** *[banlieusard, homme d'affaires]* to commute between; *[véhicule]* to operate a shuttle (service) between; *[bateau]* to ply between; *[projet de loi, circulaire]* to be sent backwards and forwards between; **elle fait la ~ entre la cuisine et la chambre** she comes and goes between the kitchen and the bedroom; **faire faire la ~ à qn/qch** to have sb/sth going back and forth (*entre* between). c (*Espace*) **~ spatiale** space shuttle.

navette[2] [navɛt] **nf** (*Bot*) rape.

navetteur, -euse [navetœʀ, øz] **nm,f** (*Belgique*) commuter.

navigabilité [navigabilite] **nf** *[rivière]* navigability; *[bateau]* seaworthiness; *[avion]* airworthiness.

navigable [navigabl] **adj** *rivière* navigable.

navigant, e [navigɑ̃, ɑ̃t] **adj, nm: le personnel ~, les ~s** (*Aviat*) flying personnel; (*Naut*) seagoing personnel.

navigateur, -trice [navigatœʀ, tʀis] **nm,f** (*littér, Naut: marin*) navigator, sailor; (*Aut, Aviat: copilote*) navigator. **~ solitaire** single-handed sailor.

navigation [navigasjɔ̃] **nf** a (*Naut*) sailing (*NonC*), navigation (*NonC*); (*trafic*) (sea) traffic (*NonC*); (*pilotage*) navigation, sailing (*NonC*). **les récifs rendent la ~ dangereuse/difficile** the reefs make sailing *ou* navigation dangerous/difficult; **canal ouvert/fermé *ou* interdit à la ~** canal open/closed to shipping *ou* ships; **~ côtière/intérieure** coastal/inland navigation; **~ de plaisance** (pleasure) sailing; **~ à voiles** sailing, yachting; **compagnie de ~** shipping company; **terme de ~** nautical term.

b (*Aviat*) (*trafic*) (air) traffic (*NonC*); (*pilotage*) navigation, flying (*NonC*). **~ aérienne** aerial navigation; **compagnie de ~ aérienne** airline company; **~ spatiale** space navigation.

naviguer [navige] [1] **vi** a (*voyager*) *[bateau, passager, marin]* to sail; *[avion, passager, pilote]* to fly. **~ à la voile** to sail; **ce bateau/marin a beaucoup/n'a jamais navigué** this ship/sailor has been to sea a lot *ou* has done a lot of sailing/has never been to sea *ou* has never sailed; **bateau en état de ~** seaworthy ship; **~ à 800 mètres d'altitude** to fly at an altitude of 800 metres.

b (*piloter*) *[marin]* to navigate, sail; *[aviateur]* to navigate, fly. **~ au compas/aux instruments/à l'estime** to navigate by (the) compass/by instruments/by dead reckoning; **~ à travers Glasgow** (*en voiture*) to find one's way through *ou* make one's way across Glasgow; (*fig*) **pour réussir ici, il faut savoir ~** to succeed here you need to know how to get around *ou* you need to know the ropes.

c (*: *errer*) **c'est un type qui a beaucoup navigué** he's a guy* who has been around a lot *ou* who has knocked about quite a bit*; **après avoir navigué pendant une heure entre les rayons du supermarché** after having spent an hour finding one's way around the supermarket shelves; **le dossier a navigué de bureau en bureau** the file found its way from office to office, the file went the rounds of the offices.

navire [naviʀ] **nm** (*bateau*) ship; (*Jur*) vessel. **~ amiral** flagship; **~-citerne** tanker; **~ marchand *ou* de commerce** merchant ship, merchantman; **~-école** training ship; **~ de guerre** warship; **~-hôpital** hospital ship; **~-jumeau** sister ship; **~-usine** factory ship.

navrant, e [navʀɑ̃, ɑ̃t] **adj** (*voir* **navrer**) distressing, upsetting; (most) annoying. **tu es ~!** you're hopeless!

navré, e [navʀe] (**ptp de navrer**) **adj** sorry (*de* to). **je suis (vraiment) ~** I'm (so *ou* terribly) sorry; **~ de vous décevoir mais ...** sorry to disappoint you but ...; **avoir l'air ~** (*pour s'excuser, compatir*) to look sorry; (*d'une nouvelle*) to look distressed *ou* upset; **d'un ton ~** (*pour s'excuser*) in an apologetic tone, apologetically; (*pour compatir*) in a sympathetic tone; (*par l'émotion*) in a distressed *ou* an upset voice.

navrer [navʀe] [1] **vt** (*désoler*) *[spectacle, conduite, nouvelle]* to grieve, distress, upset; *[contretemps, malentendu]* to annoy.

nazaréen, enne [nazaʀeɛ̃, ɛn] 1 **adj** Nazarene. 2 **nm,f: N~(ne)** Nazarene.

Nazareth [nazaʀɛt] **n** Nazareth.

naze‡ [nɑz] **adj** = **nase**‡.

nazi, e [nazi] **adj, nm,f** Nazi.

nazisme [nazism] **nm** Nazism.

N.B. [ɛnbe] **nm** (**abrév de nota bene**) N.B.

N.-D. (**abrév de Notre-Dame**) *voir* **notre.**

N'Djamena [nʒamena] **n** Ndjamena.

N.D.L.R. (**abrév de note de la rédaction**) *voir* **note.**

ne [n(ə)] **adv nég, n'** *devant voyelles et h muet* a (*valeur nég: avec nég avant ou après*) **il n'a rien dit** he didn't say anything, he said nothing; **elle ~ nous a pas vus** she didn't *ou* did not see us, she hasn't *ou* has not seen us; **personne *ou* (*frm*) nul n'a compris** nobody *ou* no one *ou* not a soul understood; **il n'y a aucun mal à ça** there's no harm *ou* there's nothing wrong in that; **il n'est pas du tout *ou* nullement idiot** he's no fool, he is by no means stupid; **s'il n'est jamais monté en avion ce n'est pas qu'il n'en ait jamais eu l'occasion** if he has never been up in an aeroplane it's not that he has never had the opportunity *ou* it's not for lack of opportunities; **je n'ai pas *ou* († *ou hum*) point d'argent** I have no money, I haven't (got) any money; **il ~ sait plus ce qu'il dit** he no longer knows what he's saying; **plus rien ~ l'intéresse, rien ~ l'intéresse plus** nothing interests him any more, he's not interested in anything any more; **~ me dérangez pas** don't *ou* do not disturb me; **je ~ connais ni son fils ni sa fille** I know neither his son nor his daughter, I don't know (either) his son or his daughter; **je n'ai pas du tout *ou* aucunement l'intention de refuser** I have not the slightest *ou* least intention of refusing; **je n'ai guère le temps** I have scarcely *ou* hardly the time; **il ~ sait pas parler** he can't *ou* cannot speak; **pas un seul ~ savait sa leçon** not (a single) one (of them) knew his lesson.

b (*valeur nég: sans autre nég: gén littér*) **il ~ cesse de se plaindre** he's constantly complaining, he keeps on complaining, he does not stop complaining; **je ~ sais qui a eu cette idée** I do not know who had that idea; **elle ~ peut jouer du violon sans qu'un voisin (~) proteste** she cannot play her violin without some neighbour's objecting; **il n'a que faire de vos conseils** he has no use for your advice, he's not interested in your advice; **que n'a-t-il songé à me prévenir** if only he had thought to warn me; **n'était la situation internationale, il serait parti** had it not been for *ou* were it not for the international situation he would have left; **il n'est de paysage qui ~ soit maintenant gâché** nowadays not a patch of countryside remains unspoilt *ou* there is no unspoilt countryside left; **il n'est de jour qu'elle ~ se plaigne** not a day goes by but she complains (about something), not a day goes by without her complaining; **cela fait des années que je n'ai été au cinéma** it's years since I (last) went to the cinema; **il a vieilli depuis que je ~ l'ai vu** he has aged since I (last) saw him; **si je ~ me trompe** if I'm not mistaken; *voir*

cure[2], **empêcher, importer**[2].

c ~ ... **que** only; **elle n'a confiance qu'en nous** she trusts only us, she only has confidence in us; **c'est mauvais de ~ manger que des conserves** it is bad to eat only tinned foods *ou* nothing but tinned foods; **il n'a que trop d'assurance** he is only too self-assured; **il n'a d'autre idée en tête que de se lancer dans la politique** his (one and) only thought is to embark upon politics; **il n'y a que lui pour dire des choses pareilles!** only he *ou* nobody but he would say such things!; **il n'y a pas que vous qui le dites!** you're not the only one who says so! *ou* to say this!; **et il n'y a pas que ça!** and that's not all!; *voir* **demander.**

d (*explétif sans valeur nég, gén omis dans la langue parlée*) **je crains** *ou* **j'ai peur** *ou* **j'appréhende qu'il ~ vienne** I am afraid *ou* I fear (that) he is coming *ou* (that) he will come; **je ~ doute pas/je ~ nie pas qu'il ~ soit compétent** I don't doubt/deny that he is competent; **empêche que les enfants ~ touchent aux animaux** stop the children touching *ou* prevent the children from touching the animals; **mangez avant que la viande ~ refroidisse** do eat before the meat gets cold; **j'irai la voir avant qu'il/à moins qu'il ~ pleuve** I shall go and see her before/unless it rains; **il est parti avant que je ~ l'aie remercié** he left before I had thanked him; **il est parti sans que je ~ l'aie remercié** he left without my having thanked him; **peu s'en faut qu'il n'ait oublié la réunion** he all but *ou* he very nearly forgot the meeting; **il est plus/moins malin qu'on ~ pense** he is more cunning than/not as cunning as you think.

né, e [ne] (**ptp de naître**) **adj, nm,f** born; (*fig: causé*) caused (*de* by), due (*de* to). **orateur-/acteur-~** born orator/actor; **bien/mal ~** of noble *ou* high/humble *ou* low birth; **Paul est son premier-/dernier-~** Paul is her first-/last-born *ou* her first/last child; **Mme Durand, ~e Dupont** Mme Durand née Dupont; *voir* **mort**[2], **naître, nouveau.**

néanmoins [neɑ̃mwɛ̃] **adv** (*pourtant*) nevertheless, yet. **il était malade, il est ~ venu** he was ill, (and) nevertheless *ou* (and) yet he came; **c'est incroyable mais ~ vrai** it's incredible but nonetheless true *ou* but it's true nevertheless; **il est agressif et ~ patient** he is aggressive yet patient, he is aggressive but nevertheless patient.

néant [neɑ̃] **nm: le ~** nothingness (*NonC*); **le ~ de la vie/de l'homme** the emptiness of life/man; **et après c'est le ~** then there's a total blank; **signes particuliers: ~** distinguishing marks: none; *voir* **réduire.**

Nébraska [nebʀaska] **nm** Nebraska.

nébuleuse[1] [nebyløz] **nf** (*Astron*) nebula.

nébuleusement [nebyløzmɑ̃] **adv** nebulously, vaguely.

nébuleux, -euse[2] [nebylø, øz] **adj** (*lit*) *ciel* cloudy, overcast; (*fig*) *écrivain* nebulous, obscure; *projet, idée, discours* nebulous, vague, woolly.

nébuliseur [nebylizœʀ] **nm** spray.

nébulosité [nebylozite] **nf** *[ciel]* cloud covering, nebulosity (*SPÉC*); *[discours]* obscureness, vagueness, woolliness.

nécessaire [nesesɛʀ] 1 **adj** a (*gén, Math, Philos*) necessary. **il est ~ de le faire** it needs to be done, it has (got) to be done, it must be done, it's necessary to do it; **il est ~ qu'on le fasse** we need to do it, we have (got) to do it, we must do it, it's necessary *ou* essential for us to do it; **est-ce (bien) ~ (de le faire)?** have we (really) got to (do it)?, do we (really) need *ou* have to (do it)?, is it (really) necessary (for us to do it)?; **non, ce n'est pas ~ (de le faire)** no, there's no need to (do it), no, you don't need *ou* have to (do it), it's not (really) necessary (for you to do it); **l'eau est ~ à la vie/aux hommes/pour vivre** water is necessary for life/to man/to live; **un bon repos vous est ~** you need a good rest; **cette attitude lui est ~ pour réussir** he has to have *ou* maintain this attitude to succeed; **cette attitude est ~ pour réussir** this is a necessary attitude *ou* this attitude is necessary *ou* needed if one wants to get on; **c'est une condition ~** it's a necessary condition (*pour faire* for doing; *de qch* for sth); **c'est une conséquence ~** it's a necessary consequence (*de qch* of sth); **avoir le talent/le temps/l'argent ~ (pour qch/pour faire)** to have the (necessary *ou* requisite) talent/time/money (for sth/to do), have the talent/time/money (required) (for sth/to do); **a-t-il les moyens ~s?** does he have the necessary *ou* requisite means?, does he have the means required?; **faire les démarches ~s** to take the necessary *ou* requisite steps.

b *personne* indispensable (*à* to). **se sentir ~** to feel indispensable.

2 **nm** a (*l'indispensable*) **as-tu emporté le ~?** have you got all *ou* everything we need?; **je n'ai pas le ~ pour le faire** I haven't got what's needed *ou* the necessary stuff to do it; **il peut faire froid, prenez le ~** it may be cold so take the necessary clothes *ou* so take what's needed to keep warm; **emporter le strict ~** to take the bare *ou* absolute necessities *ou* essentials; **il faut d'abord penser au ~** one must first consider the essentials; **manquer du ~** to lack the (basic) necessities of life; **faire le ~** to do what is necessary *ou* what has to be done; **j'ai fait le ~** I've settled it *ou* seen to it, I've done what was necessary; **je vais faire le ~ (pour que)** I'll see to it (that), I'll make the necessary arrangements (so that), I'll do the necessary* (so that).

b (*Philos*) **le ~** the necessary.

3 **comp ▸nécessaire à couture** (pocket) sewing kit **▸nécessaire à ongles** manicure set **▸nécessaire à ouvrage** = **nécessaire à couture ▸nécessaire de toilette** travel pack (of toiletries) **▸nécessaire de voyage** overnight bag, grip.

nécessairement [nesesɛʀmɑ̃] **adv** necessarily. **dois-je ~ m'en aller?** is it (really) necessary for me to go?, must I (really) go?, do I (really) have to go?; **passeras-tu par Londres? — oui, ~** will you go via London? — yes, it's unavoidable *ou* you have to; **il devra ~ s'y faire** he will (just) have to get used to it; **il ne m'a pas ~ vu** I (*ou* we *etc*) can't be sure (that) he saw me; **il y a ~ une raison** there must (needs) be a reason; **ce n'est pas ~ faux** it isn't necessarily wrong; **s'il s'y prend ainsi, il va ~ échouer** if he sets about it this way, he's bound to fail *ou* he'll inevitably fail; (*Philos*) **causes et effets sont liés ~** causes and effects are necessarily linked *ou* are of necessity linked.

nécessité [nesesite] **nf** a (*obligation*) necessity. **c'est une ~ absolue** it's an absolute necessity; **sévère sans ~** unnecessarily severe; **je ne vois pas la ~ de le faire** I don't see the necessity of doing that *ou* the need for (doing) that; **se trouver** *ou* **être dans la ~ de faire qch** to have no choice *ou* alternative but to do sth; **mettre qn dans la ~ de faire** to make it necessary for sb to do; **la ~ où je suis de faire cela** having no choice *ou* alternative but to do that; **la ~ d'être le lendemain à Paris nous fit partir de très bonne heure** the need to be *ou* our having to be in Paris the next day made us leave very early.

b **les ~s de la vie** the necessities *ou* essentials of life; **les ~s du service** the demands *ou* requirements of the job; **~s financières** (financial) liabilities; **articles de première ~** bare necessities *ou* essentials.

c (*Philos*) **la ~** necessity; **la ~ de mourir** the inevitability of death.

d (††: *pauvreté*) destitution. **être dans la ~** to be in need, be poverty-stricken.

e (*loc*) **je l'ai fait par ~** I did it because I had to *ou* because I had no choice; **faire de ~ vertu** to make a virtue of necessity; (*Prov*) **~ fait loi** necessity knows no law (*Prov*).

nécessiter [nesesite] [1] **vt** (*requérir*) to require, necessitate, make necessary, call for.

nécessiteux, -euse [nesesitø, øz] 1 **adj** needy, necessitous. 2 **nm,f** needy person. **les ~** the needy, the poor.

nec plus ultra [nɛkplysyltʀa] **nm: c'est le ~** it's the last word (*de* in).

nécrologie [nekʀɔlɔʒi] **nf** (*liste*) obituary column; (*notice biographique*) obituary.

nécrologique [nekʀɔlɔʒik] **adj** obituary (*épith*).

nécromancie [nekʀɔmɑ̃si] **nf** necromancy.

nécromancien, -ienne [nekʀɔmɑ̃sjɛ̃, jɛn] **nm,f** necromancer.

nécrophage [nekʀɔfaʒ] **adj** necrophagous.

nécrophile [nekʀɔfil] 1 **adj** necrophilic. 2 **nmf** necrophiliac.

nécrophilie [nekʀɔfili] **nf** necrophilia.

nécropole [nekʀɔpɔl] **nf** necropolis.

nécrose [nekʀoz] **nf** necrosis.

nécroser vt, se nécroser vpr [nekʀoze] [1] to necrose.

nectar [nɛktaʀ] **nm** (*Bot, Myth, boisson, fig*) nectar.

nectarine [nɛktaʀin] **nf** nectarine.

néerlandais, e [neɛʀlɑ̃dɛ, ɛz] 1 **adj** Dutch, of the Netherlands. 2 **nm** a **N~** Dutchman; **les N~** the Dutch. b (*Ling*) Dutch. 3 **Néerlandaise nf** Dutchwoman.

nef [nɛf] **nf** a (*Archit*) nave. **~ latérale** side aisle. b (†† *ou littér: bateau*) vessel, ship.

néfaste [nefast] **adj** (*nuisible*) harmful (*à* to); (*funeste*) ill-fated, unlucky. **cela lui fut ~** it had disastrous consequences for him.

nèfle [nɛfl] **nf** medlar. **des ~s!**‡ nothing doing!*, not likely!*

néflier [neflije] **nm** medlar (tree).

négateur, -trice [negatœʀ, tʀis] (*littér*) 1 **adj** given to denying, contradictory. 2 **nm,f** denier.

négatif, -ive [negatif, iv] 1 **adj** negative; *quantité, nombre* negative, minus (*épith*). **particule ~ive** negative particle. 2 **nm** (*Phot, Ling*) negative. **au ~** in the negative. 3 **adv: vous êtes prêts? — ~!*** are you ready? — negative!* 4 **négative nf: répondre par la ~ive** to reply in the negative; **dans la ~ive** if not.

négation [negasjɔ̃] **nf** (*gén*) negation; (*Ling*) negative. **double ~** double negative.

négativement [negativmɑ̃] **adv** negatively. **répondre ~** to reply in the negative.

négativisme [negativism] **nm** negativism, negativity.

négativité [negativite] **nf** (*Phys*) negativity; *[attitude]* negativeness, negativity.

négaton [negatɔ̃] **nm** negatron.

négligé, e [negliʒe] (**ptp de négliger**) 1 **adj** *épouse, ami* neglected; *personne, tenue* slovenly, sloppy; *ongles* uncared-for, neglected; *travail* slapdash, careless; *style* slipshod; *occasion* missed (*épith*). 2 **nm** (*laisser-aller*) slovenliness; (*vêtement*) négligée. **je suis en ~** I'm not smartly dressed; **il était en ~** he was casually dressed *ou* wearing casual clothes; **le ~ de sa tenue** the slovenliness of his dress.

négligeable [negliʒabl] **adj** (*gén*) negligible; *détail* unimportant, trivial, trifling; *adversaire* insignificant. **qui n'est pas ~, non ~** *facteur, élément* not inconsiderable; *adversaire, aide, offre* which (*ou* who) is not to be sneezed at; *détail, rôle* not insignificant; *voir* **quantité.**

négligemment [negliʒamɑ̃] **adv** (*sans soin*) carelessly, negligently, in a slovenly way; (*nonchalamment*) casually.

négligence [negliʒɑ̃s] **nf** (*manque de soin*) negligence, slovenliness; (*faute, erreur*) omission, act of negligence; (*Jur*) criminal negligence. **il**

est d'une (telle) ~! he's so careless!; **c'est une ~ de ma part** it's an oversight *ou* a careless mistake on my part; **par ~** out of carelessness; **~ (de style)** stylistic blunder, carelessness (*NonC*) of style.

négligent, e [neglizɑ̃, ɑ̃t] **adj** (*sans soin*) negligent, careless; (*nonchalant*) casual.

négliger [neglize] 3 1 **vt** a (*gén*) to neglect; *style, tenue* to be careless about; *conseil* to neglect, pay no attention *ou* no heed to, disregard; *occasion* to miss, fail to grasp, pass up*; *rhume, plaie* to ignore. **il néglige ses amis** he neglects his friends; **une plaie négligée peut s'infecter** a wound if neglected *ou* if left unattended can become infected, if you don't attend to a wound it can become infected; **ce n'est pas à ~** (*offre*) it's not to be sneezed at; (*difficulté*) it mustn't be overlooked; **rien n'a été négligé** nothing has been missed, no stone has been left unturned, nothing has been left to chance (*pour* to); **ne rien ~ pour réussir** to leave no stone unturned *ou* leave nothing to chance in an effort to succeed.

b (*ne pas prendre la peine de*) **~ de** to neglect to; **il a négligé de le faire** he did not bother *ou* he neglected to do it; **ne négligez pas de prendre vos papiers** be sure to *ou* don't neglect to take your papers.

2 **se négliger vpr** (*santé*) to neglect o.s., not to look after o.s.; (*tenue*) to neglect *ou* not to look after one's appearance.

négoce [negɔs] **nm** (†: *commerce*) trade, commerce, business. **faire du ~** to be in business; **faire du ~ avec un pays** to trade with a country; **dans mon ~** in my trade *ou* business; **il fait le ~ de** he trades *ou* deals in; **il tenait un ~ de fruits et légumes** he had a greengrocery business, he dealt in fruit and vegetables.

négociabilité [negɔsjabilite] **nf** negotiability.

négociable [negɔsjabl] **adj** negotiable.

négociant, e [negɔsjɑ̃, jɑ̃t] **nm,f** merchant. **~ en gros** wholesaler; **~ en vin** wine merchant.

négociateur, -trice [negɔsjatœr, tris] **nm,f** (*Comm, Pol*) negotiator.

négociation [negɔsjasjɔ̃] **nf** (*Comm, Pol*) negotiation. **engager des ~s** to enter into negotiations; **~s commerciales** trade talks.

négocier [negɔsje] 7 1 **vi** (*Pol*) to negotiate; (†† *Comm*) to trade. 2 **vt** (*Fin, Pol*) to negotiate. **~ un virage** to negotiate a bend.

nègre [nɛgr] 1 **nm** (†*** *indigène*) Negro***; (*péj: écrivain*) ghost (writer). **travailler comme un ~*** to work like a slave *ou* a nigger***; **~ blanc*** white Negro***; (*Culin*) **~ en chemise** chocolate and cream dessert. 2 **adj** a (†***) *tribu, art* Negro*** (*épith*). b *couleur* nigger brown (*Brit*), dark brown; *voir* **petit**.

négresse†*** [negrɛs] **nf** Negress***. **~ blanche** white Negress***; **~ à plateaux** Negress*** with lip disc.

négrier [negrije] **nm** (*marchand d'esclaves*) slave trader; (*fig péj: patron*) slave driver*. **(bateau) ~** slave ship; **(capitaine) ~** slave-ship captain.

négrillon* [negrijɔ̃] **nm** piccaninny†***, Negro boy***.

négrillonne* [negrijɔn] **nf** piccaninny†***, Negro girl***.

négritude [negrityd] **nf** negritude.

négro†*** [negro] **nm** nigger***, negro***.

négroïde* [negrɔid] **adj** negroid***.

negro-spiritual, **pl negro-spirituals** [negrospiritɥɔl] **nm** Negro spiritual.

Néguev [negɛv] **nm**: **le désert du ~** the Negev desert.

négus [negys] **nm** (*titre*) Negus.

neige [nɛʒ] 1 **nf** (*Mét*) snow; (*arg Drogue: cocaïne*) snow (*arg*). **le temps est à la ~** it looks like (it's going to) snow; **aller à la ~*** to go to the ski resorts, go on a skiing holiday; **cheveux/teint de ~** snow-white hair/complexion. 2 **comp** ► **neige artificielle** artificial snow ► **neige carbonique** dry ice ► **neiges éternelles** eternal *ou* everlasting snow(s) ► **neige fondue** (*pluie*) sleet; (*par terre*) slush ► **neige poudreuse** powder snow ► **neige de printemps** spring snow; *voir* **bonhomme, œuf, train.**

neiger [neʒe] 3 **vb impers** to snow, be snowing.

neigeux, -euse [nɛʒø, øz] **adj** *sommet* snow-covered, snow-clad; *temps* snowy; *aspect* snowy.

nem [nɛm] **nm** (Vietnamese) small spring roll.

Némésis [nemezis] **nf** Nemesis.

néné* [nene] **nm** boob*, tit***.

nénette* [nenɛt] **nf** (*jeune femme*) chick*, bird* (*Brit*).

nenni [neni] **adv** (†† *ou dial: non*) nay.

nénuphar [nenyfar] **nm** water lily.

néo- [neo] **préf** neo-.

néo-calédonien, -ienne [neokaledɔnjɛ̃, jɛn] 1 **adj** New Caledonian. 2 **nm,f**: **N~-C~(ne)** New Caledonian.

néo-canadien, -ienne [neokanadjɛ̃, jɛn] 1 **adj** New Canadian. 2 **nm,f**: **N~-C~(ne)** New Canadian.

néo-capitalisme [neokapitalism] **nm** neocapitalism.

néo-capitaliste [neokapitalist] **adj** neocapitalist.

néo-classicisme [neoklasisism] **nm** neoclassicism.

néo-classique [neoklasik] **adj** neoclassic(al).

néo-colonialisme [neokɔlɔnjalism] **nm** neocolonialism.

néo-colonialiste [neokɔlɔnjalist] **adj** neocolonialist.

Néo-Écossais, e [neoekɔsɛ, ɛz] **nm,f** Nova Scotian.

néo-gothique [neogɔtik] **adj, nm** neogothic.

néo-libéralisme [neoliberalism] **nm** neoliberalism.

néolithique [neɔlitik] **adj, nm** neolithic.

néologie [neɔlɔʒi] **nf** neology.

néologique [neɔlɔʒik] **adj** neological.

néologisme [neɔlɔʒism] **nm** neologism.

néon [neɔ̃] **nm** (*gaz*) neon; (*éclairage*) neon lighting (*NonC*).

néo-natal, e, **mpl néo-natals** [neonatal] **adj** neonatal.

néonazi, e [neonazi] **adj, nm,f** neo-Nazi.

néonazisme [neonazism] **nm** neo-Nazism.

néophyte [neɔfit] **nmf** (*Rel*) neophyte; (*fig*) novice, neophyte (*frm*).

néoplasique [neoplazik] **adj** neoplastic.

néoplasme [neoplasm] **nm** neoplasm.

néo-platonicien, -ienne [neoplatɔnisjɛ̃, jɛn] 1 **adj** neoplatonic. 2 **nm,f** neoplatonist.

néo-platonisme [neoplatɔnism] **nm** Neo-Platonism.

néo-positivisme [neopozitivism] **nm** logical positivism.

néo-positiviste [neopozitivist] **adj, nmf** logical positivist.

néoprène [neɔprɛn] **nm**: **colle au ~** neoprene glue.

Néo-québécois, e [neokebekwa, waz] **nm,f** New-Quebec(k)er, New Québécois.

néo-réalisme [neorealism] **nm** neorealism.

néo-réaliste [neorealist] **adj** neorealist.

néo-zélandais, e [neoʒelɑ̃dɛ, ɛz] 1 **adj** New Zealand (*épith*). 2 **nm,f**: **N~-Z~(e)** New Zealander.

Népal [nepal] **nm** Nepal.

népalais, e [nepalɛ, ɛz] 1 **adj** Nepalese, Nepali. 2 **nm** (*Ling*) Nepalese, Nepali. 3 **nm,f**: **N~(e)** Nepalese, Nepali.

néphrétique [nefretik] **adj, nmf** nephritic; *voir* **colique.**

néphrite [nefrit] **nf** a (*Méd*) nephritis. **avoir une ~** to have nephritis. b (*jade*) nephrite.

néphrologie [nefrɔlɔʒi] **nf** nephrology.

néphrologue [nefrɔlɔg] **nmf** nephrologist, kidney specialist.

népotisme [nepɔtism] **nm** nepotism.

Neptune [nɛptyn] **nm** Neptune.

neptunium [nɛptynjɔm] **nm** neptunium.

néréide [nereid] **nf** (*Myth, Zool*) nereid.

nerf [nɛr] 1 **nm** a (*Anat*) nerve.

b **~s: avoir les ~s malades** to suffer with one's nerves *ou* from nerves; **avoir les ~s fragiles** to have sensitive nerves; **avoir les ~s à vif** to be very nervy (*Brit*) *ou* edgy, be on edge; **avoir les ~s à fleur de peau** to be very nervy (*Brit*) *ou* excitable; **avoir les ~s en boule*** *ou* **en pelote*** to be very tensed up *ou* tense *ou* edgy, be in a nervy (*Brit*) state; **avoir les ~s à toute épreuve** *ou* **des ~s d'acier** to have nerves of steel; **avoir ses ~s** to have an attack *ou* a fit of nerves, have a temperamental outburst; **être sur les ~s** to be all keyed up*; **vivre sur les ~s** to live on one's nerves; **porter** *ou* **taper* sur les ~s de qn** to get on sb's nerves; **passer ses ~s sur qn** to take it out on sb; **ça me met les ~s à vif** that gets on my nerves; **ça va te calmer les ~s** that will calm you down, that will calm *ou* settle your nerves; **ses ~s ont été ébranlés** that shook him *ou* his nerve; **ses ~s ont craqué*** *ou* **lâché*** his nerves have gone to pieces, he has cracked up*; *voir* **bout, crise, guerre.**

c (*vigueur*) **allons du ~!** *ou* **un peu de ~!** come on, buck up!* *ou* show some spirit!; **ça a du ~** it has really got some go* about it; **ça manque de ~** it has got no go* about it; **l'argent est le ~ de la guerre** money is the sinews of war.

d (*: *tendon*) nerve. *[viande]* **~s** gristle (*NonC*).

e (*Typ*) cord.

2 **comp** ► **nerf de bœuf** cosh (*Brit*), ≃ blackjack (*US*) ► **nerf centrifuge** centrifugal nerve ► **nerf centripète** centripetal nerve ► **nerf gustatif** gustatory nerve ► **nerf moteur** motor nerve ► **nerf optique** optic nerve ► **nerf pneumogastrique** vagus ► **nerf sensitif** sensory nerve ► **nerf vague** vagus.

Néron [nerɔ̃] **nm** Nero.

nerveusement [nɛrvøzmɑ̃] **adv** (*d'une manière excitée*) nervously, tensely; (*de façon irritable*) irritably, touchily, nervily; (*avec vigueur*) energetically, vigorously. **ébranlé ~** shaken, with shaken nerves.

nerveux, -euse [nɛrvø, øz] **adj** a (*Méd*) *tension, dépression, fatigue* nervous; (*Anat*) *cellule, centre, tissu* nerve (*épith*). **système ~** nervous system; **grossesse ~euse** false pregnancy, phantom pregnancy.

b (*agité*) *personne, animal, rire* nervous, tense; (*irritable*) irritable, touchy, nervy (*Brit*), nervous. **ça me rend ~** it makes me nervous; **c'est un grand ~** he's very highly strung.

c (*vigoureux*) *corps* energetic, vigorous; *animal* spirited, energetic, skittish; *moteur, voiture* responsive; *style* energetic, vigorous. **pas très ~ dans ce qu'il fait**not very energetic in what he does, not doing anything with very much dash *ou* spirit.

d (*sec*) *personne, main* wiry; *viande* gristly.

nervi [nɛrvi] **nm** (*gén pl*) bully boy, hatchet man.

nervosité [nɛrvozite] **nf** a (*agitation*) (*permanente*) nervousness, excitability; (*passagère*) agitation, tension. **dans un état de grande ~** in a state of great agitation *ou* tension. b (*irritabilité*) (*permanente*) irritability; (*passagère*) irritability, nerviness, touchiness. c *[moteur]* responsiveness. **manque de ~** sluggishness.

nervure [nɛrvyr] **nf** (*Bot, Zool*) nervure, vein; (*Archit, Tech*) rib;

(*Typ*) raised band.

nervuré, e [nɛʀvyʀe] adj *feuille, aile* veined; *couvercle, voûte* ribbed.

Nescafé [nɛskafe] nm ® Nescafé ®, instant coffee.

n'est-ce pas [nɛspɑ] adv a (*appelant l'acquiescement*) isn't it?, doesn't he? *etc* (*selon le verbe qui précède*). **il est fort, ~?** he is strong, isn't he?; **c'est bon, ~?** it's nice, isn't it? *ou* don't you think?; **il n'est pas trop tard, ~?** it's not too late, is it? b (*intensif*) **~ que c'est bon/difficile?** it is nice/difficult, isn't it?; (*iro*) **eux, ~, ils peuvent se le permettre** of course THEY can afford to do it; **le problème, ~, c'est qu'il s'en fiche** the problem is (that) he doesn't care, you see.

net¹, nette [nɛt] 1 adj a (*propre*) (*après n*) *surface, ongles, mains* clean; *intérieur, travail, copie* clean, neat, tidy. **elle est toujours très nette (dans sa tenue)** she is always neatly dressed *ou* turned out, she is always very neat and tidy; **avoir la conscience nette** to have a clear conscience; **mettre au ~** *rapport, devoir* to copy out, make a neat *ou* fair copy of; *plan, travail* to tidy up; **mise au ~** copying out; tidying up; *voir* **cœur, place.**

b (*Comm, Fin*) (*après n*) *bénéfice, prix, poids* net. **~ de** free of; **emprunt ~ de tout impôt** tax-free loan; **revenu ~** disposable income.

c (*clair, précis*) (*après n*) *idée, explication, esprit* clear; (*sans équivoque*) *réponse* straight, clear, plain; *refus* flat (*épith*); *situation, position* clear-cut. **je serai ~ avec vous** I shall be (quite) plain *ou* straight *ou* candid *ou* frank with you; **sa conduite** *ou* **son attitude dans cette affaire n'est pas très nette** his behaviour *ou* attitude in this matter is slightly questionable; **ce type n'est pas très ~*** (*bizarre*) this guy is slightly odd *ou* strange*; (*fou*) this guy is slightly mad*.

d (*marqué, évident*) *différence, amélioration etc* marked, distinct, sharp; *distinction* marked, sharp, clear(-cut). **il y a une très nette odeur** *ou* **une odeur très nette de brûlé** there's a distinct *ou* a very definite smell of burning; **il est très ~ qu'il n'a aucune intention de venir** it is quite clear *ou* obvious *ou* plain that he does not intend to come *ou* has no intention of coming.

e (*distinct*) (*après n*) *dessin, écriture* clear; *ligne, contour,* (*Phot*) *image* sharp; *voix, son* clear, distinct; *cassure, coupure* clean. **j'ai un souvenir très ~ de sa visite** I have a very clear *ou* vivid memory of his visit.

2 adv a (*brusquement*) *s'arrêter* dead. **se casser ~** to snap *ou* break clean through; **il a été tué ~** he was killed outright.

b (*franchement, carrément*) bluntly; *dire, parler* frankly, bluntly; *refuser* flatly. **il (m')a dit tout ~ que** he made it quite clear (to me) that, he told me frankly *ou* bluntly that; **je vous le dis tout ~** I'm telling you *ou* I'm giving it to you straight*, I'm telling you bluntly *ou* frankly; **pour vous** *ou* **à parler ~** to be blunt *ou* frank with you.

c (*Comm*) net. **il reste 200 F ~** there remains 200 francs net; **cela pèse 2 kg ~** it weighs 2 kg net.

net² [nɛt] 1 adj inv (*Tennis*) net (*épith*). 2 nm net shot.

nettement [nɛtmɑ̃] adv a (*clairement, sans ambiguïté*) *expliquer, répondre* clearly. **il refusa ~** he flatly refused, he refused point-blank; **je lui ai dit ~ ce que j'en pensais** I told him bluntly *ou* frankly *ou* plainly *ou* straight* what I thought of it; **il a ~ pris position contre nous** he has clearly *ou* quite obviously taken up a stance against us.

b (*distinctement*) *apercevoir, entendre* clearly, distinctly; *se détacher, apparaître* clearly, distinctly, sharply; *se souvenir* clearly, distinctly.

c (*incontestablement*) *s'améliorer, se différencier* markedly, decidedly, distinctly; *mériter* decidedly, distinctly. **j'aurais ~ préféré ne pas venir** I would have definitely *ou* distinctly preferred not to come; **ça va ~ mieux** things are going decidedly *ou* distinctly better; **~ fautif** distinctly *ou* decidedly faulty; **~ meilleur/plus grand** markedly *ou* decidedly *ou* distinctly better/bigger.

netteté [nɛtte] nf a (*propreté*) *[tenue, travail]* neatness. b (*clarté*) *[explication, expression, esprit, idées]* clearness, clarity. c (*caractère distinct*) *[dessin, écriture]* clearness; *[contour, image]* sharpness, clarity, clearness; *[souvenir, voix, son]* clearness, clarity; *[cassure]* cleanness.

nettoiement [netwamɑ̃] nm *[rues]* cleaning; (*Agr*) *[terre]* clearing. **service du ~** refuse disposal *ou* collection service, cleansing department.

nettoyable [netwajabl] adj *surfaces* washable; *vêtement* cleanable. **~ à sec** dry-cleanable.

nettoyage [netwajaʒ] nm (*gén*) cleaning; (*Mil, Police*) cleaning up, cleaning out. **faire le ~ par le vide*** to throw everything out; **~ de printemps** spring-cleaning; **~ à sec** dry cleaning; **un ~ complet** a thorough cleanup; (*Mil*) **opération de ~** mopping-up operation; **entreprise de ~** cleaning firm.

nettoyant, e [netwajɑ̃, ɑ̃t] 1 adj cleaning (*épith*). 2 nm cleaner.

nettoyer [netwaje] [8] vt a (*gén*) *objet* to clean; *jardin* to clear; *canal etc* to clean up. **~ au chiffon** *ou* **avec un chiffon** to dust; **~ au balai** to sweep (out); **~ à l'eau/avec du savon** to wash in water/with soap; **~ à la brosse** to brush (out); **~ à l'éponge** to sponge (down); **~ à sec** to dry-clean; **~ une maison à fond** to clean a house from top to bottom; **nettoyez-vous les mains au robinet** wash *ou* run your hands under the tap, give your hands a rinse under the tap; (*hum*) **~ son assiette** to clean one's plate; (*hum*) **le chien avait nettoyé le réfrigérateur*** the dog had cleaned out *ou* emptied the fridge; **l'orage a nettoyé le ciel** the storm has cleared away the clouds.

b (*) *personne* (*tuer*) to kill, finish off*; (*ruiner*) to clean out; (*fatiguer*) to wear out. **il a été nettoyé en 15 jours par la grippe** the flu finished him off* *ou* did for him* in a fortnight; **~ son compte en banque** to clear one's bank account; **se faire ~ au jeu** to be cleaned out at gambling.

c (*Mil, Police*) to clean out *ou* up.

nettoyeur, -euse [netwajœʀ, øz] nm,f cleaner.

Neuchâtel [nøʃatɛl] n Neuchâtel. **le lac de ~** Neuchâtel Lake.

neuf¹ [nœf] adj inv, nm inv (*chiffre*) nine. (*Myth*) **les N~ Sœurs** the (nine) Muses; *pour loc voir* **six** *et* **preuve.**

neuf², neuve [nœf, nœv] 1 adj (*gén*) new; *vision, esprit, pensée* fresh, new, original; *pays* young, new. **quelque chose de ~** something new; **regarder qch avec un œil ~** to look at sth with a new *ou* fresh eye; **être ~ dans le métier/en affaires** to be new to the trade/to business; **à l'état ~, comme ~** as good as new, as new; *voir* **flambant, peau, tout.**

2 nm new. **il y a du ~** something new has turned up, there has been a new development; **quoi de/rien de ~?** what's/nothing new?; **faire du ~** (*politique*) to introduce new *ou* fresh ideas; (*artisanat*) to make new things; **être vêtu** *ou* **habillé de ~** to be dressed in new clothes, be wearing new clothes, have new clothes on; **son appartement est meublé de ~** all the furniture in his flat is new; **remettre** *ou* **refaire à ~** to do up like new *ou* as good as new; **repeindre un appartement à ~** to redecorate a flat; **on ne peut pas faire du ~ avec du vieux** you can't make new things out of old.

neufchâtel [nøʃatɛl] nm *type of soft cream cheese.*

neurasthénie [nøʀasteni] nf (*gén*) depression; (*Méd*) neurasthenia (*SPÉC*). **faire de la ~** to be depressed, be suffering from depression.

neurasthénique [nøʀastenik] 1 adj depressed, depressive; (*Méd*) neurasthenic (*SPÉC*). 2 nmf depressed person, depressive; (*Méd*) neurasthenic (*SPÉC*).

neuro... [nøʀɔ] préf neuro... .

neurobiologie [nøʀobjɔlɔʒi] nf neurobiology.

neurochimie [nøʀoʃimi] nf neurochemistry.

neurochirurgical, e, mpl **-aux** [nøʀoʃiʀyʀʒikal, o] adj neurosurgical.

neurochirurgie [nøʀoʃiʀyʀʒi] nf neurosurgery.

neurochirurgien, -ienne [nøʀoʃiʀyʀʒjɛ̃, jɛn] nm,f neurosurgeon.

neuroleptique [nøʀɔlɛptik] adj, nm neuroleptic.

neurologie [nøʀɔlɔʒi] nf neurology.

neurologique [nøʀɔlɔʒik] adj neurological.

neurologiste [nøʀɔlɔʒist] nmf, **neurologue** [nøʀɔlɔg] nmf neurologist.

neuromédiateur [nøʀomedjatœʀ] nm neurotransmitter.

neuromusculaire [nøʀomyskylɛʀ] adj neuromuscular.

neuronal, e, mpl **-aux** [nøʀɔnal, o] adj neuronic.

neurone [nøʀɔn] nm neuron.

neuropathie [nøʀopati] nf neuropathy.

neuropathologie [nøʀopatɔlɔʒi] nf neuropathology.

neurophysiologie [nøʀofizjɔlɔʒi] nf neurophysiology.

neurophysiologique [nøʀofizjɔlɔʒik] adj neurophysiological.

neurophysiologiste [nøʀofizjɔlɔʒist] nmf neurophysiologist.

neuropsychiatre [nøʀopsikjatʀ] nmf neuropsychiatrist.

neuropsychiatrie [nøʀopsikjatʀi] nf neuropsychiatry.

neuropsychiatrique [nøʀopsikjatʀik] adj neuropsychiatric.

neuropsychologie [nøʀopsikɔlɔʒi] nf neuropsychology.

neuropsychologue [nøʀopsikɔlɔg] nmf neuropsychologist.

neurosciences [nøʀosjɑ̃s] nfpl neuroscience.

neurotransmetteur [nøʀotʀɑ̃smetœʀ] nm neurotransmitter.

neutralisation [nøtʀalizasjɔ̃] nf neutralization.

neutraliser [nøtʀalize] [1] vt (*Mil, Pol, Sci*) to neutralize. **les deux influences/produits se neutralisent** the two influences/products neutralize each other *ou* cancel each other out.

neutralisme [nøtʀalism] nm neutralism.

neutraliste [nøtʀalist] adj, nmf neutralist.

neutralité [nøtʀalite] nf neutrality. **rester dans la ~** to remain neutral.

neutre [nøtʀ] 1 adj (*gén, Chim, Élec, Pol, Phon*) neutral; (*Ling, Zool*) neuter; *style* neutral, colourless; (*sans excès*) *solution* middle-of-the-road. **rester ~ (dans)** to remain neutral (in), not to take sides (in). 2 nm (*Ling*) (*genre*) neuter; (*nom*) neuter noun; (*Élec*) neutral; (*Zool*) neuter (animal); (*Pol*) neutral (country). **les ~s** the neutral nations.

neutron [nøtʀɔ̃] nm neutron.

neuvaine [nœvɛn] nf novena. **faire une ~** to make a novena.

neuvième [nœvjɛm] adj, nmf ninth; *pour loc voir* **sixième.**

neuvièmement [nœvjɛmmɑ̃] adv ninthly, in the ninth place; *pour loc voir* **sixièmement.**

Nevada [nevada] nm Nevada.

névé [neve] nm névé, firn.

neveu, pl **~x** [n(ə)vø] nm nephew; (*††: descendant*) descendant. **un peu, mon ~!*** you bet!*, of course!, and how!*

névralgie [nevʀalʒi] nf neuralgia. **~ dentaire** dental neuralgia; **avoir des ~s** to suffer from neuralgia.

névralgique [nevʀalʒik] adj neuralgic. **centre** *ou* **point ~** (*Méd*) nerve centre; (*fig*) (*point sensible*) sensitive spot; (*point capital*) nerve centre.

névrite [nevʀit] nf neuritis.
névritique [nevʀitik] adj neuritic.
névropathe [nevʀɔpat] 1 adj neuropathic, neurotic. 2 nmf neuropath, neurotic.
névropathie [nevʀɔpati] nf neuropathy.
névrose [nevʀoz] nf neurosis. ~ **obsessionnelle** obsessional neurosis; ~ **phobique** phobia.
névrosé, e [nevʀoze] adj, nm,f neurotic.
névrotique [nevʀɔtik] adj neurotic.
New Delhi [njudɛli] n New Delhi.
New Hampshire [njuɑ̃pʃəʀ] nm New Hampshire.
New Jersey [njuʒɛʀze] nm New Jersey.
new-look* [njuluk] adj, nm inv new look.
Newton [njutɔn] nm (*savant*) Newton. (*unité*) **n~** newton.
newtonien, -ienne [njutɔnjɛ̃, jɛn] adj Newtonian.
New York [njujɔʀk] 1 n (*ville*) New York. 2 nm: **l'État de ~** New York State.
new-yorkais, e [njujɔʀkɛ, ɛz] 1 adj of *ou* from New York. 2 nm,f: **N~-Y~(e)** New Yorker.
nez [ne] nm a (*organe*) nose. **avoir le ~ grec/aquilin** to have a Grecian/an aquiline nose; ~ **épaté** *ou* **écrasé** *ou* **aplati** flat nose; ~ **en trompette** turned-up nose; ~ **en pied de marmite** bulbous turned-up nose; **ton ~ remue, tu mens** I can tell by looking at you that you're fibbing*; **parler du ~** to talk through one's nose; **cela se voit comme le ~ au milieu du visage** *ou* **de la figure** it's as plain as the nose on your face *ou* as a pikestaff, it sticks out a mile; **cela sent le brûlé à plein ~** there's a strong smell of burning.
b (*visage, face*) **le ~ en l'air** with one's nose in the air; **où est mon sac? — tu as le ~ dessus!** *ou* **sous ton ~!** where's my bag? — under your nose!; **baisser/lever le ~** to bow/raise one's head; **il ne lève jamais le ~ de son travail** he never looks up from his work; **mettre le ~** *ou* **son ~ à la fenêtre/au bureau** to show one's face at the window/at the office; **je n'ai pas mis le ~ dehors hier** I didn't put my nose outside the door yesterday; **il fait un temps à ne pas mettre le ~ dehors** it's weather you wouldn't put a dog out in; **rire/fermer la porte au ~ de qn** to laugh/shut the door in sb's face; (*au téléphone*) **elle m'a raccroché au ~** (*couper la communication*) she hung up on me; (*avec colère*) she slammed the phone down on me; **faire qch au ~ et à la barbe de qn** to do sth under sb's very nose; **regarder qn sous le ~** to stare sb in the face; **sous son ~** (right) under his nose, under his (very) nose; **se trouver ~ à ~ avec qn** to find o.s. face to face with sb; **faire un (drôle de) ~** to pull a (funny) face.
c (*flair*) flair. **avoir du ~, avoir le ~ fin** to have flair; **j'ai eu le ~ creux de m'en aller*** I was quite right to leave, I did well to leave; *voir* **vue**[2].
d (*Aviat, Naut*) nose. (*Naut*) **sur le ~** down at the bows; *voir* **piquer**.
e (*créateur de parfums*) nose.
f (*loc*) **avoir qn dans le ~*** to have something against sb; **il m'a dans le ~*** he can't stand me*, he has got something against me; **avoir un verre** *ou* **un coup dans le ~*** to have had one too many*, have had a drop too much*; **se manger** *ou* **se bouffer le ~*** to be at each others' throats; **mettre** *ou* **fourrer* le** *ou* **son ~ dans qch** to poke *ou* stick* one's nose into sth, nose *ou* pry into sth; **l'affaire lui est passée sous le ~*** the bargain slipped through his fingers; **se promener le ~ au vent** to walk along aimlessly; *voir* **bout, casser, doigt**.
NF a (abrév de **norme française**) **avoir le label ~** to have the mark of the approved French standard of manufacture, ≃ have the Kite mark (*Brit*). b abrév de **nouveau(x) franc(s)**.
ni [ni] conj (*après la négation*) nor, or. **ni ... ni ...** neither ... nor ...; **il ne boit ~ ne fume** he doesn't drink or smoke, he neither drinks nor smokes; **il ne pouvait (~) parler ~ entendre** he could neither speak nor hear, he couldn't speak or hear; **il ne pouvait pas parler ~ son frère entendre** he couldn't speak nor could his brother hear; **personne ne l'a (jamais) aidé ~ (même) encouragé** nobody (ever) helped or (even) encouraged him; **je ne veux ~ ne peux accepter** I neither wish to nor can accept, I don't wish to accept, nor can I; **elle est secrétaire, ~ plus ~ moins** she's just a secretary, no more no less; **il n'est ~ plus bête ~ plus paresseux qu'un autre** he is neither more stupid nor lazier than anyone else, he's no more stupid and no lazier than anyone else; **il ne veut pas, ~ moi non plus** he doesn't want to and neither do I *ou* and nor do I; **~ lui ~ moi** neither he nor I, neither of us, neither him nor me*; **~ l'un ~ l'autre** neither one nor the other, neither of them; **~ d'un côté ~ de l'autre** on neither one side nor the other, on neither side; **il n'a dit ~ oui ~ non** he didn't say either yes or no; **~ vu ~ connu (je t'embrouille)*** no one'll be any the wiser*; **cela ne me fait ~ chaud ~ froid** it makes no odds to me, I don't feel strongly (about it) one way or the other; *voir* **feu**[1], **foi**.
niable [njabl] adj deniable. **cela n'est pas ~** that cannot be denied, you can't deny that.
Niagara [njagaʀa] nm Niagara. **le ~** the Niagara (river); *voir* **chute**.
niais, niaise [njɛ, njɛz] 1 adj *personne* silly, simple; *air, sourire* simple; *rire* silly, inane. 2 nm,f simpleton. **pauvre ~** poor innocent *ou* fool.
niaisement [njɛzmɑ̃] adv *rire* inanely.
niaiserie [njɛzʀi] nf (*voir* **niais**) silliness; simpleness; inaneness; (*action*) foolish *ou* inane behaviour (*NonC*); (*parole*) foolish *ou* inane talk (*NonC*). **dire des ~s** to talk rubbish *ou* twaddle (*Brit*) *ou* nonsense.
Niamey [niamɛ] n Niamey.
niaule* [njol] nf = **gnôle***.
Nicaragua [nikaʀagwa] nm Nicaragua.
nicaraguayen, -enne [nikaʀagwajɛ̃, jɛn] 1 adj Nicaraguan. 2 nm,f: **N~(ne)** Nicaraguan.
niche [niʃ] nf a (*alcôve*) niche, recess; *[chien]* kennel. **à la ~!** (*à un chien*) (into your) kennel!; (* *hum: d'une personne*) scram!*, make yourself scarce!*; ~ **écologique** ecological niche. b (*farce*) trick, hoax. **faire des ~s à qn** to play tricks on sb.
nichée [niʃe] nf *[oiseaux]* brood. ~ **de chiens** litter of puppies; **une ~ de pinsons** a nest *ou* brood of chaffinches; **la mère/l'instituteur et toute sa ~ (d'enfants)*** the mother/teacher and her/his entire brood.
nicher [niʃe] [1] 1 vi *[oiseau]* to nest; (*) *[personne]* to hang out*. 2 **se nicher** vpr *[oiseau]* to nest; (*littér: se blottir*) *[village etc]* to nestle (*dans* in); (*: *se cacher*) *[personne]* to stick* *ou* put o.s.; *[objet]* to lodge itself. (*hum*) **où la vertu va-t-elle se ~!** of all the unlikely places to find such virtue!; **les cerises nichées dans les feuilles** the cherries nestling among the leaves.
nichon* [niʃɔ̃] nm tit**, boob*.
nickel [nikɛl] 1 nm nickel. 2 adj (*: *impeccable*) **chez eux, c'est ~** their home is always spick and span.
nickelage [niklaʒ] nm nickel-plating.
nickeler [nikle] [4] vt to nickel-plate. **en acier nickelé** nickel-plated steel.
Nicodème [nikɔdɛm] nm Nicodemus.
niçois, e [niswa, waz] 1 adj of *ou* from Nice; *voir* **salade**. 2 nm,f: **N~(e)** inhabitant *ou* native of Nice; (*Culin*) **à la ~e** with tomatoes and garlic (*attrib*).
Nicolas [nikɔla] nm Nicholas.
Nicosie [nikɔzi] n Nicosia.
nicotine [nikɔtin] nf nicotine.
nid [ni] 1 nm a (*Zool*) nest. ~ **d'oiseau/de vipères/de guêpes** bird's/vipers'/wasps' nest.
b (*fig: abri*) (*foyer*) cosy little nest; (*repaire*) den. **trouver le ~ vide** to find the bird has *ou* the birds have flown, find the nest empty; **surprendre qn au ~, trouver l'oiseau au ~** to find *ou* catch sb at home *ou* in.
2 comp ►**nid(s) d'abeilles** (*point*) honeycomb stitch; (*tissu*) waffle cloth; **radiateur en nid(s) d'abeilles** cellular radiator ►**nid d'aigle** (*Zool, fig*) eyrie ►**nid d'amoureux** love nest ►**nid d'ange** ≃ (baby) nest ►**nid de brigands** robbers' den ►**nids d'hirondelles** (*Culin*) birds' nest; **potage aux nids d'hirondelles** birds' nest soup ►**nid de mitrailleuses** nest of machine guns ►**nid de pie** (*Naut*) crow's-nest ►**nid de poule** pothole ►**nid à poussière** dust trap ►**nid de résistance** (*Mil*) pocket of resistance.
nidification [nidifikasjɔ̃] nf nesting.
nidifier [nidifje] [7] vi to nest.
nièce [njɛs] nf niece.
nielle [njɛl] 1 nf (*Agr*) (*plante*) corn-cockle. (*maladie*) ~ **(du blé)** blight. 2 nm (*incrustation*) niello.
nieller [njele] [1] vt (*Agr*) to blight; (*Tech*) to niello.
niellure [njelyʀ] nf (*Agr*) blight; (*Tech*) niello.
n-ième [ɛnjɛm] adj nth. **x à la ~ puissance** x to the power (of) n, x to the nth power; **je te le dis pour la ~ fois** I'm telling you for the nth *ou* umpteenth time.
nier [nje] [7] vt (*gén*) to deny; (*Jur* ††: *désavouer*) *dette, fait* to repudiate. **il nie l'avoir fait** he denies having done it; ~ **l'évidence** to deny the obvious; **je ne (le) nie pas** I'm not denying it, I don't deny it; **on ne peut ~ que** one cannot deny that; **l'accusé nia** the accused denied the charges.
nietzschéen, -enne [nitʃeɛ̃, ɛn] adj, nm,f Nietzschean.
nigaud, e [nigo, od] 1 adj silly, simple. 2 nm,f simpleton. **grand** *ou* **gros ~!** big silly!, big ninny!*
nigauderie [nigodʀi] nf (*caractère*) silliness, simpleness; (*action*) silly action.
Niger [niʒɛʀ] nm: **le ~** the Niger.
Nigéria [niʒeʀja] nm ou f Nigeria.
nigérian, e [niʒeʀjɑ̃, an] 1 adj Nigerian. 2 nm,f: **N~(e)** Nigerian.
nigérien, -ienne [niʒeʀjɛ̃, jɛn] 1 adj of *ou* from Niger. 2 nm,f: **N~(ne)** inhabitant *ou* native of Niger.
night-club, pl **night-clubs** [najtklœb] nm nightclub.
nihilisme [niilism] nm nihilism.
nihiliste [niilist(ə)] 1 adj nihilistic. 2 nmf nihilist.
Nil [nil] nm: **le ~** the Nile; **le ~ Blanc/Bleu** the White/Blue Nile.
nilotique [nilɔtik] adj of *ou* from the Nile, Nile (*épith*).
nimbe [nɛ̃b] nm (*Rel, fig*) nimbus, halo.
nimber [nɛ̃be] [1] vt (*auréoler*) to halo. **nimbé de lumière** radiant *ou* suffused with light.
nimbo-stratus [nɛ̃bostʀatys] nm inv nimbostratus.
nimbus [nɛ̃bys] nm (*Mét*) nimbus.
n'importe [nɛ̃pɔʀt(ə)] *voir* **importer**[2].
ninas [ninas] nm small cigar.
niobium [njɔbjɔm] nm niobium.

niôle* [njol] nf = **gnôle***.
nippe* [nip] nf (old) thing* ou rag*. ~s togs* (*Brit*), gear*; **de vieilles ~** old togs* (*Brit*), old clothes.
nipper* [nipe] [1] 1 vt (*habiller*) to tog out* (*Brit*), deck out. **bien/mal nippé** well/badly got up*, in a nice/an awful getup* ou rig-out*. 2 **se nipper** vpr to get togged up* (*Brit*), get decked out.
nippon, e ou **-onne** [nipɔ̃, ɔn] 1 adj Japanese, Nippon(ese). 2 nm,f: **N~(e), N~(ne)** Japanese, Nippon(ese). 3 nm (*pays*) **N~** Nippon.
nique [nik] nf (†: *lit, fig*) **faire la ~ à qn** to thumb one's nose at sb, cock a snook at sb.
niquedouille* [nikduj] = **nigaud**.
niquer** [nike] vt (*sexuellement*) to fuck**, screw**; (*abîmer*) *machine, ordinateur* to bugger**, knacker**. (*fig*) **se faire ~** to get screwed**.
nirvana [niʀvana] nm nirvana.
nitouche [nituʃ] nf *voir* **saint**.
nitrate [nitʀat] nm nitrate. **~ d'argent** silver nitrate.
nitreux, -euse [nitʀø, øz] adj nitrous.
nitrifier [nitʀifje] [7] vt to nitrify.
nitrique [nitʀik] adj nitric.
nitrite [nitʀit] nm nitrite.
nitrobenzène [nitʀobɛ̃zɛn] nm nitrobenzene.
nitroglycérine [nitʀogliseʀin] nf nitroglycerine.
nival, e, mpl **-aux** [nival, o] adj nival.
niveau, pl **~x** [nivo] 1 nm a (*hauteur*) [*huile, eau*] level; [*bâtiment*] level, floor. **le ~ de l'eau** the water level; **au ~ de l'eau/du sol** at water/ground level; **~ de la mer** sea level; **cent mètres au-dessus du ~ de la mer** a hundred metres above sea level; **l'eau est arrivée au ~ du quai** the water has risen to the level of the embankment; **la neige m'arrivait au ~ des genoux** the snow came up to my knees ou was knee-deep; **une tache au ~ du coude** a mark at the elbow; **serré au ~ de la taille** tight at the waist; **il avait une cicatrice sur la joue au ~ de la bouche** he had a scar on his cheek about level with his mouth; **au ~ du village, il s'arrêta** once level with the village, he stopped; **de ~ avec, au même ~ que** level with; **les deux vases sont au même ~** the two vases are level ou at the same height; **de ~** level; **mettre qch de ou à ~** to make sth level; **le plancher n'est pas de ~** the floor isn't level; **les deux pièces ne sont pas de ~** the two rooms are not on a level; *voir* **courbe, passage.**
b (*degré*) [*connaissances, études*] standard; [*intelligence, qualité*] level. **le ~ des études en France** the standard of French education; **le ~ d'instruction baisse** educational standards are falling; **cet élève est d'un bon ~** this pupil keeps up a good level of attainment ou a good standard; **son anglais est d'un bon ~** his English is of a good standard; **ils ne sont pas du même ~** they're not (of) the same standard, they're not on a par ou on the same level; **le ~ intellectuel de la classe moyenne** the intellectual level of the lower middle class; **le franc a atteint son ~ le plus haut/bas depuis 3 ans** the franc has reached its highest/lowest point for 3 years; **la production littéraire a atteint son ~ le plus bas** literary production has reached its lowest ebb ou level; (*Scol*) **au ~** up to standard; **les cours ne sont pas à son ~** the classes aren't up to his standard; **il faut se mettre au ~ des enfants** you have to put yourself on the same level as the children; (*Écon, Pol*) **au ~ de l'usine/des gouvernements** at factory/government level; **au ~ européen** at the European level; **négociations au plus haut ~** top-level negotiations; **cela exige un haut ~ de concentration** it demands a high level ou degree of concentration; **athlète/cadre de haut ~** top athlete/executive.
c (*objet*) (*Constr*) level; (*Aut: jauge*) gauge.
2 comp ►**niveau de base** (*Géog*) base level ►**niveau à bulle (d'air)** (*Tech*) spirit level ►**niveau d'eau** (*Tech*) water level ►**niveau d'énergie** (*Phys*) energy level ►**niveau hydrostatique** water table ►**niveau de langue** (*Ling*) register ►**niveau de maçon** (*Constr*) plumb level ►**niveau mental** (*Psych*) mental age ►**niveau social** (*Écon*) social standing ou rank ►**niveau de vie** (*Écon*) standard of living; **le niveau de vie a monté/baissé** the standard of living has gone up ou risen/gone down ou dropped.
nivelage [niv(ə)laʒ] nm (*voir* **niveler**) levelling; levelling out, evening out, equalizing.
niveler [niv(ə)le] [4] vt a (*égaliser*) *surface* to level; *fortunes, conditions sociales* to level ou even out, equalize. **l'érosion nivelle les montagnes** erosion wears down ou wears away the mountains; **sommets nivelés** mountain tops worn down ou worn away by erosion; **~ par le bas/le haut** to level down/up. b (*mesurer avec un niveau*) to measure with a spirit level, level.
niveleuse [niv(ə)løz] nf (*Constr*) grader.
nivellement [nivɛlmɑ̃] nm a (*voir* **niveler**) levelling; levelling out, evening out, equalizing. **~ par le bas** levelling down. b (*mesure*) surveying.
nivo-glaciaire [nivoglasjɛʀ] adj snow and ice (*épith*).
nivo-pluvial, e, mpl **-iaux** [nivoplyvjal, jo] adj snow and rain (*épith*).
nivôse [nivoz] nm Nivôse, *fourth month of French Republican calendar.*
NN (abrév de **nouvelles normes**) *revised standard of hotel classification.*
N° (abrév de **numéro**) no.
Nobel [nɔbɛl] nm: **le (prix) ~** the Nobel prize.
nobélisable [nɔbelizabl] 1 adj potential Nobel prize-winning (*épith*). 2 nmf potential Nobel prize-winner.
nobélium [nɔbeljɔm] nm nobelium.
nobiliaire [nɔbiljɛʀ] 1 adj nobiliary. 2 nm (*livre*) peerage list.
noble [nɔbl] 1 adj a (*de haute naissance*) noble. (*fig*) **l'or est une matière ~** gold is a noble metal. b (*généreux, digne*) *ton, attitude* noble, dignified. **une âme/un cœur ~** a noble spirit/heart; **le ~ art (de la boxe)** the noble art (of boxing). 2 nm a (*personne*) nobleman. **les ~s** the nobility. b (*monnaie*) noble. 3 nf noblewoman.
noblement [nɔbləmɑ̃] adv (*généreusement*) nobly; (*dignement*) with dignity.
noblesse [nɔblɛs] nf a (*générosité, dignité*) nobleness, nobility. **~ d'esprit/de cœur** nobleness ou nobility of spirit/heart. b (*caste*) **la ~** the nobility; **la ~ d'épée** the old nobility ou aristocracy; **la ~ de robe** the noblesse de robe; **la ~ de cour** the courtiers, the nobility at court; **la haute ~** the nobility; **~ oblige** noblesse oblige; **la petite ~** minor nobility; **~ terrienne** landed gentry.
nobliau, pl **~x** [nɔblijo] nm (*péj*) one of the lesser nobility, petty noble.
noce [nɔs] nf a (*cérémonie*) wedding; (*cortège, participants*) wedding party. (*frm*) **~s** wedding, nuptials (*frm*); **être de la ~** to be a member of the wedding party, be among the wedding guests; **être de ~** to be invited to a wedding; **aller à la ~ de qn** to go to sb's wedding; **repas/robe/nuit** *etc* **de ~(s)** wedding banquet/dress/night *etc*; **~s d'argent/d'or/de diamant** silver/golden/diamond wedding; (*Bible*) **les ~s de Cana** the wedding at Cana; **il l'avait épousée en premières/secondes ~s** she was his first/second wife; (†, *hum*) **épouser qn en justes ~s** to take sb as one's lawful wedded wife; *voir* **convoler, voyage.**
b (*loc*) **faire la ~*** to live it up*, have a wild time; **je n'étais pas à la ~*** I wasn't exactly enjoying myself, I was having a pretty uncomfortable time; **il n'avait jamais été à pareille ~** he'd never been so happy, he was having the time of his life.
noceur, -euse* [nɔsœʀ, øz] nm,f fast liver, reveller. **il est assez ~** he likes to live it up*.
nocif, -ive [nɔsif, iv] adj noxious, harmful.
nocivité [nɔsivite] nf noxiousness, harmfulness.
noctambule [nɔktɑ̃byl] 1 adj: **il est ~** (*gén*) he's a night owl ou night hawk; (††: *somnambule*) he's a sleepwalker; **des viveurs ~s** night revellers. 2 nmf (*noceur*) night reveller; (*qui veille la nuit*) night bird, night owl; (††: *somnambule*) noctambulist†.
noctambulisme [nɔktɑ̃bylism] nm (*rare: débauche*) night-time revelling, night revels; (*habitudes nocturnes*) nocturnal habits; (††: *somnambulisme*) noctambulism†.
nocturne [nɔktyʀn] 1 adj nocturnal, night (*épith*); *voir* **tapage.** 2 nm a (*oiseau*) night hunter. b (*Rel*) nocturn. c (*Mus*) nocturne; (*Peinture*) nocturne, night scene. 3 nf ou m (*Sport*) evening fixture; [*magasin*] late night opening. **réunion en ~** evening meeting; (*Sport*) **la rencontre sera jouée en ~** the game will be played under floodlights; **le magasin fait ~** ou **est ouvert en ~ le vendredi** the shop is open ou the shop opens late on Fridays.
nodal, e, mpl **-aux** [nɔdal, o] adj (*Phys, Ling*) nodal.
nodosité [nɔdozite] nf (*corps dur*) node, nodule; (*état*) knottiness, nodosity (*SPÉC*).
nodule [nɔdyl] nm nodule. **~ polymétallique** polymetalic nodule.
Noé [noe] nm Noah.
Noël [nɔɛl] nm (*fête*) Christmas; (*chant*) (Christmas) carol. (*cadeau*) **n~** Christmas present; **à la (fête de) ~** at Christmas (time); **que faites-vous pour (la) ~?** what are you doing for ou at Christmas?; **pendant (l'époque de) ~** during Christmas ou the Christmas period; **que veux-tu pour ton (petit) n~?** what would you like for Christmas?; **joyeux ~!** merry ou happy Christmas!; **~ au balcon, Pâques au tison** a warm Christmas means a cold Easter; *voir* **bûche, sapin, veille.**
Noémi [nɔemi] nf Naomi.
nœud [nø] 1 nm a (*gén: pour attacher etc*) knot; (*ornemental: de ruban*) bow. **faire/défaire un ~** to make ou tie/untie ou undo a knot ou bow; **la fillette avait des ~s dans les cheveux** the little girl had bows ou ribbons in her hair; **fais un ~ à ton mouchoir!** tie ou make a knot in your hanky!; (*fig*) **avoir un ~ dans la gorge** to have a lump in one's throat; (*fig*) **il y a un ~!*** there's a hitch! ou snag!; **les ~s d'un serpent** the coils of a snake; **~ de perles/de diamants** pearl/diamond knot; *voir* **corde.**
b (*Naut: vitesse*) knot; *voir* **filer.**
c (*protubérance*) [*planche, canne*] knot; [*branche, tige*] knot, node.
d (*fig*) **le ~ de** *problème, débat* the crux ou nub of; (*Littérat, Théât*) **le ~ de l'intrigue** the knot of the intrigue.
e (*littér: lien*) **le (saint) ~ du mariage** the bonds of (holy) wedlock; **les ~s de l'amitié** the bonds ou ties of friendship.
f (*Astron, Élec, Géog, Ling, Phys, Tech*) node.
g (**: *pénis*) cock**, dick**, prick**.
2 comp ►**nœud coulant** slipknot, running knot ►**nœud de cravate** tie knot; **faire son nœud de cravate** to knot one's tie ►**nœud ferroviaire** (*ville*) rail junction ►**nœud gordien** Gordian knot; **couper ou trancher le nœud gordien** to cut the Gordian knot ►**nœud pap***, **nœud papillon** bow tie ►**nœud plat** reef knot ►**nœud routier** (*ville*) crossroad(s) ►**nœud de vache** granny knot ►**nœud de**

vipères nest of vipers ▸**nœud vital** nerve centre.

noir, e [nwaʀ] 1 adj a (*couleur*) black; *peau, personne* (*par le soleil*) tanned; (*par les coups etc*) black and blue (*attrib*); *yeux, cheveux* dark; *fumée, mer, ciel, nuage, temps* black, dark. ~ **comme du jais/de l'encre** jet/ink(y) black, black as jet/ink; ~ **comme du cirage** as black as boot-polish *ou* as soot; ~ **comme l'ébène** jet-black; **mets-moi ça** ~ **sur blanc** put it down in black and white for me; **je l'ai vu/c'est écrit** ~ **sur blanc** I saw it/it is (down) in black and white; **les murs étaient** ~**s de saleté/suie** the walls were black with dirt/soot; **avoir les mains** ~**es** to have dirty *ou* grubby hands; *voir* **beurre, blé, lunette.**
b *personne, race* black, coloured. **l'Afrique** ~**e** black Africa; **le problème** ~ the colour problem; *voir* **musique.**
c (*obscur*) dark. **il faisait** ~ **comme dans un four*** it was as black as pitch; **il faisait nuit** ~**e** it was pitch-dark *ou* pitch-black; **dans/à la nuit** ~**e** in the/at dead of night; (*fig*) **rue** ~**e de monde** street teeming *ou* swarming with people; *voir* **chambre.**
d (*fig*) *désespoir* black, deep; *humeur, pressentiment, colère* black; *idée* gloomy, sombre; (*macabre*) *film* macabre. **faire un tableau assez** ~ **de la situation** to paint a rather black *ou* gloomy picture of the situation; **plongé dans le plus** ~ **désespoir** *ou* **le désespoir le plus** ~ plunged in the depths of despair; **être dans la misère** ~**e** to be in utter *ou* abject poverty; *voir* **bête, humour, série.**
e (*hostile, mauvais*) *âme, ingratitude, trahison* black; *regard* black. **regarder qn d'un œil** ~ to give sb a black look; **il se trame un** ~ **complot** some dark plot is being hatched; *voir* **magie, messe.**
f (*: *ivre*) drunk, sloshed‡, tight.
2 nm a (*couleur*) black, blackness; (*matière colorante*) black. **photo/télévision en** ~ **et blanc** black and white *ou* monochrome photo/television (set); **film en** ~ **et blanc** black and white film; **le** ~ **et blanc** black and white *ou* monochrome photography; **le** ~ **de ses cheveux accentuait sa pâleur** her dark *ou* black hair accentuated her pallor, the blackness of her hair accentuated her pallor; **la mer était d'un** ~ **d'encre** the sea was inky black; **elle avait du** ~ **sur le menton** she had a black mark *ou* smudge on her chin; **se mettre du** ~ **aux yeux** to put on eye make-up; ~ **de fumée** lampblack.
b (*Habillement*) **elle ne porte jamais de** ~**, elle n'est jamais en** ~ she never wears black; **elle est en** ~ she is in *ou* is wearing black; (*en deuil*) she is in mourning.
c (*obscurité*) dark, darkness. **avoir peur du** ~ to be afraid of the dark; **dans le** ~ in the dark *ou* darkness.
d (*pessimisme*) **peindre les choses en** ~ to paint things black, paint a black picture; **voir les choses en** ~ to look on the black side (of things); *voir* **broyer, pousser, voir.**
e (*: *café*) black coffee.
f (*illégalement*) **acheter/vendre au** ~ to buy/sell on the black market; **travailler au** ~ to work on the side, moonlight*; **le travail au** ~ moonlighting*.
g **N**~ black; **les N**~**s d'Amérique** the blacks of America.
3 **noire** nf a (*personne*) **Noire** black, black woman.
b (*Mus*) crotchet (*Brit*), quarter note (*US*).

noirâtre [nwaʀɑtʀ] adj blackish.

noiraud, e [nwaʀo, od] 1 adj dark, swarthy. 2 nm,f dark *ou* swarthy person.

noirceur [nwaʀsœʀ] nf (*littér*) a (*NonC: voir* **noir**) blackness; darkness. b (*acte perfide*) black *ou* evil deed.

noircir [nwaʀsiʀ] 2 1 vt a (*salir*) [*fumée*] to blacken; [*encre, charbon*] to dirty. (*fig*) ~ **du papier** to write page after page. b (*colorer*) to blacken; (*à la cire, peinture*) to darken. **le soleil l'a noirci/lui a noirci le visage** the sun has tanned him/his face. c (*fig*) *réputation* to blacken. ~ **qn** to blacken sb's reputation *ou* name; ~ **la situation** to paint a black picture of the situation. 2 vi [*personne, peau*] to tan; [*fruit*] (*se tacher*) to go black; [*ciel*] to darken, grow black *ou* dark; [*couleur*] to darken. 3 **se noircir** vpr [*ciel*] to darken, grow black *ou* dark; [*temps*] to turn stormy; [*couleur, bois*] to darken; (‡: *s'enivrer*) to get plastered‡.

noircissement [nwaʀsismɑ̃] nm (*voir* **noircir**) blackening; dirtying; darkening.

noircissure [nwaʀsisyʀ] nf black smudge.

noise [nwaz] nf: **chercher** ~ *ou* **des** ~**s à qn** to try to pick a quarrel with sb.

noisetier [nwaz(ə)tje] nm hazel tree.

noisette [nwazɛt] 1 adj inv hazel. 2 nf (*fruit*) hazel(nut). (*morceau*) ~ **de beurre** knob of butter; (*Culin*) ~ **d'agneau** noisette of lamb.

noix [nwa] 1 nf (*fruit*) walnut; (‡: *idiot*) nut*; (*Culin*) [*côtelette*] eye. **à la** ~* rubbishy, crummy‡; *voir* **brou, coquille, gîte**[1]. 2 comp ▸**noix de beurre** knob of butter ▸**noix du Brésil** Brazil nut ▸**noix de cajou** cashew nut ▸**noix de coco** coconut ▸**noix de galle** oak apple, oak-gall ▸**noix (de) muscade** nutmeg ▸**noix pâtissière, noix de veau** cushion of veal ▸**noix vomique** nux vomica.

noliser [nɔlize] 1 vt to charter. **avion nolisé** charter plane.

nom [nɔ̃] 1 nm a (*nom propre*) name. **vos** ~ **et prénom?** your surname and first name, please?; **Henri le troisième du** ~ Henry III; **un homme du** ~ **de Dupont** *ou* **qui a (pour)** ~ **Dupont** a man called Dupont, a man with *ou* by the name of Dupont; **il ne connaît pas ses élèves par leur** ~ he doesn't know his pupils by (their) name; **je le connais de** ~ I know him by name; **il écrit sous le** ~ **de X** he writes under the name of X; **c'est un** ~ *ou* **ce n'est qu'un** ~ **pour moi!** he *ou* it is just a name to me!; (* *péj*) **un** ~ **à coucher dehors** an unpronounceable *ou* an impossible-sounding name; (*péj*) ~ **à charnière** *ou* **à rallonge** *ou* **à tiroirs** double-barrelled name; **sous un** ~ **d'emprunt** under an assumed name; *voir* **faux**[2]**, petit, répondre.**
b (*désignation*) name. **quel est le** ~ **de cet arbre?** what is the name of this tree?, what's this tree called?; **c'est une sorte de fascisme qui n'ose pas dire son** ~ it's fascism of a kind hiding under *ou* behind another name; **c'est du dirigisme qui n'ose pas dire son** ~ it's covert *ou* disguised state control; **comme son** ~ **l'indique** as is indicated by its *ou* his name, as the name indicates; **il appelle les choses par leur** ~ he's not afraid to call a spade a spade *ou* to call things by their proper name; **le** ~ **ne fait rien à la chose** what's in a name?; **les beaux** ~**s de justice, de liberté** these fine-sounding words of justice and liberty; **il n'est spécialiste que de** ~ he is only nominally a specialist, he is a specialist in name only; **un crime sans** ~ an unspeakable crime; **ce qu'il a fait n'a pas de** ~ what he did was unspeakable.
c (*célébrité*) name; (*noblesse*) name. **se faire un** ~ to make a name for o.s.; **laisser un** ~ to make one's mark; **c'est un (grand)** ~ **dans l'histoire** he's one of the great names of history.
d (*Gram*) noun; *voir* **complément.**
e (*loc*) **en mon/votre** ~ in my/your name; **il a parlé au** ~ **de tous les employés** he spoke for all *ou* on behalf of all the employees; **au** ~ **de la loi, ouvrez** open up in the name of the law; **au** ~ **de quoi vous permettez-vous ...?** whatever gives you the right to ...?; **au** ~ **du Père, du Fils ...** in the name of the Father and of the Son ...; **au** ~ **du ciel!** in heaven's name!; **au** ~ **de ce que vous avez de plus cher** in the name of everything you hold most dear; ~ **de Dieu!**‡ bloody hell!*‡ (*Brit*), God damn it!‡; ~ **de** ~ *ou* **d'un chien** *ou* **d'une pipe** *ou* **d'un petit bonhomme*** jings!* (*Brit*), heck!*, blimey!* (*Brit*), strewth!* (*Brit*); **donner à qn des** ~**s d'oiseaux** to call sb names; **traiter qn de tous les** ~**s** to call sb everything under the sun.
2 comp ▸**nom de baptême** Christian name, given name (*US*) ▸**nom de chose** concrete noun ▸**nom commercial** (company) name ▸**nom commun** common noun ▸**nom composé** compound (word *ou* noun) ▸**nom déposé** (registered) trade name ▸**nom d'emprunt** (*gén*) alias, assumed name; [*écrivain*] pen name, nom de plume ▸**nom de famille** surname ▸**nom de femme mariée** married name ▸**nom de fille/garçon** girl's/boy's name ▸**nom de guerre** nom de guerre ▸**nom de jeune fille** maiden name ▸**nom de lieu** place name ▸**nom de marque** trade name ▸**nom propre** proper noun ▸**nom de rue** street name ▸**nom de théâtre** stage name.

nomade [nɔmad] 1 adj nomadic; (*Zool*) migratory. 2 nmf nomad.

nomadisme [nɔmadism] nm nomadism.

no man's land [nomanslɑ̃d] nm no-man's-land.

nombrable [nɔ̃bʀabl] adj countable, numerable. **difficilement** ~ difficult to count.

nombre [nɔ̃bʀ] 1 nm a (*Ling, Math*) number. (*Bible*) **les N**~**s** (the Book of) Numbers; (*Gram*) **s'accorder en** ~ to agree in number.
b (*quantité*) number. **le** ~ **des victimes** the number of victims; **un certain/grand** ~ **de** a certain/great number of; **(un) bon** ~ **de** a good *ou* fair number of; **je lui ai dit** ~ **de fois que ...** I've told him many *ou* a number of times that ...; **depuis** ~ **d'années** for many years, for a number of years; **les gagnants sont au** ~ **de 3** there are 3 winners, the winners are 3 in number; **être supérieur en** ~ to be superior in numbers; **être en** ~ **suffisant** to be in sufficient number *ou* sufficient in number; **ils sont en** ~ **égal** their numbers are equal *ou* even, they are equal in number; **des ennemis sans** ~ innumerable *ou* countless enemies.
c (*masse*) numbers. **être/venir en** ~ to be/come in large numbers; **faire** ~ to make up the numbers; **être submergé par le** ~**, succomber sous le** ~ to be overcome by sheer weight of *ou* force of numbers; **il y en avait dans le** ~ **qui riaient** there were some among them who were laughing; **ça ne se verra pas dans le** ~ it won't be seen among all the rest *ou* when they're all together; **le (plus) grand** ~ the (great) majority (of people).
d **au** ~ **de, du** ~ **de** (*parmi*): **je le compte au** ~ **de mes amis** I count him as *ou* consider him one of my friends, I number him among my friends; **il n'est plus du** ~ **des vivants** he is no longer of this world; **est-il du** ~ **des reçus?** is he among those who passed?, he is one of the ones who passed?
2 comp ▸**nombre aléatoire** (*Ordin*) random number ▸**nombre atomique** atomic number ▸**nombre complexe** complex number ▸**nombre entier** whole number, integer ▸**nombre au hasard** (*Ordin*) random number ▸**nombre imaginaire** imaginary number ▸**nombre de Mach** Mach number ▸**nombre d'or** golden section ▸**nombre parfait** perfect number ▸**nombre premier** prime number.

nombrer [nɔ̃bʀe] 1 vt (†, *littér*) to number†, count.

nombreux, -euse [nɔ̃bʀø, øz] adj a (*en grand nombre*) **être** ~ [*exemples, visiteurs*] to be numerous; [*accidents*] to be numerous *ou* frequent; ~ **furent ceux qui ...** there were many who ...; **les gens étaient venus** ~ a great number of people had come, people had come in great numbers; venez ~! all welcome!; certains, et ils sont ~ certain people, and there are quite a few of them; peu ~ few; le public était moins/plus ~ hier there were fewer/more spectators yesterday; nous ne sommes pas si ~ there aren't so many of us; les visiteurs arrivaient sans cesse plus ~/de plus en plus ~ visitors kept on arriving in greater *ou* increasing numbers/in greater and greater *ou* in ever-increasing numbers; ils étaient plus ~ que nousthey outnumbered us, there were more of them.

b (*le grand nombre de*) numerous, many. parmi les ~euses personnalités amongst the numerous *ou* many personalities.

c (*un grand nombre de*) de ~ many, numerous; de ~ accidents se sont produits many *ou* numerous accidents have occurred; ça se voit à de ~ exemples many *ou* numerous examples illustrate this.

d (*important*) *foule, assistance, collection* large.

e (*littér: harmonieux*) *vers, style* harmonious, rounded, rich.

nombril [nɔ̃bʀi(l)] nm *[personne]* navel, belly button*. il se prend pour le ~ du monde* he thinks he is the cat's whiskers* *ou* God's gift to mankind; se regarder le ~* to contemplate one's navel.

nombrilisme* [nɔ̃bʀilism] nm (*péj*) faire du ~ to be self-centred, be wrapped up in o.s.

nombriliste* [nɔ̃bʀilist] adj, nmf: être ~ to be self-centred, be wrapped up in o.s.

nomenclature [nɔmɑ̃klatyʀ] nf (*gén: liste*) list; (*Ling, Sci*) nomenclature; *[dictionnaire]* word list.

nominal, e, mpl -aux [nɔminal, o] 1 adj (*gén*) nominal; (*Ling*) *groupe, phrase* noun (*épith*). liste ~e list of names; procéder à l'appel ~ to call the register *ou* the roll, do the roll call; expression ~e nominal expression; syntagme ~ noun phrase; (*Fin*) valeur ~e face value. 2 nm (*Ling*) pronoun.

nominalement [nɔminalmɑ̃] adv (*gén, Ling*) nominally. appeler qn ~ to call sb by name.

nominalisation [nɔminalizasjɔ̃] nf nominalization.

nominaliser [nɔminalize] 1 vt to nominalize.

nominalisme [nɔminalism] nm nominalism.

nominaliste [nɔminalist] adj, nmf nominalist.

nominatif, -ive [nɔminatif, iv] 1 adj (*Fin*) *titre, action* registered. (*Comm*) état ~ list of items; liste ~ive list of names; l'invitation n'est pas ~ive the invitation doesn't specify a name. 2 nm (*Ling*) nominative.

nomination [nɔminasjɔ̃] nf (*promotion*) appointment, nomination (*à* to); (*titre, acte*) appointment *ou* nomination papers. obtenir sa ~ to be nominated *ou* appointed (*au poste de* to the post of).

nominativement [nɔminativmɑ̃] adv by name.

nominé, e [nɔmine] adj *film, acteur, auteur* nominated. être ~ à qch to be nominated *ou* shortlisted for sth.

nommément [nɔmemɑ̃] adv a (*par son nom*) by name. b (*spécialement*) notably, especially, particularly.

nommer [nɔme] 1 1 vt a (*promouvoir*) *fonctionnaire* to appoint; *candidat* to nominate. ~ qn à un poste to appoint *ou* nominate sb to a post; ~ qn son héritier to name *ou* appoint sb (as) one's heir; il a été nommé gérant/ministre he was appointed *ou* made manager/minister.

b (*appeler*) *personne* to call, name; (*dénommer*) *découverte, produit* to name, give a name to. ils l'ont nommé Richard they called *ou* named him Richard, they gave him the name of Richard; un homme nommé Martin a man named *ou* called *ou* by the name of Martin; le nommé Martin the man named *ou* called Martin; ce que nous nommons le bonheur what we name *ou* call happiness; *voir* point[1].

c (*citer*) *fleuves, batailles, auteurs, complices* to name, give the name(s) of. (*hum*) M. Sartin, pour ne pas le ~, ... without mentioning any names, Mr Sartin ...; quelqu'un que je ne nommerai pas somebody who shall remain nameless, somebody whose name I shall not mention.

2 se nommer vpr a (*s'appeler*) to be called. comment se nomme-t-il? what is he called?, what is his name?; il se nomme Paul he's called Paul, his name is Paul.

b (*se présenter*) to introduce o.s. il entra et se nomma he came in and gave his name *ou* introduced himself.

non [nɔ̃] 1 adv a (*réponse négative*) no. le connaissez-vous? — ~ do you know him? — no (I don't); est-elle chez elle? — ~ is she at home? — no (she isn't *ou* she's not); je vais ouvrir la fenêtre — ~ il y aura des courants d'air I'll open the window — no (don't), it'll make a draught; il n'a pas encore dit ~! he hasn't said no yet!, he hasn't refused (as) yet; je ne dis pas ~ (*ce n'est pas de refus*) I wouldn't say no; (*je n'en disconviens pas*) I don't disagree; ah ça ~! certainly *ou* definitely not!, I should say not!; ~ et ~! no, no, no!, absolutely not!; que ~! I should say not!, definitely not!; ~ merci! no thank you!; certes ~! most certainly *ou* definitely not!, indeed no!, no indeed!; vous n'y allez pas? — mais ~! *ou* bien sûr que ~! aren't you going? — of course not! *ou* I (most) certainly shall not! *ou* I should think not!; répondre (par) ~ à toutes les questions to answer no *ou* answer in the negative to all the questions; faire ~ de la tête to shake one's head; dire/répondre que ~ to say/answer it isn't (*ou* it won't *etc, selon le contexte*).

b (*remplaçant une proposition*) not. faire signe que ~ (*de la main*) to make a gesture of refusal (*ou* disagreement *ou* disapproval); (*de la tête*) to shake one's head; est-ce que c'est nécessaire? — je pense *ou* crois que ~ is that necessary? — I don't think so *ou* I don't think it is *ou* I think not; je crains que ~ I fear not, I am afraid not; il nous quitte? — j'espère que ~ is he leaving us? — I hope not *ou* I hope he isn't; je le crois — moi ~ I believe him — I (*emphatique*) don't *ou* not me*; vous avez aimé le film? — moi ~ mais les autres oui did you like the film? — (no) I didn't *ou* not me* but the others did; il l'aime bien, moi ~ he likes him but I don't *ou* not me*; j'ai demandé si elle était venue, lui dit que ~ I asked if she had been — he says not *ou* he says no *ou* he says she hasn't; ah ~? really?, no?; partez-vous ou ~? are you going or not?, are you going or aren't you?; il se demandait s'il irait ou ~ he wondered whether to go or not; erreur ou ~/qu'il l'ait voulu ou ~ le mal est fait mistake or no mistake/whether he meant it or not the damage is done.

c (*frm: pas*) not. c'est par paresse et ~ (pas) par prudence que ... it is through laziness and not caution that ...; je veux bien de leur aide mais ~ (pas) de leur argent I am willing to accept their help but not their money *ou* but I want none of their money; c'est mon avis ~ (pas) le vôtre it's my opinion not yours; ~ (pas) que ... not that ...; ~ (pas) qu'il eût peur mais ... not that he was frightened but ...; il n'a pas reculé, ~ plus qu'eux d'ailleurs he didn't go back any more than they did in fact.

d (*exprimant l'impatience, l'indignation*) tu vas cesser de pleurer ~? will you stop crying?, just stop that crying (will you?); ~ par exemple! for goodness sake!, good gracious!; ~ mais alors!*, ~ mais (des fois)!* for goodness sake!*, honestly!; ~ mais des fois, tu me prends pour qui?* look here* *ou* for God's sake‡ what do you take me for?

e (*exprimant le doute*) no? il me l'a dit lui-même — ~? he told me so himself — no?; c'est bon ~? it's good isn't it?

f ~ plus neither, not either; il ne l'a pas vu ni moi ~ plus he didn't see him — (and) neither did I *ou* (and) I didn't either; nous ne l'avons pas vu — nous ~ plus we didn't see him — neither did we *ou* we didn't either; nous ~ plus nous ne l'avons pas vu we didn't see him either; il n'a pas compris lui ~ plus he didn't understand either; il parle ~ plus en médecin mais en ami he is talking now not as a doctor but as a friend.

g (*modifiant adv*) not. ~ loin de là il y a ... not far from there there's ...; c'est une expérience ~ moins intéressante it's an experience that is no less interesting; je l'aime ~ moins que toi I love him no less than you (do), I do not love him less than you (do); un homme ~ pas érudit mais instruit a man (who is) not (at all) erudite but well-informed; il a continué ~ plus en auto mais en train he continued on his way not by car (any more) but by train; il l'a fait ~ sans raison/~ sans peine he did it not without reason/difficulty; il y est allé ~ sans protester he went (but) not without protest *ou* protesting; ~ seulement il est impoli mais ... not only is he *ou* he is not only impolite but ...; ~ seulement il ne travaille pas mais (encore) il empêche les autres de travailler not only does he not work but he (also) stops the others working too; ~ seulement le directeur mais aussi *ou* encore les employés not only the manager but the employees too *ou* as well.

h (*modifiant adj ou participe*) les objets ~ réclamés unclaimed items; une quantité ~ négligeable an appreciable amount; toutes les places ~ réservées all the unreserved seats, all seats not reserved; les travaux ~ terminés the unfinished work; ~ coupable not guilty.

2 nm inv no. répondre par un ~ catégorique to reply with a categorical no; il y a eu 30 ~ there were 30 votes against *ou* 30 noes; *voir* oui.

3 préf non-, un-. ~ ferreux/gazeux non-ferrous/-gaseous; ~ vérifié unverified; ~ spécialisé unspecialized, non-specialized.

4 comp (*le préfixe* non *reste invariable au pluriel*) ►**non accompli, e** adj (*Ling*) continuous ►**non-activité** nf inactivity ►**non-agression** nf non-aggression ►**non aligné, e** adj nonaligned ►**non-alignement** nm nonalignment ►**non-appartenance** nf non-membership ►**non arrondi, e** adj (*Phon*) spread ►**non-assistance** (*Jur*) nf: non-assistance à personne en danger failure to render assistance to a person in danger ►**non-belligérance** nf nonbelligerence ►**non belligérant, e** adj, nm,f nonbelligerent ►**non-combattant, e** adj, nm,f noncombatant ►**non-comparution** nf (*Jur*) nonappearance ►**non-conformisme** nm nonconformism ►**non conformiste** adj, nm,f nonconformist ►**non-conformité** nf nonconformity ►**non-croyant, e** nm,f unbeliever, non-believer ►**non-cumul** nm: il y a non-cumul de peines sentences run concurrently; le principe du non-cumul des fonctions the rule prohibiting anyone from holding more than one post at a time ►**non dénombrable** adj (*Ling*) uncountable ►**non directif, -ive** adj *entretien, questionnaire* with no leading questions; *thérapie* nondirective ►**non-discrimination** nf nondiscrimination ►**non-dit** nm what is unspoken, unspoken *ou* unvoiced comment ►**non engagé, e** adj *artiste* with no political commitment; *pays* neutral, nonaligned ►**non-engagement** nm *[artiste]* lack of political commitment; *[pays]* nonalignment ►**non-être** nm (*Philos*) non-being ►**non-événement** nm nonevent ►**non-exécution** nf *[contrat]* non-completion ►**non existant, e** adj nonexistent ►**non-existence** nf nonexistence ►**non figuratif, -ive** adj nonrepresentational ►**non-fumeur, -euse** adj no-smoking (*épith*) ◊ nm,f non-smoker ►**non-ingérence** nf noninterference ►**non-initié, e** nm,f lay person ►**non-inscrit, e** adj (*Pol*) independent ◊ nm,f independent (member) ►**non-intervention** nf nonintervention ►**non-interventionniste** adj, nmf noninterventionist ►**non-jouissance** nf

(*Jur*) nonenjoyment ▸**non-lieu** (*Jur*) nm: **bénéficier d'un non-lieu** to be discharged *ou* have one's case dismissed for lack of evidence ▸**non lucratif, -ive** adj: **à but non lucratif** non-profit-making ▸**non marqué, e** adj (*Ling*) unmarked ▸**non-moi** nm (*Philos*) nonego ▸**non-paiement** nm nonpayment ▸**non-partant** nm (*Sport*) non-runner ▸**non-parution** nf failure to appear *ou* be published ▸**non polluant, e** adj non-polluting (*épith*) ▸**non-prolifération** nf nonproliferation ▸**non-recevoir** nm *voir* **fin²** ▸**non-résident, e** nm,f nonresident ▸**non-retour** nm no return (*voir* **point¹**) ▸**non-rétroactivité** nf (*Jur*) nonretroactivity ▸**non-salarié, e** nm,f self-employed person ▸**non-sens** nm inv (*absurdité*) (piece of) nonsense; (*erreur de traduction*) meaningless word (*ou* phrase *etc*) ▸**non stop** adj inv, adv nonstop ▸**non-syndiqué, e** adj nonunion(ized) ◊ nm,f nonunion member, nonmember (of a *ou* the union) ▸**non-valeur** nf (*Jur*) unproductiveness; (*Fin*) bad debt; (*fig*) nonproductive asset, wasted asset ▸**non-violence** nf nonviolence ▸**non-violent, e** adj nonviolent ◊ nmf advocate *ou* supporter of nonviolence ▸**non voisé, e** adj (*Phon*) unvoiced, voiceless ▸**non-voyant, e** adj, nm,f unsighted.

nonagénaire [nɔnaʒenɛʀ] adj, nmf nonagenarian, ninety-year-old.

nonante [nɔnɑ̃t] adj (*Belgique, Suisse*) ninety.

nonantième [nɔnɑ̃tjɛm] adj (*Belgique, Suisse*) ninetieth.

nonce [nɔ̃s] nm nuncio. ~ **apostolique** apostolic nuncio.

nonchalamment [nɔ̃ʃalamɑ̃] adv nonchalantly.

nonchalance [nɔ̃ʃalɑ̃s] nf nonchalance.

nonchalant, e [nɔ̃ʃalɑ̃, ɑ̃t] adj nonchalant.

nonciature [nɔ̃sjatyʀ] nf nunciature.

nonne [nɔn] nf (††, *hum*) nun.

nonnette [nɔnɛt] nf (*Culin*) spiced bun (*made of pain d'épice*).

nonobstant [nɔnɔpstɑ̃] 1 prép († *ou Jur: malgré*) notwithstanding, despite, in spite of. 2 adv (†: *néanmoins*) notwithstanding†, nevertheless.

nonpareil, -eille†† [nɔ̃paʀɛj] adj nonpareil, peerless.

noosphère [nɔɔsfɛʀ] nf noosphere.

nord [nɔʀ] 1 nm a (*point cardinal*) north. ~ **géographique/magnétique** true/magnetic north; **le vent du** ~ the north wind; **un vent du** ~ (*gén*) a north(erly) wind; (*Naut*) a northerly; **le vent tourne/est au** ~ the wind is veering north(-wards) *ou* towards the north/is blowing from the north; **regarder vers le** ~ *ou* **dans la direction du** ~ to look north(wards) *ou* towards the north; **au** ~ (*situation*) in the north; (*direction*) to the north, north(wards); **au** ~ **de** north of, to the north of; **l'appartement est (exposé) au** ~**/en plein** ~ the flat faces (the) north *ou* northwards/due north, the flat looks north(wards)/due north; **l'Europe/l'Italie/la Bourgogne du** ~ Northern Europe/Italy/Burgundy; *voir* **mer, perdre.**

b (*partie, régions septentrionales*) north. **pays/peuples du** ~ northern countries/peoples, countries/peoples of the north; **le** ~ **de la France, le N**~ the North (of France); *voir* **grand.**

2 adj inv *région, partie* northern (*épith*); *entrée, paroi* north (*épith*); *versant, côte* north(ern) (*épith*); *côté* north(ward) (*épith*); *direction* northward (*épith*), northerly (*Mét*); *voir* **hémisphère, latitude, pôle.**

3 comp ▸**nord-africain, e** adj North African ▸**Nord-Africain, e** nm,f (**mpl Nord-Africains**) North African ▸**nord-américain, e** adj North American ▸**Nord-Américain, e** nm,f (**mpl Nord-Américains**) North American ▸**nord-coréen, -enne** adj North Korean ▸**Nord-Coréen, -enne** nm,f (**mpl Nord-Coréens**) North Korean ▸**nord-est** adj inv, nm north-east ▸**nord-nord-est** adj inv, nm north-north-east ▸**nord-nord-ouest** adj inv, nm north-north-west ▸**nord-ouest** adj inv, nm north-west ▸**nord-vietnamien, -ienne** adj North Vietnamese ▸**Nord-Vietnamien, -ienne** nm,f (**mpl Nord-Vietnamiens**) North Vietnamese.

nordique [nɔʀdik] 1 adj *pays, race* Nordic; *langues* Scandinavian, Nordic; *voir* **ski.** 2 nmf: **N**~ Scandinavian.

nordiste [nɔʀdist] (*Hist USA*) 1 adj Northern, Yankee. 2 nmf: **N**~ Northerner, Yankee.

noria [nɔʀja] nf noria, bucket waterwheel. (*fig*) **une** ~ **d'hélicoptères a transporté les blessés vers les hôpitaux** a fleet of helicopters shuttled *ou* ferried the wounded to the hospitals.

normal, e, mpl **-aux** [nɔʀmal, o] 1 adj (*gén, Chim, Math, Méd*) normal; (*courant, habituel*) normal, usual. **de dimension** ~**e** normal-sized, standard-sized; **c'est une chose très** ~**e, ça n'a rien que de très** ~ that's quite usual *ou* normal, it's quite the usual thing, it's the normal thing; **il n'est pas** ~ he's not normal, there's something wrong with him; **c'est** ~! it's (quite) natural!; **ce n'est pas** ~ there must be something wrong; *voir* **école, état, temps¹.**

2 **normale** nf a **s'écarter de la** ~**e** to diverge from the norm; **revenir à la** ~**e** to return to normality, get back to normal; **au-dessus de la** ~**e** above average; **température voisine des** ~**es saisonnières** temperature close to the seasonal average.

b (*Math*) normal (*à* to).

c **N**~**e (sup)** (**abrév de École normale supérieure**) *voir* **école.**

normalement [nɔʀmalmɑ̃] adv (*comme prévu*) normally; (*habituellement*) normally, usually, ordinarily. ~, **il devrait être là demain** normally he'd be there tomorrow, in the usual *ou* ordinary course of events he'd be there tomorrow; ~ **il vient le jeudi** as a rule *ou* normally *ou* generally he comes on a Thursday.

normalien, -ienne [nɔʀmaljɛ̃, jɛn] nm,f (*instituteur*) student at teachers' training college; (*professeur*) student at the *École normale supérieure*.

normalisation [nɔʀmalizasjɔ̃] nf (*voir* **normaliser**) normalization; standardization.

normaliser [nɔʀmalize] 1 vt *situation, relations* to normalize; *produit* to standardize.

normalité [nɔʀmalite] nf normality.

normand, e [nɔʀmɑ̃, ɑ̃d] 1 adj (*de Normandie*) Norman; (*Hist: scandinave*) Norse; *voir* **armoire, trou.** 2 nm a (*Ling*) Norman (French). b **N**~ (*de Normandie*) Norman; (*Hist: Scandinave*) Norseman, Northman; *voir* **réponse.** 3 nf: **N**~**e** Norman; Norsewoman.

Normandie [nɔʀmɑ̃di] nf Normandy.

normatif, -ive [nɔʀmatif, iv] adj prescriptive, normative.

normativisme [nɔʀmativism] nm prescriptivism.

norme [nɔʀm] nf (*Math, gén*) norm; (*Tech*) standard. ~**s de fabrication** standards of manufacture, manufacturing standards; ~**s de sécurité** safety standards; **ce produit n'est pas conforme aux** ~**s françaises/allemandes** this product doesn't conform to French/German standards; **tant que ça reste dans la** ~ as long as it is kept within limits; **pourvu que vous restiez dans la** ~ provided you do not overdo it *ou* you don't overstep the limits, provided you keep within the norm.

normé, e [nɔʀme] adj (*Math*) normed.

normographe [nɔʀmɔgʀaf] nm stencil.

norois¹, e [nɔʀwa, waz] adj, nm Old Norse.

norois², noroît [nɔʀwa] nm (*vent*) northwester.

Norvège [nɔʀvɛʒ] nf Norway.

norvégien, -ienne [nɔʀveʒjɛ̃, jɛn] 1 adj Norwegian; *voir* **marmite, omelette.** 2 nm (*Ling*) Norwegian. 3 nm,f: **N**~**(ne)** Norwegian.

nos [no] adj poss *voir* **notre.**

nostalgie [nɔstalʒi] nf nostalgia. **avoir la** ~ **de** to feel nostalgia for; **garder la** ~ **de** to retain a nostalgia for.

nostalgique [nɔstalʒik] 1 adj nostalgic. 2 nmf: **les** ~**s du nazisme** those who long for the return of the Nazis.

nota (bene) [nɔta (bene)] nm inv nota bene.

notabilité [nɔtabilite] nf notability.

notable [nɔtabl] 1 adj *fait* notable, noteworthy; *changement, progrès* notable. **c'est quelqu'un de** ~ he's somebody of note. 2 nm notable, worthy.

notablement [nɔtabləmɑ̃] adv notably.

notaire [nɔtɛʀ] nm ≃ lawyer, solicitor (*Brit*).

notamment [nɔtamɑ̃] adv (*entre autres*) notably, among others; (*plus particulièrement*) notably, in particular, particularly.

notarial, e, mpl **-iaux** [nɔtaʀjal, jo] adj notarial.

notariat [nɔtaʀja] nm (*fonction*) profession of (a) notary (public); (*corps des notaires*) body of notaries (public).

notarié, e [nɔtaʀje] adj drawn up by a notary (public) *ou* by a solicitor, notarized (*SPÉC*).

notation [nɔtasjɔ̃] nf a (*symboles, système*) notation. b (*touche, note*) *[couleurs]* touch; *[sons]* variation. (*Littérat*) **une** ~ **intéressante** an interesting touch *ou* variation. c (*transcription*) *[sentiment, geste, son]* expression. d (*jugement*) *[devoir]* marking, grading; *[employé]* assessment.

note [nɔt] 1 nf a (*remarque, communication*) note. ~ **diplomatique/officielle** diplomatic/official note; **prendre des** ~**s** to take notes; **prendre (bonne)** ~ **de qch** to take (good) note of sth; **prendre qch en** ~ to make a note of sth, write sth down; (*hâtivement*) to jot sth down; **relire ses** ~**s** to read over one's notes *ou* jottings; **remarque en** ~ marginal comment, comment in the margin; **c'est écrit en** ~ it's written in the margin.

b (*appréciation chiffrée*) mark, grade. **mettre une** ~ **à** *dissertation* to mark, grade (*US*); *élève* to give a mark to (*Brit*), grade (*US*); *employé* to assess; **avoir de bonnes/mauvaises** ~**s** to have good/bad marks *ou* grades; **avoir une bonne/mauvaise** ~ **à un devoir/en histoire** to have a good/bad mark for a homework exercise/for *ou* in history; (*fig*) **c'est une mauvaise** ~ **pour lui** it's a black mark against him.

c (*compte*) *[gaz, blanchisserie]* bill, account; *[restaurant, hôtel]* bill, check (*US*). **demander/présenter/régler la** ~ to ask for/present/settle the bill (*Brit*) *ou* check (*US*); **vous me donnerez la** ~**, s'il vous plaît** may I have the bill (*Brit*) *ou* check (*US*) please?, I'd like my bill (*Brit*) *ou* check (*US*) please; **je vais vous faire la** ~ I'll make out the bill (*Brit*) *ou* check (*US*) for you; **mettez-le sur ma** ~ put it on my bill (*Brit*) *ou* check (*US*); ~ **de frais** (*bulletin*) claim form (for expenses); (*argent dépensé*) expenses; ~ **d'honoraires** (doctor's *ou* lawyer's) account.

d (*Mus, fig*) note. **donner la** ~ (*Mus*) to give the key; (*fig*) to set the tone; **la** ~ **juste** the right note; **c'est tout à fait dans la** ~ it fits in perfectly with the rest; **ses paroles étaient tout à fait dans la** ~**/n'étaient pas dans la** ~ his words struck exactly the right note/struck the wrong note (altogether); **ce n'est pas dans la** ~ it doesn't strike the right note at all; *voir* **faux², forcer.**

e (*trace, touche*) note, touch. **mettre une** ~ **triste** *ou* **de tristesse dans qch** to lend a touch *ou* note of sadness to sth; **une** ~ **d'anxiété/de fierté perçait sous ses paroles** a note of anxiety/pride was discernible in his words; *[parfum]* **une** ~ **de santal** a hint of sandalwood.

2 comp ▸ **note de l'auteur** author's note ▸ **note en bas de page** footnote ▸ **note marginale** marginal note, note in the margin ▸ **note de passage** (*Mus*) passing note ▸ **note de la rédaction** editor's note ▸ **note de service** memorandum.

noter [nɔte] 1 vt a (*inscrire*) *adresse, rendez-vous* to write down, note down, make a note of; *idées* to jot down, write down, note down; (*Mus*) *air* to write down, take down. **si vous pouviez le ~ quelque part** could you make a note of it *ou* write it down somewhere; **notez que nous serons absents** note that we'll be away.

b (*remarquer*) *faute, progrès* to notice. **notez la précision du bas-relief** note the fine bas relief work; **notez (bien) que je n'ai rien dit, je n'ai rien dit notez-le** *ou* **notez (bien)** note that I didn't say anything, mark you, I didn't say anything; **il faut ~ qu'il a des excuses** admittedly he has an excuse, he has an excuse mark you *ou* mind you; **ceci est à ~** *ou* **mérite d'être noté** this is worth noting, this should be noted.

c (*cocher, souligner*) *citation, passage* to mark. **~ d'une croix** to mark with a cross, put a cross against (*Brit*), check off.

d (*juger*) *devoir* to mark, grade (*US*); *élève* to give a mark to, grade (*US*); *employé* to assess. **~ sur 10/20** to mark out of 10/20; **devoir bien/mal noté** homework with a good/bad mark *ou* grade; **employé bien/mal noté** highly/poorly rated employee, employee with a good/bad record; **elle note sévèrement/large** she is a strict/lenient marker.

notice [nɔtis] nf (*préface*) note; (*résumé*) note; (*mode d'emploi*) directions, instructions. **~ biographique/bibliographique** biographical/bibliographical note; **~ explicative** *ou* **d'emploi** directions for use, explanatory leaflet; **~ nécrologique** obituary.

notificatif, -ive [nɔtifikatif, iv] adj notifying. **lettre ~ive** letter of notification.

notification [nɔtifikasjɔ̃] nf (*Admin*) notification. **~ vous a été envoyée de vous présenter** notification has been sent to you to present yourself; **recevoir ~ de** to be notified of, receive notification of; (*Jur*) **~ d'actes** service of documents.

notifier [nɔtifje] 7 vt to notify. **~ qch à qn** to notify sb of sth, notify sth to sb; **on lui a notifié que ...** he was notified that ..., he received notice that ... .

notion [nosjɔ̃] nf a (*conscience*) notion. **je n'ai pas la moindre ~ de** I haven't the faintest notion of; **perdre la ~ du temps** *ou* **de l'heure** to lose all notion *ou* idea of time. b (*connaissances*) **~s** notion, elementary knowledge; **avoir quelques ~s de grammaire** to have some notion of grammar, have a smattering of grammar; (*titre*) **~s d'algèbre/d'histoire** algebra/history primer.

notionnel, -elle [nosjɔnɛl] adj notional.

notoire [nɔtwaʀ] adj *criminel, méchanceté* notorious; *fait, vérité* well-known, acknowledged (*épith*). **il est ~ que** it is common *ou* public knowledge that, it's an acknowledged fact that.

notoirement [nɔtwaʀmɑ̃] adv: **c'est ~ reconnu** it's generally recognized, it's well known; **il est ~ malhonnête** he's notoriously dishonest.

notoriété [nɔtɔʀjete] nf *[fait]* notoriety; (*renommée*) fame. **c'est de ~ publique** that's common *ou* public knowledge.

notre [nɔtʀ], pl **nos** [no] adj poss a (*possession, relation*) our; (*emphatique*) our own; (*majesté ou modestie de convention* = **mon, ma, mes**) our; (*emphatique*) our own. **~ fils et ~ fille** our son and daughter; **nous avons tous laissé ~ manteau et ~ chapeau au vestiaire** we have all left our coats and hats in the cloakroom; **~ bonne ville de Tours est en fête** our fine city of Tours is celebrating; **car tel est ~ bon plaisir** for such is our wish, for so it pleases us; **dans cet exposé ~ intention est de ...** in this essay we intend to ...; *pour autres exemples voir* **son**[1].

b (*valeur affective, ironique, intensive*) **et comment va ~ malade aujourd'hui?** and how's the *ou* our patient today?; **~ héros décide alors ...** and so our hero decides ...; **~ homme a filé sans demander son reste** the chap *ou* fellow has run off without asking for his due; **voilà ~ bon Martin!** here's good old Martin!; (*dial*) **~ maître** the master; *voir* **son**[1].

c (*représentant la généralité des hommes*) **~ planète** our planet; **~ corps/esprit** our bodies/minds; **~ maître à tous** our master, the master of us all; **N~ Seigneur/Père** Our Lord/Father; **N~-Dame** Our Lady; (*église*) Notre Dame, Our Lady; **N~-Dame de Paris** Notre Dame of Paris; **N~-Dame de Chartres/Lourdes** Our Lady of Chartres/Lourdes; **le N~ Père** the Lord's Prayer, Our Father.

nôtre [notʀ] 1 pron poss: **le ~, la ~, les ~s** ours, our own; **cette voiture n'est pas la ~** this car is not ours, this is not our car; **leurs enfants sont sortis avec les ~s** their children are out with ours *ou* our own; **à la (bonne) ~!** our good health!, here's to us!; *pour autres exemples voir* **sien.**

2 nm a **nous y mettrons du ~** we'll pull our weight, we'll do our bit*; *voir aussi* **sien.**

b **les ~s** (*famille*) our family, our (own) folks*; (*partisans*) our own people; **j'espère que vous serez des ~s ce soir** I hope you will join our party *ou* join us tonight.

3 adj poss (*littér*) ours, our own. **ces idées ne sont plus exclusivement ~s** these ideas are no longer ours alone *ou* exclusively; **ces principes, nous les avons faits ~s** we have made these principles our own.

Nouakchott [nwakʃɔt] n Nouakchott.

nouba‡ [nuba] nf: **faire la ~** to live it up*, have a rave-up‡.

nouer [nwe] 1 1 vt a (*faire un nœud avec*) *ficelle* to tie, knot; *ceinture* to fasten; *lacets, foulard* to tie; *cravate* to knot, fasten. **~ les bras autour de la taille de qn** to put one's arms round sb's waist; **l'émotion lui nouait la gorge** his throat was tight with emotion; **avoir la gorge nouée (par l'émotion)** to have a lump in one's throat.

b (*entourer d'une ficelle*) *bouquet, paquet* to tie up, do up; *cheveux* to tie up *ou* back.

c (*former*) *complot* to hatch; *alliance* to make, form; *relations* to strike up; *amitié* to form, build up. **~ conversation avec qn** to start (up) *ou* strike up a conversation with sb.

d (*Tech*) **~ la chaîne/la trame** to splice the warp/weft.

e (*Littérat*) *action, intrigue* to build up, bring to a head *ou* climax.

2 vi (*Bot*) to set.

3 **se nouer** vpr a (*s'unir*) *[mains]* to join together. **sa gorge se noua** a lump came to his throat.

b (*se former*) *[complot]* to be hatched; *[alliance]* to be made, be formed; *[amitié]* to be formed, build up; *[conversation]* to start, be started.

c (*pièce de théâtre*) **c'est là où l'intrigue se noue** it's at that point that the plot takes shape.

noueux, -euse [nwø, øz] adj *branche* knotty, gnarled; *main* gnarled; *vieillard* wizened.

nougat [nuga] nm (*Culin*) nougat. (*pieds*) **~s‡** feet; **c'est du ~*** it's dead easy* (*Brit*), it's a cinch* *ou* a piece of cake* (*Brit*); **c'est pas du ~*** it's not so easy.

nougatine [nugatin] nf nougatine.

nouille [nuj] nf a (*Culin*) piece *ou* bit of pasta. **~s** pasta, noodles; (*Art*) **style ~** Art Nouveau. b (*) (*imbécile*) noodle* (*Brit*), idiot; (*mollasson*) big lump*. **ce que c'est ~*** how idiotic (it is).

noumène [numɛn] nm noumenon.

nounou* [nunu] nf nanny.

nounours [nunuʀs] nm teddy (bear).

nourri, e [nuʀi] (ptp de **nourrir**) adj *fusillade* heavy; *applaudissements* hearty, prolonged; *conversation* lively; *style* rich.

nourrice [nuʀis] nf a (*gardienne*) child-minder, nanny; (*qui allaite*) wet nurse. **~ sèche†** dry nurse; **mettre un enfant en ~** to put a child out to nurse *ou* in the care of a nurse; **prendre un enfant en ~** to look after a child; *voir* **épingle.** b (*bidon*) jerrycan (*Brit*), can (*US*).

nourricier, -ière [nuʀisje, jɛʀ] 1 adj (*Anat*) *canal, artère* nutrient; (*Bot*) *suc, sève* nutritive; (††: *adoptif*) *mère, père* foster (*épith*). (*littér*) **la terre ~ière** the nourishing earth. 2 nm foster father. **les ~s** the foster parents.

nourrir [nuʀiʀ] 2 1 vt a (*alimenter*) *animal, personne* to feed; *feu* to stoke; *récit, devoir* to fill out; *cuir, peau* to nourish. **~ au biberon** to bottle-feed; **~ au sein** to breast-feed; **~ à la cuiller** to spoon-feed; **~ un oiseau au grain** to feed a bird (on) seed; **les régions qui nourrissent la capitale** the areas which provide food for the capital *ou* provide the capital with food; **bien/mal nourri** well-/poorly-fed; *voir* **logé.**

b (*faire vivre*) *famille, pays* to feed, provide for. **cette entreprise nourrit 10 000 ouvriers** this firm gives work to *ou* provides work for 10,000 workers; **ce métier ne nourrit pas son homme** this job doesn't earn a man his bread *ou* doesn't give a man a living wage.

c (*fig: caresser*) *projet* to nurse; *désir, espoir, illusion* to nourish, nurture, cherish, foster; *haine* to nourish, harbour a feeling of; *vengeance* to nourish, harbour thoughts of.

d (*littér: former*) **être nourri dans les bons principes** to be nurtured on good principles; **la lecture nourrit l'esprit** reading improves the mind.

2 vi to be nourishing.

3 **se nourrir** vpr to eat. **se ~ de** *viande* to feed (o.s.) on, eat; *illusions* to feed on, live on; (*fig*) **il se nourrit de romans** novels are his staple diet.

nourrissant, e [nuʀisɑ̃, ɑ̃t] adj *aliment* nourishing, nutritious; *crème, cosmétique* nourishing (*épith*).

nourrisson [nuʀisɔ̃] nm (unweaned) infant, nursling (*littér*).

nourriture [nuʀityʀ] nf a (*aliments, fig*) food. **assurer la ~ de qn** to provide sb's meals *ou* sb with food. b (*alimentation*) food. **il lui faut une ~ saine** he needs a healthy diet; **la ~ des poissons se compose de ...** the food of fish is made up of ...; **la lecture est une bonne ~ pour l'esprit** reading is good nourishment for the mind.

nous [nu] 1 pron pers a (*sujet*) we. **~ vous écrirons** we'll write to you; **~ avons bien ri tous les deux** the two of us had a good laugh, we both had a good laugh; **eux ont accepté, ~ non** *ou* **pas ~** they accepted but we didn't, they accepted but not us*; **c'est enfin ~, ~ voilà enfin** here we are at last; **qui l'a vu? — ~/pas ~** who saw him? — we did/we didn't *ou* us/not us*; **~ accepter?, jamais!** us accept that?, never!, you expect us to accept that?, never!; *voir aussi* **même.**

b (*objet dir ou indir, complément*) us. **aide-~** help us, give us a hand; **donne-~ ton livre** give us your book, give your book to us; **si vous étiez ~ que feriez-vous?** if you were us *ou* if you were in our shoes what would you do?; **donne-le-~** give it to us, give us it; **écoutez-~** listen to us; **il n'obéit qu'à ~** we are the only ones he obeys, he obeys only us.

c (*emphatique: insistance*) (*sujet*) we, we ourselves; (*objet*) us. ~, **nous le connaissons bien — mais ~ aussi** we know him well ourselves — but so do we *ou* we do too; **pourquoi ne le ferait-il pas?, nous l'avons bien fait,** ~ why shouldn't he do it?, we did it (all right); **alors ~, nous restons pour compte?** and what about us, are we to be left out?; ~, **elle nous déteste** she hates us; **elle nous connaît bien,** ~ she knows us all right.

d (*emphatique avec qui, que*) (*sujet*) we; (*objet*) us. **c'est ~ qui sommes fautifs** we are the culprits, we are the ones to blame; **merci — c'est ~ qui vous remercions** thank you — it's we who should thank you; **et ~ (tous) qui vous parlons l'avons vu** we (all) saw him personally; **est-ce ~ qui devons vous le dire?** do we have to tell you?; **et ~ qui n'avions pas le sou!** and there were we without a penny!, and to think we didn't have a penny!; **~ que le théâtre passionne, nous n'avons jamais vu cette pièce** great theatre lovers that we are we have still never seen that play, even we with all our great love for the theatre have never seen that play; **il nous dit cela à ~ qui l'avons tant aidé** and that's what he says to us who have helped him so much; **c'est ~ qu'elle veut voir** it's us she wants to see.

e (*avec prép*) us. **à ~ cinq, nous devrions pouvoir soulever ça** between the 5 of us we should be able to lift that; **cette maison est à ~** this house belongs to us *ou* is ours; **nous avons une maison à ~** we have a house of our own, we have our own house; **avec/sans ~** with/without us; **c'est à ~ de décider** it's up to us *ou* to ourselves to decide; **elle l'a appris par ~** she heard about it through *ou* from us; **un élève à ~** one of our pupils; **l'un de ~ ou d'entre ~ doit le savoir** one of us must know (it); **nos enfants à ~** our children; **l'idée vient de ~** the idea comes from us *ou* is ours; **elle veut une photo de ~ tous** she wants a photo of us all *ou* of all of us.

f (*dans comparaisons*) we, us. **il est aussi fort que ~** he is as strong as we are *ou* as us*; **il mange plus/moins que ~** he eats more/less than we do *ou* than us*; **faites comme ~** do as we do, do like us*, do the same as us*; **il vous connaît aussi bien que ~** (*aussi bien que nous vous connaissons*) he knows you as well as we do *ou* as us*; (*aussi bien qu'il nous connaît*) he knows you as well as (he knows *ou* does) us.

g (*avec vpr*) **~ ~ sommes bien amusés** we had a good time, we thoroughly enjoyed ourselves; **(lui et moi) ~ ~ connaissons depuis le lycée** we have known each other since we were at school; **~ ~ détestons** we hate (the sight of) each other; **asseyons-~ donc** let's sit down, shall we sit down?; **~ ~ écrirons** we'll write to each other.

h (*pl de majesté, modestie etc* = **moi**) we. ~, **préfet de X, décidons que** we, (the) prefect of X, decide that; **dans cet exposé, ~ essaierons d'expliquer** in this paper, we shall try to explain.

2 **nm: le ~ de majesté** the royal we.

nous-même, **pl nous-mêmes** [numɛm] **pron** *voir* **même.**

nouveau, nouvelle [nuvo, nuvɛl], **nouvel** [nuvɛl] *devant nm commençant par une voyelle ou h muet*), **mpl nouveaux** [nuvo] 1 **adj** a (*gén après n: qui apparaît pour la première fois*) new. **pommes de terre nouvelles** new potatoes; **vin ~** new wine; **carottes nouvelles** spring carrots; **la mode nouvelle** the latest fashion; **la mode nouvelle du printemps** the new spring fashion(s); **un sentiment si ~ pour moi** such a new feeling for me; **montrez-moi le chemin, je suis ~ ici** show me the way, I'm new here; **ce rôle est ~ pour lui** this is a new role for him; *voir* **art, quoi, tout.**

b (*après n: original*) *idée* novel, new, original; *style* new, original; (*moderne*) *méthode* new, up-to-date, new-fangled (*péj*). **le dernier de ses romans, et le plus ~** his latest and most original novel; **présenter qch sous un jour ~** to present sth in a new light; **c'est tout ~, ce projet** this project is brand-new; **il n'y a rien de/ce n'est pas ~!** there's/it's nothing new!

c (*inexpérimenté*) new (*en, dans* to). **il est ~ en affaires** he's new to business.

d (*avant n: qui succède*) new; (*qui s'ajoute*) new, fresh. **le ~ président** the new president, the newly-elected president; **le nouvel élu** the newly-elected representative; **nous avons un ~ président/une nouvelle voiture** we have a new president/car; **avez-vous lu son ~ livre?** have you read his new *ou* latest book?; **un ~ Napoléon** a second Napoleon; **les nouveaux philosophes** the new philosophers; **les nouveaux pauvres** the new poor; **les nouveaux parents** today's parents, the parents of today; **il y a eu un ~ tremblement de terre** there has been a further *ou* a new *ou* a fresh earthquake; **c'est là une nouvelle preuve que** it's fresh proof *ou* further proof that; **je ferai un nouvel essai** I'll make another *ou* a new *ou* a fresh attempt; **avec une ardeur/énergie nouvelle** with renewed ardour/energy; **il y eut un ~ silence** there was another silence; (*fig*) **c'est la nouvelle mode maintenant** it's the new fashion now, it's the latest thing *ou* fashion; *voir* **jusque.**

2 **nm** a (*homme, ouvrier etc*) new man; (*Scol*) new boy.

b **du ~: y a-t-il du ~ à ce sujet?** is there anything new on this?; **il y a du ~ dans cette affaire** there has been a fresh *ou* new *ou* further development in this business; **le public veut sans cesse du ~** the public always wants something new; **il n'y a rien de ~ sous le soleil** there's nothing new under the sun.

c (*loc*) **de ~** again; **faire qch de ~** to do sth again, repeat sth; **à ~** (*d'une manière différente*) anew, afresh, again; (*encore une fois*) again; **nous examinerons la question à ~** we'll examine the question anew *ou* afresh *ou* again.

3 **nouvelle nf** a (*femme, ouvrière etc*) new woman *ou* girl; (*Scol*) new girl.

b (*écho*) news (*NonC*). **une nouvelle** a piece of news; **une bonne/mauvaise nouvelle** some good/bad news; **ce n'est pas une nouvelle!** that's not news!, that's nothing new!; **vous connaissez la nouvelle?** have you heard the news?; **la nouvelle de cet événement nous a surpris** we were surprised by the news of this event; **annoncer/apprendre la nouvelle de la mort de qn** to announce/hear the news of sb's death; **aller aux nouvelles** to go and find out what is (*ou* was *etc*) happening; *voir* **dernier, faux[2], premier.**

c **nouvelles** news (*NonC*); **avez-vous de ses nouvelles?** (*de sa propre main*) have you heard from him?, have you had any news from him?; (*par un tiers*) have you heard anything about *ou* of him?, have you had any news of him?; **j'irai prendre de ses nouvelles** I'll go and see how he's getting on (*Brit*) *ou* how he's doing; **il a fait prendre de mes nouvelles (par qn)** he asked for news of me (from sb); **il ne donne plus de ses nouvelles** you never hear from him any more; **je suis sans nouvelles (de lui) depuis huit jours** I haven't heard anything (of him) for a week, I've had no news (of him) for a week; **pas de nouvelles, bonnes nouvelles** no news is good news; **il aura ou entendra de mes nouvelles!*** I'll give him a piece of my mind!*, I'll give him what for!*; **(goûtez mon vin) vous m'en direz des nouvelles*** (taste my wine,) I'm sure you'll like it.

d (*Presse, Rad, TV*) **les nouvelles** the news (*NonC*); **écouter/entendre les nouvelles** to listen to/hear the news; **voici les nouvelles** here is the news; **les nouvelles sont bonnes** the news is good.

e (*court récit*) short story.

4 **comp ►Nouvel An, Nouvelle Année** New Year; **pour le/au Nouvel An** for/at New Year; **le Nouvel An juif** the Jewish New Year **►Nouvelle-Angleterre nf** New England **►Nouveau-Brunswick nm** New Brunswick **►Nouvelle-Calédonie nf** New Caledonia **►nouvelle cuisine** nouvelle cuisine **►Nouvelle-Écosse nf** Nova Scotia **►Nouvelle-Galles du Sud nf** New South Wales **►Nouvelle-Guinée nf** New Guinea **►Nouvelles-Hébrides nfpl** New Hebrides **►nouvelle lune** new moon **►nouveaux mariés** newly-weds, newly married couple **►Nouveau-Mexique nm** New Mexico **►Nouveau Monde** New World **►nouveau-né, f nouveau-née (mpl nouveau-nés) adj** newborn ◊ **nm,f** newborn child; (*voiture*) new *ou* latest model; (*produit*) new *ou* latest addition **►La Nouvelle-Orléans** New Orleans **►nouveaux pays industrialisés** newly industrialized countries **►nouveau riche** nouveau riche **►Nouveau Testament** New Testament **►nouvelle vague adj** (*gén*) with-it*; (*Ciné*) nouvelle vague ◊ **nf** (*nouvelle génération*) new generation; (*Ciné*) nouvelle vague **►nouveau venu, nouvelle venue (mpl nouveaux venus)** newcomer (*à, dans* to) **►Nouvelle-Zélande nf** New Zealand.

nouveauté [nuvote] **nf** a (*actualité*) novelty, newness; (*originalité*) novelty; (*chose*) new thing, something new. **il n'aime pas la ~** he hates anything new *ou* new ideas, he hates change; **il travaille? c'est une ~!** he's working? that's new! *ou* that's a new departure!

b (*Habillement*) **~s de printemps** new spring fashions; **le commerce de la ~†** the fashion trade; **magasin de ~s†** draper's shop (*Brit*), fabric store (*US*).

c (*objet*) new thing *ou* article. **les ~s du mois** (*disque*) the month's new releases; (*livre*) the month's new titles; (*machine, voiture*) **les ~s du salon** the new models of the show; **la grande ~ de cet automne** the latest thing this autumn; **une ~ en matière électronique** a new thing in electronics, a new electronic invention.

nouvel [nuvɛl] **adj m** *voir* **nouveau.**

nouvellement [nuvɛlmɑ̃] **adv** recently, newly.

nouvelliste [nuvelist] **nmf** short story writer, writer of short stories.

nova [nɔva], **pl novæ** [nɔve] **nf** nova.

novateur, -trice [nɔvatœʀ, tʀis] 1 **adj** innovatory, innovative. 2 **nm,f** innovator.

novembre [nɔvɑ̃bʀ] **nm** November; *pour loc voir* **septembre** *et* **onze.**

novice [nɔvis] 1 **adj** inexperienced (*dans* in), green* (*dans* at). 2 **nmf** (*débutant*) novice, beginner, greenhorn*; (*Rel*) novice, probationer.

noviciat [nɔvisja] **nm** (*bâtiment, période*) noviciate, novitiate. (*Rel*) **de ~** probationary.

Novocaïne [nɔvɔkain] **nf** ® Novocaine ®.

novotique [nɔvɔtik] **nf** new technology.

noyade [nwajad] **nf** drowning; (*événement*) drowning accident, death by drowning. **il y a eu de nombreuses ~s à cet endroit** there have been many drowning accidents *ou* many deaths by drowning *ou* many people drowned at this spot; **sauver qn de la ~** to save sb from drowning.

noyau, **pl ~x** [nwajo] **nm** a (*lit*) *[fruit]* stone, pit; (*Astron, Bio, Phys*) nucleus; (*Géol*) core; (*Ling*) kernel, nucleus; (*Ordin*) kernel; (*Art*) centre, core; (*Élec*) core (*of induction coil etc*); (*Constr*) newel. **enlevez les ~x** remove the stones (from the fruit), pit the fruit.

b (*fig*) *[personnes]* (*cellule originelle*) nucleus; (*groupe de fidèles*) circle; (*groupe de manifestants*) small group; (*groupe d'opposants*) cell, small group. **il ne restait maintenant qu'un ~ d'opposants** now there only remained a hard core of opponents *ou* a pocket of resistance; ~ **dur** (*Écon*) hard core shareholders; *[groupe]* (*irréductibles*) hard core; (*éléments essentiels*) kernel; ~ **de résistance** centre of resistance.

noyautage [nwajotaʒ] nm (*Pol*) infiltration.

noyauter [nwajote] [1] vt (*Pol*) to infiltrate.

noyé, e [nwaje] (ptp de **noyer**[2]) 1 adj a (*fig: ne pas comprendre*) **être ~** to be out of one's depth, be all at sea (*en* in). b **avoir le regard ~** to have a faraway *ou* vague look in one's eyes; **regard ~ de larmes** tearful look, eyes swimming with tears. 2 nm,f drowned person. **il y a eu beaucoup de ~s ici** a lot of people have drowned here.

noyer[1] [nwaje] nm (*arbre*) walnut (tree); (*bois*) walnut.

noyer[2] [nwaje] [8] 1 vt a (*gén*) *personne, animal, flamme* to drown; (*Aut*) *moteur* to flood. **la crue a noyé les champs riverains** the high water has flooded *ou* drowned *ou* swamped the riverside fields; **il avait les yeux noyés de larmes** his eyes were brimming *ou* swimming with tears; **la nuit noyait la campagne** darkness shrouded the countryside; ~ **une révolte dans le sang** to put down a revolt violently, spill blood in quelling a revolt; (*Mil*) ~ **la poudre** to wet the powder; ~ **son chagrin dans l'alcool** to drown one's sorrows; (*fig*) ~ **le poisson** to duck *ou* sidestep the question, introduce a red herring into the discussion.

b (*gén pass: perdre*) ~ **qn sous un déluge d'explications** to swamp sb with explanations; **quelques bonnes idées noyées dans des détails inutiles** a few good ideas lost in *ou* buried in *ou* swamped by a mass of irrelevant detail; **être noyé dans l'obscurité** to be shrouded in darkness; **être noyé dans la foule** to be lost in the crowd; **noyé dans la masse, cet écrivain n'arrive pas à percer** because he's (just) one amongst (so) many, this writer can't manage to make a name for himself; **cette dépense ne se verra pas, noyée dans la masse** this expense won't be noticed when it's lumped *ou* put together with the rest; **ses paroles furent noyées par** *ou* **dans le vacarme** his words were drowned in the din.

c (*Culin*) *alcool, vin* to water down; *sauce* to thin too much, make too thin.

d (*Tech*) *clou* to drive right in; *pilier* to embed. **noyé dans la masse** embedded.

e (*effacer*) *contours, couleur* to blur.

2 **se noyer** vpr a (*lit*) (*accidentellement*) to drown; (*volontairement*) to drown o.s. **une personne qui se noie** a drowning person; **il s'est noyé** (*accidentellement*) he drowned *ou* was drowned; (*volontairement*) he drowned himself.

b (*fig*) **se ~ dans un raisonnement** to become tangled up *ou* bogged down in an argument; **se ~ dans les détails** to get bogged down in details; **se ~ dans un verre d'eau** to make a mountain out of a molehill, make heavy weather of the simplest thing; **se ~ l'estomac** to overfill one's stomach (*by drinking too much liquid*).

NPI [ɛnpei] nmpl (abrév de **nouveaux pays industriels**) NIC.

N.-S. J.-C. abrév de **Notre-Seigneur Jésus-Christ**.

NU (abrév de **Nations Unies**) UN.

nu, e[1] [ny] 1 adj a (*sans vêtement*) *personne* naked, nude, bare; *torse, membres* naked, bare; *crâne* bald. **~-pieds, (les) pieds ~s** barefoot, with bare feet; **~-tête, (la) tête ~e** bareheaded; **~-jambes, (les) jambes ~es** barelegged, with bare legs; **(les) bras ~s** barearmed, with bare arms; **(le) torse ~, ~ jusqu'à la ceinture** stripped to the waist, naked from the waist up; **à moitié ~, à demi ~** half-naked; **il est ~ comme un ver** *ou* **comme la main** he is as naked as the day he was born; **tout ~** stark naked; **se mettre ~** to strip (off), take one's clothes off; **se montrer ~ à l'écran** to appear in the nude on the screen; *voir* **épée, main, œil.**

b (*sans ornement*) *mur, chambre* bare; *arbre, pays, plaine* bare, naked; *style* plain; *vérité* plain, naked; (*non protégé*) *fil électrique* bare.

c (*Bot, Zool*) naked.

d (*loc*) **à ~**: **mettre à ~** *fil électrique* to strip; *erreurs, vices* to expose, lay bare; **mettre son cœur à ~** to lay bare one's heart *ou* soul; **monter un cheval à ~** to ride bareback.

2 nm (*Peinture, Phot*) nude.

3 comp ▸**nu-pieds** nmpl (*sandales*) beach sandals, flip-flops (*Brit*) ▸**nu-propriétaire, nue-propriétaire** nm,f (*Jur*) owner without usufruct ▸**nue-propriété** nf: **avoir un bien en nue-propriété** to have property without usufruct.

nuage [nɥaʒ] nm (*lit, fig*) cloud. **~ de grêle/de pluie** hail/rain cloud; **~ de fumée/de tulle/de poussière/de sauterelles** cloud of smoke/tulle/dust/locusts; **~ radioactif** radioactive cloud; (*lit, fig*) **il y a des ~s noirs à l'horizon** there are dark clouds on the horizon; **le ciel se couvre de ~s/est couvert de ~s** the sky is clouding over/is cloudy *ou* overcast *ou* has clouded over; **juste un ~ (de lait)** just a drop (of milk); (*fig*) **il est (perdu) dans les ~s** he has his head *ou* he is in the clouds; **sans ~s** *ciel* cloudless; *bonheur* unmarred, unclouded; **une amitié qui n'est pas sans ~s** a friendship which is not entirely untroubled *ou* is not entirely quarrelfree.

nuageux, -euse [nɥaʒø, øz] adj a *temps* cloudy; *ciel* cloudy, overcast; *zone, bande* cloud (*épith*). **système ~** cloud system. b (*vague*) nebulous, hazy.

nuance [nɥɑ̃s] nf a *[couleur]* shade, hue; (*Littérat, Mus*) nuance. **~ de sens** shade of meaning, nuance; **~ de style** nuance of style; **d'une ~ politique différente** of a different shade of political opinion; **de toutes les ~s politiques** of all shades of political opinion.

b (*différence*) slight difference. **il y a une ~ entre mentir et se taire** there's a slight difference between lying and keeping quiet; **je ne lui ai pas dit non, ~! je lui ai dit peut-être** I didn't say no to him, understand, I said perhaps, I didn't say no to him, I said perhaps and there's a difference between the two; **tu vois** *ou* **saisis la ~?** do you see the difference?

c (*subtilité, variation*) **les ~s du cœur/de l'amour** the subtleties of the heart/of love; **apporter des ~s à une affirmation** to qualify a statement; **faire ressortir les ~s** to bring out the finer *ou* subtler points; **tout en ~s** *esprit, discours, personne* very subtle, full of nuances; **sans ~** *discours* unsubtle, cut and dried; *esprit, personne* unsubtle.

d (*petit élément*) touch. **avec une ~ de tristesse** with a touch *ou* a slight note of sadness.

nuancé, e [nɥɑ̃se] (ptp de **nuancer**) adj *tableau* finely shaded; *opinion* qualified; *attitude* balanced; (*Mus*) nuanced.

nuancer [nɥɑ̃se] [3] vt *tableau* to shade; *opinion* to qualify; (*Mus*) to nuance.

nuancier [nɥɑ̃sje] nm (display of) make-up testers.

Nubie [nybi] nf Nubia.

nubile [nybil] adj nubile.

nubilité [nybilite] nf nubility.

nucléaire [nykleɛʀ] 1 adj nuclear. 2 nm: **le ~** (*énergie*) nuclear energy; (*technologie*) nuclear technology.

nucléariser [nykleaʀize] [1] vt *pays* to equip with nuclear weapons; *ressources énergétiques* to apply nuclear energy to the production of.

nucléé, e [nyklee] adj nucleate(d).

nucléine [nyklein] nf nuclein.

nucléique [nykleik] adj nucleic.

nucléon [nykleɔ̃] nm nucleon.

nudisme [nydism] nm nudism. **faire du ~** to practise nudism.

nudiste [nydist] adj, nmf nudist.

nudité [nydite] nf *[personne]* nakedness, nudity; (*fig*) *[mur]* bareness; (*Art*) nude. **la laideur des gens s'étale dans toute sa ~** people are exposed in all their ugliness, people's ugliness is laid bare for all to see.

nue[2] [ny] nf a (†† *ou littér*) (*nuage*) **~, ~s** clouds; (*ciel*) **la ~, les ~s** the skies. b **porter** *ou* **mettre qn aux ~s** to praise sb to the skies; **tomber des ~s** to be completely taken aback *ou* flabbergasted; **je suis tombé des ~s** you could have knocked me down with a feather, I was completely taken aback.

nuée [nɥe] nf a (*littér: nuage*) thick cloud. **~s d'orage** storm clouds; **~ ardente** nuée ardente, glowing cloud. b (*multitude*) *[insectes]* cloud, horde; *[flèches]* cloud; *[photographes, spectateurs, ennemis]* horde, host. (*fig*) **comme une ~ de sauterelles** like a plague *ou* swarm of locusts.

nuer [nɥe] [1] vt (*littér*) *couleurs* to blend *ou* match the different shades of.

nuire [nɥiʀ] [38] 1 **nuire à** vt indir (*desservir*) *personne* to harm, injure; *santé, réputation* to damage, harm, injure; *action* to prejudice. **sa laideur lui nuit beaucoup** his ugliness is very much against him *ou* is a great disadvantage to him; **il a voulu le faire mais ça va lui ~** he wanted to do it, but it will go against him *ou* it will do him harm; **chercher à ~ à qn** to try to harm sb, try to do *ou* run sb down; **cela risque de ~ à nos projets** there's a risk that it will damage *ou* harm our plans; **c'est pratique et, ce qui ne nuit pas, très bon marché** it's practical and what's more it's very cheap.

2 **se nuire** vpr (*à soi-même*) to do o.s. a lot of harm; (*l'un l'autre*) to work against each other's interests, harm each other.

nuisance [nɥizɑ̃s] nf (*gén pl*) (environmental) pollution (*NonC*) *ou* nuisance (*NonC*). **les ~s (sonores)** noise pollution.

nuisette [nɥizɛt] nf very short nightdress *ou* nightie*.

nuisible [nɥizibl] adj *climat, temps* harmful, injurious (*à* to); *influence, gaz* harmful, noxious (*à* to). **animaux ~s** vermin, pests; **insectes ~s** pests; **~ à la santé** harmful *ou* injurious to (the) health.

nuit [nɥi] 1 nf a (*obscurité*) darkness, night. **il fait ~** it is dark; **il fait ~ à 5 heures** it gets dark at 5 o'clock; **il fait ~ noire** it's pitch dark *ou* black; **une ~ d'encre** a pitch dark *ou* black night; **la ~ tombe** it's getting dark, night is falling; **à la ~ tombante** at nightfall, at dusk; **pris** *ou* **surpris par la ~** overtaken by darkness *ou* night; **rentrer avant la ~** to come home before dark; **rentrer à la ~** to come home in the dark; **la ~ polaire** the polar night *ou* darkness; (*Prov*) **la ~ tous les chats sont gris** every cat in the twilight is grey.

b (*espace de temps*) night. **cette ~** (*passée*) last night; (*qui vient*) tonight; **j'ai passé la ~ chez eux** I spent the night at their house; **dans la ~ de jeudi** during Thursday night; **dans la ~ de jeudi à vendredi** during Thursday night, during the night of Thursday to Friday; **souhaiter (une) bonne ~ à qn** to wish sb goodnight; (*Prov*) **la ~ porte conseil** let's (let them *etc*) sleep on it; **une ~ blanche** *ou* **sans sommeil** a sleepless night; **faire sa ~*** to go through the night; **~ et jour** night and day; **au milieu de la ~, en pleine ~** in the middle of the night, at dead of night; **elle part cette ~** *ou* **dans la ~** she's leaving tonight; **ouvert la ~** open at night; **sortir/travailler la ~** to go out/work at night; **rouler** *ou* **conduire la ~** *ou* **de ~** to drive at night; **conduire la ~ ne me gêne pas** I don't mind night-driving *ou* driving at night; **de ~** *service, travail, garde, infirmière etc* night (*épith*).

c (*littér*) darkness. **dans la ~ de ses souvenirs** in the darkness of his memories; **ça se perd dans la ~ des temps** it is lost in the mists of time; **ça remonte à la ~ des temps** that goes back to the dawn of time, that's as old as the hills; **la ~ du tombeau/de la mort** the darkness of the grave/of death.

2 **comp ▸ nuit bleue** night of terror **▸ nuit d'hôtel** night spent in a hotel room, overnight stay in a hotel; **payer sa nuit (d'hôtel)** to pay one's hotel bill **▸ nuit de noces** wedding night **▸ nuit de Noël** Christmas Eve **▸ la nuit des Rois** Twelfth Night.

nuitamment [nɥitamɑ̃] **adv** by night.

nuitée [nɥite] **nf** (*gén pl*) **~s** overnight stays, beds occupied (*in statistics for tourism*); **3 ~s** 3 nights (in a hotel room).

nul, nulle [nyl] 1 **adj indéf** a (*aucun: devant n*) no. **il n'avait ~ besoin/nulle envie de sortir** he had no need/no desire to go out at all; **~ doute qu'elle ne l'ait vu** there is no doubt (whatsoever) that she saw him; **~ autre que lui (n'aurait pu le faire)** no one (else) but he (could have done it); **il ne l'a trouvé nulle part** he couldn't find it anywhere, he could find it nowhere; **sans ~ doute/nulle exception** without any doubt/any exception.

b (*après n*) (*proche de zéro*) *résultat, différence, risque* nil (*attrib*); (*invalidé*) *testament, élection* null and void (*attrib*); (*inexistant*) *récolte etc* non-existent. (*Sport*) **le résultat** *ou* **le score est ~** (*zéro à zéro*) the result is a goalless *ou* a nil draw; (*2 à 2 etc*) the result is a draw, the match ended in a draw; (*Math*) **pour toute valeur non nulle de x** where x is not equal to zero; (*Jur*) **~ et non avenu** invalid, null and void; (*Jur*) **rendre ~** to annul, nullify; **nombre ~/non-~** zero/non-zero number; *voir* **match**.

c (*qui ne vaut rien*) *film, livre, personne* useless, hopeless; *intelligence* nil; *travail* worthless, useless. **être ~ en géographie** to be hopeless *ou* useless at geography; **il est ~ pour** *ou* **dans tout ce qui est manuel** he's hopeless *ou* useless at anything manual; **ce devoir est ~** this piece of work is worth nothing *ou* doesn't deserve any marks.

2 **pron indéf** (*sujet sg: personne, aucun*) no one. (*Prov*) **~ n'est prophète en son pays** no man is a prophet in his own country; **~ n'est censé ignorer la loi** ignorance of the law is no excuse; **~ d'entre vous n'ignore que ...** none of you is ignorant of the fact that ...; *voir* **à**.

nullard, e* [nylaʀ, aʀd] 1 **adj** hopeless, useless (*en* at). 2 **nm,f** dunce, numskull. **c'est un ~** he's a complete numskull, he's a dead loss*.

nullement [nylmɑ̃] **adv** not at all, not in the least.

nullité [nylite] **nf** a (*Jur*) nullity; *[personne]* uselessness; incompetence; *[raisonnement, objection]* invalidity; *voir* **entacher**. b (*personne*) nonentity, wash-out*.

nûment [nymɑ̃] **adv** (*littér*) (*sans fard*) plainly, frankly; (*crûment*) bluntly. **dire (tout) ~ que ...** to say (quite) frankly that ... .

numéraire [nymeʀɛʀ] 1 **adj: pierres ~s** milestones; **espèces ~s** legal tender *ou* currency; **valeur ~** face value. 2 **nm** specie (*SPÉC*), cash. **paiement en ~** cash payment, payment in specie (*SPÉC*).

numéral, e, mpl -aux [nymeʀal, o] **adj, nm** numeral.

numérateur [nymeʀatœʀ] **nm** numerator.

numération [nymeʀasjɔ̃] **nf** (*comptage*) numeration; (*code*) notation. (*Méd*) **~ globulaire** blood count; (*Math, Ordin*) **~ binaire** binary notation.

numérique [nymeʀik] **adj** (*gén, Math*) numerical; (*Ordin*) *affichage* digital.

numériquement [nymeʀikmɑ̃] **adv** numerically.

numériser [nymeʀize] 1 **vt** to digitize.

numériseur [nymeʀizœʀ] **nm** digitizer.

numéro [nymeʀo] **nm** a (*gén, Aut, Phys*) number. **j'habite au ~ 6** I live at number 6; **~ atomique** atomic number; **~ d'ordre** queue ticket (*Brit*), number; **~ minéralogique** *ou* **d'immatriculation** *ou* **de police** registration (*Brit*) *ou* license (*US*) number, car number; **~ d'immatriculation à la Sécurité sociale** National Insurance number (*Brit*), Social Security number (*US*); **~ (de téléphone), ~ d'appel** (tele)phone number; **~ vert** *ou* **d'appel gratuit** Freefone ® (*Brit*) *ou* toll-free (*US*) number; **faire** *ou* **composer un ~** to dial a number; (*Suisse*) **~ postal** post code; **pour eux, je ne suis qu'un ~** I'm just (another) number to them; **notre ennemi/problème ~ un** our number one enemy/problem; **le ~ un/deux du textile** the number one/two textile producer *ou* manufacturer; **le ~ un soviétique**the Soviet number one.

b *[billet de loterie]* number. **tirer le bon ~** (*lit*) to draw the lucky number; (*fig*) to strike lucky; (*fig*) **tirer le mauvais ~** to draw the short straw; **~ gagnant**winning number.

c (*Presse*) issue, number. **le ~ du jour** the day's issue; **vieux ~** back number, back issue; *voir* **suite**.

d (*spectacle*) *[chant, danse]* number; *[cirque, music-hall]* act, turn, number. (*fig*) **il nous a fait son ~ habituel** *ou* **son petit ~** he gave us *ou* put on his usual (little) act.

e (*personne*) **quel ~!*, c'est un drôle de ~!*, c'est un sacré ~!*** what a character!

numérologie [nymeʀɔlɔʒi] **nf** numerology.

numérotage [nymeʀɔtaʒ] **nm** numbering, numeration.

numérotation [nymeʀɔtasjɔ̃] **nf** numbering, numeration. **~ téléphonique** telephone number system.

numéroter [nymeʀɔte] 1 **vt** to number. **si tu continues, tu as intérêt à ~ tes abattis!*** if you go on like this you'll get what's coming to you!*

numerus clausus [nymeʀys klozys] **nm** restricted intake.

numide [nymid] 1 **adj** Numidian. 2 **nmf: N~** Numidian.

Numidie [nymidi] **nf** Numidia.

numismate [nymismat] **nmf** numismatist.

numismatique [nymismatik] 1 **adj** numismatic. 2 **nf** numismatics (*NonC*), numismatology.

nunuche* [nynyʃ] **adj** namby-pamby*.

nuptial, e, mpl -iaux [nypsjal, jo] **adj** *bénédiction, messe* nuptial (*littér*); *robe, marche, anneau, cérémonie* wedding (*épith*); *lit, chambre* bridal, nuptial (*littér*).

nuptialité [nypsjalite] **nf: (taux de) ~** marriage rate.

nuque [nyk] **nf** nape of the neck.

nurse [nœʀs] **nf** nanny, (children's) nurse.

nutriment [nytʀimɑ̃] **nm** nutriment.

nutritif, -ive [nytʀitif, iv] **adj** (*nourrissant*) nourishing, nutritious; (*Méd*) *besoins, fonction, appareil* nutritive. (*Bio*) **qualité** *ou* **valeur ~ive** food value, nutritional value.

nutrition [nytʀisjɔ̃] **nf** nutrition.

nutritionnel, -elle [nytʀisjɔnɛl] **adj** nutritional.

nutritionniste [nytʀisjɔnist] **nmf** nutritionist.

Nuuk [nyk] **n** Nuuk.

Nyasaland, Nyassaland [njasalɑ̃d] **nm** Nyasaland.

nyctalope [niktalɔp] 1 **adj** day-blind, hemeralopic (*SPÉC*). 2 **nmf** day-blind *ou* hemeralopic (*SPÉC*) person. **les chats sont ~s** cats see well in the dark.

nyctalopie [niktalɔpi] **nf** day blindness, hemeralopia (*SPÉC*).

nylon [nilɔ̃] **nm** ® nylon. **bas (de) ~ (pl)** nylons, nylon stockings.

nymphe [nɛ̃f] **nf** (*Myth, fig*) nymph; (*Zool*) nymph, nympha, pupa; (*Anat*) nymphae, labia minora.

nymphéa [nɛ̃fea] **nm** white water lily.

nymphomane [nɛ̃fɔman] **adj, nf** nymphomaniac.

nymphomanie [nɛ̃fɔmani] **nf** nymphomania.

O

O¹, o [o] **nm** (*lettre*) O, o.
O² (**abrév de Ouest**) O.
ô [o] **excl** oh!, O!
OAS [oaɛs] **nf** (**abrév de Organisation de l'armée secrète**) OAS, *illegal military organization supporting French rule of Algeria.*
oasis [ɔazis] **nf** (*lit*) oasis; (*fig*) oasis, haven. ~ **de paix** haven of peace.
obédience [ɔbedjɑ̃s] **nf** a (*appartenance*) **d'~ communiste** of Communist allegiance; **de même ~ religieuse** of the same religious persuasion. b (*Rel, littér: obéissance*) obedience.
obéir [ɔbeiʀ] 2 **obéir à vt indir** a *personne* to obey; *ordre* to obey, comply with; *loi, principe* to obey. **il sait se faire ~ de ses élèves** he knows how to command *ou* exact obedience from his pupils *ou* how to get his pupils to obey him *ou* how to make his pupils obey him; **on lui obéit** *ou* **il est obéi au doigt et à l'œil** he commands strict obedience; **je lui ai dit de le faire mais il n'a pas obéi** I told him to do it but he took no notice *ou* didn't obey (me); **ici, il faut ~** you have to toe the line *ou* obey orders here.
b (*fig*) ~ **à** *conscience, mode* to follow the dictates of; ~ **à une impulsion** to act on an impulse; **obéissant à un sentiment de pitié** prompted *ou* moved by a feeling of pity; ~ **à ses instincts** to submit to *ou* obey one's instincts.
c *[voilier, moteur, monture]* to respond to. **le cheval obéit au mors** the horse responds to the bit; **le moteur/voilier obéit bien** the engine/boat responds well.
obéissance [ɔbeisɑ̃s] **nf** *[animal, personne]* obedience (*à* to). **le refus d'~ est puni** any refusal to obey will be punished.
obéissant, e [ɔbeisɑ̃, ɑ̃t] **adj** obedient (*à* to, towards).
obélisque [ɔbelisk] **nm** (*monument*) obelisk.
obérer [ɔbeʀe] 6 **vt** (*frm*) to burden with debt. **obéré (de dettes)** burdened with debt.
obèse [ɔbɛz] 1 **adj** obese. 2 **nm** obese man. 3 **nf** obese woman.
obésité [ɔbezite] **nf** obesity.
objecter [ɔbʒɛkte] 1 **vt** a (*à une suggestion ou opinion*) ~ **une raison à un argument** to put forward a reason against an argument; **il m'objecta une très bonne raison, à savoir que** ... against that he argued convincingly that ..., he gave me *ou* he put forward a very sound reason against (doing) that, namely that ...; ~ **que** ... to object that ...; **il m'objecta que** ... he objected to me that ..., the objection he mentioned *ou* raised to me was that ...; **je n'ai rien à ~** I have no objection (to make); **elle a toujours quelque chose à ~** she always has some objection or other (to make), she always raises some objection or other.
b (*à une demande*) **il objecta le manque de temps/la fatigue pour ne pas y aller** he pleaded lack of time/tiredness to save himself going; **quand je lui ai demandé de m'emmener, il m'a objecté mon manque d'expérience/le manque de place** when I asked him to take me with him, he objected on the grounds of my lack of experience/on the grounds that there was not enough space *ou* he objected that I lacked experience/that there was not enough space.
objecteur [ɔbʒɛktœʀ] **nm:** ~ **(de conscience)** conscientious objector.
objectif, -ive [ɔbʒɛktif, iv] 1 **adj** a *article, jugement, observateur* objective, unbiased. b (*Ling, Philos*) objective; (*Méd*) *symptôme* objective. 2 **nm** a (*but*) objective, purpose; (*Mil: cible*) objective, target. ~ **de vente** sales target. b *[télescope, lunette]* objective, object glass, lens; *[caméra]* lens, objective. ~ **grand-angulaire** *ou* **(à) grand angle** wide-angle lens; ~ **traité** coated lens; **braquer son ~ sur** to train one's camera on.
objection [ɔbʒɛksjɔ̃] **nf** objection. **faire une ~** to raise *ou* make an objection, object; **si vous n'y voyez aucune ~** if you have no objection (to that); (*Jur*) ~ **(votre Honneur)!** objection (your Honour)!; ~ **de conscience** conscientious objection.
objectivement [ɔbʒɛktivmɑ̃] **adv** objectively.
objectiver [ɔbʒɛktive] 1 **vt** to objectivize.
objectivisme [ɔbʒɛktivism] **nm** objectivism.
objectivité [ɔbʒɛktivite] **nf** objectivity.
objet [ɔbʒɛ] 1 **nm** a (*article*) object, thing. **emporter quelques ~s de première nécessité** to take a few basic essentials *ou* a few essential items *ou* things; **femme-/homme-~** woman/man as a sex object; ~ **sexuel** sex object; *voir* **bureau.**
b (*sujet*) *[méditation, rêve, désir]* object; *[discussion, recherches, science]* subject. **l'~ de la psychologie est le comportement humain** human behaviour forms the subject matter of psychology, psychology is the study of human behaviour.
c (*cible*) **un ~ de raillerie/de grande admiration** an object of fun/great admiration; **il était l'~ de la curiosité/de l'envie des autres** he was an object of curiosity/an object of envy to (the) others.
d **faire** *ou* **être l'~ de** *discussion, recherches* to be *ou* form the subject of; *surveillance, enquête* to be subjected to; *soins, dévouement* to be given *ou* shown; **les prisonniers font l'~ d'une surveillance constante** the prisoners are subject *ou* subjected to constant supervision; **le malade fit** *ou* **fut l'~ d'un dévouement de tous les instants** the patient was shown *ou* was given every care and attention; **les marchandises faisant l'~ de cette facture** goods covered by this invoice.
e (*but*) *[visite, réunion, démarche]* object, purpose. **cette enquête a rempli son ~** the investigation has achieved its purpose *ou* object *ou* objective; **craintes sans ~** unfounded *ou* groundless fears; **votre plainte est dès lors sans ~** your complaint therefore no longer applies *ou* is no longer applicable.
f (*Ling, Philos*) object; *voir* **complément.**
g (*Jur*) *[procès, litige]* **l'~ du litige** the matter at issue, the subject of the case.
2 **comp** ▸ **l'objet aimé** (†† *ou hum*) the beloved one ▸ **objet d'art** objet d'art ▸ **objet social** (*Comm*) business ▸ **objets de toilette** toilet requisites *ou* articles ▸ **objets trouvés** lost property (office) (*Brit*), lost and found (*US*) ▸ **objets de valeur** valuables.
objurgations [ɔbʒyʀgasjɔ̃] **nfpl** (*littér*) (*exhortations*) objurgations (*frm*); (*prières*) pleas, entreaties.
oblat, e [ɔbla, at] **nm,f** oblate.
oblation [ɔblasjɔ̃] **nf** oblation.
obligataire [ɔbligatɛʀ] 1 **adj** *marché* debenture (*épith*). 2 **nmf** debenture holder.
obligation [ɔbligasjɔ̃] **nf** a (*devoir moral ou réglementaire*) obligation. **il faudrait les inviter — ce n'est pas une ~** we should invite them — we don't have to; **avoir l'~ de faire** to be under an obligation to do, be obliged to do; **il se fait une ~ de cette visite/lui rendre visite** he feels himself obliged *ou* he feels he is under an obligation to make this visit/to visit him; **être** *ou* **se trouver dans l'~ de faire** to be obliged to do; **sans ~ d'achat** with no *ou* without obligation to buy; **c'est sans ~ de votre part** there's no obligation on your part, you're under no obligation.
b (*gén pl: devoirs*) obligation, duty. **~s sociales/professionnelles** social/professional obligations; **~s de citoyen/de chrétien** one's obligations *ou* responsibilities *ou* duties as a citizen/Christian; **~s militaires** military obligations *ou* duties, duties *ou* obligations as a soldier; **être dégagé des ~s militaires** to have completed one's military service; ~ **scolaire** *legal obligation to provide an education for children;* **~s scolaires** *[professeur]* teaching obligations; *[élève]* obligations *ou* duties as a pupil; **~s familiales** family obligations *ou* responsibilities; **avoir des ~s envers une autre firme** to have a commitment to another firm; (*Pol*) **remplir ses ~s vis à vis d'un autre pays** to discharge one's commitments towards another country.
c (*littér: devoir de reconnaissance*) **~(s)** obligation; **avoir de l'~ à qn** to be under an obligation to sb.
d (*Jur*) obligation; (*dette*) obligation. **faire face à ses ~s (financières)** to meet one's liabilities; ~ **légale** legal obligation; ~ **alimentaire** maintenance obligation; **contracter une ~ envers qn** to contract an obligation towards sb.
e (*Fin: titre*) bond, debenture. ~ **d'État** government bond.
obligatoire [ɔbligatwaʀ] **adj** a compulsory, obligatory, mandatory. **le**

service militaire est ~ pour tous military service is obligatory *ou* compulsory for all. b (*: *inévitable*) **il est arrivé en retard? — c'était ~!** he arrived late? – he was bound to! *ou* it was inevitable!; **c'était ~ qu'il rate son examen** it was inevitable *ou* a foregone conclusion that he would fail his exam, he was bound to fail his exam.

obligatoirement [ɔbligatwaʀmɑ̃] adv a (*nécessairement*) necessarily, obligatorily (*frm*). **devoir ~ faire** to be obliged to do; **la réunion se tiendra ~ ici** the meeting will have to be held here; **pas ~** not necessarily. b (*: *sans doute*) inevitably. **il aura ~ des ennuis s'il continue comme ça** he's bound to *ou* he'll be bound to *ou* he'll inevitably make trouble for himself if he carries on like that.

obligé, e [ɔbliʒe] (ptp de **obliger**) 1 adj a (*forcé de*) **~ de faire** obliged *ou* compelled to do; **j'étais bien ~** I was forced to, I had to.
b (*frm: redevable*) **être ~ à qn** to be (most) obliged to sb, be indebted to sb (*de qch* for sth; *d'avoir fait* for having done, for doing).
c (*inévitable*) *conséquence* inevitable. **c'est ~!** it's inevitable!; **c'était ~** it had to happen!, it was sure *ou* bound to happen!
d (*indispensable*) necessary, required. **le parcours ~ pour devenir ministre** the track record necessary *ou* required in order to become a (government) minister, the required track record of a (government) minister.
2 nm,f a (*Jur*) obligee, debtor. (*Jur*) **le principal ~** the principal obligee.
b (*frm*) **être l'~ de qn** to be under an obligation to sb.

obligeamment [ɔbliʒamɑ̃] adv obligingly.

obligeance [ɔbliʒɑ̃s] nf: **ayez l'~ de vous taire pendant que je parle** (kindly) oblige me by keeping quiet while I'm speaking, have the goodness *ou* be good enough to keep quiet while I'm speaking; **il a eu l'~ de me reconduire en voiture** he was obliging *ou* kind enough to take me back in the car *ou* to drive me back.

obligeant, e [ɔbliʒɑ̃, ɑ̃t] adj *offre* kind, helpful; *personne, paroles, termes* kind, obliging, helpful.

obliger [ɔbliʒe] 3 vt a (*forcer*) **~ qn à faire** *[règlement, autorités]* to require sb to do, make it compulsory for sb to do; *[principes moraux]* to oblige sb to do; *[circonstances, parents, agresseur]* to force *ou* oblige sb to do; **le règlement vous y oblige** you are required to *ou* bound to by the regulation; **mes principes m'y obligent** I'm bound by my principles (to do it); **l'honneur m'y oblige** I'm honour bound to do it; **quand le temps l'y oblige, il travaille dans sa chambre** when forced *ou* obliged to by the weather, he works in his room; **ses parents l'obligent à aller à la messe** her parents make her go *ou* force her to go to mass; **rien ne l'oblige à partir** nothing's forcing him to leave, he's under no obligation to leave; **le manque d'argent l'a obligé à emprunter** lack of money obliged *ou* compelled *ou* forced him to borrow; **je suis obligé de vous laisser** I have to *ou* I must leave you, I'm obliged to leave you; **il va accepter? — il (y) est bien obligé** is he going to accept? – he has no choice! *ou* alternative! *ou* he jolly* (*Brit*) *ou* damned‡ well has to!; **tu vas m'~ à me mettre en colère** you'll force me to lose my temper; *voir* **noblesse**.
b (*Jur*) to bind.
c (*rendre service à*) to oblige. **vous m'obligeriez en acceptant** *ou* **si vous acceptiez** you would greatly oblige me by accepting *ou* if you accepted; (*formule de politesse*) **je vous serais très obligé de bien vouloir** I should be greatly obliged if you would kindly; **nous vous serions obligés de bien vouloir nous répondre dans les plus brefs délais** we should appreciate an early reply, we should be grateful to receive an early reply; **entre voisins, il faut bien s'~** neighbours have to help each other *ou* be of service to each other.

oblique [ɔblik] 1 adj (*gén, Ling, Math*) oblique. **regard ~** sidelong *ou* side glance; **en ~** obliquely; **il a traversé la rue en ~** he crossed the street diagonally. 2 nf (*Math*) oblique line.

obliquement [ɔblikmɑ̃] adv *planter, fixer* at an angle, slantwise, obliquely; *se diriger, se mouvoir* obliquely. **regarder qn ~** to look sideways *ou* sidelong at sb, give sb a sidelong look *ou* glance.

obliquer [ɔblike] 1 vi: **obliquez juste avant l'église** turn off just before the church; **~ à droite** to turn off *ou* bear right; **obliquez en direction de la ferme** (*à travers champs*) cut across towards the farm; (*sur un sentier*) turn off towards the farm.

obliquité [ɔblik(ɥ)ite] nf *[rayon]* (*Math*) obliqueness, obliquity; (*Astron*) obliquity.

oblitérateur [ɔbliteʀatœʀ] nm canceller.

oblitération [ɔbliteʀasjɔ̃] nf (*voir* **oblitérer**) cancelling, cancellation; obliteration; obstruction. (*Poste*) **cachet d'~** postmark.

oblitérer [ɔbliteʀe] 6 vt a *timbre* to cancel. b († *ou littér: effacer*) to obliterate. c (*Méd*) *artère* to obstruct.

oblong, -ongue [ɔblɔ̃, ɔ̃g] adj oblong.

obnubiler [ɔbnybile] 1 vt to obsess. **se laisser ~ par** to become obsessed by; **elle a l'esprit obnubilé par l'idée que** her mind is obsessed with the idea that, she is possessed with the idea that.

obole [ɔbɔl] nf a (*contribution*) mite, offering. **verser** *ou* **apporter son ~ à qch** to make one's small (financial) contribution to sth. b (*monnaie française*) obole; (*monnaie grecque*) obol.

obscène [ɔpsɛn] adj *film, propos, geste* obscene, lewd.

obscénité [ɔpsenite] nf a (*caractère: voir* **obscène**) obscenity, lewdness. b (*propos, écrit*) obscenity. **dire des ~s** to make obscene remarks.

obscur, e [ɔpskyʀ] adj a (*sombre*) dark; *voir* **salle**. b (*fig*) (*incompréhensible*) obscure; (*vague*) *malaise* vague; *pressentiment* vague, dim; (*méconnu*) *œuvre, auteur* obscure; (*humble*) *vie, situation, besogne* obscure, humble, lowly. **des gens ~s** humble folk; **de naissance ~e** of obscure *ou* lowly *ou* humble birth.

obscurantisme [ɔpskyʀɑ̃tism] nm obscurantism.

obscurantiste [ɔpskyʀɑ̃tist] adj, nmf obscurantist.

obscurcir [ɔpskyʀsiʀ] 2 1 vt a (*rendre obscur*) to darken. **ce tapis obscurcit la pièce** this carpet makes the room (look) dark *ou* darkens the room; **des nuages obscurcissent le ciel** clouds darken the sky. b (*rendre inintelligible*) to obscure. **ce critique aime ~ les choses les plus simples** this critic likes to obscure *ou* cloud the simplest issues; **cela obscurcit encore plus l'énigme** that deepens the mystery even more; **le vin obscurcit les idées** wine muddles one's brain. 2 **s'obscurcir** vpr a *[ciel]* to darken, grow dark; *[temps, jour]* to grow dark. b *[style]* to become obscure; *[esprit]* to become confused; *[vue]* to grow dim.

obscurcissement [ɔpskyʀsismɑ̃] nm (*voir* **obscurcir, s'obscurcir**) darkening; obscuring; confusing; dimming.

obscurément [ɔpskyʀemɑ̃] adv obscurely. **il sentait ~ que** he felt in an obscure way *ou* a vague (sort of) way that, he felt obscurely that.

obscurité [ɔpskyʀite] nf a (*voir* **obscur**) darkness; obscurity. (*lit*) **dans l'~** in the dark, in darkness; (*fig*) **vivre/travailler dans l'~** to live/work in obscurity; **il a laissé cet aspect du problème dans l'~** he did not cast *ou* throw any light on that aspect of the problem, he passed over *ou* neglected that aspect of the problem. b (*littér: passage peu clair*) obscurity.

obsédant, e [ɔpsedɑ̃, ɑ̃t] adj *musique, souvenir* haunting, obsessive; *question, idée* obsessive.

obsédé, e [ɔpsede] (ptp de **obséder**) nm,f obsessive. (*Psych, hum*) **un ~ (sexuel)** a sex maniac; (*hum*) **un ~ du tennis/de l'alpinisme** a tennis/climbing fanatic.

obséder [ɔpsede] 6 vt a (*obnubiler*) to haunt, obsess. **le remords l'obsédait** he was haunted *ou* obsessed by remorse; **être obsédé par** *souvenir, peur* to be haunted *ou* obsessed by; *idée, problème* to be obsessed with *ou* by; (*sexuellement*) **il est obsédé** he's obsessed (with sex), he's got a one-track mind*. b (*littér: importuner*) **~ qn de ses assiduités** to pester *ou* importune sb with one's attentions.

obsèques [ɔpsɛk] nfpl funeral. **~ civiles/religieuses/nationales** civil/religious/state funeral.

obséquieusement [ɔpsekjøzmɑ̃] adv obsequiously.

obséquieux, -ieuse [ɔpsekjø, jøz] adj obsequious.

obséquiosité [ɔpsekjozite] nf obsequiousness.

observable [ɔpsɛʀvabl] adj observable.

observance [ɔpsɛʀvɑ̃s] nf observance.

observateur, -trice [ɔpsɛʀvatœʀ, tʀis] 1 adj *personne, esprit, regard* observant, perceptive. 2 nm,f observer. **avoir des talents d'~** to have a talent for observation.

observation [ɔpsɛʀvasjɔ̃] nf a (*obéissance*) *[règle]* observance.
b (*examen, surveillance*) observation. (*Méd*) **être/mettre en ~** to be/put under observation; (*Mil*) **~ aérienne** aerial observation; (*Sport*) **round/set d'~** round/set in which one plays a guarded *ou* a wait-and-see game; *voir* **poste², satellite**.
c (*chose observée*) *[savant, auteur]* observation. **il consignait ses ~s dans son carnet** he noted down his observations *ou* what he had observed in his notebook.
d (*remarque*) observation, remark; (*objection*) remark; (*reproche*) reproof; (*Scol*) warning. **il fit quelques ~s judicieuses** he made one or two judicious remarks *ou* observations; **je lui en fis l'~** I pointed it out to him; **ce film appelle quelques ~s** this film calls for some comment; **pas d'~s je vous prie** no remarks *ou* comments please; **faire une ~ à qn** to reprove sb; (*Scol*) **~s** teacher's comments.

observatoire [ɔpsɛʀvatwaʀ] nm a (*Astron*) observatory. b (*Mil, gén: lieu*) observation *ou* look-out post.

observer [ɔpsɛʀve] 1 1 vt a (*gén: regarder*) to observe, watch; *adversaire, proie* to watch; (*Sci*) *phénomène, réaction* to observe; (*au microscope*) to examine. **les invités s'observaient avec hostilité** the guests examined *ou* observed each other hostilely; **se sentant observée, ella se retourna** feeling she was being watched *ou* observed she turned round; **il ne dit pas grand-chose mais il observe** he doesn't say much but he observes what goes on around him *ou* he watches keenly what goes on around him.
b (*contrôler*) **~ ses manières/ses gestes** to be mindful of *ou* watch one's manners/one's gestures.
c (*remarquer*) to notice, observe. **elle n'observe jamais rien** she never notices anything; **faire ~ que** to point out *ou* remark *ou* observe that; **faire ~ un détail à qn** to point out a detail to sb, bring a detail to sb's attention; **je vous ferai ~ que vous n'avez pas le droit de fumer ici** I should like to *ou* I must point out (to you) that you're not allowed to smoke here.
d (*dire*) to observe, remark. **vous êtes en retard, observa-t-il** you're late, he observed *ou* remarked.
e (*respecter*) *règlement* to observe, abide by; *fête, jeûne* to keep, observe; *coutume* to observe. **~ une minute de silence** to observe a

minute's silence.
f (*littér*) *attitude, maintien* to keep (up), maintain.
2 **s'observer** **vpr** (*surveiller sa tenue, son langage*) to keep a check on o.s., be careful of one's behaviour. **il ne s'observe pas assez en public** he's not careful enough of his behaviour in public, he doesn't keep sufficient check on himself in public.

obsession [ɔpsesjɔ̃] **nf** obsession. **il avait l'~ de la mort/l'argent** he had an obsession with death/money, he was obsessed by death/money; **je veux aller à Londres — c'est une ~!** I want to go to London — you're obsessed!

obsessionnel, -elle [ɔpsesjɔnɛl] **adj** obsessional.

obsidienne [ɔpsidjɛn] **nf** obsidian, volcanic glass.

obsolescence [ɔpsɔlesɑ̃s] **nf** (*Tech, littér*) obsolescence.

obsolescent, e [ɔpsɔlesɑ̃, ɑ̃t] **adj** (*Tech, littér*) obsolescent.

obsolète [ɔpsɔlɛt] **adj** obsolete.

obstacle [ɔpstakl] **nm** (*gén*) obstacle; (*Hippisme*) fence; (*Équitation*) jump, fence. **course d'~s** obstacle race; **faire ~ à la lumière** to block (out) *ou* obstruct the light; (*fig*) **faire ~ à un projet** to hinder a plan, put obstacles *ou* an obstacle in the way of a plan; **tourner l'~** (*Équitation*) to go round *ou* outside the jump; (*fig*) to get round the obstacle *ou* difficulty; (*lit, fig*) **progresser sans rencontrer d'~s** to make progress without meeting any obstacles *ou* hitches; **son âge n'est pas un ~ pour s'engager dans ce métier** his age is no impediment *ou* obstacle to his taking on this job; *voir* **refuser**.

obstétrical, e, **mpl -aux** [ɔpstetʀikal, o] **adj** obstetric(al).

obstétricien, -ienne [ɔpstetʀisjɛ̃, jɛn] **nm,f** obstetrician.

obstétrique [ɔpstetʀik] 1 **adj** obstetric(al). **clinique ~** obstetric clinic. 2 **nf** obstetrics (*sg*).

obstination [ɔpstinasjɔ̃] **nf** [*personne, caractère*] obstinacy, stubbornness. **~ à faire** obstinate *ou* stubborn determination to do; **son ~ au refus** his persistency in refusing, his persistent refusal.

obstiné, e [ɔpstine] (**ptp de s'obstiner**) **adj** *personne, caractère* obstinate, stubborn, unyielding, mulish (*péj*); *efforts, résistance* obstinate, dogged, persistent; *refus* stubborn; *travail, demandes* persistent, obstinate; (*fig*) *brouillard, pluie, malchance* persistent, unyielding, relentless.

obstinément [ɔpstinemɑ̃] **adv** (*voir* **obstiné**) obstinately; stubbornly; doggedly; persistently; relentlessly.

obstiner (s') [ɔpstine] 1 **vpr** to insist, dig one's heels in (*fig*). **s'~ sur un problème** to keep working *ou* labour away stubbornly at a problem; **s'~ dans une opinion** to cling stubbornly *ou* doggedly to an opinion; **s'~ dans son refus (de faire qch)** to refuse categorically *ou* absolutely (to do sth); **s'~ à faire** to persist obstinately *ou* stubbornly in doing, obstinately *ou* stubbornly insist on doing; **s'~ au silence** to remain obstinately silent, maintain an obstinate *ou* a stubborn silence; **j'ai dit non mais il s'obstine!** I said no but he insists!

obstruction [ɔpstʀyksjɔ̃] **nf** a (*blocage: voir* **obstruer**) obstruction, blockage. b (*tactique*) obstruction. **faire de l'~** (*Pol*) to obstruct (the passage of) legislation; (*gén*) to use obstructive tactics, be obstructive; (*Ftbl*) to obstruct; **faire de l'~ parlementaire** to filibuster.

obstructionnisme [ɔpstʀyksjɔnism] **nm** obstructionism, filibustering.

obstructionniste [ɔpstʀyksjɔnist] 1 **adj** obstructionist, filibustering (*épith*). 2 **nmf** obstructionist, filibuster, filibusterer.

obstruer [ɔpstʀye] 1 1 **vt** *passage, circulation, artère* to obstruct, block. **~ la vue/le passage** to block *ou* obstruct the view/the way. 2 **s'obstruer** **vpr** [*passage*] to get blocked up; [*artère*] to become blocked.

obtempérer [ɔptɑ̃peʀe] 6 **obtempérer à** **vt indir** to obey, comply with. **il refusa d'~** he refused to comply *ou* obey.

obtenir [ɔptəniʀ] 22 **vt** a *permission, explication, diplôme* to obtain, get. **~ satisfaction** to obtain satisfaction; **~ la main de qn** to gain *ou* win sb's hand; **je peux vous ~ ce livre rapidement** I can get you this book promptly, I can obtain this book promptly for you; **il m'a fait ~** *ou* **il m'a obtenu de l'avancement** he got promotion for me, he got me promoted; **il obtint de lui parler** he was (finally) allowed to speak to him; **elle a obtenu qu'il paie** she got him to pay up, she managed to make him pay up; **j'ai obtenu de lui qu'il ne dise rien** I managed to induce him *ou* to get him to agree not to say anything.
b *résultat, température* to achieve, obtain; *total* to reach, arrive at. **~ un corps à l'état gazeux** to obtain a body in the gaseous state; **~ un succès aux élections** to have *ou* achieve a success in the elections; **cette couleur s'obtient par un mélange** this colour is obtained through *ou* by mixing; **en additionnant ces quantités, on obtient 2 000** when you add these amounts together you arrive at *ou* get 2,000.

obtention [ɔptɑ̃sjɔ̃] **nf** (*voir* **obtenir**) obtaining; achievement. **pour l'~ du visa** to obtain the visa; (*Culin*) **mélangez le tout jusqu'à (l')~ d'une pâte onctueuse** mix everything together until the mixture is smooth.

obturateur, -trice [ɔptyʀatœʀ, tʀis] 1 **adj** (*Tech*) *plaque* obturating; *membrane, muscle* obturator (*épith*). 2 **nm** a (*Phot*) shutter. **~ à secteur** rotary shutter; **~ à rideau** focal plane shutter; **~ à tambour** *ou* **à boisseaux** drum shutter. b (*Tech*) obturator; [*fusil*] gas check.

obturation [ɔptyʀasjɔ̃] **nf** a (*voir* **obturer**) closing (up), sealing; filling. **faire une ~ (dentaire)** to fill a tooth, do a filling. b (*Phot*) **vitesse d'~** shutter speed.

obturer [ɔptyʀe] 1 **vt** *conduit, ouverture* to close (up), seal; *fuite* to seal *ou* block off; *dent* to fill.

obtus, e [ɔpty, yz] **adj** (*Math*) *angle* obtuse; (*fig: stupide*) dull-witted, obtuse.

obus [ɔby] **nm** shell. **~ explosif** high-explosive shell; **~ fumigène** smoke bomb; **~ incendiaire** incendiary *ou* fire bomb; **~ de mortier** mortar shell; **~ perforant** armour-piercing shell; *voir* **éclat, trou.**

obusier [ɔbyzje] **nm** howitzer. **~ de campagne** field howitzer.

obvier [ɔbvje] 7 **obvier à** **vt indir** *danger, mal* to take precautions against, obviate (*frm*); *inconvénient* to overcome, obviate (*frm*).

OC (**abrév de ondes courtes**) SW.

oc [ɔk] **nm** *voir* **langue.**

ocarina [ɔkaʀina] **nm** ocarina.

occase* [ɔkɑz] **nf abrév de occasion.** a (*article usagé*) second-hand buy; (*achat avantageux*) bargain, snip* (*Brit*). **d'~ (adj)** second-hand, used (*surtout US*); **(adv)** second-hand. b (*conjoncture favorable*) (lucky) chance.

occasion [ɔkazjɔ̃] **nf** a (*circonstance*) occasion; (*conjoncture favorable*) opportunity, chance. **avoir l'~ de faire** to have the *ou* a chance *ou* the *ou* an opportunity of doing *ou* to do; **sauter sur*** *ou* **saisir l'~** to jump at *ou* seize *ou* grab* the opportunity *ou* chance; **laisser échapper** *ou* **passer l'~** to let the opportunity pass one by *ou* slip; (*iro*) **tu as manqué une belle ~ de te taire** you should have held your tongue, why couldn't you have kept quiet *ou* kept your mouth shut; **cela a été l'~ d'une grande discussion** it gave rise to *ou* occasioned a great discussion; **à l'~ de** on the occasion of; **à cette ~** on that occasion; **si l'~ se présente** if the opportunity arises, should the opportunity arise; **je l'ai rencontré à plusieurs ~s** I've met him on several occasions; **dans/pour les grandes ~s** on/for important *ou* special occasions; **la bouteille/la robe des grandes ~s** the bottle put by/the dress kept for special *ou* great occasions.
b (*Comm*) second-hand buy; (*: *acquisition très avantageuse*) bargain, snip* (*Brit*). **(le marché de) l'~** the second-hand market; **faire le neuf et l'~** to deal in new and second-hand goods; **d'~ (adj)** second-hand, used (*surtout US*); **(adv)** second-hand.
c (*loc*) **à l'~** sometimes, on occasions; **à l'~ venez dîner** come and have dinner some time; **à la première ~** at the earliest *ou* first opportunity; **d'~** *amitié, rencontre* casual; (*frm*) **passer par ~** to chance *ou* pass by, happen to be passing by; (*Prov*) **l'~ fait le larron** opportunity makes the thief.

occasionnel, -elle [ɔkazjɔnɛl] **adj** a (*non régulier*) *rencontres, disputes* occasional (*épith*); *client, visiteur* casual, occasional (*épith*); (*fortuit*) *incidents, rencontre* chance (*épith*). b (*Philos*) occasional.

occasionnellement [ɔkazjɔnɛlmɑ̃] **adv** occasionally, from time to time.

occasionner [ɔkazjɔne] 1 **vt** *frais, dérangement* to occasion, cause; *accident* to cause, bring about. **en espérant ne pas vous ~ trop de dérangement** hoping not to put you to *ou* to cause you a great deal of trouble; **cet accident va m'~ beaucoup de frais** this accident is going to involve me in *ou* to cause me a great deal of expense.

occident [ɔksidɑ̃] **nm** (*littér: ouest*) west. **l'O~** the West, the Occident (*littér*); *voir* **empire.**

occidental, e, **mpl -aux** [ɔksidɑ̃tal, o] 1 **adj** (*littér: d'ouest*) western; (*Pol*) *pays, peuple* Western, Occidental (*littér*). **les Indes ~es** the West Indies. 2 **nm,f: O~(e)** Westerner, Occidental (*littér*).

occidentaliser [ɔksidɑ̃talize] 1 **vt** to westernize.

occipital, e, **mpl -aux** [ɔksipital, o] 1 **adj** occipital. 2 **nm** occipital bone.

occiput [ɔksipyt] **nm** back of the head, occiput (SPÉC).

occire [ɔksiʀ] **vt** (†† *ou hum*) to slay.

occitan, e [ɔksitɑ̃, an] **adj** *littérature* of the langue d'oc, of Provençal French.

occitaniste [ɔksitanist] **nmf** specialist in (the literature of) the langue d'oc.

occlure [ɔklyʀ] 35 **vt** (*Chim, Méd*) to occlude.

occlusif, -ive [ɔklyzif, iv] **adj, nf** (*Ling*) occlusive, plosive. **(consonne) ~ive** occlusive, stop (consonant).

occlusion [ɔklyzjɔ̃] **nf** (*Ling, Méd, Mét, Tech*) occlusion. (*Méd*) **~ intestinale** intestinal blockage, obstruction of the bowels *ou* intestines, ileus (SPÉC).

occultation [ɔkyltasjɔ̃] **nf** (*Astron*) occultation; (*fig*) overshadowing, eclipse. **l'~ du problème du chômage pendant la campagne électorale** the temporary eclipse of the issue of unemployment during the election campaign.

occulte [ɔkylt] **adj** a (*surnaturel*) supernatural, occult. **les sciences ~s** the occult, the occult sciences. b (*secret*) hidden, secret.

occulter [ɔkylte] 1 **vt** (*Astron, Tech*) to occult; (*fig*) to overshadow, eclipse. **n'essayez pas d'~ le problème** don't try to mask the problem.

occultisme [ɔkyltism] **nm** occultism.

occultiste [ɔkyltist] **adj, nmf** occultist.

occupant, e [ɔkypɑ̃, ɑ̃t] 1 **adj** (*Pol*) *autorité, puissance* occupying. **l'armée ~e** the army of occupation, the occupying army. 2 **nm,f** [*maison*] occupant, occupier; [*place, compartiment, voiture*] occupant. (*gén, Jur*) **le premier ~** the first occupier. 3 **nm: l'~** the occupying forces.

occupation [ɔkypasjɔ̃] **nf** a (*Mil, Pol*) occupation. **les forces/l'armée**

d'~ the forces/army of occupation, the occupying forces/army; **durant l'O~** during the Occupation; **grève avec ~ des locaux** sit-in, sit-down strike. **b** (*Jur*) *[logement]* occupancy, occupation. **c** (*passe-temps*) occupation; (*emploi*) occupation, job. **vaquer à ses ~s** to go about one's business, attend to one's affairs; **une ~ fixe/temporaire** a permanent/temporary job *ou* occupation.

occupé, e [ɔkype] (**ptp de occuper**) **adj** **a** (*affairé*) busy; (*non disponible*) busy, engaged. **je suis très ~ en ce moment** I'm very busy at present; **il ne peut pas vous recevoir, il est ~** he cannot see you as he is busy *ou* engaged. **b** *ligne téléphonique* engaged (*Brit*) (*attrib*), busy (*US*) (*attrib*); *toilettes* engaged (*attrib*) (*Brit*), occupied; *places, sièges* taken (*attrib*). **c'est ~** it's engaged; it's taken. **c** (*Mil, Pol*) *zone, usine* occupied.

occuper [ɔkype] 1 **1 vt** **a** *endroit, appartement* to occupy; *place, surface* to occupy, take up. **le bureau occupait le coin de la pièce** the desk stood in *ou* occupied the corner of the room; **leurs bureaux occupent tout l'étage** their offices take up *ou* occupy the whole floor; **le piano occupe très peu/trop de place** the piano takes up very little/too much room; **l'appartement qu'ils occupent est trop exigu** the flat they are living in *ou* occupying is too small.

b *moment, période* (*prendre*) to occupy, fill, take up; (*faire passer*) to occupy, spend, employ. **cette besogne occupait le reste de la journée** this task took (up) *ou* occupied the rest of the day; **la lecture occupe une trop petite/très grande part de mon temps** reading takes up *ou* fills *ou* occupies far too little/a great deal of my time; **comment ~ ses loisirs?** how should one spend *ou* occupy *ou* employ one's free time?

c *poste, fonction* to hold, occupy; *rang* to hold, have.

d (*absorber*) *personne, enfant* to occupy, keep occupied; (*employer*) *main d'œuvre* to employ. **mon travail m'occupe beaucoup** my work keeps me very busy; **la ganterie occupait naguère un millier d'ouvriers dans cette région** the glove industry used to employ *ou* give employment to about a thousand workers in this area; **le sujet qui nous occupe aujourd'hui** the matter which concerns us today, the matter we are dealing with today, the matter before us today.

e (*Mil, Pol*) (*envahir*) to take over, occupy; (*être maître de*) to occupy. **ils ont occupé tout le pays/l'immeuble** they took over *ou* occupied the whole country/the whole building; **les forces qui occupaient le pays** the forces occupying the country; (*Comm*) **~ le terrain (avec un produit)** to be present in the market (with a product).

2 s'occuper vpr **a s'~ de qch** (*se charger de*) to deal with sth, take care *ou* charge of sth; (*être chargé de*) to be in charge of sth, be dealing with *ou* taking care of sth; (*s'intéresser à*) to take an interest in sth, interest o.s. in sth; **je vais m'~ de ce problème/cette affaire** I'll deal with *ou* take care of this problem/this matter; **c'est lui qui s'occupe de cette affaire** he's the one in charge of *ou* who is dealing with this matter; **il s'occupe de vous trouver un emploi** he is undertaking to find you a job, he'll see about finding you a job; **je vais m'~ de rassembler les documents nécessaires** I'll set about *ou* see about gathering (together) the necessary documents, I'll undertake to get the necessary documents together; **il s'occupe un peu de politique** he takes a bit of an interest *ou* he dabbles a bit in politics; **je m'occupe de tout** I'll see to everything, I'll take care of everything; **il veut s'~ de trop de choses à la fois** he tries to take on *ou* to do too many things at once; **occupe-toi de tes affaires* *ou* oignons*** mind your own business; **t'occupe (pas)!‡** none of your business!‡, mind your own business!‡, keep your nose out of it!‡

b s'~ de (*se charger de*) *enfants, malades* to take charge *ou* care of, look after; *client* to attend to; (*être responsable de*) *enfants, malades* to be in charge of, look after; **je vais m'~ des enfants** I'll take charge *ou* care of *ou* I'll look after the children; **qui s'occupe des malades?** who is in charge of *ou* looks after the patients?; **un instant et je m'occupe de vous** one moment and I'll attend to you *ou* and I'll be with you; **est-ce qu'on s'occupe de vous Madame?** is someone serving you?, are you being attended to? *ou* served?

c (*s'affairer*) to occupy o.s., keep o.s. busy. **s'~ à faire qch/à qch** to busy o.s. doing sth/with sth; **il a trouvé à s'~** he has found something to do *ou* to occupy his time *ou* to fill his time with; **il y a de quoi s'~** there is plenty to do *ou* to keep one busy *ou* occupied; **je ne sais pas à quoi m'~** I don't know what to do with myself *ou* how to keep myself busy *ou* occupied; **s'~ l'esprit** to keep one's mind occupied.

occurrence [ɔkyʀɑ̃s] **nf** **a** (*frm*) instance, case. **en cette/toute autre ~** in this/in any other instance; **en l'~** in this case; **en pareille ~** in such circumstances, in such a case; (*frm*) **suivant *ou* selon l'~** according to the circumstances. **b** (*Ling*) occurrence, token.

OCDE [ɔsedeə] **nf** (**abrév de Organisation de coopération et de développement économique**) OECD.

océan [ɔseɑ̃] **nm** (*lit*) ocean. (*comparé à la Méditerranée*) **l'O~** the Atlantic (Ocean); **un ~ de verdure/de sable** a sea of greenery/sand; **l'~ Antarctique *ou* Austral** the Antarctic (Ocean); **l'~ Arctique** the Arctic (Ocean); **l'~ Atlantique** the Atlantic (Ocean); **l'~ glacial** the polar sea; **l'~ Indien** the Indian Ocean; **l'~ Pacifique** the Pacific (Ocean).

océanaute [ɔseanot] **nm** deep-sea diver.

Océanie [ɔseani] **nf: l'~** Oceania, the South Sea Islands.

océanien, -ienne [ɔseanjɛ̃, jɛn] **1 adj** Oceanian, Oceanic. **2 nm,f** Oceanian, South Sea Islander.

océanique [ɔseanik] **adj** oceanic.

océanographe [ɔseanɔgʀaf] **nm,f** oceanographer.

océanographie [ɔseanɔgʀafi] **nf** oceanography.

océanographique [ɔseanɔgʀafik] **adj** oceanographical.

océanologie [ɔseanɔlɔʒi] **nf** oceanology.

ocelot [ɔs(ə)lo] **nm** (*Zool*) ocelot; (*fourrure*) ocelot fur.

ocre [ɔkʀ] **nf, adj inv** ochre.

ocré, e [ɔkʀe] **adj** ochred.

ocreux, -euse [ɔkʀø, øz] **adj** (*littér*) ochreous.

octaèdre [ɔktaɛdʀ] **1 adj** octahedral. **2 nm** octahedron.

octaédrique [ɔktaedʀik] **adj** octahedral.

octal [ɔktal] **nm** octal notation.

octane [ɔktan] **nm** octane; *voir* **indice**.

octante [ɔktɑ̃t] **adj inv** (*dial*) eighty.

octave [ɔktav] **nf** **a** (*Mus*) octave. **jouer à l'~** to play an octave higher (*ou* lower). **b** (*Escrime, Rel*) octave.

octet [ɔktɛ] **nm** byte.

octobre [ɔktɔbʀ] **nm** October; *pour loc voir* **septembre**.

octogénaire [ɔktɔʒenɛʀ] **adj, nmf** octogenarian.

octogonal, e, mpl -aux [ɔktɔgɔnal, o] **adj** octagonal, eight-sided.

octogone [ɔktɔgɔn] **nm** octagon.

octopode [ɔktɔpɔd] **1 adj** (*Zool*) octopod. **2 nm** octopod. **~s** Octopoda.

octosyllabe [ɔktosi(l)lab] **1 adj** octosyllabic. **2 nm** octosyllable.

octosyllabique [ɔktosi(l)labik] **adj** octosyllabic.

octroi [ɔktʀwa] **nm** **a** (*voir* **octroyer**) granting; bestowing. **b** (*Hist*) octroi, city toll.

octroyer [ɔktʀwaje] 8 **1 vt** (*frm*) *charte* to grant (*à* to); *faveur, pardon* to bestow (*à* on, upon), grant (*à* to); *répit, permission* to grant (*à* to). **2 s'octroyer vpr** *répit, vacances* to treat o.s. to, grant o.s.

octuor [ɔktɥɔʀ] **nm** (*Mus*) octet.

oculaire [ɔkylɛʀ] **1 adj** (*Anat*) ocular; *voir* **globe, témoin**. **2 nm** (*Opt*) eyepiece, ocular (*SPÉC*).

oculiste [ɔkylist] **nmf** eye specialist, oculist, eye doctor (*US*).

odalisque [ɔdalisk] **nf** odalisque.

ode [ɔd] **nf** ode.

odeur [ɔdœʀ] **nf** **a** (*gén: bonne ou mauvaise*) smell, odour (*frm*); (*agréable*) *[fleurs etc]* fragrance, scent. **sans ~** odourless, which has no smell; **produit qui combat les (mauvaises) ~s** air freshener; **mauvaise ~** bad *ou* unpleasant smell; **~ suave/délicieuse** sweet/delicious smell *ou* scent; **à l'~ fétide** stinking, evil-smelling; **~ de brûlé/de moisi** smell of burning/of damp; **~ de renfermé** musty *ou* fusty smell; **avoir une bonne/une mauvaise ~** to smell nice/bad; *voir* **argent**.

b (*loc*) **être en ~ de sainteté auprès de qn** to be in sb's good graces; **ne pas être en ~ de sainteté auprès de qn** not to be well looked upon by sb, be out of favour with sb; (*Rel*) **mourir en ~ de sainteté** to die in the odour of sanctity.

odieusement [ɔdjøzmɑ̃] **adv** (*voir* **odieux**) hatefully; obnoxiously; odiously.

odieux, -ieuse [ɔdjø, jøz] **adj** **a** (*infâme*) *personne, caractère, tâche* hateful, obnoxious, odious; *conduite* odious, obnoxious, *crime* heinous, odious. **tu as été ~ avec elle** you were obnoxious *ou* horrible to her. **b** (*insupportable*) *gamin, élève* obnoxious, unbearable. **la vie m'est ~euse** life is unbearable to me; **cette personne m'est ~euse** I cannot bear this person, I find this person (quite) unbearable.

odontologie [ɔdɔ̃tɔlɔʒi] **nf** odontology.

odontologique [ɔdɔ̃tɔlɔʒik] **adj** odontological.

odontologiste [ɔdɔ̃tɔlɔʒist] **nmf** odontologist.

odorant, e [ɔdɔʀɑ̃, ɑ̃t] **adj** (*gén*) scented; (*plus agréable*) fragrant, sweet-smelling, odorous (*littér*).

odorat [ɔdɔʀa] **nm** (sense of) smell. **avoir l'~ fin** to have a keen sense of smell.

odoriférant, e [ɔdɔʀifeʀɑ̃, ɑ̃t] **adj** sweet-smelling, fragrant, odoriferous (*littér*).

odyssée [ɔdise] **nf** odyssey. (*littér*) **l'O~** the Odyssey.

OEA [ɔəa] **nf** (**abrév de Organisation des États américains**) OAS.

OECE [ɔəseə] **nf** (**abrév de Organisation européenne de coopération économique**) OEEC.

œcuménique [ekymenik] **adj** ecumenical; *voir* **concile**.

œcuménisme [ekymenism] **nm** ecumenicalism, ecumenism.

œcuméniste [ekymenist] **adj, nmf** ecumenist.

œdémateux, -euse [edematø, øz] **adj** oedematous, oedematose.

œdème [edɛm] **nm** oedema. **~ du poumon** pulmonary oedema.

Œdipe [edip] **nm** Oedipus; *voir* **complexe**.

œil [œj], **pl yeux** [jø] **1 nm** **a** (*Anat*) eye. **avoir les yeux bleus/bridés** to have blue/slit *ou* slant(ing) eyes; **il a les yeux bleus** he has blue eyes, his eyes are blue; **aux yeux bleus** blue-eyed, with blue eyes; **avoir les yeux faits** to have make-up on one's eyes; **aux grands yeux** wide-eyed, with big eyes; **des yeux de biche *ou* de gazelle** doe eyes; **je vois mal de cet ~** I don't see well with this eye; **avoir de bons/mauvais yeux** to have good/bad eyes *ou* eyesight; **regarde-moi dans les yeux** look me in the eye; (*fig*) **les yeux lui sortaient de la tête** his eyes were (nearly) popping out of his head, his eyes were out on stalks* (*Brit*); **je l'ai vu**

de mes (propres) yeux I saw it with my own eyes; **visible à l'~ nu** visible to the naked eye; **avoir un ~ au beurre noir** *ou* **un ~ poché*** to have a black eye; **avoir un ~ qui dit zut*** *ou* **merde*** **à l'autre, avoir les yeux qui se croisent (les bras)*** to be cross-eyed* *ou* boss-eyed*, have a squint.

b (*fig: expression*) look. **il a un ~ malin/spirituel/méchant** there's a mischievous/humorous/malicious look in his eye; **il a l'~ vif** he has a lively look about him *ou* a lively expression; **il le regardait l'~ méchant** *ou* **d'un ~ méchant** he fixed him with a threatening stare *ou* look, he looked *ou* stared at him threateningly.

c (*fig: jugement*) **considérer** *ou* **voir qch d'un bon/mauvais ~** to look on *ou* view sth favourably/unfavourably, view sth in a favourable/unfavourable light; **je ne l'ai vu** *ou* **considéré que d'un ~** I just took *ou* had (*Brit*) a glance *ou* a quick look at it; **considérer qch d'un ~ critique** to consider sth with a critical eye, look at sth critically; **il ne voit pas cela du même ~ qu'elle** he doesn't see *ou* view that in the same light as she does, he doesn't take the same view of that as she does.

d (*fig: coup d'œil*) **avoir l'~ du spécialiste/du maître** to have a trained/an expert eye, have the eye of a specialist/an expert; **il a l'~** he has sharp *ou* keen eyes; **avoir l'~ américain** to have a quick eye; **jeter un ~* à qn/qch** to have a squint at sb/sth*; **avoir un ~** *ou* **des yeux de lynx** *ou* **d'aigle** (*avoir une très bonne vue*) to have eyes like a hawk; (*fig*) to be eagle-eyed; **risquer un ~ au dehors/par-dessus la barrière** to take a peep *ou* a quick look outside/over the fence, poke one's nose outside/over the fence; *voir* **compas.**

e (*fig: regard*) **se consulter de l'~** to exchange glances, glance questioningly at one another; **attirer** *ou* **tirer l'~ (de qn)** to catch the eye (of sb); **sous l'~ (vigilant/inquiet) de** under the (watchful/anxious) eye *ou* gaze of; **ils jouaient sous l'~ de leur mère** they played under the watchful eye of their mother *ou* with their mother looking on; **faire qch aux yeux de tous** to do sth in full view of everyone; **sous les yeux de** before the very eyes of; **cela s'est passé devant** *ou* **sous nos yeux** it happened in front of *ou* before our very eyes; **vous avez l'article sous les yeux** you have the article there before you *ou* right in front of you *ou* your eyes; **couver/dévorer qn des yeux** to gaze devotedly/hungrily at sb, fix sb with a devoted/hungry look; **chercher qn des yeux** to glance *ou* look (a)round for sb; **suivre qn des yeux** to watch sb; **n'avoir d'yeux que pour qch/qn** to have eyes only for sth/sb, have eyes for nothing/nobody else but sth/sb; **se regarder les yeux dans les yeux** to gaze into each other's eyes.

f *[aiguille, marteau]* eye; *[porte d'entrée]* spyglass; (*Typ*) *[caractère]* (*pl* **œils**) face; *[fromage, pain]* eye, hole; *[pomme de terre]* eye; (*Bot: bourgeon*) bud; (*Naut: boucle*) eye, loop. **les yeux du bouillon** the globules *ou* droplets of fat in the stock; **l'~ du cyclone** (*Mét*) the eye of the cyclone *ou* hurricane; (*fig*) the eye of the storm.

g **coup d'~** glance, quick look; **il y a un beau coup d'~ d'ici** there's a lovely view from here; **ça vaut le coup d'~** it's worth seeing; **jeter** *ou* **lancer un coup d'~ à qn** to glance at sb, look quickly at sb; **jeter un coup d'~ à** *texte, objet* to glance at, have (*Brit*) *ou* take a glance *ou* quick look at; **allons jeter un coup d'~** let's go and take *ou* have (*Brit*) a look; (*fig*) **avoir le coup d'~ pour** to have an eye for.

h (*loc avec* **œil**) **à l'~*** (*gratuitement*) for nothing, for free*; **mon ~!*** (*je n'y crois pas*) my eye!*, my foot!*; (*je ne le donnerai pas*) nothing doing!*, not likely!*; **avoir l'~ à qch** to keep an eye on sth; **garder l'~ ouvert** to keep one's eyes open, stay on the alert; **avoir** *ou* **tenir qn à l'~** to keep a watch *ou* an eye on sb; **je vous ai à l'~!** I've got my eye on you!; **faire de l'~ à qn** to make eyes at sb, give sb the eye*; (*Prov*) **~ pour ~, dent pour dent** an eye for an eye, a tooth for a tooth (*Prov*); *voir* **clin, coin, rincer** *etc.*

i (*loc avec* **yeux**) **être tout yeux*** to be all eyes*; **à ses yeux, cela n'a aucune valeur** in his eyes that has no value; **faire** *ou* **ouvrir de grands yeux** to look surprised, stare in amazement; **coûter/payer les yeux de la tête** to cost/pay the earth *ou* a (small) fortune; (*fig*) **faire/acheter qch les yeux fermés** to do/buy sth with one's eyes closed *ou* shut; **il a les yeux plus grands** *ou* **gros que le ventre** *[affamé]* his eyes are bigger than his belly *ou* stomach; *[ambitieux]* he has bitten off more than he can chew; **voir avec** *ou* **avoir les yeux de la foi** to see with the eyes of a believer; **ne pas avoir les yeux dans sa poche** to be very observant; **il n'a pas les yeux en face des trous** he's half asleep, he's not thinking straight; **faire des yeux de velours à qn, faire les yeux doux à qn** to make sheep's eyes at sb; **faire** *ou* **ouvrir des yeux comme des soucoupes** to stare with eyes like saucers; **faire** *ou* **ouvrir des yeux ronds** to stare round-eyed *ou* wide-eyed; **avoir les yeux battus** to have blue rings under one's eyes; **regarder qn avec des yeux de merlan frit*** *ou* **de crapaud mort d'amour*** to look at sb like a lovesick puppy; **entre quatre yeux*, entre quat-z-yeux*** (*directement*) face to face; (*en privé*) in private.

2 **comp** ▸**œil-de-bœuf** **nm** (**pl œils-de-bœuf**) bull's-eye (window), œil-de-bœuf ▸**œil cathodique** cathode eye, magic eye ▸**œil-de-chat** **nm** (*Minér*) (**pl œils-de-chat**) tiger's eye ▸**œil électrique** electric eye ▸**œil magique**† = **œil cathodique** ▸**œil-de-perdrix** **nm** (**pl œils-de-perdrix**) (*cor, au pied*) soft corn ▸**œil-de-pie** **nm** (*Naut*) (**pl œils-de-pie**) eyelet ▸**œil-de-tigre** **nm** (**pl œils-de-tigre**) = **œil-de-chat** ▸**œil de verre** glass eye.

œillade [œjad] **nf** wink. **faire des ~s à qn** to make eyes at sb, give sb the eye*; **jeter** *ou* **décocher une ~ à qn** to wink at sb, give sb a wink.

œillère [œjɛʀ] **nf** a ~s *[cheval]* blinkers; (*fig péj*) **avoir des ~s** to wear blinkers, be blinkered. b (*Méd*) eyebath, eyecup.

œillet [œjɛ] **nm** a *[fleur]* carnation. **~ d'Inde** French marigold; **~ mignardise** pink; **~ de poète** sweet william. b (*petit trou*) eyelet; (*bordure*) grommet.

œilleton [œjtɔ̃] **nm** *[télescope]* eyepiece.

œnologie [enɔlɔʒi] **nf** oenology.

œnologique [enɔlɔʒik] **adj** oenological.

œnologue [enɔlɔg] **nmf** oenologist.

œsophage [ezɔfaʒ] **nm** oesophagus.

œsophagien, -ienne [ezɔfaʒjɛ̃, jɛn] **adj, œsophagique** [ezɔfaʒik] **adj** oesophageal.

œstral, e, **mpl -aux** [ɛstʀal, o] **adj: cycle ~** oestrous cycle.

œstrogène [ɛstʀɔʒɛn] **nm** oestrogen.

œstrus [ɛstʀys] **nm** oestrus.

œuf, **pl ~s** [œf, ø] 1 **nm** a (*Bio, Culin*) egg. **~ du jour/frais** new-laid/fresh egg; **en (forme d')~** egg-shaped; **~s de marbre/de faïence** marble/china eggs; *voir* **blanc, jaune.**

b (*idiot*) **quel ~ ce type!** what a blockhead* this fellow is!

c (*télécabine*) telecabine.

d (*loc*) **étouffer** *ou* **écraser** *ou* **détruire qch dans l'~** to nip sth in the bud; **mettre tous ses ~s dans le même panier** to put all one's eggs in one basket; **c'est comme l'~ de Colomb (fallait y penser)!** it's simple when you know how!, it's easy once you think of it!; **va te faire cuire un ~!*** (go and) take a running jump!*, get stuffed!*; *voir* **marcher, omelette.**

2 **comp** ▸**œufs brouillés** scrambled eggs ▸**œuf en chocolat** chocolate egg ▸**œuf à la coque** (soft-)boiled egg ▸**œuf dur** hard-boiled egg ▸**œufs au lait** ≃ egg custard ▸**œufs de lump** lumpfish roe ▸**œufs mimosa** eggs mimosa (*hors d'œuvre made with chopped egg yolks*) ▸**œuf (au) miroir** = **œuf sur le plat** *ou* **au plat** ▸**œuf mollet** soft-boiled egg ▸**œufs à la neige** œufs à la neige, floating islands ▸**œufs montés** *ou* **battus en neige** beaten *ou* stiff egg whites; **battre des œufs en neige** to whip (up) *ou* beat (up) egg whites until they are stiff ▸**œuf de Pâques** Easter egg ▸**œuf de pigeon*** bump (on the head) ▸**œuf sur le plat** *ou* **au plat** fried egg ▸**œuf poché** poached egg ▸**œuf à repriser** darning egg.

œuvre [œvʀ] 1 **nf** a (*livre, tableau etc*) work; (*production artistique ou littéraire*) works. **c'est une ~ de jeunesse** it's an early work; **toute l'~ de Picasso** Picasso's entire works; **les ~s complètes/choisies de Victor Hugo** the complete/selected works of Victor Hugo; **l'~ romanesque de Balzac** the novels of Balzac, Balzac's works of fiction; *voir* **chef**[1].

b (*tâche*) undertaking, task; (*travail achevé*) work. **ce sera une ~ de longue haleine** it will be a long-term task *ou* undertaking; **admirant leur ~** admiring their work; **la satisfaction de l'~ accomplie** the satisfaction of seeing the *ou* a task complete *ou* well done; **ce beau gâchis, c'est l'~ des enfants** this fine mess is the children's doing *ou* work; **ces formations sont l'~ du vent et de l'eau** these formations are the work of wind and water; *voir* **main, maître, pied.**

c (*acte*) **~(s)** deed, work; **être jugé selon ses ~s** to be judged by one's works *ou* deeds; (*frm, hum*) **enceinte de ses ~s** with child by him, bearing his child; **(bonnes) ~s** good *ou* charitable works; (*littér*) **faire ~ pie** to do a pious deed; **aide-le, ce sera une bonne ~** help him, that will be a kind act *ou* an act of kindness; *voir* **fils.**

d (*organisation*) **~ (de bienfaisance** *ou* **de charité)** charitable organization, charity; **les ~s** charity, charities.

e (*loc*) **être/se mettre à l'~** to be at/get down to work; **voir qn à l'~** (*lit*) to see sb at work; (*iro*) to see sb in action; **faire ~ utile** to do worthwhile *ou* valuable work; **faire ~ de pionnier/médiateur** to act as a pioneer/mediator; **la mort avait fait son ~** death had (already) claimed its own; **le feu avait fait son ~** the fire had wrought its havoc *ou* had done its work; **faire ~ durable** to create a work of lasting significance *ou* importance; **faire ~ utile** to do something worthwhile *ou* useful; **mettre en ~** *moyens* to implement, make use of, bring into play; **il avait tout mis en ~ pour éviter la dévaluation/pour les aider** he had done everything possible *ou* had taken all possible steps to avoid devaluation/to help them; **la mise en ~ d'importants moyens** the implementation *ou* the bringing into play of considerable resources; (*Prov*) **à l'~ on** *ou* **c'est à l'~ qu'on connaît l'ouvrier** a man is judged *ou* known by his works *ou* by the work he does.

2 **nm** (*littér*) **l'~ gravé/sculpté de Picasso** the etchings/sculptures of Picasso; *voir* **grand, gros.**

3 **comp** ▸**œuvre d'art** (*lit, fig*) work of art ▸**œuvres mortes** (*Naut*) deadwork ▸**œuvres sociales** (*Jur*) company benefit scheme ▸**œuvres vives** (*Naut*) quickwork; (*fig littér*) vitals.

œuvrer [œvʀe] 1 **vi** (*littér ou hum*) to strive (*à* for).

off [ɔf] **adj inv** (*Ciné*) *voix, son* off; *concert, festival* fringe, alternative. **dire qch en voix ~** to say sth in a voice off.

offensant, e [ɔfɑ̃sɑ̃, ɑ̃t] **adj** insulting, offensive.

offense [ɔfɑ̃s] **nf** a (*frm: affront*) insult. **faire ~ à** to offend, insult; (*hum*) **il n'y a pas d'~*** no offence (taken); (*frm*) **soit dit sans ~** let this not be taken amiss. b (*Rel: péché*) transgression, trespass, offence. **pardonnez-nous nos ~s** forgive us our trespasses; **~ à** *ou* envers *chef d'État* libel against; *Dieu* offence against.

offensé, e [ɔfɑ̃se] (ptp de **offenser**) 1 adj offended, hurt, insulted. 2 nm,f offended *ou* injured party.

offenser [ɔfɑ̃se] [1] 1 vt a *personne* to offend, hurt (the feelings of), insult, give offence to. **je n'ai pas voulu vous ~** I didn't mean to give offence (to you) *ou* to offend you; **~ Dieu** to offend *ou* trespass against God. b (*littér*) *sentiments, souvenir* to offend, insult; *personne, bon goût* to offend; *règles, principes* to offend against. 2 **s'offenser** vpr to take offence (*de qch* at sth).

offenseur [ɔfɑ̃sœʀ] nm offender.

offensif, -ive [ɔfɑ̃sif, iv] 1 adj (*Mil, Pol*) offensive; (*Sport*) forceful, aggressive.

2 **offensive** nf offensive. **prendre l'~ive** to take the offensive; **passer à l'~ive** to go onto the attack *ou* offensive; **lancer une ~ive** to launch an offensive (*contre* against); (*fig*) **l'~ive de l'hiver/du froid** the onslaught of winter/of the cold; **~ive diplomatique/de paix** diplomatic/peace offensive; **une ~ive commerciale de grande envergure** a large-scale commercial offensive.

offertoire [ɔfɛʀtwaʀ] nm (*Rel*) offertory.

office [ɔfis] 1 nm a (*littér: tâche*) duties, office; (*Hist*) charge, office; (*Admin*) office. **remplir l'~ de directeur/chauffeur** to hold the office *ou* post of manager/chauffeur; **~ ministériel** ministerial office; **~ d'avoué** office of solicitor; **le bourreau a fait *ou* rempli son ~** the executioner carried out his duties.

b (*usage*) **faire ~ de** to act *ou* serve as; **faire ~ de chauffeur** to act as (a) chauffeur; *[appareil, loi]* **remplir son ~** to fulfil its function, do its job*.

c (*bureau*) office, bureau, agency. **~ national/départemental** national/regional office; **~ de publicité** advertising agency *ou* organization; **~ des changes** foreign exchange bureau; **~ de commerce** trade organization; **~ du tourisme** tourist information (centre), tourist office.

d (*Rel*) (*messe*) (church) service; (*prières*) prayers. **l'~ (divin)** the (divine) office; **l'~ des morts** the office *ou* service for the dead; **aller à/manquer l'~** to go to/miss church *ou* the church service.

e (*loc*) **d'~**: **être nommé/mis à la retraite d'~** to be appointed/retired automatically *ou* as a matter of course; **faire qch d'~** (*Admin*) to do sth automatically; (*gén*) to do sth as a matter of course *ou* automatically; **avocat/expert (commis) d'~** officially appointed lawyer/expert.

f (*littér: service*) office. (*Pol*) **bons ~s** good offices; **Monsieur bons ~s*** mediator.

2 nm ou nf (*cuisine*) pantry, staff dining quarters.

officialisation [ɔfisjalizasjɔ̃] nf officializing, officialization.

officialiser [ɔfisjalize] [1] vt to make official, officialize.

officiant, e [ɔfisjɑ̃, jɑ̃t] (*Rel*) 1 adj m, nm: **(prêtre) ~** officiant, officiating priest. 2 adj f, nf **(sœur) ~e** officiating sister.

officiel, -elle [ɔfisjɛl] 1 adj (*gén*) official. **(c'est) ~!*** it's no joke!, it's for sure!*; **rendre ~** to make official *ou* public; *voir* **journal**. 2 nm,f official.

officiellement [ɔfisjɛlmɑ̃] adv officially.

officier¹ [ɔfisje] nm officer. **~ subalterne/supérieur/général** junior/field/general officer; **~ de marine** naval officer; **~ marinier** petty officer; **~ mécanicien** engineer officer; **~ d'ordonnance** aide-de-camp; **~ de paix** (police) inspector (*Brit*), lieutenant (*US*); **~ de police** senior police officer; **~ de police judiciaire** *official empowered to make arrests and act as a policeman*; **~ de semaine** ≃ orderly officer; **~ ministériel** member of the legal profession; **~ de l'état civil** (mayor considered in his capacity as) registrar; **~ technicien** technical officer.

officier² [ɔfisje] [7] vi (*Rel, hum*) to officiate.

officieusement [ɔfisjøzmɑ̃] adv unofficially.

officieux, -ieuse [ɔfisjø, jøz] adj unofficial. **à titre ~** unofficially, in an unofficial capacity.

officinal, e, mpl **-aux** [ɔfisinal, o] adj *plante* medicinal.

officine [ɔfisin] nf *[pharmacie]* dispensary; (*Admin, Jur: pharmacie*) pharmacy; (*péj: repaire*) headquarters, agency.

offrande [ɔfʀɑ̃d] nf (*don*) offering. (*Rel: cérémonie*) **l'~** the offertory.

offrant [ɔfʀɑ̃] nm (*Jur, Fin*) offerer, bidder. **au plus ~** to the highest bidder; (*petites annonces*) **"au plus ~"** "highest offer secures sale".

offre [ɔfʀ] nf (*gén*) offer; (*aux enchères*) bid; (*Admin: soumission*) tender. (*Écon*) **l'~ et la demande** supply and demand; **appel d'~s** invitation to tender; **il m'a fait une ~ (de prix *ou* d'emploi)** he made me an offer; **as-tu regardé les ~s d'emploi?** have you checked the situations vacant column? *ou* the job ads?*; **il y avait plusieurs ~s d'emploi pour des ingénieurs** there were several jobs advertised for engineers, there were several advertisements *ou* ads* for engineering jobs; (*Fin*) **~ publique d'achat** takeover bid (*Brit*), tender offer (*US*); (*Fin*) **~ publique d'échange** public offer of exchange; **~ publique de vente** offer for sale; (*frm*) **~(s) de service** offer of service; (*Comm*) **~ spéciale** special offer (*Brit*), special (*US*); (*Pol*) **~s de paix** peace overtures; (*Écon*) **théorie de l'~** supply-side economics.

offrir [ɔfʀiʀ] [18] 1 vt a (*donner*) to give (*à* to); (*acheter*) to buy (*à* for). **c'est pour ~?** is it for a present? *ou* a gift?; **la joie d'~** the joy of giving; **il lui a offert un bracelet** he gave her a bracelet, he presented her with a bracelet; **il nous a offert à boire** (*chez lui*) he gave us a drink; (*au café*) he bought *ou* stood us a drink.

b (*proposer*) *aide, marchandise, excuse* to offer; *sacrifice* to offer up; *choix, possibilité* to offer, give; *démission* to tender, offer. **puis-je vous ~ à boire/une cigarette?** can I offer you a drink/a cigarette?; **~ l'hospitalité à qn** to offer sb hospitality; **~ le mariage à qn** to offer to marry sb; **il m'offrit un fauteuil** he offered me a chair; **~ son bras à qn** to offer sb one's arm; **~ ses services à qn** (*gén, Comm*) to offer sb one's services; **~ de faire** to offer to do; **combien m'en offrez-vous?** how much will you give me for it? *ou* will you offer for it?; **~ sa vie à la patrie/à Dieu** to offer up one's life to the homeland/to God.

c (*présenter*) *spectacle, image* to present, offer; *vue* to offer. **~ son corps aux regards** to reveal *ou* expose one's body to the world at large; **~ sa poitrine aux balles** to proffer (*frm*) *ou* present one's chest to the bullets; **le paysage n'offrait rien de particulier** the countryside had no particular features.

d (*apporter*) *avantage, inconvénient* to offer, present; *exemple, explication* to provide, afford (*frm*); *analogie* to offer, have; *échappatoire* to offer. **~ de la résistance** *[coffre-fort]* to resist, offer resistance; *[personne]* to put up *ou* offer resistance (*à* to).

2 **s'offrir** vpr a *[femme]* to offer o.s. **s'~ à Dieu** to offer o.s. (up) to God; **s'~ aux regards** *[personne]* to expose *ou* reveal o.s. to the public gaze; *[spectacle]* to present itself to the gaze, meet *ou* greet our (*ou* your *etc*) eyes; **la première idée qui s'est offerte à mon esprit** the first idea that occurred to me *ou* that came into my mind; **s'~ comme guide** to volunteer to act as a guide; **s'~ aux coups** to let the blows rain down on one, submit to the blows.

b *repas, vacances* to treat o.s. to; *disque* to buy o.s., treat o.s. to.

c **s'~ à faire qch** to offer *ou* volunteer to do sth.

offset [ɔfsɛt] nm, adj inv (*Typ*) offset. **journal tiré en ~** offset (litho-) printed newspaper.

off-shore [ɔfʃɔʀ] 1 adj inv *plate-forme, exploitation, pétrole* offshore; (*Fin*) *fonds* offshore. 2 nm inv (*Sport*) (*bateau*) powerboat; (*activité*) powerboat racing. **faire du ~** to go powerboat racing.

offusquer [ɔfyske] [1] 1 vt to offend. **ses manières offusquent beaucoup de gens** his manners offend many people. 2 **s'offusquer** vpr to take offence *ou* umbrage (*de* at), be offended (*de* at, by).

oflag [ɔflag] nm oflag.

ogival, e, mpl **-aux** [ɔʒival, o] adj *voûte* rib (*épith*), ogival (*SPÉC*); *arc* pointed, ogival (*SPÉC*); *architecture, art* gothic (*medieval*).

ogive [ɔʒiv] nf a (*Archit*) diagonal rib. **croisée d'~s** intersection of the ribs (*of a vault*); **arc d'~s** pointed *ou* equilateral arch; **voûte en ~** rib vault; **arc en ~** lancet arch. b (*Mil*) *[fusée etc]* nose cone. **~ nucléaire** nuclear warhead.

ogre [ɔgʀ] nm ogre. **manger comme un ~, être un vrai ~** to eat like a horse.

ogresse [ɔgʀɛs] nf ogress. **elle a un appétit d'~** she's got an appetite like a horse.

oh [o] excl oh! **pousser des ~** to exclaim.

ohé [ɔe] excl hey (there)! **~ du bateau!** ahoy (there)!, hey (there)!, hullo (there)!

Ohio [ɔjɔ] nm Ohio.

ohm [om] nm ohm.

ohmmètre [ommɛtʀ] nm ohmmeter.

oïdium [ɔidjɔm] nm powdery mildew.

oie [wa] nf (*Zool*) goose; (*péj: niaise*) silly goose. **~ cendrée** greylag goose; **~ sauvage** wild goose; **~ des neiges** snow goose; (*péj*) **~ blanche** innocent young thing; *voir* **caca, jeu, patte** *etc*.

oignon [ɔɲɔ̃] nm (*légume*) onion; *[tulipe etc]* bulb; (*Méd*) bunion; (*montre*) turnip watch. **petits ~s** pickling onions; **aux petits ~s** (*Culin*) with (pickling) onions; (*fig*) **être soigné aux petits ~s** to be looked after really well; (*fig*) **c'était aux petits ~s*** it was the last word in luxury (*ou* comfort *etc*); **ce n'est pas *ou* ce ne sont pas mes ~s**‡ it's no business of mine, it's nothing to do with me; **mêle-toi *ou* occupe-toi de tes ~s**‡ mind your own business; *voir* **pelure, rang**.

oïl [ɔjl] nm *voir* **langue**.

oindre [wɛ̃dʀ] [49] vt to anoint.

oint, ointe [wɛ̃, wɛ̃t] (ptp de **oindre**) adj anointed.

oiseau, pl **~x** [wazo] 1 nm (*Zool*) bird; (*gén péj: personne*) customer*, fellow*. **être comme l'~ sur la branche** to be here today and gone tomorrow, be very unsettled (*in a place*); **trouver l'~ rare** to find the man (*ou* woman) in a million; (*fig*) **l'~ s'est envolé** the bird has flown; **drôle d'~** queer fish* (*Brit*) *ou* bird* *ou* customer*; *voir* **appétit, cervelle, petit, vol**.

2 comp ▸**oiseau chanteur** songbird ▸**oiseau des îles** exotic bird ▸**oiseau-lyre** nm (pl **oiseaux-lyres**) lyrebird ▸**oiseau de malheur** *ou* **de mauvais augure** (*fig*) bird of ill omen ▸**oiseau migrateur** migratory bird, migrant ▸**oiseau-mouche** nm (pl **oiseaux-mouches**) hummingbird ▸**oiseau de nuit** bird of the night, night-bird ▸**oiseau de paradis** bird of paradise ▸**oiseau de proie** bird of prey.

oiseleur [waz(ə)lœʀ] nm bird-catcher.

oiselier, -ière [wazəlje, jɛʀ] nm,f bird-seller.

oisellerie [wazɛlʀi] nf (*magasin*) birdshop; (*commerce*) bird-selling.

oiseux, -euse [wazø, øz] adj *dispute, digression, commentaire* pointless; *propos* idle (*épith*), pointless; *question* trivial, trifling.

oisif, -ive [wazif, iv] 1 adj idle. **une vie ~ive** a life of leisure, an idle

life. 2 **nm,f** man (*ou* woman) of leisure. **les ~s** (*gén*) the idle; (*Écon: non-actifs*) those not in active employment.
oisillon [wazijɔ̃] **nm** young bird, fledgling.
oisivement [wazivmɑ̃] **adv** idly. **vivre ~** to live a life of leisure *ou* idleness.
oisiveté [wazivte] **nf** idleness. (*Prov*) **l'~ est la mère de tous les vices** idleness is the root of all evil (*Prov*); **~ forcée** forced idleness *ou* inactivity.
oison [wazɔ̃] **nm** gosling.
OIT [ɔite] **nf** (**abrév de Organisation internationale du travail**) ILO.
OK* [oke] 1 **excl** O.K.!*, right-oh! 2 **adj inv** OK, fine (*attrib*).
okapi [ɔkapi] **nm** okapi.
Oklahoma [ɔklaɔma] **nm** Oklahoma.
okoumé [ɔkume] **nm** gaboon (mahogany).
OL (**abrév de ondes longues**) LW.
olé [ɔle] 1 **excl** olé! 2 **adj inv**: **~ ~*** (*excentrique*) *personne* wacky‡; (*osé*) *film, livre* risqué; *vêtement, personne* OTT*, over the top*.
oléacée [ɔlease] **nf** member of the Oleaceae family. **~s** Oleaceae.
oléagineux, -euse [ɔleaʒinø, øz] 1 **adj** oil-producing, oleaginous (*SPÉC*). 2 **nm** oil-producing *ou* oleaginous (*SPÉC*) plant.
oléfine [ɔlefin] **nf** olefine, alkene.
oléiculteur, -trice [ɔleikyltœʀ, tʀis] **nm** olive grower.
oléiculture [ɔleikyltyʀ] **nf** olive growing.
oléifère [ɔleifɛʀ] **adj** oil-producing, oleiferous (*SPÉC*).
oléine [ɔlein] **nf** olein, triolein.
oléoduc [ɔleɔdyk] **nm** oil pipeline.
oléum [ɔleɔm] **nm** oleum.
olfactif, -ive [ɔlfaktif, iv] **adj** olfactory.
olfaction [ɔlfaksjɔ̃] **nf** olfaction.
olibrius [ɔlibʀijys] **nm** (*péj*) (queer) customer* *ou* fellow*.
olifant [ɔlifɑ̃] **nm** (ivory) horn.
oligarchie [ɔligaʀʃi] **nf** oligarchy.
oligarchique [ɔligaʀʃik] **adj** oligarchic.
oligarque [ɔligaʀk] **nm** oligarch.
oligo-élément, **pl oligo-éléments** [ɔligoelemɑ̃] **nm** trace element.
oligopole [ɔligɔpɔl] **nm** oligopoly.
olivaie [ɔlivɛ] **nf** = **oliveraie**.
olivâtre [ɔlivɑtʀ] **adj** (*gén*) olive-greenish; *teint* sallow.
olive [ɔliv] 1 **nf** a (*fruit*) olive. **~ noire/verte** black/green olive; *voir* **huile**. b (*ornement*) bead *ou* pearl moulding; (*interrupteur*) switch. c (*Anat*) olivary body. 2 **adj inv** olive(-green).
oliveraie [ɔlivʀɛ] **nf** olive grove.
olivette [ɔlivɛt] **nf** plum tomato.
Olivier [ɔlivje] **nm** Oliver.
olivier [ɔlivje] **nm** (*arbre*) olive tree; (*bois*) olive (wood); *voir* **jardin, mont, rameau**.
olivine [ɔlivin] **nf** olivine.
olographe [ɔlɔgʀaf] **adj** *voir* **testament**.
OLP [ɔɛlpe] **nf** (**abrév de Organisation de libération de la Palestine**) PLO.
Olympe¹ [ɔlɛ̃p] **nm** Mount Olympus.
Olympe² [ɔlɛ̃p] **nf** Olympia.
olympiade [ɔlɛ̃pjad] **nf** Olympiad.
olympien, -ienne [ɔlɛ̃pjɛ̃, jɛn] **adj** (*Myth*) **les dieux ~s** the Olympic gods; (*fig*) **un calme ~** an Olympian calm; (*fig*) **un air ~** an air of Olympian aloofness.
olympique [ɔlɛ̃pik] **adj** Olympic; *voir* **jeu**.
OM (**abrév de ondes moyennes**) MW.
Oman [ɔman] **nm**: (**le Sultanat d'**)**~** (the Sultanate of) Oman.
omanais, e [ɔmanɛ, ɛz] 1 **adj** Omani. 2 **nm,f**: **O~(e)** Omani.
ombelle [ɔ̃bɛl] **nf** umbel. **en ~** umbellate (*SPÉC*), parasol-shaped.
ombellifère [ɔ̃belifɛʀ] 1 **adj** umbelliferous. 2 **nf** member of the Umbelliferae family. **~s** Umbelliferae.
ombilic [ɔ̃bilik] **nm** a (*nombril*) umbilicus, navel. b (*plante*) navelwort. c (*Bot*) hilum; (*renflement*) *[bouclier etc]* boss; (*Math*) umbilic.
ombilical, e, **mpl -aux** [ɔ̃bilikal, o] **adj** (*Anat*) umbilical; (*Sci, Tech*) navel-like; *voir* **cordon**.
omble(-chevalier), **pl ombles(-chevaliers)** [ɔ̃bl(ə)(ʃ(ə)valje)] **nm** char(r) (*fish*).
ombrage [ɔ̃bʀaʒ] **nm** a (*ombre*) shade. (*feuillage*) **sous les ~s (du parc)** in the shade of the trees (in the park), in the leafy shade (of the park). b (*loc frm*) **prendre ~ de qch** to take umbrage *ou* offence at sth; **porter ~ à qn**, († *ou littér*) **causer** *ou* **donner de l'~ à qn** to offend sb.
ombragé, e [ɔ̃bʀaʒe] (**ptp de ombrager**) **adj** shaded, shady.
ombrager [ɔ̃bʀaʒe] 3 **vt** *[arbres]* to shade. (*fig littér*) **une mèche ombrageait son front** a lock of hair shaded his brow.
ombrageux, -euse [ɔ̃bʀaʒø, øz] **adj** a *personne* touchy, prickly, quick to take offence (*attrib*), easily offended; *caractère* touchy, prickly. b *âne, cheval* skittish, nervous.
ombre¹ [ɔ̃bʀ] 1 **nf** a (*lit*) shade (*NonC*); (*ombre portée*) shadow; (*littér: obscurité*) darkness. **25° à l'~** 25° in the shade; **dans l'~ de l'arbre/du vestibule** in the shade of the tree/of the hall; **ces arbres font de l'~** these trees give (us) shade; **enlève-toi, tu me fais de l'~** get out of my light, move – you're in my light; **places sans ~/pleines d'~** shadeless/shady squares; **tapi dans l'~** crouching in the darkness *ou* in the shadows; *voir* **théâtre**.
b (*forme vague*) shadow, shadowy figure *ou* shape.
c (*fig*) (*anonymat*) obscurity; (*secret, incertitude*) dark. **laisser une question dans l'~** to leave a question in the dark, deliberately ignore a question; **tramer quelque chose dans l'~** to plot something in the dark; **travailler dans l'~** to work behind the scenes; **sortir de l'~** *[auteur]* to emerge from one's obscurity; *[terroriste]* to come out into the open; **rester dans l'~** *[artiste]* to remain in obscurity; *[meneur]* to keep in the background; *[détail]* to be still obscure, remain unclear.
d (*soupçon*) **une ~ de moustache** a hint *ou* suspicion of a moustache; **il n'y a pas l'~ d'un doute** there's not the (slightest) shadow of a doubt; **tu n'as pas l'~ d'une chance** you haven't got a ghost of a chance; (*littér*) **une ~ de tristesse passa sur son visage** a shadow of sadness passed over his face; (*littér*) **il y avait dans sa voix l'~ d'un reproche** there was a hint of reproach in his voice.
e (*fantôme*) shade.
f (*loc*) **à l'~ de** (*tout près de*) in the shadow of, close beside; (*à l'abri de*) in the shade of; **vivre dans l'~ de qn** to live in the shadow of sb; **être l'~ de qn** to be sb's (little) shadow; (*fig*) **faire de l'~ à qn** to overshadow sb; **mettre qn à l'~*** to put sb behind bars, lock sb up; **il y a une ~ au tableau** there's a fly in the ointment; **n'être plus que l'~ de soi-même** to be the mere shadow of one's former self; *voir* **peur, proie, suivre**.
2 **comp** ▸**ombres chinoises** (*improvisées*) shadowgraph; (*spectacle*) shadow show *ou* pantomime ▸**ombre méridienne** noonday shadow ▸**ombre à paupières** eye shadow ▸**ombre portée** shadow.
ombre² [ɔ̃bʀ] **nm** (*poisson*) grayling.
ombre³ [ɔ̃bʀ] **nf** (*terre, couleur*) umber. **terre d'~** umber.
ombrelle [ɔ̃bʀɛl] **nf** (*parasol*) parasol, sunshade; (*Zool*) *[méduse]* umbrella.
ombrer [ɔ̃bʀe] 1 **vt** *dessin* to shade. **~ ses paupières** to put eye shadow on.
ombreux, -euse [ɔ̃bʀø, øz] **adj** (*littér*) *pièce, forêt* shady.
Ombrie [ɔ̃bʀi] **nf** Umbria.
ombrien, -ienne [ɔ̃bʀijɛ̃, ijɛn] **adj** Umbrian.
oméga [ɔmega] **nm** omega; *voir* **alpha**.
omelette [ɔmlɛt] **nf** omelette. **~ aux fines herbes** omelette with herbs; **~ aux champignons/au fromage** mushroom/cheese omelette; **~ baveuse** runny omelette; **~ norvégienne** baked Alaska; (*Prov*) **on ne fait pas d'~ sans casser des œufs** you can't make an omelette without breaking eggs.
omettre [ɔmɛtʀ] 56 **vt** to leave out, miss out, omit. **~ de faire qch** to fail *ou* omit *ou* neglect to do sth.
omission [ɔmisjɔ̃] **nf** (*action*) omission; (*chose oubliée*) omission, oversight. **pécher par ~** to commit the sin of omission.
omnibus [ɔmnibys] **nm** (*aussi* **train ~**) slow *ou* local train; (*Hist: bus*) omnibus. **le train est ~ jusqu'à Paris** the train stops at every station before *ou* until Paris.
omnidirectionnel, -elle [ɔmnidiʀɛksjɔnɛl] **adj** omnidirectional.
omnipotence [ɔmnipɔtɑ̃s] **nf** omnipotence.
omnipotent, e [ɔmnipɔtɑ̃, ɑ̃t] **adj** omnipotent, all-powerful.
omnipraticien, -ienne [ɔmnipʀatisjɛ̃, jɛn] **nm,f** general practitioner.
omniprésence [ɔmnipʀezɑ̃s] **nf** omnipresence.
omniprésent, e [ɔmnipʀezɑ̃, ɑ̃t] **adj** omnipresent.
omniscience [ɔmnisjɑ̃s] **nf** omniscience.
omniscient, e [ɔmnisjɑ̃, jɑ̃t] **adj** omniscient.
omnisports [ɔmnispɔʀ] **adj inv** *terrain* general-purpose (*épith*). **association ~** (general) sports club; **salle ~** games hall; **palais ~** sports centre.
omnium [ɔmnjɔm] **nm** a (*Cyclisme*) prime; (*Courses*) open handicap. b (*Comm*) corporation.
omnivore [ɔmnivɔʀ] 1 **adj** omnivorous. 2 **nm** omnivorous creature, omnivore (*SPÉC*).
omoplate [ɔmɔplat] **nf** shoulder blade, scapula (*SPÉC*).
OMS [ɔɛmɛs] **nf** (**abrév de Organisation mondiale de la santé**) WHO.
OMT [ɔɛmte] **nf** (**abrév de Organisation mondiale du tourisme**) WTO.
on [ɔ̃] **pron** a (*indétermination: souvent traduit par pass*) **~ les interrogea sans témoins** they were questioned without (any) witnesses; **~ va encore augmenter l'essence** (the price of) petrol is going up again, they are putting up the price of petrol again; (*annonce*) **~ demande jeune fille** young girl wanted *ou* required; **~ ne nous a pas demandé notre avis** nobody asked our opinion, our opinion wasn't asked; **~ ne devrait pas poser des questions si ambiguës** you *ou* one shouldn't ask such ambiguous questions; **dans cet hôtel ~ ne vous permet pas d'avoir des chiens** you aren't allowed to *ou* they won't let you keep a dog in this hotel; **~ prétend que** they say that, it is said that; **~ se précipita sur les places vides** there was a rush for the empty seats; (*Prov*) **~ n'est jamais si bien servi que par soi-même** a job is never so well done as when you do it yourself; *voir* **dire**.
b (*quelqu'un*) someone, anyone. **~ a déposé ce paquet pendant que vous étiez sorti** someone left this parcel *ou* this parcel was left while you were out; **qu'est-ce que je dis si (l')~ demande à vous parler?** what shall I say if someone *ou* anyone asks to speak to you?; **~ vous demande au**

téléphone you're wanted on the phone, there's someone on the phone for you; **~ frappa à la porte** there was a knock at the door; **est-ce qu'~ est venu réparer la porte?** has anyone *ou* someone been to repair the door?; **~ peut très bien aimer la pluie** some people may well like the rain; **je n'admets pas qu'~** *ou* **que l'~ ne sache pas nager** I can't understand how (some) people can't swim.

c (*indéf: celui qui parle*) you, one, we. **~ ne dort pas par cette chaleur** you (*ou* one) can't sleep in this heat; **est-ce qu'~ est censé s'habiller pour le dîner?** is one *ou* are we expected to dress for dinner?; **~ aimerait être sur que ...** one *ou* we would like to be sure that ...; **de nos fenêtres, ~ voit les collines** from our windows you (*ou* we) can see the hills; **~ a trop chaud ici** it's too hot here; **quand ~ est inquiet rien ne peut vous** *ou* **nous distraire** when you are (*ou* one is) worried nothing can take your (*ou* one's) mind off it; **~ comprend difficilement pourquoi** it is difficult to understand why; **~ ne pense jamais à tout** one (*ou* you) can't think of everything; **~ ne lui donnerait pas 70 ans** you wouldn't think she was 70; **~ ne dirait pas que** you wouldn't think that.

d (*éloignement dans temps, espace*) they, people. **autrefois, ~ se préoccupait peu de l'hygiène** years ago, they (*ou* people) didn't worry about hygiene; **en Chine ~ mange avec des baguettes** in China they eat with chopsticks; **dans aucun pays ~ ne semble pouvoir arrêter l'inflation** it doesn't seem as if inflation can be stopped in any country, no country seems (to be) able to stop inflation.

e (**: nous*) we. **~ a décidé tous les trois de partir chacun de son côté** the three of us decided to go (each) our separate ways; **chez nous ~ mange beaucoup de pain** we eat a lot of bread in our family; **lui et moi ~ n'est pas d'accord** we don't see eye to eye, him and me*; **nous, ~ a amené notre chien** we've brought along the dog; **nous, ~ a tous réclamé une augmentation** we all (of us) demanded a rise; **~ fait ce qu'~ peut** *ou* **de son mieux** you can only do your best; **il faut bien qu'~ vive** a fellow (*ou* a girl) has got to eat*; **dans ce chapitre ~ essaiera de prouver** in this chapter we (*frm*) shall attempt to prove.

f (*gén langue parlée: familiarité, reproche etc*) **~ est bien sage aujourd'hui!** aren't we a good boy (*ou* girl) today!, we are a good boy (*ou* girl) today!; **alors ~ ne dit plus bonjour aux amis!** don't we say hello to our friends any more?; **alors, ~ est content?** well, are you pleased?; (*iro*) **~ n'a pas un sou mais ~ s'achète une voiture!** he hasn't (*ou* they haven't *etc*) a penny to his (*ou* their *etc*) name but he goes and buys (*ou* they go and buy *etc*) a car!; **~ parle ~ parle et puis ~ finit par dire des sottises** talk, talk, talk and it's all nonsense in the end.

g (*intensif*) **c'est ~ ne peut plus beau/ridicule** it couldn't be lovelier/ more ridiculous; **je suis ~ ne peut plus heureux de vous voir** I couldn't be more delighted to see you, I'm absolutely delighted to see you.

onagre[1] [ɔnagʀ] nm (*Archéol, Zool*) onager.

onagre[2] [ɔnagʀ] nf (*Bot*) oenothera (*SPÉC*), evening primrose.

onanisme [ɔnanism] nm onanism.

once[1] [ɔ̃s] nf (*mesure, aussi Can*) ounce. **il n'a pas une ~ de bon sens** he hasn't an ounce of common sense.

once[2] [ɔ̃s] nf (*Zool*) ounce, snow leopard.

oncial, e, mpl **-iaux** [ɔ̃sjal, jo] 1 adj uncial. 2 **onciale** nf uncial.

oncle [ɔ̃kl] nm uncle. (*fig*) **~ d'Amérique** rich uncle; **l'O~ Sam** Uncle Sam; **l'O~ Tom** Uncle Tom; *voir* **héritage**.

oncogène [ɔ̃kɔʒɛn] 1 adj oncogenic, oncogenous. 2 nm oncogene.

oncologie [ɔ̃kɔlɔʒi] nf oncology.

oncologiste [ɔ̃kɔlɔʒist] nmf, **oncologue** [ɔ̃kɔlɔg] nmf oncologist.

oncques†† [ɔ̃k] adv never.

onction [ɔ̃ksjɔ̃] nf (*Rel, fig*) unction. **~ des malades** anointing of the sick; *voir* **extrême**.

onctueusement [ɔ̃ktɥøzmɑ̃] adv *couler* unctuously; *parler* with unction, suavely.

onctueux, -euse [ɔ̃ktɥø, øz] adj *crème* smooth, creamy, unctuous; *manières, voix* unctuous, smooth.

onctuosité [ɔ̃ktɥozite] nf (*voir* **onctueux**) unctuousness, smoothness, creaminess.

onde [ɔ̃d] nf a (*gén, Phys*) wave. **~s herziennes** *ou* **radioélectriques/ sonores** Hertzian *ou* radio/sound waves; (*Rad*) **~s courtes** short waves; **petites ~s, ~s moyennes** medium waves; **grandes ~s** long waves; **transmettre sur ~s courtes/petites ~s/grandes ~s** to broadcast on short/ medium/long wave; (*lit, fig*) **~ de choc** shock wave; *voir* **longueur**.

b (*loc Rad*) **sur les ~s et dans la presse** on the radio and in the press; **nous espérons vous retrouver sur les ~s demain à 6 heures** we hope to join you again on the air tomorrow at 6 o'clock; **il passe sur les ~s demain** he's going on the air tomorrow; **mettre en ~s** *pièce etc* to produce for the radio; **par ordre d'entrée en ~s** in order of appearance.

c (*littér: lac, mer*) **l'~** the waters; **l'~ amère** the briny deep (*littér*).

ondé, e[1] [ɔ̃de] adj (*littér*) *tissu* watered; *cheveux* wavy.

ondée[2] [ɔ̃de] nf shower (*of rain*).

ondin, e [ɔ̃dɛ̃, in] nm,f water sprite.

on-dit [ɔ̃di] nm inv rumour, hearsay (*NonC*). **ce ne sont que des ~** it's only hearsay.

ondoiement [ɔ̃dwamɑ̃] nm a (*littér*) *[blés, surface moirée]* undulation. b (*Rel*) provisional baptism.

ondoyant, e [ɔ̃dwajɑ̃, ɑ̃t] adj a *eaux, blés* undulating; *flamme* wavering; *reflet* shimmering; *démarche* swaying, supple. b († *ou littér*) *caractère, personne* unstable, changeable.

ondoyer [ɔ̃dwaje] 8 1 vi *[blé]* to undulate, ripple; *[drapeau]* to wave, ripple. 2 vt (*Rel*) to baptize (*in an emergency*).

ondulant, e [ɔ̃dylɑ̃, ɑ̃t] adj a *démarche* swaying, supple; *ligne, profil, surface* undulating. b (*Méd*) *pouls* uneven.

ondulation [ɔ̃dylasjɔ̃] nf *[vagues, blés, terrain]* undulation. **~s** *[sol]* undulations; *[cheveux]* waves.

ondulatoire [ɔ̃dylatwaʀ] adj (*Phys*) undulatory, wave (*épith*); *voir* **mécanique**.

ondulé, e [ɔ̃dyle] (ptp de **onduler**) adj *surface* undulating; *chevelure* wavy; *carton, tôle* corrugated.

onduler [ɔ̃dyle] 1 1 vi (*gén*) to undulate; *[drapeau]* to ripple, wave; *[route]* to snake up and down, undulate; *[cheveux]* to be wavy, wave. 2 vt (†) *cheveux* to wave.

onduleux, -euse [ɔ̃dylø, øz] adj *courbe, ligne* wavy; *plaine* undulating; *silhouette, démarche* sinuous, swaying, supple.

onéreux, -euse [ɔneʀø, øz] adj expensive, costly; *voir* **titre**.

ONG [ɔɛnʒe] nf (abrév de **organisation non gouvernementale**) NGO.

ongle [ɔ̃gl] nm *[personne]* (finger)nail; *[animal]* claw. **~ des pieds** toenail; **~ incarné** ingrowing *ou* ingrown nail; **porter** *ou* **avoir les ~s longs** to have long nails; **vernis/ciseaux à ~s** nail varnish/scissors; **avoir les ~s en deuil*** to have dirty (finger)nails; **avoir bec et ~s** *ou* **dents et ~s** to be well-equipped to hit back; **avoir les ~s faits** to have painted nails; *voir* **bout, payer**.

onglée [ɔ̃gle] nf: **avoir l'~** to have fingers numb with cold.

onglet [ɔ̃glɛ] nm a *[tranche de livre]* (*dépassant*) tab; (*en creux*) thumb index. **dictionnaire à ~s** dictionary with a thumb index. b *[lame de canif]* (thumbnail) groove. c (*Menuiserie*) mitre, mitred angle. **boîte à ~s** mitre box. d (*Math*) ungula; (*Bot*) unguis; (*Reliure*) guard. e (*Boucherie*) prime cut of beef.

onglier [ɔ̃glije] 1 nm manicure set. 2 nmpl: **~s** nail scissors.

onguent [ɔ̃gɑ̃] nm a (*Pharm*) ointment, salve. b (†: *parfum*) unguent.

ongulé, e [ɔ̃gyle] 1 adj hoofed, ungulate (*SPÉC*). 2 nm hoofed *ou* ungulate (*SPÉC*) animal. **~s** ungulata.

onirique [ɔniʀik] adj (*Art, Littérat*) dreamlike, dream (*attrib*).

onirisme [ɔniʀism] nm (*Psych*) hallucinosis; (*Littérat*) fantasizing.

onomasiologie [ɔnɔmazjɔlɔʒi] nf onomasiology.

onomastique [ɔnɔmastik] 1 adj onomastic. 2 nf onomastics (*sg*).

onomatopée [ɔnɔmatɔpe] nf onomatopoeia.

onomatopéique [ɔnɔmatɔpeik] adj onomatopoeic.

onques†† [ɔ̃k] adv = **oncques††**.

ontarien, -ienne [ɔ̃taʀjɛ̃, jɛn] 1 adj Ontarian. 2 nm,f: **O~(ne)** Ontarian.

Ontario [ɔ̃taʀjo] nm Ontario. **le lac ~** Lake Ontario.

ontogenèse [ɔ̃tɔʒənɛz] nf, **ontogénie** [ɔ̃tɔʒeni] nf ontogeny, ontogenesis.

ontogénétique [ɔ̃tɔʒenetik] adj, **ontogénique** [ɔ̃tɔʒenik] adj ontogenetic, ontogenic.

ontologie [ɔ̃tɔlɔʒi] nf ontology.

ontologique [ɔ̃tɔlɔʒik] adj ontological.

ONU [ɔny] nf (abrév de **Organisation des Nations Unies**) UNO. **l'~** the UN, the UNO.

onusien, -ienne [ɔnyzjɛ̃, jɛn] 1 adj of the UN. **la diplomatie ~ne** UN diplomacy. 2 nm,f UN official.

onyx [ɔniks] nm onyx.

onze ['ɔ̃z] 1 adj inv eleven. **le ~ novembre** Armistice Day; *pour autres loc voir* **six**. 2 nm inv (*Sport*) **le ~ de France** the French eleven *ou* team; *pour autres loc voir* **six**.

onzième ['ɔ̃zjɛm] adj, nmf eleventh. (*péj*) **les ouvriers de la ~ heure** last-minute helpers; *pour autres loc voir* **sixième**.

onzièmement ['ɔ̃zjɛmmɑ̃] adv in the eleventh place; *pour loc voir* **sixièmement**.

oocyte [ɔɔsit] nm = **ovocyte**.

oolithe [ɔɔlit] nm oolite.

oolithique [ɔɔlitik] adj oolitic.

OPA [ɔpea] nf (abrév de **offre publique d'achat**) *voir* **offre**.

opacifier [ɔpasifje] 7 vt to make opaque.

opacité [ɔpasite] nf (*voir* **opaque**) opaqueness; impenetrableness.

opale [ɔpal] nf opal.

opalescence [ɔpalesɑ̃s] nf opalescence.

opalescent, e [ɔpalesɑ̃, ɑ̃t] adj opalescent.

opalin, e[1] [ɔpalɛ̃, in] adj opaline.

opaline[2] [ɔpalin] nf opaline.

opaque [ɔpak] adj *verre, corps* opaque (*à* to); *brouillard, nuit* impenetrable; (*fig*) opaque.

op' art [ɔpaʀt] nm op art.

op. cit (abrév de **opere citato**) op. cit.

OPE [ɔpeə] nf (abrév de **offre publique d'échange**) *voir* **offre**.

opéable [ɔpeabl] 1 adj liable to be taken over (*attrib*). 2 nf firm liable to be taken over.

open [ɔpɛn] adj inv, nm open. (*Sport*) **(tournoi) ~** open (tournament).

OPEP [ɔpɛp] nf (abrév de **Organisation des pays exportateurs de pétrole**) OPEC.

opéra [ɔpeʀa] nm (*œuvre, genre, spectacle*) opera; (*édifice*) opera house. ~ **bouffe** opéra bouffe, comic opera; **grand** ~ grand opera; **~-ballet** opéra ballet; **~-comique** light opera, opéra comique.

opérable [ɔpeʀabl] adj operable. **le malade est-il ~?** can the patient be operated on?; **ce cancer n'est plus ~** this cancer is too far advanced for an operation *ou* to be operable.

opérande [ɔpeʀɑ̃d] nm (*Math, Ordin*) operand.

opérant, e [ɔpeʀɑ̃, ɑ̃t] adj (*efficace*) effective.

opérateur, -trice [ɔpeʀatœʀ, tʀis] 1 nm,f a (*sur machine*) operator. ~ **(de prise de vue)** cameraman; ~ **de saisie** keyboard operator, keyboarder. b (*Bourse*) dealer, trader, operator. 2 nm a (*Math, Ordin*) operator. b *[calculateur]* processing unit. c (*Bourse, Fin*) operator.

opération [ɔpeʀasjɔ̃] nf a (*Méd*) operation. ~ **à cœur ouvert** open heart surgery (*NonC*); **salle/table d'~** operating theatre/table.

b (*Math*) operation. **les ~s fondamentales** the fundamental operations; **ça peut se résoudre en 2 ou 3 ~s** that can be solved in 2 or 3 calculations *ou* operations.

c (*Mil, gén*) operation. ~ **de police/de sauvetage** police/rescue operation; *voir* **théâtre**.

d (*Comm*) (*campagne*) campaign, drive; (*action*) operation. ~ **promotionnelle** promotional campaign; **"~ baisse des prix"** "cut-price sale"; ~ **ville morte** one-day strike by small shopkeepers; ~ **porte ouverte** open house; ~ **escargot** go-slow (*Brit*), slow-down (*US*).

e (*tractation*) (*Comm*) deal; (*Bourse*) deal, transaction, operation. ~ **financière/commerciale** financial/commercial deal; **~s de Bourse** stock-exchange dealings; **notre équipe a réalisé une bonne ~** our team got a good deal.

f (*Tech, gén*) process, operation. **les diverses ~s de la fabrication du papier** the different operations *ou* processes in the making of paper; **l'~ de la digestion** the operation of the digestive system; **les ~s de la raison** the processes of thought; **par l'~ du Saint-Esprit** (*Rel*) through the workings of the Holy Spirit; (*iro*) by magic.

opérationnel, -elle [ɔpeʀasjɔnɛl] adj operational.

opératoire [ɔpeʀatwaʀ] adj (*Méd*) *méthodes, techniques* operating; *maladie, commotion, dépression* post-operative; *voir* **bloc**.

opercule [ɔpɛʀkyl] nm (*Bot, Zool*) operculum; (*Tech*) protective cap *ou* cover.

opéré, e [ɔpeʀe] (ptp de **opérer**) nm,f (*Méd*) patient (*who has undergone an operation*).

opérer [ɔpeʀe] 6 1 vt a (*Méd*) *malade, organe* to operate on (*de* for); *tumeur* to remove. **on l'a opéré d'une tumeur** he had an operation for a tumour *ou* to remove a tumour; ~ **qn de l'appendicite** to operate on sb for appendicitis, take sb's appendix out; **se faire ~** to have an operation, have surgery; **se faire ~ des amygdales** to have one's tonsils removed *ou* out*; **il faut ~** we'll have to operate.

b (*exécuter*) *transformation, réforme* to carry out, implement; *choix* to make. **la Bourse a opéré un redressement spectaculaire** the Stock Exchange made a spectacular recovery; **cette méthode a opéré des miracles** this method has worked wonders; **seule la foi peut ~ le salut des fidèles** faith alone can bring about the salvation of the faithful; **ce traitement a opéré sur lui un changement remarquable** this treatment has brought about an amazing change in him; **un changement considérable s'était opéré** a major change had taken place *ou* occurred.

2 vi (*agir*) *[remède]* to act, work, take effect; *[charme]* to work, take effect; (*procéder*) *[photographe, technicien etc]* to proceed. **comment faut-il ~ pour nettoyer le moteur?** how does one go about *ou* what's the procedure for cleaning the engine?, how does one proceed to clean the engine?

opérette [ɔpeʀɛt] nf operetta, light opera.

Ophélie [ɔfeli] nf Ophelia.

ophidien [ɔfidjɛ̃] nm ophidian. **~s** Ophidia.

ophtalmie [ɔftalmi] nf ophthalmia. ~ **des neiges** snow blindness.

ophtalmique [ɔftalmik] adj ophthalmic.

ophtalmo* [ɔftalmo] nmf abrév de **ophtalmologiste**.

ophtalmologie [ɔftalmɔlɔʒi] nf ophthalmology.

ophtalmologique [ɔftalmɔlɔʒik] adj ophthalmological.

ophtalmologiste [ɔftalmɔlɔʒist] nmf, **ophtalmologue** [ɔftalmɔlɔg] nmf ophthalmologist (*SPÉC*), optician.

ophtalmoscope [ɔftalmɔskɔp] nm ophthalmoscope.

ophtalmoscopie [ɔftalmɔskɔpi] nf ophthalmoscopy.

opiacé, e [ɔpjase] adj *médicament, substance* opiate, opium-containing. **odeur ~e** smell of *ou* like opium.

opimes [ɔpim] adj pl (*hum, littér*) **dépouilles ~** rich booty *ou* spoils.

opinel [ɔpinɛl] nm ® (wooden-handled) pen-knife.

opiner [ɔpine] 1 vi (*littér*) (*se prononcer*) ~ **pour/contre qch** to come out in favour of/come out against sth, pronounce o.s. in favour of/against sth; (*acquiescer*) ~ **de la tête** to nod one's agreement, nod assent; (*hum*) ~ **du bonnet** *ou* **du chef** to nod (in agreement); ~ **à qch** to give one's consent to sth.

opiniâtre [ɔpinjɑtʀ] adj *personne, caractère* stubborn, obstinate; *efforts, haine* unrelenting, persistent; *résistance* stubborn, dogged (*épith*), obstinate, persistent; *fièvre* persistent; *toux* persistent, stubborn.

opiniâtrement [ɔpinjɑtʀəmɑ̃] adv (*voir* **opiniâtre**) stubbornly; obstinately; unrelentingly; persistently; doggedly.

opiniâtrer (s') [ɔpinjɑtʀe] 1 vpr († *ou littér*) **s'~ dans son erreur/dans un projet** to persist in one's mistaken belief/in pursuing a project.

opiniâtreté [ɔpinjɑtʀəte] nf (*voir* **opiniâtre**) stubbornness; obstinacy; unrelentingness; persistency; doggedness.

opinion [ɔpinjɔ̃] nf a (*jugement, conviction, idée*) opinion (*sur* on, about). **~s politiques/religieuses** political/religious beliefs *ou* convictions; **avoir une ~/des ~s** to have an opinion *ou* a point of view/(definite) opinions *ou* views *ou* points of view; **se faire une ~** to form an opinion (*sur* on), make up one's mind (*sur* about); **mon ~ est faite sur son compte** I've made up my mind about him; **c'est une affaire d'~** it's a matter of opinion; **j'ai la même ~** I hold *ou* I am of the same opinion *ou* view, I agree with your (*ou* their *etc*) views; **avoir l'~** *ou* **être de l'~ que** to be of the opinion that; **être de l'~ du dernier qui a parlé** to agree with whoever spoke last; **avoir bonne/mauvaise ~ de qn/de soi** to have a good/bad opinion of sb/o.s.; **j'ai piètre ~ de lui** I've a very low *ou* poor opinion of him; **~s toutes faites** cut-and-dried opinions, uncritical opinions.

b (*manière générale de penser*) **l'~ publique** public opinion; **l'~ ouvrière** working-class opinion; **l'~ française** French public opinion; **informer l'~** to inform the public; **braver l'~** to defy public opinion; **l'~ est unanime/divisée** opinion is unanimous/divided; **il se moque de l'~ des autres** he doesn't care what (other) people think; **avoir l'~ pour soi** to have public opinion on one's side; *voir* **presse**.

c (*dans les sondages*) **le nombre d'~s favorables** those who agreed *ou* said yes; **les sans-~** the don't knows.

opiomane [ɔpjɔman] nmf opium addict.

opiomanie [ɔpjɔmani] nf opium addiction.

opium [ɔpjɔm] nm opium. (*fig*) **l'~ du peuple** the opium of the people.

opossum [ɔpɔsɔm] nm opossum.

opportun, e [ɔpɔʀtœ̃, yn] adj *démarche, visite, remarque* timely, opportune. **il serait ~ de faire** it would be appropriate *ou* advisable to do; **nous le ferons en temps ~** we shall do it at the appropriate *ou* right time.

opportunément [ɔpɔʀtynemɑ̃] adv opportunely. **il est arrivé ~** his arrival was timely *ou* opportune, he arrived opportunely *ou* just at the right time.

opportunisme [ɔpɔʀtynism] nm opportunism.

opportuniste [ɔpɔʀtynist] adj, nmf opportunist.

opportunité [ɔpɔʀtynite] nf *[mesure, démarche]* (*qui vient au bon moment*) timeliness, opportuneness; (*qui est approprié*) appropriateness.

opposabilité [ɔpozabilite] nf (*Jur*) opposability.

opposable [ɔpozabl] adj opposable (*à* to).

opposant, e [ɔpozɑ̃, ɑ̃t] 1 nm,f opponent (*à* of). 2 adj a *minorité*, (*Jur*) *partie* opposing (*épith*). b (*Anat*) *muscle* opponent.

opposé, e [ɔpoze] (ptp de **opposer**) 1 adj a *rive, direction* opposite; *parti, équipe* opposing (*épith*). **venant en sens ~** coming in the opposite *ou* other direction; **garé en sens ~** parked facing the wrong way, parked on the wrong side of the road; **la maison ~e à la nôtre** the house opposite *ou* facing ours; **l'équipe ~e à la nôtre** the team playing against ours.

b (*contraire*) *intérêts* conflicting, opposing; *opinions* conflicting; *caractères* opposite; *forces, pressions* opposing; *couleurs, styles* contrasting; (*Math*) *nombres, angles* opposite. ~ **à** conflicting *ou* contrasting with, opposed to; **opinions totalement ~es** totally conflicting *ou* opposed opinions, opinions totally at variance; **ils sont d'un avis ~** (*au nôtre*) they are of a different *ou* the opposite opinion; (*l'un à l'autre*) they are of conflicting opinions, their opinions are at variance with each other; (*Math*) **angles ~s par le sommet** vertically opposite angles; *voir* **diamétralement**.

c (*hostile à*) ~ **à** opposed to, against; **je suis ~ à la publicité/à ce mariage** I am opposed to *ou* I am against advertising/this marriage.

2 nm a (*contraire*) **l'~** the opposite, the reverse; **il fait tout l'~ de ce qu'on lui dit** he does the opposite *ou* the reverse of what he is told; **à l'~, il serait faux de dire ...** on the other hand *ou* conversely it would be wrong to say ...; **ils sont vraiment à l'~ l'un de l'autre** they are totally unalike; **à l'~ de Paul, je pense que ...** contrary to *ou* unlike Paul, I think that ... .

b (*direction*) **à l'~** (*dans l'autre direction*) the other *ou* opposite way (*de* from); (*de l'autre côté*) on the other *ou* opposite side (*de* from).

opposer [ɔpoze] 1 1 vt a *équipes, boxeurs* to bring together; *rivaux, pays* to bring into conflict (*à* with); *idées, personnages* to contrast (*à* with); *couleurs* to contrast (*à* with); *objets, meubles* to place opposite each other. **le match opposant l'équipe de Lyon et** *ou* **à celle de Reims** the match bringing together the team from Lyons and the team from Rheims; **on m'a opposé à un finaliste olympique** they pitted me *ou* put me against an Olympic finalist; **des questions d'intérêts les ont opposés/les opposent** matters of personal interest have brought them into conflict/divide them; **quel orateur peut-on ~ à Cicéron?** what orator could be put *ou* set beside Cicero?; ~ **un vase à une statue** to place *ou* set a vase opposite a statue.

b (*utiliser comme défense contre*) ~ **à qn/qch** *armée, tactique* to set against sb/sth; ~ **son refus le plus net** to give an absolute refusal (*à* to); ~ **de véhémentes protestations à une accusation** to protest vehemently at an accusation; **opposant son calme à leurs insultes** setting his calmness against their insults; **il nous opposa une résistance farouche** he put up a fierce resistance to us; **il n'y a rien à ~ à cela** there's nothing you can say (*ou* do) against that, there's no answer to that; ~ **la force à la force** to match strength with strength.

c (*objecter*) ~ **des raisons à** to put forward objections to, raise objections to; ~ **des prétextes à** to put forward pretexts for; **que va-t-il ~ à notre propositions/nous ~?** what objections will he make *ou* raise to our proposals/to us?; **il nous opposa que cela coûtait cher** he objected that it was expensive.

2 **s'opposer** **vpr** a *[équipes, boxeurs]* to confront each other, meet; *[rivaux, partis]* to clash (*à* with); *[opinions, théories]* to conflict; *[couleurs, styles]* to contrast (*à* with); *[immeubles]* to face each other. **haut s'oppose à bas** high is the opposite of low; (*dans un combat*) **il s'est opposé à plus fort que lui** he took on *ou* he pitted himself against an opponent who was stronger than him.

b (*se dresser contre*) **s'~ à parents** to rebel against; *mesure, mariage, progrès* to oppose; **je m'oppose à lui en tout** I am opposed to him in everything; **rien ne s'oppose à leur bonheur** nothing stands in the way of their happiness; **je m'oppose formellement à ce que vous y alliez** I am strongly opposed to *ou* I am strongly against your going there; **ma conscience s'y oppose** it goes against my conscience; **sa religion s'y oppose** it is against his religion, his religion doesn't allow it; **votre état de santé s'oppose à tout excès** your state of health makes any excess extremely inadvisable.

opposite [ɔpozit] **nm** (*frm*) **à l'~** on the other *ou* opposite side (*de* from).

opposition [ɔpozisjɔ̃] 1 **nf** a (*résistance*) opposition (*à* to). **faire de l'~ systématique (à tout ce qu'on propose)** to oppose systematically (everything that is put forward); (*Jur, Pol*) **loi passée sans ~** law passed unopposed.

b (*conflit, contraste*) (*gén*) opposition; *[idées, intérêts]* conflict; *[couleurs, styles, caractères]* contrast. **l'~ des 2 partis en cette circonstance ...** (*divergence de vue*) the opposition between the 2 parties on that occasion ...; (*affrontement*) the clash *ou* confrontation between the 2 parties on that occasion ...; **l'~ du gris et du noir a permis de ...** contrasting grey with *ou* and black has made it possible to ...; **mettre 2 styles/théories en ~** to oppose *ou* contrast 2 styles/theories.

c (*Pol*) **l'O~** the opposition; **les partis de l'~** the opposition parties; **les élus de l'~** the members of the opposition parties (*surtout Brit*), opposition MPs; **l'~ parlementaire** the parliamentary opposition, the opposition in parliament.

d (*loc*) **entrer en ~ sur un point** to come into conflict over a point; **en ~ avec** (*contraste, divergence*) in opposition to, at variance with; (*résistance, rébellion*) in conflict with; (*situation dans l'espace*) in apposition to; **agir en ~ avec ses principes** to act contrary to one's principles; **ceci est en ~ avec les faits** this conflicts with the facts; **faire** *ou* **mettre ~ à** *loi, décision* to oppose; *chèque* to stop; **par ~** in contrast; **par ~ à** as opposed to, in contrast with.

2 **comp** ►**opposition à mariage** (*Jur*) objection to a marriage ►**opposition à paiement** (*Jur*) *objection by unpaid creditor to payment being made to debtor*.

oppositionnel, -elle [ɔpozisjɔnɛl] 1 **adj** oppositional. 2 **nm,f** oppositionist.

oppressant, e [ɔpʀesɑ̃, ɑ̃t] **adj** *temps, souvenirs, ambiance, chaleur* oppressive.

oppresser [ɔpʀese] 1 **vt** *[chaleur, ambiance, souvenirs]* to oppress; *[poids, vêtement serré]* to suffocate; *[remords, angoisse]* to oppress, weigh heavily on, weigh down. **avoir une respiration oppressée** to have difficulty with one's breathing; **se sentir oppressé** to feel suffocated.

oppresseur [ɔpʀesœʀ] 1 **nm** oppressor. 2 **adj** oppressive.

oppressif, -ive [ɔpʀesif, iv] **adj** oppressive.

oppression [ɔpʀesjɔ̃] **nf** (*asservissement*) oppression; (*gêne, malaise*) feeling of suffocation *ou* oppression.

opprimer [ɔpʀime] 1 **vt** a *peuple* to oppress; *opinion, liberté* to suppress, stifle. **les opprimés** (*gén*) the oppressed; (*socialement*) the downtrodden, the oppressed classes. b (*oppresser*) *[chaleur etc]* to suffocate, oppress.

opprobre [ɔpʀɔbʀ] **nm** (*littér: honte*) opprobrium (*littér*), obloquy (*littér*), disgrace. **accabler** *ou* **couvrir qn d'~** to cover sb with opprobrium; **jeter l'~ sur** to heap opprobrium on; **être l'~ de la famille** to be a source of shame to the family; **vivre dans l'~** to live in infamy.

optatif, -ive [ɔptatif, iv] **adj, nm** optative.

opter [ɔpte] 1 **vi** (*se décider*) ~ **pour** *carrière, solution* to opt for, decide upon; (*choisir*) ~ **entre** *nationalité* to choose *ou* decide between.

opticien, -ienne [ɔptisjɛ̃, jɛn] **nm,f** (dispensing) optician.

optimal, e, **mpl -aux** [ɔptimal, o] **adj** optimal, optimum (*épith*).

optimisation [ɔptimizasjɔ̃] **nf** optimization.

optimiser [ɔptimize] 1 **vt** to optimize.

optimisme [ɔptimism] **nm** optimism.

optimiste [ɔptimist] 1 **adj** optimistic. 2 **nmf** optimist.

optimum, **pl ~s** *ou* **optima** [ɔptimɔm, a] 1 **nm** optimum. 2 **adj** optimum (*épith*), optimal.

option [ɔpsjɔ̃] 1 **nf** (*littér: choix*) option, choice; (*Comm, Jur, Scol*) option; (*accessoire auto*) optional extra. (*Scol*) **matière à ~** optional subject (*Brit*), option (*Brit*), elective (*US*); **texte à ~** optional text; (*Scol*) **avec ~ mathématique(s)** with a mathematical option, with optional mathematics; (*Fin*) **prendre une ~ sur** to take (out) an option on; (*Pol*) **l'~ zéro** the zero option; (*Aut*) **boîte 5 vitesses (vendue) en ~** 5-speed gearbox available as an optional extra. 2 **comp** ►**option d'achat** (*Fin*) option to buy *ou* call ►**option de vente** (*Fin*) option to sell *ou* put.

optionnel, -elle [ɔpsjɔnɛl] **adj** optional. **matière ~le** optional subject (*Brit*), option (*Brit*), elective (*US*).

optique [ɔptik] 1 **adj** *verre* optical; *nerf* optic. **une bonne qualité ~** a good optical quality; *voir* **angle, télégraphie.**

2 **nf** a (*science, technique, commerce*) optics (*sg*). ~ **médicale/photographique** medical/photographic optics; **instrument d'~** optical instrument; *voir* **illusion.**

b (*lentilles etc*) *[caméra, microscope]* optics (*pl*).

c (*manière de voir*) perspective. **il faut situer ses arguments dans une ~ sociologique** we must situate his arguments in a sociological perspective; **voir qch avec** *ou* **dans une certaine ~** to look at sth from a certain angle *ou* viewpoint; **j'ai une tout autre ~ que la sienne** my way of looking at things is quite different from his, I have a completely different perspective from his.

opulence [ɔpylɑ̃s] **nf** a (*richesse*) (*voir* **opulent**) wealthiness; richness; opulence. **vivre dans l'~** to live an opulent life. b ~ **des formes** richness *ou* fullness of form; **l'~ de sa poitrine** the ampleness of her bosom.

opulent, e [ɔpylɑ̃, ɑ̃t] **adj** a (*riche*) *province, région, pays* wealthy, rich; *prairie* rich; *personne* opulent, wealthy, rich; *luxe, vie* opulent. b *femme* buxom; *poitrine* ample, generous.

opus [ɔpys] **nm** opus.

opuscule [ɔpyskyl] **nm** (*pamphlet*) opuscule.

OPV [ɔpeve] **nf** (**abrév de offre publique de vente**) *voir* **offre.**

or¹ [ɔʀ] **nm** a (*métal*) gold; (*dorure*) gilt, gilding, gold. ~ **blanc** *ou* **gris** white gold; ~ **fin** fine gold; ~ **massif** solid gold; **bijoux en ~ massif** solid gold jewellery, jewellery in solid gold; ~ **jaune/rouge** yellow/red gold; (*fig: pétrole*) ~ **noir** oil, black gold; (*fig: agriculture*) ~ **vert** agricultural wealth; **en lettres d'~** in gilt *ou* gold lettering; **ses cheveux d'~** his golden hair; **les blés d'~** the golden cornfields; **les ~s des coupoles/de l'automne** the golden tints of the cupolas/of autumn; **peinture/étalon/franc ~** gold paint/standard/franc; *voir* **cœur, cousu, étalon, lingot** *etc.*

b (*loc*) **en ~** *objet* gold; *occasion* golden (*épith*); *mari, enfant, sujet* marvellous, wonderful; **c'est une affaire en ~** (*achat*) it's a real bargain!; (*commerce, magasin*) it's a gold mine; **c'est de l'~ en barre** (*commerce, investissement*) it's a rock-solid investment, it's as safe as houses (*Brit*); **pour (tout) l'~ du monde** for all the money in the world, for all the tea in China (*hum*); **faire des affaires d'~** to run a gold mine; *voir* **pesant, pont, rouler** *etc.*

or² [ɔʀ] **conj** (*gén*) now; (*dans un syllogisme*) *non traduit.* **ceci n'aurait pas manqué de provoquer des jalousies, ~ nous ne désirions nullement nous brouiller avec eux** this would unfailingly have led to jealousy, when in fact *ou* whereas we had not the slightest wish to quarrel with them; († *ou frm*) ~ **donc** thus, therefore.

oracle [ɔʀɑkl] **nm** (*gén*) oracle. **rendre un ~** to pronounce an oracle; (*hum*) **l'oncle Jean était l'~ de la famille** Uncle John was the oracle of the family; **il parlait en ~** *ou* **comme un ~** he talked like an oracle.

orage [ɔʀaʒ] 1 **nm** a (*tempête*) thunderstorm, (electric) storm. **pluie/temps d'~** thundery *ou* stormy shower/weather; **vent d'~** stormy wind; **il va y avoir de l'~** *ou* **un ~** there's going to be a (thunder)storm.

b (*fig: dispute*) upset. **laisser passer l'~** to let the storm blow over; **elle sentait venir l'~** she could sense the storm brewing.

c (*fig littér: tumulte*) **les ~s de la vie** the turmoils of life; **les ~s des passions** the tumult *ou* storm of the passions.

d (*loc*) **il y a de l'~ dans l'air** (*lit*) there is a (thunder)storm brewing; (*fig*) there is trouble *ou* a storm brewing; **le temps est à l'~** there's thunder in the air, the weather is thundery; **sa voix est à l'~** his tone is ominous.

2 **comp** ►**orage de chaleur** heat storm ►**orage magnétique** magnetic storm.

orageusement [ɔʀaʒøzmɑ̃] **adv** (*fig*) tempestuously.

orageux, -euse [ɔʀaʒø, øz] **adj** a (*lit*) *ciel* stormy, lowering (*épith*); *région, saison* stormy; *pluie, chaleur, atmosphère* thundery. **temps ~** thundery weather, threatening weather. b (*fig: mouvementé*) *époque, vie, adolescence, discussion* turbulent, stormy, tempestuous.

oraison [ɔʀɛzɔ̃] **nf** orison, prayer. **l'~ dominicale** the Lord's Prayer; ~ **funèbre** funeral oration.

oral, e, **mpl -aux** [ɔʀal, o] 1 **adj** *tradition, littérature, épreuve* oral; *confession, déposition* verbal, oral; (*Ling, Méd, Psych*) oral; *voir* **stade, voie.** 2 **nm** (*Scol*) oral, viva (voce).

oralement [ɔʀalmɑ̃] **adv** *transmettre des contes, des rumeurs* orally, by word of mouth; *conclure un accord, confesser* verbally, orally; (*Méd, Scol*) orally.

oralité [ɔʀalite] **nf** oral character.

orange [ɔʀɑ̃ʒ] 1 **nf** (*fruit*) orange. (*hum*) **je t'apporterai des ~s** I'll come and visit you in prison *ou* in hospital. 2 **nm** (*couleur*) orange. (*feu de signalisation*) **l'~** amber, the amber light; **le feu était à l'~** the lights were at amber. 3 **adj inv** orange; *feu de signalisation* amber. 4 **comp** ▸**orange amère** bitter orange ▸**orange douce** sweet orange ▸**orange sanguine** blood orange.

orangé, e [ɔʀɑ̃ʒe] 1 **adj** orangey, orange-coloured. 2 **nm** orangey colour. **l'~ de ces rideaux ...** the orangey shade of these curtains ... .

orangeade [ɔʀɑ̃ʒad] **nf** orangeade.

oranger [ɔʀɑ̃ʒe] **nm** orange tree; *voir* **fleur.**

orangeraie [ɔʀɑ̃ʒʀɛ] **nf** orange grove.

orangerie [ɔʀɑ̃ʒʀi] **nf** (*serre*) orangery.

Orangiste [ɔʀɑ̃ʒist] (*Hist, Pol*) 1 **nm** Orangeman. 2 **nf** Orangewoman.

orang-outan(g), **pl orangs-outan(g)s** [ɔʀɑ̃utɑ̃] **nm** orang-outang.

orateur, -trice [ɔʀatœʀ, tʀis] **nm,f** (*homme politique, tribun*) orator, speaker; (*à un banquet etc*) speaker; (*Can*) Speaker (of House of Commons).

oratoire [ɔʀatwaʀ] 1 **adj** *art, morceau* oratorical, of oratory; *ton, style* oratorical; *voir* **joute, précaution.** 2 **nm** (*lieu, chapelle*) oratory, small chapel; (*au bord du chemin*) (wayside) shrine.

oratorio [ɔʀatɔʀjo] **nm** oratorio.

orbe[1] [ɔʀb] **nm** (*littér: globe*) orb; (*Astron*) (*surface*) plane of orbit; (*orbite*) orbit.

orbe[2] [ɔʀb] **adj: mur ~** blind wall.

orbital, e, **mpl -aux** [ɔʀbital, o] **adj** orbital.

orbite [ɔʀbit] **nf** a (*Anat*) (eye-)socket, orbit (SPÉC). **aux yeux enfoncés dans les ~s** with sunken eyes.

b (*Astron, Phys*) orbit. **mettre** *ou* **placer sur ~, mettre en ~** *satellite* to put into orbit; **la mise en** *ou* **sur ~ d'un satellite** the putting into orbit of a satellite, putting a satellite into orbit; **être sur** *ou* **en ~** *[satellite]* to be in orbit.

c (*fig: sphère d'influence*) sphere of influence, orbit. **être/entrer dans l'~ de** to be in/enter the sphere of influence of; **vivre dans l'~ de** to live in the sphere of influence of; **attirer qn dans son ~** to draw sb into one's orbit.

d (*loc*) **mettre** *ou* **placer sur ~** *auteur, projet, produit* to launch; **être sur ~** *[auteur, produit, méthode, projet]* to be successfully launched; **se mettre** *ou* **se placer sur ~** *[auteur, région]* to launch o.s. *ou* itself.

orbiter [ɔʀbite] 1 **vt** *[satellite]* to orbit.

orbiteur [ɔʀbitœʀ] **nm** orbiter.

Orcades [ɔʀkad] **nfpl: les ~** Orkney, the Orkneys, the Orkney Islands.

orchestral, e, **mpl -aux** [ɔʀkɛstʀal, o] **adj** orchestral.

orchestrateur, -trice [ɔʀkɛstʀatœʀ, tʀis] **nm,f** orchestrator.

orchestration [ɔʀkɛstʀasjɔ̃] **nf** (*voir* **orchestrer**) orchestration; scoring; organization. (*Mus*) **une bonne ~** good scoring, a good orchestration.

orchestre [ɔʀkɛstʀ] 1 **nm** a (*musiciens*) *[grande musique, bal]* orchestra; *[jazz, danse]* band. **grand ~** full orchestra; *voir* **chef[1], homme.**

b (*Ciné, Théât: emplacement*) stalls (*Brit*), orchestra (*US*); (*fauteuil*) seat in the (orchestra) stalls (*Brit*), seat in the orchestra (*US*). **l'~ applaudissait** applause came from the stalls (*Brit*) *ou* orchestra (*US*); *voir* **fauteuil, fosse.** 2 **comp** ▸**orchestre de chambre** chamber orchestra ▸**orchestre à cordes** string orchestra ▸**orchestre de danse** dance band ▸**orchestre de jazz** jazz band ▸**orchestre symphonique** symphony orchestra.

orchestrer [ɔʀkɛstʀe] 1 **vt** a (*Mus*) (*composer*) to orchestrate; (*adapter*) to orchestrate, score. b (*fig*) *couleurs* to orchestrate; *manifestation, propagande* to organize, orchestrate. **l'opération a été bien orchestrée** the operation was well organized.

orchidée [ɔʀkide] **nf** orchid.

ordalie [ɔʀdali] **nf** (*Hist*) ordeal.

ordinaire [ɔʀdinɛʀ] 1 **adj** a (*habituel*) ordinary, normal; (*Jur*) *session* ordinary. **avec sa maladresse ~** with his customary *ou* usual clumsiness; **personnage/fait peu ~** unusual character/fact; **avec un courage pas** *ou* **peu ~*** with incredible *ou* extraordinary courage; **ça alors, ce n'est pas ~!*** that's (really) unusual *ou* out of the ordinary.

b (*courant*) *vin* ordinary; *vêtement* ordinary, everyday (*épith*); *service de table* everyday (*épith*); *qualité* standard; *essence* two-star (*Brit*), 2-star (*Brit*), regular (*US*).

c (*péj: commun*) *personne, manière* common; *conversation* ordinary, run-of-the-mill. **un vin très ~** a very indifferent wine; **mener une existence très ~** to lead a humdrum existence.

2 **nm** a (*la banalité*) **l'~** the ordinary; **qui sort de l'~** which is out of the ordinary.

b (*nourriture, menu ordinaire*) **l'~** ordinary *ou* everyday fare.

c (*loc*) (*littér*) **à l'~** usually, ordinarily; **comme à l'~** as usual; **d'~** ordinarily, usually, normally, as a rule; **il fait plus chaud que d'~** *ou* **qu'à l'~** it's warmer than usual; **il a une intelligence très au-dessus de l'~** he is of far higher than average *ou* of much above average intelligence; **(comme) à son/mon ~** in his/my usual way, as was his/my wont (*littér, hum*).

3 **comp** ▸**l'ordinaire de la messe** the ordinary of the Mass.

ordinairement [ɔʀdinɛʀmɑ̃] **adv** ordinarily, usually, normally, as a rule.

ordinal, e, **mpl -aux** [ɔʀdinal, o] 1 **adj** ordinal. 2 **nm** ordinal number.

ordinateur [ɔʀdinatœʀ] **nm** computer. **~ individuel** *ou* **personnel** personal computer; **~ portable** portable *ou* laptop (computer); **~ familial** *ou* **domestique** home computer; **~ central** mainframe computer; **~ de première/seconde génération** first/second generation computer; **mettre sur ~** to computerize, put onto a computer; **mise sur ~** computerization; **la facturation est faite à l'~** the invoicing is computerized *ou* done by computer.

ordination [ɔʀdinasjɔ̃] **nf** (*Rel*) ordination.

ordinogramme [ɔʀdinɔgʀam] **nm** flow chart *ou* sheet.

ordonnance [ɔʀdɔnɑ̃s] 1 **nf** a (*Méd*) prescription. **préparer une ~** to make up a prescription; **ce médicament n'est délivré que sur ~** this medicine is only available on prescription.

b (*Jur: arrêté*) *[gouvernement]* order, edict; *[juge]* (judge's) order, ruling. **par ~ du 2-2-92** in the edict of 2/2/92.

c (*disposition*) *[poème, phrase, tableau]* organization, layout; *[bâtiment]* plan, layout; *[cérémonie]* organization; *[repas]* order.

2 **nm ou nf** (*Mil*) a (*subalterne*) orderly, batman (*Brit*).

b **d'~** *revolver, tunique* regulation (*épith*); *voir* **officier.**

3 **comp** ▸**ordonnance de paiement** authorization of payment ▸**ordonnance de police** police regulation ▸**ordonnance royale** royal decree *ou* edict.

ordonnancement [ɔʀdɔnɑ̃smɑ̃] **nm** a (*Fin*) order to pay. b (*disposition*) *[phrase, tableau]* organization, layout; *[cérémonie]* organization.

ordonnancer [ɔʀdɔnɑ̃se] 3 **vt** a (*Fin*) *dépense* to authorize. b (*agencer*) *phrase, tableau* to put together; *cérémonie* to organize.

ordonnateur, -trice [ɔʀdɔnatœʀ, tʀis] **nm,f** a *[fête, cérémonie]* organizer, arranger. **~ des pompes funèbres** funeral director (*in charge of events at the funeral itself*). b (*Fin*) official with power to authorize expenditure. (*Hist Mil*) **commissaire ~** ≃ ordnance officer.

ordonné, e [ɔʀdɔne] (**ptp de ordonner**) 1 **adj** a (*méthodique*) *enfant* tidy; *employé* methodical. b (*bien arrangé*) *maison* orderly, tidy; *vie* (well-)ordered, orderly; *idées, discours* well-ordered; *voir* **charité.** c (*Math*) ordered. **couple ~** ordered pair. 2 **ordonnée** **nf** (*Math*) ordinate, Y-axis.

ordonner [ɔʀdɔne] 1 1 **vt** a (*arranger*) *espace, idées, éléments* to arrange, organize; *discours, texte* to organize; (*Math*) *polynôme* to arrange in (*ascending or descending*) order. **il avait ordonné sa vie de telle façon que ...** he had arranged *ou* organized his life in such a way that ... .

b (*commander*) (*Méd*) *traitement, médicament* to prescribe; (*Jur*) *huis-clos etc* to order. **~ à qn de faire qch** to order sb to do sth, give sb orders to do sth; **il nous ordonna le silence** he ordered us to be quiet; **ils ordonnèrent la fermeture des cafés** *ou* **qu'on fermât les cafés** they ordered the closure of the cafés *ou* that the cafés be closed; **le travail qui m'a été ordonné** the work which I've been ordered to do; **je vais ~ que cela soit fait immédiatement** I'm going to order that that be done immediately.

c (*Rel*) *prêtre* to ordain. **être ordonné prêtre** to be ordained priest.

2 **s'ordonner** **vpr** *[idées, faits]* to organize themselves. **les idées s'ordonnaient dans sa tête** the ideas began to organize themselves *ou* sort themselves out in his head.

ordre[1] [ɔʀdʀ] **nm** a (*succession régulière*) order. (*Ling*) **l'~ des mots** word order; **par ~ alphabétique** in alphabetical order; **par ~ d'ancienneté/de mérite** in order of seniority/of merit; **alignez-vous par ~ de grandeur** line up in order of height *ou* size; **par ~ d'importance** in order of importance; **dans l'~** in order; **dans le bon ~** in the right order; **par ~** *ou* **dans l'~ d'entrée en scène** in order of appearance; (*Sport*) **~ de départ/d'arrivée** order (of competitors) at the starting/finishing line *ou* post; (*Mil*) **en ~ de bataille/de marche** in battle/marching order; **en ~ dispersé** (*Mil*) in extended order; (*fig*) without a common line *ou* plan of action; (*Jur*) **~ des descendants** *ou* **héritiers** order of descent; *voir* **numéro, procéder.**

b (*Archit, Bio: catégorie*) order. (*Archit*) **l'~ ionique/dorique** Ionic/Doric order.

c (*nature, catégorie*) **dans le même ~ d'idées** similarly; **dans un autre ~ d'idées** in a different *ou* another connection; **pour des motifs d'~ personnel/différent** for reasons of a personal/different nature; **c'est dans l'~ des choses** it's in the nature *ou* order of things; **une affaire/un chiffre du même ~** a matter/figure of the same nature *ou* order; **un chiffre de l'~ de 2 millions** a figure in the region of *ou* of the order of 2 million; **avec une somme de cet ~** with a sum of this order; (*prix*) **donnez-nous un ~ de grandeur** give us a rough estimate *ou* a rough idea; **dans cet ~ de grandeur** in this region; **de premier/deuxième/troisième ~** first-/second-/third-rate; **de dernier ~** third-rate; **considérations d'~ pratique/général** considerations of a practical/general nature.

d (*légalité*) **l'~** order; **l'~ établi** the established order; **l'~ public** law and order; **le maintien de l'~ (public)** the maintenance of law and order *ou* of public order; **quand tout fut rentré dans l'~** when order had been restored, when all was back to order; **le parti de l'~** the party of law and order; **un partisan de l'~** a supporter of law and order; **la remise en ~ du pays** restoring the country to order; *voir* **force, rappeler, service.**

e (*méthode, bonne organisation*) *[personne, chambre]* tidiness, orderliness. **sans ~** untidy, disorderly; **avoir de l'~** (*rangements*) to be tidy *ou* orderly; (*travail*) to have method, be systematic *ou* methodical; **manquer d'~** to be untidy *ou* disorderly; to have no method, be unsystematic *ou* unmethodical; **en ~** *tiroir, maison, bureau* tidy, orderly; *comptes* in order; **tenir en ~** *chambre* to keep tidy; *comptes* to keep in order; **(re)mettre en ~, (re)mettre de l'~ dans** *affaires* to set *ou* put in order, tidy up; *papiers, bureau* to tidy (up), clear up; **mettre bon ~ à qch** to put sth to rights, sort out sth; **défiler en ~** to go past in an orderly manner; **travailler avec ~ et méthode** to work in an orderly *ou* a methodical *ou* systematic way; **un homme d'~** a man of order; *voir* **rentrer**.

f (*condition, état*) **en ~ de marche** in (full) working order.

g (*association, congrégation*) order; *[profession libérale]* ≃ professional association. **les ~s de chevalerie** the orders of knighthood; **les ~s monastiques** the monastic orders; **les ~s mendiants** the mendicant orders; **l'~ de la jarretière/du mérite** the Order of the Garter/of Merit; (*Rel*) **les ~s** (holy) orders; (*Rel*) **les ~s majeurs/mineurs** major/minor orders; (*Rel*) **entrer dans les ~s** to take (holy) orders, go into the Church; **l'~ des architectes** *etc* the association of architects *etc;* **l'~ des avocats** the association of barristers, ≃ the Bar (*Brit*), ≃ the American Bar Association (*US*); **l'~ des médecins** the medical association, ≃ the British Medical Association (*Brit*), ≃ the American Medical Association (*US*); *[dentiste etc]* **être rayé de l'~** to be struck off the list *ou* register.

h **~ du jour** *[conférence etc]* agenda; (*en fin de programme*) **"autres questions à l'~ du jour"** "any other business"; (*Admin*) **l'~ du jour de l'assemblée** the business before the meeting; **passons à l'~ du jour** let us turn to the business of the day; **inscrit à l'~ du jour** on the agenda; **être à l'~ du jour** (*lit*) to be on the agenda; (*fig: être d'actualité*) to be (very) topical; *voir aussi* **ordre[2]**.

ordre[2] [ɔʀdʀ] 1 nm a (*commandement, directive*) (*gén*) order; (*Mil*) order, command. **donner (l')~ de** to give an order *ou* the order to, give orders to; **par ~** *ou* **sur les ~s du ministre** by order of the minister, on the orders of the minister; **j'ai reçu des ~s formels** I have formal instructions; **j'ai reçu l'~ de ...** I've been given orders to ...; **je n'ai d'~ à recevoir de personne** I don't take orders from anyone; **être aux ~s de qn** to be at sb's disposal; (*formule de politesse*) **je suis à vos ~s** I am at your service; **dis donc, je ne suis pas à tes ~s!** you can't give me orders!, I don't take orders from you!, I'm not at your beck and call!; (*Mil*) **à vos ~s!** yes sir!; **être/combattre sous les ~s de qn** to be/fight under sb's command; *voir* **désir, jusque, mot**.

b (*Comm, Fin*) order. **à l'~ de** payable to, to the order of; **chèque à mon ~** cheque made out to me; *voir* **billet, chèque, citer**.

2 comp ▸**ordre d'achat** (*Fin*) buying order ▸**ordre d'appel** (*Mil*) call-up papers (*Brit*), draft notice (*US*) ▸**ordre de Bourse** (*Fin*) Stock Exchange order ▸**ordre de grève** strike call ▸**ordre du jour** (*Mil*) order of the day; **citer qn à l'ordre du jour** to mention sb in dispatches ▸**ordre de mission** (*Mil*) orders (*for a mission*) ▸**ordre de route** (*Mil*) marching orders (*pl*) ▸**ordre de vente** (*Fin*) sale order ▸**ordre de virement** (*Fin*) transfer order.

ordure [ɔʀdyʀ] nf a (*saleté, immondices*) dirt (*NonC*), filth (*NonC*). **les chiens qui font leurs ~s sur le trottoir** dogs which leave their dirt *ou* messes on the pavement.

b (*détritus*) **~s** rubbish (*NonC*) (*Brit*), refuse (*NonC*), garbage (*NonC*) (*US*); **~s ménagères** household refuse; **l'enlèvement** *ou* **le ramassage des ~s** refuse *ou* rubbish (*Brit*) *ou* garbage (*US*) collection; **jeter** *ou* **mettre qch aux ~s** to throw *ou* put sth into the dustbin (*Brit*) *ou* rubbish bin (*Brit*) *ou* garbage can (*US*); **c'est juste bon à mettre aux ~s** it's fit for the dustbin (*Brit*) *ou* rubbish bin (*Brit*) *ou* garbage can (*US*); *voir* **boîte, vider**.

c (*‡: chose, personne abjecte*) **ce film est une ~** this film is pure filth; **ce type est une belle ~** this guy is a real bastard‡; **cette ~ a fait tirer dans la foule** this bastard‡ had them shoot into the crowd.

d (*grossièretés*) **~s** obscenities, filth; **dire des ~s** to utter obscenities, talk filth; **écrire des ~s** to write filth.

e (*littér: abjection*) mire (*littér*). **il aime à se vautrer dans l'~** he likes to wallow in filth.

ordurier, -ière [ɔʀdyʀje, jɛʀ] adj lewd, filthy.

orée [ɔʀe] nf (*littér*) *[bois]* edge.

Oregon [ɔʀegɔ̃] nm Oregon.

oreillard [ɔʀɛjaʀ] nm (*chauve-souris*) long-eared bat.

oreille [ɔʀɛj] nf a (*Anat*) ear. **l'~ moyenne/interne** the middle/inner ear; **l'~ externe** the outer *ou* external ear, the auricle (*SPÉC*); **~s décollées** protruding *ou* sticking-out ears; **~s en feuille de chou** big flappy ears; **~ en choux-fleur** cauliflower ears; **le béret sur l'~** his beret cocked over one ear *ou* tilted to one side; (*fig hum*) **les ~s ont dû lui tinter** his ears must have been burning; **animal aux longues ~s** long-eared animal; **aux ~s pointues** with pointed ears; *voir* **boucher[1], boucle, dresser** *etc*.

b (*ouïe*) hearing, ear. **avoir l'~ fine** to be sharp of hearing, have a sharp ear; **avoir de l'~** to have a good ear (for music); **ne pas avoir d'~** to have no ear for music; *voir* **casser, écorcher, écouter**.

c (*comme organe de communication*) ear. **avoir l'~ de qn** to have sb's ear; **écouter de toutes ses ~s** to be all ears; **porter qch/venir aux ~s de qn** to let sth be/come to be known to sb, bring sth/come to sb's attention; **dire qch à l'~ de qn, dire qch à qn dans le creux** *ou* **dans le tuyau de l'~** to have a word in sb's ear about sth; **cela entre par une ~ et ressort par l'autre** it goes in (at) one ear and out (at) the other; **n'écouter que d'une ~, écouter d'une ~ distraite** to only half listen, listen with (only) one ear; *voir* **bouche, prêter, sourd**.

d *[écrou, fauteuil]* wing; *[soupière]* handle; *[casquette]* earflap.

e (*loc*) **avoir les ~s rebattues de qch** to have heard enough of sth, be sick of hearing sth; **tirer les ~s à qn** (*lit*) to pull *ou* tweak sb's ears; (*fig*) to give sb a (good) telling off*, tell sb off*; (*fig*) **se faire tirer l'~** to take *ou* need a lot of persuading; **ouvre tes ~s** (will you) listen to what you are told; **l'~ basse** crestfallen, (with) one's tail between one's legs; **ferme tes ~s** don't (you) listen!; *voir* **échauffer, montrer, puce**.

oreiller [ɔʀeje] nm pillow. **se raccommoder sur l'~** to make it up in bed; *voir* **confidence, taie**.

oreillette [ɔʀɛjɛt] nf *[cœur]* auricle; *[casquette]* earflap. **orifice de l'~** atrium.

oreillon [ɔʀɛjɔ̃] nm a *[abricot]* (apricot) half. b (*Méd*) **les ~s** (the) mumps.

ores [ɔʀ] adv: **d'~ et déjà** already.

Oreste [ɔʀɛst] nm Orestes.

orfèvre [ɔʀfɛvʀ] nm silversmith, goldsmith. (*fig*) **M. X, qui est ~ en la matière, va nous éclairer** Mr X, who's an expert (on the subject) is going to enlighten us.

orfèvrerie [ɔʀfɛvʀəʀi] nf (*art, commerce*) silversmith's (*ou* goldsmith's) trade; (*magasin*) silversmith's (*ou* goldsmith's) shop; (*ouvrage*) (silver) plate, (gold) plate.

orfraie [ɔʀfʀɛ] nf white-tailed eagle.

organdi [ɔʀgɑ̃di] nm organdie.

organe [ɔʀgan] 1 nm a (*Anat, Physiol*) organ. **~s des sens/sexuels** sense/sexual organs; *voir* **fonction, greffe[1]**. b (*fig*) (*véhicule, instrument*) instrument, medium, organ; (*institution, organisme*) organ. **le juge est l'~ de la loi** the judge is the instrument of the law; **la parole est l'~ de la pensée** speech is the medium *ou* vehicle of thought; **un des ~s du gouvernement** one of the organs of government. c (*porte-parole*) (*magistrat, fonctionnaire*) representative, spokesman; (*journal*) mouthpiece, organ. d († *ou littér: voix*) voice. 2 comp ▸**organes de commande** controls ▸**organes de transmission** transmission system.

organigramme [ɔʀganigʀam] nm (*tableau hiérarchique, structurel*) organization chart; (*tableau des opérations, de synchronisation, Ordin*) flow chart *ou* diagram *ou* sheet.

organique [ɔʀganik] adj (*Chim, Jur, Méd*) organic; *voir* **chimie**.

organiquement [ɔʀganikmɑ̃] adv organically.

organisateur, -trice [ɔʀganizatœʀ, tʀis] 1 adj *faculté, puissance* organizing (*épith*). 2 nm,f organizer.

organisation [ɔʀganizasjɔ̃] 1 nf a (*action*) (*voir* **organiser**) organization; arranging; getting up; setting up; setting out. **il a l'esprit d'~** he has an organizing mind *ou* a mind for organization.

b (*arrangement*) *[soirée, manifestation]* organization.

c (*structure*) *[service]* organization, setup; *[armée, travail]* organization; *[texte]* organization, layout. **une ~ sociale encore primitive** a still primitive social setup; **l'~ infiniment complexe du corps humain** the infinitely complex organization of the human body; **~ scientifique du travail** scientific management.

d (*parti, syndicat*) organization. **~ non gouvernementale** non-governmental organization; **~ syndicale** trade(s) union.

2 comp ▸**Organisation de coopération et de développement économique** Organization for Economic Cooperation and Development ▸**Organisation des États américains** Organization of American States ▸**Organisation européenne de coopération économique** Organization for European Economic Cooperation ▸**Organisation internationale du travail** International Labour Organization ▸**Organisation de libération de la Palestine** Palestine Liberation Organization ▸**Organisation mondiale de la santé** World Health Organization ▸**Organisation mondiale du tourisme** World Tourism Organization ▸**Organisation des Nations Unies** United Nations Organization ▸**Organisation des pays exportateurs de pétrole** Organization of Petroleum Exporting Countries ▸**Organisation du Traité de l'Atlantique Nord** North Atlantic Treaty Organization ▸**Organisation des territoires de l'Asie du Sud-Est** South-East Asia Treaty Organization ▸**Organisation de l'unité africaine** Organization of African Unity.

organisationnel, -elle [ɔʀganizasjɔnɛl] adj *problème, moyens* organizational.

organisé, e [ɔʀganize] (ptp de **organiser**) adj *foule, groupe, citoyens* organized; *travail, affaire* organized; *esprit* organized, methodical. **personne bien ~e** well-organized person; (*fig*) **c'est du vol ~!** it's organized robbery!; *voir* **voyage**.

organiser [ɔʀganize] [1] 1 vt a (*préparer*) *voyage, fête, réunion* to organize, arrange; *campagne* to organize; *pétition* to organize, get up; *service, coopérative* to organize, set up. b (*structurer*) *travail, opérations, armée, parti* to organize; *emploi du temps* to organize, set out; *journée* to organize. 2 **s'organiser** vpr *[personne, société]* to organize o.s. (*ou* itself), get (o.s. *ou* itself) organized. **il ne sait pas s'~** he does not know how to organize himself, he can't get (himself) organized.

organisme [ɔʀganism] nm a (*organes, corps*) body, organism (*SPÉC*). **les besoins/les fonctions de l'~** the needs/functions of the body *ou* organism, bodily needs/functions. b (*Zool: individu*) organism. **un pays est un ~ vivant** a country is a living organism. c (*institution, bureaux*) body, organism. **un ~ nouvellement mis sur pied** a recently established body *ou* organism; **~ de droit public** statutory body.
organiste [ɔʀganist] nmf organist.
orgasme [ɔʀgasm] nm orgasm, climax.
orge [ɔʀʒ] nf barley; *voir* **sucre**.
orgeat [ɔʀʒa] nm orgeat; *voir* **sirop**.
orgelet [ɔʀʒəlɛ] nm (*Méd*) sty(e).
orgiaque [ɔʀʒjak] adj orgiastic.
orgie [ɔʀʒi] nf a (*Hist, repas*) orgy; (*beuverie*) drinking orgy. **faire une ~** to have an orgy; **faire des ~s de gâteaux** to have an orgy of cakes *ou* of cake-eating. b (*fig*) **~ de** profusion of; **~ de fleurs** profusion of flowers; **~ de couleurs** riot of colour.
orgue [ɔʀg] nm (*voir aussi* **orgues**) organ. **tenir l'~** to play the organ; **~ de chœur/de cinéma/électrique/portatif** choir/theatre/electric/portable organ; **~ de Barbarie** barrel organ, hurdy-gurdy; *voir* **point**[1].
orgueil [ɔʀgœj] nm a (*défaut: fierté exagérée*) pride, arrogance; (*justifiable: amour-propre*) pride. **gonflé d'~** puffed up *ou* bursting with pride; **~ démesuré** overweening pride *ou* arrogance; **il a l'~ de son rang** he has all the arrogance associated with his rank; **avec l'~ légitime du vainqueur** with the victor's legitimate pride; **par ~ il ne l'a pas fait** it was his pride which stopped him doing it; **le péché d'~** the sin of pride.
b (*loc*) **ce tableau, ~ de la collection** this picture, pride of the collection; **l'~ de se voir confier les clefs lui fit oublier sa colère** his pride at being entrusted with the keys made him forget his anger; **avoir l'~ de qch** to take pride in sth, pride o.s. on sth; **tirer ~ de qch** to take pride in sth; **mettre son ~ à faire qch** to take a pride in doing sth.
orgueilleusement [ɔʀgøjøzmɑ̃] adv (*voir* **orgueilleux**) proudly, arrogantly.
orgueilleux, -euse [ɔʀgøjø, øz] adj (*défaut*) proud, arrogant; (*qualité*) proud. **~ comme un paon** as proud as a peacock; **c'est un ~** he's a (very) proud man; **c'est une ~euse** she's a (very) proud woman; (*littér*) **un chêne ~** a proud oak.
orgues [ɔʀg] nfpl a (*Mus*) organ. **les grandes ~** the great organs; **les petites ~** the small pipe organ. b (*Géol*) **~ basaltiques** basalt columns. c (*Mil*) **~ de Staline** rocket launcher (*mounted on truck*).
oriel [ɔʀjɛl] nm oriel window.
orient [ɔʀjɑ̃] nm a (*littér: est*) orient (*littér*), east. **l'O~** the Orient (*littér*), the East; **les pays d'O~** the countries of the Orient (*littér*), the oriental countries; *voir* **extrême, moyen, proche**. b [*perle*] orient. c *voir* **grand**.
orientable [ɔʀjɑ̃tabl] adj *bras d'une machine* swivelling, rotating; *lampe, antenne, lamelles de store* adjustable.
oriental, e, mpl **-aux** [ɔʀjɑ̃tal, o] 1 adj *côte, frontière, région* eastern; *langue, produits* oriental; *musique, arts* oriental, eastern; *voir* **Inde**. 2 nm: **O~** Oriental. 3 nf: **O~e** Oriental woman.
orientalisme [ɔʀjɑ̃talism] nm orientalism.
orientaliste [ɔʀjɑ̃talist] nmf, adj orientalist.
orientation [ɔʀjɑ̃tasjɔ̃] nf a (*voir* **orienter**) positioning; adjusting, adjustment; directing; orientating, orientation. (*Scol*) **l'~** advice *ou* guidance on careers and on courses; **l'~ professionnelle** careers advising *ou* guidance (*Brit*); **l'~ scolaire** guidance (*Brit*) *ou* advice on courses to be followed; *voir* **conseiller**[2]**, course, cycle**.
b (*voir* **s'orienter**) **~ vers** [*science*] trend towards; [*parti*] move towards; [*étudiant*] specializing in, turning to; *voir* **sens, table**.
c (*position*) [*maison*] aspect; [*phare, antenne*] direction. **l'~ du jardin au sud** the garden's southern aspect *ou* the fact that the garden faces south.
d (*tendance, direction*) (*Bourse*) trend; [*science*] trends, orientation; [*magazine*] leanings, (political) tendencies. **l'~ générale de notre enquête/de ses recherches** the general direction *ou* orientation of our inquiry/of his research; **~ à la hausse** upward trend, upturn; **~ à la baisse** downward trend, downturn.
orienté, e [ɔʀjɑ̃te] (ptp de **orienter**) adj a (*disposé*) **~ à l'est/au sud** *maison* facing east/south, with an eastern/a southern aspect; *antenne* directed *ou* turned towards the east/the south; **bien/mal ~** *maison* well/badly positioned; *antenne* properly/badly directed. b (*tendancieux, partial*) *article, question* slanted, biased. c (*marqué*) *plan, carte* orientated; (*Math*) *droite, vecteur* oriented. d (*Bourse*) *marché* on a rising/falling trend. **valeurs bien ~es** shares which are on the up.
orienter [ɔʀjɑ̃te] [1] 1 vt a (*disposer*) *maison* to position; *lampe, phare* to adjust; *miroir, bras de machine* to position, adjust; *antenne* to direct, adjust, turn. **~ un transistor pour améliorer la réception** to turn a transistor round to get better reception; **~ vers** to turn (on)to; **~ une maison vers le** *ou* **au sud** to build a house facing south; **~ une antenne vers le** *ou* **au nord** to turn *ou* direct an aerial towards the north; **~ la lampe** *ou* **la lumière vers** *ou* **sur son livre** to turn *ou* direct the light onto one's book; **la lampe peut s'~ dans toutes les positions** the lamp can be put into any position, the light can be turned in all directions.
b (*guider*) *touristes, voyageurs* to direct (*vers* to); *science, recherches* to direct (*vers* towards). **~ un élève** to advise a pupil on what courses to follow *ou* what subjects to specialize in; **le patient a été orienté vers un service de cardiologie** the patient was referred to a cardiology unit; **~ la conversation vers un sujet** to turn the conversation onto a subject.
c (*marquer*) *carte* to orientate; (*Math*) *droite* to orient.
d (*Naut*) *voiles* to trim.
2 **s'orienter** vpr a (*trouver son chemin*) [*touriste, voyageur*] to find one's bearings.
b (*se diriger vers*) **s'~ vers** (*lit*) to turn towards; (*fig*) [*science, goûts*] to turn towards; [*chercheur, parti, société*] to move towards; [*étudiant*] **s'~ vers les sciences** to specialize in science, turn to science.
c (*Bourse*) **le marché s'oriente à la hausse/la baisse** the market is on a rising/falling trend, the market is trending upward/downward (*US*).
orienteur, -euse [ɔʀjɑ̃tœʀ, øz] 1 nm,f (*Scol*) careers adviser. 2 nm (*Tech*) orientator.
orifice [ɔʀifis] nm [*mur de caverne, digue*] opening, orifice, aperture; [*puits, gouffre, four, tuyau, canalisation*] opening, mouth; [*organe*] orifice; (*Phon*) cavity. (*Tech*) **~ d'admission/d'échappement (des gaz)** intake/exhaust port.
oriflamme [ɔʀiflɑm] nf (*bannière*) banner, standard; (*Hist*) oriflamme.
origami [ɔʀigami] nm origami, (Japanese) paper-folding.
origan [ɔʀigɑ̃] nm oregano.
originaire [ɔʀiʒinɛʀ] adj a **~ de** (*natif de*) *famille, personne* originating from; (*provenant de*) *plante, coutume, mets* native to; **il est ~ de** he is a native of, he was born in. b (*originel*) *titulaire, propriétaire* original, first; *vice, défaut* innate, inherent.
originairement [ɔʀiʒinɛʀmɑ̃] adv originally, at first.
original, e, mpl **-aux** [ɔʀiʒinal, o] 1 adj (*premier, originel*) original; (*neuf, personnel*) *idée, décor* original, novel; *artiste, talent* original; (*péj: bizarre*) eccentric, odd, freaky*. **édition ~e** original *ou* first edition; *voir* **version**. 2 nm,f (*péj: excentrique*) eccentric; (*fantaisiste*) clown*, joker*. **c'est un ~** he's a (real) character *ou* a bit of an eccentric. 3 nm (*exemplaire premier*) (*ouvrage, tableau*) original; (*document*) original (copy); (*texte dactylographié*) top copy, original (*US*). **l'~ de ce personnage** the model for *ou* the original of this character.
originalement [ɔʀiʒinalmɑ̃] adv (*de façon personnelle*) originally, in an original way; (*originellement*) originally.
originalité [ɔʀiʒinalite] nf a (*caractère: voir* **original**) originality; novelty; eccentricity, oddness. b (*élément, caractéristique*) original aspect *ou* feature; (*action*) eccentric behaviour (*NonC*).
origine [ɔʀiʒin] nf a (*gén*) origin; (*commencement*) origin, beginning. **les ~s de la vie** the origins of life; **tirer son ~ de, avoir son ~ dans** to have one's origins in, originate in; (*titre d'ouvrage*) **"l'Automobile, des ~s à nos jours"** "the Motor Car, from its Origins to the Present Day"; **ce coup de chance, ainsi que ses relations, sont à l'~ de sa fortune** this lucky break, as well as his connections, are at the origin *ou* root of his wealth; **quelle est l'~ de ce coup de téléphone?** who made this phonecall?
b **d'~** *nationalité, pays, appellation, région de production* of origin; *pneus, garniture* original; (*Sci*) *méridien* prime, zero; **d'~ française/noble** of French/noble origin *ou* extraction; **être d'~ paysanne/ouvrière** to come of farming/working-class stock; **mot d'~ française** word of French origin; **coutume d'~ ancienne** long-standing custom, custom of long standing.
c (*loc*) **à l'~** originally, to begin with; **dès l'~** at *ou* from the outset, at *ou* from the very beginning; **à l'~ de** *maladie, évolution* at the origin of; **souvent de telles rencontres sont à l'~ d'une vocation** such encounters are often the origin of a vocation.
originel, -elle [ɔʀiʒinɛl] adj *innocence, pureté, beauté* original, primeval; *état, sens* original; *voir* **péché**.
originellement [ɔʀiʒinɛlmɑ̃] adv (*primitivement*) originally; (*dès le début*) from the (very) beginning, from the outset.
orignal, pl **-aux** [ɔʀiɲal, o] nm moose, Canadian elk.
oripeaux [ɔʀipo] nmpl (*haillons*) rags; (*guenilles clinquantes*) showy *ou* flashy rags.
ORL [oɛʀɛl] 1 nf (abrév de **oto-rhino-laryngologie**) ENT. 2 nmf (abrév de **oto-rhino-laryngologiste**) ENT doctor *ou* specialist.
Orlon [ɔʀlɔ̃] nm ® Orlon ®.
orme [ɔʀm] nm elm; *voir* **attendre**.
ormeau, pl **~x** [ɔʀmo] nm (*Bot*) (young) elm; (*Zool*) ormer, abalone, ear shell.
orné, e [ɔʀne] (ptp de **orner**) adj *style* ornate, florid. **lettres ~es** illuminated letters.
ornement [ɔʀnəmɑ̃] nm (*gén*) ornament; (*Archit, Art*) embellishment, adornment; (*Mus*) grace note(s), ornament. **sans ~(s)** *élégance, toilette, style* plain, unadorned; **d'~** *arbre, jardin* ornamental; **les ~s du style** the ornaments *ou* ornamentation of style; (*Rel*) **~s sacerdotaux** vestments.
ornemental, e, mpl **-aux** [ɔʀnəmɑ̃tal, o] adj *style, plante* ornamental; *motif* decorative.
ornementation [ɔʀnəmɑ̃tasjɔ̃] nf ornamentation.
ornementer [ɔʀnəmɑ̃te] [1] vt to ornament.
orner [ɔʀne] [1] vt a (*décorer*) *chambre, vêtement* to decorate (*de*

with); (*embellir*) *discours, récit* to embellish (*de* with). ~ **une rue de drapeaux** to deck out a street with flags; **sa robe était ornée d'un galon** her dress was trimmed with braid; **discours orné de citations** speech embellished with quotations; **livre orné de dessins** book illustrated with drawings; (*littér*) ~ **la vérité** to adorn *ou* embellish the truth; (*littér*) ~ **son esprit** to enrich one's mind.

b (*servir d'ornement à*) to adorn, decorate, embellish. **la fleur qui ornait sa boutonnière** the flower which adorned *ou* decorated his buttonhole; **les sculptures qui ornaient la façade** the sculpture which adorned *ou* decorated *ou* embellished the façade.

ornière [ɔʀnjɛʀ] **nf** (*lit*) rut. (*fig*) **il est sorti de l'~ maintenant** he's out of the wood(s) now.

ornithologie [ɔʀnitɔlɔʒi] **nf** ornithology.

ornithologique [ɔʀnitɔlɔʒik] **adj** ornithological.

ornithologiste [ɔʀnitɔlɔʒist] **nmf**, **ornithologue** [ɔʀnitɔlɔg] **nmf** ornithologist.

ornithorynque [ɔʀnitɔʀɛ̃k] **nm** duck-billed platypus, ornithorhynchus (SPÉC).

orogénèse [ɔʀɔʒenɛz] **nf** (*processus*) orogenesis; (*période*) orogeny.

orogénie [ɔʀɔʒeni] **nf** orogeny.

orogénique [ɔʀɔʒenik] **adj** orogenic, orogenetic.

orographie [ɔʀɔgʀafi] **nf** or(e)ography.

orographique [ɔʀɔgʀafik] **adj** or(e)ographic(al).

oronge [ɔʀɔ̃ʒ] **nf** agaric. ~ **vraie** imperial mushroom; **fausse** ~ fly agaric.

orpaillage [ɔʀpajaʒ] **nm** gold washing.

orpailleur [ɔʀpajœʀ] **nm** gold washer.

Orphée [ɔʀfe] **nm** Orpheus.

orphelin, e [ɔʀfəlɛ̃, in] 1 **adj** orphan(ed). 2 **nm,f** orphan. **être ~ de père/de mère** to be fatherless/motherless, have lost one's father/mother; *voir* **veuf.**

orphelinat [ɔʀfəlina] **nm** (*lieu*) orphanage; (*orphelins*) children of the orphanage.

orphéon [ɔʀfeɔ̃] **nm** (*fanfare*) (village *ou* town) band.

orphie [ɔʀfi] **nf** garfish.

orpin [ɔʀpɛ̃] **nm** (*Bot*) stonecrop.

orque [ɔʀk] **nm** killer whale.

ORSEC [ɔʀsɛk] **nf** (**abrév de Organisation des secours**) *voir* **plan.**

orteil [ɔʀtɛj] **nm** toe. **gros/petit** ~ big/little toe.

ORTF† [ɔɛʀteɛf] **nf** (**abrév de Office de radiodiffusion-télévision française**) *French broadcasting service.*

orthocentre [ɔʀtosɑ̃tʀ] **nm** orthocentre.

orthodontie [ɔʀtodɔ̃ti] **nf** orthodontics (*sg*), dental orthopaedics (*sg*).

orthodontique [ɔʀtodɔ̃tik] **adj** orthodontic.

orthodontiste [ɔʀtodɔ̃tist] **nmf** orthodontist.

orthodoxe [ɔʀtɔdɔks] 1 **adj** a (*Rel, gén*) orthodox; *voir* **église.** b **peu ~, pas très ~** rather unorthodox, not very orthodox. 2 **nmf** (*Rel*) orthodox; (*Pol*) one who follows the orthodox (party) line. **les ~s grecs/russes** the Greek/Russian orthodox.

orthodoxie [ɔʀtɔdɔksi] **nf** orthodoxy.

orthogénèse [ɔʀtoʒenɛz] **nf** orthogenesis.

orthogénie [ɔʀtoʒeni] **nf** family planning. **centre d'~** family planning *ou* birth control centre.

orthogonal, e, **mpl -aux** [ɔʀtɔgɔnal, o] **adj** orthogonal.

orthographe [ɔʀtɔgʀaf] **nf** (*gén*) spelling, orthography (SPÉC); (*forme écrite correcte*) spelling; (*système*) spelling (system). **réforme de l'~** spelling *ou* orthographical reform, reform of the spelling system; **quelle est l'~ de votre nom?** how is your name spelt?, what is the spelling of your name?; **ce mot a 2 ~s** this word has 2 different spellings *ou* can be spelt 2 (different) ways; ~ **d'usage** spelling; ~ **d'accord** *spelling of grammatical agreements*; *voir* **faute.**

orthographier [ɔʀtɔgʀafje] 7 **vt** to spell (*in writing*). **un mot mal orthographié** a word incorrectly *ou* wrongly spelt.

orthographique [ɔʀtɔgʀafik] **adj** (*Ling*) spelling (*épith*), orthographical. **signe ~** orthographical sign.

orthonormé, e [ɔʀtonɔʀme] **adj** orthonormal.

orthopédie [ɔʀtɔpedi] **nf** orthopaedics (*sg*).

orthopédique [ɔʀtɔpedik] **adj** orthopaedic.

orthopédiste [ɔʀtɔpedist] **nmf** orthopaedic specialist, orthopaedist. **chirurgien ~** orthopaedic surgeon.

orthophonie [ɔʀtɔfɔni] **nf** (*Ling: prononciation correcte*) correct pronunciation; (*Méd: traitement*) speech therapy.

orthophoniste [ɔʀtɔfɔnist] **nmf** speech therapist.

ortie [ɔʀti] **nf** (stinging) nettle. ~ **blanche** white dead-nettle; *voir* **jeter, piqûre.**

ortolan [ɔʀtɔlɑ̃] **nm** ortolan (bunting).

orvet [ɔʀvɛ] **nm** slow worm.

os [ɔs] 1 **nm** a (*gén*) bone. **avoir de petits/gros ~** to be small-boned/big-boned; **viande avec ~** meat on the bone; **viande sans ~** boned meat, meat off the bone; **fait en ~** made of bone; **jetons/manche en ~** bone counters/handle; **à manche en ~** bone-handled.

b (*loc*) **c'est un paquet** *ou* **sac d'~** he's a bag of bones, he's (mere) skin and bone(s); **mouillé** *ou* **trempé jusqu'aux ~** soaked to the skin, wet through; **donner** *ou* **jeter un ~ à ronger à qn** to give sb something to keep him occupied *ou* quiet; **ils t'ont eu** *ou* **possédé jusqu'à l'~*** they had you good and proper*; **l'avoir dans l'~*** (*être roulé*) to be done* (*Brit*) *ou* had*; (*être bredouille*) to get egg all over one's face*; **il y a un ~*** there's a snag *ou* hitch; **il va trouver un** *ou* **tomber sur un ~*** he'll come across *ou* hit* a snag; *voir* **chair, rompre, vieux.**

2 **comp** ▶ **os à moelle** marrowbone ▶ **os de seiche** cuttlebone.

OS [oɛs] **nm** (**abrév de ouvrier spécialisé**) *voir* **ouvrier.**

oscar [ɔskaʀ] **nm** (*Ciné*) Oscar; (*autres domaines*) prize, award (*de* for). **l'~ du meilleur film/scénario** the Oscar for best film/screenplay.

oscillateur [ɔsilatœʀ] **nm** (*Phys*) oscillator.

oscillation [ɔsilasjɔ̃] **nf** (*Élec, Phys*) oscillation; *[pendule]* swinging (*NonC*), oscillation; *[navire]* rocking (*NonC*); *[température, grandeur variable, opinion]* fluctuation, variation (*de* in). **les ~s de son esprit** his (mental) fluctuations.

oscillatoire [ɔsilatwaʀ] **adj** (*Sci*) oscillatory; *mouvement* swinging, oscillatory (SPÉC).

osciller [ɔsile] 1 **vi** (*Sci*) to oscillate; *[pendule]* to swing, oscillate; *[navire]* to rock. **le vent fit ~ la flamme/la statue** the wind made the flame flicker/made the statue rock; **sa tête oscillait de droite à gauche** his head rocked from side to side; **il oscillait sur ses pieds** he rocked on his feet; (*fig*) ~ **entre** *[personne]* to waver *ou* oscillate between; *[prix, température]* to fluctuate *ou* vary between.

oscillogramme [ɔsilɔgʀam] **nm** oscillogram.

oscillographe [ɔsilɔgʀaf] **nm** oscillograph.

oscilloscope [ɔsilɔskɔp] **nm** oscilloscope.

osé, e [oze] (**ptp de oser**) **adj** *tentative, démarche, toilette* bold, daring; *sujet, plaisanterie* risqué, daring.

Osée [oze] **nm** Hosea.

oseille [ozɛj] **nf** a (*Bot*) sorrel. b (*: *argent*) dough*, dosh* (*surtout Brit*), lolly* (*Brit*), bread*. **avoir de l'~** to be in the money*, have plenty of dough* *ou* dosh (*surtout Brit*) *ou* bread*.

oser [oze] 1 **vt** a to dare. **il faut ~!** one must take risks; ~ **faire qch** to dare (to) do sth; (*littér*) ~ **qch** to dare sth; **il n'osait (pas) bouger** he did not dare (to) move; **je voudrais bien mais je n'ose pas** I'd like to but I don't dare *ou* I daren't; **ose le répéter!** I dare you to repeat it!; **approche si tu l'oses!** come over here if you dare!; **il a osé m'insulter** he dared *ou* presumed to insult me; **comment osez-vous!** how dare you!; *voir* **qui.**

b (*loc*) **si j'ose dire** if I may say so, if I may make so bold; **si j'ose m'exprimer ainsi** if I can put it that way, if you'll pardon the expression; **j'ose espérer/croire que** I like to hope/think that; **j'ose l'espérer** I like to hope so; **je n'ose y croire** I dare not *ou* daren't *ou* don't dare believe it; **j'oserais même dire que** I'd even venture to *ou* go as far as to say that.

oseraie [ozʀɛ] **nf** osier plantation.

osier [ozje] **nm** (*Bot*) willow, osier; (*fibres*) wicker (*NonC*). **corbeille en ~** wicker(work) basket; **fauteuil en ~** wicker(work) chair, basket chair; *voir* **brin.**

Osiris [oziʀis] **nm** Osiris.

Oslo [ɔslo] **n** Oslo.

osmium [ɔsmjɔm] **nm** osmium.

osmose [ɔsmoz] **nf** (*lit, fig*) osmosis. **vivre en ~ avec** to live in harmony with.

osmotique [ɔsmɔtik] **adj** osmotic.

ossature [ɔsatyʀ] **nf** *[corps]* frame, skeletal structure (SPÉC); *[tête, visage]* bone structure; *[machine, appareil, immeuble]* framework; *[voûte]* frame(work); (*fig*) *[société, texte, discours]* framework, structure. **à ~ grêle/robuste** slender-/heavy-framed.

osselet [ɔslɛ] **nm** a (*jeu*) **~s** knucklebones. b (*Anat*) *[oreille]* ossicle. c (*Vét*) osselet.

ossements [ɔsmɑ̃] **nmpl** (*squelettes*) bones.

osseux, -euse [ɔsø, øz] **adj** a (*Anat*) *tissu* bone (*épith*), osseus (SPÉC); *charpente, carapace* bony; (*Biol*) *poisson* bony; (*Méd*) *greffe* bone (*épith*); *maladie* bone (*épith*), of the bones. b (*maigre*) *main, visage* bony.

ossification [ɔsifikasjɔ̃] **nf** ossification (*Méd*).

ossifier **vt**, **s'ossifier** **vpr** [ɔsifje] 7 (*lit, fig*) to ossify.

ossu, e [ɔsy] **adj** (*littér*) large-boned.

ossuaire [ɔsɥɛʀ] **nm** (*lieu*) ossuary.

ostéite [ɔsteit] **nf** osteitis.

Ostende [ɔstɑ̃d] **n** Ostend.

ostensible [ɔstɑ̃sibl] **adj** (*bien visible*) *mépris, indifférence* conspicuous, patent; *charité, compassion, attitude, geste* conspicuous. **de façon ~** conspicuously.

ostensiblement [ɔstɑ̃sibləmɑ̃] **adv** conspicuously.

ostensoir [ɔstɑ̃swaʀ] **nm** monstrance.

ostentation [ɔstɑ̃tasjɔ̃] **nf** ostentation. **il détestait toute ~** he hated all ostentation *ou* show, he hated all manner of ostentation *ou* display; **agir avec ~** to act with ostentation *ou* ostentatiously; **courage/élégance sans ~** unostentatious courage/elegance; **faire qch sans ~** to do sth without ostentation *ou* unostentatiously; (*littér*) **faire ~ de qch** to make a display *ou* show of sth, parade sth.

ostentatoire [ɔstɑ̃tatwaʀ] **adj** (*littér*) ostentatious.

ostéoblaste [ɔsteɔblast] **nm** osteoblast.

ostéogenèse [ɔsteoʒənɛz] nf, **ostéogénie** [ɔsteoʒeni] nf osteogenesis.
ostéologie [ɔsteɔlɔʒi] nf osteology.
ostéomalacie [ɔsteomalasi] nf osteomalacia.
ostéomyélite [ɔsteomjelit] nf osteomyelitis.
ostéopathe [ɔsteɔpat] nmf osteopath.
ostéopathie [ɔsteɔpati] nf osteopathy.
ostéophyte [ɔsteɔfit] nm osteophyte.
ostéoplastie [ɔsteɔplasti] nf osteoplasty.
ostéoporose [ɔsteɔpɔʀoz] nf osteoporosis.
ostéotomie [ɔsteɔtɔmi] nf osteotomy.
osto* [ɔsto] nm = **hosto***.
ostraciser [ɔstʀasize] [1] vt to ostracize.
ostracisme [ɔstʀasism] nm ostracism. **être frappé d'~** to be ostracized; **leur ~ m'était indifférent** being ostracized by them didn't bother me.
ostréicole [ɔstʀeikɔl] adj oyster-farming (*épith*).
ostréiculteur, -trice [ɔstʀeikyltœʀ, tʀis] nm,f oyster-farmer, ostreiculturist (*SPÉC*).
ostréiculture [ɔstʀeikyltyʀ] nf oyster-farming, ostreiculture (*SPÉC*).
ostrogot(h), e [ɔstʀɔgo, gɔt] 1 adj Ostrogothic. 2 nm,f: **O~(e)** Ostrogoth. 3 nm († *ou hum*) (*mal élevé*) barbarian; (*original, olibrius*) queer fish* *ou* fellow.
otage [ɔtaʒ] nm hostage. **prendre qn en** *ou* **comme ~** to take sb hostage; *voir* **prise**.
OTAN [ɔtɑ̃] nf (abrév de **Organisation du Traité de l'Atlantique Nord**) NATO.
otarie [ɔtaʀi] nf sea-lion, otary (*SPÉC*), eared seal (*SPÉC*).
OTASE [ɔtaz] nf (abrév de **Organisation des territoires de l'Asie du Sud-Est**) SEATO.
ôter [ote] [1] 1 vt a (*enlever*) *ornement* to take away, remove (*de* from); *lunettes, vêtement* to take off, remove; *arêtes, épine* to take out (*de* of), remove (*de* from); *tache* to take out (*de* of), remove (*de* from), lift (*de* from); *hésitation, scrupule* to remove, take away; *remords* to take away. **ôte les assiettes (de la table)** clear the table, clear the dishes off the table; **un produit qui ôte l'acidité (à une** *ou* **d'une substance)** a product which removes the acidity (from a substance); **ôte tes mains de la porte!** take your hands off the door!; **ôte tes pieds de là!** get your feet off there!; **cela lui a ôté un gros poids (de dessus la poitrine)** that took a great weight off his chest *ou* lifted a great weight from his chest; **comment est-ce que ça s'ôte?** how do you remove it? *ou* take it off?; **on lui ôta ses menottes** they took his handcuffs off, they unhandcuffed him.
b (*retrancher*) *somme* to take away; *paragraphe* to remove, cut out (*de* from). **~ un nom d'une liste** to remove a name from a list, take a name off a list; **5 ôté de 8 égale 3** 5 (taken away) from 8 equals *ou* leaves 3.
c (*prendre*) **~ qch à qn** to take sth (away) from sb; **~ un enfant à sa mère** to take a child (away) from its mother; **s'~ la vie** to take one's (own) life; **~ à qn ses illusions** to rid *ou* deprive sb of his illusions; **~ à qn ses forces/son courage** to deprive sb of his strength/courage; **ça lui ôtera toute envie de recommencer** that will stop him wanting to do it again, that will rid him of any desire to do it again; **ôte-lui le couteau, ôte-lui le couteau des mains** take the knife (away) from him, take the knife out of *ou* from his hands; **on ne m'ôtera pas de l'idée que ..., je ne peux m'~ de l'idée que ...** I can't get it out of my mind *ou* head that ...; **il faut absolument lui ~ cette idée de la tête** we must get this idea out of his head; *voir* **pain**.
2 **s'ôter** vpr: **ôtez-vous de là** move yourself!, get out of there!; **ôtez-vous de la lumière,** (*hum*) **ôte-toi de mon soleil** get out of my light; (*pousse-toi*) (*hum*) **ôte-toi de là (que je m'y mette)!*** (get) out of the way!, move *ou* shift* out of the way (and give me some room)!
Othon [ɔtɔ̃] nm = **Otton**.
otite [ɔtit] nf ear infection, otitis (*SPÉC*). **~ moyenne/interne** otitis media/interna.
oto-rhino, pl **oto-rhinos** [ɔtɔʀino] nmf = **oto-rhino-laryngologiste**.
oto-rhino-laryngologie [ɔtɔʀinolaʀɛ̃gɔlɔʒi] nf oto(rhino)laryngology.
oto-rhino-laryngologiste, pl **oto-rhino-laryngologistes** [ɔtɔʀinolaʀɛ̃gɔlɔʒist] nmf ear, nose and throat specialist.
otoscope [ɔtɔskɔp] nm otoscope.
Ottawa [ɔtawa] n Ottawa.
ottoman, e [ɔtɔmɑ̃, an] 1 adj Ottoman. 2 nm a (*personne*) **O~** Ottoman. b (*tissu*) ottoman. 3 **ottomane** nf a (*personne*) **O~e** Ottoman woman. b (*canapé*) ottoman.
Otton [ɔtɔ̃] nm Otto.
ou [u] conj a (*alternative*) or. **est-ce qu'il doit venir aujourd'hui ~ demain?** is he coming today or tomorrow?; **il faut qu'il vienne aujourd'hui ~ demain** he must come (either) today or tomorrow; **vous le préférez avec ~ sans sucre?** do you prefer it with or without sugar?; **que vous alliez chez cet épicier ~ chez l'autre, c'est le même prix** it's the same price whether you go to this grocer or (to) the other one; **un kilo de plus ~ de moins, cela ne se sent pas** one kilo more or less doesn't show up; **que vous le vouliez ~ non** whether you like it or not; **jolie ~ non elle plaît** (whether she's) pretty or not, she's attractive; **est-ce qu'elle veut se lever ~ préfère-t-elle attendre demain?** does she want to get up or does she prefer to wait until tomorrow?; **il nous faut 3 pièces, ~ plutôt/~ même 4** we need 3 rooms, or preferably/or even 4; **apportez-moi une bière, ~ plutôt non, un café** bring me a beer, or rather a coffee, bring me a beer or no, a coffee instead; **~ pour mieux dire** or rather, or I should say.
b (*approximation*) or. **à 5 ~ 6 km d'ici** 5 or 6 km from here; **ils étaient 10 ~ 12 (à vouloir parler à la fois)** there were (some) 10 or 12 of them (wanting to speak at the same time).
c (*alternative avec exclusion*) **~ ... ~** either ... or; **~ il est malade ~ (bien) il est fou** he's either sick or mad, either he's sick or (else) he's mad; **~ (bien) tu m'attends ~ (bien) alors tu pars à pied** either you wait for me or (else) you'll have to walk, you (can) either wait for me or (else) go on foot; **il faut qu'il travaille ~ (bien) il échouera à son examen** he'll have to work or (else) *ou* otherwise he'll fail his exam; **donne-moi ça ~ je me fâche** give me that or I'll get cross; *voir* **tôt**.
où [u] 1 pron a (*lit: situation, direction*) where. **l'endroit ~ je vais/je suis** the place where I'm going/I am, the place I'm going to/I'm in; **l'endroit idéal ~ s'établir** the ideal place to settle; **je cherche un endroit ~ m'asseoir** I'm looking for a place to sit down *ou* for somewhere to sit; **la ville ~ j'habite** the town I live in *ou* where I live; **la maison ~ j'habite** the house I live in; **le mur ~ il est accoudé** the wall he's leaning against; **le tiroir ~ tu as rangé le livre** the drawer you put the book in *ou* where you put the book; **le tiroir ~ tu a pris le livre** the drawer (where) you took the book from; **le livre ~ il a trouvé ce renseignement** the book where *ou* in which he found this piece of information; **le livre ~ il a copié ceci** the book he copied this from *ou* from which he copied this; **le chemin par ~ il est passé** the road he went along *ou* he took; **le village par ~ il est passé** the village he went through; **l'endroit d'~ je viens** the place I've come from; **la pièce d'~ il sort** the room he's come out of; **la crevasse d'~ on l'a retiré** the crevasse they pulled him out of; **une chambre d'~ s'échappent des gémissements** a room from which moans are coming; **l'endroit jusqu'~ ils ont grimpé** the place (where) they have climbed to *ou* to which they've climbed; *voir* **là, partout**.
b (*antécédent abstrait: institution, groupe, état, condition*) **la famille ~ il est entré** the family he has become part of, the family he has joined; **la famille/la firme d'~ il sort** the family/firm he comes *ou* has come from; **la ville d'~ il vient** (*origine*) the town he comes from; **l'école ~ il est inscrit** the school where *ou* in which he is enrolled; **les mathématiques, branche ~ je ne suis guère compétent** mathematics, a branch in which I have little skill; **dans l'état ~ il est** in the state he is in *ou* in which he is; **la colère ~ il est entré** the rage he went into; **l'obligation ~ il se trouve de partir** the fact that he finds himself obliged to leave; **dans l'embarras ~ j'étais** in the embarrassed state I was in; **les conditions ~ ils travaillent** the conditions they work in *ou* in which they work; **la rêverie ~ il est plongé/d'~ je l'ai tiré** the daydream he's in/from which I roused him; **les extrêmes ~ il s'égare** the extremes into which he is straying; **le but ~ tout homme tend** the goal towards which all men strive; **la mélancolie ~ il se complaît** the melancholy in which he wallows; **au rythme/train ~ ça va** at the speed/rate it's going; **au prix ~ c'est** at the price it is; **au tarif ~ ils font payer ça** at the rate they charge for it; **à l'allure ~ ils vont** at the rate they're going; **voilà ~ nous en sommes** that's the position to date *ou* so far, that's where we're at*; *voir* **prix, train**; *pour autres constructions voir verbes appropriés.*
c (*temporel*) **le siècle ~ se passe cette histoire** the century in which this story takes place; **le jour ~ je l'ai rencontré** the day (on which) I met him; **à l'instant ~ il est arrivé** the moment he arrived; **mais là ~ je me suis fâché c'est quand il a recommencé** but what (finally) made me explode was when he started doing it again; *voir* **moment**.
2 adv rel a (*situation et direction*) where. **j'irai ~ il veut** I'll go where *ou* wherever he wants; **s'établir ~ l'on veut** to settle where one likes; **je ne sais pas d'~ il vient** I don't know where he comes from; **on ne peut pas passer par ~ on veut** you can't just go where you like; **d'~ je suis on voit la mer** you can see the sea from where I am; **~ que l'on aille/soit** wherever one goes/is; **d'~ que l'on vienne** wherever one comes from; **par ~ que l'on passe** wherever one goes.
b (*abstrait*) **~ cela devient grave, c'est lorsqu'il prétend que ...** where it gets serious is when he claims that ...; **savoir ~ s'arrêter** to know where *ou* when to stop; **d'~ l'on peut conclure que ...** from which one may conclude that ...; **d'~ son silence/ma méfiance** hence his silence/my wariness; (*titre de chapitre*) "**~ l'on voit que ...**" "in which the reader sees *ou* learns that ..."; (*littér*) **les récriminations sont vaines ~ les malheurs viennent de notre propre incurie** recrimination is in vain when misfortune comes of our own negligence; (*Prov*) **~ il y a de la gêne, il n'y a pas de plaisir** comfort comes first, there's no sense in being uncomfortable; (*péj*) talk about making yourself at home!, some people think only of their own comfort.
3 adv interrog a (*situation et direction*) where. **~ vas-tu/es-tu/l'as-tu mis?** where are you going/are you/did you put it?; **d'~ viens-tu?** where have you come from?; **par ~ y aller?** which way should we (*ou* I *etc*) go?; **~ aller?** where should I (*ou* he *etc*) go?; **~ ça?*** where's that?
b (*abstrait*) **~ en étais-je?** where was I?, where had I got to?; **~ en êtes-vous?** where are you up to?; **~ allons-nous?** where are we going?; **d'~ vient cette attitude?** what's the reason for this attitude?; **d'~ vient qu'il n'a pas répondu?** how come he hasn't replied?*, what's the reason

for his not having replied?; **d'~ le tenez-vous?** where did you hear that?; **~ voulez-vous en venir?** what are you leading up to? *ou* getting at?

OUA [ɔya] **nf** (**abrév de Organisation de l'unité africaine**) OAU.

Ouagadougou [wagadugu] **n** Ouagadougou.

ouah* ['wa] **excl** wow!*, ooh!*

ouailles [wɑj] **nfpl** (*Rel, hum*) flock. **l'une de ses ~** one of his flock.

ouais* ['wɛ] **excl** (*oui*) yeah*, yep*; (*sceptique*) oh yeah?*

ouananiche [wananiʃ] **nm** (*Can*) lake trout *ou* salmon.

ouaouaron* [wawaʀɔ̃] **nm** (*Can*) bull frog.

ouate ['wat] **1 nf a** (*pour pansement*) cotton wool (*Brit*), cotton (*US*). (*fig*) **élever un enfant dans de la ~** *ou* **dans l'~** to keep a child (wrapped up) in cotton wool (*Brit*) *ou* in cotton (*US*). **b** (*pour rembourrage*) padding, wadding. **doublé d'~** quilted. **2 comp ▸ouate hydrophile** cotton wool (*Brit*), absorbent cotton (*US*) **▸ouate thermogène** Thermogene ®.

ouaté, e ['wate] (**ptp de ouater**) **adj a** (*lit*) *pansement* cotton-wool (*épith*) (*Brit*), cotton (*US*); *vêtement* quilted. **b** (*fig*) *pas, bruit* muffled; *ambiance* cocoon-like.

ouater ['wate] **1 vt** *manteau, couverture* to quilt. **les collines ouatées de neige** the hills covered *ou* blanketed in snow.

ouatine [watin] **nf** wadding, padding.

ouatiner [watine] **1 vt** to quilt.

oubli [ubli] **nm a** (*voir* **oublier**) forgetting; leaving behind; missing; leaving-out; neglecting. **l'~ de cette date/cet objet a eu des conséquences graves** forgetting this date/forgetting *ou* leaving behind this thing has had serious repercussions; **l'~ de soi(-même)** self-effacement, self-negation; **l'~ de tout problème matériel** disregard for all material problems.

b (*trou de mémoire, omission*) lapse of memory. **ses ~s répétés m'inquiètent** his constant lapses of memory worry me, his constant forgetfulness worries me; **réparer un ~** to make up for having forgotten something *ou* for a lapse of memory; **cet ~ lui coûta la vie** this omission *ou* oversight cost him his life; **il y a des ~s dans ce récit** there are gaps *ou* things missed out in this account.

c l'~ oblivion, forgetfulness; **tirer qch de l'~** to bring sth out of oblivion; **tomber dans l'~** to sink into oblivion; **l'~ guérit toutes les blessures** oblivion *ou* forgetfulness heals all wounds.

oublier [ublije] **7 vt a** (*ne pas se souvenir de*) to forget; (*ne plus penser à*) *soucis, chagrin, client, visiteur* to forget (about). **~ de faire/pourquoi** to forget to do/why; **ça s'oublie facilement** it's easily forgotten; **j'ai oublié qui je dois prévenir** I can't remember who (it is) *ou* I've forgotten who (it is) I should warn; **j'ai complètement oublié l'heure** I completely forgot about the time; **j'ai oublié si j'ai bien éteint le gaz** I forget *ou* I can't remember if I turned off the gas; **n'oublie pas que nous sortons ce soir** remember *ou* don't forget we're going out tonight; **il oubliera avec le temps** he'll forget in time, time will help him forget; **oublions le passé** let's forget about the past, let's let bygones be bygones; **j'avais complètement oublié sa présence** I had completely forgotten that he was there *ou* forgotten his presence; **sa gentillesse fait ~ sa laideur** his niceness makes you forget (about) his ugliness; **il essaie de se faire ~** he's trying to keep out of the limelight; **mourir oublié** to die forgotten.

b (*laisser*) *chose* to forget, leave behind; *fautes d'orthographe* to miss; *virgule, phrase* to leave out. **tu as oublié (de laver) une vitre** you forgot *ou* have forgotten (to wash) one of the panes.

c (*négliger*) *famille, devoir, travail, promesse* to forget, neglect. **~ les règles de la politesse** to forget *ou* neglect the rules of etiquette; **n'oubliez pas le guide!** don't forget the guide!; **il ne faut pas ~ que c'est un pays pauvre** we must not lose sight of the fact *ou* forget that it's a poor country; **~ qn dans son testament** to leave sb out of one's will, forget (to include) sb in one's will; **~ qn dans ses pensées** to forget (to include) sb in one's thoughts, forget to think about sb; **il ne vous oublie pas** he hasn't forgotten (about) you; **on l'a oublié sur la liste** he's been left off the list; (*iro*) **il ne s'est pas oublié (dans le partage)** he didn't forget himself (in the share-out); **vous vous oubliez!** you're forgetting yourself!; **le chat s'est oublié sur la moquette** the cat had an accident on the carpet.

oubliettes [ublijɛt] **nfpl** oubliettes. (*fig*) **jeter** *ou* **mettre aux ~** *projet* to shelve; (*fig*) **tomber dans les ~ (de l'histoire)** *[déclaration, procès]* to sink into oblivion; **ce livre/projet est tombé aux ~** this book/plan has been forgotten.

oublieux, -ieuse [ublijø, ijøz] **adj** deliberately forgetful. **~ de** *bienfaits* quick to forget; *obligations, devoirs* neglectful of.

oued [wɛd] **nm** wadi.

ouest [wɛst] **1 nm a** (*point cardinal*) west. **le vent d'~** the west wind; **un vent d'~** a west(erly) wind, a westerly (*SPÉC*); **le vent tourne/est à l'~** the wind is veering west(wards) *ou* towards the west/is blowing from the west; **regarder vers l'~** *ou* **dans la direction de l'~** to look west(wards) *ou* towards the west; **à l'~** (*situation*) in the west; (*direction*) to the west, west(wards); **le soleil se couche à l'~** the sun sets in the west; **à l'~ de** west of, to the west of; **la maison est (exposée) à l'~/exposée plein ~** the house faces (the) west *ou* westwards/due west, the house looks west(wards)/due west; **l'Europe/la France/la Bourgogne de l'~** Western Europe/France/Burgundy; *voir* **Allemagne.**

b (*partie, régions occidentales*) west. (*Pol*) **l'O~** the West; **l'~ de la France, l'O~** the West of France; **les rapports entre l'Est et l'O~** East-West relations, relations between the East and the West.

2 adj inv *région, partie* western; *entrée, paroi* west; *versant, côte* west(ern); *côté* west(ward); *direction* westward, westerly; *voir* **longitude.**

3 comp ▸ouest-allemand, e adj West German **▸Ouest-Allemand, e nm,f** West German **▸ouest-nord-ouest adj inv, nm** west-north-west **▸ouest-sud-ouest adj inv, nm** west-south-west.

ouf ['uf] **excl** phew!, whew! **ils ont dû repartir sans avoir le temps de dire ~*** they had to leave again before they had time to catch their breath *ou* before they knew where they were.

Ouganda [ugɑ̃da] **nm** Uganda.

ougandais, e [ugɑ̃dɛ, ɛz] **1 adj** Ugandan. **2 nm,f: O~(e)** Ugandan.

ougrien, -ienne [ugʀijɛ̃, ijɛn] *voir* **finno-ougrien.**

oui ['wi] **1 adv a** (*réponse affirmative*) yes, aye (*Naut, régional*), yea (†† *ou littér*). **le connaissez-vous? — ~** do you know him? — yes (I do); **est-elle chez elle? — ~** is she at home? — yes (she is); **vous avez aimé le film? — ~ et non** did you like the film? — yes and no *ou* I did and I didn't; **je vais ouvrir la fenêtre — ~ cela fera un peu d'air** I'll open the window — yes (do), we could do with some fresh air; **il n'a pas encore dit ~!** he hasn't said yes yet, he hasn't agreed *ou* accepted (as) yet; (*mariage*) **dire ~** to say "I do"; **ah, ça ~!** you can say that again!*, and how!*; **que ~!** rather! (*Brit*), I should say so!; **certes ~!** (yes) most definitely *ou* certainly, yes indeed; **vous en voulez? — mais ~!** *ou* **bien sûr que ~** *ou* **~, bien sûr** do you want some? — of course (I do) *ou* I most certainly do; **~ mais, il y a un obstacle** yes but there is a difficulty; **eh bien ~, j'avoue** all right (then), I confess; **contraception ~, avortement non** yes to contraception, no to abortion, contraception — yes, abortion — no; **répondre (par) ~ à toutes les questions** to answer yes *ou* answer in the affirmative to all the questions; **répondez par ~ ou par non** answer yes or no; **faire ~ de la tête, faire signe que ~** to nod (one's head); **ah ~?** really?, yes?; (†, *hum*) **~-da** yes indeed, absolutely; (*Naut*) **~, capitaine** aye aye captain.

b (*remplaçant une proposition*) **est-il chez lui?/est-ce qu'il travaille? — je pense** *ou* **crois que ~** is he at home?/is he working? — (yes) I think so *ou* believe he is; **il nous quitte? — je crains bien/j'espère que ~** is he leaving us? — I am afraid so *ou* I am afraid he is/I hope so *ou* I hope he is; **est-ce qu'elle sort souvent? — j'ai l'impression que ~** does she often go out? — I have an idea *ou* the impression that she does; **tu as aimé ce film? — moi ~/moi non** did you like the film? — I did/I didn't; **j'ai demandé si elle était venue, lui dit que ~** I asked if she had been and he says she has.

c (*intensif*) **je suis surprise, ~ très surprise** I'm surprised — indeed very surprised; **c'est un escroc, ~, un escroc** he's a rogue, an absolute rogue; **~ vraiment, il a répondu ça?** (really), did he really answer that?; **tu vas cesser de pleurer, ~?** have you quite finished crying?, will you stop crying?; **~ (évidemment), c'est toujours bien facile de critiquer** of course it's always easy enough to criticize; **c'est bon, ~?** isn't that good?; **il va accepter, ~ ou non?** is he or isn't he going to accept?; **tu te presses, ~ ou non?** will you please hurry up, will you hurry up?; **tu te décides ~ ou merde!**⁑ are you going to damn well decide or not?⁑, make up your bloody mind!⁑ (*Brit*).

2 nm inv yes, aye. **il y a eu 30 ~** there were 30 votes for, there were 30 ayes; **j'aimerais un ~ plus ferme** I should prefer a more definite yes; **il ne dit ni ~ ni non** he's not saying either yes or no, he's not committing himself either way; **pleurer/réclamer/se disputer pour un ~ (ou) pour un non** to cry/complain/quarrel over the slightest thing.

ouï-dire ['widiʀ] **nm inv: par ~** by hearsay.

ouïe[1] ['uj] **excl = ouille.**

ouïe[2] [wi] **nf** hearing (*NonC*). **avoir l'~ fine** to have sharp hearing, have a keen sense of hearing; **être tout ~** to be all ears.

ouïes [wi] **nfpl** (*Zool*) gills; (*Mus*) sound holes.

ouille ['uj] **excl** ouch!

ouïr [wiʀ] **10 vt** (††, *littér, hum*) to hear; (*Jur*) *témoins* to hear. **j'ai ouï dire à mon père que ...** I've heard my father say that ...; **j'ai ouï dire que** it has come to my ears that, I've heard it said that; (*hum*) **oyez!** hark! (†† *ou hum*), hear ye! (†† *ou hum*).

ouistiti ['wistiti] **nm** (*Zool*) marmoset. (*type*) **un drôle de ~*** a queer bird*.

oukase [ukaz] **nm = ukase.**

Oulan-Bator [ulanbatɔʀ] **n** Ulan Bator.

ouléma [ulema] **nm = uléma.**

ouragan [uʀagɑ̃] **nm a** (*lit*) hurricane. **b** (*fig*) storm. **cet homme est un véritable ~** he's like a whirlwind, he's a human tornado; **ce livre va déchaîner un ~** this book is going to create a storm; **arriver en** *ou* **comme un ~** to arrive like a whirlwind *ou* tornado.

Oural [uʀal] **nm** (*fleuve*) **l'~** the Ural; **l'~, les monts ~** the Urals, the Ural Mountains.

ouralo-altaïque [uʀalɔaltaik] **adj, nm** Ural-Altaic.

ourdir [uʀdiʀ] **2 vt** *complot* to hatch; *intrigue* to weave.

ourdou [uʀdu] **1 adj inv** Urdu. **2 nm** (*Ling*) Urdu.

ourlé, e [uʀle] (ptp de **ourler**) adj hemmed. **oreilles délicatement ~es** delicately rimmed ears; **lèvres bien ~es** well-defined lips.
ourler [uʀle] 1 vt (*Couture*) to hem. (*fig littér*) **~ de** to fringe with.
ourlet [uʀlɛ] nm a (*Couture*) hem. **faux ~** false hem; **faire un ~ à** to hem. b (*Tech*) hem. c (*Anat*) *[oreille]* rim, helix (*SPÉC*).
ours [uʀs] 1 nm a (*Zool*) bear. **être** *ou* **tourner comme un ~ en cage** to pace up and down like a caged animal; *voir* **fosse, montreur, vendre.** b (*jouet*) **~ (en peluche)** teddy bear. c (*péj: misanthrope*) (old) bear. **vivre comme un** *ou* **en ~** to live at odds with the world; **elle est un peu ~** she's a bit of a bear *ou* a gruff individual. d (*arg Presse*) ≃ credits (*for written publications*). 2 comp ► **ours blanc** polar bear ► **ours brun** brown bear ► **ours mal léché** (*péj*) uncouth fellow ► **ours marin** fur-seal ► **ours polaire** = **ours blanc** ► **ours savant** trained *ou* performing bear.
ourse [uʀs] nf a (*Zool*) she-bear. b (*Astron*) **la Petite O~** the Little Bear, Ursa Minor, the Little Dipper (*US*); **la Grande O~** the Great Bear, Ursa Major, the Plough (*Brit*), the Big Dipper (*US*).
oursin [uʀsɛ̃] nm sea urchin, sea hedgehog.
ourson [uʀsɔ̃] nm bear cub.
oust(e)* ['ust] excl hop it!* (*Brit*), buzz off!*, off with you!
out ['aut] adj inv *personne* out of touch* (*attrib*); (*Tennis*) out.
outarde [utaʀd] nf bustard; (*Can: bernache*) Canada goose.
outil [uti] nm (*lit, fig*) tool; (*agricole, de jardin*) implement, tool. **~ de travail** tool; **~ pédagogique** teaching aid; (*Ordin*) **~ de programmation** programming tool; *voir* **machine³, mauvais.**
outillage [utijaʒ] nm *[mécanicien, bricoleur]* (set of) tools; *[fermier, jardinier]* implements (*pl*), equipment (*NonC*); *[atelier, usine]* equipment (*NonC*).
outiller [utije] 1 vt *ouvrier* to supply *ou* provide with tools, equip, kit out (*Brit*), outfit (*US*); *atelier* to fit out, equip. **je suis bien/mal outillé pour ce genre de travail** I'm well-/badly-equipped for this kind of work; **pour ce travail, il faudra qu'on s'outille** to do this job, we'll have to kit ourselves out (*Brit*) *ou* equip ourselves properly; **les ouvriers s'outillent à leurs frais** the workers buy their own tools.
outilleur [utijœʀ] nm tool-maker.
outrage [utʀaʒ] 1 nm insult. **accabler qn d'~s** to heap insults on sb; **faire ~ à** *réputation, mémoire* to dishonour; *pudeur, honneur* to outrage, be an outrage to; (*fig*) **~ au bon sens/à la raison** insult to common sense/reason; (*fig littér*) **les ~s du temps** the ravages of time; *voir* **dernier.** 2 comp ► **outrage à agent** (*Jur*) insulting behaviour (*to police officer*) ► **outrage aux bonnes mœurs** (*Jur*) outrage *ou* affront to public decency ► **outrage à magistrat** (*Jur*) contempt of court ► **outrage public à la pudeur** (*Jur*) indecent exposure (*NonC*).
outragé, e [utʀaʒe] (ptp de **outrager**) adj *air, personne* gravely offended.
outrageant, e [utʀaʒɑ̃, ɑ̃t] adj offensive.
outrager [utʀaʒe] 3 vt (*littér*) *personne* to offend gravely; *mœurs, morale* to outrage; *bon sens, raison* to insult. **outragée dans son honneur** with outraged honour.
outrageusement [utʀaʒøzmɑ̃] adv (*excessivement*) outrageously, excessively.
outrageux, -euse [utʀaʒø, øz] adj (*excessif*) outrageous, excessive. **de manière ~euse** outrageously, excessively.
outrance [utʀɑ̃s] nf a (*caractère*) extravagance. **pousser le raffinement jusqu'à l'~** to take refinement to extremes *ou* to excess.
b (*excès*) excess. **il y a des ~s dans ce roman** there are some extravagant passages in this novel; **ses ~s de langage** his outrageous language.
c **à ~: raffiner à ~** to refine excessively *ou* to excess; **dévot/méticuleux à ~** excessively pious/meticulous, pious/meticulous in the extreme *ou* to excess; *voir* **guerre.**
outrancier, -ière [utʀɑ̃sje, jɛʀ] adj *personne, propos* extreme. **son caractère ~** the extreme nature of his character, the extremeness of his character.
outre¹ [utʀ] nf goatskin, wine *ou* water skin. **gonflé** *ou* **plein comme une ~** full to bursting.
outre² [utʀ] 1 prép a (*en plus de*) as well as, besides. **~ sa cargaison, le bateau transportait des passagers** besides *ou* as well as its cargo the boat was carrying passengers; **~ son salaire, il a des pourboires** on top of *ou* in addition to his salary, he gets tips; **~ le fait que** as well as *ou* besides the fact that.
b (*loc*) **en ~** moreover, besides, further(more); **en ~ de** over and above, on top of; **~ mesure** to excess, overmuch, inordinately; **manger/boire ~ mesure** to eat/drink to excess *ou* immoderately; **cela ne lui plaît pas ~ mesure** he doesn't like that overmuch, he's not overkeen on that (*Brit*); **cet auteur a été louangé ~ mesure** this author has been praised overmuch *ou* unduly; **passer ~** to carry on regardless, let it pass; **passer ~ à un ordre** to disregard an order, carry on regardless of an order; **~ qu'il a le temps, il a les capacités pour le faire** not only does he have the time but he also has the ability to do it, apart from having the time *ou* besides having the time he also has the ability to do it; (†) **d'~ en ~** through and through.
2 comp ► **outre-Atlantique** across the Atlantic ► **outre-Manche** across the Channel ► **outre-mer** overseas ► **les territoires d'outre-mer** overseas territories ► **outre-Rhin** across the Rhine ► **les pays d'outre-rideau de fer** the iron curtain countries, the countries behind the iron curtain ► **outre-tombe** beyond the grave; **d'une voix d'outre-tombe** in a lugubrious voice; *voir* **outrecuidance, outremer, outrepasser.**
outré, e [utʀe] (ptp de **outrer**) adj a (*littér: exagéré*) *éloges, flatterie* excessive, exaggerated, overdone (*attrib*); *description* exaggerated, extravagant, overdone (*attrib*). b (*indigné*) outraged (*de, par* at, by).
outrecuidance [utʀəkɥidɑ̃s] nf a (*littér: présomption*) presumptuousness. **parler avec ~** to speak presumptuously. b (*effronterie*) impertinence. **répondre à qn avec ~** to answer sb impertinently; **~s** impudence (*NonC*), impertinences.
outrecuidant, e [utʀəkɥidɑ̃, ɑ̃t] adj a (*présomptueux*) presumptuous. b (*effronté*) *attitude, réponse* impertinent.
outremer [utʀəmɛʀ] 1 nm (*pierre*) lapis lazuli; (*couleur*) ultramarine. 2 adj inv ultramarine.
outrepassé [utʀəpɑse] (ptp de **outrepasser**) adj *voir* **arc.**
outrepasser [utʀəpɑse] 1 vt *droits* to go beyond; *pouvoir, ordres* to exceed; *limites* to go beyond, overstep.
outrer [utʀe] 1 vt a (*littér*) (*exagérer*) to exaggerate. **cet acteur outre son jeu** this actor overacts. b (*indigner*) to outrage. **votre ingratitude m'a outré** your ingratitude has outraged me, I am outraged at *ou* by your ingratitude.
outsider [autsajdœʀ] nm (*Sport, fig*) outsider.
ouvert, e [uvɛʀ, ɛʀt] (ptp de **ouvrir**) adj a *porte, magasin, valise, lieu, espace* open; *voiture* open, unlocked; (*Ling*) *voyelle, syllabe* open; *angle* wide; *série, ensemble* open-ended; *robinet* on, running; *col, chemise* open, undone (*attrib*). **la bouche ~e** open-mouthed, with open mouth; **entrez, c'est ~!** come in, the door isn't locked! *ou* the door's open!; **~ au public** open to the public; **bibliothèque ~e à tous** library open to all members of the public; **le magasin restera ~ pendant les travaux** the shop will remain open (for business) during the alterations; (*Comm*) **je suis ~ jusqu'à Noël*** I'm open till Christmas; **~ à la circulation** open to traffic; **le col du Simplon est ~** the Simplon pass is open (to traffic); **~ à la navigation** open to ships *ou* for sailing; **une rose trop ~e** a rose which is too (far) open; **elle est partie en laissant le robinet/gaz ~** she went away leaving the tap *ou* the water on *ou* running/the gas on; *voir* **bras, ciel** *etc.*
b (*commencé*) open. **la chasse/pêche est ~e** the shooting season/fishing season is open; *voir* **pari.**
c (*percé, incisé*) *plaie* open. **il a le crâne/le bras ~** he has a gaping wound in his head/arm; *voir* **cœur, fracture.**
d *débat,* (*Sport*) *compétition* open. **une partie très ~e** an open-ended game; **pratiquer un jeu ~** to play an open game.
e (*déclaré, non dissimulé*) *guerre, haine* open. **de façon ~e** openly, overtly.
f (*communicatif, franc*) *personne, caractère* open, frank; *visage, physionomie* open; (*éveillé, accessible*) *esprit, intelligence, milieu* open. **à l'esprit ~** open-minded.
ouvertement [uvɛʀtəmɑ̃] adv *dire, avouer* openly; *agir* openly, overtly.
ouverture [uvɛʀtyʀ] nf a (*action: voir* **ouvrir**) opening; unlocking; opening up; opening out; unfastening; cutting open; starting up; turning on; switching on. (*Comm*) **jours d'~** days of opening; (*Comm*) **heures d'~** *[magasin]* opening hours, hours of business *ou* of opening; *[musée]* opening hours, hours of opening; **le client était là dès l'~** the customer was there as soon as the shop opened; **"~ de 10 h à 15 h"** "open from 10 till 3"; **à l'heure d'~, à l'~** at opening time; **l'~ de la porte est automatique** the door opens *ou* is operated automatically; **cérémonie d'~** opening ceremony; **c'est demain l'~ de la chasse** tomorrow sees the opening of *ou* the first day of the shooting season; (*Chasse*) **faire l'~** to go on *ou* be at the first shoot; **en ~ du festival** to open the festival.
b (*passage, issue, accès*) opening; *[puits]* mouth, opening. **toutes les ~s sont gardées** all the openings *ou* all means of access (*ou* exit) are guarded, all the access points (*ou* exit points) are guarded.
c (*avances*) **~s** overtures; **faire des ~s à qn** to make overtures to sb; **faire des ~s de paix/conciliation** to make peace/conciliatory overtures; **faire des ~s de négociation** to make steps towards instigating negotiations.
d (*fig: largeur, compréhension*) open-mindedness. (*Pol*) **l'~** the opening up of the political spectrum; **il a une grande ~ d'esprit** he is extremely open-minded; (*Pol*) **être partisan de l'~ au centre** to be in favour of an alliance with the centre; **adopter une politique de plus grande ~ avec l'Est** to develop a more open relationship with the East; **le besoin d'(une) ~ sur le monde** the need for an opening onto the world.
e (*Mus*) overture. **l'O~ solennelle** the 1812 Overture.
f (*Math*) *[angle]* magnitude; *[compas]* degree of opening; (*Phot*) aperture.
g (*Cartes*) opening. (*Échecs*) **avoir l'~** to have the first *ou* opening move.
h (*Ftbl*) through-ball; (*Rugby*) pass (*by the stand-off half to the three-quarter backs*). **faire une ~** (*Ftbl*) to hit *ou* play a through-ball; (*Rugby*) to pass the ball to the three-quarter backs; *voir* **demi².**
ouvrable [uvʀabl] adj: **jour ~** weekday, working day; **heures ~s** business hours.

ouvrage [uvʀaʒ] 1 nm a (*travail*) work (*NonC*). **se mettre à l'~** to set to *ou* get (down) to *ou* start work; (*littér*) **l'~ du temps/du hasard** the work of time/chance; *voir* **cœur**.
b (*objet produit*) piece of work; (*Couture*) work (*NonC*). **~ d'orfèvrerie** piece of goldwork; **~ à l'aiguille** (piece of) needlework; *voir* **boîte, corbeille, panier** *etc*.
c (*livre*) (*œuvre, écrit*) work; (*volume*) book.
d (*Constr*) work.
2 nf (†, *hum: travail*) **de la belle ~** a nice piece of work.
3 comp ►**ouvrage d'art** (*Génie Civil*) structure (*bridge or tunnel etc*) ►**ouvrage avancé** (*Mil*) outwork ►**ouvrage de dames** fancy work (*NonC*) ►**ouvrage défensif** (*Mil*) defences, defence work(s) ►**ouvrage de maçonnerie** masonry work ►**ouvrage militaire** fortification.

ouvragé, e [uvʀaʒe] adj *meuble, bois* (finely) carved; *napperon* (finely) embroidered; *signature* elaborate; *métal, bijou* finely worked.

ouvrant, e [uvʀɑ̃, ɑ̃t] adj *panneau* which opens (*attrib*); *voir* **toit**.

ouvré, e [uvʀe] adj a (*Tech, littér*) *meuble, bois* (finely) carved; *napperon* (finely) embroidered; *métal, bijou* finely worked. b **jour ~** working day.

ouvre-boîte, pl **ouvre-boîtes** [uvʀəbwat] nm tin-opener (*Brit*), can-opener.

ouvre-bouteille, pl **ouvre-bouteilles** [uvʀəbutɛj] nm bottle opener.

ouvre-huître, pl **ouvre-huîtres** [uvʀ(ə)ɥitʀ] nm oyster knife.

ouvreur, -euse [uvʀœʀ, øz] 1 nm,f (*Cartes*) opener; (*Ski*) forerunner. 2 **ouvreuse** nf *[cinéma, théâtre]* usherette.

ouvrier, -ière [uvʀije, ijɛʀ] 1 adj *enfance, éducation, quartier* working-class; *conflit, agitation, législation* industrial (*épith*), labour (*épith*); *questions, mouvement* labour (*épith*). **association ~ière** workers' *ou* working men's association; *voir* **cité, classe, syndicat**.
2 nm (*gén, Pol, Sociol*) worker; (*membre du personnel*) workman. **les revendications des ~s** the workers' claims; **il a 15 ~s** he has 15 workmen, he has 15 men working for him; **des mains d'~** workman's hands; **150 ~s ont été mis en chômage technique** 150 men *ou* workers have been laid off; **comme ~, dans un petit atelier, il ...** as a workman *ou* worker in a small workshop, he ...; (*fig*) **l'~ de cette réforme** the author of this reform; *voir* **mauvais, œuvre**.
3 **ouvrière** nf a (*gén, Admin*) female worker. **~ière (d'usine)** female factory worker *ou* factory hand; (*jeune*) factory girl, young factory hand; **il allait à l'usine attendre la sortie des ~ières** he went to the factory to wait for the women *ou* girls to come out.
b (*Zool*) **(abeille) ~ière** worker (bee).
4 comp ►**ouvrier agricole** agricultural *ou* farm worker, farm labourer, farmhand ►**ouvrier de chantier** labourer ►**ouvrier à façon** pieceworker, jobber ►**ouvrier hautement qualifié** highly-skilled worker ►**ouvrier à la journée** day labourer ►**ouvrier qualifié** skilled workman ►**ouvrier spécialisé** unskilled *ou* semi-skilled worker ►**ouvrier d'usine** factory worker *ou* hand.

ouvriérisme [uvʀijeʀism] nm worker control, worker power.

ouvriériste [uvʀijeʀist] 1 adj *doctrine, attitude* which gives power to the workers *ou* supports control by the workers. 2 nmf supporter of control by the workers.

ouvrir [uvʀiʀ] [18] 1 vt a *fenêtre, porte, tiroir, paquet, bouteille, magasin, chambre, frontière* to open; *rideaux* to open, draw back; *verrou, porte fermée à clef* to unlock; *huîtres, coquillages* to open (up). **~ par** *ou* **avec effraction** *porte, coffre* to break open; **~ la porte toute grande/le portail tout grand** to open the door/gate wide; **il a ouvert brusquement la porte** he opened the door abruptly, he threw *ou* flung the door open; (*fig*) **~ sa porte** *ou* **sa maison à qn** to throw open one's doors *ou* one's house to sb; (*fig*) **ça lui a ouvert toutes les portes** this opened all doors to him; (*fig*) **~ la porte toute grande aux abus/excès** to throw the door wide open to abuses/excesses; **on a frappé: va ~!** there was a knock: go and open *ou* answer the door!; **ouvrez, au nom de la loi!** open up, in the name of the law!; **n'ouvre à personne!** don't open the door to anybody!; **fais-toi ~ par la concierge** ask *ou* get the caretaker to let you in; **le boulanger ouvre de 7 heures à 19 heures** the baker('s shop) is open *ou* opens from 7 a.m. till 7 p.m.; **ils ouvrent leur maison au public tous les étés** they open up their house to the public every summer, they throw their house open to the public every summer; *voir* **parenthèse**.
b *bouche, yeux, paupières* to open. **~ le bec, l'~**‡ to open one's trap‡; **~ la** *ou* **sa gueule**‡ to open one's gob‡ (*Brit*) *ou* trap‡; (*fig*) **~ l'œil** to keep one's eyes open (*fig*); (*lit*) **~ les yeux** to open one's eyes; (*fig*) **ce voyage en Asie m'a ouvert les yeux** this trip through Asia opened my eyes *ou* was an eye-opener (to me); **ouvre l'œil, et le bon!*** keep your eyes peeled!*; **~ les oreilles** to pin back one's ears; **elle m'a ouvert son cœur** she opened her heart to me; **ça m'a ouvert l'appétit** that whetted my appetite; **ce séjour à l'étranger lui a ouvert l'esprit** this spell abroad has enlarged *ou* widened his horizons.
c *journal, couteau* to open; *parapluie* to open (out), put up; *éventail, bras, ailes, main* to open (out); *manteau, gilet* to undo, unfasten, open; *lit, drap* to turn down. (*Mil*) **ouvrez les rangs!** dress!; (*fig*) **~ ses rangs à qn** to welcome sb among one's ranks; (*fig*) **~ sa bourse (à qn)** to put one's hand in one's pocket (to help sb).
d (*faire un trou dans*) *chaussée, mur* to open up; *membre, ventre* to open up, cut open. **les roches lui ont ouvert la jambe** he has cut his leg open on the rocks; **le médecin pense qu'il faudra ~*** the doctor thinks that they will have to open him (*ou* her *etc*) up*.
e (*faire, construire*) *porte, passage* to open up, make; *autoroute* to build; (*fig*) *horizons, perspectives* to open up. **il a fallu ~ une porte dans ce mur** a doorway had to be opened up *ou* made in this wall; **~ un passage dans le roc à la dynamite** to open up *ou* blast a passage in the rock with dynamite; **cette autoroute a été ouverte pour desservir la nouvelle banlieue** this motorway has been built to serve the new suburb; **ils lui ont ouvert un passage** *ou* **le passage dans la foule** they made way for him through the crowd; **s'~ un passage à travers la forêt** to open up *ou* cut a path for o.s. through the forest; (*fig*) **~ des horizons à qn** to open up new horizons for sb.
f (*débloquer*) *chemin, passage* to open. **le chasse-neige a ouvert la route** the snowplough opened up the road; (*Sport*) **~ le jeu** to open up the game; (*fig*) **~ la voie (à qn)** to lead the way (for sb).
g (*autoriser l'accès de*) *route, col, frontière* to open (up).
h (*commencer l'exploitation de*) *restaurant, théâtre, magasin* to open (up), start up; *école, succursale* to open (up).
i (*constituer*) *souscription, compte bancaire, enquête* to open; *emprunt* to take out; (*inaugurer*) *festival, exposition, bal* to open. **~ un compte à un client** to open an account for a customer *ou* in a customer's name; **~ les hostilités** to start up *ou* begin hostilities; **~ le feu** to open fire, open up; (*Ski*) **~ la piste** to open the piste *ou* run; (*Cartes*) **~ le jeu** to open play; (*Cartes*) **il a ouvert à pique** he opened on *ou* with spades; (*Ftbl*) **~ la marque à la 16ᵉ minute du jeu** to open the scoring after 16 minutes of play; (*Ftbl, Rugby*) **il ouvre toujours sur un joueur faible** he always passes to a weak player.
j (*être au début de*) *liste, œuvre* to head; *procession* to lead. **~ la marche** to take the lead, walk in front; **~ la danse** to lead off the dance.
k *électricité, gaz, radio* to turn on, switch on, put on; *eau, robinet* to turn on; *vanne* to open.
2 vi a *[fenêtre, porte]* to open. **cette fenêtre ouvre sur la cour** this window opens onto the yard; **la porte de derrière n'ouvre pas** the back door doesn't open.
b *[magasin]* to open. **ça ouvre de 2 à 5** they open *ou* are open from 2 to 5.
c (*commencer*) to open. **la pièce ouvre par un discours du vainqueur** the play opens with a speech from the victor.
3 **s'ouvrir** vpr a *[porte, fenêtre, parapluie, livre]* to open; *[fleur, coquillage]* to open (out); *[bouche, yeux]* to open; *[bras, main, ailes]* to open (out); *[esprit]* to open out; *[gouffre]* to open. **robe qui s'ouvre par devant** dress that undoes *ou* unfastens at the front; **sa robe s'est ouverte** her dress came undone *ou* unfastened; **la fenêtre s'ouvre sur une cour** the window opens (out) onto a courtyard; **la foule s'ouvrit pour le laisser passer** the crowd parted to let him through; **la porte s'ouvrit violemment** the door flew open *ou* was flung open *ou* was thrown open; **la porte/boîte a dû s'~** the door/box must have come open.
b (*commencer*) *[récit, séance, exposition]* to open (*par* with). **la séance s'ouvrit par un chahut** the meeting opened in (an) uproar *ou* with an uproar.
c (*se présenter*) **s'~ devant** *[paysage, vie]* to open in front of *ou* before; **un chemin poussiéreux s'ouvrit devant eux** a dusty path opened in front of *ou* before them; **la vie qui s'ouvre devant elle est pleine d'embûches** the life which is opening in front of *ou* before her is full of pitfalls.
d (*béer*) to open (up). **la terre s'ouvrit devant eux** the ground opened up before them; **le gouffre s'ouvrait à leurs pieds** the chasm lay open *ou* gaped at their feet.
e (*devenir sensible à*) **s'~ à** *amour, art, problèmes économiques* to open one's mind to, become aware of; **pays qui s'ouvre sur le monde extérieur** country which is opening up to the outside world; **son esprit s'est ouvert aux souffrances d'autrui** his mind opened to *ou* he became aware of others' suffering.
f (*se confier*) **s'~ à qn de** to open one's heart to sb about; **il s'en est ouvert à son confesseur** he opened his heart to his confessor about it.
g (*se blesser*) to cut open. **elle s'est ouvert les veines** she slashed *ou* cut her wrists; **il s'ouvrit la jambe en tombant sur une faux** he cut open his leg by falling on a scythe.

ouvroir [uvʀwaʀ] nm *[couvent]* workroom; *[paroisse]* sewing room.

ouzbek [uzbɛk] 1 adj Uzbek. 2 nm (*Ling*) Uzbek. 3 nmf: **O~** Uzbek.

Ouzbékistan [uzbekistɑ̃] nm Uzbekistan.

ovaire [ɔvɛʀ] nm ovary.

ovale [ɔval] 1 adj *table, surface* oval; *volume* egg-shaped; *voir* **ballon**. 2 nm oval. **l'~ du visage** the oval of the face; **en ~** oval(-shaped).

ovariectomie [ɔvaʀjɛktɔmi] nf ovariectomy, oophorectomy.

ovarien, -ienne [ɔvaʀjɛ̃, jɛn] adj ovarian.

ovariotomie [ɔvaʀjɔtɔmi] nf ovariotomy.

ovarite [ɔvaʀit] nf ovaritis, oophoritis.

ovation [ɔvasjɔ̃] nf ovation. **faire une ~ à qn** to give sb an ovation; **ils se levèrent pour lui faire une ~** they gave him a standing ovation; **sous les ~s du public** to the rapturous applause of the audience (*ou* crowd *etc*).

ovationner [ɔvasjɔne] [1] vt: **~ qn** to give sb an ovation.

ove [ɔv] nm ovum (*Archit*).
ové, e [ɔve] adj egg-shaped.
overdose [ɔvœʀdoz] nf (*Méd*) (drug) overdose; [*: *musique, informations*] overdose. **c'est l'~*!** it's overkill!*
overdrive [ɔvœʀdʀajv] nm overdrive.
Ovide [ɔvid] nm Ovid.
ovin, e [ɔvɛ̃, in] 1 adj ovine. 2 nm: **les ~s** the ovine race.
ovipare [ɔvipaʀ] 1 adj oviparous. 2 nm oviparous animal. **~s** ovipara.
ovni [ɔvni] nm (**abrév de objet volant non identifié**) UFO.
ovocyte [ɔvɔsit] nm oocyte.
ovoïde [ɔvɔid] adj egg-shaped, ovoid (*SPÉC*).
ovulaire [ɔvylɛʀ] adj ovular.
ovulation [ɔvylasjɔ̃] nf ovulation.
ovule [ɔvyl] nm (*Physiol*) ovum; (*Bot*) ovule; (*Pharm*) pessary.
ovuler [ɔvyle] [1] vi to ovulate.
oxacide [ɔksasid] nm oxyacid, oxygen acid.
Oxford [ɔksfɔʀd] n Oxford.
oxford [ɔksfɔʀ(d)] nm (*Tex*) oxford.
oxfordien, -ienne [ɔksfɔʀdjɛ̃, jɛn] 1 adj Oxonian. 2 nm,f: **O~(-ne)** Oxonian.
oxhydrique [ɔksidʀik] adj oxyhydrogen (*épith*).
oxonien, -ienne [ɔksɔnjɛ̃, jɛn] 1 adj Oxonian. 2 nm,f: **O~(ne)** Oxonian.
oxyacétylénique [ɔksiasetilenik] adj oxyacetylene (*épith*).
oxydable [ɔksidabl] adj liable to rust, oxidizible (*SPÉC*).
oxydant, e [ɔksidɑ̃, ɑ̃t] 1 adj oxidizing. 2 nm oxidizer, oxidizing agent.
oxydase [ɔksidɑz] nf oxidase.
oxydation [ɔksidasjɔ̃] nf oxidization, oxidation.
oxyde [ɔksid] nm oxide. **~ de carbone** carbon monoxide; **~ de plomb** lead oxide *ou* monoxide; **~ de cuivre/de fer** copper/iron oxide.
oxyder [ɔkside] [1] 1 vt to oxidize. 2 **s'oxyder** vpr to become oxidized.
oxydoréduction [ɔksidɔʀedyksjɔ̃] nf oxidation-reduction.
oxygénation [ɔksiʒenasjɔ̃] nf oxygenation.
oxygène [ɔksiʒɛn] nm oxygen. **masque/tente à ~** oxygen mask/tent.
oxygéner [ɔksiʒene] [6] vt (*Chim*) to oxygenate; *cheveux* to peroxide, bleach. **s'~ (les poumons)*** to get some fresh air (into one's lungs); *voir* **blond, eau**.
oxyhémoglobine [ɔksiemɔglɔbin] nf oxyhaemoglobin.
oxymore [ɔksimɔʀ] nm, **oxymoron** [ɔksimɔʀɔ̃] nm oxymoron.
oyez [ɔje] *voir* **ouïr**.
ozone [ozon] nm ozone. **la couche d'~** the ozone layer; (*sur emballage*) **"préserve la couche d'~"** "ozone-friendly".
ozonisation [ozonizasjɔ̃] nf ozonization.
ozoniser [ozonize] [1] vt to ozonize.

P

P, p [pe] **nm** a (*lettre*) P, p. b (**abrév de page**) p.
PAC [pak] **nf** (**abrév de politique agricole commune**) CAP.
pacage [pakaʒ] **nm** pasture *ou* grazing (land).
pacager [pakaʒe] 3 1 **vt** to pasture, graze. 2 **vi** to graze.
pacane [pakan] **nf**: **(noix de)** ~ pecan (nut).
pacemaker [pɛsmɛkœʀ] **nm** pacemaker.
pacha [paʃa] **nm** pasha. **mener une vie de** ~, **faire le** ~ (*vivre richement*) to live like a lord; (*se prélasser*) to live a life of ease.
pachyderme [paʃidɛʀm] **nm** (*éléphant*) elephant; (*ongulé*) pachyderm (*SPÉC*). (*fig*) **de** ~ elephantine, heavy.
pacificateur, -trice [pasifikatœʀ, tʀis] 1 **adj** pacificatory. 2 **nm,f** (*personne*) peacemaker; (*chose*) pacifier.
pacification [pasifikasjɔ̃] **nf** pacification. **mesures de** ~ pacification *ou* pacificatory measures.
pacifier [pasifje] 7 **vt** *pays* to pacify, bring peace to; (*fig*) *esprits* to pacify.
pacifique [pasifik] 1 **adj** a *coexistence, manifestation, règlement* peaceful; *humeur* peaceable; *personne, peuple* peace-loving, peaceable; *mesure, intention* pacific. **utilisé à des fins ~s** used for peaceful purposes. b (*Géog*) Pacific. 2 **nm** (*Géog*) **le P~** the Pacific; **îles du P~** Pacific Islands.
pacifiquement [pasifikmɑ̃] **adv** (*voir* **pacifique**) peacefully; peaceably; pacifically.
pacifisme [pasifism] **nm** pacifism.
pacifiste [pasifist] 1 **nmf** pacifist. 2 **adj** *doctrine* pacifistic, pacifist. **manifestation** ~ (*en faveur de la paix*) peace march *ou* demonstration.
pack [pak] **nm** a (*Rugby*) pack. b (*Comm*) pack. ~ **de bière/yaourts** pack of beer/yoghurts.
pacotille [pakɔtij] **nf** a (*de mauvaise qualité*) cheap junk *ou* trash, cheap and nasty goods; (*clinquant*) showy stuff. (*péj*) **c'est de la** ~ it's rubbishy stuff, it's cheap rubbish; **meubles/bijoux de** ~ cheap(-jack) furniture/jewellery. b (*Hist*) *goods carried free of freightage.*
pacson‡ [paksɔ̃] **nm** packet.
pacte [pakt] **nm** pact, treaty. ~ **d'alliance** treaty of alliance; ~ **de non-agression** non-aggression pact; **faire** *ou* **conclure** *ou* **signer un** ~ **avec** to sign a pact *ou* treaty with; **il a signé un** ~ **avec le Diable** he made a pact with the Devil.
pactiser [paktize] 1 **vt** (*péj*) (*se liguer*) to take sides (*avec* with); (*transiger*) to come to terms (*avec* with). **c'est** ~ **avec le crime** it amounts to supporting crime.
pactole [paktɔl] **nm** (*fig: source de richesses*) gold mine; (**: argent*) fortune. **un bon** ~ a tidy sum* *ou* packet*; **un petit** ~ a tidy little sum*, a small fortune; (*Géog*) **le P~** the Pactolus.
paddock [padɔk] **nm** a *[champ de courses]* paddock. b (*‡: lit*) bed. **aller au** ~ to hit the sack* *ou* the hay*, turn in*.
Padoue [padu] **n** Padua.
paella [paela] **nf** paella.
paf [paf] 1 **excl** (*chute*) bam!; (*gifle*) slap!, wham! 2 **adj inv** (*‡: ivre*) tight*. **complètement** ~ plastered‡.
PAF [paf] 1 **nm** (**abrév de paysage audiovisuel français**) *voir* **paysage.** 2 **nf** (**abrév de police de l'air et des frontières**) *voir* **police.**
pagaie [pagɛ] **nf** paddle.
pagaïe, pagaille [pagaj] **nf** a (*objets en désordre*) mess, shambles (*NonC*); (*cohue, manque d'organisation*) chaos (*NonC*). **quelle** ~ **dans la pièce!** what a mess this room is in!, what a shambles in this room!; **c'est la** ~ **sur les routes/dans le gouvernement!** there is (complete) chaos on the roads/in the government!; **il a mis** *ou* **semé la** ~ **dans mes affaires/dans la réunion** he has messed up all my things/the meeting. b (*beaucoup*) **il y en a en ~*** there are loads* *ou* masses of them.
paganiser [paganize] 1 **vt** to paganize, heathenize.
paganisme [paganism] **nm** paganism, heathenism.
pagaye [pagaj] **nf** = **pagaïe.**
pagayer [pageje] 8 **vi** to paddle.
pagayeur, -euse [pagɛjœʀ, øz] **nm,f** paddler.
page¹ [paʒ] 1 **nf** a (*feuillet*) page; (*fig*) (*passage*) passage, page; (*événement*) page, chapter, episode. **(à la)** ~ **35** (on) page 35; (*Typ*) **belle/fausse** ~ right-hand/left-hand page; **une** ~ **d'écriture** a page of writing; **les plus belles ~s de Corneille** the finest passages of Corneille; **une** ~ **glorieuse de l'histoire de France** a glorious page *ou* chapter in the history of France; **une** ~ **est tournée** a page has been turned; (*Typ*) **mettre en** ~ to make up (into pages); (*Ordin*) ~ **suivante/précédente** page down/up; *voir* **mise², tourner.**
b (*loc*) **être à la** ~ (*mode*) to be up-to-date *ou* with it*; (*actualité*) to keep in touch *ou* up-to-date, keep up with what's new; **ne plus être à la** ~ to be out of touch *ou* behind the times; **mettre qn à la** ~ to put sb in the picture.
2 **comp** ►**page blanche** blank page ►**page-écran** **nf** (**pl pages-écrans**) (*Ordin*) screenful ►**page de garde** flyleaf ►**pages jaunes (de l'annuaire)** yellow pages (*Brit*) ►**page des petites annonces** (*Presse*) small-ads page ►**page de publicité** (*TV, Radio*) commercials ►**page de titre** title page.
page² [paʒ] **nm** (*Hist*) page (boy).
page³‡ [paʒ] **nm, pageot‡** [paʒo] **nm** bed. **se mettre au** ~ to hit the sack* *ou* the hay*, turn in*.
pageoter (se)‡ [paʒɔte] 1 **vpr** to turn in*, hit the sack* *ou* the hay*.
pagination [paʒinasjɔ̃] **nf** (*gén*) pagination; (*Ordin*) paging.
paginer [paʒine] 1 **vt** (*gén*) to paginate; (*Ordin*) to page.
pagne [paɲ] **nm** (*en tissu*) loincloth; (*en paille etc*) grass skirt.
pagode [pagɔd] **nf** pagoda. **manche** ~ pagoda sleeve.
paie [pɛ] **nf** *[militaire]* pay; *[ouvrier]* pay, wages. **jour de** ~ payday; **bulletin** *ou* **feuille de** ~ payslip; **toucher sa** ~ to be paid, get one's wages; (*fig*) **il y a** *ou* **ça fait une** ~ **que nous ne nous sommes pas vus*** it's ages *ou* donkey's years* (*Brit*) since we last saw each other, we haven't seen each other for yonks‡.
paiement [pɛmɑ̃] **nm** payment (*de* for). **faire un** ~ to make a payment; ~ **à la commande** payment *ou* cash with order; ~ **à la livraison** cash on delivery; ~ **comptant** payment in full; ~ **échelonné** payment by *ou* in instalments; ~ **en liquide** cash payment; ~ **par chèque/d'avance** payment by cheque/in advance; ~ **électronique** electronic payment; *voir* **facilité.**
païen, païenne [pajɛ̃, pajɛn] **adj, nm,f** pagan, heathen.
paierie [pɛʀi] **nf**: ~ **(générale)** local office of the treasury (*paying salaries, state bills etc*).
paillage [pɑjaʒ] **nm** mulching.
paillard, e* [pajaʀ, aʀd] **adj** *personne* bawdy, coarse; *histoire* bawdy, lewd, dirty. **chanson ~e** bawdy song.
paillardise [pajaʀdiz] **nf** (*débauche*) bawdiness; (*plaisanterie*) dirty *ou* lewd joke (*ou* story *ou* remark *etc*).
paillasse¹ [pajas] **nf** a (*matelas*) straw mattress. **crever la** ~ **à qn*** to do sb in*. b *[évier]* draining board (*Brit*), drainboard (*US*); *[laboratoire]* (tiled) work surface. c (*†: prostituée*) trollop†.
paillasse² [pajas] **nm** (*clown*) clown.
paillasson [pajasɔ̃] **nm** *[porte]* doormat; (*péj: personne*) doormat (*fig*); (*Agr*) matting; *voir* **clef.**
paille [pɑj] 1 **nf** a straw; (*pour boire*) (drinking) straw. **chapeau/panier de** ~ straw hat/basket; **botte de** ~ bale of straw; **boire avec une** ~ to drink through a straw.
b (*loc*) **être sur la** ~ to be penniless; **mettre sur la** ~ to reduce to poverty; **mourir sur la** ~ to die penniless *ou* in poverty; **voir la** ~ **dans l'œil du prochain (mais pas la poutre dans le sien)** to see the mote in one's neighbour's *ou* one's brother's eye (but not the beam in one's own); **c'est la** ~ **et la poutre** it's the pot calling the kettle black; **2 millions de francs? une ~!*** 2 million francs? that's peanuts!*; *voir* **court¹, feu, homme.**
c (*Tech: défaut*) flaw.
2 **adj inv** straw-coloured.
3 **comp** ►**paille de fer** steel wool ►**paille de riz** straw; **balai en paille de riz** straw broom.

pailler [paje] 1 **vt** *chaise* to put a straw bottom in; *arbre, fraisier* to mulch. **chaise paillée** straw-bottomed chair.
pailleté, e [paj(ə)te] (**ptp de pailleter**) **adj** *robe* sequined. **yeux noisette ~s d'or** hazel eyes speckled with gold.
pailleter [paj(ə)te] 4 **vt** (*gén*) to spangle; *robe* to sew sequins on.
paillette [pajɛt] **nf** a (*Habillement*) sequin, spangle. **corsage à ~s** sequined blouse, blouse with sequins *ou* spangles on it. b *[or]* speck; *[mica, lessive]* flake. **savon en ~s** soapflakes. c *[maquillage]* **~s** glitter (*NonC*).
paillis [paji] **nm** mulch.
paillon [pajɔ̃] **nm** *[bouteille]* straw case *ou* wrapping.
paillote [pajɔt] **nf** straw hut.
pain [pɛ̃] 1 **nm** a (*substance*) bread (*NonC*). **du gros ~** bread sold by weight; **du ~ frais/dur/rassis** fresh/dry/stale bread; **~ de ménage/de boulanger** home-made/baker's bread; (*Rel*) **le ~ et le vin** the bread and wine; **notre ~ quotidien** our daily bread; **mettre qn au ~ sec** to put sb on dry bread.
b (*miche*) loaf. **un ~ (de 2 livres)** a (2-lb) loaf; **un ~ long/rond** a long/round loaf; **2 ~s** two loaves (of bread).
c (*en forme de pain*) *[cire]* bar; *[savon]* bar, cake. (*Culin*) **~ de poisson/de légumes** *etc* fish/vegetable *etc* loaf; **~ de glace** block of ice; **le liquide s'est pris en ~ (dans le congélateur)** the liquid has frozen into a block of ice in the deep-freeze; **~ dermatologique** hypoallergenic cleansing bar.
d (**: gifle*) clip on the ear*.
e (*loc*) **avoir du ~ sur la planche*** to have a lot to do, have a lot on one's plate (*Brit*); **il reste du ~ sur la planche** there's still a lot to do *ou* to be done; **ôter** *ou* **retirer le ~ de la bouche de qn** to take the bread out of sb's mouth; **ôter** *ou* **faire passer le goût du ~ à qn*** to do sb in*; *voir* **bouchée, manger, petit** *etc*.
2 **comp ▸pain azyme** unleavened bread **▸pain bénit** consecrated bread; (*fig*) **c'est pain bénit** it's a godsend (*pour* for) **▸pain bis** brown bread **▸pain brioché** brioche bread; (*miche*) brioche loaf **▸pain brûlé adj inv** deep golden brown **▸pain à cacheter** bar of sealing wax **▸pain de campagne** farmhouse bread; (*miche*) farmhouse loaf **▸pain au chocolat** chocolate-filled pastry **▸pain complet** wholemeal (*Brit*) *ou* wholewheat bread; (*miche*) wholemeal (*Brit*) *ou* wholewheat loaf **▸pain d'épice(s)** *kind of cake made with honey, rye, aniseed etc*, ≃ gingerbread **▸pain de Gênes** sponge cake **▸pain grillé** toast **▸pain de gruau = pain viennois ▸pain au lait** *kind of sweet bun* **▸pain au levain** leavened bread **▸pain de mie** sandwich bread; (*miche*) sandwich loaf **▸pain parisien** *long loaf of bread* **▸pain perdu** French toast **▸pain de plastic** stick of gelignite **▸pain aux raisins** currant (*Brit*) *ou* raisin bun **▸pain de seigle** rye bread; (*miche*) rye loaf **▸pain de son = pain complet ▸pain de sucre** sugar loaf; **montagne en pain de sucre** sugar-loaf mountain; **tête en pain de sucre** egg-shaped head **▸pain viennois** Vienna bread; (*miche*) Vienna loaf.
pair[1] [pɛʀ] **nm** a (*dignitaire*) peer. b (*égaux*) **~s** peers. c (*Fin*) par. **valeur remboursée au ~** stock repayable at par; **cours au ~** par rate. d **travailler au ~** to work in exchange for board and lodging; **jeune fille/jeune homme au ~** au pair girl/boy. e **ces 2 conditions/qualités vont** *ou* **marchent de ~** these 2 conditions/qualities go hand in hand *ou* go together; **ça va de ~ avec** it goes hand in hand with; *voir* **hors**.
pair[2]**, e**[1] [pɛʀ] **adj** *nombre* even. **le côté ~ de la rue** the even-numbers side of the street; **jours ~s** even dates; **jouer ~** to bet on the even numbers.
paire[2] [pɛʀ] **nf** a *[ciseaux, lunettes, tenailles, chaussures]* pair; *[bœufs]* yoke; *[pistolets, pigeons]* brace. **ils forment une ~ d'amis** the two of them are great friends; **une belle ~ d'escrocs** a real pair of crooks; **donner une ~ de gifles à qn** to box sb's ears; **avoir une bonne ~ de joues** to be chubby-cheeked. b (*loc*) **les deux font la ~** they're two of a kind; **ils font la ~ ces deux-là!*** they're a right pair!*; **c'est une autre ~ de manches*** that's another story; **se faire la ~‡** to clear off‡, beat it‡.
pairesse [pɛʀɛs] **nf** peeress.
pairie [peʀi] **nf** peerage.
paisible [pezibl] **adj** a (*sans remous*) peaceful, calm, quiet; (*sans agressivité*) peaceful, peaceable, quiet. **dormir d'un sommeil ~** to be sleeping peacefully. b (*Jur*) untroubled.
paisiblement [pezibləmɑ̃] **adv** (*voir* **paisible**) peacefully; calmly; quietly; peaceably.
paître [pɛtʀ] 57 1 **vi** to graze. **le pâturage où ils font ~ leur troupeau pendant l'été** the pasture where they graze their herd in the summer; **envoyer ~ qn‡** to send sb packing*. 2 **vt** *herbe* to graze on; *feuilles, fruits* to feed on. **~ l'herbe d'un pré** to graze in a meadow.
paix [pɛ] **nf** a (*Mil, Pol*) peace. **~ armée** armed peace; **~ séparée** separate peace agreement; **demander la ~** to sue for peace; **signer la ~** to sign the *ou* a peace treaty; **en temps de ~** in peacetime; **traité/pourparlers de ~** peace treaty/talks; **soldats de la ~** peacekeeping force; **Mouvement pour la ~** Peace Movement; (*Prov*) **si tu veux la ~, prépare la guerre** if you wish to have peace, prepare for war.
b (*état d'accord*) peace. **ramener la ~ entre** to make peace between; **il a fait la ~ avec son frère** he has made his peace with his brother, he and his brother have made it up (*Brit*) *ou* made up (*US*); (*hum*) **être pour la ~ des ménages** to believe in domestic harmony; *voir* **baiser, gardien, juge**.
c (*tranquillité*) peace, quiet; (*silence*) stillness, peacefulness. **tout le monde est sorti, quelle ~ dans la maison!** how peaceful *ou* quiet it is in the house now everyone has gone out!; **est-ce qu'on pourrait avoir la ~?** could we have a bit of peace and quiet? *ou* a bit of hush?* (*Brit*).
d (*calme intérieur*) peace. **la ~ de l'âme** inner peace; (*Rel*) **allez** *ou* **partez en ~** go in peace; (*hum*) **~ à sa mémoire** *ou* **à son âme** *ou* **à ses cendres** God rest his soul; **avoir la conscience en ~, être en ~ avec sa conscience** to have a clear conscience, be at peace with one's conscience; **qu'il repose en ~** may he rest in peace; **laisser qn en ~, laisser la ~ à qn** to leave sb alone *ou* in peace; **fous-moi‡** *ou* **fiche-moi* la ~!** stop pestering me!, clear off!‡; **la ~!** shut up!*, quiet!
Pakistan [pakistɑ̃] **nm** Pakistan.
pakistanais, e [pakistanɛ, ɛz] 1 **adj** Pakistani. 2 **nm,f**: **P~(e)** Pakistani.
PAL [pal] **nm** (**abrév de Phase Alternative Line**) PAL.
pal, pl ~s [pal] **nm** (*Hér*) pale; (*pieu*) stake. **le (supplice du) ~** torture by impalement.
palabrer [palabʀe] 1 **vi** (*parlementer*) to palaver, argue endlessly; (*bavarder*) to chat, waffle on* (*Brit*).
palabres [palabʀ] **nmpl ou nfpl** palaver, never-ending discussions.
palace [palas] **nm** luxury hotel.
paladin [paladɛ̃] **nm** paladin.
palais [palɛ] 1 **nm** a (*édifice*) palace; *voir* **révolution**. b (*Jur*) law courts. **en argot du P~, en termes de P~** in legal parlance. c (*Anat*) palate. **~ dur/mou** hard/soft palate; **avoir le ~ desséché** to be parched, be dying of thirst; (*fig*) **avoir le ~ fin** to have a delicate palate; (*Méd*) **~ fendu** cleft palate; *voir* **flatter, voile**[2]. 2 **comp ▸le palais-bourbon** *the seat of the French National Assembly* **▸le Palais Brogniard** the Paris Stock Exchange **▸palais des expositions** exhibition centre **▸le palais de Justice** the Law Courts **▸le palais du Luxembourg** *the seat of the French Senate* **▸palais des sports** sports stadium.
palan [palɑ̃] **nm** hoist.
palanque [palɑ̃k] **nf** stockade.
palanquin [palɑ̃kɛ̃] **nm** palanquin, palankeen.
palatal, e, mpl -aux [palatal, o] 1 **adj** (*Ling*) *consonne* palatal (*épith*); *voyelle* front (*épith*); (*Anat*) palatal. 2 **palatale nf** (*consonne*) palatal consonant; (*voyelle*) front vowel.
palatalisation [palatalizasjɔ̃] **nf** palatalization.
palataliser [palatalize] 1 **vt** to palatalize.
palatin, e [palatɛ̃, in] 1 **adj** a (*Hist*) Palatine. **le Comte/l'Électeur ~** the Count/Elector Palatine. b (*Géog*) **le (mont) P~** the Palatine Hill. 2 **nm** (*Hist*) palatine.
Palatinat [palatina] **nm**: **le ~** the Palatinate.
pale [pal] **nf** *[hélice, rame]* blade; *[roue, écluse]* paddle.
pâle [pɑl] **adj** a *teint, personne* pale; (*maladif*) pallid, pale. **~ comme un linge** as white as a sheet; **~ comme la mort** deathly pale *ou* white; **~ de peur** white with fear; **~ de colère** white *ou* livid with anger; **se faire porter ~‡** to report *ou* go* sick; *voir* **visage**. b *lueur* pale, weak, faint; *couleur, soleil, ciel* pale. c *style* weak; *imitation* pale, poor; *sourire* faint, wan. (*péj*) **un ~ crétin** a downright *ou* an utter fool.
palefrenier [palfʀənje] **nm** *[auberge]* ostler; *[château]* groom.
palefroi [palfʀwa] **nm** (*Hist*) palfrey.
paléochrétien, -ienne [paleokʀetjɛ̃, jɛn] **adj** early Christian.
paléographe [paleɔgʀaf] **nmf** paleographer.
paléographie [paleɔgʀafi] **nf** paleography.
paléographique [paleɔgʀafik] **adj** paleographic(al).
paléolithique [paleɔlitik] 1 **adj** Paleolithic. 2 **nm** Paleolithic (age).
paléomagnétisme [paleomaɲetism] **nm** paleomagnetism.
paléontologie [paleɔ̃tɔlɔʒi] **nf** paleontology.
paléontologique [paleɔ̃tɔlɔʒik] **adj** paleontologic(al).
paléontologiste [paleɔ̃tɔlɔʒist] **nmf**, **paléontologue** [paleɔ̃tɔlɔg] **nmf** paleontologist.
paléozoïque [paleozɔik] **adj** Paleozoic.
Palerme [palɛʀm] **n** Palermo.
paleron [palʀɔ̃] **nm** (*Boucherie*) chuck.
Palestine [palɛstin] **nf** Palestine.
palestinien, -ienne [palɛstinjɛ̃, jɛn] 1 **adj** Palestinian. 2 **nm,f**: **P~(ne)** Palestinian.
palet [palɛ] **nm** (*gén*) (metal *ou* stone) disc; *[hockey]* puck.
paletot [palto] **nm** (thick) cardigan. **il m'est tombé** *ou* **m'a sauté sur le ~‡** he jumped on me.
palette [palɛt] **nf** a (*Peinture: lit, fig*) palette. b (*Boucherie*) shoulder. c (*aube de roue*) paddle; (*battoir à linge*) beetle; (*Manutention, Constr*) pallet. d *[produits, prestations]* range.
palétuvier [paletyvje] **nm** mangrove.
pâleur [pɑlœʀ] **nf** *[teint]* paleness; (*maladive*) pallor, paleness; *[couleur, ciel]* paleness.
pâlichon, -onne* [pɑliʃɔ̃, ɔn] **adj** *personne* (a bit) pale *ou* peaky* (*Brit*); *soleil* sorry-looking, weakish, watery.
palier [palje] **nm** a *[escalier]* landing. **être voisins de ~, habiter sur le même ~** to live on the same floor. b (*fig: étape*) stage; *[graphique]*

plateau. **les prix ont atteint un nouveau ~** prices have found a *ou* risen to a new level; **procéder par ~s** to proceed in stages. c *[route, voie]* level, flat. (*Aviat*) **voler en ~** to fly level. d (*Tech*) bearing. **~ de butée** thrust bearing.

palière [paljɛʀ] adj f *voir* **marche, porte.**

palinodie [palinɔdi] nf (*Littérat*) palinode. (*fig*) ~s recantations.

pâlir [pɑliʀ] 2 1 vi *[personne]* to turn *ou* go pale; *[lumière, étoiles]* to grow dim; *[ciel]* to grow pale; *[couleur, encre]* to fade; (*fig*) *[souvenir]* to fade (away), dim; *[gloire]* to dim, fade. **~ de colère** to go *ou* turn pale *ou* white *ou* livid with anger; **~ de crainte** to turn pale *ou* white with fear, blench (with fear); **faire ~ qn (d'envie)** to make sb green with envy.
2 vt to turn pale.

palissade [palisad] nf *[pieux]* fence; *[planches]* boarding; (*Mil*) stockade.

palissandre [palisɑ̃dʀ] nm rosewood.

pâlissant, e [pɑlisɑ̃, ɑ̃t] adj *teinte, lumière* wan, fading.

palladium [paladjɔm] nm (*Chim, fig*) palladium.

Pallas Athena [palasatena] nf Pallas Athena.

palliatif, -ive [paljatif, iv] 1 adj (*Méd*) palliative. 2 nm (*Méd*) palliative (*à* to, for); (*mesure*) palliative, stopgap measure; (*réparation sommaire*) makeshift repair.

pallier [palje] 7 1 vt *difficulté* to overcome, get round; *manque* to offset, compensate for, make up for; (*littér*) *défaut* to palliate, disguise. 2 **pallier à** vt indir *difficulté, manque* = **pallier.**

palmarès [palmaʀɛs] nm (*Scol*) prize list; (*Sport*) (list of) medal winners; *[athlète etc]* record (of achievements). **il a de nombreux exploits à son ~** he has a number of exploits to his credit; **tu peux ajouter cela à ton ~** you can add that to your record of achievements; **le ~ des universités françaises** *the list of top French universities;* **le ~ des émissions les plus écoutées** (the list of) the most popular programmes.

palme [palm] nf a (*Archit, Bot*) palm leaf; (*symbole*) palm (*de* of). **vin/huile de ~** palm wine/oil; **~s académiques** *decoration for services to education in France;* (*lit, fig*) **la ~ revient à ...** the prize goes to ...; **disputer la ~ à qn** to compete with sb; **remporter la ~** to win, be the winner; **pour ce qui est des bêtises il remporte la ~** when it comes to being silly he wins hands down *ou* he takes the biscuit* (*Brit*) *ou* the cake* (*US*); (*Ciné*) **la P~ d'or** the Palme d'or; **la ~ du martyre** the crown of martyrdom; (*Mil*) **décoration avec ~** ≃ decoration with a bar. b *[nageur]* flipper.

palmé, e [palme] adj *feuille* palmate (*SPÉC*); *patte* webbed; *oiseau* webfooted, palmate (*SPÉC*).

palmer [palmɛʀ] nm (*Tech*) micrometer.

palmeraie [palmәʀɛ] nf palm grove.

palmier [palmje] nm a (*Bot*) palm tree. **~-dattier** date palm. b (*gâteau*) *heart-shaped biscuit made of flaky pastry.*

palmipède [palmipɛd] 1 nm palmiped (*SPÉC*). 2 adj webfooted.

palmiste [palmist] adj m *voir* **chou**[1].

palois, e [palwa, waz] 1 adj of *ou* from Pau. 2 nm,f: **P~(e)** inhabitant *ou* native of Pau.

palombe [palɔ̃b] nf woodpigeon, ringdove.

palonnier [palɔnje] nm (*Aviat*) rudder bar; (*Aut*) compensator; *[cheval]* swingletree.

palot‡ [palo] nm (*baiser*) kiss.

pâlot, -otte* [pɑlo, ɔt] adj *personne* (a bit) pale *ou* peaky* (*Brit*).

palourde [paluʀd] nf clam.

palpable [palpabl] adj (*lit, fig*) palpable.

palpation [palpasjɔ̃] nf palpation.

palper [palpe] 1 vt *objet* to feel, finger; (*Méd*) to palpate; (‡) *argent* (*recevoir*) to get; (*gagner*) to make. **qu'est-ce qu'il a dû ~ (comme argent)!**‡ he must have made a fortune *ou* a mint out of it!*

palpeur [palpœʀ] nm *[chaleur, lumière]* sensor.

palpitant, e [palpitɑ̃, ɑ̃t] 1 adj a (*passionnant*) *livre, moment* thrilling, exciting; *vie* exciting. **d'un intérêt ~, ~ d'intérêt** terribly exciting, thrilling; **être ~ d'émotion** to be quivering with emotion. b *chair* quivering (*épith*), wobbly; *blessure* throbbing (*épith*). 2 nm (‡: *cœur*) ticker*.

palpitation [palpitasjɔ̃] nf *[cœur]* racing (*NonC*); *[paupières]* fluttering (*NonC*); *[lumière, flamme]* quivering (*NonC*). (*Méd*) **avoir des ~s** to have palpitations; (*fig*) **ça m'a donné des ~s** it gave me quite a turn.

palpiter [palpite] 1 vi *[cœur]* (*battre*) to beat; (*battre rapidement*) to race; *[paupières]* to flutter; *[cadavre]* to twitch; *[chair]* to quiver; *[blessure]* to throb; *[narines, lumière, flamme]* to quiver.

paltoquet [paltɔkɛ] nm (*littér péj*) (*rustre*) boor; (*freluquet*) pompous fool.

paluche‡ [palyʃ] nf (*main*) hand, paw*. **serrer la ~ à qn** to shake hands with sb, shake sb's hand.

paludéen, -enne [palydeɛ̃, ɛn] adj (*gén, Méd*) paludal.

paludisme [palydism] nm paludism (*SPÉC*), malaria.

palustre [palystʀ] adj (*gén, Méd*) paludal.

pâmer (se) [pɑme] 1 vpr (*littér*) to swoon†. (*fig*) **se ~ *ou* être pâmé devant qch** to swoon *ou* be in raptures *ou* be ecstatic over sth; **se ~ d'admiration/d'amour** to be overcome with admiration/love; **se ~ de rire** to be convulsed with laughter.

pâmoison [pɑmwazɔ̃] nf (*littér, hum*) swoon. (*lit*) **tomber en ~** to swoon†; (*fig*) **tomber en ~ devant un tableau** to swoon over *ou* go into raptures over a painting.

pampa [pɑ̃pa] nf pampas (*pl*).

pamphlet [pɑ̃flɛ] nm satirical tract, lampoon.

pamphlétaire [pɑ̃fletɛʀ] nmf lampoonist.

pampille [pɑ̃pij] nf *[lustre]* pendant.

pamplemousse [pɑ̃plәmus] nm grapefruit.

pamplemoussier [pɑ̃plәmusje] nm grapefruit tree.

pampre [pɑ̃pʀ] nm (*littér*) vine branch.

Pan [pɑ̃] nm Pan.

pan[1] [pɑ̃] 1 nm (*lit, fig: morceau*) piece; (*basque*) tail; (*face, côté*) side, face; *[toit]* side; *[nappe]* overhanging part. **~ de rideau** curtain; **un ~ de ma vie s'est écroulé** a chapter of my life has come to an end.
2 comp ▸ **pan de chemise** shirt tail; **se promener en pans de chemise** to wander about in (one's) shirt-tails *ou* with just one's shirt on ▸ **pan de ciel** patch of sky ▸ **pan coupé** cut-off corner (*of room*); **maison en pan coupé** house with a slanting *ou* cut-off corner; **mur en pan coupé** wall with a cut-off corner ▸ **pan de mur** (section of) wall.

pan[2] [pɑ̃] excl *[coup de feu]* bang!; *[gifle]* slap!, whack!; (*langage enfantin*) **je vais te faire ~ ~ (les fesses)** you'll get your bottom smacked.

panacée [panase] nf panacea, cure-all.

panachage [panaʃaʒ] nm a (*Pol*) *voting for candidates from different parties instead of for the set list of one party.* b (*mélange*) *[couleurs]* combination; *[programmes, plats]* selection.

panache [panaʃ] nm a (*plumet*) plume, panache. (*fig*) **~ de fumée** plume of smoke.
b (*héroïsme*) gallantry. **se battre avec ~** to fight gallantly, put up a spirited resistance.
c (*éclat*) *[discours, style]* panache.

panaché, e [panaʃe] (ptp de **panacher**) 1 adj a *fleur, feuilles* variegated, many-coloured. **pétunias blancs ~s de rouge** white petunias with splashes of red *ou* with red stripes.
b *foule, assortiment* motley; *glace* two- *ou* mixed-flavour (*épith*); *salade* mixed. **bière ~e** shandy.
2 nm (*boisson*) shandy.

panacher [panaʃe] 1 vt (*mélanger*) *couleurs, fleurs* to put together; *genres* to mix, combine; *plantes* to cross; *biscuits, bonbons* to make an assortment *ou* a selection of; (*varier*) *programmes, exercices* to vary. **dois-je prendre l'un des menus ou puis-je ~ (les plats)?** do I have to take a set menu or can I make my own selection (of courses)?; **~ une liste électorale** *to vote for candidates from different parties instead of for the set list of one party.*

panachure [panaʃyʀ] nf (*gén pl*) motley colours.

panade [panad] nf bread soup. (*fig*) **être dans la ~**‡ (*avoir des ennuis*) to be in the soup*, be in a sticky situation; (*avoir des ennuis d'argent*) to be on one's beam-ends* (*Brit*), be down to one's last dollar (*US*).

panafricain, e [panafʀikɛ̃, ɛn] adj Pan-African.

panafricanisme [panafʀikanism] nm Pan-Africanism.

panais [panɛ] nm parsnip.

panama [panama] nm a (*Géog*) **P~** Panama. b (*chapeau*) Panama hat.

panaméen, -enne [panameɛ̃, ɛn] 1 adj Panamanian. 2 nm,f: **P~(ne)** Panamanian.

panaméricain, e [panameʀikɛ̃, ɛn] adj Pan-American. **route ~e** Pan-American Highway.

panaméricanisme [panameʀikanism] nm Pan-Americanism.

panarabe [panaʀab] adj Pan-Arab(ic).

panarabisme [panaʀabism] nm Pan-Arabism.

panard‡ [panaʀ] nm foot, hoof‡. **~s** plates of meat‡ (*Brit*), hooves‡. **c'est le ~!** it's magic‡ *ou* ace‡!

panaris [panaʀi] nm whitlow.

pan-bagnat, pl **pans-bagnats** [pɑ̃baɲa] nm open sandwich (*with tomatoes, lettuce, hard-boiled eggs, tuna and anchovies, seasoned with olive oil*).

pancarte [pɑ̃kaʀt] nf (*gén*) sign, notice; (*Aut*) (road)sign; *[manifestant]* placard.

pancréas [pɑ̃kʀeɑs] nm pancreas.

pancréatique [pɑ̃kʀeatik] adj pancreatic.

panda [pɑ̃da] nm panda.

pandit [pɑ̃di(t)] nm pandit, pundit.

Pandore [pɑ̃dɔʀ] nf (*Myth*) Pandora. **boîte de ~** Pandora's box.

pandore*† [pɑ̃dɔʀ] nm (*gendarme*) cop*, gendarme.

panégyrique [paneʒiʀik] nm (*frm*) panegyric. **faire le ~ de qn** to extol sb's merits; (*fig hum*) **quel ~ de sa belle-mère il a fait!** what a tribute to pay to his mother-in-law!

panégyriste [paneʒiʀist] nmf panegyrist.

panel [panɛl] nm (*jury*) panel; (*échantillon*) sample group.

paner [pane] 1 vt to coat *ou* dress with breadcrumbs. **escalope panée** escalope (coated) with breadcrumbs, breaded escalope.

pangermanisme [pɑ̃ʒɛʀmanism] nm Pan-Germanism.

pangermaniste [pɑ̃ʒɛʀmanist] 1 nmf Pan-German. 2 adj Pan-

German(ic).
panhellénique [panelenik] **adj** Panhellenic.
panhellénisme [panelenism] **nm** Panhellenism.
panier [panje] 1 **nm** a (*gén, Sport*) basket; (*contenu*) basket(ful). (*fig*) **ils sont tous à mettre dans le même ~** they are all much of a muchness (*Brit*), there's not much to choose between them; (*fig*) **ne les mets pas tous dans le même ~** don't lump them all together; **mettre** *ou* **jeter au ~** to throw out, throw in the wastepaper basket; (*Sport*) **réussir** *ou* **marquer un ~** to score *ou* make a basket; *voir* **anse, dessus, œuf.**
b (*Phot: pour diapositives*) magazine. **~ circulaire** rotary magazine.
c (*vêtement*) pannier. **robe à ~s** dress with panniers.
2 **comp ▸panier à bouteilles** bottle-carrier **▸panier de crabes:** (*fig*) **c'est un panier de crabes** they're always fighting among themselves, they're always at each other's throats **▸panier à frites** chip basket (*Brit*), fry basket (*US*) **▸panier à linge** linen basket **▸le panier de la ménagère** (*Écon*) the housewife's shopping basket **▸panier à ouvrage** workbasket **▸panier percé:** (*fig*) **c'est un panier percé** he's a spendthrift **▸panier à provisions** shopping basket **▸panier-repas nm (pl paniers-repas)** packed lunch **▸panier à salade** (*Culin*) salad shaker *ou* basket; (* *fig*) police van, Black Maria* (*Brit*), paddy waggon‡ (*US*).
panière [panjɛʀ] **nf** large basket.
panifiable [panifjabl] **adj** (suitable for) bread-making (*épith*).
panification [panifikasjɔ̃] **nf** bread-making.
panifier [panifje] 7 **vt** to make bread from.
paniquant, e* [panikɑ̃, ɑ̃t] **adj** scary*.
paniquard* [panikaʀ] **nm** (*péj*) coward, yellow belly‡.
panique [panik] 1 **nf** panic. **pris de ~** panic-stricken; **un vent de ~** a wave of panic; **c'est la ~!** everything's in a state of panic *ou* chaos!; **pas de ~!*** no need to panic!; **c'était la ~ générale*** it was panic stations* *ou* panic all round*. 2 **adj** panic. **terreur** *ou* **peur ~** panic fear.
paniquer* [panike] 1 1 **vt: ~ qn** to put the wind up sb*, give sb a scare; **il a essayé de me ~** he tried to put the wind up me*. 2 **vi, se paniquer vpr** to panic, get the wind up*. **commencer à ~** *ou* **à se ~** to get panicky; **il n'a pas paniqué, il ne s'est pas paniqué** he didn't panic, he kept his head; **être paniqué** to be in a panic; **être paniqué à l'idée de faire qch** to be scared stiff at the idea of doing sth.
panislamique [panislamik] **adj** Panislamic.
panislamisme [panislamism] **nm** Panislamism.
panne¹ [pan] **nf** a (*incident*) breakdown. *[machine]* **être** *ou* **tomber en ~** to break down; **je suis tombé en ~ (de moteur)** my car has broken down; **je suis tombé en ~ sèche** *ou* **en ~ d'essence** I have run out of petrol (*Brit*) *ou* gas (*US*); **je suis en ~ de réfrigérateur/radio** my refrigerator/radio is broken; **~ de courant** *ou* **d'électricité** power *ou* electrical failure; *[avion, voiture de course]* **~ de moteur** engine failure; **il n'a pas trouvé la ~** he couldn't find the fault *ou* problem; (*hum: sexuellement*) **il a eu une ~** he couldn't rise to the occasion (*hum*); **il m'a fait le coup de la ~** he tried on the old trick about the car breaking down.
b (* *fig*) **être en ~** *[orateur]* to be out of words, be *ou* get stuck; **je suis en ~ de cigarettes/d'idées** I've run out of *ou* I'm out of* cigarettes/ideas; **rester en ~ devant une difficulté** to be stumped* (by a problem), stick at a difficulty; **les travaux sont en ~** work has come to a halt; **ce projet est en ~** work is at a standstill *ou* has come to a halt on this project; **laisser qn en ~** to leave sb in the lurch, let sb down.
c (*Naut*) **mettre en ~** to bring to.
panne² [pan] **nf** a (*graisse*) fat. b (*étoffe*) panne. c (*poutre*) purlin.
panneau, **pl ~x** [pano] 1 **nm** (*Art, Couture, Menuiserie*) panel; (*écriteau*) sign, notice; (*Constr*) prefabricated section; (*Basketball*) backboard. **les ~x qui ornent la salle** the panelling round the room; **à ~x** panelled; (*fig*) **tomber** *ou* **donner dans le ~*** to fall *ou* walk (right) into the trap, fall for it*. 2 **comp ▸panneau d'affichage** (*pour résultats etc*) notice board (*Brit*), bulletin board (*US*); (*pour publicité*) hoarding (*Brit*), billboard (*US*) **▸panneau d'écoutille** (*Naut*) hatch cover **▸panneaux électoraux** *notice boards for election posters* **▸panneau indicateur** signpost **▸panneau de particules** chipboard (*NonC*) **▸panneau publicitaire, panneau-réclame nm (pl panneaux-réclame)** hoarding (*Brit*), billboard (*US*) **▸panneau de signalisation** roadsign **▸panneau solaire** solar panel **▸panneau de stop** stop sign **▸panneau vitré** glass panel.
panonceau, **pl ~x** [panɔ̃so] **nm** (*plaque de médecin*) plaque; (*écriteau publicitaire*) sign.
panoplie [panɔpli] **nf** a (*jouet*) outfit. **~ d'Indien** Red Indian outfit; **~ d'armes** (*sur un mur*) display of weapons; *[gangster, policier]* armoury; (*hum: instruments*) **il a sorti toute sa ~** he brought out all his equipment. b (*fig: gamme*) *[arguments, médicaments, sanctions]* range; *[mesures]* package, range.
panorama [panɔʀama] **nm** (*lit, fig*) panorama.
panoramique [panɔʀamik] 1 **adj** *vue* panoramic; *restaurant* with a panoramic view; *carrosserie* with panoramic *ou* wraparound windows; *car, voiture* with wraparound windscreen. (*Ciné*) **écran ~** wide *ou* panoramic screen; **wagon ~** observation car. 2 **nm** (*Ciné, TV*) panoramic shot.
panse [pɑ̃s] **nf** *[ruminant]* paunch; (*) *[personne]* paunch, belly‡; (*fig*) *[bouteille]* belly. **s'en mettre plein la ~*** to stuff o.s.* *ou* one's face*; **je me suis bien rempli la ~*** I've eaten my fill, I'm full to busting*; **manger à s'en faire crever** *ou* **éclater la ~*** to eat until one's fit to burst, stuff o.s.* *ou* one's face*.
pansement [pɑ̃smɑ̃] **nm** (*voir* **panser**) dressing; bandage; plaster. **faire un ~** to dress a wound; **refaire un ~** to put a clean dressing on a wound; **(tout) couvert de ~s** (all) bandaged up; **~ adhésif** sticking *ou* adhesive plaster (*Brit*), Band Aid ® (*US*).
panser [pɑ̃se] 1 **vt** a (*Méd*) *dent* to fill temporarily; *plaie* to dress; *bras, jambe* to put a dressing on; (*avec un bandage*) to bandage; (*avec du sparadrap*) to put a plaster (*Brit*) *ou* a Band Aid ® (*US*) on; *blessé* to dress the wounds of. (*fig*) **le temps panse les blessures (du cœur)** time heals the wounds of the heart; (*fig*) **~ ses blessures** to lick one's wounds. b *cheval* to groom.
panseur, euse [pɑ̃sœʀ, øz] **nm,f** *nurse who applies bandages etc.*
panslavisme [pɑ̃slavism] **nm** Pan-Slavism.
panslaviste [pɑ̃slavist] 1 **adj** Pan-Slav(onic). 2 **nmf** Pan-Slavist.
pansu, e [pɑ̃sy] **adj** *personne* potbellied, paunchy; *vase* potbellied.
pantagruélique [pɑ̃tagʀyelik] **adj** pantagruelian.
pantalon [pɑ̃talɔ̃] **nm** a (*Habillement*) *[homme]* (pair of) trousers (*Brit*), (pair of) pants (*US*); *[femme]* (pair of) trousers (*Brit*) *ou* pants (*US*) *ou* slacks; (†: *sous-vêtement*) knickers. **un ~ neuf** a new pair of trousers (*Brit*) *ou* pants (*US*), new trousers (*Brit*) *ou* pants (*US*); **10 ~s** 10 pairs of trousers (*Brit*) *ou* pants (*US*); **~ court** short trousers *ou* pants; **~ de pyjama** pyjama (*Brit*) *ou* pajama (*US*) bottoms; **~ de ski** ski pants; *voir* **porter.** b (*Théât*) **P~** Pantaloon.
pantalonnade [pɑ̃talɔnad] **nf** (*Théât*) knockabout farce (*Brit*), slapstick comedy; (*péj*) tomfoolery (*NonC*).
pantelant, e [pɑ̃t(ə)lɑ̃, ɑ̃t] **adj** *personne* gasping for breath (*attrib*), panting (*attrib*); *gorge* heaving; *cadavre, animal* twitching; *chair* throbbing, heaving. **~ de peur** panting with fear.
panthéisme [pɑ̃teism] **nm** pantheism.
panthéiste [pɑ̃teist] 1 **nmf** pantheist. 2 **adj** pantheistic.
panthéon [pɑ̃teɔ̃] **nm** pantheon.
panthère [pɑ̃tɛʀ] **nf** panther. **sa femme est une vraie ~** his wife is a real hellcat*; (*Zool*) **~ noire** black panther; (*Hist US*) **P~s noires** Black Panthers.
pantin [pɑ̃tɛ̃] **nm** (*jouet*) jumping jack; (*péj: personne*) puppet.
pantographe [pɑ̃tɔgʀaf] **nm** pantograph.
pantois [pɑ̃twa] **adj m** stunned. **j'en suis resté ~** I was stunned.
pantomime [pɑ̃tɔmim] **nf** (*art*) mime (*NonC*); (*spectacle*) mime show; (*fig*) pantomime, scene, fuss (*NonC*). **il nous a fait la ~ pour avoir un vélo** he made a great pantomime *ou* fuss about having a bike.
pantouflard, e* [pɑ̃tuflaʀ, aʀd] 1 **adj** *personne, caractère* stay-at-home (*épith*); *vie* quiet, uneventful, humdrum. 2 **nm,f** stay-at-home.
pantoufle [pɑ̃tufl] **nf** slipper. **il était en ~s** he was in his slippers.
pantoufler [pɑ̃tufle] 1 **vi** a (*arg Fonctionnaire*) to transfer to the private sector. b (*: *paresser*) to laze *ou* lounge around (at home).
panure [panyʀ] **nf** breadcrumb dressing, breadcrumbs.
Panurge [panyʀʒ] **nm** *voir* **mouton.**
PAO [peao] (**abrév de publication assistée par ordinateur**) DTP.
paon [pɑ̃] **nm** peacock. **fier** *ou* **vaniteux comme un ~** proud as a peacock; *voir* **parer¹.**
paonne [pan] **nf** peahen.
papa [papa] **nm** (*gén*) dad; (*langage enfantin*) daddy; (*langage de bébé*) dada. **la musique/les voitures de ~*** old-fashioned music/cars; **c'est vraiment l'usine de ~!*** this factory is really antiquated! *ou* behind the times!; **conduire à la ~*** to potter along, drive at a snail's pace; **alors ~, tu avances?*** come on grandad, get a move on*; **jouer au ~ et à la maman** to play mummies and daddies; **c'est un ~ gâteau** he spoils his (grand)children; **~-poule** doting father; *voir* **fils.**
papal, e, **mpl -aux** [papal, o] **adj** papal.
papauté [papote] **nf** papacy.
papaye [papaj] **nf** pawpaw, papaya.
papayer [papaje] **nm** pawpaw *ou* papaya (tree).
pape [pap] **nm** pope; (*fig*) *[école littéraire etc]* leading light. **le ~ Jean XXIII** Pope John XXIII; **du ~** papal.
Papeete [papɛt] **n** Papeete.
papelard¹* [paplaʀ] **nm** (*feuille*) (bit of) paper; (*article de journal*) article; (*journal*) paper. (*papiers d'identité*) **~s** papers.
papelard², e [paplaʀ, aʀd] **adj** (*littér*) suave, smarmy (*Brit*).
papelardise [paplaʀdiz] **nf** (*littér*) suavity, suaveness, smarminess (*Brit*).
paperasse [papʀas] **nf** (*péj*) **~(s)** (wretched) papers; (*à remplir*) forms; **je n'ai pas le temps de lire toutes les ~s** *ou* **toute la ~ qu'on m'envoie** I've no time to read all the bumf‡ (*Brit*) *ou* stuff* that people send me; **j'ai des ~s** *ou* **de la ~ à faire** I've some (wretched) paperwork to do.
paperasserie [papʀasʀi] **nf** (*péj*) (*à lire*) bumf‡ (*Brit*); (*à remplir*) forms; (*tracasserie, routine*) red tape. **il y a trop de ~ à faire dans ce travail** there's too much paperwork in this job.
paperassier, -ière [papʀasje, jɛʀ] (*péj*) 1 **adj** *personne* fond of red tape *ou* paperwork; *administration* cluttered with red tape (*attrib*), obsessed with form filling (*attrib*). 2 **nm,f** (*bureaucrate*) penpusher

(*péj*). **quel ~!** he's forever poring over his old papers *ou* scribbling away on his papers.

papeterie [papɛtʀi] **nf** (*magasin*) stationer's (shop); (*fourniture*) stationery; (*fabrique*) paper mill; (*fabrication*) paper-making industry; (*commerce*) stationery trade.

papetier, -ière [pap(ə)tje, jɛʀ] **nm,f** (*vendeur*) stationer; (*fabricant*) paper-maker. **~-libraire** stationer and bookseller.

papi [papi] **nm** (*langage enfantin*) grandad*, grandpa*; (*: *vieil homme*) old guy*.

papier [papje] 1 **nm** a (*matière*) paper. **morceau/bout de ~** piece/bit *ou* slip of paper; **de** *ou* **en ~** paper (*épith*); **mets-moi cela sur ~** (*pour ne pas oublier*) write that down for me; (*pour confirmation écrite*) let me have that in writing; **sur le ~** (*en projet, théoriquement*) on paper; **jeter une idée sur le ~** to jot down an idea; *voir* **noircir, pâte.**

b (*feuille écrite*) paper; (*feuille blanche*) sheet *ou* piece of paper; (*Presse: article*) article. **~ personnels/d'affaires** personal/business papers; **un ~ à signer/à remplir** a form to be signed/filled in; (*Presse: article*) **faire un ~ sur qn** to do an article on sb.

c (*emballage*) paper; *[bonbon]* paper, wrapper.

d **~s (d'identité)** (identity) papers; **vos ~s, s'il vous plaît!** could I see your identity papers, please?; (*Aut*) may I see your driving licence (*Brit*) *ou* driver's license (*US*), please?; **ses ~s ne sont pas en règle** his papers are not in order; (*fig*) **rayez cela de vos ~s!** you can forget about that!; *voir* **petit.**

2 **comp** ►**papier aluminium** aluminium (*Brit*) *ou* aluminum (*US*) foil, tinfoil ►**papier d'argent** silver foil *ou* paper, tinfoil ►**papier d'Arménie** incense paper ►**papier bible** bible paper, India paper ►**papier (de) brouillon** rough paper ►**papier buvard** blotting paper ►**papier cadeau** gift wrap, wrapping paper ►**papier calque** tracing paper ►**papier carbone** carbon paper ►**papier chiffon** rag paper ►**papier à cigarettes** cigarette paper ►**papier collant** gummed paper; (*transparent*) Sellotape ® (*Brit*), Scotch tape (*US*), sticky tape ►**papier collé** (*Art*) (paper) collage ►**papier en continu** (*Ordin*) continuous stationery ►**papier couché** art paper ►**papier crépon** crêpe paper ►**papier cul**‡ bog paper‡ (*Brit*), TP* (*US*) ►**papier à dessin** drawing paper ►**papier d'emballage** wrapping paper ►**papier doré** gold paper ►**papier-émeri** emery paper ►**papier à en-tête** headed notepaper, letterhead (*Comm*) ►**papier d'étain** tinfoil, silver paper ►**papier filtre** filter paper ►**papier glacé** glazed paper ►**papiers gras** (*ordures*) litter, rubbish ►**papier hygiénique** toilet paper ►**papier journal** newspaper ►**papier kraft** ® brown wrapping paper ►**papier à lettres** writing paper, notepaper ►**papier libre** plain unheaded paper ►**papier mâché** papier-mâché; (*fig*) **mine de papier mâché** pasty complexion ►**papier machine** typing paper ►**papiers militaires** army papers ►**papier millimétré** graph paper ►**papier ministre** official paper (*approx quarto size*); **écrit sur papier ministre** written on official paper ►**papier monnaie** paper money ►**papier à musique** manuscript (*Brit*) *ou* music (*US*) paper ►**papier paraffiné** (*gén*) wax paper; (*Culin*) greaseproof (*Brit*) *ou* wax (*US*) paper ►**papier peint** wallpaper ►**papier pelure** India paper ►**papier sensible** (*Phot*) bromide paper ►**papier de soie** tissue paper ►**papier sulfurisé** = **papier paraffiné** ►**papier timbré** stamped paper ►**papier toilette** toilet paper ►**papier de tournesol** litmus paper ►**papier de verre** glass-paper, sandpaper.

papille [papij] **nf** papilla. **~s gustatives** taste buds.

papillon [papijɔ̃] **nm** (*insecte*) butterfly; (*fig: personne*) fickle person; (*Tech: écrou*) wing *ou* butterfly nut; (*: *contravention*) (parking) ticket; (*autocollant*) sticker. (*nage*) **(brasse) ~** butterfly (stroke); **~ de nuit** moth; (*Aut*) **~ des gaz** throttle valve; *voir* **minute, nœud.**

papillonnant, e [papijɔnɑ̃, ɑ̃t] **adj** *personne* fickle(-minded). **esprit ~** butterfly mind.

papillonnement [papijɔnmɑ̃] **nm** (*voir* **papillonner**) flitting about *ou* around; chopping and changing (*Brit*), hopping around (from one thing to another).

papillonner [papijɔne] 1 **vi** (*entre personnes, objets*) to flit about *ou* around (*entre* between); (*entre activités diverses*) to chop and change (*Brit*) (*entre* between), hop around from one thing to another. **~ d'un sujet/d'une femme à l'autre** to flit from one subject/woman to another; **~ autour d'une femme** to hover round a woman.

papillote [papijɔt] **nf** (*bigoudi*) curlpaper; *[bonbon]* (*sweet* (*Brit*) *ou candy* (*US*)) paper, (sweet) wrapper (*Brit*); *[gigot]* frill; (*papier beurré*) buttered paper; (*papier aluminium*) tinfoil. **poisson en ~** fish cooked in tinfoil.

papillotement [papijɔtmɑ̃] **nm** (*voir* **papilloter**) twinkling; sparkling; fluttering, flickering; blinking.

papilloter [papijɔte] 1 **vi** *[lumière, étoiles]* to twinkle; *[reflets]* to sparkle; *[paupières]* to flutter, flicker; *[yeux]* to blink.

papisme [papism] **nm** papism, popery.

papiste [papist] **nmf** papist.

papotage [papɔtaʒ] **nm** (*action*) chattering (*NonC*); (*propos*) (idle) chatter (*NonC*).

papoter [papɔte] 1 **vi** to chatter, have a natter* (*Brit*).

papou, e [papu] 1 **adj** Papuan. 2 **nm** (*Ling*) Papuan. 3 **nm,f**: **P~(e)** Papuan.

papouan-néo-guinéen, -enne [papwɑ̃neɔgineɛ̃, ɛn] 1 **adj** Papua-New-Guinean, (of) Papua New Guinea 2 **nm,f**: **Papouan-Néo-Guinéen(ne)** Papua-New-Guinean.

Papouasie-Nouvelle-Guinée [papwazinuvɛlgine] **nf** Papua New Guinea.

papouille* [papuj] **nf** tickling (*NonC*). **faire des ~s à qn** to tickle sb.

paprika [papʀika] **nm** paprika (pepper).

papule [papyl] **nf** papule, papula.

papy [papi] **nm** = **papi.**

papyrus [papiʀys] **nm** papyrus.

paqson‡ [paksɔ̃] **nm** = **pacson.**

pâque [pɑk] **nf**: **la ~** Passover; *voir aussi* **Pâques.**

paquebot [pak(ə)bo] **nm** liner, (steam)ship.

pâquerette [pɑkʀɛt] **nf** daisy.

Pâques [pɑk] 1 **nm** Easter. (*fig*) **à ~ ou à la Trinité** some fine day (*iro*); **le lundi/la semaine de ~** Easter Monday/week; *voir* **dimanche, île, œuf.** 2 **nfpl**: **bonnes ou joyeuses ~** Happy Easter; **faire ses ~** to go to Easter mass (and take communion).

paquet [pakɛ] **nm** a (*pour emballer etc*) *[sucre, café]* bag; *[cigarettes]* packet, pack (*US*); *[cartes]* pack; *[linge]* bundle. **il fume deux ~s par jour** he smokes forty a day (*Brit*), he smokes two packs a day (*US*); (*fig*) **porter qn comme un ~ de linge sale** to carry sb like a sack of potatoes; **~-cadeau** gift-wrapped parcel; **faites moi un ~-cadeau** put it in gift-wrapping for me, gift-wrap it for me; (*fig*) **c'est un vrai ~ de nerfs** he's a bag *ou* bundle of nerves; **c'est un vrai ~ d'os** he's a bag of bones.

b (*colis*) parcel. **mettre en ~** to parcel up, bundle up; **faire un ~** to make up a parcel.

c (*fig: tas*) **~ de** *neige* pile *ou* mass of; *boue* lump of; *billets, actions* wad of; *eau* masses of; **par ~s** in waves.

d (*Rugby*) **~ (d'avants)** pack (of forwards).

e (*Naut*) **~ de mer** heavy sea (*NonC*), big wave.

f (* *loc*) **faire son ~** *ou* **ses ~s** to pack one's bags; **y mettre le ~** (*argent*) to spare no expense; (*efforts*) to give all one has got; **lâcher son ~ à qn** to tell sb a few home truths; **gagner/coûter un ~** to win/cost a small fortune; **il a touché un bon ~** he got a tidy sum*; **ils lui ont donné un bon petit ~ pour qu'il se taise** they gave him a tidy little sum to keep him quiet; **600 F par personne, ça fait un ~** 600 francs each, that's a fortune; *voir* **risquer.**

paquetage [pak(ə)taʒ] **nm** (*Mil*) pack, kit. **faire son ~** to get one's pack *ou* kit ready.

par[1] [paʀ] **prép** a (*agent, cause*) by. **le carreau a été cassé ~ l'orage/un enfant** the pane was broken by the storm/a child; **accablé ~ le désespoir** overwhelmed with despair; **elle nous a fait porter des fraises ~ son jardinier** she got her gardener to bring us some strawberries, she had her gardener bring us some strawberries; **il a appris la nouvelle ~ le journal/~ un ami** he learned the news from the paper/from *ou* through a friend; **elle veut tout faire ~ elle-même** she wants to do everything (for) herself; **la découverte ~ Fleming de la pénicilline** Fleming's discovery of penicillin, the discovery of penicillin by Fleming.

b (*manière, moyen*) by, with, through. **obtenir qch ~ la force/la torture/la persuasion/la ruse** to obtain sth by force/by torture/with persuasion/by *ou* through cunning; **essayer ~ tous les moyens** to try every possible means; **arriver ~ l'intelligence/le travail** to succeed through intelligence/hard work; **la porte ferme ~ un verrou** the gate is locked with *ou* by means of a bolt; **prendre qn ~ le bras/la main/la taille** to take sb by the arm/hand/waist; **payer ~ chèque** to pay by cheque; **prendre qn ~ les sentiments** to appeal to sb's feelings; **~ le train/l'avion** by rail *ou* train/air *ou* plane; **~ la poste** by post *ou* mail, through the post; **ils se ressemblent ~ leur sens de l'humour** they are alike in their sense of humour; **il descend des Bourbons ~ sa mère** he is descended from the Bourbons through his mother *ou* on his mother's side; **ils diffèrent ~ bien des côtés** they are different *ou* they differ in many ways *ou* aspects; **il est honnête ~ nature** he is honest by nature, he is naturally honest; **il ne jure que ~ elle** he swears by her alone; *voir* **cœur, excellence, mégarde** *etc.*

c (*gén sans art: cause, motif etc*) through, out of, from, by. **étonnant ~ son érudition** amazing for his learning; **~ manque de temps** owing to lack of time, because time is (*ou* was) short *ou* lacking; **~ habitude** by *ou* out of *ou* from (sheer) habit; **faire qch ~ plaisir/pitié** to do sth for pleasure/out of pity; **~ souci d'exactitude** for the sake of accuracy, out of a concern for accuracy; **~ hasard/erreur** by chance/mistake; **~ pure bêtise/négligence** through *ou* out of sheer stupidity/negligence; *voir* **principe.**

d (*lit, fig: lieu, direction*) by (way of), through, across, along. **il est sorti ~ la fenêtre** he went out by (way of) *ou* through the window; **il est venu ~ le chemin le plus court** he came (by) the shortest way; **je dois passer ~ le bureau avant de rentrer** I must drop in at the office on my way home; **nous sommes venus ~ la côte/~ Lyon/~ l'Espagne** we came along (by) the coast/via *ou* by way of Lyons/via *ou* through Spain; **~ terre ou ~ mer** by land or (by) sea; **se promener ~ les rues/les champs** to walk through the streets/through *ou* across the fields; **~ tout le pays** throughout *ou* all over the (entire) country; **il habite ~ ici** he lives round *ou* around here *ou* here somewhere; **sortez ~ ici/là** go out this/

that way; ~ **où sont-ils entrés?** which way *ou* how did they get in?; ~ **où est-il venu?** which way did he come (by)?; **passer ~ de dures épreuves** to go through some very trying times; **la rumeur s'était répandue ~ la ville** the rumour had spread (a)round the town; **elle est passée ~ toutes les couleurs de l'arc-en-ciel** she went through all the colours of the rainbow; ~ **5 mètres de fond** at a depth of 5 metres; ~ **10° de latitude sud** at a latitude of 10° south; **arriver ~ le nord/la gauche/le haut** *ou* **en haut** to arrive from the north/the left/the top; *voir* **ailleurs, mont** *etc et aussi* **par-devant** *etc.*

e (*distribution, mesure*) a, per, by. **marcher 2 ~ 2/3 ~ 3** to walk 2 by 2/3 by 3 *ou* in 2's/3's; **faites-les entrer un ~ un** let them in one at a time *ou* one by one; **nous avons payé 90 F ~ personne** we paid 90 francs per person *ou* a head *ou* apiece; **3 fois ~ jour/semaine/mois** 3 times daily *ou* a day/weekly *ou* a week/monthly *ou* a month; **6 étudiants ~ appartement** 6 students to a flat *ou* per flat; **gagner tant ~ semaine/mois** to earn so much a *ou* per week/month; ~ **an** a *ou* per year, per annum; **ils déduisent 20 F ~ enfant** they take off 20 francs for each child *ou* per child; ~ **moments** *ou* **instants, je crois rêver** at times I think I'm dreaming; **ils s'abattirent sur les plantes ~ milliers** they swooped down onto the plants in their thousands; **il y en avait ~ milliers** there were thousands of them; ~ **poignées/charretées** in handfuls/cartloads, by the handful/cartload; ~ **3 fois, on lui a demandé** 3 times he has been asked.

f (*atmosphère*) in, on; (*moment*) on. ~ **une belle nuit d'été** on a beautiful summer('s) night; **il partit ~ une pluvieuse journée de mars** he left on a rainy *ou* wet March day; **ne restez pas dehors ~ ce froid/cette chaleur** don't stay out in this cold/heat; **évitez cette route ~ temps de pluie/de brouillard** avoid that road in wet weather/in fog *ou* when it's wet/foggy; **sortir ~ moins 10°** to go out when it's minus 10°; ~ **les temps qui courent** these days.

g (*avec finir, commencer etc*) with, by. **commencer ~ qch/~ faire** to begin with sth/by doing; **il a fini ~ ennuyer tout le monde** he ended up *ou* finished up boring everyone; ~ **où allons-nous commencer?** where shall we begin?; **on a clôturé la séance ~ des élections** elections brought the meeting to a close, the meeting closed with elections; **il finit ~ m'agacer avec ses plaisanteries!** I've really had enough of his jokes!

h (*dans exclamations, serments*) by. ~ **tous les dieux du ciel** by *ou* in the name of heaven; ~ **tout ce que j'ai de plus cher, je vous promets** I promise you by all that I hold most dear; *voir* **jurer, pitié** *etc.*

i (*loc frm*) ~ **trop** far too, excessively; **de ~ le roi** in the name of the king, by order of the king; **de ~ le monde** throughout the world, the world over.

par² [paʀ] **nm** (*Golf*) par.

para* [paʀa] **nm** (**abrév de parachutiste**) para*.

parabellum [paʀabelɔm] **nm** big automatic pistol.

parabole [paʀabɔl] **nf** (*Math*) parabola; (*Rel*) parable.

parabolique [paʀabɔlik] 1 **adj** parabolic. **antenne ~** parabolic *ou* dish aerial. 2 **nm** (*radiateur*) electric fire.

paracentèse [paʀasɛ̃tɛz] **nf** paracentesis.

paracetamol [paʀasetamɔl] **nm** paracetamol.

parachèvement [paʀaʃɛvmɑ̃] **nm** perfection, perfecting.

parachever [paʀaʃ(ə)ve] 5 **vt** to perfect, put the finishing touches to.

parachutage [paʀaʃytaʒ] **nm** parachuting, dropping *ou* landing by parachute. **les électeurs n'ont pas apprécié le ~ d'un ministre dans leur département** the voters in that region didn't like the way a minister was suddenly landed on them.

parachute [paʀaʃyt] **nm** parachute. ~ **ventral/dorsal** lap-pack/back-type parachute; **descendre en ~** to parachute down; **faire du ~ ascensionnel** to go parascending.

parachuter [paʀaʃyte] 1 **vt** a (*Mil, Sport*) to parachute, drop *ou* land by parachute.

b (**: désigner*) ~ **qn à un poste** to pitchfork sb into a job; ~ **qn dans une circonscription** to dispatch sb to an area; **ils nous ont parachuté un nouveau directeur de Paris** a new manager from Paris has suddenly been landed on us.

parachutisme [paʀaʃytism] **nm** parachuting. ~ **ascensionnel** parascending; **faire du ~** to go parachuting; **faire du ~ en chute libre** to skydive, do skydiving.

parachutiste [paʀaʃytist] 1 **nmf** (*Sport*) parachutist; (*Mil*) paratrooper. **nos unités de ~s** our paratroops. 2 **adj** *unité* paratrooper (*épith*).

parade [paʀad] **nf** a (*ostentation*) show, ostentation. **faire ~ de** *érudition* to parade, display, show off; *relations* to boast about, brag about; **de ~** *uniforme, épée* ceremonial; (*péj*) **afficher une générosité de ~** to make an outward *ou* a superficial show *ou* display of generosity; **ce n'est que de la ~** it's just done for show.

b (*spectacle*) parade. ~ **militaire/foraine** military/circus parade; **les troupes s'avancèrent comme à la ~** the troops moved forward as if they were (still) on the parade ground *ou* on parade.

c (*Équitation*) pulling up.

d (*Escrime*) parry, parade; (*Boxe*) parry; (*Ftbl*) dummy; (*fig*) answer, reply; (*orale*) riposte, rejoinder. **trouver la (bonne) ~ (à une attaque/un argument)** to find the (right) answer *ou* reply (to an attack/ an argument); **on n'a pas encore trouvé la ~ contre cette maladie** an answer to this disease has still to be found.

parader [paʀade] 1 **vi** (*péj*) to strut about, show off; (*Mil*) to parade.

paradigmatique [paʀadigmatik] 1 **adj** paradigmatic. 2 **nf** study of paradigmatic relationships.

paradigme [paʀadigm] **nm** paradigm.

paradis [paʀadi] **nm** a (*lit, fig*) paradise, heaven. **le P~ terrestre** (*Bible*) the Garden of Eden; (*fig*) heaven on earth; **aller au** *ou* **en ~** to go to heaven; **c'est le ~ des enfants/chasseurs ici** it's a children's/hunters' paradise here; ~ **fiscal** tax haven; *voir* **emporter, oiseau.** b (*Théât* †*) **le ~** the gods* (*Brit*), the gallery.

paradisiaque [paʀadizjak] **adj** heavenly, paradisiacal.

paradisier [paʀadizje] **nm** bird of paradise.

paradoxal, e, **mpl -aux** [paʀadɔksal, o] **adj** paradoxical.

paradoxalement [paʀadɔksalmɑ̃] **adv** paradoxically.

paradoxe [paʀadɔks] **nm** paradox.

parafe [paʀaf] **nm** = **paraphe.**

parafer [paʀafe] 1 **vt** = **parapher.**

parafeur [paʀafœʀ] **nm** = **parapheur.**

paraffinage [paʀafinaʒ] **nm** paraffining.

paraffine [paʀafin] **nf** (*gén: solide*) paraffin wax; (*Chim*) paraffin.

paraffiner [paʀafine] 1 **vt** to paraffin(e); *voir* **papier.**

parafiscal, e, **mpl -aux** [paʀafiskal, o] **adj: taxe ~e** additional levy (*road-fund tax, stamp duty etc*).

parages [paʀaʒ] **nmpl** a **dans les ~** (*dans la région*) in the area, in the vicinity; (**: pas très loin*) round about; **dans ces ~** in these parts; **dans les ~ de** near, round about, in the vicinity of. b (*Naut*) waters, region.

paragraphe [paʀagʀaf] **nm** paragraph; (*Typ*) section (mark).

paragrêle [paʀagʀɛl] **adj** anti-hail (*épith*).

Paraguay [paʀagwɛ] **nm** Paraguay.

paraguayen, -enne [paʀagwajɛ̃, ɛn] 1 **adj** Paraguayan. 2 **nm,f: P~(ne)** Paraguayan.

paraître [paʀɛtʀ] 57 1 **vi** a (*se montrer*) (*gén*) to appear; *[personne]* to appear, make one's appearance. ~ **en scène/à** *ou* **sur l'écran/au balcon** to appear on stage/on the screen/on the balcony; **il n'a pas paru de la journée** I (*ou* we *etc*) haven't seen him all day, he hasn't shown up* *ou* appeared all day; **il n'a pas paru à la réunion** he didn't appear *ou* turn up *ou* show up* at the meeting; ~ **en public** to appear in public, make a public appearance; **un sourire parut sur ses lèvres** a smile appeared on his lips.

b (*Presse*) to appear, be published, come out. **faire ~ qch** *[éditeur]* to bring out *ou* publish sth; *[auteur]* to have sth published; **"vient de ~"** "just out", "just published"; **"à ~"** "forthcoming".

c (*briller*) to be noticed. **chercher à ~** to show off; **le désir de ~** the desire to be noticed *ou* to show off.

d (*être visible*) to show (through). **il en paraît toujours quelque chose** one can always see some sign of it *ou* traces of it; **il n'y paraîtra bientôt plus** (*tache, cicatrice*) there will soon be no trace left of it *ou* nothing left to show (of it); (*maladie*) soon no one will ever know you've had it; **laisser ~ ses sentiments/son irritation** to let one's feelings/one's annoyance show; **sans qu'il n'y paraisse rien** without anything being obvious, without letting anything show; **sans qu'il y paraisse, elle a obtenu ce qu'elle voulait** without it appearing so, she got what she wanted.

e (*sembler*) to look, seem, appear. **elle paraît heureuse** she seems (to be) happy; **cela me paraît être une erreur** it looks *ou* seems like a mistake to me; **elle paraissait l'aimer** she seemed *ou* appeared to love him; **il paraît 20 ans** (*il est plus jeune*) he looks (at least) 20; (*il est plus âgé*) he only looks 20; **le voyage a paru long** the journey seemed long; **cette robe la fait ~ plus grande** that dress makes her look taller; **essayer de ~ ce que l'on n'est pas** to try to appear to be what *ou* something one isn't.

2 **vb impers** a (*il semble*) **il me paraît difficile qu'elle puisse venir** it seems to me that it will be difficult for her to come; **il ne lui paraît pas essentiel qu'elle sache** he doesn't think it essential for her to know; **il lui paraissait impossible de refuser** he didn't see how he could refuse; **il paraîtrait ridicule de s'offenser** it would seem stupid to take offence.

b (*le bruit court*) **il va se marier, paraît-il** *ou* **à ce qu'il paraît** he's apparently getting married; **il paraît** *ou* **il paraîtrait qu'on va construire une autoroute** apparently *ou* it seems they're going to build a motorway, they're going to build a motorway, so they say; **il paraît que oui** so it seems *ou* appears, apparently so.

3 **nm: le ~** appearance(s).

paralangage [paʀalɑ̃gaʒ] **nm** paralanguage.

paralinguistique [paʀalɛ̃gɥistik] **adj** paralinguistic.

paralittérature [paʀaliteʀatyʀ] **nf** marginal literature.

parallactique [paʀalaktik] **adj** parallactic.

parallaxe [paʀalaks] **nf** parallax.

parallèle [paʀalɛl] 1 **adj** a (*Math*) parallel (*à* to); *voir* **barre.**

b (*fig*) (*comparable*) parallel, similar; (*indépendant*) separate; (*non officiel*) *marché, cours, police* unofficial; *énergie, société* alternative. **mener une action ~** to take similar action, act on *ou* along the same lines; (*Comm*) **circuits ~s de distribution** parallel distribution circuits.

2 nf (*Math*) parallel (line). (*Élec*) **monté en ~** wired (up) in parallel.

3 nm (*Géog, fig*) parallel. **~ de latitude** parallel of latitude; **établir un ~ entre 2 textes** to draw a parallel between 2 texts; **faire** *ou* **mettre en ~** *choses opposées* to compare; *choses semblables* to parallel; **mettre en ~ deux problèmes** to parallel one problem with another; *[projets]* **avancer en ~** to move along at the same pace.

parallèlement [paʀalɛlmɑ̃] **adv** (*lit*) parallel (*à* to); (*fig*) (*ensemble*) at the same time; (*similairement*) in the same way.

parallélépipède [paʀalelepipɛd] **nm** parallelepiped.

parallélisme [paʀalelism] **nm** (*lit, fig*) parallelism; (*Aut*) wheel alignment. **faire vérifier le ~ de ses roues** to have one's wheels aligned.

parallélogramme [paʀalelɔgʀam] **nm** parallelogram.

paralysé, e [paʀalize] (**ptp de paralyser**) 1 **adj** paralyzed. **rester ~** to be left paralyzed; **il est ~ des jambes** his legs are paralyzed; *[aéroport]* **~ par le brouillard** fogbound; **~ par la neige** snowbound; **~ par la grève** *[gare]* strike-bound; *[hôpital]* crippled by the strike. 2 **nm,f** paralytic.

paralyser [paʀalize] 1 **vt** (*Méd, fig*) to paralyze.

paralysie [paʀalizi] **nf** (*Méd, fig*) paralysis; (*Bible*) palsy. **~ infantile** infantile paralysis; **être frappé de ~** to be struck down with paralysis.

paralytique [paʀalitik] **adj, nmf** paralytic.

Paramaribo [paʀamaʀibo] **n** Paramaribo.

paramécie [paʀamesi] **nf** paramecium.

paramédical, e, mpl -aux [paʀamedikal, o] **adj** paramedical.

paramètre [paʀamɛtʀ] **nm** parameter.

paramétrer [paʀametʀe] 1 **vt** to parametrize.

paramilitaire [paʀamilitɛʀ] **adj** paramilitary.

parangon [paʀɑ̃gɔ̃] **nm** paragon. **~ de vertu** paragon of virtue.

parano* [paʀano] 1 **adj abrév de paranoïaque.** 2 **nf abrév de paranoïa.**

paranoïa [paʀanɔja] **nf** paranoia.

paranoïaque [paʀanɔjak] **adj, nmf** paranoiac, paranoid.

paranoïde [paʀanɔid] **adj** paranoid.

paranormal, e, mpl -aux [paʀanɔʀmal, o] **adj** paranormal. **le ~** the paranormal.

parapente [paʀapɑ̃t] **nm** parapente. **faire du ~** to go parapenting.

parapet [paʀapɛ] **nm** parapet.

paraphe [paʀaf] **nm** (*trait*) paraph, flourish; (*initiales*) initials; (*littér: signature*) signature.

parapher [paʀafe] 1 **vt** (*Admin*) to initial; (*littér: signer*) to sign.

parapheur [paʀafœʀ] **nm** signature book.

paraphrase [paʀafʀɑz] **nf** paraphrase. **faire de la ~** to paraphrase.

paraphraser [paʀafʀɑze] 1 **vt** to paraphrase.

paraphrastique [paʀafʀastik] **adj** paraphrastic.

paraplégie [paʀapleʒi] **nf** paraplegia.

paraplégique [paʀapleʒik] **adj, nmf** paraplegic.

parapluie [paʀaplɥi] **nm** umbrella. **~ atomique** *ou* **nucléaire** nuclear shield *ou* umbrella; (*fig*) **ouvrir le ~** to take cover (*from criticism*).

parapsychique [paʀapsiʃik] **adj** parapsychological.

parapsychologie [paʀapsikɔlɔʒi] **nf** parapsychology.

parapsychologue [paʀapsikɔlɔg] **nmf** parapsychologist.

parascolaire [paʀaskɔlɛʀ] **adj** extracurricular.

parasismique [paʀasismik] **adj** earthquake-resistant.

parasitaire [paʀazitɛʀ] **adj** parasitic(al).

parasite [paʀazit] 1 **nm** a (*Bot, Vét*) parasite; (*fig: personne*) parasite, sponger‡, scrounger*. b **~s** (*électricité statique*) atmospherics, static; (*Rad, TV*) interference; **la machine à laver fait des ~s dans la télévision** the washing machine causes interference on the television. 2 **adj** parasitic(al). (*Rad, TV*) **bruits ~s** interference; (*électricité statique*) atmospherics, static.

parasiter [paʀazite] 1 **vt** (*Bot, Vét*) to live as a parasite on; (*Rad, TV*) to cause interference on.

parasitique [paʀazitik] **adj** parasitic(al).

parasitisme [paʀazitism] **nm** parasitism.

parasitose [paʀazitoz] **nf** parasitosis.

parasol [paʀasɔl] **nm** *[plage]* beach umbrella, parasol; *[café, terrasse]* sunshade, parasol; (†: *ombrelle*) parasol, sunshade; *voir* **pin.**

parasympathique [paʀasɛ̃patik] **adj** parasympathetic.

parataxe [paʀataks] **nf** parataxis.

parathyroïde [paʀatiʀɔid] **nf** parathyroid (gland).

paratonnerre [paʀatɔnɛʀ] **nm** lightning conductor.

paratyphique [paʀatifik] **adj** paratyphoid.

paratyphoïde [paʀatifɔid] **nf** paratyphoid fever.

paravent [paʀavɑ̃] **nm** folding screen *ou* partition; (*fig*) screen.

parbleu†† [paʀblø] **excl** of course!

parc [paʀk] 1 **nm** (*jardin public*) park; (*jardin de château*) grounds; (*Mil: entrepôt*) depot; (*fig, Écon: ensemble*) stock. **le ~ français des ordinateurs individuels** the total number of personal computers owned in France.

2 **comp** ▸**parc à l'anglaise** landscaped garden ▸**parc animalier** safari park ▸**parc d'attractions** amusement park ▸**parc automobile** *[pays]* number of vehicles on the road; *[entreprise]* car (*ou* bus *etc*) fleet ▸**parc à bébé** playpen ▸**parc à bestiaux** cattle pen *ou* enclosure ▸**parc ferroviaire** rolling stock ▸**parc à la française** formal garden (in the French style) ▸**parc à huîtres** oyster bed ▸**parc industriel** (*Can*) industrial estate (*Brit*) *ou* park (*US*) ▸**parc de loisirs** leisure park ▸**parc à moules** mussel bed ▸**parc à moutons** sheep pen, sheepfold ▸**parc national** national park ▸**parc naturel** nature reserve ▸**parc régional** country park ▸**parc scientifique** science park ▸**parc de stationnement** car park (*Brit*), parking lot (*US*) ▸**parc à thème** theme park ▸**parc zoologique** zoological gardens.

parcage [paʀkaʒ] **nm** *[moutons]* penning; *[voitures]* parking.

parcellaire [paʀsɛlɛʀ] **adj** (*fig: fragmentaire*) *plan, travail* fragmented, bitty* (*Brit*).

parcelle [paʀsɛl] **nf** fragment, particle, bit; (*sur un cadastre*) parcel (*of land*). **~ de terre** plot of land; **~ de vérité/bon sens** grain of truth/commonsense; **pas la moindre ~ de vérité** not a grain *ou* scrap of truth; **une ~ de bonheur/gloire** a bit of happiness/fame.

parcellisation [paʀselizasjɔ̃] **nf** *[tâche]* breakdown into individual operations; *[terrain]* dividing up, division.

parcelliser [paʀselize] 1 **vt** *tâche* to break down into individual operations; *terrain* to divide up.

parce que [paʀs(ə)kə] **conj** because. **Robert, de mauvaise humeur ~ fatigué, répondit que ...** Robert, being tired, was in a temper and replied that ..., Robert was in a temper because he was tired and replied that ...; **pourquoi n'y vas-tu pas? — ~!** why aren't you going? — (just) because (I'm not!).

parchemin [paʀʃəmɛ̃] **nm** parchment (*NonC*), piece of parchment; (*Univ fig*) diploma, degree.

parcheminé, e [paʀʃəmine] (**ptp de parcheminer**) **adj** *peau* wrinkled; *visage* wizened.

parcheminer [paʀʃəmine] 1 1 **vt** to give a parchment finish to. 2 **se parcheminer vpr** to wrinkle up.

parcimonie [paʀsimɔni] **nf** parsimony, parsimoniousness. **distribuer qch avec ~** (*par économie*) to dole sth out sparingly *ou* parsimoniously; (*à contrecœur*) to dole sth out grudgingly.

parcimonieusement [paʀsimɔnjøzmɑ̃] **adv** (*voir* **parcimonie**) parsimoniously; sparingly; grudgingly.

parcimonieux, -ieuse [paʀsimɔnjø, jøz] **adj** *personne* parsimonious; *distribution* miserly, ungenerous.

par-ci par-là [paʀsipaʀla] **adv** (*espace*) here and there; (*temps*) now and then, from time to time. **il m'agace avec ses bien sûr par-ci, bien sûr par-là** he gets on my nerves saying of course, right, left and centre.

parcmètre [paʀkmɛtʀ] **nm, parcomètre** [paʀkɔmɛtʀ] **nm** (parking) meter.

parcourir [paʀkuʀiʀ] 11 **vt** a *trajet, distance* to cover, travel; (*en tous sens*) *lieu* to go all over; *pays* to travel up and down. **ils ont parcouru toute la région en un mois** they travelled the length and breadth of the region *ou* they've covered the whole region in a month; **~ la ville à la recherche de qch** to search for sth all over (the) town, scour the town for sth; **les navires parcourent les mers** ships sail all over the seas; **un frisson parcourut tout son corps** a shiver ran through his body; **le ruisseau parcourt toute la vallée** the stream runs along *ou* through the whole valley *ou* right along the valley; **l'obus parcourut le ciel** the shell flew through *ou* across the sky.

b (*regarder rapidement*) *lettre, livre* to glance *ou* skim through. **il parcourut la foule des yeux** he ran his eye over the crowd.

parcours [paʀkuʀ] **nm** a (*distance*) distance; (*trajet*) journey; (*itinéraire*) route; *[fleuve]* course. **le prix du ~** the fare. b (*Sport*) course. **sur un ~ difficile** over a difficult course; **~ de golf** (*terrain*) golf course; (*partie, trajet*) round of golf; **faire un ~ sans faute** (*Équitation, Trial*) to have a clear round; (*dans un jeu*) to get round; (*dans une carrière*) to have a model career; **~ du combattant** (*Mil*) assault course; (*fig*) obstacle course; (*Mil*) **faire le ~ du combattant** to go round an assault course; *voir* **accident, incident.** c *[carrière]* route, path.

par-delà [paʀdəla] **prép** beyond. **~ les montagnes/les mers** beyond the mountains/the seas; **~ les querelles, la solidarité demeure** there is a feeling of solidarity which goes beyond the quarrels, underneath the quarrelling there remains a feeling of solidarity.

par-derrière [paʀdɛʀjɛʀ] 1 **prép** (round) behind, round the back of. 2 **adv** *passer* round the back; *attaquer, emboutir* from behind, from the rear; *être endommagé* at the back *ou* rear; *se boutonner* at the back. **dire du mal de qn ~** to speak ill of sb behind his back.

par-dessous [paʀd(ə)su] **prép, adv** under(neath); *voir* **jambe.**

pardessus [paʀdəsy] **nm** overcoat.

par-dessus [paʀd(ə)sy] 1 **prép** over (the top of). **il a mis un pullover ~ sa chemise** he has put a pullover over *ou* on top of his shirt; **sauter ~ une barrière/un mur** to jump over a barrier/a wall; **~ tout** above all; **j'en ai ~ la tête de toutes ces histoires** I'm sick and tired of all this business; **~ le marché** into the bargain, on top of all that; **~ bord** overboard; *voir* **jambe.** 2 **adv** over (the top).

par-devant [paʀd(ə)vɑ̃] 1 **prép** (*Jur*) **~ notaire** in the presence of *ou* before a lawyer. 2 **adv** *passer* round the front; *attaquer, emboutir* from the front; *être abîmé, se boutonner* at the front.

par-devers [paʀdəvɛʀ] **prép** (*Jur*) before. (*frm*) **~ soi** (*en sa possession*) in one's possession; (*fig: dans son for intérieur*) to *ou* within oneself.

pardi† [paʀdi] **excl** of course!

pardieu†† [paʀdjø] excl of course!

pardon [paʀdɔ̃] nm a (*grâce*) forgiveness, pardon (*frm, Jur*).
b (*en Bretagne*) pardon (*religious festival*).
c (*intensif*) **et puis ~!* il travaille dur** he works hard, I'm telling you *ou* I can tell you *ou* you can take it from me*; **je suis peut-être un imbécile mais alors lui, ~!*** maybe I'm stupid but he's even worse! *ou* he takes the biscuit!* (*Brit*) *ou* cake!* (*US*); **j'ai une belle voiture mais alors celle de mon frère ~!*** I've got a nice car but wow* - you should see my brother's (one)!; **elle a un œil au beurre noir, ~!*** she's got one hell of a black eye!*
d (*loc*) **demander ~ à qn d'avoir fait qch** to apologize to sb for doing *ou* having done sth; **demande ~!** say you're sorry!; **(je vous demande) ~** (I'm) sorry, I beg your pardon, excuse me; **c'est Martin — ~?** it's Martin — pardon?, (I'm) sorry?, what did you say?; **~ Monsieur, avez-vous l'heure?** excuse me, have you got the time?; **tu n'y es pas allé — (je te demande bien) ~, j'y suis allé ce matin** you didn't go — oh yes I did *ou* excuse me, I went this morning *ou* I certainly did go this morning.

pardonnable [paʀdɔnabl] adj pardonable, forgivable, excusable. **il l'a oublié mais c'est ~** he can be forgiven *ou* excused for forgetting it, he has forgotten it but you have to forgive *ou* excuse him.

pardonner [paʀdɔne] 1 1 vt *péché* to forgive, pardon; *indiscrétion* to forgive, excuse. **~ (à) qn** to forgive sb, let sb off; **~ qch à qn/à qn d'avoir fait qch** to forgive sb for sth/for doing sth; **pour se faire ~ son erreur** to try to win forgiveness for his mistake, so as to be forgiven for his mistake; **pardonnez-moi de vous avoir dérangé** I'm sorry to have disturbed you, excuse me for disturbing you, excuse my disturbing you; **vous êtes tout pardonné** I'll let you off, you're forgiven (*hum*); **on lui pardonne tout** he gets away with everything; **je ne me le pardonnerai jamais** I'll never forgive myself; **ce genre d'erreur ne se pardonne pas** this is an unforgivable *ou* inexcusable mistake; **pardonnez-moi, mais je crois que ...** excuse me but I think that ...; *voir* **faute**.
2 vi to forgive. **il faut savoir ~** you have to forgive and forget; (*fig*) **c'est une maladie/une erreur qui ne pardonne pas** it's a fatal illness/mistake.

pare- [paʀ] préf *voir* **parer²**.

paré, e [paʀe] (ptp de **parer²**) adj (*prêt*) ready, all set; (*préparé*) prepared. **être ~ contre le froid** to be prepared for the cold weather.

parégorique [paʀegɔʀik] adj, nm paregoric; *voir* **élixir**.

pareil, -eille [paʀɛj] 1 adj a (*identique*) the same, similar, alike (*attrib*). **il n'y en a pas deux ~s** there aren't two the same *ou* alike; **~ que, ~ à** the same as, similar to, just like; **comment va-t-elle? — c'est toujours ~** how is she? — (she's) just the same (as ever) *ou* there's no change (in her); **c'est toujours ~, il ne peut pas être à l'heure** it's always the same, he never manages to be on time; **il est ~ à lui-même** he doesn't change, he's the same as ever; **tu as vu son sac? j'en ai un ~/presque ~** have you seen her bag? I've got one the same *ou* one just like it/one very similar *ou* almost identical; (*littér*) **à nul autre ~** peerless (*littér, épith*), unrivalled, unmatched; **l'an dernier à ~eille époque** this time last year.
b (*tel*) such (a), of the sort. **je n'ai jamais entendu ~ discours *ou* un discours ~** I've never heard such a speech *ou* a speech like it *ou* a speech of the sort (*péj*); **en ~ cas** in such a case; **en ~eille occasion** on such an occasion; **à ~eille heure, il devrait être debout** he ought to be up at this hour; **se coucher à une heure ~eille!** what a time to be going to bed (at)!
2 nm,f: **nos ~s** (*semblables*) our fellow men; (*égaux*) our equals *ou* peers; **je ne retrouverai jamais son ~** (*chose*) I'll never find another one like it; (*employé*) I'll never find another one like him *ou* to match him; **ne pas avoir son ~ (*ou* sa ~eille)** to be second to none; **il n'a pas son ~ pour faire la mayonnaise** no-one can beat his mayonnaise, no-one makes mayonnaise as well as he does; **vous et vos ~s** you and your kind, people like you; **sans ~** unparalleled, unequalled, without compare (*attrib*); **c'est du ~ au même*** it doesn't make the slightest difference, it comes to the same thing, it makes no odds, it's six (of one) and half-a-dozen (of the other); *voir* **rendre**.
3 adv (*) *s'habiller* the same, in the same way, alike. **faire ~** to do the same thing (*que* as).

pareillement [paʀɛjmɑ̃] adv (*de la même manière*) *s'habiller* in the same way (*à* as); (*également*) likewise, also, equally. **cela m'a ~ surpris** it surprised me also *ou* too; **~ heureux** equally happy; **mon père va bien et ma mère ~** my father is well and so is my mother *ou* and my mother too; **à vous ~!** the same to you!

parement [paʀmɑ̃] nm (*Constr, Habillement*) facing.

parenchyme [paʀɑ̃ʃim] nm parenchyma.

parent, e [paʀɑ̃, ɑ̃t] 1 adj related (*de* to).
2 nm,f a relative, relation. **être ~ de qn** to be related to *ou* a relative of sb; **nous sommes ~s par alliance/par ma mère** we are related by marriage/on my mother's side; **~s en ligne directe** blood relations; **~s proches** close relations *ou* relatives; **~s et amis** friends and relations *ou* relatives; **nous ne sommes pas ~s** we aren't related; (*fig*) **~ pauvre** poor relation (*de* to).
b (*Bio*) parent.
3 nmpl: **~s** (*père et mère*) parents; (*littér: ancêtres*) ancestors, forefathers; **les devoirs des ~s** parental duties; **accompagné de l'un de ses ~s** accompanied by one parent *ou* one of his parents; **nos premiers ~s** our first parents, Adam and Eve.

parental, e, mpl **-aux** [paʀɑ̃tal, o] adj parental. **retrait d'autorité ~e** loss of parental rights; **participation ~e** parental involvement.

parenté [paʀɑ̃te] nf (*rapport*) relationship, kinship; (*ensemble des parents*) relations, relatives, kith and kin (*pl*). **ces deux langues n'ont aucune ~** these two languages are not in any way related *ou* have no common roots.

parenthèse [paʀɑ̃tɛz] nf (*digression*) parenthesis, digression; (*signe*) bracket (*Brit*), parenthesis. (*lit*) **ouvrir/fermer la ~** to open/close the brackets (*Brit*) *ou* parentheses; **mettre qch entre ~s** to put sth in *ou* between brackets (*Brit*) *ou* parentheses; **entre ~s** (*lit*) in brackets (*Brit*) *ou* parentheses; (*fig*) incidentally, in parenthesis; **il vaut mieux mettre cet aspect entre ~s** it would be better to leave that aspect aside; **par ~** incidentally, in passing; **soit dit par ~, elle aurait mieux fait de rester** it could be said incidentally *ou* in passing that she would have done better to stay; (*fig*) **ouvrir une ~** to digress, make a digression; **je me permets d'ouvrir une ~ pour dire ...** may I interrupt *ou* digress for a moment to say ...; (*fig*) **je ferme la ~** (but) to get back to the subject.

parenthétisation [paʀɑ̃tetizasjɔ̃] nf bracketing (*Brit*), parenthesizing.

paréo [paʀeo] nm pareu.

parer¹ [paʀe] 1 1 vt a (*orner*) *chose* to adorn, bedeck; *personne* to adorn, deck out (*de* with). **robe richement parée** richly trimmed *ou* ornamented dress; (*fig*) **~ qn de toutes les vertus** to attribute every virtue to sb. b (*préparer*) *viande* to dress, trim; *cuir* to dress. 2 **se parer** vpr (*littér: se faire beau*) to put on all one's finery. **se ~ de** *bijoux* to adorn o.s. with; *robe* to attire o.s. in; (*péj*) *faux titre* to assume, invest o.s. with; (*fig*) **se ~ des plumes du paon** to take all the credit (for o.s.).

parer² [paʀe] 1 1 vt (*se protéger de*) *coup* to ward off, stave off, fend off; (*Boxe, Escrime*) to parry; (*Ftbl*) *tir* to deflect; (*fig*) *attaque* to stave off, parry.
2 **parer à** vt indir a (*remédier*) *inconvénient* to deal with, remedy, overcome; *danger* to ward off.
b (*pourvoir à*) *éventualité* to prepare for, be prepared for. **~ au plus pressé** to attend to the most urgent things first; **il faut ~ au plus pressé** first things first.
3 comp ►**pare-avalanches** nm inv avalanche barrier ►**pare-balles** nm inv bullet shield; (*adj inv*) bulletproof ►**pare-boue** nm inv mud flap ►**pare-brise** nm inv windscreen (*Brit*), windshield (*US*) ►**pare-chocs** nm inv (*Aut*) bumper (*Brit*), fender (*US*) ►**pare-étincelles** nm inv fireguard ►**pare-feu** nm inv *[forêt]* firebreak; *[foyer]* fireguard; **porte pare-feu** fire door ►**pare-soleil** nm inv sun visor.

paresse [paʀɛs] nf (*voir* **paresseux**) laziness; idleness; slowness; sluggishness; (*défaut*) laziness; (*péché*) sloth. **~ intellectuelle *ou* d'esprit** laziness *ou* sluggishness of mind; **~ intestinale** sluggishness of the digestive system.

paresser [paʀese] 1 vi to laze about *ou* around. **~ au lit** to laze in bed.

paresseusement [paʀesøzmɑ̃] adv (*voir* **paresseux**) lazily; idly; sluggishly.

paresseux, -euse [paʀesø, øz] 1 adj *personne* lazy, idle; *esprit* slow; *allure, pose* lazy; *estomac, intestin* sluggish; *fleuve* lazy, sluggish. **solution ~euse** easy way out, line of least resistance; **~ comme une couleuvre* *ou* un loir* *ou* un lézard*** bone-idle* (*Brit*), lazy; **il est ~ pour se lever** he's not very good at getting up, he's a bit of a lie-abed*. 2 nm,f lazy *ou* idle person, lazybones*. 3 nm (*Zool*) sloth.

parfaire [paʀfɛʀ] 60 vt *travail* to perfect, bring to perfection; *connaissances* to perfect, round off; *décor, impression* to complete, put the finishing touches to; *somme* to make up.

parfait, e [paʀfɛ, ɛt] (ptp de **parfaire**) 1 adj a (*impeccable*) (*gén*) *travail, condition, exemple, crime* perfect; *exécution, raisonnement* perfect, flawless; *manières* perfect, faultless; *voir* **filer**.
b (*absolu*) *bonne foi, tranquillité* complete, total, perfect; *ressemblance* perfect. **il a été d'une discrétion ~e *ou* (*frm*) ~ de discrétion** he has shown absolute discretion, he has been the soul of discretion; **dans la plus ~e ignorance** in total *ou* utter *ou* complete ignorance; **en ~ accord avec** in perfect *ou* total agreement with; **en ~e harmonie** in perfect harmony.
c (*accompli, achevé*) *élève, employé* perfect; (*péj*) *crétin, crapule* utter, downright, perfect. **le type même du ~ mari** the epitome of the perfect husband; **~ homme du monde** perfect gentleman.
d (*à son plein développement*) *fleur, insecte* perfect; *voir* **accord, gaz, nombre**.
e (*très bon*) **(c'est) ~!** (that's) perfect! *ou* excellent! *ou* great!*; (*iro*) (that's) marvellous! *ou* great!*; **vous refusez? (voilà qui est) ~, vous l'aurez voulu!** you won't? (that's) fine — it's your own affair!; **vous avez été ~!** you were fantastic!
2 nm a (*Culin*) parfait. **~ au café** coffee parfait.
b (*Ling*) perfect.

parfaitement [paʀfɛtmɑ̃] adv a (*très bien*) *connaître* perfectly. **je comprends ~** I quite understand, I understand perfectly.
b (*tout à fait*) *heureux, clair, exact* perfectly, quite; *hermétique, étanche* completely; *idiot* utterly, absolutely, perfectly. **cela m'est ~ égal**

that makes absolutely no difference to me, it's all the same to me; **vous avez ~ le droit de le garder** you have a perfect right to keep it, you're perfectly entitled to keep it.

c (*certainement*) (most) certainly, oh yes. **tu as fait ce tableau tout seul?** — **~!** you did this picture all on your own? — I (most) certainly did! *ou* I did indeed!; **tu ne vas pas partir sans moi!** — **~!** you're not going to leave without me! — oh yes *ou* indeed I am!; **je refuse d'obéir, ~, et j'en suis fier** I'm refusing to obey, most certainly *ou* definitely, and I'm proud of it.

parfois [paʀfwa] **adv** (*dans certains cas*) sometimes; (*de temps en temps*) sometimes, occasionally, at times. **~ je lis, ~ je sors** sometimes I (may) read, other times I (may) go out; **il y a ~ du brouillard en hiver** occasionally *ou* sometimes there's fog in winter.

parfum [paʀfœ̃] **nm** a (*substance*) perfume, scent, fragrance. b (*odeur*) *[fleur, herbe]* scent, fragrance; *[tabac, vin, café]* aroma; *[glace]* flavour (*Brit*), flavor (*US*); *[savon]* scent, fragrance; *[fruit]* smell; (*fig littér*) *[louanges, vertu]* odour. (*fig*) **ceci a un ~ de scandale/d'hérésie** that has a whiff of scandal/heresy about it. c (*loc*) **être au ~** to be in the know*; **mettre qn au ~** to put sb in the picture*, give sb the low-down (on sth)*, gen sb up* (*Brit*).

parfumé, e [paʀfyme] (**ptp de parfumer**) **adj** *papier à lettres, savon* scented; *air, fleur* scented, fragrant, sweet-smelling; *vin* fragrant; *effluves* aromatic. **femme trop ~e** woman wearing too much scent; **~ au citron** *glace* lemon-flavour(ed) (*Brit*), lemon-flavor(ed) (*US*); *savon* lemon-scented; **fraises très ~es** very sweet-smelling strawberries.

parfumer [paʀfyme] [1] 1 **vt** *pièce, air [fleurs]* to perfume, scent; *[café, tabac]* to fill with its aroma; *mouchoir* to put scent *ou* perfume on; (*Culin*) to flavour (*Brit*) *ou* flavor (*US*) (*à* with). **pour ~ son linge** to make one's linen smell nice. 2 **se parfumer vpr** to use *ou* wear perfume *ou* scent. **elle se parfuma rapidement** she quickly put *ou* dabbed some scent *ou* perfume on.

parfumerie [paʀfymʀi] **nf** (*usine, industrie*) perfumery; (*boutique*) perfume shop; (*rayon*) perfumery (department); (*produits*) perfumery, perfumes, fragrances.

parfumeur, -euse [paʀfymœʀ, øz] **nm, f** perfumer.

pari [paʀi] **nm** bet, wager; (*Sport*) bet; (*activité*) betting. **faire/tenir un ~** to make *ou* lay/take up a bet; **~ mutuel (urbain)** ≃ tote, parimutuel; (*fig*) **les ~s sont ouverts** there's no knowing, it's anyone's bet*.

paria [paʀja] **nm** (social) outcast, pariah; (*en Inde*) Pariah.

parier [paʀje] [7] **vt** a (*gager*) to bet, wager. **je (te) parie que c'est lui/tout ce que tu veux** I bet you it's him/anything you like; **tu ne le feras pas — qu'est-ce que tu paries?** you won't do it — what do you bet?; **il y a gros à ~ que ...** the odds are that ..., ten to one it's ...; **je l'aurais parié** I might have known; **tu as faim, je parie** I bet you're hungry.

b (*Courses*) *argent* to bet, lay, stake. **~ 100 F sur le favori** to bet *ou* lay 100 francs on the favourite; **~ gros sur un cheval** to bet heavily on *ou* lay a big bet on a horse; (*emploi absolu*) **~ sur un cheval** to bet on a horse, back a horse; **~ aux courses** to bet on the races.

pariétal, e, mpl -aux [paʀjetal, o] 1 **adj** (*Anat*) parietal; (*Art*) wall (*épith*). 2 **nm** parietal bone.

parieur, -ieuse [paʀjœʀ, jøz] **nm,f** punter.

parigot, e* [paʀigo, ɔt] 1 **adj** Parisian. 2 **nm,f: P~(e)** Parisian.

Paris [paʀi] **n** Paris.

paris-brest [paʀibʀɛst] **nm** *pastry filled with praline-flavoured cream.*

parisianisme [paʀizjanism] **nm** (*habitude*) Parisian habit; (*façon de parler*) Parisian way of speaking; (*importance donnée à Paris*) Paris bias. **faire du ~** to focus excessively on Paris.

parisien, -ienne [paʀizjɛ̃, jɛn] 1 **adj** (*gén*) Paris (*épith*), of Paris; *société, goûts, ambiance* Parisian. **le Bassin ~** the Paris basin; **la région ~ne** the Paris region *ou* area, the region *ou* area around Paris; **la vie ~ne** Paris *ou* Parisian life, life in Paris; *voir* **pain**. 2 **nm,f: P~(ne)** Parisian.

paritaire [paʀitɛʀ] **adj** *commission* joint (*épith*), with equal representation of both sides; *représentation* equal.

parité [paʀite] **nf** parity. **la ~ des changes** exchange parity; **réclamer la ~ des *ou* entre les salaires** to demand equal pay.

parjure [paʀʒyʀ] 1 **adj** *personne* faithless, disloyal; *serment* false. 2 **nm** (*violation de serment*) betrayal. 3 **nmf** traitor.

parjurer (se) [paʀʒyʀe] [1] **vpr** (*voir* **parjure**) to be faithless *ou* a traitor to one's oath *ou* promise.

parka [paʀka] **nm ou f** parka.

parking [paʀkiŋ] 1 **nm** (*lieu*) car park (*Brit*), parking lot (*US*); (*action*) parking. **~ souterrain/à étages** underground/multistorey car park (*Brit*) *ou* parking lot (*US*); **~ payant** paying car park (*Brit*) *ou* parking lot (*US*). 2 **adj** (*péj*) dead-end (*épith*), which leads nowhere (*attrib*). **section-~** dead-end department; **stage-~** dead-end training course, training course which leads nowhere.

Parkinson [paʀkinsɔn] **nm: la maladie de ~** Parkinson's disease.

parkinsonien, -ienne [paʀkinsɔnjɛ̃, jɛn] 1 **adj** associated with Parkinson's disease. 2 **nm,f** patient suffering from Parkinson's disease.

parlant, e [paʀlɑ̃, ɑ̃t] 1 **adj** a (*doué de parole*) speaking (*épith*), talking (*épith*). **il n'est pas très ~** he's not very talkative; *voir* **cinéma**. b (*fig*) *portrait* lifelike; *comparaison, description* graphic, vivid; *geste, regard* eloquent, meaningful. **les chiffres sont ~s** the figures speak for themselves. 2 **adv: scientifiquement/économiquement** *etc* **~** scientifically/economically *etc* speaking.

parlé, e [paʀle] (**ptp de parler**) 1 **adj** *langue* spoken; *voir* **chaîne, journal**. 2 **nm** (*Théât*) spoken part.

parlement [paʀləmɑ̃] **nm** parliament. **le P~ (britannique)** Parliament; **le ~ américain** the American parliament, the US Congress; **le P~ européen** the European Parliament.

parlementaire [paʀləmɑ̃tɛʀ] 1 **adj** (*Pol*) parliamentary. 2 **nmf** a (*Pol*) member of Parliament; (*aux USA*) member of Congress; (*Brit Hist: partisan*) Parliamentarian. b (*négociateur*) negociator, mediator.

parlementairement [paʀləmɑ̃tɛʀmɑ̃] **adv** parliamentarily.

parlementarisme [paʀləmɑ̃taʀism] **nm** parliamentary government.

parlementer [paʀləmɑ̃te] [1] **vi** (*négocier*) to parley; (**: discuter*) to argue things over. (*hum: palabrer*) **~ avec qn** to argue endlessly with sb.

parler [paʀle] [1] 1 **vi** a (*faculté physique*) to talk, speak. **il a commencé à ~ à 2 ans** he started talking when he was 2; **votre perroquet parle?** can your parrot talk?; **~ du nez** to talk through one's nose; **~ distinctement** to speak distinctly; **il parle entre ses dents** he talks between his teeth, he mumbles; **je n'aime pas sa façon de ~** I don't like the way he talks *ou* speaks; **parlez plus fort!** talk *ou* speak louder!, speak up!; *voir* **façon**.

b (*exprimer sa pensée*) to speak; (*bavarder*) to talk. **~ franc/crûment** to speak frankly/bluntly; **~ bien/mal** to be a good/not to be a (very) good speaker; **~ d'or** to speak words of wisdom; **~ avec les mains** to speak with one's hands; (*péj*) **~ comme un livre** to talk like a book; **~ par paraboles *ou* par énigmes** to talk *ou* speak in riddles; **il aime s'écouter ~** he likes the sound of his own voice; **~ pour qn** to speak for sb; (*iro*) **parle pour toi!** speak for yourself!; (*Cartes*) **c'est à vous de ~** it's your bid; **au lieu de ~ en l'air, renseigne-toi/agis** instead of coming out with a lot of vague talk, find out/do something; **plutôt que de ~ en l'air, allons lui demander** instead of talking (wildly) let's go and ask him; **~ à tort et à travers** to blether, talk drivel*, talk through one's hat; **~ pour ne rien dire** to talk for the sake of talking *ou* say nothing at great length; **voilà qui est (bien) parlé!** hear hear!, well said!

c (*converser*) **~ à qn** to talk *ou* speak to sb; **il faut que je lui parle** I must talk to him *ou* have a word with him; **nous ne nous parlons pas** we're not on speaking terms; **moi qui vous parle** I myself; **mais je parle, je parle et toi, comment vas-tu?** but that's enough about me — how are you (doing)?; (*fig*) **trouver à qui ~** to meet one's match; (*fig*) **c'est ~ à un mur** it's like talking to a (brick) wall; **se ~ à soi-même** to talk to o.s.

d (*s'entretenir*) **~ de qch/qn** to talk about sth/sb; (*fig*) **~ de la pluie et du beau temps, ~ de choses et d'autres** to talk about the weather (*fig*), talk of this and that; **faire ~ de soi** to get o.s. talked about; **~ mal de qn** to speak ill of sb; **on parle beaucoup de lui comme ministre** he is being talked about *ou* spoken of as a possible *ou* future minister, he's tipped as a likely minister; **on ne parle que de ça** it's the only topic of conversation, it's the only thing people are talking about; **tout le monde en parle** everybody's talking about it; **toute la ville en parle** it's the talk of the town; **il n'en parle jamais** he never mentions it *ou* refers to it *ou* talks about it; **quand on parle du loup (on en voit la queue)** talk (*Brit*) *ou* speak of the devil (and he will appear).

e (*entretenir*) **~ de qch à qn** to tell sb about sth; **parlez-nous de vos vacances/projets** tell us about your holidays/plans; **on m'avait parlé d'une vieille maison** I had been told about an old house; **je lui parlerai de cette affaire** I'll speak to him *ou* I'll have a word with him about this business; (*soutenir*) **il a parlé de moi au patron** he put in a word for me with the boss; **on m'a beaucoup parlé de vous** I've heard a lot about you.

f (*annoncer l'intention*) **~ de faire qch** to talk of doing sth; **elle a parlé d'aller voir un docteur** she has talked of going to see a doctor; **on parle de construire une route** they're talking of building a road, there is talk of a road being built *ou* of building a road.

g (*fig*) **~ par gestes** to use sign language; **~ aux yeux/à l'imagination** to appeal to the eye/the imagination; **~ au cœur** to speak to the heart; **ce tableau/cette œuvre me parle** this painting/work really speaks to me; **les faits parlent (d'eux-mêmes)** the facts speak for themselves; **faire ~ la poudre** (*se battre*) to start a gunfight; (*faire la guerre*) to resort to war; **de quoi ça parle, ton livre? — ça parle de bateaux** what is your book about? — it's about ships; **le jardin lui parlait de son enfance** the garden brought back memories of his childhood (to him); **tout ici me parle de toi** everything here reminds me of you; **le devoir a parlé** I (*ou* he *etc*) heard the call of duty, duty called; **son cœur a parlé** he heeded the call of his heart.

h (*révéler les faits*) to talk. **faire ~** *suspect* to make talk, loosen the tongue of; *introverti, timide* to draw out.

j (*loc*) **tu parles!*, vous parlez!*** (*bien sûr*) you're telling me!*, you bet!*; (*iro*) no chance!*, you must be joking!*; **tu as été dédommagé, non? — parlons-en!** (*ça ne change rien*) you've been compensated, haven't you? — some good *ou* a lot of use that is (to me)!*; (*pas du tout*) you've been compensated, haven't you? — not likely!* *ou* you must be joking!*; **tu parles *ou* vous parlez d'une brute!** talk about a brute!; **leur proposition, tu parles si on s'en fiche!*** a fat lot we think of their idea!*; (*iro*) **tu parles si ça nous aide/c'est pratique*** that helps us/it's very helpful and I don't think!*; **ne m'en parlez pas!** you're telling me!*, I don't need telling!*; **n'en parlons plus!** let's forget (about) it, let's not mention it again; **sans ~ de ...** not to mention ..., to say nothing of ..., let alone ...; **tu peux ~!*** you can talk!*; **vous n'avez qu'à ~** just say the word, you've only to say the word.

2 **vt** a *langue* to speak. **~ (l')anglais** to speak English.

b **~ politique/affaires** to talk politics/business; **~ chiffon*/boutique*** to talk clothes/shop; (*hum*) **si nous parlions finances?** how about talking cash?*

3 **nm** a (*manière de parler*) speech. **le ~ vrai** straight talking; **le ~ de tous les jours** everyday speech, common parlance; **il a un ~ vulgaire** he has a coarse way of speaking; *voir* **franc**[1].

b (*langue régionale*) dialect.

parleur [paʀlœʀ] **nm**; *voir* **beau**.

parloir [paʀlwaʀ] **nm** *[école, prison]* visiting room; *[couvent]* parlour.

parlot(t)e* [paʀlɔt] **nf** chitchat* (*NonC*). **toutes ces ~s ne mènent à rien** all this chitchat* is a waste of time; **c'est de la ~ tout ça** that's all just talk.

Parme [paʀm] 1 **n** (*ville*) Parma. 2 **nm: (jambon de) ~** Parma ham. 3 **adj** (*couleur*) **p~** violet.

Parmentier [paʀmɑ̃tje] **adj inv** *voir* **hachis**.

parmesan [paʀməzɑ̃] **nm** (*Culin*) Parmesan (cheese).

parmi [paʀmi] **prép** among(st). **~ la foule** among *ou* in the crowd; **venez ici ~ nous** come over here with us; **c'est un cas ~ d'autres** it's one case among many, it's one of many cases; **allant ~ les ruelles désertes** going through the deserted alleys.

Parnasse [paʀnɑs] **nm** Parnassus. **le Mont ~** (Mount) Parnassus.

parnassien, -ienne [paʀnasjɛ̃, jɛn] **adj, nm,f** Parnassian.

parodie [paʀɔdi] **nf** parody. (*fig*) **une ~ de procès** a parody *ou* travesty of a trial; (*fig*) **une ~ de démocratie/d'élection** a travesty of a democracy/an election.

parodier [paʀɔdje] [7] **vt** to parody.

parodique [paʀɔdik] **adj** *style* parodic(al).

parodiste [paʀɔdist] **nmf** parodist.

paroi [paʀwa] **nf** (*gén, Anat, Bot*) wall; *[récipient]* (inside) surface, (inner) wall; *[véhicule, baignoire]* side; (*cloison*) partition. **~ rocheuse** rock face.

paroisse [paʀwas] **nf** parish.

paroissial, e, **mpl -iaux** [paʀwasjal, jo] **adj** parish (*épith*). **salle ~e** church hall; **à l'échelon ~** at the parochial *ou* parish level.

paroissien, -ienne [paʀwasjɛ̃, jɛn] 1 **nm,f** parishioner. (*fig*) **un drôle de ~*** a funny customer*. 2 **nm** (*missel*) prayer book, missal.

parole [paʀɔl] **nf** a (*mot*) word. **comprenez-vous le sens de ses ~s?** can you understand (the meaning of) what he says?; **assez de ~s, des actes!** enough talking, now it's time to act!; (*Prov*) **les ~s s'envolent, les écrits restent** verba volant, scripta manent; (*hum*) **voilà une bonne ~!** sound thinking!, that's what I like to hear!; **la ~ de Dieu** the word of God; **c'est ~ d'évangile** it's the gospel truth, it's gospel*; (*iro*) **de belles ~s** fair *ou* fine words! (*iro*); **~ célèbre** famous words *ou* saying; **prononcer une ~ historique** to make a historic remark; **ce sont des ~s en l'air** it's just idle talk; **il est surtout courageux en ~s** he's brave enough when it's just a matter of words *ou* talking about it; **tout cela est bien joli en ~s mais ...** this sounds all very well but ...; *voir* **boire, moulin, payer**.

b (*texte*) **~s** *[chanson]* words, lyrics; *[dessin]* words; **histoire sans ~s** wordless cartoon; (*légende*) **"sans ~s"** "no caption".

c (*promesse*) word. **tenir ~** to keep one's word; **il a tenu ~** he kept his word, he was as good as his word; **c'est un homme de ~, il est de ~, il n'a qu'une ~** he's a man of his word, his word is his bond; **il n'a aucune ~** you (just) can't trust a word he says; **je l'ai cru sur ~** I took his word for it; **(je vous donne** *ou* **vous avez ma) ~ d'honneur!** I give you *ou* you have my word (of honour), cross my heart!*; **~ de scout/marin** *etc* scout's/sailor's *etc* honour; **manquer à sa ~** to fail to keep one's word, go back on one's word; (*fig*) **ma ~!*** (upon) my word!; **tu es fou ma ~!** heavens-you're mad!; **prisonnier sur ~** prisoner on parole.

d (*faculté d'expression*) speech. **l'homme est doué de ~** man is endowed with speech; **avoir la ~ facile** to be a fluent speaker, have the gift of the gab*; **avoir le don de la ~** to be a gifted speaker; (*Prov*) **la ~ est d'argent, le silence est d'or** speech is silver, silence is golden; *[animal]* **il ne lui manque que la ~** it *ou* he does everything but talk; **perdre/retrouver la ~** to lose/recover one's speech; (*fig*) to lose/find one's tongue*; **il n'a jamais droit à la ~** he's never allowed to get a word in edgeways.

e (*Ling*) speech, parole (*SPÉC*). **acte de ~** speech act.

f (*Cartes*) **~!** (I) pass!

g (*dans un débat*) **droit de ~** right to speak; **temps de ~** speaking time; **vous avez la ~** you have the floor, over to you*; **la ~ est à la défense** it is the turn of the defence to speak; **passer** *ou* **céder la ~ à qn** to hand over to sb; **prendre la ~** to speak; **prendre la ~ pour dire** to take the floor to say.

parolier, -ière [paʀɔlje, jɛʀ] **nm,f** *[chanson]* lyric writer.

paronyme [paʀɔnim] **nm** paronym.

paronymie [paʀɔnimi] **nf** paronymy.

paronymique [paʀɔnimik] **adj** paronymic.

parotide [paʀɔtid] **nf: (glande) ~** parotid gland.

paroxysme [paʀɔksism] **nm** *[maladie]* crisis (point); *[crise, sensation, sentiment]* paroxysm, height. **être au ~ de la joie/colère** to be in a paroxysm of joy/anger, be beside o.s. with joy/anger; **le bruit était à son ~** the noise was at its height; **son désespoir était à son ~** he was at the height of his despair; **l'incendie/la douleur avait atteint son ~** the fire/pain was at its height *ou* at its fiercest; **le combat avait atteint son ~** the fight had reached fever pitch *ou* its height *ou* a climax.

parpaillot, e [paʀpajo, ɔt] **nm,f** (*Hist, péj*) Protestant.

parpaing [paʀpɛ̃] **nm** (*pierre pleine*) perpend (*Brit*), parpen (*US*); (*aggloméré*) breeze-block.

Parque [paʀk] **nf** (*Myth*) Fate. **les ~s** the Parcae, the Fates.

parquer [paʀke] [1] 1 **vt** *voiture, artillerie* to park; *moutons, bétail* to pen (in *ou* up); (*fig*) *personnes* to pen *ou* pack in; (*à l'intérieur*) to pack in, shut up. 2 **se parquer vpr** (*Aut*) to park.

parquet [paʀkɛ] **nm** a (*plancher*) (wooden *ou* parquet) floor, floorboards. b (*Jur*) public prosecutor's department *ou* office. c (*Bourse*) **le ~** (*enceinte*) the (dealing) floor; (*agents*) the stock exchange *ou* market.

parqueter [paʀkəte] [4] **vt** to lay a wooden *ou* parquet floor in. **pièce parquetée** room with a (polished) wooden *ou* parquet floor.

parrain [paʀɛ̃] **nm** a (*Rel, fig*) godfather. **accepter d'être le ~ d'un enfant** to agree to be a child's godfather *ou* to stand godfather to a child; **un ~ de la Mafia** a godfather in the Mafia. b (*dans un cercle, une société*) (*qui introduit*) proposer; (*qui aide financièrement*) sponsor; *[navire]* christener, namer; *[entreprise, initiative]* promoter; *[œuvre, fondation]* patron.

parrainage [paʀɛnaʒ] **nm** (*voir* **parrain**) sponsorship, proposing (for membership); christening, naming; promoting; patronage. **~ publicitaire** advertising sponsorship.

parrainer [paʀene] [1] **vt** (*voir* **parrain**) to sponsor, propose (for membership); to christen, name; to promote; to patronize. **se faire ~ par qn** *[personne]* to be proposed by sb; *[association]* to be sponsored by sb.

parricide [paʀisid] 1 **adj** parricidal. 2 **nmf** parricide. 3 **nm** (*crime*) parricide.

parsec [paʀsɛk] **nm** parsec.

parsemer [paʀsəme] [5] **vt** a (*répandre*) **~ de** to sprinkle with, strew with; **~ le sol de fleurs** to scatter flowers over the ground, strew the ground with flowers; **~ un tissu de paillettes d'or** to sprinkle material with gold sequins, strew gold sequins over material; (*fig*) **~ un texte de citations** to scatter quotations through a text.

b (*être répandu sur*) to be scattered *ou* sprinkled over. **les feuilles qui parsèment le gazon** the leaves which are scattered *ou* which lie scattered over the lawn; **ciel parsemé d'étoiles** sky sprinkled *ou* strewn *ou* studded with stars; **champ parsemé de fleurs** field dotted with flowers; (*fig*) **parsemé de difficultés/de fautes** riddled with difficulties/mistakes.

parsi, e [paʀsi] 1 **adj** Parsee. 2 **nm** (*Ling*) Parsee. 3 **nm,f: P~(e)** Parsee.

part [paʀ] **nf** a (*dans un partage*) share; (*portion*) portion; (*tranche*) slice. **~ d'héritage/de soucis** his share of the inheritance/of worries; **faire 8 ~s dans un gâteau** to cut a cake into 8 (slices); **c'est 12 F la ~ de gâteau** it's 12 francs a slice; (*fig*) **vouloir sa ~ du gâteau** to want one's slice *ou* share of the cake, want one's share of the spoils; **la ~ du lion** the lion's share; **~ à deux!** share and share alike!; **chacun paie sa ~** everyone pays his share, everyone chips in*.

b (*participation*) part. **prendre ~ à** *travail* to take part in, join in, collaborate in; *frais* to share in, contribute to; *manifestation* to join in, take part in; **cela prend une grande ~ dans sa vie** it plays a great part in his life; **il a pris une ~ importante dans l'élaboration du projet** he played an important part in the development of the project; **prendre ~ à un débat** to participate in *ou* take part in a debate; **"prenez ~ au développement de votre ville!"** "help to develop your town!"; **je prends ~ à vos soucis** I share (in) your worries; **avoir ~ à** to have a share in; **faire la ~ de la fatigue/du hasard** to take tiredness/chance into account *ou* consideration, allow for *ou* make allowance(s) for tiredness/chance; **il faut faire la ~ du vrai et du faux dans ce qu'elle dit** you can't believe everything she says; **faire la ~ des choses** to take things into account *ou* consideration, make allowances; (*fig*) **faire la ~ du feu** to cut one's losses; **faire la ~ belle à qn** to give sb more than his (*ou* her) due.

c (*partie*) part, portion. **c'est une toute petite ~ de sa fortune** it's only a tiny fraction *ou* part of his fortune; **pour une bonne** *ou* **large ~** largely, to a great extent; **pour une ~** partly, to some extent; **pour une petite ~** in a small way.

d (*Fin*) ≃ share (*giving right to participate in profits but not running of firm*); (*Impôts*) ≃ tax unit.

e **à ~** (*de côté*) aside, on one side; (*séparément*) separately, on its (*ou* their) own; (*excepté*) except for, apart from, aside from (*surtout US*); (*exceptionnel*) special, extraordinary; **nous mettrons ces livres à ~ pour vous** we'll put these books aside *ou* on one side for you; **prendre qn à ~** to take sb aside; **étudier chaque problème à ~** to study each problem separately *ou* on its own; **à ~ vous, je ne connais personne ici** apart from *ou* aside from *ou* except for you I don't know anyone here; **à ~ cela** apart *ou* aside from that, otherwise; **plaisanterie à ~** joking apart *ou* aside; **c'est un homme à ~** he's an extraordinary man, he's in a class of his own; **un cas/une place à ~** a special case/place; **il est vraiment à ~*** there aren't many like him around, he's one on his own*; (*littér*) **garder qch à ~ soi** to keep sth to o.s.; (*littér*) **je pensais à ~ moi** I thought within *ou* to myself; *voir* **bande[2], chambre.**

f (*loc*) **faire ~ de qch à qn** to announce sth to sb, inform sb of sth, let sb know *ou* tell sb about sth; **de la ~ de** (*provenance*) from; (*au nom de*) on behalf of; **il vient de la ~ de X** he has been sent by X; **cette machine demande un peu de bon sens de la ~ de l'utilisateur** this machine requires a little commonsense on the part of the user *ou* from the user; **cela m'étonne de sa ~** I'm surprised at that (coming) from him; **pour ma ~** as for me, for my part (*frm*), as far as I'm concerned; **dites-lui bonjour de ma ~** give him my regards; **c'est gentil de sa ~** that's nice of him; (*Téléc*) **c'est de la ~ de qui?** who's calling? *ou* speaking?; **prendre qch en bonne ~** to take sth in good part; **prendre qch en mauvaise ~** to take sth amiss, take offence at sth; **de toute(s) ~(s)** from all sides *ou* quarters; **d'autre ~** (*de plus*) moreover; **d'une ~ ..., d'autre ~** on the one hand ... on the other hand; **de ~ et d'autre** on both sides, on either side; **de ~ en ~** right through; **membre/citoyen à ~ entière** full member/citizen; **Français à ~ entière** person with full French citizenship, fully-fledged French citizen; **artiste à ~ entière** artist in his (*ou* her) own right; **l'Europe sera le partenaire à ~ entière des USA** Europe will be a fully-committed partner with the USA; *voir* **nul, quelque.**

partage [paʀtaʒ] **nm** a (*fractionnement, division*) *[terrain, surface]* dividing up, division; *[gâteau]* cutting; (*Math*) *[nombre]* factorizing. **faire le ~ de qch** to divide sth up; **le ~ du pays en 2 camps** the division of the country into 2 camps; *voir* **ligne[1].**

b (*distribution*) *[butin, héritage]* sharing out. **procéder au ~ de qch** to share sth out; **le ~ n'est pas juste** the way it's shared out isn't fair, it isn't fairly shared out; **j'ai été oublié dans le ~** I've been forgotten in the share-out; **quel a été le ~ des voix entre les candidats?** how were the votes divided among the candidates?; (*Pol*) **en cas de ~ des voix** in the event of a tie in the voting.

c (*participation*) sharing. **l'enquête a conclu au ~ des responsabilités** the inquiry came to the conclusion that the responsibility was shared; **le ~ du pouvoir avec nos adversaires** the sharing of power with our opponents; (*fig*) **fidélité sans ~** undivided loyalty.

d (*part*) share; (*fig: sort*) portion, lot. **donner/recevoir qch en ~** to give/receive sth in a will; **la maison lui échut en ~** the house came to him in the will; (*fig*) **le bon sens qu'il a reçu en ~** the common sense with which he has been endowed.

partagé, e [paʀtaʒe] (**ptp de partager**) **adj** a (*divisé*) *avis, opinions* divided. **les experts sont ~s sur la question** the experts are divided on the question. b (*littér: doté*) endowed. **il est bien/mal ~ par le sort** fate has been/has not been kind to him; *voir* **temps[1].**

partageable [paʀtaʒabl] **adj** divisible, which can be shared out *ou* divided up. **frais ~s entre tous** costs that are shared by all; **votre gaieté est difficilement ~** it is difficult to share (in) your merriment.

partager [paʀtaʒe] [3] 1 **vt** a (*fractionner*) *terrain, feuille, gâteau* to divide up. **~ en 2/en 2 bouts/par moitié** to divide in 2/into 2 pieces *ou* bits/in half.

b (*distribuer, répartir*) *butin, gâteau* to share (out) (*entre 2/plusieurs personnes* between 2/among several people); *frais* to share. **il partage son temps entre son travail et sa famille** he divides his time between his work and his family; **il partage son affection entre plusieurs personnes** several people have to share his affections.

c (*avoir une part de, avoir en commun*) *héritage, gâteau, appartement, sort* to share (*avec* with). **voulez-vous ~ notre repas?** will you share our meal?; **~ le lit de qn** to share sb's bed; **il n'aime pas ~** he doesn't like sharing; **les torts sont partagés** both (*ou* all) parties are at fault, there are faults on both (*ou* all) sides.

d (*s'associer à*) *sentiments, bonheur, goûts* to share (in); *opinion, idée* to share, agree with. **je partage votre douleur/bonheur/surprise** I share your sorrow/happiness/surprise; **amour partagé** mutual love.

e (*fig: diviser*) *[problème, conflit]* to divide. **partagé entre l'amour et la haine** torn between love and hatred.

f (*frm: douer*) to endow. **la nature l'a bien partagé** Nature has been generous to him.

2 **se partager vpr** a (*se fractionner*) to be divided. **ça peut facilement se ~ en 3/en 3 morceaux** it can easily be divided (up) *ou* cut in 3/into 3 pieces *ou* bits; *[vote]* **se ~ entre diverses tendances** to be divided between different groups; **le monde se partage en deux: les bons et les méchants** the world falls *ou* can be divided into two groups: the good and the wicked; **à l'endroit où les branches se partagent** where the branches fork *ou* divide; **le reste des voix s'est partagé entre les autres candidats** the remaining votes are distributed *ou* shared among the other candidates; **le pouvoir ne se partage pas** power is not something which can be shared; **il se partage entre son travail et son jardin** he divides his time between his work and his garden.

b (*se distribuer*) **se ~ qch** to share *ou* divide sth between *ou* among themselves; (*fig*) **se ~ le gâteau** to share out the cake; **ils se sont partagé le butin** they shared the booty between them; **nous nous sommes partagé le travail** we shared the work between us; **les 3 candidats se sont partagé les suffrages** the votes were divided among the 3 candidates; **se ~ les faveurs du public** to vie for the public's favour.

partageur, -euse [paʀtaʒœʀ, øz] **adj** ready *ou* willing to share. **il n'est pas ~** he doesn't like sharing (his things), he's not a good sharer.

partageux, -euse† [paʀtaʒø, øz] **nm,f** distributionist.

partance [paʀtɑ̃s] **nf: en ~** *train* due to leave; *avion* outward bound; *bateau* sailing (*attrib*), outward bound; **en ~ pour Londres** *train, avion* for London, London (*épith*); *bateau* bound *ou* sailing for London (*attrib*); (*passager*) (bound) for London (*attrib*).

partant[1], e [paʀtɑ̃, ɑ̃t] 1 **nm,f** a (*coureur*) starter; (*cheval*) runner. **tous ~s** all horses running; **non-~** non-runner. b (*personne*) person leaving, departing traveller *ou* visitor *etc.* **les ~s et les arrivants** the departures and arrivals. 2 **adj: je suis ~** I'm quite prepared to join in; **il est toujours ~ pour un bon repas*** he's always ready for a good meal; **si c'est comme ça, je ne suis plus ~** if that's how it is (you can) count me out.

partant[2] [paʀtɑ̃] **conj** (*littér*) hence, therefore, consequently.

partenaire [paʀtənɛʀ] **nmf** partner. **~s sociaux** ≃ unions and management, management and labour; **~s commerciaux** trading partners.

partenariat [paʀtənaʀja] **nm** partnership.

parterre [paʀtɛʀ] **nm** a (*plate-bande*) border, (flower)bed; (**: plancher*) floor. b (*Théât*) (*emplacement*) stalls (*Brit*), orchestra (*US*); (*public*) (audience in the) stalls (*Brit*) *ou* orchestra (*US*).

Parthe [paʀt] **nm** Parthian; *voir* **flèche[1].**

parthénogénèse [paʀtenoʒenɛz] **nf** parthenogenesis.

parthénogénétique [paʀtenoʒenetik] **adj** parthenogenetic.

parthénogénétiquement [paʀtenoʒenetikmɑ̃] **adv** parthenogenetically.

Parthénon [paʀtenɔ̃] **nm: le ~** the Parthenon.

parti[1] [paʀti] 1 **nm** a (*groupe*) (*gén, Pol*) party. **le ~ des mécontents** the malcontents; **le ~ de la défaite** the defeatists; **le ~ (communiste)** the Communist party.

b (*solution*) option, course of action. **hésiter entre 2 ~s** to wonder which of 2 courses *ou* which course to follow; **prendre un ~** to come to *ou* make a decision, make up one's mind; **prendre le ~ de faire** to make up one's mind to do, decide *ou* resolve to do; **mon ~ est pris** my mind is made up; **crois-tu que c'est le meilleur ~ (à prendre)?** do you think that's the best course (to take)? *ou* the best idea?; **prendre le ~ de qn, prendre ~ pour qn** (*se mettre du côté de qn*) to side with sb, take sb's side; (*donner raison à qn*) to stand up for sb; **prendre ~ (dans une affaire)** (*se rallier*) to take sides (on *ou* in a matter); (*dire ce qu'on pense*) to take a stand (on a matter); **prendre son ~ de qch** to come to terms with sth, reconcile o.s. to sth; **il faut bien en prendre son ~** you just have to come to terms with it *ou* put up with it.

c (*personne à marier*) match. **beau** *ou* **bon** *ou* **riche ~** good match.

d (*loc*) **tirer ~ de** *situation, occasion, information* to take advantage of, turn to (good) account; *outil, ressources* to put to (good) use; *victoire* to take advantage of; **tirer le meilleur ~ possible d'une situation** to turn a situation to best account, get the most one can out of a situation; **il sait tirer ~ de tout** (*situation*) he can turn anything to his advantage, he can make capital out of anything; (*objets*) he can put everything to good use; **faire un mauvais ~ à qn** to beat sb up, give sb rough treatment.

2 **comp ▸ parti pris** prejudice, bias; **je crois, sans parti pris ...** I think without bias (on my part) ... *ou* being quite objective about it ...; **juger sans parti pris** to take an unbiased *ou* objective view; **être de/éviter le parti pris** to be/avoid being prejudiced *ou* biased.

parti[2], e[1]* [paʀti] (**ptp de partir**) **adj** (*ivre*) tipsy, tight*. **il est bien ~** he's well away*.

partial, e, mpl -iaux [paʀsjal, jo] **adj** biased, prejudiced, partial. **être ~ envers qn** to be biased *ou* prejudiced against sb.

partialement [paʀsjalmɑ̃] **adv** in a biased way. **juger qch ~** to take a biased view of sth.

partialité [paʀsjalite] **nf: ~ (envers** *ou* **contre qn)** bias (against sb); **faire preuve de ~ envers** *ou* **contre qn** to be unfair to sb, be biased against sb, show bias against sb; **elle a montré dans cette affaire une regrettable ~** her attitude was dreadfully biased in that business.

participant, e [paʀtisipɑ̃, ɑ̃t] 1 **adj** participant, participating. 2 **nm,f** (*à un concours, une course*) entrant (*à* in); (*à un débat, un projet*) participant, person taking part (*à* in); (*à une association*) member (*à* of); (*à une cérémonie, un complot*) person taking part (*à* in). **~s aux bénéfices** those sharing in the profits; **les ~s à la manifestation/au concours** those taking part in the demonstration/competition.

participatif, ive [paʀtisipatif, iv] **adj: gestion ~ive** participative management; **titre ~** non-voting share (*in a public sector company*).

participation [paʀtisipasjɔ̃] **nf** a (*action: voir* **participer**) **~ à** taking part in; participation in; joining in; appearance in; involvement in; **la réunion aura lieu sans leur ~** the meeting will take place without their taking part *ou* without them; **peu importe l'habileté: c'est la ~ qui compte** skill doesn't really matter: what counts is taking part *ou* joining in; nous nous sommes assurés la ~ de 2 équilibristes we have arranged for 2 tightrope walkers to appear; c'est la ~ de X qui va attirer les spectateurs it's X (performing) who'll draw the crowds, it's the fact that X is appearing ou performing that will draw the crowds; ce soir grand gala avec la ~ de plusieurs vedettes tonight, grand gala with appearances by several stars; (Ciné) avec la ~ de X with guest appearance by X, with (special) guest star X; ~ électorale turnout at the polls (Brit), voter turnout (US); fort/faible taux de ~ électorale high/low turnout at the polls.

b (Écon) (détention d'actions) interest. prendre une ~ majoritaire dans une firme to acquire a majority interest in a firm; la ~ (ouvrière) worker participation; ~ aux bénéfices profit-sharing; ~ du personnel à la marche d'une entreprise staff participation ou involvement in the running of a firm.

c (financière) contribution. ~ aux frais: 50 F contribution towards costs: 50 francs; nous demandons une petite ~ (de 15 F) we request a small donation (of 15 francs).

participe [paʀtisip] nm participle.

participer [paʀtisipe] 1 1 participer à vt indir a (prendre part à) concours, colloque, cérémonie to take part in. je compte ~ au concours/à l'épreuve de fond I intend to take part in ou enter the competition/the long-distance event; peu d'électeurs ont participé au scrutin there was a low turnout at the polls, there was a low poll (Brit), there was a low voter turnout (US).

b (prendre une part active à) entreprise, discussion, jeu to participate in, take part in, join in; spectacle [artiste] to appear in; aventure, complot, escroquerie to take part in, be involved in. en sport, l'important n'est pas de gagner mais de ~ in sport the important thing is not winning but taking part ou but joining in; ~ à la joie/au chagrin de qn to share sb's joy/sorrow; ils ont participé à l'allégresse générale they joined in the general mood of joyfulness; on demande aux élèves de ~ davantage pendant le cours pupils are asked to be more actively involved during the class.

c (payer sa part de) frais, dépenses to share in, contribute to. ~ (financièrement) à entreprise, projet to cooperate in.

d (avoir part à) profits, pertes, succès to share (in).

2 participer de vt indir (littér: tenir de) to partake of (frm), have something of the nature of.

participial, e, mpl -iaux [paʀtisipjal, jo] 1 adj participial. 2 participiale nf participial phrase ou clause.

particularisation [paʀtikylaʀizasjɔ̃] nf particularization.

particulariser [paʀtikylaʀize] 1 1 vt to particularize. 2 se particulariser vpr to be distinguished ou characterized (par by).

particularisme [paʀtikylaʀism] nm a (Pol: attitude) sense of identity. (particularité) ~(s) specific (local) character (NonC), specific characteristic(s); (Pol, Sociol) ~s régionaux regional idiosyncracies. b (Rel) particularism.

particularité [paʀtikylaʀite] nf a (caractéristique) [individu, caractère, religion] particularity, (distinctive) characteristic; [texte, paysage] (distinctive) characteristic ou feature; [appareil, modèle] (distinctive) feature. ces modèles ont en commun la ~ d'être ... these models all have the distinctive feature of being ..., these models are all distinguished by being ...; cet animal présente la ~ d'être herbivore a distinctive feature ou characteristic of this animal is that it is herbivorous. b (†, littér: détail) particular. c (littér: unicité) particularity.

particule [paʀtikyl] nf (Ling, Phys) particle. ~ (nobiliaire) nobiliary particle; nom à ~ ≃ name with a handle, name with a "de" usually belonging to a noble family; il a un nom à ~ he has a handle to his name.

particulier, -ière [paʀtikylje, jɛʀ] 1 adj a (spécifique) aspect, point, exemple particular, specific; trait, style, manière de parler characteristic, distinctive. dans ce cas ~ in this particular case; il n'avait pas d'aptitudes ~ières he had no particular ou special aptitudes; cette habitude lui est ~ière this habit is peculiar to him; signes ~s (gén) distinctive signs; (sur un passeport) distinguishing marks.

b (spécial) exceptional, special, particular. la situation est un peu ~ière the situation is rather exceptional; ce que j'ai à dire est un peu ~ what I have to say is slightly unusual; cela constitue un cas ~ this is a special ou an unusual ou an exceptional case; rien de ~ à signaler nothing in particular, nothing unusual to report; je l'ai préparé avec un soin tout ~ I prepared it with very special care ou with particular care.

c (étrange) mœurs peculiar, odd; goût, odeur strange, odd. il a toujours été un peu ~ he has always been a bit peculiar ou odd.

d (privé) voiture, secrétaire, conversation, intérêt private. l'entreprise a son service ~ de livraison the company has its own delivery service; intervenir à titre ~ to intervene in a private capacity; voir hôtel, leçon.

e en ~ (en privé) parler in private; (séparément) examiner separately; (surtout) in particular, particularly, especially; (entre autres choses) in particular.

2 nm a (personne) person; (Admin, Comm) private individual. comme un simple ~ like any ordinary person; (petites annonces) vente/location de ~ à ~ private sale/let (Brit) ou rental (US).

b (*: individu) individual, character. un drôle de ~ an odd character ou individual.

c (chose) le ~ the particular; du général au ~ from the general to the particular.

particulièrement [paʀtikyljɛʀmɑ̃] adv particularly, especially, specially. ~ bon/évolué particularly ou specially good/developed; je ne le connais pas ~ I don't know him very ou particularly well; il aime tous les arts et tout ~ la peinture he is keen on all the arts, especially ou specially painting; une tâche ~ difficile a particularly ou specially difficult task; je voudrais plus ~ vous faire remarquer ce détail I'd particularly like to draw your attention to this detail; voulez-vous du café? — je n'y tiens pas ~ would you like a coffee? — not particularly ou specially.

partie[2] [paʀti] 1 nf a (portion, fraction) part; (quantité) part, amount. diviser en trois ~s to divide into three parts; il y a des ~s amusantes dans le film the film is funny in parts, the film has its funny moments; il ne possède qu'une ~ du terrain he only owns (one) part of the land; (Constr) ~s communes/privatives communal parts/privately-owned areas; une petite ~ de l'argent a small part ou amount of the money; une grande ou bonne ~ du travail a large ou good part of ou a good deal of the work; la majeure ou plus grande ~ du temps/du pays most of ou the greater ou the best part of the time/the country; la majeure ~ des gens the majority of people, most people; la plus grande ~ de ce que l'on vous a dit the greater part ou most of what you were told; tout ou ~ de all or part of; en ~ partly, in part; en grande ou majeure ~ largely, in large part, mainly, for the most part; faire ~ de ensemble, obligations, risques to be part of; club, association to belong to, be a member of; catégorie, famille to belong to; élus, gagnants to be among, be one of; la rivière fait ~ du domaine the river is part of the estate; les villes faisant ~ de ma circonscription the towns that make up my constituency; elle fait ~ de notre groupe she belongs to our group, she's one of our group; faire ~ intégrante de to be an integral part of, be part and parcel of.

b (spécialité) field, subject. moi qui suis de la ~ knowing the field ou subject as I do; il n'est pas dans ou de la ~ it's not his line ou field; quand on lui parle électricité, il est dans sa ~ when it's a matter of electricity, he knows what he's talking about; demande à ton frère, c'est sa ~ ou il est de la ~ ask your brother — it's his field ou his line.

c (Cartes, Sport) game; (Golf) round; (fig: lutte) struggle, fight. faisons une ~ de ... let's have a game of ...; on a fait une bonne ~ we had a good game; (fig) abandonner la ~ to give up the fight; la ~ est délicate it's a tricky situation ou business; la ~ n'est pas égale it's an unequal ou uneven match, it's not a fair match.

d (Jur) [contrat] party; [procès] litigant; (Mil: adversaire) opponent. la ~ adverse the opposing party; les ~s en présence the parties; les ~s belligérantes the warring factions; avoir affaire à forte ~ to have no mean opponent ou a tough opponent to contend with; être ~ prenante dans une négociation to be a party to a negotiation; voir juge.

e (Mus) part.

f (Anat euph) ~s sexuelles ou génitales, ~s honteuses† private parts; ~s viriles male organs; les ~s* the privates*.

g (loc) avoir la ~ belle to be sitting pretty*; se mettre de la ~ to join in; je veux être de la ~ I don't want to miss this, I want to be in on this*; (littér) avoir ~ liée (avec qn) to be hand in glove (with sb); ce n'est que ~ remise it will be for another time, we'll take a raincheck on it* (US); prendre qn à ~ (apostropher) to take sb to task; (malmener) to set on sb; (lit, fig) la ~ immergée de l'iceberg the invisible part of the iceberg; (Comm) comptabilité en ~ simple/double single-/double-entry book-keeping.

2 comp ►partie de campagne day ou outing in the country ►partie carrée wife-swapping party ►partie de chasse shooting party ou expedition ►partie civile (Jur) private party associating in a court action with public prosecutor; se porter ou se constituer partie civile to associate in a court action with the public prosecutor ►partie du discours (Ling) part of speech ►partie fine pleasure party ►partie de jambes en l'air: tout ce qui l'intéresse, c'est une partie de jambes en l'air* all he's interested in is getting his leg over** ►partie de pêche fishing party ou trip ►partie de plaisir: (fig) ce n'est pas une partie de plaisir! it's no picnic! ou vacation! (US), it's not my idea of fun!

partiel, -elle [paʀsjɛl] 1 adj (gén) partial. paiement ~ part payment; voir élection. 2 nm (Univ) class exam.

partiellement [paʀsjɛlmɑ̃] adv partially, partly.

partir[1] [paʀtiʀ] 16 vi a (quitter un lieu) to go, leave; (se mettre en route) to leave, set off, set out; (s'éloigner) to go away ou off; (disparaître) to go. pars, tu vas être en retard go ou off you go, you're going to be late; pars, tu m'embêtes go away, you're annoying me; es-tu prêt à ~? are you ready to go?; allez, je pars I'm off now; il est parti sans laisser d'adresse he left without leaving an address; nos voisins sont partis il y a 6 mois our neighbours left ou moved ou went (away) 6 months ago; (euph: mourir) depuis que mon pauvre mari est parti since my poor husband passed on, since the departure of my poor husband; ma lettre ne partira pas ce soir my letter won't go this evening; quand partez-vous (pour Paris)? when are you going off (to Paris)? ou leaving (for Paris)?, when are you off (to Paris)?*; ~ pour le bureau to leave ou set off for the office; elle est partie de Nice à 9 heures she left Nice *ou* set off from Nice at 9 o'clock; **sa femme est partie de la maison** his wife has left home; **sa femme est partie avec un autre** his wife has gone off with another man; **le mauvais temps a fait ~ les touristes** the bad weather has driven the tourists away; **j'espère que je ne vous fais pas ~** I hope I'm not chasing you away; **ceux-là, quand ils viennent bavarder, c'est dur de les faire ~** when that lot come round to talk, it's a hard job to get rid of them*; **~, c'est mourir un peu** to leave is to die a little; **fais ~ le chat de ma chaise** get the cat off my chair.

b (*aller*) to go. **il est parti dans sa chambre/acheter du pain** he has gone to his room/to buy some bread; **~ faire des courses/se promener** to go (out) shopping/for a walk; **pars devant acheter les billets** go on ahead and buy the tickets; **~ à la chasse/à la pêche** to go shooting/fishing; **~ en vacances/en voyage** to go (off) on holiday/on a journey; **~ à pied** to set off on foot; **tu pars en avion ou en voiture?** are you flying or driving?, are you going by plane or by car?; **~ à la guerre/au front** to go (off) to the war/to the front.

c (*démarrer*) *[moteur]* to start; *[avion]* to take off; *[train]* to leave; *[coureur]* to be off; *[plante]* to take. **la voiture partit sous son nez** the car started up *ou* drove off and left him standing; **il partit en courant** he dashed *ou* ran off; **il partit en trombe** *ou* **comme une flèche** he was off *ou* set off like a shot; **attention, le train va ~** look out, the train's leaving; **l'avion va ~ dans quelques minutes** the plane is taking off in a few minutes; **ce cheval est bien/mal parti** that horse got off to a good/bad start; **~ gagnant** to begin as if one is sure of success; **les voilà partis!** they're off!; **attention, prêts? partez!** ready, steady, go!, on your marks, get set, go!; (*fig*) **il faut ~ du bon pied** one must set off on the right foot; **c'est parti mon kiki!*** here we go!*; **faire ~ une voiture/un moteur** to start (up) a car/an engine.

d (*être lancé*) *[fusée]* to go off *ou* up; *[fusil, coup de feu]* to go off; *[bouchon]* to pop *ou* shoot out. **le coup est parti tout seul** the gun went off on its own; **le coup ne partit pas** the shot didn't go off, the shot misfired; **le bouchon est parti au plafond** the cork shot up to the ceiling; **ces cris partaient de la foule** these cries came from the crowd; **l'obus qui part du canon** the shell fired from the gun; **le pétard n'a pas voulu ~** the banger wouldn't go off; **le mot partit malgré lui** the word came out before he could stop it; **le ballon partit comme un boulet de canon** the ball shot off like a bullet; **faire ~** *fusée* to launch; *pétard* to set off, light.

e (*être engagé*) **~ sur une idée fausse/une mauvaise piste** to start off with the wrong idea/on the wrong track; **~ bien/mal** to be *ou* get off to a good/bad start, start (off) well/badly; **le pays est mal parti** the country is in a bad way *ou* in a mess *ou* in a sorry state; **nous sommes mal partis pour arriver à l'heure** we've made a bad start as far as arriving on time is concerned; **son affaire est bien partie** his business has got off to a good start; **il est bien parti pour gagner** he's all set to win; **~ dans des digressions sans fin** to wander off *ou* launch into endless digressions; **quand ils sont partis à discuter, il y en a pour des heures*** once they're off* *ou* launched on one of their discussions, they'll be at it for hours*; **~ à rire*** *ou* **d'un éclat de rire** to burst out laughing; **il est (bien) parti pour parler deux heures** the way he's going, he'll be talking for *ou* he looks all set to talk for two hours; **la pluie est partie pour (durer) toute la journée** the rain has set in for the day; **on est parti pour ne pas déjeuner** at this rate *ou* the way things are going, we won't get any lunch.

f (*commencer*) **~ de** *[contrat, vacances]* to begin on, run from; *[course, excursion]* to start *ou* leave from; **l'autoroute part de Lille** the motorway starts at Lille; **un chemin qui part de l'église** a path going from *ou* leaving the church; **les branches qui partent du tronc** the branches going out from the trunk; **cet industriel est parti de rien** *ou* **de zéro** this industrialist started from scratch *ou* from *ou* with nothing; **cette rumeur est partie de rien** this rumour grew up out of nothing; **notre analyse part de cette constatation** our analysis is based on this observation *ou* takes this observation as its starting point; **partons de l'hypothèse que** let's assume that; **si tu pars du principe que tu as toujours raison/qu'ils ne peuvent pas gagner** if you start from the notion that *ou* if you start off by assuming that you're always right/that they can't win, if you take as your starting point the idea that you're always right/that they can't win; **en partant de ce principe, rien n'est digne d'intérêt** on that basis, nothing's worthy of interest; **en partant de là, on peut faire n'importe quoi** looking at things that way, one can do anything.

g (*provenir*) **~ de** to come from; **mot qui part du cœur** word which comes from the heart; **cela part d'un bon sentiment/d'un bon naturel** that comes from his (*ou* her *etc*) kindness/good nature.

h (*disparaître*) *[tache]* to go, come out; *[bouton, crochet]* to go, come off; *[douleur]* to go; *[rougeurs, boutons]* to go, clear up; *[odeur]* to go, clear. **la tache est partie au lavage** the stain has come out in the wash *ou* has washed out; **toute la couleur est partie** all the colour has gone *ou* faded; **faire ~** *tache* to remove; *odeur* to clear, get rid of; **lessive qui fait ~ la couleur** washing powder which fades *ou* destroys the colours.

i (*loc*) **à ~ de** from; **à ~ d'aujourd'hui** (as) from today, from today onwards; **à ~ de maintenant** from now on; **à ~ de 4 heures** from 4 o'clock on(wards); **à ~ d'ici le pays est plat** from here on(wards) the land is flat; **à ~ de** *ou* **en partant de la gauche, c'est le troisième** it is (the) third along from the left; **pantalons à ~ de 300 F** trousers from 300 francs (upwards); **lire à ~ de la page 5** to start reading at page 5; **allez jusqu'à la poste et, à ~ de là, c'est tout droit** go as far as the post office and after that it's straight ahead; **à ~ de ces 3 couleurs vous pouvez obtenir toutes les nuances** with *ou* from these 3 colours you can get any shade; **c'est fait à ~ de produits chimiques** it's made from chemicals; **à ~ de ce moment-là, ça ne sert à rien de discuter plus longtemps** once you've reached that stage, it's no use discussing things any further.

partir[2] [paʀtiʀ] **vt** *voir* **maille.**

partisan, e [paʀtizɑ̃, an] 1 **adj** a (*partial*) partisan. b **être ~ de qch/de faire qch** to be in favour of sth/of doing sth; **être ~ du moindre effort** to be a believer in (taking) the line of least resistance. 2 **nm,f** *[personne, thèse, régime]* supporter; *[action]* supporter, advocate, proponent; *[doctrine, réforme]* partisan, supporter, advocate; (*Mil*) partisan. **c'est un ~ de la fermeté** he's an advocate of *ou* a believer in firm measures, he supports *ou* advocates firm measures.

partita [paʀtita] **nf** (*Mus*) partita.

partitif, -ive [paʀtitif, iv] 1 **adj** partitive. 2 **nm** partitive (article).

partition [paʀtisjɔ̃] **nf** a (*Mus*) score. **as-tu ta ~?** have you got your score? *ou* music?*; **grande ~** full score. b (*frm, gén Pol: division*) partition.

partouse‡ [paʀtuz] **nf** orgy.

partouser‡ [paʀtuze] 1 **vi** to have an orgy.

partout [paʀtu] **adv** everywhere, everyplace (*US*). **~ où** everywhere (that), wherever; **avoir mal ~** to ache all over; **tu as mis des papiers ~** you've put papers all over the place; (*Sport*) **2/15 ~** 2/15 all; (*Tennis*) **40 ~** deuce.

partouze‡ [paʀtuz] **nf** = **partouse**‡.

parturiente [paʀtyʀjɑ̃t] **adjf** parturient.

parturition [paʀtyʀisjɔ̃] **nf** parturition.

parure [paʀyʀ] **nf** a (*toilette*) costume, finery (*NonC*); (*bijoux*) jewels; (*sous-vêtements*) set of lingerie; (*fig littér*) finery, livery (*littér*). **~ de table/de lit** set of table/bed linen; **~ de diamants** set of diamonds, diamond ornament; (*littér*) **les arbres ont revêtu leur ~ de feuilles** the trees have put on their leafy finery (*littér*). b (*déchet*) trimming.

parution [paʀysjɔ̃] **nf** appearance, publication.

parvenir [paʀvəniʀ] 22 1 **parvenir à vt indir** a (*arriver*) *sommet* to get to, reach; *honneurs* to achieve; *état, âge* to reach. **~ aux oreilles de qn** to reach sb's ears; **~ à maturité** to become ripe; **ma lettre lui est parvenue** my letter reached him, he got my letter; **ses ordres nous sont parvenus** his orders reached us; **faire ~ qch à qn** to send sth to sb; **~ à ses fins** to achieve one's ends; **sa renommée est parvenue jusqu'à notre époque** *ou* **nous** his fame has come down to our own day *ou* to us.

b (*réussir*) **~ à faire qch** to manage to do sth, succeed in doing sth; **il y est parvenu** he managed it; **il n'y parvient pas tout seul** he can't manage on his own.

2 **vi** (*parfois péj: faire fortune*) to succeed *ou* get on in life, arrive.

parvenu, e [paʀvəny] (**ptp de parvenir**) 1 **adj** upstart. 2 **adj, nm,f** (*péj*) parvenu, upstart.

parvis [paʀvi] **nm** square (*in front of church or public building*).

pas[1] [pɑ] 1 **nm** a (*gén*) step; (*bruit*) footstep; (*trace*) footprint. **faire un ~ en arrière/en avant, reculer/avancer d'un ~** to step back/forward, take a step *ou* a pace back/forward; **faire de grands/petits ~** to take long strides/short steps; **la politique des petits ~** the policy of taking things one step at a time; **marcher à grands ~** to stride along; **il reconnut son ~ dans le couloir** he recognized his footsteps *ou* his step in the corridor; **revenir** *ou* **retourner sur ses ~** to retrace one's steps *ou* path; **je vais là où me conduisent mes ~** I am going where my steps take me; **à ~ mesurés** *ou* **comptés** with measured steps; (*lit, fig*) **~ à ~** step by step; (*lit, fig*) **à chaque ~** at every step; **il ne peut pas faire un ~ sans elle/sans la rencontrer** he can't go anywhere without her/without meeting her; **ne le quittez pas d'un ~** follow him wherever he goes; **arriver sur les ~ de qn** to arrive just after sb, follow close on sb's heels; *voir* **marcher.**

b (*distance*) pace. **à 20 ~** at 20 paces; **c'est à deux ~ d'ici** it's only a minute away, it's just a stone's throw from here.

c (*vitesse*) pace; (*Mil*) step; *[cheval]* walk. **aller bon ~, aller** *ou* **marcher d'un bon ~** to walk at a good *ou* brisk pace; **marcher d'un ~ lent** to walk slowly; **changer de ~** to change step; **allonger** *ou* **hâter** *ou* **presser le ~** to hurry on, quicken one's step *ou* pace; **ralentir le ~** to slow down; **marcher au ~** to march; **se mettre au ~** to get in step; **mettre son cheval au ~** to walk one's horse; (*Aut*) **rouler** *ou* **aller au ~** to crawl along, go dead slow (*Brit*), go at a walking pace; **au ~ cadencé** in quick time; **au ~ de charge** at the charge; **au ~ de course** at a run; **au ~ de gymnastique** at a jog trot; **au ~ redoublé** in double time, double-quick.

d (*démarche*) tread. **d'un ~ lourd** *ou* **pesant** with a heavy tread; **~ d'éléphant** elephantine tread.

e (*Danse*) step. **~ de danse/valse** dance/waltz step; *voir* **esquisser.**

f (*Géog: passage*) *[montagne]* pass; *[mer]* strait.

g (*Tech*) *[vis, écrou]* thread.

h (*loc*) **faire un grand ~ en avant** to take a big step *ou* a great leap forward; **la science avance à grands ~/à ~ de géant** science is taking great/gigantic steps forward, science is striding foward/advancing by leaps and bounds; **à ~ de loup, à ~ feutrés** stealthily, with (a) stealthy tread; **d'un ~ léger** (*agilement*) with an airy tread; (*avec insouciance*) airily, blithely; (*joyeusement*) with a spring in one's step; **j'y vais de ce ~** I'll go straightaway *ou* at once; **mettre qn au ~** to bring sb to heel, make sb toe the line; **avoir le ~ sur qn** to rank before sb; **prendre le ~ sur** *considérations, préoccupations* to override; *théorie, méthode* to supplant; *personne* to steal a lead over; **franchir** *ou* **sauter le ~** to take the plunge; **du mensonge à la calomnie il n'y a qu'un ~** it's a short *ou* small step from lies to slander; *voir* **céder, cent[1], faux[2], premier** *etc*.

2 **comp ►pas battu** (*Danse*) pas battu **►le pas de Calais** (*détroit*) the Straits of Dover **►le Pas-de-Calais** (*département*) the Pas-de-Calais **►pas de clerc** (*littér*) blunder **►pas de deux** (*Danse*) pas de deux **►pas de l'oie** (*Mil*) goose-step; (*Mil*) **faire le pas de l'oie** to goose-step **►pas-de-porte** (*Jur*) ≃ key money (*for shop etc*) **►pas de la porte** doorstep; **sur le pas de la porte** (*lit*) on the doorstep, in the doorway **►pas de tir** *[champ de tir]* shooting range; (*Espace*) launching pad **►pas de vis** thread.

pas[2] [pɑ] 1 **adv nég** a (*avec ne: formant nég verbale*) not, n't (*dans la langue courante*). **je ne vais ~ à l'école** (*aujourd'hui*) I'm not *ou* I am not going to school; (*habituellement*) I don't *ou* I do not go to school; **ce n'est ~ vrai, c'est ~ vrai*** it isn't *ou* it's not *ou* it is not true; **je ne suis ~/il n'est ~ allé à l'école** I/he didn't *ou* did not go to school; **je ne trouve ~ mon sac** I can't *ou* cannot find my bag; **je ne vois ~** I can't *ou* cannot *ou* don't see; **c'est ~ vrai!*** no kidding!*, you don't say!*; **je ne prends ~/je ne veux ~ de pain** I won't have/I don't want any bread; **ils n'ont ~ de voiture/d'enfants** they don't have *ou* haven't got a car/any children, they have no car/children; **il m'a dit de (ne) ~ le faire** he told me not to do it; **ça me serait insupportable de ne ~ le voir, ne ~ le voir me serait insupportable** it would be unbearable not to see him, not to see him would be unbearable; **je pense qu'il ne viendra ~** I don't think he'll come; **ce n'est ~ sans peine que je l'ai convaincu** it was not without (some) difficulty that I convinced him; **non ~** *ou* **ce n'est ~ qu'il soit bête** (it's) not that he's a fool; **ce n'est ~ que je refuse** it's not that I refuse; **il n'y a ~ que ça** it's not just that; **il n'y a ~ que lui** he's not the only one; **je n'en sais ~ plus que vous** I know no more *ou* I don't know any more about it than you (do); **il n'y avait ~ plus de 20 personnes** there weren't *ou* were not more than 20 people; **il n'est ~ plus/moins intelligent que vous** he is no more/no less intelligent than you.

b (*indiquant ou renforçant opposition*) **elle travaille, (mais) lui ~** she works, but he doesn't; **il aime ça, ~ toi?** he likes it, don't you?; **ils sont 4 et non (~) 3** there are 4 of them, not 3; **vient-il ou (ne vient-il) ~?** is he coming or (is he) not?, is he coming or isn't he?; **leur maison est chauffée, la nôtre ~** their house is heated but ours isn't *ou* is not.

c (*dans réponses négatives*) not. **~ de sucre, merci!** no sugar, thanks!; **~ du tout** not at all, not a bit; **il t'a remercié, au moins? — ~ du tout** *ou* **absolument ~** he did at least thank you? — he certainly didn't *ou* did not; **~ encore** not yet; **~ plus que ça** so-so*; **~ tellement*, ~ tant que ça** not (all) that much*, not so very much; **~ des masses*** not a lot*, not an awful lot*; **qui l'a prévenu? — ~ moi/elle** *etc* who told him? — not me/she *etc ou* I didn't/she didn't *etc*.

d (*devant adj, n, dans excl, souvent* *) **ce sont des gens ~ fiers** they're not proud people; **il est dans une situation ~ banale** *ou* **ordinaire** he's in an unusual situation; **~ un n'est venu** not one *ou* none (of them) came; **~ possible!** no!, you don't say!*; **~ de chance*** hard *ou* bad luck*!, too bad*; **~ vrai?*** isn't that so?, (isn't that) right?; **tu es content, ~ vrai?!*** you're pleased, aren't you? *ou* admit it; **t'es ~ un peu fou?*** you must be *ou* you are off (*Brit*) *ou* out of (*US*) your head!*; **~ d'histoires** *ou* **de blagues, il faut absolument que j'arrive à l'heure** (now) no nonsense, I absolutely must be on time; **(c'est) ~ bête, cette idée!** that's not a bad idea (at all)!; **si c'est ~ malheureux!*** *ou* **honteux!*** isn't that *ou* it a shame!; **tu viendras, ~?*** you're coming, aren't you?, you'll come, won't you?; **~ de ça!** we'll have none of that!; *voir* **falloir, fou.**

2 **comp ►pas grand-chose** (*péj*) **nmf inv** good-for-nothing.

pascal[1], e, mpl **-aux** [paskal, o] **adj** *agneau* paschal; *messe* Easter.

pascal[2], pl **~s** [paskal] **nm** (*Phys*) pascal; (*: *billet*) 500 francs note.

pascalien, -ienne [paskaljɛ̃, jɛn] **adj** of Pascal.

passable [pɑsabl] **adj** passable, tolerable; (*sur copie d'élève*) fair. (*Univ*) **mention ~** ≃ pass(mark); **à peine ~** barely passable, not so good (*attrib*).

passablement [pɑsabləmɑ̃] **adv** (*moyennement*) *jouer, travailler* tolerably *ou* reasonably well; (*assez*) *irritant, long* rather, fairly, pretty*; (*beaucoup*) quite a lot *ou* a bit*. **il faut ~ de courage pour ...** it requires a fair amount of courage to ... .

passade [pɑsad] **nf** passing fancy, whim, fad; (*amoureuse*) passing fancy.

passage [pɑsaʒ] 1 **nm** a (*venue*) **guetter le ~ du facteur** to watch for the postman to come by, be on the look-out for the postman; **attendre le ~ de l'autobus** to wait for the bus to come; **agrandir une voie pour permettre le ~ de gros camions** to widen a road to allow heavy vehicles to use it *ou* to allow heavy vehicles through; **observer le ~ des oiseaux dans le ciel** to watch the birds fly by *ou* over; **pour empêcher le ~ de l'air sous la porte** to stop draughts (coming in) under the door; **lors de votre ~ à la douane** when you go *ou* pass through customs; **lors d'un récent ~ à Paris** when I (*ou* he *etc*) was in *ou* visiting Paris recently, on a recent trip to Paris; **la navette d'autobus fait 4 ~s par jour** the bus goes past *ou* does a shuttle service 4 times a day; **prochain ~ de notre représentant le 8 mai** our representative will call next *ou* will next be in the area on May 8th; **"~ de troupeaux"** "cattle crossing"; **livrer ~** to make way; **il y a beaucoup de ~ l'été** there are a lot of people passing *ou* coming through here in the summer; **commerçant qui travaille avec le ~** *ou* **les clients de ~** shopkeeper catering for passing trade *ou* the casual trade; **il est de ~ à Paris** he is in *ou* visiting *ou* passing through Paris at the moment; **amours/amants de ~** casual *ou* passing affairs/lovers; **je l'ai saisi au ~** (*je passais devant*) I grabbed him as I went by *ou* past; (*il passait devant*) I grabbed him as he went by *ou* past; *voir* **lieu.**

b (*transfert*) **le ~ de l'état solide à l'état gazeux** the change from the solid to the gaseous state; **le ~ de l'enfance à l'adolescence** the transition *ou* passage from childhood to adolescence; **le ~ du jour à la nuit** the change from day to night; **le ~ du grade de capitaine à celui de commandant** promotion from captain to major; **le ~ de l'alcool dans le sang** the entry of alcohol into the bloodstream; **son ~ en classe supérieure est problématique** there are problems about his moving up (*Brit*) *ou* promotion (*US*) to the next class (*Brit*) *ou* grade (*US*); **~ à l'acte** taking action, acting; *voir* **examen.**

c (*lieu*) passage; (*chemin*) way, passage; (*itinéraire*) route; (*rue*) passage(way), alley(way). **un ~ dangereux sur la falaise** a dangerous section on the cliff; **il faut trouver un ~ dans ces broussailles** we must find a way through this undergrowth; **on a mis des barrières sur le ~ de la procession** barriers have been put up along the route of the procession *ou* taken by the procession; **on se retourne sur son ~** people turn round and look when he goes past; **l'ennemi dévasta tout sur son ~** the enemy left total devastation in their wake; **barrer le ~ à qn** to block sb's way; **laisser le ~ à qn** to let sb pass *ou* past; **va plus loin, tu gênes le ~** move along, you're in the way; **ne laissez pas vos valises dans le ~** don't leave your cases in the passage; **~ du Nord-Ouest** North-West Passage; *voir* **frayer.**

d (*Naut*) **payer son ~** to pay for one's passage, pay one's fare.

e (*fragment*) *[livre, symphonie]* passage.

f (*traversée*) *[rivière, limite, montagnes]* crossing. (*Naut*) **le ~ de la ligne** crossing the Line.

g (*loc*) **il a eu un ~ à vide** (*syncope*) he felt a bit faint; (*baisse de forme*) he went through a bad patch *ou* spell; **j'ai toujours un petit ~ à vide vers 16 h** I always start to lose concentration *ou* have a short lapse of concentration around 4 o'clock.

2 **comp ►passage clouté** pedestrian crossing (*Brit*), ≃ zebra crossing (*Brit*), crosswalk (*US*) **►"passage interdit"** "no entry", "no thoroughfare" **►passage à niveau** level crossing (*Brit*), grade crossing (*US*) **►passage (pour) piétons** pedestrian walkway **►passage protégé** (*Aut*) priority *ou* right of way over secondary roads **►passage souterrain** subway (*Brit*), underpass **►passage à tabac** beating up.

passager, -ère [pɑsaʒe, ɛʀ] 1 **adj** a (*de courte durée*) *malaise* passing (*épith*), brief; *inconvénient* temporary; *bonheur, beauté* passing (*épith*), transient, ephemeral. **j'avais cru à un malaise ~** I thought this malaise would quickly pass over, I thought this would be a temporary malaise; **pluies ~ères** intermittent *ou* occasional showers *ou* rain. b *rue* busy. 2 **nm,f** passenger. **~ clandestin** stowaway.

passagèrement [pɑsaʒɛʀmɑ̃] **adv** for a short while, temporarily.

passant, e [pɑsɑ̃, ɑ̃t] 1 **adj** *rue* busy. 2 **nm,f** passer-by. 3 **nm** *[ceinture]* loop.

passation [pɑsasjɔ̃] **nf** *[contrat]* signing; (*Comm*) *[écriture]* entry. **~ de pouvoirs** handing over of office *ou* power, transfer of power.

passavant [pɑsavɑ̃] **nm** a (*Comm, Jur*) transire, carnet. b (*Naut*) catwalk.

passe[1] [pɑs] 1 **nf** a (*Escrime, Ftbl, Tauromachie*) pass. **faire une ~** to pass (*à* to); **~ en retrait/en avant** back/forward pass; (*Ftbl*) **~ croisée** cross; **faire une ~ croisée à qn** to cross to sb.

b *[magnétiseur]* pass.

c (*Roulette*) passe.

d (*Naut: chenal*) pass, channel.

e *[prostituée]* **c'est 200 F la ~** it is 200 francs a time *ou* go; **faire 20 ~s par jour** to have 20 clients *ou* customers a day; *voir* **hôtel, maison.**

f (*loc*) **être en ~ de faire** to be on one's *ou* the way to doing; **il est en ~ de réussir** he is poised to succeed; **cette espèce est en ~ de disparaître** this species is on the way to dying out *ou* looks likely to die out; **être dans une bonne ~** to be in a healthy situation; **être dans** *ou* **traverser une mauvaise ~** (*gén*) to be going through a bad patch (*Brit*), be having a rough time; (*santé*) to be in a poor state; **est-ce qu'il va sortir de cette mauvaise ~?** will he manage to pull through (this time)?; *voir* **mot.**

2 **comp ►passe d'armes** (*fig*) heated exchange **►passe de caisse** (*Comm*) *sum allowed for cashier's errors* **►passes magnétiques**

hypnotic passes.

passe²* [pɑs] nm (abrév de **passe-partout**) *voir* **passer**.

passe- [pɑs] préf *voir* **passer**.

passé, e [pɑse] (ptp de **passer**) 1 adj a (*dernier*) last. **c'est arrivé le mois ~ /l'année ~e** it happened last month/last year; **au cours des semaines/années ~es** over these last *ou* the past (few) weeks/years.

b (*révolu*) *action, conduite* past. **~ de mode** out of fashion, out of date; **songeant à sa gloire/ses angoisses ~e(s)** thinking of his past *ou* former glory/distress; **regrettant sa jeunesse/sa beauté ~e** yearning for her departed *ou* vanished youth/beauty; **si l'on se penche sur les événements ~s** if one looks back over past events; **cette époque est ~e maintenant** that era is now over; **ce qui est ~ est ~** what is past is dead and gone, what is over is over; **où sont mes années ~es?** where has my life gone?; **il se rappelait le temps ~** he was thinking back to days *ou* time gone by.

c (*fané*) *couleur, fleur* faded. **tissu ~ de ton** material that has lost its colour, faded material.

d (*plus de*) **il est 8 heures ~es** it's past *ou* gone (*Brit*) 8 o'clock; **il est rentré à 9 heures ~es** it was past *ou* gone (*Brit*) 9 o'clock when he got back; **ça fait une heure ~e que je t'attends** I've been waiting for you for more than *ou* over an hour.

2 nm a **le ~** the past; **il faut oublier le ~** the past should be forgotten; **c'est du ~, n'en parlons plus** it's (all) in the past now, let's not say any more about it; **il est revenu nous voir comme par le ~** he came back to see us as he used to in the past; **il a eu plusieurs condamnations dans le ~** he had several previous convictions.

b (*vie écoulée*) past. **pays fier de son ~** country proud of its past; **bandit au ~ chargé** gangster with a past; **son ~ m'est inconnu** I know nothing of his past.

c (*Gram*) past tense. **les temps du ~** the past tenses; **mettez cette phrase au ~** put this sentence into the past (tense); **~ antérieur** past anterior; **~ composé** perfect; **~ simple** past historic, preterite.

3 prép after. **~ 6 heures on ne sert plus les clients** after 6 o'clock we stop serving (customers); **~ cette maison, on quitte le village** after this house, you are out of the village.

passéisme [pɑseism] nm (*péj*) attachment to the past.

passéiste [pɑseist] 1 adj (*péj*) backward-looking. 2 nmf (*péj*) devotee of the past.

passement [pɑsmɑ̃] nm braid (*NonC*).

passementer [pɑsmɑ̃te] [1] vt to braid.

passementerie [pɑsmɑ̃tʀi] nf (*objets*) braid (*NonC*), trimmings; (*commerce*) sale of furnishing *etc* trimmings. **rayon de ~** department selling furnishing *etc* trimmings.

passementier, -ière [pɑsmɑ̃tje, jɛʀ] 1 adj: **industrie ~ière** furnishing trimmings industry. 2 nm,f (*fabricant*) manufacturer of furnishing *etc* trimmings; (*vendeur*) salesman (*ou* woman) specializing in furnishing trimmings.

passepoil [pɑspwal] nm piping.

passepoilé, e [pɑspwale] adj piped.

passeport [pɑspɔʀ] nm passport.

passer [pɑse] [1] 1 vi (*avec aux être*) a to pass, go *ou* come past. **~ en courant** to run past; **~ à pas lents** to go slowly past; **les camions ne passent pas dans notre rue** lorries don't come along *ou* down our street; **il passait dans la rue avec son chien/en voiture** he was walking down the street with his dog/driving down the street; **le train va bientôt ~** the train will soon come past; **où passe la route?** where does the road go?; **la Seine passe à Paris** the Seine flows through Paris; **la balle/flèche n'est pas passée loin** the bullet/arrow didn't miss by much; **le fil passe dans ce tuyau** the wire goes down *ou* through this pipe; **faire ~ les piétons** to let the pedestrians cross; **une lueur cruelle passa dans son regard** a cruel gleam came into his eyes; *voir* **bouche, coup, main**.

b (*faire une halte rapide*) **~ au bureau/chez un ami** to call (in *ou* by) *ou* drop in *ou* by at the office/at a friend's; **je ne fais que ~** I'm not stopping*, I can't stay, I'm just calling in; **~ à la radio/à la visite médicale** to go for an X-ray/one's medical *ou* physical (examination); **~ à la douane** to go *ou* pass through customs, clear customs; **~ chercher *ou* prendre qn** to call for sb, (go *ou* come and) pick sb up; **~ voir qn *ou* rendre visite à qn** to call (in) on sb, call to see sb; **puis-je ~ te voir en vitesse?** can I pop round (to see you)?; **le facteur est passé** the postman has been; **à quelle heure passe le laitier?** what time does the milkman come?; **le releveur du gaz passera demain** the gasman will call tomorrow; **j'irai le voir en passant** I'll call to see him *ou* I'll call in and see him on my way.

c (*changer de lieu, d'attitude, d'état*) to go. **~ d'une pièce dans une autre** to go from one room to another; **si nous passions au salon?** shall we go into the sitting room?; **~ à table** to sit down to eat; **~ en Belgique** to go over to Belgium; **~ à l'ennemi/l'opposition** to go over *ou* defect to the enemy/the opposition; **la photo passa de main en main** the photo was passed *ou* handed round; **~ d'un extrême à l'autre** to go from one extreme to the other; **~ de l'état solide à l'état liquide** to pass *ou* change from the solid to the liquid state; **~ du rire aux larmes** to switch from laughter to tears; **~ à un ton plus sévère** to take a harsher tone; **~ à l'action, ~ aux actes** to go into action; **~ aux ordres** to collect one's orders; **~ dans les mœurs/les habitudes** to become the custom/the habit; **~ dans la langue** to pass *ou* come into the language; **~ en proverbe** to become proverbial; **son argent de poche passe en bonbons *ou* dans les bonbons** his pocket money (all) goes on sweets; **l'alcool passe dans le sang** alcohol enters the bloodstream; **le restant des légumes est passé dans le potage** the left-over vegetables went into the soup.

d (*franchir un obstacle*) *[véhicule]* to get through; *[cheval, sauteur]* to get over; (*Alpinisme*) to get up. (*Aut: en manœuvrant*) **ça passe?** can I make it?, do I have enough room (to turn *etc*)?

e *[temps]* to go by, pass. **comme le temps passe (vite)!** how time flies!; **cela fait ~ le temps** it passes the time.

f *[liquide]* to go *ou* come through, seep through; *[café]* to go through; *[courant électrique]* to get through.

g (*être digéré, avalé*) to go down. **mon déjeuner ne passe pas** my lunch won't settle; **prendre un cachet pour faire ~ le déjeuner** to take a tablet to help one's lunch down; **prends de l'eau pour faire ~ le gâteau** have some water to wash down the cake; **ce vin passe bien** this wine goes down nicely.

h (*être accepté*) *[demande, proposition]* to pass. **je ne pense pas que ce projet de loi passera** I don't think this bill will be passed *ou* will go through; **cette plaisanterie ne passe pas dans certains milieux** that joke doesn't go down well *ou* isn't appreciated in some circles; **il y a des plaisanteries/des erreurs qui passent dans certaines circonstances mais pas dans d'autres** there are some jokes/mistakes which are all right in some circumstances but not in others; **le gouvernement se demande comment faire ~ les hausses de prix** the government is concerned at how to get (an) acceptance of the price increases *ou* how to get the price increases through; **il est passé de justesse à l'examen** he only just scraped through *ou* passed the exam; **il est passé dans la classe supérieure** he's moved up to the next class (*Brit*), he's passed *ou* been promoted to the next grade (*US*); (*Sport*) **l'équipe est passée en 2ᵉ division** (*progrès*) the team were promoted to the second division; (*recul*) the team have been relegated to the second division; **ça passe ou ça casse** it'll make us (*ou* him *etc*) *ou* break us (*ou* him *etc*).

i (*devenir*) to become. **~ directeur/président** to become *ou* be appointed director/president.

j (*Ciné*) *[film]* to be showing, be on; (*TV*) *[émission]* to be on; *[personne]* to be on, appear. **~ à la radio/à la télé*** to be on the radio/on TV*; **~ à l'antenne** to go on the air.

k (*dépasser*) **le panier est trop petit, la queue du chat passe** the basket is too small — the cat's tail is sticking out; **son manteau est trop court, la robe passe** her coat is too short — her dress shows underneath *ou* below (it); **ne laisse pas ~ ton bras par la portière** don't put your arm out of the window.

l (*disparaître*) *[couleur]* to fade; *[mode]* to die out; *[douleur]* to pass (off), wear off; *[colère]* to die down; (*lit, fig*) *[orage]* to blow over, die down; *[beauté]* to fade; *[jeunesse]* to pass; (*mourir*) *[personne]* to pass on *ou* away. **faire ~ à qn le goût *ou* l'envie de faire** to cure sb of doing, make sb give up doing; **il voulait être pompier mais ça lui a passé** he wanted to be a fireman but he got over it; **cela fera ~ votre rhume** that will get you over your cold *ou* get rid of your cold for you; **le plus dur est passé** the worst is over now; (*fig*) **ça lui passera!*** (*habitude*) he'll get over it!; (*sentiment*) he'll grow out of it!

m (*Cartes*) to pass.

n (*Jur, Parl: être présenté*) to come up. **le projet de loi va ~ devant la Chambre** the bill will come *ou* be put before Parliament; **il est passé devant le conseil de discipline de l'école** he came up *ou* was brought up before the school disciplinary committee; **~ en justice** to (come) up before the courts.

o (*Aut*) **~ en première/marche arrière** to go into first/reverse; **~ en seconde/quatrième** to change into second/fourth; **les vitesses passent mal** the gears are stiff.

p **~ par** *lieu* to go *ou* come through; *intermédiaire* to go through; *expérience* to go through, undergo; **je passe par Amiens pour y aller** I go *ou* pass through Amiens to get there, I go there via Amiens; **par où êtes-vous passé?** which way did you go? *ou* come?; **le chien est trop gros pour ~ par le trou** the dog is too big to get through the hole; **~ par l'université/par un collège technique** to go through university/technical school; **pour lui parler, j'ai dû ~ par sa secrétaire** I had to go through *ou* via his secretary *ou* I had to see his secretary before I could speak to him; **pour téléphoner, il faut ~ par le standard** you have to go through the switchboard to make a call; **~ par des difficultés** to have difficulties *ou* a difficult time; **il est passé par des moments difficiles** he had some hard times; **nous sommes tous passés par là** we've all been through that, that's happened to all of us; **il faudra bien en ~ par là** there's no way round it; **il faudra bien en ~ par ce qu'il demande** we'll have to give him what he wants, we'll have to comply with *ou* give in to his request; **une idée m'est passée par la tête** an idea occurred to me; **elle dit tout ce qui lui passe par la tête** she says whatever comes into her head; **ça fait du bien par où ça passe!**** that's just what the doctor ordered!*

q **~ pour: je ne voudrais pas ~ pour un imbécile** I wouldn't like to be taken for a fool; **il pourrait ~ pour un Allemand** you could take him for a German, he could pass as a German; **auprès de ses amis, il passait pour un séducteur/un excentrique** he was regarded by his friends as (being) a lady's man/an eccentric; **il passe pour intelligent** he is thought of as intelligent, he's supposed to be intelligent; **il passe pour beau auprès de certaines femmes** some women think *ou* find him good-looking, he's considered good-looking by some women; **cela passe pour vrai** it's thought to be true; **se faire ~ pour** to pass o.s. off as; **il s'est fait ~ pour fou pour se faire réformer** he pretended to be mad so he could be declared unfit for service; **faire ~ qn pour** to make sb out to be; **tu veux me faire ~ pour un idiot!** do you want to make me look stupid or what?

r **~ sous/sur/devant/derrière** *etc* to go under/over/in front of/behind *etc;* **~ devant la maison/sous les fenêtres de qn** to pass *ou* go past sb's house/sb's window; **l'air passe sous la porte** a draught comes in under the door; **la voie ferrée passe le long du fleuve** the railway line runs alongside the river; **je passe devant vous pour vous montrer le chemin** I'll go in front to show you the way; **passez donc devant** you go first; **l'autobus lui est passé dessus, il est passé sous l'autobus** he was run over by the bus; **le travail passe avant tout/avant les loisirs** work comes first/before leisure; **~ devant un jury** to go before a jury; (*fig*) **~ devant Monsieur le maire** to get married or hitched*; **ma famille passe en premier** my family comes first; **le confort, ça passe après** comfort is less important *ou* comes second; **les poissons sont passés au travers du filet** the fish slipped through the net; (*fig*) **~ sur** *faute* to pass over, overlook; *détail inutile ou scabreux* to pass over; **je veux bien ~ sur cette erreur** I'm willing to pass over *ou* overlook this mistake; **je passe sur les détails** I shall pass over *ou* leave out *ou* skip the details; *voir* **corps, côté, nez, ventre.**

s **y ~*: on a eu la grippe, tout le monde y est passé** we've had the flu and everybody got it *ou* nobody escaped it; **si tu conduis comme ça, on va tous y ~** if you go on driving like that, we've all had it*; **toute sa fortune y est passée** he spent all his fortune on it, his whole fortune went on it.

t **laisser ~** *air, lumière* to let in; *personne, procession* to let through (*ou* past, in, out *etc*); *erreur* to overlook, miss; *occasion* to let slip, miss; **s'écarter pour laisser ~ qn** to move back to let sb (get) through *ou* past; **nous ne pouvons pas laisser ~ cette affaire sans protester** we cannot let this matter pass without a protest, we can't let this matter rest there — we must make a protest.

u (*loc*) **en passant** (*accessoirement*) in passing, by the way; **soit dit en passant** let me say in passing; **qu'il soit menteur, passe (encore), mais voleur c'est plus grave** he may be a liar, that's one thing but a thief, that's more serious; **passe pour cette erreur, mais une malhonnêteté, c'est impardonnable** a mistake is one thing, but being dishonest is unforgivable; **passons** let's say no more (about it).

2 **vt** (*avec aux avoir*) a *rivière, frontière, seuil* to cross; *porte* to go through; *haie* to jump *ou* get over. **~ une rivière à la nage/en bac** to swim across/take the ferry across a river.

b *examen* to sit, take; *douane* to go through, clear. **~ son permis (de conduire)** to take one's driving test; **~ une visite médicale** to have a medical (examination); **~ un examen avec succès** to pass an exam.

c *temps, vacances* to spend. **~ le temps/sa vie à faire** to spend the time/one's life doing; **~ son temps à ne rien faire** to idle one's time away; **(faire qch) pour ~ le temps** (to do sth) to while away *ou* pass the time; **~ la soirée chez qn** to spend the evening at sb's (house); *voir* **mauvais.**

d (*assouvir*) **~ sa colère/sa mauvaise humeur sur qn** to work off *ou* vent one's anger/one's bad temper on sb; **~ son envie de gâteaux** to satisfy one's urge for cakes.

e (*omettre*) *mot, ligne* to miss out (*Brit*), leave out. **~ son tour** to miss one's turn; **et j'en passe!** and that's not all!; **j'en passe, et des meilleures!** and that's not all — I could go on!, and that's the least of them!; *voir* **silence.**

f (*permettre*) **~ une faute à qn** to overlook sb's mistake; **~ un caprice à qn** to humour *ou* indulge sb's whim; **on lui passe tout** *bêtises* he gets away with anything; *désirs* he gets everything he wants; **il faut bien se ~ quelques fantaisies** you've got to allow yourself a few *ou* indulge in a few extravagances; **passez-moi l'expression** (if you'll) pardon the expression.

g (*transmettre*) *consigne, message, maladie* to pass on; (*Sport*) *ballon* to pass. **~ qch à qn** to give *ou* hand sth to sb; **tu (le) fais ~** pass *ou* hand it round; **~ une affaire/un travail à qn** to hand a matter/a job over to sb; **passe-moi une cigarette** pass *ou* give me a cigarette; **passez-moi du feu** give me a light; **il m'a passé un livre** he's lent me a book; **je suis fatigué, je vous passe le volant** I am tired, you take the wheel *ou* you drive; (*au téléphone*) **je vous passe M. X** (*standard*) I'm putting you through to Mr X; (*je lui passe l'appareil*) here's Mr X; **passe-lui un coup de fil** give him a ring (*Brit*) *ou* call, phone *ou* ring (*Brit*) *ou* call him (up); **passez-moi tous vos paquets** let me have all your parcels.

h (*Douane*) **~ des marchandises en transit** to carry goods in transit; **~ qch en fraude** to smuggle sth (in, out, through *etc*); **~ des faux billets** to pass forged notes.

i (*enfiler*) *pull* to slip on; *robe* to slip into. **~ une bague au doigt de qn** to slip a ring on sb's finger; **~ un lacet dans qch** to thread a lace through sth; **~ la corde au cou de qn** to put the rope round sb's neck.

j **~ la tête à la porte** to poke one's head round the door; **~ la main/la tête à travers les barreaux** to stick one's hand/head through the bars.

k (*dépasser*) *gare, maison* to pass, go past. **~ le poteau** to pass the post, cross the finishing line; **~ les limites *ou* les bornes** to go too far (*fig*); **tu as passé l'âge (de ces jeux)** you are too old (for these games); **il ne passera pas la nuit/la semaine** he won't last the night/the week *ou* see the night/week out; *voir* **cap.**

l (*Culin*) *thé* to strain; *café* to pour the water on. **~ la soupe** (*à la passoire*) to strain the soup; (*au mixer*) to blend the soup, put the soup through the blender.

m (*Aut*) **~ la seconde/la troisième** to go *ou* change (up *ou* down) into second/third (gear).

n *film, diapositives* to show; *disque* to put on, play. **que passent-ils au cinéma?** what's on *ou* showing at the cinema?

o (*Comm*) *écriture* to enter; *commande* to place; *marché, accord* to reach, come to; *contrat* to sign. (*lit, fig*) **~ qch aux profits et pertes** to write sth off.

p (*faire subir une action*) **~ le balai/l'aspirateur/le chiffon** to sweep up/hoover ® (*Brit*) *ou* vacuum/dust; **passe le chiffon dans le salon** dust the sitting room, give the sitting room a dust; **~ une pièce à l'aspirateur** to hoover ® (*Brit*) *ou* vacuum a room, go over a room with the vacuum cleaner; **~ la serpillière dans la cuisine, ~ la cuisine à la serpillière** to wash (down) the kitchen floor; **~ une couche de peinture sur qch** to give sth a coat of paint; **~ un mur à la chaux** to whitewash a wall; **~ qch sous le robinet** to rinse *ou* run sth under the tap; **elle lui passa la main dans les cheveux** she ran her hand through his hair; **se ~ les mains à l'eau** to rinse one's hands; **passe-toi de l'eau sur le visage** give your face a (quick) wash; **qu'est-ce qu'il lui a passé (comme savon)!*** he gave him a really rough time!*, he really laid into him!*; *voir* **arme, éponge, menotte, revue, tabac.**

3 **se passer vpr** a (*avoir lieu*) to take place; (*arriver*) to happen. **la scène se passe à Paris** the scene takes place in Paris; **qu'est-ce qui s'est passé?** what (has) happened?; **que se passe-t-il?, qu'est-ce qu'il se passe?** what's going on?; **ça ne s'est pas passé comme je l'espérais** it didn't work out as I'd hoped; **tout s'est bien passé** everything went off smoothly; **ça s'est mal passé** it turned out badly, it went off badly; **je ne sais pas ce qui se passe en lui** I don't know what's the matter with him *ou* what's come over him *ou* what's got into him; **cela ne se passera pas ainsi!** I shan't stand for that!, I shan't let it rest at that!; **il ne se passe pas un seul jour sans qu'il ne pleuve** not a day goes by *ou* passes without it *ou* its raining.

b (*finir*) to pass off, be over. **il faut attendre que ça se passe** you'll have to wait till it passes off *ou* is over.

c **se ~ de qch** to do without sth; **on peut se ~ d'aller au théâtre** we can do without going to the theatre; **se ~ de qn** to manage without sb; **je peux me ~ de ta présence** I can manage without you around; **je me passerais bien d'y aller!** I could do without having to go; **s'il n'y en a plus, je m'en passerai** if there isn't any more, I'll do without; **nous nous voyons dans l'obligation de nous ~ de vos services** we find ourselves obliged to dispense with your services; **je me passe de tes conseils!** I can do without your advice!; **il se passerait de manger plutôt que de faire la cuisine** he'd go without eating *ou* without food rather than cook; (*iro*) **tu pourrais te ~ de fumer** you could refrain from smoking; **la citation se passe de commentaires** the quotation needs no comment *ou* speaks for itself.

4 **comp ▸passe-crassane nf (pl passe-crassanes)** *type of winter pear* **▸passe-droit nm (pl passe-droits)** (undeserved) privilege, favour; **il a eu un passe-droit** he got preferential treatment **▸passe-lacet nm (pl passe-lacets)** bodkin (*voir* **raide**) **▸passe-montagne nm (pl passe-montagnes)** balaclava **▸passe-partout** (*clef*) master *ou* skeleton key; *tenue* for all occasions, all-purpose (*épith*); *formule* all-purpose (*épith*), catch-all (*épith*) **▸passe-plat nm (pl passe-plats)** serving hatch **▸passe-rose nf (pl passe-roses)** hollyhock **▸passe-temps nm inv** pastime; **ses passe-temps préférés** his favourite outside interests *ou* pastimes **▸passe-thé nm inv** tea strainer **▸passe-vues nm inv** slide changer; *voir* **tour.**

passereau, pl ~x [pasʀo] **nm** (*Orn*) passerine; (†: *moineau*) sparrow.

passerelle [pasʀɛl] **nf** (*pont*) footbridge; (*Naut: pont supérieur*) bridge; (*Aviat, Naut: voie d'accès*) gangway; (*fig: passage*) (inter)link. (*Scol*) **(classe) ~** reorientation class (*facilitating change of course at school*).

passette [pasɛt] **nf** (small) tea strainer.

passeur [pasœʀ] **nm** *[rivière]* ferryman, boatman; *[frontière]* smuggler (*of drugs, refugees etc*).

passible [pasibl] **adj: ~ d'une amende/peine** *personne* liable to a fine/penalty; *délit* punishable by a fine/penalty; **~ d'un impôt** liable for (a) tax; (*Comm*) **~ de droits** liable to duty.

passif, -ive [pasif, iv] 1 **adj** (*gén*) passive. **rester ~ devant une situation** to remain passive in the face of a situation; *voir* **défense**[1]. 2 **nm** a (*Ling*) passive. **au ~** in the passive voice. b (*Fin*) liabilities. **le ~ d'une succession** the liabilities on an estate; (*fig*) **mettre qch au ~ de qn** to add sth to sb's list of weak points.

passiflore [pasiflɔʀ] **nf** passionflower.

passing-shot, pl passing-shots [pasiŋʃɔt] **nm** passing shot. **faire un ~** to play a passing shot.

passion [pasjɔ̃] nf **a** (*goût*) passion. **avoir la ~ du jeu/des voitures** to have a passion for gambling/cars; **le sport est sa ~ ou est une ~ chez lui** he is mad* *ou* crazy* about sport, his one passion is sport.

b (*amour*) passion. **déclarer sa ~** to declare one's love; **aimer à la ou avec ~** to love passionately.

c (*émotion, colère*) passion. **emporté par la ~** carried away by passion; **discuter avec/sans ~** to argue passionately *ou* heatedly/dispassionately *ou* coolly; **débat sans ~** lifeless debate; **œuvre pleine de ~** work full of passion.

d (*Mus, Rel*) **P~** Passion; **le dimanche de la P~** Passion Sunday; **le jour de la P~** the day of the Passion; **la semaine de la P~** Passion week; **la P~ selon saint Matthieu** (*Rel*) the Passion according to St Matthew; (*Mus*) the St Matthew Passion; *voir* **fruit**.

passionnant, e [pasjɔnɑ̃, ɑ̃t] adj *personne* fascinating; *livre, match, film* fascinating, gripping, enthralling, exciting; *métier* fascinating, exciting.

passionné, e [pasjɔne] (ptp de **passionner**) **1** adj *personne, tempérament, haine* passionate; *description, orateur, jugement* impassioned. **être ~ de ou pour** to have a passion for; **un photographe ~** a (mad*) keen photographer; **débat ~** heated *ou* impassioned debate. **2** nm,f **a** (*personne exaltée*) passionate person. **b ~ de: c'est un ~ de voitures de course** he's a racing car fanatic.

passionnel, -elle [pasjɔnɛl] adj *relation, sentiment* passionate; *crime* of passion.

passionnément [pasjɔnemɑ̃] adv passionately, with passion. **~ amoureux de** madly *ou* passionately in love with.

passionner [pasjɔne] [1] **1** vt *personne [mystère, match]* to fascinate, grip; *[livre, sujet]* to fascinate; *[sport, science]* to be a passion with; *débat* to inflame. **ce film/ce roman m'a passionné** I found that film/novel fascinating; **la musique le passionne** music is his passion, he has a passion for music; **j'ai un métier qui me passionne** I have a fascinating *ou* exciting job. **2 se passionner** vpr: **se ~ pour** *livre, mystère* to be fascinated by; *sport, science* to have a passion for, be mad keen on*; *métier* to be fascinated *ou* really excited by.

passivement [pasivmɑ̃] adv passively.

passivité [pasivite] nf passivity, passiveness.

passoire [pɑswaʀ] nf (*gén*) sieve; *[thé]* strainer; *[légumes]* colander. (*fig*) **être une (vraie) ~** to be like a sieve; **quelle ~ ce gardien de but!** what a useless goalkeeper – he lets everything in!; **avoir la tête ou la mémoire comme une ~** to have a memory like a sieve; **troué comme une ~** with as many holes as a sieve.

pastel [pastɛl] **1** nm (*Bot*) woad, pastel; (*teinture bleue*) pastel; (*bâtonnet de couleur*) pastel (crayon); (*œuvre*) pastel. **au ~** in pastels. **2** adj inv *tons* pastel. **un bleu/vert ~** a pastel blue/green.

pastelliste [pastelist] nmf pastellist.

pastenague [pastənag] nf stingray.

pastèque [pastɛk] nf watermelon.

pasteur [pastœʀ] nm **a** (*Rel: prêtre*) minister, pastor, clergyman, preacher (*US*). **b** (*littér, Rel: berger*) shepherd. **le Bon P~** the Good Shepherd.

pasteurisation [pastœʀizasjɔ̃] nf pasteurization.

pasteuriser [pastœʀize] [1] vt to pasteurize.

pastiche [pastiʃ] nm (*imitation*) pastiche.

pasticher [pastiʃe] [1] vt to do (*ou* write *etc*) a pastiche of.

pasticheur, -euse [pastiʃœʀ, øz] nm,f (*gén*) imitator; (*auteur*) author of pastiches.

pastille [pastij] nf *[médicament, sucre]* pastille, lozenge; *[encens, couleur]* block; *[papier, tissu]* disc. **~s de menthe** mints; **~s pour la toux** cough pastilles (*Brit*) *ou* drops *ou* lozenges; **~s pour la gorge** throat pastilles (*Brit*) *ou* lozenges; **~ de silicium** silicon chip.

pastis [pastis] nm (*boisson*) pastis; (‡ *dial: ennui*) fix*. **être dans le ~** to be in a fix* *ou* a jam*.

pastoral, e, mpl **-aux** [pastɔʀal, o] **1** adj (*gén*) pastoral. **2 pastorale** nf (*Littérat, Peinture, Rel*) pastoral; (*Mus*) pastorale.

pastorat [pastɔʀa] nm pastorate.

pastoureau, pl **~x** [pastuʀo] nm (*littér*) shepherd boy.

pastourelle [pastuʀɛl] nf (*littér*) shepherd girl; (*Mus*) pastourelle.

pat [pat] **1** adj inv stalemate(d). **2** nm: **le ~** stalemate; **faire ~** to end in (a) stalemate; **faire qn ~** to stalemate sb.

patachon [pataʃɔ̃] nm *voir* **vie**.

patagon, -onne [patagɔ̃, ɔn] **1** adj Patagonian. **2** nm,f: **P~(-ne)** Patagonian.

Patagonie [patagɔni] nf Patagonia.

patagonien, -ienne [patagɔnjɛ̃, jɛn] **1** adj Patagonian. **2** nm,f: **P~(-ne)** Patagonian.

pataphysique [patafizik] nf pataphysics (*sg*).

patapouf [patapuf] **1** excl (*langage enfantin*) whoops! **faire ~** to tumble (down). **2** nmf (*) fatty*.

pataquès [patakɛs] nm **a** (*faute de liaison*) mistaken elision; (*faute de langage*) malapropism. **b** (*péj: discours*) incoherent jumble; (*confusion*) muddle. **il a fait un ~** (*discours*) his speech was an incoherent jumble; (*confusion*) he made a real muddle, he muddled things up.

patata* [patata] excl *voir* **patati***.

patate [patat] nf (*: *pomme de terre*) spud*; (‡: *imbécile*) fathead‡, chump*, clot‡. (*Bot*) **~ (douce)** sweet potato; *voir* **gros**.

patati* [patati] excl: **et ~ et patata** and so on and so forth.

patatras [patatʀa] excl crash!

pataud, e [pato, od] **1** adj lumpish (*Brit*), clumsy. **2** nm,f lump. **3** nm (*chien*) pup(py) (*with large paws*).

pataugeoire [patoʒwaʀ] nf paddling pool.

patauger [patoʒe] [3] vi **a** (*marcher*) (*avec effort*) to wade about; (*avec plaisir*) to splash about; **on a dû ~ dans la boue pour y aller** we had to wade *ou* flounder *ou* squelch (*Brit*) through the mud to get there. **b** (*fig*) (*dans un discours*) to get bogged down; (*dans une matière*) to flounder. **notre projet patauge** our project is getting nowhere.

patchouli [patʃuli] nm patchouli.

patchwork [patʃwœʀk] nm patchwork. **couverture en ~** patchwork blanket.

pâte [pɑt] **1** nf **a** (*Culin*) (*à tarte*) pastry; (*à gâteaux*) mixture; (*à pain*) dough; (*à frire*) batter. (*fig*) **il est de la ~ dont sont faits les héros*** he's (of) the stuff heroes are made of; *voir* **bon¹, coq¹, main**.

b *[fromage]* cheese. **(fromage à) ~ dure/molle/cuite/fermentée** hard/soft/cooked/fermented cheese.

c ~s (alimentaires) pasta; (*dans la soupe*) noodles.

d (*gén: substance*) paste; (*crème*) cream.

e (*Art*) paste.

2 comp ►**pâte d'amandes** almond paste, marzipan ►**pâte brisée** shortcrust (*Brit*) *ou* pie crust (*US*) pastry ►**pâte à choux** choux pastry ►**pâte à crêpes** pancake batter ►**pâte dentifrice** toothpaste ►**pâte feuilletée** puff *ou* flaky (*Brit*) pastry ►**pâte à frire** batter ►**pâte de fruits** crystallized fruit (*NonC*); **2 pâtes de fruits** 2 pieces of fruit jelly; **une framboise en pâte de fruit** a raspberry jelly ►**pâte à modeler** modelling clay, Plasticine ® ►**pâte molle** (*péj*) milksop, spineless individual ►**pâte à pain** (bread) dough ►**pâte à papier** wood pulp ►**pâtes pectorales** cough drops *ou* pastilles (*Brit*) ►**pâte sablée** sablé (*Brit*) *ou* sugar crust (*US*) pastry ►**pâte de verre** molten glass.

pâté [pɑte] nm **a** (*Culin*) pâté. **~ en croûte** ≈ meat pie; **petit ~** meat patty, small pork pie; **~ de campagne** pâté de campagne, farmhouse pâté; **~ de foie** liver pâté. **b** (*tache d'encre*) (ink) blot. **c ~ de maisons** block (of houses). **d ~ (de sable)** sandpie, sandcastle.

pâtée [pɑte] nf **a** *[chien, volaille]* mash (*NonC*), feed (*NonC*); *[porcs]* swill (*NonC*). **b** (*: *punition, défaite*) hiding*. **recevoir la ou une ~** to get a hiding*; **donner la ou une ~ à qn** to give sb a hiding*.

patelin¹* [patlɛ̃] nm village; (*péj*) godforsaken place*.

patelin², e [patlɛ̃, in] adj (*littér péj*) bland, smooth, ingratiating.

patelinerie [patlinʀi] nf (*littér péj*) blandness (*NonC*), smoothness (*NonC*).

patelle [patɛl] nf (*Zool*) limpet.

patène [patɛn] nf paten.

patenôtre [pat(ə)notʀ(ə)] nf (†, *péj*) (*prière*) paternoster, oraison (†: *littér*); (*marmonnement*) gibberish (*NonC*).

patent, e¹ [patɑ̃, ɑ̃t] adj obvious, manifest, patent (*frm*). **il est ~ que** it is patently obvious that; *voir* **lettre**.

patentable [patɑ̃tabl] adj (*Comm*) liable to trading dues, subject to a (trading) licence.

patente² [patɑ̃t] nf (*Comm*) trading dues *ou* licence; (*Naut*) bill of health.

patenté, e [patɑ̃te] adj (*Comm*) licensed; (*fig hum: attitré*) established, officially recognized. **c'est un menteur ~** he's a thoroughgoing liar.

pater [patɛʀ] nm inv **a** (‡: *père*) old man‡, pater* (*Brit*), governor† (*Brit hum*). **b** (*Rel*) **P~** pater, paternoster. **c** (*Antiq, fig*) **~ familias** paterfamilias.

patère [patɛʀ] nf (hat- *ou* coat-)peg.

paternalisme [patɛʀnalism] nm paternalism.

paternaliste [patɛʀnalist] adj paternalistic.

paterne [patɛʀn] adj (*littér*) fatherly, avuncular.

paternel, -elle [patɛʀnɛl] **1** adj *autorité, descendance* paternal; (*bienveillant*) *personne, regard, conseil* fatherly. **quitter le domicile ~** to leave one's father's house; **du côté ~** on one's father's side, on the paternal side; **ma tante ~elle** my aunt on my father's side, my paternal aunt. **2** nm (‡) old man‡, pater* (*Brit*), governor† (*Brit hum*).

paternellement [patɛʀnɛlmɑ̃] adv (*voir* **paternel**) paternally; in a fatherly way.

paternité [patɛʀnite] nf (*lit*) paternity, fatherhood; (*fig*) *[roman]* paternity, authorship; *[invention, théorie]* paternity.

pâteux, -euse [pɑtø, øz] adj (*gén*) pasty; *pain* doughy; *encre* thick; *langue* coated, furred (*Brit*); *voix* thick; *style* woolly. **avoir la bouche ~euse** to have a furred (*Brit*) *ou* coated tongue.

pathétique [patetik] **1** adj moving, pathetic; (*Anat*) pathetic. **2** nm pathos.

pathétiquement [patetikmɑ̃] adv movingly, pathetically.

pathétisme [patetism] nm (*littér*) pathos.

pathogène [patɔʒɛn] adj pathogenic.

pathologie [patɔlɔʒi] nf pathology.

pathologique [patɔlɔʒik] adj pathological.
pathologiquement [patɔlɔʒikmɑ̃] adv pathologically.
pathologiste [patɔlɔʒist] nmf pathologist.
pathos [patos] nm (overdone) pathos, emotionalism. **rédigé avec un ~ irritant** written with irritating pathos *ou* emotionalism; **l'avocat faisait du ~** the lawyer was making a strong emotional appeal.
patibulaire [patibylɛʀ] adj sinister. **avoir une mine ~** to be sinister-looking.
patiemment [pasjamɑ̃] adv patiently.
patience[1] [pasjɑ̃s] nf a (*gén*) patience; (*résignation*) long-suffering. **souffrir avec ~** to bear one's sufferings with patience *ou* patiently; **perdre ~** to lose (one's) patience; **prendre** *ou* **s'armer de ~** to be patient, have patience; **il faut avoir une ~ d'ange pour le supporter** it takes the patience of a saint *ou* of Job to put up with him; **je suis à bout de ~** my patience is exhausted, I'm at the end of my patience; **ma ~ a des limites!** there are limits to my patience!; *voir* **mal.**
b (*Cartes*) (*jeu*) patience (*Brit*) (*NonC*), solitaire (*US*) (*NonC*); (*partie*) game of patience (*Brit*) *ou* solitaire (*US*). **faire des ~s** to play patience (*Brit*) *ou* solitaire (*US*).
c (*loc*) **~, j'arrive** wait a minute! *ou* hang on!*, I'm coming; **~, il est bientôt l'heure** be patient – it's almost time; **encore un peu de ~** not long now – hold on; **~, j'aurai ma revanche** I'll get even in the end.
patience[2] [pasjɑ̃s] nf (*Bot*) (patience) dock.
patient, e [pasjɑ̃, jɑ̃t] 1 adj patient; *travail* patient, laborious. 2 nm,f (*Méd*) patient.
patienter [pasjɑ̃te] 1 vi to wait. **faites-le ~** (*pour un rendez-vous*) ask him to wait, have him wait; (*au téléphone*) ask him to hold; **si vous voulez ~ un instant** could you wait *ou* hang on* *ou* hold on* a moment?; **lisez ce journal, ça vous fera ~** read this paper to fill in *ou* pass the time; **pour ~, il regardait les tableaux** to fill in *ou* pass the time, he looked at the paintings; **patientez encore un peu** not long now – hold on.
patin [patɛ̃] nm a [*patineur*] skate; [*luge*] runner; [*rail*] base; (*pour le parquet*) cloth pad (*used as slippers on polished wood floors*). **~ (de frein)** brake block; **~s à glace** iceskates; **~s à roulettes** roller skates; **faire du ~ à glace/à roulettes** to go ice-skating/roller-skating. b (‡: *baiser*) French kiss; *voir* **rouler.**
patinage[1] [patinaʒ] nm (*Sport*) skating; (*Aut*) [*roue*] spinning; [*embrayage*] slipping. **~ artistique** figure skating; **~ à roulettes** roller-skating; **~ de vitesse** speed skating.
patinage[2] [patinaʒ] nm (*Tech*) patination.
patine [patin] nf patina, sheen.
patiner[1] [patine] 1 vi (*Sport*) to skate; (*Aut*) [*roue*] to spin; [*embrayage*] to slip. **la voiture patina sur la chaussée verglacée** the wheels of the car spun on the icy road; **faire ~ l'embrayage** to slip the clutch; **ça patine sur la route** the roads are very slippery.
patiner[2] [patine] 1 vt (*naturellement*) *bois, bronze, pierre* to give a sheen to; (*artificiellement*) to patinate, give a patina to.
patinette [patinɛt] nf scooter. **~ à pédale** pedal scooter.
patineur, -euse [patinœʀ, øz] nm,f skater.
patinoire [patinwaʀ] nf skating rink, ice rink. (*fig*) **cette route est une vraie ~** this road is like an ice rink *ou* a skidpan (*Brit*).
patio [pasjo] nm patio.
pâtir [pɑtiʀ] 2 vi (*littér*) to suffer (*de* because of, on account of).
pâtisserie [pɑtisʀi] nf a (*magasin*) cake shop, confectioner's; (*gâteau*) cake, pastry; (*art ménager*) cake-making, pastry-making, baking; (*métier, commerce*) confectionery. **apprendre la ~** (*comme métier*) to learn to be a pastrycook, learn confectionery; **faire de la ~** (*en amateur*) to do some baking, make cakes and pastries; **~ industrielle** (*gâteaux*) bought cakes; (*usine*) bakery, cake factory; **moule/ustensiles à ~** pastry dish/utensils; *voir* **rouleau.** b (*stuc*) fancy (plaster) moulding.
pâtissier, -ière [pɑtisje, jɛʀ] nm,f (*de métier*) confectioner, pastrycook; (*amateur*) baker. **~-glacier** confectioner and ice-cream maker; *voir* **crème.**
patois, e [patwa, waz] 1 adj patois (*épith*), dialectal, dialect (*épith*). 2 nm patois, (provincial) dialect. **parler (en) ~** to speak (in) patois.
patoisant, e [patwazɑ̃, ɑ̃t] 1 adj patois-speaking, dialect-speaking. 2 nm,f patois *ou* dialect speaker.
patoiser [patwaze] 1 vi to speak (in) dialect *ou* patois.
patraque* [patʀak] adj peaky* (*Brit*), off-colour (*Brit*) (*attrib*), peaked* (*US*), out of sorts (*attrib*).
pâtre [pɑtʀ] nm (*littér*) shepherd.
patriarcal, e, mpl **-aux** [patʀijaʀkal, o] adj patriarchal.
patriarcat [patʀijaʀka] nm (*Rel*) patriarchate; (*Sociol*) patriarchy, patriarchate.
patriarche [patʀijaʀʃ] nm patriarch.
Patrice [patʀis] nm Patrick.
patricien, -ienne [patʀisjɛ̃, jɛn] adj, nm,f patrician.
Patrick [patʀik] nm Patrick.
patrie [patʀi] nf homeland, fatherland; (*berceau*) homeland, home. **mourir pour la ~** to die for one's homeland *ou* country; **la Grèce, ~ de l'art** Greece, the homeland of art; **Limoges, ~ de la porcelaine** Limoges, the home of porcelain.
patrimoine [patʀimwan] nm (*gén*) inheritance, patrimony (*frm*); (*Jur*) patrimony; (*Fin: biens*) property; (*bien commun*) (*fig*) heritage, patrimony (*frm*). (*Bio*) **~ héréditaire** *ou* **génétique** genetic inheritance, genotype; **~ national** national heritage; **~ culturel** cultural heritage.
patriotard, e [patʀijɔtaʀ, aʀd] (*péj*) 1 adj jingoistic. 2 nm,f jingoist.
patriote [patʀijɔt] 1 adj patriotic. 2 nmf (*gén*) patriot. (*Hist*) **les ~s** the Patriots.
patriotique [patʀijɔtik] adj patriotic.
patriotiquement [patʀijɔtikmɑ̃] adv patriotically.
patriotisme [patʀijɔtism] nm patriotism.
patron[1] [patʀɔ̃] 1 nm a (*propriétaire*) owner, boss*; (*gérant*) manager, boss*; (*employeur*) employer. **le ~ est là?** is the boss* *ou* governor‡ (*Brit*) in?; **le ~ de l'usine** the factory owner *ou* manager; **le ~ du restaurant** the proprietor of the restaurant, the restaurant owner; **il est ~ d'hôtel** he's a hotel proprietor; **la bonne garde la maison quand ses ~s sont absents** the maid looks after the house when her employers are away; **c'est le grand ~*** he's (*ou* she's) the big boss!; **un petit ~** a boss of a small (*ou* medium-sized) company; **~ boulanger/boucher** master baker/butcher.
b (*Hist, Rel: protecteur*) patron. **saint ~** patron saint.
c (*: *mari*) (old) man‡. **il est là, le ~?** is your (old) man in?‡
d (*Hôpital*) ≃ senior consultant (*of teaching hospital*).
2 comp ► **patron (pêcheur)** (*Naut*) skipper ► **patron de presse** press baron *ou* tycoon *ou* magnate ► **patron de thèse** (*Univ*) supervisor *ou* director of postgraduate doctorate.
patron[2] [patʀɔ̃] nm (*Couture*) pattern; (*pochoir*) stencil. **~ de robe** dress pattern; **(taille) demi-~/~/grand ~** small/medium/large (size).
patronage [patʀɔnaʒ] nm a (*protection*) patronage. **sous le (haut) ~ de** under the patronage of. b (*organisation*) youth club; (*Rel*) youth fellowship.
patronal, e, mpl **-aux** [patʀɔnal, o] adj (*Ind*) *responsabilité, cotisation* employer's, employers'; (*Rel*) *fête* patronal.
patronat [patʀɔna] nm (*Ind*) **le ~** the employers.
patronne [patʀɔn] nf a (*voir* **patron**) (lady) owner, boss*; (lady) manager; (lady) employer; proprietress. b (*: *épouse*) missus‡, old lady‡. c (*sainte*) patron saint.
patronner [patʀɔne] 1 vt *personne* to patronize, sponsor; *entreprise* to patronize, support; *candidature* to support.
patronnesse [patʀɔnɛs] nf *voir* **dame.**
patronyme [patʀɔnim] nm patronymic.
patronymique [patʀɔnimik] adj patronymic.
patrouille [patʀuj] nf patrol. **partir** *ou* **aller en/être de ~** to go/be on patrol; **~ de reconnaissance/de chasse** reconnaissance/fighter patrol.
patrouiller [patʀuje] 1 vi to patrol, be on patrol. **~ dans les rues** to patrol the streets.
patrouilleur [patʀujœʀ] nm (*soldat*) soldier on patrol (duty), patroller; (*Naut*) patrol boat; (*Aviat*) patrol *ou* scout plane.
patte [pat] 1 nf a (*jambe d'animal*) leg; (*pied*) [*chat, chien*] paw; [*oiseau*] foot. **~s de devant** forelegs, forefeet; **~s de derrière** hindlegs, hind feet; **coup de ~** [*animal*] blow of its paw; (*fig*) cutting remark; **donner un coup de ~ à** [*animal*] to hit with its paw; [*fig*] to make a cutting remark to; **le chien tendit la ~** the dog put its paw out *ou* gave a paw; **faire ~ de velours** [*chat*] to draw in *ou* sheathe its claws; [*personne*] to be all sweetness and light*; (*fig*) **ça ne va** *ou* **ne marche que sur trois ~s** [*affaire, projet*] it limps along; [*relation amoureuse*] it struggles along; *voir* **bas[1], mille[1], mouton[1],** *etc.*
b (‡: *jambe*) leg. **nous avons 50 km dans les ~s** we've walked 50 km; **à ~s** on foot; **nous y sommes allés à ~s** we walked *ou* hoofed‡ it, we went on Shanks' pony* (*Brit*) *ou* mare* (*US*); **bas** *ou* **court sur ~s** *personne* short-legged; *table, véhicule* low; **tirer** *ou* **traîner la ~** to drag one's leg; **il est toujours dans mes ~s** he's always under my feet.
c (‡: *main*) hand, paw*. **s'il me tombe sous la ~, gare à lui!** if I get my hands *ou* paws* on him he'd better look out!; **tomber dans les/se tirer des ~s de qn** to fall into/get out of sb's clutches.
d (*fig: style*) [*auteur, peintre*] style. **elle a un bon coup de ~** she has a nice style *ou* touch.
e [*ancre*] palm, fluke; (*languette*) [*poche*] flap; [*vêtement*] strap; (*sur l'épaule*) epaulette; [*porte-feuilles*] tongue; [*chaussure*] tongue.
f (*favoris*) **~s (de lapin)** sideburns; *voir* **fil, graisser, quatre** *etc.*
2 comp ► **pantalon (à) pattes d'éléphant** bell-bottom *ou* flared trousers, bell-bottoms, flares ► **patte folle** gammy (*Brit*) *ou* game leg ► **patte à glace** mirror clamp ► **patte(s) de mouche** spidery scrawl; **faire des pattes de mouche** to write (in) a spidery scrawl ► **patte-d'oie** nf (pl **pattes-d'oie**) (*à l'œil*) crow's-foot; (*carrefour*) branching crossroads *ou* junction.
pattemouille [patmuj] nf damp cloth (*for ironing*).
pâturage [pɑtyʀaʒ] nm (*lieu*) pasture; (*action*) grazing, pasturage; (*droits*) grazing rights.
pâture [pɑtyʀ] nf a (*nourriture*) food. (*fig*) **il fait sa ~ de romans noirs** he is an avid reader of detective stories, detective stories form his usual reading matter; (*fig*) **les dessins animés qu'on donne en ~ à nos enfants** the cartoons served up to our children; (*fig*) **donner une nouvelle en ~ aux journalistes** to feed a story to journalists; (*lit, fig*) **donner qn en ~ aux fauves** to throw sb to the lions. b (*pâturage*)

pasture.

pâturer [patyʀe] 1 1 vi to graze. 2 vt: ~ l'herbe to graze.

paturon [patyʀɔ̃] nm pastern.

Paul [pɔl] nm Paul.

Paule [pol] nf Paula.

Pauline [polin] nf Pauline.

paulinien, -ienne [polinjɛ̃, jɛn] adj of Saint Paul, Pauline.

paulownia [polonja] nm paulownia.

paume [pom] nf *[main]* palm. (*Sport*) jeu de ~ (*sport*) real *ou* royal tennis; (*lieu*) real-tennis *ou* royal-tennis court; jouer à la ~ to play real *ou* royal tennis.

paumé, e‡ [pome] (ptp de paumer) adj (*péj*) (*dans un lieu*) lost; (*dans une explication*) lost, at sea*; (*dans un milieu inconnu*) bewildered. un pauvre ~ a poor bum*‡; habiter un bled *ou* trou ~* (*isolé*) to live in a godforsaken place *ou* hole‡; (*sans attrait*) to live in a real dump *ou* a godforsaken hole‡; (*fig: socialement inadapté*) la jeunesse ~e d'aujourd'hui the young wasters* *ou* drop-outs* of today; il est complètement ~ he's all screwed up‡.

paumelle [pomɛl] nf (*gond*) split hinge.

paumer‡ [pome] 1 1 vt (*perdre*) to lose. 2 **se paumer** vpr to get lost.

paupérisation [popeʀizasjɔ̃] nf pauperization, impoverishment.

paupériser [popeʀize] 1 vt to pauperize, impoverish.

paupérisme [popeʀism] nm pauperism.

paupière [popjɛʀ] nf eyelid.

paupiette [popjɛt] nf (*Culin*) ~ de veau veal olive.

pause [poz] nf (*arrêt*) break; (*en parlant*) pause; (*Mus*) pause; (*Sport*) half-time. faire une ~ to have a break, break off; ~-café/-thé coffee/tea break; ~-cigarette break (for a cigarette); faire une ~-cigarette to stop for a cigarette; ~ publicitaire commercial break.

pauser*† [poze] vi: faire ~ qn to keep sb waiting.

pauvre [povʀ] 1 adj a *personne, pays, sol* poor; *végétation* sparse; *minerai, gisement* poor; *style, (Aut) mélange* weak; *mobilier, vêtements* cheap-looking; *nourriture, salaire* meagre, poor. minerai ~ en cuivre ore with a low copper content, ore poor in copper; air ~ en oxygène air low in oxygen; pays ~ en ressources/en hommes country short of *ou* lacking resources/men; nourriture ~ en calcium (*par manque*) diet lacking in calcium; (*par ordonnance*) low-calcium diet; un village ~ en distractions a village which is lacking in *ou* short of amusements; ~ comme Job as poor as a church mouse; les couches ~s de la population the poorer *ou* deprived sections of the population; je suis ~ en vaisselle I don't have much crockery; *voir* rime.

b (*avant n: piètre*) *excuse, argument* weak, pathetic; *devoir* poor; *orateur* weak, bad. de ~s chances de succès only a slim *ou* slender chance of success; il esquissa un ~ sourire he smiled weakly *ou* gave a weak smile.

c (*avant n: malheureux*) poor. ~ type* (*pauvre, malheureux*) poor chap* (*Brit*) *ou* guy*; (*paumé*) poor bum‡; (*minable*) dead loss*; (*salaud*) swine‡; (*crétin*) poor sod*‡ (*Brit*) *ou* bastard*‡; ~ con!*‡ you poor sod!*‡ (*Brit*) *ou* bastard*‡; (*littér, hum*) ~ hère down-and-out; ~ d'esprit (*simple d'esprit*) half-wit; (*Rel*) les ~s d'esprit the poor in spirit; comme disait mon ~ mari as my poor (dear) husband used to say; (*hum*) ~ de moi! poor (little) me!; mon ~ ami my dear friend; elle me faisait pitié, avec son ~ petit air I felt sorry for her, she looked so wretched *ou* miserable.

2 nmf a (*personne pauvre*) poor man *ou* woman, pauper††. les ~s the poor; ce pays compte encore beaucoup de ~s there's still a lot of poverty *ou* there are still many poor people in this country; le caviar du ~ (the) poor man's caviar.

b (**: marquant dédain ou commisération*) mon (*ou* ma) ~, si tu voyais comment ça se passe ... but my dear fellow (*ou* girl *etc*) *ou* friend, if you saw what goes on ...; le ~, il a dû en voir! the poor chap* (*Brit*) *ou* guy*, he must have had a hard time of it!

pauvrement [povʀəmɑ̃] adv *meublé, éclairé, vivre* poorly; *vêtu* poorly, shabbily.

pauvresse† [povʀɛs] nf poor woman *ou* wretch.

pauvret, -ette [povʀɛ, ɛt] nm,f poor (little) thing.

pauvreté [povʀəte] nf *[personne]* poverty; *[mobilier]* cheapness; *[langage]* weakness, poorness; *[sol]* poverty, poorness. (*Prov*) ~ n'est pas vice poverty is not a vice, there is no shame in being poor; *voir* vœu.

pavage [pavaʒ] nm (*voir* paver) (*action*) paving; cobbling; (*revêtement*) paving; cobbles.

pavane [pavan] nf pavane.

pavaner (se) [pavane] 1 vpr to strut about. se ~ comme un dindon to strut about like a turkey-cock.

pavé [pave] nm a *[chaussée]* cobblestone; *[cour]* paving stone; (*fig péj: livre*) hefty tome*. déraper sur le ~ *ou* les ~s to skid on the cobbles; être sur le ~ (*sans domicile*) to be on the streets, be homeless; (*sans emploi*) to be out of a job; mettre *ou* jeter qn sur le ~ (*domicile*) to turn *ou* throw sb out (onto the streets); (*emploi*) to give sb the sack*, throw sb out; j'ai l'impression d'avoir un ~ sur l'estomac* I feel as if I've got a great *ou* lead weight in my stomach; (*fig*) c'est l'histoire du ~ de l'ours it's another example of misguided zeal; (*fig*) jeter un ~ dans la mare to set the cat among the pigeons; *voir* battre, brûler, haut.

b (*Culin*) *thickly-cut steak*.

pavement [pavmɑ̃] nm ornamental tiling.

paver [pave] 1 vt *cour* to pave; *chaussée* to cobble. cour pavée paved yard; *voir* enfer.

paveur [pavœʀ] nm paver.

pavillon [pavijɔ̃] 1 nm a (*villa*) house; (*loge de gardien*) lodge; (*section d'hôpital*) ward, pavilion; (*corps de bâtiment*) wing, pavilion.

b (*Naut*) flag. sous ~ panaméen *etc* under the Panamanian *etc* flag; *voir* baisser, battre. c (*Mus*) *[instrument]* bell; *[phonographe]* horn. d *[oreille]* pavilion, pinna. 2 comp ►pavillon de banlieue house in the suburbs ►pavillon de chasse hunting lodge ►pavillon de complaisance flag of convenience ►pavillon de détresse flag of distress ►pavillon de guerre war flag ►pavillon noir Jolly Roger ►pavillon de quarantaine yellow flag ►pavillon à tête de mort skull and crossbones ►pavillon de verdure leafy arbour *ou* bower.

pavillonnaire [pavijɔnɛʀ] adj: lotissement ~ private housing estate; banlieue ~ residential suburb (with exclusively low-rise housing).

pavlovien, -ienne [pavlɔvjɛ̃, jɛn] adj Pavlovian.

pavois [pavwa] nm (*Naut: bordage*) bulwark; (*Hist: bouclier*) shield. hisser le grand ~ to dress over all *ou* full; hisser le petit ~ to dress with masthead flags; hisser qn sur le ~ to carry sb shoulder-high.

pavoiser [pavwaze] 1 1 vt *navire* to dress; *monument* to deck with flags. 2 vi to put out flags; (*fig: Sport*) *[supporters]* to rejoice, wave the banners, exult. toute la ville a pavoisé there were flags out all over the town; (*fig*) il pavoise maintenant qu'on lui a donné raison publiquement he's rejoicing openly now that he has been publicly acknowledged to be in the right; il n'y a pas de quoi ~! it's nothing to write home about *ou* to get too excited about!

pavot [pavo] nm poppy.

payable [pɛjabl] adj payable. ~ en 3 fois *somme* payable in *ou* that must *ou* may be paid in 3 instalments; *objet* that must *ou* can be paid for in 3 instalments; l'impôt est ~ par tous taxes must be paid by everyone; (*Fin*) billet ~ à vue bill payable at sight; appareil ~ à crédit piece of equipment which can be paid for on credit.

payant, e [pɛjɑ̃, ɑ̃t] adj *spectateur* who pays (for his seat); *billet, place* which one must pay for, not free (*attrib*); *spectacle* where one must pay to go in, where there is a charge for admission; (*rentable*) *affaire* profitable; *politique, conduite, effort* which pays off. "entrée ~e" admission fee payable; c'est ~? do you have to pay (to get in)?

paye [pɛj] nf = paie.

payement [pɛjmɑ̃] nm = paiement.

payer [peje] 8 1 vt a *somme, cotisation, intérêt* to pay; *facture, dette* to pay, settle. ~ comptant to pay cash; ~ rubis sur l'ongle† to pay cash on the nail; c'est lui qui paie he's paying; *voir* qui.

b *employé* to pay; *tueur* to hire; *entrepreneur* to pay, settle up with. être payé par chèque/en espèces/en nature/à l'heure to be paid by cheque/in cash/in kind/by the hour; être payé à la pièce to be on piecework; ~ qn de *ou* en paroles/promesses to fob sb off with (empty) words/promises; je ne suis pas payé pour ça* that's not what I'm paid for; (*fig iro*) il a payé pour le savoir he has learnt the hard way, he has learnt that to his cost.

c *travail, service, maison, marchandise* to pay for. je l'ai payé de ma poche I paid for it out of my own pocket; les réparations ne sont pas encore payées the repairs haven't been paid for yet; il m'a fait ~ 50 F he charged me 50 francs (*pour* for); ~ le déplacement de qn to pay sb's travelling expenses; ~ la casse *ou* les pots cassés (*lit*) to pay for the damage; (** fig*) to pick up the pieces, carry the can* (*Brit*); travail bien/mal payé well-paid/badly-paid work; *voir* congé.

d (**: offrir*) ~ qch à qn to buy sth for sb; c'est moi qui paie (à boire) the drinks are on me*, have this one on me*; ~ des vacances/un voyage à qn to pay for sb to go on holiday/on a trip; ~ à boire à qn to stand *ou* buy sb a drink; sa mère lui a payé une voiture his mother bought him a car.

e (*récompenser*) to reward. le succès le paie de tous ses efforts his success makes all his efforts worthwhile *ou* rewards him for all his efforts; il l'aimait et elle le payait de retour he loved her and she returned his love.

f (*expier*) *faute, crime* to pay for. ~ qch de 5 ans de prison to get 5 years in jail for sth; il l'a payé de sa vie/santé it cost him his life/health; il a payé cher son imprudence he paid dearly for his rashness, his rashness cost him dearly; (*en menace*) il me le paiera! he'll pay for this!, I'll make him pay for this!

2 vi a *[effort, tactique]* to pay off; *[métier]* to be well-paid. le crime ne paie pas crime doesn't pay; ~ pour qn (*lit*) to pay for sb; (*fig*) to pick up the pieces (for sb), carry the can (*Brit*) for sb*.

b ~ de: pour y parvenir il a dû ~ de sa personne he had to sacrifice himself in order to succeed; ce poisson ne paie pas de mine this fish isn't much to look at *ou* doesn't look very appetizing; l'hôtel ne paie pas de mine the hotel isn't much to look at; ~ d'audace to take a gamble *ou* a risk.

3 **se payer** vpr a payez-vous et rendez-moi la monnaie take what is owed to you and give me the change; tout se paie (*lit*) everything must be paid for; (*fig*) everything has its price.

b (*: *s'offrir*) *objet* to buy o.s., treat o.s. to. **on va se ~ un bon dîner/le restaurant** we're going to treat ourselves to a slap-up* meal/to a meal out; **se ~ une pinte de bon sang**† to have a good laugh*; **se ~ la tête de qn** (*ridiculiser*) to put sb down*, take the mickey* out of sb (*Brit*); (*tromper*) to have sb on*, take sb for a ride‡; **se ~ une bonne grippe** to get a bad dose of flu; **il s'est payé un arbre/le trottoir/un piéton** he has wrapped his car round a tree/run into the pavement/ mown a pedestrian down; **j'ai glissé et je me suis payé la chaise** I slipped and banged *ou* crashed into the chair; **ils s'en sont drôlement payé, ils s'en sont payé une bonne tranche** they had (themselves) a good time *ou* a whale of a time*; *voir* **luxe.**

c **se ~ d'illusions** to delude o.s.; **se ~ de culot** to use one's nerve; **il se paie de mots** he's talking a lot of hot air*.

payeur, -euse [pɛjœʀ, øz] 1 **adj: organisme/service ~** claims department/office; *[chèque]* **établissement ~** paying bank. 2 **nm,f** payer; (*Mil, Naut*) paymaster. **mauvais ~** bad debtor; *voir* **conseilleur.**

pays[1] [pei] 1 **nm** a (*contrée, habitants*) country. **des ~ lointains** far-off countries *ou* lands; **les ~ membres du marché commun** the countries which are members of *ou* the member countries of the Common Market; **la France est le ~ du vin** France is the land of wine; *voir* **mal.**

b (*région*) region. **il est du ~** he's from these parts *ou* this area; **les gens du ~** the local people, the locals; **revenir au ~** to go back home; **un ~ de légumes, d'élevage et de lait** a vegetable-growing, cattle-breeding and dairy region; **c'est le ~ de la tomate** it's famous tomato-growing country; **nous sommes en plein ~ du vin** we're in the heart of the wine country; **vin de** *ou* **du ~** local wine, vin de pays (*Brit*); **melons/pêches de** *ou* **du ~** local-grown melons/peaches.

c (*village*) village.

d (*loc*) (*fig*) **le ~ des rêves** *ou* **des songes** the land of dreams, dreamland; **voir du ~** to travel around; **se comporter comme en ~ conquis** to lord it over everyone, act all high and mighty; **être en ~ de connaissance** (*dans une réunion*) to be among friends *ou* familiar faces; (*sur un sujet, dans un lieu*) to be on home ground *ou* on familiar territory.

2 **comp ►pays d'accueil** *[conférences, jeux]* host country; *[réfugiés]* country of refuge **►le Pays basque** the Basque country **►pays de cocagne** land of plenty, land of milk and honey **►pays développé** developed country *ou* nation **►le pays de Galles** Wales **►pays industrialisé** industrialized country *ou* nation **►les pays les moins avancés** the less developed countries **►pays en voie de développement** developing country **►pays en voie d'industrialisation** industrializing country.

pays[2], **e** [pei, peiz] **nm,f** (*dial: compatriote*) **nous sommes ~** we come from the same village *ou* region *ou* part of the country; **elle est ma ~e** she comes from the same village *ou* region *ou* part of the country as me.

paysage [peizaʒ] **nm** (*gén*) landscape, scenery (*NonC*); (*Peinture*) landscape (painting). **on découvrait un ~ magnifique/un ~ de montagne** a magnificent/mountainous landscape lay before us; **nous avons traversé des ~s magnifiques** we drove through (some) magnificent scenery; **les ~s orientaux** the landscape *ou* the scenery of the East; **le ~ urbain** the urban landscape; **le ~ politique/associatif** the political/ community scene; **le ~ audiovisuel français** *the French broadcasting scene*; (*gén iro*) **ça fait bien dans le ~!** it's all part of the image!, it fits the image!

paysagé, e [peizaʒe] **adj: bureau ~** open-plan office; **jardin ~** landscaped garden.

paysager, -ère [peizaʒe, ɛʀ] **adj: parc ~** landscaped garden.

paysagiste [peizaʒist] **nmf** (*Peinture*) landscape painter. (*Agr*) **architecte/jardinier ~** landscape architect/gardener.

paysan, -anne [peizɑ̃, an] 1 **adj** (*agricole*) *monde, problème* farming (*épith*); *agitation, revendications* farmers', of the farmers; (*rural*) *vie, coutumes* country (*épith*); (*péj*) *air, manières* peasant (*épith*), rustic. 2 **nm** countryman, farmer; (*Hist*) peasant; (*péj*) peasant. 3 **paysanne nf** peasant woman, countrywoman; (*Hist*) peasant (woman); (*péj*) peasant.

paysannerie [peizanʀi] **nf** peasantry, farmers.

Pays-Bas [peiba] **nmpl: les ~** the Netherlands.

PC [pese] **nm** a (**abrév de parti communiste**) *voir* **parti**[1]. b (**abrév de poste de commandement**) *voir* **poste**[2]. c (*Ordin*) PC.

Pcc (**abrév de pour copie conforme**) *voir* **copie.**

PCF [peseɛf] **nm abrév de parti communiste français.**

PCV [peseve] **nm** (*Télec*) (**abrév de percevoir**) **(appel en) ~** reverse-charge call (*Brit*), collect call (*US*); **appeler en ~** to make a reverse-charge call (*Brit*), call collect (*US*).

P.D.G. [pedeʒe] **nm inv** (**abrév de président-directeur général**) *voir* **président.**

PE nm (**abrév de Parlement européen**) EP.

péage [peaʒ] **nm** (*droit*) toll; (*barrière*) tollgate. **autoroute à ~** toll motorway (*Brit*) *ou* expressway (*US*); **pont à ~** toll bridge; **poste de ~** tollbooth; (*TV*) **chaîne/télévision à ~** pay channel/TV.

péagiste [peaʒist] **nmf** tollbooth attendant.

peau, pl ~x [po] 1 **nf** a *[personne]* skin. **avoir une ~ de pêche** to have a peach-like complexion; **soins de la/maladie de ~** skin care/disease; **les ~x mortes** (the) dead skin; **n'avoir que la ~ et les os** to be all skin and bones; **attraper qn par la ~ du cou** *ou* **du dos** *ou* **des fesses**‡ (*empoigner rudement*) to grab sb by the scruff of the neck; (*s'en saisir à temps*) to grab hold of sb in the nick of time; **faire ~ neuve** *[parti politique, administration]* to adopt *ou* find a new image; *[personne]* (*en changeant d'habit*) to change (one's clothes); (*en changeant de conduite*) to turn over a new leaf; *voir* **coûter, fleur.**

b (*: *corps, vie*) **jouer** *ou* **risquer sa ~** to risk one's neck* *ou* hide*; **sauver sa ~** to save one's skin *ou* hide*; **tenir à sa ~** to value one's life; (*il sera tué*) **sa ~ ne vaut pas cher, je ne donnerai pas cher de sa ~** he's dead meat*; **se faire crever** *ou* **trouer la ~**‡ to get killed, get a bullet in one's hide*; **recevoir 12 balles dans la ~** to be gunned down by a firing squad *ou* an execution squad; **on lui fera la ~**‡ we'll bump him off‡; **je veux/j'aurai sa ~!** I'm out to get him!*, I'll have his hide for this!*; **être bien/mal dans sa ~** (*physiquement*) to feel great*/awful; (*mentalement*) to be quite at ease/ill-at-ease, be at peace/at odds with o.s.; **avoir qn dans la ~*** to be crazy about sb*; **avoir le jeu** *etc* **dans la ~** to have gambling *etc* in one's blood; **se mettre dans la ~ de qn** to put o.s. in sb's place *ou* shoes; **entrer dans la ~ du personnage** to get (right) into the part; **je ne voudrais pas être dans sa ~** I wouldn't like to be in his shoes *ou* place; **avoir la ~ dure*** (*être solide*) to be hardy; (*résister à la critique*) *[personne]* to be thick-skinned, have a thick skin; *[idées, préjugés]* to be difficult to get rid of *ou* to overcome.

c *[animal]* (*gén*) skin; (*cuir*) hide; (*fourrure*) pelt; *[éléphant, buffle]* hide. **gants/vêtements de ~** leather gloves/clothes; *voir* **vendre.**

d *[fruit, lait, peinture]* skin; *[fromage]* rind; (*épluchure*) peel. (*lit, fig*) **glisser sur une ~ de banane** to slip on a banana skin; **enlever la ~ de** *fruit* to peel; *fromage* to take the rind off.

e **~ de balle!**‡ nothing doing!*, not a chance!*, no way!‡

2 **comp ►peau d'âne**† (*diplôme*) diploma, sheepskin (*US*) **►peau de chagrin** (*lit*) shagreen; (*fig*) **diminuer comme une peau de chagrin** to shrink away **►peau de chamois** chamois leather, shammy **►peau lainée** treated sheepskin **►peau de mouton** sheepskin; **en peau de mouton** sheepskin (*épith*) **►peau de porc** pigskin **►peau d'orange** (*Physiol*) orange peel effect **►Peau-Rouge nmf (pl Peaux-Rouges)** Red Indian, redskin **►peau de serpent** snakeskin **►peau de tambour** drumskin **►peau de vache*** (*homme*) bastard‡; (*femme*) bitch‡ **►peau de zénana** *ou* **de zébi: c'est en peau de zénana** *ou* **de zébi** it's made of some sort of cheap stuff.

peaucier [posje] **adj m, nm: (muscle) ~** platysma.

peaufiner [pofine] [1] **vt** *travail* to polish up, put the finishing touches to; *style* to polish (up).

peausserie [posʀi] **nf** (*articles*) leatherwear (*NonC*); (*commerce*) skin trade; (*boutique*) suede and leatherware shop.

peaussier [posje] 1 **adj m** leather (*épith*). 2 **nm** (*ouvrier*) leatherworker; (*commerçant*) leather dealer, fellmonger.

pébroc*, pébroque* [pebʀɔk] **nm** brolly* (*Brit*), umbrella.

pécari [pekaʀi] **nm** peccary.

peccadille [pekadij] **nf** (*vétille*) trifle; (*faute*) peccadillo.

pechblende [pɛʃblɛ̃d] **nf** pitchblende.

pêche[1] [pɛʃ] **nf** a (*fruit*) peach. **~-abricot, ~ jaune** *ou* **abricotée** yellow peach; **~ blanche** white peach; **~ de vigne** bush peach; *voir* **fendre, melba, peau.** b (*: *vitalité*) go*, oomph*. **avoir la ~** to be on form; **ça donne la ~** it gets you going. c (‡: *coup*) punch, clout*. **donner une ~ à qn** to punch sb in the face, clout sb across the face.

pêche[2] [pɛʃ] **nf** a (*activité*) fishing; (*saison*) fishing season. **la ~ à la ligne** (*mer*) line fishing; (*rivière*) angling; **la ~ à la baleine** whaling; **grande ~ au large** deep-sea fishing; **la ~ au harpon** harpoon fishing; **la ~ à la crevette** shrimp fishing; **la ~ à la truite** trout fishing; **la ~ aux moules** mussel gathering; **aller à la ~** (*lit*) to go fishing, go angling; (*fig*) **aller à la ~ aux informations** to go fishing for information; **aller à la ~ aux voix** to canvass, go vote-catching*; **filet/barque de ~** fishing net/boat; *voir* **canne.** b (*poissons*) catch. **faire une belle ~** to have *ou* make a good catch; (*Rel*) **la ~ miraculeuse** the miraculous draught of fishes; (*fête foraine*) the bran tub (*Brit*), the lucky dip.

péché [peʃe] 1 **nm** sin. **pour mes ~s** for my sins; **à tout ~ miséricorde** every sin can be forgiven *ou* pardoned; **vivre dans le ~** (*gén*) to lead a sinful life; (*sans être marié*) to live in sin; **mourir en état de ~** to die a sinner; **commettre un ~** to sin, commit a sin. 2 **comp ►péché capital** deadly sin; **les sept péchés capitaux** the seven deadly sins **►péché de chair**† sin of the flesh **►péché de jeunesse** youthful indiscretion **►péché mignon: c'est son péché mignon** he is partial to it, he has a weakness for it **►péché mortel** mortal sin **►le péché d'orgueil** the sin of pride **►le péché originel** original sin **►péché véniel** venial sin.

pécher [peʃe] [6] **vi** a (*Rel*) to sin. **~ par orgueil** to commit the sin of pride. b **~ contre la politesse/l'hospitalité** to break the rules of courtesy/hospitality; **~ par négligence/imprudence** to be too careless/ reckless; **~ par ignorance** to err through ignorance; **~ par excès de prudence/d'optimisme** to be over-careful/over-optimistic, err on the side of caution/optimism; **ça pèche par bien des points** *ou* **sur bien des côtés** it has a lot of weaknesses *ou* shortcomings.

pêcher[1] [peʃe] [1] 1 **vt** (*être pêcheur de*) to fish for; (*attraper*) to catch, land. **~ des coquillages** to gather shellfish; **~ la baleine/la crevette** to go whaling/shrimping; **~ la truite/la morue** to fish for trout/

cod, go trout-/cod-fishing; ~ **qch à la ligne/à l'asticot** to fish for *ou* catch sth with rod and line/with maggots; ~ **qch au chalut** to trawl for sth; (*fig*) **où as-tu été ~ cette idée/cette boîte?*** where did you dig that idea/box up from?*; **où a-t-il été ~ que ...?*** where did he dig up the idea that ...?

2 **vi** to go fishing; (*avec un chalut*) to trawl, go trawling. ~ **à la ligne** to go angling; ~ **à l'asticot** to fish with maggots; ~ **à la mouche** to fly-fish; (*fig*) ~ **en eau trouble** to fish in troubled waters.

pêcher² [peʃe] **nm** (*arbre*) peach tree.

pécheresse [peʃʀɛs] **nf** *voir* **pécheur**.

pêcherie [pɛʃʀi] **nf** fishery, fishing ground.

pécheur, pécheresse [peʃœʀ, peʃʀɛs] 1 **adj** sinful. 2 **nm, f** sinner.

pêcheur [pɛʃœʀ] 1 **nm** fisherman; (*à la ligne*) angler. ~ **de crevettes** shrimper; ~ **de baleines** whaler; ~ **de perles** pearl diver; ~ **de corail** coral fisherman; **c'est un ~ de coquillages** he gathers shellfish. 2 **adj** *bateau* fishing.

pêcheuse [pɛʃøz] **nf** fisherwoman; (*à la ligne*) (woman) angler.

pecnot [pɛkno] **nm** = **péquenot**.

pécore* [pekɔʀ] 1 **nf** (*péj: imbécile*) silly goose*. 2 **nmf** (*péj: paysan*) country bumpkin, yokel, hick* (*US*).

pectine [pɛktin] **nf** pectin.

pectique [pɛktik] **adj** pectic.

pectoral, e, mpl -aux [pɛktɔʀal, o] 1 **adj** a (*Anat, Zool*) pectoral. b (*Méd*) *sirop, pastille* throat (*épith*), cough (*épith*), expectorant (*SPÉC*) (*épith*). 2 **nm** (*Anat*) pectoral muscle.

pécule [pekyl] **nm** (*économies*) savings, nest egg; *[détenu, soldat]* earnings, wages (*paid on release or discharge*). **se faire** *ou* **se constituer un petit ~** to build up a little nest egg.

pécuniaire [pekynjɛʀ] **adj** *embarras* financial, pecuniary (*frm*); *aide, avantage, situation* financial.

pécuniairement [pekynjɛʀmɑ̃] **adv** financially.

pédagogie [pedagɔʒi] **nf** (*éducation*) education; (*art d'enseigner*) teaching skills; (*méthodes d'enseignement*) educational methods. **avoir beaucoup de ~** to have great teaching skills, be a skilled teacher; ~ **de la réussite/de l'échec** positive/negative teaching attitude.

pédagogique [pedagɔʒik] **adj** *intérêt, contenu, théorie* educational; *moyens, méthodes* educational. **stage (de formation) ~** teacher-training course; **il a fait un exposé très ~** he gave a very clear lecture; **sens ~** teaching ability; **cet instituteur a un grand sens ~** this teacher is very skilled at his job.

pédagogiquement [pedagɔʒikmɑ̃] **adv** (*voir* **pédagogique**) pedagogically (*SPÉC*); from an educational standpoint; clearly.

pédagogue [pedagɔg] **nmf** (*professeur*) teacher; (*spécialiste*) teaching specialist, educationalist. **c'est un bon ~, il est bon ~** he's a good teacher.

pédale [pedal] **nf** a *[bicyclette, piano, voiture]* pedal; *[machine à coudre, tour]* treadle. (*Mus*) ~ **douce/forte** soft/sustaining pedal; (*fig*) **mettre la ~ douce*** to soft-pedal*, go easy*; *voir* **perdre**. b (‡ *péj: homosexuel*) queer‡, poof‡, fag‡ (*US*). **être de la ~** to be (a) queer‡ *ou* a poof‡ (*Brit*) *ou* a fag‡ (*US*).

pédaler [pedale] 1 **vi** to pedal; (* *fig: se dépêcher*) to hurry. ~ **dans la choucroute‡** *ou* **la semoule‡** *ou* **le yaourt‡** (*ne rien comprendre*) to be all at sea, be at a complete loss; (*ne pas progresser*) to get nowhere (fast)*.

pédaleur, -euse [pedalœʀ, øz] **nm,f** (*Cyclisme*) pedaler.

pédalier [pedalje] **nm** *[bicyclette]* pedal and gear mechanism; *[orgue]* pedal-board, pedals.

pédalo [pedalo] **nm** ® pedalo, pedal-boat.

pédant, e [pedɑ̃, ɑ̃t] 1 **adj** pedantic. 2 **nm,f** pedant.

pédanterie [pedɑ̃tʀi] **nf** (*littér*) pedantry.

pédantesque [pedɑ̃tɛsk] **adj** pedantic.

pédantisme [pedɑ̃tism] **nm** pedantry.

pédé‡ [pede] **nm** (**abrév de pédéraste**) queer‡, poof‡, fag‡ *US*. **être ~** to be (a) queer‡ *ou* a poof‡ (*Brit*) *ou* fag‡ (*US*).

pédéraste [pedeʀast] **nm** pederast; (*par extension*) homosexual.

pédérastie [pedeʀasti] **nf** pederasty; (*par extension*) homosexuality.

pédérastique [pedeʀastik] **adj** pederast; (*par extension*) homosexual.

pédestre [pedɛstʀ] **adj** (*littér, hum*) **promenade** *ou* **circuit ~** walk, ramble, hike; **sentier ~** pedestrian footpath.

pédestrement [pedɛstʀəmɑ̃] **adv** (*littér, hum*) on foot.

pédiatre [pedjatʀ] **nmf** paediatrician.

pédiatrie [pedjatʀi] **nf** paediatrics (*sg*).

pedibus (cum jambis) [pedibys(kumʒɑ̃bis)] **adv** on foot, on Shanks' pony* (*Brit*) *ou* mare* (*US*).

pédicule [pedikyl] **nm** (*Anat*) pedicle; (*Bot, Zool*) peduncle.

pédicure [pedikyʀ] **nmf** chiropodist.

pedigree [pedigʀe] **nm** pedigree.

pédologie [pedɔlɔʒi] **nf** a (*Géol*) pedology. b (*Méd*) p(a)edology.

pédologique [pedɔlɔʒik] **adj** (*Géol*) pedological.

pédologue [pedɔlɔg] **nmf** (*Géol*) pedologist.

pédoncule [pedɔ̃kyl] **nm** (*Anat, Bot, Zool*) peduncle.

pédonculé, e [pedɔ̃kyle] **adj** pedunculate(d).

pédophile [pedɔfil] 1 **nm** p(a)edophile, p(a)edophiliac. 2 **adj** p(a)edophile (*épith*).

pédophilie [pedɔfili] **nf** p(a)edophilia.

pedzouille‡ [pɛdzuj] **nm** (*péj*) peasant, country bumpkin.

peeling [piliŋ] **nm** (*Méd*) skin peeling treatment; (*Cosmétique*) peeling face mask.

Pégase [pegaz] **nm** Pegasus.

P.E.G.C. [peəʒese] **nm** (**abrév de professeur d'enseignement général des collèges**) *voir* **professeur**.

pègre [pɛgʀ] **nf**: **la ~** the underworld; **membre de la ~** gangster, mobster.

peignage [pɛɲaʒ] **nm** *[laine]* carding; *[lin, chanvre]* carding, hackling.

peigne [pɛɲ] **nm** *[cheveux]* comb; (*Tex*) *[laine]* card; *[lin, chanvre]* card, hackle; *[métier]* reed. ~ **de poche** pocket comb; (*fig*) **passer qch au ~ fin** to go through sth with a fine-tooth comb; **se donner un coup de ~** to run a comb through one's hair.

peigne-cul‡, **pl peigne-culs** [pɛɲky] **nm** (*péj*) (*mesquin*) creep‡; (*inculte*) yob‡ (*Brit*), lout, boor.

peignée* [peɲe] **nf** (*raclée*) thrashing, hiding*. **donner/recevoir une** *ou* **la ~** to give/get a thrashing *ou* hiding*.

peigner [peɲe] 1 1 **vt** *cheveux* to comb; *enfant* to comb the hair of; (*Tex*) *laine* to card; *lin, chanvre* to card, hackle. **être bien peigné** *personne* to have a neat hairstyle; *cheveux* to be immaculate; **mal peigné** dishevelled, tousled; **laine peignée** *[pantalon, veston]* worsted wool; *[pull]* combed wool; (*hum*) **faire ça ou ~ la girafe** it's either that or some other pointless task. 2 **se peigner vpr** to comb one's hair, give one's hair a comb.

peignoir [pɛɲwaʀ] **nm** (*robe de chambre*) dressing gown; *[boxeur]* (boxer's) dressing gown. ~ **(de bain)** bathrobe.

peinard, e* [pɛnaʀ, aʀd] **adj** a (*sans tracas*) *travail, vie* cushy‡ (*Brit*), easy. **on est ~ dans l'armée** it's a cushy‡ (*Brit*) *ou* soft life in the army; **il fait ses 35 heures, ~** he does his 35 hours and that's it; **rester** *ou* **se tenir ~** to keep out of trouble, keep one's nose clean‡. b (*au calme*) *coin* quiet, peaceful. **on va être ~** (*pour se reposer*) we'll have a bit of peace, we can take it easy; (*pour agir*) we'll be left in peace.

peinardement* [pɛnaʀdəmɑ̃] **adv** quietly.

peindre [pɛ̃dʀ] 52 1 **vt** (*gén*) to paint; (*fig*) *mœurs* to paint, depict. ~ **qch en jaune** to paint sth yellow; ~ **à la chaux** to whitewash; **tableau peint à l'huile** picture painted in oils; ~ **au pinceau/au rouleau** to paint with a brush/a roller; **se faire ~ par X** to have one's portrait painted by X; (*fig*) **romancier qui sait bien ~ ses personnages** novelist who portrays his characters well; **il l'avait peint sous les traits d'un vieillard dans son livre** he had depicted *ou* portrayed him as an old man in his book.

2 **se peindre vpr** (*se décrire*) to portray o.s. **Montaigne s'est peint dans "Les Essais"** "Les Essais" are a self-portrayal of Montaigne; **la consternation/le désespoir se peignait sur leur visage** dismay/despair was written on their faces; **la cruauté était peinte sur ses traits** cruelty was reflected in his features.

peine [pɛn] **nf** a (*chagrin*) sorrow, sadness (*NonC*). **avoir de la ~** to be sad *ou* (*moins fort*) upset; **être dans la ~** to be grief-stricken; **faire de la ~ à qn** to upset sb, make sb sad, distress sb; **elle m'a fait de la ~ et je lui ai donné de l'argent** I felt sorry for her and gave her some money; **je ne voudrais pas te faire de (la) ~*, mais ...** I don't want to disappoint you but ...; **avoir des ~s de cœur** to have an unhappy love life; **cela fait ~ à voir** it hurts to see it; **il faisait ~ à voir** he looked a sorry *ou* pitiful sight; *voir* **âme**.

b (*effort*) effort, trouble (*NonC*). **il faut se donner de la ~, cela demande de la ~** that requires an effort, you have to make an effort; **se donner de la ~ pour faire** to go to a lot of trouble to do; **si tu te mettais seulement en ~ d'essayer, si tu te donnais seulement la ~ d'essayer** if you would only bother to try *ou* take the trouble to try; **il ne se donne aucune ~** he just doesn't try *ou* bother; (*formule de politesse*) **donnez-vous** *ou* **prenez donc la ~ d'entrer/de vous asseoir** please *ou* do come in/sit down; **ne vous donnez pas la ~ de venir me chercher** please don't bother to come and collect me; **est-ce que c'est la ~ d'y aller?** is it worth going?; **ce n'est pas la ~ de me le répéter** there's no point in repeating that, you've no need to repeat that; **ce n'est pas la ~** don't bother; (*iro*) **c'était bien la ~ de sortir!** *ou* **qu'il sorte!** it was a waste of time (his) going out, he wasted his time going out; **c'est ~ perdue** it's a waste of time (and effort); **on lui a donné 500 F pour sa ~** he was given 500 francs for his trouble; **en être pour sa ~** to get nothing for one's pains *ou* trouble; **tu as été sage, pour la ~, tu auras un bonbon** here's a sweet for being good; **ne vous mettez pas en ~ pour moi** don't go to *ou* put yourself to any trouble for me; *voir* **bout, mourir, valoir**.

c (*difficulté*) difficulty. **il a eu de la ~ à finir son repas/la course** he had difficulty finishing his meal/the race; **il a eu de la ~ mais il y est arrivé** it wasn't easy (for him) but he managed it; **avoir de la ~ à faire** to have difficulty in doing, find it difficult *ou* hard to do; **j'avais (de la) ~ à croire** I found it hard to believe, I could hardly believe it; **avec ~** with difficulty; **à grand-~** with great difficulty; **sans ~** without (any) difficulty, easily; **il n'est pas en ~ pour trouver des secrétaires** he has no difficulty *ou* trouble finding secretaries; **j'ai eu toutes les ~s du monde à le convaincre/à démarrer** I had a real job convincing him/getting the car started; **je serais bien en ~ de vous le dire/d'en trouver** I'd be hard pushed* *ou* hard pressed to tell you/to find any.

d (*punition*) punishment, penalty; (*Jur*) sentence. ~ **capitale** *ou* **de mort** capital punishment, death sentence *ou* penalty; ~ **de prison** prison sentence; ~ **alternative** *ou* **de substitution** alternative sentence; **sous ~ de mort** on pain of death; **défense d'afficher sous ~ d'amende** billposters will be fined; **défense d'entrer sous ~ de poursuites** trespassers will be prosecuted; **la ~ n'est pas toujours proportionnée au délit** the punishment does not always fit the crime; **on ne peut rien lui dire, sous ~ d'être renvoyé** you daren't *ou* can't say anything to him for fear of dismissal *ou* the sack*; **pour la** *ou* **ta ~ tu mettras la table** for that you can set the table.

e **à ~** hardly, only just, scarcely, barely; **il est à ~ 2 heures** it's only just 2 o'clock, it's only just turned 2 (*Brit*); **il leur reste à ~ de quoi manger** they've scarcely *ou* hardly any food left; **il gagne à ~ de quoi vivre** he hardly earns enough to keep body and soul together; **il parle à ~** *[personne silencieuse]* he hardly says anything; *[enfant]* he can hardly *ou* barely talk; **il était à ~ rentré qu'il a dû ressortir** he had only just got in *ou* scarcely got in when he had to go out again; **à ~ dans la voiture, il s'est endormi** no sooner had he got in the car than he fell asleep; **c'est à ~ si on l'entend** you can hardly hear him; **il était à ~ aimable** he was barely *ou* scarcely civil.

peiner [pene] [1] 1 vi *[personne]* to work hard, toil; *[moteur]* to labour; *[voiture, plante]* to struggle. ~ **sur un problème** to toil *ou* struggle with a problem; **le coureur peinait dans les derniers mètres** the runner had a hard time *ou* was struggling *ou* toiling over the last few metres; **le chien peine quand il fait chaud** the dog suffers when it is hot. 2 vt to grieve, sadden. **j'ai été peiné de l'apprendre** I was upset *ou* saddened to hear it; **dit-il d'un ton peiné** (*gén*) he said in a sad tone; (*vexé*) he said in a hurt *ou* an aggrieved tone; **il avait un air peiné** he looked upset.

peintre [pɛ̃tʀ] nmf (*lit*) painter; (*fig: écrivain*) portrayer. ~ **en bâtiment** house painter, painter and decorator; **~-décorateur** painter and decorator.

peinture [pɛ̃tyʀ] 1 nf a (*action, art*) painting. **faire de la ~ (à l'huile/à l'eau)** to paint (in oils/in watercolours).

b (*ouvrage*) painting, picture. **vendre sa ~** to sell one's paintings. *voir* **voir**.

c (*surface peinte*) paintwork (*NonC*). **toutes les ~s sont à refaire** all the paintwork needs re-doing.

d (*matière*) paint. **attention à la ~!, ~ fraîche!** wet paint!

e (*fig*) (*action*) portrayal; (*résultat*) portrait. **c'est une ~ des mœurs de l'époque** it is the portrait of *ou* it portrays *ou* depicts the social customs of the period.

2 comp ▸**peinture abstraite** (*NonC*) abstract art; (*tableau*) abstract (painting) ▸**peinture en bâtiment** house painting, painting and decorating ▸**peinture brillante** gloss paint ▸**peinture à l'eau** (*tableau, matière*) watercolour; (*pour le bâtiment*) water paint ▸**peinture à l'huile** (*tableau*) oil painting; (*matière*) oil paint; (*pour le bâtiment*) oil-based paint ▸**peinture laquée** gloss paint ▸**peinture mate** matt emulsion (paint) ▸**peinture métallisée** metallic paint ▸**peinture murale** mural ▸**peinture au pinceau** painting with a brush ▸**peinture au pistolet** spray painting ▸**peinture au rouleau** roller painting ▸**peinture satinée** satin-finish paint.

peinturer [pɛ̃tyʀe] [1] vt a (*) to slap paint on. b (*Can*) to paint.

peinturlurer [pɛ̃tyʀlyʀe] [1] vt to daub (with paint). ~ **qch de bleu** to daub sth with blue paint; **visage peinturluré** painted face; **lèvres peinturlurées en rouge** lips with a slash of red across them; **se ~ le visage** to slap make-up on one's face.

péjoratif, -ive [peʒɔʀatif, iv] 1 adj derogatory, pejorative. 2 nm (*Ling*) pejorative word.

péjoration [peʒɔʀasjɔ̃] nf pejoration.

péjorativement [peʒɔʀativmɑ̃] adv in a derogatory fashion, pejoratively.

Pékin [pekɛ̃] n Peking.

pékin [pekɛ̃] nm (*arg Mil*) civvy (*arg*), mufti (*arg*). **s'habiller en ~** to dress in civvies *ou* mufti.

pékinois, e [pekinwa, waz] 1 adj Pekinese. 2 nm a (*chien*) pekinese, peke*. b (*Ling*) Mandarin (Chinese), Pekinese. 3 nm,f: **P~(e)** Pekinese.

PEL [peəɛl] nm (abrév de **plan d'épargne-logement**) *voir* **plan**.

pelade [pəlad] nf alopecia.

pelage [pəlaʒ] nm coat, fur.

pélagique [pelaʒik] adj pelagic.

pélargonium [pelaʀgɔnjɔm] nm pelargonium.

pelé, e [pəle] (ptp de **peler**) 1 adj *personne* bald(-headed); *animal* hairless; *vêtement* threadbare; *terrain, montagne* bare. 2 nm (*) bald-headed man, baldie‡. (*fig*) **il n'y avait que trois** *ou* **quatre ~s et un tondu** there was hardly anyone there, there was only a handful of people there.

pêle-mêle [pɛlmɛl] 1 adv any old how, higgledy-piggledy*. **ils s'entassaient ~ dans l'autobus** they piled into the bus one on top of the other; **on y trouvait ~ des chapeaux, des rubans, des colliers** there were hats, ribbons and necklaces all mixed *ou* jumbled up together; **un roman où l'on trouve ~ une rencontre avec Charlemagne, un voyage sur Mars ...** a novel containing a hotchpotch of meetings with Charlemagne, trips to Mars ... . 2 nm inv (*cadre*) *photo frame with cutouts to put photos behind.*

peler [pəle] [5] vti (*gén*) to peel. **ce fruit se pèle bien** this fruit peels easily *ou* is easy to peel; **on pèle (de froid) ici!‡** it is damn cold here!‡, it is blooming freezing here!‡ (*Brit*).

pèlerin [pɛlʀɛ̃] nm pilgrim. **(faucon) ~** peregrine falcon; **(requin) ~** basking shark.

pèlerinage [pɛlʀinaʒ] nm (*voyage*) pilgrimage. **(lieu de) ~** place of pilgrimage, shrine; **aller en** *ou* **faire un ~ à** to go on a pilgrimage to.

pèlerine [pɛlʀin] nf cape.

pélican [pelikɑ̃] nm pelican.

pelisse [pəlis] nf pelisse.

pellagre [pelagʀ] nf pellagra.

pelle [pɛl] 1 nf (*gén*) shovel; *[enfant, terrassier]* spade. (*lit*) **ramasser à la ~** to shovel up; (*fig*) **on en ramasse** *ou* **il y en a à la ~** there are loads of them*; (*fig*) **avoir de l'argent** *ou* **remuer l'argent à la ~** to have pots* *ou* loads* of money, be rolling (in money)*; **ramasser** *ou* **prendre une ~‡** (*tomber*) to fall flat on one's back *ou* face, come a cropper* (*Brit*); (*échouer*) to come a cropper* (*Brit*), fall flat on one's face; (*après avoir demandé qch*) to be sent packing*; *voir* **rouler**. 2 comp ▸**pelle à charbon** coal shovel ▸**pelle mécanique** mechanical shovel *ou* digger ▸**pelle à ordures** dustpan ▸**pelle à tarte** cake *ou* pie server.

pelletée [pɛlte] nf (*voir* **pelle**) shovelful; spadeful.

pelleter [pɛlte] [4] vt to shovel (up).

pelleterie [pɛltʀi] nf (*commerce*) fur trade, furriery; (*préparation*) fur dressing; (*peau*) pelt.

pelleteur [pɛltœʀ] nm workman (*who does the digging*).

pelleteuse [pɛltøz] nf mechanical shovel *ou* digger, excavator.

pelletier, -ière [pɛltje, jɛʀ] nm,f furrier.

pellicule [pelikyl] nf a (*couche fine*) film, thin layer; (*Phot*) film. (*Phot*) ~ **couleur/noir et blanc** colour/black and white film; **ne gâche pas de la ~** don't waste film (on that). b (*Méd*) **~s** dandruff (*NonC*); **lotion contre les ~s** dandruff lotion.

Péloponnèse [pelɔpɔnɛz] nm: **le ~** the Peloponnese; **la guerre du ~** the Peloponnesian War.

pelotage* [p(ə)lɔtaʒ] nm petting* (*NonC*).

pelotari [p(ə)lɔtaʀi] nm pelota player.

pelote [p(ə)lɔt] nf a *[laine]* ball. **mettre de la laine en ~** to wind wool into a ball; (*fig*) **faire sa ~†** to feather one's nest, make one's pile*; **~ d'épingles** pin cushion; (*fig*) **c'est une vraie ~ d'épingles** he (*ou* she) is really prickly; *voir* **nerf**. b (*Sport*) **~ (basque)** pelota.

peloter* [p(ə)lɔte] [1] vt to pet*, paw*, touch up*. **arrêtez de me ~!** stop pawing me!*, keep your hands to yourself!; **ils se pelotaient** they were petting* *ou* necking* *ou* snogging‡ (*Brit*).

peloteur, -euse* [p(ə)lɔtœʀ, øz] 1 adj **il a des gestes ~s** *ou* **des mains ~euses** he can't keep his hands to himself. 2 nm,f (*) perv‡, groper*. **c'est un ~** he can't keep his hands to himself.

peloton [p(ə)lɔtɔ̃] 1 nm a *[laine]* small ball. b (*groupe*) cluster, group; *[pompiers, gendarmes]* squad; (*Mil*) platoon; (*Sport*) pack, main body of runners *ou* riders *etc*. 2 comp ▸**peloton d'exécution** firing squad ▸**peloton de tête** (*Sport*) leaders, leading runners *ou* riders *etc*; **être dans le peloton de tête** (*Sport*) to be up with the leaders; (*en classe*) to be among the top few; *[pays, entreprise]* to be one of the front runners.

pelotonner [p(ə)lɔtɔne] [1] 1 vt *laine* to wind into a ball. 2 **se pelotonner** vpr to curl (o.s.) up. **se ~ contre qn** to snuggle up to sb, nestle close to sb; **il s'est pelotonné entre mes bras** he snuggled up in my arms.

pelouse [p(ə)luz] nf lawn; (*Courses*) *area for spectators inside racetrack;* (*Ftbl, Rugby*) field, ground. **"~ interdite"** "keep off the grass".

peluche [p(ə)lyʃ] nf a (*Tex*) plush; (*poil*) fluff (*NonC*), bit of fluff. **ce pull fait des ~s** this jumper pills. b **(jouet en) ~** soft *ou* cuddly toy; **chien/lapin en ~** fluffy (*Brit*) *ou* stuffed dog/rabbit; *voir* **ours**.

pelucher [p(ə)lyʃe] [1] vi (*par l'aspect*) to become *ou* go fluffy; (*perdre des poils*) to leave fluff.

pelucheux, -euse [p(ə)lyʃø, øz] adj fluffy.

pelure [p(ə)lyʀ] nf a (*épluchure*) peel (*NonC*), peeling, piece of peel; (‡: *manteau*) (over)coat. ~ **d'oignon** (*Bot*) onion skin; (*vin*) pelure d'oignon. b **(papier) ~** flimsy (paper), copy *ou* bank paper; (*feuille*) flimsy (copy).

pelvien, -ienne [pɛlvjɛ̃, jɛn] adj pelvic; *voir* **ceinture**.

pelvis [pɛlvis] nm pelvis.

pénal, e, mpl **-aux** [penal, o] adj penal. **le droit ~** (the) criminal law; **poursuivre qn au ~** to sue sb, take legal action against sb; *voir* **clause, code**.

pénalisation [penalizasjɔ̃] nf (*Sport*) (*action*) penalization; (*sanction*) penalty. **points de ~** penalty points.

pénaliser [penalize] [1] vt *contrevenant, faute, joueur* to penalize.

pénalité [penalite] nf (*Fin, Sport: sanction*) penalty. (*Rugby*) **coup de pied de ~** penalty kick.

penalty [penalti], pl **penalties** [penaltiz] nm (*Ftbl*) (*coup de pied*) penalty (kick); (*sanction*) penalty. **siffler le** *ou* **un ~** to award a penalty; **marquer sur ~** to score from a penalty; **tirer un ~** to take a penalty (kick); (*endroit*) **point de ~** penalty spot.

pénard, e* [penaʀ, aʀd] **adj = peinard.**

pénardement* [penaʀdəmɑ̃] **adv = peinardement.**

pénates [penat] **nmpl** (*Myth*) Penates; (*fig hum*) home. **regagner ses ~** to go back home; **emporter** *ou* **aller planter ses ~ ailleurs** to set up home *ou* settle down elsewhere.

penaud, e [pəno, od] **adj** sheepish, contrite. **d'un air ~** sheepishly, contritely; **il en est resté tout ~** he became quite sheepish *ou* contrite.

pence [pɛns] **nmpl** pence.

penchant [pɑ̃ʃɑ̃] **nm** (*tendance*) tendency, propensity (*à faire* to do); (*faible*) liking, fondness (*pour qch* for sth). **avoir un ~ à faire qch** to be inclined *ou* have a tendency to do sth; **avoir un ~ pour qch** to be fond of *ou* have a liking *ou* fondness for sth; **avoir un ~ pour la boisson** to be partial to drink; (*littér*) **avoir du ~ pour qn** to be in love with sb; **le ~ qu'ils ont l'un pour l'autre** the fondness they have for each other; **mauvais ~s** baser instincts.

penché, e [pɑ̃ʃe] (**ptp de pencher**) **adj** *tableau* slanting, tilted, lop-sided; *mur, poteau* slanting, leaning over (*attrib*); *objet déséquilibré* tilting, tipping; *écriture* sloping, slanting; *tête* tilted (to one side). **le corps ~ en avant/arrière** leaning forward/back(ward); *[personne]* **être ~ sur ses livres** to be bent over one's books; *voir* **tour**[1].

pencher [pɑ̃ʃe] [1] **1 vt** *meuble, bouteille* to tip up, tilt. **~ son assiette** to tip one's plate up; **~ la tête** (*en avant*) to bend one's head forward; (*sur le côté*) to lean *ou* tilt one's head to one side.

2 vi a (*être incliné*) *[mur]* to lean over, be slanting; *[arbre]* to tilt, lean over; *[navire]* to list; *[objet en déséquilibre]* to tilt, tip (to one side). **le tableau penche un peu de ce côté** the picture is slanting *ou* tilting a bit this way; (*fig*) **faire ~ la balance** to tip the scales.

b (*être porté à*) **je penche pour la première hypothèse** I'm inclined to favour the first hypothesis; **je penche à croire qu'il est sincère** I'm inclined to believe he is sincere.

3 se pencher vpr a (*s'incliner*) to lean over; (*se baisser*) to bend down. **se ~ en avant** to lean forward; **se ~ par-dessus bord** to lean overboard; **se ~ sur un livre** to bend over a book; **défense de se ~ au dehors** *ou* **par la fenêtre** do not lean out, do not lean out of the window.

b (*examiner*) **se ~ sur un problème/cas** to study *ou* look into a problem/case; **se ~ sur les malheurs de qn** to turn one's attention to sb's misfortunes.

pendable [pɑ̃dabl] **adj** *voir* **cas, tour**[2].

pendaison [pɑ̃dɛzɔ̃] **nf** hanging. **~ de crémaillère** house warming, house-warming party.

pendant[1]**, e** [pɑ̃dɑ̃, ɑ̃t] **adj a** (*qui pend*) *bras, jambes* hanging, dangling; *langue* hanging out (*attrib*); *joue* sagging; *oreilles* drooping; (*Jur*) *fruits* on the tree (*attrib*). **ne reste pas là les bras ~s** don't just stand there (with your arms at your sides); **assis sur le mur les jambes ~es** sitting on the wall with his legs hanging down; **le chien haletait la langue ~e** the dog was panting with its tongue hanging out; **chien aux oreilles ~es** dog with drooping ears, lop-eared dog; **les branches ~es du saule** the hanging *ou* drooping branches of the willow.

b (*Admin: en instance*) *question* outstanding, in abeyance (*attrib*); *affaire* pending (*attrib*); (*Jur*) *procès* pending (*attrib*).

pendant[2] [pɑ̃dɑ̃] **nm a** (*objet*) **~ (d'oreille)** drop earring, pendant earring; **~ d'épée** frog. **b** (*contrepartie*) **le ~ de** *œuvre d'art, meuble* the matching piece to; *personne, institution* the counterpart of; **faire ~ à** to match, be matched by; to be the counterpart of, parallel; **se faire ~** to match; to be counterparts, parallel each other; **j'ai un chandelier et je cherche le ~** I've got a candlestick and I'm looking for one to match it *ou* and I'm trying to make up a pair.

pendant[3] [pɑ̃dɑ̃] **1 prép** (*au cours de*) during; (*indique la durée*) for. **~ la journée/son séjour** during the day/his stay; **~ ce temps Paul attendait** during this time *ou* meanwhile Paul was waiting; **qu'est-ce qu'il faisait ~ ce temps-là?** what was he doing during that time? *ou* meanwhile? *ou* in the meantime?; *[médicament]* **à prendre ~ le repas** to be taken at mealtimes *ou* during meals; **on a marché ~ des kilomètres** we walked for miles; **il a vécu en France ~ plusieurs années** he lived in France for several years; **~ quelques mois, il n'a pas pu travailler** for several months he was unable to work; **on est resté sans nouvelles de lui ~ longtemps** we had no news from him for a long time; **~ un moment on a cru qu'il ne reviendrait pas** for a while we thought he would not return; **avant la guerre et ~, il ...** before and during the war, he ..., before the war and while it was on*, he ...; **il n'a pas fait ses devoirs après les cours, mais ~!** he didn't do his homework after school but in class!

2 : ~ que conj while, whilst (*frm*); **~ qu'elle se reposait, il écoutait la radio** while she was resting he would listen to the radio; **~ que vous serez à Paris, pourriez-vous aller le voir?** while you're in Paris could you go and see him?; **~ que j'y pense, n'oubliez pas de fermer la porte à clef** while I think of it, don't forget to lock the door; **arrosez le jardin et, ~ que vous y êtes, arrachez les mauvaises herbes** water the garden and do some weeding while you're at *ou* about it; (*iro*) **finissez le plat ~ que vous y êtes** why don't you eat it all (up) while you're at it (*iro*); **dire que des gens doivent suivre un régime pour maigrir ~ que des enfants meurent de faim** to think that some people have to go on a diet to lose weight while there are children dying of hunger.

pendard, e [pɑ̃daʀ, aʀd] **nm,f** (††, *hum*) scoundrel.

pendeloque [pɑ̃d(ə)lɔk] **nf** *[boucles d'oreilles]* pendant; *[lustre]* lustre, pendant.

pendentif [pɑ̃dɑ̃tif] **nm** (*bijou*) pendant; (*Archit*) pendentive.

penderie [pɑ̃dʀi] **nf** (*meuble*) wardrobe (*only for hanging things up*); (*barre*) clothes rail. **le placard du couloir nous sert de ~** we hang our clothes in the hall cupboard (*Brit*) *ou* closet (*US*); **le côté ~ de l'armoire** the hanging section in the wardrobe.

pendiller [pɑ̃dije] [1] **vi** *[clefs, boucles d'oreilles, corde]* to dangle; *[linge]* to flap gently.

Pendjab [pɛ̃dʒab] **nm: le ~** the Punjab.

pendouiller* [pɑ̃duje] [1] **vi** to dangle (about *ou* down), hang down.

pendre [pɑ̃dʀ] [41] **1 vt a** *rideau* to hang, put up (*à* at); *tableau, manteau* to hang (up) (*à* on); *lustre* to hang (up) (*à* from). **~ le linge pour le faire sécher** (*dans la maison*) to hang up the washing to dry; (*dehors*) to hang out the washing to dry; **~ la crémaillère** to have a house-warming party *ou* a house warming.

b *criminel* to hang. (*Hist*) **~ qn haut et court** to hang sb; **~ qn en effigie** to hang sb in effigy; **qu'il aille se faire ~ ailleurs!*** he can go hang!*, he can take a running jump!*; **je veux être pendu si ...** I'll be hanged if ...; **dussé-je être pendu** over my dead body; *voir* **pis**[2].

2 vi a (*être suspendu*) to hang (down). **des fruits pendaient aux branches** there was fruit hanging from the branches; **cela lui pend au nez*** he's got it coming to him*.

b (*fig*) *[bras, jambes]* to dangle; *[joue]* to sag; *[langue]* to hang out; *[robe]* to dip, hang down; *[cheveux]* to hang down. **un lambeau de papier pendait** a strip of wallpaper was hanging off; **laisser ~ ses jambes** to dangle one's legs.

3 se pendre vpr a (*se tuer*) to hang o.s.

b (*se suspendre*) **se ~ à une branche** to hang from a branch; **se ~ au cou de qn** to throw one's arms round sb *ou* sb's neck.

pendu, e [pɑ̃dy] (**ptp de pendre**) **1 adj a** *chose* hung up, hanging up. **~ à** hanging from; *voir* **langue**.

b *personne* hanged. **être toujours ~ aux basques de qn** to keep pestering sb; **il est toujours ~ aux jupes** *ou* **jupons de sa mère** he's always clinging to his mother's skirts *ou* to his mother's apron strings; **~ au bras de qn** holding on to sb's arm; **elle est toujours ~e au téléphone*** she spends all her time on the phone; **ça fait deux heures qu'il est ~ au téléphone** that is two hours he has been on the phone; **être ~ aux lèvres de qn** to drink in sb's words, hang on sb's every word.

2 nm,f hanged man (*ou* woman). **le (jeu du) ~** (the game of) hangman; **jouer au ~** to play hangman.

pendulaire [pɑ̃dylɛʀ] **adj** pendular.

pendule [pɑ̃dyl] **1 nf** clock. **~ à coucou** cuckoo clock; (*fig*) **remettre les ~s à l'heure*** to set the record straight; **il en a fait une ~*** he made a song and dance about it. **2 nm** pendulum. *[alpiniste]* **faire un ~** to do a pendule *ou* pendulum.

pendulette [pɑ̃dylɛt] **nf** small clock. **~ de voyage** travelling clock.

pêne [pɛn] **nm** bolt (*of lock*).

Pénélope [penelɔp] **nf** Penelope. **c'est un travail de ~** it's a never-ending task.

pénéplaine [penepIɛn] **nf** peneplain, peneplane.

pénétrabilité [penetʀabilite] **nf** penetrability.

pénétrable [penetʀabl] **adj** *matière* penetrable (*à* by); (*fig*) *mystère, mobile* penetrable, understandable (*à* by). **peu** *ou* **difficilement ~** difficult to penetrate; (*fig*) impenetrable, enigmatic.

pénétrant, e [penetʀɑ̃, ɑ̃t] **1 adj a** (*lit*) *pluie* drenching, that soaks right through you; *froid* piercing, biting, bitter; *odeur* penetrating, pervasive; *crème* penetrating. **b** (*fig*) *regard* penetrating, searching, piercing; *esprit* penetrating, keen, shrewd; *analyse, remarque* penetrating, shrewd; *personne* shrewd. **2 pénétrante nf** urban motorway (*Brit*) *ou* freeway (*US*) (*linking centre of town to inter-city routes*).

pénétration [penetʀasjɔ̃] **nf a** (*action*) penetration. (*Mil*) **force de ~** force of penetration; **la ~ des mobiles/pensées d'autrui** the divination of others' motives/thoughts; **la ~ des idées nouvelles** the establishment *ou* penetration of new ideas. **b** (*sagacité*) penetration, perception. **c** *Comm* penetration. **taux de ~** penetration rate. **d** (*sexuelle*) penetration.

pénétré, e [penetʀe] (**ptp de pénétrer**) **adj a** (*convaincu*) **être ~ de son importance** *ou* **de soi-même** to be full of one's own importance, be full of o.s.; **être ~ de ses obligations/de la nécessité de faire** to be (fully) alive to *ou* highly conscious of one's obligations/of the need to do. **b** (*sérieux*) *air, ton* earnest, of deep conviction.

pénétrer [penetʀe] [6] **1 vi a** *[personne, véhicule]* **~ dans** *pièce, bâtiment, pays* to enter; *jungle* to penetrate into; (*fig*) *groupe, milieu* to penetrate. **personne ne doit ~ ici** nobody must be allowed to enter; **~ chez qn par la force** to force an entry *ou* one's way into sb's home; **les envahisseurs/les troupes ont pénétré dans le pays** the invaders/the troops have entered the country; **il est difficile de ~ dans les milieux de la finance** it is hard to penetrate financial circles; **faire ~ qn dans le salon** to show *ou* let sb into the lounge; **des voleurs ont pénétré dans la maison en son absence** thieves broke into his house while he was away; **l'habitude n'a pas encore pénétré dans les mœurs** the habit hasn't established itself yet *ou* made its way into general behaviour yet; **faire ~**

une idée dans la tête de qn to instil an idea in sb, get an idea into sb's head.

b *[soleil]* to shine *ou* come in; *[vent]* to blow *ou* come in; *[air, liquide, insecte]* to come *ou* get in. ~ **dans** to shine into; to come into; to blow into; to get into; **la lumière pénétrait dans la cellule (par une lucarne)** light came into *ou* entered the cell (through a skylight); **le liquide pénètre à travers une membrane** the liquid comes *ou* penetrates through a membrane; **la fumée/l'odeur pénètre par tous les interstices** the smoke/ the smell comes *ou* gets in through all the gaps; **faire ~ de l'air (dans)** to let fresh air in(to).

c (*en s'enfonçant*) ~ **dans** *[crème, balle, verre]* to penetrate; *[aiguille]* to go in, penetrate; *[habitude]* to make its way into; *[huile, encre]* to soak into. **ce vernis pénètre dans le bois** this varnish soaks (down) into the wood; **faire ~ une crème (dans la peau)** to rub a cream in(to the skin).

2 **vt** a (*percer*) *[froid, air]* to penetrate; *[odeur]* to spread through, fill; *[liquide]* to penetrate, soak through; *[regard]* to penetrate, go through. **le froid les pénétrait jusqu'aux os** the cold cut *ou* went right through them.

b (*découvrir*) *mystère, secret* to penetrate, fathom; *intentions, idées, plans* to penetrate, fathom, perceive. **il est difficile à ~** it is difficult to fathom him.

c (*fig*) **son sang-froid me pénètre d'admiration** his composure fills me with admiration; **il se sentait pénétré de pitié/d'effroi** he was filled with pity/fright; **le remords pénétra sa conscience** he was filled with remorse, he was conscience-stricken.

d *Comm marché* to penetrate, break into.

e (*sexuellement*) to penetrate.

3 **se pénétrer vpr** a **se ~ d'une idée** to get an idea firmly fixed *ou* set in one's mind; **s'étant pénétré de l'importance de qch** firmly convinced of *ou* with a clear realization of the importance of sth; **il faut bien vous ~ du fait que ...** you must be absolutely clear in your mind that *ou* have it firmly in your mind that ...; **j'ai du mal à me ~ de l'utilité de cette mesure** I find it difficult to convince myself of the usefulness of this measure.

b (*s'imbiber*) **se ~ d'eau/de gaz** to become permeated with water/ gas.

pénibilité [penibilite] **nf** hardness.

pénible [penibl] **adj** a (*fatigant, difficile*) *travail, voyage, ascension* hard; *personne* tiresome. ~ **à lire/supporter** hard *ou* difficult to read/ bear; **les derniers kilomètres ont été ~s (à parcourir)** the last few kilometres were heavy going *ou* hard going; **l'hiver a été ~** the winter has been unpleasant; **tout effort lui est ~** any effort is difficult for him, he finds it hard to make the slightest effort; **il est vraiment ~** *[enfant]* he's a real nuisance; *[personne]* he's a real pain in the neck*.

b (*douloureux*) *sujet, séparation, moment, maladie* painful (*à* to); *nouvelle, spectacle* sad, painful; *respiration* laboured. **la lumière violente lui est ~** bright light hurts his eyes, he finds bright light painful (to his eyes); **ce bruit est ~ à supporter** this noise is unpleasant *ou* painful to listen to; **il m'est ~ de constater/d'avoir à vous dire que** I am sorry to find/to have to tell you that.

péniblement [peniblǝmɑ̃] **adv** (*difficilement*) with difficulty; (*tristement*) painfully; (*tout juste*) just about, only just.

péniche [peniʃ] **nf** (*bateau*) barge. (*Mil*) ~ **de débarquement** landing craft; (*: *grosse voiture*) **il a une vraie ~*** he has a great boat of a car.

pénicilline [penisilin] **nf** penicillin.

pénil [penil] **nm** mons pubis.

péninsulaire [penɛ̃sylɛʀ] **adj** peninsular.

péninsule [penɛ̃syl] **nf** peninsula. **la ~ Ibérique** the Iberian Peninsula; **la ~ Balkanique** the Balkan Peninsula.

pénis [penis] **nm** penis.

pénitence [penitɑ̃s] **nf** a (*Rel*) (*repentir*) penitence; (*peine, sacrement*) penance. **faire ~** to repent (*de* of); **pour votre ~** as a penance. b (*gén, Scol: châtiment*) punishment. **infliger une ~ à qn** to punish sb; **mettre qn en ~** to make sb stand in the corner; **pour ta ~** as a punishment (to you). c *[jeux]* forfeit.

pénitencier [penitɑ̃sje] **nm** a (*prison*) prison, penitentiary (*US*). b (*Rel*) penitentiary.

pénitent, e [penitɑ̃, ɑ̃t] **adj, nm,f** penitent.

pénitentiaire [penitɑ̃sjɛʀ] **adj** penitentiary, prison (*épith*). **établissement ~** penal establishment, prison; *voir* **colonie**.

penne [pɛn] **nf** (*Zool*) large feather, penna (*SPÉC*); *[flèche]* flight.

Pennine [penin] 1 **adj f: chaîne ~** Pennine Chain *ou* Range. 2 **Pennines nfpl** Pennines.

Pennsylvanie [pɛnsilvani] **nf** Pennsylvania.

penny, pl pennies [peni] **nm** penny.

pénombre [penɔ̃bʀ] **nf** (*faible clarté*) half-light, shadowy light; (*obscurité*) darkness; (*Astron*) penumbra. (*fig*) **demeurer dans la ~** to stay in the background.

pensable [pɑ̃sabl] **adj** thinkable. **ce n'est pas ~** it's unthinkable.

pensant, e [pɑ̃sɑ̃, ɑ̃t] **adj** thinking; *voir* **bien, mal**.

pense-bête, pl pense-bêtes [pɑ̃sbɛt] **nm** (*gén*) reminder; (*objet*) note *ou* memo board.

pensée¹ [pɑ̃se] **nf** a (*ce que l'on pense*) thought. **sans déguiser sa ~** without hiding one's thoughts *ou* feelings; **je l'ai fait dans la seule ~ de vous être utile** I only did it thinking it would help you, my only thought in doing it was to help you; **recevez mes plus affectueuses ~s** with fondest love; **saisir/deviner les ~s de qn** to grasp/guess sb's thoughts *ou* what sb is thinking (about); **plongé dans ses ~s** deep in thought; **avoir une ~ pour qn** to think of sb; (*hum*) **j'ai eu une ~ émue pour toi** I spared a thought for you (*hum*); **si vous voulez connaître le fond de ma ~** if you want to know what I really think (about it) *ou* how I really feel about it; **à la ~ de faire qch** at the thought of doing sth; **à la ~ que ...** to think that ..., when one thinks that ... .

b (*faculté, fait de penser*) thought. **la dignité de l'homme est dans la ~** human dignity lies in man's capacity for thought; (*littér*) **arrêter sa ~ sur qch** to pause to think about sth.

c (*manière de penser*) thinking. ~ **claire/obscure** clear/muddled thinking.

d (*esprit*) thought, mind. **venir à la ~ de qn** to occur to sb; **se représenter qch par la ~** *ou* **en ~** to imagine sth in one's mind, conjure up a mental picture of sth; **les soucis qui hantent sa ~** the worries that haunt his thoughts *ou* his mind; **transportons-nous par la ~ au 16ᵉ siècle** let's travel back in our minds to the 16th century, let's imagine ourselves back in the 16th century.

e (*doctrine*) thought, thinking. **la ~ marxiste** Marxist thinking; **la ~ de Gandhi** the thought of Gandhi; **la ~ de cet auteur est difficile à comprendre** it is difficult to understand what this author is trying to say.

f (*maxime*) thought. **les ~s de Pascal** the thoughts of Pascal.

pensée² [pɑ̃se] **nf** (*Bot*) pansy. ~ **sauvage** wild pansy.

penser [pɑ̃se] [1] 1 **vi** a (*réfléchir*) to think. **façon de ~** way of thinking; **une nouvelle qui donne** *ou* **laisse à ~** a piece of news which makes you (stop and) think *ou* which gives (you) food for thought; ~ **tout haut** to think out loud.

b ~ **à** (*songer à*) *ami* to think of *ou* about; (*réfléchir à*) *problème, offre* to think about *ou* over, turn over in one's mind; **pensez donc à ce que vous dites** just think about what you're saying; ~ **aux autres/aux malheureux** to think of others/of those who are unhappy; **vous pensez à quelqu'un de précis pour ce travail?** do you have anyone (in) particular in mind for this job?; **tu vois à qui/quoi je pense?** you know who/what I'm thinking of?; **faire ~ à** to make one think of, remind one of; **cette mélodie fait ~ à Debussy** this tune reminds you of Debussy *ou* is reminiscent of Debussy; **il ne pense qu'à jouer** playing is all he ever thinks about; **pensez-y avant d'accepter** think it over *ou* give it some thought before you accept; (*hum*) **il ne pense qu'à ça*** he's got a one-track mind*; **il lui a donné un coup de pied où je pense*** he gave him a kick you know where*; **faire/dire qch sans y ~** to do/say sth without thinking about it; **n'y pensons plus!** let's forget it!, let's not dwell on it!; **c'est simple mais il fallait y ~** it's simple when you think of it but the idea has to occur to you first.

c ~ **à** (*prévoir*) to think of; (*se souvenir de*) to remember; **il pense à tout** he thinks of everything; ~ **à l'avenir/aux conséquences** to think of the future/of the consequences; **a-t-il pensé à rapporter du pain?** did he think of bringing *ou* did he remember to bring some bread?; **pense à l'anniversaire de ta mère** remember *ou* don't forget your mother's birthday; **fais m'y ~** remind me about that, don't let me forget; **il suffisait d'y ~** it was just a matter of thinking of it; **voyons, pense un peu au danger!** just think of *ou* consider the danger!; *voir aussi* **mal 3e**.

d (*loc excl*) **il vient? — penses-tu!** *ou* **pensez-vous!** is he coming? — is he heck!* *ou* you must be joking!*; **tu penses!** *ou* **vous pensez! je le connais trop bien pour le croire** not likely!* I know him too well to believe him; **il va accepter? — je pense bien!** will he accept? — of course he will! *ou* I should think so! *ou* I should think he will!

2 **vt** a (*avoir une opinion*) to think (*de* of, about). ~ **du bien/du mal de qch/qn** to have a high/poor opinion of sth/sb, think highly/not think much of sth/sb; **que pense-t-il du film?** what does he think of the film?; **que pensez-vous de ce projet?** what do you think *ou* how do you feel about this plan?; **il est difficile de savoir ce qu'il pense** it's difficult to know what he's thinking *ou* what's in his mind; **je pense comme toi** I agree with you; **je ne dis rien mais je n'en pense pas moins** I am not saying anything but that doesn't mean that I agree with it; **que penseriez-vous d'un voyage à Rome?** what would you say to *ou* how would you fancy *ou* how about a trip to Rome?

b (*supposer*) to think, suppose, believe; (*imaginer*) to think, expect, imagine. **il n'aurait jamais pensé qu'elle ferait cela** he would never have thought *ou* imagined *ou* dreamt she would do that, he would never have expected her to do that; **quand on lui dit musique, il pense ennui** when you mention the word music to him it just spells boredom to him *ou* his only thought is that it's boring; **je pense que non** I don't think so, I think not; **je pense que oui** I think so; **ce n'est pas si bête qu'on le pense** it's not such a silly idea as you might think *ou* suppose; **pensez-vous qu'il vienne?** *ou* **viendra?** do you think he'll come?, are you expecting him to come?; **je vous laisse à ~ s'il était content** you can imagine how pleased he was; **pensez qu'il est encore si jeune!** to think that he's still so young!; **ils pensent avoir trouvé une maison** they think *ou* believe they've found a house; **c'est bien ce que je pensais!** I thought as much!, just as *ou* what I thought!; **vous pensez bien qu'elle a refusé** you can well imagine (that) she refused, as you may well expect, she refused; **j'ai pensé mourir/m'évanouir** I thought I was going to die/faint; **tout laisse à ~ qu'elle l'a quitté** there is every indication that she has left him.

c ~ **faire** (*avoir l'intention de*) to be thinking of doing, consider doing; (*espérer*) to hope *ou* expect to do; **il pense partir jeudi** he's thinking of going *ou* he intends to leave on Thursday; **elle pense arriver demain** she's hoping *ou* expecting to arrive tomorrow.

d (*concevoir*) *problème, projet, machine* to think out. **c'est bien/fortement pensé** it's well/very well thought out.

3 **nm** (*littér*) thought.

penseur [pɑ̃sœʀ] 1 **nm** thinker; *voir* **libre**. 2 **adj m** (†) thoughtful.

pensif, -ive [pɑ̃sif, iv] **adj** pensive, thoughtful.

pension [pɑ̃sjɔ̃] 1 **nf** a (*allocation*) pension. ~ **de guerre** war pension; ~ **d'invalidité** disablement pension; ~ **de retraite** old age pension, retirement pension; **toucher sa ~** to draw one's pension.

b (*hôtel*) boarding house; *[chiens, chats etc]* (boarding) kennels; *[chevaux]* (boarding) stables.

c (*Scol*) (boarding) school. **mettre qn en ~** to send sb to boarding school.

d (*hébergement*) *[personne]* board and lodging, bed and board. **la ~ coûte 80 F par jour** board and lodging is 80 francs a day; **être en ~ chez qn** to board with sb *ou* at sb's, be in digs* at sb's; **prendre ~ chez qn** (*lit*) to take board and lodging at sb's; (*hum*) to take up residence at sb's; **prendre qn en ~** to take sb (in) as a lodger, board sb; **chambre sans ~** room (*with no meals provided*); **chambre avec ~ complète** full board; **avoir en ~** *cheval, chien etc* to look after; *voir* **demi-**.

2 **comp** ▸**pension alimentaire** *[étudiant]* living allowance; *[divorcée]* alimony, maintenance allowance ▸**pension de famille** ≃ boarding house, guesthouse.

pensionnaire [pɑ̃sjɔnɛʀ] **nmf** (*Scol*) boarder; *[famille]* lodger; *[hôtel]* resident; *[sanatorium]* patient; *voir* **demi-**.

pensionnat [pɑ̃sjɔna] **nm** (boarding) school.

pensionné, e [pɑ̃sjɔne] (**ptp de pensionner**) 1 **adj** who gets *ou* draws a pension. 2 **nm,f** pensioner.

pensionner [pɑ̃sjɔne] 1 **vt** to give a pension to.

pensivement [pɑ̃sivmɑ̃] **adv** pensively, thoughtfully.

pensum [pɛ̃sɔm] **nm** (*Scol* †) lines (*Brit*), punishment; (*fig*) chore.

pentaèdre [pɛ̃taɛdʀ] 1 **nm** pentahedron. 2 **adj** pentahedral.

pentagonal, e, **mpl -aux** [pɛ̃tagɔnal, o] **adj** pentagonal.

pentagone [pɛ̃tagɔn] **nm** pentagon. (*Mil*) **le P~** the Pentagon.

pentamètre [pɛ̃tamɛtʀ] **adj, nm** pentameter.

Pentateuque [pɛ̃tatøk] **nm** Pentateuch.

pentathlon [pɛ̃tatlɔ̃] **nm** pentathlon.

pentatonique [pɛ̃tatɔnik] **adj** pentatonic.

pente [pɑ̃t] **nf** a (*gén*) slope. **être en ~ douce/raide** to slope (down) gently/steeply; **la ~ d'un toit** the pitch *ou* slope of a roof; **en ~** *toit* sloping; *allée, pelouse* on a slope (*attrib*); **de petites rues en ~ raide** steep little streets; **garé dans une rue en ~** parked on a slope; *[route]* **~ à 4 %** gradient of 1 in 25, 4% incline (*US*). b (*loc*) **être sur une** *ou* **la mauvaise ~** to be going downhill, be on a downward path; (*fig*) **remonter la ~** to get on one's feet again, fight one's way back again; (*fig*) **être sur une ~ glissante** *ou* **dangereuse** *ou* **savonneuse** to be on a slippery slope (*fig*); **suivre sa ~ naturelle** to follow one's natural bent *ou* inclination; *voir* **dalle, rupture**.

Pentecôte [pɑ̃tkot] **nf** a (*Rel: dimanche*) Whit Sunday, Pentecost; (*gén: période*) Whit(suntide), Whitsun. **lundi de ~** Whit Monday; **de la ~** Pentecostal, Whit (*épith*). b (*fête juive*) Pentecost.

penthotal [pɛ̃tɔtal] **nm** ® pentothal ®.

pentu, e [pɑ̃ty] **adj** sloping.

penture [pɑ̃tyʀ] **nf** *[volet, porte]* strap hinge.

pénultième [penyltjɛm] 1 **adj** penultimate. 2 **nf** penultimate (syllable).

pénurie [penyʀi] **nf** shortage. ~ **de** shortage *ou* lack of; ~ **de main-d'œuvre/sucre** labour/sugar shortage; **on ne peut guère qu'organiser la ~** we must just make the best of a bad job* *ou* the best of what we've got.

pépé* [pepe] **nm** grandad*, grandpa*.

pépée* [pepe] **nf** (*fille*) bird* (*Brit*), chick*.

pépère* [pepɛʀ] 1 **nm** a (*pépé*) grandad*, grandpa*. b **un gros ~** (*enfant*) a bonny (*Brit*) *ou* cute (*US*) child; (*homme*) an old fatty*; **un petit ~ à vélo** a little (old) man on a bike. 2 **adj** *vie* quiet, uneventful; (*Aut*) *conduite* pottering, dawdling; *travail* cushy* (*Brit*), easy. **un petit coin ~** a nice quiet spot.

pépettes* [pepɛt] **nfpl** dough*, lolly* (*Brit*), bread*.

pépie [pepi] **nf** (*Orn*) pip. (*fig*) **avoir la ~** to have a terrible thirst, be parched*.

pépiement [pepimɑ̃] **nm** chirping (*NonC*), chirruping (*NonC*), tweeting (*NonC*).

pépier [pepje] 7 **vi** to chirp, chirrup, tweet.

pépin [pepɛ̃] **nm** a (*Bot*) pip. **sans ~s** seedless. b (*: *ennui*) snag, hitch. **avoir un ~** to hit a snag*, have a spot of bother (*Brit*); **j'ai eu un ~ avec ma voiture** I had a problem with my car; **gros/petit ~ de santé** major/slight health problem; **c'est un gros ~ pour l'entreprise** it's a major setback for the company. c (*: *parapluie*) brolly* (*Brit*), umbrella.

pépinière [pepinjɛʀ] **nf** (*lit*) tree nursery; (*fig*) breeding-ground, nursery (*de* for).

pépiniériste [pepinjeʀist] 1 **nm** nurseryman. 2 **nf** nurserywoman.

pépite [pepit] **nf** nugget.

péplum [peplɔm] **nm** peplos.

pepsine [pɛpsin] **nf** pepsin.

peptide [pɛptid] **nm** peptide.

peptique [pɛptik] **adj** peptic.

péquenaud, e* [pɛkno, od] 1 **adj** peasant (*épith*). 2 **nm,f** country bumpkin.

péquenot [pɛkno] **adj, nm** = **péquenaud**.

péquin [pekɛ̃] **nm** (*arg Mil*) = **pékin**.

péquiste [pekist] (*Québec*) 1 **adj** of the Parti québécois. 2 **nmf** member of the Parti québécois.

PER [peəɛʀ] **nm** (**abrév de plan d'épargne-retraite**) *voir* **plan**.

perborate [pɛʀbɔʀat] **nm** perborate.

perçage [pɛʀsaʒ] **nm** *[trou]* boring, drilling; *[matériau]* boring through.

percale [pɛʀkal] **nf** percale.

percaline [pɛʀkalin] **nf** percaline.

perçant, e [pɛʀsɑ̃, ɑ̃t] **adj** *cri, voix* piercing, shrill; *froid* piercing, biting, bitter; *vue* sharp, keen; (*fig*) *regard* piercing; *esprit* penetrating.

perce [pɛʀs] **nf**: **mettre en ~** *tonneau* to broach, tap.

perce- [pɛʀs] **préf** *voir* **percer**.

percée [pɛʀse] **nf** (*dans une forêt*) opening, clearing; (*dans un mur*) breach, gap; (*Mil, Sci, Écon*) breakthrough; (*Rugby*) break.

percement [pɛʀsəmɑ̃] **nm** *[trou]* piercing; (*avec perceuse*) drilling, boring; *[rue, tunnel]* building, driving; *[fenêtre]* making.

percepteur, -trice [pɛʀsɛptœʀ, tʀis] 1 **adj** perceptive, of perception. 2 **nm** tax collector, tax man*.

perceptibilité [pɛʀsɛptibilite] **nf** perceptibility.

perceptible [pɛʀsɛptibl] **adj** a *son, ironie* perceptible (*à* to). b *impôt* collectable, payable.

perceptiblement [pɛʀsɛptibləmɑ̃] **adv** perceptibly.

perceptif, -ive [pɛʀsɛptif, iv] **adj** perceptive.

perception [pɛʀsɛpsjɔ̃] **nf** a (*sensation*) perception. ~ **extrasensorielle** extrasensory perception. b *[impôt, amende, péage]* collection; (*bureau*) tax (collector's) office.

percer [pɛʀse] 3 1 **vt** a (*gén: perforer*) to pierce, make a hole in; (*avec perceuse*) to drill *ou* bore through, drill *ou* bore a hole in; *lobe d'oreille* to pierce; *chaussette, chaussure* to wear a hole in; *coffre-fort* to break open, crack*; *tonneau* to broach, tap; (*Méd*) *abcès* to lance, burst; *tympan* to burst. **avoir une poche/une chaussure percée** to have a hole in one's pocket/shoe; **percé de trous** full of holes, riddled with holes; **la rouille avait percé le métal** rust had eaten into the metal; **on a retrouvé son corps percé de coups de couteau** his body was found full of stab wounds; *voir* **chaise, panier**.

b *fenêtre, ouverture* to pierce, make; *canal* to build; *tunnel* to build, bore, drive (*dans* through). ~ **un trou dans** to pierce *ou* make a hole in; (*avec perceuse*) to drill *ou* bore a hole through *ou* in; **ils ont percé une nouvelle route à travers la forêt** they have driven *ou* built a new road through the forest; ~ **une porte dans un mur** to make *ou* open a doorway in a wall; **mur percé de petites fenêtres** wall with (a number of) small windows set in it.

c (*fig: traverser*) ~ **l'air/le silence** to pierce the air/the silence; ~ **les nuages/le front ennemi** to pierce *ou* break through the clouds/the enemy lines; ~ **la foule** to force *ou* elbow one's way through the crowd; **bruit qui perce les oreilles** ear-piercing *ou* ear-splitting noise; ~ **qn du regard** to give sb a piercing look; **ses yeux essayaient de ~ l'obscurité** he tried to peer through the darkness; **cela m'a percé le cœur** it cut me to the heart.

d (*découvrir*) *mystère* to penetrate; *complot* to uncover. ~ **qch à jour** to see (right) through sth.

e ~ **des** *ou* **ses dents** to be teething, cut one's teeth; **il a percé 2 dents** he has cut 2 teeth, he has got 2 teeth through.

2 **vi** a *[abcès]* to burst; *[plante]* to come up; *[soleil]* to come out, break through; (*Mil*) to break through; (*Sport*) to make a break. **il a une dent qui perce** he's cutting a tooth; (*Comm*) ~ **sur un nouveau marché** to break into a new market.

b *[sentiment, émotion]* to show; *[nouvelle]* to filter through *ou* out. **rien n'a percé des négociations** no news of the negotiations has filtered through; **il ne laisse jamais ~ ses sentiments** he never lets his feelings show; **un ton où perçait l'ironie** a tone tinged with irony.

c (*réussir, acquérir la notoriété*) to make a name for o.s., become famous.

3 **comp** ▸**perce-neige** **nm inv** snowdrop ▸**perce-oreille** **nm** (**pl perce-oreilles**) earwig.

perceur [pɛʀsœʀ] **nm** driller. ~ **de muraille*** burglar; ~ **de coffre-fort*** safe-breaker.

perceuse [pɛʀsøz] **nf** drill. ~ **à percussion** hammer drill.

percevable [pɛʀsəvabl] **adj** *impôt* collectable, payable.

percevoir [pɛʀsəvwaʀ] 28 **vt** a (*ressentir*) to perceive, detect, sense, make out. b (*comprendre*) *problème* to appreciate, understand; *personne* to understand. **son action a été bien/mal perçue** his action was well/badly received *ou* was perceived as something positive/negative. c (*faire payer*) *taxe, loyer* to collect; (*recevoir*) *indemnité* to receive, be paid, get.

perche[1] [pɛʀʃ] **nf** (*poisson*) perch. ~ **de mer** sea perch.

perche[2] [pɛʀʃ] **nf** a (*gén*) pole; *[tuteur]* stick; (*Ciné, Rad, TV*) boom; *voir* **saut, tendre**[1]. b (*: *personne*) **(grande)** ~ beanpole*.

percher [pɛʀʃe] 1 1 **vi** *[oiseau]* to perch; *[volailles]* to roost; (‡) *[personne]* to live, hang out‡; (*pour la nuit*) to stay, kip* (*Brit*), crash‡; *voir* **chat.** 2 **vt** to stick. ~ **qch sur une armoire** to stick sth up on top of a cupboard; **la valise est perchée sur l'armoire** the case is perched up on top of the wardrobe; **village perché sur la montagne** village set high up *ou* perched in the mountains. 3 **se percher vpr** *[oiseau]* to perch; (*: *se jucher*) to perch.

percheron, -onne [pɛʀʃəʀɔ̃, ɔn] 1 **adj** of *ou* from the Perche. 2 **nm, f: P~(-ne)** inhabitant *ou* native of the Perche. 3 **nm** (*cheval*) Percheron.

percheur, -euse [pɛʀʃœʀ, øz] **adj: oiseau** ~ perching bird.

perchiste [pɛʀʃist] **nmf** (*Sport*) pole vaulter; (*Ciné, Rad, TV*) boom operator; *[téléski]* ski lift *ou* ski tow attendant.

perchoir [pɛʀʃwaʀ] **nm** (*lit, fig*) perch; *[volailles]* roost; (*Pol*) *seat of the president of the French National Assembly.*

perclus, e [pɛʀkly, yz] **adj** (*paralysé*) crippled, paralyzed (*de* with); (*ankylosé*) stiff; (*fig*) paralyzed.

percolateur [pɛʀkɔlatœʀ] **nm** coffee machine (*for making expresso, cappuccino etc*).

perçu, e [pɛʀsy] **ptp de percevoir;** *voir* **trop-perçu.**

percussion [pɛʀkysjɔ̃] **nf** (*Méd, Mus, Phys*) percussion. **instrument à** *ou* **de** ~ percussion instrument.

percussionniste [pɛʀkysjɔnist] **nmf** percussionist.

percutané, e [pɛʀkytane] **adj** percutaneous.

percutant, e [pɛʀkytɑ̃, ɑ̃t] **adj** a (*Mil*) percussion (*épith*); (*Phys*) percussive. b (*fig*) *remarque* which has a strong impact; *argument, discours, pensée* forceful, powerful; *publicité, livre, témoignage* striking.

percuter [pɛʀkyte] 1 1 **vt** (*Mil, Phys*) to strike; (*Méd*) to percuss. ~ **un arbre** *[voiture]* to smash into *ou* strike a tree. 2 **vi:** ~ **contre** *[avion, voiture]* to crash into; *[obus]* to strike, thud into.

percuteur [pɛʀkytœʀ] **nm** firing pin, hammer.

perdant, e [pɛʀdɑ̃, ɑ̃t] 1 **adj** *numéro, cheval* losing (*épith*). **je suis** ~ (*gén*) I lose out*; (*financièrement*) I'm out of pocket, I've lost out; **tu es loin d'être** ~ (*gén*) you're certainly not losing out; (*financièrement*) you're certainly not out of pocket *ou* not losing out. 2 **nm,f** loser. **partir** ~ to have lost before one starts.

perdition [pɛʀdisjɔ̃] **nf** a (*Rel*) perdition. **lieu de** ~ den of vice *ou* iniquity. b (*Naut*) **en** ~ in distress.

perdre [pɛʀdʀ(ə)] 41 1 **vt** a *match, guerre, procès* to lose; *métier, avantage* to lose; *habitude* to lose, get out of; (*volontairement*) to break, get out of. **il a perdu son père à la guerre** he lost his father in the war; **ce quartier est en train de** ~ **son cachet** this district is losing its distinctive charm; ~ **qn/qch de vue** to lose sight of sb/sth; ~**/ne pas** ~ **un ami de vue** to lose touch/keep in touch with a friend; **j'ai perdu le goût de rire/de manger** I've lost all interest in jokes and laughter/food, I don't feel like laughing/eating any longer; (*fig*) **n'avoir rien à** ~ to have nothing to lose; (*Tennis*) ~ **un set/son service** to drop *ou* lose a set/one's serve; **le Président perd 3 points dans le dernier sondage** the President is down 3 points in the latest poll.

b *objet* (*ne plus trouver*) to lose; (*égarer*) to mislay; (*oublier*) *nom, date* to forget. ~ **sa page** (*en lisant*) to lose one's place; ~ **son chemin** to lose one's way; **j'ai perdu le nom de cet auteur** I've forgotten *ou* I can't recall the name of this author.

c *bras, cheveux, dent* to lose. ~ **du poids** to lose weight; ~ **l'appétit/la mémoire/la vie** to lose one's appetite/one's memory/one's life; **il perd la vue** his sight is failing; **il a perdu le souffle** he's out of breath; **courir à** ~ **haleine** to run as fast as one can; ~ **la parole** to lose the power of speech; **ce tableau a perdu beaucoup de valeur** this painting has lost a lot of its value; ~ **l'équilibre** to lose one's balance; ~ **espoir/patience** to lose hope/(one's) patience; ~ **l'esprit** *ou* **la raison** to go out of one's mind, take leave of one's senses; ~ **connaissance** to lose consciousness, pass out; ~ **courage** to lose heart, be downhearted; ~ **confiance** to lose one's confidence; (*Méd*) **elle a perdu les eaux** her waters have broken; (*hum*) **as-tu perdu ta langue?** have you lost your tongue?; **la voiture perd de la vitesse** the car is losing speed.

d *feuille, pétale, pelage, corne* to lose, shed. **il perd son pantalon** his trousers are falling down; **il perd sa chemise** his shirt is sticking out (of his trousers); **ce réservoir perd beaucoup d'eau** this tank leaks badly *ou* loses a lot of water.

e (*gaspiller*) *temps, peine, souffle, argent* to waste (*à qch* on sth); (*abîmer*) *aliments* to spoil. **il a perdu une heure à la chercher** he wasted an hour looking for her; **vous n'avez pas une minute à** ~ you haven't (got) a minute to lose; **sans** ~ **une minute** without wasting a minute.

f (*manquer*) *occasion* to lose, miss. **tu ne l'as jamais vu? tu n'y perds rien!** you've never seen him? you haven't missed anything!; **il n'a pas perdu un mot/une miette de la conversation** he didn't miss a single word/syllable of the conversation; **elle a perdu l'occasion de se taire** she'd have done better to keep quiet, it was a pity she didn't keep quiet; **il ne perd rien pour attendre!** he won't get off lightly when I get hold of him!

g (*causer préjudice à*) to ruin, be the ruin of. ~ **qn dans l'esprit de qn** to send sb down in sb's esteem; **son ambition l'a perdu** ambition was his downfall *ou* the ruin of him, ambition proved his undoing; **c'est le témoignage de son cousin qui l'a perdu** it was his cousin's evidence which was his undoing; (*iro*) **ta bonté te perdra!** you're too kind! (*iro*).

h (*loc fig*) ~ **la boule*** *ou* **la boussole*** to go round the bend* (*Brit*), go crazy*, lose one's marbles*; ~ **le fil*** to lose the thread (*of an explanation*), lose one's train of thought, forget where one is up to (*Brit*); ~ **le nord*** to lose the place*; **il ne perd pas le nord*** he keeps his wits about him; **tu ne perds pas le nord toi!*** you don't miss a trick!; ~ **les pédales*** (*dans une explication*) to get all mixed up; (*s'affoler*) to lose one's head *ou* one's grip; *[vieillard]* to lose one's marbles*; **j'y perds mon latin** I can't make head nor tail of it; ~ **ses moyens** to crack up*; ~ **pied** (*en nageant, fig*) to be *ou* get out of one's depth; (*en montagne*) to lose one's footing; ~ **la tête** (*s'affoler*) to lose one's head; (*devenir fou*) to go mad *ou* crazy*; *[vieillard]* to lose one's marbles*; *voir* **face, terrain.**

2 **vi** a (*gén*) to lose. (*Comm*) ~ **sur un article** to lose on an article, sell an article at a loss; **vous y perdez** you lose on *ou* by it, you lose out on it; **tu as perdu en ne venant pas** you missed something by not coming; **tu ne perds pas au change** you get the better of the deal; **il a perdu au change** he lost out (on the deal), he came off worst.

b *[citerne, réservoir]* to leak.

3 **se perdre vpr** a (*s'égarer*) to get lost, lose one's way.

b (*fig*) **se** ~ **dans les détails/dans ses explications** to get bogged down *ou* get lost in the details/in one's explanations; **se** ~ **en conjectures** to become lost in conjecture; **se** ~ **dans ses pensées** to be lost in thought; **il y a trop de chiffres, je m'y perds** there are too many figures, I'm all confused *ou* all at sea*.

c (*disparaître*) to disappear, vanish; *[coutume]* to be dying out; (*Naut*) to sink, be wrecked. **se** ~ **dans la foule** to disappear *ou* vanish into the crowd; **son cri se perdit dans le vacarme** his shout was lost in the din *ou* was drowned by the din; **leurs silhouettes se perdirent dans la nuit** their figures vanished into the night *ou* were swallowed up by the darkness; **ce sens s'est perdu** this meaning has died out *ou* has been lost.

d (*devenir inutilisable*) to be wasted, go to waste; *[denrées]* to go bad. (*fig*) **il y a des gifles/des coups de pied qui se perdent*** he (*ou* she *etc*) deserves to be slapped *ou* a good slap/deserves a kick in the pants*.

perdreau, pl ~**x** [pɛʀdʀo] **nm** (young) partridge.

perdrix [pɛʀdʀi] **nf** partridge.

perdu, e [pɛʀdy] (**ptp de perdre**) 1 **adj** a *bataille, cause, réputation, aventurier* lost; *malade* done for (*attrib*). **je suis** ~! I'm done for!, it's all up with me!* (*Brit*); **quand il se vit** ~ when he saw he was lost *ou* done for; **tout est** ~ all is lost; **rien n'est** ~ nothing's lost, there's no harm done; *voir* **corps.**

b (*égaré*) *personne, objet* lost; *balle, chien* stray. **ce n'est pas** ~ **pour tout le monde** somebody's made good use of it, somebody's been glad to get their hands on it; **une de** ~**e, dix de retrouvées** there are lots of *ou* plenty of good fish in the sea, there are plenty more as good as her; *voir* **salle.**

c (*gaspillé*) *occasion* lost, wasted, missed; *temps* wasted. **c'était une soirée de** ~**e** it was a waste of an evening; **c'est de l'argent** ~ it's money down the drain; **il y a trop de place** ~**e** there's too much space wasted; **pendant ses moments** ~**s, à temps** ~ in his spare time; *voir* **pain, peine.**

d (*abîmé*) *aliment* spoilt, wasted. **ma récolte est** ~**e** my harvest is ruined.

e (*écarté*) *pays, endroit* out-of-the-way, isolated, miles from anywhere (*attrib*).

f (*non consigné*) *emballage, verre* non-returnable, no-deposit (*épith*).

g *personne* (*embrouillé*) lost, all at sea* (*attrib*); (*absorbé*) lost, plunged (*dans* in).

2 **nm** (††) madman. **crier/rire comme un** ~ to shout/laugh like a madman.

perdurer [pɛʀdyʀe] 1 **vi** (*littér*) *tradition* to endure.

père [pɛʀ] 1 **nm** a father. **marié et** ~ **de 3 enfants** married with 3 children *ou* and father of 3 children; **il est** ~ **depuis hier** he became a father yesterday; **Martin (le)** ~ Martin senior; **de** ~ **en fils** from father to son, from one generation to the next; **ils sont bouchers de** ~ **en fils** they've been butchers for generations; *voir* **tel.**

b (*pl: ancêtres*) ~**s** forefathers, ancestors.

c (*fondateur*) father.

d (*Zool*) *[animal]* sire.

e (*Rel*) father. **le P~ X** Father X; **mon P~** Father; *voir* **dieu.**

f (*: *monsieur*) **le** ~ **Benoit** old (man) Benoit*; **le** ~ **Hugo** old

Hugo*; **un gros ~** (*enfant*) a bonny (*Brit*) *ou* cute (*US*) child; (*homme*) a big fat guy*, a lump of a fellow*; **dis-donc, petit ~** tell me old man (*Brit*) *ou* buddy*.

g (*: *enfant*) **un brave petit ~** a fine little fellow*; **un bon gros ~** a fine chubby fellow*.

2 **comp** ►**père abbé** (*Rel*) abbot ►**les Pères de l'Église** (*Rel*) the Church Fathers ►**le Père éternel** (*Rel*) our Heavenly Father ►**père de famille** (*Jur*) father; **tu es père de famille, ne prends pas de risques** you have a wife and family to think about *ou* you're a family man, don't take risks; **en bon père de famille, il s'occupait de l'éducation de ses enfants** as a good father should, he looked after his children's upbringing; (*hum*) **maintenant, c'est le vrai père de famille** now he's the sober head of the family *ou* the serious family man ►**le père Fouettard** Mr Bogeyman ►**père François: le coup du père François*** a stab in the back ►**le père Noël** Father Christmas, Santa Claus ►**père peinard, père tranquille: sous ses allures de père tranquille** *ou* **de père peinard, c'était en fait un redoutable malfaiteur** he seemed on the surface a genial *ou* benign sort of fellow but was in fact a fearsome criminal ►**père spirituel** *[groupe]* spiritual leader; *[personne]* spiritual father; *voir* **croire, placement, valeur.**

pérégrination [peʀegʀinasjɔ̃] **nf** (*surtout pl*) peregrination.

péremption [peʀɑ̃psjɔ̃] **nf** lapsing. **date de ~** expiry date.

péremptoire [peʀɑ̃ptwaʀ] **adj** *argument, ton* peremptory.

péremptoirement [peʀɑ̃ptwaʀmɑ̃] **adv** peremptorily.

pérenniser [peʀenize] [1] **vt** to perpetuate.

pérennité [peʀenite] **nf** *[institution, goûts]* durability; *[tradition]* continuity, perpetuity; *[lignée]* continuity.

péréquation [peʀekwasjɔ̃] **nf** *[prix, impôts]* balancing out, evening out; *[notes]* coordination, adjustment; *[salaires]* adjustment, realignment.

perestroïka [peʀɛstʀɔika] **nf** perestroïka.

perfectibilité [pɛʀfɛktibilite] **nf** perfectibility.

perfectible [pɛʀfɛktibl] **adj** perfectible.

perfectif, -ive [pɛʀfɛktif, iv] **adj, nm** perfective.

perfection [pɛʀfɛksjɔ̃] **nf** perfection. **à la ~** to perfection; **c'est une ~!** it's (just) perfect!

perfectionné, e [pɛʀfɛksjɔne] (**ptp de perfectionner**) **adj** *dispositif, machine* advanced, sophisticated.

perfectionnement [pɛʀfɛksjɔnmɑ̃] **nm** perfection, perfecting (*NonC*) (*de* of); improvement (*de* in). **cours de ~** proficiency course.

perfectionner [pɛʀfɛksjɔne] [1] 1 **vt** (*améliorer*) to improve, perfect. 2 **se perfectionner vpr** *[chose]* to improve; *[personne]* to improve o.s. **se ~ en anglais** to improve one's English.

perfectionnisme [pɛʀfɛksjɔnism] **nm** perfectionism.

perfectionniste [pɛʀfɛksjɔnist] **nmf** perfectionist.

perfide [pɛʀfid] 1 **adj** (*littér*) *personne, manœuvre, promesse* perfidious, treacherous, deceitful, false; *chose* treacherous. 2 **nmf** (*littér*) traitor; (*en amour*) perfidious *ou* false-hearted person.

perfidement [pɛʀfidmɑ̃] **adv** (*littér*) perfidiously, treacherously.

perfidie [pɛʀfidi] **nf** (*caractère*) perfidy, treachery; (*acte*) act of perfidy *ou* treachery.

perforage [pɛʀfɔʀaʒ] **nm** (*voir* **perforer**) punching; perforation.

perforant, e [pɛʀfɔʀɑ̃, ɑ̃t] **adj** *instrument* perforating; *balle, obus* armour-piercing.

perforateur, -trice [pɛʀfɔʀatœʀ, tʀis] 1 **adj** perforating. 2 **nm,f** (*ouvrier*) punch-card operator. 3 **nm** (*Méd*) perforator. 4 **perforatrice nf** (*perceuse*) drilling *ou* boring machine; (*Ordin*) card punch. **~ à clavier** key punch; **~ à air comprimé** compressed-air drill.

perforation [pɛʀfɔʀasjɔ̃] **nf** (*gén, Méd*) perforation; (*Ordin*) punch.

perforer [pɛʀfɔʀe] [1] **vt** (*trouer*) to pierce; (*poinçonner*) to punch; (*Méd*) to perforate. (*Ordin*) **carte perforée** punch card; **bande/feuille perforée** punched tape/sheet.

perforeuse [pɛʀfɔʀøz] **nf** card punch.

performance [pɛʀfɔʀmɑ̃s] **nf** a (*résultat*) result, performance (*NonC*); (*exploit*) feat, achievement. **ses ~s en anglais** his results *ou* performance in English; **s'il y parvient, ce sera une ~ remarquable** if he manages it that will be an outstanding feat *ou* achievement; **réussir une bonne ~** to achieve a good result. b *[voiture, machine, économie, industrie]* performance (*NonC*). c (*Ling*) **la ~** performance.

performant, e [pɛʀfɔʀmɑ̃, ɑ̃t] **adj** *machine, voiture* high-performance (*épith*); *résultat* outstanding, impressive; *entreprise, économie* successful; *investissement* high-return (*épith*); *administrateur, procédé* effective.

performatif, -ive [pɛʀfɔʀmatif, iv] **adj, nm** performative.

perfuser [pɛʀfyze] [1] **vt** *patient* to put on a drip.

perfusion [pɛʀfyzjɔ̃] **nf** (*Méd*) drip, IV (*US*), perfusion. **mettre qn/être sous ~** to put sb/be on a drip *ou* an IV (*US*).

pergola [pɛʀgɔla] **nf** pergola.

péri [peʀi] **adj m, nm: (marin) ~ en mer** sailor lost at sea; **au profit des ~s en mer** in aid of those lost at sea.

périanthe [peʀjɑ̃t] **nm** (*Bot*) perianth.

péricarde [peʀikaʀd] **nm** pericardium.

péricarpe [peʀikaʀp] **nm** (*Bot*) pericarp.

péricliter [peʀiklite] [1] **vi** *[affaire]* to be in a state of collapse, collapse.

péridot [peʀido] **nm** peridot.

péridural, e, mpl -aux [peʀidyʀal, o] 1 **adj** epidural. 2 **péridurale nf** epidural.

périf* [peʀif] (**abrév de (boulevard) périphérique**) *voir* **périphérique.**

périgée [peʀiʒe] **nm** perigee.

périglaciaire [peʀiglasjɛʀ] **adj** periglacial.

périgourdin, e [peʀiguʀdɛ̃, in] 1 **adj** of *ou* from the Perigord. 2 **nm,f: P~(e)** inhabitant *ou* native of the Perigord.

péri-informatique [peʀiɛ̃fɔʀmatik] 1 **adj** peripheral. 2 **nf** computer peripherals.

péril [peʀil] **nm** (*littér*) peril, danger. **en ~** *monument, institution* in peril; **mettre en ~** to imperil, endanger, jeopardize; **au ~ de sa vie** at the risk of one's life; (*fig*) **il n'y a pas ~ en la demeure** there's no great need to hurry; **il y a ~ à faire** it is perilous to do; **le ~ rouge/jaune** the red/yellow peril; *voir* **risque.**

périlleusement [peʀijøzmɑ̃] **adv** (*littér*) perilously.

périlleux, -euse [peʀijø, øz] **adj** perilous; *voir* **saut.**

périmé, e [peʀime] (**ptp de périmer**) **adj** *billet, bon* out-of-date (*épith*), expired, no longer valid (*attrib*); *idée* dated, outdated. **ce billet/bon est ~** this ticket/voucher is out of date *ou* has expired.

périmer [peʀime] [1] 1 **vi: laisser ~ un passeport/un billet** to let a passport/ticket expire. 2 **se périmer vpr** (*Jur*) to lapse; *[passeport, billet]* to expire; *[idée]* to date, become outdated.

périmètre [peʀimɛtʀ] **nm** (*Math*) perimeter; (*zone*) area. **dans un ~ de 3 km** within a 3 km radius.

périnatal, e, mpl ~s [peʀinatal] **adj** perinatal.

périnéal, e, mpl -aux [peʀineal, o] **adj** perineal.

périnée [peʀine] **nm** perineum.

période [peʀjɔd] **nf** (*gén*) period; (*Math*) *[fraction]* repetend. **pendant la ~ des vacances** during the holiday period; **une ~ de chaleur** a hot spell, a heat wave; **pendant la ~ électorale** at election time; (*Mil*) **~ (d'instruction)** training (*NonC*); **~ d'essai** trial period; (*Phys*) **~ radioactive** half-life; **elle a traversé une ~ difficile** she has been through a difficult period *ou* patch; **~ ensoleillée/de chaleur** sunny/warm spell *ou* period; **c'est la bonne ~ pour les champignons** it's the right time for mushrooms; **j'ai eu une ~ concert/théâtre*** I went through a period *ou* phase of going to concerts/the theatre a lot; **par ~s** from time to time.

périodicité [peʀjɔdisite] **nf** periodicity.

périodique [peʀjɔdik] 1 **adj** (*gén, Chim, Phys*) periodic; (*Presse*) periodical; (*Méd*) *fièvre* recurring. (*Math*) **fraction ~** recurring decimal; (*Math*) **fonction ~** periodic function; *voir* **garniture.** 2 **nm** (*Presse*) periodical.

périodiquement [peʀjɔdikmɑ̃] **adv** periodically.

périoste [peʀjɔst] **nm** periosteum.

péripatéticien, -ienne [peʀipatetisjɛ̃, jɛn] 1 **adj, nm,f** (*Philos*) peripatetic. 2 **péripatéticienne nf** (*hum: prostituée*) streetwalker.

péripétie [peʀipesi] **nf** a (*épisode*) event, episode. **les ~s d'une révolution/d'une exploration** the turns taken by a revolution/an exploration; **après bien des ~s** after all sorts of incidents; **voyage plein de ~s** eventful journey. b (*Littérat*) peripeteia.

périph* [peʀif] = **périf.**

périphérie [peʀifeʀi] **nf** (*limite*) periphery; (*banlieue*) outskirts.

périphérique [peʀifeʀik] 1 **adj** (*Anat, Math*) peripheral; *quartier* outlying (*épith*); *activités* associated. **poste** *ou* **radio** *ou* **station ~** private radio station (*broadcasting from a neighbouring country*). 2 **nm** a (*Ordin*) peripheral. b **(boulevard) ~** ring road (*Brit*), circular route (*US*); **(boulevard) ~ intérieur/extérieur** inner/outer ring road (*Brit*) *ou* circular route (*US*); (*Ordin*) **~ entrée-sortie** input-output device.

périphrase [peʀifʀɑz] **nf** circumlocution, periphrasis (SPÉC), periphrase (SPÉC).

périphrastique [peʀifʀastik] **adj** circumlocutory, periphrastic.

périple [peʀipl] **nm** (*par mer*) voyage; (*par terre*) tour, trip, journey. **au cours de son ~ américain** during his tour of the U.S.A.

périr [peʀiʀ] [2] **vi** (*littér*) to perish (*littér*), die; *[navire]* to go down, sink; *[empire]* to perish, fall. **~ noyé** to drown, be drowned; **faire ~** *personne, plante* to kill; **son souvenir ne périra jamais** his memory will never die *ou* perish (*littér*); (*fig*) **~ d'ennui** to die of boredom.

périscolaire [peʀiskɔlɛʀ] **adj** extracurricular.

périscope [peʀiskɔp] **nm** periscope.

périscopique [peʀiskɔpik] **adj** periscopic.

périssable [peʀisabl] **adj** perishable. **denrées ~s** perishable goods, perishables.

périssoire [peʀiswaʀ] **nf** canoe.

péristaltisme [peʀistaltism] **nm** peristalsis.

péristyle [peʀistil] **nm** peristyle.

péritel [peʀitɛl] **adj f, nf** ® **(prise) ~** SCART (socket).

péritoine [peʀitwan] **nm** peritoneum.

péritonite [peʀitɔnit] **nf** peritonitis.

perle [pɛʀl] 1 **nf** a (*bijou*) pearl; (*boule*) bead. **des dents de ~** pearly teeth; **jeter** *ou* **donner des ~s aux pourceaux** to cast pearls before swine; *voir* **enfiler.** b (*littér: goutte*) *[eau, sang]* drop(let); *[sueur]* bead. c (*fig: personne, chose de valeur*) gem. **la cuisinière est une ~** the cook is an absolute gem *ou* a perfect treasure; **c'est la ~ des maris** he's the best of husbands, you couldn't hope for a better husband; **vous êtes une ~** you're a (real) gem; **la ~ d'une collection** the gem of a collection. d (*erreur*) gem, howler. 2 **comp ▸perle de culture** cultured pearl **▸perle fine, perle naturelle** natural pearl **▸perle de rosée** dewdrop.

perlé, e [pɛʀle] (**ptp de perler**) **adj** *orge* pearl (*épith*); *riz* polished; *coton, laine* pearlized; *tissu* beaded; *travail* perfect, exquisite; *rire* rippling; *voir* **grève**.

perler [pɛʀle] [1] 1 **vi** *[sueur]* to form. **la sueur perlait sur son front** beads of sweat stood out *ou* formed on his forehead. 2 **vt** †: *travail* to take great pains over.

perlier, -ière [pɛʀlje, jɛʀ] **adj** pearl (*épith*).

perlimpinpin [pɛʀlɛ̃pɛ̃pɛ̃] **nm** *voir* **poudre**.

perlouse‡, perlouze‡ [pɛʀluz] **nf** (*grande perle*) flashy‡ pearl, dazzler*; (*pet*) smelly fart‡.

perm* [pɛʀm] **nf** a **abrév de permanence c.** b **abrév de permission.**

permanence [pɛʀmanɑ̃s] **nf** a (*durée*) permanence, permanency. **en ~** *siéger* permanently; *crier* continuously; **dans ce pays ce sont des émeutes/c'est la guerre en ~** in that country there are constant *ou* continuous riots/there is a permanent state of war. b (*service*) **être de ~** to be on duty *ou* on call; **une ~ est assurée le dimanche** there is someone on duty on Sundays, the office is manned on Sundays. c (*bureau*) (duty) office; (*Pol*) committee room; (*Scol*) study room *ou* hall (*US*). (*Scol*) **heure de ~** private study period.

permanent, e [pɛʀmanɑ̃, ɑ̃t] 1 **adj** (*gén*) permanent; *armée, comité* standing (*épith*); *spectacle* continuous; (*Presse*) *envoyé, correspondant* permanent; (*Phys*) *aimantation, gaz* permanent. (*Ciné*) **~ de 2 heures à minuit** continuous showings from 2 o'clock to midnight; **cinéma ~** cinema showing a continuous programme. 2 **nm** (*Pol*) (paid) official (*of union, political party*). **un ~ du parti** a party worker. 3 **permanente nf** (*Coiffure*) perm, permanent wave.

permanenter [pɛʀmanɑ̃te] [1] **vt** to perm. **se faire ~** to have a perm; **cheveux permanentés** permed hair.

permanganate [pɛʀmɑ̃ganat] **nm** permanganate.

perme [pɛʀm] **nf** (*arg Mil*) leave.

perméabilité [pɛʀmeabilite] **nf** (*lit*) (*Phys*) permeability; (*à l'eau*) perviousness, permeability; (*fig*) *[personne]* receptiveness, openness; *[frontière etc]* openness.

perméable [pɛʀmeabl] **adj** (*voir* **perméabilité**) permeable; pervious; receptive, open (*à* to). **trop ~ à leur influence** too easily influenced by them.

permettre [pɛʀmɛtʀ] [56] 1 **vt** a (*tolérer*) to allow, permit. **~ à qn de faire, ~ que qn fasse** to allow *ou* permit sb to do, let sb do; **la loi le permet** it is allowed *ou* permitted by law, the law allows *ou* permits it; **le docteur me permet l'alcool** the doctor allows *ou* permits me to drink *ou* lets me drink; **il se croit tout permis** he thinks he can do what he likes *ou* as he pleases; **est-il permis d'être aussi bête!** how can anyone be so stupid!; **il est permis à tout le monde de se tromper!** anyone can make a mistake!; **le professeur lui a permis de ne pas aller à l'école aujourd'hui** the teacher has given him permission to stay off school *ou* not to go to school today.

b (*rendre possible*) to allow, permit. **ce diplôme va lui ~ de trouver du travail** this qualification will allow *ou* enable *ou* permit him to find a job; **mes moyens ne me le permettent pas** I cannot afford it; **mes occupations ne me le permettent pas** I'm too busy to be able to do it; **sa santé ne le lui permet pas** his health doesn't allow *ou* permit him to do it; **son attitude permet tous les soupçons** his attitude gives cause for suspicion *ou* reinforces one's suspicions; **si le temps le permet** weather permitting; **autant qu'il est permis d'en juger** as far as one can tell.

c (*donner le droit*) to entitle. **cette carte lui permet d'obtenir des réductions** this card entitles *ou* enables him to get reductions; **être majeur permet de voter** being over 18 entitles one *ou* makes one eligible to vote; **qu'est-ce qui te permet de me juger?** what gives you the right to pass judgement on me?

d (*idée de sollicitation*) **vous permettez?** may I?; **permettez-moi de vous présenter ma sœur/de vous interrompre** may I introduce my sister/interrupt (you)?; **s'il m'est permis de faire une objection** if I may *ou* might (be allowed to) raise an objection; **vous permettez que je fume?** do you mind if I smoke?; **vous permettez que je passe!*** if you don't mind I'd like to come past!, do you mind if I come past!; **permettez! je ne suis pas d'accord** if you don't mind! *ou* pardon me! I disagree; **permets-moi de te le dire** let me tell you.

2 **se permettre vpr** a (*s'offrir*) *fantaisie, excès* to allow o.s., indulge o.s. in. **je ne peux pas me ~ d'acheter ce manteau** I can't afford to buy this coat.

b (*risquer*) *grossièreté, plaisanterie* to allow o.s. to make, dare to make. **ce sont des plaisanteries qu'on ne peut se ~ qu'entre amis** these jokes are only acceptable among friends; **je me suis permis de sourire** *ou* **un sourire** I had *ou* gave *ou* ventured a smile, I ventured to *ou* allowed myself to smile; **il s'est permis de partir sans permission** he took the liberty of going without permission; **il se permet bien des choses** he takes a lot of liberties; **je me permettrai de vous faire remarquer que ...** I'd like to point out (to you) that ...; **puis-je me ~ de vous offrir un whisky?** will you have a whisky?; (*formule épistolaire*) **je me permets de vous écrire au sujet de ...** I am writing to you in connection with ... .

permien, -ienne [pɛʀmjɛ̃, jɛn] 1 **adj** permian. 2 **nm: le ~** the Permian era.

permis, e [pɛʀmi, iz] (**ptp de permettre**) 1 **adj** *limites* permitted. (*frm*) **il est ~ de s'interroger sur la nécessité de ...** one might *ou* may well question the necessity of ... . 2 **nm** permit, licence. **~ de chasse** hunting permit; **~ (de conduire)** (*carte*) driving licence (*Brit*), driver's license (*US*); (*épreuve*) driving test; **~ de construire** planning permission; **~ d'inhumer** burial certificate; **~ moto** motorbike licence; **~ de pêche** fishing permit; **~ poids lourd** heavy-goods vehicle licence; **~ de séjour** residence permit; **~ de travail** work permit.

permissif, -ive [pɛʀmisif, iv] **adj** permissive.

permission [pɛʀmisjɔ̃] **nf** a permission. **avec votre ~** with your permission; **accorder à qn la ~ de faire** to give sb permission to do; **demander la ~** to ask permission (*de* to); **demander à qn la ~** to ask sb his permission (*de* to); **est-ce qu'il t'a donné la ~ (de le faire)?** did he give you permission (to do it)? b (*Mil*) (*congé*) leave; (*certificat*) pass. **en ~** on leave; **~ de minuit** late pass.

permissionnaire [pɛʀmisjɔnɛʀ] **nm** soldier on leave.

permissivité [pɛʀmisivite] **nf** permissiveness.

permutabilité [pɛʀmytabilite] **nf** permutability.

permutable [pɛʀmytabl] **adj** which can be changed *ou* swapped *ou* switched round; (*Math*) permutable.

permutation [pɛʀmytasjɔ̃] **nf** permutation.

permuter [pɛʀmyte] [1] 1 **vt** (*gén*) to change *ou* swap *ou* switch round, permutate; (*Math*) to permutate, permute. 2 **vi** to change, swap, switch (seats *ou* positions *ou* jobs *etc*).

pernicieusement [pɛʀnisjøzmɑ̃] **adv** (*littér*) perniciously.

pernicieux, -ieuse [pɛʀnisjø, jøz] **adj** (*gén, Méd*) pernicious. **~ pour** injurious *ou* harmful to.

péroné [peʀɔne] **nm** fibula.

péroniste [peʀɔnist] 1 **adj** Peronist. 2 **nmf: P~** Peronist.

péronnelle [peʀɔnɛl] **nf** (*péj*) silly goose* (*péj*).

péroraison [peʀɔʀɛzɔ̃] **nf** (*Littérat: conclusion*) peroration, summing up; (*péj: discours*) windy discourse (*péj*).

pérorer [peʀɔʀe] [1] **vi** to hold forth (*péj*), declaim (*péj*).

Pérou [peʀu] **nm** Peru. (*fig*) **ce qu'il gagne, ce n'est pas le ~** it's no great fortune what he earns; (*iro*) **on a 300 F? c'est le ~!** we've got 300 francs? we're loaded* *ou* we're rolling in it*! (*iro*).

Pérouse [peʀuz] **n** Perugia.

peroxyde [pɛʀɔksid] **nm** peroxide. **~ d'hydrogène** hydrogen peroxide.

perpendiculaire [pɛʀpɑ̃dikylɛʀ] **adj, nf** perpendicular (*à* to).

perpendiculairement [pɛʀpɑ̃dikylɛʀmɑ̃] **adv** perpendicularly. **~ à** at right angles to, perpendicular to.

perpète [pɛʀpɛt] **nf** (*arg Prison: perpétuité*) **il a eu la ~** he got life (*arg*); (*loin*) **à ~*** miles away*; (*longtemps*) **jusqu'à ~*** till doomsday*, till the cows come home*.

perpétration [pɛʀpetʀasjɔ̃] **nf** perpetration.

perpétrer [pɛʀpetʀe] [6] **vt** to perpetrate.

perpette [pɛʀpɛt] **nf** = **perpète.**

perpétuation [pɛʀpetɥasjɔ̃] **nf** (*littér*) perpetuation.

perpétuel, -uelle [pɛʀpetɥɛl] **adj** (*pour toujours*) perpetual, everlasting; (*incessant*) perpetual, never-ending; *fonction, secrétaire* permanent; *rente* life (*épith*), for life (*attrib*); *voir* **calendrier, mouvement.**

perpétuellement [pɛʀpetɥɛlmɑ̃] **adv** perpetually.

perpétuer [pɛʀpetɥe] [1] 1 **vt** (*immortaliser*) to perpetuate; (*maintenir*) to perpetuate, carry on. 2 **se perpétuer vpr** *[usage, abus]* to be perpetuated, be carried on; *[espèce]* to survive. **se ~ dans son œuvre/dans ses enfants** to live on in one's work/children.

perpétuité [pɛʀpetɥite] **nf** perpetuity, perpetuation. **à ~** *condamnation* for life; *concession* in perpetuity.

perplexe [pɛʀplɛks] **adj** perplexed, confused, puzzled. **rendre** *ou* **laisser ~** to perplex, confuse, puzzle.

perplexité [pɛʀplɛksite] **nf** perplexity, confusion. **je suis dans une grande ~** I just don't know what to think, I'm greatly perplexed *ou* highly confused; **être dans la plus complète ~** to be completely baffled *ou* utterly perplexed *ou* confused, be at an absolute loss (to know what to think).

perquisition [pɛʀkizisjɔ̃] **nf** (*Police*) search. **ils ont fait une ~** they've carried out *ou* made a search, they've searched the premises; *voir* **mandat.**

perquisitionner [pɛʀkizisjɔne] [1] 1 **vi** to carry out a search, make a search. **~ au domicile de qn** to search sb's house, carry out *ou* make a search of sb's house. 2 **vt** (*) to search.

perron [peʀɔ̃] **nm** steps (*leading to entrance*), perron (SPÉC).

perroquet [peʀɔkɛ] **nm** a (*Orn, fig*) parrot. **~ de mer** puffin; **répéter qch comme un ~** to repeat sth parrot fashion. b (*Naut*) topgallant (sail). c (*boisson*) *apéritif made of pastis and mint syrup.*

perruche [peʀyʃ] **nf** a (*Orn*) budgerigar, budgie*; (*femelle du perroquet*) female parrot; (*fig: femme bavarde*) chatterbox*, gas bag‡ (*péj*), windbag‡ (*péj*). b (*Naut*) mizzen topgallant (sail).

perruque [peʀyk] **nf** (*coiffure*) wig; (*Hist*) wig, periwig, peruke; (*Pêche*: enchevêtrement*) bird's nest.

perruquier, -ière [peʀykje, jɛʀ] nm,f wigmaker.

pers [pɛʀ] adj *yeux* greenish-blue, blue-green.

persan, e [pɛʀsɑ̃, an] 1 adj Persian. **(chat)** ~ Persian (cat); *voir* **tapis**. 2 nm (*Ling*) Persian. 3 nm,f: **P~(e)** Persian.

perse [pɛʀs] 1 adj Persian. 2 nm (*Ling*) Persian. 3 nmf: **P~** Persian. 4 nf (*Géog*) **P~** Persia.

persécuter [pɛʀsekyte] 1 vt (*opprimer*) to persecute; (*harceler*) to harass, plague.

persécuteur, -trice [pɛʀsekytœʀ, tʀis] 1 adj persecuting. 2 nm,f persecutor.

persécution [pɛʀsekysjɔ̃] nf persecution. **délire** *ou* **folie de ~** persecution mania.

Persée [pɛʀse] nm Perseus.

Perséphone [pɛʀsefɔn] nf Persephone.

persévérance [pɛʀseveʀɑ̃s] nf perseverance.

persévérant, e [pɛʀseveʀɑ̃, ɑ̃t] adj persevering. **être ~** to persevere, be persevering.

persévérer [pɛʀseveʀe] 6 vi to persevere. **~ dans** *effort, entreprise, recherches* to persevere with *ou* in, persist in; *erreur, voie* to persevere in; **je persévère à le croire coupable** I continue to believe he's guilty.

persienne [pɛʀsjɛn] nf (louvred) shutter.

persiflage [pɛʀsiflaʒ] nm mockery (*NonC*).

persifler [pɛʀsifle] 1 vt to mock, make mock of (*littér*), make fun of.

persifleur, -euse [pɛʀsiflœʀ, øz] 1 adj mocking. 2 nm,f mocker.

persil [pɛʀsi] nm parsley. **~ plat/frisé** flat-leaved/curly parsley.

persillade [pɛʀsijad] nf (*sauce*) parsley vinaigrette; (*viande*) *cold beef served with parsley vinaigrette*.

persillé, e [pɛʀsije] adj *plat* sprinkled with chopped parsley; *viande* marbled; *fromage* veined.

persique [pɛʀsik] adj Persian; *voir* **golfe**.

persistance [pɛʀsistɑ̃s] nf *[pluie, fièvre, douleur, odeur]* persistence; *[personne]* persistence, persistency (*à faire* in doing). **sa ~ dans l'erreur** his persistently mistaken attitude; **cette ~ dans le mensonge** this persistence in lying, this persistent lying; **avec ~** (*tout le temps*) persistently; (*avec obstination*) persistently, doggedly, stubbornly.

persistant, e [pɛʀsistɑ̃, ɑ̃t] adj (*gén*) persistent; *feuilles* evergreen, persistent (*SPÉC*). **arbre à feuillage ~** evergreen (tree).

persister [pɛʀsiste] 1 vi *[pluie]* to persist, keep up; *[fièvre, douleur, odeur]* to persist, linger; *[symptôme, personne]* to persist. **la pluie/la douleur n'a pas persisté** the rain/the pain didn't last *ou* persist; **~ dans qch/à faire** to persist in sth/in doing; **il persiste dans son refus** he won't go back on *ou* he persists in his refusal; **~ dans son opinion/ses projets** to stick to one's opinion/one's plans; **il persiste dans son silence** he persists in keeping quiet; **il persiste à faire cela** he persists in doing *ou* keeps (on) doing that, he does that persistently; **je persiste à croire que ...** I still believe that ...; (*fig*) **c'est non, je persiste et signe!** the answer is no, and that's final!; **il persistait une odeur de moisi** a musty smell persisted; **il persiste un doute** a doubt remains.

perso* [pɛʀso] adj (**abrév de personnel 1**) (*privé*) personnal; (*égoïste*) selfish.

persona [pɛʀsɔna] nf: **~ grata/non grata** persona grata/non grata.

personnage [pɛʀsɔnaʒ] nm a (*individu*) character, individual.

b (*célébrité*) (very) important person, personage (*frm, hum*). **~ influent/haut placé** influential/highly placed person; **~ connu** celebrity, well-known person *ou* personage (*frm, hum*); **~ officiel** V.I.P.; **un grand ~** a great figure; **grands ~s de l'État** State dignitaries; **~s de l'Antiquité/historiques** great names of Antiquity/of history; **il est devenu un ~** he's become a very important person *ou* a big name*; **il se prend pour un grand ~** he really thinks he is someone important, he really thinks he's somebody*.

c (*Littérat*) character. **liste des ~s** dramatis personae, list of characters; **~ principal** principal character; (*lit, fig*) **jouer un ~** to play a part, act a part *ou* role; *voir* **peau**.

d (*Art*) *[tableau]* figure.

personnalisation [pɛʀsɔnalizasjɔ̃] nf personalization.

personnaliser [pɛʀsɔnalize] 1 vt (*gén*) to personalize; *voiture, appartement* to give a personal touch to, personalize. **service personnalisé** personalized service.

personnalité [pɛʀsɔnalite] nf (*gén*) personality. **avoir une forte ~/de la ~** to have a strong personality/lots of personality; **un être sans ~** somebody who is lacking in personality; **il y aura de nombreuses ~s pour l'inauguration** there will be a number of key figures *ou* personalities at the opening.

personne [pɛʀsɔn] 1 nf a (*être humain*) person. **deux ~s** two people; **le respect de la ~ humaine** respect for human dignity; (*Jur*) **les droits de la ~** the rights of the individual; **les ~s qui ...** those who ..., the people who ...; **c'est une ~ sympathique** he *ou* she is a very pleasant person; **une ~ de connaissance m'a dit** someone *ou* a person I know told me; **il n'y a pas ~ plus discrète que lui** there is no one more discreet than he; **c'est une drôle de petite/une jolie ~**† she's a funny little/a pretty little thing; **3 gâteaux par ~** 3 cakes per person, 3 cakes each; **100 F par ~** 100 francs each *ou* per head *ou* a head *ou* per person; **par ~ interposée** through an intermediary, through a third party *ou* person; *voir* **grand, tierce**[2].

b (*personnalité*) **toute sa ~ inspire confiance** his whole being inspires confidence; **j'admire son œuvre mais je le méprise en tant que ~** I admire his works but I have no opinion of him *ou* I have no time for him as a person; **la ~ et l'œuvre de Balzac** Balzac, the man and his work.

c (*corps*) **être bien (fait) de sa ~** to be good-looking; **exposer** *ou* **risquer sa ~** to risk one's life *ou* one's neck; **sur ma ~** on my person; **il semble toujours très content de sa petite ~** he always seems very pleased with his little self *ou* with himself; **il prend soin de sa petite ~** he looks after himself; **je l'ai vu en ~** I saw him in person; **je m'en occupe en ~** I'll see to it personally; **c'est la paresse/la bonté en ~** he's *ou* she's laziness/kindness itself *ou* personified; *voir* **payer**.

d (*Gram*) person. **à la première/troisième ~** in the first/third person.

2 pron a (*quelqu'un*) anyone, anybody. **elle le sait mieux que ~ (au monde)** she knows that better than anyone *ou* anybody (else); **il est entré sans que ~ le voie** he came in without anyone *ou* anybody seeing him; **~ de blessé?** is anyone *ou* anybody injured?, no one hurt?; **elle sait faire le café comme ~** she makes better coffee than anyone (else).

b (*avec ne: aucun*) no one, nobody. **presque ~** hardly anyone *ou* anybody, practically no one *ou* nobody; **~ (d'autre) ne l'a vu** no one *ou* nobody (else) saw him; **il n'a vu ~ (d'autre)** he didn't see anyone *ou* anybody (else), he saw no one *ou* nobody (else); **~ d'autre que lui** no one *ou* nobody but he; **il n'y a ~** there's no one *ou* nobody in, there isn't anyone *ou* anybody in; **il n'y a eu ~ de blessé** no one *ou* nobody was injured, there wasn't anyone *ou* anybody injured; **à qui as-tu demandé? — à ~** who did you ask? — no one *ou* nobody *ou* I didn't ask anyone *ou* anybody; **ce n'est la faute de ~** it's no one's *ou* nobody's fault; **il n'y avait ~ d'intéressant à qui parler** there was no one *ou* nobody interesting to talk to; **il n'y est pour ~** he doesn't want to see anyone *ou* anybody; (*iro*) **pour le travail, il n'y a plus ~*** as soon as there's a bit of work to be done, everyone disappears *ou* clears off* *ou* there's suddenly no one *ou* nobody around; **n'y a-t-il ~ qui sache où il est?** doesn't anyone *ou* anybody know where he is?

3 comp ►**personne âgée** elderly person; **mesure en faveur des personnes âgées** measure benefiting the elderly ►**personne à charge** dependent ►**personne civile** (*Jur*) legal entity ►**personnes déplacées** (*Pol*) displaced persons ►**personne morale** (*Jur*) = **personne civile** ►**personne physique** (*Jur*) individual.

personnel, -elle [pɛʀsɔnɛl] 1 adj a (*particulier, privé*) personal. **fortune ~elle** personal *ou* private fortune; **strictement ~** *lettre* highly confidential, private and personal; *billet* not transferable (*attrib*); **il a des idées/des opinions très ~elles sur la question** he has (clear) ideas/opinions of his own *ou* he has his own ideas/opinions on the subject; **critiques ~elles** personal criticism.

b (*égoïste*) selfish, self-centred; (*Sport*) *joueur* selfish.

c (*Gram*) *pronom, nom, verbe* personal; *mode* finite.

2 nm *[école]* staff; *[château, hôtel]* staff, employees; *[usine]* workforce, employees, personnel; *[service public]* personnel, employees. **manquer de ~** to be shortstaffed *ou* understaffed; **il y a trop de ~ dans ce service** this department is overstaffed; **faire partie du ~** to be on the staff; **l'usine a 60 membres de ~** *ou* **un ~ de 60** the factory has 60 people on the payroll, the factory has a workforce *ou* payroll of 60; (*Aviat, Mil*) **~ à terre/navigant** ground/flight personnel *ou* staff; **~ en civil/en tenue** plain-clothes/uniformed staff; **bureau/chef du ~** personnel office/officer.

personnellement [pɛʀsɔnɛlmɑ̃] adv personally. **je lui dirai ~** I'll tell him myself *ou* personally; **~ je veux bien** personally I don't mind, I for one don't mind.

personnification [pɛʀsɔnifikasjɔ̃] nf personification. **c'est la ~ de la cruauté** he's the personification *ou* the embodiment of cruelty.

personnifier [pɛʀsɔnifje] 7 vt to personify. **cet homme personnifie le mal** this man is the embodiment of evil *ou* is evil itself *ou* is evil personified; **être la bêtise personnifiée** to be stupidity itself *ou* personified; **il personnifie son époque** he personifies *ou* typifies his age, he's the embodiment of his age.

perspectif, -ive [pɛʀspɛktif, iv] 1 adj perspective. 2 **perspective** nf a (*Art*) perspective. b (*point de vue*) (*lit*) view; (*fig*) angle, viewpoint. **dans une ~ive historique** from a historical angle *ou* viewpoint, in a historical perspective; **examiner une question sous des ~ives différentes** to examine a question from different angles *ou* viewpoints. c (*événement en puissance*) prospect; (*idée*) prospect, thought. **en ~ive** in prospect; **des ~ives d'avenir** future prospects; **quelle ~ive!** what a thought! *ou* prospect!; **à la ~ive de** at the prospect *ou* thought *ou* idea of.

perspicace [pɛʀspikas] adj clear-sighted, penetrating, perspicacious.

perspicacité [pɛʀspikasite] nf clear-sightedness, insight, perspicacity.

persuader [pɛʀsɥade] 1 1 vt (*convaincre*) to persuade, convince (*qn de qch* sb of sth). **~ qn (de faire qch)** to persuade sb (to do sth); **il les a persuadés que tout irait bien** he persuaded *ou* convinced them that all would be well; **on l'a persuadé de partir** he was persuaded to leave; **j'en suis persuadé** I'm quite sure *ou* convinced (of it); **il sait ~** he's very persuasive, he knows how to convince people.

2 vi (*littér*) **~ à qn (de faire)** to persuade sb (to do); **on lui a persuadé de rester** he was persuaded to stay.

3 **se persuader** vpr to be persuaded, be convinced. **il s'est persuadé qu'on le déteste** he is persuaded *ou* convinced that everyone hates him, he has convinced *ou* persuaded himself that everyone hates him; **elle s'est persuadée de l'inutilité de ses efforts** she has persuaded *ou* convinced herself of the uselessness of her efforts.

persuasif, -ive [pɛʀsɥazif, iv] adj *ton, éloquence* persuasive; *argument, orateur* persuasive, convincing.

persuasion [pɛʀsɥazjɔ̃] nf (*action, art*) persuasion; (*croyance*) conviction, belief.

perte [pɛʀt] 1 nf a (*gén*) loss, losing (*NonC*); (*Comm*) loss. **vendre à ~** to sell at a loss; **la ~ d'une bataille/d'un procès** the loss of a battle/court case, losing a battle/court case; **essuyer une ~ importante** to suffer heavy losses; (*Mil*) **de lourdes ~s (en hommes)** heavy losses (in men); **ce n'est pas une grosse ~** it's not a serious loss; **la ~ cruelle d'un être cher** the cruel *ou* grievous loss of a loved one; *voir* **profit**.
b (*ruine*) ruin. **il a juré sa ~** he has sworn to ruin him; **il court à sa ~** he is on the road to ruin.
c (*déperdition*) loss; (*gaspillage*) waste. **~ de chaleur/d'énergie** loss of heat/energy, heat/energy loss; **~ de lumière** loss of light; **c'est une ~ de temps** it's a waste of time; **il devrait s'économiser: c'est une ~ d'énergie** he ought to save his efforts: he's wasting energy *ou* it's a waste of energy.
d (*loc*) **à ~ de vue** (*lit*) as far as the eye can see; (*fig*) interminably; **mis à la porte avec ~ et fracas** thrown out.
2 comp ▸**pertes blanches** (*Méd*) vaginal discharge, leucorrhœa (*SPÉC*) ▸**perte de charge** pressure drop, drop in *ou* loss of pressure ▸**perte de connaissance** loss of consciousness, fainting (*NonC*) ▸**perte de mémoire** loss of memory, memory loss ▸**pertes de sang** (*Méd*) heavy bleeding ▸**perte sèche** (*Fin*) dead loss (*Fin*), absolute loss ▸**perte à la terre** (*Élec*) earth (*Brit*) *ou* ground (*US*) leakage ▸**être en perte de vitesse** (*Aviat*) to lose lift; (*fig*) *[mouvement]* to be losing momentum; *[entreprise, vedette]* to be going downhill.

pertinemment [pɛʀtinamɑ̃] adv *parler* pertinently, to the point. **il a répondu ~** his reply was to the point; **savoir ~ que** to know full well that, know for a fact that.

pertinence [pɛʀtinɑ̃s] nf (*voir* **pertinent**) aptness, pertinence, appositeness; judiciousness; relevance; significance, distinctive nature.

pertinent, e [pɛʀtinɑ̃, ɑ̃t] adj *remarque* apt, pertinent, apposite; *analyse, jugement, esprit* judicious, discerning; *idée* relevant, apt, pertinent; (*Ling*) significant, distinctive.

pertuis [pɛʀtɥi] nm (*détroit*) strait(s), channel; *[fleuve]* narrows.

pertuisane [pɛʀtɥizan] nf partisan (*weapon*).

perturbateur, -trice [pɛʀtyʀbatœʀ, tʀis] 1 adj disruptive. 2 nm,f (*gén*) troublemaker, rowdy; (*dans un débat*) heckler.

perturbation [pɛʀtyʀbasjɔ̃] nf a (*voir* **perturber**) disruption, disturbance; perturbation. **jeter la ~ dans** to disrupt; to disturb; **facteur de ~** disruptive factor; **~s dans l'acheminement du courrier** disruption(s) of the mail. b (*Mét*) **~ (atmosphérique)** (atmospheric) disturbance.

perturber [pɛʀtyʀbe] 1 vt *services publics, travaux* to disrupt; *cérémonie, réunion* to disrupt, disturb; (*Rad, TV*) *transmission* to disrupt; *personne* to perturb, disturb; (*Astron*) to perturb; (*Mét*) to disturb. **elle est très perturbée en ce moment** she's very perturbed at the moment.

péruvien, -ienne [peʀyvjɛ̃, jɛn] 1 adj Peruvian. 2 nm (*Ling*) Peruvian. 3 nm,f: **P~(-ienne)** Peruvian.

pervenche [pɛʀvɑ̃ʃ] 1 nf (*Bot*) periwinkle; (**: contractuelle*) female traffic warden (*Brit*), meter maid (*US*). 2 adj inv periwinkle blue.

pervers, e [pɛʀvɛʀ, ɛʀs] 1 adj (*littér: diabolique*) perverse; (*vicieux*) perverted, depraved. 2 nm,f pervert. (*hum*) **~ sexuel** sexual pervert.

perversion [pɛʀvɛʀsjɔ̃] nf perversion, corruption; (*Méd, Psych*) perversion.

perversité [pɛʀvɛʀsite] nf perversity, depravity.

pervertir [pɛʀvɛʀtiʀ] 2 1 vt (*dépraver*) to corrupt, pervert, deprave; (*altérer*) to pervert. 2 **se pervertir** vpr to become corrupt(ed) *ou* perverted *ou* depraved.

pesage [pəzaʒ] nm weighing; *[jockey]* weigh-in; (*salle*) weighing room; (*enceinte*) enclosure.

pesamment [pəzamɑ̃] adv *chargé, tomber* heavily; *marcher* with a heavy step *ou* tread, heavily.

pesant, e [pəzɑ̃, ɑ̃t] 1 adj *paquet* heavy, weighty; (*lit, fig*) *fardeau, joug, charge* heavy; *sommeil* deep; *démarche, pas* heavy; *esprit* slow, sluggish; *architecture* massive; *style, ton* heavy, weighty, ponderous; *présence* burdensome; *silence* heavy. 2 nm: **valoir son ~ d'or** to be worth its (*ou* one's) weight in gold.

pesanteur [pəzɑ̃tœʀ] nf a (*Phys*) gravity. b (*lourdeur: voir* **pesant**) heaviness; weightiness; depth; slowness, sluggishness; massiveness; ponderousness; burdensomeness. **avoir des ~s d'estomac** to have problems with one's digestion.

pèse- [pɛz] préf *voir* **peser**.

pesée [pəze] nf (*action*) *[objet]* weighing; (*Sport*) weight; (*fig*) *[motifs, termes]* weighing up; (*pression, poussée*) push, thrust. **effectuer une ~** to carry out a weighing operation; (*sportif*) **aller à la ~** to weigh in.

peser [pəze] 5 1 vt a *objet, personne* to weigh. **~ qch dans sa main** to feel the weight of sth (in one's hand); **se ~** to weigh o.s.; (*sportif*) **se faire ~** to get weighed in; (*fig*) **il pèse 3 millions** he is worth 3 million.
b (*évaluer*) to weigh (up). **~ le pour et le contre** to weigh (up) the pros and cons; **~ ses mots/chances** to weigh one's words/chances; **tout bien pesé** having weighed everything up, everything considered; **ce qu'il dit est toujours pesé** what he says is always carefully weighed up.
2 vi a (*gén*) to weigh; *[sportif]* to weigh in. **cela pèse beaucoup** it weighs a lot; **cela pèse peu** it doesn't weigh much; **~ 60 kg** (*gén*) to weigh 60 kg; *[sportif]* to weigh in at 60 kg; **~ lourd** to be heavy; (*fig*) **ce ministre ne pèse pas lourd*** this minister doesn't carry much weight *ou* doesn't count for much; (*fig*) **il n'a pas pesé lourd (devant son adversaire)** he was no match (for his opponent).
b (*appuyer*) to press, push; (*fig*) to weigh heavy. **~ sur/contre qch (de tout son poids)** to press *ou* push down on/against sth (with all one's weight); (*fig*) *[aliment, repas]* **~ sur l'estomac** to lie (heavy) on the stomach; (*fig*) **cela lui pèse sur le cœur** that makes him heavy-hearted; **les remords lui pèsent sur la conscience** remorse lies heavy on his conscience, his conscience is weighed down by remorse; **le soupçon/l'accusation qui pèse sur lui** the suspicion/the accusation which hangs over him; **la menace/sentence qui pèse sur sa tête** the threat/sentence which hangs over his head; **toute la responsabilité pèse sur lui** *ou* **sur ses épaules** all the responsibility is on him *ou* on his shoulders, he has to shoulder all the responsibility.
c (*accabler*) **~ à qn** to weigh sb down, weigh heavy on sb; **le silence/la solitude lui pèse** the silence/solitude is getting him down* *ou* weighs heavy on him; **le temps lui pèse** time hangs heavy on his hands; **ses responsabilités de maire lui pèsent** he feels the weight of *ou* weighed down by his responsibilities as mayor, his responsibilities as mayor weigh heavy on him.
d (*avoir de l'importance*) to carry weight. **cela va ~ (dans la balance)** that will carry some weight; **sa timidité a pesé dans leur décision** his shyness influenced their decision.
3 comp ▸**pèse-acide** nm (pl **pèse-acides**) acidimeter ▸**pèse-alcool** nm (pl **pèse-alcools**) alcoholometer ▸**pèse-bébé** nm (pl **pèse-bébés**) (baby) scales ▸**pèse-lait** nm (pl **pèse-laits**) lactometer ▸**pèse-lettre** nm (pl **pèse-lettres**) letter scales ▸**pèse-personne** nm (pl **pèse-personnes**) scales; *[salle de bains]* (bathroom) scales.

peseta [pezeta] nf peseta.

pessaire [pesɛʀ] nm pessary.

pessimisme [pesimism] nm pessimism.

pessimiste [pesimist] 1 adj pessimistic (*sur* about). 2 nmf pessimist.

peste [pɛst] 1 nf (*Méd*) plague; (*fig: personne*) pest, nuisance, menace. **la ~ bubonique** the bubonic plague; **la ~ noire** the Black Death; (*fig*) **fuir qch/qn comme la ~** to avoid sth/sb like the plague. 2 excl (*littér*) good gracious! **~ soit de ...** a plague on ... .

pester [pɛste] 1 vi to curse. **~ contre qn/qch** to curse sb/sth.

pesticide [pɛstisid] 1 adj pesticidal. 2 nm pesticide.

pestiféré, e [pɛstifeʀe] 1 adj plague-stricken. 2 nm,f plague victim. (*fig*) **fuir qn comme un ~** to avoid sb like the plague.

pestilence [pɛstilɑ̃s] nf stench.

pestilentiel, -elle [pɛstilɑ̃sjɛl] adj stinking, foul(-smelling).

pet [pɛ] 1 nm a (*‡: gaz*) fart‡*. **faire** *ou* **lâcher un ~** to fart‡*. b **faire le ~*** to be on (the) watch *ou* on (the) look-out; **~! les voilà!*** look out! here they come!; **ça va faire du ~, il va y avoir du ~** there'll be a big stink‡; *voir* **valoir**. 2 comp ▸**pet-de-nonne** nm (pl **pets-de-nonne**) fritter (*made with choux pastry*) ▸**pet-en-l'air**† bumfreezer*.

pétainiste [petenist] 1 adj Pétain (*épith*). 2 nmf: **P~** Pétain supporter.

pétale [petal] nm petal.

pétanque [petɑ̃k] nf petanque, *type of bowls played in the South of France*.

pétant, e* [petɑ̃, ɑ̃t] adj: **à 2 heures ~(es)** at 2 on the dot*, on the dot of 2*.

pétaradant, e [petaʀadɑ̃, ɑ̃t] adj *moto* noisy, spluttering, back-firing.

pétarade [petaʀad] nf *[moteur, véhicule]* backfire (*NonC*); *[feu d'artifice, fusillade]* crackling.

pétarader [petaʀade] 1 vi *[moteur, véhicule]* to backfire; *[feu d'artifice]* to go off. **il les entendait ~ dans la cour** he could hear them revving up their engines in the backyard.

pétard [petaʀ] nm a (*feu d'artifice*) banger (*Brit*), firecracker; (*accessoire de cotillon*) cracker; (*Rail*) detonator (*Brit*), torpedo (*US*); (*Mil*) petard, explosive charge. **tirer** *ou* **faire partir un ~** to let off a banger (*Brit*) *ou* firecracker; (*fig*) **lancer un ~** to drop a bombshell; **c'était un ~ mouillé** it was a damp squib.
b (*‡: tapage*) din*, racket*, row*. **il va y avoir du ~** sparks will fly, there's going to be a hell of a row‡; **faire du ~** *[nouvelle]* to cause a stir, raise a stink‡; *[personne]* to kick up a row* *ou* fuss* *ou* stink‡; **être en ~** to be raging mad*, be in a flaming temper (*contre* at).
c (*‡: revolver*) gun.
d (*‡: derrière*) bum‡ (*Brit*), ass‡ (*US*), bottom*, rump*.
e (*arg Drogue*) joint‡, reefer‡.

pétasse‡ [petas] nf stupid (*ou* ugly *etc*) tart‡.

pétaudière [petodjɛʀ] nf bedlam, bear garden.

péter [pete] [6] 1 **vi** a (‡) to fart**. (*fig*) **il veut ~ plus haut que son derrière** *ou* **son cul**** he's got ideas above his station, he thinks he's it*; (*fig*) **il m'a envoyé ~** he told me to go to hell‡ *ou* to bugger off** (*Brit*) *ou* fuck off**; **~ dans la soie** to ponce around‡ in fine clothes.

b (*) *[détonation]* to go off; *[tuyau]* to burst, bust; *[ballon]* to pop, burst; *[ficelle]* to bust*, snap. **la bombe lui a pété à la figure** the bomb went off *ou* blew up in his face; **l'affaire lui a pété dans la main** the deal fell through.

2 **vt** (*) a *ficelle* to bust*, snap; *transistor, vase* to bust*. **je me suis pété une cheville** I bust my ankle*, I did my ankle in‡; **se ~ la gueule‡** (*tomber*) to fall flat on one's face; (*s'enivrer*) to get blitzed‡ *ou* plastered‡; **c'est un coup à se ~ la gueule** you'll (*ou* he'll *etc*) break your (*ou* his *etc*) neck doing that; **il s'est pété la gueule en vélo‡** he smashed himself up when he came off his bike‡; (*saoul*) **il est complètement pété‡** he's pissed out of his brains‡.

b (*fig*) **~ du** *ou* **le feu** *ou* **des flammes** *[personne]* to be full of go* *ou* beans*; **~ la** *ou* **de santé** to be bursting with health; **ça va ~ des flammes** there's going to be a heck of a row*.

pète-sec* [pɛtsɛk] **nmf inv, adj inv: c'est un ~, il est très ~** he has a very abrupt manner, he is very sharp-tongued.

péteux, -euse* [petø, øz] 1 **adj** cowardly, yellow(-bellied)‡. 2 **nm,f** coward, yellowbelly‡.

pétillant, e [petijɑ̃, ɑ̃t] **adj** *eau* bubbly, (slightly) fizzy; *vin* bubbly, sparkling; *yeux* sparkling, twinkling. **discours ~ d'esprit** speech sparkling with wit.

pétillement [petijmɑ̃] **nm** (*action: voir* **pétiller**) crackling; bubbling; sparkling; twinkling. **entendre des ~s** to hear crackling *ou* crackles *ou* a crackle; **ce ~ de malice qui animait son regard** this mischievous sparkle in his eye.

pétiller [petije] [1] **vi** *[feu]* to crackle; *[champagne, vin, eau]* to bubble; *[joie]* to sparkle (*dans* in); *[yeux]* (*de malice*) to sparkle, glisten; (*de joie*) to sparkle, twinkle (*de* with). **ses yeux pétillaient de malice** his eyes were sparkling mischievously; **il pétillait de bonne humeur** he was bubbling (over) with good humour; **~ d'esprit** to sparkle with wit.

pétiole [pesjɔl] **nm** leafstalk, petiole (*SPÉC*).

petiot, e* [pətjo, jɔt] 1 **adj** weeny (little)*, teenyweeny*, tiny (little). 2 **nm** little laddie*. 3 **petiote nf** little lassie*.

petit, e [p(ə)ti, it] 1 **adj** a (*gén*) *main, personne, objet, colline* small, little (*épith*); *pointure* small. **~ et mince** short and thin; **~ et carré** squat; **~ et rond** dumpy; **il est tout ~** he's very small *ou* a very small man; (*nuance affective*) he's a little *ou* a tiny (little) man; (*fig*) **se faire tout ~** to try not to be noticed, make o.s. as inconspicuous as possible; **être de ~e taille** to be short *ou* small; **un ~ vieux** a little old man; **ces chaussures sont un peu/trop ~es pour moi** these shoes are a bit small *ou* rather a small fit/too small for me.

b (*mince*) *personne, taille* slim, slender; *membre* thin, slender. **avoir de ~s os** to be small-boned *ou* slight-boned; **avoir une ~e figure/de ~s bras** to have a thin face/slender *ou* thin arms; **une ~e pluie (fine) tombait** a (fine) drizzle was falling.

c (*jeune*) small, young; (*avec nuance affective*) little. **quand il était ~** when he was small *ou* little; **son ~ frère** his younger *ou* little brother, (*très petit*) his baby *ou* little brother; **~ chat/chien** (little) kitten/puppy; **un ~ Anglais** an English boy; **les ~s Anglais** English children; **~ lion/tigre/ours** little lion/tiger/bear, lion/tiger/bear cub; **dans sa ~e enfance** when he was very small, in his early childhood; **le ~ Jésus** Infant Jesus, baby Jesus; **comment va la ~e famille?** how are the young ones?; **tout ce ~ monde s'amusait** all these youngsters were enjoying themselves; (*péj*) **je vous préviens mon ~ ami** *ou* **monsieur** I warn you my good man *ou* dear fellow.

d (*court*) *promenade, voyage* short, little. **par ~es étapes** in short *ou* easy stages; **sur une ~e distance** over a short distance; **il est resté deux (pauvres) ~es heures** he only stayed for 2 short hours; **il en a pour une ~e heure** it will take him an hour at the most, it won't take him more than an hour; **attendez une ~e minute** can you wait just a *ou* half a minute?; **j'en ai pour un ~ moment** (*longtemps*) it'll take me quite a while; (*peu de temps*) it won't take me long, I shan't be long over it; **elle est sortie pour un bon ~ moment** she won't be back for a (good) while *ou* for quite a while yet; **écrivez-lui un ~ mot** write him a (short) note *ou* a line; **c'est à un ~ kilomètre d'ici** it's no more than *ou* just under a kilometre from here.

e (*faible*) *bruit* faint, slight; *cri* little, faint; *coup, tape* light, gentle; *pente* gentle, slight; *somme d'argent* small. **on entendit 2 ~s coups à la porte** we heard 2 light *ou* gentle knocks on the door; **il a un ~ appétit** he has a small appetite, he hasn't much of an appetite; **avoir une ~e santé** to be in poor health, be frail; **c'est une ~e nature** he's (*ou* she's) slightly built; **une toute ~e voix** a tiny voice.

f (*minime*) *opération, détail* small, minor; *inconvénient* slight, minor; *espoir, chance* faint, slight; *cadeau, bibelot* little; *odeur, rhume* slight. **avec un ~ effort** with a bit of an *ou* with a little effort; **ce n'est pas une ~e affaire que de le faire obéir** getting him to obey is no easy matter *ou* no mean task; **ce n'est qu'une ~e robe d'été** it's just a light summer dress.

g (*peu important*) *commerçant, pays, firme* small; *fonctionnaire, employé, romancier* minor; *soirée, réception* little. **la ~e industrie** light industry; **le ~ commerce** small businesses; **les ~es et moyennes entreprises** small and medium-sized businesses; **il est entré dans la firme par la ~e porte** he started work for the firm on the bottom rung of the ladder, he started out doing a very humble job in the firm; **les ~es gens** ordinary people; **le ~ épicier du coin** the small street-corner grocer('s); **la ~e noblesse** minor nobility; **la ~e histoire** the footnotes of history.

h (*peu nombreux*) *groupe* small. **cela n'affecte qu'un ~ nombre** it only affects a small number of people *ou* a few people.

i (*péj: mesquin*) *attitude, action* mean, petty, low; *personne* petty. **c'est ~ ce qu'il a fait là** that was a mean thing to do, that was mean of him.

j (*avec nuance affective ou euph*) little. **vous prendrez bien un ~ dessert/verre** you'll have a little dessert/drink won't you?; **faire une ~e partie de cartes** to play a little game of cards; **juste une ~e signature** can I just have your signature; **un ~ coup de rouge*** a (little) glass of red wine; **comment va la ~e santé?** how are you keeping?*; **ma ~e maman** my mummy; **mon ~ papa** my daddy; **mon ~ chou** *ou* **rat** *etc* (my little) pet*, darling; **un ~ coin tranquille** a nice quiet spot; **on va se faire un bon ~ souper** we'll make ourselves a nice little (bit of) supper; (*euph*) **le ~ coin** *ou* **endroit** the bathroom (*euph*); (*euph*) **faire son ~ besoin** *ou* **sa ~e commission** to spend a penny (*Brit*), go to the toilet; **un ~ chapeau ravissant** a lovely little hat; **avoir ses ~es habitudes/manies** to have one's little habits/ways; **espèce de ~ impertinent** you cheeky little so-and-so*; **cela coûte une ~e fortune** it costs a small fortune.

k (*loc*) (*fig hum*) **le ~ oiseau va sortir!** watch the birdie!; **être/ne pas être dans les ~s papiers de qn** to be in sb's good/bad books; **c'est de la ~e bière** it's small beer (*Brit*), it's small potatoes (*US*); **ce n'est pas de la ~e bière** it's not without importance; **se réunir en ~ comité** to have a small get-together; **à ~s pas** (*lit*) with short steps; (*fig*) slowly but surely; **un ~ peu** a little (bit); **un Balzac/un Versailles au ~ pied** a poor man's Balzac/Versailles; **mettre les ~s plats dans les grands** to lay on a first-rate meal, go to town on the meal*; **à la ~e semaine (adj)** small-time; **être aux ~s soins pour qn** to dance attendance on sb, lavish attention on sb, wait on sb hand and foot; **être dans ses ~s souliers** to be shaking in one's shoes; (*fig*) **~ poisson deviendra grand** from tiny acorns great *ou* mighty oaks grow; (*Prov*) **les ~s ruisseaux font les grandes rivières** little streams make big rivers; *voir* **tenu** *etc*.

2 **adv: ~ à ~** little by little, gradually.

3 **nm** a (*enfant*) (little) boy; (*Scol*) junior (boy). **les ~s** children; **viens ici, ~** come here, son; **pauvre ~** poor little thing; **le ~ Durand** young Durand, the Durand boy; **les ~s Durand** the Durand children; **les tout-~s** the very young, the tiny tots; (*Scol*) the infants; **jeu pour ~s et grands** game for old and young (alike).

b (*jeune animal*) (*gén*) young. **la chatte et ses ~s** the cat and her kittens; **la lionne et ses ~s** the lioness and her young *ou* cubs; **faire des ~s** to have little kittens (*ou* puppies *ou* lambs *etc*); (*fig*) **son argent a fait des ~s** his money has made more money.

c (*personne de petite taille*) small man; (*personne inférieure*) little man. **les ~s** small people; **c'est toujours le ~ qui a tort** it's always the little man who's in the wrong.

d **une cour d'école, c'est le monde en ~** a school playground is the world in miniature.

4 **petite nf** (*enfant*) (little) girl; (*femme*) small woman. **la ~e Durand** (*la fillette des Durand*) the Durand's daughter; (*péj: Mlle Durand*) the Durand girl; **pauvre ~e** poor little thing; **viens ici, ~e** come here little one.

5 **comp** ▸**petit ami** boyfriend ▸**petite amie** girlfriend ▸**petit banc** low bench ▸**petit-beurre nm (pl petits-beurre)** petit beurre biscuit (*Brit*), butter cookie (*US*) ▸**les petits blancs** poor white settlers ▸**petit bleu†** wire (*telegram*) ▸**petit bois** kindling (*NonC*) ▸**petit-bourgeois, petite-bourgeoise (mpl petits-bourgeois) adj** petit-bourgeois, middle-class ◊ **nm** petit-bourgeois, middle-class man ◊ **nf** petit-bourgeois *ou* middle-class woman ▸**"le Petit Chaperon rouge"** "Little Red Riding Hood" ▸**petits chevaux: jouer aux petits chevaux** to play ludo (*Brit*) ▸**petite classe** junior form (*Brit*), lower grade (*US*) ▸**les petites classes** the junior *ou* lower school ▸**le petit coin** (*euph*) the smallest room (*euph*), the toilet ▸**petit cousin, petite cousine** (*enfant*) little *ou* young cousin; (*enfant du cousin germain*) second cousin; (*parent éloigné*) distant cousin ▸**petit déjeuner** breakfast ▸**le petit doigt** the little finger; **mon petit doigt me l'a dit** a little bird told me ▸**le petit écran** television, TV ▸**petit-enfant nm (pl petits-enfants)** grandchild ▸**le petit endroit** (*euph*) = **le petit coin** ▸**petite-fille nf (pl petites-filles)** granddaughter ▸**petit-fils nm (pl petits-fils)** grandson ▸**petit four** petit four ▸**petit garçon** little boy; **il fait très petit garçon** there's something of the little boy about him; (*fig*) **à côté de lui, c'est un petit garçon** next to him, he's a babe in arms ▸**petit gâteau (sec)** biscuit ▸**petit-gris nm (pl petits-gris)** (*escargot*) garden snail; (*écureuil*) Siberian squirrel; (*fourrure*) squirrel fur ▸**petit-lait nm** whey (*voir* **boire**) ▸**petit-maître†† nm (pl petits-maîtres)** dandy, toff† (*Brit*), fop† ▸**petit-nègre** (*péj*) **nm** pidgin French; (*péj: galimatias*) gibberish, gobbledygook* ▸**petit-neveu nm (pl petits-neveux)** great-nephew, grand-nephew ▸**petite-nièce nf (pl petites-nièces)**

great-niece, grand-niece ▸**petit nom*** Christian name (*Brit*), first name ▸**petit pain** ≃ bread roll; **ça part** *ou* **se vend comme des petits pains*** it is selling like hot cakes* ▸**petit point** (*Couture*) petit point ▸**petit-pois nm (pl petits-pois)** (garden) pea ▸**"le Petit Poucet"** "Tom Thumb" ▸**la petite reine** (*fig*) the bicycle ▸**petit salé** (*Culin*) salted pork ▸**petit-suisse nm (pl petits-suisses)** petit-suisse (*kind of cream cheese eaten as a dessert*) ▸**la petite vérole** smallpox ▸**petite voiture (d'infirme)** (*gén*) wheelchair; (*à moteur*) invalid carriage.

petitement [pətitmɑ̃] **adv** (*chichement*) poorly; (*mesquinement*) meanly, pettily. **nous sommes ~ logés** our accommodation is cramped.

petitesse [p(ə)titɛs] **nf** *[taille, endroit]* smallness, small size; *[somme]* smallness, modesty; (*fig*) *[esprit, acte]* meanness (*NonC*), pettiness (*NonC*).

pétition [petisjɔ̃] **nf** a petition. **faire une ~ auprès de qn** to petition sb; **faire signer une ~** to set up a petition. b (*Philos*) **~ de principe** petitio principii (*SPÉC*), begging the question (*NonC*).

pétitionnaire [petisjɔnɛʀ] **nmf** petitioner.

pétochard, e‡ [petɔʃaʀ, aʀd] 1 **adj** cowardly, yellow-bellied‡. 2 **nm,f** funker‡, coward, yellow-belly‡.

pétoche‡ [petɔʃ] **nf**: **avoir la ~** to be scared silly* *ou* witless, be in a blue funk‡ (*Brit*), have the wind up‡ (*Brit*); **flanquer la ~ à qn** to scare the living daylights out of sb*, put the wind up sb‡ (*Brit*).

pétoire [petwaʀ] **nf** (*sarbacane*) peashooter; (*vieux fusil*) blunderbuss; (*péj: fusil*) peashooter (*péj*), popgun (*péj*); (*cyclomoteur*) (motor) scooter.

peton* [pətɔ̃] **nm** (*pied*) foot, tootsy*.

pétoncle [petɔ̃kl] **nm** queen scallop.

Pétrarque [petʀaʀk] **nm** Petrarch.

pétrarquisme [petʀaʀkism] **nm** Petrarchism.

pétrel [petʀɛl] **nm** (stormy) petrel.

pétri, e [petʀi] (**ptp de pétrir**) **adj**: **~ d'orgueil** filled with pride; **~ d'ignorance** steeped in ignorance; **~ de contradictions** full of contradictions; **~ de culture orientale/littérature slave** steeped in Eastern culture/Slavic literature.

pétrifiant, e [petʀifjɑ̃, jɑ̃t] **adj** *eau* petrifactive; *spectacle* petrifying; *nouvelle* horrifying.

pétrification [petʀifikasjɔ̃] **nf** a (*Géol*) petrifaction, petrification. b (*fig*) *[cœur]* hardening; *[idées]* fossilization.

pétrifier [petʀifje] [7] 1 **vt** a (*Géol*) to petrify. b (*fig*) *personne* to paralyze, transfix; *cœur* to freeze; *idées* to fossilize, ossify. **être pétrifié de terreur** to be petrified (with terror), be paralyzed *ou* transfixed with terror. 2 **se pétrifier vpr** a (*Géol*) to petrify, become petrified. b (*fig*) *[sourire]* to freeze; *[personne]* to be paralyzed *ou* transfixed; *[cœur]* to freeze; *[idées]* to become fossilized *ou* ossified.

pétrin [petʀɛ̃] **nm** a (*: *ennui*) mess*, jam*, fix*. **tirer qn du ~** to get sb out of a mess* *ou* fix* *ou* tight spot*; **laisser qn dans le ~** to leave sb in a mess* *ou* jam* *ou* fix*; **se mettre dans un beau ~** to get (o.s.) into a fine mess*; **être dans le ~** to be in a mess* *ou* jam* *ou* fix*. b (*Boulangerie*) kneading-trough; (*mécanique*) kneading-machine.

pétrir [petʀiʀ] [2] **vt** *pâte, argile* to knead; *muscle, main* to knead; *personne, esprit* to mould, shape.

pétrochimie [petʀoʃimi] **nf** petrochemistry.

pétrochimique [petʀoʃimik] **adj** petrochemical.

pétrochimiste [petʀoʃimist] **nmf** petrochemist.

pétrodollar [petʀodɔlaʀ] **nm** petrodollar.

pétrographie [petʀɔgʀafi] **nf** petrography.

pétrographique [petʀɔgʀafik] **adj** petrographic(al).

pétrole [petʀɔl] **nm** (*brut*) oil, petroleum. **~ (lampant)** paraffin (oil) (*Brit*), kerosene (*US*); **~ brut** crude (oil), petroleum; **puits de ~** oil well; **gisement de ~** oilfield; **lampe/réchaud à ~** paraffin (*Brit*) *ou* kerosene (*US*) *ou* oil lamp/heater.

pétrolette† [petʀɔlɛt] **nf** moped.

pétroleuse [petʀɔløz] **nf** (*Hist*) pétroleuse, *female fire-raiser during the Commune;* (*fig*) agitator.

pétrolier, -ière [petʀɔlje, jɛʀ] 1 **adj** *industrie, produits* petroleum (*épith*), oil (*épith*); *société* oil (*épith*); *pays* oil-producing (*épith*). 2 **nm** (*navire*) (oil) tanker; (*personne*) (*financier*) oil magnate, oilman; (*technicien*) petroleum engineer.

pétrolifère [petʀɔlifɛʀ] **adj** *roches, couches* oil-bearing. **gisement ~** oilfield.

pétulance [petylɑ̃s] **nf** exuberance, vivacity.

pétulant, e [petylɑ̃, ɑ̃t] **adj** exuberant, vivacious.

pétunia [petynja] **nm** petunia.

peu [pø] 1 **adv** a (*petite quantité*) little, not much. **il gagne/mange/lit (assez) ~** he doesn't earn/eat/read (very) much; **il gagne/mange/lit très ~** he earns/eats/reads very little *ou* precious little*; **il s'intéresse ~ à la peinture** he isn't very *ou* greatly interested in painting, he takes little interest in painting; **il se contente de ~** he is satisfied with little, it doesn't take much to satisfy him; **il a donné 50 F, c'est ~** he gave 50 francs, which isn't (very) much; **il y a (bien) ~ à faire/à voir ici** there's very little *ou* precious little* to do/see here, there's not much (at all) to do/see here; **il mange trop ~** he doesn't eat (nearly) enough; **je le connais trop ~ pour le juger** I don't know him (nearly) well enough to judge him.

b (*modifiant adj etc*) (a) little, not very. **il est (très) ~ sociable** he is not very sociable (at all), he is (very) unsociable; **fort ~ intéressant** decidedly uninteresting, of very little interest; **il conduit ~ prudemment** he drives carelessly *ou* with little care, he doesn't drive very carefully; **ils sont (bien) trop ~ nombreux** there are (far) too few of them; **un auteur assez ~ connu** a relatively little-known *ou* relatively unknown author; **c'est un ~ grand/petit** it's a little *ou* a bit (too) big/small; **quelque ~ grivois** a touch risqué; **elle n'est pas ~ soulagée d'être reçue** she's more than a little relieved *ou* not a little relieved at passing her exam; **~ avant** shortly before, a little while earlier.

c **~ de** (*quantité*) little, not much; (*nombre*) few, not (very) many; **nous avons eu (très) ~ de soleil/d'orages** we had (very) little sunshine/(very) few storms, we didn't have (very) much sunshine/(very) many storms; **je peux vous céder du pain, bien qu'il m'en reste ~** I can let you have some bread though I haven't (very) much left; **on attendait des touristes mais il en est venu (très) ~** we expected tourists but not (very) many came *ou* but (very) few came; **~ de monde** *ou* **de gens** few people, not many people; **il est ici depuis ~ de temps** he hasn't been here long, he has been here (only) for a short while *ou* time; **il est ici pour ~ de temps** he isn't here for long, he is here for (only) a short time *ou* while; **en ~ de mots** briefly, in a few words; **cela a ~ d'importance** that's not (very) important, that doesn't matter (very) much, that's of little importance.

d (*employé seul: personnes*) **ils sont ~ à croire que** few believe that, there are few *ou* there aren't many who believe that; **bien ~/trop ~ le savent** very few/too few (people) know; **~ d'entre eux sont restés** few (of them) stayed, not many (of them) stayed.

e **de ~**: **il est le plus âgé de ~** he is slightly *ou* a little older, he is just older; **il l'a battu de ~** he just beat him; **il a manqué le train de ~** he just missed the train; *voir* **falloir**.

f (*loc*) **à ~ près** (just) about, near enough*; **à ~ près terminé/cuit** almost finished/cooked, more or less finished/cooked; **à ~ près 10 minutes/kilos** roughly *ou* approximately 10 minutes/kilos; **rester dans l'à ~ près** to remain vague; **c'est terminé à ~ de chose près** it's more or less *ou* pretty well* finished, it's finished as near as damn it‡ (*Brit*); **(c'est) ~ de chose** it's nothing; **c'est pas ~ dire!*** and that's saying something!; (*littér*) **c'est ~ dire que** it is an understatement to say that; **~ à ~** gradually, little by little; (*littér*) **~ ou prou** to a greater or lesser degree, more or less; *voir* **avant, depuis, si**[1] *etc*.

2 **nm** a little. **j'ai oublié le ~ (de français) que j'avais appris** I have forgotten the little (French) I had learnt; **elle se contente du ~ (d'argent) qu'elle a** she is satisfied with what little (money) *ou* the little (money) she has; **son ~ de compréhension/patience lui a nui** his lack of understanding/patience has done him harm; **elle s'est aliéné le ~ d'amis qu'elle avait** she has alienated the few friends *ou* the one or two friends she had; **le ~ de cheveux qui lui restent sont blancs** the bit of hair he has left is white.

b **un ~** (*avec vb, modifiant adv mieux, moins, plus, trop etc*) a little, slightly, a bit; **un (tout) petit ~** a little bit, a trifle; **essaie de manger un ~** try to eat a little *ou* a bit; **il boite un ~** he limps slightly *ou* a little *ou* a bit, he is slightly *ou* a bit lame; **elle va un tout petit ~ mieux** she is a trifle better, she is ever so slightly better; **il est un ~ artiste** he's a bit of an artist, he's something of an artist; **il travaille un ~ trop/un ~ trop lentement** he works a little *ou* a bit too much/too slowly; **restez encore un ~** stay a little longer; **il y a un ~ moins de bruit** it is slightly *ou* a little less noisy, there's slightly *ou* a little less noise; **nous avons un ~ moins/plus de clients aujourd'hui** we have slightly fewer/more customers today; (*en effeuillant la marguerite*) **un ~, beaucoup, passionnément, pas du tout** he loves me, he loves me not; **un ~ plus il écrasait le chien/oubliait son rendez-vous** he all but *ou* he very nearly ran over the dog/forgot his appointment; **pour un ~ il m'aurait accusé d'avoir volé** he all but *ou* just about* accused me of stealing; **pour un ~ je l'aurais giflé** for two pins (*Brit*) *ou* cents (*US*) I'd have slapped his face.

c **un ~ de** a little, a bit of; **un ~ d'eau** a little water, a drop of water; **un ~ de patience** a little patience, a bit of patience; **un ~ de silence/de calme, s'il vous plaît!** let's have some quiet *ou* a bit of quiet/some peace *ou* a bit of peace please!; **il a un ~ de sinusite/bronchite** he has a touch of sinusitis/bronchitis.

d (*: *intensif*) **un ~!** and how!* ; **tu as vraiment vu l'accident? — un ~!** *ou* **un ~ mon neveu!‡†** did you really see the accident? — you bet!* *ou* and how!* *ou* I sure did!* (*US*); **je me demande un ~ où sont les enfants** I just wonder where the children are *ou* can be; **montre-moi donc un ~ comment tu fais** just (you) show me then how you do it; **va-t-en voir un ~ si c'est vrai!** just you go and see if it's true!; **comme menteur il est** *ou* **se pose un ~ là!** as liars go, he must be hard to beat!*; **un ~ qu'il nous a menti!** he didn't half lie to us!* (*Brit*), I'll say he lied to us!*; **on en trouve un ~ partout** you find them just about everywhere; **c'est un ~ beaucoup*** that's a bit much*.

peuchère [pøʃɛʀ] **excl** (*dial Midi*) well! well!

peuh [pø] **excl** pooh!, bah!, phooey* (*US*).

peuplade [pœplad] **nf** (small) tribe, people.

peuple [pœpl] **nm** a (*Pol, Rel: communauté*) people, nation. **les ~s**

d'Europe the peoples *ou* nations of Europe; (*Rel*) **le ~ élu** the chosen people. **b** (*prolétariat*) **le ~** the people; **les gens du ~** the common people, ordinary people; (††, *péj*) **le bas** *ou* **petit ~** the lower classes (*péj*); (*fig*) **il se moque** *ou* **se fiche du ~** who does he think he is?; (*péj*) **faire ~** (*ne pas être distingué*) to be common (*péj*); (*vouloir paraître simple*) to try to appear working-class. **c** (*foule*) crowd (of people). (*littér*) **un ~ de badauds/d'admirateurs** a crowd of onlookers/of admirers; **il y a du ~!*** there's a big crowd!

peuplé, e [pœple] (**ptp de peupler**) **adj** *ville, région* populated, inhabited. **très/peu/sous-~** densely-/sparsely-/underpopulated.

peuplement [pœpləmɑ̃] **nm** **a** (*action*) *[colonie]* populating; *[étang]* stocking; *[forêt]* planting (with trees). **b** (*population*) population.

peupler [pœple] [1] **1 vt a** (*pourvoir d'une population*) *colonie* to populate; *étang* to stock; *forêt* to plant out, plant with trees; (*fig littér*) to fill (*de* with). **les rêves/les souvenirs qui peuplent mon esprit** the dreams/memories that dwell in my mind (*littér*) *ou* that fill my mind; **les cauchemars/monstres qui peuplent ses nuits** the nightmares/monsters which haunt his nights *ou* which fill his mind at night.

b (*habiter*) *terre* to inhabit, populate; *maison* to live in, inhabit. **maison peuplée de souvenirs** house filled with *ou* full of memories; **tous ceux qui peuplent nos prisons** all those who fill our prisons.

2 se peupler vpr *[ville, région]* to become populated; (*fig: s'animer*) to fill (up), be filled (*de* with). **la rue se peuplait de cris/de boutiques** the street filled with shouts/shops.

peupleraie [pøplərɛ] **nf** poplar grove.

peuplier [pøplije] **nm** poplar (tree).

peur [pœʀ] **nf a la ~** fear; **inspirer de la ~** to cause *ou* inspire fear; **ressentir de la ~** to feel fear; **la ~ lui donnait des ailes** fear lent him wings; **être vert** *ou* **mort de ~** to be frightened *ou* scared out of one's wits, be petrified (with fear); **la ~ de la punition/de mourir/du qu'en-dira-t-on** (the) fear of punishment/of dying/of what people might say; **prendre ~** to take fright; **la ~ du gendarme*** the fear of being caught; **cacher sa ~** to hide one's fear; **sans ~** (**adj**) fearless (*de* of); (**adv**) fearlessly.

b une ~ a fear; **une ~ irraisonnée de se blesser s'empara de lui** he was seized by *ou* with an irrational fear of injuring himself; **des ~s enfantines** childish fears; **je n'ai qu'une ~, c'est qu'il ne revienne pas** I have only one fear, that he doesn't *ou* won't come back; **il a eu une ~ bleue** he had a bad fright *ou* scare; **il a une ~ bleue de sa femme** he's scared stiff* of his wife, he goes *ou* lives in fear and trembling of his wife; **il m'a fait une de ces ~s!** he gave me a dreadful fright *ou* scare, he didn't half* give me a fright! *ou* scare! (*Brit*).

c avoir ~ to be frightened *ou* afraid *ou* scared (*de* of); **avoir ~ pour qn** to be afraid for sb *ou* on sb's behalf, fear for sb; **n'ayez pas ~** (*craindre*) don't be afraid *ou* frightened *ou* scared; (*s'inquiéter*) have no fear; **il sera puni, n'aie pas ~!** he will be punished — don't worry!; **il veut faire ce voyage en 2 jours, il n'a pas ~, lui au moins!*** he wants to do the trip in 2 days — you can't say he hasn't got nerve!; **il prétend qu'il a téléphoné, il n'a pas ~, lui au moins!*** he says he phoned — he has some nerve! *ou* you can't say he hasn't got nerve!; **n'ayez pas ~ de dire la vérité** don't be afraid *ou* frightened *ou* scared to tell *ou* of telling the truth; **il n'a ~ de rien** he's afraid of nothing, nothing frightens him; **avoir ~ d'un rien** to frighten easily; **avoir ~ de son ombre** to be frightened *ou* scared of one's own shadow; **je n'ai pas ~ des mots** I'm not afraid of using plain language; **j'ai bien ~/très ~ qu'il ne pleuve** I'm afraid/very much afraid it's going to rain *ou* it might rain; **il va échouer? — j'en ai (bien) ~** is he going to fail? — I'm (very much) afraid so *ou* I'm afraid he is; **j'ai ~ qu'il ne vous ait menti/que cela ne vous gêne** I'm afraid *ou* worried *ou* I fear that he might have lied to you/that it might inconvenience you; **je n'ai pas ~ qu'il dise la vérité** I'm not afraid *ou* frightened of his telling the truth; **il a eu plus de ~ que de mal** he was more frightened than hurt, he wasn't hurt so much as frightened; **il y a eu** *ou* **ça a fait plus de ~ que de mal** it caused more fright than real harm, it was more frightening than anything else.

d faire ~ à qn (*intimider*) to frighten *ou* scare sb; (*causer une frayeur à*) to give sb a fright, frighten *ou* scare sb; **pour faire ~ aux oiseaux** to frighten *ou* scare the birds away *ou* off; **l'idée de l'examen lui fait ~** the idea of sitting the exam frightens *ou* scares him, he's frightened *ou* scared at the idea of sitting the exam; **cette pensée fait ~** the thought is frightening, it's a frightening thought; **tout lui fait ~** he's afraid *ou* frightened *ou* scared of everything; **le travail ne lui fait pas ~** he's not scared *ou* afraid of hard work; **laid** *ou* **hideux à faire ~** frighteningly ugly; (*iro*) **il fait chaud, ça fait ~!** it's not exactly roasting!* (*iro*).

e de ~ de faire for fear of doing, for fear that one might *ou* should do, lest one should do (*littér*); **il a couru de ~ de manquer le train** he ran for fear of missing the train, he ran for fear that he might *ou* should miss the train, he ran because he was afraid he might miss the train; **il a accepté de ~ de les vexer** he accepted for fear of annoying them *ou* lest he (should) annoy them (*littér*); **j'ai fermé la porte, de ~ qu'elle ne prenne froid** I closed the door so that she doesn't catch cold; **il renonça, de ~ du ridicule** he gave up for fear of ridicule.

peureusement [pøʀøzmɑ̃] **adv** fearfully, timorously.

peureux, -euse [pøʀø, øz] **1 adj** fearful, timorous. **2 nm,f** fearful *ou* timorous person.

peut-être [pøtɛtʀ] **adv** perhaps, maybe. **il est ~ intelligent, ~ est-il intelligent** he's perhaps clever, perhaps he's clever, he may *ou* might (well) be clever, maybe he's clever; **il n'est ~ pas beau mais il est intelligent** he may *ou* might not be handsome but he is clever, perhaps *ou* maybe he's not handsome but he's clever; **c'est ~ encore plus petit** it is if anything even smaller; **~ bien** perhaps (so), it could well be; **~ pas** perhaps *ou* maybe not; **~ bien mais ...** that's as may be *ou* perhaps so but ...; **~ que ...** perhaps ...; **~ bien qu'il pleuvra** it may well rain; **~ que oui** perhaps so, perhaps he will (*ou* they are *etc*); **je ne sais pas conduire ~?** who's (doing the) driving? (*iro*), I do know how to drive, you know!; **tu le sais mieux que moi ~?** so (you think) you know more about it than I do, do you?, I do know more about it than you, you know!

p.ex. (**abrév de par exemple**) e.g.

pèze‡ [pɛz] **nm** (*argent*) dough‡, bread‡.

pff(t) [pf(t)] **excl**, **pfut** [pfyt] **excl** pooh!, bah!

pH [peaʃ] **nm** pH.

phacochère [fakɔʃɛʀ] **nm** wart hog.

phaéton [faetɔ̃] **nm** (*calèche*) phaeton. (*Myth*) **P~** Phaeton.

phagocyte [fagɔsit] **nm** phagocyte.

phagocyter [fagɔsite] [1] **vt** (*Bio*) to phagocytose; (*fig*) to absorb, engulf.

phagocytose [fagɔsitoz] **nf** phagocytosis.

phalange [falɑ̃ʒ] **nf** (*Anat*) phalanx; (*Antiq, littér: armée*) phalanx. (*Pol espagnole*) **la ~** the Falange.

phalangien, -ienne [falɑ̃ʒjɛ̃, jɛn] **adj** (*Anat*) phalangeal.

phalangiste [falɑ̃ʒist] **adj, nmf** Falangist.

phalanstère [falɑ̃stɛʀ] **nm** phalanstery.

phalène [falɛn] **nf** emerald, geometrid (*SPÉC*).

phallique [falik] **adj** phallic.

phallocrate [falɔkʀat] **nm** male chauvinist pig*.

phallocratie [falɔkʀasi] **nf** male chauvinism.

phalloïde [falɔid] **adj** phalloid; *voir* **amanite**.

phallus [falys] **nm** phallus.

phantasme [fɑ̃tasm] **nm** = **fantasme**.

pharamineux, -euse [faʀaminø, øz] **adj** = **faramineux**.

pharaon [faʀaɔ̃] **nm** (*Antiq*) Pharaoh.

pharaonien, -ienne [faʀaɔnjɛ̃, jɛn] **adj**, **pharaonique** [faʀaɔnik] **adj** Pharaonic.

phare [faʀ] **1 nm a** (*tour*) lighthouse; (*Aviat, fig*) beacon. (*Naut*) **~ à feu fixe/tournant** fixed/revolving light *ou* beacon.

b (*Aut*) headlight, headlamp. **rouler pleins ~s** *ou* **en ~s** to drive on full beam (*Brit*) *ou* high beams (*US*) *ou* on full headlights *ou* with headlights full on; **mettre ses ~s en veilleuse** to switch to sidelights; **mettre ses ~s en code** to dip one's headlights (*Brit*), put on the low beams (*US*); **~s code** dipped headlights (*Brit*), low beams (*US*); **~ antibrouillard** fog lamp; **~s longue portée** high intensity lights; **~ de recul** reversing light (*Brit*), back-up light (*US*); **~ à iodes** quartz halogen lamp; *voir* **appel**.

2 adj inv *produit, secteur* leading; *élément* key (*épith*).

pharisaïque [faʀizaik] **adj** (*Hist*) Pharisaic; (*fig*) pharisaic(al).

pharisaïsme [faʀizaism] **nm** (*Hist*) Pharisaism, Phariseeism; (*fig*) pharisaism, phariseeism.

pharisien, -ienne [faʀizjɛ̃, jɛn] **nm,f** (*Hist*) Pharisee; (*fig*) pharisee.

pharmaceutique [faʀmasøtik] **adj** pharmaceutical, pharmaceutic.

pharmacie [faʀmasi] **nf a** (*magasin*) chemist's (shop) (*Brit*), pharmacy, drugstore (*Can, US*); (*officine*) dispensary; *[hôpital]* dispensary, pharmacy (*Brit*), formulary (*US*). **b** (*science*) pharmacology; (*profession*) pharmacy. **laboratoire de ~** pharmaceutical laboratory; **préparateur en ~** pharmacist. **c** (*produits*) pharmaceuticals, medicines. **(armoire à) ~** medicine chest *ou* cabinet *ou* cupboard, first-aid cabinet *ou* cupboard.

pharmacien, -ienne [faʀmasjɛ̃, jɛn] **nm,f** (*qui tient une pharmacie*) (dispensing) chemist (*Brit*), pharmacist, druggist (*US*); (*préparateur*) pharmacist, chemist (*Brit*).

pharmacodépendance [faʀmakodepɑ̃dɑ̃s] **nf** drug dependency.

pharmacologie [faʀmakɔlɔʒi] **nf** pharmacology.

pharmacologique [faʀmakɔlɔʒik] **adj** pharmacological.

pharmacopée [faʀmakɔpe] **nf** pharmacopoeia.

pharyngal, e, mpl -aux [faʀɛ̃gal, o] **1 adj** pharyngeal. **2 pharyngale nf** (*Ling*) pharyngeal.

pharyngé, e [faʀɛ̃ʒe] **adj**, **pharyngien, -ienne** [faʀɛ̃ʒjɛ̃, jɛn] **adj** pharyngeal, pharyngal.

pharyngite [faʀɛ̃ʒit] **nf** pharyngitis (*NonC*). **il a fait 3 ~s** he had 3 bouts of pharyngitis.

pharynx [faʀɛ̃ks] **nm** pharynx.

phase [fɑz] **nf** (*gén, Méd*) phase, stage; (*Astron, Chim, Phys*) phase. (*Élec*) **la ~** the live wire; **être en ~** (*Phys*) to be in phase; (*fig*) *[personnes]* to be on the same wavelength; *[projets]* to be in line (*avec* with).

Phébus [febys] **nm** Phoebus.

Phèdre [fɛdʀ] **nf** Phaedra.

Phénicie [fenisi] nf Phoenicia.
phénicien, -ienne [fenisjɛ̃, jɛn] 1 adj Phoenician. 2 nm (*Ling*) Phoenician. 3 nm,f: **P~(ne)** Phoenician.
phénix [feniks] nm (*Myth*) phoenix; (*fig* †, *littér*) paragon. **ce n'est pas un ~*** he (*ou* she) is not so wonderful.
phénobarbital, pl ~s [fenɔbaʀbital] nm phenobarbital, phenobarbitone.
phénol [fenɔl] nm carbolic acid, phenol.
phénoménal, e, mpl -aux [fenɔmenal, o] adj (*gén*) phenomenal.
phénoménalement [fenɔmenalmɑ̃] adv phenomenally.
phénomène [fenɔmɛn] nm (*gén, Philos*) phenomenon; (*monstre de foire*) freak (of nature); (*: *personne*) (*génial*) phenomenon; (*excentrique*) character*; (*anormal*) freak*. **son petit dernier est un sacré ~!** his youngest is a real devil!*
phénoménologie [fenɔmenɔlɔʒi] nf phenomenology.
phénoménologique [fenɔmenɔlɔʒik] adj phenomenological.
phénoménologue [fenɔmenɔlɔg] nmf phenomenologist.
phénotype [fenɔtip] nm phenotype.
phéromone [feʀɔmɔn] nf, **phérormone** [feʀɔʀmɔn] nf pheromone.
philanthrope [filɑ̃tʀɔp] nmf philanthropist.
philanthropie [filɑ̃tʀɔpi] nf philanthropy.
philanthropique [filɑ̃tʀɔpik] adj philanthropic(al).
philatélie [filateli] nf philately, stamp collecting.
philatélique [filatelik] adj philatelic.
philatéliste [filatelist] nmf philatelist, stamp collector.
Philémon [filemɔ̃] nm Philemon.
philharmonie [filaʀmɔni] nf (local) philharmonic society.
philharmonique [filaʀmɔnik] adj philharmonic.
philhellène [filelɛn] 1 adj philhellenic. 2 nmf philhellene, philhellenist.
philhellénique [filelenik] adj philhellenic.
philhellénisme [filelenism] nm philhellenism.
Philippe [filip] nm Philip.
philippin, e [filipɛ̃, in] 1 adj Philippine. 2 nm,f: **P~(e)** Filipino.
Philippines [filipin] nfpl: **les ~** the Philippines.
philippique [filipik] nf (*littér*) diatribe, philippic (*littér*).
philistin [filistɛ̃] adj m, nm (*Hist*) Philistine; (*fig*) philistine.
philistinisme [filistinism] nm philistinism.
philo [filo] nf (*arg Scol*) abrév de **philosophie.**
philodendron [filɔdɛ̃dʀɔ̃] nm philodendron.
philologie [filɔlɔʒi] nf philology.
philologique [filɔlɔʒik] adj philological.
philologiquement [filɔlɔʒikmɑ̃] adv philologically.
philologue [filɔlɔg] nmf philologist.
philosophale [filɔzɔfal] adj f *voir* **pierre.**
philosophe [filɔzɔf] 1 nmf philosopher. 2 adj philosophical.
philosopher [filɔzɔfe] [1] vi to philosophize.
philosophie [filɔzɔfi] nf philosophy; (*Scol*) (*enseignement*) philosophical studies; (†: *classe*) philosophy class, ≃ arts sixth (form) (*Brit*), senior humanities class (*US*). **accepter qch avec ~** to accept sth philosophically.
philosophique [filɔzɔfik] adj philosophical.
philosophiquement [filɔzɔfikmɑ̃] adv philosophically.
philtre [filtʀ] nm philtre. **~ d'amour** love potion.
phlébite [flebit] nf phlebitis.
phlébologie [flebɔlɔʒi] nf phlebology.
phlébologue [flebɔlɔg] nmf vein specialist.
phlébotomie [flebɔtɔmi] nf phlebotomy.
phlegmon [flɛgmɔ̃] nm abscess, phlegmon (SPÉC).
phlox [flɔks] nm inv phlox.
Phnom Penh [pnɔmpɛn] n Phnom Penh.
phobie [fɔbi] nf phobia. **avoir la ~ de** to have a phobia about.
phobique [fɔbik] adj, nmf phobic.
phocéen, -enne [fɔseɛ̃, ɛn] 1 adj Phocaean. **la cité ~ne** Marseilles. 2 nm,f: **P~(ne)** Phocaean.
phonateur, -trice [fɔnatœʀ, tʀis] adj phonatory.
phonation [fɔnasjɔ̃] nf phonation.
phonatoire [fɔnatwaʀ] adj = **phonateur.**
phone [fɔn] nm phone.
phonématique [fɔnematik] nf phonology, phonemics (*sg*).
phonème [fɔnɛm] nm phoneme.
phonémique [fɔnemik] 1 adj phonemic. 2 nf = **phonématique.**
phonéticien, -ienne [fɔnetisjɛ̃, jɛn] nm, f phonetician.
phonétique [fɔnetik] 1 nf phonetics (*sg*). **~ articulatoire/acoustique/auditoire** articulatory/acoustic/auditory phonetics. 2 adj phonetic. **changement/loi/système ~** sound change/law/system.
phonétiquement [fɔnetikmɑ̃] adv phonetically.
phoniatre [fɔnjatʀ] nmf speech therapist.
phoniatrie [fɔnjatʀi] nf speech therapy.
phonie [fɔni] nf wireless telegraphy (*Brit*), radiotelegraphy.
phonique [fɔnik] adj phonic.
phono [fono] nm (abrév de **phonographe**) (*phonographe*) (wind-up) gramophone (*Brit*), phonograph (*US*); (*électrophone*) record player.
phonographe [fɔnɔgʀaf] nm (wind-up) gramophone (*Brit*), phonograph (*US*).
phonographique [fɔnɔgʀafik] adj phonographic.
phonologie [fɔnɔlɔʒi] nf phonology.
phonologique [fɔnɔlɔʒik] adj phonological.
phonologue [fɔnɔlɔg] nmf phonologist.
phonothèque [fɔnɔtɛk] nf sound archives.
phoque [fɔk] nm (*animal*) seal; (*fourrure*) sealskin; *voir* **souffler.**
phosphatage [fɔsfataʒ] nm treating with phosphates.
phosphate [fɔsfat] nm phosphate.
phosphaté, e [fɔsfate] (ptp de **phosphater**) adj phosphatic, phosphated. **engrais ~s** phosphate-enriched fertilizers.
phosphater [fɔsfate] [1] vt to phosphate, treat with phosphates.
phosphène [fɔsfɛn] nm phosphene.
phosphine [fɔsfin] nf phosphine.
phosphore [fɔsfɔʀ] nm phosphorus.
phosphoré, e [fɔsfɔʀe] adj phosphorous.
phosphorer* [fɔsfɔʀe] [1] vi to think hard.
phosphorescence [fɔsfɔʀesɑ̃s] nf luminosity, phosphorescence (SPÉC).
phosphorescent, e [fɔsfɔʀesɑ̃, ɑ̃t] adj luminous, phosphorescent (SPÉC).
phosphoreux, -euse [fɔsfɔʀø, øz] adj *acide* phosphorous; *bronze* phosphor (*épith*).
phosphorique [fɔsfɔʀik] adj phosphoric.
phosphure [fɔsfyʀ] nm phosphide.
phot [fɔt] nm (*Phys*) phot.
photo [fɔto] nf (abrév de **photographie**) (*image*) photo, snap(shot), shot. **faire une ~ de, prendre en ~** to take a photo *ou* snap(shot) *ou* shot of; **en ~ ça rend bien** it looks good in *ou* on a photo; **elle est bien en ~** she looks good in photos; **tu veux ma ~?*** have I got two heads or something? (*iro*); *voir* **appareil.**
photochimie [fɔtoʃimi] nf photochemistry.
photochimique [fɔtoʃimik] adj photochemical.
photocomposer [fɔtokɔ̃poze] [1] vt to photocompose, filmset.
photocomposeur [fɔtokɔ̃pozœʀ] nm = **photocompositeur.**
photocomposeuse [fɔtokɔ̃pozøz] nf (*machine*) photocomposer, filmsetter.
photocompositeur [fɔtokɔ̃pozitœʀ] nm (photo)typesetter.
photocomposition [fɔtokɔ̃pozisjɔ̃] nf photocomposition, filmsetting.
photoconducteur, -trice [fɔtokɔ̃dyktœʀ, tʀis] adj photoconductive.
photocopie [fɔtɔkɔpi] nf (*action*) photocopying, photostatting; (*copie*) photocopy, photostat (copy).
photocopier [fɔtɔkɔpje] [7] vt to photocopy, photostat.
photocopieur [fɔtɔkɔpjœʀ] nm, **photocopieuse** [fɔtɔkɔpjøz] nf photocopier, photostat.
photodissociation [fɔtodisɔsjasjɔ̃] nf photodistintegration.
photoélasticimétrie [fɔtoelastisimetʀi] nf photoelasticity.
photoélectricité [fɔtoelɛktʀisite] nf photoelectricity.
photoélectrique [fɔtoelɛktʀik] adj photoelectric. **cellule ~** photoelectric cell, photocell.
photo-finish [fɔtofiniʃ] nf: **l'arrivée de la deuxième course a dû être contrôlée au ~** the second race was a photo finish.
photogénique [fɔtɔʒenik] adj photogenic.
photographe [fɔtɔgʀaf] nmf (*artiste*) photographer; (*commerçant*) camera dealer. **vous trouverez cet article chez un ~** you will find this item at a camera shop (*Brit*) *ou* store (*US*).
photographie [fɔtɔgʀafi] nf a (*art*) photography. **faire de la ~** (*comme passe-temps*) to be an amateur photographer, take photographs; (*en vacances*) to take photographs. b (*image*) photograph. **~ d'identité/en couleurs/aérienne** passport/colour/aerial photograph; **prendre une ~** to take a photograph *ou* a picture; **prendre qn en ~** to take a photograph *ou* a picture of sb, photograph sb.
photographier [fɔtɔgʀafje] [7] vt to photograph, take a photo(graph) of, take a picture of. **se faire ~** to have one's photo(graph) *ou* picture taken; (*fig: mémoriser*) **il avait photographié l'endroit** he had got the place firmly fixed in his mind *ou* in his mind's eye.
photographique [fɔtɔgʀafik] adj photographic; *voir* **appareil.**
photographiquement [fɔtɔgʀafikmɑ̃] adv photographically.
photograveur [fɔtɔgʀavœʀ] nm photoengraver.
photogravure [fɔtɔgʀavyʀ] nf photoengraving.
photojournalisme [fɔtoʒuʀnalism] nm photojournalism.
photolithographie [fɔtolitɔgʀafi] nf photolithography.
photoluminescence [fɔtolyminesɑ̃s] nf photoluminescence.
photolyse [fɔtɔliz] nf photolysis.
Photomaton [fɔtɔmatɔ̃] 1 nm ® automatic photo booth, five-minute photo machine. 2 nf (photo booth) photo. **se faire faire des ~s** to get one's pictures taken (in a photo booth).
photomètre [fɔtɔmɛtʀ] nm photometer.
photométrie [fɔtɔmetʀi] nf photometry.
photométrique [fɔtɔmetʀik] adj photometric(al).
photomontage [fɔtomɔ̃taʒ] nm photomontage.
photomultiplicateur [fɔtomyltiplikatœʀ] nm photomultiplier.
photon [fɔtɔ̃] nm photon.
photopériode [fɔtopeʀjɔd] nf photoperiod.
photopériodique [fɔtopeʀjɔdik] adj photoperiodic.

photopériodisme [fɔtopeʀjɔdism] nm photoperiodism.
photophobie [fɔtɔfɔbi] nf photophobia.
photopile [fɔtopil] nf solar cell.
photoréalisme [fɔtoʀealism] nm photorealism.
photoreportage [fɔtoʀəpɔʀtaʒ] nm photo story.
photoroman [fɔtoʀɔmɑ̃] nm photo love story.
photosensible [fɔtosɑ̃sibl] adj photosensitive. **dispositif ~** photosensor.
photostat [fɔtɔsta] nm photostat.
photostoppeur, -euse [fɔtɔstɔpœʀ, øz] nm,f street photographer.
photostyle [fɔtɔstil] nm light pen.
photosynthèse [fɔtosɛ̃tɛz] nf photosynthesis.
photothèque [fɔtɔtɛk] nf photographic library, picture library.
phrase [fʀɑz] nf (*Ling*) sentence; (*propos*) phrase; (*Mus*) phrase. **faire des ~s** to talk in flowery language; **assez de grandes ~s!** enough of the rhetoric *ou* fine words!; **~ toute faite** stock phrase; **citer une ~ célèbre** to quote a famous phrase *ou* saying; **sans ~s** without mincing matters; (*Ling*) **~ clivée/-noyau** *ou* **nucléaire** cleft/kernel sentence; (*Pol*) **les petites ~s de la semaine** the sayings of the week; *voir* **membre**.
phrasé [fʀɑze] nm (*Mus*) phrasing.
phraséologie [fʀazeɔlɔʒi] nf (*vocabulaire spécifique*) phraseology; (*péj*) fine words (*péj*), high-flown language (*péj*).
phraséologique [fʀazeɔlɔʒik] adj *dictionnaire* of phrases; (*péj*) *style* high-flown (*péj*), pretentious.
phraser [fʀɑze] [1] 1 vt (*Mus*) to phrase. 2 vi (*péj*) to use fine words (*péj*) *ou* high-flown language (*péj*).
phraseur, -euse [fʀɑzœʀ, øz] nm,f man (*ou* woman) of fine words (*péj*).
phrastique [fʀastik] adj phrasal.
phréatique [fʀeatik] adj *voir* **nappe**.
phrénique [fʀenik] adj phrenic.
phrénologie [fʀenɔlɔʒi] nf phrenology.
phrénologue [fʀenɔlɔg] nmf, **phrénologiste** [fʀenɔlɔʒist] nmf phrenologist.
Phrygie [fʀiʒi] nf Phrygia.
phrygien, -ienne [fʀiʒjɛ̃, jɛn] 1 adj Phrygian; *voir* **bonnet**. 2 nm,f: **P~(ne)** Phrygian.
phtaléine [ftalein] nf phthalein.
phtisie [ftizi] nf consumption, phthisis (*SPÉC*). **~ galopante** galloping consumption.
phtisiologie [ftizjɔlɔʒi] nf phthisiology.
phtisiologue [ftizjɔlɔg] nmf phthisiologist.
phtisique [ftizik] adj consumptive, phthisical (*SPÉC*).
phycologie [fikɔlɔʒi] nf phycology.
phylactère [filaktɛʀ] nm phylactery.
phylloxéra [filɔkseʀa] nm phylloxera.
phylogenèse [filoʒənɛz] nf phylogenesis.
phylogénique [filɔʒenik] adj phylogenetic, phyletic.
physicien, -ienne [fizisjɛ̃, jɛn] nm,f physicist. **~ atomiste** *ou* **nucléaire** atomic *ou* nuclear physicist.
physico-chimie [fizikoʃimi] nf physical chemistry.
physico-chimique [fizikoʃimik] adj physico-chemical.
physico-mathématique [fizikomatematik] adj of mathematical physics.
physiocrate [fizjɔkʀat] 1 nmf physiocrat. 2 adj physiocratic.
physiocratie [fizjɔkʀasi] nf physiocracy.
physiologie [fizjɔlɔʒi] nf physiology.
physiologique [fizjɔlɔʒik] adj physiological.
physiologiquement [fizjɔlɔʒikmɑ̃] adv physiologically.
physiologiste [fizjɔlɔʒist] 1 nmf physiologist. 2 adj physiological.
physionomie [fizjɔnɔmi] nf (*traits du visage*) facial appearance (*NonC*), physiognomy (*frm*); (*expression*) countenance (*frm*), face; (*fig: aspect*) face. **d'après la ~ des événements** according to the look of events, the way events are looking.
physionomiste [fizjɔnɔmist] adj, nmf: **c'est un ~, il est ~** (*bon jugement*) he's a good judge of faces; (*bonne mémoire*) he has a good memory for faces.
physiothérapie [fizjoteʀapi] nf natural medicine.
physique [fizik] 1 adj a (*gén*) physical; *voir* **amour, culture, personne**. b (*athlétique*) *joueur, match, jeu* physical. 2 nm (*aspect*) physique; (*visage*) face. **au ~** physically; **avoir un ~ agréable** to be quite good-looking; **avoir le ~ de l'emploi** to look the part. 3 nf physics (*sg*). **~ mathématique** mathematical physics; **~ nucléaire** atomic *ou* nuclear physics.
physiquement [fizikmɑ̃] adv physically. **il est plutôt bien ~** physically he's quite attractive.
phytobiologie [fitobjɔlɔʒi] nf phytology.
phytogéographie [fitoʒeɔgʀafi] nf phytogeography.
phytopathologie [fitopatɔlɔʒi] nf phytopathology.
phytoplancton [fitoplɑ̃ktɔ̃] nm phytoplankton.
phytothérapie [fitoteʀapi] nf herbal medicine.
pi [pi] nm (*lettre, Math*) pi.
p.i. (abrév de **par intérim**) acting, actg.
piaf* [pjaf] nm sparrow.
piaffement [pjafmɑ̃] nm *[cheval]* stamping, pawing.
piaffer [pjafe] [1] vi *[cheval]* to stamp, paw the ground; *[personne]* **~ d'impatience** to fidget with impatience *ou* impatiently.
piaillard, e* [pjɑjaʀ, aʀd] (*voir* **piailler**) 1 adj squawking (*épith*); screeching (*épith*); squealing (*épith*). 2 nm,f squawker, squealer.
piaillement* [pjɑjmɑ̃] nm (*voir* **piailler**) squawking (*NonC*); screeching (*NonC*); squealing (*NonC*).
piailler* [pjɑje] [1] vi *[oiseau]* to squawk, screech; *[personne]* to squawk, squeal.
piaillerie* [pjɑjʀi] nf = **piaillement***.
piailleur, -euse* [pjɑjœʀ, øz] = **piaillard***.
piane-piane* [pjanpjan] adv gently. **allez-y ~** go gently *ou* easy*, easy *ou* gently does it*; **le projet avance ~** the project is coming along slowly but surely.
pianiste [pjanist] nmf pianist, piano player.
pianistique [pjanistik] adj pianistic.
piano [pjano] 1 nm piano. **~ droit/à queue/de concert/demi-queue/quart de queue/crapaud** upright/grand/concert grand/baby grand/miniature grand/boudoir grand (piano); **~ mécanique** player piano, Pianola ®; **~ électronique** electric piano; (*hum*) **~ à bretelles** squeeze-box*; **se mettre au ~** (*apprendre*) to take up *ou* start the piano; (*s'asseoir*) to sit down at the piano; **~-bar** piano bar. 2 adv (*Mus*) piano; (** fig*) gently. **allez-y ~** easy *ou* gently does it*, go easy* *ou* gently.
piano(-)forte [pjanofɔʀte] nm pianoforte.
pianotage [pjanɔtaʒ] nm (*voir* **pianoter**) tinkling (at the piano *ou* typewriter *etc*); drumming.
pianoter [pjanɔte] [1] 1 vi (*sur un clavier*) to tinkle away (at the piano *ou* typewriter *etc*); (*fig*) to drum one's fingers. 2 vt *signal, code* to tap out. **~ un air** to strum (out) *ou* tinkle out a tune on the piano.
piastre [pjastʀ] nf piastre; (*Can: dollar*) (Canadian) dollar.
piaule* [pjol] nf pad‡.
piaulement [pjolmɑ̃] nm (*voir* **piauler**) cheeping (*NonC*); whimpering (*NonC*).
piauler [pjole] [1] vi *[oiseau]* to cheep; *[enfant]* to whimper.
P.I.B. [peibe] nm (abrév de **produit intérieur brut**) GDP.
pic [pik] nm a (*montagne, cime*) peak. b (*pioche*) pick(axe). **~ à glace** ice pick. c (*oiseau*) **~(vert)** (green) woodpecker. d (*loc*) **à ~** (adv) vertically, sheer, straight down; (adj) sheer; **couler à ~** to go straight down; (*fig*) **arriver** *ou* **tomber à ~*** to come just at the right time *ou* moment; **vous arrivez à ~*** you couldn't have come at a better time *ou* moment, you've come just at the right time *ou* moment.
pica [pika] nm (*Typ*) pica.
picaillons* [pikajɔ̃] nmpl cash* (*NonC*).
picard, e [pikaʀ, aʀd] 1 adj Picardy. 2 nm (*Ling*) Picardy dialect. 3 nm,f: **P~(e)** inhabitant *ou* native of Picardy.
Picardie [pikaʀdi] nf Picardy.
picaresque [pikaʀɛsk] adj picaresque.
piccolo [pikɔlo] nm piccolo.
pichenette* [piʃnɛt] nf flick. **faire tomber d'une ~** to flick off *ou* away.
pichet [piʃɛ] nm pitcher, jug.
pickpocket [pikpɔkɛt] nm pickpocket.
pick-up*† [pikœp] nm inv (*bras*) pickup; (*électrophone*) record player.
pico- [piko] préf pico. **~seconde** picosecond.
picoler‡ [pikɔle] [1] vi to booze‡, knock it back‡, tipple*. **qu'est-ce qu'il peut ~!** he fairly knocks it back!‡ (*Brit*), he sure can knock it back!‡ (*US*); **~ dur** to hit the bottle* (*Brit*) *ou* sauce* (*US*).
picoleur, -euse‡ [pikɔlœʀ, øz] nm,f tippler*, boozer‡.
picorer [pikɔʀe] [1] 1 vi to peck (about); (*manger très peu*) to nibble. 2 vt to peck, peck (away) at.
picot [piko] nm *[dentelle]* picot; *[planche]* burr; (*petite pointe*) spike. (*Ordin*) **dispositif d'entraînement à ~s** tractor drive.
picotement [pikɔtmɑ̃] nm *[gorge]* tickle (*NonC*), tickling (*NonC*); *[peau, membres]* smarting (*NonC*), prickling (*NonC*); *[yeux]* smarting (*NonC*), stinging (*NonC*).
picoter [pikɔte] [1] 1 vt a (*piquer*) *gorge* to tickle; *peau* to make smart *ou* prickle; *yeux* to make smart, sting; (*avec une épingle*) to prick. **la fumée lui picote les yeux** the smoke is making his eyes smart *ou* is stinging his eyes; **j'ai les yeux qui me picotent** my eyes are smarting *ou* stinging. b (*picorer*) to peck, peck (away) at. 2 vi *[gorge]* to tickle; *[peau]* to smart, prickle; *[yeux]* to smart, sting.
picotin [pikɔtɛ̃] nm (*ration d'avoine*) oats (*pl*), ration of oats; (*mesure*) peck.
picouse* [pikuz] nf (*piqûre*) shot*, jab* (*Brit*).
picrate* [pikʀat] nm (*péj*) plonk* (*Brit*), cheap wine.
picrique [pikʀik] adj: **acide ~** picric acid.
Pictes [pikt] nmpl Picts.
pictogramme [piktɔgʀam] nm pictogram.
pictographie [piktɔgʀafi] nf pictography.
pictographique [piktɔgʀafik] adj pictographic.
pictural, e, mpl **-aux** [piktyʀal, o] adj pictorial.
pidgin [pidʒin] nm pidgin. **~-english** pidgin English.
Pie [pi] nm Pius.
pie¹ [pi] 1 nf (*oiseau*) magpie; (** fig: bavarde*) chatterbox*, gasbag* (*péj*), windbag*. 2 adj inv *cheval* piebald; *vache* black and white; *voir* **voiture**.

pie² [pi] adj f *voir* **œuvre**.

pièce [pjɛs] 1 nf a (*fragment*) piece. **en ~s** in pieces; **mettre en ~s** (*lit*) (*casser*) to smash to pieces; (*déchirer*) to pull *ou* tear to pieces; (*fig*) to tear *ou* pull to pieces; **c'est inventé** *ou* **forgé de toutes ~s** it's made up from start to finish, it's a complete fabrication; **fait d'une seule ~** made in one piece; **fait de ~s et de morceaux** (*lit*) made with *ou* of bits and pieces; (*fig péj*) cobbled together; **il est tout d'une ~** he's very cut and dried about things; *voir* **tailler, tout**.

b (*gén: unité, objet*) piece; *[jeu d'échecs, de dames]* piece; *[tissu, drap]* length, piece; (*Mil*) gun; (*Chasse, Pêche: prise*) specimen. (*Comm*) **se vendre à la ~** to be sold separately *ou* individually; **2 F (la) ~** 2 francs each *ou* apiece; **travail à la ~** *ou* **aux ~s** piecework; **payé à la ~** *ou* **aux ~s** on piece(work) rate, on piecework; (*fig*) **on n'est pas aux ~s!** there's no rush!; (*Habillement*) **un deux-~s** (*costume, tailleur*) a two-piece (suit); (*maillot de bain*) a two-piece (swimsuit); *voir* **chef¹**.

c *[machine, voiture]* part, component. **~s (de rechange)** spares, (spare) parts; **~ d'origine** guaranteed genuine spare part.

d (*document*) paper, document. **avez-vous toutes les ~s nécessaires?** have you got all the necessary papers? *ou* documents?; **juger/décider sur ~s** to judge/decide on actual evidence; **avec ~s à l'appui** with supporting documents; (*Admin, Jur*) **les plaintes doivent être accompagnées de ~s justificatives** complaints must be documented *ou* accompanied by written proof *ou* evidence.

e (*Couture*) patch. **mettre une ~ à qch** to put a patch on sth.

f *[maison]* room. **appartement de 5 ~s** 5-room(ed) flat; **un deux ~s (cuisine)** a 2-room(ed) flat (*Brit*) *ou* apartment (*US*) (with kitchen).

g (*Théât*) play; (*Littérat, Mus*) piece. **jouer** *ou* **monter une ~ de Racine** to put on a play by Racine; **une ~ pour hautbois** a piece for oboe.

h **~ (de monnaie)** coin; **~ d'argent/d'or** silver/gold coin; **une ~ de 5 francs/de 50 centimes** a 5-franc/50-centime piece *ou* coin; **donner la ~ à qn*** to give *ou* slip* sb a tip, tip sb; *voir* **rendre**.

2 comp ▸**pièce d'artifice** firework ▸**pièce d'artillerie** piece of ordnance ▸**pièce de bétail** head of cattle; **50 pièces de bétail** 50 head of cattle ▸**pièce de blé** wheat field, cornfield (*Brit*) ▸**pièce de bois** piece of wood *ou* timber (*for joinery etc*) ▸**pièce de charpente** member ▸**pièce de collection** collector's item *ou* piece ▸**pièce comptable** accounting record ▸**pièce à conviction** (*Jur*) exhibit ▸**pièce détachée** spare, (spare) part; **livré en pièces détachées** (delivered) in kit form ▸**pièce d'eau** ornamental lake *ou* pond ▸**pièce d'identité** identity paper; **avez-vous une pièce d'identité?** have you (got) any identification? *ou* some means of identification? ▸**pièces jointes** (*Admin*) enclosures ▸**pièce montée** (*Culin*) *elaborately constructed and decorated cake*, ≃ tiered cake; (*à une noce*) wedding cake ▸**pièce de musée** museum piece ▸**pièce rapportée** (*Couture*) patch; *[marqueterie, mosaïque]* insert, piece; (* *hum*) (*belle-sœur, beau-frère etc*) outsider (*hum*); (*dans un groupe*) late addition ▸**pièce de résistance** main dish, pièce de résistance ▸**pièce de terre** piece *ou* patch of land ▸**pièce de théâtre** play ▸**pièce de vers** piece of poetry, short poem ▸**pièce de viande** side of meat ▸**pièce de vin** cask of wine.

piécette [pjesɛt] nf small coin.

pied [pje] 1 nm a (*gén*) *[personne, animal]* foot; (*sabot*) *[cheval, bœuf]* hoof; (*Zool*) *[mollusque]* foot. **bétail sur ~** beef (*ou* mutton *etc*) on the hoof; **aller ~s nus** *ou* **nu-pieds** to go barefoot(ed); **avoir les ~s plats** to have flat feet, be flatfooted; **avoir les ~s en dedans/dehors** to have turned-in/turned-out feet, be pigeon-toed/splay-footed; **marcher les ~s en dedans/dehors** to walk with one's feet turned in/turned out, walk pigeon-toed/splay-footed; **à ~s joints** with one's feet together; **le ~ lui a manqué** he lost his footing, his foot slipped; **aller à ~** to go on foot, walk; **nous avons fait tout le chemin à ~** we walked all the way, we came all the way on foot; **il est incapable de mettre un ~ devant l'autre** he can't walk straight, he can't put one foot in front of the other; **il ne tient pas sur ses ~s** (*alcool*) he can hardly stand up; (*maladie*) he's dead on his feet; **sauter d'un ~ sur l'autre** to hop from one foot to the other; (*lit, fig*) **~s et poings liés** tied *ou* bound hand and foot; **coup de ~** (*gén, Sport*) kick; **donner un coup de ~ à** *ou* **dans** to kick; **il a reçu un coup de ~** he was kicked; (*fig*) **un coup de ~ au derrière*** a kick in the pants* *ou* up the backside*.

b *[table]* leg; *[arbre, colline, échelle, lit, mur]* foot, bottom; *[appareil-photo]* stand, tripod; *[lampe]* base; *[lampadaire]* stand; *[verre]* stem; *[colonne]* base, foot; *[chaussette]* foot; (*Math*) *[perpendiculaire]* foot.

c (*Agr*) *[salade, tomate]* plant. **~ de laitue** lettuce (plant); **~ de céleri** head of celery; **~ de vigne** vine; **blé sur ~** standing *ou* uncut corn (*Brit*) *ou* wheat (*US*).

d (*Culin*) *[porc, mouton, veau]* trotter.

e (*mesure*) foot. **un poteau de 6 ~s** a 6-foot pole; **j'aurai voulu être à 100 ~s sous terre** I wished the ground would open up (and swallow me), I could have died*.

f (*Poésie*) foot.

g (*niveau*) **vivre sur un grand ~** to live in (great *ou* grand) style; **sur un ~ d'amitié** on a friendly footing; **sur un ~ d'égalité** on an equal footing, as equals.

h (*‡: idiot*) twit* (*Brit*), idiot. **quel ~!** what a useless twit!* (*Brit*), what an idiot!; **jouer comme un ~** to be a useless* *ou* lousy‡ player; **il s'y prend comme un ~** he hasn't a clue how to go about it*; **il conduit/chante comme un ~** he hasn't a clue about driving/singing*.

i (‡) **c'est le ~, quel ~** it's brilliant* *ou* great*; **ce n'est pas le ~** it's no picnic* *ou* fun; **c'est une solution mais ce n'est pas le ~** it is a solution but it's not brilliant* *ou* great*; **prendre son ~** (*s'amuser*) to get one's kicks‡ (*avec* with); (*sexuellement*) to have a steamy session‡ (*avec* with).

j (*loc: avec prép*) **~ à ~** *se défendre, lutter* every inch of the way; **au ~ de la lettre** literally; **remplacer qn au ~ levé** to stand in for sb at a moment's notice; **à ~ d'œuvre** ready to get down to the job; **à ~ sec** without getting one's feet wet; **de ~ ferme** resolutely; **en ~** *portrait* full-length; *statue* full-scale, full-size; **se jeter aux ~s de qn** to throw o.s. at sb's feet; **des ~s à la tête** from head to foot; **de ~ en cap** from head to foot, from top to toe; **sur le ~ de guerre** (all) ready to go, ready for action; *voir* **petit**.

k (*loc: avec verbes*) **avoir ~** to be able to touch the bottom (*in swimming*); **je n'ai plus ~** I'm out of my depth (*lit*); **perdre ~** (*lit: en nageant, aussi fig*) to be *ou* get out of one's depth; (*en montagne*) to lose one's footing; **avoir bon ~ bon œil** to be as fit as a fiddle, be fighting fit; **avoir le ~ léger** to be light of step; **avoir le ~ marin** to be a good sailor; **avoir les (deux) ~s sur terre** to have one's feet firmly (planted) on the ground; **avoir le ~ à l'étrier** to be well on the way; **mettre le ~ à l'étrier à qn** to give sb a leg up (*Brit*) *ou* a boost; (*fig*) **prendre ~ sur un marché** to gain *ou* get a foothold in a market; (*fig*) **avoir un ~ dans la firme** to have a foothold *ou* a toehold in the firm; **avoir un ~ dans la tombe** to have one foot in the grave; **être sur ~** *[projet]* to be under way; *[malade]* to be up and about; **mettre qch sur ~** to set sth up; **remettre qn sur ~** to set sb back on his feet again; **faire du ~ à qn** (*prévenir*) to give sb a warning kick; (*galamment*) to play footsy with sb*; **faire le ~ de grue** to stand about (waiting), kick one's heels (*Brit*); **faire des ~s et des mains pour faire qch*** to move heaven and earth to do sth, pull out all the stops to do sth*; **faire un ~ de nez à qn** to thumb one's nose at sb, cock a snook at sb (*Brit*); **cela lui fera les ~s*** that'll teach him (a thing or two)*; **mettre qn à ~** to dismiss sb; **mettre ~ à terre** to dismount; **mettre les ~s chez qn** to set foot in sb's house; **je n'y remettrai jamais le(s) ~(s)** I'll never set foot (in) there again; **je n'ai pas mis les ~s dehors aujourd'hui** I haven't stepped *ou* been outside all day; **mettre qn au ~ du mur** to get sb with his back to the wall (*fig*); **mettre les ~s dans le plat*** (*se fâcher*) to put one's foot down; (*gaffer*) to boob‡, put one's foot in it; (*mourir*) **partir** *ou* **sortir les ~s devant*** to go out feet first; **prendre ~ dans/sur** to get a foothold in/on; (*sur une annonce*) **"les ~s dans l'eau"** "on the waterfront"; *voir* **casser, deux, lâcher, retomber** *etc*.

2 comp ▸**pied-d'alouette** nm (*Bot*) (pl **pieds-d'alouette**) larkspur ▸**pied d'athlète** (*Méd*) athlete's foot ▸**pied-de-biche** nm (pl **pieds-de-biche**) *[machine à coudre]* presser foot; *[meuble]* cabriole leg; (*levier*) claw ▸**pied-bot** nm (pl **pieds-bots**) person with a club-foot ▸**pied-de-cheval** nm (pl **pieds-de-cheval**) native oyster ▸**pied à coulisse** calliper rule ▸**pied de fer** (cobbler's) last ▸**pied de lit** footboard ▸**pied-de-loup** nm (*Bot*) (pl **pieds-de-loup**) club moss ▸**pied de nivellement** *ou* **autoréglable** (*sur un meuble*) self-levelling foot ▸**pied-noir** nm (pl **pieds-noirs**) pied-noir, *Algerian-born Frenchman or woman* ▸**pied-d'oiseau** nm (*Bot*) (pl **pieds-d'oiseau**) bird's foot ▸**pied-plat** nm (pl **pieds-plats**) (*littér*) lout ▸**pied-de-poule** adj inv hound's-tooth ◊ nm (pl **pieds-de-poule**) hound's-tooth cloth (*NonC*) *ou* material (*NonC*) ▸**pied-de-roi** nm (*Can*) (pl **pieds-de-roi**) folding foot-rule ▸**pied-à-terre** nm inv pied-à-terre ▸**pied-de-veau** nm (*Bot*) (pl **pieds-de-veau**) lords and ladies, cuckoopint.

piédestal, pl **-aux** [pjedɛstal, o] nm (*lit, fig*) pedestal.

piège [pjɛʒ] nm (*lit, fig*) trap; (*fosse*) pit; (*collet*) snare. **les ~s d'une version/dictée** the pitfalls of a translation/dictation; **~ à rats/à moineaux** rat-/sparrow-trap; **~ à loups** mantrap; **prendre au ~** to (catch in a) trap; **être pris à son propre ~** to be caught in *ou* fall into one's own trap; **tendre un ~ (à qn)** to set a trap (for sb); **traduction pleine de ~s** translation full of tricks *ou* traps; **donner** *ou* **tomber dans le ~** to fall into the trap, be trapped.

piégé, e [pjeʒe] (ptp de **piéger**) adj: **engin ~** booby trap; **lettre ~e** letter bomb; **colis ~** parcel *ou* mail bomb; **voiture ~e** car bomb.

piégeage [pjeʒaʒ] nm (*voir* **piéger**) trapping; setting of booby traps (*de* in).

piéger [pjeʒe] 3 vt a *animal*, (*fig*) *personne* to trap. **se faire ~** to be trapped, find o.s. in a trap; **se faire ~ par un radar** to get caught in a radar trap. b *bois, arbre* to set a trap *ou* traps in; (*avec des explosifs*) *engin, porte* to booby-trap.

pie-grièche, pl **pies-grièches** [pigʀijɛʃ] nf shrike.

pie-mère, pl **pies-mères** [pimɛʀ] nf pia mater.

Piémont [pjemɔ̃] nm Piedmont.

piémontais, e [pjemɔ̃tɛ, ɛz] 1 adj Piedmontese. 2 nm (*Ling*) Piedmontese. 3 nm,f: **P~(e)** Piedmontese.

piéride [pjeʀid] nf pierid, pieridine butterfly. **~ du chou** cabbage white (butterfly).

pierraille [pjeʀɑj] nf *[route, sentier]* loose stones (*pl*), chippings (*pl*); *[pente, montagne]* scree (*NonC*), loose stones (*pl*), chippings (*pl*).

Pierre [pjɛʀ] nm Peter.

pierre [pjɛʀ] 1 nf a (*gén, Méd*) stone. *[fruits]* ~s† grit (*NonC*); **maison de** *ou* **en** ~ stone(-built) house, house built of stone; **attaquer qn à coups de ~s** to throw stones at sb, stone sb; (*fig*) **il resta** *ou* **son visage resta de** ~ he remained stony-faced; (*fig*) **cœur de** ~ heart of stone, stony heart; *voir* **âge, casseur, jeter** *etc.*
b (*fig: immobilier*) **la** ~ bricks and mortar; **investir dans la** ~ to invest in bricks and mortar.
c (*loc*) **faire d'une** ~ **deux coups** to kill two birds with one stone; (*Prov*) ~ **qui roule n'amasse pas mousse** a rolling stone gathers no moss (*Prov*); **c'est une** ~ **dans son jardin** it is a black mark against him; **jour à marquer d'une** ~ **blanche** red-letter day; **jour à marquer d'une** ~ **noire** black day; **bâtir qch** ~ **à** ~ to build sth up piece by piece *ou* stone by stone; **ils n'ont pas laissé** ~ **sur** ~ they didn't leave a stone standing; **apporter sa** ~ **à qch** to add one's contribution to sth; **aimer les vieilles ~s** to like old buildings.
2 comp ►**pierre d'achoppement** stumbling block ►**pierre à aiguiser** whetstone ►**pierre angulaire** (*lit, fig*) cornerstone ►**pierre à bâtir** building stone ►**pierre à briquet** flint ►**pierre à chaux** limestone ►**pierre à feu** flint ►**pierre fine** semiprecious stone ►**pierre funéraire** tombstone, gravestone ►**pierre à fusil** gunflint ►**pierre de lard** French chalk, tailor's chalk ►**pierre levée** standing stone ►**pierre de lune** moonstone ►**pierre ollaire** soapstone, steatite (*SPÉC*) ►**pierre philosophale** philosopher's stone ►**pierre ponce** pumice stone, pumice (*NonC*) ►**pierre précieuse** precious stone, gem ►**mur en pierres sèches** drystone wall *ou* dyke ►**pierre de taille** freestone ►**pierre tombale** tombstone, gravestone ►**pierre de touche** (*lit, fig*) touchstone.

pierreries [pjɛʀʀi] nfpl gems, precious stones.

pierreux, -euse [pjeʀø, øz] adj *terrain* stony; *fruit* gritty; (*Méd*) calculous (*SPÉC*).

Pierrot [pjɛʀo] nm a (*prénom*) Pete. b (*Théât*) Pierrot.

pierrot [pjeʀo] nm (*Orn*) sparrow.

pietà [pjeta] nf pietà.

piétaille [pjetɑj] nf (*Mil péj*) rank and file; (*fig: subalternes*) rank and file, menials; (*fig: piétons*) pedestrians.

piété [pjete] nf (*Rel*) piety; (*attachement*) devotion, reverence. ~ **filiale** filial devotion *ou* respect; **articles/livre de** ~ devotional articles/book; **images de** ~ pious images; *voir* **mont.**

piètement [pjɛtmɑ̃] nm *[meuble]* base.

piétinement [pjetinmɑ̃] nm a (*stagnation*) **le** ~ **de la discussion** the fact that the discussion is not (*ou* was not) making (any) progress; **vu le** ~ **de l'enquête** given that the investigation is (*ou* was) at a virtual standstill. b (*marche sur place*) standing about. **le** ~ **auquel nous contraignait la foule** being forced to stand about because of the crowd. c (*bruit*) stamping.

piétiner [pjetine] [1] 1 vi a (*trépigner*) to stamp (one's foot *ou* feet). ~ **de colère/d'impatience** to stamp (one's feet) angrily/impatiently.
b (*ne pas avancer*) *[personne]* to stand about; *[cortège]* to mark time; *[discussion]* to make no progress; *[affaire, enquête]* to be at a virtual standstill, hang fire, make no headway; *[économie, science]* to stagnate, be at a standstill. ~ **dans la boue** to trudge through the mud.
2 vt *sol* to trample on; *victime,* (*fig*) *adversaire* to trample underfoot; *parterres, fleurs* to trample on, trample underfoot, tread on. **plusieurs personnes furent piétinées** several people were trampled on *ou* trampled underfoot; (*fig*) ~ **les principes de qn** to trample sb's principles underfoot, ride roughshod over sb's principles; *voir* **plat[1]**.

piétisme [pjetism] nm pietism.

piétiste [pjetist] 1 adj pietistic. 2 nmf pietist.

piéton[1] [pjetɔ̃] nm pedestrian.

piéton[2], -onne [pjetɔ̃, ɔn] adj, **piétonnier, -ière** [pjetɔnje, jɛʀ] adj pedestrian (*épith*). **rue ~onne** *ou* **~ière** pedestrianized street; **zone ~onne** *ou* **~ière** pedestrian precinct, mall (*US*).

piètre [pjɛtʀ] adj (*frm*) *adversaire, écrivain, roman* very poor, mediocre; *excuse* paltry, lame. **c'est une** ~ **consolation** it's small *ou* little comfort; **faire** ~ **figure** to cut a sorry figure; **avoir** ~ **allure** to be a sorry *ou* wretched sight.

piètrement [pjɛtʀəmɑ̃] adv very poorly, mediocrely.

pieu, pl ~x [pjø] nm a (*poteau*) post; (*pointu*) stake, pale; (*Constr*) pile. b (‡: *lit*) bed. **se mettre au** ~ to hit the hay* *ou* sack*, turn in*.

pieusement [pjøzmɑ̃] adv (*Rel*) piously; (*respectueusement*) reverently. (*hum*) **un vieux tricot qu'il avait** ~ **conservé** an old sweater which he had religiously kept.

pieuter‡ [pjøte] [1] 1 vi: **(aller)** ~ **chez qn** to kip (*Brit*) *ou* crash at sb's place‡. 2 **se pieuter** vpr to hit the hay* *ou* sack*, turn in*.

pieuvre [pjœvʀ] nf (*animal*) octopus; (*sandow*) spider. **cette entreprise est une** ~ this company has got its tentacles into everything; **cette ville est une** ~ this town engulfs everything (around it).

pieux, pieuse [pjø, pjøz] adj *personne* (*religieux*) pious, devout; (*dévoué*) devoted, dutiful; *pensée, souvenir, lecture, image* pious; *silence* reverent, respectful. ~ **mensonge** white lie (*told out of pity etc*).

piézo-électricité [pjezoelɛktʀisite] nf piezoelectricity.

piézo-électrique [pjezoelɛktʀik] adj piezoelectric.

piézomètre [pjezɔmɛtʀ] nm piezometer.

pif[1]‡ [pif] nm (*nez*) conk‡ (*Brit*), hooter‡ (*Brit*), beak‡. **au** ~ (*approximativement*) at a rough guess; (*au hasard*) *répondre, choisir* at random; *plan, exercice, recette* **faire au** ~ to do by guesswork.

pif[2] [pif] excl: ~! *ou* **paf!** (*explosion*) bang! bang!; (*gifle*) smack! smack!, slap! slap!

pif(f)er‡ [pife] vt: **je ne peux pas le** ~ I can't stand‡ *ou* stick‡ (*Brit*) him.

pifomètre‡ [pifɔmɛtʀ] nm intuition, instinct. **au** ~ at a rough guess; **faire qch au** ~ to do sth by guesswork; **aller (quelque part) au** ~ to follow one's nose*.

pifrer‡ [pifʀe] [1] = **pif(f)er.**

pige [piʒ] nf a (‡: *année*) **il a 50 ~s** he is 50, he has 50 years behind him; **à 60 ~s** at 60, when one is 60. b (*Presse, Typ*) **être payé à la** ~ *[typographe]* to be paid at piecework rates; *[journaliste]* to be paid by the line; *[artiste]* to be paid per commission. c (‡: *réussir*) **il nous fait la** ~ he leaves us standing*, he puts us all in the shade.

pigeon [piʒɔ̃] 1 nm (*oiseau*) pigeon; (*: *dupe*) mug‡, sucker‡. 2 comp ►**pigeon d'argile** clay pigeon ►**pigeon ramier** woodpigeon, ring dove ►**pigeon vole** (*jeu*) ≃ Simon says (*game of forfeits*) ►**pigeon voyageur** carrier *ou* homing pigeon; **par pigeon voyageur** by pigeon post.

pigeonnant, e [piʒɔnɑ̃, ɑ̃t] adj *soutien-gorge* uplift (*épith*). **poitrine ~e** high rounded bust.

pigeonne [piʒɔn] nf hen-pigeon.

pigeonneau, pl ~x [piʒɔno] nm young pigeon, squab (*SPÉC*).

pigeonner‡ [piʒɔne] [1] vt: ~ **qn** to do sb‡, take sb for a ride‡; **se laisser** *ou* **se faire** ~ to be done‡, be taken for a ride‡, be had*.

pigeonnier [piʒɔnje] nm pigeon house *ou* loft, dovecot(e); (*: *logement*) garret, attic room.

piger‡ [piʒe] [3] vi (*comprendre*) to twig‡ (*Brit*), get it*. **il a pigé** he has twigged‡ (*Brit*), the penny has dropped* (*Brit*), he has cottoned on* (*Brit*) *ou* caught on*; **tu piges?** (d'you) get it?*, dig?‡; **je ne pige pas** I don't get it*, I don't twig‡; **je ne pige rien à la chimie** chemistry's all Greek* *ou* double Dutch* (*Brit*) to me, chemistry just doesn't register with me*; **je n'y pige rien** I just don't get it (at all)*, I can't make head nor tail of it; **tu y piges quelque chose, toi?** do you get it?*, can you make anything of it?

pigiste [piʒist] nmf (*typographe*) (piecework) typesetter; (*journaliste*) freelance journalist (*paid by the line*); (*artiste*) freelance artist.

pigment [pigmɑ̃] nm pigment.

pigmentaire [pigmɑ̃tɛʀ] adj pigmentary, pigmental.

pigmentation [pigmɑ̃tasjɔ̃] nf pigmentation.

pigmenter [pigmɑ̃te] [1] vt to pigment.

pigne [piɲ] nf (*cône*) pine cone; (*graine*) pine kernel *ou* nut.

pignocher [piɲɔʃe] [1] vi to pick *ou* nibble at one's food.

pignon [piɲɔ̃] nm a (*Archit*) gable. **à** ~ gabled; (*fig*) **avoir** ~ **sur rue** to be prosperous and highly respected. b (*roue dentée*) cog(wheel), gearwheel; (*petite roue*) pinion. c (*Bot*) ~ **(de pin)** pine kernel *ou* nut.

pignouf‡ [piɲuf] nm peasant*, boor.

pilaf [pilaf] nm pilaf(f), pilau.

pilage [pilaʒ] nm crushing, pounding.

pilastre [pilastʀ] nm pilaster.

Pilate [pilat] nm Pilate.

pilchard [pilʃaʀ] nm pilchard.

pile [pil] 1 nf a (*tas*) pile, stack.
b *[pont]* support, pile, pier.
c (*Élec*) battery. **à ~(s)** battery (*épith*), battery-operated; ~ **sèche** dry cell *ou* battery; ~ **bâton** pencil battery; ~ **rechargeable** rechargeable battery; ~ **atomique** nuclear reactor, (atomic) pile; ~ **solaire** solar cell; **appareil à ~s** *ou* **fonctionnant sur ~s** battery-operated *ou* battery-driven appliance, cordless appliance.
d (‡) (*volée*) belting‡, hammering‡; (*défaite*) hammering‡, thrashing*, licking*. **donner une** ~ **à qn** (*rosser*) to give sb a belting‡ *ou* hammering‡, lay into sb‡; (*vaincre*) to lick sb*, beat sb hollow* (*Brit*); **prendre** *ou* **recevoir une** ~ (*volée*) to get a belting‡ *ou* hammering‡; (*défaite*) to be licked*, be beaten hollow* (*Brit*).
e *[pièce]* **c'est tombé sur (le côté)** ~ it came down tails; ~ **ou face?** heads or tails?; ~ **c'est moi, face c'est toi** tails it's me, heads it's you; **sur le côté** ~ **il y a ...** on the reverse side there's ...; **on va jouer** *ou* **tirer ça à** ~ **ou face** we'll toss up for it, we'll toss up to decide that; **tirer à** ~ **ou face pour savoir si ...** to toss up to find out if ... .
2 adv (*) (*net*) dead*; (*juste*) just, right. **s'arrêter** ~ to stop dead*; **ça l'a arrêté** ~ it stopped him dead* *ou* in his tracks, it brought him up short*; **tomber** ~: *[personne]* **vous êtes tombé** ~ **en m'offrant ce cadeau** you've chosen exactly the right present for me; **j'ai ouvert le bottin et je suis tombé** ~ **sur le numéro** I opened the directory and came straight (*Brit*) *ou* right upon the number *ou* came up with* the number straight away (*Brit*) *ou* right away; *[chose]* **il lâcha sa gomme qui tomba** ~ **dans l'encrier** he let go of his rubber which fell straight *ou* right into the inkwell; **ça tombe** ~! that's just *ou* exactly what I (*ou* we *etc*) need(ed)!; **on est 6 et il y en a 12 — ça tombe** ~ there are 6 of us and 12 of them — that works out exactly *ou* evenly; **son mariage tombe** ~ **le jour de son anniversaire** her wedding is on (exactly) the same day as her birthday; (*survenir*) **tomber** *ou* **arriver** ~ *[personne]* to turn up* just at the

right moment ou time; [chose] to come just at the right moment ou time; à 2 heures ~ (at) dead on 2*, at 2 on the dot*, on the dot of 2*; il est 11 heures ~ it's dead on 11*, it's 11 o'clock exactly.

piler [pile] 1 1 vt a (lit) to crush, pound. b (* fig) ~ qn (rosser) to lay into sb⁑, give sb a hammering⁑ ou belting⁑; (vaincre) to beat sb hollow* (Brit), lick sb*. 2 vi (*: freiner) to jam on the brakes.

pileux, -euse [pilø, øz] adj follicule hair (épith); voir système.

pilier [pilje] nm (Anat, Constr, fig) pillar; (Rugby) prop (forward). c'est un ~ de cabaret ou de bistro he spends his life propping up the bar, he spends his life in the pub, he's a bar fly* (US).

pillage [pijaʒ] nm (voir piller) pillaging; plundering; looting; fleecing; wholesale borrowing (de from); plagiarizing; pirating. mettre au ~ to pillage; to plunder; to loot; to borrow wholesale from; to plagiarize; to pirate.

pillard, e [pijaʀ, aʀd] (voir piller) 1 adj nomades, troupes pillaging (épith); looting (épith); oiseau thieving (épith). 2 nm,f pillager; plunderer; looter.

piller [pije] 1 vt ville to pillage, plunder, loot; magasin, maison to loot; (voler) objets to plunder, take as booty; personne to fleece; (fig: plagier) ouvrage, auteur to borrow wholesale from, plagiarize, pirate.

pilleur, -euse [pijœʀ, øz] (voir piller) 1 adj pillaging; plundering; looting. 2 nm,f pillager; plunderer; looter; (†) literary pirate, plagiarist. ~ d'épaves looter (of wrecked ships).

pilon [pilɔ̃] nm (instrument) pestle; (jambe) wooden leg, pegleg*; [poulet] drumstick. (Typ) mettre un livre au ~ to pulp a book.

pilonnage [pilɔnaʒ] nm (voir pilonner) pounding; crushing; shelling, bombardment.

pilonner [pilɔne] 1 vt (Culin, Pharm) to pound, crush; (Mil) to pound, shell, bombard; (Typ) to pulp.

pilori [pilɔʀi] nm pillory, stocks (pl). mettre ou clouer au ~ (lit) to put in the stocks; (fig) to pillory; être condamné au ~ to be put in the stocks.

pilosité [pilozite] nf pilosity.

pilotage [pilɔtaʒ] nm (Aviat) piloting, flying; (Naut) piloting. école de ~ (Aviat) flying school; (Aut) driving school (specializing in lessons for licensed drivers on driving in difficult road conditions); ~ automatique automatic piloting; véhicule à ~ automatique self-steering vehicle; ~ sans visibilité flying blind; voir poste².

pilote [pilɔt] 1 adj (expérimental) école, ferme, réalisation experimental; (Comm) magasin cut-price (épith); produit low-priced. projet ~ pilot project; voir bateau. 2 nm (Aviat, Naut) pilot; (Aut) driver; (poisson) pilotfish; (fig: guide) guide. servir de ~ à qn to show ou guide sb round, serve as a guide for sb. 3 comp ►pilote automatique automatic pilot, autopilot ►pilote automobile racing driver ►pilote de chasse fighter pilot ►pilote de course = pilote automobile ►pilote d'essai test pilot ►pilote de guerre fighter pilot ►pilote de ligne airline pilot.

piloter [pilɔte] 1 vt avion to pilot, fly; navire to pilot; voiture to drive. (fig) ~ qn to show ou guide ou pilot sb round.

pilotis [pilɔti] nm pile, pilotis (SPÉC). sur ~ on piles.

pilou [pilu] nm flannelette.

pilule [pilyl] nf pill. prendre la ~ (contraceptive) to be on ou take the pill; ~ du lendemain morning-after pill; (⁑ fig) prendre une ou la ~ to take a hammering⁑, be thrashed*; (fig) avaler la ~ (expérience pénible) to swallow the bitter pill; (mensonge) to swallow it (whole); elle a trouvé la ~ un peu amère she found it a bitter pill to swallow; (fig) faire qch pour faire passer la ~ to do sth to sweeten ou sugar the pill; voir dorer.

pimbêche [pɛ̃bɛʃ] 1 adj f stuck-up*, full of herself (attrib). 2 nf stuck-up thing*. c'est une horrible ~ she is full of herself ou is horribly stuck-up*.

pimbina [pɛ̃bina] nm (Can) pembina (Can), type of cranberry.

piment [pimɑ̃] nm a (plante) pepper, capsicum. (Culin) ~ rouge chilli, hot red pepper; ~ doux pepper, capsicum; ~ vert green chilli pepper. b (fig) spice, piquancy. avoir du ~ to be spicy ou piquant; donner du ~ à une situation to add ou give spice to a situation; ça donne du ~ à la vie it spices up life, it adds a bit of spice to life, it makes life more exciting; trouver du ~ à qch to find sth spicy ou piquant.

pimenté, e [pimɑ̃te] (ptp de pimenter) adj plat hot, spicy; (fig) récit spicy.

pimenter [pimɑ̃te] 1 vt (Culin) to put chillis in; (fig) to add ou give spice to.

pimpant, e [pɛ̃pɑ̃, ɑ̃t] adj robe, femme spruce.

pimprenelle [pɛ̃pʀənɛl] nf (à fleurs verdâtres) (salad) burnet; (à fleurs rouges) great burnet.

pin [pɛ̃] nm (arbre) pine (tree); (bois) pine(wood). ~ maritime/parasol ou pignon maritime/umbrella pine; ~ sylvestre Scotch fir, Scots pine; voir aiguille, pomme.

pinacle [pinakl] nm (Archit) pinnacle. (fig) être au ~ to be at the top; (fig) porter qn au ~ to praise sb to the skies.

pinacothèque [pinakɔtɛk] nf art gallery.

pinaillage* [pinɑjaʒ] nm hair-splitting, quibbling.

pinailler* [pinɑje] 1 vi to quibble, split hairs. ~ sur to pick holes in*.

pinailleur, -euse* [pinɑjœʀ, øz] 1 adj pernickety, fussy, nitpicking* (épith), hair-splitting (épith). 2 nm,f nitpicker*, quibbler, fusspot*.

pinard⁑ [pinaʀ] nm (gén) wine; (péj) plonk* (Brit), cheap wine.

pinardier [pinaʀdje] nm wine tanker.

pince [pɛ̃s] 1 nf a (outil) ~(s) (gén) pair of pliers, pliers (pl); (à charbon), [forgeron] pair of tongs, tongs (pl).
b (levier) crowbar.
c (Zool) [crabe] pincer, claw.
d (Couture) dart. faire des ~s à to put darts in; ~ de poitrine bust darts.
e (⁑: main) mitt⁑, paw⁑. je lui ai serré la ~ I shook hands with him.
f (⁑: jambe) leg. aller à ~s to foot* ou hoof⁑ it; j'ai fait 15 km à ~s I footed it for 15 km*.
2 comp ►pince à billets note (Brit) ou bill (US) clip ►pince à cheveux hair clip (Brit), bobby pin (US) ►pince crocodile crocodile clips (pl) ►pince de cycliste bicycle clip ►pince à dénuder wire strippers (pl), wire stripping pliers (pl) ►pince à épiler (eyebrow) tweezers (pl) ►pince à escargots escargot pincers ►pince à glace ice tongs (pl) ►pince à linge clothes peg ►pince-monseigneur nf (pl pinces-monseigneur) jemmy (Brit), crowbar ►pince multiprise = pince crocodile ►pince à ongles nail clippers (pl) ►pince à sucre sugar tongs (pl) ►pince universelle (universal) pliers (pl).

pince- [pɛ̃s] préf voir pincer.

pincé, e¹ [pɛ̃se] (ptp de pincer) adj personne, air stiff, starchy; sourire stiff, tight-lipped; ton stiff. d'un air ~ stiffly; les lèvres ~es with pursed lips, tight-lipped; (minces) thin-lipped; (Mus) instrument à cordes ~es plucked stringed instrument.

pinceau, pl ~x [pɛ̃so] nm (gén) brush; (Peinture) (paint)brush; (fig: manière de peindre) brushwork; (⁑: pied) foot, hoof⁑. ~ à colle paste brush; ~ lumineux pencil of light; donner un coup de ~ à to give a lick of paint to; en quelques coups de ~ with a quick dab of the paintbrush; (lit, fig) s'embrouiller ou s'emmêler les ~x* to trip o.s. up.

pincée² [pɛ̃se] nf [sel, poivre] pinch.

pincement [pɛ̃smɑ̃] nm (Mus) plucking; (Agr) pinching out. elle a eu un ~ de cœur she felt a twinge of sorrow.

pincer [pɛ̃se] 3 1 vt a (accidentellement, pour faire mal) to pinch, nip; [froid, chien] to nip. je me suis pincé dans la porte/avec l'ouvre-boîte I caught myself in the door/with the can opener; se ~ le doigt to catch one's finger; se ~ le doigt dans la porte to trap ou catch one's finger in the door; ~ son manteau dans la porte to catch one's coat in the door; il s'est fait ~ par un crabe/un chien he was nipped by a crab/a dog.
b (tenir, serrer) to grip. ~ les lèvres to purse (up) one's lips; se ~ le nez to hold one's nose; une robe qui pince la taille a dress which is tight at the waist.
c (Mus) to pluck.
d (Couture) veste to put darts in.
e (* fig: arrêter, prendre) to catch, cop⁑; [police] to nick⁑ (Brit), cop⁑, catch.
f (Agr) to pinch out.
g en ~ pour qn⁑ to be stuck on sb⁑, be mad about sb*; il est pincé* he's hooked*.
2 vi (⁑) ça pince (dur) it's freezing (cold), it's biting ou hellish⁑ cold.
3 comp ►pince-fesse(s)⁑ nm inv dance, hop* ►pince-nez nm inv pince-nez ►pince-sans-rire nm inv: c'est un pince-sans-rire he's the deadpan type; adj inv deadpan.

pincette [pɛ̃sɛt] nf (gén pl) (pour le feu) pair of (fire) tongs, (fire) tongs; [horloger] pair of tweezers, tweezers. il n'est pas à toucher ou prendre avec des ~s (sale) he's filthy dirty; (mécontent) he's like a bear with a sore head.

pinçon [pɛ̃sɔ̃] nm pinch-mark.

Pindare [pɛ̃daʀ] nm Pindar.

pindarique [pɛ̃daʀik] adj Pindaric.

pine⁂ [pin] nf cock⁂, prick⁂.

pinède [pinɛd] nf, **pineraie** [pinʀɛ] nf pinewood, pine forest.

pingouin [pɛ̃gwɛ̃] nm [arctique] auk; (emploi gén) penguin. (petit) ~ razorbill.

Ping-Pong [piŋpɔ̃g] nm ® table tennis, ping-pong.

pingre [pɛ̃gʀ] (péj) 1 adj stingy, niggardly. 2 nmf skinflint, niggard.

pingrerie [pɛ̃gʀəʀi] nf (péj) stinginess, niggardliness.

Pinocchio [pinɔkjo] nm Pinocchio.

pin-pon [pɛ̃pɔ̃] excl sound made by two-tone siren.

pin's [pins] nm inv lapel badge.

pinson [pɛ̃sɔ̃] nm chaffinch. ~ du nord brambling; voir gai.

pintade [pɛ̃tad] nf guinea-fowl.

pintadeau, pl ~x [pɛ̃tado] nm young guinea-fowl, guinea-poult (SPÉC).

pinte [pɛ̃t] nf a (ancienne mesure) ≃ quart (0,93 litre); (mesure anglo-saxonne) pint; (Can) quart (1,136 litre). (fig) se payer une ~ de bon sang (s'amuser) to have a good time; (rire) to have a good laugh.
b (Suisse: débit de boissons) bar.

pinté, e⁑ [pɛ̃te] (ptp de pinter) adj sloshed⁑, smashed⁑, plastered⁑.

pinter⁑ [pɛ̃te] 1 1 vi, **se pinter⁑** vpr to booze⁑, liquor up⁑ (US). on s'est pinté au whisky we got smashed⁑ ou plastered⁑ ou pissed⁂ on whisky. 2 vt to knock back⁑.

pin up [pinœp] **nf inv** (*personne*) sexy-looking bird* (*Brit*) *ou* chick* (*US*); (*photo*) pinup.

pioche [pjɔʃ] **nf** a (*à deux pointes*) pick, pickaxe; (*à pointe et à houe*) mattock, pickaxe; *voir* **tête**. b (*tas de dominos, cartes*) stack, pile.

piocher [pjɔʃe] 1 **1 vt** *terre* to dig up *ou* over (with a pick), use a pick on; (*) *sujet* to swot at* (*Brit*), cram for, slave *ou* slog away at*; *examen* to swot (*Brit*) *ou* cram for*; (*Jeux*) *carte, domino, numéro* to take (from the stack *ou* pile). **2 vi** (*creuser*) to dig (with a pick); (*: *bûcher*) to swot* (*Brit*), slave* *ou* slog* away; (*Jeux*) to pick up *ou* take a card (*ou* domino) (from the stack *ou* pile). **~ dans le tas** (*nourriture*) to dig in; (*objets*) to dig into the pile; **~ dans ses économies** to dip into *ou* dig into one's savings.

piocheur, -euse* [pjɔʃœʀ, øz] **1 adj** hard-working. **2 nm,f** swot* (*Brit*), crammer, slogger*.

piolet [pjɔlɛ] **nm** ice axe; *voir* **marteau**.

pion [pjɔ̃] **nm** a (*Échecs*) pawn; (*Dames*) piece, draught (*Brit*), checker (*US*). (*fig*) **n'être qu'un ~ (sur l'échiquier)** to be nothing but a pawn; *voir* **damer**. b (*Scol: surveillant*) supervisor, *student paid to supervise schoolchildren*.

pioncer‡ [pjɔ̃se] 3 **vi** to get some shut-eye‡. **je n'ai pas pioncé de la nuit** I didn't sleep a wink last night; **laisse-le ~** leave him to his kip‡ (*Brit*), let him have his sleep; **je vais ~** I'm going for some shut-eye‡.

pionne [pjɔn] **nf** (*Scol: voir* **pion**) (female) supervisor.

pionnier [pjɔnje] **nm** (*lit, fig*) pioneer.

pioupiou*† [pjupju] **nm** young soldier, tommy*† (*Brit*).

pipe [pip] **nf** a pipe. **fumer la ~** (*gén*) to smoke a pipe; (*habituellement*) to be a pipe-smoker; **~ de bruyère/de terre** briar/clay pipe; *voir* **casser, fendre, tête**. b **‡** blow job**‡**.

pipeau, **pl ~x** [pipo] **nm** (*Mus*) (reed-)pipe; *[oiseleur]* bird call. (*gluaux*) **~x** limed twigs. **c'est du ~*** that's a load of rubbish*.

pipelet, -ette* [piplɛ, ɛt] **nm,f** (*péj*) concierge.

pipe-line, **pl pipe-lines** [piplin] **nm** pipeline.

piper [pipe] 1 **vt** *cartes* to mark; *dés* to load. (*fig*) **les dés sont pipés** the dice are loaded; **ne pas ~ (mot)*** not to breathe a word, keep mum*.

piperade [pipeʀad] **nf** piperade, *kind of omelette with tomatoes and peppers*.

pipette [pipɛt] **nf** pipette.

pipi* [pipi] **nm** wee(wee) (* *ou langage enfantin*). **faire ~: va faire ~** go and (have a) wee(wee)*; **j'irais bien faire ~** I want to go to the loo* (*Brit*) *ou* john* (*US*); **faire ~ au lit** to wet the bed; **le chien a fait ~ sur le tapis** the dog has made a puddle* on *ou* has done a wee* on the carpet; (*fig*) **c'est du ~ de chat** *[boisson]* it's just coloured water, it's absolute dishwater*; *[livre, film, théorie]* it's pathetic*, it's a waste of time; *voir* **dame**.

pipi-room* [pipiʀum] **nm** loo* (*Brit*), restroom (*US*). **aller au ~** to go and spend a penny* (*Brit*), go to the restroom (*US*).

pipit [pipit] **nm** pipit. **~ des arbres** tree pipit.

piquage [pikaʒ] **nm** (*Couture*) sewing up, stitching, machining.

piquant, e [pikɑ̃, ɑ̃t] **1 adj** a *barbe* prickly; (*Bot*) *tige* thorny, prickly.

b *sauce, moutarde* hot, pungent; *goût, odeur, fromage* pungent; *vin* sour, tart; *radis* hot. **eau ~e*** fizzy water (*hum*), soda water; (*Culin*) **sauce ~e** sauce piquante, piquant sauce.

c *air, froid* biting.

d *détail* titillating; *description, style* racy, piquant, titillating; *conversation, charme, beauté* piquant, titillating.

e (*mordant*) *mot, réplique* biting, cutting.

2 nm a *[hérisson]* quill, spine; *[oursin]* spine, prickle; *[rosier]* thorn, prickle; *[chardon]* prickle; *[barbelé]* barb.

b (*fig*) *[style, description]* raciness; *[conversation]* piquancy; *[aventure]* spice. **le ~ de l'histoire, c'est que ..., et, détail qui ne manque pas de ~, ...** the most entertaining thing (about it) is that ... .

pique [pik] **1 nf** (*arme*) pike; *[picador]* lance; (*fig: parole blessante*) dig, cutting remark. **lancer des ~s à qn** to make cutting remarks to sb. **2 nm** (*carte*) spade; (*couleur*) spades (*pl*).

pique- [pik] **préf** *voir* **piquer**.

piqué, e [pike] (**ptp de piquer**) **1 adj** a (*Couture*) (*cousu*) (machine-)stitched; *couvre-lit* quilted.

b (*marqué*) *glace, livre, linge* mildewed, mildewy; *meuble* worm-eaten; (*aigre*) *vin* sour. **visage ~ de taches de rousseur** freckled face, face dotted with freckles; **~ par la rouille** *métal* pitted with rust; *linge* covered in rust spots; **~ par l'acide** pitted with acid marks; (*fig*) **pas piqué des hannetons*** *ou* **des vers*** (*excellent*) brilliant*, great*; (*excentrique*) wild*; **son article n'est pas piqué des hannetons*** *ou* **des vers** his article doesn't miss the mark *ou* touches a nerve; **ce problème n'était pas ~ des hannetons!*** *ou* **des vers!*** it was one heck of a problem!*

c (*: *fou*) nuts*, barmy* (*Brit*). **il est ~, c'est un ~** he's a nutter* (*Brit*), he's nuts* *ou* barmy* (*Brit*).

d (*Mus*) *note* staccato.

2 nm a (*Aviat*) dive. **attaque en ~** (*bombardement*) dive bombing run; (*à la mitrailleuse*) strafing run; **bombardement en ~** dive bombing; **faire un ~** to (go into a) dive.

b (*tissu*) piqué.

piquer [pike] 1 **1 vt** a *[guêpe]* to sting; *[moustique, serpent]* to bite; (*avec une épingle, une pointe*) to prick; (*Méd*) to give an injection to, give a jab* (*Brit*) *ou* shot* to. **se faire ~ contre la variole** to have a smallpox injection *ou* jab* (*Brit*) *ou* shot*; **faire ~ qn contre qch** to have sb vaccinated *ou* inoculated against sth; (*euph*) **faire ~ un chat/un chien** to have a cat/dog put down (*Brit euph*) *ou* put to sleep (*euph*); **se ~ le doigt** to prick one's finger; **les ronces, ça pique** brambles prickle *ou* scratch; (*drogue*) **se ~** to shoot up; *voir* **mouche**.

b *aiguille, fourche, fléchette* to stick, stab, jab (*dans* into). **rôti piqué d'ail** joint stuck with cloves of garlic; **piqué de lardons** larded; **~ la viande avec une fourchette** to prick the meat with a fork; **~ des petits pois avec une fourchette** to stab peas with a fork; **~ qch au mur** to put *ou* stick sth up on the wall; **~ une fleur sur un corsage** to pin a flower on(to) a blouse; **~ une fleur dans ses cheveux** to stick a flower in one's hair; **des papillons piqués sur une planche** butterflies pinned on a board; **~ (une frite/un haricot) dans le plat*** to help o.s. (to a chip/a bean or two); **~ au hasard*** *ou* **dans le tas*** to choose *ou* pick at random.

c (*Couture*) **~ qch (à la machine)** to machine sth, (machine) stitch sth, sew sth up; **ta mère sait-elle ~?** can your mother use a sewing machine?

d *[barbe]* to prick, prickle; *[ortie]* to sting. **tissu qui pique (la peau)** prickly cloth, cloth that prickles the skin *ou* is prickly on the skin; **moutarde/liqueur qui pique la gorge** mustard/liqueur which burns the throat; **la fumée me pique les yeux** the smoke is stinging my eyes *ou* making my eyes smart; **le froid/le vent nous piquait le** *ou* **au visage** the cold/the wind was biting *ou* stinging our faces; *[démangeaison]* **ça (me) pique** it's itching *ou* itchy, it's making me itch; **les yeux me piquent, j'ai les yeux qui piquent** my eyes are smarting *ou* stinging; **ma gorge me pique** my throat's burning; **tu piques avec ta barbe** you're all prickly with that beard of yours, your beard prickles *ou* is prickly; **attention, ça pique** *[alcool sur une plaie]* careful, it's going to sting; *[liquide dans la bouche]* careful, it burns your throat; *voir* **qui**.

e (*exciter*) *bœufs* to goad; *curiosité* to arouse, excite; *intérêt* to arouse, stir up; (†: *vexer*) *personne* to pique, nettle; *amour-propre* to pique, hurt. **~ qn au vif** to cut sb to the quick.

f (*: *faire brusquement*) **~ un cent mètres** *ou* **un sprint** to (put on a) sprint, put on a burst of speed; **~ un roupillon** *ou* **un somme** to have forty winks* *ou* a nap, get a bit of shut-eye‡; **~ un galop** to break into a gallop; **~ une** *ou* **sa crise** to throw a fit; **~ une crise de larmes** to have a fit of tears; **~ une colère** to fly into a rage, have a fit*; **~ un soleil** *ou* **un fard** to go (bright) red; **~ une suée** to break out in a sweat; **~ un plongeon** to dive; **~ une tête dans la piscine** to dive (headfirst) into the pool.

g (*: *attraper*) *manie, maladie* to pick up, catch, get.

h (*: *voler*) *portefeuille* to pinch*, swipe*, nick‡ (*Brit*), whip‡ (*Brit*); *idée* to pinch*, steal (*à qn* from sb).

i (‡: *arrêter*) *voleur* to cop‡, nab‡, nick‡ (*Brit*).

j (*Mus*) to play staccato.

2 vi a *[avion]* to go into a dive; *[oiseau]* to swoop down. **le cavalier piqua droit sur nous** the horseman came straight towards us; **il faudrait ~ vers le village** we'll have to head towards the village; **~ du nez** *[avion]* to go into a nose-dive; *[bateau]* to dip her head; *[fleurs]* to droop; *[personne]* to fall headfirst; **~ du nez dans son assiette*** (*de sommeil*) to nod off* *ou* doze off* (during a meal); (*de honte*) to hang one's head in shame; **~ des deux** to go full tilt.

b *[moutarde, radis]* to be hot; *[vin]* to be sour, have a sour taste; *[fromage]* to be pungent. **eau qui pique*** aerated water, fizzy water (*hum*), soda water.

3 se piquer vpr a (*se blesser*) (*avec une aiguille*) to prick o.s.; (*dans les orties*) to get stung, sting o.s.

b *[morphinomane]* to shoot up, give o.s. a shot of *ou* inject o.s. with heroin (*ou* morphine *etc*); *[diabétique]* to give o.s. an injection, inject o.s.

c *[livres, miroir, bois, linge]* to go mildewed *ou* mildewy; *[métal]* to be pitted; *[vin, cidre]* to go *ou* turn sour.

d (*avoir la prétention*) **se ~ de littérature/psychologie** to like to think one knows a lot about literature/psychology, pride o.s. on one's knowledge of literature/psychology; **se ~ de faire qch** to pride o.s. on one's ability to do sth.

e (*se vexer*) to take offence.

f (*loc*) **il s'est piqué au jeu** he became quite taken with it (*Brit*); **c'est quelqu'un qui se pique le nez‡** he's a real boozer‡, he's on the bottle*; **il se pique le nez toute la journée‡** he knocks it back‡ *ou* boozes‡ all day long.

4 comp ► **pique-assiette*** **nmf inv** scrounger*, sponger* (*for a free meal*) ► **pique-feu** **nm inv** poker ► **pique-fleurs** **nm inv** flower-holder ► **pique-fruit(s)** **nm inv** cocktail stick ► **pique-nique** **nm (pl pique-niques)** picnic; **faire un pique-nique** to have a picnic, picnic; **demain nous allons faire un pique-nique** tomorrow we're going for *ou* on a picnic ► **pique-niquer** to have a picnic, picnic ► **pique-niqueur, -euse** **nm,f (mpl pique-niqueurs)** picnicker.

piquet [pikɛ] **nm** a (*pieu*) post, stake, picket; *[tente]* peg; (*Ski*) (marker) pole; *voir* **raide.** b (*Ind*) ~ **(de grève)** (strike-)picket, picket line; **organiser un ~ de grève** to organize a picket line; **il y a un ~ de grève à l'usine** there is a picket line at the factory; (*Mil*) ~ **d'incendie** fire-fighting squad. c (*Scol*) **mettre qn au ~** to make sb stand *ou* put sb in the corner. d (*Cartes*) piquet.

piquetage [pik(ə)taʒ] nm staking (out).

piqueter [pik(ə)te] 4 vt a *allée* to stake out, put stakes along. b (*moucheter*) to dot (*de* with). **ciel piqueté d'étoiles** star-studded *ou* star-spangled sky, sky studded with stars.

piquette [pikɛt] nf a (*cru local*) local wine; (*mauvais vin*) cheap wine, plonk* (*Brit*). b (*‡: défaite*) hammering‡, licking*, thrashing*. **prendre une ~** to be hammered‡ *ou* thrashed* *ou* licked*.

piqueur, -euse [pikœʀ, øz] 1 adj *insecte* stinging (*épith*). 2 nm a *[écurie]* groom; (*Chasse*) whip. b (*mineur*) hewer. c (*surveillant*) foreman. d (**: voleur*) thief. 3 nm,f (*Couture*) machinist.

piquier [pikje] nm pikeman.

piqûre [pikyʀ] nf a *[épingle]* prick; *[guêpe, ortie]* sting; *[moustique]* bite. ~ **d'épingle** pinprick; (*plaie*) **la ~ faite par l'aiguille** the hole made by the needle; (*fig*) ~ **d'amour-propre** injury to one's pride. b (*Méd*) injection, jab* (*Brit*), shot*. **faire une ~ à qn** to give sb an injection *ou* a jab* (*Brit*) *ou* shot*; **se faire faire une ~** to have an injection *ou* a jab* (*Brit*). c *[miroir, papier]* spot of mildew, mildew (*NonC*); *[métal]* hole, pitting (*NonC*); *[bois]* hole. ~ **de ver** wormhole. d (*Couture*) (*point*) (straight) stitch; (*rang*) (straight) stitching (*NonC*). **rang de ~s** row *ou* line of straight stitching.

piranha [piʀana] nm piranha.

piratage [piʀataʒ] nm pirating, piracy.

pirate [piʀat] 1 adj *bateau, émission, disque* pirate (*épith*). 2 nm pirate; (*fig: escroc*) swindler, shark*. ~ **de l'air** hijacker, skyjacker*; ~ **(informatique)** hacker*.

pirater [piʀate] 1 vt (*film, logiciel*) to pirate.

piraterie [piʀatʀi] nf (*NonC*) piracy; (*acte*) act of piracy; (*fig*) swindle, swindling (*NonC*). ~ **commerciale** illegal copying, forgery (*of famous brand name goods*); **acte de ~** act of piracy; ~ **aérienne** hijacking, skyjacking*; **c'est de la ~!** it's daylight robbery!

piraya [piʀaja] nm = **piranha.**

pire [piʀ] 1 adj a (*compar*) worse. **c'est bien ~** it's even worse; **quelque chose de ~** something worse; **il y a quelque chose de ~** there is worse; **c'est ~ que jamais** it's worse than ever; **il y a ~ comme chef** you could do worse for a boss; (*Prov*) **il n'est ~ eau que l'eau qui dort** still waters run deep (*Prov*); (*Prov*) **il n'est ~ sourd que celui qui ne veut pas entendre** there is none so deaf as he who will not hear (*Prov*).

b (*superl*) **le ~, la ~** the worst.

2 nm: **le ~** the worst; **le ~ de tout c'est de ...** the worst thing of all is to ...; **le ~ c'est que ...** the worst of it (all) is that ...; **pour le meilleur et pour le ~** for better or for worse; **(en mettant les choses) au ~** at (the very) worst, if the worst comes to the worst; **je m'attends au ~** I expect the worst; *voir* **politique.**

Pirée [piʀe] nm: **le ~** Piraeus.

piriforme [piʀifɔʀm] adj pear-shaped.

pirogue [piʀɔg] nf dugout (canoe), pirogue.

piroguier [piʀɔgje] nm boatman (*in a pirogue*).

pirouette [piʀwɛt] nf *[danseuse]* pirouette; (*fig: volte-face*) about-turn (*fig*); (*fig: faux-fuyant*) evasive reply. (*fig*) **répondre par une ~** to cleverly side-step *ou* evade the question.

pirouetter [piʀwete] 1 vi to pirouette.

pis¹ [pi] nm *[vache]* udder.

pis² [pi] (*littér*) 1 adj worse. **qui ~ est** what is worse. 2 adv worse. **aller de ~ en ~** to get worse and worse; **dire ~ que pendre de qn** to sling mud at sb (*fig*), have nothing good to say about sb; *voir* **mal, tant.** 3 nm: **le ~** the worst (thing); **au ~ aller** if the worst comes to the worst. 4 comp ▸**pis-aller** nm inv (*personne, solution*) last resort, stopgap; (*chose*) makeshift, stopgap; (*mesure*) stopgap measure.

piscicole [pisikɔl] adj piscicultural (*SPÉC*), fish-breeding (*épith*).

pisciculteur [pisikyltœʀ] nm pisciculturist (*SPÉC*), fish breeder *ou* farmer.

pisciculture [pisikyltyʀ] nf pisciculture (*SPÉC*), fish breeding *ou* farming.

pisciforme [pisifɔʀm] adj pisciform.

piscine [pisin] nf swimming pool; (*publique*) (swimming) baths (*pl*), swimming pool.

piscivore [pisivɔʀ] 1 adj fish-eating (*épith*), piscivorous (*SPÉC*). 2 nm fish eater.

Pise [piz] n Pisa.

pisé [pize] nm cob (*Brit*), adobe, pisé (*SPÉC*).

pisse‡ [pis] nf pee‡, piss*‡. (*fig*) **de la ~ d'âne** duck's *ou* cat's piss*‡ (*fig*), a disgusting brew.

pisse-froid‡ [pisfʀwa] nm inv wet blanket*.

pissement [pismɑ̃] nm (‡) peeing‡, pissing*‡. ~ **de sang** passing of blood (with the urine).

pissenlit [pisɑ̃li] nm dandelion. **manger les ~s par la racine** to be pushing up the daisies, be dead and buried.

pisser‡ [pise] 1 1 vi (*uriner*) *[personne]* to (have a) pee‡ *ou* piss*‡; *[animal]* to pee‡, piss*‡; (*couler*) to gush; (*fuir*) to gush out, piss out*‡ **je vais ~ un coup** I'm going out for a pee‡ *ou* a slash*‡ (*Brit*) *ou* a piss*‡; **il a pissé dans sa culotte** he wet his trousers, he peed in his pants‡; ~ **au lit** to wet the *ou* one's bed, pee in the bed‡; **ça pisse** (*il pleut*) it's chucking it down* (*Brit*), it's coming down in buckets*, it's pissing down*‡ (*Brit*); **ça l'a pris comme une envie de ~** he suddenly got an urge to do it*; **les principes, je leur pisse dessus!** principles, I spit on them!; **c'est comme si on pissait dans un violon** it's like banging your head against a brick wall; **laisse ~ (le mérinos)** forget it!*, let him (*ou* them *etc*) get on with it!

2 vt ~ **du sang** to pass blood (with the urine); **son nez pisse le sang** his nose is gushing *ou* pouring blood, blood's gushing from his nose; **il pissait le sang** the blood was gushing out of him; **réservoir qui pisse l'eau** tank which is gushing *ou* pissing‡ out water.

pissette* [pisɛt] nf (*filet de liquide*) trickle.

pisseur, -euse¹ [pisœʀ, øz] 1 nm,f (‡) weak-bladdered individual, person who is always going for a pee‡ *ou* a piss*‡ 2 **pisseuse‡** nf female (*péj*). 3 comp ▸**pisseur de copie*** *writer (or journalist etc) who churns out rubbish.*

pisseux, -euse²* [pisø, øz] adj *couleur* wishy-washy*, insipid; *aspect* tatty*, scruffy*. **odeur ~euse** smell of pee‡ *ou* piss*‡.

pisse-vinaigre‡ [pisvinɛgʀ] nm inv (*rabat-joie*) wet blanket; (*avare*) skinflint.

pissoir [piswaʀ] nm (*dial*) urinal.

pissotière‡ [pisɔtjɛʀ] nf (street) urinal, ≃ (public) loo* (*Brit*) *ou* john* (*US*) *ou* bog‡ (*Brit*).

pistache [pistaʃ] 1 nf pistachio (nut). 2 adj inv pistachio (green).

pistachier [pistaʃje] nm pistachio (tree).

pistage [pistaʒ] nm (*voir* **pister**) tracking; trailing; tailing, tagging.

pistard [pistaʀ] nm track cyclist, track racer *ou* specialist.

piste [pist] nf a (*traces*) *[animal, suspect]* track, tracks, trail. **suivre/perdre la ~** to follow/lose the trail; **être/mettre qn sur la (bonne) ~** to be/put sb on the right track; **être sur/perdre la ~ du meurtrier** to be on/lose the murderer's trail; **se lancer sur la ~ de qn** to follow sb's trail, set out to track sb down; *voir* **brouiller, faux², jeu.**

b (*Police: indice*) lead. **nous avons plusieurs ~s** we have several leads.

c *[hippodrome]* course; *[vélodrome, autodrome, stade]* track; *[patinage]* rink; *[danse]* (dance) floor; (*Ski*) (ski) run, piste; (*ski de fond*) trail; *[cirque]* ring. (*Ski*) ~ **artificielle** dry ski slope; ~ **cavalière** bridle path; ~ **cyclable** cycle track, bikeway (*US*); (*Ski*) ~ **pour débutants** nursery slope; (*Ski*) **il y a 30 km de ~ dans cette station** there are 30 km of pistes *ou* ski runs at this resort; (*Ski*) ~ **rouge/noire** red/black piste *ou* ski run; **en ~!** (*lit*) into the ring!; (*fig*) set to it!; (*fig*) **se mettre en ~** to get down to it.

d (*Aviat*) runway; *[petit aéroport]* airstrip. ~ **d'atterrissage/d'envol** landing/takeoff runway.

e (*sentier*) track; *[désert]* trail.

f *[magnétophone]* track. **à 2/4 ~s** 2/4 track; (*Ciné*) ~ **sonore** sound track.

pister [piste] 1 vt *gibier* to track, trail; *[police] personne* to tail, tag.

pisteur [pistœʀ] nm (member of the) ski patrol. **les ~s** the ski patrol.

pistil [pistil] nm pistil.

pistole [pistɔl] nf pistole.

pistolet [pistɔlɛ] 1 nm (*arme*) pistol, gun; (*jouet*) (toy) pistol, (toy) gun; *[peintre]* spray gun; (**: urinal*) bed-bottle. **peindre au ~** to spray-paint; (* *fig*) **un drôle de ~** a queer fish* (*Brit*) *ou* duck* (*US*) *ou* customer*.

2 comp ▸**pistolet à air comprimé** airgun ▸**pistolet d'alarme** alarm gun ▸**pistolet d'arçon** horse pistol ▸**pistolet à bouchon** popgun ▸**pistolet à capsules** cap gun ▸**pistolet à eau** water pistol ▸**pistolet-mitrailleur** nm (pl **pistolets-mitrailleurs**) submachine gun, sten gun (*Brit*), tommy gun.

piston [pistɔ̃] nm a (*Tech*) piston. b (*) string-pulling*. **avoir du ~** to have friends in the right places* *ou* who can pull strings*; **il a eu le poste par ~** someone pulled strings to get him the job*, he got the job through a bit of string-pulling*. c (*Mus*) (*valve*) valve; (*instrument*) cornet.

pistonner* [pistɔne] 1 vt to pull strings for* (*auprès de* with). **se faire ~** to get sb to pull (some) strings (for one)*.

pistou [pistu] nm: **soupe au ~** *vegetable soup with basil and garlic.*

pitance [pitɑ̃s] nf (*péj*, †) (means of) sustenance (†, *frm*).

pitchpin [pitʃpɛ̃] nm pitch pine.

piteusement [pitøzmɑ̃] adv pathetically; *échouer* miserably.

piteux, -euse [pitø, øz] adj (*minable*) *apparence* sorry (*épith*), pitiful, pathetic; *résultats* pitiful, pathetic; (*honteux*) *personne, air* ashamed, shamefaced. **en ~ état** in a sorry *ou* pitiful state; **faire ~euse figure** to cut a sorry figure, be a sorry *ou* pitiful sight; **avoir ~euse mine** to be shabby-looking.

pithécanthrope [pitekɑ̃tʀɔp] nm pithecanthrope.

pithiviers [pitivje] nm *cake with an almond paste filling.*

pitié [pitje] nf a (*compassion*) pity. **avoir ~ de qn** pity sb, feel pity for sb; **prendre qn/le sort de qn en ~** to take pity on sb/sb's fate, pity sb/sb's fate; **faire ~ à qn** to inspire pity in sb; **il me fait ~** I feel sorry for him, I pity him; **cela nous faisait ~ de les voir si mal vêtus** we felt great pity to see them so badly dressed; **son sort me fit ~** I pitied his fate; **c'est (une vraie) ~** *ou* **quelle ~ de voir ça** it's pitiful to see (that); **il était si maigre que c'en était ~** *ou* **que c'était à faire ~** he was so thin it was pitiful (to see him), he was pitifully *ou* pathetically thin; **chanter à faire ~** to sing pitifully *ou* pathetically.

b (*miséricorde*) pity, mercy. **avoir ~ d'un ennemi** to take pity on an enemy, have pity *ou* mercy on an enemy; **~!** (*lit: grâce*) (have) mercy!; (**: assez*) for goodness' *ou* pity's *ou* Pete's sake!*; **par ~!** for pity's sake!; **sans ~** *agir* pitilessly, mercilessly, ruthlessly; *regarder* pitilessly; **il est sans ~** he's pitiless *ou* merciless *ou* ruthless.

piton [pitɔ̃] **nm** a (*à anneau*) eye; (*à crochet*) hook; (*Alpinisme*) piton, peg. b (*Géog*) peak.

pitoyable [pitwajabl] **adj** (*gén*) pitiful, pitiable.

pitoyablement [pitwajabləmɑ̃] **adv** pitifully.

pitre [pitʀ] **nm** (*lit, fig*) clown. **faire le ~** to clown *ou* fool about *ou* around, act the fool.

pitrerie [pitʀəʀi] **nf** tomfoolery (*NonC*). **il n'arrête pas de faire des ~s** he's always *ou* he never stops clowning around *ou* acting the fool; **arrête de faire des ~s** stop your silly antics.

pittoresque [pitɔʀɛsk] 1 **adj** *site* picturesque; *personnage, tenu* picturesque, colourful; *récit, style, détail* colourful, picturesque, vivid. 2 **nm**: **le ~** the picturesque; **le ~ de qch** the picturesque quality of sth; the colourfulness *ou* vividness of sth; (*fig*) **le ~ dans tout cela** ... the amusing *ou* ironic thing about all that ... .

pittoresquement [pitɔʀɛskəmɑ̃] **adv** picturesquely.

pivert [pivɛʀ] **nm** green woodpecker.

pivoine [pivwan] **nf** peony; *voir* **rouge**.

pivot [pivo] **nm** (*gén, Sport, Mil*) pivot; (*fig*) mainspring, pivot; *[dent]* post; (*Bot*) taproot. (*Écon*) **cours ~** central rate.

pivotant, e [pivɔtɑ̃, ɑ̃t] **adj** *bras, panneau* pivoting (*épith*), revolving (*épith*); *fauteuil* swivel (*épith*); *voir* **racine**.

pivoter [pivɔte] 1 **vi** *[porte]* to revolve, pivot; (*Mil*) to wheel round. *[personne]* **~ (sur ses talons)** to turn *ou* swivel round, turn on one's heels; **faire ~ qch** to pivot *ou* swivel sth round.

pixel [piksɛl] **nm** pixel.

pizza [pidza] **nf** pizza.

pizzeria [pidzeʀja] **nf** pizzeria.

pizzicato [pidzikato], **pl ~s, pizzicati** [pidzikati] **nm** pizzicato.

PJ (**abrév de pièce(s) jointe(s)**) enc, encl.

P.J. [peʒi] **nf** (**abrév de police judiciaire**) ≃ C.I.D. (*Brit*), FBI (*US*).

Pl. (**abrév de place**) Pl.

P.L. (**abrév de poids lourd**) LGC (*Brit*), HGV (*Brit*); *voir* **poids**.

placage [plakaʒ] **nm** a (*en bois*) veneering (*NonC*), veneer; (*en marbre, pierre*) facing. **~ en acajou** mahogany veneer. b (*Rugby*) = **plaquage**.

placard [plakaʀ] **nm** a (*armoire*) cupboard. **~ à balai/de cuisine** broom/kitchen cupboard. b (*affiche*) poster, notice. *[journal]* **~ publicitaire** display advertisement; (*fig péj*) **écrire un grand ~ sur qch** to write screeds *ou* a great tome about sth. c (*Typ*) galley (proof). d (**: couche*) thick layer, thick coating (*NonC*). e (*loc*) **mettre qn au ~*** (*en prison*) to put sb away*, send sb down*; (*renvoyer*) to fire sb, give sb the push*; (*mettre à l'écart*) to push sb to one side; (*arg Police*) **3 ans de ~** 3 years inside* *ou* in the clink (*arg*); **mettre qch au ~** to shelve sth.

placarder [plakaʀde] 1 **vt** to stick up, put up; *mur* to stick posters on, placard. **mur placardé d'affiches** wall covered with *ou* placarded with posters.

place [plas] **nf** a (*esplanade*) square. **la p~ Rouge** Red Square; (*fig*) **étaler ses divergences sur la ~ publique** to wash one's dirty linen in public; (*fig*) **clamer qch sur la ~ publique** to proclaim sth from the rooftops.

b *[objet]* place. **remettre qch à sa ~** *ou* **en ~** to put sth back where it belongs *ou* in its proper place; **la ~ des mots dans la phrase** word order in sentences; **changer la ~ de qch** to move *ou* shift sth, put sth in a different place, change the place of sth; (*Prov*) **une ~ pour chaque chose et chaque chose à sa ~** a place for everything and everything in its place (*Prov*).

c *[personne]* (*lit, fig*) place; (*assise*) seat. **~ d'honneur** place *ou* seat of honour; **à vos ~s!, en ~!** to your places! *ou* seats!; **tout le monde est en ~** everyone is in (his) place *ou* is seated; **prenez ~** take your place *ou* seat; **prendre la ~ de qn** to take sb's place; (*remplacer*) to take over from sb, take sb's place; **il ne tient pas en ~** he can't keep still, he's always fidgeting; (*fig*) **remettre qn à sa ~** to put sb in his place; **laisser la ~ à qn** (*lit*) to give (up) one's seat to sb; (*fig*) to hand over to sb; **savoir rester à sa ~** to know one's place; **tenir sa ~** (*faire bonne figure*) to put up a good show, hold one's own; **il n'est pas à sa ~ dans ce milieu** he feels out of place in this setting; **se faire une ~ dans le monde/dans la littérature** to carve out a place *ou* niche for o.s. in society/in literature; **avoir sa ~ dans la littérature** to have found a place in literature; **se faire une ~ au soleil** to find o.s. a place in the sun (*fig*); **avoir sa ~ dans le cœur de qn** to have a place in sb's heart; **elle tient une grande ~ dans ma vie** she means a great deal *ou* a lot to me; **trouver** *ou* **prendre ~ parmi/dans** to find a place (for o.s.) among/in; **il ne donnerait pas sa ~ pour un empire** *ou* **pour un boulet de canon*** he wouldn't change places with anyone for all the tea in China* *ou* for the world; **être en bonne ~ pour gagner** to be well-placed *ou* in a good position to win; **se mettre à la ~ de qn** to put o.s. in sb's place *ou* in sb's shoes; **à votre/sa ~** if I were you/him *ou* he (*frm*), in your/his place; *voir* **qui**.

d (*espace libre*) room, space. **tenir** *ou* **prendre de la ~** to take up a lot of room *ou* space; **faire de la ~** to make room *ou* space; **j'ai trouvé une ~** *ou* **de la ~ pour me garer** I've found room *ou* (a) space to park; **pouvez-vous me faire une petite ~?** can you make a bit of room for me?; **on n'a pas de ~ pour se retourner** there's no room to move *ou* not enough room to swing a cat* (*Brit*).

e (*siège, billet*) seat; (*prix, trajet*) fare; (*emplacement réservé*) space. **louer** *ou* **réserver sa ~** to book one's seat; **il n'a pas payé sa ~** he hasn't paid for his seat; he hasn't paid his fare; **payer ~ entière** (*au cinéma etc*) to pay full price; (*dans le tram etc*) to pay full fare; **~ de parking** parking space, stall (*US*); **parking de 500 ~s** parking (space) for 500 cars; **cinéma de 400 ~s** cinema seating 400 (people) *ou* with a seating capacity of 400; **~ assise** seat; **~s assises 20, ~s debout 40** seating capacity 20, standing passengers 40; **il n'y a que des ~s debout** it's standing room only; **une (voiture de) 4 ~s** a 4-seater (car); (*Aut*) **la ~ du mort** the (front) seat beside the driver; **tente à 4 ~s** tent that sleeps 4, 4-man tent; **j'ai 3 ~s dans ma voiture** I've room for 3 in my car.

f (*rang*) (*Scol*) place (in class); (*Sport*) place, placing. **il a eu une bonne ~** he got a good place, he got a good placing; **être reçu dans les premières ~s** to get one of the top places, be amongst the top; **il a eu une 2ᵉ ~** *ou* **une ~ de 2ᵉ en histoire** he came (*Brit*) *ou* came out *ou* was 2nd in history.

g (*emploi*) job; *[domestique]* position, situation. **une ~ d'employé/de dactylo** a job as a clerk/a typist; *[domestique]* **être en ~** to be in service (*chez* with); (*Pol*) **les gens en ~** influential people, people with influence.

h (*Mil*) **~ (forte** *ou* **de guerre)** fortified town; **le commandant de la ~** the fortress commander; **s'introduire/avoir des contacts dans la ~** to get/have contacts on the inside; (*fig*) **maintenant il est dans la ~** now he's on the inside; **~ d'armes** parade ground.

i (*Comm, Fin*) market. **vous n'en trouverez pas de moins cher sur la ~ de Paris** you won't find cheaper on the Paris market; **dans toutes les ~s financières du monde** in all the money markets of the world.

j (*loc*) **par ~s, de ~ en ~** here and there, in places; **rester sur/se rendre sur ~** to stay on/go to the spot, stay/go there; **on peut faire la réparation sur ~** we can repair it right here *ou* on the spot; **être cloué sur ~** to be *ou* stand rooted to the spot; **faire du sur ~*** *[cycliste]* to balance; *[automobilistes]* to move at a snail's pace; *[enquête]* to hang fire, mark time; **à la ~ (de)** (*en échange*) instead (of), in place (of); **faire une démarche à la ~ de qn** to take steps on sb's behalf; **répondre à la ~ de qn** to reply in sb's place *ou* on sb's behalf; **être en ~** *[plan]* to be ready; *[forces de l'ordre]* to be in place *ou* stationed; **mettre en ~** *plan* to set up, organize; *marchandises* to put on the shelves; *service d'ordre* to deploy; *mécanisme* to install; **mise en ~** *[plan]* setting up; *[service d'ordre]* deployment; **faire ~ à qch** to give way to sth; **faire ~ à qn** (*lit*) to let sb pass; (*fig*) to give way to sb; **faire ~ nette** to make a clean sweep; **~ aux jeunes!** make way for the young!; **pour entrer dans cette université les ~s sont chères** it's difficult to get into this university.

placé, e [plase] (**ptp de placer**) **adj** a (*gén*) **la fenêtre/leur maison est ~e à gauche** the window/their house is (situated) on the left; **je suis** *ou* **je me trouve ~ dans une position délicate** I am (placed) in *ou* I find myself (placed) in a tricky position; **être bien/mal ~** *[terrain]* to be well/badly situated, be favourably/unfavourably situated; *[objet]* to be well/badly placed; *[spectateur]* to have a good/a poor seat; *[concurrent]* to be in a good/bad position, be well/badly placed; **leur confiance a été bien/mal ~e** their trust was justified/misplaced; **sa fierté est mal ~e** his pride is misplaced *ou* out of place; **il est bien ~ pour gagner** he is in a good position *ou* well placed to win; **il est bien ~ pour le savoir** he is in a position to know; **je suis bien/mal ~ pour vous répondre** I'm in a/in no position to answer; **tu es mal ~ pour te plaindre!*** you've got nothing to complain about!, you have scarcely cause for complaint!; *voir* **haut**.

b (*Courses*) **arriver ~** to be placed; **jouer (un cheval) ~** to back a horse each way (*Brit*) *ou* to win, put an each-way (*Brit*) bet on (a horse).

placebo [plasebo] **nm** placebo. **effet ~** placebo effect.

placement [plasmɑ̃] **nm** a (*Fin*) investment. **faire un ~ d'argent** to invest (some) money; **~ de père de famille** gilt-edged investment, safe investment. b *[employés]* placing. **l'école assure le ~ des élèves** the school ensures that the pupils find employment; *voir* **bureau**.

placenta [plasɛ̃ta] **nm** placenta; (*arrière-faix*) afterbirth, placenta.

placentaire [plasɛ̃tɛʀ] **adj** placental.

placer [plase] 3 1 **vt** a (*assigner une place à*) *objet, personne* to place, put; *invité* to seat, put; *spectateur* to seat, give a seat to, put; *sentinelle* to post, station; (*Ftbl*) *balle* to place; (*Boxe*) *coup* to land, place; (*Tech: installer*) to put in, fit in. **vous me placez dans une situation délicate** you're placing *ou* putting me in a tricky position; **~ sa voix** to pitch one's voice; **~ ses affaires bien en ordre** to put one's things

tidy *ou* straight.
b (*situer*) to place, set, put. **il a placé l'action de son roman en Provence** he has set *ou* situated the action of his novel in Provence; **où placez-vous Lyon?** whereabouts do you think Lyons is?, where would you put Lyons?; **~ l'honnêteté avant l'intelligence** to set *ou* put *ou* place honesty above intelligence; **~ le bonheur dans la vie familiale** to consider that happiness is found in family life; **~ un nom sur un visage** to put a name to a face; **je ne peux pas ~ de nom sur son visage** I can't place him *ou* his face, I can't put a name to his face *ou* to him; **~ ses espérances en qn/qch** to set *ou* pin one's hopes on sb/sth.
c (*introduire*) *remarque, anecdote, plaisanterie* to come out with, put in, get in. **il n'a pas pu ~ un mot** he couldn't get a word in (edgeways).
d *ouvrier, malade, écolier* to place (*dans* in). **~ qn comme vendeur/chez X** to get *ou* find sb a job as a salesman/with X; **~ qn comme apprenti (chez X)** to apprentice sb (to X); **~ qn à la comptabilité** to give sb a job *ou* place sb in the accounts department; **~ qn à la tête d'une entreprise** to put sb at the head of a business, put sb in charge of a business; (*hum*) **ils n'ont pas encore pu ~ leur fille** they've still not been able to marry off their daughter (*hum*) *ou* to get their daughter off their hands (*hum*); **~ qn/qch sous l'autorité/les ordres de** to place *ou* put sb/sth under the authority/orders of.
e (*Comm: vendre*) *marchandise* to place, sell. (*fig hum*) **elle a réussi à ~ sa vieille machine à laver** she managed to find a home (*hum*) *ou* a buyer for her old washing machine.
f *argent* (*à la Bourse*) to invest; (*à la Caisse d'Épargne, sur un compte*) to deposit. **~ une somme sur son compte** to put *ou* pay a sum into one's account.
2 **se placer** **vpr** a *[personne]* to take up a position; (*debout*) to stand; (*assis*) to sit (down); *[événement, action]* to take place. **se ~ de face/contre le mur/en cercle** to stand face on/against the wall/in a circle; **se ~ sur le chemin de qn** to stand in sb's path; **cette démarche se place dans le cadre de nos revendications** these steps should be seen in the context of our claims; (*fig*) **si nous nous plaçons à ce point de vue** *ou* **dans cette perspective** if we look at things from this point of view, if we view the situation in this way; **plaçons-nous dans le cas où cela arriverait** let us suppose that this happens, let us put ourselves in the situation where this actually happens.
b *[cheval]* to be placed. (*Scol, Sport*) **se ~ 2ᵉ** to be *ou* come 2nd, be in 2nd place; **il s'est bien placé dans la course** he was well placed in the race; **se ~ parmi les premiers** to be in the first few.
c (*prendre une place*) **se ~ comme vendeuse** to get *ou* find a job as a salesgirl; **retraité qui voudrait bien se ~ (dans une institution)** pensioner who would like to find a place in a home; (*hum*) **ce célibataire n'a pas encore réussi à se ~** this bachelor still hasn't been able to find anyone willing to marry him *ou* give him a home (*hum*).

placet [plasɛ] **nm** (*Hist, Jur*) petition.

placeur [plasœʀ] **nm** *[spectateurs, invités]* usher; *[domestiques]* (domestic) employment agent.

placeuse [plasøz] **nf** *[spectateurs]* usherette; *[domestiques]* (domestic) employment agent.

placide [plasid] **adj** placid, calm.

placidement [plasidmɑ̃] **adv** placidly, calmly.

placidité [plasidite] **nf** placidity, placidness, calmness.

placier [plasje] **nm** travelling salesman, traveller. **~ en assurances** insurance broker.

Placoplâtre [plakoplɑtʀ] **nm** ® plasterboard.

plafond [plafɔ̃] **nm** a (*lit*) *[salle]* ceiling; *[voiture, caverne]* roof. **~ à caissons** coffered ceiling; **pièce haute/basse de ~** high-ceilinged/low-ceilinged room, room with a high/low ceiling; *voir* **araignée**. b (*fig: limite*) *[prix, loyer]* ceiling; (*Mét: nuages*) ceiling, cloud cover; (*Aviat*) ceiling, maximum height; (*Aut*) top *ou* maximum speed. **niveau/prix-~** ceiling, ceiling *ou* maximum limit/price; **âge(-)~** maximum age; **~ de crédit** lending *ou* credit limit; (*Mét*) **le ~ est bas** the cloud cover is low.

plafonnement [plafɔnmɑ̃] **nm**: **il y a un ~ des salaires/cotisations** there is an upper limit on salaries/contributions.

plafonner [plafɔne] [1] 1 **vi** *[prix, écolier, salaire]* to reach a ceiling *ou* maximum; (*Aviat*) to reach one's ceiling; (*Aut*) to reach one's top speed *ou* maximum speed. **les ventes plafonnent** sales have reached their *ou* a ceiling (limit); **la voiture plafonne à 100 km/h** the car can't do more than 100 km/h. 2 **vt** a (*Constr*) to put a ceiling in. **grenier plafonné** loft which has had a ceiling put in. b *salaires* to put an upper limit on. **cotisations plafonnées à 1 500 F** contributions which have had their ceiling *ou* upper limit fixed at 1.500 francs.

plafonnier [plafɔnje] **nm** *[voiture]* courtesy *ou* interior light; *[chambre]* ceiling light *ou* lamp.

plagal, e, **mpl -aux** [plagal, o] **adj** plagal.

plage [plaʒ] 1 **nf** a *[mer, rivière, lac]* beach. **~ de sable/de galets** sandy/pebble beach; **sac/serviette/robe de ~** beach bag/towel/robe. b (*ville*) (seaside) resort. c (*zone*) (*dans un barème, une progression*) range, bracket; (*dans un horaire etc*) (time) segment. **~ d'ombre** band of shadow (*fig*), shadowy area (*fig*); **temps d'écoute divisé en ~s (horaires)** listening time divided into segments; (*Scol*) **~ horaire** slot (in timetable); **~ de prix** price range *ou* bracket. d *[disque]* track. 2 **comp** ▸**plage arrière** (*Naut*) quarter-deck; (*Aut*) parcel *ou* back shelf ▸**plage avant** (*Naut*) forecastle (head *ou* deck), fo'c'sle ▸**plage lumineuse** illuminated area.

plagiaire [plaʒjɛʀ] **nmf** plagiarist, plagiarizer.

plagiat [plaʒja] **nm** plagiarism, plagiary. **c'est un véritable ~** it's absolute plagiarism; **faire du ~** to plagiarize.

plagier [plaʒje] [7] **vt** to plagiarize.

plagiste [plaʒist] **nm** beach manager *ou* attendant.

plaid [plɛd] **nm** (tartan) car rug, lap robe (*US*).

plaidant, e [plɛdɑ̃, ɑ̃t] **adj** *partie* litigant; *avocat* pleading.

plaider [plede] [1] 1 **vt** to plead. **~ coupable/non coupable/la légitime défense** to plead guilty/not guilty/self-defence; **~ la cause de qn** (*fig*) to plead sb's cause, argue *ou* speak in favour of sb; (*Jur*) to plead for sb, plead sb's case, defend sb; **~ sa propre cause** to speak in one's own defence; (*fig*) **~ le faux pour savoir le vrai** to tell a lie (in order) to get at the truth; **l'affaire s'est plaidée à Paris/à huis clos** the case was heard in Paris/in closed court *ou* in camera. 2 **vi** a *[avocat]* to plead (*pour* for, on behalf of, *contre* against). b (*intenter un procès*) to go to court, litigate. **~ contre qn** to take sb to court, take (out) proceedings against sb; **ils ont plaidé pendant des années** their case has dragged on for years. c (*fig*) **~ pour** *ou* **en faveur de qn** *[personne]* to speak for sb, defend sb; *[mérites, qualités]* to be a point in sb's favour.

plaideur, -euse [plɛdœʀ, øz] **nm,f** litigant.

plaidoirie [plɛdwaʀi] **nf** (*Jur*) speech for the defence, defence speech; (*fig*) plea, appeal (*en faveur de* on behalf of).

plaidoyer [plɛdwaje] **nm** (*Jur*) speech for the defence; (*fig*) defence, plea. (*fig*) **~ en faveur de/contre qch** plea for/against sth.

plaie [plɛ] **nf** (*physique, morale*) wound; (*coupure*) cut; (*fig: fléau*) scourge. (*fig*) **rouvrir une ~** to reopen an old sore; **quelle ~!*** (*personne*) what a bind* (*Brit*) *ou* nuisance he is!, what a pest* (he is)!; (*chose*) what a bind!* (*Brit*) *ou* pest!* *ou* nuisance (it is)!; **remuer** *ou* **tourner le couteau** *ou* **le fer dans la ~** to twist *ou* turn the knife in the wound; (*Prov*) **~ d'argent n'est pas mortelle** money isn't everything; (*Bible*) **les ~s d'Égypte** the plagues of Egypt; *voir* **rêver**.

plaignant, e [plɛɲɑ̃, ɑ̃t] 1 **adj** *partie* litigant. 2 **nm,f** plaintiff, complainant.

plain [plɛ̃] **nm** (*Naut*) **le ~** high tide.

plain-chant, **pl plains-chants** [plɛ̃ʃɑ̃] **nm** plainchant (*NonC*), plainsong (*NonC*).

plaindre [plɛ̃dʀ] [52] 1 **vt** a *personne* to pity, feel sorry for. **aimer se faire ~** to like to be pitied; **il est bien à ~** he is to be pitied; **elle n'est pas à ~** (*c'est bien fait*) she doesn't deserve (any) sympathy, she doesn't deserve to be pitied; (*elle a de la chance*) she's got nothing to complain about; **je vous plains de vivre avec lui** I pity you *ou* I sympathize with you (for) having to live with him.
b (**: donner chichement*) to begrudge, grudge. **donne-moi plus de papier, on dirait que tu le plains** give me some more paper — anybody would think you begrudged it (me); **il ne plaint pas son temps/sa peine** he doesn't grudge his time/his efforts.
2 **se plaindre** **vpr** (*gémir*) to moan; (*protester*) to complain, grumble, moan* (*de* about); (*frm, Jur: réclamer*) to make a complaint (*de* about, *auprès de* to). (*souffrir*) **se ~ de** *maux de tête etc* to complain of; **se ~ de qn/qch à qn** to complain to sb about sb/sth; **de quoi te plains-tu?** (*lit*) what are you complaining *ou* grumbling *ou* moaning* about?; (*iro*) what have you got to complain *ou* grumble *ou* moan* about?; **il se plaint que les prix montent** he's complaining about rising prices *ou* that prices are going up; **ne viens pas te ~ si tu es puni** don't come and complain *ou* moan* (to me) if you're punished; **se ~ à qui de droit** to make a complaint *ou* to complain to the appropriate person.

plaine [plɛn] **nf** plain. **c'est de la ~** it is flat open country; **en ~** in the plains; **haute ~** high plain.

plain-pied [plɛ̃pje] **adv**: **de ~** (*pièce*) on the same level (*avec* as); (*maison*) (built) at street-level; (*fig*) **entrer de ~ dans le sujet** to come straight to the point; (*fig*) **être de ~ avec qn** to be on an equal footing with sb.

plainte [plɛ̃t] **nf** a (*gémissement*) moan, groan; (*littér*) *[vent]* moaning. b (*doléance*) complaint, moaning (*NonC: péj*). c (*Jur*) complaint. **porter ~** *ou* **déposer une ~ contre qn** to lodge a complaint against *ou* about sb.

plaintif, -ive [plɛ̃tif, iv] **adj** plaintive, sorrowful, doleful.

plaintivement [plɛ̃tivmɑ̃] **adv** plaintively, sorrowfully, dolefully.

plaire [plɛʀ] [54] 1 **vi** a (*être apprécié*) **ce garçon me plaît** I like that boy; **ce garçon ne me plaît pas** I don't like that boy, I don't care for that boy; **ce spectacle/dîner/livre m'a plu** I liked *ou* enjoyed that show/dinner/book; **ce genre de musique ne me plaît pas beaucoup** I'm not (very *ou* terribly) keen on (*Brit*) *ou* I don't (really) care for *ou* go for* that kind of music, that kind of music doesn't appeal to me very much; **ton nouveau travail te plaît?** (how) do you like your new job?, how are you enjoying your new job?; **les brunes me plaisent** I like *ou* go for* dark-haired girls, dark-haired girls appeal to me; **tu ne me plais pas avec cette coiffure** I don't like you with your hair like that *ou* with that hairstyle; **c'est une chose qui me plairait beaucoup à faire** it's something I'd very much like to do *ou* I'd love to do; **on ne peut pas ~**

à tout le monde one cannot be liked by everyone; il cherche à ~ à tout le monde he tries to please everyone; il cherchait à ~ à toutes les femmes he was trying to impress all the women *ou* appeal to all the women; c'est le genre d'homme qui plaît aux femmes he's the sort of man that women like *ou* who appeals to women; le désir de ~ the desire to please; c'est le genre de personne qui plaît en société he's the type of person who gets on well with people *ou* that people like; (*iro*) tu commences à me ~ (avec tes questions)!* (you and your questions –) you know how to please me! (*iro*).

b (*convenir à*) ce plan me plaît this plan suits me; ça te plairait d'aller au cinéma? would you like to go to the pictures?, do you fancy* (*Brit*) *ou* do you feel like going to the pictures?; ce qui vous plaira le mieux whichever *ou* whatever suits you best; j'irai si ça me plaît I'll go if I feel like it *ou* if it suits me; je travaille quand ça me plaît I work when I feel like it *ou* when it suits me *ou* when the fancy takes me* (*Brit*); je fais ce qui me plaît I do what I like *ou* as I please; si ça ne te plaît pas c'est le même prix!* if you don't like it (that's just) too bad!* *ou* that's tough!*

c (*réussir*) fais un gâteau, cela plaît toujours make a cake, it's always welcome *ou* popular; achète des fleurs, cela plaît toujours buy some flowers, they're always appreciated *ou* welcome; la pièce a plu the play was a success *ou* hit* *ou* went down well *ou* was well-received; cette réponse a plu this reply went down well *ou* was appreciated *ou* was well-received.

2 vb impers a ici, je fais ce qu'il me plaît I do as I please *ou* like here; et s'il me plaît d'y aller? and what if I want to go?; vous plairait-il de venir dîner ce soir? would you care *ou* like to come for dinner this evening?; (*littér*) il lui plaît de croire que ... he likes to think that ...; comme il vous plaira just as you like *ou* please *ou* choose.

b (*loc*) s'il te plaît, s'il vous plaît please; et elle a un manteau de vison, s'il vous plaît!* and she's got a mink coat if you please! *ou* no less!; (*littér*) plaise *ou* plût à Dieu *ou* au ciel, qu'il réussisse! please God that *ou* would to God that *ou* heaven grant that he succeeds! (*littér*); (*frm*) plaît-il? I beg your pardon? (*frm*); *voir* dieu.

3 se plaire vpr a (*se sentir bien, à l'aise*) il se plaît à Londres he likes *ou* enjoys being in London, he likes it in London; j'espère qu'il s'y plaira I hope he'll like it there; se ~ avec qn to enjoy being with sb, enjoy sb's company; te plais-tu avec tes nouveaux amis? do you like being with your new friends?; les fougères se plaisent dans les sous-bois ferns do *ou* grow well *ou* thrive *ou* flourish in the undergrowth.

b (*s'apprécier*) je me plais en robe longue I like myself in *ou* I like wearing a long dress; tu te plais avec ton chapeau? do you like *ou* fancy* (*Brit*) yourself in your hat?; ces deux-là se plaisent those two get on well together *ou* are drawn to each other, those two (have) hit it off (together)*.

c (*littér: prendre plaisir à*) se ~ à lire to take pleasure in reading, like *ou* be fond of reading; se ~ à tout critiquer to delight in criticizing everything.

plaisamment [plɛzamɑ̃] adv (*voir* plaisant) pleasantly; attractively; agreeably; amusingly; laughably, ridiculously.

plaisance [plɛzɑ̃s] nf: la (navigation de) ~ boating; (*à voile*) sailing, yachting; bateau de ~ yacht; port de ~ (*bassin*) sailing *ou* yachting harbour; (*ville*) sailing *ou* yachting resort; maison de ~ country cottage.

plaisancier [plɛzɑ̃sje] nm (*amateur*) sailor, yachtsman.

plaisant, e [plɛzɑ̃, ɑ̃t] adj a (*agréable*) *personne, séjour* pleasant, agreeable; *maison* attractive, pleasant; *souvenir* pleasant, agreeable. ~ à l'œil pleasing to *ou* on the eye, nice *ou* attractive to look at; ce n'est guère ~ it's not exactly pleasant, it's not very nice; *voir* mauvais. b (*amusant*) *histoire, aventure* amusing, funny. le ~ de la chose the funny side *ou* part of it, the funny thing about it. c (*ridicule*) laughable, ridiculous. d (†*: bizarre*) bizarre, singular. voilà qui est ~! it's quite bizarre!; je vous trouve bien ~ de parler de la sorte I consider it most bizarre *ou* singular of you to speak in that way.

plaisanter [plɛzɑ̃te] [1] 1 vi to joke, have a joke (*sur* about). je ne suis pas d'humeur à ~ I'm in no mood for jokes *ou* joking, I'm not in a joking mood; et je ne plaisante pas! and I mean it!, and I'm not joking!, and I'm serious!; c'est quelqu'un qui ne plaisante pas he's not the sort you can have a joke with; vous plaisantez you must be joking *ou* kidding*, you're joking *ou* kidding*; pour ~ for fun *ou* a joke *ou* a laugh*; on ne plaisante pas avec cela it's no joking *ou* laughing matter, this is a serious matter; il ne faut pas ~ avec les médicaments you shouldn't mess around* with medicines; il ne plaisante pas sur la discipline/cette question there's no joking with him over matters of discipline/this subject; on ne plaisante pas avec la police there's no joking where the police are concerned, the police are not to be trifled with.

2 vt to make fun of, tease. ~ qn sur qch to tease sb about sth.

plaisanterie [plɛzɑ̃tʀi] nf a (*blague*) joke (*sur* about). aimer la ~ to be fond of a joke; ~ de corps de garde barrack-room joke; par ~ for fun *ou* a joke *ou* a laugh*; faire une ~ to tell *ou* crack a joke; tourner qch en ~ to make a joke of sth, laugh sth off.

b (*raillerie*) joke. il est en butte aux ~s de ses amis his friends are always making fun of him *ou* poking fun at him, his friends treat him as a figure of fun; faire des ~s sur to joke *ou* make jokes about *ou* at the expense of; il comprend *ou* prend bien la ~ he knows how to *ou* he can take a joke; il ne faudrait pas pousser la ~ trop loin we mustn't take the joke too far.

c (*farce*) (practical) joke, prank; *voir* mauvais.

d (*loc fig*) c'est une ~ pour lui de résoudre ce problème/gagner la course he could solve this problem/win the race with his eyes shut *ou* standing on his head*; lui, se lever tôt? c'est une ~! him, get up early? what a joke! *ou* you must be joking! *ou* you must be kidding!*

plaisantin [plɛzɑ̃tɛ̃] nm a (*blagueur*) joker. c'est un petit ~ he's quite a joker. b (*fumiste*) phoney*.

plaisir [pleziʀ] nm a (*joie*) pleasure. avoir du ~ *ou* prendre ~ à faire qch to find *ou* take pleasure in doing sth, delight in doing sth; prendre (un malin) ~ à faire qch to take (a mischievous) delight in doing sth; j'ai le ~ de vous annoncer que ... it is with great pleasure that I am able to announce that ...; M. et Mme X ont le ~ de vous faire part de ... Mr and Mrs X have pleasure in announcing ..., Mr and Mrs X are pleased to announce ...; c'est un ~ de le voir it's a pleasure to see him; par ~, pour le ~ (*gén*) for pleasure; *bricoler, peindre* as a hobby; ranger pour le ~ de ranger to tidy up just for the sake of it; (*iro*) je vous souhaite bien du ~! good luck to you! (*iro*), I wish you (the best of) luck! (*iro*); (*iro*) ça nous promet du ~ (en perspective) I can hardly wait! (*iro*); avec (le plus grand) ~ with (the greatest of) pleasure; au ~ de vous revoir, au ~* (I'll) see you again sometime, (I'll) be seeing you*; le ~ solitaire self-abuse; les ~s de la chair the pleasures of the flesh; *voir* durer, gêne.

b (*distraction*) pleasure. les ~s de la vie life's (little) pleasures; courir après les ~s to be a pleasure-seeker; le tennis est un ~ coûteux tennis is an expensive hobby *ou* pleasure; lieu de ~ house of pleasure.

c (*littér: volonté*) pleasure (*littér*), wish. si c'est votre (bon) ~ if such is your will *ou* wish, if you so desire; les faits ont été grossis à ~ the facts have been wildly exaggerated; il s'inquiète à ~ he seems to take a perverse delight in worrying himself; il ment à ~ he lies for the sake of lying *ou* for the sake of it.

d (*loc*) faire ~ à qn to please sb; ce cadeau m'a fait ~ I was very pleased with this gift, this gift gave me great pleasure; cela me fait ~ de vous entendre dire cela I'm pleased *ou* delighted to hear you say that, it gives me great pleasure to hear you say that; mine/appétit qui fait ~ à voir healthy face/appetite that is a pleasure to see *ou* to behold; pour me faire ~ (just) to please me; fais-moi ~: mange ta soupe/arrête la radio do me a favour, eat your soup/turn off the radio, be a dear and eat your soup/turn off the radio; (*frm*) voulez-vous me faire le ~ de venir dîner? I should be most pleased if you would come to dinner, would you do me the pleasure of dining with me (*ou* us)? (*frm*); fais-moi le ~ de te taire! would you mind just being quiet!, do me a favour and shut up!*; il se fera un ~ de vous reconduire he'll be (only too) pleased *ou* glad to drive you back, it will be a pleasure for him to drive you back; bon, c'est bien pour vous faire ~ *ou* si cela peut vous faire ~ all right, if it will make you happy *ou* give you pleasure; j'irai, mais c'est bien pour vous faire ~ I'll go (just) to keep you happy.

plan[1] [plɑ̃] 1 nm a [*maison*] plan, blueprint; [*machine*] plan, scale drawing; [*ville, métro*] map, plan; [*région*] map. acheter une maison sur ~ to buy a house while it's still only a plan on paper; faire *ou* tracer *ou* tirer un ~ to draw a plan; (*fig*) tirer des ~s sur la comète* to build castles in the air.

b (*Math, Phys: surface*) plane.

c (*Ciné, Phot*) shot. (*Peinture, Phot*) premier ~ foreground; dernier ~ background; au second ~ in the background; (*Peinture*) au deuxième ~ in the middle distance; (*Ciné*) ~ américain medium close shot; *voir* gros.

d (*fig: niveau*) plane, level. mettre qch au deuxième ~ to consider sth of secondary importance; ce problème est au premier ~ de nos préoccupations this problem is uppermost in our minds *ou* is one of our foremost preoccupations; parmi toutes ces questions, l'inflation vient au premier ~ *ou* nous mettons l'inflation au premier ~ of all these questions, inflation is the key *ou* priority issue *ou* we consider inflation to be the most important; personnalité de premier ~ key figure; personnalité de second ~ minor figure; un savant de tout premier ~ a scientist of the first rank, one of our foremost scientists; au premier ~ de l'actualité at the forefront of the news, very much in the news; mettre sur le même ~ to put on the same plane *ou* level; au ~ national/international at the national/international level; sur le ~ du confort as far as comfort is concerned, as regards comfort; sur le ~ moral/intellectuel morally/intellectually speaking, on the moral/intellectual plane; sur tous les ~s in every way, on all fronts; *voir* arrière.

e (*projet*) plan, project; (*Écon*) plan, programme. avoir/exécuter un ~ to have/carry out a plan; ~ de carrière career path; ~ de cinq ans five-year plan; ~ de relance de l'économie plan to reflate the economy; ~ d'action plan of action; (*Comm*) ~ d'attaque plan of attack; ~ de modernisation modernization plan; ~ de développement économique et social economic and social development plan.

f (**: idée*) plan, idea, scheme. tu as un ~ pour les vacances? have you any plans for the holidays?; c'est un super ~ *ou* un ~ d'enfer! it's a great idea!; il a toujours des ~s foireux** celui-là he is full of crap** ideas *ou* schemes.

g *[livre, dissertation, devoir]* plan, outline, framework. **faire un ~ de qch** to make a plan for sth, plan sth out.

h (**loc*) **rester en ~** *[personne]* to be left stranded, be left high and dry; *[voiture]* to be abandoned *ou* ditched*; *[projets]* to be abandoned in midstream, be left (hanging) in mid air; **laisser en ~** *personne* to leave in the lurch *ou* high and dry *ou* stranded; *voiture* to leave (behind), abandon, ditch*; *affaires* to abandon; *projet, travail* to drop, abandon; **il a tout laissé en ~ pour venir me voir** he dropped everything to come and see me.

2 **comp** ▸**plan d'amortissement** (*pour un bien, un investissement*) depreciation schedule; (*pour un emprunt*) redemption plan ▸**plan directeur** (*Mil*) *map of the combat area;* (*Écon*) blueprint, master plan ▸**plan d'eau** (*lac*) lake; (*sur un cours d'eau*) stretch of smooth water ▸**plan d'épargne logement** ≃ building society savings plan ▸**plan d'épargne populaire** individual savings plan ▸**plan d'épargne retraite** personal pension plan *ou* scheme ▸**plan d'équipement** industrial development programme ▸**plan d'études** study plan *ou* programme ▸**plan de faille** fault plane ▸**plan de financement** financing plan ▸**plan fixe** (*Ciné*) static shot ▸**plan incliné** inclined plane; **en plan incliné** sloping ▸**plan d'occupation des sols** zoning regulations *ou* ordinances (*US*) ▸**plan ORSEC** *scheme set up to deal with major civil emergencies* ▸**plan rapproché** (*Ciné*) close-up (shot) ▸**plan séquence** (*Ciné*) sequence shot ▸**plan de travail** (*dans une cuisine*) work-top, work(ing) surface; (*planning*) work plan *ou* programme *ou* schedule ▸**plan de vol** flight plan; *voir* **plan-concave, plan-convexe.**

plan², plane [plɑ̃, plan] **adj** *miroir* flat; *surface* flat, level, plane; (*Math*) *angle, géométrie* plane.

planche [plɑ̃ʃ] 1 **nf** a (*en bois*) plank; (*plus large*) board; (*rayon*) shelf; (*Naut: passerelle*) gangplank; (*plongeoir*) diving board; (**: ski*) ski. **cabine/sol en ~s** wooden hut/floor; **dormir sur une ~** to sleep on a wooden board; *voir* **pain.**

b (*Typ, illustration*) plate.

c (*Horticulture*) bed.

d (*Théât*) **les ~s** the boards, the stage (*NonC*); **monter sur les ~s** (*entrer en scène*) to go on stage; (*faire du théâtre*) to go on the stage; *voir* **brûler.**

e (*Natation*) floating (on one's back). **faire la ~** to float on one's back.

2 **comp** ▸**planche à billets** banknote plate; **faire marcher la planche à billets*** to print money ▸**planche à découper** *[cuisinière]* chopping board; *[boucher]* chopping block ▸**planche à dessin** *ou* **à dessiner** drawing board ▸**planche à laver** washboard ▸**planche à pain** (*lit*) breadboard; (*péj*) flat-chested woman, woman who is as flat as a board (*péj*) ▸**planche à pâtisserie** pastry board ▸**planche à repasser** ironing board ▸**planche à roulettes** (*objet*) skateboard; (*sport*) skateboarding; **faire de la planche à roulettes** to skateboard, go skateboarding ▸**planche de salut** (*appui*) mainstay; (*dernier espoir*) last hope, sheet anchor (*Brit*) ▸**planche à voile** (*objet*) windsurfing-board, sailboard; (*sport*) windsurfing; **faire de la planche à voile** to windsurf, go windsurfing.

planchéié, e [plɑ̃ʃeje] **adj** floored (*lit*).

plancher¹ [plɑ̃ʃe] **nm** a (*Constr*) floor. (*Aut*) **mettre le pied au ~** to put one's foot down to the floor, step on it* *ou* on the gas*; (*fig*) **le ~ des vaches*** dry land; **faux ~** false floor; *voir* **débarrasser.** b (*limite*) lower limit. **~ des cotisations** lower limit on contributions; **prix ~** minimum *ou* floor *ou* bottom price. c (*Anat*) floor. **~ pelvien** pelvic floor.

plancher² [plɑ̃ʃe] [1] **vi** (*arg Scol*) to talk, spout* (*Brit*). **sur quoi as-tu planché?** what did they get you to talk on *ou* spout (*Brit*) on?*; **~ sur un rapport** to work on a report.

planchette [plɑ̃ʃɛt] **nf** (*gén*) (small) board; (*rayon*) (small) shelf.

planchiste [plɑ̃ʃist] **nmf** windsurfer.

plan-concave [plɑ̃kɔ̃kav] **adj** plano-concave.

plan-convexe [plɑ̃kɔ̃vɛks] **adj** plano-convex.

plancton [plɑ̃ktɔ̃] **nm** plankton.

planéité [planeite] **nf** (*voir* **plan²**) flatness; levelness; planeness.

planer [plane] [1] **vi** a *[oiseau]* to glide, soar; (*en tournoyant*) to hover; *[avion]* to glide, volplane; *[fumée]* to float, hover; *voir* **vol.**

b *[danger, soupçons]* **~ sur** to hang *ou* hover over; **laisser ~ le mystère (sur)** to let mystery hang (over).

c (*se détacher*) *[savant]* to have no sense of reality, be divorced from reality; *[rêveur]* to have one's head in the clouds. **~ au-dessus de** *querelles, détails* to be above; **il plane dans un univers de rêve** he is lost in a dream world.

d (*littér*) *[regard]* **~ sur** to look down on *ou* over; **le regard planait au loin sur la mer** one had a commanding view over the sea.

e (*arg Drogue*) to be high* *ou* stoned*. **musique/spectacle qui fait ~** music/show which sends you‡.

planétaire [planetɛʀ] **adj** (*Astron, Tech*) planetary.

planétarium [planetaʀjɔm] **nm** planetarium.

planète [planɛt] **nf** planet. **la ~ bleue** the Earth.

planétologie [planetɔlɔʒi] **nf** planetology.

planeur [planœʀ] **nm** (*Aviat*) glider. **faire du ~** to go gliding.

planificateur, -trice [planifikatœʀ, tʀis] (*Écon*) 1 **adj** economic. 2 **nm,f** planner.

planification [planifikasjɔ̃] **nf** (economic) planning. **~ démographique** population planning.

planifier [planifje] [7] **vt** to plan. **économie planifiée** planned *ou* controlled economy.

planimétrie [planimetʀi] **nf** planimetry.

planimétrique [planimetʀik] **adj** planimetric(al).

planisphère [planisfɛʀ] **nm** planisphere.

planning [planiŋ] **nm** (*Écon, Ind*) programme, schedule. **~ familial** family planning.

planque‡ [plɑ̃k] **nf** (*cachette*) hideaway, hideout, hidey-hole* (*Brit*); (*Police*) hideout; (*travail tranquille*) cushy job*, cushy *ou* soft (*Brit*) *ou* real easy number‡. **c'est la ~!** it's dead cushy!‡, it's a real cushy number!‡

planqué [plɑ̃ke] **nm** (*arg Mil*) funker* (*Brit*).

planquer‡ [plɑ̃ke] [1] 1 **vt** to hide (away), stash away*. 2 **se planquer vpr** to hide.

plant [plɑ̃] **nm** (*plante*) *[légume]* seedling, young plant; *[fleur]* bedding plant; (*plantation*) *[légumes]* bed, (vegetable) patch; *[fleurs]* (flower) bed; *[arbres]* plantation. **un ~ de salade** a lettuce seedling, a young lettuce (plant); **un ~ de vigne/de bégonia** a young vine/begonia.

Plantagenêt [plɑ̃taʒnɛ] **nmf** Plantagenet.

plantain [plɑ̃tɛ̃] **nm** plantain.

plantaire [plɑ̃tɛʀ] **adj** plantar. **verrue ~** verruca on the sole of the foot (*Brit*), plantar wart (*US*); *voir* **voûte.**

plantation [plɑ̃tasjɔ̃] **nf** a (*Horticulture*) (*action*) planting; (*culture*) plant; (*terrain*) *[légumes]* bed, (vegetable) patch; *[fleurs]* (flower) bed; *[arbres, café, coton]* plantation. **faire des ~s de fleurs** to plant flowers (out). b (*exploitation agricole*) plantation. c (*Théât*) *[décor]* setting up.

plante¹ [plɑ̃t] **nf** (*Bot*) plant. **~ annuelle** annual (plant); **~ d'appartement** *ou* **d'agrément** house *ou* pot plant; **~ à fleurs** flowering plant; **~ fourragère** fodder plant; **~ grasse** succulent (plant); **~ grimpante** creeper; **~s médicinales** medicinal plants; **~ de serre** (*lit*) greenhouse *ou* hothouse plant; (*fig*) hothouse plant, delicate flower; **~ textile** fibre plant; **~ verte** house plant, green (foliage) plant; (*fig*) **c'est une belle ~** she's a lovely *ou* fine specimen.

plante² [plɑ̃t] **nf** (*Anat*) **~ (des pieds)** sole (of the foot).

planté, e [plɑ̃te] (**ptp de planter**) **adj: bien ~** *dents* straight; **mal ~** *dents* uneven; **ses cheveux sont ~s très bas** he has a very low hairline; **être bien ~ (sur ses jambes)** to be sturdily built; **il est resté ~ au milieu de la rue** he stood stock-still in the middle of the road; **ne restez pas ~ (debout** *ou* **comme un piquet) à ne rien faire!** don't just stand there doing nothing!; **rester ~ devant une vitrine** to stand looking in a shop window.

planter [plɑ̃te] [1] 1 **vt** a *plante, graine* to plant, put in; *jardin* to put plants in; (*repiquer*) to plant out. **~ une région en vignes** to plant a region with vines; **~ un terrain en gazon** to plant out a piece of ground with grass, grass a piece of ground; **avenue plantée d'arbres** tree-lined avenue; (*fig*) **aller ~ ses choux** to retire to the country.

b (*enfoncer*) *clou* to hammer in, knock in; *pieu* to drive in. **~ un poignard dans le dos de qn** to stick a knife into sb's back, knife *ou* stab sb in the back; **l'ours planta ses griffes dans le bras de l'enfant** the bear stuck its claws into the child's arm; **se ~ une épine dans le doigt** to get a thorn stuck in one's finger; **la flèche se planta dans la cible** the arrow sank into the target.

c (*mettre*) to stick, put. **~ son chapeau sur sa tête** to stick one's hat on one's head; **il a planté sa voiture au milieu de la rue et il est parti** he stuck *ou* dumped* his car in the middle of the road and went off; **il nous a plantés sur le trottoir pour aller chercher un journal** he left us hanging about* *ou* standing on the pavement while he went to get a paper; **~ un baiser sur la joue de qn** to plant a kiss on sb's cheek; **~ son regard** *ou* **ses yeux sur qn** to fix one's eyes on sb; **il se planta devant moi** he planted *ou* plonked* himself in front of me; **~ là** (*laisser sur place*) *personne* to dump*, leave behind; *voiture* to dump*, ditch*; *travail, outils* to dump*, drop; (*délaisser*) *épouse* to walk out on*, ditch*; *travail* to pack in.

d (*installer*) *échelle, drapeau* to put up; *tente* to put up, pitch; (*Théât*) *décors* to put *ou* set up. **~ une échelle contre un mur** to put a ladder (up) *ou* stand a ladder (up) against a wall; (*fig*) **cet auteur sait ~ ses personnages** this author is good at characterization, this author knows how to build up *ou* give substance to his characters.

2 **se planter* vpr** (*se tromper*) to get it all wrong. **il s'est planté dans ses calculs** he got his calculations wrong, he was way out* in his calculations.

planteur [plɑ̃tœʀ] **nm** (*colon*) planter.

planteuse [plɑ̃tøz] **nf** (*Agr*) (potato) planter.

plantigrade [plɑ̃tigʀad] **adj, nm** plantigrade.

plantoir [plɑ̃twaʀ] **nm** dibble.

planton [plɑ̃tɔ̃] **nm** (*Mil*) orderly. **être de ~** to be on orderly duty; (*fig*) **faire le ~*** to hang about*, stand around *ou* about (waiting).

plantureusement [plɑ̃tyʀøzmɑ̃] **adv** *manger, boire* copiously.

plantureux, -euse [plɑ̃tyʀø, øz] **adj** a *repas* copious, lavish; *femme* buxom; *poitrine* ample. b *région, terre* fertile. **récolte/année ~euse** bumper crop/year.

plaquage [plakaʒ] **nm** a (*Rugby*) tackling (*NonC*), tackle. **~ à retardement** late tackle. b (*‡: abandon: voir* **plaquer**) jilting*; ditching*; chucking (in *ou* up)*; packing in.

plaque [plak] 1 **nf** a *[métal, verre]* sheet, plate; *[marbre]* slab; *[chocolat]* block, slab; (*revêtement*) plate, cover(ing); *voir* **côté**.
b *[verglas]* sheet, patch; *[boue]* patch.
c (*tache sur la peau*) patch, blotch, plaque (*SPÉC*); *[eczéma]* patch; *voir* **sclérose**.
d (*portant une inscription*) plaque; (*insigne*) badge; (*au casino*) chip. *[médecin, avocat]* **poser** *ou* **visser sa ~** to set up in practice.
e (*Élec, Phot*) plate.
f (*Géol*) plate.
2 **comp** ►**plaque de blindage** armour-plate (*NonC*), armour-plating (*NonC*) ►**plaque chauffante** *ou* **de cuisson** (*Culin*) hotplate ►**plaque de cheminée** fireback ►**plaque commémorative** commemorative plaque *ou* plate ►**plaque dentaire** dental plaque ►**plaque d'égout** manhole cover ►**plaque de four** baking tray ►**plaque d'identité** *[soldat]* identity disc; *[chien]* name tag, identity disc; *[bracelet]* nameplate ►**plaque d'immatriculation** *ou* **minéralogique** *ou* **de police** (*Aut*) number plate, registration plate (*Brit*), license plate (*US*) ►**plaque de propreté** fingerplate ►**plaque sensible** (*Phot*) sensitive plate ►**plaque tournante** (*Rail*) turntable; (*fig*) (*lieu*) hub; (*personne*) linchpin.

plaqué, e [plake] (**ptp de plaquer**) 1 **adj** *bracelet* plated; *poches* patch (*épith*); *accord* non-arpeggiated. **~ or/argent** gold-/silver-plated; **~ chêne** oak-veneered. 2 **nm** plate. **en ~** plated; **c'est du ~** it's plated.

plaquer [plake] [1] **vt** a *bois* to veneer; *bijoux* to plate. **~ du métal sur du bois** to plate wood with metal; **~ des bijoux d'or/d'argent** to plate jewellery with gold/silver, gold-plate/silver-plate jewellery; (*fig*) **ce passage semble plaqué sur le reste du texte** this passage seems to be stuck on *ou* tacked on to the rest of the text; **elle lui plaqua un baiser sur la joue** she planted a kiss on his cheek.
b (*‡: abandonner*) *fiancé* to jilt*, ditch*, chuck*; *épouse* to ditch*, chuck*, walk out on; *emploi* to chuck (in *ou* up)*, pack in* (*Brit*). **elle a tout plaqué pour le suivre** she chucked up* *ou* packed in* everything to follow him.
c (*aplatir*) *cheveux* to plaster down. **la sueur plaquait sa chemise contre son corps** the sweat made his shirt cling *ou* stick to his body; **~ une personne contre un mur/au sol** to pin a person to a wall/to the ground; **se ~ les cheveux** to plaster one's hair down (*sur* on, over); **se ~ au sol/contre un mur** to flatten o.s. on the ground/against a wall; **le vent plaquait la neige contre le mur** the wind was flattening *ou* plastering the snow up against the wall.
d (*Rugby*) to tackle, bring down.
e (*Mus*) *accord* to strike, play.

plaquette [plakɛt] **nf** a (*petite plaque*) *[métal]* plaque; *[marbre]* tablet; *[chocolat]* block, bar; *[sang]* platelet; *[pilules]* blister *ou* bubble pack *ou* package. (*Aut*) **~ de frein** brake pad. b (*livre*) small volume.

plasma [plasma] **nm** (*Anat, Phys*) plasma. **~ sanguin** blood plasma.

plastic [plastik] **nm** gelignite.

plasticage [plastikaʒ] **nm** bombing (*de* of), bomb attack (*de* on).

plasticien [plastisjɛ̃] **nm** (*chirurgien*) plastic surgeon.

plasticité [plastisite] **nf** (*lit*) plasticity; (*fig*) malleability, plasticity.

plastie [plasti] **nf** plastic surgery. **elle a subi une ~ des doigts** she had plastic surgery on her fingers.

plastifiant, e [plastifjɑ̃, jɑ̃t] 1 **adj** plasticizing. 2 **nm** plasticizer.

plastification [plastifikasjɔ̃] **nf**: **~ de documents** plastic coating of documents.

plastifier [plastifje] [7] **vt** to coat with plastic. **plastifié** plastic-coated.

plastiquage [plastikaʒ] **nm** = **plasticage**.

plastique [plastik] 1 **adj** a (*Art*) plastic. **chirurgie ~** plastic surgery. b (*malléable*) malleable, plastic. **en matière ~** plastic. 2 **nm** plastic. **en ~** plastic. 3 **nf** *[sculpteur]* art of modelling, plastic art; *[statue]* modelling; (*arts*) plastic arts (*pl*).

plastiquement [plastikmɑ̃] **adv** from the point of view of form, plastically (*SPÉC*).

plastiquer [plastike] [1] **vt** to blow up, carry out a bomb attack on.

plastiqueur [plastikœʀ] **nm** terrorist (*planting a plastic bomb*).

plastoc* [plastɔk] **nm** plastic. **en ~** plastic (*épith*).

plastron [plastʀɔ̃] **nm** (*Habillement*) *[corsage]* front; *[chemise]* shirt front; (*amovible*) false shirt front, dicky*; *[escrimeur]* plastron; *[armure]* plastron, breastplate.

plastronner [plastʀɔne] [1] 1 **vi** to swagger. 2 **vt** to put a plastron on.

plat[1], plate [pla, plat] 1 **adj** a *surface, pays, couture, pli* flat; *mer* smooth, still; *eau* plain, non-fizzy; (*Géom*) *angle* straight; *encéphalogramme* flat; *ventre, poitrine* flat; *cheveux* straight. **bateau à fond ~** flat-bottomed boat; **chaussure plate** *ou* **à talon ~** flat(-heeled) *ou* low(-heeled) shoe; **elle est plate de poitrine, elle a la poitrine plate** she is flat-chested; **elle est plate comme une galette*** *ou* **une limande*** *ou* **une planche à pain*** she's as flat as a board*; *voir* **assiette, battre**.
b (*fade*) *style* flat, dull, unimaginative; *dissertation, livre* dull, unremarkable, unimaginative; *adaptation* unimaginative, unremarkable; *voix* flat, dull; *vin* weak-tasting, flat; *personne, vie* dull, uninteresting. **ce qu'il écrit est très ~** what he writes is very dull *ou* flat.
c (*obséquieux*) *personne* obsequious, ingratiating (*épith*). **il nous a fait ses plus plates excuses** he made the humblest of apologies to us.
d **à ~**: **mettre** *ou* **poser qch à ~** to lay sth (down) flat; **posez le ruban bien à ~** put the ribbon in nice and flat; (*fig*) **mettre qch à ~** to have a close look at things; (*fig*) **remettre qch à ~** to send sth back to the drawing board; **poser la main à ~ sur qch** to lay one's hand flat on sth; **être à ~** *[pneu, batterie]* to be flat; *[personne]* to be washed out* *ou* run down; **la grippe l'a mis à ~*** he was laid low by (the) flu; (*Aut*) **être/rouler à ~** to have a/drive on a flat (tyre); (*fig*) **tomber à ~** *[remarque, plaisanterie, pièce]* to fall flat; **tomber à ~ ventre** to fall flat on one's face, fall full-length; **se mettre à ~ ventre** to lie face down; (*fig*) **se mettre à ~ ventre devant qn** to crawl *ou* grovel *ou* toady to sb.
2 **nm** (*partie plate*) flat (part); *[main]* flat. **il y a 15 km de ~ avant la montagne** there is a 15 km flat stretch before the mountain; **une course de ~** a flat race; (*Natation*) **faire un ~** to (do a) belly flop; (*fig*) **faire du ~ à*** *supérieur* to crawl *ou* grovel *ou* toady to; *femme* to chat up* (*Brit*), sweet-talk*.
3 **plate nf** (*bateau*) punt, flat-bottomed boat.
4 **comp** ►**plate-bande nf (pl plates-bandes)** (*Horticulture*) flower bed; (*fig*) **marcher sur** *ou* **piétiner les plates-bandes de qn*** to trespass on sb's preserves, tread on sb else's patch ►**plat-bord nm (pl plats-bords)** gunwale ►**plat de côtes, plates côtes** middle *ou* best rib ►**plate-forme nf (pl plates-formes)** (*gén: terrasse, estrade*) platform; *[autobus]* platform; (*Rail: wagon*) flat wagon (*Brit*) *ou* car (*US*); (*Pol, fig*) platform; **toit en plate-forme** flat roof; (*Géog*) **plate-forme continentale** continental shelf; (*Pol*) **plate-forme électorale** election platform; **plate-forme (de forage en mer)** (off-shore) oil rig; **plate-forme flottante** floating rig.

plat[2] [pla] 1 **nm** (*récipient, mets*) dish; (*partie du repas*) course; (*contenu*) dish, plate(ful). **~ à légumes/à poisson** vegetable/fish dish; **on en était au ~ de viande** we had reached the meat course; **2 ~s de viande au choix** a choice of 2 meat dishes *ou* courses; (*fig*) **il en a fait tout un ~*** he made a song and dance* *ou* a great fuss* about it; **il voudrait qu'on lui apporte tout sur un ~ (d'argent)** he wants everything handed to him on a plate, he expects to be waited on hand and foot; **mettre les petits ~s dans les grands** to put on a first-rate meal, go to town on the meal*; **elle lui prépare de bons petits ~s** she makes tasty little dishes for him; (*Bible, fig*) **pour un ~ de lentilles** for a mess of potage; *voir* **œuf, pied**.
2 **comp** ►**plat à barbe** shaving mug ►**plat cuisiné** (*chez un traiteur*) ready-made meal ►**plat garni** main course (served with vegetables) ►**plat du jour** today's special, ≃ (today's) set menu, plat du jour ►**plat de résistance** main course; (*fig*) pièce de résistance.

platane [platan] **nm** plane tree. (*Aut*) **rentrer dans un ~** to crash into a tree.

plateau, pl ~x [plato] 1 **nm** a tray. **~ de fromages** cheese-board, choice of cheeses (*on a menu*); **~ d'huîtres/de fruits de mer** plate of oysters/seafood; (*fig*) **il faut tout lui apporter sur un ~ (d'argent)** he needs everything to be handed to him on a plate, he needs to be waited on hand and foot; *voir* **négresse**.
b *[balance]* pan; *[électrophone]* turntable, deck; *[table]* top; *[graphique]* plateau, tableland (*NonC*). **la courbe fait un ~ avant de redescendre** the curve levels off *ou* reaches a plateau before falling again; (*fig*) **mettre dans** *ou* **sur les ~x de la balance** to weigh up (*fig*).
c (*Géog*) plateau. **haut ~** high plateau.
d (*Théât*) stage; (*Ciné, TV*) set. (*invités*) **nous avons un ~ exceptionnel ce soir** we have an exceptional line-up this evening.
e (*Rail: wagon*) flat wagon (*Brit*) *ou* car (*US*); (*plate-forme roulante*) trailer.
2 **comp** ►**plateau continental** continental shelf ►**plateau d'embrayage** (*Aut*) pressure plate ►**plateau-repas nm (pl plateaux-repas)** tray meal ►**plateau sous-marin** submarine plateau ►**plateau de tournage** (*Ciné*) film set.

platée [plate] **nf** (*Culin*) dish(ful), plate(ful).

platement [platmɑ̃] **adv** *écrire, s'exprimer* dully, unimaginatively; *s'excuser* humbly.

platine[1] [platin] 1 **nm** platinum. **~ iridié** platinum-iridium alloy. 2 **adj inv** (*couleur*) platinum (*épith*). **blond ~** platinum blond.

platine[2] [platin] **nf** *[électrophone]* deck, turntable; *[microscope]* stage; *[presse]* platen; *[montre, serrure]* plate; *[machine à coudre]* throat plate. **~ laser** laser disk player.

platiné, e [platine] **adj** *cheveux* platinum (*épith*). **une blonde ~e** a platinum blonde; *voir* **vis[1]**.

platitude [platityd] **nf** a *[style]* flatness, dullness; *[livre, film, discours, remarque]* dullness, lack of imagination (*de* in, of); *[vie, personnage]* dullness. b (*propos*) platitude. **dire des ~s** to make trite remarks, utter platitudes. c (*†: servilité*) *[personne]* obsequiousness; *[excuse]* humility; (*acte*) obsequiousness (*NonC*).

Platon [platɔ̃] **nm** Plato.

platonicien, -ienne [platɔnisjɛ̃, jɛn] 1 **adj** Platonic. 2 **nm,f** Platonist.

platonique [platɔnik] **adj** *amour* platonic; *protestation* futile, vain (épith).

platoniquement [platɔnikmɑ̃] adv (voir platonique) platonically; vainly.

platonisme [platɔnism] nm Platonism.

plâtrage [plɑtʀaʒ] nm (voir plâtrer) plastering; liming; setting ou putting in plaster; lining.

plâtras [plɑtʀɑ] nm (débris) rubble; (morceau de plâtre) chunk ou lump of plaster.

plâtre [plɑtʀ] nm a (matière) (Chirurgie, Constr, Sculp) plaster; (Agr) lime. (Méd) mettre dans le ~ to put ou set in plaster; (fig: fromage) c'est du ~! it's like chalk!; voir battre. b (Chirurgie, Sculp: objet) plaster cast. (Constr) les ~s the plasterwork (NonC); (Chirurgie) ~ de marche walking plaster (Brit) ou cast (US); voir essuyer.

plâtrer [plɑtʀe] 1 vt mur to plaster; prairie to lime; jambe to set ou put in plaster; estomac to line. jambe plâtrée leg in plaster.

plâtrerie [plɑtʀəʀi] nf (usine) plaster works.

plâtreux, -euse [plɑtʀø, øz] adj sol limey, chalky; surface plastered, coated with plaster; (fig) fromage chalky(-textured).

plâtrier [plɑtʀije] nm plasterer.

plâtrière [plɑtʀijɛʀ] nf (carrière) gypsum ou lime quarry; (four) gypsum kiln.

plausibilité [plozibilite] nf plausibility, plausibleness.

plausible [plozibl] adj plausible.

plausiblement [plozibləmɑ̃] adv plausibly.

Plaute [plot] nm Plautus.

playback [plɛbak] nm miming. c'est du ~ they (ou he etc) are just miming (to a prerecorded tape); chanter en ~ to mime to a prerecorded tape.

playboy [plɛbɔj] nm playboy.

plèbe [plɛb] nf (péj) plebs, proles. (Hist) la ~ the plebeians (pl).

plébéien, -ienne [plebejɛ̃, jɛn] 1 adj (Hist) plebeian; goûts plebeian, common. 2 nm,f plebeian.

plébiscitaire [plebisitɛʀ] adj of a plebiscite.

plébiscite [plebisit] nm plebiscite. faire ou organiser un ~ to hold a referendum.

plébisciter [plebisite] 1 vt (Pol) to elect by plebiscite; (fig: approuver) to elect by an overwhelming majority. se faire ~ to be elected by an overwhelming majority, have a landslide victory.

plectre [plɛktʀ] nm plectrum.

pléiade [plejad] nf a (groupe) group, pleiad. (Littérat) la P~ the Pléiade; une ~ d'artistes a whole host of stars. b (Astron) P~ Pleiad; la P~ the Pleiades.

plein, pleine [plɛ̃, plɛn] 1 adj a (rempli) boîte full; bus, salle full (up); joue, visage full, plump; crustacé, coquillage full; vie, journée full, busy. ~ à déborder full to overflowing; ~ à craquer valise full to bursting, crammed full; salle, bus, train packed (out), crammed full, full to bursting; un ~ verre de vin a full glass of wine; un ~ panier de pommes a whole basketful of apples, a full basket of apples; j'ai les mains pleines my hands are full, I've got my hands full; parler la bouche pleine to speak with one's mouth full; avoir l'estomac ou le ventre ~* to be full, have eaten one's fill; ~ comme un œuf* tiroir chock-a-block* (Brit), chock-full*; estomac full to bursting; nez stuffed up; être ~ aux as** to be rolling in money* ou in it*, be filthy rich**; (péj) un gros ~ de soupe* a big fat slob** (péj).

b ~ de bonne volonté, admiration, idées, attentions, fautes, vie full of; taches, graisse covered in ou with; salle pleine de monde room full of people, crowded room; journée pleine d'événements day packed ou crowded with events, eventful day; entreprise pleine de risques undertaking fraught with risk(s); voilà une remarque pleine de finesse that's a very shrewd remark; il est ~ de santé/d'idées he's bursting with health/ideas; il est ~ de son sujet/de sa nouvelle voiture he's full of his subject/his new car; mets ~ de saveur dish full of flavour, flavourful (Brit) ou flavorful (US) dish; être ~ de soi to be full of o.s. ou of one's own importance; être ~ d'égards pour qn to shower attention on sb.

c (complet) succès complete; confiance complete, total; satisfaction full, complete, total. vous avez mon accord ~ et entier you have my wholehearted consent ou approval; absent un jour ~ absent for a whole day; à ~ temps, à temps ~ travailler, emploi full-time; il a ~ pouvoir pour agir he has full power ou authority to act; avoir les ~s pouvoirs to have full powers; être membre de ~ droit to be a member in one's own right; voir arc.

d lune full. la mer est pleine, c'est la pleine mer the tide is in, it is high tide.

e (non creux) paroi, porte, pneu, roue solid; trait unbroken, continuous; son solid; voix rich, sonorous. avec reliure pleine peau fully bound in leather; manteau de fourrure pleine peau fur coat made of solid ou full skins; (fig) mot employé dans son sens ~ word used in its full sense ou meaning.

f (**: ivre) stoned**, plastered**. ~ comme une barrique as drunk as a lord*.

g (Vét) pregnant, in calf (ou foal, lamb etc).

h (indiquant l'intensité) la pleine lumière le fatiguait he found the bright light tiring; avoir pleine conscience de qch to be fully aware of sth; en pleine possession de ses moyens in full possession of one's faculties; être en pleine forme* to be in ou on top form; les heures pleines peak periods ou hours; de son ~ gré of one's own free will; réclamer qch de ~ droit to claim sth as one's right; heurter qch de ~ fouet to crash headlong into sth; entreprise qui marche à ~ rendement business that is working at full capacity; à ~ régime (Aut) at maximum revs; (fig) la production/l'économie marche à ~ régime production/the economy is going flat out*; rouler (à) ~s gaz* ou tubes**, rouler ~ pot* to drive flat out*; rouler ~s phares to drive on full beam (Brit) ou full headlights (Brit) ou high beams (US); payer ~ pot to pay the full whack*; rincer le sol à ~s seaux to rinse the floor with bucketfuls of water; embrasser qn à pleine bouche to kiss sb full on the mouth; ça sent l'ammoniaque à ~ nez there's a terrible smell of ammonia, it reeks of ammonia; rire à pleine gorge to laugh heartily, laugh one's head off; crier à ~s poumons ou à ~ gosier to shout at the top of one's voice, shout one's head off; respirer l'air frais à ~s poumons to take deep breaths of fresh air, fill one's lungs with fresh air; ramasser qch à ~s bras/à pleines mains to pick up armfuls/handfuls of sth; prendre qch à pleines mains to lay a firm hold on sth, grasp sth firmly.

i (au milieu de, au plus fort de) en ~ milieu right ou bang* ou slap* in the middle; en pleine poitrine full ou right in the chest; en pleine tête right in the head; arriver en ~ (milieu du) cours/en pleine répétition to arrive (right) in the middle of the class/rehearsal; oiseau en ~ vol bird in full flight; tué en pleine jeunesse killed in the bloom ou fullness of youth; c'est arrivé en ~ Paris/en pleine rue it happened in the middle of Paris/in the middle of the street; en ~ midi (à l'heure du déjeuner) in the middle of the lunch hour; (en plein zénith) at the height of noon ou at high noon; (exposé plein sud) facing due south, south-facing; en ~ jour in broad daylight; en pleine nuit in the middle of the night, at dead of night; en ~ hiver in the depths ou middle of winter; rester en ~ soleil to stay (out) in the heat of the sun; le jardin est en ~ soleil the garden is in full sun, the sun is shining right on(to) the garden; son visage était en pleine lumière the light was shining straight into his face ou at him; enfant en pleine croissance child who is growing fast ou shooting up; affaire en ~ essor ou en pleine croissance rapidly expanding ou growing business; en ~ vent right in the wind; arbre planté en pleine terre tree planted in open ground ou out in the open; en pleine saison at the height ou peak of the season; (touristique) when the season is (ou was) in full swing, at the middle ou peak of the (tourist) season; je suis en ~ travail I'm in the middle of (my) work, I'm hard at work; en pleine obscurité in complete ou utter darkness; arriver en ~ drame to arrive in the middle of a crisis.

2 adv a avoir des bonbons ~ les poches to have one's pockets full of ou stuffed with sweets; avoir de l'encre ~ les mains to have ink all over one's hands ou one's hands covered in ink; avoir de l'argent ~ les poches to have plenty of money, be rolling in money*, be a moneybags*; il a des jouets ~ un placard he's got a cupboardful ou a cupboard full of toys; se diriger/donner ~ ouest to head/face due west; en avoir ~ la bouche de qn/qch to be full of sb/sth, talk of nothing but sb/sth; en avoir ~ le dos* ou le cul*** de qch to be fed up with sth*, be sick and tired of sth*, be pissed off*** with sth; en avoir ~ les jambes* ou les bottes* ou les pattes* to be all-in*, have walked one's legs off*; il a voulu nous en mettre ~ la vue* he wanted to dazzle us; on s'en est mis ~ la lampe* we had a slap-up meal* ou a real blow-out**; voir tout.

b (*: beaucoup de) ~ de lots of, loads of*; il y a ~ de bouteilles dans la cave/de gens dans la rue the cellar/street is full of bottles/people, there are lots ou loads* of bottles in the cellar/people in the street; un gâteau avec ~ de crème a cake filled with lots of ou plenty of cream; il a mis ~ de chocolat sur sa veste he has got chocolate all over his jacket.

c en ~: la lumière frappait son visage en ~ the light was shining straight ou right into his face; en ~ devant toi right ou straight ou bang* in front of you; en ~ dans l'eau/l'œil right ou straight in the water/eye; mettre en ~ dans le mille (lit) to strike right ou (slap-)bang* in (the middle of) the bull's-eye; (fig) to hit the nail on the head.

d (au maximum) à ~ at full capacity; entreprise qui tourne à ~ business that is working at full capacity ou flat out*; les légumes donnent à ~ it is the height of the vegetable season; utiliser à ~ son potentiel/une machine/ses connaissances to use one's potential/a machine/one's knowledge to the full, make full use of one's potential/a machine/one's knowledge; cet argument a porté à ~ this argument struck home ou made its point.

3 nm a faire le ~ (d'essence) to fill up; (faites) le ~, s'il vous plaît fill it ou her* up please; on a fait 2 ~s pour descendre jusqu'à Nice it took 2 tankfuls to get down to Nice, we had to fill up twice to get down to Nice; faire le ~ d'eau/d'huile to top up the water/oil; faire le ~ de soleil to get a good dose of the sun; (fig) théâtre qui fait le ~ (de monde) tous les soirs theatre which has a full house every night; (fig) la gauche a fait le ~ des voix aux élections the left got their maximum possible vote in the elections; tu as acheté beaucoup de conserves/livres — oui, j'ai fait le ~* you bought lots of tins/books — yes I stocked up.

b (plénitude) [animation, fête] height; voir battre.

c (Archit) solid; (Calligraphie) downstroke.

4 comp ▸**plein air** open air; (*Scol*) **les enfants ont plein air le mercredi** the children have games *ou* sport on Wednesdays; **jeux de plein air** outdoor games; **en plein air** *spectacle, cirque* open-air (*épith*); *s'asseoir* (out) in the open (air) ▸**plein-emploi** nm full employment ▸**pleine mer** (*le large*) open sea; (*la marée haute*) high tide; **en pleine mer** out at sea, on the open sea.

pleinement [plɛnmɑ̃] adv *vivre, jouir* to the full; *approuver* wholeheartedly, fully. **utiliser qch ~** to make full use of sth, use sth to the full *ou* fully; **~ responsable/satisfait de** wholly *ou* entirely *ou* fully responsible for/satisfied with; **~ rassuré** completely *ou* totally reassured.

pléistocène [pleistɔsɛn] adj, nm Pleistocene.

plénier, -ière [plenje, jɛʀ] adj plenary.

plénipotentiaire [plenipɔtɑ̃sjɛʀ] adj, nm plenipotentiary; *voir* **ministre**.

plénitude [plenityd] nf *[forme]* plenitude (*littér*), fullness; *[son]* fullness, richness; *[droit]* completeness. **réaliser ses désirs dans leur ~** to realize one's desires in their entirety; **vivre la vie avec ~** to live one's life to the full; **dans la ~ de sa jeunesse/de sa beauté** in the fullness of his youth/beauty (*littér*).

plenum [plenɔm] nm plenary session *ou* meeting.

pléonasme [pleɔnasm] nm pleonasm.

pléonastique [pleɔnastik] adj pleonastic.

plésiosaure [plezjɔzɔʀ] nm plesiosaurus.

pléthore [pletɔʀ] nf overabundance, plethora.

pléthorique [pletɔʀik] adj *nombre* excessive; *effectifs, documentation* overabundant; *classe* overcrowded.

pleur [plœʀ] nm **a** (*littér*) (*larme*) tear; (*sanglot*) sob. (*hum*) **verser un ~** to shed a tear. **b** (*loc*) **en ~s** in tears; **il y aura des ~s et des grincements de dents quand ...** there'll be much wailing and gnashing of teeth when ...; **essuyer** *ou* **sécher les ~s de qn** to wipe away *ou* dry sb's tears.

pleurage [plœʀaʒ] nm (*Élec*) wow.

pleural, e, mpl **-aux** [plœʀal, o] adj pleural.

pleurard, e [plœʀaʀ, aʀd] (*péj*) **1** adj *enfant* whining (*épith*), who never stops crying; *ton* whimpering (*épith*), whining (*épith*), grizzling* (*Brit*) (*épith*). **2** nm, f crybaby*, whiner, grizzler* (*Brit*).

pleurer [plœʀe] 1 **1** vi **a** (*larmoyer*) *[personne]* to cry, weep; *[yeux]* to water, run. **s'endormir en pleurant** to cry oneself to sleep; **~ bruyamment** to cry noisily, howl*, bawl‡; **~ de rire** to shed tears of laughter, laugh until one cries; **~ de rage** to weep *ou* cry with rage, shed tears of rage; **~ de joie** to cry *ou* weep for joy, shed tears of joy; **~ d'avoir fait qch** to cry *ou* weep at *ou* over having done sth; **j'ai perdu mon sac, j'en aurais pleuré** I lost my bag — I could have cried *ou* wept; **il vaut mieux en rire que d'en ~** it's better to laugh (about it) than cry about *ou* over it; **faire ~ qn** to make sb cry, bring tears to sb's eyes; **les oignons me font ~** onions make my eyes water *ou* make me cry *ou* bring tears to my eyes; **~ comme un veau** (*péj*) *ou* **une madeleine** *ou* **à chaudes larmes** to cry one's eyes *ou* one's heart out; **être sur le point de ~** to be almost in tears, be on the point *ou* verge of tears; **aller ~ dans le gilet de qn*** to run crying to sb; **triste à (faire) ~** dreadfully *ou* terribly sad; **bête à (faire) ~** pitifully stupid; **c'est bête à (faire) ~** it's enough to make you weep.

b ~ sur to lament (over); **~ sur son propre sort** to feel sorry for o.s., bemoan one's lot.

c (*péj: réclamer*) **elle est tout le temps à ~** she's always whining *ou* begging for something; **~ après qch** to shout for sth; **il a été ~ à la direction pour obtenir une augmentation** he has been moaning *ou* complaining to the management about getting a rise.

d (*littér*) *[sirène, violon]* to wail.

2 vt **a** *personne* to mourn (for); *chose* to bemoan; *faute* to bewail, bemoan, lament. **mourir sans être pleuré** to die unlamented *ou* unmourned; **~ des larmes de joie** to weep *ou* shed tears of joy, weep for joy; **~ des larmes de sang** to shed tears of blood; **~ tout son soûl** to have a good cry; **~ toutes les larmes de son corps** to cry one's eyes out; **~ misère** to bewail *ou* bemoan one's destitution *ou* impoverished state; **~ sa jeunesse** to mourn *ou* lament the loss of one's youth, mourn for one's lost youth.

b (*péj*) (*quémander*) *augmentation, objet* to beg for; (*lésiner sur*) *nourriture, fournitures* to begrudge, stint. **il ne pleure pas sa peine*** he spares no effort, he doesn't stint his efforts; **il ne pleure pas son argent*** he doesn't stint his money.

pleurésie [plœʀezi] nf pleurisy. **avoir une ~** to have pleurisy.

pleurétique [plœʀetik] adj pleuritic.

pleureur, -euse [plœʀœʀ, øz] **1** adj *enfant* whining (*épith*), always crying (*attrib*); *ton* tearful, whimpering (*épith*). **c'est un ~/une ~euse** (*pleurard*) he/she is always crying; (*péj: quémandeur*) he/she is always begging for something; *voir* **saule**. **2 pleureuse** nf (hired) mourner.

pleurnichard, e [plœʀniʃaʀ, aʀd] = **pleurnicheur**.

pleurnichement [plœʀniʃmɑ̃] nm = **pleurnicherie**.

pleurnicher [plœʀniʃe] 1 vi to snivel*, grizzle* (*Brit*), whine.

pleurnicherie [plœʀniʃʀi] nf snivelling* (*NonC*), grizzling* (*Brit*) (*NonC*), whining (*NonC*).

pleurnicheur, -euse [plœʀniʃœʀ, øz] **1** adj *enfant* snivelling* (*épith*), grizzling* (*Brit*) (*épith*), whining (*épith*); *ton* whining (*épith*), grizzling* (*Brit*) (*épith*). **2** nm, f crybaby*, grizzler* (*Brit*), whiner.

pleuropneumonie [plœʀopnømɔni] nf pleuropneumonia.

pleurote [plœʀɔt] nf pleurotus.

pleurotomie [plœʀɔtɔmi] nf pleurotomy.

pleutre [pløtʀ] (*littér*) **1** adj cowardly. **2** nm coward.

pleutrerie [pløtʀəʀi] nf (*littér*) (*caractère*) cowardice; (*acte*) act of cowardice.

pleuvasser [pløvase] vi, **pleuviner** [pløvine] vi 1 (*crachiner*) to drizzle, spit (with rain); (*par averses*) to be showery.

pleuvoir [pløvwaʀ] 23 **1** vb impers to rain. **il pleut** it's raining; **les jours où il pleut** on rainy days; **on dirait qu'il va ~** it looks like rain; **il pleut à grosses gouttes** heavy drops of rain are falling; **il pleut à flots** *ou* **à torrents** *ou* **à seaux** *ou* **à verse, il pleut des cordes** *ou* **des hallebardes, il pleut comme vache qui pisse*** it's pouring (down) *ou* it's teeming down (*Brit*) (with rain), it's raining cats and dogs*; **qu'il pleuve ou qu'il vente** rain or shine, come wind or foul weather; **il a reçu des cadeaux comme s'il en pleuvait** he was showered with presents; **il ramasse de l'argent comme s'il en pleuvait*** he's raking it in*, he's raking in the money*; (*hum*) **tu vas faire ~!** (*à une personne qui chante mal*) you'll shatter the (glass in the) windows! (*hum*).

2 vi *[coups, projectiles]* to rain down; *[critiques, invitations]* to shower down. **faire ~ des coups sur qn** to rain blows (up)on sb; **faire ~ des injures sur qn** to shower insults (up)on sb, subject sb to a torrent of insults *ou* abuse; **les invitations pleuvaient sur lui** he was showered with invitations, invitations were showered (up)on him.

pleuvoter [pløvɔte] 1 vi = **pleuvasser**.

plèvre [plɛvʀ] nf pleura.

Plexiglass [plɛksiglas] nm ® Plexiglass ®.

plexus [plɛksys] nm plexus. **~ solaire** solar plexus.

pli [pli] **1** nm **a** *[tissu, rideau, ourlet, accordéon]* fold; (*Couture*) pleat. **(faux) ~** crease; **faire un ~ à un pantalon** (*au fer*) to put a crease in a pair of trousers, press a pair of trousers; (*par négligence*) to crease a pair of trousers; **jupe/robe à ~s** pleated skirt/dress; **son manteau est plein de ~s** his coat is all creased; **ton manteau fait un ~ dans le dos** your coat has a crease at the back, your coat creases (up) at the back; **son corsage est trop étroit, il fait des ~s** her blouse is too tight — it's all puckered (up); **les ~s et les replis de sa cape** the many folds of her cloak; (*fig*) **il va refuser, cela ne fait pas un ~*** he'll refuse, no doubt about it; **j'avais dit qu'elle oublierait, ça n'a pas fait de ~!** I had said she would forget and she did! *ou* and I was right!

b (*jointure*) *[genou, bras]* bend; (*bourrelet*) *[menton, ventre]* (skin-) fold; (*ligne*) *[bouche, yeux]* crease; (*ride*) *[front]* crease, furrow, line. **sa peau faisait des ~s au coin des yeux/sur son ventre** his skin was creased round his eyes/made folds on his stomach; **le ~ de l'aine** the (fold of the) groin; **les ~s et les replis de son menton** the many folds under his chin, his quadruple chin (*hum*).

c (*forme*) *[vêtement]* shape. **suspends ton manteau pour qu'il garde un beau ~** hang up your coat so that it will keep its shape; **garder un bon ~** to keep its shape; **prendre un mauvais ~** *[vêtement]* to get crushed; *[cheveux]* to twist *ou* curl the wrong way; *voir* **mise²**.

d (*fig: habitude*) habit. **prendre le ~ de faire** to get into the habit of doing; **il a pris un mauvais ~** he has got into a bad habit; **c'est un ~ à prendre!** you get used to it!

e (*enveloppe*) envelope; (*Admin: lettre*) letter. **sous ce ~** enclosed, herewith; **sous ~ cacheté** in a sealed envelope.

f (*Cartes*) trick. **faire un ~** to win a trick, take a trick.

g (*Géol*) fold.

2 comp ▸**pli d'aisance** (*Couture*) inverted pleat ▸**pli creux** (*Couture*) box pleat ▸**pli de pantalon** trouser crease ▸**pli plat** (*Couture*) flat pleat ▸**pli de terrain** fold in the ground, undulation.

pliable [plijabl] adj pliable, flexible.

pliage [plijaʒ] nm folding.

pliant, e [plijɑ̃, ɑ̃t] **1** adj *lit, table, vélo* collapsible, folding (*épith*); *mètre* folding (*épith*); *canot* collapsible. **2** nm folding *ou* collapsible (canvas) stool, campstool.

plie [pli] nf plaice.

plier [plije] 7 **1** vt **a** *papier, tissu* (*gén*) to fold; (*ranger*) to fold up. **~ le coin d'une page** to fold over *ou* fold down *ou* turn down the corner of a page.

b (*rabattre*) *lit, table, tente* to fold up; *éventail* to fold; *livre, cahier* to close (up); *volets* to fold back. (*fig*) **~ bagage** to pack up (and go); **on leur fit rapidement ~ bagage** we quickly sent them packing *ou* made them clear out*.

c (*ployer*) *branche* to bend; *genou, bras* to bend, flex. (*fig*) **~ le genou devant qn** to bow before sb, bend the knee before sb; **être plié par l'âge** to be bent (double) with age; **être plié (en deux), être plié de rire** to be doubled up with laughter; **être plié de douleur** to be doubled up with pain.

d ~ qn à une discipline to force a discipline upon sb; **~ qn à sa volonté** to bend sb to one's will; **~ qn à sa loi** to lay down the law to sb; **~ ses désirs à la situation** to adjust *ou* adapt one's desires to suit the situation.

e (**: endommager*) *voiture* to wreck.

2 vi **a** *[arbre, branche]* to bend (over); *[plancher, paroi]* to sag, bend over. **les branches pliant sous le poids des pêches** the branches bending *ou* sagging under the weight of the peaches; **faire ~ le plancher sous son poids** to make the floor sag beneath one's weight; **~ sous le poids des soucis/des ans** to be weighed down by worry/years.

b (*céder*) *[personne]* to yield, give in, knuckle under; *[armée]* to give way, lose ground; *[résistance]* to give way. **~ devant l'autorité** to give in *ou* yield *ou* bow to authority; **faire ~ qn** to make sb give in *ou* knuckle under; (*Sport*) **notre défense plie mais ne rompt pas** our defence is weakening but isn't breaking down completely.

3 **se plier** vpr a *[lit, chaise]* to fold (up).

b **se ~ à** *règle* to submit to, abide by; *discipline* to submit o.s. to; *circonstances* to bow to, submit to, yield to; *désirs, caprices de qn* to give in to, submit to.

Pline [plin] nm Pliny.

plinthe [plɛ̃t] nf (*gén*) skirting (board); (*Archit*) plinth.

pliocène [plijɔsɛn] adj, nm Pliocene.

plissage [plisaʒ] nm pleating.

plissé, e [plise] (ptp de **plisser**) 1 adj *jupe* pleated; *terrain* folded; *peau* creased, wrinkled. 2 nm pleats. **~ soleil** sunray pleats.

plissement [plismɑ̃] nm (*voir* **plisser**) puckering (up); screwing up; creasing; folding. (*Géol*) **~ de terrain** fold; **le ~ alpin** the folding of the Alps.

plisser [plise] 1 1 vt a (*froncer*) *jupe* to pleat, put pleats in; *papier* to fold (over). b (*rider*) *lèvres* to pucker (up); *yeux* to screw up; *front* to crease. **un sourire plissa son visage** his face creased into a smile; **il plissa le front** he knit *ou* creased his brow; **une ride lui plissa le front** a wrinkle furrowed his brow. c (*chiffonner*) to crease. d (*Géol*) to fold. 2 vi to become creased. 3 **se plisser** vpr *[front]* to crease, furrow; *[lèvres]* to pucker (up).

plissure [plisyʀ] nf pleats.

pliure [plijyʀ] nf fold; *[bras, genou]* bend; (*Typ*) folding.

ploc [plɔk] excl plop!, plip plop!, plop plop!

ploiement [plwamɑ̃] nm bending.

plomb [plɔ̃] nm a (*métal*) lead. **de ~** *tuyau* lead; *soldat* tin; *ciel* leaden; *soleil* blazing; *sommeil* deep, heavy; *[essence]* **sans ~** unleaded, lead-free; **j'ai des jambes de ~** my legs are *ou* feel like lead; **il n'a pas de ~ dans la tête** *ou* **la cervelle** he's featherbrained; **cela lui mettra du ~ dans la tête** *ou* **la cervelle** that will knock some sense into him; **avoir du ~ dans** *ou* **sur l'estomac** to have something lying heavy on one's stomach, have a lump in one's stomach.

b (*Chasse*) (lead) shot (*NonC*). **j'ai trouvé 2 ~s dans le lièvre en le mangeant** I found 2 pieces of (lead) shot in the hare when I was eating it; **du gros ~** buckshot; **du petit ~** small shot; (*fig*) **avoir du ~ dans l'aile** to be in a bad way.

c (*Pêche*) sinker; (*Typ*) type; *[vitrail]* lead; (*sceau*) (lead) seal; (*Élec: fusible*) fuse; (*Couture*) lead weight. (*Naut*) **~ (de sonde)** sounding lead.

d (*loc*) **mettre un mur à ~** to plumb a wall; **le soleil tombe à ~** the sun is blazing straight down.

plombage [plɔ̃baʒ] nm a (*action: voir* **plomber**) weighting (with lead); filling, stopping; sealing (with lead). b (*sur une dent*) filling.

plombe‡ [plɔ̃b] nf hour. **ça fait 2 ~s que j'attends** I've been waiting 2 hours now; **à 3 ~s du matin** at 3 o'clock in the morning.

plombé, e [plɔ̃be] (ptp de **plomber**) 1 adj *teint, couleur, ciel* leaden; *essence* leaded. **canne ~e** *ou* **à bout ~** walking stick with a lead(en) tip. 2 **plombée** nf (*arme*) bludgeon; (*Pêche*) sinkers, weights.

plomber [plɔ̃be] 1 1 vt *canne, ligne* to weight (with lead); *dent* to fill, stop, put a filling in; *colis* to seal (with lead), put a lead seal on; *mur* to plumb; (*Agr*) to roll; (*colorer*) to turn leaden. (*Pêche*) **ligne pas assez plombée** insufficiently weighted line, line that hasn't enough weights on it. 2 **se plomber** vpr to turn leaden.

plomberie [plɔ̃bʀi] nf (*métier, installations*) plumbing; (*atelier*) plumber's (work)shop; (*industrie*) lead industry. **faire de la ~** to do some plumbing.

plombier [plɔ̃bje] nm plumber. **c'est le ~!** plumber!

plombières [plɔ̃bjɛʀ] nf inv tutti-frutti (ice cream).

plombifère [plɔ̃bifɛʀ] adj plumbiferous.

plonge [plɔ̃ʒ] nf washing-up (*Brit*), dishwashing (*in restaurant*). **faire la ~** to be a washer-up (*Brit*) *ou* dishwasher.

plongé, e[1] [plɔ̃ʒe] (ptp de **plonger**) adj: **~ dans** *obscurité, désespoir, misère* plunged in; *vice* steeped in; *méditation, pensées* immersed in, deep in; **~ dans la lecture d'un livre** engrossed in reading a book, buried *ou* immersed in a book; **~ dans le sommeil** sound asleep, in a deep sleep.

plongeant, e [plɔ̃ʒɑ̃, ɑ̃t] adj *décolleté, tir* plunging. **vue ~e** view from above.

plongée[2] [plɔ̃ʒe] nf a (*action*) *[nageur]* diving; *[sous-marin]* submersion. **effectuer plusieurs ~s** to make several dives; to carry out several submersions; **sous-marin en ~** submerged submarine; **~ sous-marine** (*gén*) diving; (*sans scaphandre*) skin diving, scuba diving; **~ de haut vol** platform high diving; **l'avion a fait une ~ sur la ville** the plane swooped down over the town. b (*Ciné: prise de vue*) high angle shot. **faire une ~ sur qch** to take a high angle shot of sth.

plongeoir [plɔ̃ʒwaʀ] nm diving board.

plongeon [plɔ̃ʒɔ̃] nm a (*Ftbl, Natation*) dive. **faire un ~** *[nageur]* to dive; *[gardien de but]* to make a dive, dive; (*tomber*) to go head over heels; (*fig*) **faire le ~** *[société]* to go under suddenly; *[prix, valeurs]* to nose-dive, take a nose dive. b (*oiseau*) diver.

plonger [plɔ̃ʒe] 3 1 vi a (*gén*) *[personne, sous-marin, avion]* to dive (*dans* into, *sur* on, onto). **avion qui plonge sur son objectif** plane that dives (down) onto its target; **oiseau qui plonge sur sa proie** bird that dives *ou* plunges onto its prey; **il plongea sa main dans sa poche pour prendre son mouchoir** he plunged his hand *ou* he dived into his pocket to get his handkerchief out.

b (*fig*) *[route, terrain]* to plunge (down), dip (sharply *ou* steeply); *[racines]* to go down. **~ dans le sommeil** to fall (straight) into a deep sleep; **mon regard plongeait sur la vallée** I cast my eyes down upon the valley.

c (*Fin*) *[société]* to go under suddenly; *[prix, valeurs]* to nose-dive, take a nose dive.

d (*arg Crime*) *[truand]* to get done* (*Brit*) *ou* busted* (*US*) (*pour* for).

2 vt: **~ qch dans** *sac* to plunge *ou* thrust sth into; *eau* to plunge sth into; **~ qn dans** *obscurité, misère* to plunge sb into; *désespoir* to throw *ou* plunge sb into; *sommeil, méditation, vice* to plunge sb into; **~ qn dans la surprise** to surprise sb greatly; **vous me plongez dans l'embarras** you have thrown me into a difficult position; **il lui plongea un poignard dans le cœur** he plunged *ou* thrust a dagger into his heart; **plante qui plonge ses racines dans le sol** plant that thrusts its roots deep into the ground; **~ son regard sur/vers** to cast one's eyes at/towards; **il plongea son regard dans mes yeux** he looked deeply into my eyes.

3 **se plonger** vpr: **se ~ dans** *études, lecture* to bury *ou* immerse o.s. in, throw o.s. into, plunge into; *dossier, eau, bain* to plunge into, immerse o.s. in; **se ~ dans le vice** to throw *ou* hurl o.s. into a life of vice.

plongeur, -euse [plɔ̃ʒœʀ, øz] 1 adj diving. 2 nm, f a (*Sport*) diver. **~ sous-marin** (*gén*) diver; (*sans scaphandre*) skin diver; *voir* **cloche**. b *[restaurant]* washer-up (*Brit*), dishwasher. 3 nm (*Orn*) diver.

plosive [ploziv] nf plosive.

plot [plo] nm (*Élec*) contact; (*butée*) pin.

plouc* [pluk] 1 nm (*péj*) (*paysan*) country bumpkin; (*crétin*) ninny*. 2 adj: **il est ~** he's a ninny*; **sa robe fait ~** her dress looks dowdy.

plouf [pluf] excl splash! **il est tombé dans l'eau avec un gros ~** he slipped and fell into the water with a splash; **la pierre a fait ~ en tombant dans l'eau** the stone made a splash as it fell into the water.

ploutocrate [plutɔkʀat] nm plutocrat.

ploutocratie [plutɔkʀasi] nf plutocracy.

ploutocratique [plutɔkʀatik] adj plutocratic.

ployer [plwaje] 8 (*littér*) 1 vi *[branche, dos]* to bend; *[poutre, plancher]* to sag; *[genoux, jambes]* to give way, bend; *[armée]* to yield, give in; *[résistance]* to give way. **faire ~ le plancher sous son poids** to make the floor sag beneath one's weight; **~ sous l'impôt** to be weighed down by taxes; (*Sport*) **notre défense ploie mais ne rompt pas** our defence is weakening but not breaking down completely; (*fig*) **~ sous le joug** to bend beneath the yoke. 2 vt to bend. **~ un pays sous son autorité** to make a country bow down *ou* submit to one's authority.

plucher [plyʃe] 1 vi = **pelucher**.

pluches [plyʃ] nfpl (*arg Mil*) potato-peeling, spud-bashing (*Brit arg*). **être de (corvée de) ~** to be on potato-peeling *ou* spud-bashing (*Brit arg*).

plucheux, -euse [plyʃø, øz] adj = **pelucheux**.

pluie [plɥi] nf a rain; (*averse*) shower (of rain). **les ~s** the rains; **la saison des ~s** the rainy season; **le temps est à la ~** we're in for rain, it looks like rain; **jour/temps de ~** wet *ou* rainy day/weather; **sous la ~** in the rain; **~ battante** driving *ou* lashing rain; **~ diluvienne** pouring rain (*NonC*), downpour; **~ fine** drizzle; **une ~ fine tombait** it was drizzling; **~ jaune/acide** yellow/acid rain.

b (*fig*) *[cadeaux, cendres]* shower; *[balles, pierres, coups]* hail, shower. **en ~** in a shower; **tomber en ~** to shower down; (*Culin*) **jeter le riz en ~** to sprinkle in *ou* on the rice.

c (*loc*) **après la ~ (vient) le beau temps** (*lit*) the sun is shining again after the rain; (*fig*) everything's fine again; (*fig*) **faire la ~ et le beau temps** to rule the roost; **il n'est pas né** *ou* **tombé de la dernière ~** he wasn't born yesterday; *voir* **ennuyeux, parler**.

plum-pudding [plumpudiŋ] nm (rich) fruit cake.

plumage [plymaʒ] nm plumage (*NonC*), feathers (*pl*).

plumard‡ [plymaʀ] nm bed. **aller au ~** to turn in*, hit the hay* *ou* the sack*.

plume [plym] 1 nf a *[oiseau]* feather. **chapeau à ~s** feathered hat, hat with feathers; **oreiller/lit de ~s** feather pillow/bed; **être aussi léger qu'une ~, ne pas peser plus lourd qu'une ~** to be as light as a feather; **soulever qch comme une ~** to lift sth up as if it were a featherweight; **il y a laissé des ~s*** (*gén*) he came off badly; (*financièrement*) he got his fingers burnt; (*hum*) **il perd ses ~s*** his hair is falling out, he's going bald; *voir* **gibier, poids, voler**.

b (*pour écrire*) (*d'oiseau*) quill (pen); (*en acier*) (pen) nib. **~ d'oie** goose quill; **dessin à la ~** pen-and-ink drawing; **écrire au fil** *ou* **courant de la ~** to write just as the ideas come to one *ou* come into one's head; **il a la ~ facile** writing comes easy to him; **vivre de sa ~** to live by writing *ou* by one's pen; **prendre la ~ pour ...** to take up one's pen to ..., put pen to paper to ...; (*dans une lettre*) **je lui passe la ~** I'll hand over to him, I'll let him carry on; (*fig*) **tremper sa ~ dans le poison** to steep one's pen in venom; *voir* **homme**.

2 **nm** = **plumard**.

3 **comp** ►**plume à vaccin** vaccine point.

plumeau, pl ~x [plymo] **nm** feather duster.

plumer [plyme] 1 **vt** *volaille* to pluck; (‡ *fig*) *personne* to fleece*.

plumet [plymɛ] **nm** plume.

plumetis [plym(ə)ti] **nm** (*tissu*) Swiss muslin; (*broderie*) raised satin stitch.

plumeux, -euse [plymø, øz] **adj** feathery.

plumier [plymje] **nm** pencil box.

plumitif [plymitif] **nm** (*péj*) (*employé*) penpusher (*péj*); (*écrivain*) scribbler (*péj*).

plupart [plypaʀ] **nf**: **la ~**: **la ~ des gens** most people, the majority of people; **la ~ des gens qui se trouvaient là** most of the people there; **la ~ (d'entre eux) pensent que ...** most (of them) *ou* the majority (of them) think that ...; **dans la ~ des cas** in most cases, in the majority of cases; **pour la ~** mostly, for the most part; **ces gens qui, pour la ~, avaient tout perdu** these people who, for the most part, had lost everything, these people, most of whom had *ou* who had mostly lost everything; **la ~ du temps** most of the time; **la ~ de mon temps** most of my time, the greater part of my time.

plural, e, mpl **-aux** [plyʀal, o] **adj** *vote* plural.

pluralisme [plyʀalism] **nm** pluralism.

pluraliste [plyʀalist] 1 **adj** pluralistic. 2 **nmf** pluralist.

pluralité [plyʀalite] **nf** multiplicity, plurality.

pluriannuel, -elle [plyʀianɥɛl] **adj** which lasts several years.

pluridisciplinaire [plyʀidisiplinɛʀ] **adj** (*Scol*) pluridisciplinary, multidisciplinary.

pluridisciplinarité [plyʀidisiplinaʀite] **nf** pluridisciplinarity, multidisciplinary system.

pluriel, -elle [plyʀjɛl] 1 **adj** plural. *[livre, pièce de théâtre]* **c'est une œuvre ~le** it is a work with many levels, it is a work which can be read (*ou* understood *etc*) on many different levels. 2 **nm** plural. **au ~** in the plural; **la première personne du ~** the first person plural; **le ~ de majesté** the royal plural, the royal "we"; **le ~ de "cheval" est "chevaux"** the plural of "cheval" is "chevaux".

plurifonctionnalité [plyʀifɔ̃ksjɔnalite] **nf** *[appareil, salle]* multifunctionality, ability to be used for many different functions.

plurilatéral, e, mpl **-aux** [plyʀilateʀal, o] **adj** multilateral.

plurilingue [plyʀilɛ̃g] **adj** multilingual.

plurilinguisme [plyʀilɛ̃gɥism] **nm** multilingualism.

pluripartisme [plyʀipaʀtism] **nm** (*Pol*) multi-party system.

plurivalent, e [plyʀivalɑ̃, ɑ̃t] **adj** multivalent, polyvalent.

plus 1 **adv nég** [ply] a (*temps*) **ne ... ~** not any longer *ou* any more, no longer; **il ne la voit ~** he no longer sees her, he doesn't see her any more; **je ne reviendrai ~/~ jamais** I shan't/I'll never come back again *ou* any more; **il n'a ~ besoin de son parapluie** he doesn't need his umbrella any longer *ou* any more; **il n'a ~ à s'inquiéter/travailler maintenant** he does not need to worry/work any more now; **il n'a ~ dit un mot** he didn't say another word (after that); **il n'est ~ là** he's gone (away); (*euph*) **son père n'est ~** his father has passed away (*euph*); **elle n'est ~ très jeune** she's not as young as she was, she's getting on in years; **~ de doute** no doubt now, no longer any doubt about it; **~ besoin de rester*** no need to stay now; (*hum*) **il n'y a ~ d'enfants/de jeunesse!** children/young people aren't what they used to be.

b (*quantité*) **ne ... ~** no more, not any more; **elle n'a ~ de pain/d'argent** she's got no more *ou* she hasn't got any more bread/money, she's got no (more) bread/money left; **elle ne veut ~ de pain** she doesn't want any more bread; **des fruits? il n'y en a ~** fruit? there is none left *ou* there isn't any (more) left; **~ de vin, merci** no more wine, thank you; **(il n'y a) ~ personne à la maison** there's no one left in the house, they've all left the house, they've all gone (away); **il n'y a ~ rien** there's nothing left; **il n'y a ~ rien d'autre à faire** there's nothing else to do; **il n'y a ~ guère *ou* beaucoup de pain** there's hardly any bread left; **on n'y voit presque ~ rien** you can hardly see anything now; *voir* **non**.

c (*avec que: seulement*) **il n'y a ~ que des miettes** there are only crumbs left, there's nothing left but crumbs; **cela ne tient ~ qu'à elle** it's up to her now; **il n'y a (guère) ~ que huit jours avant les vacances** there's only (about) a week to go before the holidays; **~ que 5 km à faire** only another 5 km to go.

2 **adv** *emploi comparatif*: [ply] *devant consonne*, [plyz] *devant voyelle*, [plys] *à la finale* a (*avec adj*) **il est ~ intelligent (que vous/moi)** he is more intelligent (than you (are)/than me *ou* than I am *ou* than I (*frm*)); **elle n'est pas ~ grande (que sa sœur)** she isn't any taller *ou* she is no taller (than her sister); **il est ~ bête que méchant** he's stupid rather than malicious; **il est ~ vieux qu'elle de 10 ans** he's 10 years older than her *ou* than she is *ou* than she (*frm*); **il est 2 fois ~ âgé qu'elle** he's twice as old as her, he's twice her age; **2 ou 3 fois ~ cher que ...** 2 or 3 times more expensive than ... *ou* as expensive as ...; **il est ~ qu'intelligent** he's clever to say the least, he isn't just intelligent; **un résultat ~ qu'honorable** an honourable result to say the least.

b (*avec adv*) **il court ~ vite (qu'elle)** he runs faster (than her *ou* than she does); **beaucoup ~ facilement** much more *ou* a lot more easily; **une heure ~ tôt/tard** an hour earlier/later; **ne venez pas ~ tard que 6 heures** don't come any later than 6 o'clock; **2 fois ~ souvent que ...** twice as often as ...; **j'en ai ~ qu'assez!** I've had more than enough!

c [ply(s)] (*avec vb*) **vous travaillez ~ (que nous)** you work more *ou* harder (than us); **il ne gagne pas ~ (que vous)** he doesn't earn any more (than you); **j'aime la poésie ~ que tout au monde** I like poetry more than anything (else) in the world; **j'aime 10 fois ~ le théâtre que le cinéma** I like the theatre 10 times better than the cinema.

d [ply(s)] (*davantage de*) **~ de: (un peu) ~ de pain** (a little *ou* a bit) more bread; **j'ai ~ de pain que vous** I've got more bread than you (have); **il y aura (beaucoup) ~ de monde demain** there will be (a lot *ou* many) more people tomorrow; **il n'y aura pas ~ de monde demain** there won't be any more people tomorrow.

e [ply] (*au-delà de*) **~ de: il y aura ~ de 100 personnes** there will be more than *ou* over 100 people; **à ~ de 100 mètres d'ici** more than *ou* over 100 metres from here; **les enfants de ~ de 4 ans** children over 4; **les ~ de 30/40 ans** the over 30s/40s; **il n'y avait pas ~ de 10 personnes** there were no more than 10 people; **il est ~ de 9 heures** it's after *ou* past 9 o'clock; **100 000 F et ~** [ply(s)] 100,000 francs and more *ou* and over; **~ d'un** more than one; **~ d'un aurait refusé** many would have refused.

f [ply], *devant voyelle* [plyz] **~ ... ~: ~ on est de fous, ~ on rit *ou* s'amuse** the more the merrier; **~ il en a, ~ il en veut** the more he has, the more he wants; **~ on boit, ~ on a soif** the more you drink, the thirstier you get; **~ il gagne, moins il est content** the more he earns, the less happy he is.

g [ply(s)] **de ~, en ~: elle a 10 ans de ~ (que lui)** she's 10 years older (than him); **il y a 10 personnes de ~ qu'hier** there are 10 more people than yesterday; **une fois de ~** once more, once again; **les frais de poste en ~** postal charges extra *ou* on top of that *ou* not included; **on nous a donné 2 verres de ~ *ou* en ~** we were given 2 more *ou* extra glasses; (*de trop*) we were given 2 glasses too many; **en ~ de son travail, il prend des cours du soir** on top of *ou* besides his work, he's taking evening classes; **en ~ de cela** on top of (all) that, in addition to that, into the bargain.

h (*loc*) **de ~ en ~** more and more; **il fait de ~ en ~ beau chaque jour** the weather gets better and better every day; **aller de ~ en ~ vite** to go faster and faster; **~ ou moins** more or less; **il a réussi ~ ou moins bien** he didn't manage too badly, he just about managed; **~ que jamais** more than ever; **qui ~ est, de ~** furthermore, what is more, moreover, into the bargain; (*Prov*) **~ fait douceur que violence** kindness succeeds where force will fail; *voir* **autant, raison, tant**.

3 [ply] **adv** *emploi superlatif* a (*avec adj*) **le ~ beau de tous mes livres** the most beautiful of all my books; **le ~ intelligent des deux** the cleverer *ou* the more intelligent of the two; **le ~ intelligent de tous** the cleverest *ou* most intelligent of all; **l'enfant le ~ doué que je connaisse/de la classe** the most gifted child I've (ever) met/in the class; **il était dans une situation des ~ embarrassantes** he was in a most embarrassing situation *ou* the most embarrassing of situations; **la ~ grande partie de son temps** most of his time, the best part of his time; **c'est ce que j'ai de ~ précieux** it's the most precious thing I possess; **la ~ belle fille du monde ne peut donner que ce qu'elle a** one can only give as much as one has got.

b (*avec adv*) **c'est le livre que je lis le ~ souvent** it's the book I read most often; **il a couru le ~ vite** he ran the fastest; **il a couru le ~ vite possible** he ran as fast as possible *ou* as fast as he could; **prends-en le ~ possible** [ply(s)] take as much (*ou* as many) as possible *ou* as you can.

c [ply(s)] (*avec vb*) **c'est le livre que j'aime le ~** it's the book I most like *ou* I like (the) most *ou* (the) best; **ce qui nous frappe le ~** what strikes us most.

d [ply(s)] **le ~ de: c'est nous qui avons cueilli le ~ de fleurs** we've picked the most flowers; **c'est le samedi qu'il y a le ~ de monde** it's on Saturdays that there are (the) most people; **prends le ~ possible de livres/de beurre** take as many books/as much butter as possible.

e [ply(s)] **au ~** at the most *ou* outside; **tout au ~** at the very most.

4 [plys] **conj** a (*addition*) plus, and. **deux ~ deux font quatre** two and two are four, two plus two make four; **tous les voisins, ~ leurs enfants** all the neighbours, plus their children *ou* and their children (as well); **il paie sa chambre, ~ le gaz et l'électricité** he pays for his room, plus gas and electricity.

b (*avec un chiffre*) plus. **il fait ~ deux aujourd'hui** it's plus two (degrees) today, it's two above freezing today; (*Math*) **~ cinq** plus five.

5 [plys] **nm** a (*Math*) **(signe) ~** plus (sign).

b (*avantage*) plus.

6 **comp** ►**plus petit commun multiple** lowest common multiple ►**plus-que-parfait** [plyskəpaʀfɛ] **nm** (*Gram*) pluperfect (tense), past perfect ►**plus-value** [plyvaly] **nf** (**pl plus-values**) *[investissement, terrain]* appreciation (*NonC*), increase in value; (*excédent*) *[budget]* surplus; (*bénéfice*) profit, surplus; *voir* **impôt**.

plusieurs [plyzjœʀ] 1 **adj indéf pl** several. **on ne peut pas être en ~ endroits à la fois** you can't be in more than one place at once; **ils sont ~** there are several (of them), there are a number of them; **un ou ~** one or more; **payer en ~ fois** to pay in instalments. 2 **pron indéf pl** several (people). ~ **(d'entre eux)** several (of them); **ils se sont mis à ~ pour ...** several people banded *ou* got together to ...; **nous nous sommes mis à ~ pour ...** several of us got together to ... .

Plutarque [plytaʀk] **nm** Plutarch.

Pluton [plytɔ̃] **nm** (*Astron, Myth*) Pluto.

plutonium [plytɔnjɔm] **nm** plutonium.

plutôt [plyto] **adv** a (*de préférence*) rather; (*à la place*) instead. **ne lis pas ce livre, prends ~ celui-ci** don't read that book but rather take this one *ou* take this one instead; **prends ce livre ~ que celui-là** take this book rather than *ou* instead of that one; **cette maladie affecte ~ les enfants** this illness affects children for the most part *ou* tends to affect children; **je préfère ~ celui-ci** (*je voudrais de préférence*) I'd rather *ou* sooner have this one; (*j'aime mieux*) I prefer this one, I like this one better; **~ souffrir que mourir** it is better to suffer (rather) than to die; **~ que de me regarder, viens m'aider** rather than *ou* instead of (just) watching me, come and help; **n'importe quoi ~ que cela!** anything but that!, anything rather than that!
b (*plus exactement*) rather. **il n'est pas paresseux mais ~ apathique** he's apathetic rather than *ou* more than lazy, he's not so much lazy as apathetic; **il est ignorant ~ que sot** he's ignorant rather *ou* more than stupid, he's more ignorant than stupid, he's not so much stupid as ignorant; **ou ~, c'est ce qu'il pense** or rather that's what he thinks; **c'est un journaliste ~ qu'un romancier** he's more of a journalist than a novelist, he's a journalist more *ou* rather than a novelist; **il s'y habitue ~ qu'il n'oublie** he's getting used to it rather than *ou* more than forgetting about it.
c (*assez*) *chaud, bon* rather, quite, fairly, pretty*. **il remange, c'est ~ bon signe** he's eating again — that's quite *ou* rather a good sign; **nos vacances sont ~ compromises avec cet événement** our holidays are rather *ou* somewhat in the balance because of this incident; **un homme brun, ~ petit** a dark man, rather *ou* somewhat on the short side *ou* rather short; **il est ~ pénible, celui-là!** he's a bit of a pain in the neck, that fellow!*; **il faisait beau? — non, il faisait ~ frais** was the weather good? — no, it was cool if anything; **qu'est-ce qu'il est pénible, celui-là — ah oui, ~!*** what a pain in the neck he is!* — you said it!* *ou* you're telling me!*

pluvial, e, **mpl -iaux** [plyvjal, jo] **adj** *régime, écoulement* pluvial. **eau ~e** rainwater.

pluvier [plyvje] **nm** plover. **~ guignard** dotterel.

pluvieux, -ieuse [plyvjø, jøz] **adj** rainy, wet.

pluviner [plyvine] 1 **vi** = **pleuvasser.**

pluviomètre [plyvjɔmɛtʀ] **nm** pluviometer (*SPÉC*), rain gauge.

pluviométrie [plyvjɔmetʀi] **nf** pluviometry.

pluviométrique [plyvjɔmetʀik] **adj** pluviometric(al). **carte ~** isopluvial map; **courbe ~** rainfall graph.

pluviôse [plyvjoz] **nm** Pluviôse, *fifth month in the French Republican calendar.*

pluviosité [plyvjozite] **nf** *[temps, saison]* raininess, wetness; (*pluie tombée*) (average) rainfall.

PM [peɛm] 1 **nf** a (**abrév de préparation militaire**) *voir* **préparation.** b (**abrév de police militaire**) MP. 2 **nm** a (**abrév de pistolet-mitrailleur**) *voir* **pistolet.** b (**abrév de poids moléculaire**) *voir* **poids.**

PMA [peɛma] **nmpl** (**abrév de pays les moins avancés**) LDCs.

PME [peɛmə] **nf (pl)** (**abrév de petite(s) et moyenne(s) entreprise(s)**) SME(s).

PMI [peɛmi] **nfpl** (**abrév de petite(s) et moyenne(s) industrie(s)**) *voir* **industrie.**

PMU [peɛmy] **nm** (**abrév de Pari mutuel urbain**) pari-mutuel, ≃ tote* (*Brit*). **jouer au ~** to bet on the horses, ≃ bet on the tote* (*Brit*); **le bureau du ~** the betting office.

PNB [peɛnbe] **nm** (**abrév de Produit national brut**) GNP.

pneu [pnø] *nm* (**abrév de pneumatique**) a *[véhicule]* tyre (*Brit*), tire (*US*). **~ clouté** *ou* **à clous** studded tyre (*Brit*) *ou* tire (*US*); **~ sans chambre** *ou* **tubeless** tubeless tyre (*Brit*) *ou* tire (*US*); **~-neige** snow tyre (*Brit*) *ou* tire (*US*); **~ plein** solid tyre (*Brit*) *ou* tire (*US*). b (*message*) letter sent by pneumatic despatch *ou* tube. **par ~** by pneumatic dispatch *ou* tube.

pneumatique [pnømatik] 1 **adj** (*Sci*) pneumatic; (*gonflable*) inflatable; *voir* **canot, marteau, matelas.** 2 **nf** pneumatics *(sg)*. 3 **nm** = **pneu.**

pneumectomie [pnømɛktomi] **nf** pneumectomy.

pneumoconiose [pnømokɔnjoz] **nf** pneumoconiosis.

pneumocoque [pnømɔkɔk] **nm** pneumococcus.

pneumogastrique [pnømogastʀik] 1 **adj** pneumogastric. 2 **nm** vagus nerve.

pneumologie [pnømɔlɔʒi] **nf** pneumology.

pneumologue [pnømɔlɔg] **nmf** lung specialist.

pneumonectomie [pnømɔnɛktɔmi] **nf** pneumonectomy.

pneumonie [pnømɔni] **nf** pneumonia (*NonC*). **faire** *ou* **avoir une ~** to have pneumonia.

pneumonique [pnømɔnik] 1 **adj** pneumonic. 2 **nmf** pneumonia patient.

pneumothorax [pnømotɔʀaks] **nm** pneumothorax; (*Chirurgie*) artificial pneumothorax.

Pnom-Penh [pnɔmpɛn] **n** Phnom Penh.

P.O. (**abrév de petites ondes**) SW.

Pô [po] **nm: le ~** the Po.

pochade [pɔʃad] **nf** (*dessin*) quick sketch (in colour); (*histoire*) humorous piece.

pochard, e* [pɔʃaʀ, aʀd] **nm, f** drunk, soak*, tippler*.

poche[1] [pɔʃ] **nf** a *[vêtement, cartable, portefeuille]* pocket. **~ revolver/intérieure** hip/inside pocket; **~ de pantalon** trouser pocket; **~ appliquée** *ou* **plaquée** patch pocket; **fausse ~** false pocket; **sans diplôme en ~, on ne peut rien faire** you can't do anything without qualifications; **s'en mettre plein les ~s*, se remplir les ~s*** to line one's pockets; **de ~** *sous-marin, couteau, mouchoir* pocket (*épith*); *collection, livre* paperback (*épith*); **format de ~** pocket-size; **j'avais 10 F/je n'avais pas un sou en ~** I had 10 francs/I hadn't a penny on me; **en être de sa ~*** to be out of pocket, lose out* (financially); **il a payé de sa ~** it came *ou* he paid for it out of his (own) pocket; (*fig*) **il a mis le maire dans sa ~** he has the mayor in his pocket, he has the mayor eating out of his hand; **il a sa nomination en ~** his appointment is in the bag*; **c'est dans la ~!*** it's in the bag!*; **ce n'est pas dans la ~!*** it's not in the bag yet!*; **faire les ~s à qn*** to go through *ou* rifle sb's pockets; **connaître un endroit comme sa ~** to know a place like the back of one's hand *ou* inside out; **mets ça dans ta ~ (et ton mouchoir par-dessus)** (*somme d'argent*) put that in your pocket (and forget about it); (*renseignement*) keep it under your hat*; *voir* **argent, langue** *etc.*
b (*déformation*) **faire des ~s** *[veste]* to go out of shape; *[pantalon]* to go baggy; **avoir des ~s sous les yeux** to have bags *ou* pouches under one's eyes.
c (*Comm: sac*) (paper *ou* plastic) bag. d *[kangourou]* pouch.
e (*cavité*) pocket. **~ d'air** air pocket; **~ d'eau** pocket of water; **~ de pus** pus sac; **~ de sang** haematoma; **~ des eaux** amniotic sac.
f (*Culin*) **~ à douille** piping bag.

poche[2] [pɔʃ] **nm** (*livre*) paperback.

pocher [pɔʃe] 1 **vt** (*Culin*) to poach. **~ un œil à qn** to give sb a black eye.

pochetée* [pɔʃte] **nf** oaf, twit* (*Brit*).

pochette [pɔʃɛt] **nf** (*mouchoir*) (breast) pocket handkerchief; (*petite poche*) breast pocket; (*sac*) clutch *ou* envelope bag; *[timbres, photos]* wallet, envelope; *[serviette, aiguilles]* case; *[disque]* sleeve. **~ surprise** lucky bag, ≃ Cracker Jack ® (*US*); (*hum*) **il a eu son permis/diplôme dans une ~ surprise*** he won his licence/degree in a lucky dip (*Brit*) *ou* a raffle; **~ d'allumettes** book of matches.

pocheuse [pɔʃøz] **nf** (egg)poacher.

pochoir [pɔʃwaʀ] **nm** (*cache*) stencil; (*tampon*) transfer.

podagre [pɔdagʀ] 1 **nf** (††) gout. 2 **adj** (†) suffering from gout.

podium [pɔdjɔm] **nm** podium. **monter sur le ~** to mount the podium.

podologie [pɔdɔlɔʒi] **nf** chiropody, podiatry (*US*).

podologue [pɔdɔlɔg] **nmf** chiropodist, podiatrist (*US*).

podomètre [pɔdɔmɛtʀ] **nm** pedometer.

poêle[1] [pwal] **nf: ~ (à frire)** frying pan; (**: détecteur de métaux*) metal detector; **passer à la ~** to fry.

poêle[2], **poële** [pwal] **nm** stove. **~ à mazout/à pétrole** oil/paraffin (*Brit*) *ou* kerosene (*US*) stove; **~ à bois** wood(-burning) stove.

poêle[3] [pwal] **nm** *[cercueil]* pall.

poêlée [pwale] **nf: une ~ de** a frying pan full of.

poêler [pwale] 1 **vt** to fry.

poêlon [pwalɔ̃] **nm** casserole.

poème [pɔɛm] **nm** poem. **~ en prose/symphonique** prose/symphonic poem; **c'est tout un ~*** (*c'est compliqué*) it's a real palaver*, what a carry-on* (*Brit*); (*c'est indescriptible*) it defies description.

poésie [pɔezi] **nf** (*art, qualité*) poetry; (*poème*) poem, piece of poetry. **faire de la ~** to write poetry.

poète [pɔɛt] 1 **nm** poet; (*fig: rêveur*) poet, dreamer; *voir* **œillet.** 2 **adj** *tempérament* poetic. **être ~** to be a poet; **femme ~** poetess.

poétesse [pɔetɛs] **nf** poetess.

poétique [pɔetik] 1 **adj** poetic(al). 2 **nf** poetics *(sg)*.

poétiquement [pɔetikmɑ̃] **adv** poetically.

poétisation [pɔetizasjɔ̃] **nf** (*action*) poetizing; (*résultat*) poetic depiction.

poétiser [pɔetize] 1 **vt** to poetize.

pogne* [pɔɲ] **nf** mitt*, paw*. **être à la ~ de qn** to be under sb's thumb; **avoir qn à sa ~** to have sb under one's thumb.

pognon* [pɔɲɔ̃] **nm** dough*, lolly* (*Brit*), bread*.

pogrom(e) [pɔgʀɔm] **nm** pogrom.

poids [pwɑ] 1 **nm** a (*gén*) weight. **prendre/perdre du ~** to gain/lose weight; **Georges a encore pris du ~** George has been putting on *ou* gaining weight again; **vendu au ~** sold by weight; **quel ~ fait-il?** what weight is he?, what does he weigh?, what's his weight?; **quel ~ cela pèse!** what a weight this is!; **ces bijoux d'argent seront vendus au ~ du métal** this silver jewellery will be sold by the weight of the metal; **la branche pliait sous le ~ des fruits** the branch was weighed down with (the) fruit *ou* was bending beneath the weight of the fruit; **elle s'appuyait contre lui de tout son ~** she leaned against him with all her weight; **elle a ajouté une pomme pour faire le ~** she put in an extra apple to make up the weight; *[acteur, homme politique]* **il ne fait vraiment pas le ~** he really doesn't measure up; **il ne fait pas le ~ face**

à son adversaire he's no match for his opponent; *voir* bon[1].
b (*objet*) *[balance, horloge etc]* weight; (*Sport*) shot. (*Sport*) lancer le ~ to put(t) the shot; *voir* deux.
c (*fig: charge*) weight. tout le ~ de l'entreprise repose sur lui he carries the weight of the whole business on his shoulders; syndicat qui a beaucoup de ~ union which has a lot of muscle *ou* which carries a lot of weight; plier sous le ~ des soucis/des impôts to be weighed down by worries/taxes, be bent beneath the weight of one's worries/of taxes; être courbé sous le ~ des ans to be weighed down by (the weight of) years; (*hum*) c'est le ~ des ans old age never comes alone (*hum*); enlever un ~ (de la conscience) à qn to take a weight *ou* a load off sb's mind; c'est un ~ sur sa conscience it's a weight on his conscience, it lies *ou* weighs heavy on his conscience; (*fig*) avoir *ou* se sentir un ~ sur l'estomac to have something lying heavy on one's stomach; j'ai un ~ sur la poitrine my chest feels tight, I have difficulty breathing.
d (*force, influence*) weight. argument de ~ weighty *ou* forceful argument, argument of great weight; homme de ~ man who carries weight (*fig*); cela donne du ~ à son hypothèse that gives *ou* lends weight to his hypothesis.
e (*boxeur*) ~ mi-mouche light flyweight; ~ mouche flyweight; ~ coq bantamweight; ~ plume featherweight; ~ léger lightweight; ~ super-léger light welterweight; ~ welter *ou* mi-moyen welterweight; ~ super-welter *ou* super-mi-moyen light middleweight; ~ moyen middleweight; ~ mi-lourd light heavyweight; ~ lourd (*lit, fig* *) heavyweight; le championnat du monde (des) ~ lourds the world heavyweight championship.
2 comp ►poids atomique† atomic weight ►poids brut gross weight ►poids et haltères (*Sport*) nmpl weightlifting; faire des poids et haltères (*spécialité*) to be a weightlifter; (*pour s'entraîner*) to do weight training *ou* weightlifting ►poids lourd nm (*camion*) lorry (*Brit*), truck (*US*), large *ou* heavy goods vehicle (*Brit*) ►poids et mesures nmpl weights and measures ►poids moléculaire molecular weight ►poids mort (*Tech, fig*) dead weight; (*fig péj*) cet employé est un poids mort this employee is not pulling his weight *ou* is a dead weight ►poids net net weight ►poids net égoutté drained weight ►poids spécifique specific gravity ►poids total en charge gross weight ►poids utile net weight ►poids à vide *[véhicule]* tare.

poignant, e [pwaɲɑ̃, ɑ̃t] adj *récit, spectacle, chagrin* poignant, heartrending, agonizing, harrowing.

poignard [pwaɲaʀ] nm dagger. coup de ~ stab; frappé d'un coup de ~ en plein cœur stabbed in *ou* through the heart.

poignarder [pwaɲaʀde] [1] vt to stab, knife. (*lit, fig*) ~ qn dans le dos to stab sb in the back; la jalousie/la douleur le poignardait he felt stabs of jealousy/pain, jealousy/pain cut through him like a knife.

poigne [pwaɲ] nf (*étreinte*) grip; (*main*) hand; (*fig: autorité*) firm-handedness. avoir de la ~ (*lit*) to have a strong grip; (*fig*) to rule with a firm hand; à ~ *personne, gouvernement* firm-handed.

poignée [pwaɲe] nf a (*lit: quantité*) handful, fistful; (*fig: petit nombre*) handful. à *ou* par ~s in handfuls; ajoutez une ~ de sel add a handful of salt. b *[porte, tiroir, valise]* handle; *[épée]* handle, hilt. c ~ de main handshake; donner une ~ de main à qn to shake hands with sb, shake sb's hand *ou* sb by the hand.

poignet [pwaɲɛ] nm (*Anat*) wrist; (*Habillement*) cuff; *voir* force.

poil [pwal] 1 nm a (*Anat*) hair. avoir du ~ *ou* des ~s sur la poitrine to have hairs on one's chest, have a hairy chest; les ~s de sa barbe (*entretenue*) the bristles *ou* hairs of his beard; (*mal rasée*) the stubble on his face; sans ~s *poitrine, bras* hairless; il n'a pas un ~ sur le caillou* he's as bald as a coot* *ou* an egg*; il n'a pas un ~ de sec* (*pluie*) he's drenched, he's soaked to the skin; (*sueur*) he's sweating in streams* *ou* like a pig**.
b *[animal]* hair; (*pelage*) coat. monter un cheval à ~†† to ride a horse bareback; en ~ de chèvre goatskin (*épith*); en ~ de lapin rabbitskin (*épith*); en ~ de chameau camelhair (*épith*); caresser dans le sens du ~ *chat* to stroke the right way; (*fig*) *personne* to rub up the right way; *voir* gibier.
c *[brosse à dents, pinceau]* bristle; *[tapis, étoffe]* strand; (*Bot*) *[plante]* down (*NonC*); *[artichaut]* choke (*NonC*). les ~s d'un tapis the pile of a carpet; les ~s d'un tissu the pile *ou* nap of a fabric.
d (*: *un petit peu*) s'il avait un ~ de bon sens if he had an iota *ou* an ounce of good sense; à un ~ près, l'armoire ne passait pas dans la porte a fraction more and the cupboard wouldn't have gone through the doorway; ça mesure environ un mètre, à un ~ près it measures one metre as near as makes no difference; il n'y a pas un ~ de différence entre les deux there isn't the slightest difference between the two (of them); pousser qch d'un ~ to shift sth a fraction; il s'en est fallu d'un ~ it was a near *ou* close thing *ou* a close shave*; *voir* quart.
e (*loc*) (*nu*) à ~** starkers** (*Brit*), in the altogether*, in one's birthday suit*; à ~!** (*à chanteur, orateur*) get off!*; (*déshabillez-vous*) get 'em off!**; se mettre à ~** to strip off; au (quart de) ~* (*magnifique*) great*, fantastic*; (*précisément*) *réglé, convenir* perfectly; tu arrives au ~, j'allais partir you've come just at the right moment — I was just about to leave; ça me va au ~* it suits me fine* *ou* to a T*; de tout ~ of all kinds, of all shapes and sizes; avoir un ~ dans la main* to be bone-idle*; (*péj*) un jeune blanc-bec qui n'a même pas de ~ au menton* a lad who's still wet behind the ears* (*péj*), a babe in arms (*péj*); tu parleras quand tu auras du ~ au menton you can have your say when you're out of short pants*; être de bon/de mauvais ~* to be in a good/bad mood; avoir qn sur le ~* to have sb breathing down one's neck (*fig*); tomber sur le ~ à qn* (*agresser*) to go for* *ou* lay into* sb; *[police]* to jump sb*; *[fisc]* to come down on sb; reprendre du ~ de la bête *[malade, plante]* to pick up (again), regain strength; *[rebelles, mouvement]* to regain strength, be on the way up again.
2 comp ►poil de carotte *personne* red-haired, red-headed; *cheveux* red, carroty ►poils follets down (*NonC*) ►poil à gratter itching powder.

poilant, e** [pwalɑ̃, ɑ̃t] adj killing**, killingly funny*.

poiler (se)** [pwale] [1] vpr to kill o.s. (laughing)**.

poilu, e [pwaly] 1 adj hairy. 2 nm poilu, French soldier in First World War.

poinçon [pwɛ̃sɔ̃] nm a (*outil*) *[cordonnier]* awl; *[menuisier]* awl, bradawl; *[brodeuse]* bodkin; *[graveur]* style; *[bijou, or]* die, stamp. b (*estampille*) hallmark. c (*matrice*) pattern.

poinçonnage [pwɛ̃sɔnaʒ] nm, poinçonnement [pwɛ̃sɔnmɑ̃] nm (*voir* poinçonner) stamping; hallmarking; punching, clipping.

poinçonner [pwɛ̃sɔne] [1] vt *marchandise* to stamp; *pièce d'orfèvrerie* to hallmark; *billet* to punch (a hole in), clip.

poinçonneur, -euse [pwɛ̃sɔnœʀ, øz] 1 nm, f (*Hist: personne*) ticket-puncher. 2 poinçonneuse nf (*machine*) punching machine, punch press.

poindre [pwɛ̃dʀ] [49] 1 vi (*littér*) *[jour]* to break, dawn; *[aube]* to break; *[plante]* to come up, peep through. 2 vt (†) *[tristesse]* to afflict; *[douleur, amour]* to sting (*littér*).

poing [pwɛ̃] nm fist. taper du ~ *ou* donner des coups de ~ sur la table to thump the table (with one's fist), bang *ou* thump one's fist on the table; les ~s sur les hanches with (one's) hands on (one's) hips, with (one's) arms akimbo; revolver au ~ revolver in hand; coup de ~ punch; donner un coup de ~ à qn to punch sb; il a reçu *ou* pris un coup de ~ dans la figure he was punched in the face; faire le coup de ~ avec qn to fight alongside sb; (*arme*) coup-de-~ américain* knuckle-duster(s); je vais t'envoyer *ou* te coller* mon ~ dans la figure you'll get my fist in your face*, I'm going to thump* *ou* punch you; montrer les ~s to shake one's fist; menacer qn du ~ to shake one's fist at sb; *voir* dormir, lever, pied, serrer.

point[1] [pwɛ̃] 1 nm a (*endroit*) point, place, spot; (*Astron, Géom*) point; (*fig: situation*) point, stage. pour aller d'un ~ à un autre to go from one point *ou* place *ou* spot to another; fixer un ~ précis dans l'espace to stare at a fixed point in space; déborder en plusieurs ~s to overflow at several points *ou* in several places; ils étaient venus de tous les ~s de l'horizon they had come from all corners of the earth *ou* from all the points of the compass; je reprends mon discours au ~ où je l'ai laissé I take up my speech where *ou* at the point at which I left off; avoir atteint le ~ où ..., en être arrivé au ~ où ... to have reached the point *ou* stage where ...; nous en sommes toujours au même ~ we haven't got any further, we're no further forward; c'est bête d'en être (arrivé) à ce ~-là et de ne pas finir it's silly to have got so far *ou* to have reached this point *ou* stage and not to finish; au ~ où on en est, cela ne changera pas grand-chose considering the situation we're in, it won't make much difference; on continue? — au ~ où l'on en est shall we go on? — we've got this far.
b (*degré*) (*Sci*) point; (*fig: niveau*) point, stage. ~ d'ébullition/de congélation boiling/freezing point; jusqu'à un certain ~ to some extent *ou* degree, up to a point, to a certain extent; au plus haut ~ *détester, admirer* intensely; se méfier au plus haut ~ de qch to be extremely mistrustful of *ou* highly sceptical about sth; être au plus haut ~ de la gloire to be at the peak *ou* summit of glory; est-il possible d'être bête à ce ~(-là)! how can anyone be so (incredibly) stupid?, how stupid can you get?*; vous voyez à quel ~ il est généreux you see how (very) generous he is *ou* the extent of his generosity; il ne pleut pas au ~ de mettre des bottes it isn't raining enough for you to put boots on, it isn't raining so much that you need boots; tirer sur une corde au ~ de la casser to pull on a rope so much that it breaks, pull a rope to the point where it breaks; sa colère avait atteint un ~ tel *ou* un tel ~ que ... he was so (very) angry that ..., his anger was such that ...; il en était arrivé à ce ~ *ou* à un tel ~ d'avarice que ... he had become so miserly that ..., his avarice had reached such proportions that ...; il a mangé au ~ de se rendre malade he ate so much that he was sick; c'était à ce ~ absurde que ... it was so (very) absurd that ... .
c (*aspect, détail, subdivision*) point. exposé en 3/4 ~s 3/4 point exposé; ~ de théologie/de philosophie point of theology/philosophy; passons au ~ suivant de l'ordre du jour let us move on to the next item on the agenda; ~ d'accord/de désaccord point of agreement/disagreement; ~ mineur *ou* de détail minor point, point of detail; voilà déjà un ~ acquis *ou* de réglé that's one thing *ou* point settled; avoir des ~s communs to have things in common; je n'ai aucun ~ commun avec elle I have nothing in common with her; ils sont d'accord sur ce ~/sur tous les ~s they are agreed on this point *ou* score/on all points *ou* scores *ou* counts; se ressembler en tout ~ to resemble each other in every respect; nous avons repris la question ~ par ~ we went over the

question point by point; **de ~ en ~** point by point, in every detail, down to the last detail.

d (*position*) (*Aviat, Naut*) position. **recevoir le ~ par radio** to be given one's position by radio; (*Naut*) **faire le ~** to take a bearing, plot one's position; (*Mil*) **faire le ~ cartographique** *ou* **géographique** to take a bearing; **faire le ~ horaire** to give regular bulletins, have regular updates; **nous allons maintenant faire le ~ horaire** let's have an update (on the situation); **faire le ~ de la situation** to take stock of the situation, review the situation; (*faire un compte rendu*) to sum up the situation.

e (*marque*) (*gén, Mus, en morse, sur i*) dot; (*ponctuation*) full stop (*Brit*), period; (*tache*) spot, speck; [*dé*] pip. **le bateau n'était plus qu'un ~ à l'horizon** the ship was now nothing but a dot *ou* speck *ou* spot on the horizon; (*fig*) **mettre les ~s sur les i** to dot one's i's (and cross one's t's), spell it out; **~, à la ligne** (*lit*) new paragraph; (*fig*) full stop (*Brit*), period (*US*); **tu n'iras pas, un ~ c'est tout** you're not going and that's all there is to it *ou* and that's that, you're not going — period *ou* full stop; *voir* **deux**.

f [*score*] (*Cartes, Sport*) point; (*Scol, Univ*) mark, point; [*retraite*] unit; [*salaire*] point. (*Boxe*) **aux ~s** on points; **il a échoué d'un ~** he failed by one mark *ou* point; **la partie se joue en 15 ~s** the winner is the first person to get to *ou* to score 15 (points); (*esp Tennis*) **faire** *ou* **marquer le ~** to win the point; (*fig*) **donner** *ou* **rendre des ~s à qn** to give sb points, give sb a (head) start; **bon/mauvais ~** (*Scol*) good/bad mark (*for conduct etc*); (*fig*) plus/minus (mark); **enlever un ~ par faute** to take a mark *ou* point off for every mistake; *voir* **bon, compter, marquer**.

g (*Écon, Bourse*) point. **sa cote de popularité a baissé de 3 ~s** his popularity rating has fallen (by) 3 points *ou* is down 3 points.

h (*Méd*) **avoir un ~ dans le dos** to have a twinge (of pain) in one's back; **vous avez un ~ de congestion là** you have a spot of congestion there.

i (*Typ, TV, Phot*) point.

j (*loc*) (*Culin*) **à ~** *viande* medium; *fruit* just ripe (*attrib*), nicely ripe; *fromage* just right for eating (*attrib*); **arriver à ~ (nommé)** to arrive just at the right moment *ou* just when needed; **cela tombe à ~** that comes just at the right moment, that's just *ou* exactly what I (*ou* we *etc*) need; **au ~** *image, photo* in focus; *affaire* completely finalized *ou* settled; *procédé, technique, machine* perfected; *discours, ouvrage* up to scratch (*attrib*), in its final form; **mettre au ~** to (bring into) focus; to finalize; to settle; to perfect; **mettre une affaire au ~ avec qn** to finalize *ou* settle all the details of a matter with sb; [*machine, spectacle*] **ce n'est pas encore au ~** it isn't quite up to scratch yet; **être sur le ~ de faire qch** to be (just) about to do sth, be just going to do sth, be on the point of doing sth; **j'étais sur le ~ de faire du café** I was just going to *ou* (just) about to make some coffee; *voir* **mal, mise**[2].

2 comp ▸**point d'accès** (*Ordin*) access point ▸**point d'ancrage** (*Aut*) anchorage point; (*fig*) [*politique*] foundation stone ▸**points d'annonce** (*Cartes*) thirteen points necessary for bidding ▸**point d'appui** (*Mil*) base of operations; [*levier*] fulcrum; [*personne*] something to lean on; **chercher un point d'appui** to look for something to lean on; **chercher un point d'appui pour placer une échelle** to look for somewhere to lean a ladder *ou* something to lean a ladder on *ou* against; **l'échelle a glissé de son point d'appui** the ladder slipped from where it was leaning *ou* from its resting place ▸**point d'attache** [*bateau*] mooring (post); (*fig*) base ▸**point d'avantage** (*Tennis*) break point ▸**point aveugle** (*Anat*) blind spot ▸**points cardinaux** points of the compass, cardinal points ▸**point chaud** (*Mil*) trouble spot, hot spot; (*fig: endroit*) trouble spot; (*fait*) **c'est un des points chauds de l'actualité** it's one of today's talking points *ou* major issues ▸**point de chute** (*lit*) landing place; (*fig*) stopping-off place ▸**point de contrôle** checkpoint ▸**point de côté** stitch (*pain in the side*) ▸**point critique** (*Phys, fig*) critical point ▸**point culminant** [*gloire, réussite, panique, épidémie*] height; [*affaire, scandale*] climax, culmination; [*montagne*] peak, summit; [*carrière*] height, zenith ▸**point de départ** [*train, autobus*] point of departure; [*science, réussite, aventure*] starting point; [*enquête*] point of departure, starting point; (*Sport*) start; **revenir à son point de départ** to come back to where it (*ou* one) started; (*fig*) **nous voilà revenus au point de départ** (so) we're back to square one*, we're back where we started ▸**point de droit** point of law ▸**point d'eau** (*source*) watering place; [*camping*] water (supply) point ▸**point d'exclamation** exclamation mark (*Brit*) *ou* point (*US*) ▸**point faible** weak point ▸**point de fait** point of fact ▸**point final** (*lit*) full stop (*Brit*), period (*US*); (*fig*) **je refuse, point final** I refuse, period (*US*), I refuse and that's final; (*fig*) **mettre un point final à qch** to put an end to sth, bring sth to an end ▸**point fort** strong point ▸**point d'honneur** point of honour; **mettre un point d'honneur à** *ou* **se faire un point d'honneur de faire qch** to make it a point of honour to do sth ▸**point d'impact** point of impact ▸**point d'information** point of information ▸**point d'interrogation** question mark; **qui sera élu, c'est là le point d'interrogation** who will be elected — that's the big question (mark) *ou* that's the 64,000-dollar question* ▸**point d'intersection** point of intersection ▸**point du jour** daybreak, break of day ▸**point lumineux** dot *ou* spot of light ▸**point de mire** (*lit*) target; (*fig*) focal point ▸**point mort** (*Tech*) dead centre; (*Aut*) neutral; (*Fin*) break-even point; **au point mort** (*Aut*) in neutral; [*négociations, affaires*] at a standstill ▸**point névralgique** (*Méd*) nerve centre; (*fig*) sensitive spot ▸**point noir** [*visage*] blackhead; (*fig: problème*) problem, difficulty; (*Aut: lieu d'accidents*) blackspot ▸**point de non-retour** point of no return ▸**point d'ordre** point of order ▸**point d'orgue** (*Mus*) pause; (*fig*) [*festival, conférence*] break ▸**point de ralliement** rallying point ▸**point de rassemblement** (*à l'aéroport etc*) meeting point; (*Naut*) muster station ▸**point de ravitaillement** (*en nourriture*) refreshment point, staging point; (*en essence*) refuelling point ▸**point de rencontre** meeting point ▸**point de repère** (*dans l'espace*) landmark; (*dans le temps*) point of reference ▸**points de reprise** (*Mus*) repeat marks ▸**point de rouille** spot *ou* speck of rust ▸**point de rupture** (*gén*) breaking point; (*Ordin*) breakpoint ▸**point de saturation** (*Sci, fig*) saturation point ▸**point sensible** (*sur la peau*) tender spot; (*Mil*) trouble spot; (*fig*) sensitive area, sore point ▸**point de soudure** spot *ou* blob of solder ▸**point stratégique** key point ▸**points de suspension** (*gén*) suspension points; (*en dictant*) "dot, dot, dot" ▸**point de tangence** tangential point ▸**point de vente** (*Comm*) point of sale, sales outlet; **"points de vente dans toute la France"** "on sale throughout France"; **liste des points de vente** list of stockists *ou* retailers ▸**point-virgule** (pl **points-virgules**) semicolon ▸**point voyelle** (*Ling*) vowel point ▸**point de vue** (*lit*) view(point); (*fig*) point of view, standpoint; **du** *ou* **au point de vue argent** from the financial point of view *ou* standpoint *ou* viewpoint, as regards money, moneywise*; **nous aimerions connaître votre point de vue sur ce sujet** we should like to know your point of view *ou* standpoint *ou* where you stand in this matter.

point[2] [pwɛ̃] **1** nm (*Couture, Tricot*) stitch. **bâtir à grands ~s** to tack; **coudre à grands ~s** to sew *ou* stitch using a long stitch; **faire un (petit) ~ à qch** to put a stitch in sth.

2 comp ▸**point d'Alençon** Alençon lace ▸**point d'arrêt** finishing-off stitch ▸**point arrière** backstitch ▸**point de chaînette** chain stitch ▸**point de chausson** (*Couture*) blind hem stitch; (*Broderie*) closed herringbone stitch ▸**point de couture** stitch ▸**point de croix** cross-stitch ▸**point devant** running stitch ▸**point d'épine** feather stitch ▸**point de feston** blanket stitch ▸**point de jersey** stocking stitch ▸**point mousse** garter stitch ▸**point d'ourlet** hem-stitch ▸**point de riz** (*Tricot*) moss stitch ▸**point de suture** (*Med*) stitch; **faire des points de suture à** to put stitches in, stitch up ▸**point de tapisserie** canvas stitch ▸**point de tige** stem stitch ▸**point de torsade** cable stitch ▸**point de tricot** (*gén*) knitting stitch; (*maille à l'endroit*) knit stitch ▸**point de Venise** rose point.

point[3] [pwɛ̃] adv (*littér, hum*) = **pas**[2].

pointage [pwɛ̃taʒ] nm **a** (*action: voir* **pointer**[1]) ticking *ou* checking *ou* marking off; checking in; checking out; pointing, aiming, levelling; training; directing; dotting; starting off; clocking in; clocking out. **b** (*contrôle*) check.

pointe [pwɛ̃t] **1** nf **a** (*extrémité*) [*aiguille, épée*] point; [*flèche, lance*] head, point; [*couteau, crayon, clocher, clou*] point, tip; [*canne*] (pointed) end, tip, point; [*montagne*] peak, top; [*menton, nez, langue, ski*] tip; [*moustache, seins, col*] point; [*chaussure*] toe. **à la ~ de l'île** at the tip of the island; **chasser l'ennemi à la ~ de l'épée/de la baïonnette** to chase away the enemy with swords drawn/at bayonet point.

b (*partie saillante*) [*grillage*] spike; [*côte*] headland. **la côte forme une ~** *ou* **s'avance en ~ à cet endroit** the coast juts out (into the sea) *ou* forms a headland at that point; **objet qui forme une ~** object that tapers (in)to a point; (*Danse*) **faire des ~s** to dance on points; **en ~** *barbe* in a point, pointed; *col* pointed; **décolleté en ~** V-neckline; **tailler en ~** *arbre, barbe* to cut *ou* trim into a point; *crayon* to sharpen (in)to a point; **clocher/canne qui se termine en ~** bell-tower/stick with a pointed tip *ou* that ends in a point.

c (*clou*) tack; (*Sport*) [*chaussure*] spike; (*outil pointu*) point. **tu cours avec des tennis ou avec des ~s?** do you run in trainers or spikes?

d (*foulard*) triangular (neck)scarf; (*couche de bébé*) (triangular-)shaped nappy (*Brit*) *ou* diaper (*US*).

e (*allusion ironique*) pointed remark; (*trait d'esprit*) witticism.

f (*petite quantité*) **~ de** *ail* touch *ou* dash *ou* hint of; *ironie, jalousie* touch *ou* tinge *ou* hint of; **il a une ~ d'accent** he has a hint of an accent.

g (*maximum*) peak. (*Aut*) **faire des ~s (de vitesse) de 140** to have the occasional burst of 140 km/h; **faire** *ou* **pousser une ~ jusqu'à Paris** to push *ou* press on as far as Paris; **faire** *ou* **pousser une ~ de vitesse** [*athlète, cycliste, automobiliste*] to put on a burst of speed, put on a spurt, step on it*; (*Aut*) **faire du 200 km/h en ~** to have a top *ou* maximum speed of 200 km/h; **à la ~ du combat** in the forefront of (the) battle; **à la ~ de l'actualité** in the forefront of current affairs *ou* of the news; **à la ~ du progrès** in the forefront *ou* the front line *ou* at the leading edge of progress; **de ~** *industrie* leading, high-tech; *technique* latest, ultramodern, advanced; *vitesse* top, maximum; **heure** *ou* **période de ~** [*gaz, électricité*] peak period; [*circulation*] rush *ou* peak hour.

h (*Naut*) [*compas*] point.

2 comp ▸**pointe d'asperge** asparagus tip *ou* spear ▸**pointe Bic** ® Biro ® (*Brit*), ball-point (pen), ball pen ▸**pointes de feu** (*Méd*) ignipuncture (*Brit*); **faire des pointes de feu à qn** to perform

ignipuncture (*Brit*) on sb ▸**pointe fibre** (*stylo*) fibre-tip (pen) ▸**pointe du jour** (*littér*) daybreak ▸**la pointe des pieds** the toes; **(se mettre) sur la pointe des pieds** (to stand) on tiptoe *ou* on one's toes; **marcher/entrer sur la pointe des pieds** to walk/come in on tiptoe *ou* on one's toes, tiptoe in/out; (*fig*) **il faut y aller sur la pointe des pieds (avec lui)** you have to tread very carefully (when dealing with him) ▸**pointe sèche** (*Art*) dry-point; **gravure à la pointe sèche** dry-point engraving ▸**pointe de terre** spit *ou* tongue of land, headland.

pointeau, pl ~**x** [pwɛ̃to] **nm** a *[carburateur, graveur]* needle. b (*Ind: surveillant*) timekeeper.

pointer¹ [pwɛ̃te] 1 1 **vt** a (*cocher*) to tick off, check off, mark off. (*Naut*) ~ **(sa position sur) la carte** to prick off *ou* plot one's position; *voir* **zéro**.

b (*Ind*) *employé* (*à l'arrivée*) to clock in, check in; (*au départ*) to clock out, check out.

c (*braquer*) *fusil* to point, aim, level (*vers, sur* at); *jumelles* to train (*vers, sur* on); *lampe* to direct (*vers, sur* towards); *boule* (*de pétanque*) to roll (*as opposed to throw*). **il pointa vers elle un index accusateur** he pointed *ou* directed an accusing finger at her.

d (*Mus*) *note* to dot. **notes pointées** dotted rhythm.

e (*Tech*) *trou de vis* to start off.

2 **vi** *[employé]* (*arrivée*) to clock in, check in; (*départ*) to clock out, check out.

3 **se pointer* vpr** (*arriver*) to turn up*, show up*.

pointer² [pwɛ̃te] 1 1 **vt** a (*piquer*) to stick. **il lui pointa sa lance dans le dos** he stuck his lance into his back. b (*dresser*) **église qui pointe ses tours vers le ciel** church whose towers soar (up) into the sky; **chien qui pointe les oreilles** dog which pricks up its ears. 2 **vi** (*littér*) a (*s'élever*) *[tour]* to soar up. b (*apparaître*) *[plante]* to peep out; (*fig*) *[ironie]* to pierce through. **ses seins pointaient sous la robe** the points of her breasts showed beneath her dress; **le jour pointait** day was breaking *ou* dawning; **le bateau pointait à l'horizon** the boat appeared as a dot on the horizon.

pointer³ [pwɛ̃tœʀ] **nm** (*chien*) pointer.

pointeur [pwɛ̃tœʀ] **nm** (*Ind, Sport*) timekeeper; (*Ordin*) pointer; *[boules] player who rolls the bowl (as opposed to throwing it)*; *[canon]* gun-layer.

pointeuse [pwɛ̃tøz] **nf: (horloge)** ~ time clock.

pointillage [pwɛ̃tijaʒ] **nm** stipple, stippling.

pointillé, e [pwɛ̃tije] (**ptp de pointiller**) 1 **adj** dotted. 2 **nm** a (*Art*) (*procédé*) stipple, stippling; (*gravure*) stipple. b (*trait*) dotted line; (*perforations*) perforation(s). **en** ~ (*lit*) dotted; (*fig*) (*sous-entendu*) hinted at; (*discontinu*) *carrière, vie* marked by stops and starts; **"détacher suivant le** ~**"** "tear along the dotted line".

pointillement [pwɛ̃tijmɑ̃] **nm** = **pointillage**.

pointiller [pwɛ̃tije] 1 (*Art*) 1 **vi** to draw (*ou* engrave) in stipple. 2 **vt** to stipple.

pointilleux, -euse [pwɛ̃tijø, øz] **adj** particular, pernickety (*péj*), fussy (*péj*) (*sur* about).

pointillisme [pwɛ̃tijism] **nm** pointillism.

pointilliste [pwɛ̃tijist] **adj, nmf** pointillist.

pointu, e [pwɛ̃ty] 1 **adj** a (*lit*) (*en forme de pointe*) pointed; (*aiguisé*) sharp. b (*péj*) *air* touchy, peevish, peeved; *caractère* touchy, peevish, crabbed; *voix, ton* shrill. **accent** ~ northern accent (*expression used by people from South of France*). c (*fig*) *analyse* in-depth; *sujet* specialized. 2 **adv: parler** ~ to speak with *ou* have a northern accent.

pointure [pwɛ̃tyʀ] **nf** *[gant, chaussure]* size. **quelle est votre** ~**?, quelle** ~ **faites-vous?** what size do you take *ou* are you?; (*fig*) **c'est une (grande)** ~ **dans la chanson/ce domaine*** he is a big name in songwriting/this field*.

poire [pwaʀ] 1 **nf** a (*fruit*) pear. **il m'a dit cela entre la** ~ **et le fromage** ≈ he told me that (casually) over coffee (*at the end of a meal*); *voir* **couper, garder**.

b (*: *tête*) mug‡, face. **il a une bonne** ~ he's got a nice enough face; **se ficher de** *ou* **se payer la** ~ **de qn** (*ridiculiser*) to have a good laugh at sb's expense; (*tromper*) to take sb for a ride*; **en pleine** ~ right in the face.

c (*: *dupe*) mug* (*Brit*), sucker*. **c'est une bonne** ~ he's a real mug* (*Brit*) *ou* sucker*; **et moi, bonne** ~**, j'ai dit oui** and like a mug* (*Brit*) *ou* sucker* I said yes.

d *[vaporisateur]* squeezer.

2 **adj: être** ~* to be a mug* (*Brit*) *ou* a sucker*.

3 **comp** ▸**poire électrique** (pear-shaped) switch ▸**poire à injections** syringe ▸**poire à lavement** enema ▸**poire à poudre** powder horn.

poiré [pwaʀe] **nm** perry.

poireau, pl ~**x** [pwaʀo] **nm** leek. (*fig*) **faire le** ~* to hang about*; **elle m'a fait faire le** ~ **pendant 2 heures*** she kept *ou* left me hanging about for 2 hours.

poireauter* [pwaʀote] 1 **vi** to be left kicking *ou* cooling one's heels*. **faire** ~ **qn** to leave sb to kick *ou* cool his (*ou* her) heels*, leave sb kicking *ou* cooling his (*ou* her) heels*.

poirée [pwaʀe] **nf** (*bette*) Chinese leaves (*pl*).

poirier [pwaʀje] **nm** pear tree. (*fig*) **faire le** ~ to do a headstand.

poiroter* [pwaʀote] = **poireauter.**

pois [pwɑ] 1 **nm** a (*légume*) pea. **petits** ~ (garden) peas. b (*Habillement*) (polka) dot, spot. **robe à** ~ dotted *ou* spotted *ou* polka dot dress; *voir* **purée.** 2 **comp** ▸**pois cassés** split peas ▸**pois chiche** chickpea, garbanzo ▸**pois de senteur** sweet pea.

poiscaille* [pwaskaj] **nm ou f** (*souvent péj*) fish.

poison [pwazɔ̃] 1 **nm** (*lit, fig*) poison. **on a mis du** ~ **dans sa soupe** his soup was poisoned. 2 **nmf** (* *fig: personne*) misery*, misery-guts‡; (*enfant*) little horror*; (*chose*) drag*, bind* (*Brit*).

poissard, e [pwasaʀ, aʀd] 1 **adj** *accent, langage* vulgar, coarse. 2 **poissarde nf: parler comme une** ~**e** to talk like a fishwife.

poisse‡ [pwas] **nf** rotten luck*, bad luck. **avoir la** ~ to have rotten* *ou* bad luck; **quelle** ~**!, c'est la** ~**!** just my (*ou* our) (rotten) luck!*; **ne le fais pas, ça porte la** ~ don't do that – it's bad luck *ou* it's unlucky; **ça leur a porté la** ~ that brought them bad luck.

poisser [pwase] 1 **vt** a (‡: *attraper*) to nab‡, cop‡. b (*salir*) to make sticky; (*engluer*) *cordage* to pitch. **ça poisse** it is all sticky.

poisseux, -euse [pwasø, øz] **adj** *mains, surface* sticky.

poisson [pwasɔ̃] 1 **nm** a fish. **pêcher du** ~ to fish; **2/3** ~**s** 2/3 fish *ou* fishes; **fourchette/couteau à** ~ fish fork/knife; **être (heureux) comme un** ~ **dans l'eau** to be in one's element, be as happy as a sandboy; **être comme un** ~ **hors de l'eau** to be like a fish out of water; **engueuler qn comme du** ~ **pourri‡** to call sb all the names under the sun, bawl at sb; *voir* **petit, queue.**

b (*Astron*) **les P**~**s** Pisces, the Fishes; **être (un) P**~**s** to be Pisces *ou* a Piscean.

2 **comp** ▸**poisson d'argent** silverfish ▸**poisson d'avril excl** April fool! ◊ **nm** (*blague*) April fool's trick ▸**poisson(-)chat nm (pl poissons (-)chats)** catfish ▸**poisson d'eau douce** freshwater fish ▸**poisson épée** swordfish ▸**poisson lune** sunfish ▸**poisson de mer** saltwater fish ▸**poisson perroquet** parrotfish ▸**poisson pilote** pilotfish ▸**poisson plat** flatfish ▸**poisson rouge** goldfish ▸**poisson scie** sawfish ▸**poisson volant** flying fish.

poissonnerie [pwasɔnʀi] **nf** (*boutique*) fishmonger's (shop) (*esp Brit*), fish shop; (*métier*) fish trade.

poissonneux, -euse [pwasɔnø, øz] **adj** full of fish (*attrib*), well-stocked with fish, abounding in fish (*attrib*).

poissonnier [pwasɔnje] **nm** fishmonger (*esp Brit*), fish merchant (*US*).

poissonnière [pwasɔnjɛʀ] **nf** a (*personne*) (woman) fishmonger (*esp Brit*), fish merchant (*US*). b (*ustensile*) fish kettle.

poitevin, e [pwat(ə)vɛ̃, in] 1 **adj** Poitou (*épith*), of Poitou; Poitiers (*épith*), of Poitiers. 2 **nm, f: P**~**(e)** inhabitant *ou* native of Poitou *ou* Poitiers.

poitrail [pwatʀaj] **nm** (*Zool*) breast; (*hum: poitrine*) chest.

poitrinaire† [pwatʀinɛʀ] 1 **adj: être** ~ to have TB, be tuberculous (*SPÉC*). 2 **nmf** tuberculosis sufferer.

poitrine [pwatʀin] **nf** (*gén*) chest, breast (*littér*); (*seins*) bust, bosom; (*Culin*) *[veau, mouton]* breast; *[porc]* belly. ~ **salée (***ou* **fumée)** ≈ streaky bacon; ~ **de bœuf** brisket (of beef); **maladie de** ~**†** chest complaint; **elle a beaucoup de** ~ she has a big bust *ou* bosom, she's big-busted; **elle n'a pas de** ~ she's flat-chested, she has no bust; *voir* **fluxion, tour², voix.**

poivrade [pwavʀad] **nf** (*Culin*) vinaigrette (sauce) with pepper. **(à la)** ~ with salt and pepper.

poivre [pwavʀ] 1 **nm** pepper; *voir* **moulin, steak.** 2 **comp** ▸**poivre blanc** white pepper ▸**poivre de Cayenne** Cayenne pepper ▸**poivre en grains** whole pepper, peppercorns (*pl*) ▸**poivre gris** black pepper ▸**poivre moulu** ground pepper ▸**poivre noir** black pepper ▸**poivre en poudre** = **poivre moulu** ▸**poivre rouge** red pepper ▸**poivre et sel adj inv** *cheveux* pepper-and-salt ▸**poivre vert** green pepper (*spice*).

poivré, e [pwavʀe] (**ptp de poivrer**) **adj** *plat, goût, odeur* peppery; (*fig*) *histoire* spicy, juicy*, saucy*; (‡: *soûl*) pickled‡, plastered‡.

poivrer [pwavʀe] 1 1 **vt** to pepper, put pepper in *ou* on. 2 **se poivrer‡ vpr** (*se soûler*) to get pickled‡ *ou* plastered‡.

poivrier [pwavʀije] **nm** a (*Bot*) pepper plant. b (*Culin*) pepperpot, pepper shaker (*US*).

poivrière [pwavʀijɛʀ] **nf** a (*Culin*) pepperpot, pepper shaker (*US*). b (*plantation*) pepper plantation. c (*Archit*) pepper-box.

poivron [pwavʀɔ̃] **nm:** ~ **(vert)** green pepper, capsicum; ~ **rouge** red pepper, capsicum.

poivrot, e* [pwavʀo, ɔt] **nm, f** drunkard, wino‡, tippler*, boozer‡.

poix [pwa] **nf** pitch (*tar*).

poker [pɔkɛʀ] **nm** (*Cartes*) (*jeu*) poker; (*partie*) game of poker. **faire un** ~ to have a game of poker; ~ **d'as/de dames** four aces/queens; ~ **d'as** (*jeu*) poker dice; ~ **menteur** bluff; (*fig*) **coup de** ~ gamble.

polaire [pɔlɛʀ] 1 **adj** (*Chim, Géog, Math*) polar. **froid** ~ arctic cold; *voir* **cercle, étoile.** 2 **nf** (*Math*) polar.

polaque [pɔlak] **nm** (*péj*) Polack (*péj*).

polar* [pɔlaʀ] **nm** (*roman*) whodunnit*, thriller.

polard, e [pɔlaʀ, aʀd] **nm, f** (*péj, arg Scol*) swot*.

polarisant, e [pɔlaʀizɑ̃, ɑ̃t] **adj** (*Élec, Phys*) polarizing.

polarisation [pɔlaʀizasjɔ̃] **nf** (*Élec, Phys*) polarization; (*fig*) focusing.

polariser [pɔlaʀize] 1 1 **vt** a (*Élec, Phys*) to polarize. b (*fig: faire converger sur soi*) *attention, regards* to attract. **problème qui polarise**

toute l'activité/tout le mécontentement problem around *ou* upon which all the activity/discontent centres *ou* is centred. c (*fig: concentrer*) ~ **son attention/ses efforts sur qch** to focus *ou* centre one's attention/efforts on sth; ~ **son énergie sur qch** to bring all one's energies to bear on sth. 2 **se polariser** **vpr** (*Phys*) to polarize. **se ~ *ou* être polarisé sur qch** *[mécontentement, critiques]* to be centred (a)round *ou* upon sth, be focused upon sth; *[personne]* to focus *ou* centre one's attention on sth.

polariseur [pɔlaʀizœʀ] **adj, nm: (prisme)** ~ polarizer.

polarité [pɔlaʀite] **nf** (*Bio, Ling, Math, Phys*) polarity.

Polaroïd [pɔlaʀɔid] **nm** ® Polaroid ®. **(appareil-photo) polaroid** ® Polaroid ® (camera).

polder [pɔldɛʀ] **nm** polder.

pôle [pol] **nm** (*Sci, fig*) pole. ~ **Nord/Sud** North/South Pole; ~ **magnétique** magnetic pole; (*fig*) ~ **d'attraction** centre of attraction; (*Écon*) ~ **de conversion** relocation area; ~ **de développement** pole of development.

polémique [pɔlemik] 1 **adj** controversial, polemic(al). 2 **nf** controversy, argument, polemic. **engager une ~ avec qn** to enter into an argument with sb; **chercher à faire de la ~** to try to be controversial; (*débat*) **une grande ~ s'est engagée sur ...** a great debate has been started about *ou* on ... .

polémiquer [pɔlemike] [1] **vi** to be involved in controversy.

polémiste [pɔlemist] **nmf** polemist, polemicist.

polémologie [pɔlemɔlɔʒi] **nf** study of war.

pole position [polpozisjɔ̃] **nf** (*Aut, fig*) pole position.

poli, e[1] [pɔli] **adj** polite. **être ~ avec qn** to be polite to sb; **il est trop ~ pour être honnête** his politeness makes me suspicious of his motives, he's so polite I smell a rat; **soyez ~!** don't be so rude!

poli, e[2] [pɔli] (**ptp de polir**) 1 **adj** *bois, ivoire* polished; *métal* burnished, polished; *caillou* smooth. 2 **nm** shine. **donner du ~ à** to put a shine on, polish (up).

police[1] [pɔlis] 1 **nf** a (*corps*) police (*NonC*), police force. **voiture de ~** police car; **être dans *ou* de la ~** to be in the police (force), be a policeman; **la ~ est à ses trousses** the police are after him *ou* are on his tail; **la guerre des ~s** the rivalry between different branches of the police; **toutes les ~s de France** the police throughout France; **après avoir passé la douane et les formalités de ~** once you've gone through customs and immigration; *voir* **plaque, salle.**

b (*maintien de l'ordre*) policing, enforcement of (law and) order. **les pouvoirs de ~ dans la société** powers to enforce *ou* maintain law and order in society; **exercer *ou* faire la ~** to keep (law and) order; **faire la ~ dans une classe** to police a class, keep order in a class, keep a class in order; **faire sa propre ~** to do one's own policing, keep (law and) order for o.s.

c (*règlements*) regulations (*pl*). ~ **intérieure d'un lycée** internal regulations of a school.

d (*tribunal*) **passer en simple ~** to be tried in a police *ou* magistrates' court; *voir* **tribunal.**

2 **comp** ▸**police de l'air et des frontières** border police ▸**police de la circulation** traffic police ▸**police judiciaire** ≈ Criminal Investigation Department ▸**police des mœurs *ou* mondaine** ≈ vice squad ▸**police montée *ou* à cheval** (*Can*) mounted police, mounties* ▸**police nationale** national police force ▸**police parallèle** ≈ secret police ▸**la police des polices** Complaints and Discipline Branch (*Brit*), Internal Affairs (*US*) ▸**police privée** private police force ▸**police de la route** traffic police (*Brit*), state highway patrol (*US*) ▸**police secours** police (*special service for emergencies*), ≈ emergency services (*pl*); **appeler police secours** ≈ to dial 999 (*Brit*) *ou* 911 (*US*), ≈ call the emergency services ▸**police secrète** secret police.

police[2] [pɔlis] **nf** a (*Assurances*) (insurance) policy. ~ **d'assurance vie** life insurance *ou* assurance policy; ~ **d'assurance contre l'incendie** fire insurance policy. b (*Typ*) ~ **(de caractères)** fount (*Brit*), font (*esp US*).

policer [pɔlise] [3] **vt** (*littér*, ††) to civilize.

polichinelle [pɔliʃinɛl] **nm** a (*Théât*) **P~** Punchinello; *voir* **secret.** b (*marionnette*) Punch. c (*fig péj: personne*) buffoon. **faire le ~** to act the buffoon. d (‡: *être enceinte*) **avoir un ~ dans le tiroir** to have a bun in the oven‡.

policier, -ière [pɔlisje, jɛʀ] 1 **adj** *chien, enquête, régime* police (*épith*); *film, roman* detective (*épith*). 2 **nm** a (*agent*) policeman, police officer. **femme ~** policewoman, woman police officer. b (*roman*) detective novel; (*film*) detective film.

policlinique [pɔliklinik] **nf** out-patients' clinic.

poliment [pɔlimɑ̃] **adv** politely.

polio [pɔljo] 1 **nf** (**abrév de poliomyélite**) (*maladie*) polio. 2 **nmf*** (**abrév de poliomyélitique**) polio victim.

poliomyélite [pɔljɔmjelit] **nf** poliomyelitis.

poliomyélitique [pɔljɔmjelitik] 1 **adj** suffering from polio. 2 **nmf** polio victim.

polir [pɔliʀ] [2] **vt** a *meuble, objet, souliers* to polish (up), put a polish *ou* shine on; *pierre, verre* to polish; *métal* to polish, burnish, buff; *ongles* to polish, buff. b (*fig*) *discours* to polish (up); *style* to polish; *manières* to polish, refine.

polissage [pɔlisaʒ] **nm** (*voir* **polir**) polishing; shining; burnishing; buffing.

polisseur, -euse [pɔlisœʀ, øz] **nm, f** polisher.

polissoir [pɔliswaʀ] **nm** polisher, polishing machine. ~ **à ongles** nail buffer.

polisson, -onne [pɔlisɔ̃, ɔn] 1 **adj** a (*espiègle*) *enfant, air* naughty, mischievous. b (*grivois*) *chanson* naughty, saucy; *regard* saucy, randy*. 2 **nm, f** (*enfant*) (little) rascal, (little) devil*, mischief*; (*personne égrillarde*) saucy *ou* randy devil*; (††: *petit vagabond*) street urchin.

polissonner† [pɔlisɔne] [1] **vi** to be naughty.

polissonnerie [pɔlisɔnʀi] **nf** a (*espièglerie*) naughty trick. b (*grivoiserie*) (*parole*) naughty *ou* saucy remark; (*action*) naughty thing.

politesse [pɔlitɛs] **nf** a (*savoir-vivre*) politeness, courtesy. **par ~** out of politeness, to be polite; (*Ling*) **conditionnel de ~** polite conditional (form); (*Ling*) **pluriel de ~** polite plural (form); *voir* **brûler, formule, visite.** b (*parole*) polite remark; (*action*) polite gesture. **rendre une ~** to return a favour; **se faire des ~s** (*paroles*) to exchange polite remarks; (*actions*) to make polite gestures to one another; **ce serait la moindre des ~s** it is the least you can do.

politicaillerie* [pɔlitikajʀi] **nf** (*péj*) politicking (*péj*).

politicard [pɔlitikaʀ] **nm** (*péj*) politician, political schemer.

politicien, -ienne [pɔlitisjɛ̃, jɛn] (*péj*) 1 **adj** politicking (*péj*). (*péj*) **la politique ~ne** politicking, politics for its own sake. 2 **nm,f** politician, political schemer.

politico- [pɔlitiko] **préf** politico-.

politique [pɔlitik] 1 **adj** a *institutions, économie, parti, prisonnier, pouvoir, réfugié* political; *carrière* political, in politics. **homme ~** politician; **compte rendu de la semaine ~** report on the week in politics; *voir* **science.**

b (*littér: habile*) *personne* diplomatic; *acte, invitation* diplomatic, politic.

2 **nf** a (*science, carrière*) politics (*sg*). **parler ~** to talk politics; **faire de la ~** (*militantisme*) to be a political activist; (*métier*) to be in politics.

b (*Pol, fig: ligne de conduite*) policy; (*manière de gouverner*) policies. **la ~ extérieure/intérieure du gouvernement** the government's foreign/domestic policy; **l'opposition se plaint de la ~ du gouvernement** the opposition is complaining about the government's policies; **avoir une ~ de gauche/droite** to follow left-/right-wing policies; ~ **des prix et des revenus** prices and incomes policy; ~ **agricole commune** Common Agricultural Policy; (*fig*) **il est de bonne ~ de faire** it is good policy to do; **la ~ du moindre effort** the principle of least effort; **la ~ du pire** the policy of adopting the worst possible line in order to attain one's own ends; **faire *ou* pratiquer la ~ de la chaise vide** to make a show of non-attendance; **pratiquer la ~ de l'autruche** to bury one's head in the sand; **c'est la ~ de l'autruche** it's like burying one's head in the sand; **~-fiction** political fantasy.

3 **nm** (*politicien*) politician; (*aspects politiques*) politics, the political side of things.

politiquement [pɔlitikmɑ̃] **adv** (*lit*) politically; (*fig littér*) diplomatically.

politiquer*† [pɔlitike] [1] **vi** to talk (about) politics.

politisation [pɔlitizasjɔ̃] **nf** politicization.

politiser [pɔlitize] [1] 1 **vt** *débat* to politicize, bring politics into; *événement* to make a political issue of; *personne, mouvement, action* to politicize. *personne* **très politisé** highly politicized, politically aware. 2 **se politiser** **vpr** *[action, mouvement, débat]* to become politicized; *[personne]* to become politicized *ou* politically aware.

politologie [pɔlitɔlɔʒi] **nf** political science.

politologue [pɔlitɔlɔg] **nmf** political pundit *ou* analyst *ou* expert.

polka [pɔlka] **nf** polka.

pollen [pɔlɛn] **nm** pollen.

polluant, e [pɔlɥɑ̃, ɑ̃t] **adj** polluting. **produit ~** pollutant, polluting agent.

polluer [pɔlɥe] [1] **vt** to pollute.

pollueur, -euse [pɔlɥœʀ, øz] 1 **adj** polluting. 2 **nm, f** (*substance*) pollutant, polluting agent; (*industrie, personne*) polluter.

pollution [pɔlysjɔ̃] **nf** pollution. ~ **atmosphérique/acoustique** atmospheric/noise pollution; ~ **de l'air/des eaux/de l'environnement** air/water/environmental pollution; (*Méd*) **~s nocturnes** wet dreams.

polo [pɔlo] **nm** a (*Sport*) polo. b (*chemise*) sports shirt.

polochon* [pɔlɔʃɔ̃] **nm** bolster. **sac ~** duffel bag.

Pologne [pɔlɔɲ] **nf** Poland.

polonais, e [pɔlɔnɛ, ɛz] 1 **adj** Polish. 2 **nm** a **P~** Pole; *voir* **soûl.** b (*Ling*) Polish. 3 **polonaise** **nf** a **P~e** Pole. b (*Mus, danse*) polonaise. c (*gâteau*) polonaise, *meringue-covered sponge cake containing preserved fruit.*

polonium [pɔlɔnjɔm] **nm** polonium.

poltron, -onne [pɔltʀɔ̃, ɔn] 1 **adj** cowardly, craven (*littér*). 2 **nm, f** coward.

poltronnerie [pɔltʀɔnʀi] **nf** cowardice.

poly... [pɔli] **préf** poly... .

polyacide [pɔliasid] **adj, nm** polyacid.

polyamide [pɔliamid] nm polyamide.
polyandre [pɔljɑ̃dʀ] adj *femme, plante* polyandrous.
polyandrie [pɔliɑ̃dʀi] nf polyandry.
polyarchie [pɔljaʀʃi] nf polyarchy.
polyarthrite [pɔliaʀtʀit] nf polyarthritis.
polycarburant [pɔlikaʀbyʀɑ̃] adj m *moteur* multifuel (*épith*).
polychrome [pɔlikʀom] adj polychrome, polychromatic.
polyclinique [pɔliklinik] nf private general hospital.
polycopie [pɔlikɔpi] nf duplication, stencilling. **tiré à la ~** duplicated, stencilled.
polycopié [pɔlikɔpje] nm (*Univ*) (*payant*) duplicated lecture notes (*sold to students*); (*gratuit*) handout.
polycopier [pɔlikɔpje] 7 vt to duplicate, stencil. **cours polycopiés** duplicated lecture notes (*sold to students*); **machine à ~** duplicator.
polyculture [pɔlikyltyʀ] nf mixed farming.
polyèdre [pɔljɛdʀ] 1 adj *angle, solide* polyhedral. 2 nm polyhedron.
polyédrique [pɔljedʀik] adj polyhedral.
polyester [pɔliɛstɛʀ] nm polyester.
polyéthylène [pɔlietilɛn] nm polyethylene.
polygame [pɔligam] 1 adj polygamous. 2 nm polygamist.
polygamie [pɔligami] nf polygamy.
polyglotte [pɔliglɔt] adj, nmf polyglot.
polygonal, e, mpl **-aux** [pɔligɔnal, o] adj polygonal, many-sided.
polygone [pɔligɔn] nm (*Math*) polygon; (*fig: zone*) area, zone. (*Mil*) **~ de tir** rifle range.
polygraphe [pɔligʀaf] nmf polygraph.
poly-insaturé, e [poliɛ̃satyʀe] adj polyunsaturated.
polymère [pɔlimɛʀ] 1 adj polymeric. 2 nm polymer.
polymérisation [pɔlimeʀizasjɔ̃] nf polymerization.
polymériser vt, **se polymériser** vpr [pɔlimeʀize] 1 to polymerize.
polymorphe [pɔlimɔʀf] adj polymorphous, polymorphic.
polymorphie [pɔlimɔʀfi] nf, **polymorphisme** [pɔlimɔʀfism] nm polymorphism
Polynésie [pɔlinezi] nf Polynesia.
polynésien, -ienne [pɔlinezjɛ̃, jɛn] 1 adj Polynesian. 2 nm (*Ling*) Polynesian. 3 nm, f: **P~(-ienne)** Polynesian.
polynévrite [pɔlinevʀit] nf polyneuritis.
Polynice [pɔlinis] nm Polynices.
polynôme [pɔlinom] nm polynomial (*Math*).
polynucléaire [pɔlinykleɛʀ] 1 adj polynuclear, multinuclear. 2 nm polymorphonuclear leucocyte.
polype [pɔlip] n (*Zool*) polyp; (*Méd*) polyp, polypus.
polyphasé, e [pɔlifɑze] adj polyphase.
Polyphème [pɔlifɛm] nm Polyphemus.
polyphonie [pɔlifɔni] nf polyphony (*Mus*).
polyphonique [pɔlifɔnik] adj polyphonic (*Mus*).
polypier [pɔlipje] nm polypary.
polypore [pɔlipɔʀ] nm polyporus.
polysémie [pɔlisemi] nf polysemy.
polysémique [pɔlisemik] adj polysemous, polysemic.
polystyrène [pɔlistiʀɛn] nm polystyrene. **~ expansé** expanded polystyrene.
polysyllabe [pɔlisi(l)lab] 1 adj polysyllabic. 2 nm polysyllable.
polysyllabique [pɔlisi(l)labik] adj polysyllabic. **mot ~** polysyllable.
polytechnicien, -ienne [pɔlitɛknisjɛ̃, jɛn] nm,f polytechnicien, *student or ex-student at the École polytechnique*.
polytechnique [pɔlitɛknik] adj (†) polytechnic. **(l'École) ~** ou **Polytechnique** École polytechnique.
polythéisme [pɔliteism] nm polytheism.
polythéiste [pɔliteist] 1 adj polytheistic. 2 nmf polytheist.
polyvalence [pɔlivalɑ̃s] nf (*Chim, Méd*) polyvalency; *[personne, mot]* versatility.
polyvalent, e [pɔlivalɑ̃, ɑ̃t] 1 adj (*Chim*) *corps* polyvalent; (*Méd*) *sérum, vaccin* polyvalent; (*fig*) *rôle, traitement* varied; *attributions, usages* various, many; *salle* multi-purpose; *personne, mot* versatile. **enseignement ~** comprehensive education. 2 nm tax inspector (*sent to examine company's books*).
polyvinylique [pɔlivinilik] adj polyvinyl (*épith*).
pomélo [pɔmelo] nm grapefruit, pomelo (*US*).
Poméranie [pɔmeʀani] nf Pomerania; *voir* **loulou**[1].
pommade [pɔmad] nf *[peau]* ointment; *[cheveux]* cream, pomade. (*fig*) **passer de la ~ à qn*** to butter sb up*, soft-soap sb*.
pommader [pɔmade] 1 vt *cheveux* to pomade.
pomme [pɔm] 1 nf a (*fruit*) apple; (*pomme de terre*) potato. (*fig*) **grand** ou **haut comme trois ~s*** knee-high to a grasshopper*; (*fig*) **tomber dans les ~s*** to faint, pass out; (*fig*) **elle est restée longtemps dans les ~s*** she was out for some time.
b *[chou, laitue]* heart; *[canne, lit]* knob; *[arrosoir, douche]* rose; *[mât]* truck.
c (*) (*tête*) head, nut*; (*visage*) face, mug‡. **c'est pour ma ~** (*gén*) it's for me ou for yours truly*; (*qch de désagréable*) it's for muggins here‡ (*Brit*) ou for yours truly*; **je m'occupe d'abord de ma ~** I'm looking after number one*; **c'est pour ta ~** (*gén*) it's for you; (*iro*) it's for your lordship* (ou ladyship*) (*Brit*) ou for you.
d (*: *naïf, indulgent*) mug* (*Brit*), sucker*. **et moi, bonne ~, j'ai dit oui** and like a mug* (*Brit*) ou sucker* I said yes.
2 comp ►**pomme d'Adam** Adam's apple ►**pommes allumettes** matchstick potatoes ►**pomme d'api** *type of small apple* ►**pomme cannelle** sweetsop (*Brit*), custard apple ►**(pommes) chips** (potato) crisps (*Brit*) ou chips (*US*) ►**pomme à cidre** cider apple ►**pomme à couteau** eating apple ►**pomme à cuire** cooking apple, cooker* ►**pommes dauphine** Pommes Dauphine, ≃ potato croquettes (*without breadcrumbs*) ►**pomme de discorde** (*fig*) bone of contention ►**pommes frites** (*gén*) chips (*Brit*), French fries; (*au restaurant*) French fried potatoes; **bifteck (aux) pommes frites** steak and chips (*Brit*) ou French fries ►**pomme golden** golden delicious (apple) ►**pommes mousseline** mashed potatoes ►**pommes noisettes** ≃ mini potato croquettes (*without breadcrumbs*) ►**pommes paille** straw potatoes, ≃ shoestring potatoes (*US*) ►**pomme de pin** pine ou fir cone ►**pomme (de) reinette** Cox's orange pippin (*Brit*) ►**pomme sauvage** crab apple ►**pomme de terre** potato ►**pommes vapeur** boiled potatoes.
pommé, e [pɔme] (ptp de **pommer**) adj *chou* firm and round; *laitue* with a good heart.
pommeau, pl **~x** [pɔmo] nm *[épée, selle]* pommel; *[canne]* knob.
pommelé, e [pɔm(ə)le] (ptp de **pommeler**) adj *cheval* dappled; *ciel* full of fluffy ou fleecy clouds, mackerel (*épith*). **gris ~** dapple-grey.
pommeler (se) [pɔm(ə)le] 4 vpr *[ciel]* to become full of fluffy ou fleecy clouds; *[chou, laitue]* to form a head ou heart.
pommelle [pɔmɛl] nf filter (*over a pipe*).
pommer [pɔme] 1 vi (*Bot*) to form a head ou heart.
pommeraie [pɔm(ə)ʀɛ] nf apple orchard.
pommette [pɔmɛt] nf cheekbone. **le rouge lui monta aux ~s** a flush came to his cheeks; **~s saillantes** high cheekbones.
pommier [pɔmje] nm apple tree. **~ sauvage** crab-apple tree.
Pomone [pɔmɔn] nf Pomona.
pompage [pɔ̃paʒ] nm pumping.
pompe[1] [pɔ̃p] 1 nf a (*machine*) pump. **~ à air/à vide/de bicyclette** air/vacuum/bicycle pump; *voir* **bateau, château**.
b (* *fig: chaussure*) shoe. **être à l'aise** ou **bien dans ses ~s** to have got it together*; **il est toujours bien dans ses ~s** he's a very together kind of guy*; **être mal dans ses ~s** to be mixed-up*; *voir* **côté**.
c (**loc*) **à toute ~** at top speed, flat out*; (*Mil*) **(soldat de) deuxième ~** private; (*Sport*) **faire des ~s** to do press-ups (*Brit*) ou push-ups (*US*); **c'est juste un petit coup de ~*** I'm (ou we're) just feeling a bit drained; **j'ai eu un** ou **le coup de ~*** I felt drained, I was shattered*.
2 comp ►**pompe aspirante** suction ou lift pump; **pompe aspirante et foulante** suction and force pump ►**pompe à chaleur** heat pump ►**pompe à essence** (*distributeur*) petrol (*Brit*) ou gasoline (*US*) pump; (*station*) petrol station (*Brit*), gas station (*US*) ►**pompe foulante** force pump ►**pompe à incendie** fire engine (*apparatus*).
pompe[2] [pɔ̃p] nf a (*littér: solennité*) pomp. **en grande ~** with great pomp. b (*Rel: vanités*) **~s** pomps and vanities; **renoncer au monde et à ses ~s** to renounce the world and all its pomps and vanities. c **~s funèbres** funeral director's (*Brit*), undertaker's, mortician's (*US*); **entreprise de ~s funèbres** funeral director's (*Brit*), funeral parlor (*US*) ou home (*US*); **employé des ~s funèbres** undertaker's (*Brit*) ou mortician's (*US*) assistant.
pompé, e‡ [pɔ̃pe] (ptp de **pomper**) adj (*fatigué*) whacked‡ (*Brit*), pooped‡ (*US*), dead-beat‡, all-in*.
Pompée [pɔ̃pe] nm Pompey.
Pompéi [pɔ̃pei] n Pompeii.
pompéien, -ienne [pɔ̃pejɛ̃, jɛn] 1 adj Pompeiian. 2 nm, f: **P~(ne)** Pompeiian.
pomper [pɔ̃pe] 1 vt a *air, liquide* to pump; *[moustique]* to suck (up); (*évacuer*) to pump out; (*faire monter*) to pump up. **~ de l'eau** to get water from the pump, pump water out; **tu me pompes (l'air)‡** you're getting on my nerves, I'm getting fed up with you‡. b *[éponge, buvard]* to soak up. c (*arg Scol: copier*) to crib* (*sur* from). d (‡: *boire*) to swill down‡, knock back‡. **qu'est-ce qu'il pompe!** he can't half (*Brit*) ou he sure can (*US*) knock it back!‡ e (‡: *épuiser*) to wear out, tire out. **tout ce travail m'a pompé** I'm worn out* ou whacked‡ (*Brit*) ou pooped‡ (*US*) after (doing) all that work.
pompette* [pɔ̃pɛt] adj tipsy*.
pompeusement [pɔ̃pøzmɑ̃] adv pompously, pretentiously.
pompeux, -euse [pɔ̃pø, øz] adj (*ampoulé*) pompous, pretentious; (*imposant*) solemn.
pompier, -ière [pɔ̃pje, jɛʀ] 1 adj (*) *style, écrivain* pompous, pretentious; *morceau de musique* slushy*; *art* kitsch. 2 nm a fireman (*Brit*), firefighter. **appeler les ~s** to call the fire brigade (*Brit*) ou department (*US*); *voir* **fumer**. b (**) blow job**.
pompiste [pɔ̃pist] nmf petrol (*Brit*) ou gasoline (*US*) pump attendant.
pompon [pɔ̃pɔ̃] nm *[chapeau, coussin]* pompom; *[frange, instrument]* bobble. **avoir son ~†*** to be tipsy*; (*fig iro*) **avoir** ou **tenir le ~** to take the biscuit* (*Brit*) ou cake*, be the limit*; **c'est le ~!** it's the last straw!, that beats everything!*, that's the limit!*; *voir* **rose**.
pomponner [pɔ̃pɔne] 1 1 vt to titivate, doll up*; *bébé* to dress up.

bien pomponné all dolled up* *ou* dressed up. 2 **se pomponner** vpr to titivate (o.s.), doll o.s. up*, get dolled up* *ou* dressed up.

ponant [pɔnɑ̃] nm (*littér*) west.

ponçage [pɔ̃saʒ] nm (*voir* **poncer**) sanding (down); rubbing down; sandpapering; pumicing.

ponce [pɔ̃s] nf a **(pierre)** ~ pumice (stone). b (*Art*) pounce box.

Ponce Pilate [pɔ̃spilat] nm Pontius Pilate.

poncer [pɔ̃se] 3 vt a (*décaper*) (*avec du papier de verre*) to sand (down), rub down, sandpaper; (*avec une ponceuse*) to sand (down), rub down; (*avec une pierre ponce*) to pumice. **il faut ~ d'abord** it needs sanding down first. b (*Art*) *dessin* to pounce.

ponceuse [pɔ̃søz] nf sander.

poncho [pɔ̃(t)ʃo] nm (*cape*) poncho; (*chaussette*) slipper sock, Afghan slipper.

poncif [pɔ̃sif] nm (*cliché*) commonplace, cliché; (*Art*) stencil (*for pouncing*).

ponction [pɔ̃ksjɔ̃] nf (*lombaire*) puncture; (*pulmonaire*) tapping; *[argent]* draining. **par de fréquentes ~s il a épuisé son capital** he has dipped into *ou* drawn on his capital so often he has used it all up; **faire une sérieuse ~ dans ses économies** *[impôt]* to make a large hole in *ou* make serious inroads into one's savings; (*pour vacances etc*) to draw heavily on one's savings; (*hum*) **faire une ~ dans les bonbons** to raid the sweets; (*hum*) **faire une ~ dans une bouteille** to help o.s. to plenty out of a bottle.

ponctionner [pɔ̃ksjɔne] 1 vt *région lombaire* to puncture; *poumon* to tap; *réserves* to tap; *contribuable, entreprise* to bleed.

ponctualité [pɔ̃ktɥalite] nf (*exactitude*) punctuality; (*assiduité*) punctiliousness (*frm*), meticulousness.

ponctuation [pɔ̃ktɥasjɔ̃] nf punctuation.

ponctuel, -elle [pɔ̃ktɥɛl] adj a (*à l'heure*) punctual; (*scrupuleux*) punctilious (*frm*), meticulous. b (*Phys*) punctual; (*fig: isolé*) limited; *intervention* selective; *contrôles* selective; (*aspect d'un verbe*) punctual. **ces terroristes se livrent à des actions ~elles** these terrorists strike selectively.

ponctuellement [pɔ̃ktɥɛlmɑ̃] adv (*voir* **ponctuel**) punctually; punctiliously (*frm*), meticulously; selectively.

ponctuer [pɔ̃ktɥe] 1 vt (*lit, fig*) to punctuate (*de* with); (*Mus*) to phrase.

pondéral, e, mpl **-aux** [pɔ̃deʀal, o] adj weight (*épith*). **surcharge ~e** excess weight.

pondérateur, -trice [pɔ̃deʀatœʀ, tʀis] adj *influence* stabilizing, steadying.

pondération [pɔ̃deʀasjɔ̃] nf a *[personne]* level-headedness. b (*équilibrage*) balancing; (*Écon*) weighting. ~ **des pouvoirs** balance of powers.

pondéré, e [pɔ̃deʀe] (ptp de **pondérer**) adj a *personne, attitude* level-headed. b (*Écon*) **indice ~** weighed index.

pondérer [pɔ̃deʀe] 6 vt (*équilibrer*) to balance; (*compenser*) to counterbalance (*par* by); (*Écon*) *indice* to weight.

pondéreux, -euse [pɔ̃deʀø, øz] 1 adj *marchandises, produits* heavy. 2 nmpl: **les ~** heavy goods.

pondeur [pɔ̃dœʀ] nm (*péj*) ~ **de romans** writer who churns out books.

pondeuse [pɔdøz] nf: **(poule)** ~ good layer; ~ **(d'enfants)*** prolific child-bearer (*hum*).

pondre [pɔ̃dʀ] 41 1 vt *œuf* to lay; (*) *enfant* to produce; *devoir, texte* to produce, turn out*. **œuf frais pondu** new-laid egg. 2 vi *[poule]* to lay; *[poisson, insecte]* to lay its eggs.

poney [pɔnɛ] nm pony.

pongé(e) [pɔ̃ʒe] nm (*Tex*) pongee.

pongiste [pɔ̃ʒist] nmf table tennis player.

pont [pɔ̃] 1 nm a (*Constr*) bridge; (*acrobatie*) bridge; (*fig: lien*) bridge, link. **passer un ~** to go over *ou* cross a bridge; **vivre** *ou* **coucher sous les ~s** to be a tramp; *[acrobate]* **faire le ~** to do a bridge; **se porter comme le P~-Neuf*** to be hale and hearty; **faire un ~ d'or à qn (pour l'employer)** to offer sb a fortune to take on a job; *voir* **couper, eau, jeter.**
b (*Naut*) deck. ~ **avant/arrière/supérieur** fore/rear/upper *ou* top deck; **navire à 2/3 ~s** 2/3 decker.
c (*Aut*) axle. ~ **avant/arrière** front/rear axle.
d (*vacances*) extra day(s) off (*taken between two public holidays or a public holiday and a weekend*). **on a un ~ de 3 jours pour Noël** we have 3 extra days (off) for *ou* at Christmas; **faire le ~** to take the extra day (off), make a long weekend of it.
e (*Antiq*) **(royaume du) P~** Pontus.
f (*Ftbl*) **petit ~** nutmeg; **faire un petit ~ à qn** to nutmeg sb.
2 comp ►**pont aérien** airlift ►**pont aux ânes** pons asinorum; (*fig*) **c'est le ~ aux ânes** any fool knows that ►**pont basculant** bascule bridge ►**pont de bateaux** floating bridge, pontoon bridge ►**pont-canal** nm (pl **ponts-canaux**) canal bridge ►**les Ponts et Chaussées** (*service*) the highways department, department of civil engineering; (*école*) school of civil engineering; **ingénieur des ponts et chaussées** civil engineer ►**pont élévateur** (*Aut*) hydraulic ramp ►**pont d'envol** (*Naut*) flight deck ►**le Pont-Euxin** (*Antiq*) the Euxine Sea ►**pont-l'évêque** pont-l'évêque cheese ►**pont de glace** (*Can*) ice bridge *ou* road ►**pont de graissage** (*Aut*) ramp (*in a garage*) ►**pont-levis** nm (pl **ponts-levis**) drawbridge ►**pont mobile** movable bridge ►**pont à péage** tollbridge ►**pont promenade** (*Naut*) promenade deck ►**pont roulant** (*Rail*) travelling crane ►**pont suspendu** suspension bridge ►**pont tournant** swing bridge ►**pont transbordeur** transporter bridge.

pontage [pɔ̃taʒ] nm (*Naut*) decking. (*Méd*) ~ **(cardiaque)** (heart) bypass operation.

ponte¹ [pɔ̃t] nf (*action*) laying (of eggs); (*œufs*) eggs, clutch; (*saison*) (egg-)laying season. ~ **ovulaire** ovulation.

ponte² [pɔ̃t] nm a (*: *pontife*) big shot*, big noise* (*de* in). b (*Jeux*) punter.

ponter¹ [pɔ̃te] 1 vt (*Naut*) to deck, lay the deck of.

ponter² [pɔ̃te] 1 (*Jeux*) 1 vi to punt. 2 vt to bet.

pontife [pɔ̃tif] nm a (*Rel*) pontiff; *voir* **souverain.** b (* *fig*) big shot*, pundit*.

pontifiant, e* [pɔ̃tifjɑ̃, jɑ̃t] adj *personne, ton* pontificating.

pontifical, e, mpl **-aux** [pɔ̃tifikal, o] adj (*Antiq*) pontifical; (*Rel*) *messe* pontifical; *siège, gardes, états* papal.

pontificat [pɔ̃tifika] nm pontificate.

pontifier* [pɔ̃tifje] 7 vi to pontificate.

ponton [pɔ̃tɔ̃] nm (*plate-forme*) pontoon, (floating) landing stage; (*chaland*) lighter; (*navire*) hulk.

pontonnier [pɔ̃tɔnje] nm (*Mil*) pontoneer, pontonier.

pool [pul] nm *[producteurs, dactylos]* pool. ~ **bancaire** banking pool.

pop [pɔp] 1 adj inv *musique, art* pop. 2 nm (*musique*) pop (music); (*art*) pop art.

pop-corn [pɔpkɔʀn] nm inv popcorn.

pope [pɔp] nm (Orthodox) priest.

popeline [pɔplin] nf poplin.

popote [pɔpɔt] 1 nf a (*: *cuisine*) cooking. **faire la ~** to cook. b (*Mil*) mess, canteen. 2 adj inv (*) stay-at-home (*épith*), home-loving. **il est très ~** he likes his home comforts.

popotin* [pɔpɔtɛ̃] nm bottom*; *voir* **magner.**

populace [pɔpylas] nf (*péj*) rabble, mob.

populaire [pɔpylɛʀ] adj a (*du peuple*) *gouvernement, front, croyance, tradition* popular; *démocratie* popular, people's; *république* people's; *mouvement, manifestation* mass, of the people. **la République populaire de ...** the People's Republic of ... . b (*pour la masse*) *roman, art, chanson* popular; *édition* cheap; *voir* **bal, soupe.** c (*plébéien*) *goût* common; (*ouvrier*) *milieu, quartier, origines* working-class. **les classes ~s** the working classes. d (*qui plaît*) popular, well-liked. **très ~ auprès des jeunes** very popular with young people, greatly liked by young people. e (*Ling*) *mot, expression* vernacular; *étymologie* popular; *latin* popular.

populairement [pɔpylɛʀmɑ̃] adv (*gén*) popularly; *parler* in the vernacular.

populariser [pɔpylaʀize] 1 vt to popularize.

popularité [pɔpylaʀite] nf popularity.

population [pɔpylasjɔ̃] nf (*gén, Bot, Zool*) population. **région à ~ dense/faible** densely/sparsely populated region *ou* area; ~ **active/agricole** working/farming population; **la ~ du globe** the world's population, world population; **la ~ scolaire** the school population.

populeux, -euse [pɔpylø, øz] adj *pays, ville* densely populated, populous; *rue* crowded.

populisme [pɔpylism] nm (*Littérat*) populisme, *a literary movement of the 1920s and 1930s which sets out to describe the lives of ordinary people.*

populiste [pɔpylist] adj, nmf (*voir* **populisme**) populiste.

populo‡ [pɔpylo] nm (*péj: peuple*) ordinary people *ou* folks*; (*foule*) crowd (of people).

porc [pɔʀ] nm (*animal*) pig, hog (*US*); (*viande*) pork; (*péj: personne*) pig; (*peau*) pigskin.

porcelaine [pɔʀsəlɛn] nf a (*matière*) porcelain, china; (*objet*) piece of porcelain. ~ **tendre** bone china; ~ **vitreuse** vitreous china; ~ **de Saxe/de Sèvres** Dresden/Sèvres china; ~ **de Limoges** Limoges porcelain *ou* china(ware); **de** *ou* **en ~** china, porcelain. b (*Zool*) cowrie.

porcelainier, -ière [pɔʀsəlenje, jɛʀ] 1 adj china (*épith*), porcelain (*épith*). 2 nm (*fabricant*) porcelain *ou* china manufacturer.

porcelet [pɔʀsəlɛ] nm piglet.

porc-épic, pl **porcs-épics** [pɔʀkepik] nm porcupine; (*fig: personne irritable*) prickly customer* *ou* person. (*homme mal rasé*) **tu es un vrai ~** you're all bristly.

porche [pɔʀʃ] nm porch. **sous le ~ de l'immeuble** in the porch *ou* porchway of the flats.

porcher, -ère [pɔʀʃe, ɛʀ] nm,f pig-keeper, swineherd†.

porcherie [pɔʀʃəʀi] nf (*lit, fig*) pigsty (*Brit*), pigpen (*US*).

porcin, e [pɔʀsɛ̃, in] 1 adj (*lit*) porcine; (*fig*) piglike. 2 nm pig. **les ~s** swine, pigs.

pore [pɔʀ] nm pore. **il sue l'arrogance par tous les ~s** he exudes arrogance from every pore.

poreux, -euse [pɔʀø, øz] adj porous.

porno* [pɔʀno] (abrév de **pornographique**) 1 adj pornographic. **film/revue/cinema ~** porn(o) film/magazine/cinema*. 2 nm porn*.

pornographe [pɔʀnɔgʀaf] 1 nmf pornographer. 2 adj of pornography (*attrib*), pornographic.

pornographie [pɔʀnɔgʀafi] nf pornography.
pornographique [pɔʀnɔgʀafik] adj pornographic.
porosité [pɔʀozite] nf porosity.
porphyre [pɔʀfiʀ] nm porphyry.
porphyrique [pɔʀfiʀik] adj porphyritic.
port¹ [pɔʀ] 1 nm a (*bassin*) harbour, port; (*Comm*) port; (*ville*) port; (*fig, littér: abri*) port, haven. **sortir du ~** to leave port *ou* harbour; **arriver au ~** (*Naut*) to dock; (*fig*) to reach the finishing straight (*Brit*), reach the last stretch; **arriver à bon ~** to arrive intact, arrive safe and sound; **~ de commerce/de pêche/de guerre** commercial port/fishing port/naval base; (*fig*) **un ~ dans la tempête** a port in a storm. b *[Pyrénées]* pass. c (*Ordin*) port. 2 comp ▸**port artificiel** artificial harbour ▸**port d'attache** (*Naut*) port of registry; (*fig*) home base ▸**port fluvial** river port ▸**port franc** free port ▸**port maritime** seaport; *voir* **plaisance**.
port² [pɔʀ] nm a (*fait de porter*) *[objet]* carrying; *[habit, barbe, décoration]* wearing. **le ~ du casque est obligatoire** safety helmets *ou* crash helmets (*Aut*) must be worn; **~ d'armes prohibées** illegal carrying of firearms; (*Mil*) **se mettre au ~ d'armes** to shoulder arms. b (*prix*) (*poste*) postage; (*transport*) carriage. **franco** *ou* **franc de ~** carriage paid; **(en) ~ dû/payé** postage due/paid. c (*comportement*) bearing, carriage. **elle a un ~ majestueux** *ou* **de reine** she has a noble *ou* majestic *ou* queenly bearing; **elle a un joli ~ de tête** she holds her head very nicely. d (*Mus*) **~ de voix** portamento.
portable [pɔʀtabl] 1 adj *vêtement* wearable; (*portatif*) portable; *logiciel* portable. 2 nm (*Ordin*) (*gén*) portable; (*qui tient sur les genoux*) laptop.
portage [pɔʀtaʒ] nm a *[marchandise]* porterage; (*Naut, Can*) portage. b (*Ordin*) port. **travailler au ~ du logiciel** to work on porting the software, work on a port of the software (*sous* to).
portager [pɔʀtaʒe] 3 vi (*Can*) to portage.
portail [pɔʀtaj] nm portal.
portance [pɔʀtɑ̃s] nf (*Aviat*) lift.
portant, e [pɔʀtɑ̃, ɑ̃t] 1 adj a *mur* structural, supporting; *roue* running. (*Aviat*) **surface ~e** aerofoil (*Brit*), airfoil (*US*). b **être bien/mal ~** to be healthy *ou* in good health/in poor health; *voir* **bout**. 2 nm (*anse*) handle; (*Théât*) upright.
portatif, -ive [pɔʀtatif, iv] adj portable.
Port-au-Prince [pɔʀopʀɛ̃s] n Port-au-Prince.
porte [pɔʀt] 1 nf a *[maison, voiture, meuble]* door; *[forteresse, jardin, stade, ville]* gate; (*seuil*) doorstep; (*embrasure*) doorway. **~ pliante/coulissante** folding/sliding door; **franchir** *ou* **passer la ~** to go through *ou* come through the door(way); **sonner à la ~** to ring the (door)bell; **c'est à ma ~** it's close by, it's on the doorstep; **le bus me descend** *ou* **met à ma ~** the bus stops at my (front) door *ou* takes me to my door; **j'ai trouvé ce colis à ma ~** I found this parcel on my doorstep; **ils se réfugièrent sous la ~** they took shelter in the doorway; **une (voiture) 3/5 ~s** a 3-door/5-door (car); **il y a 100 km/j'ai mis 2 heures de ~ à ~** it's 100 km/it took me 2 hours from door to door; **de ~ en ~** from house to house; **faire du ~ à ~** (*vendre*) to sell from door to door, be a door-to-door salesman, do doorstep selling (*Brit*); (*chercher du travail*) to go from firm to firm, go round all the firms; **l'ennemi est à nos ~s** the enemy is at our gate(s); **Dijon, ~ de la Bourgogne** Dijon, the gateway to Burgundy; *voir* **casser, clef** *etc*.
b *[aéroport]* gate.
c *[écluse]* (lock) gate; (*Ski*) gate.
d (*loc*) **c'est/ce n'est pas la ~ à côté*** it's practically/it's not exactly on our (*ou* my *etc*) doorstep; **la ~!*** (shut the) door!; **(à) la ~!** (get) out!; **être à la ~** to be locked out; **mettre** *ou* **flanquer* qn à la ~** (*licencier*) to sack sb* (*Brit*), fire sb*, give sb the sack* (*Brit*); (*Scol*) to expel sb; (*Univ*) to send sb down (*Brit*), flunk sb out* (*US*); (*éjecter*) to throw *ou* boot* (*Brit*) sb out; **être mis à la ~** to get the chop‡; **claquer/fermer la ~ au nez de qn** to slam/shut the door in sb's face; (*fig*) **entrer** *ou* **passer par la petite ~/la grande ~** to start at the bottom/at the top; **fermer** *ou* **refuser sa ~ à qn** to close the door to sb, bar sb from one's house; (*fig*) **fermer la ~ à qch** to close the door on sth; **j'ai trouvé ~ close** *ou* (*Belgique*) **de bois** (*maison*) no one answered the door; (*magasin, bâtiment public*) it was closed; **frapper** *ou* **sonner à la bonne ~** to strike lucky, hit on *ou* get hold of the right person; **frapper** *ou* **sonner à la mauvaise ~** to be out of luck, get hold of the wrong person; **c'est la ~ ouverte** *ou* **c'est ouvrir la ~ à tous les abus** it means leaving the door wide open *ou* the way open to all sorts of abuses, if that happens it'll mean anything goes*; **toutes les ~s lui sont ouvertes** every door is open to him; **laisser la ~ ouverte à un compromis** to leave the door open for a compromise; **journée ~(s) ouverte(s)** open day (*Brit*), open house (*US*); **aux ~s de la mort** at death's door; **parler à qn entre deux ~s** to have a quick word with sb, speak to sb very briefly *ou* in passing; **recevoir qn entre deux ~s** to meet sb very briefly *ou* in passing; **prendre la ~** to go away, leave; **aimable** *ou* **souriant comme une ~ de prison** like a bear with a sore head.
2 adj: **veine ~** portal vein.
3 comp ▸**porte accordéon** concertina folding door ▸**portes du Ciel** gates of Heaven ▸**porte cochère** carriage entrance, porte-cochère ▸**porte à deux battants** double door *ou* gate ▸**porte d'embarquement** (*Aviat*) departure gate ▸**portes de l'Enfer** gates of Hell ▸**porte d'entrée** front door ▸**porte-fenêtre** nf (pl **portes-fenêtres**) French window ▸**les Portes de Fer** (*Géog*) the Iron Gate(s) ▸**porte palière** landing door, door opening onto the landing ▸**porte de secours** emergency exit *ou* door ▸**porte de service** tradesman's (*surtout Brit*) *ou* rear entrance ▸**porte de sortie** (*lit*) exit, way out; (*fig*) way out, let-out*.
porte- [pɔʀt] préf *voir* **porter**.
porté, e¹ [pɔʀte] (ptp de **porter**) adj: **être ~ à faire** to be apt *ou* inclined to do, tend to do; **nous sommes ~s à croire que ...** we are inclined to believe that ...; **être ~ à la colère/à l'exagération** to be prone to anger/exaggeration; **être ~ sur qch** to be keen on (*Brit*) *ou* fond of sth, be partial to sth; **être ~ sur la chose*** to be always at it* (*Brit*), have a one-track mind, be a randy one*.
portée² [pɔʀte] nf a (*distance*) range, reach; *[fusil, radar]* range; *[cri, voix]* carrying-distance, reach. **canon à faible/longue ~** short-/long-range gun; **missile de moyenne ~** intermediate-range weapon; **à ~ de la main** within (arm's) reach, at *ou* on hand; **restez à ~ de voix** stay within earshot; **restez à ~ de vue** don't go out of sight; (*fig*) **cet hôtel est/n'est pas à la ~ de toutes les bourses** this hotel is/is not within everyone's means *ou* reach, this hotel suits/does not suit everyone's purse; **ne laissez pas les médicaments à ~ de main** *ou* **à la ~ des enfants** keep medicines out of reach of children; **hors de ~** out of reach *ou* range; **hors de ~ de fusil/de voix** out of rifle range/earshot.
b (*capacité*) *[intelligence]* reach, scope, capacity; (*niveau*) level. **ce concept dépasse la ~ de l'intelligence ordinaire** this concept is beyond the reach *ou* scope *ou* capacity of the average mind; **être à la ~ de qn** to be understandable to sb, be at sb's level, be within sb's capability; **il faut savoir se mettre à la ~ des enfants** you have to be able to come down to a child's level.
c (*effet*) *[parole, écrit]* impact, import; *[acte]* significance, consequences. **il ne mesure pas la ~ de ses paroles/ses actes** he doesn't think about the import of what he's saying/the consequences of his actions; **la ~ de cet événement est incalculable** this event will have far-reaching consequences *ou* incalculable repercussions; **sans ~ pratique** of no practical consequence *ou* importance *ou* significance.
d (*Archit*) (*poussée*) loading; (*distance*) span.
e (*Mus*) stave, staff.
f (*Vét*) litter.
portefaix†† [pɔʀtəfɛ] nm inv porter.
portefeuille [pɔʀtəfœj] nm *[argent]* wallet, pocketbook (*US*), billfold (*US*); (*Assurances, Bourse, Pol*) portfolio. **avoir un ~ bien garni** to be well-off; *voir* **lit, ministre**.
portemanteau, pl **~x** [pɔʀt(ə)mɑ̃to] nm a (*cintre*) coat hanger; (*accroché au mur*) coat rack; (*sur pied*) hat stand. **accrocher une veste au ~** to hang up a jacket. b (*††: malle*) portmanteau.
porter [pɔʀte] 1 1 vt a *parapluie, paquet, valise* to carry; (*fig*) *responsabilité* to bear, carry; (*Comm*) *marché* to boost. **~ un enfant dans ses bras/sur son dos** to carry a child in one's arms/on one's back; **pouvez-vous me ~ ma valise?** can you carry my case for me?; **laisse-toi ~ par la vague pour bien nager** to swim well let yourself be carried by the waves; **ses jambes ne le portent plus** his legs can no longer carry him; **ce pont n'est pas fait pour ~ des camions** this bridge isn't meant to carry lorries *ou* meant for lorries *ou* can't take the weight of a lorry; (*Mil*) **portez ... arme!** present ... arms!; **la tige qui porte la fleur** the stem which bears the flower; **cette poutre porte tout le poids du plafond** this beam bears *ou* carries *ou* takes the whole weight of the ceiling; (*fig*) **~ sa croix** to carry *ou* bear one's cross; (*fig*) **~ le poids de ses fautes** to bear the weight of one's mistakes.
b (*amener*) to take. **~ qch à qn** to take sth to sb; **porte-lui ce livre** take this book to him, take him this book; **~ des lettres/un colis à qn** to deliver letters/a parcel to sb; **je vais ~ la lettre à la boîte** I'm going to take the letter to the postbox, I'm going to put this letter in the postbox; **~ les plats sur la table** to put the dishes on the table; **~ qn sur le lit** to put *ou* lay sb on the bed; **~ la main à son front** to put one's hand to one's brow; **~ la main à son chapeau** to lift one's hand to one's hat; **~ la main sur qn** to raise one's hand to sb; **~ qch à sa bouche** to lift *ou* put sth to one's lips; **~ de l'argent à la banque** to take some money to the bank; **se faire ~ à manger** to have food brought (to one); **~ l'affaire sur la place publique/devant les tribunaux** to take *ou* carry the matter into the public arena/before the courts; **~ la nouvelle à qn** to take *ou* carry the news to sb, let sb know *ou* have the news; (*Ciné, Théât*) **~ une œuvre à l'écran/à la scène** to transfer a work to the screen/to the stage; **cela porte bonheur** it brings good fortune, it's lucky; **~ chance/malheur (à qn)** to be lucky/unlucky (for sb), bring (sb) (good) luck/misfortune; **~ bonheur à qn** to be lucky for sb, bring sb luck; (*Prov*) **~ de l'eau à la rivière** to carry coals to Newcastle; (*littér*) **portant partout la terreur et la mort** carrying fear and death everywhere.
c *vêtement, bague, laine, lunettes* to wear; *armes héraldiques* to bear; *barbe* to have, wear; *nom* to have, bear. **~ les cheveux longs** to wear one's hair long, have long hair; **~ le nom d'une fleur** to be called after a flower, bear the name of a flower (*frm*); **~ le nom de Jérôme** to be called Jerome; **il porte bien son nom** his name suits him; **elle porte bien son âge** she's wearing well; **elle porte bien le pantalon** trousers

suit her; (*fig*) **c'est elle qui porte le pantalon** *ou* **la culotte** she is the one that wears the trousers (*Brit*) *ou* pants (*US*); **le chameau porte deux bosses** the camel has two humps; **les jupes se portent très courtes** very short skirts are in fashion *ou* are the fashion, skirts are being worn very short; **cela ne se porte plus** that's out of fashion, nobody wears that any more; **les T-shirts sont très portés en ce moment** T-shirts are very popular at the moment; (*fig*) **je ne veux pas ~ le chapeau*** I don't want to carry the can* *ou* take the rap* (*pour* for); **on lui a fait ~ le chapeau*** he carried the can* *ou* took the rap*.

d (*tenir*) to hold, keep. **~ la tête haute** (*lit*) to hold *ou* keep one's head up; (*fig*) to hold one's head high; **~ le corps en avant** to lean *ou* stoop forward.

e (*montrer*) *signe, trace* to show, bear; *blessure, cicatrice* to bear; *inscription, date* to bear. **il porte la bonté sur son visage** he has a very kind(-looking) face, his face is a picture of kindness; **ce livre porte un beau titre** this book has a fine title; **la lettre porte la date du 12 mai** the letter bears the date of *ou* is dated May 12th; (*Ling*) **~ la marque de** to be marked for.

f (*inscrire*) *nom* to write down, put down (*sur* on, in); (*Comm*) *somme* to enter (*sur* in). **~ de l'argent au crédit d'un compte** to credit an account with some money; **nous portons cette somme à votre débit** we are debiting this sum to your account; **se faire ~ absent** to go absent; **se faire ~ malade** to report *ou* go sick; **~ qn absent** (*Mil*) to report sb absent; (*Scol*) to mark sb absent; **porté disparu au nombre des morts** reported missing/dead; **porté manquant** unaccounted for.

g (*diriger*) *regard* to direct, turn (*sur, vers* towards); *choix* to direct (*sur* towards); *attention* to turn, give (*sur* to), focus (*sur* on); *effort* to direct (*sur* towards); *pas* to turn (*vers* towards); *coup* to deal (*à* to); *accusation* to make (*contre* against); *attaque* to make (*contre* on). **il fit ~ son attention sur ce détail** he turned *ou* focused his attention on this detail; **il fit ~ son choix sur ce livre** his choice fell on this book.

h (*ressentir*) *amour, haine* to have, feel, bear (*à* for); *reconnaissance* to feel (*à* to, towards). **~ de l'amitié à qn** to feel friendship towards sb.

i (*faire arriver*) to bring. **~ qn au pouvoir** to bring *ou* carry sb to power; **~ qch à sa perfection/à son paroxysme/à l'apogée** to bring sth to perfection/to a peak/to a climax; **~ la température à 800°/le salaire à 16 000 F/la vitesse à 30 nœuds** to bring the temperature up to 800°/the salary up to 16,000 francs/the speed up to 30 knots; **cela porte le nombre de blessés à 20** that brings the number of casualties (up) to 20.

j (*inciter*) **~ qn à faire qch** to prompt *ou* induce *ou* lead sb to do sth; **cela le portera à l'indulgence** that will prompt him to be indulgent, that will make him indulgent; **tout (nous) porte à croire que ...** everything leads us to believe that ...; *voir* **porté**.

k (*Méd*) *enfant* to carry; (*Vét*) *petits* to carry; (*Fin*) *intérêts* to yield; (*Bot*) *graines, fruit* to bear; *récolte, moisson* to yield. **cette ardeur/haine qu'il portait en lui** this ardour/hatred which he carried with him; **je ne le porte pas dans mon cœur** I am not exactly fond of him; **idée qui porte en soi les germes de sa propre destruction** idea which carries (within itself) *ou* bears the seeds of its own destruction; (*fig*) **~ ses fruits** to bear fruit.

l (*conduire*) to carry; (*entraîner*) *[foi]* to carry along; *[vent]* to carry away. **se laisser ~ par la foule** to (let o.s.) be carried away by the crowd.

m (*Ordin*) *logiciel* to port (*sous* to).

2 **vi** a *[bruit, voix, canon]* to carry. **le son/le coup a porté à 500 mètres** the sound/the shot carried 500 metres; **le fusil porte à 300 mètres** the rifle has a range of 300 metres.

b *[reproche, coup]* **~ (juste)** to hit *ou* strike home; **tous les coups portaient** every blow told; **un coup qui porte** a telling blow; **ses conseils ont porté** his advice had some effect *ou* was of some use.

c (*Méd*) *[femme]* to carry her child *ou* baby; (*Vét*) *[animal]* to carry its young.

d **~ sur** *[édifice, pilier]* to be supported by *ou* on; (*fig*) *[débat, cours]* to turn on, revolve around, be about; *[revendications, objection]* to concern; *[étude, effort, action]* to be concerned with, focus on; *[accent]* to fall on. **tout le poids du plafond porte sur cette poutre** the whole weight of the ceiling falls on *ou* is supported by this beam; **la question portait sur des auteurs au programme** the question was on some of the authors on the syllabus; **il a fait ~ son exposé sur la situation économique** in his talk he concentrated *ou* focused on the economic situation.

e (*frapper*) **sa tête a porté sur le bord du trottoir** his head struck the edge of the pavement; **c'est la tête qui a porté** his head took the blow.

f **~ à faux** *[mur]* to be out of plumb *ou* true; *[rocher]* to be precariously balanced; (*fig*) *[remarque]* to come *ou* go amiss, be out of place.

3 **se porter vpr** a *[personne]* **se ~ bien/mal** to be well/unwell; **comment vous portez-vous? — je me porte bien** how are you? — I'm fine *ou* I'm very well; **se ~ comme un charme** to be fighting fit, be as fit as a fiddle*; **buvez moins, vous ne vous en porterez que mieux** drink less and you'll feel better for it; **et je ne m'en suis pas plus mal porté** and I didn't come off any worse for it, and I was no worse off for it; *voir* **pont**.

b (*se présenter comme*) **se ~ candidat** to put o.s. up *ou* stand (*Brit*) *ou* run as a candidate; **se ~ acquéreur (de)** to put in a bid (for); *voir* **caution** *etc*.

c (*se diriger*) *[soupçon, choix]* **se ~ sur** to fall on; **son regard se porta sur moi** his eyes fell on me, his gaze focused on me; **son attention se porta sur ce point** he focused *ou* concentrated his attention on this point.

d (*aller*) to go. **se ~ à la rencontre** *ou* **au-devant de qn** to go to meet sb.

e (*se laisser aller*) **se ~ à** *voies de fait, violences* to commit; **se ~ à des extrémités** to go to extremes.

4 **comp ▸porte-aéronefs nm inv** aircraft carrier **▸porte-aiguilles nm inv** needle case **▸porte-avions nm inv** aircraft carrier **▸porte-bagages nm inv** (luggage) rack **▸porte-bébé nm (pl porte-bébés)** baby sling, baby carrier **▸porte-bonheur nm inv** lucky charm; **acheter du muguet porte-bonheur** to buy lily of the valley for good luck **▸porte-bouteilles nm inv** (*à anse*) bottle-carrier; (*à casiers*) wine rack; (*hérisson*) bottle-drainer **▸porte-carte(s) nm inv** *[cartes d'identité]* card wallet *ou* holder; *[cartes géographiques]* map wallet **▸porte-cigares nm inv** cigar case **▸porte-cigarettes nm inv** cigarette case **▸porte-clefs nm inv** (*anneau*) key ring; (*étui*) key case; (*††: geôlier*) turnkey†† **▸porte-conteneurs** (*Naut*) **nm inv** container ship **▸porte-couteau nm (pl porte-couteau(x))** knife rest **▸porte-crayon nm (pl porte-crayon(s))** pencil holder **▸porte-documents nm inv** briefcase, attaché case, document case **▸porte-drapeau** (*lit, fig*) **nm (pl porte-drapeau(x))** standard bearer **▸porte-étendard†† nm inv** standard bearer **▸porte-à-faux nm inv** *[mur]* slant; *[rocher]* precarious balance, overhang; (*Archit*) cantilever; **en porte-à-faux** slanting, out of plumb; precariously balanced, overhanging; cantilevered; (*fig*) *personne* in an awkward position (*fig*) **▸porte-fusibles nm inv** fuse box **▸porte-greffe nm (pl porte-greffe(s))** stock (*for graft*) **▸porte-hélicoptères nm inv** helicopter carrier **▸porte-jarretelles nm inv** suspender belt (*Brit*), garter belt (*US*) **▸porte-jupe nm (pl porte-jupe(s))** skirt hanger **▸porte-menu nm inv** menu holder **▸porte-mine nm (pl porte-mine(s))** propelling pencil **▸porte-monnaie nm inv** (*gén*) purse (*Brit*), coin purse (*US*); (*pour hommes*) wallet; **faire appel au porte-monnaie de qn** to ask sb to dip into his pocket; **avoir le porte-monnaie bien garni** to be well-off **▸porte-musique nm inv** music case **▸porte-outil nm (pl porte-outil(s))** chuck (*Tech*) **▸porte-parapluies nm inv** umbrella stand **▸porte-parole nm inv** (*gén*) spokesperson; (*homme*) spokesman; (*femme*) spokeswoman; **se faire le porte-parole de qn** to act as spokesman for sb, speak on sb's behalf; **journal qui est le porte-parole d'un parti** newspaper which is the mouthpiece *ou* organ of a party **▸porte-plume nm inv** penholder **▸porte-revues nm inv** magazine rack **▸porte-savon nm (pl porte-savon(s))** soapdish **▸porte-serviettes nm inv** towel rail **▸porte-skis** (*Aut*) **nm inv** ski rack **▸porte-valise nm (pl porte-valise(s))** luggage stand **▸porte-vélos** (*Aut*) **nm inv** bicycle rack **▸porte-voix nm inv** megaphone; (*électrique*) loudhailer; **mettre ses mains en porte-voix** to cup one's hands round one's mouth.

porteur, -euse [pɔʀtœʀ, øz] 1 **adj** *fusée* booster; *courant* carrier; (*Écon*) *marché, créneau* strong, buoyant. **onde ~euse** carrier (wave); *voir* **mère**.

2 **nm, f** a *[valise, colis]* porter; *[message]* messenger; *[chèque]* bearer; *[titre, actions]* holder. **~ d'eau** water carrier; **~ de journaux** newsboy, paper boy; **le ~ du message** the bearer of the message; **il arriva ~ d'une lettre/d'une nouvelle alarmante** he came bearing *ou* bringing a letter/an alarming piece of news; **il était ~ de faux papiers** he was carrying forged papers; **le ~ du ballon** the person with the ball *ou* who has (possession of) the ball; **payable au ~** payable to bearer; (*Fin*) **les petits/gros ~s** small/big shareholders.

b (*Méd*) carrier. **~ de germes** germ carrier; **~ sain** carrier; **il est ~ du virus** he is carrying the virus.

portier [pɔʀtje] **nm** commissionaire (*Brit, Can*), porter. (*Rel*) **(frère) ~** porter; **~ de nuit** night porter; **~ électrique** entrance intercom, entry phone.

portière [pɔʀtjɛʀ] **nf** a (*Aut, Rail*) door. b (*rideau*) portiere. c (*Rel*) **(sœur) ~** portress.

portillon [pɔʀtijɔ̃] **nm** gate; *[métro]* gate, barrier; *voir* **bousculer**.

portion [pɔʀsjɔ̃] **nf** *[héritage]* portion, share; (*Culin*) portion, helping; (*partie*) portion, section, part. **fromage en ~s** cheese portions (*pl*); (*fig*) **être réduit à la ~ congrue** to get the smallest *ou* meanest share; **bonne/mauvaise ~ de route** good/bad stretch of road.

portique [pɔʀtik] **nm** (*Archit*) portico; (*Sport*) crossbar and stands (*for holding gymnastic apparatus*). (*à l'aéroport*) **~ électronique** *ou* **de sécurité** *ou* **de détection** diver's gate (*SPÉC*), metal detector; (*Rail*) **~ à signaux** signal gantry.

Port-Louis [pɔʀlui] **n** Port-Louis.

Port Moresby [pɔʀmɔʀɛsbi] **n** Port Moresby.

Porto [pɔʀto] **n** Oporto.

porto [pɔʀto] **nm** port (wine).

Port of Spain [pɔʀɔfspɛjn] **n** Port of Spain.

Porto-Novo [pɔʀtonovo] **n** Porto Novo.

portoricain, e [pɔʀtɔʀikɛ̃, ɛn] 1 **adj** Puerto Rican. 2 **nm, f: P~(e)** Puerto Rican.

Porto Rico [pɔʀtɔʀiko] **nf** Puerto Rico.

portrait [pɔʀtʀɛ] **nm** a (*peinture*) portrait; (*photo*) photograph; (*:

visage) face, mug*. ~ **fidèle** good likeness; (*Police*) **~-robot** Identikit picture ®, Photofit ® (picture); (*fig*) **faire le ~-robot du Français moyen** to draw the profile of the average Frenchman; ~ **en pied/en buste** full-length/head-and-shoulders portrait; **c'est tout le ~ de son père** he's the spitting image *ou* the very spit* (*Brit*) of his father; **faire le ~ de qn** (*lit*) to paint sb's portrait; **se faire tirer le ~*** to have one's photograph taken; **se faire abîmer** *ou* **esquinter le ~*** to get one's face *ou* head bashed in* *ou* smashed in*; **il t'a bien abîmé le ~!*** he made a real mess of your face!

b (*description*) *[personne]* portrait, description; *[situation]* picture. **faire** *ou* **tracer le ~ de qn** to draw a portrait of *ou* describe sb; **elle en a fait un ~ flatteur** she painted a flattering picture of him; **~-charge** caricature; **jouer au ~** to play twenty questions.

c (*genre*) **le ~** portraiture.

portraitiste [pɔʀtʀetist] **nmf** portrait painter, portraitist.

portraiturer [pɔʀtʀetyʀe] [1] **vt** (*lit, fig*) to portray.

port-salut [pɔʀsaly] **nm** port-salut (cheese).

Port Stanley [pɔʀstanlɛ] **n** (Port) Stanley.

portuaire [pɔʀtɥɛʀ] **adj** port (*épith*), harbour (*épith*).

portugais, e [pɔʀtygɛ, ɛz] 1 **adj** Portuguese. 2 **nm** a **P~** Portuguese. b (*Ling*) Portuguese. 3 **portugaise nf** a **P~e** Portuguese. b (*huître*) Portuguese oyster. (*: *oreille*) **il a les ~es ensablées** he's a real cloth-ears* (*Brit*), he's as deaf as a post.

Portugal [pɔʀtygal] **nm** Portugal.

P.O.S. [peoɛs] **nm** (**abrév de plan d'occupation des sols**) *voir* **plan**.

pose [poz] **nf** a (*installation*) *[tableau, rideaux]* hanging, putting up; *[tapis]* laying, putting down; *[moquette]* fitting, laying; *[vitre]* putting in, fixing (in); *[serrure]* fixing (on), fitting; *[chauffage]* installation, putting in; *[gaz, électricité]* laying on, installation; *[canalisations]* laying, putting in; *[fondations, mines, voie ferrée]* laying.

b (*attitude*) pose, posture; (*Art*) pose. **garder la ~** to hold the pose; **prendre une ~** to strike a pose; **faire prendre une ~ à qn** to pose sb.

c (*Phot*) (*vue*) exposure. **un film (de) 36 ~s** a 36-exposure film; **déterminer le temps de ~** to decide on the exposure (time); **indice de ~** exposure index; **mettre le bouton sur ~** to set the button to time exposure; **prendre une photo en ~** *ou* **à la ~** to take a photo in time exposure.

d (*fig: affectation*) posing, pretention. **parler avec/sans ~** to speak pretentiously/quite unpretentiously *ou* naturally.

posé, e [poze] (**ptp de poser**) **adj** a (*pondéré*) *personne, caractère, air* serious, sedate, staid; *attitude, allure* steady, sober. **c'est un garçon ~** he has his head firmly on his shoulders, he's level-headed; **d'un ton ~ mais ferme** calmly but firmly. b (*Mus*) **bien/mal ~** *voix* steady/unsteady.

Poséidon [pɔseidɔ̃] **nm** Poseidon.

posément [pozemɑ̃] **adv** *parler* calmly, deliberately, steadily; *agir* calmly, unhurriedly.

posemètre [pozmɛtʀ] **nm** exposure meter.

poser [poze] [1] 1 **vt** a (*placer*) *objet* to put (down), lay (down), set down; (*debout*) to stand (up), put (up); (*Math*) *opération, chiffres* to write, set down. (*ôter*) **~ son manteau/chapeau** to take off one's coat/hat; **~ qch sur une table/par terre** to put sth (down) on the table/on the floor; **~ sa main/tête sur l'épaule de qn** to put *ou* lay one's hand/head on sb's shoulder; **~ sa tête sur l'oreiller** to lay one's head on the pillow; **~ une échelle contre un mur** to lean *ou* stand *ou* put (up) a ladder against a wall; **où ai-je posé mes lunettes?** where have I put my glasses?; (*fig*) **il a posé son regard** *ou* **les yeux sur la fille** he looked at the girl, his gaze came to rest on the girl; **le pilote posa son avion en douceur** the pilot brought his plane down *ou* landed his plane gently; (*Mus*) **~ la voix de qn** to train sb's voice; (*Math*) **je pose 4 et je retiens 3** (I) put down 4 and carry 3, 4 and 3 to carry; **~ un lapin à qn*** to stand sb up*.

b (*installer*) *tableau, rideaux* to hang, put up; *tapis, carrelage* to lay, put down; *moquette* to fit, lay; *vitre* to put in, fix in; *serrure* to fix on, fit; *chauffage* to put in, install; *gaz, électricité* to lay on, install; *canalisations* to lay, put in; *fondations, mines, voie ferrée* to lay; *bombe* to plant. (*lit, fig*) **~ la première pierre** to lay the foundation stone; **~ des étagères au mur** to fix *ou* put some shelves *ou* shelving on the wall, fix *ou* put up some wall-shelves; **~ des jalons** (*lit*) to put stakes up; (*fig*) to prepare the ground, pave the way.

c (*fig: énoncer*) *principe, condition* to lay *ou* set down, set out, state; *question* to ask; (*à un examen*) to set; *devinette* to set, ask. **le prof nous a posé un problème difficile** the teacher set us a difficult problem; (*formuler*) **il a bien su ~ le problème** he put *ou* formulated the problem well; **ce retard pose un problème** this delay poses a problem *ou* confronts us with a problem; **son admission au club pose des problèmes** his joining the club is problematic *ou* is not straightforward; **son cas nous pose un sérieux problème** his case poses a difficult problem for us, his case presents us with a difficult problem; **~ une question à qn** to ask sb a question, put a question to sb; **l'ambiguïté de son attitude pose la question de son honnêteté** his ambivalent attitude makes you wonder how honest he is *ou* leads one to question his honesty; **la question me semble mal posée** I think the question is badly put; (*Pol*) **~ la question de confiance** to ask for a vote of confidence; **~ sa candidature à un poste** to apply for a post, submit an application for a post; (*Pol*) **~ sa candidature** to put o.s. up *ou* run (*US*) for election; **dire cela, c'est ~ que ...** in saying that, one is supposing that *ou* taking it for granted that ...; **ceci posé** supposing that this is (*ou* was *etc*) the case, assuming this to be the case; **posons que ...** let us suppose *ou* assume *ou* take it that ... .

d (*donner de l'importance*) to give standing to; (*professionnellement*) to establish the reputation of. **voilà ce qui pose un homme** that's what sets a man up; **avoir un frère ministre, ça vous pose!*** having a brother who's a cabinet minister really makes people look up to you! *ou* gives you real status!; **une maison comme ça, ça (vous) pose*** with a house like that people really think you are somebody.

2 **vi** a (*Art, Phot*) to pose, sit (*pour* for); (*fig*) to swank (*Brit*), show off, put on airs. (*hum*) **~ pour la postérité** to pose for posterity; (*fig*) **~ pour la galerie** to play to the gallery; (*faire attendre*) **faire ~ qn*** to keep sb hanging about* *ou* around*.

b (*jouer à*) **~ au grand patron/à l'artiste** to play *ou* act *ou* come* the big businessman/the artist, pretend to be a big businessman/an artist.

c (*Constr*) *[poutre]* **~ sur** to bear *ou* rest on, be supported by.

3 **se poser vpr** a *[insecte, oiseau]* to land, settle, alight (*sur* on); *[avion]* to land, touch down; *[regard]* to (come to) rest, settle, fix (*sur* on). (*Aviat*) **se ~ en catastrophe/sur le ventre** to make an emergency landing/a belly-landing; **son regard se posa sur la pendule** he turned his eyes to the clock, his glance fell on the clock; **une main se posa soudain sur son épaule** a hand was suddenly laid on his shoulder; **pose-toi là*** sit down here.

b *[personne]* **se ~ comme** *ou* **en tant que victime** to pretend *ou* claim to be a victim; **se ~ en chef/en expert** to pass o.s. off as *ou* pose as a leader/an expert.

c *[question, problème]* to come up, crop up, arise. **la question qui se pose** the question which must be asked *ou* considered; **le problème qui se pose** the problem we are faced with *ou* we must face; **si tu viens en voiture, le problème ne se pose pas** if you come by car the problem doesn't arise; **le problème ne se pose pas dans ces termes** the problem shouldn't be stated in these terms; **il se pose la question des passeports** the question of passports arises, there's the question of passports; **il se pose la question de savoir s'il viendra** there's the question of (knowing) whether he'll come; **je me pose la question** that's the question, that's what I'm wondering; **il commence à se ~ des questions** he's beginning to wonder *ou* to have his doubts; **il y a une question que je me pose** there's one thing I'd like to know, there's one question I ask myself.

d (**loc*) **se ~ là: comme menteur, vous vous posez (un peu) là!** you're a terrible *ou* an awful liar!; **comme erreur, ça se posait (un peu) là!** that was (quite) some mistake!*; **tu as vu leur chien/père? — il se pose là!** have you seen their dog/father? — it's/he's enormous *ou* huge *ou* massive!

poseur, -euse [pozœʀ, øz] 1 **adj** affected. 2 **nm, f** a (*péj*) show-off, poseur. b (*ouvrier*) **~ de carrelage/de tuyaux** tile/pipe layer; **~ d'affiches** billsticker (*Brit*), billposter; **~ de bombes** bomb planter.

positif, -ive [pozitif, iv] 1 **adj** (*gén, Ling, Sci*) positive; *cuti* positive; *fait, preuve* positive, definite; *personne, esprit* pragmatic, down-to-earth; *action, idée* positive, constructive; *avantage* positive, real. (*sang*) **Rhésus ~** Rhesus positive. 2 **nm** a (*réel*) positive, concrete. **je veux du ~!** I want something positive! b (*Mus*) (*clavier d'un orgue*) choir organ (*division of organ*); (*instrument*) positive organ. c (*Phot*) positive. d (*Ling*) positive (degree). **au ~** in the positive (form).

position [pozisjɔ̃] **nf** a (*gén, Ling, Mil: emplacement*) position; *[navire]* bearings, position; (*Comm*) *[produit]* position. **~ de défense/fortifiée** defensive/fortified position; (*lit*) **rester sur ses ~s** to stand one's ground; (*fig*) **rester** *ou* **camper sur ses ~s** to stand one's ground, stick to one's guns *ou* line; **abandonner ses ~s** to retreat, abandon one's position, withdraw; **se replier** *ou* **se retirer sur des ~s préparées à l'avance** to fall back on positions prepared in advance; **avoir une ~ de repli** (*Mil*) to have a position to fall back on; (*fig*) to have secondary proposals to make, have other proposals to fall back on *ou* other proposals in reserve; **la ville jouit d'une ~ idéale** the town is ideally situated; **les joueurs ont changé de ~** the players have changed position(s); **être en première/seconde/dernière ~** (*dans une course*) to be in the lead/in second place/last; (*sur une liste*) to be at the top of the list/second on the list/at the bottom *ou* end of the list; **arriver en première/deuxième/dernière ~** to come first/second/last; (*Ling*) **syllabe en ~ forte/faible** stressed/unstressed syllable, syllable in (a) stressed/(an) unstressed position; (*Ling*) **voyelle en ~ forte/faible** stressed *ou* strong/unstressed *ou* weak vowel; *voir* **feu[1], guerre**.

b (*posture*) position. **dormir dans une mauvaise ~** to sleep in the wrong position; (*Mil, gén*) **se mettre en ~** to take up (one's) position(s), get into position; **en ~!** (get to your) positions!; **en ~ de combat** in a fighting position; **en ~ allongée/assise/verticale** in a reclining/sitting/vertical *ou* upright position; **la ~ du missionnaire** the missionary position.

c (*fig: situation*) position, situation; (*dans la société*) position. **être dans une ~ délicate/fausse** to be in a difficult *ou* an awkward position/in a false position; **être en ~ de force pour négocier** to be bargaining from (a position of) strength; **être en ~ de faire** to be in a position to do;

dans sa ~ il ne peut se permettre une incartade a man in his position dare not commit an indiscretion; **il occupe une ~ importante** he holds an important position; (†, *hum*) **femme dans une ~ intéressante** woman in a certain condition (*hum, euph*).

d (*attitude*) position, stance. **le gouvernement doit définir sa ~ sur cette question** the government must make its position *ou* stance on this question clear; **prendre ~** to take a stand, declare o.s.; **prendre (fermement) ~ en faveur de qch** to come down (strongly) in favour of sth; *voir* **pris.**

e (*Fin*) *[compte bancaire]* position, balance. **demander sa ~** to ask for the balance of one's account.

positionnement [pozisjɔnmɑ̃] **nm** *[objet, produit, entreprise]* positioning.

positionner [pozisjɔne] 1 1 **vt** a (*placer*) (*gén, Mil*) to position; *Comm produit* to position. b (*repérer*) *navire, troupes* to locate. c *compte bancaire* to establish the position *ou* balance of. 2 **se positionner vpr** (*gén*) to position o.s.; *troupe* to take up (one's) position, get into position. **comment se positionne ce produit sur le marché?** what slot does this product fill in the market?

positivement [pozitivmɑ̃] **adv** (*gén, Sci*) positively. **je ne le sais pas ~** I'm not positive about it.

positivisme [pozitivism] **nm** positivism.

positiviste [pozitivist] **adj, nmf** positivist.

positivité [pozitivite] **nf** positivity.

positon [pozitɔ̃] **nm, positron** [pozitʀɔ̃] **nm** (*Phys*) positron.

posologie [pozɔlɔʒi] **nf** (*étude*) posology; (*indications*) directions for use, dosage.

possédant, e [pɔsedɑ̃, ɑ̃t] 1 **adj** propertied, wealthy. 2 **nmpl: les ~s** the wealthy, the propertied, the moneyed.

possédé, e [pɔsede] (**ptp de posséder**) 1 **adj** possessed (*de* by). **~ du démon** possessed by the devil. 2 **nm, f** person possessed. **crier comme un ~** to cry like one possessed.

posséder [pɔsede] 6 1 **vt** a *bien, maison, fortune* to possess, own, have. **c'est tout ce que je possède** it's all I possess *ou* all I've got; (*fig*) **~ une femme** to possess a woman; **pour ~ le cœur d'une femme** to capture a woman's heart.

b *caractéristique, qualité, territoire* to have, possess; *expérience* to have (had); *diplôme, titre* to have, hold. **cette maison possède une vue magnifique/2 entrées** this house has a magnificent view/2 entrances; **il croit ~ la vérité** he believes that he is in possession of truth *ou* that he possesses the truth.

c (*bien connaître*) *métier* to have a thorough knowledge of, know inside out; *technique* to have mastered; *langue* to have a good command of. **elle possède parfaitement l'anglais** she has a perfect command of English; **~ la clef de l'énigme** to possess *ou* have the key to the mystery; **bien ~ son rôle** to be really on top of *ou* into* one's role *ou* part.

d (*égarer*) *[démon]* to possess. **la fureur/jalousie le possède** he is beside himself with *ou* he is overcome *ou* consumed with rage/jealousy; **quel démon *ou* quelle rage te possède?** what's got into you?*, what's come over you?; *voir* **possédé.**

e (**: duper*) **~ qn** to take sb in*; **se faire ~** to be taken in*, be had*.

2 **se posséder vpr: elle ne se possédait plus de joie** she was beside herself *ou* was overcome with joy; **lorsqu'il est en colère, il ne se possède pas** when he's angry he loses all self-control.

possesseur [pɔsesœʀ] **nm** *[bien]* possessor, owner; *[diplôme, titre, secret]* holder, possessor; *[billet de loterie]* holder. **être ~ de** *objet* to have; *diplôme* to hold; *secret* to possess, have.

possessif, -ive [pɔsesif, iv] 1 **adj** (*gén, Ling*) possessive. 2 **nm** (*Ling*) possessive.

possession [pɔsesjɔ̃] **nf** a (*fait de posséder*) *[bien]* possession, ownership; *[diplôme, titre]* holding, possession; *[billet de loterie]* holding. **la ~ d'une arme/de cet avantage le rendait confiant** having a weapon/this advantage made him feel confident; **~ vaut titre** possession amounts to title; **avoir qch en sa ~** to have sth in one's possession; **être en ~ de qch** to be in possession of sth; **tomber en la ~ de qn** to come into sb's possession; **prendre ~ de, entrer en ~ de** *fonction* to take up; *bien, héritage* to take possession of, enter into possession of; *appartement* to take possession of; *voiture* to take delivery of; **être en ~ de toutes ses facultés** to be in possession of all one's faculties; **il était en pleine ~ de ses moyens** his intellectual (*ou* physical) powers were at their peak.

b (*chose possédée*) possession. **nos ~s à l'étranger** our overseas possessions.

c (*maîtrise*) **~ de soi** self-control; **reprendre ~ de soi-même** to regain one's self-control *ou* one's composure.

d (*connaissance*) *[langue]* command, mastery.

e (*Rel: envoûtement*) possession.

possessivité [pɔsesivite] **nf** possessiveness.

possibilité [pɔsibilite] **nf** (*gén*) possibility. **il y a plusieurs ~s** there are several possibilities; **je ne vois pas d'autre ~ (que de faire)** I don't see any other possibility (than to do); **ai-je la ~ de faire du feu/de parler librement?** is it possible for me to light a fire/speak freely?, is there the possibility of (my) lighting a fire/speaking freely?; **~s** (*moyens*) means; (*potentiel*) possibilities, potential; **quelles sont vos ~s financières?** how much money can you put up?, what is your financial situation?; **quelles sont vos ~s de logement?** how many people can you accommodate? *ou* put up?; **les ~s d'une découverte/d'un pays neuf** the possibilities *ou* potential of a discovery/of a new country; *[entreprise, projet]* **~ (de réalisation)** feasibility.

possible [pɔsibl] 1 **adj** a (*faisable*) *solution* possible; *projet, entreprise* feasible. **il est ~/il n'est pas ~ de faire** it is possible/impossible to do; **nous avons fait tout ce qu'il était humainement ~ de faire** we've done everything that was humanly possible; **lui serait-il ~ d'arriver plus tôt?** could he possibly *ou* would it be possible for him to come earlier?; **arrivez tôt si (c'est) ~** arrive early if possible *ou* if you can; **c'est parfaitement ~** it's perfectly possible *ou* feasible; **ce n'est pas ~ autrement** there's no other way, otherwise it's impossible; **il n'est pas ~ qu'il soit aussi bête qu'il en a l'air** he can't possibly be as stupid as he looks; **c'est dans les choses ~s** it's a possibility; **la paix a rendu ~ leur rencontre** peace has made a meeting between them possible *ou* has made it possible for them to meet.

b (*éventuel*) (*gén*) possible; *danger* possible, potential. **une erreur est toujours ~** a mistake is always possible; **il est ~ qu'il vienne/qu'il ne vienne pas** he may *ou* might (possibly) come/not come, it's possible (that) he'll come/he won't come; **il est bien ~ qu'il se soit perdu en route** he may very well have *ou* it could well be *ou* it's quite possible that he has lost his way; **c'est (bien) ~/très ~** possibly/very possibly.

c (*indiquant une limite*) possible. **dans le meilleur des mondes ~s** in the best of all possible worlds; **il a essayé tous les moyens ~s** he tried every possible means *ou* every means possible; **il a eu toutes les difficultés ~s et imaginables à obtenir un visa** he had all kinds of problems getting a visa, he had every possible difficulty getting a visa; **venez aussi vite/aussitôt que ~** come as quickly as possible *ou* as you (possibly) can/as soon as possible *ou* as you (possibly) can; **venez le plus longtemps ~** come for as long as you (possibly) can; **venez le plus vite/tôt ~** come as quickly/as soon as you (possibly) can; **il sort le plus (souvent)/le moins (souvent) ~** he goes out as often/as little as possible *ou* as he can; **il a acheté la valise la plus légère ~** he bought the lightest possible suitcase *ou* the lightest suitcase possible; **le plus grand nombre ~ de personnes** as many people as possible, the greatest possible number of people; *voir* **autant.**

d (**: nég: acceptable*) **cette situation n'est plus ~** this situation has become impossible *ou* intolerable *ou* unbearable; **il n'est pas ~ de travailler dans ce bruit** it just isn't possible *ou* it's (quite) impossible to work in this noise; **un bruit/une puanteur pas ~!** an incredible racket*/stink!

e (*loc*) **est-ce ~!** I don't believe it!; **c'est pas ~!*** (*faux*) that can't be true! *ou* right!; (*étonnant*) well I never!*; (*irréalisable*) it's out of the question!, it's impossible!; **ce n'est pas ~ d'être aussi bête!** how can anyone be so stupid!, how stupid can you get!*; **elle voudrait vous parler — c'est (bien) ~, mais il faut que je parte** she'd like a word with you — that's as may be *ou* quite possibly, but I've got to go; **il devrait se reposer! — c'est (bien) ~, mais il n'a pas le temps** he ought to take a rest! — maybe (he should), but he's too busy.

2 **nm** a (*gén*) what is possible. **il fera le ~ et l'impossible pour avoir la paix** he will move heaven and earth *ou* he'll do anything possible to get some peace; **c'est dans le ~ *ou* dans les limites du ~** it is within the realms of possibility; **faire (tout) son ~** to do one's utmost *ou* one's best, do all one can (*pour* to, *pour que* to make sure that); **il a été grossier/aimable au ~** he couldn't have been ruder/nicer (if he'd tried), he was as rude/nice as it's possible to be; **c'est énervant au ~** it's extremely annoying; *voir* **mesure.**

b (*Sport*) possible.

post- [pɔst] **préf** post-. **~électoral/surréaliste** *etc* post-election/-surrealist *etc; voir* **postdater** *etc.*

postal, e, **mpl -aux** [pɔstal, o] **adj** *service, taxe, voiture* postal (*Brit*), mail; *train, avion* mail; *colis* sent by post (*Brit*) *ou* mail. **code ~** postcode (*Brit*), zip code (*US*); **sac ~** postbag, mailbag; *voir* **carte, chèque, franchise.**

postcure [pɔstkyʀ] **nf** aftercare.

postdater [pɔstdate] 1 **vt** to postdate.

poste[1] [pɔst] 1 **nf** a (*administration, bureau*) post office. **employé/ingénieur des ~s** post office worker/engineer; **les Postes, Télécommunications et Télédiffusion** *the French post office and telephone service;* **la grande ~, la ~ principale, le bureau de ~ principal** the main *ou* head post office.

b (*service postal*) post (*Brit*), postal (*Brit*) *ou* mail service. **envoyer qch par la ~** to send sth by post (*Brit*) *ou* mail; **mettre une lettre à la ~** to post (*Brit*) *ou* mail a letter; *voir* **cachet.**

c (*Hist*) post. **maître de ~** postmaster; **cheval de ~** post horse; **courir la ~** to go posthaste; *voir* **chaise, voiture.**

2 **comp ►poste aérienne** airmail **►poste auxiliaire** sub post office **►poste restante** poste restante (*Brit*), general delivery (*US*).

poste[2] [pɔst] 1 **nm** a (*emplacement*) post. **~ de douane** customs post; **être/rester à son ~** to be/stay at one's post; **mourir à son ~** to die at one's post; **à vos ~s!** to your stations! *ou* posts!; **à vos ~s de combat!** action stations!; (*fig*) **être solide au ~** to be hale and hearty;

(*fig*) **toujours fidèle au ~?*** still manning the fort?*

b (*Police*) ~ **(de police)** (police) station; **conduire** *ou* **emmener qn au** ~ to take sb to the police station; **il a passé la nuit au** ~ he spent the night in the cells.

c (*emploi*) (*gén*) job; *[fonctionnaire]* post, appointment (*frm*); (*dans une hiérarchie*) position; (*nomination*) appointment. **être en ~ à Paris/à l'étranger** to hold an appointment *ou* a post in Paris/abroad; **il a trouvé un ~ de bibliothécaire** he has found a post *ou* job as a librarian; **il a un ~ de professeur/en fac** he is a teacher/a university lecturer; **la liste des ~s vacants** the list of positions available *ou* of unfilled appointments; ~ **d'enseignant** teaching position *ou* post *ou* job.

d (*Rad, TV*) set. ~ **émetteur/récepteur** transmitting/receiving set, transmitter/receiver; ~ **de radio/de télévision** radio/television (set); **ils l'ont dit au ~*** they said so on TV* *ou* on the radio.

e (*Téléc*) ~ **23** extension 23.

f (*Fin*) (*opération*) item, entry; *[budget]* item, element.

g (*Ind*) shift. ~ **de 8 heures** 8-hour shift.

2 **comp** ▸**poste d'aiguillage** (*Rail*) signal box ▸**poste avancé** (*Mil*) advanced post ▸**poste budgétaire** budget heading ▸**poste de commandement** headquarters ▸**poste de contrôle** checkpoint ▸**poste d'équipage** (*Naut*) crew's quarters ▸**poste d'essence** petrol *ou* filling station, gas station (*US*) ▸**poste frontière** border *ou* frontier post ▸**poste de garde** (*Mil*) guardroom ▸**poste d'incendie** fire point ▸**poste de lavage** (*Aut*) car wash ▸**poste d'observation** observation post ▸**poste de pilotage** (*Aviat*) cockpit ▸**poste de police** (*Police*) police station; (*Mil*) guard-room, guardhouse ▸**poste de secours** first-aid post ▸**poste téléphonique** telephone ▸**poste de travail** (*Ordin*) work station.

posté, e [pɔste] (**ptp de poster**) **adj**: **travail/travailleur** ~ shift work/worker.

poster¹ [pɔste] 1 **1 vt a** *lettre* to post (*Brit*), mail. **b** *sentinelle* to post, station. **2 se poster vpr** to take up (a) position, position o.s., station o.s.

poster² [pɔstɛʀ] **nm** poster.

postérieur, e [pɔsteʀjœʀ] **1 adj** (*dans le temps*) *date, document* later; *événement* subsequent, later; (*dans l'espace*) *partie* back, posterior (*frm*); *membre* hind, rear, back; *voyelle* back. **ce document est légèrement/très ~ à cette date** this document dates from slightly later/much later; **l'événement est ~ à 1850** the event took place later than *ou* after 1850; ~ **à 1800** after 1800. **2 nm** (*) behind*, rear, posterior (*hum*).

postérieurement [pɔsteʀjœʀmɑ̃] **adv** later, subsequently. ~ **à** after.

posteriori [pɔsteʀjɔʀi] **loc adv**: **a** ~ a posteriori.

postériorité [pɔsteʀjɔʀite] **nf** posteriority.

postérité [pɔsteʀite] **nf** (*descendants*) descendants, posterity; (*avenir*) posterity. (*frm*) **mourir sans** ~ to die without issue; **être jugé par la** ~ to be judged by posterity; **entrer dans la ~, passer à la** ~ to go down to posterity.

postface [pɔstfas] **nf** postscript, postface.

postglaciaire [pɔstglasjɛʀ] **adj** postglacial.

posthume [pɔstym] **adj** posthumous.

postiche [pɔstiʃ] **1 adj** *cheveux, moustache* false; (*fig*) *ornement, fioriture* postiche, superadded; *sentiment* pretended; (*Ling*) *élément, symbole* dummy. **2 nm** (*pour homme*) toupee; (*pour femme*) hairpiece, postiche.

postier, -ière [pɔstje, jɛʀ] **nm, f** post office worker. **grève des ~s** postal (*Brit*) *ou* mail strike.

postillon [pɔstijɔ̃] **nm** (*Hist: cocher*) postilion; (*: *salive*) sputter. **envoyer des ~s** to sputter, splutter.

postillonner* [pɔstijɔne] 1 **vi** to sputter, splutter.

post(-)industriel, -elle [pɔstɛ̃dystʀijɛl] **adj** post-industrial.

postnatal, e, mpl ~s [pɔstnatal] **adj** postnatal.

postopératoire [pɔstɔpeʀatwaʀ] **adj** post-operative.

postposer [pɔstpoze] 1 **vt** to place after. **sujet postposé** postpositive subject, subject placed after the verb.

postposition [pɔstpozisjɔ̃] **nf** postposition. **verbe à ~** phrasal verb.

postscolaire [pɔstskɔlɛʀ] **adj** *enseignement* further (*épith*), continuing (*épith*).

post-scriptum [pɔstskʀiptɔm] **nm inv** postscript.

postsonorisation [pɔstsɔnɔʀizasjɔ̃] **nf** dubbing.

postsonoriser [pɔstsɔnɔʀize] 1 **vt** to dub.

postsynchronisation [pɔstsɛ̃kʀɔnizasjɔ̃] **nf** dubbing (*of a film*).

postsynchroniser [pɔstsɛ̃kʀɔnize] 1 **vt** to dub (*a film*).

postulant, e [pɔstylɑ̃, ɑ̃t] **nm,f** applicant; (*Rel*) postulant.

postulat [pɔstyla] **nm** postulate.

postuler [pɔstyle] 1 **1 vt a** *emploi* to apply for, put in for. **b** *principe* to postulate. **2 vi a** ~ **à** *ou* **pour un emploi** to apply for a job. **b** (*Jur*) ~ **pour** to represent.

posture [pɔstyʀ] **nf** posture, position. **être en bonne** ~ to be in a good position; **être en très mauvaise** ~ to be in a really bad position *ou* a tight corner; (†, *littér*) **en ~ de faire** in a position to do.

pot [po] **1 nm a** (*récipient*) (*en verre*) jar; (*en terre*) pot; (*en métal*) tin (*Brit*), can; (*en carton*) carton. **petit ~ pour bébé** jar of baby food; ~ **à confiture** jamjar, jampot (*Brit*); ~ **de confiture** jar *ou* pot (*Brit*) of jam; **mettre en** ~ *fleur* to pot; *confiture* to put in jars, pot (*Brit*); **plantes en** ~ pot plants; **mettre un enfant sur le** ~ to put a child on the potty, pot a child.

b (*) (*boisson*) drink, jar* (*Brit*); (*réunion*) drinks party. **tu viens prendre** *ou* **boire un ~?*** are you coming for a drink? *ou* for a jar?* (*Brit*); *voir* **cuiller, découvrir, fortune.**

c (*: *chance*) luck. **avoir du** ~ to be lucky *ou* in luck; **manquer de** ~ to be unlucky *ou* out of luck; **pas de** *ou* **manque de ~!** just his (*ou* your *etc*) luck!; **tu as du ~!** some people have all the luck!, you're a lucky begger!* *ou* blighter!* (*Brit*); **c'est un vrai coup de ~!** what a stroke of luck!

d (*Cartes*) (*enjeu*) kitty; (*restant*) pile.

2 **comp** ▸**pot à bière** (*en verre*) beer mug; (*en terre ou en métal*) tankard ▸**pot catalytique** catalytic converter ▸**pot de chambre** chamberpot ▸**pot de colle** (*lit*) pot of glue; (*péj: crampon*) leech; **il est du genre pot de colle!** you just can't shake him off!, he sticks like a leech! ▸**pot à eau** (*pour se laver*) water jug, pitcher; (*pour boire*) water jug ▸**pot d'échappement** exhaust pipe; (*silencieux*) silencer (*Brit*), muffler (*US*) ▸**pot-au-feu nm inv** (*plat*) (beef) stew; (*viande*) stewing beef ◊ **adj inv** (*) stay-at-home, home-loving ▸**pot de fleurs** (*récipient*) plant pot, flowerpot; (*fleurs*) pot plant, flowering plant ▸**pot à lait** (*pour transporter*) milk can; (*sur la table*) milk jug ▸**pot-pourri nm (pl pots-pourris)** (*fleurs*) pot-pourri; (*Mus*) potpourri, medley ▸**pot à tabac** (*lit*) tobacco jar; (*fig*) dumpy little person ▸**pot de terre** earthenware pot; **un particulier qui se bat contre l'administration c'est le pot de terre contre le pot de fer** one individual struggling against the authorities can't hope to win ▸**pot-de-vin nm (pl pots-de-vin)** bribe, backhander* (*Brit*), payola (*US*); **donner un pot-de-vin à qn** to bribe sb, give sb a backhander* (*Brit*), grease sb's palm.

potable [pɔtabl] **adj** (*lit*) drinkable; (* *fig*) reasonable, passable, decent. **eau ~** drinking water; **eau non ~** water which is not for drinking, non-drinking water; **il ne peut pas faire un travail ~** he can't do a decent piece of work; **le film est ~** the film isn't bad; **ce travail est tout juste ~** this piece of work is barely passable *ou* acceptable.

potache* [pɔtaʃ] **nm** schoolboy, schoolkid*.

potage [pɔtaʒ] **nm** soup.

potager, -ère [pɔtaʒe, ɛʀ] **1 adj** *plante* vegetable (*épith*), edible; *jardin* kitchen (*épith*), vegetable (*épith*). **2 nm** kitchen *ou* vegetable garden.

potasse [pɔtas] **nf** (*hydroxide*) potassium hydroxide, caustic potash; (*carbonate*) potash, *impure potassium carbonate*.

potasser* [pɔtase] 1 **1 vt** *livre, discours* to swot up* (*Brit*) *ou* cram *ou* bone up‡ for; *examen* to swot* (*Brit*) *ou* cram *ou* bone up‡ for; *sujet* swot up (on)* (*Brit*), bone up (on)‡. **2 vi** to swot* (*Brit*), cram.

potassique [pɔtasik] **adj** potassic.

potassium [pɔtasjɔm] **nm** potassium.

pote* [pɔt] **nm** pal*, mate* (*Brit*), chum*, buddy* (*US*). **salut, mon ~!** hi there!*, hi, buster!‡ (*US*).

poteau, pl ~x [pɔto] **1 nm a** post. (*Courses*) **rester au** ~ to be left at the (starting) post; **elle a les jambes comme des ~x*** she's got legs like tree trunks*. **b** ~ **(d'exécution)** execution post, stake (*for execution by shooting*); **envoyer au** ~ to sentence to execution by firing squad; **au ~!** lynch him!, string him up!*; **le directeur au ~!** down with the boss! **c** (*†: *ami*) pal*, buddy* (*US*). **2 comp** ▸**poteau d'arrivée** winning *ou* finishing post ▸**poteau de but** goal-post ▸**poteau de départ** starting post ▸**poteau indicateur** signpost ▸**poteau télégraphique** telegraph post *ou* pole ▸**poteau de torture** torture post.

potée [pɔte] **nf** (*Culin*) ≃ hotpot (*of pork and cabbage*).

potelé, e [pɔt(ə)le] **adj** *enfant* plump, chubby; *bras* plump.

potence [pɔtɑ̃s] **nf a** (*gibet*) gallows (*sg*); *voir* **gibier. b** (*support*) bracket. **en** ~ (*en équerre*) L-shaped; (*en T*) T-shaped.

potentat [pɔtɑ̃ta] **nm** (*lit*) potentate; (*fig péj*) despot.

potentialité [pɔtɑ̃sjalite] **nf** potentiality.

potentiel, -elle [pɔtɑ̃sjɛl] **adj, nm** (*gén*) potential.

potentiellement [pɔtɑ̃sjɛlmɑ̃] **adv** potentially.

potentille [pɔtɑ̃tij] **nf** potentilla.

potentiomètre [pɔtɑ̃sjɔmɛtʀ] **nm** potentiometer.

poterie [pɔtʀi] **nf** (*atelier, art*) pottery; (*objet*) earthenware bowl (*ou* dish *ou* jug *etc*), piece of pottery. **~s** earthenware, pieces of pottery.

poterne [pɔtɛʀn] **nf** postern.

potiche [pɔtiʃ] **nf** (large) oriental vase; (*fig*) figurehead.

potier, -ière [pɔtje, jɛʀ] **nm,f** potter.

potin* [pɔtɛ̃] **nm a** (*vacarme*) din*, racket*. **faire du** ~ (*lit*) to make a noise; (*fig*) to kick up a fuss*; **ça va faire du** ~ (*lit*) there'll be a lot of noise, it'll be noisy; (*fig*) this is going to stir things up*, there'll be quite a rumpus (over this). **b** (*commérage*) **~s** gossip, tittle-tattle.

potiner [pɔtine] 1 **vi** to gossip.

potion [posjɔ̃] **nf** (*lit*) potion. (*fig*) ~ **(amère)** bitter pill.

potiron [pɔtiʀɔ̃] **nm** pumpkin.

potron-minet* [pɔtʀɔ̃minɛ] **nm**: **dès** ~ at the crack of dawn, at daybreak.

pou, pl ~x [pu] **nm** louse. ~ **du pubis** pubic louse, crab (louse)‡; **couvert de ~x** covered in lice, lice-ridden; *voir* **chercher, laid.**

pouah [pwa] **excl** ugh!, yuk!

poubelle [pubɛl] nf *[ordures]* (dust) bin (*Brit*), trash *ou* garbage can (*US*). **c'est bon à mettre à la ~** it's only fit for the dustbin (*Brit*) *ou* trash can (*US*).

pouce [pus] nm **a** (*Anat*) *[main]* thumb; *[pied]* big toe. **se tourner** *ou* **se rouler les ~s** to twiddle one's thumbs; **mettre les ~s*** to give in *ou* up; (*au jeu*) ~! pax! (*Brit*), truce!; **on a déjeuné** *ou* **on a pris un morceau sur le ~*** we had a quick snack *ou* a bite to eat*; (*Can* *) **faire du ~, voyager sur le ~** to thumb* a lift, hitch*, hitch-hike; **coup de ~** (*pour aider qn*) nudge in the right direction; **donner un coup de ~ aux ventes** to give sales a bit of a boost; **donner un coup de ~ à un projet** to help a project along.
b (*mesure, aussi Can*) inch. (*fig*) **il n'a pas avancé d'un ~** he refused to budge, he wouldn't budge an inch; **son travail n'a pas avancé d'un ~** his work hasn't progressed at all; **un ~ de terrain** a tiny plot of land; **et le ~!*** and a bit more besides!

Poucet [pusɛ] nm: **le Petit ~** Tom Thumb.

Pouchkine [puʃkin] nm Pushkin.

pouding [pudiŋ] nm = **pudding**.

poudingue [pudɛ̃g] nm (*Géol*) conglomerate.

poudre [pudʀ] **1** nf (*gén*) powder; (*poussière*) dust; (*fard*) (face) powder; (*explosif*) (gun) powder; (*Méd*) powder; (*arg Drogue: héroïne*) stuff*, smack‡, H (*arg*). **~ d'or/de diamant** gold/diamond dust; **réduire qch en ~** to reduce *ou* grind sth to powder, powder sth; **en ~** *lait, œufs* dried, powdered; *chocolat* drinking (*épith*); **se mettre de la ~** to powder one's face *ou* nose; **se mettre de la ~ sur** to powder; **~ libre/compacte** loose/pressed powder; **prendre la ~ d'escampette*** to take to one's heels, skedaddle*; **de la ~ de perlimpinpin** the universal remedy (*iro*), a magic cure-all; *voir* **feu**[1], **inventer, jeter.**
2 comp ▸**poudre à canon** gunpowder ▸**poudre dentifrice** tooth powder ▸**poudre à éternuer** sneezing powder ▸**poudre à laver** washing powder (*Brit*), soap powder ▸**poudre à récurer** scouring powder ▸**poudre de riz** face powder.

poudrer [pudʀe] [1] **1** vt to powder. **2** vi (*Can*) *[neige]* to drift. **3 se poudrer** vpr to powder one's face *ou* nose.

poudrerie [pudʀəʀi] nf gunpowder *ou* explosives factory; (*Can*) blizzard, drifting snow.

poudreux, -euse [pudʀø, øz] **1** adj (*poussiéreux*) dusty. **neige ~euse** powder snow; (*Can*) drifting snow. **2 poudreuse** nf powder snow.

poudrier [pudʀije] nm (powder) compact.

poudrière [pudʀijɛʀ] nf powder magazine; (*fig*) powder keg (*fig*).

poudroiement [pudʀwamɑ̃] nm dust haze.

poudroyer [pudʀwaje] [8] vi *[poussière]* to rise in clouds; *[neige]* to rise in a flurry. **la route poudroie** clouds of dust rise up from the road.

pouf [puf] **1** nm pouffe. **2** excl thud! **faire ~** to tumble (over).

pouffer [pufe] [1] vi: **~ (de rire)** to burst out laughing.

pouffiasse‡ [pufjas] nf (*péj*) (*grosse femme*) fat bag‡ *ou* broad‡ (*US*); (*femme que l'on déteste*) tart‡, slag‡ (*Brit*); (*prostituée*) whore (*péj*), tart‡.

pouh [pu] excl pooh!

pouillerie [pujʀi] nf squalor.

pouilleux, -euse [pujø, øz] **1** adj **a** (*lit*) lousy, flea-ridden, verminous. **b** (*fig: sordide*) *quartier, endroit* squalid, seedy, shabby; *personne* dirty, filthy. **2** nm, f (*pauvre*) down-and-out; (*couvert de poux*) flea-ridden *ou* lice-ridden *ou* verminous person.

pouillot [pujo] nm warbler. **~ fitis** willow warbler; **~ véloce** chiffchaff.

poujadisme [puʒadism] nm Poujadism.

poujadiste [puʒadist] adj, nmf Poujadist.

poulailler [pulɑje] nm henhouse. (*Théât*) **le ~*** the gods* (*Brit*), the gallery.

poulain [pulɛ̃] nm foal; (*fig*) promising young athlete (*ou* writer *ou* singer *etc*); (*protégé*) protégé.

poulaine [pulɛn] nf (*Hist: soulier*) poulaine, long pointed shoe.

poularde [pulaʀd] nf fatted chicken. (*Culin*) **~ demi-deuil** poularde demi-deuil.

poulbot [pulbo] nm street urchin (*in Montmartre*).

poule[1] [pul] **1** nf **a** (*Zool*) hen; (*Culin*) (boiling) fowl. (*fig*) **se lever avec les ~s** to get up with the lark (*Brit*) *ou* birds (*US*), be an early riser; **se coucher avec les ~s** to go to bed early; **quand les ~s auront des dents** when pigs can fly *ou* have wings; **être comme une ~ qui a trouvé un couteau** to be at a complete loss; *voir* **chair, cul, lait.**
b (‡) (*maîtresse*) mistress, bit on the side‡; (*fille*) bird* (*Brit*), broad‡ (*US*), chick*; (*prostituée*) whore, tart‡, hooker‡ (*US*). **ma ~** (my) pet.
2 comp ▸**poule d'eau** moorhen ▸**poule faisane** hen pheasant ▸**poule mouillée** softy*, coward ▸**la poule aux œufs d'or** the goose that lays the golden eggs ▸**poule pondeuse** laying hen, layer ▸**poule au pot** (*Culin*) boiled chicken; (*Hist*) **la poule au pot tous les dimanches** a chicken in the pot every Sunday ▸**poule au riz** chicken and rice.

poule[2] [pul] nf **a** (*enjeu*) pool, kitty. **b** (*tournoi*) (*gén*) tournament; (*Escrime*) pool; (*Rugby*) group.

poulet [pulɛ] nm (*Culin, Zool*) chicken; (‡: *flic*) cop‡; (††: *billet doux*) love letter. **~ de grain/fermier** corn-fed/free-range (*Brit*) chicken; (*fig*) **mon (petit) ~!*** (my) pet! *ou* love!

poulette [pulɛt] nf (*Zool*) pullet; (*: *fille*) girl, lass*, bird* (*Brit*), chick* (*US*). (*fig*) **ma ~!*** (my) pet! *ou* love!; (*Culin*) **sauce ~** sauce poulette.

pouliche [puliʃ] nf filly.

poulie [puli] nf pulley; (*avec sa caisse*) block. **~ simple/double/fixe** single/double/fixed block; **~ folle** loose pulley.

pouliner [puline] [1] vi to foal.

poulinière [pulinjɛʀ] adj f, nf: **(jument) ~** brood mare.

poulot, -otte†* [pulo, ɔt] nm, f: **mon ~!, ma ~te!** poppet!*, (my) pet! *ou* love! (*said to a child*).

poulpe [pulp] nm octopus.

pouls [pu] nm pulse. **prendre** *ou* **tâter le ~ de qn** (*lit*) to feel *ou* take sb's pulse; (*fig*) to sound sb (out); (*fig*) **prendre** *ou* **tâter le ~ de** *opinion publique* to test, sound out; *économie* to feel the pulse of.

poumon [pumɔ̃] nm lung. **respirer à pleins ~s** to breathe in deeply, take deep breaths; **chanter/crier à pleins ~s** to sing/shout at the top of one's voice; **avoir des ~s** *[chanteur, coureur]* to have a good pair of lungs; **~ artificiel/d'acier** artificial/iron lung.

poupard [pupaʀ] **1** adj (†) chubby(-cheeked). **2** nm bonny (*Brit*) baby, bouncing baby.

poupe [pup] nf (*Naut*) stern; *voir* **vent.**

poupée [pupe] nf **a** (*jouet*) doll, dolly*. **~(s) gigogne(s)** *ou* **russe(s)** nest of dolls, Russian dolls; **~ gonflable** inflatable doll; **elle joue à la ~** she's playing with her doll(s); *voir* **maison. b** (* *fig*) (*femme jolie ou pomponnée*) doll*; (*fille, maîtresse*) bird* (*Brit*), chick* (*US*). **bonjour, ~** hullo, sweetie*. **c** (*pansement*) finger bandage. **faire une ~ à qn** to bandage sb's finger.

poupin, e [pupɛ̃, in] adj chubby.

poupon [pupɔ̃] nm little baby, babe-in-arms.

pouponner [pupɔne] [1] vi to play mother. **tu vas bientôt (pouvoir) ~** soon you'll be fussing around like a fond mother (*ou* father *etc*).

pouponnière [pupɔnjɛʀ] nf day nursery, crèche.

pour [puʀ] **1** prép **a** (*direction*) for, to. **partir ~ l'Espagne** to leave for Spain; **il part ~ l'Espagne demain** he leaves for Spain *ou* he is off to Spain tomorrow; **partir ~ l'étranger** to go abroad; **le train ~ Londres** the London train, the train for London.
b (*temps*) for. **demander/promettre qch ~ le mois prochain/~ dans huit jours/~ après les vacances** to ask for/promise sth for next month/for next week/for after the holidays; **il lui faut sa voiture ~ demain** he must have his car for *ou* by tomorrow; **ne m'attendez pas, j'en ai encore ~ une heure** don't wait for me, I'll be another hour (yet); **~ le moment** *ou* **l'instant** for the moment; **~ toujours** for ever; (*iro*) **c'est ~ aujourd'hui ou ~ demain?** are we getting it *ou* is it coming today?, shall we have it this side of Christmas?; **ce sera ~ des jours meilleurs** we'll have to wait for better days; **garder le meilleur ~ la fin** to keep the best till last *ou* till the end.
c (*intention, destination*) for. **faire qch ~ qn** to do sth for sb; **il ferait tout ~ elle/sa mère** he would do anything for her/his mother *ou* for her sake/his mother's sake; **faire qch ~ la gloire/le plaisir** to do sth for the glory/for the pleasure of it *ou* for pleasure; **c'est fait ~** that's what it's meant *ou* made for; **son amour ~ les bêtes** his love of animals; **quêter ~ les hôpitaux** to collect for *ou* in aid of hospitals; **il travaille ~ un cabinet d'architectes** he works for a firm of architects; **ce n'est pas un livre ~ (les) enfants** it's not a book for children, it's not a children's book; **coiffeur ~ dames** ladies' hairdresser; **c'est mauvais/bon ~ vous/~ la santé** it's bad/good for you/for the health; **il a été très gentil ~ ma mère** he was very kind to my mother; **sirop ~ la toux** cough mixture (*Brit*) *ou* syrup (*US*); **pastilles ~ la gorge** throat tablets; **il n'est pas fait ~ le travail de bureau** he's not made for office work; **le plombier est venu/a téléphoné ~ la chaudière** the plumber came/phoned about the boiler; **~ le meilleur et ~ le pire** for better or for worse; **l'art ~ l'art** art for art's sake; *voir* **amour, craindre.**
d (*approbation*) for, in favour of. **être ~ la peine de mort** to be for *ou* in favour of the death penalty; **il est ~ protester** he's in favour of protesting, he's (all) for protesting*; **je suis ~!*** I'm all for it!*, I'm all in favour (of it)!; *voir* **voter.**
e (*point de vue*) **~ moi, le projet n'est pas réalisable** as I see it *ou* in my opinion *ou* in my view the plan cannot be carried out; **~ moi, je suis d'accord** personally *ou* for my part I agree; **ce n'est un secret ~ personne** it's no secret from anyone; **sa fille est tout ~ lui** his daughter is everything to him; **c'est trop compliqué ~ elle** it's too complicated for her.
f (*cause*) **être condamné ~ vol** to be convicted for theft; **il a été félicité ~ son audace** he was congratulated on his boldness; **fermé ~ cause de maladie** closed owing to *ou* because of *ou* on account of illness; **fermé ~ réparations** closed for repairs; **quelle histoire ~ si peu** what a fuss *ou* to-do* over *ou* about such a little thing; **il n'en est pas plus heureux ~ cela!** he is none the happier for all that!, he is no happier for all that!; **il est furieux et ~ cause!** he's furious and with good reason!; **pourquoi se faire du souci ~ cela?** why worry about that?; **il est ~ quelque chose/~ beaucoup dans le succès de la pièce** he is partly/largely responsible for the success of the play, he had something/a lot to do with the play's success; *voir* **beau, oui.**
g (*à la place de, en échange de*) **payer ~ qn** to pay for sb; **signez ~**

moi sign in my place *ou* for me; (*Comm etc*) **~ le directeur** p.p. Manager; **il a parlé ~ nous tous** he spoke on behalf of all of us *ou* on our behalf, he spoke for all of us; **en avoir ~ son argent** to have *ou* get one's money's worth; **donnez-moi ~ 200 F d'essence** give me 200 francs' worth of petrol; **il l'a eu ~ 5 F/une bouchée de pain** he got it for 5 francs/for a song; *voir* **chacun**.

h (*rapport, comparaison*) for. **~ cent/mille** per cent/thousand; **il est petit ~ son âge** he is small for his age; **il fait chaud ~ la saison** it's warm for the time of year; **~ un Anglais, il parle bien le français** he speaks French well for an Englishman; **~ un qui s'intéresse, il y en a 6 qui bâillent** for every one that takes an interest there are 6 (who are) yawning; **c'est mot ~ mot ce qu'il a déjà dit** it's word for word what he has already said; **jour/heure ~ jour/heure** to the (very) day/hour; **mourir ~ mourir, je préfère que ce soit ici** if I have to die I should prefer it to be here; *voir* **coup, œil**.

i (*rapport d'équivalence: comme*) for, as. **prendre qn ~ femme** to take sb as one's wife; **prendre qn ~ un imbécile** to take sb for an idiot; **il a ~ adjoint son cousin** he has his cousin as his deputy; **il passe ~ filou** he's said to be a crook; **il s'est fait passer ~ fou/~ son patron** he passed himself off as a madman/as his boss; **il a ~ principe/méthode de faire ...** it is his principle/method to do ..., his principle /method is to do ...; **cela a eu ~ effet de** that had the effect of; **~ de bon* *ou* de vrai*** truly, really, for real*; *voir* **compter, laisser**.

j (*emphatique*) **~ (ce qui est de) notre voyage, il faut y renoncer** as for our journey *ou* as far as our journey goes, we'll have to forget it, we'll have to give up all idea of going on that journey; **~ une malchance c'est une malchance!** of all the unfortunate things (to happen)!, that was unfortunate and no mistake!; **~ être furieux, je le suis!** talk about furious, I really am!*; **~ sûr†*** for sure *ou* certain.

k (+ *infin: but, succession*) to. **trouvez un argument ~ le convaincre** find an argument to convince him *ou* that will convince him; **il est d'accord ~ nous aider** he agrees *ou* he has agreed to help us; **nous avons assez d'argent ~ l'aider** we have enough money to help him; **~ mûrir, les tomates ont besoin de soleil** tomatoes need sunshine to ripen; **je n'ai rien dit ~ ne pas le blesser** I didn't say anything so as not to hurt him; **je n'ai rien dit ~ le blesser** I said nothing to hurt him; **creuser ~ trouver de l'eau/du pétrole** to dig for water/oil; **elle se pencha ~ ramasser son gant** she bent down to pick up her glove; **il étendit le bras ~ prendre la boîte** he reached for the box; **il finissait le soir tard ~ reprendre le travail tôt le lendemain** he used to finish work late at night only to start again early the next morning; **il y a des gens assez innocents ~ le croire** some people are unsuspecting enough to believe him; **le travail n'est pas ~ l'effrayer *ou* ~ lui faire peur** he's not afraid of hard work *ou* of working hard; **ce n'est pas ~ arranger les choses** this isn't going to help matters, this will only make things worse; **il a dit ça ~ rire *ou* ~ plaisanter** he said it in fun *ou* as a joke; **il est parti ~ ne plus revenir** he left never to return, he left and never came back again; **j'étais ~ partir*** I was just going, I was just about to go, I was on the point of leaving; *voir* **assez, trop**.

l (+ *infin: cause, concession*) **elle a été punie ~ avoir menti** she was punished for lying *ou* having lied; **~ avoir réussi, il n'en est pas plus riche** he's no richer *ou* none the richer for having succeeded *ou* for his success.

m ~ que + *subj* so that, in order that (*frm*); **écris vite ta lettre ~ qu'elle parte ce soir** write your letter quickly so (that) it will go *ou* it goes this evening; **il a mis une barrière ~ que les enfants ne sortent pas** he has put up a fence so that the children won't get out; **il est trop tard ~ qu'on le prévienne** it's too late to warn him *ou* for him to be warned; (*iro*) **c'est ça, laisse ton sac là ~ qu'on te le vole!** that's right, leave your bag there for someone to steal it! *ou* so that someone steals it!; **elle est assez grande ~ qu'on puisse la laisser seule** she is old enough (for her) to be left on her own.

n (*restriction, concession*) **~ riche qu'il soit, il n'est pas généreux** (as) rich as he is *ou* rich though he is, he's not generous; **~ peu qu'il soit sorti sans sa clef ...** if he should have come out without his key ...; **~ autant que je sache** as far as I know *ou* am aware, to the best of my knowledge.

2 nm: le ~ et le contre the arguments for and against, the pros and the cons; **il y a du ~ et du contre** there are arguments on both sides *ou* arguments for and against.

pourboire [puʀbwaʀ] **nm** tip. **~ interdit** no gratuities, our staff do not accept gratuities; **donner un ~ de 10 F à qn, donner 10 F de ~ à qn** to tip sb 10 francs, give sb a 10 francs tip.

pourceau, *pl* **~x** [puʀso] **nm** (*littér, péj*) pig, swine (*inv, littér*); *voir* **perle**.

pour-cent [puʀsɑ̃] **nm inv** (*commission*) percentage, cut*.

pourcentage [puʀsɑ̃taʒ] **nm** percentage; (*Comm*) percentage, cut*. **travailler au ~** to work on commission; **côte à fort ~** steep slope.

pourchasser [puʀʃase] [1] **vt** *[police, chasseur, ennemi]* to pursue, hunt down; *[créancier]* to hound, harry; *[importun]* to hound. **~ la misère/le crime** to hunt out *ou* seek out poverty/crime; **~ les fautes d'orthographe** to hunt out the spelling mistakes.

pourfendeur [puʀfɑ̃dœʀ] **nm** (*hum*) destroyer.

pourfendre [puʀfɑ̃dʀ] [41] **vt** (*littér*) *adversaire* to set about, assail; (*fig*) *abus* to fight against, combat.

pourlécher (se) [puʀleʃe] [6] **vpr** (*lit, fig*) to lick one's lips. **je m'en pourlèche déjà** (*lit*) my mouth is watering already; (*fig*) I can hardly wait; **se ~ les babines*** (*lit*) to lick one's chops*; (*fig*) to lick *ou* smack one's lips.

pourparlers [puʀpaʀle] **nmpl** talks, negotiations, discussions. **entrer en ~ avec** to start negotiations *ou* discussions with, enter into talks with; **être en ~ avec** to negotiate with, have talks *ou* discussions with.

pourpier [puʀpje] **nm** portulaca; (*comestible*) purslane.

pourpoint [puʀpwɛ̃] **nm** doublet, pourpoint.

pourpre [puʀpʀ] **1 adj** crimson. **il devint ~** (*furieux*) he went purple (in the face), he went *ou* turned crimson; (*gêné*) he turned crimson *ou* scarlet. **2 nm** (*couleur*) crimson. **le ~ de la honte** the crimson (colour) of shame; **~ rétinien** visual purple. **3 nf a** (*matière colorante, étoffe, symbole*) purple; (*couleur*) scarlet. **~ royale** royal purple; **accéder à la ~ cardinalice *ou* romaine** to be given the red hat; **né dans la ~** born in the purple. **b** (*Zool*) murex.

pourpré, e [puʀpʀe] **adj** (*littér*) crimson.

pourquoi [puʀkwa] **1 conj** why. **~ est-il venu?** why did he come?, what did he come for?; **~ les avoir oubliés?** why did he (*ou* they *etc*) forget them?; **c'est *ou* voilà ~ il n'est pas venu** that's (the reason) why he didn't come. **2 adv** why. **tu me le prêtes? — ~ (donc)?** can you lend me it? — why? *ou* what for?; **tu viens? — ~ pas?** are you coming? — why not? *ou* why shouldn't I?; **il a réussi, ~ pas vous?** (*dans le futur*) he succeeded so why shouldn't you?; (*dans le passé*) he succeeded so why didn't you? *ou* so how come you didn't?*; **je vais vous dire ~** I'll tell you why; **il faut que ça marche, ou que ça dise ~*** it had better work or else ...*, it had better work, or I'll want to know why (not); **allez savoir *ou* comprendre ~*, je vous demande bien ~** I didn't know why, I just can't imagine why!, don't ask me!, search me!* **3 nm inv** (*raison*) reason (*de* for); (*question*) question. **le ~ de son attitude** the reason for his attitude; **il veut toujours savoir le ~ et le comment** he always wants to know the whys and wherefores; **il est difficile de répondre à tous les ~ des enfants** it isn't easy to find an answer for everything children ask you.

pourri, e [puʀi] (**ptp de pourrir**) **1 adj a** *fruit* rotten, bad, spoilt; *bois* rotten; *feuille* decayed, rotting; *viande* bad; *œuf* rotten, addled, bad; *enfant* thoroughly spoilt; *cadavre* decomposed, putrefied. **être ~** *[pomme]* to have gone rotten *ou* bad; *[œuf]* to have gone bad; *voir* **poisson**.

b *roche* crumbling, rotten; *neige* melting, half-melted.

c (*mauvais*) *temps, été* wet, rainy; *personne, société* rotten, corrupt. **flic ~‡** bent copper* (*Brit*), dirty *ou* bad cop* (*US*); **~ de fric‡** stinking‡ *ou* filthy‡ rich, lousy with money‡; **~ de défauts** full of *ou* riddled with faults; **~ de talent*** oozing with talent.

2 nm a enlever le ~ (*d'un fruit etc*) to take out the rotten *ou* bad part; **sentir le ~** to smell rotten *ou* bad.

b (‡: *crapule*) swine‡, sod‡* (*Brit*). **bande de ~s!** (you) bastards!‡, (you) lousy sods!‡* (*Brit*).

c (‡: *policier corrompu*) bent copper* (*Brit*), dirty *ou* bad cop* (*US*).

pourrir [puʀiʀ] [2] **1 vi** *[fruit]* to go rotten *ou* bad, spoil; *[bois]* to rot (away); *[œuf]* to go bad; *[cadavre]* to rot away; *[corps, membre]* to be eaten away; *[relations]* to deteriorate. **récolte qui pourrit sur pied** harvest which is rotting on the stalk; (*fig*) **~ dans la misère** to languish in poverty; **~ en prison** to rot (away) in prison; **laisser ~ la situation** to let the situation deteriorate *ou* get worse; **laisser ~ une grève** to let a strike drag on.

2 vt a *fruit* to make rotten, rot, spoil; *bois* to make rotten, rot; (*infecter*) *corps* to eat away (at).

b (*fig*) (*gâter*) *enfant* to spoil through and through, ruin; (*corrompre*) *personne* to corrupt, spoil. **les ennuis qui pourrissent notre vie** the worries which spoil our lives.

3 se pourrir vpr *[fruit]* to go rotten *ou* bad, spoil; *[bois]* to rot (away); *[relations, situation]* to deteriorate, get worse.

pourrissement [puʀismɑ̃] **nm** *[situation]* deterioration, worsening (*de* in, of).

pourriture [puʀityʀ] **nf a** (*lit, Agr*) rot; *[société]* rottenness. **odeur de ~** putrid smell. **b** (*péj: personne*) louse*, swine‡.

pour-soi [puʀswa] **nm** (*Philos*) pour-soi.

poursuite [puʀsɥit] **nf a** *[voleur, animal]* chase (*de* after), pursuit (*de* of); (*fig*) *[bonheur, gloire]* pursuit (*de* of). **se mettre *ou* se lancer à la ~ de qn** to chase *ou* run after sb, go in pursuit of sb. **b** (*Jur*) **~s (judiciaires)** legal proceedings; **engager des ~s contre** to start legal proceedings against, take legal action against; **s'exposer à des ~s** to lay o.s. open to *ou* run the risk of prosecution. **c** (*continuation*) continuation. **ils ont voté/décidé la ~ de la grève** they voted/decided to continue the strike. **d (course) ~** (*Sport*) track race; (*Police*) chase, pursuit; **~ individuelle** individual pursuit.

poursuiteur [puʀsɥitœʀ] **nm** track rider, track cyclist.

poursuivant, e [puʀsɥivɑ̃, ɑ̃t] **1 adj** (*Jur*) **partie ~e** plaintiff. **2 nm, f** (*ennemi*) pursuer; (*Jur*) plaintiff.

poursuivre [puʀsɥivʀ] [40] **1 vt a** (*courir après*) *fugitif, ennemi* to pursue; *animal* to chase (after), hunt down, pursue; *malfaiteur* to chase (after), pursue. **un enfant poursuivi par un chien** a child (being) chased *ou* pursued by a dog; **les motards poursuivaient la voiture** the police motorcyclists were chasing the car *ou* were in pursuit of the car.

b (*harceler*) *[importun, souvenir]* to hound. **être poursuivi par ses créanciers** to be hounded *ou* harried by one's creditors; ~ **qn de sa colère/de sa haine** to hound sb through anger/hatred; ~ **une femme de ses assiduités** to force one's attentions on a woman; **cette idée le poursuit** he can't get this idea out of his mind, he's haunted by this idea; **les photographes ont poursuivi l'actrice jusque chez elle** the photographers followed the actress all the way home.

c (*chercher à atteindre*) *fortune, gloire* to seek (after); *vérité* to pursue, seek (after); *rêve* to pursue, follow; *but, idéal* to strive towards, pursue.

d (*continuer*) (*gén*) to continue, go *ou* carry on with; *avantage* to follow up, pursue. ~ **sa marche** to keep going, walk on, carry on walking, continue on one's way.

e (*Jur*) ~ **qn (en justice)** (*au criminel*) to prosecute sb, bring proceedings against sb; (*au civil*) to sue sb, bring proceedings against sb; **être poursuivi pour vol** to be prosecuted for theft.

2 vi a (*continuer*) to carry on, go on, continue. **poursuivez, cela m'intéresse** go on *ou* tell me more, it interests me; **puis il poursuivit: voici pourquoi ...** then he went on *ou* continued: that's why ... .

b (*persévérer*) to keep at it, keep it up.

3 **se poursuivre** vpr *[négociations, débats]* to go on, continue; *[enquête, recherches, travail]* to be going on, be carried out. **les débats se sont poursuivis jusqu'au matin** discussions went on *ou* continued until morning.

pourtant [puʀtɑ̃] adv (*néanmoins, en dépit de cela*) yet, nevertheless, all the same, even so; (*cependant*) (and) yet. **et** ~ and yet, but nevertheless; **frêle mais** ~ **résistant** frail but nevertheless *ou* but even so *ou* but all the same *ou* (and *ou* but) yet resilient; **il faut** ~ **le faire** it's got to be done all the same *ou* even so *ou* nevertheless, (and) yet it's got to be done; **il n'est** ~ **pas très intelligent** (and) yet he's not very clever, he's not very clever though; (*intensif*) **c'est** ~ **facile!** but it's easy!, but it's not difficult!; **on lui a** ~ **dit de faire attention** (and) yet we told him *ou* did tell him to be careful.

pourtour [puʀtuʀ] nm *[cercle]* circumference; *[rectangle]* perimeter; (*bord*) surround. **sur le** ~ **de** around, on the sides of.

pourvoi [puʀvwa] nm (*Jur*) appeal. ~ **en grâce** appeal for clemency; **former un** ~ **en cassation** to (lodge an) appeal.

pourvoir [puʀvwaʀ] 25 1 vt a ~ **qn de qch** to provide *ou* equip *ou* supply sb with sth, provide sth for sb; ~ **un enfant de vêtements chauds** to provide a child with warm clothes, provide warm clothes for a child; **la nature l'a pourvu d'une grande intelligence** nature has endowed him with great intelligence, he is gifted with great natural intelligence; **la nature l'a pourvue d'une grande beauté** she is graced with great natural beauty; ~ **sa maison de tout le confort moderne** to fit one's house out *ou* equip one's house with all modern conveniences; ~ **sa cave de vin** to stock one's cellar with wine; *voir* **pourvu**[1].

b *poste* to fill. **il y a 2 postes à** ~ there are 2 posts to fill.

2 **pourvoir à** vt indir *éventualité* to provide for, cater for; *emploi* to fill. ~ **aux besoins de qn** to provide for *ou* cater for *ou* supply sb's needs; ~ **à l'entretien du ménage** to provide for the upkeep of the household; **j'y pourvoirai** I'll see to it *ou* deal with it.

3 **se pourvoir** vpr a **se** ~ **de** *argent, vêtements* to provide o.s. with; *provisions, munitions* to provide o.s. with, equip o.s. with, supply o.s. with.

b (*Jur*) to appeal, lodge an appeal. **se** ~ **en appel** to take one's case to the Court of Appeal; **se** ~ **en cassation** to (lodge an) appeal.

pourvoyeur, -euse [puʀvwajœʀ, øz] 1 nm, f supplier, purveyor; *[drogue]* supplier, pusher*. 2 nm (*Mil: servant de pièce*) artilleryman.

pourvu[1]**, e** [puʀvy] (ptp de **pourvoir**) adj a *[personne]* **être** ~ **de** *intelligence, imagination* to be gifted with, be endowed with; *beauté* to be endowed with, be graced with; **avec ces provisions nous voilà** ~**s pour l'hiver** with these provisions we're stocked up *ou* well provided for for the winter; **nous sommes très bien/très mal** ~**s en commerçants** we're very well-off/very badly off for shops, we're very well/very badly provided with shops; **après l'héritage qu'il a fait c'est quelqu'un de bien** ~ with the inheritance he's received, he's very well-off *ou* very well provided for.

b *[chose]* **être** ~ **de** to be equipped *ou* fitted with; **feuille de papier** ~**e d'une marge** sheet of paper with a margin; **animal (qui est)** ~ **d'écailles** animal which has scales *ou* which is equipped with scales.

pourvu[2] [puʀvy] conj: ~ **que** (*souhait*) let's hope; (*condition*) provided (that), so long as; ~ **que ça dure!** let's hope it lasts!, here's hoping it lasts!*

poussa(h) [pusa] nm (*jouet*) tumbler; (*péj: homme*) potbellied man.

pousse [pus] nf a (*bourgeon*) shoot. ~**s de bambou** bamboo shoots; **la plante fait des** ~**s** the plant is growing shoots. b (*action*) *[feuilles]* sprouting; *[dents, cheveux]* growth.

poussé, e[1] [puse] (ptp de **pousser**) 1 adj *études* advanced; *enquête* extensive, exhaustive; *interrogatoire* intensive; *moteur* souped-up. **très** ~ *organisation, technique, dessin* elaborate; *précision* high-level (*épith*), advanced; **il n'a pas eu une formation/éducation très** ~**e** he hasn't had much training/education; **une plaisanterie un peu** ~**e** a joke which goes a bit too far. 2 nm (*Mus*) up-bow.

pousse-au-crime* [pusokʀim] nm inv (*boisson*) firewater*. (*fig*) **c'est du** ~! it's an invitation!

pousse-café* [puskafe] nm inv liqueur.

poussée[2] [puse] nf a (*pression*) *[foule]* pressure, pushing, shoving; (*Archit, Géol, Phys*) thrust (*NonC*). **sous la** ~ under the pressure. b (*coup*) push, shove; *[ennemi]* thrust. **écarter qn d'une** ~ to thrust *ou* push *ou* shove sb aside; **enfoncer une porte d'une** ~ **violente** to break a door down with a violent heave *ou* shove. c (*éruption*) *[acné]* attack, eruption; *[prix]* rise, upsurge, increase. ~ **de fièvre** (sudden) high temperature; **la** ~ **de la gauche/droite aux élections** the upsurge of the left/right in the elections; **la** ~ **révolutionnaire de 1789** the revolutionary upsurge of 1789.

pousse-pousse [puspus] nm inv rickshaw.

pousser [puse] 1 1 vt a (*gén*) *charrette, meuble, personne* to push; *brouette, landau* to push, wheel; *verrou* (*ouvrir*) to slide, push back; (*fermer*) to slide, push to *ou* home; *objet gênant* to move, shift, push aside. ~ **une chaise contre le mur/près de la fenêtre/dehors** to push a chair (up) against the wall/(over) near the window/outside; ~ **les gens vers la porte** to push the people towards *ou* to the door; **il me poussa du genou/du coude** he nudged me with his knee/(with his elbow); ~ **un animal devant soi** to drive an animal (in front of one); ~ **l'aiguille** to sew; ~ **la porte/la fenêtre** (*fermer*) to push the door/window to *ou* shut; (*ouvrir*) to push the door/window open; ~ **un caillou du pied** to kick a stone (along); **le vent nous poussait vers la côte** the wind was blowing *ou* pushing us towards the shore; **le courant poussait le bateau vers les rochers** the current was carrying the boat towards the rocks; (*balançoire*) **peux-tu me** ~? can you give me a push?; **peux-tu** ~ **ta voiture?** can you move *ou* shift your car (out of the way)?; **pousse tes fesses!**⁑ shift your backside!⁑, shove over!⁑; **(ne) poussez pas, il y a des enfants!** don't push *ou* stop pushing, there are children here!; **il m'a poussé** he pushed *ou* jostled me; (*fig*) **faut pas** ~ **(grand-mère dans les orties)!**⁑ that *ou* this is going a bit far!, you (*ou* he) must be kidding!⁑; (*fig*) ~ **un peu loin le bouchon** to push it*, go a bit far; **ne pousse pas le bouchon trop loin** don't push it*, don't push your luck; *voir* **pointe**.

b (*stimuler*) *élève, ouvrier* to urge on, egg on, push; *cheval* to ride hard, push; *moteur* (*techniquement*) to soup up, hot up, hop up (*US*); (*en accélérant*) to flog* (*surtout Brit*), drive hard; *voiture* to drive hard *ou* fast; *machine* to work hard; *feu* to stoke up; *chauffage* to turn up; (*mettre en valeur*) *candidat, protégé* to push; *dossier* to help along. **c'est l'ambition qui le pousse** he is driven by ambition, it's ambition which drives him on; **dans ce lycée on pousse trop les élèves** the pupils are worked *ou* driven *ou* pushed too hard in this school; **ce prof l'a beaucoup poussé en maths** this teacher has really pushed him *ou* made him get on in maths.

c ~ **qn à faire qch** *[faim, curiosité]* to drive sb to do sth; *[personne]* (*inciter*) to urge *ou* press sb to do sth; (*persuader*) to persuade *ou* induce sb to do sth, talk sb into doing sth; **ses parents le poussent à entrer à l'université/vers une carrière médicale** his parents are urging *ou* encouraging *ou* pushing him to go to university/to take up a career in medicine; **c'est elle qui l'a poussé à acheter cette maison** she talked him into *ou* pushed him into buying this house, she induced him to buy this house; **son échec nous pousse à croire que ...** his failure leads us to think that ..., because of his failure we're tempted to think that ...; ~ **qn au crime/au désespoir** to drive sb to crime/to despair; ~ **qn à la consommation** to encourage sb to buy (*ou* eat *ou* drink *etc*) more than he wants; ~ **qn à la dépense** to encourage sb to spend (more) money, drive sb into spending (more) money; **le sentiment qui le poussait vers sa bien-aimée** the feeling which drove him to his beloved; ~ **qn sur un sujet** to get sb onto a subject.

d (*poursuivre*) *études, discussion* to continue, carry on (with), go *ou* press on with; *avantage* to press (home), follow up; *affaire* to follow up, pursue; *marche, progression* to continue, carry on with. ~ **l'enquête/les recherches plus loin** to carry on *ou* press on with the inquiry/research; ~ **la curiosité/la plaisanterie un peu (trop) loin** to carry *ou* take curiosity/the joke a bit (too) far; ~ **les choses au noir** always to look on the black side, always take a black view of things; ~ **qch à la perfection** to carry *ou* bring sth to perfection; **il a poussé le dévouement/la gentillesse/la malhonnêteté jusqu'à faire** he was devoted/kind/dishonest enough to do, his devotion/kindness/dishonesty was such that he did; ~ **l'indulgence jusqu'à la faiblesse** to carry indulgence to the point of weakness; ~ **qn dans ses derniers retranchements** to get sb up against a wall *ou* with his back to the wall; ~ **qn à bout** to push sb to breaking point, drive sb to his wits' end *ou* the limit.

e *cri, hurlement* to let out, utter, give; *soupir* to heave, give. ~ **des cris** to shout, scream; ~ **des rugissements** to roar; **les enfants poussaient des cris perçants** the children were shrieking; **le chien poussait de petits jappements plaintifs** the dog was yelping pitifully; **pousser des cris d'orfraie** to cry out in fear (*ou* in indignation *etc*); ~ **une gueulante**⁑ (*douleur*) to be screaming with pain; (*colère*) to be shouting and bawling (with anger); (*hum*) ~ **la chansonnette** *ou* **sa chanson** *ou* **la romance, en** ~ **une*** to sing a song.

2 vi a (*grandir*) *[barbe, enfant]* to grow; *[dent]* to come through;

[ville] to grow, expand; *[plante]* (*sortir de terre*) to sprout; (*se développer*) to grow. *[enfant]* ~ **bien** *ou* **comme un champignon** to be growing well, be shooting up; **alors, les enfants, ça pousse?** and how are the kids doing?*; **mes choux poussent bien** my cabbages are coming on *ou* doing nicely *ou* well; **tout pousse bien dans cette région** everything grows well in this region; **ils font ~ des tomates par ici** they grow tomatoes in these parts, this is a tomato-growing area; **la pluie fait ~ les mauvaises herbes** the rain makes the weeds grow; **ça pousse comme du chiendent** they grow like weeds; **il se fait** *ou* **se laisse ~ la barbe** he's growing a beard; **il se fait** *ou* **se laisse ~ les cheveux** he's letting his hair grow; **il a une dent qui pousse** he's cutting a tooth, he's got a tooth coming through; **de nouvelles villes poussaient comme des champignons** new towns were springing up *ou* sprouting like mushrooms, new towns were mushrooming.

b (*faire un effort*) (*pour accoucher, aller à la selle*) to push. (*fig*) ~ **à la roue** to do a bit of pushing, push a bit; ~ **(à la roue) pour que qn fasse qch** to keep nudging *ou* pushing sb to get him to do sth; (*Fin*) ~ **à la hausse** to push prices up; (*Fin*) ~ **à la baisse** to force prices down.

c (*aller*) **nous allons ~ un peu plus avant** we're going to go on *ou* push on a bit further; ~ **jusqu'à Lyon** to go on *ou* push on as far as *ou* carry on to Lyons; **l'ennemi poussait droit sur nous** the enemy was coming straight for *ou* towards us.

d (‡: *exagérer*) to go too far, overdo it. **tu pousses!** that's going a bit far!; **faut pas ~!** that *ou* this is going a bit far!, that *ou* this is overdoing it a bit!

3 **se pousser** vpr (*se déplacer*) to move, shift; (*faire de la place*) to move *ou* shift over (*ou* up *ou* along *ou* down); (*en voiture*) to move. (*fig*) **se ~ (dans la société)** to make one's way *ou* push o.s. up in society *ou* in the world.

poussette [pusɛt] nf push chair. **~-canne** baby buggy, (folding) stroller (*US*).

poussier [pusje] nm coaldust, screenings (*SPÉC*).

poussière [pusjɛʀ] nf dust. ~ **de charbon** coaldust; ~ **d'étoiles** stardust; ~ **d'or** gold dust; **faire** *ou* **soulever de la ~** to raise a dust; **couvert de ~** dusty, covered in dust; **avoir une ~ dans l'œil** to have a speck of dust in one's eye; (*frm*) **leur ~ repose dans ces tombes** their ashes *ou* mortal remains lie in these tombs; (*fig*) **3 F et des ~s*** just over 3 francs, 3 and a bit francs*; (*fig*) **une ~ de** a myriad of; ~ **radioactive** radioactive particles *ou* dust (*NonC*); ~ **volcanique** volcanic ash (*NonC*) *ou* dust (*NonC*); **réduire/tomber en ~** to reduce to/crumble into dust.

poussiéreux, -euse [pusjeʀø, øz] adj (*lit*) dusty; (*fig*) fusty.

poussif, -ive [pusif, iv] adj *personne* wheezy, short-winded; *cheval* broken-winded; *moteur* puffing, wheezing; *style* flabby, tame.

poussin [pusɛ̃] nm a (*Zool*) chick. (*fig*) **mon ~!*** pet!, poppet!* b (*Sport*) under eleven, junior. c (*arg Mil*) *first-year cadet in the air force*.

poussivement [pusivmɑ̃] adv: **il monta ~ la côte/l'escalier** he wheezed up *ou* puffed up the hill/the stairs.

poussoir [puswaʀ] nm *[sonnette]* button. (*Aut*) ~ **(de soupape)** tappet.

poutre [putʀ] nf (*en bois*) beam; (*en métal*) girder; (*Gym*) beam. **~s apparentes** exposed beams; *voir* **paille**.

poutrelle [putʀɛl] nf girder.

pouvoir¹ [puvwaʀ] 33 1 vb aux a (*permission*) can, may (*frm*), to be allowed to. **il ne peut pas venir** he can't *ou* cannot *ou* may not (*frm*) come, he isn't allowed to come; **peut-il/ne peut-il pas venir?** can he/can't he come?, may he/may he not come? (*frm*); **il peut ne pas venir** he doesn't have to come, he's not bound to come; **il pourra venir** he will be able *ou* allowed to come; **il pourrait venir s'il nous prévenait** he could come *ou* he would be able *ou* allowed to come if he notified us; **il pouvait venir, il a pu venir** he could come, he was allowed *ou* able to come; **il aurait pu venir** he could have come, he would have been allowed *ou* able to come; **s'il avait pu venir** if he could have come, if he had been allowed *ou* able to come; **les élèves peuvent se promener le dimanche** the pupils may *ou* can go *ou* are allowed to go for walks on Sundays; **maintenant, tu peux aller jouer** now you can *ou* may go and play; **est-ce qu'on peut fermer la fenêtre?** may *ou* can we *ou* do you mind if we shut the window?; **on ne peut pas laisser ces enfants seuls** we can't leave these children on their own; **dans la famille victorienne, on ne pouvait pas jouer du piano le dimanche** in Victorian families, you weren't allowed to *ou* could not play the piano on Sundays.

b (*possibilité*) can, to be able to; (*: *réussir*) to manage to. **il ne peut pas venir** he can't come, he isn't able to *ou* is unable to come; **peut-il venir?** can he *ou* is he able to come?; **ne peut-il pas venir?** can't he *ou* isn't he able to *ou* is he unable to come?; **il ne peut pas ne pas venir** he can't not come, he has to *ou* he must come; (*littér*) **je puis venir** I can come; **il aurait pu venir** he could have come, he would have been able to come; **s'il avait pu venir** if he could have come, if he had been able to come; **il n'a (pas) pu** *ou* (*littér*) **ne put venir** he couldn't *ou* wasn't able to *ou* was unable to come; **il ne peut pas s'empêcher de tousser** he can't help coughing; **peut-il marcher sans canne?** can he (manage to) walk *ou* is he able to walk without a stick?; **il peut bien faire cela** that's the least he can do; **venez si vous pouvez/dès que vous pourrez** come if/as soon as you can (manage) *ou* are able; **puis-je vous être utile?** can I be of any help (to you)?, can *ou* may I be of assistance?; **la salle peut contenir 100 personnes** the room can seat *ou* hold 100 people *ou* has a seating capacity of 100; **comme il pouvait comprendre la fiche technique, il a pu réparer le poste** since he could understand the technical information he was able to *ou* he managed to repair the set; **il ne pourra jamais plus marcher** he will never be able to walk again; **il pourrait venir demain si vous aviez besoin de lui** he could come tomorrow if you needed him; **pourriez-vous nous apporter du thé?** could you bring us some tea?

c (*éventualité*) **il peut être français** he may *ou* might *ou* could be French; **il ne peut pas être français** he can't be French; **peut-il être français?** could *ou* might he be French?; **ne peut-il pas être français?** couldn't *ou* mightn't he *ou* may he not (*frm*) be French?; **il peut ne pas être français** he may *ou* might not be French; **il ne peut pas ne pas être français** he must be French; **il pourrait être français** he might *ou* could be French; **il aurait pu être français** he might *ou* could have been French; **quel âge peut-il (bien) avoir?** (just) how old might he be?; **l'émeute peut éclater d'un moment à l'autre** rioting may *ou* might *ou* could break out any minute; **qu'est-ce que cela peut bien lui faire?*** what's that (got) to do with him?*; **il peut être très méchant, parfois** he can be very nasty at times; **où ai-je bien pu mettre mon stylo?** where on earth can I have put my pen?; **vous pourrez en avoir besoin** you may *ou* might need it; **les cambrioleurs ont pu entrer par la fenêtre** the burglars could *ou* may *ou* might have got in through the window; **il a très bien pu entrer sans qu'on le voie** he may very well *ou* he could easily have come in unseen; **songez un peu à ce qui pourrait arriver** just imagine what might *ou* could happen; **cela pourrait se faire** that might *ou* could be arranged; **ceci pourrait bien constituer une des questions les plus importantes** this is potentially one of the key issues, this could well be one of the most important issues.

d (*suggestion*) might, could. **elle pourrait arriver à l'heure!** she might *ou* could (at least) be punctual!; **il aurait pu me dire cela plus tôt!** he might *ou* could have told me sooner!; **vous pouvez bien lui prêter votre livre** you can lend him your book, can't you?, surely you can lend him your book!

e (*littér: souhait*) **puisse Dieu/le ciel les aider!** may God/Heaven help them!; **puisse-t-il guérir rapidement!** would to God (*littér*) *ou* let us hope he recovers soon!, may he soon recover (*littér*); **puissiez-vous dire vrai!** let us pray *ou* hope you're right!

2 vb impers may, might, could, to be possible. **il peut** *ou* **pourrait pleuvoir** it may *ou* might *ou* could rain, it is possible that it will rain; **il pourrait y avoir du monde** there may *ou* might *ou* could be a lot of people there; **il aurait pu y avoir un accident!** there could *ou* might have been an accident!; **il pourrait se faire qu'elle ne soit pas chez elle** she may *ou* might well not be at home, it may *ou* might well be that she isn't at home.

3 vt a can, to be able to. **est-ce qu'on peut quelque chose pour lui?** is there anything we can do for him?; **il partira dès qu'il le pourra** he will leave as soon as he can *ou* is able (to); **il fait ce qu'il peut** he does what he can, he does the best he can; **il a fait tout ce qu'il a pu** he did all he could *ou* all that was in his power; **il peut beaucoup** he's very capable; (*frm*) **que puis-je pour vous?** what can I do for you?, can I do anything to assist you?; **personne ne peut rien sur lui** he won't listen to anyone, no one has any hold on him.

b (+ *adj ou adv compar*) **il a été on ne peut plus aimable/compréhensif/impoli** he couldn't have been kinder/more understanding/ruder, he was as kind/understanding/rude as it's possible to be; **elle le connaît on ne peut mieux** she knows him as well as it's possible to know anyone, no one knows him better than she does; **ils sont on ne peut plus mal avec leurs voisins** they couldn't (possibly) be on worse terms with their neighbours, they're on the worst possible terms with their neighbours.

c (*loc*) **je n'en peux plus** I can't stand it any longer; **je n'en peux plus d'attendre** I can wait no longer, I can't stand the strain of waiting any longer; **il n'en peut plus** (*fatigué*) he's all-in* *ou* tired out; (*à bout de nerfs*) he can't go on, he's had enough, he can't take any more; **je n'en peux plus de fatigue** I'm all-in* *ou* tired out *ou* worn out; (*littér*) **il n'en pouvait mais** there was nothing he could do about it, he could do nothing about it; **qu'y pouvons-nous? — on n'y peut rien** what can we do about it? — there's nothing we can do (about it); **je m'excuse, mais je n'y peux rien** I'm sorry, but it can't be helped *ou* there's nothing I can do *ou* there's nothing to be done.

4 **se pouvoir** vpr: **il se peut/se pourrait qu'elle vienne** she may *ou* could/might *ou* could (well) come; **se peut-il que ...?** is it possible that ...?, could *ou* might it be that ...?; **il se peut, éventuellement, que ...** it may possibly be that ...; **cela se pourrait bien** that's quite possible, that may *ou* could well be, that's a clear possibility; **ça se peut*** possibly, perhaps, maybe, could be*; **ça ne se peut pas*** that's impossible, that's not possible, that can't be so; *voir* **autant**.

pouvoir² [puvwaʀ] 1 nm a (*faculté*) (*gén*) power; (*capacité*) ability, capacity; (*Phys, gén: propriété*) power. **avoir le ~ de faire** to have the power *ou* ability to do; **il a le ~ de se faire des amis partout** he has the ability *ou* he is able to make friends everywhere; **il a un extraordinaire ~ d'éloquence/de conviction** he has remarkable *ou* exceptional powers of oratory/persuasion; **ce n'est pas en mon ~** it is not within *ou* in my power, it is beyond my power; **il n'est pas en son ~ de vous aider** it is beyond *ou* it does not lie within his power to help you; **il fera tout ce qui est en son ~** he will do everything (that is) in his power *ou* all that he possibly can; **~ couvrant/éclairant** covering/lighting power; **~ absorbant** absorption power, absorption factor (*SPÉC*).

b (*autorité*) power; (*influence*) influence. **avoir beaucoup de ~** to have a lot of power *ou* influence, be very powerful *ou* influential; **avoir du ~ sur qn** to have influence *ou* power over sb, exert an influence over sb; **le père a ~ sur ses enfants** a father has power over his children; **tenir qn en son ~** to hold sb in one's power; **le pays entier est en son ~** the whole country is in his power, he has the whole country in his power; **avoir du ~ sur soi-même** to have self-control.

c (*droit, attribution*) power. **dépasser ses ~s** to exceed one's powers; **en vertu des ~s qui me sont conférés** by virtue of the power which has been vested in me; **séparation des ~s** division of powers; **avoir ~ de faire** (*autorisation*) to have authority to do; (*droit*) to have the right to do; **je n'ai pas ~ pour vous répondre** I have no authority to reply to you; *voir* **plein**.

d (*Pol*) **le ~** (*direction des pays*) power; (*dirigeants*) the government; **le parti (politique) au ~** the (political) party in power *ou* in office, the ruling party; **avoir le ~** to have *ou* hold power; **exercer le ~** to exercise power, rule, govern; **prendre le ~** (*légalement*) to come to power *ou* into office; (*illégalement*) to seize power; **des milieux proches du ~** sources close to the government; **le ~ actuel, dans ce pays** the present régime, in this country; **l'opinion et le ~** public opinion and the authorities, us and them*.

e (*Jur: procuration*) proxy. **~ par-devant notaire** power of attorney; **donner ~ à qn de faire** to give sb proxy to do (*Jur*), empower sb to do, give sb authority to do.

2 comp ►**pouvoir d'achat** purchasing power ►**pouvoir de concentration** powers of concentration ►**pouvoirs constitués** powers that be ►**pouvoir de décision** decision-making power(s) ►**pouvoir disciplinaire** disciplinary power(s) ►**pouvoirs exceptionnels** emergency powers ►**pouvoir exécutif** executive power ►**pouvoir judiciaire** judiciary, judicial power ►**pouvoir législatif** legislative power ►**pouvoirs publics** authorities ►**pouvoir spirituel** spiritual power ►**pouvoir temporel** temporal power.

pp. (**abrév de pages**) pp.

p.p. (**abrév de per procurationem**) p.p.

ppcm (**abrév de plus petit commun multiple**) LCM; *voir* **plus 6**.

PQ [peky] 1 **abrév de Province de Québec**. 2 **nm**(‡) bog paper‡ (*Brit*), loo paper* (*Brit*), TP* (*US*).

PR [peɛʀ] 1 **nm** (**abrév de parti républicain**) *French political party*. 2 **nf** (**abrév de poste restante**) *voir* **poste**.

Pr. (**abrév de professeur**) Prof.

praesidium [pʀezidjɔm] **nm** praesidium. **le ~ suprême** the praesidium of the Supreme Soviet.

pragmatique [pʀagmatik] 1 **adj** pragmatic. 2 **nf** pragmatics (*sg*).

pragmatisme [pʀagmatism] **nm** pragmatism.

pragmatiste [pʀagmatist] 1 **adj** pragmatic, pragmatist. 2 **nmf** pragmatist.

Prague [pʀag] **n** Prague.

Praia [pʀaja] **n** Praia.

praire [pʀɛʀ] **nf** clam.

prairial [pʀɛʀjal] **nm** Prairial, *9th month of French Republican calendar*.

prairie [pʀeʀi] **nf** meadow. (*aux USA*) **la ~** the prairie; **des hectares de ~** acres of grassland.

pralin [pʀalɛ̃] **nm** praline (*filling for chocolates*).

praline [pʀalin] **nf** (*bonbon*) praline, sugared almond; (*Belgique: chocolat*) chocolate.

praliné, e [pʀaline] 1 **adj** *amande* sugared; *glace, crème* praline-flavoured. 2 **nm** praline-flavoured ice cream.

prame [pʀam] **nf** (*Naut*) pram, praam.

praséodyme [pʀazeɔdim] **nm** praseodymium.

praticable [pʀatikabl] 1 **adj** a *projet, moyen, opération* practicable, feasible; *chemin* passable, negotiable, practicable. **route difficilement ~ en hiver** road which is almost impassable in winter. b (*Théât*) *porte, décor* practicable. 2 **nm** (*Théât: décor*) practicable scenery; (*Ciné: plate-forme*) gantry; (*Sport*) large surface gymnastics mat.

praticien, -ienne [pʀatisjɛ̃, jɛn] **nm, f** (*gén, Méd*) practitioner.

pratiquant, e [pʀatikɑ̃, ɑ̃t] 1 **adj** practising (*épith*). **il est très/peu ~** he goes to *ou* attends church regularly/infrequently, he's a regular/an infrequent attender at church *ou* churchgoer. 2 **nm, f** (regular) churchgoer, practising Christian (*ou* Catholic *etc*); (*adepte*) follower. **cette religion compte 30 millions de ~s** this faith has 30 million followers *ou* 30 million faithful.

pratique [pʀatik] 1 **adj** a (*non théorique*) *jugement, philosophe, connaissance* practical; (*Scol*) *exercice, cours* practical. **considération d'ordre ~** practical consideration; *voir* **travail**[1].

b (*réaliste*) *personne* practical(-minded). **il faut être ~ dans la vie** you have to be practical in life; **avoir le sens ~** to be practical-minded; **avoir l'esprit ~** to have a practical turn of mind.

c (*commode*) *livre, moyen, vêtement, solution* practical; *instrument* practical, handy; *emploi du temps* convenient. **c'est très ~, j'habite à côté du bureau** it's very convenient *ou* handy, I live next door to the office.

2 **nf** a (*application*) practice. **dans la ~** in (actual) practice; **dans la ~ de tous les jours** in the ordinary run of things, in the normal course of events; **en ~** in practice; **mettre qch en ~** to put sth into practice.

b (*expérience*) practical experience. **il a une longue ~ des élèves** he has a long practical experience of teaching, he is well-practised at teaching; **il a perdu la ~** he is out of practice, he's lost the knack; **avoir la ~ du monde††** to be well-versed in *ou* have a knowledge of *ou* be familiar with the ways of society.

c (*coutume, procédé*) practice. **c'est une ~ générale** it is a widespread practice; **des ~s malhonnêtes** dishonest practices, sharp practice; **~s religieuses** religious practices.

d (*exercice, observance*) *[règle]* observance; *[médecine]* practising, exercise; *[sport]* practising; *[vertu]* exercise, practice. **la ~ de l'escrime/du cheval/du golf développe les réflexes** fencing/horse-riding/golfing *ou* (playing) golf develops the reflexes; **la ~ du yoga** the practice of yoga; **~ (religieuse)** church attendance; **condamné pour ~ illégale de la médecine** convicted of the illegal practising of medicine.

e (*††: clientèle*) *[commerçant]* custom (*NonC*), clientèle (*NonC*); *[avocat]* practice, clientèle (*NonC*). **donner sa ~ à un commerçant** to give a tradesman one's custom.

f (*††: client*) *[commerçant]* customer; *[avocat]* client.

g (*††: fréquentation*) *[personne, société]* frequenting, frequentation; *[auteur]* close study.

pratiquement [pʀatikmɑ̃] **adv** (*en pratique*) in practice; (*en réalité*) in (actual) practice; (*presque*) practically, virtually. **c'est ~ la même chose, ça revient ~ au même** it's basically the same (thing).

pratiquer [pʀatike] [1] 1 **vt** a (*mettre en pratique*) *philosophie, politique* to practise (*Brit*), practice (*US*), put into practice; *règle* to observe; *vertu, charité* to practise, exercise; *religion* to practise.

b (*exercer*) *profession, art* to practise; *football, golf* to play. **~ l'escrime/le cheval/la pêche** to go (in for) fencing/horse-riding/fishing; **~ la photo** to go in for photography; **ils pratiquent l'exploitation systématique du touriste** they systematically exploit *ou* make a practice of systematically exploiting the tourist; **il est recommandé de ~ un sport** it is considered advisable to play *ou* practise *ou* do a sport.

c (*faire*) *ouverture* to make; *trou* to pierce, bore, open up; *route* to make, build, open up; (*Méd*) *intervention* to carry out (*sur* on).

d (*utiliser*) *méthode* to practise, use; *système* to use. **~ le chantage/le bluff** to use blackmail/bluff.

e (*††: fréquenter*) *auteur* to study closely; *personne, haute société* to frequent.

2 **vi** a (*Rel*) to go to church, be a churchgoer, be a practising Christian *etc*.

b (*Méd*) to be in practice, have a practice.

3 **se pratiquer vpr** *[méthode]* to be the practice; *[religion]* to be practised. **cela se pratique encore dans les villages** it is still the practice in the villages; **comme cela se pratique en général** as is the usual practice; **les prix qui se pratiquent à Paris** prices which prevail *ou* are current in Paris; **le vaudou se pratique encore dans cette région** voodoo is still practised in this region.

praxis [pʀaksis] **nf** praxis.

Praxitèle [pʀaksitɛl] **nm** Praxiteles.

pré [pʀe] 1 **nm** meadow. **aller sur le ~** to fight a duel. 2 **comp** ►**pré-salé nm (pl prés-salés)** (*mouton*) salt meadow sheep; (*viande*) (salt meadow) lamb.

pré... [pʀe] **préf** pre... .

préadolescent, e [pʀeadɔlesɑ̃, ɑ̃t] **nm,f, adj** preadolescent.

préalable [pʀealabl] 1 **adj** *entretien, condition* preliminary; *accord, avis* prior, previous. **~ à** preceding; **lors des entretiens ~s aux négociations** during (the) discussions (which took place) prior to the negotiations; **vous ne pouvez pas partir sans l'accord ~ du directeur** you cannot leave without first obtaining *ou* having obtained the agreement of the director *ou* without the prior *ou* previous agreement of the director; **ceci n'allait pas sans une certaine inquiétude ~** a certain initial anxiety was experienced; **sans avis ~** without prior *ou* previous notice.

2 **nm** (*condition*) precondition, prerequisite; (*†: préparation*) preliminary. **au ~** first, beforehand.

préalablement [pʀealabləmɑ̃] **adv** first, beforehand. **~ à** prior to; **~ à toute négociation** before any negotiation can take place, prior to any negotiation.

Préalpes [pʀealp] **nfpl: les ~** the Pre-Alps.

préalpin, e [pʀealpɛ̃, in] **adj** of the Pre-Alps.

préambule [pʀeɑ̃byl] **nm** *[discours, loi]* preamble (*de* to); *[contrat]* recitals (*pl*); (*fig: prélude*) prelude (*à* to). **sans ~** without any preliminaries, straight off.

préau, pl ~x [pʀeo] **nm** *[école]* covered playground; *[prison]* (exercise) yard; *[couvent]* inner courtyard.

préavis [pʀeavi] **nm** (advance) notice. **un ~ d'un mois** a month's notice *ou* warning; **~ de licenciement** notice of termination; **~ de grève** strike notice; **déposer un ~ de grève** to give notice *ou* warning of strike action; **sans ~** *faire grève, partir* without (previous) notice, without advance warning; *retirer de l'argent* on demand, without advance *ou* previous notice.

prébende [pʀebɑ̃d] **nf** (*Rel*) prebend; (*péj*) emoluments, payment (*NonC*).

prébendé, e [pʀebɑ̃de] **adj** prebendal.

prébendier [pʀebɑ̃dje] **nm** prebendary.

précaire [pʀekɛʀ] **adj** *position, situation, bonheur, emploi* precarious; *santé* shaky, precarious; *abri* makeshift. (*Jur*) **possesseur/possession (à titre) ~** precarious holder/tenure.

précairement [pʀekɛʀmɑ̃] **adv** precariously.

précambrien, -ienne [pʀekɑ̃bʀijɛ̃, ijɛn] **adj, nm** Precambrian.

précariser [pʀekaʀize] [1] **vt** *situation* to jeopardize.

précarité [pʀekaʀite] **nf** (*gén, Jur*) precariousness.

précaution [pʀekosjɔ̃] **nf** a (*disposition*) precaution. **prendre des** *ou* **ses ~s** to take precautions; **s'entourer de ~s** to take a lot of precautions; **~s oratoires** carefully phrased remarks; **faire qch avec les plus grandes ~s** to do sth with the utmost care *ou* the greatest precaution. b (*prudence*) caution, care. **par ~** as a precaution (*contre* against); **par mesure de ~** as a precautionary measure; **pour plus de ~** to be on the safe side; **avec ~** cautiously.

précautionner (se) [pʀekosjɔne] [1] **vpr** to take precautions (*contre* against).

précautionneusement [pʀekosjɔnøzmɑ̃] **adv** (*par précaution*) cautiously; (*avec soin*) carefully.

précautionneux, -euse [pʀekosjɔnø, øz] **adj** (*prudent*) cautious; (*soigneux*) careful.

précédemment [pʀesedamɑ̃] **adv** before, previously.

précédent, e [pʀesedɑ̃, ɑ̃t] 1 **adj** previous. **un discours/article ~** a previous *ou* an earlier speech/article; **le discours/film ~** the preceding *ou* previous speech/film; **le jour/mois ~** the previous day/month, the day/month before. 2 **nm** (*fait, décision*) precedent. **sans ~** unprecedented, without precedent; **créer un ~** to create *ou* set a precedent.

précéder [pʀesede] [6] 1 **vt** a (*venir avant*) (*dans le temps, une hiérarchie*) to precede, come before; (*dans l'espace*) to precede, be in front of, come before; (*dans une file de véhicules*) to be in front *ou* ahead of, precede. **les jours qui ont précédé le coup d'État** the days preceding *ou* leading up to *ou* which led up to the coup d'état; **être précédé de** (*gén*) to be preceded by; *[discours]* to be preceded by, be prefaced with; **faire ~ son discours d'un préambule** to precede one's speech by *ou* preface one's speech with an introduction, give a short introduction at the start of one's speech.

b (*devancer*) (*dans le temps, l'espace*) to precede, go in front *ou* ahead of; (*dans une carrière etc*) to precede, get ahead of. **quand j'y suis arrivé, j'ai vu que quelqu'un m'avait précédé** when I got there I saw that someone had got there before me *ou* ahead of me *ou* had preceded me; **il le précéda dans la chambre** he went into the room in front of him, he entered the room ahead of *ou* in front of him; **il m'a précédé de 5 minutes** he got there 5 minutes before me *ou* ahead of me.

2 **vi** to precede, go before. **les jours qui ont précédé** the preceding days; **dans tout ce qui a précédé** in all that has been said (*ou* written *etc*) before *ou* so far; **dans le chapitre/la semaine qui précède** in the preceding chapter/week.

précepte [pʀesɛpt] **nm** precept.

précepteur [pʀesɛptœʀ] **nm** private tutor.

préceptorat [pʀesɛptɔʀa] **nm** tutorship, tutorage (*frm*).

préceptrice [pʀesɛptʀis] **nf** governess.

préchauffer [pʀeʃofe] [1] **vt** *four* to preheat.

prêche [pʀɛʃ] **nm** (*lit, fig*) sermon.

prêcher [pʀeʃe] [1] 1 **vt** (*Rel, fig*) to preach; *personne* to preach to. **~ un converti** to preach to the converted; (*hum*) **~ la bonne parole** to spread the good word. 2 **vi** (*Rel*) to preach; (*fig*) to preach, preachify, sermonize. (*fig*) **~ dans le désert** to preach in the wilderness; **~ d'exemple** to practise what one preaches, preach by example; **~ pour son saint** *ou* **sa paroisse** to look after one's own interests, look after *ou* take care of number one*.

prêcheur, -euse [pʀɛʃœʀ, øz] 1 **adj** *personne, ton* moralizing. **frères ~s** preaching friars. 2 **nm, f** (*Rel*) preacher; (*fig*) moralizer.

prêchi-prêcha [pʀeʃipʀeʃa] **nm inv** (*péj*) preachifying (*NonC*), continuous moralizing (*NonC*) *ou* sermonizing (*NonC*).

précieusement [pʀesjøzmɑ̃] **adv** (*voir* **précieux**) preciously; in an affected way.

précieux, -ieuse [pʀesjø, jøz] 1 **adj** a *pierre, métal, temps, qualité, objet* precious; *collaborateur, aide, conseil* invaluable (*à* to); *ami* valued, precious. b (*Littérat*) *écrivain, salon* précieux, precious; (*fig: affecté*) precious, mannered, affected. 2 **précieuse nf** précieuse.

préciosité [pʀesjozite] **nf** a **la ~** (*Littérat*) preciosity; (*affectation*) preciosity, affectation. b (*formule, trait*) stylistic affectation, euphuism.

précipice [pʀesipis] **nm** a (*gouffre*) chasm; (*paroi abrupte*) precipice. **un ~ de plusieurs centaines de mètres** a drop of several hundred metres; **la voiture s'immobilisa au bord du ~/tomba dans le ~** the car stopped at the very edge *ou* brink of the precipice/went over the precipice; **d'affreux ~s s'ouvraient de tous côtés** frightful chasms opened up on all sides; **ne t'aventure pas près du ~** you mustn't go too near the edge (of the precipice). b (*fig*) abyss. **être au bord du ~** to be at the edge of the abyss.

précipitamment [pʀesipitamɑ̃] **adv** hurriedly, hastily, precipitately. **sortir ~** to rush *ou* dash out.

précipitation [pʀesipitasjɔ̃] **nf** a (*hâte*) haste; (*hâte excessive*) great haste, violent hurry. **dans ma ~, je l'ai oublié chez moi** in my haste, I left it at home; **avec ~** in great haste, in a great rush *ou* hurry. b (*Chim*) precipitation. c (*Mét*) **~s** precipitation.

précipité, e [pʀesipite] (**ptp de précipiter**) 1 **adj** *départ, décision* hurried, hasty, precipitate; *fuite* headlong; *pas* hurried; *pouls, respiration* fast, rapid; *rythme* rapid, fast, swift. **tout cela est trop ~** it's all happening too fast, it's all far too hasty. 2 **nm** (*Chim*) precipitate.

précipiter [pʀesipite] [1] 1 **vt** a (*jeter*) *personne* to throw (down), hurl (down), push headlong; *objet* to throw, hurl (*contre* against, at, *vers* towards, at). **~ qn du haut d'une falaise** to hurl *ou* throw sb (down) from the top of a cliff, push sb headlong off a cliff; (*fig*) **~ qn dans le malheur** to plunge sb into misfortune.

b (*hâter*) *pas* to quicken, speed up; *événement* to hasten, precipitate; *départ* to hasten. **il ne faut rien ~** we mustn't be hasty, we mustn't rush (into) things.

c (*Chim*) to precipitate.

2 **vi** (*Chim*) to precipitate.

3 **se précipiter vpr** a (*se jeter*) *[personne]* **se ~ dans le vide** to hurl o.s. *ou* plunge (headlong) into space; **se ~ du haut d'une falaise** to throw o.s. off the edge of *ou* over a cliff.

b (*se ruer*) to rush over *ou* forward. **se ~ vers** to rush *ou* race towards; **se ~ sur** to rush at; **se ~ contre** *[personne]* to rush at, throw o.s. against; *[voiture]* to tear into, smash into; **se ~ au devant de qn/aux pieds de qn** to throw o.s. in front of sb/at sb's feet; **se ~ sur l'ennemi** to rush at *ou* hurl o.s. on *ou* at the enemy; **elle se précipita dans ses bras** she rushed into *ou* threw herself into *ou* flew into his arms; **il se précipita à la porte pour ouvrir** he rushed to open the door; **il se précipita sur le balcon** he raced *ou* dashed *ou* rushed out onto the balcony.

c (*s'accélérer*) *[rythme]* to speed up; *[pouls]* to quicken, speed up. **les choses** *ou* **événements se précipitaient** things began to happen all at once *ou* in a great rush, events started to move fast *ou* faster.

d (*se dépêcher*) to hurry, rush. **ne nous précipitons pas** let's not rush things.

précis, e [pʀesi, iz] 1 **adj** a (*juste*) *style, témoignage, vocabulaire* precise; *sens* precise, exact; *description, indication* precise, exact, clear, accurate; *instrument, tir* precise, accurate.

b (*défini*) *idée, donnée, règle* precise, definite; *heure* precise; *ordre, demande* precise; *fait, raison* precise, particular, specific. **sans raison ~e** for no particular *ou* precise reason; **je ne pense à rien de ~** I'm not thinking of anything in particular; **à cet instant ~** at that precise *ou* very moment; **à 4 heures ~es** at 4 o'clock sharp *ou* on the dot*, at 4 o'clock precisely; **sans que l'on puisse dire de façon ~e ...** although we can't say precisely *ou* with any precision ...; **se référer à un texte de façon ~e** to make precise reference to a text.

c (*net*) *point* precise, exact; *contours* precise, distinct; *geste, esprit* precise; *trait* distinct.

2 **nm** (*résumé*) précis, summary; (*manuel*) handbook.

précisément [pʀesizemɑ̃] **adv** a (*avec précision: voir* **précis**) precisely; exactly; clearly, accurately; distinctly. **ou plus ~** or more precisely *ou* exactly, or to be more precise.

b (*justement*) **je venais ~ de sortir** I had in fact just gone out, as it happened I'd just gone out; **c'est lui ~ qui m'avait conseillé de le faire** as a matter of fact it was he *ou* it so happens that it was he who advised me to do it; **c'est ~ la raison pour laquelle** *ou* **c'est ~ pour cela que je viens vous voir** that's precisely *ou* just why I've come to see you, it's for that very *ou* precise reason that I've come to see you; **il fallait ~ ne rien lui dire** in actual fact he shouldn't have been told anything; **mais je ne l'ai pas vu! — ~!** but I didn't see him! — precisely! *ou* exactly! *ou* that's just it! *ou* that's just the point!

c (*exactement*) exactly, precisely. **c'est ~ ce que je cherchais** that's exactly *ou* precisely *ou* just what I was looking for; **il est arrivé ~ à ce moment-là** he arrived right *ou* just at that moment *ou* at that exact *ou* precise *ou* very moment; **ce n'est pas ~ ce que j'appelle un chef-d'œuvre** it's not exactly what I'd call a masterpiece.

préciser [pʀesize] [1] 1 **vt** *idée, intention* to specify, make clear, clarify; *fait, point* to be more specific about, clarify. **je vous préciserai la date de la réunion plus tard** I'll let you know the exact date of the meeting *ou* precisely when the meeting is later; **il a précisé que ...** he explained that ..., he made it clear that ...; **je dois ~ que ...** I must point out *ou* add that ..., I must be specific that ...; **pourriez-vous ~ quand cela est arrivé?** could you be more exact *ou* specific about when it happened?; **pourriez-vous ~?** could you be more precise? *ou* specific? *ou* explicit?

2 **se préciser vpr** *[idée]* to take shape; *[danger, intention]* to become clear *ou* clearer. **la situation commence à se ~** we are beginning to see

the situation more clearly.

précision [pʀesizjɔ̃] nf **a** (*gén*) precision, preciseness; *[description, instrument]* precision, preciseness, accuracy; *[contours]* precision, preciseness, distinctness; *[trait]* distinctness. **avec ~** precisely, with precision; **de ~** precision (*épith*). **b** (*détail*) point, piece of information. **j'aimerais vous demander une ~/des ~s** I'd like to ask you to explain one thing/for further explanation *ou* information; **il a apporté des ~s intéressantes** he revealed some interesting points *ou* facts *ou* information; **encore une ~** one more point *ou* thing.

précité, e [pʀesite] adj aforesaid, aforementioned; (*par écrit*) aforesaid, above(-mentioned).

précoce [pʀekɔs] adj *fruit, saison, gelée* early; *plante* early-flowering, early-fruiting, precocious (*SPÉC*); *calvitie, sénilité* premature; *mariage* young (*épith*), early (*épith*); *enfant* (*intellectuellement*) precocious, advanced for his *ou* her age (*attrib*); (*sexuellement*) sexually precocious *ou* forward.

précocement [pʀekɔsmɑ̃] adv precociously.

précocité [pʀekɔsite] nf *[fruit, saison]* earliness; *[enfant]* (*intellectuelle*) precocity, precociousness; (*sexuelle*) sexual precocity, sexual precociousness.

précolombien, -ienne [pʀekɔlɔ̃bjɛ̃, jɛn] adj pre-Colombian.

précombustion [pʀekɔ̃bystjɔ̃] nf precombustion.

précompte [pʀekɔ̃t] nm deduction (from sb's pay).

précompter [pʀekɔ̃te] 1 vt to deduct (*sur* from).

préconception [pʀekɔ̃sɛpsjɔ̃] nf preconception.

préconçu, e [pʀekɔ̃sy] adj preconceived. **idée ~e** preconceived idea.

préconisation [pʀekɔnizasjɔ̃] nf recommendation.

préconiser [pʀekɔnize] 1 vt *remède* to recommend; *méthode, mode de vie* to advocate; *plan, solution* to advocate, push.

précontraint, e [pʀekɔ̃tʀɛ̃, ɛ̃t] adj, nm: **(béton) ~** prestressed concrete.

précuit, e [pʀekɥi, it] adj precooked.

précurseur [pʀekyʀsœʀ] **1** adj m precursory. **~ de** preceding; *voir* **signe**. **2** nm forerunner, precursor.

prédateur, -trice [pʀedatœʀ, tʀis] **1** adj predatory. **2** nm predator.

prédation [pʀedasjɔ̃] nf predation.

prédécesseur [pʀedesesœʀ] nm predecessor.

prédestination [pʀedɛstinasjɔ̃] nf predestination.

prédestiné, e [pʀedɛstine] (ptp de **prédestiner**) adj predestined (*à qch* for sth, *à faire* to do), fated (*à faire* to do).

prédestiner [pʀedɛstine] 1 vt to predestine (*à qch* for sth, *à faire* to do).

prédétermination [pʀedetɛʀminasjɔ̃] nf predetermination.

prédéterminer [pʀedetɛʀmine] 1 vt to predetermine.

prédicant [pʀedikɑ̃] nm preacher.

prédicat [pʀedika] nm predicate.

prédicateur [pʀedikatœʀ] nm preacher.

prédicatif, -ive [pʀedikatif, iv] adj predicative.

prédication [pʀedikasjɔ̃] nf (*activité*) preaching; (*sermon*) sermon.

prédiction [pʀediksjɔ̃] nf prediction.

prédigéré, e [pʀediʒeʀe] adj predigested.

prédilection [pʀedilɛksjɔ̃] nf (*pour qn, qch*) predilection, partiality (*pour* for). **avoir une ~ pour la cuisine française** to have a partiality for *ou* be partial to French cooking; **de ~** favourite, preferred (*frm*).

prédire [pʀediʀ] 37 vt *[prophète]* to foretell; (*gén*) to predict. **~ l'avenir** to tell *ou* predict the future; **~ qch à qn** to predict sth for sb; **il m'a prédit que je ...** he predicted (that) I ..., he told me (that) I ... .

prédisposer [pʀedispoze] 1 vt to predispose (*à qch* to sth, *à faire* to do). **être prédisposé à une maladie** to be predisposed *ou* prone to an illness; **être prédisposé en faveur de qn** to be predisposed in sb's favour.

prédisposition [pʀedispozisjɔ̃] nf predisposition (*à qch* to sth, *à faire* to do).

prédominance [pʀedɔminɑ̃s] nf (*gén*) predominance, predominancy; *[couleur]* predominance, prominence.

prédominant, e [pʀedɔminɑ̃, ɑ̃t] adj (*gén*) predominant, most dominant; *avis, impression* prevailing; *couleur* predominant, most prominent.

prédominer [pʀedɔmine] 1 vi (*gén*) to predominate, be most dominant; *[avis, impression]* to prevail; *[couleur]* to predominate, be most prominent. **le souci qui prédomine dans mon esprit** the worry which is uppermost in my mind.

pré-électoral, e, mpl **-aux** [pʀeelɛktɔʀal, o] adj pre-election (*épith*).

pré-emballé, e [pʀeɑ̃bale] adj prepacked, prepackaged.

prééminence [pʀeeminɑ̃s] nf pre-eminence.

prééminent, e [pʀeeminɑ̃, ɑ̃t] adj pre-eminent.

préemption [pʀeɑ̃psjɔ̃] nf pre-emption. **droit de ~** pre-emptive right.

préencollé, e [pʀeɑ̃kɔle] adj pre-pasted. **papier peint ~** pre-pasted *ou* ready-pasted wallpaper.

préétablir [pʀeetabliʀ] 2 vt to pre-establish.

préexistant, e [pʀeɛgzistɑ̃, ɑ̃t] adj pre-existent, pre-existing.

préexistence [pʀeɛgzistɑ̃s] nf pre-existence.

préexister [pʀeɛgziste] 1 vi to pre-exist. **~ à** to exist before.

préfabrication [pʀefabʀikasjɔ̃] nf prefabrication.

préfabriqué, e [pʀefabʀike] **1** adj prefabricated. **2** nm (*maison*) prefabricated house, prefab*; (*matériau*) prefabricated material.

préface [pʀefas] nf preface; (*fig: prélude*) preface, prelude (*à* to).

préfacer [pʀefase] 3 vt *livre* to write a preface for, preface.

préfacier [pʀefasje] nm preface writer.

préfectoral, e, mpl **-aux** [pʀefɛktɔʀal, o] adj (*Admin française, Antiq*) prefectorial, prefectural; *voir* **arrêté**.

préfecture [pʀefɛktyʀ] nf (*Admin française, Antiq*) prefecture. **~ de police** Paris police headquarters.

préférable [pʀefeʀabl] adj preferable (*à qch* to sth), better (*à qch* than sth). **il est ~ que je parte** it is preferable *ou* better that I should leave *ou* for me to leave; **il serait ~ d'y aller *ou* que vous y alliez** it would be better if you went *ou* for you to go; **il est ~ de faire** it is preferable *ou* better to do.

préférablement [pʀefeʀabləmɑ̃] adv preferably. **~ à** in preference to.

préféré, e [pʀefeʀe] (ptp de **préférer**) **1** adj favourite, pet* (*épith*), preferred (*frm*). **2** nm, f favourite, pet*. **le ~ du professeur** the teacher's pet*.

préférence [pʀefeʀɑ̃s] nf preference. **de ~** preferably; **de ~ à** in preference to, rather than; **donner la ~ à** to give preference to; **avoir une ~ marquée pour ...** to have a marked preference for ...; **avoir la ~ sur** to have preference over; **je n'ai pas de ~** I have no preference, I don't mind; **par ordre de ~** in order of preference.

préférentiel, -ielle [pʀefeʀɑ̃sjɛl] adj preferential. **tarif ~** preferential *ou* special rate.

préférentiellement [pʀefeʀɑ̃sjɛlmɑ̃] adv preferentially.

préférer [pʀefeʀe] 6 vt to prefer (*à* to). **je préfère ce manteau à l'autre** I prefer this coat to that, I like this coat better than that one *ou* the other; **je te préfère avec les cheveux courts** I like you better *ou* prefer you with short hair; **je préfère aller au cinéma** I prefer to go *ou* I would rather go to the cinema; **il préfère que ce soit vous qui le fassiez** he prefers that you should do it, he would rather you did it; **nous avons préféré attendre avant de vous le dire** we preferred to wait *ou* we thought it better to wait before telling you; **nous avons préféré attendre que d'y aller tout de suite** we preferred to wait *ou* thought it better to wait rather than go straight away; **que préférez-vous: du thé ou du café?** what would you rather have *ou* would you prefer – tea or coffee?; **si tu préfères** if you prefer, if you like, if you'd rather; **comme vous préférez** as you prefer *ou* like *ou* wish *ou* please.

préfet [pʀefɛ] nm (*Admin française, Antiq*) prefect. **~ de police** prefect of police, chief of police.

préfète [pʀefɛt] nf (*femme préfet*) (female *ou* woman) prefect; (*femme du préfet*) prefect's wife.

préfiguration [pʀefigyʀasjɔ̃] nf prefiguration, foreshadowing.

préfigurer [pʀefigyʀe] 1 vt to prefigure, foreshadow.

préfixal, e, mpl **-aux** [pʀefiksal, o] adj prefixal.

préfixation [pʀefiksasjɔ̃] nf prefixation.

préfixe [pʀefiks] nm prefix.

préfixer [pʀefikse] 1 vt to prefix.

préglaciaire [pʀeglasjɛʀ] adj preglacial.

prégnant, e [pʀegnɑ̃, ɑ̃t] adj (*littér*) pregnant.

préhenseur [pʀeɑ̃sœʀ] adj m prehensile.

préhensile [pʀeɑ̃sil] adj prehensile.

préhension [pʀeɑ̃sjɔ̃] nf prehension.

préhistoire [pʀeistwaʀ] nf prehistory.

préhistorique [pʀeistɔʀik] adj prehistoric; (*fig: suranné*) antediluvian, ancient.

préjudice [pʀeʒydis] nm (*matériel, financier*) loss; (*moral*) harm (*NonC*), damage (*NonC*), wrong. **subir un ~** (*matériel*) to suffer a loss; (*moral*) to be wronged; **porter ~ à qn** (*gén*) to do sb harm, harm sb, do sb a disservice; *[décision]* to be detrimental to sb *ou* to sb's interests; **ce supermarché a porté ~ aux petits commerçants** this supermarket was detrimental to (the interests of) small tradesmen; **je ne voudrais pas vous porter ~ en leur racontant cela** I wouldn't like to harm you *ou* your case *ou* make difficulties for you by telling them about this; **au ~ de sa santé/de la vérité** to the prejudice (*frm*) *ou* at the expense *ou* at the cost of his health/the truth; **au ~ de M. X** to the prejudice (*frm*) *ou* at the expense of Mr X; **~ moral** moral wrong; **~ matériel** material loss *ou* damage; **~ financier** financial loss; **sans ~ de** without prejudice to.

préjudiciable [pʀeʒydisjabl] adj prejudicial, detrimental, harmful (*à* to).

préjugé [pʀeʒyʒe] nm prejudice. **avoir un ~ contre** to be prejudiced *ou* biased against; **sans ~** unprejudiced, unbiased; **bénéficier d'un ~ favorable** to be favourably considered; **~s de classe** class bias; **~ de race** racial prejudice.

préjuger [pʀeʒyʒe] vt, **préjuger (de)** vt indir 3 to prejudge. **~ d'une réaction** to foresee a reaction, judge what a reaction might be; **autant qu'on peut le ~, à ce qu'on en peut ~** as far as it is possible to judge in advance.

prélasser (se) [pʀelɑse] 1 vpr (*dans un fauteuil*) to sprawl, lounge; (*au soleil*) to bask.

prélat [pʀela] nm prelate.

prélature [pʀelatyʀ] nf prelacy.

prélavage [pʀelavaʒ] nm prewash.

prélaver [pʀelave] 1 vt to prewash.

prélèvement [pʀelɛvmɑ̃] **nm** (*voir* **prélever**) taking (*NonC*); levying (*NonC*), levy, imposition; deduction; withdrawal, drawing out (*NonC*); removal. **faire un ~ de sang** to take a blood sample; **~ automatique** (*somme fixe*) standing order; (*somme variable*) direct debit; **~ bancaire** standing *ou* banker's order (*Brit*), automatic deduction (*US*); **~ fiscal/compensatoire/sur le capital/à l'importation** tax/compensatory/capital/import levy.

prélever [pʀel(ə)ve] 5 **vt** *échantillon* to take (*sur* from); *impôt* to levy, impose (*sur* on); *retenue, montant* to deduct (*sur* from); *argent* (*sur un compte*) to withdraw, draw out (*sur* from); (*Méd*) *sang* to take (a sample of); *organe* to remove. **ses factures d'électricité sont automatiquement prélevées sur son compte** his electricity bills are automatically deducted from his account.

préliminaire [pʀeliminɛʀ] 1 **adj** (*gén*) preliminary; *discours* introductory. 2 **nmpl: ~s** preliminaries; [*négociations*] preliminary talks.

prélude [pʀelyd] **nm** (*Mus*) (*morceau*) prelude; (*pour se préparer*) warm-up; (*fig*) prelude (*à* to).

préluder [pʀelyde] 1 1 **vi** (*Mus*) to warm up. **~ par** to begin with. 2 **préluder à vt indir** to be a prelude to, lead up to, prelude.

prématuré, e [pʀematyʀe] 1 **adj** *bébé, nouvelle* premature; *mort* untimely, premature. **il est ~ de** it is premature to, it's too early to; **~ de 3 semaines** 3 weeks premature *ou* early. 2 **nm, f** premature baby.

prématurément [pʀematyʀemɑ̃] **adv** prematurely. **une cruelle maladie l'a enlevé ~ à notre affection** a grievous illness took him too soon from his loving family *ou* brought his untimely departure from our midst.

prémédication [pʀemedikasjɔ̃] **nf** premedication, premed*.

préméditation [pʀemeditasjɔ̃] **nf** premeditation. **avec ~** *crime* premeditated; *tuer* with intent, with malice aforethought†.

préméditer [pʀemedite] 1 **vt** to premeditate. **~ de faire** to plan to do.

prémenstruel, -elle [pʀemɑ̃stʀyɛl] **adj** premenstrual. **syndrome ~** premenstrual tension *ou* syndrome.

prémices [pʀemis] **nfpl** (*littér*) beginnings; [*récolte*] first fruits; [*animaux*] first-born (animals).

premier, -ière [pʀəmje, jɛʀ] 1 **adj** a (*dans le temps, l'espace*) (*gén*) first; *impression* first, initial; *enfance, jeunesse* early; *rang* front; *ébauche, projet* first, rough; *branche* lower, bottom; *barreau d'échelle* bottom. **arriver/être ~** to arrive/be first; **arriver bon ~** to get there well ahead of the others; (*dans une course*) to come an easy first; **dans le ~ café venu** in the first café they came to; **la ~ière fille venue** the first girl to come along; (*Sport*) **être en/venir en ~ière position** to be in/come into the lead; (*Équitation*) **en ~ière position: Brutus** (and it's) Brutus leading *ou* in the lead; (*Presse*) **en ~ière page** on the front page; **les 100 ~ières pages** the first 100 pages; **la ~ière marche de l'escalier** (*en bas*) the bottom step; (*en haut*) the top step; **le ~ barreau de l'échelle** the bottom *ou* first *ou* lowest rung of the ladder; **le ~ mouchoir de la pile** the first handkerchief in the pile, the top handkerchief in the pile; **les ~ières heures du jour** the early hours (of the morning), the (wee) small hours*; **dès les ~s jours** from the very first days; **ses ~s poèmes** his first *ou* early poems; **les ~s habitants de la terre** the earliest *ou* first inhabitants of the earth; **les ~ières années de sa vie** the first few *ou* the early years of his life; **lire qch de la ~ière à la dernière ligne** to read sth from beginning to end *ou* from cover to cover; **c'est la ~ière et la dernière fois que je suis tes conseils** it's the first and last time I follow your advice; **acheter une voiture de ~ière main** to buy a car which has only had one owner; **au ~ signe de résistance** at the first *ou* slightest sign of resistance; **à mon ~ signal** at the first signal from me, as soon as you see my signal; *voir* **lit, sixième, tête**.

b (*dans un ordre*) first; (*à un examen*) first, top; (*en importance*) leading, foremost, top*. **~ secrétaire/lieutenant** first secretary/lieutenant; **~ commis/clerc** chief shop assistant/clerk; **~ danseur/rôle** leading dancer/part; **article de ~ière qualité** top quality article, article of the first *ou* highest quality; **de ~ ordre** first-rate; (*Rail*) **~ière classe** first-class; (*Boucherie*) **morceau de ~ choix** prime cut; **affaire à traiter en ~ière urgence** question to be dealt with as a matter of the utmost urgency *ou* as (a) top priority; (*Gram*) **à la ~ière personne (du singulier)** in the first person (singular); **être reçu ~** to come first *ou* top; **il est toujours ~ en classe** he's always top of the class *ou* first in the class; **avoir le ~ prix** to get *ou* win first prize; (*Mus*) **c'est un ~ prix du conservatoire de Paris** he won first prize at the Paris Conservatoire; **un événement/document de ~ière importance** an event/a document of paramount *ou* prime *ou* the highest *ou* the first importance; **de ~ière nécessité** absolutely essential; **objets de ~ière nécessité** basic essentials; **cela m'intéresse au ~ chef** it's of the greatest *ou* utmost interest to me; **c'est lui le ~ intéressé dans cette histoire** he's the one who has most at stake in this business; **le ~ constructeur automobile du monde** the world's leading car manufacturer; **c'est le ~ écrivain français vivant** he's the leading *ou* greatest *ou* foremost *ou* top* French writer alive today; **le ~ personnage de l'État** the country's leading *ou* most senior statesman; **la ~ière dame de France** France's first lady.

c (*du début*) *échelon, grade, prix* bottom. **c'était le ~ prix** it was the cheapest; **apprendre les ~s rudiments d'une science** to learn the first *ou* basic rudiments of a science.

d (*après n: originel, fondamental*) *cause, donnée* basic; *principe* first, basic; *objectif* basic, primary, prime; *état* initial, original. **la qualité ~ière d'un chef d'État est ...** the prime *ou* essential quality of a head of state is ...; **retrouver sa vivacité ~ière/son éclat ~** to regain one's former *ou* initial liveliness/sparkle; *voir* **matière, nombre, vérité**.

e (*loc*) **au ~ abord** at first sight, to begin with; **au *ou* du ~ coup** at the first attempt *ou* go *ou* try; **demain, à la ~ière heure** tomorrow at first light; **il n'est plus de la ~ière jeunesse** he's not as young as he was *ou* as he used to be, he's not in the first flush of youth; **en ~ lieu** in the first place; **il veut acheter une maison mais il n'en a pas le ~ sou** he wants to buy a house but he hasn't got two pennies (*Brit*) *ou* cents (*US*) to rub together *ou* a penny (*Brit*) *ou* a cent (*US*) (to his name); **il n'en connaît *ou* n'en sait pas le ~ mot** he doesn't know the first thing about it; **il s'en moque *ou* fiche comme de sa ~ière chemise*** he doesn't give a damn about it**, he doesn't care a fig* *ou* a rap* *ou* two hoots* about it; **~ière nouvelle!** that's the first I've heard about it!, it's news to me!; **à la ~ière occasion** at the first opportunity, as soon as one can; **il a fait ses ~ières armes dans le métier en 1960/comme manœuvre** he started out on the job in 1960/as an unskilled worker; **faire ses ~s pas** to start walking; **faire les ~s pas** to take the initiative, make the first move; **il n'y a que le ~ pas qui coûte** the first step is the hardest; **dans un ~ temps** to start *ou* begin with, as a first step, at first; **dans les ~s temps** at the outset, at first; **à ~ière vue** at first sight.

2 **nm, f** first (one). **parler/passer/sortir le ~** to speak/go/go out first; **arriver les ~s** to arrive (the) first; **les ~s arrivés seront les ~s servis** first come, first served; **Pierre et Paul sont cousins, le ~ est médecin** Peter and Paul are cousins, the former is a doctor; **il a été le ~ à reconnaître ses torts** he was the first to admit that he was in the wrong; **elle sera servie la ~ière** she will be served first; **au ~ de ces messieurs** next gentleman please; (*Scol, Univ*) **il a été reçu dans *ou* parmi les ~s** he was in the top *ou* first few; **il est le ~ de sa classe** he is top of his class; **les ~s seront les derniers** the last shall be first, and the first last; **les ~s venus** (*lit*) the first to come *ou* to arrive; (*fig*) anybody, anybody who happens by; **il n'est pas le ~ venu** he isn't just anyone; **elle n'épousera pas le ~ venu** she won't marry the first man that comes along; **le ~ semble mieux** (*entre deux*) the first one seems better; (*dans une série*) the first one seems best; *voir* **jeune, né**.

3 **nm** (*gén*) first; (*étage*) first floor (*Brit*), second floor (*US*). (*enfant*) **c'est leur ~** it's their first child; **le ~ de l'an** New Year's Day; (*charade*) **mon ~ est ...** my first is in ...; **il était arrivé en ~** he had arrived first; **en ~ je dirai que ...** firstly *ou* first *ou* in the first place *ou* to start with I'd like to say that ... .

4 **première nf** a (*gén*) first; (*Aut*) first (gear); (*Hippisme*) first (race). (*Aut*) **être en/passer la ~ière** to be in/go into first (gear).

b (*Théât*) first night; (*Ciné*) première; (*gén: exploit*) first; (*Alpinisme*) first ascent. **le public des grandes ~ières** firstnighters; **~ière mondiale** (*Ciné*) world première; (*gén*) world first.

c (*Aviat, Rail etc*) first class. **voyager en ~ière** to travel first-class; **billet de ~ière** first-class ticket.

d (*Scol*) ≃ lower sixth.

e (*Couture*) head seamstress.

f (*semelle*) insole.

g (**loc*) **c'est de ~ière!** it's first-class!; **il est de ~ière pour trouver les bons restaurants/pour les gaffes!** he's got a great knack* for *ou* he's great* at finding good restaurants/making blunders!

5 **comp** ▸**le premier âge** the first 3 months ▸**le premier avril** the first of April, April Fool's Day, All Fools' Day ▸**premiers balcons** (*Théât*) lower circle ▸**premier chantre** (*Rel*) precentor ▸**première classe** (*Mil*) **nm** ≃ private (*Brit*), private first class (*US*) ▸**premier communiant/première communiante** young boy/girl making his/her first communion ▸**première communion** first communion; **faire sa première communion** to make one's first communion ▸**premier cor** principal horn ▸**premier de cordée** (*Alpinisme*) leader ▸**première épreuve** (*Typ*) first proof ▸**premier jet** first *ou* rough draft ▸**premier jour** [*exposition*] first *ou* opening day ▸**premières loges** (*Théât*) first-tier boxes; (*fig*) **être aux premières loges** to have a front seat (*fig*) ▸**le Premier Mai** the first of May, May Day ▸**premier-maître nm** (**pl premier-maîtres**) (*Naut*) chief petty officer ▸**Premier ministre** Prime Minister, Premier ▸**premier plan** (*Phot*) foreground; (*fig*) forefront; **personnage/rôle de (tout) premier plan** principal character/role ▸**premier rôle** (*Théât*) leading role *ou* part; (*fig*) **avoir le premier rôle dans une affaire** to play the leading part in an affair ▸**les premiers secours** first aid ▸**premier violon** (*chef*) leader (*Brit*), concert master (*US*) ▸**les premiers violons** (*groupe*) the first violins.

premièrement [pʀəmjɛʀmɑ̃] **adv** (*d'abord*) first(ly); (*en premier lieu*) in the first place; (*introduisant une objection*) firstly, for a start. **~ il ne m'a rien dit** to begin with *ou* first of all *ou* at first he didn't say anything to me.

prémisse [pʀemis] **nf** premise, premiss.

prémolaire [pʀemɔlɛʀ] **nf** premolar (tooth).

prémonition [pʀemɔnisjɔ̃] **nf** premonition.

prémonitoire [pʀemɔnitwaʀ] **adj** premonitory.

prémunir [pʀemyniʀ] 2 1 **vt** (*littér*) (*mettre en garde*) to warn; (*protéger*) to protect (*contre* against). 2 **se prémunir vpr** to protect o.s. (*contre* from), guard (*contre* against).

prenable [pʀənabl] **adj** *ville* pregnable.
prénaissance [pʀenɛsɑ̃s] **nf** pregnancy.
prenant, e [pʀənɑ̃, ɑ̃t] **adj** a (*captivant*) *film, livre* absorbing, engrossing, compelling; *voix* fascinating, captivating. b (*absorbant*) *activité* absorbing, engrossing. **ce travail est trop ~** this job is too absorbing *ou* is over-absorbing. c (*Zool*) *queue* prehensile.
prénatal, e, mpl ~s [pʀenatal] **adj** antenatal; *allocation* maternity (*épith*).
prendre [pʀɑ̃dʀ] 58 1 **vt** a (*saisir*) *objet* to take. **prends-le dans le placard/sur l'étagère** take it out of the cupboard/off *ou* (down) from the shelf; **il l'a pris dans le tiroir** he took *ou* got it out of the drawer; **il prit un journal/son crayon sur la table** he picked up *ou* took a newspaper/his pencil from the table; **prends tes lunettes pour lire** put your glasses on to read; **il la prit par le cou/par la taille** he put his arms round her neck/round her waist; **ils se prirent par le cou/par la taille** they put their arms round one another('s necks/waists); **il y a plusieurs livres, lequel prends-tu?** there are several books — which one are you going to take? *ou* which one do you want?; **il a pris le bleu** he took the blue one; **~ qch des mains de qn** (*débarrasser*) to take sth out of sb's hands; (*enlever*) to take sth off sb *ou* away from sb.
b (*aller chercher*) *chose* to pick up, get, fetch (*Brit*); *personne* to pick up; (*emmener*) to take. **passer ~ qn à son bureau** to pick sb up *ou* call for sb at his office; **je passerai les ~ chez toi** I'll come and collect *ou* get them *ou* I'll call in for them at your place; **pouvez-vous me ~ (dans votre voiture)?** can you give me a lift?; **si tu sors, prends ton parapluie** if you go out, take your umbrella (with you); **as-tu pris les valises?** have you brought the suitcases?; **je ne veux plus de ce manteau, tu peux le ~** I don't want this coat any more so you can take *ou* have it; **prends ta chaise et viens t'asseoir ici** bring your chair and come and sit over here; **prends du beurre dans le frigo** go and get *ou* go and fetch (*Brit*) some butter from the fridge, get some butter out of the fridge.
c (*s'emparer de*) *poisson, voleur* to catch; *argent, place, otage* to take; (*Mil*) *ville* to take, capture; (*Cartes, Échecs*) to take. **un voleur lui a pris son portefeuille** a thief has taken *ou* stolen his wallet *ou* has robbed him of his wallet; **il m'a pris mon idée** he has taken *ou* used *ou* pinched* (*Brit*) my idea; **il prend tout ce qui lui tombe sous la main** he takes *ou* grabs everything he can lay his hands on; **le voleur s'est fait ~** the robber was caught; **~ une femme** to take a woman; (*Tennis*) **~ le service de qn** to break sb's service.
d (*surprendre*) to catch; (*duper*) to take in. **~ qn à faire qch** to catch sb doing sth; **je vous y prends!** caught you!; (*menace*) **si je t'y prends (encore), que je t'y prenne** just *ou* don't let me catch you doing that (again) *ou* at it (again); **~ qn sur le fait** to catch sb in the act *ou* red-handed; **le brouillard nous a pris dans la descente** we were caught in the fog *ou* overtaken by the fog on the way down the hill; **on ne m'y prendra plus** I won't be taken in again, I won't be had a second time*; **se laisser ~ à des paroles aimables** to let o.s. be taken in by soft talk.
e *boisson, repas* to have; *médicament* to take; *bain, douche* to take, have. **est-ce que vous prenez du sucre?** do you take sugar?; **est-ce que vous prendrez du café?** will you have *ou* would you like (some) coffee?; **fais-lui ~ son médicament** give him his medicine; **à ~ avant les repas** to be taken before meals; **ce médicament se prend dans de l'eau** this medicine must be taken in water; **as-tu pris de ce bon gâteau?** have you had some of this nice cake?; **il n'a rien pris depuis hier** he hasn't eaten anything since yesterday; **le docteur m'interdit de ~ de l'alcool** the doctor won't allow me *ou* has forbidden me (to drink) alcohol.
f (*voyager par*) *métro, taxi* to take, travel *ou* go *ou* come by; *voiture* to take; (*s'engager dans*) *direction, rue* to take. **il prit le train puis l'avion de Paris à Londres** he took the train *ou* went by train then flew from Paris to London; **je prends l'avion/le train de 4 heures** I'm catching the 4 o'clock plane/train; (*d'habitude*) I catch the 4 o'clock plane/train; **je préfère ~ ma voiture** I'd rather take the car *ou* go in the car; **~ la mauvaise direction** to take the wrong direction, go the wrong way; **ils prirent un chemin défoncé** they went down a bumpy lane.
g (*se procurer*) *billet, essence* to get; (*acheter*) *voiture* to buy; (*réserver*) *couchette, place* to book. **il prend toujours son pain à côté** he always gets *ou* buys his bread from the shop next door; **peux-tu me ~ du pain?** can you get me some bread?; **nous avons pris une maison** (*loué*) we have taken *ou* rented a house; (*acheté*) we have bought a house.
h (*accepter*) *client* to take; *passager* to pick up; *locataire* to take (in); *personnel* to take on; *domestique* to engage, take on. **l'école ne prend plus de pensionnaires** the school no longer takes boarders; **ce train ne prend pas de voyageurs** this train does not pick up passengers; **il l'a prise comme interprète** he took her on as an interpreter.
i *photo, film* to take. **~ qn en photo/en film** to take a photo *ou* snap*/a film of sb, photograph/film sb.
j (*noter*) *renseignement, adresse, nom, rendez-vous* to write down, take down, jot down, make a note of; *mesures, température, empreintes* to take; (*sous la dictée*) *lettre* to take (down). **~ des notes** to take notes.
k (*adopter, choisir*) *air, ton* to put on, assume; *décision* to take, make, come to; *risque, mesure* to take; *attitude* to strike, take up. **il prit un ton menaçant** a threatening note crept into his voice, his voice took on a threatening tone.
l (*acquérir*) *assurance* to gain. **~ du ventre** to get fat; **~ du poids** *[adulte]* to put on weight; *[bébé]* to gain weight; **~ de l'autorité** to gain authority; **cela prend un sens** it's beginning to make sense; **les feuilles prenaient une couleur dorée** the leaves were turning golden-brown *ou* taking on a golden-brown colour.
m (*Méd*) *maladie* to catch. **~ froid** to catch cold; **~ un rhume** to catch a cold.
n (*s'accorder*) *congé* to take; *vacances* to take, have, go on; *repos* to have, take. **il a pris son temps!** he took his time (over *ou* about it)!; **~ le temps de faire** to find time to do.
o (*coûter*) *temps, place, argent* to take. **cela me prend tout mon temps** it takes up all my time; **la réparation a pris des heures** the repair took hours *ou* ages.
p (*faire payer*) to charge. **ils (m')ont pris 100 F pour une petite réparation** they charged (me) 100 francs for a minor repair; **ce spécialiste prend très cher** this specialist charges very high fees, this specialist's charges *ou* fees are very high; **ce plombier prend cher de l'heure** this plumber's hourly rate is high.
q (*prélever*) *pourcentage* to take. **ils prennent un pourcentage sur la vente** they charge a commission on the sale, they take a percentage on the sale; **il prend sa commission sur la vente** he takes his commission on the sale; **~ de l'argent à la banque/sur son compte** to draw (out) *ou* withdraw money from the bank/from one's account; **la cotisation à la retraite est prise sur le salaire** the pension contribution is taken off one's salary *ou* deducted from one's salary; **il a dû ~ sur ses économies pour payer les dégâts** he had to dip into *ou* go into his savings to pay for the damage; **il a pris sur son temps pour venir m'aider** he gave up some of his time to help me.
r (**: recevoir, subir*) *coup, choc* to get, receive. **il a pris la porte en pleine figure** the door hit *ou* got* him right in the face; **nous avons pris l'averse sur le dos** we got caught in the shower; **on a pris toute l'averse** we got drenched; **qu'est-ce qu'on a pris!, on en a pris plein la tronche‡!** (*reproches*) we didn't half catch* *ou* cop‡ (*Brit*) it!; (*défaite*) we got hammered!‡; (*averse*) we got drenched!; (*emploi absolu*) **il a pris pour les autres** he took the rap*; **le seau d'eau s'est renversé et c'est moi qui ai tout pris** the bucket of water tipped over and I caught the lot* (*Brit*) *ou* I caught the whole thing.
s (*manier*) *personne* to handle; *problème* to handle, tackle, deal with, cope with. **~ qn par la douceur** to use gentle persuasion on sb; **~ qn par son point faible** to get sb by his weak spot; **elle m'a pris par les sentiments** she appealed to my feelings; **elle sait le ~** she knows how to handle *ou* approach *ou* get round him; **on ne sait jamais par quel bout le ~** you never know how to handle him *ou* how he's going to react; **il y a plusieurs façons de ~ le problème** there are several ways of going about *ou* tackling the problem.
t (*réagir à*) *nouvelle* to take. **il a bien/mal pris la chose, il l'a bien/mal pris** he took it well/badly; **si vous le prenez ainsi ...** if that's how you want it ...; **~ qch avec bonne humeur** to take sth good-humouredly *ou* in good part; **~ les choses comme elles sont/la vie comme elle vient** to take things as they come/life as it comes.
u **~ qn/qch pour** (*considérer*) to take sb/sth for; (*se servir de*) to take sb/sth as; **pour qui me prenez-vous?** what do you take me for?, what do you think I am?; **~ qn pour un autre** to take sb for *ou* think sb is somebody else, mistake sb for somebody else; **je n'aime pas qu'on me prenne pour un imbécile** I don't like being taken for a fool; **~ qch pour prétexte/pour cible** to take sth as a pretext/target.
v (*assaillir*) *[colère]* to come over; *[fièvre]* to strike; *[doute]* to seize, sweep over; *[douleur]* to strike, get*. **la colère le prit soudain** he was suddenly overcome with anger, anger suddenly came over him; **être pris de vertige** to come over* (*Brit*) *ou* go (*Brit*) *ou* get dizzy; **être pris de remords** to be stricken by remorse; **être pris de panique** to be panic-stricken; **l'envie me prend** *ou* **il me prend l'envie de faire** I feel like doing, I've got an urge to do; **la douleur m'a pris au genou** the pain got* me in the knee; **les douleurs la prirent** her labour pains started; **qu'est-ce qui te prend?*** what's the matter *ou* what's up* with you?, what's come over you?*; **ça te prend souvent?‡** are you often like that? (*iro*), do you often get these fits?* (*iro*); **quand le froid vous prend** when the cold hits you; **ça vous prend aux tripes‡** it gets you right there, it hits you right in the guts‡; **ça me prend la tête‡, les maths!** maths does my head in‡; **il me prend la tête‡, ce type!** that guy drives me nuts* *ou* mad.
w (*accrocher, coincer*) to catch, trap. **le chat s'est pris la patte dans un piège** the cat got its paw trapped, the cat caught its paw in a trap; **le rideau se prend dans la fenêtre** the curtain gets caught (up) *ou* stuck in the window; **j'ai pris mon manteau dans la porte, mon manteau s'est pris dans la porte** I caught *ou* trapped my coat in the door, my coat got stuck *ou* trapped *ou* caught in the door; **se ~ les pieds dans le tapis** (*lit*) to catch one's foot in the rug, trip on the rug; (*fig*) to trip oneself up.
x (*loc*) **à tout ~** on the whole, all in all; **c'est à ~ ou à laisser** (you can) take it or leave it; **avec lui j'en prends et j'en laisse** I take everything he says with a pinch of salt; **c'est toujours ça** *ou* **autant de pris** that's something at least; **~ qch sur soi** to take sth upon o.s.; **~ sur soi**

de faire qch to take it upon o.s. to do sth.

2 **vi** a (*durcir*) [*ciment, pâte, crème*] to set.

b (*réussir*) [*plante*] to take (root); [*vaccin*] to take; [*mouvement, mode*] to catch on; [*livre, spectacle*] to be a success. **la plaisanterie a pris** the joke was a great success; **avec moi, ça ne prend pas*** it won't wash with me* (*Brit*), it doesn't work with me*.

c [*feu*] (*foyer*) to go; [*incendie*] to start; [*allumette*] to light; [*bois*] to catch fire. **le feu ne veut pas ~** the fire won't go; **le feu a pris au toit** the fire took hold in the roof.

d (*se diriger*) to go. **~ à gauche** to go *ou* turn *ou* bear left; **~ par les petites rues** to take to *ou* go along *ou* keep to the side streets.

3 **se prendre vpr** a (*se considérer*) **se ~ au sérieux** to take o.s. seriously; **il se prend pour un intellectuel** he thinks *ou* likes to think he's an intellectual; **pour qui se prend-il?** (just) who does he think he is?

b (*littér: commencer*) **se ~ à faire qch** to begin to do *ou* begin doing sth, start doing sth; **se ~ d'amitié pour qn** to take a liking to sb.

c **s'y ~** to set about (doing) it; **il fallait s'y ~ à temps** you should have set about it *ou* started before it was too late; **s'y ~ bien/mal pour faire qch** to set about doing sth the right/wrong way; **il s'y est pris drôlement pour le faire** he chose the oddest way of doing it, he went about it in the strangest way; **s'y ~ à deux fois/plusieurs fois pour faire qch** to try twice/several times to do sth, take two/several attempts to do sth; **il faut s'y ~ à deux** it needs two of us (to do it); **il ne sait pas s'y ~** he doesn't know how to do it *ou* set about it; **je ne sais pas comment tu t'y prends** I don't know how you manage it; **il ne s'y serait pas pris autrement s'il avait voulu tout faire échouer** he couldn't have done better if he had actually set out to ruin the whole thing; **s'y ~ bien** *ou* **savoir s'y ~ avec qn** to handle sb the right way; **il faut s'y ~ à l'avance** you have to do it ahead of time *ou* in advance.

d **s'en ~ à** *personne* (*agresser*) to lay into*, set about; (*passer sa colère sur*) to take it out on; (*blâmer*) to lay *ou* put the blame on, attack; *tradition, préjugé* (*remettre en question*) to challenge; *autorité, organisation* (*critiquer*) to attack, take on; **s'en ~ à qch** to take it out on sth*; **tu ne peux t'en ~ qu'à toi** you've only got yourself to blame; **s'en ~ aux traditions** to let fly at tradition.

e (*se solidifier*) to set hard. **l'eau s'est prise en glace** the water has frozen over.

preneur, -euse [pʀənœʀ, øz] **nm, f** (*acheteur*) buyer; (*locataire*) lessee (*Jur*), taker, tenant. (*Ciné*) **~ de son** sound-man; **trouver ~** to find a buyer; (*fig*) **ces restes de gâteau vont vite trouver ~** someone will soon eat (up) what's left of this cake, there'll be no problem finding a taker for the rest of this cake; **je suis ~ à 100 F** I'll buy *ou* take it for 100 francs.

prénom [pʀenɔ̃] **nm** (*gén*) Christian name (*Brit*), first name; (*Admin*) forename, given name (*US*). **~ usuel** name by which one is known.

prénommé, e [pʀenɔme] (**ptp de prénommer**) 1 **adj: le ~ Paul** the said Paul. 2 **nm, f** (*Jur*) above-named.

prénommer [pʀenɔme] [1] 1 **vt** to call, name, give a (first) name to. **on l'a prénommé comme son oncle** he was called *ou* named after his uncle, he was given the same name as his uncle. 2 **se prénommer vpr** to be called *ou* named.

prénuptial, e, mpl -aux [pʀenypsjal, o] **adj** premarital.

préoccupant, e [pʀeɔkypɑ̃, ɑ̃t] **adj** worrying.

préoccupation [pʀeɔkypasjɔ̃] **nf** a (*souci*) worry, anxiety. **sa mauvaise santé était une ~ supplémentaire pour ses parents** his ill health was a further worry to *ou* cause for concern to his parents. b (*priorité*) preoccupation, concern. **sa seule ~ était de** his one concern *ou* preoccupation was to.

préoccupé, e [pʀeɔkype] (**ptp de préoccuper**) **adj** (*absorbé*) preoccupied (*de qch* with sth, *de faire* with doing); (*soucieux*) concerned (*de qch* about sth, *de faire* to do), worried (*de qch* about sth, *de faire* over doing). **tu as l'air ~** you look worried.

préoccuper [pʀeɔkype] [1] 1 **vt** a (*inquiéter*) to worry. **il y a quelque chose qui le préoccupe** something is worrying *ou* bothering him, he has something on his mind; **l'avenir de son fils le préoccupe** he is concerned *ou* anxious *ou* bothered about his son's future.

b (*absorber*) to preoccupy. **cette idée lui préoccupe l'esprit** *ou* **le préoccupe** he is preoccupied with that idea; **il est uniquement préoccupé de sa petite personne** he only thinks about himself *ou* number one*, he's totally wrapped up in himself.

2 **se préoccuper vpr** to concern o.s. (*de* with), be concerned (*de* with); to worry (*de* about). **se ~ de la santé de qn** to show (great) concern about sb's health; **il ne se préoccupe pas beaucoup de notre sort** he isn't greatly concerned *ou* very worried *ou* he doesn't care very much about what happens to us; **il ne s'en préoccupe guère** he hardly gives it a thought.

préopératoire [pʀeɔpeʀatwaʀ] **adj** preoperative.

prépa [pʀepa] **nf** (*arg Scol*) (**abrév de classe préparatoire**) *voir* **préparatoire**.

préparateur, -trice [pʀepaʀatœʀ, tʀis] **nm, f** (*gén*) assistant; (*Univ*) demonstrator. **~ en pharmacie** pharmaceutical *ou* chemist's (*Brit*) assistant.

préparatifs [pʀepaʀatif] **nmpl** preparations (*de* for). **nous en sommes aux ~ de départ** we're getting ready *ou* we're preparing to leave.

préparation [pʀepaʀasjɔ̃] **nf** a (*confection*) (*gén*) preparation; [*repas*] preparation, making; [*médicament*] preparation, making up; [*complot*] laying, hatching; [*plan*] preparation, working out, drawing up. **plat dont la ~ demande des soins minutieux** dish which requires very careful preparation.

b (*apprêt*) (*gén*) preparation; [*table*] laying, getting ready; [*peaux, poisson, volaille*] dressing; [*attaque, départ, voyage*] preparation (*de* for). **la ~ de l'avenir** preparing *ou* preparation for the future; **attaque après ~ d'artillerie** attack following initial assault by the artillery; (*fig*) **~ du terrain** preparing the ground; **auteur qui a plusieurs livres en ~** author who has several books in hand *ou* in preparation.

c (*étude*) [*examen*] preparation, getting ready (*de* for).

d (*entraînement*) [*personne*] (*à un examen*) preparation (*à* for); (*à une épreuve sportive*) preparation, training (*à* for). **annoncer quelque chose sans ~** to announce something abruptly *ou* without preparation, spring something on someone.

e (*Chim, Pharm*) preparation.

f (*Scol*) (*classe préparatoire*) **faire une ~ à Polytechnique** to prepare for entrance to the École Polytechnique (*in one of the classes préparatoires*); (*devoir*) **une ~ française** a French exercise, a piece of French homework; **faire sa ~ militaire** to do a training course in preparation for one's military service.

préparatoire [pʀepaʀatwaʀ] **adj** *travail, démarche, conversation* preparatory, preliminary. **classe ~ (aux Grandes Écoles)** *class which prepares students for the entry exams to the Grandes Écoles; voir* **cours**.

préparer [pʀepaʀe] [1] 1 **vt** a (*confectionner*) (*gén*) to prepare; *repas* to prepare, make; *médicament* to prepare, make up; *piège, complot* to lay, hatch; *plan* to draw up, work out, prepare; *cours, discours* to prepare; *thèse* to be doing, be working on, prepare. **elle nous prépare une tasse de thé** she's making a cup of tea for us, she's getting us a cup of tea; **elle lui prépare de bons petits plats** she makes *ou* cooks *ou* prepares tasty dishes for him; **acheter un plat tout préparé** to buy a ready-cooked *ou* pre-cooked dish.

b (*apprêter*) (*gén*) to prepare; *table* to lay, get ready; *affaires, bagages, chambre* to prepare, get ready; *peaux, poisson, volaille* to dress; (*Agr*) *terre* to prepare; *attaque, rentrée, voyage* to prepare (for), get ready for; *transition* to prepare for. **~ le départ** to get ready *ou* prepare to leave, make ready for one's departure; **~ l'avenir** to prepare for the future; **~ ses effets** to time one's effects carefully, prepare one's effects; **il a préparé la rencontre des 2 ministres** he made the preparations for *ou* he organized *ou* he set up the meeting of the 2 ministers; **l'attaque avait été soigneusement préparée** the attack had been carefully prepared *ou* organized; **le coup avait été préparé de longue main** they (*ou* he *etc*) had been preparing for it for a long time; (*Mil, fig*) **~ le terrain** to prepare the ground.

c (*Scol*) *examen* to prepare for, study for. **~ Normale Sup** to study for entrance to the École normale supérieure.

d (*habituer, entraîner*) **~ qn à qch/à faire qch** to prepare sb for sth/to do sth; **~ les esprits** to prepare people's minds (*à qch* for sth); **~ qn à un examen** to prepare *ou* coach sb for an exam; **il a essayé de la ~ à la triste nouvelle** he tried to prepare her for the sad news; **je n'y étais pas préparé** I wasn't prepared for it, I wasn't expecting it.

e (*réserver*) **~ qch à qn** to have sth in store for sb; **je me demande ce qu'elle nous prépare** I wonder what she's cooking up for us; **on ne sait pas ce que l'avenir nous prépare** we don't know what the future holds (in store) for us *ou* has in store for us; **il nous prépare une surprise** he has a surprise in store for us, he's got a surprise up his sleeve; (*iro*) **ce temps nous prépare de joyeuses vacances!** if this weather continues, the holidays will be just great!*, this weather bodes well for our holidays! (*iro*); **il nous prépare un bon rhume** he's in for a cold.

2 **se préparer vpr** a (*s'apprêter*) to prepare (o.s.), get ready (*à qch* for sth, *à faire* to do). **attendez, elle se prépare** wait a minute, she's getting ready; **se ~ à une mauvaise nouvelle** to prepare o.s. *ou* be prepared for some bad news; **se ~ au combat** *ou* **à combattre** to prepare to fight *ou* to do battle; **se ~ pour les Jeux olympiques** to prepare *ou* train for the Olympics; **préparez-vous au pire** prepare yourself for the worst; **je ne m'y étais pas préparé** I hadn't prepared myself for it, I wasn't expecting it; **se ~ pour le bal/pour sortir dîner en ville** to get ready *ou* dressed for the dance/to go out to dinner; **préparez-vous à être appelé d'urgence** be prepared to be called out urgently; **vous vous préparez des ennuis** you are storing up problems for yourself.

b (*approcher*) [*orage*] to be brewing. **il se prépare une bagarre** there's going to be a fight, there's a fight brewing; **il se prépare quelque chose de louche** there's something fishy in the air.

prépayé, e [pʀepeje] **adj** *billet* prepaid, paid in advance.

prépondérance [pʀepɔ̃deʀɑ̃s] **nf** [*nation, groupe*] ascendancy, preponderance, supremacy; [*idée, croyance, théorie*] supremacy; [*trait de caractère*] domination.

prépondérant, e [pʀepɔ̃deʀɑ̃, ɑ̃t] **adj** *rôle* dominating, preponderant. **voix ~e** casting vote.

préposé [pʀepoze] **nm** (*gén*) employee; (*facteur*) postman (*Brit*), mailman (*US*); [*douane*] official, officer; [*vestiaire*] attendant.

préposée [pʀepoze] **nf** (*gén*) employee; (*factrice*) postwoman (*Brit*), mailwoman (*US*); [*vestiaire*] attendant.

préposer [prepoze] 1 vt to appoint (*à* to). **être préposé à** to be in charge of.

prépositif, -ive [prepozitif, iv] adj prepositional.

préposition [prepozisjɔ̃] nf preposition.

prépositionnel, -elle [prepozisjɔnɛl] adj prepositional.

prépositivement [prepozitivmɑ̃] adv prepositionally, as a preposition.

préprogrammé, e [preprɔgrame] adj (*Ordin*) preprogrammed.

prépuce [prepys] nm foreskin, prepuce (*SPÉC*).

préraphaélisme [prerafaelism] nm Pre-Raphaelitism.

préraphaélite [prerafaelit] adj, nm Pre-Raphaelite.

prérentrée [prerɑ̃tre] nf (*Scol*) *preparatory day before school term for teachers*.

préretraite [prer(ə)trɛt] nf (*état*) early retirement; (*pension*) early retirement pension. **être mis en** ~ to be given early retirement, be retired early.

préretraité, e [prerətrete] nm, f person who takes early retirement.

prérogative [prerɔgativ] nf prerogative.

préromantique [prerɔmɑ̃tik] adj pre-Romantic. **les ~s** the pre-Romantics, the pre-Romantic poets.

préromantisme [prerɔmɑ̃tism] nm pre-Romanticism.

près [prɛ] 1 adv a (*dans l'espace*) near(by), close (by), near *ou* close at hand; (*dans le temps*) near, close. **la gare est tout** ~ we're very close to the station, the station is very near by *ou* close at hand; **il habite assez/tout** ~ he lives quite/very near *ou* close (by) *ou* near at hand *ou* close at hand; **ne te mets pas trop** ~ don't get (*ou* sit *ou* stand *etc*) too close *ou* near; **c'est plus/moins** ~ **que je ne croyais** (*espace*) it's nearer *ou* closer than/further than I thought *ou* not as near *ou* close as I thought; (*temps*) it's nearer *ou* sooner *ou* closer than/not as near *ou* soon as I thought *ou* further off than I thought; **Noël est très** ~ **maintenant** Christmas is (getting) very near *ou* close now, it'll very soon be Christmas now.

b ~ **de** (*dans le temps*) close to; (*dans l'espace*) close to, near (to); (*approximativement*) nearly, almost; **leur maison est** ~ **de l'église** their house is close to *ou* near the church; **le plus/moins** ~ **possible de la porte/de Noël** as close *ou* near to/as far away as possible from the door/Christmas; **une robe** ~ **du corps** a slim-fitting dress; **ils étaient très** ~ **l'un de l'autre** (*lit*) they were very close to each other; (*fig*) *[candidats]* they were very close (to each other); *[enfants]* they were very close (to each other) in age; **il est** ~ **de minuit** it is close to *ou* on midnight, it's nearly midnight; **elle est** ~ **de sa mère** she's with her mother; **être très** ~ **du but** to be very close *ou* near to one's goal; **être très** ~ **d'avoir trouvé la solution** to have almost *ou* nearly found the solution; **il est** ~ **de la retraite** he is close to *ou* nearing retirement; **arriver** ~ **de la fin d'un voyage/des vacances** to be nearing the end *ou* coming near *ou* close to the end of a journey/the holidays; **il est** ~ **de la cinquantaine** he's nearly *ou* almost fifty, he's coming up to fifty (*Brit*), he's going on fifty; **il a dépensé** ~ **de la moitié de son mois** he has spent nearly *ou* almost half his month's salary; **il y a** ~ **de 5 ans qu'ils sont partis** they left nearly *ou* close on 5 years ago, it's nearly 5 years since they left; **elle a été très** ~ **de refuser** she was on the point of *ou* on the verge of refusing *ou* about to refuse; **je suis très** ~ **de croire que** ... I'm (almost) beginning to think that ...; (*iro*) **je ne suis pas** ~ **de partir/réussir** at this rate, I'm not likely to be going (yet)/to succeed; (*iro*) **je ne suis pas** ~ **d'y retourner/de recommencer** I shan't go back there/do that again in a hurry, you won't catch me going back there/doing that again in a hurry; (*fig*) **être** ~ **de son argent** *ou* **de ses sous*** to be close-fisted, be tight-fisted.

c **de (très)** ~ (very) closely; **le coup a été tiré de** ~ the shot was fired at close range; **il voit mal/bien de** ~ he can't see very well/he can see all right close to; **surveiller qn de** ~ to keep a close watch on sb, watch carefully over sb; **il faudra examiner cette affaire de plus** ~ we must have *ou* take a closer look at *ou* look more closely into this business; **il a vu la mort de** ~ he has stared *ou* looked death in the face; **on a frôlé de très** ~ **la catastrophe** we came within an inch *ou* ace of disaster, we had a close shave *ou* a narrow escape; *voir* **connaître, rasé, regarder.**

d (*loc*) **à peu de chose(s)** ~ more or less (*voir aussi* **peu**); **ce n'est pas aussi bon, à beaucoup** ~ it's nothing like *ou* nowhere near as good, it's not as good by a long way *ou* chalk (*Brit*); **ils sont identiques, à la couleur** ~ they are identical apart from *ou* except for the colour, colour apart, they are identical; **à cela** ~ **que** ... if it weren't for *ou* apart from *ou* aside from the fact that ...; **je vais vous donner le chiffre à un franc/à un centimètre** ~ I'll give you the figure to within about a franc/a centimetre; **cela fait 100 F à quelque chose** *ou* **à peu de chose(s)** ~ that comes to 100 francs, as near as makes no difference *ou* as near as damn it* (*Brit*); **il n'en est pas à 100 F** ~ he's not going to quibble over an odd *ou* a mere 100 francs, he can spare (another) 100 francs, (another) 100 francs isn't going to ruin him; **il a raté le bus à une minute** ~ he missed the bus by a minute or so; **il n'est pas à 10 minutes/à un kilo de sucre** ~ he can spare 10 minutes/a kilo of sugar; **il n'est pas à un crime** ~ he won't let a crime stop him; **il n'est plus à 10 minutes** ~ he can wait another 10 minutes.

2 prép (*littér, Admin*) *lieu* near. **ambassadeur** ~ **le roi de** ambassador to the king of.

présage [prezaʒ] nm omen, sign, forewarning, presage (*littér*), portent (*littér*). **mauvais** ~ ill omen; ~ **de malheur** sign of misfortune.

présager [prezaʒe] 3 vt (*annoncer*) to be a sign *ou* an omen of, presage (*littér*), portend (*littér*); (*prévoir*) to predict, foresee. **cela ne présage rien de bon** nothing good will come of it, that's an ominous sign; **cela nous laisse** ~ **que** it leads us to predict *ou* expect that; **rien ne laissait** ~ **la catastrophe** there was no inkling *ou* hint of the disaster; **rien ne laissait** ~ **que** there was nothing to hint that.

présalé [presale] nm = **pré-salé**; *voir* **pré.**

presbyte [prɛsbit] adj long-sighted, far-sighted (*US*), presbyopic (*SPÉC*).

presbytère [prɛsbitɛr] nm presbytery.

presbytérianisme [prɛsbiterjanism] nm Presbyterianism.

presbytérien, -ienne [prɛsbiterjɛ̃, jɛn] adj, nm, f Presbyterian.

presbytie [prɛsbisi] nf long-sightedness, far-sightedness (*US*), presbyopia (*SPÉC*).

prescience [presjɑ̃s] nf prescience, foresight.

prescient, e [presjɑ̃, jɑ̃t] adj prescient, far-sighted.

préscolaire [preskɔlɛr] adj preschool (*épith*). **enfant d'âge** ~ preschool child.

prescripteur, -trice [prɛskriptœr, tris] nm, f: **(médecin)** ~ consultant.

prescriptible [prɛskriptibl] adj prescriptible.

prescription [prɛskripsjɔ̃] nf (*Méd*) prescription, directions; (*Jur*) prescription; (*ordre*) (*gén*) order, instruction; *[morale, règlement]* dictate.

prescrire [prɛskrir] 39 vt (*Méd*) to prescribe; (*Jur*) *droit* to prescribe; *objet, méthode, livre*) to strongly recommend; *[morale, honneur, loi]* to stipulate, lay down; (*ordonner*) to order, command. **à la date prescrite** on the prescribed date, on the date stipulated; (*Méd*) **ne pas dépasser la dose prescrite** do not exceed the prescribed dose; *[peine, dette]* **être prescrit, se** ~ to lapse.

préséance [preseɑ̃s] nf precedence (*NonC*).

présélecteur [preselɛktœr] nm preselector.

présélection [preselɛksjɔ̃] nf (*gén*) preselection; *[candidats]* short-listing (*Brit*). (*Aut*) **boîte de vitesses à** ~ preselector (gearbox); (*Rad*) **bouton de** ~ preset switch.

présélectionner [preselɛksjɔne] 1 vt *chaîne de radio* to preset; *candidats* to short-list (*Brit*).

présence [prezɑ̃s] 1 nf a *[personne, chose, pays]* presence; (*au bureau, à l'école*) attendance; (*Rel*) presence. **la** ~ **aux cours est obligatoire** attendance at classes is compulsory; **fuir la** ~ **de qn** to avoid sb, keep well away from sb; (*frm*) **Monsieur le maire a honoré la cérémonie de sa** ~ the Mayor honoured them with his presence at the ceremony; **j'ai juste à faire de la** ~ I just have to be there; ~ **assidue au bureau** regular attendance at the office; ~ **policière** police presence; *voir* **acte, feuille, jeton.**

b (*personnalité*) presence. **avoir de la** ~ to have (a) great presence.

c (*être*) **sentir une** ~ to be aware of sb's presence *ou* of a presence.

d (*loc*) **en** ~ *armées* opposing (each other); *personnes* face to face (with each other); **mettre 2 personnes en** ~ to bring 2 people together *ou* face to face; (*Jur*) **les parties en** ~ the litigants, the opposing parties; **en** ~ **de** in the presence of; **cela s'est produit en ma/hors de ma** ~ it happened while I was there *ou* in my presence/while I was not there *ou* in my absence; **en** ~ **de tels incidents** faced with *ou* in the face of such incidents; **mettre qn en** ~ **de qn/qch** to bring sb face to face with sb/sth.

2 comp ▸ **présence d'esprit** presence of mind.

présent[1]**, e** [prezɑ̃, ɑ̃t] 1 adj a *personne* present; (*Rel*) present. (*frm*) **les personnes ici ~es** the persons here present (*frm*), the people here present; **les personnes (qui étaient) ~es au moment de l'incident** the people who were present *ou* there when the incident occurred; **être** ~ **à une cérémonie** to be present at *ou* attend a ceremony; **être** ~ **à l'appel** to be present at roll call; **~!** present!; (*hum*) **pour un bon repas, il est toujours ~!** you can always count on him to be there for a good meal, he's always around* *ou* there when there's a good meal on the go!; **je suis** ~ **en pensée** my thoughts are with you (*ou* him *etc*), I'm thinking of you (*ou* him *etc*).

b *chose* present. **métal** ~ **dans un minerai** metal present *ou* found in an ore; **son pessimisme est partout** ~ **dans son dernier roman** his pessimism runs right through *ou* is evident throughout his latest novel; **sa gentillesse est ~e dans chacun de ses actes** his kindness is evident in *ou* is to be found in everything he does; **avoir qch** ~ **à l'esprit** to have sth fresh in one's mind, not to forget about sth; **je n'ai pas les chiffres ~s à l'esprit** I can't bring the figures to mind, I can't remember the figures offhand; **j'aurai toujours ce souvenir** ~ **à l'esprit** this memory will be ever-present in my mind *ou* will always be fresh in my mind; **gardez ceci** ~ **à l'esprit** keep *ou* bear this in mind.

c (*actuel*) *circonstances, état, heure, époque* present. **le 15 du mois** ~ on the 15th instant (*Brit Admin*) *ou* of this month.

d (*Gram*) *temps, participe* present.

e (*dont il est question*) present. **le** ~ **récit** the present account, this account; (*Admin*) **par la ~e lettre** by the present letter, by this letter.

2 nm a (*époque*) **le** ~ the present.

b (*Gram*) present (tense). **au** ~ in the present (tense); ~ **de**

l'indicatif present indicative; ~ **historique** *ou* **de narration** historic(al) present.

c (*personne*) **les ~s et les absents** those present and those absent; **il n'y avait que 5 ~s** there were only 5 people present *ou* there.

d (*loc*) **à ~** (*en ce moment*) at present, presently (*US*); (*maintenant*) now; (*de nos jours*) now, nowadays; **à ~ que nous savons** now that we know; **la jeunesse/les gens d'à ~** youngsters/people of today, youngsters/people nowadays; *voir* **dès, jusque.**

3 **présente** nf (*Admin: lettre*) **veuillez recevoir par la ~e** please accept by the present letter *ou* by this letter.

présent[2] [pʀezɑ̃] nm (*littér*) gift, present. **faire ~ de qch à qn** to present sb with sth.

présentable [pʀezɑ̃tabl] adj *plat, personne* presentable.

présentateur, -trice [pʀezɑ̃tatœʀ, tʀis] nm,f (*Rad, TV*) *[jeu, causerie, variétés]* host, compere; *[débat]* presenter; *[nouvelles]* newscaster, newsreader.

présentation [pʀezɑ̃tasjɔ̃] nf a (*gén*) presentation. **sur ~ d'une pièce d'identité** on presentation of proof of identity.

b *[nouveau venu, conférencier]* introduction; (*frm: à la cour*) presentation. **faire les ~s** to make the introductions, introduce people to one another.

c (*au public*) *[tableaux, pièce]* presentation; *[marchandises]* presentation, display; *[film]* presentation, showing; (*Rad, TV*) *[émission]* presentation, introduction. **~ de mode** fashion show.

d (*manière de présenter*) *[idées, produit, travail]* presentation. (*fig*) *[personne]* **avoir une bonne/mauvaise ~** to have a good *ou* pleasant/an unattractive *ou* off-putting (*Brit*) appearance.

e (*Rel*) **la P~** the Presentation.

f (*Méd*) *[fœtus]* presentation. **~ par la tête/le siège** head/breech presentation.

présentement [pʀezɑ̃tmɑ̃] adv (*en ce moment*) at present, presently (*US*); (*maintenant*) now.

présenter [pʀezɑ̃te] [1] 1 vt a (*introduire*) *connaissance, conférencier* to introduce (*à* to, *dans* into); (*au roi, à la cour*) to present (*à* to). **je vous présente ma femme** this is my wife, have you met my wife?, may I introduce my wife (to you)?

b (*proposer au public*) *marchandises* to present, display (*à* to), set out (*à* before); (*Théât*) *acteur, pièce* to present; (*Rad, TV*) *émission* to present, introduce, compere; *modes, tableaux* to present. (*TV*) **c'est lui qui présente les nouvelles** he presents *ou* reports the news.

c (*exposer*) *problème* to set out, explain; *idées* to present, set *ou* lay out; *théorie* to expound, set out. **c'est un travail bien/mal présenté** it's a well-/badly presented *ou* well/badly laid-out piece of work; **~ qch sous un jour favorable** to present sth in a favourable light; **présentez-lui cela avec tact** explain it to him *ou* put it to him tactfully; **il nous a présenté son ami comme un héros** he spoke of his friend as a hero.

d (*montrer*) *billet, passeport* to present, show, produce. **il présentait un tel air de consternation** he presented such a picture of consternation; **il présenta sa joue au baiser de sa mère** he presented *ou* offered his cheek for his mother to kiss.

e (*tourner*) to turn. **~ le flanc à l'ennemi** to turn one's flank towards the enemy; **bateau qui présente le travers au vent** ship which turns *ou* sails broadside on to the wind.

f (*exprimer*) *excuses* to present, offer, make; *condoléances, félicitations* to present, offer; *respects* to present, pay; *objection* to raise.

g (*laisser paraître*) *avantage, intérêt* to present, afford; *différences* to reveal, present; *danger, difficulté, obstacle* to present. **cette route présente beaucoup de détours** there are a lot of bends on this road; **ce malade présente des symptômes de tuberculose** this patient presents *ou* shows symptoms of tuberculosis; **ce vase présente de nombreux défauts** this vase has *ou* shows a number of flaws.

h (*offrir*) *plat* to present, hold out; *rafraîchissements* to offer, hand round; *bouquet* to present. **~ son bras à qn** to offer one's arm to sb.

i (*soumettre*) *addition, facture, devis* to present, submit; *thèse* to submit; *motion* to move; *projet de loi* to present, introduce; *rapport, requête* to present, put in, submit. **~ sa candidature à un poste** to apply for *ou* put in for a job; **~ un candidat à un concours** to put a candidate in *ou* enter a candidate for a competitive examination; (*Scol*) **~ un texte de Camus à un examen** to choose *ou* do a text by Camus for an exam.

j (*Mil*) *armes* to present; *troupes* to present (*for inspection*). **présentez armes!** present arms!

k (*Tech: placer*) to position, line up.

2 vi *[personne]* **~ bien/mal** to have a good *ou* pleasant/an unattractive *ou* off-putting (*Brit*) appearance, be of good/poor appearance.

3 **se présenter** vpr a (*se rendre*) to go, come, appear. **se ~ chez qn** to go to sb's house; **il ose encore se ~ chez toi!** does he still dare to show himself *ou* to appear at your house!; **il ne s'est présenté personne** no one turned up *ou* came *ou* appeared; **je ne peux pas me ~ dans cette tenue** I can't appear dressed like this; (*dans une annonce*) **ne pas écrire, se ~** (interested) applicants should apply in person; (*Jur*) **se ~ à l'audience** to appear in court, make a court appearance.

b (*être candidat*) to come forward. **se ~ pour un emploi** to put in for a job; **se ~ à** *élection* to stand at (*Brit*), run for (*surtout US*); *examen* to sit (*Brit*), take; *concours* to go in for, enter (for); **se ~ comme candidat** (*à un poste*) to apply, be an applicant (*à* for); (*aux élections*) to be a candidate, stand (*Brit*) *ou* run (*surtout US*) as a candidate (*à* at).

c (*se faire connaître*) (*gén*) to introduce o.s.; (*à un patron*) to introduce o.s., report (*à* to).

d (*surgir*) *[occasion]* to arise, present itself; *[difficulté]* to crop *ou* come up, arise, present itself; *[solution]* to come to mind, present itself. **un problème se présente à nous** we are faced *ou* confronted with a problem; **il lit tout ce qui se présente** he reads everything he can get his hands on, he reads anything that's going*; **il faut attendre que quelque chose se présente** we must wait until something turns up; **deux noms se présentent à l'esprit** two names come *ou* spring to mind; **un spectacle magnifique se présenta à ses yeux** a magnificent sight met his eyes; **profiter de l'occasion qui se présente** to take advantage of the opportunity that has arisen *ou* that presents itself.

e (*apparaître*) **cela se présente sous forme de cachets** it's presented *ou* it comes in the form of tablets; **l'affaire se présente bien/mal** things are looking good/aren't looking too good; **le problème se présente sous un nouveau jour** the problem takes on (quite) a different aspect *ou* complexion *ou* appears in a new light; **comment le problème se présente-t-il?** what exactly is the problem?, what is the nature of the problem?; (*Méd*) **comment l'enfant se présente-t-il?** how is the baby presenting?; **comment cela se présente-t-il?** (*lit*) what does it look like?; (* *fig*) how's it going?*

présentoir [pʀezɑ̃twaʀ] nm (*étagère*) display shelf.

préserie [pʀeseʀi] nf pilot production.

préservateur, -trice [pʀezɛʀvatœʀ, tʀis] adj preventive, protective.

préservatif, -ive [pʀezɛʀvatif, iv] 1 adj preventive, protective. 2 nm condom, sheath.

préservation [pʀezɛʀvasjɔ̃] nf preservation, protection.

préserver [pʀezɛʀve] [1] vt (*protéger*) to protect (*de* from, against); (*sauver*) to save (*de* from); (*sauvegarder*) to protect, safeguard. **se ~ du soleil** to protect o.s. from the sun; **le ciel** *ou* **Dieu m'en préserve!** Heaven preserve me! *ou* forbid!

présidence [pʀezidɑ̃s] nf a *[état, tribunal]* presidency; *[comité, réunion]* chairmanship; *[firme]* chairmanship, directorship; *[université]* vice-chancellorship (*Brit*), presidency (*US*). (*Pol*) **candidat à la ~** presidential candidate. b (*résidence*) presidential residence *ou* palace.

président [pʀezidɑ̃] 1 nm a (*Pol*) president. **Monsieur le ~** (*gén*) Mr President; (*Jur*) Your Honour. b *[comité, réunion]* chairman; *[club, société savante]* president; *[commission]* convener; *[firme]* chairman, president; *[jury d'examen]* chairman, chief examiner; *[université]* vice-chancellor (*Brit*), president (*US*), chancellor (*US*). c (*Jur*) *[tribunal]* presiding judge *ou* magistrate; *[jury]* foreman. 2 comp ▸ **président du Conseil** (*Hist*) prime minister ▸ **président-directeur général** chairman and managing director (*Brit*), chairman and chief executive officer (*US*) ▸ **le président Mao** Chairman Mao ▸ **président à vie** life president.

présidente [pʀezidɑ̃t] nf a (*en titre: voir* **président**) (lady *ou* woman) president; chairwoman; presiding judge *ou* magistrate. b (*épouse: voir* **président**) president's wife, first lady; president's *ou* chairman's wife.

présidentiable [pʀezidɑ̃sjabl] adj: **être ~** to be a possible *ou* potential presidential candidate.

présidentialisme [pʀezidɑ̃sjalism] nm presidentialism.

présidentiel, -elle [pʀezidɑ̃sjɛl] 1 adj presidential. 2 **présidentielles** nfpl presidential election(s).

présider [pʀezide] [1] 1 vt *tribunal, conseil, assemblée* to preside over; *comité, débat, séance* to chair. **~ un dîner** to be the guest of honour at a dinner; **c'est X qui préside** (*séance*) X is in *ou* taking the chair, X is chairing; (*club*) X is the president, X is presiding. 2 **présider à** vt indir *préparatifs, décisions, exécution* to direct, be in charge *ou* command of; *destinées* to rule over; *cérémonie* to preside over. **règles qui président à qch** rules which govern sth; **la volonté de conciliation a présidé aux discussions** a conciliatory spirit prevailed throughout the talks.

présidium [pʀezidjɔm] nm presidium.

présomptif, -ive [pʀezɔ̃ptif, iv] adj: **héritier ~** heir apparent.

présomption [pʀezɔ̃psjɔ̃] nf a (*supposition*) presumption, assumption; (*Jur*) presumption. **de lourdes ~s pèsent sur lui** he is heavily suspected. b (*prétention*) presumptuousness, presumption.

présomptueusement [pʀezɔ̃ptɥøzmɑ̃] adv presumptuously.

présomptueux, -euse [pʀezɔ̃ptɥø, øz] adj presumptuous, self-assured. **ton/air ~** presumptuous *ou* brash tone/air.

presque [pʀɛsk] adv a almost, nearly, virtually. **j'ai ~ terminé** I've almost *ou* nearly *ou* virtually *ou* as good as finished; **~ à chaque pas** at almost every step; **une espèce d'inquiétude, ~ d'angoisse** a kind of anxiety — almost anguish; **c'est ~ de la folie** it's little short of madness; **c'est ~ impossible** it's almost *ou* next to *ou* virtually *ou* well-nigh impossible; **c'est sûr ou ~** it's almost *ou* practically *ou* virtually certain.

b (*contexte négatif*) hardly, scarcely, almost, virtually. **personne/**

rien ou ~, ~ personne/rien hardly *ou* scarcely anyone/anything, almost nobody/nothing, next to nobody/nothing; **as-tu trouvé des fautes? — ~ pas** did you find any mistakes? – only a few *ou* – no, hardly *ou* scarcely any *ou* – no, practically *ou* virtually none; **a-t-il dormi? — ~ pas** has he had a sleep? – no, not really, did he sleep? – no, hardly *ou* scarcely at all *ou* no, not really; **je ne l'ai ~ pas entendu** I hardly *ou* scarcely heard him; **il n'y a ~ plus de vin** there's almost no *ou* hardly *ou* scarcely any wine left, the wine has nearly all gone; **ça n'arrive ~ jamais** it hardly *ou* scarcely ever happens, it almost *ou* practically never happens.

c (*avant n*) **dans la ~ obscurité** in the near darkness; **la ~ totalité des lecteurs** almost *ou* nearly all the readers; **j'en ai la ~ certitude** I'm almost *ou* virtually certain.

presqu'île [pʀɛskil] **nf** peninsula.

pressage [pʀesaʒ] **nm** *[disque, raisin]* pressing.

pressant, e [pʀesɑ̃, ɑ̃t] **adj** *besoin, danger, invitation* urgent, pressing (*épith*); *situation, travail, désir* urgent; *demande, personne* insistent, urgent. **demander qch de façon ~e** to ask for sth urgently; **le créancier a été/s'est fait ~** the creditor was insistent/started to insist *ou* started to press him (*ou* me *etc*); (*euph*) **avoir un besoin ~** to need to spend a penny (*euph*) (*Brit*) *ou* go to the restroom (*US*).

presse [pʀɛs] **nf** a (*institution*) press; (*journaux*) (news)papers. **la grande ~, la ~ à grand tirage** the popular press; **c'est dans toute la ~** it's in all the papers; **la ~ périodique** periodicals, journals; **~ régionale/mensuelle** regional/monthly press *ou* papers; **~ féminine/automobile** women's/car magazines; **~ d'opinion** papers specializing in political *etc* analysis and commentary; **~ d'information** newspapers; **~ à scandale** *ou* **à sensation** gutter press; **~ du cœur** romance magazines (*pl*); **avoir bonne/mauvaise ~** (*lit*) to get *ou* have a good/bad press; (*fig*) to be well/badly thought of; **agence/attaché/conférence de ~** press agency/attaché/conference; *voir* **délit, liberté, service.**

b (*appareil*) (*gén*) press; (*Typ*) (printing) press. **~ à cylindres/à bras** cylinder/hand press; **mettre sous ~** *livre* to send to press; *journal* to put to bed; **le livre a été mis sous ~** the book has gone to press; **le journal a été mis sous ~** the (news)paper has gone to bed; **livre sous ~** book in press; **correct au moment de la mise sous ~** correct at the time of going to press.

c (*littér: foule*) throng (*littér*), press (*littér*).

d (*urgence*) **pendant les moments de ~** when things get busy; **il n'y a pas de ~*** there's no rush *ou* hurry.

presse- [pʀɛs] **préf** *voir* **presser.**

pressé, e [pʀese] (**ptp de presser**) **adj** a *pas* hurried. **avoir un air ~** to look as though one is in a hurry; **marcher d'un pas ~** to hurry along; **je suis (très) ~/ne suis pas ~** I'm in a (great) hurry *ou* (very) pressed for time/in no hurry; **être ~ de partir** to be in a hurry to leave.

b (*urgent*) *travail, lettre* urgent. **c'est ~?** is it urgent?, are you in a hurry for it?; **il n'a eu rien de plus ~ que de faire ...** he wasted no time doing ..., he just couldn't wait to do ...; **si tu n'as rien de plus ~ à faire que de ...** if you have nothing more urgent to do than ...; **il faut parer au plus ~** we must do the most urgent thing(s) first, first things first.

c **citron ~/orange ~e** freshly-squeezed lemon/orange juice.

pressentiment [pʀesɑ̃timɑ̃] **nm** (*intuition*) foreboding, presentiment, premonition; (*idée*) feeling. **j'ai comme un ~ qu'il ne viendra pas** I've got a feeling *ou* a premonition he won't come; **avoir le ~ de qch/que ...** to have a premonition of sth/that ... .

pressentir [pʀesɑ̃tiʀ] 16 **vt** a *danger* to sense, have a foreboding *ou* a premonition of. **~ que ...** to have a feeling *ou* a premonition that ...; **j'avais pressenti quelque chose** I had sensed something; **il n'a rien laissé ~ de ses projets** he gave no hint of his plans; **rien ne laissait ~ une mort si soudaine** there was nothing to forewarn of *ou* to hint at such a sudden death. b *personne* to sound out, approach. **il a été pressenti pour le poste** he has been sounded out *ou* approached about taking the job; **ministre pressenti** prospective minister.

presser [pʀese] 1 1 **vt** a *éponge* to squeeze; *fruit* to squeeze (the juice out of); *raisin* to press. (*fig*) **on presse l'orange** *ou* **le citron et on jette l'écorce** you use people as long as they can be of service to you and then you cast them aside.

b (*serrer*) *objet* to squeeze. **les gens étaient pressés les uns contre les autres** people were squashed up *ou* crushed up against one another; **~ qn dans ses bras** to squeeze sb in one's arms, hug sb; **~ qn contre sa poitrine** to clasp sb to one's chest; **~ la main de** *ou* **à qn** to squeeze sb's hand, give sb's hand a squeeze.

c (*appuyer sur*) *bouton, sonnette* to press, push. **~ une matrice dans la cire** to press a mould into the wax; **il faut ~ ici** you must press here.

d (*façonner*) *disque, pli de pantalon* to press.

e (*inciter à*) **~ qn de faire** to urge *ou* press sb to do.

f (*hâter*) *affaire* to speed up; *départ* to hasten, speed up. **(faire) ~ qn** to hurry sb (up); **(faire) ~ les choses** to speed things up; **~ le pas** *ou* **l'allure** to speed up, hurry on; **il fit ~ l'allure** he quickened *ou* speeded up the pace; **qu'est-ce qui vous presse?** what's the hurry?; **rien ne vous presse** there's no hurry, we're in no rush.

g (*harceler*) *débiteur* to press; (*littér: Mil*) *ennemi* to press. **être pressé par le besoin** to be driven *ou* pressed by need; (*littér*) **le désir qui le presse** the desire which drives him; (*fig*) **~ qn de questions** to bombard *ou* ply sb with questions.

2 **vi** (*être urgent*) to be urgent. **l'affaire presse** it's urgent; **le temps presse** time is short, time presses; **cela ne presse pas, rien ne presse** there's no hurry *ou* rush *ou* urgency, there's no need to rush *ou* hurry.

3 **se presser vpr** a (*se serrer*) **se ~ contre qn** to squeeze up against sb; **les gens se pressaient pour entrer** people were pushing to get in, there was a crush to get in; **les gens se pressaient autour de la vedette** people were pressing *ou* crowding round the star.

b (*se hâter*) to hurry (up). **ils allaient/travaillaient sans se ~** they went/were working without hurrying *ou* at a leisurely pace; **pressez-vous, il est tard** hurry up *ou* get a move on*, it's getting late; **il faut se ~** we must hurry up *ou* get cracking* *ou* get a move on*; **presse-toi de partir** hurry up and go; **allons, pressons(-nous)!** come on, come on!, come on, we must hurry!

4 **comp ▸presse-agrumes nm inv** lemon squeezer **▸presse-ail nm inv** garlic press **▸presse-bouton adj inv** push-button **▸presse-citron nm inv** lemon squeezer **▸presse-livres nm inv** book-ends **▸presse-papiers nm inv** paperweight **▸presse-purée nm inv** potato-masher **▸presse-raquette nm inv** racket press.

pressing [pʀesiŋ] **nm** a (*repassage*) steam-pressing; (*établissement*) dry-cleaner's. b (*Sport*) pressure. **faire le ~** to put the pressure on (*sur qn* sb).

pression [pʀesjɔ̃] **nf** a (*action*) pressure. **je sentais la ~ de sa main sur la mienne** I could feel the pressure of his hand on mine *ou* his hand pressing on mine; **une simple ~ du doigt suffit** one push with the finger is all that is needed; **faire ~ sur le couvercle d'une boîte** (*pour fermer*) to press (down) on the lid of a box; (*pour ouvrir*) to push up the lid of a box; **il inséra le levier sous la pierre et fit ~ pour la lever** he inserted the lever under the stone and pressed on it to lift the stone.

b (*Méd, Phys*) pressure. **~ artérielle/atmosphérique** blood/atmospheric pressure; **à haute/basse ~** high/low pressure (*épith*); **être sous ~** *[machine]* to be under pressure, be at full pressure; *[cabine]* to be pressurized; (*fig: être tendu*) to be keyed up, be tense; **mettre sous ~** to pressurize; (*excès de travail*) **je suis sous ~ en ce moment** I am under pressure just now; (*fig*) **faire monter la ~** to increase the pressure.

c (*fig: contrainte*) pressure. **~ sociale/fiscale** social/tax pressure; **sous la ~ des événements** under the pressure of events; **faire ~** *ou* **exercer une ~ sur qn (pour qu'il fasse qch)** to put pressure on sb (to do sth), bring pressure to bear on sb (to do sth), pressurize sb (into doing sth); **être soumis à des ~s** to be subject to pressures, be under pressure; *voir* **groupe.**

d **bière à la ~** draught (*Brit*) *ou* draft (*US*) beer, beer on draught (*Brit*) *ou* draft (*US*); **deux ~(s)* s'il vous plaît** two (draught) beers, please.

e (*bouton*) press stud (*Brit*), snap (fastener) (*US*), popper* (*Brit*).

pressoir [pʀeswaʀ] **nm** a (*appareil*) *[vin]* wine press; *[cidre]* cider press; *[huile]* oil press. b (*local*) press-house.

pressurage [pʀesyʀaʒ] **nm** *[fruit]* pressing.

pressurer [pʀesyʀe] 1 **vt** *fruit* to press; (*fig: exploiter*) *personne* to squeeze.

pressurisation [pʀesyʀizasjɔ̃] **nf** pressurization.

pressuriser [pʀesyʀize] 1 **vt** to pressurize. **cabine pressurisée** pressurized cabin.

prestance [pʀɛstɑ̃s] **nf** imposing bearing, presence. **avoir de la ~** to have great presence.

prestataire [pʀɛstatɛʀ] **nm** person receiving benefits *ou* allowances. **~ de service** provider of a service.

prestation [pʀɛstasjɔ̃] 1 **nf** a (*allocation*) *[assurance]* benefit. b (*gén pl: services*) *[hôtel, restaurant]* service; *[maison]* unique features. c (*performance*) *[artiste, sportif]* performance. **faire une bonne ~** to put up a good performance, perform well.

2 **comp ▸prestations familiales** State benefits paid to the family (*maternity benefit, family income supplement, rent rebate etc*) **▸prestation d'invalidité** disablement benefit *ou* allowance **▸prestation en nature** payment in kind **▸prestation de serment** taking the oath; **la prestation de serment du président a eu lieu hier** the president was sworn in yesterday **▸prestations sociales** social security benefits, welfare payments **▸prestation de service** provision of a service **▸prestation de vieillesse** old age pension.

preste [pʀɛst] **adj** (*littér*) nimble.

prestement [pʀɛstəmɑ̃] **adv** (*littér*) nimbly.

prestesse [pʀɛstɛs] **nf** (*littér*) nimbleness.

prestidigitateur, -trice [pʀɛstidiʒitatœʀ, tʀis] **nm,f** conjurer, magician.

prestidigitation [pʀɛstidiʒitasjɔ̃] **nf** conjuring. **tour de ~** conjuring trick; (*fig*) **c'est de la ~!** it's like a conjuring trick!

prestige [pʀɛstiʒ] **nm** (*gén*) prestige. **le ~ de l'uniforme** the glamour of uniforms; **de ~** *politique, opération, voiture* prestige (*épith*).

prestigieux, -ieuse [pʀɛstiʒjø, jøz] **adj** prestigious; (*Comm*) renowned, prestigious. **X est une marque ~euse de voiture** X is a famous *ou* prestigious make of car *ou* name in cars.

presto [pʀɛsto] **adv** (*Mus*) presto; (* *fig*) double-quick*.

présumable [pʀezymabl] **adj** presumable.

présumer [pʀezyme] 1 1 vt to presume, assume. **présumé innocent** presumed innocent; **l'auteur présumé du livre** the presumed author of the book. 2 **présumer de** vt indir: **trop ~ de qch/qn** to overestimate *ou* overrate sth/sb; **trop ~ de ses forces** to overestimate one's strength.

présupposé [pʀesypoze] nm presupposition.

présupposer [pʀesypoze] 1 vt to presuppose.

présupposition [pʀesypozisjɔ̃] nf presupposition.

présure [pʀezyʀ] nf rennet.

prêt¹, prête [pʀɛ, pʀɛt] 1 adj a (*préparé*) *personne, repas* ready. **~ à** *ou* **pour qch/à** *ou* **pour faire qch** ready for sth/to do sth; **~ à fonctionner** ready for use; **~ à l'emploi** ready for use; **poulet ~ à cuire** *ou* **rôtir** oven-ready chicken; **~ au départ** *ou* **à partir** ready to go *ou* leave, ready for off* (*Brit*); **être fin ~ (au départ)** to be all set, be raring* to go; **tout est (fin) ~** everything is (quite) ready *ou* is at the ready, everything is in readiness; **se tenir ~ à qch/à faire qch** to hold o.s. *ou* be ready for sth/to do sth; **tiens ta monnaie ~e pour payer** have your money ready to pay; *[criminel]* **il est ~ à tout** he will do anything, he will stop at nothing; **on m'a averti: je suis ~ à tout** they've warned me and I'm ready for anything; *voir* **marque**.

b (*disposé*) **~ à** ready *ou* prepared *ou* willing to; **être tout ~ à faire qch** to be quite ready *ou* prepared *ou* willing to do sth.

2 comp ▸**prêt-à-coudre** nm (pl **prêts-à-coudre**) ready-to-sew garment ▸**prêt-à-manger** nm (pl **prêts-à-manger**) ready-made meal ▸**prêt-à-monter** nm (pl **prêts-à-monter**) kit.

prêt² [pʀɛ] 1 nm a (*action*) loaning, lending; (*somme*) loan. **le service de ~ d'une bibliothèque** the lending department of a library; **~ sur gages** (*service*) pawnbroking; (*somme*) loan against security; *voir* **bibliothèque**. b (*Mil*) pay. c (*avance*) advance. 2 comp ▸**prêt-bail** leasing ▸**prêt bancaire** bank loan ▸**prêt à la construction** building loan ▸**prêt d'honneur** (*government*) *loan made with no guarantee of repayment* ▸**prêt immobilier** mortgage (loan), real-estate loan (*US*) ▸**prêt privilégié** guaranteed loan ▸**prêt relais** bridging loan.

prêt-à-porter [pʀɛtapɔʀte] nm ready-to-wear (clothes). **acheter qch en ~** to buy sth ready to wear *ou* off the peg (*Brit*); **je n'achète que du ~** I only buy off-the-peg (*Brit*) clothes *ou* ready-to-wear clothes.

prêté [pʀete] nm: **c'est un ~ (pour un) rendu** it's tit for tat.

prétendant, e [pʀetɑ̃dɑ̃, ɑ̃t] 1 nm (*prince*) pretender; (*littér: galant*) suitor. 2 nm, f (*candidat*) candidate (*à* for).

prétendre [pʀetɑ̃dʀ] 41 1 vt a (*affirmer*) to claim, maintain, assert, say. **il prétend être** *ou* **qu'il est le premier à avoir trouvé la réponse** he claims to be the first to have found the answer, he claims *ou* maintains *ou* asserts (that) he's the first to have found the answer; **il se prétend insulté/médecin** he makes out *ou* claims he's been insulted/he's a doctor; **je ne prétends pas qu'il l'ait fait** I don't say *ou* I'm not saying he did it; **on le prétend très riche** he is said *ou* alleged to be very rich; **en prétendant qu'il venait chercher un livre** on the pretence of coming to get a book, making out *ou* claiming that he had come to get a book; **à ce qu'il prétend** according to him *ou* to what he says, if what he says is true; **à ce qu'on prétend** allegedly, according to what people say.

b (*avoir la prétention de*) to claim. **il prétend savoir jouer du piano** he claims he can play the piano; **tu ne prétends pas le faire tout seul?** you don't pretend *ou* expect to do it on your own?; **je ne prétends pas me défendre** I don't pretend *ou* I'm not trying to justify myself.

c (*littér*) (*vouloir*) to want; (*avoir l'intention de*) to mean, intend. **que prétendez-vous de moi?** what do you want of me? (*littér*); **que prétend-il faire?** what does he mean *ou* intend to do?; **je prétends être obéi** *ou* **qu'on m'obéisse** I mean to be obeyed.

2 **prétendre à** vt indir *honneurs, emploi* to lay claim to, aspire to; *femme* to aspire to. **~ à faire** to aspire to do.

prétendu, e [pʀetɑ̃dy] (ptp de **prétendre**) 1 adj *ami, expert* so-called, supposed; *alibi, preuves, déclaration* alleged. 2 nm, f (†: *fiancé*) intended (†, *littér*).

prétendument [pʀetɑ̃dymɑ̃] adv supposedly, allegedly.

prête-nom, pl **prête-noms** [pʀɛtnɔ̃] nm figurehead.

prétentaine† [pʀetɑ̃tɛn] nf: **courir la ~** to go gallivanting.

prétentieusement [pʀetɑ̃sjøzmɑ̃] adv pretentiously.

prétentieux, -ieuse [pʀetɑ̃sjø, jøz] adj *personne, manières, ton* pretentious, conceited; *appellation* pretentious, fancy; *maison* pretentious, showy. **c'est un petit ~!** he's a conceited little blighter!* (*Brit*) *ou* jerk*.

prétention [pʀetɑ̃sjɔ̃] nf a (*exigence*) claim. (*salaire*) **~s** expected salary; **avoir des ~s à** *ou* **sur** to lay claim to; **quelles sont vos ~s?** what sort of salary do you expect? *ou* are you looking for?*

b (*ambition*) pretension, claim (*à* to). **avoir la ~ de faire** to claim to be able to do, (like to) think one can do; **je n'ai pas la ~ de rivaliser avec lui** I don't claim *ou* expect *ou* pretend (to be able) to compete with him; **il n'a pas la ~ de tout savoir** he makes no pretence of knowing everything, he doesn't pretend *ou* claim to know everything; **sa ~ à l'élégance** her claims *ou* pretensions to elegance; **sans ~** *maison, repas* unpretentious; *robe* simple.

c (*vanité*) pretentiousness, pretension, conceitedness. **avec ~** pretentiously, conceitedly.

prêter [pʀete] 1 1 vt a *objet, argent* to lend. **~ qch à qn** to lend sth to sb, lend sb sth; **peux-tu me ~ ton stylo?** can you lend me your pen, can I borrow your pen?; **ils prêtent à 10 %** they lend (money) at 10 %, they give loans at 10 %; **ils m'ont prêté 100 F** they lent me 100 francs; **~ sur gages** to lend against security; (*Prov*) **on ne prête qu'aux riches** reputations shape reactions.

b (*attribuer*) *sentiment, facultés* to attribute, ascribe. **on lui prête l'intention de démissionner** he is alleged *ou* claimed to be intending *ou* going to resign, he is said *ou* supposed to be going to resign; **on me prête des paroles que je n'ai pas dites** people attribute *ou* ascribe to me words that I never said, people put words in my mouth that I never said, people say I said things that I didn't; **nous prêtons une grande importance à ces problèmes** we consider these problems of great importance, we accord a great deal of importance to these problems.

c (*apporter, offrir*) *aide, appui* to give, lend. **~ assistance/secours à qn** to go to sb's assistance/aid; **~ main forte à qn** to lend sb a hand, go to sb's help; **~ son concours à** to give one's assistance to; **~ sa voix à une cause** to speak on behalf of *ou* in support of a cause; **~ sa voix pour un gala** to sing at a gala performance; **dans cette émission il prêtait sa voix à Napoléon** in this broadcast he played *ou* spoke the part of Napoleon; **~ son nom à** to lend one's name to; **~ la main à une entreprise/un complot** to be *ou* get involved in *ou* take part in an undertaking/a plot; **~ attention à** to pay attention to, take notice of; **il faut ~ la plus grande attention à mes paroles** you must listen very closely *ou* you must pay very close attention to what I have to say; **~ le flanc à la critique** to lay o.s. open to criticism, invite criticism; **~ l'oreille** to listen, lend an ear (*à* to); **~ serment** to take an *ou* the oath; **faire ~ serment à qn** to administer the oath to sb; (*hum*) **si Dieu me prête vie** if God grants me life, if I am spared (*hum*).

2 **prêter à** vt indir: **son attitude prête à équivoque/à la critique/aux commentaires** his attitude is ambiguous/is open to *ou* gives rise to *ou* invites criticism/makes people talk; **décision qui prête à (la) discussion** decision which is open to debate, debatable *ou* controversial decision; **sa conduite prête à rire** his behaviour makes you (want to) laugh *ou* is ridiculous *ou* laughable.

3 vi *[tissu, cuir]* to give, stretch.

4 **se prêter** vpr a (*consentir*) **se ~ à** *expérience, arrangement* to lend o.s. to; *projet, jeu* to fall in with, go along with; **il n'a pas voulu se ~ à leurs manœuvres** he didn't want any part in *ou* wouldn't lend himself to *ou* refused to have anything to do with their schemes.

b (*s'adapter*) *[chaussures, cuir]* to give, stretch. **se ~ (bien) à qch** to lend itself (well) to sth; **la salle se prête mal à une réunion intime** the room doesn't lend itself to an informal meeting.

prétérit [pʀeteʀit] nm preterite (tense). **au ~** in the preterite (tense).

prétérition [pʀeteʀisjɔ̃] nf paralipsis, paraleipsis.

préteur [pʀetœʀ] nm (*Antiq*) praetor.

prêteur, -euse [pʀɛtœʀ, øz] 1 adj unselfish. **il n'est pas ~** *[enfant]* he's possessive about his toys *ou* belongings, he doesn't like lending his things; *[adulte]* he isn't willing to lend things, he doesn't believe in lending (things). 2 nm, f (money) lender. **~ sur gages** pawnbroker.

prétexte [pʀetɛkst] nm pretext, pretence, excuse. **mauvais ~** poor *ou* lame excuse; **sous ~ d'aider son frère** on the pretext *ou* pretence *ou* under (the) pretext of helping his brother; **sous (le) ~ que ...** on *ou* under the pretext that ..., on the pretence that ...; **sous ~ qu'elle est jeune on lui passe tout** just because she's young she gets away with everything; **sous aucun ~** on no account; **il a pris ~ du froid** *ou* **il a donné le froid comme ~ pour rester chez lui** he used *ou* took the cold weather as a pretext *ou* an excuse for staying at home; **servir de ~ à qch/à faire qch** to be a pretext *ou* an excuse for sth/to do sth; **ça lui a servi de ~** *ou* **ça lui a donné un ~ pour refuser** it provided him with an excuse to refuse *ou* with a pretext for refusing; **il saisit le premier ~ venu pour partir** he made the first excuse he could think of for leaving; **ce n'est qu'un ~** it's just an excuse.

prétexter [pʀetɛkste] 1 vt to give as a pretext *ou* an excuse. **il a prétexté/en prétextant qu'il était trop fatigué** he said *ou* he gave as a pretext *ou* as his excuse/on the pretext *ou* excuse that he was too tired; **~ une angine pour refuser une invitation** to plead a bad throat to excuse oneself from an invitation.

prétoire [pʀetwaʀ] nm (*Antiq*) praetorium; (*Jur: frm*) court.

Pretoria [pʀetɔʀja] n Pretoria.

prétorien, -ienne [pʀetɔʀjɛ̃, jɛn] adj, nm (*Antiq*) praetorian.

prêtraille [pʀɛtʀɑj] nf (*péj*) **la ~** priests, the clergy.

prêtre [pʀɛtʀ] nm priest.

prêtre-ouvrier, pl **prêtres-ouvriers** [pʀɛtʀuvʀije] nm worker priest.

prêtresse [pʀɛtʀɛs] nf priestess.

prêtrise [pʀɛtʀiz] nf priesthood.

preuve [pʀœv] 1 nf a (*démonstration*) proof, evidence. **faire la ~ de qch/que** to prove sth/that; **avoir la ~ de/que** to have proof *ou* evidence of/that; **sur la ~ de son identité** on proof of one's identity; **pouvez-vous apporter la ~ de ce que vous dites?** can you prove *ou* can you produce proof *ou* evidence of what you're saying?; **c'est la ~ que** that proves that; **j'avais prévu cela, la ~, j'ai déjà mon billet*** I'd thought of that, witness the fact that *ou* and to prove it I've already got my ticket; **jusqu'à ~ (du) contraire** until we find proof *ou* evidence to the contrary, until there's proof *ou* evidence that it's not the case; **n'importe qui peut**

conduire, à ~ ma femme* anyone can drive, just look at *ou* take my wife (for instance); **il a réussi, à ~ qu'il ne faut jamais désespérer*** he succeeded, which just goes to show *ou* prove you should never give up hope.

b (*indice*) proof, piece of evidence, evidence (*NonC*). **je n'ai pas de ~s** I have no proof *ou* evidence; **c'est une ~ supplémentaire de sa culpabilité** it's (a) further proof *ou* it's further evidence of his guilt; **il y a 3 ~s irréfutables qu'il ment** there are 3 definite pieces of evidence to show that he's lying *ou* which prove quite clearly that he's lying; **affirmer qch ~s en mains** to back up a statement with concrete proof *ou* evidence.

c (*marque*) proof. **c'est une ~ de bonne volonté/d'amour** it's (a) proof of his good intentions/of his love.

d (*Math*) *[opération]* proof. **faire la ~ par neuf** to cast out the nines.

e (*loc*) **faire ~ de** to show; **faire ses ~s** *[personne]* to prove o.s., show one's ability; *[technique]* to be well-tried, be tried and tested; *[voiture]* to prove itself; **cette nouvelle technique n'a pas encore fait ses ~s** this new technique hasn't yet been thoroughly tested *ou* fully tried and tested; **professeur qui a fait ses ~s** experienced teacher.

2 **comp** ►**preuve par l'absurde** reductio ad absurdum ►**preuve concluante** conclusive *ou* positive proof ►**preuve a contrario** a contrario proof ►**preuve matérielle** material evidence (*NonC*).

preux†† [pʀø] 1 **adj** valiant†, gallant†. 2 **nm** valiant knight†.

prévaloir [pʀevalwaʀ] [29] 1 **vi** (*littér*) to prevail (*sur* over, *contre* against). **faire ~ ses droits** to insist upon one's rights; **faire ~ son opinion** to win agreement *ou* acceptance for one's opinion; **son opinion a prévalu sur celle de ses collègues** his opinion prevailed against *ou* overrode that of his colleagues; **rien ne peut ~ contre ses préjugés** nothing can overcome his prejudices. 2 **se prévaloir vpr** a (*se flatter*) **se ~ de** to pride o.s. on. b (*profiter*) **se ~ de** to take advantage of.

prévaricateur, -trice [pʀevaʀikatœʀ, tʀis] 1 **adj** corrupt. 2 **nm, f** corrupt official.

prévarication [pʀevaʀikasjɔ̃] **nf** corrupt practices.

prévariquer [pʀevaʀike] [1] **vi** to be guilty of corrupt practices.

prévenance [pʀev(ə)nɑ̃s] **nf** thoughtfulness (*NonC*), consideration (*NonC*), kindness (*NonC*). **toutes les ~s que vous avez eues pour moi** all the consideration *ou* kindness you've shown me; **entourer qn de ~s** to be very considerate to *ou* towards sb; **il n'a aucune ~ pour les autres** he shows *ou* has no consideration for others, he is quite thoughtless of others.

prévenant, e [pʀev(ə)nɑ̃, ɑ̃t] **adj** *personne* considerate, kind (*envers* to), thoughtful; *manières* kind, attentive.

prévenir [pʀev(ə)niʀ] [22] **vt** a (*avertir*) to warn (*de qch* about *ou* against sth); (*aviser*) to inform, tell, let know (*de qch* about sth). **qui faut-il ~ en cas d'accident?** who should be informed *ou* told if there's an accident?; **~ le médecin/la police** to call the doctor/the police; **tu es prévenu!** you've been warned!; **partir sans ~** to leave without warning, leave without telling anyone; **il aurait pu ~** he could have let us know.

b (*empêcher*) *accident, catastrophe* to prevent, avert, avoid; *maladie* to prevent, guard against; *danger* to avert, avoid; *malheur* to ward off, avoid, provide against; *voir* **mieux.**

c (*devancer*) *besoin, désir* to anticipate; *question, objection* to forestall. (*littér*) **il voulait arriver le premier mais son frère l'avait prévenu** he wanted to be the first to arrive but his brother had anticipated him *ou* had got there before him.

d (*frm: influencer*) **~ qn contre qn** to prejudice *ou* bias sb against sb; **~ qn en faveur de qn** to prejudice *ou* predispose sb in sb's favour.

préventif, -ive [pʀevɑ̃tif, iv] **adj** *mesure, médecine* preventive. **à titre ~** as a precaution *ou* preventive; *voir* **détention.**

prévention [pʀevɑ̃sjɔ̃] **nf** a *[accident, crime]* prevention. **~ routière** road safety. b (*Jur*) custody, detention. **mettre en ~** to detain, remand in *ou* take into custody. c (*préjugé*) prejudice (*contre* against). **considérer qch sans ~** to take an unprejudiced *ou* unbiased view of sth.

préventivement [pʀevɑ̃tivmɑ̃] **adv** *agir* preventively, as a precaution *ou* preventive. (*Jur*) **être incarcéré ~** to be remanded *ou* held in custody *ou* detention (awaiting trial).

préventorium [pʀevɑ̃tɔʀjɔm] **nm** tuberculosis sanatorium.

prévenu, e [pʀev(ə)ny] (**ptp de prévenir**) 1 **adj** (*Jur*) charged. **être ~ d'un délit** to be charged with *ou* accused of a crime. 2 **nm, f** (*Jur*) defendant, accused (person).

préverbe [pʀevɛʀb] **nm** verbal prefix.

prévisibilité [pʀevizibilite] **nf** foreseeable nature.

prévisible [pʀevizibl] **adj** foreseeable. **difficilement ~** difficult to foresee.

prévision [pʀevizjɔ̃] **nf** a (*gén pl: prédiction*) prediction, expectation; (*Fin*) forecast, estimate, prediction. **~s budgétaires** budget estimates; **~s météorologiques** weather forecast; **~ à court/long terme** short-term/long-term forecast; **il a réussi au-delà de toute ~** he has succeeded beyond all *ou* the wildest expectations.

b (*action*) **la ~ du temps** weather forecasting, forecasting of the weather; **la ~ de ses réactions est impossible** predicting his reactions is quite impossible, it's impossible to predict his reactions *ou* to foresee what his reactions will be; **en ~ de son arrivée/d'une augmentation du trafic** in anticipation *ou* expectation of his arrival/of an increase in the traffic.

prévisionnel, -elle [pʀevizjɔnɛl] **adj** *mesure, plan* forward-looking; *budget* projected.

prévisionniste [pʀevizjɔnist] **nmf** (economic) forecaster.

prévoir [pʀevwaʀ] [24] **vt** a (*anticiper*) *événement, conséquence* to foresee, anticipate; *temps* to forecast; *réaction, contretemps* to expect, reckon on, anticipate. **~ le pire** to expect the worst; **il faut ~ les erreurs éventuelles** we must allow for *ou* make provision for possible errors; **nous n'avions pas prévu qu'il refuserait** we hadn't reckoned on his refusing, we hadn't anticipated *ou* foreseen (that) he'd refuse; **cela fait *ou* laisse ~ un malheur** it bodes ill; **rien ne laisse ~ une amélioration rapide** there's no prospect *ou* suggestion of a quick improvement; **tout laisse ~ une issue rapide/qu'il refusera** everything points *ou* all the signs point to a rapid solution/to his refusing; **rien ne faisait *ou* ne laissait ~ que ...** there was nothing to suggest *ou* to make us think that ...; **on ne peut pas tout ~** you can't think of everything; **plus tôt que prévu** earlier than expected *ou* anticipated; **ce n'était pas prévu au programme*** we weren't expecting that (to happen) *ou* reckoning on that (happening); **elle n'était pas prévue au programme*** she wasn't expected to appear.

b (*projeter*) *voyage, construction* to plan. **~ de faire qch** to plan to do *ou* on doing sth; **pour quand prévoyez-vous votre arrivée?** when do you plan to arrive?; **au moment prévu** at the appointed *ou* scheduled *ou* prescribed time; **comme prévu** as planned, according to plan; *[autoroute]* **ouverture prévue pour la fin de l'année** scheduled to open at the end of the year.

c (*préparer, envisager*) to allow. **il faudra ~ des trous pour l'écoulement des eaux** you must leave *ou* provide some holes for the water to drain away; **prévoyez de l'argent en plus pour les faux frais** allow some extra money *ou* put some money on one side for incidental expenses; **il vaut mieux ~ quelques couvertures en plus** you'd better allow a few extra blankets *ou* bring (along) a few extra blankets; **il faudrait ~ un repas** you ought to make plans for *ou* to organize a meal; **tout est prévu pour l'arrivée de nos hôtes** everything is in hand *ou* organized for the arrival of our guests; **cette voiture est prévue pour 4 personnes** this car is designed *ou* supposed to take 4 people; **vous avez prévu grand** you've allowed a lot of (extra) space, you've planned things on a grand scale; **déposez vos lettres dans la boîte prévue à cet effet** put your letters in the box provided; **on a prévu des douches** (*à installer*) they have made provision for showers to be built; (*déjà installées*) they have laid on *ou* provided showers.

d (*Jur*) *[loi, règlement]* to provide for, make provision for. **c'est prévu à l'article 8** article 8 makes provision for that, it's provided for in article 8; **le code pénal prévoit que ...** the penal code holds that ...; **la loi prévoit une peine de prison** the law makes provision for a prison sentence; **ce n'est pas prévu dans le contrat** it is not provided for in the contract, the contract makes no provision for it.

prévôt [pʀevo] **nm** (*Hist, Rel*) provost; (*Mil*) provost marshal.

prévôtal, e, mpl -aux [pʀevotal, o] **adj** of a provost.

prévôté [pʀevote] **nf** (*Hist*) provostship; (*Mil*) military police.

prévoyance [pʀevwajɑ̃s] **nf** foresight, forethought. **caisse de ~** contingency fund; **société de ~** provident society.

prévoyant, e [pʀevwajɑ̃, ɑ̃t] **adj** provident.

Priam [pʀijam] **nm** Priam.

priapisme [pʀijapism] **nm** priapism.

prie-Dieu [pʀidjø] **nm inv** prie-dieu.

prier [pʀije] [7] 1 **vt** a *Dieu, saint* to pray to. **~ Dieu de faire un miracle** to pray for a miracle; **je prie Dieu que cela soit vrai** pray God that it is true.

b (*implorer*) to beg, beseech (*littér*). **elle le pria de rester** she begged *ou* urged *ou* pressed him to stay; **je vous prie de me pardonner** I beg you to forgive me, please forgive me; **dites oui, je vous en prie** please say yes, say yes I beg *ou* beseech you; **Pierre, je t'en prie, calme-toi** Peter, for heaven's sake, calm down; **je t'en prie, ça suffit!** please, that's quite enough!

c (*inviter*) to invite, ask; (*frm*) to request (*frm*). **il m'a prié à déjeuner *ou* de venir déjeuner** he has invited *ou* asked me to lunch; **vous êtes prié de vous présenter à 9 heures** you are requested to present yourself at 9 o'clock; **on l'a prié d'assister à la cérémonie** he was invited to be present *ou* his presence was requested at the ceremony; **nous vous prions d'honorer de votre présence la cérémonie** we request the honour *ou* pleasure of your company at the ceremony.

d (*ordonner*) **je vous prie de sortir** will you please leave the room; **vous êtes prié de répondre quand on vous parle/de rester assis** please reply when spoken to/remain seated; **taisez-vous, je vous prie** would you please be quiet.

e (*formules de politesse*) **je vous en prie** (*faites donc*) please do, of course; (*après vous*) after you; (*idée d'irritation*) would you mind!; **excusez-moi — je vous en prie** I'm sorry — don't mention it *ou* not at all; **voulez-vous ouvrir la fenêtre je vous prie?** would you mind opening the window please?, would you be so kind as to open the window please?; (*formule épistolaire*) **je vous prie d'agréer mes sentiments les meilleurs** yours sincerely.

f (*loc*) **se faire ~: il s'est fait ~** he needed coaxing *ou* persuading; **il ne s'est pas fait ~** he didn't need persuading, he didn't wait to be asked twice, he was only too willing (to do it); **il a accepté l'offre sans se faire ~** he accepted the offer without hesitation.

2 **vi** to pray (*pour* for). **prions, mes frères** brothers, let us pray.

prière [pʀijɛʀ] **nf** a (*Rel: oraison, office*) prayer. **être en ~** to be praying *ou* at prayer; **dire** *ou* **faire ses ~s** to say one's prayers; **se rendre à la ~** to go to prayer; (*fig*) **ne m'oubliez pas dans vos ~s*** remember me in your prayers, pray for me; *voir* **livre**[1], **moulin**.

b (*demande*) plea, entreaty. **céder aux ~s de qn** to give in to sb's requests; **à la ~ de qn** at sb's request *ou* behest (*littér*); **j'ai une ~ à vous adresser** I have a request to make to you; **il est resté sourd à mes ~s** he turned a deaf ear to my pleas *ou* entreaties.

c (*loc*) **~ de: ~ de répondre par retour du courrier** please reply by return of post; **~ de vous présenter à 9 heures** you are requested to present yourself *ou* please present yourself at 9 o'clock; **~ de ne pas fumer** no smoking (please); **~ de ne pas se pencher à la fenêtre** (please) do not lean out of the window; (*Édition*) **~ d'insérer** please insert.

prieur [pʀijœʀ] **nm: (père) ~** prior.

prieure [pʀijœʀ] **nf: (mère) ~** prioress.

prieuré [pʀijœʀe] **nm** (*couvent*) priory; (*église*) priory (church).

prima donna [pʀimadɔna] **nf** prima donna.

primaire [pʀimɛʀ] 1 **adj** a (*Écon, Élec, Méd, Pol, Scol*) primary; (*Géol*) *ère* primary, palaeozoic; (*Psych*) *personne, caractère, fonction* primary (*SPÉC*); *élection* primary. **délinquant ~** first offender. b (*péj: simpliste*) *personne* simple-minded, of limited outlook, limited*; *raisonnement* simplistic. 2 **nm** (*Scol*) primary school *ou* education; (*Élec*) primary; (*Géol*) Primary, Palaeozoic. (*Scol*) **être en ~** to be in primary school. 3 **nf** (*Pol*) primary (election).

primal [pʀimal] **adjm: cri ~** primal scream.

primarité [pʀimaʀite] **nf** primarity.

primat [pʀima] **nm** a (*Rel*) primate. b (*littér: primauté*) primacy.

primate [pʀimat] **nm** (*Zool*) primate.

primauté [pʀimote] **nf** (*Rel*) primacy; (*fig*) primacy, pre-eminence (*sur* over).

prime[1] [pʀim] **nf** a (*cadeau*) free gift. **objet donné en ~ avec qch** object given away *ou* given as a free gift with sth; (*iro*) **cette année il a eu la rougeole, la varicelle et les oreillons en ~** this year he had (the) measles, chickenpox and (the) mumps to boot!

b (*bonus*) bonus; (*subvention*) premium, subsidy; (*indemnité*) allowance. **~ de fin d'année/de rendement** Christmas/productivity bonus; **~ d'ancienneté** seniority bonus *ou* pay; **~ de licenciement** severance pay, termination bonus, redundancy payment *ou* money; **~ à l'exportation** export premium *ou* subsidy; **~ de transport** transport allowance; **~ d'allaitement** nursing mother's allowance; (*fig*) **c'est donner une ~ à la paresse!** it's like actively encouraging laziness!

c (*Assurances, Bourse*) premium. **~ d'émission** issuing share *ou* premium; **~ de remboursement** redemption premium; *voir* **marché**.

d **faire ~** to be at a premium.

prime[2] [pʀim] **adj** a **de ~ abord** at first glance, at the outset; **dès sa ~ jeunesse** from his earliest youth; **il n'est plus de ~ jeunesse** he's no longer in the prime *ou* first flush of youth, he's past his first youth. b (*Math*) prime. **n ~** n prime.

prime[3] [pʀim] **nf** (*Escrime, Rel*) prime.

primer [pʀime] [1] 1 **vt** a (*surpasser*) to outdo, prevail over, take precedence over *ou* of. **chez elle, l'intelligence prime la sagesse** in her case, intelligence is more in evidence *ou* to the fore than wisdom.

b (*récompenser*) to award a prize to; (*subventionner*) to subsidize. **invention primée dans un concours** prize-winning invention in a competition; **bête primée** prize(-winning) animal.

2 **vi** (*dominer*) to be the prime *ou* dominant feature, dominate; (*compter, valoir*) to be of prime importance, take first place. **c'est le bleu qui prime dans ce tableau** blue is the prime *ou* dominant colour in this picture; **pour moi ce sont les qualités de cœur qui priment** the qualities of the heart are what take first place for me *ou* are of prime importance to me.

primerose [pʀimʀoz] **nf** hollyhock.

primesautier, -ière [pʀimsotje, jɛʀ] **adj** impulsive. **être d'humeur ~ière** to have an impulsive temperament *ou* nature.

primeur [pʀimœʀ] 1 **nfpl** (*Comm*) **~s** early fruit and vegetables; **marchand de ~s** greengrocer (*Brit*) (*specializing in early produce*). 2 **nf** a (*Presse: nouvelle*) scoop. **avoir la ~ d'une nouvelle** to be the first to hear a piece of news; **je vous réserve la ~ de mon manuscrit** I'll let you be the first to read my manuscript. b **vin (de) ~** nouveau wine, wine of the latest vintage.

primevère [pʀimvɛʀ] **nf** (*sauvage*) primrose; (*cultivée*) primula; (*jaune*) primrose.

primigeste [pʀimiʒɛst] **nf** primigravida.

primipare [pʀimipaʀ] 1 **adj** primiparous. 2 **nf** primipara.

primitif, -ive [pʀimitif, iv] 1 **adj** a (*originel*) *forme, état* original, primitive; *projet, question, préoccupation* original, first; *église* primitive, early; *peintre* primitive; (*Logique*) *proposition, concept* basic; (*Art*) *couleurs* primary; (*Géol*) *terrain* primitive, primeval. **ville construite sur le site ~ d'une cité romaine** town built on the original site of a Roman city; **je préfère revenir à mon projet ~/à mon idée ~ive** I'd rather revert to my original *ou* initial *ou* first plan/idea.

b (*Sociol*) *peuple, art, mœurs* primitive.

c (*sommaire*) *installation* primitive, crude.

d (*Ling*) *temps, langue* basic; *mot* primitive; *sens* original.

e (*Math*) **fonction ~ive** primitive.

2 **nm, f** (*Art, Sociol*) primitive.

3 **primitive nf** (*Math*) primitive.

primitivement [pʀimitivmɑ̃] **adv** originally.

primo [pʀimo] **adv** first (of all), firstly.

primogéniture [pʀimoʒenityʀ] **nf** primogeniture.

primo-infection, **pl primo-infections** [pʀimoɛ̃fɛksjɔ̃] **nf** primary infection.

primordial, e, **mpl -iaux** [pʀimɔʀdjal, jo] **adj** a (*vital*) essential, primordial. **d'une importance ~e** of the utmost *ou* of paramount *ou* primordial importance. b (*littér: originel*) primordial.

primordialement [pʀimɔʀdjalmɑ̃] **adv** essentially.

prince [pʀɛ̃s] 1 **nm** a (*lit*) prince. (*fig*) **le ~ des chanteurs** *etc* the prince *ou* king of singers *etc; voir* **fait**[2]. b (*loc*) **être bon ~** to be magnanimous *ou* generous, behave generously; **être habillé comme un ~** to be dressed like a prince. 2 **comp ▸ prince des apôtres** Prince of the apostles **▸ prince charmant** Prince Charming **▸ prince consort** Prince Consort **▸ prince des démons** prince of darkness **▸ prince de l'Église** prince of the Church **▸ prince de Galles** Prince of Wales; (*tissu*) check cloth **▸ prince héritier** crown prince **▸ prince du sang** prince of royal blood.

princeps [pʀɛ̃sɛps] **adj** *édition* first.

princesse [pʀɛ̃sɛs] **nf** princess. **faire la** *ou* **sa ~, prendre des airs de ~** to put on airs and graces; *voir* **frais**[2].

princier, -ière [pʀɛ̃sje, jɛʀ] **adj** (*lit, fig*) princely.

princièrement [pʀɛ̃sjɛʀmɑ̃] **adv** in (a) princely fashion.

principal, e, **mpl -aux** [pʀɛ̃sipal, o] 1 **adj** a *entrée, bâtiment, résidence* main; *clerc, employé* chief, head; *question* main, principal; *raison, but* principal, main; *personnage, rôle* leading, main, principal. **elle a eu l'un des rôles ~aux dans l'affaire** she played a major role *ou* she was one of the leading *ou* main figures in the business. b (*Gram*) *proposition* main. 2 **nm** a (*Fin*) principal. b (*Scol*) head(master) (*Brit*), principal (*of a college*); (*Admin*) chief clerk. c (*chose importante*) most important thing, main point. **c'est le ~** that's the main thing. 3 **principale nf** a (*Gram*) main clause. b (*Scol*) head(mistress) (*Brit*), principal (*of a college*).

principalement [pʀɛ̃sipalmɑ̃] **adv** principally, mainly, chiefly.

principat [pʀɛ̃sipa] **nm** princedom.

principauté [pʀɛ̃sipote] **nf** principality.

principe [pʀɛ̃sip] **nm** a (*règle*) *[science, géométrie]* principle. **il nous a expliqué le ~ de la machine** he explained to us the principle on which the machine worked; **le ~ d'Archimède** Archimedes' principle; *voir* **pétition**.

b (*hypothèse*) principle, assumption. **partir du ~ que ..., poser comme ~ que ...** to work on the principle *ou* assumption that ...; *voir* **accord**.

c (*règle morale*) principle. **il a des ~s** he's a man of principle, he's got principles; **il n'a pas de ~s** he is unprincipled, he has no principles; **avoir pour ~ de faire** to make it a principle to do, make a point of doing; **je ne mens pas, c'est un ~ chez moi** I make a point of not telling lies, it's a rule with me that I don't tell lies; **il n'est pas dans mes ~s de ...** I make it a principle not to ...; **il a manqué à ses ~s** he has abandoned his principles, he has failed to stick to his principles.

d (*origine*) principle. **remonter jusqu'au ~ des choses** to go back to first principles.

e (*élément*) principle, element, constituent. **~ nécessaire à la nutrition** necessary principle of nutrition.

f (*rudiment*) **~s** rudiments, principles.

g (*loc*) **par ~** on principle; **en ~** (*d'habitude, en général*) as a rule; (*théoriquement*) in principle, theoretically; **de ~** mechanical, automatic; **faire qch pour le ~** to do sth on principle *ou* for the sake of (doing) it.

printanier, -ière [pʀɛ̃tanje, jɛʀ] **adj** *soleil, couleur* spring; *temps* spring(-like); *vêtement, atmosphère* spring-like.

printemps [pʀɛ̃tɑ̃] **nm** spring. **au ~** in (the) spring(time); (*littér*) **au ~ de la vie** in the springtime of (one's) life; (*hum*) **mes 40 ~s** my 40 summers (*hum*).

priorat [pʀijɔʀa] **nm** priorate.

priori [pʀijɔʀi] *voir* **a priori**.

prioritaire [pʀijɔʀitɛʀ] 1 **adj** a *projet* having priority, priority (*épith*); *personne* having priority. b (*Aut*) *véhicule, personne* having priority *ou* right of way. **il était sur une route ~** he had right of way, he was on the main road. 2 **nmf** (*Aut*) person who has right of way *ou* priority.

priorité [pʀijɔʀite] **nf** a (*gén*) priority. **discuter qch en ~** to discuss sth as a (matter of) priority; **venir en ~** to come first; **l'une des choses à faire en grande ~, l'une des ~s essentielles** one of the first *ou* top priorities; **il nous faudrait en ~ des vivres** first and foremost we need supplies, we need supplies as a matter of urgency.

b (*Aut*) priority, right of way. **avoir la ~** to have right of way; **avoir**

~ **sur un autre véhicule** to have right of way over another vehicle; ~ **à droite** (*principe*) *system of giving priority ou right of way to traffic coming from the right;* (*panneau*) give way to the vehicles on your right; **laisser** *ou* **céder la** ~ **à qn** to give way to sb; *voir* **refus.**

pris, prise [pʀi, pʀiz] (**ptp de prendre**) 1 **adj** a *place* taken. **avoir les mains prises** to have one's hands full; **tous les billets sont** ~ the tickets are sold out, all the tickets have been sold; **toutes les places sont prises** all the seats are taken *ou* have gone; **toute ma journée est prise** I'm busy all day, I have engagements all day.

b *personne* busy, engaged (*frm*). **le directeur est très ~ cette semaine** the manager is very busy this week; **si vous n'êtes pas ~ ce soir ...** if you're free *ou* if you've got nothing on this evening* ...; **désolé, je suis** ~ I'm sorry, but I've got something on*.

c (*Méd*) *nez* stuffy, stuffed-up; *gorge* hoarse. **j'ai le nez** ~ my nose is stuffed up; **j'ai la gorge prise** my throat is hoarse; **la paralysie gagne, le bras droit est** ~ the paralysis is spreading, and has reached *ou* taken hold of the right arm; **les poumons sont** ~ the lungs are (now) affected.

d **avoir la taille bien prise**† to have a neat waist; **la taille prise dans un manteau de bonne coupe** wearing a well-cut coat to show off a neat waist.

e (*fig*) (*Culin*) *crème, mayonnaise* set; (*gelé*) *eau* frozen.

f ~ **de peur/remords** stricken with *ou* by fear/remorse; ~ **d'une inquiétude soudaine/d'une envie** seized by a sudden anxiety/a fancy; ~ **de boisson** under the influence*, the worse for drink.

2 **prise nf** a (*moyen d'empoigner, de prendre*) hold (*NonC*), grip (*NonC*); (*pour soulever, faire levier*) purchase (*NonC*); (*Catch, Judo*) hold; (*Alpinisme*) hold; (*Sport: sur raquette, club, batte*) grip. **faire une prise de judo à qn** to get sb in a judo hold; **on n'a pas de prise pour soulever la caisse** there's no purchase to lift the chest, you can't get a hold on this chest to lift it; **cette construction offre trop de prise au vent** this building catches the wind very badly; *voir* **lâcher.**

b (*Chasse, Pêche: butin*) catch; (*Mil: capture*) capture, seizure; (*Dames, Échecs*) capture. **la prise de la Bastille** the storming of the Bastille.

c (*Aut*) **être/mettre en prise** to be in/put the car into gear; **en prise (directe)** in direct drive; (*fig*) **en prise directe avec, en prise (directe) sur** tuned in to.

d (*Élec*) **prise (de courant)** (*mâle*) plug; (*femelle*) socket, point, power point (SPÉC); (*boîtier*) socket. **prise multiple** adaptor; **prise pour rasoir électrique** razor point.

e *[tabac]* pinch of snuff.

f (*Méd*) dose. **à administrer en plusieurs prises par jour** to be given *ou* administered at intervals throughout the day.

g *[drogue]* snort‡.

h (*loc*) **avoir prise sur** to have a hold on *ou* over; **personne n'a aucune prise sur lui** no one has any hold *ou* influence over him; **les passions n'ont que trop de prise sur elle** her passions have all too great a hold on *ou* over her; **donner prise à** to give rise to, lay one open to; **son attitude donne prise aux soupçons** his attitude gives rise to *ou* lays him open to suspicion; **être** *ou* **se trouver aux prises avec des difficultés** to be battling *ou* grappling with difficulties; **être** *ou* **se trouver aux prises avec un créancier** to be battling against *ou* doing battle with a creditor; **on les a mis/laissés aux prises** we set them by the ears/left them to fight it out.

3 **comp** ►**prise d'air** air inlet *ou* intake ►**prise d'armes** military review *ou* parade ►**prise de bec*** row*, set-to*; **avoir une prise de bec avec qn** to have a row* *ou* a set-to* with sb, fall out with sb ►**prise de bénéfices** profit-taking ►**prise en charge** (*par taxi*) *[passager]* picking up; (*taxe*) pick-up charge; (*par Sécurité sociale etc*) *undertaking to reimburse medical expenses* ►**prise de conscience** awareness, realization; **il faut qu'il y ait une prise de conscience du problème** people must be made aware of *ou* must be alive to the problem, a new awareness *ou* full realization of the problem is needed ►**prise en considération: la prise en considération de qch** taking sth into consideration *ou* account ►**prise de contact** initial contact *ou* meeting ►**prise de contrôle** (*Fin*) takeover ►**prise de corps** (*Jur*) arrest ►**prise de courant** *voir* **2d** ►**prise d'eau** water (supply) point; (*robinet*) tap (*Brit*), faucet (*US*) ►**prise de guerre** spoils of war (*pl*) ►**prise d'habit** (*Rel*) taking the cloth (*NonC*) ►**prise d'otages** taking *ou* seizure of hostages, hostage-taking (*NonC*) ►**prise de parole** speech ►**prise de participations** (*Fin*) acquisition of holdings ►**prise à partie** (*Jur*) *action against a judge* ►**prise de position** taking a stand (*NonC*), stand ►**prise de possession** taking possession, taking over ►**prise du pouvoir** (*Pol*) seizure of power, political takeover ►**prise de risques** risk-taking ►**prise de sang** blood test; **faire une prise de sang à qn** to take a blood sample from sb ►**prise de son** (*Ciné, Rad, TV*) sound recording; **prise de son J. Dupont** sound (engineer) J. Dupont ►**prise de terre** (*Élec, Rad*) earth (*Brit*), ground (*US*) ►**prise de voile** (*Rel*) taking the veil ►**prise de vue(s)** (*opération: Ciné, TV*) filming, shooting; **prise de vue(s) J. Dupont** camera(work) J. Dupont ►**prise de vue** (*photographie*) shot.

priser[1] [pʀize] 1 **vt** (*littér*) to prize, value. **je prise fort peu ce genre de plaisanterie** I don't appreciate this sort of joke at all.

priser[2] [pʀize] 1 1 **vt** *tabac* to take; *drogue* to take, snort‡; *voir* **tabac.** 2 **vi** to take snuff.

priseur, -euse [pʀizœʀ, øz] **nm, f** snuff taker; *voir* **commissaire.**

prismatique [pʀismatik] **adj** prismatic.

prisme [pʀism] **nm** prism.

prison [pʀizɔ̃] **nf** a (*lieu*) prison, jail, penitentiary (*US*); (*fig: demeure sombre*) prison. (*Hist*) ~ **pour dettes** debtors' prison; **mettre en** ~ to send to prison *ou* jail, imprison; ~ **ouverte** open prison; *voir* **porte.** b (*emprisonnement*) imprisonment, prison, jail. **peine de** ~ prison sentence; **faire de la** ~ to go to *ou* be in prison; **faire 6 mois de** ~ to spend 6 months in jail *ou* prison; **condamné à 3 mois de ~ ferme/à la ~ à vie** sentenced to 3 months' imprisonment/to life imprisonment; **faire de la ~ préventive** to be remanded in custody.

prisonnier, -ière [pʀizɔnje, jɛʀ] 1 **adj** *soldat* captive. **être** ~ (*enfermé*) to be trapped, be a prisoner; (*en prison*) to be imprisoned, be a prisoner; **être ~ de ses vêtements** to be imprisoned in *ou* hampered by one's clothes; **être ~ de ses préjugés/de l'ennemi** to be a prisoner of one's prejudices/of the enemy. 2 **nm, f** prisoner. ~ **d'opinion** prisoner of conscience; ~ **politique** political prisoner; **faire/retenir qn** ~ to take/hold sb prisoner; ~ **de guerre** prisoner of war; *voir* **camp, constituer.**

Prisunic [pʀizynik] **nm** ® department store (*for inexpensive goods*), ≃ Woolworth's ® (*Brit*), ≃ five and ten (*US*).

privatif, -ive [pʀivatif, iv] 1 **adj** a (*Gram*) privative. b (*Jur: qui prive*) which deprives of rights (*ou* liberties *etc*). c (*Jur: privé*) private. **avec jardin** ~ with private garden; (*sur annonce*) **"jardin ~"** "own garden". 2 **nm** (*Gram*) privative (prefix *ou* element).

privation [pʀivasjɔ̃] **nf** a (*suppression*) deprivation, deprival. (*Jur*) **la ~ des droits civiques** the forfeiture *ou* deprival *ou* deprivation of civil rights; **la ~ de liberté** the loss of liberty; **la ~ de la vue/d'un membre** the loss of one's sight/a limb. b (*gén pl: sacrifice*) privation, hardship. **les ~s que je me suis imposées** the things I went *ou* did *ou* managed without, the hardships I bore.

privatisation [pʀivatizasjɔ̃] **nf** privatization.

privatiser [pʀivatize] 1 **vt** *entreprise* to privatize.

privautés [pʀivote] **nfpl** liberties. **prendre des ~ avec** to take liberties with; ~ **de langage** familiar *ou* coarse language.

privé, e [pʀive] 1 **adj** (*gén*) private; (*Presse*) *source* unofficial; (*Jur*) *droit* civil; *télévision, radio* independent. **personne ~e** private person; **en séjour (à titre)** ~ on a private visit. 2 **nm** (*vie*) private life; (*Comm: secteur*) private sector; (**: détective*) private eye*, private detective. **dans le** ~ (*gén*) in (one's) private life; (*Comm*) in the private sector; **en** ~ *conversation, réunion* private, in private (*attrib*); *parler* privately, in private.

privément [pʀivemɑ̃] **adv** (*littér*) privately.

priver [pʀive] 1 1 **vt** a (*délibérément, pour punir*) ~ **qn de** to deprive sb of; **il a été privé de dessert** he was deprived of dessert, he had to go without his dessert; **il a été privé de récréation** he was kept in at playtime; **on l'a privé de sa liberté/de ses droits** he was deprived of his freedom/his rights.

b (*faire perdre*) ~ **qn de ses moyens** to deprive sb of *ou* strip sb of his means; **cette perte m'a privé de ma seule joie** this loss has deprived me of my only joy *ou* has taken my only joy from me; **l'accident l'a privé d'un bras** he lost an arm in the accident; **privé de connaissance** unconscious; **privé de voix** speechless, unable to speak; **un discours privé de l'essentiel** a speech from which the main content had been removed *ou* which was stripped of its essential content.

c (*démunir*) **nous avons été privés d'électricité pendant 3 jours** we were without *ou* we had no *ou* we were deprived of electricity for 3 days; **il a été privé de sommeil** he didn't get any sleep; **on m'interdit le sel, ça me prive beaucoup** I'm not allowed salt and I must say I miss it *ou* and I don't like having to go *ou* do without it; **cela ne me prive pas du tout** (*de vous le donner*) I can spare it (quite easily); (*de ne plus en manger*) I don't miss it at all; (*de ne pas y aller*) I don't mind at all.

2 **se priver vpr** a (*par économie*) to go without, do without. **se ~ de qch** to go without sth, do without sth, manage without sth; **ils ont dû se ~ pour leurs enfants** they had to go *ou* do without because of their children; **je n'ai pas l'intention de me** ~ I've no intention of going *ou* doing without, I don't intend to go short (*Brit*).

b (*se passer de*) **se ~ de** to manage without, do without, deny o.s., forego; **il se prive de dessert par crainte de grossir** he does without dessert *ou* he misses out on the dessert* for fear of putting on weight; **se ~ de cigarettes** to deny o.s. cigarettes; **ils ont dû se ~ d'une partie de leur personnel** they had to manage without *ou* do without some of their staff; **tu te prives d'un beau spectacle en refusant d'y aller** you'll miss out on* *ou* you'll deprive yourself of a fine show by not going.

c (*gén nég: se retenir*) **il ne s'est pas privé de le dire/le critiquer** he made no bones about *ou* he had no hesitation in saying it/criticizing him; **j'aime bien manger et quand j'en ai l'occasion je ne m'en prive pas** I love eating and whenever I get the chance I don't hold back; **si tu veux y aller, ne t'en prive pas pour moi** if you want to go don't hold back for me *ou* don't deny yourself *ou* stop yourself because of me.

privilège [pʀivilɛʒ] **nm** (*gén*) privilege. **j'ai eu le ~ d'assister à la**

cérémonie I had the privilege of attending *ou* I was privileged to attend the ceremony; **avoir le triste ~ de faire** to have the unhappy privilege of doing.

privilégié, e [privileʒje] (**ptp de privilégier**) 1 **adj** *personne* privileged, favoured; *site, climat* privileged; (*Fin*) *action* preference (*épith*); *créancier* preferential. **~ par le sort** fortunate, lucky; **il a été ~ par la nature** he has been favoured by nature; **les classes ~es** the privileged classes. 2 **nm,f** privileged person. **c'est un ~** he is fortunate *ou* lucky; **quelques ~s** a privileged *ou* lucky few.

privilégier [privileʒje] 7 **vt** to favour, give greater place *ou* importance to.

prix [pri] 1 **nm** a (*coût*) *[objet]* price; *[location, transport]* cost; (*étiquette*) price tag. **le ~ du pain** the price of bread; **le ~ d'un billet Paris-Lyon** the fare between Paris and Lyons, the price of a ticket between Paris and Lyons; **à quel ~ vend-il/sont ses tapis?** what price is he asking for/are his carpets?, how much is he charging *ou* asking for/are his carpets?; **quel ~ veut-elle de sa maison?** what (price) is she asking *ou* how much does she want for her house?; **quels sont vos ~?** (*pour service*) what are your rates?; (*pour objet*) what sort of prices do you charge?; **je l'ai payé 600 F! — c'est le ~** I paid 600 francs for it! — that's the going rate; **10 000 francs ~ à débattre** 10,000 francs or nearest offer, 10,000 francs o.n.o. (*Brit*); **au ~ que ça coûte** for what it costs, for the price it is; **au ~ où sont les choses** *ou* **où est le beurre!*** with prices what they are!; **votre ~ sera le mien** name *ou* state your price; **acheter qch à ~ d'or** to pay a (small) fortune for sth; **au ~ fort** at the highest possible price, for a tremendous price; **ça n'a pas de ~** it is priceless; **je vous fais un ~ (d'ami)** I'll let you have it cheap *ou* at a reduced price, I'll knock a bit off for you*; **"~ sacrifiés", "~ écrasés"** "prices slashed", "rock bottom prices"; **j'y ai mis le ~ (qu'il fallait)** I had to pay a lot *ou* quite a price for it, it cost me a lot; **il faut y mettre le ~** you have to be prepared to pay for it; **il n'a pas voulu y mettre le ~** he didn't want to pay that much; **je cherche une robe — dans quels ~?** I'm looking for a dress — in what price range?; **c'est dans mes ~** that's affordable *ou* within my price range; (*enchères*) **mettre qch à ~** to set a reserve price (*Brit*) *ou* an upset price (*US*) on sth; **mettre à ~ la tête de qn** to put a price on sb's head, offer a reward for sb's capture; **objet de ~** expensive *ou* pricey object; *voir* **bas[1], hors, premier.**

b (*fig*) price. **le ~ du succès/de la gloire** the price of success/glory; **j'apprécie votre geste à son juste ~** I appreciate your gesture for what it's worth; **son amitié n'a pas de ~ pour moi** I cannot put a price on his friendship; **donner du ~ à** *exploit, aide* to make (even) more worthwhile *ou* impressive; **leur pauvreté donne encore plus de ~ à leur cadeau** their poverty makes their present even more precious *ou* impressive, their poverty increases the value *ou* worth of their gift even more; **à tout ~** at all costs, at any price; **à aucun ~** on no account, not at any price; **au ~ de grands efforts/sacrifices** at the expense of great efforts/sacrifices.

c (*Scol, gén: récompense*) prize. (*Scol*) **(livre de) ~** prize (-book); **le ~ Nobel de la paix** the Nobel Peace Prize.

d (*vainqueur*) (*personne*) prizewinner; (*livre*) prizewinning book. **premier ~ du Conservatoire** first prizewinner at the Conservatoire; **as-tu lu le dernier ~ Goncourt?** have you read the book that won the last *ou* latest Prix Goncourt?

e (*Courses*) race. (*Aut*) **Grand P~ (automobile)** Grand Prix.

2 **comp** ►**prix d'achat** purchase price ►**prix actuel** going price (*de* for) ►**prix conseillé** manufacturer's recommended price, recommended retail price ►**prix coûtant** cost price ►**prix de départ** asking price ►**prix de détail** retail price ►**prix d'encouragement** special *ou* consolation prize (*for promising entrant*) ►**prix d'excellence** (*Scol*) prize for coming first in the class *ou* for being top of the form ►**prix de fabrique** factory price ►**prix fixe** (*gén*) set price; (*menu*) set (price) menu; **(repas à) prix fixe** set (price) meal ►**prix forfaitaire** contract price ►**prix de gros** wholesale price ►**prix imposé** (*Comm*) regulation price ►**prix d'interprétation** (*Ciné, Théât*) *prize for the interpretation of a role* ►**prix d'intervention** intervention price ►**prix de lancement** introductory price ►**prix marqué** marked price ►**prix à la production** *ou* **au producteur** farm gate price ►**prix public** retail *ou* list price ►**prix de revient** cost price ►**prix sortie d'usine** factory price ►**prix de vente** selling price, sale price ►**prix de vertu** paragon of virtue.

pro* [pro] **nmf** (**abrév de professionnel**) pro.

pro- [pro] **préf** pro-. **~américain/chinois** pro-American/-Chinese.

probabilisme [prɔbabilism] **nm** probabilism.

probabiliste [prɔbabilist] **adj** (*Statistique*) probability (*épith*).

probabilité [prɔbabilite] **nf** (*voir* **probable**) probability; likelihood; (*chance*) probability. **selon toute ~, il est perdu** in all probability *ou* likelihood it has been lost, the chances are it has been lost.

probable [prɔbabl] **adj** *événement, hypothèse* probable, likely; (*Math, Statistique*) probable. **il est ~ qu'il gagnera** it is likely *ou* probable that he will win, he is likely to win, the chances are (that) he'll win; **il est peu ~ qu'il vienne** he is unlikely to come, there is little chance of his coming, the chances are (that) he won't come; **il est fort ~ qu'il ait raison** in all likelihood he is right, it is highly likely that he's right; **c'est (très) ~** it's (very *ou* highly) probable, (very) probably, it's (highly) likely.

probablement [prɔbabləmɑ̃] **adv** probably. **il viendra ~** he's likely to come, he'll probably come; **~ pas** probably not.

probant, e [prɔbɑ̃, ɑ̃t] **adj** *argument, expérience* convincing; (*Jur*) probative.

probation [prɔbasjɔ̃] **nf** (*Jur, Rel*) probation. **stage de ~** trial *ou* probationary period.

probatoire [prɔbatwar] **adj** *examen, test* grading, preliminary. **stage ~** trial *ou* probationary period.

probe [prɔb] **adj** (*littér*) upright, honest.

probité [prɔbite] **nf** probity, integrity.

problématique [prɔblematik] 1 **adj** problematic(al). 2 **nf** (*problème*) problem; (*science*) problematics *(sg)*.

problème [prɔblɛm] **nm** (*difficulté*) problem; (*question débattue*) problem, issue; (*Math*) problem. (*Scol*) **~s de robinets** sums about the volume of water in containers; **c'est tout un ~** it's a real problem; **le ~ du logement** the housing problem, the problem of housing; **enfant/cheveux à ~s** problem child/hair; **faire ~** to pose problems; **(il n'y a) pas de ~!*** no problem!; *voir* **faux[2]**.

procédé [prɔsede] **nm** a (*méthode*) process. **~ de fabrication** manufacturing process. b (*conduite*) behaviour (*NonC*), conduct (*NonC*). **avoir recours à un ~ malhonnête** to do sth in a dishonest way, resort to dishonest behaviour; **ce sont là des ~s peu recommandables** that's pretty disreputable behaviour; *voir* **échange.** c (*Billard*) tip.

procéder [prɔsede] 6 1 **vi** (*agir*) to proceed; (*moralement*) to behave. **~ par ordre** to take things one by one, do one thing at a time; **~ avec prudence/par élimination** to proceed with caution/by elimination; **je n'aime pas sa façon de ~ (envers les gens)** I don't like the way he behaves (towards people).

2 **procéder à vt indir** (*opérer*) *enquête, expérience* to conduct, carry out; *dépouillement* to start. **~ à l'ouverture du coffre** to proceed to open the chest, set about *ou* start opening the chest; **nous avons fait ~ à une étude sur** we have initiated *ou* set up a study on; **~ au vote (sur)** to take a vote (on); **~ à une élection** to hold an election; **~ à l'élection du nouveau président** to hold an election for the new president, elect the new president.

3 **procéder de vt indir** (*frm: provenir de*) to come from, proceed from, originate in; (*Rel*) to proceed from. **cette philosophie procède de celle de Platon** this philosophy originates in *ou* is a development from that of Plato; **cela procède d'une mauvaise organisation** it comes from *ou* is due to bad organization.

procédural, e, mpl -aux [prɔsedyral, o] **adj** *problème* procedural.

procédure [prɔsedyr] **nf** a (*marche à suivre*) procedure. **quelle ~ doit-on suivre pour obtenir ...?** what procedure must one follow to obtain ...?, what's the (usual) procedure for obtaining ...? b (*Jur: règles*) procedure; (*procès*) proceedings. **~ accélérée** expeditious procedure; **~ de conciliation** conciliation procedure; **~ civile** civil (law) procedure; **~ pénale** criminal (law) procedure; **problème de ~** procedural problem.

procédurier, -ière [prɔsedyrje, jɛr] **adj** (*péj*) *tempérament, attitude* quibbling (*épith*), pettifogging (*épith*), nit-picking* (*épith*).

procès [prɔsɛ] 1 **nm** a (*Jur*) (*poursuite*) (legal) proceedings, (court) action, lawsuit; *[cour d'assises]* trial. **faire/intenter un ~ à qn** to take/start *ou* institute (*frm*) (legal) proceedings against sb; **engager un ~ contre qn** to take (court) action against sb, bring an action against sb, take sb to court, sue sb; **intenter un ~ en divorce** to institute divorce proceedings; **être en ~ avec qn** to be involved in a lawsuit with sb; **gagner/perdre son ~** to win/lose one's case; **réviser un ~** to review a case *ou* judgment.

b (*fig*) **faire le ~ de qn/la société capitaliste** to put sb/capitalism on trial *ou* in the dock; **faire le ~ de qch** to pick holes in sth, criticize sth; **faire un ~ d'intention à qn** to accuse sb on the basis of his supposed intentions, make a case against sb based on assumptions not facts; **vous me faites un mauvais ~** you're making unfounded *ou* groundless accusations against me; *voir* **forme.**

c (*Anat*) process.

d (*Ling*) process.

2 **comp** ►**procès civil** civil proceedings *ou* action ►**procès criminel** criminal proceedings *ou* trial ►**procès-verbal nm (pl procès-verbaux)** (*compte rendu*) minutes; (*Jur: constat*) report, statement; (*de contravention*) statement; **dresser un procès-verbal contre un automobiliste** to book (*Brit*) *ou* give a ticket to a motorist.

processeur [prɔsesœr] **nm** processor.

procession [prɔsesjɔ̃] **nf** (*gén*) procession. **marcher en ~** to walk in procession.

processionnaire [prɔsesjɔnɛr] 1 **adj** processionary. 2 **nf** processionary caterpillar.

processionnel, -elle [prɔsesjɔnɛl] **adj** processional.

processionnellement [prɔsesjɔnɛlmɑ̃] **adv** in procession.

processus [prɔsesys] **nm** a (*gén*) process; *[maladie]* progress. **~ économique** economic process. b (*Anat*) process.

prochain, e [prɔʃɛ̃, ɛn] 1 **adj** a (*suivant*) *réunion, numéro, semaine* next. **lundi/le mois ~** next Monday/month; **le 8 septembre ~** on the 8th

September of this year; **la ~e rencontre aura lieu à Paris** the next meeting will take place in Paris; **la ~e fois que tu viendras** (the) next time you come; **la ~e fois** *ou* **la fois ~e, je le saurai** I'll know next time; **à la ~e occasion** at the next *ou* first opportunity; **à la ~e!*** be seeing you!*; **au revoir, à une ~e fois!** goodbye, see you again!*; **je ne peux pas rester dîner aujourd'hui, ce sera pour une ~e fois** I can't stay for dinner today – it'll have to be *ou* I'll have to come some other time; **je descends à la ~e*** I'm getting off at the next stop (*ou* station *etc*); **au ~ (client)!** next (one) please!

b (*proche*) *arrivée, départ* impending, imminent; *mort* imminent; *avenir* near, immediate. **un jour ~** soon, in the near future; **un de ces ~s jours** one of these days, before long.

c *village* (*suivant*) next; (*voisin*) neighbouring, nearby; (*plus près*) nearest.

d (*littér*) *cause* immediate.

2 **nm** fellow man; (*Rel*) neighbour.

prochainement [pʀɔʃɛnmɑ̃] **adv** soon, shortly. (*Ciné*) **~ (sur vos écrans)** ... coming soon ... *ou* shortly ... .

proche [pʀɔʃ] 1 **adj** a (*dans l'espace*) *village* neighbouring (*épith*), nearby (*épith*); *rue* nearby (*épith*). **être (tout) ~** to be (very) near *ou* close, be (quite) close by; **~ de la ville** near the town, close to the town; **le magasin le plus ~** the nearest shop; **les maisons sont très ~s les unes des autres** the houses are very close together; **de ~ en ~** step by step, gradually; **la nouvelle se répandit de ~ en ~** the news spread from one person to the next.

b (*imminent*) *mort* close (*attrib*), at hand (*attrib*); *départ* imminent, at hand (*attrib*). **dans un ~ avenir** in the near *ou* immediate future; **être ~** *[fin, but]* to be drawing near, be near at hand; **être ~ de** *fin, victoire* to be nearing, be close to; *dénouement* to be reaching, be drawing close to; **être ~ de la mort** to be near death *ou* close to death; **la nuit est ~** it's nearly nightfall; **l'heure est ~ où** ... the time is at hand when ...; *voir* **futur**.

c (*récent*) *événement* close (*attrib*), recent.

d *parent* close, near. **mes plus ~s parents** my nearest *ou* closest relatives, my next of kin (*Admin*).

e *ami* close. **je me sens très ~ d'elle** I feel very close to her.

f **~ de** (*avoisinant*) close to; (*parent de*) closely related to; **l'italien est ~ du latin** Italian is closely related to Latin; **une désinvolture ~ de l'insolence** an offhandedness verging on insolence.

2 **nmpl**: **~s** close relations, nearest and dearest*, next of kin (*Admin*).

3 **comp** ▸**le Proche-Orient** the Near East; **du Proche-Orient** Near Eastern, in *ou* from the Near East.

proclamateur, -trice [pʀɔklamatœʀ, tʀis] **nm,f** proclaimer.

proclamation [pʀɔklamasjɔ̃] **nf** (*voir* **proclamer**) proclamation; declaration; announcement; (*écrite*) proclamation.

proclamer [pʀɔklame] 1 **vt** a (*affirmer*) *conviction, vérité* to proclaim. **~ son innocence** to proclaim *ou* declare one's innocence; **~ que** to proclaim *ou* declare *ou* assert that; **il se proclamait le sauveur du pays** he proclaimed *ou* declared himself (to be) the saviour of the country; (*littér*) **chez eux, tout proclamait la pauvreté** everything in their house proclaimed their poverty. b *république, état d'urgence* to proclaim, declare; *décret* to publish; *verdict, résultats d'élection* to declare, announce; *résultats d'examen* to announce. **~ qn roi** to proclaim sb king.

proclitique [pʀɔklitik] **adj, nm** proclitic.

proconsul [pʀokɔ̃syl] **nm** proconsul.

procrastination [pʀɔkʀastinasjɔ̃] **nf** procrastination.

procréateur, -trice [pʀɔkʀeatœʀ, tʀis] (*littér*) 1 **adj** procreative. 2 **nm,f** procreator.

procréation [pʀɔkʀeasjɔ̃] **nf** (*littér*) procreation. **~ artificielle** *ou* **(médicalement) assistée** artificial insemination.

procréer [pʀɔkʀee] 1 **vt** (*littér*) to procreate.

procuration [pʀɔkyʀasjɔ̃] **nf** (*Jur*) (*pour voter, représenter qn*) proxy; (*pour toucher de l'argent*) power of attorney. **par ~** by proxy; **avoir (une) ~** to have power of attorney *ou* an authorization; **avoir ~ sur un compte en banque** to have power of attorney over a bank account; **donner (une) ~ à qn** to give sb power of attorney, authorize sb.

procurer [pʀɔkyʀe] 1 1 **vt** a (*faire obtenir*) **~ qch à qn** to get *ou* obtain sth for sb, find sth for sb, provide sb with sth. b (*apporter*) *joie, ennuis* to bring; *avantage* to bring, give, procure. **le plaisir que procure le jardinage** the pleasure that gardening brings *ou* that one gets from gardening. 2 **se procurer vpr** (*obtenir*) to get, procure, obtain (for o.s.); (*trouver*) to find, come by; (*acheter*) to get, buy (o.s.).

procureur [pʀɔkyʀœʀ] **nm** (*Jur*) **~ (de la République)** public *ou* state prosecutor; **~ général** public prosecutor (*in appeal courts*); (*Can*) **~ général, juge en chef** Attorney General, Chief Justice (*Can*); (*Can*) **~ de la Couronne** Crown attorney (*Can*).

prodigalité [pʀɔdigalite] **nf** a (*caractère*) prodigality, extravagance. b (*dépenses*) **~s** extravagance, extravagant expenditure (*NonC*). c (*littér: profusion*) *[détails]* abundance, profusion, wealth.

prodige [pʀɔdiʒ] 1 **nm** (*événement*) marvel, wonder; (*personne*) prodigy. **un ~ de la nature/science** a wonder of nature/science; **tenir du ~** to be astounding *ou* extraordinary; **faire des ~s** to work wonders; **grâce à des ~s de courage/patience** thanks to his (*ou* her *etc*) prodigious *ou* extraordinary courage/patience. 2 **adj**: **enfant ~** child prodigy.

prodigieusement [pʀɔdiʒjøzmɑ̃] **adv** prodigiously, fantastically, incredibly, phenomenally, tremendously.

prodigieux, -ieuse [pʀɔdiʒjø, jøz] **adj** *foule, force, bêtise* prodigious, fantastic, incredible, phenomenal; *personne, génie* prodigious, phenomenal; *effort* prodigious, tremendous, fantastic.

prodigue [pʀɔdig] 1 **adj** (*dépensier*) extravagant, wasteful, prodigal; (*généreux*) generous. **être ~ de ses compliments** to be lavish with one's praise; **être ~ de conseils** to be full of advice *ou* free with one's advice; **lui en général si peu ~ de compliments/conseils** he who is usually so sparing of compliments/advice; **être ~ de son temps** to be unsparing *ou* unstinting of one's time; **être ~ de son bien** to be lavish with one's money; (*Rel*) **l'enfant** *ou* **le fils ~** the prodigal son. 2 **nmf** spendthrift.

prodiguer [pʀɔdige] 1 **vt** *énergie, talent* to be unsparing *ou* unstinting of; *compliments, conseils* to be full of, pour out; *argent* to be lavish with. **~ des compliments/conseils à qn** to lavish compliments/advice on sb, pour out compliments/advice to sb; **elle me prodigua ses soins** she lavished care on me; **malgré les soins que le médecin lui a prodigués** in spite of the care *ou* treatment the doctor gave him; **se ~ sans compter** to spare no efforts, give unsparingly *ou* unstintingly of o.s.

producteur, -trice [pʀɔdyktœʀ, tʀis] 1 **adj** producing (*épith*), growing (*épith*). **pays ~ de pétrole** oil-producing country, oil producer; **pays ~ de blé** wheat-growing country, wheat producer; (*Ciné*) **société ~trice** film company. 2 **nm, f** a (*Comm*) producer; (*Agr*) *[œufs]* producer; *[blé, tomates]* grower, producer. **du ~ au consommateur** from the producer to the consumer. b (*Ciné, TV*) producer. (*TV*) **~-réalisateur** producer and director.

productible [pʀɔdyktibl] **adj** producible.

productif, -ive [pʀɔdyktif, iv] **adj** productive. (*Fin*) **~ d'intérêts** that bears interest, interest-bearing.

production [pʀɔdyksjɔ̃] **nf** a (*action: voir* **produire**) production; generation; growing; writing; painting. b (*rendement, fabrication, récolte*) (*Ind*) production, output; (*Agr*) production, yield. **notre ~ est inférieure à nos besoins**: our output is lower than our needs; **restreindre la ~** to restrict output *ou* production; **~ brute** gross output; **la ~ cinématographique/dramatique du 20e siècle** 20th-century cinema/plays; *voir* **moyen**. c (*produit*) product. **~s** (*Agr*) produce; (*Comm, Ind*) goods; **les ~s de l'esprit** creations of the mind. d (*Ciné*) production.

productique [pʀɔdyktik] **nf** factory *ou* industrial automation.

productivité [pʀɔdyktivite] **nf** productivity, productiveness; (*Écon, Ind: rendement*) productivity.

produire [pʀɔdɥiʀ] 38 1 **vt** a (*fabriquer*) *acier, voiture* to produce, make, turn out; *électricité* to produce, generate; *maïs, tomates* to produce, grow; *charbon, pétrole* to produce; *rouille, humidité, son* to produce, make; *roman* to produce, write, turn out; *tableau* to produce, paint, turn out; (*Fin*) *intérêt* to yield, return. **arbre/terre qui produit de bons fruits** tree/soil which yields *ou* produces good fruit; **certains sols produisent plus que d'autres** some soils are more productive *ou* give a better yield than others; **un poète qui ne produit pas beaucoup** a poet who doesn't write much *ou* turn out very much; **cette école a produit plusieurs savants** this school has produced several scientists; **pays qui produit du pétrole** oil-producing country, country which produces oil.

b (*causer*) *effet* to produce, have; *changement* to produce, bring about; *résultat* to produce, give; *sensation* to cause, create. **~ une bonne/mauvaise impression sur qn** to produce *ou* make a good/bad impression on sb; **il a produit une forte impression sur les examinateurs** he made a great impression on the examiners, the examiners were highly impressed by him.

c (*présenter*) *document, témoin* to produce.

d (*Ciné*) *film* to produce.

2 **se produire vpr** a (*survenir*) to happen, occur, take place. **il s'est produit un revirement dans l'opinion** there has been a complete change in public opinion; **le changement qui s'est produit en lui** the change that has come over him *ou* taken place in him.

b *[acteur]* to perform, give a performance, appear. **se ~ sur scène** to appear on the stage; **se ~ en public** to appear in public, give a public performance.

produit [pʀɔdɥi] 1 **nm** a (*denrée, article*) product. **~s** (*Agr*) produce; (*Comm, Ind*) goods, products; **~s finis/semi-finis, ~s ouvrés/semi-ouvrés** finished/semi-finished goods *ou* products; **~ de substitution** alternative product; **il faudrait acheter un ~ pour nettoyer les carreaux** we'll have to buy something to clean the windows (with); **chef** *ou* **responsable (de) ~** product manager, brand manager; (*fig*) **un ~ typique de notre université** a typical product of our university.

b (*rapport*) product, yield; (*bénéfice*) profit; (*revenu*) income. **le ~ de la collecte sera donné à une bonne œuvre** the proceeds *ou* takings from the collection will be given to charity; **vivre du ~ de sa terre** to live on the produce of *ou* the income from one's land.

c (*Math*) product.

d (*Chim*) product, chemical.

e (*Zool: petit*) offspring (*inv*).

2 **comp** ▸**produits agricoles** agricultural *ou* farm produce ▸**produits alimentaires** foodstuffs ▸**produit bancaire** banking

product ►**produits de beauté** cosmetics, beauty products ►**produit brut** (*bénéfice*) gross profit; (*objet*) unfinished product ►**produit chimique** chemical ►**produit de consommation** consumable; **produit de consommation courante** basic consumable; **produits de grande consommation** consumer goods ►**produit d'entretien** clean(s)ing product ►**produit de l'impôt** tax yield ►**produits industriels** industrial goods *ou* products ►**produit intérieur brut** gross domestic product ►**produits manufacturés** manufactured goods ►**produit national brut** gross national product ►**produit net** net profit ►**produit pétrolier** oil product ►**produit pharmaceutique** pharmaceutical (product) ►**produits de toilette** toiletries ►**produit pour la vaisselle** washing-up (*Brit*) *ou* dishwashing (*US*) liquid ►**produit des ventes** income *ou* proceeds from sales.

proéminence [pʀɔeminɑ̃s] **nf** prominence, protuberance.

proéminent, e [pʀɔeminɑ̃, ɑ̃t] **adj** prominent, protuberant.

prof* [pʀɔf] **nmf** (**abrév de professeur**) (*Scol*) teacher; (*Univ*) ≃ lecturer (*Brit*), instructor (*US*), prof* (*US*); (*avec chaire*) prof*.

profanateur, -trice [pʀɔfanatœʀ, tʀis] **1 adj** profaning (*épith*), profane. **2 nm,f** profaner.

profanation [pʀɔfanasjɔ̃] **nf** (*voir* **profaner**) desecration; profanation; violation; defilement; debasement; prostitution.

profane [pʀɔfan] **1 adj a** (*non spécialiste*) **je suis ~ en la matière** I'm a layman in the field, I don't know anything about the subject. **b** *fête* secular; *auteur, littérature, musique* secular, profane (*littér*). **2 nmf a** (*gén*) layman, lay person. **aux yeux du ~** to the layman *ou* the uninitiated; **un ~ en art** a person who is uninitiated in the field of art, a person who knows nothing about art. **b** (*Rel*) non-believer. **3 nm** (*Rel*) **le ~** the secular, the profane (*littér*).

profaner [pʀɔfane] 1 **vt** *église* to desecrate, profane; *tombe* to desecrate, violate, profane; *sentiments, souvenir, nom* to defile, profane; *institution* to debase; *talent* to prostitute, debase.

proférer [pʀɔfeʀe] 6 **vt** *parole* to utter; *injures* to utter, pour out.

professer [pʀɔfese] 1 **vt a** *opinion* to profess, declare, state; *théorie* to profess; *sentiment* to profess, declare. **~ que ...** to profess *ou* declare *ou* claim that ... . **b** (*Scol*) to teach.

professeur [pʀɔfesœʀ] **1 nm** (*gén*) teacher; [*lycée, collège*] (school) teacher; (*Univ*) ≃ lecturer (*Brit*), instructor (*US*); (*avec chaire*) professor. **elle est ~** she's a (school)teacher *ou* schoolmistress (*Brit*); (*Univ*) **(Monsieur) le ~ X** Professor X; **~ de piano/de chant** piano/singing teacher *ou* master (*Brit*) *ou* mistress (*Brit*); **~ de droit** lecturer in law; professor of law; **l'ensemble des ~s** the teaching staff.

2 comp ►**professeur adjoint** (*Can Univ*) assistant professor ►**professeur agrégé** (*gén*) qualified schoolteacher (*who has passed the agrégation*); (*en médecine*) professor of medicine (*holder of the agrégation*); (*Can Univ*) associate professor ►**professeur certifié** qualified schoolteacher (*who has passed the CAPES*) ►**professeur d'enseignement général des collèges** basic-grade schoolteacher (*in a college*) ►**professeur principal** ≃ class teacher (*Brit*), form tutor (*Brit*), homeroom teacher (*US*) ►**professeur titulaire** (*Can Univ*) full professor.

profession [pʀɔfesjɔ̃] **1 nf a** (*gén*) occupation; (*manuelle*) trade; (*libérale*) profession. **exercer la ~ de médecin** to be a doctor by profession, practise as a doctor (*Brit*), practice medicine (*US*); **menuisier de ~** carpenter by *ou* to trade; (*fig*) **menteur de ~** professional liar; (*Admin*) **"sans ~"** (*gén*) "unemployed"; (*femme mariée*) "housewife".

b (*personnes*) **(les gens de) la ~** (*gén, artisans*) the people in the trade; (*professions libérales*) the people in the profession.

c faire ~ de non-conformisme to profess nonconformism; **faire ~ d'être non conformiste** to profess *ou* declare o.s. a nonconformist.

2 comp ►**profession de foi** (*Rel, fig*) profession of faith ►**profession libérale** (liberal) profession; **les membres des professions libérales** professional people, the members of the (liberal) professions.

professionnaliser [pʀɔfesjɔnalize] 1 **1 vt** (*Sport*) to professionalize. **sportif professionnalisé** professional. **2 se professionnaliser vpr** (*Sport*) to become professionalized; [*sportif*] to turn professional.

professionnalisme [pʀɔfesjɔnalism] **nm** professionalism.

professionnel, -elle [pʀɔfesjɔnɛl] **1 adj a** *activité, maladie* occupational (*épith*); *école* technical (*épith*). **faute ~elle** (professional) negligence (*NonC*); (*Méd*) malpractice; **formation/orientation ~elle** vocational training/guidance; **cours ~** vocational training course; **frais ~s** business expenses; **(être tenu par) le secret ~** (to be bound by) professional secrecy; *voir* **certificat, conscience, déformation**.

b *écrivain, sportif,* (*fig*) *menteur* professional.

2 nm,f a (*gén, Sport*) professional. **c'est un travail de ~** it's a job for a professional; (*bien fait*) it's a professional job; **passer ~** to turn professional; **les ~s du tourisme** people working in the tourist industry. **b** (*Ind*) skilled worker.

professionnellement [pʀɔfesjɔnɛlmɑ̃] **adv** professionally.

professoral, e, mpl -aux [pʀɔfesɔʀal, o] **adj** *ton, attitude* professorial. **le corps ~** (*gén*) (the) teachers, the teaching profession; (*d'une école*) the teaching staff.

professorat [pʀɔfesɔʀa] **nm: le ~** the teaching profession; **le ~ de français** French teaching, the teaching of French.

profil [pʀɔfil] **nm a** (*silhouette*) [*personne*] profile; [*édifice*] outline, profile, contour; [*voiture*] line, contour. **de ~** *dessiner* in profile; *regarder* sideways on, in profile; (*fig*) **un ~ de médaille** a finely chiselled profile; **garder le ~ bas, prendre** *ou* **adopter un ~ bas** to keep a low profile. **b** (*coupe*) [*bâtiment, route*] profile; (*Géol*) [*sol*] section. **c** (*Psych*) profile. **~ de carrière** career profile; **le ~ d'un étudiant** the profile of a student's performance; **il a le bon ~ pour le métier** his previous experience *ou* his career to date *ou* his career profile seems right for the job.

profilé, e [pʀɔfile] (**ptp de profiler**) **1 adj** (*gén*) shaped; (*aérodynamique*) streamlined. **2 nm** (*Tech*) **~ (métallique)** metal section.

profiler [pʀɔfile] 1 **1 vt a** (*Tech*) (*dessiner*) to profile, represent in profile; (*fabriquer*) to shape; (*rendre aérodynamique*) to streamline. **b** (*faire ressortir*) **la cathédrale profile ses tours contre le ciel** the cathedral towers stand out *ou* stand outlined *ou* are silhouetted against the sky. **2 se profiler vpr** [*objet*] to stand out (in profile), be outlined (*sur, contre* against); (*fig*) [*ennuis, solution*] to emerge. **les obstacles qui se profilent à l'horizon** the obstacles which are looming *ou* emerging *ou* which stand out on the horizon.

profit [pʀɔfi] **nm a** (*Comm, Fin: gain*) profit. **c'est une source illimitée de ~** it's an endless source of profit; **compte de ~s et pertes** profit and loss account; (*fig*) **faire passer qch aux ~s et pertes** to write sth off (as a loss).

b (*avantage*) benefit, advantage, profit. **être d'un grand ~ à qn** to be of great benefit *ou* most useful to sb; **faire du ~** (*gén*) to be economical, be good value (for money); (*) [*vêtement*] to wear well; [*rôti*] to go a long way; **ce rôti n'a pas fait de ~** that roast didn't go very far; **ses vacances lui ont fait beaucoup de ~** *ou* **lui ont été d'un grand ~** his holiday greatly benefited him *ou* did him a lot of good, he greatly benefited from his holiday; **vous avez ~ à faire cela** it's in your interest *ou* to your advantage to do that; **s'il le fait, c'est qu'il y trouve son ~** if he does it, it's because it's to his advantage *ou* in his interest *ou* because he's getting something out of it*; **il a suivi les cours sans (en tirer) aucun ~/avec ~** he attended the classes without deriving any benefit *ou* advantage *ou* profit from them/and got a lot out of them *ou* and gained a lot from them; **tirer ~ de** *leçon, affaire* to profit *ou* benefit from; **tirer ~ du malheur des autres** to profit from *ou* take advantage of other people's misfortune; **collecte au ~ des aveugles** collection in aid of the blind; **il fait (son) ~ de tout** he turns everything to (his) advantage; **mettre à ~** *idée, invention* to turn to (good) account; *jeunesse, temps libre, sa beauté* to make the most of, take advantage of; **tourner qch à ~** to turn sth to good account; **il a mis à ~ le mauvais temps pour ranger le grenier** he made the most of *ou* took advantage of the bad weather to tidy the attic, he turned the bad weather to (good) account by tidying (up) the attic.

profitabilité [pʀɔfitabilite] **nf** profitability.

profitable [pʀɔfitabl] **adj** (*utile*) beneficial, of benefit (*attrib*); (*lucratif*) profitable (*à* to).

profitablement [pʀɔfitabləmɑ̃] **adv** profitably.

profiter [pʀɔfite] 1 **1 profiter de vt indir** (*tirer avantage*) *situation, privilège, occasion, crédulité* to take advantage of; *jeunesse, vacances* to make the most of, take advantage of. **ils ont profité de ce que le professeur était sorti pour se battre** they took advantage of the teacher's being absent *ou* of the fact that the teacher had gone out to have a fight.

2 profiter à vt indir (*rapporter*) **~ à qn** [*affaire, circonstances*] to be profitable *ou* of benefit to sb, be to sb's advantage; [*repos*] to benefit sb, be beneficial to sb; [*conseil*] to benefit *ou* profit sb, be of benefit to sb; **à qui cela profite-t-il?** who stands to gain by it?, who will that help?; *voir* **bien**.

3 vi (*) (*se développer*) [*enfant*] to thrive, grow; (*être économique*) [*plat*] to go a long way, be economical; [*vêtement*] to wear well.

profiterole [pʀɔfitʀɔl] **nf** profiterole.

profiteur, -euse [pʀɔfitœʀ, øz] **nm,f** profiteer. **~ de guerre** war profiteer.

profond, e [pʀɔfɔ̃, ɔ̃d] **1 adj a** (*lit*) deep. **peu ~** *eau, vallée, puits* shallow; *coupure* superficial; **~ de 3 mètres** 3 metres deep.

b (*grand, extrême*) *soupir* deep, heavy; *sommeil* deep, sound; *coma* deep; *silence, mystère* deep, profound; (*littér*) *nuit* deep (*littér*), dark; *joie, foi, différence, influence, erreur* profound; *ignorance* profound, extreme; *intérêt, sentiment* profound, keen; *ennui* profound, acute; *forage* penetrating; *révérence* low, deep.

c (*caché, secret*) *cause, signification* underlying, deeper; (*Ling*) *structure* deep; *tendance* deep-seated, underlying. **la France ~e** the broad mass of French people.

d (*pénétrant*) *penseur, réflexion* profound, deep; *esprit, remarque* profound.

e *voix, couleur, regard* deep.

2 nm: au plus ~ de *forêt, désespoir* in the depths of; **au plus ~ de la mer** at the (very) bottom of the sea, in the depths of the sea; **au plus ~ de la nuit** at dead of night; **au plus ~ de mon être** in the depths of my being, in my deepest being.

3 adv *creuser* deep; *planter* deep (down).

profondément [pʀɔfɔ̃demɑ̃] **adv** *ému, choqué* deeply, profoundly; *convaincu* deeply, utterly; *différent* profoundly, vastly; *influencer, se tromper* profoundly; *réfléchir* deeply, profoundly; *aimer, ressentir* deeply; *respirer* deep(ly); *creuser, pénétrer* deep; *s'incliner* low. **il dort ~** (*en général*) he sleeps soundly, he is a sound sleeper; (*en ce moment*) he is sound *ou* fast asleep; **s'ennuyer ~** to be utterly *ou* acutely *ou* profoundly bored; **idée ~ ancrée dans les esprits** idea deeply rooted in people's minds; **ça m'est ~ égal** I really couldn't care less.

profondeur [pʀɔfɔ̃dœʀ] **nf** a (*lit*) *[trou, boîte, mer]* depth; *[plaie]* deepness, depth. **à cause du peu de ~** because of the shallowness; **cela manque de ~** it's not deep enough; **creuser en ~** to dig deep; **creuser jusqu'à 3 mètres de ~** to dig down to a depth of 3 metres; **avoir 10 mètres de ~** to be 10 metres deep *ou* in depth; **à 10 mètres de ~** 10 metres down, at a depth of 10 metres; **cette pommade agit en ~** this cream works deep into the skin; (*Phot*) **~ de champ** depth of field.
b (*fond*) *[mine, métro, poche]* **~s** depths; (*fig*) **les ~s de l'être** the depths of the human psyche.
c (*fig*) *[personne]* profoundness, profundity, depth; *[esprit, remarque]* profoundness, profundity; *[sentiment]* depth, keenness; *[sommeil]* soundness, depth; *[regard]* depth; *[couleur, voix]* deepness. **en ~** *agir, exprimer* in depth; *nettoyage* thorough; **c'est une réforme en ~ qu'il faut** what is needed is a radical *ou* thorough(going) reform.

pro forma [pʀofɔʀma] **adj inv: facture ~** pro forma invoice.

profus, e [pʀɔfy, yz] **adj** (*littér*) profuse.

profusément [pʀɔfyzemɑ̃] **adv** (*littér*) profusely, abundantly.

profusion [pʀɔfyzjɔ̃] **nf** *[fleurs, lumière]* profusion; *[idées, conseils]* wealth, abundance, profusion. **il y a des fruits à ~ sur le marché** there is fruit galore* *ou* in plenty *ou* there is plenty of fruit on the market; **nous en avons à ~** we've got plenty *ou* masses*.

progéniture [pʀɔʒenityʀ] **nf** *[homme, animal]* offspring, progeny (*littér*); (*hum: famille*) offspring (*hum*).

progestatif [pʀɔʒɛstatif] **nm** progestogen, progestin.

progestérone [pʀɔʒɛsteʀɔn] **nf** progesterone.

progiciel [pʀɔʒisjɛl] **nm** software package.

programmable [pʀɔgʀamabl] **adj** programmable. **touche ~** user-definable key.

programmateur, -trice [pʀɔgʀamatœʀ, tʀis] 1 **nm,f** (*Rad, TV*) programme planner. 2 **nm** (*appareil*) (*gén*) time switch; *[four]* autotimer.

programmation [pʀɔgʀamasjɔ̃] **nf** (*Rad, TV*) programming, programme planning; (*Ordin*) programming.

programme [pʀɔgʀam] **nm** a *[concert, spectacle, télévision, radio]* programme (*Brit*), program (*US*). **au ~** in the programme; **numéro hors ~** item not (billed *ou* announced) in the programme; (*Rad, TV*) **voici le ~ de la matinée** here is a rundown of the morning's programmes; (*Rad, TV*) **~ minimum** restricted service (*during a strike*); (*Rad, TV*) **fin de nos ~s à minuit** close-down will be at midnight (*Brit*), we will be closing down at midnight (*Brit*), our programmes will end at midnight; **cette excursion n'est pas prévue au ~** this trip is not on the programme; **changement de ~** change in (the) *ou* of programme.
b (*calendrier*) programme (*Brit*), program (*US*). **quel est le ~ de la journée? *ou* des réjouissances?*** what's the programme for the day?, what's on the agenda?*; **j'ai un ~ très chargé** I have a very busy timetable.
c (*Scol*) *[matière]* syllabus; *[classe, école]* curriculum. **le ~ de français** the French syllabus; **quel est le ~ en sixième?** what's (on) the curriculum in the first year?; **les œuvres du ~** the set (*Brit*) *ou* assigned (*US*) books *ou* works, the books on the syllabus; **~ de sensibilisation** awareness programme.
d (*projet, Pol*) programme (*Brit*), program (*US*). **~ d'action/de travail** programme of action/work; **il y a un changement de ~** there's a change of plan *ou* programme; **c'est tout un ~!** that'll take some doing!
e *[ordinateur]* (computer) program; *[machine à laver]* programme.

programmé, e [pʀɔgʀame] (**ptp de programmer**) **adj** *opération,* (*Typ*) *composition* computerized. **~ à l'avance** pre-programmed; *voir* **enseignement**.

programmer [pʀɔgʀame] 1 **vt** *émission* to schedule; *machine* to programme (*Brit*), program (*US*); *ordinateur* to program; (*: *prévoir*) *vacances* to plan.

programmeur, -euse [pʀɔgʀamœʀ, øz] **nm,f** (computer) programmer.

progrès [pʀɔgʀɛ] **nm** a (*amélioration*) progress (*NonC*). **faire des ~/de petits ~** to make progress/a little progress; **élève en ~** pupil who is making progress *ou* who is progressing *ou* getting on (well); **il y a du ~** there is some progress *ou* improvement; **c'est un grand ~** it's a great advance, much progress has been made; **il a fait de grands ~** he has made great progress *ou* shown (a) great improvement; **~ scolaires** academic progress; **~ social** social progress.
b (*évolution*) progress (*NonC*). **croire au ~** to believe in progress; **suivre les ~ de** to follow the progress of; **c'est le ~!** that's progress!
c (*progression*) *[incendie, inondation]* spread, progress; *[maladie]* progression, progress; *[armée]* progress, advance.

progresser [pʀɔgʀese] 1 **vi** a (*s'améliorer*) *[malade, élève]* to progress, make progress, get *ou* come on (well). b (*avancer*) *[explorateurs, sauveteurs, ennemi]* to advance, make headway *ou* progress; *[maladie]* to progress; *[science, recherches]* to advance, progress; *[projet]* to progress; *[prix, ventes]* to rise, increase; *[idée, théorie]* to gain ground, make headway. **afin que notre monde/la science progresse** so that our world/science goes forward *ou* progresses *ou* makes progress; **les salaires progressent moins vite que les prix** salaries are going up *ou* are rising more slowly than prices.

progressif, -ive [pʀɔgʀesif, iv] **adj** (*gén, Ling*) progressive.

progression [pʀɔgʀesjɔ̃] **nf** a *[élève, explorateurs]* progress; *[ennemi]* advance; *[maladie]* progression, spread; *[science]* progress, advance. **la ~ très rapide de ces idées** the rapid spread *ou* advance of these ideas.
b (*Math, Mus*) progression. **~ arithmétique/géométrique** arithmetic/geometric progression; **~ économique** economic advance; **ventes en ~** rising *ou* increasing sales.

progressiste [pʀɔgʀesist] **adj, nmf** progressive.

progressivement [pʀɔgʀesivmɑ̃] **adv** progressively.

progressivité [pʀɔgʀesivite] **nf** progressiveness.

prohibé, e [pʀɔibe] (**ptp de prohiber**) **adj** *marchandise, action* prohibited, forbidden; *arme* illegal.

prohiber [pʀɔibe] 1 **vt** to prohibit, ban, forbid.

prohibitif, -ive [pʀɔibitif, iv] **adj** *prix* prohibitive; *mesure* prohibitory, prohibitive.

prohibition [pʀɔibisjɔ̃] **nf** (*gén, Hist USA*) prohibition (*de* on). **la ~ du port d'armes** a ban on the carrying of weapons.

prohibitionnisme [pʀɔibisjɔnism] **nm** prohibitionism.

prohibitionniste [pʀɔibisjɔnist] **adj, nmf** prohibitionist.

proie [pʀwɑ] **nf** a (*lit*) prey (*NonC*); *voir* **oiseau**.
b (*fig*) prey. *[personne]* **être la ~ de** to fall (a) prey *ou* victim to, be the prey of; **le pays fut la ~ des envahisseurs** the country fell (a) prey to invaders; **la maison était la ~ des flammes** the house fell (a) prey to *ou* was claimed by the flames; **c'est une ~ facile pour des escrocs** he's (*ou* she's) easy prey *ou* game* *ou* meat* for swindlers.
c (*loc*) **être en ~ à** *maladie* to be a victim of; *douleur* to be racked *ou* tortured by; *doute, émotion* to be (a) prey to; **il était en ~ au remords** he was (a) prey to remorse, remorse preyed on him; **en ~ au désespoir** racked by despair, a prey to despair; **lâcher *ou* laisser la ~ pour l'ombre** to give up what one has (already) for some uncertain *ou* fanciful alternative.

projecteur [pʀɔʒɛktœʀ] **nm** a *[diapositive, film]* projector. **~ sonore** sound projector. b (*lumière*) *[théâtre]* spotlight; *[prison, bateau]* searchlight; *[monument public, stade]* floodlight; (*Aut*) headlamp unit *ou* assembly, headlight. (*fig*) **sous les ~s de l'actualité, sous les feux des ~s** in the limelight, in the public eye.

projectif, -ive [pʀɔʒɛktif, iv] **adj** projective.

projectile [pʀɔʒɛktil] **nm** (*gén*) missile; (*Mil, Tech*) projectile.

projection [pʀɔʒɛksjɔ̃] **nf** a *[ombre]* casting, projection, throwing; *[film]* (*action*) projection; (*séance*) showing. **appareil de ~** projector, projection equipment (*NonC*); **salle de ~** film theatre; **cabine de ~** projection room; **conférence avec des ~s (de diapositives)** lecture (illustrated) with slides. b (*lancement*) *[liquide, vapeur]* discharge, ejection; *[pierre]* throwing (*NonC*). (*Géol*) **~s volcaniques** volcanic ejections *ou* ejecta. c (*Math, Psych*) projection (*sur* onto).

projectionniste [pʀɔʒɛksjɔnist] **nmf** projectionist.

projet [pʀɔʒɛ] **nm** a (*dessein*) plan. **~s criminels/de vacances** criminal/holiday plans; **faire des ~s d'avenir** to make plans for the future, make future plans; **faire *ou* former le ~ de faire** to make plans to do; **ce ~ de livre/d'agrandissement** this plan for a book/for an extension; **quels sont vos ~s pour le mois prochain?** what are your plans *ou* what plans have you for next month?; **ce n'est encore qu'un ~, c'est encore à l'état de ~ *ou* encore en ~** it's still only at the planning stage.
b (*ébauche*) *[roman]* (preliminary) draft; *[maison, ville]* plan. **~ de loi** bill; **établir un ~ d'accord/de contrat** to draft an agreement/a contract, produce a draft agreement/contract.

projeter [pʀɔʒ(ə)te] 4 1 **vt** a (*envisager*) to plan (*de faire* to do). **as-tu projeté quelque chose pour les vacances?** have you made any plans *ou* have you planned anything for your holidays?
b (*jeter*) *gravillons* to throw up; *étincelles* to throw off; *fumée* to send out, discharge; *lave* to eject, throw out. **attention! la poêle projette de la graisse** careful! the frying pan is spitting (out) fat; **être projeté hors de** to be thrown *ou* hurled *ou* flung out of; **on lui a projeté de l'eau dans les yeux** water was thrown *ou* flung into his eyes.
c (*envoyer*) *ombre, reflet* to cast, project, throw; *film, diapositive* to project; (*montrer*) to show. **on peut ~ ce film sur un petit écran** this film may be projected onto a small screen; **on nous a projeté des diapositives** we were shown some slides.
d (*Math, Psych*) to project (*sur* onto).
2 **se projeter vpr** *[ombre]* to be cast, fall (*sur* on).

projeteur [pʀɔʒ(ə)tœʀ] **nm** project manager.

projo* [pʀɔʒo] **nm abrév de projecteur**.

prolapsus [pʀɔlapsys] **nm** prolapse.

prolégomènes [pʀɔlegɔmɛn] **nmpl** prolegomena.

prolepse [pʀɔlɛps] **nf** (*Littérat*) prolepsis.

prolétaire [pʀɔletɛʀ] 1 **adj** proletarian. 2 **nmf** proletarian. **les enfants de ~s** children of working-class people; **~s de tous les pays unissez-**

vous! workers of the world unite!
prolétariat [pRɔletaRja] **nm** proletariat.
prolétarien, -ienne [pRɔletaRjɛ̃, jɛn] **adj** proletarian.
prolétarisation [pRɔletaRizasjɔ̃] **nf** proletarianization.
prolétariser [pRɔletaRize] 1 **vt** to proletarianize.
prolifération [pRɔlifeRasjɔ̃] **nf** proliferation.
proliférer [pRɔlifeRe] 6 **vi** to proliferate.
prolifique [pRɔlifik] **adj** prolific.
prolixe [pRɔliks] **adj** *orateur, discours* verbose, prolix (*frm*), wordy.
prolixement [pRɔliksəmɑ̃] **adv** verbosely, prolixly (*frm*), wordily.
prolixité [pRɔliksite] **nf** verbosity, prolixity (*frm*), wordiness.
prolo* [pRolo] 1 **nmf** (**abrév de prolétaire**) pleb* (*péj*), prole* (*péj*). 2 **adj** common-looking, plebby*.
prologue [pRɔlɔg] **nm** prologue (*à* to).
prolongateur [pRɔlɔ̃gatœR] **nm** extension cable *ou* lead.
prolongation [pRɔlɔ̃gasjɔ̃] **nf** (*voir* **prolonger**) prolongation; extension. (*Ftbl*) **~s** extra time (*NonC*); (*Ftbl*) **ils ont joué les ~s** they played extra time, the game *ou* they went into extra time.
prolonge [pRɔlɔ̃ʒ] **nf**: **~ d'artillerie** gun carriage.
prolongé, e [pRɔlɔ̃ʒe] (**ptp de prolonger**) **adj** *débat, séjour* prolonged, lengthy; *rire, cri* prolonged; *effort* prolonged, sustained. **exposition ~e au soleil** prolonged exposure to the sun; (*hum*) **jeune fille ~e**† old maid, girl left on the shelf; **rue de la Paix ~e** continuation of Rue de la Paix; **en cas d'arrêt ~** in case of prolonged stoppage.
prolongement [pRɔlɔ̃ʒmɑ̃] **nm** a *[route]* continuation; *[bâtiment]* extension; (*fig*) *[affaire, politique]* extension. **décider le ~ d'une route** to decide to extend *ou* continue a road; **cette rue se trouve dans le ~ de l'autre** this street runs on from the other *ou* is the continuation of the other; **l'outil doit être un ~ du bras** the tool should be an extension of one's arm. b (*suites*) **~s** repercussions, effects.
prolonger [pRɔlɔ̃ʒe] 3 1 **vt** a (*dans le temps*) *séjour, trêve, séance* to prolong, extend; *billet* to extend; *vie, maladie* to prolong; (*Mus*) *note* to prolong. **nous ne pouvons ~ notre séjour** we cannot stay any longer, we cannot prolong our stay any longer.
b (*dans l'espace*) *rue* to extend, continue; (*Math*) *ligne* to prolong, produce. **on a prolongé le mur jusqu'au garage** we extended *ou* continued the wall as far as *ou* up to the garage; **ce bâtiment prolonge l'aile principale** this building is the *ou* an extension *ou* a continuation of the main wing.
2 **se prolonger vpr** a (*persister*) *[attente]* to go on; *[situation]* to go on, last, persist; *[effet]* to last, persist; *[débat]* to last, go on, carry on; *[maladie]* to continue, persist. **il voudrait se ~ dans ses enfants** he would like to live on in his children.
b (*s'étendre*) *[rue, chemin]* to go on, carry on (*Brit*), continue.
promenade [pRɔm(ə)nad] **nf** a (*à pied*) walk, stroll; (*en voiture*) drive, ride, spin*; (*en bateau*) sail; (*en vélo, à cheval*) ride. **partir en ~, faire une ~** to go for a walk *ou* stroll (*ou* drive *etc*); **être en ~** to be out walking *ou* out for a walk; **faire faire une ~ à qn** to take sb (out) for a walk; (*Sport*) **cette course a été une vraie ~ pour lui** this race was a real walkover for him; **ça n'a pas été une ~ de santé** it has been no picnic*. b (*avenue*) walk, esplanade; (*front de mer*) promenade.
promener [pRɔm(ə)ne] 5 1 **vt** a **(emmener) ~ qn** to take sb (out) for a walk *ou* stroll; **~ le chien** to walk the dog, take the dog out (for a walk); **~ des amis à travers une ville** to show *ou* take friends round a town; **cela te promènera** that will get you out for a while; **il promène son nounours partout*** he trails his teddy bear (around) everywhere with him; **est-ce qu'il va nous ~ encore longtemps à travers ces bureaux?*** is he going to trail us round these offices much longer?; *voir* **envoyer**.
b (*fig*) **~ ses regards sur qch** to run *ou* cast one's eyes over sth; **~ ses doigts sur qch** to run *ou* pass one's fingers over sth; **~ sa tristesse** to carry one's sadness around with one.
2 **se promener vpr** a (*voir* **promenade**) to go for a walk *ou* stroll (*ou* drive *etc*). **aller se ~** to go (out) for a walk *ou* stroll (*ou* drive *etc*); **viens te ~ avec maman** come for a walk with mummy; **se ~ dans sa chambre** to walk *ou* pace up and down in one's room; **allez vous ~!*** go and take a running jump!*, (go and) get lost!*; **je ne vais pas laisser tes chiens se ~ dans mon jardin** I'm not going to let your dogs wander round my garden; (*Sport*) **il s'est vraiment promené dans cette course** this race was a real walkover for him.
b (*fig*) *[pensées, regards, doigts]* to wander. **son crayon se promenait sur le papier** he let his pencil wander over the paper, his pencil wandered over the paper; **ses affaires se promènent toujours partout*** his things are always lying around all over the place *ou* are always scattered about the place.
promeneur, -euse [pRɔm(ə)nœR, øz] **nm,f** walker, stroller. **les ~s du dimanche** Sunday strollers, people out for a Sunday walk *ou* stroll.
promenoir [pRɔm(ə)nwaR] **nm** (†: *Théât*) promenade (gallery), standing gallery; *[école, prison]* (covered) walk.
promesse [pRɔmɛs] **nf** (*assurance*) promise; (*parole*) promise, word; (*Comm*) commitment, undertaking. **~ de mariage** promise of marriage; **~ en l'air** *ou* **d'ivrogne** *ou* **de Gascon** empty *ou* vain promise; **~ d'achat/de vente** commitment to buy/to sell; **faire une ~** to make a promise, give one's word; **il m'en a fait la ~** he gave me his word for it; **tenir/manquer à sa ~** to keep/break one's promise *ou* word; **j'ai sa ~** I have his word for it, he has promised me; (*fig*) **auteur plein de ~s** writer showing much promise *ou* full of promise, very promising writer; **sourire plein de ~s** smile that promised (*ou* promises) much.
Prométhée [pRɔmete] **nm** Prometheus.
prométhium [pRɔmetjɔm] **nm** promethium.
prometteur, -euse [pRɔmetœR, øz] **adj** *début, signe* promising; *acteur, politicien* up-and-coming, promising.
promettre [pRɔmɛtR] 56 1 **vt** a *chose, aide* to promise. **je lui ai promis un cadeau** I promised him a present; **je te le promets** I promise (you); **il n'a rien osé ~** he couldn't promise anything, he didn't dare commit himself; **il a promis de venir** he promised to come; **il m'a promis de venir** *ou* **qu'il viendrait** he promised me that he would come; **~ la lune, ~ monts et merveilles** to promise the moon *ou* the earth; **tu as promis, il faut y aller** you've promised *ou* you've given your word so you have to go; **il ne faut pas ~ quand on ne peut pas tenir** one mustn't make promises that one cannot keep; **~ le secret** to promise to keep a secret; **~ son cœur/sa main/son amour** to pledge one's heart/hand/love.
b (*prédire*) to promise. **je vous promets qu'il ne recommencera pas** I (can) promise you he won't do that again; **il sera furieux, je te le promets** he will be furious, I (can) promise you *ou* I can tell you; **on nous promet du beau temps/un été pluvieux** we are promised *ou* we are in for* some fine weather/a rainy summer; **ces nuages nous promettent de la pluie** these clouds mean *ou* promise rain; **cela ne nous promet rien de bon** this promises to be pretty bad for us, this doesn't look at all hopeful for us.
c (*faire espérer*) to promise. **le spectacle/dîner promet d'être réussi** the show/dinner promises to be a success; **cet enfant promet** this child shows promise *ou* is promising, he's (*ou* she's) a promising child; (*iro*) this child shows great promise (*iro*); (*iro*) **ça promet!** that's a good start! (*iro*), that's promising! (*iro*); (*iro*) **ça promet pour l'avenir/pour l'hiver!** that bodes well for the future/(the) winter! (*iro*).
2 **se promettre vpr: se ~ de faire qch** to mean *ou* resolve to do sth; **se ~ du bon temps** *ou* **du plaisir** to promise o.s. a good time; **je me suis promis un petit voyage** I've promised myself a little trip; **je me suis bien promis de ne jamais plus l'inviter** I vowed never to invite him again.
promis, e [pRɔmi, iz] (**ptp de promettre**) 1 **adj** a (*assuré*) **tu le feras? — ~(, juré)!** you will do it? — yes, I promise! b (*destiné*) **être ~ à qch** to be destined *ou* set for sth; *voir* **chose, terre.** 2 **nm,f** (††, *dial*) betrothed††.
promiscuité [pRɔmiskɥite] **nf** *[lieu public]* crowding (*NonC*) (*de* in); *[chambre]* (degrading) lack of privacy (*NonC*) (*de* in). **~ sexuelle** (sexual) promiscuity.
promo* [pRɔmo] **nf** (**abrév de promotion**) year (*Brit*), class (*US*).
promontoire [pRɔmɔ̃twaR] **nm** (*Géog*) headland, promontory.
promoteur, -trice [pRɔmɔtœR, tRis] **nm,f** (*instigateur*) instigator, promoter; (*Chim*) promoter. **~ (immobilier)** property developer.
promotion [pRɔmosjɔ̃] **nf** a (*avancement*) promotion (*à un poste* to a job). **~ sociale** social advancement. b (*Scol*) year (*Brit*), class (*US*). **être le premier de sa ~** to be first in one's year (*Brit*) *ou* class (*US*).
c (*Comm: réclame*) promotion. **notre ~ de la semaine** this week's special offer; **article en ~** item on special offer; **il y a une ~ sur les chemises** shirts are on special offer, there's a special on shirts (*US*); (*Comm*) **~ des ventes** sales promotion. d (*encouragement*) promotion. **faire la ~ de** *politique, idée, technique* to promote.
promotionnel, -elle [pRɔmosjɔnɛl] **adj** *article* on (special) offer; *vente* promotional. **matériel ~** publicity material.
promouvoir [pRɔmuvwaR] 27 **vt** *personne* to promote, upgrade (*à* to); *politique, recherche, idée, technique* to promote; (*Comm*) *produit* to promote. **il a été promu directeur** he was promoted *ou* upgraded to (the rank of) manager.
prompt, prompte [pRɔ̃(pt), pRɔ̃(p)t] **adj** (*gén*) swift, rapid, speedy, quick; *repartie* ready (*épith*), quick; *esprit* ready (*épith*), quick, sharp; *réaction* prompt, swift; *départ, changement* sudden. **~ rétablissement!** get well soon!, I (*ou* we) wish you a speedy recovery; **~ à l'injure/aux excuses/à se décider** quick to insult/to apologize/to make up one's mind; **avoir le geste ~** to be quick to act; **avoir la main prompte** to be quick to raise one's hand; **~ comme l'éclair** *ou* **la foudre** as quick as lightning; (*Comm*) **dans l'espoir d'une prompte réponse** hoping for an early reply.
promptement [pRɔ̃ptmɑ̃] **adv** (*voir* **prompt**) swiftly; rapidly; speedily; quickly; promptly; suddenly.
prompteur [pRɔ̃ptœR] **nm** ® teleprompter ®.
promptitude [pRɔ̃(p)tityd] **nf** (*voir* **prompt**) swiftness; rapidity; speed; quickness; promptness, promptitude (*frm*); suddenness.
promulgation [pRɔmylgasjɔ̃] **nf** promulgation.
promulguer [pRɔmylge] 1 **vt** to promulgate.
pronateur [pRɔnatœR] **adj, nm: (muscle) ~** pronator.
pronation [pRɔnasjɔ̃] **nf** pronation.
prône [pRon] **nm** sermon.
prôner [pRone] 1 **vt** (*vanter*) to laud, extol; (*préconiser*) to advocate, commend.
pronom [pRɔnɔ̃] **nm** pronoun.
pronominal, e, mpl -aux [pRɔnɔminal, o] **adj** pronominal. **(verbe) ~**

pronominal (verb).

pronominalement [pRɔnɔminalmɑ̃] adv (*voir* **pronominal**) pronominally; reflexively.

prononçable [pRɔnɔ̃sabl] adj pronounceable.

prononcé, e [pRɔnɔ̃se] (ptp de **prononcer**) 1 adj *accent, goût, trait* marked, pronounced, strong. 2 nm (*Jur*) pronouncement.

prononcer [pRɔnɔ̃se] 3 1 vt a (*articuler*) *mot, son* to pronounce. **son nom est impossible à ~** his name is impossible to pronounce *ou* is unpronounceable; **comment est-ce que ça se prononce?** how is it pronounced?, how do you pronounce it?; **cette lettre ne se prononce pas** that letter is silent *ou* is not pronounced; **tu prononces mal** your pronunciation is bad; **mal ~ un mot** to mispronounce a word, pronounce a word badly; **~ distinctement** to speak clearly, pronounce one's words clearly.
b (*dire*) *parole, nom* to utter; *souhait* to utter, make; *discours* to make, deliver. **sortir sans ~ un mot** to go out without uttering a word; **ne prononcez plus jamais ce nom!** don't you ever mention *ou* utter that name again!; (*Rel*) **~ ses vœux** to take one's vows.
c *sentence* to pronounce, pass; *dissolution, excommunication* to pronounce. **~ le huis clos** to order that a case (should) be heard in camera.
2 vi (*Jur*) to deliver *ou* give a verdict. (*littér*) **~ en faveur de/contre** to come down *ou* pronounce in favour of/against.
3 **se prononcer** vpr (*se décider*) (*gén*) to reach *ou* come to a decision (*sur* on, about); (*Jur*) to reach a verdict (*sur* on); (*s'exprimer*) (*avis*) to give *ou* express an opinion (*sur* on); (*décision*) to give a decision (*sur* on); (*Jur*) to give a verdict (*sur* on). **le médecin ne s'est toujours pas prononcé** the doctor still hasn't given a verdict *ou* a firm opinion; **se ~ en faveur de qn/pour qch** to come down *ou* pronounce o.s. in favour of sb/in favour of sth; **se ~ contre une décision** to declare one's opposition to *ou* pronounce o.s. against a decision.

prononciation [pRɔnɔ̃sjasjɔ̃] nf a (*Ling*) pronunciation. **il a une bonne/mauvaise ~** he speaks/doesn't speak clearly, he pronounces/does not pronounce his words clearly; (*dans une langue étrangère*) he has a good/bad pronunciation; **faute** *ou* **erreur de ~** error of pronunciation; **faire une faute de ~** to mispronounce a word (*ou* a sound *etc*); **défaut** *ou* **vice de ~** speech impediment *ou* defect. b (*Jur*) pronouncement.

pronostic [pRɔnɔstik] nm (*gén*) forecast, prognostication (*frm*); (*Méd*) prognosis; (*Courses*) tip; (*Sport*) forecast. **quels sont vos ~s?** what is your forecast?; **au ~ infaillible** unerring in his (*ou* her *etc*) forecasts; **elle a fait le bon ~** (*gén*) her prediction proved correct; (*Méd*) she made the right prognosis; (*gén*) **se tromper dans ses ~s** to get one's forecasts wrong; (*Courses*) **mes ~s donnaient le 11 gagnant** I tipped number 11 to win; **faire des ~s sur les matchs de football** to forecast the football results.

pronostiquer [pRɔnɔstike] 1 vt (*prédire*) to forecast, prognosticate (*frm*); (*être le signe de*) to foretell, be a sign of; (*Courses*) to tip.

pronostiqueur, -euse [pRɔnɔstikœR, øz] nm,f (*gén*) forecaster, prognosticator (*frm*); (*Courses*) tipster.

pronunciamiento [pRɔnunsjamjɛnto] nm pronunciamento.

propagande [pRɔpagɑ̃d] nf propaganda. **film/discours de ~** propaganda film/speech; **faire de la ~ pour qch/qn** to push *ou* plug* sth/sb; **je ne ferai pas de ~ pour ce commerçant/ce produit** I certainly shan't be doing any advertising for this trader/product; **~ électorale** electioneering propaganda; **discours de ~ (électorale)** electioneering speech; **journal de ~** paper of political propaganda, propaganda sheet; **~ de guerre** war propaganda.

propagandiste [pRɔpagɑ̃dist] nmf propagandist.

propagateur, -trice [pRɔpagatœR, tRis] nm,f [*méthode, religion, théorie*] propagator; [*nouvelle*] spreader.

propagation [pRɔpagasjɔ̃] nf a (*voir* **propager**) propagation; spreading (abroad); putting about (*Brit*). **la ~ de l'espèce** the propagation of the species. b (*voir* **se propager**) spread, spreading; propagation.

propager [pRɔpaʒe] 3 1 vt a *foi, idée* to propagate; *nouvelle* to spread (abroad); *maladie* to spread; *fausse nouvelle* to spread (abroad), put about (*Brit*); (*Phys*) *son* to propagate. b (*Bio*) *espèce* to propagate. 2 **se propager** vpr [*incendie, idée, nouvelle, maladie*] to spread; (*Phys*) [*onde*] to be propagated; (*Bio*) [*espèce*] to propagate.

propane [pRɔpan] nm propane.

propédeutique† [pRɔpedøtik] nf (*Univ*) *foundation course for first-year university students.*

propène [pRɔpɛn] nm propene.

propension [pRɔpɑ̃sjɔ̃] nf proclivity (*frm*) (*à qch* to *ou* towards sth, *à faire* to do), propensity (*à qch* for sth, *à faire* to do). (*Écon*) **~ à consommer/économiser** propensity to spend/save.

propergol [pRɔpɛRgɔl] nm [*fusée*] propellant, propellent.

prophète [pRɔfɛt] nm (*gén*) prophet, seer; (*Rel*) prophet. **~ de malheur** prophet of doom, Jeremiah; *voir* **nul**.

prophétesse [pRɔfetɛs] nf (*gén*) prophetess, seer; (*Rel*) prophetess.

prophétie [pRɔfesi] nf (*Rel, gén*) prophecy.

prophétique [pRɔfetik] adj prophetic.

prophétiquement [pRɔfetikmɑ̃] adv prophetically.

prophétiser [pRɔfetize] 1 vt to prophesy.

prophylactique [pRɔfilaktik] adj prophylactic.

prophylaxie [pRɔfilaksi] nf disease prevention, prophylaxis (*SPÉC*).

propice [pRɔpis] adj *circonstance, occasion* favourable, auspicious, propitious; *milieu, terrain* favourable. **attendre le moment ~** to wait for the right moment, wait for a favourable *ou* an opportune moment; **être ~ à qch** to favour sth, be favourable to sth; (*littér, hum*) **que les dieux vous soient ~s!** may the gods look kindly *ou* smile upon you! (*littér, hum*).

propitiation [pRɔpisjasjɔ̃] nf propitiation. **victime de ~** propitiatory victim.

propitiatoire [pRɔpisjatwaR] adj propitiatory.

proportion [pRɔpɔRsjɔ̃] nf a (*gén, Art, Math*) proportion. **selon** *ou* **dans une ~ de 100 contre** *ou* **pour 1** in a proportion of 100 to 1; **quelle est la ~ entre la hauteur et la largeur?** *ou* **de la hauteur et de la largeur?** what is the proportion *ou* relation of height to width?, what's the ratio between height and width?; **~ égale de réussites et d'échecs** equal proportion of successes and failures, equal ratio of successes to failures; **il n'y a aucune ~ entre la faute et la peine** the punishment is out of all proportion to the offence, the punishment bears no relation to the offence.
b (*taille, importance*) **~s** proportions; **de vastes ~s** of vast proportions; **édifice de belles ~s** well-proportioned building; **cela a pris des ~s considérables** it took on considerable proportions; **réduire qch à de plus justes ~s** to cut sth down to size; **augmenter/réduire qch dans de sérieuses ~s** to increase/reduce sth drastically.
c (*loc*) **à ~ de** in proportion to, proportionally to; **en ~ de** (adj) in proportion *ou* relation to, proportional to; (adv) in proportion *ou* relation to, proportionally to; **en ~** in proportion; **on lui a donné un poste élevé et un salaire en ~** he was given a high position and a salary in proportion; **quand on veut avoir des domestiques, il faut avoir des revenus en ~** when you want to have servants you must have a commensurate income *ou* an income to match; **hors de (toute) ~** out of (all) proportion (*avec* to); **toute(s) ~(s) gardée(s)** relatively speaking, making due allowance(s).

proportionnalité [pRɔpɔRsjɔnalite] nf proportionality; (*Pol*) proportional representation. **~ de l'impôt** proportional taxation (system).

proportionné, e [pRɔpɔRsjɔne] (ptp de **proportionner**) adj: **~ à** proportional *ou* proportionate to; **bien ~** well-proportioned; **admirablement ~** admirably well-proportioned.

proportionnel, -elle [pRɔpɔRsjɔnɛl] 1 adj (*gén, Math, Pol*) proportional; *impôt, retraite* proportional. **~ à** proportional *ou* proportionate to, in proportion to *ou* with; **directement/inversement ~ à** directly/inversely proportional to, in direct/inverse proportion to. 2 **proportionnelle** nf (*Math*) proportional. (*Pol*) **la ~** proportional representation.

proportionnellement [pRɔpɔRsjɔnɛlmɑ̃] adv proportionally, proportionately. **~ plus grand** proportionally *ou* proportionately bigger; **~ à** in proportion to, proportionally to.

proportionner [pRɔpɔRsjɔne] 1 vt to proportion, make proportional, adjust (*à* to).

propos [pRɔpo] nm a (*gén pl*) talk (*NonC*), remarks (*pl*), words (*pl*). **ce sont des ~ en l'air** it's just empty *ou* idle talk *ou* hot air*; **tenir des ~ blessants** to say hurtful things, make hurtful remarks; (*péj*) **des ~ de femme soûle** drunken ramblings; *voir* **avant**.
b (*littér: intention*) intention, aim. **mon ~ est de vous expliquer ...** my intention *ou* aim is to explain to you ...; **il n'entre pas dans mon ~ de** it is not my intention to; **tel n'était pas mon ~** that was not my intention; **avoir le ferme ~ de faire** to have the firm intention of doing; **faire qch de ~ délibéré** to do sth deliberately *ou* on purpose.
c (*sujet*) **à quel ~ voulait-il me voir?** what did he want to see me about?; **à quel ~ est-il venu?** what was his reason for coming?, what brought him?*; **c'est à quel ~?** what is it about?, what is it in connection with?; **à ~ de ta voiture** about your car, on the subject of your car; **je vous écris à ~ de l'annonce** I am writing regarding *ou* concerning the advertisement *ou* in connection with the advertisement; **il se plaint à tout ~** he complains at the slightest (little) thing; **il se met en colère à ~ de tout et de rien** *ou* **à tout ~** he loses his temper at the drop of a hat *ou* at the slightest (little) thing *ou* for no reason at all; **à ce ~** in this connection, (while) on this subject; *voir* **hors**.
d **à ~** *décision* well-timed, opportune, timely; *remarque* apt, pertinent, apposite; *arriver* at the right moment *ou* time; **tomber** *ou* **arriver mal à ~** to happen (just) at the wrong moment *ou* time; **voilà qui tombe à ~/mal à ~!** it couldn't have come at a better/worse time! *ou* moment!; **il a jugé à ~ de nous prévenir** he thought it right to let us know, he thought *ou* saw fit to let us know; **à ~, dis-moi ...** incidentally *ou* by the way, tell me ... .

proposable [pRɔpozabl] adj which may be proposed.

proposer [pRɔpoze] 1 1 vt a (*suggérer*) *arrangement, interprétation, projet, appellation* to suggest, propose; *solution, interprétation* to suggest, put forward, propose; *candidat* to propose, nominate, put forward; (*Scol, Univ*) *sujet, texte* to set (*Brit*), assign (*US*); (*Pol*) *loi* to move, propose. **on a proposé mon nom pour ce poste** my name has been put forward for this post; **~ qch à qn** to suggest *ou* put sth to sb; **~ de faire qch** to suggest *ou* propose doing sth; (*TV*) **le film que nous vous proposons (de voir) ce soir** the film which you will be able to watch *ou* which we are showing this evening; **l'homme propose, Dieu dispose**

man proposes, God disposes (*Prov*); **je vous propose de passer me voir** I suggest that you come round and see me; **~ qu'une motion soit mise aux voix** to move that a motion be put to the vote; **~ qu'un comité soit établi** to propose the setting-up of a committee, move *ou* propose that a committee be set up.

b (*offrir*) *aide, prix, situation* to offer. **~ qch à qn** to offer sth to sb, offer sb sth; **~ de faire qch** to offer to do sth; **on me propose une nouvelle voiture** I am being offered *ou* I have the offer of a new car; **je lui ai proposé de la raccompagner** I offered to see her home.

2 **se proposer** **vpr** a (*offrir ses services*) to offer one's services. **elle s'est proposée pour garder les enfants** she offered to look after the children.

b (*envisager*) *but, tâche* to set o.s. **se ~ de faire qch** to intend *ou* mean *ou* propose to do sth; **il se proposait de prouver que ...** he set out to prove that ... .

proposition [pʀɔpozisjɔ̃] **nf** a (*suggestion, offre*) suggestion, proposal, proposition; (*Pol: recommandation*) proposal. **~s de paix** peace proposals; (*Pol*) **~ de loi** private bill, private member's bill (*Brit*); **sur (la) ~ de** at the suggestion of, on the proposal of; **sur sa ~, il a été décidé d'attendre** at his suggestion, it was decided to wait; **la ~ de qn à un grade supérieur** putting sb forward for *ou* the nomination of sb to a higher grade; **faire des ~s (malhonnêtes) à une femme** to proposition a woman; *voir* **contre.**

b (*Math, Philos: postulat*) proposition; (*déclaration*) proposition, assertion.

c (*Gram*) clause. **~ principale/subordonnée/indépendante** main/ subordinate/independent clause; **~ consécutive** *ou* **de conséquence** consecutive *ou* result clause.

propositionnel, -elle [pʀɔpozisjɔnɛl] **adj** propositional.

propre¹ [pʀɔpʀ] 1 **adj** a (*pas sali*) *linge, mains, maison* clean; (*net*) *personne, vêtement* neat, tidy; *travail, exécution d'un morceau de musique* neat, neatly done; (*Scol*) *cahier, copie* neat. **~ comme un sou neuf** as neat *ou* clean as a new pin; **leurs enfants sont toujours (tenus) très ~s** their children are always very neat and tidy *ou* very neatly turned out; **ce n'est pas ~ de manger avec les doigts** it's messy *ou* dirty to eat with your fingers; **nous voilà ~s*!** now we're in a fine *ou* proper mess*!

b (*qui ne salit pas*) *chien, chat* house-trained; *enfant* toilet-trained, potty-trained*, clean (*Brit*); (*non polluant*) *moteur, voiture* clean. **il n'est pas encore ~** he still isn't clean (*Brit*) *ou* toilet-trained *ou* potty-trained*.

c (*honnête*) *personne* honest, decent; *affaire, argent* honest; *mœurs* decent. **il n'a jamais rien fait de ~** he's never done a decent *ou* an honest thing in his life; **une affaire pas très ~** a slightly suspect *ou* shady piece of business; **ce garçon-là, ce n'est pas grand-chose de ~** that young man hasn't got much to recommend him *ou* isn't up to much*.

2 **nm**: **sentir le ~** to smell clean; (*Scol*) **mettre** *ou* **recopier qch au ~** to make a fair copy of sth, copy sth out neatly; **c'est du ~!*** (*gâchis*) what a mess!, what a shambles!*; (*comportement*) what a way to behave!, it's an absolute disgrace!

propre² [pʀɔpʀ] 1 **adj** a (*intensif possessif*) own. **il a sa ~ voiture** he's got *ou* he has his own car *ou* a car of his own; **par ses ~s moyens** *réussir* on one's own, by oneself; *rentrer* under one's own steam; **ce sont ses ~s mots** those are his own *ou* his very *ou* his actual words; **de mes ~s yeux** with my own (two) eyes; **de sa ~ initiative** on his own initiative; (*frm*) **de son ~ chef** on his own initiative, on his own authority; **ils ont leurs caractères/qualités ~s** they have their own (specific) *ou* their particular characters/qualities; **au lieu de critiquer nos enfants, il devrait surveiller les siens ~s** instead of criticizing our children, he ought to keep his own in order; *voir* **amour, main.**

b (*particulier, spécifique*) **c'est un trait qui lui est ~** it's a trait which is peculiar to him, it's a distinctive *ou* specific characteristic of his; **les coutumes ~s à certaines régions** the customs peculiar to *ou* characteristic of *ou* proper to (*frm*) certain regions; (*Jur*) **biens ~s** personal property; *voir* **nom, sens.**

c (*qui convient*) suitable, appropriate (*à* for). **le mot ~** the right *ou* proper word; **ce n'est pas un lieu ~ à la conversation** it isn't a suitable *ou* an appropriate place for talking; **sol ~ à la culture du blé** soil suitable for *ou* suited to wheat-growing; **on l'a jugé ~ à s'occuper de l'affaire** he was considered the right man for *ou* suitable for the job.

d (*de nature à*) **un poste ~ à lui apporter des satisfactions** a job likely to bring him satisfaction; **exercice ~ à développer les muscles des épaules** exercise that will develop the shoulder muscles; **c'est bien ~ à vous dégoûter de la politique** it's (exactly) the sort of thing that turns you *ou* to turn you right off politics, it's guaranteed to put you off politics.

2 **nm** a (*qualité distinctive*) peculiarity, (exclusive *ou* distinctive) feature. **la raison est le ~ de l'homme** reason is a peculiarity *ou* (distinctive) feature of man, reason is peculiar to man; **le rire/la parole est le ~ de l'homme** laughter/speech is man's special gift *ou* attribute; **c'est le ~ de ce système d'éducation de fabriquer des paresseux** it's a peculiarity *ou* feature of this educational system that it turns out idlers; **c'est le ~ des ambitieux de vouloir réussir à tout prix** it's a peculiarity *ou* (specific) feature of ambitious people to want to succeed at any price; **avoir un domaine en ~** to be the sole owner of an estate, have exclusive possession of an estate; **cette caractéristique que la France possède en ~** this feature which is peculiar *ou* exclusive to France.

b (*Ling*) **au ~** in the literal sense *ou* meaning, literally.

propre-à-rien, **pl propres-à-rien** [pʀɔpʀaʀjɛ̃] **nmf** good-for-nothing, ne'er-do-well, waster.

proprement [pʀɔpʀəmɑ̃] **adv** a (*avec propreté*) cleanly; (*avec netteté*) neatly, tidily; (*comme il faut*) properly; (*fig: décemment*) decently. **tenir une maison très ~** to keep a house very clean; **mange ~!** don't make such a mess (when you're eating)!, eat properly!; **se conduire ~** to behave properly *ou* correctly.

b (*exactement*) exactly, literally; (*exclusivement*) specifically, strictly; (*vraiment*) absolutely. **à ~ parler** strictly speaking; **le village ~ dit** the actual village, the village itself; **la linguistique ~ dite** linguistics proper; **c'est un problème ~ français** it's a specifically French problem; **c'est ~ scandaleux** it's absolutely disgraceful; **il m'a ~ fermé la porte au nez** he simply *ou* jolly well* (*Brit*) shut the door in my face; **on l'a ~ rossé** he was well and truly beaten up.

propret, -ette [pʀɔpʀɛ, ɛt] **adj** *personne* neat (and tidy), spruce; *chose* neat (and tidy), spick-and-span (*attrib*).

propreté [pʀɔpʀəte] **nf** (*voir* **propre¹**) cleanliness, cleanness; neatness; tidiness. **ils n'ont aucune notion de ~** they have no notion of hygiene; **l'apprentissage de la ~ chez l'enfant** toilet-training in the child.

propriétaire [pʀɔpʀijetɛʀ] 1 **nm** a (*gén*) *[voiture, chien, maison]* owner; *[hôtel, entreprise]* proprietor, owner. **il est ~ (de sa maison)** he owns his (own) house; **quand on est ~, il faut ...** when one is a home-owner *ou* house-owner *ou* householder one has to ...; **faire le tour du ~** to look *ou* go round *ou* over one's property; **je vais te faire faire le tour du ~** I'll show you over *ou* round the place.

b *[location]* landlord, owner. **mis à la porte par son ~** thrown out by one's landlord.

c *[terres, immeubles etc]* landowner, owner. **~-éleveur** breeder; **~ récoltant** grower; **achat direct au ~** direct purchase from the grower; **~ terrien** landowner; **~ foncier** property owner; **les petits ~s** (the) smallholders.

2 **nf** (*gén*) owner; *[hôtel, entreprise]* proprietress, owner; *[location]* landlady, owner.

propriété [pʀɔpʀijete] 1 **nf** a (*droit*) ownership, property (*frm, Jur*); (*possession*) property. **~ de l'État/collective** state/collective ownership; **posséder en toute ~** to be the sole owner of, have sole ownership of; **accession à la ~** possibility of home-ownership; **la ~ c'est le vol** property is theft; *voir* **titre.**

b (*immeuble, maison*) property; (*terres*) property (*gén NonC*), land (*gén NonC*), estate. **revenu d'une ~** revenue from a property *ou* a piece of land.

c (*gén, Chim, Phys: qualité*) property.

d (*correction*) *[mot]* appropriateness, suitability, correctness.

2 **comp** ► **propriété artistique** artistic copyright ► **propriété bâtie** developed property ► **propriété commerciale** security of tenure (*of industrial or commercial tenant*) ► **propriété foncière** property ownership ► **propriétés immobilières** real estate (*NonC*), realty (*NonC*) (*Jur*) ► **propriété industrielle** patent rights ► **propriété littéraire** author's copyright ► **propriété non bâtie** undeveloped *ou* unbuilt-on property ► **propriété privée** private property ► **propriété publique** public property.

proprio* [pʀɔpʀijo] **nm** (**abrév de propriétaire**) (*homme*) landlord; (*femme*) landlady.

propulser [pʀɔpylse] [1] 1 **vt** a *voiture* to propel, drive (along *ou* forward); *missile* to propel, power. b (*projeter*) to hurl, fling. (*fig*) **on l'a propulsé chef de service** he was propelled speedily up the ladder to departmental head. 2 **se propulser*** **vpr** (*aller*) to trot*; (*se hâter*) to shoot*.

propulseur [pʀɔpylsœʀ] 1 **adj** propulsive, driving (*épith*). 2 **nm** propeller.

propulsif, -ive [pʀɔpylsif, iv] **adj** propelling, propellent.

propulsion [pʀɔpylsjɔ̃] **nf** propulsion. **à ~ atomique/nucléaire** atomic-/ nuclear-powered.

propylène [pʀɔpilɛn] **nm** propylene.

prorata [pʀɔʀata] **nm inv** proportional share, proportion. **au ~ de** in proportion to, on the basis of.

prorogatif, -ive [pʀɔʀɔgatif, iv] **adj** (*voir* **proroger**) extending; deferring.

prorogation [pʀɔʀɔgasjɔ̃] **nf** (*voir* **proroger**) extension; putting back, deferment; adjournment; prorogation.

proroger [pʀɔʀɔʒe] [3] **vt** a *délai, durée* to extend; *échéance* to put back, defer. b *séance* to adjourn; (*Parl*) to prorogue.

prosaïque [pʀozaik] **adj** *esprit, personne, vie* mundane, prosaic; *style* pedestrian, mundane, prosaic; *remarque, détail* mundane, prosaic; *goûts* mundane, commonplace.

prosaïquement [pʀozaikmɑ̃] **adv** mundanely, prosaically. **vivre ~** to lead a mundane life *ou* a prosaic existence.

prosaïsme [pʀozaism] **nm** (*voir* **prosaïque**) mundaneness; prosaicness;

pedestrianism.
prosateur [pʀozatœʀ] nm prose-writer, writer of prose.
proscription [pʀɔskʀipsjɔ̃] nf (*voir* **proscrire**) banning; prohibition; proscription; outlawing (*NonC*); banishment, exiling (*NonC*).
proscrire [pʀɔskʀiʀ] 39 vt *idéologie, activité* to ban, prohibit, proscribe; *drogue, mot* to ban, prohibit the use of, proscribe; *personne* (*mettre hors la loi*) to outlaw, proscribe (*littér*); (*exiler*) to banish, exile. ~ **une expression de son style** to banish an expression from one's style.
proscrit, e [pʀɔskʀi, it] (ptp de **proscrire**) nm, f (*hors-la-loi*) outlaw; (*exilé*) exile.
prose [pʀoz] nf (*gén*) prose; (*style*) prose (style). **poème/tragédie en** ~ prose poem/tragedy; **écrire en** ~ to write in prose; **faire de la** ~ to write prose; (*péj*) **la** ~ **administrative** officialese; (*péj*) **je viens de lire sa** ~ (*lettre*) I've just read his epistle (*hum*); (*devoir, roman*) I've just read his great work (*iro, hum*).
prosélyte [pʀozelit] nmf proselyte (*frm*), convert. **les** ~**s du parapente** converts to parapente.
prosélytisme [pʀozelitism] nm proselytism. **faire du** ~ to proselytize, preach.
prosodie [pʀɔzɔdi] nf prosody.
prosodique [pʀɔzɔdik] adj prosodic. **trait** ~ prosodic feature.
prosopopée [pʀɔzɔpɔpe] nf prosopopoeia, prosopopeia.
prospecter [pʀɔspɛkte] 1 vt (*Min*) to prospect; (*Comm*) to canvass.
prospecteur, -trice [pʀɔspɛktœʀ, tʀis] nm, f prospector. ~**-placier** ≈ job-placement officer (*Brit*), *civil servant responsible for finding jobs for the unemployed*.
prospectif, -ive [pʀɔspɛktif, iv] 1 adj prospective. 2 **prospective** nf futurology.
prospection [pʀɔspɛksjɔ̃] nf (*voir* **prospecter**) prospecting; canvassing. (*Comm*) **faire de la** ~ to canvass for business; **ils font de la** ~ **pétrolière** they are prospecting for oil.
prospectus [pʀɔspɛktys] nm (*feuille*) handbill, leaflet, handout; (*dépliant*) prospectus, brochure, leaflet.
prospère [pʀɔspɛʀ] adj a *commerce, pays, collectivité* prosperous, thriving, flourishing; *période* prosperous. b *santé, mine* flourishing; *personne* in flourishing health (*attrib*), blooming with health (*attrib*).
prospérer [pʀɔspeʀe] 6 vi [*commerce*] to prosper, thrive, flourish; [*personne*] to prosper; [*animal, activité, plante*] to thrive, flourish.
prospérité [pʀɔspeʀite] nf a (*matérielle*) prosperity; (*économique*) prosperity, affluence. b (*santé*) (flourishing) health.
prostaglandine [pʀɔstaglɑ̃din] nf prostaglandin.
prostate [pʀɔstat] nf prostate (gland).
prostatectomie [pʀɔstatɛktɔmi] nf prostatectomy.
prostatique [pʀɔstatik] 1 adj prostatic. 2 nm prostate sufferer.
prosternation [pʀɔstɛʀnasjɔ̃] nf prostration.
prosterné, e [pʀɔstɛʀne] (ptp de **prosterner**) adj prostrate.
prosternement [pʀɔstɛʀnəmɑ̃] nm (*action*) prostration; (*attitude*) prostrate attitude; (*fig*) grovelling.
prosterner [pʀɔstɛʀne] 1 1 vt (*littér*) to bow low. **il prosterna le corps** he prostrated himself. 2 **se prosterner** vpr (*s'incliner*) to bow low, bow down, prostrate o.s. (*devant* before); (*fig: s'humilier*) to grovel (*devant* before), kowtow (*devant* to).
prostitué [pʀɔstitɥe] nm male prostitute.
prostituée [pʀɔstitɥe] nf prostitute.
prostituer [pʀɔstitɥe] 1 1 vt (*lit*) ~ **qn** to make a prostitute of sb; ~ **qn (à qn)** to prostitute sb (to sb); (*fig*) to prostitute. 2 **se prostituer** vpr (*lit, fig*) to prostitute o.s.
prostitution [pʀɔstitysjɔ̃] nf (*lit, fig*) prostitution.
prostration [pʀɔstʀasjɔ̃] nf (*Méd, Rel*) prostration.
prostré, e [pʀɔstʀe] adj (*fig*) prostrate, prostrated; (*Méd*) prostrate.
protactinium [pʀɔtaktinjɔm] nm protactinium.
protagoniste [pʀɔtagɔnist] nm protagonist.
protecteur, -trice [pʀɔtɛktœʀ, tʀis] 1 adj a (*gén, Chim, Écon*) protective (*de* of); *voir* **société**. b *ton, air* patronizing. 2 nm,f (*défenseur*) protector, guardian; [*arts*] patron. 3 nm [*femme*] (*souteneur*) pimp (*péj*); (†: *galant*) fancy man†. (*au Québec*) ~ **du citoyen** ombudsman.
protection [pʀɔtɛksjɔ̃] 1 nf a (*défense*) protection (*contre* against, from). **mesures de** ~ protective measures; **sous la** ~ **de** under the protection of; **prendre qn sous sa** ~ to give sb one's protection, take sb under one's wing; **assurer la** ~ **de** to protect; **assurer la** ~ **rapprochée du chef de l'État** to ensure the personal safety of the head of state; **il a demandé à bénéficier d'une** ~ **rapprochée** he asked for 24-hour police protection.
b (*patronage*) patronage. **prendre qn sous sa** ~ to give sb one's patronage, take sb under one's wing; **obtenir une place par** ~ to get a post by pulling strings; **je l'avais pris chez moi par** ~ I'd taken him on to do him a good turn; **air/sourire de** ~ protective air/smile.
c (*blindage*) [*navire*] armour(-plating).
d (*Ordin*) protection.
2 comp ▸**protection civile** *state-financed civilian rescue organization* ▸**protection du consommateur** consumer protection ▸**protection de l'emploi** job protection ▸**protection de l'enfance** child welfare ▸**protection de l'environnement** protection of the environment, environmental protection ▸**protection maternelle et infantile** *regional organization providing for the welfare of mothers-to-be and infants* ▸**protection de la nature** preservation *ou* protection of the countryside ▸**protection des sites** preservation *ou* protection of beauty spots ▸**protection sociale** social welfare.
protectionnisme [pʀɔtɛksjɔnism] nm protectionism.
protectionniste [pʀɔtɛksjɔnist] adj, nmf protectionist.
protectorat [pʀɔtɛktɔʀa] nm protectorate.
protège- [pʀɔtɛʒ] préf *voir* **protéger**.
protégé, e [pʀɔteʒe] (ptp de **protéger**) 1 adj a (*Ordin*) *disquette* write-protected; *logiciel* copy-protected. ~ **en écriture** write-protected. b (*pour handicapé*) **atelier** ~ sheltered workshop; **emploi** ~ job in a sheltered workshop; *voir* **passage**. 2 nm protégé; (**: chouchou*) favourite, pet*. 3 **protégée** nf protégée; (**: favorite*) favourite, pet*.
protéger [pʀɔteʒe] 6 et 3 1 vt a *personne* (*veiller à la sécurité de*) to protect, guard; (*abriter*) to protect, shield; (*moralement*) to protect, guard, shield; *plantes, lieu* (*des éléments*) to protect, shelter; *équipement, matériel, membres* (*des chocs etc*) to protect; *institution, tradition* to protect (*de, contre* from). ~ **les intérêts de qn** to protect sb's interests; **se** ~ **du froid/contre les piqûres d'insectes** to protect o.s. from the cold/against insect bites; **crème qui protège contre le soleil** cream that gives protection against the sun.
b (*patronner*) *personne* to be a patron of; *carrière* to further; *arts, sports, artisanat* to patronize.
c (*Comm*) *produits locaux* to protect.
d (*Ordin*) to protect.
2 comp ▸**protège-cahier** nm (pl **protège-cahiers**) exercise-book cover ▸**protège-dents** nm inv gum-shield ▸**protège-slip** nm (pl **protège-slips**) panty liner ▸**protège-tibia** nm (pl **protège-tibias**) shin guard.
protéiforme [pʀɔteifɔʀm] adj protean.
protéine [pʀɔtein] nf protein.
protéique [pʀɔteik] adj protein (*épith*), proteinic.
protestable [pʀɔtɛstabl] adj protestable, which may be protested.
protestant, e [pʀɔtɛstɑ̃, ɑ̃t] adj, nm, f Protestant.
protestantisme [pʀɔtɛstɑ̃tism] nm Protestantism.
protestataire [pʀɔtɛstatɛʀ] 1 adj *personne* protesting (*épith*); *marche, mesure* protest (*épith*). 2 nmf protestor, protester.
protestation [pʀɔtɛstasjɔ̃] nf (*plainte*) protest; (*déclaration*) protestation, profession; (*Jur*) protesting, protestation. **en signe de** ~ as a (sign of) protest; **faire des** ~**s d'amitié à qn** to profess one's friendship to sb.
protester [pʀɔtɛste] 1 1 vi to protest (*contre* against, about). ~ **de son innocence/de sa loyauté** to protest one's innocence/loyalty; **"mais non", protesta-t-il** "no" he protested. 2 vt (*Jur*) to protest; (*frm: déclarer*) to declare, affirm, profess. (*frm*) **il protesta la plus vive admiration pour elle** he declared that he had the keenest admiration for her.
protêt [pʀɔtɛ] nm (*Comm, Jur*) protest.
prothèse [pʀɔtɛz] nf (*appareil*) prosthesis; (*science, technique*) prosthetics (*gén sg*), prosthesis. ~ **(dentaire)** denture, dentures (*pl*), false teeth (*pl*); **(appareil de)** ~ artificial limb (*ou* hand *ou* arm *etc*), prosthesis (*SPÉC*).
prothésiste [pʀɔtezist] nmf prosthetic technician. ~ **(dentaire)** dental technician.
protide [pʀɔtid] nm protein.
proto... [pʀɔtɔ] préf proto... .
protocolaire [pʀɔtɔkɔlɛʀ] adj *invitation, cérémonie* formal. **question** ~ question of protocol; **ce n'est pas très** ~! it's not showing much regard for etiquette!
protocole [pʀɔtɔkɔl] nm a (*étiquette*) etiquette; (*Pol, Ordin, Sci*) protocol. b (*procès-verbal*) protocol. **établir un** ~ **d'accord** to draw up a draft treaty.
proton [pʀɔtɔ̃] nm proton.
protoplasma [pʀɔtɔplasma] nm, **protoplasme** [pʀɔtɔplasm] nm protoplasm.
protoplasmique [pʀɔtɔplasmik] adj protoplasmic.
prototype [pʀɔtɔtip] nm prototype. ~ **d'avion** prototype aircraft.
protoxyde [pʀɔtɔksid] nm protoxide.
protozoaire [pʀɔtɔzɔɛʀ] nm protozoon. ~**s** protozoa.
protubérance [pʀɔtybeʀɑ̃s] nf bulge, protuberance.
protubérant, e [pʀɔtybeʀɑ̃, ɑ̃t] adj *ventre, yeux* bulging, protuberant, protruding; *nez, menton* protuberant, protruding.
prou [pʀu] adv *voir* **peu**.
proue [pʀu] nf bow, bows (*pl*), prow; *voir* **figure**.
prouesse [pʀuɛs] nf (*littér*) feat. (*fig*) **il a fallu faire des** ~**s pour le convaincre** we had to work minor miracles *ou* stand on our heads to convince him.
proustien, -ienne [pʀustjɛ̃, jɛn] adj Proustian, Proust (*épith*).
prout* [pʀut] nm: **faire** ~ to let off*.
prouvable [pʀuvabl] adj provable. **allégations difficilement** ~**s** allegations which are difficult to prove.
prouver [pʀuve] 1 vt (*gén*) to prove. ~ **qch par l'absurde** to prove sth by reducing it to the absurd; **les faits ont prouvé qu'il avait raison/qu'il**

était innocent the facts proved him (to be) right/innocent *ou* proved that he was right/innocent; **il est prouvé que ...** it has been proved that ...; **cela prouve que ...** it proves *ou* shows that ...; **il n'est pas prouvé qu'il soit coupable** there is no proof that he is guilty *ou* of his guilt; **cela n'est pas prouvé** there's no proof of it, that hasn't been proved, that remains to be proved; **cette réponse prouve de l'esprit** that answer gives proof of his (*ou* her *etc*) wit *ou* shows wit; **comment vous ~ ma reconnaissance?** how can I show *ou* demonstrate my gratitude to you?; **il a voulu se ~ (à lui-même) qu'il en était capable** he wanted to prove to himself that he was capable of it; **son efficacité n'est plus à ~** its effectiveness is no longer in doubt *ou* in question.

provenance [pʀɔv(ə)nɑ̃s] **nf** *[produit, objet, famille]* origin, provenance (*frm*); *[mot, coutume]* source, provenance (*frm*). **j'ignore la ~ de cette lettre** I don't know where this letter comes *ou* came *ou* was sent from; **pays de ~** country of origin; **des objets de toutes ~s** articles of every possible origin; **de ~ étrangère** of foreign origin; **en ~ de l'Angleterre** from England.

provençal, e, mpl **-aux** [pʀɔvɑ̃sal, o] 1 **adj** Provençal. (*Culin*) **(à la) ~e** (à la) Provençale. 2 **nm** (*Ling*) Provençal. 3 **nmf: P~(e)** Provençal.

Provence [pʀɔvɑ̃s] **nf** Provence.

provenir [pʀɔv(ə)niʀ] [22] provenir de **vt indir** (*venir de*) *pays* to come from, be from; (*résulter de*) *cause* to be due to, be the result of. **son genre de vie provient de son éducation** his life style is the result of his upbringing; **mot qui provient d'une racine grecque** word which comes *ou* derives from a Greek root *ou* source; **fortune qui provient d'une lointaine cousine** fortune whose source is a distant cousin *ou* that comes from a distant cousin; **vase provenant de Chine** vase (that comes) from China; **je me demande d'où provient sa fortune** I wonder where he got his money from, I wonder how he came by so much money.

proverbe [pʀɔvɛʀb] **nm** proverb. **comme dit le ~** as the saying goes; (*Bible*) **le livre des P~s** (the Book of) Proverbs.

proverbial, e, mpl **-iaux** [pʀɔvɛʀbjal, jo] **adj** proverbial.

proverbialement [pʀɔvɛʀbjalmɑ̃] **adv** proverbially.

providence [pʀɔvidɑ̃s] **nf** (*Rel*) providence; (*fig: sauveur*) guardian angel. (*fig*) **cette bouteille d'eau a été notre ~** that bottle of water was our salvation *ou* was a lifesaver; **vous êtes ma ~!** you're my salvation!; *voir* **état.**

providentiel, -elle [pʀɔvidɑ̃sjɛl] **adj** providential.

providentiellement [pʀɔvidɑ̃sjɛlmɑ̃] **adv** providentially.

province [pʀɔvɛ̃s] **nf** a (*région*) province. **Paris et la ~** Paris and the provinces; **vivre en ~** to live in the provinces; **ville de ~** provincial town; (*péj*) **il arrive de sa ~** where has he been?; (*péj*) **elle fait très ~** she is very provincial; (*Hist: Hollande*) **les P~s Unies** the United Provinces. b (*Can Pol*) province, *main political division.* **les P~s maritimes** the Maritime Provinces, the Maritimes (*Can*); **habitant des P~s maritimes** Maritimer; **les P~s des prairies** the Prairie Provinces (*Can*); **la Belle P~** Quebec.

provincial, e, mpl **-iaux** [pʀɔvɛ̃sjal, jo] 1 **adj** a (*gén, Rel*) provincial. b (*Can Pol*) **gouvernement ~** Provincial government. 2 **nm,f** provincial. **les ~iaux** people who live in the provinces, provincials. 3 **nm** a (*Rel*) Provincial. b (*Can*) **le ~** the Provincial Government.

provincialisme [pʀɔvɛ̃sjalism] **nm** provincialism.

proviseur [pʀɔvizœʀ] **nm** head(master) (*Brit*), principal (*of a lycée*).

provision [pʀɔvizjɔ̃] **nf** a (*réserve*) *[vivres, cartouches]* stock, supply; *[eau]* supply. **faire (une) ~ de** *nourriture, papier* to stock up with, lay *ou* get in a stock of; *énergie, courage* to build up a stock of; **j'ai acheté toute une ~ de bonbons** I've bought in a whole supply *ou* stock of sweets; **j'ai une bonne ~ de conserves** I have a good stock of canned food, I've plenty of canned food in; **avoir une bonne ~ de courage** to have a good stock of courage.

b (*vivres*) **~s** provisions, food (*NonC*); **faire ses ~s, aller aux ~s*** to go shopping (for groceries *ou* food); **elle posa ses ~s sur la table** she put her groceries on the table; **faire des ~s pour l'hiver** (*lit*) to buy in food *ou* provisions for the winter, stock up (with food *ou* provisions) for the winter; (*hum*) (*financièrement*) to put something away for a rainy day; (*hum: trop manger*) **tu fais des ~s pour l'hiver?** are you fattening yourself up for the winter?; **~s de guerre** war supplies; **~s de bouche** provisions; **filet/panier à ~s** shopping bag/basket; **armoire** *ou* **placard à ~s** food cupboard.

c (*arrhes*) (*chez un avocat*) retainer, retaining fee; (*pour un achat*) deposit. (*Banque*) **y a-t-il ~ au compte?** are there sufficient funds in the account?; (*immeuble d'habitation*) **~s sur charges** interim payment for maintenance *ou* service charges; *voir* **chèque.**

provisionnel, -elle [pʀɔvizjɔnɛl] **adj** (*Jur*) provisional. **acompte** *ou* **tiers ~** provisional payment (*towards one's income tax*).

provisoire [pʀɔvizwaʀ] 1 **adj** *arrêt, jugement* provisional; *mesure, solution* provisional, temporary; *bonheur, liaison* temporary; *installation* temporary; *adjoint* temporary, acting (*épith*); *gouvernement* provisional, interim (*épith*). **à titre ~** temporarily, provisionally; *voir* **liberté.** 2 **nm: c'est du ~** it's a temporary *ou* provisional arrangement.

provisoirement [pʀɔvizwaʀmɑ̃] **adv** (*pour l'instant*) for the time being.

provitamine [pʀɔvitamin] **nf** provitamin.

provocant, e [pʀɔvɔkɑ̃, ɑ̃t] **adj** provocative.

provocateur, -trice [pʀɔvɔkatœʀ, tʀis] 1 **adj** provocative; *voir* **agent.** 2 **nm** agitator.

provocation [pʀɔvɔkasjɔ̃] **nf** provocation. **~ à (faire) qch** incitement to (do) sth; **~ en duel** challenge to a duel; **manifestants qui font de la ~** demonstrators who use tactics of provocation.

provoquer [pʀɔvɔke] [1] **vt** a (*inciter, pousser à*) **~ qn à** to incite sb to.

b (*défier*) to provoke. **~ qn en duel** to challenge sb to a duel; **elle aime ~ les hommes** she likes to provoke men; **les 2 adversaires s'étaient provoqués** the 2 opponents had provoked each other.

c (*causer*) *accident, incendie, explosion* to cause; *réaction, changement d'attitude* to provoke, prompt, produce; *courant d'air* to create, cause; *révolte* to cause, bring about, instigate; *commentaires* to give rise to, provoke, prompt; *colère* to arouse, spark off; *curiosité* to arouse, excite, prompt; *gaieté* to cause, give rise to, provoke; *aveux, explications* to prompt. **blessures qui ont provoqué la mort** injuries which led to *ou* brought about death; **médicament qui provoque le sommeil** medicine which brings on *ou* induces sleep; **le malade est sous sommeil/évanouissement provoqué** the patient is in an induced sleep/a state of induced unconsciousness; (*Chim*) **l'élévation de température a provoqué cette réaction** the rise in temperature brought about *ou* triggered off *ou* started up this reaction.

proxénète [pʀɔksenɛt] **nm** procurer.

proxénétisme [pʀɔksenetism] **nm** procuring.

proximité [pʀɔksimite] **nf** (*dans l'espace*) nearness, closeness, proximity; (*dans le temps*) imminence, closeness. **à ~** near *ou* close by, near *ou* close at hand; **à ~ de** near (to), close to, in the vicinity of, in proximity to.

pruche [pʀyʃ] **nf** (*Can*) hemlock spruce.

prude [pʀyd] 1 **adj** prudish. 2 **nf** prude.

prudemment [pʀydamɑ̃] **adv** (*voir* **prudent**) carefully; cautiously; prudently; wisely, sensibly; cagily. **garder ~ le silence** to keep a cautious silence.

prudence [pʀydɑ̃s] **nf** (*voir* **prudent**) care; caution, cautiousness; prudence; wisdom; caginess. **~! ça glisse** careful! it's slippery; **manquer de ~** not to be careful *ou* cautious enough; **par (mesure de) ~** as a precaution; **il a eu la ~ de partir** he had the good sense *ou* he was wise *ou* sensible enough to leave; **il faudra lui annoncer la nouvelle avec beaucoup de ~** the news must be broken to him very carefully; (*Prov*) **~ est mère de sûreté** safety is born of caution.

prudent, e [pʀydɑ̃, ɑ̃t] **adj** (*circonspect*) careful, cautious, prudent; (*sage*) wise, sensible; (*réservé*) cautious, cagey. **il est ~ de faire** it is wise *ou* advisable *ou* a good idea to do; **il serait ~ de vous munir d'un parapluie** it would be wise *ou* sensible *ou* a good idea to take an umbrella, you would be well-advised to take an umbrella; **ce n'est pas ~** it's not advisable, it's not a good idea; **ce n'est pas ~ de boire avant de conduire** it's not prudent *ou* sensible *ou* wise *ou* advisable to drink before driving; **c'est plus ~** it's wiser *ou* safer *ou* more sensible; **soyez ~!** be careful!, take care!; **il s'est montré très ~ au sujet du résultat** he was very cautious *ou* cagey about the result; **il jugea plus ~ de se taire** he thought it prudent *ou* wiser *ou* more sensible to keep quiet; **c'est un ~** he's a careful *ou* cautious *ou* prudent type.

pruderie [pʀydʀi] **nf** (*littér*) prudishness (*NonC*), prudery.

prud'homal, e, mpl **-aux** [pʀydɔmal, o] **adj** of an industrial tribunal.

prud'homie [pʀydɔmi] **nf** (*voir* **prud'homme**) jurisdiction of an industrial tribunal.

prud'homme [pʀydɔm] **nm: conseil de ~s** ≃ industrial tribunal (*with wider administrative and advisory powers*).

prudhommerie [pʀydɔmʀi] **nf** sententiousness, pomposity.

prudhommesque [pʀydɔmɛsk] **adj** sententious, pompous.

prune [pʀyn] 1 **nf** (*fruit*) plum; (*alcool*) plum brandy; (†*: *coup*) clout*. (*fig*) **pour des ~s*** for nothing; **des ~s!*** not likely!*, not on your life!*, no way!*; **filer une ~ à qn*†** to give sb a clout*, clout* sb. 2 **adj inv** plum-coloured.

pruneau, pl **~x** [pʀyno] **nm** (*sec*) prune; (*Suisse: quetsche*) *kind of dark-red plum;* (*: *balle*) slug*.

prunelle [pʀynɛl] **nf** a (*Bot*) sloe; (*eau-de-vie*) sloe gin. b (*Anat: pupille*) pupil; (*œil*) eye. **il y tient comme à la ~ de ses yeux** (*objet*) he treasures *ou* cherishes it; (*personne*) she (*ou* he) is the apple of his eye, she (*ou* he) is very precious to him; **il/elle jouait de la ~*** he/she was giving her/him the eye*.

prunellier [pʀynəlje] **nm** sloe, blackthorn.

prunier [pʀynje] **nm** plum tree; *voir* **secouer.**

prunus [pʀynys] **nm** prunus, Japanese flowering cherry.

prurigineux, -euse [pʀyʀiʒinø, øz] **adj** pruriginous.

prurigo [pʀyʀigo] **nm** prurigo.

prurit [pʀyʀit] **nm** pruritus.

Prusse [pʀys] **nf** Prussia; *voir* **bleu.**

prussien, -ienne [pʀysjɛ̃, jɛn] 1 **adj** Prussian. 2 **nm,f: P~(ne)** Prussian.

prussique [pʀysik] **adjm: acide ~** prussic acid.

prytanée [pʀitane] **nm: ~ militaire** military academy.

PS [peɛs] **nm abrév de parti socialiste.**

P-S [peɛs] nm (abrév de **post-scriptum**) p.s.
psallette [psalɛt] nf choir.
psalmiste [psalmist] nm psalmist.
psalmodie [psalmɔdi] nf (*Rel*) psalmody, chant; (*fig littér*) drone.
psalmodier [psalmɔdje] 7 1 vt (*Rel*) to chant; (*fig littér*) to drone out. 2 vi to chant; to drone (on *ou* away).
psaume [psom] nm psalm. (*Bible*) **le livre des P~s** the Book of Psalms.
psautier [psotje] nm psalter.
pseudo- [psødɔ] préf (*gén*) pseudo-; *employé, officier* bogus.
pseudonyme [psødɔnim] nm (*gén*) assumed *ou* fictitious name; *[écrivain]* pen name, pseudonym; *[comédien]* stage name; (*Jur, hum*) alias.
psi [psi] nm psi.
psitt [psit] excl ps(s)t!
psittacisme [psitasism] nm (*répétition mécanique*) parrotry; (*Psych*) psittacism.
psittacose [psitakoz] nf psittacosis.
psoriasis [psɔʀjazis] nm psoriasis.
PSV [peɛsve] (abrév de **pilotage sans visibilité**) *voir* **pilotage**.
psy* [psi] 1 nmf (abrév de **psychiatre**) shrink*. 2 adj inv (abrév de **psychologique**) psychological.
psychanalyse [psikanaliz] nf *[personne]* psychoanalysis, analysis (*esp US*); *[texte]* psychoanalytical study.
psychanalyser [psikanalize] 1 vt *personne* to psychoanalyze; *texte* to study from a psychoanalytical viewpoint. **se faire ~** to have o.s. psychoanalyzed.
psychanalyste [psikanalist] nmf psychoanalyst, analyst (*esp US*).
psychanalytique [psikanalitik] adj psychoanalytic(al).
psyché [psiʃe] nf a (*Psych*) psyche. b (*miroir*) cheval glass, swing mirror. c (*Myth*) **P~** Psyche.
psychédélique [psikedelik] adj psychedelic.
psychédélisme [psikedelism] nm psychedelic state.
psychiatre [psikjatʀ] nmf psychiatrist.
psychiatrie [psikjatʀi] nf psychiatry.
psychiatrique [psikjatʀik] adj *troubles* psychiatric; *hôpital* psychiatric, mental (*épith*).
psychique [psiʃik] adj psychological, psychic(al).
psychisme [psiʃism] nm psyche, mind.
psycho* [psiko] nf abrév de **psychologie**.
psychodrame [psikɔdʀam] nm psychodrama.
psychogène [psikɔʒɛn] adj psychogenic.
psychokinésie [psikokinezi] nf psychokinesis.
psycholinguistique [psikolɛ̃gɥistik] 1 adj psycholinguistic. 2 nf psycholinguistics (*sg*).
psychologie [psikɔlɔʒi] nf psychology. **~ de l'enfant** child psychology; **la ~ des foules/du comportement** crowd/behavioural psychology.
psychologique [psikɔlɔʒik] adj psychological. **tu sais, mon vieux, c'est ~!** it's psychological *ou* it's all in the mind, old boy!; *voir* **moment**.
psychologiquement [psikɔlɔʒikmɑ̃] adv psychologically.
psychologue [psikɔlɔg] 1 adj: (*intuitif*) **il est ~** he is a good psychologist; **il n'est pas (très) ~** he's not much of a psychologist. 2 nmf psychologist. **~ d'entreprise** industrial psychologist; **~ scolaire** educational psychologist.
psychométrie [psikɔmetʀi] nf psychometry, psychometrics (*sg*).
psychométrique [psikɔmetʀik] adj psychometric.
psychomoteur, -trice [psikomɔtœʀ, tʀis] adj psychomotor.
psychopathe [psikɔpat] nmf person who is mentally ill; (*agressif, criminel*) psychopath.
psychopathie [psikɔpati] nf mental illness; psychopathy.
psychopathologie [psikopatɔlɔʒi] nf psychopathology.
psychopédagogie [psikopedagɔʒi] nf educational psychology.
psychopédagogique [psikopedagɔʒik] adj: **études ~s** studies in educational psychology.
psychophysiologie [psikofizjɔlɔʒi] nf psychophysiology.
psychophysiologique [psikofizjɔlɔʒik] adj psychophysiological.
psychose [psikoz] nf (*Psych*) psychosis; (*fig: obsession*) obsessive fear (*de* of).
psychosensoriel, -elle [psikosɑ̃sɔʀjɛl] adj psychosensory.
psychosocial, e, mpl **-iaux** [psikosɔsjal, jo] adj psychosocial.
psychosociologie [psikosɔsjɔlɔʒi] nf psychosociology.
psychosomatique [psikosɔmatik] 1 adj psychosomatic. 2 nf psychosomatics (*sg*).
psychotechnicien, -ienne [psikotɛknisjɛ̃, jɛn] nm,f psychotechnician, psychotechnologist.
psychotechnique [psikotɛknik] 1 adj psychotechnical, psychotechnological. 2 nf psychotechnics (*sg*), psychotechnology.
psychothérapeute [psikoteʀapøt] nmf psychotherapist.
psychothérapie [psikoteʀapi] nf psychotherapy. **~ de soutien** supportive therapy.
psychothérapique [psikoteʀapik] adj psychotherapeutic.
psychotique [psikɔtik] adj, nmf psychotic.
Pte abrév de **porte**.
ptérodactyle [pteʀɔdaktil] nm pterodactyl.
Ptolémée [ptɔleme] nm Ptolemy.
ptose [ptoz] nf ptosis.
P.T.T. [petete] nfpl (abrév de **Postes, Télécommunications et Télédiffusion**) *voir* **poste**[1].
ptyaline [ptjalin] nf ptyalin.
puant, puante [pɥɑ̃, pɥɑ̃t] adj (*lit*) stinking, foul-smelling; (*fig*) *personne, attitude* bumptious, overweening. **il est ~, c'est un type ~** he's full of himself, he's a bumptious *ou* an overweening character; **~ d'orgueil** bloated with pride.
puanteur [pɥɑ̃tœʀ] nf stink, stench.
pub[1] [pœb] nm (*bar*) pub.
pub[2]* [pyb] nf (*annonce*) ad*, advert* (*Brit*); (*Ciné, TV*) commercial, ad*, advert* (*Brit*). (*métier*) **la ~** advertising; **faire de la ~ pour qch** to plug sth*, give sth a plug*.
pubère [pybɛʀ] adj pubescent.
puberté [pybɛʀte] nf puberty.
pubien, -ienne [pybjɛ̃, jɛn] adj pubic. **région ~ne** pubic region, pubes.
pubis [pybis] nm (*os*) pubis; (*bas-ventre*) pubes. **os ~** pubic bone.
publiable [pyblijabl] adj publishable. **ce n'est pas ~** it's not fit for publication.
public, -ique [pyblik] 1 adj a (*non privé*) *intérêt, lieu, opinion, vie* public; *vente, réunion* public, open to the public (*attrib*). **danger/ennemi/homme ~** public danger/enemy/figure; **la nouvelle est maintenant ~ique** the news is now common knowledge *ou* public knowledge; **la nouvelle a été rendue ~ique hier** the news was made public *ou* was released yesterday; *voir* **domaine, droit**[3]**, notoriété**.
b (*de l'État*) *services, secteur, finances* public; *école, instruction* State (*Brit*) (*épith*), public (*US*); *voir* **charge, chose, dette** *etc.*
2 nm a (*population*) (general) public. **interdit au ~** no admittance to the public.
b (*audience, assistance*) audience. **œuvre conçue pour un jeune ~** work written for a young audience; **en matière d'opéra, le ~ parisien est très exigeant** the opera-going public of Paris is very demanding, where opera is concerned Paris audiences are very demanding; **des huées s'élevèrent du ~** boos rose from the audience *ou* public; **cet écrivain s'adresse à un vaste ~** this author writes for a large readership; **cet acteur a son ~** this actor has his fans *ou* followers; **cet ouvrage plaira à tous les ~s** this work will be appreciated by all types of readership *ou* reading public; **un ~ clairsemé assistait au match** the match was attended by very few spectators; **le ~ est informé que ...** the public is advised that ...; **en ~** in public; **le grand ~** the general public; **roman destiné au grand ~** novel written for the general reader *ou* public; **appareils électroniques grand ~** consumer electronics; **film grand ~** film with mass appeal; (*fig*) **il lui faut toujours un ~** he always needs an audience; **ses romans ont conquis un vaste ~** his novels have won a vast readership; **être bon/mauvais ~** to be a good/poor audience.
c (*secteur*) **le ~** the public sector.
publicain [pyblikɛ̃] nm (*Hist romaine*) publican, tax-gatherer.
publication [pyblikasjɔ̃] nf (*action*) publication, publishing; (*écrit publié*) publication. **~ assistée par ordinateur** desktop publishing.
publiciste [pyblisist] nmf a (*: *publicitaire*) advertising executive, adman*. **il est ~** he's in advertising, he's an adman*. b (*Jur*) public law specialist.
publicitaire [pyblisitɛʀ] 1 adj *budget, affiche, agence, campagne* advertising (*épith*); *film, voiture* promotional. **annonce ~** advertisement; **échantillon ~** give-away *ou* free sample; **grande vente ~** big promotional sale; **matériel ~** publicity material; **rédacteur ~** copywriter. 2 nmf adman*, advertising executive, advertising agent.
publicité [pyblisite] nf a (*Comm: méthode, profession*) advertising. (*Comm*) **matériel de ~** publicity material; (*Comm, fig*) **faire de la ~ pour qch** to advertise sth; **il sait bien faire sa propre ~** he's good at doing his own advertising; **cette marque fait beaucoup de ~** this make does a lot of advertising; **~ de rappel** reminder advertising; **~ mensongère** misleading advertising; **~ sur les lieux de vente** point-of-sale advertising; *voir* **agence** *etc.* b (*annonce*) advertisement, ad*, advert* (*Brit*); (*Ciné, TV*) commercial, advertisement. c (*révélations*) publicity. **on a fait trop de ~ autour de cette affaire** this affair has had *ou* has been given too much publicity. d (*Jur*) **la ~ des débats** the public nature of the proceedings.
publier [pyblije] 7 vt a *livre [auteur]* to publish; *[éditeur]* to publish, bring out. b *bans, décret* to publish; (*littér*) *nouvelle* to publish (abroad) (*littér*), make public. **ça vient d'être publié** it's just out, it has just come out *ou* been published; **~ un communiqué (au sujet de *ou* concernant)** to release a statement (about).
publiphone [pyblifɔn] nm ® public telephone, payphone. **~ à carte** card phone.
publipostage [pyblipɔstaʒ] nm mailshot, mass mailing.
publiquement [pyblikmɑ̃] adv publicly.
publireportage [pybliʀ(ə)pɔʀtaʒ] nm advertorial.
puce [pys] 1 nf a (*Zool*) flea. **~ de mer *ou* de sable** sand flea; **~ d'eau** water flea; (*fig*) **cela m'a mis la ~ à l'oreille** that started me thinking; **les ~s, le marché aux ~s** the flea market; **oui, ma ~*** yes, pet* *ou* lovie*; (*fig*) **c'est une vraie ~** he's (*ou* she's) a real midget; *voir* **secouer**. b **jeu de ~s** tiddlywinks; **jouer aux ~s** to play

tiddlywinks. c (*Ordin*) (silicon) chip. ~ **électronique** microchip; ~ **mémoire** memory chip. 2 adj inv puce.

puceau*, pl ~x [pyso] 1 adjm: **être** ~ to be a virgin. 2 nm virgin.

pucelage* [pys(ə)laʒ] nm virginity.

pucelle [pysɛl] (††, *hum*,*) 1 adjf: **être** ~ to be a virgin; **elle n'est plus** ~ she has lost her virginity, she's not a virgin. 2 nf virgin, maid(en) (*littér*). (*Hist*) **la** ~ **d'Orléans** the Maid of Orleans.

puceron [pys(ə)ʀɔ̃] nm aphid, greenfly.

pucier‡ [pysje] nm bed.

pudding [pudiŋ] nm plum pudding.

puddlage [pydlaʒ] nm puddling.

pudeur [pydœʀ] nf a (*sexuelle*) (sense of) modesty, sense of decency. **elle a beaucoup de** ~ she has a keen sense of modesty *ou* decency; **sans** ~ (adj) immodest; (adv) immodestly, unblushingly; *voir* **attentat, outrage.** b (*délicatesse*) sense of propriety. **agir sans** ~ to act with no regard to propriety.

pudibond, e [pydibɔ̃, ɔ̃d] adj (excessively) prudish, prim and proper.

pudibonderie [pydibɔ̃dʀi] nf (excessive) prudishness, (excessive) primness.

pudicité [pydisite] nf (*littér: voir* **pudique**) modesty; discretion.

pudique [pydik] adj (*chaste*) modest; (*discret*) discreet.

pudiquement [pydikmɑ̃] adv (*voir* **pudique**) modestly; discreetly. **ils détournaient les yeux** ~ they looked away discreetly *ou* out of a sense of decency.

puer [pɥe] 1 1 vi to stink, reek, smell foul. (*fig*) **il pue de vanité** he is bloated with vanity. 2 vt to stink *ou* reek of.

puéricultrice [pɥeʀikyltʀis] nf (*infirmière*) paediatric nurse; (*institutrice*) nursery nurse.

puériculture [pɥeʀikyltyʀ] nf (*voir* **puéricultrice**) paediatric nursing; nursery nursing. **donner des cours de** ~ **aux mamans** to give courses on infant care to mothers.

puéril, e [pɥeʀil] adj puerile, childish.

puérilement [pɥeʀilmɑ̃] adv childishly, puerilely.

puérilité [pɥeʀilite] nf (*caractère*) puerility, childishness; (*acte*) childish act.

puerpéral, e, mpl **-aux** [pɥɛʀpeʀal, o] adj puerperal.

pugilat [pyʒila] nm (fist) fight.

pugiliste [pyʒilist] nm (*littér*) pugilist (*littér*).

pugilistique [pyʒilistik] adj (*littér*) pugilistic (*littér, frm*).

pugnace [pygnas] adj pugnacious.

pugnacité [pygnasite] nf (*littér*) pugnacity.

puîné, e† [pɥine] 1 adj (*de deux*) younger; (*de plusieurs*) youngest. 2 nm,f younger; youngest.

puis [pɥi] adv (*ensuite*) then; (*dans une énumération*) then, next. (*en outre*) **et** ~ and besides; **et** ~ **ensuite** and then, and after that; **et** ~ **c'est tout** and that's all *ou* that's it; **et** ~ **après tout** and after all; **et** ~ **après?** *ou* **ensuite?** (*ensuite*) and what next?, and then (what)?; (*et alors?*) so what?, what of it?; **et** ~ **quoi?** (*quoi d'autre*) well, what?, and then what?; (*et alors?*) so what?, what of it?

puisage [pɥizaʒ] nm drawing (of water).

puisard [pɥizaʀ] nm (*gén*) cesspool, sink; (*Naut*) well; (*Min*) sump.

puisatier [pɥizatje] nm well-digger.

puiser [pɥize] 1 vt (*lit*) *eau* to draw (*dans* from); (*fig*) *exemple, renseignement* to draw, take (*dans* from). ~ **des exemples dans un auteur** to draw examples from an author, draw on an author for one's examples; ~ **dans son sac/ses économies** to dip into one's bag/one's savings.

puisque [pɥisk(ə)] conj a (*du moment que*) since, seeing that. **ces animaux sont donc des mammifères, puisqu'ils allaitent leurs petits** these animals are therefore mammals, seeing that *ou* since they suckle their young; **ça doit être vrai, puisqu'il le dit** it must be true since he says so. b (*comme*) as, since, seeing that. ~ **vous êtes là, venez m'aider** as *ou* since *ou* seeing that you're here come and help me; **ces escrocs, puisqu'il faut les appeler ainsi ...** these crooks — as *ou* since one must call them that ... . c (*valeur intensive*) ~ **je te le dis!** I'm telling you (so)!; ~ **je te dis que c'est vrai!** I'm telling you it's true!

puissamment [pɥisamɑ̃] adv (*fortement*) powerfully; (*beaucoup*) greatly. (*iro*) ~ **raisonné!** powerfully reasoned! (*iro*), what brilliant reasoning! (*iro*).

puissance [pɥisɑ̃s] 1 nf a (*force*) *[armée, muscle, impulsion]* power, strength; *[moteur]* power; *[haut-parleur, chaîne hi-fi]* power, output; *[éclairage]* brightness, power; *[vent]* strength, force. **avoir une grande** ~ **de travail** to have a great capacity for work; **avoir une grande** ~ **d'imagination** to have a very powerful imagination *ou* great powers of imagination; **la** ~ **de son regard** the power of his gaze; **grâce à la** ~ **de sa volonté** thanks to his willpower *ou* his strength of will. b (*pouvoir*) *[classe sociale, pays, argent]* power; (*efficacité*) *[exemple]* power. **une grande** ~ **de séduction/suggestion** great seductive/suggestive power(s), great powers of seduction/suggestion; **user de sa** ~ **pour faire qch** to use one's power to do sth; **l'or/le pétrole est une** ~ gold/oil confers power; **les** ~**s qui agissent sur le monde** the powers that influence the world. c (*Pol: état*) power. **les grandes** ~**s** the great powers. d (*Élec, Phys*) power; (*Opt*) *[microscope]* (magnifying) power. (*Math*) **élever un nombre à la** ~ **10** to raise a number to the power of 10; **10** ~ **4** 10 to the power of 4, 10 to the 4th. e (*Jur, hum*) **être en** ~ **de mari** to be under a husband's authority. f (*loc*) **en** ~ *adj* potential; **exister en** ~ to have a potential existence; **c'est là en** ~ it is potentially present; **l'homme est en** ~ **dans l'enfant** the man is latent in the child. 2 comp ►**puissance administrative** (*Aut*) engine rating ►**les puissances d'argent** the forces of money ►**puissance de feu** (*Mil*) fire power ►**puissance fiscale** (*Aut*) engine rating ►**puissance au frein** (*Aut*) brake horsepower ►**puissance maritale** (*Jur*) marital rights ►**les puissances occultes** unseen *ou* hidden powers ►**puissance paternelle** (*Jur*) parental rights *ou* authority; **exercer/être déchu de sa puissance paternelle** to exercise/have lost one's parental rights ►**les puissances des ténèbres** the powers of darkness.

puissant, e [pɥisɑ̃, ɑ̃t] 1 adj (*gén*) powerful; *drogue, remède* potent, powerful; *grammaire* powerful. 2 nm: **les** ~**s** the mighty *ou* powerful.

puits [pɥi] 1 nm *[eau, pétrole]* well; (*Min*) shaft; (*Constr*) well, shaft. 2 comp ►**puits d'aérage** *ou* **d'aération** ventilation shaft ►**puits artésien** artesian well ►**puits à ciel ouvert** (*Min*) opencast mine ►**puits d'érudition** (*fig*) = **puits de science** ►**puits d'extraction** winding shaft ►**puits de mine** mine shaft ►**puits perdu** cesspool, sink ►**puits de pétrole** oil well ►**puits de science** (*fig*) well of erudition *ou* learning.

pull [pyl] nm sweater, jumper (*Brit*), jersey, pullover.

pullman [pulman] nm Pullman (car).

pull-over, pl **pull-overs** [pylɔvɛʀ] nm sweater, jumper (*Brit*), jersey, pullover.

pullulation [pylylasjɔ̃] nf, **pullulement** [pylylmɑ̃] nm (*action*) proliferation; (*profusion*) *[fourmis, moustiques]* swarm, multitude; *[erreurs]* abundance, multitude.

pulluler [pylyle] 1 vi (*se reproduire*) to proliferate, multiply, pullulate (*frm*); (*grouiller*) to swarm, pullulate (*frm*); (*fig*) *[erreurs, contrefaçons]* to abound, pullulate (*frm*). **la ville pullule de touristes** the town is swarming with tourists; **la rivière pullule de truites** the river is teeming with trout.

pulmonaire [pylmɔnɛʀ] adj *maladie* pulmonary, lung (*épith*); *artère* pulmonary. **congestion** ~ congestion of the lungs.

pulpe [pylp] nf *[fruit, dent, bois]* pulp.

pulpeux, -euse [pylpø, øz] adj *fruit* pulpy; *lèvres* full; *blonde* curvaceous.

pulsar [pylsaʀ] nm pulsar.

pulsation [pylsasjɔ̃] nf (*Méd*) *[cœur, pouls]* beating (*NonC*), beat, pulsation (*SPÉC*); (*Phys*) pulsation; (*Élec*) pulsatance. ~**s (du cœur)** (*rythme cardiaque*) heartbeat; (*battements*) heartbeats.

pulsé [pylse] adjm: **chauffage à air** ~ warm-air heating.

pulsion [pylsjɔ̃] nf (*Psych*) drive, urge. **la** ~ **sexuelle** the sex drive; ~**s sexuelles** sexual urges.

pulvérisable [pylveʀizabl] adj pulverable.

pulvérisateur [pylveʀizatœʀ] nm (*à parfum*) spray, atomizer; (*à peinture*) spray; (*pour médicament*) spray, vaporizer.

pulvérisation [pylveʀizasjɔ̃] nf (*voir* **pulvériser**) pulverizing, pulverization; spraying; demolition, demolishing; shattering*, smashing*. (*Méd*) **"trois** ~**s dans chaque narine"** "spray three times into each nostril"; (*Méd*) **le médecin a ordonné des** ~**s (nasales)** the doctor prescribed a nasal spray.

pulvériser [pylveʀize] 1 vt a *solide* to pulverize, reduce to powder; *liquide* to spray. b (*fig: anéantir*) *adversaire* to pulverize, demolish; *record* to shatter*, smash*; *argument* to demolish, pull to pieces. **bâtiment pulvérisé par l'explosion** building reduced to rubble by the explosion.

pulvériseur [pylveʀizœʀ] nm disc harrow.

pulvérulence [pylveʀylɑ̃s] nf pulverulence.

pulvérulent, e [pylveʀylɑ̃, ɑ̃t] adj pulverulent.

puma [pyma] nm puma, cougar, mountain lion.

punaise [pynɛz] nf a (*Zool*) bug. (*péj*) **c'est une vraie** ~ he's a real mischief-maker; (*excl*) ~**!*** blimey!* (*Brit*), well!; (*péj*) ~ **de sacristie*** church hen. b (*clou*) drawing pin (*Brit*), thumbtack (*US*).

punaiser [pyneze] 1 vt to pin up (*ou* down *ou* on *etc*). ~ **une affiche au mur** to pin up a poster, pin a poster up on the wall.

punch¹ [pɔ̃ʃ] nm (*boisson*) punch.

punch² [pœnʃ] nm (*Boxe*) punching ability; (*fig*) punch. **avoir du** ~ (*Boxe*) to pack *ou* have a good punch; (*fig*) to have punch *ou* muscle.

puncheur [pœnʃœʀ] nm good puncher, hard hitter.

punching-ball, pl **punching-balls** [pœnʃiŋbol] nm punchball.

punique [pynik] adj Punic.

punir [pyniʀ] 2 vt a *criminel, enfant* to punish (*pour* for). **être puni de prison/de mort** to be sentenced to prison/death. b (*faire souffrir*) to punish. **il a été puni de son imprudence** he was punished for his recklessness, he suffered for his recklessness; **tu as été malade, ça te punira de ta gourmandise** you've been ill — that will teach you not to be greedy *ou* that serves you right for being greedy *ou* it's no more than you deserve for being greedy; **il est orgueilleux, et l'en voilà bien puni** he is paying the penalty for *ou* being made to suffer

for his pride; **il est puni par où il a péché** he has got his (just) deserts, he is paying for his sins.
c (*sanctionner*) *faute, infraction, crime* to punish. **tout abus sera puni (de prison)** all abuses are punishable *ou* will be punished (by prison); **ce crime est puni par la loi/puni de mort** this crime is punishable by law/by death.
punissable [pynisabl] adj punishable (*de* by).
punitif, -ive [pynitif, iv] adj *expédition* punitive.
punition [pynisjɔ̃] nf punishment (*de qch* for sth). (*Scol*) **avoir une ~** to be given a punishment; **~ corporelle** corporal punishment (*NonC*); **en ~ de ses fautes** in punishment for his mistakes; **pour ta ~** for your punishment.
punk [pœ̃k] adj inv, nmf inv punk. **le rock ~** punk rock.
pupille[1] [pypij] nf (*Anat*) pupil.
pupille[2] [pypij] nmf (*enfant*) ward. **~ de l'État** child in (local authority) care; **~ de la Nation** war orphan.
pupitre [pypitʀ] nm (*Scol*) desk; (*Rel*) lectern; (*Mus*) *[musicien]* music stand; *[piano]* music rest; *[chef d'orchestre]* rostrum; (*Ordin*) console. (*Mus*) **au ~, Henri Dupont** at the rostrum – Henri Dupont, conducting – Henri Dupont; (*Mus*) **chef de ~** head of section.
pupitreur, -euse [pypitʀœʀ, øz] nm,f computer operator, keyboard operator, keyboarder.
pur, e [pyʀ] 1 adj a (*sans mélange*) *alcool, eau, race, métal, voix, style* pure; *vin* undiluted; *whisky, gin* neat, straight; *ciel* clear, pure; *voyelle* pure; *diamant* flawless. **~e laine** pure wool; **boire son vin ~** to drink one's wine without water *ou* undiluted; (*Chim*) **à l'état ~** in the pure state; **~ sang** thoroughbred, purebred; **l'air ~ de la campagne** the pure *ou* fresh country air; *voir* **pur-sang**.
b (*innocent*) *âme, cœur, fille* pure; *homme* pure-hearted; *intentions* pure, honourable, honest; *regard* frank. **~ de tout soupçon** free of *ou* above all suspicion; **~ de toute tache** free of all blemish, unblemished, unsullied.
c (*valeur intensive*) **c'est de la folie ~e** it's pure *ou* sheer *ou* utter madness; **c'est de la poésie/de l'imagination toute ~e** it's pure *ou* sheer poetry/imagination; **c'est de l'insubordination ~e et simple** it's insubordination pure and simple; **c'était du racisme ~ et simple** *ou* **à l'état ~** it was straight *ou* plain racism; **il donna sa démission ~e et simple** he purely and simply gave in his notice; **œuvre de ~e imagination** work of pure imagination; **c'est une question de ~e forme** it's merely *ou* purely a formal question; **c'est par ~ hasard que je l'ai vu** I saw it by sheer chance *ou* purely by chance; **c'est la ~e vérité** it's the plain *ou* simple (unadulterated) truth; **en ~e perte** for absolutely nothing, fruitlessly; **il a travaillé en ~e perte** he worked for absolutely nothing, his work was fruitless; (*Pol*) **~ et dur, ~ jus** hard-line.
2 nm,f (*Pol*) **~ (et dur)** hard-liner.
purée [pyʀe] nf: **~ (de pommes de terre)** mashed potato(es); **~ de marrons/de tomates** chestnut/tomato purée; (*fig*) **de la ~ de pois** peasoup, a peasouper; (*fig*) **être dans la ~**‡ to be in a real mess*; **~, je l'ai oublié!*** darn (it)*, I forgot!
purement [pyʀmɑ̃] adv purely. **~ et simplement** purely and simply.
pureté [pyʀte] nf a (*perfection*) *[race, style, métal]* purity; *[air, eau, son]* purity, pureness; *[diamant]* flawlessness. b (*innocence: voir* **pur**) purity; honourableness, honesty; frankness.
purgatif, -ive [pyʀgatif, iv] 1 adj purgative. 2 nm purgative, purge.
purgation [pyʀgasjɔ̃] nf (*Méd*) (*action*) purgation; (*remède*) purgative, purge.
purgatoire [pyʀgatwaʀ] nm (*Rel, fig*) purgatory.
purge [pyʀʒ] nf (*Méd*) purge, purgative; (*Pol*) purge; (*Tech*) *[conduite]* flushing out, draining; *[freins]* bleeding.
purger [pyʀʒe] 3 1 vt a (*vidanger*) *conduite, radiateur* to bleed, flush (out), drain; *circuit hydraulique, freins* to bleed. b (*Méd*) to purge, give a purgative to. c (*Jur*) *peine* to serve. d (*débarrasser*) to purge, cleanse, rid (*de* of). 2 **se purger** vpr to take a purgative *ou* purge.
purgeur [pyʀʒœʀ] nm *[tuyauterie]* drain-cock, tap (*Brit*); *[radiateur]* bleed-tap.
purifiant, e [pyʀifjɑ̃, jɑ̃t] adj purifying, cleansing.
purificateur, -trice [pyʀifikatœʀ, tʀis] 1 adj purifying, cleansing, purificatory. 2 nm (*appareil*) (air) purifier.
purification [pyʀifikasjɔ̃] nf (*voir* **purifier**) purification, purifying; cleansing; refinement; purging; **~ ethnique** ethnic cleansing.
purificatoire [pyʀifikatwaʀ] adj (*littér*) purificatory, purifying, cleansing.
purifier [pyʀifje] 7 1 vt (*gén*) to purify, cleanse; *air, langue, liquide* to purify; *métal* to refine; *âme* to cleanse, purge. 2 **se purifier** vpr to cleanse o.s.
purin [pyʀɛ̃] nm liquid manure.
purisme [pyʀism] nm purism.
puriste [pyʀist] adj, nmf purist.
puritain, e [pyʀitɛ̃, ɛn] 1 adj puritan(ical); (*Hist*) Puritan. 2 nm,f puritan; (*Hist*) Puritan.
puritanisme [pyʀitanism] nm puritanism; (*Hist*) Puritanism.
purpurin, e [pyʀpyʀɛ̃, in] adj (*littér*) crimson.
pur-sang [pyʀsɑ̃] nm inv thoroughbred, purebred.
purulence [pyʀylɑ̃s] nf purulence, purulency.
purulent, e [pyʀylɑ̃, ɑ̃t] adj purulent.
pus [py] nm pus.
pusillanime [pyzi(l)lanim] adj (*littér*) pusillanimous (*littér*), fainthearted.
pusillanimité [pyzi(l)lanimite] nf (*littér*) pusillanimity (*littér*), faintheartedness.
pustule [pystyl] nf pustule.
pustuleux, -euse [pystylø, øz] adj pustular.
putain‡ [pytɛ̃] nf (*prostituée*) whore, hustler‡ (*US*), hooker‡ (*US*), tart‡; (*fille facile*) whore, tart‡, tramp‡. **faire la ~**‡ (*lit*) to be a whore *ou* hustler‡ (*US*) *ou* hooker‡ (*US*) *ou* tart‡, turn tricks‡ (*US*); (*fig*) to sell one's soul; **ce ~ de réveil!**‡ that goddamn‡ alarm clock!; **~!** bloody hell!** (*Brit*), bugger me!** (*Brit*), goddamn it!‡; **quel ~ de vent!** what a damned awful wind!‡
putassier, -ière‡ [pytasje, jɛʀ] adj *personne, langage, mœurs* sluttish; *maquillage, tenue* tarty‡. **avoir des mœurs ~ières/un langage ~** to carry on/talk like a whore *ou* hustler‡ (*US*) *ou* hooker‡ (*US*) *ou* tart‡; (*fig: servilité*) **comportement ~** arse-licking** (*Brit*), ass-licking** (*US*), bootlicking.
putatif, -ive [pytatif, iv] adj putative, presumed. **père ~** putative father.
pute** [pyt] nf whore, hustler‡ (*US*), hooker‡ (*US*), tart‡.
putois [pytwa] nm (*animal*) polecat; (*fourrure*) polecat (fur); *voir* **crier**.
putréfaction [pytʀefaksjɔ̃] nf putrefaction. **cadavre en ~** body in a state of putrefaction, putrefying *ou* rotting body.
putréfiable [pytʀefjabl] adj putrefiable.
putréfier [pytʀefje] 7 1 vt to putrefy, rot. 2 **se putréfier** vpr to putrefy, rot, go rotten.
putrescence [pytʀesɑ̃s] nf putrescence.
putrescent, e [pytʀesɑ̃, ɑ̃t] adj putrescent.
putrescible [pytʀesibl] adj putrescible.
putride [pytʀid] adj putrid.
putridité [pytʀidite] nf putridity, putridness.
putsch [putʃ] nm putsch.
putschiste [putʃist] nm putschist.
puzzle [pœzl] nm (*lit*) jigsaw (puzzle); (*fig*) jigsaw.
P.-V. [peve] nm (abrév de **procès-verbal**) *voir* **procès**.
pygargue [pigaʀg] nm white-tailed eagle.
Pygmalion [pigmaljɔ̃] nm Pygmalion.
pygmée [pigme] nm pygmy, pigmy. (*fig, péj*) **c'est un vrai ~** he's just a little squirt* (*péj*), he's a little runt* (*péj*).
pyjama [piʒama] nm pyjamas (*pl*), pajamas (*pl*) (*US*). **il était en ~(s)** he was in his pyjamas; **acheter un ~** to buy a pair of pyjamas, buy some pyjamas; **2 ~s** 2 pairs of pyjamas; *voir* **veste**.
pylône [pilon] nm pylon.
pylore [pilɔʀ] nm pylorus.
pylorique [pilɔʀik] adj pyloric.
pyorrhée [pjɔʀe] nf pyorrhoea, pyorrhea.
pyramidal, e, mpl **-aux** [piʀamidal, o] adj pyramid-shaped, pyramid-like, pyramidal (*SPÉC*).
pyramide [piʀamid] nf (*Anat, Archit, Géom, fig*) pyramid. **~ humaine** human pyramid; **~ des âges** *pyramid-shaped diagram representing population by age-groups.*
pyrénéen, -enne [piʀeneɛ̃, ɛn] 1 adj Pyrenean. 2 nm,f: **P~(ne)** inhabitant *ou* native of the Pyrenees, Pyrenean.
Pyrénées [piʀene] nfpl: **les ~** the Pyrenees.
pyrex [piʀɛks] nm ® Pyrex ®. **assiette en ~** Pyrex plate.
pyrite [piʀit] nf pyrites.
pyrograver [piʀɔgʀave] 1 vt to do pyrography *ou* poker-work.
pyrograveur, -euse [piʀɔgʀavœʀ, øz] nm,f pyrographer.
pyrogravure [piʀɔgʀavyʀ] nf (*Art*) pyrography, poker-work; (*objet*) pyrograph.
pyrolyse [piʀɔliz] nf pyrolysis.
pyromane [piʀɔman] nmf (*Méd*) pyromaniac; (*gén, Jur*) arsonist, fire raiser.
pyromanie [piʀɔmani] nf pyromania.
pyromètre [piʀɔmɛtʀ] nm pyrometer.
pyrométrie [piʀɔmetʀi] nf pyrometry.
pyrométrique [piʀɔmetʀik] adj pyrometric.
pyrotechnie [piʀɔtɛkni] nf pyrotechnics (*sg*), pyrotechny.
pyrotechnique [piʀɔtɛknik] adj pyrotechnic.
Pyrrhon [piʀɔ̃] nm Pyrrho.
pyrrhonien, -ienne [piʀɔnjɛ̃, jɛn] 1 adj Pyrrhonic, Pyrrhonian. 2 nm,f Pyrrhonist, Pyrrhonian.
pyrrhonisme [piʀɔnism] nm Pyrrhonism.
Pyrrhus [piʀys] nm Pyrrhus; *voir* **victoire**.
Pythagore [pitagɔʀ] nm Pythagoras.
pythagoricien, -ienne [pitagɔʀisjɛ̃, jɛn] adj, nm,f Pythagorean.
pythagorique [pitagɔʀik] adj Pythagorean.
pythagorisme [pitagɔʀism] nm Pythagoreanism, Pythagorism.
Pythie [piti] nf Pythia. (*fig: devineresse*) **p~** prophetess.
python [pitɔ̃] nm python.
pythonisse [pitɔnis] nf prophetess.

Q

Q, q [ky] nm (*lettre*) Q, q.
Qatar [kataʀ] nm Qatar.
qatarien, -ienne [kataʀjɛ̃, jɛn] 1 adj Qatar (*épith*). 2 nm,f: **Q~(ne)** Qatar.
qch (abrév de **quelque chose**) sth.
qcm [kyseɛm] nm (abrév de **questionnaire à choix multiple**) *voir* **questionnaire**.
QF [kyɛf] nm (abrév de **quotient familial**) *voir* **quotient**.
QG [kyʒe] nm (abrév de **quartier général**) HQ.
QHS [kyaʃɛs] nm (abrév de **quartier de haute sécurité**) *voir* **quartier**.
QI [kyi] nm (abrév de **quotient intellectuel**) IQ.
qn (abrév de **quelqu'un**) sb.
qq abrév de **quelque**.
qu' [k] *voir* **que**.
quadragénaire [k(w)adʀaʒenɛʀ] 1 adj (*de quarante ans*) forty-year-old (*épith*). (*de quarante à cinquante ans*) **il est ~** he is in his forties; (*hum*) **maintenant que tu es ~** now that you're forty (years old), now that you've reached forty. 2 nmf forty-year-old man (*ou* woman).
Quadragésime [kwadʀaʒezim] nf Quadragesima.
quadrangle [k(w)adʀɑ̃gl] nm (*Géom*) quadrangle.
quadrangulaire [k(w)adʀɑ̃gylɛʀ] adj quadrangular.
quadrant [kadʀɑ̃] nm quadrant.
quadrature [k(w)adʀatyʀ] nf (*gén*) quadrature. (*Math*) **~ du cercle** quadrature *ou* squaring of the circle; (*fig*) **c'est la ~ du cercle** it's like trying to square the circle, it's attempting the impossible.
quadriceps [k(w)adʀisɛps] nm quadriceps.
quadrichromie [k(w)adʀikʀɔmi] nf four-colour (printing) process.
quadriennal, e, mpl **-aux** [k(w)adʀijenal, o] adj four-year (*épith*), quadrennial. (*Agr*) **assolement ~** four-year rotation.
quadrijumeaux [k(w)adʀiʒymo] adj mpl: **tubercules ~** corpora quadrigemina, quadrigeminal *ou* quadrigeminate bodies.
quadrilatère [k(w)adʀilatɛʀ] nm (*Géom, Mil*) quadrilateral.
quadrillage [kadʀijaʒ] nm a (*action*) (*Mil, Police*) covering, control(ling); (*Admin, Écon*) covering. **la police a établi un ~ serré du quartier** the police have set up a tight control over the area. b (*dessin*) *[papier]* square pattern; *[tissu]* check pattern; *[rues]* criss-cross *ou* grid pattern *ou* layout.
quadrille [kadʀij] nm (*danse, danseurs*) quadrille. **~ des lanciers** lancers.
quadrillé, e [kadʀije] (ptp de **quadriller**) adj *papier, feuille* squared.
quadriller [kadʀije] 1 vt (*Mil, Police*) to cover, control; (*Admin, Écon*) to cover; *papier* to mark out in squares. **la ville est étroitement quadrillée par la police** the town is well covered by the police, the town is under close *ou* tight police control, the police are positioned throughout the whole town; **la ville est quadrillée par un réseau de rues** the town is criss-crossed by a network of streets, the town has a criss-cross network *ou* a grid pattern of streets.
quadrillion [k(w)adʀiljɔ̃] nm quadrillion (*Brit*), septillion (*US*).
quadrimoteur [kadʀimɔtœʀ] 1 adj m four-engined. 2 nm four-engined plane.
quadriparti, e [k(w)adʀipaʀti] adj, **quadripartite** [k(w)adʀipaʀtit] adj (*Bot*) quadripartite. (*Pol*) **conférence quadripartite** *[pays]* four-power conference; *[partis]* four-party conference.
quadriphonie [k(w)adʀifɔni] nf quadraphony.
quadriphonique [k(w)adʀifɔnik] adj quadraphonic.
quadriréacteur [k(w)adʀiʀeaktœʀ] nm four-engined jet.
quadrisyllabe [k(w)adʀisi(l)lab] nm quadrisyllable.
quadrisyllabique [k(w)adʀisi(l)labik] adj quadrisyllabic.
quadrumane [k(w)adʀyman] 1 adj quadrumanous. 2 nm quadrumane.
quadrupède [k(w)adʀypɛd] 1 adj fourfooted, quadruped. 2 nm quadruped.
quadruple [k(w)adʀypl] 1 adj *quantité, rangée, nombre* quadruple. **une quantité ~ de l'autre** a quantity four times (as great as) the other; **en ~ exemplaire/partie** in four copies/parts; *voir* **croche**. 2 nm (*Math, gén*) quadruple. **je l'ai payé le ~/le ~ de l'autre** I paid four times as much for it/four times as much as the other for it; **je vous le rendrai au ~** I'll repay you four times over; **augmenter au ~** to increase fourfold.
quadrupler [k(w)adʀyple] 1 vti to quadruple, increase fourfold.
quadruplés, -ées [k(w)adʀyple] (ptp de **quadrupler**) nm,f pl quadruplets, quads*.
quadruplex [k(w)adʀyplɛks] nm (*Téléc*) quadruplex system.
quai [ke] 1 nm *[port]* (*gén*) quay; (*pour marchandises*) wharf, quay; *[gare]* platform; *[rivière]* embankment. **être à ~** *[bateau]* to be alongside (the quay); *[train]* to be in (the station); **sur les ~s de la Seine** on the banks *ou* embankments of the Seine; *voir* **accès, billet.** 2 comp ►**le Quai des Orfèvres** the police headquarters (*in Paris*), ≃ (New) Scotland Yard (*Brit*), ≃ the FBI (*US*) ►**le Quai (d'Orsay)** *the French Foreign Office*.
quaker, quakeresse [kwɛkœʀ, kwɛkʀɛs] nm,f Quaker.
quakerisme [kwɛkœʀism] nm Quakerism.
qualifiable [kalifjabl] adj: **une telle conduite n'est pas ~** such behaviour is beyond description *ou* defies description.
qualificateur [kalifikatœʀ] nm (*Ling*) qualifier.
qualificatif, -ive [kalifikatif, iv] 1 adj *adjectif* qualifying. 2 nm (*Ling*) qualifier; (*fig: terme, mot*) term.
qualification [kalifikasjɔ̃] nf a (*nom*) label, description. b (*Sport*) **obtenir sa ~** to qualify (*en, pour* for); **épreuves de ~** qualifying heats *ou* rounds; **la ~ de notre équipe demeure incertaine** it's still not certain whether our team will qualify. c (*aptitude*) qualification. **~ professionnelle** professional qualification. d (*Ling*) qualification.
qualifié, e [kalifje] (ptp de **qualifier**) adj a (*compétent*) (*gén*) qualified; (*Ind*) *main d'œuvre, ouvrier* skilled. **non ~** unskilled. b (*Jur*) *vol, délit* aggravated. (*fig*) **c'est de l'hypocrisie ~e** it's blatant hypocrisy; (*fig*) **c'est du vol ~** it's daylight *ou* sheer robbery.
qualifier [kalifje] 7 1 vt a *conduite, projets* to describe (*de* as). **~ qn de menteur** to call *ou* label sb a liar, describe sb as a liar; **sa maison qu'il qualifiait pompeusement (de) manoir** his house which he described pompously as a manor, his house which he pompously labelled *ou* termed *ou* dubbed manor. b (*Sport, gén: rendre apte*) to qualify (*pour* for). c (*Ling*) to qualify. 2 **se qualifier** vpr (*Sport*) to qualify (*pour* for). (*hum*) **il se qualifie d'artiste** he labels *ou* qualifies himself as an artist, he calls himself an artist.
qualitatif, -ive [kalitatif, iv] adj qualitative.
qualitativement [kalitativmɑ̃] adv qualitatively.
qualité [kalite] nf a *[marchandise]* quality. **de bonne/mauvaise ~** of good *ou* high/bad *ou* poor quality; **produits de (haute) ~** (high-)quality products; **fruits de ~ supérieure** fruit of superior quality, superior-quality fruit; **~ courrier** near letter-quality; **~ courante** draft mode; **la ~ de la vie** the quality of life.

b *[personne]* (*vertu*) quality; (*don*) skill. **ses ~s de cœur l'ont fait aimer de tous** his noble-heartedness made everyone like him; **il a les ~s requises pour faire ce travail** he has the necessary skills for this job; **cette œuvre a de grandes ~s littéraires** this work has great literary qualities.

c (*fonction*) position; (*††: noblesse*) quality. **sa ~ de directeur** his position as manager; **en sa ~ de maire** in his capacity as mayor; (*Admin*) **vos nom, prénom et ~** surname, forename and occupation; (*Jur*) **avoir ~ pour** to have authority to; (*frm*) **ès ~s** in an official capacity; **homme de ~††** man of quality.
quand [kɑ̃] 1 conj a (*lorsque*) when. **~ ce sera fini, nous irons prendre un café** when it's finished we'll go and have a coffee; **prête-le-moi pour ~ j'en aurai besoin** lend it to me for when I'll (next) need it; **sais-tu de ~ était sa dernière lettre?** do you know when his last letter was written? *ou* what was the date of his last letter?; **~ je te le disais!** didn't I tell you so!, I told you so!; **~ je pense que ...!** when I think that ...; (*hum*) **~ les poules auront des dents** when pigs learn to fly, when pigs have wings; (*Prov*) **~ le vin est tiré, il faut le boire** once the wine is drawn it

must be drunk, once the first step is taken there's no going back; (*Prov*) ~ **le chat n'est pas là, les souris dansent** when the cat's away the mice will play (*Prov*); (*Prov*) ~ **on parle du loup, on en voit la queue** talk of the devil.

b (*alors que*) when. **pourquoi ne pas acheter une voiture ~ nous pouvons nous le permettre?** why not buy a car when we can afford it?; **pourquoi vivre ici ~ tu pourrais avoir une belle maison?** why live here when you could have a beautiful house?

c ~ **bien même** even though *ou* if; ~ **bien même tu aurais raison, je n'irais pas** even though *ou* even if you were right, I wouldn't go.

d ~ **même: malgré tous ses défauts elle est ~ même gentille** in spite of all her faults she's still nice *ou* she's nice nonetheless; **tu aurais ~ même pu me le dire!** even so, you might have told me; ~ **même, il exagère!** really, he overdoes it!; **quel crétin ~ même!** what a downright idiot!, really, what an idiot!; (*lit, hum*) **merci ~ même** thanks all the same *ou* just the same; **tu aurais pu venir ~ même** even so you could have come, you could have come all the same *ou* just the same.

2 **adv** when. ~ **pars-tu?**, ~ **est-ce que tu pars?, tu pars ~?*** when are you leaving?; **dis-moi ~ tu pars** tell me when you're leaving *ou* when you'll be leaving; **à ~ le voyage?** when is the journey?; **c'est pour ~?** *[devoir]* when is it due? *ou* for?; *[rendez-vous]* when is it?; *[naissance]* when is it to be?; **ça date de ~?** *[événement]* when did it take place?; *[lettre]* what's the date of it?, when was it written?; *voir* **depuis, importer**[2]**, jusque.**

quant [kɑ̃] 1 **adv:** ~ **à** (*pour ce qui est de*) as for, as to; (*au sujet de*) as regards, regarding; ~ **à moi** as for me; ~ **à affirmer cela** ... as for stating that ...; **je n'ai rien su ~ à ce qui s'est passé** I knew nothing about *ou* of what happened; ~ **à cela, tu peux en être sûr** you can be quite sure about that; ~ **à cela, je n'en sais rien** as to that *ou* as regards that *ou* as far as that goes, I know nothing about it. 2 **comp** ▸**quant-à-moi nm inv, quant-à-soi nm inv** reserve; **il est resté sur son quant-à-soi** he remained aloof, he kept his reserve, he held himself *ou* kept himself aloof.

quanta [k(w)ɑ̃ta] **nmpl de quantum.**

quantième [kɑ̃tjɛm] **nm** (*Admin*) day (*of the month*).

quantifiable [kɑ̃tifjabl] **adj** quantifiable. **facteurs non ~s** factors which cannot be quantified, unquantifiable factors.

quantificateur [kɑ̃tifikatœʀ] **nm** quantifier.

quantification [kɑ̃tifikasjɔ̃] **nf** (*voir* **quantifier**) quantification; quantization.

quantifier [kɑ̃tifje] 7 **vt** (*gén, Philos*) to quantify; (*Phys*) to quantize.

quantifieur [kɑ̃tifjœʀ] **nm = quantificateur.**

quantique [k(w)ɑ̃tik] **adj** quantum (*épith*).

quantitatif, -ive [kɑ̃titatif, iv] **adj** quantitative.

quantitativement [kɑ̃titativmɑ̃] **adv** quantitatively.

quantité [kɑ̃tite] **nf** a (*somme, nombre*) quantity, amount. **la ~ d'eau nécessaire à l'organisme** the amount *ou* quantity of water necessary for the body; **il s'indignait de la ~ de gens qui ne paient pas leurs impôts** he was outraged by the number of people who don't pay their taxes; **en ~s industrielles** in massive *ou* huge amounts.

b (*grand nombre*) **(une) ~ de** *raisons, personnes* a great many, a lot of; **des ~s *ou* (une) ~ de gens croient que** a great many people *ou* a lot of people believe that; ~ **d'indices révèlent que** many signs *ou* a (great) number of signs indicate that; **il y a des fruits en (grande) ~** there is fruit in plenty, fruit is in good supply; **il y a eu des accidents en ~** there have been a great number of *ou* a lot of *ou* a great many accidents; **du travail en ~** a great deal of work.

c (*Ling, Sci*) quantity. (*Sci*) ~ **négligeable** negligible quantity *ou* amount; (*fig*) **considérer qn comme ~ négligeable** to consider sb as totally insignificant, consider sb of minimal importance, disregard sb.

quantum [k(w)ɑ̃tɔm], **pl quanta nm** (*Jur, Phys*) quantum. **la théorie des quanta** the quantum theory.

quarantaine [kaʀɑ̃tɛn] **nf** a (*âge, nombre*) about forty; *voir* **soixantaine.** b (*Méd, Naut*) quarantine. **mettre en ~** (*lit*) *malade, animal, navire* to quarantine, put in quarantine; (*fig: ostraciser*) to send to Coventry; *voir* **pavillon.**

quarante [kaʀɑ̃t] **adj, nm inv** forty. **les Q~** *the members of the French Academy;* (*disque*) **un ~-cinq tours** a single, a forty-five; *pour loc voir* **soixante, an.**

quarantenaire [kaʀɑ̃tnɛʀ] 1 **adj** *période* forty-year (*épith*); (*Méd, Naut*) quarantine (*épith*). 2 **nm** (*anniversaire*) fortieth anniversary.

quarantième [kaʀɑ̃tjɛm] **adj, nmf** fortieth. (*Naut*) **les ~s rugissants** the Roaring Forties.

quarantièmement [kaʀɑ̃tjɛmmɑ̃] **adv** in the fortieth place.

quark [kwaʀk] **nm** quark.

quart [kaʀ] 1 **nm** a (*fraction*) quarter. **un ~ de poulet/de fromage** a quarter chicken/cheese; **un ~ de beurre** a quarter (kilo) of butter; **un ~ de vin** a quarter-litre bottle of wine; **un ~ de siècle** a quarter century; **un kilo/une livre un ~ *ou* et ~** a kilo/a pound and a quarter; **on n'a pas fait le ~ du travail** we haven't done a quarter of the work; **au ~ de poil*** *travail* perfect; *travailler* perfectly; *voir* **quatre, tiers, trois.**

b (*Mil: gobelet*) beaker (*of 1/4 litre capacity*).

c ~ **d'heure** quarter of an hour; **3 heures moins le ~** (a) quarter to 3; **3 heures et ~, 3 heures un ~** (a) quarter past 3; **il est le ~/moins le ~** it's (a) quarter past/(a) quarter to; **de ~ d'heure en ~ d'heure** every quarter of an hour; **passer un mauvais *ou* sale ~ d'heure** to have a bad *ou* nasty time of it; **il lui a fait passer un mauvais ~ d'heure** he gave him a bad time; **un ~ de seconde** (*lit*) a quarter of a second; (*fig*) a split second; **en un ~ de seconde** (*lit*) in a quarter of a second; (*fig*) in no time at all.

d (*Naut*) watch. **être de ~** to keep the watch; **prendre le ~** to take the watch; **de ~** *homme, matelot* on watch; **officier de ~** officer of the watch; **petit ~** dogwatch; **grand ~** six-hour watch.

2 **comp** ▸**quart de cercle** quarter-circle ▸**quarts de finale** (*Sport*) quarter finals; **être en quarts de finale** to be in the quarter finals ▸**le quart(-)monde nm** the Fourth World ▸**quart-de-rond nm (pl quarts-de-rond)** ovolo, quarter round ▸**quart de soupir** (*Mus*) semi-quaver rest (*Brit*), sixteenth rest (*US*) ▸**quart de ton** (*Mus*) quarter tone ▸**quart de tour** quarter turn; **donner un quart de tour à un bouton** to turn a knob round a quarter (of the way), give a knob a quarter turn; (*Aut*) **partir *ou* démarrer au quart de tour** to start (up) first time; **comprendre au quart de tour*** to understand first time off *ou* straight off*, be quick on the uptake.

quarte [k(w)aʀt] 1 **nf** (*Escrime*) quarte; (*Cartes*) quart; (*Mus*) fourth; (*Hist: deux pintes*) quart. 2 **adj f** *voir* **fièvre.**

quarté [k(w)aʀte] **nm** *French system of forecast betting on four horses in a race.*

quarteron, -onne [kaʀtəʀɔ̃, ɔn] 1 **nm,f** (*métis*) quadroon. 2 **nm** (*péj: groupe*) small *ou* insignificant band, minor group.

quartette [k(w)aʀtɛt] **nm** (*Mus*) jazz quartet(te).

quartier [kaʀtje] 1 **nm** a *[ville]* (*Admin: division*) district, area; (*gén: partie*) neighbourhood, district, area, quarter. ~ **commerçant/résidentiel** shopping/residential area *ou* quarter; **les vieux ~s de la ville** the old quarter *ou* part of the town; **les gens du ~** the local people, the people of the area *ou* district *ou* neighbourhood; **vous êtes du ~?** do you come from the area? *ou* district? *ou* neighbourhood?, are you (a) local?*; **de ~** *cinéma, épicier* local (*épith*); **le ~ est/ouest de la ville** the east/west end *ou* side of (the) town; **le ~ des affaires** the business district *ou* quarter; **le ~ latin** the Latin Quarter; *voir* **bas**[1]**, beau.**

b (*Mil*) ~(s) quarters; **rentrer au(x) ~(s)** to return to quarters; **avoir ~(s) libre(s)** (*Mil*) to have leave from barracks; (*Scol*) to be free *ou* off (for a few hours); (*lit, fig*) **prendre ses ~s d'hiver** to go into winter quarters; (*fig*) **c'est là que nous tenons nos ~s** here's where we have our headquarters (*fig*) *ou* where we hang out‡.

c (*portion*) *[bœuf]* quarter; *[viande]* large piece, chunk; *[fruit]* piece, segment. (*lit, fig*) **mettre en ~s** to tear to pieces.

d (*Astron, Hér*) quarter.

e (†: *grâce, pitié*) quarter†. **demander/faire ~** to ask for/give quarter; **ne pas faire de ~** to give no quarter; **pas de ~!** show no mercy!

2 **comp** ▸**quartier général** (*Mil, fig*) headquarters; (*Mil*) **grand quartier général** general headquarters ▸**quartier de haute sécurité** *[prison]* high *ou* maximum *ou* top security wing ▸**quartier-maître nm (pl quartiers-maîtres)** (*Naut*) ≃ leading seaman; **quartier-maître de 1re classe** leading rating (*Brit*), petty officer third class (*US*) ▸**quartier de noblesse** (*lit*) degree of noble lineage (*representing one generation*); (*fig*) **avoir ses quartiers de noblesse** to be well established and respected, have earned one's colours ▸**quartier réservé** red-light district.

quartile [kwaʀtil] **nm** quartile.

quarto [kwaʀto] **adv** fourthly.

quartz [kwaʀts] **nm** quartz. **montre** *etc* **à ~** quartz watch *etc.*

quartzite [kwaʀtsit] **nm** quartzite.

quasar [kazaʀ] **nm** quasar.

quasi[1] [kazi] **nm** (*Culin*) *cut of meat from upper part of leg of veal.*

quasi[2] [kazi] 1 **adv** almost, nearly. 2 **préf** near, quasi- (*surtout US*). **~-certitude/-obscurité** near certainty/darkness; (*Aviat*) **~-collision** near miss. **la ~-totalité des dépenses** almost all (of) the expenditure; **~-contrat** quasi-contract; **~-délit** technical offence (*Brit*) *ou* offense (*US*).

quasiment [kazimɑ̃] **adv** almost, nearly. **c'est ~ fait** it's almost *ou* nearly done, it's as good as done, it's just about done.

Quasimodo [kazimɔdo] **nf: la ~, le dimanche de ~** Low Sunday.

quaternaire [kwatɛʀnɛʀ] 1 **adj** (*gén, Chim*) quaternary; (*Géol*) Quaternary. 2 **nm** (*Géol*) Quaternary.

quatorze [katɔʀz] **adj, nm inv** fourteen. **avant/après (la guerre de) ~** before/after the First World War; **le ~ juillet** the Fourteenth of July, Bastille Day, *French national holiday; pour autres loc voir* **six, chercher.**

quatorzième [katɔʀzjɛm] **adj, nmf** fourteenth; *pour loc voir* **sixième.**

quatorzièmement [katɔʀzjɛmmɑ̃] **adv** in the fourteenth place, fourteenthly.

quatrain [katʀɛ̃] **nm** quatrain.

quatre [katʀ] 1 **adj, nm inv** four. **une robe de ~ sous** a cheap dress; **il avait ~ sous d'économies** he had a modest amount of savings; **s'il avait ~ sous de bon sens** if he had a scrap *ou* modicum of common sense; **jouer aux ~ coins** to play "the four corners" game (*the player who is "he" must try to gain possession of one of the corners*); (*lit, fig*) **aux ~ coins de** in the four corners of; (*Mus*) **à ~ mains (adj)** *morceau* for four hands, four-handed; **(adv)** *jouer* four-handed; **à ~ pattes** on all fours; **se**

disperser aux ~ vents to scatter to the four winds; **être tiré à ~ épingles** to be dressed up to the nines; **un de ces ~ (matins)*** one of these (fine) days; **faire les ~ cents coups** to sow one's wild oats, get into a lot of trouble; **tomber les ~ fers en l'air** to fall flat on one's back; **faire ses ~ volontés** to do exactly as one pleases; **faire les ~ volontés de qn** to satisfy sb's every whim; **dire à qn ses ~ vérités** to tell sb a few plain *ou* home truths; (*Pol*) **les ~ grands** the Big Four; **monter/descendre (l'escalier) ~ à ~** to rush up/down the stairs four at a time; **manger comme ~** to eat like a wolf *ou* enough for four (people); **se mettre** *ou* **se couper en ~ pour qn** to go to a great deal of trouble for sb, bend over backwards to help sb*, go out of one's way for sb, put o.s. out for sb; **elle se tenait à ~ pour ne pas rire/pour ne pas le gifler** it was all she could do *ou* she was doing all she could to keep from laughing/ smacking him; **ne pas y aller par ~ chemins** not to beat about the bush, make no bones about it; **entre ~ murs** within *ou* between four walls; *voir* **couper, entre, trèfle** *etc; pour autres loc voir* **six.**

2 **comp** ▶**quatre barré** **nm** (*Naut*) coxed four ▶**quatre(-cent)-vingt-et-un** (*Dés*) **nm** *dice game in casinos and cafés* ▶**quatre-épices** **nm inv** allspice ▶**quatre heures** **nm inv** (children's) afternoon tea (*Brit*) *ou* snack ▶**(mesure à) quatre-huit** **nm inv** (*Mus*) common time ▶**quatre-mâts** **nm inv** four-master ▶**quatre-quarts** **nm inv** (*Culin*) pound cake ▶**quatre-quatre** **adj inv, nm inv** four-wheel drive ▶**quatre sans barreur** (*Naut*) coxless four ▶**quatre-vingt-dix** **adj, nm inv** ninety ▶**quatre-vingt-dixième** **adj, nmf** ninetieth ▶**quatre-vingtième** **adj, nmf** eightieth ▶**quatre-vingt-onze** **adj, nm inv** ninety-one ▶**quatre-vingt-onzième** **adj, nmf** ninety-first ▶**quatre-vingts** **adj, nm inv** eighty ▶**quatre-vingt-un** **adj, nm inv** eighty-one ▶**quatre-vingt-unième** **adj, nmf** eighty-first.

quatrième [katʀijɛm] 1 **adj** fourth. **le ~ pouvoir** the fourth estate; (*fig*) **faire qch en ~ vitesse** to do sth at great speed. 2 **nmf** (*joueur de cartes*) fourth player. 3 **nf** (*Aut: vitesse*) fourth gear; (*Cartes: quarte*) quart; (*Scol: classe*) ≃ third form *ou* year (*Brit*), third year (in junior high school) (*US*); *[livre]* **~ de couverture** back cover; *pour autres loc voir* **sixième.**

quatrièmement [katʀijɛmmɑ̃] **adv** fourthly, in the fourth place.

quatrillion [k(w)atʀiljɔ̃] **nm** quadrillion (*Brit*), septillion (*US*).

quattrocento [kwatʀotʃɛnto] **nm: le ~** quattrocento.

quatuor [kwatɥɔʀ] **nm** (*œuvre, musiciens, fig*) quartet(te). **~ à cordes** string quartet.

que [kə] 1 **conj** a (*introduisant subordonnée complétive*) that (*souvent omis; avec vb de volonté on emploie la proposition infinitive*). **elle sait ~ tu es prêt** she knows (that) you're ready; **il est agréable qu'il fasse beau** it's nice that the weather's fine; **il est possible qu'elle vienne** she may be coming, it's possible (that) she'll come; **c'est dommage qu'il pleuve** it's a pity (that) it's raining; **l'idée qu'il pourrait échouer** the idea of him *ou* his failing, the idea that he might fail; **je veux/j'aimerais qu'il vienne** I want him/would like him to come; **je ne veux pas qu'il vienne** I don't want him to come; **j'aimerais qu'il ne vienne pas** I'd rather he didn't come; *voir* **craindre, douter, peur** *etc.*

b (*remplaçant si, quand, comme etc: non traduit*) **si vous êtes sages et qu'il fasse beau, nous sortirons** if you are good and the weather is fine, we'll go out; **si vous le voyez ou ~ vous lui téléphoniez ...** if you see him or phone him ...; **il vous recevra quand il rentrera et qu'il aura déjeuné** he'll see you when he comes home and he's had a meal; **comme la maison était petite et qu'il n'y avait pas de jardin** as the house was small and there was no garden; **bien qu'il soit en retard et ~ nous soyons pressés** although he's late and we're in a hurry.

c (*hypothèse*) **il ira qu'il le veuille ou non, il ira qu'il le veuille ou qu'il ne le veuille pas** he'll go whether he wants to or not *ou* whether he likes it or not; (*conséquence*) **il cria si fort qu'on le fit sortir** he shouted so loudly that he was sent out; **la classe n'est pas si avancée qu'il ne puisse suivre** the class is not too advanced for him to keep up *ou* is not so advanced that he can't keep up; (*but*) **tenez-le qu'il ne tombe pas** hold him in case he falls *ou* so that he won't fall; **venez ~ nous causions** come along and we'll have *ou* so that we can have a chat; (*temps*) **elle venait à peine de sortir qu'il se mit à pleuvoir** she had no sooner gone out than it started raining, she had hardly *ou* just gone out when it started raining; **ils ne se connaissaient pas depuis 10 minutes qu'ils étaient déjà amis** they had known each other for only 10 minutes and already they were friends; **ça fait 2 ans qu'il est là** he has been here (for) 2 years; **ça fait 2 ans qu'il est parti** it is 2 years since he left, he left 2 years ago; *voir* **attendre, ne.**

d (*3e personne: ordre, souhait, résignation etc*) **qu'il se taise!** I wish he would be quiet!; **~ la lumière soit** let there be light; **~ la guerre finisse!** if only the war would end!; **eh bien, qu'il vienne!** all right, he can come *ou* let him come; **~ m'importe!** what do I care?, I don't care!; **~ le Seigneur ait pitié de lui!** (may) the Lord have mercy upon him.

e (*comparaison*) (*avec plus, moins*) than; (*avec aussi, autant, tel*) as. **la campagne est plus reposante ~ la mer** the country is more restful than the sea; **il est plus petit qu'elle** he's smaller than her *ou* than she is; **elle est tout aussi capable ~ vous** she's just as capable as you (are); **j'ai laissé la maison telle ~ je l'avais trouvée** I left the house (just) as I found it; *voir* **bien, condition, moins** *etc.*

2 **adv** a (*excl*) (*devant adj, adv*) how; (*devant n sg*) what a; (*devant npl*) what a lot of. **~ tu es lent!** aren't you slow!; **ce ~ tu es lent!*** you're so slow!; **qu'est-ce ~ tu es lent!** how slow you are!; **~ de monde, ce qu'il y a du monde*, qu'est-ce qu'il y a comme monde** what a crowd (there is)!, what a lot of people!; **~ de mal vous vous donnez!** what a lot of trouble you're taking!; **qu'il joue bien!, ce qu'il joue bien!*, qu'est-ce qu'il joue bien!** doesn't he play well!, what a good player he is!

b (*avec ne: excl ou interrog*) why. **~ n'es-tu venu me voir?** why didn't you come to see me?

3 **pron** a (*relatif: objet direct*) (*personne*) that, whom (*frm*); (*chose, animal*) which, that (*gén omis*); (*temps*) when. **Paul, ~ je ne voyais même pas, m'a appelé** Paul, who *ou* whom I couldn't even see, called me; **les enfants ~ tu vois jouer dans la rue** the children (that *ou* whom) you see playing in the street; **c'est le concert le plus beau ~ j'aie jamais entendu** it's the finest concert (that) I have ever heard; **l'étiquette, ~ j'avais pourtant bien collée, est tombée** the label, which I stuck on properly, fell off all the same; **la raison qu'il a donnée** the reason (that *ou* which) he gave; **tu te souviens de l'hiver qu'il a fait si froid?*** do you remember the winter (when) it was so cold?; **un jour/ un été ~*** one day/one summer when.

b (*attrib*) **quel homme charmant ~ votre voisin!** what a charming man your neighbour is; **distrait qu'il est, il n'a rien vu** dreamy as he is, he didn't notice anything; **pour ignorante qu'elle soit** ignorant though she may be, however ignorant she is *ou* may be; **c'est un inconvénient ~ de ne pas avoir de voiture** it's inconvenient not having a car; **plein d'attentions qu'il était ce jeune homme*** he was so considerate that young man was*; **de brune qu'elle était, elle est devenue blonde** once brunette *ou* brunette at one time, she has now turned blonde; **en bon fils qu'il est** being the good son (that) he is.

c (*interrog: dir, indir*) what; (*discriminatif*) which. **~ fais-tu?, qu'est-ce ~ tu fais?** what are you doing?; **qu'est-ce qui vous prend?** what has come over you?; **qu'en sais-tu?** what do you know?; **qu'est-ce qu'il y a?, qu'est-ce?** what is it?, what's the matter?; **qu'est-ce ~ c'est ~ cette histoire?** what's all this about?, what's it all about?; **il ne dit pas ce qu'il fait** he doesn't say what he's doing; **je pense ~ oui/non** I think/ don't think so; **mais il n'a pas de voiture! — il dit ~ si** but he has no car! — he says he has; **qu'est-ce ~ tu préfères, le rouge ou le noir?** which (one) do you prefer, the red or the black?; *voir* **ce, depuis, voici.**

d (*loc*) **je ne l'y ai pas autorisé, ~ je sache** I didn't give him permission to do so, as far as I know, I don't know that *ou* I'm not aware that I gave him permission to do so; **(il n'est pas venu) ~ je sache** (he didn't come) as far as I know *ou* am aware; **qu'il dit!*** that's what he says!, that's his story!, so he says!; **~ tu crois!*** that's what you think!; **~ oui!** yes indeed!, quite so!; **~ non!** certainly not!, not at all!; **mais il n'en veut pas! — ~ si/non** but he doesn't want any! — yes, he does/no, he doesn't.

Québec [kebɛk] 1 **n** (*ville*) Quebec. 2 **nm** (*province*) **le ~** Quebec.

québécisme [kebesism] **nm** *expression (or word etc) used in Quebec.*

québécois, e [kebekwa, waz] 1 **adj** Quebec (*épith*). **le Parti ~** the Parti Québécois. 2 **nm** (*Ling*) Quebec French. 3 **nm,f: Q~(e)** Quebecker, Quebecer, Québécois (*Can*).

Queensland [kwinzlɑ̃d] **nm** Queensland.

quel, quelle [kɛl] 1 **adj** a (*interrog: dir, indir*) (*être animé: attrib*) who; (*être animé: épith*) what; (*chose*) what. **~ est cet auteur?** who is that author?; **sur ~ auteur va-t-il parler?** what author is he going to talk about?; **quelles ont été les raisons de son départ?** what were the reasons for his leaving? *ou* departure?; **dans ~s pays êtes-vous allé?** what countries have you been to?; **lui avez-vous dit à quelle adresse (il faut) envoyer la lettre?** have you told him the *ou* what address to send the letter to?; **j'ignore ~ est l'auteur de ces poèmes** I don't know who wrote these poems *ou* who the author of these poems is.

b (*interrog discriminatif*) which. **~ acteur préférez-vous?** which actor do you prefer?; **~ est le vin le moins cher des trois?** which wine is the cheapest of the three?

c (*excl*) what. **quelle surprise/coïncidence!** what a surprise/ coincidence!; **~ courage/temps!** what courage/weather!; **~s charmants enfants!** what charming children!; **~ dommage qu'il soit parti!** what a pity he's gone!; **~ imbécile je suis!** what a fool I am!; **quelle chance!** what (a stroke of) luck!; **~ toupet!*** what (a) nerve!; **~ sale temps!** what rotten weather!; **il a vu ~s amis fidèles il avait** he saw what faithful friends he had; **j'ai remarqué avec quelle attention ils écoutaient** I noticed how attentively they were listening.

d (*relatif*) (*être animé*) whoever; (*chose*) whatever; (*discriminatif*) whichever, whatever. **quelle que soit** *ou* **quelle que puisse être votre décision, écrivez-nous** write to us whatever your decision (may be) *ou* whatever you decide; **~ que soit le train que vous preniez, vous arriverez trop tard** whichever *ou* whatever train you take, you will be too late; **quelles que soient les conséquences** whatever the consequences (may be); **quelle que soit la personne qui vous répondra** whoever answers you, whichever person answers you; **~ qu'il soit, le prix sera toujours trop élevé** whatever the price (is), it will still be too high; **les hommes, ~s qu'ils soient** men, whoever they may be.

2 pron interrog which. **de tous ces enfants, ~ est le plus intelligent?** of all these children which (one) is the most intelligent?; **des deux solutions quelle est celle que vous préférez?** of the two solutions, which (one) do you prefer?

quelconque [kɛlkɔ̃k] adj a (*n'importe quel*) some (or other), any. **une lettre envoyée par un ami ~ ou par un ~ de ses amis** a letter sent by some friend of his *ou* by some friend or other (of his); **choisis un stylo ~ parmi ceux-là** choose any pen from among those; **sous un prétexte ~** on some pretext or other; **pour une raison ~** for some reason (or other); **à partir d'un point ~ du cercle** from any point on the circle; *voir* **triangle**.

b (*moindre*) **un** *ou* **une ~** any, the least *ou* slightest; **il n'a pas manifesté un désir ~ d'y aller** he didn't show the slightest *ou* least desire *ou* any desire to go; **avez-vous une ~ idée de l'endroit où ça se trouve?** have you any idea where it might be?

c (*médiocre*) *repas* poor, indifferent; *élève, devoir* poor; *acteur* poor, second-rate. **c'est un repas/devoir ~** this meal/piece of homework isn't up to much*, this is a poor meal/piece of homework; **c'est quelqu'un de très ~** (*laid*) he's a very plain-looking *ou* ordinary-looking sort of person; (*ordinaire*) he's a very ordinary *ou* nondescript sort of person.

quelque [kɛlk(ə)] 1 adj indéf a (*NonC*) some. **il habite à ~ distance d'ici** he lives some distance *ou* way from here; **cela fait ~ temps que je ne l'ai vu** I haven't seen him for some time *ou* for a while, it's some time *ou* a while since I've seen him; **il faut trouver ~ autre solution** we'll have to find some other solution; **j'ai ~ peine à croire cela** I find it rather *ou* somewhat *ou* a little difficult to believe; **avec ~ impatience/inquiétude** with some impatience/anxiety; **désirez-vous ~ autre chose?** would you like something *ou* anything else?

b (*pl*) **~s** a few, some; **M. Dupont va vous dire ~s mots** Mr Dupont is going to say a few words (to you); **~s milliers (de)** a few thousand; **il ne peut rester que ~s instants** he can only stay (for) a few moments; **~s autres** some *ou* a few others; **avez-vous ~s feuilles de papier à me passer?** have you any *ou* some *ou* a few sheets of paper you could let me have?

c (*pl avec art: petit nombre*) few. **les ~s enfants qui étaient venus** the few children who had come; **ces ~s poèmes** these few poems; **les ~s centaines/milliers de personnes qui ...** the few hundred/thousand people who ... .

d **~ ... que** whatever; (*discriminatif*) whichever, whatever; **de ~ façon que l'on envisage le problème** whatever *ou* whichever way you look at the problem; **par ~ temps qu'il fasse** whatever the weather (may be *ou* is like).

e **~ part** somewhere; **posez votre paquet ~ part dans un coin** put your parcel down in a corner somewhere; (*euph:* = **W.-C.**) **je vais ~ part** I'm going to wash my hands (*euph*); (* *euph: derrière*) **tu veux mon pied ~ part?** do you want a kick somewhere where it hurts?* (*euph*) *ou* you know where?* (*euph*).

f **en ~ sorte** (*pour ainsi dire*) as it were, so to speak; (*bref*) in a word; (*d'une certaine manière*) in a way; **le liquide s'était en ~ sorte solidifié** the liquid had solidified as it were *ou* so to speak; **en ~ sorte, tu refuses** in a word, you refuse; **on pourrait dire en ~ sorte que ...** you could say in a way that ... .

2 adv a (*environ, à peu près*) some, about. **il y a ~ 20 ans qu'il enseigne ici** he has been teaching here for some *ou* about 20 years *ou* for 20 years or so; **ça a augmenté de ~ 50 F** it's gone up by about 50 francs *ou* by 50 francs or so *ou* by some 50 francs.

b **et ~s*: 20 kg et ~s** a bit over 20 kg*; **il doit être 3 heures et ~s** it must be a bit after 3*.

c **~ peu** rather, somewhat; **~ peu déçu** rather *ou* somewhat disappointed; **il est ~ peu menteur** he is something of *ou* a bit of a liar.

d (*littér*) **~ ... que** however; **~ lourde que soit la tâche** however heavy the task may be.

quelque chose [kɛlkəʃoz] pron indéf a something; (*avec interrog*) anything, something. **~ d'extraordinaire** something extraordinary; **~ d'autre** something else; **puis-je faire ~ pour vous?** is there anything *ou* something I can do for you?; **il a ~ (qui ne va pas)** (*maladie*) there's something wrong *ou* the matter with him; (*ennuis*) there's something the matter (with him); **vous prendrez bien ~ (à boire)** you'll have something to drink; **il est ~ aux PTT*** he has some sort of a job in the Post Office, he's got something to do with the Post Office; **il/ça y est pour ~** he/it has got something to do with it; **il y a ~ comme une semaine** something like a week ago, a week or so ago.

b (*: *intensif*) **il a plu ~!** it rained something dreadful!*, it didn't half rain!* (*Brit*); **je tiens ~ (de bien) comme rhume!** I've got a really dreadful cold, I don't half have a (dreadful) cold* (*Brit*); **il se prend pour ~** he thinks he's quite something.

c (*loc*) (*lit, fig*) **faire ~ à qn** to have an effect on sb; **ça alors, c'est ~!** that's (a bit) too much!, that's a bit stiff!*; **je t'ai apporté un petit ~** I've brought you a little something; *voir* **déjà, dire**.

quelquefois [kɛlkəfwa] adv sometimes, occasionally, at times.

quelques-uns, -unes [kɛlkəzœ̃, yn] pron indéf pl some, a few. **~ de nos lecteurs/ses amis** some *ou* a few of our readers/his friends; **privilège réservé à ~** privilege reserved for a very few.

quelqu'un [kɛlkœ̃] pron indéf somebody, someone; (*avec interrog*) anybody, anyone. **~ d'autre** somebody *ou* someone else; **c'est ~ de sûr/d'important** he's a reliable/an important person, he's someone reliable/important; **il faudrait ~ de plus** one more person *ou* somebody *ou* someone else would be needed; **~ pourrait-il répondre?** could somebody answer?; **ce savant, c'est ~** this scientist is (a) somebody; **ça alors, c'est ~!*†** that's (a bit) too much!, that's a bit stiff!*

quémander [kemɑ̃de] 1 vt *argent, faveur* to beg for; *louanges* to beg *ou* fish *ou* angle for.

quémandeur, -euse [kemɑ̃dœʀ, øz] nm,f (*littér*) beggar.

qu'en-dira-t-on [kɑ̃diʀatɔ̃] nm inv (*commérage*) gossip. **il se moque du ~** he doesn't care what people say *ou* about gossip.

quenelle [kənɛl] nf (*Culin*) quenelle.

quenotte [kənɔt] nf (*langage enfantin*) tooth, toothy-peg (*Brit langage enfantin*).

quenouille [kənuj] nf distaff; *voir* **tomber**.

quéquette‡ [kekɛt] nf willy‡, penis.

querelle [kəʀɛl] nf a (*dispute*) quarrel. **~ d'amoureux** lovers' tiff; **~ d'ivrognes** drunken row; **~ d'Allemand, mauvaise ~** quarrel over nothing, unreasonable quarrel; **chercher une ~ d'Allemand** *ou* **une mauvaise ~ à qn** to pick a quarrel with sb for nothing *ou* for no reason at all; **~ de famille** *ou* **familiale** family quarrel *ou* squabble; (*Pol*) **la ~ sur l'avortement** the abortion debate *ou* issue; *voir* **chercher, vider.** b (*††, littér: cause, parti*) cause, quarrel†. **épouser** *ou* **embrasser la ~ de qn** to take up *ou* fight sb's cause, fight sb's quarrels.

quereller [kəʀele] 1 1 vt (*†: gronder*) to scold. 2 **se quereller** vpr to quarrel (with one another). **se ~ au sujet** *ou* **à propos de qch** to quarrel *ou* squabble over *ou* about sth.

querelleur, -euse [kəʀelœʀ, øz] adj quarrelsome.

quérir [keʀiʀ] 21 vt (*littér: chercher*) **envoyer** *ou* **faire ~ qn** to summon sb, bid sb (to) come†; **aller ~ qn** to go seek sb†, go in quest of sb†.

questeur [kɛstœʀ] nm (*Antiq*) quaestor; (*Pol française*) questeur, *administrative and financial officer elected to the French Parliament*.

question [kɛstjɔ̃] nf a (*demande*) (*gén*) question; (*pour lever un doute*) query, question. (*Pol*) **~ écrite/orale** written/oral question; **sans (poser de) ~s** without asking any questions; without raising any queries; **évidemment! cette ~!** *ou* **quelle ~!** obviously! what a question!; **~ piège** (*d'apparence facile*) trick question; (*pour nuire à qn*) loaded question; **~ subsidiaire** tiebreaker, *decisive question in a competition;* (*Pol*) **poser la ~ de confiance** to ask for a vote of confidence.

b (*problème*) question, matter, issue. **la ~ est délicate** it's a delicate question *ou* matter; **la ~ est de savoir si** the question is whether; **~s économiques/sociales** economic/social questions *ou* matters *ou* issues; (*Presse*) **~ d'actualité** topical question; **la ~ sociale** the social question *ou* issue; **sortir de la ~** to stray *ou* wander from the point; **la ~ n'est pas là** that's not the point; **c'est toute la ~, c'est la grosse ~*** that's the big question, that's the crux of the matter, that's the whole point; **il n'y a pas de ~, c'est lui le meilleur** he is indisputably *ou* unquestionably the best, without question he's the best, there's no question about it — he's the best; **cela ne fait pas ~** there's no question about it; **c'est une ~ de temps** it's a question *ou* matter of time; **c'est une ~ d'heures/de vie ou de mort/d'habitude** it's a matter *ou* question of hours/of life or death/of habit; (*ordre du jour*) **"autres ~s"** "any other business"; *voir* **autre**.

c (*: *en ce qui concerne*) **~ argent** as far as money goes, moneywise*; **l'aider oui, mais ~ de tout faire, sûrement pas** help him I will but as for doing everything for him, I certainly won't.

d **de quoi est-il ~?** what is it about?; **il fut d'abord ~ du budget** first they spoke about *ou* discussed the budget; **il est ~ de lui comme ministre** *ou* **qu'il soit ministre** there's some question *ou* talk of his being *ou* becoming a minister; **il n'est plus ~ de ce fait dans la suite** no further mention of this fact is made subsequently, there is no further reference to this fact thereafter; **il n'est pas ~ que nous y renoncions/d'y renoncer** there's no question of our *ou* us giving it up/of giving it up; **il n'en est pas ~!** there's no question of it!; **moi y aller? pas ~!*** me go? nothing doing!* *ou* no way!*

e **en ~** in question; **hors de ~** out of the question; **la personne/le livre en ~** the person/book in question; **mettre** *ou* **remettre en ~** *autorité* to question, challenge; *science* to question, call *ou* bring in(to) question; **c'est notre vie même qui est en ~ ici** it's our very lives that are at stake here; **tout est remis en ~ à cause du mauvais temps** there is a question mark over the whole plan because of the bad weather, the bad weather throws the whole thing back into question; **le projet a été remis en ~ une fois de plus** the scheme was back in the melting pot *ou* was called into doubt yet again; **la remise en ~ de nos accords** the renewed doubt surrounding our agreements, the fact that our agreements are once again in doubt *ou* being called into question; **ils veulent remettre en ~ l'entrée de ce pays dans la CEE** they want to revive *ou* reopen the issue of this country's joining the EEC.

f (*Hist: torture*) question. **soumettre qn à la ~, infliger la ~ à qn** to put sb to the question.

questionnaire [kɛstjɔnɛʀ] nm questionnaire. (*Scol etc*) **~ à choix multiple** multiple choice question paper.

questionner [kɛstjɔne] 1 vt (*interroger*) to question (*sur* about). **arrête de ~ toujours comme ça** stop pestering me with questions all the time, stop questioning me all the time.

questionneur, -euse [kɛstjɔnœʀ, øz] nm,f questioner.

quête [kɛt] nf a (*collecte*) collection. **faire la ~** *[prêtre]* to take (the) collection; *[jongleur]* to go round with the hat; *[quêteur]* to collect for charity. b (*littér: recherche*) *[Graal]* quest (*de* for); *[absolu]* pursuit (*de* of). **âme en ~ d'absolu** soul in pursuit *ou* quest *ou* search of the absolute. c **se mettre en ~ de** *pain* to set out to look for *ou* to find, go in search of; *appartement* to (go on the) hunt for; **être en ~ de travail** to be looking for *ou* seeking work.

quêter [kete] 1 1 vi (*à l'église*) to take the collection; (*dans la rue*) to collect money. **~ pour les aveugles** to collect for the blind. 2 vt *louanges* to seek (after), fish *ou* angle for; *suffrages* to seek; *sourire, regard* to seek, try to win.

quêteur, -euse [kɛtœʀ, øz] nm,f (*dans la rue, à l'église*) collector.

quetsche [kwɛtʃ] nf *kind of dark-red plum.*

queue [kø] 1 nf a *[animal, lettre, note, avion, comète]* tail; *[orage]* tail end; *[classement]* bottom; *[casserole, poêle]* handle; *[fruit, feuille]* stalk; *[fleur]* stem, stalk; *[train, colonne]* rear. **en ~ de phrase** at the end of the sentence; **en ~ de liste/classe** at the bottom of the list/class; **en ~ (de train)** at the rear of the train; **compartiments de ~** rear compartments; **commencer par la ~** to begin at the end; *voir* **diable**.

b (*file de personnes*) queue (*Brit*), line (*US*). **faire la ~** to queue (up) (*Brit*), stand in line (*US*); **il y a 2 heures de ~** there's 2 hours' queuing (*Brit*) *ou* standing in line (*US*); **mettez-vous à la ~** join the queue (*Brit*) *ou* line (*US*); **à la ~** in the queue (*Brit*), in line (*US*).

c (***: pénis*) tool**, cock**, prick**.

d (*loc*) **la ~ basse*** *ou* **entre les jambes*** with one's tail between one's legs; **à la ~ leu leu** *marcher, arriver* in single *ou* Indian (*Brit*) file; *venir se plaindre* one after the other; **il n'y en avait pas la ~ d'un*** there wasn't the sniff *ou* glimmer of one*; (*Aut*) **faire une ~ de poisson à qn** to cut in front of sb; **finir en ~ de poisson** to finish up in the air, come to an abrupt end; **histoire sans ~ ni tête*** cock-and-bull story; *[marchand]* **mettre des ~s aux zéros** to overcharge; **pour des ~s de cerises*** *travailler* for peanuts*, for next to nothing; *acheter* for next to nothing; (*Billard*) **faire une fausse ~** to miscue.

2 comp ▸**queue d'aronde** dovetail; **assemblage en queue d'aronde** dovetail joint ▸**queue de billard** (billiard) cue ▸**queue de cheval** ponytail ▸**queue-de-morue** nf (pl **queues-de-morue**) (*pinceau*) (medium) paintbrush; (*habit*) tails (*pl*), tail coat ▸**queue-de-pie** nf (pl **queues-de-pie**) (*basques*) tails (*pl*); (*habit*) tails (*pl*), tail coat ▸**queue-de-rat** nf (pl **queues-de-rat**) round file ▸**queue de vache** adj inv *couleur, cheveux* reddish-brown.

queuter** [køte] 1 vi to go wrong, backfire. **~ à un examen** to fail *ou* flunk* an exam, come down in an exam.

queux [kø] nm *voir* **maître**.

qui [ki] 1 pron a (*interrog sujet*) who. **~ *ou* est-ce ~ l'a vu?** who saw him?; **~ est-il/elle?** who is he/she?; **on m'a raconté ... — ~ ça?** somebody told me ... — who was that?; **~ d'entre eux/parmi vous saurait?** which of them/of you would know?; **~ va là?** (*Mil*) who goes there?; (*gén*) who's there?; *voir* **que**.

b (*interrog objet*) who, whom. **elle a vu ~?*, ~ est-ce qu'elle a vu?*** who did she see?; **~ a-t-elle vu?** who *ou* whom (*frm*) did she see?; (*surprise*) **elle a vu ~?** she saw who?, who did she see?; **à *ou* avec ~ voulez-vous parler?** who would you like to *ou* do you wish to speak to?, who is it you want to speak to?, to whom (*frm*) do you wish to speak?; **à ~ est ce sac?** whose bag is this?, who does this bag belong to?, whose is this bag?; **à ~ donc parlais-tu?** who was it you were talking to?, who were you talking to?; **de ~ est la pièce?** who is the play by?; **chez ~ allez-vous?** whose house are you going to?

c (*interrog indir*) (*sujet*) who; (*objet*) who, whom (*frm*). **je me demande ~ est là/~ il a invité** I wonder who's there/who *ou* whom (*frm*) he has invited; **elle ne sait à ~ se plaindre/pour ~ voter** she doesn't know who to complain to/who to vote for, she doesn't know to whom to complain/for whom to vote (*frm*); **vous devinez ~ me l'a dit!** you can guess who told me!

d (*relatif sujet*) (*être animé*) who, that*; (*chose*) which, that. **Paul, ~ traversait le pont, trébucha** Paul, who was crossing the bridge, tripped, Paul was crossing the bridge and tripped; **les amis ~ viennent ce soir sont américains** the friends who *ou* that* are coming tonight are American; **il a un perroquet ~ parle** he's got a talking parrot, he's got a parrot which *ou* that talks; **c'est le plus grand peintre ~ ait jamais vécu** he is the greatest painter that ever lived; **prenez les assiettes ~ sont sur la table** take the plates (which *ou* that are) on the table; **la table, ~ était en acajou, était très lourde** the table, which was mahogany, was very heavy; **je la vis ~ nageait vers le rivage** I saw her (as she was) swimming towards the bank; **j'en connais ~ seraient heureux ...** I know some who would be happy ...; **montre-nous, toi ~ sais tout** show us, since you know it all *ou* since you're so clever; *voir* **ce, moi, voici**.

e (*relatif avec prép*) **l'ami de ~ je vous ai parlé** the friend (that *ou* who* *ou* whom (*frm*)) I spoke to you about; **l'auteur sur l'œuvre de ~ elle a écrit une thèse** the author whose work she wrote a thesis on *ou* on whose work she wrote a thesis, the author on the work of whom she wrote a thesis (*frm*); **le patron pour ~ il travaille** the employer (that *ou* who* *ou* whom (*frm*)) he works for, the employer for whom he works (*frm*); **les docteurs sans ~ il n'aurait pu être sauvé** the doctors without whom he couldn't have been saved.

f (*relatif sans antécédent: être animé*) whoever, anyone who. **amenez ~ vous voulez** bring along whoever *ou* anyone *ou* who you like *ou* please; **cela m'a été dit par ~ vous savez** I was told that by you-know-who*; **ira ~ voudra** let whoever wants *ou* anyone who wants to go go; **c'est à ~ des deux mangera le plus vite** each tries to eat faster than the other, they try to outdo each other in the speed they eat; **il a dit à ~ voulait l'écouter *ou* l'entendre que ...** he told anyone who *ou* whoever would listen *ou* cared to listen that ...; **je le dirai à ~ de droit** I will tell whoever is concerned *ou* is the proper authority; **j'interdis à ~ que ce soit d'entrer ici** I'm not letting anybody (come) in here, I forbid anyone to come in here; **(~ que ce soit) ~ a fait cette faute ne va pas aller le dire!** whoever (the person is who) made this mistake is not going to say so!; **~ les verrait ensemble ne devinerait jamais qu'ils se détestent** anyone seeing them together would never guess (that) they can't stand one another; **à ~ mieux mieux** (*gén*) each one more so than the other; *crier* each one louder than the other; *frapper* each one harder than the other; **ils ont sauvé des flammes tout ce qu'ils ont pu: ~ une chaise, ~ une table, ~ une radio** they saved whatever they could from the fire: some took a chair, some a table, others a radio.

g (*Prov*) **~ m'aime me suive** come all ye faithful (*hum*), come along you folks; **~ m'aime aime mon chien** love me love my dog; **~ va lentement va sûrement** more haste less speed (*Prov*); **~ vivra verra** what will be will be (*Prov*); **~ a bu boira** a leopard never changes its spots (*Prov*), once a thief always a thief (*Prov*); **~ aime bien châtie bien** spare the rod and spoil the child (*Prov*); **~ donne aux pauvres prête à Dieu** charity will be rewarded in heaven; **~ dort dîne** he who sleeps forgets his hunger; **~ ne dit mot consent** silence gives consent; **~ ne risque rien *ou* n'ose rien n'a rien** nothing venture(d) nothing gain(ed); **~ paie ses dettes s'enrichit** the rich man is the one who pays his debts; **~ peut le plus peut le moins** he who can do more can do less; **~ casse les verres les paye** you pay for your mistakes; **~ sème le vent récolte la tempête** he who sows the wind shall reap the whirlwind; **~ se ressemble s'assemble** birds of a feather flock together (*Prov*); **~ se sent morveux, qu'il se mouche** if the cap *ou* shoe (*US*) fits, wear it (*Prov*); **~ s'y frotte s'y pique** beware the man who crosses swords with us; **~ trop embrasse mal étreint** he who grasps at too much loses everything; **~ va à la chasse perd sa place** he who leaves his place loses it; **~ veut voyager loin ménage sa monture** he who takes it slow and steady goes a long way; **~ veut la fin veut les moyens** he who wills the end wills the means; **~ veut noyer son chien l'accuse de la rage** give a dog a bad name and hang him; **~ n'entend qu'une cloche n'entend qu'un son** one should hear both sides of a question; **~ vole un œuf vole un bœuf** he that will steal a pin will steal a pound (*surtout Brit*).

2 comp ▸**qui-vive?** excl who goes there?; **être sur le qui-vive** to be on the alert.

quia [kɥija] adv: **mettre à ~** to confound sb†, nonplus sb; **être à ~** to be at a loss for an answer.

quiche [kiʃ] nf: **~ (lorraine)** quiche (Lorraine).

quiconque [kikɔ̃k] (*frm*) 1 pron rel (*celui qui*) whoever, anyone who, whosoever†. **~ a tué sera jugé** whoever has killed will be judged; **la loi punit ~ est coupable** the law punishes anyone who is guilty. 2 pron indéf (*n'importe qui, personne*) anyone, anybody. **je le sais mieux que ~** I know better than anyone (else); **il ne veut recevoir d'ordres de ~** he won't take orders from anyone *ou* anybody.

quidam [k(ɥ)idam] nm (†, *hum: individu*) fellow, chap (*Brit*), cove (*Brit:* †, *hum*).

quiet, quiète [kjɛ, kjɛt] adj (*littér,* ††) calm, tranquil.

quiétisme [kjetism] nm quietism.

quiétiste [kjetist] adj, nmf quietist.

quiétude [kjetyd] nf (*littér*) *[lieu]* quiet, tranquility; *[personne]* peace (of mind). **en toute ~** (*sans soucis*) with complete peace of mind; (*sans obstacle*) in (complete) peace; **les voleurs ont pu opérer en toute ~** the thieves were able to go about their business undisturbed.

quignon [kiɲɔ̃] nm: **~ (de pain)** (*croûton*) crust (of bread), heel of the loaf; (*morceau*) hunk *ou* chunk of bread.

quille [kij] nf a skittle. **(jeu de) ~s** ninepins, skittles; *voir* **chien**. b (**: jambe*) pin*. (*arg Mil*) **la ~** demob (*arg Brit*). c (*Naut*) keel. **la ~ en l'air** bottom up(wards), keel up.

quincaillerie [kɛ̃kajʀi] nf (*ustensiles, métier*) hardware, ironmongery (*Brit*); (*magasin*) hardware shop *ou* store, ironmonger's (shop) (*Brit*); (*fig péj: bijoux*) cheap(-looking) jewellery. **elle a sorti toute sa ~** she has decked herself out with every available piece of jewellery.

quincaillier, -ière [kɛ̃kaje, jɛʀ] nm,f hardware dealer, ironmonger (*Brit*).

quinconce [kɛ̃kɔ̃s] nm: **en ~** in staggered rows.

quinine [kinin] nf quinine.

quinquagénaire [kɛ̃kaʒenɛʀ] 1 adj (*de cinquante ans*) fifty-year-old (*épith*). (*de cinquante à soixante ans*) **il est ~** he is in his fifties; (*hum*) **maintenant que tu es ~** now that you're fifty (years old), now that you've reached fifty. 2 nmf fifty-year-old man (*ou* woman).

Quinquagésime [kɥɛ̃kwaʒezim] nf Quinquagesima.

quinquennal, e, mpl **-aux** [kɛ̃kenal, o] adj five-year (*épith*), quinquennial. (*Agr*) **assolement ~** five-year rotation.

quinquennat [kɛ̃kena] **nm** *(Pol)* five year term (of office).

quinquet [kɛ̃kɛ] **nm** *(Hist)* oil lamp. *(yeux)* **~s*** peepers* *(hum)*.

quinquina [kɛ̃kina] **nm** *(Bot, Pharm)* cinchona. **(apéritif au)** ~ *quinine tonic wine.*

quint, quinte[1] [kɛ̃, kɛ̃t] **adj** *voir* **Charles.**

quintal, **pl -aux** [kɛ̃tal, o] **nm** quintal *(100 kg)*; *(Can)* hundredweight.

quinte[2] [kɛ̃t] **nf** a *(Méd)* ~ **(de toux)** coughing fit. b *(Mus)* fifth; *(Escrime)* quinte; *(Cartes)* quint.

quinté [kɛ̃te] **nm** *French system of forecast betting on five horses.*

quintessence [kɛ̃tesɑ̃s] **nf** *(Chim, Philos, fig)* quintessence. *(hum)* **abstracteur de** ~ hair-splitter.

quintette [k(ɥ)ɛ̃tɛt] **nm** *(morceau, musiciens)* quintet(te). ~ **à cordes/à vent** string/wind quintet.

quinteux, -euse [kɛ̃tø, øz] **adj** *(††, littér) vieillard* crotchety, crabbed†.

quintillion [kɛ̃tiljɔ̃] **nm** quintillion *(Brit)*, nonillion *(US)*.

quintuple [kɛ̃typl] 1 **adj** *quantité, rangée, nombre* quintuple. **une quantité ~ de l'autre** a quantity five times (as great as) the other; **en ~ exemplaire/partie** in five copies/parts.
2 **nm** *(Math, gén)* quintuple *(de* of). **je l'ai payé le ~/le ~ de l'autre** I paid five times as much for it/five times as much as the other for it; **je vous le rendrai au ~** I'll repay you five times over; **augmenter au ~** to increase fivefold.

quintupler [kɛ̃typle] [1] **vti** to quintuple, increase fivefold.

quintuplés, -ées [kɛ̃typle] **(ptp de quintupler) nm,f pl** quintuplets, quins* *(Brit)*, quints* *(US)*.

quinzaine [kɛ̃zɛn] **nf** *(nombre)* about fifteen, fifteen or so; *(salaire)* fortnightly *(Brit) ou* fortnight's *(Brit) ou* two weeks' pay. *(deux semaines)* ~ **(de jours)** fortnight *(Brit)*, two weeks; ~ **publicitaire** *ou* **commerciale** (two-week) sale; **la ~ du blanc** (two-week) white *ou* linen sale; **"~ des soldes"** "two-week sale", "sales fortnight" *(Brit)*.

quinze [kɛ̃z] 1 **nm inv** fifteen. *(Rugby)* **le ~ de France** the French fifteen; *pour autres loc voir* **six.** 2 **adj inv** fifteen. **le ~ août** the 15th August, Assumption; **demain en ~** a fortnight tomorrow *(Brit)*, two weeks from tomorrow *(US)*; **lundi en ~** a fortnight on Monday *(Brit)*, two weeks from Monday *(US)*; **dans ~ jours** in a fortnight *(Brit)*, in a fortnight's time *(Brit)*, in two weeks, in two weeks' time; **tous les ~ jours** every fortnight *(Brit)*, every two weeks.

quinzième [kɛ̃zjɛm] **adj, nmf** fifteenth; *pour loc voir* **sixième.**

quinzièmement [kɛ̃zjɛmmɑ̃] **adv** in the fifteenth place, fifteenthly.

quiproquo [kipʀɔko] **nm** a *(méprise sur une personne)* mistake; *(malentendu sur un sujet)* misunderstanding. **le ~ durait depuis un quart d'heure, sans qu'ils s'en rendent compte** they had been talking at cross-purposes for a quarter of an hour without realizing it. b *(Théât)* (case of) mistaken identity.

Quito [kito] **n** Quito.

quittance [kitɑ̃s] **nf** *(reçu)* receipt; *(facture)* bill. ~ **d'électricité** receipt *(to show one has paid one's electricity bill)*; ~ **de loyer** rent receipt; *(frm)* **donner ~ à qn de qch** to acquit sb of sth *(frm)*.

quitte [kit] **adj** a **être ~ envers qn** to be quits *ou* all square with sb, be no longer in sb's debt; **être ~ envers sa patrie** to have served one's country; **être ~ envers la société** to have paid one's debt to society; **nous sommes ~s** *(dette)* we're quits *ou* all square; *(méchanceté)* we're even *ou* quits *ou* all square; **tu es ~ pour cette fois** I'll let you off this time, I'll let you get off *ou* away with it this time, you'll get off *ou* away with it this time; **je ne vous tiens pas ~** I don't consider your debt paid.
b **être/tenir qn ~ d'une dette/obligation** to be/consider sb rid *ou* clear of a debt/an obligation; **je suis ~ de mes dettes envers vous** I'm clear as far as my debts to you are concerned, all my debts to you are clear *ou* are paid off; **tu en es ~ à bon compte** you got off lightly; **nous en sommes ~s pour la peur/un bain glacé** we got off with a fright/an icy dip.
c ~ **à** even if it means *ou* does mean, although it may mean; ~ **à s'ennuyer, ils préfèrent rester chez eux** they prefer to stay (at) home even if it means *ou* does mean getting bored *ou* although it may mean getting bored.
d ~ **ou double** *(jeu)* double or quits, go for broke; *(fig)* **c'est du ~ ou double, c'est jouer à ~ ou double** it's a big gamble, it's risking a lot.

quitter [kite] [1] **vt** a *personne, pays, école* to leave; *métier* to leave, quit, give up. **il n'a pas quitté la maison depuis 3 jours** he hasn't been outside *ou* set foot outside the house for 3 days, he hasn't left the house for 3 days; **je suis pressé, il faut que je vous quitte** I'm in a hurry so I must leave you *ou* I must be off*; **il a quitté sa femme** he's left his wife; **ne pas ~ la chambre** to be confined to one's room; **les clients sont priés de ~ la chambre avant 11 heures** guests are requested to vacate their rooms before 11 o'clock; ~ **l'autoroute** *etc* **à Lyon** to turn off *ou* leave the motorway *etc* at Lyons; **le camion a quitté la route** the lorry ran off *ou* left the road; **le train a quitté la voie** *ou* **les rails** the train derailed *ou* jumped the rails; **se ~** *[couple, interlocuteurs]* to part; **nous nous sommes quittés bons amis** we parted good friends; *(†, hum)* **il a quitté ce monde** he has departed this world; *(fig)* ~ **la place** to withdraw, retire; **ne pas ~ qn d'un pas** *ou* **d'une semelle** not to leave sb for a second; *voir* **lieu.**
b *(fig) (renoncer à) espoir, illusion* to give up, forsake; *(abandonner) [crainte, énergie]* to leave, desert. **tout son courage l'a quitté** all his courage left *ou* deserted him.
c *(enlever) vêtement* to take off. ~ **le deuil** to come out of mourning; *(fig)* ~ **l'habit** *ou* **la robe** to leave the priesthood; *(Mil)* ~ **l'uniforme** to leave the army *(ou* navy *etc)*.
d *(Ordin)* to quit, exit.
e *(loc)* **si je le quitte des yeux une seconde** if I take my eyes off him for a second, if I let him out of my sight for a second; *(Téléc)* **ne quittez pas** hold the line, hold on a moment; **ils ne se quittent pas** they are always together, you never see them apart.

quitus [kitys] **nm** *(Comm)* full discharge, quietus.

quoi [kwa] **pron** a *(interrog)* what. **de ~ parles-tu?, tu parles de ~?*** what are you talking about?, what are you on about?* *(Brit)*; **on joue ~ au cinéma?*** what's on at the cinema?; **en ~ puis-je vous aider?** how can I help you?; **en ~ est cette statue?** what is this statue made of?; **vers ~ allons-nous?** what are we heading for?; **à ~ reconnaissez-vous le cristal?** how can you tell (that) it is crystal?; ~ **faire/lui dire?** what are we (going) to do/to say to him?; ~ **encore?** what else?; *(exaspération)* what is it now?; ~ **de plus beau que ...?** what can be more beautiful than ...?; ~ **de neuf?** *ou* **de nouveau?** any news?, what's the news?, what's new?; **à ~ bon?** what's the use? *(faire* of doing).
b *(interrog indir)* what. **dites-nous à ~ cela sert** tell us what that's for; **il voudrait savoir de ~ il est question/en ~ cela le concerne** he would like to know what it's about/what that's got to do with him; **je ne vois pas avec ~/sur ~ vous allez écrire** I don't see what you are going to write with/on; **devinez ~ j'ai mangé*** guess what I've eaten; **je ne sais ~ lui donner** I don't know what to give him.
c *(relatif)* **je sais à ~ tu fais allusion** I know what (it is) you're referring to; **c'est en ~ tu te trompes** that's where you're wrong; **as-tu de ~ écrire?** have you got anything to write with?; **ils n'ont même pas de ~ vivre** they haven't even got enough to live on; **il n'y a pas de ~ rire** it's no laughing matter, there's nothing to laugh about; **il n'y a pas de ~ pleurer** it's not worth crying over *ou* about, there's nothing to cry about; **il n'y a pas de ~ s'étonner** there's nothing surprising about *ou* in that; **il n'y a pas de ~ fouetter un chat** it's not worth making a fuss about; **ils ont de ~ occuper leurs vacances** they've got enough *ou* plenty to occupy them on their holiday; **avoir/emporter de ~ écrire/manger** to have/take something to write with/to eat; *voir* **ce, comme, sans.**
d ~ **qu'il arrive** whatever happens; ~ **qu'il en soit** be that as it may, however that may be; ~ **qu'on en dise/qu'elle fasse** whatever *ou* no matter what people say/she does; **si vous avez besoin de ~ que ce soit** if there's anything (at all) you need.
e *(loc) (excl)* **~! tu oses l'accuser?** what! you dare to accuse him!; *(pour faire répéter)* **~? qu'est-ce qu'il a dit?** what was it *ou* what was that he said?; *(iro)* **et puis ~ encore!** what next! *(iro)*; **puisque je te le dis, ~!*** damn it all! I'm telling you!‡; **de ~ (de ~)!‡** what's all this nonsense!; **merci beaucoup! — il n'y a pas de ~** many thanks! — don't mention it *ou* (it's) a pleasure *ou* not at all *ou* you're welcome; **ils n'ont pas de ~ s'acheter une voiture** they can't afford to buy a car, they haven't the means *ou* the wherewithal to buy a car; **avoir de ~** to have means; **des gens qui ont de ~** people of means.

quoique [kwak(ə)] **conj** *(bien que)* although, though. **quoiqu'il soit malade et qu'il n'ait pas d'argent** although *ou* though he is ill and has no money.

quolibet† [kɔlibɛ] **nm** *(raillerie)* gibe, jeer. **couvrir qn de ~s** to gibe *ou* jeer at sb.

quorum [k(w)ɔʀɔm] **nm** quorum. **le ~ a/n'a pas été atteint** there was/was not a quorum, we *(ou* they *etc)* had/did not have a quorum.

quota [k(w)ɔta] **nm** *(Admin)* quota.

quote-part, **pl quotes-parts** [kɔtpaʀ] **nf** *(lit, fig)* share.

quotidien, -ienne [kɔtidjɛ̃, jɛn] 1 **adj** *(journalier) travail, trajet, nourriture* daily *(épith)*; *(banal) incident* everyday *(épith)*, daily *(épith)*; *existence* everyday *(épith)*, humdrum. **dans la vie ~ne** in everyday *ou* daily life; *voir* **pain.** 2 **nm** a *(journal)* daily (paper), (news)paper. **les grands ~s** the big national dailies. b *(routine)* **le ~** everyday life; **la pratique médicale/l'enseignement au ~** day-to-day medical practice/teaching.

quotidiennement [kɔtidjɛnmɑ̃] **adv** daily, every day.

quotidienneté [kɔtidjɛnte] **nf** everyday nature.

quotient [kɔsjɑ̃] **nm** *(Math)* quotient. ~ **intellectuel** intelligence quotient, IQ; *(impôts)* ~ **familial** dependents' allowance set against tax.

quotité [kɔtite] **nf** *(Fin)* quota. *(Jur)* ~ **disponible** *portion of estate of which testator may dispose at his discretion.*

R

R, r [ɛʀ] **nm** (*lettre*) R, r; *voir* **mois.**

rab‡ [ʀab] **nm abrév de rabiot‡.**

rabâchage [ʀabɑʃaʒ] **nm** constant harping on (*NonC*).

rabâcher [ʀabɑʃe] 1 **1 vt** (*ressasser*) *histoire* to rehearse, harp on*, keep (on) repeating; (*réviser*) *leçon* to go over and over, keep going back over (*à qn* for sb). **il rabâche toujours la même chose** he keeps rambling *ou* harping on about the same (old) thing*. **2 vi** (*radoter*) to keep on, keep harping on*, keep repeating o.s.

rabâcheur, -euse [ʀabɑʃœʀ, øz] **nm,f** repetitive *ou* repetitious bore. **il est du genre ~** he's the type who never stops repeating himself *ou* harping on*.

rabais [ʀabɛ] **nm** reduction, discount. **10 F de ~, ~ de 10 F** reduction *ou* discount of 10 francs, 10 francs off; **faire un ~ de 20 F sur qch** to give a reduction *ou* discount of 20 francs on sth, knock 20 francs off (the price of) sth; **au ~** *acheter, vendre* at a reduced price, (on the) cheap; (*péj*) *acteur, journaliste* third-rate; (*péj*) *enseignement, médecine* cheap-rate, on the cheap (*attrib*); (*péj*) **je ne veux pas travailler au ~** I won't work for a pittance *ou* do underpaid work.

rabaissant, e [ʀabɛsɑ̃, ɑ̃t] **adj** *remarque* disparaging, derogatory; *métier* degrading.

rabaisser [ʀabese] 1 **1 vt a** (*dénigrer*) *personne* to humble, belittle, disparage; *efforts, talent, travail* to belittle, disparage.
b (*réduire*) *pouvoirs* to reduce, decrease; *orgueil* to humble; *exigences* to moderate, reduce. **ces défauts rabaissent la qualité de l'ensemble** these defects impair the quality of the whole; **il voulait 50 000 F par mois, mais il a dû ~ ses prétentions** he wanted 50,000 francs a month but he had to lower his sights; *voir* **caquet.**
c (*diminuer*) *prix* to reduce, knock down, bring down.
d (*baisser*) *robe, store* to pull (back) down.
2 se rabaisser vpr to belittle o.s. **elle se rabaisse toujours** she never gives herself enough credit, she always belittles herself; **se ~ devant qn** to humble o.s. *ou* bow before sb.

rabane [ʀaban] **nf** raffia fabric.

rabat [ʀaba] **nm a** *[table]* flap, leaf; *[poche, enveloppe]* flap; *[drap]* fold (*over the covers*); *[avocat, prêtre]* bands. **poche à ~** flapped pocket. **b = rabattage.**

rabat-joie [ʀabaʒwa] **nm inv** killjoy, spoilsport, wet blanket. **faire le ~** to spoil the fun, act like *ou* be a spoilsport, be a wet blanket; **il est drôlement ~** he's an awful killjoy *ou* spoilsport *ou* wet blanket.

rabattage [ʀabataʒ] **nm** (*Chasse*) beating.

rabatteur, -euse [ʀabatœʀ, øz] **1 nm,f** (*Chasse*) beater; (*fig péj*) tout; *[prostituée]* procurer, pimp. **le ~ de l'hôtel** the hotel tout. **2 nm** *[moissonneuse]* reel.

rabattre [ʀabatʀ] 41 **1 vt a** *capot, clapet* to close *ou* shut down; *couvercle* to put on, close; *drap* to fold over *ou* back; *col* to turn down; *bord de chapeau* to turn *ou* pull down; *strapontin* (*ouvrir*) to pull down; (*fermer*) to put up; *jupe* to pull down. **le vent rabat la fumée** the wind blows the smoke back down; **il rabattit ses cheveux sur son front** he brushed his hair down over his forehead; **le chapeau rabattu/les cheveux rabattus sur les yeux** his hat pulled down/hair brushed down over his eyes; **~ les couvertures** (*se couvrir*) to pull the blankets up; (*se découvrir*) to push *ou* throw back the blankets.
b (*diminuer*) to reduce; (*déduire*) to deduct, take off. **il n'a pas voulu ~ un centime (du prix)** he wouldn't take *ou* knock a centime off (the price), he wouldn't come down (by) one centime (on the price); **~ l'orgueil de qn** to humble sb's pride; **en ~** (*de ses prétentions*) to climb down, come down off one's high horse; (*de ses illusions*) to lose one's illusions; *voir* **caquet.**
c (*Chasse*) *gibier* to drive; *terrain* to beat. **~ des clients*** to tout for customers.
d (*Tricot*) **~ des mailles** to cast off; (*Couture*) **~ une couture** to stitch down a seam.
2 se rabattre vpr a *[voiture]* to cut in; *[coureur]* to cut in, cut across. **se ~ devant qn** *[voiture]* to cut *ou* pull in front of sb; *[coureur]* to cut *ou* swing in front of *ou* across sb; **le coureur s'est rabattu à la corde** the runner cut *ou* swung across to the inside lane.
b (*prendre faute de mieux*) **se ~ sur** *marchandise, personne* to fall back on, make do with.
c (*se refermer*) *[porte]* to fall *ou* slam shut; *[couvercle]* to close; *[dossier]* to fold down, fold away. **la porte se rabattit sur lui** the door closed *ou* shut on *ou* behind him.

rabattu, e [ʀabaty] (**ptp de rabattre**) **adj** *col, bords* turned down; *poche* flapped; *voir* **couture.**

rabbin [ʀabɛ̃] **nm** rabbi. **grand ~** chief rabbi.

rabbinat [ʀabina] **nm** rabbinate.

rabbinique [ʀabinik] **adj** rabbinic(al).

rabbinisme [ʀabinism] **nm** rabbinism.

rabelaisien, -ienne [ʀablɛzjɛ̃, jɛn] **adj** Rabelaisian.

rabibochage* [ʀabibɔʃaʒ] **nm** (*réconciliation*) reconciliation.

rabibocher* [ʀabibɔʃe] 1 **1 vt** (*réconcilier*) *amis, époux* to bring together (again), reconcile, patch things up between. **2 se rabibocher vpr** to make it up, patch things up (*avec* with).

rabiot‡ [ʀabjo] **nm** (*supplément*) **a** *[nourriture]* extra. **est-ce qu'il y a du ~?** is there any extra (left)?, is there any extra food (left)?; **qui veut du ~?** anyone for extras?* *ou* seconds?; **va me chercher du ~ de viande** go and get me some extra meat *ou* seconds* of meat; **il reste un ~ de viande, il reste de la viande en ~** there is still (some) extra meat left (over); **que font-ils du ~?** what do they do with the extra (food)?
b *[temps]* (*Mil*) extra time. **un ~ de 5 minutes** *ou* **5 minutes de ~ pour finir le devoir** 5 minutes' extra time *ou* 5 minutes extra to finish off the exercise; **faire du ~** (*travail*) to do *ou* work extra time; (*Mil*) to do *ou* serve extra time.

rabioter‡ [ʀabjɔte] 1 **vt a** (*s'approprier*) to scrounge* (*qch à qn* sth from sb). **il a rabioté tout le vin** he scrounged* all the extra wine; **~ 5 minutes de sommeil** to snatch 5 minutes' extra sleep. **b** (*voler*) *temps, argent* to fiddle* (*Brit*). **l'ouvrier m'a rabioté 10 F/un quart d'heure** the workman swindled *ou* did* me out of 10 francs/a quarter of an hour; **commerçant qui rabiote** shopkeeper who fiddles* (*Brit*) a bit extra *ou* makes a bit extra on the side; **~ sur la quantité** to give short measure.

rabioteur, -euse‡ [ʀabjɔtœʀ, øz] **nm,f** (*voir* **rabioter**) scrounger*; fiddler* (*Brit*).

rabique [ʀabik] **adj** rabies (*épith*).

râble [ʀɑbl] **nm** *[lapin, lièvre]* back; (*‡: dos*) small of the back. **tomber** *ou* **sauter sur le ~ de qn‡** to set on sb*, go for sb*; (*Culin*) **~ de lièvre** saddle of hare.

râblé, e [ʀɑble] **adj** *homme* well-set (*Brit*), heavy-set (*US*), stocky; *cheval* broad-backed.

rabot [ʀabo] **nm** plane. **passer qch au ~** to plane sth (down).

rabotage [ʀabɔtaʒ] **nm** planing (down).

raboter [ʀabɔte] 1 **vt a** (*Menuiserie*) to plane (down). **b** (**: racler*) *chaussure, objet* to scrape, rub; *main* to graze, scrape. **ne rabote pas le mur avec ton manteau** don't brush *ou* rub your coat along the wall; **baisse-toi si tu ne veux pas te ~ la tête contre le plafond** bend down if you don't want to graze your head on the ceiling.

raboteur [ʀabɔtœʀ] **nm** (*ouvrier*) planer.

raboteuse¹ [ʀabɔtøz] **nf** (*machine*) planing machine.

raboteux, -euse² [ʀabɔtø, øz] **adj** (*rugueux*) *surface, arête* uneven, rough; *chemin* rugged, uneven, bumpy; (*littér*) *style* rough, rugged; *voix* rough.

rabougri, e [ʀabugʀi] (**ptp de rabougrir**) **adj** (*chétif*) *plante* stunted, scraggy; *personne* stunted, puny; (*desséché*) *plante* shrivelled; *vieillard* wizened, shrivelled.

rabougrir [ʀabugʀiʀ] 2 **1 vt** *personne* to (cause to) shrivel up; *plante* (*dessécher*) to shrivel (up); (*étioler*) to stunt. **2 se rabougrir vpr** *[personne]* to become shrivelled (with age), become wizened; *[plante]* to shrivel (up), become stunted.

rabougrissement [ʀabugʀismɑ̃] **nm** (*action*) stunting, shrivelling (up); (*résultat*) scragginess, stunted appearance, shrivelled appearance.

rabouter [ʀabute] 1 vt *tubes, planches* to join (together) (end to end); *étoffes* to seam *ou* sew together.

rabrouer [ʀabʀue] 1 vt to snub, rebuff. **elle me rabroue tout le temps** she rebuffs me all the time; **se faire ~** to be rebuffed.

racaille [ʀakɑj] nf rabble, riffraff, scum.

raccommodable [ʀakɔmɔdabl] adj *vêtement* repairable, mendable.

raccommodage [ʀakɔmɔdaʒ] nm a (*action*) *[vêtement, accroc, filet]* mending, repairing; *[chaussettes]* darning, mending. **faire du ~** *ou* **des ~s** (*pour soi*) to do some mending; (*comme métier*) to take in mending. b (*endroit réparé*) mend; repair; darn.

raccommodement [ʀakɔmɔdmɑ̃] nm (*réconciliation*) reconciliation.

raccommoder [ʀakɔmɔde] 1 1 vt a *vêtements, accroc* to mend, repair; *chaussette* to darn, mend. b (*) *ennemis* to bring together again, patch things up between. 2 **se raccommoder*** vpr to make it up, be reconciled.

raccommodeur, -euse [ʀakɔmɔdœʀ, øz] nm,f *[linge, filets]* mender. **~ de porcelaines**†† china mender *ou* restorer.

raccompagner [ʀakɔ̃paɲe] 1 vt to take *ou* see back (*à* to). **~ qn (chez lui)** to take *ou* see *ou* accompany sb home; **~ qn au bureau en voiture/à pied** to drive sb back/walk back with sb to the office; **~ qn à la gare** to see sb off at *ou* take sb (back) to the station; **~ qn (jusqu'à la porte** to see sb to the door; **il l'a raccompagnée jusqu'à sa voiture** he walked *ou* saw her to her car.

raccord [ʀakɔʀ] nm a *[papier peint]* join. **~ (de maçonnerie)** pointing (*NonC*); **~ (de peinture)** (*liaison*) join (*in the paintwork*); (*retouche*) touch up; **on ne voit pas les ~s (de peinture)** you can't see where the paint has been touched up; **elle procéda à un rapide ~ (de maquillage)** she quickly touched up her make-up; **papier peint sans ~s** random match wallpaper. b *[texte, discours]* link, join; (*Ciné*) (*séquence*) continuity; (*scène*) link scene. (*Ciné*) **à cause des coupures, nous avons dû faire des ~s** because of the cuts, we had to do some link shots. c (*pièce, joint*) link.

raccordement [ʀakɔʀdəmɑ̃] nm a (*voir* **raccorder**) linking; joining; connecting. (*Téléc*) **~ (au réseau)** connection (of one's phone); **ils sont venus faire le ~** they've come to connect the (*ou* our *etc*) phone; *voir* **bretelle, ligne¹, taxe, voie.** b (*soudure, épissure*) join; (*tunnel, passage*) connecting passage; (*carrefour*) junction.

raccorder [ʀakɔʀde] 1 1 vt *routes, bâtiments* to link up, join (up), connect (*à* with, to); *fils électriques* to join; *tuyaux* to join, link (*à* to); (*Ciné*) *plans* to link up. (*fig*) **~ à** *faits* to link (up) with, tie up with; (*Téléc*) **~ qn au réseau** to connect sb's phone; **quand les 2 tuyaux seront raccordés** when the 2 pipes are joined *ou* linked (up) *ou* connected together. 2 **se raccorder** vpr *[routes]* to link *ou* join up (*à* with). *[faits]* **se ~ à** to tie up *ou* in with.

raccourci [ʀakuʀsi] nm a (*chemin*) short cut. b (*fig: formule frappante*) compressed turn of phrase; (*résumé*) summary. **en ~** (*en miniature*) in miniature; (*dans les grandes lignes*) in (broad) outline; (*en bref*) in a nutshell, in brief. c (*Art*) foreshortening. **figure en ~** foreshortened figure; *voir* **bras.**

raccourcir [ʀakuʀsiʀ] 2 1 vt *distance, temps* to shorten; *vêtement* to shorten, take up; *vacances, textes* to shorten, curtail, cut short. **passons par là, ça (nous) raccourcit** let's go this way, it's shorter *ou* quicker *ou* it cuts a bit off; **~ qn**⁑ to chop sb's head off; **les vêtements larges raccourcissent la silhouette** wide clothes make people look shorter. 2 vi *[jours]* to grow shorter, draw in; *[vêtement]* (*au lavage*) to shrink. (*Mode*) **les jupes ont raccourci cette année** skirts are shorter *ou* have got shorter this year.

raccourcissement [ʀakuʀsismɑ̃] nm a (*voir* **raccourcir**) shortening; curtailing, curtailment. b *[jour]* shortening, drawing in; *[vêtement]* (*au lavage*) shrinkage.

raccoutumer [ʀakutyme] 1 vt = **réaccoutumer.**

raccroc [ʀakʀo] nm (*frm*) **par ~** (*par hasard*) by chance; (*par un heureux hasard*) by a stroke of good fortune.

raccrocher [ʀakʀɔʃe] 1 1 vi a (*Téléc*) to hang up, ring off (*surtout Brit*). **ne raccroche pas** hold on, don't hang up *ou* ring off (*surtout Brit*).
b (*arg Sport*) to retire.
2 vt a *vêtement, tableau* to hang back up, put back on the hook; *écouteur* to put down. (*arg Sport*) **~ les gants/chaussures** to hang up one's gloves/boots (*arg*).
b (*racoler*) *[vendeur, portier]* to tout for. *[prostituée]* **~ le client** to solicit, accost customers.
c (*attraper*) *personne, bonne affaire* to grab *ou* get hold of. **il m'a raccroché dans la rue** he stopped *ou* waylaid *ou* buttonholed me in the street.
d (*relier*) *wagons, faits* to link, connect (*à* to, with).
e (**: rattraper*) *affaire, contrat* to save, rescue.
3 **se raccrocher** vpr: **se ~ à** *branche* to catch *ou* grab (hold of); *espoir, personne* to cling to, hang on to; **cette idée se raccroche à la précédente** this idea links with *ou* ties in with the previous one.

race [ʀas] nf a (*ethnique*) race. **être de ~ indienne** to be of Indian stock *ou* blood; **la ~ humaine** the human race. b (*Zool*) breed. **de ~** (*gén*) pedigree (*épith*), purebred (*épith*); *cheval* thoroughbred; **avoir de la ~** to be of good stock; *voir* **bon¹, chien.** c (*ancêtres*) stock, race. **être de ~ noble** to be of noble stock *ou* blood *ou* race; **avoir de la ~** to have a certain (natural) distinction *ou* breeding. d (*catégorie*) breed. **lui et les gens de sa ~** him and people of the same breed, him and the likes of him*; **les cordonniers, c'est une ~ qui disparaît** cobblers are a dying breed *ou* race.

racé, e [ʀase] adj *animal* purebred (*épith*), pedigree (*épith*); *cheval* thoroughbred; *personne* thoroughbred, of natural distinction *ou* breeding; (*fig*) *voiture, ligne* thoroughbred.

rachat [ʀaʃa] nm (*voir* **racheter**) buying back; repurchase; purchase; buying up *ou* out *ou* over; redemption; ransom; ransoming; atonement, expiation. **~ d'entreprise (par les salariés)** (management) buyout; **option** *ou* **possibilité de ~** buy-back option.

Rachel [ʀaʃɛl] nf Rachel.

rachetable [ʀaʃ(ə)tabl] adj *dette, rente* redeemable; *péché* expiable; *pécheur* redeemable. **cette faute n'est pas ~** you can't make up for this mistake.

racheter [ʀaʃ(ə)te] 5 1 vt a *objet que l'on possédait avant* to buy back, repurchase; *nouvel objet* to buy *ou* purchase another; *pain, lait* to buy some more; *objet d'occasion* to buy, purchase; *usine en faillite* to buy up *ou* out *ou* over. **je lui ai racheté son vieux transistor** I've bought his old transistor from *ou* off* him; **il a racheté toutes les parts de son associé** he bought his partner out, he bought up all his partner's shares; **j'ai dû ~ du tissu** I had to buy more material.
b (*se libérer de*) *dette, rente* to redeem.
c *esclave, otage* to ransom, pay a ransom for; (*Rel*) *pécheur* to redeem. **il n'y en a pas un pour ~ l'autre*** they're both (just) as bad as each other.
d (*réparer*) *péché, crime* to atone for, expiate; *mauvaise conduite, faute* to make amends for, make up for; *imperfection* to make up *ou* compensate for (*par* by).
e (*Archit*) to modify.
2 **se racheter** vpr *[pécheur]* to redeem o.s.; *[criminel]* to make amends. **essaie de te ~ en t'excusant** try and make up for it *ou* try to make amends by apologizing.

rachidien, -ienne [ʀaʃidjɛ̃, jɛn] adj of the spinal column, rachidian (*SPÉC*).

rachitique [ʀaʃitik] adj (*Méd*) *personne* suffering from rickets, rachitic (*SPÉC*), rickety; *arbre, poulet* scraggy, scrawny. **c'est un ~, il est ~** he suffers from rickets.

rachitisme [ʀaʃitism] nm rickets (*sg*), rachitis (*SPÉC*). **faire du ~** to have rickets.

racial, e, mpl **-iaux** [ʀasjal, jo] adj racial.

racine [ʀasin] 1 nf a (*gén*) root. (*Bot*) **la carotte est une ~** the carrot is a root *ou* root vegetable, carrots are a root crop; (*fig: attaches*) **~s** roots; (*fig*) **il est sans ~s** he's rootless, he belongs nowhere; **prendre le mal à la ~, s'attaquer aux ~s du mal** to deal with the problem at source; **prendre ~** (*lit*) to take *ou* strike root(s), put out roots; (*s'établir*) to put down (one's) roots (*fig*); (**: chez qn, à attendre*) to take root*; *voir* **rougir.**
b (*Math*) *[équation]* root. *[nombre]* **~ carrée/cubique/dixième** square/cube/tenth root; **prendre** *ou* **extraire la ~ de** to take the root of.
c (*Ling*) *[mot]* root.
2 comp ►**racine adventive** adventitious root ►**racine aérienne** aerial root ►**racine pivotante** taproot.

racinien, -ienne [ʀasinjɛ̃, jɛn] adj Racinian.

racisme [ʀasism] nm racialism, racism. **~ antijeunes** anti-youth prejudice.

raciste [ʀasist] adj, nmf racialist, racist.

racket [ʀakɛt] nm (*action*) racketeering (*NonC*); (*vol*) racket (*extortion through blackmail etc*).

racketter, racketteur [ʀakɛtœʀ] nm racketeer.

raclage [ʀɑklaʒ] nm (*Tech*) scraping.

raclée* [ʀɑkle] nf (*coups*) hiding, thrashing; (*défaite*) hiding*, thrashing*, licking*. **il a pris une ~ à l'élection** he got thrashed* *ou* licked* in the election, he got a licking* *ou* a hiding* in the election.

raclement [ʀɑkləmɑ̃] nm (*bruit*) scraping (noise). **il émit un ~ de gorge** he cleared his throat noisily *ou* raucously.

racler [ʀɑkle] 1 1 vt a (*gén, Méd, Tech*) to scrape; *fond de casserole* to scrape out; *parquet* to scrape (down). **ce vin racle le gosier** this wine is harsh *ou* rough on the throat, this wine burns your throat; *voir* **fond.** b (*ratisser*) *allée, gravier, sable* to rake. c (*enlever*) *tache, croûte* to scrape away *ou* off; *peinture, écailles* to scrape off. **~ la boue de ses semelles** to scrape the mud off one's shoes. d (*péj*) *violon* to scrape *ou* saw (a tune) on; *guitare* to strum (a tune) on. 2 **se racler** vpr: **se ~ la gorge** to clear one's throat.

raclette [ʀɑklɛt] nf a (*outil*) scraper. b (*Culin*) raclette (*Swiss cheese dish*).

racloir [ʀɑklwaʀ] nm scraper.

raclure [ʀɑklyʀ] nf (*gén pl: déchet*) scraping.

racolage [ʀakɔlaʒ] nm (*voir* **racoler**) soliciting; touting. **faire du ~** to solicit; to tout.

racoler [ʀakɔle] 1 vt *[prostituée]* to accost; (*fig péj*) *[agent électoral, portier, vendeur]* to solicit, tout for. **elle racolait** she was soliciting; she was touting for *ou* accosting customers.

racoleur, -euse [ʀakɔlœʀ, øz] 1 nm tout. 2 **racoleuse** nf (*prostituée*) streetwalker, whore. 3 adj *slogan, publicité* (*gén*) eye-catching, enticing; (*Pol*) vote-catching.

racontable [ʀakɔ̃tabl] adj tellable, relatable.

racontar [ʀakɔ̃taʀ] nm story, lie.

raconter [ʀakɔ̃te] [1] 1 vt a (*relater*) *histoire, légende* to tell, relate, recount; *vacances, malheurs* to tell about, relate, recount. ~ **qch à qn** to tell sb sth, relate *ou* recount sth to sb; ~ **sa vie** to tell one's life story; ~ **que** to tell that; **on raconte que** people say that, it is said that, the story goes that; ~ **ce qui s'est passé** to say *ou* relate *ou* recount what happened; ~ **à qn ce qui s'est passé** to tell sb *ou* relate *ou* recount to sb what happened; **alors, qu'est-ce que tu racontes ces temps-ci?*** what's new with you (these days)?*, how are things with you (these days)?*
b (*dire de mauvaise foi*) to tell, say. **qu'est-ce que tu racontes?** what on earth do you think you're talking about? *ou* saying?; **il raconte n'importe quoi** he's talking rubbish *ou* nonsense *ou* through his hat* (*fig*); ~ **des histoires, en** ~ to tell stories, spin yarns; **il a été** ~ **qu'on allait divorcer** he's been (going around) telling people we're going to get divorced.
2 **se raconter** vpr *[écrivain]* to talk about o.s.

raconteur, -euse [ʀakɔ̃tœʀ, øz] nm,f storyteller. ~ **de** narrator of.

racornir [ʀakɔʀniʀ] [2] 1 vt (*durcir*) to toughen, harden; (*dessécher*) to shrivel (up). **cuir racorni** hardened *ou* dried-up leather; **vieillard racorni** shrivelled(-up) *ou* wizened old man; **dans son cœur racorni** in his hard heart. 2 **se racornir** vpr to become tough *ou* hard; to shrivel (up), become shrivelled (up).

racornissement [ʀakɔʀnismɑ̃] nm (*voir* **racornir**) toughening, hardening; shrivelling (up).

rad [ʀad] nm rad.

radar [ʀadaʀ] nm radar. **système/écran** ~ radar system/screen; (*Aut*) **contrôle** ~ speed check; **il s'est fait prendre au** ~* he was caught by a speed trap*; (*fig*) **marcher** *ou* **fonctionner au** ~* to be on automatic pilot*.

radariste [ʀadaʀist] nmf radar operator.

rade [ʀad] nf a (*port*) (natural) harbour, roads (*SPÉC*), roadstead (*SPÉC*). **en** ~ in harbour, in the roads (*SPÉC*); **en** ~ **de Brest** in Brest harbour. b (**loc*) **laisser en** ~ *personne* to leave in the lurch, leave high and dry, leave stranded *ou* behind; *projet* to forget about, drop, shelve; *voiture* to leave behind; **elle/sa voiture est restée en** ~ she/her car was left stranded *ou* behind; **tomber en** ~ (*panne d'essence*) to run out of petrol (*Brit*) *ou* gas (*US*); (*ennuis mécaniques*) to break down.

radeau, pl ~**x** [ʀado] nm raft; (*train de bois*) timber float *ou* raft. ~ **de sauvetage/pneumatique** rescue/inflatable raft.

radial, e, mpl **-iaux** [ʀadjal, jo] 1 adj (*gén*) radial. 2 **radiale** nf (*route*) urban motorway (*Brit*) *ou* highway (*US*).

radian [ʀadjɑ̃] nm radian.

radiant, e [ʀadjɑ̃, jɑ̃t] adj *énergie* radiant. (*Astron*) **(point)** ~ radiant.

radiateur [ʀadjatœʀ] nm (*à eau, à huile*) radiator; (*à gaz, à barres chauffantes*) heater; *[voiture]* radiator. ~ **à accumulation** storage radiator *ou* heater; ~ **électrique** electric heater; ~ **soufflant** fan heater; ~ **parabolique** electric fire.

radiation [ʀadjasjɔ̃] nf a (*Phys*) radiation. b *[nom, mention]* crossing *ou* striking off. **sa** ~ **du club** his being struck off the club register, his removal from the club register.

radical, e, mpl **-aux** [ʀadikal, o] 1 adj (*gén, Bot, Math*) radical; (*Hist, Pol*) Radical. **essayez ce remède, c'est** ~* try this remedy, it works like a charm *ou* it really does the trick*; **une heure d'aérobic et tu es mort, c'est** ~**!*** an hour of aerobics and you're exhausted, it never fails!; (*Ling*) **voyelle** ~**e** stem *ou* radical vowel. 2 nm *[mot]* stem, radical, root; (*Pol*) radical; (*Chim*) radical; (*Math*) radical sign. 3 comp ►**radical-socialisme** nm radical-socialism ►**radical-socialiste** adj, nmf (mpl **radicaux-socialistes**) radical-socialist.

radicalement [ʀadikalmɑ̃] adv *modifier* radically; *guérir* completely. ~ **faux** completely wrong; ~ **opposé à** radically opposed to.

radicalisation [ʀadikalizasjɔ̃] nf (*voir* **radicaliser**) toughening; intensification; radicalization.

radicaliser vt, **se radicaliser** vpr [ʀadikalize] [1] *position* to toughen, harden; *conflit* to intensify; *régime* to radicalize.

radicalisme [ʀadikalism] nm (*Pol*) radicalism.

radicelle [ʀadisɛl] nf rootlet, radicle (*SPÉC*).

radiculaire [ʀadikylɛʀ] adj radicular.

radicule [ʀadikyl] nf radicule.

radié, e [ʀadje] (ptp de **radier**) adj (*rayonné*) rayed, radiate.

radier [ʀadje] [7] vt *mention, nom* to cross off, strike off. **ce médecin a été radié** this doctor has been struck off (the list).

radiesthésie [ʀadjɛstezi] nf (power of) divination, dowsing (*based on the detection of radiation emitted by various bodies*).

radiesthésiste [ʀadjɛstezist] nmf diviner, dowser.

radieusement [ʀadjøzmɑ̃] adv radiantly. ~ **beau** *femme* radiantly *ou* dazzlingly beautiful; *temps* brilliantly *ou* gloriously fine.

radieux, -ieuse [ʀadjø, jøz] adj *personne* (*de joie*) glowing *ou* radiant with happiness, beaming *ou* radiant with joy; (*de beauté*) radiantly *ou* dazzlingly beautiful; *air, sourire* radiant, beaming (*épith*); *soleil, beauté* radiant, dazzling; *journée, temps* brilliant, glorious.

radin, e* [ʀadɛ̃, in] 1 adj stingy, tight-fisted. 2 nm,f skinflint.

radiner‡ vi, **se radiner‡** vpr [ʀadine] [1] (*arriver*) to turn up, show up*, roll up*; (*accourir*) to rush over, dash over. **allez, radine(-toi)!** come on, step on it!* *ou* get your skates on!*

radinerie* [ʀadinʀi] nf stinginess (*NonC*), tight-fistedness (*NonC*).

radio [ʀadjo] 1 nf a (*poste*) radio (set), wireless (set)† (*surtout Brit*). **mets la** ~ turn on *ou* put on the radio; *voir* **poste**[2].
b (*radiodiffusion*) **la** ~ (the) radio; **avoir la** ~ to have a radio; **parler à la** ~ to speak on the radio, broadcast; **passer à la** ~ to be on the radio *ou* on the air; **travailler à la** ~ to work in broadcasting *ou* on the radio.
c (*station*) radio station. ~ **pirate** pirate radio station; **la** ~ **du Caire** Cairo radio; ~ **libre** independent local radio station.
d (*radiotéléphonie*) radio. **message** ~ radio message; **la** ~ **de bord du navire** the ship's radio.
e (*radiographie*) X-ray (photograph). **passer une** ~ to have an X-ray (taken), be X-rayed.
2 nm (*opérateur*) radio operator; (*message*) radiogram, radiotelegram.

radioactif, -ive [ʀadjoaktif, iv] adj radioactive.

radioactivité [ʀadjoaktivite] nf radioactivity.

radioalignement [ʀadjoaliɲmɑ̃] nm radio navigation system.

radioamateur [ʀadjoamatœʀ] nm radio ham*.

radioastronome [ʀadjoastʀɔnɔm] nmf radio astronomer.

radioastronomie [ʀadjoastʀɔnɔmi] nf radio astronomy.

radiobalisage [ʀadjobalizaʒ] nm radio beacon signalling.

radiobalise [ʀadjobaliz] nf radio beacon.

radiobaliser [ʀadjobalize] [1] vt to equip with a radio beacon system.

radiobiologie [ʀadjobjɔlɔʒi] nf radiobiology.

radiocarbone [ʀadjokaʀbɔn] nm radiocarbon, radioactive carbon.

radiocassette [ʀadjokasɛt] nm cassette radio, radio cassette player.

radiocobalt [ʀadjokɔbalt] nm radio cobalt, radioactive cobalt.

radiocommunication [ʀadjokɔmynikasjɔ̃] nf radio communication.

radiocompas [ʀadjokɔ̃pɑ] nm radio compass.

radioconducteur [ʀadjokɔ̃dyktœʀ] nm detector.

radiodiagnostic [ʀadjodjagnɔstik] nm radiodiagnosis.

radiodiffuser [ʀadjodifyze] [1] vt to broadcast (*by radio*). **interview radiodiffusé** broadcast *ou* radio interview.

radiodiffusion [ʀadjodifyzjɔ̃] nf broadcasting (*by radio*).

radioélectricien, -ienne [ʀadjoelɛktʀisjɛ̃, jɛn] nm,f radio-engineer.

radioélectricité [ʀadjoelɛktʀisite] nf radio-engineering.

radioélectrique [ʀadjoelɛktʀik] adj radio (*épith*).

radioélément [ʀadjoelemɑ̃] nm radio-element.

radiofréquence [ʀadjofʀekɑ̃s] nf radio frequency.

radiogénique [ʀadjoʒenik] adj radiogenic.

radiogoniomètre [ʀadjogɔnjɔmɛtʀ] nm direction finder, radiogoniometer.

radiogoniométrie [ʀadjogɔnjɔmetʀi] nf radio direction finding, radiogoniometry.

radiogramme [ʀadjɔgʀam] nm (*télégramme*) radiogram, radiotelegram; (*film*) radiograph, radiogram.

radiographie [ʀadjɔgʀafi] nf a (*technique*) radiography, X-ray photography. **passer une** ~ to have an X-ray (taken). b (*photographie*) X-ray (photograph), radiograph.

radiographier [ʀadjɔgʀafje] [7] vt to X-ray.

radiographique [ʀadjɔgʀafik] adj X-ray (*épith*).

radioguidage [ʀadjogidaʒ] nm (*Aviat*) radio control, radiodirection. (*Rad*) **le** ~ **des automobilistes** broadcasting traffic reports to motorists.

radioguidé, e [ʀadjogide] adj radio-controlled.

radio-isotope, pl **radio-isotopes** [ʀadjoizɔtɔp] nm radio-isotope.

radiologie [ʀadjɔlɔʒi] nf radiology.

radiologique [ʀadjɔlɔʒik] adj radiological.

radiologiste [ʀadjɔlɔʒist] nmf, **radiologue** [ʀadjɔlɔg] nmf radiologist.

radiomètre [ʀadjɔmɛtʀ] nm radiometer.

radionavigant [ʀadjonavigɑ̃] nm radio officer.

radionavigation [ʀadjonavigasjɔ̃] nf radio navigation.

radiophare [ʀadjofaʀ] nm radio beacon.

radiophonie [ʀadjɔfɔni] nf radiotelephony.

radiophonique [ʀadjɔfɔnik] adj radio (*épith*).

radioreportage [ʀadjoʀ(ə)pɔʀtaʒ] nm radio report; *voir* **car**[1].

radioreporter [ʀadjoʀ(ə)pɔʀtɛʀ] nm radio reporter.

radio-réveil, pl **radio-réveils** [ʀadjoʀevɛj] nm radio-alarm, clock-radio.

radioscopie [ʀadjɔskɔpi] nf radioscopy.

radioscopique [ʀadjɔskɔpik] adj radioscopic.

radiosondage [ʀadjosɔ̃daʒ] nm (*Mét*) radiosonde exploration; (*Géol*) seismic prospecting.

radiosonde [ʀadjosɔ̃d] nf radiosonde.

radiosource [ʀadjosuʀs] nf radio source, star source.

radio-taxi, pl **radio-taxis** [ʀadjotaksi] nm radio taxi, radio cab.

radiotechnique [ʀadjotɛknik] 1 nf radio technology. 2 adj radiotechnological.

radiotélégraphie [ʀadjotelegʀafi] nf radiotelegraphy, wireless telegraphy.

radiotélégraphique [ʀadjotelegʀafik] adj radiotelegraphic.
radiotélégraphiste [ʀadjotelegʀafist] nmf radiotelegrapher.
radiotéléphone [ʀadjotelefɔn] nm radiotelephone.
radiotéléphonie [ʀadjotelefɔni] nf radiotelephony, wireless telephony.
radiotélescope [ʀadjotelɛskɔp] nm radio telescope.
radiotélévisé, e [ʀadjotelevize] adj broadcast on both radio and television, broadcast and televised.
radiothérapeute [ʀadjoteʀapøt] nmf radiotherapist.
radiothérapie [ʀadjoteʀapi] nf radiotherapy.
radis [ʀadi] nm a radish. ~ **noir** horseradish. b (*‡: sou*) penny (*Brit*), cent (*US*). **je n'ai pas un ~** I haven't got a penny (to my name)* *ou* a cent (*US*) *ou* a bean*; **ça ne vaut pas un ~** it's not worth a penny *ou* a bean*.
radium [ʀadjɔm] nm radium.
radius [ʀadjys] nm (*Anat*) radius.
radjah [ʀadʒa] nm = **rajah**.
radome [ʀadom] nm radome.
radon [ʀadɔ̃] nm radon.
radotage [ʀadɔtaʒ] nm (*péj*) drivel (*NonC*), rambling.
radoter [ʀadɔte] 1 vi (*péj*) to ramble on *ou* drivel (on) (in a senile way). **tu radotes‡** you're talking a load of drivel‡.
radoteur, -euse [ʀadɔtœʀ, øz] nm,f (*péj*) drivelling (old) fool, (old) driveller.
radoub [ʀadu] nm (*Naut*) refitting. **navire au ~** ship under repair *ou* undergoing a refit; *voir* **bassin**.
radouber [ʀadube] 1 vt *navire* to repair, refit; *filet de pêche* to repair, mend.
radoucir [ʀadusiʀ] 2 1 vt *personne, voix, ton, attitude* to soften; *temps* to make milder. **tu t'en vas déjà? dit-il soudain radouci** leaving already? he said, suddenly meek. 2 **se radoucir** vpr [*personne*] (*après une colère*) to calm down, be mollified; (*avec l'âge*) to mellow; [*voix*] to soften, become milder; [*temps*] to become milder.
radoucissement [ʀadusismɑ̃] nm a (*Mét*) **à cause du ~ (du temps)** because of the milder weather; **~ (de la température)** rise in (the) temperature; **on prévoit pour demain un léger/net ~** slightly/distinctly milder weather *ou* a slightly/distinctly milder spell (of weather) is forecast *ou* slightly/distinctly higher temperatures are forecast for tomorrow. b [*ton, attitude*] softening; [*personne*] calming down.
rafale [ʀafal] nf [*vent*] gust, blast; [*pluie*] gust; [*mitrailleuse*] burst; [*neige*] flurry. **une soudaine ~ (de vent)** a sudden gust *ou* blast of wind, a sudden squall; **en *ou* par ~s** in gusts; in bursts; **une ~ *ou* des ~s de balles** a hail of bullets.
raffermir [ʀafɛʀmiʀ] 2 1 vt *muscle* to harden, tone up; *chair, sol* to firm up, make firm(er); *peau* to tone up; *voix* to steady; *gouvernement, popularité* to strengthen, reinforce; *courage, résolution* to fortify, strengthen. 2 **se raffermir** vpr [*muscle*] to harden; [*chair, sol*] to firm up, become firm(er); [*autorité*] to strengthen, become strengthened *ou* reinforced; [*prix*] to strengthen; [*voix*] to become steady *ou* steadier. **ma résolution se raffermit** my resolution grew stronger; **son visage se raffermit** his face became *ou* he looked more composed; **se ~ dans ses intentions** to strengthen one's resolve.
raffermissement [ʀafɛʀmismɑ̃] nm (*voir* **raffermir**) strengthening; firming; steadying; reinforcement; fortifying.
raffinage [ʀafinaʒ] nm (*gén*) refining.
raffiné, e [ʀafine] (ptp de **raffiner**) adj a *pétrole, sucre* refined. b *personne, mœurs, style* refined, polished, sophisticated; *esprit, goûts, gourmet* discriminating, refined; *élégance, cuisine* refined.
raffinement [ʀafinmɑ̃] nm a (*caractère: voir* **raffiné**) refinement, sophistication. b (*gén pl: détail*) [*langage etc*] nicety, subtlety, refinement. c (*exagération*) **c'est du ~** that's being oversubtle. d (*surenchère*) **~ de** refinement of; **avec un ~ de luxe/de cruauté** with refinements of luxury/cruelty.
raffiner [ʀafine] 1 1 vt a *pétrole, sucre, papier* to refine. b *langage, manières* to refine, polish. 2 vi (*dans le raisonnement*) to be oversubtle; (*sur les détails*) to be (over)meticulous.
raffinerie [ʀafinʀi] nf refinery. **~ de pétrole** oil refinery.
raffineur, -euse [ʀafinœʀ, øz] nm,f refiner.
raffoler [ʀafɔle] 1 raffoler de vt indir to be very keen on (*Brit*), be fond of, be wild about*.
raffut* [ʀafy] nm (*vacarme*) row, racket, din. **faire du ~** (*être bruyant*) to kick up* *ou* make a row *ou* racket *ou* din; (*protester*) to kick up* a row *ou* fuss *ou* stink‡; **sa démission va faire du ~** his resignation will cause a row *ou* stink‡.
rafiot [ʀafjo] nm (*péj: bateau*) (old) tub (*péj*).
rafistolage* [ʀafistɔlaʒ] nm (*action: lit, fig*) patching up. **ce n'est qu'un ~** (*lit*) it's only a patched-up *ou* makeshift repair; (*fig*) it's only a patched-up *ou* makeshift solution.
rafistoler* [ʀafistɔle] 1 vt (*réparer*) to patch up.
rafle [ʀɑfl] nf (police) roundup *ou* raid, swoop. **la police a fait une ~** the police made a roundup (of suspects); (*fig*) **les voleurs ont fait une ~ chez le bijoutier/sur les montres** the thieves cleaned out the jewellery shop/cleaned out *ou* made a clean sweep of all the watches.
rafler* [ʀɑfle] 1 vt *récompenses, bijoux* to run off with, swipe‡; *place* to bag*, grab, swipe‡. **les ménagères avaient tout raflé** the housewives had swept up *ou* snaffled* everything; **elle a raflé tous les prix** she ran away *ou* off with all the prizes, she made a clean sweep of the prizes.
rafraîchir [ʀafʀeʃiʀ] 2 1 vt a (*refroidir*) *air* to cool (down), freshen; *vin* to chill; *boisson* to cool, make cooler. **fruits rafraîchis** fruit salad.
b (*revivifier*) *visage, corps* to freshen (up); [*boisson*] to refresh.
c (*rénover*) *vêtement* to smarten up, brighten up; *tableau, couleur* to brighten up, freshen up; *appartement* to do up, brighten up; *connaissances* to brush up. **se faire ~ les cheveux** to have a trim, have one's hair trimmed; (*fig*) **~ la mémoire *ou* les idées de qn** to jog *ou* refresh sb's memory.
2 vi [*vin etc*] to cool (down). **mettre à ~** *vin, dessert* to chill.
3 **se rafraîchir** vpr a (*Mét*) **le temps/ça* se rafraîchit** the weather/it's getting cooler *ou* colder.
b (*en se lavant*) to freshen (o.s.) up; (*en buvant*) to refresh o.s. **on se rafraîchirait volontiers** a cool drink would be most acceptable.
rafraîchissant, e [ʀafʀeʃisɑ̃, ɑ̃t] adj *vent* refreshing, cooling; *boisson* refreshing; (*fig*) *idée, œuvre* refreshing.
rafraîchissement [ʀafʀeʃismɑ̃] nm a [*température*] cooling. **dû au ~ de la température** due to the cooler weather *ou* the cooling of the weather; **on s'attend à un ~ rapide de la température** we expect the weather to get rapidly cooler. b (*boisson*) cool *ou* cold drink. (*glaces, fruits*) **~s** refreshments.
ragaillardir [ʀagajaʀdiʀ] 2 vt to perk up, buck up*. **tout ragaillardi par cette nouvelle** bucked up by this news*.
rage [ʀaʒ] nf a (*colère*) rage, fury. **la ~ au cœur** seething with rage *ou* anger, seething inwardly; **mettre qn en ~** to infuriate *ou* enrage sb, make sb's blood boil; **être dans une ~ folle, être ivre *ou* fou de ~** to be mad with rage, be in a furious rage *ou* a raging temper; **suffoquer *ou* étouffer de ~** to choke with anger *ou* rage; **dans sa ~ de ne pouvoir l'obtenir** in his rage *ou* fury at not being able to obtain it; *voir* **amour**.
b (*manie*) **avoir la ~ de faire/qch** to have a mania for doing/sth; **la ~ de vivre qui l'habite** the will to live which possesses him.
c **faire ~** [*bataille, incendie, tempête*] to rage.
d (*Méd*) **la ~** rabies (*sg*).
e **~ de dents** raging toothache.
rageant, e* [ʀaʒɑ̃, ɑ̃t] adj infuriating, maddening.
rager [ʀaʒe] 3 vi to fume. **ça (me) fait ~!** it makes me fume! *ou* furious! *ou* mad!; **rageant de voir que les autres n'étaient pas punis** furious *ou* fuming that the others weren't punished.
rageur, -euse [ʀaʒœʀ, øz] adj *enfant* hot-tempered, quick-tempered; *ton, voix, geste* bad-tempered, angry. **il était ~** he was furious *ou* livid.
rageusement [ʀaʒøzmɑ̃] adv angrily.
raglan [ʀaglɑ̃] nm, adj inv raglan.
ragondin [ʀagɔ̃dɛ̃] nm (*animal*) coypu; (*fourrure*) nutria.
ragot* [ʀago] nm piece of (malicious) gossip *ou* tittle-tattle. **~s** gossip, tittle-tattle.
ragougnasse* [ʀaguɲas] nf (*péj*) pigswill (*fig: NonC*).
ragoût [ʀagu] nm stew. **viande en ~** meat stew.
ragoûtant, e [ʀagutɑ̃, ɑ̃t] adj: **peu ~** *mets* unappetizing, unsavoury, unpalatable; *individu* unsavoury; *travail* unwholesome, unpalatable, unappetizing; **ce n'est guère ~** that's not very inviting *ou* tempting.
ragrafer [ʀagʀafe] 1 vt to do up. **elle se ragrafa** she did herself up (again).
rag-time [ʀagtajm] nm ragtime.
rahat-loukoum [ʀaatlukum] nm = **loukoum**.
rai [ʀɛ] nm (*littér: rayon*) ray; (*Tech*) spoke (*of wooden wheel*).
raid [ʀɛd] nm (*Mil*) raid, hit-and-run attack. (*Mil*) **~ aérien** air raid; (*Sport: parcours*) **~ automobile/à skis** long-distance car/ski trek; (*Fin*) **~ boursier** raid; (*Mil, Fin*) **faire un ~ sur** to raid.
raide [ʀɛd] 1 adj a (*rigide*) *corps, membre, geste, étoffe* stiff; *cheveux* straight; *câble* taut, tight. **être *ou* se tenir ~ comme un échalas *ou* un piquet *ou* la justice** to be (as) stiff as a poker; **assis ~ sur sa chaise** sitting bolt upright on his chair; *voir* **corde**.
b (*abrupt*) steep, abrupt.
c (*inflexible*) *attitude, morale, personne* rigid, inflexible; (*guindé*) *manières* stiff, starchy; *démarche* stiff.
d (*fort, âpre*) *alcool* rough.
e (**: difficile à croire*) **l'histoire est un peu ~** that's a bit hard to swallow *ou* a bit far-fetched; **elle est ~ celle-là** (*je n'y crois pas*) that's a bit hard to swallow, that's a bit far-fetched; (*ils vont trop loin*) that's a bit steep* *ou* stiff*; **il en a vu de ~s** he's seen a thing or two.
f (*osé*) **assez *ou* un peu ~** *propos, passage, scène* daring, bold; **il s'en passe de ~s, chez eux** all sorts of things go on at their place; **il en raconte de ~s** he's always telling pretty daring stories.
g (*‡: sans argent*) broke*. **être ~ comme un passe-lacet** to be stony (*Brit*) *ou* stone (*US*) *ou* flat broke*.
2 adv a (*en pente*) **ça montait/descendait ~** [*ascension*] it was a steep climb/climb down; [*pente*] it climbed/fell steeply.
b (*net*) **tomber ~** to drop to the ground *ou* floor; **tomber ~ mort** to drop *ou* fall down dead *ou* stone dead (*Brit*); **tuer qn ~** to kill sb outright *ou* stone dead (*Brit*); **il l'a étendu ~ (mort)*** he laid him out cold*.
raider [ʀɛdœʀ] nm (*Bourse*) raider.
raideur [ʀɛdœʀ] nf (*voir* **raide**) stiffness; straightness; tautness, tightness; steepness, abruptness; rigidity, inflexibility; starchiness; rough-

ness. **avec ~** *répondre* stiffly, abruptly; *marcher* stiffly.

raidillon [ʀedijɔ̃] **nm** steep path.

raidir [ʀediʀ] [2] **1 vt** *drap, tissu* to stiffen; *corde, fil de fer* to pull taut *ou* tight, tighten. **~ ses muscles** to tense *ou* stiffen one's muscles; **le corps raidi par la mort** his body stiffened by death; (*fig*) **~ sa position** to harden *ou* toughen one's position, take a hard(er) *ou* tough(er) line. **2 se raidir vpr a** *[toile, tissu]* to stiffen, become stiff(er); *[corde]* to grow taut; (*fig*) *[position]* to harden. **b** *[personne]* (*perdre sa souplesse*) to become stiff(er); (*bander ses muscles*) to tense *ou* stiffen o.s.; (*se préparer moralement*) to brace *ou* steel o.s.; (*s'entêter*) to take a hard *ou* tough line.

raidissement [ʀedismɑ̃] **nm** (*perte de souplesse*) stiffening. (*fig: intransigeance*) **ce ~ soudain du parti adverse** this sudden tough line taken by the opposing party.

raidisseur [ʀedisœʀ] **nm** (*tendeur*) tightener.

raie[1] [ʀɛ] **nf a** (*trait*) line; (*Agr: sillon*) furrow; (*éraflure*) mark, scratch. **faire une ~** to draw a line; **attention, tu vas faire des ~s** careful, you'll make marks *ou* scratches; **la ~ des fesses** the cleft between the buttocks. **b** (*bande*) stripe. **chemise avec des ~s** striped *ou* stripy (*Brit*) shirt; **les ~s de son pelage** the stripes on its fur; (*Phys*) **~ d'absorption/d'émission** absorption/emission line. **c** (*Coiffure*) parting (*Brit*), part (*US*). **avoir la ~ au milieu/sur le côté** to have a centre/side parting, have one's hair parted in the middle/to the side.

raie[2] [ʀɛ] **nf** (*Zool*) skate, ray. **~ bouclée** thornback ray; **~ électrique** electric ray; *voir* **gueule**.

raifort [ʀɛfɔʀ] **nm** (*aromate*) horseradish; (*radis noir*) black winter radish.

rail [ʀɑj] **nm** rail. (*voie*) **les ~s** the rails, the track; **~ conducteur** live rail; **le ~ est plus pratique que la route** the railway (*Brit*) *ou* railroad (*US*) is more practical than the road, rail is more practical than road; (*fig*) **être sur les ~s** to be under way; (*lit, fig*) **remettre sur les ~s** to put back on the rails; **quitter les ~s, sortir des ~s** to jump the rails, go off the rails; **transport ~-route** road-rail transport.

railler [ʀɑje] [1] **1 vt** (*frm: se moquer de*) *personne, chose* to scoff at, jeer at, mock at. **2 vi** (*††: plaisanter*) to jest. **..., dit-il en raillant ...,** he said in jest. **3 se railler vpr: se ~ de††** to scoff at, jeer at, mock at.

raillerie [ʀɑjʀi] **nf** (*frm*) (*ironie*) mockery, scoffing; (*remarque*) gibe, scoff. **il sortit de scène sous les ~s du public** he left the stage to the booing *ou* catcalls of the audience.

railleur, -euse [ʀɑjœʀ, øz] **1 adj** mocking, derisive, scoffing. **2 nmpl: les ~s** the scoffers, the mockers.

railleusement [ʀɑjøzmɑ̃] **adv** *répondre, suggérer* mockingly, derisively, scoffingly.

rainer [ʀene] [1] **vt** to groove.

rainette [ʀɛnɛt] **nf a** (*grenouille*) tree frog. **b** = **reinette**.

rainurage [ʀenyʀaʒ] **nm** grooved surface.

rainure [ʀenyʀ] **nf** (*gén: longue, formant glissière*) groove; (*courte, pour emboîtage*) slot.

rainurer [ʀenyʀe] [1] **vt** to groove.

rais [ʀɛ] **nm** = **rai**.

raïs [ʀais] **nm** head of state (*of an Arab country*).

raisin [ʀɛzɛ̃] **1 nm a** (*gén*) **~(s)** grapes; **~ noir/blanc** black/white grape; **c'est un ~ qui donne du bon vin** it's a grape that yields a good wine; *voir* **grain, grappe, jus**. **b** (*papier*) ≃ royal. **2 comp ►raisins de Corinthe** currants **►raisins secs** raisins **►raisins de Smyrne** sultanas **►raisins de table** dessert *ou* eating grapes.

raisiné [ʀezine] **nm** (*jus*) grape jelly; (*confiture*) *pear or quince jam made with grape jelly*; (*‡†: sang*) claret‡, blood.

raison [ʀɛzɔ̃] **1 nf a** (*gén, Philos: faculté de discernement*) reason. **seul l'homme est doué de ~** man alone is endowed with reason; **conforme à la ~** within the bounds of reason; **contraire à la ~** contrary to reason; **il n'a plus sa ~, il a perdu la ~** he has lost his reason, he has taken leave of his senses, he is not in his right mind; **si tu avais toute ta ~ tu verrais que ...** if you were in your right mind *ou* right senses, you would see that ...; **manger/boire plus que de ~** to eat/drink more than is sensible *ou* more than one should *ou* more than is good for one; *voir* **âge, mariage, rime**.

b (*motif*) reason. **la ~ pour laquelle je suis venu** the reason (why *ou* that *ou* for which) I came; **pour quelles ~s l'avez-vous renvoyé?** on what grounds did you sack him?, what were your reasons for sacking him?; **la ~ de cette réaction** the reason for this reaction; **il n'y a pas de ~ de s'arrêter** there's no reason to stop; **j'ai mes ~s** I have my reasons; **pour des ~s politiques/de famille** for political/family reasons; **pour ~s de santé** for reasons of health, on grounds of (ill) health, for health reasons; **~s cachées** hidden motives *ou* reasons; **il a refusé pour la simple ~ que ...** he refused simply on the grounds that ..., he refused simply because ...; **les ~s en sont les suivantes** the reasons (for it) are as follows.

c (*argument, explication, excuse*) reason. **sans ~** without reason; **sans ~ valable** for no valid reason; (*iro*) **il a toujours de bonnes ~s!** he's always got a good excuse! *ou* reason!; (*Prov*) **la ~ du plus fort est toujours la meilleure** might is right; **ce n'est pas une ~!** that's no excuse! *ou* reason!; *voir* **comparaison, rendre**.

d (*Math*) ratio. **~ directe/inverse** direct/inverse ratio *ou* proportion.

e (*loc*) **avec (juste) ~** rightly, justifiably, with good reason; **~ de plus** all the more reason (*pour faire* for doing); **à plus forte ~, je n'irai pas** all the more reason for me not to go; **comme de ~** as one might expect; **pour une ~ ou pour une autre** for one *ou* some reason or other *ou* another; **rire sans ~** to laugh for no reason; **non sans ~** not without reason; **avoir ~** to be right (*de faire* in doing, to do); **avoir ~ de qn/qch** to get the better of sb/sth; **donner ~ à qn** *[événement]* to prove sb right; **tu donnes toujours ~ à ta fille** you're always siding with your daughter; **se faire une ~** to accept it, put up with it; **entendre ~, se rendre à la ~** to see reason; **faire entendre ~ à qn, ramener qn à la ~** to make sb see reason; **mettre qn à la ~** to bring sb to his senses, make sb see reason, talk (some) sense into sb; (*†, littér*) **demander ~ à qn de offense** to demand satisfaction from sb for (*†, littér*); **en ~ du froid** because of *ou* owing to the cold weather; **en ~ de son jeune âge** because of *ou* on the grounds of his youth; **on est payé en ~ du travail fourni** we are paid according to *ou* in proportion to the work produced; **à ~ de 100 F par caisse** at the rate of 100 francs per crate; **payé à ~ de 40 lignes par page** paid on the basis of 40 lines a page; **à ~ de 3 fois par semaine** 3 times a week.

2 comp ►raison d'État reason of State **►raison d'être: cet enfant est toute sa raison d'être** this child is her whole life *ou* her entire reason for living *ou* her entire raison d'être; **cette association n'a aucune raison d'être** this association has no reason for being *ou* no grounds for existence *ou* no raison d'être **►raison sociale** (*Comm*) corporate name.

raisonnable [ʀɛzɔnabl] **adj a** (*sensé*) *personne* sensible, reasonable; *conseil* sensible, sound, sane; *opinion, propos, conduite* sensible, sane. **soyez ~** be reasonable; **elle devrait être plus ~ à son âge** she should know better *ou* she should have more sense at her age; **réaction bien peu ~** very unreasonable reaction; **ce n'est vraiment pas ~** it's not really sensible *ou* reasonable at all.

b (*décent*) *prix, demande, salaire, quantité* reasonable, fair; *heure* reasonable. **ils vous accordent une liberté ~** they grant you reasonable freedom, they grant you a reasonable *ou* fair *ou* tolerable amount of freedom.

c (*littér: doué de raison*) rational, reasoning.

raisonnablement [ʀɛzɔnabləmɑ̃] **adv** *conseiller* sensibly, soundly; *agir* sensibly, reasonably; *boire* in moderation; *dépenser* moderately; *travailler, rétribuer* reasonably *ou* fairly well. **on peut ~ espérer que ...** one can reasonably hope that ... .

raisonné, e [ʀɛzɔne] (**ptp de raisonner**) **adj a** (*mûri, réfléchi*) *attitude, projet* well thought-out, reasoned. **bien ~!** well argued!, well reasoned! **b** (*systématique*) **grammaire/méthode ~e de français** reasoned grammar/primer of French.

raisonnement [ʀɛzɔnmɑ̃] **nm a** (*façon de réfléchir*) reasoning (*NonC*); (*faculté de penser*) power *ou* faculty of reasoning; (*cheminement de la pensée*) thought process. **~ analogique/par déduction** analogical/deductive reasoning; **prouver qch par le ~** to prove sth by one's reasoning *ou* by the use of reason; **ses ~s m'étonnent** his reasoning surprises me. **b** (*argumentation*) argument. **un ~ logique** a logical argument, a logical line *ou* chain of reasoning. **c** (*péj: ergotages*) **~s** arguing, argument, quibbling; **tous les ~s ne changeront pas ma décision** no amount of arguing *ou* argument will alter my decision.

raisonner [ʀɛzɔne] [1] **1 vi a** (*penser, réfléchir*) to reason (*sur* about). **~ par induction/déduction** to reason by induction/deduction; **il raisonne mal** he doesn't reason very well, his reasoning *ou* way of reasoning isn't very sound; **il raisonne juste** his reasoning is sound; **il raisonne comme un panier percé*** *ou* **une pantoufle*** he can't follow his own argument; **c'est bien raisonné** it's well *ou* soundly reasoned *ou* argued.

b (*discourir, argumenter*) to argue (*sur* about). **on ne peut pas ~ avec lui** you (just) can't argue *ou* reason with him.

c (*péj: ergoter*) to argue, quibble (*avec* with).

d ~ de† *question, problème* to argue about.

2 vt a (*sermonner*) to reason with. **inutile d'essayer de le ~** it's useless to try and reason with him, it's useless to try and make him listen to *ou* see reason.

b (*justifier par la raison*) *croyance, conduite, démarche* to reason out. **explication bien raisonnée** well-reasoned explanation.

3 se raisonner vpr to reason with o.s., make o.s. see reason. **raisonne-toi** try to be reasonable *ou* to make yourself see reason; **l'amour ne se raisonne pas** love cannot be reasoned *ou* knows no reason.

raisonneur, -euse [ʀɛzɔnœʀ, øz] **1 adj** (*péj*) quibbling (*épith*), argumentative; (*réfléchi*) reasoning (*épith*). **2 nm,f a** (*péj: ergoteur*) arguer, quibbler. **c'est un ~** he's always arguing *ou* quibbling, he's an arguer *ou* a quibbler; **ne fais pas le ~** stop arguing *ou* quibbling. **b** (*penseur*) reasoner.

rajah [ʀa(d)ʒa] **nm** rajah.

rajeunir [ʀaʒœniʀ] [2] **1 vt a ~ qn** *[cure]* to rejuvenate sb; *[repos, expérience]* to make sb feel younger; *[soins de beauté, vêtement]* to make sb look younger; **l'amour/ce chapeau la rajeunit de 10 ans** love/this hat takes 10 years off her* *ou* makes her look 10 years younger; **tu le rajeunis (de 5 ans), il est né en 1950** you're making him (5 years) younger than he is – he was born in 1950; (*hum*) **ça ne nous rajeunit pas!** that makes you realize we're not getting any younger!

b *manuel* to update, bring up to date; *institution* to modernize; *installation, mobilier* to modernize, give a new look to; *vieux habits* to give a new look to, brighten up; *personnel* to infuse *ou* bring new *ou* young blood into, recruit younger people into; *thème, théorie* to inject new life into. **firme qui a besoin d'être rajeunie** firm that needs new *ou* young blood (brought *ou* infused into it) *ou* that needs an injection of new blood *ou* an influx of new people.

2 **vi** *[personne]* (*se sentir plus jeune*) to feel younger; (*paraître plus jeune*) to look younger; *[institution, quartier]* (*modernisation*) to be modernized; (*membres plus jeunes*) to take on a younger air. **avec les enfants, la vieille demeure rajeunissait** with the children around, the old house seemed to take on a younger air *ou* had a younger atmosphere about it.

3 **se rajeunir vpr** (*se prétendre moins âgé*) to make o.s. younger; (*se faire paraître moins âgé*) to make o.s. look younger.

rajeunissant, e [ʀaʒœnisɑ̃, ɑ̃t] **adj** *traitement, crème* rejuvenating.

rajeunissement [ʀaʒœnismɑ̃] **nm** *[personne]* rejuvenation; *[manuel]* updating; *[installation, mobilier]* modernization; *[vieux habits]* brightening up. ~ **du personnel** infusion *ou* injection of new *ou* young blood into the staff.

rajout [ʀaʒu] **nm** addition (*sur* to).

rajouter [ʀaʒute] 1 **vt** *sel, sucre* to put on *ou* put in *ou* add (some) more; *commentaire* to add another. **il rajouta que ...** he added that ...; (*fig*) **en** ~* to lay it on (thick)*, exaggerate; **il ne faut pas croire tout ce qu'il dit, il en rajoute toujours** you mustn't believe everything he says, he always exaggerates; **ayant déjà donné 50 F, il rajouta 10 F** having already given 50 francs he added another 10.

rajustement [ʀaʒystəmɑ̃] **nm** *[salaires, prix]* adjustment.

rajuster [ʀaʒyste] 1 1 **vt** a (*remettre en place*) *mécanisme* to readjust; *vêtement* to straighten (out), tidy; *cravate, lunettes* to straighten, adjust; *coiffure* to rearrange, tidy. **elle rajusta sa toilette** she tidied *ou* arranged herself (*ou* her dress). b (*recentrer*) *tir* to (re)adjust; (*fig*) *prix, salaire* to adjust. 2 **se rajuster vpr** *[personne]* to tidy *ou* straighten o.s. up, rearrange o.s.

raki [ʀaki] **nm** raki.

râlant, e* [ʀɑlɑ̃, ɑ̃t] **adj** infuriating.

râle[1] [ʀɑl] **nm** a *[blessé]* groan; *[mourant]* (death) rattle. ~ **d'agonie** *ou* **de la mort** death rattle. b (*Méd*) rale.

râle[2] [ʀɑl] **nm** (*Orn*) rail. ~ **(des genêts)** corncrake; ~ **(d'eau)** water rail.

ralenti, e [ʀalɑ̃ti] (**ptp de ralentir**) 1 **adj** *vie* slow-moving, easy-paced, slow; *mouvement* slow. 2 **nm** a (*Ciné*) slow motion. **en** *ou* **au** ~ *filmer, projeter* in slow motion. b (*Aut*) **régler le** ~ to adjust the tick-over (*Brit*) *ou* the idle; **le moteur est un peu faible au** ~ the engine doesn't tick over (*Brit*) *ou* doesn't idle too well; **tourner au** ~ to tick over (*Brit*), idle. c (*fig*) **vivre au** ~ to live at a slower pace; **cette existence paisible, au** ~ that peaceful slow *ou* easy-paced existence; **usine qui tourne au** ~ factory which is just ticking over (*Brit*) *ou* idling; (*péj*) **ça tourne au** ~ **chez lui!** he's a bit slow!*

ralentir [ʀalɑ̃tiʀ] 2 1 **vt** *processus, véhicule* to slow down; *mouvement, expansion* to slow down *ou* up; (*Mil*) *avance* to check, hold up; *effort, zèle* to slacken. ~ **l'allure** to slow down *ou* up, reduce speed; ~ **sa marche** *ou* **le pas** to slacken one's *ou* the pace, slow down. 2 **vi** *[marcheur]* to slow down, slacken one's pace; *[véhicule, automobiliste]* to slow down, reduce speed. (*Aut*) "~" "slow", "reduce speed now". 3 **se ralentir vpr** *[production]* to slow down *ou* up, slacken (off), fall off; (*Mil*) *[offensive]* to let up, ease off; *[ardeur, zèle]* to flag; (*Physiol*) *[fonctions]* to slow up.

ralentissement [ʀalɑ̃tismɑ̃] **nm** a (*voir* **ralentir**) slowing down; slowing up; checking, holding up; slackening. b *[marcheur, véhicule, automobiliste]* slowing down. **un ~ sur 3 km** a 3 km tailback (*Brit*) *ou* hold-up (*US*). c (*voir* **se ralentir**) slowing down; slowing up; slackening (off), falling off; letting up, easing off; flagging.

ralentisseur [ʀalɑ̃tisœʀ] **nm** (*sur route*) sleeping policeman (*Brit*), speed bump (*US*).

râler [ʀɑle] 1 **vi** a *[blessé]* to groan, moan; *[mourant]* to give the death rattle. b (**: rouspéter*) to grouse*, moan (and groan)*. **il est allé ~ chez le prof** he went to grouse* *ou* moan* to the teacher; **faire ~ qn** to infuriate sb; **ça (vous) fait** ~ it makes you fume, it makes you want to blow your top*; **qu'as tu à ~?** what have you got to grouse* *ou* moan* about?

râleur, -euse* [ʀɑlœʀ, øz] 1 **adj** grousing* (*épith*). **il est (trop)** ~ he's (too much of) a grouser* *ou* moaner*. 2 **nm,f** grouser*, moaner*.

ralingue [ʀalɛ̃g] **nf** boltrope.

ralliement [ʀalimɑ̃] **nm** a (*voir* **rallier**) rallying; winning over; uniting. **le ~ des troupes** the rallying *ou* rally of troops. b (*voir* **se rallier**) ~ **à** joining; going over to, siding with; rallying round *ou* to; coming over *ou* round (*Brit*) to; being won over to; **je suis étonné de son ~ (à notre cause)** I am surprised by the fact that he joined (our cause). c (*Mil*) rallying, rally. **signe/cri de** ~ rallying sign/cry.

rallier [ʀalje] 7 1 **vt** a (*Chasse, Mil, Naut: regrouper*) to rally.

b (*gagner*) *personne, groupe* to win over, rally (*à* to); *suffrages* to bring in, win. ~ **qn à son avis** to bring sb round (*Brit*) *ou* win sb over to one's opinion.

c (*unir*) *groupe, parti* to rally, unite. **groupe rallié autour d'un idéal** group united by an ideal.

d (*rejoindre: Mil, Naut*) to rejoin. (*Pol*) ~ **la majorité** to rejoin the majority; (*Naut*) ~ **le bord** to rejoin ship.

2 **se rallier vpr** a (*suivre*) **se ~ à** *parti* to join; *ennemi* to go over to, side with; *chef* to rally round *ou* to; *avis* to come over *ou* round (*Brit*) to; *doctrine* to be won over to; *cause* to join, rally to, be won over to.

b (*Mil, Naut: se regrouper*) to rally.

rallonge [ʀalɔ̃ʒ] **nf** a *[table]* (extra) leaf; *[fil électrique]* extension lead *ou* cable (*Brit*) *ou* cord (*US*); *[vêtement]* piece (*used to lengthen an item of clothing*); *[compas]* extension arm; *[perche]* extension piece. **table à ~(s)** extendable table. b (**: supplément*) **une ~ d'argent/de vacances** a bit of extra *ou* some extra money/holiday; **obtenir une ~ de crédit** to get an extension of credit; **une ~ de deux jours** an extra two days, a two-day extension. c (*péj*) **histoire à** ~ never-ending story; **nom à** ~ (*gén*) long, complicated surname; (*en deux mots*) double-barrelled name.

rallongement [ʀalɔ̃ʒmɑ̃] **nm** (*voir* **rallonger**) lengthening; letting down; extension.

rallonger [ʀalɔ̃ʒe] 3 1 **vt** *vêtement* (*en ajoutant*) to lengthen, make longer; (*en défaisant l'ourlet*) to let down; *texte, service militaire, piste* to lengthen, extend, make longer; *vacances, fil, table, bâtiment* to extend. **par ce chemin/en bus, ça me rallonge de 10 minutes** this way/by bus, it takes me 10 minutes longer. 2 **vi** (*) **les jours rallongent** the days are getting longer.

rallumer [ʀalyme] 1 1 **vt** a (*lit*) *feu* to light (up) again, relight, rekindle; *cigarette* to relight, light up again; *lampe* to switch *ou* turn *ou* put on again, relight. ~ **(l'électricité** *ou* **la lumière)** to switch *ou* turn *ou* put the light(s) on again; ~ **(dans) le bureau** to switch *ou* turn *ou* put the light(s) on again in the office.

b (*fig*) *courage, haine, querelle* to revive, rekindle; *conflit, guerre* to stir up again, revive, rekindle.

2 **se rallumer vpr** a *[incendie]* to flare up again; *[lampe]* to come on again. **le bureau se ralluma** the light(s) in the office went *ou* came on again.

b *[guerre, querelle]* to flare up again; *[haine, courage]* to revive, be revived.

rallye [ʀali] **nm**: ~ **(automobile)** (car) rally.

RAM [ʀam] **nf** (*Ordin*) RAM.

ramadan [ʀamadɑ̃] **nm**: **(R)**~ Ramadan.

ramage [ʀamaʒ] **nm** a (*littér: chant*) song, warbling (*NonC*). b (*branchages, dessin*) **~(s)** foliage; **tissu à ~s** fabric *ou* material with a leafy design *ou* pattern.

ramassage [ʀamɑsaʒ] **nm** a (*gén*) collection. ~ **des pommes de terre** lifting *ou* digging up of potatoes; ~ **scolaire** (*service*) school bus service; (*action*) picking up of pupils; **point de** ~ pick-up point. b (*cueillette*) *[bois mort, coquillages, foin]* gathering; *[épis, fruits tombés]* gathering (up); *[champignons]* picking, gathering; *[pommes de terres]* digging up, lifting; *[balles de tennis]* picking up.

ramasse- [ʀamɑs] **préf** *voir* **ramasser**.

ramassé, e [ʀamɑse] (**ptp de ramasser**) **adj** (*pour se protéger*) huddled (up); (*pour bondir*) crouched; (*trapu*) squat, stocky; (*concis*) compact, condensed. **le petit village ~ dans le fond de la vallée** the little village nestling in the heart of the valley.

ramasser [ʀamɑse] 1 1 **vt** a (*lit, fig: prendre*) *objet, personne* to pick up. **il l'a ramassée dans le ruisseau** he picked her up out of the gutter; **se faire ~ dans une manif*** to get picked up at a demo*; **on l'a ramassé à la petite cuiller*** they had to scrape him off the ground; ~ **une bûche*** *ou* **une pelle*** to come a cropper* (*Brit*), fall headlong, fall flat on one's face.

b (*collecter*) *objets épars* to pick up, gather up; *cartes* to pick up; *élèves* to pick up, collect; *copies, cahiers* to collect, take in, gather up; *cotisations, ordures* to collect; (*) *idée* to pick up; (*) *argent* to pick up, pocket*. (*fig*) ~ **ses forces** to gather *ou* muster one's strength.

c (*récolter*) *bois, feuilles, coquillages* to gather, collect; *fruits tombés* to gather (up); *foin* to gather; *pommes de terre* to lift, dig up; *champignons* to pick, gather. ~ **à la pelle** (*lit*) to shovel up; (*fig: en abondance*) to get loads* *ou* stacks* of.

d (*resserrer*) *jupons, draps* to gather (up); (*fig*) *style* to condense.

e (**: attraper*) *rhume, maladie* to pick up, catch, get; *réprimande, coups* to collect, get; *amende* to pick up, collect, get. **il va se faire ~ par sa mère** he'll get told off *ou* ticked off (*Brit*) by his mother*; **il a ramassé 100 F (d'amende)** he picked up *ou* collected a 100-franc fine, he was done for 100 francs* (*Brit*).

2 **se ramasser vpr** (*se pelotonner*) to curl up; (*pour bondir*) to crouch; (**: se relever*) to pick o.s. up; (*‡: tomber*) to come a cropper* (*Brit*), fall over *ou* down; (**: échouer*) *[candidat]* to come a cropper* (*Brit*), take a flat beating (*US*). **se faire ~*** *[candidat]* to be failed; *[dragueur]* to get the cold shoulder*.

3 **comp ►ramasse-miettes nm inv** table tidy (*Brit*), silent butler (*US*) **►ramasse-monnaie nm inv** (change-)tray.

ramasseur, -euse [ʀamɑsœʀ, øz] 1 **nm,f** (*personne*) collector. ~ **de**

lait milk collector; ~ **de balles (de tennis)** (*garçon*) ballboy; (*fille*) ballgirl; ~ **de mégots** collector of cigarette ends *ou* butts; ~ **de pommes de terre** potato-picker. 2 **nm** (*outil*) *[machine]* pickup. 3 **ramasseuse nf** (*machine*) ~**euse-presse** baler.

ramassis [ʀamɑsi] **nm** (*péj*) ~ **de** *voyous* pack *ou* bunch *ou* horde of; *doctrines, objets* jumble of.

rambarde [ʀɑ̃baʀd] **nf** guardrail.

ramdam‡ [ʀamdam] **nm** (*tapage*) hullabaloo*, row, racket; (*protestation*) row. **faire du** ~ (*bruit*) to kick up* *ou* make a racket *ou* row; (*protestation*) to kick up a row*; (*scandale*) to cause a stir.

rame [ʀam] **nf** a (*aviron*) oar. **aller à la** ~ to row; (*littér*) **faire force de** ~**s** to ply the oars (*littér*), row hard; **il n'en fiche pas une** ~‡ he doesn't do a damned‡ *ou* ruddy‡ (*Brit*) thing. b (*Rail*) train. ~ **(de métro)** (underground (*Brit*) *ou* subway (*US*)) train. c (*Typ*) ream; (*Tex*) tenter; (*Agr*) stake, stick; *voir* **haricot**.

rameau, **pl** ~**x** [ʀamo] **nm** (*lit*) (small) branch; (*fig*) branch; (*Anat*) ramification. (*lit, fig*) ~ **d'olivier** olive branch; (*Rel*) **(dimanche des) R~x** Palm Sunday.

ramée [ʀame] **nf** (*littér: feuillage*) leafy boughs (*littér*); (*coupé*) leafy *ou* green branches. **il n'en fiche pas une** ~‡ he doesn't do a damned‡ *ou* ruddy‡ (*Brit*) thing.

ramener [ʀam(ə)ne] 5 1 **vt** a *personne, objet* to bring back, take back; *paix, ordre* to bring back, restore. **je vais te** ~ **en voiture** I'll drive you back (home), I'll take you back (home) in the car; **ramène du pain/les enfants** bring *ou* fetch (*Brit*) some bread/the children back (*de* from); **ça l'a ramené en prison** it sent him back to prison, it put *ou* landed* him back in prison; **l'été a ramené les accidents/la mode des chapeaux** summer has brought the return of accidents/has brought back *ou* brought the return of the fashion for hats.

b (*tirer*) *voile* to draw; *couverture* to pull, draw. ~ **ses cheveux sur son front** to brush down one's hair onto *ou* over one's forehead; ~ **ses cheveux en arrière** to brush one's hair back; ~ **ses jambes/épaules en arrière** to draw back one's legs/shoulders.

c (*faire revenir à*) ~ **à** to bring back to; ~ **à la vie** *personne* to revive, bring back to life; *région* to revitalize, bring back to life; ~ **qn à la raison** to bring sb to reason *ou* to his senses; ~ **le compteur à zéro** to put the meter back to zero, reset the meter at zero; ~ **les prix à un juste niveau** to bring prices back (down) *ou* restore prices to a reasonable level; ~ **la conversation sur un sujet** to bring *ou* steer *ou* lead the conversation back (on)to a subject; ~ **son cheval au pas** to rein in one's horse to a walk; **il ramène toujours tout à lui** he always relates everything to himself; **cela nous ramène 20 ans en arrière** it takes us back 20 years; ~ **un incident à de plus justes proportions** to get *ou* bring an incident into proportion; **ils ont ramené ces bagarres au rang de simple incident** they played down the fighting, passing it off as a mere incident.

d (*réduire à*) ~ **à** to reduce to; ~ **l'inflation à moins de 3%** to reduce inflation to less than 3%, bring inflation back down to below 3%.

e (*loc*) ~ **sa fraise‡, la** ~‡ (*protester*) to kick up* a row *ou* fuss; (*intervenir*) to put *ou* shove one's oar in* (*Brit*), put in one's opinion.

2 **se ramener vpr** a (*se réduire à*) **se** ~ **à** *[problèmes]* to come down to, boil down to; (*Math*) *[fraction]* to reduce to, be reduced to.

b (‡: *arriver*) to roll up*, turn up*.

ramequin [ʀamkɛ̃] **nm** ramekin, ramequin.

ramer¹ [ʀame] 1 **vi** a (*Sport*) to row. ~ **en couple** to scull. b (*peiner*) to work hard.

ramer² [ʀame] 1 **vt** (*Agr*) to stake.

ramette [ʀamɛt] **nf** *[papier à lettres]* ream.

rameur [ʀamœʀ] **nm** (*sportif*) oarsman, rower; (*galérien*) rower.

rameuse [ʀamøz] **nf** (*sportive*) oarswoman, rower.

rameuter [ʀamøte] 1 **vt** *foule, partisans* to gather together, round up; *chiens* to round up, form into a pack again. **les gens s'étaient rameutés** people had gathered (themselves) together (again).

rami [ʀami] **nm** rummy.

ramier [ʀamje] **nm: (pigeon)** ~ woodpigeon, ringdove.

ramification [ʀamifikasjɔ̃] **nf** (*gén*) ramification.

ramifier (se) [ʀamifje] 7 **vpr** *[veines]* to ramify; *[routes, branches, famille]* to branch out (*en* into). **cette science s'est ramifiée en plusieurs autres** this science has branched out into several others.

ramille [ʀamij] **nf** (*brindille*) twig.

ramolli, e [ʀamɔli] (**ptp de ramollir**) 1 **adj** *biscuit, beurre* soft; *personne* (*avachi*) soft; (*stupide*) soft (in the head), soft-headed. (*péj*) **il a le cerveau** ~ he is *ou* has gone soft in the head. 2 **nm,f** (*péj*) soft-headed fool.

ramollir [ʀamɔliʀ] 2 1 **vt** *matière* to soften; (*fig*) *courage, résolution* to weaken. ~ **qn** *[plaisir]* to soften sb, make sb soft; *[climat]* to enervate sb. 2 **vi, se ramollir vpr** *[beurre, argile]* to soften (up), go soft. (*hum*) **son cerveau se ramollit** he's going soft in the head*.

ramollissement [ʀamɔlismɑ̃] **nm** softening. ~ **cérébral** softening of the brain.

ramollo* [ʀamɔlo] **adj** (*avachi*) droopy*; (*gâteux*) soft (in the head), soft-headed.

ramonage [ʀamɔnaʒ] **nm** chimney-sweeping; (*Alpinisme*) chimney-climbing.

ramoner [ʀamɔne] 1 1 **vt** *cheminée* to sweep; *pipe* to clean out. 2 **vi** (*Alpinisme*) to climb a chimney.

ramoneur [ʀamɔnœʀ] **nm** (chimney) sweep.

rampant, e [ʀɑ̃pɑ̃, ɑ̃t] 1 **adj** a *animal* crawling, creeping; *plante* creeping; *caractère, employé* grovelling, cringing; *inflation* creeping. (*arg Aviat*) **personnel** ~ ground crew *ou* staff; *voir* **arc.** b (*Hér*) rampant. 2 **nm** a (*arg Aviat*) member of the ground crew *ou* staff. **les** ~**s** the ground crew *ou* staff. b (*Archit*) pitch.

rampe [ʀɑ̃p] 1 **nf** a (*voie d'accès*) ramp, slope; (*côte*) slope, incline, gradient. b *[escalier]* banister(s); *[chemin, escarpe etc]* handrail. c (*Théât: projecteurs*) **la** ~ the footlights, the floats (*Brit*). d (*loc*) (*fig*) **tenez bon la** ~* hold on to your hat*; **elle tient bon la** ~* she's still going strong; (*fig*) **lâcher la** ~* to kick the bucket‡; **passer la** ~ to get across to the audience. 2 **comp** ►**rampe d'accès** approach ramp ►**rampe de balisage** runway lights ►**rampe de débarquement** disembarcation ramp ►**rampe de graissage** oil gallery ►**rampe de lancement** launching pad.

ramper [ʀɑ̃pe] 1 **vi** a *[serpent]* to crawl, slither, slide (along); *[quadrupède, homme]* to crawl; *[plante, ombre, feu]* to creep; *[sentiment, brouillard, mal, maladie]* to lurk. **entrer/sortir en rampant** to crawl in/out; **le lierre rampe contre le mur** the ivy creeps up the wall. b (*fig péj: s'abaisser*) to grovel (*devant* before), crawl, cringe (*devant* to).

ramponneau‡, **pl** ~**x** [ʀɑ̃pɔno] **nm** poke, bump, knock. **donner un** ~ **à qn** to poke *ou* bump *ou* knock sb.

ramure [ʀamyʀ] **nf** *[cerf]* antlers; *[arbre]* boughs, foliage.

rancard‡ [ʀɑ̃kaʀ] **nm** a (*tuyau*) tip; (*explication*) gen* (*Brit*) (*NonC*), info* (*NonC*). **il m'avait donné le** ~ he had tipped me the wink*, he had given me the tip-off. b (*rendez-vous*) (*gén*) meeting, date; (*amoureux*) date. **donner (un)** ~ **à qn** to arrange to meet sb, make a date with sb; **avoir (un)** ~ **avec qn** to have a meeting with sb, have a date with sb.

rancarder‡ [ʀɑ̃kaʀde] 1 **vt** (*voir* **rancard**) to tip off; to give the gen* (*Brit*) *ou* info* to; to arrange to meet; to make a date with*. (*s'informer*) **se** ~ **sur** to get the info* *ou* gen* (*Brit*) about.

rancart¹‡ [ʀɑ̃kaʀ] **nm** = **rancard‡.**

rancart²‡ [ʀɑ̃kaʀ] **nm: mettre au** ~ *objet, idée, projet* to chuck out‡, sling out‡, get shot of‡ (*Brit*), scrap; **bon à mettre au** ~ ready for the scrap heap.

rance [ʀɑ̃s] **adj** *beurre* rancid; *odeur* rank, rancid; (*fig*) stale. **sentir le** ~ to smell rancid *ou* rank *ou* off* (*Brit*); **odeur de** ~ rank *ou* rancid smell.

ranch [ʀɑ̃tʃ] **nm** ranch.

rancir [ʀɑ̃siʀ] 2 **vi** *[lard, beurre]* to go rancid *ou* off* (*Brit*); (*fig*) to grow stale.

rancœur [ʀɑ̃kœʀ] **nf** (*frm*) rancour (*NonC*), resentment (*NonC*). **avoir de la** ~ **contre qn** to be full of rancour against sb, feel resentment against sb.

rançon [ʀɑ̃sɔ̃] **nf** (*lit*) ransom. (*fig*) **c'est la** ~ **de la gloire/du progrès** that's the price you have to pay for being famous/for progress, that's the price of fame/of progress; (*littér*) **mettre à** ~ to hold to ransom.

rançonnement [ʀɑ̃sɔnmɑ̃] **nm** (*voir* **rançonner**) demanding a ransom (*de* from); fleecing; holding to ransom.

rançonner [ʀɑ̃sɔne] 1 **vt** a (*voler*) *convoi, voyageurs* to demand *ou* exact a ransom from; (*fig*) *contribuables, locataires, clients* to fleece. b (†: *exiger une rançon*) *prisonnier* to hold to ransom.

rançonneur, -euse [ʀɑ̃sɔnœʀ, øz] **nm,f** (*lit*) person demanding a ransom, ransomer; (*fig*) extortioner, extortionist.

rancune [ʀɑ̃kyn] **nf** grudge, rancour (*NonC: littér*). **avoir** *ou* **nourrir de la** ~ **à l'égard de** *ou* **contre qn** to harbour a grudge *ou* harbour feelings of rancour against sb; **garder** ~ **à qn (de qch)** to hold a grudge against sb (for sth), bear sb a grudge (for sth); **sans** ~! no hard *ou* ill feelings!

rancunier, -ière [ʀɑ̃kynje, jɛʀ] **adj** vindictive, rancorous (*littér*), spiteful.

randonnée [ʀɑ̃dɔne] **nf** a (*promenade*) (*en voiture*) drive, ride. ~ **(à bicyclette)** (bike) ride; ~ **pédestre** *ou* **à pied** (*courte, à la campagne*) walk, ramble; (*longue, en montagne etc*) hike; ~ **à ski** cross-country ski run; ~ **équestre** *ou* **à cheval** pony trek; **partir en** ~ (*courte*) to go for a walk, go (off) for a ramble; (*longue*) to go hiking; **faire une** ~ **en voiture** to go for a drive; **cette** ~ **nocturne se termina mal** this night escapade ended badly. b (*activité*) **la** ~ (*à pied*) rambling, hiking; **la** ~ **équestre** pony trekking; *voir* **sentier.**

randonneur, -euse [ʀɑ̃dɔnœʀ, øz] **nm,f** hiker, walker, rambler.

rang [ʀɑ̃] **nm** a (*rangée*) *[maisons]* row, line; *[personnes, objets, tricot]* row. **collier à 3** ~**s (de perles)** necklace with 3 rows of pearls; **porter un** ~ **de perles** to wear a string *ou* rope *ou* row of pearls; **en** ~ **d'oignons** in a row *ou* line.

b (*Scol*) row; (*Mil*) rank. **en** ~**s serrés** in close order, in serried ranks; **en** ~ **par 2/4** 2/4 abreast; **sur 2/4** ~**s** 2/4 deep; **se mettre sur un** ~ to get into *ou* form a line; (*fig*) **grossir les** ~**s de** to swell the ranks of; **se mettre en** ~**s par 4** (*Scol*) to line up in fours; (*Mil*) to form fours; **plusieurs personnes sont sur** *ou* **se sont mises sur les** ~**s pour l'acheter** several people are in the running *ou* have got themselves lined up to buy it, several people have indicated an interest in buying it;

(*Mil*) **servir dans les ~s de** to serve in the ranks of; (*Mil*) **à vos ~s, marche!** fall in!; (*Mil, fig*) **sortir du ~** to come up *ou* rise *ou* be promoted from the ranks; *voir* **rentrer, rompre, serrer.**

c (*Can*) country road (*bordered by farms at right angles*), concession road (*in Quebec*). **les ~s** the country.

d (*condition*) station. **du plus haut ~** of the highest standing *ou* station; **tenir** *ou* **garder son ~** to maintain one's rank.

e (*hiérarchique, grade, place*) rank. **avoir ~ de** to hold the rank of; **avoir ~ parmi** to rank among; **par ~ d'âge/de taille** in order of age/size *ou* height; **13e, c'est un bon ~** that's not bad – 13th place, 13th – that's a good position; **être placé au deuxième ~** to be ranked *ou* placed second; **mettre un écrivain au ~ des plus grands** to rank a writer among the greatest; **c'est au premier/dernier ~ de mes préoccupations** that's the first/last thing on my mind; **il est au premier ~ des artistes contemporains** he is one of the highest ranking of *ou* he ranks among the best of contemporary artists.

rangé, e¹ [Rɑ̃ʒe] (**ptp de ranger**) **adj** (*ordonné*) orderly; (*sans excès*) settled, steady. **il est ~** *ou* **il est ~ des voitures‡ maintenant** he has settled *ou* steadied down now; **petite vie bien ~e** well-ordered existence; **jeune fille ~e** well-behaved young lady; *voir* **bataille.**

rangée² [Rɑ̃ʒe] **nf** *[maisons, arbres]* row, line; *[objets, spectateurs, perles]* row.

rangement [Rɑ̃ʒmɑ̃] **nm** a (*action*) *[objets, linge]* putting away; *[pièce, meuble]* tidying (up). **faire du ~** *ou* **des ~s** to do some tidying (up). b (*espace*) *[appartement]* cupboard space; *[remise]* storage space. **capacité de ~ d'une bibliothèque** shelf space of a bookcase; **la maison manque d'espaces de ~** the house lacks storage *ou* cupboard space; *voir* **meuble.** c (*arrangement*) arrangement.

ranger¹ [Rɑ̃ʒe] [3] **1 vt** a (*mettre en ordre*) *tiroir, maison* to tidy (up); *dossiers, papiers* to tidy (up), arrange; *mots, chiffres* to arrange, order. **tout est toujours bien rangé chez elle** it's always (nice and) tidy at her place; **rangé par ordre alphabétique** listed *ou* arranged alphabetically *ou* in alphabetical order.

b (*mettre à sa place*) *papiers, vêtements* to put away; *bateau* to moor, berth; *voiture, vélo* (*au garage*) to put away, park; (*dans la rue*) to park. **où se rangent les tasses?** where do the cups go? *ou* belong?; **je le range parmi les meilleurs** I rank *ou* put it among the best; **ce roman est à ~ parmi les meilleurs** this novel ranks *ou* is to be ranked among the best.

c (*disposer*) *écoliers* to line up, put *ou* form into rows; *soldats* to draw up; *invités* to place. (*fig*) **~ qn sous son autorité** to bring sb under one's authority.

2 se ranger vpr a *[automobiliste]* (*stationner*) to park; (*venir s'arrêter*) to pull in, draw up. **la voiture se rangea contre le trottoir** the car pulled in *ou* drew up at the kerb; **le navire se rangea contre le quai** the ship moored *ou* berthed *ou* came alongside the quay.

b (*s'écarter*) *[piéton]* to step *ou* stand aside, make way; *[véhicule]* to pull over. **il se rangea pour la laisser passer** he stepped *ou* stood aside to let her go by *ou* past, he made way for her (to get by *ou* past).

c (*se mettre en rang*) to line up, get into line *ou* rows. **se ~ par deux/par quatre** to line up in twos/fours, get into rows of two/four.

d (*se rallier à*) **se ~ à** *décision* to go along with, abide by; *avis* to come round *ou* over to, fall in with; **se ~ du côté de qn** to side with *ou* take sides with sb.

e (*: *se caser*) to settle down; *voir* **rangé.**

ranger² [Rɑ̃dʒɛR] **nm** (*soldat*) ranger; (*scout*) rover; (*chaussure*) canvas walking boot.

rani [Rani] **nf** rani, ranee.

ranimation [Ranimasjɔ̃] **nf** = **réanimation.**

ranimer [Ranime] [1] **1 vt** *blessé* to revive, restore to consciousness, bring round (*Brit*), bring to; *feu, braises* to rekindle; *région, souvenir, époque, conversation* to revive, bring back to life; *rancune, querelle* to rake up, revive; *forces, ardeur* to renew, restore; *amour, haine* to rekindle, renew; *douleur* to revive, renew; *espoir* to reawaken, rekindle, renew; *couleurs* to brighten up, revive. **2 se ranimer vpr** (*voir* **ranimer**) to revive, be revived; to come round (*Brit*), come to; to rekindle, be rekindled; to come back to life; to be raked up; to be renewed; to be restored; to reawaken, be reawakened.

Raoul [Raul] **nm** Ralph.

raout† [Raut] **nm** (*réception*) rout††.

rap [Rap] **nm** (*musique*) rap (music); (*technique*) rapping.

rapace [Rapas] **1 nm** (*Orn*) bird of prey, raptor (*SPÉC*). **2 adj** predatory, raptorial (*SPÉC*); (*fig*) rapacious, grasping, money-grubbing.

rapacité [Rapasite] **nf** (*lit, fig*) rapaciousness, rapacity.

râpage [Rɑpaʒ] **nm** (*voir* **râper**) grating; rasping; grinding.

rapatrié, e [RapatRije] (**ptp de rapatrier**) **1 adj** repatriated. **2 nm,f** repatriate. **les ~s d'Algérie** the repatriated settlers from Algeria.

rapatriement [RapatRimɑ̃] **nm** repatriation. **~ sanitaire** repatriation on medical grounds.

rapatrier [RapatRije] [7] **vt** *personne* to repatriate; *capital, objet* to bring back (home).

râpe [Rɑp] **nf** (*voir* **râper**) grater; rasp; grinder.

râpé, e [Rɑpe] (**ptp de râper**) **1 adj** (*usé*) *veste, coude* threadbare, worn to threads (*attrib*); *carottes, fromage* grated. (*: *raté*) **c'est ~ pour ce soir** we've had it for tonight*. **2 nm** (*fromage*) grated cheese.

râper [Rɑpe] [1] **vt** *carottes, fromage* to grate; *bois* to rasp; *tabac* to grind. (*fig*) **vin qui râpe la gorge** wine that's rough on the throat.

rapetassage* [Rap(ə)tasaʒ] **nm** patching up.

rapetasser* [Rap(ə)tase] [1] **vt** to patch up.

rapetissement [Rap(ə)tismɑ̃] **nm** (*voir* **rapetisser**) taking up, shortening; taking in; shrinking; belittling; dwarfing. **le ~ des objets dû à la distance** the reduction in the size of objects when seen from a distance.

rapetisser [Rap(ə)tise] [1] **1 vt** a (*raccourcir*) *manteau* to take up, shorten; *taille, encolure* to take in; *objet* to shorten. (*fig*) **l'âge l'avait rapetissé** he had shrunk with age (*fig*).

b (*dénigrer*) to belittle.

c (*faire paraître plus petit*) to make seem *ou* look small(er). **le château rapetissait toutes les maisons qui l'entouraient** the castle dwarfed all the surrounding houses, the castle made all the surrounding houses look *ou* seem small in *ou* by comparison.

2 vi, se rapetisser vpr a *[vieillard]* to shrink, grow shorter *ou* smaller; (*) *[jours]* to get shorter. **les objets rapetissent à distance** objects look smaller at a distance.

b **se ~ aux yeux de qn** to belittle o.s. in sb's eyes.

râpeux, -euse [Rɑpø, øz] **adj** (*gén*) rough.

Raphaël [Rafaɛl] **nm** Raphael.

raphaélique [Rafaelik] **adj** Raphaelesque.

raphia [Rafja] **nm** raffia.

rapiat, e [Rapja, jat] (*péj*) **1 adj** niggardly, stingy, tight-fisted. **2 nm,f** niggard, skinflint.

rapide [Rapid] **1 adj** a (*en déplacement*) *coureur, marche, pas* fast, quick, rapid, swift, speedy; *véhicule, route* fast; *animal* fast(-moving), swift; *fleuve* fast(-flowing), swift-flowing, rapid. **~ comme l'éclair** (as) quick as a flash; **il est ~ à la course** he's a good *ou* fast runner.

b (*dans le temps*) *travail, guérison, progrès, remède, réponse* speedy, quick, rapid, swift, fast; *accord* speedy, swift, rapid; *fortune, recette* quick. **examen (trop) ~ de qch** cursory examination of sth; **décision trop ~** hasty decision.

c (*vif*) *mouvement* quick, brisk, rapid, swift; *coup d'œil* rapid, quick, swift; *intelligence* quick, lively, nimble; *travailleur* quick, rapid, fast, swift, speedy. **d'une main ~** (*vite*) quickly, rapidly, swiftly; (*adroitement*) deftly; **tu n'es pas très ~ ce matin** you're not very bright *ou* you're not on the ball* this morning; **c'est une ~** (*qui agit vite*) she's a fast worker; (*qui comprend vite*) she's quick on the uptake*.

d (*en fréquence*) *pouls, rythme, respiration* fast, rapid.

e (*concis*) *style, récit* brisk, lively, fast-flowing.

f (*raide*) *pente* steep, abrupt.

g (*Tech*) *film* fast; *ciment* quick-setting.

2 nm a (*train*) express (train), fast train. **le ~ Paris-Nice** the Paris-Nice express.

b *[rivière]* rapid.

rapidement [Rapidmɑ̃] **adv** (*voir* **rapide**) fast; quickly; rapidly; swiftly; speedily; cursorily; hastily; deftly; steeply; abruptly.

rapidité [Rapidite] **nf** (*gén*) speed; *[allure, pas, coup d'œil]* speed, rapidity, quickness; *[opération, remède, réponse]* speed, speediness, swiftness, quickness; *[geste, travailleur]* speed, quickness; *[pouls, rythme]* speed, rapidity; *[style]* briskness, liveliness.

rapiéçage [Rapjesaʒ] **nm, rapiècement** [Rapjɛsmɑ̃] **nm** a (*voir* **rapiécer**) patching (up); mending, repairing. b (*pièce*) patch.

rapiécer [Rapjese] [3] *et* [6] **vt** *vêtement, pneu* to patch (up), put a patch in; *chaussure* to mend, repair.

rapière [RapjɛR] **nf** rapier.

rapin [Rapɛ̃] **nm** († *ou péj: artiste peintre*) painter, dauber.

rapine [Rapin] **nf** (*littér*) plundering, plunder. **vivre de ~(s)** to live by plunder.

rapiner [Rapine] [1] **vti** (*littér*) to plunder.

raplapla‡ [Raplapla] **adj inv** (*fatigué*) washed out*, done in*, tuckered out‡; (*plat*) flat.

raplatir* [RaplatiR] [2] **vt** (*aplatir*) to flatten out.

rappareiller [RapaReje] [1] **vt** to match up.

rapparier [RapaRje] [7] **vt** to pair up, match up.

rappel [Rapɛl] **nm** a *[ambassadeur]* recall, recalling; (*Mil*) *[réservistes]* recall; *[marchandises défectueuses]* callback. (*Théât*) **il y a eu 3 ~s** there were 3 curtain calls; *voir* **battre.**

b *[événement]* reminder; (*Comm*) *[référence]* quote; (*Admin: deuxième avis*) reminder; (*Admin: somme due*) back pay (*NonC*); (*Méd: vaccination*) booster. **rougissant au ~ de cette bévue** blushing at being reminded of that blunder; **toucher un ~ (de salaire)** to get some back pay; (*Aut*) **~ de limitation de vitesse** speed limit sign, reminder of the speed limit; **~ à l'ordre** call to order; **~ de couleur** repeat of colour.

c (*Tech*) *[pièce, levier]* return. (*Alpinisme*) **~ (de corde)** (*technique*) abseiling, roping down; (*opération*) abseil; **faire un ~, descendre en ~** to abseil, rope down; (*Naut*) **faire du ~** to sit out; (*Tech*) **ressort de ~** return spring; *voir* **descente.**

rappelé [Rap(ə)le] **nm** recalled soldier.

rappeler [Rap(ə)le] [4] **1 vt** a (*faire revenir*) *personne* to call back; (*Mil*) *réservistes, classe* to recall, call up (again); *diplomate* to recall;

acteur to bring back, call back; *chien* to call back. ~ **qn au chevet d'un malade** *ou* **auprès d'un malade** to call *ou* summon sb back to a sick man's bedside; (*frm*) **Dieu l'a rappelé à lui** he (has) departed this world *ou* life; (*Mil*) ~ **des réservistes au front** to recall reservists to the front; (*Ordin*) ~ **un dossier (à l'écran)** to call up a file (on the screen).

b ~ **qch à qn** (*évoquer*) to recall sth to sb, remind sb of sth; (*remettre en mémoire*) to remind sb of sth; **il rappela les qualités du défunt** he evoked *ou* mentioned the qualities of the deceased, he reminded the audience of the qualities of the deceased; **faut-il ~ que ...** must I remind you that ..., must it be repeated that ...; **ces dessins rappellent l'art arabe** those drawings are reminiscent of *ou* remind one of Arabian art; **le motif des poches rappelle celui du bas de la robe** the design on the pockets is repeated round the hem of the dress; **cela ne te rappelle rien?** doesn't that remind you of anything?, doesn't that bring anything to mind?; **tu me rappelles ma tante** you remind me of my aunt; **rappelle-moi mon rendez-vous** remind me about my appointment; **rappelez-moi votre nom** sorry – could you tell me your name again?; **attends, ça me rappelle quelque chose** wait, it rings a bell; (*frm*) **rappelez-moi à son bon souvenir** kindly remember me to him, please give him my kind regards.

c ~ **qn à la vie** *ou* **à lui** to bring sb back to life, bring sb to *ou* round (*Brit*), revive sb; ~ **qn à l'ordre** to call sb to order; ~ **qn à son devoir** to remind sb of his duty; ~ **qn aux bienséances** to recall sb to a sense of propriety; ~ **qn à de meilleurs sentiments** to bring sb round to (*Brit*) *ou* put sb in a better frame of mind.

d (*retéléphoner à*) to call *ou* ring (*Brit*) *ou* phone back. **il vient de ~** he's just called *ou* rung (*Brit*) *ou* phoned back.

e (*Comm*) *référence* to quote.

f (*tirer*) (*Tech*) *pièce, levier* to return; (*Alpinisme*) *corde* to pull to *ou* through.

2 **se rappeler** vpr (*gén*) to remember, recollect, recall. **se ~ que** to remember *ou* recall *ou* recollect that; (*frm*) **je me permets de me ~ à votre bon souvenir** I am sending you my kindest regards (*frm*); **rappelle-toi que ton honneur est en jeu** remember (that) your honour is at stake; **il ne se rappelle plus (rien)** he doesn't *ou* can't remember *ou* recall anything *ou* a thing.

rappliquer* [ʀaplike] 1 vi (*revenir*) to come back; (*arriver*) to turn up, show up*. **rapplique tout de suite à la maison!** come home right away!, (better) get yourself back here right away!*

rapport [ʀapɔʀ] nm a (*lien, corrélation*) connection, relationship, link. ~ **de parenté** relationship, tie of kinship (*frm*); **il y a un ~ de parenté entre nous** we're related; **établir un ~/des ~s entre deux incidents** to establish a link *ou* connection *ou* relation/links *ou* connections between two incidents; **avoir un certain ~/beaucoup de ~ avec qch** to have something/a lot to do with sth, have some/a definite connection with sth; **n'avoir aucun ~ avec** *ou* **être sans ~ avec qch** to bear no relation to sth, have nothing to do *ou* no connection with sth; **avoir ~ à qch** to bear some relation to sth, have something to do *ou* some connection with sth; **les deux incidents n'ont aucun ~** the two incidents have nothing to do with each other *ou* have no connection (with each other), the two incidents are unconnected *ou* unrelated; **être en ~ avec qch** to be in keeping with sth; **une situation en ~ avec ses goûts** a job in keeping *ou* in harmony *ou* in line with his tastes; **son train de vie n'est pas en ~ avec son salaire** his lifestyle doesn't match *ou* isn't in keeping with his salary.

b ~**s** (*relations*) relations; **ses ~s avec les autres sont difficiles** she has lots of problems with relationships *ou* in dealing with *ou* getting on with people; **entretenir de bons/mauvais ~s avec qn** to be on good/bad terms *ou* have good/bad relations with sb; **avoir des ~s (sexuels)** to have (sexual) intercourse *ou* sexual relations *ou* sex; **les ~s d'amitié entre les deux peuples** the friendly relations *ou* ties of friendship between the two nations; **les ~s entre les professeurs et les étudiants** relations between teachers and students, student-teacher *ou* student-staff relations.

c (*exposé, compte rendu*) report; (*Mil: réunion*) (post-exercise) conference. ~ **de police** police report.

d (*revenu, profit*) yield, return, revenue. **vivre du ~ d'une terre** to live from the yield *ou* revenue of *ou* on a piece of land, live from the return on a piece of land; *[tiercé]* ~**s** winnings; **être d'un bon ~** to give a good profit, have a good yield, give a good return; **ces champs sont en plein ~** these fields are bringing in a full yield; *voir* **immeuble, maison.**

e (*Math, Tech*) ratio. **dans le ~ de 1 à 100/de 100 contre 1** in a *ou* the ratio of 1 to 100/of 100 to 1; **le ~ qualité-prix** the quality-price ratio; **ce n'est pas d'un bon ~ qualité-prix** it's not good value for money.

f (*loc*) **être en ~ avec qn** to be in touch with sb, have dealings with sb; **nous n'avons jamais été en ~ avec cette compagnie** we have never had any dealings *ou* anything to do with that company; **se mettre en ~ avec qn** to get in touch *ou* contact with sb; **mettre qn en ~ avec qn d'autre** to put sb in touch *ou* contact with sb else; **par ~ à** (*comparé à*) in comparison with, in relation to; (*en fonction de*) in relation to; (*envers*) with respect *ou* regard to, towards; **la force de la livre par ~ au dollar** the strength of the pound against the dollar; **le ~ de** *ou* **des forces entre les 2 blocs** the balance of power between the 2 blocs; **envisager des relations sous l'angle d'un ~ de forces** to see relationships in terms of a power struggle; ~ **à*** about, in connection with, concerning; **je viens vous voir ~ à votre annonce*** I've come (to see you) about your advertisement; **il n'y a aucune inquiétude à avoir sous le ~ de l'honnêteté** from the point of view of honesty *ou* as far as honesty is concerned there's nothing to worry about; **sous tous les ~s** in every respect.

rapportage [ʀapɔʀtaʒ] nm (*arg Scol: mouchardage*) tale-telling (*NonC*), tattling (*NonC*) (*US*).

rapporter [ʀapɔʀte] 1 1 vt a (*apporter*) *objet, souvenir, réponse* to bring back; *[chien] gibier* to retrieve. ~ **qch à qn** to bring *ou* take sth back to sb; **n'oublie pas de lui ~ son parapluie** don't forget to bring *ou* take him back *ou* return him his umbrella; **il rapportera le pain en rentrant** he'll bring home the bread when he comes in; ~ **une bonne impression de qch** to come back *ou* come away with a good impression of sth; **quand doit-il ~ la réponse?** when does he have to come *ou* be back with the answer?

b (*Fin, fig: produire un gain*) *[actions, terre]* to yield (a return of), bring in (a yield *ou* revenue of); *[métier]* to bring in; *[vente]* to bring in (a profit *ou* revenue of). **placement qui rapporte 5%** investment that yields (a return of) 5% *ou* that brings in (a yield *ou* revenue of) 5%; **ça rapporte beaucoup d'argent** it's extremely profitable, it brings in a lot of money, it gives a high return; **cette mauvaise action ne lui rapportera rien** that bad deed won't do him any good; **ça leur a rapporté 100 F net** they netted 100 francs, it brought them in 100 francs net.

c (*faire un compte rendu de*) *fait* to report; (*mentionner*) to mention; (*citer*) *mot célèbre* to quote; (*répéter pour dénoncer*) to report. **on nous a rapporté que son projet n'avait pas été bien accueilli** we were told that *ou* we heard that *ou* it was reported to us that his project hadn't been well received; ~ **à qn les actions de qn** to report sb's actions to sb; **il a rapporté à la maîtresse ce qu'avaient dit ses camarades** he told the teacher what his classmates had said, he reported what his classmates had said to the teacher.

d (*ajouter*) (*gén*) to add; *bande de tissu, poche* to sew on. ~ **une aile à une maison** to annex a wing to a house; ~ **un peu de terre pour surélever le sol** to bank up with earth *ou* pile up some earth to raise the level of the ground; **c'est un élément rapporté** this element has been added on; **poches rapportées** patch pockets; *voir* **pièce.**

e (*rattacher à*) ~ **à** to relate to; **il faut tout ~ à la même échelle de valeurs** everything has to be related *ou* referred to the same scale of values; **on lui rapporte des découvertes dues à d'autres savants** discoveries are attributed *ou* ascribed to him which have been made by other learned men; **il rapporte tout à lui** he sees everything in relation to himself, he views everything in terms of himself, he brings everything back to himself.

f (*annuler*) *décret, décision, mesure* to revoke.

g (*Math*) ~ **un angle** to plot an angle.

2 vi a (*Chasse*) *[chien]* to retrieve.

b (*Fin*) *[investissement]* to give a good return *ou* yield. **ça rapporte bien** *ou* **gros** it brings in a lot of money, it pays very well, it's very profitable.

c (*arg Scol: moucharder*) ~ **(sur ses camarades)** to tell tales *ou* sneak* (on one's friends), tell on* (*Brit*) *ou* sneak on* *ou* tattle on* (*US*) one's friends.

3 **se rapporter** vpr a **se ~ à qch** to relate to sth; **se ~ à** (*Gram*) *antécédent* to relate *ou* refer to; **ce paragraphe ne se rapporte pas du tout au sujet** this paragraph bears no relation *ou* connection at all to the subject, this paragraph is totally irrelevant to *ou* unconnected with the subject; **ça se rapporte à ce que je disais tout à l'heure** that ties *ou* links up with *ou* relates to what I was saying just now.

b **s'en ~ à qn** to rely on sb; **s'en ~ au jugement/au témoignage de qn** to rely on sb's judgment/account.

rapporteur, -euse [ʀapɔʀtœʀ, øz] 1 nm,f (*mouchard*) telltale, sneak*, talebearer (*Brit*), tattler* (*US*). **elle est ~euse** she's a telltale *ou* sneak* *ou* talebearer (*Brit*) *ou* tattler* (*US*). 2 nm a (*Jur*) *[tribunal]* (court) reporter; *[commission]* rapporteur, reporter (*member acting as spokesman*). b (*Géom*) protractor.

rapprendre [ʀapʀɑ̃dʀ] 58 vt = **réapprendre.**

rapproché, e [ʀapʀɔʃe] (ptp de **rapprocher**) adj a *échéance* which is near *ou* close at hand; (*proche*) *objet, date* which is close *ou* near; *bruit* which is close. **l'objet le plus ~ de toi** the object closest *ou* nearest to you; **à une date ~e, dans un avenir ~** in the near *ou* not too distant future; *voir* **combat, protection.**

b (*répété*) *crises, bruits* (increasingly) frequent. **des crises de plus en plus ~es** increasingly frequent crises, crises which have become more and more frequent; **à intervalles ~s** at (increasingly) frequent intervals, at short *ou* close intervals; **grossesses ~es** (a series of) pregnancies at short *ou* close intervals; **échecs ~s** (a series of) failures in close succession.

rapprochement [ʀapʀɔʃmɑ̃] nm a (*action: voir* **rapprocher**) *[objet, meuble etc]* bringing closer *ou* nearer; *[objets, meubles]* bringing closer *ou* nearer to each other; (*fig*) *[personnes brouillées, ennemis]* bringing together, reconciliation; *[partis, factions]* bringing together; *[points de vue, textes]* comparison, bringing together, comparing. (*Méd*) **le ~ des**

lèvres d'une plaie joining the edges of a wound, closing (the lips of) a wound.

b (*action: voir* **se rapprocher**) *[bruit]* coming closer; *[ennemis, famille]* coming together, reconciliation; *[partis, factions]* coming together, rapprochement. (*Pol*) **ce ~ avec la droite nous inquiète** their moving closer to the right worries us; **le ~ des bruits de pas** the noise of footsteps drawing *ou* coming closer.

c (*lien, rapport*) parallel. **je n'avais pas fait le ~ (entre ces deux affaires)** I hadn't made *ou* established the connection *ou* link (between these two matters); **il y a de nombreux ~s intéressants/troublants** there are numerous interesting/disquieting parallels *ou* comparisons.

rapprocher [RapRɔʃe] ⟦1⟧ **1** **vt** **a** (*approcher*) to bring closer *ou* nearer (*de* to). **~ sa chaise (de la table)** to pull *ou* draw one's chair up (to the table); **~ deux objets l'un de l'autre** to move two objects (closer) together; **~ les lèvres d'une plaie** to join the edges of a wound, close (the lips of) a wound; **il a changé d'emploi: ça le rapproche de chez lui** he has changed jobs — that brings him closer *ou* nearer to home.

b (*réconcilier, réunir*) *ennemis* to bring together. **nous nous sentions rapprochés par un malheur commun** we felt drawn together by a common misfortune, we felt that a common misfortune had brought *ou* drawn us together; **leur amour de la chasse les rapproche** their love of hunting brings them together *ou* draws them to *ou* towards each other.

c (*mettre en parallèle, confronter*) *indices, textes* to put together *ou* side by side, compare, bring together; (*établir un lien entre, assimiler*) *indices, textes* to establish a *ou* the connection *ou* link *ou* parallel between. **essayons de ~ ces indices de ceux-là** let's try and put *ou* bring these two sets of clues together, let's try and compare these two sets of clues; **on peut ~ cela du poème de Villon** we can relate *ou* connect that to Villon's poem, we can establish a *ou* the connection *ou* link *ou* parallel between that and Villon's poem; **c'est à ~ de ce qu'on disait tout à l'heure** that ties up *ou* connects with *ou* relates to what was being said earlier.

2 **se rapprocher** **vpr** **a** (*approcher*) *[échéance, personne, véhicule, orage]* to get closer *ou* nearer, approach. **rapproche-toi (de moi)** come *ou* move *ou* draw closer *ou* nearer (to me); **il se rapprocha d'elle sur la banquette** he edged his way towards her *ou* drew closer to her on the bench; **pour se ~ de chez lui, il a changé d'emploi** to get closer *ou* nearer to home he changed jobs; **plus on se rapprochait de l'examen** the closer *ou* nearer we came *ou* got to the exam, the nearer *ou* closer the exam got *ou* came; **se ~ de la vérité** to come close *ou* get near *ou* close to the truth; **les bruits se rapprochèrent** the noises got closer *ou* nearer.

b (*dans le temps*) *[crises, bruits]* to become more frequent.

c (*se réconcilier*) *[ennemis]* to come together, be reconciled; (*trouver un terrain d'entente*) *[points de vue]* to draw closer together. **il s'est rapproché de ses parents** he became *ou* drew closer to his parents; (*Pol*) **il a essayé de se ~ de la droite** he tried to move *ou* draw closer to the right; **leur position s'est rapprochée de la nôtre** their position has drawn closer to ours.

d (*s'apparenter à*) to be close to. **ça se rapproche de ce qu'on disait tout à l'heure** that's close to *ou* ties up *ou* connects with what was being said earlier; **ses opinions se rapprochent beaucoup des miennes** his opinions are very close *ou* similar to mine.

rapprovisionnement [RapRɔvizjɔnmɑ̃] **nm** = **réapprovisionnement**.

rapprovisionner [RapRɔvizjɔne] ⟦1⟧ = **réapprovisionner**.

rapsode [Rapsɔd] **nm** = **rhapsode**.

rapsodie [Rapsɔdi] **nf** = **rhapsodie**.

rapt [Rapt] **nm** (*enlèvement*) abduction.

raquer‡ [Rake] ⟦1⟧ **vti** (*payer*) to cough up*, fork out*.

raquette [Rakɛt] **nf** **a** (*Tennis*) racket; (*Ping-Pong*) bat. **c'est une bonne ~** he's a good tennis player. **b** (*à neige*) snowshoe. **c** (*Bot*) nopal, prickly pear.

raquetteur, -euse [RaketœR, øz] **nm,f** (*Can*) snowshoer.

rare [RɑR] **adj** **a** (*peu commun*) *objet, mot, édition* rare. **ça n'a rien de ~** there's nothing uncommon *ou* unusual about it, it's not a rare occurrence; **il était ~ qu'il ne sache pas** he rarely *ou* seldom did not know; **il n'était pas ~ de le rencontrer** it was not unusual *ou* uncommon to meet him; **c'est ~ de le voir fatigué** it's rare *ou* unusual to see him tired, one rarely *ou* seldom sees him tired; **c'est bien ~ s'il ne vient pas*** I'd be surprised *ou* it would be unusual if he doesn't *ou* didn't come; *voir* **oiseau**.

b (*peu nombreux*) *cas, exemples* rare, few; *visites* rare; *passants, voitures* few. **les ~s voitures qui passaient** the few *ou* odd cars that went by; **les ~s amis qui lui restent** the few friends still left to him; **à de ~s intervalles** at rare intervals; **il est l'un des ~s qui** he's one of the few (people) who; **à cette heure les clients sont ~s** at this time of day customers are scarce *ou* are few and far between; **à de ~s exceptions près** with one or two odd exceptions.

c (*peu abondant*) *nourriture, main d'œuvre* scarce; *barbe, cheveux* thin, sparse; *végétation* sparse; *gaz* rare. **il a le cheveu ~** he's rather thin on top; **se faire ~** *[argent]* to become scarce, be tight; *[légumes]* to become scarce, be in short supply; (*hum*) **vous vous faites ~** we haven't seen a lot of you recently, we rarely see you these days.

d (*exceptionnel*) *talent, qualité, sentiment, beauté* rare; *homme, énergie* exceptional, singular; *saveur, moment* exquisite; (*hum*) *imbécile, imprudence* singular. **avec un ~ courage** with rare *ou* singular *ou* exceptional courage.

raréfaction [RaRefaksjɔ̃] **nf** *[oxygène]* rarefaction; *[nourriture]* (*action*) increased scarcity; (*résultat*) scarcity, short supply.

raréfiable [RaRefjabl] **adj** rarefiable.

raréfier [RaRefje] ⟦7⟧ **1** **vt** *air* to rarefy. **2** **se raréfier** **vpr** *[oxygène]* to rarefy; *[argent, nourriture]* to grow *ou* become scarce, become in short supply.

rarement [RɑRmɑ̃] **adv** rarely, seldom.

rareté [RɑRte] **nf** **a** *[édition, objet]* rarity; *[mot, cas]* rareness, rarity; *[vivres, argent]* scarcity. **la ~ des touristes/visiteurs** the small *ou* scattered numbers of tourists/visitors; **se plaindre de la ~ des lettres/visites de qn** to complain of the infrequency of sb's letters/visits. **b** (*objet précieux etc*) rarity, rare object. **une telle erreur de sa part, c'est une ~** it's a rare *ou* an unusual occurrence for him to make a mistake like that.

rarissime [RaRisim] **adj** extremely rare.

ras[1] [Rɑs] **nm** (*titre éthiopien*) ras.

ras[2], **e** [Rɑ, Rɑz] **adj** **a** *poil, herbe* short; *cheveux* close-cropped; *étoffe* with a short pile; *mesure* full. **il avait la tête ~e** he had close-cropped hair; **à poil ~** *chien* short-haired; *étoffe* with a short pile.

b **ongles/cheveux coupés ~** *ou* **à ~** nails/hair cut short; **à ~ de terre, au ~ de la terre** level with the ground; **au ~ de l'eau** level with the water; **arbre coupé à ~ de terre** tree cut down to the ground; **voler au ~ de la terre/au ~ de l'eau** to fly close to *ou* just above the ground/water, skim the ground/water; **le projectile lui est passé au ~ de la tête/du visage** the projectile skimmed his head/face; **ses cheveux lui arrivent au ~ des fesses** her hair is right down her back; *[discours]* **c'est au ~ des pâquerettes*** (*sans prétentions intellectuelles*) it's pretty lowbrow; (*pratique et concret*) it's down-to-earth.

c **à ~ bords** to the brim; **remplir un verre à ~ bords** to fill a glass to the brim *ou* top; **plein à ~ bords** *verre* full to the brim, brimful; *baignoire* full to overflowing *ou* to the brim; **en ~e campagne** in open country; **pull ~ du cou** crew-neck sweater, round-neck sweater; **j'en ai ~ le bol*** *ou* **la casquette*** **(de tout ça)** I've had a bellyful‡, I'm fed up to the back teeth (with all that)‡; **le ~-le-bol étudiant*** the students' discontent *ou* dissatisfaction, student unrest; *voir* **bord, table**.

R.A.S. [ɛRaɛs] (**abrév de rien à signaler**) *voir* **rien**.

rasade [Rɑzad] **nf** glassful.

rasage [Rɑzaʒ] **nm** **a** *[barbe]* shaving; *voir* **lotion**. **b** (*Tex*) shearing.

rasant, e [Rɑzɑ̃, ɑ̃t] **adj** **a** (**: ennuyeux*) boring. **qu'il est ~!** he's a (real) bore! *ou* drag!* **b** *lumière* low-angled; (*Mil*) *fortification* low-built. (*Mil*) **tir ~** grazing fire.

rascasse [Raskas] **nf** scorpion fish.

rasé, e [Rɑze] (**ptp de raser**) **adj** *menton* (clean-)shaven; *tête* shaven. **être bien/mal ~** to be shaven/unshaven; **~ de près** close-shaven; **avoir les cheveux ~s** to have one's hair shaved off *ou* a shaven head.

rase-mottes [Rɑzmɔt] **nm inv** hedgehopping. **faire du ~, voler en ~** to hedgehop; **vol en ~** hedgehopping flight.

raser [Rɑze] ⟦1⟧ **1** **vt** **a** (*tondre*) *barbe, cheveux* to shave off; *menton, tête* to shave; *malade etc* to shave. **~ un prêtre/condamné** to shave a priest's/convict's head; **se faire ~ la tête** to have one's head shaved; *voir* **crème**. **b** (*effleurer*) *[projectile, véhicule]* to graze, scrape; *[oiseau, balle de tennis]* to skim (over). **~ les murs** to hug the walls. **c** (*abattre*) *maison* to raze (to the ground). **d** (**: ennuyer*) to bore. **ça me rase!** it bores me stiff*, it bores me to tears*. **e** (*Tech*) *mesure à grains* to strike; *velours* to shear. **2** **se raser** **vpr** **a** (*toilette*) to shave, have a shave. **se ~ la tête/les jambes** to shave one's head/legs. **b** (**: s'ennuyer*) to be bored stiff* *ou* to tears*.

raseur, -euse* [RɑzœR, øz] **adj, nm,f** (*importun*) bore. **qu'il est ~!** he's a (real) bore *ou* drag*.

rasibus‡ [Rɑzibys] **adv** *couper* very close *ou* fine. **passer ~** *[projectile]* to whizz past very close; **avoir un examen ~** to pass an exam by the skin of one's teeth*.

rasoir [RɑzwaR] **1** **nm** razor. **~ électrique** (electric) shaver, electric razor; **~ mécanique** *ou* **de sûreté** safety razor; **~ à main** *ou* **de coiffeur** cut-throat *ou* straight razor; *voir* **feu**[1], **fil** *etc.* **2** **adj** (**: ennuyeux*) *film, livre* dead boring*. **qu'il est ~!** what a bore *ou* drag* he is!

Raspoutine [Rasputin] **nm** Rasputin.

rassasier [Rasazje] ⟦7⟧ (*frm*) **1** **vt** **a** (*assouvir*) *faim, curiosité, désirs* to satisfy.

b (*nourrir*) **~ qn** *[aliment]* to satisfy sb *ou* sb's appetite *ou* sb's hunger; *[hôte, aubergiste]* to satisfy sb's appetite *ou* hunger, nourish sb (*frm*); **~ qn de qch** (*lui en donner suffisamment*) to satisfy sb with sth *ou* sb's appetite *ou* hunger with sth; (*lui en donner trop*) to overfeed sb with sth, surfeit sb with sth; **être rassasié** (*n'avoir plus faim*) to be satisfied, have eaten one's fill; (*en être dégoûté*) to be satiated *ou* sated, have had more than enough; **je suis rassasié de toutes ces histoires!** I've had quite enough of *ou* I've had more than my fill of all these stories!; **on ne peut pas le ~ de chocolats** you can't give him too many chocolates; (*fig*) **~ ses yeux d'un spectacle** to tire one's eyes of a sight.

2 **se rassasier** **vpr** (*se nourrir*) to satisfy one's hunger, eat one's fill. **se ~ d'un spectacle** to tire of a sight; **je ne me rassasierai jamais**

de ... I'll never tire *ou* have enough of ... .

rassemblement [ʀasɑ̃bləmɑ̃] nm a (*action*) (*voir* **rassembler**) rallying; rounding up; gathering, collecting, assembling; (*voir* **se rassembler**) gathering. (*Mil*) **le ~ a lieu à 8 heures** parade is at 8 o'clock; (*Mil*) ~! fall in!; **~ à 9 heures sur le quai** we'll meet at 9 o'clock on the platform; *voir* **point.** b (*groupe*) gathering; (*parti, organisation*) union.

rassembler [ʀasɑ̃ble] 1 1 vt a (*regrouper*) *troupes* to rally; *troupeau* to round up; *sympathisants* to round up, rally; *objets épars* to gather together, collect, assemble. **il rassembla les élèves dans la cour** he gathered *ou* assembled the pupils in the playground.

b (*accumuler*) *documents, manuscrits, notes* to gather together, collect, assemble.

c (*fig: faire appel à, reprendre*) *idées* to collect; *courage, forces* to summon up, muster (up), gather. **~ ses esprits** to collect one's thoughts.

d (*après démontage*) *pièces, mécanisme* to put back together, reassemble.

e (*Équitation*) *cheval* to collect.

2 **se rassembler** vpr [*foule, badauds*] to gather; [*soldats, participants*] to assemble, gather. **rassemblés autour du feu** gathered round the fire; **toute la famille rassemblée** the whole family gathered together.

rassembleur, -euse [ʀasɑ̃blœʀ, øz] nm,f unifier.

rasseoir [ʀaswaʀ] 26 1 vt *bébé* to sit back up (straight); *objet* to put back up straight. 2 **se rasseoir** vpr to sit down again. **faire (se) ~ qn** to make sb sit down again.

rasséréné, e [ʀaseʀene] (ptp de **rasséréner**) adj *ciel, personne, visage* serene.

rasséréner [ʀaseʀene] 6 1 vt to make serene again. 2 **se rasséréner** vpr [*personne, visage, ciel*] to become serene again, recover one's *ou* its serenity.

rassir vi, **se rassir** vpr [ʀasiʀ] 2 to go stale.

rassis, e [ʀasi, iz] (ptp de **rassir, rasseoir**) adj a *pain* stale. b *personne* (*pondéré*) composed, sober, calm; (*péj*) stale.

rassortiment [ʀasɔʀtimɑ̃] nm = **réassortiment.**

rassortir [ʀasɔʀtiʀ] 2 = **réassortir.**

rassurant, e [ʀasyʀɑ̃, ɑ̃t] adj *nouvelle* reassuring, comforting, cheering; *voix* reassuring, comforting; *visage* reassuring; *indice* encouraging. (*iro*) **c'est ~!** that's very reassuring! (*iro*), that's a fat lot of comfort!* (*Brit*).

rassurer [ʀasyʀe] 1 1 vt: **~ qn** to put sb's mind at ease *ou* rest, reassure sb; **je ne me sentais pas rassuré dans sa voiture** I didn't feel easy *ou* at ease in his car; **te voilà rassuré maintenant** you've got nothing to worry about now, your mind's at ease *ou* at rest now, you're reassured now. 2 **se rassurer** vpr: **à cette nouvelle il se rassura** his mind was put at ease *ou* rest *ou* he felt reassured on hearing the news; **il essayait de se ~ en se disant que c'était impossible** he tried to put his mind at ease *ou* rest *ou* to reassure himself by saying it was impossible; **rassure-toi** put your mind at ease *ou* rest, don't worry.

rasta(fari) [ʀasta(faʀi)] adj, nm Rasta(farian).

rastaquouère [ʀastakwɛʀ] nm (*péj*) flashy wog** (*Brit péj*), flashy foreigner (*péj*).

rat [ʀa] 1 nm (*Zool*) rat; (*péj: avare*) miser. **c'est un vrai ~, ce type** he's re[a]lly stingy* *ou* he's a real skinflint, that fellow; **il est fait comme un ~** he's cornered, he has no escape; (*fig*) **quand il y a du danger, les ~s quittent le navire** in times of danger the rats leave the sinking ship; **s'ennuyer** *ou* **s'emmerder‡ comme un ~ mort** to be bored stiff* *ou* to death*; (*terme d'affection*) **mon (petit) ~** pet, darling; **petit rat de l'Opéra** pupil of the Opéra de Paris ballet class (*working as an extra*); *voir* **à, mort².**

2 comp ►**rat d'Amérique** musquash (*Brit*), muskrat ►**rat de bibliothèque** bookworm (*who spends all his time in libraries*) ►**rat de cave** wax taper (*used for lighting one's way in a cellar or on a staircase*) ►**rat des champs** fieldmouse ►**rat d'eau** water vole ►**rat d'égout** sewer rat ►**rat d'hôtel** hotel thief ►**rat musqué** muskrat, musquash (*Brit*).

rata [ʀata] nm (*arg Mil*) (*nourriture*) grub*; (*ragoût*) stew.

ratafia [ʀatafja] nm (*liqueur*) ratafia.

ratage* [ʀataʒ] nm (*action: voir* **rater**) missing; messing up, spoiling, botching, bungling; failing, flunking*. **ces ~s successifs** these successive failures.

rataplan [ʀataplɑ̃], **rantanplan** [ʀɑ̃tɑ̃plɑ̃] excl, nm rat-a-tat-tat.

ratatiner [ʀatatine] 1 1 vt a *pomme* to dry up, shrivel; *visage, personne* to wrinkle, make wrinkled *ou* wizened *ou* shrivelled.

b (‡: *détruire*) *maison* to knock to bits *ou* pieces, wreck; *machine, voiture* to smash to bits *ou* pieces. **se faire ~** (*battre*) to get thrashed *ou* a thrashing; (*tuer*) to get done in‡ *ou* bumped off‡ (*Brit*); **sa voiture a été complètement ratatinée** his car was completely smashed up *ou* written off, his car was a complete write-off, his car was totaled* (*US*).

2 **se ratatiner** vpr [*pomme*] to shrivel *ou* dry up; [*visage*] to become wrinkled *ou* shrivelled *ou* wizened; [*personne*] (*par l'âge*) to become wrinkled *ou* shrivelled *ou* wizened; (*pour tenir moins de place*) to curl up.

ratatouille [ʀatatuj] nf (*Culin*) ~ **(niçoise)** ratatouille (*aubergines, courgettes, peppers, tomatoes etc cooked in olive oil*); (*péj*) (*ragoût*) bad stew; (*cuisine*) lousy* food.

rate¹ [ʀat] nf (*organe*) spleen; *voir* **dilater, fouler.**

rate² [ʀat] nf (*animal*) she-rat.

raté, e [ʀate] (ptp de **rater**) 1 nm,f (*: *personne*) failure. 2 nm a (*Aut: gén pl*) misfiring (*NonC*). **avoir des ~s** to misfire; (*fig*) **il y a eu des ~s dans la conduite de cette affaire** there were some hiccups in the handling of this matter. b [*arme à feu*] misfire.

râteau, pl **~x** [ʀɑto] nm (*Agr, Roulette*) rake; [*métier à tisser*] comb.

râtelier [ʀɑtəlje] nm [*bétail*] rack; [*armes, outils*] rack; (*: *dentier*) (set of) false teeth. **~ à pipes** pipe rack; *voir* **manger.**

rater [ʀate] 1 1 vi [*arme, coup*] to misfire, fail to go off; [*projet, affaire*] to go wrong, backfire, misfire. **ce contretemps/cette erreur risque de tout faire ~** this hitch/mistake could well ruin everything; **je t'avais dit qu'elle y allait: ça n'a pas raté*** I told you she'd go and I was dead right* (*Brit*) *ou* and (so) she did.

2 vt (*) a (*ne pas attraper ou saisir*) *balle, cible, occasion, train* to miss. **raté!** missed!; (*iro*) **il n'en rate pas une** he's always putting his foot in it*; **tu crois être le plus fort mais je ne te raterai pas!** you think you're the toughest but don't you worry, I'll get you!* *ou* I'll show you!; **il voulait faire le malin mais je ne l'ai pas raté** he tried to be smart but I soon sorted him out* (*Brit*) *ou* I didn't let him get away with it; **il ne t'a pas raté!** he really got you there*!; **si tu croyais m'impressionner, c'est raté** if you were trying to impress me, it hasn't worked!

b (*ne pas réussir*) *travail, affaire* to mess up, spoil, botch, bungle; *mayonnaise, sauce* to spoil; *examen* to fail, flunk*. **~ son effet** to spoil one's effect; **~ sa vie** to mess up *ou* make a mess of one's life; **il a raté son coup** he didn't bring *ou* carry *ou* pull it off; **il a raté son suicide, il s'est raté** he failed in *ou* he bungled his suicide attempt *ou* bid.

ratiboiser‡ [ʀatibwaze] 1 vt a (*rafler*) **~ qch à qn** (*au jeu*) to clean sb out of sth*; (*en le volant*) to nick‡ (*Brit*) *ou* pinch* *ou* swipe* sth from sb; **on lui a ratiboisé son portefeuille, il s'est fait ~ son portefeuille** he got his wallet nicked‡ (*Brit*) *ou* pinched* *ou* swiped*. b (*dépouiller*) **~ qn** to skin sb (alive)‡, pluck sb‡, clean sb out*. c (*abattre*) *maison* to knock to bits *ou* pieces, wreck. [*personne*] **il a été ratiboisé en moins de deux** he was done for in no time. d (*couper les cheveux à*) *personne* to scalp* (*fig*). **se faire ~** to be scalped*, have a baldie‡ (*Brit*).

raticide [ʀatisid] nm rat poison.

ratier [ʀatje] nm: **(chien)** ~ ratter.

ratière [ʀatjɛʀ] nf rattrap.

ratification [ʀatifikasjɔ̃] nf (*Admin, Jur*) ratification. **~ de vente** sales confirmation.

ratifier [ʀatifje] 7 vt (*Admin, Jur*) to ratify; (*littér: confirmer*) to confirm, ratify.

ratine [ʀatin] nf (*Tex*) ratine.

ratio [ʀasjo] nm ratio.

ratiocination [ʀasjɔsinasjɔ̃] nf (*littér péj*) (*action*) hair-splitting, quibbling; (*raisonnement*) hair-splitting argument, quibbling (*NonC*).

ratiociner [ʀasjɔsine] 1 vi (*littér péj*) to split hairs, quibble (*sur* over).

ration [ʀasjɔ̃] nf a [*soldat*] rations (*pl*); [*animal*] (feed) intake; [*organisme*] ration, (food) intake. **~ alimentaire** *ou* **d'entretien** food intake; (*Mil etc*) **toucher une ~ réduite** to be on *ou* get short rations; **~ de survie** survival rations. b (*portion*) ration. **~ de viande/fourrage** meat/fodder ration; (*fig*) **il a eu sa ~ d'épreuves/de soucis** he had his share of trials/quota *ou* share of worries.

rationalisation [ʀasjɔnalizasjɔ̃] nf rationalization.

rationaliser [ʀasjɔnalize] 1 vt to rationalize.

rationalisme [ʀasjɔnalism] nm rationalism.

rationaliste [ʀasjɔnalist] adj, nmf rationalist.

rationalité [ʀasjɔnalite] nf rationality.

rationnel, -elle [ʀasjɔnɛl] adj rational.

rationnellement [ʀasjɔnɛlmɑ̃] adv rationally.

rationnement [ʀasjɔnmɑ̃] nm rationing; *voir* **carte.**

rationner [ʀasjɔne] 1 1 vt *pain, charbon* to ration; *personne* (*lit*) to put on rations; (*fig hum: ne pas donner assez*) to give short rations to. 2 **se rationner** vpr to ration o.s.

ratissage [ʀatisaʒ] nm (*Agr*) raking; (*Mil, Police*) combing.

ratisser [ʀatise] 1 vt *gravier* to rake; *feuilles* to rake up; (*Mil, Police*) to comb; (*Rugby*) *ballon* to heel; (*: *dépouiller au jeu*) to clean out*. **~ large** to cast the net wide; **il s'est fait ~ (au jeu)** he was cleaned out* *ou* he lost everything at the gambling table.

raton [ʀatɔ̃] nm a (*Zool*) young rat. **~ laveur** racoon. b (*péj*) *term applied to North African in France,* ≃ coon** (*péj*). c (*terme d'affection*) **mon ~!** (my) pet!

raton(n)ade [ʀatɔnad] nf attack on immigrants.

RATP [ɛʀatepe] nf (abrév de **Régie autonome des transports parisiens**) *voir* **régie.**

rattachement [ʀataʃmɑ̃] nm (*Admin, Pol*) uniting (*à* with), joining (*à* to). **quel est votre service de ~?** which service are you attached to?

rattacher [ʀataʃe] 1 vt a (*attacher de nouveau*) *animal, prisonnier, colis* to tie up again; *ceinture, lacets, jupe* to do up *ou* fasten again.

b (*annexer, incorporer*) *territoire, commune, service* to join (*à* to), unite (*à* with); *employé, fonctionnaire* to attach (*à* to).

c (*comparer, rapprocher*) *problème, question* to link, connect, tie up (*à* with); *fait* to relate (*à* to). **cela peut se ~ au premier problème** that can be related to *ou* tied up with the first problem; **on peut ~ cette langue au groupe slave** this language can be related to *ou* linked with the Slavonic group.

d (*relier*) *personne* to bind, tie (*à* to). **rien ne le rattache plus à sa famille** he has no more ties with his family, nothing binds *ou* ties him to his family any more.

rattrapable [RatRapabl] **adj** which can be put right.

rattrapage [RatRapaʒ] **nm** *[maille]* picking up; *[erreur]* making good; *[candidat d'examen]* passing. **le ~ d'une bêtise/d'un oubli** making up for something silly/an omission; **le ~ des salaires sur les prix** an increase in salaries to keep up with *ou* keep pace with prices; **le ~ du retard** *[élève]* catching up, making up (for) lost time; *[conducteur]* making up (for) lost time; **~ scolaire** remedial teaching *ou* classes; **cours de ~** remedial class *ou* course; **suivre des cours de ~** to go to remedial classes; (*Scol*) **examen de ~** *additional exam for borderline cases.*

rattraper [RatRape] 1 **1 vt** a (*reprendre*) *animal échappé, prisonnier* to recapture.

b (*retenir*) *objet, enfant qui tombe* to catch (hold of).

c (*réparer*) *maille* to pick up; *mayonnaise* to salvage; *erreur* to make good, make up for; *bêtise, parole malheureuse, oubli* to make up for.

d (*regagner*) *argent perdu* to recover, get back, recoup; *sommeil* to catch up on; *temps perdu* to make up for. **le conducteur a rattrapé son retard** the driver made up (for) lost time; **cet élève ne pourra jamais ~ son retard** this pupil will never be able to make up (for) lost time *ou* catch up; **ce qu'il perd d'un côté, il le rattrape de l'autre** what he loses on the swings he gains on the roundabouts (*Brit*), what he loses in one way he gains in another.

e (*rejoindre*) (*lit, fig*) **~ qn** to catch sb up, catch up with sb; **le coût de la vie a rattrapé l'augmentation de salaire** the cost of living has caught up with the increase in salaries.

f (*Scol: repêcher*) **~ qn** to allow sb to pass, pass sb, let sb get through.

2 **se rattraper vpr** a (*reprendre son équilibre*) to stop o.s. falling, catch o.s. (just) in time. **se ~ à une branche/à qn** to stop o.s. falling by catching hold of a branch/sb.

b (*prendre une compensation*) to make up for it. **j'ai dû passer trois nuits sans dormir, mais hier je me suis rattrapé** I had to spend three sleepless nights, but I made up for it last night.

c (*se ressaisir*) to make good, make up for it. **il avait perdu gros, mais il s'est rattrapé en un soir à la roulette** he had lost heavily but he pulled back (his losses) *ou* recovered his losses *ou* made up for it in one evening at roulette; **le joueur français avait perdu les deux premiers sets, mais il s'est rattrapé au troisième** the French player had lost the first two sets but he pulled back *ou* made up for it *ou* caught up in the third.

rature [RatyR] **nf** deletion, erasure, crossing out. **faire une ~** to make a deletion *ou* an erasure; (*Admin*) **sans ~s ni surcharges** without deletions or alterations.

raturer [RatyRe] 1 **vt** (*corriger*) *mot, phrase, texte* to make an alteration *ou* alterations to; (*barrer*) *lettre, mot* to cross out, erase, delete.

RAU† [ɛRay] **nf** (**abrév de République Arabe Unie**) UAR†.

raugmenter* [Rɔgmɑ̃te] 1 **vi** (*augmenter*) to go up again. **le beurre a raugmenté** butter is up again*, butter has gone up again.

rauque [Rok] **adj** *voix* (*gén*) hoarse; *[chanteuse de blues etc]* husky, throaty; *cri* raucous.

rauwolfia [Rovɔlfja] **nf** rauwolfia.

ravage [Ravaʒ] **nm** a (*littér: action*) *[pays, ville]* laying waste, ravaging, devastation. b (*gén pl: dévastation*) *[guerre, maladie]* ravages (*pl*), devastation (*NonC*); *[vieillesse]* ravages (*pl*). **la grêle a fait du ~ dans les vignes** the hailstorm has wrought havoc in the vineyards *ou* played havoc with the vines; **l'épidémie a fait de terribles ~s parmi les jeunes** the epidemic has caused terrible loss among *ou* has destroyed huge numbers of young people; (*fig hum*) **faire des ~s** *[séducteur]* to break hearts (*fig*); *[doctrine]* to gain (too much) ground, win huge numbers of new converts.

ravagé, e [Ravaʒe] (**ptp de ravager**) **adj** a (*tourmenté*) *visage* harrowed, haggard. **avoir les traits ~s** to have harrowed *ou* ravaged *ou* haggard features; **visage ~ par la maladie** face ravaged by illness. b (‡: *fou*) **il est complètement ~** he's completely nuts* *ou* bonkers‡ (*Brit*), he's off his head‡.

ravager [Ravaʒe] 3 **vt** *pays* to lay waste, ravage, devastate; *maison, ville* to ravage, devastate; *visage [maladie]* to ravage; *[chagrin, soucis]* to harrow; *personne, vie* to wreak havoc upon.

ravageur, -euse [RavaʒœR, øz] 1 **adj** *passion* devastating. **animaux/insectes ~s** animals/insects which cause damage to *ou* which devastate the crops. 2 **nm,f** (*pillard*) ravager, devastator.

ravalement [Ravalmɑ̃] **nm** a (*voir* **ravaler**) cleaning; restoration; face lift*. **faire le ~ de** to clean; to restore; to give a face lift to*. b (*littér: avilissement*) lowering.

ravaler [Ravale] 1 **vt** a (*Constr*) (*nettoyer*) to clean; (*remettre en état*) *façade, mur* to restore; *immeuble* to give a face lift to*. (*se maquiller*) **se ~ la façade**‡ to slap on some make-up; (*se faire faire un lifting*) **se faire ~ la façade**‡ to have a facelift. b (*avaler*) *salive* to swallow; *sanglots* to swallow, choke back; *colère* to stifle; *larmes* to hold *ou* choke back. (*fig*) **faire ~ ses paroles à qn** to make sb take back *ou* swallow his words. c (*littér: rabaisser*) *dignité, personne, mérite* to lower. **~ qn au niveau de la brute** to reduce *ou* lower sb to the level of a brute; **se ~** to lower o.s.

ravaleur [RavalœR] **nm** (*maçon*) stone restorer.

ravaudage [Ravodaʒ] **nm** *[vêtement]* mending, repairing; *[chaussette]* darning; *[objet]* makeshift repair. **faire du ~** to mend; to darn.

ravauder [Ravode] 1 **vt** (*littér: repriser*) *vêtement* to repair, mend; *chaussette* to darn.

rave [Rav] **nf** (*Bot*) rape; *voir* **céleri, chou**[1].

ravenelle [Ravnɛl] **nf** (*giroflée*) wallflower; (*radis*) wild radish.

Ravenne [Ravɛn] **n** Ravenna.

ravi, e [Ravi] (**ptp de ravir**) **adj** (*enchanté*) delighted. **~ de vous connaître** delighted *ou* pleased to meet you.

ravier [Ravje] **nm** hors d'oeuvres dish.

ravigote [Ravigɔt] **nf** (*vinaigrette*) (oil and vinegar) dressing (*with hard-boiled eggs, shallot and herbs*).

ravigoter* [Ravigɔte] 1 **vt** *[alcool]* to buck up*, pick up; *[repas, douche, nouvelle, chaleur]* to buck up*, put new life into. **(tout) ravigoté par une bonne nuit** feeling refreshed after a good night's sleep; **ce vin est ravigotant** this wine bucks you up* *ou* puts new life into you.

ravin [Ravɛ̃] **nm** (*gén*) gully; (*assez encaissé*) ravine.

ravine [Ravin] **nf** (small) ravine, gully.

ravinement [Ravinmɑ̃] **nm** (*action*) gullying (*Géog*). (*rigoles, ravins*) **~s** gullies; (*aspect*) **le ~ de ces pentes** the (numerous) gullies furrowing these slopes; **le ~ affecte particulièrement ces sols** gully erosion *ou* gullying affects these kinds of soil in particular.

raviner [Ravine] 1 **vt** *versant* to gully (*Géog*); *visage* to furrow. **les bords ravinés de la rivière** the gullied (*Géog*) *ou* furrowed banks of the river.

ravioli [Ravjɔli] **nmpl** ravioli.

ravir [RaviR] 2 **vt** (*littér*) a (*charmer*) to delight. **cela lui va à ~** that suits her beautifully, she looks delightful in it. b (*enlever*) **~ à qn** *trésor, être aimé, honneur* to rob sb of, take (away) from sb. c (†: *kidnapper*) to ravish†, abduct.

raviser (se) [Ravize] 1 **vpr** to change one's mind, decide otherwise. **après avoir dit oui, il s'est ravisé** after saying yes he changed his mind *ou* decided otherwise *ou* decided against it; **il s'est ravisé** he decided against it, he thought better of it.

ravissant, e [Ravisɑ̃, ɑ̃t] **adj** *beauté* ravishing; *femme, robe* ravishing, beautiful; *maison, tableau* delightful, beautiful.

ravissement [Ravismɑ̃] **nm** a (*gén, Rel*) rapture. **plonger qn dans le ~** to send sb into raptures; **plongé dans le ~** in raptures; **regarder qn avec ~** to look at sb rapturously. b († *ou littér: enlèvement*) ravishing†, abduction.

ravisseur, -euse [RavisœR, øz] **nm,f** kidnapper, abductor.

ravitaillement [Ravitajmɑ̃] **nm** a (*action: voir* **ravitailler**) resupplying; refuelling. **~ en vol** in-flight refuelling; **le ~ des troupes (en vivres/munitions)** resupplying the troops (with food/ammunition), the provision *ou* providing of the troops with fresh supplies (of food/ammunition); **aller au ~** (*Mil*) to go for fresh supplies; (*fig*) *[campeur, ménagère]* to go and stock up, go for fresh supplies. b (*réserves*) supplies.

ravitailler [Ravitaje] 1 **1 vt** (*en vivres, munitions*) *armée, ville, navire* to provide with fresh supplies, resupply; *coureurs, skieurs* to give fresh supplies to; (*en carburant*) *véhicule, avion, embarcation* to refuel. **~ une ville en combustible** to provide a town with fresh supplies of fuel, resupply a town with fuel; **~ un avion en vol** to refuel an aircraft in flight. 2 **se ravitailler vpr** *[ville, armée]* to get fresh supplies, be resupplied; *[coureurs, skieurs]* to take on fresh supplies; (*fig hum*) *[campeur, ménagère]* to stock up (*à* at); *[véhicule, avion]* to refuel. (*Sport*) **se ~ à l'étape** to take on fresh supplies at the next leg.

ravitailleur [RavitajœR] 1 **nm** (*Mil*) (*navire*) supply ship; (*avion*) supply plane; (*véhicule*) supply vehicle. **~ en vol** aerial tanker. 2 **adj** *navire, avion, véhicule* supply (*épith*).

raviver [Ravive] 1 **vt** *feu, sentiment, douleur* to revive, rekindle; *couleur* to brighten up; *souvenir* to revive, bring back to life; (*Méd*) *plaie* to reopen. **sa douleur/sa jalousie s'est ravivée** his grief/jealousy was revived *ou* rekindled.

ravoir [RavwaR] **vt** a (*recouvrer*) to have *ou* get back. b (*: *nettoyer: gén nég*) *tissu, métal* to get clean.

rayage [Rɛjaʒ] **nm** a *[nom]* crossing *ou* scoring out. b *[canon]* rifling.

rayé, e [Reje] (**ptp de rayer**) **adj** a *tissu, pelage* striped; *papier à lettres etc* ruled, lined. b *surface* scratched; *disque* scratched, scratchy. c (*Tech*) *canon* rifled.

rayer [Reje] 8 **vt** a (*marquer de raies*) *papier à lettres etc* to rule, line. **des cicatrices lui rayaient le visage** scars lined *ou* scored his face; (*fig*) **le fouet lui raya le visage** the whip lashed his face. b (*érafler*) to scratch. c (*Tech*) *canon* to rifle. d (*biffer*) to cross *ou* score out. e (*exclure*) **~ qn de** to cross sb *ou* sb's name off; **il a été rayé de la liste** he *ou* his name has been crossed *ou* struck off the list; **~ qch de sa**

mémoire to blot out *ou* erase sth from one's memory; (*fig*) ~ **un pays/une ville de la carte** to wipe a country/town off the face of the earth.

rayon [ʀɛjɔ̃] 1 nm a (*gén: trait, faisceau*) (*Opt, Phys*) ray; *[astre]* ray; *[lumière, jour]* ray, beam; *[phare]* beam.

b (*radiations*) ~**s** radiation; ~**s infrarouges/ultraviolets** infrared/ultraviolet rays; ~**s X** X-rays; **traitement par les** ~**s** radiation treatment; **passer aux** ~**s X**† to be X-rayed.

c (*fig: lueur*) ray. ~ **d'espoir** ray *ou* gleam of hope.

d (*Math*) radius.

e *[roue]* spoke.

f (*planche*) shelf; *[bibliothèque]* (book)shelf. **le livre n'est pas en** ~ the book is not on display *ou* on the shelves.

g (*Comm*) (*section*) department; (*petit: comptoir*) counter. **le** ~ **(de l')alimentation/(de la) parfumerie** the food/perfume counter; the food/perfume department; **le** ~ **enfants** the children's department; (*fig: spécialité*) **c'est (de) son** ~**/ce n'est pas son** ~ that's/that isn't his line; (*fig: responsabilité*) **c'est son** ~ that's his concern *ou* responsibility *ou* department* (*fig*); **ce n'est pas son** ~ that's not his concern *ou* responsibility *ou* department* (*fig*), that's nothing to do with him; (*fig*) **il en connaît un** ~* he knows masses about it*, he's really clued up about it*.

h *[ruche]* (honey)comb.

i (*périmètre*) radius. **dans un** ~ **de 10 km** within a radius of 10 km *ou* a 10-km radius; **il continuait ses excursions, dans le** ~ **restreint auquel le limitait son grand âge** he continued his walks within the limited range imposed on him by his great age.

j (*Agr*) drill.

2 comp ►**rayon d'action** (*lit*) range; (*fig*) field of action, scope, range; **engin à grand rayon d'action** long-range missile ►**rayon de braquage** (*Aut*) turning circle, (steering) lock (*Brit*) ►**rayon cathodique** (*Élec*) cathode ray ►**rayons cosmiques** cosmic rays ►**rayons gamma** gamma rays *ou* radiation ►**rayon laser** (*Phys*) laser beam ►**rayon de lune** moonbeam ►**le rayon de la mort** the death ray ►**rayon de soleil** (*lit*) ray of sunlight *ou* sunshine, sunbeam; (*fig*) ray of sunshine ►**rayon visuel** (*Opt*) line of vision *ou* sight.

rayonnage [ʀɛjɔnaʒ] nm set of shelves, shelving (*NonC*). ~**s** (sets of) shelves, shelving.

rayonnant, e [ʀɛjɔnɑ̃, ɑ̃t] adj a (*radieux*) *beauté, air, personne* radiant; *sourire* radiant, beaming (*épith*); *visage* wreathed in smiles, beaming. **visage** ~ **de joie/santé** face radiant with joy/glowing *ou* radiant with health. b (*en étoile*) *motif, fleur* radiating. **le style (gothique)** ~ High Gothic; **chapelles** ~**es** radiating chapels. c (*Phys*) *énergie, chaleur* radiant; (*Méd*) *douleur* spreading.

rayonne [ʀɛjɔn] nf rayon.

rayonnement [ʀɛjɔnmɑ̃] nm a (*influence bénéfique*) *[culture, civilisation]* influence; *[influence]* extension; (*magnétisme*) *[personnalité]* radiance. **le** ~ **de la culture hellénique s'étendit au monde entier** the influence of Greek culture extended over *ou* made itself felt over the whole world. b (*éclat*) *[jeunesse, beauté]* radiance. **dans tout le** ~ **de sa jeunesse** in the full radiance of his youth; **le** ~ **de son bonheur** his radiant happiness. c (*lumière*) *[astre, soleil]* radiance. d (*radiations*) *[chaleur, lumière, astre]* radiation.

rayonner [ʀɛjɔne] 1 vi a (*étinceler*) *[influence, culture, personnalité]* to shine forth. (*se répandre*) ~ **sur/dans** *[influence, prestige]* to extend over/in, make itself felt over/in; *[culture]* to extend over/in, be influential over/in, exert its influence over/in; *[personnalité]* to be influential over/in.

b (*être éclatant*) *[joie, bonheur]* to shine *ou* beam forth; *[beauté]* to shine forth, be radiant; *[visage, personne]* (*de joie, de beauté*) to be radiant (*de* with). **le bonheur faisait** ~ **son visage** his face glowed with happiness; **l'amour rayonne dans ses yeux** love shines *ou* sparkles in his eyes; ~ **de bonheur** to be radiant *ou* glowing *ou* beaming with happiness; ~ **de beauté** to be radiant *ou* dazzling with beauty.

c (*littér: briller*) *[lumière, astre]* to shine (forth), be radiant.

d (*Phys: émettre un rayonnement*) *[chaleur, énergie, lumière]* to radiate.

e (*faire un circuit*) ~ **autour d'une ville** *[touristes]* to use a town as a base for touring (around a region); *[cars]* to service the area around a town; ~ **dans une région** *[touristes]* to tour around a region (from a base); *[cars]* to service a region.

f (*aller en rayons*) *[avenues, lignes]* to radiate (*autour de* from, out from).

rayure [ʀejyʀ] nf (*dessin*) stripe; (*éraflure*) scratch; *[fusil]* groove. **papier/tissu à** ~**s** striped paper/material; **à** ~**s noires** with black stripes, black-striped.

raz-de-marée [ʀɑdmaʀe] nm inv (*Géog, fig*) tidal wave. ~ **électoral** big swing (*to a party in an election*); **le** ~ **communiste** *ou* **le** ~ **électoral en faveur des communistes qui s'est produit aux dernières élections** the big swing to the Communists in the last elections, the massive Communist vote *ou* the Communist landslide vote in the last elections.

razzia [ʀa(d)zja] nf raid, foray, razzia. (*fig*) **faire une** ~ **dans une maison/le frigo*** to raid *ou* plunder a house/the fridge.

razzier [ʀa(d)zje] 7 vt (*lit, fig: piller*) to raid, plunder.

RDA† [ɛʀdea] nf (abrév de **République démocratique allemande**) GDR†.

rdc abrév de **rez-de-chaussée**.

ré [ʀe] nm (*Mus*) D; (*en chantant la gamme*) re, ray. **en** ~ **mineur** in D minor.

réabonnement [ʀeabɔnmɑ̃] nm renewal of subscription. **le** ~ **doit se faire dans les huit jours** renewal of subscription must be made within a week, subscriptions must be renewed within a week.

réabonner [ʀeabɔne] 1 1 vt: ~ **qn** to renew sb's subscription (*à* to). 2 **se réabonner** vpr to renew one's subscription, take out a new subscription (*à* to).

réabsorber [ʀeapsɔʀbe] 1 vt to reabsorb.

réabsorption [ʀeapsɔʀpsjɔ̃] nf reabsorption.

réac* [ʀeak] abrév de **réactionnaire**.

réaccoutumer [ʀeakutyme] 1 1 vt to reaccustom. 2 **se réaccoutumer** vpr to reaccustom o.s., become reaccustomed (*à* to).

réacteur [ʀeaktœʀ] nm (*Aviat*) jet engine; (*Chim, Phys nucléaire*) reactor. ~ **thermique** thermal reactor.

réactif, -ive [ʀeaktif, iv] 1 adj reactive. **papier** ~ reagent *ou* test paper. 2 nm (*Chim, fig*) reagent.

réaction [ʀeaksjɔ̃] nf a (*gén*) reaction. **être** *ou* **rester sans** ~ to show no reaction; **être en** ~ **contre** to be in reaction against; ~ **de défense/en chaîne** defence/chain reaction; (*Méd*) **faire à qn des** ~**s de floculation** to test sb for a flocculation reaction; **temps de** ~ reaction time; *voir* **cuti-réaction**. b (*Pol*) **la** ~ reaction; **les forces de la** ~ the forces of reaction. c (*Aviat*) **moteur à/propulsion par** ~ jet engine/propulsion (*voir* **avion**); **cette voiture a de bonnes** ~**s** this car responds well.

réactionnaire [ʀeaksjɔnɛʀ] adj, nmf reactionary.

réactionnel, -elle [ʀeaksjɔnɛl] adj reactional.

réactivation [ʀeaktivasjɔ̃] nf reactivation.

réactiver [ʀeaktive] 1 vt to reactivate.

réactualisation [ʀeaktɥalizasjɔ̃] nf updating, bringing up to date.

réactualiser [ʀeaktɥalize] 1 vt to update, bring up to date.

réadaptation [ʀeadaptasjɔ̃] nf (*voir* **réadapter**) readjustment; rehabilitation; re-education.

réadapter [ʀeadapte] 1 1 vt *personne* to readjust (*à* to); (*Méd*) to rehabilitate; *muscle* to re-educate. 2 **se réadapter** vpr to readjust, become readjusted (*à* to).

réadmettre [ʀeadmɛtʀ] 56 vt to readmit.

réadmission [ʀeadmisjɔ̃] nf readmission, readmittance.

réaffirmer [ʀeafiʀme] 1 vt to reaffirm, reassert.

réagir [ʀeaʒiʀ] 2 vi to react (*à* to, *contre* against, *sur* upon). **il a réagi de manière exagérée** he overreacted, he went over the top*.

réajustement [ʀeaʒystəmɑ̃] nm = **rajustement**.

réajuster [ʀeaʒyste] 1 vt = **rajuster**.

réalisable [ʀealizabl] adj (*fig*) *rêve* attainable; (*Fin*) *capital* realizable; *projet* workable, feasible.

réalisateur, -trice [ʀealizatœʀ, tʀis] nm,f (*Ciné*) (film) director, film-maker; (*Rad, TV*) director; *[plan]* realizer.

réalisation [ʀealizasjɔ̃] nf a (*action*) (*voir* **réaliser**) *[projet]* realization; carrying out; *[rêve]* fulfilment, realization; *[exploit]* achievement; *[valeurs, fortune]* realization; (*Comm*) *[vente, contrat]* conclusion; (*voir* **se réaliser**) *[projet, rêve]* fulfilment, realization. **plusieurs projets sont déjà en cours de** ~ several projects are already in the pipeline *ou* are already under way. b (*ouvrage*) achievement, creation. c (*Ciné*) production.

réaliser [ʀealize] 1 1 vt a (*concrétiser*) *ambition, rêve* to realize, fulfil; *effort* to make, exercise; *exploit* to achieve, carry off; *projet* to carry out, carry through, realize. **il réalise (en soi) le meilleur exemple de** he is the best (material) example of.

b (**: se rendre compte de*) to realize. ~ **l'importance de qch** to realize the importance of sth; **je n'ai pas encore réalisé** it hasn't sunk in yet.

c (*Ciné*) to produce.

d (*Comm*) to realize; *achat, vente, bénéfice* to make; *contrat* to conclude. **l'entreprise réalise un chiffre d'affaires de 100 000 F par semaine** the firm turns over 100,000 F a week.

e (*Fin*) *capital* to realize. **la banque a réalisé une partie de son portefeuille** part of the bank's portfolio was liquidated.

f (*Mus*) to realize.

2 **se réaliser** vpr a (*se concrétiser*) *[rêve]* to come true, be realized; *[projet]* to be carried out, be achieved, be realized.

b (*s'épanouir*) *[caractère, personnalité]* to fulfil o.s.

réalisme [ʀealism] nm realism.

réaliste [ʀealist] 1 adj *description, négociateur* realistic; (*Art, Littérat*) realist. 2 nmf realist.

réalité [ʀealite] nf a (*existence effective*) reality (*NonC*). **différentes** ~**s** different types of reality; **en** ~ in (actual) fact, in reality; **parfois la** ~ **dépasse la fiction** (sometimes) truth can be stranger than fiction.

b (*chose réelle*) reality. **ce que je dis est une** ~, **pas une chose fictive** what I say is reality *ou* fact, not fiction; **oublieux des** ~**s de la vie en communauté** neglecting the realities *ou* facts of communal life; **détaché des** ~**s de ce monde** divorced from the realities of this world; **ce sont les dures** ~**s de la vie** those are the harsh realities of life; **son rêve est devenu (une)** ~ his dream became (a) reality *ou* came true;

voir **désir, sens.**

réaménagement [reamenaʒmɑ̃] nm reorganization, restructuring.

réaménager [reamenaʒe] 3 vt to reorganize, restructure.

réanimateur, -trice [reanimatœʀ, tʀis] 1 nm,f (*personne*) resuscitator. 2 nm (*respirateur*) ventilator, respirator.

réanimation [reanimasjɔ̃] nf resuscitation. **être en (service de)** ~ to be in the intensive care unit, be in intensive care.

réanimer [reanime] 1 vt to resuscitate, revive.

réapparaître [reapaʀɛtʀ] 57 vi to reappear.

réapparition [reapaʀisjɔ̃] nf reappearance.

réapprendre [reapʀɑ̃dʀ] 58 vt (*gén*) to relearn, learn again; (*littér*) *solitude, liberté* to get to know again, relearn (*littér*), learn again (*littér*). ~ **qch à qn** to teach sth to sb again, teach sb sth again; ~ **à faire qch** to learn to do sth again.

réapprentissage [reapʀɑ̃tisaʒ] nm (*voir* **réapprendre**) **le ~ de qch** relearning sth, learning sth again; getting to know sth again; **cela va demander un long ~** that will take a long time to relearn *ou* to learn again.

réapprovisionnement [reapʀɔvizjɔnmɑ̃] nm (*voir* **réapprovisionner**) restocking; stocking up again.

réapprovisionner [reapʀɔvizjɔne] 1 1 vt to restock (*en* with). 2 **se réapprovisionner** vpr to stock up again (*en* with).

réargenter [reaʀʒɑ̃te] 1 1 vt to resilver. 2 **se réargenter*** vpr (*se renflouer*) to replenish the coffers, get back on a sound financial footing.

réarmement [reaʀməmɑ̃] nm (*voir* **réarmer**) winding on; refitting; rearmament.

réarmer [reaʀme] 1 1 vt *appareil-photo* to wind on (again); *bateau* to refit. 2 vi, **se réarmer** vpr *[pays]* to rearm.

réarrangement [reaʀɑ̃ʒmɑ̃] nm rearrangement. (*Phys*) ~ **moléculaire** molecular rearrangement.

réarranger [reaʀɑ̃ʒe] 3 vt *coiffure, fleurs, chambre* to rearrange; *cravate, jupe* to straighten (up) again; *entrevue* to rearrange.

réassignation [reasiɲasjɔ̃] nf (*Jur*) resummons (*sg*); (*Fin*) reallocation.

réassigner [reasiɲe] 1 vt (*gén*) to reassign; (*Jur*) to resummon; (*Fin*) to reallocate (*pay from other monies*).

réassort [reasɔʀ] nm restocking.

réassortiment [reasɔʀtimɑ̃] nm *[stock]* replenishment; *[verres]* replacement, matching (up); *[service de table, tissu]* matching (up); *[marchandises]* new *ou* fresh stock.

réassortir [reasɔʀtiʀ] 2 1 vt *magasin* to restock (*en* with); *stock* to replenish; *service de table* to match (up); *verres* to replace, match (up). 2 **se réassortir** vpr (*Comm*) to stock up again (*de* with), replenish one's stock(s) (*de* of).

réassurance [reasyʀɑ̃s] nf reinsurance.

réassurer vt, **se réassurer** vpr [reasyʀe] 1 to reinsure.

réassureur [reasyʀœʀ] nm reinsurer, reinsurance underwriter.

rebaisser [ʀ(ə)bese] 1 1 vi *[prix]* to go down again; *[température, niveau d'eau]* to fall again. 2 vt *prix* to bring back down *ou* down again, lower again; *radio, son, chauffage* to turn down again; *store, levier* to pull down again, lower again.

rebaptiser [ʀ(ə)batize] 1 vt *enfant* to rebaptize; *rue* to rename; *navire* to rechristen.

rébarbatif, -ive [ʀebaʀbatif, iv] adj (*rebutant*) *mine* forbidding, unprepossessing; *sujet, tâche* daunting, forbidding; *style* crabbed, off-putting (*Brit*).

rebâtir [ʀ(ə)bɑtiʀ] 2 vt to rebuild.

rebattre [ʀ(ə)batʀ] 41 vt a (*Cartes*) to reshuffle. b **il m'a rebattu les oreilles de son succès** he kept harping on about his success; **il en parlait toute la journée, j'en avais les oreilles rebattues** he talked of it all day long until I was sick and tired of hearing about it*.

rebattu, e [ʀ(ə)baty] (ptp de **rebattre**) adj *sujet, citation* hackneyed.

rebec [ʀəbɛk] nm rebec(k).

Rébecca [ʀebeka] nf Rebecca.

rebelle [ʀəbɛl] 1 adj a *troupes, soldat* rebel (*épith*); *enfant, cheval* rebellious, refractory; *esprit* intractable, rebellious; (*fig*) *fièvre, maladie* stubborn; (*fig*) *mèche, cheveux* unruly; (*fig hum*) *cœur* rebellious; (*fig*) *matière* unworkable, refractory, stubborn. (*fig hum*) **découragé par un steak ~, il passa aux légumes** disheartened by a steak which refused to allow itself to be cut *ou* which resisted all attempts at being eaten, he turned his attention to the vegetables.
b ~ **à** *patrie, souverain* unwilling to serve; *discipline* unamenable to; **il est ~ à la géographie/au latin** (*il n'y comprend rien*) geography/Latin is double Dutch to him; (*il ne veut pas apprendre*) he doesn't want to know about geography/Latin; **virus ~ à certains remèdes** virus resistant to certain medicines; **cheveux ~s à la brosse** hair which won't be brushed smooth *ou* which a brush cannot tame.
2 nmf rebel.

rebeller (se) [ʀ(ə)bele] 1 vpr to rebel (*contre* against).

rébellion [ʀebeljɔ̃] nf (*révolte*) rebellion. (*rebelles*) **la ~** the rebels.

rebiffer (se)* [ʀ(ə)bife] 1 vpr (*résister*) *[personne]* to hit *ou* strike back (*contre* at); (*fig*) *[corps, conscience]* to rebel (*contre* against).

rebiquer* [ʀ(ə)bike] 1 vi (*se redresser*) *[mèche de cheveux]* to stick up; *[chaussures, col]* to curl up at the ends.

reblanchir [ʀ(ə)blɑ̃ʃiʀ] 2 vt (*gén*) to rewhiten; *mur* to rewhitewash.

reblochon [ʀəblɔʃɔ̃] nm *kind of cheese from Savoie.*

reboisement [ʀ(ə)bwɑzmɑ̃] nm reafforestation.

reboiser [ʀ(ə)bwɑze] 1 vt to reafforest.

rebond [ʀ(ə)bɔ̃] nm (*voir* **rebondir**) bounce; rebound. ~ **heureux/malheureux** lucky/unlucky bounce; **faux ~** bad bounce.

rebondi, e [ʀ(ə)bɔ̃di] (ptp de **rebondir**) adj *objet, bouteille, forme* potbellied; *croupe* rounded; *poitrine* well-developed; *ventre* fat; *joues, visage* chubby, plump, fat; *femme* curvaceous, amply proportioned; *homme* portly, corpulent; *porte-monnaie* well-lined. **elle avait des formes ~es** she was amply proportioned; **il a un ventre ~** he has a paunch *ou* a corporation (*Brit*), he has a fat stomach.

rebondir [ʀ(ə)bɔ̃diʀ] 2 vi a *[balle]* (*sur le sol*) to bounce; (*contre un mur etc*) to rebound. b (*être relancé*) *[conversation]* to get going *ou* moving again, spring to life again; *[scandale, affaire, procès]* to be revived; (*Théât*) *[action, intrigue]* to get moving again, spring to life again, take off again. **faire ~** *conversation* to give new impetus to, set *ou* get going again; *action d'une tragédie* to get *ou* set moving again; *scandale, procès* to revive.

rebondissement [ʀ(ə)bɔ̃dismɑ̃] nm *[affaire]* (sudden new) development (*de* in), sudden revival (*NonC*) (*de* of).

rebord [ʀ(ə)bɔʀ] nm a *[assiette, tuyau, plat, pot]* rim; *[puits, falaise]* edge; *[corniche, table, buffet]* (projecting) edge. **le ~ de la cheminée** the mantelpiece *ou* mantelshelf; **le ~ de la fenêtre** the windowsill, the window ledge. b *[vêtement]* hem.

reborder [ʀ(ə)bɔʀde] 1 vt *vêtement* to put a new edging on; *enfant* to tuck in again.

reboucher [ʀ(ə)buʃe] 1 1 vt *trou* to fill in again; *bouteille* to recork; *carafe* to restopper; *tube* to put the cap back on. 2 **se reboucher** vpr *[tuyau]* to get blocked again.

rebours [ʀ(ə)buʀ] nm: **à ~** a (*à rebrousse-poil*) **caresser un chat à ~** to stroke a cat the wrong way; **lisser un tissu à ~** to smooth out a fabric against the nap *ou* pile; (*fig*) **prendre qn à ~** to rub sb up the wrong way.
b (*à l'envers*) **faire un trajet à ~** to make a journey *ou* trip the other way round; **prendre une rue en sens unique à ~** to go the wrong way up a one-way street; **feuilleter un magazine à ~** to flip through a magazine from back to front; **compter à ~** to count backwards; (*Mil*) **prendre l'ennemi à ~** to surprise the enemy from behind; *voir* **compte.**
c (*de travers*) **comprendre à ~** to misunderstand, get the wrong idea, get the wrong end of the stick* (*Brit*); **faire tout à ~** to do everything the wrong way round *ou* back to front *ou* upside down.
d (*à l'opposé de*) **à ~ de** against; **aller à ~ de la tendance générale** to go against *ou* run counter to the general trend; **c'est à ~ du bon sens!** it goes against *ou* flies in the face of common sense!

rebouteur, -euse [ʀ(ə)butœʀ, øz] nm,f, **rebouteux, -euse** [ʀ(ə)butø, øz] nm,f bonesetter.

reboutonner [ʀ(ə)butɔne] 1 1 vt to button up again, rebutton. 2 **se reboutonner** vpr to do o.s. up again, do up one's buttons again.

rebrousse- [ʀ(ə)bʀus] préf *voir* **rebrousser.**

rebrousser [ʀ(ə)bʀuse] 1 1 vt a ~ **chemin** to turn back, turn round and go back. b *poil* to brush up; *cheveux* to brush back. **tu as les cheveux tout rebroussés par le vent** your hair is all ruffled up *ou* tousled by the wind. 2 comp ▸**à rebrousse-poil** *caresser* the wrong way; **lisser un tissu à rebrousse-poil** to smooth out a fabric against the pile *ou* nap; (*fig*) **prendre qn à rebrousse-poil** to rub sb up the wrong way.

rebuffade [ʀ(ə)byfad] nf rebuff. **essuyer une ~** to suffer a rebuff.

rébus [ʀebys] nm rebus. (*fig*) **sa lettre est un vrai ~** reading his letter is a real puzzle.

rebut [ʀəby] nm a (*déchets*) scrap. **c'est du ~** (*objets*) it's scrap; (*vêtements*) they're just cast-offs; **c'est le ~ de la cave** it's what's to be thrown out of the cellar, it's all the unwanted stuff in the cellar; **mettre** *ou* **jeter au ~** to put on the scrap heap *ou* rubbish heap; *objets* to scrap, throw out, discard; *vêtements* to discard, throw out; **ces vieux journaux vont aller au ~** these old papers are going to be thrown out *ou* discarded *ou* are going to be put on the rubbish heap; **marchandises de ~** trash goods; **bois de ~** old wood. b (*péj: racaille*) **le ~ de la société** the scum *ou* dregs of society. c (*Poste*) **~s** dead letters.

rebutant, e [ʀ(ə)bytɑ̃, ɑ̃t] adj (*dégoûtant*) repellent; (*décourageant*) off-putting (*Brit*), disheartening.

rebuter [ʀ(ə)byte] 1 vt (*décourager*) to put off (*Brit*), dishearten, discourage; (*répugner*) to repel; (*littér: repousser durement*) to repulse. **il ne faut pas te ~ tout de suite** don't be deterred *ou* put off (*Brit*) straight away.

recacheter [ʀ(ə)kaʃ(ə)te] 4 vt to reseal.

recalage [ʀ(ə)kalaʒ] nm (*Scol*) *[candidat]* failure.

récalcitrant, e [ʀekalsitʀɑ̃, ɑ̃t] 1 adj (*indocile*) *animal* refractory, stubborn; *personne* recalcitrant, refractory; (*fig*) *appareil, pièce* unmanageable. 2 nm,f recalcitrant.

recaler [ʀ(ə)kale] 1 vt (*Scol: ajourner*) to fail. **se faire ~ (en histoire)** to fail *ou* flunk* (history); **j'ai été recalé en histoire** I failed (in) *ou* flunked* history; **les recalés** the failed candidates, the failures.

récapitulatif, -ive [ʀekapitylatif, iv] adj *chapitre* recapitulative, recapitulatory; *état, tableau* summary (*épith*). **dresser un état ~ (d'un compte** *etc***)** to draw up a summary statement (of an account *etc*).

récapitulation [ʀekapitylasjɔ̃] **nf** recapitulation, summing up, recap*. **faire la ~ de** to recapitulate, sum up, recap*.

récapituler [ʀekapityle] 1 **vt** to recapitulate, sum up, recap*.

recarreler [ʀ(ə)kaʀle] 4 **vt** to retile.

recaser* [ʀ(ə)kɑze] 1 **vt** a *travailleur* to find a new job for; *résident* to rehouse. **il a été recasé** *[chômeur]* he has been found a new job; **il a pu se ~** *[veuf, divorcé]* he managed to get hitched* again *ou* to find himself someone new; *[chômeur]* he managed to find a new job. b (*refiler*) **~ qch à qn** to palm sth off on sb*.

recauser* [ʀ(ə)koze] 1 **vi: ~ de qch** to talk about sth again; **je vous en recauserai** we'll talk about it again.

recéder [ʀ(ə)sede] 6 **vt** (*rétrocéder*) to give *ou* sell back; (*vendre*) to resell.

recel [ʀəsɛl] **nm: ~ (d'objets volés)** (*action*) receiving stolen goods, receiving (SPÉC); (*résultat*) possession of *ou* possessing stolen goods; **~ de malfaiteur** harbouring a wrongdoer; **condamné pour ~** sentenced for possession of *ou* for receiving stolen goods *ou* for receiving (SPÉC).

receler [ʀ(ə)səle] 5 **vt** a (*Jur*) *objet volé* to receive; *voleur* to harbour. b (*contenir*) *secret, erreur, trésor* to conceal.

receleur, -euse [ʀ(ə)səlœʀ, øz] **nm,f** (*Jur*) receiver.

récemment [ʀesamɑ̃] **adv** a (*depuis peu*) recently. **la pluie ~ tombée rendait la route glissante** the rain which had fallen recently *ou* had just fallen made the road slippery; **ce livre, ~ publié** *ou* **publié ~** this book which has been published recently *ou* which has just been published. b (*dernièrement*) recently, lately (*gén dans phrases nég ou interrog*). **l'as-tu vu ~?** have you seen him lately? *ou* recently?; **encore ~ il était très en forme** just recently *ou* even quite recently he was still in tiptop form.

recensement [ʀ(ə)sɑ̃smɑ̃] **nm** *[population]* census; *[objets]* inventory. (*Mil*) **~ du contingent** *registration of young men eligible for French military service, carried out by a mayor;* **faire le ~** to take a *ou* the census of the population, make *ou* take a population census.

recenser [ʀ(ə)sɑ̃se] 1 **vt** *population* to take a *ou* the census of, make a census of; *objets* to make *ou* take an inventory of; *futurs conscrits* to compile a register of.

recenseur [ʀ(ə)sɑ̃sœʀ] **adj m, nm: (agent) ~** census taker.

récent, e [ʀesɑ̃, ɑ̃t] **adj** (*survenu récemment*) *événement, traces* recent; (*nouveau, de fraîche date*) *propriétaire, bourgeois* new.

recentrage [ʀ(ə)sɑ̃tʀaʒ] **nm** *[parti]* movement towards the centre; *[politique]* redefinition, reorientation.

recentrer [ʀ(ə)sɑ̃tʀe] 1 **vt** (*Ftbl*) to cross again; *politique* to redefine, reorient.

récépissé [ʀesepise] **nm** (*reçu*) (acknowledgement of) receipt.

réceptacle [ʀesɛptakl] **nm** (*Bot*) *[fleur]* receptacle; (*déversoir*) (*gén*) receptacle; (*Géog*) catchment basin; (*fig*) gathering place; (*péj*) dumping place.

récepteur, -trice [ʀesɛptœʀ, tʀis] 1 **adj** receiving. **poste ~** receiving set, receiver. 2 **nm** (*gén, Téléc*) receiver; (*Rad, TV*) (receiving) set, receiver; (*Physiol*) receptor. **~ (de télévision)** television receiver *ou* (receiving) set.

réceptif, -ive [ʀesɛptif, iv] **adj** receptive (*à* to).

réception [ʀesɛpsjɔ̃] **nf** a (*réunion, gala*) reception; *voir* **jour**. b (*accueil*) reception, welcome. **faire bonne/mauvaise ~ à qn** to give a good/bad reception *ou* welcome to sb; **un discours de ~ (à un nouveau sociétaire)** a welcoming speech *ou* an address of welcome (given to a new member of a society). c (*entrée, salon*) *[appartement, villa]* reception room; *[hôtel]* entrance hall; (*bureau*) *[hôtel]* reception desk, reception. **salle de ~** function room, stateroom; **salons de ~** reception rooms. d (*action de recevoir*) *[paquet, lettre]* receipt; (*Bio, Rad, TV*) reception. **à la ~ de sa lettre** on receipt of *ou* on receiving his letter; **c'est lui qui s'occupe de la ~ des marchandises** he is the one who takes delivery of the goods; (*Rad*) **la ~ est mauvaise aujourd'hui** reception is bad *ou* poor today; *voir* **accusé, accuser**. e (*Sport*) (*prise, blocage*) *[ballon]* trapping, catching; (*atterrissage*) *[sauteur, parachutiste]* landing. **le footballeur manqua sa ~ et le ballon roula en touche** the footballer failed to trap *ou* catch the ball and it rolled into touch; **après une bonne ~ du ballon** after trapping *ou* catching the ball well; **le sauteur manqua sa ~** the jumper made a bad landing *ou* landed badly. f (*Constr*) **~ des travaux** acceptance of work done (*after verification*).

réceptionnaire [ʀesɛpsjɔnɛʀ] **nmf** *[hôtel]* head of reception; (*Comm*) *[marchandises]* receiving clerk; (*Jur*) receiving agent.

réceptionner [ʀesɛpsjɔne] 1 **vt** *marchandises* to receive, take delivery of, check and sign for; *client* to receive, welcome; (*Sport*) *balle* to receive.

réceptionniste [ʀesɛpsjɔnist] **nmf** receptionist. **~-standardiste** receptionist-telephonist.

réceptivité [ʀesɛptivite] **nf** (*gén*) receptivity, receptiveness; (*Méd*) sensitivity, liability (*à* to).

récessif, -ive [ʀesesif, iv] **adj** (*Bio*) recessive.

récession [ʀesesjɔ̃] **nf** recession. **de ~** recessionary; **~ avec inflation** slumpflation.

récessionniste [ʀesesjɔnist] **adj** recessionary. **tendance ~** recessionary trend.

récessivité [ʀesesivite] **nf** recessiveness.

recette [ʀ(ə)sɛt] **nf** a (*Culin*) recipe; (*Chim*) *[teinture, produit]* formula; (*fig: truc, secret*) formula, recipe (*de* for). b (*encaisse*) takings (*pl*). **aujourd'hui, j'ai fait une bonne ~** I've made a good day's takings, today the takings were good; (*fig: avoir du succès*) **faire ~** to be a big success, be a winner. c (*rentrées d'argent*) **~s** receipts; **l'excédent des ~s sur les dépenses** the excess of receipts *ou* revenue over expenses *ou* outlay. d (*Impôts*) (*fonction*) position of tax *ou* revenue collector; (*bureau*) tax (collector's) office, revenue office. **~ municipale** rates office; **~-perception** tax office; **~ principale** main tax office. e (*recouvrement*) collection. **faire la ~ des sommes dues** to collect the money due; *voir* **garçon**.

recevabilité [ʀ(ə)səvabilite] **nf** (*Jur*) *[pourvoi, témoignage]* admissibility.

recevable [ʀ(ə)səvabl] (*Jur*) **adj** *demande, appel, pourvoi* admissible, allowable; *personne* competent. **témoignage non ~** inadmissible evidence.

receveur [ʀ(ə)səvœʀ] **nm** a (*Méd*) recipient. **~ universel** universal recipient. b **~ (d'autobus)** conductor; **~ (des contributions)** tax collector *ou* officer; **~ (des postes)** postmaster; **~ municipal** rate collector.

receveuse [ʀ(ə)səvøz] **nf** a (*Méd*) recipient. **~ universelle** universal recipient. b **~ (d'autobus)** conductress; **~ (des contributions)** tax collector *ou* officer; **~ (des postes)** postmistress.

recevoir [ʀ(ə)səvwaʀ] 28 1 **vt** a (*gén*) *lettre, ordre, argent, blessure, ovation, compliment etc* to receive, get; *approbation, refus* to meet with, receive, get; *modifications* to undergo, receive; *émission, station de radio* to get, receive; (*Rel*) *confession* to hear; (*Rel*) *vœux, sacrement* to receive. (*Rel*) **~ les ordres** to take holy orders; **nous avons bien reçu votre lettre du 15 juillet** we acknowledge *ou* confirm receipt of your letter of July 15th; (*Rad, fig*) **je vous reçois cinq sur cinq** I'm reading *ou* receiving you loud and clear; **je n'ai d'ordre à ~ de personne** I don't take orders from anyone; **je n'ai pas de leçon à ~ de lui!** I don't need to take any lessons from him!; **procédé qui a reçu le nom de son inventeur** process which has taken *ou* got its name from the inventor; **l'affaire recevra toute notre attention** the matter will receive our full attention; **nous avons reçu la pluie** we got *ou* had rain; **j'ai reçu le caillou sur la tête** the stone hit me on the head, I got hit on the head by the stone; **il a reçu un coup de pied/un coup de poing dans la figure** he got kicked/punched in the face, he got a kick/punch in the face; **c'est lui qui a tout reçu** (*blâme, coups*) he got the worst of it, he bore *ou* got the brunt of it; (*sauce, éclaboussures*) he got the worst of it; (*formule épistolaire*) **recevez, cher Monsieur (***ou* **chère Madame) l'expression de mes sentiments distingués/mes salutations sincères/l'assurance de mon dévouement** yours faithfully (*Brit*) *ou* truly (*US*)/sincerely/truly. b *invité* (*accueillir*) to receive, welcome, greet; (*traiter*) to entertain; (*loger*) to take in, receive; *Jeux olympiques, championnat* to host; (*Admin*) *employé, demandeur* to see; *demande, déposition, plainte* to receive, admit. **~ qn à dîner** to entertain *ou* invite sb to dinner; **ils ont reçu le roi** they entertained the king, they were host to the king; **être bien/mal reçu** *[proposition, nouvelles]* to be well/badly received; *[personne]* to receive a good/bad welcome, get a good/bad reception; *[invités]* to be entertained well/badly; **il est reçu partout dans la haute société** all doors are open to him in society; **les Dupont reçoivent beaucoup** the Duponts entertain a lot; **la baronne reçoit le jeudi** the baroness is at home (to visitors) on Thursdays; **le directeur reçoit le jeudi** the principal receives visitors on Thursdays; **le docteur reçoit de 10 h à 12 h** the doctor's surgery (*Brit*) *ou* office (*US*) is from 10 a.m. till noon; **~ la visite de qn/d'un cambrioleur** to receive *ou* have a visit from sb/from a burglar; **elles se connaissent mais ne se reçoivent pas** they know each other but they are not on visiting terms; *voir* **chien**. c (*Scol, Univ etc*) *candidat* to pass. **être reçu à un examen** to pass an exam, be successful in an exam; **il a été reçu dans les premiers/dans les derniers** he was near the top/bottom in the exam; **il a été reçu premier/deuxième/dernier** he came first/second/last *ou* bottom in the exam; *voir* **reçu**. d (*contenir*) *[hôtel, lycée]* to take, hold, accommodate; (*récolter*) *[gouttière]* to collect. **par manque de locaux on n'a pas pu ~ plus d'élèves cette année** lack of space prevented us from taking *ou* admitting more pupils this year; (*Géog*) **~ un affluent** to be joined by a tributary; **leur chambre ne reçoit jamais le soleil** their room never gets any sun. e (*Tech*) *pièce mobile* to take, receive. **cette encoche reçoit le crochet qui assure la fermeture de la porte** this notch receives *ou* takes the hook which keeps the door shut.

2 **se recevoir vpr** (*tomber*) to land. **se ~ sur une jambe/sur les mains** to land on one leg/on one's hands; **il s'est mal reçu** he landed badly.

rechange [ʀ(ə)ʃɑ̃ʒ] **nm** a **~ (de vêtements)** change of clothes; **as-tu ton ~?** have you got a change of clothes? b **de ~** (*de remplacement*) *solution, politique* alternative; (*de secours*) *outil* spare; **avoir du linge de ~** to have a change of clothes; **j'ai apporté des chaussures de ~** I brought a spare *ou* an extra pair of shoes; *voir* **pièce**.

rechanger [R(ə)ʃɑ̃ʒe] 3 vt to change again.

rechanter [R(ə)ʃɑ̃te] 1 vt to sing again.

rechapage [R(ə)ʃapaʒ] nm retreading, remoulding (*Brit*). **le ~ n'a pas duré** the retread *ou* remould (*Brit*) didn't last long.

rechaper [R(ə)ʃape] 1 vt *pneu* to retread, remould (*Brit*). **pneus rechapés** remoulds (*Brit*), retreads.

réchapper [Reʃape] 1 vi: **~ de** *ou* **à** *accident, maladie* to come through; **tu as eu de la chance d'en ~** you were lucky to escape with your life; **si jamais j'en réchappe** if ever I come through this.

recharge [R(ə)ʃaRʒ] nf a (*action*) (*Élec*) recharging; (*Mil*) reloading. b (*cartouche*) *[arme]* reload; *[stylo]* refill.

rechargeable [R(ə)ʃaRʒabl] adj (*voir* **recharger**) reloadable; refillable; rechargeable.

rechargement [R(ə)ʃaRʒəmɑ̃] nm (*voir* **recharger**) reloading; refilling; recharging; refuelling; remetalling; relaying.

recharger [R(ə)ʃaRʒe] 3 vt *véhicule, arme, appareil-photo* to reload; *stylo* to refill; *briquet* to refill, recharge; *accumulateur* to recharge; *poêle* to refuel; (*Tech*) *route* to remetal; (*Tech*) *voie, rails* to relay. (*fig*) **~ ses batteries** *ou* **ses accus*** to recharge one's batteries.

réchaud [Reʃo] nm a (portable) stove. b (*chauffe-plat*) platewarmer. c (*cassolette*) burner (*for incense etc*).

réchauffage [Reʃofaʒ] nm *[aliment]* reheating.

réchauffé, e [Reʃofe] (ptp de **réchauffer**) adj *nourriture* reheated, warmed-up, rehashed (*péj*); (*péj*) *plaisanterie* stale, old hat (*attrib*); *théories* rehashed, old hat (*attrib*). **c'est du ~** *[ragoût]* it's reheated *ou* warmed-up *ou* rehashed (*péj*); *[politique]* it's stale *ou* rehashed *ou* old hat.

réchauffement [Reʃofmɑ̃] nm *[eau, membres, personne]* warming (up). **le ~ de la planète** global warming; **on constate un ~ de la température** we notice a rise *ou* an increase in the temperature, we notice the weather's gone warmer; **on espère un ~ de la température pour la moisson** we're hoping for warmer weather for the harvest.

réchauffer [Reʃofe] 1 1 vt a (*Culin*) *aliment* to reheat, heat *ou* warm up again. **réchauffe** *ou* **fais ~ la soupe, mets la soupe à ~** reheat the soup, heat *ou* warm the soup up again.

b *personne* to warm up. **une bonne soupe, ça réchauffe** a good soup warms you up; (*littér, hum*) **~ un serpent dans son sein** to nurse a viper in one's bosom.

c (*réconforter*) *cœur* to warm; (*ranimer*) *courage* to stir up, rekindle.

d *[soleil]* to heat up, warm up. **le soleil réchauffe la terre** the sun heats up the land; **ce rayon de soleil va ~ l'atmosphère** this ray of sunshine will warm up the air; **les tons bruns réchauffent la pièce** browns make a room seem warmer.

2 **se réchauffer** vpr a *[temps, température]* to get warmer, warm up. **on dirait que ça se réchauffe** it feels as if it's getting warmer *ou* warming up.

b *[personne]* to warm o.s. (up). **alors tu te réchauffes un peu?** are you warming up now? *ou* feeling a bit warmer now?; **se ~ les doigts, ~ ses doigts** to warm one's fingers (up).

réchauffeur [Reʃofœr] nm heater.

rechausser [R(ə)ʃose] 1 1 vt: **~ un enfant** (*chaussures enlevées*) to put a child's shoes back on; (*chaussures neuves*) to buy a child new shoes; **~ une voiture** to put new tyres (*Brit*) *ou* tires (*US*) on a car. 2 **se rechausser** vpr to put one's shoes back on; to buy (o.s.) new shoes.

rêche [Rɛʃ] adj (*au toucher*) *tissu, peau* rough, harsh; (*au goût*) *vin* rough; *fruit vert* harsh; (*péj*) *personne* abrasive.

recherche [R(ə)ʃɛRʃ] nf a (*action de rechercher*) search (*de* for). **la ~ de ce papier m'a pris plusieurs heures** the search for this paper took me several hours; **la ~ de l'albumine dans le sang est faite en laboratoire** tests to detect albumin in the blood are performed in the laboratory; **à la ~ de** in search of; (*Littérat*) **A la ~ du temps perdu** In Search of Time Lost; **être/se mettre à la ~ de qch/qn** to be/go in search of sth/sb, search for sth/sb; **je suis à la ~ de mes lunettes** I'm searching *ou* hunting *ou* looking for my glasses; **ils sont à la ~ d'un appartement/d'une maison** they are flat-hunting (*Brit*) *ou* apartment-hunting (*US*)/house-hunting, they're looking for *ou* on the look-out for a flat (*Brit*) *ou* apartment (*US*)/house; **nous avons fait toute la ville à la ~ d'un livre sur la Norvège** we hunted the town for a book on Norway; **il a dû se mettre à la ~ d'une nouvelle situation** he had to start looking *ou* hunting for a new job; **il est toujours à la ~ d'une bonne excuse** he's always on the look-out for a good excuse, he's always trying to come up with *ou* find a good excuse.

b (*enquête*) **~s** investigations; **faire des ~s** to make *ou* pursue investigations; **malgré toutes leurs ~s, ils n'ont pas trouvé le document nécessaire** in spite of all their searching *ou* hunting they haven't found the necessary document; **toutes nos ~s pour retrouver l'enfant sont demeurées sans résultat** all our investigations *ou* attempts to find the child remained fruitless; **jusqu'ici il a échappé aux ~s de la police** until now he has escaped the police hunt *ou* search.

c (*fig: poursuite*) pursuit (*de* of), search (*de* for). **la ~ des plaisirs** the pursuit of pleasure, pleasure-seeking; **la ~ de la gloire** the pursuit of glory; **la ~ de la perfection** the search *ou* quest for perfection.

d (*Scol, Univ*) (*métier, spécialité*) **la ~** research; (*études, enquêtes*) **~s** research; **faire des ~s sur un sujet** to do *ou* carry out research into a subject; **que fait-il comme ~s?** what (kind of) research does he do?, what is he doing research on? *ou* in?; **être dans la ~, faire de la ~** to be (engaged) in research, do research (work); **il fait de la ~ en maths** he's doing research in maths; **bourse/étudiant de ~** research grant/student; **c'est un travail de ~** it's a piece of research (work); **~ fondamentale** basic research; **~ opérationnelle** operational research.

e (*raffinement*) *[tenue, ameublement]* meticulousness, studied elegance; (*péj: affectation*) affectation. **être habillé avec ~** to be dressed with studied elegance; **être habillé sans ~** to be dressed carelessly.

f (*Ordin*) search.

recherché, e [R(ə)ʃɛRʃe] (ptp de **rechercher**) adj a *édition, tableau, livre* much sought-after; (*très demandé*) *produits, acteur, conférencier* in great demand (*attrib*), much sought-after; (*apprécié des connaisseurs*) *morceau délicat, plaisir* choice (*épith*), exquisite. **c'est quelqu'un de très ~** he's in great demand, he's much sought-after. b (*étudié, soigné*) *style* mannered; *expression* studied; *vocabulaire* recherché, carefully chosen; *tenue* meticulous; (*péj*) affected, studied.

rechercher [R(ə)ʃɛRʃe] 1 vt a (*chercher à trouver*) *objet égaré ou désiré, enfant perdu* to search for, hunt for; *coupable, témoin* to try to trace *ou* find, look for, seek; *cause d'accident* to try to determine *ou* find out *ou* ascertain, inquire into. **~ l'albumine dans le sang** to look for (evidence of *ou* the presence of) albumin in the blood; **~ comment/pourquoi** to try to find out how/why; **~ qch dans sa mémoire** to search one's memory for sth; **il faudra ~ ce document dans tous les vieux dossiers** we'll have to search through all the old files to find this document; (*Ordin*) **~ un mot dans un dossier** to search a file for a word; (*dans une annonce*) **"on recherche femme de ménage"** "cleaning lady required"; **recherché pour meurtre** wanted for murder; **les policiers le recherchent depuis 2 ans** the police have been looking for him *ou* have been after him for 2 years; **la police recherche ...** the police want to interview ... .

b (*viser à*) *honneurs, compliment* to seek; *danger* to court, seek; *succès, plaisir* to pursue. **~ la perfection** to strive for *ou* seek perfection; **~ l'amitié/la compagnie de qn** to seek sb's friendship/company; **un écrivain qui recherche l'insolite** a writer who strives to capture the unusual.

c (*chercher à nouveau*) to search for *ou* look for again. **il faudra que je recherche dans mon sac** I must have another look (for it) in my bag, I must look in *ou* search my bag again; **recherche donc cette lettre** search *ou* look for that letter again, have another look *ou* search for that letter.

rechigner [R(ə)ʃiɲe] 1 vi (*renâcler*) to balk, jib. **quand je lui ai dit de m'aider, il a rechigné** when I told him to help me he balked *ou* jibbed *ou* made a sour face; **faire qch en rechignant** to do sth with bad grace *ou* with a sour face; **il m'a obéi sans trop ~** he obeyed me without making too much fuss; **~ à faire qch** to balk *ou* jib at doing sth; **~ à** *ou* **devant qch** to balk *ou* jib at sth.

rechute [R(ə)ʃyt] nf (*Méd*) relapse; (*fig: dans l'erreur, le vice*) lapse (*dans* into). (*Méd*) **faire** *ou* **avoir une ~** to have a relapse.

rechuter [R(ə)ʃyte] 1 vi (*Méd*) to relapse, have a relapse.

récidivant, e [Residivɑ̃, ɑ̃t] adj (*Méd*) recurring.

récidive [Residiv] nf a (*Jur*) second *ou* subsequent offence (*Brit*) *ou* offense (*US*), second *ou* subsequent crime. **en cas de ~** in the event of a second *ou* subsequent offence, in the event of a repetition of the offence; **escroquerie avec ~** second offence of fraud; **être en ~** to reoffend, be a recidivist; **les cas de ~ se multiplient chez les jeunes délinquants** reoffending *ou* recidivism is on the increase among juvenile delinquents; **à la première ~, je le fiche à la porte** at the first (sign of) repetition *ou* if he repeats that once again, I shall throw him out. b (*Méd*) recurrence; (*fig: nouvelle incartade*) repetition (*of one's bad ways*).

récidiver [Residive] 1 vi (*Jur*) to reoffend, commit a second *ou* subsequent offence (*Brit*) *ou* offense (*US*) *ou* crime; (*fig*) *[enfant, élève]* to do it again; (*Méd*) to recur. (*hum*) **il a récidivé 15 minutes plus tard avec un second but** and did it again* 15 minutes later with a second goal.

récidivisme [Residivism] nm reoffending, recidivism (*frm*).

récidiviste [Residivist] nmf second offender, recidivist (*SPÉC*); (*plusieurs répétitions*) habitual offender, recidivist (*SPÉC*). **un condamné ~** a recidivist.

récidivité [Residivite] nf (*Méd*) recurring nature.

récif [Resif] nm reef. **~ de corail** coral reef; **~ frangeant** fringing reef; **~-barrière** barrier reef.

récipiendaire [Resipjɑ̃dɛR] nm (*Univ*) recipient (*of a diploma*); *[société]* newly elected member, member elect.

récipient [Resipjɑ̃] nm container, receptacle.

réciprocité [ResipRɔsite] nf reciprocity.

réciproque [ResipRɔk] 1 adj *sentiments, confiance, tolérance, concessions* reciprocal, mutual; (*Math*) *figure, transformation* reciprocal; (*Ling*) *adjectif, verbe, pronom* reciprocal. (*Logique*)

propositions ~s converse propositions.

2 **nf: la ~** (*l'inverse*) (*Logique*) the converse; (*gén*) the opposite, the reverse; (*la pareille*) the same (treatment); **il me déteste mais la ~ n'est pas vraie** he hates me but the opposite *ou* reverse isn't true, he hates me but conversely I don't hate him; **il m'a joué un sale tour, mais je lui rendrai la ~** he played a dirty trick on me, but I'll be quits with him yet *ou* I'll pay him back (in kind *ou* in his own coin); **encore merci, j'espère qu'un jour j'aurai l'occasion de vous rendre la ~** thanks again, I hope that one day I'll have the opportunity to do the same for you *ou* to pay you back; **s'attendre à la ~** to expect the same (treatment) *ou* to be paid back.

réciproquement [ʀesipʀɔkmɑ̃] **adv** a (*l'un l'autre*) each other, one another, mutually. **ils se félicitaient ~** they congratulated each other *ou* one another. b (*vice versa*) vice versa. **il me déteste et ~** he hates me and vice versa *ou* and it's mutual; **un employé doit avoir de l'estime pour son chef et ~** an employee must have regard for his boss and the other way round *ou* and vice versa.

réciproquer [ʀesipʀɔke] [1] **vt** (*Belgique*) *vœux, aide* to reciprocate.

récit [ʀesi] **nm** a (*action de raconter*) account, story; (*histoire*) story; (*genre*) narrative. **~ d'aventures** adventure story; **faire le ~ de** to give an account of, tell the story of; **au ~ de ces exploits** on hearing an *ou* the account of *ou* the story of these exploits. b (*Théât: monologue*) (narrative) monologue. c (*Mus*) solo.

récital, pl ~s [ʀesital] **nm** recital. **~ poétique** poetry recital.

récitant, e [ʀesitɑ̃, ɑ̃t] 1 **adj** (*Mus*) solo. 2 **nm,f** (*Mus, Rad, Théât, TV*) narrator.

récitatif [ʀesitatif] **nm** recitative.

récitation [ʀesitasjɔ̃] **nf** a (*matière, classe*) recitation. **composition de ~** recitation test; **leçon de ~** lesson to be recited by heart. b (*texte, poème*) recitation, piece (to be recited). c (*action*) recital, reciting.

réciter [ʀesite] [1] **vt** a *leçon, chapelet, prière* to recite. b (*péj*) *profession de foi, témoignage* to trot out, recite.

réclamation [ʀeklɑmasjɔ̃] **nf** a (*plainte*) complaint; (*Sport*) objection. **faire une ~** to make *ou* lodge a complaint; **adressez vos ~s à, pour toute ~ s'adresser à** all complaints should be referred to; **"(bureau des) ~s"** "complaints department *ou* office"; (*Téléc*) **téléphonez aux ~s** ring the engineers. b (*récrimination*) protest, complaint.

réclame [ʀeklɑm] **nf** (*annonce publicitaire*) advertisement, advert (*Brit*), ad*. (*publicité*) **la ~** advertising, publicity; **faire de la ~ pour un produit** to advertise *ou* publicize a product; **ça ne leur fait pas de ~** that's no advert for them; (*fig*) **je ne vais pas lui faire de la ~** I'm not going to boost his business for him *ou* spread his name around (for him), I'm not going to give him free publicity; **en ~** on (special) offer; **article ~** special offer; **~ lumineuse** neon sign.

réclamer [ʀeklɑme] [1] 1 **vt** a (*solliciter*) *silence, paix, aide* to ask *ou* call for; *argent* to ask for; *pain* to ask *ou* beg for. **~ l'indulgence de qn** to beg *ou* crave sb's indulgence; **je réclame la parole!** I ask *ou* beg to speak!; **il m'a réclamé à boire/un jouet** he asked me for a drink/a toy; **je n'aime pas les enfants qui réclament** I don't like children who are always asking for things; **l'enfant malade réclame sa mère** the sick child is calling *ou* asking for his mother, the sick child wants his mother.

b (*revendiquer*) *augmentation, droit, dû* to claim, demand; *part* to claim, lay claim to. **je lui ai réclamé le stylo que je lui avais prêté** I asked him for the pen back *ou* I reclaimed the pen which I had lent him.

c (*nécessiter*) *patience, soin* to call for, demand, require.

2 **vi** (*protester*) to complain. **si vous n'êtes pas content, allez ~ ailleurs** if you're not happy, go and complain *ou* make your complaints elsewhere; **~ contre** to cry out against.

3 **se réclamer vpr: se ~ de ses ancêtres** to call on the spirit of one's ancestors; **doctrine politique qui se réclame de la Révolution française** political doctrine that claims to go back to the spirit of *ou* that claims to have its roots in the French Revolution; **il se réclame de l'école romantique** he claims to draw *ou* take his inspiration from the romantic school; **il s'est réclamé du ministre pour obtenir ce poste** he used the minister's name (as a reference) to obtain this position; **je me réclame de Descartes quand je dis cela** I use Descartes as my authority when I say that.

reclassement [ʀ(ə)klɑsmɑ̃] **nm** (*voir* **reclasser**) placement; rehabilitation; regrading; reclassifying.

reclasser [ʀ(ə)klɑse] [1] **vt** *chômeur* to place, find a new placement for; *ex-prisonnier* to rehabilitate; *fonctionnaire* to regrade; *objet* to reclassify.

reclouer [ʀ(ə)klue] [1] **vt** to nail back on, nail back together.

reclus, e [ʀəkly, yz] 1 **adj** cloistered. **elle vit ~e, elle a** *ou* **mène une vie ~e** she leads the life of a recluse, she leads a cloistered life. 2 **nm,f** recluse.

réclusion [ʀeklyzjɔ̃] **nf** (*littér*) reclusion (*littér*). (*Jur*) **~ (criminelle)** imprisonment; **~ criminelle à perpétuité** life imprisonment.

réclusionnaire [ʀeklyzjɔnɛʀ] **nmf** (*Jur*) convict.

recoiffer [ʀ(ə)kwafe] [1] 1 **vt: ~ ses cheveux** to do one's hair; **~ qn** to do sb's hair. 2 **se recoiffer vpr** (*se peigner*) to do one's hair; (*remettre son chapeau*) to put one's hat back on.

recoin [ʀəkwɛ̃] **nm** (*lit*) nook; (*fig*) hidden *ou* innermost recess. **les ~s du grenier** the nooks and crannies of the attic; **dans les ~s de sa mémoire** in the recesses of his mind.

recollage [ʀ(ə)kɔlaʒ] **nm, recollement** [ʀ(ə)kɔlmɑ̃] **nm** (*voir* **recoller**) resticking; sticking back together again.

recoller [ʀ(ə)kɔle] [1] 1 **vt** a (*lit*) *étiquette* to stick back on *ou* down, restick; *morceau, vase* to stick back together; *enveloppe* to stick back down, restick. (*fig*) **le coureur recolla au peloton** the runner closed the gap with the rest of the bunch; (*fig: réconcilier*) **~ les morceaux** to patch things up.

b (*remettre*) **~ son oreille à la porte** to stick one's ear against *ou* to the door again; **~ qn en prison*** to stick sb back in prison*; **ne recolle pas tes affaires dans ce coin!*** don't stick your things back down in that corner!*

c (*: *redonner*) **~ une amende** *etc* **à qn** to give another fine *etc* to sb; **je ne veux pas qu'on nous recolle le grand-père!** I don't want them to dump *ou* palm off grandfather on us again!*

2 **se recoller vpr** a *[os]* to mend, knit (together).

b (*: *subir*) **il a fallu se ~ la vaisselle** we had to take on washing the dishes again.

c (*: *se remettre*) **on va se ~ au boulot** let's knuckle down to the job again*, let's get back down to the job.

d (*: *se remettre en ménage*) to go back (to live) together. **après leur brouille ils se sont recollés (ensemble)** after their quarrel they went back (to live) together.

récoltable [ʀekɔltabl] **adj** which can be harvested *ou* gathered.

récoltant, e [ʀekɔltɑ̃, ɑ̃t] **adj, nm,f: (propriétaire) ~** farmer (*who harvests his own crop*), grower.

récolte [ʀekɔlt] **nf** a (*action*) (*voir* **récolter**) harvesting; gathering (in); collecting. **faire la ~ des pommes de terre** to harvest *ou* gather (in) the potatoes *ou* the potato crop; **la saison des ~s** the harvest *ou* harvesting season. b (*produit*) *[blé, pommes de terre]* harvest, crop; *[miel]* crop. **cette année, on a fait une excellente ~ (de fruits)** this year we had an excellent *ou* a bumper crop (of fruit); **~ sur pied** standing crop. c (*fig*) *[documents, souvenirs]* collection, crop (*fig*); (*argent récolté*) takings (*pl*); (*observations récoltées*) findings (*pl*).

récolter [ʀekɔlte] [1] **vt** a *blé, pommes de terre* to harvest, gather (in); *miel* to collect, gather. (*fig*) **~ ce qu'on a semé** to reap what one has sown; *voir* **qui.** b (*recueillir*) *souvenirs, documents, signatures* to collect, gather; *argent* to collect; (*) *contravention, coups* to get, collect*. **je n'ai récolté que des ennuis** all I got was a lot of trouble.

recommandable [ʀ(ə)kɔmɑ̃dabl] **adj** (*estimable*) commendable. **peu ~** not very commendable.

recommandation [ʀ(ə)kɔmɑ̃dasjɔ̃] **nf** a (*conseil: gén, Pol*) recommendation. **faire des ~s à qn** to make recommendations to sb. b (*louange*) *[hôtel, livre]* recommendation. **je l'ai acheté sur sa ~** I bought it on his recommendation. c (*appui*) recommendation. **sur la ~ de qn** on sb's recommendation; **donner une ~ à qn pour un patron** to give sb a recommendation for an employer; *voir* **lettre.** d (*Poste: voir* **recommander**) recording; registration.

recommandé, e [ʀ(ə)kɔmɑ̃de] (**ptp de recommander**) **adj** a (*Poste: voir* **recommander**) recorded; registered. **"envoi ~"** "recorded delivery" (*Brit*); (*avec valeur assurée*) "registered post" (*Brit*), "registered mail"; **envoyer qch en ~** to send sth recorded delivery (*Brit*); (*avec valeur assurée*) to send sth by registered post (*Brit*) *ou* mail; *voir* **lettre.** b (*conseillé*) *produit* recommended; *hôtel* approved, recommended; *mesure, initiative* advisable, recommended. **est-ce bien ~?** is it advisable? *ou* recommended? (*de faire* to do); **ce n'est pas très ~** it's not very *ou* really advisable, it's not really recommended.

recommander [ʀ(ə)kɔmɑ̃de] [1] 1 **vt** a (*appuyer*) *candidat* to recommend (*à* to). **est-il recommandé?** has he been recommended?; **un savant que sa probité intellectuelle recommande autant que ses découvertes** a scholar whose intellectual honesty commends him as much as (do) his discoveries.

b (*conseiller*) *hôtel, livre, produit* to recommend (*à* to). **~ à qn de faire** to recommend *ou* advise sb to do; **le médecin lui recommande le repos** the doctor advises *ou* recommends (him to) rest; **je te recommande la modération/la discrétion** I advise you to be moderate/discreet, I recommend that you be moderate/discreet; **je te recommande (de lire) ce livre** I recommend you (to read) this book, I recommend that you read this book; (*ton de menace*) **je te recommande de partir** I strongly advise you to leave; **est-ce bien à ~?** is it to be recommended?, is it advisable?

c (*Rel*) **~ son âme à Dieu** to commend one's soul to God.

d (*tournure impersonnelle*) **il est recommandé de** it's advisable *ou* recommended to.

e (*Poste*) *lettre* (*pour attester sa remise*) to record; (*pour assurer sa valeur*) *lettre, paquet* to register.

2 **se recommander vpr: se ~ de qn** to give sb's name as a reference; **se ~ à qn/Dieu** to commend o.s. to sb/God; **il se recommande par son talent/son ambition** his talent/ambition commends him.

recommencement [ʀ(ə)kɔmɑ̃smɑ̃] **nm: le ~ des hostilités/combats** the renewal of hostilities/(the) fighting; **l'histoire est un perpétuel ~** history is a process of constant renewal *ou* a series of new beginnings; **les ~s sont toujours difficiles** beginning again *ou* making a fresh start is always difficult.

recommencer [ʀ(ə)kɔmɑ̃se] 3 1 vt a (*continuer*) *récit, lecture* to begin *ou* start again, resume; *lutte, combat* to start up again, start afresh, renew, resume. **soyez attentifs, ça fait la 3e fois que je recommence** pay attention, that's the 3rd time I've had to start *ou* begin again.
b (*refaire*) *travail, expérience* to start (over) again, start afresh. ~ **sa vie** to make a fresh start (in life), start *ou* begin one's life (over) again; **si c'était à** ~ if I could start *ou* have it over again; **tout est à** ~ everything has to begin again *ou* be begun again.
c (*répéter*) *erreur* to make *ou* commit again.
2 vi *[pluie, orage]* to begin *ou* start again; *[combat]* to start up again, start afresh, resume. **la pluie recommence** it's beginning *ou* starting to rain again, the rain is beginning *ou* starting again; **en septembre, l'école recommence** in September school begins *ou* starts again *ou* resumes; **année après année, les saisons recommencent** year after year the seasons begin afresh *ou* anew; **je leur ai dit de se taire, et voilà que ça recommence!** I told them to be quiet and yet there they go again!; ~ **à** *ou* **de faire** to begin *ou* start to do again, begin *ou* start doing again; **tu ne vas pas** ~ **de sitôt!** you won't do that again in a hurry!*; **on lui dit de ne pas le faire, mais deux minutes plus tard, il recommence (à le faire)** he is told not to do it but two minutes later he does it again *ou* he's at it again.

recomparaître [ʀ(ə)kɔ̃paʀɛtʀ] 57 vi (*Jur*) to appear (in court) again.

récompense [ʀekɔ̃pɑ̃s] nf (*action, chose*) reward; (*prix*) award. **en** ~ **de** in return for, as a reward for; **en** ~ **de vos services** in return for your services; **je me sacrifie et voilà ma** ~ I make sacrifices and that's all the reward I get.

récompenser [ʀekɔ̃pɑ̃se] 1 vt to reward, recompense. **être récompensé d'avoir fait qch** to be rewarded *ou* recompensed for having done sth.

recomposer [ʀ(ə)kɔ̃poze] 1 vt *puzzle* to put together again, reconstruct; (*Chim*) to recompose; (*Téléc*) *numéro* to dial again, redial; (*Typ*) *ligne* to reset. **il parvint à** ~ **la scène** (*par la mémoire*) he succeeded in reconstructing the scene; **l'œil/la télévision recompose l'image** the eye/television reconstitutes the image.

recomposition [ʀ(ə)kɔ̃pozisjɔ̃] nf (*voir* **recomposer**) reconstruction; recomposition; redialling; resetting; reconstitution.

recompter [ʀ(ə)kɔ̃te] 1 vt to count again, recount.

réconciliateur, -trice [ʀekɔ̃siljatœʀ, tʀis] nm,f reconciler.

réconciliation [ʀekɔ̃siljasjɔ̃] nf reconciliation.

réconcilier [ʀekɔ̃silje] 7 1 vt *personnes, théories* to reconcile (*avec* with). ~ **qn avec une idée** to reconcile sb to an idea. 2 **se réconcilier** vpr to be *ou* become reconciled (*avec* with). **ils se sont réconciliés** they have been reconciled, they have made their peace with one another; **se** ~ **avec soi-même** to feel *ou* be at peace with o.s.

reconductible [ʀ(ə)kɔ̃dyktibl] adj renewable.

reconduction [ʀ(ə)kɔ̃dyksjɔ̃] nf renewal. **tacite** ~ renewal by tacit agreement.

reconduire [ʀ(ə)kɔ̃dɥiʀ] 38 vt a (*continuer*) *politique, budget, bail* to renew. **commande tacitement reconduite** order renewed by tacit agreement. b (*raccompagner*) ~ **qn chez lui/à la gare** to see *ou* take *ou* escort sb (back) home/to the station; **il a été reconduit à la frontière par les policiers** he was escorted (back) to the frontier by the police; ~ **qn à pied/en voiture chez lui** to walk/drive sb (back) home; **il m'a reconduit à la porte** he showed me to the door.

réconfort [ʀekɔ̃fɔʀ] nm comfort.

réconfortant, e [ʀekɔ̃fɔʀtɑ̃, ɑ̃t] adj (*rassurant*) *parole, idée* comforting; (*stimulant*) *remède* tonic (*épith*), fortifying; *aliment* fortifying.

réconforter [ʀekɔ̃fɔʀte] 1 1 vt *[paroles, présence]* to comfort; *[alcool, aliment, remède]* to fortify. 2 **se réconforter** vpr (*boire, manger*) to have *ou* take some refreshment.

reconnaissable [ʀ(ə)kɔnɛsabl] adj recognizable (*à* by, from). **il n'était pas** ~ he was unrecognizable, you wouldn't have recognized him.

reconnaissance [ʀ(ə)kɔnɛsɑ̃s] 1 nf a (*gratitude*) gratitude, gratefulness (*à qn* to *ou* towards sb). **avoir/éprouver de la** ~ **pour qn** to be/feel grateful to sb; **en** ~ **de ses services/de son aide** in recognition of *ou* acknowledgement of *ou* gratitude for his services/his help; **être pénétré de** ~ **pour la générosité de qn** to be filled with gratitude to sb for his generosity; (*hum*) **il a la** ~ **du ventre** he's grateful for what he's been given.
b (*Pol: d'un état*) recognition; (*Jur: d'un droit*) recognition, acknowledgement.
c (*exploration*) reconnaissance, survey; (*Mil*) reconnaissance, recce*. (*lit, fig*) **envoyer en** ~ to send (out) on reconnaissance *ou* on a recce*; (*lit, fig*) **partir en** ~ to go and reconnoitre (the ground); (*Mil*) **faire** *ou* **pousser une** ~ to make a reconnaissance, go on reconnaissance; **mission/patrouille de** ~ reconnaissance mission/patrol.
d (*action de reconnaître*) recognition. **il lui fit un petit signe de** ~ he gave her a little sign of recognition; **il tenait un journal en signe de** ~ he was carrying a newspaper so that he could be recognized *ou* identified.
e (*littér: aveu*) acknowledgement, admission.
f (*Ordin*) recognition. ~ **de la parole** speech recognition.
2 comp ▸**reconnaissance de dette** acknowledgement of a debt, IOU ▸**reconnaissance d'enfant** legal recognition of a child ▸**reconnaissance du mont-de-piété** pawn ticket.

reconnaissant, e [ʀ(ə)kɔnɛsɑ̃, ɑ̃t] adj grateful (*à qn de qch* to sb for sth). **je vous serais** ~ **de me répondre rapidement** I would be grateful if you would reply quickly *ou* for a speedy reply.

reconnaître [ʀ(ə)kɔnɛtʀ] 57 1 vt a (*gén: identifier*) to recognize. **je l'ai reconnu à sa voix** I recognized him *ou* I knew it was him *ou* I could tell it was him from *ou* by (the sound of) his voice; **je le reconnaîtrais entre mille** I'd recognize him *ou* pick him out anywhere; **elle reconnut l'enfant à son foulard rouge** she recognized the child by his red scarf; ~ **la voix/le pas de qn** to recognize sb's voice/walk; **ces jumeaux sont impossibles à** ~ these twins are impossible to tell apart, it's impossible to tell which of these twins is which; **on reconnaît un fumeur à ses doigts jaunis** you can tell *ou* recognize *ou* spot a smoker by his stained fingers; **on reconnaît bien là sa paresse** that's just typical of him and his lazy ways, that's just typical of his laziness; **je le reconnais bien là** that's just like him, that's him all over!; **méfiez-vous, il sait** ~ **un mensonge** be careful – he knows *ou* recognizes *ou* he can spot a lie when he hears one; **on ne le reconnaît plus** you wouldn't know *ou* recognize him now.
b (*convenir de*) *innocence, supériorité, valeur* to recognize, acknowledge; (*avouer*) *torts* to recognize, acknowledge, admit. **il reconnut peu à peu la difficulté de la tâche** he gradually came to realize *ou* recognize the difficulty of the task; **il faut** ~ **les faits** we must face *ou* recognize the facts; **on lui reconnaît une qualité, il est honnête** he is recognized as having one quality – he is honest; **il faut** ~ **qu'il faisait très froid** admittedly it was very cold, you must admit it was very cold; **il a reconnu s'être trompé/qu'il s'était trompé** he admitted to *ou* acknowledged making a mistake/that he had made a mistake; **je reconnais que j'avais tout à fait oublié ce rendez-vous** I must confess *ou* admit (that) I had completely forgotten this appointment.
c (*admettre*) *maître, chef* to recognize; (*Pol*) *état, gouvernement* to recognize; (*Jur*) *enfant* to recognize legally, acknowledge; *dette* to acknowledge. ~ **qn pour** *ou* **comme chef** to acknowledge *ou* recognize sb as (one's) leader; (*Jur*) ~ **la compétence d'un tribunal** to acknowledge *ou* recognize the competence of a court; (*Jur*) ~ **qn coupable** to find sb guilty; ~ **sa signature** to acknowledge one's signature; **il ne reconnaît à personne le droit d'intervenir** he doesn't recognize in anyone the right to intervene, he doesn't acknowledge that anyone has the right to intervene.
d (*Mil*) *terrain, île, côte* to reconnoitre. **on va aller** ~ **les lieux** *ou* **le terrain** we're going to see how the land lies, we're going to reconnoitre (the ground); **les gangsters étaient certainement venus** ~ **les lieux auparavant** the gangsters had certainly been to look over the place *ou* spy out (*Brit*) the land beforehand.
e (*littér: montrer de la gratitude*) to recognize, acknowledge.
2 **se reconnaître** vpr a (*dans la glace*) to recognize o.s.; (*entre personnes*) to recognize each other. **elle ne se reconnaît pas du tout dans ses filles** she (just) can't see any likeness between herself and her daughters.
b (*lit, fig: se retrouver*) to find one's way about *ou* around. **je ne m'y reconnais plus** I'm completely lost; **je commence à me** ~ I'm beginning to find my bearings.
c (*être reconnaissable*) to be recognizable (*à* by). **le pêcher se reconnaît à ses fleurs roses** the peach tree is recognizable by its pink flowers, you can tell a peach tree by its pink flowers.
d (*s'avouer*) **se** ~ **vaincu** to admit *ou* acknowledge defeat; **se** ~ **coupable** to admit *ou* acknowledge one's guilt.

reconnu, e [ʀ(ə)kɔny] (ptp de **reconnaître**) adj *fait* recognized, accepted; *auteur, chef* recognized. **c'est un fait** ~ **que** ... it's a recognized *ou* an accepted fact that ...; **il est** ~ **que** ... it is recognized *ou* accepted *ou* acknowledged that ... .

reconquérir [ʀ(ə)kɔ̃keʀiʀ] 21 vt (*Mil*) to reconquer, recapture, capture back; *femme* to win back; *dignité, liberté* to recover, win back.

reconquête [ʀ(ə)kɔ̃kɛt] nf (*Mil*) reconquest, recapture; *[droit, liberté]* recovery.

reconsidérer [ʀ(ə)kɔ̃sideʀe] 6 vt to reconsider.

reconstituant, e [ʀ(ə)kɔ̃stitɥɑ̃, ɑ̃t] 1 adj *aliment, régime* which builds up *ou* boosts (up) one's strength. 2 nm energy-giving food, energizer.

reconstituer [ʀ(ə)kɔ̃stitɥe] 1 vt a *parti, armée* to re-form, reconstitute; *fortune* to build up again, rebuild; *crime, faits, puzzle, histoire* to reconstruct, piece together; *texte* to restore, reconstitute; *édifice, vieux quartier* to restore, reconstruct; *objet brisé* to put *ou* piece together again. **le parti s'est reconstitué** the party was re-formed *ou* reconstituted. b (*Bio*) *organisme* to regenerate.

reconstitution [ʀ(ə)kɔ̃stitysjɔ̃] nf (*voir* **reconstituer**) reformation; reconstitution; rebuilding; reconstruction; piecing together; restoration; regeneration. ~ **historique** reconstruction *ou* recreation of history; (*Scol*) ~ **d'un texte** text reconstitution, rewriting exercise; **la** ~ **du crime** reconstruction at the scene of the crime (*in the presence of the examining magistrate and the accused*).

reconstruction [R(ə)kɔ̃stRyksjɔ̃] nf (*voir* **reconstruire**) rebuilding; reconstruction.
reconstruire [R(ə)kɔ̃stRɥiR] 38 vt *maison* to rebuild, reconstruct; *fortune* to build up again, rebuild.
reconversion [R(ə)kɔ̃vɛRsjɔ̃] nf (*voir* **reconvertir, se reconvertir**) reconversion; redeployment, retraining. **stage de ~** retraining course.
reconvertir [R(ə)kɔ̃vɛRtiR] 2 1 vt *usine* to reconvert (*en* to); *personnel* to redeploy, retrain. 2 **se reconvertir** vpr *[usine]* to be reconverted, be turned over to a new type of production; *[personne]* to move into *ou* turn to a new type of employment. **il s'est reconverti dans le secrétariat** he has given up his old job and gone into secretarial work; **nous nous sommes reconvertis dans le textile** we have moved over *ou* gone over into textiles.
recopier [R(ə)kɔpje] 7 vt (*transcrire*) to copy out, write out; (*recommencer*) to copy out *ou* write out again. **~ ses notes au propre** to write up one's notes, make a fair copy of one's notes.
record [R(ə)kɔR] 1 nm (*Sport*) record. **~ masculin/féminin** men's/women's record; **l'indice des valeurs boursières a atteint un nouveau ~ à la hausse/à la baisse** the share index has reached an all-time high/low; **j'ai lu 2 livres en une semaine, c'est mon ~** I read 2 books within a week, it's a personal record; *voir* **battre 1b.** 2 adj inv *chiffre, production* record (*épith*). **en un temps ~** in record time.
recorder [R(ə)kɔRde] 1 vt *raquette* to restring.
recordman [R(ə)kɔRdman], pl **recordmen** [R(ə)kɔRdmɛn] nm (men's) record holder.
recordwoman [R(ə)kɔRdwuman], pl **recordwomen** [R(ə)kɔRdwɔmɛn] nf (women's) record holder.
recorriger [Rəkɔriʒe] 3 vt to recorrect, correct again; (*Scol*) to mark again, re-mark.
recors [R(ə)kɔR] nm (*Hist*) bailiff's assistant.
recoucher [R(ə)kuʃe] 1 1 vt *enfant* to put back to bed; *objet* to lay *ou* put down again. 2 **se recoucher** vpr to go back to bed.
recoudre [R(ə)kudR] 48 vt (*Couture*) *ourlet* to sew up again; *bouton* to sew back on, sew on again; (*Méd*) *plaie* to stitch up (again), put stitches (back) in; *opéré* to stitch (back) up.
recoupement [R(ə)kupmɑ̃] nm crosscheck, crosschecking (*NonC*). **par ~** by crosschecking; **faire un ~** to crosscheck.
recouper [R(ə)kupe] 1 1 vt a (*gén*) to cut again; *vêtement* to recut; *vin* to blend; *route* to intersect. **~ du pain** to cut (some) more bread; **elle m'a recoupé une tranche de viande** she cut me another slice of meat. b *[témoignage]* to tie up *ou* match up with, confirm, support. 2 vi (*Cartes*) to cut again. 3 **se recouper** vpr *[faits]* to tie *ou* match up, confirm *ou* support one another; *[droites, cercles]* to intersect; *[chiffres, résultats]* to add up.
recourbé, e [R(ə)kuRbe] (ptp de **recourber**) adj (*gén*) curved; (*accidentellement*) bent; *bec* curved, hooked. **nez ~** hooknose.
recourbement [R(ə)kuRbəmɑ̃] nm bending.
recourber [R(ə)kuRbe] 1 1 vt *bois* to bend (over); *métal* to bend, curve. 2 **se recourber** vpr to curve (up), bend (up).
recourir [R(ə)kuRiR] 11 1 vt (*Sport*) to run again. 2 **recourir à** vt indir *opération, emprunt* to resort to, have recourse to; *force* to resort to; *personne* to turn to, appeal to. **j'ai recouru à son aide** I turned *ou* appealed to him for help. 3 vi a (*Sport*) to race again, run again. **j'ai recouru le chercher*** I ran back *ou* raced back *ou* nipped back* (*Brit*) to get it. b (*Jur*) **~ contre qn** to (lodge an) appeal against sb.
recours [R(ə)kuR] 1 nm resort, recourse; (*Jur*) appeal. **le ~ à la violence ne sert à rien** resorting to violence doesn't do any good; **en dernier ~** as a last resort, in the last resort; **nous n'avons plus qu'un ~** we've only got one resort *ou* recourse left, there's only one course (of action) left open to us; **il n'y a aucun ~ contre cette décision** there is no way of changing this decision, there is no appeal possible *ou* no recourse against this decision; **il n'y a aucun ~ contre cette maladie** there is no cure *ou* remedy for this disease; **la situation est sans ~** there's nothing we can do about the situation, there's no way out of the situation; **avoir ~ à** *mesure, solution* to resort to, have recourse to; *force* to resort to; *personne* to turn to, appeal to.
2 comp ►**recours en cassation** appeal to the supreme court ►**recours contentieux** *submission for a legal settlement* ►**recours en grâce** (*remise de peine*) plea for pardon; (*commutation de peine*) plea for clemency ►**recours gracieux** *submission for an out-of-court settlement* ►**recours hiérarchique** disciplinary complaint.
recouvrable [R(ə)kuvRabl] adj a *impôt* collectable, which can be collected; *créance* recoverable, reclaimable, retrievable. b *peinture* **"~ après 24 heures"** "allow to dry 24 hours *ou* leave 24 hours before applying a second coat".
recouvrement [R(ə)kuvRəmɑ̃] nm a (*couverture: action*) covering (up); (*résultat*) cover. (*Constr*) **assemblage à ~** lap joint. b (*Fin*) *[cotisations]* collection, payment; *[impôt]* collection, levying; (*littér*) *[créance]* recovery. c (*littér*) *[forces, santé]* recovery.
recouvrer [R(ə)kuvRe] 1 vt a *santé, vue* to recover, regain; *liberté* to regain; *amitié* to win back. **~ la raison** to recover one's senses, come back to one's senses. b (*Fin*) *cotisation* to collect; *impôt* to collect, levy; (*littér*) *créance* to recover.
recouvrir [R(ə)kuvRiR] 18 1 vt a (*entièrement*) to cover. **la neige recouvre le sol** snow covers the ground; **recouvert d'écailles/d'eau** covered in *ou* with scales/water; **~ un mur de papier peint/de carreaux** to paper/tile a wall; **le sol était recouvert d'un tapis** the floor was carpeted, there was a carpet on the floor; **les ouvriers recouvrirent la maison** the workmen put the roof on the house *ou* roofed over the house; **recouvre la casserole/les haricots** put the lid on the saucepan/on *ou* over the beans.
b (*à nouveau*) *fauteuil, livre* to re-cover, put a new cover on; *casserole* to put the lid back on. **~ un enfant qui dort** to cover (up) a sleeping child again.
c (*cacher*) *intentions* to conceal, hide, mask; (*englober*) *aspects, questions* to cover.
2 **se recouvrir** vpr: **se ~ d'eau/de terre** to become covered in *ou* with water/earth; **le ciel se recouvre** the sky is getting cloudy *ou* becoming overcast again; **les deux feuilles se recouvrent partiellement** the two sheets overlap slightly.
recracher [R(ə)kRaʃe] 1 1 vt to spit out (again). 2 vi to spit again.
récré [RekRe] nf (*arg Scol*) abrév de **récréation**.
récréatif, -ive [RekReatif, iv] adj *lecture* light (*épith*). **soirée ~ive** evening's recreation *ou* entertainment.
récréation [RekReasjɔ̃] nf a (*Scol*) (*au lycée*) break; (*à l'école primaire*) playtime (*Brit*), break, recess (*US*). **aller en ~** to go out for (the) break; **les enfants sont en ~** the children are having their playtime (*Brit*) *ou* break; *voir* **cour.** b (*gén: détente*) recreation, relaxation.
recréer [R(ə)kRee] 1 vt to re-create.
récréer [RekRee] 1 (*littér*) 1 vt to entertain, amuse. 2 **se récréer** vpr to amuse o.s.
recrépir [R(ə)kRepiR] 2 vt to resurface (with roughcast *ou* pebble dash). **faire ~ sa maison** to have the roughcast *ou* pebble dash redone on one's house.
recreuser [R(ə)kRøze] 1 vt (*lit*) (*de nouveau*) to dig again; (*davantage*) to dig deeper; (*fig*) to go further *ou* deeper into, dig deeper into.
récrier (se) [RekRije] 7 vpr to exclaim, cry out in admiration (*ou* indignation, surprise *etc*).
récriminateur, -trice [RekRiminatœR, tRis] adj remonstrative, complaining.
récrimination [RekRiminasjɔ̃] nf recrimination, remonstration, complaint.
récriminatoire [RekRiminatwaR] adj *discours, propos* remonstrative.
récriminer [RekRimine] 1 vi to recriminate, remonstrate (*contre* against), complain bitterly (*contre* about).
récrire [RekRiR] 39 vt *roman, inscription* to rewrite; *lettre* to write again. **il m'a récrit** he has written to me again, he has written me another letter.
recroqueviller (se) [R(ə)kRɔk(ə)vije] 1 vpr *[papier, fleur]* to shrivel up, curl up; *[personne]* to huddle *ou* curl o.s. up. **il était tout recroquevillé dans un coin** he was all hunched up *ou* huddled up in a corner.
recru, e[1] [Rəkry] adj (*littér*) **~ (de fatigue)** exhausted, tired out.
recrudescence [R(ə)kRydesɑ̃s] nf *[criminalité, combats]* (fresh) upsurge, new and more serious wave *ou* outburst; *[épidémie]* (fresh) upsurge, further and more serious outbreak *ou* outburst. **devant la ~ des vols** in view of the upsurge in thefts; **il y a eu une ~ de froid** the cold weather suddenly set in even worse than before, there was another spell of even colder weather.
recrudescent, e [R(ə)kRydesɑ̃, ɑ̃t] adj (*littér*) recrudescent. **épidémie ~e** epidemic which is on the increase *ou* upsurge again.
recrue[2] [RəkRy] nf (*Mil*) recruit; (*fig*) recruit, new member. (*fig*) **faire une (nouvelle) ~** to gain a (new) recruit, recruit a new member.
recrutement [R(ə)kRytmɑ̃] nm (*action*) recruiting, recruitment; (*recrues*) recruits. **agence de ~** recruitment agency.
recruter [R(ə)kRyte] 1 vt (*Mil, fig*) to recruit. **se ~ dans** *ou* **parmi** to be recruited from; *[agence]* **~ des cadres pour une entreprise** to headhunt for a company.
recruteur, -euse [R(ə)kRytœR, øz] 1 nm,f (*Mil*) recruiting officer; (*pour cadres*) headhunter. 2 adj recruiting. **agent ~** recruiting agent.
recta* [Rɛkta] adv *payer* promptly, on the nail*; *arriver* on the dot*. **quand j'ai les pieds mouillés, c'est ~, j'attrape un rhume** whenever I get my feet wet that's it*, I catch a cold *ou* I catch a cold straight off (*Brit*) *ou* right off*.
rectal, e, mpl **-aux** [Rɛktal, o] adj rectal.
rectangle [Rɛktɑ̃gl] 1 nm (*gén*) rectangle, oblong; (*Math*) rectangle. (*TV*) **~ blanc** "suitable for adults only" sign. 2 adj right-angled.
rectangulaire [Rɛktɑ̃gylɛR] adj rectangular, oblong.
recteur [RɛktœR] nm a **~ (d'académie)** ≈ chief education officer (*Brit*), director of education (*Brit*), commissioner of education (*US*). b (*Rel*) (*prêtre*) priest; (*directeur*) rector.
rectifiable [Rɛktifjabl] adj *erreur* rectifiable, which can be put right *ou* corrected; *alcool* rectifiable.
rectificateur [RɛktifikatœR] nm (*Chim*) rectifier.
rectificatif, -ive [Rɛktifikatif, iv] 1 adj *compte* rectified, corrected. **acte ~, note ~ive** correction. 2 nm correction.

rectification [ʀɛktifikasjɔ̃] **nf** (*voir* **rectifier**) rectification; correction; straightening.

rectifier [ʀɛktifje] 7 **vt** *calcul* (*corriger*) to rectify, correct; (*ajuster*) to adjust; *erreur* to rectify, correct, put right; *paroles* to correct; *route, tracé* to straighten; *virage* to straighten (out); *mauvaise position* to correct; (*Tech*) *pièce* to true (up), adjust; (*Chim, Math*) to rectify. **il rectifia la position du rétroviseur/son chapeau** he adjusted *ou* straightened his driving mirror/his hat; **"non, ils étaient deux", rectifia-t-il** "no, there were two of them" he added, correcting himself; (*Mil*) ~ **la position/l'alignement** to correct one's stance/the alignment; ~ **le tir** (*lit*) to adjust the fire; (*fig*) to get one's aim right; (*fig: tuer*) **il a été rectifié*, il s'est fait ~*** they did away with him*, he got himself killed *ou* bumped off‡ (*Brit*).

rectifieur, -ieuse [ʀɛktifjœʀ, jøz] 1 **nm,f** (*ouvrier*) grinding machine operator. 2 **rectifieuse nf** (*machine*) grinding machine.

rectiligne [ʀɛktiliɲ] 1 **adj** (*gén*) straight; *mouvement* rectilinear; (*Géom*) rectilinear. 2 **nm** (*Géom*) rectilinear angle.

rectitude [ʀɛktityd] **nf** *[caractère]* rectitude, uprightness; *[jugement]* soundness, rectitude; (*littér*) *[ligne]* straightness.

recto [ʀɛkto] **nm** front (of a page), first side, recto (*frm*). ~ **verso** on both sides (of the page); **voir au** ~ see on first *ou* other side.

rectoral, e, *pl* **-aux** [ʀɛktɔʀal, o] **adj** of the Education Offices.

rectorat [ʀɛktɔʀa] **nm** (*bureaux*) Education Offices.

rectum [ʀɛktɔm] **nm** rectum.

reçu, e [ʀ(ə)sy] (*ptp de* **recevoir**) 1 **adj** a *usages, coutumes* accepted; *voir* **idée**. b *candidat* successful. **les ~s** the successful candidates; **il y a eu 50 ~s** there were 50 passes *ou* successful candidates. 2 **nm** (*quittance*) receipt, chit.

recueil [ʀəkœj] **nm** (*gén*) book, collection; *[documents]* compendium. ~ **de poèmes** anthology *ou* collection of poems; ~ **de morceaux choisis** anthology; (*fig*) ~ **de faits** collection of facts.

recueillement [ʀ(ə)kœjmɑ̃] **nm** (*Rel, gén*) meditation, contemplation. **écouter avec un grand** ~ to listen reverently; **écouter avec un ~ quasi religieux** to listen with an almost religious respect *ou* reverence.

recueilli, e [ʀ(ə)kœji] (*ptp de* **recueillir**) **adj** meditative, contemplative.

recueillir [ʀ(ə)kœjiʀ] 12 1 **vt** a (*récolter*) *graines* to gather, collect; *argent, documents* to collect; *liquide* to collect, catch; *suffrages* to win; *héritage* to inherit. ~ **le fruit de ses efforts** to reap the rewards of one's efforts; *[orateur, discours]* ~ **de vifs applaudissements** to be enthusiastically *ou* warmly applauded; **il a recueilli 100 voix** he got *ou* polled 100 votes.

b (*accueillir*) *réfugié* to take in. ~ **qn sous son toit** to receive sb in one's home, welcome sb into one's home.

c (*enregistrer*) *déposition, chansons anciennes* to take down, take note of; *opinion* to record.

2 **se recueillir vpr** (*Rel, gén*) to collect *ou* gather one's thoughts, commune with o.s. **aller se ~ sur la tombe de qn** to go and meditate at sb's grave.

recuire [ʀ(ə)kɥiʀ] 38 1 **vt** *viande* to recook, cook again; *pain, gâteaux* to rebake, bake again; *poterie* to bake *ou* fire again; (*Tech*) *métal* to anneal. 2 **vi** *[viande]* to cook for a further length of time. **faire** ~ to recook; to rebake.

recul [ʀ(ə)kyl] **nm** a (*retraite*) *[armée]* retreat; *[patron, négociateur]* climb-down* (*par rapport à* from). **j'ai été étonné de son ~ devant la menace de grève** I was amazed at how he retreated *ou* climbed down* at the threat of strike action; **avoir un mouvement de** ~ to recoil, start back, shrink back (*devant, par rapport à* from).

b (*déclin*) *[épidémie, maladie]* recession; *[civilisation, langue]* decline; *[valeur boursière]* decline. **être en** ~ *[épidémie]* to be on the decline, be subsiding; *[chômage]* to be on the decline, be going down *ou* subsiding; *[monnaie]* to be falling; *[parti]* to be losing ground; (*Pol*) ~ **de la majorité aux élections** setback for the government in the election; ~ **du franc sur les marchés internationaux** setback for the franc *ou* drop in the franc on the international markets; **le dollar est en net ~ par rapport à hier** the dollar has dropped sharply since yesterday; **le ~ de l'influence française en Afrique** the decline in French influence in Africa.

c (*éloignement dans le temps, l'espace*) distance. **avec le ~ (du temps), on juge mieux les événements** with the passing of time one can stand back and judge events better; **le village paraissait plus petit avec le** ~ from a distance *ou* from further away the village looked smaller; **prendre du** ~ (*lit*) to step back, stand back; (*fig*) to stand back (*par rapport à* from); **avec du** *ou* **le** ~ with (the benefit of) hindsight; **cette salle n'a pas assez de** ~ there isn't enough room to move back in this room, you can't move back *ou* get back far enough in this room.

d *[arme à feu]* recoil, kick.

e (*report*) *[échéance]* postponement.

f (*déplacement*) *[véhicule]* backward movement; *voir* **phare**.

reculade [ʀ(ə)kylad] **nf** (*Mil*) retreat, withdrawal; (*fig péj*) retreat, climb-down*. **c'est la ~ générale** they're all backing down.

reculé, e [ʀ(ə)kyle] (*ptp de* **reculer**) **adj** *époque* remote, distant; *ville, maison* remote, out-of-the-way (*épith*), out of the way (*attrib*).

reculer [ʀ(ə)kyle] 1 1 **vi** a *[personne]* to move *ou* step back; (*par peur*) to draw back, back away; *[automobiliste, automobile]* to reverse (*Brit*), back (up), move back; *[cheval]* to back; (*Mil*) to retreat. ~ **de 2 pas** to go back *ou* move back 2 paces, take 2 paces back; ~ **devant l'ennemi** to retreat from *ou* draw back from the enemy; ~ **d'horreur** to draw back *ou* shrink back in horror; (*fig*) **c'est ~ pour mieux sauter** it's just putting off the evil day *ou* delaying the day of reckoning; **faire** ~ *foule* to move back, force back; *cheval* to move back; *ennemi* to push *ou* force back; **ce spectacle le fit** ~ this sight made him draw back *ou* made him back away.

b (*hésiter*) to shrink back; (*changer d'avis*) to back down, back out. **tu ne peux plus ~ maintenant** you can't back out *ou* back down now; ~ **devant la dépense/difficulté** to shrink from the expense/difficulty; **je ne reculerai devant rien, rien ne me fera** ~ I'll stop *ou* stick at nothing, nothing will stop me; **il ne faut pas ~ devant ses obligations** you mustn't shrink from your obligations; **il ne recule pas devant la dénonciation** he doesn't flinch at informing on people, he doesn't shrink from informing on people; **cette condition ferait ~ de plus braves** this condition would make braver men (than I *ou* you *etc*) draw back *ou* hesitate.

c (*diminuer*) (*gén*) to be on the decline; *[patois]* to be on the decline, lose ground; *[chômage]* to decline, subside, go down; *[eaux]* to subside, recede, go down; *[incendie]* to subside, lose ground; *[élève, science, civilisation]* to be on the downgrade, decline. **faire ~ l'épidémie** to get the epidemic under control; **faire ~ le chômage** to reduce the number of unemployed; **faire ~ l'inflation** to curb inflation; (*Bourse*) **les mines d'or ont reculé d'un point** gold shares fell back a point.

d *[arme à feu]* to recoil.

2 **vt** *chaise, meuble* to move back, push back; *véhicule* to reverse (*Brit*), back (up); *frontières* to extend, push *ou* move back; *livraison, date* to put back, postpone; *décision* to put off, defer, postpone; *échéance* to defer, postpone.

3 **se reculer vpr** to stand *ou* step *ou* move back, take a step back. **se ~ d'horreur** to draw back *ou* shrink back in horror, back away *ou* off in horror.

reculons [ʀ(ə)kylɔ̃] **loc adv: à ~: aller à** ~ (*lit*) to go backwards; (*fig*) to move *ou* go backwards; **sortir à ~ d'une pièce/d'un garage** to back out of a room/a garage.

récupérable [ʀekypeʀabl] **adj** *créance* recoverable; *heures* which can be made up; *ferraille* which can be salvaged; *vieux habits* retrievable, which are worth rescuing. **délinquant qui n'est plus** ~ irredeemable delinquent, delinquent who is beyond redemption.

récupérateur [ʀekypeʀatœʀ] 1 **nm** *[chaleur]* recuperator, regenerator; *[arme]* recuperator. 2 **adj m** (*péj*) *procédé, discours* designed to win over dissenting opinion *ou* groups *etc*.

récupération [ʀekypeʀasjɔ̃] **nf** a *[argent, biens, forces]* recovery; (*Ordin*) retrieval. **la capacité de ~ de l'organisme** the body's powers of recuperation *ou* recovery. b *[ferraille]* salvage, reprocessing; *[chiffons]* reprocessing; *[chaleur]* recovery; *[délinquant]* rehabilitation. **matériel de** ~ salvage equipment. c *[journées de travail]* making up. **deux jours de** ~ two days to make up. d (*Pol: péj*) **assister à la ~ du mouvement anarchique par le gouvernement** to watch the takeover *ou* harnessing of the anarchist movement by the government.

récupérer [ʀekypeʀe] 6 1 **vt** a *argent, biens* to get back, recover; *forces* to recover, get back, regain; (*Ordin*) to retrieve. ~ **son enfant à la sortie de l'école** to pick up *ou* collect one's child when school finishes for the day.

b *ferraille* to salvage, reprocess; *chiffons* to reprocess; *chaleur* to recover; *délinquant* to rehabilitate; (* *fig*) *bonbon, gifle* to get. **toutes les pêches étaient pourries, je n'ai rien pu** ~ all the peaches were rotten and I wasn't able to save *ou* rescue a single one; **regarde si tu peux ~ quelque chose dans ces vieux habits** have a look and see if there's anything you can rescue *ou* retrieve from among these old clothes; **où es-tu allé ~ ce chat?*** wherever did you pick up *ou* get that cat (from)? *ou* find that cat?

c *journées de travail* to make up. **on récupérera samedi** we'll make it up *ou* we'll make the time up on Saturday.

d (*Pol: péj*) *personne, mouvement* to take over, harness, bring into line. **se faire ~ par la gauche/droite** to find o.s. taken over *ou* won over by the left/the right.

2 **vi** (*après des efforts*) to recover, recuperate.

récurage [ʀekyʀaʒ] **nm** scouring.

récurant, e [ʀekyʀɑ̃, ɑ̃t] **adj** *produit* cleaning.

récurer [ʀekyʀe] 1 **vt** to scour; *voir* **poudre**.

récurrence [ʀekyʀɑ̃s] **nf** (*littér: répétition*) recurrence.

récurrent, e [ʀekyʀɑ̃, ɑ̃t] **adj** (*Anat, Méd*) recurrent. (*Math*) **série ~e** recursion series.

récursif, -ive [ʀekyʀsif, iv] **adj** recursive.

récursivité [ʀekyʀsivite] **nf** recursiveness.

récusable [ʀekyzabl] **adj** *témoin* challengeable; *témoignage* impugnable.

récusation [ʀekyzasjɔ̃] **nf** (*voir* **récusable**) challenging (*NonC*), challenge; impugnment.

récuser [ʀekyze] 1 1 **vt** *témoin* to challenge; *témoignage* to impugn, challenge. (*Jur*) ~ **un argument** to make objection to an argument. 2 **se récuser vpr** to decline to give an opinion *ou* accept responsibility *etc*.

recyclable [ʀ(ə)siklabl] adj recyclable.
recyclage [ʀ(ə)siklaʒ] nm (voir **recycler**) reorientation; retraining; recycling.
recycler [ʀ(ə)sikle] 1 **1** vt **a** *élève* to reorientate; *professeur, ingénieur* (*perfectionner*) to send on a refresher course, retrain; (*reconvertir*) to retrain. **b** (*Tech*) to recycle. **papier recyclé** recycled paper. **2 se recycler** vpr to retrain; to go on a refresher course. **je ne peux pas me ~ à mon âge** I can't learn a new job *ou* trade at my age; **se ~ en permanence** to be constantly updating one's skills.
rédacteur, -trice [ʀedaktœʀ, tʀis] **1** nm,f (*Presse*) sub-editor; *[article]* writer; *[loi]* drafter; *[encyclopédie, dictionnaire]* compiler, editor. **~ politique/économique** political/economics editor; **~ sportif** sportswriter, sports editor. **2** comp ▸**rédacteur en chef** chief editor ▸**rédacteur publicitaire** copywriter.
rédaction [ʀedaksjɔ̃] nf **a** *[contrat, projet]* drafting, drawing up; *[thèse, article]* writing; *[encyclopédie, dictionnaire]* compiling, compilation; (*Jur, Admin*) wording. **ce n'est que la première ~** it's only the first draft. **b** (*Presse*) (*personnel*) editorial staff; (*bureaux*) editorial offices; voir **salle, secrétaire**. **c** (*Scol*) essay, composition (*Brit*), theme (*US*).
rédactionnel, -elle [ʀedaksjɔnɛl] adj editorial.
reddition [ʀedisjɔ̃] nf (*Mil*) surrender; (*Admin*) rendering. **~ sans conditions** unconditional surrender.
redécoupage [ʀədekupaʒ] nm: **effectuer un ~ électoral** to make constituency boundary changes.
redécouverte [ʀ(ə)dekuvɛʀt] nf rediscovery.
redécouvrir [ʀ(ə)dekuvʀiʀ] 18 vt to rediscover.
redéfaire [ʀ(ə)defɛʀ] 60 vt *paquet, lacet* to undo again; *manteau* to take off again; *couture* to unpick again. **le nœud s'est redéfait** the knot has come undone *ou* come untied again.
redéfinir [ʀ(ə)definiʀ] 2 vt to redefine.
redemander [ʀədmɑ̃de] 1 vt *adresse* to ask again for; *aliment* to ask for more; *bouteille etc* to ask for another. **redemande-le-lui** (*une nouvelle fois*) ask him for it again; (*récupère-le*) ask him to give it back to you, ask him for it back; **~ du poulet** to ask for more chicken *ou* another helping of chicken.
redémarrage [ʀ(ə)demaʀaʒ] nm *[économie]* takeoff, resurgence.
redémarrer [ʀ(ə)demaʀe] 1 vi *[économie]* to get going again, take off again.
rédempteur, -trice [ʀedɑ̃ptœʀ, tʀis] **1** adj redemptive, redeeming. **2** nm,f redeemer.
rédemption [ʀedɑ̃psjɔ̃] nf **a** (*Rel*) redemption. **b** (*Jur*) *[rente]* redemption; *[droit]* recovery.
redéploiement [ʀ(ə)deplwamɑ̃] nm redeployment.
redescendre [ʀ(ə)desɑ̃dʀ] 41 **1** vt (*avec aux avoir*) **a** *escalier* to go *ou* come (back) down again. **la balle a redescendu la pente** the ball rolled down the slope again *ou* rolled back down the slope.
b *objet* (*à la cave*) to take downstairs again; (*du grenier*) to bring downstairs again; (*d'un rayon*) to get *ou* lift (back) down again; (*d'un crochet*) to take (back) down again. **~ qch d'un cran** to put sth one notch lower down.
2 vi (*avec aux être*) **a** (*dans l'escalier*) to go *ou* come (back) downstairs again; (*d'une colline*) to go *ou* come (back) down again. **l'alpiniste redescend** (*à pied*) the mountaineer climbs down again; (*avec une corde*) the mountaineer ropes down again; **~ de voiture** to get *ou* climb out of the car again.
b *[ascenseur, avion]* to go down again; *[marée]* to go out again, go back out; *[chemin]* to go *ou* slope down again; *[baromètre, fièvre]* to fall again.
redevable [ʀ(ə)dəvabl] adj **a** (*Fin*) **être ~ de 10 F à qn** to owe sb 10 francs; **~ de l'impôt** liable for tax. **b ~ à qn de** *aide, service* indebted to sb for; **je vous suis ~ de la vie** I owe you my life.
redevance [ʀ(ə)dəvɑ̃s] nf (*gén: impôt*) tax; (*Rad, TV*) licence fee (*Brit*); (*Téléc*) rental charge; (*bail, rente*) dues, fees; *[inventeur]* royalties.
redevenir [ʀ(ə)dəv(ə)niʀ] 22 vi to become again. **le temps est redevenu glacial** the weather has become *ou* gone very cold again; **il est redevenu lui-même** he is his old self again.
redevoir [ʀ(ə)dəvwaʀ] 28 vt: **il me redoit 10 000 F** he still owes me 10,000 francs.
rédhibitoire [ʀedibitwaʀ] adj *défaut* crippling, damning. **sa mauvaise foi est vraiment ~** his insincerity puts him quite beyond the pale; **il est un peu menteur, mais ce n'est pas ~** he's a bit of a liar but that doesn't rule him out altogether; (*Jur*) **vice ~** redhibitory defect.
rediffuser [ʀ(ə)difyze] 1 vt *émission* to repeat, rerun.
rediffusion [ʀ(ə)difyzjɔ̃] nf repeat, rerun.
rédiger [ʀediʒe] 3 vt *article, lettre* to write, compose; (*à partir de notes*) to write up; *encyclopédie, dictionnaire* to compile, write; *contrat* to draw up, draft. **bien rédigé** well-written.
redingote [ʀ(ə)dɛ̃gɔt] nf (*Hist*) frock coat. *[femme]* **manteau ~** fitted coat.
rédintégration [ʀedɛ̃tegʀasjɔ̃] nf redintegration.
redire [ʀ(ə)diʀ] 37 vt **a** *affirmation* to say again, repeat; *histoire* to tell again, repeat; *médisance* to (go and) tell, repeat. **~ qch à qn** to say sth to sb again, tell sb sth again, repeat sth to sb; **il redit toujours la même chose** he's always saying *ou* he keeps saying the same thing; **je te l'ai dit et redit** I've told you that over and over again *ou* time and time again; **je lui ai redit cent fois que ...** I've told him countless times that ...; **redis-le après moi** repeat after me; **ne le lui redites pas** don't go and tell him *ou* don't go and repeat (to him) what I've said; **elle ne se le fait pas ~ deux fois** she doesn't need telling *ou* to be told twice.
b (*loc*) **avoir** *ou* **trouver à ~ à qch** to find fault with sth; **je ne vois rien à ~ (à cela)** I've no complaint with that, I can't see anything wrong with that, I have no quarrel with that.
rediscuter [ʀ(ə)diskyte] 1 vt to discuss again, have further discussion on.
redistribuer [ʀ(ə)distʀibɥe] 1 vt *biens* to redistribute; *cartes* to deal again.
redistribution [ʀ(ə)distʀibysjɔ̃] nf (*gén, Écon, Pol*) redistribution.
redite [ʀ(ə)dit] nf (needless) repetition.
redondance [ʀ(ə)dɔ̃dɑ̃s] nf **a** *[style]* redundancy (*NonC*), diffuseness (*NonC*); (*Ling*) redundancy (*NonC*). **b** (*expression*) unnecessary *ou* superfluous expression.
redondant, e [ʀ(ə)dɔ̃dɑ̃, ɑ̃t] adj *mot* superfluous, redundant; *style* redundant, diffuse; (*Ling*) redundant.
redonner [ʀ(ə)dɔne] 1 **1** vt **a** (*rendre*) *objet, bien* to give back, return; *forme, idéal* to give back, give again; *espoir, énergie* to restore, give back. **l'air frais te redonnera des couleurs** the fresh air will put some colour back in your cheeks *ou* bring some colour back to your cheeks; **~ de la confiance/du courage à qn** to give sb new *ou* fresh confidence/courage, restore sb's confidence/courage; **ça a redonné le même résultat** that gave the same result again; **cela te redonnera des forces** that will build your strength back up *ou* put new strength into you *ou* restore your strength.
b (*resservir*) *boisson, pain* to give more; *légumes, viande* to give more, give a further *ou* another helping of. **~ une couche de peinture** to give another coat of paint; **redonne-lui un coup de peigne** give his hair another quick comb, run a comb through his hair again quickly.
c (*Théât*) to put on again.
2 vi (*frm*) **~ dans** to fall *ou* lapse back into.
redorer [ʀ(ə)dɔʀe] 1 vt to regild. **~ son blason** *[famille]* to boost the family fortunes by marrying into money; *[entreprise, émission]* to regain prestige.
redormir [ʀ(ə)dɔʀmiʀ] 16 vi to sleep again, sleep for a further length of time.
redoublant, e [ʀ(ə)dublɑ̃, ɑ̃t] nm,f (*Scol*) pupil who is repeating (*ou* has repeated) a year at school, repeater (*US*).
redoublement [ʀ(ə)dubləmɑ̃] nm (*Ling*) reduplication; (*accroissement*) increase (*de* in), intensification (*de* of). **je vous demande un ~ d'attention** I need you to pay even closer attention, I need your increased attention; **avec un ~ de larmes** with a fresh flood of tears; (*Scol*) **le ~ permet aux élèves faibles de rattraper** repeating a year *ou* a grade (*US*) *ou* being kept down (*Brit*) *ou* held back a year helps the weaker pupils to catch up.
redoubler [ʀ(ə)duble] 1 **1** vt **a** (*accroître*) *joie, douleur, craintes* to increase, intensify; *efforts* to step up, redouble. **frapper à coups redoublés** to bang twice as hard, bang even harder; **hurler à cris redoublés** to yell twice as loud.
b (*Ling*) *syllabe* to reduplicate; (*Couture*) *vêtement* to reline. (*Scol*) **~ (une classe)** to repeat a year *ou* a grade (*US*), be kept down (*Brit*) *ou* held back a year.
2 redoubler de vt indir: **~ d'efforts** to step up *ou* redouble one's efforts, try extra hard; **~ de prudence/de patience** to be extra careful/patient, be doubly careful/patient; **~ de larmes** to cry even harder; **le vent redouble de violence** the wind is getting even stronger *ou* is blowing even more strongly.
3 vi (*gén*) to increase, intensify; *[froid, douleur]* to become twice as bad, get even worse; *[vent]* to become twice as strong; *[joie]* to become twice as great; *[larmes]* to flow *ou* fall even faster; *[cris]* to get even louder *ou* twice as loud.
redoutable [ʀ(ə)dutabl] adj *arme, adversaire* redoubtable, fearsome, formidable; *maladie, concurrence* fearsome, fearful.
redoute [ʀədut] nf (*Mil*) redoubt.
redouter [ʀ(ə)dute] 1 vt *ennemi, avenir, conséquence* to dread, fear. **je redoute de l'apprendre** I dread finding out about it; **je redoute qu'il ne l'apprenne** I dread his finding out about it.
redoux [ʀədu] nm (*temps plus chaud*) spell of milder weather; (*dégel*) thaw.
redresse* [ʀ(ə)dʀɛs] nf *personne* **à la ~** tough.
redressement [ʀ(ə)dʀɛsmɑ̃] nm **a** *[poteau]* setting upright, righting; *[tige]* straightening (up); *[tôle]* straightening out, knocking out; (*Élec*) *[courant]* rectification; *[buste, corps]* straightening up. **b** *[bateau]* righting; *[roue, voiture, avion]* straightening up. **c** *[situation]* (*action*) putting right; (*résultat*) recovery. **d** *[économie]* recovery, upturn; *[entreprise]* recovery, turnaround. **plan de ~** recovery pactage. **e** *[erreur]* righting, putting right; *[abus, torts]* righting, redress; *[jugement]* correcting. (*Fin*) **~ fiscal** tax adjustment *ou* reappraisal; voir **maison**.
redresser [ʀ(ə)dʀese] 1 **1** vt **a** (*relever*) *arbre, statue, poteau* to

right, set upright; *tige, poutre* to straighten (up); *tôle cabossée* to straighten out, knock out; (*Élec*) *courant* to rectify; (*Opt*) *image* to straighten. ~ **un malade sur son oreiller** to sit *ou* prop a patient up against his pillow; ~ **les épaules** to straighten one's shoulders, throw one's shoulders back; ~ **le corps (en arrière)** to stand up straight, straighten up; ~ **la tête** (*lit*) to hold up *ou* lift (up) one's head; (*fig: être fier*) to hold one's head up high; (*fig: se révolter*) to show signs of rebellion.

b (*rediriger*) *barre, bateau* to right; *avion* to lift the nose of, straighten up; *roue, voiture* to straighten up. **redresse!** straighten up!

c (*rétablir*) *économie* to redress, put *ou* set right; *entreprise déficitaire* to turn round; *situation* to put right, straighten out. ~ **le pays** to get *ou* put the country on its feet again.

d (*littér: corriger*) *erreur* to rectify, put right, redress; *torts, abus* to right, redress. ~ **le jugement de qn** to correct sb's opinion.

2 **se redresser** vpr a (*se mettre assis*) to sit up; (*se mettre debout*) to stand up; (*se mettre droit*) to stand up straight; (*après s'être courbé*) to straighten up; (*fig: être fier*) to hold one's head up high.

b *[bateau]* to right itself; *[avion]* to flatten out, straighten up; *[voiture]* to straighten up; *[pays, économie]* to recover; *[situation]* to correct itself, put itself to rights.

c *[coin replié, cheveux]* to stick up. **les blés, couchés par le vent, se redressèrent** the corn which had been blown flat by the wind straightened up again *ou* stood up straight again.

redresseur [ʀ(ə)dʀesœʀ] 1 nm a (*Hist iro*) ~ **de torts** righter of wrongs. b (*Élec*) rectifier. 2 adj m *muscle* erector; *prisme* erecting.

réducteur, -trice [ʀedyktœʀ, tʀis] 1 adj a (*Chim*) reducing; (*Tech*) *engrenage* reduction. b (*péj: simplificateur*) *analyse, concept* simplistic. 2 nm (*Chim*) reducing agent; (*Phot*) reducer. (*Tech*) ~ **(de vitesse)** speed reducer; ~ **de tête** head shrinker (*lit*).

réductibilité [ʀedyktibilite] nf reducibility.

réductible [ʀedyktibl] adj (*Chim, Math*) reducible (*en, à* to); (*Méd*) which can be reduced (SPÉC) *ou* set; *quantité* which can be reduced. **leur philosophie n'est pas ~ à la nôtre** their philosophy can't be simplified to ours.

réduction [ʀedyksjɔ̃] nf a (*diminution*) *[dépenses, impôts, production]* reduction, cut (*de* in). ~ **de salaire/d'impôts** wage/tax cut, cut in wages/taxes; **obtenir une ~ de peine** to get a reduction in one's sentence, get one's sentence cut; **il faut s'attendre à une ~ du personnel** we must expect a reduction in staff *ou* expect staff cuts; **ils voudraient obtenir une ~ des heures de travail** they would like a reduction *ou* a cut in working hours.

b (*rabais*) discount, reduction. **faire/obtenir une ~** to give/get a discount *ou* a reduction; (*Comm*) **carte de ~** discount card; **bénéficier d'une carte de ~ dans les transports** to have a concessionary fare *ou* a discount travel card.

c (*reproduction*) *[plan, photo]* reduction. (*fig*) **un adulte en ~** a miniature adult, an adult in miniature.

d (*Méd*) *[fracture]* reduction (SPÉC), setting; (*Bio, Chim, Math*) reduction.

e (*Culin*) reduction (by boiling).

f (*Mil*) *[ville]* capture; *[rebelles]* quelling.

réduire [ʀedɥiʀ] 38 1 vt a (*diminuer*) *peine, impôt, consommation* to reduce, cut; *hauteur, vitesse* to reduce; *prix* to reduce, cut, bring down; *pression* to reduce, lessen; *texte* to shorten, cut; *production* to reduce, cut (back), lower; *dépenses* to reduce, cut, cut down *ou* back (on); *tête coupée* to shrink. **il va falloir ~ notre train de vie** we'll have to cut down *ou* curb our spending; ~ **petit à petit l'autorité de qn/la portée d'une loi** to chip away at sb's authority/a law.

b (*reproduire*) *dessin, plan* to reduce, scale down; *photographie* to reduce, make smaller; *figure géométrique* to scale down.

c (*contraindre*) ~ **à** *soumission, désespoir* to reduce to; ~ **qn au silence/à l'obéissance/en esclavage** to reduce sb to silence/to obedience/ to slavery; **après son accident, il a été réduit à l'inaction** since his accident he has been reduced to idleness; **il en est réduit à mendier** he has been reduced to begging.

d ~ **à** (*ramener à*) to reduce to, bring down to; (*limiter à*) to limit to, confine to; ~ **des fractions à un dénominateur commun** to reduce *ou* bring down fractions to a common denominator; ~ **des éléments différents à un type commun** to reduce different elements to one general type; **je réduirai mon étude à quelques aspects** I shall limit *ou* confine my study to a few aspects; ~ **à sa plus simple expression** (*Math*) *polynôme* to reduce to its simplest expression; (*fig*) *mobilier, repas* to reduce to the absolute *ou* bare minimum; ~ **qch à néant** *ou* **à rien** *ou* **à zéro** to reduce sth to nothing.

e (*transformer*) ~ **en** to reduce to; **réduisez les grammes en milligrammes** convert the grammes to milligrammes; ~ **qch en miettes/ morceaux** to smash sth to tiny pieces/to pieces; ~ **qch en bouillie** to crush *ou* reduce sth to pulp; ~ **des grains en poudre** to grind *ou* reduce seeds to powder; **sa maison était réduite en cendres** his house was reduced to ashes *ou* burnt to the ground; **les cadavres étaient réduits en charpie** the bodies were torn to shreds.

f (*Méd*) *fracture* to set, reduce (SPÉC); (*Chim*) *minerai, oxyde* to reduce; (*Culin*) *sauce* to reduce (by boiling).

g (*Mil*) *place forte* to capture; *rebelles* to quell. ~ **l'opposition** to silence the opposition.

2 vi (*Culin*) *[sauce]* to reduce. **faire** *ou* **laisser ~ la sauce** to cook *ou* simmer the sauce to reduce it; **les épinards réduisent à la cuisson** spinach shrinks when you cook it.

3 **se réduire** vpr a **se ~ à** *[affaire, incident]* to boil down to, amount to; *[somme, quantité]* to amount to; **mon profit se réduit à bien peu de chose** my profit amounts to very little; **notre action ne se réduit pas à quelques discours** the action we are taking involves more than *ou* isn't just a matter of a few speeches; **je me réduirai à quelques exemples** I'll limit *ou* confine myself to a few examples, I'll just select *ou* quote a few examples.

b **se ~ en** to be reduced to; **se ~ en cendres** to be burnt *ou* reduced to ashes; **se ~ en poussière** to be reduced *ou* crumble away *ou* turn to dust; **se ~ en bouillie** to be crushed to pulp.

c (*dépenser moins*) to cut down on one's spending *ou* expenditure.

réduit, e [ʀedɥi, it] (ptp de **réduire**) 1 adj a *mécanisme, objet* (*à petite échelle*) small-scale, scaled-down; (*en miniature*) miniature; (*miniaturisé*) miniaturized. **reproduction à échelle ~e** small-scale reproduction; **tête ~e** shrunken head; *voir* **modèle**. b *tarif, prix* reduced; *moyens, débouchés* limited. **livres à prix ~s** cut-price books, books at a reduced price *ou* at reduced prices; **avancer à vitesse ~e** to move forward at low speed *ou* at a reduced speed *ou* at a crawl. 2 nm (*pièce*) tiny room; (*péj*) cubbyhole, poky little hole; (*recoin*) recess; (*Mil*) *[maquisards]* hideout.

rééchelonnement [ʀeeʃ(ə)lɔnmɑ̃] nm *[dettes]* rescheduling.

rééchelonner [ʀeeʃ(ə)lɔne] 1 vt *dettes* to reschedule.

réécrire [ʀeekʀiʀ] 39 vt = **récrire**.

réécriture [ʀeekʀityʀ] nf rewriting. (*Ling*) **règle de ~** rewrite *ou* rewriting rule.

réédification [ʀeedifikasjɔ̃] nf rebuilding, reconstruction.

réédifier [ʀeedifje] 7 vt to rebuild, reconstruct; (*fig*) to rebuild.

rééditer [ʀeedite] 1 vt (*Typ*) to republish; (* *fig*) to repeat.

réédition [ʀeedisjɔ̃] nf (*Typ*) new edition; (* *fig*) repetition, repeat.

rééducation [ʀeedykasjɔ̃] nf a (*Méd*) *[malade]* rehabilitation; *[membre]* re-education; (*spécialité médicale*) physiotherapy. **faire de la ~** to undergo *ou* have physiotherapy, have physical therapy (*US*); **exercice/ centre de ~** physiotherapy exercise/clinic; ~ **de la parole** speech therapy; **centre de ~** rehabilitation centre. b (*gén, lit*) re-education; *[délinquant]* rehabilitation.

rééduquer [ʀeedyke] 1 vt a (*Méd*) *malade* to rehabilitate; *membre* to re-educate. b (*gén, Pol, lit*) to re-educate; *délinquant* to rehabilitate.

réel, -elle [ʀeɛl] 1 adj a *fait, chef, existence, avantage* real; *besoin, cause* real, true; *danger, plaisir, amélioration, douleur* real, genuine. **faire de réelles économies** to make significant *ou* real savings; **son héros est très ~** his hero is very lifelike *ou* realistic. b (*Math, Opt, Philos, Phys*) real; (*Fin*) *valeur, salaire* real, actual. **taux d'intérêt ~** effective interest rate. 2 nm: **le ~** reality.

réélection [ʀeelɛksjɔ̃] nf re-election.

rééligibilité [ʀeeliʒibilite] nf re-eligibility.

rééligible [ʀeeliʒibl] adj re-eligible.

réélire [ʀeeliʀ] 43 vt to re-elect. **ne pas ~ qn** to vote sb out.

réellement [ʀeɛlmɑ̃] adv really, truly. **je suis ~ désolé** I'm really *ou* truly sorry; **ça m'a ~ consterné/aidé** that really worried/helped me, that was a genuine worry/help to me; **~, tu exagères!** really *ou* honestly, you go too far!

réembarquer [ʀeɑ̃baʀke] 1 vti = **rembarquer**.

réembaucher [ʀeɑ̃boʃe] 1 vt to take on again, re-employ.

réembobiner [ʀeɑ̃bɔbine] 1 vt = **rembobiner**.

réemploi [ʀeɑ̃plwa] nm (*voir* **réemployer**) re-use; reinvestment; re-employment.

réemployer [ʀeɑ̃plwaje] 8 vt *méthode, produit* to re-use; *argent* to re-invest; *ouvrier* to re-employ, take back on.

réengagement [ʀeɑ̃gaʒmɑ̃] nm = **rengagement**.

réengager [ʀeɑ̃gaʒe] 3 vt = **rengager**.

réentendre [ʀeɑ̃tɑ̃dʀ] 41 vt to hear again.

rééquilibrage [ʀeekilibʀaʒ] nm (*gén, Pol*) readjustment.

rééquilibrer [ʀeekilibʀe] 1 vt to restabilize, find a new equilibrium for.

réescompte [ʀeɛskɔ̃t] nm rediscount.

réescompter [ʀeɛskɔ̃te] 1 vt to rediscount.

réessayage [ʀeesɛjaʒ] nm second fitting.

réessayer [ʀeeseje] 8 vt *robe* to try on again, have a second fitting of.

réévaluation [ʀeevalɥasjɔ̃] nf revaluation.

réévaluer [ʀeevalɥe] 1 vt *monnaie* to revalue; *salaire* to upgrade.

réexamen [ʀeɛgzamɛ̃] nm (*voir* **réexaminer**) re-examination; reconsideration.

réexaminer [ʀeɛgzamine] 1 vt *étudiant, candidature, malade* to re-examine; *problème, situation* to examine again, reconsider.

réexpédier [ʀeɛkspedje] 7 vt (*à l'envoyeur*) to return, send back; (*au destinataire*) to send on, forward.

réexpédition [ʀeɛkspedisjɔ̃] nf (*voir* **réexpédier**) return; forwarding.

réexportation [ʀeɛkspɔʀtasjɔ̃] nf re-export.

réexporter [ʀeɛkspɔʀte] [1] vt to re-export.

réf abrév de **référence**.

refaçonner [ʀ(ə)fasɔne] [1] vt to refashion, remodel, reshape.

réfaction [ʀefaksjɔ̃] nf (*Comm*) allowance, rebate.

refaire [ʀ(ə)fɛʀ] [60] 1 vt a (*recommencer*) (*gén*) *travail, dessin, maquillage* to redo, do again; *voyage* to make *ou* do again; *pansement* to put on *ou* do up again, renew; *article, devoir* to rewrite; *nœud, paquet* to do up again, tie again, retie. **elle a refait sa vie avec lui** she started a new life *ou* she made a fresh start (in life) with him; **il m'a refait une visite** he paid me another call, he called on me again *ou* on another occasion; **il refait du soleil** the sun is shining *ou* is out again; **tu refais toujours la même faute** you always make *ou* you keep on making *ou* repeating the same mistake; **il a refait de la fièvre/de l'asthme** he has had another bout of fever/another dose *ou* bout of asthma; **il refait du vélo** he has taken up cycling again; **il va falloir tout ~ depuis le début** it will have to be done all over again, we'll have to start again from scratch; **si vous refaites du bruit** if you start making a noise again, if there's any further noise from you; **il va falloir ~ de la soupe** we'll have to make some more soup; **son éducation est à ~** he'll have to be re-educated; **si c'était à ~!** if I had to do it again! *ou* begin again!; (*Cartes*) **à ~** re-deal.

b (*retaper*) *toit* to redo, renew; *meuble* to do up, renovate, restore; *chambre* (*gén*) to do up, renovate, redecorate; (*en peinture*) to repaint; (*en papier*) to repaper. **on refera les peintures/les papiers au printemps** we'll repaint/repaper in the spring, we'll redo the paintwork/the wallpaper in the spring; **~ qch à neuf** to do sth up like new; (*fig*) **~ ses forces/sa santé** to recover one's strength/health; **à son âge, tu ne la referas pas** at her age, you won't change her.

c (*: *duper*) to take in. **il a été refait, il s'est fait ~** he has been taken in *ou* had*; **il m'a refait** *ou* **je me suis fait ~ de 5 F** he did* *ou* diddled* (*Brit*) me out of 5 francs, I was done* *ou* diddled (*Brit*) out of 5 francs.

2 **se refaire** vpr (*retrouver la santé*) to recuperate, recover; (*regagner son argent*) to make up one's losses. **se ~ (la santé) dans le Midi** to (go and) recuperate in the south of France, recover *ou* regain one's health in the south of France; **que voulez-vous, on ne se refait pas!** what can you expect – you can't change how you're made!* *ou* you can't change your own character!

réfection [ʀefɛksjɔ̃] nf *[route]* repairing, remaking; *[mur, maison]* rebuilding, repairing. **la ~ de la route va durer 3 semaines** the road repairs *ou* the repairs to the road will take 3 weeks.

réfectoire [ʀefɛktwaʀ] nm (*Scol*) dining hall, canteen; (*Rel*) refectory; *[usine]* canteen.

référé [ʀefeʀe] nm (*Jur*) **procédure/arrêt en ~** *emergency interim proceedings/ruling*.

référence [ʀefeʀɑ̃s] nf a (*renvoi*) reference; (*en bas de page*) reference, footnote. **par ~ à** in reference to; **ouvrage/numéro de ~** reference book/number; **prendre qch comme point/année de ~** to use sth as a point/year of reference; **faire ~ à** to refer to, make (a) reference to; (*Fin*) **année de ~** base year.

b (*recommandation*) (*gén*) reference. **cet employé a-t-il des ~s?** (*d'un employeur*) has this employee got a reference? *ou* a testimonial? (*Brit*); (*de plusieurs employeurs*) has this employee got references? *ou* testimonials? (*Brit*); **il a un doctorat, c'est quand même une ~** he has a doctorate which is not a bad recommendation *ou* which is something to go by; (*iro*) **ce n'est pas une ~** that's no recommendation; **lettre de ~** letter of reference *ou* testimonial (*Brit*).

c (*Ling*) reference.

référencer [ʀefeʀɑ̃se] [3] vt to reference.

référendaire [ʀefeʀɑ̃dɛʀ] 1 adj (*pour un référendum*) referendum (*épith*). 2 nm: **(conseiller) ~** ≃ public auditor.

référendum [ʀefeʀɛ̃dɔm] nm referendum. **faire** *ou* **organiser un ~** to hold a referendum.

référent [ʀefeʀɑ̃] nm referent.

référentiel, -elle [ʀefeʀɑ̃sjɛl] 1 adj referential. 2 nm system of reference.

référer [ʀefeʀe] [6] 1 **en référer à** vt indir: **en ~ à qn** to refer *ou* submit a matter *ou* question to sb. 2 **se référer** vpr: **se ~ à** (*consulter*) to consult; (*faire référence à*) to refer to; (*s'en remettre à*) to refer to; **s'en ~ à qn** to refer *ou* submit a question *ou* matter to sb.

refermer [ʀ(ə)fɛʀme] [1] 1 vt to close *ou* shut again. **peux-tu ~ la porte?** can you close *ou* shut the door (again)? 2 **se refermer** vpr *[plaie]* to close up, heal up; *[fleur]* to close up (again); *[porte, fenêtre]* to close *ou* shut (again). **le piège se referma sur lui** the trap closed *ou* shut on him.

refiler‡ [ʀ(ə)file] [1] vt to palm off*, fob off* (*à qn* on sb). **refile-moi ton livre** let me have your book, give me your book; **il m'a refilé la rougeole** I've caught measles off him, he has passed his measles on to me; **il s'est fait ~ une fausse pièce** someone has palmed *ou* fobbed a forged coin off on him*.

réfléchi, e [ʀefleʃi] (ptp de **réfléchir**) 1 adj a (*pondéré*) *action* well-thought-out (*épith*), well thought-out (*attrib*), well-considered; *personne* reflective, thoughtful; *air* thoughtful. **tout bien ~** after careful consideration *ou* thought, having weighed up all the pros and cons; **c'est tout ~** my mind is made up, I've made my mind up. b (*Gram*) reflexive. c (*Opt*) reflected. 2 nm (*Gram*) reflexive.

réfléchir [ʀefleʃiʀ] [2] 1 vi to think, reflect. **prends le temps de ~** take time to reflect *ou* to think about it *ou* to consider it; **cela donne à ~** that gives you food for thought, that makes you think; **je demande à ~** I must have time to consider it *ou* to think things over; **la prochaine fois, tâche de ~** next time just try and think a bit *ou* try and use your brains a bit.

2 **réfléchir à** *ou* **sur** vt indir: **~ à** *ou* **sur qch** to think about sth, turn sth over in one's mind; **réfléchissez-y** think about it, think it over; **réfléchis à ce que tu vas faire** think about what you're going to do.

3 vt a **~ que** to realize that; **il n'avait pas réfléchi qu'il ne pourrait pas venir** he hadn't thought *ou* realized that *ou* it hadn't occurred to him that he wouldn't be able to come.

b *lumière, son* to reflect. **les arbres se réfléchissent dans le lac** the trees are reflected in the lake, you can see the reflection of the trees in the lake.

réfléchissant, e [ʀefleʃisɑ̃, ɑ̃t] adj reflective.

réflecteur, -trice [ʀeflɛktœʀ, tʀis] 1 adj reflecting. 2 nm (*gén*) reflector.

reflet [ʀ(ə)flɛ] nm a (*éclat*) (*gén*) reflection; *[cheveux]* (*naturel*) glint, light; (*artificiel*) highlight. **~s moirés de la soie** shimmering play of light on silk; **~s du soleil sur la mer** reflection *ou* glint *ou* flash of the sun on the sea; **la lame projetait des ~s sur le mur** the reflection of the blade shone on the wall, the blade threw a reflection onto the wall; **se faire faire des ~s (dans les cheveux)** to have one's hair highlighted.

b (*lit: image*) reflection. **le ~ de son visage dans le lac** the reflection of his face in the lake.

c (*fig: représentation*) reflection. **les habits sont le ~ d'une époque/d'une personnalité** clothes reflect *ou* are the reflection of an era/one's personality; **c'est le pâle ~ de son prédécesseur** he's a pale reflection of his predecessor; **c'est le ~ de son père** he's the image of his father.

refléter [ʀ(ə)flete] [6] 1 vt (*lit, fig*) to reflect, mirror. **son visage reflète la bonté** goodness shines in his face. 2 **se refléter** vpr to be reflected; to be mirrored.

refleurir [ʀ(ə)flœʀiʀ] [2] 1 vi (*Bot*) to flower *ou* blossom again; (*renaître*) to flourish *ou* blossom again. 2 vt *tombe* to put fresh flowers on.

reflex [ʀeflɛks] 1 adj reflex. 2 nm reflex camera. **~ à un objectif/à deux objectifs** single-lens/twin-lens reflex (camera).

réflexe [ʀeflɛks] 1 adj reflex. 2 nm reflex. **~ rotulien** knee jerk; **~ conditionné** conditioned reflex; **avoir de bons/mauvais ~s** to have quick *ou* good/slow *ou* poor reflexes; **il eut le ~ de couper l'électricité** his immediate *ou* instant reaction was to switch off the electricity, he instinctively switched off the electricity; **manquer de ~** to be slow to react.

réflexibilité [ʀeflɛksibilite] nf reflexibility.

réflexible [ʀeflɛksibl] adj reflexible.

réflexif, -ive [ʀeflɛksif, iv] adj (*Math*) reflexive; (*Psych*) introspective.

réflexion [ʀeflɛksjɔ̃] nf a (*méditation*) thought, reflection (*NonC*). **plongé** *ou* **absorbé dans ses ~s** deep *ou* lost in thought *ou* reflection, absorbed in thought *ou* in one's thoughts; **ceci donne matière à ~** this gives (you) food for thought, this gives you something to think about; **ceci mérite ~** *[offre]* this is worth thinking about *ou* considering; *[problème]* this needs thinking about *ou* over; **ceci nécessite une ~ plus approfondie sur les problèmes** further thought needs to be given to the problems; **avec ~** thoughtfully; **laissez-moi un moment de ~** let me think about it for a moment, let me have a moment's reflection; **~ faite** *ou* **à la ~, je reste** on reflection *ou* on second thoughts, I'll stay; **à la ~, on s'aperçoit que c'est faux** when you think about it you can see that it's wrong; (*Pol*) **centre** *ou* **cellule** *ou* **cercle de ~** think tank; (*Comm*) **délai de ~** cooling-off period.

b (*remarque*) remark, reflection; (*idée*) thought, reflection. **consigner ses ~s dans un cahier** to write down one's thoughts *ou* reflections in a notebook; **je ne me suis pas fait cette ~** I didn't think of that; **garde tes ~s pour toi** keep your remarks *ou* reflections *ou* comments to yourself; **les clients commencent à faire des ~s** the customers are beginning to pass *ou* make remarks; **on m'a fait des ~s sur son travail** people have complained to me *ou* made complaints to me about his work.

c (*Phys*) reflection.

réflexivité [ʀeflɛksivite] nf reflexiveness; (*Math*) reflexivity.

refluer [ʀ(ə)flye] [1] vi *[liquide]* to flow back; *[marée]* to go back, ebb; *[foule]* to pour *ou* surge back; *[sang]* to rush back; *[fumée]* to blow back down; *[souvenirs]* to rush *ou* flood back. **faire ~ la foule** to push *ou* force the crowd back.

reflux [ʀəfly] nm *[foule]* backward surge; *[marée]* ebb; *voir* **flux**.

refondre [ʀ(ə)fɔ̃dʀ] [41] 1 vt *métal* to remelt, melt down again; *cloche* to recast; *texte* to recast; *dictionnaire* to revise; *système, programme* to overhaul. 2 vi to melt again.

refonte [ʀ(ə)fɔ̃t] nf (*voir* **refondre**) remelting; recasting; revision; overhaul.

réformable [ʀefɔʀmabl] adj (*gén*) reformable; *jugement* which may be reversed; *loi* which may be amended *ou* reformed.

reformater [ʀ(ə)fɔʀmate] [1] vt to reformate.
réformateur, -trice [ʀefɔʀmatœʀ, tʀis] 1 adj reforming. 2 nm,f reformer.
réformation [ʀefɔʀmasjɔ̃] nf reformation, reform. **la R~** the Reformation.
réforme [ʀefɔʀm] nf a (*changement*) reform. **~ agraire/de l'orthographe** land/spelling reform. b (*Mil*) *[appelé]* declaration of unfitness for service; *[soldat]* discharge. **mettre à la ~** (*Mil, fig*) *objets* to scrap; *cheval* to put out to grass; **mise à la ~** *[soldat]* discharge; *[objets]* scrapping. c (*Rel*) reformation.
réformé, e [ʀefɔʀme] (ptp de **réformer**) 1 adj (*Rel*) reformed; (*Mil*) *appelé* declared unfit for service; *soldat* discharged, invalided out (*Brit*). 2 nm,f (*Rel*) Protestant.
reformer [ʀ(ə)fɔʀme] [1] 1 vt to re-form. (*Mil*) **~ les rangs** to fall in again, fall into line again. 2 **se reformer** vpr *[armée, nuage]* to re-form; *[parti]* to re-form, be re-formed; *[groupe, rangs]* to form up again.
réformer [ʀefɔʀme] [1] 1 vt a (*améliorer*) *loi, mœurs, religion* to reform; *abus* to correct, (put) right, reform; *méthode* to improve, reform; *administration* to reform, overhaul. b (*Jur*) *jugement* to reverse, quash. c (*Mil*) *appelé* to declare unfit for service; *soldat* to discharge, invalid out (*Brit*); *matériel* to scrap. **il s'est fait ~** he got himself declared unfit for service; he got himself discharged on health grounds *ou* invalided out (*Brit*). 2 **se réformer** vpr to change one's ways, turn over a new leaf.
réformette* [ʀefɔʀmɛt] nf so-called reform.
réformisme [ʀefɔʀmism] nm reformism.
réformiste [ʀefɔʀmist] adj, nmf reformist.
reformuler [ʀ(ə)fɔʀmyle] [1] vt to reformulate.
refoulé, e [ʀ(ə)fule] (ptp de **refouler**) adj *personne* repressed, frustrated, inhibited.
refoulement [ʀ(ə)fulmɑ̃] nm a (*voir* **refouler**) driving back; repulsing; turning back; forcing back; holding back; repression; suppression; backing, reversing, reversal *ou* inversion of the flow of; stemming. b (*Psych: complexe*) repression.
refouler [ʀ(ə)fule] [1] vt a *envahisseur, attaque* to drive back, repulse; *immigrant, étranger* to turn back. b *larmes* to force *ou* hold back, repress; *personnalité, désir, souvenir* to repress, suppress; *colère* to repress, hold in check; *sanglots* to choke back, force back. c (*Rail*) to back, reverse. d *liquide* to force back, reverse *ou* invert the flow of. e (*Naut*) to stem.
réfractaire [ʀefʀaktɛʀ] 1 adj a **~ à** *autorité, virus, influence* resistant to; *musique* impervious to; **maladie ~** stubborn illness; **je suis ~ à la poésie** poetry is a closed book to me; **être ~ à la discipline** to resist discipline; **prêtre ~** non-juring priest. b *métal* refractory; *brique, argile* fire (*épith*); *plat* ovenproof, heat-resistant. 2 nm (*Hist Mil*) draft dodger, draft evader.
réfracter [ʀefʀakte] [1] 1 vt to refract. 2 **se réfracter** vpr to be refracted.
réfracteur, -trice [ʀefʀaktœʀ, tʀis] adj refractive, refracting (*épith*).
réfraction [ʀefʀaksjɔ̃] nf refraction.
réfractomètre [ʀefʀaktɔmɛtʀ] nm refractometer.
refrain [ʀ(ə)fʀɛ̃] nm (*Mus: en fin de couplet*) refrain, chorus; (*chanson monotone*) strains (*pl*), refrain. **c'est toujours le même ~*** it's always the same old story; **change de ~!** put another record on!*
refréner [ʀ(ə)fʀene] [6] vt *désir, impatience, envie* to curb, hold in check, check.
réfrigérant, e [ʀefʀiʒeʀɑ̃, ɑ̃t] 1 adj *fluide* refrigerant, refrigerating; *accueil, personne* icy, frosty; *voir* **mélange**. 2 nm (*Tech*) cooler.
réfrigérateur [ʀefʀiʒeʀatœʀ] nm refrigerator, fridge*. (*fig*) **mettre un projet au ~** to put a plan in cold storage *ou* on ice.
réfrigération [ʀefʀiʒeʀasjɔ̃] nf refrigeration; (*Tech*) cooling.
réfrigérer [ʀefʀiʒeʀe] [6] vt a (*gén*) to refrigerate; (*Tech*) to cool; *local* to cool. **véhicule réfrigéré** refrigerated vehicle; **je suis réfrigéré*** I'm frozen stiff*. b (*fig*) *enthousiasme* to put a damper on, cool; *personne* to have a cooling *ou* dampening effect on.
réfringence [ʀefʀɛ̃ʒɑ̃s] nf refringence.
réfringent, e [ʀefʀɛ̃ʒɑ̃, ɑ̃t] adj refringent.
refroidir [ʀ(ə)fʀwadiʀ] [2] 1 vt a *nourriture* to cool (down).
b (*fig*) *personne* to put off, have a cooling effect on; *zèle* to cool, put a damper on, dampen.
c (*‡: tuer*) to do in‡, bump off‡ (*Brit*).
2 vi (*cesser d'être trop chaud*) to cool (down); (*devenir trop froid*) to get cold. **laisser** *ou* **faire ~** *mets trop chaud* to leave to cool, let cool (down); (*involontairement*) to let get cold; *moteur* to let cool; (*péj*) *projet* to let slide *ou* slip; **mettre qch à ~** to put sth to cool (down); (*jeu*) **tu refroidis!** you're getting cold!
3 **se refroidir** vpr *[ardeur]* to cool (off); *[mets]* to get cold; *[temps]* to get cooler *ou* colder; *[personne]* (*avoir froid*) to get *ou* catch cold; (*attraper un rhume*) to catch a chill.
refroidissement [ʀ(ə)fʀwadismɑ̃] nm a *[air, liquide]* cooling. **~ par air/eau** air-/water-cooling; **~ de la température** drop in the temperature; **on observe un ~ du temps** the weather appears to be getting cooler *ou* colder. b (*Méd*) chill. **prendre un ~** to catch a chill. c *[passion]* cooling (off).
refroidisseur, -euse [ʀ(ə)fʀwadisœʀ, øz] 1 adj cooling. 2 nm cooler; (*en industrie*) cooling tower.
refuge [ʀ(ə)fyʒ] nm (*gén*) refuge; (*pour piétons*) refuge, (traffic) island; (*en montagne*) refuge, (mountain) hut. **lieu de ~** place of refuge *ou* safety; (*Bourse*) **valeur ~** safe investment.
réfugié, e [ʀefyʒje] (ptp de **se réfugier**) adj, nm,f refugee. **~ politique** political refugee.
réfugier (se) [ʀefyʒje] [7] vpr (*lit, fig*) to take refuge.
refus [ʀ(ə)fy] nm refusal. (*Jur*) **~ de comparaître** refusal to appear (in court); (*Aut*) **~ de priorité** refusal to give way (*Brit*) *ou* to yield (*US*); **~ d'obéissance** refusal to obey; (*Mil*) insubordination; **ce n'est pas de ~*** I won't say no (to that).
refusable [ʀ(ə)fyzabl] adj which can be refused.
refuser [ʀ(ə)fyze] [1] 1 vt a (*ne pas accepter*) *cadeau* to refuse; *offre* to refuse, decline, turn down, reject; *invitation* to refuse, decline, turn down; *manuscrit* to reject, turn down, refuse; *marchandise, racisme, inégalité* to reject, refuse to accept; *politique, méthodes* to refuse, reject. **il l'a demandée en mariage mais il a été refusé** he asked her to marry him but she turned him down *ou* refused him; **~ la lutte** *ou* **le combat** to refuse battle; **le cheval a refusé (l'obstacle)** the horse balked at the fence *ou* refused (the fence); **~ le risque** to refuse to take risks; **il a toujours refusé la vie routinière** he has always refused to accept a routine life.
b (*ne pas accorder*) *permission, entrée, consentement* to refuse; *demande* to refuse, turn down; *compétence, qualité* to deny. **~ l'entrée à qn** to refuse admittance *ou* entry to sb, turn sb away; **~ sa porte à qn** to bar one's door to sb; **je me suis vu ~ un verre d'eau** I was refused a glass of water; **on lui a refusé l'accès aux archives** he was refused *ou* denied access to the records; (*Aut*) **il m'a refusé la priorité** he didn't give me right of way (*Brit*), he didn't yield to me (*US*); **elle est si gentille, on ne peut rien lui ~** she's so nice, you just can't say no to her; **je lui refuse toute générosité** I refuse to accept *ou* admit that he has any generosity.
c *client* to turn away; *candidat* (*à un examen*) to fail; (*à un poste*) to turn down. **il s'est fait ~ au permis de conduire** he failed his driving test; **on a dû ~ du monde** they had to turn people away.
d **~ de faire qch** to refuse to do sth; **il a refusé net (de le faire)** he refused point-blank (to do it); **la voiture refuse de démarrer** the car won't start.
2 **se refuser** vpr a (*se priver de*) to refuse o.s., deny o.s. (*iro*) **tu ne te refuses rien!** you don't stint yourself! (*iro*), you don't let yourself go short! (*iro*).
b (*être décliné*) **ça ne se refuse pas** *[offre]* it is not to be turned down *ou* refused; *[apéritif]* I wouldn't say no (to it).
c **se ~ à** *méthode, solution* to refuse (to accept), reject; **se ~ à l'évidence** to refuse to accept *ou* admit the obvious; **se ~ à tout commentaire** to refuse to make any comment; **elle s'est refusée à lui** she refused to give herself to him; **se ~ à faire qch** to refuse to do sth.
réfutable [ʀefytabl] adj refutable, which can be disproved *ou* refuted. **facilement ~** easily refuted *ou* disproved.
réfutation [ʀefytasjɔ̃] nf refutation. **fait qui apporte la ~ d'une allégation** fact which refutes *ou* disproves an allegation.
réfuter [ʀefyte] [1] vt to refute, disprove.
regagner [ʀ(ə)gaɲe] [1] vt a (*récupérer*) *amitié, faveur* to regain, win *ou* gain back; *argent* to win back, get back. **~ le temps perdu** to make up (for) lost time; (*Mil, fig*) **~ du terrain** to regain ground, win *ou* gain ground again; **~ le terrain perdu** to win back lost ground. b (*arriver à*) *lieu* to get *ou* go back to; *pays* to arrive back in, get back to. **il regagna enfin sa maison** he finally arrived back home *ou* got back home *ou* reached home again; **~ sa place** to regain one's place, return to one's place.
regain [ʀəgɛ̃] nm a **~ de** *jeunesse* renewal of; *popularité* revival of; *activité, influence* renewal *ou* revival of; **~ de vie** new lease of life; **provoquer un ~ d'intérêt** to bring about *ou* prompt renewed interest; **parfait! dit-il avec un ~ de bonne humeur** perfect!, he said with renewed good humour. b (*Agr*) aftermath†, second crop of hay.
régal, pl **~s** [ʀegal] nm delight, treat. **ce gâteau est un ~** this cake is absolutely delicious; **c'est un ~ pour les yeux** it is a sight for sore eyes, it is a delight *ou* treat to look at; **quel ~ de manger des cerises** what a treat to have cherries (to eat).
régalade [ʀegalad] nf: **boire à la ~** to drink without letting one's lips touch the bottle (*ou* glass *etc*).
régaler [ʀegale] [1] 1 vt *personne* to treat to a slap-up* (*Brit*) *ou* delicious meal. **c'est moi qui régale** I'm treating everyone, it's my treat; **c'est le patron qui régale** it's on the house; **chaque soir, il nous régalait de ses histoires** in the evenings he would regale us with his stories.
2 **se régaler** vpr (*bien manger*) to have a delicious *ou* a slap-up* (*Brit*) meal; (*éprouver du plaisir*) to have a great time*. **se ~ de gâteaux** to treat o.s. to some delicious cakes; **on s'est (bien) régalé** (*au repas*) it was delicious; (*au cinéma, théâtre*) we had a great time*, we really enjoyed ourselves; (*fig péj*) **il y en a qui se sont régalés dans cette vente** some people made a packet* (*Brit*) *ou* did really well out of that sale; (*hum, péj*) **les cafetiers se régalent avec cette vague de**

chaleur the café owners are coining it in* (*Brit*) *ou* making a mint* *ou* doing really well in this heatwave; **se ~ de romans** (*habituellement*) to be very keen on *ou* be a keen reader of novels; (*en vacances etc*) to gorge o.s. on novels, have a feast of novel-reading.

régalien, -ienne [ʀegaljɛ̃, jɛn] **adj** *droits* kingly.

regard [ʀ(ə)gaʀ] **nm** a (*vue*) glance, eye. **parcourir qch du ~, promener son ~ sur qch** to cast a glance *ou* an eye over sth; **son ~ se posa sur moi** his glance *ou* eye *ou* gaze came to rest on me; **soustraire qch aux ~s** to hide sth from sight *ou* from view, put sth out of sight; **cela attire tous les ~s** it catches everyone's eye *ou* attention; **nos ~s sont fixés sur vous** our eyes are turned on you.

b (*expression*) look *ou* expression (in one's eye). **son ~ était dur/tendre** the look *ou* expression in his eye was hard/tender, he had a hard/tender look *ou* expression in his eye; **~ fixe/perçant** fixed/penetrating stare; **dévorer/menacer qn du ~** to look hungrily/threateningly at sb, fix sb with a hungry/threatening look *ou* stare.

c (*coup d'œil*) look, glance. **échanger des ~s avec qn** to exchange looks *ou* glances with sb; **échanger des ~s d'intelligence** to exchange knowing looks; **lancer un ~ de colère à qn** to glare at sb, cast an angry look *ou* glare *ou* glance at sb; **au premier ~** at first glance *ou* sight; **~ en coulisse** sideways *ou* sidelong glance; **~ noir** black look.

d *[égout]* manhole; *[four]* peephole, window.

e (*loc*) **au ~ de la loi** in the eyes *ou* the sight of the law, from the legal viewpoint; **texte avec photos en ~** text with photos on the opposite page *ou* facing; **en ~ de ce qu'il gagne** compared with *ou* in comparison with what he earns; *voir* **droit²**.

regardant, e [ʀ(ə)gaʀdɑ̃, ɑ̃t] **adj** careful with money. **il n'est pas ~** he's quite free with his money; **ils sont/ne sont pas ~s sur l'argent de poche** they are not very/they are quite generous with pocket money; **il n'est pas très ~ sur la propreté/les manières** he's not very particular about cleanliness/manners.

regarder [ʀ(ə)gaʀde] 1 1 **vt** a *paysage, scène* to look at; *action en déroulement, film, match* to watch. **elle regardait les voitures sur le parking** she was looking at the cars in the car park; **elle regardait les voitures défiler** *ou* **qui défilaient** she was watching the cars driving past *ou* the cars as they drove past; **~ tomber la pluie** *ou* **la pluie tomber** to watch the rain falling; **il regarda sa montre** he looked at *ou* had a look at his watch; **regarde, il pleut** look, it's raining; **regarde bien, il va sauter** watch *ou* look, he's going to jump; **~ la télévision/une émission à la télévision** to watch television/a programme on television; **~ le journal** to look at *ou* have a look at the paper; **~ sur le livre de qn** (*partager*) to share sb's book; (*tricher*) to look *ou* peep at sb's book; **~ par la fenêtre** (*du dedans*) to look out of the window; (*du dehors*) to look in through the window; **regarde les oiseaux par la fenêtre** look through *ou* out of the window at the birds, watch the birds through *ou* out of the window; **regarde devant toi/derrière toi** look in front of you/behind you; **regarde où tu marches*** watch *ou* look where you're going *ou* putting your feet; **regarde voir dans l'armoire** take *ou* have a look in the wardrobe; **regarde voir s'il arrive** look *ou* have a look and see if he's coming; **attends, je vais ~** hang on, I'll go and look *ou* I'll take a look; **regardez-moi ça/son écriture*** just (take a) look at that/at his writing; **vous ne m'avez pas regardé!*** what do you take me for!*, who do you think I am!*; **j'ai regardé partout, je n'ai rien trouvé** I looked everywhere but I couldn't find anything; **regarde à la pendule quelle heure il est** look at the clock to see what time it is, look and see what time it is by the clock; **regardez-le faire** (*gén*) watch him *ou* look at him do it; (*pour apprendre*) watch *ou* look how he does it; **elles sont allées ~ les vitrines/les magasins** they've gone to do some window-shopping/to have a look around the shops; **sans ~** *traverser* without looking; *payer* regardless of cost *ou* the expense; *voir* **chien**.

b (*rapidement*) to glance at, have a glance *ou* a (quick) look at; (*longuement*) to gaze at; (*fixement*) to stare at. **~ un texte rapidement** to glance at *ou* through a text, have a quick look *ou* glance at *ou* through a text; **~ (qch) par le trou de la serrure** to peep *ou* look (at sth) through the keyhole; **~ de près/de plus près** to have a close/closer look at, look closely/more closely at; **~ sans voir** to look with unseeing eyes; **~ bouche bée** to gape at; **~ à la dérobée** *ou* **par en-dessous** to steal a glance at, glance sidelong at; **~ qn avec colère** to glare angrily at sb; **~ qn avec méfiance** to look at *ou* eye sb suspiciously; **~ qn du coin de l'œil** to look at *ou* watch sb from the corner of one's eye; **~ qn sous le nez** to look at sb defiantly; **~ qn de travers** to scowl at sb; **~ qn/qch d'un bon/mauvais œil** to look favourably/unfavourably upon sb/sth, view sb/sth favourably/unfavourably; **~ qn de haut** to give sb a scornful look, look scornfully at sb; (*lit, fig*) **~ qn droit dans les yeux/bien en face** to look sb straight in the eye/straight in the face; **~ qn dans le blanc des yeux** to look sb straight in the face *ou* eye; **~ la vie/le danger en face** to look life/danger in the face, face up to life/danger.

c (*vérifier*) *appareil, malade* to look at; *huile, essence* to look at, check. **regarde la lampe, elle ne marche pas** have *ou* take a look at the lamp – it doesn't work; **~ dans l'annuaire** to look in the phone book; **~ un mot dans le dictionnaire** to look up *ou* check a word in the dictionary.

d (*envisager*) *situation, problème* to view. **~ l'avenir avec appréhension** to view the future with trepidation; **il ne regarde que son propre intérêt** he is only concerned with *ou* he only thinks about his own interests; **nous le regardons comme un ami** we look upon him *ou* we regard him *ou* we consider him as a friend.

e (*concerner*) to concern. **cette affaire me regarde quand même un peu** this business does concern me a bit *ou* is a little bit my concern; **en quoi cela te regarde-t-il?** (*se mêler de*) what business is it of yours?, what has it to do with you?; (*être touché par*) how does it affect *ou* concern you?; **fais ce que je te dis, la suite me regarde** do what I tell you and I'll take care of what happens next *ou* and what happens next is my concern *ou* business; **que vas-tu faire? – cela me regarde** what will you do? – that's my business *ou* my concern; **non mais, ça vous regarde!*** really is it any of your business?, really what business is it of yours?; **cela ne le regarde pas, cela ne le regarde en rien** that's none of his business, that's no concern *ou* business of his; **mêlez-vous de ce qui vous regarde** mind your own business.

f *[maison]* **~ (vers)** to face.

2 **regarder à vt indir** to think of *ou* about. **y ~ à deux fois avant de faire qch** to think twice before doing sth; **il n'y regarde pas de si près** he's not that fussy *ou* particular; **à y bien ~** on thinking it over; **c'est quelqu'un qui va ~ à 2 F** he's the sort of person who will niggle over 2 francs *ou* worry about 2 francs; **il regarde à s'acheter un costume neuf** he (always) thinks twice before laying out money for a new suit; **quand il fait un cadeau, il ne regarde pas à la dépense** when he gives (somebody) a present he doesn't worry how much he spends *ou* he spares no expense *ou* expense is no object for him; **acheter qch sans ~ à la dépense** to buy sth without thought for expense *ou* without bothering about the expense.

3 **se regarder vpr** a **se ~ dans une glace** to look at o.s. in a mirror; (*iro*) **il ne s'est pas regardé!** he should take a look at himself!

b *[personnes]* to look at each other *ou* one another; *[maisons]* to face each other *ou* one another. **les deux enfants restaient là à se ~ en chiens de faïence** the two children sat (*ou* stood) glaring at each other *ou* one another.

regarnir [ʀ(ə)gaʀniʀ] 2 **vt** *magasin, rayon* to stock up again, restock; *trousse* to refill, replenish; *plat* to fill (up) again; *coussin* to refill.

régate [ʀegat] **nf**: **~(s)** regatta.

regeler [ʀəʒ(ə)le] 5 **vt, vb impers** to freeze again.

régence [ʀeʒɑ̃s] 1 **nf** (*Pol*) regency. (*Hist*) **la R~** the Regency. 2 **adj inv** *meuble* (*en France*) (French) Regency; (*en Grande-Bretagne*) Regency; (*fig*) *personne, mœurs* overrefined.

régénérateur, -trice [ʀeʒeneʀatœʀ, tʀis] 1 **adj** regenerative. 2 **nm,f** regenerator.

régénération [ʀeʒeneʀasjɔ̃] **nf** regeneration.

régénérer [ʀeʒeneʀe] 6 **vt** (*Bio, Rel*) to regenerate; *personne, forces* to revive, restore.

régent, e [ʀeʒɑ̃, ɑ̃t] 1 **adj** regent. **prince ~** prince regent. 2 **nm,f** (*Pol*) regent; (††: *professeur*) master; (*Admin: directeur*) manager.

régenter [ʀeʒɑ̃te] 1 **vt** (*gén*) to rule over; *personne* to dictate to. **il veut tout ~** he wants to run the whole show*.

reggae [ʀege] **nm** reggae.

régicide [ʀeʒisid] 1 **adj** regicidal. 2 **nmf** (*personne*) regicide. 3 **nm** (*crime*) regicide.

régie [ʀeʒi] **nf** a (*gestion*) *[État]* state control; *[commune]* local government control (*de* over). **en ~** under state (*ou* local government) control. b (*compagnie*) **~ (d'État)** state-owned company, government corporation; **la R~ française des tabacs** *the French national tobacco company;* **la R~ autonome des transports parisiens** *the Paris city transport authority.* c (*Ciné, Théât, TV*) production department; (*Rad, TV: salle de contrôle*) control room.

regimber [ʀ(ə)ʒɛ̃be] 1 **vi** *[personne]* to rebel (*contre* against); *[cheval]* to jib. **fais-le sans ~** do it without grumbling; **quand je lui ai demandé de le faire, il a regimbé** when I asked him to do it he jibbed at the idea.

régime¹ [ʀeʒim] **nm** a (*Pol*) (*mode*) system (of government); (*gouvernement*) government; (*péj*) régime. **~ monarchique/républicain** monarchical/republican system (of government); **les opposants au ~** the opponents of the régime; *voir* **ancien**.

b (*Admin*) (*système*) scheme, system; (*règlements*) regulations. **~ douanier/des hôpitaux** customs/hospital system; customs/hospital regulations; **~ de la Sécurité sociale** Social Security system; **~ maladie** health insurance scheme; **~ vieillesse** pension scheme.

c (*Jur*) **~ (matrimonial)** marriage settlement; **se marier sous le ~ de la communauté/de la séparation de biens** to opt for a marriage settlement based on joint ownership of property/on separate ownership of property; **~ complémentaire** supplementary scheme.

d (*Méd*) diet. **être/mettre qn au ~** to be/put sb on a diet; **suivre un ~** (*gén*) to be on a diet; (*scrupuleusement*) to follow a *ou* keep to a diet; **~ sans sel/sec/lacté/basses calories/amaigrissant** salt-free/alcohol-free/milk/low-calorie/slimming (*Brit*) *ou* reducing (*US*) diet; **se mettre au ~ jockey*** to go on a starvation diet.

e *[moteur]* (engine *ou* running) speed. **ce moteur est bruyant à haut ~** this engine is noisy when it is revving hard; **~ de croisière** cruising speed; (*Tech, fig*) **marcher** *ou* **aller à plein ~** to go (at) full speed, go flat out; (*fig*) **à ce ~, nous n'aurons bientôt plus d'argent** (if we go on) at this rate *ou* at the rate we're going we'll soon have no money left.

f (*Géog, Mét*) régime.
g (*Gram*) object. ~ **direct/indirect** direct/indirect object; **cas** ~ objective case.
h (*Phys*) *[écoulement]* rate of flow.

régime² [ʀeʒim] **nm** *[dattes]* cluster, bunch; *[bananes]* bunch, hand.

régiment [ʀeʒimɑ̃] **nm** a (*Mil*) (*corps*) regiment; (**: service militaire*) military *ou* national service. **être au** ~* to be doing (one's) national *ou* military service; **aller au** ~* to go into the army, be called up. b (**: masse*) *[personnes]* regiment, army; *[choses]* mass(es), loads. **il y en a pour tout un** ~ there's enough for a whole army.

régimentaire [ʀeʒimɑ̃tɛʀ] **adj** regimental.

région [ʀeʒjɔ̃] **nf** (*Admin, Géog*) (*étendue*) region; (*limitée*) area; (*Anat*) region, area; (*fig: domaine*) region. ~**s polaires/équatoriales** polar/equatorial regions; **la** ~ **parisienne/londonienne** the Paris/London area *ou* region; **ça se trouve dans la** ~ **de Lyon** it's in the Lyons area *ou* around Lyons *ou* in the region of Lyons; **si vous passez dans la** ~, **allez les voir** if you are in the area *ou* in those parts *ou* if you go that way, go and see them; **dans nos** ~**s** in these regions, in the regions we live in.

régional, e, **mpl -aux** [ʀeʒjɔnal, o] **adj** regional.

régionalisation [ʀeʒjɔnalizasjɔ̃] **nf** regionalization.

régionaliser [ʀeʒjɔnalize] 1 **vt** to regionalize.

régionalisme [ʀeʒjɔnalism] **nm** regionalism.

régionaliste [ʀeʒjɔnalist] 1 **adj** regionalist(ic). 2 **nmf** regionalist.

régir [ʀeʒiʀ] 2 **vt** (*gén, Ling*) to govern.

régisseur [ʀeʒisœʀ] **nm** a (*Théât*) stage manager; (*Ciné, TV*) assistant director. ~ **de plateau** studio director. b *[propriété]* steward.

registre [ʀəʒistʀ] 1 **nm** a (*livre*) register. ~ **maritime/d'hôtel/du commerce** shipping/hotel/trade register; (*Scol*) ~ **de notes** mark book (*Brit*), grades register *ou* book (*US*); (*Scol*) ~ **d'absences** attendance register.
b (*Mus*) *[orgue]* stop; *[voix]* (*étage*) register; (*étendue*) register, range.
c (*Ling*) (*niveau*) register, level (of language); (*style*) register, style.
d (*Tech*) *[fourneau]* damper, register; (*Ordin, Typ*) register.
e (*fig: genre, ton*) mood, vein. *[écrivain]* **il a complètement changé de** ~ he's completely changed his style.
2 **comp** ►**registre de comptabilité** ledger ►**registre de l'état civil** register of births, marriages and deaths ►**registre mortuaire** register of deaths ►**registre de vapeur** throttle valve.

réglable [ʀeglabl] **adj** adjustable. **siège à dossier** ~ reclining seat.

réglage [ʀeglaʒ] **nm** a *[mécanisme, débit]* regulation, adjustment; *[moteur]* tuning; *[allumage, thermostat]* setting, adjustment; *[dossier, tir]* adjustment. b *[papier]* ruling.

règle [ʀɛgl] **nf** a (*loi, principe, Rel*) rule. ~ **de conduite** rule of conduct; ~ **de 3** rule of 3; **les** ~**s de la bienséance/de l'honneur** the rules of propriety/honour; ~**s de sécurité** safety regulations; **sa parole nous sert de** ~ his word is our rule; **me lever à 7 heures tous les jours, j'en ai fait une** ~ **de vie** I've made it a rule to always get up at 7 in the morning; **ils ont pour** ~ **de se réunir chaque jour** they make it a rule to meet every day; (*lit, fig*) **c'est la** ~ **du jeu** it's one of the rules of the game, those are the rules of the game; (*lit, fig*) **se plier aux** ~**s du jeu** to play the game according to the rules; **c'est la** ~ **(de la maison)!** that's the rule (of the house)!; **cela n'échappe pas à la** ~ that's no exception to the rule; (*Sport*) **laisser jouer la** ~ **de l'avantage** to play the advantage rule.
b (*instrument*) ruler. **trait tiré à la** ~ line drawn with a ruler; ~ **à calcul** *ou* **à calculer** slide rule.
c (*menstruation*) ~**s** period(s); **avoir ses** ~**s** to have one's period(s).
d (*loc*) **il est de** ~ **qu'on fasse un cadeau** it's usual *ou* it's standard practice *ou* the done thing to give a present; **en** ~ *comptabilité, papiers* in order; *avertissement* given according to the rules; *réclamation* made according to the rules; **bataille en** ~ proper *ou* right old* (*Brit*) fight; **il lui fait une cour en** ~ he's courting her according to the rule book *ou* by the book; **être en** ~ **avec les autorités** to be straight with *ou* in order with the authorities; **se mettre en** ~ **avec les autorités** to sort out *ou* straighten out one's position with the authorities; **je ne suis pas en** ~ I'm not straight with the authorities, my papers *etc* are not in order; **en** ~ **générale** as a (general) rule; **il faut faire la demande dans** *ou* **selon les** ~**s** you must make the request through the proper channels *ou* according to the rules *ou* the proper procedures; (*hum*) **dans les** ~**s de l'art** according to the rule book.

réglé, e [ʀegle] (**ptp de régler**) **adj** a (*régulier*) *vie* (well-)ordered, regular; *personne* steady, stable. **c'est** ~ **comme du papier à musique*, il arrive tous les jours à 8 heures** he arrives at 8 o'clock every day, as regular as clockwork. b *fille* pubescent, who has reached puberty. **femme (bien)** ~**e** woman whose periods are regular. c *papier* ruled, lined.

règlement [ʀɛgləmɑ̃] **nm** a (*Admin, Police, Univ*) (*règle*) regulation; (*réglementation*) rules, regulations. ~ **de service** administrative rule *ou* regulation; ~ **intérieur** (*Scol*) school rules; *[entreprise]* policies and procedures (manual). b *[affaire, conflit]* settlement, settling; *[facture, dette]* settlement, payment. **faire un** ~ **par chèque** to pay *ou* make a payment by cheque; (*Jur*) ~ **judiciaire** (compulsory) liquidation; (*Jur*) ~ **(à l')amiable** amicable settlement, out-of-court settlement; (*fig*) ~ **de compte(s)** settling of scores; (*de gangsters*) gangland killing.

réglementaire [ʀɛgləmɑ̃tɛʀ] **adj** *uniforme, taille* regulation (*épith*); *procédure* statutory, laid down in the regulations. **ça n'est pas très** ~ that isn't really allowed, that's really against the rules; **dans le temps** ~ in the prescribed time; **ce certificat n'est pas** ~ this certificate doesn't conform to the regulations; **dispositions** ~**s** regulations; **pouvoir** ~ power to make regulations.

réglementairement [ʀɛgləmɑ̃tɛʀmɑ̃] **adv** in accordance with *ou* according to the regulations, statutorily.

réglementation [ʀɛgləmɑ̃tasjɔ̃] **nf** (*règles*) regulations; (*contrôle*) *[prix, loyers]* control, regulation. ~ **des changes** exchange control regulations.

réglementer [ʀɛgləmɑ̃te] 1 **vt** to regulate, control. **la vente des médicaments est très réglementée** the sale of medicines is strictly controlled.

régler [ʀegle] 6 **vt** a (*conclure*) *affaire, conflit* to settle; *problème* to settle, sort out. ~ **qch à l'amiable** (*gén*) to settle sth amicably; (*Jur*) to settle sth out of court; **alors, c'est une affaire réglée** *ou* **c'est réglé, vous acceptez?** that's (it) settled then – do you accept?; **on va** ~ **ça tout de suite** we'll get that settled *ou* sorted out straightaway.
b (*payer*) *note, dette* to settle (up), pay (up); *compte* to settle; *commerçant, créancier* to settle up with, pay; *travaux* to settle up for, pay for. **est-ce que je peux** ~? can I settle up (with you)? *ou* settle *ou* pay the bill?; **je viens** ~ **mes dettes** I've come to settle my debts *ou* to square up with you*; **est-ce que je peux (vous)** ~ **par chèque?** can I make you a cheque out?, can I pay you by cheque?; **j'ai un compte à** ~ **avec lui** I've got a score to settle with him, I've got a bone to pick with him; **on lui a réglé son compte!*** they've settled his hash* *ou* settled him.
c *mécanisme, débit, machine* to regulate, adjust; *dossier, tir* to adjust; *moteur* to tune; *allumage, ralenti* to set, adjust; *réveil* to set. ~ **le thermostat à 18°** to set the thermostat to *ou* at 18°; ~ **une montre** (*mettre à l'heure*) to put a watch right (*sur* by); (*réparer*) to regulate a watch; **le carburateur est mal réglé** the carburettor is badly tuned.
d (*fixer*) *modalités, date, programme* to settle (on), fix (up), decide on; *conduite, réactions* to determine. ~ **l'ordre d'une cérémonie** to settle *ou* fix (up) the order of (a) ceremony; **il ne sait pas** ~ **l'emploi de ses journées** he is incapable of planning out *ou* organizing his daily routine; ~ **le sort de qn** to decide *ou* determine sb's fate.
e (*prendre comme modèle*) ~ **qch sur** to model sth on, adjust sth to; ~ **sa vie sur (celle de) son père** to model one's life on that of one's father; ~ **sa conduite sur les circonstances** to adjust one's conduct *ou* behaviour to the circumstances; **se** ~ **sur qn d'autre** to model o.s. on sb else; **il essaya de** ~ **son pas sur celui de son père** he tried to walk in step with his father; ~ **sa vitesse sur celle de l'autre voiture** to adjust *ou* match one's speed to that of the other car.
f *papier* to rule (lines on).

réglette [ʀeglɛt] **nf** (*Typ*) setting stick.

régleur, -euse [ʀeglœʀ, øz] 1 **nm,f** (*ouvrier*) setter, adjuster. 2 **régleuse nf** ruling machine.

réglisse [ʀeglis] **nf ou nm** liquorice. **bâton de** ~ liquorice stick.

réglo* [ʀeglo] **adj inv** *personne* straight*, honest, dependable. **c'est** ~ it's O.K.*, it's in order; **ce n'est pas très** ~ it's not really allowed, it's not really on*.

régnant, e [ʀeɲɑ̃, ɑ̃t] **adj** *famille, prince* reigning (*épith*); *théorie, idée* reigning (*épith*), prevailing (*épith*).

règne [ʀɛɲ] **nm** a *[roi, tyran]* (*période*) reign; (*domination*) rule, reign. **sous le** ~ **de Louis XIV** (*période*) in the reign of Louis XIV; (*domination*) under the reign *ou* rule of Louis XIV. b *[mode, banquiers]* reign; *[justice, liberté]* reign, rule. c (*Bot, Zool etc*) kingdom. ~ **animal/végétal/minéral** animal/vegetable/mineral kingdom.

régner [ʀeɲe] 6 **vi** a (*être sur le trône*) to reign; (*exercer sa domination*) to rule (*sur* over). **les 20 ans qu'il a régné** during the 20 years of his reign; (*fig*) **il règne (en maître) sur le village** he reigns *ou* rules (supreme) over the village; **elle règne dans la cuisine** she reigns over *ou* rules in the kitchen; (*littér*) ~ **sur nos passions** to rule over *ou* govern our passions; *voir* **diviser**.
b (*prédominer*) *[paix, silence]* to reign, prevail (*sur* over); *[accord, confiance, opinion]* to prevail; *[peur]* to reign, hold sway (*sur* over). **la confusion la plus totale régnait dans la chambre** utter confusion prevailed in the room, the room was in utter confusion; **maison où l'ordre règne** house where order reigns; **faire** ~ **l'ordre** to maintain law and order; **faire** ~ **la terreur/le silence** to make terror/silence reign; (*iro*) **la confiance règne!** that's *ou* there's confidence *ou* trust for you! (*iro*).

regonflage [ʀ(ə)gɔ̃flaʒ] **nm, regonflement** [ʀ(ə)gɔ̃fləmɑ̃] **nm** (*voir* **regonfler**) blowing up (again); reinflation; pumping up (again).

regonfler [ʀ(ə)gɔ̃fle] 1 1 **vt** a (*gonfler à nouveau*) *pneu de voiture* to blow up again, reinflate; *pneu de vélo, matelas, ballon* to blow up again; (*avec pompe à main*) to pump up again. b (*gonfler davantage*) to blow up harder, put some more air in, pump up further. c (*) *personne* to cheer up, bolster up. **il est regonflé (à bloc)** he's back on top of things*; ~ **le moral de qn** to bolster up sb's spirits, bolster sb up. 2

vi *[rivière]* to swell *ou* rise again; (*Méd*) to swell (up) again.

regorgement [R(ə)gɔRʒəmɑ̃] **nm** overflow.

regorger [R(ə)gɔRʒe] 3 **vi** a ~ **de** *[région, pays]* to abound in, be abundant in, overflow with; *[maison, magasin]* to be packed *ou* crammed with, overflow with; *[rue]* to be swarming *ou* milling *ou* bursting with; **la région regorge d'ananas** the region abounds in *ou* is abundant in pineapples, there is an abundance of pineapples in the region; **cette année le marché regorge de fruits** this year there is a glut of fruit *ou* there is an abundance of fruit on the market; **le pays regorge d'argent** the country has fantastic wealth *ou* has enormous financial assets; **sa maison regorgeait de livres/d'invités** his house was packed with *ou* crammed with *ou* cram-full of books/guests; **son livre regorge de bonnes idées/fautes** his book is (jam-)packed *ou* crammed with good ideas/is riddled with mistakes; **il regorge d'argent** he is rolling in money*, he has got plenty of money.

b *[liquide]* to overflow.

régresser [RegRese] 1 **vi** *[science, enfant]* to regress; *[douleur, épidémie]* to recede, diminish, decrease.

régressif, -ive [RegResif, iv] **adj** *évolution, raisonnement* regressive; *marche* backward (*épith*); (*Phon*) anticipatory. (*Géol*) **érosion ~ive** headward erosion; **forme ~ive** regressive *ou* recessive form; (*Ling*) **dérivation ~ive** back formation.

régression [RegResjɔ̃] **nf** (*gén*) regression, decline; (*Bio, Psych*) regression. **être en (voie de)** ~ to be on the decline *ou* decrease, be declining *ou* decreasing; (*Géol*) ~ **marine** marine regression.

regret [R(ə)gRɛ] **nm** a *[décision, faute]* regret (*de* for); *[passé]* regret (*de* about). **le ~ d'une occasion manquée la faisait pleurer** she wept with regret at the lost opportunity, she wept in regret at losing the opportunity; **les ~s causés par une occasion manquée** the regrets felt at *ou* for a missed opportunity; **le ~ du pays natal** homesickness; **le ~ d'avoir échoué** the regret that he had failed *ou* at having failed; **vivre dans le ~ d'une faute** to spend one's life regretting a mistake; **le ~ de sa jeunesse/de son ami mort le rendait triste** his heart was heavy with the sorrow *ou* grief he felt for his lost youth/his departed friend, he grieved for the sad loss of his youth/his friend; **c'est avec ~ que je vous le dis** I'm sorry *ou* I regret to have to tell you this; **sans ~** with no regrets; **je te le donne – sans ~s?** take this – are you (really) sure?; (*sur une tombe*) **~s éternels** sorely missed.

b (*loc*) **à ~** *partir* with regret, regretfully; *accepter, donner* with regret, reluctantly; **je suis au ~ de ne pouvoir ...** I'm sorry *ou* I regret that I am unable to ...; **j'ai le ~ de vous informer que ...** I regret to have to point out that ..., I must regretfully inform you that ... (*frm*); **à mon grand ~** to my great regret.

regrettable [R(ə)gRetabl] **adj** *incident, conséquence* regrettable, unfortunate. **il est ~ que** it's unfortunate *ou* regrettable that.

regrettablement [R(ə)gRetabləmɑ̃] **adv** (*littér*) regrettably.

regretter [R(ə)gRete] 1 **vt** a *personne, pays natal* to miss; *jeunesse* to miss, regret; *occasion manquée, temps perdu* to regret. **nous avons beaucoup regretté votre absence** we were very sorry *ou* we greatly regretted that you weren't able to join us; **il regrette son argent** he regrets the expense, he wishes he had his money back; **c'était cher, mais je ne regrette pas mon argent** it was expensive but I don't regret buying it *ou* spending the money; **notre regretté président** our late lamented president; **on le regrette beaucoup dans le village** he is greatly *ou* sadly missed in the village.

b (*se repentir de*) *décision, imprudence, péché* to regret. **tu le regretteras** you'll regret it, you'll be sorry for it; **tu ne le regretteras pas** you won't regret it; **je ne regrette rien** I have no regrets; **je regrette mon geste** I'm sorry I did that, I regret doing that.

c (*désapprouver*) *mesure, décision hostile* to regret, deplore.

d (*être désolé*) to be sorry, regret. **je regrette, mais il est trop tard** I'm sorry, but it's too late, I'm afraid it's too late; **ah non! je regrette, il était avec moi** no! I'm sorry *ou* excuse me (but) he was with me, I'm sorry to contradict you but he was with me; **nous regrettons qu'il soit malade** we regret *ou* are sorry that he is ill; **je regrette de ne pas lui avoir écrit** I'm sorry *ou* I regret that I didn't write to him, I regret not writing *ou* not having written to him; **je regrette de vous avoir fait attendre** I'm sorry to have kept you waiting; **je ne regrette pas d'être venu** I'm not sorry *ou* I'm glad I came.

regrimper [R(ə)gRɛ̃pe] 1 1 **vt** *pente, escalier* to climb (up) again. 2 **vi** *[route]* to climb (up) again; *[fièvre]* to go up *ou* rise again; *[prix]* to go up again, climb again. ~ **dans le train** to climb back into the train; **ça va faire ~ les prix/la fièvre** it'll put up prices/his temperature again.

regrossir [R(ə)gRosiR] 2 **vi** to put on weight again, put weight back on.

regroupement [R(ə)gRupmɑ̃] **nm** (*voir* **regrouper**) grouping together; bringing *ou* gathering together; reassembly; roundup; bunching together; loose scrum. (*Fin, Jur*) **~s de sociétés** groupings of companies; ~ **familial** family reunion.

regrouper [R(ə)gRupe] 1 1 **vt** a (*réunir*) *objets* to put *ou* group together; *pièces de collection* to bring *ou* gather together; *industries, partis* to unite, group together; *parcelles* to group together. b (*réunir de nouveau*) *armée, personnes* to reassemble; *parti* to regroup; *bétail* to round up, herd together. 2 **se regrouper** **vpr** (*gén*) to gather (together), assemble (*autour de* (a)round, *derrière* behind); *[coureurs]* to bunch together again; *[rugbymen]* to form a loose scrum.

régularisation [RegylaRizasjɔ̃] **nf** (*voir* **régulariser**) regularization; straightening out; putting in order; regulation.

régulariser [RegylaRize] 1 **vt** a *position* to regularize, straighten out, sort out; *passeport* to put in order. ~ **sa situation** (*gén*) to regularize *ou* straighten out *ou* sort out one's position; (*se marier*) to regularize *ou* legalize one's situation; **il a régularisé la situation en l'épousant** he made an honest woman out of her (*hum*); **faire ~ ses papiers** to have one's papers put in order *ou* sorted out. b (*régler*) *mécanisme, débit* to regulate. c (*Fin*) *monnaie* to equalize.

régularité [RegylaRite] **nf** (*voir* **régulier**) regularity; steadiness; evenness; consistency; neatness; equability. **contester la ~ d'une élection/d'un jugement/d'une opération** to question the lawfulness *ou* legality of an election/a sentence/an operation.

régulateur, -trice [RegylatœR, tRis] 1 **adj** regulating. 2 **nm** (*Tech, fig*) regulator. ~ **de vitesse/de température** speed/temperature control *ou* regulator.

régulation [Regylasjɔ̃] **nf** *[économie, trafic]* regulation; *[mécanisme]* regulation, adjustment; *[circulation, naissances]* control. (*Physiol*) ~ **thermique** regulation of body temperature, thermotaxis (*SPÉC*).

régulier, -ière [Regylje, jɛR] 1 **adj** a (*fixe, constant*) *pouls, travail, effort, élève* regular, steady; *qualité, résultats* steady, even, consistent; *habitudes, vie* regular; *vitesse, vent* steady; *paiement, visites, service de car* regular; *train, avion* regular, scheduled. **rivière ~ière** river which has a regular *ou* steady flow; **frapper qch à coups ~s** to strike sth with regular *ou* steady blows; **à intervalles ~s** at regular intervals; **il est ~ dans son travail** he's steady in his work, he's a regular *ou* steady worker; **exercer une pression ~ière sur qch** to press steadily *ou* exert a steady pressure on sth; **la compagnie a 13 lignes ~ières avec le/vols ~s au Moyen-Orient** the airline has 13 scheduled services/scheduled flights to the Middle East; **être en correspondance ~ière avec qn** to be in regular correspondence with sb.

b (*égal*) *répartition, couche, ligne* even; *façade* regular; *traits, paysage* regular, even; *écriture* regular, neat; (*Math*) *polygone* regular; (*fig*) *humeur* steady, even, equable. **avoir un visage ~** to have regular features; **il faut que la pression soit bien ~ière partout** the pressure must be evenly distributed over the whole area.

c (*légal*) *gouvernement* legitimate; *élection, procédure* in order (*attrib*); *jugement* regular, in order (*attrib*); *tribunal* legal, official. **être en situation ~ière** to be in line with *ou* straight with the law.

d (*honnête*) *opération, coup* aboveboard (*attrib*), on the level (*attrib*); *homme d'affaires* on the level (*attrib*), straightforward, straight (*attrib*). **vous me faites faire quelque chose qui n'est pas très ~** you're getting me into something that is not quite on the level *ou* aboveboard; **être ~ en affaires** to be straight *ou* honest in business; **coup ~** (*Boxe*) fair blow; (*Échecs*) correct move.

e (*Mil*) *troupes* regular; *armée* regular, standing; (*Rel*) *clergé, ordre* regular.

f *vers, verbe* regular.

g (*Can: normal*) normal, regular (*US*).

2 **nm** (*Mil, Rel, client*) regular.

3 **régulière** **nf** a (*‡: femme*) missus‡, old woman‡; (*: *maîtresse*) lady-love (*hum*).

b *battre* **à la ~ière*** fair and square.

régulièrement [RegyljɛRmɑ̃] **adv** a (*voir* **régulier**) regularly; steadily; evenly; consistently; neatly; equably; lawfully. **élu ~** properly elected, elected in accordance with the rules; **opération effectuée ~** operation carried out in the correct *ou* proper fashion; **coup porté ~** fairly dealt blow. b (*en principe*) normally, in principle; (*d'habitude*) normally, usually.

régurgitation [RegyRʒitasjɔ̃] **nf** regurgitation.

régurgiter [RegyRʒite] 1 **vt** to regurgitate.

réhabilitation [Reabilitasjɔ̃] **nf** (*voir* **réhabiliter**) clearing (the name of); rehabilitation; discharge; restoring to favour; restoration; reinstatement. **obtenir la ~ de qn** to get sb's name cleared, get sb rehabilitated; to obtain a discharge for sb.

réhabiliter [Reabilite] 1 1 **vt** *condamné* to clear (the name of), rehabilitate; *failli* to discharge; *profession, art* to bring back into favour, restore to favour; *quartier de ville, immeuble* to restore, rehabilitate. ~ **la mémoire de qn** to restore sb's good name; ~ **qn dans ses fonctions** to reinstate sb (in his job); ~ **qn dans ses droits** to restore sb's rights (to him). 2 **se réhabiliter** **vpr** *[condamné, criminel]* to rehabilitate o.s.; (*fig*) *[candidat etc]* to redeem o.s.

réhabituer [Reabitɥe] 1 1 **vt**: ~ **qn à (faire) qch** to get sb used to (doing) sth again, reaccustom sb to (doing) sth. 2 **se réhabituer** **vpr**: **se ~ à (faire) qch** to get used to (doing) sth again, reaccustom o.s. to (doing) sth; **ça va être dur de se ~** it will be difficult to get used to it again.

rehaussement [Rəosmɑ̃] **nm** (*voir* **rehausser**) heightening; raising.

rehausser [Rəose] 1 **vt** a (*relever*) *mur, clôture* to heighten, make *ou* build higher; *plafond, chaise* to raise, heighten. b (*fig: souligner*) *beauté, couleur* to set off, enhance; *goût* to emphasize, bring out; *mérite, prestige* to enhance, increase; *courage* to underline, increase; *détail* to bring out, emphasize, accentuate, underline; *tableau, robe* to

brighten up, liven up. **rehaussé de** embellished with.
réification [ʀeifikasjɔ̃] nf reification.
réifier [ʀeifje] 7 vt to reify.
réimperméabilisation [ʀeɛ̃pɛʀmeabilizasjɔ̃] nf reproofing.
réimperméabiliser [ʀeɛ̃pɛʀmeabilize] 1 vt to reproof.
réimplanter [ʀeɛ̃plɑ̃te] 1 vt *entreprise* (*gén*) to relocate; (*nouvelle*) to set up.
réimportation [ʀeɛ̃pɔʀtasjɔ̃] nf reimportation.
réimporter [ʀeɛ̃pɔʀte] 1 vt to reimport.
réimposer [ʀeɛ̃poze] 1 vt a (*Fin*) to impose a new *ou* further tax on. b (*Typ*) to reimpose.
réimposition [ʀeɛ̃pozisjɔ̃] nf (*voir* **réimposer**) further taxation; reimposition.
réimpression [ʀeɛ̃pʀesjɔ̃] nf (*action*) reprinting, reimpression; (*livre*) reprint.
réimprimer [ʀeɛ̃pʀime] 1 vt to reprint.
Reims [ʀɛ̃s] n Rheims.
rein [ʀɛ̃] nm a (*organe*) kidney. ~ **artificiel** kidney machine. b (*région*) ~s small of the back, loins (*littér*); (*taille*) waist; **avoir mal aux ~s** to have backache (*low down in one's back*), have an ache in the small of one's back; **ses cheveux tombent sur ses ~s** her hair is right down to the small of her back; **il donna un coup de ~s pour se relever** he heaved himself up; **donner un coup de ~s pour soulever qch** to heave sth up; **avoir les ~s solides** (*lit*) to have a strong *ou* sturdy back; (*fig*) to be on a sound (financial) footing, have a solid financial backing; (*fig*) **casser** *ou* **briser les ~s à qn** to ruin *ou* break sb; (*fig*) **il m'a mis l'épée dans les ~s** he forced me to work to a very tight schedule *ou* deadline; *voir* **creux** *etc.*
réincarcération [ʀeɛ̃kaʀseʀasjɔ̃] nf reimprisonment, reincarceration.
réincarcérer [ʀeɛ̃kaʀseʀe] 6 vt to reimprison, reincarcerate.
réincarnation [ʀeɛ̃kaʀnasjɔ̃] nf reincarnation.
réincarner (se) [ʀeɛ̃kaʀne] 1 vpr to be reincarnated.
réincorporer [ʀeɛ̃kɔʀpɔʀe] 1 vt *soldat* to re-enlist. ~ **son régiment** to re-enlist in one's regiment.
reine [ʀɛn] 1 nf (*Échecs, Pol, Zool, fig*) queen. **la ~ d'Angleterre** the Queen of England; **la ~ Élisabeth** Queen Elizabeth; **la ~ mère** (*lit*) the Queen mother; (* *fig*) her ladyship*; **la ~ du bal** the queen *ou* the belle of the ball; ~ **de beauté** beauty queen; **la ~ des abeilles/des fourmis** the queen bee/ant; **comme une ~** *vivre* in the lap of luxury; *traiter* like a queen; **être vêtue comme une ~** to look like a queen; *voir* **bouchée, petit, port**[2]. 2 comp ▸**reine-claude** nf (pl **reine(s)-claudes**) greengage ▸**reine-marguerite** nf (pl **reines-marguerites**) (China) aster ▸**reine-des-prés** nf (pl **reines-des-prés**) meadowsweet ▸**reine des reinettes** rennet.
reinette [ʀɛnɛt] nf rennet, pippin. ~ **grise** russet.
réinfecter [ʀeɛ̃fɛkte] 1 vt to reinfect. **la plaie s'est réinfectée** the wound has become infected again.
réinfection [ʀeɛ̃fɛksjɔ̃] nf reinfection.
réinitialiser [ʀeinisjalize] 1 vt (*Ordin*) to reboot.
réinscription [ʀeɛ̃skʀipsjɔ̃] nf reregistration, re-enrolment (*Brit*).
réinscrire [ʀeɛ̃skʀiʀ] 39 1 vt *épitaphe* to reinscribe; *date, nom* to put down again; *élève* to re-enrol (*Brit*), reregister. **je n'ai pas réinscrit** *ou* **fait ~ mon fils à la cantine cette année** I haven't reregistered my son for school meals this year. 2 **se réinscrire** vpr to re-enrol (*Brit*), reregister (*à* for).
réinsérer [ʀeɛ̃seʀe] 6 vt *publicité, feuillet* to reinsert; *délinquant, handicapé* to reintegrate, rehabilitate. **se ~ dans la société** to rehabilitate o.s. *ou* become reintegrated in society.
réinsertion [ʀeɛ̃sɛʀsjɔ̃] nf (*voir* **réinsérer**) reinsertion; reintegration, rehabilitation. **la ~ sociale des anciens détenus** the (social) rehabilitation of ex-prisoners.
réinstallation [ʀeɛ̃stalasjɔ̃] nf (*voir* **réinstaller**) putting back; reinstallation; putting up again; connecting up again. **notre ~ à Paris/dans l'appartement va poser des problèmes** (our) settling back in Paris/into the flat is going to create problems.
réinstaller [ʀeɛ̃stale] 1 1 vt *cuisinière* to put back, reinstall; *étagère* to put back up, put up again, reinstall; *téléphone* to reconnect, put back in, reinstall. ~ **qn chez lui** to reinstall sb in *ou* move sb back into his (own) home; ~ **qn dans ses fonctions** to reinstate sb (in his job), give sb his job back. 2 **se réinstaller** vpr (*dans un fauteuil*) to settle down again (*dans* in); (*dans une maison*) to settle back (*dans* into). **il s'est réinstallé à Paris** (*gén*) he has gone back to live in Paris; *[commerçant]* he has set up in business again in Paris.
réintégration [ʀeɛ̃tegʀasjɔ̃] nf (*voir* **réintégrer**) reinstatement (*dans* in); return (*de* to).
réintégrer [ʀeɛ̃tegʀe] 6 vt a ~ **qn (dans ses fonctions)** to reinstate sb (in his job), restore sb to his (former) position. b *lieu* to return to, go back to. ~ **le domicile conjugal** to return to the marital home.
réintroduction [ʀeɛ̃tʀɔdyksjɔ̃] nf (*voir* **réintroduire**) reintroduction; putting back.
réintroduire [ʀeɛ̃tʀɔdɥiʀ] 38 vt *personne, mode* to reintroduce, introduce again. ~ **qch dans une lettre** to put sth back in a letter; ~ **des erreurs dans un texte** to reintroduce errors *ou* put errors back into a text.
réinventer [ʀeɛ̃vɑ̃te] 1 vt to reinvent.
réinviter [ʀeɛ̃vite] 1 vt to invite back, ask back again, reinvite.
réitératif, -ive [ʀeiteʀatif, iv] adj reiterative.
réitération [ʀeiteʀasjɔ̃] nf reiteration, repetition.
réitérer [ʀeiteʀe] 6 vt *promesse, ordre, question* to reiterate, repeat; *demande, exploit* to repeat. **attaques réitérées** repeated attacks; **le criminel a réitéré** the criminal has repeated his crime *ou* has done it again.
reître [ʀɛtʀ] nm (*littér*) ruffianly *ou* roughneck soldier.
rejaillir [ʀ(ə)ʒajiʀ] 2 vi *[liquide]* to splash back *ou* up (*sur* onto, at); (*avec force*) to spurt back *ou* up (*sur* onto, at); *[boue]* to splash up (*sur* onto, at). ~ **sur qn** *[scandale, honte]* to rebound on sb; *[gloire]* to be reflected on sb; **l'huile bouillante m'a rejailli à la figure** the boiling oil splashed up in my face; **les bienfaits de cette invention rejailliront sur tous** the benefits of this invention will fall upon everyone, everyone will have a share in the benefits of this invention; **sa renommée a rejailli sur ses collègues** his fame brought his colleagues some reflected glory.
rejaillissement [ʀ(ə)ʒajismɑ̃] nm (*voir* **rejaillir**) splashing up; spurting up; rebounding; reflection.
rejet [ʀəʒɛ] nm a (*action: voir* **rejeter**) bringing *ou* throwing up, vomiting; spewing out; throwing out, casting up, washing up; discharge; pushing back, driving back, repulsion; casting out, expulsion; rejection; dismissal; throwing back, tossing back. **en anglais, le ~ de la préposition à la fin de la phrase est courant** putting the preposition at the end of the sentence is quite usual *ou* is common practice in English. b (*Bot*) shoot; (*Littérat*) enjamb(e)ment, rejet; (*Méd*) *[greffe]* rejection. c (*Ordin*) reject.
rejeter [ʀəʒ(ə)te] 4 1 vt a (*relancer*) *objet* to throw back (*à* to). b (*vomir, recracher*) *nourriture, dîner, sang* to bring *ou* throw up, vomit. **il** *ou* **son estomac rejette toute nourriture** his stomach rejects everything, he can't keep anything down; **le volcan rejette de la lave** the volcano is spewing *ou* throwing out lava; **le cadavre a été rejeté par la mer** the corpse was cast up *ou* washed up by the sea; **les déchets que rejettent les usines polluent les rivières** the waste thrown out *ou* discharged by factories pollutes the rivers.
c (*repousser*) *envahisseur* to push back, drive back, repulse; *indésirable* to cast out, expel; *domination* to reject; *projet de loi* to reject, throw out; *offre, demande, conseil* to reject, turn down; *recours en grâce, hypothèse* to reject, dismiss. **la machine rejette les mauvaises pièces de monnaie** the machine rejects *ou* refuses invalid coins; **le village l'a rejeté après ce dernier scandale** the village has rejected him *ou* cast him out after this latest scandal; ~ **d'un parti les éléments suspects** to cast out *ou* eject *ou* expel the suspicious elements from a party.
d ~ **une faute sur qn/qch** to shift *ou* transfer the blame *ou* responsibility for a mistake onto sb/sth; **il rejette la responsabilité sur moi** he lays the responsibility at my door.
e (*placer*) **la préposition est rejetée à la fin** the preposition is put at the end; ~ **la tête en arrière** to throw *ou* toss one's head back; ~ **ses cheveux en arrière** (*avec la main*) to push one's hair back; (*en se coiffant*) to comb *ou* brush one's hair back; (*d'un mouvement de la tête*) to toss one's hair back; ~ **les épaules en arrière pour se tenir droit** to pull one's shoulders back to stand up straight; **le chapeau rejeté en arrière** with his hat tilted back; ~ **la terre en dehors d'une tranchée** to throw the earth out of a trench.
f (*Ordin*) to reject.
2 **se rejeter** vpr a **se ~ sur qch** to fall back on sth; **faute de viande, on se rejette sur le fromage*** as there is no meat we'll have to fall back on cheese.
b **se ~ en arrière** to jump *ou* leap back(wards); **il s'est rejeté dans l'eau** he jumped back *ou* threw himself back into the water; **ils se rejettent (l'un l'autre) la responsabilité de la rupture** they lay the responsibility for the break-up at each other's door, each wants the other to take responsibility for the break-up.
rejeton [ʀəʒ(ə)tɔ̃] nm a (*: *enfant*) kid*. **il veut que son ~ soit dentiste** he wants his son and heir (*hum*) *ou* his kid* to be a dentist; **la mère et ses ~s** the mother and her kids* *ou* her offspring (*hum*). b (*Bot*) shoot; (*fig*) offshoot.
rejoindre [ʀ(ə)ʒwɛ̃dʀ] 49 1 vt a (*regagner, retrouver*) *lieu* to get (back) to; *route* to (re)join, get (back) (on)to; *personne* to (re)join, meet (again); *poste, régiment* to rejoin, return to. **la route rejoint la voie ferrée à X** the road meets (up with) *ou* (re)joins the railway line at X.
b (*rattraper*) to catch up (with). **je n'arrive pas à le ~** I can't manage to catch up with him *ou* to catch him up.
c (*se rallier à*) *parti* to join; *point de vue* to agree with. **je vous rejoins sur ce point** I agree with you *ou* I'm at one with you on that point; **mon idée rejoint la vôtre** my idea is closely akin to yours *ou* is very much like yours; **c'est ici que la prudence rejoint la lâcheté** this is where prudence comes close to *ou* is closely akin to cowardice.
d (*réunir*) *personnes* to reunite, bring back together; *choses* to bring together (again); *lèvres d'une plaie* to close.
2 **se rejoindre** vpr *[routes]* to join, meet; *[idées]* to concur, be closely akin to each other; *[personnes]* (*pour rendez-vous*) to meet (up)

(again); (*sur point de vue*) to agree, be at one.

rejointoyer [ʀ(ə)ʒwɛ̃twaje] 8 **vt** to repoint, regrout.

rejouer [ʀ(ə)ʒwe] 1 1 **vt** (*gén*) to play again; *match* to replay. (*Cartes*) ~ **cœur** to lead hearts again; **on rejoue une partie?** shall we have *ou* play another game?; ~ **une pièce** *[acteurs]* to perform a play again, give another performance of a play; *[théâtre]* to put on a play again; **nous rejouons demain à Marseille** *[acteurs]* we're performing again tomorrow at Marseilles; *[joueurs]* we're playing again tomorrow at Marseilles. 2 **vi** *[enfants, joueurs]* to play again; *[musicien]* to play *ou* perform again. **acteur qui ne pourra plus jamais** ~ actor who will never be able to act *ou* perform again.

réjoui, e [ʀeʒwi] (**ptp de réjouir**) **adj** *air, mine* joyful, joyous.

réjouir [ʀeʒwiʀ] 2 1 **vt** *personne, regard, estomac* to delight; *cœur* to gladden. **cette perspective le réjouit** this prospect delights *ou* thrills him, he is delighted *ou* thrilled at this prospect; **cette idée ne me réjouit pas beaucoup** I don't find the thought of it particularly appealing.

2 **se réjouir vpr** to be delighted *ou* thrilled (*de faire* to do). **se** ~ **de** *nouvelle, événement* to be delighted *ou* thrilled about *ou* at; *malheur* to take delight in, rejoice over; **vous avez gagné et je m'en réjouis pour vous** you've won and I'm delighted for you; **se** ~ **(à la pensée) que** to be delighted *ou* thrilled (at the thought) that; **je me réjouis à l'avance de les voir** I am greatly looking forward to seeing them; **réjouissez-vous!** rejoice!; **je me réjouis que tu aies réussi** I'm delighted *ou* thrilled that you've succeeded.

réjouissance [ʀeʒwisɑ̃s] **nf** rejoicing. ~**s** festivities, merrymaking (*NonC*); (*fig hum*) **quel est le programme des** ~**s pour la journée?** what delights are in store (for us) today? (*hum*), what's on the agenda for today?*

réjouissant, e [ʀeʒwisɑ̃, ɑ̃t] **adj** *histoire* amusing, entertaining; *nouvelle* cheering, cheerful, joyful. (*iro*) **quelle perspective** ~**e!** what a delightful *ou* heartening prospect! (*iro*); **ce n'est pas** ~! it's no joke!; (*iro*) **c'est** ~! that's great!* (*iro*).

relâche [ʀ(ə)lɑʃ] 1 **nm ou nf** a (*littér: répit*) respite, rest. **prendre un peu de** ~ to take a short rest *ou* break; **se donner** ~ to give o.s. a rest *ou* a break; **sans** ~ without (a) respite. b (*Théât*) closure. **faire** ~ to be closed, close; "~" "no performance(s) (today *ou* this week *etc*)"; **le lundi est le jour de** ~ **du cinéma local** the local cinema is closed on Monday(s). 2 **nf** (*Naut*) port of call. **faire** ~ **dans un port** to put in at *ou* call at a port.

relâché, e [ʀ(ə)lɑʃe] (**ptp de relâcher**) **adj** *style* loose, limp; *conduite, mœurs* loose, lax; *discipline, autorité* lax, slack; *prononciation* lax.

relâchement [ʀ(ə)lɑʃmɑ̃] **nm** (*voir* **relâcher**) relaxation; loosening; slackening; release; laxity; flagging. **il y a du** ~ **dans la discipline** discipline is getting lax *ou* slack, there is some slackening *ou* relaxation of discipline; ~ **des mœurs** loosening *ou* slackening of moral standards.

relâcher [ʀ(ə)lɑʃe] 1 1 **vt** a (*desserrer*) *étreinte* to relax, loosen; *lien* to loosen, slacken (off); *muscle* to relax; *ressort* to release. ~ **les intestins** to loosen the bowels.

b (*affaiblir*) *attention, discipline, effort* to relax, slacken; *surveillance* to relax.

c (*libérer*) *prisonnier, otage, gibier* to release, let go, set free.

d (*refaire tomber*) *objet* to drop again, let go of again; *corde* to let go of again. **ne relâche pas la corde** don't let go of the rope again.

2 **vi** (*Naut*) ~ **(dans un port)** to put into port.

3 **se relâcher vpr** a *[courroie]* to loosen, go *ou* get loose *ou* slack; *[muscle]* to relax.

b *[surveillance, discipline]* to become *ou* get lax *ou* slack; *[mœurs]* to become *ou* get lax *ou* loose; *[style]* to become loose *ou* limp; *[courage, attention]* to flag; *[effort, zèle]* to slacken, flag, fall off. **il se relâche** he's growing slack; **ne te relâche pas maintenant!** don't let up *ou* slack(en) off now!; **il se relâche dans son travail** he's growing slack in his work, his work is getting slack.

relais [ʀ(ə)lɛ] **nm** a (*Sport*) relay (race); (*Alpinisme*) stance. ~ **4 fois 100 mètres** 4 by 100 metres (relay); **passer le** ~ **à son coéquipier** to hand over to one's team-mate.

b (*Ind*) **travailler par** ~ to work shifts, do shift work; **ouvriers/équipe de** ~ shift workers/team; **passer le** ~ **à qn** to hand over to sb; **prendre le** ~ **(de qn)** to take over (from sb); (*Fin*) **prêt** *ou* **crédit** ~ bridging loan; (*fig*) **la pluie ayant cessé, c'est la neige qui a pris le** ~ once the rain had stopped the snow took over *ou* set in.

c (*chevaux, chiens*) relay. ~ **(de poste)** (*Hist: auberge*) post house, coaching inn; (*Mil*) staging post; ~ **routier** transport café; *voir* **cheval**.

d (*Élec, Rad, Téléc*) (*action*) relaying; (*dispositif*) relay. ~ **de télévision** television relay station; **avion/satellite de** ~ relay plane/satellite.

relance [ʀ(ə)lɑ̃s] **nf** a (*action: reprise*) *[économie, industrie]* boosting, stimulation; *[idée, projet]* revival, relaunching; (*Fin*) reflation. (*résultat*) **la** ~ **de l'économie n'a pas duré** the boost (given) to the economy did not last; **la** ~ **du terrorisme est due à ...** the fresh outburst of *ou* upsurge in terrorism is due to ...; **provoquer la** ~ **de** *économie* to give a boost to, boost, stimulate; *projet* to revive, relaunch; **mesures/politique de** ~ reflationary measures/policy. b (*Poker*) **faire une** ~ to raise the stakes, make a higher bid; **limiter la** ~ to limit the stakes. c *[débiteur]* chasing up. **lettre de** ~ reminder.

relancer [ʀ(ə)lɑ̃se] 3 **vt** a (*renvoyer*) *objet, ballon* to throw back (again). b (*faire repartir*) *gibier* to start (again); *moteur* to restart; *idée, projet* to revive, relaunch; *économie, industrie* to boost, give a boost to, stimulate. ~ **la machine économique** to boost *ou* reflate *ou* revitalize the economy. c (*harceler*) *débiteur* to chase up; *femme* to harass, pester, chase after. d (*Cartes*) *enjeu* to raise.

relaps, e [ʀəlaps] 1 **adj** relapsed. 2 **nm,f** relapsed heretic.

rélargir [ʀelaʀʒiʀ] 2 **vt** a (*agrandir*) *rue* to widen further; *vêtement* to let out further *ou* more. b (*à nouveau*) to widen again; to let out again.

rélargissement [ʀelaʀʒismɑ̃] **nm** *[route]* widening.

relater [ʀ(ə)late] 1 **vt** (*littér*) *événement, aventure* to relate, recount; (*Jur*) *pièce, fait* to record. **le journaliste relate que** the journalist says that *ou* tells us that; **pourriez-vous** ~ **les faits tels que vous les avez observés** could you state *ou* recount the facts exactly as you observed them.

relatif, -ive [ʀ(ə)latif, iv] 1 **adj** (*gén, Gram, Mus*) relative; *silence, luxe* relative, comparative. **tout est** ~ everything is relative; **discussions** ~**ives à un sujet** discussions relative to *ou* relating to *ou* connected with a subject; (*Mus*) **(ton) majeur/mineur** ~ relative major/minor (key). 2 **nm** a (*Gram*) relative pronoun. b **avoir le sens du** ~ to have a sense of proportion. 3 **relative nf** (*Gram*) relative clause.

relation [ʀ(ə)lasjɔ̃] **nf** a (*gén, Math, Philos*) relation(ship). ~ **de cause à effet** relation(ship) of cause and effect; **la** ~ **entre l'homme et l'environnement** the relation(ship) between man and the environment; **il y a une** ~ **évidente entre** there is an obvious connection *ou* relation(ship) between; **c'est sans** ~ *ou* **cela n'a aucune** ~ **avec** it has no connection with, it bears no relation to; ~ **causale** causal relation(ship).

b (*rapports*) ~**s** (*gén*) relations; (*sur le plan personnel*) relationship, relations; ~**s diplomatiques/culturelles/publiques** diplomatic/cultural/public relations; **les** ~**s sont tendues/cordiales entre nous** relations between us are strained/cordial, the relationship between us *ou* our relationship is strained/cordial; **avoir des** ~**s avec une femme** to have sexual relations *ou* intercourse with a woman; **avoir des** ~**s amoureuses avec qn** to have an affair *ou* a love affair with sb; **avoir de bonnes** ~**s/des** ~**s amicales avec qn** to be on good/friendly terms with sb, have a good/friendly relationship with sb; **avoir des** ~**s de bon voisinage avec qn** to be on neighbourly terms with sb; **être en** ~**s d'affaires avec qn** to have business relations *ou* business dealings *ou* a business relationship with sb; ~**s patrons-ouvriers** labour-management relations; ~**s patronat-syndicats** union-management relations; **être/rester en** ~**(s) avec qn** to be/keep in touch *ou* contact with sb; **entrer** *ou* **se mettre en** ~**(s) avec qn** to get in touch *ou* make contact with sb; **être en** ~**s épistolaires avec qn** to be in correspondence with sb; **nous sommes en** ~**s suivies** we have frequent contact with each other, we are in constant *ou* close contact *ou* touch (with each other); **être dans les** ~**s publiques** to be in public relations.

c (*connaissance*) acquaintance. **une de mes** ~**s** an acquaintance of mine, someone I know; **trouver un poste par** ~**s** to find a job through one's connections, find a job by knowing somebody *ou* by knowing the right people; **avoir des** ~**s** to have (influential) connections, know (all) the right people.

d (*récit*) account, report. ~ **orale/écrite** oral/written account *ou* report; **d'après la** ~ **d'un témoin** according to a witness's account; **faire la** ~ **des événements/de son voyage** to give an account of *ou* relate the events/one's journey.

relationnel, -elle [ʀ(ə)lasjɔnɛl] **adj** *grammaire* relational; (*Psych*) *problèmes* relationship (*épith*). (*Ordin*) **base de données** ~**les** relational data base.

relativement [ʀ(ə)lativmɑ̃] **adv** a *facile, honnête, rare* relatively, comparatively. b ~ **à** (*par comparaison*) in relation to, compared to; (*concernant*) with regard to, concerning.

relativisation [ʀəlativizasjɔ̃] **nf** relativization.

relativiser [ʀəlativize] 1 **vt** to relativize.

relativisme [ʀ(ə)lativism] **nm** relativism.

relativiste [ʀ(ə)lativist] 1 **adj** relativistic. 2 **nmf** relativist.

relativité [ʀ(ə)lativite] **nf** relativity.

relaver [ʀ(ə)lave] 1 **vt** to wash again, rewash.

relax* [ʀəlaks] = **relaxe**[2]*.

relaxant, e [ʀ(ə)laksɑ̃, ɑ̃t] **adj** relaxing.

relaxation [ʀ(ə)laksasjɔ̃] **nf** (*gén*) relaxation. **j'ai besoin de** ~ I need to relax, I need a bit of relaxation.

relaxe[1] [ʀəlaks] **nf** (*voir* **relaxer**) acquittal, discharge; release.

relaxe[2]* [ʀəlaks] **adj** *ambiance* relaxed, informal, laid back*; *tenue* informal, casual; *personne* relaxed, easy-going, laid-back*; *vacances* relaxing. **siège** *ou* **fauteuil** ~ reclining chair.

relaxer[1] [ʀ(ə)lakse] 1 **vt** (*acquitter*) *prisonnier* to acquit, discharge; (*relâcher*) to release.

relaxer[2] [ʀ(ə)lɔkse] 1 1 **vt** *muscles* to relax. 2 **se relaxer vpr** to relax.

relayer [ʀ(ə)leje] 8 1 **vt** a *personne* to relieve, take over from; *appareil* to replace; *initiative* to take over. **se faire** ~ to get somebody to take over, hand over to somebody else. b (*Rad, TV*) to relay. 2 **se**

relayer vpr to take turns (*pour faire* to do, at doing), take it in turns (*pour faire* to do); (*dans un relais*) to take over from one another.

relayeur, -euse [ʀ(ə)lɛjœʀ, øz] nm,f relay runner.

relecture [ʀ(ə)lɛktyʀ] nf rereading.

relégation [ʀ(ə)legasjɔ̃] nf (*voir* **reléguer**) relegation; banishment.

reléguer [ʀ(ə)lege] 6 vt a (*confiner*) *personne, problème* to relegate (*à* to); *objet* to consign, relegate (*à, dans* to); (*Sport*) to relegate (*en* to). **~ qch/qn au second plan** to relegate sth/sb to a position of secondary importance. b (*Jur: exiler*) to relegate, banish.

relent [ʀəlɑ̃] nm foul smell, stench (*NonC*). **un ~ ou des ~s de poisson pourri** the *ou* a stench *ou* foul smell of rotten fish, the reek of rotten fish; (*fig*) **ça a des ~s de vengeance** it reeks of vengeance, it has a strong whiff of vengeance about it.

relevable [ʀəl(ə)vabl] adj *siège* tip-up (*épith*), fold-away (*épith*).

relève [ʀ(ə)lɛv] nf a (*personne*) relief; (*travailleurs*) relief (team); (*troupe*) relief (troops); (*sentinelles*) relief (guard). b (*action*) relief. **la ~ de la garde** the changing of the guards; **assurer** *ou* **prendre la ~ de qn** (*lit*) to relieve sb, take over from sb; (*fig*) to take over (from sb).

relevé, e [ʀəl(ə)ve] (ptp de **relever**) 1 adj a *col* turned-up; *virage* banked; *manches* rolled-up; *tête* (*lit*) held up; (*fig*) held high. **chapeau à bords ~s** hat with a turned-up brim; **porter les cheveux ~s** to wear one's hair up.

b (*noble*) *style, langue, sentiments* elevated, lofty. **cette expression n'est pas très ~e** it's not a very choice *ou* refined expression.

c (*Culin*) *sauce, mets* highly-seasoned, spicy, hot.

2 nm *[dépenses]* summary, statement; (*repérage, résumé*) *[cote]* plotting; (*liste*) *[citations, adresses]* list; (*facture*) bill. **faire un ~ de** *citations, erreurs* to list, note down; *notes* to take down; *compteur* to read; **prochain ~ du compteur dans deux mois** next meter reading *ou* reading of the meter in two months; **~ de gaz/de téléphone** gas/telephone bill; **~ bancaire, ~ de compte** bank statement; **~ de condamnations** police record; **~ d'identité bancaire** particulars of one's bank account; **~ d'identité postal** particulars of one's post-office bank account; **~ de notes** marks sheet (*Brit*), grade sheet (*US*).

relèvement [ʀ(ə)lɛvmɑ̃] nm (*voir* **relever**) standing up again; picking up; righting; setting upright; banking; turning up; raising; tipping up; folding away; lifting up; rebuilding; putting back on its feet; rise (*de* in); increase (*de* in); putting up; plotting. **le ~ du salaire minimum** (*action*) the raising of the minimum wage; (*résultat*) the rise in the minimum wage; **on assiste à un ~ spectaculaire du pays/de l'économie** we are witnessing a spectacular recovery of the country/economy; (*Naut*) **faire un ~ de sa position** to plot one's position.

relever [ʀəl(ə)ve] 5 1 vt a (*redresser*) *statue, meuble* to stand up again; *chaise* to stand up (again), pick up; *véhicule* to right, set upright again; *bateau* to right; *personne* to help (back) up, help (back) to his feet; *blessé* to pick up; (*Aut*) *virage* to bank. **~ une vieille dame tombée dans la rue** to help up an old lady who has fallen in the street; **~ la tête** (*lit*) to lift *ou* hold up one's head; (*fig: se rebeller*) to raise one's head, show signs of rebelling; (*fig: être fier*) to hold one's head up *ou* high.

b (*remonter*) *col* to turn up; *chaussettes* to pull up; *jupe* to raise, lift; *manche, pantalon* to roll up; *cheveux* to put up; *mur, étagère, plafond* to raise, heighten; *vitre* (*en poussant*) to push up; (*avec manivelle*) to wind up; *store* to roll up, raise; *niveau* to raise, bring up; *siège* to tip up, fold away; *couvercle* to lift (up). **elle releva son voile** she lifted *ou* raised her veil; **lorsqu'il releva les yeux** when he lifted (up) *ou* raised his eyes, when he looked up.

c (*remettre en état*) *mur en ruines* to rebuild; *économie* to rebuild, restore; *pays, entreprise* to put back on its feet. (*fig*) **~ le courage de qn** to restore sb's courage; (*fig*) **~ le moral de qn** to boost *ou* raise sb's spirits, cheer sb up.

d (*augmenter*) *salaire, impôts* to raise, increase, put up; *niveau de vie* to raise; *chiffre d'affaires* to increase. **les devoirs étaient si mauvais que j'ai dû ~ toutes les notes de 2 points** the exercises were so badly done that I had to put up *ou* raise *ou* increase all the marks by 2 points; **cela ne l'a pas relevé dans mon estime** that didn't raise him in my esteem *ou* estimation, that didn't improve my opinion of him, that did nothing to heighten my opinion of him; (*péj*) **il n'y en a pas un pour ~ l'autre*** they're both (just) as bad as each other.

e *sauce, plat* to season, add seasoning *ou* spice to. **~ le goût d'un mets avec des épices** to pep up *ou* bring out the flavour of a dish with spice *ou* by adding spice; **ce plat aurait pu être un peu plus relevé** this dish could have done with a bit more seasoning; (*fig*) **mettre des touches de couleurs claires pour ~ un tableau un peu terne** to add dabs of light colour to brighten *ou* liven up a rather dull picture; (*fig*) **bijoux qui relèvent la beauté d'une femme** jewellery that sets off *ou* enhances a woman's beauty.

f (*relayer*) *sentinelle* to relieve, take over from. **à quelle heure viendra-t-on me ~?** when will I be relieved?, when is someone coming to take over from me?; **~ la garde** to change the guard.

g (*remarquer*) *faute* to pick out, find; *empreintes, faits* to find, discover. (*Jur*) **les charges relevées contre l'accusé** the charges laid against the accused.

h (*inscrire*) *adresse, renseignement* to take down, note (down); *notes* to take down; *plan* to copy out, sketch; (*Naut*) *point* to plot; *compteur, électricité* to read. **j'ai fait ~ le nom des témoins** I had the name of the witnesses noted (down) *ou* taken down; **~ une cote** to plot an altitude; *[proxénète]* **~ les compteurs**‡ to collect the takings.

i *injure, calomnie* to react to, reply to; *défi* to accept, take up, answer. **je n'ai pas relevé cette insinuation** I ignored this insinuation, I did not react *ou* reply to this insinuation; **il a dit un gros mot mais je n'ai pas relevé** he said a rude word but I didn't react *ou* I ignored it; **~ le gant** to take up the gauntlet.

j (*ramasser*) *copies, cahiers* to collect (in), take in; (††) *mouchoir, gerbe* to pick up.

k **~ qn de qch** to release sb from sth; **je te relève de ta promesse** I release you from your promise; **~ un fonctionnaire de ses fonctions** to relieve an official of his duties.

2 **relever de** vt indir a (*se rétablir*) **~ de maladie** to recover from *ou* get over an illness, get back on one's feet (after an illness); **~ de couches** to recover from *ou* get over one's confinement.

b (*être du ressort de*) to be a matter for, be the concern of; (*être sous la tutelle de*) to come under. **cela relève de la Sécurité sociale** that is a matter for *ou* the concern of the Social Security; **cela relève de la théologie** that is a matter for the theologians, that comes *ou* falls within the province of theology; **ce service relève du ministère de l'Intérieur** this service comes under the Home Office; **cette affaire ne relève pas de ma compétence** this matter does not come within my remit; **ça relève de l'imagination la plus fantaisiste** that is a product of the wildest imagination.

3 vi (*remonter*) *[vêtement]* to pull up, go up. **jupe qui relève par devant** skirt that rides up at the front.

4 **se relever** vpr a (*se remettre debout*) to stand *ou* get up (again), get back (on)to one's feet (again). **le boxeur se releva** the boxer got up again *ou* got back to his feet *ou* picked himself up; **l'arbitre a fait (se) ~ les joueurs** the referee made the players get up.

b (*sortir du lit*) to get up; (*ressortir du lit*) to get up again. (*lit, euph*) **se ~ la nuit** to get up in the night; **il m'a fait (me) ~ pour que je lui apporte à boire** he made me get up to fetch him a drink.

c (*remonter*) *[col]* to turn up, be turned up; *[strapontin]* to tip up, fold away; *[couvercle, tête de lit]* to lift up. **ses lèvres se relevaient dans un sourire** his mouth turned up in a smile; **est-ce que cette fenêtre se relève?** does this window go up?; **à l'heure où tous les stores de magasins se relèvent** when all the shop-blinds are going up.

d (*se remettre de*) **se ~ de** *deuil, chagrin, honte* to recover from, get over; **se ~ de ses ruines/cendres** to rise from its ruins/ashes.

releveur [ʀəl(ə)vœʀ] 1 adj m: **muscle ~** levator (muscle). 2 nm a (*Anat*) levator. b *[compteur]* meter reader, meter man*. **~ du gaz** gas meter reader.

relief [ʀəljɛf] nm a (*Géog*) relief. **avoir un ~ accidenté** to be hilly; **région de peu de ~** fairly flat region; **le ~ sous-marin** the relief of the sea bed.

b (*saillies*) *[visage]* contours; *[médaille]* relief, embossed *ou* raised design; (*Art*) relief. **la pierre ne présentait aucun ~** the stone was quite smooth.

c (*profondeur, contraste*) *[dessin]* relief, depth; *[style]* relief. **portrait/photographie qui a beaucoup de ~** portrait/photograph which has plenty of relief *ou* depth; **~ acoustique** *ou* **sonore** depth of sound; **personnage qui manque de ~** rather flat *ou* uninteresting character; **votre dissertation manque de ~** your essay is lacking in relief *ou* is rather flat.

d **en ~** *motif* in relief, raised; *caractères* raised, embossed; *photographie, cinéma* three-dimensional, 3-D*, stereoscopic; **l'impression est en ~** the printing stands out in relief; **carte en ~** relief map; **mettre en ~** *intelligence* to bring out; *beauté, qualités* to set *ou* show off, enhance, accentuate; *idée* to bring out, accentuate; **l'éclairage mettait en ~ les imperfections de son visage** the lighting brought out *ou* accentuated *ou* showed off the imperfections of her face; **je tiens à mettre ce point en ~** I wish to underline *ou* stress *ou* emphasize this point; **il essayait de se mettre en ~ en monopolisant la conversation** he was trying to draw attention to himself *ou* to get himself noticed by monopolizing the conversation.

e **~s** (*littér: d'un repas*) remains, left-overs; (*littér*) **les ~s de sa gloire** the remnants of his glory.

relier [ʀəlje] 7 vt a *points, mots* to join *ou* link up *ou* together; (*Élec*) to connect (up); *villes* to link (up); *idées* to link (up *ou* together); *faits* to connect (together), link (up *ou* together). **~ deux choses entre elles** to link *ou* join up two things, link *ou* join two things together; **des vols fréquents relient Paris à New York** frequent flights link *ou* connect Paris and *ou* with New York; **nous sommes reliés au studio par voiture-radio** we have a radio-car link to the studio; (*Téléc*) **nous sommes reliés à Paris par l'automatique** we are linked to Paris by the automatic dialling system; **ce verbe est relié à son complément par une préposition** this verb is linked to its complement by a preposition; **~ le passé au présent** to link the past to the present, link the past and the present (together).

b *livre* to bind; *tonneau* to hoop. **livre relié** bound volume, hardback (book); **livre relié (en) cuir** leather-bound book, book bound in leather.

relieur, -ieuse [ʀəljœʀ, jøz] nm,f (book)binder.

religieusement [ʀ(ə)liʒjøzmɑ̃] adv (*Rel, fig*) religiously; *écouter* religiously, reverently; *tenir sa parole* scrupulously, religiously. **vivre ~** to lead a religious life.

religieux, -ieuse [ʀ(ə)liʒjø, jøz] 1 adj a (*Rel*) *édifice, secte, cérémonie, opinion* religious; *art* sacred; *école, mariage, musique* church (*épith*); *vie, ordres, personne* religious. **l'habit ~** the monk's (*ou* nun's) habit. b (*fig*) *respect, soin* religious; *silence* religious, reverent; *voir* **mante.** 2 nm (*gén*) religious figure; (*moine*) monk, friar. 3 **religieuse** nf a (*nonne*) nun. b (*Culin*) iced (*Brit*) *ou* frosted (*US*) cream puff (*made with choux pastry*).

religion [ʀ(ə)liʒjɔ̃] nf a (*ensemble de croyances*) **la ~** religion. b (*culte*) (*Rel*) religion, (religious) faith; (*fig*) religion. **la ~ musulmane** the Islamic religion *ou* faith; **la ~ réformée** Calvinism; **se faire une ~ de qch** to make a religion of sth; **elle a la ~ de la propreté** cleanliness is a religion with her. c (*foi*) (religious) faith. **sa ~ est profonde** he (*ou* she) is a person of great (religious) faith; (*frm*) **avoir de la ~** to be religious. d (*vie monastique*) monastic life. **elle est entrée en ~** she has taken her vows, she has become a nun.

religiosité [ʀ(ə)liʒjozite] nf religiosity.

reliquaire [ʀəlikɛʀ] nm reliquary.

reliquat [ʀəlika] nm *[dette]* remainder, outstanding amount *ou* balance; *[compte]* balance; *[somme]* remainder. **il subsiste un ~ très important/un petit ~** there's a very large/a small amount left (over) *ou* remaining; **arrangez-vous pour qu'il n'y ait pas de ~** work it so that there is nothing left over.

relique [ʀəlik] nf (*Rel, fig*) relic. **garder** *ou* **conserver qch comme une ~** to treasure sth.

relire [ʀ(ə)liʀ] 43 vt *roman* to read again, reread; *manuscrit* to read through again, read over (again), reread. **je n'arrive pas à me ~** I can't manage to reread *ou* to read back what I've written.

reliure [ʀəljyʀ] nf (*couverture*) binding; (*art, action*) (book)binding. **~ pleine** full binding; **donner un livre à la ~** to send a book for binding *ou* to the binder('s).

relogement [ʀ(ə)lɔʒmɑ̃] nm rehousing.

reloger [ʀ(ə)lɔʒe] 3 vt to rehouse.

relouer [ʀəlwe] 1 vt *[locataire]* to rent again; *[propriétaire]* to relet (*Brit*), rent out again. **cette année je reloue dans le Midi** I'm renting a place in the South of France again this year.

reluire [ʀ(ə)lɥiʀ] 38 vi *[meuble, chaussures]* to shine, gleam; *[métal, carrosserie]* (*au soleil*) to gleam, shine; (*sous la pluie*) to glisten. **faire ~ qch** to polish *ou* shine sth up, make sth shine; *voir* **brosse.**

reluisant, e [ʀ(ə)lɥizɑ̃, ɑ̃t] adj a *meubles, parquet, cuivres* shining, shiny, gleaming. **~ de graisse** shiny with grease; **~ de pluie** glistening in the rain; **~ de propreté** *pièce* spotless. b (*fig iro*) **peu ~** *avenir, résultat, situation* far from brilliant (*attrib*); *personne* despicable.

reluquer* [ʀ(ə)lyke] 1 vt *femme* to eye (up)*, ogle⁑; *passant* to eye, squint at*; *objet, poste* to have one's eye on.

rem [ʀɛm] nm rem.

remâcher [ʀ(ə)mɑʃe] 1 vt *[ruminant]* to ruminate; *[personne] passé, soucis, échec* to ruminate over *ou* on, chew over, brood on *ou* over; *colère* to nurse.

remailler [ʀ(ə)mɑje] 1 vt = **remmailler.**

remake [ʀimɛk] nm (*Ciné*) remake; *[livre, spectacle]* new version.

rémanence [ʀemanɑ̃s] nf (*Phys*) remanence. **~ des images visuelles** after-imagery.

rémanent, e [ʀemanɑ̃, ɑ̃t] adj *magnétisme* residual; *pesticide* persistent. **image ~e** after-image.

remanger [ʀ(ə)mɑ̃ʒe] 3 1 vt (*manger de nouveau*) to have again; (*reprendre*) to have *ou* eat some more. **on a remangé du poulet aujourd'hui** we had chicken again today; **j'en remangerais bien** I'd like to have that again, I could eat that again. 2 vi to eat again, have something to eat again.

remaniement [ʀ(ə)manimɑ̃] nm (*voir* **remanier**) revision; reshaping, recasting; modification, reorganization, amendment; reshuffle. (*Pol*) **~ ministériel** cabinet reshuffle; **apporter un ~ à** to revise; to reshape, recast; to modify, reorganize; to amend; to reshuffle.

remanier [ʀ(ə)manje] 7 vt *roman, discours* to revise, reshape, recast; *encyclopédie* to revise; *programme* to modify, reorganize; *plan, constitution* to revise, amend; *cabinet, ministère* to reshuffle.

remaquiller [ʀ(ə)makije] 1 1 vt: **~ qn** to make sb up again. 2 **se remaquiller** vpr (*complètement*) to make o.s. up again, redo one's face; (*rapidement*) to touch up one's make-up.

remarcher [ʀ(ə)maʀʃe] 1 vi *[personne]* to walk again; *[appareil]* to work again.

remariage [ʀ(ə)maʀjaʒ] nm second marriage, remarriage.

remarier [ʀ(ə)maʀje] 7 1 vt: **~ sa fille** to remarry one's daughter; **il cherche à ~ sa fille** he is trying to find another husband for his daughter. 2 **se remarier** vpr to remarry, marry again.

remarquable [ʀ(ə)maʀkabl] adj *personne, exploit, réussite* remarkable, outstanding; *événement, fait* striking, noteworthy, remarkable. **il est ~ par sa taille** he is notable for *ou* he stands out because of his height; **elle est ~ par son intelligence** she is outstandingly intelligent.

remarquablement [ʀ(ə)maʀkabləmɑ̃] adv *beau, doué* remarkably, outstandingly; *réussir, jouer* remarkably *ou* outstandingly well.

remarque [ʀ(ə)maʀk] nf a (*observation*) remark, comment; (*critique*) critical remark; (*annotation*) note. **il m'en a fait la ~** he remarked *ou* commented on it to me, he made *ou* passed a remark *ou* made a comment about it to me; **je m'en suis moi-même fait la ~** that occurred to me as well, I thought that myself; **faire une ~ à qn** to make a critical remark to sb, criticize sb; **il m'a fait des ~s sur ma tenue** he passed comment *ou* he remarked on the way I was dressed. b (†, *littér*) **digne de ~** worthy of note, noteworthy.

remarqué, e [ʀ(ə)maʀke] (ptp de **remarquer**) adj *entrée, absence* conspicuous. **il a fait une intervention très ~e** his speech attracted a lot of attention.

remarquer [ʀ(ə)maʀke] 1 vt a (*apercevoir*) to notice. **je l'ai remarqué dans la foule** I caught sight of *ou* noticed him in the crowd; **avec ce chapeau, comment ne pas la ~!** with that hat on, how can you fail to notice her?; **l'impresario avait remarqué la jeune actrice lors d'une audition** the impresario had noticed the young actress at an audition, the young actress had come to the notice of the impresario at an audition; **il entra sans être remarqué** *ou* **sans se faire ~** he came in unnoticed *ou* without being noticed *ou* without drawing attention to himself; **cette tache se remarque beaucoup/à peine** this stain is quite/hardly noticeable, this stain shows badly/hardly shows; **sa jalousie se remarque beaucoup** his jealousy is very obvious *ou* is very noticeable; **ça ne se remarquera pas** no one will notice it; **c'est une femme qui cherche à/aime se faire ~** she's a woman who tries/likes to be noticed *ou* to draw attention to herself; **je remarque que vous avez une cravate** I notice *ou* see *ou* note that you are wearing a tie; **je remarque que vous ne vous êtes pas excusé** I note that you did not apologize; **ça finirait par se ~** people would start to notice *ou* start noticing.
b (*faire une remarque*) to remark, observe. **tu es sot, remarqua son frère** you're stupid, his brother remarked *ou* observed; **il remarqua qu'il faisait froid** he remarked *ou* commented *ou* observed that it was cold; **remarquez (bien) que je n'en sais rien** mark you *ou* mind you I don't know; **ça m'est tout à fait égal, remarque!** I couldn't care less, mark you! *ou* mind you!* *ou* I can tell you!
c **faire ~** *détail, erreur* to point out, draw attention to; **il me fit ~ qu'il faisait nuit/qu'il était tard** he pointed out to me that *ou* he drew my attention to the fact that it was dark/late; **il me fit ~ qu'il était d'accord avec moi** he pointed out (to me) that he agreed with me; **je te ferai seulement ~ que tu n'as pas de preuves** I should just like to point out (to you) that you have no proof.
d (*marquer de nouveau*) to remark, mark again.

remballage [ʀɑ̃balaʒ] nm (*voir* **remballer**) packing (up) again; rewrapping.

remballer [ʀɑ̃bale] 1 vt to pack (up) again; (*dans du papier*) to rewrap. **remballe ta marchandise!⁑** you can clear off and take that stuff with you!⁑; **tu n'as qu'à ~ tes commentaires!⁑** you know what you can do with your remarks!*, you can stuff your remarks!⁑ (*Brit*); **on s'est fait ~⁑** we were sent packing*, we were told to get lost⁑.

rembarquement [ʀɑ̃baʀkəmɑ̃] nm (*voir* **rembarquer**) re-embarkation; reloading.

rembarquer [ʀɑ̃baʀke] 1 1 vt *passagers* to re-embark; *marchandises* to reload. 2 vi to re-embark, go back on board (ship). **faire ~ les passagers** to re-embark the passengers. 3 **se rembarquer** vpr to re-embark, go back on board (ship).

rembarrer* [ʀɑ̃bɑʀe] 1 vt: **~ qn** (*recevoir avec froideur*) to brush sb aside, rebuff sb; (*remettre à sa place*) to put sb in his place, take sb down a peg or two; **on s'est fait ~⁑** we were sent packing*, we were told to get lost⁑.

remblai [ʀɑ̃blɛ] nm (*Rail, pour route*) embankment; (*Constr*) cut. **(terre de) ~** (*Rail*) ballast, remblai; (*pour route*) hard core; (*Constr*) backfill; **travaux de ~** (*Rail, pour route*) embankment work; (*Constr*) cutting work; (*Aut*) **~s récents** soft verges.

remblaver [ʀɑ̃blave] 1 vt (*Agr*) to resow.

remblayage [ʀɑ̃blɛjaʒ] nm (*voir* **remblayer**) banking up; filling in *ou* up.

remblayer [ʀɑ̃bleje] 8 vt *route, voie ferrée* to bank up; *fossé* to fill in *ou* up.

rembobiner [ʀɑ̃bɔbine] 1 vt *film, bande magnétique* to rewind, wind back; *fil* to rewind, wind up again.

remboîtage [ʀɑ̃bwataʒ] nm, **remboîtement** [ʀɑ̃bwatmɑ̃] nm (*voir* **remboîter**) fitting together; putting back; reassembly; recasing.

remboîter [ʀɑ̃bwate] 1 vt *tuyaux* to fit together again, reassemble; *os* to put back into place; *livre* to recase.

rembourrage [ʀɑ̃buʀaʒ] nm (*voir* **rembourrer**) stuffing; padding.

rembourrer [ʀɑ̃buʀe] 1 vt *fauteuil, matelas* to stuff; *vêtement* to pad. **bien rembourré** *coussin* well-filled, well-padded; *personne** well-padded; (*hum*) **mal rembourré, rembourré avec des noyaux de pêches** as hard as rock *ou* iron.

remboursable [ʀɑ̃buʀsabl] adj *billet* refundable; *emprunt* repayable.

remboursement [ʀɑ̃buʀsəmɑ̃] nm (*voir* **rembourser**) repayment; settlement; reimbursement. **obtenir le ~ de son repas** to get one's money back for one's meal, get a refund on one's meal; **envoi contre ~** cash with order.

rembourser [ʀɑ̃buʀse] 1 vt *dette* to pay back *ou* off, repay, settle (up); *emprunt* to pay back *ou* off, repay; *somme* to reimburse, repay, pay back; *créancier* to pay back *ou* off, repay, reimburse. ~ **qn de qch** to reimburse sth to sb, reimburse sb for sth, repay sb sth; ~ **qn de ses dépenses** to refund *ou* reimburse sb's expenses; ~ **la différence** to refund the difference; **je te rembourserai demain** I'll pay you back *ou* repay you tomorrow, I'll settle *ou* square up with you tomorrow; **je me suis fait ~ mon repas/mon voyage** I got my money back for my meal/journey, I got back the cost of my meal/journey, I got the cost of my meal/journey refunded; **est-ce remboursé par la Sécurité sociale?** ≃ can we get our (*ou* can I get my *etc*) money back from the NHS (*Brit*) *ou* from Medicaid (*US*)?; ~ **un billet de loterie** to refund the price of a lottery ticket; (*Théât*) **remboursez!** we want our money back! *ou* a refund!; **puisqu'il n'avait pas l'argent qu'il me devait, je me suis remboursé en prenant son manteau!** since he didn't have the money he owed me, I helped myself to his coat by way of repayment!

rembrunir (se) [ʀɑ̃bʀyniʀ] 2 vpr *[visage, traits]* to darken, cloud (over); *[personne]* to bristle, stiffen; *[ciel]* to become overcast, darken, cloud over. **le temps se rembrunit** it's clouding over, it's going cloudy.

rembrunissement [ʀɑ̃bʀynismɑ̃] nm (*littér*) *[visage, front]* darkening.

remède [ʀ(ə)mɛd] nm a (*Méd*) (*traitement*) remedy, cure; (*médicament*) medicine. **prescrire/prendre un ~ pour un lumbago** to give/take something *ou* some medicine for lumbago; ~ **de bonne femme** old wives' *ou* folk cure *ou* remedy; ~ **souverain/de cheval*** sovereign/drastic remedy; ~ **universel** cure-all, universal cure.

b (*fig*) remedy, cure. **porter ~ à qch** to cure sth, find a cure for sth, remedy sth; **la situation est sans ~** there is no remedy for the situation, the situation cannot be remedied *ou* is beyond remedy; **le ~ est pire que le mal** the cure is worse than the disease, the solution is even worse than the evil it is designed to remedy; **c'est un ~ à** *ou* **contre l'amour!*** *[personne]* she's (*ou* he's) enough to put you off the opposite sex altogether!*; *[chose]* it's enough to put *ou* turn you off; *voir* **à**.

remédiable [ʀ(ə)medjabl] adj *mal* that can be remedied *ou* cured, remediable.

remédier [ʀ(ə)medje] 7 remédier à vt indir (*lit*) *maladie* to cure; (*fig*) *mal, situation* to remedy, put right; *abus* to remedy, right; *perte* to remedy, make good; *besoin* to remedy; *inconvénient* to remedy, find a remedy for; *difficulté* to find a solution for, solve.

remembrement [ʀ(ə)mɑ̃bʀəmɑ̃] nm regrouping of lands.

remembrer [ʀ(ə)mɑ̃bʀe] 1 vt *terres* to regroup; *exploitation* to regroup the lands of.

remémoration [ʀ(ə)memɔʀasjɔ̃] nf recall, recollection.

remémorer (se) [ʀ(ə)memɔʀe] 1 vpr to recall, recollect.

remerciement [ʀ(ə)mɛʀsimɑ̃] nm a ~s thanks; (*dans un livre, film etc*) acknowledgements; **avec tous mes ~s** with many thanks, with my grateful thanks; **faire ses ~s à qn** to thank sb, express one's thanks to sb. b (*action*) thanks (*pl*), thanking. **il lui fit un ~ embarrassé** he thanked him in an embarrassed way, he said an embarrassed thank you to him; **lettre de ~** thank-you letter, letter of thanks; **lire un ~ à qn** to read a message of thanks to sb.

remercier [ʀ(ə)mɛʀsje] 7 vt a (*dire merci*) to thank (*qn de ou pour qch* sb for sth, *qn d'avoir fait qch* sb for doing sth). ~ **le ciel** *ou* **Dieu** to thank God; ~ **qn par un cadeau/d'un pourboire** to thank sb with a present/with a tip, give sb a present/a tip by way of thanks; **je ne sais comment vous ~** I can't thank you enough, I don't know how to thank you; **il me remercia d'un sourire** he thanked me with a smile, he smiled his thanks; **je vous remercie** (I) thank you; **tu peux me ~!** you've got me to thank for that!; (*iro*) **je te remercie de tes conseils** thanks for the advice (*iro*), I can do without your advice (thank you) (*iro*).

b (*refuser poliment*) **vous voulez boire? — je vous remercie** would you like a drink? — no thank you.

c (*euph: renvoyer*) *employé* to dismiss (*from his job*).

remettant [ʀ(ə)metɑ̃] nm (*Fin*) remitter.

remettre [ʀ(ə)mɛtʀ] 56 1 vt a (*replacer*) *objet* to put back, replace (*dans* in(to), *sur* on); *os luxé* to put back in place. ~ **un enfant au lit** to put a child back (in)to bed; ~ **un enfant à l'école** to send a child back to school; ~ **qch à cuire** to put sth on to cook again; ~ **debout** *enfant* to stand back on his feet; *objet* to stand up again; ~ **qch droit** to put *ou* set sth straight again; ~ **un bouton à une veste** to sew *ou* put a button back on a jacket; **il a remis l'étagère/la porte qu'il avait enlevée** he put the shelf back up/rehung the door that he had taken down; **je ne veux plus ~ les pieds ici!** I never want to set foot in here again!; ~ **qn sur la bonne voie** to put sb back on the right track; (*fig: rembarrer*) ~ **qn à sa place** to take sb down a peg or two, put sb in his place; ~ **un enfant insolent à sa place** to put an insolent child in his place; (*fig: recommencer*) ~ **le couvert*** to go at it* again (straight away).

b (*porter de nouveau*) *vêtement, chapeau* to put back on, put on again. **j'ai remis mon manteau d'hiver** I'm wearing my winter coat again.

c (*replacer dans une situation*) ~ **un appareil en marche** to restart a machine, start a machine (up) again, set a machine going again; ~ **le moteur en marche** to start up the engine again; ~ **une coutume en usage** to revive a custom; ~ **en question** *institution, autorité* to (call into) question, challenge; *projet, accord* to cast doubt over, throw back into question; **tout est remis en question à cause du mauvais temps** everything's in the balance again because of the bad weather, the bad weather throws the whole thing back into question; ~ **une pendule à l'heure** to put (*Brit*) *ou* set a clock right; (*fig*) ~ **les pendules à l'heure*** to set the record straight; ~ **qch à neuf** to make sth as good as new again; ~ **qch en état** to repair *ou* mend sth; **le repos l'a remise (sur pied)** the rest has set her back on her feet; ~ **de l'ordre dans qch** (*ranger*) to tidy sth up, sort sth out; (*classer*) to sort sth out.

d (*donner*) *lettre, paquet* to hand over, deliver; *clefs* to hand in *ou* over, give in, return; *récompense* to present; *devoir* to hand in, give in; *rançon* to hand over; *démission* to hand in, give in, tender (*à* to). **il s'est fait ~ les clefs par la concierge** he got the keys from the concierge, he had the keys given to him by the concierge; ~ **un enfant à ses parents** to return a child to his parents; ~ **un criminel à la justice** to hand a criminal over to the law; ~ **à qn un porte-monnaie volé** to hand *ou* give back *ou* return a stolen purse to sb.

e (*ajourner*) *réunion* to put off, postpone (*à* until), put back (*Brit*) (*à* to); (*Jur*) to adjourn (*à* until); *décision* to put off, postpone, defer (*à* until); *date* to put back (*Brit*), postpone (*à* to). **une visite qui ne peut se ~ (à plus tard)** a visit that can't be postponed *ou* put off; ~ **un rendez-vous à jeudi/au 8** to put off *ou* postpone an appointment till Thursday/the 8th; (*Prov*) **il ne faut jamais ~ à demain** *ou* **au lendemain ce qu'on peut faire le jour même** procrastination is the thief of time, never put off till tomorrow what you can do today.

f (*se rappeler*) to remember. **je vous remets très bien** I remember you very well; **je ne (me) le remets pas** I can't place him, I don't remember him; (*rappeler*) ~ **qch en esprit** *ou* **en mémoire à qn** to remind sb of sth, recall sth to sb; **ce livre m'a remis ces événements en mémoire** this book reminded me of these events *ou* brought these events to mind.

g (*rajouter*) *vinaigre, sel* to add more, put in (some) more; *verre, coussin* to add; *maquillage* to put on (some) more. **j'ai froid, je vais ~ un tricot** I'm cold — I'll go and put another jersey on; ~ **de l'huile dans le moteur** to top up the engine with oil; **en remettant un peu d'argent, vous pourriez avoir le grand modèle** if you put a little more (money) to it you could have the large size; **il faut ~ de l'argent sur le compte, nous sommes débiteurs** we'll have to put some money into the account as we're overdrawn; **en ~*** to overdo it, lay it on a bit thick*.

h *radio, chauffage* to put *ou* turn *ou* switch on again. **il y a eu une coupure mais le courant a été remis à midi** there was a power cut but the electricity came back on again *ou* was put back on again at midday; ~ **le contact** to turn the ignition on again.

i (*faire grâce de*) *dette, peine* to remit; *péché* to forgive, pardon, remit. ~ **une dette à qn** to remit sb's debt, let sb off a debt; ~ **une peine à un condamné** to remit a prisoner's sentence.

j (*confier*) ~ **son sort/sa vie entre les mains de qn** to put one's fate/life into sb's hands; ~ **son âme à Dieu** to commit one's soul to God *ou* into God's keeping.

k ~ **ça***: (*démarches*) **dire qu'il va falloir ~ ça!** to think that we'll have to go through all that again! *ou* through a repeat performance!*; **quand est-ce qu'on remet ça?** when will the next time be?; **on remet ça?** (*partie de cartes*) shall we have another game?; (*au café*) shall we have another drink? *ou* round?; (*travail*) let's get back to it*, let's get down to it again, let's get going again*; **garçon remettez-nous ça!** (the) same again please!*; (*bruit, commentaires*) **les voilà qui remettent ça!** here *ou* there they go again!*, they're at it again!*; **tu ne vas pas ~ ça avec tes critiques** no more of your criticism(s); **le gouvernement va ~ ça avec les économies d'énergie** the government is going to get going on energy saving again*.

2 **se remettre** vpr a (*recouvrer la santé*) to recover, get better, pick up; (*psychologiquement*) to cheer up. **se ~ d'une maladie/d'un accident** to recover from *ou* get over an illness/an accident; **remettez-vous!** pull yourself together!; **elle ne s'en remettra pas** she won't get over it.

b (*recommencer*) **se ~ à (faire) qch** to start (doing) sth again; **se ~ à fumer** to take up *ou* start smoking again; **il s'est remis au tennis/au latin** he has taken up tennis/Latin again; **après son départ il se remit à travailler** *ou* **au travail** after she had gone he started working again *ou* went back *ou* got back to work; **il se remet à faire froid** the weather *ou* it is getting *ou* turning cold again; **le temps s'est remis au beau** the weather has turned fine again, the weather has picked up again; **se ~ en selle** to remount, get back on one's horse; **se ~ debout** to get back to one's feet, get (back) up again, stand up again.

c (*se confier*) **se ~ entre les mains de qn** to put o.s. in sb's hands; **je m'en remets à vous** I'll leave it (up) to you, I'll leave the matter in your hands; **s'en ~ à la décision de qn** to leave it to sb to decide; **s'en ~ à la discrétion de qn** to leave it to sb's discretion.

d (*se réconcilier*) **se ~ avec qn** to make it up with sb, make *ou* patch up one's differences with sb; **ils se sont remis ensemble** they've come back *ou* they are back together again.

remeubler [ʀ(ə)mœble] 1 1 vt to refurnish. 2 **se remeubler** vpr to refurnish one's house, get new furniture.

rémige [ʀemiʒ] nf remix.

remilitarisation [ʀ(ə)militaʀizasjɔ̃] nf remilitarization.

remilitariser [ʀ(ə)militaʀize] [1] vt to remilitarize.

réminiscence [ʀeminisɑ̃s] nf (*faculté mentale: Philos, Psych*) reminiscence; (*souvenir*) reminiscence, vague recollection. **sa conversation était truffée de ~s littéraires** literary influences were constantly in evidence in his conversation; **mon latin est bien rouillé, mais j'ai encore quelques ~s** my Latin is very rusty but I've retained *ou* I still recollect a little; **on trouve des ~s de Rabelais dans l'œuvre de cet auteur** there are echoes of Rabelais in this author's work, parts of this author's work are reminiscent of Rabelais.

remisage [ʀ(ə)mizaʒ] nm *[outil, voiture]* putting away.

remise [ʀ(ə)miz] 1 nf a (*livraison*) *[lettre, paquet]* delivery; *[clefs]* handing over; *[récompense]* presentation; *[devoir]* handing in; *[rançon]* handing over, hand-over. (*Jur*) ~ **de parts** transfer *ou* conveyance of legacy.

b (*grâce*) *[péchés]* remission, forgiveness, pardon; *[peine]* remission, reduction (*de* of, in). **le condamné a bénéficié d'une importante ~ de peine** the prisoner was granted a large reduction in his sentence.

c (*Comm: rabais*) discount, reduction. **ils font une ~ de 5% sur les livres scolaires** they're giving *ou* allowing (a) 5% discount *ou* reduction on school books; (*Fin*) ~ **de dette** condonation, remission of a debt.

d (*local: pour outils, véhicules*) shed.

e (*ajournement*) *[réunion]* postponement, deferment, putting off *ou* back (*Brit*); *[décision]* putting off. ~ **à quinzaine d'un débat** postponement of a debate for a fortnight.

2 comp ►**remise en cause** calling into question ►**remise en état** *[machine]* repair(ing); *[tableau, meuble ancien]* restoration ►**remise en jeu** (*Sport*) (*Hockey*) face-off; (*Ftbl*) throw-in ►**remise en jeu (à la touche)** (*Rugby*) throw-in ►**remise à jour** updating, bringing up to date ►**remise en marche** restarting, starting (up) again ►**remise à neuf** restoration ►**remise en ordre** reordering, sorting out ►**remise en place** *[os, étagère]* putting back in place ►**remise en question** calling into question ►**remise en touche** (*Ftbl*) = **remise en jeu**.

remiser [ʀ(ə)mize] [1] 1 vt a *voiture, outil, valise* to put away. b (**: rembarrer*) *personne* to send sb packing*. 2 vi (*Jeux*) to make another bet, bet again. 3 **se remiser** vpr *[gibier]* to take cover.

rémissible [ʀemisibl] adj remissible.

rémission [ʀemisjɔ̃] nf a *[péchés]* remission, forgiveness; (*Jur*) remission. b (*Méd*) *[maladie]* remission; *[douleur]* subsidence, abatement; *[fièvre]* subsidence, lowering, abatement; (*fig littér: dans la tempête, le travail*) lull. c **sans ~** *travailler, torturer, poursuivre* unremittingly, relentlessly; *payer* without fail; *mal, maladie* irremediable; **si tu recommences tu seras puni sans ~** if you do it again you'll be punished without fail.

remmailler [ʀɑ̃mɑje] [1] vt *tricot, bas* to darn; *filet* to mend.

remmailleuse [ʀɑ̃mɑjøz] nf darner.

remmailloter [ʀɑ̃mɑjɔte] [1] vt *bébé* to change.

remmancher [ʀɑ̃mɑ̃ʃe] [1] vt *couteau, balai* (*remettre le manche*) to put the handle back on; (*remplacer le manche*) to put a new handle on.

remmener [ʀɑ̃m(ə)ne] [5] vt to take back, bring back. ~ **qn chez lui** to take sb back home; ~ **qn à pied** to walk sb back; ~ **qn en voiture** to give sb a lift back, drive sb back.

remodelage [ʀ(ə)mɔd(ə)laʒ] nm (*voir* **remodeler**) remodelling; replanning; reorganization, restructuring.

remodeler [ʀ(ə)mɔd(ə)le] [5] vt *visage* to remodel; *ville* to remodel, replan; *profession, organisation* to reorganize, restructure.

rémois, e [ʀemwa, waz] 1 adj of *ou* from Rheims. 2 nm,f: **R~(e)** inhabitant *ou* native of Rheims.

remontage [ʀ(ə)mɔ̃taʒ] nm *[montre]* rewinding, winding up; *[machine, meuble]* reassembly, putting back together; *[tuyau]* putting back.

remontant, e [ʀ(ə)mɔ̃tɑ̃, ɑ̃t] 1 adj a *boisson* invigorating, fortifying. b (*Horticulture*) *rosier* reflowering, remontant (SPÉC); *fraisier, framboisier* double-cropping *ou* -fruiting. **rosier fortement/faiblement ~** rosebush which has a strong/poor second flowering. 2 nm tonic, pick-me-up*.

remonte [ʀ(ə)mɔ̃t] nf a *[bateau]* sailing upstream, ascent; *[poissons]* run. b (*Équitation*) (*fourniture de chevaux*) remount; (*service*) remount department.

remontée [ʀ(ə)mɔ̃te] nf *[côte]* ascent, climbing; *[rivière]* ascent; *[eaux]* rising. **la ~ des mineurs par l'ascenseur** bringing miners up by lift; **il ne faut pas que la ~ du plongeur soit trop rapide** the diver must not go back up *ou* rise too quickly; **la ~ de l'or à la Bourse** the rise in the price *ou* value of gold on the Stock Exchange; **faire une (belle) ~** to catch up the lost ground (well), make a (good) recovery; **faire une ~ spectaculaire (de la 30e à la 2e place)** to make a spectacular recovery (from 30th to 2nd place); (*Sport*) ~ **mécanique** ski lift.

remonte-pente, pl **remonte-pentes** [ʀ(ə)mɔ̃tpɑ̃t] nm ski tow.

remonter [ʀ(ə)mɔ̃te] [1] 1 vi (*avec aux être*) a (*monter à nouveau*) to go *ou* come back up. **il remonta à pied** he walked back up; **remonte me voir** come back up and see me; **je remonte demain à Paris (en voiture)** I'm driving back up to Paris tomorrow; **il remonta sur la table** he climbed back (up) onto the table; ~ **sur le trône** to come back *ou* return to the throne; (*Théât*) ~ **sur les planches** to go back on the stage *ou* the boards.

b (*dans un moyen de transport*) ~ **en voiture** to get back into one's car, get into one's car again; ~ **à cheval** (*se remettre en selle*) to remount (one's horse), get back on(to) one's horse; (*se remettre à faire du cheval*) to take up riding again; (*Naut*) ~ **à bord** to go back on board (ship).

c (*s'élever de nouveau*) *[marée]* to come in again; *[prix, température, baromètre]* to rise again, go up again; *[colline, route]* to go up again, rise again. **la mer remonte** the tide is coming in again; **la fièvre remonte** his temperature is rising *ou* going up again, the fever is getting worse again; **les bénéfices ont remonté au dernier trimestre** profits were up again in the last quarter; **les prix ont remonté en flèche** prices shot up *ou* rocketed again; (*fig*) **ses actions remontent** things are looking up for him (again), his fortunes are picking up (again); **il remonte dans mon estime** my opinion of him is growing again, he is redeeming himself in my eyes; **il est remonté de la 7e à la 3e place** he has come up *ou* recovered from 7th to 3rd place.

d *[vêtement]* to go up, pull up. **sa robe remonte sur le côté** her dress goes *ou* pulls up at the side *ou* is higher on one side; **sa jupe remonte quand elle s'assoit** her skirt rides up *ou* pulls up *ou* goes up when she sits down.

e (*réapparaître*) to come back. **les souvenirs qui remontent à ma mémoire** memories which come back to me *ou* to my mind; ~ **à la surface** to come back up to the surface, resurface; **sous-marin qui remonte en surface** submarine which is coming back up to the surface *ou* which is resurfacing; **une mauvaise odeur remontait de l'égout** a bad smell was coming *ou* wafting up out of the drain.

f (*retourner*) to return, go back. ~ **à la source/cause** to go back *ou* return to the source/cause; ~ **de l'effet à la cause** to go back from the effect to the cause; (*Naut*) ~ **au vent** *ou* **dans le vent** to tack close to the wind; **il faut ~ plus haut** *ou* **plus loin pour comprendre l'affaire** you must go *ou* look further back to understand this business; ~ **jusqu'au coupable** to trace right back to the guilty person; **aussi loin que remontent ses souvenirs** as far back as he can remember; ~ **dans le temps** to go back in time; **cette histoire remonte à une époque reculée/à plusieurs années** this story dates back *ou* goes back a very long time/several years; (*hum*) **tout cela remonte au déluge!** (*c'est vieux comme le monde*) all that's as old as the hills!; (*c'est passé depuis longtemps*) all that was ages ago! *ou* donkey's years ago!* (*Brit hum*); **on ne va pas ~ au déluge!** we're not going back over ancient history again!; **la famille remonte aux croisades** the family goes *ou* dates back to the time of the Crusades.

2 vt (*avec aux avoir*) a *étage, côte, marche* to go *ou* climb back up; *rue* to go *ou* come back up. ~ **l'escalier en courant** to rush *ou* run back upstairs; ~ **la rue à pas lents** to walk slowly (back) up the street; ~ **le courant/une rivière** (*à la nage*) to swim (back) upstream/up a river; (*en barque*) to sail *ou* row (back) upstream/up a river; (*fig*) ~ **le courant** *ou* **la pente** to begin to get back on one's feet again *ou* pick up again.

b (*rattraper*) *adversaire* to catch up with. ~ **la procession** to move up towards *ou* work one's way towards the front of the procession; **se faire ~ par un adversaire** to let o.s. be caught up by an opponent; **il a 15 points/places à ~ pour être 2e** he has 15 marks/places to catch up in order to be 2nd.

c (*relever*) *mur* to raise, heighten; *tableau, étagère* to raise, put higher up; *vitre* (*en poussant*) to push up; (*avec manivelle*) to wind up; *store* to roll up, raise; *pantalon, manche* to pull up; (*en roulant*) to roll up; (*d'une saccade*) to hitch up; *chaussettes* to pull up; *col* to turn up; *jupe* to pick up, raise; (*fig*) *mauvaise note* to put up, raise. (*fig*) ~ **les bretelles à qn*** to give sb a piece of one's mind* *ou* a dressing-down; **il s'est fait ~ les bretelles par le patron*** the boss gave him a real tongue-lashing *ou* dressing-down.

d (*reporter*) to take *ou* bring back up. ~ **une malle au grenier** to take *ou* carry a trunk back up to the attic.

e *montre, mécanisme* to wind up. (*fig*) **il est remonté** (*dynamique*) he's got plenty of get-up-and-go*, he's a real live wire*; (*en colère*) he's in a foul mood *ou* temper; **il est remonté à bloc aujourd'hui** he's on top form today; **être remonté contre qn*** to be livid* *ou* mad* *ou* furious with sb; **être remonté contre qch*** to be wound up about sth*.

f (*réinstaller*) *machine, moteur, meuble* to put together again, put back together (again), reassemble; *robinet, tuyau* to put back. **ils ont remonté une usine à Lyon** they have set up *ou* built a factory in Lyons again; **il a eu du mal à ~ les roues de sa bicyclette** he had a job putting *ou* getting the wheels back on his bicycle.

g (*réassortir*) *garde-robe* to renew, replenish; *magasin* to restock. **mon père nous a remontés en vaisselle** my father has given us a whole new stock of crockery; ~ **son ménage** (*meubles*) to buy all new furniture, refurnish one's house; (*linge*) to buy all new linen.

h (*remettre en état*) *personne* (*physiquement*) to set *ou* buck* up (again); (*moralement*) to cheer *ou* buck* up (again); *entreprise* to put *ou* set back on its feet; *mur en ruines* to rebuild. ~ **le moral de qn** to raise sb's spirits, cheer *ou* buck* sb up; **le nouveau directeur a bien remonté cette firme** the new manager has really got this firm back on its feet; **ce contrat remonterait bien mes affaires** this contract would really give a boost to business for me.

i (*Théât*) *pièce* to restage, put on again.

3 **se remonter** vpr **a** **se ~ en boîtes de conserves** to get in (further) stocks of canned food, replenish one's stocks of canned food; **se ~ en linge** to build up one's stock of linen again; **se ~ en chaussures** to get some new shoes; **tu as besoin de te ~ en chemises** you need a few new shirts.

b (*physiquement*) to buck* *ou* set o.s. up (again). (*moralement*) **se ~ (le moral)** to raise (one's spirits), cheer *ou* buck* o.s. up.

remontoir [R(ə)mɔ̃twaR] nm *[montre]* winder; *[jouet, horloge]* winding mechanism.

remontrance [R(ə)mɔ̃tRɑ̃s] nf **a** remonstrance, reproof, reprimand, admonition (*frm*). **faire des ~s à qn (au sujet de qch)** to remonstrate with sb (about sth), reprove *ou* reprimand *ou* admonish (*frm*) sb (for sth). **b** (*Hist*) remonstrance.

remontrer [R(ə)mɔ̃tRe] 1 vt **a** (*montrer de nouveau*) to show again. **remontrez-moi la bleue** show me the blue one again, let me have another look at the blue one; **ne te remontre plus ici** don't show your face *ou* yourself here again.

b **en ~ à qn: dans ce domaine, il pourrait t'en ~** he could teach you a thing or two in this field; **il a voulu m'en ~, mais je l'ai remis à sa place** he wanted to prove his superiority to me *ou* to show he knew better than I but I soon put him in his place; **ce n'est pas la peine de m'en ~, je connais cela mieux que toi** don't bother trying to teach me anything – I know all that better than you, it's no use your trying to prove you know better than I – you can't teach me anything about that.

c (†, *littér*) *faute* to point out (*à* to).

remordre [R(ə)mɔRdR] 41 vt (*lit*) to bite again. (*fig*) **~ à** *peinture, sport* to take to again; *travail* to tackle again; (*fig*) **~ à l'hameçon** to rise to the bait again.

remords [R(ə)mɔR] nm remorse (*NonC*). **j'éprouve quelques ~ à l'avoir laissé seul** I am somewhat conscience-stricken *ou* I feel some remorse at having left him alone; **j'ai eu un ~ de conscience, je suis allé vérifier** I had second thoughts *ou* I thought better of it and went to check; **~ cuisants** agonies of remorse; **avoir des ~** to feel remorse, be smitten with remorse, be conscience-stricken; **n'avoir aucun ~** to have no (feeling of) remorse, feel no remorse; **je le tuerais sans (le moindre) ~** I should kill him without (the slightest) compunction *ou* remorse; **je te le donne – (c'est) sans ~?** here you are – are you sure?

remorquage [R(ə)mɔRkaʒ] nm (*voir* **remorquer**) towing; pulling, hauling; tugging.

remorque [R(ə)mɔRk] nf **a** (*véhicule*) trailer; (*câble*) towrope, towline; *voir* **camion, semi-**. **b** (*loc*) **prendre une voiture en ~** to tow a car; **"en ~"** "on tow"; (*péj*) **être à la ~ de** (*lit, fig*) to tag behind; **quand ils vont se promener ils ont toujours la belle-mère en ~** whenever they go for a walk they always have the mother-in-law in tow *ou* tagging along *ou* they always drag along the mother-in-law; *[pays]* **être à la ~ d'une grande puissance** to trail behind a great power.

remorquer [R(ə)mɔRke] 1 vt *voiture, caravane* to tow; *train* to pull, haul; *bateau, navire* to tow, tug. **je suis tombé en panne et j'ai dû me faire ~ jusqu'au village** I had a breakdown and had to get a tow *ou* get myself towed as far as the village; (*fig*) **~ toute la famille derrière soi** to have the whole family in tow, trail *ou* drag the whole family along (with one).

remorqueur [R(ə)mɔRkœR] nm (*bateau*) tug(boat).

remoudre [R(ə)mudR] 47 vt *café, poivre* to regrind, grind again.

remouiller [R(ə)muje] 1 vt **a** to wet again. **~ du linge à repasser** to (re)dampen washing ready for ironing; **se faire ~ (par la pluie)** to get wet (in the rain) again; **je viens de m'essuyer les mains, je ne veux pas me les ~** I've just dried my hands and I don't want to get them wet *ou* to wet them again. **b** (*Naut*) **~ (l'ancre)** to drop anchor again.

rémoulade [Remulad] nf remoulade, rémoulade (*dressing containing mustard and herbs*); *voir* **céleri**.

remoulage [R(ə)mulaʒ] nm **a** (*Art*) recasting. **b** (*Tech*) *[café]* regrinding; *[farine]* remilling.

remouler [R(ə)mule] 1 vt *statue* to recast.

rémouleur [RemulœR] nm (knife- *ou* scissor-)grinder.

remous [Rəmu] nm **a** *[bateau]* (back)wash (*NonC*); *[eau]* swirl, eddy; *[air]* eddy; (*fig*) *[foule]* bustle (*NonC*), bustling. **emporté par les ~ de la foule** swept along by the bustling *ou* milling crowd *ou* by the bustle of the crowd. **b** (*agitation*) upheaval, stir (*NonC*). **~ d'idées** whirl *ou* swirl of ideas; **les ~ provoqués par ce divorce** the stir caused by this divorce.

rempaillage [Rɑ̃pajaʒ] nm reseating, rebottoming (*with straw*).

rempailler [Rɑ̃paje] 1 vt *chaise* to reseat, rebottom (*with straw*).

rempailleur, -euse [Rɑ̃pajœR, øz] nm,f *[chaise]* chair-bottomer.

rempaqueter [Rɑ̃pak(ə)te] 4 vt to wrap up again, rewrap.

rempart [Rɑ̃paR] nm **a** (*Mil*) rampart. **~s** *[ville]* city walls, ramparts; *[château fort]* battlements, ramparts. **b** (*fig*) defence, bastion, rampart (*littér*). **faire à qn un ~ de son corps** to shield sb with one's (own) body.

rempiler [Rɑ̃pile] 1 **1** vt to pile *ou* stack up again. **2** vi (*arg Mil*) to join up again, re-enlist, re-up‡ (*US*).

remplaçable [Rɑ̃plasabl] adj replaceable.

remplaçant, e [Rɑ̃plasɑ̃, ɑ̃t] nm,f replacement, substitute; (*Méd*) locum (*Brit*); (*Sport*) reserve; (*pendant un match*) substitute; (*Théât*) understudy; (*Scol*) supply (*Brit*) *ou* substitute (*US*) teacher. **être le ~ de qn** to stand in for sb; **trouver un ~ à un professeur malade** to get sb to stand in *ou* substitute for a sick teacher; **il faut lui trouver un ~** we must find a replacement *ou* a substitute for him.

remplacement [Rɑ̃plasmɑ̃] nm **a** (*intérim: voir* **remplacer**) standing in (*de* for); substitution (*de* for), deputizing (*de* for). **assurer le ~ d'un collègue pendant sa maladie** to stand in *ou* deputize (*Brit*) for a colleague during his illness; **faire des ~s** *[secrétaire]* to temp*, do temporary work; *[professeur]* to do supply teaching, work as a supply (*Brit*) *ou* substitute (*US*) teacher; **j'ai fait 3 ~s cette semaine** I've had 3 temporary replacement jobs this week.

b (*substitution, changement: voir* **remplacer**) replacement (*de* of); taking over (*de* from); acting as a substitute (*de* for), acting as an alternative (*de* to). **effectuer le ~ d'une pièce défectueuse** to replace a faulty part; **film présenté en ~ d'une émission annulée** film shown as a replacement *ou* substitute for a cancelled programme; **je n'ai plus de stylos à billes, en ~ je vous donne un marqueur** I have no more ball-point pens so I'll give you a felt tip instead; **le ~ du nom par le pronom** the replacement of the noun by the pronoun; **il va falloir trouver une solution de ~** we'll have to find an alternative (solution); **produit de ~** substitute (product).

remplacer [Rɑ̃plase] 3 vt **a** (*assurer l'intérim de*) *acteur malade* to stand in for; *joueur, professeur malade* to stand in for, substitute for, deputize for (*Brit*); *médecin en vacances* to stand in for, do a locum for (*Brit*). **je me suis fait ~** I found myself a deputy (*Brit*) *ou* a stand-in, I got someone to stand in for me.

b (*substitution: succéder à*) to replace, take over from, take the place of. **le train a maintenant remplacé la diligence** the train has now replaced *ou* taken the place of the stagecoach; **son fils l'a remplacé comme directeur** his son has taken over from him *ou* has taken his place *ou* has replaced him as director; **~ une sentinelle** to take over from *ou* relieve a sentry.

c (*substitution: tenir lieu de*) to take the place of, act as a substitute for, act as an alternative to, replace. **le miel peut ~ le sucre** honey can be used in place of *ou* as a substitute for sugar *ou* can take the place of sugar; **le pronom remplace le nom dans la phrase** the pronoun stands for *ou* takes the place of *ou* replaces the noun in the sentence; **quand on n'a pas d'alcool, on peut le ~ par de l'eau de Cologne** when you have no alcohol you can use eau de Cologne in its place *ou* you can substitute eau de Cologne.

d (*changer*) *employé démissionnaire* to replace; *objet usagé* to replace, change. **~ le vieux lit par un neuf** to replace the old bed with a new one, change the old bed for a new one; **les pièces défectueuses seront remplacées gratuitement** faulty parts will be replaced free; **~ un carreau cassé** to replace a broken windowpane; **~ les pointillés par des pronoms** to replace the dotted lines by *ou* with pronouns, put pronouns in place of the dotted lines.

rempli, e [Rɑ̃pli] (ptp de **remplir**) **1** adj *théâtre, récipient* full (*de* of), filled (*de* with); *joue, visage* full, plump; *journée, vie* full, busy. **il est ~ de son importance** he's full of his own importance; **avoir l'estomac bien ~** to have a full stomach, have eaten one's fill; **texte ~ de fautes** text riddled *ou* packed with mistakes; **sa tête était ~e de souvenirs** his mind was filled with *ou* full of memories. **2** nm (*Couture*) tuck.

remplir [Rɑ̃pliR] 2 **1** vt **a** (*gén*) to fill (*de* with); *récipient* to fill (up); (*à nouveau*) to refill; *questionnaire* to fill in *ou* out. **~ qch à moitié** to half fill sth, fill sth half full; **il en a rempli 15 pages** he filled 15 pages with it, he wrote 15 pages on it; **ce chanteur ne remplira pas la salle** this singer won't fill the hall *ou* won't get a full house; **ces tâches routinières ont rempli sa vie** these routine tasks have filled his life, his life has been filled with these routine tasks; **ça remplit la première page des journaux** it fills *ou* covers the front page of the newspapers; **ce résultat me remplit d'admiration** this result fills me with admiration, I am filled with admiration at this result; **~ son temps** to fill one's time; **il remplit bien ses journées** he gets a lot done in (the course of) a day, he packs a lot into his days.

b (*s'acquitter de*) *promesse* to fulfil; *devoir* to fulfil, carry out, do; *contrat, mission* to fulfil, carry out; *travail* to carry out, do; *rôle* to fill, play; *besoin* to fulfil, answer, meet, satisfy. **objet qui remplit une fonction précise** object that fulfils a precise purpose; **vous ne remplissez pas les conditions** you do not fulfil *ou* satisfy *ou* meet the conditions; **~ ses fonctions** to do *ou* carry out one's job, carry out *ou* perform one's functions.

2 **se remplir** vpr *[récipient, salle]* to fill (up) (*de* with). **se ~ les poches*** to line one's pockets; **on s'est bien rempli la panse*** we had a good stuff-out‡ (*Brit*), we stuffed ourselves*.

remplissage [Rɑ̃plisaʒ] nm *[tonneau, bassin]* filling (up); (*péj: dans un livre*) padding. **faire du ~** to pad out one's work (*ou* speech *etc*).

remploi [Rɑ̃plwa] nm = **réemploi**.

remployer [Rɑ̃plwaje] 8 vt = **réemployer**.

remplumer* (se) [Rɑ̃plyme] 1 vpr (*physiquement*) to fill out again, get a bit of flesh on one's bones again; (*financièrement*) to get back on one's feet financially, have some money in one's pocket again.

rempocher [Rɑ̃pɔʃe] 1 vt to repocket, put back in one's pocket.

rempoissonnement [ʀɑ̃pwasɔnmɑ̃] **nm** restocking (with fish).

rempoissonner [ʀɑ̃pwasɔne] 1 **vt** to restock (with fish).

remporter [ʀɑ̃pɔʀte] 1 **vt** a (*reprendre*) to take away (again), take back. **remportez ce plat!** take this dish away! b *victoire, championnat* to win; *prix* to carry off, win. ~ **un (vif) succès** to achieve (a great) success.

rempotage [ʀɑ̃pɔtaʒ] **nm** repotting.

rempoter [ʀɑ̃pɔte] 1 **vt** to repot.

remprunter [ʀɑ̃pʀœ̃te] 1 **vt** (*une nouvelle fois*) to borrow again; (*davantage*) to borrow more.

remuant, e [ʀəmɥɑ̃, ɑ̃t] **adj** *enfant* restless, fidgety, always on the go (*attrib*).

remue-ménage [ʀ(ə)mymenaʒ] **nm inv** (*bruit*) commotion (*NonC*); (*activité*) hurly-burly (*NonC*), commotion (*NonC*), bustle (*NonC*). **il y a du ~ chez les voisins** the neighbours are making a great commotion; **faire du ~** to make a commotion; **le ~ électoral** the electoral hurly-burly.

remue-méninges [ʀ(ə)mymenɛ̃ʒ] **nm inv** brainstorming.

remuement [ʀ(ə)mymɑ̃] **nm** moving, movement.

remuer [ʀəmɥe] 1 1 **vt** a (*bouger*) *tête, bras, lèvres* to move; *oreille* to twitch. ~ **la queue** *[vache, écureuil]* to flick its tail; *[chien]* to wag its tail; ~ **les bras** *ou* **les mains en parlant** to wave one's arms about *ou* gesticulate as one speaks; ~ **les épaules/les hanches en marchant** to swing *ou* sway one's shoulders/hips as one walks; (*fig*) **il n'a pas remué le petit doigt** he didn't lift a finger (to help).

b *objet* (*déplacer*) to move, shift; (*secouer*) to shake. **il essaya de ~ la pierre** he tried to move *ou* shift the stone; **sa valise est si lourde que je ne peux même pas la ~** his case is so heavy that I can't even shift *ou* move *ou* budge it; **arrête de ~ ta chaise** stop moving your chair about; **ne remue pas** *ou* **ne fais pas ~ la table, je suis en train d'écrire** don't shake *ou* move *ou* wobble the table – I'm trying to write.

c (*brasser*) *café, sauce* to stir; *braises* to poke, stir; *sable* to stir up; *salade* to toss; *terre* to dig *ou* turn over. **il a remué la sauce/les braises** he gave the sauce a stir/the fire a poke, he stirred the sauce/poked the fire; **il a tout remué dans le tiroir** he turned the whole drawer *ou* everything in the drawer upside down; (*fig*) ~ **de l'argent (à la pelle)** to deal with *ou* handle vast amounts of money; (*fig*) ~ **la boue** *ou* **l'ordure** to rake *ou* stir up dirt *ou* muck; (*fig*) ~ **ciel et terre pour** to move heaven and earth (in order) to; (*fig*) ~ **des souvenirs** *[personne nostalgique]* to turn *ou* go over old memories in one's mind; *[évocation]* to stir up *ou* arouse old memories; **une odeur de terre remuée** a smell of fresh earth *ou* of freshly turned *ou* dug earth.

d (*émouvoir*) *personne* to move. **ça vous remue les tripes*** it really tugs at your heartstrings.

2 **vi** a (*bouger*) *[personne]* to move; *[dent, tuile]* to be loose. **cesse de ~!** keep still!, stop fidgeting!; **le vent faisait ~ les branchages** the wind was stirring the branches, the branches were stirring *ou* swaying in the wind; **ça a remué pendant la traversée*** the crossing was pretty rough*; **il a remué toute la nuit** he tossed and turned all night; *voir* **nez**.

b (*fig: se rebeller*) to show signs of unrest.

3 **se remuer vpr** a (*bouger*) to move; (*se déplacer*) to move about.

b (*) (*se mettre en route*) to get going; (*s'activer*) to shift *ou* stir o.s.*, get a move on*. **il s'est beaucoup remué pour leur trouver une maison** he's gone to a lot of trouble to find them a house; **il ne s'est pas beaucoup remué** he didn't stir *ou* strain himself much (*iro*).

rémunérateur, -trice [ʀemyneʀatœʀ, tʀis] **adj** *emploi* remunerative, lucrative.

rémunération [ʀemyneʀasjɔ̃] **nf** remuneration, payment (*de* for).

rémunérer [ʀemyneʀe] 6 **vt** *personne* to remunerate, pay. ~ **le travail de qn** to remunerate *ou* pay sb for his work; **travail mal rémunéré** badly-paid job.

renâcler [ʀ(ə)nɑkle] 1 **vi** *[animal]* to snort; (*fig*) *[personne]* to grumble, complain, show (one's) reluctance. ~ **à la besogne** *ou* **à la tâche** to grumble *ou* complain (about having to do a job); ~ **à faire qch** to grumble at having to do sth, do sth reluctantly *ou* grudgingly; **sans ~** uncomplainingly, without grumbling; **faire qch en renâclant** to do sth grudgingly *ou* with (a) bad grace.

renaissance [ʀ(ə)nɛsɑ̃s] 1 **nf** (*Rel, fig*) rebirth. (*Hist*) **la R~** the Renaissance. 2 **adj inv** *mobilier, style* Renaissance.

renaissant, e [ʀ(ə)nɛsɑ̃, ɑ̃t] **adj** a *forces* returning; *économie* reviving, recovering. **toujours** *ou* **sans cesse ~** *difficultés* constantly recurring, that keep cropping up; *obstacles* that keep cropping up; *intérêt, hésitations, doutes* constantly renewed. b (*Hist*) Renaissance (*épith*).

renaître [ʀ(ə)nɛtʀ] 59 **vi** a *[joie]* to spring up again, be revived (*dans* in); *[espoir, doute]* to be revived (*dans* in), be reborn (*littér*); *[conflit]* to spring up again, break out again; *[difficulté]* to recur, crop up again; *[économie]* to revive, recover; *[sourire]* to return (*sur* to), reappear (*sur* on); *[plante]* to come *ou* spring up again; *[jour]* to dawn, break. **le printemps renaît** spring is reawakening; **la nature renaît au printemps** nature comes back to life in spring; **faire ~** *sentiment, passé* to bring back, revive; *problème, sourire* to bring back; *espoir, conflit* to revive.

b (*revivre*) (*gén*) to come to life again; (*Rel*) to be born again (*en* in). (*Myth, fig*) ~ **de ses cendres** to rise from one's ashes; **je me sens ~** I feel as if I've been given a new lease of life.

c (*littér*) ~ **au bonheur** to find happiness again; ~ **à l'espérance** to find fresh hope; ~ **à la vie** to take on a new lease of life.

rénal, e, mpl -aux [ʀenal, o] **adj** renal (SPÉC), kidney (*épith*).

renard [ʀ(ə)naʀ] **nm** (*Zool*) fox; (*fourrure*) fox(-fur). (*fig*) **c'est un fin ~** he's a crafty *ou* sly fox *ou* dog; ~ **argenté/bleu** silver/blue fox.

renarde [ʀ(ə)naʀd] **nf** vixen.

renardeau, pl ~x [ʀ(ə)naʀdo] **nm** fox cub.

renardière [ʀ(ə)naʀdjɛʀ] **nf** (*terrier*) fox's den; (*Can*) fox farm.

renauder*† [ʀənode] 1 **vi** to grumble, grouse*, grouch*.

rencaisser [ʀɑ̃kese] 1 **vt** a (*Comm*) *argent* to put back in the till. b (*Horticulture*) to rebox.

rencard‡, rencart‡ [ʀɑ̃kaʀ] **nm = rancard‡.**

renchérir [ʀɑ̃ʃeʀiʀ] 2 **vi** a (*en paroles*) to go further, add something, go one better (*péj*); (*en actes*) to go further, go one better (*péj*). ~ **sur ce que qn dit** to add something to what sb says, go further *ou* one better (*péj*) than sb; ~ **sur ce que qn fait** to go further than sb; **"et je n'en ai nul besoin" renchérit-il** "and I don't need it in the least" he added (further); **il faut toujours qu'il renchérisse (sur ce qu'on dit)** he always has to add something (to what anyone says), he always has to go one better (than anyone else) (*péj*).

b *[prix]* to get dearer *ou* more expensive. **la vie renchérit** the cost of living is going up *ou* rising.

c (*dans une vente*) (*sur l'offre de qn*) to bid higher (*sur* than); (*sur son offre*) to raise one's bid.

renchérissement [ʀɑ̃ʃeʀismɑ̃] **nm** *[marchandises]* rise *ou* increase in (the) price (*de* of); *[loyers]* rise, increase (*de* in). **le ~ de la vie** the rise *ou* increase in the cost of living.

rencogner* [ʀɑ̃kɔɲe] 1 1 **vt** to corner. 2 **se rencogner vpr** to huddle up, curl up (in a corner).

rencontre [ʀɑ̃kɔ̃tʀ] **nf** a *[amis, diplomates, étrangers]* meeting; (*imprévue*) encounter, meeting. **faire la ~ de qn** to meet sb; (*imprévue*) to meet sb, run into sb, encounter sb (*frm*); **j'ai peur que dans ces milieux il ne fasse de mauvaises ~s** I am afraid that in these circles he might meet (up with) *ou* fall in with the wrong sort of people; **faire une ~ inattendue/une mauvaise ~** to have an unexpected/unpleasant encounter; **le hasard d'une ~ a changé ma vie** a chance encounter *ou* meeting has changed my life; ~ **au sommet** summit meeting.

b (*gén*) *[éléments]* conjunction; *[rivières]* confluence; *[routes]* junction; *[voitures]* collision; *[voyelles]* juxtaposition. **la ~ des deux lignes/routes/rivières se fait ici** the two lines/roads/rivers meet *ou* join here; *voir* **point[1]**.

c (*Athlétisme*) meeting; (*Ftbl etc*) fixture, game. **la ~ (des 2 équipes) aura lieu le 15** the 2 teams will meet on the 15th; ~ **de boxe** boxing match.

d (*Mil*) skirmish, encounter, engagement; (*duel*) encounter, meeting.

e (*loc*) **aller à la ~ de qn** to go and meet sb, go to meet sb; **(partir) à la ~ des Incas** (to go) in search of the Incas; **amours de ~** casual love affairs; **compagnons/voyageurs de ~** chance/travelling companions.

rencontrer [ʀɑ̃kɔ̃tʀe] 1 1 **vt** a (*gén*) to meet; (*par hasard*) to meet, run *ou* bump into*, encounter (*frm*). **j'ai rencontré Paul en ville** I met *ou* ran into* *ou* bumped into* Paul in town; **le Premier ministre a rencontré son homologue allemand** the Prime Minister has had a meeting with *ou* has met his German counterpart; **mon regard rencontra le sien** our eyes met, my eyes met his.

b (*trouver*) *expression* to find, come across; *occasion* to meet with. **des gens/sites comme on n'en rencontre plus** the sort of people/places you don't find any more; **arrête-toi au premier garage que nous rencontrerons** stop at the first garage you come across *ou* find; **avec lui, j'ai rencontré le bonheur** with him I have found happiness.

c (*heurter*) to strike; (*toucher*) to meet (with). **la lame rencontra un os** the blade struck a bone; **sa main ne rencontra que le vide** his hand met with nothing but empty space.

d *obstacle, difficulté, opposition* to meet with, encounter, come up against; *résistance* to meet with, come up against.

e (*Sport*) *équipe* to meet, play (against); *boxeur* to meet, fight (against).

2 **se rencontrer vpr** a *[personnes, regards]* to meet; *[rivières, routes]* to meet, join; *[équipes]* to meet, play (each other); *[boxeurs]* to meet, fight (each other); *[véhicules]* to collide (with each other). **faire se ~ deux personnes** to arrange for two people to meet, arrange a meeting between two people; (*frm*) **je me suis déjà rencontré avec lui** I have already met him; **nous nous sommes déjà rencontrés** we have already met.

b (*avoir les mêmes idées*) to be at one, be of the same opinion *ou* mind. **se ~ avec qn** to be at one with sb, be of the same opinion *ou* mind as sb; *voir* **grand**.

c (*exister*) *[coïncidence, curiosité]* to be found. **cela ne se rencontre plus de nos jours** that isn't found *ou* one doesn't come across that any more nowadays; **il se rencontre des gens qui ...** you do find people who ..., people are to be found who ... .

rendement [ʀɑ̃dmɑ̃] **nm** *[champ]* yield; *[machine]* output; *[entreprise]* (*productivité*) productivity; (*production*) output; *[personne]* output; *[investissement]* return (*de* on), yield (*de* of); (*Phys*) efficiency. **il travaille beaucoup, mais il n'a pas de ~*** he works hard but he hasn't *ou* there isn't much to show for it* *ou* but he isn't very productive; **champ/placement qui est d'un mauvais ~** low-yield field/investment.

rendez-vous [ʀɑ̃devu] **nm inv** a (*rencontre*) appointment; (*d'amoureux*) date. **donner** *ou* **fixer un ~ à qn, prendre ~ avec qn** to make an appointment with sb, arrange to see *ou* meet sb; **j'ai (un) ~ à 10 heures** I have an appointment *ou* I have to meet someone at 10 o'clock; **ma parole, vous vous êtes donné ~** my goodness, you must have seen each other coming!; (*littér*) **avoir ~ avec la mort** to have a date with death; **~ d'affaires** business appointment; **~ galant** amorous meeting; **~ spatial** docking (in space); **prendre un ~ chez le dentiste/coiffeur** to make a dental/hair appointment; **le médecin ne reçoit que sur ~** the doctor only sees patients by appointment.

b (*lieu*) meeting place. **~ de chasse** meet; *voir* **maison**.

rendormir [ʀɑ̃dɔʀmiʀ] 16 1 **vt** to put to sleep again, put back to sleep. 2 **se rendormir vpr** to go back to sleep, fall asleep again.

rendosser [ʀɑ̃dose] 1 **vt** to put on again.

rendre [ʀɑ̃dʀ] 41 1 **vt** a (*restituer*) (*gén*) to give back, return, take *ou* bring back; *marchandises défectueuses, bouteille vide* to return, take back; *argent* to pay *ou* give back, return; *objet volé* to give back, return, restore; *otage* to return; *cadeau, bague* to return, give back; (*Scol*) *copie* to hand in. **quand pourriez-vous me ~ votre réponse?** when will you be able to give me *ou* let me have your reply?; **~ son devoir en retard** to hand *ou* give in one's homework late; **~ à qn sa parole** to release sb from a promise, let sb off (his promise); **~ la liberté à qn** to set sb free, give sb his freedom; **~ la santé à qn** to restore sb to health; **~ la vue à qn** to restore sb's sight, give sb back his sight; **cela lui a rendu toutes ses forces/son courage** that gave him back *ou* restored all his strength/courage; **~ la vie à qn** to save sb's life (*fig*); **rendu à la vie civile** restored to *ou* back in civilian life; (*fig*) **~ son tablier** to give (in) one's notice; **~ à César ce qui est à César** to render unto Caesar the things which are Caesar's.

b (*Jur*) *justice* to administer, dispense; *jugement, arrêt* to pronounce, render; *verdict* to return. (*fig*) **~ justice à qn** to do justice to sb; **il faut lui ~ cette justice qu'il a essayé** he did try — (we must) grant *ou* give him that.

c (*donner en retour*) *hospitalité, invitation* to return, repay; *salut, coup, baiser* to return. **je lui ai rendu sa visite** I returned *ou* repaid his visit; **~ coup pour coup** to return blow for blow; **il m'a joué un sale tour, mais je le lui rendrai** he played a dirty trick on me, but I'll get even with him *ou* I'll get my own back on him*; **je lui ai rendu injure pour injure** I answered insult by insult, I gave him as good as I got; **il la déteste, et elle le lui rend bien** he hates her and she returns his feelings *ou* and she feels exactly the same (way) about him; **~ la monnaie à qn** to give sb his change; **il m'a donné 10 F et je lui en ai rendu 5** he gave me 10 francs and I gave him 5 francs back *ou* 5 francs change; (*fig*) **~ à qn la monnaie de sa pièce, ~ la pareille à qn** to pay sb back in his own coin; **je lui rendrai la monnaie de sa pièce** I'll be quits *ou* even with him yet.

d (+ *adj*) to make. **~ qn heureux** to make sb happy; **~ qch public** to make sth public; **~ qn responsable de** to make sb responsible for; **son discours l'a rendu célèbre** his speech has made him famous; **c'est à vous ~ fou!** it's enough to drive you mad!; **se ~ utile/indispensable** to make o.s. useful/indispensable; **il se rend ridicule** he's making himself ridiculous, he's making a fool of himself, he's making himself look foolish.

e *expression, traduction* to render. **cela ne rend pas bien sa pensée** that doesn't render *ou* convey his thoughts very well; **le portrait ne rend pas son expression** this portrait has not caught his expression.

f (*produire*) *liquide* to give out; *son* to produce, make. **le concombre rend beaucoup d'eau** cucumbers give out a lot of water; (*fig*) **l'enquête n'a rien rendu** the inquiry drew a blank *ou* didn't come to anything *ou* produced nothing; **ça ne rend pas grand-chose** (*photo, décor, musique*) it's a bit disappointing; **ça rend mal en photo** a photograph doesn't do it justice.

g (*vomir*) *bile* to vomit, bring up; *déjeuner* to vomit, bring back *ou* up. **~ tripes et boyaux*** to be as sick as a dog*; **~ du sang (par la bouche)** to cough up *ou* vomit blood; **~ du sang par le nez** to bleed from the nose.

h (*Sport*) *[cheval]* **~ du poids** to have a weight handicap; **~ 3 kg** to give *ou* carry 3 kg; *[coureur]* **~ de la distance** to have a handicap; **~ 100 mètres** to have a 100-metre handicap; (*fig*) **~ des points à qn** to give sb points *ou* a head start.

i (*Mil*) *place forte* to surrender. **~ les armes** to lay down one's arms.

j (*loc*) *[personne]* **~ l'âme** *ou* **le dernier soupir** to breathe one's last, give up the ghost; **ma voiture/mon frigo a rendu l'âme*** my car/my fridge has given up the ghost*; **~ un culte à** to worship; **~ gloire à** *Dieu* to glorify; *hommes* to pay homage to; **~ gorge** to restitute ill-gotten gains; **~ grâces à** to render (*frm*) *ou* give thanks to; **~ hommage/honneur à** to pay homage/tribute to; **le régiment rendait les honneurs** the regiment was paying honour; **~ les derniers honneurs à qn** to pay the last tributes to sb; (*frm*) **~ raison de qch à qn** to give sb an explanation for sth; **cela m'a bien rendu service** that was a great help to me; **ce petit couteau rend bien des services** this little knife comes in *ou* is very handy (for a variety of purposes); *voir* **compte, service, visite**.

2 **vi** a *[arbres, terre]* to yield, be productive. **les pommiers ont bien rendu** the apple trees have given a good yield *ou* crop; **la pêche a bien rendu** we have got a good catch (of fish); (*fig*) **ma petite expérience n'a pas rendu** my little experiment didn't pay off *ou* didn't come to anything.

b (*vomir*) to be sick, vomit. **avoir envie de ~** to feel sick.

3 **se rendre vpr** a (*céder*) *[soldat, criminel]* to give o.s. up, surrender; *[troupe]* to surrender. **se ~ aux ordres de qn** to comply with *ou* obey sb's orders; **se ~ à l'avis de qn** to bow to sb's opinion; **se ~ à l'évidence** (*regarder les choses en face*) to face facts; (*admettre son tort*) to bow before the evidence; **se ~ aux prières de qn** to give way *ou* give in *ou* yield to sb's pleas; **se ~ aux raisons de qn** to bow to *ou* accept sb's reasons.

b (*aller*) **se ~ à** to go to; **il se rend à son travail à pied/en voiture** he walks/drives to work, he goes to work on foot/by car; **alors qu'il se rendait à ...** as he was on his way to ... *ou* going to ...; **la police s'est rendue sur les lieux** the police went to *ou* arrived on the scene; **se ~ à l'appel de qn** to respond to sb's appeal; *voir* **lieu**.

c **se ~ compte de qch** to realize sth, be aware of sth; **se ~ compte que** to realize that, be aware that; **je me rends très bien compte de la situation** I am very well aware of the situation; **est-ce que tu te rends vraiment compte de ce que tu dis/fais?** do you really realize *ou* are you really aware of what you are saying/doing?; **tu ne te rends pas compte du travail que ça représente** you have no idea of the amount of work *ou* you just don't realize how much work that represents; **rendez-vous compte!** just imagine! *ou* think!; **il a osé me dire ça, à moi, tu te rends compte!** he dared say that to me — can you imagine!

rendu, e [ʀɑ̃dy] (**ptp de rendre**) 1 **adj** a (*arrivé*) **être ~** to have arrived; **nous voilà ~s!** here we are then!; **on est plus vite ~ par le train** you get there quicker by train. b (*remis*) **~ à domicile** delivered to the house. c (*fatigué*) exhausted, tired out, worn out. 2 **nm** (*Comm*) return; *voir* **prêté**.

rêne [ʀɛn] **nf** rein. (*fig*) **prendre les ~s d'une affaire** to take over a business, assume control *ou* take control of a business; **lâcher les ~s** (*lit*) to loose *ou* slacken the reins; (*fig*) to let go; (*fig*) **c'est lui qui tient les ~s du gouvernement** it's he who holds the reins of government *ou* who is in the saddle.

renégat, e [ʀənega, at] **nm,f** (*Rel*) renegade; (*Pol, gén*) renegade, turncoat.

reneiger [ʀ(ə)neʒe] 3 **vb impers** to snow again.

renfermé, e [ʀɑ̃fɛʀme] (**ptp de renfermer**) 1 **adj** withdrawn, uncommunicative, closed in upon oneself (*attrib*). 2 **nm: odeur de ~** fusty *ou* stale smell; **ça sent le ~** it smells stuffy *ou* fusty (in here), it's stuffy in here.

renfermer [ʀɑ̃fɛʀme] 1 1 **vt** a (*contenir*) *trésors* to contain, hold; *vérités, erreurs* to contain. **phrase qui renferme plusieurs idées** sentence that encompasses *ou* contains several ideas. b (†: *à clef*) to lock again, lock back up. 2 **se renfermer vpr: se ~ (en soi-même)** to withdraw into o.s.; **se ~ dans sa coquille** to withdraw into one's shell.

renfiler [ʀɑ̃file] 1 **vt** *perles* to restring; *aiguille* to thread again, rethread; *bas, manteau* to slip back into.

renflammer [ʀɑ̃flɑme] 1 **vt** to rekindle.

renflé, e [ʀɑ̃fle] (**ptp de renfler**) **adj** bulging (*épith*), bulbous.

renflement [ʀɑ̃fləmɑ̃] **nm** bulge.

renfler [ʀɑ̃fle] 1 1 **vt** to make a bulge in; *joues* to blow out. 2 **se renfler vpr** to bulge (out).

renflouage [ʀɑ̃fluaʒ] **nm, renflouement** [ʀɑ̃flumɑ̃] **nm** (*voir* **renflouer**) refloating; bailing out.

renflouer [ʀɑ̃flue] 1 1 **vt** *bateau* to refloat; (*fig*) *entreprise* to refloat, bail out; *personne* to set back on his feet again, bail out. 2 **se renflouer vpr** (*fig*) to get back on one's feet again (financially), get back on a sound financial footing again.

renfoncement [ʀɑ̃fɔ̃smɑ̃] **nm** recess. **caché dans le ~ d'une porte** hidden in a doorway.

renfoncer [ʀɑ̃fɔ̃se] 3 **vt** a *clou* to knock further in; *bouchon* to push further in. **il renfonça son chapeau (sur sa tête)** he pulled his hat down (further). b (*Typ*) to indent.

renforçateur [ʀɑ̃fɔʀsatœʀ] **nm** (*Phot*) intensifier.

renforcement [ʀɑ̃fɔʀsəmɑ̃] **nm** (*voir* **renforcer**) reinforcement; trussing; strengthening; intensification.

renforcer [ʀɑ̃fɔʀse] 3 1 **vt** a *vêtement, mur* to reinforce; *poutre* to reinforce, truss. **bas à talon renforcé** stocking with reinforced heel.

b *équipe, armée* to reinforce. **ils sont venus ~ nos effectifs** they came to strengthen *ou* swell our numbers.

c *crainte, argument, amitié* to reinforce, strengthen; *paix* to consolidate; *pression, effort* to add to, intensify; *position* to strengthen; *couleur, ton, expression* to intensify. **~ qn dans une opinion** to confirm sb's opinion, confirm sb in an opinion; **ça renforce ce que je dis** that backs up *ou* reinforces what I'm saying; (*Scol*) **(cours d')anglais renforcé** remedial English (class).

2 **se renforcer** vpr *[craintes, amitié]* to strengthen; *[pression]* to intensify. **notre équipe s'est renforcée de 2 nouveaux joueurs** our team has been strengthened by 2 new players.

renfort [rɑ̃fɔʀ] nm **a** (*gén*) help, helpers. **b** (*Mil*) ~s (*hommes*) reinforcements; (*matériel*) (further) supplies. **b** (*Tech*) reinforcement, strengthening piece. **c** (*loc*) **de** ~ *barre, toile* strengthening; *armée* back-up, supporting; *personnel* extra, additional; **envoyer qn en** ~ to send sb as an extra *ou* sb to augment the numbers; **recevoir un** ~ **de troupes/d'artillerie, recevoir des troupes/de l'artillerie de** *ou* **en** ~ to receive more troops/guns, receive reinforcements/a further supply of guns; **embaucher du personnel de** *ou* **en** ~ to employ extra *ou* additional staff; **à grand** ~ **de gestes/d'explications** with a great many gestures/explanations.

renfrogné, e [rɑ̃fʀɔɲe] (ptp de **se renfrogner**) adj *visage* sullen, scowling (*épith*), sulky; *air* sullen, sulky; *personne* sullen *ou* sulky (looking).

renfrognement [rɑ̃fʀɔɲmɑ̃] nm scowling, sullenness.

renfrogner (se) [rɑ̃fʀɔɲe] 1 vpr *[personne]* to scowl, pull a sour face.

rengagé [rɑ̃gaʒe] **1** adj m *soldat* re-enlisted. **2** nm re-enlisted soldier.

rengagement [rɑ̃gaʒmɑ̃] nm (*voir* **rengager**) starting up again; reinvestment; re-engagement; repawning; re-enlistment.

rengager [rɑ̃gaʒe] 3 **1** vt *discussion* to start up again; *fonds* to reinvest; *combat* to re-engage; *bijoux* to repawn; *soldat* to re-enlist; *ouvrier* to take on *ou* engage again, re-engage. ~ **la clef dans la serrure** to insert the key back *ou* reinsert the key into the lock; ~ **sa voiture dans une rue** to drive (back) into a street again. **2** vi (*Mil*) to join up again, re-enlist. **3** **se rengager** vpr (*Mil*) to join up again, re-enlist; *[discussion]* to start up again. **se** ~ **dans une rue** to enter a street again.

rengaine [rɑ̃gɛn] nf (*formule*) hackneyed expression; (*chanson*) old (repetitive) song *ou* melody. (*fig*) **c'est toujours la même** ~* it's always the same old chorus (*Brit*) *ou* refrain* (*Brit*) *ou* song* (*US*).

rengainer [rɑ̃gene] 1 vt **a** (*) *compliment* to save, withhold; *sentiments* to contain, hold back. **rengaine tes beaux discours!** (you can) save *ou* keep your fine speeches! **b** *épée* to sheathe, put up; *revolver* to put back in its holster.

rengorgement [rɑ̃gɔʀʒəmɑ̃] nm puffed-up pride.

rengorger (se) [rɑ̃gɔʀʒe] 3 vpr *[oiseau]* to puff out its throat; *[personne]* to puff o.s. up. **se** ~ **d'avoir fait qch** to be full of o.s. for having done sth.

rengraisser [rɑ̃gʀese] 1 vi to put on weight again, put (some) weight back on.

reniement [ʀənimɑ̃] nm (*voir* **renier**) renunciation; disowning, repudiation; breaking; denial.

renier [ʀənje] 7 **1** vt *foi, opinion* to renounce; *frère, patrie, signature, son passé* to disown, repudiate; *promesse* to go back on, break. (*Rel*) **il renia Jésus Christ** he denied Christ; ~ **Dieu** to renounce God. **2** **se renier** vpr to go back on what one has said *ou* done.

reniflement [ʀ(ə)nifləmɑ̃] nm (*voir* **renifler**) (*action*) sniffing (*NonC*); snorting (*NonC*); sniffling (*NonC*); snuffling (*NonC*); (*bruit*) sniff; snort; sniffle, snuffle.

renifler [ʀ(ə)nifle] 1 **1** vt *tabac* to sniff up, take a sniff of; *fleur, objet* to sniff (at); (* *fig*) *bonne affaire* to sniff out*. (*fig*) ~ **quelque chose de louche** to smell a rat. **2** vi *[personne]* to sniff; *[cheval]* to snort. **arrête de** ~**, mouche-toi!** stop sniffling *ou* snuffling and blow your nose!

renifleur, -euse [ʀ(ə)niflœʀ, øz] **1** adj sniffling, snuffling. **2** nm,f (*) sniffler, snuffler; *voir* **avion**.

rennais, e [ʀɛnɛ, ɛz] **1** adj of *ou* from Rennes. **2** nm,f: **R~(e)** inhabitant *ou* native of Rennes.

renne [ʀɛn] nm reindeer.

renom [ʀənɔ̃] nm **a** (*notoriété*) renown, repute, fame. **vin de grand** ~ celebrated *ou* renowned *ou* famous wine, wine of high renown *ou* repute; **restaurant en** ~ celebrated *ou* renowned *ou* famous restaurant; **acquérir du** ~ to win renown, become famous; **avoir du** ~ to be famous *ou* renowned. **b** (*frm: réputation*) reputation. **son** ~ **de sévérité** his reputation for severity; **bon/mauvais** ~ good/bad reputation *ou* name.

renommé, e [ʀ(ə)nɔme] (ptp de **renommer**) **1** adj celebrated, renowned, famous. ~ **pour** renowned *ou* famed for. **2** **renommée** nf **a** (*célébrité*) fame, renown. **marque/savant de** ~ **mondiale** world-famous make/scholar. **b** (*littér: opinion publique*) public report. **c** (*littér: réputation*) reputation. **bonne/mauvaise** ~ good/bad reputation *ou* name; *voir* **bon[1]**.

renommer [ʀ(ə)nɔme] 1 vt to reappoint.

renonce [ʀ(ə)nɔ̃s] nf (*Cartes*) **faire une** ~ to revoke, renegue, fail to follow suit.

renoncement [ʀ(ə)nɔ̃smɑ̃] nm (*action*) renouncement (*à* of). (*sacrifice*) **le** ~ renunciation, abnegation; ~ **à soi-même** self-abnegation, self-renunciation; **mener une vie de** ~ to live a life of renunciation *ou* abnegation.

renoncer [ʀ(ə)nɔ̃se] 3 **1** **renoncer à** vt indir (*gén*) to give up, renounce; *héritage, titre, pouvoir* to renounce, relinquish; *habitude* to give up; *métier* to abandon, give up. ~ **à un voyage/au mariage** to give up the idea of *ou* abandon all thought *ou* idea of a journey/of marriage; ~ **à qn** to give sb up; ~ **au tabac** to give up smoking; ~ **à lutter/à comprendre** to give up struggling/trying to understand; ~ **à se marier** to give up *ou* abandon the idea of getting married; ~ **aux plaisirs/au monde** to renounce pleasures/the world; **je** *ou* **j'y renonce** I give up; (*Cartes*) ~ **à cœur** to fail to follow (in) hearts; (*Jur*) ~ **à toute prétention** to abandon any claim.

2 vt (*littér*) *ami* to give up, withdraw one's friendship from.

renonciation [ʀənɔ̃sjasjɔ̃] nf (*voir* **renoncer**) giving up; renunciation; relinquishment; abandonment.

renoncule [ʀənɔ̃kyl] nf (*sauvage*) buttercup; (*cultivée*) globeflower, ranunculus.

renouée [ʀənwe] nf knotgrass.

renouer [ʀənwe] 1 **1** vt *lacet, nœud* to tie (up) again, re-tie; *cravate* to reknot, knot again; *conversation, liaison* to renew, resume, take up again. **2** vi: ~ **avec qn** to take up with sb again, become friends with sb again; ~ **avec une habitude** to take up a habit again; ~ **avec une tradition** to revive a tradition.

renouveau, pl ~x [ʀ(ə)nuvo] nm **a** (*transformation*) revival. **le** ~ **des sciences et des arts à la Renaissance** the revival of the sciences and the arts *ou* the renewed interest in *ou* the renewal of interest in the sciences and arts during the Renaissance. **b** (*regain*) ~ **de succès/faveur** renewed success/favour; **connaître un** ~ **de faveur** to enjoy renewed favour, come back into favour. **c** (*littér: printemps*) **le** ~ springtide (*littér*).

renouvelable [ʀ(ə)nuv(ə)labl] adj *passeport, bail, contrat, énergie* renewable; *expérience* which can be tried again *ou* repeated; *congé* which can be re-granted; *assemblée* that must be re-elected. **le mandat présidentiel est** ~ **tous les 7 ans** the president must stand (*Brit*) *ou* run for re-election every 7 years.

renouveler [ʀ(ə)nuv(ə)le] 4 **1** vt **a** (*remplacer*) *outillage, personnel* to renew, replace; *stock* to renew, replenish; *pansement* to renew, change; *conseil d'administration* to re-elect. ~ **l'air d'une salle** to air a room; ~ **l'eau d'une piscine** to renew *ou* replenish the water in a swimming pool; ~ **sa garde-robe** to renew one's wardrobe, buy some new clothes; (*Pol*) **la chambre doit être renouvelée tous les 5 ans** the house must be re-elected every 5 years.

b (*transformer*) *mode, théorie* to renew, revive. **cette découverte a complètement renouvelé notre vision des choses** this discovery has given us a whole new insight into things *ou* has cast a whole new light on things for us; **les poètes de la Pléiade renouvelèrent la langue française** the poets of the Pléiade gave new *ou* renewed life to the French language; **je préfère la pièce dans sa version renouvelée** I prefer the new version of the play.

c (*reconduire*) *passeport, contrat, abonnement* to renew; *congé* to re-grant. (*Méd*) **à** ~ to be renewed; **la chambre a renouvelé sa confiance au gouvernement** the house reaffirmed *ou* reasserted its confidence in the government.

d (*recommencer*) *candidature* to renew; *demande, offre, promesse, erreur* to renew, repeat; *expérience, exploit* to repeat, do again; (*littér*) *douleur* to renew, revive. **l'énergie sans cesse renouvelée que requiert ce métier** the constantly renewed energy which this job requires; (*dans une lettre*) **avec mes remerciements renouvelés** with renewed thanks, thanking you once more *ou* once again; (*littér*) **épisode renouvelé de l'Antiquité** episode taken *ou* borrowed from Antiquity.

e (*Rel*) *vœux* to renew.

2 **se renouveler** vpr **a** (*se répéter*) to recur, be repeated. **cette petite scène se renouvelle tous les jours** this little scene recurs *ou* is repeated every day; **et que ça ne se renouvelle plus!** and (just) don't let that happen again!

b (*être remplacé*) to be renewed *ou* replaced. **les cellules de notre corps se renouvellent constamment** the cells of our body are constantly being renewed *ou* replaced; **les hommes au pouvoir ne se renouvellent pas assez** men in power aren't replaced often enough.

c (*innover*) *[auteur, peintre]* to change one's style, try something new. *[comique]* **il ne se renouvelle pas** he never has any new jokes *ou* stories, he always tells the same old jokes *ou* stories.

renouvellement [ʀ(ə)nuvɛlmɑ̃] nm (*voir* **renouveler**) renewal; replacement; replenishment; changing; revival; repetition; recurrence. (*Pol*) **solliciter le** ~ **de son mandat** to stand (*Brit*) *ou* run for re-election; (*Rel*) **faire son** ~ to renew one's first communion promises.

rénovateur, -trice [ʀenɔvatœʀ, tʀis] **1** adj *doctrine* which seeks a renewal, reformist; *influence* renewing (*épith*), reforming (*épith*). **2** nm,f (*de la morale, Pol*) reformer. **il est considéré comme le** ~ **de cette science/de cet art** he's considered as having been the one to inject new life into this science/this art. **3** nm (*produit d'entretien*) restorer.

rénovation [ʀenɔvasjɔ̃] nf (*voir* **rénover**) renovation, modernization; redevelopment; restoration; reform; remodelling; renewal; bringing up to date.

rénover [ʀenɔve] 1 vt **a** *maison* to renovate, modernize; *quartier* to redevelop, renovate; *meuble* to restore. **b** *enseignement, institutions* to reform, remodel; *science* to renew, bring up to date; *méthodes* to reform.

renseignement [ʀɑ̃sɛɲmɑ̃] nm **a** information (*NonC*), piece of information. **un** ~ **intéressant** an interesting piece of information, some interesting information; **demander un** ~ *ou* **des** ~**s à qn** to ask sb for (some) information; **il est allé aux** ~**s** he has gone to make inquiries *ou* to see what he can find out (about it); **prendre ses** ~**s** *ou* **demander des**

~s sur qn to make inquiries *ou* ask for information *ou* for particulars about sb, try to find out about sb; **~s pris** upon inquiry; **avoir de bons ~s sur le compte de qn** to have good *ou* favourable reports about *ou* on sb; **pourriez-vous me donner un ~?** I'd like some information, could you give me some information?; **veuillez m'envoyer de plus amples ~s sur** ... please send me further details of ... *ou* further information about ...; **je peux te demander un ~?** can you give me some information?, can I ask you something?, could you tell me something?; **merci pour le ~** thanks for the information, thanks for telling me *ou* letting me know; **guichet/bureau des ~s** inquiry (*Brit*) *ou* information desk/office; (*panneau*) **"~s"** "inquiries" (*Brit*), "information"; (*Téléc*) **(service des) ~s** directory inquiries (*Brit*), information (*US*).

b (*Mil*) intelligence (*NonC*), piece of intelligence. **agent/service de ~s** intelligence agent/service; **travailler dans le ~** to work in intelligence; **les ~s généraux** *the security branch of the police force.*

renseigner [ʀɑ̃seɲe] 1 1 vt: **~ un client/un touriste** to give some information to a customer/a tourist; **~ la police/l'ennemi** to give information to the police/the enemy (*sur* about); **~ un passant/un automobiliste** (*sur le chemin à prendre*) to give directions to a passer-by/a driver, tell a passer-by/a driver the way; **qui pourrait me ~ sur le prix de la voiture/sur lui?** who could tell me the price of the car/something about him?, who could give me some information *ou* particulars about the price of the car/about him?; **il pourra peut-être te ~** perhaps he'll be able to give you some information (about it), perhaps he'll be able to tell you *ou* to help you; **document qui renseigne utilement** document which gives useful information; **ça ne nous renseigne pas beaucoup!** that doesn't get us very far!, that doesn't tell us very much! *ou* give us much to go on!; **il a l'air bien renseigné** he seems to be well informed *ou* to know a lot about it; **il est mal renseigné** he doesn't know much about it, he isn't very well informed about it; **on vous a mal renseigné** you have been misinformed.

2 **se renseigner** vpr (*demander des renseignements*) to make inquiries, ask for information (*sur* about); (*obtenir des renseignements*) to find out (*sur* about). **je vais me ~ auprès de lui** I'll ask him for information *ou* for particulars, I'll ask him about it; **j'essaierai de me ~** I'll try to find out, I'll try and get some information; **je vais me ~ sur son compte** I'll make inquiries about him, I'll find out about him; **je voudrais me ~ sur les chaînes hi-fi** I'd like some information *ou* particulars about hi-fi equipment.

rentabilisation [ʀɑ̃tabilizasjɔ̃] nf *[ligne aérienne]* making profitable. **la ~ d'une invention** the marketing *ou* commercializing of an invention.

rentabiliser [ʀɑ̃tabilize] 1 vt to make profitable, make pay.

rentabilité [ʀɑ̃tabilite] nf profitability. **~ des investissements** return on investments.

rentable [ʀɑ̃tabl] adj profitable. **c'est un exercice très ~** this is a really profitable operation, this operation really pays; **au prix où est l'essence, les transports privés ne sont pas ~s** with petrol the price it is, private transport isn't a paying *ou* viable proposition *ou* doesn't pay; (*fig*) **ce n'est plus du tout ~** it is no longer financially viable.

rentamer [ʀɑ̃tame] 1 vt *discours* to begin *ou* start again.

rente [ʀɑ̃t] nf a (*pension*) annuity, pension; (*fournie par la famille*) allowance. **~ de situation** secure *ou* guaranteed income; **~ viagère** life annuity; **faire une ~ à qn** to give an allowance to sb. b (*emprunt d'État*) government stock *ou* loan *ou* bond. **~s perpétuelles** perpetual loans, irredeemable securities. c (*loc*) **avoir des ~s** to have a private *ou* an unearned income, have private *ou* independent means; **vivre de ses ~s** to live on *ou* off one's private income; (*fig*) **cette voiture est une ~ pour le garagiste/n'est pas une ~** this car keeps the man at the garage in business*/costs me a fortune (to run).

rentier, -ière [ʀɑ̃tje, jɛʀ] nm,f person of independent *ou* private means. **c'est un petit ~** he has a small private income; **mener une vie de ~** to live a life of ease *ou* leisure.

rentrant, e [ʀɑ̃tʀɑ̃, ɑ̃t] adj *train d'atterrissage* retractable; (*Math*) *angle* reflex.

rentré, e[1] [ʀɑ̃tʀe] (ptp de **rentrer**) adj *colère* suppressed; *yeux* sunken; *joues* sunken, hollow.

rentrée[2] [ʀɑ̃tʀe] nf a **~ (scolaire)** start of the new school year, time when the schools go back; (*Univ*) start of the new academic year; (*du trimestre*) start of the new (school *ou* university) term; **acheter des cahiers pour la ~ (des classes)** to buy exercise books for the new school year; **la ~ aura lieu lundi** the new term begins on Monday, school starts again on Monday, pupils go back *ou* return to school again *ou* start school again on Monday; **la ~ s'est bien passée** the term began well; (*Comm*) **"les affaires de la ~"** "back-to-school bargains"; **à la ~ de Noël/Pâques** at the start of (the) term after the Christmas/Easter holidays, at the start of the second/third term.

b *[tribunaux]* reopening; *[parlement]* reopening, reassembly; *[députés]* return, reassembly. **la ~ parlementaire aura lieu cette semaine** parliament reassembles *ou* reopens this week, the new session of parliament starts this week; **c'est la ~ des théâtres parisiens** it's the start of the theatrical season in Paris; **la ~ littéraire** the start of the literary season *ou* calendar; **les députés font leur ~ aujourd'hui** the deputies are returning *ou* reassembling today (for the start of the new session); **faire sa ~ politique** (*après les vacances d'été*) to start the new political season, begin one's autumn campaign (*après avoir fait autre chose*) to make a *ou* one's political comeback; **la mode de la ~** the autumn fashions; **on verra ça à la ~** we'll see about that after the holidays *ou* when we come back from holiday.

c *[acteur]* (stage) comeback; *[sportif]* comeback.

d (*retour*) **pour faciliter la ~ dans la capitale** to make getting back into *ou* the return into the capital easier; **la ~ des ouvriers à l'usine le lundi matin** the workers' return to work on a Monday morning; **à l'heure des ~s dans Paris** when everyone is coming back into Paris *ou* returning to Paris, when the roads into Paris are full of returning motorists *ou* motorists on their way back home; **le concierge n'aime pas les ~s tardives** the concierge doesn't like people coming in late; (*Espace*) **~ dans l'atmosphère** re-entry into the atmosphere; **effectuer sa ~ dans l'atmosphère** to re-enter the atmosphere; (*Sport*) **~ en touche** throw-in.

e *[récolte]* bringing in. **faire la ~ du blé** to bring in the wheat.

f (*Cartes*) cards picked up.

g (*Comm*) **~s** income; **~ d'argent** sum of money (coming in); **je compte sur une ~ d'argent très prochaine** I'm expecting a sum of money *ou* some money very soon; (*Fin*) **les ~s de l'impôt** the revenue from tax.

rentrer [ʀɑ̃tʀe] 1 1 vi (*avec aux être*) a (*entrer à nouveau*) (*aller*) to go back in; (*venir*) to come back in. **il pleut trop, rentrez un instant** it's raining too hard so come back in for a while; **il était sorti sans ses clefs, il a dû ~ par la fenêtre** he'd gone out without his keys and he had to get back in through the window; **il est rentré dans la maison/la pièce** he went back (*ou* came back) into the house/the room.

b (*revenir chez soi*) to come back, come (back) home, return (home); (*s'en aller chez soi*) to go (back) home, return home; (*arriver chez soi*) to get (back) home, return home. **est-ce qu'il est rentré?** is he back?, is he (back) home?, has he got *ou* come back home?; **~ de l'école/du bureau** to come back from school/from the office, come (*ou* go) home from school/from the office; **il a dû ~ de voyage d'urgence** he had to come back *ou* come home from his trip urgently, he had to return home urgently; **~ à Paris/de Paris** to go back *ou* come back *ou* return to Paris/from Paris; (*Aviat*) **~ à sa base** to return *ou* go back to base; **je rentre en voiture** I'm driving back, I'm going back by car; **dépêche-toi de ~, ta mère a besoin de toi** hurry home *ou* back because your mother needs you; **elle est rentrée très tard hier soir** she came *ou* got in *ou* back very late last night.

c (*reprendre ses activités*) *[élèves]* to go back to school, start school again; *[université]* to start again; *[tribunaux]* to reopen; *[parlement]* to reassemble; *[députés]* to return, reassemble. **les enfants rentrent en classe** *ou* **à l'école lundi** the children go back to school *ou* start school again on Monday, school resumes *ou* starts again *ou* goes back on Monday; **le trimestre prochain, on rentrera un lundi** next term starts *ou* next term we start on a Monday.

d (*entrer*) *[personne]* to go in; to come in; *[chose]* to go in. **les voleurs sont rentrés par la fenêtre** the thieves got in by the window; **il pleuvait, nous sommes rentrés dans un café** it was raining so we went into a cafe; **il faut trouver une clef qui rentre dans cette serrure** we must find a key that goes *ou* fits into this lock; **cette clef ne rentre pas (dans la serrure)** this key doesn't fit (into the lock), I can't get this key in (the lock) *ou* into the lock; (*fig*) **il a le cou qui lui rentre dans les épaules** he is very short-necked, he has a very short neck; **il était exténué, les jambes lui rentraient dans le corps** he was so exhausted his legs were giving way under him *ou* he was ready to drop; **tout cela ne rentrera pas dans la valise** that won't all go *ou* fit into the suitcase, you (*ou* we *etc*) won't get all that into the suitcase; **pour les enfants, il y a des cubes qui rentrent les uns dans les autres** there are cubes that fit into one another *ou* one inside the other for children.

e (*travailler dans*) **~ dans** *police, firme, fonction publique* to join, go into; *industrie, banque* to go into; **c'est son père qui l'a fait ~ dans l'usine** his father helped him (to) get a job in the factory *ou* (to) get into the factory.

f (*se jeter dans*) **~ dans** to crash into, collide with; **sa voiture a dérapé, il est rentré dans un arbre** his car skidded and he crashed into a tree; **furieux, il voulait lui ~ dedans**‡ *ou* **lui ~ dans le chou**‡ he was furious and he felt like pitching into him *ou* smashing his head in*; **rentrez-leur dedans!**‡ sock it to them!‡; **il lui est rentré dans le lard**‡ *ou* **le mou**‡ *ou* **le buffet**‡ he beat him up*; **les deux voitures se sont rentrées dedans à grande vitesse** the two cars crashed into each other *ou* collided (with each other) at high speed.

g (*être compris dans*) **~ dans** to be included in, be part of; **cela ne rentre pas dans ses attributions** that is not included in *ou* part of his duties; **les frais de déplacement ne devraient pas ~ dans la note** travelling expenses should not be included in the bill *ou* should not be put on the bill; **~ dans une catégorie** to fall into *ou* come into *ou* go under a category.

h *[argent]* to come in. **l'argent ne rentre pas en ce moment** the money isn't coming in at the moment; **l'argent rentre difficilement/bien en ce moment** there isn't much money/there's plenty of money coming in at the moment; **faire ~ les impôts/les fonds** to collect the taxes/the funds; **faire ~ l'argent** to get the money in.

i (*) *[connaissances]* **la grammaire/les maths, ça ne rentre pas** he can't take grammar/maths in, he can't get the hang of grammar/maths*; **l'anglais, ça commence à ~** English is beginning to sink in; **faire ~ qch dans la tête de qn** to drum *ou* get sth into sb *ou* sb's head; **vous aurez du mal à lui faire ~ cela dans la tête** you'll have a job drumming that into him *ou* making him take that in *ou* getting that into his head.

j (*loc*) **~ dans sa coquille** to go back into one's shell; **~ dans ses droits** to recover one's rights; **~ dans son argent/dans ses frais** to recover *ou* get back one's money/expenses; **~ dans ses fonds** to recoup one's costs; **tout est rentré dans l'ordre** (*dans son état normal*) everything is back to normal again, everything is straight again *ou* in order again; (*dans le calme*) order has returned, order has been restored; (*tout a été clarifié*) everything is sorted out now; **~ dans le rang** to come *ou* fall back into line, toe the line; **~ en grâce** *ou* **faveur auprès de qn** to get back into sb's good graces; **j'aurais voulu ~ sous terre** I wished the ground could have opened and swallowed me up.

2 **vt** (*avec aux avoir*) a *foins, moisson* to bring in, get in; *marchandises, animaux* (*en venant*) to bring in; (*en allant*) to take in. **~ sa voiture (au garage)** to put the car away (in the garage), put the car in the garage; **ne laisse pas ta bicyclette à la pluie, rentre-la** don't leave your bicycle out in the rain, put it away *ou* bring it in; **~ les bêtes à l'étable** to bring the cattle into the cowshed, bring in the cattle, put the cattle in the cowshed.

b *train d'atterrissage* to raise; (*lit, fig*) *griffes* to draw in. **~ sa chemise (dans son pantalon)** to tuck one's shirt in (one's trousers); **~ le cou dans les épaules** to hunch up one's shoulders; **ne me rentre pas ton coude dans le ventre** don't jab *ou* stick your elbow in(to) my stomach; **~ le ventre** to pull one's stomach in; **~ ses larmes** to hold back *ou* choke back (one's) tears, fight back tears; **~ sa rage** to hold back *ou* suppress one's anger; (*Sport*) **~ un but** to score a goal.

renvelopper [ʀɑ̃vlɔpe] [1] **vt** to rewrap, wrap up again.

renversable [ʀɑ̃vɛʀsabl] **adj** *obstacle* (*lit*) which can be knocked down; (*fig*) which can be overcome; *ordre établi* which can be overthrown; *termes* which can be reversed; *fraction* which can be inverted. **facilement ~** *objet* easily overturned, easily knocked over; *canot* easily overturned *ou* capsized.

renversant, e* [ʀɑ̃vɛʀsɑ̃, ɑ̃t] **adj** *nouvelle* staggering*, astounding; *personne* amazing, incredible.

renverse [ʀɑ̃vɛʀs] **nf: à la ~** on one's back; **tomber à la ~** to fall backwards; (*fig*) **il y a de quoi tomber à la ~!** it's astounding! *ou* staggering!*

renversé, e [ʀɑ̃vɛʀse] (**ptp de renverser**) **adj** a (*à l'envers*) upside down (*attrib*); *fraction* inverted; *image* inverted, reversed; *voir* **crème**. b (*stupéfait*) **être ~** to be bowled over, be staggered*. c (*penché*) *écriture* backhand (*épith*).

renversement [ʀɑ̃vɛʀsəmɑ̃] **nm** a *[image, fraction]* inversion; *[ordre des mots]* inversion, reversal; *[vapeur]* reversing; *[situation]* reversal; (*Mus*) *[intervalles, accord]* inversion. b *[alliances, valeurs]* reversal; *[ministre]* removal from office; *[gouvernement]* (*par un coup d'État*) overthrow; (*par un vote*) defeat, voting *ou* turning out of office. **un ~ de tendance de l'opinion publique** a shift *ou* swing (in the opposite direction) in public opinion. c *[buste, tête]* tilting *ou* tipping back. d *[courant]* changing of direction; *[marée, vent]* turning, changing of direction.

renverser [ʀɑ̃vɛʀse] [1] 1 **vt** a (*faire tomber*) *personne* to knock over *ou* down; *chaise* to knock down, overturn; *vase, bouteille* to knock over, upset, overturn; (*Aut*) *piéton* to knock over *ou* down, run over. **il l'a renversé d'un coup de poing** he gave it a blow that knocked it over; **le cheval a renversé son cavalier** the horse threw *ou* unseated its rider; **un camion a renversé son chargement sur la route** a lorry has shed its load on the road.

b (*répandre*) *liquide* to spill, upset. **~ du vin sur la nappe** to spill *ou* upset some wine on the tablecloth.

c (*mettre à l'envers*) to turn upside down. **~ un seau (pour monter dessus)** to turn a bucket upside down (so as to stand on it).

d (*abattre*) *obstacles* (*lit*) to knock down; (*fig*) to overcome; *ordre établi, tradition, royauté* to overthrow; *ministre* to put *ou* throw out of office, remove from office. **~ le gouvernement** (*par un coup d'État*) to overthrow *ou* overturn *ou* topple the government; (*par un vote*) to defeat the government, vote *ou* throw the government out of office.

e (*pencher*) **~ la tête en arrière** to tip *ou* tilt one's head back; **~ le corps en arrière** to lean back; **elle lui renversa la tête en arrière** she tipped *ou* put his head back.

f (*inverser*) *ordre des mots, courant* to reverse; *fraction* to invert; (*Opt*) *image* to invert, reverse. **~ la situation** to reverse the situation, turn things (a)round; **~ la vapeur** (*lit*) to reverse steam; (*fig*) to change course*.

g (**: étonner*) to bowl over, stagger. **il ne faudrait pas ~ les rôles** don't try to turn the situation round on me (*ou* us *etc*); **la nouvelle l'a renversé** the news bowled him over *ou* staggered him, he couldn't get over the news.

2 **se renverser vpr** a **se ~ en arrière** to lean back; **se ~ sur le dos** to lie down (on one's back); **se ~ sur sa chaise** to tilt *ou* tip *ou* lean back on one's chair, tilt *ou* tip one's chair back.

b *[voiture, camion]* to overturn; *[bateau]* to overturn, capsize; *[verre, vase]* to fall over, be overturned.

renvoi [ʀɑ̃vwa] **nm** a (*voir* **renvoyer**) dismissal; sacking (*Brit*); expulsion; suspension; discharge; sending back; return; kicking back; throwing back; referral; postponement. **menacer de ~** *employé* to threaten with dismissal; (*Scol*) to threaten to expel *ou* with expulsion; **le ~ d'un projet de loi en commission** sending a bill to a committee *ou* for further discussion; (*Sport*) **à la suite d'un mauvais ~ du gardien, la balle fut interceptée par l'équipe adverse** as a result of a poor return *ou* throw by the goalkeeper the ball was intercepted by the opposing team; (*Rugby*) **~ aux 22 mètres** drop-out; (*Jur*) **demande de ~ devant une autre juridiction** application for transfer of proceedings.

b (*référence*) cross-reference; (*en bas de page*) footnote. **faire un ~ aux notes de l'appendice** to cross-refer to the notes in the appendix.

c (*rot*) belch. **avoir un ~** to belch; **avoir des ~s** to have wind (*Brit*) *ou* gas (*US*); **ça me donne des ~s** it gives me wind (*Brit*), it repeats on me (*Brit*), it makes me belch.

d (*Tech*) **levier de ~** reversing lever; **poulie de ~** return pulley.

e (*Mus*) repeat mark *ou* sign.

renvoyer [ʀɑ̃vwaje] [8] **vt** a (*congédier*) *employé* to dismiss, sack (*Brit*); *élève* (*définitivement*) to expel; (*temporairement*) to suspend; *étudiant* to expel, send down (*Brit*). **il s'est fait ~ de son travail** he was dismissed *ou* sacked (*Brit*) from his job; (*fig : vomir*) **~ la classe*** to throw up*.

b (*faire retourner*) to send back; (*faire repartir*) to send away; (*libérer*) *accusé, troupes* to discharge. **je l'ai renvoyé chez lui** I sent him back home; **~ les soldats dans leurs foyers** to discharge soldiers, send soldiers back home; **~ le projet de loi en commission** to refer the bill back *ou* send the bill for further discussion, send the bill to a committee; **ils se renvoient les clients de service en service** they send the customers *ou* hand on the customers from one office to the next.

c (*réexpédier*) *lettre, colis* to send back, return; *bague de fiançailles* to return, give back.

d (*relancer*) *balle* (*gén*) to send back; (*au pied*) to kick back; (*à la main*) to throw back; (*Tennis*) to return (*à* to). **il m'a renvoyé la balle** (*argument*) he threw the *ou* my argument back at me, he came back at me with the same argument; (*responsabilité*) he handed the responsibility over to me, he left it up to me, he passed the buck to me*; **ils se renvoient la balle** (*argument*) they throw the same argument at each other, they come back at each other with the same argument; (*responsabilité*) they each refuse to take the responsibility, they each want to off-load the responsibility, they're each trying to pass the buck*; (*fig*) **~ l'ascenseur** to return the favour.

e (*référer*) *lecteur* to refer (*à* to). **~ aux notes de l'appendice** to (cross-)refer to notes in the appendix; **~ un procès en Haute cour** to refer a case to the high court; **~ le prévenu en cour d'assises** to send the accused for trial by the Crown Court.

f (*différer*) *rendez-vous* to postpone, put off. (*Jur*) **l'affaire a été renvoyée à huitaine** the case was postponed *ou* put off for a week; **~ qch aux calendes grecques** to postpone sth *ou* put sth off indefinitely.

g (*réfléchir*) *son* to echo; *lumière, chaleur, image* to reflect.

h (*Cartes*) **~ carreau/pique** to play diamonds/spades again, lead diamonds/spades again.

réoccupation [ʀeɔkypasjɔ̃] **nf** reoccupation.

réoccuper [ʀeɔkype] [1] **vt** *territoire* to reoccupy; *fonction* to take up again; *local* to take over again.

réopérer [ʀeɔpeʀe] [1] **vt** to operate again. **elle s'est fait ~** she had another operation, she was operated on again.

réorchestration [ʀeɔʀkɛstʀasjɔ̃] **nf** reorchestration.

réorchestrer [ʀeɔʀkɛstʀe] [1] **vt** to reorchestrate.

réorganisateur, -trice [ʀeɔʀganizatœʀ, tʀis] **nm,f** reorganizer.

réorganisation [ʀeɔʀganizasjɔ̃] **nf** reorganization.

réorganiser [ʀeɔʀganize] [1] 1 **vt** to reorganize. 2 **se réorganiser vpr** *[pays, parti]* to be reorganized. **il faudrait qu'on se réorganise** we must get reorganized, we must reorganize ourselves.

réorientation [ʀeɔʀjɑ̃tasjɔ̃] **nf** *[politique]* redirecting, reorientation. **~ scolaire** restreaming (*Brit*), *regrouping according to ability*.

réorienter [ʀeɔʀjɑ̃te] [1] **vt** *politique* to redirect, reorient(ate); (*Scol*) *élève* to restream (*Brit*), *regroup according to ability*.

réouverture [ʀeuvɛʀtyʀ] **nf** *[magasin, théâtre]* reopening; *[débat]* resumption, reopening.

repaire [ʀ(ə)pɛʀ] **nm** (*Zool*) den, lair; (*fig*) den, hideout. **cette taverne est un ~ de brigands** this inn is a thieves' den *ou* a haunt of robbers.

repaître [ʀəpɛtʀ] [57] 1 **vt** (*littér*) **~ ses yeux de qch** to feast one's eyes on sth; **~ son esprit de lectures** to feed one's mind on books. 2 **se repaître vpr** a (*fig*) **se ~ de** *crimes* to wallow in; *lectures, films* to revel in; *illusions* to revel in, feed on. b (*manger*) *[animal]* to eat its fill; *[personne]* to eat one's fill. **se ~ de viande crue** to gorge o.s. on raw meat.

répandre [ʀepɑ̃dʀ] [41] 1 **vt** a (*renverser*) *soupe, vin* to spill; *grains* to scatter; (*volontairement*) *sciure, produit* to spread. **le camion a répandu son chargement sur la chaussée** the lorry shed *ou* spilled its load in the road; **~ du sable sur le sol** to spread *ou* sprinkle sand on the ground; ~ **sa petite monnaie (sur la table) pour la compter** to spread one's change out (on the table) to count it; **la rivière répand ses eaux dans la vallée** the waters of the river spread over *ou* out across the valley.

b (*littér*) *larmes* to shed. ~ **son sang** to shed one's blood; ~ **le sang** to spill *ou* shed blood; **beaucoup de sang a été répandu** a lot of blood was shed *ou* spilled, there was a lot of bloodshed.

c (*être source de*) *lumière* to shed, give out; *odeur* to give off; *chaleur* to give out *ou* off. ~ **de la fumée** *[cheminée]* to give out smoke; *[feu]* to give off *ou* out smoke.

d (*fig: propager*) *nouvelle, mode, joie, terreur* to spread; *dons* to lavish, pour out.

2 **se répandre** vpr a (*couler*) *[liquide]* to spill, be spilled; *[grains]* to scatter, be scattered (*sur* over). **le verre a débordé, et le vin s'est répandu par terre** the glass overflowed and the wine spilled onto the floor; **le sang se répand dans les tissus** blood spreads through the tissues; **la foule se répand dans les rues** the crowd spills out *ou* pours out into the streets.

b (*se dégager*) *[chaleur, odeur, lumière]* to spread; *[son]* to carry (*dans* through). **il se répandit une forte odeur de caoutchouc brûlé** a strong smell of burning rubber was given off.

c (*se propager*) *[doctrine, mode, nouvelle]* to spread (*dans, à travers* through); *[opinion, méthode]* to become widespread (*dans, parmi* among); *[coutume, pratique]* to take hold, become widespread. **la peur se répandit sur son visage** fear spread over his face; **l'horreur/la nouvelle se répandit à travers la ville comme une traînée de poudre** horror/the news spread round *ou* through the town like wildfire.

d **se** ~ **en calomnies/condoléances/excuses/menaces** to pour out *ou* pour forth slanderous remarks/condolences/excuses/threats; **se** ~ **en invectives** to let out a torrent of abuse, pour out a stream of abuse.

répandu, e [repɑ̃dy] (**ptp de répandre**) adj *opinion, préjugé* widespread; *méthode* widespread, widely used. **c'est une idée très ~e** it's a widely *ou* commonly held idea.

réparable [reparabl] adj *objet* repairable, which can be repaired *ou* mended; *erreur* which can be put right *ou* corrected; *perte, faute* which can be made up for. **ce n'est pas** ~ *[objet]* it is beyond repair; *[faute]* there's no way of making up for it; *[erreur]* it can't be put right.

reparaître [r(ə)parɛtr] 57 vi *[personne, trait héréditaire]* to reappear; *[lune]* to reappear, come out again.

réparateur, -trice [reparatœr, tris] 1 adj *sommeil* refreshing. 2 nm,f repairer. ~ **d'objets d'art** restorer of works of art; ~ **de porcelaine** porcelain restorer; ~ **de télévision** television *ou* TV repairman *ou* engineer.

réparation [reparasjɔ̃] nf a (*remise en état*) (*action: voir* **réparer**) mending; repairing; fixing; restoring, restoration; (*résultat*) repair. **la voiture est en** ~ the car is under repair *ou* is being repaired; **on va faire des ~s dans la maison** we're going to have some repair work *ou* some repairs done in the house; **pendant les ~s** during the repairs, while the repairs are (*ou* were) being carried out; **atelier de** ~ repair shop.

b (*correction*) *[erreur]* correction; *[oubli, négligence]* putting right, rectification.

c (*compensation*) *[faute, offense]* atonement (*de* for); *[tort]* redress (*de* for); *[perte]* compensation (*de* for). **en ~ du dommage causé** to make up for *ou* compensate for *ou* make amends for the harm that has been done; **obtenir ~ (d'un affront)** to obtain redress (for an insult); **demander ~ par les armes** to demand a duel.

d (*Ftbl*) **coup de pied/surface de** ~ penalty kick/area.

e (*régénérescence*) *[forces]* restoring, restoration, recovery. **la ~ des tissus sera longue** the tissues will take a long time to heal.

f (*dommages-intérêts*) damages, compensation. (*Hist*) **~s** reparations.

réparer [repare] 1 vt a (*remettre en état*) (*gén*) to mend; *chaussure, machine* to mend, repair, fix; *déchirure, fuite* to mend; *maison* to repair, have repairs done to; *objet d'art* to restore, repair. **donner qch à** ~ to take sth to be mended *ou* repaired; **faire ~ qch** to get *ou* have sth mended *ou* repaired; ~ **qch sommairement** to patch sth up, do a temporary repair job on sth.

b (*corriger*) *erreur* to correct, put right; *oubli, négligence* to put right, rectify.

c (*compenser*) *faute* to make up for, make amends for; *tort* to put right, redress; *offense* to atone for, make up for; *perte* to make good, make up for, compensate for. **tu ne pourras jamais ~ le mal que tu m'as fait** you can never put right *ou* never undo the harm you've done me; **comment pourrais-je ~ ma bêtise?** how could I make amends for *ou* make up for my stupidity?; **cela ne pourra jamais ~ le dommage que j'ai subi** that'll never make up for *ou* compensate for the harm I've suffered; **vous devez ~ en l'épousant** you'll have to make amends by marrying her; **comment pourrais-je ~?** what could I do to make up for it? *ou* to make amends (for it)?

d (*régénérer*) *forces, santé* to restore.

e (*loc*) **il va falloir ~ les dégâts** (*lit*) we'll have to repair the damage; (* *fig*) we'll have to repair the damage *ou* pick up the pieces; (*littér*) ~ **le désordre de sa toilette** to straighten *ou* tidy one's dress.

reparler [r(ə)parle] 1 1 vi: ~ **de qch** to talk about sth again; ~ **à qn** to speak to sb again; **nous en reparlerons** we'll talk about it again *ou* discuss it again later. 2 **se reparler** vpr to speak to each other again, be on speaking terms again, be back on speaking terms.

repartie [reparti] nf retort. **avoir de la ~, avoir la ~ facile** to be good *ou* quick at repartee.

repartir[1] [repartir] 16 vt (*littér: répliquer*) to retort, reply.

repartir[2] [r(ə)partir] 16 vi *[voyageur]* to set *ou* start off again; *[machine]* to start (up) again, restart; *[affaire, discussion]* to get going again, pick up again, get under way again. ~ **chez soi** to go back *ou* return home; **il est reparti hier** he left again yesterday; ~ **à zéro** to start from scratch again, go back to square one (*Brit*); **heureusement, c'est bien reparti** fortunately, things are going smoothly *ou* have got off to a good start this time; *[discussion]* **c'est reparti!*** they're off again!*, they're at it again!*, there they go again!

répartir [repartir] 2 1 vt a (*diviser*) *ressources, travail* to share out, divide up (*en* into, *entre* among), allocate, distribute (*entre* among); *impôts, charges* to share out (*en* into, *entre* among), apportion, allot, allocate (*entre* among); (*distribuer*) *butin, récompenses, rôles* to share out, divide up, distribute (*entre* among). **on avait réparti les joueurs en 2 groupes** the players had been divided *ou* split (up) into 2 groups.

b (*étaler*) *poids, masses, chaleur* to distribute; *paiement, cours, horaire* to spread (*sur* over). **on a mal réparti les bagages dans le coffre** the luggage has been badly *ou* unevenly distributed *ou* hasn't been evenly distributed in the boot; **les troupes sont réparties le long de la frontière** troops are spread out *ou* distributed *ou* scattered along the frontier; **le programme est réparti sur 2 ans** the programme is spread (out) over 2 years.

2 **se répartir** vpr: **les charges se répartissent comme suit** the expenses are divided up as follows *ou* in the following way; **ils se répartissent en 2 ensembles** they can be divided into 2 sets; **ils se sont répartis en 2 groupes** they divided themselves *ou* they split into 2 groups; **ils se sont réparti le travail** they shared the work out *ou* divided the work up among themselves.

répartiteur, -trice [repartitœr, tris] nm,f (*gén: littér*) distributor, apportioner; *[impôt]* assessor. ~ **d'avaries** averager, average adjuster.

répartition [repartisjɔ̃] nf a (*action: voir* **répartir**) sharing out (*NonC*), share-out; dividing up (*NonC*); allocation (*NonC*); distribution (*NonC*); apportionment (*NonC*); allotment (*NonC*); spreading (*NonC*); (*Comm*) dispatching. **cette ~ est injuste et favorise certains** this is a very unfair way to share things out because it gives some more than others; **il a fallu procéder à une deuxième ~ des tâches** the tasks had to be divided up *ou* shared out again. b (*résultat*) *[population, flore, richesses]* distribution; *[pièces, salles]* layout, distribution.

repas [r(ə)pɑ] nm meal. ~ **léger** light meal, snack; ~ **scolaire** school lunch; ~ **de midi** midday *ou* noon (*US*) meal, lunch; ~ **de noces** wedding meal *ou* breakfast; ~ **de Noël** Christmas dinner; **faire son ~ d'un œuf et d'un fruit** to eat an egg and a piece of fruit for one's meal, dine off an egg and a piece of fruit (*frm, hum*); **il prend tous ses ~ au restaurant** he has all his meals at the restaurant, he always eats (out) at the restaurant, he always eats out; **assister au ~ des fauves** to watch the big cats being fed; **à l'heure du** ~ at mealtimes, at our mealtime; **aux heures des** ~ at mealtimes; **panier-~** lunch *ou* dinner *ou* picnic basket, packed lunch; **plateau-~** meal tray; **ticket-~** luncheon voucher (*Brit*), meal ticket (*surtout US*); ~ **à prix fixe** fixed-price meal.

repassage [r(ə)pɑsaʒ] nm *[linge]* ironing; *[couteau]* sharpening. **faire le** ~ to do the ironing. (*sur une étiquette*) ~ **superflu** wash-and-wear, non-iron.

repasser [r(ə)pɑse] 1 1 vt a *rivière, montagne, frontière* to cross again, go *ou* come back across.

b *examen* to resit (*Brit*), take again; *permis de conduire* to take again; *visite médicale* to undergo again.

c *plat* to hand round again; *film* to show again; *émission* to repeat; *disque, chanson* to play again. ~ **un plat au four** to put a dish in the oven again *ou* back in the oven.

d (*au fer à repasser*) to iron; (*à la pattemouille*) to press. **le nylon ne se repasse pas** nylon doesn't need ironing *ou* must not be ironed; **planche/table à** ~ ironing board/table; *voir* **fer**.

e *couteau, lame* to sharpen (up).

f *souvenir, leçon, rôle* to go (back) over, go over again. ~ **qch dans son esprit** to go over sth again *ou* go back over sth in one's mind.

g (*: *transmettre*) *affaire, travail* to hand over *ou* on; *maladie* to pass on (*à qn* to sb). **il m'a repassé le tuyau** he passed *ou* handed me on the tip; **je te repasse ta mère** (*au téléphone*) I'm handing you back to your mother; **je vous repasse le standard** I'll put you back through to the operator.

2 vi a (*retourner*) to come back, go back. **je repasserai** I'll come *ou* call back, I'll call (in) again; **si vous repassez par Paris** (*au retour*) if you come back through Paris; (*une autre fois*) if you're passing through Paris again; **ils sont repassés en Belgique** they crossed back *ou* went back over into Belgium; **il va falloir que je repasse sur le billard* pour une autre opération** I've got to go through another operation, they want to open me up again*; **tu peux toujours ~!**‡ you've got a hope!* (*Brit*), not on your nelly!‡ (*Brit*), you haven't a prayer! (*US*).

b (*devant un même lieu*) to go *ou* come past again; (*sur un même trait*) to go over again, go back over. **je passai et repassai devant la vitrine** I kept walking backwards and forwards in front of the shop window; **souvenirs qui repassent dans la mémoire** memories that are running through one's mind; (*fig*) **quand elle fait un travail, il faut toujours ~ derrière elle** when she does some work it always has to be done again *ou* gone over again afterwards.

repasseur [R(ə)pɑsœR] **nm** (*rémouleur*) knife-grinder *ou* -sharpener.

repasseuse [R(ə)pɑsøz] **nf** (*femme*) ironer; (*machine*) ironer, ironing machine.

repavage [R(ə)pavaʒ] **nm, repavement** [R(ə)pavmɑ̃] **nm** repaving.

repaver [R(ə)pave] 1 **vt** to repave.

repayer [R(ə)peje] 8 **vt** to pay again.

repêchage [R(ə)pɛʃaʒ] **nm** (*voir* **repêcher**) recovery; fishing out; recovery of the body of; letting through; passing. **épreuve/question de ~** exam/question to give candidates a second chance.

repêcher [R(ə)peʃe] 1 **vt** a *corps* to recover, fish out; *noyé* to recover the body of, fish out. **je suis allé ~ la lettre dans la poubelle** I went and fished the letter out of the bin. b (*Scol*) *candidat* to let through, pass (*with less than the official pass mark*); *athlète* to give a second chance to. **élève repêché à l'oral** student who scrapes through *ou* just gets a pass thanks to the oral exam.

repeindre [R(ə)pɛ̃dR] 52 **vt** to repaint.

rependre [R(ə)pɑ̃dR] 41 **vt** to re-hang, hang again.

repenser [R(ə)pɑ̃se] 1 1 **repenser à vt indir:** ~ **à qch** to think about sth again; **plus j'y repense** the more I think of it; **je n'y ai plus repensé** (*plus avant*) I haven't thought about it again (since), I haven't given it any further thought (since); (*j'ai oublié*) it completely slipped my mind; **j'y repenserai** I'll think about it again, I'll have another think about it. 2 **vt** *concept* to rethink. **il faut ~ tout l'enseignement** the whole issue of education will have to be rethought; ~ **la question** to rethink the question, think the question out again, have a second think about the question.

repentant, e [R(ə)pɑ̃tɑ̃, ɑ̃t] **adj** repentant, penitent.

repenti, e [R(ə)pɑ̃ti] (**ptp de se repentir**) **adj** repentant, penitent.

repentir[1] **(se)** [R(ə)pɑ̃tiR] 16 **vpr** a (*Rel*) to repent. **se ~ d'une faute/d'avoir commis une faute** to repent of a fault/of having committed a fault. b (*regretter*) **se ~ de qch/d'avoir fait qch** to regret sth/having done sth, be sorry for sth/for having done sth; **tu t'en repentiras!** you'll be sorry (for that), you'll regret that.

repentir[2] [R(ə)pɑ̃tiR] **nm** (*Rel*) repentance (*NonC*); (*regret*) regret.

repérable [R(ə)peRabl] **adj** which can be spotted. **un chapeau rouge ~ de loin** a red hat easily spotted from a distance; **difficilement ~** difficult to spot; (*Mil*) difficult to locate.

repérage [R(ə)peRaʒ] **nm** (*Aviat, Mil*) location. **le ~ d'un point sur la carte** locating *ou* spotting a point on the map, pinpointing a spot on the map; (*Ciné*) **faire des ~s** to research locations.

répercussion [RepɛRkysjɔ̃] **nf** (*gén*) repercussion (*sur, dans* on). (*Fin*) **la ~ d'une taxe sur le client** passing a tax on *ou* along (*US*) to the customer.

répercuter [RepɛRkyte] 1 1 **vt** a *son* to echo; *écho* to send back, throw back; *lumière* to reflect. b (*transmettre*) ~ **des charges/une augmentation sur le client** to pass the cost of sth/an increase in cost on to the customer; ~ **un impôt sur le consommateur** to pass on *ou* along (*US*) a tax to the consumer. 2 **se répercuter vpr** a *[son]* to reverberate, echo; *[lumière]* to be reflected, reflect. b **se ~ sur** to have repercussions on, affect.

reperdre [R(ə)pɛRdR] 41 **vt** to lose again.

repère [R(ə)pɛR] **nm** (*gén: marque, trait*) line, mark; (*jalon, balise*) marker, indicator; (*monument, accident de terrain etc*) landmark; (*événement*) landmark; (*date*) reference point. **j'ai laissé des branches comme ~s pour retrouver notre chemin** I've left branches as markers *ou* to mark our way so that we can find the way back again; ~ **de niveau** bench mark; *voir* **point**[1].

repérer [R(ə)peRe] 6 1 **vt** a (**: localiser*) *personne, erreur* to spot, pick out; *endroit, chemin* to discover, locate, find. **se faire** ~ (*lit*) to be spotted, be picked out; (*fig*) to be found out, get caught; **il avait repéré un petit restaurant où l'on mange bien** he had discovered *ou* located *ou* tracked down a little restaurant where the food was good; **tu vas nous faire ~** we'll be noticed *ou* spotted because of you, you'll get us caught.

b (*Mil*) to locate, pinpoint.

c (*Tech*) *niveau, alignement* to mark out *ou* off, stake out.

2 **se repérer vpr** (*gén: se diriger*) to find one's way about *ou* around; (*établir sa position*) to find *ou* get one's bearings. (*fig*) **j'ai du mal à me ~ dans cette intrigue** I have difficulty getting my bearings in this plot.

répertoire [RepɛRtwaR] 1 **nm** a (*carnet*) index notebook, notebook with alphabetical thumb index; (*liste*) (alphabetical) list; (*catalogue*) catalogue. **noter un mot dans un ~** to write a word down in an alphabetical index, index a word.

b (*Théât*) repertoire, repertory; *[chanteur, musicien]* repertoire. **jouer une pièce du ~** to put on a stock play; **elle n'a que 2 chansons à son ~** she's only got 2 songs in her repertoire; (*fig*) **elle a tout un ~ de jurons/d'histoires drôles** she has quite a repertoire of swearwords/jokes.

2 **comp** ►**répertoire d'adresses** address book ►**répertoire alphabétique** alphabetical index *ou* list ►**répertoire des rues** (*sur un plan*) street index.

répertorier [RepɛRtɔRje] 7 **vt** to itemize, make a list of, list.

repeser [R(ə)pəze] 5 **vt** to reweigh, weigh again.

répéter [Repete] 6 1 **vt** a (*redire*) *explication, question* to repeat; *mot* to repeat, say again; *histoire* to repeat, retell. ~ **à qn que** to tell sb again that, repeat that; **pourriez-vous me ~ cette phrase?** could you repeat that sentence?, could you say that sentence (to me) again?; **je l'ai répété/je te l'ai répété dix fois** I've said that/I've told you that a dozen times; **il répète toujours la même chose** he keeps saying *ou* repeating the same thing; (*ton de menace*) **répète!** just you dare repeat that! *ou* say that again!; **il ne se l'est pas fait ~** he didn't have to be told *ou* asked twice, he didn't need asking *ou* telling twice.

b (*rapporter*) *calomnie* to repeat, spread about; *histoire* to repeat. **elle est allée tout ~ à son père** she went and related *ou* repeated everything to her father, she went and told her father everything; **je vais vous ~ exactement ce qu'il m'a dit** I'll repeat exactly what he said; **c'est un secret, ne le répétez pas!** it's a secret, don't repeat it! *ou* don't tell anyone!; **il m'a répété tous les détails de l'événement** he went over all the details of the event for me, he related all the details of the event to me.

c (*refaire*) *expérience, exploit* to repeat, do again; *proposition* to repeat, renew; *essai* to repeat. **nous répéterons une nouvelle fois la tentative** we'll repeat the attempt one more time, we'll have another try (at it), we'll try (it) again one more time; **tentatives répétées de suicide** repeated attempts at suicide; **tentatives répétées d'évasion** repeated escape attempts, repeated attempts to escape.

d *pièce, symphonie, émission* to rehearse; *rôle, leçon* to learn, go over; *morceau de piano* to practise. **nous répétons à 4 heures** we rehearse at 4 o'clock, the rehearsal is at 4 o'clock; **ma mère m'a fait ~ ma leçon/mon rôle** I had to go over my homework/my part with my mother.

e (*reproduire*) *motif* to repeat; (*Mus*) *thème* to repeat, restate. **les miroirs répétaient son image** his image was reflected again and again in the mirrors.

2 **se répéter vpr** a (*redire, radoter*) to repeat o.s. **se ~ qch à soi-même** to repeat sth to o.s.; **la nouvelle que toute la ville se répète** the news that everyone in town is passing round, the news which is being repeated all round the town; **je ne voudrais pas me ~, mais ...** I don't want to repeat myself *ou* say the same thing twice, but ... .

b (*se reproduire*) to be repeated, reoccur, recur. **ces incidents se répétèrent fréquemment** these incidents were frequently repeated, these incidents kept recurring *ou* occurred repeatedly; **que cela ne se répète pas!** (just) don't let that happen again!; **l'histoire ne se répète jamais** history never repeats itself.

répétiteur, -trice [RepetitœR, tRis] **nm,f** (*Scol*) tutor, coach.

répétitif, -ive [Repetitif, iv] **adj** repetitive.

répétition [Repetisjɔ̃] **nf** a (*redite*) repetition. **il y a beaucoup de ~s** there is a lot of repetition, there are numerous repetitions.

b (*Théât: représentation, fig*) rehearsal. ~ **générale** (final) dress rehearsal.

c (*action*) (*gén*) repetition; *[pièce, symphonie]* rehearsal; *[rôle]* learning; *[morceau de piano]* practising. **pour éviter la ~ d'une telle mésaventure** to prevent the repetition *ou* the recurrence of such a mishap, to prevent such a mishap recurring; **la ~ d'un tel exploit est difficile** repeating a feat like that *ou* doing a feat like that again is difficult; **la chorale est en ~** the choir is rehearsing *ou* practising.

d (*Hist Scol*) private lesson, private coaching (*NonC*).

e (*Tech*) **fusil/montre à ~** repeater rifle/watch.

repeuplement [R(ə)pœpləmɑ̃] **nm** (*voir* **repeupler**) repopulation; restocking; replanting.

repeupler [R(ə)pœple] 1 1 **vt** *région* to repopulate; *bassin, chasse* to restock (*de* with); *forêt* to replant (*de* with). 2 **se repeupler vpr** to be *ou* become repopulated.

repincer [R(ə)pɛ̃se] 3 **vt** (*lit*) to pinch *ou* nip again; (** fig*) to catch again, nab* again. **se faire ~** to get nabbed* again.

repiquage [R(ə)pikaʒ] **nm** (*voir* **repiquer**) planting *ou* pricking *ou* bedding out; subculturing; touching up, retouching; rerecording; recording, taping.

repiquer [R(ə)pike] 1 1 **vt** a (*Bot*) to plant out, prick out, bed (out); (*Bio*) to subculture. **plantes à ~** bedding plants. b (*Phot*) to touch up, retouch; *enregistrement* to rerecord; *disque* to record, tape. c (**: attraper*) to nab* again. d *[moustique]* to bite again; *[épine]* to prick again. (*Couture*) ~ **un vêtement à la machine** to restitch a garment. 2 **repiquer à*** **vt indir:** ~ **au plat** to take a second helping; ~ **au truc** to go back to one's old ways, be at it again*.

répit [Repi] **nm** (*rémission*) respite; (*repos*) respite, rest. **la douleur ne lui laisse pas de ~** he never has any respite from the pain, the pain never gives him any respite; **s'accorder un peu de ~** to take a bit of a rest *ou* a breather*; **accordez-nous 5 minutes de ~** give us 5 minutes' rest *ou* respite; **travailler sans ~** to work continuously *ou* without respite; **harceler qn sans ~** to harass sb relentlessly; **donnez-moi un petit ~ pour vous payer** give me some breathing space to pay you.

replacement [ʀ(ə)plasmɑ̃] nm (*voir* **replacer**) replacing, putting back; redeployment.

replacer [ʀ(ə)plase] [3] 1 vt *objet* to replace, put back (in its place); *employé* to find a new job for, redeploy. **il faut ~ les choses dans leur contexte** we must put things back in their context. 2 **se replacer** vpr *[employé]* to find a new job. **se ~ dans les mêmes conditions** to put o.s. in the same situation; **replaçons-nous au 16e siècle** let's go *ou* look back to the 16th century.

replanter [ʀ(ə)plɑ̃te] [1] vt *plante* to replant, plant out; *forêt, arbre* to replant. **~ un bois en conifères** to replant a wood with conifers.

replat [ʀəpla] nm projecting ledge *ou* shelf.

replâtrage [ʀ(ə)plɑtʀaʒ] nm (*voir* **replâtrer**) replastering; patching up. (*Pol*) **~ ministériel*** patching together *ou* patch-up of the cabinet.

replâtrer [ʀ(ə)plɑtʀe] [1] vt a *mur* to replaster. b (*) *amitié* to patch up; *gouvernement* to patch up.

replet, -ète [ʀəplɛ, ɛt] adj *personne* podgy, fat; *visage* chubby.

réplétion [ʀeplesjɔ̃] nf (*frm*) repletion (*frm*).

repleuvoir [ʀ(ə)plœvwaʀ] [23] vb impers to rain again, start raining again. **il repleut** it is raining again, it has started raining again.

repli [ʀəpli] nm a *[terrain, papier]* fold; *[intestin, serpent]* coil, fold; *[rivière]* bend, twist, winding (*NonC*); *[peau]* (*de l'âge*) wrinkle; (*de l'embonpoint*) fold (*de* in).

b (*Couture*) *[ourlet, étoffe]* fold, turn (*de* in).

c (*Mil*) withdrawal, falling back. (*Mil, fig*) **position de ~** fallback position.

d (*Bourse*) drop, fall, downturn. **le cours de l'étain a accentué son ~** the price of tin has weakened further; **le dollar est en ~ à 5 F** the dollar has fallen back to 5 francs.

e (*réserve*) withdrawal. **~ sur soi-même** withdrawal into oneself *ou* into one's shell, turning in on oneself.

f (*recoin*) *[cœur, conscience]* hidden *ou* innermost recess, innermost reaches.

repliable [ʀ(ə)plijabl] adj folding.

repliement [ʀ(ə)plimɑ̃] nm: **~ (sur soi-même)** withdrawal (into oneself), turning in on oneself.

replier [ʀ(ə)plije] [7] 1 vt a *carte, journal, robe* to fold up (again), fold back up; *manche, bas de pantalon* to roll up, fold up; *coin de feuille* to fold over; *ailes* to fold (back); *jambes* to tuck up; *couteau* to close. **les jambes repliées sous lui** sitting back with his legs tucked under him; **~ le drap sur la couverture** to fold the sheet back over *ou* down over the blanket.

b (*Mil*) *troupes* to withdraw; *civils* to move back *ou* away.

2 **se replier** vpr *[serpent]* to curl up, coil up; *[chat]* to curl up; *[lame de couteau]* to fold back; (*Mil*) to fall back, withdraw (*sur* to); (*Bourse*) *[valeurs]* to fall (back), drop. **se ~ (sur soi-même)** to withdraw into oneself, turn in on oneself; **la province est repliée sur elle-même** the provinces are very inward-looking.

réplique [ʀeplik] nf a (*réponse*) reply, retort, rejoinder. **il a la ~ facile** he's always ready with a quick answer, he's never at a loss for an answer *ou* a reply; **et pas de ~!** and don't answer back!, and let's not have any backchat!* (*Brit*); **obéis sans ~!** do as you're told without a word! *ou* without argument!; **argument sans ~** unanswerable *ou* irrefutable argument; **il n'y a pas de ~ à cela** there's no answer to that.

b (*contre-attaque*) counter-attack. **la ~ ne se fit pas attendre: ils attaquèrent** they weren't slow to retaliate and attacked at once.

c (*Théât*) line. **dialogue aux ~s spirituelles** dialogue with some witty lines; **oublier sa ~** to forget one's lines *ou* words; **l'acteur a manqué sa ~** the actor missed his cue; **c'est X qui vous donnera la ~** (*pour répéter*) X will give you your cue; (*dans une scène*) X will play opposite you; (*fig*) **je saurai lui donner la ~** I can match him (in an argument), I can give as good as I get; **les deux orateurs se donnent la ~** the two speakers indulge in a bit of verbal sparring.

d (*Art*) replica. (*fig*) **il est la ~ de son jumeau** he is the (spitting) image of his twin brother.

répliquer [ʀeplike] [1] 1 vt to reply. **il (lui) répliqua que** he replied *ou* retorted that; **il n'y a rien à ~ à cela** what can we say to that?, there's no answer to that; **il trouve toujours quelque chose à ~** he always has a ready answer, he's always got an answer for everything. 2 vi a (*répondre*) to reply. **~ à la critique** to reply to criticism; **et ne réplique pas!** (*insolence*) and don't answer back!; (*protestation*) and no protests! *ou* objections! b (*contre-attaquer*) to retaliate. **il répliqua par des coups de poing/des injures** he retaliated with his fists/with foul language.

replonger [ʀ(ə)plɔ̃ʒe] [3] 1 vt *rame, cuiller* to dip back (*dans* into). **replongé dans la pauvreté/la guerre/l'obscurité** plunged into poverty/war/obscurity again, plunged back into poverty/war/obscurity; **replongeant sa main dans l'eau** plunging *ou* putting *ou* sticking his hand into the water again *ou* back in(to) the water.

2 vi (*dans une piscine*) to dive back, dive again (*dans* into).

3 **se replonger** vpr to dive back *ou* dive again (*dans* into). **il se replongea dans sa lecture** he immersed himself in his book *ou* his reading again, he went back to his reading; **se ~ dans les études** to take up studying seriously again, throw oneself into one's studies again.

repolir [ʀ(ə)pɔliʀ] [2] vt *objet* to repolish; (*fig*) *discours* to polish up again, touch up again.

répondant, e [ʀepɔ̃dɑ̃, ɑ̃t] 1 nm,f guarantor, surety. **servir de ~ à qn** (*Fin*) to stand surety for sb, be sb's guarantor; (*fig*) to vouch for sb. 2 nm a (*Fin*) **il a du ~** (*compte approvisionné*) he has money behind him; (*: *beaucoup d'argent*) he has something *ou* plenty to fall back on. b (*Rel*) server.

répondeur, -euse [ʀepɔ̃dœʀ, øz] 1 adj (*) impertinent, cheeky* (*Brit*), sassy* (*US*). **je n'aime pas les enfants ~s** I don't like children who answer back. 2 nm: **~ (téléphonique)** (telephone) answering machine (*simply giving a recorded message*); **~ (enregistreur)** (telephone) answering machine, answerphone (*on which you can leave a message*); **je suis tombé sur un ~** I got a recorded message.

répondre [ʀepɔ̃dʀ] [41] 1 vt a to answer, reply. **il a répondu une grossièreté** he replied with a rude remark, he made a rude remark in reply; **il m'a répondu une lettre** he sent me a letter in reply; **il a répondu qu'il le savait** he answered *ou* replied that he knew, he said in reply that he knew; **il m'a répondu qu'il viendrait** he told me (in reply) that he would come; **je lui ai répondu de se taire** *ou* **qu'il se taise** I told him to be quiet; **vous me demandez si j'accepte, je (vous) réponds que non** you're asking me if I accept and I'm telling you I don't *ou* won't *ou* and my answer is no *ou* that I won't; **je me suis vu ~ que, il me fut répondu que** I was told that; **~ présent à l'appel** (*lit*) to answer present at roll call; (*fig*) to come forward, make oneself known, volunteer; **réponds quelque chose, même si c'est faux** give an answer (of some sort), even if it's wrong; **(c'est) bien répondu!** well answered *ou* said!; **qu'avez-vous à ~?** what have you got to say in reply?; **il n'y a rien à ~** there's no reply *ou* answer to that; **qu'est-ce que vous voulez ~ à cela?** what can you reply *ou* say to that?

b (*Rel*) **~ la messe** to serve (at) mass.

2 vi a to answer, reply. **réponds donc!** well answer (then)!; **~ en claquant la porte** to slam the door by way of reply *ou* by way of an answer; **~ à qn/à une question/à une convocation** to reply to *ou* answer sb/a question/a summons; **seul l'écho lui répondit** only the echo answered him; **je ne lui ai pas encore répondu** I haven't yet replied to his letter *ou* answered his letter *ou* written back to him; **je lui répondrai par écrit** I'll reply *ou* answer in writing, I'll let him have a written reply *ou* answer; **avez-vous répondu à son invitation?** did you reply to *ou* acknowledge his invitation?; **il répond au nom de Dick** he answers to the name of Dick; **~ par oui ou par non** to reply *ou* answer *ou* say yes or no; **~ par monosyllabes** to reply in monosyllables, give monosyllabic answers; **instruments de musique qui se répondent** musical instruments that answer each other; **~ par un sourire/en hochant la tête** to smile/nod in reply; **elle répondit à son salut par un sourire** she replied to *ou* answered his greeting with a smile, she acknowledged his greeting with a smile; **il a répondu par des injures** he replied with a string of insults, he replied by insulting us (*ou* them *etc*); (*Jur*) **prévenu qui doit ~ à plusieurs chefs d'accusation** defendant who must answer several charges *ou* who has several charges to answer.

b **~ (à la porte** *ou* **sonnette)** to answer the door; **~ (au téléphone)** to answer the telephone; **personne ne répond, ça ne répond pas** there's no answer *ou* reply, no one's answering; **on a sonné, va ~** the doorbell rang – go and see who's there, that was the bell – go and answer the door; **personne n'a répondu à mon coup de sonnette** no one answered the door *ou* the bell when I rang, I got no answer when I rang the bell.

c (*être impertinent*) to answer back. **il a répondu à la maîtresse** he answered the teacher back, he was cheeky (*Brit*) *ou* sassy* (*US*) to the teacher*.

d (*réagir*) *voiture, commandes, membres* to respond (*à* to). **son cerveau ne répond plus aux excitations** his brain no longer responds to stimuli; **les freins ne répondaient plus** the brakes were no longer working *ou* had given up *ou* had failed.

3 **répondre à** vt indir a (*correspondre à*) *besoin* to answer, meet; *signalement* to answer, fit. **ça répond tout à fait à l'idée que je m'en faisais** that corresponds exactly to *ou* fits exactly the idea I had of it; **cela répond/ne répond pas à ce que nous cherchons** this meets/doesn't meet *ou* falls short of our requirements; **ça répond/ne répond pas à mon attente** *ou* **à mes espérances** it comes up to/falls short of my expectations.

b (*payer de retour*) *attaque, avances* to respond to; *amour, affection, salut* to return; *politesse, gentillesse, invitation* to repay, pay back. **peu de gens ont répondu à cet appel** few people responded to this appeal *ou* heeded this appeal, there was little response to this appeal; **~ à la force par la force** to answer *ou* meet force with force; **s'ils lancent une attaque, nous saurons y ~** if they launch an attack we'll fight back *ou* retaliate.

c (*être identique à*) *dessin, façade* to match. **les deux ailes du bâtiment se répondent** the two wings of the building match (each other).

4 **répondre de** vt indir (*garantir*) *personne* to answer for. **~ de l'innocence/l'honnêteté de qn** to answer *ou* vouch for sb's innocence/honesty; **~ des dettes de qn** to answer for sb's debts, be answerable for sb's debts; **il viendra, je vous en réponds!** mark my words, he'll come!, he'll come all right, you can take it from me! *ou* you can take my word for it!; **si vous agissez ainsi, je ne réponds plus de rien** if you

behave like that, I'll accept no further responsibility; **je te réponds bien que cela ne se passera pas comme ça!** you can take it from me *ou* you can be sure that it won't happen like that!; (*Jur*) ~ **de ses crimes devant la cour d'assises** to answer for one's crimes in the Crown Court.

répons [ʀepɔ̃] **nm** (*Rel*) response.

réponse [ʀepɔ̃s] **nf** a (*à une lettre, demande, objection*) reply, response; (*à une question, une prière, un coup de sonnette*) answer, reply; *[problème, énigme, examen]* answer (*à, de* to); (*Mus*) answer. **en ~ à votre question** in answer *ou* reply *ou* response to your question; **le droit de ~** the right of reply; **ma lettre est restée sans ~** my letter remained unanswered; **sa demande est restée sans ~** there has been no reply *ou* response to his request; (*Mil*) **on a tiré sur l'ennemi et la ~ ne se fit pas attendre** we fired at the enemy and they were quick to fire back *ou* to return the fire; **télégramme avec ~ payée** reply-paid telegram; **bulletin-/coupon-~** reply slip/coupon.
b (*Physiol, Tech: réaction*) response; (*écho: à un appel, un sentiment*) response.
c (*loc*) **avoir ~ à tout** to have an answer for everything; (*en se justifiant*) never to be at a loss for an answer; **c'est la ~ du berger à la bergère** it's tit for tat; **il me fit une ~ de Normand** he gave me an evasive answer, he wouldn't say yes or no, he wouldn't give me a straight answer.

repopulation [ʀ(ə)pɔpylasjɔ̃] **nf** *[ville]* repopulation; *[étang]* restocking.

report [ʀəpɔʀ] **nm** (*voir* **reporter**) postponement; putting off; deferment; putting back; transfer; writing out, copying out; posting; carrying forward *ou* over; rebetting. **les ~s de voix entre les deux partis se sont bien effectués au deuxième tour** the votes were satisfactorily transferred to the party with more votes after the first round of the election; (*Fin*) ~ **d'échéance** extension of due date; **faire le ~ de** *somme* to carry forward *ou* over; *écriture* to post; (*sur livre de compte*) "**~**" (*en bas de page*) "carried forward"; (*en haut de page*) "brought forward".

reportage [ʀ(ə)pɔʀtaʒ] **nm** a (*Presse, Rad, TV*) report (*sur* on); (*sur le vif*) *[match, événement]* (live) commentary. ~ **photographique/télévisé** illustrated/television report; ~ **en direct** live commentary; **faire un ~ sur** (*Presse*) to write a report on; (*Rad, TV*) to report on; **faire** *ou* **assurer le ~ d'une cérémonie** to cover a ceremony, do the coverage of a ceremony; **être en ~** (*Presse*) to be out on a story, be covering a story; (*Rad, TV*) to be (out) reporting; **c'était un ~ de X** that report was from X, that was X reporting.
b (*métier*) (news) reporting. **il fait du ~** he's a (news) reporter; **le grand ~** the coverage of major international events; **il a fait plusieurs grands ~s pour ...** he has covered several big stories for ... .

reporter[1] [ʀ(ə)pɔʀte] [1] **1 vt** a (*ramener*) *objet* to take back; (*par la pensée*) to take back (*à* to). **cette chanson nous reporte aux années trente** this song takes us back to the thirties.
b (*différer*) *match* to postpone, put off; *décision* to put off, defer; *date* to put off *ou* back (*Brit*), defer. **la réunion est reportée à demain** the meeting has been postponed until tomorrow; (*Jur*) **le jugement est reporté à huitaine** (the) sentence has been deferred for a week.
c (*recopier*) *chiffres, indications* to transfer (*sur* to), write out, copy out (*sur* on); (*Comm*) *écritures* to post; (*Phot*) to transfer (*sur* to). ~ **une somme sur la page suivante** to carry an amount forward *ou* over to the next page.
d (*transférer*) ~ **son affection/son vote sur** to transfer one's affection/one's vote to; ~ **son gain sur un autre cheval/numéro** to put *ou* place one's winnings on *ou* transfer one's bet to another horse/number.
2 se reporter vpr a (*se référer à*) **se ~ à** to refer to; **reportez-vous à la page 5** turn to *ou* refer to *ou* see page 5.
b (*par la pensée*) **se ~ à** to think back to, cast one's mind back to; **reportez-vous par l'esprit au début du siècle** cast your mind back to the turn of the century; **si l'on se reporte à l'Angleterre de cette époque** if one thinks back to the England of that period.

reporter[2] [ʀ(ə)pɔʀtɛʀ] **nm** reporter. **grand ~** international reporter; ~**-photographe** reporter and photographer; **~-cameraman** news reporter and cameraman; *voir* **radioreporter**.

repos [ʀ(ə)po] **nm** a (*détente*) rest. **prendre du ~/un peu de ~** to take *ou* have a rest/a bit of a rest; **il ne peut pas rester** *ou* **demeurer en ~ 5 minutes** he can't rest *ou* relax for (even) 5 minutes; **le médecin lui a ordonné le ~ complet** the doctor has ordered him to rest *ou* ordered him complete rest; **après une matinée/journée de ~ il allait mieux** after a morning's/day's rest he felt better; **respecter le ~ dominical** to observe Sunday as a day of rest; *voir* **cure**[1], **jour, maison**.
b (*congé*) **avoir droit à un jour de ~ hebdomadaire** to have the right to one day off a week; **le médecin lui a donné du ~/huit jours de ~** the doctor has given him some time off/a week off.
c (*tranquillité*) peace and quiet; (*quiétude morale*) peace of mind; (*littér: sommeil, mort*) rest, sleep. **il n'y aura pas de ~ pour lui tant que ...** he'll have no peace of mind until ..., he won't get any rest until ...; **le ~ de la tombe** the sleep of the dead; **le ~ éternel** eternal rest; **avoir la conscience en ~** to have an easy *ou* a clear conscience; **pour avoir l'esprit en ~** to put my (*ou* your *etc*) mind at rest, so that I (*ou* you *etc*) can feel easy in my (*ou* your *etc*) mind; **laisse ton frère en ~** leave your brother in peace; *voir* **lit**.
d (*pause*) *[discours]* pause; *[vers]* rest; (*Mus*) cadence.
e (*loc*) (*Mil*) ~! (stand) at ease!; **au ~** *soldat* standing at ease; *masse, machine, animal* at rest; **muscle au ~** *ou* **à l'état de ~** relaxed muscle; **sans ~** *travailler* without stopping, without taking a rest, relentlessly; *marcher* without a break *ou* a rest, without stopping; *quête* uninterrupted, relentless; **de tout ~** *situation, entreprise* secure, safe; *placement* gilt-edged, safe; **ce n'est pas de tout ~!** it's not exactly restful!, it's no picnic!*; (*Agr*) **laisser la terre en ~** to let the land lie fallow; **en hiver la nature est en ~** nature rests in winter.

reposant, e [ʀ(ə)pozɑ̃, ɑ̃t] **adj** *sommeil* refreshing; *lieu, couleur* restful; *musique, vacances* restful, relaxing. **c'est ~ pour la vue** it's (very) restful on *ou* to the eyes.

repose [ʀ(ə)poz] **nf** *[appareil]* refitting, reinstallation; *[tapis]* relaying, putting (back) down again.

repose- [ʀ(ə)poz] **préf** *voir* **reposer**.

reposé, e [ʀ(ə)poze] (**ptp de reposer**) **adj** *air, teint* fresh, rested (*attrib*); *cheval* fresh (*attrib*), rested (*attrib*). **elle avait le visage ~** she looked rested; **j'ai l'esprit ~** my mind is fresh *ou* rested; **maintenant que vous êtes bien ~** ... now (that) you have had a good rest ...; *voir* **tête**.

reposer [ʀ(ə)poze] [1] **1 vt** a (*poser à nouveau*) *verre etc* to put back down, put down again; *tapis* to relay, put back down; *objet démonté* to refit, put back. ~ **ses yeux sur qch** to look at sth again; **va ~ ce livre où tu l'as trouvé** go and put that book back where you found it; (*Mil*) **reposez armes!** order arms!
b (*soulager, délasser*) *yeux, corps, membres* to rest; *esprit* to rest, relax. **se ~ l'esprit** to rest one's mind, give one's mind *ou* brain a rest; **les lunettes de soleil reposent les yeux** *ou* **la vue** sunglasses rest the eyes, sunglasses are restful to the eyes; ~ **sa tête/sa jambe sur un coussin** to rest one's head/leg on a cushion; **cela repose de ne voir personne (pendant une journée)** it's restful not to see anyone (for a whole day); *voir* **tête**.
c (*répéter*) *question* to repeat, ask again; *problème* to bring up again, raise again. **cela va ~ le problème** that will raise the (whole) problem again *ou* bring the (whole) problem up again; **cet incident va (nous) ~ un problème** this incident is going to pose us a new problem *ou* bring up a new problem for us.
2 reposer sur vt indir *[bâtiment]* to be built on; *[route]* to rest on, be supported by; *[supposition]* to rest on, be based on; *[résultat]* to depend on. **sa théorie ne repose sur rien de précis** his theory doesn't rest on *ou* isn't based on anything specific; **tout repose sur son témoignage** everything hinges on *ou* rests on his evidence.
3 vi a (*littér*) (*être étendu*) to rest, lie (down); (*dormir*) to sleep, rest; (*être enterré*) to rest. **tout reposait dans la campagne** everything was sleeping *ou* resting in the country(side); **ici repose ...** here lies ...; **qu'il repose en paix** may he rest in peace; **l'épave repose par 20 mètres de fond** the wreck is lying 20 metres down.
b **laisser ~** *liquide* to leave to settle, let settle *ou* stand; *pâte à pain* to leave to rise, let rise; *pâte feuilletée* to (allow to) rest; *pâte à crêpes* to leave (to stand); **laisser ~ la terre** to let the earth lie fallow; **faire ~ son cheval** to rest one's horse.
4 se reposer vpr a (*se délasser*) to rest. **se ~ sur ses lauriers** to rest on one's laurels.
b **se ~ sur qn** to rely on sb; **je me repose sur vous pour régler cette affaire** I'll leave it to you *ou* I'm relying on you to sort this business out; **elle se repose sur lui pour tout** she relies on him for everything.
c (*se poser à nouveau*) *[oiseau, poussière]* to settle again; *[problème]* to crop up again.
5 comp ▸ repose-bras nm inv armrest **▸ repose-pieds nm inv** footrest **▸ repose-tête nm (pl repose-têtes)** headrest.

repositionner [ʀ(ə)pɔzisjɔne] [1] **vt** to reposition. **nous cherchons à nous ~ dans le haut de gamme** we are seeking to position ourselves further up market.

reposoir [ʀ(ə)pozwaʀ] **nm** *[église, procession]* altar of repose; *[maison privée]* temporary altar.

repoussage [ʀ(ə)pusaʒ] **nm** *[cuir, métal]* repoussé work, embossing.

repoussant, e [ʀ(ə)pusɑ̃, ɑ̃t] **adj** *odeur, saleté, visage* repulsive, repugnant; *laideur* repulsive.

repousse [ʀ(ə)pus] **nf** *[cheveux, gazon]* regrowth. **pour accélérer la ~ des cheveux** to help the hair grow again *ou* grow back in.

repousse-peaux [ʀəpuspo] **nm inv** cuticle remover.

repousser [ʀ(ə)puse] [1] **1 vt** a (*écarter, refouler*) *objet encombrant* to push out of the way, push away; *ennemi, attaque* to repel, repulse, drive back; *coups* to ward off; *soupirant, quémandeur, malheureux* to turn away, repulse. ~ **qch du pied** to kick sth out of the way, kick sth away; **il me repoussa avec brusquerie** he pushed me away *ou* out of the way roughly; **elle parvint à ~ son agresseur** she managed to repel *ou* drive off *ou* beat off her attacker; **les électrons se repoussent** electrons repel each other.
b (*fig: refuser*) *demande, conseil, aide* to turn down, reject; *hypothèse* to reject, dismiss, rule out; *tentation* to reject, resist, repel; *projet de loi* to reject; *objections, arguments* to brush aside, dismiss. **la police ne repousse pas l'hypothèse du suicide** the police do not rule out the possibility of suicide.
c (*remettre en place*) *meuble* to push back; *tiroir* to push back in;

porte to push to. ~ **la table contre le mur** to push the table back *ou* up against the wall.

d (*différer*) *date, réunion* to put off *ou* back (*Brit*), postpone, defer. **la date de l'examen a été repoussée (à huitaine/à lundi)** the date of the exam has been put back (*Brit*) (a week/till Monday), the exam has been put off *ou* postponed (for a week/till Monday).

e (*dégoûter*) to repel, repulse. **tout en lui me repousse** everything about him repels *ou* repulses me.

f (*Tech*) *cuir, métal* to emboss (by hand), work in repoussé. **en cuir/métal repoussé** in repoussé leather/metal.

2 **vi** *[feuilles, cheveux]* to grow again. **laisser ~ sa barbe** to let one's beard grow again.

repoussoir [R(ə)puswaR] **nm** a (*à cuir, métal*) snarling iron; (*à ongles*) orange stick. b (*Art*) repoussoir, high-toned foreground; (*fig: faire-valoir*) foil. **servir de ~ à qn** to act as a foil to sb. c (*péj *: personne laide*) (*homme*) ugly so-and-so*; (*femme*) dog‡, ugly so-and-so*. **c'est un ~!** he *ou* she is ugly as sin!*, he *ou* she is no oil painting!*

répréhensible [RepReɑ̃sibl] **adj** *acte, personne* reprehensible. **je ne vois pas ce qu'il y a de ~ à ça!** I don't see what's wrong with (doing) that!

reprendre [R(ə)pRɑ̃dR] 58 1 **vt** a (*récupérer*) *ville* to recapture; *prisonnier* to recapture, catch again; *employé* to take back; *objet prêté* to take back, get back. ~ **sa place** (*sur un siège*) to go back to one's seat, resume one's seat; (*dans un emploi*) to go back to work; **la photo avait repris sa place sur la cheminée** the photo was back in its (usual) place on the mantelpiece; **passer ~ qn** to go back *ou* come back for sb, go *ou* come and fetch (*Brit*) sb *ou* call for sb; **il a repris sa parole** he went back on his word; **j'irai ~ mon manteau chez le teinturier** I'll go and get *ou* fetch (*Brit*) my coat (back) from the cleaner's; ~ **son nom de jeune fille** to take one's maiden name again, go back to *ou* revert to one's maiden name.

b *pain, viande* to have *ou* take (some) more. **voulez-vous ~ des légumes?** would you like a second helping of vegetables?, would you like some more vegetables?

c (*retrouver*) *espoir, droits, forces* to regain, recover. ~ **des couleurs** to get some colour back in one's cheeks; ~ **confiance/courage** to regain *ou* recover one's confidence/courage; *[humour etc]* ~ **ses droits** to reassert itself; ~ **le dessus** *[malade]* to fight back; *[équipe]* to get back on top; ~ **ses habitudes** to get back into one's old habits, take up one's old habits again; ~ **contact avec qn** to get in touch with sb again; ~ **ses esprits** *ou* **ses sens** to come to, come round (*Brit*), regain consciousness; (*divorce*) ~ **sa liberté** to regain one's freedom; ~ **haleine** *ou* **son souffle** to regain one's breath, get one's breath back; *voir* **connaissance, conscience** *etc.*

d (*Comm*) *marchandises* to take back; (*contre un nouvel achat*) to take in part exchange; *fonds de commerce, usine* to take over. **les articles en solde ne sont pas repris** sale goods cannot be returned *ou* exchanged; **ils m'ont repris ma vieille télé** they bought my old TV set off me (in part exchange); **j'ai acheté une voiture neuve et ils ont repris la vieille** I bought a new car and traded in the old one *ou* and they took the old one in part exchange.

e (*recommencer, poursuivre*) *travaux* to resume; *études, fonctions* to take up again, resume; *livre* to pick up again, go back to; *lecture* to go back to, resume; *conversation, récit* to resume, carry on (with); *promenade* to resume, continue; *hostilités* to reopen, start again; *lutte* to take up again, resume; *pièce de théâtre* to put on again. **après déjeuner ils reprirent la route** after lunch they resumed *ou* continued their journey *ou* they set off again; ~ **la plume** to take up the pen again; **reprenez votre histoire au début** start your story from the beginning again, go back to the beginning of your story again; **reprenons les faits un par un** let's go over the facts one by one again; **il reprendra la parole après vous** he will speak again after you; ~ **le travail** (*après maladie, grève*) to go back to work, start work again; (*après le repas*) to get back to work, start work again; ~ **la route** *ou* **son chemin** to go on *ou* set off on one's way again; ~ **la mer/la route** *[marin, routier etc]* to go back to sea/back on the road again; **la vie reprend son cours** life goes on again as before *ou* as usual; *voir* **collier**.

f (*saisir à nouveau*) **son mal de gorge l'a repris** he's suffering from *ou* has got a sore throat again, his sore throat is troubling *ou* bothering him again; **ses douleurs l'ont repris** he is in pain again; (*iro*) **voilà que ça le reprend!** there he goes again!, he's off again!*; **ses doutes le reprirent** he started feeling doubtful again, he was seized with doubts once more.

g (*attraper à nouveau*) to catch again. (*fig*) **on ne m'y reprendra plus** I won't let myself be caught (out) *ou* had* again *ou* a second time; (*menace*) **que je ne t'y reprenne pas!** don't let me catch you at it *ou* catch you doing that again!

h (*Sport: rattraper*) *balle* to catch. (*Tennis*) **revers bien repris par X** backhand well returned by X.

i (*retoucher, corriger*) *tableau* to touch up; *article, chapitre* to go over again; *manteau* (*gén*) to alter; (*trop grand*) to take in; (*trop petit*) to let out; (*trop long*) to take up; (*trop court*) to let down. **il n'y a rien à ~** there's not a single correction *ou* alteration to be made; **il y a beaucoup de choses à ~ dans ce travail** there are lots of improvements to be made to this work, there are a lot of things that need tidying up *ou* improving in this work; (*Couture*) **il faut ~ un centimètre à droite** we'll have to take it in half an inch on the right.

j (*réprimander*) *personne* to reprimand, tell off*, tick off* (*Brit*); (*pour faute de langue*) to pull up. ~ **un élève qui se trompe** to correct a pupil.

k (*répéter*) *refrain* to take up; *argument, critique* to repeat. **il reprend toujours les mêmes arguments** he always repeats the same arguments, he always comes out with* *ou* trots out the same old arguments; (*Mus*) **reprenez les 5 dernières mesures** let's have *ou* take the last 5 bars again; **ils reprirent la chanson en chœur** they all joined in *ou* took up the song.

l (*se resservir de*) *idée, suggestion* to take up (again), use (again). **l'incident a été repris par les journaux** the incident was taken up by the newspapers.

2 **vi** a (*retrouver la vigueur*) *[plante]* to take again; *[affaires]* to pick up. **la vie reprenait peu à peu** life gradually returned to normal; **il a bien repris depuis son opération** he has picked up well *ou* made a good recovery since his operation.

b (*recommencer*) *[bruit, pluie]* to start again; (*Scol, Univ*) to start again, go back. **le froid a repris depuis hier** it has turned cold again since yesterday.

c (*dire*) **"ce n'est pas moi" reprit-il** "it's not me" he went on.

3 **se reprendre vpr** a (*se corriger*) to correct o.s.; (*s'interrompre*) to stop o.s. **il allait plaisanter, il s'est repris à temps** he was going to joke but he stopped himself *ou* pulled himself up in time.

b (*recommencer*) **se ~ à plusieurs fois pour faire qch** to make several attempts to do sth *ou* at doing sth; **il a dû s'y ~ à 2 fois pour ouvrir la porte** he had to make 2 attempts before he could open the door; **il se reprit à penser à elle** he started thinking *ou* he went back to thinking about her, his thoughts went back to her; **il se reprit à craindre que** once more he began to be afraid *ou* to fear that; **chacun se reprit à espérer** everyone began to hope again, everyone's hopes began to revive again.

c (*réagir*) to take a grip on o.s., pull o.s. together (again), take o.s. in hand. **après une période de découragement, il s'est repris** after a period of discouragement he's taken himself in hand *ou* got a grip on himself *ou* pulled himself together (again); **le coureur s'est bien repris sur la fin** the runner made a good recovery *ou* caught up well towards the end.

repreneur [R(ə)pRənœR] **nm** (*Ind*) (company) rescuer.

représailles [R(ə)pRezaj] **nfpl** (*Pol, fig*) reprisals, retaliation (*NonC*). **user de ~, exercer des ~** to take reprisals (*envers, contre, sur* against); **par ~** in retaliation, as a reprisal; **en ~ de** by way of reprisal for, as a reprisal for, in retaliation for; **attends-toi à des ~!** you can expect reprisals!

représentable [R(ə)pRezɑ̃tabl] **adj** *phénomène* representable, that can be represented. **c'est difficilement ~** it is difficult to represent it.

représentant, e [R(ə)pRezɑ̃tɑ̃, ɑ̃t] **nm,f** (*gén*) representative. ~ **de commerce** sales representative, travelling salesman, commercial traveller, rep* (*Brit*); ~ **des forces de l'ordre** police officer; ~ **en justice** legal representative; **il est ~ en parapluies** he's a representative *ou* a rep* (*Brit*) for an umbrella firm, he travels in umbrellas*; ~ **multicarte** sales representative acting for several firms.

représentatif, -ive [R(ə)pRezɑ̃tatif, iv] **adj** (*gén*) representative. ~ **de** (*typique de*) representative of; **signes ~s d'une fonction** signs representing *ou* which represent a function.

représentation [R(ə)pRezɑ̃tasjɔ̃] **nf** a (*notation, transcription*) *[objet, phénomène, son]* representation; *[paysage, société]* portrayal; *[faits]* representation, description. ~ **graphique** graphic(al) representation; **c'est une ~ erronée de la réalité** it's a misrepresentation of reality; (*Ling*) ~ **en arbre** tree diagram.

b (*évocation, perception*) representation. **~s visuelles/auditives** visual/auditory representations.

c (*Théât: action, séance*) performance. *troupe* **en ~** on tour; (*fig*) **on a toujours l'impression qu'il est en ~** he always seems to be playing a role.

d *[pays, citoyens, mandant]* representation; (*mandataires, délégation*) representatives. **il assure la ~ de son gouvernement auprès de notre pays** he represents his government *ou* he is his government's representative in our country; ~ **diplomatique/proportionnelle/en justice** diplomatic/proportional/legal representation.

e (*Comm*) (*métier*) commercial travelling; (*publicité, frais*) sales representation. **faire de la ~** to be a (sales) representative *ou* a commercial traveller; **la ~ entre pour beaucoup dans les frais** sales representation is a major factor in costs.

f (*réception*) entertainment. **frais de ~** entertainment allowance.

g (*frm: reproches*) **faire des ~s à** to make representations to.

représentativité [R(ə)pRezɑ̃tativite] **nf** representativeness.

représenter [R(ə)pRezɑ̃te] 1 1 **vt** a (*décrire*) *[peintre, romancier]* to depict, portray, show; *[photographie]* to represent, show. (*Théât*) **la scène représente une rue** the scene represents a street; ~ **fidèlement les faits** to describe *ou* set out the facts faithfully; **on le représente comme un escroc** he's represented as a crook, he's made out to be a crook; **il a**

voulu ~ un paysage sous la neige/la société du 19e siècle he wanted to show *ou* depict a snowy landscape/to depict *ou* portray 19th-century society.

b (*symboliser*) to represent; (*signifier*) to represent, mean. **les parents représentent l'autorité** parents represent *ou* embody authority; **ce trait représente un arbre** this stroke represents a tree; **ça va ~ beaucoup de travail** that will mean *ou* represent *ou* involve a lot of work; **ça représente une part importante des dépenses** it accounts for *ou* represents a large part of the costs; **ils représentent 12% de la population** they make up *ou* represent 12% of the population.

c (*Théât*) (*jouer*) to perform, play; (*mettre à l'affiche*) to perform, put on, stage; *superproduction, adaptation* to stage. **on va ~ 4 pièces cette année** we (*ou* they *etc*) will perform *ou* put on 4 plays this year; **Hamlet fut représenté pour la première fois en 1603** Hamlet was first performed *ou* acted *ou* staged in 1603.

d (*agir au nom de*) *ministre, pays* to represent. **il s'est fait ~ par son notaire** he was represented by his lawyer, he sent his lawyer to represent him, he had his lawyer represent him; **les personnes qui ne peuvent pas assister à la réunion doivent se faire ~ (par un tiers)** those who are unable to attend the meeting should send someone to replace them *ou* should send a stand-in *ou* a deputy.

e **~ une maison de commerce** to represent a firm, be a representative *ou* a traveller for a firm.

f (*littér*) **~ qch à qn** to point sth out to sb, (try to) impress sth on sb; **il lui représenta les inconvénients de l'affaire** he pointed out to him the drawbacks of the matter.

2 vi (*frm: en imposer*) **il représente bien** he cuts a fine figure; **le directeur est un petit bonhomme qui ne représente pas** the manager is a little fellow with no presence at all *ou* who cuts a poor *ou* sorry figure.

3 **se représenter** vpr a (*s'imaginer*) to imagine. **je ne pouvais plus me ~ son visage** I could no longer bring his face to mind *ou* recall *ou* visualize his face; **on se le représente bien en Hamlet** you can well imagine him as Hamlet; **représentez-vous cet enfant maintenant seul au monde** just think of that child now alone in the world; **tu te représentes la scène quand il a annoncé sa démission!** you can just imagine the scene when he announced his resignation!

b (*survenir à nouveau*) **l'idée se représenta à lui** the idea came back to his mind *ou* occurred to him again *ou* crossed his mind again; **si l'occasion se représente** if the occasion presents itself again, if the opportunity arises again; **le même problème va se ~** the same problem will crop up again, we'll be faced *ou* confronted with the same problem again.

c (*se présenter à nouveau*) (*Scol*) to resit (*Brit*), retake; (*Pol*) to stand again (*Brit*), run again (*surtout US*). **se ~ à un examen** to resit (*Brit*) *ou* retake an exam; **se ~ à une élection** to stand (*Brit*) *ou* run for election again, stand (*Brit*) *ou* run for re-election.

répressible [ʀepʀesibl] adj repressible.

répressif, -ive [ʀepʀesif, iv] adj repressive.

répression [ʀepʀesjɔ̃] nf *[crime, abus]* suppression; *[pulsions]* repression; *[révolte]* suppression, quelling, repression. (*Pol*) **la ~** repression; **la ~ qui a suivi le coup d'État** the repression *ou* crackdown which followed the coup; **prendre des mesures de ~ contre le crime** to crack down on crime; **le Service de la ~ des fraudes** the Fraud Squad.

réprimandable [ʀepʀimɑ̃dabl] adj reprovable.

réprimande [ʀepʀimɑ̃d] nf reprimand, rebuke. **adresser une sévère ~ à un enfant** to give a child a severe reprimand, reprimand *ou* scold *ou* rebuke a child severely; **son attitude mérite une ~** he deserves a reprimand *ou* he deserves reprimanding for his attitude; **faire des ~s à qn** to sermonize sb.

réprimander [ʀepʀimɑ̃de] 1 vt to reprimand, rebuke.

réprimer [ʀepʀime] 1 vt *insurrection* to quell, repress, suppress, put down; *crimes, abus* to curb, suppress, crack down on; *sentiment* to repress, suppress; *rire, bâillement* to suppress, stifle; *larmes, colère* to hold back, swallow, suppress.

reprisage [ʀ(ə)pʀizaʒ] nm (*voir* **repriser**) darning; mending.

repris de justice [ʀ(ə)pʀid(ə)ʒystis] nm inv ex-prisoner, ex-convict. **il s'agit d'un ~** the man has previous convictions, the man is an ex-prisoner *ou* an ex-convict. **un dangereux ~** a dangerous known criminal.

reprise [ʀ(ə)pʀiz] nf a (*recommencement*) *[activité, cours, travaux]* resumption; *[hostilités]* resumption, re-opening, renewal; *[froid]* return; (*Théât*) revival; (*Ciné*) rerun, reshowing (*NonC*); (*Mus: passage répété*) repeat; (*Rad, TV: rediffusion*) repeat. (*Mus*) **la ~ des violons** the re-entry of the violins; **la ~ des combats est imminente** fighting will begin again *ou* will be resumed again very soon; **avec la ~ du mauvais temps** with the return of the bad weather, with the bad weather setting in again, with the new spell of bad weather; **les ouvriers ont décidé la ~ du travail** the men have decided to go back to *ou* to return to work; **on espère une ~ des affaires** we're hoping for a recovery in business *ou* hoping that business will pick up again; **la ~ (économique) est assez forte dans certains secteurs** the (economic) revival *ou* recovery is quite marked in certain sectors.

b (*Aut*) **avoir de bonnes ~s** *ou* **de la ~** to have good acceleration, accelerate well; **sa voiture n'a pas de ~s** his car has no acceleration.

c (*Boxe*) round; (*Escrime*) reprise; (*Équitation*) (*pour le cavalier*) riding lesson; (*pour le cheval*) dressage lesson. (*Ftbl*) **à la ~** at the start of the second half, when play resumed (*ou* resumes) after half-time; (*Tennis*) **~ de volée** volleyed return; (*après arrêt*) **~!** time!

d (*Comm*) *[marchandise]* taking back; (*pour nouvel achat*) part exchange (*Brit*), trade-in; (*pour occuper des locaux*) key money. **valeur de ~ d'une voiture** part-exchange value (*Brit*) *ou* trade-in value of a car; **nous vous offrons une ~ de 500 F pour votre vieux téléviseur, à l'achat d'un modèle en couleur** we'll give you 500 francs for your old television when you buy a colour set *ou* when you part-exchange it (*Brit*) *ou* trade it in for a colour set; **~ des bouteilles vides** return of empties; **la maison ne fait pas de ~** goods cannot be returned *ou* exchanged; **payer une ~ de 5 000 F à l'ancien locataire** to pay the outgoing tenant 5,000 francs for improvements made to the property.

e (*réutilisation*) *[idée, suggestion]* re-using, taking up again.

f *[chaussette]* darn; *[drap, chemise]* mend. **faire une ~ perdue** to darn (*ou* mend) invisibly; **faire une ~ *ou* des ~s à un drap** to mend a sheet, stitch up the tear(s) in a sheet.

g (*loc*) **à 2 ou 3 ~s** on 2 or 3 occasions, 2 or 3 times; **à maintes/plusieurs ~s** on many/several occasions, many/several times.

repriser [ʀ(ə)pʀize] 1 vt *chaussette, lainage* to darn; *collant* to mend; *drap* to mend, stitch up (a tear in); *accroc* to mend, stitch up; *voir* **aiguille, coton**.

réprobateur, -trice [ʀepʀɔbatœʀ, tʀis] adj reproving.

réprobation [ʀepʀɔbasjɔ̃] nf a (*blâme*) reprobation. **air/ton de ~** reproving look/tone. b (*Rel*) reprobation.

reproche [ʀ(ə)pʀɔʃ] nm reproach. **faire *ou* adresser des ~s à qn** to direct *ou* level reproaches at sb, reproach *ou* blame sb; **conduite qui mérite des ~s** blameworthy *ou* reprehensible behaviour; (*frm*) **faire ~ à qn d'avoir menti** to reproach *ou* upbraid sb for having lied; **je me fais de grands ~s** I blame *ou* reproach myself bitterly; **avec ~** reproachfully; **ton/regard de ~** reproachful tone/look; **homme sans ~** man beyond *ou* above reproach; **sans ~, permettez-moi *ou* je ne vous fais pas de ~ mais permettez-moi de vous dire que ...** I'm not blaming *ou* criticizing *ou* reproaching you but let me say that ... .

reprocher [ʀ(ə)pʀɔʃe] 1 vt a **~ qch à qn** to blame *ou* reproach sb for sth; **~ à qn de faire qch** to reproach sb for *ou* with doing sth; (*Jur*) **les faits qui lui sont reprochés** the charges against him; **on lui a reproché sa maladresse** they reproached *ou* criticized him for his clumsiness; **on lui reproche de nombreuses malhonnêtetés** they are reproaching him with *ou* accusing him of several instances of dishonesty; **il me reproche mon succès/ma fortune** he reproaches me with *ou* resents my success/my good fortune, he holds my success/my good fortune against me; **je ne te reproche rien** I'm not blaming you for anything; **je n'ai rien à me ~** I've nothing to reproach myself with; **il est très minutieux mais il n'y a rien à ~ à cela** he's a bit on the meticulous side but there's nothing wrong with that *ou* but that's no bad thing.

b (*critiquer*) **qu'as-tu à ~ à mon plan/à ce tableau?** what have you got (to say) against my plan/this picture?, what don't you like about my plan/this picture?; **je reproche à ce tissu d'être trop salissant** my main criticism of this material is that it gets dirty too easily, the thing I have against this material *ou* the fault I find with this material is that it gets dirty too easily; **je ne vois rien à ~ à son travail** I can't find any faults *ou* I can't find anything to criticize in his work.

reproducteur, -trice [ʀ(ə)pʀɔdyktœʀ, tʀis] 1 adj (*Bio*) reproductive. **cheval ~** studhorse, stallion. 2 nm breeder. **~s** breeding stock (*NonC*).

reproductible [ʀ(ə)pʀɔdyktibl] adj which can be reproduced, reproducible.

reproductif, -ive [ʀ(ə)pʀɔdyktif, iv] adj reproductive.

reproduction [ʀ(ə)pʀɔdyksjɔ̃] nf (*voir* **reproduire**) reproduction; copy; repeat; duplication; reprinting; breeding. **livre contenant de nombreuses ~s** book containing many reproductions; **organes de ~** reproductive organs; **garder quelques mâles pour la ~ et vendre les autres pour la viande** to keep a few males for reproduction *ou* breeding and sell the rest for meat; (*Bio*) **~ par mitose *ou* par division cellulaire** replication; (*sur un livre, album*) **"~ interdite"** "all rights (of reproduction) reserved".

reproduire [ʀ(ə)pʀɔdɥiʀ] 38 1 vt *son* to reproduce; *modèle, tableau* to reproduce, copy; *erreur* to repeat; (*par reprographie*) to reproduce, duplicate. **essayant de ~ les gestes de son professeur** trying to copy *ou* imitate his teacher's gestures; **la photo est reproduite en page 3** the picture is shown *ou* reproduced on page 3; **le texte de la conférence sera reproduit dans notre magazine** the text of the lecture will be printed in our magazine.

2 **se reproduire** vpr (*Bio, Bot*) to reproduce, breed; *[phénomène]* to recur, re-occur; *[erreur]* to reappear, recur. **et que ça ne se reproduise plus!** and don't let that happen again!; (*Bio*) **se ~ par mitose *ou* par division cellulaire** to replicate.

reprographie [ʀ(ə)pʀɔgʀafi] nf reprography (*SPÉC*), reprographics (*SPÉC*), repro (*SPÉC*). **le service de ~** the photocopying department.

reprographier [ʀ(ə)pʀɔgʀafje] 7 vt to (photo)copy, duplicate.

reprographieur [ʀ(ə)pʀɔgʀafjœʀ] nm copying machine, photocopier.

reprographique [ʀ(ə)pʀɔgʀafik] adj photocopying, reprographic

(*SPÉC*).

réprouvé, e [ʀepʀuve] (ptp de **réprouver**) nm,f (*Rel*) reprobate; (*fig*) outcast, reprobate.

réprouver [ʀepʀuve] 1 vt a *personne* to reprove; *attitude, comportement* to reprove, condemn; *projet* to condemn, disapprove of. **des actes que la morale réprouve** acts which the moral code condemns, immoral acts. b (*Rel*) to damn, reprobate.

reps [ʀɛps] nm rep(p).

reptation [ʀɛptasjɔ̃] nf crawling.

reptile [ʀɛptil] nm (*Zool*) reptile; (*serpent*) snake; (*péj: personne*) creep* (*péj*).

reptilien, -ienne [ʀɛptiljɛ̃, jɛn] adj reptilian.

repu, e [ʀəpy] (ptp de **repaître**) adj *animal* sated, satisfied, which has gorged itself; *personne* full up* (*attrib*). **je suis ~** I'm full, I've eaten my fill; (*fig*) **il est ~ de cinéma** he has had his fill of the cinema.

républicain, e [ʀepyblikɛ̃, ɛn] adj, nm,f republican; (*US Pol*) Republican; *voir* **garde**².

republier [ʀəpyblije] 7 vt to republish.

république [ʀepyblik] nf republic. **on est en ~!*** this is *ou* it's a free country!; (*fig*) **~ des lettres** republic of letters; **la R~ française** the French Republic; **la R~ arabe unie**† the United Arab Republic†; **la R~ d'Irlande** the Irish Republic; **la R~ démocratique allemande**† the German Democratic Republic†; **la R~ fédérale d'Allemagne** the Federal Republic of Germany; **la R~ populaire de Chine** the Chinese People's Republic, the People's Republic of China; (*péj*) **~ bananière** banana republic.

répudiation [ʀepydjasjɔ̃] nf (*voir* **répudier**) repudiation; renouncement; relinquishment.

répudier [ʀepydje] 7 vt *conjoint* to repudiate; *opinion, foi* to renounce; *engagement* to renounce, go back on; (*Jur*) *nationalité, succession* to renounce, relinquish.

répugnance [ʀepyɲɑ̃s] nf a (*répulsion*) (*pour personnes*) repugnance (*pour* for), disgust (*pour* for), loathing (*pour* of); (*pour nourriture, mensonge*) disgust (*pour* for), loathing (*pour* of). **avoir de la ~ pour les épinards/le travail scolaire** to loathe *ou* have a loathing of spinach/schoolwork; **j'éprouve de la ~ à la vue de ce spectacle** this sight fills me with disgust, I find this sight quite repugnant *ou* disgusting. b (*hésitation*) reluctance (*à faire qch* to do sth). **il éprouvait une certaine ~ à nous le dire** he was rather loath *ou* reluctant to tell us; **faire qch avec ~** to do sth reluctantly, do sth unwillingly.

répugnant, e [ʀepyɲɑ̃, ɑ̃t] adj *individu* repugnant; *laideur* revolting; *action* disgusting, loathsome; *travail, odeur* disgusting, revolting, repugnant; *nourriture* disgusting, revolting.

répugner [ʀepyɲe] 1 1 **répugner à** vt indir a (*dégoûter*) to repel, disgust, be repugnant to. **cet individu me répugne profondément** I am utterly repelled by that fellow, I am filled with repugnance *ou* disgust for that fellow; **manger du poisson/vivre dans la crasse lui répugnait** it was (quite) repugnant to him to eat fish/to live in squalor, he was repelled at the notion of eating fish/a life of squalor; **cette odeur lui répugnait** the smell was repugnant to him, he was repelled by the smell; **cette idée ne lui répugnait pas du tout** he wasn't in the least repelled by *ou* disgusted at this idea, he didn't find this idea off-putting (*Brit*) *ou* repellent in the least.

b **~ à faire qch** to be loath *ou* reluctant to do sth; **il répugnait à parler en public/à accepter cette aide** he was loath *ou* reluctant to speak in public/to accept this help; **il ne répugnait pas à mentir quand cela lui semblait nécessaire** he didn't hesitate to lie *ou* he had no qualms about lying if he thought he needed to.

2 vb impers (*frm*) **il me répugne de devoir vous le dire** it's very distasteful to me to have to tell you this.

3 vt (†, *) = **1a**.

répulsif, -ive [ʀepylsif, iv] adj (*gén, Phys*) repulsive.

répulsion [ʀepylsjɔ̃] nf (*gén*) repulsion, repugnance, disgust; (*Phys*) repulsion. **éprouver** *ou* **avoir de la ~ pour** to feel repulsion for, be absolutely repelled by.

réputation [ʀepytasjɔ̃] nf a (*honneur*) reputation, good name. **préserver sa ~** to keep up *ou* protect one's reputation *ou* good name.

b (*renommée*) reputation. **se faire une ~** to make a name *ou* a reputation for o.s.; **avoir bonne/mauvaise ~** to have a good/bad reputation; **sa ~ n'est plus à faire** his reputation is not in doubt, his reputation is firmly established; **produit de ~ mondiale** product which has a world-wide reputation; **connaître qn/qch de ~ (seulement)** to know sb/sth (only) by repute; **sa ~ de gynécologue** his reputation as a gynaecologist; **il a une ~ d'avarice** he has a reputation for miserliness; **il a la ~ d'être avare** he has a reputation for *ou* of being miserly, he is reputed to be miserly.

réputé, e [ʀepyte] 1 ptp de **réputer**.

2 adj a (*célèbre*) *vin, artiste* reputable, renowned, of repute. **l'un des médecins les plus ~s de la ville** one of the town's most reputable doctors, one of the best-known doctors in the town; **c'est un fromage/vin hautement ~** it's a cheese/wine of great repute *ou* renown; **orateur ~ pour ses bons mots** speaker who is renowned for his witticisms; **ville ~e pour sa cuisine/ses monuments** town which is renowned for *ou* which has a great reputation for its cooking/its monuments; **il n'est pas ~ pour son honnêteté!** he's not exactly renowned *ou* famous for his honesty!

b (*prétendu*) **remède ~ infaillible** cure which is reputed *ou* supposed *ou* said to be infallible; **professeur ~ pour être très sévère** teacher who has the reputation of being *ou* who is reputed to be *ou* said to be very strict.

requérant, e [ʀəkeʀɑ̃, ɑ̃t] nm,f (*Jur*) applicant.

requérir [ʀəkeʀiʀ] 21 vt a (*nécessiter*) *soins, prudence* to call for, require. **ceci requiert toute notre attention** this calls for *ou* requires *ou* demands our full attention; **l'honneur requiert que vous acceptiez** honour requires *ou* demands that you accept.

b (*solliciter*) *aide, service* to request; (*exiger*) *justification* to require, necessitate, call for; (*réquisitionner*) *personne* to call upon. **~ l'intervention de la police** to require *ou* necessitate police intervention; (*frm*) **je vous requiers de me suivre** I call on you *ou* I summon you to follow me.

c (*Jur*) *peine* to call for, demand. **le procureur était en train de ~** the prosecutor was summing up *ou* making his closing speech.

requête [ʀəkɛt] nf a (*Jur*) petition. **adresser une ~ à un juge** to petition a judge; **~ en cassation** appeal; **~ civile** *appeal to a court against its judgment.* b (*supplique*) request, petition. **à** *ou* **sur la ~ de qn** at sb's request, at the request of sb.

requiem [ʀekɥijɛm] nm inv requiem.

requin [ʀəkɛ̃] nm (*Zool, fig*) shark. **~ marteau** hammerhead (shark); **~ blanc/bleu/pèlerin** white/blue/basking shark; **~-tigre** tiger shark; **~-baleine** whale shark; (*fig*) **les ~s de la finance** the sharks of the financial world.

requinquer* [ʀ(ə)kɛ̃ke] 1 1 vt to pep up*, buck up*. **un bon grog vous requinquera** a good grog will pep you up* *ou* buck you up*; **avec un peu de repos, dans 3 jours vous serez requinqué** with a bit of a rest in 3 days you'll be your old (perky) self again* *ou* you'll be back on form again. 2 **se requinquer** vpr to perk up*.

requis, e [ʀəki, iz] (ptp de **requérir**) adj a (*nécessaire*) (*gén*) required; *âge, diplôme, conditions* requisite, required. b (*réquisitionné*) **les ~** labour conscripts (*civilians*).

réquisition [ʀekizisjɔ̃] nf a *[biens]* requisition, requisitioning, commandeering; *[hommes]* requisition, requisitioning, conscription. **~ de la force armée** requisitioning of *ou* calling out of the army. b (*Jur: aussi* **~s**) closing speech for the prosecution.

réquisitionner [ʀekizisjɔne] 1 vt *biens* to requisition, commandeer; *hommes* to requisition, conscript. **j'ai été réquisitionné pour faire la vaisselle*** I have been drafted in *ou* requisitioned to do the dishes (*hum*).

réquisitoire [ʀekizitwaʀ] nm a (*Jur*) (*plaidoirie*) closing speech for the prosecution (*specifying appropriate sentence*); (*acte écrit*) instruction, brief (*to examining magistrate*). b (*fig*) indictment (*contre* of). **son discours fut un ~ contre le capitalisme** his speech was an indictment of capitalism.

RER [ɛʀøɛʀ] nm (abrév de **réseau express régional**) *voir* **réseau**.

RES [ʀɛs, ɛʀəɛs] nm (abrév de **rachat d'entreprise par les salariés**) MBO.

resaler [ʀ(ə)sale] 1 vt to add more salt to, put more salt in.

resalir [ʀ(ə)saliʀ] 2 vt *tapis, mur, sol, vêtement* to get dirty again. **ne va pas te ~** don't go and get yourself dirty *ou* in a mess again; **se ~ les mains** to get one's hands dirty again, dirty one's hands again.

rescapé, e [ʀɛskape] 1 adj *personne* surviving. 2 nm,f survivor (*de* of).

rescousse [ʀɛskus] nf: **venir** *ou* **aller à la ~ de qn** to go to sb's rescue *ou* aid; **appeler qn à la ~** to call on *ou* to sb for help; **ils arrivèrent à la ~** they came to the rescue, they rallied round.

rescrit [ʀɛskʀi] nm rescript.

réseau, pl **~x** [ʀezo] nm a (*gén, fig*) network. **~ ferroviaire/commercial/de résistance/téléphonique** rail/sales/resistance/telephone network; **~ fluvial** river system, network of rivers; **~ express régional** *high-speed train service between Paris and the suburbs;* **~ d'espionnage** spy network *ou* ring; **~ d'intrigues** network *ou* web of intrigue(s); **~ d'habitudes** pattern of habits; (*Téléc*) **les abonnés du ~ sont avisés que** telephone subscribers are advised that; **sur l'ensemble du ~** over the whole network; (*Ordin*) **~ neuronal** neural net(work); (*Ordin*) **~ local** local area network, LAN.

b (*Zool*) reticulum.

c (*Phys*) **~ de diffraction** diffraction pattern; **~ cristallin** crystal lattice.

réséda [ʀezeda] nm reseda, mignonette.

réservataire [ʀezɛʀvatɛʀ] adj, nm: (**héritier**) **~** *rightful heir to the réserve légale.*

réservation [ʀezɛʀvasjɔ̃] nf (*à l'hôtel*) reservation; (*des places*) reservation, booking; (*Jur*) reservation. (*Tourisme*) **~ de groupes** group booking; **bureau de ~** booking office; **faire une ~ dans un hôtel/restaurant** to make a booking in a hotel/restaurant, book a room (in a hotel)/a table (in a restaurant).

réserve [ʀezɛʀv] nf a (*provision*) reserve; *[marchandises]* reserve, stock. **les enfants ont une ~ énorme d'énergie** children have an enormous reserve *ou* have enormous reserves of energy; **faire des ~s de sucre** to get in *ou* lay in a stock of *ou* reserves of sugar;

heureusement ils avaient une petite ~ (d'argent) fortunately they had a little money put by *ou* a little money in reserve; (*Fin*) **monnaie de ~** reserve currency; **les ~s mondiales de pétrole** the world's oil reserves; **~s (nutritives) de l'organisme** the organism's food reserves; (*hum*) **il peut jeûner, il a des ~s!** he can afford to do without food – he's got plenty of reserves!; **avoir des provisions de** *ou* **en ~** to have provisions in reserve *ou* put by; **mettre qch en ~** to put sth by, put sth in reserve; **avoir/tenir qch en ~** (*gén*) to have/keep sth in reserve; (*Comm*) to have/keep sth in stock.

b (*restriction*) reservation, reserve. **faire** *ou* **émettre des ~s sur l'opportunité de qch** to have reservations *ou* reserves about the timeliness of sth; **sous toutes ~s** *publier* with all reserve, with all proper reserves; *dire* with reservations; **je vous le dis sous toutes ~s** I can't vouch for *ou* guarantee the truth of what I'm telling you; **tarif/horaire publié sous toute ~** no guarantee as to the accuracy of the price/timetable shown; **sous ~ de** subject to; **sans ~** *admiration, consentement* unreserved, unqualified; *approuver, accepter* unreservedly, without reservation, unhesitatingly; *dévoué* unreservedly.

c (*prudence, discrétion*) reserve. **être/demeurer** *ou* **se tenir sur la ~** to be/stay on the reserve, be/remain very reserved; **il m'a parlé sans ~** he talked to me quite unreservedly *ou* openly; **elle est d'une grande ~** she's very reserved, she keeps herself to herself.

d (*Mil*) **la ~** the reserve; **les ~s** the reserves; **officiers/armée de ~** reserve officers/army.

e (*territoire*) *[nature, animaux]* reserve; *[Indiens]* reservation. **~ de pêche/chasse** fishing/hunting preserve; **~ naturelle** nature reserve *ou* sanctuary.

f *[bibliothèque, musée]* reserve collection. **le livre est à la ~** the book is in reserve.

g (*entrepôt*) storehouse, storeroom.

h (*Jur*) **~ (héréditaire** *ou* **légale)** *part of the legacy which cannot be withheld from the rightful heirs.*

réservé, e [ʀezɛʀve] (**ptp de réserver**) **adj** *place, salle* reserved (*à qn/qch* for sb/sth); *personne, caractère* reserved. **chasse/pêche ~e** private hunting/fishing; **j'ai une table ~e** I've got a table reserved *ou* booked; **les médecins sont très ~s à son sujet** the doctors are very guarded *ou* cautious in their opinions about him; **tous droits ~s** all rights reserved; **voie ~e aux autobus** bus lane; *voir* **quartier**.

réserver [ʀezɛʀve] [1] 1 **vt** a (*mettre à part*) to keep, save, reserve (*à, pour* for); *marchandises* to keep, put aside *ou* on one side (*à* for). **il nous a réservé 2 places à côté de lui** he's kept *ou* saved us 2 seats beside him; **on vous a réservé ce bureau** we've reserved you this office, we've set this office aside for you; **~ le meilleur pour la fin** to keep *ou* save the best till last; **ils réservent ces fauteuils pour les cérémonies** they reserve *ou* keep these armchairs for (special) ceremonies; **pouvez-vous me ~ 5 mètres de ce tissu?** could you put 5 metres of that material aside *ou* on one side for me?, could you keep me 5 metres of that material?; **ces emplacements sont strictement réservés aux voitures du personnel** these parking places are strictly reserved for staff cars; **nous réservons toujours un peu d'argent pour les dépenses imprévues** we always keep *ou* put a bit of money on one side *ou* earmark a bit of money for unexpected expenses.

b (*louer*) *place, chambre, table [voyageur]* to book, reserve; *[agence]* to reserve.

c (*fig: destiner*) *dangers, désagréments, joies* to have in store (*à* for); *accueil, châtiment* to have in store, reserve (*à* for). **cette expédition devait leur ~ bien des surprises** that expedition was to have many surprises in store for them, there were to be many surprises in store for them on that expedition; **nous ne savons pas ce que l'avenir nous réserve** we don't know what the future has in store for us *ou* holds for us; **le sort qui lui est réservé est peu enviable** he has an unenviable fate in store for him *ou* reserved for him; **c'est à lui qu'il était réservé de marcher le premier sur la lune** he was to be the first to walk on the moon; **c'est à lui que fut réservé l'honneur de porter le drapeau** the honour of carrying the flag fell to him; **tu me réserves ta soirée?** are you free tonight *ou* this evening?, could we do something this evening?

d (*remettre à plus tard*) *réponse, opinion* to reserve. **le médecin préfère ~ son diagnostic** the doctor would rather reserve his diagnosis.

2 **se réserver vpr** a (*prélever*) to keep *ou* reserve for o.s. **il s'est réservé le meilleur morceau** he kept *ou* saved the best bit for himself.

b (*se ménager*) **se ~ pour une autre occasion** to save o.s. for another opportunity, save o.s. until another opportunity crops up; **il ne mange pas maintenant, il se réserve pour le banquet/pour plus tard** he isn't eating now – he's saving *ou* reserving himself for the banquet/for later; (*Sport*) **il faut savoir se ~** one must learn to hold back *ou* to conserve *ou* save one's strength.

c **se ~ de faire: il se réserve d'intervenir plus tard** he's waiting to see whether he'll need to intervene later, he's reserving the possibility of intervening later; **se ~ le droit de faire qch** to reserve the right to do sth.

réserviste [ʀezɛʀvist] **nm** reservist.

réservoir [ʀezɛʀvwaʀ] **nm** (*cuve*) tank; (*plan d'eau*) reservoir; *[poissons]* fishpond; *[usine à gaz]* gasometer, gasholder. (*fig*) **ce pays est un ~ de talents/de main-d'œuvre** this country has a wealth of talent/a huge pool of labour to draw on; **~ d'eau** (*gén, Aut*) water tank; (*pour une maison*) water cistern; (*pour eau de pluie*) (*en bois*) water butt; (*en ciment*) water tank.

résidant, e [ʀezidɑ̃, ɑ̃t] **adj** resident.

résidence [ʀezidɑ̃s] 1 **nf** (*gén*) residence; (*immeuble*) (block of) residential flats (*Brit*), residential apartment building (*US*). **établir sa ~ à** to take up residence in; **changer de ~** to move (house); (*Admin*) **en ~ à** in residence at; **en ~ surveillée** *ou* **forcée** under house arrest; (*Diplomatie*) **la ~** the residency; *voir* **assigner, certificat.** 2 **comp** ►**résidence principale** main home ►**résidence secondaire** second home ►**résidence universitaire** (university) hall(s) of residence (*Brit*), residence hall (*US*), dormitory (*US*).

résident, e [ʀezidɑ̃, ɑ̃t] **nm,f** (*étranger*) foreign national *ou* resident; (*diplomate*) resident. **ministre ~** resident minister; **avoir le statut de ~ permanent en France** to have permanent resident status in France.

résidentiel, -ielle [ʀezidɑ̃sjɛl] **adj** *quartier, banlieue* smart, posh*.

résider [ʀezide] [1] **vi** (*lit, fig*) to reside (*en, dans* in). **il réside à cet hôtel/à Dijon** he resides (*frm*) at this hotel/in Dijon; **après avoir résidé quelques temps en France** after living *ou* residing (*frm*) in France for some time, after having been resident in France for some time; **le problème réside en ceci que ...** the problem lies in the fact that ... .

résidu [ʀezidy] **nm** a (*reste*) (*Chim, fig*) residue (*NonC*); (*Math*) remainder. b (*déchets*) **~s** remnants, residue (*NonC*); **~s industriels** industrial waste.

résiduel, -elle [ʀezidɥɛl] **adj** residual.

résignation [ʀeziɲasjɔ̃] **nf** resignation (*à* to). **avec ~** with resignation, resignedly.

résigné, e [ʀeziɲe] (**ptp de résigner**) **adj** *air, geste, ton* resigned. **~ à son sort** resigned to his fate; **il est ~** he is resigned to it; **dire qch d'un air ~** to say sth resignedly.

résigner [ʀeziɲe] [1] 1 **se résigner vpr** to resign o.s. (*à* to) **il faudra s'y ~** we'll have to resign ourselves to it *ou* put up with it. 2 **vt** (*littér*) *charge, fonction* to relinquish, resign.

résiliable [ʀeziljabl] **adj** (*voir* **résilier**) which can be terminated, terminable; which can be cancelled, cancellable; which can be rescinded, rescindable.

résiliation [ʀeziljasjɔ̃] **nf** (*voir* **résilier**) termination; cancellation, rescinding.

résilience [ʀeziljɑ̃s] **nf** (*Tech*) ductility.

résilient, e [ʀeziljɑ̃, jɑ̃t] **adj** (*Tech*) ductile.

résilier [ʀezilje] [7] **vt** *contrat* (*à terme*) to terminate; (*en cours*) to cancel, rescind.

résille [ʀezij] **nf** (*gén: filet*) net, netting (*NonC*); (*pour les cheveux*) hairnet; *[vitrail]* cames (*SPÉC*), lead(s), leading (*NonC*). **bas ~** fishnet stockings.

résine [ʀezin] **nf** resin.

résiné, e [ʀezine] **adj, nm: (vin) ~** retsina.

résineux, -euse [ʀezinø, øz] 1 **adj** resinous. 2 **nm** coniferous tree. **forêt de ~** coniferous forest.

résistance [ʀezistɑ̃s] **nf** a (*opposition*) resistance (*NonC*) (*à* to). (*Hist*) **la R~** the (French) Resistance; **l'armée dut se rendre après une ~ héroïque** the army was forced to surrender after putting up a heroic resistance *ou* a heroic fight; **opposer une ~ farouche à un projet** to put up a fierce resistance to a project, make a very determined stand against a project; **cela ne se fera pas sans ~** that won't be done without some opposition *ou* resistance; **~ passive/armée** passive/armed resistance; *voir* **noyau**.

b (*endurance*) resistance, stamina. **~ à la fatigue** resistance to fatigue; **il a une grande ~** *ou* **beaucoup de ~** he has great *ou* a lot of resistance *ou* stamina; **coureur qui a de la ~/qui n'a pas de ~** runner who has lots of/who has no staying power; **ces plantes-là n'ont pas de ~** those plants have no resistance; **ce matériau offre une grande ~ au feu/aux chocs** this material is very heat-/shock-resistant; *voir* **pièce, plat**[2].

c (*Élec*) (*NonC*) resistance; *[réchaud, radiateur]* element. **unité de ~** unit of (electrical) resistance.

d (*Phys: force*) resistance. **~ d'un corps/de l'air** resistance of a body/of the air; **~ mécanique** mechanical resistance; **~ des matériaux** strength of materials; **quand il voulut ouvrir la porte, il sentit une ~** when he tried to open the door he felt some resistance.

résistant, e [ʀezistɑ̃, ɑ̃t] 1 **adj** *personne* robust, tough; *plante* hardy; *vêtements, tissu* strong, hard-wearing; *couleur* fast; *acier* resistant; *métal* resistant, strong; *bois* resistant, hard. **il est très ~** (*gén*) he is very robust, he has a lot of resistance *ou* stamina; *[athlète]* he has lots of staying power; **~ à la chaleur** heatproof, heat-resistant. 2 **nm,f** (*Hist*) (French) Resistance worker *ou* fighter.

résister [ʀeziste] [1] **résister à vt indir** a (*s'opposer à*) *ennemi, agresseur, police* to resist; *passion, tentation, argument* to resist; *attaque* to hold out against, withstand, resist. **inutile de ~** it's useless to resist, it's *ou* there's no use resisting; **~ au courant d'une rivière** to fight against *ou* hold one's own against the current of a river; **~ à la volonté de qn** to hold out against *ou* resist sb's will; **il n'ose pas ~ à sa fille** he doesn't dare (to) stand up to his daughter; **je n'aime pas que mes enfants me résistent** I don't like my children opposing me; **je n'ai pas résisté à cette petite robe** I couldn't resist (buying) this dress.

b (*surmonter*) *fatigue, émotion, privations* to stand up to, withstand; *chagrin, adversité* to withstand; *douleur* to stand, withstand. **leur amour ne résista pas à cette infidélité** their love could not stand up to *ou* could not withstand this infidelity.

c (*supporter*) *sécheresse, gelée, vent* to withstand, stand up to, resist. **ça a bien résisté à l'épreuve du temps** it has really stood the test of time, it has stood up to the passing centuries; **le plancher ne pourra pas ~ au poids** the floor won't support *ou* withstand *ou* take the weight; **la porte a résisté** the door held *ou* didn't give, the door stood firm *ou* resisted; **ça n'a pas résisté longtemps** it didn't resist *ou* hold out for long; **couleur qui résiste au lavage** colour which is fast in the wash, fast colour; **tissu qui résiste au lavage en machine** material which can be machine-washed *ou* which will stand up to machine washing; **cette vaisselle résiste au feu** this crockery is heat-resistant *ou* heatproof; **ce raisonnement ne résiste pas à l'analyse** this reasoning does not stand up to analysis.

resistivité [ʀezistivite] **nf** (*Élec*) resistance. **la ~ du cuivre est très faible** copper has a very low resistance.

résolu, e [ʀezɔly] (**ptp de résoudre**) **adj** *personne, ton, air* resolute. **il est bien ~ à partir** he is firmly resolved *ou* he is determined to leave, he is set on leaving.

résoluble [ʀezɔlybl] **adj** *problème* soluble; (*Chim*) resolvable; (*Jur*) *contrat* annullable, cancellable.

résolument [ʀezɔlymɑ̃] **adv** (*totalement*) resolutely; (*courageusement*) resolutely, steadfastly. **je suis ~ contre** I'm firmly against it, I'm resolutely opposed to it.

résolutif, -ive [ʀezɔlytif, iv] **adj, nm** resolvent.

résolution [ʀezɔlysjɔ̃] **nf** a (*gén, Pol: décision*) resolution. **prendre la ~ de faire** to make a resolution to do, resolve to do, make up one's mind to do; **ma ~ est prise** I've made my resolution; **bonnes ~s** good resolutions.

b (*énergie*) resolve, resolution, determination. **avec un visage plein de ~** his face full of resolve *ou* resolution, with a determined expression on his face.

c (*solution*) solution. **il attendait de moi la ~ de son problème** he expected me to give him a solution to his problem *ou* to solve his problem for him.

d (*Jur*) *[contrat, vente]* cancellation, annulment.

e (*Méd, Mus, Phys*) resolution. **~ de l'eau en vapeur** resolution of water into steam.

f *[image]* resolution. **image de haute ~**high-resolution image.

résolutoire [ʀezɔlytwaʀ] **adj** (*Jur*) resolutive.

résonance [ʀezɔnɑ̃s] **nf** (*gén, Élec, Phys, Phon*) resonance (*NonC*); (*fig*) echo. **être/entrer en ~** to be/start resonating; **~ magnétique nucléaire** nuclear magnetic resonance; (*littér*) **ce poème éveille en moi des ~s** this poem awakens echoes in me; *voir* **caisse**.

résonateur [ʀezɔnatœʀ] **nm** resonator. **~ nucléaire** nuclear resonator.

résonnant, e [ʀezɔnɑ̃, ɑ̃t] **adj** *voix* resonant. **cour ~e de bruits** yard resounding *ou* resonant *ou* ringing with noise.

résonner [ʀezɔne] 1 **vi** *[son]* to resonate, reverberate, resound; *[pas]* to resound; *[salle]* to be resonant. **cloche qui résonne bien/faiblement** bell which resounds well/rings feebly; **ne parle pas trop fort, ça résonne** don't speak too loudly because it *ou* the noise resonates *ou* reverberates *ou* echoes; **~ de** to resound *ou* ring *ou* resonate with.

résorber [ʀezɔʀbe] 1 1 **vt** (*Méd*) to resorb; *chômage* to bring down, reduce (gradually); *déficit, surplus* to absorb; *inflation* to bring down, reduce gradually, curb. **trouver un moyen pour ~ la crise économique** to find some way of resolving the economic crisis. 2 **se résorber vpr** (*Méd*) to be resorbed; (*fig*) *[chômage]* to be brought down *ou* reduced; *[déficit]* to be absorbed. **l'embouteillage se résorbe peu à peu** the traffic jam is gradually breaking up *ou* sorting itself out *ou* resolving itself.

résorption [ʀezɔʀpsjɔ̃] **nf** (*voir* **résorber**) resorption; bringing down, gradual reduction (*de* in); absorption; curbing.

résoudre [ʀezudʀ] 51 1 **vt** a *mystère, équation, problème de maths* to solve; *dilemme, crise* to solve, resolve; *difficultés* to solve, resolve, settle, sort out; *conflit* to settle, resolve. **j'ignore comment ce problème va se ~** *ou* **va être résolu** I can't see how this problem will be solved *ou* resolved.

b (*décider*) *exécution, mort* to decide on, determine on. **~ de faire qch** to decide *ou* resolve to do sth, make up one's mind to do sth; **~ qn à faire qch** to prevail upon sb *ou* induce sb to do sth.

c (*Méd*) *tumeur* to resolve.

d (*Jur*) *contrat, vente* to cancel, annul.

e (*Mus*) *dissonance* to resolve.

f (*transformer*) **~ qch en cendres** to reduce sth to ashes; **les nuages se résolvent en pluie/grêle** the clouds break up *ou* resolve *ou* turn into rain/hail.

2 **se résoudre vpr: se ~ à faire qch** (*se décider*) to resolve *ou* decide to do sth, make up one's mind to do sth; (*se résigner*) to resign *ou* reconcile o.s. to doing sth; **il n'a pas pu se ~ à la quitter** he couldn't bring himself to leave her.

respect [ʀɛspɛ] **nm** a respect (*de, pour* for). **avoir du ~ pour qn** to have respect for sb, hold sb in respect; **il n'a aucun ~ pour le bien d'autrui** he has no respect *ou* consideration *ou* regard for other people's property; **par ~ pour sa mémoire** out of respect *ou* consideration for his memory; **malgré le ~ que je vous dois, sauf votre ~** with (all) respect, with all due respect; **manquer de ~ à** *ou* **envers qn** to be disrespectful to(wards) sb; **le ~ humain** fear of the judgment of others; **~ de soi** self-respect.

b (*formule de politesse*) **présenter ses ~s à qn** to present one's respects to sb; **présentez mes ~s à votre femme** give my regards *ou* pay my respects to your wife; **mes ~s, mon colonel** good day to you, sir.

c (*loc*) **tenir qn en ~** (*avec une arme*) to keep sb at a respectful distance *ou* at bay; **au ~ de††** compared with, in comparison to *ou* with.

respectabilité [ʀɛspɛktabilite] **nf** respectability.

respectable [ʀɛspɛktabl] **adj** (*honorable*) respectable; (*important*) respectable, sizeable. **il avait un ventre ~*** he had quite a pot-belly*, he had a fair-sized corporation* (*Brit*).

respecter [ʀɛspɛkte] 1 1 **vt** a *personne* to respect, have respect for. **~ une femme** to respect a woman's honour; **se faire ~** to be respected, make o.s. respected (*par* by), command respect (*par* from).

b *formes, loi* to respect; *traditions* to respect, have respect for, honour. **~ les opinions/sentiments de qn** to show consideration *ou* respect for sb's opinions/feelings; **~ le sommeil de qn** to respect sb's right to get some sleep; **respectez le matériel!** treat the equipment with respect!, show some respect for the equipment!; **la jeunesse ne respecte rien** young people show no respect for anything *ou* do not respect anything; **classer des livres en respectant l'ordre alphabétique** to classify books, keeping them in alphabetical order; **faire ~ la loi** to enforce the law; **~ les termes d'un contrat** to abide by *ou* respect the terms of a contract.

2 **se respecter vpr** to respect o.s. (*hum*) **tout professeur/juge/plombier qui se respecte** any self-respecting teacher/judge/plumber; **il se respecte trop pour faire cela** he is above doing that sort of thing, he has too much self-respect to do that sort of thing.

respectif, -ive [ʀɛspɛktif, iv] **adj** respective.

respectivement [ʀɛspɛktivmɑ̃] **adv** respectively.

respectueusement [ʀɛspɛktɥøzmɑ̃] **adv** respectfully, with respect.

respectueux, -euse [ʀɛspɛktɥø, øz] 1 **adj** *silence, langage, personne* respectful (*envers, pour* to). **se montrer ~ du bien d'autrui** to show respect *ou* consideration for other people's property; **~ des traditions** respectful of traditions; **~ de la loi** respectful of the law, law-abiding; **être peu ~ des autres** to show little respect for others; **veuillez agréer mes salutations ~euses** yours respectfully; **je vous envoie mes hommages ~** yours (most) sincerely, your humble servant; *voir* **distance**. 2 **respectueuse*** **nf** (*prostituée*) tart* (*Brit*), whore, prostitute.

respirable [ʀɛspiʀabl] **adj** breathable. **l'air n'y est pas ~** the air there is unbreathable; (*fig*) **l'atmosphère n'est pas ~ dans cette famille** the atmosphere in this family is suffocating.

respirateur [ʀɛspiʀatœʀ] **nm: ~ (artificiel)** (*gén*) respirator; (*pour malade dans le coma*) ventilator.

respiration [ʀɛspiʀasjɔ̃] **nf** (*fonction, action naturelle*) breathing, respiration (*SPÉC*); (*souffle*) breath. **~ pulmonaire/cutanée/artificielle** pulmonary/cutaneous/artificial respiration; **~ difficile** difficulty in breathing; **~ entrecoupée** irregular breathing; **~ courte** shortness of breath; **avoir la ~ difficile** to have difficulty (in) *ou* trouble breathing; **avoir la ~ bruyante** to breathe heavily *ou* noisily; **retenir sa ~** to hold one's breath; **faites 3 ~s complètes** breathe in and out 3 times; **respecter les ~s d'un poème** to respect the phrasing of a poem; *voir* **couper**.

respiratoire [ʀɛspiʀatwaʀ] **adj** *système, voies* respiratory; *troubles* breathing (*épith*), respiratory.

respirer [ʀɛspiʀe] 1 1 **vi** a (*lit, Bio*) to breathe, respire (*SPÉC*). (*chez le médecin*) **"respirez"** "breathe in!", "take a deep breath!"; **~ par la bouche/le nez** to breathe through one's mouth/nose; **est-ce qu'il respire (encore)?** is he (still) breathing?; **~ avec difficulté** to have difficulty (in) *ou* trouble breathing, breathe with difficulty; **~ profondément** to breathe deeply, take a deep breath; *voir* **mentir**.

b (*fig*) (*se détendre*) to get one's breath, have a break; (*se rassurer*) to breathe again *ou* easy. **ouf, on respire** phew, we can breathe again.

2 **vt** a (*inhaler*) to breathe (in), inhale. **~ un air vicié/le grand air** to breathe in foul air/the fresh air; **faire ~ des sels à qn** to make sb inhale smelling salts.

b (*exprimer*) *calme, bonheur, santé* to radiate; *honnêteté, franchise, orgueil, ennui* to exude, emanate. **son attitude respirait la méfiance** his whole attitude was mistrustful, his attitude was clearly one of mistrust.

resplendir [ʀɛsplɑ̃diʀ] 2 **vi** *[soleil, lune]* to shine, beam; *[surface métallique]* to gleam, shine. **le lac/la neige resplendissait sous le soleil** the lake/snow gleamed *ou* shone *ou* glistened *ou* glittered in the sun; **le ciel resplendit au coucher du soleil** the sky blazes with light *ou* is radiant *ou* ablaze at sunset; **toute la cuisine resplendissait** the whole kitchen shone *ou* gleamed; (*fig*) **il resplendissait de joie/de bonheur** he was aglow *ou* radiant with joy/happiness, his face was shining *ou* glowing with joy/happiness.

resplendissant, e [ʀɛsplɑ̃disɑ̃, ɑ̃t] **adj** a (*lit: brillant*) *soleil* shining, radiant, beaming, dazzling; *lune* shining, beaming; *surface métallique* gleaming, shining; *lac, neige* gleaming, shining, glistening, glittering; *ciel* radiant (*épith*). b (*fig: éclatant*) *beauté, santé, mine* radiant (*épith*); *yeux, visage* shining. **être ~ de santé/de joie** to be aglow *ou* radiant with health/joy.

resplendissement [ʀɛsplɑ̃dismɑ̃] **nm** *[beauté, soleil]* brilliance. **le ~ de la neige sur le sommet de la montagne** the glitter of the snow on the mountain top, the dazzling white of the snow on the mountain top.

responsabiliser [ʀɛspɔ̃sabilize] 1 **vt**: **~ qn** (*rendre conscient de ses responsabilités*) to make sb aware of his responsibilities; (*donner des responsabilités*) to give sb responsibilities.

responsabilité [ʀɛspɔ̃sabilite] 1 **nf** a (*légale*) liability (*de* for); (*morale*) responsibility (*de* for); (*ministérielle*) responsibility; (*financière*) (financial) accountability. **emmener ces enfants en montagne, c'est une ~** it's a responsibility taking these children to the mountains; *voir* **assurance, société**.

b (*charge*) responsibility. **de lourdes ~s** heavy responsibilities; **assumer la ~ d'une affaire** to take on the responsibility for a matter; **avoir la ~ de qn** to take *ou* have responsibility for sb; **avoir la ~ de la gestion/de la sécurité** to be responsible for the management/for security; **il fuit les ~s** he shuns (any) responsibility; **ce poste comporte d'importantes ~s** this post involves *ou* carries considerable responsibilities; **il cherche un poste offrant plus de ~s** he wants a position with more responsibility; **avoir un poste à ~** to have *ou* hold a position of responsibility; **accéder à une haute ~** to reach a position of great responsibility.

2 **comp** ►**responsabilité atténuée** (*Jur*) diminished responsibility ►**responsabilité civile** civil liability ►**responsabilité collective** collective responsibility ►**responsabilité contractuelle** contractual liability ►**responsabilité pénale** criminal responsibility ►**responsabilité pleine et entière** (*Jur*) full and entire responsibility.

responsable [ʀɛspɔ̃sabl] 1 **adj** a (*comptable*) (*légalement*) (*de dégâts*) liable, responsible (*de* for); (*de délits*) responsible (*de* for); (*moralement*) responsible, accountable (*de* for, *devant qn* to sb). **reconnu ~ de ses actes** recognized as responsible *ou* accountable for his actions; **il n'est pas ~ des délits/dégâts commis par ses enfants** he is not responsible for the misdemeanours of/liable *ou* responsible for damage caused by his children; **un père est ~ de la santé morale de ses enfants** a father is responsible for the moral well-being of his children; **civilement/pénalement ~** liable in civil/criminal law; **le ministre est ~ de ses décisions (devant le parlement)** the minister is responsible *ou* accountable (to Parliament) for his decisions.

b (*chargé de*) **~ de** responsible for, in charge of.

c (*coupable*) responsible, to blame. **X, ~ de l'échec, a été renvoyé** X, who was responsible *ou* to blame for the failure, has been dismissed; **ils considèrent l'état défectueux des freins comme ~ (de l'accident)** they consider that defective brakes were to blame *ou* were responsible for the accident.

d (*sérieux*) *attitude, employé, étudiant* responsible. **agir de manière ~** to behave responsibly.

2 **nmf** a (*coupable*) **il s'agit de trouver et de punir le ~/les ~s (de cette action)** we must find and punish the person responsible/those responsible *ou* the person who is to blame/those who are to blame (for this act); **le seul ~ est l'alcool** alcohol alone is to blame *ou* is the culprit.

b (*personne compétente*) person in charge. **adressez-vous au ~** see the person in charge.

c (*dirigeant*) official. **les ~s d'un parti** the officials of a party; **des ~s de l'industrie** representatives *ou* leaders of industry; **~ syndical** trade union official; **~ politique** politician.

resquillage [ʀɛskijaʒ] **nm, resquille** [ʀɛskij] **nf** (*dans l'autobus*) grabbing a free ride; (*au match, cinéma*) sneaking in, getting in on the sly.

resquiller* [ʀɛskije] 1 1 **vi** (*ne pas payer*) (*dans l'autobus etc*) to sneak a free ride; (*au match, cinéma*) to get in on the sly, sneak in; (*ne pas faire la queue*) to jump the queue (*Brit*), cut in (at the beginning of) the line (*US*). 2 **vt** *place* to wangle‡, fiddle*.

resquilleur, -euse* [ʀɛskijœʀ, øz] **nm,f** (*qui n'attend pas son tour*) queue-jumper (*Brit*), *person who doesn't wait his or her turn in a queue* (*Brit*) *or line* (*US*); (*qui ne paie pas*) (*dans l'autobus etc*) fare-dodger. (*au stade etc*) **expulser les ~s** to throw out the people who have wangled their way in without paying.

ressac [ʀəsak] **nm**: **le ~** (*mouvement*) the backwash, the undertow; (*vague*) the surf.

ressaisir [ʀ(ə)seziʀ] 2 1 **vt** a *branche, bouée* to catch hold of again; *fuyard* to recapture, seize again; (*fig*) *pouvoir, occasion, prétexte* to seize again; (*Jur*) *biens* to recover possession of.

b *[peur]* to grip (once) again; *[délire, désir]* to take hold of again.

c (*Jur*) **~ un tribunal d'une affaire** to lay a matter before a court again.

2 **se ressaisir vpr** a (*reprendre son sang-froid*) to regain one's self-control; (*Sport: après avoir flanché*) to rally, recover. **ressaisissez-vous!** pull yourself together!, take a grip on yourself!; **le coureur s'est bien ressaisi sur la fin** the runner rallied *ou* recovered well towards the end.

b **se ~ de** *objet, fugitifs* to recover; *pouvoir* to seize again.

ressaisissement [ʀ(ə)sezismɑ̃] **nm** recovery.

ressassé, e [ʀ(ə)sase] (**ptp de ressasser**) **adj** *plaisanterie, thème* worn out, hackneyed.

ressasser [ʀ(ə)sase] 1 **vt** *pensées, regrets* to keep rehearsing *ou* turning over; *plaisanteries, conseil* to keep trotting out.

ressaut [ʀəso] **nm** (*Géog*) (*plan vertical*) rise; (*plan horizontal*) shelf; (*Archit*) projection.

ressauter [ʀ(ə)sote] 1 1 **vi** to jump again. 2 **vt** *obstacle* to jump (over) again.

ressayage [ʀesɛjaʒ] **nm** = **réessayage.**

ressayer [ʀeseje] 8 **vt, vi** (*gén*) to try again; (*Couture*) = **réessayer.**

ressemblance [ʀ(ə)sɑ̃blɑ̃s] **nf** a (*similitude visuelle*) resemblance, likeness; (*analogie de composition*) similarity. **~ presque parfaite entre 2 substances** near perfect similarity of 2 substances; **avoir *ou* offrir une ~ avec qch** to bear a resemblance *ou* likeness to sth; **la ~ entre père et fils/ces montagnes est frappante** the resemblance between father and son/these mountains is striking; **ce peintre s'inquiète peu de la ~** this painter cares very little about likenesses; **toute ~ avec des personnes existant *ou* ayant existé est purement fortuite** any resemblance to any person living or dead is purely accidental.

b (*trait*) resemblance; (*analogie*) similarity.

ressemblant, e [ʀ(ə)sɑ̃blɑ̃, ɑ̃t] **adj** *photo, portrait* lifelike, true to life. **vous êtes très ~ sur cette photo** this photo is very like you; **il a fait d'elle un portrait très ~** he painted a very good likeness of her.

ressembler [ʀ(ə)sɑ̃ble] 1 1 **ressembler à vt indir** a (*être semblable à*) *[personne]* (*physiquement*) to resemble, be *ou* look like; (*moralement, psychologiquement*) to resemble, be like; *[choses]* (*visuellement*) to resemble, look like; (*par la composition*) to resemble, be like; *[faits, événements]* to resemble, be like. **il me ressemble beaucoup physiquement/moralement** he is very like me *ou* he resembles me closely in looks/in character; **juste quelques accrochages, rien qui ressemble à une offensive** just a few skirmishes — nothing that would pass as *ou* that you could call a real offensive; **il ne ressemble en rien à l'image que je me faisais de lui** he's nothing like how I imagined him; **à quoi ressemble-t-il?*** what does he look like?, what's he like?; **ton fils s'est roulé dans la boue, regarde à quoi il ressemble!*** your son has been rolling in the mud — just look at the state of him!; **ça ne ressemble à rien!*** *[attitude]* that has no rhyme or reason to it, it makes no sense at all; *[peinture, objet]* it's like nothing on earth!; **à quoi ça ressemble de crier comme ça!*** what's the idea of *ou* what do you mean by shouting like that!

b (*être digne de*) **cela lui ressemble bien, de dire ça** it's just like him *ou* it's typical of him to say that; **cela te ressemble peu** that's (most) unlike you *ou* not like you.

2 **se ressembler vpr** (*physiquement, visuellement*) to look *ou* be alike, resemble each other; (*moralement, par ses éléments*) to be alike, resemble each other. **ils se ressemblent comme deux gouttes d'eau** they're as like as two peas (in a pod); **tu ne te ressembles plus depuis ton accident** you're not yourself *ou* you've changed a lot since your accident; **aucune ville ne se ressemble *ou* ne ressemble à une autre** no town is like another, no two towns are alike; **aucune maison ne se ressemble dans cette rue** no two houses look alike *ou* not one house looks like another in this street; **toutes les grandes villes se ressemblent** all big towns are *ou* look alike *ou* the same; *voir* **jour, qui.**

ressemelage [ʀ(ə)səm(ə)laʒ] **nm** soling, resoling.

ressemeler [ʀ(ə)səm(ə)le] 4 **vt** to sole, resole.

ressemer [ʀəs(ə)me] 5 1 **vt** to resow, sow again. 2 **se ressemer vpr: se ~ (tout seul)** to (re)seed itself.

ressentiment [ʀ(ə)sɑ̃timɑ̃] **nm** resentment (*contre* against, *de* at). **éprouver du ~** to feel resentful; **éprouver un ~ légitime à l'égard de qn** to feel justifiably resentful towards sb; **il en a gardé du ~** it has remained a sore point with him, he has harboured resentment over it; **avec ~** resentfully, with resentment.

ressentir [ʀ(ə)sɑ̃tiʀ] 16 1 **vt** *douleur, sentiment, coup* to feel; *sensation* to feel, experience; *perte, insulte, privation* to feel, be affected by. **il ressentit les effets de cette nuit de beuverie** he felt the effects of that night's drinking; **il ressent toute chose profondément** he feels everything deeply, he is deeply affected by anything *ou* everything.

2 **se ressentir vpr** a *[travail, qualité]* **se ~ de** to show the effects of; **la qualité/son travail s'en ressent** the quality/his work is showing the effect, it is telling on the quality/his work.

b *[personne, communauté]* **se ~ de** to feel the effects of; **il se ressentait du manque de préparation** he felt the effects of his lack of preparation, his lack of preparation told on his performance.

c (*) **s'en ~ pour** to feel up to; **il ne s'en ressent pas pour faire ça** he doesn't feel up to doing that.

resserre [ʀəsɛʀ] **nf** (*cabane*) shed; (*réduit*) store, storeroom.

resserré, e [ʀ(ə)seʀe] (**ptp de resserrer**) **adj** *chemin, vallée* narrow. **une petite maison ~e entre des immeubles** a little house squeezed between high buildings.

resserrement [ʀ(ə)sɛʀmɑ̃] **nm** a (*action*) *[nœud, étreinte]* tightening; *[pores]* closing; *[liens, amitié]* strengthening; *[vallée]* narrowing; *[crédit]* tightening. b (*goulet*) *[route, vallée]* narrow part.

resserrer [ʀ(ə)seʀe] 1 1 vt *boulon, souliers, nœud* to tighten up; *étreinte* to tighten; (*fig*) *cercle, filets* to draw tighter, tighten; (*fig*) *liens, amitié* to strengthen; (*fig*) *récit* to tighten up, compress; (*fig*) *crédits* to tighten, squeeze. **la peur resserra le cercle des fugitifs autour du feu** fear drew the group of fugitives in *ou* closer around the fire; **produit qui resserre les pores de la peau** product which helps (to) close the pores of the skin.

2 **se resserrer** vpr *[nœud, étau, étreinte]* to tighten; *[liens affectifs]* to grow stronger; *[cercle, groupe]* to draw in; *[pores, mâchoire]* to close; (*fig*) *[chemin, vallée]* to narrow. **le filet/l'enquête se resserrait autour de lui** the net/inquiry was closing in on him.

resservir [ʀ(ə)sɛʀviʀ] 14 1 vt a (*servir à nouveau*) *plat* to serve (up) again (*à* to), dish up again* (*péj*) (*à* for). **ils (nous) ont resservi la soupe de midi** they served (us) up the lunchtime soup again.

b (*servir davantage*) *dîneur* to give another *ou* a second helping to. **~ de la soupe/viande** to give another *ou* a second helping of soup/meat; **ils (nous) ont resservi de la viande** they gave (us) a second helping of meat.

c (*fig*) *thème, histoire* to trot out again (*péj*). **les thèmes qu'ils nous resservent depuis des années** the themes that they have been feeding us with *ou* trotting out to us for years.

2 vi a *[vêtement usagé, outil]* to serve again, do again. **ça peut toujours ~** it may come in handy *ou* be useful again; **cet emballage peut ~** this packaging can be used again; **ce manteau pourra te ~** you may find this coat useful again (some time).

b (*Tennis*) to serve again.

3 **se resservir** vpr a *[dîneur]* to help o.s. again, take another helping. **se ~ de fromage/viande** to help o.s. to some more cheese/meat, take another helping of cheese/meat.

b (*réutiliser*) **se ~ de** *outil* to use again; *vêtement* to wear again.

ressort[1] [ʀ(ə)sɔʀ] 1 nm a (*pièce de métal*) spring. **faire ~** to spring back; **à ~** *mécanisme, pièce* spring-loaded; *voir* **matelas, mouvoir.** b (*énergie*) spirit. **avoir du/manquer de ~** to have/lack spirit; **un être sans ~** a spiritless individual. c (*littér: motivation*) **les ~s qui le font agir** the forces which motivate him, the motivating forces behind his actions; **les ~s de l'âme** the moving forces of the soul. d (†: *élasticité*) resilience. e (†: *moyen*) means. 2 comp ▸**ressort à boudin** spiral spring ▸**ressort hélicoïdal** helical *ou* coil spring ▸**ressort à lames** leafspring ▸**ressort de montre** hairspring ▸**ressort de suspension** suspension spring ▸**ressort de traction** drawspring.

ressort[2] [ʀ(ə)sɔʀ] nm a (*Admin, Jur: de la compétence de*) **être du ~ de** to be *ou* fall within the competence of; **c'est du ~ de la justice/du chef de service** that is for the law/head of department to deal with, that is the law's/the head of department's responsibility; (*fig*) **ce n'est pas de mon ~** this is not my responsibility, this doesn't come within my province, this falls outside my scope. b (*Jur: circonscription*) jurisdiction. **dans le ~ du tribunal de Paris** in the jurisdiction of the courts of Paris; *voir* **dernier.**

ressortir[1] [ʀ(ə)sɔʀtiʀ] 2 1 vi (*avec aux être*) a (*à nouveau: voir aussi* **sortir**) *[personne]* (*aller*) to go out again, leave again; (*venir*) to come out again, leave again; (*en voiture*) to drive out again; *[objet, pièce]* to come out again. **je suis ressorti faire des courses** I went out shopping again; **ils sont ressortis du pays une troisième fois** they left the country again for the third time; **le rouge/7 est ressorti** the red/7 came out *ou* up again; **ce film ressort sur nos écrans** this film is showing again *ou* has been re-released.

b (*sortir*) *[personne]* to go (*ou* come) out (again), leave; *[objet, pièce]* to come out (again). **il a jeté un coup d'œil aux journaux et il est ressorti** he glanced at the newspapers and went (back) out again; (*fig*) **des désirs refoulés/souvenirs qui ressortent** repressed desires/memories which resurface *ou* come back up to the surface.

c (*contraster*) *[détail, couleur, qualité]* to stand out. **faire ~ qch** to make sth stand out, bring out sth.

2 **ressortir de** vt indir (*résulter*) to emerge from, be the result of. **il ressort de tout cela que personne ne savait** what emerges from all that is that no one knew.

3 vt (*avec aux avoir*) (*à nouveau: voir aussi* **sortir**) *vêtements d'hiver, outil etc* to take out again; *film* to re-release, bring out again; (*Comm*) *modèle* to bring out again. **le soleil revenant, ils ont ressorti les chaises sur la terrasse** when the sun came out again, they took *ou* brought the chairs back onto the terrace; **j'ai encore besoin du registre, ressors-le** I still need the register so take *ou* get it (back) out again; **il (nous) ressort toujours les mêmes blagues** he always trots out the same old jokes; (*fig*) **~ un vieux projet d'un tiroir** to get out an old plan again, disinter an old plan.

ressortir[2] [ʀ(ə)sɔʀtiʀ] 2 **ressortir à** vt indir (*Jur*) *cour, tribunal* to come under the jurisdiction of; (*frm*) *domaine* to be the concern *ou* province of, pertain to. (*Jur*) **ceci ressort à une autre juridiction** this comes under *ou* belongs to a separate jurisdiction.

ressortissant, e [ʀ(ə)sɔʀtisɑ̃, ɑ̃t] nm,f national. **~ français** French national *ou* citizen.

ressouder [ʀ(ə)sude] 1 1 vt *objet brisé* to solder together again; *amitié* to patch up, renew the bonds of; (*souder à nouveau*) to resolder; to reweld. 2 **se ressouder** vpr *[os, fracture]* to knit, mend; *[amitié]* to mend.

ressource [ʀ(ə)suʀs] nf a (*moyens matériels, financiers*) **~s** *[pays]* resources; *[personne, famille]* resources, means; **~s personnelles** personal finances, private means *ou* resources; **avoir de maigres ~s** to have limited *ou* slender resources *ou* means; **une famille sans ~s** a family with no means of support *ou* no resources; **les ~s en hommes d'un pays** the manpower resources of a country; **les ~s de l'État** *ou* **du Trésor** the financial resources of the state; **~s humaines** human resources; **gestionnaire/directeur des ~s humaines** human resources administrator/manager.

b (*possibilités*) **~s** *[artiste, sportif, aventurier]* resources; *[art, technique, système]* possibilities; **les ~s de son talent/imagination** the resources of one's talent/imagination; **cet appareil/cette technique/ce système a des ~s variées** this camera/technique/system has a wide range of possible applications; **les ~s de la langue française** the resources of the French language; **les ~s de la photographie** the various possibilities of photography; **être à bout de ~s** to have exhausted all the possibilities, be at the end of one's resources; **homme/femme de ~(s)** man/woman of resource, resourceful man/woman.

c (*recours*) **n'ayant pas la ~ de lui parler** having no means *ou* possibility of speaking to him; **je n'ai d'autre ~ que de lui téléphoner** the only course open to me is to phone him, I have no other option but to phone him; **sa seule/dernière ~ était de** the only way *ou* course open to him/the only way *ou* course left *ou* remaining open to him was to; **vous êtes ma dernière ~** you are my last resort; **en dernière ~** as a last resort.

d **avoir de la ~** *[sportif, cheval]* to have strength in reserve; **il y a de la ~*** there's plenty more where that came from.

ressourcer (se) [ʀ(ə)suʀse] 3 vpr to refresh one's ideas.

ressouvenir (se) [ʀ(ə)suv(ə)niʀ] 22 vpr (*littér*) **se ~ de** to remember, recall; **faire se ~ qn de qch**, (*littér*) **faire ~ qn de qch** to remind sb of sth; **ce bruit le fit se ~** *ou* (*littér*) **lui fit ~ de son accident** hearing that noise he was reminded of his accident.

ressurgir [ʀ(ə)syʀʒiʀ] 2 vi = **resurgir.**

ressusciter [ʀesysite] 1 1 vi a (*Rel*) to rise (from the dead). **le Christ ressuscité** the risen Christ; **ressuscité d'entre les morts** risen from the dead.

b (*fig: renaître*) *[malade]* to come back to life, revive; *[sentiment, souvenir]* to revive, reawaken, come alive again; *[pays]* to come back to life, get back on its feet again.

2 vt a (*lit*) *mourant* to resuscitate, restore *ou* bring back to life; (*Rel*) to raise (from the dead). **buvez ça, ça ressusciterait un mort*** drink that – it'll put new life into you; **bruit à ~ les morts** noise that would wake *ou* awaken the dead.

b (*fig: régénérer*) *malade, projet, entreprise* to bring back to life, inject new life into, revive.

c (*fig: faire revivre*) *sentiment* to revive, reawaken, bring back to life; *héros, mode* to bring back, resurrect (*péj*); *passé, coutume, loi* to revive, resurrect (*péj*).

restant, e [ʀɛstɑ̃, ɑ̃t] 1 adj remaining. **le seul cousin ~** the sole *ou* one remaining cousin, the only *ou* one cousin left *ou* remaining; *voir* **poste**[1].

2 nm a (*l'autre partie*) **le ~** the rest, the remainder; **tout le ~ des provisions était perdu** all the rest *ou* remainder of the supplies were lost; **employant le ~ de ses journées à lire** spending the rest *ou* remainder of his days reading. b (*ce qui est en trop*) **accommoder un ~ de poulet** to make a dish with some left-over chicken; **faire une écharpe dans un ~ de tissu** to make a scarf out of some left-over material.

restau* [ʀɛsto] nm (abrév de **restaurant**) restaurant. **~-U** university refectory *ou* canteen *ou* cafeteria.

restaurant [ʀɛstɔʀɑ̃] 1 nm restaurant. **on mange à la maison ou on va au ~?** shall we eat at home or shall we eat out? *ou* have a meal out?; *voir* **café, hôtel** *etc.* 2 comp ▸**restaurant d'entreprise** staff canteen, staff dining room ▸**restaurant gastronomique** gourmet restaurant ▸**restaurant libre-service** self-service restaurant, cafeteria ▸**restaurant rapide** fast-food restaurant ▸**restaurant self-service** = **restaurant libre-service** ▸**restaurant universitaire** university refectory *ou* canteen *ou* cafeteria.

restaurateur, -trice [ʀɛstɔʀatœʀ, tʀis] nm,f a *[tableau, dynastie]* restorer. b (*aubergiste*) restaurant owner, restaurateur.

restauration [ʀɛstɔʀasjɔ̃] nf a *[tableau, dynastie]* restoration; *[ville, bâtiment]* restoration, rehabilitation. (*Hist*) **la R~** the restoration (*of the Bourbons in 1830*). b (*hôtellerie*) catering. **il travaille dans la ~** he works in catering; **la ~ rapide** the fast-food industry *ou* trade.

restaurer [ʀɛstɔʀe] 1 1 vt a *tableau, dynastie, paix* to restore. b (*nourrir*) to feed. 2 **se restaurer** vpr to take some refreshment, have something to eat.

restauroute [ʀɛstoʀut] nm = **restoroute.**

reste [ʀɛst] nm a (*l'autre partie*) **le ~ de sa vie/du temps/des hommes** the rest of his life/of the time/of humanity; **j'ai lu 3 chapitres, je lirai le ~ (du livre) demain** I've read 3 chapters and I'll read the rest (of the book) tomorrow; **le ~ du lait** the rest of the milk, what is left of the milk; **préparez les bagages, je m'occupe du ~** get the luggage ready and I'll see to the rest *ou* to everything else.

b (*ce qui est en trop*) **il y a un ~ de fromage/de tissu** there's some *ou* a piece of cheese/material left over; **s'il y a un ~, je fais une omelette/une écharpe** if there's some *ou* any left *ou* left over I'll make an omelette/a scarf; **ce ~ de poulet ne suffira pas** this (piece of) left-over chicken won't be enough; **s'il y a un ~ (de laine), j'aimerais faire une écharpe** if there's some spare (wool) *ou* some (wool) to spare, I'd like to make a scarf; **un ~ de tendresse/de pitié la poussa à rester** a last trace *ou* a remnant of tenderness/pity moved her to stay.

c **les ~s** (*nourriture*) the left-overs; (*frm: dépouille mortelle*) the (mortal) remains; **les ~s de** *repas* the remains of, the left-overs from; *fortune, ville incendiée etc* the remains of, what is (*ou* was) left of; **donner les ~s au chien** to give the scraps *ou* left-overs to the dog; (*hum*) **elle a de beaux ~s** (*physiques*) she is a fine woman yet; (*intellectuels*) she's still on the ball*.

d (*Math: différence*) remainder.

e (*loc*) **avoir de l'argent/du temps de ~** to have money/time left over *ou* in hand *ou* to spare; **être** *ou* **demeurer en ~** to be outdone; **il ne voulait pas être en ~ avec eux** he didn't want to be outdone by them *ou* one down on them* (*Brit*) *ou* indebted to them; (*littér*) **au ~, du ~** (and) besides, (and) what's more; **nous la connaissons, du ~, très peu** besides *ou* moreover, we hardly know her at all; **il est parti sans attendre** *ou* **demander son ~** he left without further ado *ou* without asking (any) questions *ou* without waiting to hear more; **il est menteur, paresseux et (tout) le ~** he's untruthful, lazy and everything else as well; **avec la grève, la neige et (tout) le ~, ils ne peuvent pas venir** with the strike, the snow and everything else *ou* all the rest, they can't come; **pour le ~** *ou* **quant au ~ (nous verrons bien)** (as) for the rest (we'll have to see).

rester [ʀɛste] 1 1 **vi** a (*dans un lieu*) to stay, remain; (**: habiter*) to live. **~ au lit** *[paresseux]* to stay *ou* lie in bed; *[malade]* to stay in bed; **~ à la maison** to stay *ou* remain in the house *ou* indoors; **~ chez soi** to stay at home *ou* in; **~ au** *ou* **dans le jardin/à la campagne/à l'étranger** to stay *ou* remain in the garden/in the country/abroad; **~ (à) dîner/déjeuner** to stay for *ou* to dinner/lunch; **je ne peux ~ que 10 minutes** I can only stay *ou* stop* 10 minutes; **la voiture est restée dehors/au garage** the car stayed *ou* remained outside/in the garage; **la lettre va certainement ~ dans sa poche** the letter is sure to stay in his pocket; **un os lui est resté dans la gorge** a bone was caught *ou* got stuck in his throat; **ça m'est resté là*** *ou* **en travers de la gorge** it stuck in my throat; **mon déjeuner m'est resté sur l'estomac** my lunch is still sitting there; **restez où vous êtes** stay *ou* remain where you are; **~ à regarder la télévision** to stay watching television; **nous sommes restés 2 heures à l'attendre** we stayed there waiting for him for 2 hours; **naturellement ça reste entre nous** of course we shall keep this to ourselves *ou* this is strictly between ourselves; *[nerveux]* **il ne peut pas ~ en place** he can't keep still.

b (*dans un état*) to stay, remain. **~ éveillé/immobile** to keep *ou* stay awake/still; **~ sans bouger/sans rien dire** to stay *ou* remain motionless/silent; **~ dans l'ignorance** to remain in ignorance; **~ en fonction** to remain in office; **~ debout** (*lit*) to stand, remain standing; (*ne pas se coucher*) to stay up; **je suis resté assis/debout toute la journée** I spent the (whole) day sitting/standing, I've been sitting/standing (up) all day; **ne reste pas là les bras croisés** don't just stand there with your arms folded; **il est resté très timide** he has remained *ou* he is still very shy; **il est et restera toujours maladroit** he is clumsy and he always will be; **cette coutume est restée en honneur dans certains pays** this custom is still honoured in certain countries; *voir* **panne, plan[1]**.

c (*subsister*) to be left, remain. **rien ne reste de l'ancien château** nothing is left *ou* remains of the old castle; **c'est le seul parent qui leur reste** he's their only remaining relative, he's the only relative they have left; **c'est tout l'argent qui leur reste** that's all the money they have left; **10 km restaient à faire** there were still 10 km to go.

d (*durer*) to last, live on. **c'est une œuvre qui restera** it's a work which will live on *ou* which will last; **le désir passe, la tendresse reste** desire passes, tenderness lives on; **le surnom lui est resté** the nickname stayed with him, the nickname stuck.

e **~ sur une impression** to retain an impression; **je suis resté sur ma faim** (*après un repas*) I still felt hungry; (*à la fin d'une histoire*) I was left unsatisfied, I was left hanging*; **sa remarque m'est restée sur le cœur** his remark (still) rankles (in my mind); **ça m'est resté sur l'estomac*** it still riles me*, I still feel sore about it*, it still rankles with me.

f **en ~ à** (*ne pas dépasser*) to go no further than; **ils en sont restés à quelques baisers bien innocents/des discussions préliminaires** they got no further than a few quite innocent kisses/preliminary discussions; **les gens du village en sont restés à la bougie** the villagers never moved on from candles, the villagers are still at the stage of using candles; **ils en sont restés là des pourparlers** they only got that far *ou* that is as far as they got in their discussions; **les choses en sont restées là jusqu'à ...** nothing more happened until ... *ou* was done (about it) until ...; **où en étions-nous restés dans notre lecture?** where did we leave off in our reading?; **restons-en là** let's leave off there, let's leave it at that.

g (*‡: mourir*) **y ~** to meet one's end; **il a bien failli y ~** he nearly met his end, that was nearly the end of him.

2 **vb impers: il reste encore un peu de jour/de pain** there's still a little daylight/bread left; **il leur reste juste de quoi vivre** they've just enough left to live on; **il me reste à faire ceci** I still have this to do, there's still this for me to do; **il reste beaucoup à faire** much remains to be done, there's a lot left to do *ou* to be done, there's still a lot to do *ou* to be done; **il nous reste son souvenir** we still have our memories of him; **il ne me reste que toi** you're all I have left; **il n'est rien resté de leur maison/des provisions** nothing remained *ou* was left of their house/the supplies; **le peu de temps qu'il lui restait à vivre** the short time that he had left to live; **il ne me reste qu'à vous remercier** it only remains for me to thank you; **il restait à faire 50 km** there were 50 km still *ou* left to go; **est-ce qu'il vous reste assez de force pour terminer ce travail?** have you enough strength left to finish this job?; **quand on a été en prison il en reste toujours quelque chose** when you've been in prison something of it always stays with you; **(il) reste à savoir si/à prouver que** it remains to be seen if/to be proved that; **il reste que, il n'en reste pas moins que** the fact remains (nonetheless) that, it is nevertheless a fact that; **il reste entendu que** it remains *ou* is still quite understood that.

restituer [ʀɛstitɥe] 1 **vt** a (*rendre*) *objet volé* to return, restore (*à qn* to sb); *somme d'argent* to return, refund (*à qn* to sb). b (*reconstituer*) *fresque, texte, inscription* to reconstruct, restore. **un texte enfin restitué dans son intégralité** a text finally restored in its entirety; **appareil qui restitue fidèlement les sons** apparatus which gives faithful sound reproduction; **l'énergie emmagasinée est entièrement restituée sous forme de chaleur** the energy stored up is entirely released in the form of heat.

restitution [ʀɛstitysjɔ̃] **nf** (*voir* **restituer**) return; restoration; reconstruction; reproduction; release. **la ~ des objets volés** the return *ou* restitution of the stolen goods.

restoroute [ʀɛstoʀut] **nm** ® *[route]* roadside restaurant; *[autoroute]* motorway (*Brit*) *ou* freeway (*US*) restaurant.

restreindre [ʀɛstʀɛ̃dʀ] 52 1 **vt** *quantité, production, dépenses* to restrict, limit, cut down; *ambition* to restrict, limit, curb. **nous restreindrons notre étude à quelques exemples** we will restrict our study to a few examples; (*Fin*) **~ le crédit** to restrict credit. 2 **se restreindre vpr** a (*dans ses dépenses, sur la nourriture*) to cut down (*sur* on). b (*diminuer*) *[production, tirage]* to decrease, go down; *[espace]* to decrease, diminish; *[ambition, champ d'action]* to narrow; *[sens d'un mot]* to become more restricted. **le champ de leur enquête se restreint** the scope of their inquiry is narrowing.

restreint, e [ʀɛstʀɛ̃, ɛ̃t] (**ptp de restreindre**) **adj** *production, autorité, emploi, vocabulaire* limited, restricted; *personnel, espace, moyens, nombre* limited; *sens* restricted. **~ à** confined *ou* restricted *ou* limited to; *voir* **comité, suffrage**.

restrictif, -ive [ʀɛstʀiktif, iv] **adj** restrictive.

restriction [ʀɛstʀiksjɔ̃] **nf** a (*action*) restriction, limiting, limitation. b (*de personnel, de consommation*) **~s** restrictions; **~s d'électricité** electricity restrictions, restrictions on the use of electricity; **~s de crédit** credit restrictions. c (*condition*) qualification. (*réticence*) **~ (mentale)** mental reservation; **faire des ~s** to make qualifications, express some reservations; **avec ~** *ou* **des ~s** with some qualification(s) *ou* reservation(s); **approuver qch sans ~s** to give one's unqualified approval to sth, accept sth without reservation.

restructuration [ʀəstʀyktyʀasjɔ̃] **nf** restructuring.

restructurer [ʀəstʀyktyʀe] 1 **vt** to restructure.

resucée* [ʀ(ə)syse] **nf** (*plagiat*) rehash*.

résultante [ʀezyltɑ̃t] **nf** (*Sci*) resultant; (*fig: conséquence*) outcome, result, consequence.

résultat [ʀezylta] **nm** a (*conséquence*) result, outcome. **cette tentative a eu des ~s désastreux** this attempt had disastrous results *ou* a disastrous outcome; **cette démarche eut pour ~ une amélioration de la situation** *ou* **d'améliorer la situation** this measure resulted in *ou* led to an improvement in the situation *ou* resulted in the situation's improving; **on l'a laissé seul: ~, il a fait des bêtises** we left him alone, so what happens *ou* what's the result – he goes and does something silly.

b (*chose obtenue, réalisation*) result. **c'est un ~ remarquable** it is a remarkable result *ou* achievement; **il a promis d'obtenir des ~s** he promised to get results; (*iro*) **beau ~!** well done! (*iro*); **il essaya, sans ~, de le convaincre** he tried to convince him but to no effect *ou* avail; **le traitement fut sans ~** the treatment had no effect *ou* didn't work.

c (*solution*) *[problème, addition]* result.

d (*classement*) *[examen, élection]* results. **et maintenant les ~s sportifs** and now for the sports results; **le ~ des courses** the racing results; **voici quelques ~s partiels de l'élection** here are some of the election results so far.

e (*Fin*) (*gén*) result; (*chiffres*) figures; (*bénéfices*) profit; (*revenu*) income; (*gains*) earnings. **~s** results; **~ bénéficiaire** profit; **~ net** net profit *ou* income *ou* earnings.

résulter [ʀezylte] 1 1 **vi: ~ de** to result from, be the result of; **rien de bon ne peut en ~** no good can come of it *ou* result from it; **les avantages économiques qui en résultent** the resulting economic benefits; **ce qui a résulté de la discussion est que ...** the result *ou* outcome of the discussion was that ..., what came out of the discussion was that ... .

2 **vb impers: il résulte de tout ceci que** the result of all this is that; **il en**

résulte que c'est impossible as a result it's impossible, the result is that it's impossible; **qu'en résultera-t-il?** what will be the result? *ou* outcome?

résumé [ʀezyme] **nm** (*texte, ouvrage*) summary, résumé. **"~ des chapitres précédents"** "the story (in brief) so far"; (*TV, Radio*) **~ des informations** news roundup; **en ~** (*en bref*) in short, in brief; (*pour conclure*) to sum up; (*en miniature*) in miniature; **faire un ~ de** to sum up, give a brief summary of.

résumer [ʀezyme] 1 **1 vt** (*abréger*) to summarize; (*récapituler, aussi Jur*) to sum up; (*reproduire en petit*) to epitomize, typify. **2 se résumer vpr a** *[personne]* to sum up (one's ideas). **b** (*être contenu*) **toutes les facettes du bien et du mal se résumaient en lui** every aspect of good and evil was embodied *ou* typified in him. **c** (*se réduire à*) **se ~ à** to amount to, come down to, boil down to; **l'affaire se résume à peu de chose** the affair amounts to *ou* comes down to nothing really, that's all the affair boils down to.

résurgence [ʀezyʀʒɑ̃s] **nf** (*Géol*) reappearance (*of river*), resurgence; *[idée, mythe]* resurgence.

résurgent, e [ʀezyʀʒɑ̃, ɑ̃t] **adj** (*Géol*) *eaux* re-emergent.

resurgir [ʀ(ə)syʀʒiʀ] 2 **vi** to reappear, re-emerge.

résurrection [ʀezyʀɛksjɔ̃] **nf** *[mort]* resurrection; (*fig: renouveau*) revival. (*Rel*) **la R~** the Resurrection; **c'est une véritable ~!** he has really come back to life!

retable [ʀətabl] **nm** reredos, retable.

rétablir [ʀetabliʀ] 2 **1 vt a** (*remettre*) *courant, communications* to restore.

b (*restaurer*) *monarchie* to restore, re-establish; *droit, ordre, équilibre* to restore; *forces, santé* to restore; *fait, vérité* to re-establish.

c (*réintégrer*) to reinstate. **~ qn dans son emploi** to reinstate sb in *ou* restore sb to his post; **~ qn dans ses droits** to restore sb's rights.

d (*guérir*) **~ qn** to restore sb to health, bring about sb's recovery.

2 se rétablir vpr a (*guérir*) to recover. **après sa maladie, il s'est vite rétabli** he soon recovered after his illness.

b (*revenir*) to return, be restored. **le silence/le calme s'est rétabli** silence/calm returned *ou* was restored.

c (*faire un rétablissement*) to pull o.s. up (*onto a ledge etc*).

rétablissement [ʀetablismɑ̃] **nm a** (*action : voir* **rétablir**) restoring; re-establishment. **b** (*guérison*) recovery. **en vous souhaitant un prompt ~** with my (*ou* our) good wishes for your swift recovery, hoping you will be better soon; **tous nos vœux de prompt ~** our best wishes for a speedy recovery. **c** (*Sport*) **faire** *ou* **opérer un ~** to do a pull-up (*into a standing position, onto a ledge etc*).

retailler [ʀ(ə)tɑje] 1 **vt** *vêtement* to re-cut; *crayon* to sharpen; *arbre* to (re-)prune.

rétamage [ʀetamaʒ] **nm** re-coating, re-tinning (*of pans*).

rétamé, e‡ [ʀetame] (**ptp de rétamer**) **adj** (*fatigué*) knackered‡ (*Brit*), worn out*; (*ivre*) plastered‡, sloshed‡; (*détruit, démoli*) wiped out; (*sans argent*) broke*. (*mort*) **il a été ~ en un mois** he was dead within a month, he was a goner within a month‡.

rétamer [ʀetame] 1 **1 vt a** *casseroles* to re-coat, re-tin. **b** (‡) (*fatiguer*) to knacker‡ (*Brit*), wear out*; (*rendre ivre*) to knock out‡; (*démolir*) to wipe out; (*dépouiller au jeu*) to clean out*; (*à un examen*) to flunk‡. **se faire ~ au poker** to go broke* *ou* be cleaned out* at poker. **2 se rétamer‡ vpr** *[candidat]* to flunk‡. (*tomber*) **se ~ (par terre)** to take a dive*, crash to the ground; **la voiture s'est rétamée contre un arbre** the car crashed into a tree.

rétameur [ʀetamœʀ] **nm** tinker.

retapage [ʀ(ə)tapaʒ] **nm** *[maison, vêtement]* doing up; *[voiture]* fixing up; *[lit]* straightening.

retape‡ [ʀ(ə)tap] **nf: faire (de) la ~** *[prostituée]* to be on the game‡ (*Brit*), walk the streets*; *[agent publicitaire]* to tout (around) for business; **faire de la ~ pour une compagnie de bateaux-mouches** to tout for a pleasure boat company.

retaper [ʀ(ə)tape] 1 **1 vt a** (**: remettre en état*) *maison, vêtement* to do up; *voiture* to fix up; *lit* to straighten; (** fig*) *malade, personne fatiguée* to set up (again), buck up*. **ça m'a retapé, ce whisky** that whisky has set me up again. **b** (*dactylographier*) to retype, type again. **2 se retaper* vpr** (*guérir*) to get back on one's feet. **il va se ~ en quelques semaines** he'll get back on his feet in a few weeks.

retard [ʀ(ə)taʀ] **1 nm a** *[personne attendue]* lateness (*NonC*). **ces ~s continuels seront punis** this constant lateness will be punished; **plusieurs ~s dans la même semaine, c'est inadmissible** it won't do being late several times in one week; (*Scol*) **il a eu quatre ~s** he was late four times; **son ~ m'inquiète** I'm worried that he hasn't yet arrived *ou* by his lateness; **vous avez du ~, vous êtes en ~** you're late; **vous avez 2 heures de ~** *ou* **un ~ de 2 heures, vous êtes en ~ de 2 heures** you're 2 hours late; **ça/il m'a mis en ~** it/he made me late; **je me suis mis en ~** I made myself late; *voir* **billet**.

b *[train etc]* delay. **le train est en ~ sur l'horaire** the train is running behind schedule; **un ~ de 3 heures est annoncé sur la ligne Paris-Brest** there will be a delay of 3 hours *ou* trains will run 3 hours late on the Paris-Brest line; **le conducteur essayait de combler son ~** the driver was trying to make up the time he had lost; (*Sport*) **être en ~ (de 2 heures/2 km) sur le peloton** to be (2 hours/2 km) behind the pack; (*Sport*) **avoir 2 secondes de ~ sur le champion/record** to be 2 seconds slower than *ou* behind the champion/outside the record.

c *[montre]* **cette montre a du ~** this watch is slow; **la pendule prend du ~** the clock goes slow *ou* loses; **la pendule prend un ~ de 3 minutes par jour** the clock loses 3 minutes a day.

d (*non-observation des délais*) delay. **si l'on apporte du ~ dans l'exécution d'une commande** if one is late *ou* if there is a delay in carrying out an order; **paiement en ~** (*effectué*) late payment; (*non effectué*) overdue payment, payment overdue; **vous êtes en ~ pour les inscriptions** *ou* **pour vous inscrire** you are late (in) registering; **il est toujours en ~ sur les autres pour payer ses cotisations** he is always behind the others *ou* later than the others in paying his subscriptions; **payer/livrer qch avec ~** *ou* **en ~** to pay/deliver sth late, be late (in) paying/delivering sth; **sans ~** without delay.

e (*sur un programme*) delay. **nous sommes/les recherches sont en ~ sur le programme** we are/the research is behind schedule; **j'ai du travail/courrier en ~** I'm behind *ou* behindhand (*Brit*) with my work/mail, I have a backlog of work/mail; **il avait un ~ scolaire considérable** he had fallen well behind his age-group at school; **il doit combler son ~ en anglais** he has a lot of ground to make up in English; **j'ai pris du** *ou* **je me suis mis en ~ dans mes révisions** I have fallen behind in *ou* I am behind with my revision.

f (*infériorité*) *[peuple, pays]* backwardness. **il est en ~ pour son âge** he's backward for his age; **~ de croissance** slow development; **pays qui a 100 ans de ~ économique** *ou* **est en ~ de 100 ans du point de vue économique** country whose economy is 100 years behind *ou* which is economically 100 years behind; **~ industriel** industrial backwardness; **~ mental** backwardness; **être en ~ sur son temps** *ou* **siècle** to be behind the times; **il vit avec un siècle de ~** he's 100 years behind the times, he's living in the last century; (** hum*) **tu es en ~ d'un métro** *ou* **d'un train, tu as un métro** *ou* **un train de retard** you must have been asleep!

g (*Mus*) retardation.

2 adj inv (*Pharm*) **insuline/effet ~** delayed insulin/effect.

3 comp ▸ retard à l'allumage (*Aut*) retarded spark *ou* ignition.

retardataire [ʀ(ə)taʀdatɛʀ] **1 adj** *arrivant* late; *théorie, méthode* obsolete, outmoded. **2 nmf** latecomer.

retardateur, -trice [ʀ(ə)taʀdatœʀ, tʀis] **1 adj** (*Sci, Tech*) retarding. **2 nm** (*Phot*) self-timer.

retardé, e [ʀ(ə)taʀde] (**ptp de retarder**) **adj** (*scolairement*) backward, slow; (*intellectuellement*) retarded, backward. **classe pour ~s** remedial class.

retardement [ʀ(ə)taʀdəmɑ̃] **nm a à ~** *engin, torpille* with a timing device; *dispositif* delayed action (*épith*); (*Phot*) *mécanisme* self-timing; (*) *excuses, souhaits* belated; *voir* **bombe**. **b à ~** *comprendre, rire, se fâcher* after the event, in retrospect; (*péj*) **il comprend tout à ~** he's slow on the uptake*; (*péj*) **il rit toujours à ~** he's always slow in seeing the joke.

retarder [ʀ(ə)taʀde] 1 **1 vt a** (*mettre en retard sur un horaire*) *arrivant, arrivée* to delay, make late; *personne ou véhicule en chemin* to delay, hold up. **une visite inattendue m'a retardé** I was delayed by an unexpected visitor; **je ne veux pas vous ~** I don't want to delay you *ou* make you late; **ne te retarde pas (pour ça)** don't make yourself late for that; **il a été retardé par les grèves** he has been delayed *ou* held up by the strikes.

b (*mettre en retard sur un programme*) to hinder, set back; *opération, vendange, chercheur* to delay, hold up. **ça l'a retardé dans sa mission/ses études** this has set him back in *ou* hindered him in his mission/studies, he has been held back in his mission/studies.

c (*remettre*) *départ, opération* to delay, put back; *date* to put back; (*Aut*) *allumage* to retard. **~ son départ d'une heure** to put back one's departure by an hour, delay one's departure for an hour; **porte à ouverture retardée** door with a time lock; **parachute à ouverture retardée** parachute with fail-safe delayed opening.

d *montre, réveil* to put back. **~ l'horloge d'une heure** to put the clock back an hour.

2 vi a *[montre]* to be slow; (*d'habitude*) to lose. **je retarde (de 10 minutes)** my watch is (10 minutes) slow, I'm (10 minutes) slow.

b (*être à un stade antérieur*) **~ sur son époque** *ou* **temps** *ou* **siècle** to be behind the times.

c (*) (*être dépassé*) to be out of touch, be behind the times*. (*n'être pas au courant*) **ma voiture? tu retardes, je l'ai vendue il y a 2 ans** my car? you're a bit behind the times* *ou* you're a bit out of touch – I sold it 2 years ago.

retâter [ʀ(ə)tɑte] 1 **1 vt** *pouls, objet etc* to feel again. **2 vi: ~ de** *prison* to get another taste of; *métier* to have another go at. **3 se retâter vpr** (*après une chute*) to feel o.s. over.

reteindre [ʀ(ə)tɛ̃dʀ] 52 **vt** to dye again, redye.

retéléphoner [ʀ(ə)telefɔne] 1 **vi** to phone again, call back. **je lui retéléphonerai demain** I'll phone him again *ou* call him back tomorrow, I'll give him another call tomorrow.

retendre [ʀ(ə)tɑ̃dʀ] 41 **vt a** *câble* to stretch again, pull taut again; (*Mus*) *cordes* to retighten. **b** *piège, filets* to reset, set again. **c ~ la main à qn** to stretch out one's hand again to sb.

retenir [ʀət(ə)niʀ] 22 **1 vt a** (*lit, fig: maintenir*) *personne, objet qui* *glisse* to hold back; *chien* to hold back, check; *cheval* to rein in, hold back. ~ **qn par le bras** to hold sb back by the arm; **il allait tomber, une branche l'a retenu** he was about to fall but a branch held him back; **le barrage retient l'eau** the dam holds back the water; ~ **la foule qui se rue vers ...** to hold back the crowd rushing towards ...; **il se serait jeté par la fenêtre si on ne l'avait pas retenu** he would have thrown himself out of the window if he hadn't been held back *ou* stopped; **retenez-moi ou je fais un malheur** hold me back *ou* stop me or I'll do something I'll regret; (*fig*) **une certaine timidité le retenait** a certain shyness held him back; ~ **qn de faire qch** to keep sb from doing sth, stop sb doing sth; **je ne sais pas ce qui me retient de lui dire ce que je pense** I don't know what keeps me from *ou* stops me telling him what I think.

b (*garder*) *personne* to keep. ~ **qn à dîner** to have sb stay for dinner, keep sb for dinner; **j'ai été retenu** I was kept back *ou* detained *ou* held up; **il m'a retenu une heure** he kept me for an hour; **si tu veux partir, je ne te retiens pas** if you want to leave, I won't hold you back *ou* keep you; **c'est la maladie de sa femme qui l'a retenu à Brest** it was his wife's illness that kept *ou* detained him in Brest; **son travail le retenait ailleurs** his work kept *ou* detained him elsewhere; **la grippe l'a retenu au lit/à la maison** flu kept him in bed/kept him in *ou* indoors *ou* at home; ~ **qn prisonnier** to hold sb prisoner.

c *eau d'infiltration, odeur* to retain; *chaleur* to retain, keep in; *lumière* to reflect. **cette terre retient l'eau** this soil retains water; **le noir retient la chaleur** black retains the heat *ou* keeps in the heat.

d (*fixer*) *[clou, nœud etc]* to hold. **c'est un simple clou qui retient le tableau au mur** there's just a nail holding the picture on the wall; **un ruban retenait ses cheveux** a ribbon kept *ou* held her hair in place, her hair was tied up with a ribbon.

e ~ **l'attention de qn** to hold sb's attention; **ce détail retient l'attention** this detail holds one's attention; (*frm*) **sa demande a retenu notre attention** his request has been accorded our attention, we have noted his request.

f (*réserver, louer*) *chambre, place, table* to book, reserve; *domestique* to engage.

g (*se souvenir de*) *leçon, nom, donnée* to remember; *impression* to retain. **je n'ai pas retenu son nom/la date** I can't remember his name/the date; **je retiens de cette aventure qu'il est plus prudent de bien s'équiper** I've learnt from this adventure that it's wiser to be properly equipped; **j'en retiens qu'il est pingre et borné, c'est tout** the only thing that stands out *ou* that sticks in my mind is that he's stingy and narrow-minded; **un nom qu'on retient** a name that stays in your mind, a name you remember; **retenez bien ce qu'on vous a dit** don't forget *ou* make sure you remember what you were told; (*fig*) **celui-là, je le retiens!*** I'll remember HIM all right!, I won't forget HIM in a hurry!

h (*contenir, réprimer*) *larmes, cri* to hold back *ou* in, suppress; *colère* to hold back, restrain, suppress. ~ **son souffle** *ou* **sa respiration** to hold one's breath; **il ne put** ~ **un sourire/un rire** he could not hold back *ou* suppress a smile/a laugh, he could not help smiling/laughing; **il retint les mots qui lui venaient à la bouche** he bit back (*Brit*) *ou* held back the words that came to him.

i (*Math*) to carry. **je pose 4 et je retiens 2** 4 down and 2 to carry, put down 4 and carry 2.

j (*garder*) *salaire* to stop, withhold; *possessions, bagages d'un client* to retain.

k (*retrancher, prélever*) to deduct, keep back. **ils nous retiennent 1 000 F (sur notre salaire) pour les assurances** they deduct 1,000 francs (from our wages) for insurance; ~ **une certaine somme pour la retraite** to deduct a certain sum for retirement; ~ **les impôts à la base** to deduct taxes at source.

l (*accepter*) *proposition, plan* to accept; *nom, candidature* to retain, accept. (*Jur*) **le jury a retenu la préméditation** the jury accepted the charge of premeditation; **c'est notre projet qui a été retenu** it's our project that has been accepted.

2 **se retenir** vpr a (*s'accrocher*) to hold o.s. back. **se** ~ **pour ne pas glisser** to stop o.s. sliding; **se** ~ **à** to hold on to.

b (*se contenir*) to restrain o.s.; (*s'abstenir*) to stop o.s. (*de faire* doing); (*besoins naturels*) to hold on, hold o.s. in. **se** ~ **pour ne pas pleurer** *ou* **de pleurer** to stop o.s. crying; **malgré sa colère, il essaya de se** ~ despite his anger, he tried to restrain *ou* contain himself; **il se retint de lui faire remarquer que ...** he refrained from pointing out to him that ... .

retenter [ʀ(ə)tɑ̃te] 1 vt to try again, make another attempt at, have another go at; *saut, épreuve* to try again; *opération, action* to re-attempt. ~ **sa chance** to try one's luck again; ~ **de faire qch** to try to do sth again.

rétention [ʀetɑ̃sjɔ̃] nf (*Jur, Méd*) retention. (*Méd*) ~ **d'eau/d'urine** retention of water/urine; ~ **d'informations** witholding information.

retentir [ʀ(ə)tɑ̃tiʀ] 2 vi a *[sonnerie]* to ring; *[cris, bruit métallique]* to ring out. **ces mots retentissent encore à mes oreilles** those words are still ringing *ou* echoing in my ears. b ~ **de** (*résonner de*) to ring *ou* resound with, be full of the sound of. c (*affecter*) ~ **sur** to have an effect upon, affect.

retentissant, e [ʀ(ə)tɑ̃tisɑ̃, ɑ̃t] adj a (*fort, sonore*) *voix, son* ringing (*épith*); *choc, claque, bruit* resounding (*épith*). b (*frappant, éclatant*) *échec, succès* resounding (*épith*); *scandale* tremendous; *déclaration, discours* which causes a great stir, sensational.

retentissement [ʀ(ə)tɑ̃tismɑ̃] nm a (*répercussion*) repercussion, (after-)effect. **les ~s de l'affaire** the repercussions of the affair. b (*éclat*) stir, effect. **cette nouvelle eut un grand** ~ **dans l'opinion** this piece of news created a considerable stir in public opinion; **son œuvre fut sans grand** ~ his work went virtually unnoticed *ou* caused little stir. c (*littér*) *[son]* ringing.

retenu, e[1] [ʀət(ə)ny] (ptp de **retenir**) adj (*littér: discret*) *grâce, charme* reserved, restrained.

retenue[2] [ʀət(ə)ny] nf a (*prélèvement*) deduction, stoppage* (*Brit*). **opérer une** ~ **de 10% sur un salaire** to deduct 10% from a salary; ~ **pour la retraite/la Sécurité sociale** deductions *ou* stoppages* (*Brit*) for a pension scheme/≃ National Insurance (*Brit*) *ou* Social Security (*US*); **système de** ~ **à la source** *system of deducting income tax at source*, *[salariés]* ≃ pay-as-you-earn system (*Brit*).

b (*modération*) self-control, (self-)restraint; (*réserve*) reserve, reticence. **avoir de la** ~ to be reserved; **(rire) sans** ~ (to laugh) without restraint *ou* unrestrainedly; **il n'a aucune** ~ **dans ses propos** he shows no restraint in his speech.

c (*Math*) **n'oublie pas la** ~ don't forget what to carry (over).

d (*Scol*) detention. **être en** ~ to be in detention, be kept in; **mettre en** ~ to keep in, give detention to; **il a eu 2 heures de** ~ he got 2 hours' detention, he was kept in for 2 hours (after school).

e (*Tech*) *[barrage]* **barrage à faible** ~ low-volume dam; **bassin de** ~ balancing *ou* compensating reservoir.

f (*Aut: embouteillage*) tailback (*Brit*), (traffic) backup (*US*).

rétiaire [ʀetjɛʀ] nm (*Antiq*) retiarius.

réticence [ʀetisɑ̃s] nf a (*hésitation*) hesitation, reluctance (*NonC*), reservation. **avec** ~ reluctantly, with some reservation *ou* hesitation; **sans** ~ without (any) hesitation *ou* reservation(s). b (*littér: omission*) omission, reticence (*NonC*). **parler sans** ~ to speak openly, conceal nothing.

réticent, e [ʀetisɑ̃, ɑ̃t] adj a (*hésitant*) hesitant, reluctant. **se montrer** ~ to be hesitant *ou* reluctant (*pour faire* to do). b (*réservé*) reticent, reserved.

réticule [ʀetikyl] nm (*Opt*) reticle; (*sac*) reticule.

réticulé, e [ʀetikyle] adj (*Anat, Géol*) reticulate; (*Archit*) reticulated.

rétif, -ive [ʀetif, iv] adj *animal* stubborn; *personne* rebellious, restive.

rétine [ʀetin] nf retina.

rétinien, -ienne [ʀetinjɛ̃, jɛn] adj retinal.

retirage [ʀ(ə)tiʀaʒ] nm (*Typ*) reprint.

retiré, e [ʀ(ə)tiʀe] (ptp de **retirer**) adj a (*solitaire*) *lieu* remote, out-of-the-way; *maison* isolated; *vie* secluded. **vivre ~, mener une vie ~e** to live in isolation *ou* seclusion, lead a secluded *ou* sequestered (*littér*) life; **il vivait** ~ **du reste du monde** he lived withdrawn *ou* cut off from the rest of the world; ~ **quelque part dans le Béarn** living the quiet life somewhere in the Béarn. b (*en retraite*) retired. ~ **des affaires** retired from business.

retirer [ʀ(ə)tiʀe] 1 1 vt a (*lit, fig: enlever*) *gants, manteau, lunettes* to take off, remove. ~ **son collier au chien** to take the dog's collar off, remove the dog's collar; **retire-lui ses chaussures** take his shoes off (for him); **retire-lui ce couteau des mains (il va se blesser)** take that knife (away) from him (he's going to hurt himself); ~ **à qn son emploi** to take sb's job away (from him), deprive sb of his job; ~ **son permis (de conduire) à qn** to take away *ou* revoke sb's (driving) licence, disqualify sb from driving; ~ **une pièce de l'affiche** to take off *ou* close a play; **on lui a retiré la garde des enfants** he was deprived of custody of the children; ~ **à qn sa confiance** to withdraw one's confidence in sb; **il m'a retiré son amitié** he has deprived me of his friendship; ~ **à qn ses privilèges** to withdraw sb's privileges; ~ **la parole à qn** to make sb stand down (*Brit*), take the floor from sb (*US*).

b (*faire sortir*) to take out, remove (*de* from). ~ **un bouchon** to pull out *ou* take out *ou* remove a cork; ~ **un noyé de l'eau/qn de dessous les décombres** to pull a drowning man out of the water/sb out of *ou* out from under the rubble; ~ **un plat du four/les bagages du coffre** to take a dish out of the oven/the luggage out of the boot; **ils ont retiré leur fils du lycée** they have taken their son away from *ou* removed their son from the school; **se faire** ~ **une dent** to have a tooth out; **je ne peux pas** ~ **la clef de la serrure** I can't get the key out of the lock; ~ **un dessert d'un moule** to turn a dessert out of a mould; **retire les mains de tes poches** take your hands out of your pockets; (*fig*) **on lui retirera difficilement de l'idée** *ou* **de la tête qu'il est menacé*** we'll have difficulty *ou* a job convincing him that he's not being threatened.

c (*reprendre possession de*) *bagages, billets réservés* to collect, pick up; *argent en dépôt* to withdraw, take out; *gage* to redeem. ~ **de l'argent (de la banque)** to withdraw money (from the bank), take money out (of the bank); (*Comm*) **votre commande est prête à être retirée** your order is now awaiting collection *ou* ready for collection.

d (*ramener en arrière*) to take away, remove, withdraw. ~ **sa tête/sa main (pour éviter un coup)** to remove *ou* withdraw one's head/hand (to avoid being hit); **il retira prestement sa main** he whisked *ou* snatched his hand away.

e (*annuler*) *candidature* to withdraw; *plainte, accusation* to withdraw, take back. **je retire ce que j'ai dit** I take back what I said; (*Pol*) ~ **sa candidature** to stand down (*Brit*), withdraw one's candidature.

f (*obtenir*) ~ **des avantages de qch** to get *ou* gain *ou* derive advantages from sth; **les avantages/bénéfices qu'on en retire** the benefits/profits to be had *ou* gained from it; **il en a retiré un grand profit** he profited *ou* gained greatly by it; **il n'en a retiré que des ennuis** he only got worry out of it, he got nothing but worry from it; **tout ce qu'il en a retiré, c'est ...** the only thing he has got out of it is ..., all he has gained is ... .

g (*extraire*) *minerai, extrait, huile* to obtain. **une substance dont on retire une huile précieuse** a substance from which a valuable oil is obtained.

2 **se retirer** vpr a (*partir*) to retire, withdraw; (*aller se coucher*) to retire (to bed); (*prendre sa retraite*) to retire; (*retirer sa candidature*) to withdraw, stand down (*Brit*) (*en faveur de* in favour of). **se ~ discrètement** to withdraw discreetly; **ils se sont retirés dans un coin pour discuter affaires** they withdrew *ou* retired to a corner to talk (about) business; **se ~ dans sa chambre** to withdraw *ou* retire *ou* go to one's room; (*fig*) **se ~ dans sa tour d'ivoire** to take refuge *ou* lock o.s. up in one's ivory tower; **ils ont décidé de se ~ à la campagne** they've decided to retire to the country; **elle s'est retirée dans un couvent** she retired *ou* withdrew to a convent.

b (*reculer*) (*pour laisser passer qn, éviter un coup etc*) to move out of the way; (*Mil*) *[troupes]* to withdraw; *[mer, marée]* to recede, go back, ebb; *[eaux d'inondation]* to recede, go down; *[glacier]* to recede. **retire-toi d'ici** *ou* **de là, tu me gênes** mind *ou* get out of the way – you're bothering me, stand *ou* move back a bit – you're in my way.

c (*quitter*) **se ~ de** to withdraw from; **se ~ des affaires** to retire from business; **se ~ d'une compétition** to withdraw from a competition; **se ~ du monde** to withdraw from society; **se ~ de la partie** to drop out.

retombée [ʀ(ə)tɔ̃be] nf a **~s (radioactives** *ou* **atomiques)** (radioactive) fallout (*NonC*). b (*fig: gén pl*) (*répercussions*) consequences, effects; *[invention etc]* spin-off. c (*Archit*) spring, springing.

retomber [ʀ(ə)tɔ̃be] 1 vi a (*faire une nouvelle chute*) to fall again. **le lendemain, il est retombé dans la piscine** the next day he fell into the swimming pool again; (*fig*) ~ **dans la misère** to fall on hard times again; ~ **sous le joug de qn** to come under sb's yoke again; ~ **dans le découragement** to lose heart again; ~ **dans l'erreur/le péché** to fall back *ou* lapse into error/sin; **son roman est retombé dans l'oubli** his novel has sunk back *ou* lapsed into oblivion; **le pays retomba dans la guerre civile** the country lapsed into civil war again; **je vais retomber dans l'ennui** I shall start being bored again, boredom is going to set in again; **la conversation retomba sur le même sujet** the conversation turned once again *ou* came round again to the same subject.

b (*redevenir*) ~ **amoureux/malade** to fall in love/fall ill again; **ils sont retombés d'accord** they reached agreement again.

c *[pluie, neige]* to fall again, come down again. **la neige retombait de plus belle** the snow came down again *ou* was falling again still more heavily.

d (*tomber après s'être élevé*) *[personne]* to land; *[chose lancée, liquide]* to come down; *[abattant, capot, herse]* to fall back down; *[fusée, missile]* to land, come back to earth; (*fig*) *[conversation]* to fall away, die; (*fig*) *[intérêt]* to fall away, fall off; *[vent]* to subside, die down. **il est retombé lourdement (sur le dos)** he landed heavily (on his back); **elle saute bien mais elle ne sait pas ~** she can jump well but she doesn't know how to land; **le chat retombe toujours sur ses pattes** cats always land on their feet; (*fig*) **il retombera toujours sur ses pattes** *ou* **pieds** he'll always land *ou* fall on his feet; **les nuages retombent en pluie** the clouds come down *ou* fall again as rain; **l'eau retombait en cascades** the water fell back in cascades; (*fig*) **après quelques leçons, l'intérêt retombait** after a few lessons interest was falling away *ou* falling off; (*fig*) **ça lui est retombé sur le nez** that's rebounded on him; **le brouillard est retombé en fin de matinée** the fog fell again *ou* came down again *ou* closed in again towards lunchtime; **l'inflation est retombée à 4%** inflation has fallen to 4%; **laisser ~ le couvercle d'un bureau avec bruit** to let a desk lid fall back noisily; **se laisser ~ sur son oreiller** to fall back *ou* sink back onto one's pillow; (*Sport*) **laissez ~ les bras** let your arms drop *ou* fall (by your sides).

e (*pendre*) *[cheveux, rideaux]* to fall, hang (down). **de petites boucles blondes retombaient sur son front** little blond curls tumbled *ou* fell onto her forehead.

f (*fig: échoir à*) **le péché du père retombera sur la tête des enfants** the sin of the father will fall on the heads of the children, the sins of the fathers will be visited on the sons; **la responsabilité retombera sur toi** the responsibility will fall *ou* land* on you; **les frais retombèrent sur nous** we were landed* *ou* saddled with the expense; **faire ~ sur qn la responsabilité de qch/les frais de qch** to pass the responsibility for sth/the cost of sth on to sb, land* sb with the responsibility for sth/the cost of sth; **ça va me ~ dessus*** (*gén*) I'll get the blame *ou* take the flak* (for it); (*travail*) it'll be dumped* on me, I'll get lumbered with it* (*Brit*).

g (*loc*) **Noël retombe un samedi** Christmas falls on a Saturday again; ~ **en enfance** to lapse into second childhood; **je suis retombé sur lui le lendemain, au même endroit** I came across him again the next day in the same place; **ils nous sont retombés dessus le lendemain** they landed* on us again the next day.

retordre [ʀ(ə)tɔʀdʀ] 41 vt a (*Tech*) *câbles, fils* to twist again; *voir* **fil.** b *linge* to wring (out) again; *fil de fer* to rewind.

rétorquer [ʀetɔʀke] 1 vt to retort.

retors, e [ʀətɔʀ, ɔʀs] adj (*rusé*) sly, wily, underhand.

rétorsion [ʀetɔʀsjɔ̃] nf (*frm, Jur, Pol*) retortion, retaliation. **user de ~ envers un état** to retaliate *ou* use retortion against a state; *voir* **mesure.**

retouchable [ʀ(ə)tuʃabl] adj *photo* which can be touched up; *vêtement* which can be altered.

retouche [ʀ(ə)tuʃ] nf *[photo, peinture]* touching up (*NonC*); *[texte, vêtement]* alteration. **faire une ~ à une photo** to touch up a photo; **faire une ~** (*à une photo*) to do some touching up; (*à un vêtement*) to make an alteration.

retoucher [ʀ(ə)tuʃe] 1 1 vt a (*améliorer*) *photo, peinture* to touch up, retouch; *vêtement, texte* to alter, make alterations to. **il faudra ~ cette veste au col** this jacket will have to be altered at the neck; **on voit tout de suite que cette photo est retouchée** you can see straight away that this photo has been touched up. b (*toucher de nouveau*) to touch again; (*blesser de nouveau*) to hit again. 2 vi: ~ **à qch** to touch sth again; **s'il retouche à ma sœur, gare à lui!** if he lays hands on *ou* touches my sister again he'd better look out!

retoucheur, -euse [ʀ(ə)tuʃœʀ, øz] nm,f: ~ **(en confection)** dressmaker in charge of alterations; ~ **photographe** retoucher.

retour [ʀ(ə)tuʀ] 1 nm a (*fait d'être revenu*) (*gén*) return; (*à la maison*) homecoming, return home; (*chemin, trajet*) return (journey), way back, journey back; (*billet*) return (ticket). **il fallait déjà penser au ~** it was already time to think about going back *ou* about the return journey; **être sur le (chemin du) ~** to be on one's way back; **pendant le ~** on the way back, during the return journey, on the journey back; **elle n'a pas assez pour payer son ~** she hasn't enough to pay for her return journey; **(être) de ~ (de)** (to be) back (from); **à votre ~, écrivez-nous** write to us when you are *ou* get back; **à leur ~, ils trouvèrent la maison vide** when they got back *ou* on their return, they found the house empty; **de ~ à la maison** back home; **au ~ de notre voyage** when we got back from our journey, arriving back from our journey; **à son ~ d'Afrique/du service militaire** on his return *ou* on returning from Africa/military service; *voir* **cheval.**

b (*à un état antérieur*) ~ **à** return to; **le ~ à une vie normale** the return *ou* reversion to (a) normal life; ~ **à la nature/à la terre** return to nature/the land; ~ **aux sources** (*gén: aux origines*) return to basics; (*à la nature*) return to the basic *ou* simple life; (*à son village natal*) return to one's roots; ~ **au calme/à l'Antiquité** return to a state of calm/to Antiquity; **son ~ à la politique** his return to politics, his political comeback.

c (*réapparition*) return; (*répétition régulière*) *[thème, motif, cadence]* recurrence. **le ~ du printemps/de la paix** the return of spring/peace; **on prévoit un ~ du froid** a return of the cold weather is forecast; **un ~ offensif de la grippe** a renewed outbreak of flu.

d (*Comm, Poste*) *[emballage, récipient, objets invendus]* return. ~ **à l'envoyeur** *ou* **à l'expéditeur** return to sender; **avec faculté de ~** on approval, on sale or return; (*Fin*) **clause de ~** no protest clause.

e (*Jur*) reversion. **(droit de) ~** reversion.

f (*littér*) (*changement d'avis*) change of heart. (*revirements*) **~s** reversals; **les ~s de la fortune** the turns of fortune; **un ~ soudain dans l'opinion publique** a sudden turnabout in public opinion.

g (*Tech*) *[pièce mobile, chariot de machine]* return; (*partie de bureau*) (desk) extension. **le ~ du chariot est automatique** the carriage return is automatic.

h (*Élec*) ~ **à la terre** *ou* **à la masse** earth (*Brit*) *ou* ground (*US*) return.

i (*Tennis*) return. ~ **de service** return of service *ou* serve.

j (*Fin*) return. ~ **sur investissements** return on investments.

k (*loc*) **en ~** in return; **choc** *ou* **effet en ~** backlash; **bâtiment en ~ (d'équerre)** building constructed at right angles; (*péj*) **être sur le ~*** to be over the hill*, be a bit past it* (*Brit*); **faire ~ à** to revert to; **par un juste ~ des choses, il a été cette fois récompensé** events went his way *ou* fate was fair to him this time and he got his just reward; **par ~ (du courrier)** by return (of post); **sans ~** irredeemably, irrevocably, for ever; **voyage sans ~** journey from which there is no return; ~ **sur soi-même** soul-searching (*NonC*); **faire un ~ sur soi-même** to take stock of o.s., do some soul-searching; *voir* **payer.**

2 comp ►**retour d'âge** change of life ►**retour en arrière** (*Littérat, Ciné*) flashback; (*souvenir*) look back; (*mesure rétrograde*) retreat; **faire un retour en arrière** to take a look back, look back; (*Ciné*) to flash back ►**retour de bâton** kickback ►**retour de couches** first period (after pregnancy), return of menstruation ►**retour éternel** (*Philos*) eternal recurrence ►**retour de flamme** (*dans un moteur*) backfire; (*fig*) rekindling of passion; *[feu]* **il y a eu un retour de flamme** the flames leapt out ►**retour en force** return in strength ►**retour de manivelle** (*lit*) backfire, kick; (*fig*) **il y aura un retour de manivelle** it'll backfire (on them) ►**retour offensif** renewed attack.

retournement [ʀ(ə)tuʀnəmɑ̃] nm *[situation, opinion publique]* reversal (*de* of), turnaround (*de* in).

retourner [ʀ(ə)tuʀne] 1 **1** vt (*avec aux avoir*) **a** (*mettre dans l'autre sens*) *seau, caisse* to turn upside down; *matelas* to turn (over); *carte* to turn up *ou* over; (*Culin*) *viande, poisson, omelette* to turn over; *crêpe* (*avec une spatule*) to turn over; (*en lançant*) to toss. ~ **un tableau/une carte contre le mur** to turn a picture/a map against the wall; (*fig*) **elle l'a retourné (comme une crêpe** *ou* **un gant)*** she soon changed his mind for him; ~ **la situation** to reverse the situation, turn the situation round.
b (*en remuant, secouant*) *sol, terre* to turn over; *salade* to toss. ~ **le foin** to toss (the) hay, turn (over) the hay.
c (*mettre l'intérieur à l'extérieur*) *sac, vêtement, parapluie* to turn inside out; (*Couture*) *vêtement, col* to turn. (*fig*) ~ **sa veste** to turn one's coat; ~ **ses poches pour trouver qch** to turn one's pockets inside out *ou* turn out one's pockets to find sth; **son col/revers est retourné** (*par mégarde*) his collar/lapel is turned up.
d (*orienter dans le sens opposé*) *mot, phrase* to turn round. ~ **un argument contre qn** to turn an argument back on sb *ou* against sb; ~ **contre l'ennemi ses propres armes** to turn the enemy's own weapons on him; **il retourna le pistolet contre lui-même** he turned the gun on himself; **on pourrait vous ~ votre compliment/votre critique** one might return the compliment/your criticism.
e (*renvoyer*) *marchandise, lettre* to return, send back.
f (*fig *: bouleverser*) *pièce, maison* to turn upside down; *personne* to shake. **il a tout retourné dans la maison pour retrouver ce livre** he turned the whole house upside down to find that book; **la nouvelle l'a complètement retourné** the news has severely shaken him; **ce spectacle m'a retourné** the sight of this shook me *ou* gave me quite a turn*.
g (*tourner plusieurs fois*) ~ **une pensée/une idée dans sa tête** to turn a thought/an idea over (and over) in one's mind; (*fig*) ~ **le couteau** *ou* **le poignard dans la plaie** to twist the knife in the wound; *voir* **tourner**.
2 vi (*avec aux être*) **a** (*aller à nouveau*) to return, go back. ~ **en Italie/à la mer** to return *ou* go back to Italy/the seaside; **je devrai ~ chez le médecin** I'll have to go back to the doctor's; ~ **en arrière** *ou* **sur ses pas** to turn back, retrace one's steps; **il retourne demain à son travail/à l'école** he's going back to work/school tomorrow; (*rentrer*) **elle est retournée chez elle chercher son parapluie** she went back home to get her umbrella.
b (*à un état antérieur*) ~ **à** to return to, go back to; ~ **à la vie sauvage** to revert *ou* go back to the wild state; ~ **à Dieu** to return to God; **il est retourné à son ancien métier/à la physique** he has gone back to his old job/to physics.
3 vb impers: **nous voudrions bien savoir de quoi il retourne** we should really like to know what is going on *ou* what it's all about.
4 se retourner vpr **a** *[personne couchée]* to turn over; *[véhicule, automobiliste]* to turn over, overturn. **se ~ sur le dos/le ventre** to turn (over) onto one's back/stomach; **se ~ dans son lit toute la nuit** to toss and turn all night in bed; (*hum*) **il doit se ~ dans sa tombe!** he must be turning in his grave! (*hum*); **la voiture s'est retournée** *ou* **ils se sont retournés (dans un fossé)** the car *ou* they overturned (into a ditch); (*fig*) **laissez-lui le temps de se ~** give him time to sort himself out *ou* turn himself round *ou* to find his feet; (*fig*) **il sait se ~** he knows how to cope.
b (*tourner la tête*) to turn round. **partir sans se ~** to leave without looking back *ou* without a backward glance; **tout le monde se retournait sur son passage** everyone turned round as he went by.
c (*fig*) *[situation]* to be reversed, be turned round. **se ~ contre qn** *[personne]* to turn against sb; *[acte, situation]* to backfire on sb, rebound on sb; (*Jur: poursuivre*) to take (court) action *ou* proceedings against sb; **il ne savait vers qui se ~** he didn't know who to turn to.
d (*tordre*) *pouce* to wrench, twist.
e (*littér*) **s'en ~** (*cheminer*) to journey back; (*partir*) to depart, leave; (*fig*) **il s'en retourna comme il était venu** he left as he had come; **s'en ~ dans son pays (natal)** to return to one's native country.

retracer [ʀ(ə)tʀase] 3 vt **a** (*raconter*) *vie, histoire* to relate, recount. **b** (*tracer à nouveau*) *trait effacé* to redraw, draw again.

rétractable [ʀetʀaktabl] adj (*Jur*) revocable.

rétractation [ʀetʀaktasjɔ̃] nf *[témoignage, aveux, promesse]* retraction, withdrawal.

rétracter [ʀetʀakte] 1 **1** vt **a** (*contracter, rentrer*) *corne, griffe* to draw in, retract. **b** (*littér: revenir sur*) *parole, opinion* to retract, withdraw, take back. **2 se rétracter** vpr **a** (*se retirer*) *[griffe, antenne]* to retract. (*fig littér*) **au moindre reproche, elle se rétractait** she would shrink at the slightest reproach. **b** (*se dédire*) (*Jur*) to retract, withdraw one's statement. **je ne veux pas avoir l'air de me ~** I don't want to appear to back down.

rétractile [ʀetʀaktil] adj retractile.

rétraction [ʀetʀaksjɔ̃] nf retraction.

retraduction [ʀ(ə)tʀadyksjɔ̃] nf retranslation.

retraduire [ʀ(ə)tʀadɥiʀ] 38 vt (*traduire de nouveau*) to translate again; (*traduire dans la langue de départ*) to translate back.

retrait [ʀ(ə)tʀɛ] nm **a** (*départ*) *[mer]* ebb; *[eaux, glacier]* retreat; *[troupes, candidat]* withdrawal (*de* from).
b (*fait de retirer*) *[somme d'argent]* withdrawal; *[bagages]* collection; *[objet en gage]* redemption. **le ~ des bagages peut se faire à toute heure** luggage may be collected at all times.
c (*fait d'ôter*) *[candidature]* withdrawal. ~ **du permis (de conduire)** disqualification from driving, driving ban, revocation of a driving licence; (*Admin*) ~ **d'emploi** deprivation of office; (*Jur*) ~ **de plainte** nonsuit.
d (*rétrécissement*) *[ciment]* shrinkage, contraction; *[tissu]* shrinkage. **il y a du ~** there's some shrinkage.
e en ~: situé en ~ set back; **se tenant en ~** standing back; **en ~ de** set back from; **une petite maison, un peu en ~ de la route** a little house, set back a bit from the road; (*fig*) **rester en ~** to stay in the background; **des propositions en ~ sur les précédentes** offers which represent a retreat from the previous position *ou* which do not go as far as the earlier ones.

retraite [ʀ(ə)tʀɛt] **1** nf **a** (*Mil: déroute, fuite*) retreat. **battre/sonner la ~** to beat/sound the retreat; *voir* **battre**.
b (*cessation de travail*) retirement. **être en** *ou* **à la ~** to be retired *ou* in retirement; **en ~** retired; **travailleur en ~** retired worker, pensioner; **mettre qn à la ~** to pension sb off, superannuate sb; **mise à la ~** retirement; **mettre qn à la ~ d'office** to make sb take compulsory retirement; **mise à la ~ d'office** compulsory retirement; **prendre sa ~** to retire, go into retirement; **prendre une ~ anticipée** to retire early, take early retirement; **pour lui, c'est la ~ forcée** he has had retirement forced on him, he has had to retire early.
c (*pension*) pension. **toucher** *ou* **percevoir une petite ~** to receive *ou* draw a small pension; *voir* **caisse, maison**.
d (*littér: refuge*) *[poète, amants]* retreat, refuge; *[ours, loup]* lair; *[voleurs]* hideout, hiding place.
e (*Rel: récollection*) retreat. **faire** *ou* **suivre une ~** to be in retreat, go into retreat.
2 comp ►**retraite des cadres** management pension ►**retraite par capitalisation** self-funded retirement plan ►**retraite complémentaire** supplementary pension ►**retraite aux flambeaux** (*Mil*) torchlight procession ►**retraite par répartition** contributory pension scheme ►**retraite des vieux*** (old age) pension ►**retraite des vieux travailleurs** retirement pension.

retraité, e [ʀ(ə)tʀete] **1** adj **a** *personne* retired. **b** *déchets* reprocessed. **2** nm,f (old age) pensioner.

retraitement [ʀ(ə)tʀɛtmɑ̃] nm reprocessing. **usine de ~ des déchets nucléaires** nuclear reprocessing plant.

retraiter [ʀ(ə)tʀete] 1 vt to reprocess.

retranchement [ʀ(ə)tʀɑ̃ʃmɑ̃] nm (*Mil*) entrenchment, retrenchment. (*fig*) **poursuivre** *ou* **pourchasser qn jusque dans ses derniers ~s** to drive *ou* hound sb into a corner.

retrancher [ʀ(ə)tʀɑ̃ʃe] 1 **1** vt **a** (*enlever*) *quantité, somme* to take away, subtract (*de* from); *somme d'argent* to deduct, dock, take off; *passage, mot* to take out, remove, omit (*de* from). ~ **10 de 15** to take 10 (away) from 15, subtract 10 from 15; ~ **une somme d'un salaire** to deduct *ou* dock a sum from a salary, take a sum out of a salary; **si l'on retranche ceux qui n'ont pas de licence** if you leave out *ou* omit the non-graduates; (*hum*) **ils étaient décidés à me ~ du monde des vivants** they were set on removing me from the land of the living.
b (*littér: couper*) *chair gangrenée* to remove, cut off; *organe malade* to remove, cut out.
c (*littér: séparer*) to cut off. **son argent le retranchait des autres** his money cut him off from other people.
d (†: *Mil: fortifier*) to entrench.
2 se retrancher vpr **a** (*Mil: se fortifier*) **se ~ derrière/dans** to entrench o.s. behind/in; **se ~ sur une position** to entrench o.s. in a position.
b (*fig*) **se ~ dans son mutisme** to take refuge in silence; **se ~ dans sa douleur** to draw back into one's pain, shut o.s. off with one's pain; **se ~ derrière la loi/le secret professionnel** to take refuge behind *ou* hide behind the law/professional secrecy.

retranscription [ʀ(ə)tʀɑ̃skʀipsjɔ̃] nf retranscription.

retranscrire [ʀ(ə)tʀɑ̃skʀiʀ] 39 vt to retranscribe.

retransmetteur [ʀ(ə)tʀɑ̃smetœʀ] nm relay station.

retransmettre [ʀ(ə)tʀɑ̃smɛtʀ] 56 vt *match, émission, concert* (*Rad*) to broadcast, relay; (*TV*) to show, broadcast, relay. ~ **en différé** to broadcast a recording of; (*TV*) to show *ou* broadcast a recording of; ~ **en direct** to relay *ou* broadcast live; (*TV*) to show *ou* broadcast live.

retransmission [ʀ(ə)tʀɑ̃smisjɔ̃] nf (*voir* **retransmettre**) broadcast; showing. ~ **en direct/différé** live/recorded broadcast; live/recorded showing; **la ~ du match aura lieu à 23 heures** the match will be shown at 11 p.m.

retravailler [ʀ(ə)tʀavaje] 1 **1** vi **a** (*recommencer le travail*) to start work again. **il retravaille depuis le mois dernier** he has been back at work since last month. **b** (*se remettre à*) ~ **à qch** to start work on sth again, work at sth again. **2** vt *question* to give (some) more thought to; *discours, ouvrage* to work on again; (*Culin*) *pâte* to knead again; *argile* to work again; *minerai* to reprocess.

retraverser [ʀ(ə)tʀavɛʀse] 1 vt (*de nouveau*) to recross; (*dans l'autre sens*) to cross back over.

rétréci, e [ʀetʀesi] (ptp de **rétrécir**) adj *tricot, vêtement* shrunk, shrunken; *pupille* contracted; (*péj*) *esprit* narrow. (*Aut*) **"chaussée ~e"** "road narrows"; (*Comm, Tex*) ~ **(à la coupe)** preshrunk.

rétrécir [RetResiR] [2] 1 **vt** *vêtement* to take in; *tissu* to shrink; *pupille* to contract; *rue, conduit, orifice* to narrow, make narrower; *bague* to tighten, make smaller; (*fig*) *champ d'activité, esprit* to narrow. 2 **vi** a *[laine, tissu]* to shrink; *[pupille]* to contract; *[rue, vallée]* to narrow, become *ou* get narrower; *[esprit]* to grow narrow; *[cercle d'amis]* to grow smaller, dwindle. b **faire ~** *tissu* to shrink. 3 **se rétrécir vpr = 2a.**

rétrécissement [RetResismɑ̃] **nm** a (*le fait de se rétrécir*) *[tricot, laine]* shrinkage; *[pupille]* contraction; *[rue, vallée]* narrowing. b (*le fait de rétrécir*) *[tissu]* shrinking; *[vêtement]* taking in; *[conduit]* narrowing. c (*Méd*) *[rectum, aorte]* stricture.

retrempe [R(ə)tRɑ̃p] **nf** *[acier]* requenching.

retremper [R(ə)tRɑ̃pe] [1] 1 **vt** a (*Tech*) *acier* to requench. (*fig*) ~ **son courage aux dangers du front** to try *ou* test one's courage again in the dangers at the front. b (*réimprégner*) to resoak. 2 **se retremper vpr** *[baigneur]* to go back into the water. (*fig*) **se ~ dans l'ambiance familiale** to reimmerse o.s. in the family atmosphere.

rétribuer [RetRibɥe] [1] **vt** *ouvrier* to pay. ~ **le travail/les services de qn** to pay sb for his work/his services.

rétribution [RetRibysjɔ̃] **nf** (*paiement*) payment, remuneration (*NonC*); (*littér: récompense*) reward, recompense (*de* for).

retriever [RetRivœR] **nm** retriever.

rétro[1]* [RetRo] **nm** a **abrév de rétroviseur.** b (*Billard etc*) screw-back stroke.

rétro[2] [RetRo] 1 **adj inv: la mode/le style** ~ the pre-1940s fashions/style; **robe** ~ pre-1940s style dress. 2 **nm: le** ~ the pre-1940s style.

rétroactif, -ive [RetRoaktif, iv] **adj** *effet, action, mesure* retrospective; (*Jur*) retroactive. (*Admin*) **mesure/augmentation avec effet** ~ backdated measure/pay rise; **la loi est entrée en vigueur avec effet ~ à compter du 1er octobre** the law came into force, retroactive to October 1st.

rétroaction [RetRoaksjɔ̃] **nf** retrospective effect.

rétroactivement [RetRoaktivmɑ̃] **adv** (*gén*) retrospectively, in retrospect; (*Jur*) retroactively.

rétroactivité [RetRoaktivite] **nf** retroactivity; *voir* **non.**

rétrocéder [RetRosede] [6] **vt** (*Jur*) to retrocede, cede back.

rétrocession [RetRosesjɔ̃] **nf** (*Jur*) retrocession, retrocedence.

rétroflexe [RetRɔflɛks] **adj** retroflex.

rétrofusée [RetRofyze] **nf** retrorocket.

rétrogradation [RetRɔgRadasjɔ̃] **nf** (*littér: régression*) regression, retrogression; (*Admin*) *[officier]* demotion; *[fonctionnaire]* demotion, downgrading; (*Astron*) retrogradation.

rétrograde [RetRɔgRad] **adj** a (*péj: arriéré*) *esprit* reactionary; *mesures, idées, politique* retrograde, reactionary. b (*de recul*) *mouvement, sens* backward, retrograde; (*Littérat*) *vers, rimes* palindromic; (*Astron*) retrograde. (*Billard*) **effet** ~ screw-back.

rétrograder [RetRɔgRade] [1] 1 **vi** a (*Aut*) to change down. ~ **de troisième en seconde** to change down from third to second. b (*régresser*) (*dans une hiérarchie*) to regress, move down; (*contre le progrès*) to go backward, regress; (*perdre son avance*) to fall back; (*reculer*) to move back. c (*Astron*) to retrograde. 2 **vt** *officier* to demote, reduce in rank; *fonctionnaire* to demote, downgrade.

rétropédalage [RetRopedalaʒ] **nm** back-pedalling (*lit*).

rétroprojecteur [RetRopRɔʒɛktœR] **nm** overhead projector.

rétropropulsion [RetRopRɔpylsjɔ̃] **nf** reverse thrust.

rétrospectif, -ive [RetRɔspɛktif, iv] 1 **adj** *étude, peur* retrospective. 2 **rétrospective nf** (*Art: exposition*) retrospective. (*Ciné: projections*) **~ive Buster Keaton** Buster Keaton season.

rétrospectivement [RetRɔspɛktivmɑ̃] **adv** *apparaître* in retrospect, retrospectively; *avoir peur, être jaloux* in retrospect, looking back. **ces faits me sont apparus ~ sous un jour inquiétant** looking back on it *ou* in retrospect I saw the worrying side of these facts.

retroussé, e [R(ə)tRuse] (**ptp de retrousser**) **adj** *jupe* hitched up; *manche, pantalon* rolled *ou* turned up; *nez* turned-up, snub; *moustaches, lèvres* curled up.

retroussement [R(ə)tRusmɑ̃] **nm** (*action: voir* **retrousser**) hitching up; rolling up; curling; *[narines]* flaring.

retrousser [R(ə)tRuse] [1] 1 **vt** *jupe* to hitch up, tuck up; *manche, pantalon* to roll up; *lèvres* to curl up. (*lit, fig*) ~ **ses manches** to roll up one's sleeves. 2 **se retrousser vpr** *[femme]* to hitch up one's skirt(s); *[bords]* to turn outwards.

retroussis [R(ə)tRusi] **nm** (*littér: partie retroussée*) lip; *[lèvres]* curl.

retrouvailles [R(ə)tRuvɑj] **nfpl** reunion.

retrouver [R(ə)tRuve] [1] 1 **vt** a (*récupérer*) *objet personnel, enfant* to find (again); *fugitif, objet égaré par un tiers* to find. ~ **son chemin** to find one's way again; **on retrouva son cadavre sur une plage** his body was found on a beach; **on les a retrouvés vivants** they were found alive; **une chienne n'y retrouverait pas ses petits, une poule n'y retrouverait pas ses poussins** it's in absolute chaos, it's an absolute shambles *ou* an unholy mess*.

b (*se remémorer*) to think of, remember, recall. **je ne retrouve plus son nom** I can't think of *ou* remember *ou* recall his name.

c (*revoir*) *personne* to meet (up with) again; *endroit* to be back in, see again. **je l'ai retrouvé par hasard en Italie** I met up with him again by chance in Italy, I happened to come across him again in Italy; **je l'ai retrouvé grandi/vieilli** I found him taller/aged *ou* looking older; **et que je ne te retrouve pas ici!** and don't let me catch *ou* find you here again!; **je serai ravi de vous ~** I'll be delighted to see *ou* meet you again.

d (*rejoindre*) to join, meet (again), see (again). **je vous retrouve à 5 heures au Café de la Poste** I'll join *ou* meet *ou* see you at 5 o'clock at the Café de la Poste.

e (*recouvrer*) *forces, santé, calme* to regain; *joie, foi* to find again. ~ **le sommeil** to go *ou* get back to sleep (again); **elle mit longtemps à ~ la santé/le calme** she took a long time to regain her health/composure, it was a long time before her health/composure returned *ou* before she regained her health/composure; **très vite elle retrouva son sourire** she very soon found her smile again.

f (*redécouvrir*) *secret* to rediscover; *recette* to rediscover, uncover; *article en vente* to find again; *situation, poste* to find again. **je voudrais ~ des rideaux de la même couleur** I'd like to find curtains in the same colour again; ~ **du travail** to find work again; **il a bien cherché, mais une situation pareille ne se retrouve pas facilement** he looked around but it's not easy to come by *ou* find another job like that; **une telle occasion ne se retrouvera jamais** an opportunity like this will never occur again *ou* crop up again.

g (*reconnaître*) to recognize. **on retrouve chez Jacques le sourire de son père** you can see *ou* recognize his father's smile in Jacques, you can see Jacques has the same smile as his father *ou* has his father's smile; **je retrouve bien là mon fils!** that's my son all right!

h (*trouver, rencontrer*) to find, encounter. **on retrouve sans cesse les mêmes tournures dans ses romans** you find the same expressions all the time in his novels, you are constantly coming across *ou* meeting the same expressions in his novels; **ces caractéristiques se retrouvent aussi chez les cervidés** these characteristics are also found *ou* encountered in the deer family.

2 **se retrouver vpr** a (*se réunir*) to meet, meet up; (*se revoir après une absence*) to meet again. **après le travail, ils se sont tous retrouvés au café** after work they all met in the café; **ils se sont retrouvés par hasard à Paris** they met again by chance in Paris; **un club où l'on se retrouve entre sportifs** a club where one meets with other sportsmen *ou* where sportsmen get together; **comme on se retrouve!** fancy *ou* imagine meeting *ou* seeing you here!; (*fig*) **on se retrouvera!** I'll get even with you!, I'll get my own back! (*Brit*).

b (*être de nouveau*) to find o.s. back. **il se retrouva place de la Concorde** he found himself back at the Place de la Concorde; **se ~ dans la même situation** to find o.s. back in the same situation; **se ~ seul** (*sans amis etc*) to be left on one's own *ou* with no one; (*loin des autres, de la foule*) to be alone *ou* on one's own.

c (**: finir*) **il s'est retrouvé en prison/dans le fossé** he ended up in prison/in the ditch, he landed up* (*Brit*) *ou* wound up* in prison/in the ditch.

d (*voir clair, mettre de l'ordre*) **il ne se** *ou* **s'y retrouve pas dans ses calculs/la numération binaire** he can't make sense of his calculations/binary notation; **on a de la peine à s'y ~, dans ces digressions/ces raisonnements** it's hard to find one's way through *ou* to make sense of these digressions/arguments; **allez donc vous (y) ~ dans un désordre pareil!** let's see you try and straighten out this awful mess!; **je ne m'y retrouve plus** I'm completely lost.

e (**: rentrer dans ses frais*) **s'y ~** to break even; **les frais furent énormes mais il s'y est largement retrouvé** his costs were enormous but he made handsomely on the deal *ou* he did very well out of the deal; **tout ce que j'espère c'est qu'on s'y retrouve** all I hope is that we don't lose on it *ou* that we break even; **s'il te prête cet argent c'est qu'il s'y retrouve** if he lends you this money it's because there's something in it for him.

f (*trouver son chemin*) **se ~, s'y ~** to find one's way; **la ville où je suis né a changé et je ne m'y retrouve plus** the town where I was born has changed, and I can't find my way around any more.

g (*littér: faire un retour sur soi-même*) to find o.s. again.

rétrovirus [RetRoviRys] **nm** retrovirus.

rétroviseur [RetRɔvizœR] **nm** rear-view mirror, (driving) mirror. ~ **latéral** wing mirror (*Brit*), side-view mirror (*US*).

rets [Rɛ] **nmpl** (*littér: piège*) snare. **prendre** *ou* **attraper qn dans les ~** to ensnare sb; **se laisser prendre** *ou* **tomber dans les ~ de qn** to be ensnared by sb.

réuni, e [Reyni] (**ptp de réunir**) **adj** a (*pris ensemble*) **~s** (put) together, combined; **aussi fort que les Français et les Anglais ~s** as strong as the French and the English put together *ou* combined. b (*Comm: associés*) **~s** associated; **les Transporteurs R~s** Associated Carriers.

réunification [Reynifikasjɔ̃] **nf** reunification.

réunifier [Reynifje] [7] **vt** to reunify.

Réunion [Reynjɔ̃] **nf** (*Géog*) **la ~, l'île de la ~** Réunion (Island).

réunion [Reynjɔ̃] 1 **nf** a *[objets, faits]* collection, gathering; *[fonds]* raising; *[membres d'une famille, d'un club]* bringing together, reunion, reuniting; *[éléments, parties]* combination; (*Math*) *[ensembles]* union. ~ **d'une province à un état** the union of a province with a state.

b *[amis]* reuniting, reunion; *[compagnies]* merging; *[états]* union; *[fleuves]* confluence, merging; *[rues]* junction, joining; *[idées]* meeting.

c (*séance*) meeting. **notre prochaine ~ sera le 10** our next meeting will be on the 10th; **dans une ~** at *ou* in a meeting.

d (*journée sportive*) ~ **cycliste** cycle rally; ~ **hippique** gymkhana (*Brit*), horse show.

2 comp ▸réunion de famille family gathering **▸réunion sportive** sports meeting **▸réunion syndicale** union meeting.

réunionite* [reynjɔnit] **nf** mania for meetings.

réunionnais, e [reynjɔnɛ, ɛz] **1 adj** of *ou* from Réunion. **2 nm,f: R~(e)** inhabitant *ou* native of Réunion.

réunir [reyniʀ] **2 1 vt a** (*rassembler*) *objets* to gather *ou* collect (together); *faits, preuves* to put together. ~ **tout son linge en un paquet** to collect all one's washing into a bundle; ~ **des papiers par une épingle** to pin papers together, fix papers together with a pin.

b (*recueillir*) *fonds* to raise, get together; *preuves* to collect, gather (together); *pièces de collection, timbres* to collect.

c (*cumuler*) to combine. **ce livre réunit diverses tendances stylistiques** this book combines various styles, this book is a combination of different styles.

d (*assembler*) *participants* to gather, collect; (*convoquer*) *membres d'un parti* to call together, call a meeting of; (*inviter*) *amis, famille* to entertain, have round (*Brit*), have in; (*rapprocher*) *ennemis, antagonistes* to bring together, reunite; *anciens amis* to bring together again, reunite. **on avait réuni les participants dans la cour** they had gathered those taking part in the yard; **ce congrès a réuni des écrivains de toutes tendances** this congress gathered *ou* brought together writers of all types; **nous réunissons nos amis tous les mercredis** we have our friends round (*Brit*) *ou* in every Wednesday; **après une brouille de plusieurs années, ce deuil les a réunis** after a quarrel which lasted several years, this bereavement brought them together again *ou* reunited them.

e (*raccorder*) *parties, éléments* to join. **le couloir réunit les deux ailes du bâtiment** the corridor joins *ou* links the two wings of the building.

f (*relier*) to join (up *ou* together). ~ **deux fils** to tie two threads together; ~ **les bords d'une plaie/d'un accroc** to bring together the edges of a wound/tear.

g (*rattacher à*) ~ **à** *province etc* to unite to.

2 se réunir vpr a (*se rencontrer*) to meet, get together, have a get-together. **se ~ entre amis** to get together with (some) friends, have a friendly get-together; **le petit groupe se réunissait dans un bar** the little group would meet *ou* get together in a bar.

b (*s'associer*) *[compagnies]* to combine, merge; *[états]* to unite.

c (*se joindre*) *[états]* to unite; *[fleuves]* to flow into each other, merge; *[rues]* to join, converge; *[idées]* to unite, be united.

réussi, e [reysi] (**ptp de réussir**) **adj** (*couronné de succès*) *dîner, soirée, mariage* successful, a success (*attrib*); (*bien exécuté*) *mouvement* good, well executed (*frm*); *photo, roman* successful; *mélange, tournure* effective. **c'était vraiment très ~** it really was a great success *ou* very successful; (*iro*) **eh bien, c'est ~!** well that's just great!* (*iro*), very clever! (*iro*).

réussir [reysiʀ] **2 1 vi a** *[affaire, projet, entreprise]* to succeed, be a success, be successful; *[culture, plantation]* to thrive, do well; *[manœuvre, ruse]* to pay off. **pourquoi l'entreprise n'a-t-elle pas réussi?** why wasn't the venture a success?, why didn't the venture come off *ou* succeed?; **le culot réussit parfois où la prudence échoue** sometimes nerve succeeds *ou* works where caution fails; **la vigne ne réussit pas partout** vines don't thrive everywhere *ou* do not do well everywhere; **tout lui/rien ne lui réussit** everything/nothing goes *ou* comes right for him, everything/nothing works for him; **cela lui a mal réussi, cela ne lui a pas réussi** that didn't do him any good.

b *[personne]* (*dans une entreprise, la vie*) to succeed, be successful, be a success; (*à un examen*) to pass. ~ **dans la vie** to succeed *ou* get on in life; ~ **dans les affaires/dans ses études** to succeed *ou* do well in business/one's studies; **et leur expédition au Pôle, ont-ils réussi? — ils n'ont pas réussi** what about their expedition to the Pole, did they succeed? *ou* did they pull it off? — they didn't *ou* they failed; **il a réussi dans tout ce qu'il a entrepris** he has made a success of *ou* been successful *ou* succeeded in all his undertakings; **il a réussi à son examen** he passed his exam; **tous leurs enfants ont bien réussi** all their children have done well; **il réussit bien en maths/à l'école** he's a success at *ou* he does well at maths/school.

c ~ **à faire** to succeed in doing, manage to do; **il a réussi à les convaincre** he succeeded in convincing them, he managed to convince them; (*iro*) **cette maladroite a réussi à se brûler*** this clumsy girl has managed to burn herself *ou* has gone and burnt herself*.

d (*être bénéfique à*) ~ **à** to agree with; **l'air de la mer/la vie active lui réussit** sea air/an active life agrees with him; **le curry ne me réussit pas** curry doesn't agree with me.

2 vt a (*bien exécuter*) *film, entreprise, plat* to make a success of. ~ **sa carrière** to have a successful career; ~ **sa vie** to make a success of one's life; **elle a bien réussi sa sauce** her sauce was a great success; **vont-ils ~ leur coup?** will they manage to carry *ou* pull it off?; **il a réussi son coup: 10 000 F de raflés en 10 minutes!** he pulled the job off — 10,000 francs swiped in 10 minutes flat*; (*hum*) **je l'ai bien réussi, mon fils** I did a good job on my son (*hum*); **elle a réussi son effet** she achieved the effect she wanted.

b (*exécuter*) *but, essai* to bring off, pull off; *tâche* to bring off, manage successfully. **il a réussi 2 très jolies photos** he managed 2 very nice photographs, he took 2 very successful photographs.

réussite [reysit] **nf a** *[entreprise]* success, successful outcome; *[culture, soirée]* success. **ce fut une ~ complète** it was a complete *ou* an unqualified success. **b** *[personne]* success. **une ~ bien méritée** a well-deserved success. **c** (*Cartes*) patience. **faire une ~** to play patience.

réutiliser [reytilize] **1 vt** to re-use.

revaccination [ʀ(ə)vaksinasjɔ̃] **nf** revaccination.

revacciner [ʀ(ə)vaksine] **1 vt** to revaccinate.

revaloir [ʀ(ə)valwaʀ] **29 vt** to pay back. **je te revaudrai ça, je te le revaudrai** (*hostile*) I'll pay you back for this (*Brit*), I'll get even with you for this, I'll get back at you for this; (*reconnaissant*) I'll repay you some day.

revalorisation [ʀ(ə)valɔʀizasjɔ̃] **nf** (*voir* **revaloriser**) revaluation; raising; fresh promotion. **une ~ du mariage** a reassertion of the value of marriage.

revaloriser [ʀ(ə)valɔʀize] **1 vt** *monnaie* to revalue; *salaire* to raise; *méthode* to promote again; *valeur morale, institution* to reassert the value of.

revanchard, e [ʀ(ə)vɑ̃ʃaʀ, aʀd] (*péj*) **1 adj** *politique* of revenge (*esp against enemy country*); *politicien* who is an advocate of *ou* who advocates revenge; *pays* bent on revenge (*attrib*). **2 nm,f** advocate of revenge, revanchist (*frm*).

revanche [ʀ(ə)vɑ̃ʃ] **nf** (*après défaite, humiliation*) revenge; (*Jeux, Sport*) revenge match; (*Boxe*) return fight *ou* bout. **prendre sa ~ (sur qn)** to take one's revenge (on sb), get one's own back (on sb)* (*Brit*); **prendre une ~ éclatante (sur qn)** to take a spectacular revenge (on sb); (*Jeux, Sport*) **donner sa ~ à qn** to let sb have *ou* give sb his revenge; **le mépris est la ~ des faibles** contempt is the revenge of the weak; **en ~** on the other hand; *voir* **charge**.

revanchisme [ʀ(ə)vɑ̃ʃism] **nm** (*Pol*) revanchism.

revanchiste [ʀ(ə)vɑ̃ʃist] **adj, nmf** revanchist.

rêvasser [ʀɛvase] **1 vi** to daydream, let one's mind wander, muse (*littér*).

rêvasserie [ʀɛvasʀi] **nf** (*rêve*) daydreaming; (*chimère*) (idle) dream, (idle) fancy, daydreaming (*NonC*).

rêve [ʀɛv] **nm a** (*pendant le sommeil, chimère*) dream; (*éveillé*) dream, daydream. **le ~ et la réalité** dream and reality; (*Psych*) **le ~, les ~s** dreaming, dreams; (*Psych*) **le ~ éveillé** daydreaming; **j'ai fait un ~ affreux** I had a horrible dream; **faire des ~s** to dream, have dreams; **faites de beaux ~s!** sweet dreams!; **il est dans un ~** he's (day)dreaming; **sortir d'un ~** to come out of a dream; *voir* **mauvais**.

b (*loc*) **c'était un beau ~!** it was a lovely dream!; **c'est un de mes ~s de jeunesse** it's one of the things I've always dreamt of *ou* wanted; **une voiture/maison de ~** a dream car/house; **une créature/un silence de ~** a dream woman/silence; **la voiture/la femme de ses ~s** the car/woman of his dreams, his dream car/woman; **disparaître** *ou* **s'évanouir comme un ~** to vanish *ou* fade like a dream; **disparaître comme dans un ~** to be gone *ou* disappear in a trice; **voir/entendre qch en ~** to see/hear sth in a dream; **créer qch en ~** to dream sth up; **ça, c'est le ~*** that would be ideal *ou* (just) perfect; **une maison comme ça, ce n'est pas le ~*** it's not the sort of house you dream about.

rêvé, e [ʀeve] (**ptp de rêver**) **adj** ideal, perfect.

revêche [ʀəvɛʃ] **adj** surly, sour-tempered.

réveil [ʀevɛj] **nm a** *[dormeur]* waking (up) (*NonC*), wakening (*littér*); (*fig: retour à la réalité*) awakening. **au ~, je le trouvai déjà parti** when I woke up *ou* on waking I found he was already gone; **il a le ~ difficile** he finds it hard to wake up, he finds waking up difficult; **il eut un ~ brutal** he was rudely woken up *ou* awakened; **dès le ~, il chante** as soon as he's awake *ou* he wakes up he starts singing, he's singing from the moment he's awake; **ils assistaient au ~ du roi** they were present at the awakening of the king; **il a passé une nuit entrecoupée de ~s en sursaut** he spent a broken night, waking with a start every so often; (*fig*) **après tous ces châteaux en Espagne, le ~ fut pénible** after building all these castles in the air, he (*ou* I *etc*) had a rude awakening.

b (*fig: renaissance*) *[nature, sentiment, souvenir]* reawakening; *[volcan]* fresh stirrings; *[douleur]* return.

c (*Mil*) reveille. **sonner le ~** to sound the reveille; **battre le ~** *to wake soldiers up to the sound of drums;* ~ **en fanfare** reveille on the bugle; (*fig*) **mes enfants m'ont gratifié d'un ~ en fanfare ce matin!** my children treated me to a rowdy awakening this morning!

d (*réveille-matin*) alarm (clock). **mets le ~ à 8 heures** set the alarm for 8 (o'clock).

réveillé, e [reveje] (**ptp de réveiller**) **adj** (*à l'état de veille*) awake; (**: dégourdi*) bright, all there* (*attrib*). **à moitié ~** half asleep; **il était mal ~** he was still half asleep, he hadn't woken up properly.

réveille-matin [revejmatɛ̃] **nm inv** alarm clock.

réveiller [reveje] **1 1 vt a** *dormeur* to wake (up), waken, awaken (*littér*); (*ranimer*) personne évanouie to bring round, revive; (*ramener à la réalité*) rêveur to wake up, waken. réveillez-moi à 5 heures wake me (up) at 5 (o'clock); être réveillé en sursaut to be woken (up) with a start; faire un vacarme à ~ les morts to make a row that would waken the dead; (*Prov*) ne réveillez pas le chat qui dort let sleeping dogs lie (*Prov*).

b (*raviver*) appétit, courage to rouse, awaken; douleur (*physique*) to start up again; (*mentale*) to revive, reawaken; rancune, jalousie to reawaken, rouse.

c (*ranimer*) souvenir to awaken, revive, bring back; membre ankylosé to bring some sensation *ou* feeling back into. ~ les consciences to awaken *ou* stir people's consciences.

2 se réveiller vpr a [dormeur] to wake (up), awake, awaken (*littér*); [personne évanouie] to come round (*Brit*), come to, regain consciousness; (*fig*) [rêveur, paresseux] to wake up (*de* from). réveille-toi! wake up!; (*fig*) se réveillant de sa torpeur rousing himself from his lethargy; se ~ en sursaut to wake up *ou* come awake with a start.

b (*se raviver*) [appétit, courage] to be roused; [douleur] to return; [rancune, jalousie] to be reawakened *ou* roused; [souvenir] to return, come back, to reawaken (*littér*).

c (*se ranimer*) [nature] to reawaken; [volcan] to stir again. [membre ankylosé] mon pied se réveille the feeling's coming back into my foot, I'm getting some feeling back in my foot.

réveillon [ʀevɛjɔ̃] nm: ~ (de Noël/du Nouvel An) (*repas*) Christmas Eve/New Year's Eve dinner; (*fête*) Christmas Eve/New Year's (Eve) party; (*date*) Christmas Eve/New Year's Eve.

réveillonner [ʀevɛjɔne] [1] vi to celebrate Christmas *ou* New Year's Eve (*with a dinner and a party*).

réveillonneur [ʀevɛjɔnœʀ] nm party-goer, reveller (*on Christmas or New Year's Eve*). un des ~s proposa un jeu one of the people at the party suggested a game.

révélateur, -trice [ʀevelatœʀ, tʀis] 1 adj indice, symptôme revealing. ~ de revealing; film ~ d'une mode/d'une tendance film revealing a fashion/a tendency; c'est ~ d'un malaise profond it reveals a deep malaise. 2 nm (*Phot*) developer; (*littér: qui dévoile*) (*personne*) enlightener; (*événement, expérience*) revelation. ces manies sont un ~ de la personnalité these quirks are revealing of personality.

révélation [ʀevelasjɔ̃] nf a (*voir* révéler) [fait, projet, secret] revelation; disclosure; [artiste] revelation; (*Phot*) [image] developing. ce jeune auteur a été la ~ de l'année this young author was the discovery of the year. b [sensations, talent, tendances] revelation. c (*chose avouée*) disclosure, revelation. faire des ~s importantes to make important disclosures *ou* revelations. d (*illuminations, surprise, Rel*) revelation. ce fut une ~! it was (quite) a revelation!

révélé, e [ʀevele] (ptp de révéler) adj (*Rel*) dogme, religion revealed.

révéler [ʀevele] [6] 1 vt a (*divulguer*) fait, projet to reveal, make known, disclose; secret to disclose, give away, reveal; opinion to make known. ça l'avait révélée à elle-même this had opened her eyes to herself, this had given her a new awareness of *ou* insight into herself; je ne peux encore rien ~ I can't disclose *ou* reveal anything yet, I can't give anything away yet; ~ que to reveal that.

b (*témoigner de*) aptitude, caractère to reveal, display, show; sentiments to show. œuvre qui révèle une grande sensibilité work which reveals *ou* displays great sensitivity; sa physionomie révèle la bonté/une grande ambition his features show *ou* evince (*frm*) goodness/great ambition.

c (*faire connaître*) artiste [impresario] to discover; [œuvre] to bring to fame; (*Rel*) to reveal.

d (*Phot*) to develop.

2 se révéler vpr a (*apparaître*) [vérité, talent, tendance] to be revealed, reveal itself; (*Rel*) to reveal o.s. [artiste] il ne s'est révélé que vers la quarantaine he didn't show *ou* display his talent until he was nearly forty; des sensations nouvelles se révélaient à lui he was becoming aware of new feelings.

b (*s'avérer*) se ~ cruel/ambitieux to show o.s. *ou* prove to be cruel/ambitious; se ~ difficile/aisé to prove difficult/easy; son hypothèse se révéla fausse his hypothesis proved *ou* was shown to be false.

revenant, e [ʀ(ə)vənɑ̃, ɑ̃t] nm,f ghost. tiens, un ~!* hello stranger!*; *voir* histoire.

revendeur, -euse [ʀ(ə)vɑ̃dœʀ, øz] nm,f (*détaillant*) retailer, stockist, (*Brit*) dealer; (*d'occasion*) secondhand dealer. chez votre ~ habituel at your local stockist (*Brit*) *ou* dealer; ~ (de drogue) (drug-)pusher* *ou* dealer.

revendicateur, -trice [ʀ(ə)vɑ̃dikatœʀ, tʀis] adj: dans notre lettre ~trice in the letter stating our claims; déclaration ~trice declaration of claims.

revendicatif, -ive [ʀ(ə)vɑ̃dikatif, iv] adj mouvement, journée of protest. organiser une journée ~ive to organize a day of action *ou* protest (in support of one's claims).

revendication [ʀ(ə)vɑ̃dikasjɔ̃] nf a (*action*) claiming. b (*Pol, Syndicats: demande*) claim, demand. le parti de la ~ the claim-makers; journée de ~ day of action *ou* protest (in support of one's claims); lettre de ~ letter putting forward one's claims.

revendiquer [ʀ(ə)vɑ̃dike] [1] vt a (*demander, réclamer*) chose due, droits to claim, demand. les ouvriers ont décidé de ~ the workers have decided to put in *ou* to make a claim; ils passent leur temps à ~ they spend their time putting forward claims; ~ l'égalité des salaires to demand equal pay. b (*assumer*) responsabilité, paternité to claim; explosion, attentat to claim responsibility for. l'attentat n'a pas été revendiqué no one has claimed responsibility for the attack.

revendre [ʀ(ə)vɑ̃dʀ] [41] vt a (*vendre d'occasion*) to resell. ça se revend facilement that's easily resold, that's easily sold again. b (*vendre au détail*) to sell. c (*vendre davantage*) j'en ai vendu 2 en janvier et j'en ai revendu 4 en février I sold 2 in January and I sold another 4 in February; j'en ai vendu la semaine dernière mais je n'en ai pas revendu depuis I sold some last week but I've sold no more since then. d (*loc*) avoir de l'énergie/de l'intelligence à ~ to have energy/brains (enough and) to spare; si tu veux un tableau, on en a à ~ if you want a picture, we've got them by the score.

revenez-y [ʀəv(ə)nezi] nm inv *voir* goût.

revenir [ʀəv(ə)niʀ] [22] 1 vi a (*repasser, venir de nouveau*) to come back, come again. il doit ~ nous voir demain he's coming back to see us tomorrow, he's coming to see us again tomorrow; pouvez-vous ~ plus tard? can you come back later?

b (*réapparaître*) [saison, mode] to come back, return; [soleil, oiseaux] to return, reappear; [fête, date] to come (round) again; [calme, ordre] to return; [thème, idée] to recur, reappear. cette expression revient souvent dans sa conversation that expression often crops up in his conversation; Noël revient chaque année à la même date Christmas comes (round) on the same date every year; sa lettre est revenue parce qu'il avait changé d'adresse his letter was returned *ou* came back because he had left that address *ou* had changed his address.

c (*rentrer*) to come back, return. ~ quelque part/de quelque part to come back *ou* return (to) somewhere/from somewhere; ~ chez soi to come back *ou* return home; ~ dans son pays to come back *ou* return to one's country; ~ en bateau/avion to sail/fly back, come back by boat/air; ~ à la hâte to hurry back; ~ de voyage to return from a journey; en revenant de l'école coming back *ou* coming home from school, on the way back *ou* home from school; sa femme lui est revenue his wife has come back to him; je reviens dans un instant I'll be back in a minute, I'll be right back*.

d (*recommencer, reprendre*) ~ à études, sujet to go back to, return to; méthode, procédé to go back to, return to, revert to; ~ à la religion to come back to religion; ~ à ses premières amours to go back *ou* return to one's first love; ~ à de meilleurs sentiments to return to a better frame of mind; on y reviendra, à cette mode this fashion will come back; nous y reviendrons dans un instant we'll come back to that in a moment; n'y revenez plus! that's all you're getting!, don't bother coming back!; j'en reviens toujours là, il faut ... I still come back to this, we must ...; il n'y a pas à y ~ there's no going back on it; ~ en arrière (*gén*) to go back; (*dans le temps*) on ne peut pas ~ en arrière you can't turn *ou* put back the clock.

e (*réexaminer*) ~ sur affaire, problème to go back over; ne revenons pas là-dessus let's not go back over that; ~ sur le passé to go back over the past, hark back to the past.

f [souvenir, idée] ~ à la mémoire to recur, come back to mind; ~ à qn to come back to sb, recur to sb; son nom me revient maintenant his name has come back to me now; ça me revient! I've got it now!, it's coming back to me now!

g [courage, appétit, parole] ~ à qn to come back to sb, return (to sb); à la vue de sa résistance farouche, le courage me revint seeing his fierce resistance, my courage came back to me *ou* returned; à la vue de cette ratatouille, l'appétit m'est revenu my appetite returned at the sight of *ou* when I saw that ratatouille.

h (*se remettre de*) ~ de maladie to recover from, get over; syncope to come round from (*Brit*), come to after; égarement, surprise to get over; illusions to lose, shake off; erreurs, théories to leave behind, throw over, put *ou* cast aside; ils sont déjà revenus de ces théories they have already thrown over *ou* put aside these theories; elle est revenue de tout she's seen it all before.

i (*se dédire de*) ~ sur promesse to go back on; décision to go back on, reconsider.

j (*parvenir à la connaissance de*) ~ à qn, ~ aux oreilles de qn to reach sb's ears, get back to sb; (*frm, hum*) il m'est revenu que word has come back to me *ou* reached me that.

k [droit, honneur, responsabilité] ~ à qn (*être la prérogative de*) to fall to sb; (*échoir à*) to come *ou* pass to sb; (*être la part de*) to come *ou* go to sb; (*incomber à*) il lui revient de décider it is for him *ou* up to him to decide; ce titre lui revient de droit this title is his by right; cet honneur lui revient this honour is due to him *ou* is his by right; tout le mérite vous revient all the credit goes to you, the credit is all yours; les biens de son père sont revenus à l'État his father's property passed to the state; là-dessus, 100 F me reviennent 100 francs of that comes to me.

l (*équivaloir à*) ~ à to come down to, amount to, boil down to; cette hypothèse revient à une proposition très simple this hypothesis comes down *ou* amounts to a very simple proposition; ça revient à une question d'argent it all boils down to a question of money; cela revient à

dire que that amounts to saying that; **cela revient au même** it amounts *ou* comes to the same thing.

m (*coûter*) ~ **à** to amount to, come to, cost; **ça revient à 100 F** it comes to *ou* amounts to 100 francs; **ça revient cher** it's expensive, it's an expensive business; **à combien est-ce que cela va vous ~?** how much will that cost you?, how much will that set you back?*

n (*Culin*) **faire ~** to brown; **"faire ~ les oignons dans le beurre"** "brown *ou* fry the onions gently in the butter".

o (*Sport*) ~ **à la marque** *ou* **au score** to draw (even *ou* level); (*Cyclisme*) ~ **sur les échappés** to catch up with the breakaway;

p (*loc*) (*en réchapper*) **en ~** to pull through; **crois-tu qu'il en reviendra?** do you think he'll pull through?; ~ **à soi** to come round (*Brit*), come to; ~ **à la vie** to come back to life; **il revient de loin** it was a close shave *ou* a near thing for him, he had a close shave; **je n'en reviens pas!** I can't get over it!; **il a une tête qui ne me revient pas** I don't like the look of him; **elle ne me revient pas du tout cette fille** I don't like that girl at all; ~ **à la charge** to return to the attack; *voir* **tapis**.

2 **s'en revenir** *vpr*: **comme il s'en revenait (du village), il aperçut un aigle** as he was coming back (from the village), he noticed an eagle; **il s'en revenait la queue basse** he was coming away with his tail between his legs; **il s'en revint, le cœur plein d'allégresse** he came away with a joyful heart.

revente [ʀ(ə)vɑ̃t] *nf* resale.

revenu [ʀəv(ə)ny] 1 *nm* a *[particulier]* income (*NonC*) (*de* from); *[état]* revenue (*de* from); *[domaine, terre]* income (*de* from); *[investissement, capital]* yield (*de* from, on). ~ **annuel/brut/imposable/par habitant** annual/gross/assessed/per capita income; (*Fin*) **à ~ fixe** *valeurs* fixed yield; **les pays à ~ élevé** high-income countries; **avoir de gros ~s** to have a large income, have substantial means; **être sans ~s** to have no income *ou* means.

b (*Tech*) *[acier]* tempering.

2 *comp* ►**revenus de l'État** (*Écon*) public revenue ►**revenu intérieur brut** gross domestic income ►**revenu minimum d'insertion** *minimum welfare payment given to those who are not entitled to unemployment benefit,* ≃ *income support* (*Brit*), ≃ *welfare* (*US*) ►**revenu national** gross national product ►**revenu net d'impôts** disposable income ►**revenus publics** = **revenus de l'État** ►**revenu du travail** earned income.

rêver [ʀeve] 1 1 *vi* a *[dormeur]* to dream (*de, à* of, about). ~ **que** to dream that; **j'ai rêvé de toi** I dreamt about *ou* of you; **il en rêve la nuit*** he dreams about it at night; ~ **tout éveillé** to be lost in a daydream; **je ne rêve pas, c'est bien vrai?** I'm not imagining it *ou* dreaming, am I – it's really true!; **tu m'as appelé? – moi? tu rêves!** did you call me? – me? you must have been dreaming! *ou* you're imagining things!; **une révolution, maintenant? vous rêvez!** a revolution now? your imagination's running away with you!; **on croit ~!*** I can hardly believe it!, the mind boggles!*

b (*rêvasser*) to dream, muse (*littér*), daydream. **travaille au lieu de ~!** get on with your work instead of (day)dreaming!; ~ **à des jours meilleurs** to dream of better days.

c (*désirer*) ~ **de qch/de faire** to dream of sth/of doing; **elle rêve d'une chaumière en pleine forêt** she dreams of a cottage in the heart of a forest; ~ **de réussir** to long to succeed, long for success; ~ **de rencontrer l'épouse idéale** to dream of meeting *ou* long to meet the ideal wife.

2 *vt* a (*en dormant*) to dream. **j'ai rêvé la même chose qu'hier** I dreamt the same (thing) as last night.

b (*littér: imaginer*) to dream. **il rêve sa vie au lieu de la vivre** he's dreaming his life away instead of living it; (*péj*) **où as-tu été ~ ça?** where did you dream that up?; (*péj*) **je n'ai jamais dit ça, c'est toi qui l'as rêvé!** I never said that – you must have dreamt it!

c (*désirer*) to dream of. (*littér*) ~ **mariage/succès** to dream of marriage/success; (*littér*) **il se rêve conquérant** he dreams of being a conqueror; **il ne rêve que plaies et bosses** his mind is full of warlike *ou* heroic dreams, he lives in a dream world of bold and bloody deeds.

réverbération [ʀevɛʀbeʀasjɔ̃] *nf [son]* reverberation; *[chaleur, lumière]* reflection.

réverbère [ʀevɛʀbɛʀ] *nm* (*d'éclairage*) street lamp *ou* light; (*Tech*) reflector; *voir* **allumeur**.

réverbérer [ʀevɛʀbeʀe] 6 *vt son* to send back, reverberate; *chaleur, lumière* to reflect.

reverdir [ʀ(ə)vɛʀdiʀ] 2 1 *vi [plantes]* to grow green again. 2 *vt* (*Tech*) to soak.

révérence [ʀeveʀɑ̃s] *nf* a (*salut*) *[homme]* bow; *[femme]* curtsey. **faire une ~** to bow; to curtsey (*à qn* to sb); **tirer sa ~ (à qn)** (*lit*) to bow out (from sb's presence), make one's bow (and leave); (*fig*) to take one's leave (of sb). b (*littér: respect*) reverence (*envers, pour* for). ~ **parler**† with all due respect.

révérencieux, -ieuse [ʀeveʀɑ̃sjø, jøz] *adj* (*littér*) reverent. **être peu ~ envers** to show scant respect for.

révérend, e [ʀeveʀɑ̃, ɑ̃d] *adj, nm* reverend. **le R~ Père Martin** Reverend Father Martin.

révérendissime [ʀeveʀɑ̃disim] *adj* most reverend.

révérer [ʀeveʀe] 6 *vt* (*littér*) (*gén*) to revere; (*Rel*) to revere, reverence.

rêverie [ʀɛvʀi] *nf* a (*activité*) daydreaming, reverie (*littér*), musing (*littér*). b (*moment de rêverie*) daydream, reverie (*littér*). c (*péj: chimère*) ~**s** daydreams, delusions, illusions.

revérifier [ʀ(ə)veʀifje] 7 *vt* to double-check.

revernir [ʀ(ə)vɛʀniʀ] 2 *vt* to revarnish.

revers [ʀ(ə)vɛʀ] *nm* a *[papier, feuille]* back; *[étoffe]* wrong side. (*fig littér*) **le ~ de la charité** the reverse of charity; **le ~ de la vérité** the hidden truth; **prendre l'ennemi de** *ou* **à ~** to take the enemy from *ou* in the rear.

b *[pièce d'argent, médaille]* reverse, reverse side, back. **pièce frappée au ~ d'une effigie** coin struck with a portrait on the reverse; (*fig*) **c'est le ~ de la médaille** that's the other side of the coin; **toute médaille a son ~** every rose has its thorn.

c *[main]* back. **d'un ~ de main** with the back of one's hand.

d (*Tennis*) backhand. **faire un ~** to play a backhand shot; **volée de ~** backhand volley.

e (*Habillement*) *[veste, manteau]* lapel, revers; *[pantalon]* turn-up (*Brit*), cuff (*US*); *[bottes]* top; *[manche]* (turned-back) cuff. **bottes à ~** turned-down boots; **pantalons à ~** trousers with turn-ups (*Brit*) *ou* cuffs (*US*).

f (*coup du sort*) setback. ~ **(de fortune)** reverse (of fortune); ~**économiques/militaires** economic/military setbacks *ou* reverses.

reverser [ʀ(ə)vɛʀse] 1 *vt* a *liquide* (*verser davantage*) to pour out some more. **reverse-moi du vin/un verre de vin** pour me (out) some more wine/another glass of wine; (*remettre*) **reversez le vin dans la bouteille** pour the wine back into the bottle. b (*Fin*) *excédent, somme* to put back, pay back (*dans, sur* into).

réversibilité [ʀevɛʀsibilite] *nf [pension]* revertibility; *[mouvement]*, (*Chim*) reversibility.

réversible [ʀevɛʀsibl] *adj mouvement, vêtement, réaction chimique* reversible; (*Jur*) revertible (*sur* to). **l'histoire n'est pas ~** history cannot be undone *ou* altered.

réversion [ʀevɛʀsjɔ̃] *nf* (*Bio, Jur*) reversion. **pension de ~** reversion pension.

revêtement [ʀ(ə)vɛtmɑ̃] *nm* (*enduit*) coating; (*surface*) *[route]* surface; (*placage, garniture*) *[mur extérieur]* facing, cladding; *[mur intérieur]* covering. ~ **(du sol)** flooring (*NonC*), floor-covering (*NonC*); ~ **mural** wall-covering (*NonC*).

revêtir [ʀ(ə)vetiʀ] 20 1 *vt* a (*frm, hum: mettre*) *uniforme, habit* to don (*frm*), put on, array o.s. in (*frm*).

b (*prendre, avoir*) *caractère, importance* to take on, assume; *apparence, forme* to assume, appear in, take on. **une rencontre qui revêt une importance particulière** a meeting which takes on particular importance; **le langage humain revêt les formes les plus variées** human language appears in *ou* takes on the most varied forms.

c (*frm, hum: habiller*) *[vêtement]* to adorn. *[personne]* ~ **qn de** to dress *ou* array (*frm*) sb in; ~ **un prélat des vêtements sacerdotaux** to array (*frm*) *ou* clothe a prelate in his priestly robes.

d (*couvrir, déguiser*) ~ **qch de** to cloak sth in, cover sth with.

e (*frm: investir de*) ~ **qn de** *dignité, autorité* to endow *ou* invest sb with.

f (*Admin, Jur*) ~ **un document de sa signature/d'un sceau** to append one's signature/a seal to a document.

g (*Tech*) (*enduire*) to coat (*de* with); (*couvrir*) *route* to surface (*de* with); *mur, sol* to cover (*de* with). ~ **un mur de boiseries** to (wood-)panel a wall; ~ **un mur de carreaux** to tile a wall, cover a wall with tiles; ~ **de plâtre** to plaster; ~ **de crépi** to face with roughcast, roughcast; ~ **d'un enduit imperméable** to cover with a waterproof coating, give a waterproof coating to; **rue revêtue d'un pavage** street which has been paved over; **les falaises que la tempête avait revêtues de neige** the cliffs (which) the storm had covered in snow.

2 **se revêtir** *vpr* (*mettre*) **se ~ de** (*frm*) to array o.s. in (*frm*), don (*frm*), dress o.s. in; (*littér*) **vers l'automne les sommets se revêtent de neige** as autumn draws near, the mountain tops don their snowy mantle (*littér*) *ou* are bedecked (*frm*) with snow.

revêtu, e [ʀ(ə)vety] (*ptp de* **revêtir**) *adj* a (*habillé de*) ~ **de** dressed in, wearing. b (*Tech*) *route* surfaced. **chemin non ~** unsurfaced road. c (*Tech*) ~ **de** (*enduit de*) coated with.

rêveur, -euse [ʀɛvœʀ, øz] 1 *adj air, personne* dreamy. **il a l'esprit ~** he's inclined to be a dreamer; **ça vous laisse ~*** the mind boggles*, it makes you wonder. 2 *nm,f* (*lit, péj*) dreamer.

rêveusement [ʀɛvøzmɑ̃] *adv* (*distraitement*) dreamily, as (if) in a dream; (*avec perplexité*) distractedly.

revient [ʀəvjɛ̃] *voir* **prix**.

revigorer [ʀ(ə)vigɔʀe] 1 *vt [vent, air frais]* to invigorate; *[repas, boisson]* to revive, put new life into, buck up*; *[discours, promesse]* to cheer, invigorate, buck up*. **un petit vent frais qui revigore** a bracing *ou* an invigorating cool breeze.

revirement [ʀ(ə)viʀmɑ̃] *nm* (*changement d'avis, volte-face*) change of mind, reversal (of opinion); (*changement brusque*) *[tendances]* reversal (*de* of); *[goûts]* (abrupt) change (*de* in); *[opinions]* change, turnaround (*de* in), revulsion (*frm*) (*de* of). ~ **d'opinion** change *ou* U-turn *ou* turnaround in public opinion, revulsion (*frm*) of public opinion; **un ~**

soudain de la situation a sudden reversal of the situation.

réviser [ʀevize] 1 vt, **reviser** [ʀəvize] vt 1 a *procès, règlement, constitution* to review; (*fig*) *croyance, opinion* to review, reappraise. b *comptes* to audit; *liste* to revise; *texte, manuscrit* to revise, look over again; (*Typ*) *épreuves* to revise. **nouvelle édition complètement révisée** new and completely revised edition; *estimation* ~ **en hausse/en baisse** to revise up/down. c (*Scol*) *sujet* to revise. ~ **son histoire** to revise history, do one's history revision; **commencer à** ~ to start revising *ou* (one's) revision. d *moteur, installation* to overhaul, service; *montre* to service. **faire** ~ **sa voiture** to have one's car serviced.

réviseur [ʀevizœʀ] nm, **reviseur** [ʀəvizœʀ] nm reviser. ~**-comptable** independent auditor.

révision [ʀevizjɔ̃] nf, **revision** [ʀəvizjɔ̃] nf (*action, séance: voir* **réviser**) review; reappraisal; auditing (*NonC*); revision (*NonC*); overhaul (*NonC*); servicing (*NonC*). ~ **des listes électorales** revision *ou* revising of the electoral register; (*Scol*) **faire ses** ~**s** to do one's revision, revise; (*Aut*) **prochaine** ~ **après 10 000 km** next major service after 10,000 km.

révisionnisme [ʀevizjɔnism] nm revisionism.

révisionniste [ʀevizjɔnist] adj, nmf revisionist.

revisiter [ʀ(ə)vizite] 1 vt *ville, musée* to revisit, visit again; *théorie* to reexamine.

revisser [ʀ(ə)vise] 1 vt to screw back again.

revitalisation [ʀ(ə)vitalizasjɔ̃] nf revitalization, regeneration.

revitaliser [ʀ(ə)vitalize] 1 vt to revitalize. **crème revitalisante** revitalizing *ou* regenerative cream.

revivifier [ʀ(ə)vivifje] 7 vt (*littér*) *personne* to re-enliven, revitalize; *souvenir* to revive, bring alive again.

revivre [ʀ(ə)vivʀ] 46 1 vi a (*être ressuscité*) to live again. **on peut vraiment dire qu'il revit dans son fils** it's really true to say that he is living (over) again in his son.

b (*être revigoré*) to come alive again. **je me sentais** ~ I felt alive again, I felt a new man (*ou* woman); **ouf, je revis!** whew! what a relief!, whew! I can breathe again!*; **depuis que je n'ai plus ces soucis, je me sens** ~ ever since I've been without these worries I feel I've come alive again *ou* I've been given a new lease of life.

c (*se renouveler*) [*institution, coutumes, mode*] to be revived.

d **faire** ~ (*ressusciter*) to bring back to life, restore to life; (*revigorer*) to revive, put new life in *ou* into; (*remettre en honneur*) *mode, époque, usage* to revive; (*remettre en mémoire*) to bring back; **faire** ~ **un personnage/une époque dans un roman** to bring a character/an era back to life in a novel; **le grand air m'a fait** ~ the fresh air put new life in me; **ce spectacle faisait** ~ **tout un monde que j'avais cru oublié** this sight brought back a whole world I thought I had forgotten.

2 vt *passé, période* (*lit*) to relive, live (through) again; (*en imagination*) to relive, live (over) again.

révocabilité [ʀevɔkabilite] nf [*contrat*] revocability; [*fonctionnaire*] removability.

révocable [ʀevɔkabl] adj *legs, contrat* revocable; *fonctionnaire* removable, dismissible.

révocation [ʀevɔkasjɔ̃] nf (*voir* **révoquer**) removal (from office), dismissal; revocation. (*Hist*) **la** ~ **de l'Édit de Nantes** the Revocation of the Edict of Nantes.

revoici* [ʀ(ə)vwasi] prép, **revoilà*** [ʀ(ə)vwala] prép: ~ **Paul!** Paul's back (again)!, here's Paul again!; **me** ~! it's me again!, here I am again!; **nous** ~ **à la maison/en France** here we are, back home/in France (again); ~ **la mer** here's the sea again; **le** ~ **qui se plaint!** there he goes complaining again!

revoir [ʀ(ə)vwaʀ] 30 vt a (*retrouver*) *personne* to see *ou* meet again; *village, patrie* to see again. **je l'ai revu deux ou trois fois depuis** I've seen him two or three times since, we've met two or three times since; **quand le revois-tu?** when are you seeing *ou* meeting him again?, when are you meeting again?; **au** ~! goodbye!; **au** ~ **Monsieur/Madame** goodbye Mr X/Mrs X; **dire au** ~ **à qn** to say goodbye to sb; **faire au** ~ **de la main** to wave goodbye; **ce n'était heureusement qu'un au** ~ fortunately it was only a temporary farewell *ou* parting; *voir* **plaisir**.

b (*apercevoir de nouveau*) to see again.

c (*regarder de nouveau*) *photos* to see again, have another look at; *film, exposition* to see again. **je suis allé** ~ **ce film** I went to (see) that film again.

d (*être à nouveau témoin de*) *atrocités, scène* to witness *ou* see again; *conditions* to see again. **craignant de** ~ **s'installer le chômage** afraid of seeing unemployment settle in again.

e (*imaginer de nouveau*) to see again. **je la revois encore, dans sa cuisine** I can still see her there in her kitchen; **je me revoyais écolier, dans mon village natal** I saw myself as a schoolboy again back in the village where I was born.

f (*réviser*) *texte, édition* to revise; (*Scol*) *leçons* to revise, go over again. **édition revue et corrigée/augmentée** revised and updated/expanded edition; (*fig*) **l'histoire de France revue et corrigée par X** the history of France revised and updated *ou* given a new treatment by X; (*fig*) ~ **sa copie** to review one's plans, go back to the drawing board.

revoler[1] [ʀ(ə)vɔle] 1 vi [*pilote, oiseau*] to fly again.

revoler[2] [ʀ(ə)vɔle] 1 vt: ~ **qch** to steal sth again.

révoltant, e [ʀevɔltɑ̃, ɑ̃t] adj revolting, appalling.

révolte [ʀevɔlt] nf revolt, rebellion. **les paysans sont en** ~ **contre** the peasants are in revolt against *ou* up in arms against.

révolté, e [ʀevɔlte] (ptp de **révolter**) 1 adj a rebellious, in revolt (*attrib*). b (*outré*) outraged, incensed. 2 nm,f rebel.

révolter [ʀevɔlte] 1 1 vt (*indigner*) to revolt, outrage, appal. **ceci nous révolte** we are revolted *ou* outraged by this. 2 **se révolter** vpr a [*personne*] (*s'insurger*) to revolt, rebel, rise up (*contre* against); (*se cabrer*) to rebel (*contre* against). b (*s'indigner*) to be revolted *ou* repelled *ou* appalled (*contre* by), to rebel (*contre* against). **à cette vue tout mon être se révolte** my whole being revolts *ou* rebels at this sight; **l'esprit se révolte contre une telle propagande** the mind revolts at *ou* against *ou* is repelled *ou* revolted by such propaganda.

révolu, e [ʀevɔly] adj a (*littér: de jadis*) *jours, époque* past, bygone (*épith*), gone by. **des jours** ~**s** past *ou* bygone days, days gone by; **rêvant à l'époque** ~**e des diligences** dreaming of the bygone days of stagecoaches. b (*fini*) *époque, jours* past, in the past (*attrib*). **cette époque est** ~**e, nous devons penser à l'avenir** that era is in the past – we have to think of the future. c (*Admin: complété*) **âgé de 20 ans** ~**s** over 20 years of age; **avoir 20 ans** ~**s** to be over 20 years of age; **après 2 ans** ~**s** when two full years had (*ou* have) passed.

révolution [ʀevɔlysjɔ̃] nf a (*rotation*) revolution. b (*changement, révolte*) revolution. ~ **violente/pacifique/permanente** violent/peaceful/permanent revolution; **la R**~ **(française)** the French Revolution; **la** ~ **industrielle** the industrial revolution; **la** ~ **silencieuse/verte** the silent/green revolution; **la R**~ **culturelle** the Cultural Revolution; ~ **de palais** palace revolution *ou* coup; **la** ~ **technologique** the technological revolution, the revolution in technology. c **la** ~ (*parti, forces de la révolution*) the forces of revolution. d (*loc*) **être en** ~ to be in (a) turmoil; [*invention, procédé, idée*] **faire** ~ **dans** to revolutionize.

révolutionnaire [ʀevɔlysjɔnɛʀ] 1 adj (*gén*) revolutionary; (*Hist*) Revolutionary, of the French Revolution. 2 nmf (*gén*) revolutionary; (*Hist*) Revolutionary (*in the French Revolution*).

révolutionner [ʀevɔlysjɔne] 1 vt a (*transformer radicalement*) to revolutionize. b (*: *bouleverser*) *personnes* to stir up. **son arrivée a révolutionné le quartier** his arrival stirred up the whole neighbourhood *ou* caused a great stir in the neighbourhood.

revolver [ʀevɔlvɛʀ] nm (*pistolet*) (*gén*) pistol, (hand)gun; (*à barillet*) revolver. **microscope à** ~ microscope with a revolving nosepiece; **tour** ~ capstan lathe, turret lathe; **coup de** ~ pistol shot, gunshot; **tué de plusieurs coups de** ~ gunned down; *voir* **coup, poche**[1].

révoquer [ʀevɔke] 1 vt a (*destituer*) *magistrat, fonctionnaire* to remove from office, dismiss. b (*annuler*) *legs, contrat, édit* to revoke, repeal, rescind. c (*littér*) ~ **qch en doute** to call sth into question, question sth, cast doubt on sth.

revoter [ʀ(ə)vɔte] 1 vi to vote again.

revouloir* [ʀ(ə)vulwaʀ] 31 vt a (*désirer à nouveau*) *jouer etc* to want again. b **en** ~: **il en reveut** he wants some more; **qui en reveut?** (*gén*) who wants (some) more?; (*nourriture*) anyone for seconds?*

revoyure‡ [ʀ(ə)vwajyʀ] excl: **à la** ~! see you!‡, (I'll) be seeing you!‡

revue [ʀ(ə)vy] 1 nf a (*examen*) ~ **de** review of; **faire la** ~ **de** to review, go through; **une** ~ **de la presse hebdomadaire** a review of the weekly press.

b (*Mil: inspection des troupes*) inspection, review; (*parade*) march-past, review.

c (*magazine*) (*à fort tirage, illustré*) magazine; (*spécialisée*) journal; (*érudite*) review.

d (*spectacle*) (*satirique*) revue; (*de variétés*) variety show *ou* performance. ~ **à grand spectacle** revue spectacular.

e (*loc*) **passer en** ~ (*Mil*) to pass in review, review, inspect; (*fig: énumérer mentalement*) to go over in one's mind, pass in review, go through; **être de la** ~* to lose out.

2 comp ►**revue d'armement** (*Mil*) arms inspection ►**revue de détail** (*Mil*) kit inspection ►**revue de presse** review of the press *ou* papers.

révulsé, e [ʀevylse] (ptp de **se révulser**) adj *yeux* rolled upwards (*attrib*); *visage* contorted.

révulser [ʀevylse] 1 1 vt (*dégoûter*) to disgust. **ça me révulse** I find it repulsive *ou* disgusting. 2 **se révulser** vpr [*visage*] to contort; [*yeux*] to roll upwards.

révulsif, -ive [ʀevylsif, iv] (*Méd*) 1 adj revulsant. 2 nm revulsant, revulsive.

révulsion [ʀevylsjɔ̃] nf (*Méd, fig*) revulsion.

rewriter[1] [ʀiʀajte] 1 vt to edit, rewrite (*US*).

rewriter[2] [ʀiʀajtœʀ] nm editor, rewriter (*US*).

rewriting [ʀiʀajtiŋ] nm editing, rewriting (*US*).

Reykjavik [ʀekjavik] n Reykjavik.

rez-de-chaussée [ʀed(ə)ʃose] nm inv ground floor (*Brit*), first floor (*US*). **au** ~ on the ground floor; **habiter un** ~ to live in a ground-floor flat (*Brit*) *ou* in a first-floor apartment (*US*).

rez-de-jardin [ʀed(ə)ʒaʀdɛ̃] nm inv garden level. **appartement en** ~ garden flat (*Brit*) *ou* apartment (*US*).

RF (abrév de **République française**) *voir* **république**.

RFA [ɛʀɛfa] nf (abrév de **République fédérale d'Allemagne**) *voir* **république**.

RG [ɛʀʒe] nmpl (abrév de **renseignements généraux**) *voir* **renseignement**.
rhabiller [ʀabije] 1 1 vt a ~ qn (*lit*) to dress sb again, put sb's clothes back on; (*lui racheter des habits*) to fit sb out again, reclothe sb. b *édifice* to renovate. **un immeuble rhabillé façon moderne** a renovated and modernized building. 2 **se rhabiller** vpr to put one's clothes back on, dress (o.s.) again. **va te ~!‡, tu peux aller te ~!‡** you can forget it!*, you can (go and) take a running jump!‡
rhabituer [ʀabitɥe] 1 = **réhabituer**.
rhapsode [ʀapsɔd] nm rhapsode.
rhapsodie [ʀapsɔdi] nf rhapsody.
rhème [ʀɛm] nm rheme.
rhénan, e [ʀenɑ̃, an] adj (*Géog*) Rhine (*épith*), of the Rhine; (*Art*) Rhenish.
Rhénanie [ʀenani] nf Rhineland. **~-Palatinat** Rhineland-Palatinate.
rhénium [ʀenjɔm] nm rhenium.
rhéostat [ʀeɔsta] nm rheostat.
rhésus [ʀezys] nm a (*Méd*) rhesus. ~ **positif/négatif** rhesus *ou* Rh positive/negative; *voir* **facteur**. b (*Zool*) rhesus monkey.
rhéteur [ʀetœʀ] nm (*Hist*) rhetor.
rhétique [ʀetik] adj rhetic.
rhétoricien, -ienne [ʀetɔʀisjɛ̃, jɛn] nm,f (*lit, péj*) rhetorician.
rhétorique [ʀetɔʀik] 1 nf rhetoric; *voir* **figure, fleur**. 2 adj rhetorical.
rhéto-roman, e, pl **rhéto-romans** [ʀetoʀɔmɑ̃, an] 1 adj Rhaeto-Romanic. 2 nm (*Ling*) Rhaeto-Romanic.
Rhin [ʀɛ̃] nm: **le ~** the Rhine.
rhinite [ʀinit] nf rhinitis (*SPÉC*).
rhinocéros [ʀinɔseʀɔs] nm rhinoceros, rhino. ~ **d'Asie** Indian rhinoceros; ~ **d'Afrique** (African) white rhinoceros.
rhinolaryngite [ʀinolaʀɛ̃ʒit] nf sore throat, throat infection, rhinolaryngitis (*SPÉC*).
rhinologie [ʀinɔlɔʒi] nf rhinology.
rhinopharyngé, e [ʀinofaʀɛ̃ʒe] adj, **rhinopharyngien, -ienne** [ʀinofaʀɛ̃ʒjɛ̃, jɛn] adj nose and throat (*épith*), rhinopharyngeal (*SPÉC*).
rhinopharyngite [ʀinofaʀɛ̃ʒit] nf sore throat, throat infection, rhinopharyngitis (*SPÉC*).
rhinopharynx [ʀinofaʀɛ̃ks] nm nose and throat, rhinopharynx (*SPÉC*).
rhizome [ʀizom] nm rhizome.
rhodanien, -ienne [ʀɔdanjɛ̃, jɛn] adj Rhone (*épith*), of the Rhone.
Rhode Island [ʀɔdajlɑ̃d] nm Rhode Island.
Rhodes [ʀɔd] n Rhodes. **l'île de ~** the island of Rhodes; *voir* **colosse**.
Rhodésie [ʀɔdezi] nf Rhodesia.
rhodésien, -ienne [ʀɔdezjɛ̃, jɛn] 1 adj Rhodesian. 2 nm,f: **R~(ne)** Rhodesian.
rhodium [ʀɔdjɔm] nm rhodium.
rhododendron [ʀɔdɔdɛ̃dʀɔ̃] nm rhododendron.
rhombe [ʀɔ̃b] nm (†: *losange*) rhomb, rhombus.
rhombique [ʀɔ̃bik] adj rhombic.
rhomboïdal, e, mpl **-aux** [ʀɔ̃bɔidal, o] adj rhomboid.
rhomboïde [ʀɔ̃bɔid] nm rhomboid.
Rhône [ʀon] nm: **le ~** the (river) Rhone.
rhovyl [ʀɔvil] nm ® vinyl.
rhubarbe [ʀybaʀb] nf rhubarb.
rhum [ʀɔm] nm rum. ~ **blanc** white rum.
rhumatisant, e [ʀymatizɑ̃, ɑ̃t] adj, nm,f rheumatic.
rhumatismal, e, mpl **-aux** [ʀymatismal, o] adj rheumatic.
rhumatisme [ʀymatism] nm rheumatism (*NonC*). **avoir un ~ ou des ~s dans le bras** to have rheumatism in one's arm; ~ **articulaire** rheumatoid arthritis (*NonC*); ~ **déformant** polyarthritis.
rhumatologie [ʀymatɔlɔʒi] nf rheumatology.
rhumatologiste [ʀymatɔlɔʒist] nmf, **rhumatologue** [ʀymatɔlɔg] nmf rheumatologist.
rhume [ʀym] nm cold. **attraper un (gros) ~** to catch a (bad *ou* heavy) cold; ~ **de cerveau** head cold; ~ **des foins** hay fever.
rhumerie [ʀɔmʀi] nf (*distillerie*) rum distillery.
rhyolit(h)e [ʀjɔlit] nf rhyolite.
ria [ʀija] nf ria.
riant, riante [ʀ(i)jɑ̃, ʀ(i)jɑ̃t] adj *paysage* smiling; *atmosphère, perspective* cheerful, pleasant, happy; *visage* cheerful, smiling, happy.
RIB [ʀib] nm (abrév de **relevé d'identité bancaire**) *voir* **relevé**.
ribambelle [ʀibɑ̃bɛl] nf: ~ **de** *enfants* swarm *ou* herd *ou* flock of; *animaux* herd of; *noms* string of; *objets* row of; *choses à faire* stack(s) of.
ribaud [ʀibo] nm (†† *ou hum*) bawdy *ou* ribald fellow.
ribaude†† [ʀibod] nf trollop†‡, bawdy wench††.
riboflavine [ʀiboflavin] nf riboflavin.
ribonucléique [ʀibonykleik] adj: **acide ~** ribonucleic acid.
ribosome [ʀibozom] nm ribosom.
ribote [ʀibɔt] nf († *ou* *) merrymaking (*NonC*), revel, carousing† (*NonC*). **être en ~, faire ~** to make merry, carouse†.
ribouldingue*† [ʀibuldɛ̃g] nf spree, binge*. **deux jours de ~** two days on the spree *ou* the binge*; **faire la ~** to go on the spree *ou* the binge*.
ricain, e‡ [ʀikɛ̃, ɛn] (*péj*) 1 adj Yank(ee)* (*péj*). 2 nm,f: **R~(e)** Yank(ee)*.
ricanement [ʀikanmɑ̃] nm (*voir* **ricaner**) snigger, sniggering (*NonC*); giggle, giggling (*NonC*); nervous *ou* self-conscious *ou* embarrassed laugh *ou* laughter (*NonC*).
ricaner [ʀikane] 1 vi (*méchamment*) to snigger; (*bêtement*) to giggle (away); (*avec gêne*) to laugh nervously *ou* self-consciously, give a nervous *ou* an embarrassed laugh.
ricaneur, -euse [ʀikanœʀ, øz] (*voir* **ricaner**) 1 adj sniggering; giggling. 2 nm,f sniggerer; giggler.
Richard [ʀiʃaʀ] nm Richard. (*Hist*) ~ **Cœur de Lion** Richard (the) Lionheart.
richard, e* [ʀiʃaʀ, aʀd] nm,f (*péj*) moneybags* (*inv*).
riche [ʀiʃ] 1 adj a (*nanti*) *personne* rich, wealthy, well-off (*attrib*); *pays* rich. **il est ~ à millions** he is enormously wealthy; ~ **comme Crésus** as rich as Croesus, fabulously rich *ou* wealthy; **c'est un ~ parti** he (*ou* she) is an excellent match; **faire un ~ mariage** to marry into a wealthy family, marry (into) money; **vous savez, nous ne sommes pas ~s** we're by no means rich *ou* we're not very well-off, you know.

b (*luxueux*) *étoffes, bijoux* rich, costly; *coloris* rich; *mobilier* sumptuous, costly. **je vous donne ce stylo, mais ce n'est pas un ~ cadeau** I'll give you this pen but it's not much of a gift; **ça fait ~*** it looks plush(y)* *ou* expensive *ou* posh*.

c (*fertile, consistant*) *terre, aliment, mélange, sujet* rich. **le français est une langue ~** French is a rich language; **c'est une ~ idée** that's a great* *ou* grand idea; **c'est une ~ nature** he (*ou* she) is a person of immense resources *ou* qualities.

d (*abondant*) *moisson* rich; *végétation* rich, lush; *collection* large, rich; *vocabulaire* rich, wide. **il y a une documentation très ~ sur ce sujet** there is a wealth of *ou* a vast amount of information on this subject.

e ~ **en** *calories, gibier, monuments* rich in; ~ **de** *possibilités, espérances* full of; ~ **en protéines** with a high protein content, rich in protein, protein-rich (*épith*); **alimentation ~ en protéines/cellulose végétale** high protein/high-fibre diet; **je ne suis pas ~ en sucre** I'm not very well-off for sugar; **c'est une aventure ~ d'enseignements** you learn a great deal from this venture, this venture is a tremendous learning experience; **il est revenu, ~ de souvenirs** he returned with a wealth of memories.

2 nmf rich *ou* wealthy person. **les ~s** the rich, the wealthy; (*péj*) **voiture de ~(s)** fancy *ou* flashy car; (*péj*) **gosse de ~(s)*** rich kid*.
richelieu [ʀiʃəljø] nm (*chaussure*) Oxford.
richement [ʀiʃmɑ̃] adv *récompenser, vêtir* richly; *décoré, meublé* richly, sumptuously. **marier ~ sa fille** to marry one's daughter into a wealthy family, find a rich *ou* wealthy match *ou* husband for one's daughter; ~ **illustré** richly *ou* lavishly illustrated, with lavish *ou* copious illustrations.
richesse [ʀiʃɛs] nf a *[personne, pays]* wealth. **la ~ ne l'a pas changé** wealth *ou* being rich hasn't altered him; **vivre dans la ~** to be wealthy *ou* very comfortably off; **ce n'est pas la ~, mais c'est mieux que rien*** it's not exactly the lap of luxury but it's better than nothing.

b *[ameublement, décor]* sumptuousness, costliness, richness; *[étoffe, coloris]* richness.

c *[sol, texte, aliment, collection]* richness; *[végétation]* richness, lushness. **la ~ de son vocabulaire** the richness of his vocabulary, his wide *ou* rich vocabulary; **la ~ de cette documentation** the abundance *ou* fullness of the information; **la ~ en calcium de cet aliment** the high calcium content of this food; **la ~ en matières premières/en gibier de cette région** the abundance of raw materials/of game in this region; **la ~ en pétrole/en minéraux du pays** the country's abundant *ou* vast oil/mineral resources.

d (*fig: bien*) blessing. **la santé est une ~** good health is a great blessing *ou* is a boon, it's a blessing to be healthy.

e **~s** (*argent*) riches, wealth; (*ressources*) wealth; (*fig: trésors*) treasures; **entasser des ~s** to pile up riches; **la répartition des ~s d'un pays** the distribution of a country's wealth; **l'exploitation des ~s naturelles** the exploitation of natural resources; **découvrir les ~s d'un art/d'un musée** to discover the treasures of an art/a museum; **montrez-nous toutes vos ~s** show us all your precious possessions *ou* all your treasures.
richissime [ʀiʃisim] adj fabulously rich *ou* wealthy.
ricin [ʀisɛ̃] nm castor oil plant; *voir* **huile**.
ricocher [ʀikɔʃe] 1 vi *[balle de fusil]* to rebound, ricochet; *[pierre etc]* to rebound; (*sur l'eau*) to bounce. ~ **sur** to rebound *ou* ricochet off, rebound *ou* glance off, bounce on *ou* off; **faire ~ un caillou sur l'eau** to skim a pebble across the water, make a pebble bounce on the water.
ricochet [ʀikɔʃɛ] nm (*gén*) rebound; *[balle de fusil]* ricochet; *[caillou sur l'eau]* bounce. **faire ~** (*lit*) to rebound (*sur* off), bounce (*sur* on, off); (*fig*) to rebound; **il a été blessé par ~** he was wounded by a ricocheting bullet *ou* as the bullet rebounded; (*fig*) **par ~, il a perdu son emploi** as an indirect result he lost his job; **(s'amuser à) faire des ~s** to skim pebbles; **il a fait 4 ~s** he made the pebble bounce 4 times.
ric-rac‡ [ʀikʀak] adv (*de justesse*) by the skin of one's teeth; *payer* on the nail*. **quand on lui confie un travail, il le fait toujours ~** when you give him a job to do he's always spot on with it*.
rictus [ʀiktys] nm (*sourire grimaçant*) grin; *[animal, dément]* (snarling) grimace. ~ **moqueur/cruel** mocking *ou* sardonic/cruel grin.
ride [ʀid] nf *[peau, pomme]* wrinkle (*de* in); *[eau, sable]* ripple (*de* on,

in), ridge (*de* in). **les ~s de son front** the wrinkles *ou* lines on his forehead; **visage creusé de ~s** deeply lined face, wrinkled face; (*lit, fig*) **elle n'a pas pris une ~** she has not aged.

rideau, pl **~x** [ʀido] 1 nm a (*draperie*) curtain. **tirer les ~x** (*fermer*) to draw *ou* close the curtains *ou* drapes (*US*), draw the curtains to; (*ouvrir*) to draw the curtains, pull *ou* draw the curtains back; (*fig*) **tirer le ~ sur** *passé, défaut* to draw a veil over; **tomber en ~*** to break down; **je me suis retrouvé en ~ en pleine campagne*** there I was broken down* in the middle of nowhere.

b (*Théât*) curtain. **~ à 8 heures** the curtain rises at 8 o'clock, (the) curtain's at 8 (o'clock); **~!** (*cri des spectateurs*) curtain!; (** fig: assez*) that's enough!, I've had enough!; (*fig*) **le ~ est tombé sur leur révolte/l'affaire** the curtain come down on their revolt/the affair.

c *[boutique]* shutter; *[cheminée]* register, blower; *[secrétaire, classeur]* roll shutter; *[appareil-photo]* shutter.

d (*fig: écran*) **~ de** *arbres, verdure* curtain *ou* screen of; *policiers, troupes* curtain of; *pluie* curtain *ou* sheet of; **~ de fumée** smoke screen; **~ de feu** fire curtain.

2 comp ►**rideaux bonne femme** looped curtains *ou* drapes (*US*) ►**rideau de fer** *[boutique]* metal shutter(s); *[théâtre]* (metal) safety curtain, fire curtain; **le rideau de fer**† (*Pol*) the iron curtain†; **les pays au-delà du rideau de fer**† the iron curtain countries†, the countries behind the iron curtain† ►**rideaux de lit** bed hangings *ou* curtains.

ridelle [ʀidɛl] nf *[camion, charrette]* slatted side.

rider [ʀide] 1 1 vt *peau, fruit* to wrinkle; *front [colère, soucis]* to wrinkle; *[âge]* to line with wrinkles; *eau* to ripple, ruffle the surface of; *sable, neige* to ruffle *ou* wrinkle the surface of. *pomme* **toute ridée** all shrivelled up (*attrib*). 2 **se rider** vpr to become wrinkled, become lined with wrinkles; to ripple, become rippled. **à ces mots, son front se rida** his forehead wrinkled *ou* he wrinkled his forehead at these words.

ridicule [ʀidikyl] 1 adj a (*grotesque*) *personne, conduite, vêtement* ridiculous, ludicrous, absurd; *prétentions* ridiculous, laughable; *superstition* ridiculous, silly. **se rendre ~ aux yeux de tous** to make o.s. (look) ridiculous *ou* make a fool of o.s. *ou* make o.s. look a fool in everyone's eyes; **ça le rend ~** it makes him look ridiculous *ou* a fool; **ne sois pas ~** don't be ridiculous *ou* silly *ou* absurd.

b (*infime*) *prix* ridiculous, ridiculously low; *quantité* ridiculous, ridiculously small.

2 nm a (*absurdité*) ridiculousness, absurdity. **le ~ de la conversation ne lui échappait pas** he was well aware of the absurdity of the conversation; **je ne sais pas si vous saisissez tout le ~ de la situation** I don't know if you realize just how absurd *ou* ridiculous the situation is *ou* if you realize the full absurdity of the situation; **il y a quelque ~ à faire ...** it is rather ridiculous to do ...; **c'est d'un ~ achevé** it's perfectly *ou* utterly ridiculous; **se donner le ~ de ...** to be ridiculous enough to ...; *voir* **tourner**.

b **le ~** ridicule; **tomber dans le ~** *[personne]* to make o.s. ridiculous, become ridiculous; *[film]* to become ridiculous; **s'exposer au ~** to expose o.s. *ou* lay o.s. open to ridicule; **avoir le sens du ~** to have a sense of the ridiculous; **la peur du ~** (the) fear of ridicule *ou* of appearing ridiculous; **le ~ ne tue pas** ridicule has never been the unmaking of anyone, ridicule never killed anyone; **tourner qn/qch en ~** to ridicule sb/sth, make sb/sth an object of ridicule; **couvrir qn de ~** to heap ridicule on sb, make sb look ridiculous.

c (*travers*) **~s** silliness (*NonC*), ridiculous *ou* silly ways, absurdities; **les ~s humains** the absurdities of human nature; **les ~s d'une classe sociale** the ridiculous ways *ou* the (little) absurdities of a social class.

ridiculement [ʀidikylmɑ̃] adv *vêtu, bas* ridiculously; *marcher, chanter* in a ridiculous way.

ridiculiser [ʀidikylize] 1 1 vt *personne, défaut, doctrine* to ridicule, hold up to ridicule. 2 **se ridiculiser** vpr to make o.s. (look) ridiculous, make a fool of o.s.

rien [ʀjɛ̃] 1 pron indéf a (*avec ne*) nothing. **je n'ai ~ entendu** I didn't hear anything, I didn't hear a thing, I heard nothing; **~ ne le fera reculer** nothing will make him go back; **il n'y a ~ qui puisse m'empêcher de** there's nothing that could prevent me from; **il n'y a ~ que je ne fasse pour elle** there's nothing I wouldn't do for her; **on ne pouvait plus ~ pour elle** there was nothing more *ou* else to be done for her, nothing more could be done for her; **il n'y a plus ~** there's nothing left; **je ne crois plus à ~** I don't believe in anything any more; *voir* **comprendre, risquer, valoir**.

b **~ de** + adj, ptp nothing; **~ d'autre** nothing else; **~ de plus** nothing more *ou* else *ou* further; **~ de moins** nothing less; **~ de neuf** nothing new; **il n'y a ~ eu de volé** nothing was stolen, there was nothing stolen; **nous n'avons ~ d'autre** *ou* **de plus à ajouter** we have nothing else *ou* more *ou* further to add; **il n'est ~ de tel qu'une bonne pêche** there's nothing like *ou* nothing to beat a good peach, you can't beat a good peach*; **cela n'a ~ d'impossible** there's nothing impossible about it, that's perfectly possible; **~ de plus facile** nothing easier; **elle a fait ce qu'il fallait, ~ de plus, ~ de moins** she did all she had to, nothing more nor less *ou* nothing more, nothing less.

c **~ que: ~ que la chambre coûte déjà très cher** the room alone already costs a great deal; **la vérité, ~ que la vérité** the truth and nothing but the truth; **~ qu'à le voir, j'ai deviné** just looking at him I guessed, just looking at him was enough to let me guess; **je voudrais vous voir, ~ qu'une minute** could I see you just for a minute?; **il le fait ~ que pour l'embêter*** he does it just to annoy him.

d (*quelque chose*) anything. **avez-vous jamais ~ fait pour l'aider?** have you ever done anything to help him?; **as-tu jamais lu ~ de plus drôle?** have you ever read anything funnier?; **sans ~ qui le prouve** without anything to prove it; **sans que/avant que tu en saches ~** without your knowing/before you know anything about it; **avez-vous jamais ~ vu de pareil?** have you ever seen such a thing? *ou* anything like it? *ou* the like?

e (*intensif*) **~ au monde** nothing on earth *ou* in the world; **~ du tout** nothing at all; **~ de ~*** nothing, absolutely nothing; **il ne fait ~, mais ~ de ~*** he does nothing, and I mean nothing *ou* but nothing (at all); **je ne connais ~ au monde de plus bête** I can't think of anything more stupid, I know of nothing on earth more stupid; **deux** *ou* **trois fois ~** next to nothing.

f (*Sport*) nil, nothing; (*Tennis*) love. **~ à ~, ~ partout** (*Sport*) nothing all; (*Tennis*) love all; (*Tennis*) **15 à ~** 15 love.

g (*avec avoir, être, faire*) **n'avoir ~ contre qn** to have nothing against sb; **il n'a ~ d'un politicien/d'un dictateur** *etc* he's got nothing of the politician/dictator *etc* in *ou* about him; **il n'a ~ de son père** he is nothing *ou* not a bit like his father; **n'être ~** *[personne]* to be a nobody; *[chose]* to be nothing; **n'être ~ en comparaison de ...** to be nothing compared to ...; **il n'est ~ dans la maison** he's a nobody *ou* he's nothing in the firm; **n'être ~ à qn** to be nothing to do with sb; **il ne nous est ~** he's not connected with us, he's nothing to do with us; **n'être pour ~ dans une affaire** to have no hand in *ou* have nothing to do with an affair; **on le croyait blessé, mais il n'en est ~** we thought he was injured but he's not at all *ou* he's nothing of the sort; **élever 4 enfants, ça n'est pas ~** bringing up 4 children is not exactly a picnic* *ou* is no mean feat; **c'est ~ de le dire*** (and) that's putting it mildly*, (and) that's an understatement; **il ne fait (plus) ~** he doesn't work (any more); **huit jours sans ~ faire** a week doing nothing; **il ne nous a ~ fait** he hasn't done anything to us; **cela ne lui fait ~** he doesn't mind *ou* care, it doesn't make any odds* (*Brit*) *ou* it doesn't matter to him; **ça ne fait ~*** it doesn't matter, never mind; **~ à faire!** it's no good!, nothing doing!*, it's not on!* (*Brit*).

h (*loc*) **~ à déclarer/signaler** nothing to declare/report; **je vous remercie — de ~*** thank you — you're welcome *ou* don't mention it *ou* not at all; **c'est cela ou ~** it's that or nothing, take it or leave it; **(c'est) mieux que ~** it's better than nothing; **(c'est) moins que ~** it's nothing at all; **ce que tu fais ou ~!** your efforts are useless, you may as well not bother; **~ n'y fait!** nothing's any good; **c'est à moi, ~ qu'à moi** it's mine and mine alone, it's mine and mine only; (*iro*) **il voulait 500 F, ~ que ça!** he wanted a mere 500 francs (*iro*), he just *ou* only wanted 500 francs (*iro*); **une petite blessure de ~ (du tout)** a trifling *ou* trivial little injury, a mere scratch; **qu'est-ce que c'est que cette pomme/ce cadeau de ~ du tout?** what on earth can I (*ou* you *etc*) do with this stupid little apple/present?; (*péj*) **une fille de ~** a worthless girl; **cela ne nous gêne en ~ (du tout)** it doesn't bother us in any way *ou* in the least *ou* at all; **pour ~** (*peu cher*) for a song, for next to nothing; (*inutilement*) for nothing; **on n'a ~ pour ~** you get nothing for nothing, you get what you pay for; **(dans la vie) on n'a ~ sans ~** (in life,) you only get out (of it) what you put in(to it); **ce n'est pas pour ~ que ...** it is not without cause *ou* good reason that ..., it's not for nothing that ...; **~ moins que sûr** anything but sure, not at all sure; **il ne s'agit de ~ moins qu'un crime** it's nothing less than a crime; **il ne s'agit de ~ (de) moins que d'abattre 2 forêts** it will mean nothing less than chopping down 2 forests; (*Prov*) **~ ne sert de courir, il faut partir à point** *ou* **temps** slow and steady wins the race; **je n'en ai ~ à faire** *ou* **foutre**⁑ *ou* **cirer**⁑ *ou* **secouer**⁑ I don't give a damn⁑ *ou* toss⁑; *voir* **comme, compter, dire** *etc*.

2 nm a (*néant*) nothingness.

b **un ~** a mere nothing; **des ~s** trivia; **il a peur d'un ~, un ~ l'effraie** every little thing *ou* anything *ou* the slightest thing frightens him; **un ~ la fait rire** she laughs at every little thing *ou* at the slightest thing *ou* at anything at all; **un ~ l'habille** she looks good in the simplest thing; **il pleure pour un ~** he cries at the drop of a hat *ou* at the slightest little thing; **comme un ~*** no bother*, no trouble (at all); **il pourrait te casser le bras comme un ~*** he could break your arm, no probs* *ou* problem.

c **un ~ de** a touch *ou* hint of; **mettez-y un ~ de muscade** add a touch *ou* a tiny pinch of nutmeg; **un ~ de vin** a taste of wine; **un ~ de fantaisie** a touch of fantasy; **avec un ~ d'ironie** with a hint *ou* touch of irony; **en un ~ de temps** in no time (at all), in next to no time.

d **un ~** (*adv: gén **) a tiny bit, a shade, a fraction; **c'est un ~ bruyant ici** it's a bit *ou* a shade *ou* a fraction noisy in here; **moi pas, dit-elle un ~ insolente** I'm not, she said rather insolently.

e **c'est un/une ~ du tout** (*social*) he/she is a nobody; (*moral*) he/she is no good.

3 adv (⁑) (*très*) not half* (*Brit*), really. **c'est ~ impressionnant cette cérémonie** this ceremony isn't half impressive* (*Brit*) *ou* is tremendously impressive; **il fait ~ froid ici** it isn't half cold* (*Brit*) *ou* it's damned cold⁑ here; **ils sont ~ snobs** they aren't half snobs* (*Brit*),

they're really stuck-up*.

rieur, rieuse [ʀ(i)jœʀ, ʀ(i)jøz] 1 adj *personne* cheerful, merry; *yeux, expression* cheerful, laughing; *voir* **mouette**. 2 nm,f: **les ~s se turent** people stopped laughing; **avoir les ~s de son côté** to have the laughs on one's side, have people laughing with one rather than at one.

rififi [ʀififi] nm (*arg Crime*) trouble.

riflard*† [ʀiflaʀ] nm (*parapluie*) brolly* (*Brit*), umbrella.

Riga [ʀiga] n Riga.

rigaudon [ʀigodɔ̃] nm rigadoon.

rigide [ʀiʒid] adj a *armature, tige* rigid, stiff; *muscle* stiff; *carton* stiff. **livre à couverture ~** hardback (book), book with a stiff cover. b *caractère* rigid, inflexible; *règle* strict, rigid, hard and fast; *classification, éducation* strict; *morale, politique* strict, rigid.

rigidement [ʀiʒidmɑ̃] adv *élever un enfant* strictly; *appliquer un règlement* strictly, rigidly.

rigidifier [ʀiʒidifje] 7 vt (*lit*) to make rigid *ou* stiff; (*fig*) to rigidify.

rigidité [ʀiʒidite] nf (*voir* **rigide**) rigidity, rigidness; stiffness; inflexibility; strictness. **~ cadavérique** rigor mortis.

rigodon [ʀigɔdɔ̃] nm = **rigaudon**.

rigolade* [ʀigɔlad] nf a (*amusement*) **il aime la ~** he likes a bit of fun *ou* a laugh*; **on a eu une bonne partie** *ou* **séance de ~** it was *ou* we had a good laugh* *ou* a lot of fun; **quelle ~, quand il est entré!** what a laugh* *ou* a kill‡ (*Brit*) when he came in!; **il n'y a pas que la ~ dans la vie** having fun isn't the only thing in life; **il prend tout à la ~** he thinks everything's a big joke *ou* laugh*, he makes a joke of everything.

b (*loc*) **démonter ça, c'est une** *ou* **de la ~** taking that to pieces is child's play *ou* is a cinch*; **ce qu'il dit là, c'est de la ~** what he says is a lot of *ou* a load of hooey‡; **ce procès est une (vaste) ~** this trial is a (big) joke *ou* farce; **cette crème amaigrissante c'est de la ~** this slimming cream is a complete con‡.

rigolard, e* [ʀigɔlaʀ, aʀd] adj *personne, air* grinning. **c'est un ~** he's always ready for a laugh*, he likes a good laugh*.

rigole [ʀigɔl] nf (*canal*) channel; (*filet d'eau*) rivulet; (*Agr: sillon*) furrow. **la pluie avait creusé des ~s dans le sol** the rain had cut channels *ou* furrows in the earth; **~ d'irrigation** irrigation channel; **~ d'écoulement** drain.

rigoler* [ʀigɔle] 1 vi a (*rire*) to laugh. **quand il l'a su, il a bien rigolé** when he found out, he had a good laugh about it*; **il nous a bien fait ~** he had us all laughing *ou* in stitches*; (*iro*) **tu me fais ~** you make me laugh; (*iro*) **ne me fais pas ~** don't make me laugh; **il n'y a pas de quoi ~** that's nothing to laugh about, what's so funny?; **quand tu verras les dégâts, tu rigoleras moins** you'll be laughing on the other side of your face *ou* you won't be laughing when you see the damage.

b (*s'amuser*) to have (a bit of) fun, have a (bit of a) laugh*. **il aime ~** he likes a bit of fun *ou* a good laugh*; **on a bien rigolé, en vacances** we had great fun *ou* a good laugh* on holiday; **chez eux on ne doit pas ~ tous les jours!** it can't be much fun at home for them!

c (*plaisanter*) to joke. **tu rigoles!** you're kidding!* *ou* joking!; **je ne rigole pas** I'm not joking *ou* kidding*; **il ne faut pas ~ avec ces médicaments** you shouldn't mess about* *ou* fool about* with medicines like these; **il ne faut pas ~ avec ce genre de maladie** an illness like this has to be taken seriously *ou* can't be taken lightly; **j'ai dit ça pour ~** it was only a joke, I only said it in fun *ou* for a laugh*.

rigolo, -ote* [ʀigɔlo, ɔt] 1 adj *film, histoire* funny, killing*; *personne* funny, comical. **il est ~** (*plaisantin*) he's a laugh* *ou* a kill‡, he's funny; (*original*) he's comical *ou* funny, he's a comic; **ce qui lui est arrivé n'est pas ~** what's happened to him is no joke *ou* is not funny; (*iro*) **vous êtes ~, vous, mettez-vous à ma place!** funny aren't you?* *ou* you make me laugh – put yourself in my shoes!; **c'est ~, je n'avais jamais remarqué cela** that's funny *ou* odd, I had never noticed that.

2 nm,f (*amusant*) comic, wag; (*péj: fumiste*) fraud, phoney, chancer‡ (*Brit*). **c'est un sacré ~** he likes a good laugh*, he's a real comic *ou* scream*; (*péj*) **c'est un (petit) ~** he's a (little) chancer‡ (*Brit*) *ou* fraud.

3 nm (†‡: *revolver*) gun, rod (*US*).

rigorisme [ʀigɔʀism] nm rigorism, austerity, rigid moral standards.

rigoriste [ʀigɔʀist] 1 adj rigoristic, austere, rigid. 2 nmf rigorist, rigid moralist.

rigoureusement [ʀiguʀøzmɑ̃] adv a *punir, traiter* harshly; *raisonner, démontrer* rigorously; *appliquer, classifier* rigorously, strictly. b (*absolument*) *authentique, vrai* absolutely, utterly, entirely; *exact* rigorously; *interdit* strictly. **ce n'est pas ~ vrai** it's not entirely *ou* strictly true.

rigoureux, -euse [ʀiguʀø, øz] adj a (*sévère*) *punition, discipline* rigorous, harsh, severe; *mesures* rigorous, stringent, harsh; (*fig*) *climat* rigorous, harsh; *maître, moraliste* rigorous, strict, rigid. **hiver ~** hard *ou* harsh winter. b (*exact*) *raisonnement, style, méthode* rigorous; *définition, classification* rigorous, strict. c (*absolu*) *interdiction, sens d'un mot* strict. **observation ~euse du règlement** strict observation of the rule; **ce n'est pas une règle ~euse** it's not a hard-and-fast *ou* an absolute and unbreakable rule.

rigueur [ʀigœʀ] nf a (*sévérité*) *[condamnation, discipline]* harshness, severity, rigour; *[mesures]* harshness, stringency, rigour; *[climat, hiver]* rigour, harshness. **punir qn avec toute la ~ de la loi** to punish sb with the utmost rigour of the law; **faire preuve de ~ à l'égard de qn** to be strict *ou* harsh with sb, be hard on sb; **traiter qn avec la plus grande ~** to treat sb with the utmost rigour *ou* harshness *ou* severity; (*littér*) **les ~s du sort/de l'hiver** the rigours of fate/winter; *voir* **arrêt, délai**.

b (*austérité*) *[morale]* rigour, rigidness, strictness; *[personne]* sternness, strictness. **la politique de ~ du gouvernement** the government's austerity measures; **la ~ économique** economic austerity.

c (*précision*) *[raisonnement, style, pensée]* rigour; *[calcul]* precision, exactness; *[définition, classification]* strictness, rigour, rigorousness. **manquer de ~** to lack rigour.

d **tenir ~ à qn de n'être pas venu** to hold it against sb that he didn't come *ou* for not coming, refuse to forgive sb for not coming; **je ne vous en tiens pas ~** I don't hold it against you; **à la ~** at a pinch, if need be, in extreme circumstances (*frm*); **on peut à l'extrême ~ remplacer le curry par du poivre** at a pinch *ou* if the worst comes to the worst *ou* if need be you can use pepper instead of curry powder; **un délit, à la ~, mais un crime non: le mot est trop fort** a minor offence possibly *ou* perhaps, but not a crime – that's too strong a word; **il pourrait à la ~ avoir gagné la côte, mais j'en doute** there is a faint possibility that he made it *ou* he may just possibly have made it back to the shore but I doubt it; **il est de ~ d'envoyer un petit mot de remerciement** it is the done thing to send a note of thanks; **la tenue de ~ est ...** the dress to be worn is ..., the accepted dress *ou* attire (*frm*) is ...; **"tenue de soirée de ~"** "evening dress", "dress: formal".

rikiki* [ʀikiki] adj *voir* **riquiqui**.

rillettes [ʀijɛt] nfpl ≃ potted meat (*made from pork or goose*), rillettes.

rillons [ʀijɔ̃] nmpl *chopped pork cooked in fat and served cold.*

rimailler [ʀimɑje] 1 vi (*péj*) to write bits of verse, write poetry of a sort, versify.

rimailleur, -euse [ʀimɑjœʀ, øz] nm,f (*péj*) would-be poet, poet of a sort, rhymester, versifier.

rimaye [ʀimaj] nf bergschrund.

rimbaldien, -ienne [ʀɛ̃baldjɛ̃, jɛn] adj of Rimbaud.

rime [ʀim] nf rhyme. **~ masculine/féminine** masculine/feminine rhyme; **~ pauvre/riche** poor/rich rhyme; **~s croisées** *ou* **alternées** alternate rhymes; **~s plates** *ou* **suivies** rhyming couplets; **~s embrassées** abba rhyme scheme; **~s tiercées** terza rima; **~ pour l'œil/l'oreille** rhyme for the eye/ear; **faire qch sans ~ ni raison** to do sth without either rhyme or reason; **cela n'a ni ~ ni raison** there's neither rhyme nor reason to it.

rimer [ʀime] 1 1 vi a *[mot]* to rhyme (*avec* with). (*fig*) **cela ne rime à rien** it does not make sense, there's no sense *ou* point in it; **à quoi cela rime-t-il?** what's the point of it? *ou* sense in it?; **économie ne rime pas toujours avec profit** saving doesn't necessarily go together with profit, saving and profit don't necessarily go hand in hand. b *[poète]* to write verse *ou* poetry. 2 vt to put into verse. **poésie rimée** rhyming poetry *ou* verse.

rimeur, -euse [ʀimœʀ, øz] nm,f (*péj*) rhymester, would-be poet, versifier.

rimmel [ʀimɛl] nm ® mascara.

rinçage [ʀɛ̃saʒ] nm (*voir* **rincer**) (*action*) rinsing out *ou* through; rinsing; (*opération*) rinse. **cette machine à laver fait 3 ~s** this washing machine does 3 rinses.

rince- [ʀɛ̃s] préf *voir* **rincer**.

rinceau, pl **~x** [ʀɛ̃so] nm (*Archit*) foliage (*NonC*), foliation (*NonC*).

rincée [ʀɛ̃se] nf (*: *averse*) downpour; (‡: *défaite, volée*) thrashing*, licking*.

rincer [ʀɛ̃se] 3 1 vt (*laver*) to rinse out *ou* through; (*ôter le savon*) to rinse. **rince le verre** give the glass a rinse, rinse the glass out; (*fig*) **se faire ~*** (*par la pluie*) to get drenched *ou* soaked; (*au jeu*) to get cleaned out*. 2 **se rincer** vpr: **se ~ la bouche** to rinse out one's mouth; **se ~ les mains** to rinse one's hands; **se ~ l'œil‡** to get an eyeful*; **se ~ la dalle‡** to wet one's whistle*. 3 comp ►**rince-bouteilles** nm inv (*machine*) bottle-washing machine; (*brosse*) bottle-brush ►**rince-doigts** nm inv (*bol*) finger-bowl; (*en papier*) (disposable) finger wipe.

rincette* [ʀɛ̃sɛt] nf nip of brandy *etc*, little drop of wine (*ou* brandy *etc*).

rinçure [ʀɛ̃syʀ] nf (*eau de lavage*) rinsing water; (*péj: mauvais vin*) dishwater (*péj*), foul-tasting *ou* lousy* wine (*ou* beer).

ring [ʀiŋ] nm (boxing) ring. **les champions du ~** boxing champions; **monter sur le ~** (*pour un match*) to go into the ring; (*faire carrière*) to take up boxing.

ringard[1] [ʀɛ̃gaʀ] nm (*tisonnier*) poker.

ringard[2], e* [ʀɛ̃gaʀ, aʀd] 1 adj (*démodé*) corny*, rinky-dink* (*US*). **c'est ~** it's corny* *ou* old hat*. 2 nm,f fuddy-duddy*.

RIP [ʀip] (abrév de **relevé d'identité postal**) *voir* **relevé**.

ripaille*† [ʀipɑj] nf (*festin*) feast. **faire ~** to have a feast, have a good blow-out* (*Brit*).

ripailler*† [ʀipɑje] 1 vi (*festoyer*) to feast, have a good blow-out* (*Brit*).

ripailleur, -euse* [ʀipɑjœʀ, øz] 1 adj revelling. 2 nm,f reveller.

ripaton‡ [ʀipatɔ̃] nm (*pied*) foot, tootsy*.

riper [ʀipe] 1 1 vi (*déraper*) to slip. 2 vt (*aussi* **faire ~**: *déplacer*) *meuble, pierre, véhicule* to slide along.

riposte [ʀipɔst] **nf** (*réponse*) retort, riposte; (*contre-attaque*) counter-attack, reprisal; (*Escrime*) riposte. **il est prompt à la ~** he always has a ready answer *ou* a quick retort.

riposter [ʀipɔste] [1] **1** **vi** **a** (*répondre*) to answer back, riposte, retaliate. **~ à une insulte** to reply to an insult; **il riposta (à cela) par une insulte** he answered back *ou* retorted *ou* retaliated *ou* riposted with an insult, he flung back an insult; **~ à une accusation par une insulte** to counter an accusation by an insult. **b** (*contre-attaquer*) to counter-attack, retaliate. **~ à coups de grenades** to retaliate by throwing grenades; **~ à une attaque** to counter an attack (*par* by). **c** (*Escrime*) to riposte. **2** **vt**: **~ que** to retort *ou* riposte *ou* answer back that.

ripou, **pl ~s, ~x** [ʀipu] **nm** (*arg Police*) bent copper‡ (*Brit*), corrupt policeman.

riquiqui* [ʀikiki] **adj inv** *portion* tiny, mean, stingy*. **elle portait un chapeau ~** she was wearing a shabby little hat; **ça fait un peu ~** (*portion*) it looks a bit stingy*; (*manteau*) it looks pretty shabby *ou* grotty* (*Brit*).

rire [ʀiʀ] [36] **1** **vi** **a** to laugh. **~ aux éclats** *ou* **à gorge déployée** to roar with laughter, shake with laughter, laugh one's head off; **~ aux larmes** to laugh until one cries; **~ franchement** *ou* **de bon cœur** to laugh heartily; **~ bruyamment** to guffaw, roar with laughter; (*péj*) **~ comme un bossu** *ou* **comme une baleine** to laugh o.s. silly, be doubled up with laughter, split one's sides (laughing); **c'est à mourir** *ou* **crever* de ~** it's hilarious, it's awfully funny, you'd die laughing*; **la plaisanterie fit ~** the joke raised a laugh *ou* made everyone laugh; **ça ne me fait pas ~** I don't find it funny, I'm not amused, it doesn't make me laugh; **nous avons bien ri (de notre mésaventure)** we had a good laugh* (over our mishap); **ça m'a bien fait ~** that really made me laugh, that had me in fits*; **on va ~**: **il va essayer de sauter** we're in for a laugh* because he's going to try and jump; **il vaut mieux en ~ qu'en pleurer** it's better to look *ou* we (*ou* you *etc*) may as well look on the bright side of things; **il a pris les choses en riant** (*avec bonne humeur*) he saw the funny side of it; (*à la légère*) he laughed it off; **il n'y a pas de quoi ~** there's nothing to laugh about, it's no laughing matter; (*Prov*) **rira bien qui rira le dernier** he who laughs last laughs longest (*Brit*) *ou* best (*US*) (*Prov*).

b (*littér*) *[yeux]* to sparkle *ou* shine with happiness *ou* laughter; *[visage]* to shine with happiness.

c (*s'amuser*) to have fun, have a laugh*. **il ne pense qu'à ~** he only thinks of having fun; **il passe son temps à ~ avec ses camarades** he spends his time playing about (*Brit*) *ou* larking about (*Brit*) *ou* fooling around with his friends; **~ aux dépens de qn** to laugh *ou* have a laugh at sb's expense; **c'est un homme qui aime bien ~** he is a man who likes a bit of fun *ou* a good laugh*; **c'est maintenant qu'on va ~!** this is where the fun starts!; *voir* **histoire**.

d (*plaisanter*) **vous voulez ~!** you're joking!, you must be joking!; **et je ne ris pas** and I'm not joking!; **sans ~, c'est vrai?** joking apart *ou* aside, is it true?, seriously, is it true?; **il a dit cela pour ~** he was only joking, he said it in fun, he didn't mean it; **il a fait cela pour ~** he did it for a joke *ou* laugh*; **c'était une bagarre pour ~** it was only a pretend fight, it wasn't a real fight; *voir* **mot**.

e (*loc*) **~ dans sa barbe** *ou* **tout bas** to laugh to o.s., chuckle (away) to o.s.; **~ dans sa barbe** *ou* **sous cape** to laugh up one's sleeve, have a quiet laugh; **~ aux anges** *[personne]* to have a great beam *ou* a vacant grin on one's face, beam (away); *[bébé]* to smile happily in one's sleep; **~ au nez** *ou* **à la barbe de qn** to laugh in sb's face; **~ du bout des dents** *ou* **des lèvres** to force o.s. to laugh, laugh politely; **il faisait semblant de trouver ça drôle, mais en fait il riait jaune** he pretended he found it funny but in fact he had to force himself to laugh; **quand il apprendra la nouvelle il rira jaune** when he hears the news he'll laugh on the other side of his face (*Brit*) *ou* he won't find it funny; (*iro*) **vous me faites ~!, laissez-moi ~!** don't make me laugh!, you make me laugh! (*iro*); **elle l'a quitté – oh! sans ~?** she has left him – really?, you're joking? (*iro*).

2 **rire de** **vt indir** (*se moquer de*) *personne, défaut, crainte* to laugh at, scoff at. **il fait ~ de lui** people laugh at him *ou* make fun of him, he makes himself a laughing stock.

3 **se rire** **vpr**: **se ~ de** (*se jouer de*) *difficultés, épreuve* to make light of, take in one's stride; (*se moquer de*) *menaces, recommandations* to laugh off, laugh at; *personne* to laugh at, scoff at.

4 **nm** (*façon de rire*) laugh; (*éclat de rire*) laughter (*NonC*), laugh. **~s** laughter; **le ~** laughter; **un gros ~** a loud laugh, a guffaw; **un ~ homérique** a hearty *ou* booming laugh; **un petit ~ bête** a stupid giggle *ou* titter; **un ~ moqueur** a mocking *ou* scornful laugh; (*TV, Rad*) **~s préenregistrés** *ou* **en boîte*** canned laughter; **il y eut des ~s dans la salle quand ...** there was laughter in the room when ...; **elle a un ~ bête** she has a silly *ou* stupid laugh; **elle eut un petit ~ méchant** she gave a wicked little laugh, she laughed wickedly; **il eut un petit ~ de satisfaction** he gave a little chuckle of satisfaction, he chuckled with satisfaction; **les ~s l'obligèrent à se taire** the laughter forced him to stop speaking, he was laughed down; *voir* **éclater, fou, mourir** *etc*.

ris[1] [ʀi] **nm** **a** (*Culin*) **~ de veau** calf sweetbread. **b** (*Naut*) reef.

ris[2] [ʀi] **nm** (*littér: rire*) laugh, laughter (*NonC*).

risée [ʀize] **nf** **a** **s'exposer à la ~ générale** to lay o.s. open to ridicule; **être un objet de ~** to be a laughing stock, be an object of ridicule; **être la ~ de toute l'Europe** to be *ou* make o.s. the laughing stock of Europe. **b** (*Naut*) **~(s)** light breeze.

risette [ʀizɛt] **nf**: **faire (une) ~ à qn** to give sb a nice *ou* little smile; **fais ~ (au monsieur)** smile nicely (at the gentleman); (*fig*) **être obligé de faire des ~s au patron** to have to smile politely to the boss.

risible [ʀizibl] **adj** (*ridicule*) *attitude* laughable, ridiculous, silly; (*comique*) *aventure* laughable, funny.

risiblement [ʀiziblәmɑ̃] **adv** ridiculously, laughably.

risque [ʀisk] **nm** **a** (*gén, Jur: danger*) risk. **~ calculé** calculated risk; **une entreprise pleine de ~s** a high-risk business; **c'est un ~ à courir** it's a risk one has to take *ou* run, one has to take *ou* run the risk; **il y a du ~ à faire cela** there's a risk in doing that, it's taking a risk doing that, it's risky doing *ou* to do that; **le goût du ~** a taste for danger; **ce qui paie, c'est le ~** it pays off to take risks, taking risks pays off; **on n'a rien sans ~** you don't get anywhere without taking risks, nothing ventured, nothing gained (*Prov*); **prendre tous les ~s** to take any number of risks; **il y a un (un) ~ d'émeute/d'épidémie** there's a risk of an uprising/an epidemic; **à cause du ~ d'incendie** because of the fire risk *ou* the risk of fire; **cela constitue un ~ pour la santé** that is a health hazard *ou* health risk; **à ~** (*Sociol*) *population* at risk; (*Fin*) *placement* risky; **à haut ~** high-risk (*épith*); (*fig*) **ne prendre aucun ~** to play (it) safe, take no risks; *voir* **assurance**.

b (*loc*) (*hum*) **ce sont les ~s du métier** that's an occupational hazard (*hum*); **il n'y a pas de ~ qu'il refuse** there's no risk *ou* chance of his refusing, he isn't likely to refuse; **au ~ de le mécontenter/de se tuer/de sa vie** at the risk of displeasing him/of killing o.s./of his life; **c'est à tes ~s et périls** it's at your own risk, on your own head be it!

risqué, e [ʀiske] (**ptp de risquer**) **adj** (*hasardeux*) risky, dicey* (*Brit*); (*licencieux*) risqué, daring, coarse, off-color (*US*).

risquer [ʀiske] [1] **1** **vt** **a** (*mettre en danger*) *réputation, fortune, vie* to risk.

b (*s'exposer à*) *prison, renvoi, ennuis* to risk. **il risque la mort** he's risking death; **tu risques gros** you're taking a big risk, you're sticking your neck out*; **tu risques qu'on te le vole** you risk having it stolen; **qu'est-ce qu'on risque?** (*quels sont les risques?*) what do we risk?, what are the risks? *ou* dangers?; (*c'est sans danger*) what have we got to lose?, where's *ou* what's the risk?; **bien emballé, ce vase ne risque rien** packed like this the vase is *ou* will be quite safe; **ce vieux chapeau ne risque rien** this old hat doesn't matter at all, it doesn't matter what happens to this old hat.

c (*tenter*) to risk. **~ le tout pour le tout, ~ le paquet*** to risk *ou* chance the lot; **risquons le coup** let's chance it, let's take the chance; (*Prov*) **qui ne risque rien n'a rien** nothing ventured, nothing gained (*Prov*).

d (*hasarder*) *allusion, regard* to venture, hazard. **je ne risquerais pas un gros mot devant mon père** I wouldn't risk swearing *ou* take the risk of swearing in front of my father; **~ un œil derrière un mur** to venture a peep behind a wall; (*hum*) **~ un orteil dans l'eau** to venture a toe in the water.

e **~ de**: **tu risques de le perdre** (*éventualité*) you might (well) *ou* could (well) lose it; (*forte possibilité*) you could easily lose it; (*probabilité*) you're likely to lose it; **il risque de pleuvoir** it could *ou* may (well) rain, there's a chance of rain; **le feu risque de s'éteindre** the fire may (well) go out, there's a risk the fire may go out; **avec ces embouteillages, il risque d'être en retard** with these traffic jams he's likely to be late, these traffic jams could well make him late; **pourquoi ~ de tout perdre?** why should we risk losing *ou* take the risk of losing everything?; **ça ne risque pas (d'arriver)!** not a chance!, there's no chance *ou* danger of that (happening)!, that's not likely to happen!; **il ne risque pas de gagner** he hasn't got much chance of winning, there isn't much chance of him winning, he isn't likely to win.

2 **se risquer** **vpr**: **se ~ dans une grotte/sur une corniche** to venture inside a cave/onto a ledge; **se ~ dans une entreprise** to venture (up)on *ou* take a gamble on an enterprise; **se ~ dans une aventure dangereuse** to risk one's neck *ou* chance one's luck in a dangerous adventure; **se ~ à faire qch** to venture *ou* dare to do sth; **je vais me ~ à faire un soufflé** I'll have a try *ou* a go *ou* I'm going to try my hand at making a soufflé.

risque-tout [ʀiskәtu] **nmf inv** daredevil. **elle est ~, c'est une ~** she's a daredevil.

rissole [ʀisɔl] **nf** rissole.

rissoler [ʀisɔle] [1] **1** **vt** (*Culin: aussi* **faire ~**) to brown. **pommes rissolées** fried potatoes. **2** **vi** **a** (*Culin*) to brown. **b** (*hum: bronzer*) **se faire** *ou* **se laisser ~ sur la plage** to (lie and) roast (o.s.) on the beach.

ristourne [ʀistuʀn] **nf** (*sur achat*) discount; (*sur cotisation*) rebate; (*commission*) commission. **faire une ~ à qn** to give sb a discount.

ristourner [ʀistuʀne] [1] **vt** (*accorder une réduction de*) to give a discount of; (*rembourser un trop-perçu de*) to refund the difference of; (*donner une commission de*) to give a commission of. **ils m'ont ristourné 500 F** they gave me a 500 francs back.

rital‡ [ʀital] **nm** (*péj: Italien*) wop‡ (*péj*), Eyetie‡ (*péj*).

rite [ʀit] **nm** (*gén, Rel*) rite; (*fig: habitude*) ritual.

ritournelle [ʀituʀnɛl] **nf** (*Mus*) ritornello. (*fig*) **c'est toujours la même**

~ it's always the same (old) story *ou* tune *ou* theme, he (*ou* she *etc*) is always harping on about that.

ritualiser [ʀitɥalize] 1 vt to ritualize.

ritualisme [ʀitɥalism] nm ritualism.

ritualiste [ʀitɥalist] 1 adj ritualistic. 2 nmf ritualist.

rituel, -elle [ʀitɥɛl] adj, nm (*gén*) ritual.

rituellement [ʀitɥɛlmɑ̃] adv (*religieusement*) religiously, ritually; (*hum: invariablement*) invariably, unfailingly.

rivage [ʀivaʒ] nm shore.

rival, e, mpl -aux [ʀival, o] adj, nm,f rival. **sans ~** unrivalled.

rivaliser [ʀivalize] 1 vi: **~ avec** *[personne]* to rival, compete with, vie with, emulate; *[chose]* to hold its own against, compare with; **~ de générosité/de bons mots avec qn** to vie with sb *ou* try to outdo sb in generosity/wit, rival sb in generosity/wit; **ils rivalisaient de générosité** they vied with each other *ou* they tried to outdo each other in generosity; **il essaie de ~ avec moi** he's trying to emulate me *ou* to vie with me; **ses œuvres rivalisent avec les plus grands chefs-d'œuvre** his works rival the greatest masterpieces *ou* can hold their own against *ou* compare with the greatest masterpieces.

rivalité [ʀivalite] nf rivalry.

rive [ʀiv] nf a *[mer, lac]* shore; *[rivière]* bank. **la ~ gauche/droite de la Tamise** the north/south bank (of the Thames); **la R~ gauche** the Left Bank (*in Paris: a district noted for its student and intellectual life*). b (*Tech*) *[four]* lip.

rivé, e [ʀive] (ptp de **river**) adj: **~ à** *bureau, travail* tethered *ou* tied to; *chaise* glued *ou* riveted to; **les yeux ~s sur moi/la tache de sang** (with) his eyes riveted on me/the bloodstain; **rester ~ sur place** to be *ou* stand riveted *ou* rooted to the spot; **~ à la télé*** glued to the TV*.

river [ʀive] 1 vt a (*Tech*) *clou* to clinch; *plaques* to rivet together. (*fig*) **~ son clou à qn*** to shut sb up*. b (*littér: fixer*) **~ qch au mur/au sol** to nail sth to the wall/floor; **la poigne qui le rivait au sol** the tight grip which held him down on *ou* pinned him to the ground; **la haine/le sentiment qui les rivait ensemble** *ou* **l'un à l'autre** the hatred/the emotional bond which held them to each other.

riverain, e [ʀiv(ə)ʀɛ̃, ɛn] 1 adj (*d'un lac*) lakeside, waterside, riparian (SPÉC); (*d'une rivière*) riverside, waterside, riparian (SPÉC). (*d'une route*) **les propriétés ~es** the houses along the road; **les propriétés ~es de la Seine** the houses bordering on the Seine *ou* along the banks of the Seine. 2 nm,f lakeside resident; riverside resident; riparian (SPÉC). **les ~s se plaignent du bruit des voitures** the residents of *ou* in the street complain about the noise of cars; **"interdit sauf aux ~s"** "no entry except for access", "residents only".

rivet [ʀivɛ] nm rivet.

rivetage [ʀiv(ə)taʒ] nm riveting.

riveter [ʀiv(ə)te] 4 vt to rivet (together).

riveteuse [ʀiv(ə)tøz] nf, **riveuse** [ʀivøz] nf riveting machine.

rivière [ʀivjɛʀ] nf (*lit, fig*) river; (*Équitation*) water jump. **~ de diamants** diamond rivière; *voir* **petit.**

rixe [ʀiks] nf brawl, fight, scuffle.

Riyad [ʀijad] n Riyadh.

riz [ʀi] nm rice. **~ Caroline** *ou* **à grains longs** long-grain rice; **~ brun** *ou* **complet** brown rice; **~ au lait** rice pudding; (*Culin*) **~ créole** creole rice; *voir* **curry, gâteau, paille** *etc.*

rizerie [ʀizʀi] nf rice-processing factory.

riziculture [ʀizikyltyʀ] nf rice-growing.

rizière [ʀizjɛʀ] nf paddy-field, ricefield.

RMI [ɛʀɛmi] nm (abrév de **revenu minimum d'insertion**) *voir* **revenu.**

RMN [ɛʀɛmɛn] nf (abrév de **résonance magnétique nucléaire**) NMR.

RN [ɛʀɛn] 1 nf (abrév de **route nationale**) *voir* **route.** 2 nm (abrév de **revenu national**) *voir* **revenu.**

robe [ʀɔb] 1 nf a *[femme, fillette]* dress, frock. **~ courte/décolletée/d'été** short/low-necked/summer dress.
b *[magistrat, prélat]* robe; *[professeur]* gown. (*Hist Jur*) **la ~** the legal profession; *voir* **gens¹, homme, noblesse.**
c (*pelage*) *[cheval, fauve]* coat.
d (*peau*) *[oignon]* skin; *[fève]* husk.
e *[cigare]* wrapper, outer leaf.
f (*couleur*) *[vin]* colour.
2 comp ▸**robe bain de soleil** sundress ▸**robe de bal** ball gown *ou* dress, evening dress *ou* gown ▸**robe de baptême** christening robe ▸**robe de chambre** dressing gown; **pommes de terre en robe de chambre** *ou* **des champs** (*Culin*) jacket (*Brit*) *ou* baked potatoes, potatoes in their jackets ▸**robe chasuble** pinafore dress ▸**robe chaussette** = **robe tube** ▸**robe chemisier** shirtwaister (dress) (*Brit*), shirtwaist (*US*) ▸**robe de communion** *ou* **de communiant(e)** first communion dress ▸**robe de grossesse** maternity dress ▸**robe d'intérieur** housecoat ▸**robe-manteau** nf (pl **robes-manteaux**) coat-dress ▸**robe de mariée** wedding dress *ou* gown ▸**robe-sac** nf (pl **robes-sacs**) sack dress ▸**robe du soir** evening dress *ou* gown ▸**robe-tablier** nf (pl **robes-tabliers**) overall ▸**robe tube** tube ▸**robe tunique** smock.

Robert [ʀɔbɛʀ] nm Robert.

roberts‡ [ʀɔbɛʀ] nmpl (*seins*) tits‡, boobs‡.

robin†† [ʀɔbɛ̃] nm (*péj*) lawyer.

robinet [ʀɔbinɛ] nm *[évier, baignoire, tonneau]* tap (*Brit*), faucet (*US*). **~ d'eau chaude/froide** hot/cold (water) tap (*Brit*) *ou* faucet (*US*); **~ mélangeur, ~ mitigeur** mixer tap (*Brit*) *ou* faucet (*US*); **~ du gaz** gas tap; **~ d'arrêt** stopcock; *voir* **problème.**

robinetterie [ʀɔbinɛtʀi] nf (*installations*) taps (*Brit*), faucets (*US*), plumbing (*NonC*); (*usine*) tap (*Brit*) *ou* faucet (*US*) factory; (*commerce*) tap (*Brit*) *ou* faucet (*US*) trade.

robinier [ʀɔbinje] nm locust tree, false acacia.

roboratif, -ive [ʀɔbɔʀatif, iv] adj (*littér*) *climat* bracing; *activité* invigorating; *vin, liqueur* tonic, stimulating.

robot [ʀɔbo] nm (*lit, fig*) robot. **~ ménager, ~ de cuisine** food processor; **avion ~** remote-controlled aircraft; *voir* **photo, portrait.**

robotique [ʀɔbɔtik] nf robotics (*sg*).

robotisation [ʀɔbɔtizasjɔ̃] nf automation.

robotiser [ʀɔbɔtize] 1 vt to automate.

robre [ʀɔbʀ] nm (*Bridge*) rubber.

robusta [ʀɔbysta] nm (*café*) robusta.

robuste [ʀɔbyst] adj *personne* robust, sturdy; *santé* robust, sound; *plante* robust, hardy; *voiture* robust, sturdy; *moteur, machine* robust; *foi* firm, strong.

robustement [ʀɔbystəmɑ̃] adv robustly, sturdily.

robustesse [ʀɔbystɛs] nf (*voir* **robuste**) robustness; sturdiness; soundness; hardiness; firmness, strength.

roc¹ [ʀɔk] nm (*lit, fig*) rock; *voir* **bâtir, dur.**

roc² [ʀɔk] nm (*Myth*) (**oiseau**) **~** roc.

rocade [ʀɔkad] nf (*route*) bypass; (*Mil*) communications line.

rocaille [ʀɔkaj] 1 adj *objet, style* rocaille. 2 nf a (*cailloux*) loose stones; (*terrain*) rocky *ou* stony ground. b (*jardin*) rockery, rock garden. **plantes de ~** rock plants. c (*Constr*) **grotte/fontaine en ~** grotto/fountain in rockwork.

rocailleux, -euse [ʀɔkajø, øz] adj *terrain* rocky, stony; *style* rugged; *son, voix* harsh, grating.

rocambolesque [ʀɔkɑ̃bɔlɛsk] adj *aventures, péripéties* fantastic, incredible.

rochassier, -ière [ʀɔʃasje, jɛʀ] nm,f rock climber.

roche [ʀɔʃ] nf (*gén*) rock. **~s sédimentaires/volcaniques** sedimentary/volcanic rock(s); **~ lunaire** moon rock; (*Naut*) **fond de ~** rock bottom; *voir* **aiguille, coq¹, cristal** *etc.*

rocher [ʀɔʃe] nm a (*bloc*) rock; (*gros, lisse*) boulder; (*substance*) rock. **le ~ de Sisyphe** the rock of Sisyphus; **le ~ de Gibraltar** the Rock (of Gibraltar); (*Alpinisme*) **faire du ~** to go rock-climbing. b (*Anat*) petrosal bone. c (*en chocolat*) chocolate.

rochet [ʀɔʃɛ] nm a (*Rel*) ratchet. b (*Tech*) **roue à ~** ratchet wheel.

rocheux, -euse [ʀɔʃø, øz] 1 adj *récit, terrain, lit* rocky. **paroi ~euse** rock face; *voir* **montagne.** 2 **Rocheuses** nfpl: **les R~euses** the Rockies.

rock [ʀɔk] nm (*Myth*) = **roc².**

rock (and roll) [ʀɔk(ɛnʀɔl)] nm (*musique*) rock 'n' roll; (*danse*) jive. **ballet/comédie musicale ~** rock ballet/musical; **le ~ punk** punk rock.

rocker [ʀɔkœʀ] nm (*chanteur*) rock musician; (*admirateur*) rock fan.

rocking-chair, pl **rocking-chairs** [ʀɔkiŋ(t)ʃɛʀ] nm rocking chair.

rococo [ʀɔkɔko] 1 nm (*Art*) rococo. 2 adj inv (*Art*) rococo; (*péj*) old-fashioned, outdated.

rodage [ʀɔdaʒ] nm (*voir* **roder**) running in (*Brit*), breaking in (*US*); grinding. **"en ~"** "running in" (*Brit*), "breaking in" (*US*); **pendant le ~** during the running-in (*Brit*) *ou* breaking-in (*US*) period; **ce spectacle a demandé un certain ~** the show took a little while to get over its teething troubles *ou* get into its stride; (*Aut*) **~ de soupapes** valve grinding.

rodéo [ʀɔdeo] nm rodeo; (*fig*) free-for-all.

roder [ʀɔde] 1 vt *véhicule, moteur* to run in (*Brit*), break in (*US*); *soupape* to grind. (*fig*) **il faut ~ ce spectacle/ce nouveau service** we have to let this show/this new service get into its stride, we have to give this show/this new service time to get over its teething troubles; **il n'est pas encore rodé** *[personne]* he hasn't yet got the hang of things* *ou* got into the way of things, he is not yet broken in; *[organisme]* it hasn't yet got into its stride, it is not yet run in properly; **ce spectacle est maintenant bien rodé** the show is really running well *ou* smoothly now, all the initial problems in the show have been ironed out.

rôder [ʀode] 1 vi (*au hasard*) to roam *ou* wander about; (*de façon suspecte*) to loiter *ou* lurk (about *ou* around); (*être en maraude*) to prowl about, be on the prowl. **~ autour d'un magasin** to hang *ou* lurk around a shop; **~ autour d'une femme** to hang around a woman.

rôdeur, -euse [ʀodœʀ, øz] nm,f prowler.

Rodolphe [ʀɔdɔlf] nm Rudolph, Rudolf.

rodomontade [ʀɔdɔmɔ̃tad] nf (*littér*) (*vantarde*) bragging (*NonC*), boasting (*NonC*); (*menaçante*) sabre rattling (*NonC*).

Rogations [ʀɔgasjɔ̃] nfpl (*Rel*) Rogations.

rogatoire [ʀɔgatwaʀ] adj (*Jur*) rogatory; *voir* **commission.**

rogatons [ʀɔgatɔ̃] nmpl (*péj*) (*nourriture*) scraps (of food), left-overs; (*objets, vêtements*) old things (*not needed any more*).

Roger [ʀɔʒe] nm Roger.

rogne* [ʀɔɲ] nf anger. **être en ~** to be (hopping) mad* *ou* really ratty* (*Brit*), be in a paddy* (*Brit*); **se mettre en ~** to get (hopping) mad* *ou* really ratty* (*Brit*), blow one's top* (*contre* at); **mettre qn en ~** to make *ou* get sb (hopping) mad* *ou* really ratty* (*Brit*), get sb's temper up; **il était dans une telle ~ que** ... he was in such a (foul) temper *ou* such a paddy* (*Brit*) that ..., he was so mad* *ou* ratty* (*Brit*) that ...; **ses ~s duraient des jours** his tempers lasted for days.

rogner [ʀɔɲe] 1 vt a (*couper*) *ongle, page, plaque* to trim; *griffe* to clip, trim; *aile, pièce d'or* to clip. **~ les ailes à qn** to clip sb's wings. b (*réduire*) *prix* to whittle down, cut down; *salaire* to cut back *ou* down, whittle down. **~ sur** *dépense, prix* to cut down on, cut back on; *nourriture, sorties* to cut down on.

rognon [ʀɔɲɔ̃] nm (*Culin*) kidney; (*Géol*) nodule.

rognures [ʀɔɲyʀ] nfpl *[métal]* clippings, trimmings; *[papier, cuir]* clippings; *[ongles]* clippings, parings; *[viande]* scraps.

rogomme [ʀɔgɔm] nm: **voix de ~** hoarse *ou* rasping voice.

rogue [ʀɔg] adj offensive, haughty, arrogant.

roi [ʀwa] 1 nm a (*souverain, Cartes, Échecs*) king. (*Rel*) **les R~s** the Three Kings *ou* Wise Men; **le jour des R~s** (*gén*) Twelfth Night; (*Rel*) Epiphany; (*Bible*) **le livre des R~s** (the Book of) Kings; **tirer les ~s** to eat Twelfth Night cake; **le ~ n'est pas son cousin!** he's very full of himself *ou* very conceited (*péj*), he's as pleased *ou* as proud as Punch; **travailler pour le ~ de Prusse** to receive no reward for one's pains; *voir* **bleu, camelot** *etc.*

b (*fig*) **le ~ des animaux/de la forêt** the king of the beasts/of the forest; **~ du pétrole** oil king; **les ~s de la finance** the kings of finance; **un des ~s de la presse/du textile** one of the press/textile barons *ou* kings *ou* magnates *ou* tycoons; **X, le ~ des fromages** X, the leading *ou* first name in cheese(s), X, the cheese king (*hum*); **c'est le ~ de la resquille!*** he's a master *ou* an ace at getting something for nothing; **tu es vraiment le ~ (des imbéciles)!*** you really are a prize idiot!*, you really take the cake (for sheer stupidity)!*; **c'est le ~ des cons**⁂ he's the world's biggest bloody cretin⁂ (*Brit*), he's a total asshole⁂ (*US*); **c'est le ~ des salauds**‡ he's the world's biggest bastard⁂.

2 comp ► **les rois fainéants** (*Hist*) *the last Merovingian kings* ► **les Rois mages** (*Rel*) the Magi, the Three Wise Men ► **le Roi des Rois** the King of Kings ► **le Roi-Soleil** the Sun King.

roide [ʀwad], **roideur** [ʀwadœʀ], **roidir** [ʀwadiʀ] = **raide, raideur, raidir.**

roitelet [ʀwat(ə)lɛ] nm (*péj*) kinglet, petty king. **~ (huppé)** goldcrest.

Roland [ʀɔlɑ̃] nm Roland.

rôle [ʀol] nm a (*Théât, fig*) role, part. **premier ~** lead, leading *ou* major role *ou* part; **second/petit ~** supporting/minor role *ou* part; **~-titre** title role; **~ muet** non-speaking part; **~ de composition** character part *ou* role; **savoir son ~** to know one's part *ou* lines; **distribuer les ~s** to cast the parts; **je lui ai donné le ~ de Lear** I gave him the role *ou* part of Lear, I cast him as Lear; **jouer un ~** to play a part, act a role; (*fig*) **il joue toujours les seconds ~s** he always plays second fiddle; **il joue bien son ~ de jeune cadre** he acts his role of young executive *ou* plays the part of a young executive well; **renverser les ~s** to reverse the roles; *voir* **beau, jeu.**

b (*fonction, statut*) *[personne]* role, part; *[institution, système]* role, function; (*contribution*) part; (*travail, devoir*) job. **il a un ~ important dans l'organisation** he plays an important part *ou* he has an important part to play *ou* he has an important role in the organization; **quel a été son ~ dans cette affaire?** what part did he play in this business?; **ce n'est pas mon ~ de vous sermonner mais** ... it isn't my job *ou* place to lecture you but ...; **le ~ de la métaphore chez Lawrence** the role of metaphor *ou* the part played by metaphor in Lawrence; **la télévision a pour ~ de** ... the role *ou* function of television is to ... .

c (*registre*) (*Admin*) roll; (*Jur*) cause list. **~ d'équipage** muster (roll); **~ d'impôt** tax list *ou* roll; *voir* **tour²**.

rollmops [ʀɔlmɔps] nm rollmop.

ROM [ʀɔm] nf (*Ordin*) ROM.

romain, e [ʀɔmɛ̃, ɛn] 1 adj (*gén*) Roman. 2 nm,f: **R~(e)** Roman; *voir* **travail¹**. 3 **romaine** nf: **(laitue) ~e** cos (lettuce) (*Brit*), romaine (lettuce) (*US*); **(balance) ~e** steelyard.

romaïque [ʀɔmaik] adj, nm Romaic, demotic Greek.

roman¹ [ʀɔmɑ̃] 1 nm a (*livre*) novel; (*fig: récit*) story. (*genre*) **le ~** the novel; **ils ne publient que des ~s** they only publish novels *ou* fiction; **ça n'arrive que dans les ~s** it only happens in novels *ou* fiction *ou* stories; **sa vie est un vrai ~** his life is a real storybook *ou* is like something out of a storybook; **c'est tout un ~*** it's a long story, it's a real saga; *voir* **eau, nouveau.**

b (*Littérat: œuvre médiévale*) romance. **~ courtois** courtly romance; **le R~ de la Rose/de Renart** the Roman de la Rose/de Renart, the Romance of the Rose/of Renart.

2 comp ► **roman d'amour** (*lit*) love story; (*fig*) love story, (storybook) romance ► **roman d'analyse** psychological novel ► **roman d'anticipation** futuristic novel, science-fiction novel ► **roman d'aventures** adventure story ► **roman de cape et d'épée** historical romance ► **roman de chevalerie** tale of chivalry ► **roman à clefs** roman à clef ► **roman d'épouvante** horror story ► **roman d'espionnage** spy thriller *ou* story, cloak-and-dagger story ► **roman-feuilleton** nm (pl **romans-feuilletons**) serialized novel, serial ► **roman-fleuve** nm (pl **romans-fleuves**) roman fleuve, saga ► **roman historique** historical novel ► **roman de mœurs** social novel ► **roman noir** (*Hist*) Gothic novel; (*policier*) violent thriller ► **roman-photo** nm (pl **romans-photos**) photo romance, photo love story ► **roman policier** detective novel *ou* story, whodunit* ► **roman de science-fiction** science-fiction novel ► **roman (de) série noire** thriller.

roman², e [ʀɔmɑ̃, an] 1 adj (*Ling*) Romance (*épith*), Romanic; (*Archit*) Romanesque, (*en Grande-Bretagne*) Norman. 2 nm (*Ling*) **le ~ (commun)** late vulgar Latin; (*Archit*) **le ~** the Romanesque.

romance [ʀɔmɑ̃s] nf a (*chanson*) sentimental ballad, lovesong. **les ~s napolitaines** the Neapolitan lovesongs; *voir* **pousser.** b (*Littérat, Mus*) ballad, romance.

romancer [ʀɔmɑ̃se] 3 vt (*présenter sous forme de roman*) to make into a novel; (*agrémenter*) to romanticize; *voir* **biographie, histoire.**

romanche [ʀɔmɑ̃ʃ] adj, nm Ro(u)mansh.

romancier [ʀɔmɑ̃sje] nm novelist.

romancière [ʀɔmɑ̃sjɛʀ] nf (woman) novelist.

romand, e [ʀɔmɑ̃, ɑ̃d] adj of French-speaking Switzerland. **les R~s** the French-speaking Swiss; *voir* **suisse.**

romanesque [ʀɔmanɛsk] 1 adj a *histoire* fabulous, fantastic; *amours* storybook (*épith*); *aventures* storybook (*épith*), fabulous; *personne, tempérament, imagination* romantic. b (*Littérat*) *récit, traitement* novelistic. **la technique ~** the technique(s) of the novel; **œuvre ~** novels, fiction (*NonC*). 2 nm *[imagination, personne]* romantic side. **elle se réfugiait dans le ~** she took refuge in fancy.

romanichel, -elle⁂ [ʀɔmaniʃɛl] nm,f (*péj*) gipsy⁂ (*péj*).

romanisant, e [ʀɔmanizɑ̃, ɑ̃t] 1 adj (*Rel*) romanist; (*Ling*) specializing in Romance languages. 2 nm,f (*linguiste*) romanist, specialist in Romance languages.

romaniser [ʀɔmanize] 1 vt (*gén*) to romanize.

romaniste [ʀɔmanist] nmf (*Jur, Rel*) romanist; (*Ling*) romanist, specialist in Romance languages.

romano [ʀɔmano] nm (*péj*) gippo⁂ (*péj*).

romantique [ʀɔmɑ̃tik] 1 adj romantic. 2 nmf romantic(ist).

romantisme [ʀɔmɑ̃tism] nm romanticism. **le ~** the Romantic Movement.

romarin [ʀɔmaʀɛ̃] nm rosemary.

rombière‡ [ʀɔ̃bjɛʀ] nf (*péj*) old biddy‡ (*péj*).

Rome [ʀɔm] n Rome; *voir* **tout.**

Roméo [ʀɔmeo] nm Romeo.

rompre [ʀɔ̃pʀ] 41 1 vt a (*faire cesser*) *relations diplomatiques, fiançailles, pourparlers* to break off; *silence, monotonie, enchantement* to break; (*ne pas respecter*) *traité, marché* to break. **~ l'équilibre** to upset the balance; **~ le Carême** to break Lent *ou* the Lenten fast; (*littér*) **~ le charme** to break the spell.

b (*casser*) *branche* to break; *pain* to break (up). **il faut ~ le pain, non le couper** bread should be broken not cut; **il rompit le pain et distribua les morceaux** he broke (up) the bread and handed the pieces around; (*fig littér*) **tu nous romps la tête avec ta musique** you're deafening us with your music; (*fig littér*) **je vais lui ~ les côtes** I'm going to tan his hide; (*lit, fig*) **~ ses chaînes** to break one's chains; (*Naut*) **~ ses amarres** to break (loose from) its moorings; (*Mil*) **~ le front de l'ennemi** to break through the enemy front; **la mer a rompu les digues** the sea has broken (through) *ou* burst the dykes; *voir* **applaudir, glace¹**.

c (*littér*) **~ qn à un exercice** to break sb in to an exercise.

d (*loc*) **~ une lance** *ou* **des lances pour qn** to take up the cudgels for sb; **~ une lance** *ou* **des lances contre qn** to cross swords with sb; (*Mil*) **~ les rangs** to fall out, dismiss; (*Mil*) **rompez (les rangs)!** dismiss!, fall out!

2 vi a (*se séparer de*) **~ avec qn** to break with sb, break off one's relations with sb; **ils ont rompu (leurs fiançailles)** they've broken it off, they've broken off their engagement; **~ avec de vieilles habitudes/la tradition** to break with old habits/tradition; **il n'a pas le courage de ~** he hasn't got the courage to break it off.

b *[corde]* to break, snap; *[digue]* to burst, break.

c (*Boxe, Escrime*) to break. (*fig*) **~ en visière avec** to quarrel openly with; (*Mil*) **~ le combat** to withdraw from the engagement.

3 **se rompre** vpr (*se briser*) *[câble, corde, branche, chaîne]* to break, snap; *[digue]* to burst, break; *[veine]* to burst, rupture. **se ~ un vaisseau** to burst *ou* rupture a blood vessel; **il va se ~ les os** *ou* **le cou** he's going to break his neck.

rompu, e [ʀɔ̃py] (ptp de **rompre**) adj a (*fourbu*) **~ (de fatigue)** exhausted, worn-out, tired out; **~ de travail** exhausted by overwork. b (*expérimenté*) **~ aux affaires** with wide business experience; **~ aux privations/à la discipline** accustomed *ou* inured to hardship/discipline; **il est ~ à toutes les ficelles du métier/au maniement des armes** he is experienced in *ou* familiar with all the tricks of the trade/the handling of firearms; *voir* **bâton.**

romsteck [ʀɔmstɛk] nm (*viande*) rumpsteak (*NonC*); (*tranche*) piece of rumpsteak.

ronce [ʀɔ̃s] nf a (*branche*) bramble branch. (*buissons*) **~s** brambles, thorns; (*Bot*) **~ (des haies)** blackberry bush, bramble (bush); **il a déchiré son pantalon dans les ~s** he tore his trousers on *ou* in the brambles. b (*Menuiserie*) **~ de noyer** burr walnut; **~ d'acajou** figured mahogany.

ronceraie [ʀɔ̃sʀɛ] nf bramble patch, briar patch.

Roncevaux [ʀɔ̃s(ə)vo] n Roncesvalles.

ronchon [ʀɔ̃ʃɔ̃] 1 adj grumpy, grouchy*. 2 nm grumbler, grouch(er)*, grouser*.

ronchonnement [ʀɔ̃ʃɔnmɑ̃] nm grumbling, grousing*, grouching*.

ronchonner [ʀɔ̃ʃɔne] 1 vi to grumble, grouse*, grouch* (*après* at). **..., ronchonna-t-il** ..., he grumbled.

ronchonneur, -euse [ʀɔ̃ʃɔnœʀ, øz] 1 adj grumpy, grouchy*. 2 nm,f grumbler, grouser*, grouch*.

rond, e [ʀɔ̃, ʀɔ̃d] 1 adj a (*gén*) *objet, forme, visage* round; *pièce, lit* circular, round; *voir* **dos, table** *etc.*

b (*gras*) *visage, joue* round, chubby, plump; *fesse* plump, well-rounded; *mollet* (well-)rounded, well-turned; *poitrine* full, (well-) rounded; *ventre* plump, tubby. **une petite femme toute ~e** a plump little woman.

c (*net*) round. **chiffre ~** round number *ou* figure; **ça fait 50 F tout ~** it comes to exactly 50 francs, it comes to a round 50 francs; **ça coûte 29 F/31 F, disons 30 F pour faire un compte ~** it costs 29 francs/31 francs, let's round it up/down to 30 francs *ou* let's say 30 francs to make a round figure; **être ~ en affaires** to be straightforward *ou* straight* *ou* on the level* in business matters, do a straight deal*.

d (*: *soûl*) drunk, tight*. **être ~ comme une bille** *ou* **comme une queue de pelle** to be blind *ou* rolling drunk*.

2 nm a (*cercle dessiné*) circle, ring. **faire des ~s de fumée** to blow smoke rings; **faire des ~s dans l'eau** to make rings *ou* circular ripples in the water; **le verre a fait des ~s sur la table** the glass has made rings on the table.

b (*tranche*) *[carotte, saucisson]* slice, round (*Brit*); (*objet*) *[cuisinière]* ring. **~ de serviette** serviette (*Brit*) *ou* napkin ring; *voir* **baver, flan.**

c (*: *sou*) **~s** lolly‡ (*NonC*), cash* (*NonC*); **avoir des ~s** to be loaded*, be rolling in it*, have plenty of cash*; **il n'a pas le** *ou* **un ~** he hasn't got a penny (to his name) *ou* a cent *ou* a brass farthing (*Brit*); **il n'a plus le** *ou* **un ~** he hasn't got a penny left, he's (stony (*Brit*) *ou* stone (*US*) *ou* flat) broke*; **ça doit valoir des ~s!** that must cost a heck of a lot!*, that must be worth a penny or two (*Brit*) *ou* a mint!*; **pièce de 10/20 ~s** 10-centime/20-centime piece.

d (*loc*) **en ~** in a circle *ou* ring; **s'asseoir/danser en ~** to sit/dance in a circle *ou* ring; *voir* **empêcheur, tourner.**

3 adv: **avaler qch tout ~** to swallow sth whole; *voir* **tourner.**

4 **ronde** nf a (*tour de surveillance*) *[gardien, soldats]* rounds, patrol; *[policier]* beat, patrol, rounds; (*patrouille*) patrol. **faire sa ~e** to be on one's rounds *ou* on the beat *ou* on patrol; **sa ~e dura plus longtemps** he took longer doing his rounds; **il a fait 3 ~es aujourd'hui** he has been on his rounds 3 times today, he has covered his beat 3 times today; **~e de nuit** (*tour*) night rounds, night beat *ou* patrol; (*patrouille*) night patrol; **ils virent passer la ~e** they saw the soldiers pass on their rounds; *voir* **chemin.**

b (*danse*) round (dance), dance in a ring; (*danseurs*) circle, ring. **~e villageoise/enfantine** villagers'/children's dance (*in a ring*); **faites la ~e** dance round in a circle *ou* ring.

c (*Mus: note*) semibreve (*Brit*), whole note (*US*).

d (*Écriture*) roundhand.

e (*loc*) **à 10 km à la ~e** for 10 km round, within a 10-km radius; **à des kilomètres à la ~e** for miles around; **passer qch à la ~e** to pass sth round; **boire à la ~e** to pass *ou* hand the bottle (*ou* cup *etc*) round.

5 comp ►**ronde(-)bosse** nf (pl **rondes(-)bosses**) (sculpture in the) round ►**rond-de-cuir** (*péj*) nm (pl **ronds-de-cuir**) penpusher (*Brit*), pencil pusher (*US*) ►**rond de jambes** (*Danse*) rond de jambe; (*fig*) **faire des ronds de jambes** to bow and scrape (*péj*) ►**rond-point** nm (pl **ronds-points**) (*carrefour*) roundabout (*Brit*), traffic circle (*US*); (*dans nom de lieu: place*) circus (*Brit*).

rondeau, pl **~x** [ʀɔ̃do] nm (*Littérat*) rondeau; (*Mus*) rondo.

rondelet, -ette [ʀɔ̃dlɛ, ɛt] adj *femme* plumpish, nicely rounded; *enfant* chubby, plumpish; *bourse* well-lined; *salaire, somme* tidy (*épith*).

rondelle [ʀɔ̃dɛl] nf a (*Culin*) *[carotte, saucisson]* slice, round (*Brit*). **couper en ~s** to slice, cut into rounds (*Brit*) *ou* slices. b (*disque de carton, plastique etc*) disc; *[boulon]* washer; *[canette de bière]* ring; *[bâton de ski]* basket.

rondement [ʀɔ̃dmɑ̃] adv a (*efficacement*) briskly. **mener ~ une affaire** to deal briskly with a piece of business. b (*franchement*) frankly, outspokenly. **je vais parler ~** I shan't beat about the bush, I'm going to be frank *ou* to speak frankly.

rondeur [ʀɔ̃dœʀ] nf a *[bras, personne, joue]* plumpness, chubbiness; *[visage]* roundness, plumpness, chubbiness; *[poitrine]* fullness; *[mollet]* roundness. (*hum*) **les ~s d'une femme** (*formes*) a woman's curves *ou* curviness; (*embonpoint*) a woman's plumpness *ou* chubbiness. b *[terre]* roundness. c (*bonhomie*) friendly straightforwardness, easy-going directness. **avec ~** with (an) easy-going directness.

rondin [ʀɔ̃dɛ̃] nm log; *voir* **cabane.**

rondo [ʀɔ̃do] nm rondo.

rondouillard, e* [ʀɔ̃dujaʀ, aʀd] adj (*péj*) tubby, podgy (*Brit*), pudgy (*US*). **c'est un petit ~** he's a dumpy *ou* tubby *ou* podgy little chap (*Brit*) *ou* guy*.

Ronéo [ʀɔneo] nf ® mimeo, roneo ®.

ronéoter [ʀɔneɔte] 1 vt, **ronéotyper** [ʀɔneɔtipe] 1 vt to duplicate, roneo ®, mimeo.

ronflant, e [ʀɔ̃flɑ̃, ɑ̃t] adj (*péj*) *discours* high-flown, grand(-sounding); *titre* grand(-sounding); *style* bombastic.

ronflement [ʀɔ̃fləmɑ̃] nm (*voir* **ronfler**) snore, snoring (*NonC*); hum(ming) (*NonC*); roar, roaring (*NonC*); purr(ing) (*NonC*); throbbing (*NonC*).

ronfler [ʀɔ̃fle] 1 vi a *[dormeur]* to snore; *[toupie]* to hum; *[poêle, feu]* (*sourdement*) to hum; (*en rugissant*) to roar; *[moteur]* (*sourdement*) to purr, throb; (*en rugissant*) to roar. **faire ~ son moteur** to rev up one's engine; **il actionna le démarreur et le moteur ronfla** he pressed the starter and the engine throbbed *ou* roared into action. b (*: *dormir*) to snore away, be out for the count* (*Brit*).

ronfleur, -euse [ʀɔ̃flœʀ, øz] 1 nm,f snorer. 2 nm *[téléphone]* buzzer.

ronger [ʀɔ̃ʒe] 3 1 vt a *[souris]* to gnaw *ou* eat away at, gnaw *ou* eat into; *[rouille, acide, vers, pourriture]* to eat into; *[mer]* to wear away, eat into; *[eczéma]* to pit. **~ un os** *[chien]* to gnaw (at) a bone; *[personne]* to pick a bone, gnaw (at) a bone; **les chenilles rongent les feuilles** caterpillars are eating away *ou* are nibbling (at) the leaves; **rongé par les vers** worm-eaten; **rongé par la rouille** eaten into by rust, pitted with rust; *[cheval]*, (*fig*) **~ son frein** to champ at the bit; *voir* **os.**

b (*fig*) *[maladie]* to sap (the strength of); *[chagrin, pensée]* to gnaw *ou* eat away at. **le mal qui le ronge** the evil which is gnawing *ou* eating away at him; **rongé par la maladie** sapped by illness.

2 **se ronger** vpr: **se ~ les ongles** to bite one's nails; **se ~ de soucis, se ~ les sangs** to worry o.s., fret; **se ~ les sangs pour savoir comment faire qch** to agonize over how to do sth; **elle se ronge (de chagrin)** she is eating her heart out, she is tormented with grief.

rongeur, -euse [ʀɔ̃ʒœʀ, øz] adj, nm rodent.

ronron [ʀɔ̃ʀɔ̃] nm *[chat]* purr(ing) (*NonC*); *[moteur]* purr(ing) (*NonC*), hum(ming) (*NonC*); (*péj*) *[discours]* drone (*NonC*), droning (on) (*NonC*).

ronronnement [ʀɔ̃ʀɔnmɑ̃] nm (*voir* **ronronner**) purr (*NonC*), purring (*NonC*); hum (*NonC*), humming (*NonC*).

ronronner [ʀɔ̃ʀɔne] 1 vi *[chat]* to purr; *[moteur]* to purr, hum. (*fig*) **il ronronnait de satisfaction** he was purring with satisfaction.

roque [ʀɔk] nm (*Échecs*) castling. **grand/petit ~** castling queen's/king's site.

roquefort [ʀɔkfɔʀ] nm Roquefort (cheese).

roquer [ʀɔke] 1 vi (*Échecs*) to castle; (*Croquet*) to roquet.

roquet [ʀɔkɛ] nm (*péj*) (*chien*) (nasty little) lap-dog; (*personne*) ill-tempered little runt*.

roquette [ʀɔkɛt] nf (*Mil*) rocket; *voir* **lancer.**

rosace [ʀozas] nf *[cathédrale]* rose window, rosace; *[plafond]* (ceiling) rose; (*Broderie*) Tenerife motif; (*figure géométrique*) rosette.

rosacé, e [ʀozase] 1 adj (*Bot*) rosaceous. 2 **rosacée** nf a (*Méd*) rosacea. b (*Bot*) rosaceous plant. **~es** Rosaceae, rosaceous plants.

rosaire [ʀozɛʀ] nm rosary. **réciter son ~** to say *ou* recite the rosary, tell one's beads†.

Rosalie [ʀozali] nf Rosalyn, Rosalind, Rosalie.

rosat [ʀoza] adj inv *pommade, miel* rose (*épith*). **huile ~** oil of roses.

rosâtre [ʀozɑtʀ] adj pinkish.

rosbif [ʀɔsbif] nm a (*rôti*) roast beef (*NonC*); (*à rôtir*) roasting beef (*NonC*). **un ~** a joint of (roast) beef; a joint of (roasting) beef. b (‡ *péj: Anglais*) ≃ limey* (*péj*).

rose [ʀoz] 1 nf (*fleur*) rose; (*vitrail*) rose window; (*diamant*) rose diamond. (*Prov*) **pas de ~s sans épines** no rose without a thorn (*Prov*); *voir* **bois, bouton** *etc.*

2 nm (*couleur*) pink; *voir* **vieux.**

3 adj a (*gén*) pink; *joues, teint* pink; (*plein de santé*) rosy. **~ bonbon** candy-pink; **~ saumoné** *ou* **saumon** salmon pink; *voir* **crevette, flamant, tendre**[2].

b (*Pol*) red.

c (*érotique*) **messageries ~s, Minitel ~** sex chatlines (*on Minitel*).

d (*loc*) **tout n'est pas ~, ce n'est pas tout ~** it's not all roses *ou* all rosy, it's not a bed of roses; **voir la vie** *ou* **tout en ~** to see everything through rose-coloured *ou* rose-tinted glasses *ou* spectacles; **sa vie n'était pas bien ~** his life was not a bed of roses.

4 comp ►**Rose-croix** nf inv (*confrérie*) Rosicrucians ◊ nm inv (*membre*) Rosicrucian; (*grade de franc-maçonnerie*) Rose-croix ►**rose d'Inde** African marigold ►**rose de Noël** Christmas rose ►**rose pompon** button rose ►**rose des sables** gypsum flower ►**rose-thé** nf (pl **roses-thé**) tea rose ►**rose trémière** hollyhock ►**rose des vents** compass card.

rosé, e[1] [ʀoze] 1 adj *couleur* pinkish; *vin* rosé. 2 nm rosé (wine).

roseau, pl **~x** [ʀozo] nm reed.

rosée[2] [ʀoze] nf dew. **couvert** *ou* **humide de ~** *prés, herbe* dewy, covered in *ou* with dew; *sac de couchage, objet laissé dehors* wet with dew; *voir* **goutte.**

roséole [ʀozeɔl] nf (*Méd: éruption*) roseola.

roseraie [ʀozʀɛ] nf (*jardin*) rose garden; (*plantation*) rose-nursery.

rosette [ʀozɛt] nf (*nœud*) bow; (*insigne*) rosette; (*Archit, Art, Bot*) rosette. **avoir la ~** to be an officer of the Légion d'honneur; (*Culin*) **~ de Lyon** (*type of*) slicing sausage.

rosicrucien, -ienne [ʀozikʀysjɛ̃, jɛn] adj, nm,f Rosicrucian.
rosier [ʀozje] nm rosebush, rose tree. ~ **nain/grimpant** dwarf/climbing rose.
rosière [ʀozjɛʀ] nf (*Hist*) *village maiden publicly rewarded for her chastity;* (*hum*) innocent maiden.
rosiériste [ʀozjeʀist] nmf rose grower.
rosir [ʀoziʀ] 2 1 vi *[ciel, neige]* to grow *ou* turn pink; *[visage, personne]* (*de confusion*) to go pink, blush slightly; (*de santé*) to get one's colour back, get one's rosy cheeks back. 2 vt *ciel, neige* to give a pink(ish) hue *ou* tinge to.
rosse [ʀɔs] 1 nf a († *péj: cheval*) nag. b (* *péj: méchant*) (*homme*) beast*, swine‡; (*femme*) beast*, bitch‡. **ah les ~s!** the (rotten) swine!‡, the (rotten) beasts!* 2 adj (*péj*) *critique, chansonnier* beastly* (*Brit*), nasty, vicious; *caricature* nasty, vicious; *coup, action* lousy*, rotten*, beastly* (*Brit*); *maître, époux* beastly* (*Brit*), horrid; *femme, patronne* bitchy‡, beastly* (*Brit*), horrid. **tu as vraiment été ~ (envers lui)** you were really beastly* (*Brit*) *ou* horrid (to him).
rossée [ʀɔse] nf (*, †) thrashing, (good) hiding, hammering‡.
rosser [ʀɔse] 1 vt a (*frapper*) to thrash, give a (good) hiding to. **se faire ~** to get a (good) hiding *ou* a thrashing *ou* a hammering‡. b (*: *vaincre*) to thrash, lick*, hammer*.
rosserie [ʀɔsʀi] nf (*voir* **rosse**) a (*caractère*) beastliness* (*Brit*); nastiness, viciousness; lousiness*, rottenness*; horridness; bitchiness‡. b (*propos*) beastly* (*Brit*) *ou* nasty *ou* bitchy‡ remark; (*acte*) lousy* *ou* rotten* *ou* beastly* (*Brit*) trick.
rossignol [ʀɔsiɲɔl] nm a (*Orn*) nightingale. b (*: *invendu*) unsaleable article, piece of junk*. c (*clef*) picklock.
rossinante [ʀɔsinɑ̃t] nf (†, *hum*) (old) jade, old nag.
rostre [ʀɔstʀ] nm (*éperon*) rostrum. (*tribune*) **~s** rostrum.
rot [ʀo] nm belch, burp*; *[bébé]* burp. **faire** *ou* **lâcher un ~** to belch, burp*, let out a belch *ou* burp*; **le bébé a fait son ~** the baby has done his (little) burp *ou* has got his wind up (*Brit*).
rôt†† [ʀo] nm roast.
rotarien [ʀɔtaʀjɛ̃] nm Rotarian.
rotatif, -ive [ʀɔtatif, iv] 1 adj rotary. 2 **rotative** nf rotary press.
rotation [ʀɔtasjɔ̃] nf a (*mouvement*) rotation. **mouvement de ~** rotating movement, rotary movement *ou* motion; **corps en ~** rotating body, body in rotation; **vitesse de ~** speed of rotation. b (*alternance*) *[matériel, stock]* turnover; *[avions, bateaux]* frequency (of service). *[avions, bateaux]* **effectuer plusieurs ~s** to make several trips; **la ~ du personnel** (*à des tâches successives*) the rotation of staff; (*départs et embauche*) the turnover of staff; **médecin qui est de garde par ~ tous les mois** doctor who is on duty each month on a rota basis *ou* system; **~ des cultures** rotation of crops.
rotatoire [ʀɔtatwaʀ] adj rotatory, rotary.
roter* [ʀɔte] 1 vi to burp*, belch.
rôti [ʀoti] nm (*Culin*) (*au magasin*) joint, roasting meat (*NonC*); (*au four, sur la table*) joint, roast, roast meat (*NonC*). **~ de bœuf/porc** joint of beef/pork, roasting beef/pork (*NonC*); joint of beef/pork, roast beef/pork (*NonC*).
rôtie [ʀoti] nf (†, *dial*) piece *ou* slice of toast.
rotin [ʀɔtɛ̃] nm a (*fibre*) rattan (cane). **fauteuil de ~** cane (arm)chair. b (†, *: *sou*) penny, cent. **il n'a pas un ~** he hasn't got a penny *ou* cent to his name.
rôtir [ʀotiʀ] 2 1 vt (*Culin: aussi* **faire ~**) to roast. **poulet/agneau rôti** roast chicken/lamb. 2 vi (*Culin*) to roast; *[estivants, baigneur]* to roast, be roasting hot. **on rôtit ici!** it's roasting *ou* scorching (hot) *ou* sweltering here!, we're roasting (hot) *ou* sweltering here! 3 **se rôtir** vpr: **se ~ au soleil** to bask in the sun.
rôtisserie [ʀotisʀi] nf (*dans noms de restaurant*) rotisserie, steakhouse, grill and griddle; (*boutique*) shop selling roast meat.
rôtisseur, -euse [ʀotisœʀ, øz] nm,f (*traiteur*) seller of roast meat; (*restaurateur*) steakhouse proprietor.
rôtissoire [ʀotiswaʀ] nf rotisserie, (roasting) spit.
rotogravure [ʀɔtɔgʀavyʀ] nf rotogravure.
rotonde [ʀɔtɔ̃d] nf (*Archit*) rotunda; (*Rail*) engine shed (*Brit*), roundhouse (*US*). **édifice en ~** circular building.
rotondité [ʀɔtɔ̃dite] nf a (*sphéricité*) roundness, rotundity (*frm*). b (*hum: embonpoint*) plumpness, rotundity (*hum*). **~s** *[femme]* plump curves.
rotophare [ʀɔtɔfaʀ] nm (*Aut*) revolving *ou* flashing light (*on police car etc*).
rotoplots‡ [ʀɔtɔplo] nmpl tits‡, boobs‡, knockers‡.
rotor [ʀɔtɔʀ] nm rotor.
rotule [ʀɔtyl] nf a (*Anat*) kneecap, patella (*SPÉC*). **être sur les ~s*** to be dead beat* *ou* all in*. b (*Tech*) ball-and-socket joint.
rotulien, -ienne [ʀɔtyljɛ̃, jɛn] adj patellar.
roture [ʀɔtyʀ] nf (*absence de noblesse*) common rank. **la ~** (*roturiers*) the commoners, the common people; *[fief]* roture.
roturier, -ière [ʀɔtyʀje, jɛʀ] 1 adj (*Hist*) common, of common birth; (*fig: vulgaire*) common, plebeian. 2 nm,f commoner.
rouage [ʀwaʒ] nm *[engrenage]* cog(wheel), gearwheel; *[montre]* part. **les ~s d'une montre** the works *ou* parts of a watch; (*fig*) **il n'est qu'un ~ dans cette organisation** he's merely a cog in this organization; (*fig*) **les ~s de l'État/de l'organisation** the wheels of State/of the organization; (*fig*) **les ~s administratifs** the administrative machinery; (*fig*) **organisation aux ~s compliqués** organization with complex structures.
roubignoles*‡ [ʀubiɲɔl] nfpl balls‡, nuts‡, testicles.
roublard, e* [ʀublaʀ, aʀd] 1 adj crafty, wily, artful. 2 nm,f crafty *ou* artful devil*. **ce ~ de Paul** crafty old Paul*.
roublardise [ʀublaʀdiz] nf (*caractère*) craftiness, wiliness, artfulness; (*acte, tour*) crafty *ou* artful trick.
rouble [ʀubl] nm rouble.
roucoulade [ʀukulad] nf (*voir* **roucouler**) (*gén pl*) coo(ing) (*NonC*); (billing and) cooing (*NonC*); warble (*NonC*), warbling (*NonC*).
roucoulement [ʀukulmɑ̃] nm (*voir* **roucouler**) coo(ing) (*NonC*); (billing and) cooing (*NonC*); warble (*NonC*), warbling (*NonC*).
roucouler [ʀukule] 1 1 vi *[oiseau]* to coo; (*péj*) *[amoureux]* to bill and coo; (*péj*) *[chanteur]* to warble. **venir ~ sous la fenêtre de sa bien-aimée** to come cooing under the window of one's beloved. 2 vt (*péj*) *chanson* to warble; *mots d'amour* to coo.
roudoudou [ʀududu] nm *kind of licking toffee.*
roue [ʀu] 1 nf *[véhicule, loterie, montre]* wheel; *[engrenage]* cog(wheel), (gear)wheel; (*pirouette*) cartwheel. **véhicule à deux/quatre ~s** two-/four-wheeled vehicle; **~ avant/arrière** front/back wheel; **(supplice de) la ~** (torture of) the wheel; (*fig*) **la ~ de la Fortune** the wheel of Fortune; **faire la ~** *[paon]* to spread *ou* fan its tail; *[personne]* (*se pavaner*) to strut about, swagger (about); (*Gymnastique*) to do a cartwheel; *voir* **bâton, chapeau, cinquième** *etc.*
2 comp ▸**roue à aubes** *[bateau]* paddle wheel ▸**roue dentée** cogwheel ▸**roue à godets** bucket wheel ▸**roue de gouvernail** (*Naut*) (steering) wheel, helm ▸**roue hydraulique** waterwheel ▸**roue libre** (*Aut*) freewheel; **descendre une côte en roue libre** to freewheel *ou* coast down a hill; **pédaler en roue libre** to freewheel, coast (along); (*fig: ne pas se surmener*) **il s'est mis en roue libre*** he's taking it easy ▸**roue motrice** (*Aut*) driving wheel; **vehicule à 4 roues motrices** 4-wheel drive vehicle ▸**roue de secours** (*Aut*) spare wheel ▸**roue de transmission** driving wheel.
roué, e [ʀwe] (ptp de **rouer**) 1 adj (*rusé*) cunning, wily, sly. 2 nm,f cunning *ou* sly individual. **c'est une petite ~e** she's a cunning *ou* wily *ou* sly little minx. 3 nm (*Hist: débauché*) rake, roué. 4 **rouée** nf (*Hist: débauchée*) hussy.
rouelle [ʀwɛl] nf: **~ (de veau)** slice of calf's leg.
rouennais, e [ʀwanɛ, ɛz] 1 adj of *ou* from Rouen. 2 nm,f: **R~(e)** inhabitant *ou* native of Rouen.
rouer [ʀwe] 1 vt a **~ qn de coups** to give sb a beating *ou* thrashing, beat sb black and blue. b (*Hist*) *condamné* to put on the wheel.
rouerie [ʀuʀi] nf (*caractère*) cunning, wiliness, slyness; (*tour*) cunning *ou* wily *ou* sly trick.
rouet [ʀwɛ] nm (*à filer*) spinning wheel.
rouflaquettes* [ʀuflakɛt] nfpl (*favoris*) sideboards (*Brit*), sideburns.
rouge [ʀuʒ] 1 adj a (*gén, Pol*) red; *voir* **armée²**, **chaperon** *etc.*
b (*porté à l'incandescence*) *fer* red-hot; *tison* glowing red (*attrib*), red-hot.
c *visage, yeux* red. **~ de colère/de confusion/de honte** red *ou* flushed with anger/embarrassment/shame; **~ d'émotion** flushed with emotion; **devenir ~ comme une cerise** to blush, go quite pink, go red in the face; **il est ~ comme un coq** *ou* **un coquelicot** *ou* **une pivoine** *ou* **une écrevisse** *ou* **une tomate** he's as red as a beetroot *ou* a lobster; **il était ~ d'avoir couru** he was red in the face *ou* his face was flushed from running; *voir* **fâcher**.
d *cheveux, pelage* red.
2 nm a (*couleur*) red. (*Pol*) **voter ~** to vote Communist; (*Aut*) **le feu est au ~** the lights are red; **passer au ~** (*redémarrer trop tôt*) to jump the lights; (*ne pas s'arrêter*) to shoot the lights, go through a red light; *[feu]* to change to red; (*Fin*) **être dans le ~*** to be in the red*; *voir* **bordeaux.**
b (*signe d'émotion*) **le ~ lui monta aux joues** his cheeks flushed, he went red (in the face); **le ~ (de la confusion/de la honte) lui monta au front** his face went red *ou* flushed *ou* he blushed (with embarrassment/shame).
c (*vin*) red wine; (*: *verre de vin*) glass of red wine. **boire un coup de ~** to have a glass of red wine; *voir* **gros.**
d (*fard*) rouge†, blusher; (*à lèvres*) lipstick; *voir* **bâton, tube.**
e (*incandescence*) **fer porté au ~** red-hot iron.
3 nmf (*péj: communiste*) Red* (*péj*), Commie* (*péj*).
4 comp ▸**rouge-cerise** adj inv cherry-red ▸**rouge-gorge** nm (pl **rouges-gorges**) robin (redbreast) ▸**rouge à lèvres** lipstick ▸**rouge-queue** nm (pl **rouges-queues**) redstart ▸**rouge-sang** adj inv blood red.
rougeâtre [ʀuʒatʀ] adj reddish.
rougeaud, e [ʀuʒo, od] adj red-faced. **ce gros ~ la dégoûtait** she found this fat red-faced man repellent.
rougeoiement [ʀuʒwamɑ̃] nm *[incendie, couchant]* red *ou* reddish glow; *[ciel]* reddening.
rougeole [ʀuʒɔl] nf: **la ~** (the) measles (*sg*); **il a eu une très forte ~** he had a very bad bout of measles.
rougeoyant, e [ʀuʒwajɑ̃, ɑ̃t] adj *ciel* reddening; *cendres* glowing red (*attrib*), glowing. **des reflets ~s** a glimmering red glow.

rougeoyer [ʀuʒwaje] [8] **vi** *[feu, incendie, couchant]* to glow red; *[ciel]* to turn red, take on a reddish hue.

rouget [ʀuʒɛ] **nm** mullet. ~ **barbet** red mullet; ~ **grondin** gurnard.

rougeur [ʀuʒœʀ] **nf** a (*teinte*) redness. b *[personne]* (*due à la course, un échauffement, une émotion*) red face, flushing (*NonC*); (*due à la honte, gêne*) red face, blushing (*NonC*), blushes; *[visages, joues]* redness, flushing (*NonC*). **sa ~ a trahi son émotion/sa gêne** her red face *ou* her blushes betrayed her emotion/embarrassment; **la ~ de ses joues** his red face *ou* cheeks, his blushing; **avoir des ~s de jeune fille** to blush like a young girl; **elle était sujette à des ~s subites** she was inclined to blush *ou* to colour up suddenly. c (*Méd: tache*) red blotch *ou* patch.

rougir [ʀuʒiʀ] [2] 1 **vi** a (*de honte, gêne*) to blush, go red, redden, colour (up) (*de* with); (*de plaisir, d'émotion*) to flush, go red, redden (*de* with). **il rougit de colère** he *ou* his face flushed *ou* reddened with anger; **à ces mots, elle rougit** she blushed *ou* coloured (up) *ou* went red *ou* reddened at the words; ~ **jusqu'au blanc des yeux** *ou* **jusqu'aux yeux,** ~ **jusqu'aux oreilles,** ~ **jusqu'à la racine des cheveux** to go bright red, blush to the roots of one's hair; (*lit, fig*) **faire ~ qn** to make sb blush; **dire qch sans ~** to say sth without blushing *ou* unblushingly.

b (*fig: avoir honte*) ~ **de** to be ashamed of; **je n'ai pas à ~ de cela** that is nothing for me to be ashamed of; **il ne rougit de rien** he's quite shameless, he has no shame; **j'en rougis pour lui** I blush for him, I'm ashamed for him.

c (*après un coup de soleil*) to go red.

d *[ciel, neige, feuille]* to go *ou* turn red, redden; *[métal]* to become *ou* get red-hot; (*Culin*) *[crustacés]* to go *ou* turn red, redden; (*Agr*) *[tomates, fraises]* to redden, turn red.

2 **vt** *ciel* to turn red, give a red glow to, redden; *feuilles, arbres* to turn red, redden; *métal* to heat to red heat, make red-hot. ~ **son eau** to put a dash *ou* drop of red wine in one's water; **boire de l'eau rougie** to drink water with just a dash *ou* a few drops of red wine in it; ~ **la terre de son sang** (*lit*) to stain the ground with one's blood; (*fig*) to shed one's blood.

rougissant, e [ʀuʒisɑ̃, ɑ̃t] **adj** *visage, jeune fille* blushing; *feuille, ciel* reddening.

rougissement [ʀuʒismɑ̃] **nm** (*de honte etc*) blush, blushing (*NonC*); (*d'émotion*) flush, flushing (*NonC*).

rouille [ʀuj] 1 **nf** a (*Bot, Chim*) rust. b (*Culin*) *spicy Provençal sauce accompanying fish.* 2 **adj inv** rust(-coloured), rusty.

rouillé, e [ʀuje] (**ptp de rouiller**) **adj** a *métal* rusty, rusted; (*littér*) *roche, écorce* rust-coloured. **tout ~** rusted over. b (*fig*) *mémoire* rusty; *muscles* stiff; *athlète* rusty, out of practice (*attrib*). **j'étais ~ en latin*** my Latin was rusty. c (*Bot*) *blé* rusty.

rouiller [ʀuje] [1] 1 **vi** to rust, go *ou* get rusty. **laisser ~ qch** to let sth go *ou* get rusty. 2 **vt** *métal, esprit* to make rusty. **l'inaction rouillait les hommes** the lack of action was making the men rusty. 3 **se rouiller vpr** *[métal]* to go *ou* get rusty, rust; *[esprit, mémoire]* to become *ou* go rusty; *[corps, muscles]* to grow *ou* get stiff; *[athlète]* to get rusty, get out of practice.

rouir [ʀwiʀ] [2] **vt** (*aussi* **faire ~**) to ret.

rouissage [ʀwisaʒ] **nm** retting.

roulade [ʀulad] **nf** a (*Mus*) roulade, run; *[oiseau]* trill. b (*Culin*) rolled meat (*NonC*). ~ **de veau** rolled veal (*NonC*). c (*Sport*) roll. ~ **avant/arrière** forward/backward roll.

roulage [ʀulaʒ] **nm** (*Min, †: transport, camionnage*) haulage; (*Agr*) rolling.

roulant, e [ʀulɑ̃, ɑ̃t] 1 **adj** a (*mobile*) *meuble* on wheels; *voir* **cuisine, fauteuil, table.** b (*Rail*) **matériel ~** rolling stock; **personnel ~** train crews. c *trottoir, surface transporteuse* moving; *voir* **escalier, feu¹, pont.** d *route* fast. e (*‡: drôle*) *chose, événement* killing* (*Brit*), killingly funny* (*Brit*), hysterical (*US*). **elle est ~e!** she's a scream!*, she's killingly funny!* (*Brit*). 2 **nmpl** (*arg Rail*) **les ~s** train crews. 3 **roulante nf** (*arg Mil*) field kitchen.

roulé, e [ʀule] (**ptp de rouler**) 1 **adj** a **être bien ~*** to be shapely, have a good shape *ou* figure. b *bord de chapeau* curved; *bord de foulard, morceau de boucherie* rolled. ~ **main** hand-rolled; *voir* **col.** c (*Ling*) rolled. **r ~** trilled *ou* rolled r. 2 **nm** (*gâteau*) Swiss roll; (*pâte*) ≃ turnover; (*viande*) rolled meat (*NonC*). ~ **de veau** rolled veal (*NonC*). 3 **comp ▸ roulé-boulé** (*Sport*) **nm** (**pl roulés-boulés**) roll; **faire un roulé-boulé** to roll over, curl up; **tomber en roulé-boulé** to roll (down).

rouleau, pl ~x [ʀulo] 1 **nm** a (*bande enroulée*) roll. ~ **de papier/tissu/pellicule** roll of paper/material/film; **un ~ de cheveux blonds** a ringlet of blond hair; *voir* **bout.**

b (*cylindre*) *[tabac, pièces]* roll. ~ **de réglisse** liquorice roll.

c (*ustensile, outil*) roller; *[machine à écrire]* platen, roller. **passer une pelouse au ~** to roll a lawn; **avoir des ~x dans les cheveux** to have one's hair in curlers *ou* rollers, have curlers *ou* rollers in one's hair; **peindre au ~** to paint with a roller.

d (*vague*) roller.

e (*Sport: saut*) roll.

2 **comp ▸ rouleau compresseur** steamroller, roadroller **▸ rouleau dorsal** (*Sport*) Fosbury flop **▸ rouleau encreur** = **rouleau imprimeur ▸ rouleau essuie-mains** roller towel **▸ rouleau imprimeur** ink roller **▸ rouleau de papier hygiénique** toilet roll, roll of toilet paper *ou* tissue **▸ rouleau de parchemin** scroll *ou* roll of parchment **▸ rouleau à pâtisserie** rolling pin **▸ rouleau de printemps** (*Culin*) spring roll **▸ rouleau ventral** (*Sport*) western roll.

roulement [ʀulmɑ̃] 1 **nm** a (*rotation*) *[équipe, ouvriers]* rotation. **travailler par ~** to work on a rota basis *ou* system, work in rotation. b (*circulation*) *[voiture, train]* movement. **route usée/pneu usé par le ~** road/tyre worn through use; *voir* **bande¹.** c (*bruit*) *[train, camion]* rumble, rumbling (*NonC*); *[charrette]* rattle, rattling (*NonC*). **entendre le ~ du tonnerre** to hear the rumble *ou* peal *ou* roll of thunder, hear thunder rumbling; **il y eut un ~ de tonnerre** there was a rumble *ou* peal *ou* roll of thunder; ~ **de tambour** drum roll. e *[capitaux]* circulation; *voir* **fonds.** 2 **comp ▸ roulement (à billes)** ball bearings; **monté sur roulement à billes** mounted on ball bearings.

rouler [ʀule] [1] 1 **vt** a (*pousser*) *meuble* to wheel (along), roll (along); *chariot, brouette* to wheel (along), trundle along; *boule, tonneau* to roll (along). ~ **un bébé dans sa poussette** to wheel *ou* push a baby (along) in his pushchair.

b (*enrouler*) *tapis, tissu, carte* to roll up; *cigarette* to roll; *ficelle, fil de fer* to wind up, roll up; *viande, parapluie, mèche de cheveux* to roll (up). ~ **qn dans une couverture** to wrap *ou* roll sb (up) in a blanket; ~ **un pansement autour d'un bras** to wrap *ou* wind a bandage round an arm; ~ **ses manches jusqu'au coude** to roll up one's sleeves to one's elbows.

c (*tourner et retourner*) to roll. ~ **des boulettes dans de la farine** to roll meatballs in flour; **la mer roulait les galets sur la plage** the sea rolled the pebbles along the beach; (*fig*) **il roulait mille projets dans sa tête** he was turning thousands of plans over (and over) in his mind; (*littér*) **le fleuve roulait des flots boueux** the river flowed muddily along.

d (*passer au rouleau*) *court de tennis, pelouse* to roll; (*Culin*) *pâte* to roll out.

e (**: duper*) to con‡; (*sur le prix, le poids*) to diddle* (*Brit*), do* (*sur* over). **je l'ai bien roulé** I really conned him‡, I really took him for a ride*; **elle m'a roulé de 50 F** she's diddled* (*Brit*) *ou* done* me out of 50 francs; **se faire ~** to be conned‡ *ou* had* *ou* done* *ou* diddled* (*Brit*); **il s'est fait ~ dans la farine*** he was had*.

f ~ **les** *ou* **des épaules (en marchant)** to sway one's shoulders (when walking); ~ **des mécaniques‡** (*en marchant*) to (walk with a) swagger; (*montrer sa force, ses muscles*) to show off one's muscles; (*intellectuellement*) to show off; ~ **les** *ou* **des hanches** to wiggle one's hips; ~ **les yeux** to roll one's eyes; (*fig*) **il a roulé sa bosse** he has knocked about the world*, he has certainly been places*; ~ **une pelle** *ou* **un patin à qn‡** to give sb a French kiss.

g (*Ling*) ~ **les "r"** to roll one's r's.

2 **vi** a *[voiture, train]* to go, run. **le train roulait/roulait à vive allure à travers la campagne** the train was going along/was racing (along) through the countryside; **cette voiture a très peu/beaucoup roulé** this car has a very low/high mileage; **cette voiture a 10 ans et elle roule encore** this car is 10 years old but it's still going *ou* running; **la voiture roule bien depuis la révision** the car is running *ou* going well since its service; **les voitures ne roulent pas bien sur le sable** cars don't run well on sand; **le véhicule roulait à gauche** the vehicle was driving (along) on the left; ~ **au pas** (*prudence*) to go dead slow (*Brit*), go at a walking pace; (*dans un embouteillage*) to crawl along; **le train roulait à 150 à l'heure au moment de l'accident** the train was doing 150 *ou* going at 150 kilometres an hour at the time of the accident.

b *[passager, conducteur]* to drive. ~ **à 80 km à l'heure** to do 80 km *ou* 50 miles per hour, drive at 80 km *ou* 50 miles per hour; **on a bien roulé*** we kept up a good speed, we made good time; **ça roule/ça ne roule pas bien** the traffic is/is not flowing well; **nous roulions sur la N7 quand soudain ...** we were driving along the N7 when suddenly ...; **dans son métier, il roule beaucoup** in his job, he does a lot of driving; **il roule en 2CV** he drives a 2CV; **il roule en Rolls** he drives (around in) a Rolls; (*†, hum*) ~ **carrosse** to live in high style; (*fig: être à la solde de*) ~ **pour qn*** to work for sb.

c *[boule, bille, dé]* to roll; *[presse]* to roll, run. **allez, roulez!** let's roll it!*, off we go!; **une larme roula sur sa joue** a tear rolled down his cheek; **une secousse le fit ~ à bas de sa couchette** a jerk sent him rolling down from his couchette, a jerk made him roll off his couchette; **il a roulé en bas de l'escalier** he rolled right down the stairs; **un coup de poing l'envoya ~ dans la poussière** a punch sent him rolling in the dust; (*ivre*) **il a roulé sous la table** he was legless* *ou* under the table; **faire ~** *boule* to roll; *cerceau* to roll along; *voir* **pierre.**

d *[bateau]* to roll. **ça roulait*** the boat was rolling quite a bit.

e (**: bourlinguer*) to knock about, drift around. **il a pas mal roulé** he has knocked about *ou* drifted around quite a bit.

f *[argent, capitaux]* to turn over, circulate.

g (*faire un bruit sourd*) *[tambour]* to roll; *[tonnerre]* to roll, rumble, peal.

h *[conversation]* ~ **sur** to turn on, be centred on.

i (*‡: ça va?*) **ça roule?** how's things?*, how's life?

j ~ **sur l'or** to be rolling in money*, have pots of money*; **ils ne roulent pas sur l'or depuis qu'ils sont à la retraite** they're not exactly

living in the lap of luxury *ou* they're not terribly well-off now they've retired.
3 se rouler vpr a to roll (about). se ~ de douleur to roll about in *ou* with pain; se ~ par terre/dans l'herbe to roll on the ground/in the grass; (*fig*) se ~ par terre de rire to fall about* (laughing) (*Brit*), roll on the ground with laughter (*US*); c'est à se ~ (par terre)* it's a scream*, it's killing* (*Brit*); *voir* pouce.
b (*s'enrouler*) se ~ dans une couverture to roll *ou* wrap o.s. up in a blanket; se ~ en boule to roll o.s. (up) into a ball.

roulette [rulɛt] nf a [*meuble*] castor. fauteuil à ~s armchair on castors; ça a marché *ou* été comme sur des ~s* [*plan*] it went like clockwork *ou* very smoothly; [*soirée, interview*] it went off very smoothly *ou* like a dream; *voir* patin. b (*outil*) [*pâtissière*] pastry (cutting) wheel; [*relieur*] fillet; [*couturière*] tracing wheel. ~ de dentiste dentist's drill. c (*jeu*) roulette; (*instrument*) roulette wheel. ~ russe Russian roulette.

rouleur [rulœr] nm (*Cyclisme*) flat racer.

roulier [rulje] nm (*Hist*) cart driver, wagoner; (*Naut*) roll-on roll-off ship.

roulis [ruli] nm (*Naut*) roll(ing) (*NonC*). il y a beaucoup de ~ the ship is rolling a lot; coup de ~ roll.

roulotte [rulɔt] nf caravan (*Brit*), trailer (*US*).

roulotter [rulɔte] [1] vt (*Couture*) *ourlet* to roll; *foulard* to roll the edges of, roll a hem on.

roulure‡ [rulyr] nf (*péj*) slut (*péj*), trollop† (*péj*).

roumain, e [rumɛ̃, ɛn] 1 adj Rumanian, Romanian. 2 nm (*Ling*) Rumanian, Romanian. 3 nm,f: R~(e) Rumanian, Romanian.

Roumanie [rumani] nf Rumania, Romania.

round [raund] nm (*Boxe*) round.

roupettes‡‡ [rupɛt] nfpl (*testicules*) balls‡‡, nuts‡‡.

roupie [rupi] nf a (*monnaie*) rupee. b (†*) c'est de la ~ de sansonnet it's a load of (old) rubbish *ou* junk*, it's absolute trash*; ce n'est pas de la ~ de sansonnet it's none of your cheap rubbish *ou* junk*.

roupiller* [rupije] [1] vi (*dormir*) to sleep; (*faire un petit somme*) to have a snooze* *ou* a kip‡ (*Brit*) *ou* a nap. j'ai besoin de ~ I must get some shut-eye‡; je n'arrive pas à ~ I can't get any shut-eye‡; je vais ~ I'll be turning in*, I'm off to hit the hay*; viens ~ chez nous come and kip down (*Brit*) *ou* bed down at our place‡; secouez-vous, vous roupillez! pull yourself together – you're half asleep! *ou* you're dozing!

roupillon* [rupijɔ̃] nm snooze*, kip‡ (*Brit*), nap. piquer *ou* faire un ~ to have a snooze* *ou* a kip‡ (*Brit*) *ou* a nap.

rouquin, e* [rukɛ̃, in] 1 adj *personne* red-haired; *cheveux* red, carroty* (*péj*). 2 nm,f redhead. 3 nm (‡: *vin rouge*) red plonk* (*Brit*), (cheap) red wine.

rouscailler‡ [ruskɑje] [1] vi to moan*, bellyache‡.

rouspétance* [ruspetɑ̃s] nf (*voir* rouspéter) moaning* (*NonC*); grousing* (*NonC*), grouching* (*NonC*); grumbling (*NonC*).

rouspéter* [ruspete] [6] vi (*ronchonner*) to moan*, grouse*, grouch*; (*protester*) to moan*, grumble (*après* at).

rouspéteur, -euse* [ruspetœr, øz] 1 adj grumpy. c'est un ~ he's a proper moaner* *ou* grumbler, he's a grumpy individual. 2 nm,f (*ronchonneur*) moaner*, grouser*, grouch*; (*qui proteste*) grumbler, moaner*.

roussâtre [rusɑtr] adj reddish, russet.

rousse[1] [rus] *voir* roux.

rousse[2] [rus] nf (*arg Crime*) la ~ the fuzz (*arg*).

rousseauiste [rusoist] adj Rousseauistic.

rousserolle [rus(ə)rɔl] nf: ~ verderolle marsh warbler.

roussette [rusɛt] nf (*poisson*) dogfish; (*chauve-souris*) flying fox; (*grenouille*) common frog.

rousseur [rusœr] nf a (*couleur: voir* roux) redness; gingery colour; russet colour; *voir* tache. b (*sur le papier*) ~s brownish marks *ou* stains; (*sur la peau*) brown blotches, freckles.

roussi [rusi] nm: odeur de ~ smell of (something) burning *ou* scorching *ou* singeing; ça sent le ~! (*lit*) there's a smell of (something) burning *ou* scorching *ou* singeing; (*fig*) I can smell trouble.

roussin†† [rusɛ̃] nm horse.

roussir [rusir] [2] 1 vt [*fer à repasser*] to scorch, singe; [*flamme*] to singe. ~ l'herbe [*gelée*] to turn the grass brown *ou* yellow; [*chaleur*] to scorch the grass. 2 vi a [*feuilles, forêt*] to turn *ou* go brown *ou* russet. b (*Culin*) faire ~ to brown.

roustons‡‡ [rustɔ̃] nmpl (*testicules*) balls‡‡, nuts‡‡.

routage [rutaʒ] nm (*distribution*) sorting and mailing. entreprise de ~ mailing firm *ou* service.

routard, e* [rutar, ard] nm,f backpacker.

route [rut] nf a road. ~ nationale/départementale ≃ trunk (*Brit*) *ou* main/secondary road; ~ de montagne mountain road; prenez la ~ de Lyon take the road to Lyons *ou* the Lyons road; *voir* course, grand.
b (*moyen de transport*) la ~ road; la ~ est plus économique que le rail road is cheaper than rail; la ~ est meurtrière the road is a killer, driving is treacherous; arriver par la ~ to arrive by road; faire de la ~ to do a lot of mileage; accidents/blessés de la ~ road accidents/casualties; *voir* code.
c (*chemin à suivre*) way; (*Naut: direction, cap*) course. je ne l'emmène pas, ce n'est pas (sur) ma ~ I'm not taking him because it's not on my way; perdre/retrouver sa ~ to lose/find one's way.
d (*ligne de communication*) route. ~ aérienne/maritime air/sea route; la ~ du sel/de l'opium/des épices the salt/opium/spice route *ou* trail; la ~ des vins the wine trail; la ~ des Indes the route *ou* road to India; indiquer/montrer la ~ à qn to point out/show the way to sb; ils ont fait toute la ~ à pied/à bicyclette they did the whole journey on foot/by bicycle, they walked/cycled the whole way; la ~ sera longue (*gén*) it'll be a long journey; (*en voiture*) it'll be a long drive *ou* ride; il y a 3 heures de ~ (*en voiture*) it's a 3-hour drive *ou* ride *ou* journey; (*à bicyclette*) it's a 3-hour (cycle-)ride *ou* journey; *voir* barrer, compagnon *etc.*
e (*fig: ligne de conduite, voie*) path, road, way. la ~ à suivre the path *ou* road to follow; la ~ du bonheur the road *ou* path *ou* way to happinesss; votre ~ est toute tracée your path is set out for you; la ~ s'ouvre devant lui the road *ou* way opens (up) before him; être sur la bonne ~ (*dans la vie*) to be on the right road *ou* path; (*dans un problème*) to be on the right track; remettre qn sur la bonne ~ to put sb back on the right road *ou* path, put sb back on the right track; c'est lui qui a ouvert la ~ he's the one who opened (up) the road *ou* way.
f (*loc*) faire ~ vers (*gén*) to head towards *ou* for; [*bateau*] to steer a course for, head for; en ~ pour, faisant ~ vers bound for, heading for, on its way to; faire ~ avec qn to travel with sb; prendre la ~, se mettre en ~ to start out, set off *ou* out, get under way; en ~ on the way *ou* journey, en route; en ~! let's go!, let's be off; prendre la ~ to set off; reprendre la ~, se remettre en ~ to resume one's journey, start out again, set off *ou* out again; bonne ~! have a good journey! *ou* trip!; (*hum*) en ~, mauvaise troupe! off we go!; mettre en ~ *machine, moteur* to start (up); *affaire* to set in motion, get under way; *projet* to set up; mise en ~ starting up, setting in motion, setting up; carnet *ou* journal de ~ travel diary *ou* journal; tenir la ~ [*voiture*] to hold the road; [*matériel*] to be well-made *ou* serviceable; [*plan*] to hold together; *voir* faux, tenu.

router [rute] [1] vt *journaux* to pack and mail.

routier, -ière [rutje, jɛr] 1 adj *circulation, carte, réseau, transport* road (*épith*); *voir* gare[1]. 2 nm (*camionneur*) long-distance lorry (*Brit*) *ou* truck (*US*) driver; (*restaurant*) ≃ transport café (*Brit*), roadside café; (*cycliste*) road racer *ou* rider; (*Naut: carte*) route chart; (†: *scout*) rover; *voir* vieux. 3 routière nf (*Aut*) tourer (*Brit*), touring car. grande ~ière high-performance tourer (*Brit*) *ou* touring car.

routine [rutin] nf a (*habitude*) routine. par ~ as a matter of routine; opération/visite de ~ routine operation/visit. b (*Ordin*) routine.

routinier, -ière [rutinje, jɛr] adj *procédé, travail, vie* humdrum, routine; *personne* routine-minded, addicted to routine (*attrib*). il a l'esprit ~ he's completely tied to (his) routine; c'est un travail un peu ~ the work is a bit routine *ou* humdrum; c'est un ~ he's a creature of habit.

rouvre [ruvr] adj, nm (chêne) ~ durmast *ou* sissile oak.

rouvrir vti, **se rouvrir** vpr [ruvrir] [18] to reopen, open again. la porte se rouvrit the door opened again; ~ le débat to reopen the debate.

roux, rousse[1] [ru, rus] 1 adj *cheveux* red, auburn; (*orangé*) ginger; *barbe* red; (*orangé*) ginger; *pelage, robe, feuilles* russet, reddish-brown. il aime les rousses he likes redheads; *voir* beurre, blond, lune *etc.* 2 nm a (*couleur*) (*voir* adj) red; auburn; ginger; russet, reddish-brown. b (*Culin*) roux.

royal, e, mpl **-aux** [rwajal, o] adj a *couronne, palais, appartement* royal; *pouvoir, autorité* royal, regal; *prérogative, décret, charte* royal. la famille ~e the Royal Family *ou* royal family. b *maintien, magnificence* kingly, regal; *repas, demeure, cadeau* fit for a king (*attrib*); *salaire* princely; *voir* aigle, tigre. c (*intensif*) *indifférence, mépris* majestic, lofty, regal. il m'a fichu une paix ~e* he left me in perfect peace. d (*Culin*) lièvre à la ~e hare royale. e la R~* the French Navy.

royalement [rwajalmɑ̃] adv *vivre* in (a) royal fashion; *recevoir, traiter* royally, in (a) regal *ou* royal fashion. il se moque ~ de sa situation* he couldn't care less* *ou* he doesn't care two hoots* about his position; (*iro*) il m'a ~ offert 3 F d'augmentation* he offered me a princely 3-franc rise (*iro*).

royalisme [rwajalism] nm royalism.

royaliste [rwajalist] 1 adj royalist. être plus ~ que le roi to out-Herod Herod (*in the defence of sb or in following a doctrine etc*). 2 nmf royalist.

royalties [rwajalti] nfpl royalties (*on patent, on the use of oilfields or pipeline*).

royaume [rwajom] 1 nm (*lit*) kingdom, realm; (*fig: domaine*) realm, (private) world. le vieux grenier était son ~ the old attic was his (private) world *ou* his realm; *voir* à. 2 comp ▸le royaume céleste *ou* de Dieu the kingdom of heaven *ou* God ▸le Royaume-Uni (de Grande-Bretagne et d'Irlande du Nord) the United Kingdom (of Great Britain and Northern Ireland).

royauté [rwajote] nf (*régime*) monarchy; (*fonction, dignité*) kingship.

RP 1 nm (abrév de Révérend Père) *voir* révérend. 2 nf (abrév de recette principale) *voir* recette. 3 nfpl (abrév de relations publiques) PR.

RPR [ɛrpeɛr] nm (abrév de Rassemblement pour la République) *French political party.*

RSS† [ɛʀɛsɛs] (abrév de **République socialiste soviétique**) S.S.R†.
RSVP [ɛʀɛsvepe] (abrév de **répondez s'il vous plaît**) R.S.V.P.
Rte abrév de **route**.
RU [ʀy] nm (abrév de **restaurant universitaire**) *voir* **restaurant.**
ru† [ʀy] nm brook, rivulet (*littér*).
ruade [ʀɥad] nf kick (*of a horse's hind legs*). **tué par une ~** killed by a kick from a horse; **le cheval lui a cassé la jambe d'une ~** the horse kicked *ou* lashed out at him and broke his leg; **décocher** *ou* **lancer une ~** to lash *ou* kick out.
Ruanda [ʀwɑ̃da] nm Rwanda. (*Hist*) **~-Urundi** Ruanda-Urundi.
ruandais, e [ʀwɑ̃dɛ, ɛz] 1 adj Rwandan. 2 nm,f: **R~(e)** Rwandan.
ruban [ʀybɑ̃] 1 nm (*gén, fig*) ribbon; *[machine à écrire]* ribbon; *[téléscripteur, magnétophone]* tape; *[ourlet, couture]* binding, tape. **le ~ (de la Légion d'honneur)** the ribbon of the Légion d'Honneur; (*fig*) **le ~ argenté du Rhône** the silver ribbon of the Rhone; **le double ~ de l'autoroute** the two *ou* twin lines of the motorway; *voir* **mètre, scie.** 2 comp ►**ruban d'acier** steel band *ou* strip ►**ruban adhésif** adhesive tape, sticky tape ►**le ruban bleu** (*Naut*) the Blue Riband *or* Ribbon (*of the Atlantic*) ►**ruban de chapeau** hat band ►**ruban encreur** typewriter ribbon ►**ruban isolant** insulating tape ►**ruban perforé** (*Ordin*) paper tape.
rubato [ʀybato] adv, nm rubato.
rubéole [ʀybeɔl] nf German measles (*sg*), rubella (*SPÉC*).
Rubicon [ʀybikɔ̃] nm Rubicon; *voir* **franchir.**
rubicond, e [ʀybikɔ̃, ɔ̃d] adj rubicund, ruddy.
rubidium [ʀybidjɔm] nm rubidium.
rubis [ʀybi] 1 nm (*pierre*) ruby; (*couleur*) ruby (colour); *[horloge, montre]* jewel; *voir* **payer.** 2 adj inv ruby(-coloured).
rubrique [ʀybʀik] nf a (*article, chronique*) column. **~ sportive/littéraire/des spectacles** sports/literary/entertainments column. b (*titre, catégorie*) heading, rubric. **sous cette même ~** under the same heading *ou* rubric. c (*Rel*) rubric.
ruche [ʀyʃ] nf a (*en bois*) (bee) hive; (*essaim*) hive; (*en paille*) (bee) hive, skep (*SPÉC*). (*fig*) **l'école se transforme en ~ dès 8 heures** the school turns into a (regular) hive of activity at 8 o'clock. b (*Couture*) ruche.
ruché [ʀyʃe] nm (*Couture*) ruching (*NonC*), ruche.
rucher [ʀyʃe] nm apiary.
rude [ʀyd] adj a (*au toucher*) *surface, barbe, peau* rough; (*à l'ouïe*) *voix, sons* harsh.
b (*pénible*) *métier, vie, combat* hard, tough; *adversaire* tough; *montée* stiff, tough, hard; *climat, hiver* harsh, hard, severe. **être mis à ~ épreuve** *[personne]* to be severely tested, be put through the mill; *[tissu, métal]* to receive *ou* have rough treatment; **mes nerfs ont été mis à ~ épreuve** it was a great strain on my nerves; **il a été à ~ école dans sa jeunesse** he learned life the hard way when he was young; **en faire voir de ~s à qn** to give sb a hard *ou* tough time; **en voir de ~s** to have a hard *ou* tough time (of it).
c (*fruste*) *manières* unpolished, crude, unrefined; *traits* rugged; *montagnards* rugged, tough.
d (*sévère, bourru*) *personne, caractère* harsh, hard, severe; *manières* rough.
e (*intensif: fameux*) **un ~ gaillard** a hearty fellow; **avoir un ~ appétit/estomac** to have a hearty appetite/an iron stomach; **il a une ~ veine** he's a lucky beggar* (*Brit*) *ou* son-of-a-gun* (*US*); **ça m'a fait une ~ peur** it gave me a dreadful *ou* real fright; **recevoir un ~ coup de poing** to get a real *ou* proper* (*Brit*) thump.
rudement [ʀydmɑ̃] adv a *heurter, tomber, frapper* hard; *répondre* harshly; *traiter* roughly, harshly.
b (**: très, beaucoup*) *content, bon* terribly*, awfully*, jolly* (*Brit*); *fatigant, mauvais, cher* dreadfully, terribly, awfully. **travailler ~** to work terribly *ou* awfully *ou* jolly (*Brit*) hard; **elle danse ~ bien** she dances terribly *ou* awfully *ou* jolly (*Brit*) well, she's quite a dancer; **ça me change ~ de faire ça** it's a real change *ou* quite a change for me to do that; **elle avait ~ changé** she had really changed, she hadn't half changed* (*Brit*); **il est ~ plus généreux que toi** he's a great deal *ou* darned sight* more generous than you; **j'ai eu ~ peur** I had quite a scare, I had a dreadful *ou* an awful scare *ou* fright.
rudesse [ʀydɛs] nf (*voir* **rude**) roughness; harshness; hardness; toughness; severity; crudeness; ruggedness. **traiter qn avec ~** to treat sb roughly *ou* harshly.
rudiment [ʀydimɑ̃] nm a **~s** *[discipline]* rudiments; *[théorie, système]* principles; **~s d'algèbre** principles *ou* rudiments of algebra; **avoir quelques ~s de chimie** to have some basic *ou* rudimentary notions *ou* some basic knowledge of chemistry, have a rudimentary knowledge of chemistry; **avoir quelques ~s d'anglais** to have a smattering of English *ou* some basic knowledge of English; **nous n'en sommes qu'aux ~s** we're still on the basics; **on en est encore aux ~s** we're still at a rudimentary stage. b (*Anat, Zool*) rudiment.
rudimentaire [ʀydimɑ̃tɛʀ] adj rudimentary.
rudoiement [ʀydwamɑ̃] nm rough *ou* harsh treatment.
rudoyer [ʀydwaje] 8 vt to treat harshly.
rue¹ [ʀy] nf (*voie, habitants*) street. (*péj: populace*) **la ~** the mob; **~ à sens unique** one-way street; **~ piétonnière** *ou* **piétonne** pedestrianized street; **scènes de la ~** street scenes; **élevé dans la ~** brought up in the street(s); **être à la ~** to be on the streets; **jeter qn à la ~** to put sb out *ou* throw sb out (into the street); *voir* **chaussée, coin, combat** *etc.*
rue² [ʀy] nf (*plante*) rue.
ruée [ʀɥe] nf rush; (*péj*) stampede. **à l'ouverture, ce fut la ~ vers l'entrée du magasin** when the shop opened, there was a (great) rush *ou* a stampede for the entrance, as soon as the doors opened there was a stampede *ou* a mad scramble to get into the shop; (*fig*) **dès que quelqu'un prend sa retraite ou démissionne, c'est la ~** the moment someone retires or resigns there's a scramble for the position; **dans la ~, il fut renversé** he was knocked over in the rush *ou* stampede; **la ~ vers l'or** the gold rush.
ruelle [ʀɥɛl] nf (*rue*) alley(way); (††) *[chambre]* ruelle††, space (between bed and wall); (*Hist, Littérat*) ruelle (*room used in 17th century to hold literary salons*).
ruer [ʀɥe] 1 1 vi *[cheval]* to kick (out). **prenez garde, il rue** watch out — he kicks; (*fig*) **~ dans les brancards** to rebel, become rebellious, protest, lash out. 2 **se ruer** vpr: **se ~ sur** *personne, article en vente, nourriture* to pounce on; *emplois vacants* to fling o.s. at, pounce at; **se ~ vers** *sortie, porte* to dash *ou* rush for *ou* towards; **se ~ dans/hors de** *pièce, maison* to dash *ou* rush *ou* tear into/out of; **se ~ dans l'escalier** (*monter*) to tear *ou* dash up the stairs; (*descendre*) to tear down the stairs, hurl o.s. down the stairs; **se ~ à l'assaut** to hurl *ou* fling o.s. into the attack.
ruf(f)ian†† [ʀyfjɑ̃] nm ruffian.
rugby [ʀygbi] nm Rugby (football), rugger*. **~ à quinze** Rugby Union; **~ à treize** Rugby League.
rugbyman [ʀygbiman], pl **rugbymen** [ʀygbimɛn] nm rugby player.
rugir [ʀyʒiʀ] 2 1 vi *[fauve, mer, moteur]* to roar; *[vent, tempête]* to howl, roar. *[personne]* **~ de douleur** to howl *ou* roar with pain; **~ de colère** to bellow *ou* roar with anger. 2 vt *ordres, menaces* to roar *ou* bellow out.
rugissement [ʀyʒismɑ̃] nm (*voir* **rugir**) roar; roaring (*NonC*); howl; howling (*NonC*). **~ de douleur** howl *ou* roar of pain; **~ de colère** roar of anger.
rugosité [ʀygozite] nf a (*caractère: voir* **rugueux**) roughness; coarseness; ruggedness, bumpiness. b (*aspérité*) rough patch, bump.
rugueux, -euse [ʀygø, øz] adj (*gén*) rough; *peau, tissu* rough, coarse; *sol* rugged, rough, bumpy.
Ruhr [ʀuʀ] nf: **la ~** the Ruhr.
ruine [ʀɥin] nf a (*lit, fig: décombres, destruction*) ruin. **~s romaines** Roman ruins; **acheter une ~ à la campagne** to buy a ruin in the country; (*péj*) **~ (humaine)** (human) wreck; **en ~** in ruin(s), ruined (*épith*); **causer la ~ de** *monarchie* to bring about the ruin *ou* downfall of; *réputation, carrière, santé* to ruin, bring about the ruin of; *banquier, firme* to ruin, bring ruin upon; **c'est la ~ de tous mes espoirs** that puts paid to (*Brit*) *ou* that means the ruin of all my hopes; **courir** *ou* **aller à sa ~** to be on the road to ruin, be heading for ruin; **menacer ~** to be threatening to collapse; **tomber en ~** to fall in ruins; **50 F, ce n'est pas la ~!*** 50 francs won't break the bank!*
b (*acquisition coûteuse*) **cette voiture est une vraie ~** that car will ruin me.
ruiner [ʀɥine] 1 1 vt a *personne, pays* to ruin, cause the ruin of. **ça ne va pas te ~!*** it won't break* *ou* ruin you! b *réputation* to ruin, wreck; *espoirs* to shatter, dash, ruin; *santé* to ruin. 2 **se ruiner** vpr (*dépenser tout son argent*) to ruin *ou* bankrupt o.s.; (*fig: dépenser trop*) to spend a fortune.
ruineux, -euse [ʀɥinø, øz] adj *goût* extravagant, ruinously expensive; *dépense* ruinous; *acquisition, voiture* (*prix élevé*) ruinous, ruinously expensive; (*entretien coûteux*) expensive to run (*ou* keep *etc*). **ce n'est pas ~!** it won't break* *ou* ruin us!, it doesn't cost a fortune!
ruisseau, pl **~x** [ʀɥiso] nm a (*cours d'eau*) stream, brook. (*fig*) **des ~x de** *larmes* floods of; *lave, sang* streams of; *voir* **petit.** b (*caniveau*) gutter. (*fig*) **élevé dans le ~** brought up *ou* dragged up* in the gutter; (*fig*) **tirer qn du ~** to pull *ou* drag sb out of the gutter.
ruisselant, e [ʀɥis(ə)lɑ̃, ɑ̃t] adj *mur* streaming, running with water; *visage* streaming; *personne* dripping wet, streaming.
ruisseler [ʀɥis(ə)le] 4 vi a (*couler*) *[lumière]* to stream; *[cheveux]* to flow, stream (*sur* over); *[liquide, pluie]* to stream, flow (*sur* down). b (*être couvert d'eau*) **~ (d'eau)** *[mur]* to run with water, stream (with water); *[visage]* to stream (with water); **~ de lumière/larmes** to stream with light/tears; **~ de sueur** to drip *ou* stream with sweat; **le visage ruisselant de larmes** his face streaming with tears, with tears streaming down his face.
ruisselet [ʀɥis(ə)lɛ] nm rivulet, brooklet.
ruissellement [ʀɥisɛlmɑ̃] 1 nm: **le ~ de la pluie/de l'eau sur le mur** the rain/water streaming *ou* running *ou* flowing down the wall; **le ~ de sa chevelure sur ses épaules** her hair flowing *ou* streaming over her shoulders; **un ~ de pierreries** a glistening *ou* glittering cascade of jewels; **ébloui par ce ~ de lumière** dazzled by this stream of light. 2 comp ►**ruissellement pluvial** (*Géol*) run-off.
rumba [ʀumba] nf rumba.
rumeur [ʀymœʀ] nf a (*nouvelle imprécise*) rumour. **selon certaines ~s, elle ...** rumour has it that she ..., it is rumoured that she ...; **si l'on**

en croit la ~ publique, il ... if you believe what is publicly rumoured, he ...; **faire courir de fausses ~s** to spread rumours. b (*son*) *[vagues, vent]* murmur(ing) (*NonC*); *[ville, rue, circulation]* hum (*NonC*), rumbling; *[émeute]* hubbub (*NonC*), rumbling; *[bureau, conversation]* buzz (*NonC*), rumbling, hubbub (*NonC*). c (*protestation*) rumblings. **~ de mécontentement** rumblings of discontent; **une ~ s'éleva** *ou* **des ~s s'élevèrent de la foule** rumblings rose up from the crowd.

ruminant [ʀyminɑ̃] **nm** (*Zool*) ruminant.

rumination [ʀyminasjɔ̃] **nf** (*Zool*) rumination.

ruminer [ʀymine] 1 1 **vt** (*Zool*) to ruminate; (*fig*) *projet* to ruminate on *ou* over, chew over; *chagrin* to brood over; *vengeance* to ponder, meditate. **toujours dans son coin, à ~ (ses pensées)** always in his corner chewing the cud (*fig*) *ou* chewing things over *ou* pondering (things). 2 **vi** (*Zool*) to ruminate, chew the cud.

rumsteck [ʀɔmstɛk] = **romsteck**.

rune [ʀyn] **nf** (*Ling*) rune.

runique [ʀynik] **adj** runic.

rupestre [ʀypɛstʀ] **adj** (*Bot*) rupestrine (*SPÉC*), rock (*épith*); (*Art*) rupestrian (*SPÉC*), rupestral (*SPÉC*), rock (*épith*).

rupin, e* [ʀypɛ̃, in] **adj** *appartement, quartier* ritzy*, plush(y)*; *personne* stinking *ou* filthy rich*. **c'est un ~** he's got money to burn*, he's stinking *ou* filthy rich*, he's rolling in it*; **les ~s** the stinking *ou* filthy rich*.

rupteur [ʀyptœʀ] **nm** (contact) breaker.

rupture [ʀyptyʀ] 1 **nf** a (*annulation: action*) *[relations diplomatiques]* breaking off, severing, rupture; *[fiançailles, pourparlers]* breaking off. **la ~ du traité/contrat par ce pays** this country's breaking the treaty/contract, the breach of the treaty/contract by this country; **après la ~ des négociations** after negotiations broke down *ou* were broken off.

b (*annulation: résultat*) *[contrat, traité]* breach (*de* of); *[relations diplomatiques]* severance, rupture (*de* of); *[pourparlers]* breakdown (*de* of, in). **la ~ de leurs fiançailles l'a tué** their broken engagement killed him.

c (*séparation amoureuse*) break-up, split. **sa ~ (d')avec Louise** his split *ou* break-up with Louise; **~ passagère** temporary break-up; (*fig*) **être en ~ avec le monde/les idées de son temps** to be at odds with the world/the ideas of one's time.

d (*cassure, déchirure*) *[câble]* breaking, parting; *[poutre, branche, corde]* breaking; *[digue]* bursting, breach(ing); *[veine]* bursting, rupture; *[organe]* rupture; *[tendon]* rupture, tearing. **limite de ~** breaking point.

e (*solution de continuité*) break. **~ entre le passé et le présent** break between the past and the present; **~ de rythme** (sudden) break in (the) rhythm; **~ de ton** abrupt change in *ou* of tone.

f (*Ordin*) **~ de séquence** jump.

2 **comp** ►**rupture d'anévrisme** aneurysmal rupture ►**rupture de ban** *illegal return from banishment;* **en rupture de ban** (*Jur*) *illegally returning from banishment;* (*fig*) in defiance of the accepted code of conduct; **en rupture de ban avec la société** at odds with society ►**rupture de circuit** (*Élec*) break in the circuit ►**rupture de contrat** breach of contract ►**rupture de direction** steering failure ►**rupture d'équilibre** (*lit*) loss of balance; (*fig*) **une rupture d'équilibre est à craindre entre ces nations** an upset in the balance of power is to be feared among these states ►**rupture d'essieu** broken axle ►**rupture de pente** change of incline *ou* gradient ►**être en rupture de stock** to be out of stock.

rural, e, **mpl -aux** [ʀyʀal, o] 1 **adj** (*gén*) country (*épith*), rural; (*Admin*) rural. 2 **nm,f** country person, rustic. **les ruraux** country people, countryfolk; *voir* **exode**.

ruse [ʀyz] **nf** a (*NonC*) (*habileté*) (*pour gagner, obtenir un avantage*) cunning, craftiness, slyness; (*pour tromper*) trickery, guile. **obtenir qch par ~** to obtain sth by *ou* through trickery *ou* by guile. b (*subterfuge*) trick, ruse. (*lit, fig, hum*) **~ de guerre** stratagem, tactics; **avec des ~s de Sioux** with crafty tactics; **usant de ~s féminines** using her womanly wiles.

rusé, e [ʀyze] (**ptp de ruser**) **adj** *personne* cunning, crafty, sly, wily; *air* sly, wily. **~ comme un (vieux) renard** as sly *ou* cunning as a fox; **c'est un ~** he's a crafty *ou* sly one.

ruser [ʀyze] 1 **vi** (*voir* **ruse**) to use cunning; to use trickery. **ne ruse pas avec moi!** don't try and be clever *ou* smart* with me!

rush [ʀœʃ] **nm** (*afflux, Ciné*) rush.

russe [ʀys] 1 **adj** Russian. **œuf dur à la ~** œuf dur à la Russe; **boire à la ~** to drink (and cast one's glass aside) in the Russian style; *voir* **montagne, roulette.** 2 **nm** (*Ling*) Russian. 3 **nmf: R~** Russian; **R~ blanc(he)** White Russian.

Russie [ʀysi] **nf** Russia. **la ~ blanche** White Russia; **~ soviétique** Soviet Russia.

russification [ʀysifikasjɔ̃] **nf** russianization, russification.

russifier [ʀysifje] 7 **vt** to russianize, russify.

rustaud, e [ʀysto, od] 1 **adj** countrified, rustic. 2 **nm,f** country bumpkin, yokel, hillbilly (*US*).

rusticité [ʀystisite] **nf** a *[manières, personne]* rustic simplicity, rusticity (*littér*). b (*Agr*) hardiness.

rustine [ʀystin] **nf** ® rubber repair patch (*for bicycle tyre*).

rustique [ʀystik] 1 **adj** a *mobilier* rustic; *maçonnerie* rustic, rusticated. **bois ~** rustic wood. b (*littér*) *maison* rustic (*épith*); *vie, manières* rustic, country (*épith*). c (*Agr*) hardy. 2 **nm** (*style*) rustic style. **meubler une maison en ~** to furnish a house in the rustic style *ou* with rustic furniture.

rustre [ʀystʀ] 1 **nm** a (*péj: brute*) lout, boor. b (†: *paysan*) peasant. 2 **adj** brutish, boorish.

rut [ʀyt] **nm** (*état*) *[mâle]* rut; *[femelle]* heat; (*période*) rutting (period), heat period. **être en ~** to be rutting, be in *ou* on heat.

rutabaga [ʀytabaga] **nm** swede, rutabaga (*US*).

Ruth [ʀyt] **nf** Ruth.

ruthénium [ʀytenjɔm] **nm** ruthenium.

rutilant, e [ʀytilɑ̃, ɑ̃t] **adj** (*brillant*) brightly shining, gleaming; (*rouge ardent*) rutilant. **vêtu d'un uniforme ~** very spick and span *ou* very spruce in his (*ou* her) uniform.

rutilement [ʀytilmɑ̃] **nm** gleam.

rutiler [ʀytile] 1 **vi** to gleam, shine brightly.

rv **abrév de rendez-vous.**

Rwanda [ʀwɑ̃da] = **Ruanda.**

rythme [ʀitm] **nm** a (*Art, Littérat, Mus*) rhythm. **marquer le ~** to beat time; (*Mus*) **au ~ de** to the beat *ou* rhythm of; **avoir le sens du ~** to have a sense of rhythm; (*Théât*) **pièce qui manque de ~** play which lacks tempo, slow-moving play.

b (*cadence*) *[respiration, cœur, saisons]* rhythm. **interrompant le ~ de sa respiration** interrupting the rhythm of his breathing.

c (*vitesse*) *[respiration]* rate; *[battements du cœur]* rate, speed; *[vie, travail]* tempo, pace; *[production]* rate. **~ cardiaque** (rate of) heartbeat; **à ce ~-là, il ne va plus en rester** at that rate there won't be any left; **il n'arrive pas à suivre le ~** he can't keep up (the pace); **produire des voitures au ~ de 1 000 par jour** to produce cars at the rate of 1,000 a *ou* per day.

rythmé, e [ʀitme] (**ptp de rythmer**) **adj** rhythmic(al). **bien ~** highly rhythmic(al).

rythmer [ʀitme] 1 **vt** (*cadencer*) *prose, phrase, travail* to give rhythm to, give a certain rhythm to, punctuate. **leur marche rythmée par des chansons** their march, given rhythm by their songs; **les saisons rythmaient leur vie** the seasons gave (a certain) rhythm to their life *ou* punctuated their life.

rythmique [ʀitmik] 1 **adj** rhythmic(al); *voir* **section.** 2 **nf** (*Littérat*) rhythmics (*sg*). **la (danse) ~** rhythmics (*sg*).

S

S¹, s [ɛs] **nm** a (*lettre*) S, s. b (*figure*) zigzag; (*virages*) double bend, S bend, Z bend. **faire des s** to zigzag; **en s** *route* zigzagging *(épith)*, winding; *barre* S-shaped.
S² (**abrév de Sud**) S.
s' [s] *voir* **se, si¹**.
s/ abrév de sur.
SA [ɛsa] **nf** (**abrév de société anonyme**) (*gén*) limited company; (*ouverte au public*) public limited company. **Raymond ~** Raymond Ltd (*Brit*), Raymond Inc. (*US*); (*ouverte au public*) Raymond plc.
sa [sa] **adj poss** *voir* **son¹**.
Saba [saba] **nf** Sheba. **la reine de ~** the Queen of Sheba.
sabayon [sabajɔ̃] **nm** zabaglione.
sabbat [saba] **nm** a (*Rel*) Sabbath. b (**: bruit*) racket, row*. c *[sorcières]* (witches') sabbath.
sabbatique [sabatik] **adj** (*Rel, Univ*) sabbatical. **prendre un congé ~ d'un an** to take a year's sabbatical *ou* a year-long sabbatical.
sabin, e [sabɛ̃, in] 1 **adj** Sabine. 2 **nm, f: S~(e)** Sabine; *voir* **enlèvement.**
sabir [sabiʀ] **nm** (*parlé dans le Levant*) sabir; (*Ling*) ≃ pidgin; (*péj: jargon*) jargon. **un curieux ~ fait de français et d'arabe** a strange mixture of French and Arabic.
sablage [sablaʒ] **nm** *[allée]* sanding; *[façade]* sandblasting.
sable¹ [sɑbl] 1 **nm** sand. **de ~** *dune, vent* sand (*épith*); *fond, plage* sandy; **~s mouvants** quicksand(s); **mer de ~** sea of sand; **tempête de ~** sandstorm; (*fig*) **être sur le ~*** to be down-and-out; *voir* **bac, bâtir, grain, marchand.** 2 **adj inv** sandy, sand-coloured.
sable² [sɑbl] **nm** (*Hér*) sable.
sablé, e [sɑble] (**ptp de sabler**) 1 **adj** a *gâteau* made with shortbread dough; *voir* **pâte.** b *route* sandy, sanded. 2 **nm** shortbread biscuit (*Brit*) *ou* cookie (*US*), piece of shortbread.
sabler [sɑble] 1 **vt** a *route* to sand; *façade* to sandblast. b **~ le champagne** (*lit*) to drink *ou* have champagne; (*fig: fêter quelque chose*) to celebrate.
sableux, -euse [sɑblø, øz] 1 **adj** sandy. 2 **sableuse nf** (*machine*) sandblaster.
sablier [sɑblije] **nm** (*gén*) hourglass, sandglass; (*Culin*) egg timer.
sablière [sɑblijɛʀ] **nf** (*carrière*) sand quarry; (*Constr*) string-piece; (*Rail*) sand-box.
sablonneux, -euse [sɑblɔnø, øz] **adj** sandy.
sablonnière [sɑblɔnjɛʀ] **nf** sand quarry.
sabord [sabɔʀ] **nm** scuttle (*Naut*).
sabordage [sabɔʀdaʒ] **nm, sabordement** [sabɔʀdəmɑ̃] **nm** (*Naut*) scuppering, scuttling; (*fig*) *[entreprise]* winding up, shutting down.
saborder [sabɔʀde] 1 1 **vt** (*Naut*) to scupper, scuttle; (*fig*) *entreprise* to wind up, shut down; *négociations, projet* to put paid to, scupper. 2 **se saborder vpr** (*Naut*) to scupper *ou* scuttle one's ship; *[patron]* to wind up, shut down; *[candidat]* to write o.s. off, scupper o.s.
sabot [sabo] **nm** a (*chaussure*) clog. (*fig*) **je le vois venir avec ses gros ~s** I can see just what he's after, I can see him coming a mile off (*fig*); *voir* **baignoire, pied.** b (*Zool*) hoof. **le cheval lui donna un coup de ~** the horse kicked out at him. c (** péj*) (*bateau*) old tub*, old wreck*; (*voiture*) old heap*, old crock*; (*machine, piano*) useless heap (of rubbish)*; (*personne*) clumsy idiot *ou* oaf. **il travaille comme un ~** he's a shoddy worker, he's a real botcher; **il joue comme un ~** he's a hopeless *ou* pathetic* player. d (*toupie*) (whipping) top. e (*Tech*) *[pied de table, poteau]* ferrule. **~ de frein** brake shoe; (*Aut*) **~ (de Denver)** wheel clamp.
sabotage [sabɔtaʒ] **nm** a (*action: Mil, Pol, fig*) sabotage; (*acte*) act of sabotage. **~ industriel** industrial sabotage. b (*bâclage*) botching.
saboter [sabɔte] 1 **vt** a (*Mil, Pol, fig*) to sabotage. b (*bâcler*) to make a (proper) mess of, botch; (*abîmer*) to mess up, ruin.
saboterie [sabɔtʀi] **nf** clog factory.
saboteur, -euse [sabɔtœʀ, øz] **nm, f** (*Mil, Pol*) saboteur; (*bâcleur*) shoddy worker, botcher.
sabotier, -ière [sabɔtje, jɛʀ] **nm, f** (*fabricant*) clog-maker; (*marchand*) clog-seller.
sabra [sabʀa] **nmf** sabra.
sabre [sɑbʀ] **nm** sabre. **~ d'abordage** cutlass; **~ de cavalerie** riding sabre; **mettre ~ au clair** to draw one's sword; **charger ~ au clair** to charge with swords drawn; (*fig*) **le ~ et le goupillon** the Army and the Church; (*fig Pol*) **bruits de ~** sabre-rattling.
sabrer [sɑbʀe] 1 **vt** a (*Mil*) to sabre, cut down. **~ le champagne** (*lit*) *to open a bottle of champagne using a sword or a knife;* (*fig*) to crack open a bottle of champagne.
b (*littér: marquer*) **la ride qui sabrait son front** the line that cut *ou* was scored across his brow; **dessin sabré de coups de crayon rageurs** drawing scored *ou* plastered with angry strokes of the pencil.
c (**: biffer*) *texte* to slash (great) chunks out of*; *passage, phrase* to cut out, scrub (out)*; *projet* to axe, chop*.
d (*) (*couler*) *étudiant* to give a hammering to*; (*renvoyer*) *employé* to sack*, fire*. **se faire ~** *[étudiant]* to get a hammering*; *[employé]* to get the sack*, get fired* *ou* sacked*.
e (**: critiquer*) *devoir* to tear to pieces *ou* to shreds; *livre, pièce* to slam*, pan*.
f (**: bâcler*) *travail* to knock off* (in a rush), belt through‡.
sabretache [sɑbʀətaʃ] **nf** sabretache.
sabreur [sɑbʀœʀ] **nm** (*péj: soldat*) fighting cock (*péj*); (*escrimeur*) swordsman.
sac¹ [sak] 1 **nm** a (*gén*) bag; (*de grande taille, en toile*) sack; (*cartable*) (school) bag; (*à bretelles*) satchel. **~ à charbon** coal-sack; **~ en plastique** plastic bag; (*pour aspirateur*) **~ à poussières** dust bag; **mettre en ~(s)** to put in sacks; *voir* **course.**
b (*contenu*) bag, bagful; sack, sackful.
c (*‡: argent*) ten francs, ≃ quid* (*Brit*), two bucks* (*US*).
d (*loc*) **habillé comme un ~** dressed like a tramp; **mettre dans le même ~*** to lump together; **l'affaire est** *ou* **c'est dans le ~*** it's in the bag*; **des gens de ~ et de corde††** gallows birds; (*Rel*) **le ~ et la cendre** sackcloth and ashes; *voir* **main, tour².**
e (*Anat*) sac.
2 **comp** ►**sac à bandoulière** shoulder bag ►**sac de couchage** sleeping bag ►**sac à dos** rucksack, knapsack ►**sac d'embrouilles** web of intrigue, can of worms; **c'est un sac d'embrouilles juridique/politique** it's a legal/political minefield ►**sac à main** handbag (*Brit*), purse (*US*) ►**sac à malice** bag of tricks ►**sac de marin** kitbag ►**sac (de montagne)** rucksack; knapsack ►**sac de nœuds*** = **sac d'embrouilles*** ►**sac d'os*** bag of bones ►**sac à ouvrage** workbag ►**sac de plage** beach bag ►**sac-poubelle (pl sacs-poubelles)** bin liner (*Brit*), garbage bag (*US*) ►**sac à provisions** shopping bag; (*en papier*) (paper) carrier (*Brit*), carrier-bag (*Brit*) ►**sac reporter** organizer bag ►**sac de sable** (*Constr, Mil*) sandbag; (*Boxe*) punchbag ►**sac à viande** (*arg Camping*) sleeping bag sheet ►**sac à vin*** (old) soak*, drunkard ►**sac de voyage** overnight bag, travelling bag; (*pour l'avion*) flight bag.
sac² [sak] **nm** *[ville]* sack, sacking. **le ~ de Rome** the sack(ing) of Rome; **mettre à ~** *ville* to sack; *maison, pièce* to ransack.
saccade [sakad] **nf** jerk. **avancer par ~s** to jerk forward *ou* along, move forward *ou* along in fits and starts *ou* jerkily; **parler par ~s** to speak haltingly *ou* in short bursts; **rire par ~s** to give a jerky laugh.
saccadé, e [sakade] **adj** *démarche, gestes, rire, style* jerky; *débit, respiration* spasmodic, halting; *bruit* staccato; *sommeil* fitful.
saccage [sakaʒ] **nm** *[pièce]* havoc (*de* in); *[jardin]* havoc, devastation (*de* in).
saccager [sakaʒe] 3 **vt** a (*dévaster*) *pièce* to turn upside down, create havoc in; *jardin* to create havoc in, wreck, devastate. **ils ont tout saccagé dans la maison** they turned the whole house upside down; **les enfants saccagent tout** children wreck everything; **champ saccagé par la grêle** field laid waste *ou* devastated by the hail. b (*piller*) *ville, pays* to sack, lay waste; *maison* to ransack.

saccageur, -euse [sakaʒœʀ, øz] nm,f (*dévastateur*) vandal; (*pillard*) pillager, plunderer.
saccharification [sakaʀifikasjɔ̃] nf saccharification.
saccharifier [sakaʀifje] 7 vt to saccharify.
saccharine [sakaʀin] nf saccharin(e).
saccharose [sakaʀoz] nm sucrose, saccharose.
SACEM [sasɛm] nf (abrév de **Société des auteurs, compositeurs et éditeurs de musique**) *French body responsible for collecting and distributing music royalties*, ≃ PRS (*Brit*).
sacerdoce [sasɛʀdɔs] nm (*Rel*) priesthood; (*fig*) calling, vocation.
sacerdotal, e, mpl **-aux** [sasɛʀdɔtal, o] adj priestly, sacerdotal.
sachem [saʃɛm] nm sachem.
sachet [saʃɛ] nm *[bonbons]* bag; *[lavande, poudre]* sachet; *[soupe]* packet. **de la soupe en ~** packet soup; **~ de thé** tea bag.
sacoche [sakɔʃ] nf (*gén*) bag; (*pour outils*) toolbag; *[cycliste]* (*de selle*) saddlebag; (*de porte-bagages*) pannier; *[écolier]* (school) bag; (*à bretelles*) satchel; *[encaisseur]* (money) bag; *[facteur]* (post-)bag.
sacquer* [sake] 1 vt a *employé* to fire, kick out‡, give the sack* (*Brit*) ou push‡ ou boot‡ to. **se faire ~** to get the sack* (*Brit*) ou push‡ ou boot‡, get (o.s.) kicked out‡. b *élève* (*sanctionner*) to give a hammering to‡; (*recaler*) to plough* (*Brit*), fail. c (*détester*) **je ne peux pas le ~** I can't stand him, I hate his guts‡.
sacral, e, mpl **-aux** [sakʀal, o] adj sacred.
sacralisation [sakʀalizasjɔ̃] nf: **la ~ des loisirs/de la famille** regarding leisure time/the family as sacred.
sacraliser [sakʀalize] 1 vt to regard as sacred, make sacred. **~ la réussite sociale/la famille** to regard social success/the family as sacred.
sacramentel, -elle [sakʀamɑ̃tɛl] adj a (*fig: rituel*) ritual, ritualistic. b (*Rel*) *rite, formule* sacramental.
sacre [sakʀ] nm a *[roi]* coronation; *[évêque]* consecration. (*Mus*) **le S~ du Printemps** the Rite of Spring. b (*Orn*) saker.
sacré, e[1] [sakʀe] (ptp de **sacrer**) 1 adj a (*après n: Rel*) *lieu, objet* sacred, holy; *art, musique* sacred; *horreur, terreur* holy; *droit* hallowed, sacred. **la fête du S~-Cœur** the Feast of the Sacred Heart; **le S~ Collège** the Sacred College (of Cardinals); *voir* **feu**.
b (*après n: inviolable*) *droit, promesse* sacred. **son sommeil, c'est ~** his sleep is sacred.
c (*: *avant n: maudit*) blasted*, confounded*, damned‡. **~ nom de nom!‡** hell and damnation!‡
d (*: *avant n: considérable*) **un ~ ...** a ou one heck* ou hell‡ of a ..., a right* ...; **c'est un ~ imbécile/menteur** he's a right idiot/liar* (*Brit*), he's one heck* ou hell‡ of an idiot/a liar; **il a un ~ toupet** he's got a ou one heck* ou hell‡ of a cheek, he's got a right cheek* (*Brit*); **elle a eu une ~e chance** she was one hell of a lucky‡.
e (*: *avant n: admiration, surprise*) **~ farceur!** you old devil (you)!*; **ce ~ Paul a encore gagné aux courses** that devil Paul ou that blinking (*Brit*) Paul has gone and won on the horses again*.
2 nm: **le ~** the sacred.
sacré, e[2] [sakʀe] adj (*Anat*) sacral.
sacrebleu*†† [sakʀəblø] excl 'struth!*† (*Brit*), confound it!
sacrement [sakʀəmɑ̃] nm sacrament. **recevoir les derniers ~s** to receive the last rites ou sacraments; **il est mort, muni des ~s de l'Église** he died fortified with the (last) rites ou sacraments of the Church; *voir* **saint**.
sacrément* [sakʀemɑ̃] adv *intéressant, laid, froid* jolly* (*Brit*), damned‡, ever so*. **j'ai eu ~ peur** I was jolly* (*Brit*) ou damned‡ ou ever so* scared; **ça m'a ~ plu** I liked it ever so much*.
sacrer [sakʀe] 1 1 vt *roi* to crown; *évêque* to consecrate. (*fig*) **il fut sacré sauveur de la patrie** he was hailed as the saviour of the country. 2 vi (*††) to curse, swear.
sacrificateur, -trice [sakʀifikatœʀ, tʀis] nm,f sacrificer; (*juif*) priest.
sacrificatoire [sakʀifikatwaʀ] adj sacrificial.
sacrifice [sakʀifis] nm (*Rel, fig*) sacrifice. **faire un ~/des ~s** to make a sacrifice/sacrifices; **faire le ~ de sa vie/d'une journée de vacances** to sacrifice one's life/a day's holiday; **offrir qch en ~ à** to offer sth as a sacrifice to; **~ de soi** self-sacrifice; *voir* **saint**.
sacrificiel, -ielle [sakʀifisjɛl] adj sacrificial.
sacrifié, e [sakʀifje] (ptp de **sacrifier**) adj *peuple, troupe* sacrificed. **les jeunes sont les ~s de notre société** the young are the sacrificial victims of our society; (*Comm*) **articles ~s** give-aways*, items given away at knockdown prices; **"prix ~s"** "giveaway prices", "rock-bottom prices", "prices slashed".
sacrifier [sakʀifje] 7 1 vt (*gén*) to sacrifice (*à* to, *pour* for); (*abandonner*) to give up; (*Comm*) *marchandises* to give away (at a knockdown price). **~ sa vie pour sa patrie** to lay down ou sacrifice one's life for one's country; **~ sa carrière** to wreck ou ruin ou sacrifice one's career; **il a dû ~ ses vacances** he had to give up his holidays. 2 **sacrifier à** vt indir *préjugés, mode* to conform to. 3 **se sacrifier** vpr to sacrifice o.s. (*à* to, *pour* for).
sacrilège [sakʀilɛʒ] 1 adj (*Rel, fig*) sacrilegious. 2 nm (*Rel, fig*) sacrilege. **ce serait un ~ de ...** it would be (a) sacrilege to ... . 3 nmf sacrilegious person.
sacripant [sakʀipɑ̃] nm (††, *hum*) rogue, scoundrel.
sacristain [sakʀistɛ̃] nm (*Rel*) *[sacristie]* sacristan; *[église]* sexton.
sacristaine [sakʀistɛn] nf sacristan.
sacristie [sakʀisti] nf (*catholique*) sacristy; (*protestante*) vestry; *voir* **punaise**.
sacristine [sakʀistin] nf = **sacristaine**.
sacro-iliaque [sakʀoiljak] adj sacroiliac.
sacro-saint, e [sakʀɔsɛ̃, sɛ̃t] adj (*lit, iro*) sacrosanct.
sacrum [sakʀɔm] nm sacrum.
sadique [sadik] 1 adj sadistic. 2 nmf sadist.
sadiquement [sadikmɑ̃] adv sadistically.
sadisme [sadism] nm sadism.
sado* [sado] 1 adj sadistic. **il est ~-maso** he's into SM‡. 2 nmf sadist.
sadomasochisme [sadomazɔʃism] nm sadomasochism.
sadomasochiste [sadomazɔʃist] 1 adj sadomasochistic. 2 nmf sadomasochist.
safari [safaʀi] nm safari. **faire un ~** to go on safari; **~-photo** photographic safari.
safran [safʀɑ̃] 1 nm a (*Bot, Culin, couleur*) saffron. **riz au ~** saffron rice. b (*Naut*) rudder blade. 2 adj inv saffron(-coloured), saffron (yellow).
safrané, e [safʀane] (ptp de **safraner**) adj *plat, couleur* saffron (*épith*); *tissu* saffron(-coloured), saffron (yellow).
safraner [safʀane] 1 vt *plat* to flavour ou season with saffron.
saga [saga] nf saga.
sagace [sagas] adj (*littér*) sagacious, shrewd.
sagacité [sagasite] nf sagacity, shrewdness. **avec ~** shrewdly.
sagaie [sagɛ] nf assegai, assagai.
sage [saʒ] 1 adj a (*avisé*) *conseil* wise, sound, sensible; *personne* wise; *action, démarche* wise, sensible. **il serait plus ~ de ...** it would be wiser ou more sensible to ..., you (ou he *etc*) would be better advised to ... .
b (*chaste*) *jeune fille* good, well-behaved.
c (*docile*) *enfant, animal* good, well-behaved. **sois ~** be good, behave yourself, be a good boy (ou girl); **~ comme une image** (as) good as gold; **il a été très ~ chez son oncle** he was very well-behaved ou he behaved (himself) very well, at his uncle's.
d (*modéré, décent*) *goûts* sober, moderate; *roman* restrained, tame. **une petite robe bien ~** a sober little dress ou number*.
2 nm wise man; (*Antiq*) sage.
sage-femme, pl **sages-femmes** [saʒfam] nf midwife.
sagement [saʒmɑ̃] adv a (*avec bon sens*) *conseiller, agir* wisely, sensibly. b (*chastement*) properly. **se conduire ~** to be good, behave o.s. (properly). c (*docilement*) quietly. **il est resté ~ assis sans rien dire** he sat quietly ou he sat like a good child (ou boy) and said nothing; **va bien ~ te coucher** be a good boy (ou girl) and go to bed, off you go to bed like a good boy (ou girl). d (*modérément*) wisely, moderately. **savoir user ~ de qch** to know how to use sth wisely ou in moderation ou moderately.
sagesse [saʒɛs] nf a (*bon sens*) *[personne]* wisdom, (good) sense; *[conseil]* soundness; *[action, démarche]* wisdom; (*expérience*) wisdom. **il a eu la ~ de** he had the wisdom ou (good) sense to, he was wise ou sensible enough to; **écouter la voix de la ~** to listen to the voice of wisdom; **la ~ des nations** popular wisdom.
b (*chasteté*) properness.
c (*docilité*) *[enfant]* good behaviour. **il est la ~ même** he is the model of a well-behaved child; **il a été d'une ~ exemplaire** he has been very good, he has behaved himself very well, he has been a model child; *voir* **dent**.
d (*modération*) moderation. **savoir utiliser qch avec ~** to know how to use sth wisely ou in moderation.
Sagittaire [saʒitɛʀ] nm (*Astron*) **le ~** Sagittarius, the Archer; **être (du) ~** to be (a) Sagittarius ou a Sagittarian.
sagittal, e, mpl **-aux** [saʒital, o] adj sagittal.
sagouin, e [sagwɛ̃, in] 1 nm a (*singe*) marmoset. b (‡: *homme*) (*sale*) filthy pig‡, filthy slob‡; (*méchant*) swine‡; (*incompétent*) bungling idiot*. 2 **sagouine‡** nf (*sale*) filthy cow‡; (*méchante*) useless bitch‡; (*incompétente*) useless cow‡.
Sahara [saaʀa] nm: **le ~** the Sahara (desert); **le ~ occidental** Western Sahara.
saharien, -ienne [saaʀjɛ̃, jɛn] 1 adj (*du Sahara*) Saharan; (*très chaud*) tropical. (*costume*) **ensemble ~** safari suit. 2 **saharienne** nf (*veste*) safari jacket; (*chemise*) safari shirt.
Sahel [saɛl] nm: **le ~** the Sahel.
sahélien, -ienne [saeljɛ̃, jɛn] 1 adj Sahelian. 2 nm,f: **S~(ne)** Sahelian.
sahib [saib] nm sahib.
sahraoui, e [saʀawi] 1 adj Western Saharan. 2 nm,f: **S~(e)** Western Saharan.
saignant, e [sɛɲɑ̃, ɑ̃t] adj *plaie* (*lit*) bleeding; (*fig*) raw; *entrecôte* rare, underdone; (‡) *critique* scathing, savage, biting; *mésaventure* bloody (*Brit*) ou damned nasty‡. **je n'aime pas le ~** I don't like underdone meat.
saignée [seɲe] nf a (*Méd*) (*épanchement*) bleeding (*NonC*); (*opération*) blood letting (*NonC*), bleeding (*NonC*). **faire une ~ à qn** to bleed sb, let sb's blood. b (*fig: perte*) *[budget]* savage cut

(*à, dans* in). **les ~s que j'ai dû faire sur mon salaire/mes économies pour** ... the huge holes I had to make in my salary/savings to ...; **les ~s faites dans le pays par la guerre** the heavy losses incurred by the country in the war. c (*Anat*) **la ~ du bras** the bend of the arm. d (*sillon*) *[sol]* trench, ditch; *[mur]* groove.

saignement [sɛɲmɑ̃] **nm** bleeding (*NonC*). **~ de nez** nosebleed.

saigner [seɲe] [1] 1 **vi** a to bleed. **il saigne comme un bœuf** blood is gushing out of him; **il saignait du nez** he had (a) nosebleed, his nose was bleeding. b (*fig littér*) *[orgueil, dignité]* to sting, bleed (*littér*). **mon cœur saigne** *ou* **le cœur me saigne encore** my heart is still bleeding (*littér*). 2 **vt** a *animal* to kill (*by bleeding*); *malade* to bleed. b (*exploiter*) to bleed. **~ qn à blanc** to bleed sb white. 3 **se saigner vpr: se ~ (aux quatre veines) pour qn** to bleed o.s. white for sb, sacrifice o.s. for sb.

Saigon [saigɔ̃] **nm** Saigon.

saillant, e [sajɑ̃, ɑ̃t] 1 **adj** a *menton* prominent, protruding (*épith*), jutting (*épith*); *front, muscle, veine* protruding (*épith*), prominent, protuberant; *pommette* prominent; *yeux* bulging (*épith*), protuberant, protruding (*épith*); *corniche* projecting (*épith*); *voir* **angle.** b *événement, trait, point* salient, outstanding. 2 **nm** (*avancée*) salient.

saillie [saji] **nf** a (*aspérité*) projection. **faire ~** to project, jut out; **qui forme ~, en ~** projecting, overhanging; **rocher qui s'avance en ~** rock which sticks *ou* juts out. b (*littér: boutade*) witticism. c (*Zool: accouplement*) covering, serving.

saillir[1] [sajiʀ] [13] **vi** *[balcon, corniche]* to jut out, stick out, project; *[menton]* to jut out, protrude; *[poitrine, pommette]* to be prominent; *[muscle, veine]* to protrude, stand out; *[yeux]* to bulge, protrude.

saillir[2] [sajiʀ] [2] 1 **vi** (*littér: jaillir*) to gush forth. 2 **vt** (*Zool*) to cover, serve.

sain, saine [sɛ̃, sɛn] **adj** a (*en bonne santé*) *personne* healthy; *constitution, dents* healthy, sound. **être/arriver ~ et sauf** to be/arrive safe and sound; **il est sorti ~ et sauf de l'accident** he escaped unharmed *ou* safe and sound from the accident; **~ de corps et d'esprit** sound in body and mind; *voir* **porteur.**

b (*salubre*) *climat* healthy; *nourriture* healthy, wholesome. **il est ~ de se promener après le repas** it is good for you *ou* healthy to take a walk after meals; **il est ~ de rire de temps en temps** it's good (for one) to laugh from time to time.

c (*non abîmé*) *fruit* sound; *viande* good; *mur, fondations* sound; (*fig*) *gestion, affaire* healthy.

d (*moralement*) *personne* sane; *politique, jugement* sound, sane; *idées, goûts, humeur* healthy; *lectures* wholesome.

e (*Naut*) *rade* clear, safe.

saindoux [sɛ̃du] **nm** lard.

sainement [sɛnmɑ̃] **adv** *vivre* healthily; *manger* healthily, wholesomely; *juger* sanely; *raisonner* soundly. **être ~ logé** to have healthy accommodation.

sainfoin [sɛ̃fwɛ̃] **nm** sainfoin.

saint, sainte [sɛ̃, sɛ̃t] 1 **adj** a (*sacré*) *semaine, image* holy. **la s~e Bible** the Holy Bible; **les S~es Écritures** the Holy Scriptures, Holy Scripture; **les ~es huiles** the holy oils; **la ~e Croix/S~e Famille** the Holy Cross/Family; **s'approcher de la ~e table** to take communion; **le vendredi ~** Good Friday; **le jeudi ~** Maundy Thursday; **le mercredi/mardi ~** Wednesday/Tuesday before Easter, the Wednesday/Tuesday of Holy Week; **le samedi ~** Easter Saturday; *voir* **guerre, lieu, semaine, terre.**

b (*devant prénom*) Saint. (*apôtre*) **~ Pierre/Paul** Saint Peter/Paul; (*église*) **S~-Pierre/-Paul** Saint Peter's/Paul's; (*fête*) **ils ont fêté la S~-Pierre** they celebrated the feast of Saint Peter; (*jour*) **le jour de la S~-Pierre, à la S~-Pierre** (on) Saint Peter's day; **à la S~-Michel/-Martin** at Michaelmas/Martinmas; *voir aussi* **saint-pierre.**

c (*pieux*) *personne, pensée* saintly, godly; *vie, action* pious, saintly, holy.

d (* *loc*) **toute la ~e journée** the whole blessed day*; **avoir une ~e terreur de qch** to have a holy terror of sth*; **être saisi d'une ~e colère** to fly into an almighty rage; **il est arrivé avec tout son ~-frusquin** he has arrived with all his clobber* (*Brit*) *ou* gear*; **il y avait le frère, l'oncle, le chat et tout le ~-frusquin** there were the brother, the uncle, the cat – Old Uncle Tom Cobbly and all* (*Brit*); **à la ~-glinglin** never in a month of Sundays; **il te le rendra à la ~-glinglin** he'll never give it back to you in a month of Sundays; **attendre jusqu'à la ~-glinglin** to wait till the cows come home; **on ne va pas rester là jusqu'à la ~-glinglin** we're not going to hang around here forever*; *voir* **danse.**

2 **nm, f** (*lit, fig*) saint. **il veut se faire passer pour un (petit) ~** he wants to pass for a saint; **elle a la patience d'une ~e** she has the patience of a saint *ou* of Job; **un ~ de bois/pierre** a wooden/stone statue of a saint; **la fête de tous les ~s** All Saints' Day; (*fig*) **ce n'est pas un ~** he's no saint; *voir* **prêcher, savoir.**

3 **comp** ►**la Sainte-Alliance** (*Hist*) the Holy Alliance ►**la Saint-Barthélemy** (*Hist*) St Bartholomew's Day Massacre ►**saint-bernard nm inv** (*chien*) St Bernard; (*fig*) good Samaritan ►**le saint chrême** the chrism, the holy oil ►**Saint-Cyr** French military academy ►**saint-cyrien nm (pl saint-cyriens)** (military) cadet (*of the Saint-Cyr academy*) ►**Saint-Domingue** Santo Domingo ►**le Saint Empire romain germanique** the Holy Roman Empire ►**le Saint-Esprit** the Holy Spirit *ou* Ghost (*voir* **opération**) ►**les saints de glace** the 11th, 12th and 13th of May ►**Sainte-Hélène** St Helena ►**saint-honoré nm (pl saint-honoré(s))** Saint Honoré (gâteau) ►**Saints-Innocents: le jour des Saints-Innocents** Holy Innocents Day ►**Saint-Jacques-de-Compostelle** Santiago de Compostela ►**la Saint-Jean** Midsummer('s) Day ►**le Saint-Laurent** the St Lawrence (river) ►**Sainte-Lucie** Saint Lucia ►**Saint-Marin** San Marino ►**la Saint-Nicolas** St Nicholas's day ►**sainte nitouche** (*péj*) (pious *ou* saintly) hypocrite; **c'est une sainte nitouche** she looks as if butter wouldn't melt in her mouth; **de sainte nitouche** *attitude, air* hypocritically pious ►**le Saint-Office** the Holy Office ►**saint patron** patron saint ►**Saint-Père** Holy Father ►**Saint-Pierre-et-Miquelon** Saint Pierre and Miquelon ►**le Saint-Sacrement** the Blessed Sacrament; **porter qch comme le Saint Sacrement** to carry sth with infinite care *ou* as if it were the Crown Jewels ►**le saint sacrifice** the Holy Sacrifice of the Mass ►**le Saint des Saints** (*Rel, fig*) the Holy of Holies ►**le Saint-Sépulcre** the Holy Sepulchre ►**le Saint-Siège** the Holy See ►**saint-simonien, -ienne adj, nm, f (mpl saint-simoniens)** Saint-Simonian ►**saint-simonisme nm** Saint-Simonism ►**Sainte-Sophie nf** Saint Sophia ►**le saint suaire** the Holy Shroud; **le saint suaire de Turin** the Turin Shroud ►**la Saint-Sylvestre** New Year's Eve ►**le Saint-Synode** the holy synod ►**la sainte Trinité** the Holy Trinity ►**la Saint-Valentin** Saint Valentine's day ►**la Sainte Vierge** the Blessed Virgin ►**Saint-Vincent et (les) Grenadines npl** Saint Vincent and the Grenadines.

saintement [sɛ̃tmɑ̃] **adv** *agir, mourir* like a saint. **vivre ~** to lead a saintly *ou* holy life, live like a saint.

sainteté [sɛ̃tte] **nf** a *[personne]* saintliness, godliness; *[Évangile, Vierge]* holiness; *[lieu]* holiness, sanctity; *[mariage]* sanctity; *voir* **odeur.** b **Sa S~ (le pape)** His Holiness (the Pope).

saint-pierre [sɛ̃pjɛʀ] **nm inv** (*poisson*) dory, John Dory.

saisi [sezi] **nm** (*Jur*) distrainee.

saisie [sezi] 1 **nf** a *[biens]* seizure, distraint (*SPÉC*), distress (*SPÉC*). b *[publication, articles prohibés]* seizure, confiscation. c (*capture*) capture. d (*Ordin*) **~ de données** data capture *ou* keyboarding. 2 **comp** ►**saisie-arrêt nf (pl saisies-arrêts)** distraint, attachment ►**saisie conservatoire** seizure of goods (*to prevent sale etc*) ►**saisie-exécution nf (pl saisies-exécutions)** distraint (*for sale by court order*) ►**saisie-gagerie nf (pl saisies-gageries)** seizure of goods (*by landlord in lieu of unpaid rent*) ►**saisie immobilière** seizure of property.

saisine [sezin] **nf** a (*Jur*) submission of a case to the court. b (*Naut: cordage*) lashing.

saisir [seziʀ] [2] 1 **vt** a (*prendre*) to take hold of, catch hold of; (*s'emparer de*) to seize, grab (hold of). **~ qn à la gorge** to grab *ou* seize sb by the throat; **~ un ballon au vol** to catch a ball (in mid air); **il lui saisit le bras pour l'empêcher de sauter** he grabbed (hold of) *ou* seized his arm to stop him jumping; **ils le saisirent à bras-le-corps** they took hold of *ou* seized him bodily.

b (*fig*) *occasion* to seize; *prétexte* to seize (on). **~ une occasion/la chance au vol** to jump at the opportunity/the chance; **~ l'occasion par les cheveux*** to grasp the opportunity when it arises; **~ la balle au bond** to jump at the opportunity (while the going is good).

c (*entendre*) *mot, nom* to catch, get; (*comprendre*) *explications* to grasp, understand, get. **il a saisi quelques noms au vol** he caught *ou* overheard various names in passing; **d'un coup d'œil, il saisit ce qui se passait** at a glance he understood what was going on; **tu saisis ce que je veux dire?*** do you get it?*, do you get what I mean?

d *[peur]* to take hold of, seize, grip; *[colère, allégresse]* to take hold of, come over; *[malaise]* to come over. **le froid l'a saisi** *ou* **il a été saisi par le froid en sortant** he was struck *ou* gripped by the sudden cold as he went out; **saisi de joie** overcome with joy; **saisi de peur** seized *ou* gripped by fear, transfixed with fear; **saisi de panique/d'horreur** panic-/horror-stricken.

e (*impressionner, surprendre*) **~ qn** to bring sb up with a start; **la ressemblance entre les 2 sœurs le saisit** he was brought up short *ou* with a start by the resemblance between the 2 sisters; **être saisi par** *horreur* to be gripped by, be transfixed with; *beauté, grâce* to be captivated by; **son air de franchise a saisi tout le monde** his apparent frankness struck everybody; **elle fut tellement saisie que** ... she was so overcome that ... .

f (*Jur*) (*procéder à la saisie de*) *biens* to seize, distrain (*SPÉC*); *personne* to take into custody, seize; (*porter devant*) *juridiction* to submit *ou* refer to. **~ le Conseil de sécurité d'une affaire** to submit *ou* refer a matter to the Security Council; **~ la Cour de justice** to complain to the Court of Justice; **la cour a été saisie de l'affaire** the case has been submitted *ou* referred to the court.

g (*Culin*) *viande* to seal, fry quickly, fry over a fierce heat.

h (*Ordin*) to capture, keyboard.

2 **se saisir vpr: se ~ de qch/qn** to seize *ou* grab sth/sb.

saisissable [sezisabl] **adj** a *nuance, sensation* perceptible. b (*Jur*) seizable, distrainable (*SPÉC*).

saisissant, e [sezisɑ̃, ɑ̃t] 1 **adj** a *spectacle* gripping; *ressemblance, différence* startling, striking; *froid* biting, piercing. b (*Jur*) distraining. 2 **nm** (*Jur*) distrainer.

saisissement [sezismɑ̃] **nm** (*frisson de froid*) sudden chill; (*émotion*) (sudden) agitation, (rush of) emotion.

saison [sɛzɔ̃] **nf** a (*division de l'année*) season. **la belle/mauvaise ~** the summer/winter months; (*littér*) **la ~ nouvelle** springtide (*littér*); **en cette ~** at this time of year; **en toutes ~s** all (the) year round; **il fait un temps de ~** the weather is right *ou* what one would expect for the time of year, the weather is seasonable.
b (*époque*) season. **~ des amours/des fraises/théâtrale/touristique** mating/strawberry/theatre/tourist season; **la ~ des pluies** the rainy *ou* wet season; **la ~ des moissons/des vendanges** harvest/grape-harvest(ing) time; **les nouvelles toilettes de la ~** the new season's fashions; **nous faisons la ~ sur la Côte d'Azur** we're working on the Côte d'Azur during the season; **haute/basse ~** high/low *ou* off season; **en (haute) ~ les prix sont plus chers** in the high season *ou* at the height of the season prices are higher; *voir* **marchand, mort², voiture.**
c (*cure*) stay (*at a spa*), cure.
d (*loc*) **hors ~** *plante* out of season (*attrib*); *prix* off-season (*épith*), low-season (*épith*); **prendre ses vacances hors ~** *ou* **en basse ~** to go on holiday in the off season *ou* low season; **faire preuve d'un optimisme de ~** to show fitting optimism; (*littér*) **vos plaisanteries ne sont pas de ~** your jokes are totally out of place.

saisonnier, -ière [sɛzɔnje, jɛʀ] 1 **adj** seasonal. 2 **nm, f** (*ouvrier*) seasonal worker; (*vacancier*) holiday-maker (*Brit*), vacationer (*US*).

saké [sake] **nm** sake.

salace [salas] **adj** (*littér*) salacious.

salacité [salasite] **nf** (*littér*) salaciousness, salacity.

salade [salad] **nf** a (*plante*) (*laitue*) lettuce; (*scarole*) curly endive. **la laitue est une ~** lettuce is a salad vegetable. b (*plat*) green salad. **~ de tomates/de fruits/russe** tomato/fruit/Russian salad; **~ niçoise** salade niçoise; **~ composée** mixed salad; **haricots en ~** bean salad; *voir* **panier.** c (* *fig: confusion*) tangle, muddle. d (* *fig: mensonges*) **~s** stories*; **raconter des ~s** to spin yarns, tell stories*; *[représentant]* **vendre sa ~** to sell one's line. e *[armure]* sallet.

saladier [saladje] **nm** salad bowl.

salage [salaʒ] **nm** salting.

salaire [salɛʀ] **nm** a (*mensuel*) salary, pay; (*journalier, hebdomadaire*) wage(s), pay. **famille à ~ unique** single income family; (*allocation*) **toucher le ~ unique** ≃ to get income support (*Brit*); **~ de famine** *ou* **de misère** starvation wage; **~ minimum** minimum wage; **~ minimum agricole garanti** *guaranteed minimum agricultural wage;* **~ minimum interprofessionnel de croissance, ~ minimum interprofessionnel garanti†** (index-linked) guaranteed minimum wage; **~ de base** basic pay; **~ indirect** employer's contributions; **~ brut/net** gross/net pay, ≃ before-tax/tax-deducted *ou* disposable income; *voir* **augmentation, bulletin.**
b (*fig: récompense*) reward (*de* for); (*châtiment*) reward, retribution, recompense (*de* for); *voir* **tout.**

salaison [salɛzɔ̃] **nf** a (*procédé*) salting. b (*aliment*) (*viande*) salt meat; (*poisson*) salt fish.

salamalecs* [salamalɛk] **nmpl** (*péj*) exaggerated politeness. **faire des ~** to be ridiculously overpolite.

salamandre [salamɑ̃dʀ] **nf** a (*Zool*) salamander. b (*poêle*) slow-combustion stove.

salami [salami] **nm** salami.

Salamine [salamin] **n** Salamis.

salant [salɑ̃] **adj m** *voir* **marais.**

salarial, e, **mpl -iaux** [salaʀjal, jo] **adj** (*voir* **salaire**) salary (*épith*); pay (*épith*); wage(s) (*épith*). **conventions ~es** salary agreements; **politique ~e** pay policy; *voir* **masse.**

salariat [salaʀja] **nm** a (*voir* **salaire**) (*salariés*) salaried class; wage-earning class; (*mode de paiement*) payment by salary; payment by wages. b (*condition*) (being in) employment. **être réduit au ~ après avoir été patron** to be reduced to the ranks of the employees *ou* of the salaried staff after having been in a senior position.

salarié, e [salaʀje] 1 **adj** a (*voir* **salaire**) *travailleur* salaried (*épith*); wage-earning. b *travail* paid. 2 **nm, f** (*voir* **salaire**) salaried employee; wage-earner.

salaud‡ [salo] 1 **nm** bastard‡‡, sod‡‡ (*Brit*), swine‡. **alors mon ~, tu ne t'en fais pas!** well you old bugger – you're not exactly overdoing it!‡‡; **10 000 F? ben, mon ~!** 10,000 francs, bugger me!‡‡ (*Brit*). 2 **adj: tu es ~** you're an absolute bastard‡‡ *ou* sod‡‡ (*Brit*) *ou* swine‡; **il a été ~ avec elle** he was a real bastard to her‡‡; **c'est ~ d'avoir fait ça** that was a shitty‡ thing to do.

sale [sal] 1 **adj** a (*crasseux*) dirty. **j'ai les mains/pieds ~s** I've got dirty hands/feet, my hands/feet are dirty; **blanc ~** dirty white; **~ comme un cochon** *ou* **un porc** *ou* **un peigne** filthy (dirty); **oh la ~!** you dirty girl!; **c'est pas ~!*** it's not bad!*; *voir* **laver.**
b (*ordurier*) *histoire* dirty, filthy.
c (*: *avant n: mauvais*) nasty. **~ bête** nasty *ou* foul creature; (*fig*) **~ coup*** (*sale tour*) dirty trick*; (*choc*) real *ou* terrible blow; **~ gosse** horrible brat, nasty little brat; **~ temps** filthy* *ou* foul *ou* lousy* weather; **~ tour** dirty trick; **~ type** foul *ou* nasty character, nasty piece of work; **avoir une ~ gueule‡** to have a nasty face; **faire une ~ gueule‡** to look bloody‡ (*Brit*) *ou* damned‡ annoyed; **il m'est arrivé une ~ histoire** something really nasty *ou* rotten* happened to me; **il a un ~ caractère** he has a foul *ou* rotten* *ou* lousy* temper, he's foul-tempered.
2 **nm: mettre un vêtement au ~** to put a garment in the wash; **ta chemise est au ~** your shirt is in the wash.

salé, e [sale] (**ptp de saler**) 1 **adj** a (*contenant du sel*) *saveur, mer* salty; (*additionné de sel*) *amande, plat* salted; *gâteau* (*non sucré*) savoury; (*au goût ~*) salty; (*conservé au sel*) *poisson, viande* salt (*épith*); *beurre* salted; *voir* **eau, pré.** b (*: *grivois*) spicy, juicy, fruity‡. c (*: *sévère*) *punition* stiff; *facture* steep. 2 **nm** (*nourriture*) salty food; (*porc salé*) salt pork. **préférer le ~ au sucré** to prefer savoury *ou* salty (*US*) foods to sweet; *voir* **petit.** 3 **adv: manger ~** to like a lot of salt on one's food, like one's food well salted; **avec son régime, il ne peut pas manger trop ~** with his diet he can't have his food too salty.

salement [salmɑ̃] **adv** a (*malproprement, bassement*) dirtily. b (‡: *très*) *dur, embêtant* bloody‡ (*Brit*), damned‡. **j'ai ~ mal** it's bloody (*Brit*) *ou* damned painful‡, it hurts like mad*; **j'ai eu ~ peur** I had a *ou* one hell of a fright‡, I was bloody (*Brit*) *ou* damned scared‡.

saler [sale] 1 **vt** a *plat, soupe* to put salt in, salt; *chaussée* to salt; (*pour conserver*) to salt. **tu ne sales pas assez** you don't put enough salt in, you don't use enough salt. b (*) *client* to do*, fleece; *facture* to bump up*; *inculpé* to be tough on*.

Salerne [salɛʀn] **n** Salerno.

saleté [salte] **nf** a (*malpropreté*) *[lieu, personne]* dirtiness.
b (*crasse*) dirt, filth. **murs couverts de ~** walls covered in dirt *ou* filth; **vivre dans la ~** to live in filth *ou* squalor; **le chauffage au charbon fait de la ~** coal heating makes a lot of mess *ou* dirt, coal is a dirty *ou* messy way to heat; **tu as fait de la ~ en réparant le moteur** you've made a mess repairing the motor.
c (*ordure*) dirt (*NonC*). **il y a une ~ par terre/sur ta robe** there's some dirt *ou* muck on the floor/your dress; **j'ai une ~ dans l'œil** I've got some dirt in my eye; **tu as fait des ~s partout en perçant le mur** you've made a mess all over the place *ou* you've dirtied everything drilling the wall; **enlève tes ~s de ma chambre** get your (old) rubbish out of my room; **le chat a fait des ~s** *ou* **ses ~s dans le salon** the cat has done its business *ou* made a mess in the lounge.
d (*: *chose sans valeur*) rubbish (*NonC*), junk (*NonC*). **ce réfrigérateur est une ~** *ou* **de la vraie ~** this fridge is a load of old rubbish*; **c'est une ~ qu'ils ont achetée en vacances** it's some (old) junk *ou* rubbish *ou* trash they bought on holiday*; **chez eux, il n'y a que des ~s** (*bibelots*) there's junk *ou* trash *ou* rubbishy stuff lying about all over their place*; (*meubles*) they've just got cheap and nasty stuff *ou* (cheap) rubbish *ou* junk at their place*; **on n'a qu'à acheter une ~ quelconque au gosse** we only need to get some rubbishy toy *ou* some bit of junk *ou* rubbish *ou* trash for the kid*; **il se bourre de ~s avant le repas** he stuffs himself with junk food *ou* rubbish before meals*.
e (*: *maladie*) **je me demande où j'ai bien pu attraper cette ~-là** I wonder where on earth I could have caught this blasted thing* *ou* bug*; **cet enfant récolte toutes les ~s qui traînent** this child catches every blasted thing going*.
f (*: *obscénité*) dirty *ou* filthy thing (to say)*. **dire des ~s** to say filthy things*, talk filth*.
g (*: *méchanceté*) dirty *ou* filthy trick*. **faire une ~ à qn** to play a dirty *ou* filthy trick on sb*; **on en a vu, des ~s pendant la guerre** we saw plenty of disgusting things during the war.
h (*: *salaud*) nasty piece of work*, nasty character.

salicylate [salisilat] **nm** salicylate.

salicylique [salisilik] **adj: acide ~** salicylic acid.

salière [saljɛʀ] **nf** (*récipient*), (*) *[clavicule]* saltcellar.

salifère [salifɛʀ] **adj** saliferous.

salification [salifikasjɔ̃] **nf** salification.

salifier [salifje] 7 **vt** to salify.

saligaud‡ [saligo] **nm** (*malpropre*) dirty *ou* filthy pig‡; (*salaud*) swine‡, bastard‡‡.

salin, e [salɛ̃, in] 1 **adj** saline. 2 **nm** salt marsh. 3 **saline nf** (*entreprise*) saltworks; (*salin*) salt marsh.

salinité [salinite] **nf** salinity.

salique [salik] **adj** Salic, Salian. **loi ~** Salic law.

salir [saliʀ] 2 1 **vt** a *lieu* to (make) dirty, mess up*, make a mess in; *objet* to (make) dirty, soil. **le charbon salit** coal is messy *ou* dirty. b *imagination* to corrupt, defile; *réputation* to sully, soil, tarnish. **~ qn** to sully *ou* soil *ou* tarnish sb's reputation. 2 **se salir vpr** a *[tissu]* to get dirty *ou* soiled; *[personne]* to get dirty, dirty o.s. **le blanc se salit facilement** white shows the dirt (easily), white soils easily; (*lit, fig*) **se ~ les mains** to get one's hands dirty, dirty one's hands. b (*se déshonorer*) to sully *ou* soil *ou* tarnish one's reputation.

salissant, e [salisɑ̃, ɑ̃t] **adj** *étoffe* which shows the dirt, which soils easily; *travail* dirty, messy.

salissure [salisyʀ] **nf** (*saleté*) dirt, filth; (*tache*) dirty mark.

salivaire [salivɛʀ] **adj** salivary.

salivation [salivasjɔ̃] **nf** salivation.

salive [saliv] **nf** saliva, spittle. (*fig*) **épargne** *ou* **ne gaspille pas ta ~** save your breath, don't waste your breath; **dépenser beaucoup de ~ pour convaincre qn** to have to do a lot of talking *ou* use a lot of breath to persuade sb.

saliver [salive] 1 vi to salivate; *[animal]*, (*péj*) to drool. **ça le faisait ~** *[nourriture]* it made his mouth water; *[spectacle]* it made him drool.

salle [sal] 1 nf a *[musée, café]* room; *[château]* hall; *[restaurant]* (dining) room; *[hôpital]* ward; *voir* **fille, garçon**.
b (*Ciné, Théât*) (*auditorium*) auditorium, theatre; (*public*) audience; (*cinéma*) cinema (*Brit*), movie theater (*US*). **plusieurs ~s de quartier ont dû fermer** several local cinemas had to close down; **faire ~ comble** to have a full house, pack the house; **cinéma à plusieurs ~s** film-centre with several cinemas; **film projeté dans la ~ 3** film showing in cinema 3.
2 comp ▸**salle d'armes** arms room ▸**salle d'attente** waiting room ▸**salle d'audience** courtroom ▸**salle de bain(s)** bathroom ▸**salle de bal** ballroom ▸**salle de banquets** *[château]* banqueting hall ▸**salle de billard** billiard room ▸**salle du chapitre** (*Rel*) chapter room ▸**salle de cinéma** cinema (*Brit*), movie theater (*US*) ▸**salle de classe** classroom ▸**salle commune** *[colonie de vacances etc]* commonroom; *[hôpital]* ward ▸**salle de concert** concert hall ▸**salle de conférences** lecture *ou* conference room; (*grande*) lecture hall *ou* theatre ▸**salle de cours** classroom ▸**salle de douches** shower-room, showers (*pl*) ▸**salle d'eau** shower-room ▸**salle d'embarquement** (*Aviat*) departure lounge ▸**salle d'étude(s)** prep room ▸**salle d'exposition** (*Comm*) showroom ▸**salle des fêtes** village hall ▸**salle de garde** staff waiting room (*in hospital*) ▸**salle de jeu** (*pour enfants*) playroom; *[casino]* gaming room ▸**salle des machines** engine room ▸**salle à manger** (*pièce*) dining room; (*meubles*) dining room suite ▸**les salles obscures** the cinemas (*Brit*), the movie theaters (*US*) ▸**salle d'opération** operating theatre (*Brit*) *ou* room (*US*) ▸**salle des pas perdus** (waiting) hall ▸**salle de police** guardhouse, guardroom ▸**salle des professeurs** common room, staff room ▸**salle de projection** film theatre ▸**salle de réanimation** recovery room ▸**salle de rédaction** (newspaper) office ▸**salle de réveil** observation ward ▸**salle de séjour** living room ▸**salle de soins** treatment room ▸**salle de spectacle** theatre, cinema ▸**salle du trône** throne room ▸**salle des ventes** saleroom, auction room.

salmigondis [salmigɔ̃di] nm (*Culin, fig*) hotchpotch (*Brit*), hodgepodge (*US*).

salmis [salmi] nm salmi. **~ de perdreaux** salmi of partridges.

salmonella [salmɔnɛla] nf, **salmonelle** [salmɔnɛl] nf salmonella.

salmonellose [salmɔneloz] nf salmonellosis.

salmoniculture [salmɔnikyltyʀ] nf salmon farming.

saloir [salwaʀ] nm salting-tub.

Salomé [salɔme] nf Salome.

Salomon [salɔmɔ̃] nm Solomon. **le jugement de ~** the judgment of Solomon; **les îles ~** the Solomon Islands.

salomonien, -ienne [salomonjɛ̃, jɛn] 1 adj Solomonian. 2 **S~(ne)** nm, f Solomonian.

salon [salɔ̃] 1 nm a *[appartement, maison]* lounge (*Brit*), sitting room, living room; *[hôtel]* lounge; *[navire]* saloon, lounge.
b (*hôtel*) (*pour les clients*) lounge; (*pour conférences, réceptions*) function room.
c (*meubles*) lounge (*Brit*) *ou* living-room suite; (*de trois pièces*) three-piece suite. **~ de jardin** set of garden furniture.
d (*exposition*) exhibition, show.
e (*cercle littéraire*) salon. (*hum*) **faire ~** to have a natter*; *voir* **dernier**.
2 comp ▸**Salon des Arts ménagers** ≃ Ideal Home *ou* Modern Homes Exhibition (*Brit*) ▸**salon d'attente** waiting room ▸**Salon de l'Auto** Motor *ou* Car Show ▸**salon de beauté** beauty salon *ou* parlour ▸**salon de coiffure** hairdressing salon ▸**salon d'essayage** fitting room ▸**salon funéraire** (*Can*) funeral parlour, funeral home *ou* parlor (*US*) ▸**Salon du Livre** Book Fair ▸**salon particulier** private room ▸**salon de réception** reception room ▸**salon-salle à manger** living (room) cum dining room, living-dining room ▸**salon de thé** tearoom.

saloon [salun] nm (*Far-West*) saloon.

salop‡ [salo] nm = **salaud‡**.

salopard‡ [salɔpaʀ] nm bastard**‡, sod**‡ (*Brit*).

salope‡** [salɔp] nf (*méchante, déloyale*) bitch‡, cow‡ (*Brit*); (*dévergondée*) whore, tart‡ (*Brit*); (*sale*) slut.

saloper‡ [salɔpe] 1 vt (*bâcler*) to botch, bungle, make a mess of; (*salir*) to mess up*, muck up*.

saloperie‡ [salɔpʀi] nf a (*chose sans valeur*) trash* (*NonC*), junk (*NonC*), rubbish (*NonC*). **ce transistor est une ~ ou de la vraie ~** this transistor is absolute trash *ou* rubbish; **ils n'achètent que des ~s** they only buy trash *ou* junk *ou* rubbish.
b (*mauvaise nourriture*) muck* (*NonC*), rubbish* (*NonC*). **ils nous ont fait manger de la ~ ou des ~s** they gave us awful muck *ou* rubbish to eat*; **c'est bon, ces petites ~s** these little bits and pieces are really good.
c (*maladie*) **il a dû attraper une ~ en vacances** he must have caught something *ou* a bug* on holiday; **il récolte toutes les ~s** he gets every blasted thing going*.
d (*ordure*) dirt (*NonC*), mess (*NonC*), muck* (*NonC*). **le grenier est plein de ~s** the attic is full of junk *ou* rubbish; **quand on ramone la cheminée ça fait des ~s ou de la ~ partout** when the chimney gets swept there's dirt *ou* muck* *ou* (a) mess everywhere; **va faire tes ~s ailleurs** go and make your mess somewhere else.
e (*action*) dirty trick*; (*parole*) bitchy remark*. **faire une ~ à qn** to play a dirty *ou* a lousy trick on sb*, do the dirty on sb*.
f (*obscénités*) **~s** dirty *ou* filthy remarks*; **dire des ~s** to talk filth*, say filthy things*.
g (*crasse*) filth.

salopette [salɔpɛt] nf *[ouvrier]* overall(s); *[femme, enfant]* dungarees; (*Ski*) salopettes (*Brit*).

salpêtre [salpɛtʀ] nm saltpetre.

salpêtrer [salpetʀe] 1 vt a (*Agr*) *terre* to add saltpetre to. b *mur* to cover with saltpetre. **cave salpêtrée** cellar covered with saltpetre.

salpingite [salpɛ̃ʒit] nf salpingitis.

salsa [salsa] nf salsa.

salsifis [salsifi] nm salsify, oyster-plant.

SALT [salt] (abrév de **Strategic Arms Limitation Talks**) SALT.

saltimbanque [saltɛ̃bɑ̃k] nmf (travelling) performer;

salto [salto] nm salto. **~ avant/arrière** forward/backward somersault; **double ~** double somersault.

salubre [salybʀ] adj healthy, salubrious (*frm*).

salubrité [salybʀite] nf *[lieu, région, climat]* healthiness, salubrity (*frm*), salubriousness (*frm*). **par mesure de ~** as a health measure; **~ publique** public health.

saluer [salɥe] 1 vt a (*dire bonjour*) to greet. **se découvrir/s'incliner pour ~ qn** to raise one's hat/bow to sb (in greeting); **~ qn de la main** to wave (one's hand) to sb (in greeting); **~ qn d'un signe de tête** to nod (a greeting) to sb; **~ qn à son arrivée** to greet sb on his arrival; **~ une dame dans sa loge** to pay one's respects to a lady in her box; **saluez-le de ma part** give him my regards.
b (*dire au revoir*) to take one's leave. **il nous salua et sortit** he took his leave (of us) and went out; **~ qn à son départ** to take one's leave of sb (as one goes); **acteur qui salue (le public)** actor who bows to the audience.
c (*Mil, Naut*) *supérieur, drapeau, navire* to salute.
d (*témoigner son respect*) *ennemi vaincu, heroïsme* to salute. **nous saluons en vous l'homme qui a sauvé tant de vies** we salute you as the man who has saved so many lives; **je salue le courage des sauveteurs** I salute the courage of the rescuers.
e (*célébrer, acclamer*) *décision, événement* to greet; *arrivée* to greet, hail. **~ qn comme roi** to acclaim *ou* hail sb (as) king; (*Rel*) **"je vous salue, Marie"** "Hail, Mary"; **nous saluons la naissance d'un nouveau journal** we greet *ou* salute the birth of a new newspaper; (*hum*) **il/son arrivée fut salué(e) par des huées** he/his arrival was greeted with *ou* by booing.

salut [saly] 1 nm a (*de la main*) wave (of the hand); (*de la tête*) nod (of the head); (*du buste*) bow; (*Mil, Naut*) salute. **faire un ~** to wave (one's hand); to nod (one's head); to bow; **faire le ~ militaire** to give the military salute; **~ au drapeau** salute to the colours.
b (*sauvegarde*) *[personne]* (personal) safety; *[nation]* safety. **trouver/chercher son ~ dans la fuite** to find/seek safety in flight; **elle n'a dû son ~ qu'à son courage** only her courage saved her; **mesures de ~ public** state security measures, measures to protect national security; **ancre ou planche de ~** sheet anchor (*fig*).
c (*Rel: rédemption*) salvation; *voir* **armée[2], hors**.
2 excl a (*) (*bonjour*) hi (there)!*, hello!; (*au revoir*) see you!*, bye!*, cheerio!* (*Brit*) **~, les gars!** hi (there) lads!* (*Brit*) *ou* guys!* (*US*); (*rien à faire*) **~!** no thanks!
b (*littér*) (all) hail. **~ (à toi) puissant seigneur** (all) hail (to thee) mighty lord (*littér*); **~, forêt de mon enfance** hail (to thee), o forest of my childhood (*littér*).

salutaire [salytɛʀ] adj a *conseil* salutary (*épith*), profitable (*épith*); *choc, épreuve* salutary (*épith*); *influence* healthy (*épith*), salutary (*épith*); *dégoût* healthy (*épith*). **cette déception lui a été ~** that disappointment was good for him *ou* did him some good. b *air* healthy, salubrious (*frm*); *remède* beneficial. **ce petit repos m'a été ~** that little rest did me good *ou* was good for me.

salutairement [salytɛʀmɑ̃] adv (*littér*) *conseiller* profitably; *réagir* in a healthy way.

salutation [salytasjɔ̃] nf salutation, greeting. **veuillez agréer, Monsieur, mes ~s distinguées** yours faithfully *ou* truly.

salutiste [salytist] adj, nmf Salvationist.

Salvador [salvadɔʀ] nm: **Le ~** El Salvador.

salvadorien, -ienne [salvadɔʀjɛ̃, jɛn] 1 adj Salvadorian. 2 nm, f: **S~(ne)** Salvadorian.

salvateur, -trice [salvatœʀ, tʀis] adj (*littér*) saving (*épith*).

salve [salv] nf (*Mil*) salvo; *[applaudissements]* salvo, volley.

Salzbourg [salzbuʀ] n Salzburg.

Samarie [samaʀi] nf Samaria.

samaritain, e [samaʀitɛ̃, ɛn] 1 adj Samaritan. 2 nm, f: **S~(e)** Samaritan; *voir* **bon[1]**.

samarium [samaʀjɔm] nm samarium.

samba [sɑ̃(m)ba] nf samba.

samedi [samdi] nm Saturday. **~ nous irons** on Saturday we'll go; **~ nous sommes allés ...** on Saturday *ou* last Saturday we went ...; **~ pro-**

chain next Saturday, Saturday next; ~ **qui vient** this Saturday, next Saturday; ~ **dernier** last Saturday; **le premier/dernier** ~ **du mois** the first/last Saturday of *ou* in the month; **un** ~ **sur deux** every other *ou* second Saturday; **nous sommes** ~ **(aujourd'hui)** it's Saturday (today); ~, **le 18 décembre** Saturday December 18th; **le** ~ **23 janvier** on Saturday January 23rd; **il y a huit/quinze jours** ~ **dernier** a week/a fortnight (*Brit*) *ou* two weeks past on Saturday; **le** ~ **suivant** the following Saturday; **l'autre** ~ the Saturday before last; ~ **matin/après-midi** Saturday morning/afternoon; ~ **soir** Saturday evening *ou* night; **la nuit de** ~ Saturday night; **l'édition de** ~ *ou* **du** ~ the Saturday edition; *voir* **huit, quinze**.

samit [sami] **nm** samite.

Samoa [samɔa] **nm** Samoa.

samoan, e [samɔɑ̃, an] 1 **adj** Samoan. 2 **nm, f**: **S~(e)** Samoan.

samouraï [samuʀaj] **nm** samurai.

samovar [samɔvaʀ] **nm** samovar.

sampan(g) [sɑ̃pɑ̃] **nm** sampan.

Samson [sɑ̃sɔ̃] **nm** Samson.

SAMU [samy] **nm** (**abrév de Service d'assistance médicale d'urgence**) *voir* **service**.

Samuel [samyɛl] **nm** Samuel.

samuraï [samuʀaj] **nm** = **samouraï**.

sana* [sana] **nm abrév de sanatorium**.

Sanaa [sanaa] **n** San'a, Sanaa.

sanatorium [sanatɔʀjɔm] **nm** sanatorium (*Brit*), sanitarium (*US*).

Sancho Pança [sɑ̃ʃopɑ̃sa] **nm** Sancho Panza.

sanctificateur, -trice [sɑ̃ktifikatœʀ, tʀis] 1 **adj** sanctifying (*épith*). 2 **nm, f** sanctifier. 3 **nm**: **le S~** the Holy Spirit *ou* Ghost.

sanctification [sɑ̃ktifikasjɔ̃] **nf** sanctification.

sanctifié, e [sɑ̃ktifje] (**ptp de sanctifier**) **adj** blessed.

sanctifier [sɑ̃ktifje] [7] **vt** to sanctify, hallow, bless. ~ **le dimanche** to observe the Sabbath; (*Rel*) **"que ton nom soit sanctifié"** "hallowed be Thy name".

sanction [sɑ̃ksjɔ̃] **nf** a (*condamnation*) sanction, penalty; (*Scol*) punishment; (*fig: conséquence*) penalty (*de* for). ~**s économiques** economic sanctions; **prendre des** ~**s contre qn** to take action against sb; **imposer des** ~**s contre qn** to impose sanctions on sb. b (*ratification*) sanction (*NonC*), approval (*NonC*). **recevoir la** ~ **de qn** to obtain sb's sanction *ou* approval; (*conséquence*) **c'est la** ~ **du progrès** this is the outcome of progress.

sanctionner [sɑ̃ksjɔne] [1] **vt** a (*punir*) *faute, personne* to punish. b (*consacrer*) (*gén*) to sanction, approve; *loi* to sanction. **ce diplôme sanctionne les études secondaires** this diploma marks the successful conclusion of secondary education.

sanctuaire [sɑ̃ktɥɛʀ] **nm** a (*Rel*) (*lieu saint*) sanctuary, shrine; *[temple, église]* sanctuary. b (*fig littér*) sanctuary.

sanctus [sɑ̃ktys] **nm** sanctus.

sandale [sɑ̃dal] **nf** sandal.

sandalette [sɑ̃dalɛt] **nf** sandal.

sandiniste [sɑ̃dinist] **adj, nmf** Sandinist(a).

sandow [sɑ̃do] **nm** ® (*attache*) luggage elastic; (*Aviat*) catapult.

sandre [sɑ̃dʀ] **nm** pikeperch.

sandwich, **pl** ~**es** *ou* ~**s** [sɑ̃dwi(t)ʃ] **nm** sandwich. ~ **au jambon** ham sandwich; **(pris) en** ~ **(entre)*** sandwiched (between); **les 2 voitures l'ont pris en** ~* he was sandwiched between the 2 cars; *voir* **homme**.

sandwicherie [sɑ̃dwi(t)ʃəʀi] **nf** sandwich shop (*Brit*) *ou* bar (*US*).

San Francisco [sɑ̃ fʀɑ̃sisko] **n** San Francisco.

sang [sɑ̃] 1 **nm** a (*lit, fig*) blood. **animal à** ~ **froid/chaud** cold/warm-blooded animal; **le** ~ **a coulé** blood has flowed; **verser** *ou* **faire couler le** ~ to shed *ou* spill blood; (*fig*) **avoir du** ~ **sur les mains** to have blood on one's hands; **son** ~ **crie vengeance** his blood cries (for) vengeance; **être en** ~ to be bleeding; **pincer qn (jusqu')au** ~ to pinch sb till he bleeds *ou* till the blood comes; **payer son crime de son** ~ to pay for one's crime with one's life; **donner son** ~ **pour sa patrie** to shed one's blood for one's country; *voir* **bon**[1], **donneur, feu, mauvais, noyer, pinte**.

b (*race, famille*) blood. **de** ~ **royal** of royal blood; **avoir du** ~ **bleu** to have blue blood, be blue-blooded; **du même** ~ of the same flesh and blood; **liens du** ~ blood ties, ties of blood; *voir* **prince, voix**.

c (*loc*) **avoir le** ~ **chaud** (*s'emporter facilement*) to be hotheaded; (*être sensuel*) to be hot-blooded; (*fig*) **un apport de** ~ **frais** an injection of new *ou* fresh blood (*dans* into); **se faire un** ~ **d'encre*** to be worried stiff*; **avoir du** ~ **dans les veines** to have courage *ou* guts*; **il n'a pas de** ~ **dans les veines, il a du** ~ **de navet** *ou* **de poulet** (*manque de courage*) he's a spineless individual, he's got no guts*; (*manque d'énergie*) he's a lethargic individual; **il a le jeu/la passion de la musique dans le** ~ he's got gambling/a passion for music in his blood; **le** ~ **lui monta au visage** the blood rushed to his face; **avoir le** ~ **qui monte à la tête** to be about to burst out in anger; **coup de** ~ (*Méd*) stroke; (*fig: colère*) **attraper un coup de** ~ to fly into a rage; **mon** ~ **n'a fait qu'un tour** (*émotion, peur*) my heart missed *ou* skipped a beat; (*colère, indignation*) I saw red; **se ronger** *ou* **se manger les** ~**s** to worry (o.s.), fret; **tourner les** ~**s à qn** to shake sb up; **histoire à glacer le** ~ bloodcurdling story; *voir* **suer**.

2 **comp** ▸ **sang-froid** **nm inv** sangfroid, cool*, calm; **garder/perdre son sang-froid** to keep/lose one's head *ou* one's cool*; **faire qch de sang-froid** to do sth in cold blood *ou* cold-bloodedly; **répondre avec sang-froid** to reply coolly *ou* calmly; **meurtre accompli de sang-froid** cold-blooded murder ▸ **sang-mêlé** **nmf inv** half-caste.

sanglant, e [sɑ̃glɑ̃, ɑ̃t] **adj** a *couteau, plaie* bloody; *bandage, habits* blood-soaked, bloody; *mains, visage* covered in blood, bloody. b *combat, guerre* bloody. c *insulte, reproche* cruel, extremely hurtful; *défaite* cruel. d (*littér: couleur*) blood-red.

sangle [sɑ̃gl] **nf** (*gén*) strap; *[selle]* girth. *[siège]* ~**s** webbing; *voir* **lit**.

sangler [sɑ̃gle] [1] 1 **vt** *cheval* to girth; *colis, corps* to strap up. **sanglé dans son uniforme** done up *ou* strapped up tight in one's uniform. 2 **se sangler** **vpr** to do one's belt up tight.

sanglier [sɑ̃glije] **nm** (wild) boar.

sanglot [sɑ̃glo] **nm** sob. **avoir des** ~**s dans la voix** to have a sob in one's voice; **elle répondit dans un** ~ **que ...** she answered with a sob that ...; *voir* **éclater**.

sangloter [sɑ̃glɔte] [1] **vi** to sob.

sangria [sɑ̃gʀija] **nf** sangria.

sangsue [sɑ̃sy] **nf** (*lit, fig*) leech.

sanguin, e [sɑ̃gɛ̃, in] 1 **adj** a *caractère, homme* fiery; *visage* ruddy, sanguine (*frm*). **orange** ~**e** blood orange. b (*Anat*) blood (*épith*). 2 **sanguine** **nf** a (*Bot*) blood orange. b (*dessin*) red chalk drawing; (*crayon*) red chalk, sanguine (*SPÉC*).

sanguinaire [sɑ̃ginɛʀ] 1 **adj** *personne* bloodthirsty, sanguinary (*frm, littér*); *combat* bloody, sanguinary (*frm, littér*). 2 **nf** (*plante*) bloodroot, sanguinaria.

sanguinolent, e [sɑ̃ginɔlɑ̃, ɑ̃t] **adj** *crachat* streaked with blood. **plaie** ~**e** wound that is bleeding slightly *ou* from which blood is oozing.

Sanisette [sanizɛt] **nf** ® *coin-operated public toilet*, Superloo ® (*Brit*).

sanitaire [sanitɛʀ] 1 **adj** a (*Méd*) *services, mesures* health (*épith*); *conditions* sanitary. **campagne** ~ campaign to improve sanitary conditions; *voir* **cordon, train**. b (*Plomberie*) **l'installation** ~ **est défectueuse** the bathroom plumbing is faulty; **appareil** ~ bathroom *ou* sanitary appliance. 2 **nm**: **le** ~ bathroom installations; **les** ~**s** (*lieu*) the bathroom; (*appareils*) the bathroom (suite); (*plomberie*) the bathroom plumbing.

San José [sɑ̃ʒoze] **n** San José.

San Juan [sɑ̃ʒyɑ̃] **n** San Juan.

sans [sɑ̃] 1 **prép** a (*privation, absence*) without. **ménage** ~ **enfant** childless couple; ~ **père/mère** fatherless/motherless, with no father/mother; **il est** ~ **secrétaire en ce moment** he is without a secretary at the moment, he has no secretary at the moment; **ils sont** ~ **argent** *ou* ~**un sou** *ou* ~ **le sou*** they have no money, they are penniless; **je suis sorti** ~ **chapeau ni manteau** I went out without (a) hat or coat *ou* with no hat or coat; **repas à 60 F** ~ **le vin** meal at 60 francs exclusive of wine *ou* not including wine; **on a retrouvé le sac, mais** ~ **l'argent** they found the bag minus the money *ou* but without the money; **être** ~ **abri** to be homeless; **être** ~ **travail** *ou* ~ **emploi** to be unemployed *ou* out of work; *voir* **3**.

b (*manière, caractérisation*) without. **manger** ~ **fourchette** to eat without a fork; **boire** ~ **soif** to drink without being thirsty; **il est parti** ~ **même** *ou* ~ **seulement un mot de remerciement** he left without even a word of thanks *ou* without so much as a word of thanks; **la situation est** ~ **remède** the situation cannot be remedied *ou* is beyond *ou* past remedy, the situation is hopeless; **l'histoire n'est pas** ~ **intérêt** the story is not devoid of interest *ou* is not without interest; **nous avons trouvé sa maison** ~ **mal** we found his house with no difficulty *ou* with no trouble *ou* without difficulty; **la situation n'est pas** ~ **nous inquiéter** the situation is somewhat disturbing; **il a accepté** ~ **hésitation** he accepted unhesitatingly *ou* without hesitation; **travailler** ~ **arrêt** *ou* (*littér*) ~ **trêve** to work ceaselessly (*littér*) *ou* without a break *ou* relentlessly; **marcher** ~ **chaussures** to walk barefoot; **marcher** ~ **but** to walk aimlessly; **promenade** ~ **but** aimless walk; **il est** ~ **scrupules** he is unscrupulous, he has no scruples, he is devoid of scruple(s); **il est** ~ **préjugés** he is unprejudiced *ou* unbiased *ou* free from prejudice(s); (*fig*) **objet** ~ **prix** priceless object; **robe** ~ **manches** sleeveless dress; **pièce** ~ **tapis** uncarpeted room; (*Scol*) **dictée** ~ **fautes** error-free dictation; **je le connais,** ~ **plus** I know him but no more than that; *voir* **cesse, doute, effort** *etc*.

c (*cause ou condition négative*) but for. ~ **cette réunion, il aurait pu partir ce soir** if it had not been for *ou* were it not for *ou* but for this meeting he could have left tonight; ~ **sa présence d'esprit, il se tuait** had he not had such presence of mind *ou* without *ou* but for his presence of mind he would have killed himself.

d (*avec infin ou subj*) without. **vous n'êtes pas** ~ **savoir** you must be aware, you cannot but know (*frm*); **il est entré** ~ **faire de bruit** he came in without making a noise *ou* noiselessly; **il est entré** ~ **(même** *ou* **seulement) que je l'entende** he came in without my (even) hearing him; **je n'irai pas** ~ **être invité** I won't go without being invited *ou* unless I am invited; ~ **que cela (ne) vous dérange** as long as *ou* provided that it doesn't put you out; **il lui écrivit** ~ **plus attendre** he wrote to her without further delay; **j'y crois** ~ **y croire** I believe it and I don't; ~ **(même) que nous le sachions, il avait écrit** he had written without our (even) knowing; **je ne suis pas** ~ **avoir des doutes sur son honnêteté** I have my doubts *ou* I am not without some doubts as to his honesty; **il ne se passe pas de jour ~ qu'il lui écrive** not a day passes without his writing to him *ou* but that (*littér*) he writes to him; **il va ~ dire que** it goes without saying that; *voir* **jamais**.

e **non ~ peine** *ou* **mal** *ou* **difficulté** not without difficulty; **l'incendie a été maîtrisé, non ~ que les pompiers aient dû intervenir** the fire was brought under control but not until the fire brigade were brought in *ou* but not without the fire brigade's being brought in.

f (*) **~ ça, ~ quoi** otherwise; **si on m'offre un bon prix je vends ma voiture, ~ ça** *ou* **~ quoi je la garde** I'll sell my car if I'm offered a good price for it but otherwise *ou* if not, I'll keep it; **sois sage, ~ ça ...!** be good or else ...!, be good – otherwise ... !

2 **adv** (*) **votre parapluie! vous alliez partir ~** your umbrella! you were going to go off without it; **il a oublié ses lunettes et il ne peut pas conduire ~** he's forgotten his glasses, and he can't drive without them.

3 **comp ►sans-abri nmf inv** homeless person; **les sans-abri** the homeless **►sans-cœur adj inv** heartless ◊ **nmf inv** heartless person **►sans-culotte** (*Hist*) **nm (pl sans-culottes)** sans culotte **►sans domicile fixe adj** of no fixed abode ◊ **nmf inv** person of no fixed abode **►sans-emploi nmf inv** unemployed person; **les sans-emploi** (**nmpl**) the jobless, the unemployed, those out of work; **le nombre des sans-emploi** the number of unemployed *ou* of those out of work, the jobless figure **►sans faute loc adv** without fail; **faire un sans fautes** (*Équitation*) to do a clear round; (*fig: Pol etc*) not to put a foot wrong **►sans-fil nf** wireless telegraphy **►sans-filiste nmf (pl sans-filistes)** wireless enthusiast **►sans-gêne adj inv** inconsiderate ◊ **nm inv** lack of consideration (for others), inconsiderateness ◊ **nmf inv** inconsiderate type **►sans-logis = sans-abri ►sans-opinions nmf inv** don't-know **►sans-parti nmf inv** (*gén*) member of no political party; (*candidat*) independent **►sans-patrie nmf inv** stateless person **►sans-soin adj inv** careless ◊ **nmf inv** careless person **►sans-le-sou adj inv** penniless, broke **►sans-souci adj inv** carefree **►sans-travail nmf inv = sans-emploi**.

San Salvador [sɑ̃salvadɔʀ] **n** San Salvador.

sanscrit, e, sanskrit, e [sɑ̃skʀi, it] **adj, nm** Sanskrit.

sansonnet [sɑ̃sɔnɛ] **nm** starling; *voir* **roupie**.

santal [sɑ̃tal] **nm: (bois de) ~** sandal(wood).

santé [sɑ̃te] **nf** a *[personne, esprit, pays]* health. **~ mentale** mental health; **en bonne/mauvaise ~** in good/bad health; **c'est bon/mauvais pour la ~** it's good/bad for the health *ou* for you; **être en pleine ~** to be in perfect health; **avoir la ~** to be healthy, be in good health; (*fig: énergie*) **il a la ~!*** he must have lots of energy!*; **il n'a pas de ~, il a une petite ~** he's not a healthy type, he has poor health, he's not very strong; **avoir une ~ de fer** to have an iron constitution; **comment va la ~?*** how are you keeping?* (*Brit*) *ou* doing?* (*US*); **meilleure ~** get well soon; *voir* **maison, raison, respirer**.

b (*Admin*) **la ~ publique** public health; (*Naut*) **la ~** the quarantine service; (*Admin*) **services de ~** health services; *voir* **ministère, ministre**.

c (*en trinquant*) **à votre ~!, ~!*** cheers!*, (your) good health!; **à la ~ de Paul!** (here's to) Paul!; **boire à la ~ de qn** to drink (to) sb's health.

santiag [sɑ̃tjag] **nm** cowboy boot.

Santiago [sɑ̃tjago] **n** Santiago.

santoméen, enne [sɑ̃tɔmeɛ̃, ɛn] 1 **adj** Samoan. 2 **nm** (*langue*) Samoan. 3 **S~(ne) nm, f** Samoan.

santon [sɑ̃tɔ̃] **nm** (ornamental) figure (*at a Christmas crib*).

saoudien, -ienne [saudjɛ̃, jɛn] 1 **adj** Saudi Arabian. 2 **nm, f: S~(ne)** Saudi Arabian.

saoul, e [su, sul] = **soûl**.

saoulard, e‡ [sulaʀ, aʀd] **nm, f = soûlard‡**.

sapajou [sapaʒu] **nm** (*Zool*) sapajou.

sape [sap] **nf** a (*lit, fig: action*) undermining, sapping; (*tranchée*) approach *ou* sapping trench. **travail de ~** (*Mil*) sap; (*fig*) insidious undermining process *ou* work. b (*habits*) **~s‡** gear* (*NonC*), clobber‡ (*NonC: Brit*).

sapement [sapmɑ̃] **nm** undermining, sapping.

saper [sape] 1 1 **vt** (*lit, fig*) to undermine, sap. **~ le moral à qn*** to knock the stuffing out of sb*. 2 **se saper‡ vpr** to do o.s. up*. **il s'était sapé pour aller danser** he had done *ou* got himself up to go dancing*; **bien sapé** well-dressed.

saperlipopette [sapɛʀlipɔpɛt] **excl** († *hum*) gad! (††, *hum*), gadzooks! (††, *hum*).

sapeur [sapœʀ] 1 **nm** (*Mil*) sapper; *voir* **fumer**. 2 **comp ►sapeur-pompier nm (pl sapeurs-pompiers)** fireman, fire fighter.

saphène [safɛn] 1 **adj** saphenous. 2 **nf** saphena.

saphique [safik] **adj, nm** (*Littérat*) Sapphic.

saphir [safiʀ] 1 **nm** (*pierre*) sapphire; (*aiguille*) sapphire, needle. 2 **adj inv** sapphire.

saphisme [safism] **nm** sapphism.

sapide [sapid] **adj** sapid.

sapidité [sapidite] **nf** sapidity.

sapience† [sapjɑ̃s] **nf** sapience (*frm*), wisdom.

sapin [sapɛ̃] **nm** (*arbre*) fir (tree); (*bois*) fir. **~ de Noël** Christmas tree; **costume en ~‡** wooden overcoat‡; **une toux qui sent le ~‡** a cough which sounds as though one hasn't long to go.

sapinière [sapinjɛʀ] **nf** fir plantation *ou* forest.

saponacé, e [sapɔnase] **adj** saponaceous.

saponaire [sapɔnɛʀ] **nf** saponin.

saponification [sapɔnifikasjɔ̃] **nf** saponification.

saponifier [sapɔnifje] 7 **vt** to saponify.

sapristi*† [sapʀisti] **excl** (*colère*) for God's sake!*; (*surprise*) good grief!, great heavens!†

saprophage [sapʀɔfaʒ] 1 **adj** saprophagous. 2 **nm** saprophagous animal.

saprophyte [sapʀɔfit] 1 **adj** (*Biol, Méd*) saprophyte. 2 **nm** saprophyte.

saquer* [sake] 1 **vt = sacquer***.

S.A.R. (**abrév de Son Altesse Royale**) HRH.

sarabande [saʀabɑ̃d] **nf** (*danse*) saraband; (**: tapage*) racket, hullabaloo*; (*succession*) jumble. **faire la ~*** to make a racket *ou* a hullabaloo*; **les souvenirs/chiffres qui dansent la ~ dans ma tête** the memories/figures that are whirling around in my head.

Saragosse [saʀagɔs] **n** Saragossa.

Sara(h) [saʀa] **nf** Sarah.

Sarajevo [saʀajevo] **n** Sarajevo.

sarbacane [saʀbakan] **nf** (*arme*) blowpipe, blowgun; (*jouet*) peashooter.

sarcasme [saʀkasm] **nm** (*ironie*) sarcasm; (*remarque*) sarcastic remark.

sarcastique [saʀkastik] **adj** sarcastic.

sarcastiquement [saʀkastikmɑ̃] **adv** sarcastically.

sarcelle [saʀsɛl] **nf** teal.

sarclage [saʀklaʒ] **nm** (*voir* **sarcler**) weeding; hoeing.

sarcler [saʀkle] 1 **vt** *jardin, culture* to weed; *mauvaise herbe* to hoe.

sarclette [saʀklɛt] **nf, sarcloir** [saʀklwaʀ] **nm** spud, weeding hoe.

sarcomateux, -euse [saʀkɔmatø, øz] **adj** sarcomatoid, sarcomatous.

sarcome [saʀkom] **nm** sarcoma. **~ de Kaposi** Kaposi's Sarcoma.

sarcophage [saʀkɔfaʒ] **nm** (*cercueil*) sarcophagus.

sarcoplasme [saʀkɔplasm] **nm** sarcoplasm.

Sardaigne [saʀdɛɲ] **nf** Sardinia.

sarde [saʀd] 1 **adj** Sardinian. 2 **nm** (*Ling*) Sardinian. 3 **nmf: S~** Sardinian.

sardine [saʀdin] **nf** a sardine. **serrés** *ou* **tassés comme des ~s (en boîte)** packed *ou* squashed together like sardines (in a tin (*Brit*) *ou* can (*US*)). b (*arg Mil*) stripe.

sardinerie [saʀdinʀi] **nf** sardine cannery.

sardinier, -ière [saʀdinje, jɛʀ] 1 **adj** sardine (*épith*). 2 **nm, f** (*ouvrier*) sardine canner. 3 **nm** (*bateau*) sardine boat; (*pêcheur*) sardine fisher.

sardonique [saʀdɔnik] **adj** sardonic.

sardoniquement [saʀdɔnikmɑ̃] **adv** sardonically.

sargasse [saʀgas] **nf** sargasso, gulfweed; *voir* **mer**.

sari [saʀi] **nm** sari.

sarigue [saʀig] **nf** (o)possum.

SARL [ɛsaɛʀɛl] **nf** (**abrév de société à responsabilité limitée**) limited liability company. **Raymond ~** Raymond Ltd (*Brit*), Raymond Inc. (*US*); *voir* **société**.

sarment [saʀmɑ̃] **nm** (*tige*) twining *ou* climbing stem, bine (*SPÉC*). **~ (de vigne)** vine shoot.

sarmenteux, -euse [saʀmɑ̃tø, øz] **adj** *plante* climbing (*épith*); *tige* climbing (*épith*), twining (*épith*).

sarrasin[1], e [saʀazɛ̃, in] (*Hist*) 1 **adj** Saracen. 2 **nm, f: S~(e)** Saracen.

sarrasin[2] [saʀazɛ̃] **nm** (*Bot*) buckwheat.

sarrau [saʀo] **nm** smock.

Sarre [saʀ] **nf** (*région*) Saarland. (*rivière*) **la ~** the Saar.

sarriette [saʀjɛt] **nf** savory.

sarrois, e [saʀwa, waz] 1 **adj** Saar (*épith*). 2 **nm, f: S~(e)** inhabitant *ou* native of the Saar.

sartrien, -ienne [saʀtʀijɛ̃, jɛn] **adj** Sartrian, of Sartre.

S.A.S. [ɛsaɛs] (**abrév de Son Altesse Sérénissime**) HSH.

sas [sɑs] **nm** a (*Espace, Naut*) airlock; *[écluse]* lock. b (*tamis*) sieve, screen.

sassafras [sasafʀa] **nm** sassafras.

sasser [sɑse] 1 **vt** *farine* to sift, screen; *péniche* to pass through a lock.

Satan [satɑ̃] **nm** Satan.

satané, e* [satane] **adj** blasted*, confounded*.

satanique [satanik] **adj** (*de Satan*) satanic; (*fig*) *rire, plaisir, ruse* fiendish, satanic, wicked.

satanisme [satanism] **nm** (*culte*) Satanism; (*fig*) fiendishness, wickedness. (*fig*) **c'est du ~!** it's fiendish! *ou* wicked!

satellisation [satelizasjɔ̃] **nf** a *[fusée]* (launching and) putting into orbit. **programme de ~** satellite launching programme. b *[pays]* **la ~ de cet état est à craindre** it is to be feared that this state will become a satellite (state).

satelliser [satelize] 1 **vt** *fusée* to put into orbit (round the earth); *pays* to make a satellite of, make into a satellite.

satellite [satelit] **nm** a (*Astron, Espace, Pol*) satellite. **~ artificiel/naturel** artificial/natural satellite; **~ de communication/de télécommunications/de radiodiffusion** communications/telecommunications/broadcast satellite; ~ **météorologique** weather satellite; ~ **d'observation** monitoring satellite; **~-espion** spy satellite, spy-in-the-sky*; ~ **antisatellite**, ~ **d'intervention** killer satellite; **~-relais** = ~ **de télécommunications; pays/villes ~s** satellite countries/towns. b (*Tech*) **(pignon)** ~ bevel pinion.

satiété [sasjete] **nf** satiety, satiation. **(jusqu')à** ~ *manger, boire* to satiety *ou* satiation; *répéter* ad nauseam; **j'en ai à** ~ I've more than enough, I've enough and to spare.

satin [satɛ̃] **nm** satin. **elle avait une peau de** ~ her skin was (like) satin, she had satin(-smooth) skin; ~ **de laine/de coton** wool/cotton satin.

satiné, e [satine] (**ptp de satiner**) 1 **adj** *tissu, aspect* satiny, satin-like; *peau* satin (*épith*), satin-smooth; *peinture, papier* with a silk finish. 2 **nm** satin(-like) *ou* satiny quality.

satiner [satine] [1] **vt** *étoffe* to put a satin finish on; *photo, papier* to give a silk finish to, put a silk finish on. **la lumière satinait sa peau** the light gave her skin a satin-like quality *ou* gloss, her skin shone like satin beneath the light.

satinette [satinɛt] **nf** (*en coton et soie*) satinet; (*en coton*) sateen.

satire [satiʀ] **nf** (*gén*) satire; (*écrite*) satire, lampoon. **faire la ~ de qch** to satirize sth, lampoon sth.

satirique [satiʀik] **adj** satirical, satiric.

satiriquement [satiʀikmɑ̃] **adv** satirically.

satiriser [satiʀize] [1] **vt** (*gén*) to satirize; (*par écrit*) to satirize, lampoon.

satiriste [satiʀist] **nmf** satirist.

satisfaction [satisfaksjɔ̃] **nf** a (*assouvissement*) *[faim, passion]* satisfaction, appeasement; *[soif]* satisfaction, quenching; *[envie]* satisfaction; *[désir]* satisfaction, gratification.

b (*contentement*) satisfaction. **éprouver une certaine ~ à faire** to feel a certain satisfaction in doing, get a certain satisfaction out of doing *ou* from doing; **donner (toute** *ou* **entière)** ~ **à qn** to give (complete) satisfaction to sb, satisfy sb (completely); **je vois avec ~ que** I'm gratified to see that; **à la ~ générale** *ou* **de tous** to the general satisfaction, to everybody's satisfaction.

c **une ~: c'est une ~ qu'il pourrait m'accorder** he might grant me that satisfaction; **leur fils ne leur a donné que des ~s** their son has been a (source of) great satisfaction to them; ~ **d'amour-propre** gratification (*NonC*) of one's self-esteem.

d (*gén, Rel: réparation, gain de cause*) satisfaction. **obtenir** ~ to get *ou* obtain satisfaction; **donner ~ à qn** to give sb satisfaction; **j'aurai ~ de cette offense** I will have satisfaction for that insult.

satisfaire [satisfɛʀ] [60] 1 **vt** *personne, cœur, curiosité* to satisfy; *désir* to satisfy, gratify; *passion, faim* to satisfy, appease; *besoin* to satisfy, answer, gratify; *soif* to satisfy, quench; *demande* to satisfy, meet. **votre nouvel assistant vous satisfait-il?** are you satisfied with your new assistant?, is your new assistant satisfactory?, does your new assistant satisfy you?; **j'espère que cette solution vous satisfait** I hope you find this solution satisfactory, I hope this solution satisfies you, I hope you are satisfied *ou* happy with this solution; **je suis désolé que vous n'en soyez pas satisfait** I am sorry it was not satisfactory *ou* you were not satisfied; (*euph*) ~ **un besoin pressant** to satisfy an urgent need, attend to the call of nature (*hum*); ~ **l'attente de qn** to come up to sb's expectations; (*Ind*) **arriver à ~ la demande** to keep up with demand.

2 **satisfaire à vt indir** *désir* to satisfy, gratify; *promesse, engagement* to fulfil; *demande, revendication* to meet, satisfy; *condition* to meet, fulfil, satisfy; *goût* to satisfy; *test de qualité* to pass. **avez-vous satisfait à vos obligations militaires?** have you fulfilled the requirement for military service?; **cette installation ne satisfait pas aux normes** this installation does not comply with *ou* satisfy standard requirements.

3 **se satisfaire vpr** to be satisfied (*de* with); (*euph*) to relieve o.s. (*péj*) **se ~ de peu** to be easily satisfied; (*hum*) **tu as vu son mari?, elle se satisfait de peu!** have you seen her husband? — she's not exactly choosy.

satisfaisant, e [satisfəzɑ̃, ɑ̃t] **adj** (*acceptable*) satisfactory; (*qui fait plaisir*) satisfying.

satisfait, e [satisfɛ, ɛt] (**ptp de satisfaire**) **adj** *personne, air* satisfied. (*Comm*) **"satisfait ou remboursé"** "satisfaction or your money back"; **être ~ de qn** to be satisfied with sb; **être ~ de** *solution, décision* to be satisfied with, be happy with *ou* about; *soirée* to be pleased with; **être ~ de soi** to be self-satisfied, be satisfied with o.s.; **il est ~ de son sort** he is satisfied *ou* happy with his lot; (*iro*) **te voilà ~!** you asked for it!*

satisfecit [satisfesit] **nm inv** (*Scol*) ≃ star, merit point. (*fig*) **je lui donne un ~ pour la façon dont il a mené son affaire** I give him full marks (*Brit*) *ou* points (*US*) for the way he conducted the business.

satrape [satʀap] **nm** satrap.

saturable [satyʀabl] **adj** saturable.

saturant, e [satyʀɑ̃, ɑ̃t] **adj** saturating. **vapeur ~e** saturated vapour.

saturateur [satyʀatœʀ] **nm** *[radiateur]* humidifier; (*Sci*) saturator.

saturation [satyʀasjɔ̃] **nf** (*gén, Sci*) saturation (*de* of). **être/arriver à ~** to be at/reach saturation point; **manger à ~** to eat till one reaches saturation point; **à cause de la ~ des lignes téléphoniques** because the telephone lines are all engaged (*Brit*) *ou* busy (*US*); **j'en ai jusqu'à ~** I've had more than I can take of it.

saturer [satyʀe] [1] **vt** a (*gén, Sci*) to saturate (*de* with). (*fig*) ~ **les électeurs de promesses** to swamp the electors with promises; **la terre est saturée d'eau après la pluie** the ground is saturated (with water) *ou* sodden after the rain; **j'ai mangé tant de fraises que j'en suis saturé** I've eaten so many strawberries that I can't take any more *ou* that I've had as many as I can take; **je suis saturé de télévision/de publicité** I can't take any more television/advertising*; **l'autoroute est saturée** the motorway is badly congested; **le marché est saturé** the market is saturated.

b (*Téléc*) **être saturé** *[réseau]* to be overloaded *ou* saturated; *[standard]* to be jammed; *[lignes]* to be engaged (*Brit*) *ou* busy (*US*).

saturnales [satyʀnal] **nfpl** (*lit*) Saturnalia; (*fig*) saturnalia.

Saturne [satyʀn] 1 **nm** (*Myth*) Saturn. 2 **nf** (*Astron*) Saturn. (*Pharm*) **extrait** *ou* **sel de s~** lead acetate.

saturnien, -ienne [satyʀnjɛ̃, jɛn] **adj** (*littér*) saturnine.

saturnin, e [satyʀnɛ̃, in] **adj** saturnine.

saturnisme [satyʀnism] **nm** lead poisoning, saturnism (*SPÉC*).

satyre [satiʀ] **nm** (*: *obsédé*) sex maniac; (*Myth, Zool*) satyr.

satyrique [satiʀik] **adj** satyric.

sauce [sos] **nf** a (*Culin*) sauce; *[salade]* dressing; (*jus de viande*) gravy. **viande en ~** meat cooked in a sauce; ~ **blanche/béchamel/piquante/tomate/moutarde** white/béchamel/piquant/tomato/mustard sauce; ~ **vinaigrette** vinaigrette *ou* French dressing; ~ **à l'orange/aux câpres** orange/caper sauce; ~ **chasseur/mousseline** sauce chasseur/mousseline; ~ **madère/suprême/hollandaise** madeira/suprême/hollandaise sauce.

b (*) (*remplissage*) padding*. (*présentation*) **reprendre un vieux discours en changeant la ~** to dish up an old speech with a new slant*, take an old speech and dress it up; **c'est la même chose avec une autre ~** same meat, different gravy; **il faudrait rallonger la ~ pour ce devoir** you'll have to pad out this piece of work, you'll have to put some padding into this piece of work.

c (*loc*) **à quelle ~ allons-nous être mangés?** I wonder what fate has in store for us; **mettre qn à toutes les ~s** to make sb do any job going*; **mettre un exemple à toutes les ~s** to turn *ou* adapt an example to fit any case; **mettre la ~*** (*Aut*) to step on the gas*; (*gén: se dépêcher*) to step on it‡; (*Aut, gén*) **mettre toute la ~** to go flat out; **recevoir la ~*** to get soaked *ou* drenched.

saucée* [sose] **nf** downpour. **recevoir** *ou* **prendre une ~** to get soaked *ou* drenched.

saucer [sose] [3] **vt** a *assiette* to wipe (the sauce off); *pain* to dip in the sauce. b **se faire ~*, être saucé*** to get soaked *ou* drenched.

saucier [sosje] **nm** sauce chef *ou* cook.

saucière [sosjɛʀ] **nf** (*gén*) sauceboat; *[jus de viande]* gravy boat.

sauciflard‡ [sosiflaʀ] **nm** (slicing) sausage, ≃ salami.

saucisse [sosis] **nf** a (*Culin*) sausage. ~ **de Morteau** (type of) smoked sausage; ~ **de Strasbourg** (type of) beef sausage; ~ **de Francfort** frankfurter; *voir* **attacher, chair.** b (*Aviat*) sausage. c **(grande)** ~‡ nincompoop*, great ninny*.

saucisson [sosisɔ̃] **nm** a (*Culin*) (large) (slicing) sausage. ~ **à l'ail** garlic sausage; ~ **sec** (dry) pork and beef sausage, ≃ salami; ~ **pur porc** 100 % pork sausage; *voir* **ficeler.** b (*pain*) (cylindrical) loaf.

saucissonné, e* [sosisɔne] (**ptp de saucissonner**) **adj** trussed up.

saucissonner* [sosisɔne] [1] 1 **vi** to (have a) picnic. 2 **vt** *livre, émission* to cut up. ~ **un film avec des publicités** to insert commercial breaks into a film.

sauf[1], sauve [sof, sov] **adj** *personne* unharmed, unhurt; *honneur* saved, intact; *voir* **sain, vie.**

sauf[2] [sof] **prép** a (*à part*) except, but, save (*frm*). **tout le monde ~ lui** everyone except *ou* but *ou* save (*frm*) him; **nous sortons tout le temps ~ s'il/quand il pleut** we always go out except if/when it's raining; **le repas était excellent ~ le dessert** *ou* ~ **pour ce qui est du dessert** the meal was excellent except for *ou* but for *ou* apart from *ou* aside from (*surtout US*) the dessert; ~ **que** except that, but that (*frm*).

b (*sous réserve de*) unless. **nous irons demain, ~ s'il pleut** we'll go tomorrow unless it rains; ~ **avis contraire** unless you hear *ou* are told otherwise, unless you hear to the contrary; ~ **erreur de ma part** if I'm not mistaken; ~ **imprévu** barring the unexpected, unless anything unforeseen happens; (*Jur*) ~ **accord** *ou* **convention contraire** unless otherwise agreed; ~ **dispositions contraires** except as otherwise provided.

c (*loc*) (*littér*) **il accepte de nous aider, ~ à nous critiquer si nous échouons** he agrees to help us even if he does (reserve the right to) criticize us if we fail; (††, *hum*) ~ **le respect que je vous dois** with all due respect; (††, *hum*) ~ **votre respect** saving your presence (††, *hum*).

sauf-conduit, pl sauf-conduits [sofkɔ̃dɥi] **nm** safe-conduct.

sauge [soʒ] **nf** (*Culin*) sage; (*ornementale*) salvia.

saugrenu, e [sogʀəny] **adj** preposterous, ludicrous.

Saül [sayl] **nm** Saul.

saulaie [solɛ] **nf** willow plantation.

saule [sol] **nm** willow (tree). ~ **pleureur** weeping willow.

saumâtre [somɑtʀ] **adj** *eau, goût* brackish, briny; *plaisanterie, impression, humeur* nasty, unpleasant. **il l'a trouvée ~‡** he found it a bit off* (*Brit*), he was not amused.

saumon [somɔ̃] 1 **nm** salmon. 2 **adj inv** salmon (pink).

saumoné, e [somɔne] adj *couleur* salmon (pink); *voir* **truite**.
saumure [somyʀ] nf brine.
saumuré, e [somyʀe] adj *hareng* pickled (in brine).
sauna [sona] nm (*bain*) sauna (bath); (*établissement*) sauna.
saunier [sonje] nm (*ouvrier*) worker in a saltworks; (*exploitant*) salt merchant.
saupiquet [sopikɛ] nm (*sauce, ragoût*) *type of spicy sauce or stew*.
saupoudrage [sopudʀaʒ] nm (*voir* **saupoudrer**) sprinkling; dredging, dusting.
saupoudrer [sopudʀe] [1] vt (*gén*) to sprinkle; (*Culin*) to dredge, dust, sprinkle (*de* with).
saupoudreuse [sopudʀøz] nf (sugar *ou* flour *etc*) dredger.
saur [sɔʀ] adj m *voir* **hareng**.
saurer [sɔʀe] [1] vt *viande* to smoke, cure.
saurien [sɔʀjɛ̃] nm saurian. **~s** Sauria (*SPÉC*), saurians.
saurissage [sɔʀisaʒ] nm *[viande]* smoking, curing.
saut [so] 1 nm a (*lit, fig: bond*) jump, leap. (*Sport*) **~ avec/sans élan** running/standing jump; **faire un ~** to (make a) jump *ou* leap; **faire un ~ dans l'inconnu/le vide** to (make a) leap into the unknown/the void; **le véhicule fit un ~ de 100 mètres dans le ravin** the vehicle fell *ou* dropped 100 metres into the ravine; **se lever d'un ~** to jump *ou* leap up, jump *ou* leap to one's feet; **quittons Louis XIV et faisons un ~ d'un siècle** let us leave Louis XIV and jump a century; (*fig*) **progresser** *ou* **avancer par ~s** to go forward by *ou* in stages.
b (*Sport*) jumping. **épreuves de ~** jumping events; *voir* **triple**.
c (*Géog: cascade*) waterfall.
d (*loc*) **faire qch au ~ du lit** to do sth on getting up *ou* getting out of bed, do sth as soon as one gets up *ou* gets out of bed; **prendre qn au ~ du lit** to find sb just out of bed (when one calls); **faire le ~** to take the plunge; **faire un ~ chez qn** to pop over *ou* round (*Brit*) to sb's (place)*, drop in on sb; **il a fait un ~ jusqu'à Bordeaux** he made a flying visit to Bordeaux.
2 comp ▸**saut de l'ange** (*Natation*) swallow dive (*Brit*), swan dive (*US*) ▸**saut de carpe** jack-knife dive, pike (*Brit*) ▸**saut de chat** pas de chat ▸**saut en chute libre** (*sport*) free-fall parachuting; (*bond*) free-fall jump ▸**saut en ciseaux** scissors (jump) ▸**saut à la corde** skipping (*with a rope*) ▸**saut à l'élastique** bungee jumping ▸**saut groupé** tuck ▸**saut de haies** hurdling ▸**saut en hauteur** (*sport*) high jump; (*bond*) (high) jump ▸**saut-de-lit** nm inv negligée, housecoat ▸**saut en longueur** (*sport*) long jump; (*bond*) (long) jump ▸**saut-de-loup** nm (pl **sauts-de-loup**) (wide) ditch ▸**saut de la mort** leap of death ▸**saut-de-mouton** nm (pl **sauts-de-mouton**) flyover (*Brit*), overpass (*US*) ▸**saut en parachute** (*sport*) parachuting, parachute jumping; (*bond*) parachute jump ▸**saut à la perche** (*sport*) pole vaulting; (*bond*) (pole) vault ▸**saut périlleux** somersault ▸**saut à pieds joints** standing jump ▸**saut de puce** step (*fig*) ▸**saut en rouleau** western roll ▸**saut de séquence** (*Ordin*) jump ▸**saut à skis** (*sport*) skijumping; (*bond*) jump.
saute [sot] nf sudden change. **~ d'humeur** sudden change of mood; **~ de température** jump in temperature; (*TV*) **pour empêcher les ~s d'images** to stop the picture flickering, to keep the picture steady.
saute- [sot] préf *voir* **sauter**.
sauté, e [sote] (ptp de **sauter**) adj, nm sauté. **~ de veau** sauté of veal.
sauter [sote] [1] 1 vi a *[personne]* to jump, leap (*dans* into, *par-dessus* over); (*vers le bas*) to jump *ou* leap (down); (*vers le haut*) to jump *ou* leap (up); *[oiseau]* to hop; *[insecte]* to jump, hop; *[kangourou]* to jump. **~ à pieds joints** to jump with (the) feet together, make a standing jump; **~ à cloche-pied** to hop; **~ à la corde** to skip (*with a rope*); **~ à la perche** to pole-vault; **~ en parachute** (*gén, Sport*) to parachute, make a parachute jump; *[parachutistes]* to parachute, be dropped (*sur* over); (*en cas d'accident*) to bail out (*US*), bale out (*Brit*), make an emergency (parachute) jump; (*Sport*) **~ en ciseaux** to do a scissors jump; **faire ~ un enfant sur ses genoux** to bounce *ou* dandle a child on one's knee; **les cahots faisaient ~ les passagers** the passengers jolted *ou* bounced along over the bumps; **il sauta de la table** he jumped *ou* leapt (down) off *ou* from the table; **~ en l'air** to jump *ou* leap *ou* spring up, jump *ou* leap *ou* spring into the air; (*fig*) **~ en l'air** *ou* **au plafond** (*de colère*) to hit the roof*; (*de joie*) to jump for joy; (*de surprise, de peur*) to jump (out of one's skin), start (up); (*lit, fig*) **~ de joie** to jump for joy.
b (*se précipiter*) **~ (à bas) du lit** to jump *ou* leap *ou* spring out of bed; **~ en selle** to jump *ou* leap *ou* spring into the saddle; **~ à la gorge** *ou* **au collet de qn** to fly *ou* leap at sb's throat; **~ au cou de qn** to fly into sb's arms; **~ dans un taxi/un autobus** to jump *ou* leap *ou* spring into a taxi/onto a bus; **~ par la fenêtre** to jump *ou* leap out of the window; **~ d'un train en marche** to jump *ou* leap from a moving train; (*fig*) **~ sur une occasion/une proposition** to jump *ou* leap at an opportunity/an offer; **il m'a sauté dessus** he pounced on me, he leaped at me; (*fig*) **saute-lui dessus* quand il sortira du bureau pour lui demander ...** grab him when he comes out of the office and ask him ...; **va faire tes devoirs, et que ça saute!*** go and do your homework and get a move on!* *ou* be quick about it!; **il est malade, cela saute aux yeux** he's ill — it sticks out a mile *ou* it's (quite) obvious, *ou* it's staring you in the face, you can't miss the fact that he's ill; **sa malhonnêteté saute aux yeux** his dishonesty sticks out a mile *ou* is (quite) obvious.
c (*indiquant la discontinuité*) to jump, leap. **~ d'un sujet à l'autre** *ou* **du coq à l'âne** to jump *ou* skip from one subject to another.
d *[bouchon]* to pop *ou* fly out; *[bouton]* to fly *ou* pop off; *[chaîne de vélo]* to come off; (*) *[cours, classe]* to be cancelled. **faire ~ une crêpe** to toss a pancake; **faire ~ une serrure** to burst *ou* break open a lock.
e (*exploser*) *[bombe, pont, bâtiment]* to blow up, explode; (*Élec*) *[fil, circuit]* to fuse; *[fusible]* to blow. **faire ~** *train, édifice* to blow up; (*Élec*) *plombs* to blow; **faire ~ une mine** (*pour la détruire*) to blow up a mine; (*pour détruire un bâtiment etc*) to set off a mine; **se faire ~ avec les otages** to blow o.s. up with the hostages; **se faire ~ la cervelle*** *ou* **le caisson⁑** to blow one's brains out; (*Casino*) **faire ~ la banque** to break the bank; **les plombs ont sauté** the lights have fused, the fuses have blown *ou* gone.
f (*: *être renvoyé*) *[employé, ministère]* to get fired, get the sack* (*Brit*) *ou* the push⁑ *ou* the boot⁑, get kicked out⁑. **faire ~ qn** to fire sb, give sb the sack* (*Brit*) *ou* the push⁑ *ou* the boot⁑, kick sb out⁑.
g (*Culin*) **faire ~** to sauté, (shallow) fry.
h (*clignoter*) *[paupière]* to twitch; *[télévision]* to flicker.
2 vt a (*franchir*) *obstacle, mur* to jump (over), leap (over). **il saute 5 mètres** he can jump 5 metres; **il sauta le fossé d'un bond** he jumped *ou* cleared the ditch with one bound; (*fig*) **~ le pas** to take the plunge.
b (*omettre*) *étape, page, repas* to skip, miss (out). (*Scol*) **~ une classe** to skip a class; **faire ~ un cours** to cancel a class *ou* a lecture; **on la saute ici!⁑** we're starving to death here!*
c (⁑: *avoir des rapports sexuels*) to lay⁑, fuck*⁑, screw*⁑. **elle s'est fait ~ par le patron⁑** she had it off with the boss⁑, she got laid by the boss⁑.
3 comp ▸**saute-mouton** nm leapfrog ▸**saute-ruisseau** (*Hist*) nm inv errand boy, office boy (*in a lawyer's office*).
sauterelle [sotʀɛl] nf (*gén*) grasshopper; (*criquet*) locust. (*lit, fig*) **nuage** *ou* **nuée de ~s** plague *ou* swarm of locusts; (* *fig*) **(grande) ~** beanpole.
sauterie [sotʀi] nf party, thrash*.
sauteur, -euse [sotœʀ, øz] 1 adj *insecte* jumping (*épith*); *oiseau* hopping (*épith*); *voir* **scie**. 2 nm, f (*cheval, athlète*) jumper. 3 nm (*péj: homme*) unreliable type *ou* individual. 4 **sauteuse** nf a (*Culin*) high-sided frying pan. b (⁑ *péj: femme*) easy lay⁑, tart⁑ (*Brit*), scrubber⁑ (*Brit*). **c'est une petite** *ou* **une drôle de ~euse** she's an easy lay⁑, she's a right little tart⁑ (*Brit*) *ou* scrubber⁑ (*Brit*). 5 comp ▸**sauteur en hauteur** high jumper ▸**sauteur en longueur** long jumper ▸**sauteur à la perche** pole vaulter ▸**sauteur à skis** skijumper.
sautillant, e [sotijɑ̃, ɑ̃t] adj (*voir* **sautiller**) *mouvement* hopping (*épith*), skipping (*épith*); *oiseau* hopping (*épith*); *enfant* skipping (*épith*); hopping (*épith*); *musique* bouncy, bouncing (*épith*); *style* jumpy, jerky.
sautillement [sotijmɑ̃] nm (*voir* **sautiller**) hopping; skipping.
sautiller [sotije] [1] vi *[oiseau]* to hop; *[enfant]* to skip; (*sur un pied*) to hop.
sautoir [sotwaʀ] nm a (*Bijouterie*) chain. **~ de perles** string of pearls; **porter qch en ~** to wear sth (on a chain) round one's neck; **épées en ~** crossed swords. b (*Sport*) jumping pit.
sauvage [sovaʒ] 1 adj a (*non civilisé*) *animal, plante, lieu* wild; *peuplade* savage. **vivre à l'état ~** to live wild; *voir* **soie**[1]. b (*farouche*) *animal* wild; *personne* unsociable. c (*brutal*) *cri* wild; *conduite* savage, wild; *combat* savage. d (*illégal*) *vente* unauthorized; *concurrence* unfair; *crèche, école* unofficial; *urbanisation* unplanned; *immigration* illegal. **faire du camping ~** (*illégal*) to camp on unauthorized sites; (*dans la nature*) to camp in the wild, camp rough; *voir* **grève**. 2 nmf a (*solitaire*) unsociable type, recluse. **vivre en ~** to live a secluded life, live as a recluse. b (*brute*) brute, savage. **mœurs de ~s** brutal *ou* brutish *ou* savage ways. c (*indigène*) savage.
sauvagement [sovaʒmɑ̃] adv *frapper* savagely, wildly; *tuer* savagely, brutally.
sauvageon, -onne [sovaʒɔ̃, ɔn] 1 nm, f little savage. 2 nm wild stock (*for grafting*).
sauvagerie [sovaʒʀi] nf (*cruauté*) savagery, savageness, brutality; (*insociabilité*) unsociability, unsociableness.
sauvagin, e [sovaʒɛ̃, in] 1 adj *odeur, goût* of wildfowl. 2 **sauvagine** nf wildfowl. **chasse à la ~e** wildfowling.
sauve [sov] adj f *voir* **sauf**[1].
sauvegarde [sovgaʀd] nf (*gén*) safeguard; (*Ordin*) backup. **sous la ~ de** under the protection of; **être la ~ de** to safeguard, be the safeguard of; **clause de ~** safety clause; (*Ordin*) **faire la ~ d'un programme** to save a program, make a backup of a program.
sauvegarder [sovgaʀde] [1] vt (*gén*) to safeguard; (*Ordin*) to save.
sauve-qui-peut [sovkipø] nm inv (*cri*) (cry of) run for your life; (*panique*) stampede, mad rush.
sauver [sove] [1] 1 vt a (*épargner la mort, la faillite à*) to save; (*porter secours à, essayer de ramener etc*) to rescue. **elle est sauvée!** *[malade]* she has been saved!; *[accidentée, otage]* she has been rescued!; **nous sommes sauvés!*** we've made it!, we're home and dry!; **~ qn/une firme de** *danger, désastre* to save sb/a firm from, rescue sb/a

firm from; **un mot de lui peut tout ~** a word from him can save everything.

b (*sauvegarder*) *biens, cargaison, mobilier* to save, rescue; *honneur* to save. **~ qch de** *incendie etc* to save *ou* rescue sth from.

c (*Rel*) *âme, pécheurs* to save.

d (*fig: racheter*) to save, redeem. **ce sont les illustrations qui sauvent le livre** it's the illustrations which save *ou* redeem the book, the illustrations are the redeeming feature *ou* the saving grace of the book.

e (*loc*) **~ la vie à** *ou* **de qn** to save sb's life; **~ sa peau/tête** to save one's skin *ou* hide*/head; (*fig*) **~ les meubles** to salvage *ou* save something from the wreckage (*fig*); **~ la situation** to retrieve the situation; **~ les apparences** to keep up appearances; **~ la face** to save face; **il m'a sauvé la mise** he bailed me out, he got me out of a tight corner.

2 **se sauver** vpr a **se ~ de** *danger, mauvais pas, désastre* to save o.s. from.

b (*s'enfuir*) to run away (*de* from); (*: *partir*) to be off*, get going. **il s'est sauvé à toutes jambes** he ran away as fast as his legs could carry him; **sauve-toi*, il est déjà 8 heures** you'd better be off* *ou* get going, it's already 8 o'clock; **bon, je me sauve*** right, I'm off* *ou* I'm on my way; **vite, le lait se sauve*** quick, the milk's boiling over.

c **sauve qui peut!** run for your life!; *voir* **sauve-qui-peut**.

sauvetage [sov(ə)taʒ] nm a *[personnes]* rescue; (*moral*) salvation; *[biens]* salvaging. **le ~ des naufragés** rescuing the shipwrecked, the rescue of the shipwrecked; **opérer le ~ de** *personnes* to rescue; *biens* to salvage; **bateau** *ou* **canot de ~** lifeboat; **~ en mer/montagne** sea-/mountain-rescue; (*Écon*) **proposer un plan de ~ de la firme** to put forward a rescue plan for the firm; *voir* **bouée, ceinture** *etc*. b (*technique*) **le ~** life-saving; **épreuve/cours de ~** life-saving competition/lessons.

sauveteur [sov(ə)tœʀ] nm rescuer.

sauvette* [sovɛt] nf: **à la ~** *se marier etc* hastily, hurriedly, double-quick*; **vente à la ~** (unauthorized) street hawking *ou* peddling; **vendre à la ~** to hawk *ou* peddle on the streets (*without authorization*).

sauveur [sovœʀ] adj m, nm saviour.

SAV [ɛsave] nm (abrév de **service après-vente**) *voir* **service**.

savamment [savamɑ̃] adv (*avec érudition*) learnedly; (*adroitement*) skilfully, cleverly. (*par expérience*) **j'en parle ~** I speak knowingly.

savane [savan] nf savannah; (*Can* *) swamp.

savant, e [savɑ̃, ɑ̃t] 1 adj a (*érudit*) *personne* learned, scholarly; *édition* scholarly; *société, mot* learned. **être ~ en** to be learned in; (*hum*) **c'est trop ~ pour moi** *[livre, discussion]* it's too highbrow for me; *[problème]* it's too difficult *ou* complicated for me. b (*habile*) *stratagème, dosage, arrangement* clever, skilful. **le ~ désordre de sa tenue** the studied carelessness *ou* untidiness of his dress. c *chien, puce* performing (*épith*). 2 nm (*sciences*) scientist; (*lettres*) scholar.

savarin [savaʀɛ̃] nm (*Culin*) savarin.

savate* [savat] nf a (*pantoufle*) worn-out old slipper; (*soulier*) worn-out old shoe. **être en ~s** to be in one's slippers; *voir* **traîner**. b (*: *maladroit*) clumsy idiot *ou* oaf. c (*Sport*) French boxing.

savetier†† [sav(ə)tje] nm cobbler†.

saveur [savœʀ] nf (*lit: goût*) flavour; (*fig: piment*) savour.

Savoie [savwa] nf Savoy; *voir* **biscuit**.

savoir [savwaʀ] 32 1 vt a to know. **~ le nom/l'adresse de qn** to know sb's name/address; **c'est difficile à ~** it's difficult to ascertain *ou* know; **je ne savais quoi** *ou* **que dire/faire** I didn't know what to say/do; **oui, je (le) sais** yes I know; **je savais qu'elle était malade, je la savais malade** I knew (that) she was ill, I knew her to be ill; **on ne lui savait pas de parents/de fortune** we didn't know whether *ou* if he had any relatives/money; (*en fait il en a*) we didn't know (that) he had any relatives/money; **savez-vous quand/comment il vient?** do you know when/how he's coming?; **vous savez la nouvelle?** have you heard *ou* do you know the news?; **elle sait cela par** *ou* **de son boucher** she heard it from her butcher; **tout le village sut bientôt la catastrophe** the whole village soon knew *ou* heard *ou* learnt of *ou* about the disaster; **personne ne savait sur quel pied danser/où se mettre** nobody knew what to do/where to put themselves; **il ne savait pas s'il devait accepter** he didn't know whether to accept (or not) *ou* whether *ou* if he should accept (or not); **je crois savoir que** I believe *ou* understand that, I am led to believe *ou* understand that, I have reason to believe that; **je n'en sais rien** I don't know, I have no idea; **il ment — qu'en savez-vous?** he is lying — how do you know? *ou* what do you know about it?; **je voudrais en ~ davantage** I'd like to know more about it; **il nous a fait ~ que** he informed us *ou* let us know that; **ça se saurait si c'était vrai** it would be known if it were true, if that were true people would know about it; **ça finira bien par se ~** it will surely end up getting out *ou* getting known, it'll get out in the end.

b (*avoir des connaissances sur*) to know. **~ le grec/son rôle/sa leçon** to know Greek/one's part/one's lesson; **dites-nous ce que vous savez de l'affaire** tell us what you know about *ou* of the business; **en ~ trop (long)** to know too much; **il croit tout ~** he thinks he knows everything *ou* knows it all; (*péj*) **Monsieur (ou Madame** *ou* **Mademoiselle) je-sais-tout*** smart-alec(k)*, know-all; **tu en sais, des choses*** you certainly know a thing or two, don't you!*; **il ne sait ni A ni B, il ne sait rien de rien** he doesn't know a (single) thing, he hasn't a clue about anything.

c (*avec infin: être capable de*) to know how to. **elle sait lire et écrire** she can read and write, she knows how to read and write; **il ne sait pas nager** he can't swim, he isn't able to *ou* doesn't know how to swim; **~ plaire** to know how to please; **~ vivre** *[épicurien]* to know how to live; *[homme du monde]* to know how to behave; **il sait parler aux enfants** he's good at talking to children, he knows how to talk to children, he can talk to children; **elle saura bien se défendre** she'll be quite able to look after herself, she'll be quite capable of looking after herself, she'll know how to look after herself all right; **il a toujours su y faire** *ou* **s'y prendre** he's always known how to go about things (the right way); **il sait écouter** he's a good listener; **il faut ~ attendre/se contenter de peu** you have to learn to be patient *ou* to wait/be content with little; (*littér, hum*) **on ne saurait penser à tout** one can't think of everything; **je ne saurais vous exprimer toute ma gratitude** I shall never be able to *ou* I could never express my gratitude; **je ne saurais pas vous répondre/vous renseigner** I'm afraid I couldn't answer you *ou* give you an answer/give you any information; **ces explications ont su éclairer et rassurer** these explanations proved both enlightening and reassuring *ou* served both to enlighten and reassure.

d (*se rendre compte*) to know. **il ne sait plus ce qu'il dit** he doesn't know *ou* realize what he's saying, he isn't aware of what he's saying; **je ne sais plus ce que je dis** I no longer know what I'm saying; **il ne sait pas ce qu'il veut** he doesn't know what he wants, he doesn't know his own mind; **il se savait très malade** he knew he was very ill; **elle sait bien qu'il ment** she's well aware of the fact that *ou* she knows very well *ou* full well that he's lying; **sans le ~** (*sans s'en rendre compte*) without knowing *ou* realizing (it), unknowingly; (*sans le faire exprès*) unwittingly, unknowingly; **c'est un artiste sans le ~** he's an artist but he doesn't know it *ou* he isn't aware of the fact.

e (*loc*) **qui sait?** who knows?; **et que sais-je encore** and I don't know what else; **~ si ça va lui plaire!** how can we tell if he'll like it or not!, I don't know whether he's going to *ou* whether he'll like it (or not)!; **je sais ce que je sais** I know what I know; **et puis, tu sais, nous serons très heureux de t'aider** and then, you know, we'll be very happy to help you; **il nous a emmenés je ne sais où** he took us goodness knows where; **je ne sais qui de ses amis m'a dit que ...** one of his friends whose name I forget told me that ...; **il y a je ne sais combien de temps qu'il ne l'a vue** it's *ou* it has been I don't know how long since he (last) saw her, I don't how long it is *ou* it has been since he (last) saw her; **elle ne sait pas quoi faire** *ou* **elle ne sait que faire pour l'aider/le consoler** she's at a loss to know how to help him/comfort him; **on ne sait pas par quel bout le prendre** you just don't know how to tackle him; **il n'a rien voulu ~*** he didn't want to know; **on ne sait jamais** you never know, you *ou* one can never tell, one never knows; **(pour autant) que je sache** as far as I know, to the best of my knowledge; **pas que je sache** not as far as I know, not to my knowledge; **je ne sache pas que je vous ai invité!** I'm not aware that *ou* I don't know that I invited you!; **sachons-le bien, si ...** let's be quite clear, if ...; **sachez (bien) que jamais je n'accepterai!** I'll have you know *ou* let me tell you *ou* you may be assured that I shall never accept; **oui, mais sachez qu'à l'origine, c'est elle-même qui ne le voulait pas** yes but you should know *ou* you may as well know that at the start it was she herself who didn't want to; **à ~** that is, namely, i.e.; (*hum*) **l'objet/la personne que vous savez sera là demain** you-know-what/you-know-who will be there tomorrow (*hum*); (*frm*) **vous n'êtes pas sans ~ que** you are not *ou* will not be unaware (of the fact) that (*frm*), you will not be ignorant of the fact that (*frm*); **il m'a su gré/il ne m'a su aucun gré de l'avoir averti** he was grateful to me/he wasn't in the least grateful to me for having warned him; **il ne savait à quel saint se vouer** he didn't know which way to turn; **si je savais, j'irais la chercher** if I knew (for sure) *ou* if I could be sure, I would go and look for her; **elle ne savait où donner de la tête** she didn't know whether she was coming or going *ou* what to do first; **si j'avais su** had I known, if I had known; *voir* **dieu, qui** *etc*.

2 nm learning, knowledge.

3 comp ►**savoir-faire** nm inv know-how* ►**savoir-vivre** nm inv savoir-faire, mannerliness; **il n'a aucun savoir-vivre** he has no savoir-faire, he has no idea how to behave (in society).

savon [savɔ̃] nm a (*matière*) soap (*NonC*); (*morceau*) bar *ou* tablet *ou* cake of soap. **~ liquide/noir** liquid/soft soap; **~ à barbe/de toilette/de Marseille** shaving/toilet/household soap; **~ en paillettes/en poudre** soap flakes/powder; *voir* **bulle, pain**. b (*) **il m'a passé/j'ai reçu un (bon) ~** he gave me/I got a (good) ticking-off* (*Brit*) *ou* dressing-down*, he (really) tore a strip/I (really) got a strip torn off me* (*Brit*).

savonnage [savɔnaʒ] nm soaping (*NonC*).

savonner [savɔne] 1 vt *linge, enfant* to soap; *barbe* to lather, soap. **~ la tête de qn*** to give sb a dressing-down*, haul sb over the coals*; (*fig*) **~ la planche à qn*** to make life difficult for sb*.

savonnerie [savɔnʀi] nf a (*usine*) soap factory. b (*tapis*) Savonnerie carpet.

savonnette [savɔnɛt] nf bar *ou* tablet *ou* cake of (toilet) soap.

savonneux, -euse [savɔnø, øz] adj soapy.

savourer [savuʀe] 1 vt *plat, boisson, plaisanterie, triomphe* to savour.

savoureux, -euse [savuʀø, øz] adj *plat* tasty, flavoursome; *anecdote* juicy, spicy.

savoyard, e [savwajaʀ, aʀd] 1 adj Savoyard, of Savoie. 2 nm,f:

S~(e) Savoyard.
Saxe [saks] nf Saxony; *voir* **porcelaine**.
saxe [saks] nm Dresden china (*NonC*); (*objet*) piece of Dresden china.
saxhorn [saksɔʀn] nm saxhorn.
saxifrage [saksifʀaʒ] nm saxifrage.
saxo* [sakso] 1 nm (*instrument*) sax*. 2 nm (*musicien*) sax player*.
saxon, -onne [saksɔ̃, ɔn] 1 adj Saxon. 2 nm (*Ling*) Saxon. 3 nm, f: **S~(-onne)** Saxon.
saxophone [saksɔfɔn] nm saxophone.
saxophoniste [saksɔfɔnist] nmf saxophonist, saxophone player.
saynète [sɛnɛt] nf playlet.
sbire [sbiʀ] nm (*péj*) henchman (*péj*).
S.C. (abrév de **service compris**) *voir* **service**.
s/c (abrév de **sous couvert de**) c/o.
scabieux, -ieuse [skabjø, jøz] 1 adj scabious. 2 **scabieuse** nf scabious.
scabreux, -euse [skabʀø, øz] adj (*indécent*) improper, shocking; (*dangereux*) risky.
scalaire [skalɛʀ] 1 adj (*Math*) scalar. 2 nm (*poisson*) angel fish, scalare.
scalène [skalɛn] adj scalene.
scalp [skalp] nm (*action*) scalping; (*chevelure*) scalp.
scalpel [skalpɛl] nm scalpel.
scalper [skalpe] 1 vt to scalp.
scampi [skɑ̃pi] nmpl scampi.
scandale [skɑ̃dal] nm a (*fait choquant, affaire*) scandal. **~ financier/public** financial/public scandal; **c'est un ~!** it's scandalous! *ou* outrageous!, it's a scandal!; **sa tenue/ce livre a fait ~** his clothes/that book scandalized people, people found his clothes/that book scandalizing; **au grand ~ de mon père, j'ai voulu épouser un étranger** I wanted to marry a foreigner, which scandalized my father, much to the alarm of my father I wanted to marry a foreigner; **elle va crier au ~** she'll make a great protest about it, she'll cry out in indignation; **les gens vont crier au ~** there'll be an outcry *ou* a public outcry; **à ~** *livre, couple* controversial, headline-hitting* *(épith)*; **journal à ~** scandal sheet.
b (*scène, tapage*) scene, fuss. **faire un** *ou* **du ~** to make a scene, kick up a fuss*; **et pas de ~!** and don't make a fuss!; **condamné pour ~ sur la voie publique** fined for disturbing the peace *ou* for creating a public disturbance.
scandaleusement [skɑ̃daløzmɑ̃] adv *se comporter* scandalously, outrageously, shockingly; *cher* scandalously, outrageously, prohibitively; *laid, mauvais* appallingly; *sous-estimé, exagéré* grossly.
scandaleux, -euse [skɑ̃dalø, øz] adj *conduite, propos, prix* scandalous, outrageous, shocking; *littérature, chronique* outrageous, shocking. **vie ~euse** life of scandal, scandalous life.
scandaliser [skɑ̃dalize] 1 vt to scandalize, shock deeply. **se ~ de qch** to be deeply shocked at sth, be scandalized by sth.
scander [skɑ̃de] 1 vt *vers* to scan; *discours* to give emphasis to; *mots* to articulate separately; *nom, slogan* to chant.
scandinave [skɑ̃dinav] 1 adj Scandinavian. 2 nmf: **S~** Scandinavian.
Scandinavie [skɑ̃dinavi] nf Scandinavia.
scandium [skɑ̃djɔm] nm scandium.
scanner [skanɛʀ] nm (*Méd*) scanner; (*Opt*) (*optical*) scanner. **passer un ~*** to have a scan.
scanneur [skanœʀ] nm (*Méd*) scanner; (*Opt*) (*optical*) scanner.
scanographe [skanɔgʀaf] nm (*Méd*) scanner.
scanographie [skanɔgʀafi] nf (*science*) (body) scanning; (*photo*) scan. **~ du cerveau** brain scan.
scansion [skɑ̃sjɔ̃] nf scanning, scansion.
scaphandre [skafɑ̃dʀ] nm *[plongeur]* diving suit; *[cosmonaute]* spacesuit. **~ autonome** aqualung, scuba.
scaphandrier [skafɑ̃dʀije] nm (underwater) diver.
scapulaire [skapylɛʀ] adj, nm (*Anat, Méd, Rel*) scapular.
scarabée [skaʀabe] nm beetle, scarab (*SPÉC*).
scarificateur [skaʀifikatœʀ] nm (*Méd*) scarificator; (*Agr*) scarifier.
scarification [skaʀifikasjɔ̃] nf scarification.
scarifier [skaʀifje] 7 vt (*Agr, Méd*) to scarify.
scarlatine [skaʀlatin] nf scarlet fever, scarlatina (*SPÉC*).
scarole [skaʀɔl] nf endive.
scatologie [skatɔlɔʒi] nf scatology.
scatologique [skatɔlɔʒik] adj scatological, lavatorial.
sceau, pl **~x** [so] nm (*cachet, estampille*) seal; (*fig: marque*) stamp, mark. **mettre son ~ sur** to put one's seal to *ou* on; **apposer son ~ sur** to affix one's seal to; (*fig*) **porter le ~ du génie** to bear the stamp *ou* mark of genius; **sous le ~ du secret** under the seal of secrecy; *voir* **garde**[2].
scélérat, e [seleʀa, at] 1 adj (*littér*, ††) villainous, blackguardly††; wicked. 2 nm, f (*littér*, ††: *criminel*) villain, blackguard††. **petit ~!*** (you) little rascal!
scélératesse [seleʀatɛs] nf (*littér*, ††) (*caractère*) villainy, wickedness; (*acte*) villainy, villainous *ou* wicked *ou* blackguardly†† deed.
scellement [sɛlmɑ̃] nm (*voir* **sceller**) sealing; embedding (*NonC*).
sceller [sele] 1 vt a *pacte, document, sac* to seal. b (*Constr*) to embed.
scellés [sele] nmpl seals. **apposer** *ou* **mettre les ~ sur une porte** to put the seals on a door, affix the seals to a door; **lever les ~** to take the seals off.
scellofrais [sɛlɔfʀɛ] nm ® cling film, cling wrap.
scénario [senaʀjo] nm (*Ciné, Théât: plan*) scenario; (*Ciné: découpage et dialogues*) screenplay, (film) script, scenario. (*évolution possible*) **il y a plusieurs ~s possibles** there are several possible scenarios; (*fig*) **ça s'est déroulé selon le ~ habituel** (*attentat*) it followed the usual pattern; (*conférence de presse*) it followed the usual ritual *ou* pattern; **c'est toujours le même ~*** it's always the same old ritual *ou* carry-on* (*Brit*).
scénariste [senaʀist] nmf (*Ciné*) scriptwriter.
scène [sɛn] nf a (*estrade*) stage. **~ tournante** revolving stage; **être en ~** to be on stage; **sortir de ~** to go offstage, exit; **en ~!** on stage!; **occuper le devant de la ~** to be in the foreground; *voir* **entrée**.
b (*le théâtre*) **la ~** the stage; **les vedettes de la ~ et de l'écran** the stars of stage and screen; **à la ~ comme à la ville** (both) on stage and off, both on and off (the) stage; **porter une œuvre à la ~** to bring a work to the stage, stage a work; **adapter un film pour la ~** to adapt a film for the stage; **mettre en ~** (*Théât*) *personnage, histoire* to present, put on stage; *auteur, romancier* to stage; *pièce de théâtre* to stage, direct; (*Ciné*) *film* to direct; **ce chapitre met en ~/dans ce chapitre l'auteur met en ~ un nouveau personnage** this chapter presents/in this chap- ter the author presents a new character; *voir* **metteur, mise**[2].
c (*Ciné, Théât: division*) scene. **dans la première ~** in the first *ou* opening scene, in scene one; **~ d'amour** love scene; (*fig*) **elle m'a joué la grande ~ du deux*** she put on a great act, she acted out a big scene*.
d (*décor*) scene. **la ~ représente un salon du 18e siècle** the scene represents an 18th-century drawing room; **changement de ~** scene change.
e (*lieu de l'action*) scene. (*Ciné, Théât*) **la ~ est** *ou* **se passe à Rome** the action takes place in Rome, the scene is set in Rome; (*gén*) **arrivé sur la ~ du crime/drame** having arrived at the scene of the crime/drama.
f (*spectacle*) scene. **le témoin a assisté à toute la ~** the witness was present at *ou* during the whole scene; (*Psych*) **la ~ originaire** *ou* **primitive** the primal scene.
g (*confrontation, dispute*) scene. **une ~ de réconciliation** a scene of reconciliation; **j'ai assisté à une pénible ~ de rupture** I witnessed a distressing break-up scene; **faire une ~ d'indignation** to put on a great show of indignation; **~ de ménage** domestic fight *ou* scene; **faire une ~** to make a scene; **il m'a fait une ~ parce que j'avais oublié la clef** he made a scene because I had forgotten the key; **avoir une ~ (avec qn)** to have a scene (with sb).
h (*fig: domaine*) scene. **sur la ~ politique/universitaire/internationale** on the political/university/international scene.
i (*Art: tableau*) scene. **~ d'intérieur/mythologique** indoor/mythological scene; **~ de genre** genre painting.
scenic railway [senikʀɛlwɛ] nm roller coaster, big dipper, switchback (*Brit*).
scénique [senik] adj theatrical; *voir* **indication**.
scéniquement [senikmɑ̃] adv (*Théât*) theatrically.
scénographie [senɔgʀafi] nf (*Théât*) scenography.
scepticisme [sɛptisism] nm scepticism.
sceptique [sɛptik] 1 adj sceptical, sceptic. 2 nmf sceptic; (*Philos*) Sceptic.
sceptiquement [sɛptikmɑ̃] adv sceptically.
sceptre [sɛptʀ] nm (*lit, fig*) sceptre.
schah [ʃa] nm = **shah**.
schako [ʃako] nm = **shako**.
schapska [ʃapska] nm = **chapska**.
Schéhérazade [ʃeeʀazad] nf Sheherazade.
scheik [ʃɛk] nm = **cheik**.
schelem [ʃlɛm] nm = **chelem**.
schelling [ʃ(ə)lɛ̃] nm = **schilling**.
schéma [ʃema] nm a (*diagramme*) diagram, sketch. **~ de montage** assembly diagram *ou* instructions. b (*résumé*) outline. **faire le ~ de l'opération** to give an outline of the operation.
schématique [ʃematik] adj *dessin* diagrammatic(al), schematic; (*péj*) *interprétation, conception* oversimplified.
schématiquement [ʃematikmɑ̃] adv *représenter* diagrammatically, schematically. **il exposa l'affaire ~** he gave an outline of the affair, he outlined the affair; **très ~, voici de quoi il s'agit** ... briefly this is what it's all about ... .
schématisation [ʃematizasjɔ̃] nf schematization; (*péj*) (over)simplification.
schématiser [ʃematize] 1 vt to schematize; (*péj*) to (over)simplify.
schématisme [ʃematism] nm (*péj*) oversimplicity.
schème [ʃɛm] nm (*Philos*) schema; (*Art*) design, scheme.
scherzando [skɛʀtsando] adv scherzando.
scherzo [skɛʀdzo] 1 nm scherzo. 2 adv scherzando.
schilling [ʃiliŋ] nm schilling.
schismatique [ʃismatik] adj, nmf schismatic.

schisme [ʃism] nm (*Rel*) schism; (*Pol*) split. **faire** ~ to split away.
schiste [ʃist] nm (*métamorphique*) schist, shale. ~ **bitumineux** oil shale; **huile de** ~ shale oil.
schisteux, -euse [ʃistø, øz] adj schistose.
schizoïde [skizɔid] adj, nmf schizoid.
schizophrène [skizɔfʀɛn] adj, nmf (*Méd, fig*) schizophrenic.
schizophrénie [skizɔfʀeni] nf (*Méd, fig*) schizophrenia.
schlague [ʃlag] nf (*Mil Hist*) **la** ~ drubbing, flogging; **ils n'obéissent qu'à la** ~‡ they only obey if you really lay into them‡ *ou* if you give them what-for‡.
schlass‡ [ʃlɑs] 1 adj inv sozzled‡, plastered‡. 2 nm knife.
schlinguer‡ [ʃlɛ̃ge] 1 vi to pong‡, stink to high heaven*.
schlittage [ʃlitaʒ] nm sledging (*of wood*).
schlitte [ʃlit] nf sledge (*for transporting wood*).
schlitter [ʃlite] 1 vt to sledge (*wood*).
schnaps [ʃnaps] nm schnap(p)s.
schnock‡, schnoque‡ [ʃnɔk] nm: **(vieux)** ~ (old) fathead!‡ *ou* blockhead!‡; **eh! du** ~ hey, fathead!‡ *ou* blockhead!‡
schnouff† [ʃnuf] nf (*arg Drogue*) dope (*arg*), junk (*arg*).
schproum* [ʃpʀum] nm: **faire du** ~ to kick up a stink‡; **il va y avoir du** ~ there will be a tremendous outcry, there will be a hell of a fuss*.
Schtroumpf [ʃtʀumf] nm Smurf.
schuss [ʃus] 1 nm schuss. 2 adv: **descendre (tout)** ~ to schuss (down).
schwa [ʃva] nm schwa(h).
Schweppes [ʃwɛps] nm ® (Indian) tonic.
SCI [ɛssei] nf (abrév de **société civile immobilière**) *voir* **société**.
sciage [sjaʒ] nm *[bois, métal]* sawing.
sciatique [sjatik] 1 nf sciatica. 2 adj sciatic.
scie [si] nf a saw. ~ **à bois** wood saw; ~ **circulaire** circular saw; ~ **à chantourner** *ou* **découper** fretsaw; ~ **électrique** power saw; ~ **à métaux** hacksaw; ~ **musicale** musical saw; ~ **à ruban** bandsaw; ~ **sauteuse** jigsaw; ~ **à tronçonner** chain saw, cross-cut saw; *voir* **couteau, dent, poisson.** b (*péj*) (*chanson*) catch-tune; (*personne*) bore.
sciemment [sjamɑ̃] adv knowingly, wittingly, on purpose.
science [sjɑ̃s] 1 nf a (*domaine scientifique*) science. **les** ~**s** (*gén*) the sciences; (*Scol*) science; **la** ~ **du beau/de l'être** the science of beauty/of being; ~**s appliquées/exactes/pures/humaines/occultes** applied/exact/pure/social/occult sciences; ~**s expérimentales** experimental sciences; (*Univ*) **institut des** ~**s sociales** institute of social science; (*Scol*) ~**s naturelles** biology, natural science†; ~**s physiques** physical science; ~**s marines** *ou* **de la mer** marine science; **les** ~**s de la vie** the life sciences; ~**s d'observation** observational sciences; ~ **politique** political science; (*Univ*) **S~s Po** *French school of political science; voir* **homme.**
b (*art, habileté*) art. **la** ~ **de la guerre** the science *ou* art of war; **faire qch avec une** ~ **consommée** to do sth with consummate skill; **sa** ~ **des couleurs** his skillful use of colour.
c (*érudition*) knowledge. **avoir la** ~ **infuse** to have innate knowledge; (*Rel*) **la** ~ **du bien et du mal** the knowledge of good and evil; **savoir de** ~ **certaine que** to know for a fact *ou* for certain that; *voir* **puits.**
2 comp ▸**science-fiction** nf science fiction; **film/livre de science-fiction** science fiction film/book; **œuvre de science-fiction** work of science fiction.
scientificité [sjɑ̃tifisite] nf scientific character *ou* nature.
scientifique [sjɑ̃tifik] 1 adj scientific. 2 nmf scientist.
scientifiquement [sjɑ̃tifikmɑ̃] adv scientifically.
scientisme [sjɑ̃tism] nm scientism.
scientiste [sjɑ̃tist] 1 nmf adept of scientism. 2 adj scientistic.
scientologie [sjɑ̃tɔlɔʒi] nf Scientology.
scientologue [sjɑ̃tɔlɔg] adj, nmf Scientologist.
scier [sje] 7 vt a (*gén*) *bois, métal* to saw; *bûche* to saw (up); *partie en trop* to saw off. ~ **une branche pour faire des bûches** to saw (up) a branch into logs; (*fig*) ~ **la branche sur laquelle on est assis** to dig one's own grave. b (**: stupéfier*) **ça m'a scié!** it bowled me over!*, it staggered me!*; **c'est vraiment sciant!** it's absolutely staggering!* c (**: ennuyer*) ~ **qn** to bore sb rigid* *ou* stiff*.
scierie [siʀi] nf sawmill.
scieur [sjœʀ] nm sawyer. ~ **de long** pit sawyer.
scille [sil] nf scilla.
Scilly [sili] n: **les îles** ~ the Scilly Isles.
scinder [sɛ̃de] 1 1 vt to split (up), divide (up) (*en* in, into). 2 **se scinder** vpr to split (up) (*en* in, into).
scintigraphie [sɛ̃tigʀafi] nf scintigraphy.
scintillant, e [sɛ̃tijɑ̃, ɑ̃t] adj (*voir* **scintiller**) sparkling; glittering; twinkling; scintillating; glistening.
scintillation [sɛ̃tijasjɔ̃] nf (*Astron, Phys*) scintillation. **compteur à** ~**s** scintillation counter.
scintillement [sɛ̃tijmɑ̃] nm (*voir* **scintiller**) sparkling; glittering; twinkling; scintillating; glistening. **le** ~ **de son esprit** his scintillating mind.
scintiller [sɛ̃tije] 1 vi *[diamant]* to sparkle, glitter; *[étoile]* to twinkle, sparkle, scintillate; *[yeux]* to sparkle, glitter (*de* with); *[lumières, firmament]* to glitter, sparkle; *[goutte d'eau]* to glisten; *[esprit]* to sparkle, scintillate.
scion [sjɔ̃] nm (*Bot*) (*gén*) twig; (*greffe*) scion; (*Pêche*) top piece.
Scipion [sipjɔ̃] nm Scipio. ~ **l'Africain** Scipio Africanus.
scission [sisjɔ̃] nf a (*schisme*) split, scission (*frm*). **faire** ~ to split away, secede. b (*Écon*) demerger. c (*Bot, Phys*) fission.
scissionniste [sisjɔnist] adj, nmf secessionist.
scissipare [sisipaʀ] adj fissiparous.
scissiparité [sisipaʀite] nf scissiparity, schizogenesis.
scissure [sisyʀ] nf fissure, sulcus.
sciure [sjyʀ] nf: ~ **(de bois)** sawdust; **acheter une bague dans la** ~† to buy a ring from a street hawker.
scléreux, -euse [skleʀø, øz] adj sclerotic.
sclérosant, e [skleʀozɑ̃, ɑ̃t] adj (*fig*) ossifying.
sclérose [skleʀoz] nf a (*Méd*) sclerosis. ~ **artérielle** hardening of the arteries, arteriosclerosis (SPÉC); ~ **en plaques** multiple sclerosis. b (*fig*) ossification.
sclérosé, e [skleʀoze] (ptp de **se scléroser**) adj (*lit*) sclerosed, sclerotic; (*fig*) ossified.
scléroser (se) [skleʀoze] 1 vpr (*Méd*) to become sclerotic *ou* sclerosed, sclerose; (*fig*) to become ossified.
sclérotique [skleʀɔtik] nf sclera, sclerotic.
scolaire [skɔlɛʀ] adj a (*gén*) school (*épith*). **année** ~ school *ou* academic year; **ses succès** ~**s** his success in *ou* at school, his scholastic achievements *ou* attainments; **enfant d'âge** ~ child of school age; **progrès** ~**s** academic progress; *voir* **établissement, groupe, livret** *etc.* b (*péj*) schoolish. **son livre est un peu** ~ **par endroits** his book is a bit schoolish in places.
scolairement [skɔlɛʀmɑ̃] adv *réciter* schoolishly.
scolarisable [skɔlaʀizabl] adj educable.
scolarisation [skɔlaʀizasjɔ̃] nf *[enfant]* schooling. **la** ~ **d'une population/d'un pays** providing a population with schooling/country with schools; **taux de** ~ percentage of children in full-time education.
scolariser [skɔlaʀize] 1 vt *enfant* to provide with schooling, send to school; *pays, région* to provide with schools *ou* schooling.
scolarité [skɔlaʀite] nf schooling. **la** ~ **a été prolongée** schooling has been extended, the school-leaving age has been raised; **pendant mes années de** ~ during my school years *ou* years at school; ~ **obligatoire** compulsory school attendance, compulsory schooling; (*Univ*) **service de la** ~ registrar's office; *voir* **certificat, frais²**.
scolastique [skɔlastik] 1 adj (*Philos, péj*) scholastic. 2 nf scholasticism. 3 nm (*Philos*) scholastic, schoolman; (*péj*) scholastic.
scoliose [skɔljoz] nf curvature of the spine, scoliosis (SPÉC).
scolopendre [skɔlɔpɑ̃dʀ] nf (*Zool*) centipede, scolopendra (SPÉC); (*Bot*) hart's-tongue, scolopendrium (SPÉC).
sconse [skɔ̃s] nm skunk (fur).
scoop* [skup] nm (*Presse*) scoop.
scooter [skutœʀ] nm (motor) scooter. ~ **des mers** jet ski; ~ **des neiges** Skidoo ®.
scootériste [skuteʀist] nmf scooter rider.
scopie‡ [skɔpi] nf abrév de **radioscopie**.
scorbut [skɔʀbyt] nm scurvy.
scorbutique [skɔʀbytik] adj *symptômes* of scurvy, scorbutic (SPÉC); *personne* suffering from scurvy, scorbutic (SPÉC).
score [skɔʀ] nm (*gén, Sport*) score. (*Pol*) **faire un bon/mauvais** ~ to have a good/bad result.
scorie [skɔʀi] nf (*gén pl*) (*Ind*) slag (*NonC*), scoria (*NonC*), clinker (*NonC*); (*fig*) dross (*NonC*). (*Géol*) ~**s (volcaniques)** (volcanic) scoria.
scorpion [skɔʀpjɔ̃] nm a (*Zool*) scorpion. ~ **d'eau** water-scorpion; ~ **de mer** scorpion-fish. b (*Astron*) **le S~** Scorpio, the Scorpion; **être (du) S~** to be (a) Scorpio.
scotch [skɔtʃ] nm a (*boisson*) scotch (whisky). b **S~** ® (*adhésif*) Sellotape ® (*Brit*), Scotchtape ® (*US*).
scotcher [skɔtʃe] 1 vt ® to sellotape ® (*Brit*), stick with Scotchtape ® (*US*).
scoubidou [skubidu] nm *strip of plaited plastic threads.*
scoumoune‡ [skumun] nf (*arg Crime*) tough *ou* rotten luck*.
scout, e [skut] adj, nm scout, boyscout. (*péj*) **avoir un côté** ~ to be a bit boyscoutish*.
scoutisme [skutism] nm (*mouvement*) scout movement; (*activité*) scouting.
SCPI [ɛssepei] nf (abrév de **société civile de placement immobilier**) *voir* **société.**
Scrabble [skʀabl] nm ® Scrabble ®.
scratcher [skʀatʃe] 1 vt (*Sport*) to scratch.
scriban [skʀibɑ̃] nm (*avec cabinet*) bureau bookcase; (*sans cabinet*) slant-front bureau.
scribe [skʀib] nm (*péj: bureaucrate*) penpusher (*péj*); (*Hist*) scribe.
scribouillard, e [skʀibujaʀ, aʀd] nm, f (*péj*) penpusher (*péj*).
script [skʀipt] 1 nm a **(écriture)** ~ printing; **apprendre le** ~ to learn how to print (letters); **écrire en** ~ to print. b (*Ciné*) (shooting) script. 2 nf = **script-girl.**
scripte [skʀipt] nf (*Ciné*) continuity girl.
scripteur [skʀiptœʀ] nm (*Ling*) writer.
script-girl, pl **script-girls** [skʀiptgœʀl] nf continuity girl.
scriptural, e, mpl **-aux** [skʀiptyʀal, o] adj *voir* **monnaie.**

scrofulaire [skʀɔfylɛʀ] nf figwort.
scrofule [skʀɔfyl] nf (*Méd*) scrofula. (*Hist Méd*) **~s** scrofula, king's evil.
scrofuleux, -euse [skʀɔfylø, øz] adj *tumeur* scrofulous; *personne* scrofulous, suffering from scrofula.
scrogneugneu [skʀɔɲøɲø] excl damnation!, damn me!
scrotal, e, mpl **-aux** [skʀɔtal, o] adj scrotal.
scrotum [skʀɔtɔm] nm scrotum.
scrupule [skʀypyl] nm a scruple. **avoir des ~s** to have scruples; **avoir des ~s à** *ou* **se faire ~ de faire qch** to have scruples *ou* misgivings *ou* qualms about doing sth; **faire taire ses ~s** to silence one's qualms of conscience *ou* one's scruples; **je n'aurais aucun ~ à refuser** I wouldn't have any scruples *ou* qualms *ou* misgivings about refusing, I wouldn't scruple to refuse; **son honnêteté est poussée jusqu'au ~** his honesty is absolutely scrupulous; **il est dénué de ~s** he has no scruples, he is completely unscrupulous; **sans ~s** *personne* unscrupulous, without scruples; *agir* without scruple, unscrupulously; **vos ~s vous honorent** your scrupulousness is *ou* your scruples are a credit to you; **je comprends votre ~** *ou* **vos ~s** I understand your scruples.
b (*souci de*) **dans un** *ou* **par un ~ d'honnêteté/d'exactitude historique** in scrupulous regard for honesty/historical exactness.
scrupuleusement [skʀypyløzmɑ̃] adv scrupulously.
scrupuleux, -euse [skʀypylø, øz] adj *personne, honnêteté* scrupulous. **peu ~** unscrupulous.
scrutateur, -trice [skʀytatœʀ, tʀis] 1 adj (*littér*) *regard, caractère* searching. 2 nm (*Pol*) scrutineer (*Brit*), teller, canvasser (*US*).
scruter [skʀyte] 1 vt *horizon* to scan, search, scrutinize, examine; *objet, personne* to scrutinize, examine; *pénombre* to peer into, search.
scrutin [skʀytɛ̃] nm a (*vote*) ballot. **par voie de ~** by ballot; **voter au ~ secret** to vote by secret ballot; **il a été élu au troisième tour de ~** he was elected on *ou* at the third ballot *ou* round; **dépouiller le ~** to count the votes. b (*élection*) poll. **le jour du ~** polling day; **ouverture/clôture du ~** start/close of polling. c (*modalité*) **~ de liste** list system; **~ d'arrondissement** district election system; **~ majoritaire** election on a majority basis; **~ proportionnel** voting using the system of proportional representation; **~ de ballottage** second ballot, second round of voting; **~ uninominal** uninominal system.
sculpter [skylte] 1 vt *statue, marbre* to sculpture, sculpt; *meuble* to carve, sculpture, sculpt; *bâton, bois* to carve. **elle peint et sculpte** she paints and sculptures *ou* sculpts; **~ qch dans du bois** to carve sth out of wood.
sculpteur [skyltœʀ] nm (*homme*) sculptor; (*femme*) sculptress. **~ sur bois** woodcarver.
sculptural, e, mpl **-aux** [skyltyʀal, o] adj (*Art*) sculptural; (*fig*) *beauté, femme* statuesque.
sculpture [skyltyʀ] nf (*art, objet*) sculpture; (*Aut*) *[pneu]* tread pattern. **~ sur bois** woodcarving; **les ~s d'un pneu** the pattern on a tyre.
Scylla [sila] nf Scylla; *voir* **tomber.**
scythe [sit] 1 adj Scythian. 2 nm (*Ling*) Scythian. 3 nmf: **S~** Scythian.
scythie [siti] nf Scythia.
scythique [sitik] adj = **scythe.**
S.D.N. [ɛsdeɛn] nf (abrév de **Société des Nations**) *voir* **société.**
se [sə] pron a (*valeur strictement réfléchie*) (*sg*) (*indéfini*) oneself; (*sujet humain mâle*) himself; (*sujet humain femelle*) herself; (*sujet non humain*) itself; (*pl*) themselves. **~ regarder dans la glace** to look at o.s. in the mirror; (*action le plus souvent réfléchie: forme parfois intransitive en anglais*) **~ raser/laver** to shave/wash; **~ mouiller/salir** to get wet/dirty; **~ brûler/couper** to burn/cut o.s.; *voir* **écouter, faire.**
b (*réciproque*) each other, one another. **deux personnes qui s'aiment** two people who love each other *ou* one another; **des gens/3 frères qui ~ haïssent** people/3 brothers who hate one another *ou* each other.
c (*valeur possessive: se traduit par l'adjectif possessif*) **~ casser la jambe** to break one's leg; **il ~ lave les mains** he is washing his hands; **elle s'est coupé les cheveux** she has cut her hair.
d (*valeur passive: généralement rendu par une construction passive*) **cela ne ~ fait pas** that's not done; **cela ~ répare/recolle facilement** it can easily be repaired again/glued together again; **la vérité finira par ~ savoir** (the) truth will out (in the end), the truth will finally be found out; **l'anglais ~ parle dans le monde entier** English is spoken throughout the world; **cela ~ vend bien** it sells well; **les escargots ~ servent dans la coquille** snails are served in their shells *ou* the shell, one serves snails in the shell.
e (*en tournure impersonnelle*) **il ~ peut que** it may be that, it is possible that; **comment ~ fait-il que ...?** how is it that ...?
f (*autres emplois pronominaux*) (*exprime le devenir*) **s'améliorer** to get better; **s'élargir** to get wider; **~ développer** to develop; **~ transformer** to change; (*indique une action subie*) **~ boucher** to become *ou* get blocked; **~ casser** to break; **~ fendre** to crack; *pour tous ces cas, et les emplois purement pronominaux* (*à valeur intransitive*), *V le verbe en question.*
S.E. (abrév de **Son Excellence**) HE.
S.É. (abrév de **Son Éminence**) HE.

séance [seɑ̃s] nf a (*réunion*) *[conseil municipal]* meeting, session; *[tribunal, parlement]* session, sitting; *[comité]* séance. **~ de spiritisme** séance; **être en ~** to be in session, sit; **la ~ est levée** the meeting is ended, the meeting is at an end; **~ extraordinaire** extraordinary meeting; *voir* **suspension.**
b (*période*) session. **~ de photographie/de rééducation/de gymnastique** photographic *ou* photography/physiotherapy/gymnastics session; **~ de pose** sitting.
c (*représentation*) (*Théât*) performance. **~ privée** private showing *ou* performance; **~ de cinéma** film show; (*Ciné*) **première/dernière ~** first/last showing.
d (**: scène*) performance*. **faire une ~ à qn** to give sb a performance*.
e **~ tenante** forthwith; **nous partirons ~ tenante** we shall leave forthwith *ou* without further ado.
séant[1] [seɑ̃] nm (*hum: derrière*) posterior (*hum*). (*frm*) **se mettre sur son ~** to sit up (*from a lying position*).
séant[2]**, séante** [seɑ̃, seɑ̃t] adj (*littér: convenable*) seemly (*littér*), fitting (*littér*). **il n'est pas ~ de dire cela** it is unseemly *ou* unfitting to *ou* it is not seemly *ou* fitting to say that.
seau, pl **~x** [so] nm (*récipient*) bucket, pail; (*contenu*) bucket(ful), pail(ful). **il pleut à ~x, la pluie tombe à ~x** it's coming *ou* pouring down in buckets *ou* bucketfuls, it's raining buckets* *ou* cats and dogs; **~ à champagne/glace** champagne/ice-bucket; **~ à charbon** coal scuttle; **~ hygiénique** slop pail.
sébacé, e [sebase] adj sebaceous.
Sébastien [sebastjɛ̃] nm Sebastian.
sébile [sebil] nf (small wooden) bowl.
séborrhée [sebɔʀe] nf seborrhoea.
sébum [sebɔm] nm sebum.
sec, sèche[1] [sɛk, sɛʃ] 1 adj a *climat, temps, bois, linge, toux* dry; *raisins, figue* dried. **je n'ai plus un poil de ~*** I'm sweating like a pig*, I'm soaked through; **elle le regarda partir, l'œil ~** she watched him go, dry-eyed; (*fig*) **avoir la gorge sèche*, avoir le gosier ~*** to be parched *ou* dry; *voir* **cale**[1]**, cinq, cul** *etc.*
b (*sans graisse*) *épiderme, cheveu* dry; (*maigre*) *personne, bras* lean. **il est ~ comme un coup de trique*** *ou* **comme un hareng*** he's as thin as a rake.
c (*sans douceur*) *style, ton, vin, rire, bruit* dry; *personne* hard (-hearted), cold; *cœur* cold, hard; *réponse* curt; *tissu* harsh; *jeu* crisp. (*Sport*) **placage ~** hard tackle; **il lui a écrit une lettre très sèche** he wrote him a very curt letter; **se casser avec un bruit ~** to break with a sharp snap; *voir* **coup.**
d (*sans eau*) *alcool* neat. **il prend son whisky ~** he takes *ou* drinks his whisky neat *ou* straight.
e (*Cartes*) **atout/valet ~** singleton trumps/jack; **son valet était ~** his jack was a singleton.
f (** loc*) **je l'ai eu ~** I was cut up (about it)*; **être** *ou* **rester ~** to be stumped*; **je suis ~ sur ce sujet** I draw a blank on that subject.
2 adv *frapper* hard. **boire ~** to drink hard, be a hard *ou* heavy drinker; **démarrer ~** (*sans douceur*) to start (up) with a jolt *ou* jerk; (*rapidement*) to tear off; (*fig*) **ça démarre ~ ce soir** it's getting off to a good start this evening; **conduire ~** to drive jerkily; **aussi ~!**‡ pronto!*; **et lui, aussi ~**‡**, a répondu que ...** and he replied straight off *ou* straight away that ... .
3 nm: **tenir qch au ~** to keep sth in a dry place; **rester au ~** to stay in the dry; **un puits à ~** a dry *ou* dried-up well; **être à ~** *[torrent, puits]* to be dry *ou* dried-up; (**: sans argent*) *[personne]* to be broke* *ou* skint‡ (*Brit*); *[caisse]* to be empty; **mettre à ~ un étang** *[personne]* to drain a pond; *[soleil]* to dry up a pond; **mettre à ~ un joueur** to clean out a gambler.
sécable [sekabl] adj divisible.
SECAM [sekam] adj, nm (abrév de **séquentiel couleur à mémoire**) SECAM.
sécant, e [sekɑ̃, ɑ̃t] adj, nf secant.
sécateur [sekatœʀ] nm (pair of) secateurs, (pair of) pruning shears.
sécession [sesesjɔ̃] nf secession. **faire ~** to secede; *voir* **guerre.**
sécessionniste [sesesjɔnist] adj, nmf secessionist.
séchage [seʃaʒ] nm drying; *[bois]* seasoning.
sèche[2]* [sɛʃ] nf (*cigarette*) fag* (*Brit*), cigarette.
sèche- [sɛʃ] préf *voir* **sécher.**
sèchement [sɛʃmɑ̃] adv *disserter* drily, dryly; *répondre* (*froidement*) drily, dryly; (*brièvement*) curtly.
sécher [seʃe] 6 1 vt a (*gén*) to dry; *cours d'eau, flaque* to dry (up). **sèche tes larmes** dry your tears *ou* eyes; (*fig*) **~ les larmes** *ou* **les pleurs de qn** to wipe away sb's tears; **se ~ au soleil/avec une serviette** to dry o.s. in the sun/with a towel; **se ~ devant le feu** to dry o.s. *ou* dry (o.s.) off in front of the fire.
b (*arg Scol: manquer*) *cours* to skip*. **ce matin, je vais ~ (les cours)** this morning I'm going to skip classes*.
c (‡) **~ son verre** to drain one's glass; **~ son verre de bière** to down *ou* knock back *ou* drain one's glass of beer.
2 vi a *[surface mouillée, peinture]* to dry (off); *[substance imbibée de liquide]* to dry (out); *[linge]* to dry. **faire** *ou* **laisser ~ qch** to leave sth to dry (off *ou* out); **mettre le linge à ~** to put out the washing to dry;

"faire ~ sans essorer" "do not spin (dry)"; **"faire ~ à plat"** "dry flat".
b (*se déshydrater*) *[bois]* to dry out; *[fleur]* to dry up *ou* out. **le caoutchouc a séché** the rubber has dried up *ou* gone dry; **~ sur pied** *[plante]* to wilt on the stalk; (*fig*) *[personne]* to languish; **faire ~** *fruits, viande, fleurs* to dry; *bois* to season.
c (*arg Scol: rester sec*) to be stumped*. **j'ai séché en maths** I drew a (complete) blank *ou* I dried up* completely in maths.
3 **comp** ▸**sèche-cheveux** **nm inv** hair-drier ▸**sèche-linge** **nm inv** drying cabinet; (*machine*) tumble-dryer ▸**sèche-mains** **nm inv** hand-dryer *ou* blower.

sécheresse [sɛʃʀɛs] **nf** a *[climat, sol, ton, style]* dryness; *[réponse]* curtness; *[cœur]* coldness, hardness. b (*absence de pluie*) drought.

sécherie [sɛʃʀi] **nf** (*machine*) drier, drying machine; (*installations*) drying plant.

séchoir [seʃwaʀ] **nm** (*local*) (*pour nourriture, tabac etc*) drying shed; (*pour linge*) drying room; (*appareil*) drier. **~ à linge** (*pliant*) clothes-horse; **~ à chanvre/à tabac** hemp/tobacco drying shed; **~ à cheveux** hair-drier; **~ à tambour** tumble-dryer.

second, e[1] [s(ə)gɔ̃, ɔ̃d] 1 **adj** a (*chronologiquement*) second. **en ~ lieu** second(ly), in the second place; **je vous le dis pour la ~e fois, vous n'aurez rien** I repeat, you'll get nothing; **il a obtenu ces renseignements de ~e main** he got this information secondhand; *[chercheur]* **travailler sur des ouvrages de ~e main** to work from secondary sources; **~ violon/ténor** second violin/tenor; **le s~ Empire** the Second Empire; **~ chapitre, chapitre ~** chapter two; *voir* **noce**.
b (*hiérarchiquement*) second. **de ~ choix** (*de mauvaise qualité*) low-quality, low-grade; (*Comm: catégorie*) class two; **articles de ~ choix** seconds; **voyager en ~e classe** to travel second-class; **passer en ~** to come second; **commander en ~** to be second in command; **officier** *ou* **capitaine en ~** first mate; **intelligence/malhonnêteté à nulle autre ~e** unparalleled intelligence/dishonesty, intelligence/dishonesty which is quite without equal; **jouer les ~s rôles** (*Ciné*) to play minor parts *ou* supporting roles; (*fig: en politique etc*) to play second fiddle (*auprès de* to); (*fig*) **~ couteau** minor figure; **ce ne sont que des ~s couteaux** they're only the small fry; (*Bourse*) **~ marché** ≈ unlisted securities market; *voir* **plan**[1].
c (*autre, nouveau*) second. **une ~e jeunesse** a second youth; **dans une ~e vie** in a second life; **cet écrivain est un ~ Hugo** this writer is a second Hugo; **chez lui, c'est une ~e nature** with him it's second nature; **doué de ~e vue** gifted with second sight; **trouver son ~ souffle** (*Sport*) to get one's second wind; (*fig*) to find a new lease of life; **être dans un état ~** to be in a sort of trance; *voir* **habitude**.
d (*dérivé*) *cause* secondary.
2 **nm, f** second. **le ~ de ses fils** his second son, the second of his sons; **il a été reçu ~ (en maths)** he came *ou* was second (in maths); (*littér*) **sans ~** second to none, peerless (*littér*); (*Alpinisme*) **~ (de cordée)** second (on the rope).
3 **nm** a (*adjoint*) second in command; (*Naut*) first mate; (*en duel*) second.
b (*étage*) second floor (*Brit*), third floor (*US*). **la dame du ~** the lady on the second floor (*Brit*) *ou* the third floor (*US*).
c (*dans une charade*) second. **mon ~ est ...** my second is... .
4 **seconde** **nf** (*classe de transport*) second class; (*billet*) second-class ticket; (*Scol*) ≈ fifth form (*Brit*) (*in secondary school*), tenth grade (*US*) (*in high school*); (*Aut*) second (gear); (*Mus*) second; (*Danse*) second (position); (*Escrime*) seconde. (*Typ: épreuves*) **~es** second proofs; (*Rail*) **les ~es sont à l'avant** the second-class seats *ou* carriages are at the front *ou* in front; **voyager en ~e** to travel second-class.

secondaire [s(ə)gɔ̃dɛʀ] 1 **adj** (*gén, Chim, Scol*) secondary; (*Géol*) mesozoic, secondary†; (*Psych*) *caractère* tending not to show one's reactions. (*Littérat*) **intrigue ~** subplot; (*gén, Méd*) **effets ~s** side effects; *voir* **secteur**. 2 **nm** (*Géol*) **le ~** the Mesozoic, the Secondary Era†; (*Scol*) **le ~** secondary (school) (*Brit*) *ou* high-school (*US*) education; **les professeurs du ~** secondary school (*Brit*) *ou* high-school (*US*) teachers; (*Écon*) **le ~** the secondary sector; (*Élec*) **(enroulement) ~** secondary (winding).

secondairement [s(ə)gɔ̃dɛʀmɑ̃] **adv** secondarily.

secondarité [s(ə)gɔ̃daʀite] **nf** tendency to conceal one's reactions.

seconde[2] [s(ə)gɔ̃d] **nf** (*gén, Géom*) second. **(attends) une ~!** just a *ou* one second! *ou* sec!*; *voir* **fraction, quart**.

secondement [s(ə)gɔ̃dmɑ̃] **adv** second(ly).

seconder [s(ə)gɔ̃de] [1] **vt** (*lit, fig*) to assist, aid, help.

secouer [s(ə)kwe] [1] 1 **vt** a *arbre, salade* to shake; *poussière, miettes* to shake off; *paresse, oppression* to shake off; *tapis* to shake (out). **~ le joug de** *[tyrannie, dictature]* to throw off *ou* cast off the yoke of; **arrête de me ~ comme un prunier*** stop shaking me up and down, stop shaking me like a rag doll; **~ la tête** (*pour dire oui*) to nod (one's head); (*pour dire non*) to shake one's head; **l'explosion secoua l'hôtel** the explosion shook *ou* rocked the hotel; **on est drôlement secoué** (*dans un autocar*) you're terribly shaken about; (*dans un bateau*) you're terribly tossed about; **le vent secouait le petit bateau** the wind tossed the little boat about.
b (*traumatiser*) to shake (up). **ce deuil l'a beaucoup secoué** this bereavement has really shaken him.
c (*fig*) (*bousculer*) to shake up. **cet élève ne travaille que lorsqu'on le secoue** this pupil only works if he's shaken up *ou* given a good shake; **~ les puces à qn*** (*réprimander*) to tick* (*Brit*) *ou* tell sb off, give sb a ticking-off* (*Brit*) *ou* telling-off; (*stimuler*) to give sb a good shake(-up), shake sb up; **secoue tes puces*** *ou* **ta graisse**‡ shake yourself out of it*, shake yourself up; **~ le cocotier*** to get rid of the deadwood*.
2 **se secouer** **vpr** (*lit*) to shake o.s.; (*: *faire un effort*) to shake o.s. out of it, shake o.s. up; (*: *se dépêcher*) to get a move on. **secouez-vous si vous voulez passer l'examen** you'll have to shake your ideas up *ou* shake yourself up if you want to pass the exam.

secourable [s(ə)kuʀabl] **adj** *personne* helpful; *voir* **main**.

secourir [s(ə)kuʀiʀ] [11] **vt** *blessé, pauvre* to help, succour (*littér*), assist, aid; *misère* to help relieve *ou* ease.

secourisme [s(ə)kuʀism] **nm** first aid.

secouriste [s(ə)kuʀist] **nmf** first-aid worker.

secours [s(ə)kuʀ] **nm** a (*aide*) help, aid, assistance. **appeler qn à son ~** to call sb to one's aid *ou* assistance; **demander du ~** to ask for help *ou* assistance; **crier au ~** to shout *ou* call (out) for help; **au ~!** help!; **aller au ~ de qn** to go to sb's aid *ou* assistance; **porter ~ à qn** to give sb help *ou* assistance.
b (*aumône*) aid (*NonC*). **distribuer/recevoir des ~** to distribute/receive aid; **société de ~ mutuel** mutual aid association.
c (*sauvetage*) aid (*NonC*), assistance (*NonC*). **porter ~ à un alpiniste** to bring help *ou* aid to a mountaineer; **~ aux blessés** aid *ou* assistance for the wounded; **~ d'urgence** emergency aid *ou* assistance; **le ~ en montagne/en mer** mountain/sea rescue; **équipe de ~** rescue party *ou* team; **quand les ~ arrivèrent** when help *ou* the rescue party arrived; *voir* **poste**[2]**, premier**.
d (*Mil*) relief (*NonC*). **la colonne de ~** the relief column; **les ~ sont attendus** relief is expected.
e (*Rel*) **mourir avec/sans les ~ de la religion** to die with/without the last rites.
f (*loc*) **cela m'a été/ne m'a pas été d'un grand ~** this has been a *ou* of great help/of little help to me; **une bonne nuit te serait de meilleur ~ que ces pilules** a good night's sleep would be more help to you than these pills; **éclairage/sortie de ~** emergency lighting/exit; **batterie/roue de ~** spare battery/wheel.

secousse [s(ə)kus] **nf** a (*cahot*) *[voiture, train]* jolt, bump; *[avion]* bump. **sans une ~** *s'arrêter* without a jolt, smoothly; *transporter* smoothly; **avancer par ~s** to move jerkily *ou* in jerks. b (*choc*) jerk, jolt; (*morale*) jolt, shock; (*traction*) tug, pull. **~ (électrique)** (electric) shock; **donner des ~s à** *corde* to give a few tugs *ou* pulls to; *thermomètre* to give a few shakes to. c **~ (tellurique** *ou* **sismique)** (earth) tremor; (*fig*) **~ politique** political upheaval; **il n'en fiche pas une ~*** he never lifts a finger*; **en mettre** *ou* **ficher une (bonne) ~*** to give it all one's got*.

secret, -ète [səkʀɛ, ɛt] 1 **adj** a *document, rite* secret. **garder** *ou* **tenir qch ~** to keep sth secret *ou* dark; **des informations classées ~ètes** classified information; *voir* **agent, fonds, service**.
b (*caché*) *tiroir, porte, vie, pressentiment* secret. **nos plus ~ètes pensées** our most secret *ou* our innermost thoughts; **un charme ~** a hidden charm.
c (*renfermé*) *personne* reticent, reserved.
2 **nm** a secret. **c'est son ~** it's his secret; **il a gardé le ~ de notre projet** he kept our plan secret; **ne pas avoir de ~ pour qn** *[personne]* to have no secrets from sb, keep nothing from sb; *[sujet]* to have *ou* hold no secrets for sb; **confier un ~ à qn** to confide a secret to sb; **il n'en fait pas un ~** he makes no secret about *ou* of it; **~ d'alcôve** intimate talk; **~ de fabrication** trade secret; **~ d'État** state *ou* official secret; (*fig*) **faire de qch un ~ d'État** to make a big secret of sth, act as if sth were a state secret; **"~-défense"** "official secret"; **c'est le ~ de Polichinelle** it's an open secret; **ce n'est un ~ pour personne que ...** it's no secret that ... .
b (*moyen, mécanisme*) secret. **~ de fabrication** trade secret; **le ~ du bonheur/de la réussite/de la bonne cuisine** the secret of happiness/of success/ of good cooking; **il a trouvé le ~ pour obtenir tout ce qu'il veut** he's found the secret for getting everything he wants; **une sauce/un tour de passe-passe dont il a le ~** a sauce/conjuring trick of which he (alone) has the secret; **il a le ~ de ces plaisanteries stupides** he's got the knack of telling these stupid jokes; **tiroir à ~** drawer with a secret lock.
c (*discrétion, silence*) secrecy. **demander/exiger/promettre le ~ (absolu)** to ask for/demand/promise (absolute) secrecy; **trahir le ~** to betray the oath of secrecy; **le ~ professionnel** professional secrecy; **le ~ d'État** official secrecy; **le ~ de la confession** the seal of the confessional; **le gouvernement a gardé le ~ sur les négociations** the government has maintained silence *ou* remained silent about the negotiations; *voir* **sceau**.
d (*mystère*) secret. **les ~s de la nature** the secrets of nature, nature's secrets; **pénétrer dans le ~ des cœurs** to penetrate the secrets of the heart.
e (*loc*) **dans le ~** in secret *ou* secrecy, secretly; **négociations**

menées dans le plus grand ~ negotiations carried out in the strictest *ou* utmost secrecy; **mettre qn dans le ~** to let sb into *ou* in on the secret, let sb in on it*; **être dans le ~** to be in on the secret, be in on it*; **être dans le ~ des dieux** to share the secrets of the powers that be; **faire ~ de tout** to be secretive about everything; **en ~** (*sans témoins*) in secret *ou* secrecy, secretly; (*intérieurement*) secretly; (*Prison*) **au ~** in solitary confinement, in solitary*.

3 **secrète** nf (*Police*) the secret police; (*Rel*) the Secret.

secrétaire [s(ə)kʀetɛʀ] 1 nmf (*gén*) secretary. **~ médicale/commerciale/particulière** medical/business *ou* commercial/private secretary.

2 nm (*meuble*) writing desk, secretaire (*Brit*), secretary (*US*).

3 comp ▸**secrétaire d'ambassade** embassy secretary ▸**secrétaire de direction** private *or* personal secretary (*to a director or directors*), executive secretary ▸**secrétaire d'État** junior minister (*de* in); (*US Pol : ministre des Affaires étrangères*) Secretary of State, State Secretary; **le secrétaire d'État américain au Trésor** the Treasury Secretary ▸**secrétaire général** secretary-general ▸**secrétaire de mairie** ≃ town clerk (*in charge of records and legal business*) ▸**secrétaire de production** (*Ciné*) production secretary ▸**secrétaire de rédaction** sub-editor.

secrétariat [s(ə)kʀetaʀja] nm a (*fonction officielle*) secretaryship, post *ou* office of secretary; (*durée de fonction*) secretaryship, term (of office) as secretary; (*bureau*) secretariat. **~ d'État** (*fonction*) post of junior minister; (*bureau*) junior minister's office; **~ général des Nations Unies** post *ou* office of Secretary-General of the United Nations. b (*profession, travail*) secretarial work; (*bureaux*) *[école]* (secretary's) office; *[usine, administration]* secretarial offices; *[organisation internationale]* secretariat; (*personnel*) secretarial staff. **école de ~** secretarial college; **~ de rédaction** editorial office.

secrète [səkʀɛt] *voir* **secret**.

secrètement [səkʀɛtmɑ̃] adv secretly.

sécréter [sekʀete] 6 vt (*Bot, Physiol*) to secrete; (*fig*) *ennui* to exude.

sécréteur, -euse *ou* **-trice** [sekʀetœʀ, øz, tʀis] adj secretory.

sécrétion [sekʀesjɔ̃] nf secretion.

sécrétoire [sekʀetwaʀ] adj secretory.

sectaire [sɛktɛʀ] adj, nmf sectarian.

sectarisme [sɛktaʀism] nm sectarianism.

secte [sɛkt] nf sect.

secteur [sɛktœʀ] nm a (*gén, Mil*) sector; (*Admin*) district; (*gén: zone*) area; *[agent de police]* beat; (*fig*) (*domaine*) area; (*partie*) part. (*Mil*) **~ postal** postal area, ≃ BFPO area (*Brit*); **dans le ~*** (*ici*) round here; (*là-bas*) round there; **changer de ~*** to move elsewhere; (*Admin*) **~ sauvegardé** conservation area; (*Scol*) **~ géographique** *ou* **de recrutement scolaire** catchment area.

b (*Élec*) (*zone*) local supply area. (*circuit*) **le ~** the mains (supply); **panne de ~** local supply breakdown; **fonctionne sur pile et ~** battery or mains operated.

c (*Écon*) **~ public/semi-public/privé** public *ou* state/semi-public/private sector; **~ nationalisé** nationalized industries; **~ d'activité** branch of industry; **~ primaire** primary sector; **~ secondaire** secondary sector; **~ tertiaire** service sector, tertiary sector.

d (*Géom*) sector. **~ circulaire** sector of circle; **~ sphérique** spherical sector, sector of sphere.

section [sɛksjɔ̃] nf a (*coupe*) section. **prenons un tube de ~ double** let's get a tube which is twice the bore; **dessiner la ~ d'un os/d'une tige** to draw the section of a bone/of a stem, draw a bone/a stem in section; **la ~ (de ce câble) est toute rouillée** the end (of this cable) is all rusted.

b (*Admin*) section; (*Scol*) section, stream, division; (*Pol*) branch. **~ du Conseil d'État** department of the Council of State; **~ (du) contentieux** legal section *ou* department; **~ électorale** ward; **~ syndicale** (trade) union group; **mettre un élève en ~ littéraire/scientifique** to put a pupil into the literature/science stream *ou* section; (*Scol*) **changer de ~** ≃ to change courses.

c (*partie*) *[ouvrage]* section; *[route, rivière, voie ferrée]* section; (*en autobus*) fare stage. **de la Porte d'Orléans à ma rue, il y a 2 ~s** from the Porte d'Orléans to my street there are 2 fare stages; *voir* **fin²**.

d (*Mus*) section. **~ mélodique/rythmique** melody/rhythm section.

e (*Mil*) platoon.

f (*Math*) section. **~ conique/plane** conic/plane section.

sectionnement [sɛksjɔnmɑ̃] nm (*voir* **sectionner**) severance; division (*into sections*).

sectionner [sɛksjɔne] 1 1 vt *tube, fil, artère* to sever; *circonscription, groupe* to divide (up), split (up) (*en* into). 2 **se sectionner** vpr to be severed; to divide *ou* split (up) (into sections).

sectoriel, -ielle [sɛktɔʀjɛl] adj sector-based.

sectorisation [sɛktɔʀizasjɔ̃] nf division into sectors.

sectoriser [sɛktɔʀize] 1 vt to divide into sectors, sector.

Sécu* [seky] nf (abrév de **Sécurité sociale**) *voir* **sécurité**.

séculaire [sekylɛʀ] adj (*très vieux*) *arbre, croyance* age-old; (*qui a lieu tous les cent ans*) *fête, jeux* secular. **ces forêts/maisons sont 4 fois ~s** these forests/houses are 4 centuries old; **année ~** last year of the century.

sécularisation [sekylaʀizasjɔ̃] nf secularization.

séculariser [sekylaʀize] 1 vt to secularize.

séculier, -ière [sekylje, jɛʀ] 1 adj *clergé, autorité* secular; *voir* **bras**. 2 nm secular.

secundo [səgɔ̃do] adv second(ly), in the second place.

sécurisant, e [sekyʀizɑ̃, ɑ̃t] adj *climat* of security, reassuring. **attitude ~e** reassuring attitude, attitude which makes one feel secure.

sécuriser [sekyʀize] 1 vt: **~ qn** to give (a feeling of) security to sb, make sb feel secure.

Securit [sekyʀit] nm ® **verre ~** Triplex (glass) ®.

sécuritaire [sekyʀitɛʀ] adj: **mesures ~s** security measures.

sécurité [sekyʀite] 1 nf a (*tranquillité d'esprit*) feeling *ou* sense of security; (*absence de danger*) safety; (*conditions d'ordre, absence de troubles*) security. **être/se sentir en ~** to be/feel safe, be/feel secure; **une fausse impression de ~** a false sense of security; **cette retraite représentait pour lui une ~** this pension meant security for him; **la ~ de l'emploi** security of employment, job security; **assurer la ~ d'un personnage important/des ouvriers/des installations** to ensure the safety of an important person/of workers/of the equipment; **l'État assure la ~ des citoyens** the State looks after the security *ou* safety of its citizens; **la ~ nationale/internationale** national/international security; **mesures de ~** (*contre incendie etc*) safety measures *ou* precautions; (*contre attentat*) security measures; **des mesures de ~ très strictes avaient été prises** very strict security precautions *ou* measures had been taken, security was very tight; *voir* **ceinture, compagnie, conseil** *etc.*

b (*mécanisme*) safety catch. **de ~** *dispositif* safety (*épith*); (*Aut*) **(porte à) ~ enfants** childproof lock, child lock; *voir* **cran**.

c (*service*) security. **la ~ militaire** military security.

2 comp ▸**la sécurité publique** law and order; **agent de la sécurité publique** officer of the law ▸**la sécurité routière** road safety ▸**la Sécurité sociale** (*pour la santé*) ≃ the National Health Service (*Brit*), ≃ Medicaid (*US*); (*pour vieillesse etc*) ≃ the Social Security; **prestations de la Sécurité sociale** ≃ Social Security benefits.

sédatif, -ive [sedatif, iv] adj, nm sedative.

sédation [sedasjɔ̃] nf sedation.

sédentaire [sedɑ̃tɛʀ] adj *vie, travail, goûts, personne* sedentary; *population* settled, sedentary; (*Mil*) permanently garrisoned.

sédentairement [sedɑ̃tɛʀmɑ̃] adv sedentarily.

sédentarisation [sedɑ̃taʀizasjɔ̃] nf settling process.

sédentariser [sedɑ̃taʀize] 1 vt to settle. **population sédentarisée** settled population.

sédentarité [sedɑ̃taʀite] nf settled way of life.

sédiment [sedimɑ̃] nm (*Méd, fig*) sediment; (*Géol*) deposit, sediment.

sédimentaire [sedimɑ̃tɛʀ] adj sedimentary.

sédimentation [sedimɑ̃tasjɔ̃] nf sedimentation; *voir* **vitesse**.

sédimenter [sedimɑ̃te] 1 vi to deposit sediment.

séditieux, -ieuse [sedisjø, jøz] 1 adj (*en sédition*) *général, troupes* insurrectionary (*épith*), insurgent (*épith*); (*agitateur*) *esprit, propos, réunion* seditious. 2 nm, f insurrectionary, insurgent.

sédition [sedisjɔ̃] nf insurrection, sedition. **esprit de ~** spirit of sedition *ou* insurrection *ou* revolt.

séducteur, -trice [sedyktœʀ, tʀis] 1 adj seductive. 2 nm (*débaucheur*) seducer; (*péj: Don Juan*) womanizer (*péj*). 3 **séductrice** nf seductress.

séduction [sedyksjɔ̃] nf a (*voir* **séduire**) seduction, seducing; charming; captivation; winning over. **scène de ~** seduction scene. b (*attirance*) appeal. **troublé par la ~ de sa jeunesse** disturbed by the charm *ou* seductiveness of her youth; **exercer une forte ~ sur** to exercise a strong attraction over, have a great deal of appeal for; **les ~s de la vie estudiantine** the attractions *ou* appeal of student life.

séduire [sedɥiʀ] 38 vt a (*abuser de*) to seduce.

b (*attirer, gagner*) *[femme, tenue]* to charm, captivate; *[négociateur, charlatan]* to win over, charm. **il l'a séduite et abandonnée** he loved her and left her; **son but était de ~** her aim was to charm *ou* captivate us (*ou* him *etc*); **ils ont essayé de nous ~ avec ces propositions** they tried to win us over *ou* charm us with these proposals.

c (*plaire*) *[tenue, style, qualité, projet]* to appeal to. **une des qualités qui me séduisent le plus** one of the qualities which most appeal to me *ou* which I find most appealing; **leur projet/genre de vie me séduit mais ...** their plan/life style does appeal to me but ..., their plan/life style appeals to me *ou* does have some attraction for me but ...; **cette idée va-t-elle les ~?** is this idea going to tempt them? *ou* appeal to them?

séduisant, e [sedɥizɑ̃, ɑ̃t] adj *femme, beauté* enticing (*épith*), seductive; *homme, démarche, visage* (very) attractive; *tenue, projet, genre de vie, style* appealing, attractive.

séfarade [sefaʀad] 1 adj Sephardic. 2 nmf Sephardi.

segment [sɛgmɑ̃] nm (*gén*) segment. (*Aut*) **~ de frein** brake shoe; (*Aut*) **~ de piston** piston ring.

segmental, e, mpl **-aux** [sɛgmɑ̃tal, o] adj (*Ling*) segmental.

segmentation [sɛgmɑ̃tasjɔ̃] nf (*gén*) segmentation.

segmenter [sɛgmɑ̃te] 1 1 vt to segment. 2 **se segmenter** vpr to segment, form *ou* break into segments.

ségrégatif, -ive [segʀegatif, iv] adj segregative.

ségrégation [segʀegasjɔ̃] nf segregation.

ségrégationnisme [segʀegasjɔnism] **nm** racial segregation, segregationism.

ségrégationniste [segʀegasjɔnist] 1 **adj** *manifestant* segregationist; *problème* of segregation; *troubles* due to segregation. 2 **nmf** segregationist.

ségrégé, e [segʀeʒe], **ségrégué, e** [segʀege] **adj** segregated.

seiche [sɛʃ] **nf** (*Zool*) cuttlefish; *voir* **os.**

séide [seid] **nm** (fanatically devoted) henchman.

seigle [sɛgl] **nm** rye; *voir* **pain.**

seigneur [sɛɲœʀ] **nm** a (*Hist: suzerain, noble*) lord; (*fig: maître*) overlord. (*hum*) **mon ~ et maître** my lord and master; **se montrer grand ~ avec qn** to behave in a lordly fashion towards sb; *voir* **à, grand.** b (*Rel*) **le S~** the Lord; **Notre-S~ Jésus-Christ** Our Lord Jesus Christ; **S~ Dieu!** good Lord!; *voir* **jour, vigne.**

seigneurial, e, **mpl -iaux** [sɛɲœʀjal, jo] **adj** *château, domaine* seigniorial; *allure, luxe* lordly, stately.

seigneurie [sɛɲœʀi] **nf** a **Votre/Sa S~** your/his Lordship. b (*terre*) (lord's) domain, seigniory; (*droits féodaux*) seigniory.

sein [sɛ̃] **nm** a (*mamelle*) breast. **donner le ~ à un bébé** (*méthode*) to breast-feed (a baby), suckle† a baby; (*être en train d'allaiter*) to feed a baby (at the breast), suckle† a baby; (*présenter le sein*) to give a baby the breast; **prendre le ~** to take the breast; *plage, serveuse* **~s nus** topless; *voir* **faux², nourrir.**
b (*littér*) (*poitrine*) breast (*littér*), bosom (*littér*); (*matrice*) womb; (*fig: giron, milieu*) bosom. **pleurer dans le ~ d'un ami** to cry on a friend's breast *ou* bosom; **porter un enfant dans son ~** to carry a child in one's womb; **dans le ~ de la terre/de l'église** in the bosom of the earth/of the church; **le ~ de Dieu** the bosom of the Father; *voir* **réchauffer.**
c **au ~ de** (*parmi, dans*) *équipe, institution* within; (*littér*) *bonheur, flots* in the midst of.

Seine [sɛn] **nf: la ~** the Seine.

seine [sɛn] **nf** (*filet*) seine.

seing [sɛ̃] **nm** (††) signature. (*Jur*) **acte sous ~ privé** private agreement (*document not legally certified*).

séisme [seism] **nm** (*Géog*) earthquake, seism (*SPÉC*); (*fig*) upheaval.

séismique [seismik] **adj** = **sismique.**

séismographe [seismɔgʀaf] **nm** = **sismographe.**

séismologie [seismɔlɔʒi] **nf** = **sismologie.**

SEITA [seta] **nf** (**abrév de Société d'exploitation industrielle des tabacs et allumettes**) *French state tobacco company.*

seize [sɛz] **adj inv, nm inv** sixteen; *pour loc voir* **six.**

seizième [sɛzjɛm] **adj, nmf** sixteenth. (*Sport*) **~s de finale** first round (*of 5-round knockout competition*); **le ~ (arrondissement)** the sixteenth arrondissement, (*fashionable residential area in Paris*); *pour autres loc voir* **sixième.**

seizièmement [sɛzjɛmmɑ̃] **adv** in the sixteenth place, sixteenth.

séjour [seʒuʀ] **nm** a (*arrêt*) stay, sojourn (*littér*). **faire un ~ de 3 semaines à Paris** to stay (for) 3 weeks in Paris, have a 3-week stay in Paris; **faire un ~ forcé à Calais** to have an enforced stay in Calais; *voir* **interdit¹, permis, taxe.** b (*salon*) living room, lounge (*Brit*). **un ~ double** a through lounge (*Brit*) *ou* living room; *voir* **salle.** c (*littér: endroit*) abode (*littér*), dwelling place (*littér*); (*demeure temporaire*) sojourn (*littér*). **le ~ des dieux** the abode *ou* dwelling place of the gods.

séjourner [seʒuʀne] 1 **vi** *[personne]* to stay, sojourn (*littér*); *[neige, eau]* to lie.

sel [sɛl] 1 **nm** a (*gén, Chim*) salt. (*à respirer*) **~s** smelling salts; *voir* **esprit, gros, poivre.** b (*fig*) (*humour*) wit; (*piquant*) spice. **la remarque ne manque pas de ~** the remark has a certain wit; **c'est ce qui fait tout le ~ de l'aventure** that's what gives the adventure its spice; (*littér*) **ils sont le ~ de la terre** they are the salt of the earth; *voir* **grain.** 2 **comp** ►**sel attique** Attic salt *ou* wit ►**sels de bain** bath salts ►**sel de céleri** celery salt ►**sel de cuisine** cooking salt ►**sel fin** = **sel de table** ►**sel gemme** rock salt ►**sel marin** sea salt ►**sel de table** table salt.

sélacien, -ienne [selasjɛ̃, jɛn] **adj, nm** selachian.

select* [selɛkt] **adj inv**, **sélect, e*** [selɛkt] **adj** *personne* posh*, high-class; *clientèle, club, endroit* select, posh*.

sélecteur [selɛktœʀ] 1 **nm** *[ordinateur, poste de TV, central téléphonique]* selector; *[motocyclette]* gear lever. 2 **adj: comité ~** selection committee.

sélectif, -ive [selɛktif, iv] **adj** (*gén*) selective.

sélection [selɛksjɔ̃] **nf** a (*action*) choosing, selection, picking; (*Scol, Univ*) selective entry (*Brit*) *ou* admission (*US*). **faire** *ou* **opérer** *ou* **effectuer une ~ parmi** to make a selection from among; (*Sport*) **comité de ~** selection committee; (*Élevage, Zool*) **la ~** selection; **épreuve de ~** (selection) trial; (*Bio*) **~ (naturelle)** natural selection; **~ professionnelle** professional recruitment.
b (*choix, gamme*) *[articles, produits, œuvres]* selection. **avant d'acheter, voyez notre ~ d'appareils ménagers** before buying see our selection of household appliances.
c (*Sport*) selection. (*Ftbl, Rugby*) **avoir plus de 20 ~s (pour l'équipe nationale) à son actif** to have been capped more than 20 times, have more than 20 caps to one's credit, have been selected *ou* picked more than 20 times (to play for the national team).

sélectionné, e [selɛksjɔne] (**ptp de sélectionner**) 1 **adj** (*soigneusement choisi*) specially selected, choice (*épith*). 2 **nm, f** (*Ftbl etc*) selected player; (*Athlétisme*) selected competitor.

sélectionner [selɛksjɔne] 1 **vt** *athlètes, produits* to select, pick. (*Ftbl, Rugby*) **3 fois sélectionné pour l'équipe nationale** capped 3 times (to play for the national team), selected 3 times to play for the national team.

sélectionneur, -euse [selɛksjɔnœʀ, øz] **nm, f** (*Sport*) selector.

sélectivement [selɛktivmɑ̃] **adv** selectively.

sélectivité [selɛktivite] **nf** (*Rad*) selectivity.

sélénite [selenit] 1 **adj** moon (*épith*). 2 **nmf: S~** moon-dweller.

sélénium [selenjɔm] **nm** selenium.

self [sɛlf] 1 **nm** (*: *restaurant*) self-service (restaurant), cafeteria. 2 **nf** (*Élec*) (*propriété*) self-induction; (*bobine*) self-induction coil.

self-control [sɛlfkɔ̃tʀol] **nm** self-control.

self-inductance [sɛlfɛ̃dyktɑ̃s] **nf** self-inductance.

self-induction [sɛlfɛ̃dyksjɔ̃] **nf** self-induction.

self-made-man [sɛlfmɛdman] **nm, pl self-made-men** [sɛlfmɛdmɛn] self-made man.

self-service, **pl self-services** [sɛlfsɛʀvis] **nm** self-service (restaurant), cafeteria.

selle [sɛl] **nf** a (*Cyclisme, Équitation*) saddle. **monter sans ~** to ride bareback; **se mettre en ~** to mount, get into the saddle; **mettre qn en ~** (*lit*) to put sb in the saddle; (*fig*) to give sb a leg-up (*Brit*) *ou* a boost; **se remettre en ~** (*lit*) to remount, get back into the saddle; (*fig*) to get back in the saddle; (*lit, fig*) **être bien en ~** to be firmly in the saddle; *voir* **cheval.** b (*Boucherie*) saddle. c (*Méd*) **~s** stools, motions; **êtes-vous allé à la ~ aujourd'hui?** have you had *ou* passed a motion today?, have your bowels moved today? d (*Art*) *[sculpteur]* turntable.

seller [sele] 1 **vt** to saddle.

sellerie [sɛlʀi] **nf** (*métier, articles, selles*) saddlery; (*lieu de rangement*) tack room, harness room, saddle room.

sellette [sɛlɛt] **nf** a **être/mettre qn sur la ~** to be/put sb in the hot seat (*fig*). b (*Art*) (*pour sculpteur*) small turntable; (*pour statue, pot de fleur*) stand. c (*Constr*) cradle. d *[cheval de trait]* saddle.

sellier [selje] **nm** saddler.

selon [s(ə)lɔ̃] **prép** a (*conformément à*) in accordance with. **~ la volonté de qn** in accordance with sb's wishes; **~ une orbite elliptique** in an elliptical orbit.
b (*en proportion de, en fonction de*) according to. **vivre ~ ses moyens** to live according to one's means; **le nombre varie ~ la saison** the number varies (along) with the season, the number varies according to the season; **on répartit les enfants ~ l'âge** *ou* **leur âge/la taille** *ou* **leur taille** the children were grouped according to age/height; **c'est ~ le cas/les circonstances** it all depends on the individual case/on the circumstances; **c'est ~*** it (all) depends; **il acceptera ou n'acceptera pas, ~ son humeur** he may or may not accept, depending on *ou* according to his mood *ou* how he feels.
c (*suivant l'opinion de*) according to. **~ ses propres termes** in his own words; **~ les journaux, il aurait été assassiné** according to the papers he was murdered; **~ moi/lui, elle devrait se plaindre** in my/his opinion *ou* to my mind/according to him, she should complain; **~ les prévisions de la radio, il fera beau demain** according to the radio forecast it will be fine tomorrow.
d (*loc*) **~ toute apparence** to all appearances; **~ toute vraisemblance** in all probability; **~ que** according to *ou* depending on whether, according as (*frm*).

Seltz [sɛls] **nf** *voir* **eau.**

semailles [s(ə)mɑj] **nfpl** (*opération*) sowing (*NonC*); (*période*) sowing period; (*graine*) seed, seeds.

semaine [s(ə)mɛn] **nf** a (*gén*) week. **la première ~ de mai** the first week in *ou* of May; **en ~** during the week, on weekdays; **louer à la ~** to let by the week; **dans 2 ~s à partir d'aujourd'hui** 2 weeks *ou* a fortnight (*Brit*) (from) today; **la ~ de 39 heures** the 39-hour (working) week; **à la ~ prochaine!** I'll see you (*ou* talk to you *etc*) next week!; *voir* **courant, fin².**
b (*salaire*) week's wages *ou* pay, weekly wage *ou* pay; (*argent de poche*) week's *ou* weekly pocket money.
c (*Publicité*) week. **~ publicitaire/commerciale** publicity/business week; **la ~ du livre/du bricolage** book/do-it-yourself week; **la ~ contre la faim** feed the hungry week; **la ~ contre la tuberculose** anti-tuberculosis week; (*hum*) **c'est sa ~ de bonté!*** it's charity *ou* do-gooders' week!* (*hum*).
d (*Bijouterie*) (*bracelet*) (seven-band) bracelet; (*bague*) (seven-band) ring.
e (*loc*) **la ~ sainte** Holy Week; **il te le rendra la ~ des quatre jeudis** he'll never give it back to you in a month of Sundays; **faire la ~ anglaise** to work *ou* do a five-day week; (*Mil*) **être de ~** to be on duty (*for the week*); **officier de ~** officer on duty (*for the week*), officer of the week; *voir* **petit.**

semainier, -ière [s(ə)menje, jɛʀ] 1 **nm, f** (*personne*) person on duty (*for the week*). 2 **nm** (*agenda*) desk diary; (*meuble*) chest of (seven) drawers, semainier; (*bracelet*) (seven-band) bracelet.

sémantème [semɑ̃tɛm] nm sememe, semanteme.
sémanticien, -ienne [semɑ̃tisjɛ̃, jɛn] nm,f semantician, semanticist.
sémantique [semɑ̃tik] 1 adj semantic. 2 nf semantics *(sg)*.
sémantisme [semɑ̃tism] nm semantics *(sg)*.
sémaphore [semafɔʀ] nm *(Naut)* semaphore; *(Rail)* semaphore signal.
semblable [sɑ̃blabl] 1 adj a *(similaire)* similar. ~ **à** like, similar to; **dans un cas ~, j'aurais refusé** in a similar case I should have refused; **je ne connais rien de ~** I don't know anything like that; **maison ~ à tant d'autres** house like so many others *ou* similar to so many others; **en cette circonstance, il a été ~ à lui-même** on this occasion he remained himself.
b *(avant n: tel)* such. **de ~s calomnies sont inacceptables** such calumnies *ou* calumnies of this kind are unacceptable.
c *(qui se ressemblent)* ~s alike; **les deux frères étaient ~s (en tout)** the two brothers were alike (in everything); *voir* **triangle.**
2 nm fellow creature, fellow man. **aimer son ~** to love one's fellow creatures *ou* fellow men; *(péj)* **toi et tes ~s** you and your kind *(péj)*, you and people like you *(péj)*; **il n'a pas son ~** there's no-one like him.
semblablement [sɑ̃blabləmɑ̃] adv similarly.
semblant [sɑ̃blɑ̃] nm a *(apparence)* **un ~ de calme/de bonheur/de vie/de vérité** a semblance of calm/happiness/life/truth; **un ~ de réponse** some vague attempt at a reply, a sort of reply*; **un ~ de soleil** a glimmer of sun; **un ~ de sourire** the shadow of a smile; **nous avons un ~ de jardin** we've got the mere semblance of a garden *ou* something akin to a garden; *voir* **faux²**. b **faire ~ de dormir/lire** to pretend to be asleep/to read; **il fait ~** he's pretending; **il ne fait ~ de rien* mais il entend tout** he's pretending to take no notice but he can hear everything.
sembler [sɑ̃ble] [1] 1 vb impers a *(paraître)* **il semble** it seems; **il semble bon/inutile de faire** it seems a good idea/useless to do; **il semblerait qu'il ne soit pas venu** it would seem *ou* appear that he didn't come, it looks as though *ou* as if he didn't come.
b *(estimer)* **il me semble** it seems *ou* appears to me; **il peut te ~ démodé de ...** it may seem *ou* appear old-fashioned to you to ...; **il me semble que tu n'as pas le droit de ...** it seems *ou* appears to me (that) you don't have the right to ..., it looks to me as though *ou* as if you don't have the right to ...; **comme bon me/te semble** as I/you see fit, as I/you think best *ou* fit; **prenez qui/ce que bon vous semble** take who *ou* whom *(frm)*/what you please *ou* wish.
c *(croire)* **il me semble que** I think (that); **il me semblait bien que je l'avais posé là** I really thought *ou* did think I had put it down here; **il me semble revoir mon grand-père** it's as though I see *ou* it's like seeing my grandfather again; **il me semble vous l'avoir déjà dit** I think *ou* I have a feeling I've already told you.
d *(loc)* **je vous connais ce me semble†** methinks I know you††, it seems to me that I know you; **je suis déjà venu ici me semble-t-il** it seems to me (that) I've been here before, I seem to have been here before; **à ce qu'il me semble, notre organisation est mauvaise** to my mind *ou* it seems to me (that) our organization is bad, our organization seems bad to me; *(frm, hum)* **que vous en semble?** what do you think (of it)?
2 vi to seem. **la maison lui sembla magnifique** the house seemed magnificent to him; **ce bain lui sembla bon après cette dure journée** that bath seemed good to him after that hard day; **il semblait content/nerveux** he seemed (to be) *ou* appeared happy/nervous; **oh! vous me semblez bien pessimiste!** you do sound *ou* seem very pessimistic!; **il ne semblait pas convaincu** he didn't seem (to be) *ou* didn't look *ou* sound convinced, it *ou* he didn't look *ou* sound as though he were convinced; **les frontières de la science semblent reculer** the frontiers of science seem *ou* appear to be retreating.
sème [sɛm] nm seme.
semé, e [s(ə)me] (ptp de **semer**) adj: **questions ~es de pièges** questions bristling with traps; **parcours ~ de difficultés** route plagued with difficulties; **mer ~e d'écueils** sea dotted with reefs; **robe ~e de diamants** diamond-spangled dress, dress studded with diamonds; **récit ~ d'anecdotes** story interspersed *ou* sprinkled with anecdotes; **campagne ~e d'arbres** countryside dotted with trees; **la vie est ~e de joies et de peines** life is strewn with joys and troubles.
semelle [s(ə)mɛl] nf a sole. **~s (intérieures)** insoles, inner soles; **~s compensées** platform soles; **chaussures à ~s compensées** platform shoes; **chaussettes à ~s renforcées** socks with reinforced soles; **leur viande était de la vraie ~*** their meat was as tough as old boots* *(Brit)* *ou* shoe leather *(US)*, their meat was like leather; *voir* **battre, crêpe²**. b *(loc)* **il n'a pas avancé/reculé d'une ~** he hasn't advanced/moved back (so much as) a single inch *ou* an inch; **il ne m'a pas quitté d'une ~** he never left me by so much as a single inch *ou* an inch. c *(Tech)* *[rail]* base plate pad; *[machine]* bedplate; *[fer à repasser]* sole plate.
semence [s(ə)mɑ̃s] nf a *(Agr, fig)* seed. **blé/pommes de terre de ~** seed corn/potatoes. b *(sperme)* semen, seed *(littér)*. c *(clou)* tack. d *(Bijouterie)* **~ de diamants** diamond sparks; **~ de perles** seed pearls.
semer [s(ə)me] [5] vt a *(répandre)* *graines, mort, peur, discorde* to sow; *clous, confettis* to scatter, strew; *faux bruits* to spread, disseminate *(frm)*, sow. **~ ses propos de platitudes** to intersperse *ou* sprinkle one's remarks with platitudes; *voir* **qui.** b *(*: perdre)* *mouchoir* to lose; *poursuivant* to lose, shake off.
semestre [s(ə)mɛstʀ] nm a *(période)* half-year, six-month period; *(Univ)* semester. **taxe payée par ~** tax paid half-yearly; **pendant le premier/second ~ (de l'année)** during the first/second half of the year, during the first/second six-month period (of the year). b *(loyer)* half-yearly *ou* six months' rent. **je vous dois un ~** I owe you six months' *ou* half a year's rent.
semestriel, -ielle [s(ə)mɛstʀijɛl] adj *(voir* **semestre***)* half-yearly, six-monthly; semestral.
semestriellement [s(ə)mɛstʀijɛlmɑ̃] adv *(voir* **semestre***)* half-yearly; every *ou* each semester.
semeur, -euse [s(ə)mœʀ, øz] nm,f sower. **~ de discorde** sower of discord; **~ de faux bruits** sower *ou* disseminator *(frm)* *ou* spreader of false rumours.
semi- [səmi] 1 préf semi-.
2 comp *(le préfixe* **semi-** *est invariable dans les composés)* ►**semi-aride** adj semiarid ►**semi-automatique** adj semiautomatic ►**semi-auxiliaire** adj semiauxiliary ◊ nm semiauxiliary verb ►**semi-chenillé, e** adj half-tracked ◊ nm half-track ►**semi-circulaire** adj semicircular ►**semi-conducteur, -trice,** adj *propriétés, caractéristiques* semiconducting ◊ nm semiconductor; *(Ordin)* **semi-conducteur à oxyde métallique** metal oxide semiconductor ►**semi-conserve** nf semipreserve ►**semi-consonne** nf semivowel, semiconsonant ►**semi-final, e** adj semifinished ►**semi-fini, e** adj semifinished ►**semi-liberté** nf ≃ partial release ►**semi-nomade** adj seminomadic ◊ nmf seminomad ►**semi-nomadisme** nm seminomadism ►**semi-ouvré, e** adj = **semi-fini, e** ►**semi-perméable** adj semipermeable ►**semi-précieux, -euse** adj semiprecious ►**semi-produit** nm semi-finished product ►**semi-public, -ique** *(Jur)* adj semipublic ►**semi-remorque,** *(nf: remorque)* trailer *(Brit)*, semitrailer *(US)*; *(nm: camion)* articulated lorry *ou* truck *(Brit)*, trailer truck *(US)* ►**semi-voyelle** nf semivowel.
sémillant, e [semijɑ̃, ɑ̃t] adj *(vif, alerte) personne* vivacious, spirited; *allure, esprit* vivacious; *(fringant)* dashing *(épith)*, full of dash *(attrib)*.
séminaire [seminɛʀ] nm *(Rel)* seminary; *(Univ)* seminar.
séminal, e, mpl **-aux** [seminal, o] adj *(Bio)* seminal.
séminariste [seminaʀist] nm seminarist.
séminifère [seminifɛʀ] adj seminiferous.
sémiologie [semjɔlɔʒi] nf *(Ling, Méd)* semiology.
sémiologique [semjɔlɔʒik] adj semiological.
sémioticien, -ienne [semjɔtisjɛ̃, jɛn] nm,f semiotician.
sémiotique [semjɔtik] 1 adj semiotic. 2 nf semiotics *(sg)*.
sémique [semik] adj semic. **acte ~** semic *ou* meaningful act.
Sémiramis [semiʀamis] nf Semiramis.
semis [s(ə)mi] nm *(plante)* seedling; *(opération)* sowing; *(terrain)* seedbed, seed plot; *(motif)* pattern, motif.
sémite [semit] 1 adj Semitic. 2 nmf: **S~** Semite.
sémitique [semitik] adj Semitic.
sémitisme [semitism] nm Semitism.
semoir [səmwaʀ] nm a *(machine)* sower, seeder. **~ à engrais** muck-spreader, manure spreader. b *(sac)* seed-bag, seed-lip.
semonce [səmɔ̃s] nf reprimand. *(Naut)* **coup de ~** warning shot across the bows.
semoule [s(ə)mul] nf semolina; *voir* **gâteau, sucre.**
sempiternel, -elle [sɑ̃pitɛʀnɛl] adj *plaintes, reproches* eternal *(épith)*, never-ending, never-ceasing.
sempiternellement [sɑ̃pitɛʀnɛlmɑ̃] adv eternally.
sénat [sena] nm senate.
sénateur [senatœʀ] nm senator.
sénatorial, e, mpl **-iaux** [senatɔʀjal, jo] adj senatorial.
sénatus-consulte, pl **sénatus-consultes** [senatyskɔ̃sylt] nm *(Hist: sous Napoléon, Antiq)* senatus consultum.
séné [sene] nm senna.
sénéchal, pl **-aux** [seneʃal, o] nm *(Hist)* seneschal.
sénéchaussée [seneʃose] nf *(Hist)* *(juridiction)* seneschalsy; *(tribunal)* seneschal's court.
séneçon [sɛnsɔ̃] nm groundsel.
Sénégal [senegal] nm Senegal.
sénégalais, e [senegalɛ, ɛz] 1 adj Senegalese. 2 nm,f: **S~(e)** Senegalese.
Sénégambie [senegɑ̃bi] nf Senegambia.
Sénèque [senɛk] nm Seneca.
sénescence [senesɑ̃s] nf senescence.
sénescent, e [senesɑ̃, ɑ̃t] adj senescent.
sénevé [sɛnve] nm *(plante)* wild mustard; *(graine)* wild mustard seed.
sénile [senil] adj *(péj, Méd)* senile.
sénilité [senilite] nf senility.
senior [senjɔʀ] adj, nm *(Sport)* senior.
séniorité [senjɔʀite] nf seniority.
senne [sɛn] nf = **seine.**
sens [sɑ̃s] 1 nm a *(vue, goût etc)* sense. **les ~** the senses; **avoir le ~ de l'odorat/de l'ouïe très développé** to have a highly developed *ou* a very keen sense of smell/hearing; **reprendre ses ~** to regain consciousness; *voir* **organe.**
b *(instinct)* sense. **avoir le ~ du rythme/de l'humour/du ridicule** to

have a sense of rhythm/humour/the ridiculous; **il n'a aucun ~ moral/pratique** he has no moral/practical sense; **avoir le ~ des réalités** to be a realist; **avoir le ~ de l'orientation** to have a (good) sense of direction.

c (*raison, avis*) sense. **ce qu'il dit est plein de ~** what he is saying makes (good) sense *ou* is very sensible; **un homme de (bon) ~** a man of (good) sense; **cela n'a pas de ~** that doesn't make (any) sense, there's no sense in that; **~ commun** common sense; **il a perdu le ~ (commun)** he's lost his *ou* all common sense; **à mon ~** to my mind, to my way of thinking, in my opinion, the way I see it; *voir* **abonder, dépit, sixième, tomber.**

d (*signification*) meaning. **au ~ propre/figuré** in the literal *ou* true/figurative sense *ou* meaning; **ce qui donne un ~ à la vie/à son action?** what gives (a) meaning to life/to his action; **le ~ d'un geste** the meaning of a gesture; **qui n'a pas de ~, dépourvu de ~** meaningless, which has no meaning; **en un (certain) ~** in a (certain) sense; **en ce ~ que** in the sense that; *voir* **double, faux[2], non.**

e (*direction*) direction. **aller *ou* être dans le bon/mauvais ~** to go *ou* be in the right/wrong direction, go the right/wrong way; **mesurer/fendre qch dans le ~ de la longueur** to measure/split sth along its length *ou* lengthwise *ou* lengthways; **ça fait 10 mètres dans le ~ de la longueur** that's 10 metres in length *ou* lengthwise *ou* lengthways; **dans le ~ de la largeur** across its width, in width, widthwise; **dans le ~ (du bois)** with the grain (of the wood); **dans le ~ contraire du courant** against the stream; **arriver/venir en ~ contraire *ou* inverse** to arrive/come from the opposite direction; **aller en ~ contraire** to go in the opposite direction; **dans le ~ des aiguilles d'une montre** clockwise; **dans le ~ contraire des aiguilles d'une montre** anticlockwise (*Brit*), counterclockwise (*US*); **dans le ~ de la marche** facing the front (of the train), facing the engine; **il retourna la boîte dans tous les ~ avant de l'ouvrir** he turned the box this way and that before opening it; (*lit, fig*) **être/mettre ~ dessus dessous** to be/turn upside down; **~ devant derrière** back to front, the wrong way round; (*Aut*) **une voie de circulation a été mise en ~ inverse sur ...** there is a contraflow system in operation on ...; (*Aut*) **la circulation dans le ~ Paris-province/dans le ~ province-Paris** traffic out of Paris/into Paris.

f (*ligne directrice*) **il a répondu dans le même ~** he replied more or less the same way *ou* along the same lines; **il a agi dans le même ~** he acted along the same lines, he did more or less the same thing; **j'ai donné des directives dans ce ~** I've given instructions to that effect *ou* end; **dans quel ~ allez-vous orienter votre action?** along what lines are you going to direct your action?, what will be your general line of action?; **le ~ de l'histoire** the course of history.

2 comp ▸**sens giratoire** (*Aut*) roundabout (*Brit*), traffic circle (*US*); **la place est en sens giratoire** the square forms a roundabout ▸**sens interdit** (*Aut*) one-way street; **vous êtes en sens interdit** you are in a one-way street, you are going the wrong way (up a one-way street) ▸**sens unique** (*Aut*) one-way street; **à sens unique** *rue* one-way; *concession* one-sided.

sensass* [sɑ̃sas] adj inv fantastic*, terrific*, sensational.

sensation [sɑ̃sasjɔ̃] nf a (*perception*) sensation; (*impression*) feeling, sensation. **il eut une ~ d'étouffement** he had a feeling of suffocation, he had a suffocating feeling *ou* sensation; **éprouver une ~ de bien-être** to have a feeling of well-being; **éprouver une ~ de faim/de froid** to have a cold/hungry feeling; **j'ai la ~ de l'avoir déjà vu** I have a feeling I've seen him before; **quelle ~ cela te procure-t-il?** what do you feel?, what does it make you feel?, what kind of sensation does it give you?; **un amateur de ~s fortes** an enthusiast for sensational experiences *ou* big thrills.

b (*effet*) **faire ~** to cause *ou* create a sensation; **roman à ~** sensational novel; **la presse à ~** the gutter press.

sensation(n)alisme [sɑ̃sasjɔnalism] nm sensationalism.

sensationnel, -elle [sɑ̃sasjɔnɛl] 1 adj (**: merveilleux*) fantastic*, terrific*, sensational; (*qui fait sensation*) sensational. 2 nm: **le ~** the sensational; **à l'affût du ~** on the lookout for something sensational.

sensé, e [sɑ̃se] adj sensible.

sensément [sɑ̃semɑ̃] adv sensibly.

sensibilisateur, -trice [sɑ̃sibilizatœʀ, tʀis] 1 adj sensitizing. 2 nm sensitizer.

sensibilisation [sɑ̃sibilizasjɔ̃] nf a (*fig*) **la ~ de l'opinion publique à ce problème est récente** public opinion has only become sensitive *ou* alive to this problem in recent years; (*Pol*) **campagne de ~** awareness campaign, consciousness-raising campaign. b (*Bio, Phot*) sensitization.

sensibilisé, e [sɑ̃sibilize] (ptp de **sensibiliser**) adj: **~ à** *personne, public* sensitive *ou* alive to; **~ aux problèmes politiques/sociaux** politically/socially aware.

sensibiliser [sɑ̃sibilize] [1] vt a **~ qn** to make sb sensitive *ou* alive (*à* to); **~ l'opinion publique au problème de** to heighten public awareness of the problem of, make the public aware of the problem of. b (*Bio, Phot*) to sensitize.

sensibilité [sɑ̃sibilite] nf *[personne]* (*gén*) sensitivity, sensitiveness; (*de l'artiste*) sensibility, sensitivity; (*Tech*) *[pellicule, instrument, muscle]* sensitivity. (*Pol*) **il a une ~ de gauche/de droite** his sympathies lie with the left/right.

sensible [sɑ̃sibl] adj a (*impressionnable*) sensitive (*à* to). **pas recommandé aux personnes ~s** not recommended for people of (a) nervous disposition; **elle a le cœur ~** she is tender-hearted, she has a tender heart; **être ~ aux attentions de qn/au charme de qch** to be sensitive to sb's attentions/to the charm of sth; *voir* **âme, point.**

b (*tangible*) perceptible. **le vent était à peine ~** the wind was scarcely *ou* hardly perceptible; **~ à la vue/l'ouïe** perceptible to the eye/the ear.

c (*appréciable*) *progrès, changement, différence* appreciable, noticeable, palpable (*épith*). **la différence n'est pas ~** the difference is hardly noticeable *ou* appreciable.

d (*Physiol*) *organe, blessure* sensitive. **avoir l'ouïe/l'odorat ~** to have sensitive *ou* keen hearing/a keen sense of smell; **~ au chaud/froid** sensitive to (the) heat/cold; **elle est ~ au froid** she feels the cold, she's sensitive to (the) cold; **être ~ de la bouche/gorge** to have a sensitive mouth/throat.

e (*difficile*) *dossier, projet, secteur* sensitive.

f (*Tech*) *papier, balance, baromètre* sensitive; *voir* **corde.**

g (*Mus*) **(note) ~** leading note.

h (*Philos*) **intuition ~** sensory intuition; **être ~** sentient being; **univers ~** sensible universe.

sensiblement [sɑ̃sibləmɑ̃] adv a (*presque*) approximately, more or less. **être ~ du même âge/de la même taille** to be approximately *ou* more or less the same age/height. b (*notablement*) appreciably, noticeably, markedly.

sensiblerie [sɑ̃sibləʀi] nf (*sentimentalité*) sentimentality, mawkishness; (*impressionnabilité*) squeamishness.

sensitif, -ive [sɑ̃sitif, iv] 1 adj (*Anat*) *nerf* sensory; (*littér*) oversensitive. 2 **sensitive** nf (*Bot: mimosa*) sensitive plant.

sensoriel, -ielle [sɑ̃sɔʀjɛl] adj sensory, sensorial.

sensorimoteur, -trice [sɑ̃sɔʀimɔtœʀ, tʀis] adj sensorimotor.

sensualisme [sɑ̃sɥalism] nm (*Philos*) sensualism.

sensualiste [sɑ̃sɥalist] (*Philos*) 1 adj sensualist, sensualistic. 2 nmf sensualist.

sensualité [sɑ̃sɥalite] nf (*voir* **sensuel**) sensuality; sensuousness.

sensuel, -uelle [sɑ̃sɥɛl] adj (*porté à ou dénotant la volupté*) sensual; (*qui recherche et apprécie les sensations raffinées*) sensuous.

sensuellement [sɑ̃sɥɛlmɑ̃] adv (*voir* **sensuel**) sensually; sensuously.

sente [sɑ̃t] nf (*littér*) (foot)path.

sentence [sɑ̃tɑ̃s] nf (*verdict*) sentence; (*adage*) maxim.

sentencieusement [sɑ̃tɑ̃sjøzmɑ̃] adv sententiously.

sentencieux, -ieuse [sɑ̃tɑ̃sjø, jøz] adj sententious.

senteur [sɑ̃tœʀ] nf (*littér*) scent, perfume; *voir* **pois.**

senti, e [sɑ̃ti] (ptp de **sentir**) adj *sentiment* heartfelt, sincere. **quelques vérités bien ~es** a few home truths; **quelques mots bien ~s** (*bien choisis*) a few well-chosen *ou* well-expressed words; (*de blâme*) a few well-chosen words; **un discours bien ~** a well-delivered *ou* heartfelt speech.

sentier [sɑ̃tje] nm (*lit*) (foot)path; (*fig*) path. (*lit, fig*) **s'écarter *ou* s'éloigner des ~s battus** to go off the *ou* stray from the beaten track; (*littér*) **les ~s de la gloire** the path to glory; (*lit, fig*) **être sur le ~ de la guerre** to be on the warpath.

sentiment [sɑ̃timɑ̃] nm a (*émotion*) feeling, sentiment (*frm*). **un ~ de pitié/tendresse/haine** a feeling of pity/tenderness/hatred; **~ de culpabilité** guilt *ou* guilty feeling; **avoir de bons/mauvais ~s à l'égard de qn** to have kind/ill feelings for sb; **bons ~s** finer feelings; **dans ce cas, il faut savoir oublier les ~s** in this case, we have to put sentiment to *ou* on one side *ou* to disregard our own feelings in the matter; **prendre qn par les ~s** to appeal to sb's feelings; (*souvent iro*) **ça n'empêche pas les ~s*** that doesn't mean we (*ou* they *etc*) don't love each other.

b (*sensibilité*) **le ~** feeling, emotion; **être capable de ~** to be capable of emotion; **être dépourvu de ~** to be devoid of all feeling *ou* emotion; (*Théât etc*) **jouer/danser avec ~** to play/dance with feeling; **agir par ~** to let one's feelings guide *ou* determine one's actions; (*péj*) **faire du ~** to sentimentalize, be sentimental; **tu ne m'auras pas au ~*** sentimental appeals won't work with me.

c (*conscience*) **avoir le ~ de** to be aware of; **elle avait le ~ très vif de sa valeur** she was keenly aware of her worth, she had a keen sense of her worth; **avoir le ~ que quelque chose va arriver** to have a feeling that something is going to happen.

d (*formules de politesse*) **recevez, Monsieur, *ou* veuillez agréer, Monsieur, (l'expression de) mes ~s distingués *ou* respectueux** yours faithfully (*Brit*), yours truly (*US*); **transmettez-lui nos meilleurs ~s** give him our best wishes.

e (*littér: opinion*) feeling. **quel est votre ~?** what are your feelings *ou* what is your feeling (about that)?

sentimental, e, mpl **-aux** [sɑ̃timɑ̃tal, o] 1 adj a (*tendre*) *personne* sentimental. b (*non raisonné*) *réaction, voyage* sentimental. c (*amoureux*) *vie, aventure* love (*épith*). **il a des problèmes ~aux** he has problems with his love life. d (*péj*) *personne, chanson, film* sentimental, soppy*. **ne sois pas si ~** don't be so soft *ou* soppy* *ou* sentimental. 2 nm, f sentimentalist.

sentimentalement [sɑ̃timɑ̃talmɑ̃] adv sentimentally; (*péj*) soppily*.

sentimentalisme [sɑ̃timɑ̃talism] nm sentimentalism.

sentimentalité [sɑ̃timɑ̃talite] **nf** sentimentality; (*péj*) soppiness*.

sentinelle [sɑ̃tinɛl] **nf** sentry, sentinel (*littér*). (*Mil*) **être en ~** to be on sentry duty, stand sentry; (*fig*) **mets-toi en ~ à la fenêtre** stand guard *ou* keep watch at the window.

sentir [sɑ̃tiʀ] [16] 1 **vt** a (*percevoir*) (*par l'odorat*) to smell; (*au goût*) to taste; (*au toucher, contact*) to feel. **~ un courant d'air** to feel a draught; **~ son cœur battre/ses yeux se fermer** to feel one's heart beating/one's eyes closing; **il ne sent pas la différence entre le beurre et la margarine** he can't taste *ou* tell the difference between butter and margarine; **elle sentit une odeur de gaz/de brûlé** she smelt (*Brit*) *ou* smelled (*US*) gas/burning; **on sent qu'il y a de l'ail dans ce plat** you can taste the garlic in this dish, you can tell there's garlic in this dish; **il ne sent jamais le froid/la fatigue** he never feels the cold/feels tired; **elle sentit qu'on lui tapait sur l'épaule** she felt somebody tapping her on the shoulder; **je suis enrhumé, je ne sens plus rien** I have a cold and can't smell anything *ou* and I've lost all sense of smell; (*fig: froid*) **je ne sens plus mes doigts** I have lost all sensation in my fingers, I can't feel my fingers any longer; (*fatigue*) **je ne sens plus mes jambes** my legs are dropping off* (*Brit*), my legs are folding under me (*US*); (*fig*) **il ne peut pas le ~*** he can't stand *ou* bear (the sight of) him; (*fig*) **~ l'écurie** to get the smell *ou* scent of home in one's nostrils.

b (*avec attrib: dégager une certaine odeur*) to smell; (*avoir un certain goût*) to taste. **~ bon/mauvais** to smell good *ou* nice/bad; **~ des pieds/de la bouche** to have smelly feet/bad breath; **son manteau sent la fumée** his coat smells of smoke; **ce poisson commence à ~** this fish is beginning to smell; **ce thé sent le jasmin** (*goût*) this tea tastes of jasmine; (*odeur*) this tea smells of jasmine; **la pièce sent le renfermé/le moisi** the room smells stale/musty; **ça ne sent pas la rose!*** it's not a very nice smell, is it?

c (*fig: dénoter*) to be indicative of, reveal, smack of. **plaisanteries qui sentent la caserne** jokes with a whiff of the barrack room about them, jokes which smack of the barrack room; **plaisanteries qui sentent le potache** jokes with a touch of the schoolboy about them; **une certaine arrogance qui sent la petite bourgeoisie** a certain arrogance indicative of *ou* which reveals *ou* suggests a middle-class background.

d (*annoncer*) **ça sent le fagot/l'autoritarisme** it smacks *ou* savours of heresy/authoritarianism; **ça sent le piège** there's a trap *ou* catch in it; **ça sent la pluie/la neige** it looks *ou* feels like rain/snow; **ça sent l'orage** there's a storm in the air; **ça sent le printemps** spring is in the air; **ça sent la punition** someone's in for a telling off*, someone's going to be punished; **ça sent le roussi*** there's going to be trouble; **cela sent la poudre** things could flare up; **il sent le sapin*** he hasn't long to go.

e (*avoir conscience de*) *changement, fatigue* to feel, be aware *ou* conscious of; *importance de qch* to be aware *ou* conscious of; (*apprécier*) *beauté, élégance de qch* to appreciate; (*pressentir*) *danger, difficulté* to sense. **~ que** to feel *ou* be aware *ou* conscious that; (*pressentir*) to sense that; **il sentait la panique le gagner** he felt panic rising within him; **sentant le but proche ...** sensing the goal was at hand ...; **il ne sent pas sa force** he doesn't know *ou* realize his own strength; **elle sent maintenant le vide causé par son départ** now she is feeling the emptiness left by his departure; **sentez-vous la beauté de ce passage?** do you feel *ou* appreciate the beauty of this passage?; **le cheval sentait (venir) l'orage** the horse sensed the storm (coming); **il sentit qu'il ne reviendrait jamais** he sensed *ou* felt that he would never come back (again); **nul besoin de réfléchir, cela se sent** there's no need to think about it — you can feel *ou* sense it; **c'est sa façon de ~ (les choses)** that's his way of feeling (things), that's how he feels about things.

f **faire ~ son autorité** to make one's authority felt; **essayez de faire ~ la beauté d'une œuvre d'art** try to bring out *ou* demonstrate *ou* show the beauty of a work of art; **il m'a fait ~ que j'étais de trop** he let me know I wasn't wanted; **les effets des restrictions commencent à se faire ~** the effects of the restrictions are beginning to be felt *ou* to make themselves felt.

2 **se sentir vpr** a **se ~ mal/mieux/fatigué** to feel ill/better/ tired; **se ~ revivre/rajeunir** to feel o.s. coming alive again/growing young again; **il ne se sent pas la force/le courage de le lui dire** he doesn't feel strong/ brave enough to tell him.

b (*être perceptible*) [*effet*] to be felt, show. **cette amélioration/augmentation se sent** this improvement/increase can be felt *ou* shows; **les effets des grèves vont se ~ à la fin du mois** the effect of the strikes will be felt *ou* will show at the end of the month.

c (*se supporter*) **ils ne peuvent pas se ~*** they can't stand *ou* bear each other.

d (*loc*) **ne pas se ~ de joie** to be beside o.s. with joy; **il ne se sent plus!*** he's beside himself!; **non, mais tu ne te sens plus!*** really, have you taken leave of your senses! *ou* you're off your head!* *ou* you're out of your mind!*

seoir [swaʀ] [26] (*frm*) 1 **vi** (*convenir à*) **~ à qn** to become sb. 2 **vb impers: il sied de/que** it is proper *ou* fitting to/that; **comme il sied** as is proper *ou* fitting; **il lui sied/ne lui sied pas de faire** it befits *ou* becomes/ ill befits *ou* ill becomes him to do.

Séoul [seul] **n** Seoul.

sep [sɛp] **nm** = **cep**.

sépale [sepal] **nm** sepal.

séparable [sepaʀabl] **adj** separable (*de* from). **2 concepts difficilement ~s** 2 concepts which are difficult to separate.

séparateur, -trice [sepaʀatœʀ, tʀis] 1 **adj** separating (*épith*), separative. (*Opt*) **pouvoir ~ de l'œil/d'un instrument d'optique** resolving power of the eye/of an optical instrument. 2 **nm** (*Élec, Tech*) separator.

séparation [sepaʀasjɔ̃] **nf** a (*action: voir* **séparer**) pulling off *ou* away; separation; separating out; parting; splitting, division; driving apart; pulling apart. **nous recommandons la ~ des filles et des garçons** we recommend separating the girls and the boys *ou* splitting up the girls and the boys *ou* the separation of the girls and the boys; **mur de ~** separating *ou* dividing wall.

b (*voir* **se séparer**) parting; splitting off; separation; dispersal; breaking up; split-up*; split- *ou* break-up. (*Jur*) **~ de corps** legal separation; (*Jur*) **~ de fait** *ou* **à l'amiable** voluntary separation; **au moment de la ~** [*manifestants*] when they dispersed; [*convives*] when they parted; **des ~s déchirantes** heartrending partings.

c (*absence*) [*amis, parents*] (period of) separation. **une longue ~ avait transformé leurs rapports** a long (period of) separation had changed their relationship.

d (*disjonction*) [*pouvoirs, notions, services*] separation. (*Pol*) **la ~ des pouvoirs** the separation of powers; (*Pol*) **la ~ de l'Église et de l'État** the separation of the Church and the State; (*Jur*) **le régime de la ~ de biens** separation *ou* division of property (*type of marriage settlement*).

e (*cloison*) division, partition; (*fig*) dividing line. **il faut faire une ~ très nette entre ces problèmes** you must draw a very clear dividing line between these problems.

séparatisme [sepaʀatism] **nm** (*Pol, Rel*) separatism.

séparatiste [sepaʀatist] **adj, nmf** (*Pol*) separatist; (*Hist US: sudiste*) secessionist.

séparé, e [sepaʀe] (**ptp de séparer**) **adj** a (*distinct*) *sons, notions* separate. b *personnes* (*Jur: désuni*) separated; (*gén: éloigné*) parted (*attrib*), apart (*attrib*). **vivre ~** to live apart, be separated (*de* from).

séparément [sepaʀemɑ̃] **adv** separately.

séparer [sepaʀe] [1] 1 **vt** a (*détacher*) *écorce, peau, enveloppe* to pull off, pull away (*de* from); (*extraire*) *éléments, gaz, liquides* to separate (out) (*de* from). **~ la tête du tronc** to separate *ou* sever the head from the trunk; **~ la noix de sa coquille** to separate the nut from its shell; **~ le grain du son** to separate the grain from the bran; **~ des gaz/liquides** to separate (out) gases/liquids; **~ un minerai de ses impuretés** to separate an ore from its impurities; (*Bible*) **~ le bon grain de l'ivraie** to separate the wheat from the chaff.

b (*diviser*) to part, split, divide. **~ les cheveux par une raie** to part one's hair; **~ un territoire (en deux) par une frontière** to split *ou* divide a territory (in two) by a frontier.

c (*désunir*) *amis, alliés* to part, drive apart; *adversaires, combattants* to separate, pull apart, part. **~ deux hommes qui se battent** to separate *ou* pull apart *ou* part two men who are fighting; **~ qn et** *ou* **de qn d'autre** to separate *ou* part sb from sb else; **dans cet hôpital, ils séparent les hommes et les femmes** in this hospital they separate the men from *ou* and the women; **ils avaient séparé l'enfant de sa mère** they had separated *ou* parted the child from its mother.

d *territoires, classes sociales, générations* to separate. **une barrière sépare les spectateurs des** *ou* **et les joueurs** a barrier separates the spectators from the players; **un simple grillage nous séparait des fauves** a simple wire fence was all that separated us from *ou* was all that was between us and the big cats; **une chaîne de montagnes sépare la France et** *ou* **de l'Espagne** a chain of mountains separates France from *ou* and Spain; **un seul obstacle le séparait encore du but** only one obstacle stood *ou* remained between him and his goal; (*fig*) **tout les séparait** they were worlds apart, they had nothing in common.

e (*différencier*) *questions, aspects* to distinguish between. **~ l'érudition de** *ou* **et l'intelligence** to distinguish *ou* differentiate between learning and intelligence.

2 **se séparer vpr** a (*se défaire de*) **se ~ de** *employé, objet personnel* to part with; **en voyage, ne vous séparez jamais de votre passeport** when travelling never part with *ou* be parted from your passport.

b (*s'écarter*) to divide, part (*de* from); (*se détacher*) to split off, separate off (*de* from). **écorce qui se sépare du tronc** bark which comes away from the trunk; **l'endroit où les branches se séparent du tronc** the place where the branches split *ou* separate off from the trunk; **le premier étage de la fusée s'est séparé (de la base)** the first stage of the rocket has split off (from the base) *ou* separated (off) from the base; **à cet endroit, le fleuve se sépare en deux** at this place the river divides into two; **les routes/branches se séparent** the roads/ branches divide *ou* part.

c (*se disperser*) [*adversaires*] to separate, break apart; [*manifestants, participants*] to disperse; [*assemblée*] to break up; [*convives*] to leave each other, part; [*époux*] to part, split up, separate (*Jur*). **se ~ de son mari/sa femme** to part *ou* separate from one's husband/wife.

sépia [sepja] **nf** (*Zool: sécrétion*) cuttlefish ink, sepia; (*substance,* *couleur, dessin*) sepia. **(dessin à la)** ~ sepia (drawing).

sept [sɛt] adj inv, nm inv seven. **les ~ péchés capitaux** the seven deadly sins; **les S~ Merveilles du monde** the seven wonders of the world; *pour autres loc voir* **six**.

septain [sɛtɛ̃] nm *seven-line stanza or poem.*

septante [sɛptɑ̃t] adj inv (††, *ou Belgique, Suisse*) seventy. (*Hist Rel*) **les S~** the Seventy; (*Bible*) **la version des S~** the Septuagint.

septembre [sɛptɑ̃bʀ] nm September. **le mois de ~** the month of September; **le premier/dix ~** (nm) the first/tenth of September; (adv) on the first/tenth of September; **en ~** in September; **au mois de ~** in (the month of) September; **au début (du mois) de ~, début ~** at the beginning of September; **au milieu (du mois) de ~, à la mi-~** in the middle of September, in mid-September; **à la fin (du mois) de ~, fin ~** at the end of September; **pendant le mois de ~** during September; **vers la fin de ~** late in September, in late September, towards the end of September; **~ a été très froid** September was very cold; **~ prochain/dernier** next/last September.

septennal, e, mpl **-aux** [sɛptenal, o] adj (*durée*) *mandat, période* seven-year (*épith*); (*fréquence*) *festival* septennial.

septennat [sɛptena] nm *[président]* seven-year term (of office); *[roi]* seven-year reign.

septentrion [sɛptɑ̃tʀijɔ̃] nm (††, *littér*) north.

septentrional, e, mpl **-aux** [sɛptɑ̃tʀijɔnal, o] adj northern.

septicémie [sɛptisemi] nf (*Méd*) blood poisoning, septicaemia (*SPÉC*).

septicémique [sɛptisemik] adj septicaemic.

septicité [sɛptisite] nf septicity.

septième [sɛtjɛm] 1 adj, nm seventh. **le ~ art** the cinema; **être au ~ ciel** to be in (the) seventh heaven, be on cloud nine*; *pour autres loc voir* **sixième**. 2 nf a (*Scol*) senior form (*Brit*) *ou* grade (*US*) in primary school. b (*Mus*) seventh.

septièmement [sɛtjɛmmɑ̃] adv seventhly; *pour loc voir* **sixièmement**.

septique [sɛptik] adj *fièvre, bactérie* septic; *voir* **fosse**.

septuagénaire [sɛptɥaʒenɛʀ] 1 adj septuagenarian, seventy-year-old (*épith*). 2 nmf septuagenarian, seventy-year-old man (*ou* woman).

septuagésime [sɛptɥaʒezim] nf Septuagesima.

septum [sɛptɔm] nm septum.

septuor [sɛptɥɔʀ] nm septet(te).

septuple [sɛptypl] 1 adj sevenfold, septuple. 2 nm: **le ~ de 2** seven times 2.

septupler [sɛptyple] [1] 1 vt: **~ qch** to increase sth sevenfold. 2 vi to increase sevenfold.

sépulcral, e, mpl **-aux** [sepylkʀal, o] adj *atmosphère, voix* sepulchral; *salle* tomb-like.

sépulcre [sepylkʀ] nm sepulchre; *voir* **saint**.

sépulture [sepyltyʀ] nf a (†, *littér: inhumation*) sepulture (*littér*), burial. **être privé de ~** to be refused burial. b (*tombeau*) burial place; *voir* **violation**.

séquelles [sekɛl] nfpl *[maladie]* after-effects; *[guerre, révolution]* aftermath; *[décision]* consequences.

séquence [sekɑ̃s] nf (*Ciné, Mus, Rel*) sequence; (*Cartes*) run; (*Ling, Ordin*) sequence, string. **~ d'ADN/d'ARN** DNA/RNA sequence; *voir* **plan**.

séquenceur [sekɑ̃sœʀ] nm sequencer.

séquentiel, -ielle [sekɑ̃sjɛl] adj *programme, information* sequential. (*Ling*) **arrangement ~ de la langue** sequential ordering of language; (*Ordin*) **accès ~** sequential *ou* serial access.

séquestration [sekɛstʀasjɔ̃] nf (*voir* **séquestrer**) illegal confinement; sequestration, impoundment.

séquestre [sekɛstʀ] nm (*Jur, Pol*) (*action*) confiscation, impoundment, sequestration; (*dépositaire*) depository. **placer des biens sous ~** to sequester goods.

séquestrer [sekɛstʀe] [1] vt *personne* to confine illegally; *biens* to sequester, impound (*pending decision over ownership*).

sequin [səkɛ̃] nm (*Hist: pièce d'or*) sequin.

séquoia [sekɔja] nm sequoia, redwood.

sérac [seʀak] nm serac.

sérail [seʀaj] nm (*lit*) seraglio, serail; (*fig*) inner circle.

séraphin [seʀafɛ̃] nm seraph.

séraphique [seʀafik] adj (*Rel, fig*) seraphic.

serbe [sɛʀb] 1 adj Serbian. 2 nm (*Ling*) Serbian. 3 nmf: **S~** Serb.

Serbie [sɛʀbi] nf Serbia.

serbo-croate, pl **serbo-croates** [sɛʀbokʀɔat] 1 adj Serbo-Croat(ian). 2 nm (*Ling*) Serbo-Croat.

Sercq [sɛʀk] nm Sark.

serein, e [səʀɛ̃, ɛn] adj a (*calme*) *ciel, nuit, jour* serene, clear; *âme, foi, visage* serene, calm. b (*impartial*) *jugement, critique* calm, dispassionate.

sereinement [səʀɛnmɑ̃] adv (*voir* **serein**) serenely; clearly; calmly; dispassionately.

sérénade [seʀenad] nf a (*Mus: concert, pièce*) serenade. **donner une ~ à qn** to serenade sb. b (* *hum: charivari*) racket, hullabaloo*.

sérénissime [seʀenisim] adj: **Son Altesse ~** His (*ou* Her) Most Serene Highness; (*Hist*) **la S~ République** the Venetian Republic.

sérénité [seʀenite] nf (*voir* **serein**) serenity; clarity; calmness; dispassionateness.

séreux, -euse [seʀø, øz] 1 adj serous. 2 **séreuse** nf serous membrane, serosa.

serf, serve [sɛʀ(f), sɛʀv] 1 adj *personne* in serfdom (*attrib*). **condition serve** (state of) serfdom; **terre serve** land held in villein tenure. 2 nm, f serf.

serfouette [sɛʀfwɛt] nf hoe-fork, weeding hoe.

serge [sɛʀʒ] nf serge.

sergent[1] [sɛʀʒɑ̃] nm (*Mil*) sergeant. **~-chef** staff sergeant; **~ de ville**† policeman; **~-fourrier** quartermaster sergeant; **~ instructeur** drill sergeant; **~-major** ≃ quartermaster sergeant (*in charge of accounts etc*).

sergent[2] [sɛʀʒɑ̃] nm (*serre-joint*) cramp, clamp.

séricicole [seʀisikɔl] adj silkworm-breeding (*épith*), sericultural (*SPÉC*).

sériciculteur [seʀisikyltœʀ] nm silkworm breeder, sericulturist (*SPÉC*).

sériciculture [seʀisikyltyʀ] nf silkworm breeding, sericulture (*SPÉC*).

série [seʀi] nf a (*suite*) *[timbres]* set, series; *[clefs, casseroles, volumes]* set; *[tests]* series, battery; *[ennuis, accidents, succès]* series, string. (*beaucoup*) **(toute) une ~ de*** ... a (whole) series *ou* string of ...; **meurtres en ~** serial killings; **des attentats/accidents en ~** a series of accidents/attacks; (*hum*) **dans la ~ les ennuis continuent ...** yet another example of annoying things ...; **(ouvrages de) ~ noire** crime thrillers, whodunnits*; **ambiance/poursuite (de) ~ noire** crime-thriller atmosphere/chase; (*fig*) **c'est la ~ noire** it's one disaster following (on) another, it's one disaster after another, it's a run of bad luck *ou* a chain of disasters; **~ télévisée** television series.
b (*catégorie*) (*Naut*) class; (*Sport*) rank; (*épreuve de qualification*) qualifying heat *ou* round. **joueur de deuxième ~** player of the second rank; **film de ~ B** B film *ou* movie.
c (*Comm, Ind*) **fabrication** *ou* **production en ~** (*lit, fig*) mass production; **article/voiture de ~** standard article/car; *voir* **fin**[2], **hors**.
d (*Chim, Math, Mus, Phon*) series; (*Billard*) break. (*Élec*) **monté en ~** connected in series.

sériel, -ielle [seʀjɛl] adj *ordre* serial. (*Mus*) **musique ~ielle** serial *ou* twelve-note *ou* dodecaphonic music.

sérier [seʀje] [7] vt *problèmes, questions* to classify, arrange.

sérieusement [seʀjøzmɑ̃] adv (*voir* **sérieux**) seriously; responsibly; genuinely; considerably. **non, il l'a dit ~** no — he meant it seriously, no — he was in earnest when he said that.

sérieux, -ieuse [seʀjø, jøz] 1 adj a (*grave, ne plaisantant pas*) *personne, air* serious, earnest, solemn. **~ comme un pape** sober as a judge.
b (*digne de confiance*) *maison de commerce, tuteur* reliable, dependable; *employé, élève, apprenti* reliable, responsible; (*moralement*) *jeune homme, jeune fille* responsible, trustworthy. **vous laissez un client attendre une heure, puis vous annulez le rendez-vous, ce n'est pas ~!** you make a customer wait an hour and then you cancel the appointment — this is just not good enough!; **partir skier pendant les examens, ce n'est vraiment pas ~!** it's not taking a very responsible *ou* serious attitude *ou* it's taking a pretty flippant attitude to go off skiing during the exams.
c (*fait consciencieusement, à fond*) *études* serious; *travail, artisan* careful, painstaking.
d (*réfléchi*) *personne* serious, serious-minded.
e (*de bonne foi*) *acquéreur, promesses, raison* genuine, serious; *renseignements* genuine, reliable. **un client ~** (*hum: qui achète beaucoup*) a serious customer; **non, il était ~** no, he was serious *ou* he meant it; **c'est ~, ce que vous dites?** are you serious?, do you really mean that?; **ce n'est pas ~!, vous n'êtes pas ~!** you must be joking!; **ce n'est pas ~, il ne le fera jamais** he's not serious *ou* he doesn't really mean it *ou* it isn't a genuine threat (*ou* promise) — he'll never do it!; **"pas ~ s'abstenir"** "only genuine inquirers need apply".
f (*digne d'attention*) *conversation, livre, projet* serious. **passons aux affaires** *ou* **choses ~euses** let us move on to more serious matters.
g (*important, grave*) *situation, affaire, maladie* serious.
h (*intensif*) *raison* good; *coup* serious; *somme, différence* considerable, sizeable. **de ~ieuses chances de ...** a strong *ou* good chance of ...; **de ~ieuses raisons de ...** good reasons to ...; **ils ont une ~ieuse avance** they have a strong *ou* good *ou* sizeable lead.
2 nm (*voir adj*) seriousness; earnestness; reliability; dependability; trustworthiness; carefulness; genuineness; serious-mindedness. **garder son ~** to keep a straight face; **perdre son ~** to give way to laughter; **prendre au ~** to take seriously; **se prendre au ~** to take o.s. seriously.

sérigraphie [seʀigʀafi] nf (*technique*) silkscreen printing, serigraphy (*SPÉC*); (*estampe*) screen print, serigraph (*SPÉC*).

serin [s(ə)ʀɛ̃] nm (*Orn*) canary; († *péj: niais*) ninny*.

seriner [s(ə)ʀine] [1] vt a (*péj: rabâcher*) **~ qch à qn** to drum *ou* din sth into sb; **tais-toi, tu nous serines!*** oh, be quiet, you keep telling us the same thing over and over again! *ou* we're tired of hearing the same thing all the time! b **~ (un air à) un oiseau** to teach a bird a tune using a bird-organ.

seringa(t) [s(ə)ʀɛ̃ga] nm seringa.

seringue [s(ə)ʀɛ̃g] nf (*Méd*) syringe; *[jardinier]* garden syringe; *[pâtissier]* (icing) syringe. *[mécanicien]* **~ à graisse** grease gun.

sérique [seʀik] adj serum (*épith*).

serment [sɛʀmɑ̃] nm a (*solennel*) oath. **faire un ~** to take an oath; ~

sur l'honneur solemn oath, word of honour; **sous** ~ on *ou* under oath; ~ **d'Hippocrate** Hippocratic oath; ~ **professionnel** oath of office; *voir* **prestation, prêter.** b (*promesse*) pledge. **échanger des ~s (d'amour)** to exchange vows *ou* pledges of love; (*fig*) ~ **d'ivrogne** empty vow, vain resolve; **je te fais le ~ de ne plus jouer** I (solemnly) swear to you *ou* I'll make (you) a solemn promise that I'll never gamble again; *voir* **faux**[2].

sermon [sɛʀmɔ̃] **nm** (*Rel*) sermon; (*fig péj*) lecture, sermon.

sermonner [sɛʀmɔne] [1] **vt**: ~ **qn** to lecture sb, give sb a talking-to, sermonize sb.

sermonneur, -euse [sɛʀmɔnœʀ, øz] **nm, f** (*péj*) sermonizer, preacher.

SERNAM [sɛʀnam] **nf** (**abrév de Service national des messageries**) *French national parcels service.*

sérodiagnostic [seʀodjagnɔstik] **nm** serodiagnosis.

sérologie [seʀɔlɔʒi] **nf** serology.

sérologiste [seʀɔlɔʒist] **nmf** serologist.

séronégatif, -ive [seʀonegatif, iv] 1 **adj** HIV negative, seronegative (*SPÉC*). 2 **nm, f** person who is HIV negative *ou* seronegative (*SPÉC*).

séropositif, ive [seʀopozitif, iv] 1 **adj** HIV positive, seropositive (*SPÉC*). 2 **nm, f** person who is HIV positive *ou* seropositive (*SPÉC*), person with HIV.

sérosité [seʀozite] **nf** serous fluid, serosity.

sérothérapie [seʀoteʀapi] **nf** serotherapy.

serpe [sɛʀp] **nf** billhook, bill. (*fig*) **un visage taillé à la ~ ou à coups de ~** a craggy *ou* rugged face.

serpent [sɛʀpɑ̃] 1 **nm** a (*Zool*) snake; (*Mus*) bass horn. (*Rel*) **le ~** the serpent; **une ruse/prudence de ~** snake-like cunning/caution; *voir* **charmeur, réchauffer.** b (*fig: ruban*) ribbon. **un ~ de fumée** a ribbon of smoke; **le ~ argenté du fleuve** the silvery ribbon of the river. 2 **comp** ►**serpent d'eau** water snake ►**serpent à lunettes** Indian cobra ►**serpent de mer** (*hum Presse*) awe-inspiring *ou* alarming spectre ►**le serpent (monétaire)** (*Écon*) the (currency) snake ►**serpent à plumes** (*Myth*) plumed serpent ►**serpent à sonnettes** rattlesnake.

serpentaire [sɛʀpɑ̃tɛʀ] 1 **nm** (*Zool*) secretary bird, serpent-eater. 2 **nf** (*plante*) snakeroot.

serpenteau, pl **~x** [sɛʀpɑ̃to] **nm** (*Zool*) young snake; (*feu d'artifice*) serpent.

serpenter [sɛʀpɑ̃te] [1] **vi** *[rivière, chemin]* to snake, meander, wind; *[vallée]* to wind. **la route descendait en serpentant vers la plaine** the road snaked *ou* wound (its way) down to the plain.

serpentin, e [sɛʀpɑ̃tɛ̃, in] 1 **adj** (*gén*) serpentine. 2 **nm** (*ruban*) streamer; (*Chim*) coil. 3 **serpentine nf** (*Minér*) serpentine.

serpette [sɛʀpɛt] **nf** pruning knife.

serpillière [sɛʀpijɛʀ] **nf** floorcloth.

serpolet [sɛʀpɔlɛ] **nm** mother-of-thyme, wild thyme.

serrage [seʀaʒ] **nm** (*gén, Tech*) *[vis, écrou]* tightening; *[joint]* clamping; *[nœud]* tightening, pulling tight; *voir* **bague, collier, vis**[1].

serre[1] [sɛʀ] **nf** (*gén*) greenhouse, glasshouse; (*attenant à une maison*) conservatory. **pousser en ~** to grow under glass; ~ **chaude** hothouse; *voir* **effet.**

serre[2] [sɛʀ] **nf** (*griffe*) talon, claw.

serre- [sɛʀ] **préf** *voir* **serrer.**

serré, e [seʀe] (**ptp de serrer**) 1 **adj** a *vêtement, soulier* tight. b *passagers, spectateurs* (tightly) packed. **être ~s comme des harengs ou sardines** to be packed like sardines; **mettez-vous ailleurs, nous sommes trop ~s à cette table** sit somewhere else because we are too crowded at this table; *voir* **rang.**
c *tissu* closely woven; *réseau* dense; *mailles, écriture* close; *herbe, blés, forêt* dense; (*fig*) *style* tight, concise. **un café (bien) ~** a (good) strong coffee; **pousser en touffes ~es** to grow in thick clumps.
d (*bloqué*) **trop ~** too tight; **pas assez ~** not tight enough; *voir aussi* **serrer.**
e (*contracté*) **avoir le cœur ~** to feel a pang of anguish; **avoir la gorge ~e** to feel a tightening *ou* a lump in one's throat; **les poings ~s** with clenched fists; *voir aussi* **serrer.**
f *discussion* closely conducted, closely argued; *jeu, lutte, match* tight, close-fought; *budget* tight; *prix* keen. (*fig*) **la partie est ~e, nous jouons une partie ~e** it is a tight game, we're in a tight game; **un train de vie assez ~** a rather constrained *ou* straitened life style.
2 **adv**: **écrire ~** to write one's letters close together, write a cramped hand; (*fig*) **jouer ~** to play it tight, play a tight game; **vivre ~** to live on a tight budget.

serrement [sɛʀmɑ̃] **nm** a ~ **de main** handshake; ~ **de cœur** pang of anguish; ~ **de gorge ou à la gorge** tightening in the throat. b (*Min*) dam.

serrer [seʀe] [1] 1 **vt** a (*maintenir, presser*) to grip, hold tight. ~ **une pipe/un os entre ses dents** to clench *ou* have a pipe/a bone between one's teeth; ~ **qn dans ses bras/contre son cœur** to clasp sb in one's arms/to one's chest; ~ **la main à qn** (*la donner à qn*) to shake sb's hand, shake hands with sb; (*presser*) to squeeze *ou* press sb's hand; **se ~ la main** to shake hands; ~ **qn à la gorge** to grab sb by the throat; *voir* **kiki.**
b (*contracter*) ~ **le poing/les mâchoires** to clench one's fist/jaws; ~ **les lèvres** to set one's lips; **les mâchoires serrées** with set *ou* clenched jaws; **les lèvres serrées** with tight lips, tight-lipped; **avoir le cœur serré par l'émotion** to feel one's heart wrung by emotion; **avoir la gorge serrée par l'émotion** to be choked by emotion; **cela serre le cœur ou c'est à vous ~ le cœur de les voir si malheureux** it wrings your heart *ou* makes your heart bleed to see them so unhappy; ~ **les dents** (*lit*) to clench *ou* set one's teeth; (*fig*) to grit one's teeth; (*fig*) ~ **les fesses**‡ to be scared stiff *ou* out of one's wits*.
c (*comprimer*) to be too tight for; (*mouler*) to fit tightly. **mon pantalon me serre** my trousers are too tight (for me); **cette jupe me serre (à) la taille** this skirt is too tight round the *ou* my waist; **elle se serre la taille dans un corset pour paraître plus jeune** she wears a tight corset to make herself look younger; **ces chaussures me serrent (le pied)** these shoes are too tight; **son jersey lui serrait avantageusement le buste** the tight fit of her jersey showed her figure off to advantage.
d (*bloquer*) *vis, écrou* to tighten; *joint* to clamp; *robinet* to turn off tight; *nœud, lacet, ceinture* to tighten, pull tight; (*tendre*) *câble* to tauten, make taut, tighten; (*Naut*) *voile* to make fast, belay (*SPÉC*). ~ **le frein à main** to put on the handbrake; (*fig*) ~ **la vis à qn*** to crack down harder on sb*.
e (*se tenir près de*) (*par derrière*) to keep close behind; (*latéralement*) *automobile, concurrent* to squeeze (*contre* up against). ~ **qn de près** to follow close behind sb; ~ **une femme de près** to press up against a woman; ~ **de près l'ennemi** to pursue the enemy closely; ~ **qn dans un coin** to wedge sb in a corner; ~ **un cycliste contre le trottoir** to squeeze a cyclist against the pavement; ~ **le trottoir** to hug the kerb; (*Aut*) ~ **sa droite** to keep (well) to the right; **ne serre pas cette voiture de trop près** don't get too close to *ou* behind that car; (*fig*) ~ **une question de plus près** to study a question more closely; (*fig*) ~ **le texte** to follow the text closely, keep close to the text; (*Naut*) ~ **la côte** to sail close to the shore, hug the shore; (*Naut*) ~ **le vent** to hug the wind.
f (*rapprocher*) *objets alignés, mots, lignes* to close up, put close together. (*Mil*) ~ **les rangs** to close ranks; **serrez!** close ranks!; ~ **son style** to write concisely *ou* in a condensed *ou* concise style; **il faudra ~ les invités: la table est petite** we'll have to squeeze the guests up *ou* together since the table is small.
g (*dial*, †: *ranger*) to put away.
2 **vi** (*Aut: obliquer*) ~ **à droite/gauche** to move in to the right-/left-hand lane; **"véhicules lents serrez à droite"** "slow-moving vehicles keep to the right".
3 **se serrer vpr** a (*se rapprocher*) **se ~ contre qn** to huddle (up) against sb; (*tendrement*) to cuddle *ou* snuggle up to sb; **se ~ autour de la table/du feu** to squeeze *ou* crowd round the table/fire; **se ~ pour faire de la place** to squeeze up to make room; **serrez-vous un peu** squeeze up a bit.
b (*se contracter*) **à cette vue, son cœur se serra** at the sight of this he felt a pang of anguish; **ses poings se serrèrent, presque malgré lui** his fists clenched *ou* he clenched his fists almost in spite of himself.
c (*loc*) **se ~ les coudes**‡ to stick together, back one another up; **se ~ (la ceinture)** to tighten one's belt.
4 **comp** ►**serre-file nm** (**pl serre-files**) (*Mil*) file closer ►**serre-frein(s) nm inv** brakesman ►**serre-joint(s) nm inv** clamp, cramp ►**serre-livres nm inv** book end ►**serre-tête nm inv** (*bandeau*) headband, sweatband; (*bonnet*) *[cycliste, skieur]* skullcap; *[aviateur]* helmet.

serrure [seʀyʀ] **nf** *[poste, coffre-fort, valise]* lock. ~ **encastrée** mortise lock; ~ **de sûreté** safety lock; (*Aut*) ~ **de sécurité** safety lock, child lock; ~ **à pompe** spring lock; ~ **à combinaison** combination lock; ~ **trois points** three-point security lock; *voir* **trou.**

serrurerie [seʀyʀʀi] **nf** (*métier*) locksmithing, locksmith's trade; (*travail*) ironwork. ~ **d'art** ornamental ironwork, wrought-iron work; **grosse ~** heavy ironwork.

serrurier [seʀyʀje] **nm** *[serrures, clefs]* locksmith; *[fer forgé]* ironsmith.

sertir [sɛʀtiʀ] [2] **vt** a *pierre précieuse* to set. b (*Tech*) *pièces de tôle* to crimp.

sertissage [sɛʀtisaʒ] **nm** (*voir* **sertir**) setting; crimping.

sertisseur, -euse [sɛʀtisœʀ, øz] **nm, f** (*voir* **sertir**) setter; crimper.

sertissure [sɛʀtisyʀ] **nf** *[pierre précieuse]* (*procédé*) setting; (*objet*) bezel.

sérum [seʀɔm] **nm** a (*Physiol*) ~ **(sanguin)** (blood) serum; ~ **artificiel ou physiologique** normal *ou* physiological salt solution. b (*Méd*) serum. ~ **antidiphtérique/antitétanique/antivenimeux** anti-diphtheric/antitetanus/snakebite serum; (*fig*) ~ **de vérité** truth drug.

servage [sɛʀvaʒ] **nm** (*Hist*) serfdom; (*fig*) bondage, thraldom.

serval, pl **-s** [sɛʀval] **nm** serval.

servant, e [sɛʀvɑ̃, ɑ̃t] 1 **adj**: **chevalier ou cavalier ~** escort. 2 **nm** (*Rel*) server; (*Mil*) *[pièce d'artillerie]* server; (*Tennis*) = serveur. 3 **servante nf** a (*domestique*) servant, maidservant. b (*étagère*) sideboard; (*table*) side table; (*Tech: support*) adjustable support *ou* rest.

serve [sɛʀv] *voir* **serf.**

serveur, -euse [sɛʀvœʀ, øz] 1 **nm** a *[restaurant]* waiter; *[bar]* barman. b (*ouvrier*) *[machine]* feeder. c (*Tennis*) server. d (*Cartes*) dealer. e (*Ordin*) server. **centre ~** service centre, retrieval centre; ~ **(Minitel)** *information service provided by Minitel.* 2 **serveuse nf** *[restaurant]* waitress; *[bar]* barmaid.

serviabilité [sɛʀvjabilite] nf willingness to help.

serviable [sɛʀvjabl] adj obliging, willing to help.

service [sɛʀvis] 1 nm a (*travail, fonction*) duty. (*temps de travail*) **le ~** (the period of) duty; **un ~ de surveillance/contrôle** surveillance/checking duties; (*Mil*) **~ intérieur** barracks duty; (*Mil*) **~ de jour/semaine** day/week duty; **quel ~ fait-il cette semaine?** what duty is he on this week?; **on ne fume pas pendant le ~** smoking is not allowed during duty hours *ou* while on duty; **être à cheval sur le ~** to be strict about the rules at work; (*Admin*) **autorisation refusée dans l'intérêt du ~** permission refused on administrative grounds *ou* for administrative reasons; **heures de ~** hours of service *ou* duty; **le ~ d'un enseignant est de 15 à 20 heures en moyenne** a teacher does between 15 and 20 hours of duty *ou* service on average; **il est très ~(-)~*** he's very hot* *ou* keen (*Brit*) on the rules and regulations *ou* on doing the job properly; **prendre son ~** to come on duty; **être de ~** to be on duty; **pompier/médecin de ~** duty fireman/doctor, fireman/doctor on duty; (*Admin, Mil*) **être en ~ commandé** to be acting under orders, be on an official assignment; **avoir 25 ans de ~** to have completed 25 years' service; *voir* **note, règlement.**

b (*gén pl: prestation*) service. (*Écon*) **~s** services; (*Écon*) **les ~s** the service industries; **offrir ses ~s à qn** to offer sb one's services; **offre de ~** offer of service; **s'assurer les ~s de qn** to enlist sb's services; (*Écon*) **biens et ~s** goods and services.

c (*domesticité*) (domestic) service. **entrer/être en ~ chez qn** to go into/be in sb's service, go into/be in service with sb; **être au ~ de** *maître, Dieu* to be in the service of; **se mettre au ~ de** *maître* to enter the service of *ou* go into service with; *Dieu, nation, État* to place o.s. in the service of; **10 ans de ~ chez le même maître** 10 years in service with the same master; **prendre qn à son ~** to take sb into one's service; **escalier de ~** service *ou* servants' stairs, backstairs; **entrée de ~** service *ou* tradesman's entrance.

d (*Mil*) **le ~ (militaire)** military *ou* national service; **le ~ civil pour les objecteurs de conscience** non-military national service for conscientious objectors; **bon pour le ~** fit for military service; **faire son ~** to do one's military *ou* national service; **~ armé** combatant service; *voir* **état.**

e (*fonction, organisation d'intérêt public*) service; (*section, département*) department, section. **le ~ hospitalier/de la poste** the hospital/postal service; **les ~s de santé/postaux** health (care)/postal services; **~ du contentieux/des achats/de la publicité** legal/buying/publicity department; **les ~s d'un ministère** the departments of a ministry; **le ~ des urgences** the casualty department; **S~ d'assistance médicale d'urgence** mobile emergency medical service; **~ médico-social** medical-social work department; **~ de réanimation** intensive care unit; **les ~s publics** the (public) utilities; **les ~s sociaux** the social services; **~ régional de police judiciaire** regional crime squad; *voir* **chef[1].**

f (*Rel: office, messe*) service. **~ funèbre** funeral service.

g (*faveur, aide*) service. **rendre un petit ~ à qn** to do sb a favour, do sb a small service; **tous les ~s qu'il m'a rendus** all the favours *ou* services he has done me; **rendre ~ à qn** (*aider*) to do sb a service *ou* a good turn; (*s'avérer utile*) to come in useful *ou* handy for sb, be of use to sb; **il aime rendre ~** he likes to do good turns *ou* be helpful; (*fig*) **rendre un mauvais ~ à qn** to do sb a disservice; (*frm*) **qu'y-a-t-il pour votre ~?** how can I be of service to you?; (*frm*) **je suis à votre ~** I am at your service.

h (*à table, au restaurant*) service; (*pourboire*) service charge; (*série de repas*) sitting. **Jean fera le ~** John will serve (out); **la nourriture est bonne mais le ~ est exécrable** the food is good but the service is shocking; **laisse 10 F pour le ~** leave 10 francs for the service; **ils ont oublié de facturer le ~** they have forgotten to include the service (charge) on the bill; **~ compris/non compris** service included/not included, inclusive/exclusive of service; **premier/deuxième ~** first/second sitting; *voir* **libre, self.**

i (*assortiment*) *[couverts]* set; *[vaisselle, linge de table]* service, set. **~ de table** set of table linen; **~ à thé** tea set *ou* service; **~ à liqueurs** set of liqueur glasses; **~ à poisson** (*plats*) set of fish plates; (*couverts*) fish service; **~ à fondue** fondue set; **~ à gâteaux** (*couverts*) cake cutlery (*NonC*) *ou* set; (*vaisselle*) set of cake plates; **~ à fromage** set of cheese dishes; **~ de 12 couteaux** set of 12 knives; **un beau ~ de Limoges** a beautiful service of Limoges china.

j *[machine, installation]* operation, working. **faire le ~ d'une pièce d'artillerie** to operate *ou* work a piece of artillery.

k (*fonctionnement, usage*) **mettre en ~** *installation, usine* to put *ou* bring into service, bring on stream *ou* line; *[installation, usine]* **entrer en ~** to come on stream *ou* on line *ou* into service; **machine/vêtement qui fait un long ~** machine/garment which gives long service; *voir* **hors.**

l (*transport*) service. **un ~ d'autocars dessert ces localités** there is a coach service to these districts; **assurer le ~ entre** to provide a service between; **~ d'hiver/d'été** winter/summer service; **le ~ est interrompu sur la ligne 3** (the) service is suspended on line 3; **~ minimum** skeleton service.

m (*Tennis*) service. **être au ~** to have the service; **il a un excellent ~** he has an excellent service *ou* serve; **~ canon** bullet-like serve *ou* service.

2 comp ▸**service après-vente** after-sales service ▸**service d'ordre** (*policiers*) police contingent; (*manifestants*) team of stewards (responsible for crowd control *etc*); **pour assurer le service d'ordre** to maintain (good) order; **un important service d'ordre assurait le bon déroulement de la manifestation** a large police presence *ou* contingent ensured that the demonstration passed off smoothly ▸**service de presse** (*distribution*) distribution of review copies; (*ouvrage*) review copy; (*agence*) press relations department ▸**services secrets** secret service.

serviette [sɛʀvjɛt] 1 nf a (*en tissu*) **~ (de toilette)** (hand) towel; **~ (de table)** serviette, (table) napkin; *voir* **rond.** b (*cartable*) *[écolier, homme d'affaires]* briefcase. 2 comp ▸**serviette de bain** bath towel ▸**serviette éponge** terry towel ▸**serviette hygiénique** sanitary towel ▸**serviette en papier** paper serviette, paper (table) napkin ▸**serviette périodique** = **serviette hygiénique.**

servile [sɛʀvil] adj a (*soumis*) *homme, flatterie, obéissance* servile, cringing; *traduction, imitation* slavish. b (*littér: de serf*) *condition, travail* servile.

servilement [sɛʀvilmɑ̃] adv (*voir* **servile**) servilely; cringingly; slavishly.

servilité [sɛʀvilite] nf (*voir* **servile**) servility; slavishness.

servir [sɛʀviʀ] 14 1 vt a (*être au service de*) *pays, Dieu, État, cause* to serve; (*emploi absolu: être soldat*) to serve. (*Rel*) **~ le prêtre** to serve the priest; (*Rel*) **~ la messe** to serve mass.

b *[domestique] patron* to serve, wait on. **il sert comme chauffeur** he serves as a chauffeur; **elle aime se faire ~** she likes to be waited on; (*Prov*) **on n'est jamais si bien servi que par soi-même** if you want something done you're best to do it yourself.

c (*aider*) *personne* to be of service to, aid. **~ les ambitions/les intérêts de qn** to serve *ou* aid sb's ambitions/interests; **ceci nous sert** this serves our interests; **sa prudence l'a servi auprès des autorités** his caution served him well *ou* stood him in good stead in his dealings with the authorities; **il a été servi par les circonstances** he was aided by circumstances; **il a été servi par une bonne mémoire** he was well served *ou* aided by a good memory.

d (*dans un magasin*) *client* to serve, attend to; (*au restaurant*) *consommateur* to serve; *dîneur* to wait on; (*chez soi, à table*) to serve. **ce boucher nous sert depuis des années** this butcher has supplied us for years, we've been going to this butcher for years; **le boucher m'a bien servi** (*en qualité*) the butcher has given me good meat; (*en quantité*) the butcher has given me a good amount for my money; **on vous sert, Madame?** are you being attended to? *ou* served?; **il a faim, servez-le bien** he is hungry so give him a good helping; **prenez, n'attendez pas qu'on vous serve** help yourself — don't wait to be served; **"Madame est servie"** "dinner is served"; **pour vous ~†** at your service; **des garçons en livrée servaient** waiters in livery waited *ou* served at table; **il sert dans un café** he is a waiter in a café; (*fig*) **les paysans voulaient la pluie, ils ont été servis!** the farmers wanted rain — now their wish has been granted! *ou* well, they've got what they wanted!; (*fig*) **en fait d'ennuis, elle a été servie** as regards troubles she's had her share (and more) *ou* she's had more than her fair share; *voir* **on.**

e (*Mil*) *pièce d'artillerie* to serve.

f (*donner*) *rafraîchissement, plat* to serve. **~ qch à qn** to serve sb with sth, help sb to sth; **~ le déjeuner/dîner** to serve (up) lunch/dinner; **le vin rouge doit se ~ chambré** red wine must be served at room temperature; **"~ frais"** "serve cool"; **~ à déjeuner/dîner** to serve lunch/dinner (*à qn* to sb); **~ à boire** to serve a drink *ou* drinks; **~ à boire à qn** to serve a drink to sb; **on nous a servi le petit déjeuner au lit** we were served (our) breakfast in bed; **à table, c'est servi!** come and sit down now, it's ready!; (*fig*) **il nous sert toujours les mêmes plaisanteries** he always trots out the same old jokes *ou* treats us to the same old jokes; (*fig*) **~ la soupe à qn*** (*gén*) to do sb's work for them; *[écrivain]* to ghost for sb.

g (*procurer*) to pay. **~ une rente/une pension/des intérêts à qn** to pay sb an income/a pension/interest.

h (*Cartes*) to deal. **être servi** to stick.

i (*Tennis*) to serve. **à vous de ~** your service, it's your turn to serve.

j (*être utile*) **~ à** *personne* to be of use *ou* help to; *usage, opération* to be of use in, be useful for; **~ à faire** to be used for doing; **ça m'a servi à réparer ce meuble** I used it to mend this piece of furniture; **cela ne sert à rien** *[objet]* this is no use, this is useless; *[démarche]* there is no point in it, it serves no (useful) purpose; **cela ne sert à rien de pleurer/réclamer** it's no use *ou* there's no point crying/complaining, crying/complaining doesn't help; **à quoi sert cet objet?** what is this object used for?; **à quoi servirait de réclamer?** what use would complaining be?, what would be the point of complaining?; **cela ne servirait pas à grand-chose de dire ...** there's little point in saying ..., it wouldn't be much use saying ...; **est-ce que cela pourrait vous ~?** could this be (of) any use to you?, could you make use of this?; **vos conseils lui ont bien servi** your advice has been very useful *ou* helpful to him; **ne jette pas cette boîte, cela peut toujours ~** don't throw that box away — it may still come in handy *ou* still be of some use; **ces projecteurs servent à guider les avions** these floodlights are used to guide *ou* for guiding the planes; **cet instrument sert à beaucoup de choses** this implement has many uses *ou* is used for many things; **cela a servi à nous faire comprendre les difficultés** this served to make us understand the difficulties; *voir* **rien**.

k **~ de** *[personne]* to act as; *[ustensile, objet]* to serve as; **elle lui a servi d'interprète/de témoin** she acted as his interpreter/as a witness (for him); **cette pièce sert de chambre d'amis** this room serves as *ou* is used as a guest room; **cela pourrait te ~ de table** you could use that as a table, that would serve *ou* do as a table for you; **~ de leçon à qn** to be a lesson to sb; **~ d'exemple à qn** to serve as an example to sb.

2 **se servir** **vpr** a (*à table, dans une distribution*) to help o.s. (*chez un fournisseur*) **se ~ chez X** to buy *ou* shop at X's; **se ~ en viande chez X** to buy one's meat at X's *ou* from X, go to X's for one's meat; **servez-vous donc de viande** do help yourself to meat; (*iro*) **je t'en prie, sers-toi** go ahead, help yourself.

b **se ~ de** *outil, mot, main-d'œuvre* to use; *personne* to use, make use of; **il sait bien se ~ de cet outil** he knows how to use this tool; **t'es-tu servi de ce vêtement?** have you used this garment?; **il se sert de sa voiture pour aller au bureau** he uses his car to go to the office; **se ~ de ses relations** to make use of *ou* use one's acquaintances; **il s'est servi de moi** he used me.

serviteur [sɛʀvitœʀ] **nm** (*gén*) servant. (*hum*) **en ce qui concerne votre ~** ... as far as yours truly is concerned ... (*hum*).

servitude [sɛʀvityd] **nf** a (*esclavage*) servitude. b (*gén pl: contrainte*) constraint. c (*Jur*) easement. **~ de passage** right of way.

servocommande [sɛʀvokɔmɑ̃d] **nf** (*Tech*) servo-mechanism.

servodirection [sɛʀvodiʀɛksjɔ̃] **nf** servo(-assisted) steering.

servofrein [sɛʀvofʀɛ̃] **nm** (*Tech*) servo(-assisted) brake.

servomécanisme [sɛʀvomekanism] **nm** (*Tech*) servo system.

servomoteur [sɛʀvomɔtœʀ] **nm** (*Tech*) servo-motor.

servovalve [sɛʀvovalv] **nf** servo valve.

ses [se] **adj poss** *voir* **son**[1].

sésame [sezam] **nm** (*Bot*) sesame. (*fig*) **(S)~ ouvre-toi** open Sesame.

sessile [sesil] **adj** (*Bot*) sessile.

session [sesjɔ̃] **nf** (*Jur, Parl*) session, sitting. (*Parl*) **~ extraordinaire** special session; (*Univ*) **~ (d'examen)** university exam session; **la ~ de juin** the June exams; **la ~ de septembre, la seconde ~** the (September) resits (*Brit*).

sesterce [sɛstɛʀs] **nm** (*Hist*) sesterce, sestertius; (*mille unités*) sestertium.

set [sɛt] **nm** a (*Tennis*) set; *voir* **balle**[1]. b **~ (de table)** (*ensemble*) set of tablemats *ou* place mats; (*napperon*) tablemat, place mat.

sétacé, e [setase] **adj** setaceous.

setter [setɛʀ] **nm** setter.

seuil [sœj] **nm** a *[porte]* (*dalle etc*) door sill, doorstep; (*entrée*) doorway, threshold†; (*fig*) threshold. **se tenir sur le ~ de sa maison** to stand in the doorway of one's house; **il m'a reçu sur le ~** he kept me on the doorstep *ou* at the door, he didn't ask me in; **avoir la campagne au ~ de sa maison** to have the country on *ou* at one's doorstep; (*fig: début*) **le ~ de** *période* the threshold of; (*fig*) **au ~ de la mort** on the threshold of death, on the brink of the grave; (*fig*) **le ~ du désert** the edge of the desert.

b (*Géog, Tech*) sill.

c (*fig: limite*) threshold; (*Psych*) threshold, limen (*SPÉC*). **~ auditif** auditory threshold; **~ de rentabilité** break-even point; **~ de tolérance** threshold of tolerance; **~ de pauvreté** poverty line *ou* level.

seul, e [sœl] 1 **adj** a (*après n ou attrib*) *personne* (*sans compagnie, non accompagnée*) alone (*attrib*), on one's own (*attrib*), by oneself (*attrib*); (*isolé*) lonely; *objet, mot* alone (*attrib*), on its own (*attrib*), by itself (*attrib*). **être/rester ~** to be/remain alone *ou* on one's own *ou* by oneself; **laissez-moi ~ quelques instants** leave me alone *ou* on my own *ou* by myself for a moment; **~ avec qn/ses pensées/son chagrin** alone with sb/one's thoughts/one's grief; **ils se retrouvèrent enfin ~s** they were alone (together) *ou* on their own *ou* by themselves at last; **un homme ~/une femme ~e peut très bien se débrouiller** a man on his own/a woman on her own *ou* a single man/woman can manage perfectly well; **au bal, il y avait beaucoup d'hommes ~s** at the dance there were many men on their own; **se sentir (très) ~** to feel (very) lonely *ou* lonesome; **~ au monde** alone in the world; **les amoureux sont ~s au monde** lovers behave as if they are alone in the world *ou* are the only ones in the world; **mot employé ~** word used alone *ou* on its own *ou* by itself; **la lampe ~e ne suffit pas** the lamp alone *ou* on its own is not enough, the lamp is not enough on its own *ou* by itself; *voir* **cavalier**.

b (*avant n: unique*) **un ~ homme/livre** (*et non plusieurs*) one man/book, a single man/book; (*à l'exception de tout autre*) only one man/book; **le ~ homme/livre** the one man/book, the only man/book, the sole man/book; **les ~es personnes/conditions** the only people/conditions; **un ~ livre suffit** one book *ou* a single book will do; **un ~ homme peut vous aider: Paul** only one man can help you and that's Paul; **pour cette ~e raison** for this reason alone *ou* only, for this one reason; **son ~ souci est de ...** his only *ou* sole *ou* one concern is to ...; **un ~ moment d'inattention** one *ou* a single moment's lapse of concentration; **il n'y a qu'un ~ Dieu** there is only one God, there is one God only *ou* alone; **une ~e fois** only once, once only; **la ~e chose, c'est que ça ferme à 6 heures** the only thing is (that) it shuts at 6.

c (*en apposition*) only, alone. **~ le résultat compte** the result alone counts, only the result counts; **~s les parents sont admis** only parents are admitted; **~e Gabrielle peut le faire** only Gabrielle *ou* Gabrielle alone can do it; **~e l'imprudence peut être la cause de cet accident** only carelessness can be the cause of this accident; **lui ~ est venu en voiture** he alone *ou* only he came by car; **à eux ~s, ils ont fait plus de dégâts que ...** they did more damage by themselves *ou* on their own than ...; **je l'ai fait à moi (tout) ~** I did it (all) on my own *ou* (all) by myself, I did it single-handed.

d (*loc*) **~ et unique** one and only; **c'est la ~e et même personne** it's one and the same person; **~ de son espèce** alone of its kind, the only one of its kind; **d'un ~ coup** (*subitement*) suddenly; (*ensemble, à la fois*) in *ou* at one blow; **d'un ~ tenant** *terrain* all in one piece, lying together; **vous êtes ~ juge** you alone are the judge *ou* can judge; **à ~e fin de** with the sole purpose of; **dans la ~e intention de faire** with the one *ou* sole intention of doing; **du ~ fait que ...** by the very fact that ...; **à la ~e pensée de ...** at the mere thought of ...; **la ~e pensée d'y retourner la remplissait de frayeur** the mere thought *ou* the thought alone of going back there filled her with fear; **parler à qn ~ à ~** to speak to sb in private *ou* privately *ou* alone; **se retrouver ~ à ~ avec qn** to find o.s. alone with sb; (*fig*) **comme un ~ homme** as one man; **d'une ~e voix** with one voice.

2 **adv** a (*sans compagnie*) **parler/rire ~** to talk/laugh to oneself; **rire tout ~** to have a quiet laugh to oneself; **vivre/travailler ~** to live/work alone *ou* by oneself *ou* on one's own.

b (*sans aide*) by oneself, on one's own, unaided. **faire qch (tout) ~** to do sth (all) by oneself *ou* (all) on one's own, do sth unaided *ou* single-handed; *voir* **tout**.

3 **nm, f**: **un ~ peut le faire** (*et non plusieurs*) one man can do it, a single man can do it; (*à l'exception de tout autre*) only one man can do it; **un ~ contre tous** one (man) against all; **le ~ que j'aime** the only one I love; **vous n'êtes pas la ~e à vous plaindre** you aren't the only one to complain, you aren't alone in complaining; **une ~e de ses peintures n'a pas été détruite dans l'incendie** only one of his paintings was not destroyed in the fire; **il n'en reste pas un ~** there isn't a single *ou* solitary one left.

seulement [sœlmɑ̃] **adv** a (*quantité: pas davantage*) only. **5 personnes ~ sont venues** only 5 people came; **nous serons ~ 4** there will be only 4 of us; **je pars pour 2 jours ~** I am going away for 2 days only, I'm only going away for 2 days.

b (*exclusivement*) only, alone, solely. **on ne vit pas ~ de pain** you can't live on bread alone *ou* only *ou* solely on bread; **ce n'est pas ~ sa maladie qui le déprime** it's not only *ou* just his illness that depresses him; **50 F, c'est ~ le prix de la chambre** 50 francs is the price for just the room *ou* is the price for the room only; **on leur permet de lire ~ le soir** they are allowed to read only at night *ou* at night only; **il fait cela ~ pour nous ennuyer** he does that only *ou* solely to annoy us, he only does that to annoy us.

c (*temps: pas avant*) only. **il vient ~ d'entrer** he's only just (now) come in; **ce fut ~ vers 10 heures qu'il arriva** it was not until about 10 o'clock that he arrived; **il est parti ~ ce matin** he left only this morning, he only left this morning.

d (*en tête de proposition: mais, toutefois*) only, but. **je connais un bon chirurgien, ~ il est cher** I know a good surgeon only *ou* but he is expensive.

e (*loc*) **non ~ il a plu, mais (encore) il a fait froid** it didn't only rain but it was cold too, it not only rained but it was also cold; **pas ~** (*même pas*): **on ne nous a pas ~ donné un verre d'eau** we were not even given a glass of water, we were not given so much as a glass of water; **il n'a pas ~ de quoi se payer un costume** he hasn't even enough to buy himself a suit; **il est parti sans ~ nous prévenir** he left without so much as *ou* without even warning us; **si ~** if only; *voir* **si**[1].

seulet, -ette* [sœlɛ, ɛt] **adj** (*hum*) lonesome, lonely, all alone. **se sentir bien ~** to feel all alone *ou* very lonesome.

sève [sɛv] **nf** *[arbre]* sap; (*fig*) sap, life, vigour. **~ ascendante** *ou* **brute/descendante** *ou* **élaborée** rising *ou* crude/falling *ou* elaborated sap; **les arbres sont en pleine ~** the sap has risen in the trees; **la jeunesse est débordante de ~** young people are brimming with strength and vigour.

sévère [sevɛʀ] **adj** a *maître, juge, climat, règlement* severe, harsh; *parent, éducation, ton* strict, severe, stern; *regard, critique, jugement* severe, stern. **une morale ~** a stern *ou* severe code of morals. b *style, architecture* severe; *tenue* severe, stern. **une beauté ~** a severe beauty. c (*intensif*) *pertes, échec* severe, grave.

sévèrement [sevɛʀmɑ̃] **adv** (*voir* **sévère**) severely; harshly; strictly; sternly. **un malade ~ atteint** a severely affected patient.

sévérité [seveʀite] **nf** (*voir* **sévère**) severity; harshness; strictness; sternness; gravity.

sévices [sevis] **nmpl** (*physical*) cruelty (*NonC*), ill treatment (*NonC*). **exercer des ~ sur son enfant** to ill-treat one's child.

Séville [sevil] **n** Seville.

sévir [seviʀ] 2 **vi** a (*punir*) to act ruthlessly. **~ contre** *personne, abus, pratique* to deal ruthlessly with; **si vous continuez, je vais devoir ~** if you carry on, I shall have to deal severely with you *ou* use harsh measures. b (*lit, hum: exercer ses ravages*) *[fléau, doctrine etc]* to rage, hold sway. **la pauvreté sévissait** poverty was rampant *ou* rife; **il sévit à la télé depuis 20 ans** he's been plaguing our TV/screens for 20 years now (*hum*); **est-ce qu'il sévit encore à la Sorbonne?** is he still let loose on the students at the Sorbonne? (*hum*).

sevrage [səvʀaʒ] **nm** (*voir* **sevrer**) weaning; severing, sevrance.

sevrer [səvʀe] 5 **vt** a *nourrisson, jeune animal* to wean. b (*Horticulture*) to sever. c (*fig*) **~ qn de qch** to deprive sb of sth; **nous avons été sevrés de théâtre** we have been deprived of visits to the theatre.

Sèvres [sɛvʀ] **nm** (*porcelaine*) Sèvres porcelain; (*objet*) piece of Sèvres porcelain.

sexagénaire [sɛksaʒenɛʀ] 1 **adj** sixty-year-old (*épith*), sexagenarian. 2 **nmf** sexagenarian, sixty-year-old man (*ou* woman).

sexagésimal, e, **mpl -aux** [sɛgsaʒezimal, o] **adj** sexagesimal.

sexagésime [sɛgsaʒezim] **nf** (*Rel*) Sexagesima (Sunday).

sex-appeal [sɛksapil] **nm** sex appeal.

sexe [sɛks] **nm** a (*catégorie*) sex. **enfant du ~ masculin/féminin** child of male/female sex, male/female child; **le ~ faible/fort** the weaker/stronger sex; **le (beau) ~** the fair sex. b (*sexualité*) sex. **ce journal ne parle que de ~** this paper is full of nothing but sex. c (*organes génitaux*) genitals, sex organs; *voir* **cacher**.

sexisme [sɛksism] **nm** sexism.

sexiste [sɛksist] **adj, nmf** sexist.

sexologie [sɛksɔlɔʒi] **nf** sexology.

sexologue [sɛksɔlɔg] **nmf** sexologist, sex specialist.

sex-shop **nm, pl sex-shops** [sɛksʃɔp] sex-shop.

sextant [sɛkstɑ̃] **nm** (*instrument*) sextant; (*Math: arc*) sextant arc.

sextillion [sɛkstiljɔ̃] **nm** sextillion.

sextuor [sɛkstɥɔʀ] **nm** (*Mus*) sextet(te).

sextuple [sɛkstypl] 1 **adj** sixfold. 2 **nm: 12 est le ~ de 2** 12 is six times 2; **ils en ont reçu le ~** they have had a sixfold return.

sextupler [sɛkstyple] 1 **vti** to increase six times *ou* sixfold.

sextuplés, ées [sɛkstyple] **nm, fpl** sextuplets.

sexualiser [sɛksɥalize] 1 **vt** to sexualize.

sexualité [sɛksɥalite] **nf** sexuality. **troubles de la ~** sexual problems.

sexué, e [sɛksɥe] **adj** *mammifères, plantes* sexed, sexual; *reproduction* sexual.

sexuel, -elle [sɛksɥɛl] **adj** *caractère, instinct, plaisir* sexual; *éducation, hormone, organe* sexual, sex (*épith*). **l'acte ~** the sex act; *voir* **harcèlement, obsédé**.

sexuellement [sɛksɥɛlmɑ̃] **adv** sexually; *voir* **maladie**.

sexy* [sɛksi] **adj inv** sexy*.

seyant, e [sɛjɑ̃, ɑ̃t] **adj** *vêtement* becoming.

Seychelles [seʃɛl] **nfpl: les ~** the Seychelles.

seychellois, e [seʃelwa, az] 1 **adj** of *ou* from Seychelles. 2 **S~(e)** **nm, f** inhabitant *ou* native of Seychelles.

sézigue⁑ [sezig] **pron pers** his nibs⁑.

S.F.B. [ɛsɛfbe] **nf** (**abrév de Société française de Bourse**) *French stockbrokers' association.*

SFIO [ɛsɛfio] **nf** (**abrév de Section française de l'Internationale ouvrière**) *French political movement.*

SG [ɛsʒe] **nm** (**abrév de secrétaire général**) *voir* **secrétaire**.

S.G.B.D. [ɛsʒebede] **nm** (**abrév de système de gestion de bases de données**) *voir* **système**.

sgraffite [sgʀafit] **nm** sgraffito.

shah [ʃa] **nm** shah.

shakespearien, -ienne [ʃɛkspiʀjɛ̃, jɛn] **adj** Shakespearian.

shaker [ʃɛkœʀ] **nm** cocktail shaker.

shako [ʃako] **nm** shako.

shampooiner, shampouiner [ʃɑ̃pwine] 1 **vt** to shampoo.

shampooineur, -euse, shampouineur, -euse [ʃɑ̃pwinœʀ, øz] 1 **nm, f** (hairdressing) junior. 2 **shampooineuse** **nf** carpet shampooer.

shampooing [ʃɑ̃pwɛ̃] **nm** shampoo. **faire un ~ à qn** to give sb a shampoo, shampoo *ou* wash sb's hair; **~ colorant** tint, rinse.

Shanghai [ʃɑ̃gaj] **n** Shanghai.

shant(o)ung [ʃɑ̃tuŋ] **nm** shantung (silk).

sharia [ʃaʀja] **nf** sharia, sheria.

shekel [ʃekɛl] **nm** shekel.

shérif [ʃeʀif] **nm** sheriff.

sherpa [ʃɛʀpa] **nmf** (*guide*) Sherpa; (*Pol*) aide (*helping with preparations for summit talks*).

sherry [ʃeʀi] **nm** sherry.

shetland [ʃɛtlɑ̃d] **nm** a (*laine*) Shetland wool; (*tricot*) Shetland pullover. b **les îles S~** the Shetland Islands.

shetlandais, e [ʃɛtlɑ̃dɛ, ɛz] 1 **adj** Shetland (*épith*). 2 **nm, f: S~(e)** Shetlander.

shiite [ʃiit] **adj, nmf = chi'ite**.

shilling [ʃiliŋ] **nm** shilling.

shimmy [ʃimi] **nm** (*Aut*) shimmy.

shintô [ʃinto] **nm, shintoïsme** [ʃintɔism] **nm** Shinto, Shintoism.

shintoïste [ʃintɔist] **adj, nmf** Shintoist.

Shiva [ʃiva] **nm = Siva**.

Shoah [ʃɔa] **nf** Shoah.

shogun [ʃɔgun] **nm** shogun.

shoot [ʃut] **nm** (*Ftbl*) shot.

shooter [ʃute] 1 1 **vi** (*Ftbl*) to shoot, make a shot. 2 **vt: ~ un penalty** to take a penalty (kick *ou* shot). 3 **se shooter** **vpr** (*arg Drogue*) to fix (*arg*), shoot (up) (*arg*). **se ~ à l'héroïne** to mainline heroin, shoot up with heroin.

shopping [ʃɔpiŋ] **nm** shopping. **faire du ~** to go shopping.

short [ʃɔʀt] **nm: ~(s)** pair of shorts, shorts (*pl*); **être en ~(s)** to be in shorts *ou* wearing shorts.

show [ʃo] **nm** show.

shrapnel(l) [ʃʀapnɛl] **nm** shrapnel.

shunt [ʃœ̃t] **nm** (*Élec*) shunt.

shunter [ʃœ̃te] 1 **vt** (*Élec*) to shunt; (*) *personne, service* to bypass.

SI a (**abrév de syndicat d'initiative**) *voir* **syndicat**. b (**abrév de Système international (d'unités)**) SI.

si[1] [si] 1 **conj** a (*éventualité, condition*) if. **s'il fait beau demain (et ~ j'en ai** *ou* **et que j'en aie le temps), je sortirai** if it is fine tomorrow (and (if) I have time), I will go out.

b (*hypothèse*) if. **~ j'avais de l'argent, j'achèterais une voiture** if I had any money *ou* had I any money I would buy a car; **même s'il s'excusait, je ne lui pardonnerais pas** even if he were to apologize I should not forgive him; **~ nous n'avions pas été prévenus (et ~ nous avions attendu** *ou* **et que nous eussions attendu), nous serions arrivés** *ou* **nous arrivions trop tard** if we hadn't been warned (and (if) we had waited), we should have arrived too late; **il a déclaré que ~ on ne l'augmentait pas, il partirait** *ou* **il partait** he said that if he didn't get a rise he would leave *ou* he was leaving; **viendras-tu? ~ oui, préviens-moi à l'avance** are you coming? if so *ou* if you are, tell me in advance; *voir* **comme**.

c (*répétition: toutes les fois que*) if, when. **s'il faisait beau, il allait se promener** if *ou* when it was nice he used to go *ou* he would go for a walk; **~ je sors sans parapluie, il pleut** if *ou* whenever I go out without an umbrella it always rains.

d (*opposition*) while, whilst (*surtout Brit*). **~ lui est aimable, sa femme (par contre) est arrogante** while *ou* whereas he is very pleasant his wife (on the other hand) is arrogant.

e (*exposant un fait*) **s'il ne joue plus, c'est qu'il s'est cassé la jambe** if he doesn't play any more it's because he has broken his leg, the reason he no longer plays is that he has broken his leg; **c'est un miracle ~ la voiture n'a pas pris feu** it's a miracle (that) the car didn't catch fire; **excusez-nous** *ou* **pardonnez-nous ~ nous n'avons pas pu venir** please excuse *ou* forgive us for not being able to come.

f (*dans une interrogation indirecte*) if, whether. **il ignore/se demande ~ elle viendra** he doesn't know/is wondering whether *ou* if she will come; **il faut s'assurer ~ la voiture marche** we must make sure that *ou* if *ou* whether the car is working; **vous imaginez s'ils étaient fiers!** you can imagine how proud they were!; **~ je veux y aller! quelle question!** do I want to go! what a question!

g (*en corrélation avec proposition implicite*) if. **~ j'avais su!** if I had only known!, had I only known, had I but known!; **~ je le tenais!** if I could (only) lay my hands on him!; **et s'il refusait?** and what if he refused?, and what if he should refuse?, and supposing he refused?; **~ tu lui téléphonais?** how *ou* what about phoning him?, supposing you phoned him?; **~ nous allions nous promener?** what *ou* how about going for a walk?, what do you say to a walk?

h **~ ce n'est: qui peut le savoir, ~ ce n'est lui?** who will know if not him? *ou* apart from him?; **~ ce n'est elle, qui aurait osé?** who but she would have dared?; **~ ce n'était la crainte de les décourager** if it were not *ou* were it not for the fear of putting them off; **il n'avait rien emporté, ~ ce n'est quelques biscuits et une pomme** he had taken nothing with him apart from *ou* other than a few biscuits and an apple; **une des plus belles, ~ ce n'est la plus belle** one of the most beautiful, if not the most beautiful; **elle se porte bien, ~ ce n'est qu'elle est très fatiguée** she's quite well apart from the fact that she is very tired *ou* apart from feeling very tired.

i (*loc*) **~ tant est que ...** so long as, provided that, if ... (that is); **invite-les tous, ~ tant est que nous ayons assez de verres** invite them all, so long as we have enough glasses *ou* if we have enough glasses (that is); **s'il te** *ou* **vous plaît** please; **~ je ne me trompe,** (*frm, iro*) **~ je ne m'abuse** if I am not mistaken *ou* under a misapprehension (*frm*), unless I'm mistaken; (*frm, hum*) **~ j'ose dire** if I may say so; (*frm*) **~ je puis dire** if I may put it like that; **~ l'on peut dire** in a way, as it were, so to speak, in a manner of speaking; **~ on veut, ~ l'on veut** as it were; **~ j'ai bien compris/entendu** if I understood correctly/heard properly; **~ seulement il venait/était venu** if only he was coming/had come; **brave homme s'il en fut** a fine man if ever there was one; **~ c'est ça*, je m'en vais** if that's how it is, I'm off*.

2 **nm inv** if. **avec des ~ et des mais, on mettrait Paris dans une bouteille** if ifs and ands were pots and pans there'd be no need for tinkers.

si[2] [si] **adv** a (*affirmatif*) **vous ne venez pas? — ~/mais ~/que ~** aren't you coming? — yes I am/of course I am/indeed I am *ou* I certainly am; **vous n'avez rien mangé? — ~, une pomme** haven't you had anything to eat? – yes (I have), an apple; ~, ~, **il faut venir** oh but you must come!; **il n'a pas voulu, moi** ~ he didn't want to, but I did; **répondre que** ~ to reply that one would (*ou* did, was *etc*); **il n'a pas écrit? – il semble bien** *ou* **il paraît que** ~ hasn't he written? – yes, it seems that he has (done); **je pensais qu'il ne viendrait pas, mais quand je lui en ai parlé il m'a répondu que** ~ I thought he wouldn't come but when I mentioned it to him he told me he would; **je croyais qu'elle ne voulait pas venir, mais il m'a dit que** ~ I thought she didn't want to come but he said she did; ~ **fait**† indeed yes.

b (*intensif: tellement*) (*modifiant attrib, adv*) so. (*modifiant épith*) **un ami** ~ **gentil** such a kind friend, so kind a friend (*frm*); **des amis** ~ **gentils, de** ~ **gentils amis** such kind friends; **il parle** ~ **bas qu'on ne l'entend pas** he speaks so low *ou* in such a low voice that you can't hear him; **j'ai** ~ **faim** I'm so hungry; **elle n'est pas** ~ **stupide qu'elle ne puisse comprendre ceci** she's not so stupid that she can't understand this; (*iro*) **il est stupide, non? –** ~ **peu!** he's stupid, isn't he? – and how!*, too right!*.

c ~ **bien que** so that, so much so that, with the result that.

d (*concessif: aussi*) however. ~ **bête soit-il** *ou* **qu'il soit, il comprendra** (as) stupid as he is *ou* however stupid he is he will understand; ~ **rapidement qu'il progresse** however fast his progress is *ou* he's making progress, as fast as his progress is; ~ **adroitement qu'il ait parlé, il n'a convaincu personne** for all that he spoke very cleverly *ou* however cleverly he may have spoken he didn't convince anyone; ~ **beau qu'il fasse, il ne peut encore sortir** however good the weather is he cannot go out yet; ~ **peu que ce soit** however little it may be, little as *ou* though it may be (*frm*).

e (*égalité: aussi*) as, so. **elle n'est pas** ~ **timide que vous croyez** she's not so *ou* as shy as you think; **il ne travaille pas** ~ **lentement qu'il en a l'air** he doesn't work as slowly as he seems to; **ce n'est pas** ~ **facile** *ou* **simple** it's not as simple as that.

si[3] [si] **nm inv** (*Mus*) B; (*en chantant la gamme*) ti, te.

sial [sjal] **nm** (*Géol*) sial.

Siam [sjam] **nm** Siam.

siamois, e [sjamwa, waz] 1 **adj** (*Géog* †), *chat* Siamese. **frères/sœurs** ~**(es)** (boy/girl) Siamese twins. 2 **nm,f** a (*Géog* †) **S**~**(e)** Siamese. b (*pl: jumeaux*) Siamese twins. 3 **nm** (*chat*) Siamese.

Sibérie [sibeʀi] **nf** Siberia.

sibérien, -ienne [sibeʀjɛ̃, jɛn] 1 **adj** (*Géog, fig*) Siberian. 2 **nm,f: S**~**(ne)** Siberian.

sibilant, e [sibilɑ̃, ɑ̃t] **adj** (*Méd*) sibilant.

sibylle [sibil] **nf** sibyl.

sibyllin, e [sibilɛ̃, in] **adj** (*Myth, fig*) sibylline.

sic [sik] **adv** sic.

SICAF [sikaf] **nf** (**abrév de société d'investissement à capital fermé** *ou* **fixe**) *voir* **société**.

SICAV [sikav] **nf** (**abrév de société d'investissement à capital variable**) *voir* **société**.

siccatif, -ive [sikatif, iv] **adj, nm** siccative.

Sicile [sisil] **nf** Sicily.

sicilien, -ienne [sisiljɛ̃, jɛn] 1 **adj** Sicilian. 2 **nm** a **S**~ Sicilian. b (*dialecte*) Sicilian. 3 **sicilienne nf** a **S**~**ne** Sicilian. b (*danse*) Siciliano, Sicilienne.

SICOB [sikɔb] **nm** (**abrév de Salon des industries du commerce et de l'organisation du bureau**) ≃ Office Automation Fair.

SIDA [sida] **nm** (**abrév de syndrome immunodéficitaire acquis**) AIDS.

sidatique [sidatik] **adj, nmf** = **sidéen**.

side-car, pl side-cars [sidkaʀ] **nm** (*habitacle*) sidecar; (*véhicule entier*) (motorcycle) combination.

sidéen, -éenne [sideɛ̃, ɛn] 1 **adj** with AIDS. 2 **nm,f** AIDS sufferer.

sidéral, e, mpl -aux [sideʀal, o] **adj** sidereal.

sidérant, e* [sideʀɑ̃, ɑ̃t] **adj** staggering*, shattering*.

sidérer* [sideʀe] 6 **vt** to stagger*, shatter*.

sidérurgie [sideʀyʀʒi] **nf** (*fabrication*) iron and steel metallurgy; (*industrie*) iron and steel industry.

sidérurgique [sideʀyʀʒik] **adj** *procédé* (iron and) steel-making (*épith*); *industrie* iron and steel (*épith*).

sidérurgiste [sideʀyʀʒist] **nmf** (iron and) steel maker.

sidi [sidi] **nm** (*péj*) wog*** (*péj*), *North African immigrant (resident in France)*.

Sidon [sidɔ̃] **n** Sidon.

siècle[1] [sjɛkl] **nm** (*période de cent ans, date*) century; (*époque, âge*) age, century. **au 3e** ~ **avant Jésus-Christ/après Jésus-Christ** *ou* **de notre ère** in the 3rd century B.C./A.D.; **être de son** ~**/d'un autre** ~ to belong to one's age/to another age; **de** ~ **en** ~ from age to age, through the ages; **le** ~ **de Périclès/d'Auguste** the age of Pericles/Augustus; **le S**~ **des lumières** (the Age of) the Enlightenment; **le hold-up/match du** ~* the hold-up/match of the century; **il y a un** ~ *ou* **des** ~**s que nous ne nous sommes vus*** it has been *ou* it is years *ou* ages since we last saw each other; **cet arbre a/ces ruines ont des** ~**s** this tree is/these ruins are centuries old; *voir* **consommation, fin**[2], **grand, mal**.

siècle[2] [sjɛkl] **nm** (*Rel*) **le** ~ the world; **les plaisirs du** ~ worldly pleasures, the pleasures of the world.

siège[1] [sjɛʒ] **nm** a (*meuble, de W.-C.*) seat. ~ **de jardin/de bureau** garden/office chair; **donner/offrir un** ~ **à qn** to give/offer sb a seat; **prenez un** ~ take a seat; **Dupont, le spécialiste du** ~ **de bureau** Dupont, the specialist in office seating; (*Aut*) ~ **avant/arrière** front/back seat; (*Aviat*) ~ **éjectable** ejector seat; (*Aut*) ~ **baquet** bucket seat; (*Aut*) ~ **pour bébés** baby seat.

b (*frm, Méd: postérieur*) seat. **l'enfant se présente par le** ~ the baby's in the breech position; *voir* **bain**.

c (*Pol: fonction*) seat. ~ **vacant** vacant seat.

d (*Jur*) *[magistrat]* bench; *voir* **magistrature**.

e (*résidence principale*) *[firme]* head office; *[parti, organisation internationale]* headquarters; *[tribunal, assemblée]* seat. ~ **social** registered office; ~ **épiscopal/pontifical** episcopal/pontifical see; **cette organisation, dont le** ~ **est à Genève** this Geneva-based organization, this organization which is based in Geneva *ou* which has its headquarters in Geneva; *voir* **saint**.

f (*fig: centre*) *[maladie, passions, rébellion]* seat; (*Physiol*) *[faculté, sensation]* centre.

siège[2] [sjɛʒ] **nm** *[place forte]* siege. **mettre le** ~ **devant** to besiege; (*lit, fig*) **faire le** ~ **de** to lay siege to; *voir* **état, lever**.

siéger [sjeʒe] 3 **et** 6 **vi** *[députés, tribunal, assemblée]* to sit; (*fig*) *[maladie]* to be located; *[faculté]* to have its centre; *[passion]* to have its seat. **voilà où siège le mal** that's where the trouble lies, that's the seat of the trouble.

sien, sienne [sjɛ̃, sjɛn] 1 **pron poss: le** ~**, la sienne, les** ~**s, les siennes** *[homme]* his (own); *[femme]* hers, her own; *[chose, animal]* its own; *[nation]* its own, hers, her own; (*indéf*) one's own; **ce sac/cette robe est le** ~**/la sienne** this bag/dress is hers, this is her bag/dress; **il est parti avec une casquette qui n'est pas la sienne** he went away with a cap which isn't his (own); **le voisin est furieux parce que nos fleurs sont plus jolies que les siennes** our neighbour is furious because our flowers are nicer than his (own); **mes enfants sont sortis avec 2 des** ~**s/les 2** ~**s** my children have gone out with 2 of hers/her 2; **cet oiseau préfère les nids des autres au** ~ this bird prefers other birds' nests to its own; **je préfère mes ciseaux, les** ~**s ne coupent pas** I prefer my scissors because hers don't cut; (*emphatique*) **la sienne de voiture est plus rapide*** HIS car is faster, HIS is a faster car; **de tous les pays, on préfère toujours le** ~ of all countries one always prefers one's own.

2 **nm** a **les choses s'arrangent depuis qu'il/elle y a mis du** ~ things are beginning to sort themselves out since he/she began to pull his/her weight; **chacun doit être prêt à y mettre du** ~ everyone must be prepared to pull his weight *ou* to make some effort.

b **les** ~**s** (*famille*) one's family, one's (own) folks*; (*partisans*) one's own people; **Dieu reconnaît les** ~**s** God knows his own *ou* his people.

3 **nf: il/elle a encore fait des siennes*** he/she has (gone and) done it again*; **le mal de mer commençait à faire des siennes parmi les passagers** seasickness was beginning to claim some victims among the passengers.

4 **adj poss** († *ou littér*) **un** ~ **cousin** a cousin of his *ou* hers; **il fait siennes toutes les opinions de son père** he adopts all his father's opinions.

Sienne [sjɛn] **n** Siena; *voir* **terre**.

sierra [sjeʀa] **nf** sierra.

Sierra Leone [sjeʀa leɔn(e)] **nf** Sierra Leone.

sierra-léonien, -ienne [sjeʀaleɔnjɛ̃, jɛn] 1 **adj** Sierra Leonean. 2 **nm, f: Sierra-Léonien(ne)** Sierra Leonean.

sieste [sjɛst] **nf** (*gén*) nap, snooze; (*en Espagne etc*) siesta. **faire la** ~ to have *ou* take a nap; to have a siesta.

sieur [sjœʀ] **nm: le** ~ **X** (†† *ou Jur*) Mr X; (*péj hum*) Master X.

sifflant, e [siflɑ̃, ɑ̃t] **adj** *sonorité* whistling; *toux* wheezing; *prononciation* hissing, whistling. (*consonne*) ~**e** sibilant.

sifflement [sifləmɑ̃] **nm** a (*voir* **siffler**: *volontaire*) whistling (*NonC*); hissing (*NonC*). **un** ~ a whistle; a hiss; **un** ~ **d'admiration** a whistle of admiration; **un** ~ **mélodieux** a melodious whistle; **des** ~**s se firent entendre** one could hear whistling noises; **j'entendis le** ~ **aigu/les** ~**s de la locomotive** I heard the shrill whistle/the whistling of the locomotive.

b (*voir* **siffler**: *involontaire*) hissing (*NonC*); wheezing (*NonC*); whistling (*NonC*). **des** ~**s** whistling noises; hissing noises; ~ **d'oreilles** whistling in the ears.

siffler [sifle] 1 1 **vi** a (*volontairement*) *[personne]* to whistle; (*avec un sifflet*) to blow one's *ou* a whistle; *[oiseau, train]* to whistle; *[serpent]* to hiss. ~ **comme un merle** to whistle like a bird.

b (*involontairement*) *[vapeur, gaz, machine à vapeur]* to hiss; *[voix, respiration]* to wheeze; *[vent]* to whistle; *[projectile]* to whistle, hiss. **la balle/l'obus siffla à ses oreilles** the bullet/shell whistled *ou* hissed past his ears; **il siffle en dormant/parlant** he whistles in his sleep/when he talks; **il siffle en respirant** he wheezes.

2 **vt** a (*appeler*) *chien, enfant* to whistle for; *fille* to whistle at; *automobiliste ou joueur en faute* to blow one's whistle at; (*signaler*) *départ, faute* to blow one's whistle for. (*Ftbl*) ~ **la fin du match** to blow the final whistle, blow for time.

b (*huer*) ~ **un acteur/une pièce** to whistle one's disapproval of an actor/a play, hiss *ou* boo an actor/a play; **se faire** ~ to get hissed *ou* booed.

c (*moduler*) *air, chanson* to whistle.
d (‡: *avaler*) to guzzle*, knock back‡.

sifflet [siflɛ] nm a (*instrument, son*) whistle. ~ **à roulette** whistle; ~ **à vapeur** steam whistle; ~ **d'alarme** alarm whistle; *voir* **coup**. b ~**s** (*huées*) whistles of disapproval, hissing, booing, catcalls. c (‡: *gorge*) **serrer le** ~ **à qn** to throttle sb; *voir* **couper**.

siffleur, -euse [siflœʀ, øz] 1 adj *merle* whistling; *serpent* hissing. **(canard)** ~ widgeon. 2 nm,f (*qui sifflote*) whistler; (*qui hue*) hisser, booer.

siffleux [siflø] nm (*Can* *) groundhog, woodchuck, whistler (*US, Can*).

sifflotement [siflɔtmɑ̃] nm whistling (*NonC*).

siffloter [siflɔte] 1 1 vi to whistle (a tune). ~ **entre ses dents** to whistle under one's breath. 2 vt *air* to whistle.

sigillé, e [siʒile] adj sigillated.

sigisbée [siʒizbe] nm (†, *hum: amant*) beau†.

siglaison [siglɛzɔ̃] nf abbreviation.

sigle [sigl] nm (*prononcé lettre par lettre*) (set of) initials, abbrevation; (*acronyme*) acronym.

sigma [sigma] nm sigma.

signal, pl **-aux** [siɲal, o] nm a (*signe convenu; Psych: stimulus*) signal; (*indice*) sign. **donner le** ~ **de** (*lit*) to give the signal for; (*fig: déclencher*) to be the signal *ou* sign for, signal; **cette émeute fut le** ~ **d'une véritable révolution** the riot was the signal for the start of *ou* signalled the outbreak of a virtual revolution; **à mon** ~ **tous se levèrent** when I gave the signal *ou* sign everyone got up; **donner le** ~ **du départ** (*gén*) to give the signal for departure; (*Sport*) to give the starting signal; ~ **de détresse** distress signal.
b (*Naut, Rail: écriteau, avertisseur*) signal; (*Aut: écriteau*) (road) sign. (*feux*) **signaux (lumineux)** traffic signals *ou* lights; (*Rail*) ~ **automatique** automatic signal; (*Rail*) ~ **d'alarme** alarm; **tirer le** ~ **d'alarme** to pull the alarm, pull the communication cord (*Brit* †); ~ **sonore** *ou* **acoustique** sound *ou* acoustic signal; ~ **optique/lumineux** visual/light signal; (*Rail*) ~ **avancé** advance signal.
c (*Ling, Ordin, Téléc*) signal. ~ **horaire** time signal.

signalé, e [siɲale] (ptp de **signaler**) adj (*littér*) *service, récompense* signal (*littér*) (*épith*).

signalement [siɲalmɑ̃] nm [*personne, véhicule*] description, particulars.

signaler [siɲale] 1 1 vt a (*être l'indice de*) to indicate, be a sign of. **des empreintes qui signalent la présence de qn** footprints indicating sb's presence.
b [*sonnerie, écriteau*] to signal; [*personne*] (*faire un signe*) to signal; (*en mettant un écriteau ou une indication*) to indicate. **on signale l'arrivée d'un train au moyen d'une sonnerie** the arrival of a train is signalled by a bell ringing, a bell warns of *ou* signals the arrival of a train; **sur ma carte, on signale l'existence d'une source près du village** my map indicates that there's a spring near the village, on my map there's a spring marked near the village; **signalez que vous allez tourner à droite en tendant le bras droit** indicate *ou* signal that you are turning right by putting out your right arm.
c *erreur, détail* to indicate, point out; *fait nouveau, vol, perte* to report. **on signale la présence de l'ennemi** there are reports of the enemy's presence; **on a signalé leur présence à Paris** they are reported to be in Paris; **on signale l'arrivée du bateau** it has been reported *ou* there have been reports that the boat will arrive shortly; **rien à** ~ nothing to report; ~ **qn à l'attention de qn** to bring sb to sb's attention; ~ **qn à la vindicte publique** to expose sb to public condemnation; **nous vous signalons en outre que ...** we would further point out to you that ...; **nous vous signalons qu'il ...** for your information, he ... .
2 **se signaler** vpr a (*s'illustrer*) to distinguish o.s., stand out. **il se signale par sa bravoure** he distinguishes himself by his courage, his courage makes him stand out.
b (*attirer l'attention*) to draw attention to o.s. **se** ~ **à l'attention de qn** to attract sb's attention, bring o.s. to sb's attention.

signalétique [siɲaletik] 1 adj *détail* identifying, descriptive. **fiche** ~ identification sheet. 2 nf means of signalling.

signalisation [siɲalizasjɔ̃] nf a (*action: voir* **signaliser**) erection of (road)signs (and signals) (*de* on); laying out of runway markings and lights (*de* on); putting signals (*de* on). **erreur de** ~ (*Aut*) signposting error; (*Rail*) signalling error; **moyens de** ~ means of signalling; "~ **horizontale effacée**" "no road markings"; *voir* **feu¹**, **panneau**. b (*signaux*) signals. ~ **routière** roadsigns; **une bonne** ~ a good signal system.

signaliser [siɲalize] 1 vt *route, réseau* to put up (road)signs on; *piste* to put runway markings and lights on; *voie* to put signals on. **bien signalisé** with good roadsigns; with good (runway) markings and lights; with good signals.

signataire [siɲatɛʀ] nmf [*traité, paix*] signatory. **les** ~**s** those signing, the signatories; **pays** ~**s** signatory countries.

signature [siɲatyʀ] nf a (*action*) signing; (*marque, nom*) signature. **apposer sa** ~ to append one's signature; (*Comm*) **les fondés de pouvoir ont la** ~ the senior executives may sign for the company; **le devoir d'honorer sa** ~ the duty to honour one's signature; (*Jur*) ~ **usurpatoire/légalisée/sociale** unauthorised/authenticated/authorized signature. b (*Typ: cahier*) signature.

signe [siɲ] 1 nm a (*geste*) (*de la main*) sign, gesture; (*de l'expression*) sign. **s'exprimer par** ~**s** to use signs to communicate; **langage par** ~**s** sign language; **échanger des** ~**s d'intelligence** to exchange knowing looks; **faire un** ~ **à qn** to make a sign to sb, sign to sb; **un** ~ **de tête affirmatif/négatif** a nod/a shake of the head; **ils se faisaient des** ~**s** they were making signs to each other; **un** ~ **d'adieu/de refus** a sign of farewell/refusal.
b (*indice*) sign. ~ **précurseur** *ou* **avant-coureur** portent, omen, forewarning; **c'est un** ~ **de pluie** it's a sign it's going to rain, it's a sign of rain; **c'est** ~ **qu'il va pleuvoir/qu'il est de retour** it shows *ou* it's a sign that it's going to rain/that he's back; **c'est bon/mauvais** ~ it's a good/bad sign; (*lit, fig*) **ne pas donner** ~ **de vie** to give no sign of life; **c'est un** ~ **des temps** it's a sign of the times; **c'est un** ~ **révélateur** it's very revealing; **c'est un** ~ **qui ne trompe pas** the signs are unmistakable; **donner des** ~**s de fatigue** to show signs of tiredness; (*Méd*) ~ **clinique** clinical sign.
c (*trait*) mark. "~**s particuliers: néant**" "distinguishing marks: none".
d (*symbole: gén, Ling, Math, Mus*) sign; (*Typ*) [*correcteurs*] mark. **le** ~ **moins/plus/égal** the minus/plus/equals sign; ~ **(typographique)** character; (*Mus*) ~**s d'expression** expression marks.
e (*Astrol*) ~ **du zodiaque** sign of the zodiac; **sous quel** ~ **es-tu né?** what sign were you born under?; (*fig*) **rencontre placée sous le** ~ **de l'amitié franco-britannique** meeting where the keynote was Franco-British friendship *ou* where the dominant theme was Franco-British friendship; **ministère qui a vécu sous le** ~ **du mécontentement** term of office for the government where the dominant *ou* prevailing mood was one of discontent.
f (*loc*) **faire** ~ **à qn** (*lit*) to make a sign to sb; (*fig: contacter*) to get in touch with sb, contact sb; **faire** ~ **à qn d'entrer** to make a sign for sb to come in, sign to sb to come in; **il m'a fait** ~ **de la tête de ne pas bouger** he shook his head to tell me not to move; **il a fait** ~ **à la voiture de franchir les grilles** he waved the car through the gates; **faire** ~ **du doigt à qn** to beckon (to) sb with one's finger; **faire** ~ **que oui** to nod in agreement, nod that one will (*ou* did *etc*); **faire** ~ **que non** to shake one's head (in disagreement *ou* dissent); **en** ~ **de protestation** as a sign *ou* mark of protest; **en** ~ **de respect** as a sign *ou* mark *ou* token of respect; **en** ~ **de deuil** as a sign of mourning.
2 comp ►**signe cabalistique** cabalistic sign ►**signe de la croix** sign of the cross; **faire le signe de la croix** *ou* **un signe de croix** to make the sign of the cross, cross o.s ►**signes extérieurs de richesse** outward signs of wealth ►**signes héraldiques** coat of arms ►**signe de ponctuation** punctuation mark ►**signe de ralliement** rallying symbol.

signer [siɲe] 1 1 vt a *document, traité, œuvre d'art* to sign. ~ **la paix** to sign a peace treaty; **signez au bas de la page/en marge** sign at the bottom of the page/in the margin; ~ **un chèque en blanc** to sign a blank cheque; ~ **son nom** to sign one's name; ~ **d'une croix/de son sang/de son vrai nom** to sign with a cross/with one's blood/with one's real name; **tableau non signé** unsigned painting; **œuvre signée de la main de l'artiste** work signed by the artist; **cravate/carrosserie signée X** tie/coachwork by X; (*fig*) **c'est signé!*** it's absolutely characteristic, it's written all over it!*; (*fig*) **c'est signé Louis!*** it has Louis written all over it!*; (*fig*) **il a signé son arrêt de mort** he has signed his own death warrant.
b (*Tech*) to hallmark.
2 **se signer** vpr (*Rel*) to cross o.s.

signet [siɲɛ] nm (book) marker, bookmark.

signifiant, e [siɲifjɑ̃, jɑ̃t] 1 adj (*littér*) significative, meaningful. 2 nm (*Ling*) signifier, signifiant.

significatif, -ive [siɲifikatif, iv] adj a (*révélateur*) *mot, sourire, geste* significant, revealing. **ces oublis sont** ~**s de son état d'esprit** his forgetfulness is indicative of his state of mind. b (*expressif*) *symbole* meaningful, significant. (*Math*) **chiffres** ~**s** significant figures *ou* digits (*US*).

signification [siɲifikasjɔ̃] nf a (*sens*) [*fait*] significance (*NonC*), meaning; [*mot, symbole*] meaning. (*Ling*) **la** ~ signification. b (*Jur*) [*décision judiciaire*] notification. ~ **d'actes** service of documents.

signifié [siɲifje] nm (*Ling*) signified, signifié.

signifier [siɲifje] 7 vt a (*avoir pour sens*) to mean, signify. **que signifie ce mot/son silence?** what is the meaning of this word/his silence?, what does this word/his silence mean *ou* signify?; (*Ling*) **les symboles signifient** symbols convey meaning; **que signifie cette cérémonie?** what is the significance of this ceremony?, what does this ceremony signify?; **ses colères ne signifient rien** his tempers don't mean anything; **bonté ne signifie pas forcément faiblesse** kindness does not necessarily mean *ou* signify *ou* imply weakness *ou* is not necessarily synonymous with weakness; **l'envol des hirondelles signifie que l'automne est proche** the departure of the swallows means *ou* shows that autumn is near *ou* marks *ou* signifies the approach of autumn; **qu'est-ce que cela signifie?** (*indignation*) (*gén*) what's the meaning of this?; (*après remarque hostile*) what's that supposed to mean?
b (*frm: faire connaître*) to make known. ~ **ses intentions/sa volonté**

à qn to make one's intentions/wishes known to sb, inform sb of one's intentions/wishes; (*renvoyer*) ~ **son congé à qn** to give sb notice of dismissal, give sb his notice; **son regard me signifiait tout son mépris** his look conveyed to me his utter scorn; **signifiez-lui qu'il doit se rendre à cette convocation** inform him that he is to answer this summons.
c (*Jur*) *exploit, décision judiciaire* to serve notice of (*à* on), notify (*à* to). ~ **un acte judiciaire** to serve legal process.

Sikh [sik] nmf Sikh.

silence [silɑ̃s] nm a (*absence de bruits, de conversation*) silence. **garder le** ~ to keep silent, say nothing; **faire** ~ to be silent; **faire qch en** ~ to do sth in silence; **il n'arrive pas à faire le** ~ **dans sa classe** he can't get silence in his class *ou* get his class to be silent; **sortez vos cahiers et en** ~! get out your books and no talking!; **(faites)** ~! silence!, no talking!; (*Ciné*) ~! **on tourne** quiet everybody, action!; **il prononça son discours dans un** ~ **absolu** there was dead silence while he made his speech; **un** ~ **de mort** a deathly hush *ou* silence; *voir* **minute, parole.**
b (*pause: dans la conversation, un récit*) pause; (*Mus*) rest. ~ **radio** radio silence; **récit entrecoupé de longs** ~**s** account broken by lengthy pauses; **il y eut un** ~ **gêné** there was an embarrassed silence; **à son entrée il y eut un** ~ there was a hush when he came in.
c (*impossibilité ou refus de s'exprimer*) silence. **les journaux gardèrent le** ~ **sur cette grève** the newspapers kept silent *ou* were silent on this strike; **promets-moi un** ~ **absolu** promise me you won't breathe a word; **garder un** ~ **absolu sur qch** to say absolutely nothing about sth, keep completely quiet about sth; **contraindre l'opposition au** ~ to force the opposition to keep silent; **réduire qn au** ~ to silence sb; **passer qch sous** ~ to pass over sth in silence; **souffrir en** ~ to suffer in silence; **aimer qn en** ~ to love sb silently *ou* in silence; **surprise préparée dans le plus grand** ~ surprise prepared in the greatest secrecy; *voir* **loi.**
d (*paix*) silence, still(ness). **dans le grand** ~ **de la plaine** in the great silence *ou* stillness of the plain; **vivre dans la solitude et le** ~ to live in solitary silence.

silencieusement [silɑ̃sjøzmɑ̃] adv (*voir* **silencieux**) silently; quietly; noiselessly.

silencieux, -ieuse [silɑ̃sjø, jøz] 1 adj a *mouvement, pas, élèves, auditeurs* silent, quiet; *moteur, machine* quiet, noiseless. **le voyage du retour fut** ~ the return journey was quiet *ou* was a silent one; **rester** ~ to remain silent. b (*paisible*) *lieu, cloître* silent, still. c (*peu communicatif*) quiet; (*qui ne veut ou ne peut s'exprimer*) silent; *voir* **majorité.** 2 nm *[arme à feu]* silencer; *[pot d'échappement]* silencer (*Brit*), muffler (*US*).

Silésie [silezi] nf Silesia.

silex [silɛks] nm flint. (*Archéol*) **des (armes en)** ~ flints.

silhouettage [silwɛtaʒ] nm (*Phot*) blocking out.

silhouette [silwɛt] nf a (*profil: vu à contre-jour etc*) outline, silhouette; (*lignes, galbe*) outline. **la** ~ **du château se détache sur le couchant** the outline *ou* silhouette of the château stands out *ou* the château is silhouetted against the sunset; **on le voyait en** ~, **à contre-jour** he could be seen in outline *ou* silhouetted against the light. b (*allure*) figure. **une** ~ **un peu masculine** a slightly masculine figure. c (*figure*) figure. **des** ~**s multicolores parsemaient la neige** the snow was dotted with colourful figures; ~**s de tir** figure targets.

silhouetter [silwete] 1 1 vt a (*Art*) to outline. **l'artiste silhouetta un corps de femme** the artist outlined *ou* drew an outline of a woman's body. b (*Phot*) to block out. 2 **se silhouetter** vpr to be silhouetted. **le clocher se silhouette sur le ciel** the bell tower is silhouetted *ou* outlined against the sky.

silicate [silikat] nm silicate.

silice [silis] nf silica. ~ **fondue** *ou* **vitreuse** silica glass; **gel de** ~ silica gel.

siliceux, -euse [silisø, øz] adj siliceous, silicious.

silicium [silisjɔm] nm silicon.

silicone [silikon] nf silicone.

silicose [silikoz] nf silicosis.

sillage [sijaʒ] nm a *[embarcation]* wake; *[avion à réaction]* (*déplacement d'air*) slipstream; (*trace*) (vapour) trail; (*fig*) *[personne, animal, parfum]* trail. (*lit, fig*) **dans le** ~ **de qn** (following) in sb's wake; **aspiré dans son** ~ pulled along in his wake. b (*Phys*) wake.

sillon [sijɔ̃] nm a *[champ]* furrow. (*littér*) **les** ~**s** the (ploughed (*Brit*) *ou* plowed (*US*)) fields; b (*fig: ride, rayure*) furrow. c (*Anat*) fissure. d *[disque]* groove.

sillonner [sijɔne] 1 vt a (*traverser*) *[avion, bateau, routes]* to cut across, cross. **les canaux qui sillonnent la Hollande** the canals which cut across *ou* which criss-cross Holland; **région sillonnée de canaux/routes** region which is criss-crossed by canals/roads; **des avions ont sillonné le ciel toute la journée** planes have been droning backwards and forwards *ou* to and fro across the sky all day; **des éclairs sillonnaient le ciel** flashes of lightning criss-crossed the sky; ~ **les routes** to travel the roads; **les touristes sillonnent la France en été** tourists travel to every corner *ou* throughout the length and breadth of France in the summer.
b (*creuser*) *[rides, ravins, crevasses]* to furrow. **visage sillonné de rides** face furrowed with wrinkles; **front sillonné d'une ride profonde** deeply furrowed brow.

silo [silo] nm (*Aviat, Mil*) silo. ~ **à céréales/fourrages** grain/fodder silo; **mettre en** ~ to put in a silo, silo.

silotage [silɔtaʒ] nm (*Tech*) ensilage.

silure [silyʀ] nm silurid.

sima [sima] nm sima.

simagrée [simagʀe] nf (*gén pl*) fuss (*NonC*), playacting (*NonC*). **elle a fait beaucoup de** ~**s avant d'accepter son cadeau** she made a great fuss (about it) *ou* she put on a great show of reluctance before she accepted his present.

simien, -ienne [simjɛ̃, jɛn] adj, nm simian.

simiesque [simjɛsk] adj (*voir* **singe**) monkey-like; ape-like.

similaire [similɛʀ] adj similar. **le rouge à lèvres, le fond de teint et produits** ~**s** lipstick, foundation cream and similar products *ou* products of a similar nature *ou* type.

similarité [similaʀite] nf similarity.

simili [simili] 1 préf imitation (*épith*), artificial. ~**cuir** imitation leather, leatherette; **en** ~ **fourrure** fun fur (*épith*). 2 nm imitation. **bijoux en** ~ imitation *ou* costume jewellery. 3 nf (*) abrév de **simili-gravure.**

similigravure [similigʀavyʀ] nf half-tone engraving.

similitude [similityd] nf a similarity. **il y a certaines** ~**s entre ces méthodes** there are certain likenesses *ou* similarities between these methods. b (*Géom*) similarity.

Simon [simɔ̃] nm Simon.

simonie [simɔni] nf simony.

simoun [simun] nm simoom, simoon.

simple [sɛ̃pl] 1 adj a (*non composé*) simple; (*non multiple*) single. **billet** ~ single ticket (*Brit*), one-way ticket; **en** ~ **épaisseur** in a single layer *ou* thickness; *voir* **aller, partie**[2], **passé.**
b (*peu complexe*) simple; (*facile*) simple, straightforward. **réduit à sa plus** ~ **expression** reduced to a minimum; ~ **comme bonjour*** *ou* **chou*** easy as falling off a log* *ou* as pie*; **dans ce cas, c'est bien** ~: **je m'en vais** in that case it's quite simple *ou* straightforward — I'm leaving, in that case I'm quite simply leaving; **ce serait trop** ~! that would be too easy! *ou* too simple! *ou* too straightforward!; **ce n'est pas si** ~ it's not as simple as that; **il y a un moyen** ~ **pour ...** there is an easy way of ... .
c (*modeste*) *personne* plain (*épith*), simple, unaffected; *vie, goûts* simple; *robe, repas, style* simple, plain. **les gens** ~**s** simple folk; **il a su rester** ~ he has managed to stay unaffected; **être** ~ **dans sa mise** to dress simply *ou* plainly; (*hum*) **dans le plus** ~ **appareil** in one's birthday suit, in the altogether* (*hum*).
d (*naïf*) simple. ~ **d'esprit** (adj) simple-minded; (nmf) simpleton, simple-minded person.
e (*valeur restrictive*) simple. **un** ~ **particulier/salarié** an ordinary citizen/wage earner; **un** ~ **soldat** a private; **une** ~ **formalité** a simple formality; **un** ~ **regard/une** ~ **remarque la déconcertait** just a *ou* (even) a mere *ou* simple look/comment would upset her; **d'un** ~ **geste de la main** with a simple movement of his hand; *voir* **pur.**
2 nm a **passer du** ~ **au double** to double.
b (*Bot*) medicinal plant, simple†.
c (*Tennis*) singles. ~ **messieurs/dames** men's/ladies'singles.

simplement [sɛ̃pləmɑ̃] adv a (*voir* **simple**) simply; straightforwardly; plainly; unaffectedly. b (*seulement*) simply, merely, just. **je veux** ~ **dire que ...** I simply *ou* merely *ou* just want to say that ...; **c'est (tout)** ~ **incroyable que tu ne l'aies pas vue** it's (just) simply incredible that you didn't see her; *voir* **purement.**

simplet, -ette [sɛ̃plɛ, ɛt] adj a *personne* simple, ingenuous. b *raisonnement, question* simplistic, naïve; *roman, intrigue* simple, unsophisticated.

simplex [sɛ̃plɛks] nm (*Ordin*) simplex.

simplexe [sɛ̃plɛks] nm (*Math*) simplex.

simplicité [sɛ̃plisite] nf a (*voir* **simple**) simplicity; straightforwardness; plainness; unaffectedness; *voir* **tout.** b (*naïveté*) simpleness.

simplifiable [sɛ̃plifjabl] adj (*gén*) *méthode* that can be simplified; (*Math*) *fraction* reducible.

simplificateur, -trice [sɛ̃plifikatœʀ, tʀis] adj simplifying (*épith*).

simplification [sɛ̃plifikasjɔ̃] nf simplification.

simplifier [sɛ̃plifje] 7 vt (*gén, Math*) to simplify. **pour** ~ **la vie/cette tâche** to simplify one's existence/this job, to make life/this job simpler; **il a le travers de trop** ~ he tends to oversimplify.

simplisme [sɛ̃plism] nm (*péj*) simplism.

simpliste [sɛ̃plist] adj (*péj*) simplistic.

simulacre [simylakʀ] nm (*action simulée*) enactment. **les acteurs firent un** ~ **de sacrifice humain** the actors enacted a human sacrifice; (*péj: fausse apparence*) **un** ~ **de justice** a pretence of justice; **un** ~ **de gouvernement/de procès** a sham government/trial, a mockery of a government/a trial.

simulateur, -trice [simylatœʀ, tʀis] 1 nm,f (*gén*) shammer, pretender; (*Mil: qui feint la maladie*) malingerer. 2 nm (*Aut*) ~ **de conduite** (driving) simulator; (*Aviat*) ~ **de vol** flight simulator.

simulation [simylasjɔ̃] nf (*voir* **simuler**) feigning, simulation. **il n'est pas malade, c'est de la** ~ (*gén*) he isn't ill — it's all sham *ou* it's all put on; (*Mil*) he isn't ill — he's just malingering.

simulé, e [simyle] (ptp de **simuler**) adj (*feint*) *attaque, retraite* feigned, sham (*épith*); *amabilité, gravité* feigned, sham (*épith*), simulated (*frm*); (*imité*) *velours, colonnade* simulated; (*Tech: reproduit*) *conditions, situation* simulated.

simuler [simyle] 1 **vt** a (*feindre*) *sentiment, attaque* to feign, sham, simulate (*frm*). ~ **une maladie** to feign illness, pretend to be ill. b (*avoir l'apparence de*) to simulate. **ce papier peint simule une boiserie** this wallpaper is made to look like *ou* simulates wood panelling. c (*Tech: reproduire*) *conditions, situation* to simulate. d (*Jur*) *contrat, vente* to effect fictitiously. e (*Ordin*) to simulate.

simultané, e [simyltane] 1 **adj** simultaneous; *voir* **traduction**. 2 **simultanée nf** (*Échecs*) simultaneous, simul.

simultanéisme [simyltaneism] **nm** (*Littérat: procédé narratif*) (use of) simultaneous action.

simultanéité [simyltaneite] **nf** simultaneousness, simultaneity.

simultanément [simyltanemɑ̃] **adv** simultaneously.

Sinaï [sinai] **nm** Sinai.

sinapisé [sinapize] **adj: bain/cataplasme** ~ mustard bath/poultice.

sinapisme [sinapism] **nm** mustard poultice *ou* plaster.

sincère [sɛ̃sɛʀ] **adj** *personne, aveu, paroles* sincere; *réponse, explication* sincere, honest; *repentir, amour, partisan, admiration* sincere, genuine, true (*épith*); *élections, documents* genuine. **est-il ~ dans son amitié?** is he sincere in his friendship?, is his friendship sincere? *ou* genuine?; **un ami ~ des bêtes/arts** a true *ou* genuine friend of animals/of the arts; (*formule épistolaire*) **mes ~s condoléances** my sincere *ou* heartfelt condolences; **mes regrets les plus ~s** my sincerest regrets.

sincèrement [sɛ̃sɛʀmɑ̃] **adv** a (*voir* **sincère**) sincerely; honestly; truly; genuinely. **je suis ~ désolé que ...** I am sincerely *ou* truly *ou* genuinely sorry that ... . b (*pour parler franchement*) honestly, really. **~, vous feriez mieux de refuser** honestly *ou* really you would be better saying no.

sincérité [sɛ̃seʀite] **nf** (*voir* **sincère**) sincerity; honesty; genuineness. **en toute ~** in all sincerity.

sinécure [sinekyʀ] **nf** sinecure. **ce n'est pas une ~*** it's not exactly a rest cure.

sine die [sinedje] **adv** sine die.

sine qua non [sinekwanɔn] **adj: une condition ~** an indispensable condition, a sine qua non.

Singapour [sɛ̃gapuʀ] **nm** Singapore.

singapourien, -ienne [sɛ̃gapuʀjɛ̃, jɛn] 1 **adj** Singaporean. 2 **nm,f: S~(ne)** Singaporean.

singe [sɛ̃ʒ] **nm** a (*Zool*) monkey; (*de grande taille*) ape. **les grands ~s** the big apes. b (*fig*) (*personne laide*) horror; (*enfant espiègle*) monkey. c (*arg Mil: corned beef*) bully beef (*arg Mil*). d († *arg Typ etc: patron*) boss*. e (*loc*) **faire le ~** to monkey about (*pulling faces etc*); **être agile/malin comme un ~** to be as agile/crafty *ou* artful as a monkey; *voir* **apprendre, monnaie**.

singer [sɛ̃ʒe] 3 **vt** *personne, démarche* to ape, mimic, take off; *sentiments* to feign.

singerie [sɛ̃ʒʀi] **nf** a (*gén pl: grimaces et pitreries*) antics (*pl*), clowning (*NonC*). **faire des ~s** to clown about, play the fool. b (*simagrées*) **~s** airs and graces. c (*cage*) monkey house.

single [siŋgœl] **nm** (*Tennis*) singles game; (*chambre*) single room; (*disque 45 tours*) single.

singleton [sɛ̃glətɔ̃] **nm** singleton.

singulariser [sɛ̃gylaʀize] 1 1 **vt** to mark out, make conspicuous. 2 **se singulariser vpr** to call attention to o.s., make o.s. conspicuous.

singularité [sɛ̃gylaʀite] **nf** a (*caractère: voir* **singulier**) remarkable nature; singularity; uncommon nature. b (*exception, anomalie*) peculiarity.

singulier, -ière [sɛ̃gylje, jɛʀ] 1 **adj** a (*étonnant*) remarkable, singular (*frm*); (*littér: peu commun*) singular, remarkable, uncommon. **je trouve ~ qu'il n'ait pas jugé bon de ...** I find it (pretty) remarkable *ou* odd that he didn't see fit to ... . b (*Ling*) singular. c *voir* **combat**. 2 **nm** (*Ling*) singular.

singulièrement [sɛ̃gyljɛʀmɑ̃] **adv** a (*étrangement*) in a peculiar way, oddly, strangely. b (*beaucoup*) remarkably, singularly (*frm*). (*très*) **~ intéressant/fort** remarkably *ou* uncommonly *ou* extremely interesting/strong; **ceci m'a ~ aiguisé l'appétit** this sharpened my appetite remarkably *ou* tremendously; **il me déplaît ~ de voir ...** I find it particularly unpleasant to see ... . c (*en particulier*) particularly, especially.

sinistre [sinistʀ] 1 **adj** a (*de mauvais augure*) *bruit, endroit, projet* sinister. (*avant n: intensif*) **un ~ voyou/imbécile** an appalling lout/idiot. b (**: maussade*) *soirée, réunion* grim*, deadly (boring)*. 2 **nm** (*catastrophe*) disaster; (*incendie*) blaze; (*Assurances: cas*) accident. **l'assuré doit déclarer le ~ dans les vingt-quatre heures** any (accident) claim must be notified within 24 hours; (*Assurances*) **évaluer l'importance d'un ~** to appraise the extent of the damage *ou* loss *etc*.

sinistré, e [sinistʀe] 1 **adj** *région, pays* (disaster-)stricken (*épith*). **le département du Gard a été déclaré zone ~e après les incendies** the department of the Gard was declared a disaster area after the fires. 2 **nm,f** disaster victim.

sinistrement [sinistʀəmɑ̃] **adv** in a sinister way.

sinistrose [sinistʀoz] **nf** pessimism.

sino- [sinɔ] **préf** Sino-. **~soviétique** Sino-Soviet.

sinoc‡ [sinɔk] **adj** = **sinoque‡**.

sinologie [sinɔlɔʒi] **nf** sinology.

sinologue [sinɔlɔg] **nmf** sinologist, Pekinologist, specialist in Chinese affairs, China watcher*.

sinon [sinɔ̃] **conj** a (*frm: sauf*) except, other than, save†. **on ne possède jamais rien, ~ soi-même** there is nothing one ever possesses, except (for) *ou* other than *ou* save† oneself; **à quoi peut bien servir cette manœuvre ~ à nous intimider?** what can be the purpose of this manoeuvre other than *ou* if not to intimidate us?; **un homme courageux, ~ qu'il était un tant soit peu casse-cou†** a courageous man, save† for being a trifle reckless. b (*de concession: si ce n'est*) if not. **il faut le faire, ~ pour le plaisir, du moins par devoir** it must be done, if not for pleasure, (then) at least out of duty; **il avait leur approbation, ~ leur enthousiasme** he had their approval if not their enthusiasm; **je ne sais pas grand-chose, ~ qu'il a démissionné** I don't know much about it only that *ou* other than that he has resigned; (*frm*) **cette histoire est savoureuse, ~ très morale** this story is spicy if not very moral; (*frm*) **ils y étaient opposés, ~ hostiles** they were opposed, if not (actively) hostile, to it. c (*autrement*) otherwise, or else. **fais-le, ~ nous aurons des ennuis** do it, otherwise *ou* or else we will be in trouble; **faites-le, vous vous exposerez ~ à des ennuis** do it – you will lay yourself open to trouble otherwise; **elle doit être malade, ~ elle serait déjà venue** she must be ill, otherwise *ou* or else she would have already come; (*pour indiquer la menace*) **fais-le, ~ ...** do it, or else ... .

sinophile [sinɔfil] **adj, nmf** sinophile.

sinoque‡ [sinɔk] 1 **adj** batty*, daft* (*Brit*), loony‡, cracked‡, nutty‡. 2 **nmf** loony‡, nutcase‡, crackpot‡.

sinueux, -euse [sinɥø, øz] **adj** *route* winding (*épith*); *rivière* winding (*épith*), meandering (*épith*); *ligne* sinuous; (*fig*) *pensée* tortuous.

sinuosité [sinɥozite] **nf** a (*gén pl: courbe*) *[route]* winding (*NonC*), curve; *[rivière]* winding (*NonC*), meandering (*NonC*), curve, loop. (*fig*) **les ~s de sa pensée** his tortuous train of thought, the convolutions of his thought processes. b (*forme: voir* **sinueux**) winding; meandering; tortuousness.

sinus[1] [sinys] **nm inv** (*Anat*) sinus. **~ frontal/maxillaire** frontal/maxillary sinus.

sinus[2] [sinys] **nm** (*Math*) sine.

sinusite [sinyzit] **nf** (*Med*) sinusitis (*NonC*).

sinusoïdal, e, mpl -aux [sinyzɔidal, o] **adj** sinusoidal.

sinusoïde [sinyzɔid] **nf** sinusoid.

Sion [sjɔ̃] **n** Zion.

sionisme [sjɔnism] **nm** Zionism.

sioniste [sjɔnist] **adj, nmf** Zionist.

sioux [sju] 1 **adj inv** Sioux. 2 **nm** (*Ling*) Sioux. 3 **nmf inv: S~** Sioux; *voir* **ruse**.

siphon [sifɔ̃] **nm** (*tube, bouteille, Zool*) siphon; *[évier, W.-C.]* U-bend; (*Spéléologie*) sump.

siphonné, e [sifɔne] (**ptp de siphonner**) **adj** (*‡: fou*) batty‡, daft* (*Brit*), loony, nutty‡, cracked‡.

siphonner [sifɔne] 1 **vt** to siphon.

sire [siʀ] **nm** a (*au roi*) **S~** Sire. b (*Hist: seigneur*) lord. c **un triste ~** an unsavoury individual; **un pauvre ~†** a poor *ou* penniless fellow.

sirène [siʀɛn] **nf** a (*Myth, fig*) siren, mermaid. (*fig*) **écouter le chant des ~s** to listen to the sirens' *ou* mermaids' song. b (*appareil*) *[bateau, ambulance]* siren; *[usine]* hooter (*Brit*), siren (*US*). **~ d'alarme** (*en temps de guerre*) air-raid siren; (*en temps de paix*) fire alarm.

Sirius [siʀjys] **nm** Sirius; *voir* **point[1]**.

sirocco [siʀɔko] **nm** sirocco.

sirop [siʀo] **nm** (*pharmaceutique*) syrup, mixture; (*à diluer: pour une boisson*) syrup, squash (*Brit*), cordial (*Brit*); (*boisson*) (fruit) cordial (*Brit*) *ou* drink *ou* squash (*Brit*). **~ d'orgeat** barley water; **~ de groseille/d'ananas/de menthe** redcurrant/pineapple/mint cordial (*Brit*) *ou* beverage (*US*); **~ d'érable** maple syrup; **~ de maïs** corn syrup; **~ contre la toux** cough mixture *ou* syrup *ou* linctus (*Brit*).

siroter* [siʀɔte] 1 **vt** to sip.

sirupeux, -euse [siʀypø, øz] **adj** *liquide* syrupy; (*fig péj*) *musique* syrupy.

sis, sise [si, siz] **adj** (*Admin, Jur*) located.

sisal [sizal] **nm** sisal.

sismal, e, mpl -aux [sismal, o] **adj** (*Géog*) **ligne ~e** path of an earthquake.

sismicité [sismisite] **nf** seismicity.

sismique [sismik] **adj** seismic; *voir* **secousse**.

sismogramme [sismɔgʀam] **nm** seismogram.

sismographe [sismɔgʀaf] **nm** seismograph.

sismographie [sismɔgʀafi] **nf** seismography.

sismologie [sismɔlɔʒi] **nf** seismology.

sismothérapie [sismoteʀapi] **nf** shock therapy.

sistre [sistʀ] **nm** sistrum.

Sisyphe [sizif] **nm** Sisyphus; *voir* **rocher**.

sitar [sitaʀ] **nm** sitar.

site [sit] 1 **nm** a (*environnement*) setting; (*endroit pittoresque*) beauty spot. **construire un château dans le ~ approprié** to build a château in the right setting; **dans un ~ merveilleux/très sauvage** in a marvellous/very wild setting; **~s naturels/historiques** natural/historic sites; **les ~s pittoresques d'une région** the beauty spots of an area; **la protection des ~s** the conservation of places of interest; **un ~ classé** a conservation area; **"Beaumanoir, ses plages, ses hôtels, ses ~s"** "Beaumanoir for beaches, hotels and places to visit *ou* places of interest".

b (*emplacement*) site. **~ favorable à la construction d'un barrage** suitable site for the construction of a dam.

c (*Mil*) **(angle de) ~** (angle of) sight; **ligne de ~** line of sight.

2 comp ►**site archéologique** archeological site ►**site propre** (*voie*) bus lane.

sit-in [sitin] nm inv sit-in.

sitôt [sito] 1 adv a **~ couchée, elle s'endormit** as soon as *ou* immediately (*Brit*) she was in bed she fell asleep, she was no sooner in bed *ou* no sooner was she in bed than she fell asleep; **~ dit, ~ fait** no sooner said than done; **~ après avoir traversé la ville, ils se trouvèrent dans les collines** immediately (*Brit*) on leaving the town *ou* straight (*Brit*) *ou* right (*US*) after driving through the town they found themselves in the hills; **~ après la guerre** straight (*Brit*) *ou* right (*US*) *ou* immediately (*Brit*) after the war, immediately the war was over.

b (*avec nég*) **ce n'est pas de ~ qu'il reviendra** he won't be back for quite a while *ou* for (quite) some time, he won't be back in a hurry; **il a été si bien puni qu'il ne recommencera pas de ~!** he was so severely punished that he won't be doing that again for a while! *ou* in a hurry!

c **~ que, ~ après que** as soon as, no sooner than; **~ (après) que le docteur fut parti, elle se sentit mieux** as soon as the doctor had left she felt better, the doctor had no sooner left than she felt better; **~ qu'il sera guéri, il reprendra le travail** as soon as he is better he'll go back to work.

2 prép (*littér*) **~ la rentrée des classes, il faudra que ...** as soon as school is back, we must ...; **~ les vacances, elle partait** she would go *ou* went away as soon as the holidays started, the holidays had no sooner begun than she would go away.

sittelle [sitɛl] nf nuthatch.

situation [sitɥasjɔ̃] nf a (*emplacement*) situation, position, location. **la ~ de cette villa est excellente** this villa is excellently situated, the villa has an excellent situation.

b (*conjoncture, circonstances*) situation. (*Philos*) **étudier/montrer l'homme en ~** to study/show man in his best situation; **être en ~ de faire** to be in a position to do; (*iro*) **elle est dans une ~ intéressante*** she is in an interesting condition (*iro*) *ou* in the family way*; **~ de fait** de facto situation; **~ de famille** marital status; **~ financière/politique** financial/political situation; **dans une ~ désespérée** in a desperate plight; *voir* **comique, renverser.**

c (*emploi*) post, situation. **chercher une/perdre sa ~** to look for a/lose one's post; **se faire une belle ~** to work up to a good position.

d (*Fin: état*) statement of finances. **~ de trésorerie** cash flow statement.

situé, e [sitɥe] (ptp de **situer**) adj situated. **bien/mal ~** well/badly situated.

situer [sitɥe] [1] 1 vt a (*lit: placer, construire*) to site, situate, locate.

b (*par la pensée: localiser*) to set, place; (**: catégoriser*) *personne* to place. **on ne le situe pas bien*** you just can't figure him out*.

2 **se situer** vpr a (*emploi réfléchi*) to place o.s. **essayer de se ~ par rapport à qn/qch** to try to place o.s. in relation to sb/sth.

b (*se trouver*) (*dans l'espace*) to be situated; (*dans le temps*) to take place; (*par rapport à des notions*) to stand. **l'action/cette scène se situe à Paris** the action/this scene is set *ou* takes place in Paris; **la hausse des prix se situera entre 5 % et 10 %** prices will rise by between 5% and 10%, there will be price rises of between 5% and 10%.

Siva [ʃiva] nm Siva, Shiva.

six [sis], *devant n commençant par consonne* [si], *devant n commençant par voyelle ou h muet* [siz] 1 adj cardinal inv six. **il y avait ~ mille personnes** there were six thousand people; **ils sont ~ enfants** there are six children; **je suis resté ~ heures/jours** I stayed six hours/days; **les ~ huitièmes de cette somme** six eighths of this sum; **il a ~ ans** he is six (years old); **un enfant de ~ ans** a six-year-old (child), a child of six; **un objet de ~ F** a six-franc article, an article costing six francs; **polygone à ~ faces** six-sided polygon; **couper qch en ~ morceaux** to cut sth into six pieces; **j'en ai pris trois, il en reste ~** I've taken three (of them) and there are six (of them) left; **il est ~ heures** it's six o'clock; **il est ~ heures du soir** it's 6 p.m., it's six in the evening; **il est ~ heures du matin** it's 6 a.m., it's six in the morning; **il est trois heures moins ~** it is six minutes to three; **par vingt voix contre ~** by twenty votes to six; **cinq jours/fois sur ~** five days/times out of six; **ils sont venus tous les ~** all six of them came; **ils ont porté la table à eux ~** the six of them carried the table; **ils ont mangé le jambon à eux ~** the six of them ate the ham, they ate the ham between the six of them; **partagez cela entre vous ~** share that among the six of you; **ils viennent à ~ pour déjeuner** there are six coming to lunch; **on peut s'asseoir à ~ autour de cette table** this table can seat six (people); **ils vivent à ~ dans une seule pièce** there are six of them living in one room; **se battre à ~ contre un/à un contre ~** to fight six against one/one against six; **entrer ~ par ~** to come in by sixes *ou* six at a time *ou* six by six; **se mettre en rangs par ~** to form rows of six.

2 adj ordinal inv: **arriver le ~ septembre** to arrive on the sixth of September *ou* (on) September the sixth *ou* (on) September sixth; **Louis ~** Louis the Sixth; **chapitre/page/article ~** chapter/page/article six; **le numéro ~ gagne un lot** number six wins a prize; **il habite au numéro ~ de la rue Arthur** he lives at number six (in) Rue Arthur.

3 nm inv a six. **trente-/quarante-~** thirty-/forty-six; **quatre et deux font ~** four and two are *ou* make six; **il fait mal ses ~** he writes his sixes badly; **c'est le ~ qui a gagné** (*numéro*) (number) six has won; (*coureur*) number six has won; **il habite au ~ (de la rue)** he lives at number six; **il habite ~ rue de Paris** he lives at six Rue de Paris; **nous sommes le ~ aujourd'hui** it's the sixth today; **il est venu le ~** he came on the sixth; **il est payé le ~** *ou* **tous les ~ de chaque mois** he is paid on the sixth of each month; (*Cartes*) **le ~ de cœur** the six of hearts; (*Dominos*) **le ~ et deux** the six-two; **la facture est datée du ~** the bill is dated the 6th.

b (*Pol: jusqu'en 1973*) **les S~, l'Europe des S~** the Six, the Europe of the Six.

4 comp ►**six-huit** (*Mus*) nm inv six-eight (time); **mesure à six-huit** bar in six-eight (time) ►**les Six Jours** (*Sport*) *six-day cycling event* ►**six-mâts** (*Naut*) nm inv six-master ►**six quatre deux*** nf: **faire qch à la six quatre deux** to do sth in a slapdash way, do sth any old how* (*Brit*) *ou* any old way*.

sixain [sizɛ̃] nm = **sizain.**

sixième [sizjɛm] 1 adj sixth. **vingt-/trente-~** twenty-/thirty-sixth; **recevoir la ~ partie d'un héritage** to receive a sixth of a bequest; **demeurer dans le ~ (arrondissement)** to live in the sixth arrondissement (*in Paris*); **habiter au ~ (étage)** to live on the sixth floor.

2 nmf (*gén*) sixth (person). **se classer ~** to come sixth; **nous avons besoin d'un ~ pour compléter l'équipe** we need a sixth (person) to complete the team; **elle est arrivée (la) ~ dans la course** she came (in) sixth in the race.

3 nm (*portion*) sixth. **calculer le ~ d'un nombre** to work out the sixth of a number; **recevoir le ~** *ou* **un ~ d'une somme** to receive a sixth of a sum; **(les) deux ~s du budget seront consacrés à ...** two sixths of the budget will be given over to ... .

4 nf (*Scol*) first form (*Brit*), sixth grade (*US*). **entrer en (classe de) ~** ≃ to go into the first form (*Brit*) *ou* sixth grade (*US*); **élève de ~** ≃ first form (*Brit*) *ou* sixth-grade (*US*) pupil.

sixièmement [sizjɛmmɑ̃] adv in the sixth place, sixthly.

sixte [sikst] nf (*Mus*) sixth; (*Escrime*) sixte.

Sixtine [sikstin] adj, nf: **la (chapelle) ~** the Sistine Chapel.

sizain [sizɛ̃] nm (*Littérat*) six-line stanza; (*Cartes*) *packet of 6 packs of cards*.

ska [ska] nm ska.

Skaï [skaj] nm ® Leatherette ®.

skate(-board) [skɛt(bɔʀd)] nm skateboard. (*activité*) **le ~** skateboarding; **faire du ~** to skateboard.

sketch, pl **~es** [skɛtʃ] nm (variety) sketch; *voir* **film.**

ski [ski] 1 nm (*objet*) ski; (*sport*) skiing. **s'acheter des ~s** to buy o.s. a pair of skis *ou* some skis; **aller quelque part à** *ou* **en ~s** to go somewhere on skis, ski somewhere; **faire du ~** to ski, go skiing; **aller au ~*** to head for the slopes*, go skiing; **vacances/équipement de ~** ski(ing) holiday/equipment; **chaussures/moniteur/épreuve/station de ~** ski boots/instructor/race/resort; *voir* **piste.**

2 comp ►**ski acrobatique** hot-dogging, free-styling ►**ski alpin** Alpine skiing ►**ski artistique** ski ballet ►**ski court** short ski ►**ski de descente** downhill skiing ►**ski évolutif** short ski method, ski évolutif ►**ski de fond** cross-country skiing, ski touring (*US*), langlauf ►**ski de haute montagne** ski-mountaineering ►**ski hors piste** off-piste skiing ►**ski nautique** water-skiing ►**ski nordique** Nordic skiing ►**ski de piste** skiing on piste ►**ski de randonnée** = **ski de fond.**

skiable [skjabl] adj skiable.

ski-bob, pl **ski-bobs** [skibɔb] nm skibob. **faire du ~** to go skibobbing.

skier [skje] [7] vi to ski.

skieur, -skieuse [skjœʀ, skjøz] nm,f skier; (*ski nautique*) water-skier. **~ de fond** cross-country *ou* langlauf skier; **~ hors piste** off-piste skier; **2 ~s hors piste ont été tués** 2 skiers skiing off-piste were killed.

skiff [skif] nm skiff.

skin* [skin] nm skin*.

skinhead [skinɛd] nm skinhead.

skipper [skipœʀ] nm (*course à la voile*) skipper.

slalom [slalɔm] nm (*épreuve, piste*) slalom; (*mouvement*) slalom movement; (*fig: entre divers obstacles*) zigzag. **faire du ~ (entre ...** *ou* **parmi ...)** to slalom (between ...); **descente en ~** slalom descent; **~ géant/spécial** giant/(special) slalom.

slalomer [slalɔme] [1] vi (*Ski*) to slalom; (*fig: entre divers obstacles*) to zigzag.

slalomeur, -euse [slalɔmœʀ, øz] nm,f (*Ski*) slalom skier *ou* specialist *ou* racer.

slave [slav] 1 adj Slav(onic), Slavic; *langue* Slavic, Slavonic. **le charme ~** Slavonic charm. 2 nmf: **S~** Slav.

slavisant, e [slavizɑ̃, ɑ̃t] nm, f Slavist.
Slavonie [slavɔni] nf Slavonia.
slavophile [slavɔfil] adj, nmf Slavophile.
sleeping† [slipiŋ] nm sleeping car.
slip [slip] nm a *[homme]* briefs *(pl)*, (under)pants *(pl)*; *[femme]* pant(ie)s *(pl)*, briefs *(pl)*. ~ **de bain** *[homme]* (bathing *ou* swimming) trunks *(pl)*; (*bikini*) (bikini) briefs *(pl)*; **j'ai acheté 2 ~s** I bought 2 pairs of briefs *ou* pants; (*fig*) **se retrouver en ~*** to lose one's shirt. b (*Naut*) slipway.
slogan [slɔgɑ̃] nm slogan.
sloop [slup] nm sloop.
slovaque [slɔvak] 1 adj Slovak. 2 nmf: **S~** Slovak.
Slovaquie [slɔvaki] nf Slovakia.
slovène [slɔvɛn] 1 adj Slovene. 2 nm (*Ling*) Slovene. 3 nmf: **S~** Slovene.
Slovénie [slɔveni] nf Slovenia.
slow [slo] nm (*blues etc*) slow number; (*fox-trot*) slow fox trot.
SMAG [smag] nm (abrév de **salaire minimum agricole garanti**) *voir* **salaire**.
smala* [smala] nf (*troupe*) tribe*.
smash [sma(t)ʃ] nm (*Tennis*) smash.
smasher [sma(t)ʃe] 1 (*Tennis*) 1 vt to smash. 2 vi to smash (the ball).
SME [ɛsɛmə] nm (abrév de **système monétaire européen**) EMS.
SMIC [smik] nm (abrév de **salaire minimum interprofessionnel de croissance**) *voir* **salaire**.
smicard, e* [smikaʀ, aʀd] nm,f minimum wage earner.
SMIG† [smig] nm (abrév de **salaire minimum interprofessionnel garanti**) *voir* **salaire**.
smigard, e*† [smigaʀ, aʀd] nm,f minimum wage earner.
smocks [smɔk] nmpl smocking (*NonC*).
smoking [smɔkiŋ] nm (*costume*) dinner suit, evening suit, dress suit; (*veston*) dinner jacket, DJ* (*Brit*), tuxedo (*US*).
SMUR [smyʀ] nm (abrév de **Service médical d'urgence et de réanimation**) *mobile emergency unit.*
snack [snak] nm, **snack-bar,** [snakbaʀ] nm, pl **snack-bars** snack bar.
S.N.C. (abrév de **service non compris**) *voir* **service**.
SNCF [ɛsɛnseɛf] nf (abrév de **Société nationale des chemins de fer français**) *French national railway company.*
SNECMA [snekma] nf (abrév de **Société nationale d'études et de construction de moteurs d'avions**) *French aircraft engine research and construction company.*
sniff-sniff [snifsnif] excl boo hoo!
sniffer [snife] 1 vt (*arg Drogue*) to sniff. ~ **de la cocaïne/la colle** to sniff cocaine/glue.
snob [snɔb] 1 nmf snob. 2 adj snobbish, snobby, posh*.
snober [snɔbe] 1 vt *personne* to snub, give the cold shoulder to; *endroit, réception* to turn one's nose up at.
snobinard, e* [snɔbinaʀ, aʀd] (*péj*) 1 adj snooty*, stuck-up*, snobbish. 2 nm,f stuck-up thing*.
snobisme [snɔbism] nm snobbery, snobbishness. ~ **à l'envers** inverted snobbery.
sobre [sɔbʀ] adj *personne* sober, temperate, abstemious; *style, éloquence* sober. ~ **de gestes/en paroles** sparing of gestures/words; ~ **comme un chameau** as sober as a judge.
sobrement [sɔbʀəmɑ̃] adv (*voir* **sobre**) soberly; temperately; abstemiously.
sobriété [sɔbʀijete] nf (*voir* **sobre**) sobriety; temperance; abstemiousness. ~ **de gestes/paroles** restraint in one's gestures/words.
sobriquet [sɔbʀikɛ] nm nickname.
soc [sɔk] nm ploughshare (*Brit*), plowshare (*US*).
sociabilité [sɔsjabilite] nf (*voir* **sociable**) social nature; sociability; hospitality.
sociable [sɔsjabl] adj a (*qui vit en groupe*) social. b (*ouvert, civil*) *personne, caractère* sociable; *milieu* hospitable.
social, e, mpl **-iaux** [sɔsjal, jo] 1 adj a *animal, créature* social.
b *rapports, phénomène, conventions* social; *voir* **science**.
c *classe, conflit, questions, loi, politique, système* social; *revendications* over social conditions, for better living conditions; *voir* **cas**.
d (*Admin*) **services ~aux** social services; **prestations ~es** social security benefits; **aide ~e** welfare; (*subsides*) social security (benefits); **assurances ~es** ≃ National Insurance (*Brit*), ≃ Social Security (*US*); *voir* **assistant, avantage, sécurité**.
e (*Comm*) *voir* **capital, raison, siège**[1].
2 nm: **le ~** (*affaires*) social matters; (*questions*) social issues; (*péj*) **faire du ~** to act concerned about social issues.
3 comp ▸**social-démocrate** adj, nmf (mpl **sociaux-démocrates**) Social Democrat ▸**social-démocratie** nf (pl **social-démocraties**) social democracy.
socialement [sɔsjalmɑ̃] adv socially.
socialisant, e [sɔsjalizɑ̃, ɑ̃t] adj with socialist leanings *ou* tendencies.
socialisation [sɔsjalizasjɔ̃] nf socialization.
socialiser [sɔsjalize] 1 vt to socialize.
socialisme [sɔsjalism] nm socialism. ~ **utopique/scientifique/révolutionnaire** utopian/scientific/revolutionary socialism; ~ **d'État** state socialism.
socialiste [sɔsjalist] adj, nmf socialist.
sociétaire [sɔsjetɛʀ] nmf member (*of a society*). ~ **de la Comédie-Française** (shareholding) member of the Comédie-Française.
société [sɔsjete] 1 nf a (*groupe, communauté*) society. **la ~** society; **la vie en ~** life in society; ~ **sans classe** classless society.
b (*club*) (*littéraire*) society; (*sportive*) club. ~ **de pêche/tir** angling/shooting club; ~ **secrète/savante** secret/learned society; **la S~ protectrice des animaux** ≃ the Royal Society for the Prevention of Cruelty to Animals (*Brit*), the American Society for the Prevention of Cruelty to Animals (*US*).
c (*Comm*) company, firm. ~ **financière/d'assurance** finance/insurance company; ~ **immobilière** (*compagnie*) property (*Brit*) *ou* real estate (*US*) company; *[copropriétaires]* housing association.
d (*classes oisives*) **la ~** society; **la bonne ~** polite society; **la haute ~** high society.
e (*assemblée*) company, gathering. **il y venait une ~ assez mêlée/une ~ d'artistes et d'écrivains** a fairly mixed company *ou* gathering/a company *ou* gathering of artists and writers used to come; **toute la ~ se leva pour l'acclamer** the whole company rose to acclaim him.
f (*compagnie*) company, society (*frm, littér*). **rechercher/priser la ~ de qn** to seek/value sb's company *ou* society (*littér*) *ou* companionship; **dans la ~ de qn** in the company *ou* society (*frm, littér*) of sb; *voir* **jeu, talent**[1].
2 comp ▸**société par actions** joint-stock company ▸**société anonyme** (*gén*) ≃ limited company; (*ouverte au public*) ≃ public limited company ▸**Société des auteurs, compositeurs et éditeurs de musique** *French body responsible for collecting and distributing music royalties,* ≃ Publishing Rights Society (*Brit*) ▸**société à capital variable** company with variable capital ▸**société civile** (*Comm*) non-trading company; (*Philos*) civil society ▸**société civile immobilière** non-trading property (*Brit*) *ou* real estate (*US*) company ▸**société civile de placement immobilier** non-trading property (*Brit*) *ou* real estate (*US*) investment trust ▸**société en commandite** limited partnership ▸**société commerciale** trading company ▸**la société de consommation** the consumer society ▸**société de crédit** credit *ou* finance company ▸**société d'économie mixte** semi-public company ▸**société écran** umbrella company ▸**société d'exploitation** development company ▸**société d'investissement** investment trust; **société d'investissement à capital fermé** *ou* **fixe** closed-end investment trust; **société d'investissement à capital variable** unit trust (*Brit*), open-end investment trust (*US*), mutual fund (*US*) ▸**la société de Jésus** the Society of Jesus ▸**société en nom collectif** general partnership ▸**société en participation** joint-venture company ▸**société à responsabilité limitée** limited liability company ▸**la Société des Nations** (*Hist Pol*) the League of Nations ▸**société de services** service company; **société de services et d'ingénierie en informatique** software house ▸**société de tempérance** temperance society.
sociobiologie [sɔsjobjɔlɔʒi] nf sociobiology.
socioculturel, -elle [sɔsjokyltyʀɛl] adj sociocultural.
sociodrame [sɔsjodʀam] nm sociodrama.
socio-économique, pl **socio-économiques** [sɔsjoekɔnɔmik] adj socioeconomic.
socio-éducatif, -ive, mpl **socio-éducatifs** [sɔsjoedykatif, iv] adj socioeducational.
sociogéographique [sɔsjoʒeɔgʀafik] adj sociogeographic.
sociogramme [sɔsjogʀam] nm sociogram.
sociolinguistique [sɔsjolɛ̃gɥistik] 1 adj sociolinguistic. 2 nf sociolinguistics *(sg)*.
sociologie [sɔsjɔlɔʒi] nf sociology.
sociologique [sɔsjɔlɔʒik] adj sociological.
sociologiquement [sɔsjɔlɔʒikmɑ̃] adv sociologically.
sociologue [sɔsjɔlɔg] nmf sociologist.
sociométrie [sɔsjɔmetʀi] nf sociometry.
sociopolitique [sɔsjopɔlitik] adj sociopolitical.
socioprofessionnel, -elle [sɔsjopʀɔfesjɔnɛl] adj socio-professional.
socle [sɔkl] nm a *[statue, colonne]* plinth, pedestal, socle (*SPÉC*); *[lampe, vase]* base. b (*Géog*) platform.
socque [sɔk] nm (*sabot*) clog.
socquette [sɔkɛt] nf ankle sock (*Brit*), anklet (*US*).
Socrate [sɔkʀat] nm Socrates.
socratique [sɔkʀatik] adj Socratic.
soda [sɔda] nm fizzy drink. ~ **à l'orange** orangeade; **whisky ~** whisky and soda.
sodé, e [sɔde] adj sodium (*épith*).
sodique [sɔdik] adj sodic.
sodium [sɔdjɔm] nm sodium.
Sodome [sɔdɔm] n Sodom.
sodomie [sɔdɔmi] nf sodomy; buggery.
sodomiser [sɔdɔmize] 1 vt to bugger, have anal intercourse with.
sodomite [sɔdɔmit] nm sodomite.
sœur [sœʀ] nf a (*lit, fig*) sister. **avec un dévouement de ~** with a

sister's *ou* with sisterly devotion; **et ta ~?*** go and take a running jump*, get lost*; **la poésie, ~ de la musique** poetry, sister of *ou* to music; **peuplades/organisations ~s** sister peoples/organizations; (*littér*) **~ d'infortune** fellow sufferer; (*hum*) **j'ai trouvé la ~ de cette commode chez un antiquaire** I found the partner to this chest of drawers in an antique shop; *voir* **âme, lait.**

b (*Rel*) nun, sister; (*comme titre*) Sister. **~ Jeanne** Sister Jeanne; **elle a été élevée chez les ~s** she was convent educated; **ses parents l'ont mise en pension chez les ~s** her parents sent her to a convent (boarding) school; **les Petites S~s des pauvres** the Little Sisters of the Poor; **les ~s de la Charité** the Sisters of Charity; *voir* **bon[1]**.

sœurette* [sœʀɛt] **nf** little sister.

sofa [sɔfa] **nm** sofa.

Sofia [sɔfja] **n** Sofia.

SOFRES [sɔfʀɛs] **nf** (**abrév de Société française d'enquêtes par sondage**) *French public opinion poll institute*, ≃ Gallup, ≃ MORI (*Brit*).

soft(ware) [sɔft(waʀ)] **nm** software.

soi [swa] 1 **pron pers** a (*gén*) one(self); (*fonction d'attribut*) oneself; (*avec il(s), elle(s) comme antécédent: gén frm*, †) himself; herself; itself. **n'aimer que ~** to love only oneself; **regarder devant/derrière ~** to look in front of/behind one; **malgré ~** in spite of oneself; **avoir confiance en ~** to have confidence in oneself; **rester chez ~** to stay at home; (*faire un effort*) **prendre sur ~** to take a grip on o.s.; **prendre sur ~ de faire qch** to take it upon o.s. to do sth.

b (*loc*) **aller de ~** to be self-evident, be obvious; **cela va de ~** it's obvious, it stands to reason, that goes without saying; **il va de ~ que ...** it goes without saying *ou* it stands to reason that ...; (*intrinsèquement*) **en ~** in itself; **être/exister pour ~** to be/exist only for oneself; **dans un groupe, on peut se rendre service entre ~** in a group, people *ou* you* can help each other *ou* one another (out); (*frm*) **il n'agissait que pour ~** he was only acting for himself *ou* in his own interests; (*évite une ambiguïté*) **elle comprenait qu'il fût mécontent de ~** she understood his not being pleased with himself; **il allait droit devant ~** he was going straight ahead (of him); **être/rester ~** to be/remain oneself; *voir* **chacun, hors, maître** *etc.*

c **~-même** oneself; **on le fait ~-même** you do it yourself, one does it oneself (*frm*); **le respect de ~-même** self-respect; (*hum*) **Monsieur X? — ~-même!** Mr X? — in person! *ou* none other!; *pour autres loc voir* **même.**

2 **nm** (*Philos, littér: personnalité, conscience*) self; (*Psych: inconscient*) id. **la conscience de ~** self-awareness, awareness of self; **trouver un autre ~-même** to find another self; *voir* **en-soi, pour-soi.**

soi-disant [swadizɑ̃] 1 **adj inv: un ~ poète/professeur** a so-called *ou* would-be poet/teacher. 2 **adv** supposedly. **il était ~ parti à Rome** he had supposedly left for Rome, he was supposed to have left for Rome; **il était venu ~ pour discuter** he had come for a discussion — or so he said, he had come ostensibly for a discussion; **~ que* ...** it would appear that ..., apparently ... .

soie[1] [swa] **nf** a (*Tex*) silk. **~ sauvage** wild silk; **~ grège** raw silk; **~ lavée** washed silk; *voir* **papier, ver.** b (*poil*) *[sanglier etc]* bristle. **brosse en ~s de sanglier** (boar) bristle brush; **brosse à dents en ~s de nylon** nylon (bristle) brush, brush with nylon bristles.

soie[2] [swa] **nf** (*Tech*) *[lime, couteau]* tang.

soient [swa] *voir* **être.**

soierie [swaʀi] **nf** (*tissu*) silk; (*industrie, commerce*) silk trade; (*filature*) silk mill.

soif [swaf] **nf** a (*lit*) thirst. **avoir ~** to be thirsty; *[plante, terre]* to be dry *ou* thirsty; **donner ~** to make one thirsty; **le sel donne ~** salt makes you thirsty, salt gives one a thirst; **jusqu'à plus ~** (*lit*) till one's thirst is quenched; (*fig*) till one can take no more; **rester sur sa ~** (*lit*) to remain thirsty; (*fig*) to be left thirsting for more, be left unsatisfied; *voir* **boire, étancher, garder, mourir.** b (*fig: désir*) **~ de** *richesse, connaissances, vengeance* thirst *ou* craving for; **~ de faire qch** craving to do sth.

soiffard, e*† [swafaʀ, aʀd] (*péj*) 1 **adj** boozy*. 2 **nm,f** boozer*.

soignant, e [swaɲɑ̃, ɑ̃t] **adj** *personnel* nursing (*épith*); *voir* **aide.**

soigné, e [swaɲe] (**ptp de soigner**) **adj** a (*propre*) *personne, tenue, chevelure* well-groomed, neat; *ongles* well-groomed, well-kept; *mains* well-cared-for *(épith)*, well cared for *(attrib)*. **peu ~** *personne* untidy; *cheveux* unkempt, untidy; *ongles, mains* unkempt, neglected(-looking); **il est très ~ de sa personne** he is very well-turned out *ou* well-groomed.

b (*consciencieux*) *travail, style, présentation* careful, meticulous; *vitrine* neat, carefully laid out; *jardin* well-kept; *repas* carefully prepared. **peu ~** careless; badly laid-out; badly kept; badly prepared.

c (**: intensif*) *note* massive*, whopping* (*épith*); *punition* stiff*. **avoir un rhume (quelque chose de) ~** to have a real beauty* *ou* a whopper* of a cold; **la note était ~e** it was some bill*, it was a massive* *ou* whopping* bill.

soigner [swaɲe] 1 **vt** a *patient, maladie [médecin]* to treat; *[infirmière, mère]* to look after, nurse. **j'ai été très bien soigné dans cette clinique** I had very good treatment in this clinic, I was very well looked after in this clinic; **~ les blessés** to tend *ou* nurse the injured; **tu devrais te faire ~** you should have treatment *ou* see a doctor; **rentrez chez vous pour ~ votre rhume** go back home and look after *ou* nurse that cold (of yours); **soigne-toi bien** take good care of yourself, look after yourself properly; **je soigne mes rhumatismes avec des pilules** I'm taking pills for my rheumatism; **de nos jours, la tuberculose se soigne** these days tuberculosis can be treated.

b (*entretenir*) *chien, plantes, invité* to look after; *ongles, chevelure, outils, livres* to look after, take (good) care of; *tenue* to take care over; *cheval* to groom; *travail, repas, style, présentation* to take care over. **~ sa clientèle** to look after one's customers; **elle se soigne avec coquetterie** she takes great care over her appearance, she is tremendously interested in her appearance; (*hum*) **ils se soignent: champagne, saumon, cigares ...!** they take good care of *ou* look after themselves (all right) — champagne, salmon, cigars, the lot!

c (** loc*) **(il) faut te faire ~!** you need your brains tested!* *ou* your head seen to!* (*surtout Brit*); **35 F le café: ils nous ont soignés!** 35 francs for a coffee — they've ripped us off!* *ou* we've been had!* *ou* done!* (*Brit*); **ils lui sont tombés dessus à quatre: j'aime autant te dire qu'ils l'ont soigné** four of them laid into him — I can tell you they really let him have it*; **ça se soigne, tu sais*!** there's a cure for that, you know!; *voir* **oignon.**

soigneur [swaɲœʀ] **nm** (*Boxe*) second; (*Cyclisme, Ftbl*) trainer.

soigneusement [swaɲøzmɑ̃] **adv** (*voir* **soigneux**) tidily, neatly; carefully; painstakingly; meticulously. **~ préparé** carefully prepared, prepared with care.

soigneux, -euse [swaɲø, øz] **adj** a (*propre, ordonné*) tidy, neat. **ce garçon n'est pas assez ~** this boy isn't tidy enough. b (*appliqué*) *travailleur* careful, painstaking; *travail* careful, meticulous. **être ~ dans son travail** to be careful in one's work, take care over one's work. c **être ~ de sa santé** to be careful about one's health; **être ~ de ses affaires** to be careful with one's belongings; **être ~ de sa personne** to be careful about *ou* take care over one's appearance; **être ~ de ses vêtements** to be careful with one's clothes, take care of *ou* look after one's clothes.

soi-même [swamɛm] **pron** *voir* **même, soi.**

soin [swɛ̃] **nm** a (*application*) care; (*ordre et propreté*) tidiness, neatness. **sans ~** (**adj**) careless; untidy; (**adv**) carelessly; untidily; **faire qch avec (grand) ~** to do sth with (great) care *ou* (very) carefully; **il n'a aucun ~, il est sans ~** he is untidy; **il nous évite avec un certain ~, il met un certain ~ à nous éviter** he takes great care *ou* he goes to some lengths to avoid us, he is scrupulously avoiding us.

b (*charge, responsabilité*) care. **confier à qn le ~ de ses affaires** to entrust sb with the care of one's affairs; **confier à qn le ~ de faire** to entrust sb with the job *ou* task of doing; **je vous laisse ce ~** I leave this to you, I leave you to take care of this; **son premier ~ fut de faire ...** his first concern was to do ...; (*littér*) **le ~ de son salut/avenir l'occupait tout entier** his thoughts were filled with the care of his salvation/future (*littér*).

c **~s** (*entretien, hygiène*) care (*NonC*); (*attention*) care (and attention) (*NonC*); (*traitement*) attention (*NonC*), treatment (*NonC*); **les ~s du ménage** *ou* **domestiques** the care of the home; **l'enfant a besoin des ~s d'une mère** the child needs a mother's care (and attention); **~s de beauté** beauty care; **pour les ~s de la chevelure/des ongles utilisez ...** for hair-/nail-care use ...; **les ~s du visage** face-care, care of the complexion; **~s médicaux** medical *ou* health care; **~s dentaires** dental treatment; **son état demande des ~s** his condition needs treatment *ou* (medical) attention; **le blessé a reçu les premiers ~s** the injured man has been given first aid; **~s palliatifs** palliative care; **confier qn/qch aux (bons) ~s de** to leave sb/sth in the hands *ou* care of; (*sur lettre: frm*) **aux bons ~s de** care of, c/o; **être aux petits ~s pour qn** to lavish attention upon sb, wait on sb hand and foot, dance attendance on sb.

d (*loc*) **avoir** *ou* **prendre ~ de faire** to take care to do, make a point of doing; **avoir** *ou* **prendre ~ de qn/qch** to take care of *ou* look after sb/sth; **il prend bien ~/grand ~ de sa petite personne** he takes good care/great care of his little self *ou* of number one*; **ayez** *ou* **prenez ~ d'éteindre** take care *ou* be sure to turn out the lights, make sure you turn out the lights; **avoir ~ que ...** to make sure that ...; (*Rel*) **donner ses ~s à** to minister to.

soir [swaʀ] **nm** a evening. **les ~s d'automne/d'hiver** autumn/winter evenings; **le ~ descend** *ou* **tombe** evening is closing in; **le ~ où j'y suis allé** the evening I went; **viens nous voir un de ces ~s** come and see us one evening *ou* night; **être du ~** to be a night owl* (*fig*); (*fig littér*) **au ~ de la/sa vie** in the evening of life/his life (*littér*); *voir* **matin.**

b **repas/journal du ~** evening meal/paper; **5 heures du ~** 5 (o'clock) in the afternoon *ou* evening, 5 p.m.; **8 heures du ~** 8 (o'clock) in the evening, 8 o'clock at night, 8 p.m.; **11 heures du ~** 11 (o'clock) at night, 11 p.m.; *voir* **cours, robe.**

c (*loc: compléments de temps*) **le ~ je vais souvent les voir** in the evening I often go to see them, I often go to see them of an evening (*Brit*); **le ~, je suis allé les voir/il a plu** in the evening I went to see them/it rained; **il pleut assez souvent le ~** it quite often rains in the evening(s); **j'y vais ce ~** I'm going this evening *ou* tonight; **à ce ~!** (I'll) see you (*ou* I'll talk to you *etc*) this evening *ou* tonight!; **tous les ~s, chaque ~** every evening *ou* night; **hier ~** last night, yesterday evening; **demain ~** tomorrow evening *ou* night; **dimanche ~** Sunday evening *ou* night; **hier/le 17 au** ~ in the evening (of) yesterday/of the 17th; **la veille au** ~ the previous evening; **il est arrivé un (beau)** ~ he turned up one evening.

soirée [swaʀe] **nf** a (*soir*) evening. b (*réception*) party. ~ **dansante** dance; *voir* **tenu.** c (*Ciné, Théât: séance*) evening performance. **donner un spectacle/une pièce en** ~ to give an evening performance of a show/play.

soissons [swasɔ̃] **nmpl** (*haricots*) (variety of) dwarf beans.

soit [swa] 1 **adv** (*frm: oui*) very well, well and good, so be it (*frm*). **eh bien, ~, qu'il y aille!** very well then *ou* well and good then, let him go!; *voir* **tant.**

2 **conj** a (*d'alternative*) ~ **l'un** ~ **l'autre** (either) one or the other; ~ **avant** ~ **après** (either) before or after; ~ **timidité,** ~ **mépris** *ou* **timidité ou mépris, elle ne lui adressait jamais la parole** be it (out of) *ou* whether out of shyness or contempt she never spoke to him; ~ **que** + *subj:* ~ **qu'il soit fatigué,** ~ **qu'il en ait assez** whether he is tired or whether he has had enough; ~ **qu'il n'entende pas, ou ne veuille pas entendre** whether he cannot hear or (whether) he does not wish to hear.

b (*à savoir*) that is to say. **des détails importants,** ~ **l'approvisionnement, le transport** *etc* important details, that is to say *ou* for instance provisions, transport *etc.*

c (*Math: posons*) ~ **un rectangle ABCD** let ABCD be a rectangle.

soixantaine [swasɑ̃tɛn] **nf** a (*environ soixante*) sixty or so, (round) about sixty, sixty-odd*. **il y avait une** ~ **de personnes/de livres** there were sixty or so *ou* (round) about sixty people/books, there were sixty-odd* people/books; **la** ~ **de spectateurs qui étaient là** the sixty or so *ou* the sixty-odd* people there; **ils étaient une bonne** ~ there were a good sixty of them; **il y a une ~/une bonne** ~ **d'années** sixty or so *ou* sixty-odd*/a good sixty years ago; **ça doit coûter une** ~ **de mille (francs)** that must cost sixty thousand or so francs *ou* (round) about sixty thousand francs *ou* some sixty thousand francs.

b (*soixante unités*) sixty. **sa collection n'atteint pas encore/a dépassé la** ~ his collection has not yet reached/has passed the sixty mark, there are not yet sixty/are now over sixty in his collection.

c (*âge*) sixty. **approcher de la/atteindre la** ~ to near/reach sixty; **un homme dans la** ~ a man in his sixties; **d'une** ~ **d'années** *personne* of about sixty; *arbre* sixty or so years old; **elle a la** ~ she is sixtyish, she is in her sixties.

soixante [swasɑ̃t] **adj inv, nm inv** sixty. **à la page** ~ on page sixty; **habiter au** ~ to live at number sixty; **les années** ~ the sixties, the 60s; ~ **et un** sixty-one; ~ **et unième** sixty-first; ~**-dix** seventy; ~**-dixième** seventieth; ~ **mille** sixty thousand; (*jeu, rue*) **le (numéro)** ~ number sixty.

soixante-huitard, e, **mpl soixante-huitards** [swasɑ̃tɥitaʀ, aʀd] 1 **adj** *personne* nostalgic for the events of May 1968; *attitude, idées* which hark back to the events of May 1968. 2 **nm,f** (*en 1968*) participant in the events of May 1968; (*après 1968*) proponent of the ideals of May 1968.

soixantième [swasɑ̃tjɛm] **adj, nm** sixtieth.

soja [sɔʒa] **nm** (*plante*) soya; (*graines*) soya beans (*pl*). **germes de** ~ (soya) bean sprouts, beanshoots.

sol¹ [sɔl] 1 **nm** (*gén*) ground; (*plancher*) floor; (*revêtement*) floor, flooring (*NonC*); (*territoire, terrain: Agr, Géol*) soil. **étendu sur le** ~ spread out on the ground; **posé au** ~ *ou* **à même le** ~ (placed) on the ground (*ou* floor); ~ **carrelé/cimenté** tiled/concrete floor; **la surface du** ~ the floor surface; (*Constr*) **la pose des ~s** the laying of floors *ou* of flooring; **sur le** ~ **français** on French soil; (*Aviat*) **essais/vitesse au** ~ ground tests/speed; (*Sport*) **exercices au** ~ floor exercises. 2 **comp** ▸ **sol-air** (*Mil*) **adj inv** ground-to-air ▸ **sol-sol adj inv** ground-to-ground.

sol² [sɔl] **nm inv** (*Mus*) G; (*en chantant la gamme*) so(h); *voir* **clef.**

sol³ [sɔl] **nm** (*Chim*) sol.

sol⁴ [sɔl] **nm** (*monnaie*) sol.

solaire [sɔlɛʀ] 1 **adj** a (*Astrol, Astron*), *énergie, panneaux* solar; *crème, filtre* sun (*attrib*); *voir* **cadran, spectre, système.** b *voir* **plexus.** 2 **nm** (*énergie*) **le** ~ solar energy.

solarisation [sɔlaʀizasjɔ̃] **nf** (*chauffage*) solar heating; (*Phot*) solarization.

solarium [sɔlaʀjɔm] **nm** solarium.

soldanelle [sɔldanɛl] **nf** (*Bot*) (*primulacée*) soldanella; (*liseron*) sea bindweed.

soldat [sɔlda] **nm** (*gén*) soldier. **(simple)** ~, ~ **de 2e classe** (*armée de terre*) private; (*armée de l'air*) aircraftman (*Brit*), basic airman (*US*); ~ **de 1re classe** (*armée de terre*) ≃ private (*Brit*), private first class (*US*); (*armée de l'air*) leading aircraftman (*Brit*), airman first class (*US*); ~ **d'infanterie** infantryman; **se faire** ~ to join the army, enlist; **le S~ inconnu** the Unknown Soldier *ou* Warrior; (*fig littér*) ~ **de la liberté/du Christ** soldier of liberty/of Christ; **~s de la paix** peacekeepers; ~ **de plomb** tin *ou* toy soldier; *voir* **fille.**

soldate [sɔldat] **nf** woman soldier.

soldatesque [sɔldatɛsk] (*péj*) 1 **nf** army rabble. 2 **adj** (†) barrack-room (*épith*).

solde¹ [sɔld] **nf** a [*soldat, matelot*] pay. b (*péj*) **être à la** ~ **de** to be in the pay of; **avoir qn à sa** ~ to have sb in one's pay.

solde² [sɔld] **nm** a (*Comm: reliquat*) (*gén*) balance; (*reste à payer*) balance outstanding. **il y a un** ~ **de 10 F en votre faveur** there is a balance of 10 francs in your favour *ou* to your credit; ~ **débiteur/créditeur** debit/credit balance; ~ **de trésorerie** cash balance; **pour** ~ **de (tout) compte** in settlement.

b ~ **(de marchandises)** sale goods (*pl*); **vente de ~s** sale, sale of reduced items; ~ **de lainages** sale of woollens, woollen sale; **mettre des marchandises en** ~ to put goods in a sale; **vendre/acheter qch en** ~ to sell (off)/buy sth at sale price; **article (vendu) en** ~ sale(s) item *ou* article; **les ~s** (*parfois f*) the sales; **je l'ai acheté en** ~ *ou* **dans les ~s** I bought it in the sales; **la saison des ~s** the sales season.

solder [sɔlde] [1] 1 **vt** a *compte* (*arrêter*) to wind up, close; (*acquitter*) to pay (off) the balance of, settle, balance.

b *marchandises* to sell (off) at sale price. **ils soldent ces pantalons à 130 F** they are selling off these trousers at *ou* for 130 francs, they are selling these trousers in the sale at *ou* for 130 francs; **je vous le solde à 40 F** I'll let you have it for 40 francs, I'll knock it down* *ou* reduce it to 40 francs for you.

2 **se solder vpr: se** ~ **par** (*Comm*) [*exercice, budget*] to show; (*fig*) [*entreprise, opération*] to end in; **les comptes se soldent par un bénéfice** the accounts show a profit; **l'exercice se solde par un déficit/bénéfice de 50 millions** the end-of-year figures show a loss/profit of 50 million; **l'entreprise/la conférence s'est soldée par un échec** the undertaking/conference ended in failure *ou* came to nothing.

solderie [sɔldəʀi] **nf** discount store.

soldeur, -euse [sɔldœʀ, øz] **nm,f** discount store owner.

sole¹ [sɔl] **nf** (*poisson*) sole. (*Culin*) ~ **meunière** sole meunière.

sole² [sɔl] **nf** (*Tech*) [*four*] hearth; [*sabot, bateau*] sole.

solécisme [sɔlesism] **nm** solecism (*in language*).

soleil [sɔlɛj] **nm** a (*astre, gén*) sun. (*Astron, Myth*) **le S~** the Sun; **orienté au** ~ **levant/couchant** facing the rising/setting sun; **le** ~ **de minuit** the midnight sun; (*littér*) **les ~s pâles/brumeux de l'hiver** the pale/misty sun of winter; (*fig*) **tu es mon (rayon de)** ~ you are the sunshine of my life; *voir* **coucher, lever, rayon.**

b (*chaleur*) sun, sunshine; (*lumière*) sun, sunshine, sunlight. **au** ~ in the sun; **être assis/se mettre au** ~ to be sitting in/go into the sun(shine) *ou* sunlight; **vivre au** ~ to live in the sun; **il y a du ~, il fait du ~, il fait ~*** the sun is shining, it's sunny; **il fait un beau** ~ it's lovely and sunny; **il fait un** ~ **de plomb** the sun is blazing down, there's a blazing sun; **être en plein** ~ to be right in the sun; **des jours sans** ~ sunless days; **se chercher un coin au** ~ to look for a spot in the sun(shine) *ou* a sunny spot; **chat qui cherche le** ~ cat looking for a sunny spot; **les pays du** ~ the lands of the sun; **la couleur a passé au** ~ the colour has faded in the sun; *voir* **bain, coup, fondre.**

c (*motif, ornement*) sun.

d (*feu d'artifice*) Catherine wheel.

e (*acrobatie*) grand circle. (*fig: culbute*) **faire un** ~ to turn *ou* do a somersault, somersault.

f (*fleur*) sunflower.

g (*loc*) **se lever avec le** ~ to rise with the sun, be up with the sun *ou* the lark; (*Prov*) **le** ~ **brille pour tout le monde** nature belongs to everyone; **rien de nouveau** *ou* **neuf sous le** ~ there's nothing new under the sun; **avoir du bien** *ou* **des biens au** ~ to be the owner of property, have property; (*fig*) **se faire/avoir une place au** ~ to find oneself/have a place in the sun.

solennel, -elle [sɔlanɛl] **adj** (*gén*) solemn; *promesse, ton, occasion* solemn, formal; *séance* ceremonious; *voir* **communion.**

solennellement [sɔlanɛlmɑ̃] **adv** (*gén*) solemnly; *offrir, ouvrir* ceremoniously.

solenniser [sɔlanize] [1] **vt** to solemnize.

solennité [sɔlanite] **nf** a (*caractère*) solemnity. b (*fête*) grand *ou* formal occasion. c (*gén pl: formalité*) formality, solemnity.

solénoïde [sɔlenɔid] **nm** solenoid.

soleret [sɔlʀɛ] **nm** (*Hist*) solleret.

Solex [sɔlɛks] **nm** ® ≃ moped.

solfège [sɔlfɛʒ] **nm** (*théorie*) musical theory *ou* notation; (*livre*) (musical) theory book; (†*: gamme*) (tonic) sol-fa. **apprendre le** ~ to learn musical theory *ou* notation.

solfier [sɔlfje] [7] **vti** to sing naming the notes.

soli **npl de solo.**

solidaire [sɔlidɛʀ] **adj** a [*personnes*] **être ~s** to show solidarity, stand *ou* stick together; **pendant les grèves les ouvriers sont ~s** during strikes, workers stand *ou* stick together *ou* show solidarity; **être** ~ **de** to stand by, be behind; **nous sommes ~s du gouvernement** we stand by *ou* are behind *ou* are backing the government; **être** ~ **des victimes d'un régime** to show solidarity with *ou* stand by *ou* support the victims of a régime; **ces pays se sentent ~s** these countries feel they have each others' support *ou* feel solidarity with each other.

b *mécanismes, pièces, systèmes* interdependent. **cette pièce est** ~ **de l'autre** this part is firmly *ou* immovably attached to the other.

c (*Jur*) *contrat, engagement* binding all parties; *débiteurs* jointly liable.

solidairement [sɔlidɛʀmɑ̃] **adv** jointly, jointly and severally (*SPÉC*).

solidariser (se) [sɔlidaʀize] [1] **vpr: se** ~ **avec** to show solidarity with.

solidarité [sɔlidaʀite] **nf** a [*personnes*] solidarity. ~ **de classe/professionnelle** class/professional solidarity; ~ **ministérielle** ministerial solidarity (*whereby all ministers assume responsibility for a government's decisions*); **cesser le travail par ~ avec des grévistes** to come out in sympathy *ou* stop work in sympathy with the strikers; *voir* **grève**. b *[mécanismes, systèmes]* interdependence. c (*Jur*) joint and several liability.

solide [sɔlid] 1 **adj** a (*non liquide*) *nourriture, état, corps* solid. **ne lui donnez pas encore d'aliments ~s** don't give him any solid food *ou* any solids yet.

b (*robuste*) *matériaux* solid, sturdy, tough; *outil* solid, strong; *construction* solid, sturdy. **c'est du ~** it's solid stuff; **être ~ sur ses jambes** to be steady on one's legs; **avoir une position ~** to have a secure position.

c (*fig: durable, sérieux*) *institutions, qualités* sound, solid; *bases* solid, firm, sound; *amitié, vertus* solid; *connaissances, raisons* sound. **doué d'un ~ bon sens** possessing sound commonsense *ou* good solid commonsense; **ces opinions/raisonnements ne reposent sur rien de ~** these opinions/arguments have no solid *ou* sound foundation.

d (*fig*) *personne* (*vigoureux, en bonne santé*) sturdy, robust; (*sérieux, sûr*) reliable, solid; *poigne, jambes, bras* sturdy, solid; *santé, poumons, cœur* sound; *esprit, psychisme* sound. **avoir la tête ~** (*lit*) to have a hard head; (*fig: équilibré*) to have a good head on one's shoulders; **il n'a plus la tête bien ~** his mind's not what it was; **il n'a pas l'estomac très ~** he has a rather weak *ou* delicate stomach; *voir* **rein**.

e (*intensif*) *coup de poing* (good) hefty*; *revenus* substantial; *engueulade* good, proper* (*Brit*). **un ~ repas le remit d'aplomb** a (good) solid meal put him on his feet again.

f (*loc*) **être ~ au poste** (*Mil*) to be loyal to one's post; (*fig*) to be completely dependable *ou* reliable; **~ comme un roc** as solid as a rock; **~ comme le Pont-Neuf†** (as) strong as an ox.

2 **nm** (*Géom, Phys*) solid.

solidement [sɔlidmɑ̃] **adv** a (*lit*) *fixer, attacher, tenir* firmly; *fabriquer, construire* solidly. **résister ~** to put up a solid *ou* firm resistance. b (*fig*) *s'établir, s'installer* securely, firmly, solidly; *raisonner* soundly. **rester ~ attaché aux traditions locales** to remain firmly attached to local traditions; **être ~ attaché à qn/qch** to be deeply *ou* profoundly attached to sb/sth; **il l'a ~ engueulé*** he gave him a good *ou* proper (*Brit*) telling-off*, he told him off well and truly*.

solidification [sɔlidifikasjɔ̃] **nf** solidification.

solidifier **vt**, **se solidifier** **vpr** [sɔlidifje] 7 to solidify.

solidité [sɔlidite] **nf** (*voir* **solide**) solidity; sturdiness; toughness; soundness; robustness; reliability. *[construction, meuble]* **d'une ~ à toute épreuve** strong enough to resist anything.

soliflore [sɔliflɔʀ] **nm** slim vase (*designed to hold a single flower*).

soliloque [sɔlilɔk] **nm** soliloquy.

soliloquer [sɔlilɔke] 1 **vi** to soliloquize.

Soliman [sɔlimɑ̃] **nm**: **~ le Magnifique** Sulaiman the Magnificent.

solipède [sɔlipɛd] **adj, nm** solidungulate.

solipsisme [sɔlipsism] **nm** solipsism.

soliste [sɔlist] **nmf** soloist.

solitaire [sɔlitɛʀ] 1 **adj** a (*isolé*) *passant* solitary (*épith*), lone (*épith*); *maison, arbre, rocher* solitary (*épith*), lonely (*épith*), isolated. **là vivaient quelques chasseurs/bûcherons ~s** there lived a few solitary *ou* lone hunters/woodcutters.

b (*désert*) *parc, demeure, chemin* lonely (*épith*), deserted, solitary (*épith*).

c (*sans compagnie*) *adolescent, vieillard, vie* solitary, lonely, lonesome (*US*); *passe-temps, caractère* solitary; *voir* **plaisir**.

d *voir* **ver**.

2 **nmf** (*ermite*) solitary, recluse, hermit; (*fig: ours*) lone wolf, loner. **il préfère travailler en ~** he prefers to work on his own; **course/traversée en ~** solo race/crossing.

3 **nm** a (*sanglier*) old boar.

b (*diamant*) solitaire.

c (*jeu*) solitaire.

solitairement [sɔlitɛʀmɑ̃] **adv** *souffrir* alone. **vivre ~** to lead a solitary life, live alone.

solitude [sɔlityd] **nf** *[personne]* (*tranquillité*) solitude; (*manque de compagnie*) loneliness, lonesomeness (*US*); *[endroit]* loneliness. **~ morale** moral solitude *ou* isolation; **la ~ à deux** shared solitude; (*littér*) **les ~s glacées du Grand Nord** the icy solitudes *ou* wastes of the far North (*littér*).

solive [sɔliv] **nf** joist.

sollicitation [sɔlisitasjɔ̃] **nf** a (*démarche*) entreaty, appeal. b (*littér: gén pl: tentation*) solicitation (*littér*), enticement. c (*action exercée sur qch*) prompting. **l'engin répondait aux moindres ~s de son pilote** the craft responded to the slightest promptings of its pilot.

solliciter [sɔlisite] 1 **vt** a (*frm: demander*) *poste* to seek, solicit (*frm*); *faveur, audience, explication* to seek, request, solicit (*frm*) (*de qn* from sb).

b (*frm: faire appel à*) *personne* to appeal to. **~ qn de faire** to appeal to sb *ou* request sb to do; **je l'ai déjà sollicité à plusieurs reprises à ce sujet** I have already appealed to him *ou* approached him on several occasions over this matter; **il est très sollicité** there are many calls upon him, he's very much in demand.

c (*agir sur*) *curiosité, sens de qn* to appeal to; *attention* to attract, entice, solicit (*frm*). **les attractions qui sollicitent le touriste** the attractions that are there to tempt *ou* entice the tourist; **mille détails sollicitaient leur curiosité** a thousand details appealed to their curiosity; **le moteur répondait immédiatement lorsque le pilote le sollicitait** the engine responded immediately when the pilot prompted it; **~ un cheval** to urge a horse on.

solliciteur, -euse [sɔlisitœʀ, øz] 1 **nm,f** supplicant. 2 **nm** (*Can*) **~ général** Solicitor General.

sollicitude [sɔlisityd] **nf** concern (*NonC*), solicitude (*frm*). **toutes leurs ~s finissaient par nous agacer** we found their constant concern (for our welfare) *ou* their solicitude (*frm*) annoying in the end.

solo [sɔlo], **pl ~s** *ou* **soli** **adj inv, nm** solo. **~ de violon** violin solo; **violon ~** solo violin; **jouer/chanter en ~** to sing/play solo; **escalade en ~** solo climbing; **il a décidé d'agir en ~** he decided to go it alone.

solstice [sɔlstis] **nm** solstice. **~ d'hiver/d'été** winter/summer solstice.

solubiliser [sɔlybilize] 1 **vt** to make soluble.

solubilité [sɔlybilite] **nf** solubility.

soluble [sɔlybl] **adj** a *substance* soluble; *voir* **café**. b *problème* soluble, solvable.

soluté [sɔlyte] **nm** (*Chim, Pharm*) solution.

solution [sɔlysjɔ̃] 1 **nf** a *[problème, énigme, équation]* (*action*) solution, solving (*de* of); (*résultat*) solution, answer (*de* to).

b *[difficulté, situation]* (*issue*) solution, answer (*de* to); (*moyens employés*) solution (*de* to). **c'est une ~ de facilité** that's an easy answer *ou* the easy way out; **ce n'est pas une ~ à la crise qu'ils traversent** that's no answer to *ou* no real way out of the crisis they're in, that's no real way to resolve the crisis they're in; **ce n'est pas une ~!** that won't solve anything!; **hâter la ~ d'une crise** to hasten the resolution *ou* settling of a crisis.

c (*Chim: action, mélange*) solution. **en ~** in solution.

2 **comp** ►**solution de continuité** (*frm*) solution of continuity (*frm*) ►**la solution finale** (*Hist Pol*) the Final Solution.

solutionner [sɔlysjɔne] 1 **vt** to solve.

solvabilité [sɔlvabilite] **nf** solvency, creditworthiness.

solvable [sɔlvabl] **adj** (*Fin*) solvent, creditworthy.

solvant [sɔlvɑ̃] **nm** (*Chim*) solvent.

soma [sɔma] **nm** soma.

somali [sɔmali] 1 **nm** (*Ling*) Somali. 2 **nmpl**: **S~s** Somalis.

Somalie [sɔmali] **nf** (*région*) Somaliland; (*État*) Somalia.

somalien, -ienne [sɔmaljɛ̃, jɛn] 1 **adj** Somalian. 2 **nm,f**: **S~(ne)** Somalian.

somatique [sɔmatik] **adj** (*Bio, Psych*) somatic.

somatiser [sɔmatize] 1 **vt**: **~ une angoisse** *to transform an anxiety into a physical problem.*

sombre [sɔ̃bʀ] **adj** a (*peu éclairé, foncé*) dark. (*littér*) **de ~s abîmes** dark abysses; **il fait déjà ~** it's already dark; **bleu/vert ~** dark blue/green; *voir* **coupe²**. b (*fig*) (*mélancolique*) sombre, gloomy, dismal; (*ténébreux, funeste*) dark, sombre. **il avait le visage ~** he was looking gloomy *ou* sombre; **de ~s pensées** sombre *ou* gloomy thoughts, dark *ou* black thoughts; **un ~ avenir** a dark *ou* gloomy *ou* dismal future; **les moments** *ou* **heures ~s de notre histoire** the dark *ou* sombre moments of our history. c (*valeur intensive*) **~ idiot/brute** dreadful idiot/brute; **une ~ histoire d'enlèvement** a murky story of abduction. d (*Phon*) *voyelle* dark.

sombrement [sɔ̃bʀ(ə)mɑ̃] **adv** (*voir* **sombre**) darkly; sombrely; gloomily, dismally.

sombrer [sɔ̃bʀe] 1 **vi** *[bateau]* to sink, go down, founder; (*fig*) *[raison]* to give way; *[empire]* to founder; *[fortune]* to be swallowed up. **~ dans le désespoir/le sommeil** to sink into despair/sleep; **~ dans la folie** to give way to madness.

sombrero [sɔ̃bʀeʀo] **nm** sombrero.

sommable [sɔmabl] **adj** calculable.

sommaire [sɔmɛʀ] 1 **adj** *exposé, explication* basic, summary (*épith*), brief; *réponse* brief, summary (*épith*); *examen* brief, cursory, perfunctory; *instruction, réparation, repas* basic; *tenue, décoration* scanty; *justice, procédure, exécution* summary (*épith*). 2 **nm** (*exposé*) summary; (*résumé de chapitre*) summary, argument.

sommairement [sɔmɛʀmɑ̃] **adv** (*voir* **sommaire**) basically; summarily; briefly; cursorily; scantily. **il me l'a expliqué assez ~** he gave me a fairly basic *ou* cursory explanation of it.

sommation¹ [sɔmasjɔ̃] **nf** (*Jur*) summons (*sg*); (*frm: injonction*) demand; (*avant de faire feu*) warning. (*Jur*) **recevoir ~ de payer une dette** to be served with notice to pay a debt *ou* with a demand for payment of a debt; (*Mil, Police*) **faire les ~s d'usage** to give the standard *ou* customary warnings.

sommation² [sɔmasjɔ̃] **nf** (*Math*) summation.

somme¹ [sɔm] **nf** *voir* **bête**.

somme² [sɔm] **nm** nap, snooze. **faire un petit ~** to have a (short) nap *ou* a (little) snooze *ou* forty winks*.

somme³ [sɔm] **nf** a (*Math*) sum; (*gén*) (*pluralité*) sum total; (*quantité*) amount. **~ algébrique** algebraic sum; **la ~ totale** the grand total, the total sum; **faire la ~ de** to add up; **la ~ des dégâts est**

considérable the (total) amount of damage *ou* the total damage is considerable; **une ~ de travail énorme** an enormous amount of work.

b ~ **(d'argent)** sum *ou* amount (of money); **dépenser des ~s folles*** to spend vast amounts *ou* sums of money; (*intensif*) **c'est une ~!** it's quite a sum, it's quite a large amount.

c (*ouvrage de synthèse*) general survey. **une ~ littéraire/scientifique** a general survey of literature/of science.

d (*loc*) **en ~** (*tout bien considéré*) all in all; (*en résumé, après tout*) in sum, in short; **en ~, il ne s'agit que d'un incident sans importance** all in all, it's only an incident of minor importance; **en ~, vous n'en voulez plus?** in sum *ou* in short, you don't want any more?; (*frm*) **~ toute** when all's said and done.

sommeil [sɔmɛj] **nm** a (*état du dormeur, Physiol, Zool*) sleep; (*envie de dormir*) drowsiness, sleepiness. **avoir ~** to be *ou* feel sleepy; **tomber de ~** to be ready to drop (with tiredness *ou* sleep); **un ~ agréable l'envahissait** a pleasant drowsiness *ou* sleepiness *ou* desire to sleep was creeping over him; **huit heures de ~** 8 hours' sleep; **avoir le ~ léger** to be a light sleeper, sleep lightly; **dormir d'un ~ agité** to sleep restlessly; **un ~ profond** *ou* **de plomb** a heavy *ou* deep sleep; **~ paradoxal** paradoxical sleep; **premier ~** first hours of sleep; **nuit sans ~** sleepless night; *voir* **cure[1], dormir, maladie.**

b (*fig: gén littér: inactivité*) **le ~ de la nature** nature's sleep (*littér*), the dormant state of nature; **affaires en ~** dormant affairs, affairs in abeyance; **laisser une affaire en ~** to leave a matter (lying) dormant, leave a matter in abeyance; **le ~ de la petite ville pendant l'hiver** the sleepiness of the little town during winter; (*littér*) **le ~ éternel, le dernier ~** eternal rest; **le ~ des morts** the sleep of the dead.

sommeiller [sɔmeje] 1 **vi** [*personne*] to doze; (*fig*) [*qualité, défaut, nature*] to lie dormant; *voir* **cochon[1].**

sommelier [sɔməlje] **nm** wine waiter.

sommer[1] [sɔme] 1 **vt** (*frm: enjoindre*) **~ qn de faire** to charge *ou* enjoin sb to do (*frm*); (*Jur*) **~ qn de** *ou* **à comparaître** to summon sb to appear.

sommer[2] [sɔme] 1 **vt** (*additionner*) to sum.

sommet [sɔmɛ] **nm** a (*point culminant*) [*montagne*] summit, top; [*tour, arbre, toit, pente, hiérarchie*] top; [*vague*] crest; [*crâne*] crown, vertex (*SPÉC*); (*Géom, Math*) [*angle*] vertex; [*solide, figure, parabole*] vertex, apex. (*fig*) **les ~s de la gloire/des honneurs** the summits *ou* heights of fame/honour; (*littér, hum*) **redescendons de ces ~s** let us climb down from these lofty heights (*littér, hum*). b (*cime, montagne*) summit, mountain top. **l'air pur des ~s** the pure air of the summits *ou* the mountaintops. c (*Pol*) summit. *réunion, discussions* **au ~** summit (*épith*); *voir* **conférence.**

sommier [sɔmje] **nm** a [*lit*] **~ (à ressorts)** (*s'encastrant dans le lit, fixé au lit*) springing (*NonC*) (*Brit*), springs (*of bedstead*); (*avec pieds*) (interior-sprung) divan base (*Brit*), box springs (*US*); **~ (métallique)** mesh-springing (*Brit*); mesh-sprung divan base (*Brit*), mesh springs (*US*); **~ à lattes** slatted bed base; **~ extra-plat** metal-framed divan base. b (*Tech*) [*voûte*] impost, springer; [*clocher*] stock; [*porte, fenêtre*] transom; [*grille*] lower crossbar; [*orgue*] windchest. c (*registre*) ledger.

sommité [sɔ(m)mite] **nf** a (*personne*) prominent person, leading light (*de* in). b (*Bot*) head.

somnambule [sɔmnɑ̃byl] 1 **nmf** sleepwalker, somnambulist (*SPÉC*). **marcher/agir comme un ~** to walk/act like a sleepwalker *ou* as if in a trance. 2 **adj: être ~** to be a sleepwalker, sleepwalk.

somnambulisme [sɔmnɑ̃bylism] **nm** sleepwalking, somnambulism (*SPÉC*).

somnifère [sɔmnifɛʀ] 1 **nm** sleeping drug, soporific; (*pilule*) sleeping pill, sleeping tablet. 2 **adj** somniferous (*frm*), sleep-inducing, soporific.

somnolence [sɔmnɔlɑ̃s] **nf** sleepiness (*NonC*), drowsiness (*NonC*), somnolence (*NonC*) (*frm*); (*fig*) indolence, inertia.

somnolent, e [sɔmnɔlɑ̃, ɑ̃t] **adj** sleepy, drowsy, somnolent (*frm*); (*fig*) *vie, province* drowsy, sleepy, languid; *faculté* dormant, inert.

somnoler [sɔmnɔle] 1 **vi** (*lit*) to doze; (*fig*) to lie dormant.

somptuaire [sɔ̃ptɥɛʀ] **adj** a *loi, réforme* sumptuary. b **dépenses ~s** extravagant expenditure (*NonC*); **arts ~s** decorative arts.

somptueusement [sɔ̃ptɥøzmɑ̃] **adv** (*voir* **somptueux**) sumptuously; magnificently; lavishly; handsomely.

somptueux, -euse [sɔ̃ptɥø, øz] **adj** *habit, résidence* sumptuous, magnificent; *train de vie* lavish; *cadeau* handsome (*épith*), sumptuous; *repas, festin* sumptuous, lavish.

somptuosité [sɔ̃ptɥozite] **nf** (*voir* **somptueux**) sumptuousness (*NonC*); magnificence (*NonC*); lavishness (*NonC*); handsomeness (*NonC*).

son[1] [sɔ̃] **, sa** [sa] **, ses** [se] **adj poss** a [*homme*] his; (*emphatique*) his own; [*femme*] her; (*emphatique*) her own; [*nation*] its, her; (*emphatique*) its own, her own. **S~ Altesse Royale** (*prince*) His Royal Highness; (*princesse*) Her Royal Highness; **Sa Majesté** (*roi*) His Majesty; (*reine*) Her Majesty; **Sa Sainteté le pape** His Holiness the Pope; **ce n'est pas ~ genre** he *ou* she is not that sort, it's not like him *ou* her; **quand s'est passé ~ accident?** when did she (*ou* he) have her (*ou* his) accident?; **~ père et sa mère, ses père et mère** his (*ou* her) father and (his *ou* her) mother; (*emphatique*) **~ jardin à lui/elle est une vraie jungle** his *ou* his own/her *ou* her own garden is a real jungle; **ses date et lieu de naissance** his (*ou* her) date and place of birth; **à sa vue, elle poussa un cri** she screamed at the sight of him (*ou* her) *ou* on seeing him (*ou* her); **un de ses amis** one of his (*ou* her) friends, a friend of his (*ou* hers); **~ idiote de sœur*** that stupid sister of hers (*ou* his).

b [*objet, abstraction*] its. **l'hôtel est réputé pour sa cuisine** the hotel is famous for its food; **pour comprendre ce crime il faut chercher ~ mobile** to understand this crime we must try to find the motivation for it; **ça a ~ importance** that has its *ou* a certain importance.

c (*à valeur d'indéfini*) one's; (*après chacun, personne etc*) his, her. **faire ses études** to study; **on ne connaît pas ~ bonheur** one never knows how fortunate one is; **être satisfait de sa situation** to be satisfied with one's situation; **chacun selon ses possibilités** each according to his (own) capabilities; **personne ne sait comment finira sa vie** no one knows how his life will end.

d (**: valeur affective, ironique, intensive*) **il doit (bien) gagner ~ million par an** he must be (easily) earning a million a year; **avoir ~ samedi/dimanche** to have (one's) Saturday(s)/Sunday(s) off; **il a passé tout ~ dimanche à travailler** he spent the whole of *ou* all Sunday working; **~ M. X ne me plaît pas du tout** I don't care for his (*ou* her) Mr X at all; **avoir ses petites manies** to have one's funny little ways; **elle a ses jours!** she has her (good and bad) days!; **il a sa crise de foie** he is having one of his bilious attacks; **cet enfant ne ferme jamais ses portes** that child will never shut doors *ou* a door behind him; *voir* **sentir.**

son[2] [sɔ̃] **nm** a (*gén, Ling, Phys*) sound. **~articulé/inarticulé** articulate/inarticulate sound; **le timbre et la hauteur du ~ d'une cloche/d'un tambour/d'un avertisseur** the tone and pitch of (the sound of) a bell/a drum/an alarm; **réveillé par le ~ des cloches/tambours/klaxons** woken by the sound of bells/drums/hooters, woken by the ringing of bells/the beat of drums/the blare of horns; **défiler au ~ d'une fanfare** to march past to the music of a band; (*fig*) **n'entendre qu'un/entendre un autre ~ de cloche** to hear only one/another side of the story; *voir* **mur, qui, vitesse.**

b (*Ciné, Rad, TV*) sound. **baisser le ~** to turn down the sound *ou* volume; **équipe/ingénieur du ~** sound team/engineer; **synchroniser le ~ et l'image** to synchronize the sound and the picture; **(spectacle) ~ et lumière** son et lumière (display); *voir* **pris.**

son[3] [sɔ̃] **nm** bran. **farine de ~** bran flour; *voir* **pain, tache.**

sonal [sɔnal] **nm** jingle.

sonar [sɔnaʀ] **nm** sonar.

sonate [sɔnat] **nf** sonata; *voir* **forme.**

sonatine [sɔnatin] **nf** sonatina.

sondage [sɔ̃daʒ] **nm** (*Tech: forage*) boring, drilling; (*Mét, Naut*) sounding; (*Méd*) probing (*NonC*), probe; (*pour évacuer*) catheterization; (*fig*) sounding out of opinion (*NonC*). **~ (d'opinion)** (opinion) poll.

sonde [sɔ̃d] **nf** a (*Naut*) (*instrument*) lead line, sounding line; (*relevé: gén pl*) soundings (*pl*). **naviguer à la ~** to navigate by soundings; **jeter une ~** to cast the lead; *voir* **île.** b (*Tech: de forage*) borer, drill. c (*Méd*) probe; (*à canal central*) catheter; (*d'alimentation*) feeding tube. **mettre une ~ à qn** to put a catheter in sb; **alimenter un malade avec une ~** to feed a patient through a tube. d (*Aviat, Mét*) sonde. **~ aérienne** sounding balloon; **~ atmosphérique** sonde; **~ spatiale** space probe; *voir* **ballon.** e (*de douanier: pour fouiller*) probe; (*Comm: pour prélever*) taster; (*à avalanche*) pole (*for locating victims*). **~ à fromage** cheese taster.

sondé, e [sɔ̃de] **nm,f** *person who takes part in an opinion poll.* **la majorité des ~s était pour** the majority of those polled were in favour of the idea.

sonder [sɔ̃de] 1 **vt** a (*Naut*) to sound; (*Mét*) to probe; (*Tech*) *terrain* to bore, drill; *bagages* to probe, search (with a probe); *avalanche* to probe; (*Méd*) *plaie* to probe; *vessie, malade* to catheterize. (*littér*) **il sonda l'abîme du regard** his eyes probed the depths of the abyss. b (*fig*) *personne* (*gén*) to sound out; (*par sondage d'opinion*) to poll; *conscience, avenir* to sound out, probe. **~ les esprits** to sound out opinion; **~ l'opinion** to make a survey of (public) opinion; *voir* **terrain.**

sondeur [sɔ̃dœʀ] **nm** (*Tech*) sounder; (*sondage d'opinion*) pollster.

songe [sɔ̃ʒ] **nm** (*littér*) dream. **en ~** in a dream; **faire un ~** to have a dream; (*Prov*) **~, mensonge** dreams are just illusions.

songe-creux [sɔ̃ʒkʀø] **nm inv** (†, *littér*) visionary.

songer [sɔ̃ʒe] 3 1 **vi** (*littér: rêver*) to dream.

2 **vt: ~ que ...** to reflect *ou* consider that ...; **"ils pourraient refuser" songeait-il** "they could refuse" he reflected *ou* mused; **songez que cela peut présenter de grands dangers** remember *ou* you must be aware that it can present great dangers; **il n'avait jamais songé qu'ils puissent réussir** he had never imagined they might be successful; **cela me fait ~ que je voulais lui téléphoner** that reminds me — I wanted to phone him.

3 **songer à vt indir** (*évoquer*) to muse over *ou* upon, think over, reflect upon; (*considérer, penser à*) to consider, think over, reflect upon; (*envisager*) to contemplate, think of *ou* about; (*s'occuper de, prendre soin de*) to think of, have regard for. **~ à se marier** *ou* **au mariage** to contemplate marriage, think of getting married; **songez-y** think it over, consider it; **il ne songe qu'à son avancement** he thinks only of *ou* he has regard only for his own advancement; **~ à faire qch** to contemplate doing sth, think of *ou* about doing sth; **quand on songe à tout ce gaspillage** when you think of all this waste; **il ne faut pas y ~, inutile d'y**

~ it is no use (even) thinking about it; **vous n'y songez pas!** you must be joking!, you're not serious!; **vous me faites ~ à M. X** you remind me of Mr X; *voir* **mal 3c**.

songerie [sɔ̃ʒʀi] nf (*littér*) reverie.

songeur, -euse [sɔ̃ʒœʀ, øz] 1 adj pensive. **cela me laisse ~** I just don't know what to think. 2 nm,f dreamer.

sonique [sɔnik] adj *vitesse* sonic. **barrière ~** sound barrier.

sonnaille [sɔnɑj] nf (*cloche*) bell; (*bruit*) ringing (*NonC*).

sonnant, e [sɔnɑ̃, ɑ̃t] adj a **à 4 heures ~es** on the stroke *ou* dot of 4, at 4 (o'clock) sharp. b *voir* **espèce**. c *horloge* chiming, striking. d (*Phon*) resonant.

sonné, e [sɔne] (ptp de **sonner**) adj a **il est midi ~** it's gone (*Brit*) *ou* past twelve; **avoir trente ans bien ~s*** to be on the wrong side of thirty*. b (‡: *fou*) cracked*, off one's rocker‡ (*attrib*). c (*: *assommé*) groggy.

sonner [sɔne] 1 1 vt a *cloche* to ring; *tocsin, glas* to sound, toll; *clairon* to sound. **~ trois coups à la porte** to ring three times at the door; **se faire ~ les cloches*** to get a good ticking-off* (*Brit*) *ou* telling-off*; **~ les cloches à qn*** to give sb a roasting* *ou* a telling-off*.

b (*annoncer*) *messe, matines* to ring the bell for; *réveil, rassemblement, retraite* to sound. **~ l'alarme** to sound the alarm; (*Mil*) **~ la charge** to sound the charge; **~ l'heure** to strike the hour; **la pendule sonne 3 heures** the clock strikes 3 (o'clock).

c (*appeler*) *portier, infirmière* to ring for. **on ne t'a pas sonné!*** nobody asked you!, who rang your bell?* (*Brit*).

d (*: *étourdir*) *[chute]* to knock out; *[nouvelle]* to stagger*, take aback. **la nouvelle l'a un peu sonné** he was rather taken aback *ou* staggered* at *ou* by the news; **il a été bien sonné par sa grippe** he was really knocked flat by his bout of flu, his bout of flu really knocked him for six*.

2 vi a *[cloches, téléphone]* to ring; *[réveil]* to ring, go off; *[clairon, trompette]* to sound; *[tocsin, glas]* to sound, toll. (*Scol etc*) **la cloche a sonné** the bell has gone *ou* rung; **~ à toute volée** to peal (out); (*fig*) **les oreilles lui sonnent** his ears are ringing.

b (*son métallique*) *[marteau]* to ring; *[clefs, monnaie]* to jangle, jingle. **~ clair** to give a clear ring; **~ creux** (*lit*) to sound hollow; (*fig*) to ring hollow; **~ faux** (*lit*) to sound out of tune; (*fig*) to ring false; **~ juste** (*lit*) to sound in tune; (*fig*) to ring true; (*fig*) **~ bien/mal** to sound good/bad; **l'argent sonna sur le comptoir** the money jingled *ou* jangled onto the counter.

c (*être annoncé*) *[midi, minuit]* to strike. **3 heures venaient de ~** 3 o'clock had just struck, it had just struck 3 o'clock; **la récréation a sonné** the bell has gone for break; **la messe sonne** the bell is ringing *ou* going for mass; *voir* **heure**.

d (*actionner une sonnette*) to ring. **on a sonné** the bell has just gone, I just heard the bell, somebody just rang (the bell); **~ chez qn** to ring at sb's door, ring sb's doorbell.

e (*Phonétique*) **faire ~** to sound.

3 **sonner de** vt indir *clairon, cor* to sound.

sonnerie [sɔnʀi] nf a (*son*) *[sonnette, cloches]* ringing. **la ~ du clairon** the bugle call, the sound of the bugle; **j'ai entendu la ~ du téléphone** I heard the telephone ringing; **la ~ du téléphone l'a réveillé** he was woken by the telephone('s) ringing *ou* the telephone bell; **~ d'alarme** alarm bell. b (*Mil: air*) call. **la ~ du réveil** (the sounding of) reveille; **~ aux morts** last post. c (*mécanisme*) *[réveil]* alarm (mechanism), bell; *[pendule]* chimes (*pl*), chiming *ou* striking mechanism; (*sonnette*) bell. **~ électrique/téléphonique** electric/telephone bell.

sonnet [sɔnɛ] nm sonnet.

sonnette [sɔnɛt] nf a (*électrique, de porte*) bell; (*clochette*) (hand) bell. **~ de nuit** night bell; **~ d'alarme** alarm bell; (*fig*) **tirer la ~ d'alarme** to set off *ou* sound the alarm (bell); **tirer les ~s** (*lit: jeu d'enfants*) to ring doorbells (and run away); (*fig: démarcher*) to go knocking on doors; *voir* **coup, serpent**. b (*Tech*) pile driver.

sonneur [sɔnœʀ] nm a **~ (de cloches)** bell ringer. b pile driver operator.

sono* [sɔno] nf (abrév de **sonorisation**) *[salle de conférences]* P.A. (system); *[discothèque]* sound system. **la ~ est trop forte** the sound's too loud.

sonore [sɔnɔʀ] 1 adj a *objet, surface en métal* resonant; *voix* ringing (*épith*), sonorous, resonant; *rire* ringing (*épith*), resounding (*épith*); *baiser, gifle* resounding (*épith*). b *salle* resonant; *voûte* echoing. c (*péj*) *paroles, mots* high-sounding, sonorous. d (*Acoustique*) *vibrations* sound (*épith*). **onde ~** sound wave; **fond ~** (*bruits*) background noise; (*musique*) background music. e (*Ciné*) **film ~** sound film; **bande** *ou* **piste ~** sound track; **effets ~s** sound effects. f (*Ling*) voiced. 2 nf (*Ling*) voiced consonant.

sonorisation [sɔnɔʀizasjɔ̃] nf a (*Ciné*) adding the sound track (*de* to). b (*action*) *[salle de conférences]* fitting with a public address system; *[discothèque]* fitting with a sound system; (*équipement*) *[salle de conférences]* public address system, P.A. (system); *[discothèque]* sound system. c (*Ling*) voicing.

sonoriser [sɔnɔʀize] 1 vt a *film* to add the sound track to; *salle de conférences* to fit with a public address system *ou* a P.A. (system). b (*Ling*) to voice.

sonorité [sɔnɔʀite] nf a (*timbre, son*) *[radio, instrument de musique]* tone; *[voix]* sonority, tone. **~s** *[voix, instrument]* tones. b (*Ling*) voicing. c (*résonance*) *[air]* sonority, resonance; *[salle]* acoustics (*pl*); *[cirque rocheux, grotte]* resonance.

sonothèque [sɔnɔtɛk] nf sound (effects) library.

sonotone [sɔnɔtɔn] nm ® hearing aid.

sont [sɔ̃] *voir* **être**.

Sophie [sɔfi] nf Sophia, Sophie.

sophisme [sɔfism] nm sophism.

sophiste [sɔfist] nmf sophist.

sophistication [sɔfistikasjɔ̃] nf (*affectation*) sophistication; (*complexité*) sophistication; (†: *altération*) adulteration.

sophistique [sɔfistik] 1 adj sophistic. 2 nf sophistry.

sophistiqué, e [sɔfistike] (ptp de **sophistiquer**) adj (*gén*) sophisticated; (†: *altéré*) adulterated.

sophistiquer [sɔfistike] 1 1 vt (*raffiner*) to make (more) sophisticated; (†: *altérer*) to adulterate. 2 **se sophistiquer** vpr to become (more) sophisticated.

Sophocle [sɔfɔkl] nm Sophocles.

sophrologie [sɔfʀɔlɔʒi] nf relaxation therapy.

sophrologue [sɔfʀɔlɔg] nmf relaxation therapist.

soporifique [sɔpɔʀifik] 1 adj (*lit*) soporific, sleep-inducing; (*fig péj*) soporific. 2 nm sleeping drug, soporific.

soprano [sɔpʀano], pl **~s** *ou* **soprani** [sɔpʀani] 1 nm soprano (voice); (*voix d'enfant*) soprano, treble. 2 nmf soprano. **~ dramatique/lyrique** dramatic/lyric soprano.

sorbe [sɔʀb] nf sorb (apple).

sorbet [sɔʀbɛ] nm sorbet, water ice (*Brit*), sherbet (*US*). **~ au citron/à l'orange** lemon/orange sorbet.

sorbetière [sɔʀbətjɛʀ] nf (*Comm*) ice cream churn; (*ménagère*) ice-cream maker.

sorbier [sɔʀbje] nm service tree, sorb.

sorbitol [sɔʀbitɔl] nm sorbitol.

sorbonnard, e [sɔʀbɔnaʀ, aʀd] (*péj*) 1 adj pedantic, worthy of the Sorbonne (*attrib*). 2 nm,f *student or teacher at the Sorbonne*.

sorcellerie [sɔʀsɛlʀi] nf witchcraft, sorcery. (*fig*) **c'est de la ~!** it's magic!

sorcier [sɔʀsje] 1 nm (*lit*) sorcerer. (*fig*) **il ne faut pas être ~ pour ...** you don't have to be a wizard to ...; *voir* **apprenti**. 2 adj (*fig*) **ce n'est pas ~!*** you don't need witchcraft *ou* magic to do it (*ou* solve it *etc*)!

sorcière [sɔʀsjɛʀ] nf witch, sorceress; (*fig péj*) (old) witch, (old) hag; *voir* **chasse[1]**.

sordide [sɔʀdid] adj *ruelle, quartier* sordid, squalid; *action, mentalité* base, sordid; *gains, crime* sordid.

sordidement [sɔʀdidmɑ̃] adv (*voir* **sordide**) sordidly; squalidly; basely.

sordidité [sɔʀdidite] nf (*voir* **sordide**) sordidness; squalidness; baseness.

sorgho [sɔʀgo] nm sorghum.

Sorlingues [sɔʀlɛ̃g] nfpl: **les (îles) ~** the Scilly Isles, the Isles of Scilly, the Scillies.

sornettes† [sɔʀnɛt] nfpl twaddle, balderdash. **~!** fiddlesticks!

sort [sɔʀ] nm a (*situation, condition*) lot, fate. **c'est le ~ des paresseux d'échouer** it's the lot *ou* fate of the lazy to fail; **améliorer le ~ des malheureux/handicapés** to improve the lot of the unfortunate/the handicapped; **envier le ~ de qn** to envy sb's lot.

b (*destinée*) fate. (*hum*) **abandonner qn à son triste ~** to abandon sb to his sad fate; **sa proposition a eu** *ou* **subi le même ~ que les précédentes** his proposal met with the same fate as the previous ones; **le ~ décidera** fate will decide; **pour essayer de conjurer le (mauvais) ~** to try to ward off fate; **c'est un coup du ~** it's a stroke of fate; **faire un ~ à qch** (*mettre en valeur*) to stress sth, emphasize sth; (*: *se débarrasser de*) to get shot of sth‡ (*Brit*), get rid of sth; **faire un ~ à un plat/une bouteille*** to polish off a dish/a bottle*; *voir* **caprice, ironie**.

c (*hasard*) fate. **le ~ est tombé sur lui** he was chosen by fate, it fell to his lot; **le ~ en est jeté** the die is cast; **tirer au ~** to draw lots; **tirer qch au ~** to draw lots for sth; *voir* **tirage**.

d (*sorcellerie*) curse, spell. **il y a un ~ sur ...** there is a curse on ...; **jeter un ~ sur** to put a curse *ou* spell *ou* jinx* on.

sortable* [sɔʀtabl] adj (*gén nég*) *personne* presentable. **tu n'es pas ~!** we (*ou* I) can't take you anywhere!

sortant, e [sɔʀtɑ̃, ɑ̃t] 1 adj *député etc* outgoing (*épith*). **les numéros ~s** the numbers which come up. 2 nm (*personne: gén pl*) **les ~s** the outgoing crowd.

sorte [sɔʀt] nf a (*espèce*) sort, kind. **toutes ~s de gens/choses** all kinds *ou* sorts *ou* manner of people/things; **des vêtements de toutes (les) ~s** all kinds *ou* sorts *ou* manner of clothes; **nous avons 3 ~s de fleurs** we have 3 kinds *ou* types *ou* sorts of flower(s); **des roches de même ~** rocks of the same sort *ou* kind *ou* type.

b **une ~ de** a sort *ou* kind of; (*péj*) **une ~ de médecin/voiture** a doctor/car of sorts; **robe taillée dans une ~ de satin** dress cut out of some sort *ou* kind of satin, dress cut out of a sort *ou* kind of satin.

c (*loc*) **de la ~** (*de cette façon*) in that fashion *ou* way; **accoutré de la ~** dressed in that fashion *ou* way; **il n'a rien fait de la ~** he did nothing of the kind *ou* no such thing; **de ~ à** so as to, in order to; **en quelque ~** in a way, as it were; **vous avouez l'avoir dit, en quelque ~** you are in a way *ou* as it were admitting to having said it; **en aucune ~**† not at all, not in the least; **de (telle) ~ que** (*de façon à ce que*) so that, in such a way that; (*si bien que*) so much so that; **faites en ~ d'avoir fini demain** see to it *ou* arrange it *ou* arrange things so that you will have finished tomorrow; **faire en ~ que** to see to it that; (†, *littér*) **en ~ que** (*de façon à ce que*) so that, in such a way that; (*si bien que*) so much so that.

sortie [sɔʀti] 1 nf a (*action, moment*) *[personne]* leaving; *[véhicule, bateau, armée occupante]* departure; (*Mil: mission*) sortie; (*Théât*) exit. **à sa ~, tous se sont tus** when he went out *ou* left everybody fell silent; **à sa ~ du salon** when he went out of *ou* left the lounge; **il a fait une ~ remarquée** his departure was noticed, he was noticed as he left; **il a fait une ~ discrète** he made a discreet exit, he left discreetly; (*Aviat, Mil*) **faire une ~** to make a sortie; (*Mil*) **tenter une ~** to attempt a sortie; **à la ~ des ouvriers/bureaux/théâtres** when the workers/offices/theatres come out; **sa mère l'attend tous les jours à la ~ de l'école** his mother waits for him every day after school *ou* when school comes out *ou* finishes; **retrouvons-nous à la ~ (du concert)** let's meet at the end (of the concert); **elle attend la ~ des artistes** she's waiting for the performers to come out; **à sa ~ de prison** on his discharge from prison, when he comes (*ou* came) out of prison; **c'est sa première ~ depuis sa maladie** it's his first day *ou* time out since his illness; (*Théât*) **elle a manqué sa ~ à l'acte 2** she fluffed her exit in act 2; *voir* **faux**[2].

b (*congé*) day off; (*promenade etc*) outing; (*le soir: au théâtre etc*) evening *ou* night out. **c'est le jour de ~ de la bonne** it's the maid's day off; **c'est le jour de ~ des pensionnaires** it's the boarders' day out; *[soldat, domestique]* **il est de ~** it's his day off; **nous sommes de ~ ce soir** we're going out tonight, we're having an evening out tonight; **ils viennent déjeuner le dimanche, cela leur fait une petite ~** they come to lunch on Sundays — it gives them a little outing *ou* it's a day out for them; **elle s'est acheté une robe du soir pour leurs ~s** she's bought herself an evening dress for when they go out *ou* have a night out; (*Scol*) **~ éducative** *ou* **scolaire** school (educational) outing (*Brit*), school visit (*Brit*), field-trip.

c (*lieu*) exit, way out. **~ de secours** emergency exit; **~ des artistes** stage door; **attention, ~ d'usine/de garage** caution, factory/garage entrance *ou* exit; **~ de camions** vehicle exit; **garé devant la ~ de l'école** parked in front of the school gates *ou* entrance; **sa maison se trouve à la ~ du village** his house is on the outskirts of the village *ou* at the edge of the village; **les ~s de Paris sont encombrées** the roads out of Paris are jammed; **par ici la ~!** this way out!; (*fig*) **trouver/se ménager une (porte de) ~** to find/arrange a way out.

d (*écoulement*) *[eau, gaz]* outflow. **cela empêche la ~ des gaz** that prevents the gases from coming out *ou* escaping.

e (*emportement, algarade*) outburst; (*remarque drôle*) sally; (*remarque incongrue*) peculiar *ou* odd remark. **elle est sujette à ce genre de ~** she's given to that kind of outburst; she's always coming out with that kind of sally; she's always coming up with that kind of odd remark; **faire une ~ à qn** to let fly at sb; **faire une ~ contre qch/qn** to lash out against sth/sb.

f (*Comm: mise en vente etc*) *[voiture, modèle]* launching; *[livre]* appearance, publication; *[disque, film]* release.

g (*Comm*) *[marchandises, devises]* export. **~ (de capitaux)** outflow (of capital); **la ~ de l'or/des devises/de certains produits est contingentée** there are controls on gold/currency/certain products leaving the country *ou* on the export of gold/currency/certain products; **il y a eu d'importantes ~s de devises** large amounts of currency have been flowing out of *ou* leaving the country.

h (*Comm, Fin: somme dépensée*) item of expenditure. **il y a eu plus de ~s que de rentrées** there have been more outgoings than receipts.

i (*Ordin*) output, readout. **~ sur imprimante** print-out.

j (*Sport*) **~ en touche** going into touch; **il y a ~ en touche si le ballon touche la ligne** the ball is in touch *ou* has gone into touch if it touches the line; (*Rugby*) **ils ont marqué l'essai sur une ~ de mêlée** they scored a try straight out of the scrum; (*Ftbl*) **le ballon est allé en ~ de but** the ball has gone into touch behind the back line; *[gardien de but]* **faire une ~** to leave the goalmouth, come out of goal; **lors de la dernière ~ de l'équipe de France contre l'Angleterre** when France last played a match against England, during the last French-English encounter *ou* match; (*Aut*) **faire une ~ de route** to go off the track.

2 comp ▶ **sortie de bain** bathrobe.

sortilège [sɔʀtilɛʒ] nm (magic) spell.

sortir [sɔʀtiʀ] 16 1 vi (*avec aux être*) a (*lit*) (*gén*) (*aller*) to go out, leave; (*venir*) to come out, leave; (*à pied*) to walk out; (*en voiture*) to drive out, go *ou* come out; *[véhicule]* to drive out, go *ou* come out; (*Ordin*) to exit, log out; (*Théât*) to exit, leave (the stage). **~ en voiture/à bicyclette** to go out for a drive/a cycle (ride), go out in one's car/on one's bike; **~ de** *pièce* to go *ou* come out of, leave; *région, pays* to leave; **~ de chez qn** to go *ou* come out of sb's (house *etc*), leave sb's (house *etc*); **~ en courant** to run out; **~ en boitant** to limp out; **faire ~ la voiture du garage** to take *ou* get the car out of the garage; **il sortit discrètement (de la pièce)** he went out (of the room) *ou* left (the room) discreetly, he slipped out (of the room); **faites ~ ces gens** make these people go *ou* leave, get these people out; **sors (d'ici)!** get out (of here)!; **~ par la porte de la cave/par la fenêtre** to go *ou* get out *ou* leave by the cellar door/the window; (*Théât*) **"la servante sort"** "exit the maid"; (*Théât*) **"les 3 gardes sortent"** "exeunt 3 guards"; **laisser ~ qn** to let sb out *ou* leave; **ne laissez ~ personne** don't let anybody out *ou* leave; **laisser ~ qn de** *pièce, pays* to let sb out of, let sb leave.

b *[objet, pièce]* to come out. **le curseur est sorti de la rainure** the runner has come out of the groove; **le joint est sorti de son logement** the joint has come out of its socket.

c (*partir de chez soi*) to go out. **~ faire des courses/prendre l'air** to go out shopping/for some fresh air; **~ acheter du pain** to go out to buy *ou* for some bread; **~ dîner/déjeuner** to go out for *ou* to dinner/lunch; **ils sortent beaucoup/ne sortent pas beaucoup** they go out a lot/don't go out much; **mes parents ne me laissent pas ~** my parents don't let me (go) out; **on lui permet de ~ maintenant qu'il va mieux** he is allowed (to go) out now that he is getting better; **c'est le soir que les moustiques sortent** it's at night-time that the mosquitoes come out; **il n'est jamais sorti de son village** he has never been out of *ou* gone outside his village.

d (*Comm*) *[marchandises, devises]* to leave. **tout ce qui sort (du pays) doit être déclaré** everything going out *ou* leaving (the country) must be declared.

e (*quitter*) to leave, come out; *[élèves]* to get out. **~ du théâtre** to go out of *ou* leave the theatre; **~ de l'hôpital/de prison** to come out of hospital/prison; **quand sort-il?** (*de prison*) when does he come *ou* get out?; (*de l'hôpital*) when is he coming out? *ou* leaving?; **~ de table** to leave the table; **~ de l'eau** to come out of the water; **~ du lit** to get out of bed, get up; *[fleuve]* **~ de son lit** to overflow its banks; (*Rail*) **~ des rails** to go off the rails; **la voiture est sortie de la route** the car left *ou* came off the road; **il aura du mal à ~ de ce mauvais pas** he'll have a job getting out of this trouble; **~ de convalescence/d'un profond sommeil** to come out of *ou* emerge from convalescence/a deep sleep; **~ de son calme** to lose one's calm; **~ de son indifférence** to overcome one's indifference; **~ sain et sauf** *ou* **~ indemne d'un accident** to come out of an accident unscathed; **il a trop de copies à corriger, il ne s'en sort pas** he has too many exercises to correct — there's no end to them; (*Sport*) **~ en touche** to go into touch; **ce secret ne doit pas ~ de la famille** this secret must not go beyond *ou* outside family.

f (*fréquenter*) **~ avec qn** (*gén*) to go out with sb; (*relation stable*) to go steady with sb.

g (*marquant le passé immédiat*) **on sortait de l'hiver** it was getting near the end of winter; **il sort d'ici** he's just left; **il sort du lit** he's just got up, he's just out of bed; **on ne croirait pas qu'elle sort de chez le coiffeur!** you'd never believe she'd just come out of the hairdresser's! *ou* just had her hair done!; **il sort de maladie*** *ou* **d'être malade*** he's just been ill, he's just getting over an illness; **il sort d'une période de cafard** he's just gone through *ou* had a spell of depression; **je sors de lui parler*** I've just been talking to him.

h (*s'écarter de*) **~ du sujet/de la question** to go *ou* get off the subject/the point; **~ de la légalité** to overstep *ou* go outside *ou* go beyond the law; *[balle, ballon etc]* **~ du jeu** to go out (of play); **~ des limites de** to go beyond the bounds of, overstep the limits of; **cela sort de mon domaine/ma compétence** that's outside my field/my authority; **vous sortez de votre rôle** that is not your responsibility *ou* part of your brief; **cela sort de l'ordinaire** that's out of the ordinary; **il n'y a pas à ~ de là, nous avons besoin de lui** there's no getting away from it *ou* round it (*Brit*) — we need him; **il ne veut pas ~ de là** he won't budge.

i (*être issu de*) **~ d'une bonne famille/du peuple** to come from a good family/from the working class; **il sort du lycée X** he was (educated) at the lycée X; **il sort de l'université de X** he was *ou* he studied at the University of X; **officier sorti du rang** officer who has come up through the ranks *ou* risen from the ranks.

j (*dépasser*) to stick out; (*commencer à pousser*) *[blé, plante]* to come up; *[dent]* to come through. **les yeux lui sortaient de la tête** his eyes were popping *ou* starting out of his head.

k (*être fabriqué, publié etc*) to come out; *[disque, film]* to be released. **~ de** to come from; **tout ce qui sort de cette maison est de qualité** everything that comes from that firm is good quality; **une encyclopédie qui sort par fascicules** an encyclopaedia which comes out *ou* is published in instalments; **sa robe sort de chez un grand couturier** her dress comes from one of the great couturier's.

l (*Jeux, Loterie*) *[numéro, couleur]* to come up; (*Scol*) *[sujet d'examen]* to come up.

m (*provenir de*) **~ de** to come from; (*fig*) **sait-on ce qui sortira de ces entrevues!** who knows what'll come (out) of these talks! *ou* what these talks will lead to!; **des mots qui sortent du cœur** words which come from the heart, heartfelt words; **une odeur de brûlé sortait de la cuisine** a smell of burning came from the kitchen; **une épaisse fumée sortait par les fenêtres** thick smoke was pouring out of the windows.

n (*loc*) **~ de ses gonds** (*lit*) to come off (of) its hinges; (*fig*) to fly off the handle; **je sors d'en prendre*** I've had quite enough thank you (*iro*); **il est sorti d'affaire** (*il a été malade*) he has pulled through; (*il a eu des ennuis*) he has got over it; **on n'est pas sorti de l'auberge*** we're not out of the wood (*Brit*) *ou* woods (*US*) yet; **se croire sorti de la**

cuisse de Jupiter* to think a lot of o.s., think one is the cat's whiskers* (*Brit*) *ou* the bee's knees* (*Brit*) *ou* God's gift to mankind; **il est à peine sorti de l'œuf*** he's still wet behind the ears*; **ça me sort par les yeux (et les oreilles)*** I've had more than I can take (of it); **cela lui est sorti de la mémoire** *ou* **de l'esprit** that slipped his memory *ou* his mind; **cela m'est sorti de la tête** it went right out of my head; **mais d'où sort-il (donc)?** (*il est tout sale*) where has he been!; (*il ne sait pas la nouvelle*) where has he been (all this time)?; (*il est mal élevé*) where was he brought up? (*iro*); (*il est bête*) where did they find him? (*iro*), some mothers do have 'em!* (*Brit*).

2 **vt** (*avec aux avoir*) a (*mener dehors*) *personne, chien* to take out; (*: *accompagner lors d'une sortie*) to take out; (*expulser*) *personne* to throw out. **sortez-le!** throw him out!, get him out of here!; **va au cinéma, cela te sortira** go and see a film, that'll get you out a bit *ou* give you a change of scene; **ça nous a sortis de l'ordinaire** it was *ou* made a bit of a change for us.

b (*retirer*) to take out; (*Aviat*) *train d'atterrissage* to lower. ~ **des vêtements d'une armoire/des bijoux d'un coffret** to get *ou* take clothes out of a wardrobe/jewels out of a (jewel) box; **ils ont réussi à ~ les enfants de la grotte** they managed to get the children out of the cave; **il sortit de sa poche un mouchoir** he took *ou* brought *ou* pulled a handkerchief out of his pocket; ~ **les mains de ses poches** to take one's hands out of one's pockets; ~ **ses bras des manches** to take one's arms out of the sleeves; **il a sorti son passeport** he produced his passport; **les douaniers ont tout sorti de sa valise** the customs men took everything out of his suitcase; **quand il fait beau, on sort les fauteuils dans le jardin** when the weather's nice we take *ou* bring the armchairs out into the garden; (*lit, fig*) **il faut le ~ de là** we have to get him out of there; *voir* **affaire 1a**.

c (*Comm: plus gén* **faire ~**) *marchandises* (*par la douane*) to take out; (*en fraude*) to smuggle out.

d (*mettre en vente*) *voiture, modèle* to bring out; *livre* to bring out, publish; *disque, film [artiste]* to bring out; *[compagnie]* to release.

e (*: *dire*) to come out with*. **il vous sort de ces réflexions!** he comes out with some incredible remarks!*; **elle en a sorti une bien bonne** she came out with a good one*; **qu'est-ce qu'il va encore nous ~?** what will he come out with next?*

f (*: *éliminer d'un concours*) *concurrent, adversaire* to knock out (*fig*).

3 **se sortir** **vpr: se ~ d'une situation difficile** to manage to get out of a difficult situation *ou* to extricate o.s. from a difficult situation; **tu crois qu'il va s'en sortir?** (*il est malade*) do you think he'll pull through?; (*il est surchargé de travail*) do you think he'll ever get to *ou* see the end of it?; (*il est sur la sellette*) do you think he'll come through all right?

4 **nm** (*littér*) **au ~ de l'hiver/de l'enfance** as winter/childhood draws (*ou* drew) to a close; **au ~ de la réunion** at the end of the meeting, when the meeting broke up.

SOS. [ɛsoɛs] **nm** SOS. (*Aviat, Naut*) **lancer un ~** to put out an SOS; (*fig*) **envoyer un ~ à qn** to send an SOS to sb; ~ **médecins/dépannage** *etc* emergency medical/repair *etc* service.

sosie [sɔzi] **nm** double (*person*).

sot, sotte [so, sɔt] 1 **adj** silly, foolish, stupid. (*Prov*) **il n'y a pas de ~ métier** every trade has its value. 2 **nm,f** (†, *frm: niais*) fool; (*enfant*) (little) idiot; (*Hist Littérat: bouffon*) fool.

sotie [sɔti] **nf** (*Hist Littérat*) *satirical farce of 15th and 16th centuries.*

sottement [sɔtmɑ̃] **adv** foolishly, stupidly.

sottise [sɔtiz] **nf** a (*caractère*) stupidity, foolishness. **avoir la ~ de faire** to be foolish *ou* stupid enough to do, have the stupidity to do. b (*parole*) silly *ou* foolish remark; (*action*) silly *ou* foolish thing (to do), folly (†, *frm*). **dire des ~s** *[enfant]* to say silly *ou* stupid *ou* foolish things, make silly *ou* foolish remarks; (†, *frm*) *[philosophe, auteur]* to make foolish affirmations; **faire une ~** *[adulte]* to do a silly *ou* foolish thing, commit a folly (†); **faire des ~s** *[enfant]* to misbehave, be naughty, do naughty things.

sottisier [sɔtizje] **nm** collection of foolish quotations.

sou [su] **nm** a (*monnaie*) (*Hist*) sou, ≃ shilling (*Brit*); (†, *Suisse: cinq centimes*) 5 centimes (*pl*); (*Can* *) cent. (*Can*) **un trente ~s‡** a quarter (*US, Can*).

b (*loc*) **appareil** *ou* **machine à ~s** (*jeu*) one-armed bandit, fruit machine; (*péj, hum: distributeur*) slot machine; **donner/compter/économiser ~ à** *ou* **par ~** to give/count/save penny by penny; **il n'a pas le ~** he hasn't got a penny *ou* a cent *ou* a sou (to his name); **il est sans un** *ou* **le ~** he's penniless; **il n'a pas un ~ vaillant** he hasn't a penny to bless himself with; **dépenser jusqu'à son dernier ~** to spend every last penny; **il n'a pas pour un ~ de méchanceté/bon sens** he hasn't an ounce of unkindness/good sense (in him); **il n'est pas hypocrite/menteur pour un ~** he isn't at all *ou* the least bit hypocritical/untruthful; **propre/reluisant** *ou* **brillant comme un ~ neuf** (as) clean/bright as a new pin, spick and span; **un ~ est un ~** every penny counts; *voir* **cent, gros, près, quatre.**

soubassement [subasmɑ̃] **nm** *[maison]* base; *[murs, fenêtre]* dado; *[colonne]* crepidoma; (*Géol*) bedrock.

soubresaut [subʀəso] **nm** a (*cahot*) jolt. **le véhicule fit un ~** the vehicle gave a jolt; **sa monture fit un ~** his mount gave a sudden start. b (*tressaillement*) (*de peur*) start; (*d'agonie*) convulsive movement. **avoir un ~** to give a start, start (up); to make a convulsive movement.

soubrette [subʀɛt] **nf** (†, *hum: femme de chambre*) maid; (*Théât*) soubrette, maidservant.

souche [suʃ] **nf** a (*Bot*) *[arbre]* stump; *[vigne]* stock. **rester planté comme une ~** to stand stock-still; *voir* **dormir.** b *[famille, race]* founder. **faire ~** to found a line; **de vieille ~** of old stock. c (*Ling*) root. **mot de ~ latine** word with a Latin root; **mot ~** root word. d (*Bio*) *[bactéries, virus]* colony, clone. e (*talon*) counterfoil, stub. **carnet à ~s** counterfoil book. f (*Archit*) *[cheminée]* (chimney) stack.

souci[1] [susi] **nm: ~ (des jardins)** marigold; **~ d'eau** *ou* **des marais** marsh marigold.

souci[2] [susi] **nm** a (*inquiétude*) worry. **se faire du ~** to worry; **être sans ~** to be free of worries *ou* care(s); **cela t'éviterait bien du ~** it would spare you a lot of worry; **cela lui donne (bien) du ~** it worries him (a lot), he worries (a great deal) over it; **~s d'argent** money worries, worries about money.

b (*préoccupation*) concern (*de* for). **avoir ~ du bien-être de son prochain** to have concern for the well-being of one's neighbour; **sa carrière/le bien-être de ses enfants est son unique ~** his career/his children's well-being is his sole concern *ou* is all he worries about; **cet enfant est un ~ perpétuel pour ses parents** this child is a constant source of worry for his parents; **avoir le ~ de bien faire** to be concerned about doing things well; **dans le ~ de lui plaire** in his concern to please her; **c'est le moindre** *ou* **le cadet** *ou* **le dernier de mes ~s** that's the least of my worries.

soucier [susje] 7 1 **se soucier** **vpr: se ~ de** to care about; **se ~ des autres** to care about *ou* for others, show concern for others; **je ne m'en soucie guère** I am quite indifferent to it; **il s'en soucie comme de sa première chemise** *ou* **comme de l'an quarante*** he doesn't give *ou* care a fig *ou* a hoot* (about it)*, he couldn't care less (about it)*; (*littér*) **il se soucie peu de plaire** he cares little *ou* he doesn't bother whether he is liked or not; **il se soucie fort de ce qu'ils pensent** he cares very much what they think; (*littér*) **se ~ que** + *subj* to care that. 2 **vt** (†, *littér*) to worry, trouble.

soucieusement [susjøzmɑ̃] **adv** with concern.

soucieux, -ieuse [susjø, jøz] **adj** a (*inquiet*) *personne, air, ton* concerned, worried. **peu ~** unconcerned. b **être ~ de qch** to be concerned *ou* preoccupied with *ou* about sth; **~ de son seul intérêt** concerned *ou* preoccupied solely with *ou* about his own interests; **être ~ de faire** to be anxious to do; (*frm*) **~ que** concerned *ou* anxious that; **peu ~ qu'on le voie** caring little *ou* unconcerned whether he be *ou* is seen or not.

soucoupe [sukup] **nf** saucer. **~ volante** flying saucer; *voir* **œil.**

soudage [sudaʒ] **nm** (*avec brasure, fil à souder*) soldering; (*autogène*) welding.

soudain, e [sudɛ̃, ɛn] 1 **adj** (*gén*) sudden; *mort* sudden, unexpected. 2 **adv** (*tout à coup*) suddenly, all of a sudden. **~, il se mit à pleurer** all of a sudden he started to cry, he suddenly started to cry.

soudainement [sudɛnmɑ̃] **adv** suddenly.

soudaineté [sudɛnte] **nf** suddenness.

Soudan [sudɑ̃] **nm: le ~** (the) Sudan.

soudanais, e [sudanɛ, ɛz] 1 **adj** Sudanese, of *ou* from (the) Sudan. 2 **nm,f: S~(e)** Sudanese, inhabitant *ou* native of (the) Sudan.

soudard [sudaʀ] **nm** (*péj*) ruffianly *ou* roughneck soldier.

soude [sud] **nf** a (*industrielle*) soda. **~ caustique** caustic soda; *voir* **bicarbonate, cristal.** b (*Bot*) saltwort. (*Chim*) **(cendre de) ~†** soda ash.

soudé, e [sude] (**ptp de souder**) **adj** a *organes, pétales* joined (together). b (*fig: rivé*) **~ au plancher/à la paroi** glued to the floor/wall.

souder [sude] 1 1 **vt** a *métal* (*avec brasure, fil à souder*) to solder; (*soudure autogène*) to weld. **~ à chaud/froid** to hot-/cold-weld; *voir* **fer, fil, lampe.** b *os* to knit. c (*fig: unir*) *choses, organismes* to fuse (together); (*littér*) *cœurs, êtres* to bind *ou* knit together (*littér*), unite. 2 **se souder** **vpr** *[os]* to knit together; (*littér: s'unir*) to be knit together (*littér*).

soudeur, -euse [sudœʀ, øz] 1 **nm,f** (*voir* **souder**) solderer; welder. 2 **soudeuse** **nf** (*machine*) welder.

soudoyer [sudwaje] 8 **vt** (*péj*) to bribe, buy over.

soudure [sudyʀ] **nf** a (*Tech: voir* **souder**) (*opération*) soldering; welding; (*endroit*) soldered joint; weld; (*substance*) solder. **~ à l'arc** arc welding; **~ autogène** welding; **~ au chalumeau** torch welding. b *[os]* knitting; *[organes, pétales]* join; (*littér*) *[partis, cœurs]* binding *ou* knitting (*littér*) together, uniting. c (*loc*) **faire la ~ (entre)** to bridge the gap (between).

soufflage [suflaʒ] **nm** a **~ du verre** glass-blowing. b (*Métal*) blowing.

soufflant, e [suflɑ̃, ɑ̃t] **adj** (*: *étonnant*) staggering, stunning. **(radiateur) ~** fan heater.

souffle [sufl] **nm** a (*expiration*) (*en soufflant*) blow, puff; (*en respirant*) breath. **éteindre une bougie d'un ~ (puissant)** to put out a candle with a (hard) puff *ou* blow *ou* by blowing (hard); **il murmura mon nom dans un ~** he breathed my name; **le dernier ~ d'un agonisant** the last breath of a dying man; **pour jouer d'un instrument à vent, il faut du ~** you need a lot of breath *ou* puff* (*Brit*) to play a wind instrument.

b (*respiration*) breathing. **le ~ régulier d'un dormeur** the regular breathing of someone asleep; **on entendait un ~ dans l'obscurité** we heard (someone) breathing in the darkness; **il a du ~** (*lit*) he has a lot of breath *ou* puff* (*Brit*); (* *fig*) (*culot, témérité*) he has some nerve*; **manquer de ~** to be short of breath; **avoir le ~ court** to be short-winded; **retenir son ~** to hold one's breath; **reprendre son ~** to get one's breath back, regain one's breath; **n'avoir plus de ~, être à bout de ~** to be out of breath; (*lit*) **avoir le ~ coupé** to be winded; (*fig*) **il en a eu le ~ coupé** it (quite) took his breath away; **c'est à vous couper le ~** it's enough to take your breath away *ou* to make you gasp; *voir* **second**.

c (*déplacement d'air*) *[incendie, ventilateur, explosion]* blast.

d (*vent*) puff *ou* breath of air, puff of wind. **le ~ du vent dans les feuilles** the wind blowing through the leaves, the leaves blowing in the wind; **un ~ d'air faisait bruire le feuillage** a slight breeze was rustling the leaves; **brin d'herbe agité au moindre ~ (d'air *ou* de vent)** blade of grass blown about by the slightest puff *ou* breath of air *ou* the slightest puff (of wind); **il n'y avait pas un ~ (d'air *ou* de vent)** there was not a breath of air.

e (*fig: force créatrice*) inspiration. **le ~ du génie** the inspiration born of genius; (*Rel*) **le ~ créateur** the breath of God.

f (*Méd*) **~ cardiaque *ou* au cœur** cardiac *ou* heart murmur; *voir* **bruit**.

soufflé, e [sufle] (**ptp de souffler**) 1 **adj** a (*Culin*) soufflé (*épith*). b (*) (*surpris*) flabbergasted*, staggered*. 2 **nm** (*Culin*) soufflé. **~ au fromage** cheese soufflé.

souffler [sufle] [1] 1 **vi** a *[vent, personne]* to blow. **~ sur le feu** to blow on the fire; **~ dans un instrument à vent** to blow (into) a wind instrument; **~ sur une bougie (pour l'éteindre)** to blow a candle (to put it out), blow out a candle; **~ sur sa soupe (pour la faire refroidir)** to blow (on) one's soup (to cool it); **~ sur ses doigts (pour les réchauffer)** to blow on one's fingers (to warm them up); (*lit, fig*) **observer *ou* regarder de quel côté le vent souffle** to see which way the wind is blowing; **le vent a soufflé si fort qu'il a abattu deux arbres** the wind was so strong *ou* blew so hard (that) it brought two trees down; **le vent soufflait en rafales** the wind was blowing in gusts; **le vent soufflait en tempête** it was blowing a gale, the wind was howling; (*fig*) **il croit qu'il va y arriver en soufflant dessus*** he thinks it's going to be a cinch*.

b (*respirer avec peine*) to puff (and blow). **il ne peut monter les escaliers sans ~** he can't go up the stairs without puffing (and blowing); **~ comme un bœuf *ou* un phoque*** to puff and blow like a grampus.

c (*se reposer*) **laisser ~ qn/un animal** to give sb/an animal a breather, let sb/an animal get his/its breath back; **il ne prend jamais le temps de ~** he never lets up, he never stops to get his breath back; **donnez-lui un peu de temps pour ~** (*pour se reposer*) give him time to get his breath back, give him a breather; (*avant de payer*) give him a breather*.

2 **vt** a *bougie, feu* to blow out.

b **~ de la fumée au nez de qn** to blow smoke in(to) sb's face; **~ des odeurs d'ail au visage de qn** to breathe garlic over sb *ou* into sb's face; **le ventilateur soufflait des odeurs de graillon** the fan was blowing *ou* giving out greasy smells; **le vent leur soufflait le sable dans les yeux** the wind was blowing the sand into their eyes; (*fig*) **~ le chaud et le froid** to lay down the law.

c (*: *prendre*) to pinch*, nick** (*Brit*), swipe** (*à qn* from sb). **il lui a soufflé sa petite amie/son poste** he has swiped** *ou* pinched* his girlfriend/his job; (*Dames*) **~ un pion** to huff a draught.

d *[bombe, explosion]* **leur maison a été soufflée par une bombe** their house was destroyed by the blast from a bomb.

e (*dire*) *conseil, réponse, réplique* to whisper (*à qn* to sb). **~ sa leçon à qn** to whisper sb's lesson to him; (*Théât*) **~ son rôle à qn** to prompt sb, give sb a prompt, whisper sb's lines to him; (*Théât*) **qui est-ce qui souffle ce soir?** who's prompting this evening?; **~ qch à l'oreille de qn** to whisper sth in sb's ear; **ne pas ~ mot** not to breathe a word.

f (*: *étonner*) to flabbergast*, stagger*. **elle a été soufflée d'apprendre leur échec** she was flabbergasted* *ou* staggered* to hear of their failure; **leur toupet m'a soufflé** I was flabbergasted* *ou* staggered* at their nerve.

g (*Tech*) **~ le verre** to blow glass.

soufflerie [suflǝʀi] **nf** *[orgue, forge]* bellows; (*Tech: d'aération etc*) ventilating fan; (*Ind*) blowing engine. (*Aviat*) **~ (aérodynamique)** wind tunnel.

soufflet[1] [suflɛ] **nm** a *[forge]* bellows (*pl*). b (*Rail*) vestibule; (*Couture*) gusset; *[sac, classeur]* extendible gusset; *[appareil photographique]* bellows (*pl*).

soufflet[2] [suflɛ] **nm** (*littér*) slap in the face.

souffleter [suflǝte] [4] **vt** (*littér*) **~ qn** to give sb a slap in the face.

souffleur, -euse [suflœʀ, øz] 1 **nm,f** (*Théât*) prompter. (*Tech*) **~ de verre** glass-blower; *voir* **trou**. 2 **souffleuse nf** (*Can*) snowblower.

souffrance [sufʀɑ̃s] **nf** a (*douleur*) suffering. b (*fig*) **être en ~** *[marchandises, colis]* to be awaiting delivery, be held up; *[affaire, dossier]* to be pending, be waiting to be dealt with.

souffrant, e [sufʀɑ̃, ɑ̃t] **adj** a (*malade*) *personne* unwell, poorly*. b (*littér*) **l'humanité ~e** suffering humanity; **l'Église ~e** the Church suffering.

souffre-douleur [sufʀǝdulœʀ] **nmf inv** scapegoat, underdog. **être le ~ de qn/d'un groupe** to be sb's scapegoat/the underdog *ou* scapegoat of a group.

souffreteux, -euse [sufʀǝtø, øz] **adj** sickly.

souffrir [sufʀiʀ] [18] 1 **vi** a (*physiquement*) to suffer. **la pauvre fille souffre beaucoup** the poor girl is in great pain *ou* is suffering a great deal; **où souffrez-vous?** where is the pain?, where are you in pain?, where does it hurt?; (*lit, fig*) **~ en silence** to suffer in silence; **~ comme un damné** to suffer torture *ou* torment(s); **faire ~ qn** *[personne, blessure]* to hurt sb; **mes cors me font ~** my corns are hurting (me) *ou* are painful; **~ de la tête** to have a headache; (*habituellement*) to have headaches; **~ de l'estomac/des reins** to have stomach/kidney trouble; **il souffre d'une grave maladie/de rhumatismes** he is suffering from a serious illness/from rheumatism; **~ du froid/de la chaleur** to suffer from the cold/from the heat.

b (*moralement*) to suffer (*de* from). **faire ~ qn** *[personne]* to make sb suffer; *[attitude, événement]* to cause sb pain; **il a beaucoup souffert d'avoir été chassé de son pays** he has suffered a great deal from being chased out of his country; **je souffre de le voir si affaibli** it pains *ou* grieves me to see him so weakened; **j'en souffrais pour lui** I felt bad for him.

c (*pâtir*) to suffer. **les fraises souffrent de la chaleur** strawberries suffer in (the) heat; **les fraises ont souffert du gel tardif** the strawberries have suffered from *ou* have been hard hit by the late frost; **ils sont lents, et la productivité en souffre** they are slow and productivity is suffering; **sa réputation en a souffert** his reputation suffered by it; **ils souffrent d'un manque d'expérience certain** they suffer from a definite lack of experience; **la nation a souffert de la guerre** the nation has suffered from the war.

d (*: *éprouver de la difficulté*) **on a fini par gagner, mais ils nous ont fait ~ *ou* mais on a souffert** we won in the end but they gave us a rough time* *ou* they put us through it*; **les sciences m'ont toujours fait ~** science has always given me trouble; **j'ai souffert pour lui faire comprendre** I had enormous difficulty *ou* great trouble getting him to understand.

2 **vt** a (*éprouver*) *pertes* to endure, suffer; *tourments* to endure, undergo. **~ le martyre** to go through agonies, go through hell on earth; **sa jambe lui fait ~ le martyre** his leg gives him agonies; **~ mille morts** to go through agonies, die a thousand deaths.

b (*supporter*) *affront, mépris* to suffer, endure. **je ne peux ~ de te voir malheureux** I cannot bear *ou* endure to see you unhappy, I cannot abide seeing you unhappy; **il ne peut pas ~ le mensonge/les épinards** he can't stand *ou* bear lies/spinach; **elle ne peut pas le ~** she can't stand *ou* bear him; **il ne peut pas ~ que ...** he cannot bear that ... .

c (*littér: tolérer*) **~ que** to allow *ou* permit that; **souffrez que je vous contredise** allow *ou* permit me to contradict you; **je ne souffrirai pas que mon fils en pâtisse** I will not allow my son to suffer from it.

d (*admettre*) **cette affaire ne peut ~ aucun retard** this matter admits of *ou* allows of no delay *ou* simply cannot be delayed; **la règle souffre quelques exceptions** the rule admits of *ou* allows of a few exceptions; **la règle ne peut ~ aucune exception** the rule admits of no exception.

3 **se souffrir vpr** (*se supporter*) **ils ne peuvent pas se ~** they can't stand *ou* bear each other.

soufisme [sufism] **nm** Sufism.

soufrage [sufʀaʒ] **nm** *[vigne, laine]* sulphuration; *[allumettes]* sulphuring.

soufre [sufʀ] **nm** sulphur. **jaune ~** sulphur yellow; (*fig*) **sentir le ~** to smack of heresy.

soufrer [sufʀe] [1] **vt** *vigne* to (treat with) sulphur; *allumettes* to sulphur; *laine* to sulphurate.

soufrière [sufʀijɛʀ] **nf** sulphur mine. **la S~** the Soufrière.

souhait [swɛ] **nm** wish. **formuler des ~s pour qch** to express one's best wishes for sth; **les ~s de bonne année** New Year greetings, good wishes for the New Year; **tous nos ~s de réussite** our best wishes for your success; **à tes ~s!** bless you!; **la viande était rôtie à ~** the meat was done to perfection; **le vin était fruité à ~** the wine was delightfully fruity *ou* as fruity as one could wish; **tout marchait à ~** everything went as well as one could wish *ou* went perfectly; **tout lui réussit à ~** everything works to perfection for him, everything works like a charm for him.

souhaitable [swɛtabl] **adj** desirable.

souhaiter [swete] [1] **vt** a *réussite, changements* to wish for. **~ que** to hope that; **il est à ~ que** it is to be hoped that; **ce n'est pas à ~** we don't want that to happen; **je souhaite qu'il réussisse** I hope he succeeds, I would like him to succeed; **je souhaite réussir** I hope to succeed; **~ pouvoir *ou* (*littér*) ~ de pouvoir étudier/partir à l'étranger** to hope to be able to study/go abroad; (*littér*) **je le souhaitais mort/loin** I wished him dead/far away; **je souhaitais l'examen terminé** I wished the exam were over, I wished the exam (to be) over; **je souhaiterais vous aider** I wish I could help you.

b **~ à qn le bonheur/la réussite** to wish sb happiness/success; **je**

vous souhaite bien des choses all good wishes, every good wish; ~ **à qn de réussir** to wish sb success; (*iro*) **je vous souhaite bien du plaisir!** I wish you joy! (*iro*), I wish you luck of it!; ~ **la bonne année/bonne chance à qn** to wish sb a happy New Year/(the best of) luck; **je vous la souhaite bonne et heureuse**‡ here's hoping you have a really good New Year!*

souiller [suje] 1 **vt** (*littér*) (*lit*) *drap, vêtement* to soil, dirty; *atmosphère* to dirty; (*fig*) *réputation, pureté, âme* to soil, dirty, sully, tarnish. **souillé de boue** spattered with mud; (*fig*) **le besoin de tout ~ qu'éprouve cet auteur** this author's need to defile everything; (*fig*) ~ **ses mains du sang des innocents** to stain one's hands with the blood of innocents; (†: *fig*) ~ **la couche nuptiale** to defile the conjugal bed.

souillon [sujɔ̃] **nf** slattern, slut.

souillure [sujyʀ] **nf** (*littér*) (*lit*) stain; (*fig*) blemish, stain. **la ~ du péché** the stain of sin.

souk [suk] **nm** (*lit*) souk. (*fig*) **c'est le ~ ici!*** it's like a cattle market in here.

soul [sul] (*Mus*) 1 **adj inv** soul (*épith*). 2 **nm ou f** soul.

soûl, soûle [su, sul] 1 **adj** a (*ivre*) drunk, drunken (*épith*). ~ **comme une bourrique** *ou* **un Polonais*** (as) drunk as a lord (*surtout Brit*), blind drunk*. b (*fig*) **~s de musique/poésie après 3 jours de festival** our (*ou* their) heads reeling with music/poetry after 3 days of the festival; (*littér*) ~ **de plaisirs** surfeited *ou* satiated with pleasures.
2 **nm**: **manger tout son ~** to eat one's fill, eat to one's heart's content; **chanter tout son ~** to sing to one's heart's content; **elle a ri/pleuré tout son ~** she laughed/cried till she could laugh/cry no more.

soulagement [sulaʒmɑ̃] **nm** relief. **ça a été un ~ d'apprendre que** it was a relief *ou* I was (*ou* we were *etc*) relieved to learn that.

soulager [sulaʒe] 3 1 **vt** a *personne* (*physiquement*) to relieve; (*moralement*) to relieve, soothe; *douleur* to relieve, soothe; *maux* to relieve; *conscience* to ease. **ça le soulage de s'étendre** he finds relief in stretching out, it relieves him *ou* his pain to stretch out; **ça le soulage de prendre ces pilules** these pills bring him relief; **buvez, ça vous soulagera** drink this — it'll give you relief *ou* make you feel better; **être soulagé d'avoir fait qch** to be relieved to have done sth; **cet aveu l'a soulagé** this confession made him feel better *ou* eased his conscience *ou* took a weight off his mind; ~ **les pauvres/les déshérités** to bring relief to *ou* relieve the poor/the underprivileged; **il faut ~ la pauvreté** we must relieve poverty.
b (*décharger*) *personne* to relieve (*de* of); (*Archit*) *mur, poutre* to relieve the strain on. (*hum*) ~ **qn de son portefeuille** to relieve sb of his wallet (*hum*).
2 **se soulager vpr** a (*se décharger d'un souci*) to find relief, ease one's feelings, make o.s. feel better; (*apaiser sa conscience*) to ease one's conscience. **elle se soulageait en lui prodiguant des insultes** she found relief in *ou* eased her feelings by throwing insults at him; **leurs consciences se soulagent à bon marché** their consciences can be eased at little expense.
b (*: *euph*) to relieve o.s.

soûlant, e* [sulɑ̃, ɑ̃t] **adj** wearing. **tu es ~ avec tes questions** you're wearing me out *ou* tiring me out with your questions.

soûlard, e‡ [sulaʀ, aʀd] **nm,f**, **soûlaud, e**‡ [sulo, od] **nm,f** drunkard.

soûler [sule] 1 1 **vt** a (*: *rendre ivre*) ~ **qn** *[personne]* to get sb drunk; *[boisson]* to make sb drunk.
b (*fig*) ~ **qn** (*fatiguer*) to make sb's head spin *ou* reel; (*littér: griser*) *[parfum]* to go to sb's head, intoxicate sb; *[vent, vitesse, théories, visions]* to intoxicate *ou* inebriate sb, make sb's head spin *ou* reel.
c (*fig*) ~ **qn de** *théories, promesses* to intoxicate sb with, make sb's head spin *ou* reel with; *questions, conseils* to wear *ou* tire sb out with; *luxe, sensations* to intoxicate sb with; **chaque fois qu'il vient, il nous soûle de paroles** every time he comes his endless talking makes our heads spin.
2 **se soûler vpr** (*: *s'enivrer*) to get drunk. **se ~ la gueule**‡ to get pissed‡‡ (*Brit*) *ou* blind drunk*; (*fig*) **se ~ de** *bruit, vitesse, vent, parfums* to intoxicate o.s. with, get high* *ou* drunk on; *théories, visions, sensations* to intoxicate o.s. with, make o.s. drunk with *ou* on.

soûlerie [sulʀi] **nf** (*péj*) drunken binge.

soulèvement [sulɛvmɑ̃] **nm** a (*révolte*) uprising. b (*Géol*) upthrust, upheaval.

soulever [sul(ə)ve] 5 1 **vt** a (*lever*) *fardeau, malade, couvercle, rideau* to lift (up). ~ **qn de terre** to lift sb (up) off the ground; (*fig*) **cela me soulève le cœur** *[odeur]* it makes me feel sick *ou* want to heave, it turns my stomach; *[attitude]* it makes me sick, it turns my stomach; (*fig*) **cette déclaration a permis de ~ un coin du voile** this declaration has thrown a little light on the matter.
b (*remuer*) *poussière* to raise. **le véhicule soulevait des nuages de poussière** the vehicle made clouds of dust fly *ou* swirl up, the vehicle sent up *ou* raised clouds of dust; **le bateau soulevait de grosses vagues** the boat was sending up great waves; **le vent soulevait les vagues/le sable** the wind made the waves swell, *ou* whipped up the waves/blew *ou* whipped up the sand.
c (*indigner*) to stir up; (*pousser à la révolte*) to stir up *ou* rouse (to revolt); (*exalter*) to stir. ~ **l'opinion publique (contre qn)** to stir up *ou* rouse public opinion (against sb).
d (*provoquer*) *enthousiasme, colère* to arouse; *prostestations, applaudissements* to raise; *difficultés, questions* to raise, bring up.
e (*évoquer*) *question, problème* to raise, bring up.
f (‡: *voler*) ~ **qch (à qn)** to pinch* *ou* swipe‡ sth (from sb).
2 **se soulever vpr** a (*se lever*) to lift o.s. up. **soulève-toi pour que je redresse ton oreiller** lift yourself up *ou* sit up a bit so that I can plump up your pillow.
b (*être levé*) *[véhicule, couvercle, rideau]* to lift; (*fig*) *[vagues, mer]* to swell (up). (*fig*) **à cette vue, le cœur se soulève** the sight of it makes one's stomach turn; (*fig*) **à cette vue, son cœur se souleva** his stomach turned at the sight.
c (*s'insurger*) to rise up.

soulier [sulje] **nm** shoe. **~s bas/plats** low-heeled/flat shoes; **~s montants** boots; **~s de marche** walking shoes; (*fig*) **être dans ses petits ~s** to feel awkward.

soulignage [suliɲaʒ] **nm**, **soulignement** [suliɲmɑ̃] **nm** underlining.

souligner [suliɲe] 1 **vt** a (*lit*) to underline; (*fig: accentuer*) to accentuate, emphasize. ~ **qch d'un trait double** to double underline sth, underline sth with a double line; ~ **qch en rouge** to underline sth in red; ~ **ses yeux de noir** to accentuate one's eyes with black eye-liner; **ce tissu à rayures soulignait son embonpoint** that striped material emphasized *ou* accentuated his stoutness. b (*faire remarquer*) to underline, stress, emphasize. **il souligna l'importance de cette rencontre** he underlined *ou* stressed *ou* emphasized the importance of this meeting.

soûlographie* [sulɔgʀafi] **nf** (*hum*) drunkenness, boozing*.

soumettre [sumɛtʀ] 56 1 **vt** a (*dompter*) *pays, peuple* to subject, subjugate; *personne* to subject; *rebelles* to put down, subdue, subjugate.
b (*asservir*) ~ **qn à** *maître, loi* to subject sb to.
c (*astreindre*) ~ **qn à** *traitement, formalité, régime, impôt* to subject sb to; ~ **qch à** *traitement, essai, taxe* to subject sth to; **tout citoyen/ce revenu est soumis à l'impôt** every citizen/this income is subject to tax(ation).
d (*présenter*) *idée, cas, manuscrit* to submit (*à* to). ~ **une idée/un projet/une question à qn** to submit an idea/a plan/a matter to sb, put an idea/a plan/a matter before sb.
2 **se soumettre vpr** a (*obéir*) to submit (*à* to).
b **se ~ à** *traitement, formalité* to submit to; *entraînement, régime* to submit *ou* subject o.s. to.

soumis, e [sumi, iz] (**ptp de soumettre**) **adj** (*docile*) *personne, air* submissive; *voir* **fille**.

soumission [sumisjɔ̃] **nf** a (*obéissance*) submission (*à* to). **il est toujours d'une parfaite ~ à leur égard** he is always totally submissive to their wishes. b (*acte de reddition*) submission. **ils ont fait leur ~** they have submitted. c (*Comm*) tender.

soumissionnaire [sumisjɔnɛʀ] **nmf** (*Comm*) bidder, tenderer.

soumissionner [sumisjɔne] 1 **vt** (*Comm*) to bid for, tender for.

soupape [supap] **nf** valve. (*lit, fig*) ~ **de sûreté** *ou* **de sécurité** safety valve; (*Aut*) ~ **d'admission/d'échappement** inlet/exhaust valve; (*Aut*) **~s en tête/en chapelle** *ou* **latérale** overhead/side valves.

soupçon [supsɔ̃] **nm** a (*suspicion*) suspicion. **conduite exempte de tout ~** conduct free from all suspicion; **homme à l'abri de** *ou* **au-dessus de tout ~** man free from *ou* man above all *ou* any suspicion; **de graves ~s pèsent sur lui** he's under serious suspicion; **sa femme eut bientôt des ~s** his wife soon had her suspicions *ou* became suspicious; **éveiller les ~s de qn** to arouse sb's suspicions; **avoir ~ de qch** to suspect sth; **des difficultés dont il n'avait pas ~** difficulties of which he had no inkling *ou* no suspicion; **avoir ~ que** to suspect that, have an inkling that.
b (*petite quantité*) *[assaisonnement, maquillage, vulgarité]* hint, touch, suggestion; *[vin, lait]* drop.

soupçonnable [supsɔnabl] **adj** (*gén nég*) that arouses suspicion(s).

soupçonner [supsɔne] 1 **vt** to suspect. **il est soupçonné de vol** he is suspected of theft; **on le soupçonne d'y avoir participé, on soupçonne qu'il y a participé** he is suspected of having taken part in it; **il soupçonnait un piège** he suspected a trap; **vous ne soupçonnez pas ce que ça demande comme travail** you haven't an inkling *ou* you've no idea how much work that involves.

soupçonneusement [supsɔnøzmɑ̃] **adv** with suspicion, suspiciously.

soupçonneux, -euse [supsɔnø, øz] **adj** suspicious.

soupe [sup] **nf** a (*Culin*) soup. ~ **à l'oignon/aux légumes/de poisson** onion/vegetable/fish soup; *voir* **cheveu, gros, marchand** *etc*.
b (*hum: nourriture*) grub‡, nosh‡. **à la ~!** grub's up!‡, come and get it!
c (*: *Ski*) porridge*.
d (*Bio*) ~ **primitive** primeval soup.
e (*loc*) **avoir droit à la ~ à la grimace** to be given a frosty reception on arriving home; **il est (très) ~ au lait, c'est une ~ au lait** he flies off the handle easily, he's very quick-tempered, he's very quick to flare up; ~ **populaire** (*lit*) soup kitchen; (*fig*) **être réduit à la ~ populaire** to be on one's uppers*; **par ici la bonne ~!*** roll up! roll up! and hand over your money!; (*fig*) **aller à la ~*** to be on the lookout for a backhander*; **il est allé à la ~*** he has taken a backhander*.

soupente [supɑ̃t] **nf** cupboard (*Brit*) *ou* closet (*US*) (under the stairs).

souper [supe] 1 nm supper; (*Belgique, Can, Suisse: dîner*) dinner, supper. 2 vi 1 a to have supper; (*Belgique, Can, Suisse*) to have dinner *ou* supper. **après le spectacle, nous sommes allés ~** after the show we went for supper. b (*) **j'en ai soupé de ces histoires!** I'm sick and tired* *ou* I've had a bellyful‡ of all this fuss!

soupeser [supəze] 5 vt (*lit*) to weigh in one's hand(s), feel the weight of; (*fig*) to weigh up.

soupière [supjɛʀ] nf (soup) tureen.

soupir [supiʀ] nm a sigh. **~ de soulagement** sigh of relief; **pousser un ~ de soulagement** to heave a sigh of relief; **pousser un gros ~** to let out *ou* give a heavy sigh, sigh heavily; (*littér*) **les ~s du vent** the sighing *ou* soughing (*littér*) of the wind; *voir* **dernier.** b (*Mus*) crotchet rest (*Brit*), quarter(-note) rest (*US*); *voir* **demi-, quart.**

soupirail, pl **-aux** [supiʀaj, o] nm (small) basement window (*gen with bars*).

soupirant [supiʀɑ̃] nm († *ou hum*) suitor († *ou hum*), wooer († *ou hum*).

soupirer [supiʀe] 1 vi (*lit*) to sigh. **~ d'aise** to sigh with contentment; (*littér*) **~ après** *ou* **pour qch/qn** to sigh for sth/sb (*littér*), yearn for sth/sb; **"j'ai tout perdu" soupira-t-il** "I've lost everything" he sighed; **... dit-il en soupirant** ... he said with a sigh.

souple [supl] adj a (*flexible*) *corps, membres, matériau* supple; *branche, tige* pliable, supple; *lentilles cornéennes* soft; *col* soft, floppy. **~ comme un chat** *ou* **une chatte** as agile as a cat; *voir* **échine.** b (*fig: qui s'adapte*) *personne, caractère, esprit* flexible, adaptable; *discipline, forme d'expression, règlement* flexible. c (*gracieux, fluide*) *corps, silhouette* lithe, lissom (*littér*); *démarche, taille* lithe, supple; *style* fluid, flowing (*épith*).

souplesse [suplɛs] nf (*voir* **souple**) suppleness; pliability; flexibility; adaptability; litheness; lissomness (*littér*); fluidity. **faire qch en ~** to do sth smoothly; **un démarrage en ~** a smooth start.

souquenille [suknij] nf (*Hist*) smock.

souquer [suke] 1 1 vt to tighten. 2 vi: **~ ferme** *ou* **dur** to pull hard (at the oars).

sourate [suRat] nf sura.

source [surs] nf a (*point d'eau*) spring. **~ thermale/d'eau minérale** hot *ou* thermal/mineral spring; *voir* **couler, eau.**

b (*foyer*) **~ de chaleur/d'énergie** source of heat/energy; **~ lumineuse** *ou* **de lumière** source of light, light source; **~ sonore** source of sound.

c *[cours d'eau]* source. **cette rivière prend sa ~ dans le Massif central** this river has its source in *ou* springs up in the Massif Central.

d (*fig: origine*) source. **~ de ridicule/profits** source of ridicule/profit; **l'argent est la ~ de tous nos maux** money is the root of all our ills; **de ~ sûre, de bonne ~** from a reliable source, on good authority; **tenir qch de ~ sûre** to have sth on good authority, get sth from a reliable source; **de ~ généralement bien informée** from a usually well-informed *ou* accurate source; **de ~ autorisée** from an official source; (*Ordin*) **langage/programme ~** source language/program; (*Ling*) **langue ~** departure *ou* source language; *voir* **retenue[2], retour.**

sourcier, -ière [sursje, jɛʀ] nm,f water diviner; *voir* **baguette.**

sourcil [sursi] nm (eye)brow. **aux ~s épais** heavy-browed, beetle-browed; *voir* **froncer.**

sourcilier, -ière [sursilje, jɛʀ] adj superciliary; *voir* **arcade.**

sourciller [sursije] 1 vi: **il n'a pas sourcillé** he didn't turn a hair *ou* bat an eyelid; **écoutant sans ~ mes reproches** listening to my reproaches without turning a hair *ou* batting an eyelid.

sourcilleux, -euse [sursijø, øz] adj (*pointilleux*) finicky; (*littér: hautain*) haughty.

sourd, e [suʀ, surd] 1 adj a *personne* deaf. **~ d'une oreille** deaf in one ear; **être ~ comme un pot*** to be as deaf as a post; **faire la ~e oreille (à des supplications)** to turn a deaf ear (to entreaties); *voir* **naissance.**

b **~ à** *conseils, prières* deaf to; *vacarme, environnement* oblivious of *ou* to.

c *son* muffled, muted; *couleur* muted, toned-down, subdued; (*Phon*) *consonne* voiceless, unvoiced; *voir* **lanterne.**

d (*vague*) *douleur* dull; *désir, angoisse, inquiétude* muted, gnawing; *colère, hostilité* veiled, subdued, muted.

e (*caché*) *lutte, menées* silent, hidden. **se livrer à de ~es manigances** to be engaged in hidden manoeuvring.

2 nm,f deaf person. **les ~s** the deaf; **~(e)-muet(te),** *mpl* **~s-muets (adj)** deaf-and-dumb; (nm,f) deaf-mute; **taper** *ou* **frapper** *ou* **cogner comme un ~** to bang with all one's might; **crier** *ou* **hurler comme un ~** to yell like a deaf man *ou* at the top of one's voice; (*Prov*) **il n'est pire ~ que celui qui ne veut pas entendre** there are none so deaf as those who will not hear (*Prov*); *voir* **dialogue, pire, tomber.**

3 **sourde** nf (*Phon*) voiceless *ou* unvoiced consonant.

sourdement [surdəmɑ̃] adv (*avec un bruit assourdi*) dully; (*littér: souterrainement, secrètement*) silently. **le tonnerre grondait ~ au loin** there was a muffled rumble of thunder *ou* thunder rumbled dully in the distance.

sourdine [suRdin] nf mute. **jouer en ~** to play softly *ou* quietly; (*fig*) **faire qch en ~** to do sth on the quiet; (*fig*) **mettre une ~ à** *prétentions* to tone down; *enthousiasme* to damp.

sourdingue‡ [surdɛ̃g] adj, nmf: **il est ~, c'est un ~** he's a clothears*.

sourdre [surdʀ] vi *[source]* to rise; *[eau]* to spring up, rise; (*fig, littér*) to well up, rise.

souriant, e [surjɑ̃, jɑ̃t] adj *visage* smiling; *personne* cheerful; (*fig*) *pensée, philosophie* benign, agreeable.

souriceau, pl **~x** [suriso] nm young mouse.

souricière [surisjɛʀ] nf (*lit*) mousetrap; (*fig*) trap.

sourire [suriʀ] 1 nm smile. **le ~ aux lèvres** with a smile on his lips; **avec le ~** (*accueillir qn*) with a smile; (*exécuter une tâche*) cheerfully; **gardez le ~!** keep smiling!; (*lit, fig*) **avoir le ~** to have a smile on one's face; **faire** *ou* **adresser un ~ à qn** to give sb a smile; **faire des ~s à qn** to keep smiling at sb; **un large ~** (*chaleureux*) a broad smile; (*amusé*) a (broad) grin, a broad smile; *voir* **coin.**

2 vi 36 a to smile (*à qn* at sb). **~ à la vie** to delight in living; (*lit*) **cette remarque les fit ~** this remark made them smile *ou* brought a smile to their faces; (*fig*) **ce projet ridicule fait ~** this ridiculous project is laughable; **je souris de le voir si vaniteux** it makes me smile to see how vain he is; **il sourit de nos efforts** he laughs at our efforts, our efforts make him smile; **il ne faut pas ~ de ces menaces** these threats can't just be laughed *ou* shrugged off.

b **~ à** (*plaire à*) to appeal to; (*être favorable à*) to smile on, favour; **cette idée ne me sourit guère** that idea doesn't appeal to me, I don't fancy that idea* (*Brit*); **l'idée de faire cela ne me sourit pas** I don't relish the thought of doing that, the idea of doing that doesn't appeal to me; **la chance lui souriait** luck smiled on him.

souris[1] [suri] nf a (*Zool*) mouse. **~ blanche** white mouse (*bred for experiments*); (*fig: pour espionner*) **je voudrais bien être une petite ~** it would be interesting to be *ou* I wish I were a fly on the wall; *voir* **gris, jouer, trou.** b (‡: *femme*) bird* (*Brit*), chick* (*US*). **~ d'hôtel** sneak thief (*operating in hotels*). c *[gigot]* knuckle-joint. d (*Ordin*) mouse.

souris[2]†† [suri] nm smile.

sournois, e [surnwa, waz] 1 adj *personne, regard, air* deceitful, sly, shifty; *méthode, propos, attaque* underhand. 2 nm: **c'est un petit ~** he's a sly little devil*.

sournoisement [surnwazmɑ̃] adv (*voir* **sournois**) deceitfully; in an underhand manner; shiftily. **il s'approcha ~ de lui** he stole *ou* crept stealthily up to him.

sournoiserie [surnwazri] nf (*voir* **sournois:** *littér*) deceitfulness; underhand manner; shiftiness.

sous [su] 1 prép a (*position*) under, underneath, beneath; (*atmosphère*) in. **s'abriter ~ un arbre/un parapluie** to shelter under *ou* underneath *ou* beneath a tree/an umbrella; **porter son sac ~ son bras** to carry one's bag under one's arm; **se promener ~ la pluie/le soleil** to take a walk in the rain/in the sunshine; **le village est plus joli ~ le soleil/la lune/la clarté des étoiles** the village is prettier in the sunshine/in the *ou* by moonlight/by starlight; **le pays était ~ la neige** the country was covered with *ou* in snow; **l'Angleterre s'étendait ~ eux** England spread out beneath *ou* below them; **dormir ~ la tente** to sleep under canvas *ou* in a tent; **une mèche dépassait de ~ son chapeau** a lock of hair hung down from under her hat; **~ terre** under the ground, underground; **nager ~ l'eau** to swim under water; **rien de neuf** *ou* **rien de nouveau ~ le soleil** there's nothing new under the sun; **ils ne veulent plus vivre ~ le même toit** they don't want to live under the same roof any longer; **cela s'est passé ~ nos yeux** it happened before *ou* under our very eyes; **~ le canon** *ou* **le feu de l'ennemi** under enemy fire; (*fig*) **vous trouverez le renseignement ~ tel numéro/telle rubrique** you will find the information under such-and-such a number/heading; (*fig*) **~ des dehors frustes/une apparence paisible** beneath *ou* behind his (*ou* her *etc*) rough exterior/his (*ou* her *etc*) peaceful exterior; *voir* **cape, manteau, prétexte.**

b (*temps*) (*à l'époque de*) under; (*dans un délai de*) within. **~ le règne/le pontificat de** under *ou* during the reign/the pontificate of; **~ Charles X** under Charles X; **~ la Révolution/la VIe République** at the time of *ou* during the Revolution/the VIth Republic; **~ un régime capitaliste/socialiste** under a capitalist/socialist régime; **~ peu** shortly, before long; **~ huitaine/quinzaine** within the *ou* a week/two weeks *ou* the *ou* a fortnight (*Brit*).

c (*cause*) under. **~ l'influence de qn/qch** under the influence of sb/sth; **~ l'empire de la terreur** in the grip of terror; **le rocher s'est effrité ~ l'action du soleil/du gel** the rock has crumbled (away) due to *ou* under *ou* with the action of the sun/the frost; **il a agi ~ l'effet** *ou* **le coup de la colère** he acted in a moment of anger; **elle est encore ~ le coup de l'émotion** she's still in a state of shock *ou* reeling from the shock; **plier ~ le poids de qch** to bend beneath *ou* under the weight of sth; *voir* **faix.**

d (*manière*) **examiner une question ~ tous ses angles** *ou* **toutes ses faces** to examine every angle *ou* facet of a question, look at a question from every angle; **~ un faux nom/une identité d'emprunt** under a false name/an assumed identity; **~ certaines conditions j'accepte** I accept on certain conditions; **je ne le connaissais pas ~ ce jour-là** I hadn't seen him in that light, I didn't know that side *ou* aspect of him; **~ ce rapport** on that score, in this *ou* that respect; **il a été peint ~ les traits d'un berger** he was painted as a shepherd *ou* in the guise of a shepherd; *voir* **clef, enveloppe, garantie.**

e (*dépendance*) under. **être ~ les ordres/la protection/la garde de qn** to be under sb's orders/under *ou* in sb's protection/in sb's care; **se mettre ~ la protection/la garde de qn** to commit o.s. to *ou* into sb's protection/care; **se mettre ~ les ordres de qn** to submit (o.s.) to sb's orders; **l'affaire est ~ sa direction** he is running *ou* managing the affair, the affair is under his management; **l'affaire est ~ sa responsabilité** the affair is his responsibility *ou* comes within his responsibility; *voir* **auspice, charme, garde**[1]**, tutelle.**

f (*Méd*) ~ **anesthésie** under anaesthetic *ou* anaesthesia; **malade ~ perfusion** patient on the drip; ~ **antibiotiques** on antibiotics.

g (*Tech*) **câble ~ gaine** sheathed *ou* encased cable; **(emballé) ~ plastique** plastic-wrapped; ~ **tube** in (a) tube; **(emballé) ~ vide** vacuum-packed.

h (*Ordin*) **travailler ~ DOS ®/UNIX ®** to work in DOS ®/UNIX ®.

2 **préf** a (*infériorité*) **c'est du ~-art/du ~-Sartre/de la ~-littérature** it's pseudo-art/pseudo-Sartre/pseudo-literature; **il fait du ~-Giono** he's a sort of substandard Giono; **~-homme** subhuman.

b (*subordination*) sub-. **~-directeur/-bibliothécaire** *etc* assistant *ou* sub-manager/-librarian *etc;* **~-classe/-catégorie/-groupe** sub-class/-category/-group; (*Écon*) **~-agence** sub-branch; (*Zool*) **~-embranchement** sub-branch; (*Ordin*) **~-programme** subroutine, subprogram.

c (*insuffisance*) under ..., insufficiently. **~-alimentation** undernourishment, malnutrition; **~-alimenté** undernourished, underfed; **~-consommation** underconsumption; **~-employer** to underuse; **la région est ~-équipée** the region is underequipped; **~-équipement** lack of equipment; **~-évaluer** to underestimate, underrate; **~-industrialisé** underindustrialized; **~-peuplé** underpopulated; **~-peuplement** underpopulation; **~-production** underproduction; **les dangers de la ~-productivité** the dangers of underproductivity; **~-rémunéré** underpaid; **la région est ~-urbanisée** the region is insufficiently urbanized.

3 **comp** ▸**sous-amendement** **nm (pl sous-amendements)** amendment to an amendment ▸**sous-bois** **nm in** undergrowth ▸**sous-brigadier** **nm (pl sous-brigadiers)** deputy sergeant ▸**sous-chef** **nm (pl sous-chefs)** (*gén*) second-in-command; (*Admin*) **sous-chef de bureau** deputy chief clerk; **sous-chef de gare** deputy *ou* sub-stationmaster ▸**sous-comité** **nm (pl sous-comités)** subcommittee ▸**sous-commission** **nf (pl sous-commissions)** subcommittee ▸**sous-continent** **nm (pl sous-continents)** subcontinent ▸**sous-couche** **nf (pl sous-couches)** undercoat ▸**sous-cutané, e** **adj** subcutaneous ▸**sous-développé, e** **adj** underdeveloped; **les pays sous-développés** the underdeveloped *ou* developing *ou* emergent countries ▸**sous-développement** **nm** underdevelopment ▸**sous-diacre** (*Rel*) **nm (pl sous-diacres)** subdeacon ▸**sous-dominante** **nf (pl sous-dominantes)** subdominant ▸**sous-effectif** **nm (pl sous-effectifs)** *[armée, police]* reduced strength; *[employés]* reduced number; **en sous-effectif** (*Mil*) undermanned; *entreprise, service* understaffed ▸**sous-emploi** **nm** underemployment ▸**sous-ensemble** **nm (pl sous-ensembles)** subset ▸**sous-entendre** **vt** to imply, infer; **il faut sous-entendre que** it is to be inferred *ou* understood that ▸**sous-entendu, e** **(mpl sous-entendus) adj** implied, understood ◊ **nm** innuendo, insinuation ▸**sous-espèce** **nf (pl sous-espèces)** subspecies ▸**sous-estimation** **nf (pl sous-estimations)** underestimate ▸**sous-estimer** **vt** to underestimate ▸**sous-évaluer** **vt** *bijou, meuble etc* to undervalue; *compétence, adversaire* to underestimate ▸**sous-exploitation** **nf (pl sous-exploitations)** underexploitation, underutilization ▸**sous-exploiter** **vt** to underexploit, to underutilize ▸**sous-exposer** **vt** to underexpose ▸**sous-exposition** **nf (pl sous-expositions)** (*Phot*) under-exposure (*NonC*) ▸**sous-fifre*** **nm (pl sous-fifres)** underling ▸**sous-groupe** **nm (pl sous-groupes)** subgroup ▸**sous-jacent, e** **adj** (*lit*) subjacent, underlying; (*fig*) underlying ▸**sous-lieutenant** (*Mil*) **nm (pl sous-lieutenants)** (*armée de terre*) second lieutenant, (*marine*) sub-lieutenant; (*aviation*) pilot officer (*Brit*), second lieutenant (*US*) ▸**sous-locataire** **nmf (pl sous-locataires)** subtenant ▸**sous-location** **nf** subletting ▸**sous-louer** **vt** to sublet ▸**sous-main** **nm inv** desk blotter; (*fig*) **en sous-main** secretly ▸**sous-maîtresse** **nf (pl sous-maîtresses)** brothel-keeper, madam ▸**sous-marin, e** **(mpl sous-marins) adj** *pêche, chasse* underwater (*épith*); *végétation, faune* submarine (*épith*) ◊ **nm** (*lit*) submarine; (*fig: espion*) mole; **sous-marin nucléaire d'attaque** hunter-killer submarine; **sous-marin de poche** pocket *ou* midget submarine ▸**sous-marinier** **nm (pl sous-mariniers)** submariner ▸**sous-marque** (*Comm*) **nf (pl sous-marques)** sub-brand ▸**sous-médicalisé, e** **adj** underprovided with medical care ▸**sous-menu** (*Ordin*) **nm (pl sous-menus)** sub-menu ▸**sous-ministre** (*Can*) **nm (pl sous-ministres)** deputy minister ▸**sous-multiple** (*Math*) **nm (pl sous-multiples)** submultiple ▸**sous-nappe** **nf (pl sous-nappes)** undercloth ▸**sous-nutrition** **nf** malnutrition ▸**sous-off*** (*Mil*) **nm (pl sous-offs)** (**abrév de sous-officier**) ▸**sous-officier** **nm (pl sous-officiers)** non-commissioned officer, N.C.O ▸**sous-ordre** **nm (pl sous-ordres)** (*Zool*) suborder; (*sous-fifre*) subordinate, underling ▸**sous-payer** **vt** to underpay ▸**sous-pied** **nm (pl sous-pieds)** (under-)strap ▸**sous-préfecture** **nf (pl sous-préfectures)** sub-prefecture ▸**sous-préfet** **nm (pl sous-préfets)** sub-prefect ▸**sous-préfète** **nf (pl sous-préfètes)** sub-prefect's wife ▸**sous-produit** **nm (pl sous-produits)** (*lit*) by-product; (*fig*) pale imitation ▸**sous-prolétaire** **nmf (pl sous-prolétaires)** (underprivileged) worker ▸**sous-prolétariat** **nm** underprivileged *ou* downtrodden class ▸**sous-pull** **nm (pl sous-pulls)** thin poloneck jersey ▸**sous-race** **nf (pl sous-races)** sub-race ▸**sous-secrétaire d'État** **nm (pl sous-secrétaires d'État)** Under-Secretary ▸**sous-secrétariat** **nm (pl sous-secrétariats)** (*fonction*) post of Under-Secretary; (*bureau*) Under-Secretary's office ▸**sous-sol** **nm (pl sous-sols)** *[terre]* subsoil, substratum; *[maison]* basement; *[magasin]* basement, lower ground floor; **les richesses de notre sous-sol** our mineral resources ▸**sous-tasse** **nf (pl sous-tasses)** saucer ▸**sous-tendre** **vt** (*Géom*) to subtend; (*fig*) to underlie ▸**sous-titrage** **nm (pl sous-titrages)** subtitling (*NonC*) ▸**sous-titre** **nm (pl sous-titres)** subtitle ▸**sous-titrer** **vt** to subtitle; **en version originale sous-titrée** in the original (version) with subtitles ▸**sous-traitance** **nf** subcontracting ▸**sous-traitant** **nm (pl sous-traitants)** subcontractor ▸**sous-traiter** **vi** to become a subcontractor, be subcontracted ◊ **vt** *affaire* to subcontract, contract out ▸**sous-ventrière** **nf (pl sous-ventrières)** girth, bellyband; (*fig: manger*) **se faire péter la sous-ventrière** to eat more than one's fill ▸**sous-verre** **nm inv** (*encadrement*) glass mount; (*Phot*) photograph mounted under glass ▸**sous-vêtement** **nm** undergarment; **sous-vêtements** *mpl* underwear (*sg*), undergarments.

souscripteur, -trice [suskʀiptœʀ, tʀis] **nm,f** *[emprunt, publication]* subscriber (*de* to).

souscription [suskʀipsjɔ̃] **nf** (*action*) subscription; (*somme*) subscription, contribution. **ouvrir une ~ en faveur de ...** to start a fund in aid of ...; **livre en ~** book sold on a subscription basis; **ce livre est offert en ~ jusqu'au 15 novembre, au prix de 750 F** this book is available to subscribers until November 15th at the prepublication price of 750 francs.

souscrire [suskʀiʀ] 39 1 **souscrire à vt indir** a *emprunt, publication* to subscribe to. ~ **à la construction de** to contribute *ou* subscribe to the construction of; **il a souscrit pour 1 000 F à la construction du monument** he contributed *ou* subscribed 1,000 francs to the construction of the monument. b *idée, opinion, projet* to subscribe to. **c'est une excellente idée et j'y souscris** it's an excellent idea and I subscribe to it *ou* and I'm all in favour of it. 2 **vt** *abonnement* to take out; *billet de commerce* to sign.

souscrit, e [suskʀi, it] (**ptp de souscrire**) **adj: capital ~** subscribed capital.

soussigné, e [susiɲe] **adj, nm, f** undersigned. **je ~, Dupont Charles-Henri, déclare que ...** I the undersigned, Charles-Henri Dupont, certify that ...; **les (témoins) ~s** we the undersigned.

soustractif, -ive [sustʀaktif, iv] **adj** subtractive.

soustraction [sustʀaksjɔ̃] **nf** a (*Math*) subtraction. **faire la ~ de** *somme* to take away, subtract; **et il faut encore déduire les frais de réparation: faites la ~ vous-même** in addition you have to deduct repair costs — you can work it out for yourself *ou* you can do the sum yourself. b (*frm: vol*) removal, abstraction.

soustraire [sustʀɛʀ] 50 1 **vt** a (*gén, Math: défalquer*) to subtract, take away (*de* from). b (*frm: dérober*) to remove, abstract; (*cacher*) to conceal, shield (*à* from). ~ **qn à la justice/à la colère de qn** to shield sb from justice/from sb's anger; (*Jur*) ~ **à la compétence de** to exclude from the jurisdiction of. 2 **se soustraire vpr** (*frm*) **se ~ à** *devoir* to shirk; *obligation, corvée* to escape, shirk; *autorité* to elude, escape from; *curiosité* to conceal o.s. from, escape from; **se ~ à la justice** to elude justice; (*s'enfuir*) to abscond; **quelle corvée! comment m'y ~?** what drudgery! how shall I escape it? *ou* get out of it?

soutane [sutan] **nf** cassock, soutane. (*fig*) **prendre la ~** to enter the Church.

soute [sut] **nf** *[navire]* hold. ~ **(à bagages)** *[bateau, avion]* baggage hold; ~ **à charbon** coal bunker; ~ **à munitions** ammunition store; ~ **à mazout** oil tank; ~ **à bombes** bomb bay.

soutenable [sut(ə)nabl] **adj** *opinion* tenable, defensible. **ce film est d'une violence difficilement ~** this film is almost unbearably violent.

soutenance [sut(ə)nɑ̃s] **nf** (*Univ*) ~ **de thèse** ≃ viva, viva voce (examination).

soutènement [sutɛnmɑ̃] **nm: travaux de ~** support(ing) works; **ouvrage de ~** support(ing) structure; *voir* **mur.**

souteneur [sut(ə)nœʀ] **nm** procurer.

soutenir [sut(ə)niʀ] 22 1 **vt** a (*servir d'appui à*) *personne, toit, mur* to support, hold up; *[médicament etc]* to sustain. **on lui a fait une piqûre pour ~ le cœur** they gave him an injection to sustain his heart; **ses jambes peuvent à peine le ~** his legs can hardly support him *ou* hold him up; **prenez un peu d'alcool, cela soutient** have a little drink — it'll give you a lift* *ou* keep you going.

b (*aider*) *gouvernement, parti, candidat* to support, back; *famille* to support. ~ **le franc/l'économie** to bolster (up) the franc/the economy; **elle soutient les enfants contre leur père** she takes the children's part *ou* she stands up for the children against their father; **son amitié/il les a beaucoup soutenus dans leur épreuve** his friendship/he was a real support *ou* prop to them in their time of trouble, his friendship was something/he was someone for them to lean on in their time of trouble.

c (*faire durer*) *attention, conversation, effort* to keep up, sustain; *réputation* to keep up, maintain.

d (*résister à*) *assaut, combat* to stand up to, withstand; *regard* to bear, support. **il a bien soutenu le choc** he stood up well to the shock *ou* withstood the shock well; ~ **la comparaison avec** to bear *ou* stand comparison with, compare (favourably) with.

e (*affirmer*) *opinion, doctrine* to uphold, support; (*défendre*) *droits* to uphold, defend. (*Univ*) ~ **sa thèse** to attend *ou* have one's viva; **c'est une doctrine que je ne pourrai jamais** ~ it is a doctrine which I shall never be able to support *ou* uphold; **elle soutient toujours le contraire de ce qu'il dit** she always maintains the opposite of what he says; **il a soutenu jusqu'au bout qu'il était innocent** he maintained to the end that he was innocent.

2 **se soutenir** vpr a (*se maintenir*) (*sur ses jambes*) to hold o.s. up, support o.s.; (*dans l'eau*) to keep (o.s.) afloat *ou* up. **il n'arrivait plus à se** ~ **sur ses jambes** his legs could no longer support him, he could no longer stand on his legs.

b (*fig*) **ça peut se** ~ it's a tenable point of view; **un tel point de vue ne peut se** ~ a point of view like that is indefensible *ou* untenable; **l'intérêt se soutient jusqu'à la fin** the interest is kept up *ou* sustained *ou* maintained right to the end.

c (*s'entraider*) to stand by each other. **dans la famille, ils se soutiennent tous** the family all stand by each other *ou* stick together.

soutenu, e [sut(ə)ny] (ptp de **soutenir**) adj (*élevé, ferme*) *style, langue* elevated; (*constant, assidu*) *attention, effort* sustained, unflagging; *travail* sustained; (*intense*) *couleur* strong; *marché* buoyant.

souterrain, e [suterɛ̃, ɛn] 1 adj (*lit*) underground, subterranean; (*fig*) subterranean; *voir* **passage**. 2 nm underground *ou* subterranean passage.

soutien [sutjɛ̃] nm a (*gén: étai, aide*) support. (*Mil*) **unité de** ~ support *ou* reserve unit; (*Admin*) **être** ~ **de famille** to be the main wage-earner in the family (*exempted from military service*); (*Scol*) **cours de** ~ remedial course; ~ **en français** extra teaching in French; **apporter son** ~ **à qn/qch** to give sb/sth one's support. b (*action*) *[voûte]* supporting. ~ **des prix** price support.

soutien-gorge, pl **soutiens-gorge** [sutjɛ̃gɔʀʒ] nm bra; *voir* **armature**.

soutier [sutje] nm (*Naut*) coal-trimmer.

soutirage [sutiʀaʒ] nm *[vin]* decanting.

soutirer [sutiʀe] [1] vt a (*prendre*) ~ **qch à qn** *argent* to squeeze *ou* get sth out of sb; *promesse* to extract sth from sb, worm sth out of sb. b *vin* to decant, rack.

souvenance [suv(ə)nɑ̃s] nf (*littér*) recollection. **avoir** ~ **de** to recollect, have a recollection of; (*frm*) **à ma** ~ as I recall.

souvenir [suv(ə)niʀ] 1 nm a (*réminiscence*) memory, recollection. (*mémoires écrits*) ~**s** memoirs; **elle a gardé de lui un bon/mauvais** ~ she has good/bad memories of him; **ce n'est plus maintenant qu'un mauvais** ~ it's just a bad memory now; **je n'ai qu'un vague** ~ **de l'incident/de l'avoir rencontré** I have only a vague *ou* dim recollection of the incident/of having met him *ou* of meeting him; **raconter des** ~**s d'enfance/de guerre** to recount memories of one's childhood/of the war.

b (*littér: fait de se souvenir*) recollection, remembrance (*littér*). **avoir le** ~ **de qch** to have a memory of sth, remember sth; **garder** *ou* **conserver le** ~ **de qch** to retain the memory of sth; **perdre le** ~ **de qch** to lose all recollection of sth; (*frm*) **je n'ai pas** ~ **d'avoir ...** I have no recollection *ou* remembrance of having ...; **en** ~ **de** *personne disparue* in memory *ou* remembrance of; *occasion* in memory of; **évoquer le** ~ **de qn** to recall *ou* evoke the memory of sb.

c (*mémoire*) memory. **dans un coin de mon** ~ in a corner of my memory.

d (*objet gardé pour le souvenir*) keepsake, memento; (*pour touristes*) souvenir; (*marque, témoignage d'un événement*) souvenir. **garder qch comme** ~ **(de qn)** to keep sth as a memento (of sb); **cette cicatrice est un** ~ **de la guerre** this scar is a souvenir from the war; **boutique** *ou* **magasin de** ~**s** souvenir shop.

e (*formules de politesse*) **amical** *ou* **affectueux** ~ yours (ever); **mon bon** ~ **à X** remember me to X, (my) regards to X; **rappelez-moi au bon** ~ **de votre mère** remember me to your mother, give my (kind) regards to your mother; **croyez à mon fidèle** ~ yours ever, yours sincerely.

2 **se souvenir** [22] vpr: **se** ~ **de qn** to remember sb; **se** ~ **de qch/d'avoir fait/que ...** to remember *ou* recall *ou* recollect sth/doing sth/that ...; **il a plu tout l'été, tu t'en souviens?** *ou* **tu te souviens?*** it rained all summer, do you remember? *ou* recall?, it rained all summer, remember?*; **elle lui a donné une leçon dont il se souviendra** she taught him a lesson he won't forget in a hurry; **souvenez-vous qu'il est très puissant** bear in mind *ou* remember that he is very powerful; **souviens-toi de ta promesse!** remember your promise!; **tu m'as fait me** ~ **que ...,** (*littér*) **tu m'as fait** ~ **que ...** you have reminded me that ...; (*menace*) **je m'en souviendrai!** I won't forget!

3 vb impers (*littér*) **il me souvient d'avoir entendu raconter cette histoire** I recollect *ou* recall *ou* remember having heard *ou* hearing that story.

souvent [suvɑ̃] adv often. **le plus** ~**, cela marche bien** more often than not it works well; **faire qch plus** ~ **qu'à son (***ou* **mon** *etc***) tour** to have more than one's fair share of doing sth; **bien** ~ very often; **peu** ~ seldom; (*Prov*) ~ **femme varie (bien fol est qui s'y fie)** woman is fickle.

souverain, e [suv(ə)ʀɛ̃, ɛn] 1 adj a (*Pol*) *État, puissance* sovereign; *assemblée, cour, juge* supreme. **le** ~ **pontife** the Supreme Pontiff. b (*suprême*) **le** ~ **bien** the sovereign good; **remède** ~ **contre qch** sovereign remedy against sth. c (*intensif*) supreme. 2 nm,f a (*monarque*) sovereign, monarch. ~ **absolu/constitutionnel** absolute/constitutional monarch; **la** ~**e britannique** the British sovereign. b (*fig*) sovereign. **s'imposer en** ~ to reign supreme; **la philosophie est la** ~**e des disciplines de l'esprit** philosophy is the most noble *ou* the highest of the mental disciplines. 3 nm a (*Jur, Pol*) **le** ~ the sovereign power. b (*Hist Brit: monnaie*) sovereign.

souverainement [suv(ə)ʀɛnmɑ̃] adv a (*intensément*) supremely. **ça me déplaît** ~ I dislike it intensely. b (*en tant que souverain*) with sovereign power.

souveraineté [suv(ə)ʀɛnte] nf sovereignty.

soviet† [sɔvjɛt] nm soviet†. **le S~ suprême** the Supreme Soviet†; (*péj*) **les S~s*** the Soviets†.

soviétique [sɔvjetik] 1 adj Soviet. 2 nmf: **S~** Soviet citizen.

soviétiser [sɔvjetize] [1] vt to sovietize.

soviétologue [sɔvjetɔlɔg] nmf Kremlinologist.

sovkhoze [sɔvkoz] nm sovkhoz.

soya [sɔja] nm = **soja**.

soyeux, -euse [swajø, øz] 1 adj silky. 2 nm silk manufacturer (*of Lyons*), silk merchant (*of Lyons*).

SPA [ɛspea] nf (abrév de **Société protectrice des animaux**) ≃ R.S.P.C.A. (*Brit*), A.S.P.C.A. (*US*).

spacieusement [spasjøzmɑ̃] adv spaciously. ~ **aménagé** spaciously laid out; **nous sommes** ~ **logés** we have ample room in our accommodation *ou* where we are staying.

spacieux, -ieuse [spasjø, jøz] adj spacious, roomy.

spadassin [spadasɛ̃] nm (*littér, †: mercenaire*) hired killer *ou* assassin; (*†: bretteur*) swordsman.

SPADEM [spadɛm] nf (abrév de **Société de la propriété artistique et des dessins et modèles**) *French body governing artistic and industrial copyrights*.

spaghetti [spageti] nm (*gén pl*) ~**s** spaghetti; ~**s bolognaise** spaghetti Bolognaise; **un** ~ a strand of spaghetti; *voir* **western**.

spahi [spai] nm (*Hist Mil*) Spahi, *soldier of native cavalry corps of French army in North Africa*.

sparadrap [spaʀadʀa] nm adhesive *ou* sticking plaster (*Brit*), band-aid ® (*US*).

sparring-partner [spaʀiŋpaʀtnɛʀ] nm sparring partner.

Spartacus [spaʀtakys] nm Spartacus.

Sparte [spaʀt] nf Sparta.

spartiate [spaʀsjat] 1 adj Spartan. *éducation* **à la** ~ Spartan. 2 nmf (*Hist*) **S~** Spartan. 3 nf (*chaussures*) ~**s** Roman sandals.

spasme [spasm] nm spasm.

spasmodique [spasmɔdik] adj spasmodic.

spath [spat] nm (*Minér*) spar. ~ **fluor** fluorspar, fluorite (*US*).

spatial, e, mpl **-iaux** [spasjal, jo] adj (*opposé à temporel*) spatial; (*Espace*) space (*épith*).

spatialisation [spasjalizasjɔ̃] nf spatialization.

spatialiser [spasjalize] [1] vt to spatialize.

spatialité [spasjalite] nf spatiality.

spationaute [spasjonot] nmf astronaut, spaceman, spacewoman.

spationef [spasjonɛf] nm spaceship, spacecraft.

spatio-temporel, -elle, mpl **spatio-temporels** [spasjotɑ̃pɔʀɛl] adj spatiotemporal.

spatule [spatyl] nf a (*ustensile*) *[peintre, cuisinier]* spatula. b (*bout*) *[ski, manche de cuiller etc]* tip. c (*oiseau*) spoon-bill.

speaker [spikœʀ] nm, **speakerine** [spikʀin] nf (*Rad, TV*) (*annonceur*) announcer; (*journaliste*) newscaster, newsreader.

spécial, e, mpl **-iaux** [spesjal, jo] 1 adj (*gén*) special; (*bizarre*) peculiar. (*euph*) **il a des mœurs un peu** ~**es** he's a bit the other way inclined* (*euph*), he has certain tendencies (*euph*); *voir* **envoyé**. 2 **spéciale** nf (*huître*) top-quality oyster.

spécialement [spesjalmɑ̃] adv (*plus particulièrement*) especially, particularly; (*tout exprès*) specially. **pas** ~ **intéressant** not particularly *ou* especially interesting; **c'est très intéressant,** ~ **vers la fin** it is very interesting, especially *ou* particularly towards the end; **on l'a choisi** ~ **pour ce travail** he was specially chosen for this job; ~ **construit pour cet usage** specially built for this purpose.

spécialisation [spesjalizasjɔ̃] nf specialization.

spécialisé, e [spesjalize] (ptp de **spécialiser**) adj *travail, personne* specialized. **être** ~ **dans** *[personne]* to be a specialist in; *[firme]* to specialize in; *voir* **ouvrier**.

spécialiser [spesjalize] [1] 1 **se spécialiser** vpr to specialize (*dans* in). 2 vt: ~ **qn** to make sb into a specialist.

spécialiste [spesjalist] nmf (*gén, Méd*) specialist. **c'est un** ~ **de la gaffe*** he's always putting his foot in it*.

spécialité [spesjalite] nf (*gén, Culin*) speciality (*Brit*), specialty (*US*); (*Univ etc: branche*) specialism, special field. ~ **pharmaceutique** patent medicine; **il a la** ~ **de faire ...*** he has a special *ou* particular knack of doing..., he specializes in doing ... .

spécieusement [spesjøzmɑ̃] adv speciously.

spécieux, -ieuse [spesjø, jøz] adj specious.

spécification [spesifikasjɔ̃] nf specification.

spécificité [spesifisite] nf specificity.

spécifier [spesifje] [7] vt (*préciser son choix*) to specify, state; (*indiquer, mentionner*) to state. **veuillez** ~ **le modèle que vous désirez**

please specify the model that you require *ou* desire; **en passant votre commande, n'oubliez pas de ~ votre numéro d'arrondissement** when placing your order, don't forget to state your district number; **a-t-il spécifié l'heure?** did he specify *ou* state the time?; **j'avais bien spécifié qu'il devait venir le matin** I had stated specifically that he should come in the morning.

spécifique [spesifik] adj specific.

spécifiquement [spesifikmɑ̃] adv (*tout exprès*) specifically; (*typiquement*) typically.

spécimen [spesimɛn] nm (*gén: échantillon, exemple*) specimen; (*exemplaire publicitaire*) specimen copy, sample copy. **(numéro) ~** sample copy.

spectacle [spɛktakl] nm a (*vue, tableau*) sight; (*grandiose, magnifique*) sight, spectacle. **au ~ de** at the sight of; (*péj*) **se donner** *ou* **s'offrir en ~ (à qn)** to make a spectacle *ou* an exhibition of o.s. (in front of sb); **assister à un ~ imprévu** to see a happening; **une vieille dame qui assistait au ~ de la foule/de la rue** an old lady who was watching the crowd/the bustle of the street.
b (*représentation: Ciné, Théât etc*) show. (*branche*) **le ~** show business, entertainment, show biz*; (*rubrique*) **"~s"** "entertainment"; **le ~ va commencer** the show is about to begin; **un ~ lyrique/dramatique** a musical/dramatic entertainment; **~ de variétés** variety show; **aller au ~** to go to a show; **l'industrie du ~** the entertainment(s) industry, show biz*; *voir* **grand, salle.**

spectaculaire [spɛktakylɛʀ] adj spectacular.

spectateur, -trice [spɛktatœʀ, tʀis] nm,f *[événement, accident]* onlooker, witness; (*Sport*) spectator; (*Ciné, Théât*) member of the audience. **les ~s** the audience; (*fig*) **traverser la vie en ~** to go through life as an onlooker *ou* a spectator.

spectral, e, mpl **-aux** [spɛktʀal, o] adj a (*fantomatique*) ghostly, spectral. b (*Phys*) spectral; *voir* **analyse.**

spectre [spɛktʀ] nm a (*fantôme*) ghost; (*fig*) spectre. **comme s'il avait vu un ~** as if he'd seen a ghost; **le ~ de la guerre se dressait à l'horizon** the spectre of war loomed on the horizon. b (*Phys*) spectrum. **les couleurs du ~** the colours of the spectrum; **~ d'absorption/de masse** absorption/mass spectrum; **~ sonore** sound spectrum; **~ solaire** solar spectrum; **~ de résonance** resonance spectrum.

spectrogramme [spɛktʀɔgʀam] nm spectrogram.

spectrographe [spɛktʀɔgʀaf] nm spectrograph.

spectromètre [spɛktʀɔmɛtʀ] nm spectrometer.

spectrométrie [spɛktʀɔmetʀi] nf spectrometry.

spectroscope [spɛktʀɔskɔp] nm spectroscope.

spectroscopie [spɛktʀɔskɔpi] nf spectroscopy.

spectroscopique [spɛktʀɔskɔpik] adj spectroscopic.

spéculateur, -trice [spekylatœʀ, tʀis] nm,f speculator.

spéculatif, -ive [spekylatif, iv] adj (*Fin, Philos*) speculative.

spéculation [spekylasjɔ̃] nf speculation.

spéculer [spekyle] [1] vi (*Philos*) to speculate (*sur* on, about); (*Fin*) to speculate (*sur* in). (*fig: tabler sur*) **~ sur** to bank on, rely on.

spéculum [spekylɔm] nm speculum.

speech [spitʃ] nm († *ou* *: *laïus*) speech (*after a dinner, toast etc*). **faire un ~** to make a speech.

speedé, e* [spide] adj (*agité*) hyper*, hyped up*.

spéléo [speleo] nf, nmf abrév de **spéléologie, spéléologue.**

spéléologie [speleɔlɔʒi] nf (*étude*) speleology; (*exploration*) potholing, caving*.

spéléologique [speleɔlɔʒik] adj (*voir* **spéléologie**) speleological, potholing (*Brit, épith*), caving* (*épith*).

spéléologue [speleɔlɔg] nmf (*voir* **spéléologie**) speleologist, potholer (*Brit*), spelunker* (*US*), caver*.

spéléonaute [speleonot] nmf *person who spends long periods of time underground for scientific purposes.*

spencer [spɛnsœʀ] nm short jacket, spencer; (*Mil*) mess jacket.

spermaceti [spɛʀmaseti] nm spermaceti.

spermatique [spɛʀmatik] adj spermatic. **cordon ~** spermatic cord.

spermatogénèse [spɛʀmatɔʒenɛz] nf spermatogenesis.

spermatozoïde [spɛʀmatɔzɔid] nm sperm, spermatozoon.

sperme [spɛʀm] nm semen, sperm.

spermicide [spɛʀmisid] 1 adj spermicide (*épith*), spermicidal. 2 nm spermicide.

sphénoïde [sfenɔid] nm sphenoid bone.

sphère [sfɛʀ] nf (*Astron, fig*) sphere. **les hautes ~s de la politique** the higher realms of politics; **~ d'influence/d'attributions/d'activité** sphere of influence/competence/activity.

sphéricité [sfeʀisite] nf sphericity.

sphérique [sfeʀik] adj spherical; *voir* **calotte.**

sphéroïde [sfeʀɔid] nm spheroid.

sphincter [sfɛ̃ktɛʀ] nm sphincter.

sphinx [sfɛ̃ks] nm (*Art, Myth, fig*) sphinx; (*Zool*) hawkmoth, sphinxmoth. (*Myth*) **le S~** the Sphinx.

spi [spi] nm = **spinnaker.**

spina-bifida [spinabifida] nm inv spina bifida.

spinal, e, mpl **-aux** [spinal, o] adj spinal.

spinnaker [spinakɛʀ] nm spinnaker.

Spinoza [spinɔza] nm Spinoza.

spiral, e, mpl **-aux** [spiʀal, o] 1 adj spiral. 2 nm: **(ressort) ~** hairspring. 3 **spirale** nf spiral. **s'élever/tomber en ~e** to spiral up(wards)/down(wards); (*fig*) **la ~e de l'inflation** the inflationary spiral.

spiralé, e [spiʀale] adj spiral (*épith*).

spirante [spiʀɑ̃t] adjf, nf: **(consonne) ~** spirant, fricative.

spire [spiʀ] nf *[hélice, spirale]* (single) turn; *[coquille]* whorl; *[ressort]* spiral.

spirite [spiʀit] adj, nmf spiritualist.

spiritisme [spiʀitism] nm spiritualism.

spiritualiser [spiʀitɥalize] [1] vt to spiritualize.

spiritualisme [spiʀitɥalism] nm spiritualism.

spiritualiste [spiʀitɥalist] 1 adj spiritualist(ic). 2 nmf spiritualist.

spiritualité [spiʀitɥalite] nf spirituality.

spirituel, -elle [spiʀitɥɛl] adj a (*vif, fin*) witty. b (*Philos, Rel, gén*) spiritual. **musique ~elle** sacred music; **concert ~** concert of sacred music.

spirituellement [spiʀitɥɛlmɑ̃] adv (*voir* **spirituel**) wittily; spiritually.

spiritueux, -euse [spiʀitɥø, øz] 1 adj spirituous. 2 nm spirit. **les ~** spirits.

spiroïdal, e, mpl **-aux** [spiʀɔidal, o] adj spiroid.

spleen [splin] nm († *ou littér*) spleen (*fig littér*).

splendeur [splɑ̃dœʀ] nf a *[paysage, réception, résidence]* splendour, magnificence. **ce tapis est une ~** this carpet is quite magnificent; **les ~s de l'art africain** the splendours of African art. b (*gloire*) glory, splendour. **du temps de sa ~** in the days of its (*ou* his *etc*) glory *ou* splendour; (*iro*) **dans toute sa/leur ~** in all its/their splendour *ou* glory. c (*littér: éclat, lumière*) brilliance, splendour.

splendide [splɑ̃did] adj *temps, journée* splendid; *réception, résidence, spectacle* splendid, magnificent; *femme, bébé* magnificent, splendid-looking.

splendidement [splɑ̃didmɑ̃] adv splendidly, magnificently.

splénétique [splenetik] adj († *littér*) splenetic.

spoliateur, -trice [spɔljatœʀ, tʀis] 1 adj *loi* spoliatory. 2 nm,f despoiler.

spoliation [spɔljasjɔ̃] nf despoilment (*de* of).

spolier [spɔlje] [7] vt to despoil.

spondaïque [spɔ̃daik] adj spondaic.

spondée [spɔ̃de] nm spondee.

spongieux, -ieuse [spɔ̃ʒjø, jøz] adj (*gén, Anat*) spongy.

sponsor [spɔ̃sɔʀ] nm sponsor.

sponsoriser [spɔ̃sɔʀize] [1] vt to sponsor. **se faire ~ par une société** to get sponsorship from a company.

spontané, e [spɔ̃tane] adj (*gén*) spontaneous; *voir* **génération.**

spontanéité [spɔ̃taneite] nf spontaneity.

spontanément [spɔ̃tanemɑ̃] adv spontaneously.

Sporades [spɔʀad] nfpl: **les ~** the Sporades.

sporadicité [spɔʀadisite] nf sporadic nature *ou* occurrence.

sporadique [spɔʀadik] adj sporadic.

sporadiquement [spɔʀadikmɑ̃] adv sporadically.

sporange [spɔʀɑ̃ʒ] nm sporangium, spore case.

spore [spɔʀ] nf spore.

sport [spɔʀ] 1 nm a sport. **~ individuel/d'équipe** individual/team sport; **~ de compétition** competitive sport; **~ de combat** combat sport; **faire du ~ pour se maintenir en forme** to do sport in order to keep (o.s.) fit; **station de ~s d'hiver** winter sports resort; **aller aux ~s d'hiver** to go on a winter sports holiday, go winter sporting; **de ~** *vêtement, terrain, voiture* sports (*épith*); *voir* **terrain, voiture.** b (*) **il va y avoir du ~!** we'll see some fun!* *ou* action*; **faire ça, c'est vraiment du ~** doing that is no picnic*. 2 adj inv a *vêtement, coupe* casual. b (†: *chic, fair-play*) sporting, fair.

sportif, -ive [spɔʀtif, iv] 1 adj a *épreuve, journal, résultats* sports (*épith*); *pêche, marche* competitive (*épith*). b *personne, jeunesse* athletic, fond of sports (*attrib*); *allure, démarche* athletic. **elle a une conduite ~ive** she handles a car like a rally driver. c *attitude, mentalité, comportement* sporting, sportsmanlike. **faire preuve d'esprit ~** to show sportsmanship. 2 nm sportsman. 3 **sportive** nf sportswoman.

sportivement [spɔʀtivmɑ̃] adv sportingly.

sportivité [spɔʀtivite] nf sportsmanship.

spot [spɔt] nm a (*Phys*) light spot; (*Élec*) scanning spot. b (*lampe: Théât etc*) spotlight, spot. c **~ (publicitaire)** (*publicité*) commercial, advert* (*Brit*), ad*.

spoutnik [sputnik] nm sputnik.

sprat [spʀat] nm sprat.

spray [spʀɛ] nm (*aérosol*) spray, aerosol. **déodorant en ~** spray(-on) deodorant.

sprint [spʀint] nm (*de fin de course*) (final) sprint, final spurt; (*épreuve*) sprint. **battu au ~ (final)** beaten in the (final) sprint; *voir* **piquer 1c.**

sprinter¹ [spʀintœʀ] nm, **sprinteur, -euse** [spʀintœʀ, øz] nm,f sprinter; (*en fin de course*) fast finisher.

sprinter² [spʀinte] [1] vi to sprint; (*en fin de course*) to put on a final spurt.

squale [skwal] nm shark.

squame [skwam] **nf** (*Méd*) scale, squama (*SPÉC*).
squameux, -euse [skwamø, øz] **adj** (*Méd*) squamous, squamose; (*littér*) scaly.
square [skwaʀ] **nm** public garden(s), square (with garden).
squash [skwaʃ] **nm** squash.
squat* [skwat] **nm** (*logement*) squat.
squatter[1] [skwatœʀ] **nm** squatter.
squatter[2] [skwate] **vt**, **squattériser** [skwateʀize] **vt** [1] (*loger*) to squat in.
squaw [skwo] **nf** squaw.
squeezer [skwize] [1] **vt** a (*au bridge*) to squeeze. b (*: *voler*) *petit ami, portefeuille etc* to pinch*, nick‡ (*Brit*). c (*: *évincer*) to by-pass.
squelette [skəlɛt] **nm** (*lit, fig*) skeleton. **après sa maladie, c'était un vrai ~** after his illness he was just a bag of bones *ou* he was an absolute skeleton.
squelettique [skəletik] **adj** *personne, arbre* scrawny, skeleton-like; *exposé* sketchy, skimpy; (*Anat*) skeletal. **d'une maigreur ~** all skin and bone; **il est ~** he's scrawny, he's an absolute skeleton, he's mere skin and bone; **des effectifs ~s** a minimal staff.
Sri Lanka [sʀilɑ̃ka] **nm** Sri Lanka.
sri-lankais, e [sʀilɑ̃kɛ, ɛz] 1 **adj** Sri-Lankan. 2 **nm,f**: **Sri-Lankais(e)** Sri-Lankan.
SRPJ [ɛsɛʀpeʒi] **nm** (**abrév de service régional de la police judiciaire**) *voir* **service**.
S.S. [ɛsɛs] 1 **nf** a (**abrév de Sécurité sociale**) *voir* **sécurité**. b (**abrév de Sa Sainteté**) HH. 2 **nm** (*soldat*) SS.
St (**abrév de Saint**) St.
stabilisateur, -trice [stabilizatœʀ, tʀis] 1 **adj** stabilizing. 2 **nm** (*Tech*) *[véhicule]* anti-roll device; *[navire, vélo]* stabilizer; *[avion]* (*horizontal*) tailplane; (*vertical*) fixed fin; (*Chim*) stabilizer.
stabilisation [stabilizasjɔ̃] **nf** stabilization.
stabiliser [stabilize] [1] 1 **vt** (*gén*) to stabilize; *terrain* to consolidate. (*Aut*) **à 90 km/h en vitesse stabilisée** at a constant 90 km/h; *voir* **accotement**. 2 **se stabiliser vpr** to stabilize, become stabilized; *[courbe de graphe]* to plateau.
stabilité [stabilite] **nf** stability.
stable [stabl] **adj** *monnaie, gouvernement, personne,* (*Chim*), (*Phys*) stable; *position, échelle* stable, steady.
stabulation [stabylasjɔ̃] **nf** *[bétail]* stalling; *[chevaux]* stabling; *[poissons]* storing in tanks.
staccato [stakato] 1 **adv** staccato. 2 **nm** staccato passage.
stade [stad] **nm** a (*sportif*) stadium. b (*période, étape*) stage. **il en est resté au ~ de l'adolescence** he never got beyond adolescence *ou* the adolescent phase; (*Psych*) **~ oral/anal** oral/anal stage.
staff [staf] **nm** a (*personnel*) staff. b (*plâtre*) staff.
staffeur [stafœʀ] **nm** plasterer (*working in staff*).
stage [staʒ] **nm** (*période*) training period; (*cours*) training course; *[avocat]* articles (*pl*). **~ de perfectionnement** advanced training course; **~ de formation (professionnelle)** vocational (training) course; **~ d'initiation** introductory course; **~ pédagogique** teaching practice; **il a fait son ~ chez Maître X** he did his articles in Mr X's practice *ou* under Mr X; **faire** *ou* **suivre un ~** to undergo a period of training, go on a (training) course; *[employé]* **faire un ~ d'informatique** (*gén*) to go on a computing course; (*pris sur le temps de travail*) to have in-service *ou* in-house training in computing.
stagflation [stagflasjɔ̃] **nf** stagflation.
stagiaire [staʒjɛʀ] 1 **nmf** trainee. 2 **adj** trainee (*épith*). **professeur ~** student *ou* trainee teacher.
stagnant, e [stagnɑ̃, ɑ̃t] **adj** (*lit, fig*) stagnant.
stagnation [stagnasjɔ̃] **nf** (*lit, fig*) stagnation.
stagner [stagne] [1] **vi** (*lit, fig*) to stagnate.
stakhanovisme [stakanɔvism] **nm** Stakhanovism.
stakhanoviste [stakanɔvist] 1 **adj** Stakhanovist. 2 **nmf** Stakhanovite.
stalactite [stalaktit] **nf** stalactite.
stalag [stalag] **nm** stalag.
stalagmite [stalagmit] **nf** stalagmite.
Staline [stalin] **nm** Stalin.
stalinien, -ienne [stalinjɛ̃, jɛn] **adj, nm,f** Stalinist.
stalinisme [stalinism] **nm** Stalinism.
stalle [stal] **nf** *[cheval]* stall, box; (*Rel*) stall.
stance [stɑ̃s] **nf** (†: *strophe*) stanza. (*poème*) **~s** *type of verse form (of lyrical poem)*.
stand [stɑ̃d] **nm** *[exposition]* stand; *[foire]* stall. **~ (de tir)** *[foire]*, (*Sport*) shooting range; (*Mil*) firing range; (*Cyclisme etc*) **~ de ravitaillement** pit.
standard[1] [stɑ̃daʀ] **nm** (*Téléc*) switchboard.
standard[2] [stɑ̃daʀ] 1 **nm** (*norme*) standard. **~ de vie** standard of living. 2 **adj inv** (*Comm, Tech*) standard (*épith*); *voir* **échange**.
standardisation [stɑ̃daʀdizasjɔ̃] **nf** standardization.
standardiser [stɑ̃daʀdize] [1] **vt** to standardize.
standardiste [stɑ̃daʀdist] **nmf** switchboard operator. **demandez à la ~** ask the operator.
stand-by [stɑ̃dbaj] 1 **adj inv** stand-by (*épith*). **en ~** on stand-by. 2 **nm inv** stand-by passenger.
standing [stɑ̃diŋ] **nm** standing. (*Comm*) **immeuble de grand ~** block of luxury flats (*Brit*) *ou* apartments (*US*).
staphylocoque [stafilɔkɔk] **nm** staphylococcus.
star [staʀ] **nf** (*Ciné*) star.
starking [staʀkiŋ] **nf** starking (apple).
starlette [staʀlɛt] **nf** starlet.
star-system, pl star-systems [staʀsistɛm] **nm** star system.
START [staʀt] (**abrév de Strategic Arms Reduction Talks**) START.
starter [staʀtɛʀ] **nm** a (*Aut*) choke. **mettre le ~** to pull the choke out; **marcher au ~** to run with the choke out; **~ automatique** automatic choke. b (*Sport*) starter.
starting-block, pl starting-blocks [staʀtiŋblɔk] **nm** starting block.
starting-gate, pl starting-gates [staʀtiŋgɛt] **nm** starting gate.
stase [stɑz] **nf** stasis.
station [stasjɔ̃] 1 **nf** a (*lieu d'arrêt*) **~ (de métro)** (underground (*Brit*) *ou* subway (*US*)) station; **~ (d'autobus)** (bus) stop; **~ (de chemin de fer)** halt; **~ de taxis** taxi rank.
b (*poste, établissement*) station. **~ d'observation/de recherches** observation/research station; **~ agronomique/météorologique** agricultural research/meteorological station; **~ géodésique** geodesic *ou* geodetic station; **~ d'émission** transmitting station; **~ orbitale** orbiting station; **~ (de) radar** radar tracking station; **~ radiophonique** radio station; **~ spatiale** space station; **~ de lavage** carwash; (*Ordin*) **~ de travail** work station.
c (*site*) site; (*Bot, Zool*) station. **~ préhistorique** prehistoric site; (*Bot*) **une ~ de gentianes** a gentian station.
d (*de vacances*) resort. **~ balnéaire/climatique** sea *ou* seaside/health resort; **~ de ski** *ou* **de sports d'hiver** winter sports *ou* (winter) ski resort; **~ thermale** thermal spa.
e (*posture*) posture, stance. **~ verticale** upright position; **la ~ debout lui est pénible** standing upright is painful to him, an upright posture *ou* stance is painful to him.
f (*halte*) stop. **faire des ~s prolongées devant les vitrines** to make lengthy stops in front of the shop windows.
g (*Rel*) station. **les ~s de la Croix** the Stations of the Cross.
h (*Marine*) station.
2 **comp ▸station-service nf (pl stations-services)** service station, filling station, petrol (*Brit*) *ou* gas (*US*) station.
stationnaire [stasjɔnɛʀ] **adj** stationary.
stationnement [stasjɔnmɑ̃] **nm** (*Aut*) parking. **~ alterné** parking on alternate sides; **~ bilatéral/unilatéral** parking on both sides/on one side only; **"~ interdit"** "no parking", "no waiting"; (*sur autoroute*) "no stopping"; **"~ payant"** (*avec parcomètres*) "meter zone"; (*avec tickets*) "parking with ticket only"; *voir* **disque, feu**[1].
stationner [stasjɔne] [1] **vi** (*être garé*) to be parked; (*se garer*) to park.
statique [statik] 1 **adj** static. 2 **nf** statics (*sg*).
statiquement [statikmɑ̃] **adv** statically.
statisme [statism] **nm** stasis.
statisticien, -ienne [statistisjɛ̃, jɛn] **nm,f** statistician.
statistique [statistik] 1 **nf** (*science*) statistics (*sg*) (*données*) **des ~s** statistics (*pl*); **une ~** a statistic. 2 **adj** statistical.
statistiquement [statistikmɑ̃] **adv** statistically.
stator [statɔʀ] **nm** stator.
statuaire [statɥɛʀ] 1 **nf** statuary. 2 **adj** statuary. 3 **nm** (*littér*) sculptor.
statue [staty] **nf** statue. (*fig*) **elle était la ~ du désespoir** she was the picture of despair; (*fig*) **changé en ~ de sel** transfixed, rooted to the spot.
statuer [statɥe] [1] **vi** to give a verdict. **~ sur** to rule on, give a ruling on; **~ sur le cas de qn** to decide sb's case.
statuette [statɥɛt] **nf** statuette.
statufier [statyfje] [7] **vt** (*immortaliser*) to erect a statue to; (*pétrifier*) to transfix, root to the spot.
statu quo [statykwo] **nm** status quo.
stature [statyʀ] **nf** (*lit, fig: envergure*) stature. **de haute ~** of (great) stature.
statut [staty] **nm** a (*position*) status. b (*règlement*) **~s** statutes.
statutaire [statytɛʀ] **adj** statutory. **horaire ~** regulation *ou* statutory number of working hours.
statutairement [statytɛʀmɑ̃] **adv** in accordance with the statutes *ou* regulations, statutorily.
Ste (**abrév de Sainte**) St.
Sté abrév de société.
steak [stɛk] **nm** steak. **~ au poivre** steak au poivre.
stéarine [steaʀin] **nf** stearin.
stéatite [steatit] **nf** steatite.
steeple [stipl] **nm**: **~(-chase)** (*Athlétisme, Équitation*) steeplechase; **le 3 000 mètres ~** the 3,000 metres steeplechase.
stégosaure [stegɔzɔʀ] **nm** stegosaur(us).
stèle [stɛl] **nf** stela, stele.
stellaire [stelɛʀ] 1 **adj** stellar. 2 **nf** stitchwort.
stem(m) [stɛm] **nm** (*Ski*) stem. **faire du ~** to stem.
stencil [stɛnsil] **nm** (*pour polycopie*) stencil.
stendhalien, -ienne [stɛ̃daljɛ̃, jɛn] **adj** Stendhalian.

sténo [steno] nmf (abrév de **sténographe, sténographie**) shorthand. **prendre une lettre en** ~ to take a letter (down) in shorthand.
sténodactylo[1] [stenodaktilo] nf, **sténodactylographe**† [stenodaktilɔgʀaf] nf shorthand typist.
sténodactylo[2] [stenodaktilo] nf, **sténodactylographie**† [stenodaktilɔgʀafi] nf shorthand typing.
sténographe† [stenɔgʀaf] nmf stenographer†.
sténographie [stenɔgʀafi] nf shorthand, stenography†.
sténographier [stenɔgʀafje] 7 vt to take down in shorthand.
sténographique [stenɔgʀafik] adj shorthand (*épith*), stenographic (†).
sténopé [stenɔpe] nm (*Phot*) pinhole.
sténotype [stenɔtip] nf stenotype.
sténotypie [stenɔtipi] nf stenotypy.
sténotypiste [stenɔtipist] nmf stenotypist.
stentor [stɑ̃tɔʀ] nm: **une voix de** ~ a stentorian voice.
stéphanois, e [stefanwa, waz] 1 adj of *ou* from Saint-Étienne. 2 nm,f: **S~(e)** inhabitant *ou* native of Saint-Étienne.
steppe [stɛp] nf steppe.
stercoraire [stɛʀkɔʀɛʀ] nm skua.
stère [stɛʀ] nm stere.
stéréo [steʀeo] nf, adj inv (abrév de **stéréophonie, stéréophonique**) stereo. **émission (en)** ~ programme in stereo; **enregistrement (en) stereo** stereo recording; **c'est en** ~ it's in stereo.
stéréophonie [steʀeɔfɔni] nf stereophony.
stéréophonique [steʀeɔfɔnik] adj stereophonic.
stéréoscope [steʀeɔskɔp] nm stereoscope.
stéréoscopie [steʀeɔskɔpi] nf stereoscopy.
stéréoscopique [steʀeɔskɔpik] adj stereoscopic.
stéréotype [steʀeɔtip] nm (*lit, fig*) stereotype.
stéréotypé, e [steʀeɔtipe] adj stereotyped.
stérile [steʀil] adj *femme* infertile, sterile; *homme, union* sterile; *milieu* sterile; *terre* barren; *sujet, réflexions, pensées* sterile; *discussion, effort* fruitless, futile.
stérilet [steʀilɛ] nm coil, I.U.D., intra-uterine device.
stérilisant, e [steʀilizɑ̃, ɑ̃t] adj (*lit*) sterilizing; (*fig*) unproductive, fruitless.
stérilisateur [steʀilizatœʀ] nm sterilizer.
stérilisation [steʀilizasjɔ̃] nf sterilization.
stériliser [steʀilize] 1 vt to sterilize. **lait stérilisé** sterilized milk.
stérilité [steʀilite] nf (*NonC*: *voir* **stérile**) infertility; sterility; barrenness; fruitlessness, futileness.
sterling [stɛʀliŋ] nm sterling; *voir* **livre**[2].
sterne [stɛʀn] nf tern. ~ **arctique** Arctic tern.
sternum [stɛʀnɔm] nm breastbone, sternum (*SPÉC*).
stéroïde [steʀɔid] 1 nm steroid. 2 adj steroidal.
stéthoscope [stetɔskɔp] nm stethoscope.
steward [stiwaʀt] nm steward, flight attendant.
stewardesse† [stjuwaʀdɛs] nf stewardess.
stick [stik] nm [*colle etc*] stick; (*Hockey*) stick; (*groupe de parachutistes*) stick. **déodorant en** ~ stick deodorant.
stigmate [stigmat] nm a (*marque*) (*Méd*) mark, scar. (*Rel*) **~s** stigmata; (*fig*) **~s du vice/de la bêtise** marks of vice/folly. b (*orifice*) (*Zool*) stigma, spiracle; (*Bot*) stigma.
stigmatisation [stigmatizasjɔ̃] nf (*Rel*) stigmatization; (*blâme*) condemnation, denunciation.
stigmatiser [stigmatize] 1 vt (*blâmer*) to denounce, condemn, stigmatize.
stimulant, e [stimylɑ̃, ɑ̃t] 1 adj stimulating. 2 nm (*physique*) stimulant; (*intellectuel*) stimulus, spur, incentive; (*: *drogue*) upper*.
stimulateur [stimylatœʀ] nm: ~ **cardiaque** pacemaker.
stimulation [stimylasjɔ̃] nf stimulation.
stimuler [stimyle] 1 vt *personne* to stimulate, spur on; *appétit, zèle, économie* to stimulate.
stimulus [stimylys], pl **stimuli** [stimyli] nm (*Physiol, Psych*) stimulus.
stipendié, e [stipɑ̃dje] (ptp de **stipendier**) adj (*littér, péj*) hired.
stipendier [stipɑ̃dje] 7 vt (*littér, péj*) to hire, take into one's pay.
stipulation [stipylasjɔ̃] nf stipulation.
stipuler [stipyle] 1 vt [*clause, loi, condition*] to state, stipulate; (*faire savoir expressément*) to stipulate, specify.
stock [stɔk] nm (*Comm*) stock; (*fig*) stock, supply. ~ **d'or** gold reserves (*pl*); *voir* **rupture**.
stockage [stɔkaʒ] nm (*Comm*) stocking. **le** ~ **des déchets radio-actifs** the storage *ou* stockpiling of nuclear waste.
stock-car, pl **stock-cars** [stɔkkaʀ] nm (*Sport*) stock-car racing; (*voiture*) stock car. **une course de** ~ a stock-car race.
stocker [stɔke] 1 vt (*Comm*) to stock, keep in stock; (*péj: pour spéculer, amasser*) to stockpile. (*Ordin*) ~ **(sur mémoire)** to store (in the memory).
Stockholm [stɔkɔlm] n Stockholm.
stockiste [stɔkist] nmf (*Comm*) stockist (*Brit*), dealer (*US*); (*Aut*) agent.
stoïcien, -ienne [stɔisjɛ̃, jɛn] adj, nm,f stoic.
stoïcisme [stɔisism] nm (*Philos*) stoicism; (*fig*) stoicism.
stoïque [stɔik] adj stoical, stoic.
stoïquement [stɔikmɑ̃] adv stoically.
stomacal, e, mpl **-aux** [stɔmakal, o] adj stomach (*épith*), gastric.
stomatologie [stɔmatɔlɔʒi] nf stomatology.
stomatologiste [stɔmatɔlɔʒist] nmf, **stomatologue** [stɔmatɔlɔg] nmf stomatologist.
stop [stɔp] 1 excl a ~! stop! b (*Téléc*) stop. 2 nm a (*Aut*) (*panneau*) stop *ou* halt sign; (*feu arrière*) brake-light. b (*) (abrév de **auto-stop**) **faire du** ~ to hitch(hike); **faire le tour de l'Europe en** ~ to hitch round Europe; **il a fait du** ~ **pour rentrer chez lui, il est rentré chez lui en** ~ he hitched a lift (back) home.
stoppage [stɔpaʒ] nm invisible mending.
stopper [stɔpe] 1 1 vi to halt, stop. 2 vt a (*arrêter*) to stop, halt. b (*Couture*) *bas* to mend. **faire** ~ **un vêtement** to get a garment (invisibly) mended.
stoppeur, -euse [stɔpœʀ, øz] nm,f a (*Couture*) invisible mender. b (*: *auto-stoppeur*) hitchhiker. c (*Ftbl*) fullback.
store [stɔʀ] nm (*en plastique, tissu*) blind, shade; [*magasin*] awning, shade. ~ **vénitien** *ou* **à lamelles orientables** Venetian blind.
strabisme [stʀabism] nm squinting (*Brit*), strabismus (*SPÉC*). ~ **divergent** divergent squint; ~ **convergent** convergent strabismus (*SPÉC*); **il souffre d'un léger** ~ he has a slight squint (*Brit*), he is slightly cross-eyed, he suffers from a slight strabismus (*SPÉC*).
stradivarius [stʀadivaʀjys] nm Stradivarius.
strangulation [stʀɑ̃gylasjɔ̃] nf strangulation.
strapontin [stʀapɔ̃tɛ̃] nm (*Aut, Théât*) jump seat, foldaway seat; (*fig: position subalterne*) minor role.
Strasbourg [stʀazbuʀ] n Strasbourg.
strasbourgeois, e [stʀazbuʀʒwa, waz] 1 adj of *ou* from Strasbourg. 2 nm,f: **S~(e)** inhabitant *ou* native of Strasbourg.
strass [stʀas] nm (*lit*) paste, strass; (*fig péj*) show, gloss. **broche/collier en** ~ paste *ou* strass brooch/necklace.
stratagème [stʀataʒɛm] nm stratagem.
strate [stʀat] nf stratum.
stratège [stʀatɛʒ] nm (*Mil, fig*) strategist.
stratégie [stʀateʒi] nf (*Mil, fig*) strategy. (*Comm*) ~ **de vente** selling strategy.
stratégique [stʀateʒik] adj strategic.
stratégiquement [stʀateʒikmɑ̃] adv strategically.
stratification [stʀatifikasjɔ̃] nf stratification.
stratificationnel, -elle [stʀatifikɑsjɔnɛl] adj *grammaire* stratificational.
stratifié, e [stʀatifje] (ptp de **stratifier**) 1 adj stratified; (*Tech*) laminated. 2 nm laminate. **en** ~ laminated.
stratifier [stʀatifje] 7 vt to stratify.
strato-cumulus [stʀatokymylys] nm inv stratocumulus.
stratosphère [stʀatɔsfɛʀ] nf stratosphere.
stratosphérique [stʀatɔsfeʀik] adj stratospheric.
stratus [stʀatys] nm inv stratus.
streptocoque [stʀɛptɔkɔk] nm streptococcus.
streptomycine [stʀɛptɔmisin] nf streptomycin.
stress [stʀɛs] nm (*gén, Méd*) stress.
stressant, e [stʀesɑ̃, ɑ̃t] adj *situation* stress-inducing, stressful.
stresser [stʀese] 1 vt to cause stress in. **la femme stressée d'aujourd'hui** today's stress-ridden woman; **cette réunion m'a complètement stressé** this meeting made me feel very tense.
stretch [stʀɛtʃ] 1 adj inv stretch (*épith*), stretchy. 2 **S~** nm ® stretch fabric. **jupe en** ~ stretch skirt.
striation [stʀijasjɔ̃] nf striation.
strict, e [stʀikt] adj *discipline, maître, morale, obligation, sens* strict; *tenue, aménagement* plain; *interprétation* literal. **l'observation ~e du règlement** the strict observance of the rules; **c'est la ~e vérité** it is the plain *ou* simple truth; **c'est son droit le plus** ~ it is his most basic right; **un uniforme/costume très** ~ a very austere *ou* plain uniform/suit; **le** ~ **nécessaire/minimum** the bare essentials/minimum; **au sens** ~ **du terme** in the strict sense of the word; **dans la plus ~e intimité** strictly in private; **il est très** ~ **sur la ponctualité** he is a stickler for punctuality, he's very strict about punctuality; **il était très** ~ **avec nous** *ou* **à notre égard** he was very strict with us.
strictement [stʀiktəmɑ̃] adv (*voir* **strict**) strictly; plainly. ~ **personnel/confidentiel** strictly private/confidential.
stricto sensu [stʀiktosɛ̃sy] adv strictly speaking.
strident, e [stʀidɑ̃, ɑ̃t] adj shrill, strident; (*Phon*) strident.
stridulation [stʀidylasjɔ̃] nf stridulation, chirring.
striduler [stʀidyle] 1 vi to stridulate, chirr.
strie [stʀi] nf (*de couleur*) streak; (*en relief*) ridge; (*en creux*) groove; (*Anat, Géol*) stria.
strier [stʀije] 7 vt (*voir* **strie**) to streak; to ridge, to groove; to striate; *voir* **muscle**.
string [stʀiŋ] nm (*sous-vêtement*) G-string; (*maillot de bain*) tanga.
strip-tease, pl **strip-teases** [stʀiptiz] nm striptease.
strip-teaseuse, pl **strip-teaseuses** [stʀiptizøz] nf stripper, striptease artist.
striure [stʀijyʀ] nf [*couleurs*] streaking (*NonC*). **la** ~ *ou* **les ~s de la**

pierre the ridges *ou* grooves in the stone.
stroboscope [stʀɔbɔskɔp] **nm** stroboscope.
stroboscopique [stʀɔbɔskɔpik] **adj** stroboscopic, strobe (*épith*). **lumière ~** strobe lighting.
Stromboli [stʀɔ̃bɔli] **nm** Stromboli.
strontium [stʀɔ̃sjɔm] **nm** strontium.
strophe [stʀɔf] **nf** (*Littérat*) verse, stanza; (*Théât Grec*) strophe.
structural, e, mpl -aux [stʀyktyʀal, o] **adj** structural.
structuralisme [stʀyktyʀalism] **nm** structuralism.
structuraliste [stʀyktyʀalist] **adj, nmf** structuralist.
structurant, e [stʀyktyʀɑ̃, ɑ̃t] **adj** *principe* founding; *expérience* formative; *voir* **gel**.
structuration [stʀyktyʀasjɔ̃] **nf** structuring.
structure [stʀyktyʀ] **nf** structure. **~s d'accueil** reception facilities; (*Ling*) **~ syntagmatique/profonde/superficielle** *ou* **de surface** phrase/deep/surface structure.
structuré, e [stʀyktyʀe] (**ptp de structurer**) **adj** structured.
structurel, -elle [stʀyktyʀɛl] **adj** structural.
structurer [stʀyktyʀe] [1] **1 vt** to structure, to give structure to. **2 se structurer vpr** *[mouvement]* to develop a structure; *[enfant]* to form himself (*ou* herself).
strychnine [stʀiknin] **nf** strychnine.
stuc [styk] **nm** stucco.
studette [stydɛt] **nf** small studio flat (*Brit*) *ou* apartment (*surtout US*).
studieusement [stydjøzmɑ̃] **adv** studiously.
studieux, -ieuse [stydjø, jøz] **adj** *personne* studious; *vacances, soirée* study (*épith*).
studio [stydjo] **nm** (*Ciné, TV: de prise de vues*) studio; (*salle de cinéma*) film theatre, arts cinema; (*d'artiste*) studio; (*d'habitation*) studio flat (*Brit*) *ou* apartment (*surtout US*). (*Ciné*) **tourner en ~** to film *ou* shoot in the studio.
stupéfaction [stypefaksjɔ̃] **nf** (*étonnement*) stupefaction, amazement.
stupéfaire [stypefɛʀ] [60] **vt** to stun, astound, dumbfound.
stupéfait, e [stypefɛ, ɛt] (**ptp de stupéfaire**) **adj** stunned, dumbfounded, astounded (*de qch* at sth). **~ de voir que ...** astounded *ou* stunned to see that ... .
stupéfiant, e [stypefjɑ̃, jɑ̃t] **1 adj** (*étonnant*) stunning, astounding, staggering*; (*Méd*) stupefying, stupefacient (*SPÉC*). **2 nm** drug, narcotic, stupefacient (*SPÉC*); *voir* **brigade**.
stupéfié, e [stypefje] (**ptp de stupéfier**) **adj** stunned, staggered, dumbfounded.
stupéfier [stypefje] [7] **vt** (*étonner*) to stun, stagger, astound; (*Méd, littér*) to stupefy.
stupeur [stypœʀ] **nf** (*étonnement*) astonishment, amazement; (*Méd*) stupor.
stupide [stypid] **adj** (*inepte*) stupid, silly, foolish; (*hébété*) stunned, bemused.
stupidement [stypidmɑ̃] **adv** stupidly.
stupidité [stypidite] **nf** (*caractère*) stupidity; (*parole, acte*) stupid *ou* silly *ou* foolish thing to say (*ou* do). **c'est une vraie ~** *ou* **de la ~** that's a really stupid *ou* silly *ou* foolish thing to say (*ou* do).
stupre [stypʀ] **nm** (†, *littér*) debauchery, depravity.
stups* [styp] **nmpl** (**abrév de stupéfiants**) *voir* **brigade**.
style [stil] **1 nm a** (*gén, Art, Littérat, Sport*) style. **meubles/reliure de ~** period furniture/binding; **meubles de ~ Directoire/Louis XVI** Directoire/Louis XVI furniture; **je reconnais bien là son ~** that is just his style; **cet athlète a du ~** this athlete has style; **offensive/opération de grand ~** full-scale *ou* large-scale offensive/operation; *voir* **exercice**.
b (*Bot*) style; *[cylindre enregistreur]* stylus; *[cadran solaire]* style, gnomon; (*Hist: poinçon*) style, stylus.
2 comp ▸style direct/indirect (*Ling*) direct/indirect *ou* reported speech **▸style indirect libre** (*Ling*) indirect free speech **▸style journalistique** journalistic style, journalese (*péj*) **▸style télégraphique** telegraphese (*NonC*) **▸style de vie** lifestyle.
styler [stile] [1] **vt** *domestique etc* to train. **un domestique (bien) stylé** a well-trained servant.
stylet [stilɛ] **nm** (*poignard*) stiletto, stylet; (*Méd*) stylet; (*Zool*) proboscis, stylet.
stylisation [stilizasjɔ̃] **nf** stylization.
styliser [stilize] [1] **vt** to stylize. **colombe/fleur stylisée** stylized dove/flower.
stylisme [stilism] **nm** (*métier*) dress designing; (*snobisme*) concern for style.
styliste [stilist] **nmf** (*dessinateur industriel*) designer; (*écrivain*) stylist. **~ de mode** clothes *ou* dress designer.
stylisticien, -ienne [stilistisjɛ̃, jɛn] **nm,f** stylistician, specialist in stylistics.
stylistique [stilistik] **1 nf** stylistics (*sg*). **2 adj** *analyse, emploi* stylistic.
stylo [stilo] **nm** pen. **~-bille** *ou* **à bille** Biro ® (*Brit*), ball-point (pen); **~ à encre** *ou* **à réservoir** fountain pen; **~-feutre** felt-tip pen; **~ à cartouche** cartridge pen; **S~mine** ® propelling pencil.
stylographe† [stilɔgʀaf] **nm** fountain pen.
Styx [stiks] **nm: le ~** the Styx.

su [sy] (**ptp de savoir**) **nm: au ~ de** with the knowledge of; *voir* **vu**[1].
suaire [sɥɛʀ] **nm** (*littér: linceul*) shroud, winding sheet; (*fig*) shroud; *voir* **saint**.
suant, suante [sɥɑ̃, sɥɑ̃t] **adj** (*en sueur*) sweaty; (‡: *ennuyeux*) *livre, cours* deadly (dull)*. **ce film est ~** this film is a real drag‡ *ou* is deadly*; **ce qu'il est ~!** what a drag‡ *ou* a pain (in the neck)* he is!
suave [sɥav] **adj** *personne, manières, voix, regard* suave, smooth; *musique, parfum* sweet; *couleurs* mellow; *formes* smooth.
suavement [sɥavmɑ̃] **adv** *s'exprimer* suavely.
suavité [sɥavite] **nf** (*voir* **suave**) suavity; smoothness; sweetness; mellowness.
subaigu, uë [sybegy] **adj** subacute.
subalterne [sybaltɛʀn] **1 adj** *rôle* subordinate, subsidiary; *employé, poste* junior (*épith*). (*Mil*) **officier ~** subaltern. **2 nmf** subordinate, inferior.
subantarctique [sybɑ̃taʀktik] **adj** subantarctic.
subaquatique [sybakwatik] **adj** subaquatic, underwater (*épith*).
subarctique [sybaʀktik] **adj** subarctic.
subconscient, e [sypkɔ̃sjɑ̃, jɑ̃t] **adj, nm** subconscious.
subdélégué, e [sybdelege] (**ptp de subdéléguer**) **nm, f** subdelegate.
subdéléguer [sybdelege] [6] **vt** to subdelegate.
subdiviser [sybdivize] [1] **1 vt** to subdivide (*en* into). **2 se subdiviser vpr** to be subdivided, be further divided (*en* into).
subdivision [sybdivizjɔ̃] **nf** subdivision.
subéquatorial, e, mpl -iaux [sybekwatɔʀjal, jo] **adj** subequatorial.
subir [sybiʀ] [2] **vt a** (*être victime de*) *affront* to be subjected to, suffer; *violences, attaque, critique* to undergo, suffer, be subjected to; *perte, défaite, dégâts* to suffer, sustain. **faire ~ un affront/des tortures à qn** to subject sb to an insult/to torture; **faire ~ des pertes/une défaite à l'ennemi** to inflict losses/defeat upon the enemy.
b (*être soumis à*) *charme* to be subject to, be under the influence of; *influence* to be under; *peine de prison* to undergo, serve; *examen* to undergo, go through; *opération, interrogatoire* to undergo. **~ les effets de qch** to be affected by sth, experience the effects of sth; **~ la loi du plus fort** to be subjected to the law of the strongest; **~ les rigueurs de l'hiver** to undergo *ou* be subjected to the rigours of (the) winter; **faire ~ son influence à qn** to exert an influence over sb; **faire ~ un examen à qn** to put sb through *ou* subject sb to an examination, make sb undergo an examination.
c (*endurer*) to suffer, put up with, endure. **il faut ~ et se taire** you must suffer in silence; **il va falloir le ~ pendant toute la journée*** we're going to have to put up with him *ou* endure him all day.
d (*recevoir*) *modification, transformation* to undergo, go through.
subit, e [sybi, it] **adj** sudden.
subitement [sybitmɑ̃] **adv** suddenly, all of a sudden.
subito (presto)* [sybito(pʀɛsto)] **adv** (*brusquement*) all of a sudden; (*immédiatement*) at once.
subjectif, -ive [sybʒɛktif, iv] **adj** subjective. **un danger ~** a danger which one creates for oneself.
subjectivement [sybʒɛktivmɑ̃] **adv** subjectively.
subjectivisme [sybʒɛktivism] **nm** subjectivism.
subjectiviste [sybʒɛktivist] **1 adj** subjectivistic. **2 nmf** subjectivist.
subjectivité [sybʒɛktivite] **nf** subjectivity.
subjonctif, -ive [sybʒɔ̃ktif, iv] **adj, nm** subjunctive.
subjuguer [sybʒyge] [1] **vt** *auditoire* to captivate, enthrall; (*littér*) *esprits, personne malléable* to render powerless; (†) *peuple vaincu* to subjugate. **être subjugué par le charme/la personnalité de qn** to be captivated by sb's charm/personality.
sublimation [syblimasjɔ̃] **nf** (*Chim, Psych*) sublimation.
sublime [syblim] **1 adj** (*littér*) sublime. **~ de dévouement** sublimely dedicated; (*Hist*) **la S~ Porte** the Sublime Porte. **2 nm: le ~** the sublime.
sublimé, e [sublime] (**ptp de sublimer**) **1 adj** sublimate(d). **2 nm** sublimate.
sublimement [syblimmɑ̃] **adv** sublimely.
sublimer [syblime] [1] **vt** (*Psych*) to sublimate; (*Chim*) to sublimate, sublime.
subliminaire [sybliminɛʀ] **adj = subliminal.**
subliminal, e, mpl -aux [sybliminal, o] **adj** subliminal.
sublimité [syblimite] **nf** (*littér*) sublimeness (*NonC*), sublimity.
sublingual, e, mpl -aux [syblɛ̃gwal, o] **adj** sublingual. **comprimé ~** tablet to be dissolved under the tongue.
submergé, e [sybmɛʀʒe] (**ptp de submerger**) **adj a** *terres, plaine* flooded, submerged; *récifs* submerged. **b** (*fig: débordé, dépassé*) swamped, inundated, snowed under. **~ de** *appels téléphoniques, commandes* snowed under *ou* swamped *ou* inundated with; *douleur, plaisir, inquiétudes* overwhelmed *ou* overcome with; **nous étions complètement ~s** we were completely snowed under, we were up to our eyes (*Brit*) *ou* ears (*US*) in it*; **~ de travail** snowed under *ou* swamped with work, up to one's eyes in work*.
submerger [sybmɛʀʒe] [3] **vt** (*lit: inonder*) *terres, plaine* to flood, submerge; *barque* to submerge. (*fig*) **~ qn** *[foule]* to engulf sb; *[ennemi]* to overwhelm sb; *[émotion]* to overcome sb, overwhelm sb; **les quelques agents furent submergés par la foule** the one or two police were en-

gulfed in *ou* by the crowd; **ils nous submergeaient de travail** they swamped *ou* inundated us with work.
submersible [sybmɛʀsibl] **adj, nm** (*Naut*) submarine.
submersion [sybmɛʀsjɔ̃] **nf** *[terres]* flooding, submersion. (*Méd*) **mort par ~** death by drowning.
subodorer [sybɔdɔʀe] [1] **vt** (*hum: soupçonner*) *irrégularité, malversation* to scent. **il subodora quelque chose de pas très catholique** he smelt a rat.
subordination [sybɔʀdinasjɔ̃] **nf** subordination. **je m'élève contre la ~ de cette décision à leurs plans** I object to this decision being subject to their plans; *voir* **conjonction**.
subordonné, e [sybɔʀdɔne] (**ptp de subordonner**) **1 adj** (*gén, Ling*) subordinate (*à* to). (*Ling*) **proposition ~e** dependent clause, subordinate clause. **2 nm,f** subordinate. **3 subordonnée nf** (*Ling*) dependent *ou* subordinate clause.
subordonner [sybɔʀdɔne] [1] **vt a ~ qn à** (*dans une hiérarchie*) to subordinate sb to; **accepter de se ~ à qn** to agree to subordinate o.s. to sb, accept a subordinate position under sb. **b ~ qch à** (*placer au second rang*) to subordinate sth to; (*faire dépendre de*) **nous subordonnons notre décision à ses plans** our decision will be subject to his plans; **leur départ est subordonné au résultat des examens** their departure is subject to *ou* depends on the exam results.
subornation [sybɔʀnasjɔ̃] **nf** (*Jur*) bribing, subornation (*SPÉC*).
suborner [sybɔʀne] [1] **vt** (*Jur*) *témoins* to bribe, suborn (*SPÉC*); (*littér*) *jeune fille* to lead astray, seduce.
suborneur† [sybɔʀnœʀ] **nm** seducer.
subreptice [sybʀɛptis] **adj** surreptitious.
subrepticement [sybʀɛptismɑ̃] **adv** surreptitiously.
subrogation [sybʀɔgasjɔ̃] **nf** (*Jur*) subrogation.
subrogé, e [sybʀɔʒe] (**ptp de subroger**) **nm,f** (*Jur*) surrogate. **~(-)tuteur** surrogate guardian; (*Ling*) **langage ~** subrogate language.
subroger [sybʀɔʒe] [3] **vt** (*Jur*) to subrogate, substitute.
subséquemment [sypsekamɑ̃] **adv** (†, *Jur*) subsequently.
subséquent, e [sypsekɑ̃, ɑ̃t] **adj** (†, *Jur*) subsequent.
subside [sybzid] **nm** grant. **les modestes ~s qu'il recevait de son père** the small allowance he received from his father.
subsidiaire [sybzidjɛʀ] **adj** *raison, motif* subsidiary; *voir* **question**.
subsidiairement [sybzidjɛʀmɑ̃] **adv** subsidiarily.
subsidiarité [sybzidjaRite] **nf** (*Pol*) subsidiarity.
subsistance [sybzistɑ̃s] **nf** (*moyens d'existence*) subsistence. **assurer la ~ de sa famille/de qn** to support *ou* maintain *ou* keep one's family/sb; **assurer sa (propre) ~** to keep *ou* support o.s.; **ma ~ était assurée** I had enough to live on; **pour toute ~ *ou* tous moyens de ~, ils n'avaient que 2 chèvres** their sole means of subsistence was 2 goats; **ils tirent leur ~ de certaines racines** they live on certain root crops; **elle contribue à la ~ du ménage** she contributes towards the maintenance of the family *ou* towards the housekeeping money.
subsistant, e [sybzistɑ̃, ɑ̃t] **adj** remaining (*épith*).
subsister [sybziste] [1] **vi** *[personne]* (*ne pas périr*) to live on, survive; (*se nourrir, gagner sa vie*) to live, stay alive, subsist; *[erreur, doute, vestiges]* to remain, subsist. **ils ont tout juste de quoi ~** they have just enough to live on *ou* to keep body and soul together; **il subsiste quelques doutes quant à ...** there still remains *ou* exists some doubt as to ..., some doubt subsists *ou* remains as to ... .
subsonique [sybsɔnik] **adj** subsonic.
substance [sypstɑ̃s] **nf** (*gén, Philos*) substance. **voilà, en ~, ce qu'ils ont dit** here is, in substance, what they said, here is the gist of what they said; **la ~ de notre discussion** the substance *ou* gist of our discussion; (*Anat*) **~ blanche/grise** white/grey matter; **le lait est une ~ alimentaire** milk is a food.
substantialité [sypstɑ̃sjalite] **nf** substantiality.
substantiel, -ielle [sypstɑ̃sjɛl] **adj** (*gén, Philos*) substantial.
substantiellement [sypstɑ̃sjɛlmɑ̃] **adv** substantially.
substantif, -ive [sypstɑ̃tif, iv] **1 adj** *proposition* noun (*épith*); *emploi* nominal, substantival; *style* nominal. **2 nm** noun, substantive.
substantifique [sypstɑ̃tifik] **adj** (*hum*) **la ~ moelle** the very substance.
substantivation [sypstɑ̃tivasjɔ̃] **nf** nominalization.
substantivement [sypstɑ̃tivmɑ̃] **adv** nominally, as a noun, substantively.
substantiver [sypstɑ̃tive] [1] **vt** to nominalize.
substituer [sypstitɥe] [1] **1 vt: ~ qch/qn à** to substitute sth/sb for. **2 se substituer vpr: se ~ à qn** (*en l'évinçant*) to substitute o.s. for sb; (*en le représentant*) to substitute for sb, act as a substitute for sb; **l'adjoint s'est substitué au chef** the deputy is substituting for the boss.
substitut [sypstity] **nm** (*magistrat*) deputy public prosecutor (*Brit*), assistant district attorney (*US*); (*succédané*) substitute (*de* for). (*Psych*) **~ maternel** surrogate mother.
substitution [sypstitysjɔ̃] **nf** (*gén, Chim*) (*intentionnelle*) substitution (*à* for); (*accidentelle*) *[vêtements, bébés]* mix-up (*de* of, in). **ils s'étaient aperçus trop tard qu'il y avait eu ~ d'enfants** they realized too late that the children had been mixed up *ou* that they had got the children mixed up; **produit de ~** substitute; *voir* **mère, peine**.
substrat [sypstʀa] **nm, substratum†** [sypstʀatɔm] **nm** (*Géol, Ling, Philos*) substratum.
subsumer [sypsyme] [1] **vt** to subsume.
subterfuge [syptɛʀfyʒ] **nm** subterfuge.
subtil, e [syptil] **adj** (*sagace*) *personne, esprit* subtle, discerning; *réponse* subtle; (*raffiné*) *nuance, distinction* subtle, fine, nice; *raisonnement* subtle.
subtilement [syptilmɑ̃] **adv** subtly, in a subtle way; *laisser comprendre* subtly.
subtilisation [syptilizasjɔ̃] **nf** spiriting away.
subtiliser [syptilize] [1] **1 vt** (*dérober*) to spirit away (*hum*). **il s'est fait ~ sa valise** his suitcase has been spirited away. **2 vi** (*littér: raffiner*) to subtilize.
subtilité [syptilite] **nf** (*voir* **subtil**) subtlety; nicety. **des ~s** subtleties; niceties; **les ~s de la langue française** the subtleties of the French language.
subtropical, e, mpl -aux [sybtʀɔpikal, o] **adj** subtropical. **régions ~es** subtropics.
suburbain, e [sybyʀbɛ̃, ɛn] **adj** suburban.
subvenir [sybvəniʀ] [22] **subvenir à vt indir** *besoins* to provide for, meet; *frais* to meet, cover.
subvention [sybvɑ̃sjɔ̃] **nf** (*gén*) grant; (*aux agriculteurs*) subsidy; (*à un théâtre*) subsidy, grant.
subventionner [sybvɑ̃sjɔne] [1] **vt** (*voir* **subvention**) to grant funds to; to subsidize. **école subventionnée** grant-aided school; **théâtre subventionné** subsidized theatre.
subversif, -ive [sybvɛʀsif, iv] **adj** subversive.
subversion [sybvɛʀsjɔ̃] **nf** subversion.
subversivement [sybvɛʀsivmɑ̃] **adv** subversively.
suc [syk] **nm** *[plante]* sap; *[viande, fleur, fruit]* juice; (*fig littér*) *[œuvre]* pith, meat. **~s digestifs *ou* gastriques** gastric juices.
succédané [syksedane] **nm** (*substitut, ersatz*) substitute (*de* for); (*médicament*) substitute, succedaneum (*SPÉC*).
succéder [syksede] [6] **1 succéder à vt indir** *directeur, roi* to succeed; *jours, choses, personnes* to succeed, follow; (*Jur*) *titres, héritage* to inherit, succeed to. **~ à qn à la tête d'une entreprise** to succeed sb *ou* take over from sb at the head of a firm; **des prés succédèrent aux champs de blé** cornfields were followed *ou* replaced by meadows, cornfields gave way to meadows; **le rire succéda à la peur** fear gave way to laughter; (*frm*) **~ à la couronne** to succeed to the throne.
2 se succéder vpr to follow one another, succeed one another. **ils se succédèrent de père en fils** son followed father; **3 gouvernements se sont succédé en 3 ans** 3 governments have succeeded *ou* followed one another *ou* have come one after the other in 3 years; **les mois se succédèrent** month followed month; **les échecs se succédèrent** failure followed (upon) failure, one failure followed (upon) another.
succès [syksɛ] **nm a** (*réussite*) *[entreprise, roman]* success. **~ militaires/sportifs** military/sporting successes; **le ~ ne l'a pas changé** success hasn't changed him; **~ d'estime** succès d'estime, praise from the critics (*with poor sales*); **avoir du ~ auprès des femmes** to have success *ou* be successful with women.
b (*livre*) success, bestseller; (*chanson, disque*) success, hit*; (*film, pièce*) box-office success, hit*. **~ de librairie** bestseller; **tous ses livres ont été des ~** all his books were bestsellers *ou* a success.
c (*conquête amoureuse*) **~ (féminin)** conquest; **son charme lui vaut de nombreux ~** his charm brings him many conquests *ou* much success with women.
d (*loc*) **avec ~** successfully; **avec un égal ~** equally successfully, with equal success; **sans ~** unsuccessfully, without success; **à ~** *auteur, livre* successful, bestselling; **film à ~** hit film*, blockbuster, box-office sell-out *ou* success; **chanson/pièce à ~** hit*, successful song/play; **roman à ~** successful novel, bestseller; **avoir du ~, être un ~** to be successful, be a success; **cette pièce a eu un grand ~ *ou* beaucoup de ~ *ou* un ~ fou*** this play was a great success *ou* was very successful *ou* was a smash hit*.
successeur [syksesœʀ] **nm** (*gén*) successor.
successif, -ive [syksesif, iv] **adj** successive.
succession [syksesjɔ̃] **nf a** (*enchaînement, série*) succession. **la ~ des saisons** the succession *ou* sequence of the seasons; **toute une ~ de visiteurs/malheurs** a whole succession *ou* series of visitors/misfortunes.
b (*transmission de pouvoir*) succession; (*Jur*) (*transmission de biens*) succession; (*patrimoine*) estate, inheritance. **s'occuper d'une ~** to be occupied with a succession; **partager une ~** to share an estate *ou* an inheritance; (*Jur*) **la ~ est ouverte** ≃ the will is going through probate; **par voie de ~** by right of inheritance *ou* succession; **prendre la ~ de** *ministre, directeur* to succeed, take over from; *roi* to succeed; *maison de commerce* to take over; *voir* **droit³, guerre**.
successivement [syksesivmɑ̃] **adv** successively.
successoral, e, mpl -aux [syksesɔʀal, o] **adj: droits ~aux** inheritance tax.
succinct, e [syksɛ̃, ɛ̃t] **adj** *écrit* succinct; *repas* frugal. **soyez ~** be brief.
succinctement [syksɛ̃tmɑ̃] **adv** *raconter* succinctly; *manger* frugally.
succion [sy(k)sjɔ̃] **nf** (*Phys, Tech*) suction; (*Méd*) *[plaie]* sucking. **bruit de ~** sucking noise.
succomber [sykɔ̃be] [1] **vi a** (*mourir*) to die, succumb. **b** (*être vaincu*) to succumb; (*par tentations*) to succumb, give way. **~ sous le**

nombre to be overcome by numbers; ~ **à** *tentation* to succumb *ou* yield to; *promesses* to succumb to; *fatigue, désespoir, sommeil* to give way to, succumb to; (*littér: lit, fig*) ~ **sous le poids de** to yield *ou* give way beneath the weight of.

succube [sykyb] **nm** succubus.

succulence [sykylɑ̃s] **nf** (*littér*) succulence.

succulent, e [sykylɑ̃, ɑ̃t] **adj** (*délicieux*) *fruit, rôti* succulent; *mets, repas* delicious; *récit* juicy*; (††: *juteux*) succulent.

succursale [sykyʀsal] **nf** *[magasin, firme]* branch; *voir* **magasin.**

sucer [syse] [3] **vt** (*lit*) to suck. **toujours à ~ des bonbons** always sucking sweets; **ces pastilles se sucent** these tablets are to be sucked; ~ **son pouce** to suck one's thumb; **ce procès lui a sucé toutes ses économies‡** this lawsuit has bled him of all his savings; **se ~ la poire‡** to neck‡, kiss passionately.

sucette [sysɛt] **nf** (*bonbon*) lollipop, lolly (*Brit*); (*tétine*) dummy (*Brit*), comforter, pacifier (*US*).

suçon* [sysɔ̃] **nm** *mark made on the skin by sucking.* **elle lui fit un ~ au cou** she gave him a love bite* (*Brit*) *ou* hickey* (*US*) (on his neck).

suçoter [sysɔte] [1] **vt** to suck.

sucrage [sykʀaʒ] **nm** *[vin]* sugaring, sweetening.

sucrant, e [sykʀɑ̃, ɑ̃t] **adj** sweetening. **c'est très ~** it makes things very sweet, it's very sweet.

sucrase [sykʀɑz] **nf** sucrase.

sucre [sykʀ] 1 **nm** a (*substance*) sugar; (*morceau*) lump of sugar, sugar lump, sugar cube. **fraises au ~** strawberries sprinkled with sugar; **cet enfant n'est pas en ~ quand même!** for goodness sake, the child won't break!; **être tout ~ tout miel** to be all sweetness and light; **mon petit trésor en ~** my little honey-bun *ou* sugarplum; **prendre 2 ~s dans son café** to take 2 lumps (of sugar) *ou* 2 sugars in one's coffee; *voir* **casser, pain, pince** *etc.*

b (*unité monétaire*) sucre.

2 **comp** ►**sucre de betterave** beet sugar ►**sucre brun** brown sugar ►**sucre candi** candy sugar ►**sucre de canne** cane sugar ►**sucre cristallisé** (coarse) granulated sugar ►**sucre d'érable** (*Can* *) maple sugar ►**sucre glace** icing sugar (*Brit*), confectioners' sugar (*US*) ►**sucre en morceaux** lump sugar, cube sugar ►**sucre d'orge** (*substance*) barley sugar; (*bâton*) stick of barley sugar ►**sucre en poudre** caster sugar ►**sucre roux** = **sucre brun** ►**sucre semoule** = **sucre en poudre** ►**sucre vanillé** vanilla sugar.

sucré, e [sykʀe] (**ptp de sucrer**) 1 **adj** a *fruit, saveur, vin* sweet; *jus de fruits, lait condensé* sweetened. **ce thé est trop ~** this tea is too sweet; **prenez-vous votre café ~?** do you take sugar (in your coffee)?; **tasse de thé bien ~e** well-sweetened cup of tea, cup of nice sweet tea; **non ~** unsweetened; *voir* **eau.** b (*péj*) *ton* sugary, honeyed; *air* sickly-sweet. **faire le ~** (*ou* **la ~e**) to turn on the charm. 2 **nm: le ~ et le salé** sweet and savoury food; **je préfère le ~ au salé** I prefer sweets to savouries *ou* sweet things to savouries.

sucrer [sykʀe] [1] 1 **vt** a *boisson* to sugar, put sugar in, sweeten; *produit alimentaire* to sweeten. **le miel sucre autant que le sucre lui-même** honey sweetens as much as sugar, honey is as good a sweetener as sugar; **on peut ~ avec du miel** honey may be used as a sweetener *ou* may be used to sweeten things; **sucrez à volonté** sweeten *ou* add sugar to taste; (*fig*) ~ **les fraises‡** to be a bit doddery*.

b (‡: *supprimer*) ~ **son argent de poche à qn** to stop sb's pocket money; **il s'est fait ~ ses heures supplémentaires** he's had his overtime money stopped.

2 **se sucrer vpr** a (* *lit: prendre du sucre*) to help o.s. to sugar, have some sugar.

b (‡ *fig: s'enrichir*) to line one's pocket(s)*.

sucrerie [sykʀəʀi] **nf** a ~**s** sweets, sweet things; **aimer les ~s** to have a sweet tooth, like sweet things. b (*usine*) sugar house; (*raffinerie*) sugar refinery.

Sucrette [sykʀɛt] **nf** ® artificial sweetener.

sucrier, -ière [sykʀije, ijɛʀ] 1 **adj** *industrie, betterave* sugar (*épith*); *région* sugar-producing. 2 **nm** a (*récipient*) sugar basin, sugar bowl. ~ **(verseur)** sugar dispenser *ou* shaker. b (*industriel*) sugar producer.

sud [syd] 1 **nm** a (*point cardinal*) south. **le vent du ~** the south wind; **un vent du ~** a south(erly) wind, a southerly (*Naut*); **le vent tourne/est au ~** the wind is veering south(wards) *ou* towards the south/is blowing from the south; **regarder vers le ~** *ou* **dans la direction du ~** to look south(wards) *ou* towards the south; **au ~** (*situation*) in the south; (*direction*) to the south, south(wards); **au ~ de** south of, to the south of; **l'appartement est (exposé) au ~/exposé plein ~** the flat faces (the) south *ou* southwards/due south, the flat looks south(wards)/due south.

b (*partie, régions australes*) south. **le ~ de la France, le S~** the South of France; **l'Europe/l'Italie du S~** Southern Europe/Italy; *voir* **Amérique, Corée, croix.**

2 **adj inv** *région, partie* southern; *entrée, paroi* south; *versant, côte* south(ern); *côté* south(ward); *direction* southward, southerly (*Mét*); *voir* **hémisphère, pôle.**

3 **comp** ►**sud-africain, e adj** South African ►**Sud-Africain, e nm,f (mpl Sud-Africains)** South African ►**sud-américain, e adj** South American ►**Sud-Américain, e nm,f (mpl Sud-Américains)** South American ►**sud-coréen, -enne adj** South Korean ►**Sud-Coréen, -enne nm,f (mpl Sud-Coréens)** South Korean ►**sud-est nm, adj inv** south-east; **le Sud-Est asiatique** South-East Asia ►**sud-ouest nm, adj inv** south-west ►**sud-sud-est nm, adj inv** south-south-east ►**sud-sud-ouest nm, adj inv** south-south-west ►**sud-vietnamien, -ienne adj** South Vietnamese ►**Sud-Vietnamien, -ienne nm,f (mpl Sud-Vietnamiens)** South Vietnamese.

sudation [sydasjɔ̃] **nf** sweating, sudation (*SPÉC*).

sudatoire [sydatwaʀ] **adj** sudatory.

sudiste [sydist] (*Hist US*) 1 **nmf** Southerner. 2 **adj** Southern.

sudorifère [sydɔʀifɛʀ] **adj** = **sudoripare.**

sudorifique [sydɔʀifik] **adj, nm** sudorific.

sudoripare [sydɔʀipaʀ] **adj** sudoriferous, sudoriparous.

Suède [sɥɛd] **nf** Sweden.

suède [sɥɛd] **nm** (*peau*) suede. **en** *ou* **de ~** suede.

suédé, e [sɥede] **adj, nm** suede.

suédine [sɥedin] **nf** suedette.

suédois, e [sɥedwa, waz] 1 **adj** Swedish; *voir* **allumette, gymnastique.** 2 **nm** (*Ling*) Swedish. 3 **nm,f: S~(e)** Swede.

suée* [sɥe] **nf** sweat. **prendre** *ou* **attraper une bonne ~** to work up a good sweat*; **à l'idée de cette épreuve, j'en avais la ~** I was in a (cold) sweat at the idea of the test*; **je dois aller le voir, quelle ~!** I've got to go and see him — what a drag!‡ *ou* pain!‡

suer [sɥe] [1] 1 **vi** a (*transpirer*) to sweat; (*fig: peiner*) to sweat* (*sur* over). ~ **de peur** to sweat with fear, be in a cold sweat; ~ **à grosses gouttes** to sweat profusely; ~ **sur une dissertation** to sweat over an essay*.

b (*suinter*) *[murs]* to ooze, sweat (*de* with).

c (*Culin*) **faire ~** to sweat.

d (*loc*) **faire ~ qn** (*lit*) *[médicament]* to make sb sweat; (*péj*) **faire ~ le burnous‡** to use sweated labour, exploit native labour; **tu me fais ~*** you're a pain (in the neck)‡ *ou* a drag‡; **on se fait ~ ici*** what a drag it is here‡, we're getting really cheesed (off) here‡.

2 **vt** a *sueur, sang* to sweat. (*fig*) ~ **sang et eau à** *ou* **pour faire qch** to sweat blood to get sth done *ou* over sth.

b *humidité* to ooze.

c (*révéler, respirer*) *pauvreté, misère, avarice, lâcheté* to exude.

d (*danser*) **en ~ une‡** to shake a leg‡.

sueur [sɥœʀ] **nf** sweat (*NonC*). **en ~** in a sweat, sweating; **à la ~ de son front** by the sweat of one's brow; **donner des ~s froides à qn** to put sb in(to) a cold sweat; **j'en avais des ~s froides** I was in a cold sweat *ou* a great sweat* about it; (*fig*) **vivre de la ~ du peuple** to live off the backs of the people.

suffire [syfiʀ] [37] 1 **vi** a (*être assez*) *[somme, durée, quantité]* to be enough, be sufficient, suffice. **cette explication ne (me) suffit pas** this explanation isn't enough *ou* isn't sufficient (for me) *ou* won't do; **5 hommes suffisent (pour ce travail)** 5 men will do (for this job); **un rien suffirait pour** *ou* **à bouleverser nos plans** the smallest thing would be enough *ou* sufficient to upset our plans, it would only take the smallest thing to upset our plans; *voir* **à.**

b (*arriver à, satisfaire, combler*) ~ **à** *besoins* to meet; *personne* to be enough for; **ma femme me suffit** *ou* **suffit à mon bonheur,** my wife is all I need to make me happy, my wife is enough to make me happy; **il ne suffit pas aux besoins de la famille** he does not meet the needs of his family; **il ne peut ~ à tout** he can't manage (to do) everything, he can't cope with everything; **les week-ends, il ne suffisait plus à servir les clients** at weekends he could no longer manage to serve all the customers *ou* he could no longer cope (with serving) all the customers.

c (*loc*) **ça suffit** that's enough, that'll do; **(ça) suffit!** that's enough!, that will do!; **comme ennuis, ça suffit (comme ça)** we've had enough troubles thank you very much; **ça ne te suffit pas de l'avoir tourmentée?** isn't it enough for you to have tormented her?

2 **vb impers** a **il suffit de s'inscrire pour devenir membre** enrolling is enough *ou* sufficient to become a member; **il suffit de (la) faire réchauffer et la soupe est prête** just heat (up) the soup and it's ready (to serve); **il suffit que vous leur écriviez** it will be enough if you write to them, your writing to them will be enough *ou* will be sufficient *ou* will suffice (*frm*); **il suffit d'un accord verbal pour conclure l'affaire** a verbal agreement is sufficient *ou* is enough *ou* will suffice (*frm*) to conclude the matter; **il suffisait d'y penser**it's obvious when you think about it.

b (*intensif*) **il suffit d'un rien pour l'inquiéter** it only takes the smallest thing to worry him, the smallest thing is enough to worry him; **il lui suffit d'un regard pour comprendre** a look was enough to make him understand, he needed only a look to understand; **il suffit qu'il ouvre la bouche pour que tout le monde se taise** he has *ou* needs only to open his mouth and everyone stops talking *ou* to make everyone stop talking; **il suffit d'une fois: on n'est jamais trop prudent** once is enough — you can never be too careful.

3 **se suffire vpr: se ~ (à soi-même)** *[pays, personne]* to be self-sufficient; **la beauté se suffit (à elle-même)** beauty is sufficient unto itself (*littér*); **ils se suffisent (l'un à l'autre)** they are enough for each other.

suffisamment [syfizamɑ̃] **adv** sufficiently, enough. ~ **fort/clair** sufficiently strong/clear, strong/clear enough; **être ~ vêtu** to have sufficient *ou* enough clothes on, be adequately dressed; **lettre ~ affran-**

chie sufficiently *ou* adequately stamped letter; ~ **de nourriture/d'argent** sufficient *ou* enough food/money; **y a-t-il ~ à boire?** is there enough *ou* sufficient to drink?

suffisance [syfizɑ̃s] **nf** a (*vanité*) self-importance, bumptiousness. b (*littér*) **avoir sa ~ de qch†, avoir qch en ~** to have sth in plenty, have a sufficiency of sth; **il y en a en ~** there is sufficient of it; **des livres, il en a sa ~†** *ou* **à sa ~** he has books aplenty *ou* in abundance.

suffisant, e [syfizɑ̃, ɑ̃t] **adj** a (*adéquat*) sufficient; (*Scol*) *résultats* satisfactory. **c'est ~ pour qu'il se mette en colère** it's enough to make him lose his temper; **je n'ai pas la place/la somme ~e** I haven't got sufficient *ou* enough room/money; **500 F, c'est amplement** *ou* **plus que ~** 500 francs is more than enough; *voir* **condition, grâce.** b (*prétentieux*) *personne, ton* self-important, bumptious. **faire le ~** to give o.s. airs and graces.

suffixal, e, **mpl -aux** [syfiksal, o] **adj** suffixal.

suffixation [syfiksasjɔ̃] **nf** suffixation.

suffixe [syfiks] **nm** suffix.

suffixer [sufikse] 1 **vt** to add a suffix to.

suffocant, e [syfɔkɑ̃, ɑ̃t] **adj** a *fumée, chaleur* suffocating, stifling. b (*étonnant*) staggering*.

suffocation [syfɔkasjɔ̃] **nf** (*action*) suffocation; (*sensation*) suffocating feeling. **il avait des ~s** he had fits of choking.

suffoquer [syfɔke] 1 1 **vi** (*lit*) to choke, suffocate, stifle (*de* with). (*fig*) ~ **de** to choke with. 2 **vt** a *[fumée]* to suffocate, choke, stifle; *[colère, joie]* to choke. **les larmes la suffoquaient** she was choking with tears. b (*étonner*) *[nouvelle, comportement de qn]* to stagger*. **la nouvelle nous a suffoqués** the news took our breath away, we were staggered* by the news.

suffragant, e [syfʀagɑ̃, ɑ̃t] **adj** (*Rel*) suffragan.

suffrage [syfʀaʒ] 1 **nm** a (*Pol: voix*) vote. **~s exprimés** valid votes; **le parti obtiendra peu de/beaucoup de ~s** the party will poll badly/ heavily, the party will get a poor/good share of the vote.

b (*fig*) *[public, critique]* approval (*NonC*), approbation (*NonC*). **accorder son ~ à qn/qch** to give one's approval *ou* approbation to sb/ sth; **ce livre a remporté tous les ~s** this book met with universal approval *ou* approbation; **cette nouvelle voiture mérite tous les ~s** this new car deserves everyone's approval.

2 **comp** ► **suffrage censitaire** suffrage on the basis of property qualification ► **suffrage direct** direct suffrage ► **suffrage indirect** indirect suffrage ► **suffrage restreint** restricted suffrage ► **suffrage universel** universal suffrage *ou* franchise.

suffragette [syfʀaʒɛt] **nf** suffragette.

suggérer [sygʒeʀe] 6 **vt** (*gén*) to suggest; *solution, projet* to suggest, put forward. ~ **une réponse à qn** to suggest a reply to sb; **je lui suggérai que c'était moins facile qu'il ne pensait** I suggested to him *ou* I put it to him that it was not as easy as he thought; **~ à qn une solution** to put forward *ou* suggest *ou* put a solution to sb; **j'ai suggéré d'aller au cinéma/que nous allions au cinéma** I suggested going to the cinema/that we went to the cinema; **elle lui a suggéré de voir un médecin** she suggested he should see a doctor; **mot qui en suggère un autre** word which brings to mind another.

suggestibilité [sygʒɛstibilite] **nf** suggestibility.

suggestible [sygʒɛstibl] **adj** suggestible.

suggestif, -ive [sygʒɛstif, iv] **adj** (*évocateur, indécent*) suggestive.

suggestion [sygʒɛstjɔ̃] **nf** suggestion. **faire une ~** to make a suggestion.

suggestionner [sygʒɛstjɔne] 1 **vt** to influence by suggestion.

suggestivité [sygʒɛstivite] **nf** suggestiveness.

suicidaire [sɥisidɛʀ] 1 **adj** (*lit, fig*) suicidal. 2 **nmf** person with suicidal tendencies.

suicide [sɥisid] **nm** (*lit, fig*) suicide. (*fig*) **c'est un** *ou* **du ~!** it's suicide!; **opération** *ou* **mission ~** suicide mission; *voir* **avion 2, tentative.**

suicidé, e [sɥiside] (**ptp de se suicider**) 1 **adj: personne ~e** person who has committed suicide. 2 **nm,f** suicide (*person*).

suicider (se) [sɥiside] 1 **vpr** to commit suicide. (*iro*) **on a suicidé le témoin gênant** they have had the embarrassing witness "commit suicide".

suie [sɥi] **nf** soot; *voir* **noir.**

suif [sɥif] **nm** tallow. ~ **de mouton** mutton suet; (*arg Crime*) **chercher du ~ à qn** to needle sb*; (*arg Crime*) **il va y avoir du ~** there's going to be trouble.

sui generis [sɥiʒeneʀis] **adv, adj** sui generis. **l'odeur ~ d'une prison** the distinctive *ou* peculiar *ou* characteristic smell of a prison.

suint [sɥɛ̃] **nm** *[laine]* suint.

suintant, e [sɥɛ̃tɑ̃, ɑ̃t] **adj** *pierre, roche, mur* oozing, sweating.

suintement [sɥɛ̃tmɑ̃] **nm** (*voir* **suinter**) oozing; sweating; weeping. **des ~s sur le mur** oozing moisture on the wall.

suinter [sɥɛ̃te] 1 **vi** *[eau]* to ooze; *[mur]* to ooze, sweat; *[plaie]* to weep, ooze. (*fig*) **l'ennui suinte dans ce bureau** a feeling of boredom pervades this office.

Suisse [sɥis] 1 **nf** (*pays*) Switzerland. ~ **romande/allemande** *ou* **alémanique** French-speaking/German-speaking Switzerland. 2 **nm** (*personne*) Swiss. ~ **romand** French-speaking Swiss; **~-allemand** German-speaking Swiss, Swiss German; **boire/manger en ~** to drink/eat alone; *voir* **petit.**

suisse [sɥis] 1 **adj** Swiss. ~ **romand** Swiss French; **~-allemand** Swiss German. 2 **nm** a (*bedeau*) ≃ verger. b (*Zool*) chipmunk.

Suissesse [sɥisɛs] **nf** Swiss (woman).

suite [sɥit] **nf** a (*escorte*) retinue, suite.

b (*nouvel épisode*) continuation, following episode; (*second roman, film*) sequel; (*rebondissement d'une affaire*) follow-up; (*reste*) remainder, rest. **voici la ~ de notre feuilleton** here is the next episode in *ou* the continuation of our serial; **ce roman/film a une ~** there is a sequel to this novel/film; (*Presse*) **voici la ~ de l'affaire que nous évoquions hier** here is the follow-up to *ou* further information on the item we mentioned yesterday; **la ~ du film/du repas/de la lettre était moins bonne** the remainder *ou* the rest of the film/meal/letter was not so good; **la ~ au prochain numéro** (*journal*) to be continued (in the next issue); (*: *fig*) we'll talk about this later; **~ et fin** concluding *ou* final episode; **la ~ des événements devait lui donner raison** what followed was to prove him right; **attendons la ~** (*d'un repas*) let's wait for the next course; (*d'un discours*) let's see what comes next; (*d'un événement*) let's (wait and) see how it turns out; **lisez donc la ~** do read on, do read what follows.

c (*aboutissement*) result. (*prolongements*) **~s** *[maladie]* effects; *[accident]* results; *[affaire, incident]* consequences, repercussions; **la ~ logique de** the obvious *ou* logical result of; **il a succombé des ~s de ses blessures/sa maladie** he succumbed to the after-effects of his wounds/ illness; **cet incident a eu des ~s fâcheuses/n'a pas eu de ~s** the incident has had annoying consequences *ou* repercussions/has had no repercussions.

d (*succession*) (*Math*) series; (*Ling*) sequence. ~ **de** *personnes, maisons* succession *ou* string *ou* series of; *événements* succession *ou* train of; (*Comm*) **article sans ~** discontinued line.

e (*frm: cohérence*) coherence. **il y a beaucoup de ~ dans son raisonnement/ses réponses** there is a good deal of coherence in his reasoning/his replies; **ses propos n'avaient guère de ~** what he said lacked coherence *ou* consistency; **travailler avec ~** to work steadily; **des propos sans ~** disjointed talk; **avoir de la ~ dans les idées** (*réfléchi, décidé*) to show great single-mindedness *ou* singleness of purpose; (*iro: entêté*) not to be easily put off; *voir* **esprit.**

f (*appartement*) suite.

g (*Mus*) suite. ~ **instrumentale/orchestrale** instrumental/orchestral suite.

h (*loc*) (*Comm*) **(comme) ~ à votre lettre/notre entretien** further to your letter/our conversation; **à la ~** (*successivement*) one after the other; (*derrière*) **mettez-vous à la ~** join on at the back, go to *ou* join the back of the queue (*Brit*) *ou* line (*US*); **à la ~ de** (*derrière*) behind; (*en conséquence de*) **à la ~ de sa maladie** following his illness; **entraîner qn à sa ~** (*lit*) to drag sb along behind one; (*fig*) **entraîner qn à sa ~ dans une affaire** to drag sb into an affair; **de ~** (*immédiatement*) at once; **je reviens de ~** I'll be straight (*Brit*) *ou* right back; **boire 3 verres de ~** to drink 3 glasses in a row *ou* in succession *ou* one after the other; **pendant 3 jours de ~** (for) 3 days on end *ou* in succession; **il est venu 3 jours de ~** he came 3 days in a row *ou* 3 days running; **il n'arrive pas à dire trois mots de ~** he can't string three words together; (*à cause de*) **par ~ de** owing to, as a result of; (*par conséquent*) **par ~** consequently, therefore; (*ensuite*) **par la ~, dans la ~** afterwards, subsequently; **donner ~ à** *projet* to pursue, follow up; *demande, commande, lettre* to follow up; **ils n'ont pas donné ~ à notre lettre** they have taken no action concerning our letter, they have not followed up our letter; **faire ~ à** *événement* to follow (upon); *chapitre* to follow (after); *bâtiment* to adjoin; **prendre la ~ de** *firme, directeur* to succeed, take over from; *voir* **ainsi, tout.**

suivant¹, e [sɥivɑ̃, ɑ̃t] 1 **adj** a (*dans le temps*) following, next; (*dans une série*) next. **le mardi ~ je la revis** the following *ou* next Tuesday I saw her again; **vendredi et les jours ~s** Friday and the following days; **le malade ~ était très atteint** the next patient was very badly affected; **"voir page ~e"** "see next page".

b (*ci-après*) following. **faites l'exercice ~** do the following exercise.

2 **nm, f** a (*prochain*) (*dans une série*) next (one); (*dans le temps*) following (one), next (one). **(au) ~!** next (please)!; **cette année fut mauvaise et les ~es ne le furent guère moins** that year was bad and the following ones *ou* next ones were scarcely less so; **pas jeudi prochain, le ~** not Thursday (coming*), the one after (that); **je descends à la ~e*** I'm getting off at the next stop.

b (*littér: membre d'escorte*) attendant.

3 **suivante nf** (*Théât*) soubrette, lady's maid; (††) companion.

suivant² [sɥivɑ̃] **prép** (*selon*) according to. ~ **son habitude** as is (*ou* was) his habit *ou* wont, in keeping with his habit; **~ l'usage** in keeping *ou* conformity *ou* accordance with custom; **~ l'expression consacrée** as the saying goes, as they say; ~ **les jours/les cas** according to *ou* depending on the day/the circumstances; **découper ~ le pointillé** cut (out) along the dotted line; ~ **un axe** along an axis; **~ que** according to whether.

suiveur [sɥivœʀ] **nm** a *[course cycliste etc]* (official) follower (*of a race*). b (*imitateur*) imitator. c (†: *dragueur*) **elle se retourna, son ~ avait disparu** she turned round — the man who was following her had disappeared; **elle va me prendre pour un ~** she'll think I'm the sort (of fellow) who follows women.

suivi, e [sɥivi] (ptp de **suivre**) 1 adj a (*régulier*) *travail* steady; *correspondance* regular; (*constant*) *qualité* consistent; *effort* consistent, sustained; (*Comm*) *demande* constant, steady; (*cohérent*) *conversation, histoire, raisonnement* coherent; *politique* consistent.

b (*Comm*) *article* in general production (*attrib*).

c **très ~** *cours* well-attended; *mode, recommandation* widely adopted; *exemple, feuilleton* widely followed. **un match très ~** a match with a wide audience; **un cours peu ~** a poorly-attended course; **une mode peu ~e** a fashion which is not widely adopted; **un exemple peu ~** an example which is not widely followed; **un procès très ~** a trial that is being closely followed by the public; **un feuilleton très ~** a serial with a large following.

2 nm: **assurer le ~ de** *affaire* to follow through; *produit en stock* to go on stocking; **~ médical** medical follow-up.

suivisme [sɥivism] nm (*Pol*) follow-my-leader attitude.

suiviste [sɥivist] 1 adj *attitude, politique* follow-my-leader (*épith*). 2 nmf person with a follow-my-leader attitude.

suivre [sɥivʀ] [40] 1 vt a (*gén: accompagner, marcher derrière, venir après*) to follow. **elle le suit comme un petit chien** *ou* **un caniche** *ou* **un toutou*** she follows him (around) like a little dog; **il me suit comme mon ombre** he follows me about like my shadow; **vous marchez trop vite, je ne peux pas vous ~** you are walking too quickly and I can't keep up (with you); **partez sans moi, je vous suis** go on without me and I'll follow (on); **si vous voulez bien me ~** if you'll just follow me *ou* come this way please; **l'été suit le printemps** summer follows *ou* comes after spring; (*fig*) **son image me suit sans cesse** his image follows me everywhere *ou* is constantly with me; **il la suivit des yeux** *ou* **du regard** he followed her with his eyes, his eyes followed her; (*iro*) **certains députés, suivez mon regard, ont ...** certain deputies, without mentioning any names *ou* no names mentioned, have ...; **~ qn de près** *[garde du corps]* to stick close to sb; *[voiture]* to follow close behind sb; **suivre qn à la trace** to follow sb's tracks; (*iro*) **on peut le ~ à la trace!** there's no mistaking where he has been!; **faire ~ qn** to have sb followed; **suivez le guide!** this way, please!; *voir* **qui**.

b (*dans une série*) to follow. **la maison qui suit la mienne** the house after mine *ou* following mine; *voir* **jour**.

c (*longer*) *[personne]* to follow, keep to; *[route, itinéraire]* to follow. **suivez la N7 sur 10 km** keep to *ou* go along *ou* follow the N7 (road) for 10 km; **prenez la route qui suit la Loire** take the road which goes alongside *ou* which follows the Loire; (*fig*) **~ une piste** to follow up a clue; (*fig*) **ces deux amis ont suivi des voies bien différentes** these two friends have gone very different ways.

d (*se conformer à*) *personne, exemple, mode, conseil* to follow. **~ un traitement** to follow a course of treatment; **~ un régime** to be on a diet; **~ son instinct** to follow one's instinct *ou* one's nose*; **il suit son idée** he does things his (own) way; **il se leva et chacun suivit son exemple** he stood up and everyone followed suit *ou* followed his lead *ou* example; **on n'a pas voulu le ~** we didn't want to follow his advice; **tout le monde vous suivra** everybody will back you up *ou* support you; **la maladie/l'enquête suit son cours** the illness/the inquiry is running *ou* taking its course; **il me fait ~ un régime sévère** he has put me on a strict diet; **~ le mouvement** to follow the crowd, follow the general trend; **si les prix augmentent, les salaires doivent ~** if prices rise, salaries must do the same; *voir* **marche**[1].

e (*Scol*) *classe, cours* (*être inscrit à*) to attend, go to; (*être attentif à*) to follow, attend to; (*assimiler*) *programme* to keep up with.

f (*observer l'évolution de*) *carrière de qn, affaire, match* to follow; *feuilleton* to follow, keep up with. **~ un malade/un élève** to follow *ou* monitor the progress of a patient/pupil; **~ l'actualité** to keep up with *ou* follow the news; **c'est une affaire à ~** it's an affair worth following *ou* worth keeping an eye on; **il se fait ~** *ou* **il est suivi par un médecin** he's having treatment from a doctor, he is under the doctor*; **j'ai suivi ses articles avec intérêt** I've followed his articles with interest; **à ~** to be continued.

g (*Comm*) *article* to (continue to) stock.

h (*comprendre*) *argument, personne, exposé* to follow. **jusqu'ici je vous suis** I'm with you *ou* I follow you so far; **il parlait si vite qu'on le suivait mal** he spoke so fast he was difficult to follow; **là, je ne vous suis pas très bien** I don't really follow you *ou* I'm not really with you there.

2 vi a *[élève]* (*être attentif*) to attend, pay attention. **suivez avec votre voisin** *ou* **sur le livre de votre voisin** follow on your neighbour's book; **il ne suit jamais en classe** he never attends in class, he never pays attention in class.

b *[élève]* (*assimiler le programme*) to keep up, follow. **va-t-il pouvoir ~ l'année prochaine?** will he be able to keep up *ou* follow next year?

c (*Cartes*) to follow.

d **faire ~ son courrier** to have one's mail forwarded; (*sur enveloppe*) **"faire ~"** "please forward".

e (*venir après*) to follow. **lisez ce qui suit** read what follows; **les enfants suivent à pied** the children are following on foot.

3 vb impers: **il suit de ce que vous dites que ...** it follows from what you say that ...; **comme suit** as follows.

4 **se suivre** vpr a (*dans une série*) to follow each other. **ils se suivaient sur l'étroit sentier** (*deux personnes*) they were walking one behind the other along the narrow path; (*plusieurs personnes*) they were walking in single file along the narrow path; **leurs enfants se suivent (de près)** there is not much of an age difference between their children; **3 démissions qui se suivent** 3 resignations in a row *ou* coming one after the other, 3 resignations in close succession.

b (*dans le bon ordre*) to be in (the right) order. **les pages ne se suivent pas** the pages are not in (the right) order, the pages are in the wrong order *ou* are out of order.

c (*être cohérent*) *[argument, pensée]* to be coherent, be consistent. **dans son roman, rien ne se suit** there's no coherence *ou* consistency in his novel.

sujet, -ette [syʒɛ, ɛt] 1 adj: **~ à** *vertige, mal de mer* liable to, subject to, prone to; *lubies, sautes d'humeur* subject to, prone to; **~ aux accidents** accident-prone; **il était ~ aux accidents les plus bizarres** he was prone *ou* subject to the strangest accidents; **~ à faire** liable *ou* inclined *ou* prone to do; **il n'est pas ~ à faire des imprudences** he is not one to do anything imprudent; **~ à caution** *renseignement, nouvelle* unconfirmed; *moralité, vie privée, honnêteté* questionable; **je vous dis ça mais c'est ~ à caution** I'm telling you that but I can't guarantee it's true.

2 nm,f (*gouverné*) subject.

3 nm a (*matière, question, thème*) subject (*de* for). **un excellent ~ de conversation** an excellent topic (of conversation) *ou* subject (for conversation); **c'était devenu un ~ de plaisanterie** it had become a standing joke *ou* something to joke about; **ça ferait un bon ~ de comédie** that would be a good subject *ou* theme for a comedy; **bibliographie par ~s** bibliography arranged by subjects; **~ d'examen** examination question; **quel ~ ont-ils donné?** what subject did they give you *ou* did they set?; **distribuer les ~s** to give out the examination papers; *voir* **or**[1], **vif**.

b (*motif, cause*) **~ de** cause for, ground(s) for; **~ de mécontentement/de dispute** cause *ou* grounds for dissatisfaction/for dispute; **il n'avait vraiment pas ~ de se mettre en colère/se plaindre** he really had no cause to lose *ou* grounds for losing his temper/for complaint; **ayant tout ~ de croire à sa bonne foi** having every reason to believe in his good faith; **protester/réclamer sans ~** to protest/complain without (good) cause *ou* groundlessly.

c (*individu*) subject. (*Ling*) **le ~ parlant** the speaker; **les rats qui servent de ~s (d'expérience)** the rats which serve as experimental subjects; **son frère est un ~ brillant/un ~ d'élite** his brother is a brilliant/an exceptionally brilliant student; **un mauvais ~** (*enfant*) a bad boy; (*jeune homme*) a bad lot.

d (*Ling, Mus, Philos*) subject. **~ grammatical/réel/apparent** grammatical/real/apparent subject.

e (*à propos de*) **au ~ de** about, concerning; **que sais-tu à son ~?** what do you know about *ou* of him?; **au ~ de cette fille, je peux vous dire que ...** about *ou* concerning that girl *ou* with regard to that girl, I can tell you that ...; **à ce ~, je voulais vous dire que ...** on that subject *ou* about that*, I wanted to tell you that ...; **c'est à quel ~?** can I ask what it is about?

sujétion [syʒesjɔ̃] nf a (*asservissement*) subjection. **maintenir un peuple dans la ~** *ou* **sous sa ~** to keep a nation in subjection; **tomber sous la ~ de** to fall into sb's power *ou* under sb's sway; (*fig littér*) **~ aux passions/au désir** subjection to passions/desire. b (*obligation, contrainte*) constraint. **les enfants étaient pour elle une ~** the children were a real constraint to her *ou* were like a millstone round her neck; **des habitudes qui deviennent des ~s** habits which become compulsions.

sulfamides [sylfamid] nmpl sulpha drugs, sulphonamides (*SPÉC*).

sulfatage [sylfataʒ] nm *[vigne]* spraying with copper sulphate.

sulfate [sylfat] nm sulphate. **~ de cuivre** copper sulphate.

sulfaté, e [sylfate] (ptp de **sulfater**) adj sulphated.

sulfater [sylfate] [1] vt *vigne* to spray with copper sulphate.

sulfateuse [sylfatøz] nf a (*Agr*) copper sulphate spraying machine. b (*arg Crime: mitraillette*) machine gun, MG*.

sulfite [sylfit] nm sulphite.

sulfure [sylfyʀ] nm sulphide.

sulfuré, e [sylfyʀe] (ptp de **sulfurer**) adj sulphurated, sulphuretted. **hydrogène ~** hydrogen sulphide.

sulfurer [sylfyʀe] [1] vt to sulphurate, sulphurize.

sulfureux, -euse [sylfyʀø, øz] adj (*Chim*) sulphurous; *propos* heretical. **anhydride** *ou* **gaz ~** sulphur dioxide.

sulfurique [sylfyʀik] adj sulphuric. **anhydride ~** sulphur trioxide.

sulfurisé, e [sylfyʀize] adj: **papier ~** greaseproof paper.

sulky [sylki] nm (*Courses*) sulky.

sultan [syltɑ̃] nm sultan.

sultanat [syltana] nm sultanate.

sultane [syltan] nf a (*épouse*) sultana. b (*canapé*) (sort of) couch.

sumac [symak] nm sumach (*Brit*), sumac (*US*).

Sumatra [symatʀa] n Sumatra.

sumérien, -ienne [symeʀjɛ̃, jɛn] 1 adj Sumerian. 2 nm (*Ling*) Sumerian. 3 nm,f: **S~(ne)** Sumerian.

summum [sɔ(m)mɔm] nm *[gloire, civilisation]* acme, climax; *[bêtise, hypocrisie]* height.

sumo [symo] nm inv sumo (wrestling).

sunnisme [synism] nm Sunni.
sunnite [synit] adj, nmf Sunni.
super [sypɛʀ] 1 nm (abrév de **supercarburant**) super, four-star (petrol) (*Brit*), extra (*US*), premium (*US*), super (*US*). 2 préf (*) **~cher/chic** ultra-expensive/ultra-chic *ou* -smart, fantastically expensive/smart*; **~-bombe/-ordinateur** super-bomb/-computer*. 3 adj inv (*) terrific*, great*, fantastic*, super*.
superbe [sypɛʀb] 1 adj a (*splendide*) *temps, journée* superb, glorious; *femme, enfant* beautiful, gorgeous; *maison, cheval, corps, yeux* superb, magnificent, beautiful; *résultat, salaire, performance* magnificent, superb. **revenu de vacances avec une mine ~** back from holiday looking superbly *ou* wonderfully healthy; (*littér*) **~ d'indifférence** superbly indifferent. b (*littér: orgueilleux*) arrogant, haughty. 2 nf (*littér*) arrogance, haughtiness.
superbement [sypɛʀbəmɑ̃] adv superbly, wonderfully, beautifully.
superbénéfice [sypɛʀbenefis] nm immense profit.
supercarburant [sypɛʀkaʀbyʀɑ̃] nm high-octane petrol (*Brit*), high-octane *ou* high-test gasoline (*US*).
superchampion, -ionne [sypɛʀʃɑ̃pjɔ̃, jɔn] nm,f (sporting) superstar.
supercherie [sypɛʀʃəʀi] nf trick, trickery (*NonC*). **il s'aperçut de la ~** he saw through the trickery *ou* trick; **user de ~s pour tromper qn** to trick sb, deceive sb with trickery; **~ littéraire** literary hoax *ou* fabrication.
supérette [sypeʀɛt] nf mini-market, superette (*US*).
superfétation [sypɛʀfetasjɔ̃] nf (*littér*) superfluity.
superfétatoire [sypɛʀfetatwaʀ] adj (*littér*) superfluous, supererogatory (*littér*).
superficialité [sypɛʀfisjalite] nf superficiality.
superficie [sypɛʀfisi] nf (*aire*) (surface) area; (*surface*) surface; *[terrain]* area, acreage. **couvrir une ~ de** to cover an area of.
superficiel, -ielle [sypɛʀfisjɛl] adj (*gén*) superficial; *idées, esprit, personne* superficial, shallow; *beauté, sentiments, blessure* superficial, skin-deep (*attrib*); *modification* cosmetic; (*près de la surface*) *couche de liquide* superficial, upper; (*fin*) *couche de peinture* thin; *voir* **tension**.
superficiellement [sypɛʀfisjɛlmɑ̃] adv superficially.
superfin, e [sypɛʀfɛ̃, in] adj (*Comm*) *beurre, produit* superfine (*épith*), superquality (*épith*); *qualité* superfine (*épith*).
superflic* [sypɛʀflik] nm supercop*.
superflu, e [sypɛʀfly] 1 adj superfluous. **il est ~ d'insister** there is no point (in) insisting. 2 nm superfluity. **se débarrasser du ~** to get rid of the surplus; **le ~ est ce qui fait le charme de la vie** it is superfluity that gives life its charm.
superfluité [sypɛʀflyite] nf (*littér*) superfluity.
superforme* [sypɛʀfɔʀm] nf: **être en ~** (*moralement*) to feel great*; (*physiquement*) to be in great shape*; **c'est la ~** (*morale*) I'm (*ou* he's *etc*) feeling great*; (*physique*) I'm (*ou* he's *etc*) in great shape*.
superforteresse [sypɛʀfɔʀtəʀɛs] nf superfort(ress).
super-grand*, pl **super-grands** [sypɛʀgʀɑ̃] nm superpower.
super-huit [sypɛʀɥit] adj inv, nm inv super-eight.
supérieur, e [sypeʀjœʀ] 1 adj a (*dans l'espace*) (*gén*) upper (*épith*); *planètes* superior. **dans la partie ~e du clocher** in the highest *ou* upper *ou* top part of the belfry; **la partie ~e de l'objet** the top part of the object; **le feu a pris dans les étages ~s** fire broke out on the upper floors; **montez à l'étage ~** go to the next floor up *ou* to the floor above, go up to the next floor; **mâchoire/lèvre ~e** upper jaw/lip; **le lac S~** Lake Superior.

b (*dans un ordre*) *vitesse* higher, faster, greater; *nombre* higher, greater, bigger; *classes sociales* upper (*épith*); *niveaux, échelons* upper (*épith*), topmost; *animaux, végétaux* higher (*épith*). (*Rel*) **Père ~** Father Superior; (*Rel*) **Mère ~e** Mother Superior; **à l'échelon ~** on the next rung up; *voir* **cadre, enseignement, mathématique, officier**[1].

c (*excellent, qui prévaut*) *intérêts, principe* higher (*épith*); *intelligence, esprit* superior. **produit de qualité ~e** product of superior quality; **des considérations d'ordre ~** considerations of a higher order *ou* a high order.

d (*hautain*) *air, ton, regard* superior.

e **~ à** *nombre* greater *ou* higher than, above; *somme* greater than; *production* greater than, superior to; **intelligence/qualité ~e à la moyenne** above-average *ou* higher than average intelligence/quality; **des températures ~es à 300°** temperatures in excess of *ou* higher than *ou* of more than 300°; **parvenir à un niveau ~ à ...** to reach a higher level than ... *ou* a level higher than ...; **travail d'un niveau ~ à ...** work of a higher standard than ...; **roman/auteur ~ à un autre** novel/author superior to another; **être hiérarchiquement ~ à qn** to be higher (up) than sb *ou* be above sb in the hierarchy, be hierarchically superior to sb; **forces ~es en nombres** forces superior in number.

f (*fig: à la hauteur de*) **~ à sa tâche** more than equal to the task; **il a su se montrer ~ aux événements** he was able to rise above events; **restant ~ à la situation** remaining master of *ou* in control of the situation.

2 nm,f a (*Admin, Mil, Rel*) superior. **mon ~ hiérarchique** my immediate superior, my senior.

b (*Univ*) **le ~** higher education.
supérieurement [sypeʀjœʀmɑ̃] adv *exécuter qch, dessiner* exceptionally well. **~ doué/ennuyeux** exceptionally gifted/boring.
supériorité [sypeʀjɔʀite] nf a (*prééminence*) superiority. **nous avons la ~ du nombre** we outnumber them, we are superior in number(s); *voir* **complexe**. b (*condescendance*) superiority. **air de ~** superior air, air of superiority; **sourire de ~** superior smile.
superlatif, -ive [sypɛʀlatif, iv] 1 adj superlative. 2 nm superlative. **~ absolu/relatif** absolute/relative superlative; **au ~** in the superlative; (*fig*) **il m'ennuie au ~** I find him extremely trying.
superlativement [sypɛʀlativmɑ̃] adv superlatively.
superléger [sypɛʀleʒe] adj, nm *voir* **poids**.
supermarché [sypɛʀmaʀʃe] nm supermarket.
supernova [sypɛʀnɔva], pl **supernovae** [sypɛʀnɔve] nf supernova.
superpétrolier [sypɛʀpetʀɔlje] nm supertanker.
superphosphate [sypɛʀfɔsfat] nm superphosphate.
superposable [sypɛʀpozabl] adj (*gén*) that may be superimposed, superimposable (*à* on); (*éléments de mobilier*) stacking (*épith*).
superposé, e [sypɛʀpoze] (ptp de **superposer**) adj *couches, blocs* superposed; (*fig*) *visions, images* superimposed; *voir* **lit**.
superposer [sypɛʀpoze] [1] 1 vt a (*empiler*) *couches, blocs* to superpose (*à* on); *éléments de mobilier* to stack. (*fig*) **~ les consignes aux consignes** to heap *ou* pile order upon order. b (*faire chevaucher*) *cartes, clichés*, (*fig*) *visions* to superimpose; *figures géométriques* to superpose. **~ qch à** to superimpose sth on; to superpose sth on. 2 **se superposer** vpr a (*se recouvrir*) *[clichés photographiques, visions, images]* to be superimposed (on one another). b (*s'ajouter*) *[couches, éléments]* to be superposed.
superposition [sypɛʀpozisjɔ̃] nf a (*action: voir* **superposer**) superposing; superimposition. b (*état*) superposition; (*Phot*) superimposition. **la ~ de ces couches** the fact that these strata are superposed; **une ~ de terrasses s'élevant à l'infini** a series of terraces (one on top of the other) rising ever upwards; **la ~ de plusieurs influences** the cumulative effect of several influences.
superpréfet [sypɛʀpʀefɛ] nm superprefect (*in charge of a region*).
superproduction [sypɛʀpʀɔdyksjɔ̃] nf spectacular.
superprofit [sypɛʀpʀɔfi] nm immense profit.
superpuissance [sypɛʀpɥisɑ̃s] nf superpower.
supersonique [sypɛʀsɔnik] adj supersonic; *voir* **bang**.
superstitieusement [sypɛʀstisjøzmɑ̃] adv superstitiously.
superstitieux, -ieuse [sypɛʀstisjø, jøz] adj superstitious.
superstition [sypɛʀstisjɔ̃] nf superstition. **il a la ~ du chiffre 13** he's got a superstition about *ou* he's superstitious about the number 13.
superstrat [sypɛʀstʀa] nm (*Ling*) superstratum.
superstructure [sypɛʀstʀyktyʀ] nf (*gén*) superstructure.
supertanker [sypɛʀtɑ̃kœʀ] nm supertanker.
superviser [sypɛʀvize] [1] vt to supervise, oversee.
superviseur [sypɛʀvizœʀ] nm supervisor.
supervision [sypɛʀvizjɔ̃] nf supervision.
superwelter [sypɛʀwɛltɛʀ] adj, nm *voir* **poids**.
supin [sypɛ̃] nm supine.
supinateur [sypinatœʀ] 1 adj supine. 2 nm supinator.
supplanter [syplɑ̃te] [1] vt to supplant.
suppléance [sypleɑ̃s] nf (*remplacement*) (*poste*) supply post (*Brit*), substitute post (*US*); (*action*) temporary replacement. **professeur chargé d'une ~ dans un village** teacher appointed to a supply post (*Brit*) *ou* substitute post (*US*) in a village; **elle faisait des ~s pour gagner sa vie** she took supply posts (*Brit*) *ou* did supply (*Brit*) *ou* substitute (*US*) teaching to earn her living.
suppléant, e [sypleɑ̃, ɑ̃t] 1 adj (*gén*) deputy (*épith*), substitute (*épith*) (*US*); *professeur* supply (*épith*) (*Brit*), substitute (*épith*) (*US*). **médecin ~** locum; (*Gram*) **verbe ~** substitute verb. 2 nm,f (*professeur*) supply *ou* substitute teacher; (*juge*) deputy (judge); (*Pol*) deputy; (*médecin*) locum. **pendant les vacances, on fait appel à des ~s** during the holidays we take on relief *ou* temporary staff.
suppléer [syplee] [1] 1 vt a (*ajouter*) *mot manquant* to supply, provide; *somme complémentaire* to make up, supply. b (*compenser*) *lacune* to fill in; *manque, défaut* to make up for. c (*frm: remplacer*) *professeur* to stand in for, replace; *juge* to deputize for. (*littér*) **la machine a suppléé l'homme dans ce domaine** the machine has supplanted *ou* replaced man in this area. 2 **suppléer à** vt indir (*compenser*) *défaut, manque* to make up for, compensate for; (*remplacer*) *qualité, faculté* to substitute for. **ils suppléaient aux machines par l'abondante main-d'œuvre** they substituted a large labour force for machines.
supplément [syplemɑ̃] nm a (*surcroît*) **un ~ de travail/salaire** extra *ou* additional work/pay; **avoir droit à un ~ de 300 F sur ses allocations familiales** to be allowed a supplement of 300 francs *ou* a 300-franc supplement on one's child benefit, be allowed an extra *ou* an additional 300 francs on one's child benefit; **un ~ d'information** supplementary *ou* additional information.

b *[journal, dictionnaire]* supplement. **~ illustré** illustrated supplement.

c (*à payer*) (*au théâtre, au restaurant*) extra charge, supplement; (*dans le train*) (*pour prolongement de trajet*) excess fare; (*sur trains spéciaux*) supplement. **~ de 1re classe** supplement for travelling 1st class, 1st-class supplement; **~ de prix** additional charge, surcharge;

payer un ~ pour excès de bagages to pay extra for excess luggage, pay (for) excess luggage, pay excess on one's luggage.

d en ~ extra; le vin est en ~ wine is extra, an additional charge is made for wine; le tableau de bord en bois est en ~ the wooden dashboard is an extra *ou* comes as an extra, there is extra to pay for the wooden dashboard.

e (*Math*) *[angle]* supplement.

supplémentaire [syplemɑ̃tɛʀ] adj *dépenses, crédits, retards* additional, further (*épith*); *travail, vérifications* additional, extra (*épith*); *trains, autobus* relief (*épith*); (*Géom*) *angle* supplementary. (*Mus*) lignes ~s ledger lines; accorder un délai ~ to grant an extension of the deadline, allow additional time; *voir* heure.

supplémenter [syplemɑ̃te] 1 vt: ~ le billet de qn (*pour prolongement de trajet*) to make sb pay an excess fare; (*sur trains spéciaux*) to charge sb a supplement.

supplétif, -ive [sypletif, iv] 1 adj additional. 2 supplétifs nmpl (*Mil*) back-up troops.

suppliant, e [syplijɑ̃, ijɑ̃t] 1 adj *regard, voix* beseeching, imploring; *personne* imploring. 2 nm,f suppliant, supplicant.

supplication [syplikasjɔ̃] nf (*gén*) plea, entreaty; (*Rel*) supplication.

supplice [syplis] 1 nm a (*peine corporelle*) form of torture, torture (*NonC*). (*peine capitale*) le (dernier) ~ execution, death; le ~ de la roue (torture on) the wheel; le ~ du fouet flogging, the lash.

b (*souffrance*) torture. ~s moraux moral tortures *ou* torments; (*fig*) éprouver le ~ de l'incertitude to be tortured *ou* tormented by uncertainty, suffer the ordeal *ou* torture of uncertainty; (*fig*) cette lecture est un (vrai) ~! reading this book is (quite) an ordeal!

c (*loc*) être au ~ (*appréhension*) to be in agonies *ou* on the rack; (*gêne, douleur*) to be in misery; mettre qn au ~ to torture sb.

2 comp ►supplice chinois Chinese torture (*NonC*) ►le supplice de la Croix (*Rel*) the Crucifixion ►supplice de Tantale (*lit*) torment of Tantalus; (*fig*) soumis à un véritable supplice de Tantale tortured *ou* suffering like Tantalus.

supplicié, e [syplisje] (ptp de supplicier) nm,f victim of torture, torture victim. les corps/cris des ~s the bodies/cries of the torture victims *ou* of the tortured.

supplicier [syplisje] 7 vt (*lit, fig*) to torture; (*à mort*) to torture to death.

supplier [syplije] 7 vt to beseech, implore, entreat (*de faire* to do). ~ qn à genoux to beseech *ou* implore *ou* entreat sb on one's knees; n'insistez pas, je vous en supplie I beg of you not to insist, I implore *ou* beseech you not to insist.

supplique [syplik] nf petition. présenter une ~ au roi to petition the king, bring a petition before the king.

support [sypɔʀ] nm a (*gén: soutien*) support; (*béquille, pied*) prop, support; *[instruments de laboratoire, outils, livre]* stand. b (*moyen*) medium; (*aide*) aid. ~ publicitaire advertising medium; conférence faite à l'aide d'un ~ écrit/magnétique/visuel lecture given with the help of a written text/a tape/visual aids; ~ audio-visuel audio-visual aid; ~ visuel visual aid. c (*Peinture*) *[dessin]* support; (*Ordin*) *[information codée]* input medium. avoir un *ou* être sur ~ papier/plastique to be on paper/plastic; le symbole est le ~ du concept the symbol is the physical medium through which the concept is expressed.

supportable [sypɔʀtabl] adj *douleur* bearable; *conduite* tolerable; *température* bearable; (**: passable, pas trop mauvais*) tolerable, passable.

supporter¹ [sypɔʀte] 1 1 vt a (*servir de base à*) to support, hold up.

b (*subir*) *frais* to bear; *conséquences, affront, malheur* to suffer, endure. il m'a fait ~ les conséquences de son acte he made me suffer the consequences of his action.

c (*endurer*) *maladie, solitude, revers* to bear, endure, put up with; *douleur* to bear, endure; *conduite, ingratitude* to tolerate, put up with; *recommandations, personne* to put up with, bear. maladie courageusement supportée illness bravely borne; il ne pouvait plus ~ la vie he could endure *ou* bear life no longer; supportant ces formalités avec impatience impatiently putting up with these formalities; la mort d'un être cher est difficile à ~ the death of a loved one is hard to bear; il va falloir le ~ pendant toute la journée! we're going to have to put up with him all day long!; elle supporte tout d'eux, sans jamais rien dire she puts up with *ou* she takes anything from them without a word; je ne supporte pas ce genre de comportement/qu'on me parle sur ce ton I won't put up with *ou* stand for *ou* tolerate this sort of behaviour/being spoken to in that tone of voice; je ne peux pas ~ l'hypocrisie I can't bear *ou* abide hypocrisy; je ne peux pas les ~ I can't bear *ou* stand them; je ne supporte pas qu'elle fasse cela I won't stand for *ou* tolerate her doing that; je ne supporte pas de voir ça I can't bear seeing *ou* to see that, I can't stand seeing that.

d (*résister à*) *température, conditions atmosphériques, épreuve* to withstand. verre qui supporte la chaleur heatproof *ou* heat-resistant glass; il a bien/mal supporté l'opération he took the operation well/badly; il ne supporte pas l'alcool/l'avion he can't take alcohol/plane journeys; elle ne supporte pas la vue du sang she can't bear *ou* stand the sight of blood *ou* seeing blood; il ne supporte pas la chaleur heat doesn't agree *ou* disagrees with him, he can't take *ou* stand *ou* bear the heat; je ne supporte pas les épinards spinach doesn't agree *ou* disagrees with me; lait facile à ~ easily-digested milk; tu as de la chance de ~ l'ail you're lucky garlic agrees with you, you're lucky to be able to take garlic; ce roman ne supporte pas l'examen this novel does not stand up to analysis.

e (*Ordin, Sport*) to support.

f (*) on supporte un gilet, par ce temps you can do with a cardigan in this weather*; je pensais avoir trop chaud avec un pull, mais on le supporte I thought I'd be too hot with a pullover but I can do with it after all.

2 se supporter vpr (*se tolérer*) ils ne peuvent pas se ~ they can't stand *ou* bear each other.

supporter² [sypɔʀtɛʀ] nm (*Sport*) supporter.

supposable [sypozabl] adj supposable.

supposé, e [sypoze] (ptp de supposer) adj *nombre, total* estimated; *auteur* supposed; (*Jur*) *meurtrier* alleged.

supposer [sypoze] 1 vt a (*à titre d'hypothèse*) to suppose, assume. supposons un conflit atomique let's suppose *ou* if we suppose there were a conflict involving atomic weapons *ou* (that) a conflict involving atomic weapons were to take place; supposez que vous soyez malade suppose you were ill; en supposant que, à ~ que supposing (that), on the assumption that; (*Sci*) pour les besoins de l'expérience, la pression est supposée constante for the purposes of the experiment the pressure is taken to be *ou* assumed (to be) constant; (*Scol*) supposons une ligne A-B let us postulate a line A-B.

b (*présumer*) to suppose, assume, surmise. ~ qn amoureux/jaloux to imagine *ou* suppose sb to be in love/jealous; je lui suppose une grande ambition I imagine him to have great ambition; on vous supposait malade we thought you were ill; je ne peux que le ~ I can only make a supposition *ou* a surmise; cela laisse ~ que it leads one to suppose that; je suppose que tu es contre I take it *ou* I assume *ou* I suppose *ou* I presume you are against it.

c (*impliquer, présupposer*) to presuppose; (*suggérer, laisser deviner*) to imply. la gestation suppose la fécondation gestation presupposes fertilization; cela suppose du courage that takes courage; ta réponse suppose que tu n'as rien compris your reply implies *ou* indicates that you haven't understood a thing.

supposition [sypozisjɔ̃] nf supposition, assumption, surmise. une ~ que ...* supposing ... .

suppositoire [sypozitwaʀ] nm suppository.

suppôt [sypo] nm (*littér*) henchman. ~ de Satan hellhound.

suppression [sypʀesjɔ̃] nf (*voir* supprimer) deletion; removal; cancellation; withdrawal; abolition; suppression. faire des ~s dans un texte to make some deletions in a text; la ~ de la douleur/fatigue the elimination of pain/fatigue; la ~ des inégalités the abolition of inequalities, the ending of inequality; 7 000 ~s d'emploi 7,000 jobs axed *ou* lost; il y a deux ~s de poste two posts have been lost *ou* axed.

supprimer [sypʀime] 1 1 vt a (*enlever*) *mot, clause* to delete, remove (*de* from); *mur* to remove, knock down; *trains* to cancel; *permis de conduire* to withdraw, take away (*de* from). ~ qch à qn to deprive sb of sth; ~ les sorties/les permissions aux soldats to put a stop *ou* an end to the soldiers' outings/leave; on lui a supprimé sa prime/sa pension he's had his bonus/pension stopped, he has been deprived of his bonus/pension; plusieurs emplois ont été supprimés dans cette usine several jobs have been done away with *ou* axed in this factory.

b (*faire disparaître*) *loi* to do away with, abolish; *publication* to ban; *document* to suppress; *obstacle* to remove; *libertés* to suppress; *témoin gênant* to do away with, suppress; *discrimination, inégalité, concurrence* to do away with, put an end to, abolish. ~ qch de son alimentation to cut sth out of one's diet, eliminate sth from one's diet; il est dangereux de ~ (les effets de) la fatigue it is dangerous to suppress (the effects of) fatigue; prenez ce fortifiant pour ~ la fatigue take this tonic to eliminate *ou* banish tiredness; ce médicament supprime la douleur this medicine kills pain *ou* eliminates pain *ou* is a painkiller; on ne parviendra jamais à ~ la douleur we shall never succeed in doing away with *ou* in eliminating pain; ~ la discrimination raciale to do away with *ou* put an end to *ou* abolish racial discrimination; les grands ensembles suppriment l'individualisme housing schemes put an end to *ou* destroy individualism; l'avion supprime les distances air travel shortens long distances; cette technique supprime des opérations inutiles this technique does away with *ou* cuts out some unnecessary operations; dans l'alimentation, il faut ~ les intermédiaires in the food trade we must cut out *ou* do away with *ou* eliminate the middlemen.

2 se supprimer vpr to do away with o.s., take one's own life.

suppurant, e [sypyʀɑ̃, ɑ̃t] adj suppurating.

suppuration [sypyʀasjɔ̃] nf suppuration.

suppurer [sypyʀe] 1 vi to suppurate.

supputation [sypytasjɔ̃] nf a (*action: voir* supputer) calculation; computation. b (*pronostic*) prognostication.

supputer [sypyte] 1 vt *dépenses, frais* to calculate, compute; *chances, possibilités* to calculate.

supra¹... [sypʀa] préf supra... .

supra² [sypʀa] adv supra.

supraconducteur, -trice [sypʀakɔ̃dyktœʀ, tʀis] 1 adj superconductive, superconducting (*épith*). 2 nm superconductor.
supraconductivité [sypʀakɔ̃dyktivite] nf superconductivity.
supraliminaire [sypʀaliminɛʀ] adj supraliminal.
supranational, e, mpl -aux [sypʀanasjɔnal, o] adj supranational.
supranationalisme [sypʀanasjɔnalism] nm supranationalism.
supranationaliste [sypʀanasjɔnalist] adj supranationalist.
supranationalité [sypʀanasjɔnalite] nf supranational nature.
suprasegmental, e, mpl -aux [sypʀasɛgmɑ̃tal, o] adj suprasegmental.
suprasensible [sypʀasɑ̃sibl] adj suprasensitive.
supraterrestre [sypʀatɛʀɛstʀ] adj superterrestrial.
suprématie [sypʀemasi] nf supremacy.
suprématisme [sypʀematism] nm Suprematism.
suprême [sypʀɛm] 1 adj (*gén*) supreme. **au ~ degré** to the highest degree; **faire un effort ~** to make a supreme effort; *voir* **sauce, soviet** *etc.* 2 nm (*Culin*) supreme.
suprêmement [sypʀɛmmɑ̃] adv supremely.
sur[1] [syʀ] 1 prép a (*position*) on, upon; (*sur le haut de*) on top of, on; (*avec mouvement*) on, onto; (*dans*) on, in; (*par-dessus*) over; (*au-dessus*) above. **il y a un sac ~ la table/un tableau ~ le mur** there's a bag on the table/a picture on the wall; **mettre une annonce ~ le tableau** to put a notice (up) on the board; **il a laissé tous ses papiers ~ la table** he left all his papers (lying) on the table; **se promener ~ la rivière** to go boating on the river; **il y avait beaucoup de circulation ~ la route** there was a lot of traffic on the road; **~ ma route** *ou* **mon chemin** on my way; (*Rad*) **~ les grandes/petites ondes** on long/short wave; (*Géog*) **X-~-mer** X-upon-sea, X-on-sea; **elle rangea ses chapeaux ~ l'armoire** she put her hats away on top of the wardrobe; **pose ta valise ~ une chaise** put your case (down) on a chair; **elle a jeté son sac ~ la table** she threw her bag onto the table; **il grimpa ~ le toit** he climbed (up) onto the roof; **une chambre (qui donne) ~ la rue** a room that looks out onto the street; **il n'est jamais monté ~ un bateau** he's never been in *ou* on a boat; **~ la place (du marché)** in the (market) square; **la clef est restée ~ la porte** the key was left in the door; **lire qch ~ le journal*** to read sth in the paper; **chercher qch ~ une carte** to look for sth on a map; **un pont ~ la rivière** a bridge across *ou* on *ou* over the river; **il neige ~ Paris/~ toute l'Europe** snow is falling on *ou* in Paris/over the whole of Europe, it's snowing in Paris/all over Europe; **l'avion est passé ~ nos têtes** the aircraft flew over *ou* above our heads *ou* overhead; **mettre un linge ~ un plat/un couvercle ~ une casserole** to put a cloth over a dish/a lid on a saucepan; **pour allumer il suffit d'appuyer ~ le bouton** to light it you simply have to press the button; (*fig*) **s'endormir ~ un livre/son travail** to fall asleep over a book/over *ou* at one's work; **ne t'appuie pas ~ le mur** don't lean on *ou* against the wall; **retire tes livres de ~ la table** take your books from *ou* off the table; **je n'ai pas d'argent/la lettre ~ moi** I haven't (got) any money/the letter on *ou* with me; **elle a acheté des poires ~ le marché** she bought pears at the market; **~ terre et ~ mer** on land and (at) sea; **s'étendre ~ 3 km** to spread over 3 kms; **travaux ~ 5 km** roadworks for 5 kms; (*fig*) **vivre les uns ~ les autres** to live one on top of the other; *voir* **pied, piste, place** *etc.*

b (*direction*) to, towards. **tourner ~ la droite** to turn (to the) right; **l'église est ~ votre gauche** the church is on *ou* to your left; **revenir ~ Paris** to return to Paris; **diriger** *ou* **tourner ses regards/son attention ~ qch** to turn one's eyes/attention towards sth; **rejeter une faute ~ qn** to put the blame on sb; **se jeter ~ qn** to throw *ou* hurl o.s. upon *ou* at sb; **tirer ~ qn** to shoot at sb; **fermez bien la porte ~ vous** be sure and close the door behind *ou* after you; *voir* **loucher, sauter.**

c (*temps: proximité, approximation*) **il est arrivé ~ les 2 heures** he came (at) about *ou* (at) around 2; **il va ~ ses quinze ans/la quarantaine** he's getting on for (*Brit*) *ou* going on (*US*) fifteen/forty; **l'acte s'achève** *ou* **se termine ~ une réconciliation** the act ends with a reconciliation; **il est ~ le** *ou* **son départ, il est ~ le point de partir** he's just going, he's (just) about to leave; **il a été pris ~ le fait** he was caught in the act *ou* red-handed; **~ le moment** *ou* **sur le coup, je n'ai pas compris** at the time *ou* at first I didn't understand; **~ ce, il est sorti** whereupon *ou* upon which he went out; **~ ce, ~ ces mots** so saying, with this *ou* that; **~ ce, il faut que je vous quitte** and now I must leave you; **boire du café ~ de la bière** to drink coffee on top of beer; **~ une période de 3 mois** over a period of 3 months; **juger les résultats ~ une année** to assess the results over a year; *voir* **entrefait, parole.**

d (*cause*) on, by. **~ invitation/commande** by invitation/order; **~ présentation d'une pièce d'identité** on presentation of identification; **nous l'avons nommé ~ la recommandation/les conseils de X** we appointed him on X's recommendation/advice; **~ un signe/une remarque du patron, elle sortit** on seeing the boss's signal/at a word from the boss, she left; **croire qn ~ parole** to take sb's word for it; *voir* **juger.**

e (*moyen, manière*) on. **ils vivent ~ son traitement/ses économies** they live on *ou* off his salary/savings; **ne le prends pas ~ ce ton** don't take it like that; **prendre modèle ~ qn** to model o.s. on *ou* upon sb; **rester ~ la défensive/ses gardes** to stay on the defensive/one's guard; **chanter** *ou* **entonner qch ~ l'air de** to sing sth to the tune of; (*Mus*) **fantaisie** *etc* **~ un air de** fantasy *etc* on an air by *ou* from; (*Mus*) **~ le mode mineur** in the minor key *ou* mode; *voir* **jurer, mesure.**

f (*matière, sujet*) on, about. **causerie/conférence/renseignements ~ la Grèce/la drogue** talk/lecture/information on *ou* about Greece/drug addiction; **roman/film ~ Louis XIV** novel/film about Louis XIV; **questionner** *ou* **interroger qn ~ qch** to question sb about *ou* on sth; **gémir** *ou* **se lamenter ~ ses malheurs** to lament (over) *ou* bemoan one's misfortunes; **être ~ un travail** to be occupied with a job, be (in the process of) doing a job; **être ~ une bonne affaire/une piste/un coup**‡ to be on to a bargain/on a trail/on a job; *voir* **réfléchir** *etc.*

g (*rapport de proportion etc*) out of, in; (*mesure*) by; (*accumulation*) after. **~ 12 verres, 6 sont ébréchés** out of 12 glasses 6 are chipped; **un homme ~ 10** one man in (every) *ou* out of 10; **9 fois ~ 10** 9 times out of 10; **il a 9 chances ~ 10 de réussir** he has 9 chances out of 10 of succeeding, his chances of success are 9 out of 10; (*Scol, Univ etc*) **il mérite 7 ~ 10** he deserves 7 out of 10; **la cuisine fait 2 mètres ~ 3** the kitchen is *ou* measures 2 metres by 3; **un jour/un vendredi ~ trois** every third day/Friday; **il vient un jour/mercredi ~ deux** he comes every other day/Wednesday; **faire faute ~ faute** to make one mistake after another; **il a eu rhume ~ rhume** he's had one cold after another *ou* the other, he's had cold after cold; *voir* **coup.**

h (*influence, supériorité*) over, on. **avoir de l'influence/de l'effet ~ qn** to have influence on *ou* over/an effect on sb; **avoir des droits ~ qn/qch** to have rights over sb/to sth; **cela a influé ~ sa décision** that has influenced *ou* had an influence on his decision; **elle ne peut rien ~ lui** she can't control him, she has no control over him; **savoir prendre ~ soi** to keep a grip on o.s.; **prendre ~ soi de faire qch** to take it upon o.s. to do sth; *voir* **emporter, régner** *etc.*

2 préf: **~excité** overexcited; **~production** overproduction; **~dosage** overdose; *voir* **surabondance, surchauffer** *etc.*

3 comp ►**sur-le-champ, sur l'heure** (*littér*) *adv* immediately, at once, straightaway (*Brit*), right away (*US*) ►**sur-place** nm: **faire du sur-place** to mark time; **on a fait du sur-place jusqu'à Paris** it was stop-start all the way to Paris.

sur[2]**, e** [syʀ] adj (*aigre*) sour.
sûr, e [syʀ] 1 adj a **~ de** *résultats, succès* sure *ou* certain of; *allié, réflexes, moyens* sure of; *fait, diagnostic, affirmation* sure *ou* certain of *ou* about; **il avait le moral et était ~ du succès** he was in good spirits and was sure *ou* certain *ou* confident of success; **s'il s'entraîne régulièrement, il est ~ du succès** if he trains regularly he's sure of success; **il est ~ de son fait** he's sure of his facts, he's certain *ou* sure about it; **il est ~ de son fait** *ou* **coup*** he's sure *ou* confident he'll pull it off; **~ de soi** self-assured, self-confident, sure of oneself; **elle n'est pas ~e d'elle(-même)** she's lacking in self-assurance *ou* self-confidence, she's not very sure of herself; **j'en étais ~!** I knew it!, just as I thought!, I was sure of it!; **j'en suis ~ et certain** I'm positive (about it), I'm absolutely sure *ou* certain (of it).

b (*certain*) certain, sure. **la chose est ~e** that's certain, that's for sure *ou* certain; **ce** *ou* **il n'est pas ~ qu'elle aille au Maroc** it's not definite *ou* certain that she's going to Morocco; **est-ce si ~ qu'il gagne?** is he so certain *ou* sure to win?; **c'est ~ et certain** that's absolutely certain; **ça, c'est ~** that's for sure*, you can be sure of that; **ce n'est pas si ~*** it's not that certain *ou* clear cut, don't be so sure; **c'est le plus ~ moyen de réussir** it is the surest way to succeed; **ce qui est ~, c'est qu'ils ...** one thing is for sure – they ...; *voir* **coup, tenir.**

c (*sans danger*) *quartier, rue* safe. **peu ~** *quartier etc* unsafe; **il est plus ~ de ne pas compter sur lui** it's safer not to rely on him; **le plus ~ est de mettre sa voiture au garage le soir** the safest thing is to put your car in the garage at night; **en lieu ~** in a safe place; **en mains ~es** in safe hands.

d (*digne de confiance*) *personne, firme* reliable, trustworthy; *renseignements, diagnostic* reliable; *valeurs morales, raisonnement* sound; *remède, moyen* safe, reliable, sure; *dispositif, arme, valeurs boursières* safe; *main, pied, œil* steady; *goût, instinct* reliable, sound. **le temps n'est pas assez ~ pour une ascension** the weather's not certain *ou* reliable enough to go climbing; **avoir la main ~e** to have a steady hand; **raisonner sur des bases peu ~es** to argue on unsound *ou* shaky premises; **nous apprenons de source ~e que ...** we have been informed by a reliable source that ...; **peu ~** *allié* unreliable, untrustworthy; *renseignements* unreliable; *moyen, méthode* unreliable, unsafe.

2 adv (*) **~ qu'il y a quelque chose qui ne tourne pas rond** there must be *ou* there's definitely something wrong; **tu penses qu'il viendra? – pas ~** do you think he'll come? – maybe; *voir* **bien, pour.**

surabondamment [syʀabɔ̃damɑ̃] adv (*littér*) *expliquer* in excessive detail. **~ décoré de** overabundantly decorated with.
surabondance [syʀabɔ̃dɑ̃s] nf overabundance, superabundance. **une ~ de détails** an overabundance of details.
surabondant, e [syʀabɔ̃dɑ̃, ɑ̃t] adj overabundant, superabundant.
surabonder [syʀabɔ̃de] 1 vi a *[richesses, plantes, matière première]* to be overabundant, be superabundant, overabound. **une station où surabondent les touristes** a resort overflowing *ou* bursting with tourists; **des circulaires où surabondent les fautes d'impression** circulars littered with printing errors; **un port où surabondent les tavernes** a port with an inordinate number of taverns. b (*littér*) **~ de richesses** to have an overabundance of riches, have overabundant riches; **~ d'erreurs** to abound with errors.

suractivé, e [syʀaktive] adj superactivated.
suractivité [syʀaktivite] nf superactivity.
suraigu, -uë [syʀegy] adj very high-pitched, very shrill.
surajouter [syʀaʒute] 1 vt to add. **ornements surajoutés** superfluously added ornaments, superfluous ornaments; **raisons auxquelles se surajoutent celles-ci** reasons to which one might add the following.
suralimentation [syʀalimɑ̃tasjɔ̃] nf (*voir* **suralimenter**) overfeeding; overeating.
suralimenter [syʀalimɑ̃te] 1 1 vt *personne* to overfeed; *moteur* to give too much fuel to. 2 **se suralimenter** vpr to overeat.
suranné, e [syʀane] adj *idées, mode* outmoded, outdated, antiquated; *beauté, tournure, style* outdated, outmoded.
surarmement [syʀaʀməmɑ̃] nm massive stock of weapons.
surate [syʀat] nf = **sourate.**
surbaissé, e [syʀbese] (ptp de **surbaisser**) adj *plafond etc* lowered; (*Archit*) *voûte* surbased; *carrosserie, auto* low.
surbaissement [syʀbɛsmɑ̃] nm (*Archit*) surbasement.
surbaisser [syʀbese] 1 vt *plafond* to lower; (*Archit*) *voûte* to surbase; (*Aut*) *voiture, chassis* to make lower.
surbooking [syʀbukiŋ] nm double booking, overbooking.
surboum†* [syʀbum] nf party.
surcapacité [syʀkapasite] nf overcapacity.
surcapitalisation [syʀkapitalizasjɔ̃] nf overcapitalization.
surcharge [syʀʃaʀʒ] nf a *[véhicule]* overloading.
b (*poids en excédent*) extra load, excess load. **une tonne de ~** an extra *ou* excess load of a ton; **les passagers/marchandises en ~** the excess *ou* extra passengers/goods; **prendre des passagers en ~** to take on excess passengers; **payer un supplément pour une ~ de bagages** to pay extra for excess luggage, pay (for) excess luggage, pay excess on one's luggage.
c (*fig*) **cela me cause une ~ de travail/dépenses** this gives me extra work/expense; **il y a une ~ de détails/d'ornements** there is a surfeit *ou* an overabundance of detail/ornamentation.
d (*ajout*) *[document, chèque]* alteration; *[timbre-poste, voyage, hôtel]* surcharge.
surcharger [syʀʃaʀʒe] 3 vt *voiture, cheval, mémoire* to overload; *timbre* to surcharge; *mot écrit* to alter. **~ qn de travail/d'impôts** to overload *ou* overburden sb with work/taxes; **je suis surchargé de travail** I'm overloaded *ou* snowed under with work; **emploi du temps surchargé** crowded timetable; **programme scolaire surchargé** overloaded syllabus; **un manuscrit surchargé de corrections** a manuscript covered *ou* littered with corrections.
surchauffe [syʀʃof] nf (*Écon*) overheating; (*Tech*) superheating; (*Phys*) superheat.
surchauffer [syʀʃofe] 1 vt *pièce* to overheat; (*Phys, Tech*) to superheat. (*fig*) **les esprits étaient surchauffés** emotions were running high.
surchoix [syʀʃwa] adj inv *viande* prime (*épith*), top-quality; *produit, fruit* top-quality.
surclasser [syʀklɑse] 1 vt to outclass.
surcompensation [syʀkɔ̃pɑ̃sasjɔ̃] nf (*Psych*) overcompensation.
surcomposé, e [syʀkɔ̃poze] adj double-compound.
surcompression [syʀkɔ̃pʀesjɔ̃] nf *[gaz]* supercharging.
surcomprimer [syʀkɔ̃pʀime] 1 vt *gaz* to supercharge.
surconsommation [syʀkɔ̃sɔmasjɔ̃] nf overconsumption.
surcontrer [syʀkɔ̃tʀe] 1 vt (*Cartes*) to redouble.
surcote [syʀkɔt] nf overvaluation.
surcoter [syʀkɔte] 1 vt to overvalue.
surcouper [syʀkupe] 1 vt (*Cartes*) to overtrump.
surcoût [syʀku] nm extra *ou* additional cost *ou* expenditure.
surcroît [syʀkʀwa] nm a **cela lui a donné un ~ de travail/d'inquiétudes** that gave him additional *ou* extra work/worries; **ça lui a valu un ~ de respect** this won him added *ou* increased respect; **par (un) ~ d'honnêteté/de scrupules** through an excess of honesty/scruples, through excessive honesty/scrupulousness; **pour ~ de bonheur/malheur il vient de ...** to add to his happiness/misfortune(s) he has just ... . b (*de plus*) **de** *ou* **par ~** what is more, moreover; **avare et paresseux de** *ou* **par ~** miserly and idle to boot, miserly and — what's more — idle.
surdéveloppé, e [syʀdevlɔpe] adj overdeveloped.
surdéveloppement [syʀdevlɔpmɑ̃] nm overdevelopment.
surdi-mutité [syʀdimytite] nf deaf-and-dumbness.
surdité [syʀdite] nf deafness. **~ verbale** word deafness.
surdoué, e [syʀdwe] 1 adj *enfant* gifted (*Brit*), exceptional (*US*). 2 nm,f gifted (*Brit*) *ou* exceptional (*US*) child.
sureau, pl **~x** [syʀo] nm elder (tree). **baies de ~** elderberries.
sureffectifs [syʀefɛktif] nmpl overmanning (*NonC*), overstaffing (*NonC*).
surélévation [syʀelevasjɔ̃] nf (*action*) raising, heightening; (*état*) extra height.
surélever [syʀel(ə)ve] 5 vt *plafond, étage* to raise, heighten; *mur* to heighten. **~ une maison d'un étage** to heighten a house by one storey; **rez-de-chaussée surélevé** raised ground floor, ground floor higher than street level.
sûrement [syʀmɑ̃] adv a (*sans risques, efficacement*) *cacher qch, progresser* in safety; *attacher* securely; *fonctionner* safely. **l'expérience instruit plus ~ que les livres** experience is a surer teacher than books; *voir* **lentement.** b (*certainement*) certainly. **viendra-t-il? — ~!/~ pas!** will he be coming? — certainly!/certainly not!; **il viendra ~** he'll certainly come, he's sure to come; **~ qu'il a été retenu*** he must have been held up, he has surely been held up.
suremploi [syʀɑ̃plwa] nm overemployment.
surenchère [syʀɑ̃ʃɛʀ] nf a (*Comm*) (*sur prix fixé*) overbid; (*enchère plus élevée*) higher bid. **faire une ~ (sur)** to make a higher bid (than); **une douzaine de ~s successives firent monter le prix de la potiche que je convoitais** a dozen bids one after the other put up the price of the vase I wanted; **faire une ~ de 100 F (sur)** to bid 100 francs more *ou* higher (than), bid 100 francs over the previous bid *ou* bidder.
b (*fig: exagération, excès*) **la presse, royaume de la ~ et de la sensation** the press, domain of the overstatement and of sensationalism; **faire de la ~** to try to outbid *ou* outmatch *ou* outdo one's rivals; **la ~ électorale** outbidding tactics of rival (political) parties; **une ~ de violence** an increasing build-up of violence.
surenchérir [syʀɑ̃ʃeʀiʀ] 2 vi (*offrir plus qu'un autre*) to bid higher (*sur* than); (*élever son offre*) to raise one's bid; (*fig: lors d'élections etc*) to try to outmatch *ou* outbid each other (*de* with). **~ sur une offre** to bid higher than an offer *ou* bid, top a bid*; **~ sur qn** to bid higher than sb, outbid *ou* overbid sb.
surenchérisseur, -euse [syʀɑ̃ʃeʀisœʀ, øz] nm,f (higher) bidder.
surencombré, e [syʀɑ̃kɔ̃bʀe] adj *rue* overcrowded; *lignes téléphoniques* overloaded.
surencombrement [syʀɑ̃kɔ̃bʀəmɑ̃] nm *[rue]* overcrowding; *[lignes téléphoniques]* overloading.
surendetté, e [syʀɑ̃dete] adj overburdened with debt.
surendettement [syʀɑ̃dɛtmɑ̃] nm excessive debt.
surentraînement [syʀɑ̃tʀɛnmɑ̃] nm overtraining.
surentraîner vt, **se surentraîner** vpr [syʀɑ̃tʀene] 1 to overtrain.
suréquipement [syʀekipmɑ̃] nm overequipment.
suréquiper [syʀekipe] 1 vt to overequip.
surestarie [syʀɛstaʀi] nf (*Jur*) demurrage.
surestimation [syʀɛstimasjɔ̃] nf (*voir* **surestimer**) overestimation; overvaluation.
surestimer [syʀɛstime] 1 1 vt *importance, puissance, forces* to overestimate; *tableau, maison à vendre* to overvalue. 2 **se surestimer** vpr to overestimate one's abilities (*ou* strengths *etc*).
suret, -ette [syʀɛ, ɛt] adj *goût* sharp, tart.
sûreté [syʀte] nf a (*sécurité*) safety. **complot contre la ~ de l'État** plot against state security; **pour plus de ~** as an extra precaution, to be on the safe side; **être en ~** to be in safety, be safe; **mettre qn/qch en ~** to put sb/sth in a safe *ou* secure place; **serrure/verrou** *etc* **de ~** safety lock/bolt *etc*; **c'est une ~ supplémentaire** it's an extra precaution.
b (*exactitude, efficacité*) *[renseignements, méthode]* reliability; *voir* **cour, prudence.**
c (*précision*) *[coup d'œil, geste]* steadiness; *[goût]* reliability, soundness; *[réflexe, diagnostic]* reliability. **il a une grande ~ de main** he has a very sure hand; **~ d'exécution** sureness of touch.
d (*dispositif*) safety device. **mettre une arme à la ~** to put the safety catch *ou* lock on a gun; *voir* **cran.**
e (*garantie*) assurance, guarantee. **demander/donner des ~s à qn** to ask sb for/give sb assurances *ou* a guarantee; (*Jur*) **~ personnelle** guaranty; **~ réelle** security.
f (*Police*) **la S~ (nationale)** the (French) criminal investigation department, ≃ the CID (*Brit*), the Criminal Investigation Department (*Brit*), ≃ the FBI (*US*), the Federal Bureau of Investigation (*US*).
surévaluation [syʀevalɥasjɔ̃] nf overvaluation.
surévaluer [syʀevalɥe] 1 vt to overvalue.
surexcitable [syʀɛksitabl] adj overexcitable.
surexcitation [syʀɛksitasjɔ̃] nf overexcitement.
surexciter [syʀɛksite] 1 vt to overexcite.
surexploiter [syʀɛksplwate] 1 vt to overexploit.
surexposer [syʀɛkspoze] 1 vt to overexpose.
surexposition [syʀɛkspozisjɔ̃] nf overexposure.
surf [sœʀf] nm a (*activité*) surfing. **faire du ~** to surf, go surfing; **~ sur neige** snowboarding; **faire du ~ sur neige** to snowboard, go snowboarding. b **(planche de) ~** surfboard; **~ des neiges** snowboard.
surface [syʀfas] 1 nf (*gén, Géom*) surface; (*aire*) *[champ, chambre]* surface area. **faire ~** to surface; (*lit, fig*) **refaire ~** to resurface; **de ~** *politesse* superficial; *modifications* cosmetic; *grammaire* surface (*épith*); **navire de ~** surface vessel; **en ~** *nager, naviguer* at the surface, near the surface; (*fig*) *travailler, apprendre* superficially; *personne* **tout en ~** superficial, shallow; **ne voir que la ~ des choses** not to see below the surface of things, see only the surface of things; **l'appartement fait 100 mètres carrés de ~** the flat has a surface area of 100 square metres; (*Écon*) **~ financière** debt-equity ratio, financial situation; (*fig, Fin*) **avoir de la ~*** to have great standing; *voir* **grand, technicien.**
2 comp ►**surface de but** (*Ftbl*) goal area ►**surface de chauffe** heating-surface ►**surface corrigée** (*Admin*) amended area (*calculated on the basis of amenities etc for assessing rent*) ►**surface porteuse** (*Aviat*) aerofoil (*Brit*), airfoil (*US*) ►**surface de**

réparation (*Ftbl*) penalty area ▸ **surface de sustentation** (*Aviat*) = **surface porteuse**.

surfaire [syʀfɛʀ] [60] **vt** *réputation, auteur* to overrate; *marchandise* to overprice.

surfait, e [syʀfɛ, ɛt] (**ptp de surfaire**) **adj** *ouvrage, auteur* overrated.

surfer [sœʀfe] [1] **vi** to surf, go surfing.

surfeur, -euse [sœʀfœʀ, øz] **nm,f** surfer.

surfil [syʀfil] **nm** oversewing, overcasting.

surfilage [syʀfilaʒ] **nm** (*Couture*) oversewing, overcasting.

surfiler [syʀfile] [1] **vt** (*Couture*) to oversew, overcast.

surfin, e [syʀfɛ̃, in] **adj** *beurre, produit* superfine (*épith*), superquality (*épith*); *qualité* superfine (*épith*).

surgélation [syʀʒelasjɔ̃] **nf** deep-freezing, fast-freezing.

surgelé, e [syʀʒəle] 1 **adj** deep-frozen. 2 **nm**: **les ~s** (deep-)frozen food.

surgeler [syʀʒəle] [1] **vt** to deep-freeze, fast-freeze.

surgénérateur [syʀgeneʀatœʀ] **adjm, nm**: **(réacteur) ~** fast breeder (reactor).

surgeon [syʀʒɔ̃] **nm** (*Bot*) sucker.

surgir [syʀʒiʀ] [2] **vi** a *[animal, véhicule en mouvement, spectre]* to appear suddenly; *[montagne, navire]* to loom up (suddenly); *[plante, immeuble]* to shoot up, spring up. b *[problèmes, difficultés]* to arise, crop up; *[dilemme]* to arise.

surgissement [syʀʒismɑ̃] **nm** (*littér: voir* **surgir**) sudden appearance; sudden looming up; shooting up, springing up.

surhausser [syʀose] [1] **vt** (*gén, Archit*) to raise.

surhomme [syʀɔm] **nm** superman.

surhumain, e [syʀymɛ̃, ɛn] **adj** superhuman.

surimposé, e [syʀɛ̃poze] (**ptp de surimposer.**) **adj** (*Géol*) superimposed.

surimposer [syʀɛ̃poze] [1] **vt** (*taxer*) to overtax.

surimposition [syʀɛ̃pozisjɔ̃] **nf** (*Fin*) overtaxation. **payer une ~** to pay too much tax.

surimpression [syʀɛ̃pʀesjɔ̃] **nf** (*Phot*) double exposure; (*fig*) *[idées, visions]* superimposition. **en ~** superimposed; **on voyait, en ~, apparaître le visage de la mère** the mother's face appeared superimposed (on it).

surin‡† [syʀɛ̃] **nm** (*couteau*) knife, dagger.

Surinam [syʀinam] **nm** Surinam.

surinamais, e [syʀinamɛ, ɛz] 1 **adj** Surinamese. 2 **nm,f**: **S~(e)** Surinamese.

surinfecter (se) [syʀɛ̃fɛkte] [1] **vpr** to develop a secondary infection.

surinfection [syʀɛ̃fɛksjɔ̃] **nf** secondary infection.

surintendance [syʀɛ̃tɑ̃dɑ̃s] **nf** (*Hist*) superintendency.

surintendant [syʀɛ̃tɑ̃dɑ̃] **nm** (*Hist*) superintendent.

surinvestissement [syʀɛ̃vɛstismɑ̃] **nm** (*Écon, Psych*) overinvestment.

surir [syʀiʀ] [2] **vi** *[lait, vin]* to turn sour, (go) sour.

surjet [syʀʒɛ] **nm** overcast seam. **point de ~** overcast stitch.

surjeter [syʀʒəte] [4] **vt** (*Couture*) to overcast.

sur-le-champ [syʀləʃɑ̃] **adv** *voir* **sur**[1].

surlendemain [syʀlɑ̃d(ə)mɛ̃] **nm**: **le ~ de son arrivée** two days after his arrival; **il est mort le ~** he died two days later; **il revint le lendemain et le ~** he came back the next day and the day after (that); **le ~ matin** two days later in the morning.

surligneur [syʀliɲœʀ] **nm** highlighter (pen).

surmédicalisation [syʀmedikalizasjɔ̃] **nf** *[problème, cas]* overmedicalization; *[population, pays]* overprovision of medical care (*de* to).

surmédicaliser [syʀmedikalize] [1] **vt** *problème, cas* to overmedicalize; *population, pays* to overprovide with medical care.

surmenage [syʀmənaʒ] **nm** a (*voir* **surmener**) overworking, overtaxing. **éviter le ~ des élèves** to avoid overworking schoolchildren. b (*voir* **se surmener**) overwork(ing). **éviter à tout prix le ~** to avoid overwork(ing) *ou* overtaxing o.s. at all costs. c (*état maladif*) overwork. **souffrant de ~** suffering from (the effects of) overwork; **le ~ intellectuel** mental fatigue, brain-fag*.

surmener [syʀməne] [5] 1 **vt** *personne, animal* to overwork, overtax. 2 **se surmener vpr** to overwork *ou* overtax (o.s.).

surmoi [syʀmwa] **nm** superego.

surmontable [syʀmɔ̃tabl] **adj** surmountable. **obstacle difficilement ~** obstacle that is difficult to surmount *ou* overcome, obstacle that can be surmounted *ou* overcome only with difficulty.

surmonter [syʀmɔ̃te] [1] 1 **vt** a (*être au-dessus de*) to surmount, top. **surmonté d'un dôme/clocheton** surmounted *ou* topped by a dome/ bell-turret; **un clocheton surmontait l'édifice** the building was surmounted *ou* topped by a bell-turret. b (*vaincre*) *obstacle, difficultés* to overcome, get over, surmount; *dégoût, peur* to overcome, get the better of, fight down. **la peur peut se ~** fear can be overcome. 2 **se surmonter vpr** to master o.s., control o.s.

surmultiplié, e [syʀmyltiplije] **adj**: **vitesse ~e** overdrive.

surnager [syʀnaʒe] [3] **vi** *[huile, objet]* to float (on the surface); *[sentiment, souvenir]* to linger on.

surnaturel, -elle [syʀnatyʀɛl] 1 **adj** (*gén*) supernatural; *ambiance inquiétante* uncanny, eerie. 2 **nm**: **le ~** the supernatural.

surnom [syʀnɔ̃] **nm** nickname. **"le Courageux", ~ du roi Richard** "the Brave", the name by which King Richard was known.

surnombre [syʀnɔ̃bʀ] **nm**: (*participants etc*) **en ~** too many; **plusieurs élèves en ~** several pupils too many; **nous étions en ~ et avons dû partir** there were too many of us and so we had to leave; **Marie, qui était arrivée à l'improviste, était en ~** Marie, who had turned up unexpectedly, was one too many; **ils ont fait sortir les spectateurs en ~** they asked the excess spectators to leave.

surnommer [syʀnɔme] [1] **vt**: **~ qn "le gros"** to nickname sb "fatty"; **~ un roi "le Fort"** to give a king the name "the Strong"; **cette infirmité l'avait fait ~ "le Crapaud"** this disability had earned him the nickname of "the Toad"; **le roi Richard surnommé "le Courageux"** King Richard known as *ou* named "the Brave".

surnotation [syʀnɔtasjɔ̃] **nf** (*Scol*) overmarking (*Brit*), overgrading (*US*).

surnoter [syʀnɔte] [1] **vt** (*Scol*) to overmark (*Brit*), overgrade (*US*).

surnuméraire [syʀnymeʀɛʀ] **adj, nmf** supernumerary.

suroffre [syʀɔfʀ] **nf** (*Jur*) higher offer *ou* bid.

suroît [syʀwa] **nm** (*vent*) south-wester, sou'wester; (*chapeau*) sou'wester. **vent de ~** south-westerly wind.

surpaie [syʀpɛ] **nf** = **surpaye**.

surpassement [syʀpɑsmɑ̃] **nm** (*littér*) **~ de soi** surpassing (of) oneself.

surpasser [syʀpɑse] [1] 1 **vt** a (*l'emporter sur*) *concurrent, rival* to surpass, outdo. **~ qn en agilité/connaissances** to surpass sb in agility/ knowledge; **sa gloire surpassait en éclat celle de Napoléon** his glory outshone that of Napoleon. b (*dépasser*) to surpass. **le résultat surpasse toutes les espérances** the result surpasses *ou* is beyond all our hopes. 2 **se surpasser vpr** to surpass o.s., excel o.s. **le cuisinier s'est surpassé aujourd'hui** the cook has excelled *ou* surpassed himself today; (*iro*) **encore un échec, décidément tu te surpasses!** another failure — you're really excelling *ou* surpassing yourself!

surpaye [syʀpɛj] **nf** *[salariés, marchands]* overpayment. **la ~ des marchandises** paying too much for goods.

surpayer [syʀpeje] [8] **vt** *employé* to overpay; *marchandise* to pay too much for.

surpeuplé, e [syʀpœple] **adj** overpopulated.

surpeuplement [syʀpœpləmɑ̃] **nm** overpopulation.

surpiquer [syʀpike] [1] **vt** to topstitch.

surpiqûre [syʀpikyʀ] **nf** topstitch.

sur-place [syʀplas] **nm** *voir* **sur**[1].

surplis [syʀpli] **nm** surplice.

surplomb [syʀplɔ̃] **nm** overhang. **en ~** overhanging.

surplomber [syʀplɔ̃be] [1] 1 **vi** to overhang; (*Tech*) to be out of plumb. 2 **vt** to overhang.

surplus [syʀply] **nm** a (*excédent non écoulé*) surplus (*NonC*). **vendre le ~ de son stock** to sell off one's surplus stock; **avoir des marchandises en ~** to have surplus goods.

b (*reste non utilisé*) **il me reste un ~ de clous/de papier dont je ne me suis pas servi** I've got some nails/paper left over *ou* some surplus nails/paper that I didn't use; **avec le ~ (de bois), je vais essayer de me faire une bibliothèque** with what's left over (of the wood) *ou* with the leftover *ou* surplus (wood) I'm going to try to build myself a bookcase; **ce sont des ~ qui restent de la guerre/de l'exposition** they're *ou* it's left over *ou* it's surplus from the war/exhibition; **~ américains** American army surplus.

c (*d'ailleurs*) **au ~** moreover, what is more.

surpopulation [syʀpɔpylasjɔ̃] **nf** overpopulation.

surprenant, e [syʀpʀənɑ̃, ɑ̃t] **adj** (*étonnant*) amazing, surprising; (*remarquable*) amazing, astonishing.

surprendre [syʀpʀɑ̃dʀ] [58] 1 **vt** a (*prendre sur le fait*) *voleur* to surprise, catch in the act.

b (*découvrir*) *secret, complot* to discover; *conversation* to overhear; *regard, sourire complice* to intercept. **je crus ~ en lui de la gêne** I thought that I detected some embarrassment in him.

c (*prendre au dépourvu*) (*par attaque*) *ennemi* to surprise; (*par visite inopinée*) *amis, voisins etc* to catch unawares, catch on the hop* (*Brit*). **~ des amis chez eux** to drop in unexpectedly on friends, pay a surprise visit to friends; **espérant la ~ au bain/au lit** hoping to catch her in the bath/in bed; **je vais aller le ~ au travail** I'm going to drop in (unexpectedly) on him at work, I'm going to catch him unawares at work.

d *[pluie, marée, nuit]* to catch out. **se laisser ~ par la marée** to be caught (out) by the tide; **se laisser ~ par la pluie** to be caught in the rain *ou* caught (out) by the rain; **se laisser ~ par la nuit** to be overtaken by nightfall.

e (*étonner*) *[nouvelle, conduite]* to amaze, surprise. **tu me surprends** you amaze me; **cela me surprendrait fort** that would greatly surprise me; **cela m'a agréablement surpris** I was pleasantly surprised by that.

f (*littér*) **~ la vigilance de qn** to catch sb out; **~ la bonne foi de qn** to betray sb's good faith; **~ la confiance de qn**† to win sb's trust fraudulently.

2 **se surprendre vpr**: **se ~ à faire qch** to catch *ou* find o.s. doing sth.

surpression [syʀpʀesjɔ̃] **nf** (*Tech*) superpressure.

surprime [syʀpʀim] **nf** (*Assurances*) additional premium.

surpris, e[1] [syʀpʀi, iz] (ptp de **surprendre**) adj *air, regard* surprised. ~ **de qch** surprised *ou* amazed at sth; ~ **de me voir là/que je sois encore là** surprised *ou* amazed at seeing me there *ou* to see me there/that I was still there.

surprise[2] [syʀpʀiz] 1 nf a (*étonnement*) surprise. **regarder qn avec ~** to look at sb with *ou* in surprise; **avoir la ~ de voir que** to be surprised to see that; **à ma grande ~** much to my surprise, to my great surprise.

b (*cause d'étonnement, cadeau*) surprise. **voyage sans ~s** uneventful *ou* unremarkable journey; **prix sans ~s** (all-)inclusive price; **avec ça, pas de (mauvaises) ~s!** you'll have no nasty *ou* unpleasant surprises with this!; **il m'a apporté une petite ~** he brought me a little surprise; **quelle bonne ~!** what a nice *ou* pleasant *ou* lovely surprise!

c **par ~** *attaquer* by surprise; **il m'a pris par ~** he took me by surprise, he caught me off guard *ou* unawares, he caught me on the hop* (*Brit*).

d **visite-~** surprise visit; *[homme politique]* **voyage-~** surprise *ou* unexpected trip *ou* visit; *[coureur cycliste]* **échappée-~** sudden breakaway; **attaque-~** surprise attack; **grève-~** unofficial strike; *voir* **pochette**.

2 comp ▸ **surprise-partie** nf (pl **surprises-parties**) party.

surproduction [syʀpʀɔdyksjɔ̃] nf overproduction.

surproduire [syʀpʀɔdɥiʀ] 38 vt to overproduce.

surpuissant, e [syʀpɥisɑ̃, ɑ̃t] adj *voiture, moteur* ultra-powerful.

surréalisme [syʀʀealism] nm surrealism.

surréaliste [syʀʀealist] 1 adj *écrivain, peintre* surrealist; *tableau, poème* surrealist, surrealistic; (*bizarre*) surrealistic, way-out*. 2 nmf surrealist.

surrégénérateur [syʀʀeʒeneʀatœʀ] nm fast breeder (reactor).

surrénal, e, mpl **-aux** [sy(ʀ)ʀenal, o] 1 adj suprarenal. 2 nfpl: **~es** suprarenals.

sursalaire [syʀsalɛʀ] nm bonus, premium.

sursaut [syʀso] nm (*mouvement brusque*) start, jump. (*fig: élan, accès*) **~ d'énergie/d'indignation** (sudden) burst *ou* fit of energy/indignation; **se réveiller en ~** to wake up with a start *ou* jump; **elle a eu un ~** she gave a start, she jumped; **cela lui fit faire un ~** it made him jump *ou* start.

sursauter [syʀsote] 1 vi to start, jump, give a start. **faire ~ qn** to make sb start *ou* jump, give sb a start; **~ de peur** to jump with fright.

surseoir [syʀswaʀ] 26 **surseoir à** vt indir *publication, délibération* to defer, postpone; (*Jur*) *poursuites, jugement, exécution* to stay. **~ à l'exécution d'un condamné** to grant a stay of execution *ou* a reprieve to a condemned man.

sursis [syʀsi] nm a (*Jur*) *[condamnation à mort]* reprieve. **peine avec ~** *ou* **assortie du ~** suspended *ou* deferred sentence; **il a eu un ~/2 ans avec ~** he was given a suspended *ou* deferred sentence/a 2-year suspended *ou* deferred sentence; **~ à exécution** *ou* **d'exécution** stay of execution. b (*Mil*) **~ (d'incorporation)** deferment. c (*fig: temps de répit*) reprieve. **c'est un mort en ~** he's a condemned man, he's living under a death sentence.

sursitaire [syʀsitɛʀ] 1 adj (*Mil*) deferred (*épith*); (*Jur*) with a suspended *ou* deferred sentence. 2 nm (*Mil*) deferred conscript.

surtaxe [syʀtaks] nf surcharge; *[lettre mal affranchie]* surcharge; *[envoi exprès etc]* additional charge, surcharge. **~ à l'importation** import surcharge.

surtaxer [syʀtakse] 1 vt to surcharge.

surtension [syʀtɑ̃sjɔ̃] nf (*Élec*) overvoltage.

surtitre [syʀtitʀ] nm surtitle.

surtitrer [syʀtitʀe] 1 vt *opéra, pièce de théâtre* to surtitle. **"surtitré"** "with surtitles"; **l'opéra était surtitré** the opera had surtitles.

surtout[1] [syʀtu] adv a (*avant tout, d'abord*) above all; (*spécialement*) especially, particularly. **rapide, efficace et ~ discret** quick, efficient and above all discreet; **il est assez timide, ~ avec les femmes** he's quite shy, especially *ou* particularly with women; **j'aime ~ les romans, mais je lis aussi de la poésie** I particularly like novels *ou* above all I like novels, but I also read poetry; **dernièrement, j'ai ~ lu des romans** I have read mostly *ou* mainly novels of late; **j'aime les romans, ~ les romans policiers** I like novels, especially *ou* particularly detective novels; **le poulet, je l'aime ~ à la basquaise** I like chicken best (when) cooked the Basque way.

b **~ que*** especially as *ou* since.

c **~, motus et bouche cousue!** don't forget, mum's the word!; **~ pas maintenant** certainly not now; **je ne veux ~ pas vous déranger** the last thing I want is to disturb you, I certainly don't want to disturb you; **~ pas!** certainly not!; **~ ne vous mettez pas en frais** whatever you do, don't go to any expense.

surtout[2]† [syʀtu] nm (*manteau*) greatcoat†.

surveillance [syʀvɛjɑ̃s] 1 nf (*action: voir* **surveiller**) watch; supervision; invigilation. **exercer une ~ continuelle/une étroite ~ sur** to keep a constant/close watch over; **sous la ~ de la police** under police surveillance; **mission/service de ~** surveillance mission/personnel; **navire/avion en ~** ship/plane carrying out surveillance; **placer une maison sous ~** to put a house under surveillance; (*lit, fig*) **mettre qch sous haute ~** to keep a close *ou* tight watch on sth; **société de ~** security firm; **déjouer** *ou* **tromper la ~ de ses gardiens** to slip by *ou* evade the guards on duty.

2 comp ▸ **surveillance à distance** remote electronic surveillance ▸ **surveillance électronique** electronic surveillance; (*Méd*) electronic monitoring ▸ **surveillance légale** legal surveillance (*of impounded property*) ▸ **surveillance médicale** medical supervision ▸ **surveillance policière** police surveillance ▸ **la Direction de la surveillance du territoire** ≃ the Intelligence Service.

surveillant, e [syʀvɛjɑ̃, ɑ̃t] nm,f *[prison]* warder (*Brit* †), guard (*US*); *[usine, chantier]* supervisor, overseer; *[magasin]* shopwalker; (*Méd*) head nurse, charge nurse; (*Scol*) (*aux examens*) invigilator. **~ (d'étude)** supervisor; (*Scol*) **~ général** chief supervisor; (*Scol*) **~ d'internat** dormitory supervisor, dormitory monitor (*US*).

surveillé, e [syʀveje] (ptp de **surveiller**) adj *voir* **liberté**.

surveiller [syʀveje] 1 1 vt a (*garder*) *enfant, élève, bagages* to watch, keep an eye on; *prisonnier* to keep watch over, keep (a) watch on; *malade* to watch over, keep watch over. **il faut voir comme elle le surveille!** you should see the way she watches him!; **~ qn de près** to keep a close eye *ou* watch on sb; **~ qn du coin de l'œil** to keep half an eye on sb.

b (*contrôler*) *éducation, études de qn* to supervise; *réparation, construction* to supervise, oversee; (*Scol*) *examen* to invigilate. **surveille la soupe une minute** keep an eye on the soup a minute, watch the soup a minute.

c (*défendre*) *locaux* to keep watch on; *territoire* to watch over, keep watch over.

d (*épier*) *personne, mouvements, proie* to watch; *adversaire* (*Mil*) to keep watch on; (*Sport*) to watch. **se sentant surveillé, il partit** feeling he was being watched, he left.

e (*fig*) **~ son langage/sa ligne** to watch one's language/one's figure.

2 **se surveiller** vpr to keep a check *ou* a watch on o.s. **elle devrait se ~, elle grossit de plus en plus** she ought to keep a check *ou* watch on herself *ou* she ought to watch herself because she's getting fatter and fatter.

survenir [syʀvəniʀ] 22 vi *[événement]* to take place; *[incident, complications, retards]* to occur, arise; *[personne]* to appear, arrive (unexpectedly). **s'il survient des complications ...** should any complications arise ... .

survêt* [syʀvɛt] nm abrév de **survêtement**.

survêtement [syʀvɛtmɑ̃] nm (*sportif*) tracksuit; *[alpiniste, skieur]* overgarments.

survie [syʀvi] nf *[malade, accidenté]* survival; (*Rel: dans l'au-delà*) afterlife; (*fig*) *[auteur, amitié, institution, mode]* survival. **ce médicament lui a donné quelques mois de ~** this drug has given him a few more months of life *ou* a few more months to live; **une ~ de quelques jours, à quoi bon, dans son état?** what's the use of letting him survive *ou* live *ou* of prolonging his life for a few more days in his condition?; **équipement** *etc* **de ~** survival equipment *etc.*

survirer [syʀviʀe] 1 vi (*Aut*) to oversteer.

survireur, -euse [syʀviʀœʀ, øz] adj (*Aut*) **voiture ~euse** car which oversteers.

survitrage [syʀvitʀaʒ] nm double-glazing.

survivance [syʀvivɑ̃s] nf (*vestige*) relic, survival. **cette coutume est une ~ du passé** this custom is a survival from the past; (*littér*) **~ de l'âme** survival of the soul (after death), afterlife.

survivant, e [syʀvivɑ̃, ɑ̃t] 1 adj surviving. 2 nm,f (*rescapé, Jur*) survivor. **des sœurs, la ~e ...** the surviving sister ...; **un ~ d'un âge révolu** a survivor from a past age.

survivre [syʀvivʀ] 46 1 vi a (*continuer à vivre: lit, fig*) to survive. (*après accident etc*) **va-t-il ~?** will he live? *ou* survive?; **il n'avait aucune chance de ~** he had no chance of survival *ou* surviving; **~ à** *accident, maladie, humiliation* to survive; (*fig*) **rien ne survivait de leurs anciennes coutumes** nothing survived of their old customs. b (*vivre plus longtemps que*) **~ à** *[personne]* to outlive; *[œuvre, idée]* to outlive, outlast. 2 **se survivre** vpr a (*se perpétuer*) **se ~ dans** *œuvre, enfant, souvenir* to live on in. b (*péj*) *[auteur]* to outlive one's talent; *[aventurier]* to outlive one's time.

survol [syʀvɔl] nm (*voir* **survoler**) **le ~ de** flying over; skimming through, skipping through; skimming over; **faire un ~ à basse altitude** to make a low flight.

survoler [syʀvɔle] 1 vt (*lit*) to fly over; (*fig*) *livre* to skim through, skip through; *question* to skim over.

survoltage [syʀvɔltaʒ] nm (*Élec*) boosting.

survolté, e [syʀvɔlte] adj a (*surexcité*) worked up, over-excited. b (*Élec*) stepped up, boosted.

sus [sy(s)] adv a (*Admin*) **en ~** in addition; **en ~ de** in addition to, over and above. b (*††, hum*) **courir ~ à l'ennemi** to rush upon the enemy; **~ à l'ennemi!** at them!; **~ au tyran!** at the tyrant!

susceptibilité [sysɛptibilite] nf touchiness (*NonC*), sensitiveness (*NonC*). **afin de ménager les ~s** so as not to offend people's susceptibilities *ou* sensibilities.

susceptible [sysɛptibl] adj a (*ombrageux*) touchy, thin-skinned, sensitive.

b (*de nature à*) **ces axiomes ne sont pas ~s de démonstration** *ou* **d'être démontrés** these axioms are not susceptible of proof *ou* cannot be proved; **texte ~ d'être amélioré** *ou* **d'améliorations** text open to improvement *ou* that can be improved upon; **ces gens ne sont pas ~s**

d'éprouver du chagrin these people are not susceptible to grief; **des conférences ~s de l'intéresser** lectures liable *ou* likely to be of interest to him *ou* that may well be of interest to him.

c (*en mesure de*) **est-il ~ de le faire?** (*capacité*) is he able to do it?, is he capable of doing it?; (*hypothèse*) is he likely to do it?; **il est ~ de gagner** he may well win, he is liable to win; **un second ~ lui aussi de prendre l'initiative des opérations** a second-in-command who is also in a position to *ou* who is also able to direct operations.

susciter [sysite] 1 **vt** a (*donner naissance à*) *admiration, intérêt* to arouse; *passions, jalousies, haine* to arouse, incite; *controverse, critiques, querelle* to give rise to, provoke; *obstacles* to give rise to, create. b (*provoquer volontairement*) to create. **~ des obstacles/ennuis à qn** to create obstacles/difficulties for sb; **~ des ennemis à qn** to make enemies for sb.

suscription [syskʀipsjɔ̃] **nf** (*Admin*) address.

susdit, e [sysdi, dit] **adj** (*Jur*) foresaid.

sus-dominante [sysdɔminɑ̃t] **nf** submediant.

sushi [suʃi] **nm** sushi.

susmentionné, e [sysmɑ̃sjɔne] **adj** (*Admin*) above-mentioned, aforementioned.

susnommé, e [sysnɔme] **adj, nm, f** (*Admin, Jur*) above-named.

suspect, e [syspɛ(kt), ɛkt] 1 **adj** a (*louche*) *individu, conduite, attitude* suspicious. **sa générosité m'est** *ou* **me paraît ~e** I find his generosity suspicious, his generosity seems suspect *ou* suspicious to me.

b (*douteux*) *opinion, témoignage, citoyen* suspect. **individu ~ au régime** (individual) suspect in the eyes of the régime; **pensées ~es à la majorité conservatrice** thoughts which the conservative majority find suspect.

c **~ de** suspected of; **ils sont ~s de collusion avec l'ennemi** they are suspected of collusion with the enemy; **X, pourtant bien peu ~ de royalisme, a proposé que ...** X, hardly likely to be suspected of royalism, did however propose that ... .

2 **nm,f** suspect.

suspecter [syspɛkte] 1 **vt** *personne* to suspect; *bonne foi, honnêteté* to suspect, have (one's) suspicions about, question. **~ qn de faire** to suspect sb of doing; **on le suspecte de sympathies gauchistes** he is suspected of having leftist sympathies.

suspendre [syspɑ̃dʀ] 41 1 **vt** a (*accrocher*) *vêtements* to hang up. **~ qch à** *clou, crochet* to hang sth on.

b (*fixer*) *lampe, décoration* to hang, suspend (*à* from); *hamac* to sling (up). **~ un lustre au plafond par une chaîne** to hang *ou* suspend a chandelier from the ceiling on *ou* by *ou* with a chain; **~ un hamac à des crochets/à deux poteaux** to sling a hammock between some hooks/two posts.

c (*interrompre*) (*journal, permis de conduire etc*) to suspend; *récit* to break off; *audience, séance* to adjourn.

d (*remettre*) *jugement* to suspend, defer; *décision* to postpone, defer.

e (*destituer*) *prélat, fonctionnaire, joueur* to suspend. **~ qn de ses fonctions** to suspend sb from office.

2 **se suspendre vpr: se ~ à** *branche, barre* to hang from (*par* by).

suspendu, e [syspɑ̃dy] (**ptp de suspendre**) **adj** a (*accroché*) **vêtement** *etc* **~ à** garment *etc* hanging on; **lustre** *etc* **~ à** light *etc* hanging *ou* suspended from; **benne ~e à un câble/dans le vide** skip suspended by a cable/in mid air; **montre ~e à une chaîne** watch hanging on a chain; (*fig*) **être ~ aux lèvres de qn** to hang upon sb's every word; (*fig*) **chalets ~s au-dessus d'une gorge** chalets perched *ou* suspended over a gorge; *voir* **jardin, pont.** b (*Aut*) **voiture bien/mal ~e** car with good/poor suspension.

suspens [syspɑ̃] **nm** a (*en attente*) **en ~** *projet, travail* in abeyance; **une question laissée en ~** a question that has been shelved; **laisser une affaire en ~** to leave an affair in abeyance. b (*dans l'incertitude*) **en ~** in suspense; **tenir les lecteurs en ~** to keep the reader in suspense. c (*en suspension*) **en ~** *poussière, flocons de neige* in suspension; **en ~ dans l'air** suspended in the air. d (*littér: suspense*) suspense.

suspense [syspɛns, syspɑ̃s] **nm** *[film, roman]* suspense. **un moment de ~** a moment's suspense; **un ~ angoissant** an agonizing feeling of suspense; **film à ~** suspense film, thriller.

suspenseur [syspɑ̃sœʀ] 1 **adj m** suspensary. 2 **nm** suspensar.

suspensif, -ive [syspɑ̃sif, iv] **adj** (*Jur*) suspensive.

suspension [syspɑ̃sjɔ̃] 1 **nf** a (*action: voir* **suspendre**) hanging; suspending; suspension; breaking off; adjournment; deferment; postponement. **prononcer la ~ de qn pour 2 ans** to suspend sb for 2 years; *voir* **point[1]**.

b (*Aut*) suspension. **~ à roues indépendantes/hydro-pneumatique** independent/hydropneumatic suspension; *voir* **ressort[1]**.

c (*lustre*) light fitting *ou* fitment.

d (*installation, système*) suspension.

e (*Chim*) suspension.

f **en ~** *particule, poussière* in suspension, suspended; **en ~ dans l'air** *poussière* hanging on the air, suspended in the air; **en ~ dans l'air** *ou* **dans le vide** *personne, câble* suspended in mid air.

2 **comp** ►**suspension d'armes** suspension of fighting ►**suspension d'audience** adjournment ►**suspension des hostilités** suspension of hostilities ►**suspension de paiement** suspension of payment(s) ►**suspension de séance = suspension d'audience.**

suspensoir [syspɑ̃swaʀ] **nm** support.

suspicieusement [syspisjøzmɑ̃] **adv** suspiciously.

suspicieux, -ieuse [syspisjø, jøz] **adj** suspicious.

suspicion [syspisjɔ̃] **nf** suspicion. **avoir de la ~ à l'égard de qn** to be suspicious of sb, have one's suspicions about sb; **regard plein de ~** suspicious look.

sustentateur, -trice [systɑ̃tatœʀ, tʀis] **adj** (*Aviat*) lifting. **surface ~trice** aerofoil.

sustentation [systɑ̃tasjɔ̃] **nf** (*Aviat*) lift. (*Aviat*) **plan de ~** aerofoil; (*Géom*) **polygone** *ou* **base de ~** base.

sustenter [systɑ̃te] 1 1 **vt** (†: *nourrir*) to sustain. 2 **se sustenter vpr** (*hum, frm*) to take sustenance (*hum, frm*).

sus-tonique [systɔnik] **adj** (*Mus*) supertonic.

susurrement [sysyʀmɑ̃] **nm** (*voir* **susurrer**) whisper; whispering; murmuring.

susurrer [sysyʀe] 1 **vti** *[personne]* to whisper; *[eau]* to murmur.

susvisé, e [sysvize] **adj** (*Admin*) above-mentioned, aforementioned.

suture [sytyʀ] **nf** (*Anat, Bot, Méd*) suture; *voir* **point[2]**.

suturer [sytyʀe] 1 **vt** to suture (*SPÉC*), stitch up.

Suva [syva] **n** Suva.

suzerain, e [syz(ə)ʀɛ̃, ɛn] 1 **nm,f** suzerain, overlord. 2 **adj** suzerain.

suzeraineté [syz(ə)ʀɛnte] **nf** suzerainty.

svastika [svastika] **nm** swastika.

svelte [svɛlt] **adj** *personne* svelte, slender, slim, willowy; *édifice, silhouette* slender, slim.

sveltesse [svɛltɛs] **nf** slenderness.

SVP [ɛsvepe] (**abrév de s'il vous plaît**) please.

swahili, e [swaili] 1 **adj** Swahili(an). 2 **nm** (*Ling*) Swahili. 3 **nm,f: S~(e)** Swahili.

swazi, e [swazi] 1 **adj** Swazi. 2 **nm,f: S~(e)** Swazi.

Swaziland [swazilɑ̃d] **nm** Swaziland.

sweater [switœʀ] **nm** sweater.

sweat-shirt, pl sweat-shirts [switʃœʀt] **nm** sweatshirt.

sweepstake [swipstɛk] **nm** sweepstake.

swiftien, -ienne [swiftjɛ̃, jɛn] **adj** Swiftian.

swing [swiŋ] **nm** swing.

swinguer* [swiŋge] 1 **vi** to swing*. **ça swingue!** they are really swinging it!*

sybarite [sibaʀit] **nmf** sybarite.

sybaritique [sibaʀitik] **adj** sybaritic.

sybaritisme [sibaʀitism] **nm** sybaritism.

sycomore [sikɔmɔʀ] **nm** sycamore (tree).

sycophante [sikɔfɑ̃t] **nm** (*littér: délateur*) informer.

syllabation [si(l)labasjɔ̃] **nf** syllabication, syllabification.

syllabe [si(l)lab] **nf** syllable. **il n'a pas prononcé une ~** he didn't say a single word.

syllabique [si(l)labik] **adj** syllabic.

syllabisme [si(l)labism] **nm** syllabism.

syllogisme [silɔʒism] **nm** syllogism.

syllogistique [silɔʒistik] **adj** syllogistic.

sylphe [silf] **nm** sylph.

sylphide [silfid] **nf** sylphid; (*fig*) sylphlike creature. **sa taille de ~** her sylphlike figure.

sylvestre [silvɛstʀ] **adj** forest (*épith*), silvan (*littér*); *voir* **pin.**

Sylvestre [silvɛstʀ] **nm** Silvester.

sylvicole [silvikɔl] **adj** forestry (*épith*).

sylviculteur [silvikyltœʀ] **nm** forester.

sylviculture [silvikyltyʀ] **nf** forestry, silviculture (*SPÉC*).

Sylvie [silvi] **nf** Sylvia.

symbiose [sɛ̃bjoz] **nf** (*aussi fig*) symbiosis. **en ~** in symbiosis.

symbiotique [sɛ̃bjɔtik] **adj** symbiotic.

symbole [sɛ̃bɔl] **nm** (*gén*) symbol. **une ville-~/des années-~ de la liberté** a city that has come to symbolize/years that have come to symbolize freedom; **~ des apôtres** Apostles' Creed; **~ de saint Athanase** Athanasian Creed.

symbolique [sɛ̃bɔlik] 1 **adj** (*gén*) symbolic(al); (*fig: très modique*) *donation, augmentation, émolument, amende* token (*épith*), nominal; *cotisation, contribution, dommages-intérêts* nominal; (*sans valeur*) *solution* cosmetic. **c'est un geste purement ~** it's a purely symbolic(al) gesture, it's just a token gesture; **logique ~** symbolic logic; *voir* **franc.**

2 **nf** (*science*) symbolics (*sg*); (*système de symboles*) symbolic system. **la ~ des rêves** the symbolism of dreams, dream symbolism.

symboliquement [sɛ̃bɔlikmɑ̃] **adv** symbolically.

symbolisation [sɛ̃bɔlizasjɔ̃] **nf** symbolization.

symboliser [sɛ̃bɔlize] 1 **vt** to symbolize.

symbolisme [sɛ̃bɔlism] **nm** (*gén*) symbolism; (*Littérat*) Symbolism.

symboliste [sɛ̃bɔlist] **adj, nmf** Symbolist.

symétrie [simetʀi] **nf** (*gén*) symmetry (*par rapport à* in relation to). **centre/axe de ~** centre/axis of symmetry.

symétrique [simetʀik] 1 **adj** symmetrical (*de* to, *par rapport à* in relation to). 2 **nm** *[muscle]* symmetry. 3 **nf** *[figure plane]* symmetrical figure.

symétriquement [simetʀikmɑ̃] adv symmetrically.
sympa* [sɛ̃pa] adj inv (abrév de **sympathique**) *personne, soirée, robe* nice; *endroit, ambiance* nice, friendly. **un type vachement** ~ a nice *ou* good bloke* (*Brit*) *ou* guy*; **sois** ~, **prête-le-moi** be a pal* and lend it to me.
sympathie [sɛ̃pati] nf a (*inclination*) liking. **ressentir de la** ~ **à l'égard de qn** to (rather) like sb, have a liking for sb, feel drawn to *ou* towards sb; **j'ai beaucoup de** ~ **pour lui** I have a great liking for him, I like him a great deal; **il inspire la** ~ he's very likeable, he's a likeable sort; **n'ayant que peu de** ~ **pour cette nouvelle théorie** feeling very lukewarm about this new theory, having little time for this new theory, being unfavourable to(wards) this new theory; **accueillir une idée avec** ~ to receive an idea favourably.
b (*affinité*) fellow feeling, warmth, friendship. **la** ~ **qui existe entre eux** the fellow feeling *ou* friendship *ou* warmth there is between them, the affinity they feel for each other; **des relations de** ~ **les unissaient** they were united by a fellow feeling; **il n'y a guère de** ~ **entre ces factions/personnes** there's no love lost between these factions/people; **être en** ~ **avec qn** to be at one with sb (*frm*).
c (*frm: condoléances*) sympathy. **croyez à notre** ~ please accept our deepest *ou* most heartfelt sympathy, you have our deepest sympathy; (*pour deuil*) **témoignages de** ~ expressions of sympathy.
sympathique [sɛ̃patik] 1 adj a (*agréable, aimable*) *personne* likeable, nice; *geste, accueil* friendly, kindly; *soirée, réunion, ambiance* pleasant, friendly; *plat* good, nice; *appartement* nice, pleasant. **il m'est (très)** ~, **je le trouve (très)** ~ I like him (very much), I find him (very) likeable *ou* friendly *ou* nice; **il a une tête** ~ he has a friendly face. b (*Anat*) sympathetic. c *voir* **encre.** 2 nm (*Anat*) **le (grand)** ~ the sympathetic nervous system.
sympathiquement [sɛ̃patikmɑ̃] adv *accueillir, traiter* in a friendly manner. **ils ont** ~ **offert de nous aider** they have kindly offered to help us; **ils nous ont** ~ **reçus** they gave us a friendly reception.
sympathisant, e [sɛ̃patizɑ̃, ɑ̃t] (*Pol*) 1 adj sympathizing (*épith*). 2 nm,f sympathizer.
sympathiser [sɛ̃patize] 1 vi (*bien s'entendre*) to get on (well) (*avec* with); (*se prendre d'amitié*) to hit it off* (*avec* with). (*fréquenter*) **ils ne sympathisent pas avec les voisins** they don't have much contact with *ou* much to do with* the neighbours; **je suis heureux de voir qu'il sympathise avec Lucien** I'm pleased to see he gets on (well) with Lucien; **ils ont tout de suite sympathisé** they took to each other immediately, they hit it off* straight away.
symphonie [sɛ̃fɔni] nf (*Mus, fig*) symphony. ~ **concertante** symphonia concertante.
symphonique [sɛ̃fɔnik] adj symphonic; *voir* **orchestre, poème.**
symphoniste [sɛ̃fɔnist] nmf symphonist.
symposium [sɛ̃pozjɔm] nm symposium.
symptomatique [sɛ̃ptɔmatik] adj (*Méd*) symptomatic; (*révélateur*) significant. ~ **de** symptomatic of.
symptomatiquement [sɛ̃ptɔmatikmɑ̃] adv symptomatically.
symptomatologie [sɛ̃ptɔmatɔlɔʒi] nf symptomatology.
symptôme [sɛ̃ptom] nm (*Méd*) symptom; (*signe, indice*) sign, symptom.
synagogue [sinagɔg] nf synagogue.
synapse [sinaps] nf *[neurones]* synapse, synapsis; *[gamètes]* synapsis.
synarchie [sinaʀʃi] nf synarchy.
synchrone [sɛ̃kʀon] adj synchronous.
synchronie [sɛ̃kʀɔni] nf synchronic level, synchrony.
synchronique [sɛ̃kʀɔnik] adj *linguistique, analyse* synchronic; *voir* **tableau.**
synchroniquement [sɛ̃kʀɔnikmɑ̃] adj synchronically.
synchronisation [sɛ̃kʀɔnizasjɔ̃] nf synchronization.
synchronisé, e [sɛ̃kʀɔnize] (ptp de **synchroniser**) adj synchronized.
synchroniser [sɛ̃kʀɔnize] 1 vt to synchronize.
synchroniseur [sɛ̃kʀɔnizœʀ] nm (*Élec*) synchronizer; (*Aut*) synchromesh.
synchroniseuse [sɛ̃kʀɔnizøz] nf (*Ciné*) synchronizer.
synchronisme [sɛ̃kʀɔnism] nm *[oscillations, dates]* synchronism; (*Philos*) synchronicity. (*fig*) **avec un** ~ **parfait** with perfect synchronization.
synchrotron [sɛ̃kʀɔtʀɔ̃] nm synchrotron. **rayonnement** ~ synchrotron radiation.
synclinal, e, mpl **-aux** [sɛ̃klinal, o] 1 adj synclinal. 2 nm syncline.
syncope [sɛ̃kɔp] nf a (*évanouissement*) blackout, fainting fit, syncope (*SPÉC*). **avoir une** ~ to have a blackout, have a fainting fit; **tomber en** ~ to faint, pass out. b (*Mus*) syncopation. c (*Ling*) syncope.
syncopé, e [sɛ̃kɔpe] adj a (*Littérat, Mus*) syncopated. b (**: stupéfait*) staggered*, flabbergasted*.
syncrétique [sɛ̃kʀetik] adj syncretic.
syncrétisme [sɛ̃kʀetism] nm syncretism.
syndic [sɛ̃dik] nm (*Hist*) syndic; (*Jur*) receiver. ~ **(d'immeuble)** managing agent, factor (*Écos*); (*Jur, Fin*) ~ **de faillite** official receiver, ≃ trustee (in bankruptcy).
syndical, e, mpl **-aux** [sɛ̃dikal, o] adj (trade-)union (*épith*). **conseil** ~ **d'un immeuble** ≃ management committee of a block of flats (*Brit*) *ou* an apartment house (*US*); *voir* **central, chambre, tarif.**
syndicalisation [sɛ̃dikalizasjɔ̃] nf union membership.
syndicalisme [sɛ̃dikalism] nm (*mouvement*) trade unionism; (*activité*) union(ist) activities (*pl*); (*doctrine politique*) syndicalism. **collègue au** ~ **ardent** colleague with strongly unionist views; **faire du** ~ to participate in unionist activities, be a union activist.
syndicaliste [sɛ̃dikalist] 1 nmf (*responsable d'un syndicat*) (trade) union official, trade unionist; (*doctrinaire*) syndicalist. 2 adj *chef* trade-union (*épith*); *doctrine, idéal* unionist (*épith*).
syndicat [sɛ̃dika] 1 nm a *[travailleurs, employés]* (trade) union; *[employeurs]* union, syndicate; *[producteurs agricoles]* union. ~ **de mineurs/de journalistes** miners'/journalists' union; ~ **du crime** crime syndicate.
b (*non professionnel*) association; *voir* **2.**
2 comp ►**syndicat de communes** (*Admin*) association of communes ►**syndicat financier** syndicate of financiers ►**syndicat d'initiative** tourist (information) office *ou* bureau *ou* centre ►**syndicat interdépartemental** (*Admin*) association of regional authorities ►**syndicat de locataires** tenants' association ►**syndicat ouvrier** trade union ►**syndicat patronal** employers' syndicate, federation of employers, bosses' union* ►**syndicat de propriétaires** (*gén*) association of property owners; (*d'un même immeuble*) householders' association.
syndicataire [sɛ̃dikatɛʀ] 1 adj of a syndicate. 2 nmf syndicate member.
syndiqué, e [sɛ̃dike] (ptp de **syndiquer**) 1 adj belonging to a (trade) union. **ouvrier** ~ union member; **est-il** ~**?** is he in a *ou* the union?, is he a union man *ou* member?; **les travailleurs non** ~**s** workers who are not members of a *ou* the union, non-union *ou* non-unionized workers. 2 nm,f union member.
syndiquer [sɛ̃dike] 1 1 vt to unionize. 2 **se syndiquer** vpr (*se grouper*) to form a trade union, unionize; (*adhérer*) to join a trade union.
syndrome [sɛ̃dʀom] nm syndrome. ~ **chinois** China syndrome; **le** ~ **de Down** Down's syndrome; ~ **immuno-déficitaire acquis** acquired immuno-deficiency syndrome.
synecdoque [sinɛkdɔk] nf synecdoche.
synérèse [sineʀɛz] nf (*Ling*) synaeresis; (*Chim*) syneresis.
synergie [sinɛʀʒi] nf synergy, synergism.
synergique [sinɛʀʒik] adj synergetic.
synesthésie [sinɛstezi] nf synaesthesia.
synode [sinɔd] nm synod; *voir* **saint.**
synodique [sinɔdik] adj (*Astron*) synodic(al); (*Rel*) synod(ic)al.
synonyme [sinɔnim] 1 adj synonymous (*de* with). 2 nm synonym.
synonymie [sinɔnimi] nf synonymy.
synonymique [sinɔnimik] adj synonymic(al).
synopsis [sinɔpsis] nf ou m (*Ciné*) synopsis.
synoptique [sinɔptik] adj synoptic. **les (Évangiles)** ~**s** the synoptic gospels.
synovial, e, mpl **-iaux** [sinɔvjal, jo] adj synovial.
synovie [sinɔvi] nf synovia; *voir* **épanchement.**
synovite [sinɔvit] nf synovitis.
syntactique [sɛ̃taktik] adj = **syntaxique.**
syntagmatique [sɛ̃tagmatik] adj syntagmatic, phrasal.
syntagme [sɛ̃tagm] nm (word) group, phrase, syntagm (*SPÉC*). ~ **adjoint** adjunctive phrase, adjunct; ~ **nominal** nominal group, noun phrase; ~ **verbal** verb phrase.
syntaxe [sɛ̃taks] nf syntax.
syntaxique [sɛ̃taksik] adj syntactic.
synthé* [sɛ̃te] nm (abrév de **synthétiseur**) synth*.
synthèse [sɛ̃tɛz] nf synthesis. **faire la** ~ **d'un exposé** *etc* to summarize the major points of a talk *etc*; *sucre, arôme etc* **de** ~ synthetic; (*Chim*) **produit de** ~ product of synthesis; (*Ordin*) ~ **vocale/de la parole** voice/speech synthesis.
synthétique [sɛ̃tetik] adj synthetic.
synthétiquement [sɛ̃tetikmɑ̃] adv synthetically.
synthétiser [sɛ̃tetize] 1 vt to synthetize, synthesize.
synthétiseur [sɛ̃tetizœʀ] nm synthesizer. (*Ordin*) ~ **de (la) parole** speech synthesizer.
syntonie [sɛ̃tɔni] nf (*Psych*) syntonia; (*Phys*) syntonism.
syntoniser [sɛ̃tɔnize] 1 vt to syntonize.
syphilis [sifilis] nf syphilis.
syphilitique [sifilitik] adj, nmf syphilitic.
Syracuse [siʀakyz] n Syracuse.
Syrie [siʀi] nf Syria.
syrien, -ienne [siʀjɛ̃, jɛn] 1 adj Syrian. **République arabe** ~**ne** Syrian Arab Republic. 2 nm,f: **S~(ne)** Syrian.
systématique [sistematik] 1 adj *soutien, aide* unconditional; *opposition* systematic; *classement, esprit* systematic. **opposer un refus** ~ **à qch** to refuse sth systematically; **avec l'intention** ~ **de nuire** systematically intending to harm; **il est trop** ~ he's too narrow *ou* dogmatic, his views are too set; **chaque fois qu'elle est invitée quelque part il l'est aussi, c'est** ~ every time she's invited somewhere, he's automatically invited too. 2 nf (*gén*) systematics (*sg*); (*Bio*) taxonomy.
systématiquement [sistematikmɑ̃] adv systematically.
systématisation [sistematizasjɔ̃] nf systematization.

systématiser [sistematize] 1 1 **vt** *recherches, mesures* to systematize. **il n'a pas le sens de la nuance, il systématise (tout)** he has no sense of nuance – he systematizes everything. 2 **se systématiser vpr** to become the rule.

système [sistɛm] 1 **nm** a (*gén: théorie, structure, méthode, dispositif, réseau*) system. ~ **de vie** way of life, lifestyle; (*institution etc*) **faire partie du** ~ to be part of the system; (*Ling*) ~ **casuel** case system; (*Anat*) **troubles du** ~ systemic disorders; *voir* **esprit.**

b (*moyen*) system. **il connaît un ~ pour entrer sans payer** he's got a system for getting in without paying; **il connaît le** ~ he knows the trick *ou* system; **le meilleur ~, c'est de se relayer** the best plan *ou* system is to take turns.

c (*loc*) **par** ~ *agir* in a systematic way; *contredire* systematically; **il me tape** *ou* **court** *ou* **porte sur le** ~‡ he gets on my wick‡ (*Brit*) *ou* nerves*.

2 **comp** ►**système d'alarme** alarm system ►**système D*** resourcefulness ►**système décimal** decimal system ►**système de défense** (*Mil*) defence system; (*Physiol*) defence mechanism ►**système d'équations** system of equations ►**système expert** expert system ►**système d'exploitation** operating system ►**système de gestion de bases de données** database management system ►**système immunitaire** immune system ►**Système international d'unités** International System of Units ►**système métrique** metric system ►**système monétaire européen** European monetary system ►**système nerveux central/périphérique** central/peripheral nervous system ►**système pileux** hair ►**système respiratoire** respiratory system ►**système solaire** solar system ►**système de traitement de texte** word-processing package.

systémique [sistemik] **adj** systemic.

systole [sistɔl] **nf** systole.

systolique [sistɔlik] **adj** systolic.

syzygie [siziʒi] **nf** syzygy.

T

T, t [te] nm (*lettre*) T, t. **en T** *table, immeuble* T-shaped; **bandage/antenne/équerre en T** T-bandage/-aerial/-square.
t. (abrév de **tonne**) t.
t' [t] *voir* **te, tu.**
ta [ta] adj poss *voir* **ton**[1].
tabac [taba] 1 nm a (*plante, produit*) tobacco; (*couleur*) buff, tobacco (brown); (*magasin*) tobacconist's (shop) (*Brit*), tobacco *ou* smoke shop (*US*). **(café-)~** café (*selling tobacco and stamps*); *voir* **blague, bureau, débit.** b (**: loc*) **passer qn à ~** to beat sb up; (*arg Théât*) **faire un ~** to be a great hit *ou* a roaring success; **c'est toujours le même ~** it's always the same old thing; **quelque chose du même ~** something like that; **coup de ~** squall; *voir* **passage.** 2 adj inv buff, tobacco (brown). 3 comp ▸**tabac blond** light *ou* mild *ou* Virginia tobacco ▸**tabac brun** dark tobacco ▸**tabac à chiquer** chewing tobacco ▸**tabac gris** shag ▸**tabac à priser** snuff.
tabagie [tabaʒi] nf smoke den.
tabagique [tabaʒik] adj smoking (*épith*), nicotine (*épith*).
tabagisme [tabaʒism] nm addiction to smoking, nicotine addiction.
tabard [tabaʀ] nm tabard.
tabassée* [tabase] nf (*passage à tabac*) belting*; (*bagarre*) punch-up* (*Brit*), brawl.
tabasser* [tabase] [1] 1 vt (*passer à tabac*) **~ qn** to beat sb up, do sb over* (*Brit*); **se faire ~** to be given a beating, get one's face smashed in* (*par* by). 2 **se tabasser** vpr (*se bagarrer*) to have a punch-up* (*Brit*) *ou* fight.
tabatière [tabatjɛʀ] nf a (*boîte*) snuffbox. b (*lucarne*) skylight; *voir* **fenêtre.**
T.A.B.D.T. [teabedete] nm abrév de **vaccin antityphoïdique et antiparatyphoïdique A et B, antidiphtérique et tétanique.**
tabellion [tabeljɔ̃] nm (*hum péj: notaire*) lawyer, legal worthy (*hum péj*).
tabernacle [tabɛʀnakl] nm (*Rel*) tabernacle.
tablature [tablatyʀ] nf (*Mus*) tablature.
table [tabl] 1 nf a (*meuble*) table. **~ de salle à manger/de cuisine/de billard** dining-room/kitchen/billiard table; **~ de** *ou* **en bois/marbre** wooden/marble table; *voir* **dessous, carte, tennis.**
b (*pour le repas*) **être à ~** to be having a meal, be eating, be at table; **nous étions 8 à ~** there were 8 of us at *ou* round the table; **à ~!** come and eat!, dinner (*ou* lunch *etc*) is ready!; **mettre** *ou* (*littér*) **dresser la ~** to lay *ou* set the table; **débarrasser** *ou* (*littér*) **desservir la ~** to clear the table; **passer à ~, se mettre à ~** to sit down to eat, sit down at the table; **présider la ~** to sit at the head of the table; **recevoir qn à sa ~** to have sb to lunch (*ou* dinner *etc*); **se lever de ~** to get up *ou* rise (*frm*) from the table; **quitter la ~, sortir de ~** to leave the table; **~ de 12 couverts** table set for 12; **linge/vin/propos de ~** table linen/wine/talk.
c (*tablée*) table. **toute la ~ éclata de rire** the whole table burst out laughing; **une ~ de 4** a table for 4; **soldats et officiers mangeaient à la même ~** soldiers and officers ate at the same table.
d (*nourriture*) **une ~ frugale** frugal fare (*NonC*); **avoir une bonne ~** to keep a good table; **aimer (les plaisirs de) la ~** to enjoy one's food.
e (*tablette avec inscriptions*) **~ de marbre** marble tablet; **les T~s de la Loi** the Tables of the Law; *voir* **douze.**
f (*liste*) table. **~ de logarithmes/de multiplication** log/multiplication table; **~ de vérité** truth table; **~ alphabétique** alphabetical table.
g (*Géol: plateau*) tableland, plateau.
h (*loc*) (*Philos*) **~ rase** tabula rasa; **faire ~ rase** to make a clean sweep (*de* of); (*arg Police*) **se mettre à ~** to talk, come clean‡; **tenir ~ ouverte** to keep open house.
2 comp ▸**table à abattants** drop-leaf table ▸**table anglaise** gate-legged table ▸**table d'architecte** drawing board ▸**table d'autel** (*Rel*) altar stone ▸**table basse** coffee table, occasional table ▸**table de bridge** card *ou* bridge table ▸**table à cartes** (*Naut*) chart house ▸**table de chevet** bedside table, night stand *ou* table (*US*) ▸**table de communion** (*Rel*) communion table ▸**table de conférence** conference table ▸**table de cuisson** cooking surface ▸**table à dessin** drawing board ▸**table à digitaliser** (*Ordin*) digitizer ▸**table d'écoute** wire-tapping set; **mettre qn sur table d'écoute** to tap sb's phone ▸**tables gigognes** nest of tables ▸**table d'harmonie** (*Mus*) sounding board ▸**table d'honneur** top table; **faire table d'hôte** *to serve a buffet supper for residents* ▸**table de jeu** gaming table ▸**table de lancement** launch(ing) pad ▸**table à langer** changing table ▸**table de lecture** [*chaîne haute fidélité*] turntable ▸**table de malade** bedtable ▸**table des matières** (table of) contents ▸**table de mixage** mixing desk ▸**table de nuit** = **table de chevet** ▸**table d'opération** operating table ▸**table d'orientation** viewpoint indicator ▸**table à ouvrage** worktable ▸**table de ping-pong** table-tennis table ▸**table pliante** folding table ▸**table à rallonges** extending table, pull-out table ▸**table à repasser** ironing board ▸**table ronde** (*lit*) round table; (*fig*) round table, panel ▸**la Table ronde** (*Hist*) the Round Table ▸**table roulante** trolley ▸**table de survie** life table ▸**tables de tir** (*Mil*) range tables ▸**table de toilette** (*pour lavabo*) washstand; (*coiffeuse*) dressing table ▸**table tournante** séance table ▸**table traçante** (*Ordin*) (graph) plotter ▸**table de travail** work table *ou* desk.
tableau, pl ~x [tablo] 1 nm a (*peinture*) painting; (*reproduction, gravure*) picture; *voir* **galerie.**
b (*fig: scène*) picture, scene. **le ~ l'émut au plus haut point** he was deeply moved by the scene; **un ~ tragique/idyllique** a tragic/an idyllic picture *ou* scene; **le ~ changeant de la vallée du Rhône** the changing picture of the Rhone valley.
c (*Théât*) scene. **acte un, premier ~** act one, scene one.
d (*description*) picture. **un ~ de la guerre** a picture *ou* depiction of war; **il m'a fait un ~ très noir de la situation** he drew me a very black picture of the situation.
e (*Scol*) **~ (noir)** (black)board; **aller au ~** (*lit*) to go out *ou* up to the blackboard; (*se faire interroger*) to be asked questions (*on a school subject*).
f (*support mural*) [*sonneries*] board; [*fusibles*] box; [*clefs*] rack, board.
g (*panneau*) board; (*Rail*) train indicator; [*bateau*] escutcheon, name board. **~ des départs/arrivées** departure(s)/arrival(s) board; **~ des horaires** timetable.
h (*carte, graphique*) table, chart; (*Ordin: fait par tableur*) spreadsheet. **~ généalogique/chronologique** genealogical/chronological table *ou* chart; **~ des conjugaisons** conjugation table, table of conjugations; **présenter qch sous forme de ~** to show sth in tabular form.
i (*Admin: liste*) register, roll, list. **~ de l'ordre des avocats** ≃ register of the association of barristers; **médicament au ~ A/B/C** class A/B/C drug (*according to French classification of toxicity*).
j (*loc*) **vous voyez (d'ici) le ~!** you can (just) picture it!; **pour compléter** *ou* **achever le ~** to cap it all, to put the finishing touches, to complete the picture; (*fig*) **miser sur les deux ~x** to back both horses (*fig*); **il a gagné sur les deux/sur tous les ~x** he won on both/all counts.
2 comp ▸**tableau d'affichage** notice board ▸**tableau d'amortissement d'une dette** redemption table of a debt, sinking fund ▸**tableau d'avancement** (*Admin*) promotion table ▸**tableau de bord** [*auto*] dashboard, instrument panel; [*avion, bateau*] instrument panel ▸**tableau de chasse** (*lit, fig*) [*chasseur*] bag; (*fig*) tally; **ajouter qch à son tableau de chasse** to add sth to one's list of successes ▸**tableau clinique** (*Méd*) [*malade*] clinical picture ▸**tableau électronique** tote board ▸**tableau d'honneur** merit *ou* prize list (*Brit*), honor roll (*US*); **être inscrit au tableau d'honneur** to appear on the merit *ou* prize list (*Brit*), to make the honor roll (*US*); (*fig*) **au tableau d'honneur du sport français cette semaine, X ...** winner of all the prizes in French sport this week, X ... ▸**tableau de maître** masterpiece ▸**tableau de service** (*gén*) work notice board; (*horaire de service*) duty roster ▸**tableau synchronique** synchronic table of events *etc*

▶tableau synoptique synoptic table **▶tableau vivant** (*Théât*) tableau (vivant).
tableautin [tablotɛ̃] **nm** little picture.
tablée [table] **nf** table (*of people*). **toute la ~ éclata de rire** the whole table burst out laughing; **il y avait au restaurant une ~ de provinciaux qui** ... at the restaurant there was a party of country people who ... .
tabler [table] 1 **vi: ~ sur qch** to count *ou* reckon *ou* bank on sth; **il avait tablé sur une baisse des cours** he had counted *ou* reckoned *ou* banked on the rates going down; **table sur ton travail plutôt que sur la chance** rely on your work rather than on luck.
tablette [tablɛt] **nf** a (*plaquette*) *[chocolat]* bar; *[médicament]* tablet; *[chewing-gum]* stick; *[métal]* block. b (*planchette, rayon*) *[lavabo, radiateur, cheminée]* shelf; *[secrétaire]* flap. **~ à glissière** pull-out flap. c (*Hist: pour écrire*) tablet. **~ de cire** wax tablet; (*hum*) **je vais le marquer sur mes ~s** I'll make a note of it; (*hum*) **ce n'est pas écrit sur mes ~s** I have no record of it. d (*Ordin*) tablet.
tableur [tablœʀ] **nm** spreadsheet (program).
tablier [tablije] **nm** a (*Habillement*) (*gén*) apron; *[ménagère]* (*sans manches*) apron, pinafore; (*avec manches*) overall; *[écolier]* overall, smock; *voir* **rendre, robe.** b *[pont]* roadway. c (*Tech: plaque protectrice*) *[cheminée]* (flue-)shutter; *[magasin]* (iron *ou* steel) shutter; *[laminoir]* guard; (*Aut: entre moteur et habitacle*) bulkhead.
tabou [tabu] 1 **nm** taboo. 2 **adj** (*sacré, frappé d'interdit*) taboo; (*fig: intouchable*) *employé, auteur* untouchable.
taboulé [tabule] **nm** tabbouleh.
tabouret [tabuʀɛ] **nm** (*pour s'asseoir*) stool; (*pour les pieds*) footstool. **~ de piano/de bar** piano/bar stool.
tabulaire [tabylɛʀ] **adj** tabular.
tabulateur [tabylatœʀ] **nm** tabulator (*on typewriter*).
tabulation [tabylasjɔ̃] **nf** tabulation.
tabulatrice [tabylatʀis] **nf** tabulator (*for punched cards*).
tabuler [tabyle] 1 **vt** to tabulate, tabularize, tab.
tac [tak] **nm** a (*bruit*) tap. **le ~ ~ des mitrailleuses** the rat-a-tat(-tat) of the machine guns; *voir* **tic-tac.** b **répondre** *ou* **riposter du ~ au ~** always to have a quick retort *ou* a ready answer; **il lui a répondu du ~ au ~ que** ... he came back at him immediately *ou* quick as a flash that ... .
tache [taʃ] 1 **nf** a (*moucheture*) *[fruit]* mark; *[léopard]* spot; *[plumage, pelage]* mark(ing), spot; *[peau]* blotch, mark. (*fig*) **faire ~** to jar, stick out like a sore thumb; **les ~s des ongles** the white marks on the fingernails.
b (*salissure*) stain, mark. **~ de graisse** greasy mark, grease stain; **~ de brûlure/de suie** burn/sooty mark; **des draps couverts de ~s** sheets covered in stains; **sa robe n'avait pas une ~** her dress was spotless.
c (*littér: flétrissure*) blot, stain. **c'est une ~ à sa réputation** it's a blot *ou* stain on his reputation; **sans ~** *vie, conduite* spotless, unblemished; *naissance* untainted; *voir* **agneau, pur.**
d (*impression visuelle*) patch, spot. **~ de couleur** spot *ou* patch of colour; **le soleil parsemait la campagne de ~s d'or** the sun scattered patches *ou* flecks *ou* spots of gold over the countryside; **des ~s d'ombre çà et là** spots *ou* patches of shadow here and there.
e (*Peinture*) spot, dot, blob. **~ de couleur** spot *ou* patch of colour.
f (*‡: nullité*) jerk‡.
2 **comp ▶tache d'encre** (*sur les doigts*) ink stain; (*sur le papier*) (ink) blot *ou* blotch **▶tache d'huile** oily mark, oil stain; (*fig*) **faire tache d'huile** to spread, gain ground **▶tache jaune (de l'œil)** yellow spot (of the eye) **▶tache originelle** (*Rel*) stain of original sin **▶tache de rousseur** freckle **▶tache de sang** bloodstain **▶tache solaire** (*Astron*) sunspot **▶tache de son** = **tache de rousseur ▶tache de vin** (*sur la nappe*) wine stain; (*sur la peau: envie*) strawberry mark.
tâche [taʃ] **nf** a (*besogne*) task, work (*NonC*); (*mission*) task, job; (*Ordin*) job. **assigner une ~ à qn** to set (*Brit*) *ou* give sb a task, give sb a job to do, give sb some work to do; **s'atteler à une ~** to get down to work, get stuck in*; **mourir à la ~** to die in harness. b (*loc*) **à la ~** *payer* by the piece; **ouvrier à la ~** pieceworker; **travail à la ~** piecework; **être à la ~** to be on piecework; (*fig*) **je ne suis pas à la ~*** I'll do it in my own good time; (†, *littér*) **prendre à ~ de faire qch** to set o.s. the task of doing sth, take it upon o.s. to do sth.
tachéomètre [takeɔmɛtʀ] **nm** (*théodolite*) tacheometer, tachymeter.
tachéométrie [takeɔmetʀi] **nf** tacheometry.
tacher [taʃe] 1 1 **vt** a *[encre, vin]* to stain; *[graisse]* to mark, stain. **le café tache** coffee stains (badly) *ou* leaves a stain; **taché de sang** bloodstained. b (*littér: colorer*) *pré, robe* to spot, dot; *peau, fourrure* to spot, mark. **pelage blanc taché de noir** white coat with black spots *ou* markings. c (†: *souiller*) to stain, sully (*littér*, †). 2 **se tacher vpr** a (*se salir*) *[personne]* to get stains on one's clothes, get o.s. dirty; *[nappe, tissu]* to get stained *ou* marked. **c'est un tissu qui se tache facilement** this is a fabric that stains *ou* marks easily. b (*s'abîmer*) *[fruits]* to become marked.
tâcher [taʃe] 1 **vi** (*essayer de*) **~ de faire** to try *ou* endeavour (*frm*) to do; **tâchez de venir avant samedi** try to *ou* try and come before Saturday; **et tâche de ne pas recommencer*** and make sure *ou* mind it doesn't happen again; **tâche qu'il n'en sache rien*** see to it *ou* make sure that he doesn't know anything about it.
tâcheron [taʃ(ə)ʀɔ̃] **nm** a (*péj*) drudge, toiler. **un ~ de la littérature/politique** a literary/political drudge *ou* hack. b (*ouvrier*) (*dans le bâtiment*) jobber; (*agricole*) pieceworker.
tacheter [taʃ(ə)te] 4 **vt** *peau, fourrure* to spot, speckle; *tissu, champ* to spot, dot, speckle, fleck. **pelage blanc tacheté de brun** white coat with brown spots *ou* markings, white coat flecked with brown.
tachisme [taʃism] **nm** (*art abstrait*) action painting, abstract expressionism, tachisme.
tachiste [taʃist] **nmf** *painter of the abstract expressionist or tachisme school.*
Tachkent [taʃkɛnt] **n** Tachkent.
tachycardie [takikaʀdi] **nf** tachycardia.
tachygraphe [takigʀaf] **nm** tachograph, black box.
tachymètre [takimɛtʀ] **nm** (*Aut*) tachometer.
Tacite [tasit] **nm** Tacitus.
tacite [tasit] **adj** tacit. (*Jur*) **~ reconduction** renewal of contract by tacit agreement.
tacitement [tasitmɑ̃] **adv** tacitly.
taciturne [tasityʀn] **adj** taciturn, silent.
tacot* [tako] **nm** (*voiture*) banger* (*Brit*), crate*, jalopy*, old rattletrap*.
tact [takt] **nm** a (*délicatesse*) tact. **avoir du ~** to have tact, be tactful; **un homme de ~** a tactful man; **avec ~** tactfully, with tact; **sans ~ (adj)** tactless; **(adv)** tactlessly; **manquer de ~** to be tactless, be lacking in tact. b (†: *toucher*) touch, tact†.
tacticien, -ienne [taktisjɛ̃, jɛn] **nm,f** tactician.
tactile [taktil] **adj** tactile.
tactique [taktik] 1 **adj** tactical. 2 **nf** (*gén*) tactics (*pl*). **changer de ~** to change (one's) tactics; **il y a plusieurs ~s possibles** there are several different tactics one might adopt; **la ~ de l'adversaire est très simple** the opponent's tactics are very simple.
tadjik [tadʒik] 1 **adj** Tadzhiki. 2 **nm** (*Ling*) Tadzhiki. 3 **nmf: T~** Tadzhik, Tadjik, Tajik.
Tadjikistan [tadʒikistɑ̃] **nm** Tadzhikistan.
tadorne [tadɔʀn] **nm: ~ de Bellon** shelduck.
tænia [tenja] = **ténia.**
taffetas [tafta] **nm** (*Tex*) taffeta. **robe de ~** taffeta dress; **~ (gommé)** sticking plaster (*Brit*), bandaid ® (*US*).
tag [tag] **nm** (*graffiti*) tag.
Tage [taʒ] **nm: le ~** the Tagus.
tagine [taʒin] **nm** = **tajine.**
tagliatelles [taljatɛl] **nfpl** tagliatelli.
tagmème [tagmɛm] **nm** tagmeme.
tagmémique [tagmemik] **nf** tagmemics (*sg*).
taguer [tage] 1 **vti** (*faire des graffiti*) to tag.
tagueur [tagœʀ] **nm** tagger.
Tahiti [taiti] **nf** Tahiti.
tahitien, -ienne [taisjɛ̃, jɛn] 1 **adj** Tahitian. 2 **nm,f: T~(ne)** Tahitian.
taïaut†† [tajo] **excl** tallyho!
taie [tɛ] **nf** a **~ (d'oreiller)** pillowcase, pillowslip; **~ de traversin** bolster case. b (*Méd*) opaque spot, leucoma (*SPÉC*). (*fig littér*) **avoir une ~ sur l'œil** to be blinkered.
taïga [tajga] **nf** (*Géog*) taiga.
taillable [tɑjabl] **adj: ~ et corvéable (à merci)** (*Hist*) subject to tallage; (*fig*) *bonne, ouvrier* there to do one's master's bidding.
taillade [tɑjad] **nf** gash, slash, cut, wound.
taillader [tɑjade] 1 **vt** to slash, gash.
taillanderie [tɑjɑ̃dʀi] **nf** (*fabrication*) edge-tool making; (*outils*) edge-tools (*pl*).
taillandier [tɑjɑ̃dje] **nm** edge-tool maker.
taille¹ [tɑj] **nf** a (*hauteur*) *[personne, cheval, objet]* height. **homme de ~ moyenne** man of average height; **homme de petite ~** short man, man of small stature (*frm*); **homme de haute ~** tall man; **il doit faire une ~ de 1 mètre 70** he must be 1 metre 70 (tall); **ils sont de la même ~, ils ont la même ~** they are the same height.
b (*grosseur*) size. **de petite/moyenne ~** small-/medium-sized; **ils ont un chien de belle ~!** they have a pretty big *ou* large dog!; **le paquet est de la ~ d'une boîte à chaussures** the parcel is the size of a shoebox.
c (*Comm: mesure*) size. **les grandes/petites ~s** the large/small sizes; **~ 40** size 40; **il lui faut la ~ au-dessous/au-dessus** he needs the next size down/up, he needs one *ou* a size smaller/larger; **2 ~s au-dessous/au-dessus** 2 sizes smaller/larger; **ce pantalon n'est pas à sa ~** these trousers aren't his size, these trousers don't fit him; **avez-vous quelque chose dans ma ~?** do you have anything in my size?; **si je trouvais quelqu'un de ma ~** if I found someone my size.
d (*loc*) **à la ~ de** in keeping with; **c'est un poste/sujet à la ~ de ses capacités** *ou* **à sa ~** it's a job/subject in keeping with *ou* which matches his capabilities; **il a trouvé un adversaire à sa ~** he's met his match, he's found sb who's a match for him; **être de ~ à faire** to be up to doing, be quite capable of doing; **il n'est pas de ~** (*pour une tâche*) he isn't up *ou* equal to it; (*face à un concurrent, dans la vie*) he doesn't measure up; **de ~** *erreur, enjeu* considerable, sizeable; *objet* sizeable; **la gaffe est de ~!** it's no small blunder!; (*fig*) **de la ~ de César** of Caesar's stature.

e (*partie du corps*) waist; (*partie du vêtement*) waist, waistband. **elle n'a pas de ~** she has no waist(line), she doesn't go in at the waist; **avoir la ~ fine** to have a slim waist, be slim-waisted; **avoir une ~ de guêpe** to be wasp-waisted; **avoir la ~ mannequin** to have a perfect figure; **avoir la ~ bien prise** to have a neat waist(line); **prendre qn par la ~** to put one's arm round sb's waist; **ils se tenaient par la ~** they had their arms round each other's waist; **avoir de l'eau jusqu'à la ~** to be in water up to one's waist, to be waist-deep in water; **robe serrée à la ~** dress fitted at the waist; **robe à ~ basse/haute** low-/high-waisted dress; **pantalon (à) ~ basse** low-waisted trousers, hipsters; **robe sans ~** waistless dress; *voir* **tour²**.

taille² [tɑj] nf a (*voir* **tailler**) cutting; hewing (*frm*); carving; engraving; sharpening; cutting out; pruning, cutting back; trimming; clipping. **diamant de ~ hexagonale/en étoile** diamond with a six-sided/star-shaped cut; *voir* **pierre**. b (*taillis*) ~s coppice. c (*tranchant*) *[épée, sabre]* edge. **recevoir un coup de ~** to receive a blow from the edge of the sword; *voir* **frapper**. d (*Hist: redevance*) tallage, taille. e (*Min: galerie*) tunnel.

taillé, e [tɑje] (ptp de **tailler**) adj a (*bâti*) *personne* **bien ~** well-built; **il est ~ en athlète** he is built like an athlete, he has an athletic build. b (*destiné à*) *personne* **~ pour être/faire** cut out to be/do; **~ pour qch** cut out for sth, tailor-made for sth. c (*coupé*) *arbre* pruned; *haie* clipped, trimmed; *moustache, barbe* trimmed. **crayon ~ en pointe** pencil sharpened to a point; **costume bien ~** well-cut suit; **il avait les cheveux ~s en brosse** he had a crew-cut; (*fig*) **visage ~ à la serpe** rough-hewn *ou* craggy features; *voir* **âge**.

taille-crayon(s) [tɑjkʀɛjɔ̃] nm inv pencil sharpener.

taille-douce, pl **tailles-douces** [tɑjdus] nf (*technique, tableau*) line-engraving. **gravure en ~** line-engraving.

tailler [tɑje] 1 1 vt a (*travailler*) *pierre précieuse* to cut; *pierre* to cut, hew (*frm*); *bois* to carve; *verre* to engrave; *crayon* to sharpen; *tissu* to cut (out); *arbre, vigne* to prune, cut back; *haie* to trim, clip, cut; *barbe* to trim. **~ qch en biseau** to bevel sth; **~ qch en pointe** to cut *ou* sharpen sth to a point; **se ~ la moustache** to trim one's moustache.

b (*confectionner*) *vêtement* to make; *statue* to carve; *tartines* to cut, slice; (*Alpinisme*) *marche* to cut. (*fig*) **il a un rôle taillé à sa mesure** this role is tailor-made for him.

c (*loc*) **~ une bavette*** to have a natter* (*Brit*) *ou* a rap* (*US*); **~ des croupières à qn††** to make difficulties for sb; **~ une armée en pièces** to hack an army to pieces; **il préférerait se faire ~ en pièces plutôt que de révéler son secret** he'd go through fire *ou* he'd suffer tortures rather than reveal his secret; **il se ferait ~ en pièces pour elle** he'd go through fire *ou* he'd suffer tortures for her; **~ un costard** *ou* **une veste à qn*** tu run sb down behind his back*; **attention! tu vas te faire ~ un short*** careful! you'll get flattened*; **~ la route*** to hit the road*.

2 vi: **~ dans la chair** *ou* **dans le vif** to cut into the flesh.

3 **se tailler** vpr a (⁑: *partir*) to beat it⁑, clear off⁑, split⁑.

b (*loc*) **se ~ un beau** *ou* **franc succès** to be a great success; **se ~ la part du lion** to take the lion's share; **se ~ un empire/une place** to carve out an empire/a place for o.s.

tailleur [tɑjœʀ] 1 nm a (*couturier*) tailor. **~ pour dames** ladies' tailor. b (*costume*) (lady's) suit. **~-pantalon** trouser suit (*Brit*), pant-suit (*surtout US*); **un ~ Chanel** a Chanel suit. c **en ~** *assis, s'asseoir* cross-legged. 2 comp ►**tailleur de diamants** diamond-cutter ►**tailleur à façon** bespoke tailor (*Brit*), custom tailor (*US*) ►**tailleur de pierre(s)** stone-cutter ►**tailleur de verre** glass engraver ►**tailleur de vignes** vine pruner.

taillis [taji] nm copse, coppice, thicket. **dans les ~** in the copse *ou* coppice *ou* thicket.

tain [tɛ̃] nm a *[miroir]* silvering. **glace sans ~** two-way mirror. b (*Tech: bain*) tin bath.

T'ai-pei [tajpɛ] n Taipei, T'ai-pei.

taire [tɛʀ] 54 1 **se taire** vpr a (*être silencieux*) *[personne]* to be silent *ou* quiet; (*fig littér*) *[nature, forêt]* to be silent, be still (*littér*); *[vent]* to be still (*littér*); *[bruit]* to disappear. **les élèves se taisaient** the pupils kept *ou* were quiet *ou* silent; **taisez-vous!** be quiet!, be silent! (*frm*); **ils ne voulaient pas se ~, malgré les injonctions répétées du maître** they (just) wouldn't stop talking *ou* be quiet *ou* keep quiet in spite of the teacher's repeated instructions; **les dîneurs se sont tus** the diners stopped talking, the diners fell *ou* were silent; **l'orchestre s'était tu** the orchestra had fallen silent *ou* was silent.

b (*s'abstenir de s'exprimer*) to keep quiet, remain silent. **dans ces cas il vaut mieux se ~** in these cases it's best to keep quiet *ou* to remain silent *ou* to say nothing; **il sait se ~** he can keep a secret; **se ~ sur qch** to say nothing *ou* keep quiet about sth; **il a manqué** *ou* **perdu une bonne occasion de se ~** he'd have done much better to have kept quiet, it's a pity he didn't just keep his mouth shut; **tais-toi!*** (*ne m'en parle pas*) don't talk to me about it!, I don't wish to hear about it!

2 vt a (*celer*) *nom, fait, vérité* to hush up, not to tell. **~ la vérité, c'est déjà mentir** not to tell *ou* not telling the truth *ou* to hush up *ou* hushing up the truth is as good as lying; **il a tu le reste de l'histoire** he didn't reveal the rest of the story, he was silent about the rest of the story.

b (*refuser de dire*) *motifs, raisons* to conceal, say nothing about. **une personne dont je tairai le nom** a person who shall be *ou* remain nameless *ou* whose name I shan't mention *ou* reveal.

c (*garder pour soi*) *douleur, chagrin, amertume* to stifle, conceal, keep to o.s.

3 vi: **faire ~** *témoin gênant, opposition, récriminations* to silence; *craintes, désirs* to stifle, suppress; **fais taire les enfants** make the children keep *ou* be quiet, make the children shut up*, do shut the children up*.

Taiwan [tajwan] n Taiwan.

tajine [taʒin] nm (*récipient*) earthenware cooking pot; (*plat cuisiné*) (meat *ou* vegetable) stew.

talc [talk] nm *[toilette]* talc, talcum powder; (*Chim*) talc(um).

talé, e [tale] (ptp de **taler**) adj *fruits* bruised.

talent¹ [talɑ̃] nm a (*disposition, aptitude*) talent. **il a des ~s dans tous les domaines** he has talents in all fields; **un ~ littéraire** a literary talent; **il n'a pas le métier d'un professionnel mais un beau ~ d'amateur** he lacks professional expertise but has a fine amateur talent; **des ~s de société** society talents; (*hum*) **montrez-nous vos ~s*** show us what you can do; **décidément, vous avez tous les ~s!** what a talented young man (*ou* woman *etc*) you are!; **ses ~s d'imitateur/d'organisateur** his talents *ou* gifts as an impersonator/organizer.

b **le ~** talent; **avoir du ~** to have talent, be talented; **avoir beaucoup de ~** to have a great deal of talent, be highly talented; **un auteur de (grand) ~** a (highly) talented author.

c (*personnes douées*) **~s** talent (*NonC*); **encourager les jeunes ~s** to encourage young talent; **faire appel aux ~s disponibles** to call on (all) the available talent.

d (*iro*) **il a le ~ de se faire des ennemis** he has a gift for making enemies (*iro*), he has a great knack of making enemies.

talent² [talɑ̃] nm (*monnaie*) talent.

talentueusement [talɑ̃tɥøzmɑ̃] adv with talent.

talentueux, -euse [talɑ̃tɥø, øz] adj talented.

taler [tale] 1 vt *fruits* to bruise.

taleth [talɛt] nm tallith.

talion [taljɔ̃] nm *voir* **loi**.

talisman [talismɑ̃] nm talisman.

talismanique [talismanik] adj talismanic.

talkie-walkie, pl **talkies-walkies** [tokiwoki] nm walkie-talkie.

talle [tal] nf (*Agr*) sucker.

taller [tale] 1 vi (*Agr*) to sucker, put out suckers.

talleth [talɛt] = **taleth**.

Tallin [talin] n Tallin(n).

Talmud [talmyd] nm: **le ~** the Talmud.

talmudique [talmydik] adj Talmudic.

talmudiste [talmydist] nm Talmudist.

taloche* [talɔʃ] nf a (*: *gifle*) clout, cuff. **flanquer une ~ à qn** to clout *ou* cuff sb, give sb a clout *ou* cuff. b (*Constr*) roughcast.

talocher [talɔʃe] 1 vt a (*: *gifler*) to clout, cuff. b (*Constr*) to roughcast.

talon [talɔ̃] 1 nm a (*Anat*) *[cheval, chaussure]* heel. **montrer les ~s** to take to one's heels, show a clean pair of heels (*Brit*); **tourner les ~s** to turn on one's heel and walk away; **je préférerais voir ses ~s** I'd be glad to see the back of him; **être sur les ~s de qn** to be at *ou* (hot) on sb's heels; *voir* **estomac, pivoter**.

b (*croûton, bout*) *[jambon, fromage]* heel; *[pain]* crust, heel.

c *[pipe]* spur.

d *[chèque]* stub, counterfoil; *[carnet à souche]* stub.

e (*Cartes*) talon.

f (*Mus*) *[archet]* heel.

g *[ski]* tail.

2 comp ►**talon d'Achille** Achilles' heel ►**talons aiguilles** stiletto heels ►**talons bottier** medium heels ►**talons hauts** high heels ►**"talon-minute"** heel bar, on-the-spot shoe repairs ►**talons plats** flat heels ►**talon rouge** (*Hist*) aristocrat.

talonnade [talɔnad] nf (*Rugby*) heel; (*football*) back-heel.

talonnage [talɔnaʒ] nm heeling.

talonner [talɔne] 1 1 vt a (*suivre*) *fugitifs, coureurs* to follow (hot) on the heels of. **talonné par qn** hotly pursued by sb. b (*harceler*) *débiteur, entrepreneur* to hound; *[faim]* to gnaw at. **être talonné par un importun** to be hounded *ou* dogged *ou* pestered by an irritating individual. c (*frapper du talon*) *cheval* to kick, dig one's heels into, spur on. (*Rugby*) **~ (le ballon)** to heel (the ball). 2 vi (*Naut*) to touch *ou* scrape the bottom with the keel. **le bateau talonne** the boat is touching the bottom.

talonnette [talɔnɛt] nf *[chaussures]* heelpiece; *[pantalon]* stirrup.

talonneur [talɔnœʀ] nm (*Rugby*) hooker.

talquer [talke] 1 vt to put talcum powder *ou* talc on.

talqueux, -euse [talkø, øz] adj talcose.

talus [taly] 1 nm a *[route, voie ferrée]* embankment; *[terrassement]* bank, embankment. b (*Mil*) talus. 2 comp ►**talus continental** (*Géol*) continental slope ►**talus de déblai** excavation slope ►**talus d'éboulis** (*Géol*) scree ►**talus de remblai** embankment slope.

talweg [talvɛg] nm = **thalweg**.

tamanoir [tamanwaʀ] nm ant bear, anteater.

tamarin [tamaʀɛ̃] nm a (*Zool*) tamarin. b (*fruit*) tamarind (fruit). c = **tamarinier.** d = **tamaris.**
tamarinier [tamaʀinje] nm tamarind (*tree*).
tamaris [tamaʀis] nm tamarisk.
tambouille* [tɑ̃buj] nf (*péj: nourriture, cuisine*) grub*. **faire la** ~ to cook the grub*; **une bonne** ~ some lovely grub*.
tambour [tɑ̃buʀ] 1 nm a (*instrument de musique*) drum; *voir* **raisonner, roulement.**
b (*musicien*) drummer.
c (*à broder*) embroidery hoop, tambour.
d (*porte*) (*sas*) tambour; (*à tourniquet*) revolving door(s).
e (*cylindre*) *[machine à laver, treuil, roue de loterie]* drum; *[moulinet]* spool; *[montre]* barrel; *voir* **frein.**
f (*Archit*) *[colonne, coupole]* drum.
g (*loc*) ~ **battant** briskly; **sans** ~ **ni trompette** without any fuss, unobtrusively; **il est parti sans** ~ **ni trompette** he left quietly, he slipped away unobtrusively.
h (*Ordin*) drum. ~ **magnétique** magnetic drum.
2 comp ▸**tambour de basque** tambourine ▸**tambour d'église** tambour ▸**tambour de frein** brake drum ▸**tambour-major** nm (pl **tambours-majors**) drum major ▸**tambour plat** side drum ▸**tambour de ville** ≃ town crier ▸**tambour à timbre** snare drum.
tambourin [tɑ̃buʀɛ̃] nm (*tambour de basque*) tambourine; (*tambour haut et étroit*) tambourin.
tambourinage [tɑ̃buʀinaʒ] nm drumming (*NonC*).
tambourinaire [tɑ̃buʀinɛʀ] nm (*joueur de tambourin*) tambourin player.
tambourinement [tɑ̃buʀinmɑ̃] nm drumming (*NonC*).
tambouriner [tɑ̃buʀine] [1] 1 vi (*avec les doigts*) to drum. ~ **contre** *ou* **à/sur** to drum (one's fingers) against *ou* at/on; (*fig*) **la pluie tambourinait sur le toit** the rain was beating down *ou* drumming on the roof; ~ **à la porte** to hammer at *ou* drum on the door. 2 vt a (*jouer*) *marche* to drum *ou* beat out. b (†: *annoncer*) *nouvelle, décret* to cry (out). (*fig*) ~ **une nouvelle** to blaze a piece of news abroad, shout a piece of news from the rooftops.
Tamerlan [tamɛʀlɑ̃] nm Tamburlaine, Tamerlane.
tamil [tamil] = **tamoul.**
tamis [tami] nm (*gén*) sieve; (*à sable*) riddle, sifter; *[raquette]* head. **raquette grand** ~ large-headed racket; **passer au** ~ *farine, plâtre* to sieve, sift; *sable* to riddle, sift; (*fig*) *campagne, bois* to comb, search, scour; *personnes* to check out thoroughly; *dossier* to sift *ou* search through.
tamisage [tamizaʒ] nm (*voir* **tamiser**) sieving; riddling; sifting; filtering.
Tamise [tamiz] nf: **la** ~ the Thames.
tamisé, e [tamize] (ptp de **tamiser**) adj *terre* sifted, sieved; *lumière* (*artificielle*) subdued; (*du jour*) soft, softened.
tamiser [tamize] [1] vt *farine, plâtre* to sieve, sift; *sable* to riddle, sift; (*fig*) *lumière* to filter.
tamoul, e [tamul] 1 adj Tamil. 2 nm (*Ling*) Tamil. 3 nm,f: **T~(e)** Tamil.
tampon [tɑ̃pɔ̃] 1 nm a (*pour boucher*) (*gén*) stopper, plug; (*en bois*) plug, bung; (*en coton*) wad, plug; (*pour hémorragie, règles*) tampon; (*pour nettoyer une plaie*) swab; (*pour étendre un liquide, un vernis*) pad. **rouler qch en** ~ to roll sth (up) into a ball; *voir* **vernir.**
b (*Menuiserie: cheville*) (wall-)plug.
c (*timbre*) (*instrument*) (rubber) stamp; (*cachet*) stamp. **le** ~ **de la poste** the postmark; **apposer** *ou* **mettre un** ~ **sur qch** to stamp sth, put a stamp on sth.
d (*Rail, fig: amortisseur*) buffer. **servir de** ~ **entre deux personnes** to act as a buffer between two people.
e (*Chim*) **(solution)** ~ buffer (solution).
2 adj inv: **État/zone** ~ buffer state/zone.
3 comp ▸**tampon buvard** blotter ▸**tampon encreur** inking-pad ▸**tampon Jex** ® Brillo pad ® ▸**tampon à nettoyer** cleaning pad ▸**tampon à récurer** scouring pad, scourer.
tamponnement [tɑ̃pɔnmɑ̃] nm a (*collision*) collision, crash. b (*Méd*) *[plaie]* tamponade, tamponage. c (*Tech*) *[mur]* plugging.
tamponner [tɑ̃pɔne] [1] 1 vt a (*essuyer*) *plaie* to mop up, dab; *yeux* to dab (at); *front* to mop, dab; *surface à sécher, vernir etc* to mop, dab. b (*heurter*) *train, véhicule* to ram (into), crash into. c (*avec un timbre*) *document, lettre* to stamp. **faire** ~ **un reçu** to have a receipt stamped. d (*Tech: percer*) *mur* to plug, put (wall-)plugs in. 2 **se tamponner** vpr a (*se heurter*) (*accident*) to crash into each other; (*exprès*) to ram each other. b **s'en** ~ **(le coquillard)**⁑ not to give a damn⁑; **je m'en tamponne**⁑ I don't give a damn about it⁑.
tamponneuse [tɑ̃pɔnøz] adj f *voir* **auto.**
tamponnoir [tɑ̃pɔnwaʀ] nm masonry drill bit.
tam-tam, pl **tam-tams** [tamtam] nm a (*tambour*) tomtom. b (*fig: battage, tapage*) fuss. **faire du** ~ **autour de*** *affaire, événement* to make a lot of fuss *ou* a great ballyhoo* *ou* hullaballoo* about.
tan [tɑ̃] nm tan (*for tanning*).
tancer [tɑ̃se] [3] vt (*littér*) to scold, berate (*littér*), rebuke (*frm*).
tanche [tɑ̃ʃ] nf tench.
tandem [tɑ̃dɛm] nm (*bicyclette*) tandem; (*fig: duo*) pair, duo. **travailler** *etc* **en** ~ to work *etc* in tandem.
tandis [tɑ̃di] conj: ~ **que** (*simultanéité*) while, whilst (*frm*), as; (*marque le contraste, l'opposition*) whereas, while, whilst (*frm*).
tandoori [tɑ̃duʀi] nm tandoori. **poulet** ~ tandoori chicken.
tangage [tɑ̃gaʒ] nm (*voir* **tanguer**) pitching (and tossing); reeling. (*Naut*) **il y a du** ~ she's pitching.
Tanganyika [tɑ̃ganika] nf Tanganyika. **le lac** ~ Lake Tanganyika.
tangence [tɑ̃ʒɑ̃s] nf tangency.
tangent, e [tɑ̃ʒɑ̃, ɑ̃t] 1 adj a (*Géom*) tangent, tangential. ~ **à** tangent *ou* tangential to. b (*: *serré, de justesse*) close, touch-and-go (*attrib*). **on est passé de justesse mais c'était** ~ we just made it but it was a near *ou* close thing *ou* it was touch-and-go; **il était** ~ he was a borderline case; **il a eu son examen mais c'était** ~ he passed his exam by the skin of his teeth *ou* but it was a near thing. 2 **tangente** nf (*Géom*) tangent. (*fig*) **prendre la ~e*** (*partir*) to make off*, make o.s. scarce; (*éluder*) to dodge the issue, wriggle out of it.
tangentiel, -ielle [tɑ̃ʒɑ̃sjɛl] adj tangential.
tangentiellement [tɑ̃ʒɑ̃sjɛlmɑ̃] adv tangentially.
Tanger [tɑ̃ʒe] n Tangier(s).
tangible [tɑ̃ʒibl] adj tangible.
tangiblement [tɑ̃ʒibləmɑ̃] adv tangibly.
tango [tɑ̃go] nm tango.
tanguer [tɑ̃ge] [1] vi a *[navire, avion]* to pitch. b (*ballotter*) to pitch and toss, reel. **tout tanguait autour de lui** everything around him was reeling.
tanière [tanjɛʀ] nf *[animal]* den, lair; (*fig*) *[malfaiteur]* lair; *[poète, solitaire etc]* (*pièce*) den; (*maison*) hideaway, retreat.
tanin [tanɛ̃] nm tannin.
tank [tɑ̃k] nm (*char d'assaut, fig: voiture*) tank.
tanker [tɑ̃kœʀ] nm tanker.
tankiste [tɑ̃kist] nm member of a tank crew.
tannage [tanaʒ] nm tanning.
tannant, e [tanɑ̃, ɑ̃t] adj a (*: *ennuyeux*) maddening*, sickening*. **il est** ~ **avec ses remarques idiotes** he's maddening* *ou* he drives you mad* with his stupid remarks. b (*Tech*) tanning.
tannée* [tane] nf hammering*, thumping* (*Brit*).
tanner [tane] [1] vt a *cuir* to tan; *visage* to weather. **visage tanné** weather-beaten face; ~ **le cuir à qn**⁑ to give sb a thumping⁑, tan sb's hide*. b ~ **qn*** (*harceler*) to badger sb, pester sb; (*ennuyer*) to drive sb mad*, drive sb up the wall*.
tannerie [tanʀi] nf (*endroit*) tannery; (*activité*) tanning.
tanneur [tanœʀ] nm tanner.
tannin [tanɛ̃] nm = **tanin.**
tant [tɑ̃] adv a (*intensité: avec vb*) so much. **il mange** ~**!** he eats so much! *ou* such a lot!; **il l'aime** ~**!** he loves her so much!; **j'ai** ~ **marché que je suis épuisé** I've walked so much that I'm exhausted; (*littér*) **je n'aime rien** ~ **que l'odeur des sous-bois** there is nothing I love more than the scent of the undergrowth; **vous m'en direz** ~**!** is that really so!
b (*quantité*) ~ **de** *temps, eau, argent* so much; *livres, arbres, gens* so many; *habileté, mauvaise foi* such, so much; **il y avait** ~ **de brouillard qu'il n'est pas parti** it was so foggy *ou* there was so much fog about that he did not go; ~ **de fois** so many times, so often; **des gens comme il y en a** ~ people of the kind you come across so often; ~ **de précautions semblaient suspectes** so many precautions seemed suspicious; **fait avec** ~ **d'habileté** done with so much *ou* such skill; **elle a** ~ **de sensibilité** she has such sensitivity.
c (*avec adj, participe*) so. **il est rentré** ~ **le ciel était menaçant** he went home (because) the sky looked so overcast, the sky looked so overcast that he went home; **cet enfant** ~ **désiré** this child they had longed for so much; ~ **il est vrai que ...** since ..., as ...; **le jour** ~ **attendu arriva** the long-awaited day arrived.
d (*quantité imprécise*) so much. **gagner** ~ **par mois** to earn so much a month, earn such-and-such an amount a month; **il devrait donner** ~ **à l'un,** ~ **à l'autre** he should give so much to one, so much to the other; ~ **pour cent** so many per cent.
e (*comparaison*) **ce n'est pas** ~ **leur maison qui me plaît que leur jardin** it's not so much their house that I like as their garden; **il criait** ~ **qu'il pouvait** he shouted as much as he could *ou* for all he was worth; **les enfants,** ~ **filles que garçons** the children, both girls and boys *ou* girls as well as boys *ou* (both) girls and boys alike; **ses œuvres** ~ **politiques que lyriques** his political as well as his poetic works, both his political and his poetic works.
f ~ **que** (*aussi longtemps que*) as long as; (*pendant que*) while; ~ **qu'elle aura de la fièvre elle restera au lit** while *ou* as long as she has a temperature she'll stay in bed; ~ **que tu n'auras pas fini tes devoirs tu resteras à la maison** until you've finished your homework you'll have to stay indoors; ~ **que vous y êtes*, achetez les deux volumes** while you are about it *ou* at it, buy both volumes; ~ **que vous êtes ici*, donnez-moi un coup de main** since *ou* seeing you are here, give me a hand.
g (*loc*) **(tout va bien)** ~ **qu'on a la santé!** (you're all right) as long as you've got your health!; ~ **qu'il y a de la vie, il y a de l'espoir*** where there's life, there's hope; ~ **bien que mal** *aller, marcher* so-so, as well as can be expected (*hum*); *réussir, s'efforcer* after a fashion, in a

manner of speaking; **il est un ~ soit peu prétentieux** he is ever so slightly *ou* he's a little bit pretentious; **s'il est ~ soit peu intelligent il saura s'en tirer** if he is (even) remotely intelligent *ou* if he has the slightest grain of intelligence he'll be able to get out of it; **si vous craignez ~ soit peu le froid, restez chez vous** if you feel the cold at all *ou* the slightest bit, stay at home; **~ mieux** (*à la bonne heure*) (that's) good *ou* fine *ou* great*; (*avec une certaine réserve*) so much the better, that's fine; **~ mieux pour lui** good for him; **~ pis** (*conciliant: ça ne fait rien*) never mind, (that's) too bad; (*peu importe, qu'à cela ne tienne*) (that's just) too bad; **~ pis pour lui** (that's just) too bad for him; **~ et si bien que** so much so that, to such an extent that; **il a fait ~ et si bien qu'elle l'a quitté** he finally succeeded in making her leave him; **il y en a ~ et plus** *[eau, argent]* there is ever so much; *[objets, personnes]* there are ever so many; **il a protesté ~ et plus mais sans résultat** he protested for all he was worth *ou* over and over again but to no avail; **il gagne ~ et ~ d'argent qu'il ne sait pas quoi en faire** he earns so much money *ou* such a lot (of money) that he doesn't know what to do with it all; **~ qu'à faire, on va payer maintenant** we might *ou* may as well pay now; **~ qu'à faire, je préfère payer tout de suite** (since I have to pay) I might *ou* may as well pay right away; **~ qu'à faire, faites-le bien** if you're going to do it, do it properly; **~ qu'à marcher, allons en forêt** if we have to walk *ou* if we are walking, let's go to the forest; **~ que ça?*** that much?, as much as that?; **pas ~ que ça*** not that much; **tu la paies ~ que ça?*** do you pay her that much? *ou* as much as that?; **je ne l'ai pas vu ~ que ça pendant l'été** I didn't see him (all) that much* during the summer; **~ qu'à moi/lui/eux*** as for me/him/them; **~ s'en faut** not by a long way, far from it, not by a long chalk (*Brit*) *ou* shot; **~ s'en faut qu'il ait l'intelligence de son frère** he's not nearly as *ou* nowhere near as *ou* nothing like as intelligent as his brother, he's not as intelligent as his brother — not by a long way *ou* chalk (*Brit*) *ou* shot; (*Prov*) **~ va la cruche à l'eau qu'à la fin elle se casse** if you keep playing with fire you must expect to get burnt; **ils sont sous-payés, si ~ est qu'on les paie** they are underpaid, if they are paid at all; *voir* **en**[1], **si**[1], **tout**.

tantale [tɑ̃tal] **nm** a (*Myth*) **T~** Tantalus; *voir* **supplice**. b (*Chim*) tantalum.

tante [tɑ̃t] **nf** (*parente*) aunt, aunty*; (‡: *homosexuel*) queer‡, poof‡ (*Brit*), fairy‡, nancy-boy‡ (*Brit*), fag‡ (*US*). **la ~ Jeanne** Aunt *ou* Aunty* Jean; **~ à héritage** rich (childless) aunt; (*mont de piété*) **ma ~*** uncle's‡, the pawnshop.

tantième [tɑ̃tjɛm] 1 **nm** percentage. 2 **adj**: **la ~ partie de qch** such (and such) a proportion of sth.

tantine [tɑ̃tin] **nf** (*langage enfantin*) aunty*.

tantinet [tɑ̃tinɛ] **nm**: **un ~ fatigant/ridicule** a tiny *ou* weeny* bit tiring/ridiculous; **un ~ de** a tiny bit of.

tantôt [tɑ̃to] **adv** a (*cet après-midi*) this afternoon; (††: *tout à l'heure*) shortly. **mardi ~†*** on Tuesday afternoon. b (*parfois*) **~ à pied, ~ en voiture** sometimes on foot, sometimes by car; (*littér*) **~ riant, ~ pleurant** now laughing, now crying.

tantouse‡ [tɑ̃tuz] **nf** (*homosexuel*) queer‡, poof‡ (*Brit*), fairy‡, fag‡ (*US*).

Tanzanie [tɑ̃zani] **nf** Tanzania. **République unie de ~** United Republic of Tanzania.

tanzanien, -ienne [tɑ̃zanjɛ̃, jɛn] 1 **adj** Tanzanian. 2 **nm,f**: **T~(ne)** Tanzanian.

TAO [teao] **nf** (**abrév de traduction assistée par ordinateur**) MAT.

Tao [tao] **nm** Tao.

taoïsme [taoism] **nm** Taoism.

taoïste [taoist] **adj, nm,f** Taoist.

taon [tɑ̃] **nm** horsefly, gadfly.

tapage [tapaʒ] 1 **nm** a (*vacarme*) din, uproar, row, racket. **faire du ~** to create a din *ou* an uproar, kick up* *ou* make a row. b (*battage*) fuss, talk. **ils ont fait un tel ~ autour de cette affaire que ...** there was so much fuss made about *ou* so much talk over this affair that ... . 2 **comp** ▸**tapage nocturne** (*Jur*) disturbance of the peace (*at night*).

tapageur, -euse [tapaʒœʀ, øz] **adj** a (*bruyant*) *enfant, hôtes* noisy, rowdy. b (*peu discret, voyant*) *publicité* obtrusive; *élégance, toilette* flashy, loud, showy.

tapant, e [tapɑ̃, ɑ̃t] **adj**: **à 8 heures ~(es)** at 8 (o'clock) sharp, on the stroke of 8, at 8 o'clock on the dot*.

tape [tap] **nf** (*coup*) slap.

tape- [tap] **préf** *voir* **taper**.

tapé, e[1] [tape] (**ptp de taper**) **adj** a *fruit* (*talé*) bruised. b (*: *fou*) cracked*, bonkers‡ (*Brit*).

tapecul , tape-cul, **pl tape-culs** [tapky] **nm** (*voile*) jigger; (*: *balançoire*) see-saw; (*: *voiture*) bone-shaker (*Brit*), rattletrap*; (*: *trot assis*) close trot.

tapée[2]**‡** [tape] **nf**: **une ~ de, des ~s de** loads of*, masses of*.

tapement [tapmɑ̃] **nm** banging (*NonC*), banging noise.

tapenade [tap(ə)nad] **nf** tapenade.

taper [tape] [1] 1 **vt** a (*battre*) *tapis* to beat; (*) *enfant* to slap, clout; (*claquer*) *porte* to bang, slam. **~ le carton*** to play cards.

b (*frapper*) **~ un coup/deux coups à la porte** to knock once/twice at the door, give a knock/two knocks at the door; (*péj*) **~ un air sur le piano** to bang *ou* thump out a tune on the piano.

c **~ (à la machine)** *lettre* to type (out); **apprendre à ~ à la machine** to learn (how) to type; **elle tape bien** she types well, she's a good typist; **elle tape 60 mots à la minute** her typing speed is 60 words a minute; **tapé à la machine** typed, typewritten.

d (‡: *emprunter à, solliciter*) **~ qn (de 10 F)** to touch sb* (for 10 francs), cadge (10 francs) off sb*.

2 **vi** a (*frapper, cogner*) **~ sur un clou** to hit a nail; **~ sur la table** to bang *ou* rap on the table; (*péj*) **~ sur un piano** to bang *ou* thump away at a piano; **~ sur qn*** to thump sb*; **~ sur la gueule de qn‡** to bash sb up‡, belt sb‡; (*fig*) **~ sur le ventre de** *ou* **à* qn** to be a bit pushy with sb*, be overfamiliar with sb; **~ à la porte/au mur** to knock on the door/wall; **il tapait comme un sourd** he was thumping away for all he was worth; **il tape (dur), le salaud‡** the bastard's‡ hitting hard; **~ dans un ballon** to kick a ball about *ou* around.

b (*: *dire du mal de*) **~ sur qn** to run sb down*, have a go at sb* (behind his back).

c (*: *entamer*) **~ dans** *provisions, caisse* to dig into*.

d (*être fort, intense*) *[soleil]* to beat down; (*) *[vin]* to go to one's head.

e (‡: *sentir mauvais*) to stink*, pong‡ (*Brit*).

f (*loc*) **~ des pieds** to stamp one's feet; **~ des mains** to clap one's hands; (*fig*) **se faire ~ sur les doigts*** to be rapped over the knuckles; **il a tapé à côté*** he was wide of the mark; **~ sur les nerfs** *ou* **le système de qn*** to get on sb's nerves* *ou* wick‡ (*Brit*); **~ dans l'œil de qn*** to take sb's fancy*; **~ dans le tas** (*bagarre*) to pitch into the crowd; (*repas*) to tuck in*, dig in*; *voir* **mille**[1].

3 **se taper vpr** a (‡: *s'envoyer*) *repas* to put away*; *corvée* to do, get landed* with; *importun* to get landed* *ou* lumbered* (*Brit*) with. **on s'est tapé les 10 km à pied** we slogged it on foot for the (whole) 10 km*, we footed the whole 10 km*; (*sexuellement*) **se ~ une femme** to have it off with a woman‡, lay a woman‡.

b (*loc*) **se ~ (sur) les cuisses de contentement*** to slap one's thighs with satisfaction; **il y a de quoi se ~ le derrière*** *ou* **le cul‡ par terre** it's darned* *ou* bloody‡ (*Brit*) ridiculous; **c'est à se ~ la tête contre les murs** it's enough to drive you up the wall*; **se ~ la cloche*** to feed one's face*, have a blow-out‡ (*Brit*); **il peut toujours se ~‡** he knows what he can do‡; **se ~ sur le ventre*** to be on chummy* *ou* pally* terms; **s'en ~*** not to give a damn‡.

4 **comp** ▸**tape-à-l'œil** (*péj*) **adj inv** *décoration, élégance* flashy, showy; **c'est du tape-à-l'œil** it's all show *ou* flash* (*Brit*) *ou* razzle-dazzle*.

tapette [tapɛt] **nf** a (*pour tapis*) carpet beater; (*pour mouches*) flyswatter; (*pour souris*) mousetrap. b (†*: *langue*) **il a une bonne** *ou* **fière ~** *ou* **une de ces ~s** he's a real chatterbox*. c (‡: *homosexuel*) poof‡ (*Brit*), queer‡, fairy‡, nancy-boy‡ (*Brit*), fag‡ (*US*).

tapeur, -euse* [tapœʀ, øz] **nm,f** (*emprunteur*) cadger*.

tapin [tapɛ̃] **nm** a (‡) **faire le ~** to be on the game‡, hustle* (*US*). b (†: *tambour*) drummer.

tapiner‡ [tapine] [1] **vi** to be on the game‡, hustle* (*US*).

tapinois [tapinwa] **nm**: **en ~** *s'approcher* furtively; *agir* on the sly.

tapioca [tapjɔka] **nm** tapioca.

tapir [tapiʀ] **nm** (*Zool*) tapir.

tapir (se) [tapiʀ] [2] **vpr** (*se blottir*) to crouch; (*se cacher*) to hide away; (*s'embusquer*) to lurk. **maison tapie au fond de la vallée** house hidden away at the bottom of the valley; **ce mal tapi en lui depuis des années** this sickness that for years had lurked within him.

tapis [tapi] 1 **nm** a *[sol]* (*gén*) carpet; (*petit*) rug; (*natte*) mat; (*dans un gymnase*) mat. **~ mécanique** machine-woven carpet; *voir* **marchand**.

b *[meuble]* cloth; *[table de jeu]* baize (*NonC*), cloth, covering. **le ~ vert des tables de conférence** the green baize *ou* covering of the conference tables; (*Casino*) **le ~ brûle** place your stakes.

c (*fig*) **~ de verdure/de neige** carpet of greenery/snow.

d (*loc*) **aller au ~** to go down for the count; (*lit, fig*) **envoyer qn au ~** to floor sb; **mettre** *ou* **porter sur le ~** *affaire, question* to lay on the table, bring up for discussion; **être/revenir sur le ~** to come up/come back up for discussion.

2 **comp** ▸**tapis à bagages** (*dans un aéroport*) carousel ▸**tapis de bain** bath mat ▸**tapis de billard** billiard cloth ▸**tapis de bombes** carpet of bombs ▸**tapis-brosse nm (pl tapis-brosses)** doormat ▸**tapis de chœur** altar carpet ▸**tapis de couloir** runner ▸**tapis de haute laine** long-pile carpet ▸**tapis d'Orient** oriental carpet ▸**tapis persan** Persian carpet ▸**tapis de prière** prayer mat ▸**tapis ras** short-pile carpet ▸**tapis rouge** red carpet; **dérouler le tapis rouge** to roll out the red carpet ▸**tapis roulant** (*pour colis etc*) conveyor belt; (*pour piétons*) moving walkway, travelator; (*pour bagages*) carousel ▸**tapis de sol** groundsheet ▸**tapis de table** table cover ▸**tapis volant** flying carpet.

tapissé, e [tapise] (**ptp de tapisser**) **adj**: **sol ~ de neige/de mousse** ground carpeted with snow/moss; **mur ~ de photos/d'affiches** wall covered *ou* plastered with photos/posters; **~ de lierre/de mousse** ivy-/moss-clad; **~ de neige** snow-clad, covered in snow; **voiture ~e de cuir** car with leather interior trim *ou* leather upholstery.

tapisser [tapise] 1 vt a *[personne]* ~ **(de papier peint)** to (wall)paper; ~ **un mur/une pièce de tentures** to hang a wall/room with drapes, cover a wall/room with hangings; ~ **un mur d'affiches/de photos** to plaster *ou* cover a wall with posters/photos. b *[tenture, papier]* to cover, line; *[mousse, neige, lierre]* to carpet, cover; (*Anat, Bot*) *[membranes, tissus]* to line. **le lierre tapissait le mur** the wall was covered with ivy.

tapisserie [tapisʀi] nf a (*tenture*) tapestry; (*papier peint*) wallpaper, wall covering; (*activité*) tapestry-making. **faire ~** *[subalterne]* to stand on the sidelines; *[danseur, danseuse]* to be a wallflower, sit out; **j'ai dû faire ~ pendant que mon mari dansait** I had to sit out *ou* I was a wallflower while my husband was dancing. b (*broderie*) tapestry; (*activité*) tapestrywork. **faire de la ~** to do tapestry work; **fauteuil recouvert de ~** armchair upholstered with tapestry; **pantoufles en ~** embroidered slippers; *voir* **point²**.

tapissier, -ière [tapisje, jɛʀ] nm,f (*fabricant*) tapestry-maker; (*commerçant*) upholsterer. **~-décorateur** interior decorator.

tapon† [tapɔ̃] nm: **en ~** in a ball; **mettre en ~** to roll (up) into a ball.

tapotement [tapɔtmɑ̃] nm (*sur la table*) tapping (*NonC*); (*sur le piano*) plonking (*NonC*).

tapoter [tapɔte] 1 1 vt *joue* to pat; *baromètre* to tap. **~ sa cigarette pour faire tomber la cendre** to flick (the ash off) one's cigarette; (*péj*) **~ une valse au piano** to plonk *ou* thump out a waltz at *ou* on the piano. 2 vi: **~ sur *ou* contre** to tap on.

tapuscrit [tapyskʀi] nm typescript.

taquet [takɛ] nm (*coin, cale*) wedge; (*cheville, butée*) peg; (*pour enrouler un cordage*) cleat.

taquin, e [takɛ̃, in] adj *caractère, personne* teasing (*épith*). **c'est un ~** he's a tease *ou* a teaser.

taquiner [takine] 1 vt *[personne]* to tease; *[fait, douleur]* to bother, worry. (*hum*) **~ le goujon** to do a bit of fishing; (*hum*) **~ la muse** to dabble in poetry, court the Muse (*hum*).

taquinerie [takinʀi] nf teasing (*NonC*). **agacé par ses ~s** annoyed by his teasing.

tarabiscoté, e [taʀabiskɔte] adj *meuble* (over)-ornate, fussy; *style* involved, (over)-ornate, fussy.

tarabuster [taʀabyste] 1 vt *[personne]* to badger, pester; *[fait, idée]* to bother, worry.

tarama [taʀama] nm taramasalata.

taratata [taʀatata] excl (stuff and) nonsense!, rubbish!

taraud [taʀo] nm tap.

taraudage [taʀodaʒ] nm tapping. **~ à la machine/à la main** machine-/hand-tapping.

tarauder [taʀode] 1 vt (*Tech*) *plaque, écrou* to tap; *vis, boulon* to thread; (*fig*) *[insecte]* to bore into; *[remords, angoisse]* to pierce.

taraudeur, -euse [taʀodœʀ, øz] 1 nm,f (*ouvrier*) tapper. 2 **taraudeuse** nf (*machine*) tapping-machine; (*à fileter*) threader.

tard [taʀ] 1 adv (*dans la journée, dans la saison*) late. **plus ~** later (on); **il est ~** it's late; **il se fait ~** it's getting late; **se coucher/travailler ~** to go to bed/work late; **travailler ~ dans la nuit** to work late (on) into the night; **il vint nous voir ~ dans la matinée/journée** he came to see us late in the morning *ou* in the late morning/late in the day; **il vous faut arriver jeudi au plus ~** you must come on Thursday at the latest; **c'est un peu ~ pour t'excuser** it's a bit late in the day to be making your excuses; **pas plus ~ qu'hier** only yesterday; **pas plus ~ que la semaine dernière** just *ou* only last week, as recently as last week; **remettre qch à plus ~** to put sth off till later (on); *voir* **jamais, mieux, tôt**.

2 nm: **sur le ~** (*dans la vie*) late (on) in life, late in the day (*fig*); (*dans la journée*) late in the day.

tarder [taʀde] 1 1 vi a (*différer, traîner*) to delay. **~ à entreprendre qch** to put off *ou* delay starting sth; **ne tardez pas (à le faire)** don't be long doing it *ou* getting down to it; **~ en chemin** to loiter *ou* dawdle on the way; **sans (plus) ~** without (further) delay; **pourquoi tant ~?** why delay it *ou* put it off so long?, why be so long about it?

b (*se faire attendre*) *[réaction, moment]* to be a long time coming; *[lettre]* to take a long time (coming), be a long time coming. **l'été tarde (à venir)** summer is a long time coming *ou* is slow to appear; **ce moment tant espéré tant tardé** this much hoped-for moment had taken so long to come *ou* had been so long (in) coming.

c (*loc nég*) **ne pas ~** (*se manifester promptement*): **ça ne va pas ~** it won't be long (coming); **ça n'a pas tardé** it wasn't long (in) coming; **leur réaction ne va pas ~** their reaction won't be long (in) coming; **il est 2 heures: ils ne vont pas ~** it's 2 o'clock — they won't be long (now); **ils n'ont pas tardé à être endettés** before long they were in debt, it wasn't long before they were in debt; **il n'a pas tardé à s'en apercevoir** it didn't take him long to notice, he noticed soon enough; **ils n'ont pas tardé à réagir, leur réaction n'a pas tardé** they weren't long (in) reacting, their reaction came soon enough; **l'élève ne tarda pas à dépasser le maître** the pupil soon outstripped the teacher.

d (*sembler long*) **le temps *ou* le moment me tarde d'être en vacances** I'm longing to be on holiday, I can't wait to be on holiday.

2 vb impers (*littér*) **il me tarde de le revoir/que ces travaux soient finis** I am longing *ou* I can't wait to see him again/for this work to be finished.

tardif, -ive [taʀdif, iv] adj *apparition, maturité, rentrée, repas* late; *regrets, remords* belated, tardy (*frm*); *fruits* late.

tardivement [taʀdivmɑ̃] adv (*à une heure tardive*) *rentrer* late; (*après coup, trop tard*) *s'apercevoir de qch* belatedly, tardily (*frm*).

tare [taʀ] nf a (*contrepoids*) tare. **faire la ~** to allow for the tare. b (*défaut*) *[personne, marchandise]* defect (*de* in, of); *[société, système]* flaw (*de* in), defect (*de* of). **c'est une ~ de ne pas avoir fait de maths** it's a weakness not to have done any maths.

taré, e [taʀe] 1 adj *régime, politicien* tainted, corrupt; *enfant, animal* sickly, with a defect. (*péj*) **il faut être ~ pour faire cela*** you have to be sick to do that*. 2 nm,f (*Méd*) degenerate. (*péj*) **regardez-moi ce ~*** look at that cretin*.

tarentelle [taʀɑ̃tɛl] nf tarantella.

tarentule [taʀɑ̃tyl] nf tarantula.

tarer [taʀe] 1 vt (*Comm*) to tare, allow for the tare.

targette [taʀʒɛt] nf bolt (*on a door*); (*‡: chaussure*) shoe.

targuer (se) [taʀge] 1 vpr (*se vanter*) **se ~ de qch** to boast about sth, pride *ou* preen o.s. on sth; **se ~ de ce que ...** to boast that ...; **se ~ d'avoir fait qch** to pride o.s. on having done sth; **se targuant d'y parvenir aisément ...** boasting (that) he would easily manage it ... .

targui, e [taʀgi] 1 adj Tuareg. 2 nm,f: **T~(e)** Tuareg.

tarière [taʀjɛʀ] nf a (*Tech*) (*pour le bois*) auger; (*pour le sol*) drill. b (*Zool*) drill, ovipositor (*SPÉC*).

tarif [taʀif] 1 nm (*tableau*) price list, tariff (*Brit*); (*barème*) rate, rates (*pl*), tariff (*Brit*); (*prix*) rate. **consulter/afficher le ~ des consommations** to check/put up the price list for drinks *ou* the drinks tariff (*Brit*); **le ~ postal pour l'étranger/le ~ des taxis va augmenter** overseas postage rates/taxi fares are going up; **les ~s postaux/douaniers vont augmenter** postage/customs rates are going up; **payé au ~ syndical** paid according to union rates, paid the union rate *ou* the union scale; **quels sont vos ~s?** (*réparateur*) how much do you charge?; (*profession libérale*) what are your fees?, what fee do you charge?; **est-ce le ~ habituel?** is this the usual *ou* going rate?; **voyager à plein ~/à ~ réduit** to travel at full/reduced fare; (*hum*) **50 F d'amende/2 mois de prison, c'est le ~!*** a 50-franc fine/2 months' prison is what you get!

2 comp ▸**tarif de base** (*gén*) standard *ou* basic rate; (*Publicité*) open rate, transient rate (*US*) ▸**tarif dégressif** (*gén*) tapering charges; (*Publicité*) earned rate ▸**tarif de nuit** night *ou* off-peak rate.

tarifaire [taʀifɛʀ] adj tariff (*épith*).

tarifer [taʀife] 1 vt to fix the price *ou* rate for. **marchandises tarifées** fixed-price goods.

tarification [taʀifikasjɔ̃] nf fixing of a price scale (*de* for).

tarin [taʀɛ̃] nm (*‡: nez*) conk‡ (*Brit*), snoot‡ (*US*); (*Orn*) siskin.

tarir [taʀiʀ] 2 1 vi a *[cours d'eau, puits]* to run dry, dry up; *[larmes]* to dry (up); *[pitié, conversation]* to dry up; *[imagination, ressource]* to run dry, dry up. b *[personne]* **il ne tarit pas sur ce sujet** he can't stop talking about that, he is unstoppable* on that subject; **il ne tarit pas d'éloges sur elle** he never stops *ou* he can't stop praising her. 2 vt (*lit, fig*) to dry up. (*littér*) **~ les larmes de qn** to dry sb's tears. 3 **se tarir** vpr *[source, imagination]* to run dry, dry up.

tarissement [taʀismɑ̃] nm (*voir* **tarir, se tarir**) drying up.

tarot [taʀo] nm (*jeu*) tarot; (*paquet de cartes*) tarot (pack).

Tarse [taʀs] nm Tarsus.

tarse [taʀs] nm (*Anat, Zool*) tarsus.

tarsien, -ienne [taʀsjɛ̃, jɛn] adj tarsal.

tartan [taʀtɑ̃] nm tartan.

tartane [taʀtan] nf tartan.

tartare [taʀtaʀ] 1 adj a (*Hist*) Tartar. b (*Culin*) **sauce ~** tartar(e) sauce; **(steak) ~** steak tartare. 2 nmf (*Hist*) **T~** Tartar.

tartarin [taʀtaʀɛ̃] nm († *hum*) braggart†.

tarte [taʀt] 1 nf a (*Culin*) tart. **~ aux fruits/à la crème** fruit/cream tart; **~ Tatin** ≃ apple upside-down tart; (*fig péj*) **~ à la crème** (*formule vide*) pet theme; *comique, comédie* slapstick (*épith*), custard-pie (*épith*); **c'est pas de la ~‡** it's no joke*, its no easy matter. b (*‡: gifle*) clout, clip round the ear. 2 adj inv (*) (*laid*) plain-looking; (*bête*) daft* (*Brit*), stupid.

tartelette [taʀtəlɛt] nf tartlet, tart.

tartempion* [taʀtɑ̃pjɔ̃] nm thingumabob*, so-and-so*.

tartine [taʀtin] nf a (*beurrée*) slice of bread and butter; (*à la confiture*) slice of bread and jam; (*tranche prête à être tartinée*) slice *ou* piece of bread. **le matin, on mange des ~s** in the morning we have bread and butter; **tu as déjà mangé 3 ~s, ça suffit** you've already had 3 slices *ou* 3 pieces of bread, that's enough; **couper des tranches de pain pour faire des ~s** to cut (slices of) bread for buttering; **~ au *ou* de miel** slice *ou* piece of bread and honey; **~ grillée et beurrée** piece of toast and butter; **as-tu du pain pour les ~s?** have you got any bread to slice?

b (* *fig: lettre, article*) screed (*Brit*). **il en a mis une ~** he wrote reams *ou* a great screed* (*Brit*); **il y a une ~ dans le journal à propos de ...** there's a long screed (*Brit*) *ou* a great spread in the paper about ... .

tartiner [taʀtine] 1 vt *pain* to spread (*de* with); *beurre* to spread. **pâté de foie/fromage à ~** liver/cheese spread; **~ du pain de beurre** to butter bread, spread bread with butter.

tartre [taʀtʀ] nm *[dents]* tartar; *[chaudière, bouilloire]* fur; *[tonneau]*

tartar.
tartrique [taʀtʀik] adj: **acide** ~ tartaric acid.
tartu(f)fe [taʀtyf] 1 nm (sanctimonious) hypocrite, tartuffe. 2 adj hypocritical. **il est un peu** ~ he's something of a hypocrite *ou* tartuffe, he's a po-faced hypocrite*.
tartu(f)ferie [taʀtyfʀi] nf hypocrisy.
Tarzan [taʀzɑ̃] nm Tarzan; (* *fig*) muscleman.
tas [tɑ] 1 nm a (*amas*) pile, heap. **mettre en** ~ to make a pile of, put into a heap, heap *ou* pile up.
b (*: *beaucoup de*) **un** *ou* **des** ~ **de** loads of*, heaps of*, lots of; **il connaît un** ~ **de choses/gens** he knows loads* *ou* heaps* *ou* lots of things/people; **il m'a raconté un** ~ **de mensonges** he told me a pack of lies; ~ **de crétins*** you load *ou* bunch *ou* shower of idiots!*
c (*loc*) **tirer dans le** ~ to fire into the crowd; **foncer dans le** ~ to charge in; **dans le** ~, **on en trouvera bien un qui sache conduire** you're bound to find one out of the whole crowd who can drive; **dans le** ~ **tu trouveras bien un stylo qui marche** you're bound to find one pen that works out of that pile; **j'ai acheté des cerises, tape** *ou* **pioche dans le** ~ I've bought some cherries so dig in* *ou* so help yourself; **former qn sur le** ~ to train sb on the job; **formation sur le** ~ on-the-job training; *voir* **grève**.
2 comp ►**tas de boue** (*: *voiture*) banger* (*Brit*), heap*, wreck* ►**tas de charge** (*Archit*) tas de charge ►**tas de fumier** dung *ou* manure heap.
Tasmanie [tasmani] nf Tasmania.
tasmanien, -ienne [tasmanjɛ̃, jɛn] 1 adj Tasmanian. 2 nm,f: **T~(ne)** Tasmanian.
tasse [tɑs] nf cup. ~ **de porcelaine** china cup; ~ **à thé** teacup; ~ **à café** coffee cup; ~ **de thé** cup of tea; (*hum*) **ce n'est pas ma** ~ **de thé** it's not my cup of tea; (*fig*) **boire une** *ou* **la** ~* (*en nageant*) to swallow *ou* get a mouthful.
Tasse [tas] nm: **le** ~ Tasso.
tassé, e [tɑse] (ptp de **tasser**) adj a (*affaissé*) *façade, mur* that has settled *ou* sunk *ou* subsided; *vieillard* shrunken. ~ **sur sa chaise** slumped on his chair. b (*serrés*) *spectateurs, passagers* packed (tight). c **bien** ~* (*fort*) *whisky* stiff (*épith*); (*bien rempli*) *verre* well-filled, full to the brim (*attrib*); **café bien** ~ good strong coffee, coffee that is good and strong; **3 kilos bien** ~**s** a good 3 kilos; **il a 50 ans bien** ~**s** he's well on in his fifties, he's well over fifty.
tasseau, pl ~**x** [tɑso] nm (*morceau de bois*) piece *ou* length of wood; (*support*) bracket.
tassement [tɑsmɑ̃] nm a [*sol, neige*] packing down. b [*mur, terrain*] settling, subsidence. (*Méd*) ~ **de la colonne (vertébrale)** compression of the spinal column. c (*diminution*) **le** ~ **des voix en faveur du candidat** the drop *ou* fall-off in votes for the candidate; **un** ~ **de l'activité économique** a downturn *ou* a slowing down in economic activity.
tasser [tɑse] 1 1 vt a (*comprimer*) *sol, neige* to pack down, tamp down; *foin, paille* to pack. ~ **le contenu d'une valise** to push *ou* ram down the contents of a case; ~ **le tabac dans sa pipe** to pack *ou* tamp down the tobacco in one's pipe; ~ **des prisonniers dans un camion** to cram *ou* pack prisoners into a truck.
b (*Sport*) *concurrent* to box in.
2 **se tasser** vpr a (*s'affaisser*) [*façade, mur, terrain*] to settle, sink, subside; (*fig*) [*vieillard, corps*] to shrink.
b (*se serrer*) to bunch up. **on s'est tassé à 10 dans la voiture** 10 of us crammed into the car; **tassez-vous, il y a encore de la place** bunch *ou* squeeze up, there's still room.
c (*: *s'arranger*) to settle down. **ne vous en faites pas, ça va se** ~ don't worry – things will settle down *ou* iron themselves out*.
d (‡: *engloutir*) *petits fours, boissons* to down*, get through*.
taste-vin [tastəvɛ̃] nm inv (wine-)tasting cup.
tata [tata] nf (*langage enfantin: tante*) auntie*; (‡: *pédéraste*) poof‡ (*Brit*), queer‡, fairy‡, fag‡ (*US*).
tatami [tatami] nm tatami.
tatane‡ [tatan] nf shoe.
ta, ta, ta [tatata] excl (stuff and) nonsense!, rubbish!
tâter [tɑte] 1 1 vt a (*palper*) *objet, étoffe, pouls* to feel. ~ **qch du bout des doigts** to feel *ou* explore sth with one's fingertips; **marcher en tâtant les murs** to feel *ou* grope one's way along the walls.
b (*sonder*) *adversaire, concurrent* to try (out). ~ **l'opinion** to sound *ou* test out opinion; (*fig*) ~ **le terrain** to find out *ou* see how the land lies, find out *ou* check the lie (*Brit*) *ou* lay (*US*) of the land, take soundings, put out feelers.
2 vi a (†, *littér: goûter à*) ~ **de** *mets* to taste, try.
b (*essayer, passer par*) to sample, try out. ~ **de la prison** to sample prison life, have a taste of prison; **il a tâté de tous les métiers** he has had a go at *ou* he has tried his hand at all possible jobs.
3 **se tâter** vpr a (*après une chute*) to feel o.s. (*for injuries*); (*pensant avoir perdu qch*) to feel one's pocket(s). **il se releva, se tâta: rien de cassé** he got up and felt himself but he had nothing broken.
b (*: *hésiter*) to be in (*Brit*) *ou* of (*US*) two minds. **viendras-tu? – je ne sais pas, je me tâte** are you coming? – I don't know, I'm in (*Brit*) *ou* of (*US*) two minds (about it) *ou* I haven't made up my mind (about it).
tâte-vin [tatvɛ̃] nm inv = **taste-vin**.
tatillon, -onne [tatijɔ̃, ɔn] adj finicky, pernickety (*Brit*), persnickety (*US*), nit-picking*. **il est** ~, **c'est un** ~ he's very finicky *ou* pernickety (*Brit*), he's a nit-picker*, he's always nit-picking*.
tâtonnement [tɑtɔnmɑ̃] nm (*gén pl: essai*) trial and error (*NonC*), experimentation (*NonC*). **après bien des** ~**s** after a good deal of experimentation *ou* of trial and error; **procéder par** ~**(s)** to move forward by trial and error.
tâtonner [tɑtɔne] 1 vi a (*pour se diriger*) to grope *ou* feel one's way (along), grope along; (*pour trouver qch*) to grope *ou* feel around *ou* about. b (*fig*) to grope around; (*par méthode*) to proceed by trial and error.
tâtons [tɑtɔ̃] adv: (*lit, fig*) **avancer à** ~ to grope along, grope *ou* feel one's way along; (*lit, fig*) **chercher qch à** ~ to grope *ou* feel around for sth.
tatou [tatu] nm armadillo.
tatouage [tatwaʒ] nm (*action*) tattooing; (*dessin*) tattoo.
tatouer [tatwe] 1 vt to tattoo.
tatoueur, -euse [tatwœʀ, øz] nm,f tattooer.
taudis [todi] nm (*logement*) hovel, slum; (*pl: Admin, gén*) slums. (*fig: en désordre*) **ta chambre est un vrai** ~ your room is like a pigsty *ou* a slum.
taulard, -arde‡ [tolaʀ, aʀd] nm,f (*arg Crime*) convict, con (*arg*).
taule‡ [tol] nf a (*prison*) nick‡ (*Brit*), jug‡, clink‡. **aller en** ~ to go inside*, get banged up‡ (*Brit*); **il a fait de la** ~ he's done time *ou* a stretch*, he has been inside*; **il a eu 5 ans de** ~ he has been given a 5-year stretch* *ou* 5 years in the nick‡ (*Brit*) *ou* in clink‡. b (*chambre*) room.
taulier, -ière‡ [tolje, jɛʀ] nm,f (hotel) boss*.
taupe [top] nf a (*animal, fig: espion*) mole; (*fourrure*) moleskin. (*fig péj*) **une vieille** ~ an old crone *ou* hag (*péj*), an old bag‡ (*péj*); (*fig*) **ils vivent comme des** ~**s dans ces grands immeubles** they live closeted away *ou* completely shut up in these multi-storey blocks, they never get out to see the light of day from these multi-storey blocks; *voir* **myope**. b (*arg Scol: classe*) advanced maths class (*preparing for the Grandes Écoles*).
taupin [topɛ̃] nm a (*Zool*) click beetle, elaterida (SPÉC). b (*Scol*) maths student (*voir* **taupe**).
taupinière [topinjɛʀ] nf (*tas*) molehill; (*galeries, terrier*) mole tunnel; (*fig péj: immeuble, bureaux*) rabbit warren.
taureau, pl ~**x** [tɔʀo] nm (*Zool*) bull. (*Astron*) **le T~** Taurus, the Bull; **être (du) T~** to be Taurus *ou* a Taurean; ~ **de combat** fighting bull; **il avait une force de** ~ he was as strong as an ox; **une encolure** *ou* **un cou de** ~ a bull neck; (*fig*) **prendre le** ~ **par les cornes** to take the bull by the horns; *voir* **course**.
taurillon [tɔʀijɔ̃] nm bull-calf.
taurin, e [tɔʀɛ̃, in] adj bullfighting (*épith*).
tauromachie [tɔʀɔmaʃi] nf bullfighting.
tauromachique [tɔʀɔmaʃik] adj bullfighting (*épith*).
tautologie [totɔlɔʒi] nf tautology.
tautologique [totɔlɔʒik] adj tautological.
taux [to] nm a (*gén, Fin, Statistique*) rate. ~ **d'intérêt** interest rate, rate of interest; ~ **des salaires** wage rate; ~ **de change** exchange rate, rate of exchange; ~ **de mortalité** mortality rate; ~ **de natalité** birth rate; ~ **actuariel (brut)** annual percentage rate; ~ **officiel d'escompte** bank rate; ~ **d'escompte** discount rate; ~ **de prêt** lending rate; ~ **de croissance** growth rate; ~ **de base bancaire** minimum *ou* base lending rate; ~ **de chômage** unemployment rate. b (*niveau, degré*) [*infirmité*] degree; [*cholestérol, sucre*] level. [*moteur*] ~ **de compression** compression ratio.
tavelé, e [tav(ə)le] (ptp de **taveler**) adj *fruit* marked. **visage** ~ **de taches de son** face speckled with *ou* covered in freckles; **visage** ~ **par la petite vérole** pockmarked face, face pitted with pockmarks.
taveler [tav(ə)le] 4 1 vt *fruit* to mark; *visage* to speckle. 2 **se taveler** vpr [*fruit*] to become marked.
tavelure [tav(ə)lyʀ] nf [*fruit*] mark; [*peau*] mark, spot.
taverne [tavɛʀn] nf (*Hist*) inn, tavern; (*Can*) tavern, beer parlor (*Can*).
tavernier, -ière [tavɛʀnje, jɛʀ] nm,f (*Hist, hum*) innkeeper.
taxable [taksabl] adj (*gén*) taxable; (*à la douane*) liable to duty (*épith*), dutiable.
taxateur, -trice [taksatœʀ, tʀis] nm,f (*Admin*) taxer; (*Jur*) taxing master. **juge** ~ taxing master.
taxation [taksasjɔ̃] nf (*voir* **taxer**) taxing, taxation; fixing (the rate); fixing the price; assessment. ~ **d'office** estimation of tax(es).
taxe [taks] 1 nf a (*impôt, redevance*) tax; (*à la douane*) duty. ~**s locales/municipales** local/municipal taxes; **toutes** ~**s comprises** inclusive of tax; *voir* **hors**.
b (*Admin, Comm: tarif*) statutory price. **vendre des marchandises à la** ~**/plus cher que la** ~ to sell goods at/for more than the statutory price.
c (*Jur*) [*dépens*] taxation, assessment.
2 comp ►**taxes d'aéroport** airport tax(es) ►**taxe d'apprentissage** apprenticeship tax (*paid by French employers to finance*

apprenticeships) ▸**taxe d'habitation** ≃ property tax (*US*), ≃ council tax (*Brit*), ≃ rates (*Brit*) ▸**taxe de luxe** tax on luxury goods ▸**taxe professionnelle** local tax on businesses, ≃ business rate (*Brit*) ▸**taxe de raccordement** (*Télec*) connection fee ▸**taxe de séjour** tourist tax ▸**taxe à** *ou* **sur la valeur ajoutée** value-added tax, VAT.

taxer [takse] [1] **vt** **a** (*imposer*) *marchandises, service* to put *ou* impose a tax on, tax; (*à la douane*) to impose *ou* put duty on.
b *particuliers* to tax. ~ **qn d'office** to assess sb for tax *ou* taxation (purposes).
c (*Admin, Comm*) *valeur* to fix (the rate of); *marchandise* to fix the price of; (*Jur*) *dépens* to tax, assess.
d (*Brit*) (*‡: voler*) to pinch*, nick‡. (*‡: extorquer*) **il m'a taxé de 100 F** he got 100 francs out of me*.
f ~ **qn de qch** (*qualifier de*) to call sb sth; (*accuser de*) to tax sb with sth (*frm*), accuse sb of sth; **une méthode que l'on a taxée de charlatanisme** a method to which the term charlatanism has been applied; **il m'a taxé d'imbécile** he called me an idiot; **on le taxe d'avarice** he's accused of miserliness *ou* of being a miser.

taxi [taksi] **nm** **a** (*voiture*) taxi, (taxi)cab. ~**-brousse** bush taxi; *voir* **avion, chauffeur, station.** **b** (**: chauffeur*) cabby*, taxi driver.

taxidermie [taksidɛʀmi] **nf** taxidermy.

taxidermiste [taksidɛʀmist] **nmf** taxidermist.

taxigirl [taksigœʀl] **nf** (*danseuse*) taxigirl.

taximètre [taksimɛtʀ] **nm** (taxi)meter.

taxinomie [taksinɔmi] **nf** taxonomy.

taxinomique [taksinɔmik] **adj** taxonomic(al).

taxinomiste [taksinɔmist] **nmf** taxonomist.

taxiphone [taksifɔn] **nm** ® pay-phone, public (tele)phone.

taxiway [taksiwɛ] **nm** taxiway.

taxonomie [taksɔnɔmi] = **taxinomie.**

taylorisme [tɛlɔʀism] **nm** Taylorism.

TB (**abrév de très bien**) VG.

Tbilissi [tbilisi] **n** Tbilissi.

Tchad [tʃad] **nm: le** ~ Chad; **le lac** ~ Lake Chad.

tchadien, -ienne [tʃadjɛ̃, jɛn] **1 adj** Chad. **2 nm,f: T~(ne)** Chad.

tchador [tʃadɔʀ] **nm** chador.

Tchaikovski [tʃaikɔvski] **nm** Tchaikovsky.

tchao [tʃao] **excl** bye!, cheerio!

tchatche‡ [tʃatʃ] **nf** yacking*, yakking*, jabbering. **il a une de ces** ~! he is a real gasbag!‡, he's got verbal diarrhoea!‡ (*Brit*) *ou* diarrhea‡! (*US*).

tchatcher‡ [tʃatʃe] [1] **vi** to yack*, yak*, jabber. **il ne fait que** ~ he never stops yacking* *ou* yakking*, all he does is yak, yak, yak*.

tchécoslovaque [tʃekɔslɔvak] **adj** Czechoslovak(ian).

Tchécoslovaquie [tʃekɔslɔvaki] **nf** Czechoslovakia.

Tchekhov [tʃekɔv] **nm** Chek(h)ov.

tchèque [tʃɛk] **1 adj** Czech. **2 nm** (*Ling*) Czech. **3 nmf: T~** Czech.

tchin(-tchin)* [tʃin(tʃin)] **excl** cheers!

TD [tede] **nm** (*Univ*) (**abrév de travaux dirigés**) *voir* **travail.**

TDF [tedeɛf] **nf** (**abrév de Télédiffusion de France**) *French broadcasting authority*, ≃ IBA (*Brit*), FCC (*US*).

te [tə] **pron** (*objet direct ou indirect*) you; (*réfléchi*) yourself. ~ **l'a-t-il dit?** did he tell you?, did he tell you about it?; **t'en a-t-il parlé?** did he speak to you about it?

té¹ [te] **nm** (*règle*) T-square; (*ferrure*) T(-shaped) bracket. **fer** *etc* **en** ~ T-shaped iron *etc.*

té² [te] **excl** (*dial*) well! well!, my!

TEC [teɔse] **nf** (**abrév de tonne équivalent charbon**) TCE.

technétium [teknesjɔm] **nm** technetium.

technicien, -ienne [tɛknisjɛ̃, jɛn] **nm,f** technician. (*Admin*) ~ **de surface** cleaning operative; ~ **de (la) télévision** television technician; **c'est un** ~ **de la politique/finance** he's a political/financial expert *ou* wizard; **c'est un** ~ **du roman** he's a practitioner *ou* practician (*Brit*) of the novel.

technicité [tɛknisite] **nf** technical nature.

technico-commercial, e, **mpl -iaux** [tɛknikokɔmɛʀsjal, jo] **adj: agent** ~ technical salesman.

Technicolor [tɛknikɔlɔʀ] **nm** ® Technicolor ®. **film en** ~ Technicolor film, film in Technicolor.

technique [tɛknik] **1 nf** **a** (*méthode, procédés*) [*peintre, art*] technique. **des** ~**s nouvelles** new techniques; **manquer de** ~ to lack technique; **il n'a pas la (bonne)** ~* he hasn't got the knack* *ou* technique. **b** (*aire de la connaissance*) **la** ~ technique. **2 adj** technical; *voir* **escale, incident.** **3 nm** (*enseignement*) **le** ~ technical education, industrial arts (*US*); **il est professeur dans le** ~ he's a technical teacher.

techniquement [tɛknikmɑ̃] **adv** technically.

technocrate [tɛknɔkʀat] **nmf** technocrat.

technocratie [tɛknɔkʀasi] **nf** technocracy.

technocratique [tɛknɔkʀatik] **adj** technocratic.

technologie [tɛknɔlɔʒi] **nf** technology. ~ **de pointe** *ou* **avancée** frontier *ou* leading-edge *ou* advanced *ou* high technology; ~ **de l'information** information technology; ~ **des systèmes automatisés** automated systems technology.

technologique [tɛknɔlɔʒik] **adj** technological. **la révolution** ~ **des années 70** the technological revolution of the 70s.

technologue [tɛknɔlɔg] **nmf** technologist.

teck [tɛk] **nm** teak.

teckel [tekɛl] **nm** dachshund.

tectonique [tɛktɔnik] **1 adj** tectonic. **2 nf** tectonics (*sg*). ~ **des plaques** plate tectonics.

Te Deum [tedeɔm] **nm inv** Te Deum.

TEE [teəə] **nm abrév de Trans Europe Express.**

tee [ti] **nm** tee. **partir du** ~ to tee off.

tee(-)shirt [tiʃœʀt] **nm** T-shirt, tee shirt.

Téflon [teflɔ̃] **nm** ® Teflon ®.

Tegucigalpa [tegusigalpa] **n** Tegucigalpa.

tégument [tegymɑ̃] **nm** (*Bot, Zool*) integument.

Téhéran [teeʀɑ̃] **n** Teheran.

teigne [tɛɲ] **nf** **a** (*Zool*) moth, tinea (*SPÉC*). **b** (*Méd*) ringworm, tinea (*SPÉC*). **c** (*fig péj*) (*homme*) swine‡ (*Brit*), bastard‡; (*femme*) shrew, bitch‡, vixen. **mauvais** *ou* **méchant comme une** ~ as nasty as anything.

teigneux, -euse [tɛɲø, øz] **adj** suffering from ringworm. **il est** ~ (*lit*) he has *ou* is suffering from ringworm; (*péj: pouilleux*) he's scabby*; (*péj: acariâtre*) he's a swine‡ *ou* a nasty piece of work.

teindre [tɛ̃dʀ] [52] **1 vt** *vêtement, cheveux* to dye. **2 se teindre vpr** **a** **se** ~ **(les cheveux)** to dye one's hair; **se** ~ **la barbe/la moustache** to dye one's beard/moustache. **b** (*littér: se colorer*) **les montagnes se teignaient de pourpre** the mountains took on a purple hue *ou* tinge *ou* tint, the mountains were tinged with purple.

teint, e [tɛ̃, tɛ̃t] (**ptp de teindre**) **1 adj** *cheveux, laine* dyed. (*péj*) **elle est ~e** her hair is dyed, she has dyed her hair. **2 nm** (*permanent*) complexion, colouring; (*momentané*) colour. **avoir le** ~ **jaune** to have a sallow complexion *ou* colouring; **il revint de vacances le** ~ **frais** he came back from his holidays with a fresh *ou* good colour; *voir* **bon¹, fond, grand.** **3 teinte nf** (*nuance*) shade, hue, tint; (*couleur*) colour; (*fig*) tinge, hint. **pull aux ~es vives** brightly-coloured sweater; (*fig*) **avec une ~e de tristesse dans la voix** with a tinge *ou* hint of sadness in his voice; *voir* **demi-.**

teinté, e [tɛ̃te] (**ptp de teinter**) **adj** *bois* stained; *verre* tinted. **table ~e acajou** mahogany-stained table; **blanc** ~ **de rose** white with a hint of pink; (*fig*) **discours** ~ **de puritanisme** speech tinged with puritanism.

teinter [tɛ̃te] [1] **1 vt** *papier, verre* to tint; *meuble, bois* to stain. **un peu d'eau teintée de vin** a little water with a hint of wine *ou* just coloured with wine. **2 se teinter vpr** (*littér*) **se** ~ **d'amertume** to become tinged with bitterness; **les sommets se teintèrent de pourpre** the peaks took on a purple tinge *ou* hue, the peaks were tinged with purple.

teinture [tɛ̃tyʀ] **nf** **a** (*colorant*) dye; (*action*) dyeing. (*fig*) **une** ~ **de maths/de français** a smattering of maths/French, a nodding acquaintance with maths/French. **b** (*Pharm*) tincture. ~ **d'arnica/d'iode** tincture of arnica/iodine.

teinturerie [tɛ̃tyʀʀi] **nf** (*métier, industrie*) dyeing; (*magasin*) (dry) cleaner's.

teinturier, -ière [tɛ̃tyʀje, jɛʀ] **nm,f** (*qui nettoie*) dry cleaner; (*qui teint*) dyer.

tek [tɛk] **nm** = **teck.**

tel, telle [tɛl] **1 adj** **a** (*similitude*) (*sg: avec n concret*) such, like; (*avec n abstrait*) such; (*pl*) such. **une telle ignorance/réponse est inexcusable** such ignorance/such an answer is unpardonable; ~ **père,** ~ **fils** like father like son; **nous n'avons pas de ~s orages en Europe** we don't get such storms *ou* storms like this in Europe; **as-tu jamais rien vu de ~?** have you ever seen such a thing?, have you ever seen the like? *ou* anything like it?; **s'il n'est pas menteur, il passe pour** ~ perhaps he isn't a liar but he is taken for one *ou* but they say he is *ou* but that's the reputation he has *ou* but that's how he's thought of; **il a filé** ~ **un zèbre** he ran off as quick as an arrow *ou* a shot, he whizzed off; **~s sont ces gens que vous croyiez honnêtes** that's what they're really like — the people you thought were honest, such are those whom you believed (to be) honest; (*frm*) **prenez telles décisions qui vous sembleront nécessaires** take such decisions as you find *ou* whatever decisions you find necessary; **telles furent ses dernières paroles** such were his last words; **il est le patron, en tant que** ~ *ou* **comme** ~ **il aurait dû agir** he is the boss and as such he ought to have taken action, he's the boss and in that capacity he should have acted; ~ **il était enfant,** ~ **je le retrouve** thus he was as a child, and thus he has remained; (*littér*) **le lac** ~ **un miroir** the lake like a mirror *ou* mirror-like; *voir* **rien.**
b (*valeur d'indéfini*) such-and-such. ~ **et** ~ such-and-such; **venez** ~ **jour/à telle heure** come on such-and-such a day/at such-and-such a time; **telle quantité d'arsenic peut tuer un homme et pas un autre** a given quantity of arsenic can kill one man and not another; **telle ou telle personne vous dira que** someone *ou* somebody or other will tell you that; **j'ai lu dans** ~ **et** ~ **article que** I read in some article or other that; **l'homme en général et non** ~ **homme** man in general and not any one *ou* particular *ou* given man; ~ **enfant qui se croit menacé devient agressif** any child that feels (himself) threatened will become aggressive; **l'on sait** ~ **bureau où ...** there's *ou* I know a certain office *ou* one office where ... .

c ~ **que** like, (such *ou* the same *ou* just) as; (*énumération*) like, such as; **il est resté ~ que je le connaissais** he is still the same *ou* just as he used to be, he's stayed just as I remember him; **un homme ~ que lui doit comprendre** a man like him *ou* such a man as he (*frm*) must understand; **~ que je le connais, il ne viendra pas** if I know him *ou* if he's the man I think he is, he won't come; **~ que vous me voyez, je reviens d'Afrique** I'm just (this minute) back from Africa; **~ que vous me voyez, j'ai 72 ans** you wouldn't think it to look at me but I'm 72; **restez ~ que vous êtes** stay (just) as you are; **là il se montre ~ qu'il est** now he's showing himself in his true colours *ou* as he really is; **les métaux ~s que l'or, l'argent et le platine** metals like *ou* such as gold, silver and platinum; (*littér*) **le ciel à l'occident ~ qu'un brasier** the western sky like a fiery furnace.

d **~ quel, ~ que*: il a acheté la maison telle quelle** *ou* **telle que*** he bought the house (just) as it was *ou* stood; **laissez tous ces dossiers ~s quels** *ou* **~s que*** leave all those files as they are *ou* as you find them; (*sur objet en solde*) **"à vendre ~ quel"** "sold as seen" (*Brit*), "sold as is" (*US*); **il m'a dit: "sortez d'ici ou je vous sors" ~ que!*** he said to me "get out of here or I'll throw you out" — just like that!

e (*intensif*) (*sg: avec n concret*) such a; (*avec n abstrait*) such; (*pl*) such. **on n'a jamais vu (une) telle cohue** you've never seen such a mob; **c'est une telle joie de l'entendre!** what joy *ou* it's such a joy to hear him!

f (*avec conséquence*) **de telle façon** *ou* **manière** in such a way; **ils ont eu de ~s ennuis avec leur voiture qu'ils l'ont vendue** they had such (a lot of) trouble *ou* so much trouble with their car that they sold it; **de telle sorte que** so that; **à telle(s) enseigne(s) que** so much so that, the proof being that, indeed; *voir* **point[1]**.

2 **pron indéf: ~ vous dira qu'il faut voter oui, ~ autre ...** one will tell you you must vote yes, another ...; (*Prov*) **~ qui rit vendredi, dimanche pleurera** you can be laughing on Friday but crying by Sunday; **si ~ ou ~ vous dit que** if somebody (or other) *ou* if anybody tells you that; (*Prov*) **~ est pris qui croyait prendre** it's the biter bit; *voir* **un**.

tél. (**abrév de téléphone**) tel.

Tel-Aviv(-Jaffa) [tɛlaviv(ʒafa)] **n** Tel Aviv(-Jaffa).

télé* [tele] 1 **nf abrév de télévision. a** (*organisme*) TV. **il travaille à la ~** he works on TV. **b** (*programmes*) TV. **qu'est-ce qu'il y a à la ~ ce soir?** what's on TV *ou* telly* (*Brit*) tonight?; **la ~ du matin** breakfast TV. **c** (*chaîne*) TV channel. **nous allons avoir 20 chaînes (de) ~** *ou* **20 ~s** we're going to have 20 TV channels. **d** (*poste*) TV. **allume la ~** turn on the TV *ou* the telly* (*Brit*). 2 **nm** (**abrév de téléobjectif**) telephoto lens.

téléachat [teleaʃa] **nm** teleshopping (*NonC*), armchair shopping (*NonC*).

téléalarme [telealaʀm] **nf** remote alarm.

télébenne [telebɛn] **nf** cable car.

téléboutique [telebutik] **nf** ® phone shop.

télécabine [telekabin] **nf = télébenne.**

télécarte [telekaʀt] **nf** ® phonecard.

téléchargement [teleʃaʀʒəmɑ̃] **nm** downloading.

télécharger [teleʃaʀʒe] [3] **vt** to download.

télécinéma [telesinema] **nm** (*service*) film department (*of television channel*).

télécommande [telekɔmɑ̃d] **nf** remote control.

télécommander [telekɔmɑ̃de] [1] **vt** (*Tech*) to operate by remote control. (*fig*) **~ des menées subversives/un complot de l'étranger** to mastermind subversive activity/a plot from abroad.

télécommunication [telekɔmynikasjɔ̃] **nf** (*gén pl*) telecommunication.

téléconférence [telekɔ̃feʀɑ̃s] **nf** conference call.

télécopie [telekɔpi] **nf** (*procédé*) facsimile transmission; (*document*) fax, telefax. **transmettre par ~** to send by fax *ou* facsimile; **service de ~** facsimile service.

télécopieur [telekɔpjœʀ] **nm** fax machine, facsimile machine.

télécran [telekʀɑ̃] **nm** (large) television screen.

télédétection [teledetɛksjɔ̃] **nf** remote detection.

télédiffuser [teledifyze] [1] **vt** to broadcast by television.

télédiffusion [teledifyzjɔ̃] **nf** television broadcasting. **T~ de France** *French broadcasting authority*, ≃ Independent Broadcasting Authority (*Brit*), ≃ Federal Communications Commission (*US*).

télédistribution [teledistʀibysjɔ̃] **nf** television broadcasting by cable.

télé(-)enseignement [teleɑ̃sɛɲmɑ̃] **nm** television teaching, teaching by television.

téléférique [telefeʀik] **nm** (*installation*) cableway; (*cabine*) cable-car.

téléfilm [telefilm] **nm** television *ou* TV film.

télégénique [teleʒenik] **adj** telegenic.

télégestion [teleʒɛstjɔ̃] **nf** (*Ordin*) teleprocessing, remote processing.

télégramme [telegʀam] **nm** telegram, wire, cable.

télégraphe [telegʀaf] **nm** telegraph.

télégraphie [telegʀafi] **nf** (*technique*) telegraphy. **~ optique** signalling; **~ sans fil†** wireless telegraphy†.

télégraphier [telegʀafje] [7] **vt** *message* to telegraph, wire, cable. **tu devrais lui ~** you should send him a telegram *ou* wire *ou* cable, you should wire (to) him *ou* cable him.

télégraphique [telegʀafik] **adj a** *poteau, fils* telegraph (*épith*); *alphabet, code* Morse (*épith*); *message* telegram (*épith*), telegraphed, telegraphic. **adresse ~** telegraphic address. **b** (*fig*) *style, langage* telegraphic.

télégraphiste [telegʀafist] **nmf** (*technicien*) telegrapher, telegraphist; (*messager*) telegraph boy.

téléguidage [telegidaʒ] **nm** radio control.

téléguider [telegide] [1] **vt** (*Tech*) to radio-control; (*fig*) to control (from a distance).

téléimprimeur [teleɛ̃pʀimœʀ] **nm** teleprinter.

téléinformatique [teleɛ̃fɔʀmatik] **nf** remote-access computing.

télékinésie [telekinezi] **nf** telekinesis.

télémaintenance [telemɛ̃t(ə)nɑ̃s] **nf** remote maintenance.

télémanipulation [telemanipylasjɔ̃] **nf** remote control handling.

Télémaque [telemak] **nm** Telemachus.

télémark [telemaʀk] **nm** (*Ski*) telemark.

télématique [telematik] 1 **adj** telematic. 2 **nf** telematics (*sg*), on-line data processing.

télémètre [telemɛtʀ] **nm** (*Mil, Phot*) rangefinder.

télémétrie [telemetʀi] **nf** telemetry.

télémétrique [telemetʀik] **adj** telemetric(al).

téléobjectif [teleɔbʒɛktif] **nm** telephoto lens.

téléologie [teleɔlɔʒi] **nf** teleology.

téléologique [teleɔlɔʒik] **adj** teleologic(al).

télépathe [telepat] 1 **nmf** telepathist. 2 **adj** telepathic.

télépathie [telepati] **nf** telepathy.

télépathique [telepatik] **adj** telepathic.

téléphérage [telefeʀaʒ] **nm** transport by cableway.

téléphérique [telefeʀik] = **téléférique.**

téléphone [telefɔn] 1 **nm** (*système*) telephone; (*appareil*) (tele)phone. (*Admin*) **les T~s** the telephone service, ≃ British Telecom (*Brit*); **avoir le ~** to be on the (tele)phone; **demande-le-lui au** *ou* **par ~** phone him (and ask) about it, give him a call about it; *voir* **abonné, numéro** *etc.*

2 **comp ►téléphone arabe** bush telegraph **►téléphone automatique** automatic telephone system **►téléphone de brousse = téléphone arabe ►téléphone à cadran** dial (tele)phone **►téléphone à carte (magnétique)** cardphone **►téléphone cellulaire** cellular (tele)phone **►téléphone interne** internal telephone **►téléphone à manivelle** magneto telephone **►téléphone manuel** manually-operated telephone system **►téléphone public** public (tele)phone, pay-phone **►le téléphone rouge** (*Pol*) the hot line; **il l'a appelé par le téléphone rouge** he called him on the hot line **►téléphone sans fil** cordless (tele)phone **►téléphone à touches** push-button (tele)phone.

téléphoner [telefɔne] [1] 1 **vt** *message* to (tele)phone. **il m'a téléphoné la nouvelle** he phoned me the news; **téléphone-lui de venir** phone him and tell him to come; (*fig*) **leur manœuvre était téléphonée*** you could see their move coming a mile off*. 2 **vi: ~ à qn** to telephone sb, phone *ou* ring *ou* call sb (up); **où est Jean? — il téléphone** where's John? — he's on the phone *ou* he's phoning *ou* he's making a call; **j'étais en train de ~ à Jean** I was on the phone to John, I was busy phoning John; **je téléphone beaucoup, je n'aime pas écrire** I phone people a lot *ou* I use the phone a lot as I don't like writing.

téléphonie [telefɔni] **nf** telephony. **~ sans fil** wireless telephony, radiotelephony.

téléphonique [telefɔnik] **adj** *liaison, ligne, réseau* telephone (*épith*), telephonic (*frm*). **conversation ~** (tele)phone conversation; *voir* **appel, cabine, communication.**

téléphoniquement [telefɔnikmɑ̃] **adv** by telephone, telephonically.

téléphoniste [telefɔnist] **nmf** *[poste]* telephonist (*Brit*), (telephone) operator; *[entreprise]* switchboard operator.

téléphotographie [telefɔtɔgʀafi] **nf** telephotography.

téléprompteur [telepʀɔ̃ptœʀ] **nm** teleprompter.

téléreportage [teleʀ(ə)pɔʀtaʒ] **nm** (*activité*) television reporting. **un ~** a television report; **le car de ~** the outside-broadcast coach.

télescopage [telɛskɔpaʒ] **nm** *[véhicules]* concertinaing (*NonC*); *[trains]* telescoping, concertinaing (up).

télescope [telɛskɔp] **nm** telescope.

télescoper [telɛskɔpe] [1] 1 **vt** *véhicule* to smash up; *faits, idées* to mix up, jumble together. 2 **se télescoper vpr** *[véhicules]* to concertina; *[trains]* to telescope, concertina; *[souvenirs]* to become confused *ou* mixed up.

télescopique [telɛskɔpik] **adj** (*gén*) telescopic.

téléscripteur [teleskʀiptœʀ] **nm** teleprinter, Teletype ® (machine).

télésiège [telesjɛʒ] **nm** chairlift.

téléski [teleski] **nm** (ski) lift, (ski) tow. **~ à fourche** T-bar tow; **~ à archets** T-bar lift.

téléspectateur, -trice [telespɛktatœʀ, tʀis] **nm,f** (television *ou* TV) viewer. **les ~s** the viewing audience, the viewers.

télésurveillance [telesyʀvɛjɑ̃s] **nf** electronic surveillance.

Télétel [teletɛl] **nm** ® electronic telephone directory.

télétexte [teletɛkst] **nm** Teletext ®, Viewdata ®.

télétraitement [teletʀɛtmɑ̃] **nm** remote processing.

télétransmission [teletʀɑ̃smisjɔ̃] **nf** remote transmission.

Télétype [teletip] nm ® teleprinter, Teletype ® (machine).

télévendeur, -euse [televɑ̃dœʀ, øz] nm,f telesales operator *ou* person.

télévente [televɑ̃t] nf (*technique*) telephone selling, telesales; (*action*) telephone sales.

téléviser [televize] 1 vt to televise; *voir* **journal**.

téléviseur [televizœʀ] nm television (set).

télévision [televizjɔ̃] nf a (*organisme, technique*) television. **la ~ par satellite** satellite television; **la ~ câblée** *ou* **par câble** cable television, cablevision (*US*); **il travaille pour la ~ allemande** he works for German television; **plateau de ~** television studio set; **studio de ~** television studio.

b (*programmes*) television. **à la ~** on television; **regarder la ~** to watch television; **la ~ scolaire** schools television; **la ~ du matin** breakfast television.

c (*chaîne*) television channel. **les ~s étrangères** foreign channels; **~ payante** pay channel, subscription channel; **~ privée**independent *ou* private channel.

d (*poste*) television (set). **~ (en) noir et blanc/couleur** black and white/colour television.

télévisuel, -elle [televizɥɛl] adj television (*épith*).

télex [telɛks] nm inv telex. **envoyer par ~** to telex.

télexer [telɛkse] 1 vt to telex.

télexiste [telɛksist] nmf telex operator.

tellement [tɛlmɑ̃] adv a (*si*) (*avec adj ou adv*) so; (*avec compar*) so much. **il est ~ gentil** he's so (very) nice; **~ mieux/plus fort/plus beau** so much better/stronger/more beautiful; **j'étais ~ fatigué que je me suis couché immédiatement** I was so (very) tired (that) I went straight to bed; (*nég, avec subj: littér*) **il n'est pas ~ pauvre qu'il ne puisse ...** he's not so (very) poor that he cannot ... .

b (*tant*) so much. (*tant de*) **~ de gens** so many people; **~ de temps** so much time, so long; **il a ~ insisté que ...** he insisted so much that ..., he was so insistent that ...; **il travaille ~ qu'il se rend malade** he works so much *ou* hard (that) he is making himself ill; (*nég, avec subj: littér*) **il ne travaille pas ~ qu'il ait besoin de repos** he does not work to such an extent *ou* so very much that he needs rest.

c (*introduisant une causale: tant*) **on ne le comprend pas, ~ il parle vite** he talks so quickly (that) you can't understand him; **il trouve à peine le temps de dormir, ~ il travaille** he hardly finds time to sleep, he works so much *ou* hard.

d (*avec nég: pas très, pas beaucoup*) **pas ~ fort/lentement** not (all) that strong/slowly, not so (very) strong/slowly; **il ne travaille pas ~** he doesn't work (all) that much *ou* hard, he doesn't work so (very) much *ou* hard; **cet article n'est plus ~ demandé** this article is no longer (very) much in demand; **ce n'est plus ~ à la mode** it's not really *ou* all that fashionable any more; **cela ne se fait plus ~** it's not done (very) much *ou* all that much any more; **tu aimes le cinéma? — pas ~** do you like the cinema? — not (all) that much *ou* not particularly *ou* not especially; **y allez-vous toujours? — plus ~, maintenant qu'il y a le bébé** do you still go there? — not (very) much *ou* not all that much now (that) there's the baby; **on ne la voit plus ~** we don't really see (very) much of her any more.

tellure [telyʀ] nm tellurium.

tellurique [telyʀik] adj telluric; *voir* **secousse**.

téméraire [temeʀɛʀ] adj *action, entreprise* rash, reckless, foolhardy; *jugement* rash; *personne* reckless, foolhardy, rash. **~ dans ses jugements** rash in his judgments.

témérairement [temeʀɛʀmɑ̃] adv (*voir* **téméraire**) rashly; recklessly; foolhardily.

témérité [temeʀite] nf (*voir* **téméraire**) rashness; recklessness; foolhardiness.

témoignage [temwaɲaʒ] nm a (*en justice*) (*déclaration*) testimony (*NonC*), evidence (*NonC*); (*faits relatés*) evidence (*NonC*). **d'après le ~ de M. X** according to Mr X's testimony *ou* evidence, according to the evidence of *ou* given by Mr X; **j'étais présent lors de son ~** I was present when he gave evidence *ou* gave his testimony; **ces ~s sont contradictoires** these are contradictory pieces of evidence; **c'est un ~ écrasant/irrécusable** the evidence is overwhelming/incontestable; **appelé en ~** called as a witness, called (upon) to give evidence *ou* to testify; **porter ~ de qch** to testify to sth, bear witness to sth (*frm*); *voir* **faux²**.

b (*récit, rapport*) account, testimony. **ce livre est un merveilleux ~ sur notre époque** this book gives a marvellous account of the age we live in; **invoquer le ~ d'un voyageur** to call upon a traveller to give his (eyewitness) account *ou* his testimony.

c (*attestation*) **~ de probité/de bonne conduite** evidence (*NonC*) *ou* proof (*NonC*) of honesty/of good conduct; **invoquer le ~ de qn pour prouver sa bonne foi** to call on sb's evidence *ou* testimony to prove one's good faith; **en ~ de quoi ...** in witness whereof ... .

d (*manifestation*) **~ d'amitié/de reconnaissance** (*geste*) expression *ou* gesture of friendship/gratitude; (*cadeau*) token *ou* mark *ou* sign of friendship/gratitude; **leurs ~s de sympathie nous ont touchés** we are touched by their expressions *ou* gestures of sympathy; **en ~ de ma reconnaissance** as a token *ou* mark of my gratitude; **le ~ émouvant de leur confiance** the touching expression of their confidence.

témoigner [temwaɲe] 1 1 vi (*Jur*) to testify. **~ en faveur de/contre qn** to testify *ou* give evidence in sb's favour/against sb; **~ en justice** to testify in court; **~ de vive voix/par écrit** to give spoken/written evidence, testify in person/in writing.

2 vt a (*attester que*) **~ que** to testify that; **il a témoigné qu'il ne l'avait jamais vu** *ou* **ne l'avoir jamais vu** he testified that he had never seen him.

b (*faire preuve de, faire paraître*) to show, display; *reconnaissance* to show, evince (*frm*). **~ un goût pour qch** to show *ou* display a taste *ou* liking for sth; **~ de l'aversion à qn** to show *ou* evince (*frm*) dislike of sb.

c (*démontrer*) **~ que/de qch** to attest *ou* reveal that/sth; **son attitude témoigne de sa préoccupation** *ou* **qu'il est préoccupé** his attitude is evidence of his preoccupation, his attitude reveals his preoccupation *ou* that he is preoccupied; (*fig*) **sa mort témoigne qu'on ne peut vivre seul** his death testifies to the fact *ou* is evidence that one cannot live alone.

d (*manifester*) **~ de** to indicate, attest, bespeak (*frm*); **ce livre témoigne d'une certaine originalité** this book indicates *ou* attests *ou* bespeaks (*frm*) a certain originality.

3 **témoigner de** vt indir (*confirmer*) to testify to, bear witness to. **~ de Dieu** to bear witness to God; **je peux en ~** I can testify to that, I can bear witness to that (*frm*).

témoin [temwɛ̃] 1 nm a (*gén, Jur: personne*) witness; *[duel]* second. **~ auriculaire** earwitness; **~ oculaire** eyewitness; **~ direct/indirect** direct/indirect witness; **~ de moralité** character reference (*person*); **~ gênant** embarrassing witness; (*Jur*) **être ~ à charge/à décharge** to be (a) witness for the prosecution/for the defence; **être ~ de** *crime, scène* to witness, be a witness to; *la sincérité de qn* to vouch for; **prendre qn à ~ (de qch)** to call sb to witness (to *ou* of sth); **parler devant ~(s)** to speak in front of witnesses; **faire qch sans ~** to do sth unwitnessed; **cela doit être signé devant ~** this must be signed in front of a witness; **il a été mon ~ à notre mariage** he was (a) witness at our wedding; **que Dieu m'en soit ~** as God is my witness; **Dieu m'est ~ que je n'ai pas voulu le tuer** as God is my witness, I didn't mean to kill him; (*Rel*) **les T~s de Jéhovah** Jehovah's Witnesses; (*fig*) **ces lieux ~s de notre enfance** these places which saw *ou* witnessed our childhood; *voir* **faux²**.

b (*chose, personne: preuve*) evidence (*NonC*), testimony. **ces ruines sont le ~ de la férocité des combats** these ruins are (the) evidence of *ou* a testimony to the fierceness of the fighting; **ces aristocrates sont les ~s d'une époque révolue** these aristocrats are the surviving evidence of a bygone age; **la région est riche, ~ les constructions nouvelles qui se dressent partout** the region is rich — witness the new buildings going up everywhere.

c (*Sport*) baton. **passer le ~** to hand on *ou* pass the baton.

d (*Géol*) outlier; *[excavations]* dumpling; *voir* **butte**.

e (*Constr: posé sur une fente*) telltale.

f (*borne*) boundary marker.

2 adj (*après n*) control (*épith*). **des magasins(-)~s pour empêcher les abus** control *ou* check shops to prevent abuses; **animaux/sujets ~s** control animals/subjects; **appartement ~** show-flat (*Brit*), model apartment (*US*); **réalisation ~** pilot *ou* test development; *voir* **lampe**.

tempe [tɑ̃p] nf (*Anat*) temple. **avoir les ~s grisonnantes** to have greying temples, be going grey at the temples.

tempera [tɑ̃peʀa] nf: **a ~** in *ou* with tempera.

tempérament [tɑ̃peʀamɑ̃] nm a (*constitution*) constitution. **~ robuste/faible** strong/weak constitution; **se tuer** *ou* **s'esquinter le ~*** to wreck one's health; **~ sanguin/lymphatique** sanguine/lymphatic constitution; **~ nerveux** nervous disposition.

b (*nature, caractère*) disposition, temperament, nature. **elle a un ~ actif/réservé** she is of *ou* has an active/a reserved disposition; **~ romantique** romantic nature *ou* temperament; **moqueur par ~** naturally given to *ou* disposed to mockery, mocking by nature; **c'est un ~** he (*ou* she) has a strong personality.

c (*sensualité*) sexual nature *ou* disposition. **être de ~ ardent/froid** to have a passionate/cold nature; **avoir du ~** to be hot-blooded *ou* highly sexed.

d (*Comm*) **vente à ~** sale on deferred (payment) terms; **acheter qch à ~** to buy sth on hire purchase (*Brit*) *ou* on an installment plan (*US*); **trop d'achats à ~ l'avaient mis dans une situation difficile** too many hire purchase commitments (*Brit*) *ou* too many purchases on H.P.* (*Brit*) *ou* too many installment purchases (*US*) had got him into a difficult situation.

e (*Mus*) temperament.

tempérance [tɑ̃peʀɑ̃s] nf temperance; *voir* **société**.

tempérant, e [tɑ̃peʀɑ̃, ɑ̃t] adj temperate.

température [tɑ̃peʀatyʀ] nf a (*Mét, Phys*) temperature. **les ~s sont en hausse/en baisse** temperatures are rising/falling; (*Phys*) **~ d'ébullition/de fusion** boiling/melting point; (*Phys*) **~ absolue** *ou* **en degrés absolus** absolute temperature. b (*chaleur du corps*) temperature. **animaux à ~ fixe/variable** warm-blooded/cold-blooded animals; **avoir** *ou* **faire de la ~** to have a temperature, be running a temperature; **prendre la ~ de** *malade* to take the temperature of; (*fig*) *auditoire, groupe public* to gauge the temperature of, test *ou* get the feeling of; *voir* **courbe**,

feuille.

tempéré, e [tɑ̃peʀe] (*ptp de* **tempérer**) *adj climat, zone* temperate; (*Mus*) tempered.

tempérer [tɑ̃peʀe] 16 *vt froid, rigueur du climat* to temper; (*littér*) *peine, douleur* to soothe, ease; (*littér*) *ardeur, sévérité* to temper.

tempête [tɑ̃pɛt] *nf* a (*lit*) storm, gale, tempest (*littér*). **~ de neige** snowstorm, blizzard; **~ de sable** sandstorm; *voir* **briquet[1], lampe, qui, souffler.** b (*fig: agitation*) storm. **une ~ dans un verre d'eau** a storm in a teacup (*Brit*), a tempest in a teapot (*US*); **cela va déchaîner des ~s** that's going to cause a storm; **il est resté calme dans la ~** he remained calm in the midst of the storm *ou* while the storm raged all around him; **les ~s de l'âme** inner turmoil. c (*déchaînement*) **une ~ d'applaudissements** a storm of applause, thunderous applause (*NonC*); **une ~ d'injures** a storm of abuse.

tempêter [tɑ̃pete] 1 *vi* to rant and rave, rage.

tempétueux, -euse [tɑ̃petɥø, øz] *adj* (*littér*) *région, côte* tempestuous (*littér*), stormy; (*fig*) *vie, époque* tempestuous, stormy, turbulent.

temple [tɑ̃pl] *nm* a (*Hist, littér*) temple. b (*Rel*) (Protestant) church. c **l'Ordre du T~, le T~** the Order of the Temple.

templier [tɑ̃plije] *nm* (Knight) Templar.

tempo [tɛmpo] *nm* (*Mus*) tempo; (*fig*) tempo, pace.

temporaire [tɑ̃pɔʀɛʀ] *adj personnel, mesures, crise* temporary. **nomination à titre ~** temporary appointment, appointment on a temporary basis; *voir* **travail[1].**

temporairement [tɑ̃pɔʀɛʀmɑ̃] *adv* temporarily.

temporal, e, *mpl* **-aux** [tɑ̃pɔʀal, o] (*Anat*) 1 *adj* temporal. 2 *nm* temporal (bone).

temporalité [tɑ̃pɔʀalite] *nf* (*Ling, Philos*) temporality.

temporel, -elle [tɑ̃pɔʀɛl] *adj* a (*Rel*) (*non spirituel*) worldly, temporal; (*non éternel*) temporal. **biens ~s** temporal *ou* worldly goods, temporals. b (*Ling, Philos*) temporal.

temporellement [tɑ̃pɔʀɛlmɑ̃] *adv* temporally.

temporisateur, -trice [tɑ̃pɔʀizatœʀ, tʀis] 1 *adj* temporizing (*épith*), delaying (*épith*), stalling (*épith*). 2 *nm,f* temporizer.

temporisation [tɑ̃pɔʀizasjɔ̃] *nf* temporization, delaying, stalling, playing for time.

temporiser [tɑ̃pɔʀize] 1 *vi* to temporize, delay, stall, play for time.

temps[1] [tɑ̃] 1 *nm* a (*passage des ans*) **le ~** time; (*personnifié*) **le T~** (Old) Father Time; **l'action du ~** the action of time; *voir* **tuer.**

b (*durée*) time. **cela prend trop de ~** it takes (up) too much time; **la blessure mettra du ~ à guérir** the wound will take (some) time to heal; **il a mis beaucoup de ~ à se préparer** he took a long time to get ready; **avec le ~, ça s'oubliera** it'll all be forgotten with *ou* in time; **la jeunesse n'a qu'un ~** youth will not endure; **travailler à plein ~/à ~ partiel** to work full-time/part-time; **en peu de ~** in a short time; **peu de ~ avant/après** (*prép*) shortly before/after, a short while *ou* time before/after; (*adv*) shortly before/after(wards), a short while *ou* time before/after(wards); **dans peu de ~** before (very) long; **dans quelque ~** before too long, in a (little) while; **pour un ~** for a time *ou* while; **attendre quelque ~** to wait a while; **durant** *ou* **pendant (tout) ce ~-(là)** all this time; **je ne le vois plus depuis quelque ~** I haven't seen him for a (little) while *ou* some (little) time; *voir* **emploi, laps.**

c (*portion de temps*) time. **~ d'arrêt** pause, halt; **marquer un ~ d'arrêt** to pause (momentarily); **s'accorder un ~ de réflexion** to give o.s. time for reflection; **la plupart du ~** most of the time; **avoir le ~ (de faire)** to have time (to do); **je n'ai pas le ~** I haven't time; **je n'ai pas le ~ de le faire** I haven't the time *ou* I can't spare the time to do it; **il avait du ~ devant lui** he had time to spare, he had time on his hands; **vous avez tout votre ~** you have all the time in the world *ou* plenty of time *ou* all the time you need; **prendre le ~ de vivre** to make time to enjoy o.s.; **il n'y a pas de ~ à perdre** there's no time to lose *ou* to be lost; **le ~ presse** time is short, time presses; **prenez donc votre ~** do take your time; **cela fait gagner beaucoup de ~** it saves a lot *ou* a great deal of time, it's very time-saving; **chercher à gagner du ~** (*aller plus vite*) to try to save time; (*temporiser*) to play for time, try to gain time; **passer son ~ à la lecture** *ou* **à lire** to spend one's time reading; **il passe tout son ~ à faire .../à ceci** he spends all his time doing .../on this; **perdre du/son ~ (à faire qch)** to waste time/waste one's time (doing sth); **donnez-moi le ~ de m'habiller et je suis à vous** just give me time *ou* a moment to get dressed *ou* I'll just get dressed and I'll be with you; **je me suis arrêté en chemin juste le ~ de prendre un verre** I stopped on the way just long enough for a drink *ou* to have a drink; (*Prov*) **le ~ perdu ne se rattrape jamais** time and tide wait for no man (*Prov*); **faire son ~** *[soldat]* to serve one's time (in the army); *[prisonnier]* to do *ou* serve one's time; (*fig*) **il a fait son ~** *[auteur]* he has had his day; *[objet]* it has had its day; *voir* **clair.**

d (*moment précis*) time. **il est ~ de partir** it's time to go, it's time we left; **il est** *ou* **il serait (grand) ~ qu'il parte** it's (high) time he went, it's time for him to go; **le ~ est venu de supprimer les frontières** the time has come to abolish frontiers, it's time frontiers were abolished; **il était ~!** (*pas trop tôt*) not before time!, about time too!*; (*c'était juste*) it came in the nick of time!; **il n'est plus ~ de se lamenter** the time for bemoaning one's lot is past *ou* over.

e (*époque*) time, times (*pl*). **en ~ de guerre/paix** in wartime/peacetime; **en ~ de crise** in times of crisis; **par les ~ qui courent** these days, nowadays; **les ~ modernes** modern times; **dans les ~ anciens** in ancient times *ou* days; **en ces ~ troublés** in these troubled times; **les ~ ont bien changé** times have changed; **le ~ n'est plus où ...** gone are the days when ...; **c'était le bon ~** those were the days, those were the good times; **dans le ~** at one time, in the past, formerly; **dans le** *ou* **au bon vieux ~** in the good old days; **en ce ~-là** at that time; **en ~ normal** in normal circumstances; **les premiers ~** at the beginning, at first; **ces** *ou* **les derniers ~** *ou* **~ derniers** lately, recently, latterly; **dans un premier ~** at first; **dans un deuxième ~** subsequently; *voir* **nuit, signe.**

f (*époque délimitée*) time(s), day(s). **du ~ de Néron** in Nero's time *ou* day(s), at the time of Nero; **au ~ des Tudors** in Tudor times, in the days of the Tudors; **de mon ~** in my day *ou* time; **dans mon jeune ~** in my younger days; **être de son ~** to move with *ou* keep up with the times; **quels ~ nous vivons!** what times we're living in!; **les ~ sont durs!** times are hard!; **les jeunes de notre ~** young people of our time *ou* (of) today, young people these days.

g (*saison*) **le ~ des moissons/des vacances** harvest/holiday time; **le ~ de la chasse** the hunting season.

h (*Mus*) beat; (*Gym*) *[exercice, mouvement]* stage. **~ fort/faible** strong/weak beat; (*fig*) **les ~ forts et les ~ faibles d'un roman** the powerful and the subdued moments of a novel; (*Mus*) **~ frappé** downbeat; **à deux/trois ~** in duple/triple time; **~ de valse** waltz time.

i (*Ling*) *[verbe]* tense. **~ simple/composé** simple/compound tense; **~ surcomposé** double-compound tense; **adverbe/complément de ~** adverb/complement of time, temporal adverb/complement; *voir* **concordance.**

j (*Tech: phase*) stroke. **moteur à 4 ~** 4-stroke engine; **un 2 ~** a 2-stroke.

k (*Sport*) *[coureur, concurrent]* time. **dans les meilleurs ~** among the best times; **être dans les ~** (*Sport*) to be within the time limit; (*travail*) to be on schedule; (*fig: pas trop tard*) to be in time; **depuis le ~ qu'il essaie** he has been trying long enough; **depuis le ~ que je te le dis** I've told you often enough.

l (*loc*) **à ~** in time; **en un ~ où** at a time when; **de ~ en ~, de ~ à autre** from time to time, now and again, every now and then; **de tout ~** from time immemorial; **dans le ~** in the old days; (*littér: à l'époque où*) **du ~ que, du ~ où, dans le ~ où, au ~ où** in the days when, at the time when; (*: *pendant que*) **du ~ que tu y es, rapporte des fruits** while you're at it* *ou* about* it, get some fruit; **en ~ et lieu** in due course, at the proper time (and place); **en ~ opportun** at an appropriate time; **ce n'est ni le ~ ni le lieu de discuter** this is neither the time nor the place for discussions; **chaque chose en son ~** each thing in its proper time; **en ~ voulu** *ou* **utile** in due time *ou* course; **à ~ perdu** in one's spare time; **au ~ pour moi!** my mistake!; **il faut bien passer le ~** you've got to pass the time somehow; **cela fait passer le ~** it passes the time; (*Prov*) **le ~ c'est de l'argent** time is money (*Prov*); *voir* **deux, juste, tout.**

2 *comp* ▸**temps d'accès** (*Ordin*) access time ▸**temps d'antenne** (*Rad, TV*) airtime ▸**temps astronomique** (*Sci*) mean *ou* astronomical time ▸**temps atomique** (*Phys*) atomic time ▸**temps différé** (*Ordin*) batch mode ▸**temps libre** spare time; **comment occupes-tu ton temps libre?** what do you do in your spare time? ▸**temps mort** (*Ftbl, Rugby*) injury time (*NonC*), stoppage for injury; (*fig*) (*dans le commerce, le travail*) slack period; (*dans la conversation*) lull ▸**temps partagé** (*Ordin*) time-sharing; (*Ordin*) **utilisation en temps partagé** time-sharing ▸**temps réel** (*Ordin*) real time; **ordinateur exploité en temps réel** real-time computer ▸**temps de saignement** (*Méd*) bleeding time ▸**temps sidéral** (*Astron*) sideral time ▸**temps solaire vrai** apparent *ou* real solar time ▸**temps universel** universal time.

temps[2] [tɑ̃] *nm* (*conditions atmosphériques*) weather. **quel ~ fait-il?** what's the weather like?; **il fait beau/mauvais ~** the weather's fine/bad; **le ~ s'est mis au beau** the weather has turned fine; **le ~ se gâte** the weather is changing for the worse; **par ~ pluvieux/mauvais ~** in wet/bad weather; **sortir par tous les ~** to go out in all weathers; **avec le ~ qu'il fait!** in this weather!, with the weather we are having!; **~ de chien*** rotten* *ou* lousy* weather; **~ de saison** seasonable weather; **il faisait un beau ~ sec** (*pendant une période*) it was beautiful dry weather; (*ce jour-là*) it was a lovely dry day; **le ~ est lourd aujourd'hui** it's close today; (*fig*) **prendre le ~ comme il vient** to take things as they come; *voir* **air[1].**

tenable [t(ə)nabl] *adj* (*gén nég*) *température, situation* bearable. **il fait trop chaud ici, ce n'est pas ~** it's too warm here, it's unbearable; **quand ils sont ensemble, ce n'est plus ~** when they're together it becomes *ou* they become unbearable.

tenace [tənas] *adj* a (*persistant*) *douleur, rhume* stubborn, persistent; *croyance, préjugés* deep-rooted, stubborn, deep-seated; *souvenir* persistent; *espoir, illusions* tenacious, stubborn; *odeur* lingering, persistent. b (*têtu, obstiné*) *quémandeur* persistent; *chercheur* dogged, tenacious; *résistance, volonté* tenacious, stubborn. c *colle* firmly adhesive, strong.

tenacement [tənasmɑ̃] *adv* (*voir* **tenace**) stubbornly; persistently; tenaciously; doggedly.

ténacité [tenasite] *nf* (*voir* **tenace**) stubbornness; persistence; deep-rooted nature; tenacity; doggedness.

tenaille [t(ə)nɑj] nf a (*gén pl*) *[menuisier, bricoleur]* pliers, pincers; *[forgeron]* tongs; *[cordonnier]* nippers, pincers. b (*Mil*) *[fortification]* tenaille, tenail. (*manœuvre*) **prendre en ~** to catch in a pincer movement; **mouvement de ~** pincer movement.

tenailler [tənɑje] 1 vt *[remords, inquiétude]* to torture, torment, rack. **la faim le tenaillait** he was gnawed by hunger; **le remords/l'inquiétude le tenaillait** he was racked *ou* tortured *ou* tormented by remorse/worry.

tenancier [tənɑ̃sje] nm a *[maison de jeu, hôtel, bar]* manager. b *[ferme]* tenant farmer; (*Hist*) *[terre]* (feudal) tenant.

tenancière [tənɑ̃sjɛʀ] nf *[maison close]* brothel-keeper, madam; *[maison de jeu, hôtel, bar]* manageress.

tenant, e [tənɑ̃, ɑ̃t] 1 adj: **chemise à col ~** shirt with an attached collar *ou* with collar attached; *voir* **séance.** 2 nm a (*gén pl: partisan*) *[doctrine]* supporter, upholder (*de* of), adherent (*de* to); *[homme politique]* supporter. b (*Sport*) *[coupe]* holder. **le ~ du titre** the title-holder, the reigning champion. c (*loc*) (*fig*) **les ~s et (les) aboutissants d'une affaire** the ins and outs of a question; **d'un (seul) ~** *terrain* all in one piece, lying together; **100 hectares d'un seul ~** 100 unbroken *ou* uninterrupted hectares.

tendance [tɑ̃dɑ̃s] nf a (*inclination, Psych*) tendency. **~s refoulées/inconscientes** repressed/unconscious tendencies; **la ~ principale de son caractère est l'égoïsme** the chief tendency in his character *ou* his chief tendency is egoism; **manifester des ~s homosexuelles** to show homosexual leanings *ou* tendencies; **~ à l'exagération/à s'enivrer** tendency to exaggerate *ou* for exaggeration/to get drunk.
b (*opinions*) *[parti, politicien]* leanings (*pl*), sympathies (*pl*); *[groupe artistique, artiste]* leanings (*pl*); *[livre]* drift, tenor. **il est de ~ gauchiste/surréaliste** he has leftist/surrealist leanings; **à quelle ~ (politique) appartient-il?** what are his (political) leanings? *ou* sympathies?
c (*évolution*) *[art, langage, système économique ou politique]* trend. **~s démographiques** population trends; **~ à la hausse/baisse** *[prix]* upward/downward trend, rising/falling trend; *[température]* upward/downward trend; **la récente ~ à la baisse des valeurs mobilières** the recent downward *ou* falling trend in stocks and shares; **les ~s actuelles de l'opinion publique** the current trends in public opinion; *voir* **indicateur.**
d (*loc*) **avoir ~ à** *paresse, exagération* to have a tendency for, tend *ou* be inclined towards; **avoir ~ à s'enivrer/être impertinent** to have a tendency to get drunk/to be impertinent, tend *ou* be inclined to get drunk/to be impertinent; **cette roue a ~ à se bloquer** this wheel tends *ou* has a tendency *ou* is inclined to lock; **le temps a ~ à se gâter vers le soir** the weather tends to deteriorate towards the evening; **en période d'inflation les prix ont ~ à monter** in a period of inflation, prices tend *ou* have a tendency *ou* are inclined to go up.

tendanciel, -ielle [tɑ̃dɑ̃sjɛl] adj underlying.

tendancieusement [tɑ̃dɑ̃sjøzmɑ̃] adv tendentiously.

tendancieux, -ieuse [tɑ̃dɑ̃sjø, jøz] adj tendentious.

tender [tɑ̃dɛʀ] nm (*Rail*) tender.

tendeur [tɑ̃dœʀ] nm (*dispositif*) *[fil de fer]* wire-strainer; *[ficelle de tente]* runner; *[chaîne de bicyclette]* chain-adjuster; (*câble élastique*) elastic *ou* extensible strap. **~ de chaussures** shoe-stretcher.

tendineux, -euse [tɑ̃dinø, øz] adj *viande* stringy; (*Anat*) tendinous.

tendinite [tɑ̃dinit] nf tendinitis (*NonC*).

tendon [tɑ̃dɔ̃] nm tendon, sinew. **~ d'Achille** Achilles' tendon.

tendre[1] [tɑ̃dʀ] 41 1 vt a (*raidir*) *corde, câble, corde de raquette* to tighten, tauten; *corde d'arc* to brace, draw tight; *arc* to bend, draw back; *ressort* to set; *muscles* to tense, brace; *pièce de tissu* to stretch, pull *ou* draw tight. **~ la peau d'un tambour** to brace a drum; **~ le jarret** to flex *ou* brace one's leg muscles; (*littér*) **~ son esprit vers ...** to bend one's mind to ... .
b (*installer, poser*) *tapisserie, tenture* to hang; *piège* to set. **~ une bâche sur une remorque** to pull a tarpaulin over a trailer; **~ une chaîne entre deux poteaux** to hang *ou* fasten a chain between two posts; **~ ses filets** (*lit*) to set one's nets; (*fig*) to set one's snares; (*fig*) **~ un piège/une embuscade (à qn)** to set a trap/an ambush (for sb).
c († *littér: tapisser*) **~ une pièce de tissu** to hang a room with material; **~ une pièce de soie bleue** to put blue silk hangings in a room, line the walls of a room with blue silk.
d (*avancer*) **~ le cou** to crane one's neck; **~ l'oreille** to prick up one's ears; **~ la joue** to offer one's cheek; (*fig*) **~ l'autre joue** to turn the other cheek; (*fig*) **~ la gorge au couteau** to lay one's head on the block; **~ le poing** to raise one's fist; **~ la main** to hold out one's hand; **~ le bras** to stretch out one's arm; **il me tendit la main** he held out his hand to me; **il me tendit les bras** he stretched out his arms to me; **~ une main secourable** to offer a helping hand; **~ le dos** (*aux coups*) to brace one's back.
e (*présenter, donner*) **~ qch à qn** (*briquet, objet demandé*) to hold sth out to *ou* for sb; (*cigarette offerte, bonbon*) to offer sth to sb; **il lui tendit un paquet de cigarettes** he held out a packet of cigarettes to him; **il lui tendit un bonbon/une cigarette** he offered him a sweet/a cigarette; (*fig*) **~ la perche à qn** to throw sb a line.
2 **se tendre** vpr *[corde]* to become taut, tighten; *[rapports]* to become strained.
3 vi a (*aboutir à*) **~ à qch/à faire** to tend towards sth/to do; **le langage tend à se simplifier sans cesse** language tends to become simpler all the time; **la situation tend à s'améliorer** the situation seems to be improving; (*sens affaibli*) **ceci tend à prouver/confirmer que ...** this seems *ou* tends to prove/confirm that ... .
b (*littér: viser à*) **~ à qch/à faire** to aim at sth/to do; **cette mesure tend à faciliter les échanges** this measure aims to facilitate *ou* at facilitating exchanges; **~ à** *ou* **vers la perfection** to strive towards perfection, aim at perfection.
c (*Math*) **~ vers l'infini** to tend towards infinity.

tendre[2] [tɑ̃dʀ] 1 adj a (*délicat*) *peau, pierre, bois* soft; *pain* fresh(ly made), new; *haricots, viande* tender. *[cheval]* **avoir la bouche ~** to be tender-mouthed; (*littér*) **couché dans l'herbe ~** lying in the sweet grass *ou* the fresh young grass; (*littér*) **~s bourgeons/fleurettes** tender shoots/little flowers; **depuis sa plus ~ enfance** from his earliest days; (*hum*) **dans ma ~ enfance** in my innocent childhood days; **~ comme la rosée** wonderfully tender; *voir* **âge.**
b (*affectueux*) *ami, amour, amitié, regard* fond, tender, loving. **ne pas être ~ pour qn** to be hard on sb; **~ aveu** tender confession; *voir* **cœur.**
c *couleurs* soft, delicate. **rose/vert/bleu ~** soft *ou* delicate pink/green/blue.
2 nmf: **c'est un ~** he is soft at heart, he is tender-hearted; **en affaires, ce n'est pas un ~*** in business he is a tough customer*.

tendrement [tɑ̃dʀəmɑ̃] adv (*voir* **tendre**[2]) tenderly; lovingly; fondly. **époux ~ unis** fond *ou* loving couple.

tendresse [tɑ̃dʀɛs] nf a (*NonC: voir* **tendre**[2]) tenderness; fondness. b **la ~** tenderness; **privé de ~ maternelle** denied maternal affection; **un besoin de ~** a need for tenderness *ou* affection; **avoir de la ~ pour qn** to feel tenderness *ou* affection for sb. c (*câlineries*) **~s** tokens of affection, tenderness (*NonC*); **combler qn de ~s** to overwhelm sb with tenderness *ou* with tokens of (one's) affection; **"mille ~s"** "lots of love", "much love". d (*littér: indulgence*) **n'avoir aucune ~ pour** to have no fondness for; **il avait gardé des ~s royalistes** he had retained (his) royalist sympathies.

tendreté [tɑ̃dʀəte] nf *[viande]* tenderness; *[bois, métal]* softness.

tendron [tɑ̃dʀɔ̃] nm a (*Culin*) **~ de veau** tendron of veal (*Brit*), plate of veal (*US*). b (*pousse, bourgeon*) (tender) shoot. c († *hum: jeune fille*) young *ou* little girl.

tendu, e [tɑ̃dy] (ptp de **tendre**[1]) adj a (*raide*) *corde, toile* tight, taut; *muscles* tensed, braced; *ressort* set; (*Ling*) *voyelle, prononciation* tense. **tir ~** (*Mil*) straight shot; (*Ftbl*) straight kick; **la corde est trop ~e/bien ~e** the rope is too tight *ou* taut/is taut; **la corde est mal ~e** the rope is slack *ou* isn't tight *ou* taut enough.
b (*appliqué*) *esprit* concentrated.
c (*empreint de nervosité*) *rapports, relations* strained, fraught; *personne* tense, strained, keyed-up, uptight*; *situation* tense, fraught.
d **les bras ~s** with arms outstretched, with outstretched arms; **s'avancer la main ~e** to come forward with one's hand held out; **la politique de la main ~e à l'égard de ...** a policy of friendly cooperation with ... *ou* friendly exchanges with ...; **le poing ~** with one's fist raised.
e (*tapissé de*) **~ de** *velours, soie* hung with; **chambre ~e de bleu/de soie bleue** bedroom with blue hangings/blue silk hangings.

ténèbres [tenɛbʀ] nfpl (*littér*) *[nuit, cachot]* darkness, gloom. **plongé dans les ~** plunged in darkness; **s'avançant à tâtons dans les ~** groping his way forward in the dark(ness) *ou* gloom; **les ~ de la mort** the shades of death (*littér*); (*littér*) **le prince/l'empire des ~** the prince/world of darkness; (*fig*) **les ~ de l'ignorance** the darkness of ignorance; (*fig*) **les ~ de l'inconscient** the dark regions *ou* murky depths of the unconscious; (*fig*) **une lueur au milieu des ~** a ray of light in the darkness *ou* amidst the gloom.

ténébreux, -euse [tenebʀø, øz] adj a (*littér: obscur*) *prison, forêt* dark, gloomy; (*fig*) *conscience, intrigue, desseins* dark (*épith*); (*fig*) *époque, temps* obscure; (*fig*) *affaire, philosophie* dark (*épith*), mysterious. b (*littér*) *personne* saturnine; *voir* **beau.**

Ténéré [teneʀe] nm: **le ~** Ténéré.

Tenerife [teneʀif] n Tenerife.

teneur [tənœʀ] nf a *[traité]* terms (*pl*); *[lettre]* content, terms (*pl*); *[article]* content. b *[minerai]* grade, content; *[solution]* content. **de haute/faible ~** high-/low-grade (*épith*); **~ en cuivre/fer** copper/iron content; **la forte ~ en fer d'un minerai** the high iron content of an ore, the high percentage of iron in an ore; **la ~ en hémoglobine du sang** the haemoglobin content of the blood; *[vin, bière]* **~ en alcool** alcohol content.

tenez [təne] excl *voir* **tenir.**

ténia [tenja] nm tape worm, taenia (*SPÉC*).

tenir [t(ə)niʀ] 22 1 vt a (*lit: gén*) *[personne]* to hold. **il tenait la clef dans sa main** he was holding the key in his hand; (*fig*) **~ le bon bout** to be on the right track; *voir* **compagnie, œil, rigueur.**
b (*maintenir dans un certain état*) to keep; (*dans une certaine position*) to hold, keep. **~ les yeux fermés/les bras levés** to keep one's eyes shut/one's arms raised *ou* up; **~ un plat au chaud** to keep a dish hot; **une robe qui tient chaud** a warm dress, a dress which keeps you warm; **le café le tient éveillé** coffee keeps him awake; *[nourriture]* **~ au corps** to be filling; **elle tient ses enfants très propres** she keeps her

children very neat; ~ **qch en place/en position** to hold *ou* keep sth in place/position; **ses livres sont tenus par une courroie** his books are held (together) by a strap; ~ **un chien en laisse** to keep a dog on a leash; **il m'a tenu la tête sous l'eau** he held my head under the water; *voir* **échec**[1], **haleine, respect.**

c (*Mus: garder*) *note* to hold. ~ **l'accord** to stay in tune.

d (*avoir, détenir*) *voleur,* (*) *rhume etc* to have, have caught; *vérité, preuve* to hold, have. (*menace*) **si je le tenais!** if I could get my hands *ou* lay hands on him!; **nous le tenons** (*lit: nous l'avons attrapé*) we've got *ou* caught him; (*il ne peut se désister*) we've got him (where we want him); (*il est coincé, à notre merci*) we've got him; **je tiens un de ces rhumes!*** I've got *ou* caught a nasty cold; **nous tenons maintenant la preuve de son innocence** we now hold *ou* have proof of his innocence; **je tiens le mot de l'énigme/la clef du mystère** I've found *ou* got the secret of the riddle/the key to the mystery; **nous tenons un bon filon** we're on to a good thing *ou* something good, we've struck it rich; **parfait, je tiens mon article/mon sujet** fine, now I have my article/my subject; (*Prov*) **un tiens vaut mieux que deux tu l'auras,** (*Prov*) **mieux vaut ~ que courir** a bird in the hand is worth two in the bush (*Prov*); *voir* **main.**

e (*Comm: stocker*) *article, marchandise* to stock, keep.

f (*avoir de l'autorité sur*) *enfant, classe* to have under control, keep under control *ou* on a tight rein; *pays* to have under one's control. **il tient (bien) sa classe** he has *ou* keeps his class (well) under control, he controls his class well; **les enfants sont très tenus** the children are held very much in check *ou* are kept on a very tight rein; **les soldats tiennent la plaine** the soldiers are holding the plain, the soldiers control the plain.

g (*gérer*) *hôtel, magasin* to run, keep; *comptes, registre, maison, ménage* to keep; *voir* **barre, orgue.**

h *séance, conférence, emploi* to hold; *rôle* to fulfill. **elle a bien tenu son rôle de femme au foyer/de chef** she was the perfect housewife/manager.

i (*avoir reçu*) ~ **de qn** *renseignement, meuble, bijou* to have (got) from sb; *trait physique, de caractère* to get from sb; **il tient cela de son père** he gets that from his father; **je tiens ce renseignement d'un voisin** I have *ou* I got this information from a neighbour; *voir* **source.**

j (*occuper*) *place, largeur* to take up. **tu tiens trop de place!** you are taking up too much room!; **le camion tenait toute la largeur/la moitié de la chaussée** the lorry took up the whole width of/half the roadway; (*Aut*) **il ne tenait pas sa droite** he was not keeping to the right; (*Naut*) ~ **le large** to stand off from the coast, stand out to sea; (*fig*) ~ **une place importante** to hold *ou* have an important place; *voir* **lieu, rang.**

k (*contenir*) *[récipient]* to hold.

l (*résister à, bien se comporter*) *[souliers]* ~ **l'eau** to keep out the water; ~ **l'alcool*** to be able to hold *ou* take (*Brit*) one's drink; (*Naut*) ~ **la mer** *[bateau]* to be seaworthy; (*Aut*) ~ **la route** to hold the road; **une tente qui tient la tempête** a tent which can withstand storms.

m (*immobiliser*) **cette maladie le tient depuis 2 mois** he has had this illness for 2 months (now); **il m'a tenu dans son bureau pendant une heure** he kept me in his office for an hour; **il est très tenu par ses affaires** he's very tied (*Brit*) *ou* tied up (*US*) by his business; (*littér*) **la colère le tenait** anger had him in its grip; (*littér*) **l'envie me tenait de ...** I was filled *ou* gripped by the desire to ...; *voir* **jambe.**

n (*respecter*) *promesse* to keep; *pari* to keep to, honour. (*accepter*) **je tiens le pari** I'll take on the bet; **il avait dit qu'il arriverait premier: pari tenu!** he said he would come first and he managed it! *ou* he pulled it off!; *voir* **parole.**

o (*se livrer à*) *discours* to give; *propos* to say; *langage* to use. **il tenait un langage d'une rare grossièreté** the language he used *ou* employed (*frm*) was exceptionally coarse; ~ **des propos désobligeants à l'égard de qn** to make *ou* pass offensive remarks about sb, say offensive things about sb; **elle me tenait des discours sans fin sur la morale** she gave me endless lectures on morality, she lectured me endlessly on morality; **il aime ~ de grands discours** he likes to hold forth; **il m'a tenu ce raisonnement** he gave me this explanation; **si l'on tient le même raisonnement que lui** if you support the same view as he does; **si tu tiens ce raisonnement** if this is the view you hold *ou* take, if this is how you think.

p ~ **qn/qch pour** to regard sb/sth as, consider sb/sth (as), hold sb/sth to be (*frm*); **je le tenais pour un honnête homme** I regarded him as *ou* considered him (to be) *ou* held him to be (*frm*) an honest man; ~ **pour certain** *ou* **sûr que ...** to regard it as certain that ..., consider it certain that ...; *voir* **estime, quitte.**

q (‡: *aimer*) **en ~ pour qn** to fancy sb* (*Brit*), be keen on sb*, have a crush on sb*.

r **tiens!, tenez!** (*en donnant*) take this, here (you are); (*de surprise*) **tiens, voilà mon frère!** ah *ou* hullo, there's my brother!; **tiens, tiens*** well, well!, fancy that!; (*pour attirer l'attention*) **tenez, je vais vous expliquer** look, I'll explain to you; **tenez, ça m'écœure** you know, that sickens me.

2 vi a *[objet fixe, nœud]* to hold; *[objets empilés, échafaudage]* to stay up, hold (up). **croyez-vous que le clou tienne?** do you think the nail will hold?; **l'armoire tient au mur** the cupboard is held *ou* fixed to the wall; **ce chapeau ne tient pas sur ma tête** this hat won't stay on (my head); **la branche est cassée, mais elle tient encore bien à l'arbre** the branch is broken but it's still firmly attached to the tree; ~ **debout** *[objet]* to be upright, be standing; *[personne]* to be standing; **je n'arrive pas à faire ~ le livre debout** I can't keep the book upright, I can't make the book stand *ou* stay up; **son histoire ne tient pas debout** his story doesn't make sense *ou* doesn't hold together *ou* doesn't hold water; **cette théorie tient debout après tout** this theory holds up *ou* holds good after all; **je ne tiens plus debout** I'm dropping* *ou* ready to drop*, I can hardly stand up any more; **il tient bien sur ses jambes** he is very steady on his legs; **cet enfant ne tient pas en place** this child cannot keep *ou* stay still; *voir* **fil.**

b (*être valable*) to be on. **il n'y a pas de bal/match qui tienne** there's no question of going to any dance/match; **ça tient toujours, notre pique-nique de jeudi?*** is our picnic on Thursday still on?, does our picnic on Thursday still stand?

c (*Mil, gén: résister*) to hold out. ~ **bon** *ou* **ferme** to stand fast *ou* firm, hold out; **il fait trop chaud, on ne tient plus ici** it's too hot — we can't stand it here any longer; **furieux, il n'a pas pu ~: il a protesté violemment** in a blazing fury he couldn't contain himself and he protested vehemently.

d (*être contenu dans*) ~ **dans** *ou* **à** *ou* **en** to fit in(to); **ils ne tiendront pas dans la pièce/la voiture** the room/the car will not hold them, they will not fit into the room/the car; **nous tenons à 4 à cette table** this table seats 4, we can get 4 round this table; **son discours tient en quelques pages** his speech takes up just a few pages, his speech is just a few pages long; **ma réponse tient en un seul mot: non** my answer is just one word long: no; **est-ce que la caisse tiendra en hauteur?** will the box fit in vertically?

e (*durer*) *[accord, beau temps]* to hold; *[couleur]* to be fast; *[mariage]* to last; *[fleurs]* to last (well); *[mise en plis]* to stay in.

f (†: *littér*) **faire ~ qch à qn** *lettre etc* to transmit *ou* communicate sth to sb.

g (*être contigu*) to adjoin. **le jardin tient à la ferme** the garden adjoins the farmhouse.

3 tenir à vt indir **a** (*aimer, priser*) *réputation, opinion de qn* to value, care about; *objet aimé* to be attached to, be fond of; *personne* to be attached to, be fond of, care for. **il ne tenait plus à la vie** he felt no further attachment to life, he no longer cared about living; **voudriez-vous un peu de vin? — je n'y tiens pas** would you like some wine? — not really *ou* not particularly *ou* I'm not that keen* (*Brit*).

b (*vouloir*) ~ **à** + *infin*, ~ **à ce que** + *subj* to be anxious to, be anxious that; **il tient beaucoup à vous connaître** he is very anxious *ou* keen (*Brit*) *ou* eager to meet you; **elle a tenu absolument à parler** she insisted on speaking; **il tient à ce que nous sachions ...** he insists *ou* is anxious that we should know ...; **si vous y tenez** if you really want to, if you insist; **tu viens avec nous? — si tu y tiens** are you coming with us? — if you really want me to *ou* if you insist.

c (*avoir pour cause*) to be due to, stem from. **ça tient au climat** it's because of the climate, it's due to the climate.

4 tenir de vt indir (*ressembler à*) *parent* to take after. **il tient de son père** he takes after his father; **il a de qui ~** it runs in the family; **sa réussite tient du prodige** his success is something of a miracle; **cela tient du comique et du tragique** there's something (both) comic and tragic about it, there are elements of both the comic and the tragic in it.

5 vb impers to depend. **il ne tient qu'à vous de décider** it's up to you to decide, the decision rests with you; **il ne tient qu'à elle que cela se fasse** it's entirely up to her whether it is done; **cela ne tient pas qu'à lui** it doesn't depend on him alone; **à quoi cela tient-il qu'il n'écrive pas?** how is it *ou* why is it that he doesn't write?; **qu'à cela ne tienne** never mind (that), that needn't matter, that's no problem; **cela tient à peu de chose** it's touch and go, it's in the balance.

6 se tenir vpr **a se ~ à qch** to hold on to sth; **ils se tenaient par la taille/le cou** they had their arms round each other's waist/neck; **ils se tenaient par la main** they were holding hands *ou* holding each other by the hand; **il se tenait le ventre de douleur** he was clutching *ou* holding his stomach in pain; **l'acrobate se tenait par les pieds** the acrobat hung on by his feet.

b (*être dans une position ou un état ou un lieu*) **se ~ debout/couché/à genoux** to be standing (up)/lying (down)/kneeling (down) *ou* on one's knees; **tenez-vous prêts à partir** be ready to leave; **elle se tenait à sa fenêtre/dans un coin de la pièce** she was standing at her window/in a corner of the room; **tiens-toi tranquille** (*lit*) keep still; (*fig: ne pas agir*) lie low; **tiens-toi bien** *ou* **droit** (*debout*) stand up straight; (*assis*) sit up (straight).

c (*se conduire*) to behave. **se ~ tranquille** to be quiet; **se ~ bien/mal** to behave well/badly; (*avertissement*) **vous n'avez plus qu'à bien vous ~!** you'd better behave yourself!, you just behave yourself!; **tenez-vous-le pour dit!** you've been warned once and for all!, you won't be warned *ou* told again!; **il ne se tient pas pour battu** he doesn't consider himself beaten.

d (*réunion etc: avoir lieu*) to be held. **le marché se tient là chaque semaine** the market is held there every week.

e (*être lié*) to hang *ou* hold together. **tous les faits se tiennent** all the facts hang *ou* hold together.

f (*se retenir: gén nég*) **il ne peut se ~ de rire/critiquer** he can't help laughing/criticizing; **il ne se tenait pas de joie** he couldn't contain his joy; **se ~ à quatre pour ne pas faire qch** to struggle to stop o.s. (from) doing sth, restrain o.s. forcibly from doing sth; **tiens-toi bien!** wait till you hear the next bit!

g **s'en ~ à** (*se limiter à*) to confine o.s. to, stick to; (*se satisfaire de*) to content o.s. with; **nous nous en tiendrons là pour aujourd'hui** we'll leave it at that for today; **il aimerait savoir à quoi s'en ~** he'd like to know where he stands; **je sais à quoi m'en ~ sur son compte** I know exactly who I'm dealing with, I know just the sort of man he is.

Tennessee [tenesi] **nm** Tennessee.

tennis [tenis] 1 **nm** a (*sport*) tennis. **~ sur gazon** lawn tennis; **~ sur terre battue** hard-court tennis; **~ en salle** indoor tennis; **~ de table** table tennis. b (*terrain*) (tennis) court. c (*partie*) game of tennis. **faire un ~** to have a game of tennis, play tennis. 2 **nmpl** (*chaussures*) tennis shoes; (*par extension, chaussures de gym*) trainers, plimsolls (*Brit*), gym shoes, sneakers.

tennisman [tenisman], **pl tennismen** [tenismɛn] **nm** tennis player.

tenniswoman [teniswuman], **pl tenniswomen** [teniswumɛn] **nf** tennis player.

tenon [tənɔ̃] **nm** (*Menuiserie*) tenon. **assemblage à ~ et mortaise** mortice and tenon joint.

ténor [tenɔʀ] 1 **nm** a (*Mus*) tenor. (*Mus*) **~ léger** light tenor. b (*fig*) (*Pol*) leading light, big name (*de* in); (*Sport*) star player, big name. 2 **adj** tenor.

tenseur [tɑ̃sœʀ] 1 **nm** a (*Anat, Math*) tensor. b (*Tech: dispositif*) [*fil de fer*] wire-strainer; [*ficelle de tente*] runner; [*chaîne de bicyclette*] chain-adjuster. 2 **adj m: muscle ~** tensor muscle.

tensiomètre [tɑ̃sjɔmɛtʀ] **nm** tensiometer.

tension [tɑ̃sjɔ̃] **nf** a (*état tendu*) [*ressort, cordes de piano, muscles*] tension; [*courroie*] tightness, tautness, tension. **chaîne à ~ réglable** adjustable tension chain; **corde de ~ d'une scie** tightening-cord of a saw.

b (*Phonétique*) (*phase d'articulation*) attack; (*état d'un phonème tendu*) tension, tenseness.

c (*Élec*) voltage, tension. **~ de 110 volts** tension of 110 volts; **à haute/basse ~** high-/low-voltage *ou* -tension (*épith*); **sous ~** (*lit*) live; (*fig*) under stress; **chute de ~** voltage drop, drop in voltage; **mettre un appareil sous ~** to switch on a piece of equipment.

d (*Méd*) **~ (artérielle)** blood pressure; **avoir de la ~** *ou* **trop de ~** to have (high) blood pressure *ou* hypertension (*SPÉC*); **prendre la ~ de qn** to take sb's blood pressure.

e (*fig*) [*relations*] tension (*de* in); [*situation*] tenseness (*de* of). **dans un état de ~ nerveuse** in a state of nervous tension *ou* stress; **~ entre deux pays/personnes/groupes** strained relationship between *ou* tension between two countries/people/groups.

f (*concentration, effort*) **~ d'esprit** sustained mental effort; (*littér*) **~ vers un but/idéal** striving *ou* straining towards a goal/an ideal.

g (*Phys*) [*liquide*] tension; [*vapeur*] pressure; (*Tech*) stress. **~ superficielle** surface tension.

tentaculaire [tɑ̃takylɛʀ] **adj** (*Zool*) tentacular. (*fig*) **villes ~s** sprawling towns; **firmes ~s** monster (international) combines.

tentacule [tɑ̃takyl] **nm** (*Zool, fig*) tentacle.

tentant, e [tɑ̃tɑ̃, ɑ̃t] **adj** *plat* tempting, inviting, enticing; *offre, projet* tempting, attractive, enticing.

tentateur, -trice [tɑ̃tatœʀ, tʀis] 1 **adj** *beauté* tempting, alluring, enticing; *propos* tempting, enticing. (*Rel*) **l'esprit ~** the Tempter. 2 **nm** tempter. (*Rel*) **le T~** the Tempter. 3 **tentatrice nf** temptress.

tentation [tɑ̃tasjɔ̃] **nf** temptation. (*Rel*) **la ~ de saint Antoine** the temptation of Saint Anthony; **résister à la ~** to resist temptation; **succomber à la ~** to yield to temptation.

tentative [tɑ̃tativ] **nf** (*gén*) attempt, endeavour; (*sportive, style journalistique*) bid, attempt. **de vaines ~s** vain attempts *ou* endeavours; **~ d'évasion** attempt *ou* bid to escape, escape bid *ou* attempt; **~ de meurtre/de suicide** (*gén*) murder/suicide attempt; (*Jur*) attempted murder/suicide; **faire une ~ auprès de qn (en vue de ...)** to approach sb (with a view to ...).

tente [tɑ̃t] 1 **nf** (*gén*) tent. **~ de camping** (camping) tent; **coucher sous la ~** to sleep under canvas, sleep out, camp out; (*fig*) **se retirer sous sa ~** to go and sulk in one's corner. 2 **comp** ►**tente-abri nf** (**pl tentes-abris**) shelter tent ►**tente de cirque** circus tent, marquee ►**tente à oxygène** (*Méd*) oxygen tent ►**tente de plage** beach tent.

tenté, e [tɑ̃te] (**ptp de tenter**) **adj: être ~ de faire/croire qch** to be tempted to do/believe sth.

tenter [tɑ̃te] 1 **vt** a (*chercher à séduire*) *personne* (*gén, Rel*) to tempt. **~ qn (par une offre)** to tempt sb (with an offer); **ce n'était pas cher, elle s'est laissée ~** it wasn't expensive and she yielded *ou* succumbed to the temptation; **c'est vraiment ~ le diable** it's really tempting fate *ou* Providence; **il ne faut pas ~ le diable** don't tempt fate, don't push your luck*.

b (*risquer*) *expérience, démarche* to try, attempt. **on a tout tenté pour le sauver** they tried everything to save him; **on a tenté l'impossible pour le sauver** they attempted the impossible to save him; **~ le tout pour le tout** to risk one's all; **~ la** *ou* **sa chance** to try one's luck; **~ le coup*** to have a go* *ou* a bash*, give it a try* *ou* a whirl*; **nous allons ~ l'expérience pour voir** we shall try the experiment to see.

c (*essayer*) **~ de faire** to attempt *ou* try to do; **je vais ~ de le convaincre** I'll try *ou* attempt *ou* endeavour to convince him, I'll try and convince him.

tenture [tɑ̃tyʀ] **nf** a (*tapisserie*) hanging. **~ murale** wall covering. b (*grands rideaux*) hanging, curtain, drape (*US*); (*derrière une porte*) door curtain. c (*de deuil*) funeral hangings.

tenu, e [t(ə)ny] (**ptp de tenir**) 1 **adj** a (*entretenu*) **bien ~** *enfant* well *ou* neatly turned out; *maison* well-kept, well looked after; **mal ~** *enfant* poorly turned out, untidy; *maison* poorly kept, poorly looked after.

b (*strictement surveillé*) **leurs filles sont très ~es** their daughters are kept on a tight rein *ou* are held very much in check.

c (*obligé*) **être ~ de faire** to be obliged to do, have to do; **être ~ au secret professionnel** to be bound by professional secrecy; *voir* **à**.

d (*Mus*) *note* held, sustained.

2 **tenue nf** a [*maison*] upkeep, running; [*magasin*] running; [*classe*] handling, control; [*séance*] holding; (*Mus*) [*note*] holding, sustaining. **la ~e des livres de comptes** the book-keeping; **~e fautive de la plume** wrong way of holding one's pen.

b (*conduite*) (good) manners (*pl*), good behaviour. **bonne ~e en classe/à table** good behaviour in class/at (the) table; **avoir de la/manquer de ~e** to have/lack good manners, know/not know how to behave (o.s.); **allons! un peu de ~e!** come on, behave yourself!, come on, watch your manners!; (*Fin*) **la bonne ~e du franc face au dollar** the good performance of the franc against the dollar.

c (*qualité*) [*journal*] standard, quality. **une publication qui a de la ~e** a publication of a high standard, a quality publication; **une publication de haute ~e** a quality publication.

d (*maintien*) posture. **mauvaise ~e d'un écolier** bad posture of a schoolboy.

e (*habillement, apparence*) dress, appearance; (*vêtements, uniforme*) dress. **leur ~e négligée** their sloppy dress *ou* appearance; **en ~e négligée** wearing *ou* in casual clothes; **~e d'intérieur** indoor clothes; **en ~e légère** (*vêtements légers*) wearing *ou* in light clothing; (*tenue osée*) scantily dressed *ou* clad; **en petite ~e** *homme* scantily dressed *ou* clad; *femme* scantily dressed *ou* clad, in one's undies (*hum*); **en grande ~e** in full dress (uniform); (*Mil*) **être en ~e** to be in uniform; **les policiers en ~e** uniformed policemen, policemen in uniform; (*Mil*) **~e camouflée/de campagne** camouflage/combat dress; **des touristes en ~e estivale/d'hiver** tourists in summer/winter clothes.

3 **comp** ►**tenue de combat** (*Mil*) battle dress ►**tenue de route** (*Aut*) road holding ►**tenue de service** uniform ►**tenue de soirée** formal *ou* evening dress; **"tenue de soirée de rigueur"** ≃ "black tie" ►**tenue de sport** sports clothes, sports gear ►**tenue de ville** [*homme*] lounge suit (*Brit*), town suit (*US*); [*femme*] town dress *ou* suit ►**tenue de vol** (*Aviat*) flying gear.

ténu, e [teny] **adj** (*littér*) *point, particule* fine; *fil* slender, fine; *brume* thin; *voix* thin, reedy; *raisons* tenuous, flimsy; *nuances, causes* tenuous, subtle.

ténuité [tenɥite] **nf** (*littér*) (*voir* **ténu**) fineness; slenderness; thinness; reediness; tenuousness, tenuity; flimsiness; subtlety.

tenure [tənyʀ] **nf** (*Hist Jur*) tenure.

téorbe [teɔʀb] **nm = théorbe.**

TEP [teəpe] (**abrév de tonne équivalent pétrole**) TOE.

tequila [tekila] **nf** tequila.

ter [tɛʀ] 1 **adj: il habite au 10 ~** he lives at (number) 10 B. 2 **adv** (*Mus*) three times, ter.

tératogène [teʀatɔʒɛn] **adj** teratogenic.

tératologie [teʀatɔlɔʒi] **nf** teratology.

tératologique [teʀatɔlɔʒik] **adj** teratological.

terbium [tɛʀbjɔm] **nm** terbium.

tercet [tɛʀsɛ] **nm** (*Poésie*) tercet, triplet.

térébenthine [teʀebɑ̃tin] **nf** turpentine. **nettoyer à l'essence de ~** *ou* **à la ~** to clean with turpentine *ou* turps* (*Brit*) *ou* turp (*US*).

térébinthe [teʀebɛ̃t] **nm** terebinth.

Tergal [tɛʀgal] **nm** ® Terylene ®.

tergiversations [tɛʀʒivɛʀsasjɔ̃] **nfpl** procrastination, humming and hawing (*NonC*), shilly-shallying* (*NonC*), pussyfooting* (about *ou* around) (*NonC*).

tergiverser [tɛʀʒivɛʀse] 1 **vi** to procrastinate, hum and haw, shilly-shally*, pussyfoot* (about *ou* around).

terme [tɛʀm] **nm** a (*mot, expression, Ling*) term; (*Math, Philos: élément*) term. (*formulation*) **~s** terms; **aux ~s du contrat** according to the terms of the contract; **en ~s clairs/voilés/flatteurs** in clear/veiled/flattering terms; **en d'autres ~s** in other words; **... et le ~ est faible ...** and that's putting it mildly, ... and that's an understatement; **~ de marine/de métier** nautical/professional term; *voir* **acception, force, moyen.**

b (*date limite*) time limit, deadline; (*littér: fin*) [*vie, voyage, récit*] end, term (*littér*). **passé ce ~** after this date; **se fixer un ~ pour ...** to set o.s. a time limit *ou* a deadline for ...; **arriver à ~** [*délai*] to expire;

[opération] to reach its *ou* a conclusion; *[paiement]* to fall due; **mettre un ~ à qch** to put an end *ou* a stop to sth; **mener qch à (son) ~** to bring sth to completion, carry sth through (to completion); **arrivé au ~ de sa vie** having reached the end *ou* the term (*littér*) of his life; **prévisions/projets à court/long ~** short-term *ou* short-range/long-term *ou* long-range forecasts/plans; **à ~ c'est ce qui arrivera** this is what will happen eventually *ou* sooner or later *ou* in the long run *ou* in the end.

c (*Méd*) **à ~** *accouchement* full-term; *naître* at term; **avant ~** *naître, accoucher* prematurely; **bébé né/naissance avant ~** premature baby/birth; **un bébé né 2 mois avant ~** a baby born 2 months premature, a 2-months premature baby.

d *[loyer]* (*date*) term, date for payment; (*période*) quarter, rental term *ou* period; (*somme*) (quarterly) rent (*NonC*). **payer à ~ échu** to pay at the end of the rental term, pay a quarter *ou* term in arrears; **le (jour du) ~** the term *ou* date for payment; **il a un ~ de retard** he's one quarter *ou* one payment behind (with his rent); **devoir/payer son ~** to owe/pay one's rent.

e (*Bourse, Fin*) **à ~** forward; **transaction à ~** (*Bourse de marchandises*) forward transaction; (*Bourse des valeurs*) settlement bargain; **marché à ~†** settlement market, forward market; **crédit/emprunt à court/long ~** short-term *ou* short-dated/long-term *ou* long-dated credit/loan, short/long credit/loan.

f (*relations*) **~s** terms; **être en bons/mauvais ~s avec qn** to be on good *ou* friendly/bad terms with sb; **ils sont dans les meilleurs ~s** they are on the best of terms.

terminaison [tɛʀminɛzɔ̃] **nf** (*Ling*) ending. (*Anat*) **~s nerveuses** nerve endings.

terminal, e, **mpl -aux** [tɛʀminal, o] 1 **adj** *élément, bourgeon, phase de maladie* terminal. (*Scol*) **classe ~e** final year, ≃ upper sixth (form) (*Brit*), senior year (*US*); **malade au stade ~** terminally ill patient. 2 **nm** a (*aérogare*) (air) terminal. b *[pétrole, marchandises]* terminal. **~ pétrolier** oil terminal; **~ maritime** shipping terminal. c (*ordinateur*) terminal. **~ intelligent/passif** smart *ou* intelligent/dumb terminal; **~ de paiement électronique** electronic payment terminal; **~ point de vente** point-of-sale *ou* POS terminal. 3 **terminale nf** (*Scol*) *voir* **1**.

terminer [tɛʀmine] [1] 1 **vt** a (*clore*) *débat, séance* to bring to an end *ou* to a close, terminate.

b (*achever*) *travail* to finish (off), complete; *repas* to finish, end; *vacances, temps d'exil* to end, finish; *récit, débat* to finish, close, end. **il termina en nous réprimandant** he finished (up *ou* off) *ou* he ended by giving us a reprimand; **j'ai terminé ainsi ma journée** and so I ended my day; **nous avons terminé la journée/soirée chez un ami/par une promenade** we finished off *ou* ended the day/evening at a friend's house/with a walk; **~ ses jours à la campagne/à l'hôpital** to end one's days in the country/in hospital; **~ un repas par un café** to finish off *ou* round off *ou* end a meal with a coffee; **~ un livre par quelques conseils pratiques** to end a book with a few pieces of practical advice; **en avoir terminé avec un travail** to be finished with a job; **j'en ai terminé avec eux** I am *ou* have finished with them, I have done with them; **pour ~ je dirais que ...** in conclusion *ou* to conclude I would say that ..., and finally I would say that ...; **j'attends qu'il termine** I'm waiting for him to finish, I'm waiting till he's finished.

c (*former le dernier élément*) **le café termina le repas** the meal finished *ou* ended with coffee, coffee finished off *ou* concluded *ou* ended the meal; **un bourgeon termine la tige** the stalk ends in a bud.

2 **se terminer vpr** a (*prendre fin*) *[rue, domaine]* to end, terminate (*frm*); *[affaire, repas, vacances]* to (come to an) end. **les vacances se terminent demain** the holidays finish *ou* (come to an) end tomorrow; **le parc se termine ici** the park ends here; **ça s'est bien/mal terminé** it ended well/badly, it turned out well *ou* all right/badly (in the end); **alors ces travaux, ça se termine?** well, is the work just about complete *ou* done?; (*impatience*) when's the work going to be finished?

b (*s'achever sur*) **se ~ par** to end with; **la thèse se termine par une bibliographie** the thesis ends with a bibliography; **la soirée se termina par un jeu** the evening ended with a game; **ces verbes se terminent par le suffixe "ir"** these verbs end in the suffix "ir".

c (*finir en*) **se ~ en** to end in; **les mots qui se terminent en "ation"** words which end in "ation"; **cette comédie se termine en tragédie** this comedy ends in tragedy; **se ~ en pointe** to end in a point.

terminologie [tɛʀminɔlɔʒi] **nf** terminology.

terminologique [tɛʀminɔlɔʒik] **adj** terminological.

terminologue [tɛʀminɔlɔg] **nmf** terminologist.

terminus [tɛʀminys] **nm** *[autobus, train]* terminus. **~! tout le monde descend!** (last stop!) all change!

termite [tɛʀmit] **nm** termite, white ant.

termitière [tɛʀmitjɛʀ] **nf** ant-hill, termitary (*SPÉC*).

ternaire [tɛʀnɛʀ] **adj** compound.

terne [tɛʀn] **adj** *teint* colourless, lifeless; *regard* lifeless, lacklustre; *personne* dull, colourless, drab; *style, conversation* dull, drab, lacklustre; *couleur, journée, vie* dull, drab.

terni, e [tɛʀni] (**ptp de ternir**) **adj** *argenterie, métal, réputation* tarnished; *glace* dulled.

ternir [tɛʀniʀ] [2] 1 **vt** a (*lit*) *métal* to tarnish; *glace, meuble* to dull; *teint* to drain of colour. b (*fig*) *mémoire, honneur, réputation* to stain, tarnish, sully, besmirch. 2 **se ternir vpr** *[métal]* to tarnish, become tarnished; *[glace]* to (become) dull; *[réputation]* to become tarnished *ou* stained.

ternissement [tɛʀnismɑ̃] **nm** *[métal]* tarnishing; *[glace]* dulling.

ternissure [tɛʀnisyʀ] **nf** (*voir* **terni**) (*aspect*) tarnish, tarnished condition; dullness; (*tache*) tarnished spot; dull spot.

terrain [teʀɛ̃] 1 **nm** a (*relief*) ground, terrain (*SPÉC, littér*); (*sol*) soil, ground. **~ caillouteux/vallonné** stony/hilly ground; **~ meuble/lourd** loose/heavy soil *ou* ground; **c'est un bon ~ pour la culture** it's (a) good soil for cultivation; *voir* **accident, glissement, tout.**

b (*Ftbl, Rugby*) pitch, field; (*avec les installations*) ground; (*Courses, Golf*) course. **~ de basket-ball** basketball court; **sur le ~** on the field; **disputer un match sur ~ adverse/sur son propre ~** to play an away/a home match.

c (*Comm: étendue de terre*) land (*NonC*); (*parcelle*) plot (of land), piece of land; (*à bâtir*) site. **~ à lotir** land for dividing into plots; **chercher un ~ convenable pour un bâtiment** to look for a suitable site for a building; **"~ à bâtir"** "site *ou* building land for sale"; **une maison avec 2 hectares de ~** a house with 2 hectares of land; **le prix du ~ à Paris** the price of land in Paris.

d (*Géog, Géol: souvent pl*) formation. **les ~s primaires/glaciaires** primary/glacial formations.

e (*Mil*) (*lieu d'opérations*) terrain; (*gagné ou perdu*) ground. **en ~ ennemi** on enemy ground *ou* territory; **disputer le ~** (*Mil*) to fight for every inch of ground; (*fig*) to fight every inch of the way; (*lit, fig*) **céder/gagner/perdre du ~** to give/gain/lose ground; **céder du ~ à l'ennemi** to lose *ou* yield ground to the enemy, fall back before the enemy; *[négociateurs]* **ils finiront par céder du ~** in the end they'll make concessions; **l'épidémie cède du ~ devant les efforts des médecins** the epidemic is receding before the doctors' efforts; **la livre a cédé/gagné du ~** the pound has lost/gained ground (*par rapport à* against); **reconnaître le ~** (*lit*) to reconnoitre the terrain; (*fig*) to see how the land lies, get the lie (*Brit*) *ou* lay (*US*) of the land; (*fig*) **sonder** *ou* **tâter le ~** to test the ground, put out feelers; **avoir l'avantage du ~** (*lit*) to have territorial advantage; (*fig*) to have the advantage of being on (one's) home ground; **préparer/déblayer le ~** to prepare/clear the ground; **aller/être sur le ~** to go out into/be out in the real world *ou* in the field.

f (*fig: domaine, sujet*) ground. **être sur son ~** to be on home ground *ou* territory; **trouver un ~ d'entente** to find common ground *ou* an area of agreement; **chercher un ~ favorable à la discussion** to seek an area conducive to (useful) discussion; **je ne le suivrai pas sur ce ~** I can't go along with him there *ou* on that, I'm not with him on that; **être en** *ou* **sur un ~ mouvant** to be on uncertain ground; **être sur un ~ glissant** to be on slippery *ou* dangerous ground; **le journaliste s'aventura sur un ~ brûlant** the journalist ventured onto dangerous ground *ou* risked tackling a highly sensitive *ou* ticklish issue; **l'épidémie a trouvé un ~ très favorable chez les réfugiés** the epidemic found an ideal breeding ground amongst the refugees; (*Méd*) **~ allergique** conditions likely to produce allergies.

2 **comp** ►**terrain d'atterrissage** landing ground ►**terrain d'aviation** airfield ►**terrain de camping** campsite, camping ground ►**terrain de chasse** hunting ground ►**terrain d'exercice** training ground ►**terrain de jeu** playing field ►**terrain militaire** army ground ►**terrain de sport** sports ground ►**terrain de tir** shooting *ou* firing range ►**terrain vague** waste ground (*NonC*), wasteland (*NonC*).

terrasse [teʀas] **nf** a *[parc, jardin]* terrace. **cultures en ~s** terrace cultivation; (*Géog*) **~ fluviale** river terrace. b *[appartement]* terrace; (*sur le toit*) terrace roof. **toiture en ~, toit-~** flat roof. c *[café]* terrace, pavement (area). **j'ai aperçu Charles attablé à la ~ du Café Royal** I saw Charles sitting at the terrace of the Café Royal *ou* outside the Café Royal; **à la** *ou* **en ~** outside; **il refusa de me servir à la** *ou* **en ~** he refused to serve me outside. d (*Constr: métier*) excavation work. **faire de la ~** to do excavation work.

terrassement [teʀasmɑ̃] **nm** a (*action*) excavation. **travaux de ~** excavation works; **engins de ~** earth-moving *ou* excavating equipment. b (*terres creusées*) **~s** excavations, earthworks; *[voie ferrée]* embankments.

terrasser [teʀase] [1] **vt** a *personne [adversaire]* to floor, bring down; *[attaque]* to bring down; (*fig*) *[fatigue]* to overcome; *[émotion, nouvelle]* to overwhelm; *[maladie]* to strike down. **cette maladie l'a terrassé** this illness laid him low; **terrassé par une crise cardiaque** struck down *ou* felled by a heart attack. b (*Tech*) to excavate, dig out; (*Agr*) to dig over.

terrassier [teʀasje] **nm** unskilled road worker, navvy (*Brit*).

terre[1] [tɛʀ] 1 **nf** a (*planète*) earth; (*monde*) world. **la planète T~** the planet Earth; **Dieu créa le Ciel et la T~** God created the Heavens and the Earth, God created Heaven and Earth; **il a parcouru la ~ entière** he has travelled the world over, he has travelled all over the globe; **prendre à témoin la ~ entière** to take the world as one's witness; **tant qu'il y aura des hommes sur la ~** as long as there are men on (the) earth; **être seul sur (la) ~** to be alone in (all) the world; **il ne faut pas s'attendre au bonheur sur (cette) ~** happiness is not to be expected in this world *ou* on this earth; (*fig*) **redescendre** *ou* **revenir sur ~** to come down *ou* back to earth; *voir* **remuer, sel, ventre.**

b (*sol: surface*) ground, land; (*matière*) earth, soil; (*pour la poterie*) clay. **pipe/vase en ~** clay pipe/vase; **ne t'allonge pas par ~, la ~ est humide** don't lie on the ground – it's damp, don't lie down – the ground is damp; **une ~ fertile/aride** a fertile/an arid *ou* a barren soil; **retourner/labourer la ~** to turn over/work the soil; **travailler la ~** to work the soil *ou* land; **planter des arbres en pleine ~** to plant trees in the (open) ground; **poser qch à** *ou* **par ~** to put sth (down) on the ground; **jeter qch à** *ou* **par ~** to throw sth (down) on the ground, throw sth to the ground; **cela fiche** *ou* **flanque tous nos projets par ~*** that throws all our plans out of the window, that really messes up all our plans*, that puts paid to all our plans; **mettre qn en ~** to bury sb; **mettre qch en ~** to put sth into the soil; **5 mètres sous ~** 5 metres underground; (*fig*) **être à six pieds sous ~** to be six feet under, be pushing up the daisies*; (*fig: de honte*) **j'aurais voulu rentrer sous ~** I wished the earth would swallow me up, I could have died*; *voir* **chemin, motte, toucher, ver.**

c (*étendue, campagne*) **~(s)** land (*NonC*); **une bande** *ou* **langue de ~** a strip *ou* tongue of land; **retourner à la/aimer la ~** to return to/love the land; **des ~s à blé** corn-growing land; **il a acheté un bout** *ou* **un lopin de ~** he's bought a piece *ou* patch *ou* plot of land; **~s cultivées** cultivated land; **~s en friche** *ou* **en jachère/incultes** fallow/uncultivated land.

d (*par opposition à mer*) land (*NonC*). **sur la ~ ferme** on dry land, on terra firma; **apercevoir la ~** to sight land; (*Naut*) **~!** land ho!; (*Naut*) **aller à ~** to go ashore; **dans les ~s** inland; **aller/voyager par (voie de) ~** to go/travel by land *ou* overland; *voir* **toucher.**

e (*propriété, domaine*) land (*gén NonC*). **la ~** land; **une ~** an estate; **il a acheté une ~ en Normandie** he's bought an estate *ou* some land in Normandy; **vivre sur/de ses ~s** to live on/off one's lands *ou* estates; **se retirer sur ses ~s** to go and live on one's country estate; **la ~ est un excellent investissement** land is an excellent investment.

f (*pays, région*) land, country. **sa ~ natale** his native land *ou* country; **la France, ~ d'accueil** France, (the) land of welcome; **~s lointaines/australes** distant/southern lands; **la T~ promise** the Promised Land.

g (*Élec*) earth (*Brit*), ground (*US*). **mettre** *ou* **relier à la ~** to earth (*Brit*), ground (*US*); *voir* **pris.**

2 **comp ►la Terre Adélie** the Adélie Coast, Adélie Land **►terre battue** hard-packed surface; (*Tennis*) **jouer sur terre battue** to play on a hard court **►terre brûlée: politique de la terre brûlée** (*fig*) scorched earth policy **►terre de bruyère** heath-mould, heath-peat **►terre cuite** (*pour briques, tuiles*) baked clay; (*pour jattes, statuettes*) terracotta; **objets en terre cuite, terres cuites** terracotta ware (*NonC*); **une terre cuite** a terracotta (object) **►la Terre de Feu** Tierra del Fuego **►terre à foulon** fuller's earth **►terre glaise** clay **►terre-neuvas nm (pl terres-neuvas)** (*bateau*) fishing boat (*for fishing off Newfoundland*); (*marin*) fisherman, trawlerman (*who fishes off Newfoundland*) **►Terre-Neuve nf** Newfoundland **►terre-neuve nm inv** (*chien*) Newfoundland terrier; (*fig*) **cet homme est un vrai terre-neuve** that man's a real (good) Samaritan! **►terre-neuvien, -ienne adj** Newfoundland (*épith*) **►Terre-Neuvien(ne) nm,f (mpl Terre-Neuviens)** Newfoundlander **►terre-neuvier nm (pl terre-neuviers) = terre-neuvas ►terre noire** (*Géog*) chernozem **►terre-plein nm (pl terre-pleins)** (*Mil*) terreplein; (*Constr*) platform; (*sur chaussée*) central reservation (*Brit*), center divider strip (*US*) **►terre à potier** potter's clay **►terres rares** (*Chim*) rare earths **►la Terre sainte** the Holy Land **►terre de Sienne** sienna **►terre à terre, terre-à-terre adj inv** *esprit* down-to-earth, matter-of-fact; *personne* down-to-earth, unimaginative, prosaic; *préoccupations* mundane, workaday, prosaic **►terres vierges** virgin lands.

terre² [tɛʀ] **nf** (*poisson*) sting ray.

terreau [tɛʀo] **nm** compost. **~ de feuilles** leaf mould.

terrer [teʀe] [1] 1 **se terrer vpr** a [*personne poursuivie*] to flatten o.s., crouch down; [*criminel recherché*] to lie low, go to ground *ou* earth; [*personne peu sociable*] to hide (o.s.) away. **terrés dans la cave pendant les bombardements** hidden *ou* buried (away) in the cellar during the bombings. b [*lapin, renard*] (*dans son terrier*) to go to earth *ou* ground; (*contre terre*) to crouch down, flatten itself. 2 **vt** (*Agr*) *arbre* to earth round *ou* up; *pelouse* to spread with soil; *semis* to earth over; (*Tech*) *drap* to full.

terrestre [tɛʀɛstʀ] **adj** a *faune, flore, transports, habitat* land (*épith*); *surface, magnétisme* earth's (*épith*), terrestrial, of earth. (*Mil*) **effectifs ~s** land forces; (*Mil*) **missile ~** land-based missile; *voir* **croûte, écorce, globe.** b (*d'ici-bas*) *biens, plaisirs, vie* earthly, terrestrial; *voir* **paradis.**

terreur [tɛʀœʀ] **nf** a (*peur*) terror (*gén NonC*). **avec ~** with terror *ou* dread; **vaines ~s** vain *ou* empty fears; **le dentiste était ma grande ~** the dentist was my greatest fear, I was terrified of the dentist; **il vivait dans la ~ d'être découvert/de la police** he lived in terror of being discovered/of the police. b (*terrorisme*) terror. (*Hist*) **la T~** the (Reign of) Terror. c (* *hum: personne*) terror. **petite ~** little terror *ou* horror; **jouer les ~s** to play the tough guy*; **on l'appelait Joe la ~** he was known as Joe, the tough guy*; **c'est la ~ de la ville** he's the terror of the town.

terreux, -euse [tɛʀø, øz] **adj** a *goût, odeur* earthy. b *sabots* muddy; *mains* grubby, soiled; *salade* gritty, dirty. c *teint* sallow, muddy; *ciel* muddy, leaden, sullen.

terri [tɛʀi] **nm = terril.**

terrible [teʀibl] 1 **adj** a (*effroyable*) *accident, maladie, châtiment* terrible, dreadful, awful; *arme* terrible.

b (*terrifiant, féroce*) *guerrier, air, menaces* terrible, fearsome.

c (*intensif*) *vent, force, pression, bruit, colère* terrific, tremendous, fantastic. **c'est un ~ menteur** he's a terrible *ou* an awful liar; **c'est ~ ce qu'il peut manger** it's terrific *ou* fantastic what he can eat*.

d (*affligeant, pénible*) terrible, dreadful, awful. **c'est ~ d'en arriver là** it's terrible *ou* awful *ou* dreadful to come to this; **le ~ est qu'il refuse qu'on l'aide** the awful *ou* dreadful part about it is that he refuses to be helped; **il est ~, avec sa manie de toujours vous contredire** he's awful *ou* dreadful, the way he's always contradicting you *ou* with his habit of always contradicting you; **c'est ~ de devoir toujours tout répéter** it's awful *ou* dreadful always having to repeat everything; *voir* **enfant.**

e (*: *formidable*) *film, soirée, personne* terrific*, great*, tremendous*. **ce film n'est pas ~** this film is nothing special *ou* nothing marvellous *ou* nothing to write home about *ou* no great shakes* (*Brit*).

2 **adv** (‡) **ça marche ~** it's working fantastically (well)* *ou* really great‡.

terriblement [teʀibləmɑ̃] **adv** a (*extrêmement*) terribly, dreadfully, awfully. b (†: *affreusement*) terribly†.

terrien, -ienne [tɛʀjɛ̃, jɛn] 1 **adj** a landed (*épith*), landowning (*épith*). **propriétaire ~** landowner, landed proprietor. b **vertus ~nes** virtues of the soil *ou* land; **avoir une vieille ascendance ~ne** to come of old country stock. 2 **nm** a (*paysan*) man of the soil, countryman. b (*habitant de la Terre*) Earthman, earthling. c (*non-marin*) landsman. 3 **terrienne nf** (*voir* **2**) countrywoman; Earthwoman, earthling; landswoman.

terrier [tɛʀje] **nm** a (*tanière*) [*lapin, taupe*] burrow, hole; [*renard*] earth. b (*chien*) terrier.

terrifiant, e [tɛʀifjɑ̃, jɑ̃t] **adj** a (*effrayant*) terrifying. b (*sens affaibli*) *progrès, appétit* fearsome, incredible. **c'est ~ comme il a maigri/grandi!** it's awful *ou* frightening how much weight he has lost/how tall he has grown!

terrifier [tɛʀifje] [7] **vt** to terrify.

terril [tɛʀi(l)] **nm** (coal) tip, slag heap.

terrine [tɛʀin] **nf** (*pot*) earthenware vessel, terrine; (*Culin*) (*récipient*) terrine; (*pâté*) pâté; (‡: *tête*) head, noddle‡. **~ du chef** chef's special pâté.

territoire [tɛʀitwaʀ] **nm** (*gén, Pol, Zool*) territory; [*département, commune*] area; [*évêque, juge*] jurisdiction. **~s d'outre-mer** (French) overseas territories; *voir* **aménagement, surveillance.**

territorial, e, mpl -iaux [tɛʀitɔʀjal, jo] 1 **adj** a *puissance* land (*épith*); *intégrité, modifications* territorial. **eaux ~es** territorial waters; **armée ~e** Territorial Army. b (*Jur: opposé à personnel*) territorial. 2 **nm** (*Mil*) Territorial. 3 **territoriale nf** (*Mil*) Territorial Army.

territorialité [tɛʀitɔʀjalite] **nf** (*Jur*) territoriality.

terroir [tɛʀwaʀ] **nm** a (*Agr*) soil. **vin qui a un goût de ~** wine which has a taste *ou* tang of its soil. b (*fig: région rurale*) **accent du ~** country *ou* rural accent, brogue; **mots du ~** words with a rural flavour; **il sent son ~** he is very much of his native heath *ou* soil; **poète du ~** poet of the land.

terrorisant, e [tɛʀɔʀizɑ̃, ɑ̃t] **adj** terrifying.

terroriser [tɛʀɔʀize] [1] **vt** to terrorize.

terrorisme [tɛʀɔʀism] **nm** terrorism.

terroriste [tɛʀɔʀist] **adj, nmf** terrorist.

tertiaire [tɛʀsjɛʀ] 1 **adj** (*Géol, Méd*) tertiary. (*Écon*) **(secteur) ~** service industries, tertiary sector (*SPÉC*), tertiary industry (*SPÉC*). 2 **nm** (*Géol*) Tertiary; (*Écon*) service sector, tertiary sector, tertiary industry.

tertiarisation [tɛʀsjaʀizasjɔ̃] **nf** expansion *ou* development of the service sector.

tertio [tɛʀsjo] **adv** third(ly).

tertre [tɛʀtʀ] **nm** (*monticule*) hillock, mound, knoll (*littér*); [*sépulture*] (burial) mound.

tes [te] *voir* **ton¹.**

tessiture [tesityʀ] **nf** [*voix*] tessitura; [*instrument*] range.

tesson [tesɔ̃] **nm: ~ (de bouteille)** shard, sliver *ou* piece of broken glass *ou* bottle.

test¹ [tɛst] 1 **nm** (*gén*) test. **faire passer un ~ à qn** to give sb a test; **soumettre qn à des ~s** to subject sb to tests, test sb; **~ d'intelligence** IQ test; **~ d'orientation professionnelle** vocational *ou* occupational test; **~ d'aptitude/psychologique** *ou* **de personnalité** aptitude/personality test; **~ de grossesse** pregnancy test; **~ du SIDA** AIDS test; **~ biologique** biological test. 2 **adj: conflit-/région-~** test conflict/area.

test² [tɛst] **nm** (*Zool*) test.

test³ [tɛst] **nm = têt.**

testable [tɛstabl] **adj** testable.

testament [tɛstamɑ̃] 1 **nm** a (*Rel*) **Ancien/Nouveau T~** Old/New Testament.

b (*Jur*) will, testament (*Jur*). **mourir sans ~** to die intestate (*Jur, frm*) *ou* without leaving a will; **ceci est mon ~** this is my last will and testament; (hum) il peut faire son ~* he can ou he'd better make out his will (hum); voir coucher, léguer.

c (fig) [homme politique, artiste] legacy. le ~ politique de Jaurès Jaurès' political legacy.

2 comp ▸testament par acte public, testament authentique will dictated to notary in the presence of witnesses ▸testament mystique will written or dictated by testator, signed by him, and handed in sealed envelope, before witnesses, to notary ▸testament olographe will written, dated and signed by the testator ▸testament secret = testament mystique.

testamentaire [tɛstamɑ̃tɛʀ] adj: dispositions ~s clauses ou provisions of a will, devises (SPÉC); donation ~ bequest, legacy; héritier ~ devisee, legatee; voir exécuteur.

testateur [tɛstatœʀ] nm testator, devisor, legator.

testatrice [tɛstatʀis] nf testatrix, devisor, legator.

tester¹ [tɛste] 1 vt to test.

tester² [tɛste] 1 vi to make (out) one's will.

testicule [tɛstikyl] nm testicle, testis (SPÉC).

testostérone [tɛstɔsteʀɔn] nf testosterone.

têt [tɛ(t)] nm (Chim) ~ à rôtir roasting dish ou crucible; ~ à gaz beehive shelf.

tétanie [tetani] nf tetany.

tétanique [tetanik] adj convulsions tetanic; patient tetanus (épith), suffering from tetanus (attrib).

tétanisation [tetanizasjɔ̃] nf [muscle] tetanization.

tétaniser [tetanize] 1 vt to tetanize.

tétanos [tetanos] nm (maladie) tetanus, lockjaw; (contraction) tetanus. ~ musculaire ou physiologique tetanus (of a muscle); vaccin contre le ~ tetanus vaccine.

têtard [tɛtaʀ] nm (Zool) tadpole.

tête [tɛt] 1 nf a (gén) [homme, animal] head; (chevelure) hair (NonC). être ~ nue, n'avoir rien sur la ~ to be bareheaded, have nothing on one's head; avoir une ~ frisée to have curly hair, have a curly head of hair; avoir mal à la ~ to have a headache; j'ai la ~ lourde my head feels heavy; avoir la ~ sale/propre to have dirty/clean hair; de la ~ aux pieds from head to foot ou toe, from top to toe; veau à deux ~s two-headed calf; se tenir la ~ à deux mains to hold one's head in one's hands; rester la ~ en bas to hang upside down; coup de ~ (lit) head-butt; (fig) sudden impulse; donner un coup de ~ à qn to head-butt sb; donner des coups de ~ contre qch to bang one's head against sth; (fig) agir sur un coup de ~ to act on impulse; voir fromage, hocher.

b (fig: vie) head, neck. réclamer la ~ de qn to demand sb's head; jurer sur la ~ de qn to swear on sb's life ou head; risquer sa ~ to risk one's neck; sauver sa ~ to save one's skin ou neck; il y va de sa ~ his life is at stake.

c (visage, expression) face. il a une ~ sympathique he has a friendly face; il a une ~ sinistre he has a sinister look about him, he looks an ugly customer; il a une bonne ~ he looks a decent sort; quand il a appris la nouvelle il a fait une (drôle de) ~! he pulled a face when he heard the news!, you should have seen his face when he heard the news!; il en fait une ~! what a face!, just look at his face!; faire la ~ to sulk, have the sulks* (Brit); faire une ~ d'enterrement ou de six pieds de long to have a face as long as a fiddle; quelle (sale) ~ il a! he looks a nasty piece of work (Brit), he has a really nasty look about him; je connais cette ~-là! I know that face; mettre un nom sur une ~ to put a name to a face; il a ou c'est une ~ à claques* ou à gifles* he has got the sort of face you'd love to smack ou that just asks to be smacked.

d (unité) head. ~ couronnée crowned head; (animal) 20 ~s de bétail 20 head of cattle; des ~s vont tomber heads will roll; le repas coûtera 150 F par ~ ou par ~ de pipe** the meal will cost 150 francs a head ou 150 francs per person ou 150 francs apiece.

e (mesure) head. il a une ~ de plus he is a head taller; il a une demi-~ de plus que moi he's half a head taller than me; (Courses) gagner d'une ~ to win by a head.

f [clou, marteau] head; [arbre] top. ~ d'ail head of garlic; ~ d'artichaut artichoke head; ~ d'épingle pinhead; gros comme une ~ d'épingle no bigger than a pinhead; à la ~ du lit at the head of the bed.

g (partie antérieure) [train, procession] front, head; (Mil) [colonne, peloton] head. (Rail) voiture de ~ front coach; on monte en ~ ou en queue? shall we get on at the front or (at) the back?; être en ~ to be in the lead ou in front; ils sont entrés dans la ville, musique en ~ they came into the town led ou headed by the band; tué à la ~ de ses troupes killed leading his troops ou at the head of his troops; voir soupape.

h [page, liste, chapitre, classe] top, head. (Presse) article de ~ leading article, leader (column); en ~ de phrase at the beginning of the sentence; être ou venir en ~ de liste to head the list, come at the head ou top of the list; être à la ~ d'un mouvement/d'une affaire to be at the head of a movement/a business, head (up) a movement/a business; être la ~ d'un mouvement/d'une affaire to be the leader of a movement/a business, head up a movement/a business.

i (faculté(s) mentale(s)) avoir (toute) sa ~ to have (all) one's wits about one; n'avoir rien dans la ~ to be empty-headed; où ai-je la ~? whatever am I thinking of?; avoir une petite ~ to be dim-witted; alors, petite ~!* well, dimwit!*; avoir ou être une ~ sans cervelle ou en l'air ou de linotte to be scatterbrained, be a scatterbrain; avoir de la ~ to have a good head on one's shoulders; avoir la ~ sur les épaules to be level-headed; femme/homme de ~ level-headed ou capable woman/man; calculer qch de ~ to work sth out in one's head; je n'ai plus le chiffre/le nom en ~ I can't recall the number/the name, the number/the name has gone (clean) out of my head; chercher qch dans sa ~ to search one's memory for sth; mettre ou fourrer* qch dans la ~ de qn to put ou get ou stick* sth into sb's head; se mettre dans la ~ ou en ~ que (s'imaginer) to get it into one's head that; se mettre dans la ou en ~ de faire qch (se décider) to take it into one's head to do sth; j'ai la ~ vide my mind is a blank ou has gone blank; avoir la ~ à ce que l'on fait to have one's mind on what one is doing; avoir la ~ ailleurs to have one's mind on other matters ou elsewhere; se casser ou se creuser la ~ to rack one's brains; ils ne se sont pas cassé ou creusé la ~! they didn't exactly put themselves out! ou overexert themselves!; n'en faire qu'à sa ~ to do (exactly) as one pleases, please o.s., go one's own (sweet) way; (faire qch) à ~ reposée (to do sth) in a more leisurely moment; voir idée, perdre.

j (tempérament) avoir la ~ chaude/froide to be quick- ou fiery-tempered/cool-headed; avoir la ~ dure to be thick(headed) ou a thick-head ou blockheaded* ou a blockhead*; c'est une forte ~ he (ou she) is a rebel; avoir ou être une ~ de mule* ou de bois* ou de lard* ou de cochon*, être une ~ de pioche* to be as stubborn as a mule, be mulish ou pigheaded; il fait sa mauvaise ~ he's being awkward ou difficult; avoir la ~ près du bonnet to be quick-tempered; voir coup.

k (Ftbl) header. faire une ~ to head the ball.

l (loc) (fig) aller ou marcher la ~ haute to walk with one's head held high, carry one's head high; (fig) avoir la ~ basse to hang one's head; (lit) courir ou foncer ~ baissée to rush ou charge headlong; (fig) y aller ~ baissée to charge in blindly; (fig) se jeter ou donner ~ baissée dans entreprise, piège to rush headlong into; garder la ~ froide to keep a cool head, remain cool, keep one's head; tomber la ~ la première to fall headfirst; jeter ou lancer à la ~ de qn que ... to hurl in sb's face that ...; en avoir par-dessus la ~ to be fed up to the back teeth*; c'est à se cogner ou se taper la ~ contre les murs it's enough to drive you up the wall*; j'en donnerais ma ~ à couper I would stake my life on it; ne plus savoir où donner de la ~ not to know which way to turn; prendre la ~ to take the lead, take charge; prendre la ~ du cortège to lead the procession, take one's place at the head of the procession; il me prend la ~** he's a pain in the neck* ou arse** (Brit) ou ass** (US); faire une ~ au carré à qn** to smash sb's face in**, knock sb's block off**; tenir ~ à to stand up to; avoir ses ~s* to have one's favourites; mettre la ~ de qn à prix to put a price on sb's head; se trouver à la ~ d'une petite fortune/de 2 maisons to find o.s. the owner ou possessor of a small fortune/2 houses; voir martel, payer, tourner.

2 comp ▸tête d'affiche (Théât) top of the bill; être la tête d'affiche to head the bill, be top of the bill ▸tête-bêche adv head to foot ou tail; timbre tête-bêche tête-bêche stamp ▸tête de bielle (Aut) big end ▸tête blonde* (fig: enfant) little one ▸tête brûlée (baroudeur) desperado ▸tête chercheuse (lit) homing device; (fig) (groupe) pioneering research group; (personne) pioneering researcher; fusée à tête chercheuse homing rocket ▸tête de cuvée tête de cuvée ▸tête de Delco ® (Aut) distributor ▸tête d'écriture (Ordin) writing head ▸tête d'enregistrement recording head ▸tête d'injection (Tech) swivel ▸tête de lecture [pick-up] pickup head; [magnétophone] playback head; (Ordin) reading head; (Ordin) tête de lecture-écriture read-write head ▸tête de ligne terminus, start of the line (Rail) ▸tête de liste (Pol) chief candidate (in list system of voting) ▸tête de lit bedhead ▸tête-de-loup nf (pl têtes-de-loup) ceiling brush ▸tête de mort (emblème) death's-head; [pavillon] skull and crossbones, Jolly Roger; (Zool) death's-head moth; (Culin) Gouda cheese ▸tête-de-nègre adj inv dark brown, nigger-brown (Brit) ▸tête de nœud** prick**, dick-head** ▸tête nucléaire nuclear warhead ▸tête d'œuf (péj) egg-head ▸tête de pont (au-delà d'un fleuve) bridgehead; (au-delà de la mer) beachhead; (fig) bridgehead ▸tête-à-queue nm inv spin; faire un tête-à-queue [cheval] to turn about; [voiture] to spin round ▸tête de série (Tennis) seeded player; il était classé troisième tête de série he was seeded third; il est tête de série numéro 2 he's the number 2 seed ▸tête-à-tête nm inv (conversation) tête-à-tête, private conversation; (meuble) tête-à-tête; (service) breakfast set for two (ou tea ou coffee set for two); en tête-à-tête alone together; dîner en tête-à-tête intimate dinner for two; discussion en tête-à-tête discussion in private ▸tête de Turc whipping boy, Aunt Sally.

tétée [tete] nf (action) sucking; (repas, lait) feed (Brit), nursing (US). 5 ~s par jour 5 feeds (Brit) ou nursings (US) a day; l'heure de la ~ feeding (Brit) ou nursing (US) time (of baby).

téter [tete] 6 vt a lait to suck; biberon, sein to suck at. ~ sa mère to suck at one's mother's breast; donner à ~ à un bébé to feed a baby (at the breast), suckle a baby†. b (*) pouce to suck; pipe to suck at ou on.

têtière [tɛtjɛʀ] nf [cheval] headstall; [divan] antimacassar; [voile] head.

tétine [tetin] nf [vache] udder, dug (SPÉC); [truie] teat, dug (SPÉC);

[biberon] teat (*Brit*), nipple (*US*); (*sucette*) comforter, dummy (*Brit*), pacifier (*US*).
téton [tetɔ̃] **nm** a (*: *sein*) breast, tit** b (*Tech: saillie*) stud, nipple.
tétrachlorure [tetʀaklɔʀyʀ] **nm** tetrachloride. ~ **de carbone** carbon tetrachloride.
tétracorde [tetʀakɔʀd] **nm** tetrachord.
tétraèdre [tetʀaɛdʀ] **nm** tetrahedron.
tétraédrique [tetʀaedʀik] **adj** tetrahedral.
tétralogie [tetʀalɔʒi] **nf** tetralogy. **la T~ de Wagner** Wagner's Ring.
tétramètre [tetʀamɛtʀ] **nm** tetrameter.
tétraphonie [tetʀafɔni] **nf** quadraphonia.
tétraphonique [tetʀafɔnik] **adj** quadraphonic.
tétraplégie [tetʀapleʒi] **nf** tetraplegia.
tétrapode [tetʀapɔd] **nm** tetrapod.
tétrarque [tetʀaʀk] **nm** tetrarch.
tétras [tetʀa(s)] **nm**: **~-lyre** black grouse; **grand ~** capercaillie.
tétrasyllabe [tetʀasi(l)lab] 1 **adj** tetrasyllabic. 2 **nm** tetrasyllable.
tetrasyllabique [tetʀasi(l)labik] **adj** tetrasyllabic.
têtu, e [tety] **adj** stubborn, mulish, pigheaded. **~ comme une mule** *ou* **une bourrique** *ou* **un âne** as stubborn *ou* obstinate as a mule.
teuf-teuf, **pl teufs-teufs** [tœftœf] **nm** a (*bruit*) *[train]* puff-puff, chuff-chuff; *[voiture]* chug-chug. b (*: *automobile*) bone-shaker, rattle-trap*; (*langage enfantin: train*) chuff-chuff, puff-puff.
teuton, -onne [tøtɔ̃, ɔn] 1 **adj** (*Hist, péj*) Teutonic. 2 **nm,f**: **T~(ne)** Teuton.
teutonique [tøtɔnik] **adj** (*Hist, péj*) Teutonic.
texan, e [tɛksɑ̃, an] 1 **adj** Texan. 2 **nm,f**: **T~(e)** Texan.
Texas [tɛksas] **nm** Texas.
texte [tɛkst] **nm** a *[contrat, pièce de théâtre etc]* text. **lire Shakespeare/la Bible dans le ~ (original)** to read Shakespeare/the Bible in the original (text); (*iro*) **en français dans le ~** those were the very words used, to quote the words used; (*Théât*) **apprendre son ~** to learn one's lines; **les illustrations sont bonnes mais il y a trop de ~** the pictures are good but there is too much text.
b (*œuvre écrite*) text; (*fragment*) passage, piece. **~s choisis** selected passages; **expliquez ce ~ de Gide** comment on this passage *ou* piece from *ou* by Gide; **il y a des erreurs dans le ~** there are textual errors *ou* errors in the text; *voir* **explication**.
c (*énoncé*) *[devoir, dissertation]* subject, topic; (*Rel*) text. **amender un ~ de loi** to amend a law; *voir* **cahier**.
textile [tɛkstil] 1 **nm** a (*matière*) textile. **~s artificiels** man-made fibres; **~s synthétiques** synthetic *ou* man-made fibres. b (*Ind*) **le ~** the textile industry, textiles (*pl*). 2 **adj** textile.
texto* [tɛksto] **adj** word for word*.
textuel, -elle [tɛkstɥɛl] **adj** (*conforme au texte*) *traduction* literal, word for word; *copie* exact; *citation* verbatim (*épith*), exact; (*tiré du texte*) textual; *analyse, sens* textual. **elle m'a dit d'aller me faire cuire un œuf: ~, mon vieux!*** she told me to get lost — those were her very words!, she told me to get lost, and I quote!; **c'est ~** those were his (*ou* her *etc*) very *ou* exact words.
textuellement [tɛkstɥɛlmɑ̃] **adv** (*voir* **textuel**) literally, word for word; exactly; verbatim. **alors il m'a dit, ~, que j'étais un imbécile** so he told me, in these very words *ou* and I quote, that I was a fool.
texture [tɛkstyʀ] **nf** (*lit, fig*) texture.
tézigue* [tezig] **pron pers** you.
TF1 [teɛfœ̃] **nm** (**abrév de Télévision française un**) *French television channel.*
TG [teʒe] **nf** (**abrév de Trésorerie générale**) *voir* **trésorerie**.
TGV [teʒeve] **nm** (**abrév de train à grande vitesse**) *voir* **train**.
thaï [taj] 1 **nm** (*Ling*) Thai. 2 **adj inv** Thai.
thaïlandais, e [tajlɑ̃dɛ, ɛz] 1 **adj** Thai. 2 **nm,f**: **T~(e)** Thai.
Thaïlande [tailɑ̃d] **nf** Thailand.
thalamus [talamys] **nm** (*Anat*) thalamus.
thalassémie [talasemi] **nf** thalassemia.
thalassothérapie [talasoteʀapi] **nf** thalassatherapy.
thalle [tal] **nm** thallus.
thallium [taljɔm] **nm** thallium.
thallophytes [talɔfit] **nmpl ou nfpl** thallophytes.
thalweg [talvɛg] **nm** thalweg.
Thanatos [tanatɔs] **nm** Thanatos.
thaumaturge [tomatyʀʒ] 1 **nm** miracle-worker, thaumaturge (*SPÉC*), thaumaturgist (*SPÉC*). 2 **adj** miracle-working (*épith*), thaumaturgic(al) (*SPÉC*).
thaumaturgie [tomatyʀʒi] **nf** miracle-working, thaumaturgy (*SPÉC*).
thé [te] 1 **nm** a (*feuilles séchées, boisson*) tea. **~ de Chine** China tea; **les ~s de Ceylan** Ceylon teas; **~ vert** green tea; **~ au lait/nature** tea with milk/without milk; **~ au citron/au jasmin/à la menthe** lemon/jasmin/mint tea; **~ à la bergamote** tea scented with bergamot, ≃ Earl Grey; **faire** *ou* **préparer le ~** to make tea; **prendre le ~** to have tea; *voir* **feuille, rose, salon.** b (*arbre*) tea plant. c (*réunion*) tea party. **~ dansant** early evening dance, thé-dansant. 2 **adj inv**: **rose ~** tea rose.
théâtral, e, **mpl -aux** [teɑtʀal, o] **adj** a *œuvre, situation* theatrical, dramatic; *rubrique, chronique* stage (*épith*), theatre (*épith*); *saison* theatre (*épith*); *représentation* stage (*épith*), theatrical. **la censure ~e** stage censorship, censorship in the theatre. b (*fig péj*) *air, attitude, personne* theatrical, histrionic, dramatic, stagey*. **ses attitudes ~es m'agacent** his theatricals *ou* histrionics irritate me.
théâtralement [teɑtʀalmɑ̃] **adv** (*lit*) theatrically; (*péj*) histrionically.
théâtraliser [teɑtʀalize] 1 **vti** to dramatize.
théâtralité [teɑtʀalite] **nf** (*littér*) theatricality.
théâtre [teɑtʀ] **nm** a (*gén: comme genre artistique*) theatre; (*comme ensemble de techniques*) drama, theatre; (*comme activité, profession*) stage, theatre. **faire du ~** to be on the stage; **faire un peu de ~** to do a bit of acting; **elle a fait du ~** she has appeared on the stage, she has done some acting; **s'intéresser au ~** to be interested in drama *ou* the theatre; **elle veut faire du ~, elle se destine au ~** she wants to go on the stage; **je préfère le ~ au cinéma** I prefer the stage *ou* the theatre to films *ou* to the cinema; **je n'aime pas le ~ à la télévision** I do not like televised stage dramas *ou* stage productions on television; **c'est du ~ filmé** it's a filmed stage production, it's a film of the play; **ses pièces ne sont pas du bon ~** his plays are not good theatre *ou* drama, his plays do not stage well; **technique** *ou* **art du ~** stagecraft; **~ d'essai** experimental theatre *ou* drama; **il fait du ~ d'amateurs** he's involved in *ou* he does some amateur dramatics *ou* theatricals; **un roman adapté pour le ~** a novel adapted for the stage *ou* the theatre; *voir* **critique**[2].
b (*lieu, entreprise*) theatre. **~ de rue** street theatre; **~ de marionnettes/de verdure** puppet/open-air theatre; **~ d'ombres** shadow theatre; **~ de guignol** ≃ Punch and Judy show; **il ne va jamais au ~** he never goes to the theatre, he is not a theatregoer; **à la sortie des ~s** when the theatres come out; **le ~ est plein ce soir** it's a full house tonight, the performance is sold out tonight; *voir* **agence, jumeau.**
c **de ~** stage (*épith*), theatre (*épith*); **un homme/une femme de ~** a man/woman of the theatre *ou* stage; **les gens de ~** theatre *ou* stage people; **accessoires/costumes/décors/grimage de ~** stage props/costumes/sets/make-up; **artifices de ~** stage tricks; **directeur de ~** theatre *ou* theatrical *ou* stage director; **troupe de ~** theatre *ou* drama company; **voix/gestes de ~** theatrical *ou* histrionic *ou* stagey* voice/gestures; **coup de ~** (*Théât*) coup de théâtre; (*gén*) dramatic turn of events.
d (*genre littéraire*) drama, theatre; (*œuvres théâtrales*) plays (*pl*), dramatic works (*pl*), theatre. **le ~ de Sheridan** Sheridan's plays *ou* dramatic works, the theatre of Sheridan; **le ~ classique/élisabéthain** the classical/Elizabethan theatre, classical/Elizabethan drama; **le ~ antique** the theatre *ou* drama of antiquity; **le ~ de caractères/de situation** the theatre of character/situation; **le ~ à thèse** didactic theatre; **le ~ de l'absurde** the theatre of the absurd; **le ~ de boulevard** light comedies (*as performed in the theatres of the Paris Boulevards*); **le ~ burlesque** the theatre of burlesque, the burlesque theatre; *voir* **pièce.**
e (*fig péj*) (*exagération*) theatricals (*pl*), histrionics (*pl*); (*simulation*) playacting. **c'est du ~** it's just playacting.
f *[événement, crime]* scene. **les Flandres ont été le ~ de combats sanglants** Flanders has been the scene of bloody fighting; (*Mil*) **le ~ des opérations** the theatre of operations.
thébaïde [tebaid] **nf** (*littér*) solitary retreat.
thébain, e [tebɛ̃, ɛn] 1 **adj** Theban. 2 **nm,f**: **T~(e)** Theban.
Thèbes [tɛb] **n** Thebes.
théier [teje] **nm** tea plant.
théière [tejɛʀ] **nf** teapot.
théine [tein] **nf** theine.
théisme [teism] **nm** a (*Rel*) theism. b (*Méd*) tea poisoning.
théiste [teist] 1 **adj** theistic(al), theist. 2 **nmf** theist.
thématique [tematik] 1 **adj** (*gén*) thematic; (*Ling*) *voyelle* thematic. 2 **nf** set of themes.
thème [tɛm] **nm** a (*sujet: gén, Littérat, Mus*) theme. **le ~ de composition d'un peintre** a painter's theme; *[débat]* **~ de réflexion** theme, subject; **ce livre nous offre plusieurs ~s de réflexion** this book provides us with several points for discussion; (*Mil*) **~ tactique** tactical ground plan; (*Psych*) **~s délirants** themes of delusion.
b (*Scol: traduction*) translation (*into the foreign language*), prose (composition). **~ et version** prose (composition) and unseen (translation); **~ allemand/espagnol** German/Spanish prose (composition), translation into German/Spanish; *voir* **fort.**
c (*Ling*) stem, theme. **~ nominal/verbal** noun/verb stem *ou* theme.
d (*Astrol*) **~ astral** birth chart.
théocratie [teɔkʀasi] **nf** theocracy.
théocratique [teɔkʀatik] **adj** theocratic.
Théocrite [teɔkʀit] **nm** Theocritus.
théodicée [teɔdise] **nf** theodicy.
théodolite [teɔdɔlit] **nm** theodolite.
Théodore [teɔdɔʀ] **nm** Theodore.
théogonie [teɔgɔni] **nf** theogony.
théologal, e, **mpl -aux** [teɔlɔgal, o] *voir* **vertu.**
théologie [teɔlɔʒi] **nf** theology. **études de ~** theological studies; **faire sa ~** to study theology *ou* divinity.
théologien, -ienne [teɔlɔʒjɛ̃, jɛn] **nm,f** theologian, theologist.
théologique [teɔlɔʒik] **adj** (*Rel*) theological.
théologiquement [teɔlɔʒikmɑ̃] **adv** theologically.
Théophile [teɔfil] **nm** Theophilus.

Théophraste [teɔfʀast] **nm** Theophrastus.
théorbe [teɔʀb] **nm** theorbo.
théorème [teɔʀɛm] **nm** theorem. **le ~ de Pythagore** Pythagoras' theorem.
théoricien, -ienne [teɔʀisjɛ̃, jɛn] **nm,f** theoretician, theorist.
théorie¹ [teɔʀi] **nf** (*doctrine, hypothèse*) theory. **la ~ et la pratique** theory and practice; **en ~** in theory, on paper (*fig*); **la ~, c'est bien joli, mais ...** theory *ou* theorizing is all very well, but ...; (*Math*) **~ des ensembles** set theory; (*Math*) **~ des catastrophes** catastrophe theory.
théorie² [teɔʀi] **nf** (*littér: procession*) procession, file.
théorique [teɔʀik] **adj** theoretical, theoretic. **c'est une liberté toute ~** it's a purely theoretical freedom.
théoriquement [teɔʀikmɑ̃] **adv** theoretically. **~, c'est vrai** in theory *ou* theoretically it's true.
théorisation [teɔʀizasjɔ̃] **nf** theorization.
théoriser [teɔʀize] [1] **1 vi** to theorize (*sur* about). **2 vt** to theorize about.
théosophe [teɔzɔf] **nmf** theosophist.
théosophie [teɔzɔfi] **nf** theosophy.
théosophique [teɔzɔfik] **adj** theosophic.
thérapeute [teʀapøt] **nmf** therapist.
thérapeutique [teʀapøtik] **1 adj** therapeutic. **2 nf** (*branche de la médecine*) therapeutics (*sg*); (*traitement*) therapy.
thérapie [teʀapi] **nf: ~ de groupe** group therapy; *voir aussi* **thérapeutique.**
Thérèse [teʀɛz] **nf** Theresa, Teresa.
thermal, e, **mpl -aux** [tɛʀmal, o] **adj: cure ~e** water cure; **faire une cure ~e** to take the waters; **eaux ~es** hot (mineral) springs; **émanations ~es** thermal *ou* hot springs; **établissement ~** hydropathic *ou* water-cure establishment; **source ~e** thermal *ou* hot spring; **station ~e** spa.
thermalisme [tɛʀmalism] **nm** (*science*) balneology; (*cures*) water cures.
thermes [tɛʀm] **nmpl** (*Hist*) thermae; (*établissement thermal*) thermal baths.
thermidor [tɛʀmidɔʀ] **nm** Thermidor, *11th month of French Republican calendar.*
thermidorien, -ienne [tɛʀmidɔʀjɛ̃, jɛn] **1 adj** of the 9th Thermidor. **2 nm,f** revolutionary of the 9th Thermidor.
thermie [tɛʀmi] **nf** (*Phys*) therm.
thermique [tɛʀmik] **adj** *unité* thermal; *énergie* thermic. **moteur ~** heat engine; **carte ~** temperature map; **centrale ~** power station; **ascendance ~** thermal, thermal current; **science ~** science of heat.
thermocautère [tɛʀmɔkotɛʀ] **nm** diathermy, electro-cautery.
thermochimie [tɛʀmoʃimi] **nf** thermochemistry.
thermocouple [tɛʀmokupl] **nm** (*Phys*) thermocouple, thermoelectric couple.
thermodynamique [tɛʀmodinamik] **1 nf** thermodynamics (*sg*). **2 adj** thermodynamic(al).
thermoélectricité [tɛʀmoelɛktʀisite] **nf** thermoelectricity.
thermoélectrique [tɛʀmoelɛktʀik] **adj** thermoelectric(al). **couple ~** thermoelectric couple, thermocouple; **effet ~** thermoelectric *ou* Seebeck effect; **pile ~** thermopile, thermoelectric pile.
thermoformage [tɛʀmofɔʀmaʒ] **nm** thermal compression moulding.
thermoformé, e [tɛʀmofɔʀme] **adj** thermally moulded.
thermogène [tɛʀmɔʒɛn] *voir* **ouate.**
thermographe [tɛʀmɔgʀaf] **nm** thermograph.
thermographie [tɛʀmɔgʀafi] **nf** thermography.
thermoluminescence [tɛʀmolyminesɑ̃s] **nf** thermoluminescence.
thermomètre [tɛʀmɔmɛtʀ] **nm** thermometer. **le ~ indique 38°** the thermometer is (standing) at *ou* is showing 38°; **le ~ monte** the temperature is rising, the thermometer is showing a rise in temperature; **~ à mercure/à alcool** mercury/alcohol thermometer; **~ à maxima et minima** maximum and minimum thermometer; **~ médical** clinical thermometer; (*fig*) **le ~ de l'opinion publique** the barometer *ou* gauge of public opinion.
thermométrie [tɛʀmɔmetʀi] **nf** thermometry.
thermométrique [tɛʀmɔmetʀik] **adj** thermometric(al).
thermonucléaire [tɛʀmonykleɛʀ] **adj** thermonuclear.
thermopile [tɛʀmopil] **nf** thermopile.
thermoplastique [tɛʀmoplastik] **adj** thermoplastic.
thermopropulsion [tɛʀmopʀɔpylsjɔ̃] **nf** thermal propulsion.
Thermopyles [tɛʀmɔpil] **nfpl: les ~** Thermopylae.
thermorégulateur, -trice [tɛʀmoʀegylatœʀ, tʀis] **adj** thermotaxic, thermoregulation (*épith*).
thermorégulation [tɛʀmoʀegylasjɔ̃] **nf** thermotaxis, thermoregulation (*épith*).
thermorésistant, e [tɛʀmoʀezistɑ̃, ɑ̃t] **adj** thermosetting.
thermos [tɛʀmos] **nm ou nf** (®: *aussi* **bouteille ~**) vacuum *ou* Thermos ® flask (*Brit*) *ou* bottle (*US*).
thermoscope [tɛʀmɔskɔp] **nm** thermoscope.
thermosiphon [tɛʀmosifɔ̃] **nm** thermosiphon.
thermosphère [tɛʀmɔsfɛʀ] **nf** thermosphere.
thermostat [tɛʀmɔsta] **nm** thermostat.
thermothérapie [tɛʀmoteʀapi] **nf** (deep) heat treatment, thermotherapy.
thésard, -arde* [tezaʀ, aʀd] **nm,f** Ph.D. student.
thésaurisation [tezɔʀizasjɔ̃] **nf** hoarding (*of money*); (*Écon*) building up of capital.
thésauriser [tezɔʀize] [1] **1 vi** to hoard money. **2 vt** to hoard (up).
thésauriseur, -euse [tezɔʀizœʀ, øz] **nm,f** hoarder (*of money*).
thésaurus [tezɔʀys] **nm** thesaurus.
thèse [tɛz] **nf a** (*doctrine*) thesis, argument. (*Littérat*) **pièce/roman à ~** pièce/roman à thèse (*SPÉC*), play/novel expounding a philosophical *ou* social thesis. **b** (*Univ*) thesis. **~ de doctorat (d'État)** Ph.D., doctoral thesis (*Brit*), doctoral dissertation (*US*); **~ de 3ᵉ cycle** ≃ M.A. *ou* M.Sc. thesis, Master's thesis; *voir* **soutenance, soutenir. c** (*Philos*) thesis. **d** (*Police: théorie*) theory, possibility. **écarter la ~ du suicide** to rule out the theory of suicide.
Thésée [teze] **nm** Theseus.
Thessalie [tɛsali] **nf** Thessaly.
thessalien, -ienne [tɛsaljɛ̃, jɛn] **1 adj** Thessalian. **2 nm,f: T~(ne)** Thessalian.
Thessalonique [tesalɔnik] **n** Thessalonica.
thêta [tɛta] **nm** theta.
thibaude [tibod] **nf** anti-slip undercarpeting (*NonC*), carpet underlay (*NonC*). **moquette sur ~** fitted carpet (*Brit*) *ou* wall-to-wall carpet (*US*) with underlay.
Thibau(l)t [tibo] **nm** Theobald.
Thibet [tibɛ] **nm** = **Tibet.**
thibétain, e [tibetɛ̃, ɛn] = **tibétain.**
Thierry [tjɛʀi] **nm** Terry.
Thimbou [timbu] **n** Thimbu.
Thomas [tɔmɑ] **nm** Thomas.
thomisme [tɔmism] **nm** Thomism.
thomiste [tɔmist] **1 adj** Thomistic(al). **2 nmf** Thomist.
thon [tɔ̃] **nm** (*Zool*) tunny (fish) (*Brit*), tuna; (*en boîte*) tuna(-fish) (*NonC*). **~ blanc** long fin tuna *ou* tunny (*Brit*); **~ rouge** blue fin tuna *ou* tunny (*Brit*); **~ au naturel/à l'huile** tuna(-fish) in brine/in oil.
thonier [tɔnje] **nm** tuna boat.
Thor [tɔʀ] **nm** Thor.
Thora [tɔʀa] **nf: la ~** the Torah.
thoracique [tɔʀasik] **adj** *cavité, canal* thoracic. **cage ~** ribcage; **capacité ~** respiratory *ou* vital capacity.
thorax [tɔʀaks] **nm** thorax.
thorium [tɔʀjɔm] **nm** thorium.
Thrace [tʀas] **nf** Thrace.
thrène [tʀɛn] **nm** threnody.
thrombine [tʀɔ̃bin] **nf** thrombin.
thrombocyte [tʀɔ̃bɔsit] **nm** thrombocyte.
thrombose [tʀɔ̃boz] **nf** thrombosis.
Thucydide [tysidid] **nm** Thucydides.
Thulé [tyle] **nm** Thule.
thulium [tyljɔm] **nm** thulium.
thune [tyn] **nf a** (†*: *pièce*) 5-franc piece. **b** (‡: *argent*) **de la ~, des ~s** dosh‡ (*Brit*), cash*.
thuriféraire [tyʀifeʀɛʀ] **nm** (*Rel*) thurifier; (*fig littér*) flatterer, sycophant.
thuya [tyja] **nm** thuja.
thym [tɛ̃] **nm** thyme. **~ sauvage** wild thyme.
thymique [timik] **adj** (*Méd, Psych*) thymic.
thymus [timys] **nm** thymus.
thyroïde [tiʀɔid] **1 adj** thyroid (*épith*). **2 nf: (glande) ~** thyroid (gland).
thyroïdien, -ienne [tiʀɔidjɛ̃, jɛn] **adj** thyroid (*épith*).
thyroxine [tiʀɔksin] **nf** thyroxin.
thyrse [tiʀs] **nm** (*Bot, Myth*) thyrsus.
tiare [tjaʀ] **nf** tiara.
Tibère [tibɛʀ] **nm** Tiberius.
Tibériade [tibeʀjad] **n: le lac de ~** Lake Tiberias, the Sea of Galilee.
Tibesti [tibɛsti] **nm: le (massif du) ~** the Tibesti (Massif).
Tibet [tibɛ] **nm** Tibet.
tibétain, e [tibetɛ̃, ɛn] **1 adj** Tibetan. **2 nm** (*Ling*) Tibetan. **3 nm,f: T~(e)** Tibetan.
tibia [tibja] **nm** (*Anat: os*) tibia (*SPÉC*), shinbone; (*partie antérieure de la jambe*) shin. **donner un coup de pied dans les ~s à qn** to kick sb in the shins.
Tibre [tibʀ] **nm: le ~** the Tiber.
tic [tik] **nm a** (*facial*) (facial) twitch *ou* tic; (*du corps*) twitch, mannerism, tic; (*manie*) habit, mannerism. **~ (nerveux)** nervous twitch *ou* tic; **~ langagier** *ou* **de langage** (verbal) mannerism, verbal tic; **c'est un ~ chez lui** (*manie*) it's a habit with him; (*geste*) it's a tic he has; **il a un ~ facial inquiétant** he has a worrying facial twitch *ou* tic; **il est plein de ~s** he is ridden with tics, he never stops twitching. **b** (*Vét: déglutition*) cribbing (*NonC*), crib-biting (*NonC*).
ticket [tikɛ] **1 nm a** (*billet*) ticket. **~ de métro/consigne/vestiaire** underground (*Brit*) *ou* subway (*US*)/left-luggage/cloakroom ticket. **b** (‡†: *10 F*) 10-franc note, ≃ quid* (*Brit*), ≃ buck* (*US*). **c** (‡) **j'ai le** *ou* **un ~ avec sa sœur** I've made a hit with his sister*. **2 comp ▸ ticket**

de caisse sales slip *ou* receipt ▸**ticket modérateur** patient's contribution (*towards cost of medical treatment*) ▸**ticket de quai** platform ticket ▸**ticket de rationnement** (ration) coupon ▸**ticket-repas** *ou* **-restaurant** *voucher given to employees redeemable in restaurants*, luncheon voucher (*Brit*), ≃ meal ticket (*US*).

tic-tac [tiktak] nm ticking, tick-tock. **faire ~** to tick, go tick tock.

tie break [tajbʀɛk] nm tie break.

tiédasse [tjedas] adj (*péj*) lukewarm, tepid.

tiède [tjɛd] 1 adj a *boisson, bain* lukewarm, tepid; *vent, saison* mild, warm; *atmosphère* balmy; (*fig littér: sécurisant, enveloppant*) warm.
b (*péj*) *sentiment, foi, accueil* lukewarm, half-hearted, tepid; *chrétien, communiste* half-hearted, lukewarm.
2 nmf (*péj*) lukewarm *ou* half-hearted individual. **des mesures qui risquent d'effaroucher les ~s** measures likely to scare the half-hearted *ou* the fainthearts.
3 adv: **elle boit son café ~** she drinks her coffee lukewarm, she doesn't like her coffee too hot; **les Anglais boivent leur bière ~** the English drink their beer (luke)warm *ou* tepid; **qu'il se dépêche un peu, je n'aime pas boire ~** I wish he'd hurry up because I don't like drinking things (when they're) lukewarm.

tièdement [tjɛdmɑ̃] adv (*péj: voir* **tiède**) in a lukewarm way; half-heartedly.

tiédeur [tjedœʀ] nf (*voir* **tiède**) lukewarmness; tepidness; mildness, warmth; balminess; half-heartedness.

tiédir [tjediʀ] [2] 1 vi a (*devenir moins chaud*) to cool down; (*se réchauffer*) to grow warm(er). **faire ~ de l'eau/une boisson** to warm *ou* heat up some water/a drink. b (*fig*) *[sentiment, foi, ardeur]* to cool (off). 2 vt *[soleil, source de chaleur]* to warm (up); *[air frais]* to cool (down).

tiédissement [tjedismɑ̃] nm (*voir* **tiédir**) cooling (down); warming up; cooling (off).

tien, tienne [tjɛ̃, tjɛn] 1 pron poss: **le ~, la tienne, les ~s, les tiennes** yours, your own, (††, *Rel*) thine; **ce sac n'est pas le ~** this bag is not yours, this is not your bag; **mes fils sont stupides comparés aux ~s** my sons are stupid compared to yours *ou* your own; **à la tienne!*** your (good) health!, cheers!*; (*iro*) **tu vas faire ce travail tout seul? — à la tienne!*** are you going to do the job all by yourself? — good luck to you! *ou* rather you than me!; *pour autres exemples voir* **sien**.
2 nm a **il n'y a pas à distinguer le ~ du mien** what's mine is yours; *pour autres exemples voir* **sien**.
b **les ~s** your family, your (own) folks*; **toi et tous les ~s** you and your whole set, you and the likes of you*; *voir* **sien**.
3 adj poss (*littér*) **un ~ cousin** a cousin of yours.

tiens [tjɛ̃] excl *voir* **tenir**.

tierce[1] [tjɛʀs] 1 nf a (*Mus*) third. **~ majeure/mineure** major/minor third. b (*Cartes*) tierce. **~ majeure** tierce major. c (*Typ*) final proof. d (*Rel*) terce. e (*Escrime*) tierce. f (*unité de temps*) sixtieth of a second. 2 adj *voir* **tiers**.

tiercé, e [tjɛʀse] 1 adj (*Hér*) tiercé, tierced; *voir* **rime**. 2 nm *French system of forecast betting on three horses*, tierce (*Austral*). **réussir le ~ dans l'ordre/dans le désordre** *ou* **dans un ordre différent** to win on the tiercé with the right placings/without the right placings; **un beau ~** a good win on the tiercé; **toucher** *ou* **gagner le ~** to win the tiercé; (*fig*) **voici le ~ gagnant** here are the three winners.

tierceron [tjɛʀsəʀɔ̃] nm tierceron.

tiers, tierce[2] [tjɛʀ, tjɛʀs] 1 adj third. (*Math*) **b tierce** b triple dash; **une tierce personne** a third party, an outsider; (*Typ*) **tierce épreuve** final proof; (*Jur*) **~ porteur** endorsee; (*Jur*) **tierce opposition** opposition by third party (*to outcome of litigation*).
2 nm a (*fraction*) third. **le premier ~/les deux premiers ~ de l'année** the first third/the first two thirds of the year; **j'ai lu le** *ou* **un ~/les deux ~ du livre** I have read a third/two thirds of the book; **j'en suis au ~** I'm a third of the way through; **les deux ~ des gens pensent que** the majority of people think that; **l'article est trop long d'un ~** the article is a third too long *ou* over length, the article is too long by a third.
b (*troisième personne*) third party *ou* person; (*étranger, inconnu*) outsider; (*Jur*) third party. **il a appris la nouvelle par un ~** he learnt the news through a third party; he learnt the news through an outsider; **l'assurance ne couvre pas les ~** the insurance does not cover third party risks; **il se moque du ~ comme du quart**† he doesn't care a fig *ou* a hoot* *ou* a damn*; *voir* **assurance**.
3 comp ▸**tiers(-)arbitre** nm (pl **tiers(-)arbitres**) independent arbitrator ▸**le Tiers État** nm (*Hist*) the third estate ▸**le Tiers-Monde** nm (*Pol*) the Third World ▸**tiers-mondiste** adj Third-World (*épith*) ◊ nmf supporter of the Third-World ▸**tiers ordre** (*Rel*) third order ▸**tiers payant** direct payment by insurers (*for medical treatment*) ▸**tiers-point** nm (pl **tiers-points**) (*Archit*) crown; (*lime*) saw-file ▸**tiers provisionnel** provisional *ou* interim payment (*of tax*) ▸**tiers temps: bénéficier d'un tiers temps** (*Univ: à un examen*) to be allowed extra time to do one's exam.

tif‡ [tif] nm (*gén pl*) hair. **~s** hair.

TIG [teiʒe] nm (abrév de **travaux d'intérêt général**) *voir* **travail**[1].

tige [tiʒ] nf a (*Bot*) *[fleur, arbre]* stem; *[céréales, graminées]* stalk. **fleurs à longues ~s** long-stemmed flowers; **(arbre de) haute/basse ~** standard/half-standard tree; **~ aérienne/souterraine** overground/underground stem. b (*plant*) sapling. c (*fig*) *[colonne, plume, démarreur]* shaft; *[botte, chaussette, bas]* leg (part); *[chaussure]* ankle (part); *[clef, clou]* shank; *[pompe]* rod. **chaussures à ~** boots; **chaussures à ~ haute** knee-length boots; **chaussures à ~ basse** ankle(-length) boots; **~ de métal** metal rod; (*Aut*) **~ de culbuteur** pushrod. d (†, *littér*) *[arbre généalogique]* stock. **faire ~** to found a line. e (*: *cigarette*) fag* (*Brit*), cig*, smoke*.

tignasse [tiɲas] nf (*chevelure mal peignée*) shock of hair, mop (of hair); (*: *cheveux*) hair.

Tigre [tigʀ] nm: **le ~** the Tigris.

tigre [tigʀ] nm (*Zool, fig*) tiger. **~ royal** *ou* **du Bengale** Bengal tiger; (*fig*) **~ de papier** paper tiger.

tigré, e [tigʀe] adj a (*tacheté*) spotted (*de* with); *cheval* piebald. b (*rayé*) striped, streaked. **chat ~** tabby (cat).

tigresse [tigʀɛs] nf (*Zool*) tigress; (*fig*) tigress, hellcat*.

tilbury [tilbyʀi] nm tilbury.

tilde [tild(ə)] nm tilde.

tillac [tijak] nm (*Hist Naut*) upper deck.

tilleul [tijœl] nm (*arbre*) lime (tree), linden (tree); (*infusion*) lime(-blossom) tea. **(vert) ~** lime green.

tilt [tilt] nm (*billard électrique*) electronic billiards. **faire ~** (*lit*) to ping *ou* ring for the end of the game *ou* to mark the end of the game; (*fig: échouer*) to fail; (*fig: inspirer*) **ce mot a fait ~ dans mon esprit** this word rang a bell (in my mind).

timbale [tɛ̃bal] nf a (*Mus*) kettledrum, timp*. **les ~s** the timpani, the timps*, the kettledrums. b (*gobelet*) (metal) cup (*without handle*), (metal) tumbler. c (*Culin*) (*moule*) timbale (mould). (*mets*) **~ de langouste** lobster timbale.

timbalier [tɛ̃balje] nm timpanist.

timbrage [tɛ̃bʀaʒ] nm (*voir* **timbrer**) stamping; postmarking. **dispensé du ~** postage paid.

timbre [tɛ̃bʀ] 1 nm a (*vignette*) stamp. **~(-poste)** (postage) stamp; **~ neuf/oblitéré** new/used stamp; **marché** *ou* **bourse aux ~s** stamp market; **~s antituberculeux/anticancéreux** TB/cancer research stamps; *voir* **collection**.
b (*marque*) stamp; (*cachet de la poste*) postmark. **mettre** *ou* **apposer** *ou* **imprimer son ~ sur** to put one's stamp on, affix one's stamp to; **~ sec/humide** embossed/ink(ed) stamp; *voir* **droit**[3].
c (*instrument*) stamp. **~ de caoutchouc/de cuivre** rubber/brass stamp.
d (*Mus*) *[tambour]* snares (*pl*).
e (*son*) *[instrument, voix]* timbre, tone; *[voyelle]* timbre. **avoir le ~ voilé** to have a muffled voice; **une voix qui a du ~** a sonorous *ou* resonant voice; **une voix sans ~** a voice lacking in resonance.
f (*sonnette*) bell.
2 comp ▸**timbre-amende** nm (pl **timbres-amendes**) fine payment stamp (*proving that one has paid*) ▸**timbre d'escompte, timbre-escompte** nm (pl **timbres-escompte**) trading stamp ▸**timbre fiscal** excise *ou* revenue stamp ▸**timbre horodateur** time and date stamp ▸**timbre de quittance, timbre-quittance** nm (pl **timbres-quittance**) receipt stamp.

timbré, e [tɛ̃bʀe] (ptp de **timbrer**) 1 adj a (*Admin, Jur*) *document, acte* stamped, bearing a stamp (*attrib*); *voir* **papier**. b *voix* resonant, sonorous; *sonorité* resonant. **une voix bien ~e** a beautifully resonant voice; **mal ~** lacking in resonance. c (*: *fou*) cracked*, dotty*, nuts*, barmy* (*Brit*). 2 nm,f (*: *fou*) loony‡, nutcase‡, head case‡.

timbrer [tɛ̃bʀe] [1] vt (*apposer un cachet sur*) *document, acte* to stamp; *lettre, envoi* to postmark; (*affranchir*) *lettre, envoi* to stamp, put a stamp (*ou* stamps) on. **lettre timbrée de** *ou* **à Paris** letter with a Paris postmark, letter postmarked Paris.

timide [timid] adj a (*timoré*) *personne, critique, réponse, tentative* timid, timorous; *entreprise, style* timid. **une ~ amélioration de l'économie** a slight *ou* faint improvement in the economy. b (*emprunté*) *personne, air, sourire, voix, amoureux* shy, bashful, timid. **faussement ~** coy; **c'est un grand ~** he's awfully shy.

timidement [timidmɑ̃] adv (*voir* **timide**) timidly; timorously; shyly; bashfully.

timidité [timidite] nf (*voir* **timide**) timidity; timorousness; shyness; bashfulness.

timing [tajmiŋ] nm timing.

timon [timɔ̃] nm *[char]* shaft; *[charrue]* beam; *[embarcation]* tiller.

timonerie [timɔnʀi] nf a (*Naut*) (*poste, service*) wheelhouse; (*marins*) wheelhouse crew. b (*Aut*) steering and braking systems.

timonier [timɔnje] nm a (*Naut*) helmsman, steersman. b (*cheval*) wheel-horse, wheeler.

timoré, e [timɔʀe] adj (*gén*) *caractère, personne* timorous, fearful, timid; (*Rel, littér*) *conscience* over-scrupulous.

Timothée [timɔte] nm Timothy.

tinctorial, e, mpl **-iaux** [tɛ̃ktɔʀjal, jo] adj *opération, produit* tinctorial (*SPÉC*), dyeing (*épith*). **matières ~es** dyestuffs; **plantes ~es** plants used in dyeing.

tinette [tinɛt] nf (*pour la vidange*) sanitary tub. (*arg Mil: toilettes*) **~s**

latrines.

tintamarre [tɛ̃tamaʀ] **nm** din, racket, hullabaloo*. **faire du ~** to make a din *ou* racket; **un ~ de klaxons** the blaring *ou* din of horns.

tintement [tɛ̃tmɑ̃] **nm** (*voir* **tinter**) ringing; chiming; tinkling; jingling; chinking. **~ d'oreilles** ringing in the ears, tinnitus (*SPÉC*).

tinter [tɛ̃te] 1 **1 vi** *[cloche]* to ring, chime; *[clochette]* to tinkle, jingle; *[objets métalliques, pièces de monnaie]* to jingle, chink; *[verres entrechoqués]* to chink; *[verre frotté]* to ring. **faire ~** to ring; to make tinkle; to make jingle; to make chink; **trois coups tintèrent** the bell rang *ou* chimed three times; **les oreilles me tintent** my ears are ringing, there's a ringing in my ears; (*fig*) **les oreilles ont dû vous ~** your ears must have been burning. **2 vt** *cloche, heure, angélus* to ring; *messe* to ring for.

tintin‡ [tɛ̃tɛ̃] **excl** nothing doing!*, no go!*, you're not on!*. **faire ~** to go without.

tintinnabuler [tɛ̃tinabyle] 1 **vi** (*littér*) to tinkle, tintinnabulate (*littér*).

Tintoret [tɛ̃tɔʀɛ] **nm: le ~** Tintoretto.

tintouin* [tɛ̃twɛ̃] **nm** **a** (*tracas*) bother, worry. **quel ~ pour y aller** what a to-do *ou* what a lot of bother to get there; **donner du ~ à qn** to give sb a lot of bother; **se donner du ~** to go to a lot of bother. **b** (†: *bruit*) racket, din.

tipi [tipi] **nm** te(e)pee.

tique [tik] **nf** (*parasite*) tick.

tiquer [tike] 1 **vi** **a** *[personne]* to pull (*Brit*) *ou* make a face, raise an eyebrow. **sans ~** without turning a hair *ou* batting an eyelid *ou* raising an eyebrow. **b** *[cheval]* to crib(-bite), suck wind.

tiqueté, e [tik(ə)te] **adj** (*littér*) speckled, mottled.

TIR [tiʀ] **nmpl** (**abrév de transports internationaux routiers**) TIR.

tir [tiʀ] **1 nm** **a** (*discipline sportive ou militaire*) shooting. **~ au pistolet/à la carabine** pistol/rifle shooting; *voir* **stand**.

b (*action de tirer*) firing (*NonC*). **en position de ~** in firing position; **prêt au ~** ready for firing; **commander/déclencher le ~** to order/set off *ou* open the firing; **puissance/vitesse de ~ d'une arme** fire-power/ firing speed of a gun; **des ~s d'exercice** practice rounds; **des ~s à blanc** firing blank rounds *ou* blanks; **corriger** *ou* **rectifier le ~** (*lit*) to adjust the fire; (*fig*) to make some adjustments.

c (*manière de tirer*) firing; (*trajectoire des projectiles*) fire. **arme à ~ automatique/rapide** automatic/rapid-firing gun; **régler/ajuster le ~** to regulate/adjust the fire; **arme à ~ courbe/tendu** gun with curved/flat trajectory fire; **~ groupé/direct** grouped/direct fire; (*fig: contre politique*) combined/direct attack; **plan/angle/ligne de ~** plane/angle/ line of fire; *voir* **table**.

d (*feu, rafales*) fire (*NonC*). **stoppés par un ~ de mitrailleuses/ d'artillerie** halted by machine-gun/artillery fire.

e (*Boules*) shot (*at another bowl*); (*Ftbl*) shot. **~ au but** shot at goal.

f (*stand*) **~ (forain)** shooting gallery, rifle range.

g (*Espace: lancement*) launch.

2 comp ►**tir d'appui** = **tir de soutien** ►**tir à l'arbalète** crossbow archery ►**tir à l'arc** archery ►**tir de barrage** barrage fire ►**secteur** *ou* **zone de tir libre** free-fire zone ►**tir au pigeon** clay pigeon shooting ►**tir de soutien** support fire.

tirade [tiʀad] **nf** (*Théât*) monologue, speech; (*fig, péj*) tirade.

tirage [tiʀaʒ] **1 nm** **a** *[chèque]* drawing; *[vin]* drawing off; *[carte]* taking, drawing.

b (*Phot, Typ*) printing. **faire le ~ de clichés/d'une épreuve** to print negatives/a proof; **~ à la main** hand-printing; **un ~ sur papier glacé** a print on glazed paper; **~ par contact/inversion** contact/reversal print.

c *[journal]* circulation; *[livre]* (*nombre d'exemplaires*) (print) run; (*édition*) edition. **~ de luxe/limité** de luxe/limited edition; **cet auteur réalise de gros ~s** this author's works have huge print runs *ou* are printed in great numbers; **quel est le ~ de cet ouvrage?** how many copies of this work were printed? (*ou* are being printed?); **les gros ~s de la presse quotidienne** the high circulation figures of the daily press; **~ de 2 000 exemplaires** run *ou* impression of 2,000 copies.

d *[cheminée]* draught. **avoir du ~** to draw well, have a good draught; **cette cheminée a un bon/mauvais ~** this chimney draws well/ badly.

e (*Loterie*) draw. **le ~ des numéros gagnants** the draw for the winning numbers.

f (*: *désaccord*) friction. **il y avait du ~ entre eux** there was some friction between them.

g *[métaux]* drawing.

2 comp ►**tirage à part** off-print ►**tirage au sort** drawing lots; **procéder par tirage au sort** to draw lots; **le gagnant sera désigné par tirage au sort** the winner will be chosen by drawing lots; **le tirage au sort des équipes de football** the selection *ou* choice of the football teams by drawing lots.

tiraillement [tiʀajmɑ̃] **nm** **a** (*sur une corde etc*) tugging (*NonC*), pulling (*NonC*). **ces ~s ont causé la rupture de la corde** all this pulling *ou* tugging caused the rope to break. **b** (*douleur*) (*intestinal, stomacal*) gnawing *ou* crampy pain; (*de la peau, musculaire, sur une plaie*) stabbing pain. **~s d'estomac** gnawing pains in the stomach. **c** (*fig*) (*doutes, hésitations*) agonizing indecision (*NonC*); (*conflits, friction*) friction (*NonC*), conflict (*NonC*). **~s (de la conscience) entre devoir et ambition** friction *ou* conflict (within one's conscience) between duty and ambition.

tirailler [tiʀɑje] 1 **1 vt** **a** *corde, moustache, manche* to pull at, tug at. **les enfants tiraillaient le pauvre vieux de droite et de gauche** the children were tugging the poor old man this way and that; **~ qn par le bras** *ou* **la manche** to pull *ou* tug at sb's sleeve.

b *[douleurs]* to gnaw at, stab at. **des douleurs qui tiraillent l'estomac** gnawing pains in the stomach; **des élancements lui tiraillaient l'épaule** he had sharp *ou* shooting *ou* stabbing pains in his shoulder.

c *[doutes, remords]* to tug at, plague, pester; *[choix, contradictions]* to beset, plague. **être tiraillé entre plusieurs possibilités** to be torn between several possibilities; **la crainte et l'ambition le tiraillaient** he was torn between fear and ambition.

2 vi (*en tous sens*) to shoot wild; (*Mil: tir de harcèlement*) to fire at random. **ça tiraillait de tous côtés dans le bois** there was firing on all sides in the wood.

tirailleur [tiʀɑjœʀ] **nm** **a** (*Mil, fig*) skirmisher. **se déployer/avancer en ~s** to be deployed/advance as a skirmish contingent. **b** (*Hist Mil: dans les colonies*) soldier, infantryman (*native*).

Tirana [tiʀana] **n** Tirana.

tirant [tiʀɑ̃] **nm** **a** (*cordon*) (draw) string; (*tirette*) *[botte]* bootstrap; (*partie de la tige*) *[chaussure]* facing. **b** (*Constr*) *[arcades]* tie-rod; *[comble]* tie-beam. *[pont]* **~ d'air** headroom. **c** (*Naut*) **~ (d'eau)** draught (*Brit*), draft (*US*); **~ avant/arrière** draught (*Brit*) *ou* draft (*US*) at the bows/stern; **avoir 6 mètres de ~ (d'eau)** to draw 6 metres of water; *[navire]* **~ d'air** clearance height.

tire¹‡ [tiʀ] **nf** (*voiture*) wagon*, car. **vieille ~** old rattletrap* *ou* crate* *ou* banger* (*Brit*).

tire² [tiʀ] **nf: vol à la ~** picking pockets; **voleur à la ~** pickpocket.

tire³ [tiʀ] **nf** (*Can*) toffee, taffy (*Can, US*); molasses, maple candy. **~ d'érable** maple toffee *ou* taffy (*Can, US*); **~ sur la neige** taffy-on-the-snow (*Can, US*).

tire- [tiʀ] **préf** *voir* **tirer**.

tiré, e [tiʀe] (**ptp de tirer**) **1 adj** **a** (*tendu*) *traits, visage* drawn, haggard. **avoir les traits ~s** to look drawn *ou* haggard; **les cheveux ~s en arrière** with one's hair drawn back; **~ à quatre épingles** impeccably *ou* well turned-out, done up *ou* dressed up to the nines*; (*fig*) **~ par les cheveux** far-fetched; *voir* **couteau**. **b** (*Fin*) **la personne ~e** the drawee. **c (bas) prix ~** rock-bottom price; **pratiquer des prix ~s** to sell at rock-bottom prices. **2 nm** (*Fin*) drawee; (*Mus*) down-bow. **3 tirée*** **nf** (*long trajet*) long haul, long trek. (‡: *quantité*) **une ~e de** a load* of, heaps* *ou* tons* of. **4 comp** ►**tiré à part** **adj, nm** off-print.

tirelire [tiʀliʀ] **nf** **a** moneybox; (*en forme de cochon*) piggy bank. **casser la ~** to break open the piggy bank. **b** (‡) (*estomac, ventre*) belly‡, gut(s)‡; (*tête*) nut*, noddle*, bonce‡ (*Brit*); (*visage*) face.

tirer [tiʀe] 1 **1 vt** **a** (*amener vers soi*) *pièce mobile, poignée, corde* to pull; *manche, robe* to pull down; *chaussette* to pull up. **ne tire pas, ça risque de tomber/ça va l'étrangler** don't pull or it'll fall/strangle him; **~ les cheveux à qn** to pull sb's hair; **~ l'aiguille** to ply the needle; (*lit*) **~ qch à soi** to pull sth to(wards) one; (*fig*) **~ un texte/auteur à soi** to turn a text/an author round to suit one; *voir* **couverture, diable, langue, révérence**.

b *rideaux* to draw, pull; *tiroir* to pull open; *verrou* (*fermer*) to slide to, shoot; (*ouvrir*) to draw. **tire la porte** pull the door to; **il est tard: tire les rideaux** it's getting late so pull the curtains (to) *ou* draw the curtains; **as-tu tiré le verrou?** have you bolted the door?

c *personne* to pull. **~ qn par le bras** to pull sb's arm, pull sb by the arm; **~ qn par la manche** to tug *ou* pluck sb's sleeve; **~ qn de côté** *ou* **à l'écart** to draw sb aside, take sb on one side.

d (*haler, remorquer*) *véhicule, charge* to pull, draw; *navire, remorque* to tow; *charrue* to draw, pull. **une charrette tirée par un tracteur** a cart drawn *ou* pulled by a tractor, a tractor-drawn cart; **carrosse tiré par 8 chevaux** carriage drawn by 8 horses.

e (*retirer, extraire*) *épée, couteau* to draw, pull out; *vin, cidre* to draw; *carte, billet, numéro* to draw; (*fig*) *conclusions, morale, argument, idée, thème* to draw; (*fig*) *plaisir, satisfaction* to draw, derive (*de* from). **~ une substance d'une matière première** to extract a substance from a raw material; **~ le jus d'un citron** to extract the juice from a lemon, squeeze the juice from a lemon *ou* out of a lemon; **~ un son d'un instrument** to get a sound out of *ou* draw a sound from an instrument; **cette pièce tire son jour** *ou* **sa lumière de cette lucarne** this room gets its light from *ou* is lit by this skylight; **~ un objet d'un tiroir/d'un sac** to pull an object out of a drawer/bag; **~ son chapeau/sa casquette à qn** to raise one's hat/cap to sb; **~ de l'argent d'une activité/d'une terre** to make *ou* derive *ou* get money from an activity/a piece of land; **~ de l'argent de qn** to get money out of sb; **~ qn du sommeil** to arouse sb from sleep; **~ qn du lit** to get *ou* drag sb out of bed; **~ qn de son travail** to take *ou* drag sb away from his work; **ce bruit le tira de sa rêverie** this noise brought him out of *ou* roused him from his daydream; **~ qch de qn** to obtain sth from sb, get sth out of sb; **on ne peut rien en ~** (*enfant têtu*) you can't do anything with him; (*qui refuse de parler*) you can't get anything out of him; **~ des larmes/gémissements à qn** to draw tears/moans from sb; **savoir ~ qch de la vie/d'un moment** (to know how) to get sth out of life/a moment; (*à l'Épiphanie*) ~ **les rois** to cut the Twelfth Night cake; *voir* **avantage, clair, épingle, parti**[1].

f (*délivrer*) ~ **qn de prison/des décombres/d'une situation dangereuse** to get sb out of prison/the rubble/a dangerous situation; ~ **qn du doute** to remove *ou* dispel sb's doubts; ~ **qn de l'erreur** to disabuse sb; ~ **qn de la misère/de l'obscurité** to rescue sb from poverty/obscurity; **il faut le ~ de là** we'll have to help him out; *voir* **affaire, embarras.**

g (*indiquant l'origine*) ~ **son origine d'une vieille coutume** to have an old custom as its origin; **mots tirés du latin** words taken *ou* derived from (the) Latin; ~ **son nom de** to take one's name from; **pièce tirée d'un roman** play taken from *ou* adapted from *ou* derived from a novel; **on tire de l'huile des olives** oil is extracted from olives; **l'opium est tiré du pavot** opium is obtained from the poppy.

h (*choisir*) *billet, numéro* to draw; *carte* to take, draw; *loterie* to draw, carry out the draw for. ~ **qch au sort** to draw lots for sth; (*fig*) **il a tiré un bon/mauvais numéro** he's come up with *ou* hit a lucky/unlucky number; *voir* **carte, court**[1].

i (*Phot, Typ*) to print. **on tire ce journal à 100 000 exemplaires** this paper has a circulation of 100,000; ~ **un roman à 8 000 exemplaires** to print 8,000 copies of a novel; **tirons quelques épreuves de ce texte** let's run off *ou* print a few proofs of the text; (*fig*) **tiré à des centaines d'exemplaires** turned out *ou* churned out by the hundred; *voir* **bon**[2].

j (*tracer*) *ligne, trait* to draw; *plan* to draw up; *portrait* to do. **se faire ~ le portrait*** (*croquer*) to have one's portrait drawn; (*photographier*) to have one's photograph taken; *voir* **plan**[1].

k *coup de feu, balle* to fire; *flèche* to shoot; *boule* to throw (*so as to hit another or the jack*); *feu d'artifice* to set off; *gibier* to shoot. **il a tiré plusieurs coups de revolver sur l'agent** he fired several shots at the policeman, he shot *ou* fired at the policeman several times; **il a tiré plusieurs coups de feu et s'est enfui** he fired several times *ou* several shots and ran off; ~ **le canon** to fire the cannon; **la balle a été tirée avec un gros calibre** the bullet was fired from a large-bore gun; **il a tiré un faisan** he shot a pheasant; (*fig*) ~ **un coup**** to have a bang**, have it off**.

l *chèque, lettre de change* to draw. ~ **de l'argent sur son compte** to draw money out of one's account, withdraw money from one's account.

m (*Naut*) ~ **6 mètres** to draw 6 metres of water; ~ **un bord** *ou* **une bordée** to tack.

n (*: *passer*) to get through. **encore une heure/un mois à ~** another hour/month to get through; ~ **2 ans de prison/service** to do 2 years in prison *ou* a 2-year stretch*/2 years in the army; **voilà une semaine de tirée** that's one week over with.

o (‡: *voler*) to pinch*, nick‡ (*Brit*). **il s'est fait ~ son blouson** he got his jacket pinched* *ou* nicked‡ (*Brit*).

p (*Tech: étirer*) *métal* to draw.

q (*baisser*) ~ **ses prix** to sell at rock-bottom prices.

2 **vi** a (*faire feu*) to fire. **il leur donna l'ordre de ~** he gave the order for them to fire; **le canon tirait sans arrêt** the cannon fired continuously; ~ **en l'air** to fire into the air; ~ **à vue** to shoot on sight; ~ **à balles (réelles)/à blanc** to fire (real) bullets/blanks; ~ **sans sommation** to shoot without warning; ~ **dans le dos de qn** (*lit*) to shoot sb in the back; (*fig*) to stab sb in the back; *voir* **boulet, tas.**

b (*se servir d'une arme à feu, viser*) to shoot. **apprendre à ~** to learn to shoot; ~ **au but** to hit the target.

c (*Ftbl*) to shoot, take a shot; (*Boules*) to throw (*one "boule" at another or at the jack*). ~ **au but** to take a shot at goal, shoot at goal.

d (*Presse*) ~ **à 10 000 exemplaires** to have a circulation of 10,000.

e [*cheminée, poêle*] to draw. **la cheminée tire bien** the chimney draws well.

f [*moteur, voiture*] to pull. **le moteur tire bien en côte** the engine pulls well on hills; *voir aussi* **4.**

g [*points de suture, sparadrap*] to pull. **ma peau est très sèche et me tire** my skin is very dry and feels tight.

h (*loc*) ~ **au flanc*** *ou* **au cul**‡ to skive* (*Brit*), shirk; ~ **dans les jambes** *ou* **pattes* de qn** to make life difficult for sb; ~ **en longueur** to drag on.

3 **tirer sur vt indir** a *corde, poignée* to pull at *ou* on, tug at. ~ **sur les rênes** to pull in *ou* on the reins; (*fig*) ~ **sur la ficelle*** *ou* **la corde*** to push one's luck*, go too far, overstep the mark.

b (*approcher de*) *couleur* to border on, verge on. **il tire sur la soixantaine** he's getting on for (*Brit*) *ou* going on (*US*) sixty, he's verging on sixty.

c (*faire feu sur*) to shoot at, fire (a shot *ou* shots) at. **il m'a tiré dessus** he shot *ou* fired at me; **se ~ dessus** (*lit*) to shoot *ou* fire at each other; (*fig: se critiquer, quereller*) to shoot each other down, snipe at one another; *voir* **boulet.**

d (*aspirer*) *pipe* to pull at, draw on; *cigarette, cigare* to puff at, draw on, take a drag at*.

4 **tirer à vt indir:** ~ **à sa fin** to be drawing to a close; ~ **à conséquence** to matter; **cela ne tire pas à conséquence** it's of no consequence, it doesn't matter; **la voiture tire à gauche** the car pulls to the left.

5 **se tirer vpr** a (*s'échapper à*) **se ~ de** *danger, situation* to get (o.s.) out of; **sa voiture était en mille morceaux mais lui s'en est tiré*** his car was smashed to pieces but he escaped; **il est très malade mais je crois qu'il va s'en ~** he's very ill but I think he'll pull through; **la première fois il a eu le sursis mais cette fois il ne va pas s'en ~ si facilement** the first time he got a suspended sentence but he won't get off so lightly this time; **il s'en est tiré avec une amende/une jambe cassée** he got off with a fine/a broken leg; **il s'en est tiré à bon compte** he got off lightly; *voir* **affaire, flûte, patte.**

b (*se débrouiller*) **bien/mal se ~ de qch** *tâche* to manage *ou* handle sth well/badly, make a good/bad job of sth; **comment va-t-il se ~ de ce sujet/travail?** how will he get on with *ou* cope with this subject/job?; **les questions étaient difficiles mais il s'en est bien tiré** the questions were difficult but he managed *ou* handled them well *ou* coped very well with them; **on n'a pas beaucoup d'argent mais on s'en tire** we haven't a lot of money but we get by *ou* we manage; **on s'en tire tout juste** we just scrape by, we just (about) get by.

c (‡: *déguerpir*) to push off*, shove off‡, clear off‡. **allez, on se tire** come on — we'll be off, come on — let's push off* *ou* clear off‡.

d (*: *toucher à sa fin*) [*période, travail*] to drag towards its close. **ça se tire** the end is (at last) in sight.

e (*être tendu*) [*traits, visage*] to become drawn.

6 **comp** ▸ **à tire-d'aile(s)** **loc adv** *voler* swiftly; **passer à tire-d'aile(s)** to pass by in full flight; **s'envoler à tire-d'aile(s)** to take flight in a flurry of feathers; (*fig*) **partir à tire-d'aile(s)** to leave at top speed, take flight ▸ **tire-bonde** **nm** (**pl tire-bondes**) bung-drawer ▸ **tire-botte** **nm** (**pl tire-bottes**) (*pour se chausser*) boot-hook; (*pour se déchausser*) bootjack ▸ **tire-bouchon** **nm** (**pl tire-bouchons**) corkscrew; (*mèche de cheveux*) corkscrew curl; **en tire-bouchon** corkscrew (*épith*); **cochon avec la queue en tire-bouchon** pig with a corkscrew *ou* curly tail; **pantalon en tire-bouchon** crumpled trousers ▸ **tire-bouchonner** **vt** *mèche* to twiddle, twirl ◊ **vi** [*pantalons*] to crumple (up); **pantalon tire-bouchonné** crumpled trousers; **se tire-bouchonner**‡ ◊ **vpr** (*rire*) to fall about laughing* (*Brit*), be in stitches* ▸ **tire-clou** **nm** (**pl tire-clous**) nail puller ▸ **tire-au-cul**‡ **nmf inv** = **tire-au-flanc** ▸ **tire-fesses*** **nm inv** (*gén, à perche*) ski tow; (*à archet*) T-bar tow ▸ **tire-au-flanc*** **nmf inv** skiver* (*Brit*), layabout, shirker ▸ **tire-fond** **nm inv** (*vis*) *long screw with ring attachment* ▸ **tire-jus**‡ **nm inv** nose-wipe*, snot-rag‡ ▸ **tire-laine**†† **nm inv** footpad†† ▸ **tire-lait** **nm inv** breast-pump ▸ **à tire-larigot*** **loc adv** to one's heart's content ▸ **tire-ligne** **nm** (**pl tire-lignes**) drawing pen.

tiret [tiʀɛ] **nm** (*trait*) dash; (*en fin de ligne*, †: *trait d'union*) hyphen.

tirette [tiʀɛt] **nf** a [*bureau, table*] (*pour écrire*) (writing) leaf; (*pour ranger des crayons etc*) (pencil) tray; (*pour soutenir un abattant*) support. b [*fermeture éclair*] pull, tab. c [*cheminée*] damper. d (*cordon*) [*sonnette*] bell-pull; [*rideaux*] (curtain) cord *ou* pull.

tireur, -euse [tiʀœʀ, øz] 1 **nm** (*f rare*) a (*avec arme à feu*) **c'est le fait d'un ~ isolé** it is the work of a lone gunman *ou* gunner; (*Mil*) ~ **d'élite** marksman, sharpshooter; **c'est un bon ~** he is a good shot; **concours ouvert aux ~s débutants et entraînés** shooting competition open to beginners and advanced classes. b (*Boules*) thrower. c (*photographe*) printer. d (*escrimeur*) ~ **(d'épée** *ou* **d'armes)** swordsman, fencer. 2 **nm** (*Fin*) [*chèque, lettre de change*] drawer. 3 **tireuse nf** a **~euse de cartes** fortuneteller. b (*Tech*) (hand) pump. **bière/vin à la ~euse** hand-drawn beer/wine. c (*Phot*) contact printer.

tiroir [tiʀwaʀ] 1 **nm** a [*table, commode*] drawer. ~ **(à) secret** secret drawer; (*fig*) **roman/pièce à ~s** novel/play made up of episodes, roman/pièce à tiroirs (*SPÉC*); *voir* **fond, nom.** b (*Tech*) slide valve. 2 **comp** ▸ **tiroir-caisse** **nm** (**pl tiroirs-caisses**) till, cash register.

tisane [tizan] **nf** a (*boisson*) herb(al) tea. ~ **de tilleul/de menthe** lime(-blossom)/mint tea; (*hum*) **c'est de la ~*** it's pretty watery stuff*. b (‡: *correction*) belting‡, hiding*.

tisanière [tizanjɛʀ] **nf** teapot (*for making herbal tea*).

tison [tizɔ̃] **nm** brand; *voir* **allumette, Noël.**

tisonner [tizɔne] 1 **vt** to poke.

tisonnier [tizɔnje] **nm** poker.

tissage [tisaʒ] **nm** weaving.

tisser [tise] 1 **vt** (*lit, fig*) to weave. **l'araignée tisse sa toile** the spider spins its web; *voir* **métier.**

tisserand, e [tisʀɑ̃, ɑ̃d] **nm,f** weaver.

tisseur, -euse [tisœʀ, øz] **nm,f** weaver.

tissu[1] [tisy] 1 **nm** a (*Tex*) fabric, material, cloth. **les parois sont en ~ et non en bois** the walls are cloth not wood; **c'est un ~ très délicat** it's a very delicate fabric *ou* material; **acheter du ~/3 mètres de ~ pour faire une robe** to buy some cloth *ou* material *ou* fabric/3 metres of material *ou* fabric *ou* cloth to make a dress; **choisir un ~ pour faire une robe** to choose material to make a dress, choose a dress fabric *ou* material; ~ **imprimé/à fleurs** printed/floral-patterned material *ou* fabric; ~ **synthétique** synthetic material *ou* fabric; **~s d'ameublement** soft furnishings; **étoffe à ~ lâche/serré** loosely-/finely-woven material *ou* fabric *ou* cloth.

b (*fig péj*) **un ~ de mensonges/contradictions** a web *ou* tissue of lies/contradictions; **un ~ d'intrigues** a web of intrigue; **un ~ d'horreurs/d'obscénités/d'inepties** a jumble *ou* farrago of horrors/obscenities/stupidities.

c (*Anat, Bot*) tissue. ~ **sanguin/osseux/cicatriciel** blood/bone/scar *ou* cicatricial (SPÉC) tissue.

d (*Sociol*) **le ~ social/industriel/urbain** the social/industrial/urban fabric.

2 **comp ►tissu-éponge nm (pl tissus-éponge)** (terry) towelling (*NonC*).

tissu², e [tisy] 1 **ptp de tisser.** 2 **adj** (*littér: composé de*) **~ de contradictions/ramifications** woven *ou* shot through with contradictions/ complications.

tissulaire [tisylɛʀ] **adj** (*Bio*) tissue (*épith*). **culture ~** tissue culture.

Titan [titɑ̃] **nm** Titan. **les ~s** the Titans; (*fig*) **œuvre/travail de ~** titanic work/task.

titane [titan] **nm** titanium.

titanesque [titanɛsk] **adj, titanique** [titanik] **adj** titanic.

Tite [tit] **nm** Titus.

Tite-Live [titliv] **nm** Livy.

titi [titi] **nm: ~ (parisien)** (cocky) Parisian kid*.

Titien [tisjɛ̃] **nm** Titian.

titillation [titijasjɔ̃] **nf** (*littér, hum*) titillation.

titiller [titije] 1 **vt** (*littér, hum*) to titillate.

titrage [titʀaʒ] **nm** (*voir* **titrer**) assaying; titration; titling.

titre [titʀ(ə)] **nm** a [*œuvre*] title; [*chapitre*] heading, title; (*Jur*) [*code*] title; (*manchette de journal*) headline; (*journal*) newspaper. **les (gros) ~s** the headlines; **~ sur 5 colonnes à la une** 5-column front page headline; (*Typ*) **~ courant** running head; **les principaux ~s de la presse parisienne** the major Parisian newspapers; (*Typ*) **(page de) ~** title page; **~ budgétaire** budgetary item; *voir* **sous.**

b (*honorifique, de fonctions professionnelles*) title; (*formule de politesse*) form of address; (*littér: nom*) title, name. **~ nobiliaire** *ou* **de noblesse** title; **conférer à qn le ~ de maréchal/prince** to confer the title of marshal/prince on sb; **il ne mérite pas le ~ de citoyen/d'invité** he is unworthy of the name *ou* title of citizen/guest.

c (*Sport*) title.

d **en ~** (*Admin*) titular; (*Comm*) *fournisseur* appointed; (*hum*) *maîtresse, victime* official, recognized.

e (*document*) title; (*certificat*) certificate; (*reçu*) receipt. **~ de créance** evidence ~ proof of debt; **~ de pension** pension book; **~ de propriété** title deed; **~ de séjour** residence permit; (*Admin*) **~ de transport** ticket; **~ de paiement** order to pay, remittance; (*Admin*) **~ universel de paiement** universal payment order.

f (*Bourse, Fin*) security. **acheter/vendre des ~s** to buy/sell securities *ou* stock; **~s cotés/non cotés** listed/unlisted securities; **~ de Bourse, ~ boursier** stock-exchange security, stock certificate; **~ d'obligation** debenture (bond); **~ participatif** non-voting share (*in a public sector enterprise*); **~ au porteur** bearer bond (*ou* share); **~s d'État** government securities; **~s nominatifs** registered securities; **dollar-~** security dollar.

g (*preuve de capacité, diplôme*) (*gén*) qualification; (*Univ*) degree, qualification. **~s universitaires** academic *ou* university qualifications; **nommer/recruter sur ~s** to appoint/recruit according to qualifications; **il a tous les ~s (nécessaires) pour enseigner** he is fully qualified *ou* he has all the necessary qualifications to teach.

h (*littér, gén pl: droit, prétentions*) **avoir des ~s à la reconnaissance de qn** to have a right to sb's gratitude; **ses ~s de gloire** his claims to fame.

i [*or, argent, monnaie*] fineness; [*solution*] titre. **or/argent au ~** standard gold/silver; **~ d'alcool** *ou* **alcoolique** alcohol content.

j (*loc*) **à ce ~** (*en cette qualité*) as such; (*pour cette raison*) on this account, therefore; **à quel ~?** on what grounds?; **au même ~** in the same way; **il y a droit au même ~ que les autres** he is entitled to it in the same way as the others; **à aucun ~** on no account; **nous ne voulons de lui à aucun ~** we don't want him on any account; **à des ~s divers, à plusieurs ~s, à plus d'un ~** on several accounts, on more than one account; **à double ~** on two accounts; **à ~ privé/personnel** in a private/ personal capacity; **à ~ permanent/provisoire** on a permanent/temporary basis, permanently/provisionally; **à ~ exceptionnel** *ou* **d'exception** (*dans ce cas*) in this exceptional case; (*dans certains cas*) in exceptional cases; **à ~ d'ami/de client fidèle** as a friend/a loyal customer; **à ~ gratuit** freely, free of charge; **à ~ gracieux** free of *ou* without charge; **à ~ lucratif** for payment; **à ~ d'essai** on a trial basis; **à ~ d'exemple** as an example, by way of example; (*frm*) **à ~ onéreux** in return for remuneration (*frm*) *ou* payment; **à ~ indicatif** for information only; **il travaille à ~ de secrétaire** he works as a secretary; **à ~ consultatif** *collaborer* in an advisory *ou* a consultative capacity; **on vous donne 500 F à ~ d'indemnité** we are giving you 500 francs by way of indemnity *ou* as an indemnity; *voir* **juste.**

titré, e [titʀe] **(ptp de titrer) adj** a (*noble*) *personne* titled; *terres* carrying a title (*attrib*). b (*Tech*) *liqueur* standard.

titrer [titʀe] 1 **vt** a (*gén ptp: anoblir*) to confer a title on. b (*Chim*) *alliage* to assay; *solution* to titrate. c (*Ciné*) to title. d (*Presse*) to run as a headline. **~ sur 2/5 colonnes: "Défaite de la Gauche"** to run a 2/5-column headline: "Defeat of the Left". e [*alcool, vin*] **~ 10°/38°** to be 10°/38° proof (*on the Gay Lussac scale*), ≃ to be 17°/66° proof.

titrisation [titʀizasjɔ̃] **nf** securitization.

titubant, e [titybɑ̃, ɑ̃t] **adj** (*voir* **tituber**) staggering; reeling; unsteady.

tituber [titybe] 1 **vi** [*personne*] (*de faiblesse, fatigue*) to stagger (along); (*d'ivresse*) to stagger (along), reel (along); [*démarche*] to be unsteady. **il avançait vers nous/sortit de la cuisine en titubant** he came staggering *ou* stumbling *ou* tottering towards us/out of the kitchen, he staggered *ou* stumbled *ou* tottered towards us/out of the kitchen; **nous titubions de fatigue** we were so tired that we could hardly keep upright, we were staggering *ou* tottering *ou* stumbling along, so tired were we.

titulaire [titylɛʀ] 1 **adj** a (*Admin*) *professeur* with tenure. **être ~** to have tenure; **être ~ de** (*Univ*) *chaire* to occupy, hold; (*Pol*) *portefeuille* to hold. b (*Jur*) **(être) ~ de** *droit* (to be) entitled to; *permis, carte* (to be) the holder of. c (*Rel*) *évêque* titular (*épith*). **saint/patron ~ d'une église** (titular) saint/patron of a church. 2 **nmf** (*Admin*) [*poste*] incumbent; (*Jur*) [*droit*] person entitled (*de* to); [*permis, carte*] holder; (*Rel*) [*église*] titular saint. **~ d'une carte de crédit** credit card holder.

titularisation [titylaʀizasjɔ̃] **nf** granting of tenure (*de qn* to sb).

titulariser [titylaʀize] 1 **vt** to give tenure to. **être titularisé** to get *ou* be given tenure.

T.N.T. [teɛnte] **nm** (**abrév de trinitrotoluène**) TNT.

toast [tost] **nm** a (*pain grillé*) slice *ou* piece of toast. **un ~ beurré** a slice *ou* piece of buttered toast. b (*discours*) toast. **~ de bienvenue** welcoming toast; **porter un ~ en l'honneur de qn** to drink (a toast) to sb, toast sb.

toasteur [tostœʀ] **nm** toaster.

toboggan [tɔbɔgɑ̃] **nm** a (*traîneau*) toboggan. **faire du ~** to go tobogganing; **piste de ~** toboggan run. b (*glissière*) (*jeu*) slide; [*piscine*] chute; (*Tech: pour manutention*) chute. (*Aut: viaduc*) **T~** ® flyover (*Brit*), overpass (*US*).

toc¹ [tɔk] 1 **excl** a (*bruit: gén ~ ~*) knock knock!, rat-a-tat(-tat)! b (*: *repartie*) **et ~!** (*en s'adressant à qn*) so there!*; (*en racontant la réaction de qn*) and serves him (*ou* her *etc*) jolly (*Brit*) *ou* damned well right!* 2 **adj** (*: *gén ~ ~: idiot*) cracked*, barmy* (*Brit*), nutty*.

toc² [tɔk] 1 **nm: c'est du ~** (*imitation, faux*) it's fake; (*camelote*) it's rubbish *ou* trash *ou* junk; **en ~** *bijou, bracelet* imitation, fake; rubbishy, trashy. 2 **adv, adj: ça fait ~, c'est ~** (*imité, tape-à-l'œil*) it's a gaudy imitation; (*camelote*) it looks cheap *ou* rubbishy, it's junk.

tocante* [tɔkɑ̃t] **nf** ticker* (*Brit*), watch.

tocard, e* [tɔkaʀ, aʀd] 1 **adj** *meubles, décor* cheap and nasty, trashy*. 2 **nm** (*personne*) dead loss*, useless twit*, washout*; (*cheval*) (old) nag (*péj*).

toccata [tɔkata] **nf** toccata.

tocsin [tɔksɛ̃] **nm** alarm (bell), tocsin (*littér*). **sonner le ~** to ring the alarm, sound the tocsin (*littér*).

toge [tɔʒ] **nf** a (*Hist*) toga. **~ virile/prétexte** toga virilis/praetexta. b (*Jur, Scol*) gown.

Togo [tɔgo] **nm** Togo.

togolais, e [tɔgɔlɛ, ɛz] 1 **adj** of *ou* from Togo. 2 **nm,f: T~(e)** native of Togo.

tohu-bohu [tɔybɔy] **nm** (*désordre*) jumble, confusion; (*agitation*) hustle (and bustle); (*tumulte*) hubbub, commotion.

toi [twa] **pron pers** a (*sujet, objet*) you. **~ et lui, vous êtes tous les deux aussi têtus** you and he are as stubborn the one as the other, the two of you are (both) equally stubborn; **si j'étais ~, j'irais** if I were you *ou* in your shoes I'd go; **il n'obéit qu'à ~** you are the only one he obeys, he obeys only you; **il a accepté, ~ non** *ou* **pas ~** he accepted but you didn't *ou* but not you; **c'est enfin ~!** here you are at last!; **qui l'a vu? ~?** who saw him? (did) you?; **~ mentir? ce n'est pas possible** YOU tell a lie? I can't believe it; **~ qui sais tout, explique-moi** you're the one who knows everything so explain to me; **marche devant** *ou* **va devant, c'est ~ qui connais le chemin** you go first (since) you know the way *ou* you are the one who knows the way; **~, tu n'as pas à te plaindre** you have no cause to complain; **pourquoi ne le ferais-je pas, tu l'as bien fait ~!** why shouldn't I do it? YOU did it, didn't you? *ou* you jolly (*Brit*) well did (it)!*; **tu l'as vu, ~?** did you see him?, have you seen him?; **t'épouser, ~? jamais!** marry you? never!; **~, je te connais** I know you; **aide-moi, ~!** you there *ou* hey you, give me a hand!; **~, tu m'agaces!, tu m'agaces, ~!** (oh) you get on my nerves!; **~, pauvre innocent, tu n'as rien compris** you, poor fool, haven't understood a thing, you poor fool — you haven't understood a thing!

b (*avec vpr: souvent non traduit*) **assieds-~** sit down!; **mets-~ là!** stand over there!; **toi, tais-~!** you be quiet!; **montre-~ un peu aimable!** be a bit more pleasant!

c (*avec prép*) you, yourself. **à ~ tout seul, tu ne peux pas le faire** you can't do it on your own; **cette maison est-elle à ~?** does this house belong to you?, is this house yours?; **tu n'as même pas une chambre à ~ tout seul?** you don't even have a room of your own? *ou* a room to yourself?; **tu ne penses qu'à ~** you only think of yourself, you think only of yourself; **je compte sur ~** I'm counting on you.

d (*dans comparaisons*) you. **il me connaît mieux que ~** (*qu'il ne te connaît*) he knows me better than (he knows) you; (*que tu ne me connais*) he knows me better than you (do); **il est plus/moins fort que ~** he is stronger than/not so strong as you; **il a fait comme ~** he did what you did, he did the same as you.

toile [twal] 1 **nf** a (*tissu*) (*gén*) cloth (*NonC*); (*grossière, de chanvre*) canvas (*NonC*); (*pour pneu*) canvas (*NonC*). **grosse ~** (rough *ou* coarse) canvas; **~ de lin/de coton** linen/cotton (cloth); **en ~, de ~**

draps linen; *pantalon, blazer* (heavy) cotton; *sac* canvas; **en ~ tergal** in Terylene fabric; **~ caoutchoutée/plastifiée** rubberized/plastic-coated cloth; **relié ~** cloth bound; **~ d'amiante/métallique** asbestos/metal cloth; **~ imprimée** printed cotton, cotton print; *voir* **chanson, village.**

b (*morceau*) piece of cloth. **poser qch sur une ~** to put sth on a piece of cloth; (**: draps*) **se mettre dans les ~s** to hit the hay* *ou* the sack*.

c (*Art*) (*support*) canvas; (*œuvre*) canvas, painting. **il expose ses ~s chez X** he exhibits his canvasses *ou* paintings at X's; **une ~ de maître** an old master; **gâcher** *ou* **barbouiller de la ~** to daub on canvas.

d (*Naut: ensemble des voiles*) sails. **faire de la/réduire la ~** to make/take in sail; **navire chargé de ~s** ship under canvas, ship under full sail.

e *[araignée]* web. **la ~ de l'araignée** the spider's web; **une belle ~ d'araignée** a beautiful spider's web; **grenier plein de ~s d'araignées** attic full of cobwebs.

f (**: film*) film, movie (*surtout US*). **se faire une ~** to go and see a film, go to a movie (*surtout US*), go to the flicks* (*Brit*).

2 **comp ▸toile d'avion** aeroplane cloth *ou* linen **▸toile à bâche** tarpaulin **▸toile cirée** oilcloth **▸toile émeri** emery cloth **▸toile de fond** (*Théât*) backdrop, backcloth; (*fig*) backdrop **▸toile goudronnée** tarpaulin **▸toile de Jouy** ≃ Liberty print **▸toile de jute** hessian **▸toile à matelas** ticking **▸toile à sac** sacking, sackcloth **▸toile de tente** (*Camping*) canvas; (*Mil*) tent sheet **▸toile à voile** sailcloth.

toilerie [twalʀi] **nf** (*fabrication*) textile manufacture (*of cotton, linen, canvas etc*); (*commerce*) cotton (*ou* linen *etc*) trade; (*atelier*) cotton (*ou* linen *etc*) mill.

toilettage [twaletaʒ] **nm** *[chien]* grooming; *[texte de loi]* tidying up. (*enseigne*) **"~ pour chiens", "salon de ~"** "dogs' beauty parlour".

toilette [twalɛt] **nf** a (*ablutions*) **faire sa ~** to have a wash, get washed; (*habillage*) **être à sa ~** to be dressing, be getting ready; **faire une grande ~/une ~ rapide** *ou* **un brin de ~** to have a thorough/quick wash; **faire une ~ de chat** to give o.s. a cat-lick (*Brit*) *ou* a lick and a promise; **~ intime** personal hygiene; **elle passe des heures à sa ~** she spends hours getting ready *ou* washing and dressing *ou* at her toilet (*frm*); **la ~ des enfants prend toujours du temps** it always takes a long time to get children washed *ou* ready; **un délicieux savon pour la ~ matinale** an exquisite soap for morning skin care; **une lotion pour la ~ de bébé** a cleansing lotion for baby; **articles/nécessaire de ~** toilet articles/bag; **faire la ~ d'un mort** to lay out a corpse; **la ~ d'un condamné à mort** the washing of a prisoner before execution; *voir* **cabinet, gant, trousse.**

b (*fig: nettoyage*) *[voiture]* cleaning; *[maison, monument]* facelift. **faire la ~ de** *voiture* to clean; *monument, maison* to give a facelift to, tart up* (*Brit hum*); *texte* to tidy up, polish up.

c *[animal]* **faire sa ~** to wash itself; **faire la ~ de son chien** to groom one's dog.

d (*meuble*) washstand.

e (*habillement, parure*) clothes (*pl*). **en ~ de bal** dressed for a dance, in a dance dress; **~ de mariée** wedding *ou* bridal dress *ou* gown; **être en grande ~** to be grandly dressed, be dressed in all one's finery; **parler ~** to talk (about) clothes; **aimer la ~** to like clothes; **elle porte bien la ~** she wears her clothes well; **elle prend beaucoup de soins/dépense beaucoup pour sa ~** she takes great care over/spends a good deal on her clothes.

f (*costume*) outfit. **elle a changé 3 fois de ~!** she has changed her outfit *ou* clothes 3 times!; **"nos ~s d'été"** "summer wear *ou* outfits"; **on voit déjà les ~s d'été** you can already see people in summer outfits *ou* clothes.

g (*W.-C.*) **~s** toilet; (*publiques*) public conveniences (*Brit*) *ou* lavatory, restroom (*US*); **aller aux ~s** to go to the toilet; (*dans un café etc*) **où sont les ~s** (*gén*) where is the toilet? *ou* the restroom? (*US*); (*pour femmes*) where is the ladies?* (*Brit*) *ou* the ladies' room *ou* the powder room?; (*pour hommes*) where is the gents?* (*Brit*) *ou* men's room?

h (*†: petite pièce de toile*) small piece of cloth.

i (*Boucherie*) **~ (de porc)** *lining of pig's intestine wrapped round pieces of meat.*

toiletter [twalete] [1] **vt** *chien, chat* to groom; *texte de loi* to tidy up.

toi-même [twamɛm] **pron** *voir* **même.**

toise [twaz] **nf** a (*instrument*) height gauge. **passer à la ~ (vt)** *recrues etc* to measure the height of; **(vi)** *[recrues etc]* to have one's height measured. b (*Hist: mesure*) toise (= 6 *ft*).

toiser [twaze] [1] **vt** a (*regarder avec dédain*) to look up and down, eye scornfully (up and down). **ils se toisèrent** they eyed each other scornfully (up and down). b (*†, littér: évaluer*) to estimate.

toison [twazɔ̃] **nf** a *[mouton]* fleece. **la T~ d'or** the Golden Fleece. b (*chevelure*) (*épaisse*) mop; (*longue*) mane. c (*poils*) abundant growth.

toit [twa] **nm** a (*gén*) roof. **~ de chaume/de tuiles/d'ardoises** thatched/tiled/slate roof; **~ plat** *ou* **en terrasse/en pente** flat/sloping roof; **habiter sous le ~** *ou* **les ~s** to live under the eaves; (*fig*) **le ~ du monde** the roof of the world; (*fig*) **crier qch sur (tous) les ~s** to shout *ou* proclaim sth from the rooftops *ou* housetops; **voiture à ~ ouvrant** car with a sunroof.

b (*fig: maison*) **avoir un ~** to have a roof over one's head, have a home; **être sans ~** to have no roof over one's head, have nowhere to call home *ou* one's own; **sous le ~ de qn** under sb's roof, in sb's house; **vivre sous le même ~** to live under the same roof; **vivre sous le ~ paternel** to live in the paternal home; **recevoir qn sous son ~** to have sb as a guest in one's house.

toiture [twatyʀ] **nf** roof, roofing.

tokai, tokay [tɔkɛ] **nm, tokaï** [tɔkaj] **nm** Tokay.

Tokyo [tɔkjo] **n** Tokyo.

tôle[1] [tol] **nf** (*matériau*) sheet metal (*NonC*); (*pièce*) steel (*ou* iron) sheet. **~ d'acier/d'aluminium** sheet steel/aluminium; **~ étamée** tinplate; **~ galvanisée/émaillée** galvanized/enamelled iron; (*Aut*) **~ froissée** dented bodywork; **~ ondulée** corrugated iron; (*fig: route*) rugged dirt track.

tôle[2]‡ [tol] = **taule**‡.

Tolède [tɔlɛd] **n** Toledo.

tôlée [tole] **adj f: neige ~** crusted snow.

tolérable [tɔleʀabl] 1 **adj** *comportement, retard* tolerable; *douleur, attente* tolerable, bearable. **cette attitude n'est pas ~** this attitude is intolerable *ou* cannot be tolerated. 2 **nm: attitude à la limite du ~** barely tolerable attitude.

tolérance [tɔleʀɑ̃s] **nf** a (*compréhension, largeur d'esprit*) tolerance. b (*liberté limitée*) **c'est une ~, pas un droit** it is tolerated *ou* sanctioned rather than allowed as of right; (*Comm: produits hors taxe*) **il y a une ~ de 2 litres de spiritueux/200 cigarettes** there's an allowance of 2 litres of spirits/200 cigarettes; **~ orthographique/grammaticale** permitted departure in spelling/grammar; *voir* **maison.** c (*Méd, Tech*) tolerance; *voir* **marge.** d (*Hist, Rel*) toleration.

tolérant, e [tɔleʀɑ̃, ɑ̃t] **adj** tolerant.

tolérantisme [tɔleʀɑ̃tism] **nm** (*Hist Rel*) tolerationism.

tolérer [tɔleʀe] [6] **vt** a (*ne pas sévir contre*) *culte, pratiques, abus, infractions* to tolerate; (*autoriser*) to allow. **ils tolèrent un excédent de bagages de 15 kg** they allow 15 kg (of) excess baggage.

b (*supporter*) *comportement, excentricités, personne* to put up with, tolerate; *douleur* to bear, endure, stand. **ils ne s'aimaient guère: disons qu'ils se toléraient** they did not like each other much — you could say that they put up with *ou* tolerated each other; **je ne tolérerai pas cette impertinence/ces retards** I shall not stand for *ou* put up with *ou* tolerate this impertinence/this constant lateness; **il tolérait qu'on l'appelle par son prénom** he put up with being called by his first name, he allowed people to call him by his first name; **il ne tolère pas qu'on le contredise** he won't stand (for) *ou* tolerate being contradicted.

c (*Bio, Méd*) *[organisme]* to tolerate; (*Tech*) *[matériau, système]* to tolerate. **il ne tolère pas l'alcool** he can't tolerate *ou* take alcohol, alcohol doesn't agree with him.

tôlerie [tolʀi] **nf** a (*fabrication*) sheet metal manufacture; (*commerce*) sheet metal trade; (*atelier*) sheet metal workshop. b (*tôles*) *[auto]* panels (*pl*), coachwork (*NonC*); *[bateau, chaudière]* plates (*pl*), steel-work (*NonC*).

tolet [tɔlɛ] **nm** rowlock, thole.

tôlier[1] [tolje] **nm** (*industriel*) sheet iron *ou* steel manufacturer. **(ouvrier-)~** sheet metal worker; **~ en voitures** panel beater.

tôlier[2], -ière‡ [tolje, jɛʀ] **nm,f** = **taulier**‡.

tollé [tɔ(l)le] **nm** general outcry *ou* protest. **ce fut un ~ (général)** there was a general outcry.

Tolstoï [tɔlstɔj] **nm** Tolstoy.

toluène [tɔlɥɛn] **nm** toluene.

T.O.M. [tɔm] **nm** (**abrév de territoire d'outre-mer**) *voir* **territoire.**

tomahawk [tɔmaok] **nm** tomahawk.

tomaison [tɔmɛzɔ̃] **nf** volume numbering.

tomate [tɔmat] **nf** a (*plante*) tomato (plant); (*fruit*) tomato. **~s farcies** stuffed tomatoes; **~s (à la) provençale** tomatoes (à la) Provençale; **~s cerises** cherry tomatoes; (*fig*) **il va recevoir des ~s** he'll have a hostile reception, he'll get booed; *voir* **rouge.** b (*boisson*) *grenadine and pastis drink.*

tombal, e, mpl ~s *ou* **~aux** [tɔ̃bal, o] **adj** *dalle* funerary; (*littér: funèbre*) tomb-like, funereal (*épith*). **inscription ~e** tombstone inscription; *voir* **pierre.**

tombant, e [tɔ̃bɑ̃, ɑ̃t] **adj** *draperies* hanging (*épith*); *épaules* sloping (*épith*), drooping (*épith*); *moustaches* drooping (*épith*); *voir* **nuit.**

tombe [tɔ̃b] **nf** a (*gén*) grave; (*avec monument*) tomb; (*pierre*) gravestone, tombstone. **froid comme la ~** cold as the tomb; **silencieux comme la ~** silent as the grave *ou* tomb; *voir* **muet, recueillir, retourner.**

b (*loc*) **suivre qn dans la ~** to follow sb to the grave; **avoir un pied dans la ~** to have one foot in the grave; (*littér*) **descendre dans la ~** to go to one's grave.

tombeau, pl ~x [tɔ̃bo] **nm** a (*lit*) tomb. **mettre au ~** to commit to the grave, entomb; **mise au ~** entombment. b (*fig*) (*endroit lugubre ou solitaire*) grave, tomb; (*ruine*) *[espérances, amour]* death (*NonC*); (*lieu du trépas*) grave. (*trépas*) **jusqu'au ~** to the grave; **descendre au ~** to go to one's grave; **cette pièce est un ~** this room is like a grave *ou* tomb; (*secret*) **je serai un vrai ~** my lips are sealed, I'll be as silent as the grave. c **à ~ ouvert** at breakneck speed.

tombée [tɔ̃be] nf a **(à) la ~ de la nuit** (at) nightfall; **(à) la ~ du jour** (at) the close of the day. b (*littér*) *[neige, pluie]* fall.

tomber [tɔ̃be] 1 1 vi (*avec aux être*) a (*de la station debout*) to fall (over *ou* down). **il est tombé en courant et s'est cassé la jambe** he fell (over *ou* down) while running and broke his leg; **le chien l'a fait ~** the dog knocked him over *ou* down; **~ par terre** to fall down, fall to the ground; **~ raide mort** to fall down *ou* drop (down) dead; **~ à genoux** to fall on(to) one's knees; (*fig*) **~ aux pieds** *ou* **genoux de qn** to fall at sb's feet; (*fig*) **~ dans les bras de qn** to fall into sb's arms; **~ de tout son long** to fall headlong, go sprawling, measure one's length; **~ de tout son haut** *ou* **de toute sa hauteur** to fall *ou* crash *ou* topple to the ground; **se laisser ~ dans un fauteuil** to drop *ou* fall into an armchair; (*fig*) **~ de fatigue** to drop from exhaustion; (*fig*) **~ de sommeil** to be falling asleep on one's feet; *voir* **inanition, pomme, renverse**.

b (*de la position verticale*) *[arbre, bouteille, poteau]* to fall (over *ou* down); *[chaise, pile d'objets]* to fall (over); *[échafaudage, mur]* to fall down, collapse. **faire ~** (*gén*) to knock down; (*en renversant*) to knock over.

c (*d'un endroit élevé*) *[personne, objet]* to fall (down); *[avion]* to fall; (*fig littér: pécher*) to fall. **attention, tu vas ~** careful, you'll fall; (*fig*) **~ (bien) bas** to sink (very) low; (*fig littér*) **ne condamnez pas un homme qui est tombé** do not condemn a fallen man; **prince tombé** fallen prince; **~ d'un arbre** to fall from a tree, fall out of a tree; **~ d'une chaise/d'une échelle** to fall off a chair/(down) off a ladder; **~ du cinquième étage** to fall from the fifth floor; **~ dans** *ou* **à l'eau** to fall in *ou* into the water; **~ de bicyclette/de cheval** to fall off one's bicycle/from *ou* off one's horse; **~ à bas de son cheval** to fall from *ou* off one's horse; **il tombait des pierres** stones were falling.

d (*se détacher*) *[feuilles, fruits]* to fall; *[cheveux]* to fall (out). **ramasser des fruits tombés** to pick up fruit that has fallen, pick up windfalls; **le journal tombe (des presses) à 6 heures** the paper comes off the press at 6 o'clock; **la nouvelle vient de ~ à l'instant** the news has just this minute broken; **un télex vient de ~** a telex has just come through; **la plume me tombe des mains** the pen is falling from my hand; **faire ~** (*en lâchant*) to drop; **porte le vase sur la table sans le faire ~** carry the vase to the table without dropping it.

e *[eau, lumière]* to fall; *[neige, pluie]* to fall, come down; *[brouillard]* to come down. **il tombe de la neige** snow is falling; **qu'est-ce qu'il tombe!*** it isn't half coming down!* (*Brit*), it's coming down in buckets!*; **l'eau tombait en cascades** the water was cascading down; **il tombe quelques gouttes** it's raining slightly, there are a few drops of rain (falling), it's spotting (with rain) (*Brit*) *ou* sprinkling lightly (*US*); **la nuit tombe** night is falling *ou* coming; **la foudre est tombée deux fois/tout près** the lightning has struck twice/nearby.

f (*fig: être tué*) *[combattant]* to fall. **ils tombaient les uns après les autres** they were falling one after the other; **tombé au champ d'honneur** killed in action; *voir* **mouche**.

g (*fig*) *[ville, régime, garnison]* to fall. **faire ~ le gouvernement** to bring down the government, bring the government down; (*Cartes*) **l'as et le roi sont tombés** the ace and king have gone *ou* have been played; (*Cartes*) **faire ~ une carte** to drop.

h (*baisser*) *[fièvre]* to drop; *[vent]* to drop, abate, die down; *[baromètre]* to fall; *[jour]* to draw to a close; *[voix]* to drop, fall away; *[prix, nombre, température]* to fall, drop (*à* to, *de* by); *[colère, conversation]* to die down; *[exaltation, assurance, enthousiasme]* to fall away. **le dollar est tombé à 5 F** the dollar has fallen *ou* dropped to 5 francs; **faire ~** *température, vent, prix* to bring down.

i (*disparaître*) *[obstacle, objection]* to disappear; *[plan, projet]* to fall through; *[droit, poursuites]* to lapse.

j (*pendre, descendre*) *[draperie, robe, chevelure]* to fall, hang; *[pantalon]* to hang; *[moustaches, épaules]* to droop. **ses cheveux lui tombaient sur les épaules** his hair fell *ou* hung down onto his shoulders; **les lourds rideaux tombaient jusqu'au plancher** the heavy curtains hung down to the floor; **ce pantalon tombe bien** these trousers hang well.

k (*devenir: avec attribut, avec en: voir aussi les noms et adjectifs en question*) **~ malade** to fall ill; **~ amoureux** to fall in love (*de* with); **~ d'accord** to come to an agreement, reach agreement; **~ en disgrâce** to fall into disgrace; **~ en syncope** to faint, fall into a faint; *voir* **arrêt, désuétude**.

l (*avec dans, sous, à: se trouver: voir aussi les noms en question*) **~ dans un piège/une embuscade** to fall into a trap/an ambush; **~ dans l'oubli** to fall into oblivion; **~ dans l'excès/le ridicule** to lapse into excess/the ridiculous; **~ dans l'excès inverse** to go to the opposite extreme; **~ d'un excès dans un autre** to go from one extreme to another; **~ sous la domination de** to fall *ou* come under the domination of; **~ aux mains de l'ennemi** to fall into enemy hands; *voir* **coupe[2], dent, main**.

m (*échoir*) *[date, choix, sort]* to fall. **Pâques tombe tard cette année** Easter falls late this year; **Noël tombe un mardi** Christmas falls on a Tuesday; **les deux concerts tombent le même jour** the two concerts fall on the same day; **le choix est tombé sur lui** the choice fell on him; **et il a fallu que ça tombe sur moi** it (just) had to be me.

n (*arriver inopinément*) **il est tombé en pleine réunion/scène de ménage** he walked straight into a meeting/a domestic row.

o **laisser ~** *objet que l'on porte* to drop; *amis, activité* to drop; *métier* to drop, give up, chuck up*; *fiancé* to jilt, throw over*; *vieux parents* to let down, leave in the lurch; **il a voulu faire du droit mais il a vite laissé ~** he wanted to do law but he soon gave it up *ou* dropped it; **la famille nous a bien laissé ~** the family really let us down *ou* left us in the lurch; **laissez ~!*, laisse ~!*** (*gén*) forget it!*; (*nuance d'irritation*) give it a rest!*.

p (*‡: être arrêté*) to be *ou* get busted‡ *ou* nicked‡ (*Brit*) *ou* pinched‡.

q (*loc*) **bien/mal ~** (*avoir de la chance*) to be lucky/unlucky; **il est vraiment bien/mal tombé avec son nouveau patron** he's really lucky/unlucky *ou* in luck/out of luck with his new boss; **bien/mal ~, ~ bien/mal** (*arriver, se produire*) to come at the right/wrong moment; **ça tombe bien** that's lucky *ou* fortunate; **ça tombe à point** *ou* **à pic*** that's perfect timing; **ça ne pouvait pas mieux ~** that couldn't have come at a better time; **~ de Charybde en Scylla** to jump out of the frying pan into the fire; **~ juste** (*en devinant*) to be (exactly) right; *[calculs]* to come out right; **~ de haut** to be badly let down, be bitterly disappointed; **il n'est pas tombé de la dernière pluie** *ou* **averse*** he wasn't born yesterday; **ce n'est pas tombé dans l'oreille d'un sourd** it didn't fall on deaf ears; **il est tombé sur la tête!*** he's got a screw loose*; **~ en quenouille** to pass into female hands; (*fig*) **~ de la lune** to have dropped in from another planet; (*fig*) **~ du ciel** to be a godsend, be heaven-sent; **~ du lit** to be up bright and early; **~ des nues** to be completely taken aback; (*fig*) **~ à l'eau** *[projets, entreprise]* to fall through; **~ à plat** *[plaisanterie]* to fall flat; *[pièce de théâtre]* to be a flop; **cela tombe sous le sens** it's (perfectly) obvious, it stands to reason; *voir* **bras, cul**.

2 **tomber sur** vt indir (*avec aux être*) a (*rencontrer*) *connaissance* to run into, come across; *détail* to come across *ou* upon. **prenez cette rue, et vous tombez sur le boulevard** go along this street and you come out on the boulevard; **je suis tombé sur cet article de journal** I came across *ou* upon this newspaper article; **~ sur un bec*** *ou* **un os*** (*obstacle temporaire*) to hit a snag; (*impasse*) to be stymied; (*échec*) to come unstuck.

b (*se poser*) *[regard]* to fall *ou* light upon; *[conversation]* to come round to.

c (*) (*attaquer*) to set about*, go for*; (*critiquer*) to go for*. **il m'est tombé sur le râble‡** *ou* **le paletot‡** *ou* **le dos‡** he set on me*, he went for me*; **ils nous sont tombés dessus à 8 contre 3** 8 of them laid into the 3 of us; *voir* **bras**.

d (**: s'inviter, survenir*) to land on*. **il nous est tombé dessus le jour de ton anniversaire** he landed on us on your birthday*.

3 vt (*avec aux avoir*) a **~ qn** (*Sport*) to throw sb; (**: Pol*) to beat sb; **~ une femme‡** to lay‡ *ou* have‡ a woman.

b **~ la veste*** to slip off one's jacket.

tombereau, pl **~x** [tɔ̃bʀo] nm (*charrette*) tipcart; (*contenu*) cartload.

tombeur [tɔ̃bœʀ] nm (*lutteur*) thrower. (*fig*) **~ (de femmes)*** Don Juan, ladykiller, Casanova.

tombola [tɔ̃bɔla] nf tombola, raffle.

Tombouctou [tɔ̃buktu] n Timbuktoo.

tome [tɔm] nm (*division*) part, book; (*volume*) volume.

tomer [tɔme] 1 vt *ouvrage* to divide into parts *ou* books; *page, volume* to mark with the volume number.

tomette [tɔmɛt] nf = **tommette**.

tomme [tɔm] nf tomme (cheese).

tommette [tɔmɛt] nf (red, hexagonal) floor-tile.

tomodensitomètre [tomodɑ̃sitɔmɛtʀ] nm scanner.

tomodensitométrie [tomodɑ̃sitɔmetʀi] nf scanning.

tomographie [tɔmɔgʀafi] nf tomography.

tom-pouce* [tɔmpus] nm (*nain*) Tom Thumb, dwarf, midget.

ton[1] [tɔ̃], **ta** [ta], **tes** [te] adj poss a (*possession, relation*) your, (*emphatique*) your own; (†, *Rel*) thy. **~ fils et ta fille** your son and (your) daughter; (*Rel*) **que ta volonté soit faite** Thy will be done; *pour autres exemples voir* **son[1]**.

b (*valeur affective, ironique, intensive*) **je vois que tu connais tes classiques!** I can see that you know your classics!; **tu as de la chance d'avoir ~ samedi!*** you're lucky to have (your) Saturday(s) off!; **~ Paris est devenu très bruyant** this Paris of yours *ou* your beloved Paris is getting very noisy; **tu vas avoir ta crise de foie si tu manges ça** you'll have one of your upsets *ou* you'll upset your stomach if you eat that; **ferme donc ta porte!** shut the door behind you; *pour autres exemples voir* **son[1]**.

ton[2] [tɔ̃] nm a (*hauteur de la voix*) pitch; (*timbre*) tone; (*manière de parler*) tone (of voice). **~ aigu/grave** shrill/low pitch; **~ nasillard** nasal tone; **d'un ~ détaché/brusque/pédant** in a detached/an abrupt/a pedantic tone (of voice); **avec un ~ de supériorité** in a superior tone; **sur le ~ de la conversation/plaisanterie** in a conversational/joking tone (of voice); **hausser le ~** to raise (the tone of) one's voice *ou* one's tone; **baisser le ~** to lower one's voice, pipe down*; (*fig*) **hausser le ~** (*se fâcher*) to raise one's voice; (*être arrogant*) to adopt an arrogant tone; (*fig*) **faire baisser le ~ à qn** to make sb change his tune, bring sb down a peg (or two); (*fig*) **il devra changer de ~** he'll have to sing a different tune *ou* change his tune; (*fig*) **ne le prenez pas sur ce ~** don't take it in that way *ou* like that; (*fig*) **alors là, si vous le prenez sur ce ~** well if that's the way you're going to take it, well if you're going to take it like that; (*fig*) **dire/répéter sur tous les ~s** to say/repeat in every possible way.

b (*Mus*) (*intervalle*) tone; *[morceau]* key; *[instrument à vent]* crook; (*hauteur d'un instrument*) pitch. **le ~ de si majeur** the key of B major; **passer d'un ~ à un autre** to change from one key to another; **il y a un ~ majeur entre do et ré** there is a whole *ou* full tone between doh and ray; **prendre le ~** to tune up (*de* to); **donner le ~** to give the pitch; **sortir du ~** to go out of tune; **il/ce n'est pas dans le ~** he/it is not in tune; **le ~ est trop haut pour elle** it is set in too high a key for her, it is pitched too high for her.

c (*Ling, Phonétique*) tone. **langue à ~s** tone language.

d (*manière de s'exprimer, décrire*) tone. **le ~ précieux/soutenu de sa prose** the precious/elevated tone of his prose; **des plaisanteries** *ou* **remarques de bon ~** jokes *ou* remarks in good taste; **il est de bon ~ de faire** it is good form to do; **être dans le ~** to fit in; **il s'est vite mis dans le ~** he soon fitted in; **donner le ~** to set the tone; (*en matière de mode*) to set the fashion.

e (*couleur, nuance*) shade, tone. **être dans le ~** to tone in, match; **la ceinture n'est pas du même ~** *ou* **dans le même ~ que la robe** the belt does not match the dress; **des ~s chauds** warm tones *ou* shades; **des ~s dégradés** gradual shadings; **~ sur ~** in matching tones.

tonal, e, mpl **~s** [tɔnal] adj (*Ling, Mus*) tonal.

tonalité [tɔnalite] nf a (*Mus: système*) tonality; (*Mus: ton*) key; (*Phonétique*) *[voyelle]* tone. b (*fidélité*) *[poste, amplificateur]* tone. c (*timbre, qualité*) *[voix]* tone; (*fig*) *[texte, impression]* tone; *[couleurs]* tonality. d (*Téléc*) dialling tone. **je n'ai pas la ~** I'm not getting the dialling tone, the line has gone dead.

tondeur, -euse [tɔ̃dœʀ, øz] 1 nm,f: **~ de drap** cloth shearer; **~ de moutons** sheep shearer. 2 **tondeuse** nf (*à cheveux*) clippers (*pl*); (*pour les moutons*) shears (*pl*); (*Tex: pour les draps*) shears (*pl*). **~ (à gazon)** (lawn)mower; **~ à main/à moteur** hand-/motor-mower; **~ électrique** *[gazon]* electric (lawn)mower; *[cheveux]* electric clippers (*pl*).

tondre [tɔ̃dʀ] 41 vt a *mouton, toison* to shear; *gazon* to mow; *haie* to clip, cut; *caniche, poil* to clip; *cheveux* to crop; *drap, feutre* to shear. (*fig*) **~ un œuf** to shave an egg. b (*) **~ qn** (*couper les cheveux*) to chop* sb's hair; (*escroquer*) to fleece sb; **je vais me faire ~** I'm going to get my hair chopped*; **~ la laine sur le dos de qn**† to have the shirt off sb's back; **il ne faut pas te faire ~ la laine sur le dos** you shouldn't just allow people to fleece you *ou* to get the better of you.

tondu, e [tɔ̃dy] (ptp de **tondre**) adj *cheveux, tête* (closely-)cropped; *personne* with closely-cropped hair, close-cropped; *pelouse,* (*fig*) *sommet* closely-cropped. (*péj: aux cheveux courts*) **regardez-moi ce ~** just look at that short back and sides; *voir* **pelé.**

tongs [tɔ̃g] nfpl (*sandales*) flip-flops (*Brit*), thongs (*US*).

tonicité [tɔnisite] nf a (*Méd*) *[tissus]* tone, tonicity (*SPÉC*), tonus (*SPÉC*). b (*fig*) *[air, mer]* tonic *ou* bracing effect.

tonifiant, e [tɔnifjɑ̃, jɑ̃t] 1 adj *air* bracing, invigorating; *massage, lotion* toning (*épith*), tonic (*épith*), stimulating; *lecture, expérience* invigorating, stimulating. 2 nm tonic.

tonifier [tɔnifje] 7 vt *muscles, peau* to tone up; (*fig*) *esprit, personne* to invigorate, stimulate. **cela tonifie tout l'organisme** it tones up the whole system.

tonique [tɔnik] 1 adj a *médicament, vin, boisson* tonic (*épith*), fortifying; *lotion* toning (*épith*), tonic (*épith*). b (*fig*) *air, froid* invigorating, bracing; *idée, expérience* stimulating; *lecture* invigorating, stimulating. c (*Ling*) *syllabe, voyelle* tonic, accented; *accent* tonic. 2 nm (*Méd, fig*) tonic; (*lotion*) toning lotion. **~ du cœur** heart tonic. 3 nf (*Mus*) tonic, keynote.

tonitruant, e [tɔnitʀyɑ̃, ɑ̃t] adj *voix* thundering (*épith*), booming (*épith*).

tonitruer [tɔnitʀye] 1 vi to thunder.

Tonkin [tɔ̃kɛ̃] nm Tonkin, Tongking.

tonkinois, e [tɔ̃kinwa, waz] 1 adj Tonkinese. 2 nm,f: **T~(e)** Tonkinese.

tonnage [tɔnaʒ] nm *[navire]* tonnage, burden; *[port, pays]* tonnage. **~ brut/net** gross/net tonnage.

tonnant, e [tɔnɑ̃, ɑ̃t] adj *voix, acclamation* thunderous, thundering (*épith*).

tonne [tɔn] nf a (*unité de poids*) (metric) ton, tonne. **une ~ de bois** a ton *ou* tonne of wood; (*Statistique*) **~ kilométrique** ton kilometre; **un navire de 10 000 ~s** a 10,000-ton *ou* -tonne ship, a ship of 10,000 tons *ou* tonnes; **un (camion de) 5 ~s** a 5-ton lorry, a 5-tonner*; **~ équivalent charbon** ton coal equivalent; **~ équivalent pétrole** ton oil equivalent. b **des ~s de*** tons of*, loads of*; **il y en a des ~s** there are tons* *ou* loads* *ou* stacks* of them; **en faire des ~s*** to overdo it, go over the top*. c (*Tech: récipient*) tun; (*Naut: bouée*) nun-buoy.

tonneau, pl **~x** [tɔno] nm a (*récipient, contenu*) barrel, cask. **vin au ~** wine from the barrel *ou* cask; (*fig*) **c'est le ~ des Danaïdes** it is a Sisyphean task; (*péj*) **être du même ~*** to be of the same kind; *voir* **perce.** b (*Aviat*) hesitation flick roll (*Brit*), hesitation snap roll (*US*); *voir* **demi-.** c (*Aut*) somersault. **faire un ~** to somersault, roll over. d (*Naut*) ton. **un bateau de 1 500 ~x** a 1,500-ton ship.

tonnelet [tɔnlɛ] nm keg, (small) cask.

tonnelier [tɔnəlje] nm cooper.

tonnelle [tɔnɛl] nf (*abri*) bower, arbour; (*Archit*) barrel vault.

tonnellerie [tɔnɛlʀi] nf cooperage.

tonner [tɔne] 1 1 vi a *[canons, artillerie]* to thunder, boom, roar. b *[personne]* to thunder, rage, inveigh (*contre* against). 2 vb impers to thunder. **il tonne** it is thundering; **il a tonné vers 2 heures** there was some thunder about 2 o'clock; **il tonnait sans discontinuer** it went on thundering without a break, the thunder rumbled continuously.

tonnerre [tɔnɛʀ] 1 nm a (*détonation*) thunder; (†: *foudre*) thunderbolt. **le ~ gronde** there is a rumble of thunder; **un bruit/une voix de ~** a noise/voice like thunder, a thunderous noise/voice; (*fig*) **un ~ d'applaudissements** thunderous applause, a thunder of applause; (*fig*) **le ~ des canons** the roar *ou* the thundering of the guns; *voir* **coup.**

b (*: *valeur intensive*) **du ~** terrific*, fantastic*, stupendous, great*; **ça marchait du ~** it was going tremendously well, things were fantastic*; **un livre du ~ de Dieu** one *ou* a hell of a book‡, a fantastic book*.

2 excl: **~!*†** ye gods!*†; **mille ~s!*, ~ de Brest!*** shiver my timbers!* (†, *hum*); **~ de Dieu!‡** hell and damnation!‡, hell's bells!*

tonsure [tɔ̃syʀ] nf (*Rel*) tonsure; (*: *calvitie*) bald spot *ou* patch. **porter la ~** to wear the tonsure.

tonsuré, e [tɔ̃syʀe] (ptp de **tonsurer**) 1 adj tonsured. 2 nm (*péj: moine*) monk.

tonsurer [tɔ̃syʀe] 1 vt to tonsure.

tonte [tɔ̃t] nf a (*action*) *[moutons]* shearing; *[haie]* clipping; *[gazon]* mowing. b (*laine*) fleece. c (*époque*) shearing-time.

tontine [tɔ̃tin] nf (*Fin, Jur*) tontine.

tonton [tɔ̃tɔ̃] nm (*langage enfantin*) uncle.

tonus [tɔnys] nm a **~ musculaire** muscular tone *ou* tonus (*SPÉC*); **~ nerveux** nerve tone. b (*fig: dynamisme*) energy, dynamism; (*au travail*) drive.

top [tɔp] 1 nm a (*signal électrique*) pip. (*Rad*) **au 4ᵉ ~ il sera midi** at the 4th pip *ou* stroke it will be twelve o'clock. b (*Courses*) **donner le ~** to give the starting signal; **attention, ~, partez!/~ départ!** on your marks, get set, go! c (*Mus*) **le ~ 50** the top 50 (singles), ≃ the singles charts; **numéro un du ~ 50** number one in the charts. 2 adj: **~ secret** top secret; *[athlète, chercheur]* **être au ~ niveau** to be a top level athlete *ou* researcher *etc*).

topaze [tɔpɑz] 1 nf topaz. **~ brûlée** burnt topaz. 2 adj inv (*couleur*) topaz. **un liquide ~** a topaz-coloured liquid.

tope [tɔp] excl *voir* **toper.**

toper [tɔpe] 1 vi: **~ à qch** to shake on sth, agree to sth; **tope(-là), topez-là!** done!, you're on!*, it's a deal!*, let's shake on it!

topinambour [tɔpinɑ̃buʀ] nm Jerusalem artichoke.

topique [tɔpik] 1 adj (*frm*) *argument, explication* pertinent; *citation* apposite; (*Méd*) *remède, médicament* topical, local. 2 nm (*Méd*) topical *ou* local remedy; (*Philos*) topic. 3 nf (*Philos*) topics (*sg*).

topo* [tɔpo] nm (*exposé, rapport*) lecture, rundown*; (*péj: laïus*) spiel*. **faire un ~ sur qch** to give a rundown* on sth; **c'est toujours le même ~** it's always the same old story* *ou* spiel*.

topographe [tɔpɔgʀaf] nm topographer.

topographie [tɔpɔgʀafi] nf (*technique*) topography; (*configuration*) layout, topography; (†: *description*) topographical description; (*croquis*) topographical plan.

topographique [tɔpɔgʀafik] adj topographic(al).

topographiquement [tɔpɔgʀafikmɑ̃] adv topographically.

topologie [tɔpɔlɔʒi] nf topology.

topologique [tɔpɔlɔʒik] adj topologic(al).

topométrie [tɔpɔmetʀi] nf topometry.

toponyme [tɔpɔnim] nm place name, toponym (*SPÉC*).

toponymie [tɔpɔnimi] nf (*étude*) toponymy (*SPÉC*), study of place names; (*noms de lieux*) toponymy (*SPÉC*), place names (*pl*).

toponymique [tɔpɔnimik] adj toponymic.

toquade [tɔkad] nf (*péj*) (*pour qn*) infatuation; (*pour qch*) fad, craze. **avoir une ~ pour qn** to be infatuated with sb.

toquante‡ [tɔkɑ̃t] nf = **tocante‡.**

toquard, e‡ [tɔkaʀ, aʀd] = **tocard‡.**

toque [tɔk] nf (*en fourrure*) fur hat; *[juge, jockey]* cap. **~ de cuisinier** chef's hat.

toqué, e* [tɔke] 1 adj crazy*, cracked*, nuts* (*attrib*). **être ~ de qn** to be crazy *ou* mad *ou* nuts about sb*. 2 nm,f loony‡, nutcase* (*Brit*), nutter‡.

toquer¹* (se) [tɔke] 1 vpr: **se ~ d'une femme** to lose one's head over a woman, go crazy over a woman*.

toquer²* [tɔke] 1 vi to tap, rap. **~ (à la porte)** to tap *ou* rap at the door.

Tor [tɔʀ] nm = **Thor.**

Torah [tɔʀa] nf = **Thora.**

torche [tɔʀʃ] nf a (*flambeau*) torch. **~ électrique** (electric) torch (*Brit*), flashlight (*US*); **être transformé en ~ vivante** to be turned into a human torch; (*Parachutisme*) **se mettre en ~** to candle. b (*Ind: torchère*) flare.

torche-cul‡, pl **torche-culs** [tɔʀʃəky] nm bog-paper‡ (*Brit*), toilet paper;

(*fig*, †: *écrit*) drivel (*NonC*).
torchée* [tɔʀʃe] **nf** (*correction*) hammering, licking.
torcher [tɔʀʃe] 1 **1 vt a** (*) *assiette* to wipe (clean); *jus* to mop up. **b** (‡) *bébé, derrière* to wipe. **c** (*péj*) *travail, rapport* (*produire*) to toss off; (*bâcler*) to make a mess of, do a bad job on. **un rapport/article bien torché** a well-written report/article. **2 se torcher‡ vpr: se ~ (le derrière)** to wipe one's bottom; (*fig*) **je m'en torche*** I don't care *ou* give a damn*.
torchère [tɔʀʃɛʀ] **nf a** (*Ind*) flare. **b** (*vase*) cresset; (*candélabre*) torchère; (*chandelier*) candelabrum.
torchis [tɔʀʃi] **nm** cob (*for walls*).
torchon [tɔʀʃɔ̃] **nm a** (*gén*) cloth; (*pour épousseter*) duster; (*à vaisselle*) tea towel, dish towel. **coup de ~** (*bagarre*) dust-up* (*Brit*), scrap; (*épuration*) clear-out; **donner un coup de ~** (*ménage*) to give a room a dust, flick a duster over a room; (*vaisselle*) to give the dishes a wipe; (*fig: épuration*) to have a clear-out; (*fig*) **le ~ brûle** there's a running battle (going on) (*entre* between); *voir* **mélanger. b** (*péj*) (*devoir mal présenté*) mess; (*écrit sans valeur*) drivel (*NonC*), tripe* (*NonC*); (*mauvais journal*) rag. **ce devoir est un ~** this homework is a mess.
torchonner* [tɔʀʃɔne] 1 **vt** (*péj*) *travail* to do a rushed job on. **un devoir torchonné** a slipshod *ou* badly done piece of homework.
tordant, e* [tɔʀdɑ̃, ɑ̃t] **adj** killing*, screamingly funny*, hilarious. **il est ~** he's a scream* *ou* a kill*.
tord-boyaux*† [tɔʀbwajo] **nm inv** rotgut*, hooch‡.
tordre [tɔʀdʀ] 41 **1 vt a** (*entre ses mains*) to wring; (*pour essorer*) to wring (out); *tresses* to wind; (*Tex*) *brins, laine* to twist; *bras, poignet* to twist. (*sur étiquette*) **ne pas ~** do not wring; **~ le cou à un poulet** to wring a chicken's neck; (*fig*) **je vais lui ~ le cou*** I'll wring his neck (for him); **cet alcool vous tord les boyaux*** this drink rots your guts‡; **la peur lui tordait l'estomac** his stomach was turning over with fear, fear was churning his stomach.
b (*plier*) *barre de fer* to twist; *cuiller, branche de lunette* to bend.
c (*déformer*) *traits, visage* to contort, twist. **une joie sadique lui tordait la bouche** his mouth was twisted into a sadistic smile; **la colère lui tordait le visage** his face was twisted *ou* contorted with anger.
2 se tordre vpr a *[personne]* **se ~ de douleur** to be doubled up with pain; **se ~ (de rire)** to be doubled up *ou* creased up (*Brit*) with laughter; **c'est à se ~ (de rire)** you'd die (laughing)*, it's killing*; **ça les a fait se ~ de rire** this had them in stitches*, this absolutely convulsed them*; **mon estomac se tord** I have a gnawing pain in my stomach.
b *[barre, poteau]* to bend; *[roue]* to buckle, twist; (*littér*) *[racine, tronc]* to twist round, writhe (*littér*).
c se ~ le bras/le poignet/la cheville to sprain *ou* twist one's arm/wrist/ankle; **se ~ les mains (de désespoir)** to wring one's hands (in despair).
tordu, e [tɔʀdy] (**ptp de tordre**) **1 adj** *nez* crooked; *jambes* bent, crooked; *tronc* twisted; *règle, barre* bent; *roue* bent, buckled, twisted; *idée, raisonnement* weird, twisted. **avoir l'esprit ~** to have a warped *ou* weird mind; **être (complètement) ~‡** to be round the bend* (*Brit*) *ou* the twist‡ (*Brit*), be off one's head*. **2 nm,f** (‡) (*fou*) loony‡, nutcase*; (*crétin*) twit‡.
tore [tɔʀ] **nm** (*Géom*) torus. **~ magnétique** magnetic core; **~ de ferrite** ferrite core.
toréador [tɔʀeadɔʀ] **nm** toreador.
toréer [tɔʀee] 1 **vi** to fight *ou* work a bull.
torero [tɔʀeʀo] **nm** bullfighter, torero.
torgnole* [tɔʀɲɔl] **nf** clout, wallop*, swipe*.
toril [tɔʀil] **nm** bullpen.
tornade [tɔʀnad] **nf** tornado. **entrer comme une ~** to come in like a whirlwind.
toron [tɔʀɔ̃] **nm** (*brin*) strand.
Toronto [tɔʀɔ̃to] **n** Toronto.
torontois, e [tɔʀɔ̃twa, waz] **1 adj** Torontonian. **2 nm,f: T~(e)** Torontonian.
torpédo [tɔʀpedo] **nf** (*Hist*) open tourer (*Brit*), open touring car (*US*).
torpeur [tɔʀpœʀ] **nf** torpor. **faire sortir** *ou* **tirer qn de sa ~** to bring sb out of his torpor.
torpide [tɔʀpid] **adj** (*littér*) torpid.
torpillage [tɔʀpijaʒ] **nm** torpedoing.
torpille [tɔʀpij] **nf a** (*Mil*) (*sous-marine*) torpedo. (*bombe*) **~ (aérienne)** (aerial) torpedo; *voir* **lancer. b** (*Zool*) torpedo.
torpiller [tɔʀpije] 1 **vt** *navire*, (*fig*) *plan* to torpedo.
torpilleur [tɔʀpijœʀ] **nm** torpedo boat; *voir* **contre.**
torréfacteur [tɔʀefaktœʀ] **nm a** (*appareil: voir* **torréfier**) roaster; toasting machine. **b** (*marchand*) coffee merchant.
torréfaction [tɔʀefaksjɔ̃] **nf** (*voir* **torréfier**) roasting; toasting.
torréfier [tɔʀefje] 7 **vt** *café, malt, cacao* to roast; *tabac* to toast.
torrent [tɔʀɑ̃] **nm** (*cours d'eau*) torrent. **~ de lave** torrent *ou* flood of lava; (*fig: pluie*) **des ~s d'eau** torrential rain; **il pleut à ~s** the rain is coming down in torrents; (*fig*) **un ~ de** *injures, paroles* a torrent *ou* stream *ou* flood of; *musique* a flood of; (*fig*) **des ~s de** *fumée* a stream of, streams of; *larmes, lumière* a stream *ou* flood of, streams *ou* floods of.
torrentiel, -elle [tɔʀɑ̃sjɛl] **adj** (*Géog*) *eaux, régime* torrential; *pluie* torrential, lashing (*épith*).
torrentueux, -euse [tɔʀɑ̃tɥø, øz] **adj** (*littér*) *cours d'eau* torrential, onrushing (*épith*), surging (*épith*); (*fig*) *vie* hectic; *discours* torrent-like, onrushing (*épith*).
torride [tɔʀid] **adj** *région, climat* torrid; *journée, chaleur* scorching, torrid.
tors, torse[1] [tɔʀ, tɔʀs] *ou* **torte** [tɔʀt] **adj** *fil* twisted; *colonne* wreathed; *pied de verre* twist (*épith*); *jambes* crooked, bent.
torsade [tɔʀsad] **nf** *[fils]* twist; (*Archit*) cable moulding. **~ de cheveux** twist *ou* coil of hair; **en ~** *embrasse, cheveux* twisted; **colonne à ~s** cabled column; *voir* **point**[2].
torsader [tɔʀsade] 1 **vt** *frange, corde, cheveux* to twist. **colonne torsadée** cabled column.
torse[2] [tɔʀs] **nm** (*gén*) chest; (*Anat, Sculp*) torso. **~ nu** stripped to the waist, bare-chested; *voir* **bomber.**
torsion [tɔʀsjɔ̃] **nf** (*action*) twisting; (*Phys, Tech*) torsion. **exercer sur qn une ~ du bras** to twist sb's arm back; *voir* **couple.**
tort [tɔʀ] **nm a** (*action, attitude blâmable*) fault. **il a un ~, c'est de trop parler** he has one fault and that's talking too much; **il a le ~ d'être trop jeune** his trouble is *ou* his fault is that he's too young; **il a eu le ~ d'être impoli un jour avec le patron** he made the mistake one day of being rude to the boss; **ils ont tous les ~s de leur côté** the fault *ou* wrong is entirely on their side, they are completely in the wrong; (*Jur*) **les ~s sont du côté du mari/cycliste** the fault lies with the husband/cyclist, the husband/cyclist is at fault; **avoir des ~s envers qn** to have wronged sb; **il n'a aucun ~** he's not at fault, he's not in the wrong, he's in no way to blame; **reconnaître/regretter ses ~s** to acknowledge/be sorry for the wrong one has done *ou* for one's wrongs *ou* one's wrongdoings; **vous avez refusé? c'est un ~** did you refuse? – you were wrong (to do so) *ou* you shouldn't have (done so); **tu ne le savais pas? c'est un ~** you didn't know? – you should have *ou* that was a mistake *ou* was unfortunate.
b (*dommage, préjudice*) wrong. **redresser un ~** to right a wrong; **causer** *ou* **faire du ~ à qn, faire ~ à qn** to harm sb, do sb harm; **ça ne fait de ~ à personne** it doesn't harm *ou* hurt anybody; **il s'est fait du ~** he has harmed himself, he has done himself no good; **cette mesure va faire du ~ aux produits laitiers** this measure will harm *ou* be harmful to *ou* be detrimental to the dairy industry; *voir* **redresseur.**
c à ~ wrongly; **soupçonner/accuser qn à ~** to suspect/accuse sb wrongly; **c'est à ~ qu'on l'avait dit malade** he was wrongly *ou* mistakenly said to be ill; **à ~ ou à raison** rightly or wrongly; **dépenser à ~ et à travers** to spend wildly, spend money like water *ou* here there and everywhere; **il parle à ~ et à travers** he's blathering, he's saying any old thing*.
d être/se mettre/se sentir dans son ~ to be/put o.s./feel o.s. in the wrong; **mettre qn dans son ~** to put sb in the wrong; **être en ~** to be in the wrong *ou* at fault.
e avoir ~ to be wrong; **il a ~ de se mettre en colère** he is wrong *ou* it is wrong of him to get angry; **il n'a pas tout à fait ~ de dire que ...** he is not altogether *ou* entirely wrong in saying that ...; **elle a grand** *ou* **bien ~ de le croire** she's very wrong to believe it; **tu aurais bien ~ de te gêner!** you'd be quite wrong to bother yourself!; *voir* **absent.**
f donner ~ à qn (*blâmer*) to lay the blame on sb, blame sb; (*ne pas être d'accord avec*) to disagree with sb; **les statistiques donnent ~ à son rapport** statistics show *ou* prove his report to be wrong *ou* inaccurate; **les événements lui ont donné ~** events proved him wrong *ou* showed that he was wrong.
torte [tɔʀt] **adj f** *voir* **tors.**
torticolis [tɔʀtikɔli] **nm** stiff neck, torticollis (*SPÉC*). **avoir/attraper le ~** to have/get a stiff neck.
tortillard [tɔʀtijaʀ] **nm** (*hum, péj: train*) local train.
tortillement [tɔʀtijmɑ̃] **nm** (*voir* **se tortiller**) writhing; wriggling; squirming; fidgeting. **~ des hanches** wiggling of the hips.
tortiller [tɔʀtije] 1 **1 vt** *corde, mouchoir* to twist; *cheveux, cravate* to twiddle (with); *moustache* to twirl; *doigts* to twiddle. **2 vi: ~ des hanches** to wiggle one's hips; (*fig*) **il n'y a pas à ~*** there's no wriggling *ou* getting round it. **3 se tortiller vpr a** *[serpent]* to writhe; *[ver]* to wriggle, squirm; *[personne]* (*en dansant, en se débattant etc*) to wiggle; (*d'impatience*) to fidget, wriggle; (*par embarras, de douleur*) to squirm. **se ~ comme une anguille** *ou* **un ver** to wriggle like a worm *ou* an eel, squirm like an eel. **b** *[fumée]* to curl upwards; *[racine, tige]* to curl, writhe.
tortillon [tɔʀtijɔ̃] **nm a** (*Dessin*) stump, tortillon. **b ~ (de papier)** twist (of paper).
tortionnaire [tɔʀsjɔnɛʀ] **nm** torturer.
tortue [tɔʀty] **nf a** (*Zool*) tortoise; (*fig*) slowcoach (*Brit*), slowpoke (*US*), tortoise. **~ d'eau douce** terrapin; **~ de mer** turtle; **avancer comme une ~** *ou* **d'un pas de ~** to crawl along at a snail's pace; *voir* **île. b** (*Hist Mil*) testudo, tortoise.
tortueusement [tɔʀtɥøzmɑ̃] **adv** (*voir* **tortueux**) windingly; tortuously; meanderingly; deviously.
tortueux, -euse [tɔʀtɥø, øz] **adj a** (*lit*) *chemin, escalier* winding,

twisting, tortuous (*littér*); *rivière* winding, meandering. b (*fig péj*) *langage, discours* tortuous, involved, convoluted; *allure* tortuous; *manœuvres, conduite* devious.

torturant, e [tɔʀtyʀɑ̃, ɑ̃t] **adj** agonizing.

torture [tɔʀtyʀ] **nf** (*lit*) torture (*NonC*); (*fig*) torture, torment. **c'est une ~ atroce** it's an appalling form *ou* kind of torture; **instruments de ~** instruments of torture; **chambre** *ou* **salle des ~s** torture chamber; (*fig*) **mettre qn à la ~** to torture sb, make sb suffer; (*fig*) **les ~s de la passion** the torture *ou* torments of passion.

torturer [tɔʀtyʀe] 1 1 **vt** a (*lit*) *prisonnier, animal* to torture; (*fig*) *[faim, douleur, remords]* to rack, torment, torture; *[personne]* to torture. b (*littér: dénaturer*) *texte* to distort, torture (*littér*). **visage torturé par le chagrin** face torn *ou* racked with grief; **la poésie torturée, déchirante de X** the tormented, heartrending poetry of X. 2 **se torturer vpr** (*se faire du souci*) to agonize, fret, worry o.s. sick (*pour* over). **se ~ le cerveau** *ou* **l'esprit** to rack *ou* cudgel one's brains.

torve [tɔʀv] **adj** *regard, œil* menacing, grim.

toscan, e [tɔskɑ̃, an] 1 **adj** Tuscan. 2 **nm** (*Ling*) Tuscan.

Toscane [tɔskan] **nf** Tuscany.

tôt [to] **adv** a (*de bonne heure*) early. **se lever/se coucher (très) ~** to get up/go to bed (very) early; **il se lève ~** he is an early riser, he gets up early; (*Prov*) **l'avenir appartient à ceux qui se lèvent ~** the early bird catches the worm (*Prov*); **venez ~ dans la matinée/soirée** come early (on) in the morning/evening *ou* in the early morning/evening; **~ dans l'année** early (on) in the year, in the early part of the year; **~ le matin, il n'est pas très lucide** he's not very clear-headed first thing (in the morning) *ou* early in the morning; **il n'est pas si ~ que je croyais** it's not as early as I thought; **Pâques est plus ~ cette année** Easter falls earlier this year; **il arrive toujours ~ le jeudi** he is always early on Thursdays.
b (*vite*) soon, early. **il est (encore) un peu (trop) ~ pour le juger** it's (still) a little too soon *ou* early *ou* it's (still) rather early to judge him, it's early days yet to judge him; **~ ou tard il faudra qu'il se décide** sooner or later he will have to make up his mind; **il a eu ~ fait de s'en apercevoir!** he was quick *ou* it didn't take him long to notice it!, it wasn't long before he noticed it!; **il aura ~ fait de s'en apercevoir!** it won't be long before he notices it!, it won't take him long to notice it!; **si tu étais venu une heure plus ~, tu le rencontrais** if you had come an hour sooner *ou* earlier you would have met him; **si seulement vous me l'aviez dit plus ~!** if only you had told me sooner! *ou* earlier!; **ce n'est pas trop ~!** it's not a moment too soon!, it's not before time!, and about time too!*; **je ne m'attendais pas à le revoir si ~** I didn't expect to see him (again) so soon; **il n'était pas plus ~ parti que la voiture est tombée en panne** no sooner had he set off *ou* he had no sooner set off than the car broke down.
c **le plus ~, au plus ~: venez le plus ~ possible** come as early *ou* as soon as you can; **le plus ~ sera le mieux** the sooner the better; **il peut venir jeudi au plus ~** Thursday is the earliest *ou* soonest he can come; **c'est au plus ~ en mai qu'il prendra la décision** it'll be May at the earliest that he takes *ou* he'll take the decision, he'll decide in May at the earliest; **il faut qu'il vienne au plus ~** he must come as soon as possible *ou* as soon as he possibly can.

total, e, mpl -aux [tɔtal, o] 1 **adj** a (*absolu*) (*gén*) total; *ruine, désespoir* utter (*épith*), total; *pardon* absolute. **grève ~e** all-out strike; *voir* **guerre**.
b (*global*) *hauteur, somme, revenu* total. **la somme ~e est plus élevée que nous ne pensions** the total (sum *ou* amount) is higher than we thought.
2 **adv** (net) result, net outcome. **~, il a tout perdu** the net result *ou* outcome was that he lost everything, net result — he lost everything.
3 **nm** (*quantité*) total (number); (*résultat*) total. **le ~ s'élève à 150 F** the total amounts to 150 francs; **le ~ de la population** the total (number of the) population; (*Fin*) **le ~ général** the grand total; **faire le ~** to work out the total; (*fig*) **si on fait le ~, ils n'ont pas réalisé grand-chose** if you add it all up *ou* together they didn't achieve very much; **au ~** (*lit*) in total; (*fig*) on the whole, all things considered, all in all.
4 **totale*** **nf** (*Méd*) (total) hysterectomy. **on lui a fait la ~** she had her works out‡.

totalement [tɔtalmɑ̃] **adv** totally. **c'est ~ faux** (*en entier*) it's totally *ou* wholly wrong; (*absolument*) it's totally *ou* utterly wrong.

totalisateur, -trice [tɔtalizatœʀ, tʀis] 1 **adj** *appareil, machine* adding (*épith*). 2 **nm** adding machine; (*Ordin*) accumulator.

totalisation [tɔtalizasjɔ̃] **nf** adding up, addition.

totaliser [tɔtalize] 1 **vt** a (*additionner*) to add up, total, totalize. b (*avoir au total*) to total, have a total of. **à eux deux ils totalisent 60 ans de service** between the two of them they have a total of 60 years' service *ou* they total 60 years' service; **le candidat qui totalise le plus grand nombre de points** the candidate with the highest total *ou* who gets the highest number of points.

totalitaire [tɔtalitɛʀ] **adj** (*Pol*) *régime* totalitarian; (*Philos*) *conception* all-embracing, global.

totalitarisme [tɔtalitaʀism] **nm** totalitarianism.

totalité [tɔtalite] **nf** a (*gén*) **la ~ de** all of; **la ~ du sable/des livres** all (of) the sand/the books; **la ~ du livre/de la population** all the book/the population, the whole *ou* entire book/population; **la ~ de son salaire** his whole *ou* entire salary, all of his salary; **la ~ de ses biens** all of his possessions; **vendu en ~ aux États-Unis** all sold to the USA; **édité en ~ par X** published entirely by X; **pris dans sa ~** taken as a whole *ou* in its entirety; **j'en connais la quasi-~** I know virtually all of them *ou* just about all of them; **la presque ~ de la population** almost all the population, virtually *ou* almost the whole *ou* entire population.
b (*Philos*) totality.

totem [tɔtɛm] **nm** (*gén*) totem; (*poteau*) totem pole.

totémique [tɔtemik] **adj** totemic.

totémisme [tɔtemism] **nm** totemism.

tôt-fait, pl tôt-faits [tofɛ] **nm** ≃ sponge cake.

toto‡ [toto] **nm** (*pou*) louse, cootie* (*US*).

toton [tɔtɔ̃] **nm** teetotum.

touage [twaʒ] **nm** (*Naut*) warping, kedging.

touareg [twaʀɛg] 1 **adj** Tuareg. 2 **nm** (*Ling*) Tuareg. 3 **nmf: T~** Tuareg.

toubib* [tubib] **nm** doctor, doc*. **elle est ~** she's a doctor *ou* a medic*; **aller chez le ~** to go and see the doc* *ou* the quack*.

toucan [tukɑ̃] **nm** toucan.

touchant[1] [tuʃɑ̃] **prép** (*au sujet de*) concerning, with regard to, about.

touchant[2], e [tuʃɑ̃, ɑ̃t] **adj** (*émouvant*) *histoire, lettre, situation, adieux* touching, moving; (*attendrissant*) *geste, reconnaissance, enthousiasme* touching. **~ de naïveté/d'ignorance** touchingly naïve/ignorant.

touche [tuʃ] **nf** a *[piano, machine à écrire, ordinateur]* key; *[instrument à corde]* fingerboard; *[guitare]* fret. (*Ordin*) **~ de fonction/programmable** function/user-defined key.
b (*Peinture: tache de couleur*) touch, stroke; (*fig: style*) *[peintre, écrivain]* touch. **appliquer la couleur par petites ~s** to apply the colour with small strokes *ou* in small touches *ou* dabs, dab the colour on; **finesse de ~ d'un peintre/auteur** deftness of touch of a painter/an author; (*fig*) **une ~ exotique** an exotic touch; **une ~ de gaieté** a touch *ou* note of gaiety; **avec une ~ d'humour** with a hint *ou* suggestion *ou* touch of humour.
c (*Pêche*) bite. **faire une ~** to have a bite.
d (*Escrime*) hit, touch.
e (*Jeux de ballon*) (*gén, sortie*) touch; (*ligne*) touchline; (*remise en jeu*) (*Ftbl Hand-ball*) throw-in; (*Rugby*) line-out; (*Basket*) return to play; (*Hockey*) roll-in. **taper en ~** to kick into touch; **envoyer** *ou* **mettre la balle en ~** to put the ball into touch; **le ballon est sorti en ~** the ball has gone into touch, the ball is in touch; **rester sur la ~** to stay on the touchline; (*Ftbl*) **jouer la ~** to play for time (*by putting the ball repeatedly out of play*); *voir* **juge**.
f (**: allure*) look, appearance. **quelle drôle de ~!** what a sight!*, what does he (*ou* she *etc*) look like!*; **il a une de ces ~s!** he looks like nothing on earth!*; **il a la ~ de quelqu'un qui sort de prison** he looks as though he's just out of prison.
g (*loc*) **être mis/rester sur la ~** to be put/stay on the sidelines; (*draguer*) **faire une ~*** to make a hit*; **avoir la ~*, avoir fait une ~*** to have made a hit* (*avec* with); *voir* **pierre**.

touche-à-tout [tuʃatu] **nmf inv** (*gén enfant*) (little) meddler; (*fig: chercheur, inventeur*) dabbler. **c'est un ~** *[enfant]* he's a little meddler, his little fingers are into everything; *[inventeur]* he dabbles in everything.

toucher [tuʃe] 1 1 **vt** a (*pour sentir, prendre*) (*gén*) to touch; (*pour palper*) *fruits, tissu, enflure* to feel. **~ qch du doigt/avec un bâton** to touch sth with one's finger/a stick; (*fig*) **faire ~ qch du doigt à qn** to let sb see sth for himself; **~ la main de** *ou* **à qn** to give sb a quick handshake; **il me toucha l'épaule** he touched *ou* tapped my shoulder; **"prière de ne pas ~"** "please do not touch"; (*fig*) **il n'a pas touché un verre de vin depuis son accident** he hasn't touched a drop of wine since his accident; (*fig*) **je n'avais pas touché une raquette/une carte depuis 6 mois** I hadn't had a racket/a card in my hands for 6 months; (*fig*) **il n'a pas touché une balle pendant ce match** he didn't hit a single ball throughout the match.
b (*entrer en contact avec*) to touch. **il ne faut pas que ça touche (le mur/le plafond)** it mustn't touch (the wall/ceiling); (*Lutte*) **il lui fit ~ le sol des épaules** he got his shoulders down on the floor; **~ le fond** (*lit*) to touch the bottom; (*fig*) *[récession, productivité]* to bottom out; (*fig*) **~ le fond de l'abîme** to be utterly destitute, be in abject poverty; **~ le fond du désespoir** to be in the depths of despair; **~ terre** to land; **l'avion toucha le sol** the plane touched down *ou* landed; **les deux lignes se touchent** the two lines touch; **au football on ne doit pas ~ le ballon (de la main)** in football one mustn't touch the ball (with one's hand) *ou* one mustn't handle the ball.
c (*être proche de*) (*lit*) to adjoin; (*fig*) *[affaire]* to concern; *[personne]* to be a near relative of. **son jardin touche le nôtre** his garden (ad)joins ours *ou* is adjacent to ours; **nos deux jardins se touchent** our two gardens are adjacent (to each other) *ou* join each other; **les deux villes se sont tellement développées qu'elles se touchent presque** the two towns have been developed to such an extent that they almost meet.
d (*atteindre: lit, fig*) *adversaire, objectif* to hit. (*Boxe*) **il l'a touché au menton/foie** he hit him on the chin/stomach; **il s'affaissa, touché d'une balle en plein cœur** he slumped to the ground, hit by a bullet in the heart; **deux immeubles ont été touchés par l'explosion** two buildings

have been hit *ou* damaged by the explosion.

e (*contacter*) to reach, get in touch with, contact. **où peut-on le ~ par téléphone?** where can he be reached *ou* contacted by phone?, where can one get in touch with him by phone?

f (*faire escale à*) *port* to put in at, call at, touch.

g (*recevoir*) *pension, traitement* to draw, get; *prime* to get, receive; *chèque* to cash; (*Mil*) *ration, équipement* to draw; (*Scol*) *fournitures* to receive, get. **~ le tiercé/le gros lot** to win the tiercé/the jackpot; **il touche une petite pension** he gets a small pension; **il touche sa pension le 10 du mois** he draws *ou* gets his pension on the 10th of the month; **il est allé à la poste ~ sa pension** he went to draw (out) *ou* collect his pension at the post office; **à partir du mois prochain, ils toucheront 1 000 F par mois/des primes** as from next month they'll get *ou* they'll be paid 1,000 francs a month/bonuses; **il a fini le travail mais n'a encore rien touché** he's finished the work but he hasn't been paid anything *ou* hasn't had anything for it yet.

h (*émouvoir*) *[drame, deuil]* to affect, shake; *[scène attendrissante]* to touch, move; *[critique, reproche]* to have an effect on. **cette tragédie les a beaucoup touchés** this tragedy affected them greatly *ou* has shaken them very badly; **votre reproche l'a touché au vif** your reproach touched *ou* cut him to the quick; **rien ne le touche** there is nothing that can move him; **votre cadeau/geste nous a vivement touchés** we were deeply touched by your gift/gesture; **un style qui touche** an affecting *ou* a moving style; *voir* **corde.**

i (*concerner*) to affect. **ce problème ne nous touche pas** this problem does not affect *ou* concern us; **le chômage touche surtout les jeunes** unemployment affects the young especially; **ils n'ont pas été touchés par la dévaluation** they haven't been affected *ou* hit by the devaluation.

j (*loc*) **je vais lui en ~ un mot** I'll have a word with him about it, I'll mention it to him, I'll talk to him about it; **tu devrais ~ un mot de cette affaire au patron** you should have a word with the boss about this business, you should mention this business to the boss; **touchons du bois!*** touch wood!* (*Brit*), knock on wood!* (*US*); **pas touche!*** hands off!*; **touché!** (*Escrime, fig*) touché!; (*bataille navale*) hit!

2 **se toucher*** vpr (*euph*) (*se masturber*) to play with o.s.* (*euph*); (*se peloter*) to pet*, touch each other up‡.

3 **toucher à** vt indir a *objet dangereux, défendu* to touch; *capital, économies* to break into, touch. **n'y touche pas!** don't touch!; **prière de ne pas ~ aux objets exposés** please do not touch the exhibits, kindly refrain from handling the exhibits; **~ à tout** *[enfant]* to touch everything, fiddle with everything; *[inventeur]* to try one's hand at everything, be into everything; **elle n'a pas touché à son déjeuner/au fromage** she didn't touch her lunch/the cheese; **on n'a pas touché au fromage** we haven't touched the cheese, the cheese has been left untouched; **il n'a jamais touché à une raquette/un fusil** he has never handled a racket/rifle, he has never had a racket/rifle in his hand.

b (*malmener*) *enfant, jeune fille* to touch, lay a finger on; (*attaquer*) *réputation, légende* to question. **s'il touche à cet enfant/ma sœur, gare à lui!** if he lays a finger on *ou* touches that child/my sister, he'd better watch out!; **s'il touche à un cheveu de cet enfant, gare à lui!** if he so much as touches a hair of that child's head, he'd better watch out!; (*Pol*) **~ aux intérêts d'un pays** to interfere with a country's interests; **personne n'ose ~ à cette légende** nobody dares question that legend.

c (*modifier*) *règlement, loi, tradition* to meddle with; *mécanisme* to tamper with; *monument, site classé* to touch. **quelqu'un a touché au moteur** someone has tampered with the engine; **on peut rénover sans ~ à la façade** it's possible to renovate without touching the façade *ou* interfering with the façade; **c'est parfait, n'y touche pas** it's perfect, don't change a thing.

d (*concerner*) *intérêts* to affect; *problème, domaine* to touch, have to do with. **tout ce qui touche à l'enseignement** everything connected with *ou* to do with teaching *ou* that concerns teaching *ou* relating to teaching.

e (*aborder*) *période, but* to near, approach; *sujet, question* to broach, come onto. **je touche ici à un problème d'ordre très général** here I am coming onto *ou* broaching a problem of a very general character; **vous touchez là à une question délicate** that is a very delicate matter you have raised *ou* broached; **nous touchons au but** we're nearing our goal, our goal is in sight; **l'hiver/la guerre touche à sa fin** winter/the war is nearing its end *ou* is drawing to a close; (*fig littér*) **~ au port** to be within sight of home.

f (*être en contact avec*) to touch; (*être contigu à*) to border on, adjoin; (*confiner à*) to verge on, border on. **l'armoire touchait presque au plafond** the wardrobe almost touched *ou* reached to the ceiling; **le jardin touche à la forêt** the garden adjoins the forest *ou* borders on the forest; **cela touche à la folie/pornographie** that verges *ou* borders on madness/pornography.

g (*loc*) **avec un air de ne pas y ~, sans avoir l'air d'y ~** looking as if butter would not melt in his (*ou* her) mouth, acting the innocent*.

4 nm a (*sens*) (sense of) touch.

b (*action, manière de toucher*) touch; (*impression produite*) feel. **doux au ~** soft to the touch; **cela a le ~ de la soie** it has the feel of silk (about it), it feels like silk; **s'habituer à reconnaître les objets au ~** to become used to recognizing objects by touch *ou* feel(ing); **on reconnaît la soie au ~** you can tell silk by the feel of it.

c (*Mus*) touch.

d (*Méd*) (internal) examination. **~ rectal/vaginal** rectal/vaginal examination.

e (*Sport*) **avoir un bon ~ de balle** to have a nice touch.

touche-touche* [tuʃtuʃ] adv: **être à ~** *[trains, voitures]* to be nose to tail.

toucheur [tuʃœʀ] nm: **~ de bœufs** (cattle) drover.

touée [twe] nf (*Naut*) (*câble*) warp, cable; (*longueur de chaîne*) scope.

touer [twe] 1 vt (*Naut*) to warp, kedge.

toueur [twœʀ] nm: **(bateau) ~** warping tug.

touffe [tuf] nf *[herbe]* tuft, clump; *[arbres, buissons]* clump; *[cheveux, poils]* tuft; *[fleurs]* cluster, clump (*de* of). **~ de lavande** lavender bush, clump of lavender.

touffeur [tufœʀ] nf (†, *littér*) suffocating *ou* sweltering heat (*NonC*).

touffu, e [tufy] adj a (*épais, dense*) *barbe, sourcils* bushy; *arbres* with thick *ou* dense foliage; *haie* thick, bushy; *bois, maquis, végétation* dense, thick. b (*fig*) *roman, style* dense.

touillage* [tujaʒ] nm stirring.

touiller* [tuje] 1 vt *lessive* to stir round; *sauce, café* to stir.

toujours [tuʒuʀ] adv a (*continuité*) always; (*répétition: souvent péj*) forever, always, all the time. **je l'avais ~ cru célibataire** I (had) always thought he was a bachelor; **je t'aimerai ~** I shall always love you, I shall love you forever; **je déteste et détesterai ~ l'avion** I hate flying and always shall; **la vie se déroule ~ pareille** life goes on the same as ever *ou* forever the same; **il est ~ à*** *ou* **en train de critiquer** he is always *ou* forever criticizing, he keeps on criticizing; **une rue ~ encombrée** a street (that is) always *ou* forever *ou* constantly jammed with traffic; **les saisons ~ pareilles** the never-changing seasons; **il n'est pas ~ très ponctuel** he's not always very punctual; **il est ~ à l'heure** he's always *ou* invariably on time; **il fut ~ modeste** he was always *ou* ever (*littér*) modest; **les journaux sont ~ plus pessimistes** the newspapers are more and more pessimistic; **les jeunes veulent ~ plus d'indépendance** young people want more and more *ou* still more independence; **comme ~** as ever, as always; **ce sont des amis de ~** they are lifelong friends; **il est parti pour ~** he's gone forever *ou* for good; **presque ~** almost always; *voir* **depuis.**

b (*prolongement de l'action* = **encore**) still. **bien qu'à la retraite il travaillait ~** although he had retired he was still working *ou* he had kept on working; **j'espère ~ qu'elle viendra** I keep hoping *ou* I'm still hoping she'll come; **ils n'ont ~ pas répondu** they still haven't replied; **est-ce que X est rentré? — non il est ~ à Paris/non ~ pas** is X back? — no he is still in Paris/no not yet *ou* no he's still not back; **il est ~ le même/~ aussi désagréable** he is (still) the same as ever/(still) as unpleasant as ever.

c (*intensif*) anyway, anyhow. **écrivez ~, il vous répondra peut-être** write anyway *ou* anyhow *ou* you may as well write — he (just) might answer you; **il vient ~ un moment où** there must *ou* will (always *ou* inevitably) come a time when; **buvez ~ un verre avant de partir** have a drink at least *ou* anyway *ou* anyhow before you go; **c'est ~ pas toi qui l'auras*** at all events *ou* at any rate it won't be you that gets it*; **où est-elle? — pas chez moi ~!** where is she? — not at my place anyway! *ou* at any rate!; **je trouverai ~ (bien) une excuse** I can always think up an excuse; **passez à la gare, vous aurez ~ bien un train** go (along) to the station — you're sure *ou* bound to get a train *ou* there's bound to be a train; **tu peux ~ courir!*** *ou* **te fouiller!‡** you haven't a hope! (*Brit*) *ou* a prayer! (*US*) *ou* a chance!, you've got some hope! (*iro*), no way!*; **il aime donner des conseils mais ~ avec tact** he likes to give advice but he always does it tactfully; **vous pouvez ~ crier, il n'y a personne** shout as much as you like *ou* shout by all means — there's no one about; **~ est-il que** the fact remains that, that does not alter the fact that, be that as it may; **il était peut-être là, ~ est-il que je ne l'ai pas vu** he may well have been there, (but) the fact remains *ou* that does not alter the fact that I didn't see him; **cette politique semblait raisonnable, ~ est-il qu'elle a échoué** this policy seemed reasonable, (but) be that as it may *ou* but the fact remains it was a failure; **c'est ~ ça de pris*** that's something anyway, (well) at least that's something; **ça peut ~ servir** it'll come in handy some day, it'll always come in handy; *voir* **causer**[2].

toulousain, e [tuluzɛ̃, ɛn] 1 adj of *ou* from Toulouse. 2 nm,f: **T~(e)** inhabitant *ou* native of Toulouse.

toundra [tundʀa] nf tundra.

toupet [tupɛ] nm a **~ (de cheveux)** quiff (*Brit*), tuft (of hair). b (*: *culot*) sauce* (*Brit*), nerve, cheek (*Brit*). **avoir du ~** to have a nerve *ou* a cheek (*Brit*); **il ne manque pas d'un certain ~** he's got quite a nerve, he doesn't lack cheek (*Brit*); **quel ~!** what a nerve! *ou* cheek! (*Brit*).

toupie [tupi] nf a (*jouet*) (spinning) top. **~ à musique** humming-top; *voir* **tourner.** b **vieille ~‡** silly old trout‡. c (*Tech*) *[menuisier]* spindle moulding-machine; *[plombier]* turn-pin.

tour[1] [tuʀ] 1 nf a (*édifice*) tower; (*Hist: machine de guerre*) siege tower. **(immeuble) ~, ~ d'habitation** tower block, high-rise block; (*fig péj*) **c'est une vraie ~, il est gros comme une ~** he is massive *ou* enormous.

b (*Échecs*) castle, rook.

2 **comp ▸la tour de Babel** the Tower of Babel; (*fig*) **c'est une tour de Babel** it's a real Tower of Babel *ou* a babel of tongues **▸tour de contrôle** (*Aviat*) control tower **▸la tour Eiffel** the Eiffel Tower **▸tour de forage** drilling rig, derrick **▸tour de guet** watchtower, look-out tower **▸tour hertzienne** radio mast **▸tour d'ivoire** (*fig*) ivory tower **▸la tour de Londres** the Tower of London **▸la tour penchée de Pise** the Leaning Tower of Pisa.

tour[2] [tuʀ] 1 **nm** a (*parcours, exploration*) **faire le ~ de** *parc, pays, circuit, montagne* to go round; (*fig*) *possibilités* to explore; *magasins* to go round, look round; *problème* to consider from all angles; **~ de ville** (*pour touristes*) city tour; **le ~ du parc prend bien une heure** it takes a good hour to walk round the park; **si on faisait le ~?** shall we go round (it)? *ou* walk round (it)?; **faire le ~ du cadran** *[aiguille]* to go round the clock; *[dormeur]* to sleep (right) round the clock; **faire le ~ du monde** to go round the world; **faire un ~ d'Europe** to go on a European tour, tour Europe; **faire un ~ d'Europe en auto-stop** to hitch-hike around Europe; **un ~ du monde en bateau** a boat trip (a)round the world, a round-the-world trip by boat; **la route fait (tout) le ~ de leur propriété** the road goes (right) round their estate; **faire le ~ des invités** to do the rounds of the guests; **la bouteille/plaisanterie a fait le ~ de la table** the bottle/joke went round the table; (*dans un débat*) **procéder à un ~ de table** to seek the views of all those seated round the table.

b (*excursion*) trip, outing; (*balade*) (*à pied*) walk, stroll; (*en voiture*) run, drive, spin, ride. **faire un ~ de manège** *ou* **de chevaux de bois** to have a ride on a merry-go-round; **faire un (petit) ~** (*à pied*) to go for a (short) walk *ou* stroll; (*en voiture*) to go for a (short) run *ou* drive *ou* spin; (*en vélo*) to go for a ride *ou* spin; **faire un ~ en ville/sur le marché** to go for a walk round town/round the market; **faire un ~ en Italie** to go for a trip round Italy; **un ~ de jardin/en voiture vous fera du bien** a walk *ou* stroll round the garden/a run *ou* drive (in the car) will do you good; **faire le ~ du propriétaire** to look round *ou* go round one's property; **je vais te faire faire le ~ du propriétaire** I'll show you over *ou* round the place; (*littér*) **la rivière fait des ~s et des détours** the river meanders along *ou* winds its way in and out, the river twists and turns (along its way).

c (*succession*) turn, go. **c'est votre ~** it's your turn; **à ton ~ (de jouer)** (*gén*) (it's) your turn *ou* go; (*Échecs, Dames*) (it's) your move; **attendre/perdre son ~** to wait/miss one's turn; **prendre/passer son ~** to take/miss one's turn *ou* go; **parler à son ~** to speak in turn; **ils parleront chacun à leur ~** they will each speak in turn; **attends, tu parleras à ton ~** wait – you'll have your turn to speak; **chacun son ~!** wait your turn!; **nous le faisons chacun à notre ~** (*deux personnes*) we do it in turn, we take turns at it, we do it turn and turn about (*Brit*); (*plusieurs personnes*) we take turns at it, we do it by turns; **c'est au ~ de Marc de parler** it's Mark's turn to speak; **à qui le ~?** whose turn *ou* go is it?, who is next?; **à ~ de rôle, ~ à ~** alternately, in turn; **ils vinrent à ~ de rôle nous vanter leurs mérites** they each came in turn to sing their own praises; **le temps était ~ à ~ pluvieux et ensoleillé** the weather was alternately wet and sunny; **elle se sentait ~ à ~ optimiste et désespérée** she felt optimistic and despairing by turns; **avoir un ~ de faveur** to get in ahead of one's turn; **mon prochain ~ de garde** *ou* **service est à 8 heures** my next spell *ou* turn of duty is at 8 o'clock; (*lit, fig*) **votre ~ viendra** your turn will come; *voir* **souvent**.

d (*Pol*) **~ (de scrutin)** ballot; **au premier/second ~** in the first/second ballot *ou* round.

e (*circonférence*) *[partie du corps]* measurement; *[tronc, colonne]* girth; *[visage]* contour, outline; *[surface]* circumference; *[bouche]* outline. **~ de taille/tête** waist/head measurement; **~ de poitrine** *[homme]* chest measurement; *[femme]* bust measurement; **~ de hanches** hip measurement; **elle avait le ~ des yeux fait** she had eyeliner round her eyes; **mesurer le ~ d'une table** to measure round a table, measure the circumference of a table; **la table fait 3 mètres de ~** the table measures 3 metres round (the edge); **le tronc fait 3 mètres de ~** the trunk measures 3 metres round *ou* has a girth of 3 metres.

f (*rotation*) *[roue, manivelle]* turn, revolution; *[axe, arbre]* revolution. **un ~ de vis** a (turn of a) screw; **l'hélice a fait deux ~s** the propeller turned *ou* revolved twice; (*Aut*) **régime de 2 000 ~s (minute)** speed of 2,000 revs *ou* revolutions per minute; **il suffit d'un ~ de clef/manivelle** it just needs one turn of the key/handle; **donne encore un ~ de vis** give it another screw *ou* turn, give another turn of the screw; (*fig*) **donner un ~ de vis au crédit** to freeze credit, put a squeeze on credit; **donner un ~ de vis aux libertés** to crack down *ou* clamp down on freedom; **~ de vis militaire/politique** military/political crackdown *ou* clampdown (*à l'encontre de* on); **donner un ~ de clef** to turn the key, give the key a turn; (*Cyclisme*) **battre un concurrent d'un ~ de roue** to beat a competitor by a wheel's turn; **faire un ~/plusieurs ~s sur soi-même** to spin round once/several times (on oneself); **faire un ~ de valse** to waltz round the floor; **après quelques ~s de valse** after waltzing round the floor a few times; *voir* **double, quart**.

g (*disque*) **un 33 ~s** an LP; **un 45 ~s** a single; **un 78 ~s** a 78.

h (*tournure*) *[situation, conversation]* turn, twist. (*expression*) **~ (de phrase)** turn of phrase; **la situation prend un ~ dramatique/désagréable** the situation is taking a dramatic/an unpleasant turn *ou* twist; **il a un ~ de phrase élégant** he has an elegant turn of phrase; **un certain ~ d'esprit** a certain turn *ou* cast of mind.

i (*exercice*) *[acrobate]* feat, stunt; *[jongleur, prestidigitateur]* trick. **~ d'adresse** feat of skill, skilful trick; **~ de passe-passe** trick, sleight of hand (*NonC*); **elle a réussi cela par un simple ~ de passe-passe** she managed it by mere sleight of hand; **~s d'agilité** acrobatics; **~ de cartes** card trick; **et le ~ est joué!** and Bob's your uncle!* (*Brit*), and there you have it!; **c'est un ~ à prendre!** it's just a knack one picks up; **avoir plus d'un ~ dans son sac** to have more than one trick up one's sleeve.

j (*duperie*) trick. **faire** *ou* **jouer un ~ à qn** to play a trick on sb; **un ~ pendable** a rotten trick; **un sale ~, un ~ de cochon*** *ou* **de salaud**‡ a dirty *ou* lousy trick*, a mean trick; **je lui réserve un ~ à ma façon!** I'll pay him back in my own way!; *voir* **jouer**.

k **à ~ de bras** *frapper, taper* with all one's strength *ou* might; (*fig*) *composer, produire* prolifically; *critiquer* with a vengeance; **il écrit des chansons à ~ de bras** he writes songs by the dozen, he runs off *ou* churns out songs one after the other.

2 **comp ▸tour de chant** song recital **▸tour de cou** (*ruban*) choker; (*fourrure*) fur collar; (*mensuration*) collar measurement; **faire du 39 de tour de cou** to take a size 39 collar **▸tour de force** (*lit*) feat of strength, tour de force; (*fig*) amazing feat **▸le Tour de France** (*course cycliste*) the Tour de France; (*apprentissage*) the Tour de France (*carried out by a journeyman completing his apprenticeship*) **▸tour d'honneur** (*Sport*) lap of honour **▸tour d'horizon** (*fig*) (general) survey **▸tour de lit** (bed) valance **▸tour de main** (*adresse*) dexterity; **avoir/acquérir un tour de main** to have/pick up a knack; **en un tour de main** in the twinkling of an eye, (as) quick as a flash, in a trice, in no time at all **▸tour de piste** (*Sport*) lap; (*cirque*) circuit (of the ring) **▸tour de reins: souffrir d'un tour de reins** to suffer from a strained *ou* sprained back; **se donner un tour de reins** to strain *ou* sprain one's back.

tour[3] [tuʀ] **nm** a (*Tech*) lathe. **~ de potier** potter's wheel; **un objet fait au ~** an object turned on the lathe; **travail au ~** lathe-work; (*fig littér*) **des jambes/cuisses faites au ~** well-turned (†, *littér*) *ou* shapely legs/thighs. b (*passe-plats*) hatch.

tourangeau, -elle [tuʀɑ̃ʒo, ɛl] 1 **adj** of *ou* from Touraine *ou* Tours (*épith*), Touraine (*épith*) *ou* Tours (*épith*). 2 **nm,f: T~(-elle)** Tourangeau, *native or inhabitant of Tours or of Touraine*.

tourbe [tuʀb] **nf** (*Agr*) peat. **~ limoneuse** alluvial peat.

tourbeux, -euse [tuʀbø, øz] **adj** a *terrain* (*qui contient de la tourbe*) peat (*épith*), peaty; (*de la nature de la tourbe*) peaty. b *plante* found in peat.

tourbière [tuʀbjɛʀ] **nf** peat bog.

tourbillon [tuʀbijɔ̃] **nm** a (*atmosphérique*) **~ (de vent)** whirlwind; **~ de fumée/sable/neige** swirl *ou* eddy of smoke/sand/snow; **le sable s'élevait en ~s** the sand was swirling up. b (*dans l'eau*) whirlpool. c (*Phys*) vortex. d (*fig*) whirl. **~ de plaisirs** whirl of pleasure, giddy round of pleasure(s); **le ~ de la vie/des affaires** the hurly-burly *ou* hustle and bustle of life/business; **il regardait du balcon le ~ des danseurs** he looked down from the balcony upon the whirling *ou* swirling group of dancers.

tourbillonnant, e [tuʀbijɔnɑ̃, ɑ̃t] **adj** *vent, feuilles* whirling, swirling, eddying; *vie* whirlwind (*épith*); *jupes* swirling.

tourbillonnement [tuʀbijɔnmɑ̃] **nm** (*voir* **tourbillonner**) whirling, swirling; eddying; twirling.

tourbillonner [tuʀbijɔne] 1 **vi** *[poussière, sable, feuilles mortes]* to whirl, swirl, eddy; *[danseurs]* to whirl (round), swirl (round), twirl (round); (*fig*) *[idées]* to swirl (round), whirl (round).

tourelle [tuʀɛl] **nf** a (*petite tour*) turret. b (*Mil, Naut*) (gun) turret; *[caméra]* lens turret; *[sous-marin]* conning tower.

tourière [tuʀjɛʀ] **adj, nf: (sœur) ~** sister at the convent gate, extern sister.

tourillon [tuʀijɔ̃] **nm** *[mécanisme]* bearing, journal, pin; *[canon]* trunnion.

tourisme [tuʀism] **nm: le ~** the tourist industry *ou* trade, tourism; **faire du ~** to go touring *ou* sightseeing; **on a fait un peu de ~** we did a bit of sightseeing, we toured about a bit (*en* in); **le ~ français se porte bien** the French tourist industry *ou* trade is in good shape; **grâce au ~, l'exode rural a pu être stoppé dans cette région** thanks to tourism it has been possible to halt the drift from the country in this region; **le ~ d'hiver/d'été** winter/summer tourism, the winter/summer tourist trade *ou* industry; **avion/voiture de ~** private plane/car; **office du ~** tourist office; **agence de ~** tourist agency; *voir* **grand**.

touriste [tuʀist] **nmf** tourist. (*fig*) **faire qch en ~** to do sth half-heartedly; *voir* **classe**.

touristique [tuʀistik] **adj** *itinéraire, billet, activités, renseignements, guide* tourist (*épith*); *région, ville* with great tourist attractions, popular with (the) tourists (*attrib*), touristic (*péj*). **le menu ~** the standard *ou* set menu; **d'attrait ~ assez faible** with little to attract (the) tourists, with little tourist appeal.

tourment [tuʀmɑ̃] **nm** (*littér*) (*physique*) agony; (*moral*) agony, torment, torture (*NonC*). **les ~s de la jalousie** the torments *ou* agonies of jealousy.

tourmente [tuʀmɑ̃t] nf (*tempête*) storm, gale, tempest (*littér*); (*fig: sociale, politique*) upheaval, storm, turmoil. ~ **de neige** snowstorm, blizzard.

tourmenté, e [tuʀmɑ̃te] (ptp de **tourmenter**) adj a *personne* tormented, tortured; *expression, visage, esprit* anguished, tormented, tortured. b *paysage, formes* tortured (*littér*); *style, art* tortured, anguished. c (*littér*) *vie, mer* stormy, turbulent, tempestuous.

tourmenter [tuʀmɑ̃te] [1] 1 vt a [*personne*] to torment. **ses créanciers continuaient à le** ~ his creditors continued to harass *ou* hound him; ~ **qn de questions** to plague *ou* harass sb with questions.

b [*douleur, rhumatismes, faim*] to rack, torment; [*remords, doute*] to rack, torment, plague; [*ambition, envie, jalousie*] to torment. **ce doute le tourmente depuis longtemps** this doubt has been tormenting *ou* plaguing him for a long time; **ce qui me tourmente dans cette affaire** what worries *ou* bothers *ou* bugs* me in this business.

2 **se tourmenter** vpr to fret, worry (o.s.). **ne vous tourmentez pas, ce n'était pas de votre faute** don't distress *ou* worry yourself – it wasn't your fault; **il se tourmente à cause de son fils** he is fretting *ou* worrying about his son.

tourmenteur, -euse [tuʀmɑ̃tœʀ, øz] nm,f (*littér: persécuteur*) tormentor.

tourmentin [tuʀmɑ̃tɛ̃] nm a (*Naut: foc*) storm jib. b (*oiseau*) stormy petrel.

tournage [tuʀnaʒ] nm a (*Ciné*) shooting. **être en** ~ **en Italie** to be filming in Italy, be on a shoot* in Italy. b (*Menuiserie*) turning. **le** ~ **sur bois/métal** wood-/metal-turning. c (*Naut*) belaying cleat.

tournailler* [tuʀnɑje] [1] vi (*péj*) to wander up and down.

tournant, e [tuʀnɑ̃, ɑ̃t] 1 adj a *fauteuil, dispositif* swivel (*épith*); *feu, scène* revolving (*épith*); *voir* **grève, plaque, pont, table**.

b *mouvement, manœuvre* encircling (*épith*).

c *escalier* spiral (*épith*); (*littér*) *ruelle, couloir* winding, twisting.

2 nm a (*virage*) bend. ~ **en épingle à cheveux** hairpin bend; **prendre bien/mal son** ~ to take a bend well/badly, corner well/badly; **rattraper** *ou* **avoir qn au** ~* to get one's own back on sb (*Brit*), get even with sb; **attendre qn au** ~* to wait for the chance to trip sb up *ou* catch sb out.

b (*changement*) turning point. ~ **décisif** watershed; **les** ~**s de l'histoire/de sa vie** the turning points in history/in his life; **c'est à la 50e minute qu'a eu lieu le** ~ **du match** the decisive *ou* turning point of the match came in the 50th minute; **il arrive à un** ~ **de sa carrière** he's coming to a key *ou* decisive turning point *ou* a watershed in his career; **un** ~ **de la politique française** a watershed in French politics; **marquer un** ~ to be a turning point; **cette entreprise a bien su prendre le** ~ this company has managed the change *ou* switch well, this company has adapted well to the new circumstances.

tourné, e[1] [tuʀne] (ptp de **tourner**) adj a **bien** ~ *personne* shapely, with a good figure; *jambes* shapely; *taille* neat, trim; (*fig*) *compliment, poème, expression* well-turned; *article, lettre* well-worded, well-phrased. b **mal** ~ *article, lettre* badly expressed *ou* phrased *ou* worded; *expression* unfortunate; **avoir l'esprit mal** ~ to have a dirty mind. c *lait, vin* sour; *poisson, viande* off (*attrib*), high (*attrib*); *fruits* rotten, bad. d (*Menuiserie*) *pied, objet* turned.

tournebouler* [tuʀnəbule] [1] vt *personne* to put in a whirl. ~ **la cervelle à qn** to turn sb's head *ou* brain, put sb's head in a whirl; **il en était tourneboulé** (*mauvaise nouvelle*) he was very upset by it; (*heureuse surprise*) his head was in a whirl over it.

tournebroche [tuʀnəbʀɔʃ] nm roasting jack (*Brit*) *ou* spit, rotisserie. **poulet au** ~ chicken cooked on a rotisserie *ou* a spit.

tourne-disque, pl **tourne-disques** [tuʀnədisk] nm record player.

tournedos [tuʀnədo] nm tournedos.

tournée[2] [tuʀne] nf a (*tour*) [*conférencier, artiste*] tour; [*inspecteur, livreur, représentant*] round. **partir/être en** ~ to set off on/be on tour; to set off on/be on one's rounds; ~ **de conférences/théâtrale** lecture/theatre tour; **faire une** ~ **électorale** to do an election tour; ~ **d'inspection** round of inspection; **faire la** ~ **de** *magasins, musées, cafés* to do the rounds of, go round; **faire la** ~ **des grands ducs*** to go out on the town *ou* on a spree.

b (*consommations*) round (of drinks). **payer une/sa** ~ to buy *ou* stand a/one's round (of drinks); **c'est ma** ~ it's my round; **il a payé une** ~ **générale** he paid for drinks all round; **c'est la** ~ **du patron** the drinks are on the house.

c (*: *raclée*) hiding, thrashing.

tournemain [tuʀnəmɛ̃] nm: **en un** ~ in a trice, in the twinkling of an eye, (as) quick as a flash, in no time at all.

tourner [tuʀne] [1] 1 vt a *manivelle, clef, poignée* to turn; *sauce* to stir; *salade* to toss; *page* to turn (over). **tournez s.v.p.** please turn over, P.T.O.; ~ **et retourner** *chose* to turn over and over; *pensée, problème* to turn over and over (in one's mind), mull over.

b (*diriger, orienter*) *appareil, tête, yeux* to turn. **elle tourna son regard** *ou* **les yeux vers la fenêtre** she turned her eyes towards the window; ~ **la tête à droite/à gauche/de côté** to turn one's head to the right/to the left/sideways; **quand il m'a vu, il a tourné la tête** when he saw me he looked away *ou* he turned his head away; ~ **les pieds en dedans/en dehors** to turn one's toes *ou* feet in/out; (*lit, fig*) ~ **le dos à** to turn one's back on; **il avait le dos tourné à la porte** he had his back (turned) towards the door; **dès que j'ai le dos tourné** as soon as my back is turned; **tourne le tableau de l'autre côté/contre le mur** turn the picture the other way round/round to face the wall; ~ **ses pensées/efforts vers** to turn *ou* bend one's thoughts/efforts towards *ou* to.

c (*contourner*) (*Naut*) *cap* to round; *armée* to turn, outflank; *obstacle* to round; (*fig: éluder*) *difficulté, règlement* to get round *ou* past. ~ **la loi** to get round the law, find a loophole in the law; **il vient de** ~ **le coin de la rue** he has just turned the corner; (*Rugby*) ~ **la mêlée** to turn the scrum, wheel the scrum round.

d (*frm: exprimer*) *phrase, compliment* to turn; *demande, lettre* to phrase, express.

e (*transformer*) ~ **qch/qn en** to turn sth/sb into; ~ **qn/qch en ridicule** *ou* **dérision** to make sb/sth a laughing stock, ridicule sb/sth, hold sb/sth up to ridicule; **il a tourné l'incident en plaisanterie** he laughed off the incident, he made light of the incident, he made a joke out of the incident; **il tourne tout à son avantage** he turns everything to his (own) advantage.

f (*Ciné*) *scène* [*cinéaste*] to shoot, film; [*acteur*] to film, do; *film* (*faire les prises de vues*) to shoot; (*produire*) to make; (*jouer dans*) to make, do. **ils ont dû** ~ **en studio** they had to do the filming in the studio; **scène tournée en extérieur** scene shot on location; *voir* **silence**.

g (*Tech*) *bois, ivoire* to turn; *pot* to throw.

h (*loc*) ~ **bride** (*lit*) to turn back; (*fig*) to do an about-turn; ~ **casaque** (*fuir*) to turn tail, flee; (*changer de camp*) to turn one's coat, change sides; ~ **le cœur** *ou* **l'estomac à qn** to turn sb's stomach, make sb heave; ~ **la page** (*lit*) to turn the page; (*fig*) to turn over a new leaf, turn the page; (*littér*) ~ **ses pas vers** to wend one's way towards (*littér*); (*lit, fig*) **se** ~ **les pouces** to twiddle one's thumbs; ~ **le sang** *ou* **les sangs à qn** to shake sb up; ~ **la tête à qn** [*vin*] to go to sb's head; [*succès*] to go to *ou* turn sb's head; [*femme*] to turn sb's head; *voir* **talon**.

2 vi a [*manège, compteur, aiguille d'horloge etc*] to turn, go round; [*disque, cylindre, roue*] to turn, revolve; [*pièce sur un axe, clef, danseur*] to turn; [*toupie*] to spin; [*taximètre*] to tick away; [*usine, moteur*] to run. [*porte*] ~ **(sur ses gonds)** to turn (on its hinges); ~ **sur soi-même** to turn round on o.s.; (*très vite*) to spin round and round; **l'heure tourne** time is passing *ou* is going by *ou* on; **la grande aiguille tourne plus vite que la petite** the big hand goes round faster than the small one; **tout d'un coup, j'ai vu tout** ~ all of a sudden my head began to spin *ou* swim; **faire** ~ **le moteur** to run the engine; ~ **au ralenti** to tick over; ~ **à plein régime** to run at maximum revs; ~ **à vide** [*moteur*] to run in neutral; [*engrenage, mécanisme*] to turn without gripping; [*personne*] to be unable to think straight; **c'est lui qui va faire** ~ **l'affaire** he's going to manage *ou* run the business; (*Comm*) **représentant qui tourne sur Lyon** sales representative who covers Lyons; **les éléphants tournent sur la piste** the elephants move round the ring.

b [*programme d'ordinateur*] to work. **arriver à faire** ~ **un programme** to get a program working *ou* to work; **ça tourne sur quelles machines?** which machines does it work on?, which machines is it compatible with?

c ~ **autour de** (*gén*) to turn *ou* go round; [*terre, roue*] to revolve *ou* go round; [*chemin*] to wind *ou* go round; [*oiseau*] to wheel *ou* circle *ou* fly round; [*mouches*] to buzz *ou* fly round; [*prix*] to be around *ou* about (*Brit*); ~ **autour de la piste** to go round the track; ~ **autour de qn** (*péj: importuner*) to hang round sb; (*pour courtiser*) to hang round sb; (*par curiosité*) to hover round sb; **un individu tourne autour de la maison depuis une heure** somebody has been hanging round outside the house for an hour; [*discussion, sujet*] ~ **autour de** *ou* **sur qch** to centre *ou* focus on; **l'enquête tourne autour de ces 3 suspects/de cet indice capital** the enquiry centres on these 3 suspects/this vital clue; **la conversation a tourné sur la politique** the conversation centred *ou* focussed on politics; **le prix de cette voiture doit** ~ **autour de 80 000 F** the price of this car must be around 80,000 francs *ou* the 80,000-franc mark *ou* in the region of 80,000 francs.

d (*changer de direction*) [*vent, opinion*] to turn, shift, veer (round); [*chemin, promeneur*] to turn. **la chance a tourné** his (*ou* her *etc*) luck has turned; **la voiture a tourné à gauche** the car turned left *ou* turned off to the left; **tournez à droite au prochain feu rouge** turn right *ou* take the right(-hand) turn at the next traffic lights.

e (*évoluer*) **bien** ~ to turn out well; **mal** ~ [*farce, entreprise*] to go wrong, turn out badly; [*personne*] to go to the dogs, turn out badly; **ça va mal** ~* no good will come of it, that'll lead to trouble, it'll turn nasty; **si les choses avaient tourné autrement** if things had turned out *ou* gone differently; ~ **à l'avantage de qn** to turn to sb's advantage; **la discussion a tourné en bagarre** the argument turned *ou* degenerated into a fight; **cela risque de faire** ~ **la discussion en bagarre** it might turn the argument into a fight; **sa bronchite a tourné en pneumonie** his bronchitis has turned *ou* developed into pneumonia; **le débat tournait à la politique** the debate was turning to *ou* moving on to politics; **le temps a tourné au froid/à la pluie** the weather has turned cold/rainy *ou* wet; ~ **au vert/rouge** to turn *ou* go green/red; ~ **au drame/au tragique** to take a dramatic/tragic turn.

f *[lait]* to turn (sour); *[poisson, viande]* to go off, go bad; *[fruits]* to go rotten *ou* bad. *[vin]* ~ (au vinaigre) to turn (vinegary); faire ~ to turn sour.

g (*loc*) ~ à l'aigre *ou* au vinaigre to turn sour; *[projet, débat]* ~ court to come to a sudden end; ~ de l'œil* to pass out, faint; ~ en rond (*lit*) to walk round and round; *[discussion]* to go round in circles; *[négociations, enquête]* nous tournons en rond depuis 3 mois we've been marking time *ou* going round in circles for 3 months; ~ rond to run smoothly; ça ne tourne pas rond chez elle*, elle ne tourne pas rond* she's not quite with us*, she must be a bit touched*; qu'est-ce qui ne tourne pas rond?* what's the matter?, what's wrong?, what's up?*; (*fig*) ~ autour du pot to beat about the bush; il tourne comme un ours *ou* comme une bête en cage he paces about like a caged animal; la tête me tourne my head is spinning; ce bruit lui fit ~ la tête this noise made his head spin *ou* made him dizzy *ou* giddy; ça me fait ~ la tête *[vin]* it goes to my head; *[bruit, altitude]* it makes my head spin, it makes me dizzy *ou* giddy; (*Spiritisme*) faire ~ les tables to do table-turning; faire ~ qn en bourrique to drive sb round the bend* *ou* up the wall*.

3 se tourner vpr: se ~ du côté de *ou* vers qn/qch to turn towards sb/sth; se ~ vers qn pour lui demander de l'aide to turn to sb for help; se ~ vers une profession/la politique/une question to turn to a profession/to politics/to a question; se ~ contre qn to turn against sb; se ~ et se retourner dans son lit to toss and turn in bed; de quelque côté que l'on se tourne whichever way one turns; tourne-toi (de l'autre côté) turn round *ou* the other way.

tournesol [tuʀnəsɔl] nm a (*Bot*) sunflower; *voir* huile. b (*Chim*) litmus.

tourneur, -euse [tuʀnœʀ, øz] 1 nm,f (*Tech*) turner. ~ sur bois/métaux wood/metal turner. 2 adj *voir* derviche.

tournevis [tuʀnəvis] nm screwdriver. ~ cruciforme Phillips screwdriver.

tournicoter* [tuʀnikɔte] [1] vi, **tourniquer** [tuʀnike] vi [1] (*péj*) to wander up and down.

tourniquet [tuʀnikɛ] nm a (*barrière*) turnstile; (*porte*) revolving door. b (*Tech*) ~ (hydraulique) reaction turbine; (*d'arrosage*) (lawn-)sprinkler. c (*présentoir*) revolving stand. d (*Méd*) tourniquet. e (*arg Mil*) court-martial. passer au ~ to come up before a court-martial.

tournis [tuʀni] nm a (*Vét*) sturdy. b (*) avoir le ~ to feel dizzy *ou* giddy; cela/il me donne le ~ that/he makes my head spin, that/he makes me (feel) dizzy *ou* giddy.

tournoi [tuʀnwa] nm a (*Hist*) tournament, tourney. b (*Sport*) tournament. ~ d'échecs/de tennis chess/tennis tournament; (*fig littér*) un ~ d'éloquence/d'adresse a contest of eloquence/skill; (*Rugby*) le ~ des cinq nations the five-nation championship, the Five Nations tournament; (~) open open (tournament).

tournoiement [tuʀnwamɑ̃] nm (*voir* tournoyer) whirling, twirling; swirling; eddying; wheeling. des ~s de feuilles swirling *ou* eddying leaves; les ~s des danseurs the whirling (of the) dancers.

tournoyer [tuʀnwaje] [8] vi a (*sur place*) *[danseurs]* to whirl (round), swirl (round), twirl (round); *[eau, fumée]* to swirl, eddy, whirl. faire ~ qch to whirl *ou* twirl sth; la fumée s'élevait en tournoyant the smoke swirled *ou* spiralled up. b (*en cercles*) *[oiseaux]* to wheel (round); *[feuilles mortes]* to swirl *ou* eddy around.

tournure [tuʀnyʀ] nf a (*tour de phrase*) turn of phrase; (*forme*) form. ~ négative/impersonnelle negative/impersonal form; la ~ précieuse de ses phrases the affected way (in which) he phrases his sentences.

b (*apparence*) *[événements]* turn. la ~ des événements the turn of events; la ~ que prenaient les événements the way the situation was developing, the turn events were taking; la situation a pris une mauvaise/meilleure ~ the situation took a turn for the worse/for the better; donner une autre ~ à une affaire to put a matter in a different light, put a new face on a matter; prendre ~ to take shape.

c ~ d'esprit turn *ou* cast of mind.

d (†: *allure*) bearing. il a belle ~ he carries himself well, he has a very upright bearing.

touron [tuʀɔ̃] nm *kind of nougat.*

tour-opérateur [tuʀɔpeʀatœʀ] nm tour operator.

tourte [tuʀt] 1 adj (‡: *bête*) thick‡ (*Brit*), dense*. 2 nf (*Culin*) pie. ~ à la viande/au poisson meat/fish pie.

tourteau¹, pl ~x [tuʀto] nm (*Agr*) oilcake, cattle-cake.

tourteau², pl ~x [tuʀto] nm (*Zool*) common *ou* edible crab.

tourtereau, pl ~x [tuʀtəʀo] nm (*Zool*) young turtledove. (*fig: amoureux*) ~x lovebirds.

tourterelle [tuʀtəʀɛl] nf turtledove.

tourtière [tuʀtjɛʀ] nf (*à tourtes*) pie tin; (*à tartes*) pie dish *ou* plate.

tous [tu] *voir* tout.

toussailler [tusɑje] [1] vi to have a bit of a cough. arrête de ~! stop coughing and spluttering like that!

Toussaint [tusɛ̃] nf: la ~ All Saints' Day; il fait un temps de ~ it's real November weather, it's grim cold weather.

tousser [tuse] [1] vi a *[personne]* (*lit, pour avertir etc*) to cough. ne sors pas, tu tousses encore un peu don't go out — you've still got a bit of a cough. b (*fig*) *[moteur]* to splutter, cough, hiccup.

toussotement [tusɔtmɑ̃] nm (slight) coughing (*NonC*).

toussoter [tusɔte] [1] vi (*lit*) to have a bit of a *ou* a slight cough; (*pour avertir, signaler*) to cough softly, give a little cough. je l'entendais ~ dans la pièce à côté I could hear him coughing in the next room; cet enfant toussote: je vais lui faire prendre du sirop this child has a bit of a *ou* a slight cough — I'm going to give him some cough mixture.

tout [tu], **toute** [tut], mpl tous [tu] (adj) *ou* [tus] (pron), fpl toutes [tut] 1 adj a (*avec déterminant: complet, entier*) ~ le, toute la all (the), the whole (of the); il a plu toute la nuit it rained the whole (of the) night *ou* all night (long) *ou* throughout the night; il a plu toute cette nuit/toute une nuit it rained all (of) *ou* throughout last night/for a whole night; pendant ~ le voyage during the whole (of the) trip, throughout the trip; ~ le monde everybody, everyone; ~ le reste (all) the rest; ~ le temps all the time; il a ~ le temps/l'argent qu'il lui faut he has all the time/money he needs; avoir ~ son temps to have all the time one needs, have all the time in the world; il a dépensé ~ son argent he has spent all (of) his money; mange toute ta viande eat up your meat, eat all (of) your meat; il a passé toutes ses vacances à lire he spent the whole of *ou* all (of) his holidays reading; toute la France regardait le match the whole of *ou* all France was watching the match; c'est toute une affaire it's quite a business, it's a whole rigmarole; c'est ~ le portrait de son père he is the spitting image of his father; féliciter qn de ~ son cœur to congratulate sb wholeheartedly; je le souhaite de ~ mon cœur I wish it with all my heart, it is my heartfelt wish; il courait de toute la vitesse de ses petites jambes he was running as fast as his little legs would carry him; *voir* somme³.

b (*intensif: tout à fait*) quite. c'est ~ le contraire it's quite the opposite *ou* the very opposite; c'est ~ autre chose that's quite another matter; avec toi c'est ~ l'un ou ~ l'autre with you it's either all black or all white.

c (*seul, unique*) only. c'est ~ l'effet que cela lui fait that's all the effect *ou* the only effect it has on him; c'est là ~ le problème that's the whole problem, that's just where the problem lies; ~ le secret est dans la rapidité the whole secret lies in speed; cet enfant est toute ma joie this child is my only *ou* sole joy, all my joy in life lies with this child; pour toute réponse, il grogna his only reply was a grunt *ou* was to grunt; il avait une valise pour ~ bagage one case was all the luggage he had *ou* all he had in the way of luggage, his luggage was one single case; ils avaient pour ~ domestique une bonne one maid was all the servants they had, all they had in the way of servants was one maid.

d (*sans déterminant: complet, total*) all (of), the whole of. donner toute satisfaction to give complete satisfaction, be entirely *ou* completely satisfactory; il a lu ~ Balzac he has read the whole of *ou* all of Balzac; de toute beauté most beautiful, of the utmost beauty; elle a visité ~ Londres she has been round the whole of London; de ~ temps, de toute éternité from time immemorial, since the beginning of time; ce n'est pas un travail de ~ repos it's not an easy job; c'est un placement de ~ repos it's an absolutely secure investment, this investment is as safe as houses; à ~ prix at all costs; à toute allure *ou* vitesse at full *ou* top speed; il est parti à toute vitesse he left like a shot; il a une patience/un courage à toute épreuve his patience/courage will stand any test, he has an inexhaustible supply of patience/courage; selon toute apparence to all appearances; en toute simplicité/franchise in all simplicity/sincerity; *voir* attente, hasard, intérêt.

e (*sans déterminant: n'importe quel, chaque*) any, all. toute personne susceptible de nous aider any person *ou* anyone able to help us; toute trace d'agitation a disparu all *ou* any trace of agitation has gone; à toute heure (du jour ou de la nuit) at any time *ou* at all times (of the day or night); "restauration à toute heure" "meals served all day"; il me dérange à ~ instant he keeps on disturbing me, he's constantly *ou* continually disturbing me; ça peut se produire à ~ instant it can happen (at) any time *ou* moment; à ~ âge at any age, at all ages; ~ autre (que lui) aurait deviné anybody *ou* anyone (but him) would have guessed; pour ~ renseignement, téléphoner ... for all information, ring ...; (moto/voiture/véhicule) ~-terrain all-terrain *ou* off-road (motor)bike/car/vehicle; faire du ~-terrain (*course*) to go off-road racing; (*pour le plaisir*) to go off-road driving.

f (*en apposition: complètement*) il était ~ à son travail he was entirely taken up by *ou* absorbed in his work; un manteau ~ en laine an all wool coat; habillé ~ en noir dressed all in black, dressed entirely in black; un style ~ en nuances a very subtle style, a style full of nuances; un jeu ~ en douceur a very delicate style of play.

g tous, toutes (*l'ensemble, la totalité*) all, every; toutes les personnes que nous connaissons all the people *ou* everyone *ou* everybody (that) we know; toutes les fois que je le vois every time I see him; tous les moyens lui sont bons he'll stick at nothing, he will use any means to achieve his ends; il avait toutes les raisons d'être mécontent he had every reason to be *ou* for being displeased; tous les hommes sont mortels all men are mortal; courir dans tous les sens to run in all directions *ou* in every direction; il roulait tous feux éteints he was driving with all his lights out; film (pour) tous publics film suitable for all audiences; des individus de toutes tendances/tous bords people of all tendencies/shades of opinion; toutes sortes de all sorts of, every kind of; tous azimuts *attaquer* on all fronts.

h (*de récapitulation: littér*) **le saut en hauteur, la course, le lancer du javelot, toutes disciplines qui exigent ...** the high jump, running, throwing the javelin, all (of them) disciplines requiring ... .

i **tous** *ou* **toutes les** (*chaque*) every; **tous les jours/ans/mois** every day/year/month; **venir tous les jours** to come every day, come daily; **tous les deux jours/mois** every other *ou* second *ou* alternate day/month, every two days/months; **tous les 10 mètres** every 10 metres; **il vient tous les combien?*** how often does he come?; **toutes les 3 heures** every 3 hours, at 3-hourly intervals; (*hum*) **tous les trente-six du mois** once in a blue moon.

j (*avec numéral: ensemble*) **tous (les) deux** both (of them), the two of them, each (of them); **tous (les) 3/4** all 3/4 (of them); **tous les 5/6** *etc* all 5/6 *etc* (of them).

k (*loc*) **en ~ bien ~ honneur** with the most honourable (of) intentions; **à ~ bout de champ = à ~ propos; en ~ cas** anyway, in any case, at any rate; **~ un chacun** all and sundry, every one of us (*ou* them), everybody and anybody; (*Prov*) **tous les chemins mènent à Rome** all roads lead to Rome; **de ~ côté, de tous côtés** *chercher, regarder* on all sides, everywhere; **ça marche à tous les coups*** it works every time, it never fails; **à tous les coups, il est sorti*** he's gone out, I'm sure of it; **à tous égards** in every respect; **en ~ état de cause** anyway, in any case; **de toute façon** in any case, anyway, anyhow; **il s'est enfui à toutes jambes** he ran away as fast as his legs could carry him, he showed a clean pair of heels; **en tous lieux** everywhere; (*Prov*) **toute peine mérite salaire** the labourer is worthy of his hire (*Prov*); **faire ~ son possible** to do one's utmost (*pour* to); **toutes proportions gardées** relatively speaking, making due allowances; (*sans arrêt*) **à ~ propos** every other minute; (*Prov*) **toute vérité n'est pas bonne à dire** some truths are better left unsaid; *voir* **lettre.**

2 **pron indéf** a (*gén*) everything, all; (*sans discrimination*) anything. **il a ~ organisé** he organized everything, he organized it all; **ses enfants mangent (de) ~** her children will eat anything; **il vend de ~** he sells anything and everything; **on ne peut pas ~ faire** one can't do everything; **~ va bien** all's (going) well, everything's fine; **avec lui, c'est ~ ou rien** with him it's all or nothing; **être ~ pour qn** to be everything to sb; **son travail, ses enfants, ~ l'exaspère** his work, the children, everything annoys him; **~ lui est bon** everything *ou* all is grist to his mill (*pour* to); (*iro*) **il a ~ pour plaire*** he's got nothing going for him; *voir* **falloir.**

b **tous, toutes** all; **tous/toutes tant qu'ils/qu'elles sont** all of them, every single one of them; **tous sont arrivés** they have all arrived; **il les déteste tous** *ou* **toutes** he hates them all *ou* all of them; **nous avons tous nos défauts** we all *ou* we each of us have our faults; **nous mourrons tous** we shall all die; **vous tous qui m'écoutez** all of you who are listening to me; **écoutez bien tous!** listen, all of you!; **il s'attaque à nous tous** he's attacking us all; **tous ensemble** all together; **film pour tous** film suitable for all audiences.

c **~ ce qui, ~ ce que: ~ ce que je sais, c'est qu'il est parti** all I know is that he's gone; **c'est ~ ce qu'il m'a dit/laissé** that's all he told me/left me; **est-ce que vous avez ~ ce dont vous avez besoin?** *ou* **ce qu'il vous faut?** have you everything *ou* all (that) you need?; **ne croyez pas ~ ce qu'il raconte** don't believe everything *ou* all he tells you; **~ ce qui lui appartient** everything *ou* all that belongs to him; **~ ce que le pays compte de sportifs/savants** all the country has in the way of sportsmen/scientists, the country's entire stock of sportsmen/scientists; (*Prov*) **~ ce qui brille n'est pas or** all that glitters is not gold (*Prov*); **il a été ~ ce qu'il y a de gentil/serviable** he was most kind/obliging, he couldn't have been kinder/more obliging.

d (*loc*) **~ est bien qui finit bien** all's well that ends well; **~ est pour le mieux dans le meilleur des mondes** everything is for the best in the best of all possible worlds; **~ a une fin** there is an end to everything, everything comes to an end; **... et ~ et ~*** ... and all that sort of thing, ... and so on and so forth; **~ finit par des chansons** everything ends with a song; **~ passe, ~ casse** nothing lasts for ever; (*fig*) **~ est là** that's the whole point; **c'est ~** that's all; **c'est ~ dire** I need say no more; **ce sera ~?** will that be all?, (will there be) anything else?; **et ce n'est pas ~!** and that's not all!, and there's more to come!; **ce n'est pas ~ (que) d'en parler** there's more to it than just talking about it; **ce n'est pas ~ de partir, il faut arriver** it's not enough to set off — one must arrive as well; **c'était ~ ce qu'il y a de chic** it was the last word in chic *ou* the ultimate in chic; **il y avait des gens ~ ce qu'il y a de plus distingué(s)** there were the most distinguished people there; **à ~ prendre, ~ bien considéré** all things considered, taking everything into consideration; (*Comm*) **~ compris** inclusive, all-in; **la formule du ~ compris** inclusive *ou* all-in terms; (*péj*) **avoir ~ d'un brigand/du clown** to be an absolute *ou* a real brigand/clown; **avoir ~ d'une intrigante** to be a real schemer; **en ~** in all; **en ~ et pour ~** all in all; (*Prov*) **~ vient à point à qui sait attendre** everything comes to him who waits; *voir* **après, comme, malgré.**

3 **adv** (*s'accorde en genre et en nombre devant adj f qui commence par consonne ou h aspiré*) a (*tout à fait*) very, quite. **c'est ~ neuf** (*objet*) it's brand new; (*littér*) **son bonheur ~ neuf** his new-found happiness; **il est ~ étonné** he is very *ou* most surprised; **les toutes premières années** the very first *ou* early years; **c'est une ~ autre histoire** that's quite another story; **elles étaient ~ heureuses/toutes contentes** they were most *ou* extremely happy/pleased; **il a mangé sa viande toute crue** he ate his meat quite *ou* completely raw; **c'est ~ naturel** it's perfectly *ou* quite natural; **la ville ~ entière** the whole town; **~ (toute) nu(e)** stark naked; **~ enfant** *ou* **toute petite elle aimait la campagne** as a (very) small child she liked the country; **c'est une toute jeune femme** she's a very young woman; **il est ~ seul** he's all alone; **il était ~ seul dans un coin** he was all by himself *ou* all alone in a corner; **il l'a fait ~ seul** he did it (all) on his own *ou* all by himself *ou* single-handed *ou* unaided; **cette tasse ne s'est pas cassée toute seule!** this cup didn't break all by itself!; **cela va ~ seul** it all goes smoothly.

b (*concession: quoique*) **~ médecin qu'il soit** even though *ou* although he is a doctor, I don't care if he is a doctor; **toute malade qu'elle se dise** however ill *ou* no matter how ill she says she is; **~ grand que soit leur appartement** however large *ou* no matter how large their flat (is), large though their flat may be.

c (*intensif*) **~ près** *ou* **à côté** very near *ou* close; **~ au loin** far away, right *ou* far in the distance; **~ là-bas** right over there; **~ simplement** *ou* **bonnement** quite simply; **je vois cela ~ autrement** I see it quite differently; **je le sais ~ autant que toi** I know it as well as you do, I'm as aware of it as you are; **j'aime ça ~ aussi peu que lui** I like that as little as he does; **~ en bas de la colline** right at the bottom of the hill; **~ dans le fond/au bout** right at the bottom/at the end, at the very bottom/end; **il répondit ~ court que non** he just answered no (and that was all); **ne m'appelez pas Dupont de la Motte, pour les amis c'est Dupont ~ court** don't call me Dupont de la Motte, it's plain Dupont to my friends; **tu t'es ~ sali** you've got yourself all dirty; **tu as ~ sali tes habits** you've got your clothes all dirty; **parler ~ bas** to speak very low *ou* quietly; **il était ~ en sueur** he was in a lather of sweat *ou* running with sweat; **elle était ~ en larmes** she was in floods of tears; **le jardin est ~ en fleurs** the garden is a mass of flowers.

d **~ en** + *participe présent*: **~ en marchant/travaillant** as *ou* while you walk/work, while walking/working; **elle tricotait ~ en regardant la télévision** she was knitting while watching television; **~ en prétendant le contraire il voulait être élu** (al)though he pretended otherwise he wanted to be elected; **~ en reconnaissant ses mérites je ne suis pas d'accord avec lui** (al)though *ou* even though I recognize his strengths I don't agree with him.

e (*avec n*) **être ~ yeux/oreilles** to be all eyes/ears; (*hum*) **je suis ~ ouïe** I am all ears!; **être ~ sucre ~ miel** to be all sweetness and light; **~ laine/coton** all wool/cotton; **être ~ feu ~ flammes** to be fired with enthusiasm.

f (*déjà*) **~ prêt, ~ préparé** ready-made; **formules toutes faites** ready-made *ou* set *ou* standard phrases; **idées toutes faites** preconceived ideas, unquestioning ideas; **vendu ~ cuit** sold ready cooked *ou* pre-cooked; **c'est du ~ cuit*** it's a cinch* *ou* a pushover*; **c'est ~ vu*** it's a foregone conclusion, it's a dead cert*.

g (*loc*) **~ au plus** at the (very) most; **~ au moins** at (the very) least; **~ d'abord** first of all, in the first place; **~ de même** (*en dépit de cela*) all the same, for all that; (*très*) quite, really; (*indignation*) **~ de même!** well really!, honestly! I mean to say!; **c'est ~ de même agaçant** all the same it is annoying, it's really most annoying; **tu aurais pu nous prévenir ~ de même** all the same *ou* even so you might have told us; (*tout à fait*) **il est gentil ~ de même** he's ever so nice; **c'est ~ de même étonnant** it's quite surprising (*que* that); **~ à coup** all of a sudden, suddenly, all at once; **~ à fait** quite, entirely, altogether; **ce n'est pas ~ à fait la même chose** it's not quite the same thing; **c'est ~ à fait faux/exact** it's quite *ou* entirely wrong/right; **il est ~ à fait charmant** he's absolutely *ou* quite charming; **je suis ~ à fait d'accord avec vous** I'm in complete agreement with you, I agree completely *ou* entirely with you; **vous êtes d'accord? — ~ à fait!** do you agree? — absolutely!; **~ de go** *dire* straight out; *entrer* straight in; **~ à l'heure** (*plus tard*) later, in a short *ou* little while; (*peu avant*) just now, a short while ago, a moment ago; **~ à l'heure j'ai dit que** I said just now *ou* earlier that; **le ~-Paris** the Paris smart set, the tout-Paris; **~ de suite** straightaway, at once, immediately; **ce n'est pas pour ~ de suite** (*ce n'est pas pressé*) there's no rush; (*ce n'est pas près d'arriver*) it won't happen overnight; **il est gentil/mignon ~ plein*** he is really very *ou* really awfully* nice/sweet; **~ nouveau ~ beau** (just) wait till the novelty wears off; **c'est ~ comme*** it comes to the same thing really; **c'est ~ un** it's all one, it's one and the same thing; **être ~ d'une pièce** to be as straight as a die.

4 **nm** a whole. **tous ces éléments forment un ~** all these elements make up a whole; **acheter/vendre/prendre le ~** to buy/sell/take the (whole) lot *ou* all of it (*ou* them); (*charade*) **mon ~** my whole *ou* all; (*Rel*) **le grand T~** the Great Whole.

b (*loc*) **le ~ est qu'il parte à temps** the main *ou* most important thing is that he leaves in time; **le ~ c'est de faire vite** the main thing is to be quick about it; **il avait changé du ~ au ~** he had changed completely; **ce n'est pas le ~*** this is no good, this isn't good enough; **ce n'est pas le ~ de s'amuser, il faut travailler** we can't keep on enjoying ourselves like this — we must get down to work; **(pas) du ~** not at all; **il n'y a pas de pain du ~** there's no bread at all; **il n'y a plus du ~ de pain** there's no bread left at all; **je n'entends rien du ~** I can't hear a thing, I can't hear anything at all; *voir* **comme, risquer.**

tout-à-l'égout [tutalegu] **nm inv** mains drainage, main sewer.
Toutankhamon [tutɑ̃kamɔ̃] **nm** Tutankhamen, Tutankhamun.
toutefois [tutfwa] **adv** however. **sans ~ que cela les retarde** without that delaying them however; **si ~ il est d'accord** if he agrees however *ou* nonetheless.
tout-en-un [tutɑ̃nœ̃] **adj inv** all-in-one.
toute-puissance [tutpɥisɑ̃s] **nf** omnipotence.
tout-fou*, **pl tout-fous** [tufu] **adj m** over-excited. **il fait son ~** he's a bit over-excited.
toutim(e)* [tutim] **nm: le ~** the whole lot, everything.
toutou [tutu] **nm** (*langage enfantin*) doggie, bow-wow (*langage enfantin*). (*fig*) **suivre qn/obéir à qn comme un ~** to follow sb about/obey sb as meekly as a lamb.
tout-petit, **pl tout-petits** [tup(ə)ti] **nm** toddler, tiny tot. **un jeu pour les ~s** a game for the very young *ou* for toddlers *ou* tiny tots.
tout-puissant, **toute-puissante** [tupɥisɑ̃, tutpɥisɑ̃t] 1 **adj** almighty, omnipotent, all-powerful. 2 **nm: le Tout-Puissant** the Almighty.
tout(-)va [tuva] **adv: à ~** here, there and everywhere, all over the place.
tout-venant [tuv(ə)nɑ̃] **nm inv** (*charbon*) raw coal. (*articles, marchandises*) **le ~** the run-of-the-mill *ou* ordinary stuff.
toux [tu] **nf** cough. **~ grasse/sèche/nerveuse** loose/dry/nervous cough; *voir* **quinte**[2].
toxémie [tɔksemi] **nf** blood poisoning, toxaemia.
toxicité [tɔksisite] **nf** toxicity.
toxico* [tɔksiko] **nmf** (**abrév de toxicomane**) junkie*.
toxicologie [tɔksikɔlɔʒi] **nf** toxicology.
toxicologique [tɔksikɔlɔʒik] **adj** toxicological.
toxicologue [tɔksikɔlɔg] **nmf** toxicologist.
toxicomane [tɔksikɔman] **nmf** drug addict.
toxicomanie [tɔksikɔmani] **nf** drug addiction.
toxicose [tɔksikoz] **nf** toxicosis.
toxine [tɔksin] **nf** toxin.
toxique [tɔksik] 1 **adj** toxic, poisonous. 2 **nm** toxin, poison.
toxoplasme [tɔksoplasm] **nm** toxoplasma.
toxoplasmose [tɔksoplasmoz] **nf** toxoplasmosis.
TP [tepe] 1 **nm** (**abrév de Trésor public**) *voir* **trésor**. 2 **nmpl** a (**abrév de travaux pratiques**) *voir* **travail**[1]. b (**abrév de travaux publics**) *voir* **travail**[1].
TPE [tepeø] **nm** (**abrév de terminal de paiement électronique**) *voir* **terminal**.
TPG [tepeʒe] **nm** (**abrév de trésorier-payeur général**) *voir* **trésorier**.
TPV [tepeve] **nm** (**abrév de terminal point de vente**) POST.
trac[1] [tʀak] **nm** (*Théât, en public*) stage fright; (*aux examens etc*) nerves (*pl*). **avoir le ~** (*Théât, en public*) (*sur le moment*) to have stage fright; (*à chaque fois*) to get stage fright; (*aux examens*) (*sur le moment*) to be nervous; (*à chaque fois*) to get nervous, get (an attack *ou* fit of) nerves; **fícher le ~ à qn*** to put the wind up sb* (*Brit*), give sb a fright.
trac[2] [tʀak] **nm: tout à ~** *dire, demander* right out of the blue.
traçage [tʀasaʒ] **nm** (*voir* **tracer**) drawing; tracing; opening up; marking out.
traçant, e [tʀasɑ̃, ɑ̃t] **adj** a (*Bot*) *racine* running, creeping. b (*Mil*) *obus, balle* tracer; *voir* **table**.
tracas [tʀaka] 1 **nm** (*littér †: embarras*) bother, upset. **se donner bien du ~** to give o.s. a great deal of trouble. 2 **nmpl** (*soucis, ennuis*) worries.
tracasser [tʀakase] 1 1 **vt** (*gén*) to worry, bother; *[administration]* to harass, bother. **qu'est-ce qui te tracasse?** what's bothering *ou* worrying you? 2 **se tracasser vpr** (*se faire du souci*) to worry, fret. **ne te tracasse pas pour si peu!** don't worry *ou* fret over a little thing like that!
tracasserie [tʀakasʀi] **nf** (*gén pl*) harassment. **les ~s de l'administration** the irksome *ou* bothersome *ou* annoying aspects of officialdom.
tracassier, -ière [tʀakasje, jɛʀ] **adj** irksome, bothersome, worrisome. **une administration ~ière** bothersome *ou* irksome officialdom.
trace [tʀas] **nf** a (*empreinte*) *[animal, fugitif, pneu]* tracks (*pl*). **la ~ du renard diffère de celle de la belette** the fox's tracks differ from those of the weasel; **suivre une ~ de blaireau** to follow some badger tracks; **~s de pas** footprints; **~s de pneus** tyre tracks.

b (*chemin frayé*) track, path; (*Ski*) track. **s'ouvrir une ~ dans la brousse** to open up a track *ou* path through the undergrowth; (*Alpinisme, Ski*) **faire la ~** to be the first to ski (*ou* walk *etc*) on new snow; **on voyait leur ~ dans la face nord** we could see their tracks on the north face; (*Ski*) **~ directe** direct descent.

c (*marque*) *[sang]* trace; *[brûlure, encre]* mark; *[outil]* mark; *[blessure, maladie]* mark. **~s de freinage** brake marks; **~s de doigt** (*sur disque, meuble*) finger marks; **~s d'effraction** signs of a break-in; (*littér*) **les ~s de la souffrance** the marks of suffering; **des ~s de fatigue se lisaient sur son visage** his face showed signs of tiredness *ou* bore the marks of tiredness; **cet incident avait laissé une ~ durable/profonde dans son esprit** the incident had left an indelible/a definite mark on his mind.

d (*indice*) trace. **il n'y avait pas ~ des documents volés/du fugitif dans l'appartement** there was no trace of the stolen documents/of the fugitive in the flat; **on ne trouve pas ~ de cet événement dans les journaux** there's no trace of this event to be found in the papers.

e (*vestige: gén pl*) *[bataille, civilisation]* trace; (*indice: gén pl*) *[bagarre]* sign. **on y voyait les ~s d'une orgie/d'un passage récent** you could see the signs of an orgy/that somebody had recently passed by; **retrouver les ~s d'une civilisation disparue** to discover the traces *ou* signs of a lost civilisation.

f (*quantité minime*) *[poison, substance]* trace. **on y a trouvé de l'albumine à l'état de ~** traces of albumen have been found; (*fig*) **il ne montrait nulle ~ de repentir/de chagrin** he showed no trace of regret/sorrow *ou* no sign(s) of being sorry/of sorrow; **sans une ~ d'accent étranger** without a *ou* any trace of a foreign accent.

g (*loc*) **disparaître sans laisser de ~s** *[personne]* to disappear without trace; *[tache]* to disappear completely without leaving a mark; **suivre à la ~** *animal, fugitif* to track; (*fig*) **on peut le suivre à la ~** you can always tell when he has been here; **être sur la ~ de** *fugitif* to be on the track *ou* trail of; *complot, document* to be on the track of; **perdre la ~ d'un fugitif** to lose track of *ou* lose the trail of a fugitive; **retrouver la ~ d'un fugitif** to pick up the trail of a fugitive again; (*fig*) **marcher sur** *ou* **suivre les ~s de qn** to follow in sb's footsteps.
tracé [tʀase] **nm** a (*plan*) *[réseau routier ou ferroviaire, installations]* layout, plan. b (*parcours*) *[ligne de chemin de fer, autoroute]* route; *[rivière]* line, course; *[itinéraire]* course; (*contour*) *[côte, crête]* line. c (*graphisme*) *[dessin, écriture]* line.
tracer [tʀase] 3 1 **vt** a (*dessiner*) *ligne, triangle, plan* to draw; *courbe de graphique* to plot; (*écrire*) *chiffre, mot* to write, trace. (*fig*) **~ le tableau d'une époque** to sketch *ou* draw *ou* paint the picture of a period. b *route, piste* (*frayer*) to open up; (*baliser*) to mark out. (*fig*) **~ le chemin** *ou* **la voie à qn** to show sb the way. 2 **vi** (*‡: courir*) a to shift* (*Brit*), hurry, belt* *ou* rush along. b (*Bot*) to creep (horizontally).
traceur, -euse [tʀasœʀ, øz] 1 **adj** (*Sci*) *substance* tracer (*épith*). 2 **nm** *[appareil enregistreur]* pen; (*Sci: isotope*) tracer. (*Ordin*) **~ (de courbes)** (graph) plotter; **~ incrémentiel** incremental plotter.
trachéal, e, **mpl -aux** [tʀakeal, o] **adj** tracheal.
trachée [tʀaʃe] **nf** a (*Anat*) **~(-artère)** windpipe, trachea (SPÉC). b (*Zool*) trachea.
trachéen, -enne [tʀakeɛ̃, ɛn] **adj** (*Zool*) tracheal.
trachéite [tʀakeit] **nf** tracheitis (*NonC*). **avoir une ~, faire de la ~** to have tracheitis.
trachéotomie [tʀakeɔtɔmi] **nf** tracheotomy.
traçoir [tʀaswaʀ] **nm** *[dessinateur, graveur]* scriber; *[jardinier]* drill marker.
tract [tʀakt] **nm** pamphlet, leaflet, handout.
tractable [tʀaktabl] **adj** *caravane* towable.
tractation [tʀaktasjɔ̃] **nf** (*gén péj*) negotiation, dealings (*pl*), bargaining (*NonC*).
tracté, e [tʀakte] **adj** tractor-drawn.
tracter [tʀakte] 1 **vt** to tow.
tracteur [tʀaktœʀ] **nm** tractor.
traction [tʀaksjɔ̃] **nf** a (*Sci, gén: action, mouvement*) traction. (*Sci*) **résistance à la/effort de ~** tensile strength/stress; **faire des ~s** (*en se suspendant*) to do pull-ups; (*au sol*) to do press-ups (*Brit*) *ou* push-ups.

b (*mode d'entraînement d'un véhicule*) traction, haulage; (*Rail*) traction. **~ animale/mécanique** animal/mechanical traction *ou* haulage; **à ~ animale** drawn *ou* hauled by animals; **à ~ mécanique** mechanically drawn; **~ à vapeur/électrique** steam/electric traction; (*Aut*) **~ arrière** rear-wheel drive; (*Aut*) **~ avant** (*dispositif*) front-wheel drive; (*automobile*) car with front-wheel drive.

c (*Rail: service*) **la ~** the engine and driver section; **service du matériel et de la ~** mechanical and electrical engineer's department.
tractus [tʀaktys] **nm** (*Anat*) tract. **~ digestif** digestive tract.
tradition [tʀadisjɔ̃] **nf** a (*gén*) tradition. (*Rel*) **la T~** Tradition; (*Littérat*) **la ~ manuscrite d'une œuvre** the manuscript tradition of a work; **la ~ orale** the oral tradition; **de ~** traditional; **fidèle à la ~** true to tradition; **c'était bien dans la ~ française** it was very much in the French tradition; **il est de ~** *ou* **c'est la ~ que/de faire** it is a tradition *ou* traditional that/to do. b (*Jur*) tradition, transfer.
traditionalisme [tʀadisjɔnalism] **nm** traditionalism.
traditionaliste [tʀadisjɔnalist] 1 **adj** traditionalist(ic). 2 **nm,f** traditionalist.
traditionnel, -elle [tʀadisjɔnɛl] **adj** *pratique, interprétation, opinion* traditional; (**: habituel*) good old* (*épith*), usual. **sa ~elle robe noire*** her good old* *ou* usual black dress.
traditionnellement [tʀadisjɔnɛlmɑ̃] **adv** traditionally; (*habituellement*) as always, as usual. **~ vêtue de noir** dressed in black as always *ou* as is (*ou* was) her wont (*hum*).
traducteur, -trice [tʀadyktœʀ, tʀis] **nm,f** translator. **~-interprète** translator-interpreter.
traduction [tʀadyksjɔ̃] **nf** a (*action, opération, technique*) translation, translating (*dans, en* into); (*phrase, texte, Scol: exercice*) translation. **la ~ en arabe pose de nombreux problèmes** translation *ou* translating into Arabic presents many problems; **la ~ de ce texte a pris 3 semaines** the translation of this text *ou* translating this text took 3 weeks; **c'est une**

~ **assez libre** it's a fairly free translation *ou* rendering; **une excellente ~ de Proust** an excellent translation of Proust; ~ **fidèle** faithful *ou* accurate translation; ~ **littérale** literal translation; **la ~ automatique** machine *ou* automatic translation; ~ **assistée par ordinateur** machine-aided translation; **la ~ simultanée** simultaneous translation.

b (*fig: interprétation*) *[sentiments]* expression.

traduire [tʀadɥiʀ] 38 **vt** a *mot, texte, auteur* to translate (*en, dans* into). **traduit de l'allemand** translated from (the) German.

b (*exprimer*) to convey, render, express; (*rendre manifeste*) to be the expression of. **les mots traduisent la pensée** words convey *ou* render *ou* express thought; **ce tableau traduit un sentiment de désespoir** this picture conveys *ou* expresses a feeling of despair; **sa peur se traduisait par une grande volubilité** his fear found expression in great volubility; **cela s'est traduit par une baisse du pouvoir d'achat** the effect of this was a drop in buying power, it was translated into a drop in buying power.

c (*Jur*) ~ **qn en justice** to bring sb before the courts; ~ **qn en correctionnelle** to bring sb before the criminal court.

traduisible [tʀadɥizibl] **adj** translatable.

Trafalgar [tʀafalgaʀ] **nm** Trafalgar. **coup de ~** underhand trick.

trafic [tʀafik] **nm** a (*péj*) (*commerce clandestin*) traffic; (*activité*) trafficking; (†: *commerce*) trade (*de* in). ~ **d'armes** arms dealing, gunrunning; **faire le ~ d'armes** to be engaged in arms dealing *ou* gunrunning; ~ **de stupéfiants** *ou* **drogue** drug trafficking; **faire le ~ des stupéfiants** *ou* **de la drogue** to trafffic in drugs; **le ~ des vins/cuirs**† the wine/leather trade.

b (*fig: activités suspectes*) dealings (*pl*); (*: *micmac*) funny business*, goings-on* (*pl*). (*Hist*) ~ **des bénéfices** selling of benefices; (*Jur*) ~ **d'influence** trading of favours; (*fig péj*) **faire ~ de son honneur** to trade in one's honour; (*fig hum*) **faire (le) ~ de ses charmes** to offer one's charms for sale; **il se fait ici un drôle de ~ *** there's some funny business going on here*, there are some strange goings-on here*.

c (*Aut, Aviat, Rail*) traffic. ~ **maritime/routier/aérien/ferroviaire** sea/road/air/rail traffic; **ligne à fort ~** line carrying dense *ou* heavy traffic; ~ **(de) marchandises/(de) voyageurs** goods/passenger traffic.

traficoter* [tʀafikɔte] 1 **vti** a (*altérer*) *vin* to doctor*; *moteur* to tamper *ou* fiddle with. ~ **les comptes** to cook* (*Brit*) *ou* fiddle the books. b (*réparer*) *serrure, transistor, robinet* to patch up, mend. c (*faire*) **qu'est-ce qu'il traficote dans la cuisine?** what's he up to *ou* doing in the kitchen?

trafiquant, e [tʀafikɑ̃, ɑ̃t] **nm,f** (*péj*) trafficker. ~ **de drogue** drug trafficker; ~ **d'armes** arms dealer, gunrunner.

trafiquer [tʀafike] 1 1 **vi** (*péj*) to traffic, trade (illicitly). ~ **de son influence/ses charmes** to offer one's influence/charms for sale. 2 **vt** (*: *péj*) *vin* to doctor*; *moteur* to tamper *ou* fiddle with; *document* to tamper with.

tragédie [tʀaʒedi] **nf** (*gén, Théât*) tragedy.

tragédien [tʀaʒedjɛ̃] **nm** tragedian, tragic actor.

tragédienne [tʀaʒedjɛn] **nf** tragedienne, tragic actress.

tragi-comédie, pl tragi-comédies [tʀaʒikɔmedi] **nf** (*Théât, fig*) tragicomedy.

tragi-comique [tʀaʒikɔmik] **adj** (*Théât, fig*) tragi-comic.

tragique [tʀaʒik] 1 **adj** (*Théât, fig*) tragic. **ce n'est pas ~*** it's not the end of the world. 2 **nm** a (*auteur*) tragedian, tragic author. b (*genre*) **le ~** tragedy. c (*caractère dramatique*) *[situation]* tragedy. **la situation tourne au ~** the situation is taking a tragic turn; **prendre qch au ~** to act as if sth were a tragedy, make a tragedy out of sth.

tragiquement [tʀaʒikmɑ̃] **adv** tragically.

trahir [tʀaiʀ] 2 1 **vt** a *ami, patrie, cause*, (†) *femme* to betray. ~ **la confiance/les intérêts de qn** to betray sb's confidence/interests; (*fig*) **ses sens le trahirent: pour une fois il se trompa** his senses betrayed *ou* deceived him — for once he was mistaken; **sa rougeur la trahit** her blushes gave her away *ou* betrayed her.

b (*révéler, manifester*) *secret, émotion* to betray, give away. ~ **sa pensée** to betray *ou* reveal one's thoughts; **son intonation trahissait sa colère** his intonation betrayed his anger.

c (*lâcher*) *[forces, santé]* to fail. **ses forces l'ont trahi** his strength failed him; **ses nerfs l'ont trahi** his nerves let him down *ou* failed him.

d (*mal exprimer*) to misrepresent. **ces mots ont trahi ma pensée** those words misrepresented what I had in mind; **ce traducteur/cet interprète a trahi ma pièce** this translator/performer has given a totally false rendering of my play.

2 **se trahir vpr** to betray o.s., give o.s. away. **il s'est trahi par cette question** his question gave him away, by asking this question he gave himself away; **sa peur se trahissait par une grande volubilité** his fear betrayed itself in a great flow of words.

trahison [tʀaizɔ̃] **nf** (*gén*) betrayal, treachery (*NonC*); (*Jur, Mil: crime*) treason. **il est capable des pires ~s** he is capable of the worst treachery; *voir* **haut**.

traille [tʀɑj] **nf** (*câble*) ferry-cable; (*bac*) (cable) ferry.

train [tʀɛ̃] 1 **nm** a (*Rail*) train. ~ **omnibus/express/rapide** slow *ou* stopping/fast/express train; ~ **direct** fast *ou* non-stop *ou* express train; ~ **à vapeur/électrique** steam/electric train; ~ **de marchandises/voyageurs** goods/passenger train; ~ **auto-couchettes** car-sleeper train, ≃ Motorail (*Brit*); ~**s supplémentaires** extra trains; ~ **à supplément** fast train (*on which one has to pay a supplement*); **c'est un ~ à supplément** you have to pay a supplement on this train; **le ~ de Paris/Lyon** the Paris/Lyons train; ~ **à grande vitesse** high-speed train; **les ~s de neige** the winter-sports trains; **il est dans ce ~** he's on *ou* aboard this train; **mettre qn dans le ~** *ou* **au ~** to see sb to the train, see sb off on the train *ou* at the station; **voyager par** *ou* **prendre le ~** to travel by rail *ou* train, take the train; **attraper/rater le train de 10 h 50** to catch/miss the 10.50 train; **monter dans** *ou* **prendre le ~ en marche** (*lit*) to get on the moving train; (*fig*) to jump on *ou* climb onto the bandwagon; **la Grande-Bretagne a pris le ~ du Marché commun en marche** Great Britain has jumped on *ou* climbed onto the Common Market bandwagon.

b (*allure*) pace. **ralentir/accélérer le ~** to slow down/speed up, slow/quicken the pace; **aller son ~** to carry along; **aller son petit ~** to go along at one's own pace; **l'affaire va son petit ~** things are chugging *ou* jogging along (nicely); **aller bon ~** *[affaire, travaux]* to make good progress; *[voiture]* to go at a good pace, make good progress; **aller grand ~** to make brisk progress, move along briskly; **les langues des commères allaient bon ~** the old wives' tongues were wagging away *ou* were going nineteen to the dozen (*Brit*); **mener/suivre le ~** to set/follow the pace; (*fig: dépenser beaucoup*) **mener grand ~** to live in grand style, spend money like water; **il allait à un ~ d'enfer** he was going flat out, he was racing along; **au ~ où il travaille** (at) the rate he is working; **au** *ou* **du ~ où vont les choses, à ce ~-là** the rate things are going, at this rate; *voir* **fond**.

c **être en ~** (*en action*) to be under way; (*de bonne humeur*) to be in good spirits; **mettre qn en ~** (*l'égayer*) to put sb in good spirits; **mettre un travail en ~** to get a job under way *ou* started; **mise en ~** *[travail]* starting (up), start; (*Typ*) make-ready; (*exercices de gym*) warm-up; (*en bonne santé*) **être/se sentir en ~** to be/feel in good form *ou* shape; **elle ne se sent pas très en ~** she doesn't feel too good *ou* too bright*, she feels a bit off-colour *ou* under the weather (*Brit*).

d **être en ~ de faire qch** to be doing sth; **être en ~ de manger/regarder la télévision** to be busy eating/watching television; **j'étais juste en ~ de manger** I was (right) in the middle of eating, I was just eating; **on l'a pris en ~ de voler** he was caught stealing.

e (*file*) *[bateaux, mulets, chevaux]* train, line. (*Mil*) **le ~ (des équipages)** ≃ the (Army) Service Corps; ~ **de bois (de flottage)** timber raft; (*Espace*) ~ **spatial** space train.

f (*Tech: jeu*) ~ **d'engrenages** train of gears; ~ **de pneus** set of (four) tyres.

g (*Admin: série*) **un ~ d'arrêtés/de mesures** a batch of decrees/measures; **un premier ~ de réformes** a first batch *ou* set of reforms.

h (*partie*) (*Aut*) ~ **avant/arrière** front/rear wheel-axle unit; *[animal]* ~ **de devant** forequarters (*pl*); ~ **de derrière** hindquarters (*pl*).

i (⁑: *derrière*) backside⁑, rear (end)*. **recevoir un coup de pied dans le ~** to get a kick in the pants* *ou* up the backside⁑; *voir* **filer, magner**.

2 **comp** ▸**train d'atterrissage** (*Aviat*) undercarriage, landing gear ▸**train de maison** (†: *domestiques*) household, retainers (†) (*pl*); (*dépenses, ménage*) (household) establishment ▸**train mixte** goods and passenger train ▸**train d'ondes** (*Phys*) wave train ▸**train postal** mail train ▸**train sanitaire** (*Mil*) hospital train ▸**train de sonde** (*Tech*) drilling bit and pipe ▸**train de vie** lifestyle, style of living; **le train de vie de l'État** the government's rate of expenditure.

traînailler [tʀɛnɑje] 1 **vi** a (*être lent*) to dawdle, dillydally. b (*vagabonder*) to loaf around, loiter about, hang around, lounge about.

traînant, e [tʀɛnɑ̃, ɑ̃t] **adj** *voix, accent* drawling (*épith*); *robe, aile* trailing (*épith*); *démarche* shuffling (*épith*).

traînard, e [tʀɛnaʀ, aʀd] **nm,f** (*péj*) (*gén*) slowcoach* (*Brit*), slowpoke* (*US*); (*toujours en queue d'un groupe*) straggler.

traînasser [tʀɛnase] 1 **vi** = **traînailler**.

traîne [tʀɛn] **nf** a *[robe]* train. b (*Pêche*) dragnet. **pêche à la ~** dragnet fishing. c (*fig*) **être à la ~** (*en remorque*) to be in tow; (*: *en retard, en arrière*) to lag behind.

traîneau, pl ~x [tʀɛno] **nm** a (*véhicule*) sleigh, sledge (*Brit*), sled (*US*). **promenade en ~** sleigh ride. b (*Pêche*) dragnet.

traînée [tʀene] **nf** a (*laissée par un véhicule, un animal etc*) trail, tracks (*pl*); (*sur un mur: d'humidité, de sang etc*) streak, smear; (*bande, raie: dans le ciel, un tableau*) streak. ~**s de brouillard** wisps *ou* streaks of fog; ~ **de poudre** powder trail; **se répandre comme une ~ de poudre** to spread like wildfire. b (*péj: femme de mauvaise vie*) slut, hussy†. c (*Tech: force*) drag.

traînement [tʀɛnmɑ̃] **nm** *[jambes, pieds]* trailing, dragging; *[voix]* drawl.

traîne-misère [tʀɛnmizɛʀ] **nm inv** wretch.

traîne-patins* [tʀɛnpatɛ̃] **nm inv** = **traîne-savates***.

traîner [tʀene] 1 1 **vt** a (*tirer*) *sac, objet lourd, personne* to pull, drag; *wagon, charrette* to draw, pull, haul. ~ **un meuble à travers une pièce** to pull *ou* drag *ou* haul a piece of furniture across a room; ~ **qn par les pieds** to drag sb along by the feet; ~ **les pieds** (*lit*) to drag one's feet, shuffle along; (*fig: hésiter*) to drag one's feet; ~ **la jambe** *ou* **la patte*** to limp, hobble; **elle traînait sa poupée dans la poussière** she was trailing *ou* dragging her doll through the dust; (*fig*) ~ **ses guêtres***

to mooch around* (*Brit*), drag o.s. around; (*fig*) ~ **la savate*** to bum around‡; (*fig*) ~ **qn dans la boue** *ou* **fange** to drag sb *ou* sb's name through the mud; (*fig*) ~ **un boulet** to have a millstone round one's neck.

b (*emmener: péj*) to drag (with one). **il traîne sa femme à toutes les réunions** he drags his wife along (with him) to all the meetings; **elle est obligée de ~ ses enfants partout** she has to trail *ou* drag her children along (with her) everywhere; **il traîne toujours une vieille valise avec lui** he is always dragging *ou* lugging* an old suitcase around with him; (*fig*) ~ **de vieilles idées/des conceptions surannées** to cling to old ideas/outdated conceptions.

c (*subir*) **elle traîne cette bronchite depuis janvier** this bronchitis has been with her *ou* plaguing her since January; **elle traîne un mauvais rhume** she has a bad cold she can't get rid of *ou* shake off; ~ **une existence misérable** to drag out a wretched existence; **cette mélancolie qu'il traîna sans pouvoir s'en défaire** this feeling of melancholy which clung to him *ou* oppressed him and would not be dispelled.

d (*faire durer*) to drag out, draw out. ~ **les choses en longueur** to drag things out.

e **(faire)** ~ *mots* to drawl; *fin de phrase* to drag out, drawl; **(faire)** ~ **sa voix** to drawl.

2 vi a *[personne]* (*rester en arrière*) to lag *ou* trail behind; (*aller lentement*) to dawdle; (*péj: errer*) to hang about. ~ **en chemin** to dawdle on the way; ~ **dans les rues** to roam the streets, hang about the streets; **elle laisse ses enfants ~ dans la rue** she lets her children hang about the street(s); **il traîne pour se préparer** he dawdles when he gets dressed, he takes ages to get dressed; ~ **en peignoir dans la maison** to trail round *ou* hang about in one's dressing-gown in the house; **on est en retard, il ne s'agit plus de ~** we're late – we must stop hanging around *ou* dawdling; ~ **dans les cafés** to hang around the cafés; **après sa maladie, il a encore traîné 2 ans** after his illness he lingered on for 2 years.

b *[chose]* (*être éparpillé*) to lie about *ou* around. **ses livres traînent sur toutes les chaises** his books are lying about on all the chairs; **ne laisse pas ~ ton argent/tes affaires** don't leave your money/things lying about *ou* around; **des histoires/idées qui traînent partout** stories/ideas that float around everywhere; **elle attrape tous les microbes qui traînent** *ou* **tout ce qui traîne** she catches anything that's going.

c (*durer trop longtemps*) to drag on. **un procès qui traîne** a case which is dragging on; **une maladie qui traîne** a lingering illness, an illness which drags on; **la discussion a traîné en longueur** the discussion dragged on for ages *ou* dragged on and on; **ça n'a pas traîné!*** that wasn't long coming!; **il n'a pas traîné (à répondre)*** he was quick (with his answer), his answer wasn't long in coming, he replied immediately; **ça ne traînera pas, il vous mettra tous à la porte*** he'll throw you all out before you know what's happening *ou* where you are; **faire ~ qch** (*en longueur*) to drag sth out; **doctrine où traînent des relents de fascisme** doctrine which still has a whiff of fascism about it.

d *[robe, manteau]* to trail. **ta ceinture/ton lacet traîne par terre** your belt/shoelace is trailing *ou* hanging *ou* dragging on the ground; **des effilochures de brume qui traînent dans le ciel** wisps of mist which trail across *ou* linger in the sky.

3 **se traîner** vpr a *[personne fatiguée]* to drag o.s.; *[train, voiture]* to crawl along. **on se traînait à 20 à l'heure** we were crawling along at 20; **se ~ par terre** to crawl on the ground; **avec cette chaleur, on se traîne** it's all one can do to drag oneself around in this heat; **elle a pu se ~ jusqu'à son fauteuil** she managed to drag *ou* haul herself (over) to her chair; **je ne peux même plus me ~** I can't even drag myself about any more; (*fig*) **se ~ aux pieds de qn** to grovel at sb's feet.

b *[conversation, journée, hiver]* to drag on.

traîne-savates* [tʀɛnsavat] nm inv (*vagabond*) tramp, bum‡; (*traînard*) slowcoach (*Brit*), slowpoke (*US*).

training [tʀeniŋ] nm a (*entraînement*) training. ~ **autogène** autogenic training. b (*chaussure*) trainer. (® : *survêtement*) **T~** tracksuit top.

train-train, traintrain [tʀɛ̃tʀɛ̃] nm humdrum routine. **le ~ de la vie quotidienne** the humdrum routine of everyday life, the daily round.

traire [tʀɛʀ] [50] vt *vache* to milk; *lait* to draw. **machine à ~** milking machine.

trait [tʀɛ] 1 nm a (*ligne*) (*en dessinant*) stroke; (*en soulignant, dans un graphique*) line. **faire** *ou* **tirer** *ou* **tracer un ~** to draw a line; (*fig*) **tirer un ~ sur son passé** to make a complete break with one's past, sever all connections with one's past; **tirons un ~ sur cette affaire** let's put this business behind us, let's draw a veil over this business; **ta promotion? tu peux tirer un ~ dessus!** your promotion? you can forget about it! *ou* kiss it goodbye!*; (*technique, œuvre*) **dessin au ~** line drawing; (*Art*) **le ~ est ferme** the line is firm; (*lit, fig*) **d'un ~ de plume** with one stroke of the pen; ~ **de repère** reference mark; **biffer qch d'un ~** to score *ou* cross sth out, put a line through sth; **copier** *ou* **reproduire qch ~ pour ~** to copy sth line by line, make a line for line copy of sth; (*fig*) **ça lui ressemble ~ pour ~** that's just *ou* exactly like him, that's him to a T; **les ~s d'un dessin/portrait** the lines of a drawing/portrait; **dessiner qch à grands ~s** to sketch sth roughly, make a rough sketch of sth; (*fig*) **décrire qch à grands ~s** to describe sth in broad outline; (*fig*) **il l'a décrit en ~s vifs et émouvants** he drew a vivid and moving picture of it.

b (*élément caractéristique*) feature, trait. **c'est un ~ de cet auteur** this is a (characteristic) trait *ou* feature of this author; **les ~s dominants d'une époque/œuvre** the dominant features of an age/a work; **avoir des ~s de ressemblance avec** to have certain features in common with; **il tient ce ~ de caractère de son père** this trait (of character) comes to him from his father, he gets this characteristic from his father.

c (*acte révélateur*) ~ **de générosité/courage/perfidie** act of generosity/courage/wickedness.

d **~s** (*physionomie*) features; **avoir des ~s fins/réguliers** to have delicate/regular features; **avoir les ~s tirés/creusés** to have drawn/sunken features.

e (*†: projectile*) arrow, dart; (*littér: attaque malveillante*) taunt, gibe. **filer** *ou* **partir comme un ~** to be off like an arrow *ou* a shot; **il l'anéantit de ce ~ mordant** he crushed him with this biting taunt; **un ~ satirique/d'ironie** a shaft of satire/irony (*littér*); (*fig*) **les ~s de la calomnie** the darts of slander (*littér*).

f (*courroie*) trace.

g (*traction*) **animal** *ou* **bête/cheval de ~** draught (*Brit*) *ou* draft (*US*) animal/horse.

h (*Mus*) virtuosic passage.

i (*Rel*) tract.

j (*gorgée*) draught (*Brit*), draft (*US*), gulp. **d'un ~** *dire* in one breath; *boire* in one gulp, at one go; *dormir* uninterruptedly, without waking; **à longs ~s** in long draughts (*Brit*) *ou* drafts (*US*); **à grands ~s** in great gulps.

k (*Ling*) ~ **distinctif** distinctive feature.

l (*Échecs*) **avoir le ~** to have the move; **en début de partie les blancs ont toujours le ~** at the start of the game white always has first move; **il avait le ~** it was his move, it was his turn to move.

m (*loc*) **avoir ~ à** to relate to, be connected with, have to do with, concern; **tout ce qui a ~ à cette affaire** everything relating to *ou* connected with *ou* (having) to do with *ou* concerning this matter.

2 comp ►**trait (d'esprit)** flash *ou* shaft of wit, witticism ►**trait de génie** brainwave, flash of inspiration *ou* genius ►**trait de lumière** (*lit*) shaft *ou* ray of light; (*fig*) flash of inspiration, sudden revelation (*NonC*) ►**trait de scie** cutting-line ►**trait d'union** (*Typ*) hyphen; (*fig*) link.

traitable [tʀɛtabl] adj a (*littér*) *personne* accommodating, tractable (*frm*). b *sujet, matière* manageable.

traitant, e [tʀɛtɑ̃, ɑ̃t] adj a (*shampooing*) medicated; *voir* **médecin**. b (*Espionnage*) **(officier)** ~ contact.

traite [tʀɛt] nf a (*trafic*) ~ **des Noirs** slave trade; ~ **des Blanches** white slave trade. b (*Comm: billet*) draft, bill. **tirer/escompter une ~** to draw/discount a draft; ~ **de cavalerie** accommodation bill. c (*parcours*) stretch. **d'une (seule) ~** *parcourir* in one go, without stopping on the way; *dire* in one breath; *boire* in one gulp, at one go; *dormir* uninterruptedly, without waking. d *[vache]* milking. ~ **mécanique** machine milking; **l'heure de la ~** milking time.

traité [tʀete] nm a (*livre*) treatise; (*Rel : brochure*) tract. b (*convention*) treaty. ~ **de paix** peace treaty; **le ~ de Versailles/Paris** *etc* the Treaty of Versailles/Paris *etc*; **conclure/ratifier un ~** to conclude/ratify a treaty.

traitement [tʀɛtmɑ̃] nm a (*manière d'agir*) treatment. **mauvais ~s** ill-treatment (*NonC*); ~ **de faveur** special *ou* preferential treatment.

b (*Méd*) treatment. **suivre/prescrire un ~ douloureux** to undergo/prescribe painful treatment *ou* a painful course of treatment; **être en ~** to be having treatment (*à l'hôpital* in hospital).

c (*rémunération*) salary, wage; (*Rel*) stipend. **toucher un bon ~** to get a good wage *ou* salary.

d (*Tech*) *[matières premières]* processing, treating. **le ~ (automatique) de l'information** *ou* **des données** (automatic) data processing; (*Ordin*) ~ **de texte** (*technique*) word-processing; (*logiciel*) word-processing package; **machine** *ou* **système de ~ de texte (dédié)** word processor; ~ **par lots** batch processing; ~ **interactif** interactive computing.

traiter [tʀete] [1] 1 vt a *personne, animal* to treat; (*Méd: soigner*) *malade, maladie* to treat; (†) *invités* to entertain. ~ **qn bien/mal/comme un chien** to treat sb well/badly/like a dog; ~ **qn d'égal à égal** to treat sb as an equal; ~ **qn en enfant/malade** to treat sb as *ou* like a child/an invalid; **ils traitent leurs enfants/domestiques durement** they are hard with *ou* on their children/servants, they give their children/servants a hard time; **les congressistes ont été magnifiquement traités** the conference members were entertained magnificently; **se faire ~ pour une affection pulmonaire** to undergo treatment for *ou* be treated for lung trouble.

b (*qualifier*) ~ **qn de fou/menteur** to call sb a fool/a liar; ~ **qn de tous les noms** to call sb all the names imaginable *ou* all the names under the sun; **ils se sont traités de voleur(s)** they called each other thieves; **je me suis fait ~ d'imbécile** they called me a fool.

c (*examiner, s'occuper de*) *question* to treat, deal with; (*Art*) *thème, sujet* to treat; (*Comm*) *affaire* to handle, deal with. **il n'a pas traité le sujet** he has not dealt with the subject.

d (*Tech*) *cuir, minerai, pétrole* to treat, process; (*Ordin*) *données* to process. **non traité** untreated.

2 **traiter de** vt indir to deal with, treat of (*frm*). **le livre/romancier traite des problèmes de la drogue** the book/novelist deals with *ou* treats of (*frm*) the problems of drugs.

3 vi (*négocier, parlementer*) to negotiate, make *ou* do* a deal. ~ **avec qn** to negotiate *ou* deal with sb, have dealings with sb; **les pays doivent** ~ **entre eux** countries must deal *ou* have dealings with each other.

traiteur [tʀɛtœʀ] nm caterer. **épicier-**~ grocer and caterer.

traître, traîtresse [tʀɛtʀ, tʀɛtʀɛs] 1 adj a *personne* treacherous, traitorous; *allure* treacherous; *douceur, paroles* perfidious, treacherous. **être** ~ **à une cause/à sa patrie** to be a traitor to a cause/one's country, betray a cause/one's country. b (*fig: dangereux*) *animal* vicious; *vin* deceptive; *escalier, virage* treacherous. c (*loc*) **ne pas dire un** ~ **mot** not to breathe a (single) word. 2 nm a (*gén*) traitor; (*Théât*) villain. b (†: *perfide*) scoundrel†. c **prendre/attaquer qn en** ~ to take/attack sb off-guard, play an underhand trick/make an insidious attack on sb. 3 **traîtresse** nf traitress.

traîtreusement [tʀɛtʀøzmɑ̃] adv treacherously.

traîtrise [tʀɛtʀiz] nf a (*caractère*) treachery, treacherousness. b (*acte*) (piece of) treachery; (*danger*) treacherousness (*NonC*), peril.

trajectoire [tʀaʒɛktwaʀ] nf (*gén*) trajectory; *[projectile]* path, trajectory. **la** ~ **de la balle passe très près du cœur** the bullet passed very close to the heart.

trajet [tʀaʒɛ] nm a (*distance à parcourir*) distance; (*itinéraire*) route; (*parcours, voyage*) journey; (*par mer*) voyage. **un** ~ **de 8 km** a distance of 8 km; **choisir le** ~ **le plus long** to choose the longest route *ou* way; **elle fait à pied le court** ~ **de son bureau à la gare** she walks the short distance from her office to the station; **elle a une heure de** ~ **pour se rendre à son travail** she has an hour's travelling time to get to work, it takes her an hour to get to work; **le** ~ **aller/retour** the outward/return journey; **faire le** ~ **de Paris à Lyon en voiture/train** to do the journey from Paris to Lyons by car/train; **le** ~ **par mer est plus intéressant** the sea voyage *ou* crossing is more interesting; (*fig*) **quel** ~ **il a parcouru depuis son dernier roman!** what a distance *ou* a long way he has come since his last novel!

b (*Anat*) *[nerf, artère]* course; *[projectile]* path.

tralala* [tʀalala] 1 nm (*luxe, apprêts*) fuss (*NonC*), frills; (*accessoires*) fripperies. **faire du** ~ to make a lot of fuss; **en grand** ~ with all the works*, with a great deal of fuss; **avec tout le** ~ with all the frills *ou* trimmings. 2 excl: ~**! j'ai gagné!** hooray! I've won!

tram [tʀam] nm = **tramway**.

tramail [tʀamaj] nm trammel (net).

trame [tʀam] nf a *[tissu]* weft, woof. **usé jusqu'à la** ~ threadbare. b (*fig*) *[roman]* framework; *[vie]* web. c (*Typ: quadrillage*) screen; (*TV: lignes*) frame. d (*Géog*) network, system. **la** ~ **urbaine** the urban network *ou* system.

tramer [tʀame] 1 vt a *évasion, coup d'État* to plot; *complot* to hatch, weave. **il se trame quelque chose** there's something brewing. b (*Tex*) to weave. c (*Typ*) to screen.

tramontane [tʀamɔ̃tan] nf tramontana. **perdre la** ~† to go off one's head, lose one's wits.

tramp [tʀɑ̃p] nm (*Naut*) tramp.

trampoline [tʀɑ̃pɔlin] nm trampoline. **faire du** ~ to go *ou* do trampolining.

tramway [tʀamwɛ] nm (*moyen de transport*) tram(way); (*voiture*) tram(car) (*Brit*), streetcar (*US*).

tranchant, e [tʀɑ̃ʃɑ̃, ɑ̃t] 1 adj a *couteau, arête* sharp. **du côté** ~**/non** ~ with the sharp *ou* cutting/blunt edge. b (*fig*) *personne, ton* assertive, peremptory, curt. 2 nm a *[couteau]* sharp *ou* cutting edge. **avec le** ~ **de la main** with the edge of one's hand; *voir* **double**. b (*instrument*) *[apiculteur]* scraper; *[tanneur]* fleshing knife. c (*fig*) *[argument, réprimande]* force, impact.

tranche [tʀɑ̃ʃ] nf a (*portion*) *[pain, jambon]* slice; *[bacon]* rasher. ~ **de bœuf** beefsteak; ~ **de saumon** salmon steak; ~ **napolitaine** neapolitan slice; **en** ~**s** sliced, in slices; **couper en** ~**s** to slice, cut into slices; (*Ordin*) ~ **de silicium** silicon wafer; **ils s'en sont payé une** ~ * they had a great time* *ou* a whale of a time*, they had a lot of fun.

b (*bord*) *[livre, pièce de monnaie, planche]* edge; *voir* **doré**.

c (*section*) (*gén*) section; (*Fin*) *[actions, bons]* block, tranche; *[crédit, prêt]* instalment; (*Admin*) *[revenus]* bracket; *[imposition]* band, bracket. (*Loterie*) ~ **(d'émission)** issue; (*Admin*) ~ **d'âge/de salaires** age/wage bracket; (*TV, Rad*) ~ **horaire** (time) slot; ~ **de temps** period of time; **une** ~ **de vie** a part of sb's life; **la première** ~ **des travaux** the first phase of the work.

d (*Boucherie: morceau*) ~ **grasse** silverside; **bifteck dans la** ~ ≃ piece of silverside steak.

tranché, e¹ [tʀɑ̃ʃe] adj *couleurs* clear, distinct; *limite* clear-cut, definite; *opinion* clear-cut, cut-and-dried.

tranchée² [tʀɑ̃ʃe] nf a (*gén, Mil: fossé*) trench; *voir* **guerre**. b (*Sylviculture*) cutting.

tranchées [tʀɑ̃ʃe] nfpl (*Méd*) colic, gripes, tormina (*SPÉC*). ~ **utérines** after-pains.

tranchefile [tʀɑ̃ʃfil] nf *[reliure]* headband.

trancher [tʀɑ̃ʃe] 1 1 vt a (*couper*) *corde, nœud, lien* to cut, sever. ~ **le cou** *ou* **la tête à** *ou* **de qn** to cut off *ou* sever sb's head; ~ **la gorge à qn** to cut *ou* slit sb's throat; (*fig*) **la mort** *ou* **la Parque tranche le fil des jours** death severs *ou* the Fates sever the thread of our days; *voir* **nœud**.

b (†, *frm: mettre fin à*) *discussion* to conclude, bring to a close. ~ **court** *ou* **net** to bring things to an abrupt conclusion; **tranchons là** let's close the matter there.

c (*résoudre*) *question, difficulté* to settle, decide, resolve; (*emploi absolu: décider*) to take a decision. ~ **un différend** to settle a difference; **le juge a dû** ~**/a tranché que** the judge had to make a ruling/ruled that; **il ne faut pas avoir peur de** ~ one must not be afraid of taking decisions; **le gouvernement a tranché en faveur de ce projet** the government has decided *ou* has come out in favour of this plan.

2 vi a (*couper*) ~ **dans le vif** (*Méd*) to cut into the flesh; (*fig*) to take drastic action.

b (*contraster avec*) *[couleur]* to stand out clearly (*sur, avec* against); *[trait, qualité]* to contrast strongly *ou* sharply (*sur, avec* with). **cette vallée sombre tranche sur le paysage environnant** this dark valley stands out against the surrounding countryside; **la journée du dimanche a tranché sur une semaine très agitée** Sunday formed a sharp contrast to a very busy week; **son silence tranchait avec** *ou* **sur l'hystérie générale** his silence was in stark contrast to the general mood of hysteria.

tranchet [tʀɑ̃ʃɛ] nm *[bourrelier, sellier]* leather knife; *[plombier]* hacking knife.

tranchoir [tʀɑ̃ʃwaʀ] nm a (*Culin*) (*plateau*) trencher†, platter; (*couteau*) chopper. b (*Zool*) zanclus.

tranquille [tʀɑ̃kil] adj a (*calme*) *eau, mer, air* quiet, tranquil (*littér*); *sommeil* gentle, peaceful, tranquil (*littér*); *vie, journée, vacances, endroit* quiet, peaceful, tranquil (*littér*). **un** ~ **bien-être l'envahissait** a feeling of quiet *ou* calm well-being crept over him; **c'est l'heure la plus** ~ **de la journée** it's the quietest *ou* most peaceful time of day; **aller/entrer d'un pas** ~ to walk/enter calmly.

b (*assuré*) *courage, conviction* quiet, calm. **avec une** ~ **assurance** with quiet *ou* calm assurance.

c (*paisible*) *tempérament, personne* quiet, placid, peaceable, peaceful; *voisins, enfants, élèves* quiet. **il veut être** ~ he wants to have some peace; **rester/se tenir** ~ to keep *ou* stay/be quiet; **pour une fois qu'il est** ~ since he's quiet for once; **nous étions bien** ~**s et il a fallu qu'il nous dérange** we were having a nice quiet *ou* peaceful time and he had to come and disturb us; **ferme la porte, j'aime être** ~ **après le repas** close the door — I like (to have) some peace (and quiet) after my meal; **laisser qn** ~ to leave sb alone, to leave sb in peace, give sb a bit of peace; **laisser qch** ~ to leave sth alone *ou* in peace; **laisse-le-donc** ~**, tu vois bien qu'il travaille/qu'il est moins fort que toi** leave him alone *ou* in peace *ou* let him be — you can see he's working/not as strong as you are; **laissez-moi** ~ **avec vos questions** stop bothering me with your questions; **il est** ~ **comme Baptiste** he's got nothing to worry about; *voir* **père**.

d (*rassuré*) **être** ~ to feel *ou* be easy in one's mind; **tu peux être** ~ you needn't worry, you can set your mind at rest, you can rest easy; **il a l'esprit** ~ his mind is at rest *ou* at ease, he has an easy mind; **pour avoir l'esprit** ~ to set one's mind at rest, to feel easy in one's mind; **avoir la conscience** ~ to be at peace with one's conscience, have a clear conscience; (*lit*) **pouvoir dormir** ~ to be able to sleep easy (in one's bed); (*fig: être rassuré*) **tu peux dormir** ~ you can rest easy, you needn't worry; **comme cela, nous serons** ~**s** that way our minds will be at rest; **soyez** ~**, tout ira bien** set your mind at rest *ou* don't worry — everything will be all right; **maintenant je peux mourir** ~ now I can die in peace.

e (*: *certain*) **être** ~ **(que ...)** to be sure (that ...); (*iro*) **soyez** ~**, je me vengerai** don't (you) worry *ou* rest assured — I shall have my revenge; **il n'ira pas, je suis** ~ he won't go, I'm sure of it; **tu peux être** ~ **que ...** you may be sure that ..., rest assured that ... .

f **baume** ~ soothing balm; **vin** ~ still wine.

g (*emploi adverbial**: *facilement*) easily. **il l'a fait en 3 heures** ~ he did it in 3 hours easily *ou* no trouble; (*sans risques*) **tu peux y aller** ~ you can go there quite safely.

tranquillement [tʀɑ̃kilmɑ̃] adv (*voir* **tranquille**) quietly; tranquilly; gently, peacefully; placidly, peaceably. **il vivait** ~ **dans la plus grande abjection** he lived quietly *ou* at peace in the most utter abjection; **on peut y aller** ~**: ça ne risque plus rien*** we can go ahead safely — there's no risk now; (*sans se presser*) **vous pouvez y aller** ~ **en 2 heures** you can get there easily *ou* without hurrying in 2 hours.

tranquillisant, e [tʀɑ̃kilizɑ̃, ɑ̃t] 1 adj *nouvelle* reassuring; *effet, produit* soothing, tranquillizing. 2 nm (*Méd*) tranquillizer.

tranquilliser [tʀɑ̃kilize] 1 vt: ~ **qn** to reassure sb, set sb's mind at rest; **se** ~ to set one's mind at rest; **tranquillise-toi, il ne lui arrivera rien** calm down *ou* take it easy, nothing will happen to him; **je suis tranquillisé** I'm reassured *ou* relieved.

tranquillité [tʀɑ̃kilite] nf a (*voir* **tranquille**) quietness; tranquillity; gentleness; peacefulness. b (*paix, sérénité*) peace, tranquillity. **en toute** ~ without being bothered *ou* disturbed; **ils ont cambriolé la villa**

en toute ~ they burgled the house without being disturbed (at all) *ou* without any disturbance; **troubler la** ~ **publique** to disturb the peace; **travailler dans la** ~ to work in peace (and quiet); **il tient beaucoup à sa** ~ he sets great store by his peace and quiet. c (*absence de souci*) ~ **(d'esprit)** peace of mind; ~ **matérielle** material security; **en toute** ~ with complete peace of mind, free from all anxiety.

trans... [tʀɑ̃z] **préf** trans... .

transaction [tʀɑ̃zaksjɔ̃] **nf** a (*Comm*) transaction. **~s commerciales/financières** commercial/financial transactions *ou* dealings. b (*Jur: compromis*) settlement, compromise. c (*Ordin*) transaction.

transactionnel, -elle [tʀɑ̃zaksjɔnɛl] **adj** (*Ordin*) transactional; (*Jur*) compromise (*épith*), settlement (*épith*); **formule ~le** compromise formula; **règlement** ~ compromise settlement; (*Psych*) **analyse ~le** transactional analysis.

transafricain, e [tʀɑ̃zafʀikɛ̃, ɛn] **adj** transafrican.

transalpin, e [tʀɑ̃zalpɛ̃, in] **adj** transalpine.

transamazonien, -ienne [tʀɑ̃zamazɔnjɛ̃, jɛn] **adj** trans-Amazonian. **(autoroute) ~ienne** trans-Amazonian highway.

transaméricain, e [tʀɑ̃zameʀikɛ̃, ɛn] **adj** transamerican (*épith*).

transaminase [tʀɑ̃zaminɑz] **nf** transaminase.

transat [tʀɑ̃zat] 1 **nm abrév de transatlantique.** 2 **nf** (**abrév de course transatlantique**) ~ **en solitaire** single-handed race across the Atlantic *ou* transatlantic race; ~ **en double** two-man (*ou* tow-woman) transatlantic race.

transatlantique [tʀɑ̃zatlɑ̃tik] 1 **adj** transatlantic. **course** ~ transatlantic race. 2 **nm** (*paquebot*) transatlantic liner; (*fauteuil*) deckchair.

transbahuter* [tʀɑ̃sbayte] [1] 1 **vt** to shift, hump along* (*Brit*), lug along*. 2 **se transbahuter vpr** to traipse along*, lug o.s. along*.

transbordement [tʀɑ̃sbɔʀdəmɑ̃] **nm** (*voir* **transborder**) tran(s)shipment; transfer.

transborder [tʀɑ̃sbɔʀde] [1] **vt** (*Naut*) to tran(s)ship; (*Rail*) to transfer.

transbordeur [tʀɑ̃sbɔʀdœʀ] **nm: (pont)** ~ transporter bridge.

transcanadien, -ienne [tʀɑ̃skanadjɛ̃, jɛn] **adj** trans-Canada (*épith*).

transcendance [tʀɑ̃sɑ̃dɑ̃s] **nf** (*Philos*) transcendence, transcendency; (*littér*, †: *excellence*) transcendence (*littér*); (*fait de se surpasser*) self-transcendence (*littér*).

transcendant, e [tʀɑ̃sɑ̃dɑ̃, ɑ̃t] **adj** a (*littér: sublime*) *génie, mérite* transcendent (*littér*). *[film, livre]* **ce n'est pas ~*** it's nothing special*, it's nothing to write home about*. b (*Philos*) transcendent(al). **être ~ à** to transcend. c (*Math*) transcendental.

transcendantal, e, mpl -aux [tʀɑ̃sɑ̃dɑ̃tal, o] **adj** transcendental.

transcendantalisme [tʀɑ̃sɑ̃dɑ̃talism] **nm** transcendentalism.

transcender [tʀɑ̃sɑ̃de] [1] 1 **vt** to transcend. 2 **se transcender vpr** to transcend o.s.

transcodage [tʀɑ̃skɔdaʒ] **nm** (*Ordin*) compiling; (*TV*) transcoding.

transcoder [tʀɑ̃skɔde] [1] **vt** (*Ordin*) *programme* to compile; (*TV*) to transcode.

transcodeur [tʀɑ̃skɔdœʀ] **nm** (*Ordin*) compiler; (*TV*) transcoder.

transcontinental, e, mpl -aux [tʀɑ̃skɔ̃tinɑ̃tal, o] **adj** transcontinental.

transcripteur [tʀɑ̃skʀiptœʀ] **nm** transcriber.

transcription [tʀɑ̃skʀipsjɔ̃] **nf** a (*voir* **transcrire**) copying out; transcription; transliteration. b (*copie*) copy; (*translittération*) transcript; (*Mus, Ling*) transcription; (*Bio*) transcription. ~ **phonétique** phonetic transcription.

transcrire [tʀɑ̃skʀiʀ] [39] **vt** a (*copier*) to copy out, transcribe (*frm*). b (*translittérer*) to transcribe, transliterate. c (*Mus, Ling*) to transcribe. d (*Bio*) to transcribe.

transdisciplinaire [tʀɑ̃sdisiplinɛʀ] **adj** interdisciplinary.

transducteur [tʀɑ̃sdyktœʀ] **nm** transducer.

transduction [tʀɑ̃sdyksjɔ̃] **nf** (*Bio*) transduction.

transe [tʀɑ̃s] **nf** a (*état second*) trance. **être en** ~ to be in a trance; **entrer en** ~ (*lit*) to go into a trance; (*fig: s'énerver*) to go into a rage, see red*. b (*affres*) **~s** agony; **être dans les ~s** to be in *ou* suffer agony, go through agony; **être dans les ~s de l'attente/des examens** to be in agonies of anticipation/over the exams.

transept [tʀɑ̃sɛpt] **nm** transept.

transférable [tʀɑ̃sfeʀabl] **adj** transferable.

transfèrement [tʀɑ̃sfɛʀmɑ̃] **nm** *[prisonnier]* transfer. ~ **cellulaire** transfer by prison van.

transférer [tʀɑ̃sfeʀe] [6] **vt** a *fonctionnaire, assemblée, bureaux* to transfer, move; *prisonnier*, (*Sport*) *joueur* to transfer; (*Ordin*) to transfer; *dépouille mortelle, reliques, évêque* to transfer, translate (*littér*). ~ **la production dans une autre usine** to transfer *ou* switch production to another factory; **nos bureaux sont transférés au 5 rue de Lyon** our offices have transferred *ou* moved to 5 rue de Lyon. b *capitaux* to transfer, move; *propriété, droit* to transfer, convey (*SPÉC*); (*Comptabilité: par virement etc*) to transfer. c (*fig, Psych*) to transfer. ~ **des sentiments sur qn** to transfer feelings onto sb.

transfert [tʀɑ̃sfɛʀ] **nm** a (*voir* **transférer**) transfer; translation; conveyance. (*Écon*) ~ **de technologie** transfer of technology, technology transfer. b (*Psych*) transference. c (*décalque*) transfer (*Brit*), decal (*US*). d (*Ordin*) transfer.

transfiguration [tʀɑ̃sfigyʀasjɔ̃] **nf** transfiguration. (*Rel*) **la T~** the Transfiguration.

transfigurer [tʀɑ̃sfigyʀe] [1] **vt** (*transformer*) to transform, transfigure (*frm*); (*Rel*) to transfigure.

transfo* [tʀɑ̃sfo] **nm abrév de transformateur.**

transformable [tʀɑ̃sfɔʀmabl] **adj** *structure* convertible; *aspect* transformable; (*Rugby*) *essai* convertible.

transformateur, -trice [tʀɑ̃sfɔʀmatœʀ, tʀis] 1 **adj** *processus* transformation (*épith*); *action* transforming (*épith*). **pouvoir** ~ power to transform. 2 **nm** transformer.

transformation [tʀɑ̃sfɔʀmasjɔ̃] **nf** a (*action, résultat: voir* **transformer**) change; alteration; conversion; transformation. **travaux de ~, ~s** conversion work; **depuis son mariage, nous assistons chez lui à une véritable** ~ since he married we have seen a real transformation in him *ou* a complete change come over him; *voir* **industrie.** b (*Rugby*) conversion. c (*Géom, Math, Ling*) transformation.

transformationnel, -elle [tʀɑ̃sfɔʀmasjɔnɛl] **adj** transformational.

transformer [tʀɑ̃sfɔʀme] [1] 1 **vt** a (*modifier*) *personne, caractère* to change, alter; *magasin, matière première* to transform, convert; *vêtement* to alter, remake; (*changer radicalement, améliorer*) *personne, caractère, pays* to transform. **on a transformé toute la maison** we've made massive alterations to the house, we've transformed the whole house; **on a mis du papier peint et la pièce en a été transformée** we put on wallpaper and it has completely altered the look of the room *ou* it has transformed the room; **le bonheur/son séjour à la montagne l'a transformé** happiness/his holiday in the mountains has transformed him *ou* made a new man of him; **rêver de ~ la société/les hommes** to dream of transforming society/men; **depuis qu'il va à l'école, il est transformé** since he's been at school he has been a different child.

b ~ **qn/qch en** to turn sb/sth into; ~ **la houille en énergie** to convert coal into energy; ~ **du plomb en or** to turn *ou* change *ou* transmute lead into gold; **on a transformé la grange en atelier** the barn has been converted *ou* turned *ou* made into a studio; **elle a fait ~ son manteau en jaquette** she's had her coat made into a jacket; **elle a transformé leur maison en palais** she has transformed their house into a palace.

c (*Rugby*) *essai* to convert. (*fig*) **maintenant il faut ~ l'essai** now they must consolidate their gains *ou* ram their advantage home.

d (*Géom, Math, Ling*) to transform.

2 **se transformer vpr** (*Bot, Zool*) *[larve, embryon]* to be transformed, transform itself; (*Chim, Phys*) *[énergie, matière]* to be converted; *[personne, pays]* to change, alter; (*radicalement*) to be transformed. **se ~ en** to be transformed into; to be converted into; to change *ou* turn into; **la chenille se transforme en papillon** the caterpillar transforms itself *ou* turns into a butterfly; **il s'est transformé en agneau** he has turned *ou* been transformed into a lamb; **la manifestation risque de se ~ en émeute** the demonstration could (well) turn into a riot; **la ville s'est étonnamment transformée en 2 ans** the town has changed astonishingly in 2 years *ou* has undergone astonishing changes in 2 years; **il s'est transformé depuis qu'il a ce poste** there's been a real transformation *ou* change in him *ou* a real change has come over him since he has had this job.

transformisme [tʀɑ̃sfɔʀmism] **nm** transformism.

transformiste [tʀɑ̃sfɔʀmist] **adj, nmf** transformist.

transfrontalier, -ière [tʀɑ̃sfʀɔ̃talje, jɛʀ] **adj** cross-border (*épith*).

transfuge [tʀɑ̃sfyʒ] **nmf** (*Mil, Pol*) renegade.

transfuser [tʀɑ̃sfyze] [1] **vt** *sang, liquide* to transfuse; (*fig littér*) to transfuse (*littér*) (*à* into), instil (*à* into), impart (*à* to).

transfuseur [tʀɑ̃sfyzœʀ] **nm** transfuser.

transfusion [tʀɑ̃sfyzjɔ̃] **nf:** ~ **(sanguine)** (blood) transfusion.

transgresser [tʀɑ̃sgʀese] [1] **vt** *règle, code* to infringe, contravene, transgress (*littér*); *ordre* to disobey, go against, contravene. ~ **la loi** to break the law.

transgresseur [tʀɑ̃sgʀesœʀ] **nm** (*littér*) transgressor (*littér*).

transgression [tʀɑ̃sgʀesjɔ̃] **nf** (*voir* **transgresser**) infringement; contravention; transgression; disobedience; breaking. ~ **marine** encroachment of the sea.

transhumance [tʀɑ̃zymɑ̃s] **nf** transhumance.

transhumant, e [tʀɑ̃zymɑ̃, ɑ̃t] **adj** transhumant.

transhumer [tʀɑ̃zyme] [1] **vti** to move to summer pastures.

transi, e [tʀɑ̃zi] (**ptp de transir**) **adj: être ~ (de froid)** to be perished, be numb with cold *ou* chilled to the bone *ou* frozen to the marrow; **être ~ de peur** to be paralyzed by fear, be transfixed *ou* numb with fear; *voir* **amoureux.**

transiger [tʀɑ̃ziʒe] [3] **vi** a (*Jur, gén: dans un différend*) to compromise, come to terms *ou* an agreement. b (*fig*) ~ **avec sa conscience** to come to terms with *ou* to a compromise with *ou* make a deal with one's conscience; ~ **avec le devoir** to come to a compromise with duty; **ne pas ~ sur l'honneur/le devoir** to make no compromise in matters of honour/duty; **je me refuse à ~ sur ce point** I refuse to compromise on this point, I am adamant on this point.

transir [tʀɑ̃ziʀ] [2] **vt** (*littér*) *[froid]* to chill to the bone, numb, freeze to the marrow; *[peur]* to paralyze, transfix, numb.

transistor [tʀɑ̃zistɔʀ] **nm** (*élément, poste de radio*) transistor.

transistorisation [tʀɑ̃zistɔʀizasjɔ̃] **nf** transistorization.

transistoriser [tʀɑ̃zistɔʀize] 1 vt to transistorize. **transistorisé** transistorized.

transit [tʀɑ̃zit] nm transit. **en ~** *marchandises, voyageurs* in transit; **de ~** *document, port* transit (*épith*); **le ~ intestinal** digestion, intestinal transit time (*SPÉC*); **~ baryté** barium X-ray.

transitaire [tʀɑ̃zitɛʀ] 1 adj *pays* of transit; *commerce* which is done in transit. 2 nmf forwarding agent.

transiter [tʀɑ̃zite] 1 1 vt *marchandises* to pass *ou* convey in transit. 2 vi to pass in transit (*par* through).

transitif, -ive [tʀɑ̃zitif, iv] adj (*Ling, Math, Philos*) transitive.

transition [tʀɑ̃zisjɔ̃] nf (*gén, Art, Ciné, Mus, Sci*) transition. **de ~** *période, mesure* transitional; **sans ~** without any transition.

transitionnel, -elle [tʀɑ̃zisjɔnɛl] adj transitional.

transitivement [tʀɑ̃zitivmɑ̃] adv transitively.

transitivité [tʀɑ̃zitivite] nf (*Ling, Philos*) transitivity.

transitoire [tʀɑ̃zitwaʀ] adj a (*fugitif*) transitory, transient. b (*de transition*) *régime, mesures* transitional, provisional; *fonction* interim (*épith*), provisional.

transitoirement [tʀɑ̃zitwaʀmɑ̃] adv (*voir* **transitoire**) transitorily; transiently; provisionally.

Transjordanie [tʀɑ̃sjɔʀdani] nf: **la ~** (*Pol*) the Left Bank (of Jordan); (*Hist*) Transjordan.

translation [tʀɑ̃slasjɔ̃] nf a (*Admin*) *[tribunal, évêque]* translation (*frm*), transfer; (*Jur*) *[droit, propriété]* transfer, conveyance; (*littér*) *[dépouille, cendres]* translation (*littér*); (*Rel*) *[fête]* transfer, translation (*frm*). b (*Géom, Sci*) translation. **mouvement de ~** translatory movement.

translit(t)ération [tʀɑ̃sliteʀasjɔ̃] nf transliteration.

translit(t)érer [tʀɑ̃sliteʀe] 6 vt to transliterate.

translocation [tʀɑ̃slɔkasjɔ̃] nf (*Bio*) translocation.

translucide [tʀɑ̃slysid] adj translucent.

translucidité [tʀɑ̃slysidite] nf translucence, translucency.

transmanche [tʀɑ̃smɑ̃ʃ] adj inv cross-Channel (*épith*).

transmetteur [tʀɑ̃smetœʀ] nm (*Téléc, Bio*) transmitter. (*Naut*) **~ d'ordres** speaking tube.

transmettre [tʀɑ̃smɛtʀ] 56 vt a (*léguer*) *biens, secret, tradition, autorité* to hand down, pass on; *qualité* to pass on; (*transférer*) *biens, titre, autorité* to pass on, hand over, transmit (*frm*); (*communiquer*) *secret, recette* to pass on. **sa mère lui avait transmis le goût de la nature** his mother had passed her love of nature on to him.

b *message, ordre, renseignement* to pass on; *lettre, colis* to send on, forward; (*Téléc*) *signal* to transmit, send; (*Rad, TV*) *émission, discours* to broadcast. **~ sur ondes courtes** (*Téléc*) to transmit on short wave; (*Rad, TV*) to broadcast on short wave; **veuillez ~ mes amitiés à Paul** kindly pass on *ou* convey my best wishes to Paul; **veuillez ~ mon meilleur souvenir à Paul** kindly give my regards to *ou* remember me to Paul.

c (*Sport*) *ballon* to pass; *témoin, flambeau* to hand over, pass on.

d (*Sci*) *énergie, impulsion* to transmit; (*Méd*) *maladie* to pass on, transmit; (*Bio*) *microbe* to transmit. **une maladie qui se transmet par contact** an illness passed on *ou* transmitted by contact; **il risque de ~ son rhume aux autres** he's likely to pass on *ou* transmit his cold to others.

transmigration [tʀɑ̃smigʀasjɔ̃] nf transmigration.

transmigrer [tʀɑ̃smigʀe] 1 vi to transmigrate.

transmissibilité [tʀɑ̃smisibilite] nf transmissibility.

transmissible [tʀɑ̃smisibl] adj *patrimoine, droit, caractère* transmissible, transmittable. **maladie sexuellement ~** sexually transmitted disease.

transmission [tʀɑ̃smisjɔ̃] nf a (*voir* **transmettre**) handing down; passing on; handing over; transmission; sending on, forwarding; broadcasting; conveying; passing. (*Aut, Tech*) **les organes de ~, la ~** the parts of the transmission system, the transmission; (*Aut*) **~ automatique** automatic transmission; (*Pol*) **~ des pouvoirs** handing over *ou* transfer of power; (*Ordin*) **~ de données** data transmission; *voir* **arbre, courroie**. b (*Mil: service*) **les ~s** ≃ the Signals (corps). c **~ de pensée** thought transfer, telepathy.

transmuer [tʀɑ̃smɥe] 1 vt (*Chim, littér*) to transmute.

transmutabilité [tʀɑ̃smytabilite] nf transmutability.

transmutation [tʀɑ̃smytasjɔ̃] nf (*Chim, Phys, littér*) transmutation.

transmuter [tʀɑ̃smyte] 1 = **transmuer**.

transnational, e, mpl **-aux** [tʀɑ̃snasjɔnal, o] adj transnational.

transocéanien, -ienne [tʀɑ̃zɔseanjɛ̃, jɛn] adj, **transocéanique** [tʀɑ̃zɔseanik] adj transoceanic.

Transpac [tʀɑ̃spak] nm ® packet switch network, ≃ PSS (*Brit*).

transparaître [tʀɑ̃spaʀɛtʀ] 57 vi to show (through).

transparence [tʀɑ̃spaʀɑ̃s] nf a (*voir* **transparent**) transparency, transparence; limpidity; clearness; openness. **regarder qch par ~** to look at sth against the light; **voir qch par ~** to see sth showing through; **éclairé par ~** with the light shining through; **la ~ de cette allusion** the transparency of this allusion; **réclamer la ~ du financement des partis politiques** to call for openness in the financing of political parties; **société dotée de la ~ fiscale** ≃ partnership. b (*Ciné*) back projection.

transparent, e [tʀɑ̃spaʀɑ̃, ɑ̃t] 1 adj a (*lit*) *verre, porcelaine* transparent; *papier, tissu* transparent, see-through. b (*diaphane*) *eau, ciel* transparent, limpid; *teint, âme, personne* transparent; *regard, yeux* transparent, limpid, clear. c (*fig*) (*évident*) *allusion, sentiment, intentions* transparent, evident; (*sans secret*) *négociation, comptes* open. (*Écon*) **société ~e** ≃ partnership. 2 nm a (*écran*) transparent screen. b (*Archit*) openwork motif. c (*feuille réglée*) ruled sheet (*placed under writing paper*). d (*pour rétroprojecteur*) transparency.

transpercer [tʀɑ̃spɛʀse] 3 vt a (*gén*) to pierce; (*d'un coup d'épée*) to run through, transfix; (*d'un coup de couteau*) to stab; *[épée, lame]* to pierce; *[balle]* to go through. (*fig*) **transpercé de douleur** pierced by sorrow; (*fig*) **~ qn du regard** to give sb a piercing look.

b *[froid, pluie]* to go through, pierce. **malgré nos chandails, le froid nous transperçait** despite our sweaters, the cold was going *ou* cutting straight through us; **la pluie avait finalement transpercé ma pèlerine/la toile de tente** the rain had finally come through *ou* penetrated my cape/the tent canvas; **je suis transpercé (par la pluie)** I'm soaked through *ou* drenched (by the rain).

transpiration [tʀɑ̃spiʀasjɔ̃] nf (*processus*) perspiration, perspiring; (*Bot*) transpiration; (*sueur*) perspiration, sweat. **être en ~** to be perspiring *ou* sweating *ou* in a sweat.

transpirer [tʀɑ̃spiʀe] 1 vi a (*lit*) to perspire, sweat; (*Bot*) to transpire; (**: travailler dur*) to sweat over sth*. **il transpire des mains/pieds** his hands/feet perspire *ou* sweat, he has sweaty hands/feet; **~ à grosses gouttes** to be running *ou* streaming with sweat; **~ sur un devoir*** to sweat over an exercise*. b (*fig*) *[secret, projet, détails]* to come to light, leak out, transpire. **rien n'a transpiré** nothing came to light, nothing leaked out *ou* transpired.

transplant [tʀɑ̃splɑ̃] nm (*Bio*) transplant.

transplantable [tʀɑ̃splɑ̃tabl] adj transplantable.

transplantation [tʀɑ̃splɑ̃tasjɔ̃] nf *[arbre, peuple, traditions]* transplantation, transplanting; (*Méd*) (*technique*) transplantation; (*intervention*) transplant. **~ cardiaque/du rein** heart/kidney transplant.

transplanter [tʀɑ̃splɑ̃te] 1 vt (*Bot, Méd, fig*) to transplant. **se ~ dans un pays lointain** to uproot o.s. and move to a distant country, resettle in a distant country.

transpolaire [tʀɑ̃spɔlɛʀ] adj transpolar.

transport [tʀɑ̃spɔʀ] 1 nm a (*voir* **transporter**) carrying; moving; transport(ation), conveying; conveyance; bringing; carrying over, transposition. (*Rail*) **~ de voyageurs/marchandises** passenger/goods transportation, conveyance *ou* transport of passengers/goods; **un car se chargera du ~ des bagages** the luggage will be taken *ou* transported by coach; **pour faciliter le ~ des blessés** to facilitate the transport of the injured, to enable the injured to be moved more easily; **le ~ des blessés graves pose de nombreux problèmes** transporting *ou* moving seriously injured people poses many problems; **endommagé pendant le ~** damaged in transit; **~ maritime** *ou* **par mer** shipping, sea transport(ation), transport(ation) by sea; **~ par train** *ou* **rail** rail transport(ation), transport(ation) by rail; **~ par air** *ou* **avion** air transport(ation); (*Mil*) **~ de troupes** (*action*) troop transportation; (*navire, train*) troop transport; **matériel/frais de ~** transportation *ou* transport equipment costs; **~ de fonds** transfer of funds; *voir* **avion, moyen**.

b **les ~s** transport; **les ~s publics** *ou* **en commun** public transport; **~s urbains** city *ou* urban transport; **~s fluviaux** transport by inland waterway; **~(s) routier(s)** road haulage *ou* transport; **~(s) aérien(s)/maritime(s)** air/sea transport; **mal des ~(s)** travel-sickness (*Brit*), motion sickness (*US*); **médicament contre le mal des ~s** travel sickness drug (*Brit*), anti-motion-sickness drug (*US*); **entreprise de ~s** haulage company.

c (*littér, hum: manifestation d'émotion*) transport. **(avec) des ~s de joie/d'enthousiasme** (with) transports of delight/enthusiasm; **~ de colère** fit of rage *ou* anger; **~ au cerveau** seizure, stroke; **~s amoureux** amorous transports.

2 comp ▸**transport de justice, transport sur les lieux** (*Jur*) *visit by public prosecutor's department to scene of crime*.

transportable [tʀɑ̃spɔʀtabl] adj *marchandise* transportable; *blessé, malade* fit to be moved (*attrib*).

transporter [tʀɑ̃spɔʀte] 1 1 vt a (*à la main, à dos*) to carry, move; (*avec un véhicule*) *marchandises, voyageurs* to transport, carry, convey; (*Tech*) *énergie, son* to carry. **le train transportait les écoliers/touristes** the train was carrying schoolchildren/tourists, the train had schoolchildren/tourists on board; **le train a transporté les soldats/le matériel au camp de base** the train took *ou* conveyed the soldiers/the equipment to base camp; **on a transporté le blessé à l'hôpital** the injured man was taken *ou* transported to hospital; **on l'a transporté d'urgence à l'hôpital** he was rushed to hospital; **~ des marchandises par terre** to transport *ou* carry *ou* convey goods by land; **~ qch par mer** to ship sth, transport sth by sea; **~ des marchandises par train/avion** to transport *ou* convey goods by train/plane; **ils ont dû ~ tout le matériel à bras** they had to move all the equipment by hand; **le sable/vin est transporté par péniche** the sand/wine is transported *ou* carried by barge; **elle transportait une forte somme d'argent** she was carrying a large sum of money; (*fig*) **cette musique nous transporte dans un autre monde/siècle** this music transports us into another world/century.

b (*transférer*) *traditions, conflit* to carry, bring; *thème, idée* to carry over, transpose. ~ **la guerre/la maladie dans un autre pays** to carry *ou* spread war/disease into another country; ~ **un fait divers à l'écran** to bring a news item to the screen; **dans sa traduction, il transporte la scène à Moscou** in his translation, he shifts the scene to Moscow.

c (*littér: agiter, exalter*) to carry away, send into raptures. ~ **qn de joie/d'enthousiasme** to send sb into raptures *ou* transports (*hum*) of delight/enthusiasm; **être** *ou* **se sentir transporté de joie/d'admiration** to be in transports (*hum*) of delight/admiration, be carried away with delight/admiration; **transporté de fureur** beside o.s. with fury; **cette musique m'a transporté** this music carried me away *ou* sent me into raptures.

2 **se transporter** vpr (*se déplacer*) to betake o.s. (*frm*), repair (*frm*). (*Jur*) **le parquet s'est transporté sur les lieux** the public prosecutor's office visited the scene of the crime; **se ~ quelque part par la pensée** to transport o.s. somewhere in imagination, let one's imagination carry one away somewhere.

transporteur [tʀɑ̃spɔʀtœʀ] nm a (*entrepreneur*) haulier (*Brit*), haulage contractor, carrier; (*Jur: partie contractante*) carrier. ~ **aérien** airline company; ~ **routier** road haulier (*Brit*), road haulage contractor. b (*Tech: appareil*) conveyor. c (*Chim, Bio*) carrier.

transposable [tʀɑ̃spozabl] adj transposable.

transposée [tʀɑ̃spoze] adj f, nf (*Math*) **(matrice)** ~ transpose.

transposer [tʀɑ̃spoze] 1 vti to transpose.

transposition [tʀɑ̃spozisjɔ̃] nf transposition.

transrhénan, e [tʀɑ̃sʀenɑ̃, an] adj transrhenane.

transsaharien, -ienne [tʀɑ̃(s)saaʀjɛ̃, jɛn] adj trans-Saharan.

transsexualisme [tʀɑ̃(s)sɛksɥalism] nm transexualism.

transsexuel, -elle [tʀɑ̃(s)sɛksɥɛl] adj, nm,f transsexual.

transsibérien, -ienne [tʀɑ̃(s)sibeʀjɛ̃, jɛn] adj trans-Siberian. **le ~** the Trans-Siberian Railway.

transsubstantiation [tʀɑ̃(s)sypstɑ̃sjasjɔ̃] nf transubstantiation.

transsudation [tʀɑ̃(s)sydasjɔ̃] nf transudation.

transsuder [tʀɑ̃(s)syde] 1 vi to transude.

Transvaal [tʀɑ̃sval] nm: **le ~** the Transvaal.

transvasement [tʀɑ̃svɑzmɑ̃] nm decanting.

transvaser [tʀɑ̃svɑze] 1 vt to decant.

transversal, e, mpl **-aux** [tʀɑ̃svɛʀsal, o] adj *coupe, fibre, pièce, barre* cross (*épith*), transverse (*SPÉC*); *mur, chemin, rue* which runs across *ou* at right angles; *vallée* transverse. (*Aut, Transport*) **axe ~, liaison ~e** cross-country trunk road (*Brit*) *ou* highway (*US*), cross-country link; **moteur ~** transverse engine; (*fig*) **thème ~** cross-disciplinary theme.

transversalement [tʀɑ̃svɛʀsalmɑ̃] adv across, crosswise, transversely (*SPÉC*).

transverse [tʀɑ̃svɛʀs] adj (*Anat*) transverse.

transvestisme [tʀɑ̃svɛstism] = **travestisme**.

transvider [tʀɑ̃svide] 1 vt to transfer to another container.

Transylvanie [tʀɑ̃silvani] nf Transylvania.

trapèze [tʀapɛz] nm a (*Géom*) trapezium (*Brit*), trapezoid (*US*). b (*Sport*) trapeze. ~ **volant** flying trapeze; **faire du ~** to perform on the trapeze. c (*Anat*) **(muscle) ~** trapezius (muscle).

trapéziste [tʀapezist] nmf trapeze artist.

trapézoèdre [tʀapezɔɛdʀ] nm (*Minér*) trapezohedron.

trapézoïdal, e, mpl **-aux** [tʀapezɔidal, o] adj trapezoid (*épith*).

trapézoïde [tʀapezɔid] adj, nm: **(os) ~** trapezoid.

trappe [tʀap] nf a (*dans le plancher*) trap door; (*Tech: d'accès, d'évacuation*) hatch; (*Théât*) trap door; (*Aviat: pour parachute*) exit door. (*fig*) **mettre qn à la ~** to give sb the push*. b (*piège*) trap.

Trappe [tʀap] nf (*couvent*) Trappist monastery; (*ordre*) Trappist order.

trappeur [tʀapœʀ] nm trapper, fur trader.

trappiste [tʀapist] nm Trappist (monk).

trapu, e [tʀapy] adj a *personne* squat, stocky, thickset; *maison* squat. b (*arg Scol: calé*) *élève* brainy*, terrific*; *question, problème* tough, hard, stiff. **une question ~e** a stinker* of a question, a really tough question, a poser; **il est ~ en latin** he's terrific* at Latin.

traque [tʀak] nf: **la ~ (du gibier)** the tracking (of game).

traquenard [tʀaknaʀ] nm (*piège*) trap; (*fig*) *[grammaire, loi]* pitfall, trap.

traquer [tʀake] 1 1 vt *gibier* to track (down); *fugitif* to track down, run to earth, hunt down; (*fig littér*) *abus, injustice* to hunt down; (*harceler*) *[journalistes, percepteur etc]* to hound, pursue. **air/regard de bête traquée** look/gaze of a hunted animal; **c'était maintenant un homme traqué, aux abois** he was now at bay, a hunted man. 2 vi (**: avoir le trac*) (*Théât, en public*) (*sur le moment*) to have stage fright; (*à chaque fois*) to get stage fright; (*aux examens etc*) (*sur le moment*) to be nervous; (*à chaque fois*) to get nervous, get (an attack *ou* a fit of) nerves.

traquet [tʀakɛ] nm: ~ **(pâtre)** stonechat; ~ **(motteux)** wheatear.

traqueur, -euse [tʀakœʀ, øz] 1 nm,f (*Chasse*) tracker; (*personne anxieuse*) bag of nerves*. 2 adj nervous.

trauma [tʀoma] nm (*Méd, Psych*) trauma.

traumatique [tʀomatik] adj traumatic.

traumatisant, e [tʀomatizɑ̃, ɑ̃t] adj traumatizing.

traumatiser [tʀomatize] 1 vt to traumatize.

traumatisme [tʀomatism] nm traumatism. ~ **crânien** cranial traumatism.

traumatologie [tʀomatɔlɔʒi] nf *branch of medicine dealing with road and industrial accidents etc.* **service de ~ d'un hôpital** casualty department *ou* accident-and-emergency department of a hospital.

traumatologique [tʀomatɔlɔʒik] adj traumatological.

traumatologiste [tʀomatɔlɔʒist(ə)] nmf, **traumatologue** [tʀomatɔlɔg] nmf trauma specialist, accident and emergency specialist.

travail[1], pl **-aux** [tʀavaj, o] 1 nm a (*labeur, tâches à accomplir*) **le ~** work; ~ **intellectuel** brainwork, intellectual *ou* mental work; ~ **manuel** manual work; ~ **musculaire** heavy labour; **fatigue due au ~ scolaire** tiredness due to school work; **je n'y touche pas: c'est le ~ de l'électricien** I'm not touching it — that's the electrician's job; **observer qn au ~** to watch sb at work, watch sb working; **séance/déjeuner de ~** working session/lunch; **ce mouvement demande des semaines de ~** it takes weeks of work to perfect this movement; **avoir du ~/beaucoup de ~** to have (some) work/a lot of work to do; **se mettre au ~** to set to *ou* get down to work; **j'ai un ~ fou en ce moment*** I've got a load of work on at the moment*, I'm up to my eyes in work at the moment*, I'm snowed under with work at the moment*; **le ~ c'est la santé*** work is good for you; *voir* **cabinet, table**.

b (*tâche*) work (*NonC*), job; (*ouvrage*) work (*NonC*). **c'est un ~ de spécialiste** (*difficile à faire*) it's work for a specialist, it's a specialist's job; (*bien fait*) it's the work of a specialist; **fais-le tout seul, c'est ton ~** do it yourself, it's your job; **commencer/achever/interrompre un ~** to start/complete/interrupt a piece of work *ou* a job; **ce n'est pas du ~** that's not work!, (do you) call that work!; **les ~aux de la commission seront publiés** the committee's work *ou* deliberations *ou* findings will be published; **~aux scientifiques/de recherche** scientific/research work; **~aux sur bois** woodwork; **~aux sur métal** metalwork; **il est l'auteur d'un gros ~ sur le romantisme** he is the author of a sizeable work on romanticism; (*Mil*) **~aux d'approche/de siège** sapping *ou* approach/siege works; **~aux de réfection/de réparation/de construction** renovation/repair/building work; **faire faire des ~aux dans la maison** to have some work *ou* some jobs done in the house; **~aux de plomberie** plumbing work; **~aux d'aménagement** alterations, alteration work; **les ~aux de la ferme** farm work; **les ~aux pénibles, les gros ~aux** the heavy work *ou* tasks; **entreprendre de grands ~aux d'assainissement/d'irrigation** to undertake large-scale sanitation/irrigation work; **"pendant les ~aux, le magasin restera ouvert"** "business as usual during alterations", "the shop will remain open (as usual) during alterations"; **attention! ~aux!** caution! work in progress!; (*sur la route*) road works (*Brit*) *ou* roadwork (*US*) ahead!; **il y a des ~aux (sur la chaussée)** the road is up, there are roadworks in progress.

c (*métier, profession*) job, occupation; (*situation*) work (*NonC*), job, situation. (*activité rétribuée*) **le ~** work (*NonC*); **avoir un ~ intéressant/lucratif** to have an interesting/a highly paid occupation *ou* job; **apprendre un ~** to learn a job; **être sans ~, ne pas avoir de ~** to be out of work *ou* without a job *ou* unemployed; ~ **à mi-/plein temps** part-/full-time work; ~ **temporaire** temporary job *ou* work (*NonC*); (*Ind*) **accident/conflit/législation du ~** industrial accident/dispute/legislation; ~ **de bureau/d'équipe** office/team work; ~ **en usine** factory work, work in a factory; ~ **en atelier** work in a workshop; ~ **à la pièce** *ou* **aux pièces** piecework; ~ **à domicile** outwork (*Brit*), homework; **elle a un ~ à domicile/au dehors** she has a job at home/outside, she works at home/goes out to work; (*Ind*) **cesser le ~** to stop work, down tools; **reprendre le ~** to go back to work; *voir* **arrêt, bleu** *etc.*

d (*Écon: opposé au capital*) labour. **l'exploitation du ~** the exploitation of labour; **association capital-~** cooperation between workers and management *ou* workers and the bosses*; **les revenus du ~** earned income; **le monde du ~** the workers; *voir* **division**.

e (*facture*) work (*NonC*). **dentelle d'un ~ très fin** finely-worked lace; **sculpture d'un ~ délicat** finely-wrought sculpture; **c'est un très joli ~** it's a very nice piece of handiwork *ou* craftsmanship *ou* work; ~ **soigné** *ou* **d'artiste/d'amateur** meticulous/amateurish workmanship (*NonC*); (*iro*) **c'est du beau** *ou* **joli ~!** what a beautiful piece of work!* (*iro*), well done!* (*iro*).

f (*façonnage*) *[bois, cuir, fer]* working. (*Peinture*) **le ~ de la pâte** working the paste; **le ~ du marbre requiert une grande habileté** working with marble requires great skill.

g *[machine, organe]* work. ~ **musculaire** muscular effort, work of the muscles.

h (*effet*) *[gel, érosion, eaux]* work; (*évolution*) *[bois]* warp, warping; *[vin, cidre]* working. **le ~ de l'imagination/l'inconscient** the workings of the imagination/the unconscious; **le ~ du temps** the work of time.

i (*Phys*) work. **unité de ~** unit of work.

j (*Méd*) *[femme]* labour. **femme en ~** woman in labour; **entrer en ~** to go into *ou* start labour; **salle de ~** labour ward.

2 comp ►**travaux agricoles** agricultural *ou* farm work ►**travaux d'aiguille** needlework ►**travaux d'approche** (*fig*) (*pour faire la cour*) initial overtures (*auprès de* to); (*pour demander qch*) preliminary manœuvres *ou* moves (*auprès de* with); **faire** *ou* **entreprendre des travaux d'approche auprès du patron pour une augmentation** to broach

the subject of a rise with the boss, introduce the idea of a rise to the boss ▸**un travail de Bénédictin** (*fig*) a painstaking task ▸**travail à la chaîne** assembly line *ou* production line work ▸**travaux des champs** = **travaux agricoles** ▸**les travaux de dame** handwork ▸**travaux dirigés** (*Univ*) tutorial (class) (*Brit*), section (of a course) (*US*) ▸**travail de forçat** (*fig*) hard labour (*fig*); **c'est un travail de forçat** it's hard labour ▸**travaux forcés** hard labour; (*Jur*) **être condamné aux travaux forcés** to be sentenced to hard labour; (*fig*) **dans cette entreprise c'est vraiment les travaux forcés** it's real slave labour in this company ▸**un travail de fourmi** (*fig*) a long, painstaking job ▸**travaux d'intérêt général** *community work carried out by young offenders,* ≃ community service (*Brit*) ▸**les travaux d'Hercule** the labours of Hercules ▸**travaux manuels** (*Scol*) handicrafts ▸**travaux ménagers** housework ▸**travail au noir** moonlighting ▸**le travail posté** shift work ▸**travaux pratiques** (*Scol, Univ*) (*gén*) practical work; (*en laboratoire*) lab work (*Brit*), lab (*US*) ▸**travaux préparatoires** *[projet de loi]* preliminary documents ▸**travaux publics** civil engineering; **ingénieur des travaux publics** civil engineer; **entreprise des travaux publics** civil engineering firm ▸**un travail de Romain** a Herculean task ▸**travaux d'utilité collective** (paid) community work (*done by the unemployed*), ≃ employment training (*Brit*), ≃ YTS (*Brit*).

travail², pl **~s** [tʀavaj] **nm** (*appareil*) trave.

travaillé, e [tʀavaje] (**ptp de travailler**) **adj** a (*façonné*) *bois, cuivre* worked, wrought. b (*fignolé*) *style, phrases* polished, studied; *meuble, ornement* intricate, finely-worked. c (*tourmenté*) ~ **par le remords/la peur/la jalousie** tormented *ou* distracted by remorse/fear/jealousy.

travailler [tʀavaje] [1] 1 **vi** a (*faire sa besogne*) to work. ~ **dur** to work hard; ~ **jour et nuit** to work day and night; ~ **comme un forçat/une bête de somme** to work like a galley slave/a horse *ou* a Trojan; **il aime ~ au jardin** he likes working in the garden; **je vais ~ un peu à la bibliothèque** I'm going to do some work in the library; **faire ~ sa tête** *ou* **sa matière grise** to set one's mind *ou* the grey matter to work; **fais ~ ta tête!** get your brain working!, use your head!; **faire ~ ses bras** to exercise one's arms; ~ **du chapeau*** to be slightly dotty* *ou* a bit cracked* *ou* touched* *ou* nuts*; ~ **pour le roi de Prusse** to receive no reward for one's pains; **va ~** (go and) get on with your work.

b (*exercer un métier*) to work. ~ **en usine** to work in a factory; ~ **à domicile** to work at home; ~ **dans les assurances/l'enseignement** to work in insurance/education; ~ **aux pièces** to do piecework; ~ **au noir** to moonlight, do moonlighting; **tu pourras te l'offrir quand tu travailleras** you'll be able to buy *ou* afford it once you start work; **dans ce pays on fait ~ les enfants à 8 ans** in this country they put children to work at the age of 8 *ou* they make children work from the age of 8; **il a commencé à ~ chez X hier** he started work *ou* he went to work at X's yesterday; **sa femme travaille** his wife goes out to work, his wife works; **on finit de ~ à 17 heures** we finish *ou* stop work at 5 o'clock.

c (*s'exercer*) *[artiste, acrobate]* to practise, train; *[boxeur]* to have a workout, train; *[musicien]* to practise. *[enfant]* **son père le fait ~ tous les soirs** his father makes him work every evening; ~ **sans filet** (*lit*) to work without a safety net; (*fig*) to be out on one's own, work in the dark, work without any backup.

d (*agir, fonctionner*) *[firme, argent]* to work. **l'industrie travaille pour le pays** industry works for the country; ~ **à perte** to work *ou* be working at a loss; **faire ~ l'argent** to make one's money work for one; **le temps travaille pour/contre eux** time is on their side/against them.

e *[métal, bois]* to warp; *[vin, cidre]* to work, ferment; *[pâte]* to work, rise; (*fig*) *[imagination]* to work.

2 **vt** a (*façonner*) *matière, verre, fer* to work, shape. ~ **la terre** to work *ou* cultivate the land; ~ **la pâte** (*Culin*) to knead *ou* work the dough; (*Peinture*) to work the paste.

b (*potasser*) *branche, discipline* to work at *ou* on; *morceau de musique* to work on, practise; *rôle, scène* to work on; (*fignoler*) *style, phrase* to polish up, work on; (*Sport*) *mouvement, coup* to work on. ~ **son anglais** to work on one's English; ~ **le chant/piano** to practise singing/the piano; ~ **son piano/violon** to do one's piano/violin practice; (*Tennis*) ~ **une balle** to put some spin on a ball.

c (*agir sur*) *personne* to work on. ~ **l'opinion/les esprits** to work on public opinion/people's minds; ~ **qn au corps** (*Boxe*) to punch *ou* pummel sb around the body; (*fig*) to badger sb, give sb a hard time.

d (*faire s'exercer*) *taureau, cheval* to work.

e (*préoccuper*) *[doutes, faits]* to distract, worry; (*tourmenter*) *[douleur, fièvre]* to distract, torment. **cette idée/ce projet le travaille** this idea/plan is on his mind *ou* is preying on his mind; **le ventre me ~** I have pains in my stomach.

3 **travailler à vt indir** *livre, projet* to work on; *cause, but* to work for; (*s'efforcer d'obtenir*) to work towards. ~ **à la perte de qn** to work towards sb's downfall, endeavour to bring about sb's downfall.

travailleur, -euse [tʀavajœʀ, øz] 1 **adj** (*consciencieux*) hard-working, painstaking, diligent (*frm*).

2 **nm,f** a (*gén*) worker. **un bon/mauvais ~, une bonne/mauvaise ~euse** a good/bad worker.

b (*personne consciencieuse*) (hard) worker.

3 **nm** (*personne exerçant un métier, une profession*) worker. **les ~s** the workers, working people; **les revendications des ~s** the claims made by the workers; **il avait loué sa ferme à des ~s étrangers** he had rented his farm to immigrant workers; **le problème des ~s étrangers** the problem of immigrant labour *ou* workers.

4 **comp** ▸**travailleur agricole** agricultural *ou* farm worker ▸**travailleur à domicile** homeworker ▸**travailleuse familiale** home help ▸**travailleur de force** labourer ▸**travailleur indépendant** self-employed person, freelance worker ▸**travailleur intellectuel** non-manual *ou* intellectual worker ▸**travailleur manuel** manual worker ▸**travailleur au noir** moonlighter ▸**travailleur social** social services employee.

travaillisme [tʀavajism] **nm** Labour philosophy, Labour brand of socialism.

travailliste [tʀavajist] 1 **adj** Labour. 2 **nmf** Labour Party member. **il est ~** he is Labour, he supports Labour; **les ~s** Labour, the Labour Party.

travailloter [tʀavajɔte] [1] **vi** (*péj*) to work a little, work without over-straining o.s.

travée [tʀave] **nf** a (*section*) *[mur, voûte, rayon, nef]* bay; *[pont]* span. b (*Tech: portée*) span. c (*rangée*) *[église, amphithéâtre]* row (of benches); *[théâtre]* row (of seats). **les ~s du fond manifestèrent leur mécontentement** the back rows showed their annoyance.

traveller's chèque, traveller's check [tʀavlœʀ(s)ʃɛk] **nm** traveller's cheque (*Brit*), traveler's check (*US*).

travelling [tʀavliŋ] **nm** (*Ciné*) (*dispositif*) dolly, travelling platform; (*mouvement*) tracking. ~ **avant/arrière/latéral** tracking in/out/sideways; ~ **optique** zoom shots (*pl*).

travelo⁑ [tʀavlo] **nm** (*travesti*) drag queen⁑.

travers¹ [tʀavɛʀ] **nm** (*défaut*) failing, fault, shortcoming. **chacun a ses petits ~** everyone has his little failings *ou* faults; **tomber dans le ~ qui consiste à faire ...** to make the opposite mistake of doing ... .

travers² [tʀavɛʀ] **nm** a (*sens diagonal, transversal*) **en ~** across, crosswise; **en ~ de** across; **couper/scier en ~** to cut/saw across; **pose la planche en ~** lay the plank across *ou* crosswise; **un arbre était en ~ de la route** a tree was lying across the road; **le véhicule dérapa et se mit en ~ (de la route)** the vehicle skidded and stopped sideways on *ou* stopped across the road; (*fig*) **se mettre en ~ (des projets de qn)** to stand in the way (of sb's plans); *voir* **tort**.

b (*Naut*) *navire* **en ~, par le ~** abeam, on the beam; **vent de ~** wind on the beam; **mettre un navire en ~** to heave to; **se mettre en ~** to heave to; **s'échouer en ~** to run aground on the beam.

c **au ~** through; **au ~ de** through; **la palissade est délabrée: on voit au ~/le vent passe au ~** the fence is falling down and you can see (right) through/the wind comes (right) through; **au ~ de ses mensonges, on devine sa peur** through his lies, you can tell he's frightened; (*fig*) **passer au ~** to escape; **le truand est passé au ~** the criminal slipped through the net *ou* escaped; **passer au ~ d'une corvée** to get out of doing a chore; **tout le monde a eu la grippe mais je suis passé au ~** everyone had flu but I managed to avoid *ou* escape it.

d **de ~** (*pas droit*) crooked, askew; (*fig: à côté*) **répondre de ~** to give a silly answer; **comprendre de ~** to misunderstand; (*fig: mal*) **aller** *ou* **marcher de ~** to be going wrong; **avoir la bouche/le nez de ~** to have a crooked mouth/nose; *[ivrogne]* **marcher de ~** to stagger *ou* totter along; **planter un clou de ~** to hammer a mail in crooked; **il répond toujours de ~** he never gives a straight *ou* proper answer; **il raisonne toujours de ~** his reasoning is always unsound; *[véhicule etc]* **se mettre de ~** to stop sideways on; **elle a mis son chapeau de ~** she has put her hat on crooked, her hat is not on straight; **il a l'esprit un peu de ~** he's slightly odd; **il lui a jeté un regard** *ou* **il l'a regardé de ~** he looked askance at him, he gave him a funny look; **il a avalé sa soupe de ~, sa soupe est passée de ~** his soup has gone down the wrong way; **tout va de ~ chez eux en ce moment** everything is going wrong *ou* nothing is going right for them at the moment; **prendre qch de ~** to take sth amiss *ou* the wrong way; **il prend tout de ~** he takes everything the wrong way *ou* amiss.

e **à ~** *vitre, maille, trou, foule* through; *campagne, bois* across, through; **voir qn à ~ la vitre** to see sb through the window; **ce n'est pas opaque, on voit à ~** it's not opaque – you can see through it; **le renard est passé à ~ le grillage** the fox went through the fence; **sentir le froid à ~ un manteau** to feel the cold through a coat; **passer à ~ champs/bois** to go through *ou* across fields *ou* across country/through woods; **la couche de glace est mince, tu risques de passer à ~** the layer of ice is thin – you could fall through; **juger qn à ~ son œuvre** to judge sb through his work; **à ~ les siècles** through *ou* across the centuries; **à ~ les divers rapports, on entrevoit la vérité** through the various reports, we can get some idea of the truth; (*lit, fig*) **passer à ~ (les mailles du filet)** to slip through the net.

f (*Boucherie*) ~ **(de porc)** sparerib of pork.

traversable [tʀavɛʀsabl] **adj** which can be crossed, traversable (*frm*). **rivière ~ à gué** fordable river.

traverse [tʀavɛʀs] **nf** a (*Rail*) sleeper (*Brit*), tie (*US*). b (*pièce, barre transversale*) strut, crosspiece. c **chemin de ~, ~†** road which cuts across, shortcut.

traversée [tʀavɛʀse] 1 **nf** a *[rue, mer, pont etc]* crossing; *[ville, forêt,* *tunnel etc]* going through. **la ~ des Alpes/de l'Atlantique en avion** the crossing of the Alps/of the Atlantic by plane; **la ~ de la ville en voiture peut prendre 2 heures** driving through the town can take 2 hours, crossing the town can take 2 hours by car; **faire la ~ d'un fleuve à la nage** to swim across a river. b (*Naut: trajet*) crossing. c (*Alpinisme*) (*course*) through-route; (*passage*) traverse. (*Ski*) **descendre en ~** to traverse. 2 **comp ▸traversée du désert** (*fig*) time (spent) in the wilderness.

traverser [tʀavɛʀse] 1 **vt** a *[personne, véhicule] rue, pont* to cross; *chaîne de montagnes, mer* to cross, traverse (*littér*); *ville, forêt, tunnel* to go through. **~ une rivière à la nage** to swim across a river; **~ une rivière en bac** to take a ferry across a river, cross a river by ferry; **~ (une rivière) à gué** to ford a river, wade across a river; **il traversa le salon à grands pas** he strode across the living room; **avant de ~, assurez-vous que la chaussée est libre** before crossing, see that the road is clear.

b *[pont, route]* to cross, run across; *[tunnel]* to cross under; *[barre, trait]* to run across. **le fleuve/cette route traverse tout le pays** the river/this road runs *ou* cuts right across the country; **ce tunnel traverse les Alpes** this tunnel crosses under the Alps; **un pont traverse le Rhône en amont de Valence** a bridge crosses *ou* there is a bridge across the Rhone upstream from Valence; **une cicatrice lui traversait le front** he had a scar (right) across his forehead, a scar ran right across his forehead.

c (*percer*) *[projectile, infiltration]* to go *ou* come through. **~ qch de part en part** to go right through sth; **les clous ont traversé la semelle** the nails have come through the sole; **la pluie a traversé la tente** the rain has come through the tent; **une balle lui traversa la tête** a bullet went through his head; **il s'effondra, la cuisse traversée d'une balle** he collapsed, shot through the thigh; **une douleur lui traversa le poignet** a pain shot through his wrist; **une idée lui traversa l'esprit** an idea passed through his mind *ou* occurred to him.

d (*passer à travers*) **~ la foule** to make one's way through the crowd.

e (*fig: dans le temps*) *période* to go *ou* live through; *crise* to pass *ou* go through, undergo. **sa gloire a traversé les siècles** his glory travelled down the ages.

traversier, -ière [tʀavɛʀsje, jɛʀ] 1 **adj** a *rue* which runs across. b (*Naut*) *navire* cutting across the bows. c *voir* **flûte**. 2 **nm** (*Can*) ferryboat.

traversin [tʀavɛʀsɛ̃] **nm** *[lit]* bolster.

travertin [tʀavɛʀtɛ̃] **nm** travertin(e).

travesti, e [tʀavɛsti] (**ptp de travestir**) 1 **adj** (*gén: déguisé*) disguised; (*Théât*) *acteur* playing a female role; *rôle* female (*played by man*); *voir* **bal**. 2 **nm** a (*Théât: acteur*) actor playing a female role; (*artiste de cabaret*) female impersonator, drag artist; (*Psych: homosexuel*) transvestite. **numéro de ~** drag act. b (*déguisement*) fancy dress. **en ~** in fancy dress.

travestir [tʀavɛstiʀ] 2 1 **vt** a (*déguiser*) *personne* to dress up; *acteur* to cast in a female role. **~ un homme en femme** to dress a man up as a woman. b (*fig*) *vérité, paroles* to travesty, misrepresent, parody. 2 **se travestir vpr** (*pour un bal*) to put on fancy dress; (*Théât*) to put on a woman's costume; (*pour un numéro de cabaret*) to put on drag; (*Psych*) to dress as a woman, cross-dress. **se ~ en Arlequin** to dress up as Harlequin.

travestisme [tʀavɛstism] **nm** (*Psych*) transvestism.

travestissement [tʀavɛstismɑ̃] **nm** a (*action*) *[personne]* (*gén*) dressing-up; (*Psych*) cross-dressing; *[vérité, paroles]* travesty, misrepresentation. b (*habit*) fancy dress (*NonC*).

traviole* [tʀavjɔl] **adv: de ~** skew-whiff*, crooked; **être/mettre de ~** to be/put skew-whiff* *ou* crooked; **il comprend tout de ~** he gets hold of the wrong end of the stick every time*, he gets in a muddle about everything.

trayeur, -euse [tʀɛjœʀ, øz] 1 **nm,f** milker. 2 **trayeuse nf** (*machine*) milking machine.

trébuchant, e [tʀebyʃɑ̃, ɑ̃t] **adj** (*chancelant*) *démarche, ivrogne* tottering (*épith*), staggering (*épith*); (*fig*) *diction, voix* halting (*épith*); *voir* **espèce**.

trébucher [tʀebyʃe] 1 **vi** (*lit, fig*) to stumble. **faire ~ qn** to trip sb up; **~ sur** *ou* **contre** *racine, pierre* to stumble over, trip against; *mot, morceau difficile* to stumble over.

trébuchet [tʀebyʃɛ] **nm** a (*piège*) bird-trap. b (*balance*) assay balance.

tréfilage [tʀefilaʒ] **nm** wiredrawing.

tréfiler [tʀefile] 1 **vt** to wiredraw.

tréfilerie [tʀefilʀi] **nf** wireworks.

tréfileur [tʀefilœʀ] **nm** (*ouvrier*) wireworker, wiredrawer.

tréfileuse [tʀefiløz] **nf** (*machine*) wiredrawing machine.

trèfle [tʀɛfl] **nm** a (*Bot*) clover. **~ à quatre feuilles** four-leaf clover; **~ blanc** white clover. b (*Cartes*) clubs. **jouer ~** to play a club *ou* clubs; **le 8 de ~** the 8 of clubs. c (*Aut*) **(carrefour en) ~** cloverleaf (junction *ou* intersection). d (*Archit*) trefoil. e (*‡: argent*) lolly‡ (*Brit*), dough‡. f (*emblème de l'Irlande*) **le ~** the shamrock; (*Rugby*) **l'équipe du ~** the Irish team.

tréflière [tʀeflijɛʀ] **nf** field of clover.

tréfonds [tʀefɔ̃] **nm** (*littér*) **le ~ de** the inmost depths of; **ébranlé jusqu'au ~** deeply *ou* profoundly shaken, shaken to the core; **dans le ~ de mon cœur** deep down in my heart; **le ~ de l'homme** the inmost depths of man; **dans le ~ de son âme** deep down, in the depths of his soul.

treillage [tʀɛjaʒ] **nm** (*sur un mur*) lattice work, trellis(work); (*clôture*) trellis fence. **~ en voûte** trellis archway.

treillager [tʀɛjaʒe] 3 **vt** *mur* to trellis, lattice; *fenêtre* to lattice. **treillagé de rubans** criss-crossed with tape.

treille [tʀɛj] **nf** (*tonnelle*) vine arbour; (*vigne*) climbing vine; *voir* **jus**.

treillis[1] [tʀeji] **nm** (*en bois*) trellis; (*en métal*) wire-mesh; (*Constr*) lattice work.

treillis[2] [tʀeji] **nm** (*Tex*) canvas; (*Mil: tenue*) combat uniform.

treize [tʀɛz] **adj inv, nm inv** thirteen. **~ à la douzaine** baker's dozen; **il m'en a donné ~ à la douzaine** he gave me a baker's dozen; **vendre des huîtres ~ à la douzaine** to sell oysters at thirteen for the price of twelve; *pour autres loc voir* **six**.

treizième [tʀɛzjɛm] **adj, nmf** thirteenth. **~ mois** (*de salaire*) (bonus) thirteenth month's salary; *pour loc voir* **sixième**.

treizièmement [tʀɛzjɛmmɑ̃] **adv** in the thirteenth place.

trekking [tʀekiŋ] **nm** (*activité*) trekking (*NonC*); (*randonnée*) trek. **faire un ~** to go on a trek; **faire du ~** to go trekking.

tréma [tʀema] **nm** dieresis. **i ~** i dieresis.

trémail [tʀemaj] = **tramail**.

tremblant, e [tʀɑ̃blɑ̃, ɑ̃t] 1 **adj** *personne, membre, main* trembling, shaking; *voix* trembling, tremulous, shaky, quavering (*épith*); *lumière* trembling (*épith*), quivering (*épith*), flickering (*épith*). **il vint me trouver, ~** he came looking for me in fear and trembling; **il se présenta ~ devant son chef** he appeared trembling *ou* shaking before his boss; **~ de froid** shivering with *ou* trembling with cold; **~ de peur** trembling *ou* shaking *ou* shivering with fear. 2 **tremblante nf** (*Vét*) scrapie.

tremble [tʀɑ̃bl] **nm** aspen.

tremblé, e [tʀɑ̃ble] (**ptp de trembler**) **adj** a *écriture, dessin* shaky; *voix* trembling, shaky, tremulous, quavering (*épith*); *note* quavering (*épith*). b (*Typ*) **(filet) ~** wavy *ou* waved rule.

tremblement [tʀɑ̃bləmɑ̃] 1 **nm** a (*voir* **trembler**) shiver; trembling (*NonC*); shaking (*NonC*); fluttering (*NonC*); flickering (*NonC*); quivering (*NonC*); wavering (*NonC*); quavering (*NonC*); vibration. **un ~ le parcourut** a shiver went through him; **il fut saisi d'un ~ convulsif** he was seized with a violent fit of shivering *ou* trembling; **avec des ~s dans la voix** with a trembling *ou* quavering *ou* shaky voice. b (*loc*) **tout le ~*** (*choses ou personnes*) the whole outfit*, the whole caboodle*; (*choses*) all that jazz* *ou* guff‡. 2 **comp ▸tremblement de terre** earthquake; **léger tremblement de terre** earth tremor.

trembler [tʀɑ̃ble] 1 **vi** a *[personne]* (*de froid, de fièvre*) to shiver, tremble, shake (*de* with); (*de peur, d'indignation, de colère*) to tremble, shake (*de* with). **il tremblait de tout son corps** *ou* **de tous ses membres** he was shaking *ou* trembling all over; **~ comme une feuille** to shake *ou* tremble like a leaf.

b *[feuille]* to tremble, flutter; *[lumière]* to tremble, flicker, quiver; *[flamme]* to tremble, flicker, waver; *[voix]* to tremble, shake, quaver; *[son]* to tremble, quaver; *[main]* to tremble, shake.

c *[bâtiment, fenêtre]* to shake, tremble; *[plancher]* to tremble, vibrate; *[terre]* to shake, quake, tremble. **faire ~ le sol** to make the ground tremble, shake the ground; **la terre a tremblé** there has been an earth tremor.

d (*fig: avoir peur*) to tremble. **~ pour qn/qch** to fear for *ou* tremble for sb/sth, be anxious over sb/sth; **~ à la pensée de qch** to tremble at the (very) thought of sth; **il tremble de l'avoir perdu** he is afraid *ou* he fears that he has lost it; **je tremble qu'elle ne s'en remette pas** I fear that she may not recover; **il fait ~ ses subordonnés** he strikes fear (and trembling) into those under him, his subordinates live in dread of him.

tremblotant, e [tʀɑ̃blɔtɑ̃, ɑ̃t] **adj** *personne, main* trembling, shaking; *voix* quavering (*épith*), tremulous; *flamme* trembling (*épith*), flickering (*épith*), wavering (*épith*); *lumière* trembling (*épith*), quivering (*épith*), flickering (*épith*).

tremblote* [tʀɑ̃blɔt] **nf: avoir la ~** (*froid*) to have the shivers*; (*peur*) to have the jitters*; *[vieillard]* to have the shakes*.

tremblotement [tʀɑ̃blɔtmɑ̃] **nm** (*voir* **trembloter**) trembling (*NonC*); shaking (*NonC*); quavering (*NonC*); flickering (*NonC*). **avec un ~ dans sa voix** with a tremble in his voice.

trembloter [tʀɑ̃blɔte] 1 **vi** *[personne, mains]* to tremble *ou* shake (slightly); *[voix]* to quaver, tremble; *[lumière]* to tremble, quiver, flicker; *[flamme]* to tremble, flicker, waver.

trémie [tʀemi] **nf** a (*Tech: entonnoir*) *[concasseur, broyeur, trieuse]* hopper. b (*mangeoire*) feedbox. c (*Constr*) *[cheminée]* hearth cavity *ou* space; *[escalier]* stair cavity.

trémière [tʀemjɛʀ] **adj f** *voir* **rose**.

trémolo [tʀemɔlo] **nm** *[instrument]* tremolo; *[voix]* quaver, tremor. **avec des ~s dans la voix** with a quaver *ou* tremor in one's voice.

trémoussement [tʀemusmɑ̃] **nm** jigging about (*Brit*) (*NonC*), wiggling (*NonC*).

trémousser (se) [tʀemuse] 1 **vpr** to jig about (*Brit*), wiggle. **se ~ sur**

sa chaise to wriggle *ou* jig about (*Brit*) on one's chair; **marcher en se trémoussant** to wiggle as one walks.

trempage [tʀɑ̃paʒ] **nm** *[linge, graines, semences]* soaking; *[papier]* damping, wetting.

trempe [tʀɑ̃p] **nf** **a** (*Tech*) *[acier]* (*processus*) quenching; (*qualité*) temper. **de bonne** ~ well-tempered. **b** (*fig*) *[personne, âme]* calibre. **un homme de sa** ~ a man of his calibre *ou* of his moral fibre. **c** (*Tech: trempage*) *[papier]* damping, wetting; *[peaux]* soaking. **d** (*) (*correction*) walloping*, hiding*; (*gifle*) slap, clout*.

trempé, e [tʀɑ̃pe] (**ptp de tremper**) **adj** **a** (*mouillé*) *vêtement, personne* soaked, drenched. ~ **de sueur** bathed *ou* soaked in *ou* streaming with perspiration; ~ **jusqu'aux os** *ou* **comme une soupe*** wet through, soaked to the skin, absolutely drenched, like a drowned rat; **visage** ~ **de pleurs** face bathed in tears. **b** (*Tech*) *acier, verre* tempered. (*fig*) **caractère bien** ~ sturdy character.

tremper [tʀɑ̃pe] [1] **1 vt** **a** (*mouiller*) to soak, drench; (*gén* **faire** ~) *linge, graines* to soak; *aliments* to soak, steep; *papier* to damp, wet; *tige de fleur* to stand in water. **la pluie a trempé sa veste/le tapis** the rain has soaked *ou* drenched his jacket/the carpet.

b (*plonger*) *mouchoir, plume* to dip (*dans* into, in); *pain, biscuit* to dip, dunk (*dans* in). ~ **sa main dans l'eau** to dip one's hand in the water; ~ **ses lèvres dans une boisson** to take just a sip of a drink; **il n'aime pas qu'on lui trempe la tête dans l'eau** he doesn't like having his head ducked in the water; ~ **la soupe**† to pour soup onto bread.

c (*Tech*) *métal, lame* to quench; *voir* **acier**.

d (*littér: aguerrir, fortifier*) *personne, caractère, âme* to steel, strengthen.

2 vi **a** *[tige de fleur]* to stand in water; *[linge, graines, semences]* to soak. **mettre le linge à** ~ to soak the washing, put the washing to soak.

b (*fig péj: participer*) ~ **dans** *crime, affaire, complot* to take part in, have a hand in, be involved in.

3 se tremper vpr (*prendre un bain rapide*) to have a quick dip; (*se mouiller*) to get (o.s.) soaked *ou* soaking wet, get drenched. **je ne fais que me** ~ I'm just going for a quick dip.

trempette [tʀɑ̃pɛt] **nf** **a** (*pain trempé*) piece of bread (*for dunking*); (*sucre trempé*) sugar lump (*for dunking*). **faire** ~ to dunk one's bread; to dunk one's sugar. **b** (*baignade*) (quick) dip. **faire** ~ to have a (quick) dip.

tremplin [tʀɑ̃plɛ̃] **nm** **a** (*lit*) *[piscine]* diving-board, springboard; *[gymnase]* springboard; (*Ski*) ski-jump. **b** (*fig*) springboard. **servir de** ~ **à qn** to be a springboard for sb.

trémulation [tʀemylasjɔ̃] **nf** (*Méd*) tremor.

trentaine [tʀɑ̃tɛn] **nf** (*âge, nombre*) about thirty, thirty or so.

trente [tʀɑ̃t] **1 adj inv, nm inv** thirty; *pour loc voir* **six, tour**.

2 comp ▸trente-et-quarante nm inv (*Jeux*) trente et quarante **▸trente-six** (*lit*) thirty-six; (* *fig: beaucoup*) umpteen*; **il y en a trente-six modèles** there are umpteen* models; **il n'y a pas trente-six possibilités** there aren't all that many choices; **faire trente-six choses en même temps** *ou* **à la fois** to (try to) do too many things at once, (try to) do a hundred things at once; **tous les trente-six du mois** once in a blue moon; **j'ai trente-six mille choses à faire** I've a thousand and one things to do; **voir trente-six chandelles*** to see stars **▸trente-sixième***: **dans le trente-sixième dessous** right down (*Brit*) *ou* way down (*US*) in the dumps* **▸trente et un nm** (*lit, Cartes*) thirty-one; (*fig*) **être/se mettre sur son trente et un*** to be wearing/put on one's Sunday best *ou* one's glad rags*, be/get all dressed up to the nines*, be/get dressed to kill*; *voir* **concile, guerre**.

trentenaire [tʀɑ̃t(ə)nɛʀ] **adj** thirty-year. **concession** ~ thirty-year lease.

trentième [tʀɑ̃tjɛm] **adj, nm** thirtieth; *pour loc voir* **sixième**.

trépan [tʀepɑ̃] **nm** (*Méd*) trephine, trepan; (*Tech*) trepan.

trépanation [tʀepanasjɔ̃] **nf** (*Méd*) trephination, trepanation.

trépané, e [tʀepane] (**ptp de trépaner**) **1 nmf** (*Méd*) patient who has undergone trephination *ou* trapanation. **2 adj: être** ~ to have undergone trephination *ou* trepanation.

trépaner [tʀepane] [1] **vt** (*Méd*) to trephine, trepan.

trépas [tʀepɑ] **nm** (*littér*) demise, death; *voir* **vie**.

trépassé, e [tʀepɑse] (**ptp de trépasser**) **adj** (*littér*) deceased, dead. **les** ~**s** the departed; (*Rel*) **le jour** *ou* **la fête des T**~**s** All Souls' (Day).

trépasser [tʀepɑse] [1] **vi** (*littér*) to pass away, depart this life.

trépidant, e [tʀepidɑ̃, ɑ̃t] **adj** *plancher* vibrating, quivering; *machine* vibrating, throbbing; *rythme* pulsating (*épith*), thrilling (*épith*); *vie* hectic, busy.

trépidation [tʀepidasjɔ̃] **nf** vibration; (*fig*) *[vie]* flurry (*NonC*), whirl (*NonC*).

trépider [tʀepide] [1] **vi** *[plancher]* to vibrate, reverberate; *[machine]* to vibrate, throb.

trépied [tʀepje] **nm** (*gén*) tripod; (*dans l'âtre*) trivet.

trépignement [tʀepiɲmɑ̃] **nm** stamping (of feet) (*NonC*).

trépigner [tʀepiɲe] [1] **1 vi** to stamp one's feet. ~ **d'impatience/d'enthousiasme** to stamp (one's feet) with impatience/enthusiasm; ~ **de colère** to stamp one's feet with rage, be hopping mad*. **2 vt** to stamp *ou* trample on.

trépointe [tʀepwɛ̃t] **nf** welt.

tréponème [tʀepɔnɛm] **nm** treponema.

très [tʀɛ] **adv** (*avec adj*) very, awfully*, terribly*, most; (*avec adv*) very; (*devant certains ptp etc*) (very) much, greatly, highly. ~ **intelligent/difficile** very *ou* awfully* *ou* most *ou* pretty* *ou* terrifically* intelligent/difficult; ~ **admiré** greatly *ou* highly *ou* (very) much admired; ~ **industrialisé/automatisé** highly industrialized/automatized; **il est** ~ **conscient de ...** he is very much aware of *ou* very conscious of ...; **c'est** ~ **bien écrit/fait** it's very *ou* awfully* well written/done; ~ **peu de gens** very few people; **c'est un garçon** ~ **travailleur** he is a very *ou* most hard-working lad, he's a very *ou* an awfully* hard worker; **elle est** ~ **grande dame** she is very much the great lady *ou* every bit a great lady; **avoir** ~ **peur** to be very much afraid *ou* very *ou* terribly* *ou* dreadfully frightened; **avoir** ~ **faim** to be very *ou* terribly* *ou* dreadfully hungry; **elle a été vraiment** ~ **aimable** she was really most *ou* awfully* kind; **c'est** ~ **nécessaire** it's most *ou* absolutely essential; **ils sont** ~ **amis/**~ **liés** they are great friends/very close (friends); **je suis** ~, ~ **content** I'm very, very *ou* terribly, terribly* pleased; **j'ai** ~ **envie de le rencontrer** I would very much like to meet him, I am very *ou* most anxious to meet him; **il est** ~ **en avant/arrière** (*sur le chemin*) he is well *ou* a long way ahead/behind; (*dans une salle*) he is well forward *ou* a long way to the front/well back *ou* a long way back; **un jeune homme** ~ **comme il faut** a well brought-up young man, a very respectable young man; **être** ~ **à la page*** *ou* **dans le vent*** to be very *ou* terribly with-it*; **je ne suis jamais** ~ **à mon aise avec lui** I never feel very *ou* particularly *ou* terribly* comfortable with him; **êtes-vous fatigué?** — ~**/pas** ~ are you tired? — very *ou* terribly*/not very *ou* not terribly*; ~ **bien, si vous insistez** all right *ou* very well, if you insist; ~ **bien, je vais le lui expliquer** all right *ou* fine* *ou* very good *ou* O.K.*, I'll explain to him; **travailler le samedi?** ~ **peu pour moi!** work on Saturday? not likely!* *ou* not me!; (*Dieu*) **le T**~**-Haut** the Almighty; *voir* **peu**.

trésor [tʀezɔʀ] **nm** **a** (*richesses enfouies*) treasure (*NonC*); (*Jur: trouvé*) treasure-trove; (*fig: chose, personne, vertu précieuse*) treasure. **découvrir un** ~ to find some treasure *ou* a treasure-trove; **course** *ou* **chasse au/chercheur de** ~ treasure hunt/hunter.

b (*petit musée*) treasure-house, treasury. **le** ~ **de Notre-Dame** the treasure-house of Notre-Dame.

c (*gén pl: richesses*) treasure. **les** ~**s du Louvre/de l'océan** the treasures *ou* riches of the Louvre/the ocean; (*hum*) **je vais chercher dans mes** ~**s** I'll look through my treasures *ou* precious possessions.

d (*source*) **un** ~ **de conseils/renseignements** a mine *ou* wealth *ou* store of advice/information; (*quantité*) **des** ~**s de dévouement/de patience** a wealth of devotion/patience, boundless devotion/patience; **dépenser des** ~**s d'ingéniosité** to expend boundless ingenuity.

e (*ouvrage*) treasury.

f (*Admin, Fin: ressources*) *[roi, État]* exchequer, finances; *[organisation secrète]* finances, funds. (*service*) **le T**~ **(public)** the public revenue department, ≃ the Treasury (*Brit*), the Treasury Department (*US*); *voir* **bon**[2].

g (*affectif*) **mon (petit)** ~ my (little) treasure, my precious; **tu es un** ~ **de m'avoir acheté ce disque** you're a (real) treasure for buying me this record.

h (*Fin*) ~ **de guerre** war chest.

trésorerie [tʀezɔʀʀi] **nf** **a** (*bureaux*) *[Trésor public]* public revenue office; *[firme]* accounts department. ~ **générale** Treasury. **b** (*gestion*) accounts. **leur** ~ **est bien/mal tenue** their accounts are well/badly kept; *voir* **moyen**. **c** (*argent disponible*) finances, funds. **difficultés de** ~ cash shortage, cash (flow) problems, shortage of funds. **d** (*fonction de trésorier*) treasurership.

trésorier, -ière [tʀezɔʀje, jɛʀ] **nm,f** (*gén*) *[club, association]* treasurer. (*Admin*) ~**-payeur général** paymaster (*for a département*).

tressage [tʀesaʒ] **nm** (*voir* **tresser**) plaiting; braiding; weaving; twisting.

tressaillement [tʀesajmɑ̃] **nm** (*voir* **tressaillir**) thrill; quiver, quivering (*NonC*); shudder, shuddering (*NonC*); wince; start; twitch, twitching (*NonC*); shaking (*NonC*), vibration.

tressaillir [tʀesajiʀ] [13] **vi** **a** (*frémir*) (*de plaisir*) to thrill, quiver; (*de peur*) to shudder, shiver; (*de douleur*) to wince. **son cœur tressaillait** his heart was fluttering. **b** (*sursauter*) to start, give a start. **faire** ~ **qn** to startle sb, make sb jump. **c** (*s'agiter*) *[personne, animal, nerf]* to quiver, twitch; *[plancher, véhicule]* to shake, vibrate.

tressautement [tʀesotmɑ̃] **nm** (*voir* **tressauter**) start; jump, jumping (*NonC*); jolt, jolting (*NonC*), tossing (*NonC*); shaking (*NonC*).

tressauter [tʀesote] [1] **vi** **a** (*sursauter*) to start, jump. **faire** ~ **qn** to startle sb, make sb jump.

b (*être secoué*) *[voyageurs]* to be jolted *ou* tossed about; *[objets]* to shake about, jump about. **faire** ~ **les voyageurs** to toss the passengers about; **les tasses tressautent sur le plateau** the cups are shaking *ou* jumping *ou* jiggling about on the tray.

tresse [tʀɛs] **nf** **a** (*cheveux*) plait, braid. **b** (*cordon*) braid (*NonC*). **c** (*Archit: motif*) strapwork.

tresser [tʀese] [1] **vt** **a** *cheveux, rubans* to plait, braid; *paille* to plait. **b** *panier, guirlande* to weave; *câble, corde, cordon* to twist. (*fig*) ~ **des couronnes à qn** to laud sb to the skies, sing sb's praises.

tréteau, pl ~**x** [tʀeto] **nm** **a** trestle. **table à** ~**x** trestle table. **b** (*Théât fig*) **les** ~**x** the boards, the stage; **monter sur les** ~**x** to go on the boards *ou* the stage.

treuil [tʀœj] **nm** winch, windlass.

treuiller [tʀœje] 1 **vt** to winch up.

trêve [tʀɛv] **nf** a (*Mil, Pol*) truce. (*Hist*) ~ **de Dieu** truce of God; (*hum*) ~ **des confiseurs** Christmas *ou* New Year (political) truce. b (*fig: répit*) respite, rest. **s'accorder une** ~ to allow o.s. a (moment's) respite *ou* a rest; (*littér*) **faire** ~ **à** *disputes, travaux* to rest from. c ~ **de** (*assez de*): ~ **de plaisanteries/d'atermoiement** enough of this joking/procrastination. d **sans** ~ (*sans cesse*) unremittingly, unceasingly, relentlessly.

Trèves [tʀɛv] **n** Trier.

trévise [tʀeviz] **nf** radicchio lettuce.

tri [tʀi] **nm** a (*gén*) sorting out; *[fiches]* sorting; *[volontaires]* selection; *[wagons]* marshalling, shunting; *[lentilles]* picking over; (*calibrage*) grading; (*tamisage*) sifting. **faire le** ~ **de** to sort out; to sort; to select; to marshal; to pick over; to grade; to sift; **on a procédé à des** ~**s successifs pour sélectionner les meilleurs candidats** they used a series of selection procedures to sift out the best candidates. b (*Poste*) sorting. **le (bureau de)** ~ the sorting office.

tri... [tʀi] **préf** tri... .

triacide [tʀiasid] **nm** triacid.

triade [tʀijad] **nf** (*littér*) triad.

triage [tʀijaʒ] = **tri**; *voir* **gare**.

trial [tʀijal] **nm** motocross, scrambling (*Brit*). **faire du** ~ to do motocross, go scrambling (*Brit*); *voir* **moto**.

triangle [tʀijɑ̃gl] **nm** (*Géom, Mus*) triangle. **en** ~ in a triangle; ~ **isocèle/équilatéral/rectangle/scalène** isosceles/equilateral/right-angled/scalene triangle; ~**s semblables/égaux** similar/equal triangles; ~ **quelconque** ordinary triangle; **soit un** ~ **quelconque ABC** let ABC be any triangle; (*Aut*) ~ **de signalisation** warning triangle; **le** ~ **des Bermudes** the Bermuda Triangle; **le T~ d'Or** the golden triangle.

triangulaire [tʀijɑ̃gylɛʀ] 1 **adj** *section, voile, prisme* triangular; *débat, tournoi* three-cornered. (*Hist*) **commerce** *ou* **trafic** ~ triangular slave trade. 2 **nf: (élection)** ~ three-cornered (election) contest *ou* fight.

triangulation [tʀijɑ̃gylasjɔ̃] **nf** triangulation.

trianguler [tʀijɑ̃gyle] 1 **vt** to triangulate.

trias [tʀijɑs] **nm** (*terrain*) trias; (*période*) Triassic, Trias.

triasique [tʀijɑzik] **adj** Triassic.

triathlon [tʀi(j)atlɔ̃] **nm** triathlon.

triatomique [tʀiatɔmik] **adj** triatomic.

tribal, e, **mpl -aux** [tʀibal, o] **adj** tribal.

tribalisme [tʀibalism] **nm** (*littér*) tribalism.

tribasique [tʀibɑzik] **adj** tribasic.

tribo-électricité [tʀiboelɛktʀisite] **nf** tribo-electricity.

tribo-électrique [tʀiboelɛktʀik] **adj** triboelectric.

triboluminescence [tʀibolyminesɑ̃s] **nf** triboluminescence.

tribord [tʀibɔʀ] **nm** starboard. **à** ~ to starboard, on the starboard side.

tribu [tʀiby] **nf** (*Ethnologie, Hist, fig*) tribe.

tribulations [tʀibylasjɔ̃] **nfpl** (*mésaventures*) tribulations, trials, troubles.

tribun [tʀibœ̃] **nm** (*Hist romaine*) tribune; (*orateur*) powerful orator; (*littér: défenseur*) tribune (*littér*).

tribunal, **pl -aux** [tʀibynal, o] 1 **nm** a court. ~ **judiciaire/d'exception** judicial/special court; ~ **révolutionnaire/militaire** revolutionary/military tribunal; **porter une affaire devant les** ~**aux** to bring a case before the courts; **affaire renvoyée d'un** ~ **à l'autre** case referred from one court to another.

b (*fig*) **le** ~ **des hommes** the justice of men; **être jugé par le** ~ **suprême** *ou* **de Dieu** to appear before the judgment seat of God; **être condamné par le** ~ **de l'histoire** to be condemned by the judgment of history, be judged and condemned by history; **s'ériger en** ~ **du goût/des mœurs** to set o.s. up as an arbiter of (good) taste/morals.

2 **comp** ▸**tribunal administratif** *tribunal dealing with internal disputes in the French civil service* ▸**tribunal de commerce** commercial court ▸**tribunal des conflits** jurisdictional court ▸**tribunal correctionnel** ≃ magistrates' court (*dealing with criminal matters*) ▸**tribunal pour enfants** juvenile court ▸**tribunal de grande instance** ≃ county court ▸**tribunal d'instance** ≃ magistrates' court (*dealing with civil matters*) ▸**tribunal de police** police court ▸**tribunal de première instance**† = **tribunal de grande instance**.

tribune [tʀibyn] 1 **nf** a (*pour le public*) *[église, assemblée, tribunal]* gallery; (*gén pl*) *[stade, champ de courses]* stand. ~ **d'honneur** grandstand; **les** ~**s du public/de la presse** public/press gallery; **les applaudissements des** ~**s** applause from the stands; **il avait une** ~ he had a seat in the stand; (*Parl*) ~ **du public** visitors' gallery.

b (*pour un orateur*) platform, rostrum. **monter à la** ~ to mount the platform *ou* rostrum, stand up to speak; (*Parl: parler*) to address the House.

c (*fig: débat*) forum. ~ **radiophonique** radio forum; **offrir une** ~ **à la contestation** to offer a forum *ou* platform for protest; ~ **libre d'un journal** opinion column in *ou* of a newspaper; **organiser une** ~ **sur un sujet d'actualité** to organize an open forum *ou* a free discussion on a topic of the day; **se présenter à l'élection pour avoir une** ~ **afin de faire connaître ses vues** to stand for election to give o.s. a platform from which to publicize one's views.

2 **comp** ▸**tribune d'orgue** organ loft.

tribut [tʀiby] **nm** (*lit, fig*) tribute. **payer** ~ **au vainqueur** to pay tribute to the conqueror (*money etc*); **rendre** *ou* **payer un** ~ **d'admiration/de respect à qn** to give sb the admiration/respect due to him; (*fig*) **ils ont payé un lourd** ~ **à la maladie/guerre** disease/war has cost them dear, disease/war has taken heavy toll of *ou* among them; (*fig littér*) **payer** ~ **à la nature** to go the way of all flesh, pay the debt of nature.

tributaire [tʀibytɛʀ] **adj** a (*dépendant*) **être** ~ **de** to be dependent *ou* reliant on. b (*Géog*) **être** ~ **de** to be a tributary of, flow into. c (*Hist*) tributary. **être** ~ **de qn** to be a tributary of sb, pay tribute to sb.

tric [tʀik] = **trick**.

tricentenaire [tʀisɑ̃t(ə)nɛʀ] 1 **adj** three-hundred-year-old (*épith*). 2 **nm** tercentenary, tricentennial.

tricéphale [tʀisefal] **adj** (*littér*) three-headed.

triceps [tʀisɛps] **adj, nm: (muscle)** ~ triceps (muscle); ~ **brachial/crural** brachial/crural triceps.

triche* [tʀiʃ] **nf** cheating. **c'est de la** ~ it's cheating *ou* a cheat.

tricher [tʀiʃe] 1 **vi** (*gén*) to cheat. ~ **au jeu** to cheat at gambling; ~ **sur son âge** to lie about *ou* cheat over one's age; ~ **sur le poids/la longueur** to cheat over *ou* on the weight/the length, give short weight/short measure; ~ **sur les prix** to cheat over the price, overcharge; ~ **en affaires/en amour** to cheat in business/love; **on a dû** ~ **un peu: un des murs est en contre-plaqué** we had to cheat a bit – one of the walls is plywood.

tricherie [tʀiʃʀi] **nf** (*tromperie*) cheating (*NonC*). **gagner par** ~ to win by cheating; **c'est une** ~ *ou* **de la** ~ it's a cheat *ou* cheating; (*astuce*) **on s'en tire avec une petite** ~ we'll get round it by using a little trick to fix it, we'll cheat a bit to fix it.

tricheur, -euse [tʀiʃœʀ, øz] **nm,f** (*gén*) cheater, cheat*; (*en affaires*) swindler, trickster, cheat.

trichloréthylène [tʀiklɔʀetilɛn] **nm** trichlorethylene, trichloroethylene.

trichrome [tʀikʀom] **adj** (*Tech*) three-colour (*épith*), trichromatic.

trichromie [tʀikʀɔmi] **nf** (*Tech*) three-colour process.

trick [tʀik] **nm** (*Bridge*) seventh trick.

tricolore [tʀikɔlɔʀ] **adj** (*gén*) three-coloured, tricolour(ed) (*frm*); (*aux couleurs françaises*) red, white and blue. **le drapeau** ~ the (French) tricolour; (*fig*) **le chauvinisme** ~ French *ou* Gallic chauvinism; (*Sport*) **l'équipe** ~*, **les** ~**s*** the French team.

tricorne [tʀikɔʀn] **nm** three-cornered hat, tricorn(e).

tricot [tʀiko] **nm** a (*vêtement*) jumper (*Brit*), sweater, jersey. ~ **de corps** vest (*Brit*), undershirt (*US*); **emporte des** ~**s** take some woollens *ou* woollies* with you. b (*technique*) knitting (*NonC*); (*ouvrage*) (*gén*) knitting (*NonC*); (*Comm*) knitwear (*NonC*). **faire du** ~ to knit, do some knitting; ~ **jacquard** Jacquard knitwear; ~ **plat** ordinary knitting, knitting on 2 needles; ~ **rond** knitting on 4 needles; *voir* **point**[2]. c (*tissu*) knitted fabric. **en** ~ knitted; **vêtements de** ~ knitwear.

tricotage [tʀikɔtaʒ] **nm** knitting.

tricoter [tʀikɔte] 1 1 **vt** *vêtement, maille* to knit. 2 **vi** a to knit; ~ **serré/lâche** to be a tight/loose knitter; *voir* **aiguille, laine, machine**[3]. b (*) *[cycliste]* to twiddle* (*Brit*), pedal fast*; *[danseur]* to prance about *ou* jig about like a mad thing* (*Brit*) *ou* like crazy*. ~ **des jambes** *[fugitif]* to run like mad*; *[danseur]* to prance about *ou* jig about madly*.

tricoteur, -euse [tʀikɔtœʀ, øz] 1 **nm,f** knitter. ~ **de filets** netmaker. 2 **tricoteuse** **nf** (*machine*) knitting machine; (*meuble*) tricoteuse.

trictrac [tʀiktʀak] **nm** (*Hist*) (*jeu*) backgammon; (*partie*) game of backgammon; (*plateau*) backgammon board.

tricycle [tʀisikl] **nm** *[enfant]* tricycle; *[livreur]* delivery tricycle.

tridactyle [tʀidaktil] **adj** tridactyl, tridactylous.

trident [tʀidɑ̃] **nm** (*Myth*) trident; (*Pêche*) trident, fish-spear; (*Agr*) three-pronged fork.

tridimensionnel, -elle [tʀidimɑ̃sjɔnɛl] **adj** three-dimensional.

trièdre [tʀi(j)ɛdʀ] 1 **adj** trihedral. 2 **nm** trihedron.

triennal, e, **mpl -aux** [tʀijenal, o] **adj** *prix, foire, élection* triennial, three-yearly; *charge, mandat, plan* three-year (*épith*); *magistrat, président* elected *ou* appointed for three years. (*Agr*) **assolement** ~ 3-year rotation of crops.

triennat [tʀiɛna] **nm** three-year period of office. **durant son** ~ during his three years in office.

trier [tʀije] 7 **vt** a (*classer*) (*gén*) to sort out; *lettres, fiches* to sort; *wagons* to marshal; *fruits* to sort; (*en calibrant*) to grade. b (*sélectionner*) *grains, visiteurs* to sort out; *volontaires* to select, pick; *lentilles* to pick over; (*en tamisant*) to sift. (*fig*) **triés sur le volet** hand-picked.

Trieste [tʀijɛst] **n** Trieste.

trieur, trieuse [tʀijœʀ, tʀijøz] 1 **nm,f** (*personne*) sorter; grader. ~ **de minerai/de légumes** ore/vegetable grader. 2 **nm** (*machine*) sorter. ~ **de grains** grain sorter; ~**-calibreur** *[fruits]* sorter; *[œufs]* grader, grading machine. 3 **trieuse** **nf** (*machine*) (*gén*) sorter; *[ordinateur, photocopieur]* sorting machine.

trifolié, e [tʀifɔlje] **adj** trifoliate, trifoliated.

trifouiller* [tʀifuje] 1 1 **vt** to rummage about in, root about in. 2 **vi**

to rummage about, root about.
triglycéride [tRigliseRid] nm triglyceride.
triglyphe [tRiglif] nm triglyph.
trigonométrie [tRigɔnɔmetRi] nf trigonometry.
trigonométrique [tRigɔnɔmetRik] adj trigonometric(al).
trijumeau [tRiʒymo] adj, nm: **(nerf)** ~ trigeminal *ou* trifacial nerve.
trilatéral, e, mpl **-aux** [tRilateRal, o] adj a (*Géom*) trilateral, three-sided. b (*Écon*) *accords* tripartite. **la (commission)** ~**e** the Trilateral Commission.
trilingue [tRilɛ̃g] adj *dictionnaire, secrétaire* trilingual. **il est** ~ he's trilingual, he speaks three languages.
trille [tRij] nm *[oiseau, flûte]* trill.
trillion [tRiljɔ̃] nm trillion.
trilobé, e [tRilɔbe] adj *feuille* trilobate; *ogive* trefoil (*épith*).
trilogie [tRilɔʒi] nf trilogy.
trimaran [tRimaRɑ̃] nm trimaran.
trimard*† [tRimaR] nm road. **prendre le** ~ to take to *ou* set out on the road.
trimarder*† [tRimaRde] 1 1 vi (*vagabonder*) to walk the roads, be on the road. 2 vt (*transporter*) to lug* *ou* cart* along.
trimardeur, -euse*† [tRimaRdœR, øz] nm,f (*vagabond*) tramp (*Brit*), hobo (*US*).
trimbal(l)age [tRɛ̃balaʒ] nm, **trimbal(l)ement** [tRɛ̃balmɑ̃] nm *[bagages, marchandises]* carting *ou* lugging around*. **on en a bien pour 3 à 4 heures de** ~ we'll be carting *ou* lugging this stuff around for 3 or 4 hours*.
trimbal(l)er [tRɛ̃bale] 1 1 vt (*) *bagages, marchandises* to lug* *ou* cart* around; (*péj*) *personne* to trail along. **qu'est-ce qu'il trimballe!**‡ he's as thick (*Brit*) *ou* dumb as they come‡. 2 **se trimbal(l)er**‡ vpr to trail along. **on a dû se** ~ **en voiture jusque chez eux** we had to trail over to their place in the car; **il a fallu que je me trimballe jusqu'à la gare avec mes valises** I had to trail all the way to the station with my suitcases.
trimer* [tRime] 1 vi to slave away. **faire** ~ **qn** to keep sb's nose to the grindstone, drive sb hard, keep sb hard at it*.
trimestre [tRimɛstR] nm a (*période*) (*gén, Comm*) quarter; (*Scol*) term. (*Scol*) **premier/second/troisième** ~ autumn/winter/summer term. b (*somme*) (*loyer*) quarter, quarter's rent; (*frais de scolarité*) term's fees; (*salaire*) quarter's income.
trimestriel, -elle [tRimɛstRijɛl] adj *publication* quarterly; *paiement* three-monthly, quarterly; *fonction, charge* three-month (*épith*), for three months (*attrib*); (*Scol*) *bulletin, examen* end-of-term (*épith*), termly (*épith*).
trimestriellement [tRimɛstRijɛlmɑ̃] adv *payer* on a quarterly *ou* three-monthly basis, every quarter, every three months; *publier* quarterly; (*Scol*) once a term.
trimètre [tRimɛtR] nm trimeter.
trimoteur [tRimɔtœR] nm three-engined aircraft.
tringle [tRɛ̃gl] nf a (*Tech*) rod. ~ **à rideaux** curtain rod *ou* rail. b (*Archit: moulure*) tenia. c **se mettre la** ~‡ to tighten one's belt.
tringler [tRɛ̃gle] 1 vt a (*Tech*) to mark with a line. b (**: *sexuellement*) to lay‡, screw**, fuck**. **se faire** ~ to have it off‡ (*avec* with), get laid‡.
trinidien, -ienne [tRinidjɛ̃, jɛn] 1 adj Trinidadian. 2 nm,f: **T~(ne)** Trinidadian.
trinitaire [tRinitɛR] adj, nmf (*Rel*) Trinitarian.
trinité [tRinite] nf a (*triade*) trinity. **la T~** (*dogme*) the Trinity; (*fête*) Trinity Sunday; **à la T~** on Trinity Sunday; **la Sainte T~** the Holy Trinity; *voir* **Pâques.** b (*Géog*) **T~ et Tobago** Trinidad and Tobago; **(l'île de) la T~** Trinidad.
trinitrobenzène [tRinitRobɛ̃zɛn] nm trinitrobenzene.
trinitrotoluène [tRinitRotɔlɥɛn] nm trinitrotoluene, trinitrotoluol.
trinôme [tRinom] nm (*Math*) trinomial.
trinquer [tRɛ̃ke] 1 vi a (*porter un toast*) to clink glasses. ~ **à qch/qn** to drink to sth/sb. b (*: *écoper*) to cop it‡ (*Brit*), take the rap*. **il a trinqué pour les autres** he took the rap for the others*; **si on les prend, on va les faire** ~ if we catch them we'll give them what for* *ou* we'll really make them pay (for it). c (†*: *trop boire*) to booze*. d (†: *se heurter*) to knock *ou* bump into one another.
trinquet [tRɛ̃kɛ] nm (*Naut*) foremast.
trinquette [tRɛ̃kɛt] nf (*Naut*) fore(-topmast) staysail.
trio [tRijo] nm (*Mus*) trio; (*groupe*) threesome, trio.
triode [tRijɔd] nf triode.
triolet [tRijɔlɛ] nm (*Mus*) triplet; (*Hist Littérat*) triolet.
triomphal, e, mpl **-aux** [tRijɔ̃fal, o] adj *succès, élection* triumphal; *entrée, accueil, geste, air* triumphant; (*Hist romaine*) triumphal.
triomphalement [tRijɔ̃falmɑ̃] adv *accueillir, saluer* in triumph; *annoncer* triumphantly.
triomphalisme [tRijɔ̃falism] nm triumphalism.
triomphaliste [tRijɔ̃falist] adj triumphalist.
triomphant, e [tRijɔ̃fɑ̃, ɑ̃t] adj triumphant.
triomphateur, -trice [tRijɔ̃fatœR, tRis] 1 adj *parti, nation* triumphant. 2 nm,f (*vainqueur*) triumphant victor. 3 nm (*Hist romaine*) triumphant general.
triomphe [tRijɔ̃f] nm a (*Mil, Pol, Sport, gén*) triumph; *[maladie, mode]* victory. **le** ~ **de la mini-jupe** the victory *ou* triumph of the mini-skirt; **cet acquittement représente le** ~ **de la justice/du bon sens** this acquittal represents the triumph of *ou* is a triumph for justice/common sense.
b (*Hist romaine, gén: honneurs*) triumph. **en** ~ in triumph; **porter qn en** ~ to bear *ou* carry sb in triumph, carry sb shoulder-high (in triumph); *voir* **arc.**
c (*exultation*) triumph. **air/cri de** ~ air/cry of triumph, triumphant air/cry; **leur** ~ **fut de courte durée** their triumph was short-lived.
d (*succès*) triumph. **cette pièce/cet artiste a remporté un** ~ this play/artist has been *ou* had a triumphant success; **ce film/livre est un vrai** ~ this film/book is a triumphant success.
triompher [tRijɔ̃fe] 1 1 vi a (*militairement*) to triumph; (*aux élections, en sport, gén*) to triumph, win; *[cause, raison]* to prevail, be triumphant; *[maladie]* to claim its victim. **faire** ~ **une cause** to bring *ou* give victory to a cause; **il a fait** ~ **la mode des cheveux longs** he ensured success for the fashion for long hair; *voir* **vaincre.**
b (*crier victoire*) to exult, rejoice.
c (*exceller*) to triumph, excel. *[acteur]* ~ **dans un rôle** to give a triumphant performance in a role.
2 **triompher de** vt indir *ennemi* to beat, triumph over, vanquish; *concurrent, rival* to beat, triumph over, overcome; *obstacle, difficulté* to triumph over, surmount, overcome; *peur, timidité* to conquer, overcome.
trip* [tRip] nm (*arg Drogue*) trip (*arg*). **c'est pas mon** ~ it's not my thing*.
tripaille‡ [tRipɑj] nf (*péj*) guts*, innards.
triparti, e [tRipaRti] adj (*Bot, Pol: à trois éléments*) tripartite; (*Pol: à trois partis*) three-party (*épith*).
tripartisme [tRipaRtism] nm three-party government.
tripartite [tRipaRtit] adj = **triparti.**
tripatouillage* [tRipatujaʒ] nm (*péj: action: voir* **tripatouiller**) fiddling about*; fiddling*; messing about* (*de* with); (*opération malhonnête*) fiddle*. ~ **électoral** election fiddle* (*Brit*), electoral jiggery-pokery* (*NonC*).
tripatouiller* [tRipatuje] 1 vt (*péj*) a (*remanier*) *texte* to fiddle about with*, *comptes, résultats électoraux* to fiddle*, tamper with. b (*manier*) to fiddle *ou* mess about with*, toy with; *femme* to paw*.
tripatouilleur, -euse* [tRipatujœR, øz] nm,f (*péj*) (*touche-à-tout*) fiddler*; (*affairiste*) grafter* (*péj*).
tripe [tRip] nf a (*Culin*) ~**s** tripe; ~**s à la mode de Caen/à la lyonnaise** tripe à la mode de Caen/à la Lyonnaise. b (*: *intestins*) ~**s** guts*; **cela vous prend aux** ~**s** that gets you in the guts* *ou* right there; **rendre** ~**s et boyaux** to be as sick as a dog*. c (* *fig: fibre*) **avoir la** ~ **républicaine/royaliste** to be a republican/a royalist through and through *ou* to the core.
triperie [tRipRi] nf (*boutique*) tripe shop; (*commerce*) tripe trade.
tripette* [tRipɛt] *voir* **valoir 1h.**
triphasé, e [tRifɑze] 1 adj three-phase. 2 nm three-phase current.
triphtongue [tRiftɔ̃g] nf triphthong.
tripier, -ière [tRipje, jɛR] nm,f tripe butcher.
triplace [tRiplas] adj three-seater.
triplan [tRiplɑ̃] nm triplane.
triple [tRipl] 1 adj a (*à trois éléments ou aspects*) triple; (*trois fois plus grand*) treble, triple. **au** ~ **galop** hell for leather*; **le prix est** ~ **de ce qu'il était** the price is three times *ou* treble what it was, the price has trebled; **faire qch en** ~ **exemplaire** to make three copies of sth, do sth in triplicate; **il faut que l'épaisseur soit** ~ three thicknesses are needed, a treble thickness is needed; **avec** ~ **couture** triple stitched; **avec** ~ **semelle** with a three-layer sole; **les murs sont** ~**s** there are three thicknesses of wall, the wall is in three sections; **l'inconvénient en est** ~, **il y a un** ~ **inconvénient** there are three disadvantages, the disadvantages are threefold; ~ **naissance** birth of triplets; **prendre une** ~ **dose (de)** to take three times the dose (of), take a triple dose (of).
b (*intensif*) **c'est un** ~ **idiot** he's a prize idiot; ~ **idiot!** you great idiot! *ou* fool!
2 nm: **manger/gagner le** ~ **(de qn)** to eat/earn three times as much (as sb *ou* as sb does); **celui-ci pèse le** ~ **de l'autre** this one weighs three times as much as the other *ou* is three times *ou* treble the weight of the other; **9 est le** ~ **de 3** 9 is three times 3; **c'est le** ~ **du prix normal/de la distance Paris-Londres** it's three times *ou* treble the normal price/the distance between Paris and London; **on a mis le** ~ **de temps à le faire** it took three times as long *ou* treble the time to do it.
3 comp ►**la Triple Alliance** the Triple Alliance ►**triple croche** nf (*Mus*) demi-semiquaver (*Brit*), thirty-second note (*US*) ►**la Triple Entente** the Triple Entente ►**triple menton** nm (*péj*) row of chins ►**triple saut** nm (*Sport*) triple jump.
triplé, e [tRiple] (ptp de **tripler**) 1 nm a (*Courses de chevaux*) treble (*betting on 3 different horses in 3 different races*). b (*Sport*) *[athlète]* triple success. **il a réussi un beau** ~ he came first in three events; *[équipe]* **réussir le** ~ **dans le 4 000 mètres** to win the first three places *ou* come 1st, 2nd and 3rd in the 4,000 metres; (*fig iro*) **c'est un beau** ~**!** that's a fine catalogue of disasters! 2 **triplés** nmpl (*bébés*) triplets; (*mâles*) boy triplets. 3 **triplées** nfpl girl triplets.

triplement [tʀipləmɑ̃] 1 adv (*pour trois raisons*) in three ways; (*à un degré triple, valeur intensive*) trebly, three times over. 2 nm (*voir* **tripler**) trebling (*de* of), tripling (*de* of); threefold increase (*de* in).

tripler [tʀiple] [1] 1 vt to treble, triple. **il tripla la dose** he made the dose three times as big, he tripled *ou* trebled the dose; ∼ **la longueur/l'épaisseur de qch** to treble *ou* triple the length/thickness of sth, make sth three times as long/thick; ∼ **la couche protectrice** to put on three protective coats, give three layers of protective coating; ∼ **le service d'autobus/la garnison** to make the bus service three times as frequent/the garrison three times as large, treble the frequency of the bus service/the size of the garrison; ∼ **sa mise** to treble one's stake.
2 vi to triple, treble, increase threefold. ∼ **de valeur/de poids** to treble in value/in weight.

triplette [tʀiplɛt] nf (*Boules*) threesome.

triplex[1] [tʀiplɛks] nm (*appartement*) three-storey apartment *ou* flat (*Brit*), triplex (*US*).

Triplex[2] [tʀiplɛks] nm ® (*verre*) Triplex ® (*Brit*), laminated safety glass.

triploïde [tʀiplɔid] adj triploid.

tripode [tʀipɔd] 1 adj tripodal. **mât** ∼ tripod (mast). 2 nm tripod.

Tripoli [tʀipɔli] n Tripoli.

triporteur [tʀipɔʀtœʀ] nm delivery tricycle.

tripot [tʀipo] nm (*péj*) dive*, joint*.

tripotage [tʀipɔtaʒ] nm (*péj: action: voir* **tripoter**) playing (*de* with); speculating (*de* with); fingering; fiddling (*de* with); pawing; (*manigances*) jiggery-pokery* (*NonC*). ∼**s électoraux** election fiddles* (*Brit*), electoral jiggery-pokery*.

tripotée⁑ [tʀipɔte] nf a (*correction*) belting⁑, hiding*, thrashing. b (*grand nombre*) **une** ∼ **de** ... loads* of ...; lots of ...; **avoir toute une** ∼ **d'enfants** to have a whole string of children*.

tripoter* [tʀipɔte] [1] (*péj*) 1 vt a *fonds* to play with, speculate with. b *objet, fruit* to fiddle with, finger; (*machinalement*) *montre, stylo, bouton* to fiddle with, play with, toy with. **se** ∼ **le nez/la barbe** to fiddle with one's nose/beard.
c (⁑) *femme, partie du corps* to paw*.
2 vi a (*fouiller*) to root about, rummage about. ∼ **dans les affaires de qn/dans un tiroir** to root about *ou* rummage about in sb's things/in a drawer.
b (*trafiquer*) ∼ **en Bourse/dans l'immobilier** to be *ou* get involved in some shady business on the Stock Market/in property; **il a tripoté dans diverses affaires assez louches** he has had a hand in a few fairly shady affairs.

tripoteur, -euse* [tʀipɔtœʀ, øz] nm,f (*péj*) (*affairiste*) shark*, shady dealer*; (⁑: *peloteur*) feeler⁑, groper⁑.

tripous, tripoux [tʀipu] nmpl *dish (from Auvergne) of sheep's offal and sheep's feet.*

triptyque [tʀiptik] nm a (*Art, Littérat*) triptych. b (*Admin: classement*) triptyque.

triquard [tʀikaʀ] nm (*arg Crime*) ex-con (*arg*).

trique [tʀik] nf cudgel. **mener qn à la** ∼ to bully sb along, drive sb like a slave; **donner des coups de** ∼ **à** to cudgel, thrash; **maigre** *ou* **sec comme un coup de** ∼ as skinny as a rake.

trirectangle [tʀiʀɛktɑ̃gl] adj trirectangular.

trirème [tʀiʀɛm] nf trireme.

trisaïeul, pl ∼**s** *ou* ∼**-eux** [tʀizajœl, ø] nm great-great-grandfather. **les trisaïeux** the great-great-grandparents.

trisaïeule [tʀizajœl] nf great-great-grandmother.

trisannuel, -elle [tʀizanɥɛl] adj *fête, plante* triennial.

trisection [tʀisɛksjɔ̃] nf (*Géom*) trisection.

trisomie [tʀizɔmi] nf trisomy. ∼ **21** trisomy of chromosome 21.

trisomique [tʀizɔmik] 1 adj trisomic. 2 nmf trisome. ∼ **21** person with Down's syndrome.

trisser (se)⁑ [tʀise] [1] vpr (*partir*) to clear off*, skedaddle*.

trissyllabe [tʀisi(l)lab] adj, nm = **trisyllabe.**

trissyllabique [tʀisi(l)labik] adj = **trisyllabique.**

Tristan [tʀistɑ̃] nm Tristan, Tristram. ∼ **et Iseu(l)t** Tristan and Isolde.

triste [tʀist] adj a (*malheureux, affligé*) *personne* sad, unhappy; *regard, sourire* sad, sorrowful. **d'un air** ∼ sadly, with a sad look; **d'une voix** ∼ sadly, in a sad *ou* sorrowful voice; **un enfant à l'air** ∼ a sad-looking *ou* an unhappy-looking child; **les animaux en cage ont l'air** ∼ caged animals look sad *ou* miserable; **être** ∼ **à l'idée** *ou* **à la pensée de partir** to be sad at the idea *ou* thought of leaving; **elle était** ∼ **de voir partir ses enfants** she was sad to see her children go.
b (*sombre, maussade*) *personne, pensée* sad, gloomy, glum; *couleur, temps, journée* dreary, dismal, miserable; *paysage* sad, bleak, dreary. **il aime les chansons** ∼**s** he likes sad *ou* melancholy songs; ∼ **à pleurer** hopelessly miserable; **il est** ∼ **comme une porte de prison** *ou* **un bonnet de nuit** he's as miserable as sin; **faire** ∼ **mine** *ou* **figure à** to give a cool reception to, greet unenthusiastically; **avoir** *ou* **faire** ∼ **mine, avoir** *ou* **faire** ∼ **figure** to cut a sorry figure, look a sorry sight; *voir* **vin.**
c (*attristant, pénible*) *nouvelle, épreuve, destin* sad. **depuis ces** ∼**s événements** since these sad events took place; **c'est une** ∼ **nécessité** it is a painful necessity, it is sadly necessary; **il se lamente toujours sur son** ∼ **sort** he is always bewailing his unhappy *ou* sad fate; **ce furent des mois bien** ∼**s** these were very sad *ou* unhappy months; **il est de mon** ∼ **devoir de vous dire que** ... it is my painful duty to have to tell you that ...; ∼ **chose que** it is a sorry *ou* sad state of affairs when; **depuis son accident, il est dans un** ∼ **état** (ever) since his accident he has been in a sad *ou* sorry state; **c'est pas** ∼**!*** (*c'est difficile*) it's really tough!*, it's no joke!*; (*c'est amusant*) it's a laugh a minute!*; (*c'est la pagaille*) it's a real mess!
d (*avant n: péj: lamentable*) **quelle** ∼ **personne/époque** what a dreadful person/age; **une** ∼ **réputation/affaire** a sorry reputation/business; **un** ∼ **sire** *ou* **personnage** an unsavoury *ou* dreadful individual; **ses** ∼**s résultats à l'examen** his wretched *ou* deplorable exam results.

tristement [tʀistəmɑ̃] adv a (*d'un air triste*) sadly, sorrowfully. b (*de façon lugubre*) sadly, gloomily, glumly. c (*valeur intensive, péjorative*) sadly, regrettably. **il est** ∼ **célèbre** he is regrettably well-known; **c'est** ∼ **vrai** sadly it is only too true, it is sadly true.

tristesse [tʀistɛs] nf a (*caractère, état*) *[personne, pensée]* sadness, gloominess; *[couleur, temps, journée]* dreariness; *[paysage]* sadness, bleakness, dreariness. **il sourit toujours avec une certaine** ∼ there is always a certain sadness in his smile; **enclin à la** ∼ given to melancholy, inclined to be gloomy *ou* sad. b (*chagrin*) sadness (*NonC*), sorrow. **avoir un accès de** ∼ to be overcome by sadness; **les** ∼**s de la vie** life's sorrows, the sorrows of life; **c'est avec une grande** ∼ **que nous apprenons son décès** it is with deep sadness *ou* sorrow that we have learned of his death.

tristounet, -ette* [tʀistunɛ, ɛt] adj *temps, nouvelles* gloomy, depressing. **il avait l'air** ∼ he looked a bit down in the mouth* *ou* down in the dumps*.

trisyllabe [tʀisi(l)lab] 1 adj trisyllabic. 2 nm trisyllable.

trisyllabique [tʀisi(l)labik] adj trisyllabic.

tritium [tʀitjɔm] nm tritium.

triton[1] [tʀitɔ̃] nm (*Zool*) triton. (*Myth*) **T**∼ Triton.

triton[2] [tʀitɔ̃] nm (*Mus*) tritone, augmented fourth.

trituration [tʀityʀasjɔ̃] nf (*voir* **triturer**) grinding up, trituration (*SPÉC*); pummelling, kneading; manipulation.

triturer [tʀityʀe] [1] vt a (*broyer*) *sel, médicament, fibres* to grind up, triturate (*SPÉC*). b (*malaxer*) *pâte* to pummel, knead; (*fig: manipuler*) *objet, clef, poignée* to manipulate. **ce masseur vous triture les chairs** this masseur really pummels you; **il s'agit non plus d'influencer, mais véritablement de** ∼ **l'opinion** it's no longer a matter of influencing public opinion but of bludgeoning *ou* coercing it into changing. c **se** ∼ **la cervelle*** *ou* **les méninges*** to rack *ou* cudgel one's brains*.

triumvir [tʀijɔmviʀ] nm triumvir.

triumviral, e, mpl **-aux** [tʀijɔmviʀal, o] adj triumviral.

triumvirat [tʀijɔmviʀa] nm triumvirate.

trivalence [tʀivalɑ̃s] nf trivalence, trivalency.

trivalent, e [tʀivalɑ̃, ɑ̃t] adj trivalent.

trivalve [tʀivalv] adj trivalve.

trivial, e, mpl **-iaux** [tʀivjal, jo] adj a (*vulgaire*) *langage, plaisanterie* coarse, crude. b (*littér: ordinaire*) *objet, acte* mundane, commonplace; *détail* mundane, trivial; (†: *rebattu*) trite, commonplace.

trivialement [tʀivjalmɑ̃] adv (*voir* **trivial**) coarsely, crudely; in a mundane way; in a commonplace way; trivially; tritely.

trivialité [tʀivjalite] nf (*voir* **trivial**) a (*caractère*) coarseness, crudeness; mundane nature; commonplace nature; triviality; triteness. b (*remarque*) coarse *ou* crude remark; commonplace *ou* trite remark. c (*détail*) coarse *ou* crude detail; mundane *ou* trivial detail.

troc [tʀɔk] nm (*échange*) exchange; (*système*) barter. **faire un** ∼ **avec qn** to make an exchange with sb; **faire le** ∼ **de qch avec qch d'autre** to barter *ou* exchange *ou* swap sth for sth else.

trochaïque [tʀɔkaik] adj trochaic.

trochée [tʀɔʃe] nm trochee.

trochlée [tʀɔkle] nf trochlea.

troène [tʀɔɛn] nm privet.

troglodyte [tʀɔglɔdit] nm (*Ethnologie*) cave dweller; (*fig*) troglodyte; (*Orn*) wren.

troglodytique [tʀɔglɔditik] adj (*Ethnologie*) troglodytic (*SPÉC*), cave-dwelling (*épith*). **habitation** ∼ cave dwelling, cave-dweller's settlement.

trogne [tʀɔɲ] nf (*péj: visage*) mug⁑ (*péj*), face.

trognon [tʀɔɲɔ̃] 1 nm *[fruit]* core; *[chou]* stalk. ∼ **de pomme** apple core; **se faire avoir jusqu'au** ∼⁑ to be well and truly had⁑; **mon petit** ∼* sweetie pie*. 2 adj inv (*: *mignon*) *enfant, objet, vêtement* cute*, lovely.

Troie [tʀwa] n Troy. **la guerre/le cheval de** ∼ the Trojan War/Horse.

troïka [tʀɔika] nf (*lit, Pol*) troika.

trois [tʀwa] 1 adj inv a three; (*troisième*) third. **volume/acte** ∼ volume/act three; **le** ∼ **(janvier)** the third (of January); **Henri III** Henry the Third; *pour autres loc voir* **six** *et* **fois, ménage** *etc.*
b (*approximation*) **achète deux ou** ∼ *ou* **ou quatre citrons** buy a couple of lemons; **je pars dans** ∼ **minutes** I'm off in a couple of *ou* a few minutes; **il n'a pas dit** ∼ **mots** he hardly opened his mouth *ou* said a word; *voir* **cuiller.**
2 nm inv three; (*troisième*) third; (*Cartes, Dés*) three; *[égratignure, cadeau]* **c'est** ∼ **fois rien** it's nothing at all, it's hardly anything; **ça**

coûte ~ fois rien it costs next to nothing; et de ~! that makes three!; *pour loc voir* six.

3 comp ▸les trois coups mpl (*Théât*) the three knocks (*announcing beginning of play*) ▸trois-deux nm (*Mus*) three-two time ▸les trois dimensions fpl (*Phys*) the three dimensions; à trois dimensions three-dimensional ▸trois étoiles adj *cognac, restaurant* three-star (*épith*) ◊ nm (*restaurant*) three-star restaurant; (*hôtel*) three-star hotel ▸les trois Grâces fpl (*Myth*) the three Graces ▸trois-huit nm (*Mus*) three-eight (time); (*travail*) faire les trois-huit to operate three eight-hour shifts, operate round the clock in eight-hour shifts ▸trois-mâts nm inv (*Naut*) three-master ▸"Les Trois Mousquetaires" mpl (*Littérat*) "The Three Musketeers" ▸les trois ordres mpl (*Hist*) the three estates ▸trois-pièces nm inv (*complet*) three-piece suit; (*appartement*) three-room flat (*Brit*) *ou* apartment (*US*) ▸trois-portes nf inv (*Aut*) two-door hatchback ▸trois quarts[1] nmpl three-quarters; portrait de trois quarts three-quarter(s) portrait; j'ai fait les trois quarts du travail I've done three-quarters of the work; les trois quarts des gens l'ignorent the great majority of people *ou* most people don't know this; aux trois quarts détruit almost totally destroyed ▸trois-quarts[2] nm inv (*violon*) three-quarter violin; (*manteau*) three-quarter (length) coat; (*Rugby*) three-quarter; il joue trois-quarts aile he plays wing (three-quarter); (*Rugby*) trois-quarts centre centre (three-quarter); (*Rugby*) la ligne des trois-quarts the three-quarter line ▸trois-quatre nm (*Mus*) three-four time ▸trois temps (*Mus*) three beats to the bar; à trois temps in triple time.

troisième [tʀwazjɛm] 1 adj, nmf third. le ~ degré (*torture*) the third degree; le ~ sexe the third sex; le ~ âge (*période*) the years of retirement; (*groupe social*) senior citizens; personne du ~ âge senior citizen; ~ cycle d'université graduate school; étudiant de ~ cycle graduate *ou* post-graduate (*Brit*) student; être *ou* faire le ~ larron dans une affaire to take advantage of the other two quarrelling over some business; *pour autres loc voir* sixième. 2 nf a (*Scol*) (classe de) ~ fourth form *ou* year (*Brit*), 8th grade (*US*). b (*Aut*) third (gear). en ~ in third (gear).

troisièmement [tʀwazjɛmmɑ̃] adv third(ly), in the third place.

troll [tʀɔl] nm troll.

trolley [tʀɔlɛ] nm (*dispositif*) trolley(-wheel); (*: *bus*) trolley bus.

trolleybus [tʀɔlɛbys] nm trolley bus.

trombe [tʀɔ̃b] nf a (*Mét*) waterspout. (*fig: pluie*) une ~ d'eau, des ~s d'eau a cloudburst, a downpour; (*fig*) des ~s de lave/débris streams *ou* torrents of lava/debris. b entrer/sortir/passer en ~ to sweep in/out/by like a whirlwind.

trombine* [tʀɔ̃bin] nf (*visage*) face, mug* (*péj*); (*tête*) nut*.

trombinoscope* [tʀɔ̃binɔskɔp] nm a (*photographie collective*) group mug-shot* (*fig*). b (*annuaire de l'Assemblée nationale*) *register, with photographs, of French deputés,* ≃ rogues' gallery* of MPs (*Brit*) *ou* representatives (*US*).

tromblon [tʀɔ̃blɔ̃] nm a (*Mil*) (*Hist*) blunderbuss; [*fusil lance-roquettes*] grenade launcher. b (*: *chapeau*) hat, titfer (*Brit arg*), headgear* (*NonC*).

trombone [tʀɔ̃bɔn] nm a (*Mus*) (*instrument*) trombone; (*tromboniste*) trombonist, trombone (player). ~ à coulisse/à pistons slide/valve trombone; ~ basse bass trombone. b (*agrafe*) paper clip.

tromboniste [tʀɔ̃bɔnist] nmf trombonist, trombone (player).

trompe [tʀɔ̃p] 1 nf a (*Mus*) trumpet, horn; (†: *avertisseur, sirène*) horn. ~ de chasse hunting horn; ~ de brume fog horn; *voir* son[2]. b (*Zool*) [*éléphant*] trunk, proboscis (SPÉC); [*insecte*] proboscis; [*tapir*] snout, proboscis (SPÉC); (*: *nez*) proboscis (*hum*), snout*. c (*Tech*) ~ à eau/mercure water/mercury pump. d (*Archit*) squinch. 2 comp ▸trompe d'Eustache (*Anat*) Eustachian tube ▸trompe de Fallope *ou* utérine (*Anat*) Fallopian tube.

trompe-la-mort [tʀɔ̃plamɔʀ] nmf inv death-dodger.

trompe-l'œil [tʀɔ̃plœj] nm inv a trompe-l'œil. peinture en ~ trompe-l'œil painting; décor en ~ decor done in trompe-l'œil; peint en ~ sur un mur painted in trompe-l'œil on a wall. b (*fig: esbroufe*) eyewash*. c'est du ~ it's all eyewash*.

tromper [tʀɔ̃pe] 1 1 vt a (*duper*) to deceive, trick, fool; (*être infidèle à*) *époux* to be unfaithful to, deceive. ~ qn sur qch to deceive *ou* mislead sb about *ou* over sth; ~ sa femme avec une autre to deceive one's wife *ou* be unfaithful to one's wife with another woman; un mari trompé a husband who has been deceived; cela ne trompe personne that doesn't fool anybody.

b (*induire en erreur par accident*) [*personne*] to mislead; [*symptômes*] to deceive, mislead. les apparences trompent appearances are deceptive *ou* misleading; c'est ce qui vous trompe that's where you are mistaken *ou* wrong; c'est un signe qui ne trompe pas it's a clear *ou* an unmistakable sign, it's clear proof.

c (*déjouer*) *poursuivants* [*personne*] to elude, trick, escape from, outwit; [*manœuvre*] to fool, trick; *vigilance* to elude. il a trompé la surveillance de ses gardes et s'est enfui he evaded *ou* eluded *ou* outwitted the guards and made his escape.

d (*décevoir*) ~ l'attente/l'espoir de qn to fall short of *ou* fail to come up to *ou* deceive (*frm*) sb's expectations/hopes; être trompé dans son attente/ses espoirs to be disappointed *ou* deceived (*frm*) in one's expectations/hopes; ~ la faim/la soif to stave off one's hunger/thirst; pour ~ le temps to kill *ou* pass time, to while away the time; pour ~ leur longue attente to while away *ou* beguile (*frm*) their long wait.

2 se tromper vpr a to make a mistake, be mistaken. se ~ de 5 F dans un calcul to be 5 francs out (*Brit*) *ou* off (*US*) in one's calculations; tout le monde peut se ~ anybody can make a mistake; se ~ sur les intentions de qn to be mistaken about *ou* regarding sb's intentions, misjudge *ou* mistake sb's intentions; on pourrait s'y ~, c'est à s'y ~ you'd hardly know the difference; ne vous y trompez pas, il arrivera à ses fins make no mistake – he will obtain his ends; si je ne me trompe if I am not mistaken, unless I'm very much mistaken.

b se ~ de route/chapeau to take the wrong road/hat; se ~ d'adresse to get the wrong address; (*fig*) tu te trompes d'adresse *ou* de porte you've come to the wrong place, you've got the wrong person; se ~ de jour/date to get the day/date wrong, make a mistake about the day/date.

tromperie [tʀɔ̃pʀi] nf a (*duperie*) deception, deceit, trickery (*NonC*). b (*littér: illusion*) illusion.

trompeter [tʀɔ̃pete] 4 vt (*péj*) *nouvelle* to trumpet abroad, shout from the housetops.

trompette [tʀɔ̃pɛt] 1 nf a (*Mus*) trumpet. ~ de cavalerie bugle; ~ d'harmonie *ou* à pistons *ou* chromatique *ou* naturelle orchestral *ou* valve *ou* chromatic *ou* natural trumpet; ~ basse/bouchée bass/muted trumpet; (*Bible*) la ~ du Jugement dernier the last Trump; (*littér*) la ~ de la Renommée the Trumpet of Fame; avoir la queue en ~ to have a turned-up tail; *voir* nez, tambour. b (*Bot*) ~ de la mort *ou* des morts horn of plenty. c (*coquillage*) trumpet shell. 2 nm (*trompettiste*) trumpeter, trumpet (player); (*Mil*) bugler.

trompettiste [tʀɔ̃petist] nmf trumpet player, trumpeter.

trompeur, -euse [tʀɔ̃pœʀ, øz] 1 adj a *personne* deceitful, deceiving (*épith*); *paroles, discours* deceitful. b *apparences* deceptive, misleading; *distance, profondeur* deceptive. les apparences sont ~euses appearances are deceptive. 2 nm,f deceiver. (*Prov*) à ~, ~ et demi every rogue has his match.

trompeusement [tʀɔ̃pøzmɑ̃] adv (*voir* trompeur) deceitfully; deceptively.

tronc [tʀɔ̃] 1 nm a [*arbre*] trunk; [*colonne*] shaft, trunk; (*Géom*) [*cône, pyramide*] frustum; (*Anat*) [*nerf, vaisseau*] trunk, mainstem. ~ d'arbre tree trunk; ~ de cône/pyramide truncated cone/pyramid. b (*Anat: thorax et abdomen*) trunk; [*cadavre mutilé*] torso. c (*boîte*) (collection) box. le ~ des pauvres the poorbox. 2 comp ▸tronc commun (*Scol*) common-core syllabus.

troncation [tʀɔ̃kasjɔ̃] nf (*Ling*) truncating; (*Ordin*) truncation. recherche par ~ à droite/à gauche search by truncating a word on the right/left.

troncature [tʀɔ̃katyʀ] nf (*Minér*) truncation.

tronche* [tʀɔ̃ʃ] nf (*visage*) mug* (*péj*), face; (*tête*) nut*.

tronçon [tʀɔ̃sɔ̃] nm a [*tube, colonne, serpent*] section. b [*route, voie*] section, stretch; [*convoi, colonne*] section; [*phrase, texte*] part.

tronconique [tʀɔ̃kɔnik] adj like a flattened cone *ou* a sawn-off cone.

tronçonnage [tʀɔ̃sɔnaʒ] nm, **tronçonnement** [tʀɔ̃sɔnmɑ̃] nm (*voir* tronçonner) sawing *ou* cutting up; cutting into sections.

tronçonner [tʀɔ̃sɔne] 1 vt *tronc* to saw *ou* cut up; *tube, barre* to cut into sections.

tronçonneuse [tʀɔ̃sɔnøz] nf chain saw.

trône [tʀon] nm a (*siège, fonction*) throne. ~ pontifical papal throne; placer qn/monter sur le ~ to put sb on/come to *ou* ascend the throne; chasser du ~ to dethrone, remove from the throne; le ~ et l'autel King and Church. b (* *hum: W.-C.*) throne* (*hum*). être sur le ~ to be on the throne*.

trôner [tʀone] 1 vi a [*roi, divinité*] to sit enthroned, sit on the throne. b (*avoir la place d'honneur*) [*personne*] to sit enthroned; [*chose*] to sit imposingly; (*péj: faire l'important*) to lord it.

tronquer [tʀɔ̃ke] 1 vt a *colonne, statue* to truncate. b (*fig*) *citation, texte* to truncate, curtail, cut down, shorten; *détails, faits* to abbreviate, cut out. version tronquée shortened *ou* truncated version.

trop [tʀo] 1 adv a (*avec vb: à l'excès*) too much; (*devant adv, adj*) too. beaucoup *ou* bien ~ *manger etc* far *ou* much too much; beaucoup *ou* bien *ou* (*littér*) par ~ (*avec adj*) far too, much too; il a ~ mangé/bu he has had too much to eat/drink, he has eaten/drunk too much; je suis exténué d'avoir ~ marché I'm exhausted from having walked too far *ou* too much; il a ~ travaillé he has worked too hard, he has done too much work, he has overworked; la pièce est ~ chauffée the room is overheated; la maison est ~ grande/loin pour eux the house is too large/far for them; un ~ grand effort l'épuiserait too great an effort would exhaust him; des restrictions ~ sévères aggraveraient la situation économique too severe restrictions would aggravate the economic situation; elle en a déjà bien ~ dit she has said far *ou* much too much already; il ne faut pas ~ demander/insister one mustn't be too greedy/pressing, one mustn't be overdemanding/overinsistent; tu as conduit ~ vite/lentement you drove too fast/slowly; tu as ~ conduit you drove for too long, you have been driving (for) too long; il ne faut pas ~ aller le voir we must not go to visit him too often, we mustn't overdo the visits; vous êtes ~ (nombreux)/~ peu (nombreux) there are too many/

too few of you; **une ~ forte dose** an overdose; **en faire ~, aller beaucoup ~ loin** to go overboard*, go too far, overdo it; **elle est ~, ta copine!*** your girlfriend's too much!*; **elle en fait ~ pour qu'on la croit vraiment malade** she makes so much fuss it's difficult to believe she's really ill.

b **~ de** (*quantité*) too much; (*nombre*) too many; **j'ai acheté ~ de pain/d'oranges** I've bought too much bread/too many oranges; **n'apportez pas de pain, il y en a déjà ~** don't bring any bread – there is too much already; **n'apportez pas de verres, il y en a déjà ~** don't bring any glasses – there are too many already; **s'il te reste ~ de dollars, vends-les moi** if you have dollars left over *ou* to spare, sell them to me; **nous avons ~ de personnel** we are overstaffed; **il y a ~ de monde dans la salle** the hall is overcrowded *ou* overfull, there are too many people in the hall; **j'ai ~ de travail** I'm overworked, I have too much work (to do); **ils ne seront pas ~ de deux pour ce travail** this job will need at least the two of them (on it); **~ de bonté/d'égoïsme** excessive kindness/selfishness.

c (*avec conséquence*) too much; (*devant adj, adv*) too. **il mange beaucoup ~ pour maigrir** he eats far too much to lose any weight; **le village est ~ loin pour qu'il puisse y aller à pied** the village is too far for him to walk there; **elle a ~ de travail pour qu'on lui permette de sortir tôt** she has too much work (to do) for her to be allowed out early; **il est bien ~ idiot pour comprendre** he is far too stupid *ou* too much of an idiot to understand; **c'est ~ beau pour être vrai!** it's too good to be true; **les voyages à l'étranger sont ~ rares pour ne pas en profiter** trips abroad are too rare to be missed.

d (*superl, intensif*) too, so (very). **j'ai oublié mes papiers, c'est vraiment ~ bête** how stupid (of me) *ou* it's too stupid for words – I've forgotten my papers; **il y a vraiment par ~ de gens égoïstes** there are far too many selfish people about; **c'est par ~ injuste** it's too unfair for words; **c'est ~ drôle!** it's too funny for words!, it's hilarious!, how funny!; **il n'est pas ~ satisfait/mécontent du résultat** he's not overpleased *ou* too satisfied *ou* too pleased/not too unhappy *ou* dissatisfied with the result; **nous n'avons pas ~ de place chez nous** we haven't got (so) very much room *ou* (all) that much* room at our place; **vous êtes ~ aimable** you are too *ou* most kind; **je ne sais ~ que faire** I am not too *ou* quite sure what to do *ou* what I should do, I don't really know what to do; **il n'aime pas ~ ça*** he isn't too keen (*Brit*) *ou* overkeen (*Brit*) (on it), he doesn't like it overmuch *ou* (all) that much*; **cela n'a que ~ duré** it's gone on (far) too long already; **je ne le sais que ~** I know only too well, I am only too well aware; **je n'ai pas ~ confiance en lui** I haven't much *ou* all that much* confidence in him; **c'est ~!, c'en est ~!, ~ c'est ~!** that's going too far!, enough is enough!; **cela ne va pas ~ bien** things are not going so *ou* terribly well; **je n'en sais ~ rien** I don't really know; *voir* **tôt**.

e **de ~, en ~: il y a une personne/2 personnes de ~ *ou* en ~ dans l'ascenseur** there is one person/there are 2 people too many in the lift; **s'il y a du pain en ~, j'en emporterai** if there is any bread (left) over *ou* any bread extra *ou* any surplus bread I'll take some away; **il m'a rendu 2 F de ~ *ou* en ~** he gave me back 2 francs too much; **ces 5 F sont de ~** that's 5 francs too much; **l'argent versé en ~** the excess payment; **il pèse 3 kg de ~** he is 3 kg overweight; **ce régime vous fait perdre les kilos en ~** this diet will help you lose those extra pounds; **si je suis de ~, je peux m'en aller!** if I'm in the way *ou* not welcome I can always leave!; **cette remarque est de ~** that remark is uncalled-for; **il a bu un verre *ou* un coup* de ~** he's had a drink *ou* one* too many; **tu manges/bois de ~*** you eat/drink too much.

2 **nm** excess, surplus. **le ~ d'importance accordé à ...** the excessive importance attributed to ...; **que faire du ~ qui reste?** what is to be done with what is left (over)? *ou* with the extra?

trope [tʀɔp] **nm** (*Littérat*) trope.

trophée [tʀɔfe] **nm** trophy. **~ de chasse** hunting trophy.

tropical, e, **mpl -aux** [tʀɔpikal, o] **adj** tropical.

tropicaliser [tʀɔpikalize] [1] **vt** *matériel* to tropicalize.

tropique [tʀɔpik] 1 **adj** *année* tropical. 2 **nm** a (*Géog: ligne*) tropic. **~ du Cancer/Capricorne** tropic of Cancer/Capricorn. b (*zone*) **les ~s** the tropics; **le soleil des ~s** the tropical sun; **vivre sous les ~s** to live in the tropics.

tropisme [tʀɔpism] **nm** (*Bio*) tropism.

troposphère [tʀɔpɔsfɛʀ] **nf** troposphere.

trop-perçu, **pl trop-perçus** [tʀopɛʀsy] **nm** (*Admin, Comm*) excess (tax) payment, overpayment (of tax).

trop-plein, **pl trop-pleins** [tʀoplɛ̃] **nm** a (*excès d'eau*) *[réservoir, barrage]* overflow; *[vase]* excess water; (*tuyau d'évacuation*) overflow (pipe); (*déversoir*) overflow outlet. b (*excès de contenu: grains etc*) excess, surplus. c (*fig*) **~ d'amour/d'amitié** overflowing love/friendship; **~ de vie *ou* d'énergie** surplus *ou* boundless energy; **déverser le ~ de son cœur/âme** to pour out one's heart/soul *ou* all one's pent-up feelings.

troquer [tʀɔke] [1] **vt: ~ qch contre qch d'autre** to barter *ou* exchange *ou* trade *ou* swap sth for sth else; (*fig: remplacer*) to swap sth for sth else.

troquet‡ [tʀɔkɛ] **nm** small café.

trot [tʀo] **nm** *[cheval]* trot. **petit/grand ~** jog/full trot; **~ de manège** dressage trot; **~ assis/enlevé** close/rising trot; **course de ~ attelé** trotting race; **course de ~ monté** *trotting race under saddle;* (*lit*) **aller au ~** to trot along; (*fig*) **au ~*** at the double; **vas-y, et au ~!*** off you go, at the double *ou* and be quick about it!; (*lit, * fig*) **partir au ~** to set off at a trot; **prendre le ~** to break into a trot.

Trotski [tʀɔtski] **nm** Trotsky.

trotskisme, trotskysme [tʀɔtskism] **nm** Trotskyism.

trotskiste, trotskyste [tʀɔtskist] **adj, nmf** Trotskyist, Trotskyite (*péj*).

trotte* [tʀɔt] **nf: il y a *ou* ça fait une ~ (d'ici au village)** it's a fair step* *ou* distance (from here to the village); **on a fait une (jolie) ~** we've come a good way, we covered a good distance.

trotte-bébé [tʀɔtbebe] **nm inv** baby-walker ®.

trotter [tʀɔte] [1] 1 **vi** a *[cheval, cavalier]* to trot. b (*fig*) *[personne]* (*marcher à petits pas*) to trot about (*ou* along *etc*); (*marcher beaucoup*) to run around, run hither and thither; *[souris, enfants]* to scurry (about), scamper (about); *[bébé]* to toddle along. **un air/une idée qui vous trotte dans *ou* par la tête *ou* la cervelle** a tune/an idea which keeps running through your head. 2 **se trotter*** **vpr** (*se sauver*) to dash (off).

trotteur, -euse [tʀɔtœʀ, øz] 1 **nm,f** (*cheval*) trotter, trotting horse. 2 **nm** (*chaussure*) flat shoe. 3 **trotteuse nf** (*aiguille*) (sweep) second hand.

trottin†† [tʀɔtɛ̃] **nm** (dressmaker's) errand girl.

trottinement [tʀɔtinmɑ̃] **nm** (*voir* **trottiner**) jogging; trotting; scurrying, scampering; toddling.

trottiner [tʀɔtine] [1] **vi** *[cheval]* to jog along; *[personne]* to trot along; *[souris]* to scurry *ou* scamper about *ou* along; *[bébé]* to toddle along.

trottinette [tʀɔtinɛt] **nf** (child's) scooter.

trottoir [tʀɔtwaʀ] **nm** a pavement (*Brit*), sidewalk (*US*). **~ roulant** moving walkway, travellator (*Brit*). b (*péj*) **faire le ~*** to walk the streets, be on the game‡.

trou [tʀu] 1 **nm** a (*gén, Golf*) hole; (*terrier*) hole, burrow; *[flûte]* (finger-)hole; *[aiguille]* eye. **par le ~ de la serrure** through the keyhole; (*Théât*) **le ~ du souffleur** the prompt box; **faire un ~** (*dans le sol*) to dig *ou* make a hole; (*dans une haie*) to make a hole *ou* a gap; (*dans un mur avec une vrille*) to bore *ou* make a hole; (*en perforant: dans le cuir, papier*) to punch *ou* make a hole; (*avec des ciseaux, un couteau*) to cut a hole; (*en usant, frottant*) to wear a hole (*dans* in); (*Golf*) **faire un ~ en un** to get a hole in one; (*Golf*) **un 9/18 ~s** a 9-hole/an 18-hole course; **il a fait un ~ à son pantalon** (*usure*) he has (worn) a hole in his trousers; (*brûlure, acide*) he has burnt a hole in his trousers; (*déchirure*) he has torn a hole in his trousers; **ses chaussettes sont pleines de ~s *ou* ont des ~s partout** his socks are in holes *ou* are full of holes; **sol/rocher creusé *ou* piqué de ~s** ground/rock pitted with holes; (*fig*) **une œuvre qui a des ~s** a work with certain weaknesses *ou* weak parts.

b (*fig*) (*moment de libre*) gap; (*déficit*) deficit; (*Sport: trouée*) gap, space. **un ~ (de 10 millions) dans la comptabilité** a deficit (of 10 million) in the accounts; (*Sport*) **faire le ~** to break *ou* burst through; **il y a des ~s dans son témoignage** there are gaps in his account, there are things missing from his account; **cela a fait un gros ~ dans ses économies** it made quite a hole in his savings; **j'ai un ~ dans la matinée, venez me voir** I have a gap in my schedule during the morning so come and see me; *[professeur]* **j'ai un ~ *ou* une heure de ~** I have a free period *ou* an hour's free time; **j'ai eu un ~ (de mémoire)** my memory failed me for a moment, my mind went blank.

c (*Anat*) foramen. **~ optique** optic foramen; **~s intervertébraux** intervertebral foramina; *voir* **œil**.

d (*péj: localité*) place, hole* (*péj*). **ce village est un ~** this village is a real hole* (*péj*) *ou* dump* (*péj*); **il n'est jamais sorti de son ~** he has never been out of his own backyard; **chercher un petit ~ pas cher** to look for a little place that's not too expensive; **un ~ perdu *ou* paumé*** a dead-and-alive (little) hole* (*péj*), a god forsaken hole* *ou* dump*.

e (*loc*) (*fig*) **(se) faire son ~*** to make a niche for o.s.; (*fig*) **vivre tranquille dans son ~** to live quietly in one's little hidey-hole* (*Brit*) *ou* hideaway; (*prison*) **mettre/être au ~*** to put/be in (the) nick‡ (*Brit*) *ou* in clink‡; (*fig*) **quand on sera dans le ~*** when we're dead and buried *ou* dead and gone, when we're six feet under*; *voir* **boire**.

2 **comp ►trou d'aération** airhole, (air) vent **►trou d'air** (*Aviat*) air pocket **►trou de balle**‡‡ arse-hole‡‡ (*Brit*), asshole‡‡ (*US*); (*fig: imbécile*) berk‡ (*Brit*), twat‡‡ **►trou du chat** (*Naut*) lubber's hole **►trou du cul**‡‡ = **trou de balle**‡‡ **►trou d'homme** manhole **►trou-madame nm** (**pl trous-madame**) troll-madam, *type of bagatelle* **►trou de nez*** nostril **►trou noir** (*Astron*) black hole; (*fig: désespoir*) **c'était le trou noir** I (*ou* he *etc*) was in the depths of despair **►trou normand** *glass of spirits, often Calvados, drunk between courses of meal* **►trou d'obus** shell-hole, shell-crater **►trou de souris** mouse-hole; **elle était si gênée qu'elle serait rentrée dans un trou de souris** she was so embarrassed that she would have liked the ground to swallow her up **►trou-trou nm** (**pl trou-trous**) (*Tricot*) *row of holes through which ribbon is passed;* (*Couture*) *lace trimming through which ribbon is passed.*

troubadour [tʀubaduʀ] **nm** troubadour.

troublant, e [tʀublɑ̃, ɑ̃t] **adj** (*déconcertant*) disturbing, disquieting, unsettling; (*sexuellement provocant*) disturbing, arousing.

trouble[1] [tʀubl] 1 **adj** a *eau, vin* unclear, cloudy, turbid (*littér*);

regard misty, dull; *image* blurred, misty, indistinct; *photo* blurred, out of focus. **avoir la vue ~** to have blurred vision; *voir* **pêcher**[1]. b (*fig*) (*impur, équivoque*) *personnage, rôle* fishy, suspicious, dubious; *affaire* shady, murky, fishy; *désir* dark (*épith*); *joie* perverse (*épith*); (*vague, pas franc*) *regard* shifty, uneasy. 2 **adv: voir ~** to have blurred vision, see things dimly *ou* as if through a mist.

trouble[2] [tʀubl] **nm** a (*agitation, remue-ménage*) tumult, turmoil; (*zizanie, désunion*) discord, trouble.

b (*émeute*) **~s** unrest (*NonC*), disturbances, troubles; **~s politiques/sociaux** political/social unrest (*NonC*) *ou* disturbances *ou* upheavals; **des ~s sanglants** disturbances *ou* troubles causing bloodshed; **des ~s ont éclaté dans le sud du pays** rioting has broken out *ou* disturbances have broken out in the south of the country; *voir* **fauteur**.

c (*émoi affectif ou sensuel*) (inner) turmoil, agitation; (*inquiétude, désarroi*) distress; (*gêne, perplexité*) confusion, embarrassment. **le ~ étrange qui s'empara d'elle** the strange feeling of turmoil *ou* agitation which overcame her; **le ~ profond causé par ces événements traumatisants** the profound distress caused by these traumatic events; (*littér*) **le ~ de son âme/cœur** the tumult *ou* turmoil in his soul/heart; **le ~ de son esprit** the agitation in his mind, the turmoil his mind was in; **dominer/se laisser trahir par son ~** to overcome/give o.s. away by one's confusion *ou* embarrassment; **semer le ~ dans l'esprit des gens** to sow confusion in peoples' minds.

d (*gén pl: Méd*) trouble (*NonC*), disorder. **~s physiologiques/psychiques** physiological/psychological trouble *ou* disorders; **il a des ~s de la vision** he has trouble with his (eye)sight *ou* vision; **~s de la personnalité** *ou* **du caractère** personality problems *ou* disorders; **~s du comportement** behavioural problems; **~s du langage** speech difficulties; **ce n'est qu'un ~ passager** it's only a passing disorder.

trouble-fête [tʀubləfɛt] **nmf inv** spoilsport, killjoy.

troubler [tʀuble] [1] 1 **vt** a (*perturber*) *ordre* to disturb, disrupt; *sommeil, tranquillité, silence* to disturb; *représentation, réunion* to disrupt; *jugement, raison, esprit* to cloud. **~ l'ordre public** to disturb public order, cause a breach of public order, disturb the peace; **en ces temps troublés** in these troubled times.

b *personne* (*démonter, impressionner*) to disturb, disconcert; (*inquiéter*) to trouble, perturb; (*gêner, embrouiller*) to bother, confuse; (*d'émoi amoureux*) to disturb, agitate, arouse. **ce film/cet événement l'a profondément troublé** this film/event has disturbed him deeply; **la perspective d'un échec ne le trouble pas du tout** the prospect of failure doesn't perturb *ou* trouble him in the slightest; **il y a quand même un détail qui me trouble** there's still a detail which is bothering *ou* confusing me; **cesse de parler, tu me troubles (dans mes calculs)** stop talking — you are disturbing me *ou* putting me off (in my calculations); **~ un candidat** to disconcert a candidate, put a candidate off; **~ (les sens de) qn** to disturb *ou* agitate sb.

c (*brouiller*) *eau* to make cloudy *ou* muddy *ou* turbid (*littér*); *vin* to cloud, make cloudy; *atmosphère* to cloud; *ciel* to darken, cloud; (*TV*) *image* to upset, disturb. **les larmes lui troublaient la vue** tears clouded *ou* blurred her vision.

2 **se troubler vpr** a (*devenir trouble*) *[eau]* to cloud, become cloudy *ou* muddy *ou* turbid (*littér*); *[temps]* to become cloudy *ou* overcast; *[ciel]* to become cloudy *ou* overcast, darken.

b (*perdre contenance*) to become flustered. **il se trouble facilement aux examens/lorsqu'il a à parler** he is easily flustered *ou* disconcerted in exams/when he has to speak; **il répondit sans se ~** he replied unperturbed.

troué, e [tʀue] (**ptp de trouer**) 1 **adj: bas/sac ~** stocking/bag with a hole *ou* with holes in it; **avoir un bas (de) ~** to have a hole in one's stocking, have a stocking with a hole in it; **ce sac est ~** this bag has a hole *ou* holes (in it); **une veste toute ~e** a jacket that is full of holes; **ses chaussettes sont toutes ~es** *ou* **~es de partout** his socks are full of holes; **ce seau est ~ de partout** *ou* **comme une passoire** *ou* **comme une écumoire** this bucket has a bottom like a sieve *ou* colander, this bucket has as many holes in it as a sieve *ou* colander; **corps ~ comme une passoire** *ou* **écumoire** body riddled with bullets; **son gant ~ laissait passer son pouce** his thumb stuck *ou* poked out through a hole in his glove.

2 **trouée nf** a *[haie, forêt, nuages]* gap, break (*de* in).

b (*Mil*) breach. **faire une ~e** to make a breach, break through.

c (*Géog: défilé*) gap. **la ~e de Belfort** the Belfort Gap.

trouer [tʀue] [1] **vt** a *vêtement* to make *ou* wear a hole in; *ticket* to punch (a hole in); (*transpercer*) to pierce. **il a troué son pantalon** (*avec une cigarette*) he's burnt a hole in his trousers; (*dans les ronces*) he's torn *ou* ripped a hole in his trousers; (*par usure*) he's worn a hole in his trousers; **ces chaussettes se sont trouées très vite** these socks soon got holes in them *ou* soon went into holes (*Brit*); **~ qch de part en part** to pierce sth through, pierce a hole right through sth; **la poitrine trouée d'une balle** his chest pierced by a bullet; **~ la peau à qn‡** to put a bullet into sb*; **se faire ~ la peau‡** to get a bullet in one's hide*.

b (*fig: traverser*) *silence, nuit* to pierce. **une fusée troua l'obscurité** a rocket pierced the darkness; **le soleil troue les nuages** the sun breaks through the clouds.

c (*fig: parsemer: gén ptp*) to dot. **la plaine trouée d'ombres** the plain dotted with shadows.

troufignon‡† [tʀufiɲɔ̃] **nm** backside‡, arse** (*Brit*), ass** (*US*).

troufion* [tʀufjɔ̃] **nm** soldier. **quand j'étais ~** when I was in the army *ou* a soldier.

trouillard, e‡ [tʀujaʀ, aʀd] (*péj*) 1 **adj** yellow*, chicken* (*attrib*), yellow-bellied‡. 2 **nm,f** yellowbelly‡.

trouille‡ [tʀuj] **nf: avoir la ~** to be in a (blue) funk‡ (*Brit*), have the wind up* (*Brit*), be scared to death; **j'ai eu la ~ de ma vie** I got the fright of my life *ou* a hell of a fright*; **flanquer** *ou* **ficher la ~ à qn** to put the wind up sb* (*Brit*), scare the pants off sb‡.

trouillomètre‡ [tʀujɔmɛtʀ] **nm: avoir le ~ à zéro** to be in a blue funk‡ (*Brit*), be scared witless*.

troupe [tʀup] **nf** a (*Mil, Scoutisme*) troop. (*Mil*) **la ~** (*l'armée*) the army; (*les simples soldats*) the troops (*pl*), the rank and file; **les ~s** the troops; **~s de choc/de débarquement** shock/landing troops; **lever des ~s** to raise troops; **faire intervenir la ~** to call *ou* bring in the army; **réservé à la ~** reserved for the troops; **il y avait de la ~ cantonnée au village** there were some army units billeted in the village; *voir* **enfant, homme**. b *[chanteurs, danseurs]* troupe. *[acteurs]* **~ (de théâtre)** (theatrical) company. c *[gens, animaux]* band, group, troop. **se déplacer en ~** to go about in a band *ou* group *ou* troop.

troupeau, pl ~x [tʀupo] **nm** *[bœufs, chevaux]* (*dans un pré*) herd; (*transhumant*) drove; *[moutons, chèvres]* flock; *[éléphants, buffles, girafes]* herd; *[oies]* gaggle; (*péj*) *[touristes, prisonniers]* herd (*péj*). (*Rel*) **le ~ du Seigneur** the Lord's flock.

troupiale [tʀupjal] **nm** (*oiseau*) troupial.

troupier [tʀupje] 1 **nm** (†) private. 2 **adj** *voir* **comique**.

trousse [tʀus] **nf** a (*étui*) (*gén*) case, kit; *[médecin, chirurgien]* instrument case; *[écolier]* pencil case *ou* wallet. **~ à aiguilles** needle case; **~ à couture** sewing case *ou* kit; **~ de maquillage** (*mallette*) vanity case *ou* bag; (*sac*) make-up bag; **~ à outils** toolkit; **~ à ongles** nail kit, manicure set; **~ de toilette** *ou* **de voyage** (*sac*) toilet bag, sponge bag; (*mallette*) travelling case, grip. b (*loc*) **aux ~s de** (hot) on the heels of, on the tail of; **les créanciers/policiers étaient à ses ~s** the creditors/policemen were on his tail *ou* (hot) on his heels; **avoir la police aux ~s** to have the police on one's tail *ou* (hot) on one's heels.

trousseau, pl ~x [tʀuso] **nm** a **~ de clefs** bunch of keys. b (*vêtements, linge*) *[mariée]* trousseau; *[écolier]* outfit.

troussequin [tʀuskɛ̃] **nm** a (*Équitation*) cantle. b (*outil*) = **trusquin**.

trousser [tʀuse] [1] **vt** a (*Culin*) *volaille* to truss. b (†: *retrousser*) *robe, jupes* to pick *ou* tuck up. **se ~** to pick *ou* tuck up one's skirts. c (†, *hum*) *femme* to tumble†. d (†: *expédier*) *poème, article, discours* to dash off, throw together. **compliment bien troussé** well-phrased compliment.

trousseur [tʀusœʀ] **nm** (†, *hum*) **~ de jupons** womanizer, ladykiller.

trouvaille [tʀuvaj] **nf** (*objet*) find; (*fig: idée, métaphore, procédé*) brainwave, stroke of inspiration; (*mot*) coinage. (*iro*) **quelle est sa dernière ~?** what's his latest brainwave?

trouver [tʀuve] [1] 1 **vt** a (*en cherchant*) *objet, emploi, main-d'œuvre, renseignement* to find. **je ne le trouve pas** I can't find it; **où peut-on le ~?** where can he be found?, where is he to be found?; **on lui a trouvé une place dans un lycée** he was found a place in a lycée, they found him a place *ou* a place for him in a lycée; **est-ce qu'ils trouveront le chemin?** will they find the way? *ou* their way?; **~ le temps/l'énergie/le courage de faire qch** to find (the) time/the energy/the courage to do sth; **~ refuge** *ou* **asile/faveur auprès de qn** to find refuge/favour with sb; **comment avez-vous trouvé un secrétaire si compétent?** how did you come by *ou* find such a competent secretary?; **elle a trouvé en lui un ami sûr/un associé compétent** she has found in him a faithful friend/a competent partner; *voir* **chercher, enfant, objet**.

b (*rendre visite*) **aller/venir ~ qn** to go/come and see sb.

c (*rencontrer par hasard*) *document, information, personne* to find, come upon, come across; *difficultés* to meet with, come across, come up against. **on trouve cette plante** *ou* **cette plante se trouve sous tous les climats humides** this plant is found *ou* is to be found in all damp climates.

d (*imaginer, inventer*) *solution, prétexte, cause, moyen* to find, think out. (*énigme*) **comment as-tu fait pour ~?** how did you manage to find out?, how did you work it out?; **j'ai trouvé!** I've got it!*; **c'est tout trouvé** it's quite simple *ou* straightforward; **formule bien trouvée** clever *ou* happy phrase; (*iro*) **tu as trouvé ça tout seul!** did you think it out all by yourself? (*iro*); **où est-il allé ~ ça?** where (on earth) did he get that idea from?, whatever gave him that idea?

e (*avec à + infin*) **~ à redire (à tout)** to find fault with everything, find something to criticize (in everything); **on ne peut rien ~ à redire là-dessus** there's nothing to say *ou* you can say to that; **~ à manger/à boire** to find something to eat/to drink; **elle trouve toujours à faire dans la maison** she can always find something to do in the house; **~ à se distraire/à s'occuper** to find a way to amuse/occupy o.s., find something to amuse/occupy o.s. with; **ils trouveront bien à les loger quelque part** they will surely find a way to put them up somewhere, they will surely find somewhere to put them up.

f (*éprouver*) **~ du plaisir à qch/à faire qch** to take pleasure in sth/in doing sth; ~ **un malin plaisir à taquiner qn** to get a mischievous pleasure out of teasing sb, take a mischievous pleasure in teasing sb, derive a mischievous pleasure from teasing sb; ~ **de la difficulté à faire** to find *ou* have difficulty (in) doing; ~ **une consolation dans le travail** to find consolation in work *ou* in working.

g (*avec attribut du complément*) (*découvrir*) to find; (*penser*) to think. ~ **qch cassé/vide** to find sth broken/empty; (*estimer, juger*) ~ **qch à son goût/trop cher** to find sth to one's liking/too expensive; (*fig*) **j'ai trouvé les oiseaux envolés** I found the birds had flown; ~ **porte close** to find nobody at home *ou* in; **je l'ai trouvée en train de pleurer** I found her crying; ~ **que** to find *ou* think that; **tu ne trouves pas que j'ai raison?** don't you think I'm right?; **je trouve cela trop sucré/lourd** I find it too sweet/heavy, it's too sweet/heavy for me; **elle trouve qu'il fait trop chaud ici** she finds it too hot (in) here; **je le trouve fatigué** I think he looks tired, I find him tired-looking, I find him looking tired; **tu lui trouves bonne mine?** do you think he's looking well?; **comment l'as-tu trouvé?** what did you think of him?, how did you find him?; **vous la trouvez sympathique?** do you like her?, do you think she's nice?, do you find her a nice person?; **on ne lui trouve que des qualités** he has only virtues *ou* good qualities; **trouvez-vous cela normal?** do you think that's as it should be?; **tu trouves ça drôle!** *ou* **que c'est drôle!** so you think that's funny!, so you find that funny!; **vous trouvez?** (do) you think so?; **il a trouvé bon de nous écrire** he thought *ou* saw fit to write to us; ~ **le temps court/long** to find that time passes quickly *ou* races on/passes slowly *ou* hangs heavy *ou* heavily on one's hands.

h (*loc*) ~ **grâce auprès** *ou* **aux yeux de qn** to find favour with sb; **il a trouvé à qui parler** he met his match; **il va** ~ **à qui parler** he'll get more than he bargained for; ~ **son maître** to find one's master; **cet objet n'avait pas trouvé d'amateur** no one had expressed *ou* shown any interest in the object; **cet objet n'avait pas trouvé preneur** the object had had no takers; ~ **la mort (dans un accident)** to meet one's death (in an accident); **je la trouve mauvaise!*** *ou* **saumâtre!*** I think it's a bit off* (*Brit*), I don't like it at all; (*hum*) **trouvez-vous votre bonheur** *ou* **votre vie dans ce bric-à-brac?** can you find what you're after *ou* what you're looking for in this jumble?; **ne pas** ~ **ses mots** to be at a loss for words; ~ **le sommeil** to get to sleep, fall asleep; ~ **chaussure à son pied** to find a suitable match; (*fig*) ~ **le joint*** to come up with a solution, find an answer *ou* a way out; **il a trouvé son compte dans cette affaire** he got something out of this bit of business; (*lit*) ~ **le moyen de faire** to find some means of doing; (*fig hum*) **il a trouvé le moyen de s'égarer** he managed *ou* contrived to get (himself) lost.

2 **se trouver** *vpr* a (*être dans une situation*) *[personne]* to find o.s.; *[chose]* to be. **il se trouva nez à nez avec Paul** he found himself face to face with Paul; **la question se trouva reléguée au second plan** the question was relegated to the background; **la voiture se trouva coincée entre ...** the car was jammed between ...; **je me suis trouvé dans l'impossibilité de répondre** I found myself unable to reply; **nous nous trouvons dans une situation délicate** we are in a delicate situation; **il se trouve dans l'impossibilité de venir** he is unable to come, he is not in a position to come; **il se trouve dans l'obligation de partir** he has to *ou* is compelled to leave; **et tu te trouves malin** *ou* **intelligent!/spirituel!** I suppose you think that's clever!/funny!; **et tu te trouves beau!** I suppose you think you look good!; (*iro*) **je me suis trouvé fin!** a fine *ou* right* fool I looked!

b (*être situé*) *[personne]* to be; *[chose]* to be, be situated. **ça ne se trouve pas sur la carte** it isn't *ou* doesn't appear on the map; **son nom ne se trouve pas sur la liste** his name is not on *ou* does not appear on the list; **je me trouvais près de l'entrée** I was (standing *ou* sitting *etc*) near the entrance; **il ne fait pas bon se** ~ **dehors par ce froid** it's not pleasant to be out in this cold; **la maison se trouve au coin de la rue** the house is (situated) *ou* stands on the corner of the street; **où se trouve la poste?** where is the post office?; **les toilettes se trouvent près de l'entrée** the toilets are (situated) near the entrance; **ça ne se trouve pas sous le pas** *ou* **le sabot d'un cheval** it's not easy to find *ou* to come by.

c (*se sentir*) to feel. **se** ~ **bien** (*dans un fauteuil etc*) to feel comfortable; (*santé*) to feel well; **il se trouve mieux en montagne** he feels better in the mountains; **elle se trouvait bien dans ce pays** she was happy in this country; **se** ~ **mal** to faint, pass out; **se** ~ **bien/mal d'avoir fait qch** to have reason to be glad/to regret having done sth; **il s'en est bien trouvé** he benefited from it; **il s'en est mal trouvé** he lived to regret it.

d (*avec infin: exprime la coïncidence*) **se** ~ **être/avoir ...** to happen to be/have ...; **elles se trouvaient avoir le même chapeau** it turned out that they had *ou* they happened to have the same hat.

e (*en méditant etc*) **essayer de se** ~ to try to find o.s.

3 **se trouver** *vpr impers* a (*le fait est*) **il se trouve que c'est moi** it happens to be me, it's me as it happens; **il se trouvait que j'étais là** I happened to be there; **il se trouvait qu'elle avait menti** it turned out that she had been lying; **comme il se trouve parfois/souvent** as is sometimes/often the case, as sometimes/often happens; **et s'il se trouve qu'elles ne viennent pas?** and what if *ou* and suppose *ou* supposing they don't come?

b (*il y a*) **il se trouve toujours des gens qui disent ...** *ou* **pour dire ...** there are always people *ou* you'll always find people who will say ... .

c (*) **ils sont sortis, si ça se trouve** they may well be out, they're probably out; **si ça se trouve, il ne viendra pas** it's quite likely he won't come.

trouvère [truvɛr] *nm* trouvère.

troy [trɔj] *nm*: **le système** ~ the troy system.

troyen, -enne [trwajɛ̃, ɛn] 1 *adj* Trojan. 2 *nm,f*: **T~(ne)** Trojan.

truand, e [tryɑ̃, ɑ̃d] 1 *nm* (*gangster*) gangster, mobster (*US*); (*escroc*) crook. 2 *nm,f* (†: *mendiant*) beggar.

truander⁑ [tryɑ̃de] [1] 1 *vt* to swindle, do⁑. **se faire** ~ to be swindled *ou* done⁑. 2 *vi* to cheat (*à* at).

trublion [tryblijɔ̃] *nm* troublemaker, agitator.

truc¹ [tryk] *nm* a (*) (*moyen, combine*) way, trick; (*dispositif*) thingummy*, whatsit*. **il a trouvé le** ~ **(pour le faire)** he's found the way (of doing it), he's got the trick (of doing it); **il n'a pas encore compris le** ~ he's not yet grasped *ou* learnt the trick; **avoir le** ~ to have the knack; **cherche un** ~ **pour venir me voir** try to wangle coming to see me*, try to find some way of coming to see me; **c'est connu leur** ~*, **on le connaît leur** ~* we know what they're up to* *ou* playing at*, we're onto their little game*; **les ~s du métier** the tricks of the trade.

b (*tour*) *[prestidigitateur]* trick; (*trucage: Ciné etc*) trick, effect. **c'est impressionnant mais ce n'est qu'un** ~ it's impressive but it's only a trick *ou* an effect; **il y a un** ~! there's a trick in it!

c (*: *chose, idée*) thing. **on m'a raconté un** ~ **extraordinaire** I've been told an extraordinary thing; **j'ai pensé (à) un** ~ I've thought of something, I've had a thought; **il y a un tas de ~s à faire** there's a heap of things to do*; **il n'y a pas un** ~ **de vrai là-dedans** there's not a word of truth in it; **le ski, c'est pas mon** ~* skiing's not my thing*.

d (*: *machin*) (*dont le nom échappe*) thingumajig*, thingummy*, whatsit*; (*inconnu, jamais vu*) contraption, thing, thingumajig*; (*tableau, statue bizarre*) thing. **méfie-toi de ces ~s-là** be careful of *ou* beware of those things.

e (⁑: *personne*) **T~ (Chouette), Machin T~** what's-his-(*ou* her-) name*, what-d'you-call-him* (*ou* -her), thingummybob*.

truc² [tryk] *nm* (*Rail*) truck, waggon.

trucage [trykaʒ] *nm* = **truquage**.

truchement [tryʃmɑ̃] *nm* a **par le** ~ **de qn** through (the intervention of) sb; **par le** ~ **de qch** with the aid of sth. b (††, *littér: moyen d'expression, intermédiaire*) medium, means of expression.

trucider* [tryside] [1] *vt* (*hum*) to knock off⁑, bump off⁑.

truck [tryk] *nm* = **truc²**.

trucmuche⁑ [trykmyʃ] *nm* thingumajig*, thingummybob*, whatsit*.

truculence [trykylɑ̃s] *nf* (*voir* **truculent**) vividness; colourfulness; raciness. **la** ~ **de ce personnage** the liveliness *ou* verve of this character.

truculent, e [trykylɑ̃, ɑ̃t] *adj langage* vivid, colourful, racy; *personnage* colourful, larger-than-life (*épith*), larger than life (*attrib*).

truelle [tryɛl] *nf [maçon]* trowel. (*Culin*) ~ **à poisson** fish slice.

truffe [tryf] *nf* a (*Bot*) truffle. ~ **noire/blanche** black/white truffle. b (*Culin*) ~**s (au chocolat)** (chocolate) truffles. c (*nez du chien*) nose; (*: *nez*) conk* (*Brit*), hooter* (*Brit*). d (*: *idiot*) nitwit*, twit*.

truffer [tryfe] [1] *vt* a (*Culin*) to garnish with truffles. b (*fig: remplir*) ~ **qch de** to pepper sth with; **truffé de citations** peppered *ou* larded with quotations; **truffé de pièges** bristling with traps; **truffé de fautes** packed full of mistakes, riddled with mistakes.

truffier, -ière [tryfje, jɛr] *adj région* truffle (*épith*); *chêne* truffle-producing. **chien** ~ truffle hound.

truie [trɥi] *nf* (*Zool*) sow.

truisme [tryism] *nm* (*littér*) truism.

truite [trɥit] *nf* trout (*pl inv*). ~ **saumonée** salmon trout; ~ **de mer** sea trout; ~ **arc-en-ciel** rainbow trout; (*Culin*) ~ **meunière** truite *ou* trout meunière.

truité, e [trɥite] *adj* a (*tacheté*) *cheval* mottled, speckled; *chien* spotted, speckled. b (*craquelé*) *porcelaine* crackled.

trumeau, *pl* ~**x** [trymo] *nm* a (*pilier*) pier; (*entre portes, fenêtres*) pier; (*panneau ou glace*) pier glass; *[cheminée]* overmantel. b (*Culin*) shin of beef.

truquage [trykaʒ] *nm* a (*action: voir* **truquer**) rigging; fixing*; adapting; doctoring*; fiddling*; faking. (*Ciné*) **le** ~ **d'une scène** using special effects in a scene. b (*Ciné*) **un** ~ **très réussi** a very successful effect; ~**s optiques** optical effects *ou* illusions; ~**s de laboratoire** lab effects.

truqué, e [tryke] (*ptp de* **truquer**) *adj élections* rigged; *combat* fixed*; *cartes, dés* fixed*. (*Ciné*) **une scène** ~**e** a scene involving special effects.

truquer [tryke] [1] *vt* a *élections* to rig, fix*; (*gén ptp*) *combat* to fix. (*Ciné*) ~ **une scène** to use special effects in a scene. b *serrure, verrou* to adapt, fix*; *cartes, dés* to fix*. c (†: *falsifier*) *dossier* to doctor*; *comptes* to fiddle*; *œuvre d'art, meuble* to fake.

truqueur, -euse [trykœr, øz] *nm,f* a (*fraudeur*) cheat. b (*Ciné*) special effects man (*ou* woman).

truquiste [trykist(ə)] *nm* = **truqueur b**.

trusquin [tryskɛ̃] *nm* marking gauge.

trust [trœst] *nm* (*Écon: cartel*) trust; (*toute grande entreprise*) corporation; *voir* **antitrust**.

truster [trœste] [1] *vt* (*Écon*) *secteur du marché* to monopolize, corner;

produit to have the monopoly of, monopolize; (**: accaparer*) to monopolize. **ils ont trusté les médailles aux derniers Jeux olympiques** they carried off all the medals *ou* they made a clean sweep of the medals at the last Olympic Games.

trypanosome [tʀipanozom] **nm** trypanosom.

trypanosomiase [tʀipanozomjɑz] **nf** trypanosomiasis.

TSA [teɛsa] **nf** (**abrév de technologie des systèmes automatisés**) *voir* **technologie**.

tsar [dzaʀ] **nm** tsar, czar, tzar.

tsarévitch [dzaʀevitʃ] **nm** tsarevich, czarevich, tzarevich.

tsarine [dzaʀin] **nf** tsarina, czarina, tzarina.

tsarisme [dzaʀism] **nm** tsarism, czarism, tzarism.

tsariste [dzaʀist] **adj** tsarist, czarist, tzarist.

tsé-tsé [tsetse] **nf**: **(mouche)** ~ tsetse fly.

TSF† [teɛsɛf] **nf** (**abrév de télégraphie sans fil**) (*procédé*) wireless telegraphy; (*radio*) wireless, radio; (*poste*) wireless. **à la** ~ on the radio *ou* wireless.

T(-)shirt [tiʃœʀt] **nm** = **tee(-)shirt**.

tsigane [tsigan] 1 **adj** (Hungarian) gypsy *ou* gipsy, tzigane. **violoniste/musique** ~ (Hungarian) gypsy violinist/music. 2 **nmf**: **T~** (Hungarian) Gypsy *ou* Gipsy, Tzigane.

tsoin-tsoin‡, tsouin-tsouin‡ [tswɛ̃tswɛ̃] **excl** boom-boom!

tss-tss [tsts] **excl** tut-tut!

TSVP (**abrév de tournez s'il vous plaît**) PTO.

TTC [tetese] (**abrév de toutes taxes comprises**) *voir* **taxe**.

tu, t'* [ty, t] 1 **pron pers** you (*as opposed to "vous": familiar form of address*); (*Rel*) thou. **t'as* de la chance** you're lucky. 2 **nm**: **employer le** ~ to use the "tu" form; **dire** ~ **à qn** to address sb as "tu"; **être à** ~ **et à toi avec qn** to be on first-name terms with sb, be a great pal of sb*.

TU [tey] **nm** (**abrév de temps universel**) *voir* **temps**.

tuant, tuante [tɥɑ̃, tɥɑ̃t] **adj** (*fatigant*) killing, exhausting; (*énervant*) exasperating, tiresome.

tub [tœb] **nm** (*bassin*) (bath)tub; (*bain*) bath.

tuba [tyba] **nm** (*Mus*) tuba; (*Sport*) snorkel, breathing tube. ~ **d'orchestre** bass tuba.

tubage [tybaʒ] **nm** (*Méd*) intubation, cannulation.

tubaire [tybɛʀ] **adj** (*Méd*) tubal.

tubard, e‡ [tybaʀ, aʀd] (*péj*) (**abrév de tuberculeux**) 1 **adj** suffering from TB. 2 **nm,f** TB case.

tube [tyb] **nm** a (*tuyau*) (*gén, de mesure, en verre*) tube; (*de canalisation, tubulure, métallique*) pipe. ~ **capillaire** capillary tube; ~ **compte-gouttes** pipette; ~ **à essai** test tube; (*TV*) **~-image** cathode ray tube; ~ **à injection** hypodermic syringe; (*Mil*) ~ **lance-torpilles** torpedo tube; (*Élec*) ~ **au néon** neon tube; (*Élec*) ~ **redresseur** vacuum diode; ~ **régulateur de potentiel** triode; (*Élec, TV, Ordin*) ~ **cathodique** cathode ray tube; ~ **à vide** vacuum valve *ou* tube.

b (*emballage*) *[aspirine, comprimés, dentifrice etc]* tube. ~ **de rouge (à lèvres)** lipstick.

c (*Anat, Bot: conduit*) ~ **digestif** digestive tract, alimentary canal; **~s urinifères** uriniferous tubules; ~ **pollinique** pollen tube.

d (**: chanson à succès*) hit.

e (*vêtement*) **jupe** ~ tube skirt; **pull** ~ skinny-rib (sweater *ou* jumper).

f (**†: téléphone*) **donner un coup de** ~ **à qn** to give sb a buzz* *ou* a tinkle*.

g (*†*: haut-de-forme*) topper*.

h (*loc*) *[moteur]* **marcher à pleins ~s*** to be running full throttle *ou* at maximum revs; (*fig*) **délirer à pleins ~s*** to be raving mad*, be off one's head* *ou* rocker‡.

tubeless [tyblɛs] **adj inv, nm inv (pneu)** ~ tubeless tyre (*Brit*) *ou* tire (*US*).

tubercule [tybɛʀkyl] **nm** (*Anat, Méd*) tubercle; (*Bot*) tuber.

tuberculeux, -euse [tybɛʀkylø, øz] 1 **adj** a (*Méd*) tuberculous, tubercular. **être** ~ to suffer from tuberculosis *ou* TB, have tuberculosis *ou* TB. b (*Bot*) tuberous, tuberose. 2 **nm,f** tuberculosis *ou* tubercular *ou* TB patient.

tuberculine [tybɛʀkylin] **nf** tuberculin.

tuberculinique [tybɛʀkylinik] **adj** *test* tuberculinic, tuberculin.

tuberculose [tybɛʀkyloz] **nf** tuberculosis. ~ **pulmonaire** pulmonary tuberculosis; ~ **osseuse** tuberculosis of the bones.

tubéreux, -euse [tybeʀø, øz] 1 **adj** tuberous. 2 **tubéreuse nf** (*Bot*) tuberose.

tubérosité [tybeʀozite] **nf** (*Anat*) tuberosity.

tubulaire [tybylɛʀ] **adj** tubular.

tubulé, e [tybyle] **adj** *plante* tubulate; *flacon* tubulated.

tubuleux, -euse [tybylø, øz] **adj** tubulous, tubulate.

tubulure [tybylyʀ] **nf** a (*tube*) pipe. b (*Tech: ouverture*) tubulure. (*tubes*) **~s** piping; (*Aut*) ~ **d'échappement/d'admission** exhaust/inlet manifold; ~ **d'alimentation** feed *ou* supply pipe.

TUC [tyk] 1 **nmpl** (**abrév de travaux d'utilité collective**) *voir* **travail**. 2 **nmf** = **tuciste**.

tuciste [tysist] **nmf** (paid) community worker (*otherwise unemployed*), ≃ employment trainee (*Brit*), ≃ YTS trainee (*Brit*).

tudieu†† [tydjø] **excl** zounds!††, 'sdeath!††

tué, e [tɥe] (**ptp de tuer**) **nm,f** (*dans un accident, au combat*) person killed. **les ~s** the dead, those killed; **il y a eu 5 ~s et 4 blessés** there were 5 (people) killed *ou* 5 dead and 4 injured.

tue-mouche [tymuʃ] 1 **nm inv** (*Bot*) **(amanite)** ~ fly agaric. 2 **adj**: **papier** *ou* **ruban ~(s)** flypaper.

tuer [tɥe] [1] 1 **vt** a *personne, animal* to kill; (*à la chasse*) to shoot. (*Bible*) **tu ne tueras point** thou shalt not kill; ~ **qn à coups de pierre/de couteau** to stone/stab *ou* knife sb to death; ~ **qn d'une balle** to shoot sb dead; **l'alcool tue** alcohol can kill *ou* is a killer; **la route tue** the highway is deadly *ou* is a killer; **cet enfant me tuera** this child will be the death of me; **la honte/le déshonneur la tuerait** the shame/dishonour would kill her; (*fig*) **il est à ~!** you (*ou* I) could kill him!; **il n'a jamais tué personne!** he wouldn't hurt a fly, he's quite harmless; **quelle odeur! ça tue les mouches à 15 pas!*** what a stink!* it would kill a man at 15 paces!; (*fig*) **un coup** *ou* **une gifle à** ~ **un bœuf** a blow to fell an ox; ~ **la poule aux œufs d'or/le veau gras** to kill the goose that lays the golden eggs/the fatted calf.

b (*ruiner*) to kill; (*exténuer*) to exhaust, wear out. **la bureaucratie tue toute initiative** bureaucracy kills (off) all initiative; **les supermarchés n'ont pas tué le petit commerce** supermarkets have not killed off small traders; **ce rouge tue tout leur décor** this red kills (the effect of) their whole decor; **ces escaliers/ces querelles me tuent** these stairs/quarrels will be the death of me; ~ **qch dans l'œuf** to nip sth in the bud; ~ **le temps** to kill time.

2 **se tuer vpr** a (*accident*) to be killed. **il s'est tué en montagne/en voiture** he was killed in a mountaineering/car accident.

b (*suicide*) to kill o.s. **il s'est tué d'une balle dans la tête** he put a bullet through his head, he killed himself with a bullet through his *ou* the head.

c (*fig*) **se** ~ **à la peine** *ou* **à la tâche** *ou* **au travail** to work o.s. to death, kill o.s. with work; **se** ~ **à répéter/à essayer de faire comprendre qch à qn** to wear o.s. out repeating sth to sb/trying to make sb understand sth.

tuerie [tyʀi] **nf** (*carnage*) slaughter, carnage.

tue-tête [tytɛt] **adv**: **crier/chanter à** ~ to shout/sing at the top of one's voice, shout/sing one's head off*.

tueur, tueuse [tɥœʀ, tɥøz] 1 **nm,f** a (*assassin*) killer. ~ **(à gages)** hired *ou* professional killer, contract killer, hitman*. b (*chasseur*) ~ **de lions/d'éléphants** lion-/elephant-killer. 2 **nm** (*d'abattoir*) slaughterman, slaughterer.

tuf [tyf] **nm** (*Géol*) (*volcanique*) tuff; (*calcaire*) tufa.

tuile [tɥil] **nf** a (*lit*) tile. ~ **creuse** *ou* **romaine** *ou* **ronde** curved tile; ~ **faîtière** ridge tile; **~s mécaniques** industrial *ou* interlocking tiles; **couvrir un toit de ~s** to tile a roof; **~s de pierre/d'ardoise** stone/slate tiles; **nous préférons la** ~ **à l'ardoise** we prefer tiles to slate. b (**: coup de malchance*) blow. **quelle ~!** what a blow! c (*Culin*) (thin sweet) biscuit.

tuilerie [tɥilʀi] **nf** (*fabrique*) tilery; (*four*) tilery, tile kiln.

tuilier, -ière [tɥilje, jɛʀ] 1 **adj** tile (*épith*). 2 **nm,f** tile maker *ou* manufacturer.

tulipe [tylip] **nf** (*Bot*) tulip; (*ornement*) tulip-shaped glass (*ou* lamp *etc*).

tulipier [tylipje] **nm** tulip tree.

tulle [tyl] **nm** tulle. **robe de** ~ tulle dress; (*Méd*) ~ **gras** sofra-tulle.

tuméfaction [tymefaksjɔ̃] **nf** (*effet*) swelling *ou* puffing up, tumefaction (*SPÉC*); (*partie tuméfiée*) swelling.

tuméfier [tymefje] [7] 1 **vt** to cause to swell, tumefy (*SPÉC*). **visage/œil tuméfié** puffed-up *ou* swollen face/eye. 2 **se tuméfier vpr** to swell *ou* puff up, tumefy (*SPÉC*).

tumescence [tymesɑ̃s] **nf** tumescence.

tumescent, e [tymesɑ̃, ɑ̃t] **adj** tumescent.

tumeur [tymœʀ] **nf** tumour (*de* of), growth (*de* in). ~ **bénigne/maligne** benign/malignant tumour; ~ **au cerveau** brain tumour.

tumoral, e, mpl -aux [tymɔʀal, o] **adj** tumorous, tumoral.

tumulte [tymylt] **nm** a (*bruit*) *[foule]* commotion; *[voix]* hubbub; *[acclamations]* thunder, tumult. **un** ~ **d'applaudissements** thunderous applause, a thunder of applause; (*littér*) **le** ~ **des flots/de l'orage** the tumult of the waves/of the storm. b (*agitation*) *[affaires]* hurly-burly; *[passions]* turmoil, tumult; *[rue, ville]* hustle and bustle (*de* in, of), commotion (*de* in).

tumultueusement [tymyltɥøzmɑ̃] **adv** (*voir* **tumultueux**) stormily; turbulently; tumultuously.

tumultueux, -euse [tymyltɥø, øz] **adj** *séance* stormy, turbulent, tumultuous; *foule* turbulent, agitated; (*littér*) *flots, bouillonnement* turbulent; *vie, période* stormy, turbulent; *passion* tumultuous, turbulent.

tumulus [tymylys] **nm** burial mound, tumulus (*SPÉC*), barrow (*SPÉC*).

tuner [tynɛʀ] **nm** (*amplificateur*) tuner.

tungstène [tœ̃kstɛn] **nm** tungsten, wolfram.

tunique [tynik] **nf** a *[soldat, écolier]* tunic; *[prêtre]* tunicle, tunic; *[femme]* (*droite*) tunic; (*à forme ample*) smock; (*longue*) gown; (*de gymnastique*) gym-slip. b (*Anat*) tunic, tunica; (*Bot*) tunic. ~ **de l'œil** tunica albuginea of the eye.

Tunis [tynis] **n** Tunis.

Tunisie [tynizi] **nf** Tunisia.

tunisien, -ienne [tynizjɛ̃, jɛn] 1 **adj** Tunisian. 2 **nmf: T~(ne)** Tunisian.

tunnel [tynɛl] **nm** a (*lit, gén*) tunnel; (*Horticulture*) tunnel. **~ ferroviaire/routier** railway/road tunnel; **~ aérodynamique** wind tunnel; **le ~ sous la Manche** the Channel Tunnel, the Chunnel*. b (*fig*) tunnel. **arriver au bout** *ou* **voir le bout du ~** to come to the end of the tunnel.

tunnelier [tynəlje] **nm** (*ouvrier*) tunneller; (*machine*) mole.

TUP [typ] **nm** (**abrév de titre universel de paiement**) *voir* **titre**.

tuque [tyk] **nf** (*Can*) woollen cap, tuque (*Can*).

turban [tyʀbɑ̃] **nm** turban.

turbin‡ [tyʀbɛ̃] **nm** (*emploi*) job. **aller au ~** to go off to the daily grind*; **se remettre au ~** to get back to the slog* *ou* the grind*; **après le ~** after the day's grind*, after work.

turbine [tyʀbin] **nf** turbine. **~ hydraulique** water *ou* hydraulic turbine; **~ à réaction/à impulsion** reaction/impulse turbine; **~ à vapeur/à gaz** steam/gas turbine.

turbiner‡ [tyʀbine] [1] **vi** to graft (away)‡, slog away‡, slave away. **faire ~ qn** to make sb work, keep sb at it* *ou* with his nose to the grindstone*.

turbo [tyʀbo] **nm** (*Aut*) turbo. (*fig*) **mettre le ~*** to get a move on*, step on it*.

turbocompresseur [tyʀbokɔ̃pʀesœʀ] **nm** turbo-compressor.

turbodiesel [tyʀbodjezɛl] **adj, nm** turbodiesel.

turbomoteur [tyʀbomɔtœʀ] **nm** turbine engine.

turbopompe [tyʀbopɔ̃p] **nf** turbopump, turbine-pump.

turbopropulseur [tyʀbopʀɔpylsœʀ] **n** turboprop.

turboréacteur [tyʀboʀeaktœʀ] **nm** turbojet (engine).

turbot [tyʀbo] **nm** turbot.

turbotrain [tyʀbotʀɛ̃] **nm** turbotrain.

turbulence [tyʀbylɑ̃s] **nf** a (*agitation*) excitement. b (*dissipation*) rowdiness, boisterousness, unruliness. c (*Sci: remous*) turbulence (*NonC*). (*Aviat*) **il y a des ~s** there is (air) turbulence.

turbulent, e [tyʀbylɑ̃, ɑ̃t] **adj** a *enfant, élève* rowdy, unruly, boisterous. b (*littér: tumultueux*) *passion* turbulent, stormy; (*Sci*) turbulent.

turc, turque [tyʀk] 1 **adj** Turkish. **à la turque** *accroupi, assis* cross-legged; *cabinets* seatless; (*Mus*) alla turca; *voir* **bain, café, fort, tête.** 2 **nm** a (*personne*) **T~** Turk; (*fig*) **les jeunes T~s d'un parti** the Young Turks of a party. b (*Ling*) Turkish. 3 **nf: Turque** Turkish woman.

turf [tyʀf] **nm** (*terrain*) racecourse. (*activité*) **le ~** racing, the turf.

turfiste [tyʀfist] **nmf** racegoer.

turgescence [tyʀʒesɑ̃s] **nf** turgescence.

turgescent, e [tyʀʒesɑ̃, ɑ̃t] **adj** turgescent.

turgide [tyʀʒid] **adj** (*littér*) swollen.

Turin [tyʀɛ̃] **n** Turin.

turista* [tuʀista] **nf** ≃ Delhi belly*, ≃ Montezuma's revenge*.

turkmène [tyʀkmɛn] 1 **adj** Turkoman, Turkman. 2 **nm** (*Ling*) Turkmen, Turkoman, Turkman. 3 **nmf: T~** Turkoman, Turkman.

Turkménistan [tyʀkmenistɑ̃] **nm** Turkmenistan.

turlupiner* [tyʀlypine] [1] **vt** to bother, worry. **ce qui me turlupine** what bugs me* *ou* worries me.

turne [tyʀn] **nf** a († *péj: logement*) digs*. b (*Scol: chambre*) room.

turpitude [tyʀpityd] **nf** a (*caractère*) turpitude. b (*acte: gén pl*) base act.

turque [tyʀk] *voir* **turc**.

Turquie [tyʀki] **nf** Turkey.

turquoise [tyʀkwaz] **nf, adj inv** turquoise.

tutélaire [tytelɛʀ] **adj** (*littér: protecteur*) tutelary, protecting (*épith*); (*Jur: de la tutelle*) tutelary.

tutelle [tytɛl] **nf** a (*Jur*) *[mineur, aliéné]* guardianship. **avoir la ~ de qn, avoir qn en ~** to have the guardianship of sb; **mettre qn en ~** to put sb in the care of a guardian; **enfant en ~** child under guardianship.

b (*dépendance*) supervision; (*protection*) tutelage, protection. **sous (la) ~ américaine** under American supervision; **mettre sous ~** to put under supervision; **organisme de ~** parent organization; **sous ~ administrative/de l'État** under administrative/state supervision; **territoires sous ~** trust territories; **être sous la ~ de qn** (*dépendant*) to be under sb's supervision; (*protégé*) to be in sb's tutelage; **prendre qn sous sa ~** to take sb under one's wing.

tuteur, -trice [tytœʀ, tʀis] 1 **nm,f** (*Jur, fig littér: protecteur*) guardian. **~ légal/testamentaire** legal/testamentary guardian; **~ ad hoc** *specially appointed guardian.* 2 **nm** (*Agr*) stake, support, prop.

tuteurage [tytœʀaʒ] **nm** (*Agr*) staking.

tuteurer [tytœʀe] [1] **vt** (*Agr*) to stake (up).

tutoiement [tytwamɑ̃] **nm** use of (the familiar) "tu" (*instead of "vous"*).

tutorat [tytɔʀa] **nm** (*Scol*) pastoral care, guidance (teaching); (*Univ*) student counselling.

tutoyer [tytwaje] [8] **vt** a (*lit*) **~ qn** to use (the familiar) "tu" when speaking to sb, address sb as "tu" (*instead of "vous"*). b (*fig littér*) to be on familiar *ou* intimate terms with.

tutti quanti [tutikwɑ̃ti] **nmpl: et ~** and all the rest (of them), and all that lot* *ou* crowd*.

tutu [tyty] **nm** tutu, ballet skirt.

tuyau, **pl ~x** [tɥijo] 1 **nm** a (*gén, rigide*) pipe, length of piping; (*flexible, en caoutchouc, vendu au mètre*) length of rubber tubing, rubber tubing (*NonC*); *[pipe]* stem. (*fig*) **il me l'a dit dans le ~ de l'oreille*** he whispered it to me, he tipped me off about it.

b (*Habillement: pli*) flute.

c (*fig **) (*conseil*) tip; (*renseignement*) gen* (*NonC*). **quelques ~x pour le bricoleur** a few tips for the do-it-yourself enthusiast; **il nous a donné des ~x sur leurs activités/projets** he gave us some gen* on their activities/plans; **~ crevé** useless tip.

2 **comp** ►**tuyau d'alimentation** feeder pipe ►**tuyau d'arrosage** hosepipe, garden hose ►**tuyau de cheminée** chimney pipe *ou* flue ►**tuyau de descente** (*pluvial*) downpipe, fall pipe; *[lavabo, W.-C.]* wastepipe ►**tuyau d'échappement** exhaust (pipe) ►**tuyau d'orgue** (*Géol, Mus*) organ pipe ►**tuyau de poêle** stovepipe; (*† *fig*) **(chapeau en) tuyau de poêle** stovepipe hat ►**tuyau de pompe** pump pipe.

tuyautage [tɥijɔtaʒ] **nm** a *[linge]* fluting, goffering. b (*: *renseignement*) tipping off.

tuyauter [tɥijɔte] [1] **vt** a *linge* to flute, goffer. **un tuyauté** a fluted frill. b (*) **~ qn** (*conseiller*) to give sb a tip; (*mettre au courant*) to give sb some gen*, put sb in the know*, give sb the tip-off*.

tuyauterie [tɥijɔtʀi] **nf** *[machines, canalisations]* piping (*NonC*); *[orgue]* pipes.

tuyauteur, -euse* [tɥijɔtœʀ, øz] **nm,f** (*qui renseigne*) informant.

tuyère [tyjɛʀ] **nf** *[turbine]* nozzle; *[four, haut fourneau]* tuyère, twyer. **~ d'éjection** exhaust *ou* propulsion nozzle.

TV [teve] (**abrév de télévision**) TV.

TVA [tevea] **nf** (**abrév de taxe sur la valeur ajoutée**) VAT.

tweed [twid] **nm** tweed.

twist [twist] **nm** (*danse*) twist.

tympan [tɛ̃pɑ̃] **nm** a (*Anat*) eardrum, tympanum (*SPÉC*). **bruit à vous déchirer** *ou* **crever les ~s** earsplitting noise; *voir* **caisse.** b (*Archit*) tympan(um). c (*Tech: pignon*) pinion.

tympanique [tɛ̃panik] **adj** (*Anat*) tympanic.

tympanon [tɛ̃panɔ̃] **nm** (*Mus*) dulcimer.

type [tip] 1 **nm** a (*modèle*) type. **il y a plusieurs ~s de bicyclettes** there are several types of bicycle; **une pompe du ~ B5** a pump of type B5, a type B5 pump; **une pompe du ~ réglementaire** a regulation-type pump; **une voiture (de) ~ break** an estate-type (*Brit*) *ou* station-wagon-type (*US*) car; **des savanes (du) ~ jungle** jungle-type savannas; **certains ~s humains** certain human types; **avoir le ~ oriental/nordique** to be Oriental-/Nordic-looking, have Oriental/Nordic looks; **un beau ~ de femme/d'homme** a fine specimen of womanhood/manhood; **c'est le ~ d'homme à faire cela** he's the type *ou* sort of man who would do that; **ce** *ou* **il/elle n'est pas mon ~*** he/she is not my type *ou* sort.

b (*personne, chose: représentant*) classic example. **c'est le ~ (parfait** *ou* **même) de l'intellectuel/du vieux garçon** he's the epitome of *ou* he's the typical intellectual/old bachelor, he's a perfect *ou* classic example of the intellectual/old bachelor; **il s'était efforcé de créer un ~ de beauté** he had striven to create an ideal type of beauty; **c'est le ~ même de la machination politique** it's a classic example of political intrigue.

c (*: *individu*) guy*, chap*, bloke* (*Brit*); (†: *individu remarquable*) character; (*amant*) boyfriend. **quel sale ~!** what a rotter* *ou* swine‡ *ou* bastard‡ he is!; **c'est vraiment un ~!†** he's quite a character!

d (*Typ*) (*pièce, ensemble des caractères*) type; (*empreinte*) typeface; (*Numismatique*) type.

2 **adj inv** typical, classic; (*Statistique*) standard. **l'erreur/le politicien ~** the typical *ou* classic mistake/politician; (*Statistique*) **l'écart ~** the standard deviation; **l'exemple/la situation ~** the typical *ou* classic example/situation; **lettre/contrat ~** standard letter/contract; **un portrait ~ du Français** a picture of the classic *ou* typical Frenchman.

typer [tipe] [1] **vt** a (*caractériser*) **auteur/acteur qui type son personnage** author/actor who brings out the features of the character well; **un personnage bien typé** a character well rendered as a type; **il est japonais mais il n'est pas très typé** he's Japanese but he doesn't look very Japanese. b (*Tech*) stamp, mark.

typesse [tipɛs] **nf** (‡† *péj*) female* (*péj*).

typhique [tifik] **adj** (*du typhus*) typhous; (*de la typhoïde*) typhic. **bacille ~** typhoid bacillus.

typhoïde [tifɔid] **adj** typhoid. **la (fièvre) ~** typhoid (fever).

typhoïdique [tifɔidik] **adj** typhic.

typhon [tifɔ̃] **nm** typhoon.

typhus [tifys] **nm** typhus (fever).

typique [tipik] **adj** (*gén*) typical; (*Bio*) true to type. **~ de ...** typical of ...; **sa réaction est ~** his reaction is typical (of him) *ou* true to form *ou* type; **un cas ~ de ...** a typical case of ... .

typiquement [tipikmɑ̃] **adv** typically.

typo* [tipɔ] **nm** (**abrév de typographe**) typo*.

typographe [tipɔgʀaf] **nmf** (*gén*) typographer; (*compositeur à la main*) hand compositor.

typographie [tipɔgʀafi] **nf** a (*procédé d'impression*) letterpress (printing); (*opérations de composition, art*) typography. b (*aspect*) typography.

typographique [tipɔgʀafik] **adj** *procédé, impression* letterpress

(*épith*); *opérations, art* typographic(al). **erreur** *ou* **faute** ~ typographic(al) *ou* printer's error, misprint; **argot** ~ typographers' jargon; **cet ouvrage est une réussite** ~ this work is a success typographically *ou* as regards typography.
typographiquement [tipɔgʀafikmɑ̃] **adv** *imprimer* by letter-press. **livre** ~ **réussi** book that is a success typographically *ou* successful as regards typography.
typolithographie [tipolitɔgʀafi] **nf** typolithography.
typologie [tipɔlɔʒi] **nf** typology.
typologique [tipɔlɔʒik] **adj** typological.
Tyr [tiʀ] **n** Tyre.
tyran [tiʀɑ̃] **nm** (*lit, fig*) tyrant. **c'est un** ~ **domestique** he's a tyrant at home.
tyranneau, **pl** ~**x** [tiʀano] **nm** (*hum, péj*) petty tyrant.
tyrannie [tiʀani] **nf** (*lit, fig*) tyranny. **la** ~ **de la mode/d'un mari** the tyranny of fashion/of a husband; **exercer sa** ~ **sur qn** to tyrannize sb, wield one's tyrannical powers over sb.
tyrannique [tiʀanik] **adj** tyrannical, tyrannous.
tyranniquement [tiʀanikmɑ̃] **adv** tyrannically.
tyranniser [tiʀanize] [1] **vt** (*lit, fig*) to tyrannize.
tyrannosaure [tiʀanɔzɔʀ] **nm** tyrannosaur, tyrannosaurus.
Tyrol [tiʀɔl] **nm**: **le** ~ the Tyrol.
tyrolien, -ienne [tiʀɔljɛ̃, jɛn] **1** **adj** Tyrolean; *voir* **chapeau.** **2** **nm,f**: **T~(ne)** Tyrolean. **3** **tyrolienne** **nf** (*chant*) yodel, Tyrolienne.
Tyrrhénienne [tiʀenjɛn] **nf** *voir* **mer.**
tzar [dzaʀ] **nm**, **tzarévitch** [dzaʀevitʃ] **nm**, **tzarine** [dzaʀin] **nf** = **tsar, tsarévitch, tsarine.**
tzigane [dzigan] = **tsigane.**

U

U, u [y] nm (*lettre*) U, u. **poutre en U** U(-shaped) beam; **vallée en U** U-shaped valley.
UAL [yaɛl] nf (**abrév de unité arithmétique et logique**) ALU.
ubac [ybak] nm (*Géog*) north(-facing) side, ubac (*SPÉC*).
ubiquité [ybikɥite] nf ubiquity. **avoir le don d'~** to be ubiquitous, be everywhere at once (*hum*).
ubuesque [ybyɛsk] adj (*grotesque*) grotesque; (*Littérat*) Ubuesque.
UCE [yseə] nf (**abrév de unité de compte européenne**) EUA.
UDF [ydeɛf] nf **abrév de Union pour la démocratie française**.
UE [yə] nf (**abrév de unité d'enseignement**) *voir* **unité**.
UEFA [yefa] nf (**abrév de Union of European Football Associations**) **la coupe de l'~** the UEFA cup.
UEO [yəo] nf (**abrév de Union de l'Europe occidentale**) WEU.
UER† [yœɛʀ] nf (**abrév de Unité d'enseignement et de recherche**) *voir* **unité**.
UFR [yɛfɛʀ] nf (**abrév de Unité de formation et de recherche**) *voir* **unité**.
UHF [yaʃɛf] (**abrév de ultra-high frequency**) UHF.
uhlan [ylɑ̃] nm uhlan.
UHT [yaʃte] nf (**abrév de ultra-haute température**) UHT.
ukase [ukɑz] nm (*Hist, fig*) ukase.
Ukraine [ykʀɛn] nf Ukraine.
ukrainien, -ienne [ykʀɛnjɛ̃, jɛn] 1 adj Ukrainian. 2 nm (*Ling*) Ukrainian. 3 nm,f: **U~(ne)** Ukrainian.
ukulélé [jukulele] nm ukulele.
ulcération [ylseʀasjɔ̃] nf ulceration.
ulcère [ylsɛʀ] nm ulcer. **~ à l'estomac** stomach ulcer; **~ variqueux** varicose ulcer.
ulcérer [ylseʀe] 6 vt a (*révolter*) to sicken, appal. **être ulcéré (par l'attitude de qn)** to be sickened *ou* appalled (by sb's attitude). b (*Méd*) to ulcerate. **blessure qui s'ulcère** wound that ulcerates *ou* festers; **plaie ulcérée** festering *ou* ulcerated wound.
ulcéreux, -euse [ylseʀø, øz] adj ulcerated, ulcerous.
uléma [ylema] nm ulema.
ULM [yɛlɛm] nm (**abrév de ultra léger motorisé**) microlight, microlite.
ulmaire [ylmɛʀ] nf (*plante*) meadowsweet.
Ulster [ylstɛʀ] nm Ulster.
ultérieur, e [ylteʀjœʀ] adj later, subsequent, ulterior. **à une date ~e** at a later date; (*Comm*) **commandes ~es** further orders.
ultérieurement [ylteʀjœʀmɑ̃] adv later, subsequently.
ultimatum [yltimatɔm] nm ultimatum. **envoyer** *ou* **adresser un ~ à qn** to present sb with an ultimatum.
ultime [yltim] adj ultimate, final.
ultra [yltʀa] 1 nm (*réactionnaire*) extreme reactionary; (*extrémiste*) extremist. (*Hist*) **U~(-royaliste)** ultra(-royalist); *voir* **nec**. 2 préf: **~-chic/-rapide/-long** ultra-fashionable/-fast/-long; **crème ~-pénétrante** deep-cleansing cream; **~-court** (*gén*) ultra-short; (*Rad*) **ondes ~-courtes** ultra-high frequency; (*Aviat*) **~ léger motorisé** *nm* microlight, microlite; **~secret** top-secret; **~-sensible** *surface, balance* ultra-sensitive; *peau* highly sensitive; **film** *ou* **pellicule ~-sensible** high-speed film.
ultra-confidentiel, -ielle [yltʀakɔ̃fidɑ̃sjɛl] adj (*gén*) top secret; (*sur un dossier*) top secret, "eyes only".
ultramicroscope [yltʀamikʀɔskɔp] nm ultramicroscope.
ultramicroscopique [yltʀamikʀɔskɔpik] adj ultramicroscopic.
ultramoderne [yltʀamɔdɛʀn] adj (*gén*) ultramodern; *équipement* high tech, state-of-the-art (*épith*).
ultramontain, e [yltʀamɔ̃tɛ̃, ɛn] adj (*Hist*) ultramontane.
ultra(-)son [yltʀasɔ̃] nm ultrasonic sound. **les ~s** ultra-sonic sound, ultrasonics.
ultra(-)sonique [yltʀasɔnik] adj ultrasonic.
ultra(-)violet, -ette [yltʀavjɔlɛ, ɛt] 1 adj ultraviolet. 2 nm ultraviolet ray.
ultravirus [yltʀaviʀys] nm ultravirus.
ululation [ylylasjɔ̃] nf, **ululement** [ylylmɑ̃] nm = **hululement**.
ululer [ylyle] 1 vi = **hululer**.
Ulysse [ylis] nm Ulysses.
un, une [œ̃, yn] 1 art indéf a a, an (*devant voyelle*); (*un, une quelconque*) some. **ne venez pas ~ dimanche** don't come on a Sunday; **le témoignage d'~ enfant n'est pas valable** a child's evidence *ou* the evidence of a child is not valid; **c'est l'œuvre d'~ poète** it's the work of a poet; **retrouvons-nous dans ~ café** let's meet in a café *ou* in some café (or other); **~ jour/soir il partit** one day/evening he went away; **une fois, il est venu avec ~ ami et ...** once he came with a friend and ...; **passez ~ soir** drop in one *ou* some evening; **~ jour sur deux** every other day; **une semaine sur trois** one week in every three, every third week, one week out of three; **~ jour, tu comprendras** one day *ou* some day you'll understand; *voir* **fois, pas**[1] *etc*.

b (*avec noms abstraits*) **avec une grande sagesse/violence** with great wisdom/violence, very wisely/violently; **des hommes d'~ courage sans égal** men of unparalleled courage; *voir* **certain, rien**.

c (*avec nom propre*) a, an. **ce n'est pas ~ Picasso** (*hum: personne*) he's no Picasso, he's not exactly (a) Picasso; (*tableau*) it's not a Picasso; **~ certain M. X** a (certain) Mr X, one Mr X; **on a élu ~ (nommé)** *ou* **(certain) Dupont** a certain Dupont has been appointed, they've appointed a man called Dupont; **Monsieur Untel** Mr so-and-so; **Madame Unetelle** Mrs so-and-so; **c'est encore ~ Kennedy qui fait parler de lui** that's yet another Kennedy in the news; **il a le talent d'~ Hugo** he has the talent of a Hugo; **cet enfant sera ~ Paganini** this child will be another Paganini.

d (*intensif*) **elle a fait une scène!** *ou* **une de ces scènes!** she made a dreadful scene! *ou* such a scene!, what a scene she made!; **j'ai une faim/une soif!** *ou* **une de ces faims/une de ces soifs!** I'm so hungry/thirsty, I'm starving/terribly thirsty; **il est d'~ sale!** *ou* **d'une saleté!** he's so dirty!, he's filthy!; *voir* **besoin, comble, monde**.

2 pron a one. **prêtez-moi ~ de vos livres** lend me one of your books; **prêtez-m'en ~** lend me one (of them); **il est ~ des rares qui m'ont écrit** he's one of the few (people) who wrote to me; **j'en connais ~ qui sera content!** I know someone *ou* somebody *ou* one person who'll be pleased!; **il est ~ de ces enfants qui s'ennuient partout** he's the kind of child *ou* one of those children who gets bored wherever he goes; **j'en ai vu ~ très joli de chapeau*** I've seen a very nice hat; **~ à qui je voudrais parler c'est Jean** there's someone *ou* one person I'd like to speak to and that is John, someone *ou* one person I'd like to speak to is John.

b (*avec art déf*) **l'~** one; **les ~s** some; **l'une des meilleures chanteuses** one of the best singers; **l'~ ... l'autre** (the) one ... the other; **les ~s disent ... les autres ...** some say ... others ...; **prenez l'~ ou l'autre** take one or the other; **l'une et l'autre solution sont acceptables** either solution is acceptable, both solutions are acceptable; **elles étaient assises en face l'une de l'autre** they were sitting opposite one another *ou* each other; **ils se regardaient l'~ l'autre** they looked at one another *ou* at each other; **malgré ce que peuvent dire les ~s et les autres** despite what some *ou* other people may say; (*Bible*) **aimez-vous les ~s les autres** love one another; (*à tout prendre*) **l'~ dans l'autre** on balance, by and large; **l'~ dans l'autre, cela fera dans les 2 000 F** (what) with one thing and another it will work out at some 2,000 francs; (*loc*) **à la une, à la deux, à la trois** with a one and a two and a three.

3 adj a (*cardinal*) one. **vingt et ~** twenty-one; **il n'en reste qu'~** there's only one left; **nous sommes six contre ~** we are six against one; **~ seul** one only, only one; **pas ~ (seul)** not one; (*emphatique*) not a single one; **il n'y en a pas eu ~ pour m'aider** not a soul *ou* nobody lifted a finger to help me; **~ à ~, ~ par ~** one by one, one after another; **(l')~ des trois a dû mentir** one of the three must have been lying; **sans ~ (sou)*** penniless, broke*; **le cavalier ne faisait qu'~ avec son cheval** horse and rider were as one; **les deux frères ne font qu'~** the two brothers are like one person; **pour moi c'est tout ~** as far as I'm concerned it amounts to the same thing *ou* it's all the same; (*Prov*) **un(e) de perdu(e), dix de retrouvé(e)s** win a few — lose a few, there are plenty more fish in the sea; *voir* **fois, moins**.

b (*chiffre*) one. ~ **et** ~ **font deux** one and one are two; **compter de** ~ **à 100** to count from one to a 100; **et d'**~ **(de fait)** that's one done *ou* finished *ou* out of the way; (*d'abord*) **et d'une!*** for a start!; **personne ne t'a forcé de venir, et d'une!** no one forced you to come — that's the first thing!, for a start no one forced you to come!; **il n'a fait ni une ni deux, il a accepté** he accepted without a second's hesitation *ou* like a shot; **il n'a fait ni une ni deux et il est parti** he left there and then *ou* without further ado.

c (*ordinal*) **page/chapitre** ~ page/chapter one.

d (*formant un tout*) **le Dieu** ~ **et indivisible** the one and indivisible God.

4 **nf** (*Presse*) **la une** the front page, page one; (*TV*) **la une** channel one; (*Presse*) **sur cinq colonnes à la une** in banner headlines on the front page.

unanime [ynanim] **adj** *témoins, sentiment, vote* unanimous. ~**s pour** *ou* **à penser que** unanimous in thinking that.

unanimement [ynanimmɑ̃] **adv** unanimously, with one accord.

unanimité [ynanimite] **nf** unanimity. **vote acquis à l'**~ unanimous vote; **ils ont voté à l'**~ **pour** they voted unanimously for; **élu/voté à l'**~ elected/voted unanimously; **il y a** ~ **pour dire que** the unanimous opinion is that, everyone agrees that; **élu à l'**~ **moins une voix** elected with only one vote against *ou* with only one dissenting vote; **cette décision a fait l'**~ this decision was approved unanimously; **il fait l'**~ there is general agreement about him; **il fait l'**~ **contre lui** everyone thinks he's stupid (*ou* lazy *ou* incompetent *etc*).

UNEDIC [ynedik] **nf** (**abrév de Union nationale pour l'emploi dans l'industrie et le commerce**) *French national organization managing unemployment benefit schemes.*

UNEF [ynɛf] **nf** (**abrév de Union nationale des étudiants de France**) *French national students' union.*

UNESCO [ynɛsko] **nf** (**abrév de United Nations Educational, Scientific and Cultural Organization**) UNESCO.

uni, e [yni] (**ptp de unir**) **adj** a (*sans ornements*) *tissu, jupe* plain, self-coloured (*Brit*); *couleur* plain. **tissu de couleur** ~**e** self-coloured (*Brit*) *ou* plain fabric; **l'imprimé et l'**~ printed and plain *ou* self-coloured (*Brit*) fabrics *ou* material. b (*soudé*) *couple, amis* close; *famille* close(-knit). **ils sont** ~**s comme les deux doigts de la main, ils sont très** ~**s** they are very close; (*frm*) ~**s par les liens du mariage** joined in marriage; **présenter un front** ~ **contre l'adversaire** to present a united front to the enemy. c (*uniforme, lisse*) *surface* smooth, even; *mer* calm, unruffled. (*littér*) **une vie** ~**e et sans nuages** a serene untroubled life.

UNICEF [ynisɛf] **nf ou m** (**abrév de United Nations International Children's Emergency Fund**) UNICEF.

unicellulaire [yniselylɛʀ] **adj** unicellular.

unicité [ynisite] **nf** uniqueness, unicity (*SPÉC*).

unicolore [ynikɔlɔʀ] **adj** self-coloured (*Brit*), plain.

unidirectionnel, -elle [ynidiʀɛksjɔnɛl] **adj** unidirectional.

unième [ynjɛm] **adj: vingt/trente et** ~ twenty-/thirty-first.

unièmement [ynjɛmmɑ̃] **adv: vingt/trente et** ~ in the twenty-/thirty-first place.

unificateur, -trice [ynifikatœʀ, tʀis] **adj** unifying.

unification [ynifikasjɔ̃] **nf** (*voir* **unifier**) unification; standardization.

unifier [ynifje] 7 **vt** *pays, systèmes* to unify; *parti* to unify, unite; (*Comm*) *tarifs etc* to standardize, unify. **des pays qui s'unifient lentement** countries that slowly become unified.

uniforme [ynifɔʀm] 1 **adj** (*gén*) uniform; *vitesse, mouvement* regular, uniform, steady; *terrain, surface* even; *style* uniform, unvarying; *vie, conduite* unchanging, uniform. 2 **nm** (*lit, fig*) (*vêtement*) uniform. **en (grand)** ~ in (dress) uniform, in full regalia; **endosser/quitter l'**~ to join/leave the forces; **il y avait beaucoup d'**~**s à ce dîner** there were a great many officers at the dinner; ~ **scolaire** school uniform.

uniformément [ynifɔʀmemɑ̃] **adv** (*voir* **uniforme**) uniformly; regularly; steadily; evenly; unvaryingly; unchangingly. **le temps s'écoule** ~ time passes at a steady *ou* an unchanging pace *ou* rate, time goes steadily by; (*Phys*) **vitesse** ~ **accélérée** uniform (rate of) change of speed.

uniformisation [ynifɔʀmizasjɔ̃] **nf** standardization.

uniformiser [ynifɔʀmize] 1 **vt** *paysage, mœurs, tarifs* to standardize; *teinte* to make uniform.

uniformité [ynifɔʀmite] **nf** (*voir* **uniforme**) uniformity; regularity; steadiness; evenness.

unijambiste [yniʒɑ̃bist] 1 **adj** one-legged. 2 **nmf** one-legged man (*ou* woman).

unilatéral, e, mpl -aux [ynilateʀal, o] **adj** (*gén, Bot, Jur*) unilateral; *voir* **stationnement**.

unilatéralement [ynilateʀalmɑ̃] **adv** unilaterally.

unilingue [ynilɛ̃g] **adj** unilingual.

uniment [ynimɑ̃] **adv** (*littér: uniformément*) smoothly. (†: *simplement*) **(tout)** ~ (quite) plainly.

uninominal, e, mpl -aux [yninɔminal, o] **adj** *vote* for a single member (*attrib*).

union [ynjɔ̃] 1 **nf** a (*alliance*) *[États, partis, fortunes]* union. **en** ~ **avec** in union with; (*Prov*) **l'**~ **fait la force** strength through unity.

b (*mariage*) union.

c (*juxtaposition*) *[éléments, couleurs]* combination, blending; *voir* **trait**.

d (*groupe*) association, union. **l'U**~ **sportive de Strasbourg** *etc* Strasbourg *etc* sports club.

2 **comp** ►**union charnelle** union of the flesh ►**union conjugale** marital union ►**union de consommateurs** consumers' association ►**union douanière** customs union ►**Union de l'Europe occidentale** Western European Union ►**Union européenne** European Union ►**l'union libre** free love ►**union monogame** (*Zool*) pair-bonding ►**union mystique** (*Rel*) mystic union ►**Union des républiques socialistes soviétiques**† Union of Soviet Socialist Republics† ►**union sacrée** (*Hist*) union sacrée; (*fig*) **l'union sacrée des syndicats contre la nouvelle loi** the trade unions' united front *ou* unholy alliance (*iro*) against the new law ►**l'Union soviétique**† the Soviet Union†.

unionisme [ynjɔnism] **nm** (*gén*) unionism; (*Hist*) Unionism.

unioniste [ynjɔnist] **adj, nmf** (*gén*) unionist; (*Hist*) Unionist.

unipare [ynipaʀ] **adj** uniparous.

unipersonnel, -elle [ynipɛʀsɔnɛl] 1 **adj** (*Ling*) impersonal. 2 **nm** (*verbe*) impersonal verb.

unipolaire [ynipɔlɛʀ] **adj** unipolar.

Uniprix [ynipʀi] **nm** ® department store (*for inexpensive goods*), ≃ Woolworth's ® (*Brit*), five and ten (*US*).

unique [ynik] **adj** a (*seul*) only. **mon** ~ **souci/espoir** my only *ou* sole (*frm*) *ou* one concern/hope; **fils/fille** ~ only son/daughter; **c'est un fils/une fille** ~ he is/she is an only child; (*Pol*) **système à parti** ~ one-party system; (*Rail*) **voie** ~ single track; **route à voie** ~ single-lane road *ou* single-track; **tiré par un cheval** ~ drawn by only one *ou* by a single horse; ~ **en France/en Europe** unique *ou* the only one of its kind in France/in Europe; **deux aspects d'un même et** ~ **problème** two aspects of one and the same problem; **rayon à prix** ~ department where all items are at one price; (*dans un cinéma*) **"places: prix** ~ **30 F"** "all seats 30 francs"; *voir* **salaire, sens, seul**.

b (*après n: exceptionnel*) *livre, talent* unique. ~ **en son genre** unique of its kind; **un paysage** ~ **au monde** an absolutely unique landscape.

c (*: *impayable*) priceless*. **il est** ~ **ce gars-là!** that fellow's priceless!*

uniquement [ynikmɑ̃] **adv** a (*exclusivement*) only, solely, exclusively. **ne fais-tu que du classement? — pas** ~ are you only doing the sorting out? — not only *ou* not just that; **il était venu** ~ **pour me voir** he had come solely to see me, he had come for the sole purpose of seeing me; **il pense** ~ **à l'argent** he thinks only of money; **si** ~ **dévoué à son maître** so exclusively devoted to his master. b (*simplement*) only, merely, just. **c'était** ~ **par curiosité** it was only *ou* just *ou* merely out of curiosity.

unir [yniʀ] 2 1 **vt** a (*associer*) *États, partis, fortunes* to unite (*à* with). ~ **ses forces** to combine one's forces; **ces noms unis dans notre mémoire** these names linked in our memory; **le sentiment commun qui les unit** the common feeling which binds them together *ou* unites them.

b (*marier*) to unite, join together. ~ **en mariage** to unite *ou* join in marriage; **ils ont voulu** ~ **leurs deux destinées** they wanted to unite their destinies through marriage.

c (*juxtaposer, combiner*) *couleurs, qualités* to combine (*à* with). **il unit l'intelligence au courage** he combines intelligence with courage.

d (*relier*) *continents, villes* to link, join up.

2 **s'unir vpr** a (*s'associer*) *[pays, partis, fortunes]* to unite (*à, avec* with). **s'**~ **contre un ennemi commun** to unite against a common enemy.

b (*se marier*) to be joined (together) in marriage. **des jeunes gens qui vont s'**~ a young couple who are going to be joined (together) in marriage.

c (*s'accoupler*) **s'**~ **dans une étreinte fougueuse** to come together in a passionate embrace.

d (*se combiner*) *[mots, formes, couleurs, qualités]* to combine (*à, avec* with).

unisexe [ynisɛks] **adj inv** unisex.

unisexualité [ynisɛksɥalite] **nf** unisexuality.

unisexué, e [ynisɛksɥe] **adj** (*Bio, Bot*) unisexual.

unisson [ynisɔ̃] **nm** (*Mus*) unison. **à l'**~ *chanter* in unison; (*fig*) *penser* with one mind, identically.

unitaire [ynitɛʀ] 1 **adj** (*Comm, Math, Phys*) unitary, unit (*épith*); (*Pol*) unitarian; (*Rel*) Unitarian. **prix** ~ unit price. 2 **nmf** (*Rel*) Unitarian.

unitarien, -ienne [ynitaʀjɛ̃, jɛn] **adj, nm,f** (*Pol*) unitarian; (*Rel*) Unitarian.

unitarisme [ynitaʀism] **nm** (*Pol*) unitarianism; (*Rel*) Unitarianism.

unité [ynite] **nf** a (*cohésion*) unity. ~ **de vues** unity *ou* unanimity of views; **l'**~ **d'action des syndicats** the united action of the unions; (*Littérat*) **les trois** ~**s** the three unities; **roman qui manque d'**~ novel lacking in unity *ou* cohesion.

b (*gén, Comm, Math: élément*) unit. ~ **de mesure/de poids** unit of measure/of weight; ~ **administrative** administrative unit; ~ **monétaire** monetary unit; ~ **monétaire européenne** European monetary *ou* currency unit; ~ **de compte** unit of account; ~ **de compte européenne** European Unit of Account; ~ **de production/de fabrication** production/

manufacturing unit; ~ **lexicale** lexical item; **la colonne des ~s** the units column; **antibiotique à 100 000 ~s** antibiotic with 100,000 units; **prix de vente à l'~** unit selling price, selling price per item; **nous ne les vendons pas à l'~** we don't sell them singly *ou* individually.

c (*troupe*) unit; (*bateau*) ship. (*Mil*) **rejoindre son ~** to rejoin one's unit; ~ **mobile de police** police mobile unit; ~ **de réanimation** resuscitation unit.

d (*Univ*) ~ **de formation et de recherche,** ~ **d'enseignement et de recherche**† university department; ~ **d'enseignement,** ~ **de valeur**† ≃ credit, course.

e (*Ordin*) ~ **arithmétique et logique** arithmetic logic unit; ~ **centrale** mainframe, central processing unit; ~ **de commande** control unit; ~ **de (lecteur de) disquettes** disk drive unit; ~ **périphérique de sortie** output device.

f (*: *10 000 F*) ten thousand francs.

univalve [ynivalv] adj univalve (*épith*).

univers [ynivɛʀ] nm (*gén*) universe; (*milieu, domaine*) world, universe. **son ~ se borne à son travail** his work is his whole universe *ou* world; (*Ling*) **l'~ du discours** the universe of discourse; **l'~ mathématique** the field of mathematics; **s'exhiber aux yeux de (tout) l'~** to show o.s. to the whole wide world; **clamer qch à la face de l'~** to shout sth from the rooftops *ou* for all the world to hear.

universal, pl -aux [ynivɛʀsal, o] nm: ~ **(du langage)** (language) universal; (*Philos*) **les ~aux** the universals.

universalisation [ynivɛʀsalizasjɔ̃] nf universalization.

universaliser [ynivɛʀsalize] [1] vt to universalize.

universalisme [ynivɛʀsalism] nm (*Rel*) Universalism; (*Philos*) universalism.

universaliste [ynivɛʀsalist] adj, nmf (*Rel*) Universalist; (*Philos*) universalist.

universalité [ynivɛʀsalite] nf universality.

universel, -elle [ynivɛʀsɛl] adj a (*gén*) universal. **esprit ~** polymath; **c'est un homme ~** he is a polymath *ou* a man of vast *ou* universal knowledge; **un produit de réputation ~le** a world-famous product, a product which is universally renowned; **il a une réputation ~le d'honnêteté** he is well-known for his honesty, his honesty is universally recognized; *voir* **exposition, légataire, suffrage.** b (*aux applications multiples*) *outil, appareil* universal, all-purpose (*épith*). **remède ~** universal remedy; *voir* **pince.**

universellement [ynivɛʀsɛlmɑ̃] adv universally.

universitaire [ynivɛʀsitɛʀ] 1 adj *vie étudiante, restaurant* university (*épith*); *études, milieux, carrière, diplôme* university (*épith*), academic; *voir* **année, centre, cité.** 2 nmf academic. **une famille d'~s** a family of academics.

université [ynivɛʀsite] nf university. **l'U~ s'oppose à ...** the Universities are against ...; ~ **du troisième âge** university of the third age, post-retirement *ou* senior citizens' university; ~ **d'été** summer school.

univocité [ynivɔsite] nf (*Math, Philos*) univocity.

univoque [ynivɔk] adj *mot* univocal; *relation* one-to-one.

Untel, Unetelle [œ̃tɛl, yntɛl] nm,f *voir* **un 1c.**

upérisation [ypeʀizasjɔ̃] nf ultra heat treatment, UHT treatment.

upériser [ypeʀize] [1] vt to sterilize at ultrahigh temperature. **upérisé** ultra heat treated; **lait upérisé** UHT milk.

UPF [ypeɛf] nf (abrév de **Union pour la France**) *French political party.*

uppercut [ypɛʀkyt] nm uppercut.

uranifère [yʀanifɛʀ] adj uranium-bearing.

uranium [yʀanjɔm] nm uranium. ~ **enrichi** enriched uranium.

uranoscope [yʀanɔskɔp] nm stargazer.

Uranus [yʀanys] 1 nm (*Myth*) Uranus. 2 nf (*Astron*) Uranus.

urbain, e [yʀbɛ̃, ɛn] adj a (*de la ville*) (*gén*) urban; *transports* city (*épith*), urban. b (*littér: poli*) urbane.

urbanisation [yʀbanizasjɔ̃] nf urbanization.

urbaniser [yʀbanize] [1] vt to urbanize. **la campagne environnante s'urbanise rapidement** the surrounding countryside is quickly becoming urbanized *ou* is being quickly built up; *voir* **zone.**

urbanisme [yʀbanism] nm town planning.

urbaniste [yʀbanist] 1 nmf town planner. 2 adj = **urbanistique.**

urbanistique [yʀbanistik] adj *réglementation, impératifs* town-planning (*épith*), urbanistic. **nouvelles conceptions ~s** new concepts in town planning.

urbanité [yʀbanite] nf urbanity.

urée [yʀe] nf urea.

urémie [yʀemi] nf uraemia (*Brit*), uremia (*US*). **faire de l'~** to get uraemia (*Brit*) *ou* uremia (*US*).

urémique [yʀemik] adj uraemic (*Brit*), uremic (*US*).

uretère [yʀ(ə)tɛʀ] n ureter.

urètre [yʀɛtʀ] nm urethra.

urgence [yʀʒɑ̃s] nf a [*décision, départ, situation*] urgency. **il y a ~** it's urgent, it's a matter of (great) urgency; **y a-t-il ~ à ce que nous fassions ...?** is it urgent for us to do ...?; *mesures, situation* **d'~** emergency (*épith*); **faire qch d'~/de toute** *ou* **d'extrême ~** to do sth as a matter of urgency/with the utmost urgency; **transporté d'~ à l'hôpital** rushed to hospital (*Brit*), rushed to the hospital (*US*); **être opéré d'~** to have an emergency operation; **à envoyer d'~** to be sent immediately, for immediate dispatch; **convoquer d'~ les actionnaires** to call an emergency meeting of the shareholders; *voir* **cas, état.**

b (*cas urgent*) emergency. **service/salle des ~s** emergency department/ward.

urgent, e [yʀʒɑ̃, ɑ̃t] adj (*pressant*) urgent. **rien d'~** nothing urgent; **l'~ est de** the most urgent thing is to; **il est ~ de réparer le toit** the roof needs urgent repair; **c'est plus qu'~** it's desperately urgent.

urger* [yʀʒe] [3] vi: **ça urge!** it's urgent!

urinaire [yʀinɛʀ] adj urinary.

urinal, pl -aux [yʀinal, o] nm (bed) urinal.

urine [yʀin] nf urine (*NonC*). **sucre dans les ~s** sugar in the urine.

uriner [yʀine] [1] vi to urinate, pass *ou* make water (*SPÉC*).

urinifère [yʀinifɛʀ] adj uriniferous.

urinoir [yʀinwaʀ] n (public) urinal.

urique [yʀik] adj uric.

urne [yʀn] nf a (*Pol*) ~ **(électorale)** ballot box; **aller aux ~s** to vote, go to the polls. b (*vase*) urn. ~ **funéraire** funeral urn.

urogénital, e, mpl -aux [yʀɔʒenital, o] adj urogenital.

urographie [yʀɔgʀafi] nf intravenous pyelogram.

urologie [yʀɔlɔʒi] nf urology.

urologue [yʀɔlɔg] nmf urologist.

ursidés [yʀside] nmpl ursids.

URSS† [yʀs] nf (abrév de **Union des républiques socialistes soviétiques**) USSR†.

URSSAF [yʀsaf] nf abrév de **Union pour le recouvrement des cotisations de la Sécurité sociale et des allocations familiales.**

ursuline [yʀsylin] nf Ursuline.

urticaire [yʀtikɛʀ] nf nettle rash, hives, urticaria (*SPÉC*). (*fig*) **donner** *ou* **filer de l'~ à qn*** to bring sb out in a rash*.

urubu [yʀyby] nm buzzard.

Uruguay [yʀygwɛ] nm Uruguay.

uruguayen, -enne [yʀygwajɛ̃, ɛn] 1 adj Uruguayan. 2 nm,f: **U~(ne)** Uruguayan.

U.S. ... nf (abrév de **Union sportive de ...**) *voir* **union.**

us [ys] nmpl (††) customs. ~ **et coutumes** (habits and) customs.

US(A) [yɛs(a)] nmpl (abrév de **United States (of America)**) US(A).

usage [yzaʒ] nm a (*utilisation*) [*appareil, méthode*] use. **apprendre l'~ de la boussole** to learn how to use a compass; **il fait un ~ immodéré d'eau de toilette** he uses (far) too much *ou* an excessive amount of toilet water; **abîmé par l'~** damaged through constant use; **elle nous laisse l'~ de son jardin** she lets us use her garden, she gives us *ou* allows us the use of her garden; *voir* **faux², garanti.**

b (*exercice, pratique*) [*membre, langue*] use; [*faculté*] use, power. **perdre l'~ de ses yeux/membres** to lose the use of one's eyes/limbs; **perdre l'~ de la parole** to lose the power of speech; (*littér*) **il n'a pas l'~ du monde** he lacks savoir-faire *ou* the social graces.

c (*fonction, application*) [*instrument*] use. **outil à ~s multiples** multipurpose tool; (*Méd*) **à ~ externe/interne** for external/internal use; **servir à divers ~s** to have several uses, serve several purposes; **moquette/pile à ~ intensif** heavy-duty carpeting/battery; *voir* **valeur.**

d (*coutume habitude*) custom. **un ~ qui se perd** a vanishing custom, a custom which is dying out; **c'est l'~** it's the custom, it's what's done, it's the way things are done; **ce n'est pas l'~ (de)** it's not done (to), it's not the custom (to); **entrer dans l'~ (courant)** [*objet, mot*] to come into common *ou* current use; [*mœurs*] to become common practice; **contraire aux ~s** contrary to common practice *ou* to custom; **il n'est pas dans les ~s de la compagnie de faire cela** the company is not in the habit of doing that, it is not the usual policy of the company to do that *ou* customary for the company to do that; **il était d'~** *ou* **c'était un ~ de** it was customary *ou* a custom *ou* usual to; **formule d'~** set formula; **après les compliments/recommandations d'~** after the usual *ou* customary compliments/recommendations.

e (*Ling*) **l'~** usage; **expression consacrée par l'~** expression fixed by usage; **l'~ écrit/oral** written/spoken usage; **l'~ décide** (common) usage decides; *voir* **bon¹.**

f (*littér: politesse*) **avoir de l'~** to have breeding; **manquer d'~** to lack breeding, be lacking in the social graces.

g (*loc*) **faire ~ de** *pouvoir, droit* to exercise; *permission, avantage* to make use of; *violence, force, procédé* to use, employ; *expression* to use; *objet, thème* to make use of; **faire (un) bon/mauvais ~ de qch** to put sth to good/bad use, make good/bad use of sth; **avoir l'~ de qch** (*droit d'utiliser*) to have the use of sth; (*occasion d'utiliser*) **en aurez-vous l'~?** will you have any use for it?; **ce souliers ont fait de l'~** these shoes have lasted a long time, I've (*ou* we've *etc*) had good use out of these shoes; **vous verrez à l'~ comme c'est utile** you'll see when you use it how useful it is; **ça s'assouplira à l'~** it will soften with use; **son français s'améliorera à l'~** his French will improve with practice; **à l'~ de** for use of, for; **à son ~ personnel, pour son propre ~** for his personal use; **notice à l'~ de** notice for (the attention of); **à l'~ des écoles** *émission* for schools; *manuel* for use in schools; *dispositif, mot* **en ~** in use; *voir* **hors.**

usagé, e [yzaʒe] adj (*qui a beaucoup servi*) *pneu, habits* worn, old; (*d'occasion*) used, secondhand. **quelques ustensiles ~s** some old utensils.

usager, -ère [yzaʒe, ɛʀ] **nm,f** user. ~ **de la route** road user; ~ **de la drogue** drug user; **les ~s de la langue française** French language users, speakers of the French language.

usant, e* [yzɑ̃, ɑ̃t] **adj** (*fatigant*) *travail* exhausting, wearing; *personne* tiresome, wearing. **il est ~ avec ses discours** he wears *ou* tires you out with his talking.

usé, e [yze] (**ptp de user**) **adj** a (*détérioré*) *objet* worn; *vêtement, tapis* worn, worn-out; (*fig*) *personne* worn-out (*in health or age*). ~ **jusqu'à la corde** threadbare; *voir* **eau.** b (*banal*) *thème, expression* hackneyed, trite, well-worn; *plaisanterie* well-worn, stale, corny*.

user [yze] [1] 1 **vt** a (*détériorer*) *outil, roches* to wear away; *vêtements* to wear out. ~ **un manteau jusqu'à la corde** to wear out a coat, wear a coat threadbare; (*hum*) **ils ont usé leurs fonds de culottes sur les mêmes bancs** they were at school together.

b (*fig: épuiser*) *personne, forces* to wear out; *nerfs* to wear down; *influence* to weaken, sap. **la maladie l'avait usé** illness had worn him out.

c (*consommer*) *essence, charbon* to use, burn; *papier, huile, eau* to use. **ce poêle use trop de charbon** this stove uses *ou* burns too much coal; **il use 2 paires de chaussures par mois** he goes through 2 pairs of shoes (in) a month.

2 **vi** (*littér: se comporter*) **en ~ mal/bien avec** *ou* **à l'égard de qn** to treat *ou* use (*littér*) sb badly/well.

3 **user de vt indir** (*utiliser*) *pouvoir, patience, droit* to exercise; *permission, avantage* to make use of; *violence, force, procédé* to use, employ; *expression, mot* to use; (*littér*) *objet, thème* to make use of. **usant de douceur** using gentle means; **il en a usé et abusé** he has used and abused it.

4 **s'user vpr** [*tissu, vêtement*] to wear out. **mon manteau s'use** my coat is showing signs of wear; **elle s'use les yeux à trop lire** she's straining her eyes by reading too much; **elle s'est usée au travail** she wore herself out with work.

usinage [yzinaʒ] **nm** (*voir* **usiner**) machining; manufacturing.

usine [yzin] 1 **nf** factory. **un copain de l'~** *ou* **d'~** a mate from the works *ou* factory; **travailler en ~** to work in a factory; **travail en ~** factory work; (*fig*) **ce bureau est une vraie ~!*** this office is like a factory!; *voir* **cheminée.** 2 **comp** ►**usine atomique** atomic energy station, atomic plant ►**usine automatisée** automated factory ►**usine d'automobiles** car factory *ou* plant ►**usine à gaz** gasworks ►**usine métallurgique** ironworks ►**usine de pâte à papier** paper mill ►**usine de raffinage** refinery ►**usine sidérurgique** steelworks, steel mill ►**usine textile** textile plant *ou* factory, mill ►**usine de traitement des ordures** sewage works *ou* farm *ou* plant.

usiner [yzine] [1] **vt** (*travailler, traiter*) to machine; (*fabriquer*) to manufacture. (*travailler dur*) **ça usine dans le coin!*** they're hard at it round here!*

usinier, -ière [yzinje, jɛʀ] **adj** *industrie* factory (*épith*), manufacturing; *faubourg* working-class.

usité, e [yzite] **adj** in common use, common. **un temps très/peu ~** a very commonly-used/a rarely-used tense; **le moins ~** the least (commonly) used; **ce mot n'est plus ~** this word is no longer used *ou* in use.

ustensile [ystɑ̃sil] **nm** (*gén: outil, instrument*) implement. (*: *attirail*) **~s*** implements, tackle (*NonC*), gear (*NonC*); ~ **(de cuisine)** (kitchen) utensil; **~s de ménage** household cleaning stuff *ou* things; **~s de jardinage** gardening tools *ou* implements; **qu'est-ce que c'est que cet ~?*** what's that gadget? *ou* contraption?

usuel, -elle [yzɥɛl] 1 **adj** *objet* everyday (*épith*), ordinary; *mot, expression, vocabulaire* everyday (*épith*). **dénomination ~le d'une plante** common name for *ou* of a plant; **il est ~ de faire** it is usual to do, it is common practice to do. 2 **nm** (*livre*) book on the open shelf. **c'est un ~** it's on the open shelves.

usuellement [yzɥɛlmɑ̃] **adv** ordinarily, commonly.

usufruit [yzyfʀɥi] **nm** usufruct.

usufruitier, -ière [yzyfʀɥitje, jɛʀ] **adj, nm,f** usufructuary.

usuraire [yzyʀɛʀ] **adj** *taux, prêt* usurious.

usure¹ [yzyʀ] **nf** a (*processus*) [*vêtement*] wear (and tear); [*objet*] wear; [*terrain, roche*] wearing away; [*forces, énergie*] wearing out; (*Ling*) [*mot*] weakening. ~ **normale** fair wear and tear; **résiste à l'~** resists wear, wears well; **subir l'~ du temps** to be worn away by time; (*Pol*) **c'est l'~ du pouvoir** it's the wearing effect of being in power; ~ **de la monnaie** debasement of the currency; **on l'aura à l'~*** we'll wear him down in the end; *voir* **guerre.** b (*état*) [*objet, vêtement*] worn state.

usure² [yzyʀ] **nf** (*intérêt*) usury. **prêter à ~** to lend at usurious rates of interest; (*fig littér*) **je te le rendrai avec ~** I will pay you back (with interest), I will get my own back (on you) with interest (*Brit*).

usurier, -ière [yzyʀje, jɛʀ] **nm,f** usurer.

usurpateur, -trice [yzyʀpatœʀ, tʀis] 1 **adj** *tendance, pouvoir* usurping (*épith*). 2 **nm,f** usurper.

usurpation [yzyʀpasjɔ̃] **nf** (*voir* **usurper**) usurpation; encroachment.

usurpatoire [yzyʀpatwaʀ] **adj** usurpatory. (*Jur*) **signature ~** unauthorised signature.

usurper [yzyʀpe] [1] 1 **vt** *pouvoir, honneur* to usurp. **il a usurpé le titre de docteur en médecine** he wrongfully took *ou* assumed the title of Doctor of Medicine; **réputation usurpée** usurped reputation. 2 **vi** (*littér: empiéter*) ~ **sur** to encroach (up)on.

ut [yt] **nm** (*Mus*) (the note) C; *voir* **clef.**

Utah [yta] **nm** Utah.

utérin, e [yteʀɛ̃, in] **adj** uterine.

utérus [yteʀys] **nm** womb. **location** *ou* **prêt d'~** womb-leasing; *voir* **col.**

utile [ytil] 1 **adj** a *objet, appareil, action* useful; *aide, conseil* useful, helpful (*à qn* to *ou* for sb). **livre ~ à lire** useful book to read; **cela vous sera certainement ~** that'll certainly be of use to you; **ton parapluie m'a été bien ~ ce matin** your umbrella came in very handy (for me) this morning; **est-il vraiment ~ d'y aller** *ou* **que j'y aille?** do I really need to go?; **la vie ~ d'un bien** the productive life of an asset; *voir* **charge, temps¹, voter.** b *collaborateur, relation* useful. **il adore se rendre ~** he loves to make himself useful; **puis-je vous être ~?** can I be of help?, can I do anything for you? 2 **nm: l'~** what is useful; *voir* **joindre.**

utilement [ytilmɑ̃] **adv** (*avec profit*) profitably, usefully. **conseiller ~ qn** to give sb useful advice.

utilisable [ytilizabl] **adj** usable. **est-ce encore ~?** [*cahier, vêtement*] can it still be used?, is it still usable?; [*appareil*] is it still usable? *ou* working?

utilisateur, -trice [ytilizatœʀ, tʀis] **nm,f** [*appareil*] user. (*Ordin*) ~ **final** end user.

utilisation [ytilizasjɔ̃] **nf** (*gén*) use; (*Culin*) [*restes*] using (up).

utiliser [ytilize] [1] **vt** a (*employer*) *appareil, système* to use, utilize; *outil, produit, mot* to use; *force, moyen* to use, employ; *droit* to use; *avantage* to make use of. **savoir ~ les compétences** to know how to make the most of *ou* make use of people's abilities. b (*tirer parti de*) *personne, incident* to make use of; (*Culin*) *restes* to use (up).

utilitaire [ytilitɛʀ] 1 **adj** utilitarian; *voir* **véhicule.** 2 **nm** (*Ordin*) utility.

utilitarisme [ytilitaʀism] **nm** utilitarianism.

utilitariste [ytilitaʀist] **adj, nmf** (*Philos*) utilitarian.

utilité [ytilite] **nf** (*caractère utile*) usefulness; (*utilisation possible*) use. **je ne conteste pas l'~ de cet appareil** I don't deny the usefulness of this apparatus; **cet outil a son ~** this tool has its uses; **cet outil peut avoir son ~** this tool might come in handy *ou* useful; **d'une grande ~** very useful, of great use *ou* usefulness *ou* help (*attrib*); **ce livre ne m'est pas d'une grande ~** this book isn't much use *ou* help *ou* a great deal of use *ou* help to me; **de peu d'~** of little use *ou* help (*attrib*); **d'aucune ~** (of) no use (*attrib*) *ou* help; **sans ~** useless; **auras-tu l'~ de cet objet?** can you make use of this object?, will you have any use for this object?; **de quelle ~ est-ce que cela peut (bien) vous être?** what earthly use is it to you?, what on earth can you use it for?; (*Jur*) **reconnu** *ou* **déclaré d'~ publique** state-approved; **jouer les ~s** (*Théât*) to play small *ou* bit parts; (*fig*) to play second fiddle.

utopie [ytɔpi] **nf** a (*genre, ouvrage, idéal politique*) utopia, Utopia. b (*idée, plan chimérique*) utopian view *ou* idea *etc.* **~s** utopianism, utopian views *ou* ideas; **ceci est une véritable ~** that's sheer utopianism.

utopique [ytɔpik] **adj** utopian, Utopian; *voir* **socialisme.**

utopisme [ytɔpism] **nm** Utopianism.

utopiste [ytɔpist] **nmf** utopian, Utopian.

UV [yve] 1 **nf** (†: *Univ*) (**abrév de unité de valeur**) *voir* **unité.** 2 **nm** (**abrév de ultra-violet**) *voir* **ultra(-)violet.**

uvulaire [yvylɛʀ] **adj** uvular.

uvule [yvyl] **nf** (*luette*) uvula.

V

V[1], v[1] [ve] **nm** *(lettre)* V, v. **en V** V-shaped; **moteur en V** V-engine; **encolure en V** V-neck; **un décolleté en V** a plunging (V-)neckline; **le V de la victoire** the victory sign, the V for victory; *voir* **vitesse**.

V[2], v[2] **(abrév de voir, voyez)** V.

va [va] *voir* **aller**.

vacance [vakɑ̃s] 1 **nf** a *(Admin: poste)* vacancy.

b *(Jur)* **~ de succession** abeyance of succession; **~ du pouvoir** power vacuum.

c *(littér: disponibilité)* unencumbered state *(littér)*. **en état de ~** unencumbered *(littér)*, vacant.

2 **vacances nfpl** a *(gén: repos)* holiday *(Brit)*, vacation *(US)*; *(Scol)* holiday(s) *(Brit)*, vacation *(US)*; *(Univ)* vacation; *[salariés]* holiday(s) *(Brit)*, vacation *(US)*. **les ~s de Noël** the Christmas holidays *ou* vacation; **partir en ~s** to go away on holiday *ou* on vacation; **au moment de partir en ~s** at the time of setting off on (our) holiday *ou* on our holidays *ou* on (our) vacation; **il n'a jamais pris de ~s** he has never taken a holiday *ou* vacation; **avoir droit à 4 semaines de ~s** to be entitled to 4 weeks' holiday(s) *ou* vacation; **prendre ses ~s en une fois** to take (all) one's holiday(s) *ou* vacation at once; **être en ~s** to be on holiday *ou* vacation; **j'ai besoin de ~s/de quelques jours de ~s** I need a holiday *ou* vacation/a few days' holiday *ou* vacation; **aller en ~s en Angleterre** to go on holiday *ou* vacation to England; **~s de neige** winter sports holiday *ou* vacation; **pays/lieu de ~s** holiday country/place; **la ville est déserte pendant les ~s** the town is deserted during the holidays *ou* vacation; **~s actives/à thème** activity/special interest holiday(s) *ou* vacation; *voir* **colonie, devoir, grand**.

b *(Jur)* **~s judiciaires** recess, vacation; **~s parlementaires** parliamentary recess.

vacancier, -ière [vakɑ̃sje, jɛʀ] **nm, f** holiday-maker *(Brit)*, vacationist *(US)*.

vacant, e [vakɑ̃, ɑ̃t] **adj** a *poste, siège* vacant; *appartement* unoccupied, vacant. b *(Jur) biens, succession* in abeyance *(attrib)*. c *(fig littér)* **l'air ~** with a vacant air; **un cœur/esprit ~** an empty *ou* unencumbered *(littér)* heart/mind.

vacarme [vakaʀm] **nm** din, racket, row, pandemonium, hullabaloo*. **faire du ~** to make a din *ou* racket *ou* row; **un ~ de klaxons** the blaring of hooters; **un ~ continuel de camions/de coups de marteau** a constant roaring of lorries/thumping of hammers.

vacataire [vakatɛʀ] **nmf** temporary replacement, stand-in; *(Univ)* part-time lecturer (on contract). **il est ~** he's on a temporary contract.

vacation [vakasjɔ̃] **nf** *(Jur) [expert, notaire] (temps de travail)* session, sitting; *(honoraires)* fee. **être payé à la ~** to be paid on a sessional basis; *(Jur: vacances)* **~s** recess, vacation.

vaccin [vaksɛ̃] **nm** *(substance)* vaccine; *(vaccination)* vaccination, inoculation. **faire un ~ à qn** to give sb a vaccination *ou* inoculation; *(fig)* **un ~ contre qch** a safeguard against sth.

vaccinable [vaksinabl] **adj** able to be vaccinated *ou* inoculated, that can be vaccinated *ou* inoculated.

vaccinal, e, mpl -aux [vaksinal, o] **adj** vaccinal.

vaccinateur, -trice [vaksinatœʀ, tʀis] 1 **adj** vaccinating *(épith)*, inoculating *(épith)*. 2 **nm, f** vaccinator, inoculator.

vaccination [vaksinasjɔ̃] **nf** vaccination, inoculation.

vaccine [vaksin] **nf** *(maladie)* cowpox, vaccinia *(SPÉC)*; *(†: inoculation)* inoculation of cowpox. **fausse ~** vacinella, false vaccinia.

vacciner [vaksine] 1 **vt** *(Méd)* to vaccinate, inoculate *(contre* against). **se faire ~** to have a vaccination *ou* an inoculation, get vaccinated *ou* inoculated; *(fig)* **être vacciné contre qch*** to be cured of sth; **merci, maintenant je suis vacciné!*** thanks, I've learnt my lesson! *ou* I'm cured of that!

vaccinostyle [vaksinɔstil] **nm** scarificator.

vachard, e* [vaʃaʀ, aʀd] **adj** *(méchant)* nasty, rotten*, mean.

vache [vaʃ] 1 **nf** a *(Zool)* cow; *(cuir)* cowhide. **~ laitière** dairy cow; *voir* **lait, plancher[1]**.

b (* *péj: police*) **les ~s** the fuzz*, the bulls* *(US)*; *(hum)* **~ à roulette†** motorbike cop*.

c (*: *personne méchante*) *(femme)* bitch*, cow*; *(homme)* swine*, sod*; *voir* **peau**.

d *(loc)* **comme une ~ qui regarde passer les trains** stolidly, phlegmatically, with a gormless* *ou* vacant air; **il parle français comme une ~ espagnole** he absolutely murders the French language; **manger de la ~ enragée** to go through hard *ou* lean times; **période de ~s grasses/maigres pour l'économie française** good *ou* prosperous/lean *ou* hard times for the French economy; **donner des coups de pied en ~ à qn** to kick sb slyly; **faire un coup en ~ à qn** to pull a fast one on sb*, do the dirty on sb* *(Brit)*; **ah! les ~!*** the swine(s)*; **ah la ~!*** *(surprise, admiration)* wow!*, blimey!* *(Brit)*, I'll be jiggered!*; *(douleur, indignation)* hell!*, damn (me)!*; *(intensif)* **une ~ de surprise/bagnole*** a *ou* one hell of a surprise/car*.

2 **adj** (*: *méchant, sévère*) rotten*, mean*. **il est ~** he's a (rotten) swine* *ou* sod*, he's really rotten* *ou* mean; **elle est ~** she's a (mean *ou* rotten) cow* *ou* bitch*, she's really rotten* *ou* mean; **il n'a pas été ~ avec toi** he was quite kind *ou* good to you; **c'est ~ pour eux** it's really rotten for them*.

3 **comp** ►**vache à eau** (canvas) water bag ►**vache à lait*** *(péj)* mug* *(person) (péj)*.

vachement* [vaʃmɑ̃] **adv** a *(très)* **~ bon/difficile** damned* *ou* bloody* *(Brit)* good/hard; **on s'est ~ dépêchés** we rushed like hell*; **ça m'a ~ aidé** it helped me a hell of a lot*, it helped me no end*; **on s'est ~ trompés** we made one *ou* a hell of a mistake*; **il pleut ~** it's raining damned* *ou* bloody* *(Brit)* hard. b *(méchamment)* in a rotten* *ou* mean way.

vacher [vaʃe] **nm** cowherd.

vachère [vaʃɛʀ] **nf** cowgirl.

vacherie [vaʃʀi] **nf** a (*: *méchanceté*) *[personne, remarque]* rottenness*, meanness; *(action)* dirty trick*; *(remarque)* nasty *ou* bitchy* remark. **faire une ~ à qn** to play a dirty* *ou* mean trick on sb; **dire des ~s** to make nasty remarks. b (*: *intensif*) **c'est de la ~** it's rubbish *ou* junk*; **c'est une sacrée ~** *[appareil]* it's a dead loss*, it's a useless thing; *[maladie]* it's a nasty illness; **cette ~ d'appareil ne veut pas marcher** this damned* *ou* blasted* *ou* confounded *ou* bloody* *(Brit)* machine refuses to go; **quelle ~ de temps!** what damned* *ou* bloody* *(Brit)* awful weather! c *(†: étable)* cowshed, byre.

vacherin [vaʃʀɛ̃] **nm** *(glace)* vacherin; *(fromage)* vacherin cheese.

vachette [vaʃɛt] **nf** a *(jeune vache)* young cow. b *(cuir)* calfskin.

vacillant, e [vasijɑ̃, ɑ̃t] **adj** a *(lit) jambes, démarche* unsteady, shaky, wobbly; *lueur, flamme* flickering *(épith)*. b *(fig) santé, mémoire* shaky, failing; *raison* failing; *courage* wavering, faltering; *caractère* indecisive, wavering *(épith)*.

vacillation [vasijasjɔ̃] **nf** *[démarche]* unsteadiness, shakiness; *[flamme]* flickering. **les ~s de son esprit/sa raison** the wavering of his mind/reason, his wavering *ou* failing mind/reason.

vacillement [vasijmɑ̃] **nm** *(voir* **vaciller***)* swaying; wobbling; faltering, wavering, flickering. **ses ~s m'inquiétaient: je craignais qu'elle ne fût malade** her unsteadiness *ou* shakiness worried me and I feared that she might be ill.

vaciller [vasije] 1 **vi** a *(lit) [personne]* to sway (to and fro); *[blessé, ivrogne]* to totter, reel, stagger; *[bébé]* to wobble; *[mur, poteau]* to sway (to and fro); *[meuble]* to wobble. **~ sur ses jambes** to stand unsteadily on one's legs, sway to and fro (on one's legs); **il s'avança en vacillant vers la porte** he tottered *ou* reeled *ou* staggered towards the door. b *[flamme, lumière]* to flicker. c *(fig) [voix]* to shake; *[résolution, courage]* to falter, waver; *[raison, intelligence]* to fail; *[santé, mémoire]* to be shaky, be failing. **il vacillait dans ses résolutions** he wavered *ou* vacillated in his resolution.

va-comme-je-te-pousse [vakɔmʒtəpus] **adv: à la ~** in a slapdash manner, any old how* *ou* way *(Brit)*.

vacuité [vakɥite] **nf** *(littér: vide)* vacuity *(littér)*, emptiness; *(intellectuelle, spirituelle)* vacuity, vacuousness.

vacuole [vakɥɔl] **nf** (*Bio*) vacuole.
vade-mecum [vademekɔm] **nm inv** pocketbook, vade mecum.
vadrouille* [vadʀuj] **nf** ramble, jaunt. **être en ~** to be out on a ramble; **faire une ~** to go on a ramble *ou* jaunt.
vadrouiller* [vadʀuje] 1 **vi** to rove around *ou* about. **~ dans les rues de Paris** to knock* *ou* loaf* *ou* rove about the streets of Paris.
Vaduz [vadyz] **n** Vaduz.
va-et-vient [vaevjɛ̃] **nm inv** a *[personnes, véhicules]* comings and goings *(pl)*, to-ings and fro-ings *(pl)*; *[rue, bureau, café]* comings and goings *(pl)* (*de* in), to-ings and fro-ings *(pl)* (*de* in). b *[piston, pièce]* **(mouvement de) ~** (*gén*) to and fro (motion), backwards and forwards motion; (*verticalement*) up-and-down movement; **faire le ~ entre** *[bateau, train]* to go to and fro between, ply between; *[pièce de mécanisme]* to go to and fro between. c (*gond*) helical hinge. **porte à ~** swing door. d (*bac*) (small) ferryboat. e (*téléphérage*) jig-back. f (*Élec*) **(interrupteur de) ~** two-way switch; **circuit de ~** two-way wiring (*NonC*) *ou* wiring system.
vagabond, e [vagabɔ̃, ɔ̃d] 1 **adj** (*littér*) *peuple, vie* wandering (*épith*); *imagination* roaming (*épith*), roving (*épith*), restless. **avoir l'humeur ~e** to be in a restless mood. 2 **nm,f** (*péj: rôdeur*) tramp, vagrant, vagabond; (*littér: aventurier*) wanderer.
vagabondage [vagabɔ̃daʒ] **nm** (*errance*) wandering, roaming; (*Jur, péj: vie sans domicile fixe*) vagrancy. **leurs ~s à travers l'Europe** their wanderings *ou* roamings across Europe; **après une longue période de ~ il échoua en prison** after a long period of vagrancy he ended up in prison; **le ~ de son imagination** the rovings of his imagination.
vagabonder [vagabɔ̃de] 1 **vi** *[personne]* to roam, wander; (*fig*) *[imagination, esprit]* to roam, rove, wander. **~ à travers l'Europe** to roam the length and breadth of Europe, wander across Europe.
vagin [vaʒɛ̃] **nm** vagina.
vaginal, e, mpl -aux [vaʒinal, o] **adj** vaginal; *voir* **frottis.**
vaginite [vaʒinit] **nf** vaginitis (*NonC*).
vagir [vaʒiʀ] 2 **vi** *[bébé]* to wail, cry.
vagissant, e [vaʒisɑ̃, ɑ̃t] **adj** wailing, crying.
vagissement [vaʒismɑ̃] **nm** cry, wail.
vague[1] [vag] 1 **adj** (*imprécis*) *renseignement, geste* vague; *notion, idée* vague, hazy; *sentiment, forme* vague, indistinct; (*distrait*) *air, regard* faraway (*épith*), abstracted (*épith*); (*ample*) *robe, manteau* loose(-fitting). **un ~ cousin** some sort of distant cousin; **il avait un ~ diplôme** he had a diploma of sorts *ou* some kind of (a) diploma; **d'un air ~** with a faraway look, with an abstracted expression; **il y avait rencontré une ~ parente** there he had met someone vaguely related to him *ou* some distant relation or other; *voir* **nerf, terrain.**
2 **nm** a (*littér*) *[forme]* vagueness, indistinctness; *[passions, sentiments]* vagueness.
b **le ~** vagueness; **j'ai horreur du ~** I can't bear vagueness; **nous sommes dans le ~** things are rather unclear to us; **il est resté dans le ~** he kept it all rather vague; **regarder dans le ~** to gaze (vacantly) into space *ou* into the blue; **les yeux perdus dans le ~** with a faraway look in his eyes.
c **~ à l'âme** vague melancholy; **avoir du** *ou* **le ~ à l'âme** to feel vaguely melancholic.
vague[2] [vag] **nf** a (*lit*) wave. **~ de fond** (*lit*) ground swell (*NonC*); (*fig*) surge of opinion; (*littér*) **le gonflement de la ~** the swelling of the waves.
b (*fig: déferlement*) wave. **~ d'enthousiasme/de tendresse** wave *ou* surge of enthusiasm/tenderness; **~ d'applaudissements/de protestations** wave of applause/protest(s); **premières ~s de touristes/d'immigrants** first influxes of tourists/immigrants; (*Mil*) **~ d'assaut** wave of assault; (*Mét*) **~ de chaleur** heatwave; (*Mét*) **~ de froid** cold spell *ou* snap; **~ de criminalité** crime wave; *voir* **nouveau.**
c *[émanations]* wave. **une ~ de gaz se propagea jusqu'à nous** a smell of gas drifted *ou* wafted up to us.
d (*fig: ondulation*) (*Archit*) waved motif; *[chevelure]* wave; (*littér*) *[blés, fougères etc]* wave, undulation (*littér*). **effet de ~** ripple effect; (*complications*) **faire des ~s** to make waves; **surtout pas de ~s** above all let's avoid a scandal.
vaguelette [vaglɛt] **nf** wavelet, ripple.
vaguement [vagmɑ̃] **adv** vaguely. **un geste ~ surpris/incrédule** a gesture of vague surprise/incredulity, a vaguely surprised/incredulous gesture.
vaguemestre [vagmɛstʀ] **nm** (*Mil, Naut*) *officer responsible for the delivery of mail.*
vaguer [vage] 1 **vi** (*littér*) to wander, roam.
vahiné [vaine] **nf** vahine.
vaillamment [vajamɑ̃] **adv** (*voir* **vaillant**) bravely, courageously; valiantly, gallantly.
vaillance [vajɑ̃s] **nf** (*courage*) courage, bravery; (*au combat*) valour, gallantry, valiance.
vaillant, e [vajɑ̃, ɑ̃t] **adj** a (*courageux*) brave, courageous; (*au combat*) valiant, gallant; *voir* **à, sou.** b (*vigoureux, plein de santé*) vigorous, hale and hearty, robust. **je ne me sens pas très ~** I'm feeling (a bit) under the weather (*Brit*), I don't feel particularly great today*.
vaille que vaille [vajkəvaj] **loc adv** after a fashion, somehow (or other).
vain, e [vɛ̃, vɛn] 1 **adj** a (*futile*) *paroles, promesse* empty, hollow, vain (*épith*); *craintes, espoir, plaisirs* vain (*épith*), empty. **des gens pour qui la loyauté n'est pas un ~ mot** people for whom loyalty is not an empty word, people for whom the word loyalty really means something.
b (*frivole*) *personne, peuple* shallow, superficial.
c (*infructueux*) *effort, tentative, attente* vain (*épith*), in vain (*attrib*), futile, fruitless; (*stérile*) *regrets, discussion* vain (*épith*), useless, idle (*épith*). **son sacrifice n'aura pas été ~** his sacrifice will not have been in vain; **il est ~ d'essayer de ...** it is futile to try to ... .
d (*littér: vaniteux*) vain (*de* of). **contrairement à ce qu'un ~ peuple pense** contrary to accepted belief.
e (*loc*) **en ~** in vain; **elle essaya en ~ de s'en souvenir** she tried vainly *ou* in vain to remember; **ce ne fut pas en ~ que ...** it was not in vain that ...; **je ressayai, mais en ~** I tried again, but in vain *ou* but to no avail; (*frm*) **invoquer le nom de Dieu en ~** to take the name of God in vain.
2 **comp ▸ vaine pâture** (*Jur*) common grazing land.
vaincre [vɛ̃kʀ] 42 **vt** a *rival, concurrent* to defeat, beat; *armée, ennemi* to defeat, vanquish (*littér*), conquer. **les meilleurs ont fini par ~** the best men finally won; **sachons ~ ou sachons périr!** do or die!; (*Prov*) **à ~ sans péril, on triomphe sans gloire** triumph without peril brings no glory; **nous vaincrons** we shall overcome. b *obstacle* to overcome; *difficulté, maladie* to overcome, triumph over, conquer; *instincts, timidité, sentiment* to triumph over, conquer, overcome; *résistance* to overcome, defeat.
vaincu, e [vɛ̃ky] (**ptp de vaincre**) 1 **adj** beaten, defeated, vanquished (*littér*). **s'avouer ~** to admit defeat, confess o.s. beaten; **il part ~ d'avance** he feels he's beaten *ou* defeated before he begins. 2 **nm,f** defeated man (*ou* woman). **les ~s** the vanquished (*littér*), the defeated; **malheur aux ~s!** woe to the vanquished! (*littér*); **mentalité/attitude de ~** defeatist mentality/attitude.
vainement [vɛnmɑ̃] **adv** vainly, unavailingly. **j'ai ~ essayé de lui expliquer** I tried in vain to explain to him, I tried to explain to him (but) to no avail.
vainqueur [vɛ̃kœʀ] 1 **nm** (*à la guerre*) conqueror, victor; (*en sport*) winner. **le ~ de l'Everest** the conqueror of Everest; **les ~s de cette équipe** the conquerors of this team; **les ~s de cette compétition** the winners in *ou* of this competition; **sortir ~ d'une épreuve** to emerge (as) the winner of a contest; **arriver quelque part en ~** to arrive somewhere as a winner *ou* as conqueror. 2 **adj m** victorious, triumphant.
vair [vɛʀ] **nm** vair.
vairon [vɛʀɔ̃] 1 **nm** (*Zool*) minnow. 2 **adj m: yeux ~s** wall-eyes.
vaisseau, pl ~x [vɛso] **nm** a (*Naut*) vessel (*frm*), ship. **~ amiral** flagship; **~ de guerre** warship; **~ fantôme** ghost ship; (*Mus*) **le V~ fantôme** the Flying Dutchman; (*Aviat*) **~ spatial** spaceship; *voir* **brûler, capitaine, enseigne, lieutenant.** b (*Anat*) vessel. **~ sanguin/lymphatique/capillaire** blood/lymphatic/capillary vessel. c (*Bot*) vessel. **plante à ~x** vascular plant. d (*Archit*) nave. e (*littér: récipient*) vessel.
vaisselier [vɛsəlje] **nm** dresser (*cupboard*).
vaisselle [vɛsɛl] **nf** (*plats*) crockery; (*plats à laver*) dishes *(pl)*, crockery; (*lavage*) washing-up (*Brit*), dishes (*pl*). **~ de porcelaine/faïence** china/earthenware crockery; **~ plate** (gold *ou* silver) plate; **faire la ~** to wash up, do the washing-up (*Brit*) *ou* the dishes; **la ~ était faite en deux minutes** the washing-up (*Brit*) was *ou* the dishes were done in two minutes; *voir* **eau, essuyer, laver.**
val, pl ~s *ou* **vaux** [val, vo] **nm** (*gén dans noms de lieux*) valley. **le V~ de Loire** the Val de Loire, the Loire Valley; **le V~ d'Aoste** Valle d'Aosta; *voir* **mont.**
valable [valabl] **adj** a (*utilisable, légitime*) *contrat, passeport,* (*Jur*) valid; *excuse, raison* valid, legitimate, good (*épith*); *loi, critère, théorie, motif* valid. **elle n'a aucune raison ~ de le faire** she has no good *ou* valid reason for doing so; **ce n'est ~ que dans certains cas** it is only valid *ou* it only holds *ou* applies in certain cases; **il faut que cela soit jugé ~ par les scientifiques** it must pass muster with the scientists *ou* be accepted as valid by the scientists; (*Comm*) **offre ~ une semaine** firm offer for a week, offer which remains valid for a week.
b (*de qualité*) *œuvre, solution, commentaire* really good, worthwhile; *équipements* acceptable, decent, worthwhile; *concurrent, auteur* really good, worth his (*ou* her) salt (*attrib*); *voir* **interlocuteur.**
valablement [valabləmɑ̃] **adv** a (*légitimement: voir* **valable**) validly; legitimately. **ce billet ne peut pas être ~ utilisé** this ticket is not valid; **ne pouvant ~ soutenir que ...** not being able to uphold legitimately *ou* justifiably that ... . b (*de façon satisfaisante*) **pour en parler ~, il faut des connaissances en linguistique** to be able to say anything worthwhile *ou* valid about it one would have to know something about linguistics, to have anything worth saying *ou* any valid comments to make one would have to know something about linguistics.
Valais [valɛ] **nm: le ~** Valais.
valaisan, -anne [valɛzɑ̃, an] 1 **adj** of *ou* from Valais. 2 **nm,f: V~(ne)** inhabitant *ou* native of Valais.
valdinguer* [valdɛ̃ge] 1 **vi: aller ~** *[personne]* to go flat on one's face*, go sprawling; **les boîtes ont failli ~ (par terre)** the boxes nearly came

crashing down *ou* nearly went flying*; (*fig*) **envoyer ~ qn** to tell sb to clear off* *ou* buzz off*, send sb packing*, send sb off with a flea in his ear*; **envoyer ~ qch** to send sth flying*.

Valence [valɑ̃s] **n** (*en Espagne*) Valencia; (*en France*) Valence.

valence [valɑ̃s] **nf** (*Phys*) valency (*Brit*), valence (*US*). **~-gramme** gramme-equivalent.

valenciennes [valɑ̃sjɛn] **nf inv** Valenciennes lace.

Valentin [valɑ̃tɛ̃] **nm** Valentine.

valériane [valeʀjan] **nf** valerian.

valet [valɛ] 1 **nm** a (*domestique*) (man) servant; (*Hist*) *[seigneur]* valet; (*péj Pol*) lackey (*péj*). **premier ~ de chambre du roi** king's first valet; (*Théât*) **~ de comédie** manservant (part *ou* role); (*Théât*) **jouer les ~s** to play servant parts *ou* roles. b (*Cartes*) jack, knave. **~ de cœur** jack *ou* knave of hearts. c (*cintre*) **~ (de nuit)** valet. d (*Tech*) **~ (de menuisier)** (woodworker's) clamp. 2 **comp** ▸**valet d'âtre** companion set ▸**valet de chambre** manservant, valet ▸**valet d'écurie** groom, stableboy, stable lad (*Brit*) ▸**valet de ferme** farmhand ▸**valet de pied** footman.

valetaille [valtɑj] **nf** († *ou péj*) menials (*pl*), flunkeys† (*pl*).

valétudinaire [valetydinɛʀ] **adj, nmf** (*littér*) valetudinarian.

valeur [valœʀ] **nf** a (*prix*) value, worth; (*Fin*) *[devise, action]* value, price. (*Écon*) **~ d'usage/d'échange** usage *ou* practical/exchange value; (*Comm*) **~ marchande** market value; **~ vénale** monetary value; **vu la ~ de ces objets il faudra les faire assurer** in view of the value of these things they will have to be insured; **quelle est la ~ de cet objet?** what is this object worth?, what is the value of this object?; **prendre/perdre de la ~** to go up/down in value, lose/gain in value; **la ~ intrinsèque de qch** the intrinsic value *ou* worth of sth; **fixer la ~ d'une devise** to fix the value *ou* price of a currency; **quelle est la ~ de la livre en ce moment?** what is the pound worth *ou* what is the value of the pound at the moment?; (*jugement subjectif*) **la livre/le franc/cette pièce n'a plus de ~** the pound/franc/this coin is worthless; **estimer la ~ d'un terrain/tableau à 80 000 F** to value a piece of land/a picture at 80,000 francs, put the value *ou* estimate the value of a piece of land/of a picture at 80,000 francs; **ces tableaux sont de même ~** *ou* **ont la même ~** these pictures are of equal value *ou* have the same value *ou* are worth the same amount; (*Poste*) **en ~ déclarée** value declared; **~ faciale** *ou* **nominale** face *ou* nominal value; **~ ajoutée** added value; *voir* **taxe**.

b (*Bourse: gén pl: titre*) security. (*Bourse*) **~s (boursières)** securities, stocks and shares; (*Comm: effet*) bill (of exchange); **~s (mobilières)** transferable securities; (*Comm*) **~ en compte** value in account; **~s disponibles** liquid assets; **~s de premier ordre** *ou* **de tout repos** *ou* **de père de famille** gilt-edged *ou* blue-chip securities; **~s vedettes de la cote** leaders; *voir* **bourse, refuge**.

c (*qualité*) *[personne, auteur]* worth, merit; *[roman, tableau]* value, merit; *[science, théorie]* value. **un homme de (grande) ~** a man of great personal worth *ou* merit; **professeur/acteur de ~** teacher/actor of considerable merit; **la ~ de cette méthode/découverte reste à prouver** the value of this method/discovery is still to be proved; **estimer** *ou* **juger qn/qch à sa (juste) ~** to estimate *ou* judge sb/sth at his/its true value *ou* worth; **son œuvre n'est pas sans ~** his work is not without value *ou* merit; **je doute de la ~ de cette méthode** I am doubtful as to the value *ou* merit(s) of this method *ou* as to how valuable this method is; **ce meuble n'a qu'une ~ sentimentale** this piece of furniture has only sentimental value; **accorder** *ou* **attacher de la ~ à qch** to value sth, place value on sth; *voir* **jugement, juste**.

d **~s (morales/intellectuelles)** (moral/intellectual) values; **échelle** *ou* **hiérarchie des ~s** scale of values; **système de ~s** value system.

e (*idée de mesure, de délimitation*) *[couleur, terme, carte à jouer]* value; (*Math*) *[fonction]* value; (*Mus*) *[note]* value, length. **la ~ affective/poétique d'un mot** the emotive/poetic value of a word; (*Math*) **~ absolue** absolute value; **~ relative/absolue d'un terme** relative/absolute value of a term; **en ~ absolue/relative l'ouvrier américain gagne plus que son homologue français** in absolute/relative terms American workmen earn more than their French counterparts; (*Mus*) **la ~ d'une blanche est deux noires** one minim (*Brit*) *ou* half note (*US*) is equivalent to *ou* equals *ou* is worth two crochets (*Brit*) *ou* quarter notes (*US*); **donnez-lui la ~ d'un verre à liqueur/d'une cuiller à café** give him the equivalent of a liqueur glass/a teaspoonful.

f (*loc*) *bijou, meuble* **de ~** valuable, of value; **objets de ~** valuables, articles of value; **sans ~** *objet* valueless, worthless; *témoignage* invalid, valueless; **mettre en ~** *bien, terrain* to exploit; *capitaux* to exploit, turn to good account; *détail, caractéristique* to bring out, highlight; *objet décoratif* to set off, show (off) to advantage, highlight; *personne* to show to advantage *ou* in a flattering light; **se mettre en ~** to show o.s. off to advantage; **ce chapeau te met en ~** that hat (of yours) is very flattering *ou* becoming, that hat really suits you; *voir* **mise**[2].

valeureusement [valœʀøzmɑ̃] **adv** valorously.

valeureux, -euse [valœʀø, øz] **adj** valorous.

validation [validasjɔ̃] **nf** (*voir* **valider**) validation; authentication; ratification; stamping.

valide [valid] **adj** a *personne* (*non blessé ou handicapé*) able, able-bodied; (*en bonne santé*) fit, well (*attrib*); *membre* good (*épith*). **la population ~** the able-bodied population; **se sentir assez ~ pour faire** to feel fit *ou* well enough to do, feel up to doing. b *billet, carte d'identité* valid.

validement [validmɑ̃] **adv** (*Jur*) validly.

valider [valide] 1 **vt** *passeport, billet* to validate; *document* to authenticate; *décision* to ratify. **faire ~ un bulletin** to get a coupon validated *ou* stamped.

validité [validite] **nf** validity. **durée de ~ d'un billet** (period of) validity of a ticket.

valise [valiz] **nf** (suit)case, bag. **faire sa ~/ses ~s** to pack one's (suit)case/(suit)cases *ou* bags, pack; (*fig: partir*) **faire ses ~s** *ou* **sa ~** to pack one's bags, pack up and leave; **la ~ (diplomatique)** the diplomatic bag; *voir* **boucler, mot**.

Valkyrie [valkiʀi] **nf** Valkyrie, Walkyrie.

vallée [vale] **nf** (*Géog*) valley. **les gens de la ~** the lowland people; **~ suspendue/glaciaire** hanging/U-shaped *ou* glaciated valley; **~ sèche** *ou* **morte** dry valley; **la ~ de la Loire/du Nil** the Loire/Nile valley; (*fig littér*) **la vie est une ~ de larmes** life is a vale *ou* valley of tears (*littér*).

vallon [valɔ̃] **nm** small valley.

vallonné, e [valɔne] **adj** undulating, cut by valleys (*attrib*).

vallonnement [valɔnmɑ̃] **nm** undulation.

valoche* [valɔʃ] **nf** case, bag.

valoir [valwaʀ] 29 1 **vi** a *[propriété, bijou]* **~ (un certain prix/une certaine somme)** to be worth (a certain price/amount); **ça vaut combien?** how much is it (worth)?; **~ de l'argent** to be worth money; **ça vaut bien 50 F** (*estimation*) it must be worth 50 francs; (*jugement*) it is well worth 50 francs; **~ cher/encore plus cher** to be worth a lot/still more; **cette montre vaut-elle plus cher que l'autre? — elles se valent à peu près** is this watch worth more than the other one? — they are worth about the same (amount); *voir* **pesant**.

b (*avoir certaines qualités*) **que vaut cet auteur/cette pièce/le nouveau maire?** is this author/this play/the new mayor any good?; **sa dernière pièce ne valait pas grand-chose** his last play wasn't particularly good, his last play wasn't up to much* (*Brit*); **ils ne valent pas mieux l'un que l'autre** there's nothing to choose between them, they are two of a kind, one's as bad as the other; **leur fils ne vaut pas cher!** their son isn't much good, their son's a bit of a waster *ou* a bad egg*; **tissu/marchandise qui ne vaut rien** material/article which is no good, rubbishy *ou* trashy material/article; **prendre une chose pour ce qu'elle vaut** to take a thing for what it is; **il a conscience de ce qu'il vaut** he is aware of his worth, he knows his (own) worth *ou* value, he knows what he's worth; **ce climat ne vaut rien pour les rhumatismes** this climate is no good (at all) for rheumatism; **l'inaction ne lui vaut rien** inactivity does not suit him *ou* isn't (any) good for him *ou* does nothing for him*; **ça ne lui a rien valu** that didn't do him any good; **votre argument ne vaut rien** your argument is worthless; **cet outil ne vaut rien** this tool is useless *ou* no good *ou* no use.

c (*être valable*) to hold, apply, be valid. **ceci ne vaut que dans certains cas** this only holds *ou* applies *ou* is only valid in certain cases; **la décision vaut pour tout le monde** the decision goes for *ou* applies to *ou* is applicable to everyone; **cette pièce/cet auteur vaut surtout par son originalité** this play's/author's merit *ou* worth lies chiefly in its/his originality, the chief *ou* principal merit of this play/author lies in its/his originality; *voir aussi* **vaille**.

d (*équivaloir à*) **la campagne vaut bien la mer** the countryside is just as good *ou* is every bit as good as the seaside; (*Mus*) **une blanche vaut deux noires** one minim (*Brit*) *ou* half note (*US*) is equivalent to *ou* equals two crochets (*Brit*) *ou* quarter notes (*US*), one minim (*Brit*) *ou* half note (*US*) is worth (the same as) two crochets (*Brit*) *ou* quarter notes (*US*); **il vaut largement son frère** he is every bit as good as his brother *ou* quite the equal of his brother; **ce nouveau médicament/traitement ne vaut pas le précédent** this new medicine/treatment is not as good as *ou* isn't up to* (*Brit*) *ou* isn't a patch on* (*Brit*) the previous one; **tout cela ne vaut pas la mer/la liberté** this is all very well but it's not like the seaside/having one's freedom *ou* but give me the seaside/freedom any day!; **rien ne vaut la mer** there's nothing like the sea, there's nothing to beat the sea; **ces deux candidats/méthodes se valent** there's nothing to choose between these two applicants/methods, these two applicants/methods are of equal merit *ou* are much of a muchness*; **cette méthode en vaut une autre** it's as good a method as any (other); (*en mal*) **ces deux frères se valent** these two brothers are two of a kind *ou* are both about as bad as each other; **ça se vaut*** it's six of one and half a dozen of the other*, it's all one, it's all the same; *voir* **homme**.

e (*justifier*) to be worth. **Lyon vaut (bien) une visite/le déplacement/le voyage*** Lyons is (well) worth a visit/the journey; **le musée valait le détour** the museum was worth the detour; **cela vaut la peine** it's worth it, it's worth the trouble; **le film vaut (la peine) d'être vu** *ou* **qu'on le voie** the film is worth seeing; **cela valait la peine d'essayer** it was worth trying *ou* a try *ou* a go; **ça vaut la peine qu'il y aille** it's worth it for him to go, it's worth his while going; **cela ne vaut pas la peine d'en parler** (*c'est trop mauvais*) it's not worth wasting one's breath over, it's not worth talking about; (*c'est insignifiant*) it's hardly *ou* not worth mentioning.

f (*Comm*) **à ~** to be deducted; **paiement/acompte à ~ sur ...** payment/deposit to be deducted from ...; **j'ai 90 F à ~** *ou* **j'ai un à ~ de 90 F dans ce grand magasin** I've 90 francs' credit at this store.

g **faire ~** *domaine* to exploit; *titres, capitaux* to exploit, turn to (good) account, invest profitably; *droits* to assert; *fait, argument* to emphasize; (*mettre en vedette*) *caractéristique* to highlight, bring out; *personne* to show off to advantage; **je lui fis ~ que ...** I impressed upon him that ..., I pointed out to him that ...; **se faire ~** to push o.s. forward, get o.s. noticed; **il ne sait pas se faire ~** he doesn't know how to make sure he's noticed *ou* to show himself off to best advantage; *voir aussi* **faire.**

h (*loc*) **ça/il ne vaut pas tripette*** *ou* **un clou*** *ou* **un pet de lapin*** *ou* **un pet de coucou*** *[machine, film, auteur]* it's/he's a dead loss*; **il ne vaut pas la corde pour le pendre** let's not waste a second on him – he's not worth it; **ne faire/n'écrire rien qui vaille** to do/write nothing useful *ou* worthwhile *ou* of any use; **cela ne me dit rien qui vaille** it doesn't appeal to me in the least *ou* slightest; **ça vaut le coup** it's worth it; **c'est un spectacle qui vaut le coup** it's a show worth seeing; **ça ne vaut pas le coup de partir pour 2 jours*** it's not worth going (just) for 2 days; **il vaut mieux refuser, mieux vaut refuser** it is better to refuse; **il vaudrait mieux que vous refusiez** you had better refuse, you would do better *ou* best to refuse, you had best refuse; **avertis-le: ça vaut mieux** I would tell him if I were you, it would be better if you told him; **il vaut mieux le prévenir** we (*ou* you *etc*) had better tell him; **mieux vaut trop de travail que pas assez** too much work is better than not enough; *voir* **mieux, vaille que vaille.**

2 **vt** (*causer, coûter*) **~ qch à qn** to earn sb sth; **ceci lui a valu des louanges/des reproches** this earned *ou* brought him praise/reproaches *ou* brought praise/reproaches upon him; **les soucis/les ennuis que nous a valus cette affaire!** the worry/trouble that this business has cost *ou* brought us!; **qu'est ce qui nous vaut l'honneur de cette visite?** to what do we owe the honour of this visit?; **l'incident lui a valu d'être accusé d'imprudence** the incident earned him the accusation of carelessness; **un bon rhume, c'est tout ce que cela lui a valu de sortir sous la pluie** a bad cold is all he gained *ou* got for going out in the rain.

valorisant, e [valɔʀizɑ̃, ɑ̃t] **adj** status-enhancing (*épith*).

valorisation [valɔʀizasjɔ̃] **nf** a *[région]* (economic) development; *[produit]* enhanced value; (*Psych*) self-actualization (*SPÉC*). b *[entreprise]* valuation.

valoriser [valɔʀize] [1] 1 **vt** a (*mettre en valeur*) *région* to develop (the economy of); *produit* to enhance the value of; *conduite, personne* to increase the standing of, actualize (*SPÉC*). b (*évaluer, expertiser*) to value. 2 **se valoriser vpr** *[immeuble]* to increase in value; *[personne]* to increase one's standing, self-actualize (*SPÉC*).

valse [vals] **nf** a (*danse, air*) waltz. **~ lente/viennoise** slow/Viennese waltz; **~ musette** waltz (*to accordion accompaniment*). b (*fig: carrousel*) musical chairs. **la ~ des étiquettes** constant price rises; **la ~ des ministres** *ou* **des portefeuilles** the ministerial musical chairs; **~-hésitation** pussyfooting* (*NonC*).

valser [valse] [1] **vi** a (*danser*) to waltz. b (*: *fig*) **envoyer ~ qch/qn** (*en heurtant*) to send sth/sb flying; **envoyer ~ qn** (*rembarrer*) to send sb packing*; **il est allé ~ contre le mur** he went flying against the wall; **faire ~ l'argent** to spend money like water, throw money around; **faire ~ les chiffres** to dazzle people with figures; **faire ~ les ministres/les employés** to play musical chairs with ministerial/staff posts.

valseur, -euse [valsœʀ, øz] **nm,f** waltzer.

valve [valv] **nf** (*Bot, Élec, Tech, Zool*) valve.

valvulaire [valvylɛʀ] **adj** (*Anat, Méd*) valvular.

valvule [valvyl] **nf** (*Anat, Tech*) valve; (*Bot*) valvule. **~ mitrale** mitral valve.

vamp [vɑ̃p] **nf** vamp.

vamper* [vɑ̃pe] [1] **vt** to vamp.

vampire [vɑ̃piʀ] **nm** a (*fantôme*) vampire. b (*fig*) (†: *criminel*) vampire; (*escroc, requin*) vulture, vampire, bloodsucker. c (*Zool*) vampire bat.

vampirique [vɑ̃piʀik] **adj** vampiric.

vampiriser* [vɑ̃piʀize] [1] **vt** (*fig*) to suck the lifeblood out of.

vampirisme [vɑ̃piʀism] **nm** (*Psych*) necrophilia; (*fig: rapacité*) vampirism.

van¹ [vɑ̃] **nm** (*panier*) winnowing basket.

van² [vɑ̃] **nm** (*véhicule*) horse-box (*Brit*), horse trailer (*US*).

vanadium [vanadjɔm] **nm** vanadium.

Vancouver [vɑ̃kuvɛʀ] **n** Vancouver. **île de ~** Vancouver Island.

vandale [vɑ̃dal] 1 **nmf** vandal; (*Hist*) Vandal. 2 **adj** vandal (*épith*); (*Hist*) Vandalic.

vandalisme [vɑ̃dalism] **nm** vandalism.

vandoise [vɑ̃dwaz] **nf** dace.

vanesse [vanɛs] **nf** vanessa.

vanille [vanij] **nf** (*Bot, Culin*) vanilla. **crème/glace à la ~** vanilla cream/ice cream.

vanillé, e [vanije] **adj** vanilla (*épith*), vanilla-flavoured.

vanillier [vanije] **nm** vanilla plant.

vanilline [vanilin] **nf** vanillin.

vanité [vanite] **nf** a (*amour-propre*) vanity, conceit; (*frivolité*) shallowness, superficiality. **il avait des petites ~s d'artiste** he had the little conceits of an artist; **sans ~** without false modesty; **tirer ~ de** to pride o.s. on; **flatter/blesser qn dans sa ~** to flatter/wound sb's pride. b (*littér: futilité: voir* **vain**) emptiness; hollowness; vanity; shallowness, superficiality; futility, fruitlessness; uselessness, idleness.

vaniteusement [vanitøzmɑ̃] **adv** vainly, conceitedly.

vaniteux, -euse [vanitø, øz] 1 **adj** vain, conceited. 2 **nm,f** vain *ou* conceited person.

vannage [vanaʒ] **nm** (*Agr*) winnowing.

vanne [van] **nf** a *[écluse]* (lock) gate, sluice (gate); *[barrage, digue]* floodgate, (sluice) gate; *[moulin]* (weir) hatch; *[canalisation]* gate. (*Aut*) **~ thermostatique** thermostat; (*fig*) **ouvrir les ~s** to turn on the waterworks*. b (*: *remarque*) dig*, jibe. **envoyer une ~ à qn** to have a dig at sb*, jibe at sb.

vanneau, **pl ~x** [vano] **nm** peewit, lapwing.

vanner [vane] [1] **vt** a (*Agr*) to winnow. b (‡: *fatiguer*) to fag out* (*Brit*), do in*, knacker‡ (*Brit*). **je suis vanné** I'm dead-beat* *ou* fagged out* (*Brit*) *ou* knackered‡ (*Brit*).

vannerie [vanʀi] **nf** (*métier*) basketry, basketwork; (*objets*) wickerwork, basketwork.

vanneur, -euse [vanœʀ, øz] **nm,f** winnower.

vannier [vanje] **nm** basket maker, basket worker.

vantail, **pl -aux** [vɑ̃taj, o] **nm** *[porte]* leaf; *[armoire]* door. **porte à double ~** *ou* **à (deux) vantaux** Dutch door.

vantard, e [vɑ̃taʀ, aʀd] 1 **adj** boastful, bragging (*épith*), boasting (*épith*). 2 **nm,f** braggart, boaster.

vantardise [vɑ̃taʀdiz] **nf** (*caractère*) boastfulness; (*propos*) boast, boasting (*NonC*), bragging (*NonC*).

vanter [vɑ̃te] [1] 1 **vt** (*recommander, préconiser*) *auteur, endroit* to speak highly of, speak in praise of; *qualités* to vaunt (*frm*), praise, speak highly of, speak in praise of; *méthode, avantages, marchandises* to vaunt; (*frm: louer*) *personne, qualités* to extol (*frm*), laud (*frm*), sing the praises of. **film dont on vante les mérites** much-praised film.

2 **se vanter vpr** a (*fanfaronner*) to boast, brag. **sans (vouloir) me ~** without wishing to blow my own trumpet, without false modesty, without wishing to boast *ou* brag.

b (*se targuer*) **se ~ de** to pride o.s. on; **se ~ d'avoir fait qch** to pride o.s. on having done sth; **il se vante de (pouvoir) faire ...** he boasts he can *ou* will do ...; (*iro*) **il ne s'en est pas vanté** he kept quiet about it; **il n'y a pas de quoi se ~** there's nothing to be proud of *ou* to boast about; **et il s'en vante!** and he's proud of it!

va-nu-pieds [vanypje] **nmf inv** (*péj*) tramp, beggar.

vapes‡ [vap] **nfpl: tomber dans les ~** to fall into a dead faint, pass out; **être dans les ~** (*distrait*) to have one's head in the clouds; (*évanoui*) to be out for the count* *ou* out cold*; (*drogué, après un choc*) to be woozy* *ou* in a daze.

vapeur [vapœʀ] 1 **nf** a (*littér: brouillard*) haze (*NonC*), vapour (*NonC*).

b **~ (d'eau)** steam, (water) vapour; **~ atmosphérique** atomospheric vapour; (*Tech*) **à ~** steam (*épith*); **bateau à ~** steamship, steamer; **repassage à la ~** steam-ironing; (*Culin*) **(cuit à la) ~** steamed.

c (*émanation: Chim, Phys*) vapour. (*nocives*) **~s** fumes; **~s d'essence** petrol (*Brit*) *ou* gasoline (*US*) fumes; **~ saturante** saturated vapour; **~ sèche** dry steam.

d (†: *gén pl: malaises*) **~s** vapours†; **avoir ses ~s** (*bouffées de chaleur*) to have hot flushes; (†: *malaise*) to have the vapours†.

e (*gén pl: griserie*) **les ~s de l'ivresse/de la gloire** the heady fumes of intoxication/of glory.

f (*loc*) **aller à toute ~** *[navire]* to sail full steam ahead; (*: *fig*) to go at full speed, go full steam ahead (*fig*); **renverser la ~** (*lit*) to reverse engines; (*fig*) to go into reverse.

2 **nm** (*bateau*) steamship, steamer.

vaporeusement [vapɔʀøzmɑ̃] **adv** vaporously.

vaporeux, -euse [vapɔʀø, øz] **adj** *tissu, robe* filmy, gossamer (*épith, littér*), diaphanous; (*littér*) *lumière, atmosphère* hazy, misty, vaporous; *nuage, cheveux* gossamer (*épith, littér*). (*Art*) **lointain ~** sfumato background.

vaporisateur [vapɔʀizatœʀ] **nm** (*à parfum*) spray, atomizer; (*Agr*) spray; (*Tech*) vaporizer.

vaporisation [vapɔʀizasjɔ̃] **nf** (*voir* **vaporiser**) spraying; vaporization.

vaporiser [vapɔʀize] [1] 1 **vt** a *parfum, insecticide, surface* to spray. b (*Phys*) to vaporize, turn to vapour. 2 **se vaporiser vpr** (*Phys*) to vaporize.

vaquer [vake] [1] 1 **vaquer à vt indir** (*s'occuper de*) to attend to, see to. **~ à ses occupations** to attend to one's affairs, go about one's business. 2 **vi** a (†: *être vacant*) to stand *ou* be vacant. b (*Admin: être en vacances*) to be on vacation.

varan [vaʀɑ̃] **nm** varanus.

varappe [vaʀap] **nf** (*sport*) rock-climbing; (*ascension*) (rock) climb. **faire de la ~** to go rock-climbing.

varapper [vaʀape] [1] **vi** to rock-climb.

varappeur [vaʀapœʀ] **nm** (rock-)climber, cragsman.

varappeuse [vaʀapøz] **nf** (rock-)climber.

varech [vaʀɛk] **nm** wrack, kelp, varec.

vareuse [vaʀøz] **nf** *[pêcheur, marin]* pea jacket; (*d'uniforme*) tunic; (*de ville*) jacket.

variabilité [vaʀjabilite] **nf** a *[temps, humeur]* changeableness, variableness. b (*Math, Sci*) variability.

variable [vaʀjabl] 1 **adj** a (*incertain*) *temps* variable, changeable, unsettled; *humeur* changeable, variable; (*Mét*) *vent* variable. **le baromètre est au ~** the barometer is at *ou* reads "change"; **le temps est au ~** the weather is variable *ou* changeable *ou* unsettled.

b (*susceptible de changements*) *montant, allocation, part* variable; *dimensions, modalités, formes* adaptable, variable; (*Math, Sci*) *grandeur, quantité, facteur* variable; (*Ling*) *forme, mot* inflectional, inflected (*épith*). (*Fin*) **à revenu ~** variable yield (*épith*); **la récolte est ~: parfois bonne, parfois maigre** the harvest is variable *ou* varies: sometimes good, sometimes poor; **mot ~ en genre** word that is inflected *ou* marked for gender; *voir* **foyer, géométrie.**

c (*au pl: varié*) *résultats, réactions* varied, various, varying (*épith*). **les réactions sont très ~s: certains sont pour, d'autres sont contre** reactions are very varied *ou* vary greatly: some are for and others are against.

2 **nf** (*Chim, Ling, Math, Phys, Statistique*) variable. **~ aléatoire** random variable; (*Ordin*) **~ entière/numérique** integer/numeric variable.

variance [vaʀjɑ̃s] **nf** (*Sci*) variance.

variante [vaʀjɑ̃t] **nf** (*gén*) variant (*de* of), variation (*de* on); (*Ling, Littérat*) variant (*de* of). **une variante (d'itinéraire)** an alternative route.

variateur [vaʀjatœʀ] **nm**: **~ de vitesse** speed variator; **~ (de lumière)** dimmer.

variation [vaʀjasjɔ̃] **nf** a (*action: voir* **varier**) variation, varying; change, changing. b (*écart, changement, Sci*) variation (*de* in); (*transformation*) change (*de* in). **les ~s de la température** the variations in (the) temperature, the temperature variations; **les ~s du mode de vie au cours des siècles** the changes in life-style through the centuries; **les ~s orthographiques/phonétiques au cours des siècles/selon les régions** spelling/phonetic variations *ou* variants throughout the centuries/from region to region. c (*Mus*) variation. (*fig hum*) **~s sur un thème connu** variations on the same old theme *ou* on a well-worn theme.

varice [vaʀis] **nf** (*Méd*) varicose vein, varix (*SPÉC*). **bas à ~s** support stockings.

varicelle [vaʀisɛl] **nf** chickenpox, varicella (*SPÉC*).

varié, e [vaʀje] (**ptp de varier**) **adj** a (*non monotone*) *style, existence, paysage* varied, varying (*épith*); *programme, menu* (*qu'on change souvent*) varying (*épith*); (*diversifié*) varied. **un travail très ~** a very varied job; (*Mil*) **en terrain ~** on irregular terrain; (*Mus*) **air ~** theme with *ou* and variations; *voir* **musique.**

b (*littér: non uni*) *tissu, couleur* variegated.

c (*divers*) *résultats* various, varying (*épith*), varied; *produits, sujets, objets* various. **hors-d'œuvre ~s** selection of hors d'œuvres, hors d'œuvres variés; **ayant recours à des arguments ~s** having recourse to various arguments; **on rencontre les opinions les plus ~es** you come across the most varied *ou* diverse opinions on the subject.

varier [vaʀje] [7] 1 **vi** a (*changer*) to vary, change. (*Math*) **faire ~ une fonction** to vary a function; *voir* **souvent.**

b (*différer, présenter divers aspects ou degrés, Sci*) to vary; (*Ling*) *[mot, forme]* to be inflected. **les professeurs varient souvent dans leurs opinions au sujet de ...** teachers' opinions often vary on the subject of ...; **elle n'a jamais varié sur ce point** she has never changed her opinion on that.

2 **vt** a *style, vie* (*changer*) to vary; (*rendre moins monotone*) to vary, lend *ou* give variety to. (*iro*) **pour ~ les plaisirs** just for a pleasant change (*iro*); **ils ne font que ~ la sauce*** they only dress it up differently, they just make it look different; **elle variait souvent sa coiffure/le menu** she often varied *ou* changed her hair style/the menu *ou* rang the changes on her hair style/the menu.

b *problèmes, thèmes, produits* to vary, diversify.

variété [vaʀjete] **nf** a (*caractère: voir* **varié**) variety, diversity. **étonné par la grande ~ des produits/opinions** surprised at the great variety *ou* diversity *ou* the wide range of products/opinions; **aimer la ~** to like variety; **~ des langues** language variety.

b (*type, espèce*) variety; (*aspect, forme*) variety, type. **il cultive exclusivement cette ~ de rose** he cultivates exclusively this variety of rose; **on y rencontrait toutes les ~s de criminels/de costumes** there you could find every possible variety *ou* type of criminal/costume.

c **~s** (*Littérat*) miscellanies; (*Music hall*) variety show; (*Rad, TV: musique*) light music (*NonC*); **émission/spectacle/théâtre de ~s** variety programme/show/hall.

variole [vaʀjɔl] **nf** smallpox, variola (*SPÉC*).

variolé, e [vaʀjɔle] **adj** pockmarked.

varioleux, -euse [vaʀjɔlø, øz] 1 **adj** suffering from smallpox, variolous (*SPÉC*). 2 **nm** (*gén pl*) smallpox case, patient suffering from smallpox.

variolique [vaʀjɔlik] **adj** smallpox (*épith*), variolous (*SPÉC*).

variomètre [vaʀjɔmɛtʀ] **nm** variometer.

variqueux, -euse [vaʀikø, øz] **adj** *ulcère* varicose.

varlope [vaʀlɔp] **nf** trying-plane.

varloper [vaʀlɔpe] [1] **vt** to plane (down).

Varsovie [vaʀsɔvi] **n** Warsaw.

vasculaire [vaskylɛʀ] **adj** (*Anat, Bot*) vascular. **système ~ sanguin** blood-vascular system.

vascularisation [vaskylaʀizasjɔ̃] **nf** (*processus*) vascularization; (*réseau*) vascularity.

vascularisé, e [vaskylaʀize] **adj** vascular.

vase¹ [vɑz] 1 **nm** (*à fleurs, décoratif*) vase, bowl. (*fig*) **en ~ clos** *vivre, croître* in isolation, cut off from the world, in seclusion; *étudier, discuter* behind closed doors, in seclusion; (*Horticulture*) **taillé en ~** cut in the shape of a vase, vase-shaped; *voir* **goutte.** 2 **comp ▸vases communicants** communicating vessels **▸vase d'expansion** (*Aut*) expansion bottle *ou* tank **▸vase de nuit** chamber(pot) **▸vases sacrés** (*Rel*) sacred vessels.

vase² [vɑz] **nf** silt, mud, sludge (*on riverbed*).

vasectomie [vazɛktɔmi] **nf** vasectomy.

vaseline [vaz(ə)lin] **nf** Vaseline ®, petroleum jelly.

vaseux, -euse [vɑzø, øz] **adj** a (*) (*fatigué, drogué*) woozy*, in a daze*; (*confus*) *raisonnement* woolly*, hazy, muddled. b (*boueux*) silty, muddy, sludgy. c (*médiocre*) *astuce, plaisanterie* pathetic*, lousy‡.

vasistas [vazistɑs] **nm** *[porte]* (opening) window, fanlight; *[fenêtre]* fanlight.

vaso(-)constricteur, pl vaso(-)constricteurs [vazoykɔ̃stʀiktœʀ] 1 **adj m** vasoconstrictor (*épith*). 2 **nm** vasoconstrictor.

vaso(-)constriction [vazokɔ̃stʀiksjɔ̃] **nf** vasoconstriction.

vaso(-)dilatateur, pl vaso(-)dilatateurs [vazodilatatœʀ] 1 **adj m** vasodilator (*épith*). 2 **nm** vasodilator.

vaso(-)dilatation [vazodilatasjɔ̃] **nf** vasodil(at)ation.

vaso(-)moteur, -trice [vazomɔtœʀ, tʀis] **adj** vasomotor (*épith*).

vasouillard, e* [vazujaʀ, aʀd] **adj** *personne* woozy*, in a daze; *explication, raisonnement* woolly*, hazy, muddled.

vasouiller* [vazuje] [1] **vi** *[personne]* to flounder, struggle, fumble about; *[opération, affaire]* to struggle along, limp along; *[argument, article]* to go haywire*.

vasque [vask] **nf** (*bassin, lavabo*) basin; (*coupe*) bowl.

vassal, e, mpl -aux [vasal, o] **nm,f** (*Hist, fig*) vassal.

vassalité [vasalite] **nf, vasselage** [vaslaʒ] **nm** (*Hist, fig*) vassalage.

vaste [vast] **adj** a *surface, édifice, salle* vast, immense, enormous, huge; *vêtement* huge, enormous; *organisation, groupement* vast, huge. **à la tête d'un ~ empire industriel** at the head of a vast *ou* huge industrial empire; **de par le ~ monde** throughout the whole wide world.

b (*fig*) *connaissances, érudition, ambitions* vast, immense, enormous, far-reaching; *génie, culture* immense, enormous; *domaine, sujet* wide(-ranging), huge, vast; *problème* wide-ranging, far-reaching. **un homme d'une ~ culture** a man of immense *ou* enormous culture, a highly cultured man; **ce sujet est trop ~** this subject is far too wide(-ranging) *ou* vast.

c (**: intensif*) **c'est une ~ rigolade** *ou* **plaisanterie** *ou* **fumisterie** it's a huge *ou* an enormous joke *ou* hoax *ou* farce.

va-t-en-guerre [vatɑ̃gɛʀ] **nm inv** warmonger.

Vatican [vatikɑ̃] **nm**: **le ~** the Vatican.

Vaticane [vatikan] **adj f**: **la (bibliothèque) ~** the Vatican Library.

vaticinateur, -trice [vatisinatœʀ, tʀis] **nm,f** (*littér*) vaticinator (*frm, littér*).

vaticination [vatisinasjɔ̃] **nf** (*littér*) vaticination (*frm, littér*). (*péj*) **~s** pompous predictions *ou* prophecies.

vaticiner [vatisine] [1] **vi** (*littér: prophétiser*) to vaticinate (*frm, littér*); (*péj*) to make pompous predictions *ou* prophecies.

va-tout [vatu] **nm**: **jouer son ~** to stake *ou* risk one's all.

Vaud [vo] **nm** *voir* **canton.**

vaudeville [vod(ə)vil] **nm** vaudeville, light comedy. (*fig*) **ça tourne au ~** it's turning into a farce.

vaudevillesque [vod(ə)vilɛsk] **adj** vaudeville (*épith*); (*fig*) farcical.

vaudevilliste [vod(ə)vilist] **nm** writer of vaudeville.

vaudois, e [vodwa, waz] 1 **adj** (*Hist*) Waldensian; (*Géog*) Vaudois, of *ou* from the canton of Vaud. 2 **nm,f** (*Hist*) Waldensian. (*Géog*) **V~(e)** Vaudois.

vaudou [vodu] 1 **nm**: **le (culte du) ~** voodoo. 2 **adj inv** voodoo (*épith*).

vau-l'eau [volo] **adv**: **à ~** (*lit*) with the stream *ou* current; (*fig*) **aller** *ou* **s'en aller à ~** to be on the road to ruin, go to the dogs*; **voilà tous mes projets à ~!** there are all my plans in ruins! *ou* down the drain!* *ou* gone for a burton!* (*Brit*).

vaurien, -ienne [voʀjɛ̃, jɛn] 1 **nm,f** (*voyou*) good-for-nothing; (*garnement*) little devil*. **petit ~!** little devil!* 2 **nm** (*Naut*) small yacht *ou* sailing boat.

vaut [vo] *voir* **valoir.**

vautour [votuʀ] **nm** (*Zool, fig*) vulture.

vautrer (se) [votʀe] [1] **vpr**: **se ~ dans** *boue,* (*fig*) *vice, obscénité, oisiveté* to wallow in; *fauteuil* to loll *ou* slouch in; **se ~ sur** *tapis, canapé* to sprawl on; **vautré à plat ventre** *ou* **par terre** sprawling *ou* sprawled (flat) on the ground; **vautré dans l'herbe/sur le tapis** sprawling *ou* sprawled in the grass/on the carpet; (*fig littér*) **se ~ dans la fange** to wallow in the mire.

vauvert [vovɛʀ] *voir* **diable**.
vaux [vo] **nmpl** *voir* **val**.
va-vite* [vavit] **adv: à la ~** in a rush *ou* hurry; **faire qch à la ~** to rush sth, do sth in a rush *ou* hurry.
V.D.Q.S. (**abrév de vin délimité de qualité supérieure**) *label guaranteeing quality of wine*.
veau, pl ~x [vo] **nm** a (*Zool*) calf. **~ marin** seal; (*Bible*) **le V~ d'or** the golden calf; **adorer le V~ d'or** to worship Mammon; **tuer le ~ gras** to kill the fatted calf; *voir* **crier, pleurer**. b (*Culin*) veal. **escalope/côte/paupiettes de ~** veal escalope/chop/olives; **foie/pied/tête de ~** calf's liver/foot/head; **rôti de ~** roast veal; **~ marengo** veal marengo; *voir* **blanquette, ris[1]**. c (*cuir*) calfskin. d (*: *péj*) (*personne*) sheep; (*cheval*) nag (*péj*); (*automobile*) tank* (*péj*).
vécés* [vese] **nmpl: les ~** the toilet, the restroom (*US*).
vecteur [vɛktœʀ] 1 **adj m** (*Astron, Géom*) **rayon ~** radius vector. 2 **nm** (*Math*) vector; (*Mil: véhicule*) carrier; (*Bio: d'un virus*) carrier, vector (*SPÉC*); (*fig*) vehicle, medium.
vectoriel, -elle [vɛktɔʀjɛl] **adj** (*Math*) vectorial. **calcul ~** vector analysis.
vécu, e [veky] (**ptp de vivre**) 1 **adj** *histoire, aventure* real(-life) (*épith*), true(-life) (*épith*); *roman* real-life (*épith*), based on fact (*attrib*); (*Philos*) *temps, durée* lived. 2 **nm** (*Philos*) **le ~** that which has been lived; **ce que le lecteur veut, c'est du ~** what the reader wants is real-life *ou* actual experience.
vedettariat [vədetaʀja] **nm** (*état*) stardom; (*vedettes*) stars (*pl*). **détester le ~ politique** to hate the way politicians try to achieve stardom *ou* the way politicians behave like stars.
vedette [vədɛt] **nf** a (*artiste, fig: personnage en vue*) star. **les ~s de l'écran/du cinéma** screen/film stars; **une ~ de la diplomatie/de la politique** a leading light *ou* figure in diplomacy/politics; **joueur ~** star *ou* top player; **mannequin ~** top model; (*fig*) **produit-~** leading product, flagship (*fig*); **station-~** leading station.
b (*Ciné, Théât: première place*) **avoir la ~** to top the bill, have star billing; (*fig*) **avoir** *ou* **tenir la ~ (de l'actualité)** to be in the spotlight, make the headlines; (*fig*) **pendant toute la soirée il a eu la ~** he was in the limelight *ou* was the centre of attraction all evening; **partager la ~ avec qn** (*Théât*) to share star billing with sb, top the bill alongside sb; (*fig*) to share the limelight with sb; **mettre qn en ~** (*Ciné*) to give sb star billing; (*fig*) to push sb into the limelight, put the spotlight on sb; (*fig*) **ravir la ~** to steal the show (*à qn* from sb); **en ~ américaine** as a special guest star.
c (*embarcation*) launch; (*Mil*) patrol boat; (*munie de canons*) gun boat. **~ lance-torpilles** motor torpedo boat; **~ lance-missiles** missile-carrying launch.
d (*Mil ††: guetteur*) sentinel.
e (*Fin*) **~s de la cote** leaders.
vedettisation [vədɛtizasjɔ̃] **nf: la ~ de qn** pushing sb into the limelight, putting the spotlight on sb.
védique [vedik] **adj** Vedic.
védisme [vedism] **nm** Vedaism.
végétal, e, mpl -aux [veʒetal, o] 1 **adj** *graisses, teintures, huiles* vegetable (*épith*); *biologie, histologie, fibres, cellules* plant (*épith*); *sol* rich in humus; *ornementation* plant-like; *voir* **règne**. 2 **nm** vegetable, plant.
végétalien, -ienne [veʒetaljɛ̃, jɛn] **adj, nm,f** vegan.
végétalisme [veʒetalism] **nm** veganism.
végétarien, -ienne [veʒetaʀjɛ̃, jɛn] **adj, nm,f** vegetarian.
végétarisme [veʒetaʀism] **nm** vegetarianism.
végétatif, -ive [veʒetatif, iv] **adj** a (*Bot, Physiol*) vegetative. b (*fig péj*) vegetative, vegetable (*épith*).
végétation [veʒetasjɔ̃] **nf** a (*Bot*) vegetation. b (*Méd*) **~s (adénoïdes)** adenoids; **se faire opérer des ~s** to have one's adenoids removed *ou* out*.
végéter [veʒete] [6] **vi** a (*péj*) [*personne*] to vegetate; [*affaire*] to stagnate. b (*Agr*) (*être chétif*) to grow poorly, be stunted; (†: *pousser*) to grow, vegetate.
véhémence [veemɑ̃s] **nf** (*littér*) vehemence. **protester avec ~** to protest vehemently.
véhément, e [veemɑ̃, ɑ̃t] **adj** (*littér*) vehement.
véhémentement [veemɑ̃tmɑ̃] **adv** (*littér*) vehemently.
véhiculaire [veikylɛʀ] **adj** (*Ling*) **langue ~** lingua franca, common language.
véhicule [veikyl] **nm** a (*moyen de transport, agent de transmission*) vehicle. **~ automobile/utilitaire/industriel** motor/commercial/industrial vehicle; **~ spatial** spacecraft; **~ tout terrain** all-purpose *ou* all-roads vehicle. b (*fig*) vehicle, medium. **le langage est le ~ de la pensée** language is the vehicle *ou* medium of thought. c (*Rel*) **petit/grand ~** Hinayana/Mahayana Buddhism.
véhiculer [veikyle] [1] **vt** *marchandises, troupes* to convey, transport; (*fig*) *substance, idées* to convey, serve as a vehicle for.
veille [vɛj] **nf** a (*état*) wakefulness; (*période*) period of wakefulness. **en état de ~** in a waking state, awake; **entre la ~ et le sommeil** between waking and sleeping; **faire de la ~ technologique** to monitor technological development.
b (*garde*) (night) watch. **homme de ~** (night) watch; **prendre la ~** to take one's turn on watch.
c (*jour précédent*) **la ~** the day before; **la ~ au soir** the previous evening, the night *ou* evening before; **la ~ de Pâques/de cet examen** the day before Easter/that exam; **la ~ de Noël/du jour de l'an** Christmas/New Year's Eve; **la ~ de sa mort** on the eve of his death, on the day before his death; *voir* **demain**.
d (*fig*) **à la ~ de** *guerre, révolution* on the eve of; **être à la ~ de commettre une grave injustice/une grosse erreur** to be on the brink *ou* verge of committing a grave injustice/of making a big mistake; **ils étaient à la ~ d'être renvoyés/de manquer de vivres** they were on the point of being dismissed/of running out of supplies.
veillée [veje] **nf** a (*période*) evening (*spent in company*); (*réunion*) evening gathering *ou* meeting. **passer la ~ à jouer aux cartes** to spend the evening playing cards; **il se souvient de ces ~s d'hiver** he remembers those winter evening gatherings; **~ d'armes** (*Hist*) knightly vigil; (*fig*) night before combat (*fig*). b **~ (funèbre)** wake.
veiller [veje] [1] 1 **vi** a (*ne pas se coucher*) to stay up, sit up. **~ au chevet d'un malade** to sit up at the bedside of a sick person; **~ auprès du mort** to keep watch over the body.
b (*être de garde*) to be on watch; (*rester vigilant*) to be watchful, be vigilant.
c (*être en état de veille*) to be awake.
d (*faire la veillée*) to spend the evening in company.
2 **vt** *mort, malade* to watch over, sit up with. (*fig: obscurité*) **on veille les morts ici!** it's pitch dark in here.
3 **vt indir** a **veiller à** *intérêts, approvisionnement* to attend to, see to, look after; *bon fonctionnement, bonne marche de qch* to attend to, see to. **~ au bon fonctionnement d'une machine** to see to it that a machine is working properly, attend *ou* see to the proper working of a machine; **~ à ce que ...** to see to it that ..., make sure that ...; **veillez à ce que tout soit prêt** make sure that *ou* ensure that everything is ready; (*fig*) **~ au grain** to keep an eye open for trouble *ou* problems, look out for squalls (*fig*).
b (*surveiller*) **veiller sur** *personne, santé, bonheur de qn* to watch over, keep a watchful eye on.
veilleur [vɛjœʀ] **nm** a **~ (de nuit)** (night) watchman. b (*Mil*) look-out.
veilleuse [vɛjøz] **nf** a (*lampe*) night light; (*Aut*) sidelight. **mettre en ~** *lampe* to dim; *projet* to shelve; (*Aut*) **se mettre en ~** to put one's sidelights on; **mets-la en ~!**‡ cool it!‡ b (*flamme*) pilot light.
veinard, e* [vɛnaʀ, aʀd] 1 **adj** lucky, jammy‡ (*Brit*). 2 **nm,f** lucky devil* *ou* dog*, jammy so-and-so‡ (*Brit*).
veine [vɛn] **nf** a (*Anat*) vein. **~ coronaire/pulmonaire** coronary/pulmonary vein; **~ cave** vena cava; **~ porte** portal vein; (*fig*) **avoir du feu dans les ~s** to have fire in one's veins; *voir* **ouvrir, saigner, sang**.
b (*nervure*) vein; (*filon*) [*houille*] seam, vein; [*minerai non ferreux*] vein; [*minerai de fer*] lode, vein.
c (*fig: inspiration*) inspiration. **~ poétique/dramatique** poetic/dramatic inspiration; **sa ~ est tarie** his inspiration has dried up; **de la même ~** in the same vein; **être en ~** to be inspired, have a fit of inspiration; **être en ~ de patience/bonté/confidences** to be in a patient/benevolent/confiding mood *ou* frame of mind.
d (*: *chance*) luck. **c'est une ~** that's a bit of luck, what a bit of luck; **un coup de ~** a stroke of luck; **pas de ~!** hard *ou* bad *ou* rotten* luck!; **avoir de la ~** to be lucky; **il n'a pas de ~** (*dans la vie*) he has no luck; (*aujourd'hui*) he's out of luck; **ce type a de la ~** that fellow's a lucky devil* *ou* dog*; **avoir une ~ de cocu‡** *ou* **pendu*** to have the luck of the devil*; **il a eu de la ~ aux examens** he was lucky *ou* in luck at the exams, his luck was in at the exams; **il n'a pas eu de ~ aux examens** he was unlucky in the exams, his luck was out at the exams; (*iro*) **c'est bien ma ~** that's just my (rotten*) luck; **~ alors!** what luck!, lucky me!
veiné, e [vene] (**ptp de veiner**) **adj** a *bras, peau* veined, veiny. **bras à la peau ~e** arm with the veins apparent on the skin. b (*fig*) *bois* grained; *marbre* veined. **marbre ~ de vert** marble with green veins, green-veined marble.
veiner [vene] [1] **vt** (*pour donner l'aspect du bois*) to grain; (*pour donner l'aspect du marbre*) to vein. **les stries qui veinent une dalle de marbre** the streaks veining the surface of a marble slab; **les nervures qui veinent une feuille** the veins that appear on the surface of a leaf.
veineux, -euse [vɛnø, øz] **adj** a *système, sang* venous. b *bois* grainy; *marbre* veined.
veinule [venyl] **nf** (*Anat*) veinlet, venule (*SPÉC*); (*Bot*) venule.
veinure [venyʀ] **nf** (*voir* **veiner**) graining; veining. **admirant la ~ du marbre** admiring the veins *ou* veining of the marble.
vêlage [vɛlaʒ] **nm** (*Géog, Zool*) calving.
vélaire [velɛʀ] **adj, nf: (consonne/voyelle) ~** velar (consonant/vowel).
vélarisation [velaʀizasjɔ̃] **nf** velarization.
vélariser [velaʀize] [1] **vt** to velarize.
Velcro [vɛlkʀo] **nm** ® Velcro ®.
vêlement [vɛlmɑ̃] **nm** = **vêlage**.
vêler [vele] [1] **vi** to calve.
vélin [velɛ̃] **nm** (*peau*) vellum. **(papier) ~** vellum (paper).
véliplanchiste [veliplɑ̃ʃist] **nmf** windsurfer.

vélite [velit] **nm** (*Hist*) ~**s** velites.
velléitaire [veleitɛʀ] 1 **adj** irresolute, indecisive, wavering (*épith*). 2 **nmf** waverer.
velléité [veleite] **nf** vague desire, vague impulse. **leurs ~s révolutionnaires ne m'effrayaient guère** I was scarcely alarmed by their vague desire for revolution *ou* their vague revolutionary impulses; **une ~ de sourire/menace** a hint of a smile/threat.
vélo [velo] **nm** bike, cycle. ~ **de course** racing cycle; ~ **de santé**, ~ **d'appartement** exercise bike; ~**-cross** (*sport*) stunt-riding; (*vélo*) stunt bike; **faire du ~-cross** to go stunt-riding; ~ **tout terrain** mountain bike; **faire du ~ tout terrain** to go mountain-biking; **être à** *ou* **en** ~ to be on a bike; **venir à** *ou* **en** ~ to come by bike *ou* on a bike; **il sait faire du** ~ he can ride a bike; **je fais beaucoup de** ~ I cycle a lot, I do a lot of cycling; **on va faire un peu de** ~ we're going out (for a ride) on our bikes; **à 5 ans il allait déjà à** ~ he could already ride a bike at 5; **on y va à ~?** shall we go by bike? *ou* on our bikes?, shall we cycle there?; (*fig*) **il a un (petit) ~ dans la tête*** he's got a screw loose* (*Brit*), he isn't all there*.
véloce [velɔs] **adj** (*littér*) swift, fleet (*littér*).
vélocement [velɔsmɑ̃] **adv** (*littér*) swiftly, fleetly (*littér*).
vélocipède†† [velɔsipɛd] **nm** velocipede.
vélociste [velɔsist] **nmf** bicycle sales and repair man (*ou* woman).
vélocité [velɔsite] **nf** a (*Mus*) nimbleness, swiftness. **exercices de** ~ exercises for the agility of the fingers. b (*Tech*) velocity; (*littér: vitesse*) swiftness, fleetness (*littér*).
vélodrome [velodʀom] **nm** velodrome.
véloski [veloski] **nm** skibob.
vélomoteur [velɔmɔtœʀ] **nm** motorized bike, velosolex ®.
vélomotoriste [velɔmɔtɔʀist] **nmf** rider of a velosolex ®.
velours [v(ə)luʀ] **nm** a (*tissu*) velvet. ~ **de coton/de laine** cotton/wool velvet; ~ **côtelé** corduroy, cord; ~ **uni** velvet; *voir* **jouer, main.** b (*velouté*) velvet. **le ~ de la pêche** the bloom of the peach; **le ~ de sa joue** the velvety texture of her cheek, her velvet(y) cheek; **peau/yeux de** ~ velvet(y) skin/eyes; (*fig*) **faire des yeux de ~ à qn** to make sheep's eyes at sb; **ce potage/cette crème est un vrai** ~ this soup/cream dessert is velvety-smooth; *voir* **œil, patte.**
velouté, e [vəlute] (**ptp de velouter**) 1 **adj** a (*Tex*) brushed; (*à motifs*) with a raised velvet pattern. b (*fig: doux*) *joues* velvet (*épith*), velvety, velvet-smooth; *pêche* velvety, downy; *crème, potage* velvety, smooth; *vin* smooth, velvety; *lumière, regard* soft, mellow; *voix* velvet-smooth, mellow. 2 **nm** a (*douceur: voir adj*) velvetiness; smoothness; downiness; softness; mellowness. b (*Culin*) (*sauce*) velouté sauce; (*potage*) velouté. ~ **de tomates/d'asperges** cream of tomato/asparagus soup.
velouter [vəlute] [1] 1 **vt** a *papier* to put a velvety finish on. b *joues, pêche* to give a velvet(y) texture to; *vin, crème, potage* to make smooth; *lumière, regard* to soften, mellow; *voix* to mellow. (*fig*) **le duvet qui veloutait ses joues** the down that gave a velvet softness to her cheeks. 2 **se velouter vpr** (*voir* **velouter**) to take on a velvety texture; to become smooth; to soften; to mellow.
velouteux, -euse [vəlutø, øz] **adj** velvet-like, velvety.
Velpeau [vɛlpo] **nm** ® *voir* **bande**[1].
velu, e [vəly] **adj** *main* hairy; *plante* hairy, villous (*SPÉC*).
velum, vélum [velɔm] **nm** canopy.
venaison [vənɛzɔ̃] **nf** venison.
vénal, e, **mpl -aux** [venal, o] **adj** a *personne* venal, mercenary; *activité, affection* venal. b (*Hist*) *office* venal; *voir* **valeur.**
vénalement [venalmɑ̃] **adv** venally.
vénalité [venalite] **nf** venality.
venant [v(ə)nɑ̃] **nm** *voir* **tout.**
vendable [vɑ̃dabl] **adj** saleable, marketable.
vendange [vɑ̃dɑ̃ʒ] **nf** (*parfois pl: récolte*) wine harvest, grape harvest *ou* picking, vintage; (*raisins récoltés*) grapes (harvested), grape crop; (*gén pl: période*) grape harvest *ou* picking (time), vintage. **pendant les ~s** during the grape harvest *ou* picking (time), during the vintage; **faire la ~** *ou* **les ~s** to harvest *ou* pick the grapes.
vendangeoir [vɑ̃dɑ̃ʒwaʀ] **nm** grape-picker's basket.
vendanger [vɑ̃dɑ̃ʒe] [3] 1 **vt** *vigne* to gather *ou* pick *ou* harvest grapes from; *raisins* to pick, harvest, vintage. 2 **vi** (*faire la vendange*) to pick *ou* harvest the grapes; (*presser le raisin*) to press the grapes.
vendangeur, -euse [vɑ̃dɑ̃ʒœʀ, øz] 1 **nm,f** grape-picker, vintager. 2 **vendangeuse nf** (*machine à vendanger*) grape harvester; (*fleur*) aster.
vendéen, -enne [vɑ̃deɛ̃, ɛn] 1 **adj** of *ou* from the Vendée. 2 **nm,f: V~(ne)** inhabitant *ou* native of the Vendée.
vendémiaire [vɑ̃demjɛʀ] **nm** Vendémiaire (*1st month of French Republican calendar*).
venderesse [vɑ̃dʀɛs] **nf** vendor.
vendetta [vɑ̃deta] **nf** vendetta.
vendeur, euse [vɑ̃dœʀ, øz] 1 **nm** a (*dans un magasin*) shop assistant (*Brit*), salesman, salesclerk (*US*); *[grand magasin]* shop assistant (*Brit*), sales assistant, salesman. **"cherchons 2 ~s, rayon librairie"** "2 sales assistants required for our book department".
b (*marchand*) seller, salesman. ~ **ambulant** itinerant *ou* travelling salesman; ~ **à la sauvette** street hawker; ~ **de journaux** newsvendor, newspaper seller.
c (*Comm: chargé des ventes*) salesman. (*fig*) **c'est un excellent** ~ he is an excellent salesman, he has a flair for selling.
d (*Jur*) vendor, seller; (*Écon*) seller. **cette responsabilité incombe au** ~ this responsibility falls on the vendor *ou* seller; **je ne suis pas** ~ I'm not selling; **il serait** ~ he'd be ready *ou* willing to sell; **les pays ~s de cacao** the cocoa-selling countries.
2 **vendeuse nf** a (*dans un magasin*) shop assistant (*Brit*), saleswoman, salesclerk (*US*); *[grand magasin]* shop assistant (*Brit*), sales assistant, saleswoman; (*jeune*) salesgirl.
b (*marchande*) seller, saleswoman. ~ **de poissons/légumes** fish/vegetable seller *ou* saleswoman.
3 **adj** *slogan* which boosts sales *ou* gets things sold.
vendre [vɑ̃dʀ] [41] 1 **vt** a *marchandise, valeurs* to sell (*à* to). ~ **qch à qn** to sell sb sth *ou* sth to sb; **elle vend des foulards à 400 F** she sells scarves for *ou* at 400 francs; **il m'a vendu un tableau 3 000 F** he sold me a picture for 3,000 francs; **l'art de** ~ the art of selling; **elle vend cher** she is expensive *ou* dear (*Brit*), her prices are high; (*Comm*) **ces affiches publicitaires font** ~ these advertising posters get things sold *ou* are boosting sales; ~ **qch aux enchères** to sell sth by auction; ~ **sa part d'une affaire** to sell (out) one's share of a business; **(maison/terrain) à** ~ (house/land) for sale; (*Bible*) ~ **son droit d'aînesse pour un plat de lentilles** to sell one's birthright for a mess of potage; *voir* **crédit, perte, prix** *etc*.
b (*péj*) *droit, honneur, charge* to sell. ~ **son âme/honneur** to sell one's soul/honour; ~ **son silence** to be paid for one's silence; **il vendrait (ses) père et mère** he would sell his father and mother.
c (*fig: faire payer*) **ils nous ont vendu très cher ce droit/cet avantage** they made us pay dear *ou* dearly for this right/advantage; ~ **chèrement sa vie** *ou* **sa peau*** to sell one's life *ou* one's skin dearly.
d (**: trahir*) *personne, complice* to sell.
e (*loc*) ~ **la peau de l'ours (avant de l'avoir tué)** to count one's chickens (before they are hatched); ~ **la mèche*** (*volontairement*) to give the game *ou* show away*; (*involontairement*) to let the cat out of the bag, give the game *ou* show away*.
2 **se vendre vpr** a *[marchandise]* to sell, be sold. **se ~ à la pièce/douzaine** to be sold singly/by the dozen; **ça se vend bien/comme des petits pains** that sells well/like hot cakes; **un ouvrage/auteur qui se vend bien** a work/an author that sells well.
b *[personne]* (*aussi péj*) to sell o.s. **se ~ à un parti/l'ennemi** to sell o.s. to a party/the enemy.
vendredi [vɑ̃dʀədi] **nm** Friday. (*personnage de Robinson Crusoe*) **V~** Man Friday; ~ **saint** Good Friday; **c'était un ~ treize** it was Friday the thirteenth; *pour autres loc voir* **samedi.**
vendu, e [vɑ̃dy] (**ptp de vendre**) 1 **adj** *fonctionnaire, juge* bribed, who has sold himself for money; *voir* **adjuger.** 2 **nm** (*péj*) Judas, mercenary traitor.
venelle [vənɛl] **nf** alley.
vénéneux, -euse [venenø, øz] **adj** (*lit*) poisonous; (*fig littér*) pernicious, harmful.
vénérable [veneʀabl] 1 **adj** (*littér, hum: respectable*) venerable; (*hum: très vieux*) *personne* ancient, venerable; *chose* ancient. **une automobile d'un âge** ~ a motorcar of venerable age, an ancient motorcar. 2 **nm** (*Rel*) Venerable; (*Franc-Maçonnerie*) Worshipful Master.
vénération [veneʀasjɔ̃] **nf** (*Rel*) veneration; (*gén: grande estime*) veneration, reverence.
vénérer [veneʀe] [6] **vt** (*Rel*) to venerate; (*gén*) to venerate, revere.
vénerie [vɛnʀi] **nf** a (*art*) venery (*SPÉC*), hunting. **petite** ~ small game hunting; **grande** ~ hunting of larger animals. b (*administration*) **la** ~ the Hunt.
vénérien, -ienne [veneʀjɛ̃, jɛn] 1 **adj** a (*Méd*) venereal. **maladies ~nes** venereal diseases, V.D., sexually transmitted diseases. b (††: *sexuel*) venereal††, sexual. 2 **nm** (*gén pl: malade*) V.D. patient, person with V.D. *ou* venereal disease.
vénér(é)ologie [veneʀ(e)ɔlɔʒi] **nf** venereology.
vénér(é)ologiste [veneʀ(e)ɔlɔʒist] **nmf** venereologist.
Vénétie [venesi] **nf** Venetia.
veneur [vənœʀ] **nm** (*Hist*) huntsman, venerer††; *voir* **grand.**
Venezuela [venezɥela] **nm** Venezuela.
vénézuélien, -ienne [venezɥeljɛ̃, jɛn] 1 **adj** Venezuelan. 2 **nm,f: V~(ne)** Venezuelan.
vengeance [vɑ̃ʒɑ̃s] **nf** (*voir* **se venger**) vengeance, revenge. **tirer ~ de** to be avenged for, be revenged for; **exercer sa ~ sur** to take (one's) vengeance *ou* revenge on; **ce forfait crie** *ou* **demande** ~ this crime cries out for *ou* demands vengeance *ou* revenge; **agir par** ~ to act out of revenge; **de petites ~s** petty acts of vengeance *ou* revenge; **une ~ cruelle** cruel vengeance *ou* revenge; **la ~ divine** divine vengeance; (*Prov*) **la ~ est un plat qui se mange froid** never take revenge in the heat of the moment.
venger [vɑ̃ʒe] [3] 1 **vt** a *personne, honneur, mémoire* to avenge (*de* for).
b *injustice, affront* to avenge. **rien ne vengera cette injustice** nothing will avenge this injustice, there is no revenge for this injustice.

2 **se venger** vpr to avenge o.s., take (one's) revenge *ou* vengeance. **se ~ de qn** to take revenge *ou* vengeance on sb, get one's own back on sb (*sur qn d'autre* through sb else); **se ~ de qch** to avenge o.s. for sth, to take one's revenge for sth; **je me vengerai** I shall be avenged, I shall get *ou* have *ou* take my revenge; **je n'ai pas pris de fromage mais je me vengerai sur les fruits** I haven't had any cheese but I'll make up for it with the fruit.

vengeur, -geresse [vɑ̃ʒœʀ, ʒ(ə)ʀɛs] 1 adj *personne* (re)vengeful; *bras, lettre, pamphlet* avenging (*épith*). 2 nm,f avenger.

véniel, -elle [venjɛl] adj *faute, oubli* venial (*littér*), pardonable, excusable; *voir* **péché**.

véniellement [venjɛlmɑ̃] adv venially.

venimeux, -euse [vənimø, øz] adj a (*lit*) *serpent, piqûre* venomous, poisonous. b (*fig*) *personne, voix* venomous, vicious; *remarque, haine* venomous, envenomed, vicious. **une langue ~euse** a poisonous *ou* venomous *ou* vicious tongue.

venimosité [vənimozite] nf venomousness, venom.

venin [vənɛ̃] nm a (*lit*) venom, poison. **~ de serpent** snake venom; **crochets à ~** poison fangs; **sérum contre les ~s** anti-venom serum. b (*fig*) venom, viciousness. **jeter** *ou* **cracher son ~** to spit out one's venom; **répandre son ~ contre qn** to pour out one's venom against sb; **paroles pleines de ~** venomous *ou* envenomed words, words full of venom *ou* viciousness.

venir [v(ə)niʀ] [22] 1 vi a (*gén*) to come. **ils sont venus en voiture** they came by car, they drove (here); **ils sont venus par le train** they came by train; **ils sont venus en avion** they came by air, they flew (here); **je viens!** I'm coming!, I'm on my way!; **je viens dans un instant** I'm coming *ou* I'll be there in a moment; **le voisin est venu** the man from next door came round *ou* called; **il vint vers moi** he came up to *ou* towards me; **il venait sur nous sans nous voir/l'air furieux** he advanced upon us without seeing us/looking furious; (*s'adresser à*) **il est venu à nous plutôt qu'à son supérieur** he came to us rather than (to) his superior; **il vient chez nous tous les jeudis** he comes (round) to our house *ou* to us every Thursday; **il ne vient jamais aux réunions** he never comes to meetings; **je viens de la part de Jules** I've come *ou* I'm here on behalf of Jules; **de la part de qui venez-vous?** who asked you to come?, who sent you?, who had you come?; *voir* **aller**.

b **faire ~** *médecin, plombier* to call, send for; **tu nous as fait ~ pour rien: la réunion n'a pas eu lieu** you got us to come *ou* you made us come for nothing – the meeting didn't take place; **faire ~ son vin de Provence/ses robes de Paris** to have *ou* get one's wine sent from Provence/one's dresses sent from Paris, send to Provence for one's wine/to Paris for one's dresses; **on va prendre l'apéritif, ça les fera peut-être ~** we'll have a pre-dinner drink and perhaps that will make them come (along); **ferme la fenêtre tu vas faire ~ les moustiques** shut the window or you'll attract the mosquitoes *ou* bring in the mosquitoes; **le patron l'a fait ~ dans son bureau** the boss called him into his office; **ça me fait ~ des démangeaisons** it makes me itch.

c (*fig*) *[idées, bruit]* to come. **mot qui vient sur les lèvres/sous la plume** word that comes to the tongue/pen; **les idées ne viennent pas** the ideas aren't coming; **le bruit est venu jusqu'à nous que ...** word has reached us *ou* come to us that ...; **l'idée lui est venue de ...** the idea came *ou* occurred to him to ..., it occurred to him to ...; **ça ne me serait pas venu à l'idée** *ou* **à l'esprit** that would never have occurred to me *ou* entered my head, I should never have thought of that; **une idée m'est venue (à l'esprit)** an idea crossed my mind, an idea occurred to me; **comment (en) est-il venu au sport/à la religion?** how did he (first) come to sport/religion?

d (*survenir*) to come. **quand l'aube vint** when dawn came; **la nuit vient vite** night is coming (on) fast; **ceci vient à point/mal à propos** this comes (along) just at the right/wrong moment; *voir* **voir**.

e (*dans le temps, dans une série*) to come. **ça vient avant/après** that comes before/after; **le moment viendra où ...** the time will comes when ...; **la semaine/l'année qui vient** the coming week/year; *voir* **venu**.

f (*se développer*) *[plante]* to come along. **cette plante vient bien** this plant is coming along *ou* is doing well *ou* nicely.

g **~ de** (*provenance, cause*) to come from; (*Ling*) to derive from; **ils viennent de Paris** (*en voyage*) they're coming from Paris; (*par les origines*) they come *ou* are from Paris; **les victimes venaient de Lyon** the casualties were on their way *ou* were coming from Lyons; **ce produit vient du Maroc** this product comes from Morocco; **l'épée lui vient de son oncle** the sword has been passed down to him by his uncle; **ces troubles viennent du foie** this trouble comes *ou* stems from the liver; **ceci vient de son imprudence** this is the result of his carelessness, this comes from his carelessness; **d'où vient que ...?** how is it that ...?, what is the reason that ...?; **de là vient que ...** the result of this is that ...; **d'où vient cette hâte soudaine?** what's the reason for this sudden haste?, how come* *ou* why this sudden haste?; **ça vient de ce que ...** it comes *ou* results *ou* stems from the fact that ... .

h (*atteindre*) **~ à** (*vers le haut*) to come up to, reach (up to); (*vers le bas*) to come down to, reach (down to); (*en longueur, en superficie*) to come out to, reach; **l'eau nous vient aux genoux** the water comes up to *ou* reaches (up to) our knees, we are knee-deep in (the) water; **il me vient à l'épaule** he comes up to my shoulder; **sa jupe lui vient aux genoux** her skirt comes (down) to *ou* reaches her knees; **la forêt vient jusqu'à la route** the forest comes (right) to *ou* reaches the road.

i **en ~ à: j'en viens maintenant à votre question/à cet aspect du problème** I shall now come *ou* turn to your question/that aspect of the problem; **venons-en au fait** let's get to the point; **j'en viens à la conclusion que ...** I have come to *ou* reached the conclusion that ..., I'm coming to the conclusion that ...; **j'en viens à leur avis** I'm coming round to their opinion; **j'en viens à me demander si ...** I'm beginning to wonder if ...; **il faudra bien en ~ là** we'll have to come *ou* resort to that in the end, that's what it'll come to in the end; **il en est venu à mendier** he was reduced to begging, he had to resort to begging; **il en est venu à haïr ses parents** he has come to loathe his parents, he has got to the stage of loathing his parents; **comment les choses en sont-elles venues là?** how did things come to this? *ou* get to this stage? *ou* get into this state?; **en ~ aux mains** *ou* **coups** to come to blows; **où voulez-vous en ~?** what are you getting *ou* driving at?

j **y ~: j'y viens, mais ne me brusquez pas** I'm coming round to it *ou* to the idea, but don't hustle me; **il faudra bien qu'il y vienne** he'll just have to come round to it.

k (*loc*) **~ au monde** to come into the world, be born; **il est allé** *ou* **retourné comme il est venu** he left as he came; (*menace*) **viens-y!** just (you) come here!; (*menace*) **qu'il y vienne!** just let him come!; (*impatience*) **ça vient?** well, when are we getting it?, come on!; **alors ce dossier ça vient?** well, when am I (*ou* are we) getting this file?, how much longer must I (*ou* we *etc*) wait for this file?; **les années/générations à ~** the years/generations to come, future years/generations; **~ à bout de** *travail* to get through, get to the end of; *adversaire* to get the better of, overcome; *repas, gâteau* to get through; **je n'en viendrai jamais à bout** I'll never manage it, I'll never get through it, I'll never see the end of it; *voir* **tout**.

2 vb aux a (*se déplacer pour*) **je suis venu travailler** I have come to work; **il va ~ la voir** he's going to come to see her; **viens m'aider** come and help me; **après cela ne viens pas te plaindre!** and don't (you) come and complain *ou* come complaining afterwards!

b (*passé récent*) **~ de faire** to have just done; **il vient d'arriver** he has just arrived; **elle venait de se lever** she had just got up.

c (*éventualité*) **s'il venait à mourir** if he were to die *ou* if he should (happen to) die; **vint à passer un officier** an officer happened to pass by; **s'il venait à passer par là** if he should (happen *ou* chance to) go that way.

3 vb impers a **il vient beaucoup d'enfants** a lot of children are coming, there are a lot of children coming; **il lui est venu des boutons** he came out in spots; **il ne lui viendrait pas à l'idée** *ou* **à l'esprit que ...** it wouldn't occur to him that ..., it wouldn't enter his head that ..., it wouldn't cross his mind that ... .

b **il vient un temps/une heure où ...** the time/the hour comes when ... .

c (*éventualité*) **s'il vient à pleuvoir/neiger** if it should (happen to) rain/snow.

4 **s'en venir** vpr (*littér*, †) to come, approach. **il s'en venait tranquillement** he was coming along *ou* approaching unhurriedly; **il s'en vint nous voir** he came to see us.

Venise [vəniz] n Venice.

vénitien, -ienne [venisjɛ̃, jɛn] 1 adj Venetian; *voir* **lanterne, store**. 2 nm,f: **V~(ne)** Venetian.

vent [vɑ̃] 1 nm a wind. **~ du nord/d'ouest** North/West wind; **le ~ du large** the sea breeze; (*Astron*) **~ solaire** solar wind; **il y a** *ou* **il fait du ~** it is windy, there's a wind blowing; (*lit, fig*) **le ~ tourne** the wind is turning; **un ~ d'orage** a stormy wind; **un ~ à décorner les bœufs** a fierce gale, a howling wind; **un coup** *ou* **une rafale de ~ a emporté son chapeau** a gust of wind carried *ou* blew his hat off; **flotter au ~** to flutter in the wind; (*lit, fig*) **observer d'où vient le ~** to see how the wind blows *ou* (from) which way the wind blows; **être en plein ~** to be exposed to the wind; *voir* **coup, moulin, quatre** *etc*.

b (*fig: tendance*) **le ~ est à l'optimisme** there is a feeling of optimism, there is optimism in the air; **un ~ de révolte/contestation soufflait** a wind of revolt/protest was blowing.

c (*euph*, †*: gaz intestinal*) wind (*NonC*). **il a des ~s** he has wind; **lâcher un ~** to break wind.

d (*loc: Chasse, Naut*) **au ~ (de)** to windward (of); **sous le ~ (de)** to leeward (of); **avoir bon ~** to have a fair wind; **bon ~!** (*Naut*) fair journey!; (**: fichez le camp*) good riddance!; **prendre le ~** (*lit*) to test the wind; (*fig*) to find out *ou* see how the wind blows *ou* (from) which way the wind is blowing *ou* how the land lies; **venir au ~** to turn into the wind; **~ arrière/debout** *ou* **contraire** rear/head wind; **avoir le ~ debout** to head into the wind; **avoir le ~ arrière** *ou* **en poupe** to have the wind astern, sail *ou* run before the wind; (*fig*) **il a le ~ en poupe** he has the wind in his sails; **l'entreprise a le ~ en poupe** the company is on the roll; **aller contre le ~** to go into the wind; **chasser au ~** *ou* **dans le ~** to hunt upwind.

e (*loc*) **à tous les ~s** *ou* **aux quatre ~s** to the four winds (of heaven), to all (four) points of the compass; **être dans le ~*** to be with it* *ou* hip*, be trendy* (*Brit*); **il est dans le ~*** he's very with it* *ou* hip*; **une jeune fille/robe dans le ~*** a trendy (*Brit*) *ou* with it* girl/

dress*; (*péj*) **c'est du ~*** it's all wind *ou* hot air*; (*: *allez-vous-en*) **du ~!** away with you!; **avoir ~ de** to get wind of; **ayant eu ~ de sa nomination** having got wind of his nomination; (*gén hum*) **quel bon ~ vous amène?** to what do I (*ou* we) owe the pleasure (of seeing you *ou* of your visit)? (*hum*); **elle l'a fait contre ~s et marées** she did it against all the odds *ou* despite all the obstacles; **je le ferai contre ~s et marées** I'll do it come hell or high water; **faire du ~** *[éventail]* to create a breeze; (*sur le feu*) to fan the flame, blow up the fire; (*péj: être inefficace*) to make a lot of hot air*; (*être ivre*) **avoir du ~ dans les voiles*** to be half-seas over* (*Brit*), be under the influence*, be tiddly*; **rapide comme le ~** swift as the wind.

2 **comp** ▸**vent coulis** draught.

ventail, pl -aux [vɑ̃taj, o] **nm** ventail.

vente [vɑ̃t] 1 **nf** a (*action*) sale. **la ~ de cet article est interdite** the sale of this article is forbidden; **bureau de ~** sales office; **être en ~ libre** (*gén*) to be freely sold, have no sales restrictions; (*sans ordonnance*) to be sold without prescription; **en ~ dès demain** available *ou* on sale (as) from tomorrow; **en ~ dans toutes les pharmacies/chez votre libraire** available *ou* on sale at all chemists/at your local bookshop; **tous les articles exposés sont en ~** all (the) goods on show are for sale; **mettre en ~** *produit* to put on sale; *maison, objet personnel* to put up for sale; **mise en ~** *[maison]* putting up for sale; *[produit]* putting on sale; **les articles en ~ dans ce magasin** the goods on sale in this store; **nous n'en avons pas la ~** we have no demand *ou* sale for that, we can't sell that; **contrat/promesse de ~** sales contract/agreement; *voir* **crédit, point[1], sauvette** *etc.*

b (*Comm*) (*transaction*) sale. **la ~** (*service*) sales (*pl*); (*technique*) selling; **avoir l'expérience de la ~** to have sales experience, have experience in selling; **s'occuper de la ~** (*dans une affaire*) to deal with the sales; **il a un pourcentage sur les ~s** he gets a percentage on sales; **directeur/direction/service des ~s** sales director/management/department.

c **~ (aux enchères)** (auction) sale, auction; **courir les ~s** to do the rounds of the sales *ou* auctions; *voir* **hôtel, salle.**

d (*Bourse*) selling. **la livre vaut 10 F à la ~** the selling rate for (the pound) sterling is 10 francs.

2 **comp** ▸**vente par adjudication** sale by auction ▸**vente de charité** charity sale *ou* bazaar, jumble sale, sale of work ▸**vente par correspondance** mail-order selling ▸**vente par courtage** direct selling ▸**vente directe** direct selling *ou* sales ▸**vente à domicile** door-to-door selling ▸**vente judiciaire** auction by order of the court ▸**vente paroissiale** church sale *ou* bazaar ▸**vente publique** public sale ▸**vente par téléphone** telephone sales, telesales ▸**vente à tempérament** hire purchase (*Brit*), installment plan (*US*).

venté, e [vɑ̃te] (**ptp de venter**) **adj** windswept, windy.

venter [vɑ̃te] 1 **vb impers** (*littér*) **il vente** the wind blows *ou* is blowing, it is windy; *voir* **pleuvoir.**

venteux, -euse [vɑ̃tø, øz] **adj** windswept, windy.

ventilateur [vɑ̃tilatœʀ] **nm** (*gén*) fan; (*dans un mur, une fenêtre*) ventilator, fan. **~ électrique** electric fan; **~ à hélice** blade fan; **~ à turbine** turbine ventilator; *voir* **courroie.**

ventilation [vɑ̃tilasjɔ̃] **nf** a (*aération*) ventilation. (*Méd*) **~ respiratoire** respiratory ventilation; **il y a une bonne ~ dans cette pièce** this room is well ventilated, this room has good ventilation. b *[sommes]* breaking down; (*Jur: évaluation*) separate valuation. **voici la ~ des ventes pour l'année 1976** here is the breakdown of sales for (the year) 1976.

ventiler [vɑ̃tile] 1 **vt** a (*aérer*) *pièce, tunnel* to ventilate. **pièce bien/mal ventilée** well/poorly ventilated room. b (*décomposer*) *total, chiffre, somme* to break down; (*Jur*) *produit d'une vente* to value separately. c (*répartir*) *touristes, élèves* to divide up (into groups).

ventôse [vɑ̃toz] **nm** Ventôse (*6th month of French Republican calendar*).

ventouse [vɑ̃tuz] **nf** a (*Méd*) cupping glass. **poser des ~s à qn** to place cupping glasses on sb, cup sb. b (*Zool*) sucker. c (*dispositif adhésif*) suction disc, suction pad; (*pour déboucher*) plunger. **faire ~** to cling, adhere; **porte-savon à ~** suction-grip soap holder, self-adhering soap holder; *voir* **voiture.** d (*Tech: ouverture*) airhole, air-vent.

ventral, e, mpl -aux [vɑ̃tʀal, o] **adj** ventral; *voir* **parachute, rouleau.**

ventre [vɑ̃tʀ] **nm** a (*abdomen*) stomach, tummy* (*gén langage enfantin*), belly. **dormir/être étendu sur le ~** to sleep/be lying on one's stomach *ou* front; **avoir/prendre du ~** to have/be getting rather a paunch, have/be getting a bit of a tummy* *ou* belly; **rentrer le ~** to hold *ou* pull in one's stomach; (*fig*) **passer sur le ~ de qn** to ride roughshod over sb, walk over sb; **il faudra me passer sur le ~!** over my dead body!; *voir* **bas[1], danse, plat[1].**

b (*estomac*) stomach. **avoir le ~ creux** to have an empty stomach; **avoir le ~ plein** to be full; **avoir mal au ~, avoir des maux de ~** to have stomach ache *ou* (a) tummy ache*; (*fig*) **ça me ferait mal au ~*** it would sicken me, it would make me sick; (*Prov*) **~ affamé n'a point d'oreilles** words are wasted on a starving man; **le ~ de la terre** the bowels of the earth; *voir* **œil, reconnaissance, taper.**

c (*utérus*) womb.

d *[animal]* (under)belly.

e *[cruche, vase]* bulb, bulbous part; *[bateau]* belly, bilge; *[avion]* belly; *voir* **atterrissage.**

f (*Tech*) **faire ~** *[mur]* to bulge; *[plafond]* to sag, bulge.

g (*Phys*) *[onde]* antinode.

h (*loc*) **courir** *ou* **aller ~ à terre** to go flat out* (*Brit*) *ou* at top speed, go hell for leather* (*Brit*) *ou* hell bent for leather* (*US*); **nous allons voir s'il a quelque chose dans le ~** we'll see what he's made of, we'll see if he has guts*; **il n'a rien dans le ~** he has no guts*, he's spineless; **chercher à savoir ce que qn a dans le ~** to try and find out what is (going on) in sb's mind; (*fig*) **ouvrir sa montre pour voir ce qu'elle a dans le ~*** to open (up) one's watch to see what it has got inside *ou* what's inside it; (*fig*) **ce pays est le ~ mou de l'Europe** this country is the soft underbelly of Europe; *voir* **cœur.**

ventrebleu†† [vɑ̃tʀəblø] **excl** gadzooks!††, zounds!††

ventrée† [vɑ̃tʀe] **nf** (*repas*) stuffing* (*NonC*). **une ~ de pâtes** a good bellyful* of pasta; **on s'en est mis une bonne ~*** we pigged‡ *ou* stuffed* ourselves on it.

ventre-saint-gris†† [vɑ̃tʀəsɛ̃gʀi] **excl** gadzooks!††, zounds!††

ventriculaire [vɑ̃tʀikylɛʀ] **adj** ventricular.

ventricule [vɑ̃tʀikyl] **nm** ventricle.

ventrière [vɑ̃tʀijɛʀ] **nf** a (*sangle*) girth; (*toile de transport*) sling. b (*Constr*) purlin; (*Naut*) bilge block.

ventriloque [vɑ̃tʀilɔk] **nmf** ventriloquist. **il est ~** he can throw his voice; (*de profession*) he's a ventriloquist.

ventriloquie [vɑ̃tʀilɔki] **nf** ventriloquy, ventriloquism.

ventripotent, e [vɑ̃tʀipɔtɑ̃, ɑ̃t] **adj** potbellied.

ventru, e [vɑ̃tʀy] **adj** *personne* potbellied; *pot, commode* bulbous.

venu, e [v(ə)ny] (**ptp de venir**) 1 **adj** a (*fondé, placé*) **être bien ~ de faire** to have (good) grounds for doing; **être mal ~ de faire** to have no grounds for doing, be in no position to do; **il serait mal ~ de se plaindre/refuser** he is in no position to complain/refuse, he should be the last to complain/refuse.

b (*à propos*) **bien ~** *événement, question, remarque* timely, apposite; **mal ~** *événement, question* untimely, inapposite, out-of-place (*épith*); **sa remarque était plutôt mal ~e** his remark was rather out of place *ou* uncalled-for, his remark was a bit off*; **un empressement mal ~** unseemly *ou* unfitting haste; **il serait mal ~ de lui poser cette question** it would not be fitting *ou* it would be a bit out of place to ask him (that).

c (*développé*) **bien ~** *enfant* sturdy, sturdily built; *plante, arbre* well-developed, fine; *pièce, œuvre* well-written; **mal ~** *enfant, arbre* stunted.

d (*arrivé*) **tard ~** late; **tôt ~** early; *voir* **dernier, nouveau, premier.**

2 **venue nf** a *[personne]* coming. **à l'occasion de sa ~e nous irons ...** when he comes we'll go ...; *voir* **allée.**

b (*littér: avènement*) coming. **la ~e du printemps/du Christ** the coming of spring/of Christ; **lors de ma ~e au monde** when I came into the world.

c (*loc: littér*) **d'une seule ~e, tout d'une ~e** *arbre* straight-growing (*épith*); **d'une belle ~e** finely *ou* beautifully developed.

Vénus [venys] **nf** (*Astron, Myth*) Venus; (*Zool*) venus. (*fig: femme*) **une ~** a venus, a great beauty; *voir* **mont.**

vêpres [vɛpʀ] **nfpl** vespers. **sonner les ~** to ring the vespers bell.

ver [vɛʀ] 1 **nm** (*gén*) worm; (*larve*) grub; *[viande, fruits, fromage]* maggot; *[bois]* woodworm (*NonC*). **mangé** *ou* **rongé aux ~s** worm-eaten; (*Méd*) **avoir des ~s** to have worms; (*Agr*) **mes poireaux ont le ~** my leeks have been eaten *ou* attacked by grubs; (*fig*) **le ~ est dans le fruit** the rot has already set in; **tirer les ~s du nez à qn*** to worm information out of sb; *voir* **nu, piqué, tortiller.** 2 **comp** ▸**ver d'eau** caddis worm ▸**ver blanc** May beetle grub ▸**ver luisant** glow-worm ▸**ver de sable** sea slug ▸**ver à soie** silkworm ▸**ver solitaire** tapeworm ▸**ver de terre** (*lit*) earthworm; (*fig péj*) worm.

véracité [veʀasite] **nf** *[rapport, récit, témoin]* veracity (*frm*), truthfulness; *[déclaration, fait]* truth, veracity (*frm*). **raconter qch avec ~** to tell sth truthfully.

véranda [veʀɑ̃da] **nf** veranda(h).

verbal, e, mpl -aux [vɛʀbal, o] **adj** a (*oral*) verbal; *voir* **procès, rapport.** b (*Ling*) *adjectif, locution* verbal; *système, forme, terminaison* verb (*épith*), verbal. **groupe ~** verb phrase.

verbalement [vɛʀbalmɑ̃] **adv** *dire, faire savoir* verbally, by word of mouth; *approuver, donner son accord* verbally.

verbalisateur [vɛʀbalizatœʀ] **adj m: l'agent ~ doit toujours ...** an officer reporting an offence must always ...; **l'agent ~ a oublié de ...** the officer who booked* (*Brit*) *ou* reported me (*ou* him *etc*) forgot to ... .

verbalisation [vɛʀbalizasjɔ̃] **nf** a (*Police*) *reporting (by an officer) of an offence.* b (*Psych*) verbalization.

verbaliser [vɛʀbalize] 1 1 **vi** a (*Police*) **l'agent a dû ~** the officer had to book* (*Brit*) *ou* report him (*ou* me *etc*). b (*Psych*) to verbalize. 2 **vt** (*Psych*) to verbalize.

verbalisme [vɛʀbalism] **nm** verbalism.

verbe [vɛʀb] **nm** a (*Gram*) verb. **~ défectif/impersonnel** defective/impersonal verb; **~ transitif/intransitif** transitive/intransitive verb; **~ pronominal** pronominal verb; **~ actif/passif** active/passive verb, verb in the active/passive (voice); **~ d'action/d'état** verb of action/state; **~ fort**

strong verb; ~ **à particule** phrasal verb. b (*Rel*) **le V~** the Word; **le V~ s'est fait chair** the Word was made flesh. c (*littér: mots, langage*) language, word. **la magie du** ~ the magic of language *ou* the word. d (*littér: ton de voix*) tone (of voice). **avoir le** ~ **haut** to speak in a high and mighty tone, sound high and mighty.
verbeusement [vɛʀbøzmɑ̃] **adv** verbosely.
verbeux, -euse [vɛʀbø, øz] **adj** verbose, wordy, prolix.
verbiage [vɛʀbjaʒ] **nm** verbiage.
verbicruciste [vɛʀbikʀysist] **nmf** crossword compiler, compiler of crossword puzzles.
verbosité [vɛʀbozite] **nf** verbosity, wordiness, prolixity.
verdâtre [vɛʀdɑtʀ] **adj** greenish.
verdeur [vɛʀdœʀ] **nf** a (*jeunesse*) vigour, vitality. b *[fruit]* tartness, sharpness; *[vin]* acidity. c *[langage]* forthrightness.
verdict [vɛʀdik(t)] **nm** (*Jur, gén*) verdict. (*Jur*) ~ **de culpabilité/ d'acquittement** verdict of guilty/of not guilty; **rendre un** ~ to give a verdict, return a verdict.
verdier [vɛʀdje] **nm** greenfinch.
verdir [vɛʀdiʀ] 2 1 **vi** to turn *ou* go green. 2 **vt** to turn green.
verdoiement [vɛʀdwamɑ̃] **nm** (*état*) verdancy (*littér*), greenness. (*action*) **le** ~ **des prés au printemps** the greening of the meadows *ou* the verdant hue taken on by the meadows in spring (*littér*).
verdoyant, e [vɛʀdwajɑ̃, ɑ̃t] **adj** verdant (*littér*), green.
verdoyer [vɛʀdwaje] 8 **vi** (*être vert*) to be verdant (*littér*) *ou* green; (*devenir vert*) to become verdant (*littér*) *ou* green.
verdunisation [vɛʀdynizasjɔ̃] **nf** chlorination.
verduniser [vɛʀdynize] 1 **vt** to chlorinate.
verdure [vɛʀdyʀ] **nf** a (*végétation*) greenery (*NonC*), verdure (*NonC*) (*littér*). **tapis de** ~ greensward (*littér*); **rideau de** ~ curtain of greenery *ou* verdure (*littér*); **tapisserie de** ~ *ou* **à** ~**s** verdure (*tapestry*); **je vous mets un peu de** ~**?** (*pour un bouquet*) shall I put some greenery in for you?; *voir* **théâtre**. b (*littér: couleur*) verdure (*littér*), greenness. c (*légumes verts*) green vegetable, greenstuff (*NonC*).
véreux, -euse [veʀø, øz] **adj** a (*lit*) *aliment* maggoty, worm-eaten. b (*fig*) *agent, financier* dubious, shady*; *affaire* dubious, fishy*, shady*.
verge [vɛʀʒ] **nf** a (†: *baguette*) stick, cane, rod. (*pour fouetter*) ~**s** birch(-rod); **ce serait lui donner des** ~**s pour nous faire battre** that would be giving him a stick to beat us with. b (*Hist: insigne d'autorité*) *[huissier]* wand; *[bedeau]* rod. c (*Anat*) penis. d (*Tech: tringle*) shank. e (*Can*) yard (*0,914 m*).
vergé, e [vɛʀʒe] **adj, nm: (papier)** ~ laid paper.
verger [vɛʀʒe] **nm** orchard.
vergeté, e [vɛʀʒəte] **adj** streaked.
vergeture [vɛʀʒətyʀ] **nf** stretch mark.
verglacé, e [vɛʀglase] **adj** icy, iced-over (*attrib*).
verglas [vɛʀglɑ] **nm** (black) ice (*on road etc*).
vergogne [vɛʀgɔɲ] **nf: sans** ~ **(adj)** shameless; **(adv)** shamelessly.
vergue [vɛʀg] **nf** (*Naut*) yard. **grand-**~ main yard; ~ **de misaine** fore-yard; ~ **de hune** topsail yard.
véridique [veʀidik] **adj** *récit, témoignage* truthful, true, veracious (*frm*); *témoin* truthful, veracious (*frm*); *repentir, douleur* genuine, authentic.
véridiquement [veʀidikmɑ̃] **adv** truthfully, veraciously (*frm*).
vérifiable [veʀifjabl] **adj** verifiable. **c'est aisément** ~ it can easily be checked.
vérificateur, -trice [veʀifikatœʀ, tʀis] 1 **adj** *appareil, système* checking (*épith*), verifying (*épith*). **employé** ~ controller, checker. 2 **nm,f** controller, checker. ~ **des douanes** Customs inspector; (*Fin*) ~ **des comptes** auditor; (*Can*) ~ **général** Auditor General; (*Ordin*) ~ **orthographique** *ou* **d'orthographe** spellchecker, spelling checker. 3 **vérificatrice nf** (*Tech*) verifier.
vérificatif, -ive [veʀifikatif, iv] **adj** checking (*épith*).
vérification [veʀifikasjɔ̃] **nf** a (*contrôle*) check; (*action: voir* **vérifier a**) checking; verifying; verification; ascertaining; auditing. (*opération*) **une ou plusieurs** ~**s** one or several checks; ~ **faite, il se trouve que** ... on checking, we find that ...; (*Police*) ~ **d'identité** identity check; (*lors d'une assemblée générale*) ~ **des pouvoirs** check on proxies given to shareholders; (*Pol*) ~ **du scrutin** *ou* **des votes** scrutiny of votes. b (*preuve*) proof; (*confirmation*) confirmation; (*action: voir* **vérifier b**) establishing; confirming; proving (to be true).
vérifier [veʀifje] 7 1 **vt** a (*contrôler*) *affirmation, fait, récit* to check, verify; *adresse, renseignement* to check; *véracité, authenticité* to ascertain, verify, check; (*Fin*) *comptes* to audit; *poids, mesure, classement* to check. **ne vous faites pas de souci, cela a été vérifié et revérifié** don't worry — it has been checked and double-checked *ou* cross-checked; **vérifie que/si la porte est bien fermée** check that/if the door is properly closed; ~ **ses freins/le niveau d'huile** to check one's brakes/the oil (level).
b (*confirmer, prouver*) *affirmation, fait* to establish the truth of, confirm (the truth of), prove to be true; *axiome* to establish *ou* confirm the truth of; *témoignage* to establish the truth *ou* veracity (*frm*) of, confirm (the veracity of); *authenticité, véracité* to establish, confirm, prove; *soupçons, conjecture* to bear out, confirm; *hypothèse, théorie* to bear out, confirm, prove. **cet accident a vérifié mes craintes** this accident has borne out *ou* confirmed my fears.
2 **se vérifier vpr** *[craintes]* to be borne out, be confirmed; *[théorie]* to be borne out, be proved.
vérifieur, -ieuse [veʀifjœʀ, jøz] **nm,f** (*personne*) checker.
vérin [veʀɛ̃] **nm** jack. ~ **hydraulique/pneumatique** hydraulic/pneumatic jack; **monté sur** ~ raised on a jack.
véritable [veʀitabl] **adj** a (*authentique*) *cuir, perles, larmes, colère* real, genuine; *argent, or* real; *ami, artiste, vocation* real (*épith*), genuine, true (*épith*). **l'art/l'amour** ~ **se reconnaît d'emblée** true art/ love is immediately recognizable.
b (*épith: vrai, réel*) *identité, raisons* true, real; *nom* real. **la** ~ **religion/joie** true religion/joy; **sous son jour** ~ in its (*ou* his *etc*) true light; **ça n'a pas de** ~ **fondement** that has no real foundation.
c (*intensif: qui mérite bien son nom*) real. **un** ~ **coquin** an absolute *ou* a real *ou* a downright rogue; ~ **provocation** real *ou* downright *ou* sheer provocation; **c'est une** ~ **folie** it's absolute *ou* sheer madness; **c'est une** ~ **expédition/révolution** it's a real *ou* veritable (*frm*) expedition/revolution.
véritablement [veʀitabləmɑ̃] **adv** really. **est-il** ~ **fatigué/diplômé?** is he really *ou* truly tired/qualified?; **il l'a** ~ **fait/rencontré** he actually *ou* really did it/met him; **ce n'est pas truqué: ils traversent** ~ **les flammes** it isn't fixed — they really *ou* genuinely do go through the flames; **ce n'est pas** ~ **un roman/dictionnaire** it's not really *ou* exactly a novel/ dictionary, it's not a real *ou* proper novel/dictionary; (*intensif*) **c'est** ~ **délicieux** it's absolutely *ou* positively *ou* really delicious.
vérité [veʀite] **nf** a **la** ~ (*connaissance du vrai*) truth; (*conformité aux faits*) the truth; **nul n'est dépositaire de la** ~ no one has a monopoly of truth; **la** ~ **d'un fait/principe** the truth of a fact/principle; **c'est l'entière** ~ it is the whole truth; **c'est la** ~ **vraie*** it's the honest truth*; **la** ~ **toute nue** the naked *ou* unadorned truth; **son souci de (la)** ~ his desire for (the) truth; **dire la** ~ to tell *ou* speak the truth; (*Jur, hum*) **jurez de dire la** ~, **toute la** ~, **rien que la** ~ do you swear to tell the truth, the whole truth and nothing but the truth?; **la** ~ **historique/matérielle** historical/material truth; (*Prov*) **la** ~ **sort de la bouche des enfants** out of the mouths of babes and sucklings (comes forth truth) (*Prov*); (*Prov*) **la** ~ **n'est pas toujours bonne à dire** the truth is sometimes best left unsaid.
b (*vraisemblance, ressemblance au réel*) *[portrait]* lifelikeness, trueness to life; *[tableau, personnage]* trueness to life. **s'efforcer à la** ~ **en art** to strive to be true to life in art; **le désespoir de ce peintre était de ne pouvoir rendre la** ~ **de certains objets** it was the despair of this painter that he was unable to depict the true nature of certain objects; (*la réalité*) **la** ~ **dépasse souvent ce qu'on imagine**(the) truth often surpasses one's imaginings, truth is often stranger than fiction.
c (*sincérité, authenticité*) truthfulness, sincerity. **un air/accent de** ~ an air/a note of sincerity *ou* truthfulness, a truthful look/note; **ce jeune auteur s'exprime avec une** ~ **rafraîchissante** this young author expresses himself with refreshing sincerity *ou* truthfulness *ou* openness.
d (*fait vrai, évidence*) truth. **une** ~ **bien sentie** a heartfelt truth; ~**s éternelles/premières** eternal/first truths *ou* verities (*frm*); *voir* **quatre**.
e (*loc*) **en** ~ (*en fait*) really, actually; **c'est (bien) peu de chose, en** ~ it's really *ou* actually nothing very much; (*Bible*) **"en** ~ **je vous le dis"** "verily I say unto you"; (*frm*) **à la** ~, **en** ~ (*à dire vrai*) to tell the truth, truth to tell, to be honest; (*frm*) **à la** ~ *ou* **en** ~ **il préfère s'amuser que de travailler** to tell the truth *ou* truth to tell *ou* to be honest he prefers to enjoy himself rather than work; **plus qu'il n'en faut, en** ~, **pour en causer la ruine** in fact *ou* indeed more than enough to cause its downfall; **j'étais à la** ~ **loin de m'en douter** to tell the truth *ou* truth to tell I was far from suspecting it; **la** ~, **c'est que je n'en sais rien** the truth (of the matter) is that *ou* to tell the truth I know nothing about it; **l'heure** *ou* **la minute** *etc* **de** ~ the moment of truth; *voir* **sérum**.
verjus [vɛʀʒy] **nm** verjuice.
verlan [vɛʀlɑ̃] **nm** (back) slang.
vermeil, -eille [vɛʀmɛj] 1 **adj** *tissu, objet* vermilion, bright red; *bouche* ruby (*épith*), cherry (*épith*), ruby- *ou* cherry-red; *teint* rosy; *voir* **carte**. 2 **nm** (*métal*) vermeil.
vermicelle [vɛʀmisɛl] **nm** (*souvent pl: pâtes*) ~**(s)** vermicelli; **potage au** ~ vermicelli soup; ~ **chinois** fine Chinese rice noodles.
vermiculaire [vɛʀmikylɛʀ] **adj** (*Anat*) vermicular, vermiform. **appendice** ~ vermiform appendix; **éminence** ~ vermis; **contraction** ~ peristalsis (*NonC*).
vermiculé, e [vɛʀmikyle] **adj** vermiculated.
vermiculure [vɛʀmikylyʀ] **nf** (*gén pl*) vermiculation (*NonC*).
vermiforme [vɛʀmifɔʀm] **adj** vermiform.
vermifuge [vɛʀmifyʒ] **adj, nm** vermifuge (*SPÉC*). **poudre** ~ worm powder.
vermillon [vɛʀmijɔ̃] 1 **nm** (*poudre*) vermilion, cinnabar. (*couleur*) **(rouge)** ~ vermilion, scarlet. 2 **adj inv** vermilion, scarlet.
vermine [vɛʀmin] **nf** a (*parasites*) vermin (*NonC*). **couvert de** ~ crawling with vermin, lice-ridden. b (*littér péj: racaille*) vermin; († *péj: vaurien*) knave (†, *littér*), cur (†, *littér*).
vermisseau, **pl** ~**x** [vɛʀmiso] **nm** (*ver*) small worm, vermicule (*SPÉC*). (*fig*) **un** ~ a mere worm.

Vermont [vɛʀmɔ̃] nm Vermont.
vermoulu, e [vɛʀmuly] adj *bois* full of woodworm, worm-eaten. **cette commode est ~e** there is woodworm in this chest, this chest is full of woodworm *ou* is worm-eaten.
vermoulure [vɛʀmulyʀ] nf (*traces*) woodworm (*NonC*), worm holes (*pl*).
vermout(h) [vɛʀmut] nm vermouth.
vernaculaire [vɛʀnakylɛʀ] adj vernacular. **langue ~** vernacular.
vernal, e, mpl **-aux** [vɛʀnal, o] adj (*littér*) vernal (*littér*).
verni, e [vɛʀni] (ptp de **vernir**) adj a *bois* varnished; (*fig: luisant*) *feuilles* shiny, glossy. **cuir ~** patent leather; **souliers ~s** patent (leather) shoes; **poterie ~e** glazed earthenware. b (**: chanceux*) lucky, jammy* (*Brit*). **il est ~, c'est un ~** he's lucky *ou* jammy* (*Brit*), he's a lucky devil* *ou* dog*.
vernier [vɛʀnje] nm vernier (scale).
vernir [vɛʀniʀ] 2 vt *bois, tableau, ongles, cuir* to varnish; *poterie* to glaze. (*Ébénisterie*) **~ au tampon** to French polish.
vernis [vɛʀni] nm a *[bois, tableau, mur]* varnish; *[poterie]* glaze. **~ (à ongles)** nail varnish *ou* polish; **~ cellulosique/synthétique** cellulose/synthetic varnish; **~ au tampon** French polish. b (*éclat*) shine, gloss. **des chaussures d'un ~ éclatant** shoes with a brilliant shine *ou* a high gloss (on them). c (*fig*) veneer (*fig*). **un ~ de culture** a veneer of culture.
vernissage [vɛʀnisaʒ] nm a (*action: voir* **vernir**) varnishing; glazing; (*voir* **vernisser**) glazing. b (*exposition*) private viewing, preview (*at art gallery*).
vernissé, e [vɛʀnise] (ptp de **vernisser**) adj *poterie, tuile* glazed; (*fig: luisant*) *feuillage* shiny, glossy.
vernisser [vɛʀnise] 1 vt to glaze.
vernisseur, -euse [vɛʀnisœʀ, øz] nm,f *[bois]* varnisher; *[poterie]* glazer.
vérole [veʀɔl] nf a (*variole*) *voir* **petit**. b (**: syphilis*) pox*. **il a/il a attrapé la ~** he's got/he has caught the pox*.
vérolé, e* [veʀɔle] adj: **il est ~** he has the pox*.
véronal [veʀɔnal] nm (*Pharm*) veronal.
Vérone [veʀɔn] n Verona.
Véronique [veʀɔnik] nf Veronica.
véronique [veʀɔnik] nf (*Bot*) speedwell, veronica; (*Tauromachie*) veronica.
verrat [veʀa] nm boar.
verre [vɛʀ] 1 nm a (*substance*) glass. **~ moulé/étiré/coulé** pressed/cast/drawn glass; **cela se casse** *ou* **se brise comme du ~** it's as brittle as glass; *voir* **laine, papier, pâte**.
b (*objet*) *[vitre, cadre]* glass; *[lunettes]* lens. **mettre qch sous ~** to put sth under glass; **~ grossissant/déformant** magnifying/distorting glass; **porter des ~s** to wear glasses; *voir* **sous**.
c (*récipient, contenu*) glass. **~ à bière/liqueur** beer/liqueur glass; (*pour une recette*) **ajouter un ~ à liqueur de .../un ~ de lait** ≃ add two tablespoons of .../one cup of milk; **un ~ d'eau/de bière** a glass of water/beer; *voir* **casser, noyer²**, **tempête**.
d (*boisson alcoolique*) drink. **payer un ~ à qn** to buy *ou* offer sb a drink; **boire** *ou* **prendre un ~** to have a drink; **lever son ~** to raise one's glass; **videz vos ~s!** drink up!; **un petit ~*** a quick one*, a dram* (*Brit*); **il est toujours entre deux ~s*** he's always on the bottle*; **avoir bu un ~ de trop*, avoir un ~ dans le nez*** to have had one too many*, have had a drop too much*, have had one over the eight*.
2 comp ▸**verre armé** wired glass ▸**verre ballon** balloon glass, brandy glass ▸**verre blanc** plain glass ▸**verre cathédrale** cathedral glass ▸**verres de contact (souples/durs)** (soft/hard) contact lenses ▸**verres correcteurs** corrective lenses ▸**verre à** *ou* **de dégustation** wine-tasting glass ▸**verre à dents** tooth mug *ou* glass ▸**verre dépoli** frosted glass ▸**verre feuilleté** laminated glass ▸**verre fumé** smoked glass ▸**verres fumés** (*lunettes*) tinted lenses ▸**verre incassable** unbreakable glass ▸**verre de lampe** lamp glass, (lamp) chimney ▸**verre de montre** watch glass ▸**verre à moutarde** (glass) mustard jar ▸**verre à pied** stemmed glass ▸**verres progressifs** multifocal lenses, multifocals ▸**verre de sécurité** safety glass ▸**verre trempé** toughened glass ▸**verre à vin** wineglass ▸**verre à vitre** window glass ▸**verre à whisky** whisky glass *ou* tumbler.
verrerie [vɛʀʀi] nf (*usine*) glassworks, glass factory; (*fabrication du verre*) glass-making; (*manufacture d'objets*) glass-working; (*objets*) glassware; (*commerce*) glass trade *ou* industry.
verrier [vɛʀje] nm (*ouvrier*) glassworker; (*artiste*) glass artist, artist in glass.
verrière [vɛʀjɛʀ] nf a (*fenêtre*) *[église, édifice]* window. b (*toit vitré*) glass roof. c (*paroi vitrée*) glass wall. d (*Aviat*) canopy.
verroterie [veʀɔtʀi] nf glass jewellery. **un collier de ~** a necklace of glass beads; **en ~** glass jewellery.
verrou [veʀu] nm a *[porte]* bolt. **tire/pousse le ~** unbolt/bolt the door; **as-tu mis le ~?** have you bolted the door?; (*fig*) **mettre qn sous les ~s** to put sb under lock and key; **être sous les ~s** to be behind bars. b (*Tech*) *[aiguillage]* facing point lock; *[culasse]* bolt. c (*Géol*) constriction. d (*Mil*) stopper (*in breach*). e (*Ordin*) lock.
verrouillage [veʀujaʒ] nm a (*action: voir* **verrouiller**) bolting; locking; closing. (*Aut*) **~ automatique des portes** central (door) locking. b (*dispositif*) locking mechanism.
verrouiller [veʀuje] 1 vt *porte* to bolt; *culasse* to lock; (*Mil*) *brèche* to close; (*Ordin*) to lock. (*lit, fig*) **ses parents le verrouillent** his parents keep him locked in; **la police a verrouillé le quartier** the police cordoned off the area; (*fig*) **se ~ chez soi** to shut o.s. away at home; (*fig: vérifier*) **j'ai tout verrouillé** I've got everything under control.
verrouilleur [veʀujœʀ] nm (*Rugby*) last man in the line-out.
verrue [veʀy] nf (*lit*) wart, verruca (*SPÉC*); (*fig*) eyesore. **~ plantaire** verruca; **cette usine est une ~ au milieu du paysage** this factory is a blot on the landscape *ou* an eyesore in the middle of the countryside.
verruqueux, -euse [veʀykø, øz] adj warty, verrucose (*SPÉC*).
vers¹ [vɛʀ] prép a (*direction*) toward(s), to. **en allant ~ Aix/la gare** going to *ou* toward(s) Aix/the station; **le lieu ~ lequel il nous menait** the place he was leading us to *ou* to which he was leading us; **~ la droite, la brume se levait** to *ou* toward(s) the right the mist was rising; **la foule se dirigeait ~ la plage** the crowd was making for the beach; **"~ la plage"** "to the beach"; **elle fit un pas ~ la fenêtre** she took a step toward(s) the window; **notre chambre regarde ~ le sud/la colline** our bedroom faces *ou* looks south/faces the hills *ou* looks toward(s) the hills; **il tendit la main ~ la bouteille** he reached out for the bottle, he stretched out his hand toward(s) the bottle; **le pays se dirige droit ~ l'abîme** the country is heading straight for disaster; **c'est un pas ~ la paix/la vérité** it's a step toward(s) (establishing) peace/(finding out) the truth; (*titre*) **"V~ une sémantique de l'anglais"** "Towards a Semantics of English"; **traduire ~ le français/l'espagnol** to translate into French/Spanish.
b (*aux environs de*) around. **c'est ~ Aix que nous avons eu une panne** it was (somewhere) near Aix *ou* round about Aix that we broke down; **~ 2 000 mètres l'air est frais** at around the 2,000 metres mark *ou* at about 2,000 metres the air is cool.
c (*temps: approximation*) (at) about, (at) around. **~ quelle heure doit-il venir?** (at) around *ou* (at) about what time is he due?; **elle a commencé à lire ~ 6 ans** she started reading at about 6 *ou* around 6; **il était ~ (les) 3 heures quand je suis rentré** it was about *ou* around 3 when I came home; **~ la fin de la soirée/de l'année** toward(s) *ou* going on for (*Brit*) the end of the evening/the year; **~ 1900/le début du siècle** toward(s) *ou* about 1900/the turn of the century.
vers² [vɛʀ] nm a (*sg: ligne*) line. **au 3ᵉ ~** in line 3, in the 3rd line; **~ de dix syllabes, ~ décasyllabe** line of ten syllables, decasyllabic line; **~ blancs/libres** blank/free verse; **un ~ boiteux** a short line, a hypometric line (*SPÉC*); **je me souviens d'un ~ de Virgile** I recall a line by Virgil; **réciter quelques ~** to recite a few lines of poetry.
b (*pl: poésie*) verse (*NonC*). **~ de circonstance** occasional verse; **traduction en ~** verse translation; **faire** *ou* **écrire des ~** to write verse, versify (*péj*); **mettre en ~** to put into verse; **il fait des ~ de temps en temps** he writes a little verse from time to time; **écrire des ~ de mirliton** to write a bit of doggerel.
Versailles [vɛʀsaj] n Versailles. **le château/traité de ~** the palace/Treaty of Versailles; (*fig*) **c'est ~!** *[appartement]* it's like a palace!, it's SOME place!*; *[événement, réception]* it's really spectacular!
versant [vɛʀsɑ̃] nm *[vallée, toit]* side; *[massif]* slopes (*pl*). **les Pyrénées ont un ~ français et un ~ espagnol** the Pyrenees have a French side and a Spanish side; **le ~ nord/français de ce massif** the northern/French slopes of this range.
versatile [vɛʀsatil] adj fickle, changeable, capricious.
versatilité [vɛʀsatilite] nf fickleness, changeability, capriciousness.
verse [vɛʀs] adv: **à ~** in torrents; **il pleut à ~** it is pouring down, it's coming down in torrents *ou* in buckets*.
versé, e [vɛʀse] (ptp de **verser**) adj: **~/peu ~ dans l'histoire ancienne** (well-)versed/ill-versed in ancient history; **~/peu ~ dans l'art de l'escrime** (highly) skilled *ou* accomplished/unaccomplished in the art of fencing; **l'homme le plus ~ de France dans l'art chaldéen** the most learned man in France in the field of Chaldean art.
Verseau [vɛʀso] nm (*Astron*) **le ~** Aquarius, the Water-carrier. **être (du) ~** to be (an) Aquarius *ou* an Aquarian.
versement [vɛʀsəmɑ̃] nm payment; (*échelonné*) instalment. **le ~ d'une somme sur un compte** the payment of a sum into an account; **~ par chèque/virement** payment by cheque/credit transfer; **en ~s (échelonnés)** in *ou* by instalments; **je veux faire un ~ sur mon compte** I want to put some money into my account, I want to make a deposit into my account; **le ~ de ces sommes se fera le mois prochain** these sums will be paid next month; **~ en espèces** cash deposit; **~ à une œuvre** donation to a charity; **un premier ~** *ou* **un ~ initial de 1 000 F** a first *ou* an initial payment of 1,000 francs.
verser [vɛʀse] 1 1 vt a *liquide, grains* to pour, tip (*dans* into, *sur* onto); (*servir*) *thé, café, vin* to pour (out) (*dans* into). **~ le café dans les tasses** to pour the coffee into the cups; **~ des haricots (d'un sac) dans un bocal** to pour *ou* tip beans (from a bag) into a jar; **~ du vin à qn** to pour sb some wine; **~ un verre de vin à qn** to pour sb a glass of wine, pour a glass of wine for sb; **verse-lui/-toi à boire** pour him/yourself a drink; **veux-tu ~ à boire/le vin s'il te plaît?** will you pour (out) *ou* serve the drinks/the wine please?; *voir* **huile**.
b (*répandre*) *larmes, sang,* (*littér*) *clarté* to shed; (*déverser*) to pour

out, scatter (*sur* onto); (*littér: apporter*) *apaisement etc* to dispense, pour forth (*à qn* to sb). (*tuer*) ~ **le sang** to shed *ou* spill blood; **sans ~ une goutte de sang** without shedding *ou* spilling a drop of blood; (*littér, hum*) ~ **un pleur/quelques pleurs** to shed a tear/a few tears; **ils versaient des brouettées de fleurs devant la procession** they scattered *ou* strewed barrowfuls of flowers in front of the procession; **drogue qui verse l'oubli** drug which brings oblivion.

c (*classer*) ~ **une pièce à un dossier** to add an item to a file.

d (*payer: gén, Fin*) to pay. ~ **une somme à un compte** to pay a sum of money into an account, deposit a sum of money in an account; ~ **des intérêts à qn** to pay sb interest; ~ **des arrhes** to put down *ou* pay a deposit; ~ **une rente à qn** to pay sb a pension.

e (*affecter, incorporer*) ~ **qn dans** to assign *ou* attach sb to; **se faire ~ dans l'infanterie** to get o.s. assigned *ou* attached to the infantry.

f (*renverser: plus gén* **faire ~**) *voiture* to overturn. **le chauffeur les a versés dans la rivière** the driver tipped them into the river.

2 **vi** a (*basculer*) [*véhicule*] to overturn. **il va nous faire ~ dans le fossé** he'll tip us into the ditch, we'll end up in the ditch because of him; **il a déjà versé deux fois** he has already overturned twice.

b (*tomber dans*) ~ **dans** *sentimentalité etc* to lapse into.

verset [vɛʀsɛ] **nm** (*Rel*) (*passage de la Bible*) verse; (*prière*) versicle; (*Littérat*) verse.

verseur, -euse [vɛʀsœʀ, øz] 1 **adj: bec ~** (pouring) lip; **bouchon ~** pour-through stopper; **sucrier ~** sugar dispenser. 2 **nm** (*dispositif*) pourer. 3 **verseuse nf** (*cafetière*) coffeepot.

versicolore [vɛʀsikɔlɔʀ] **adj** versicolour.

versificateur [vɛʀsifikatœʀ] **nm** writer of verse, versifier (*péj*), rhymester (*péj*).

versification [vɛʀsifikasjɔ̃] **nf** versification.

versifier [vɛʀsifje] 7 1 **vt** to put into verse. **une œuvre versifiée** a work put into verse. 2 **vi** to write verse, versify (*péj*).

version [vɛʀsjɔ̃] **nf** a (*Scol: traduction*) translation (*into the mother tongue*), unseen (translation). ~ **grecque/anglaise** Greek/English unseen (translation), translation from Greek/English; **"Casablanca" en ~ originale (sous-titrée)** "Casablanca" in English (with French subtitles).

b (*variante*) [*œuvre, texte*] version. **film en ~ originale** film in the original language *ou* version; ~ **originale sous-titrée** original version with subtitles; **la ~ française du film** the French version of the film; **film italien en ~ française** Italian film dubbed in French; (*Aut*) ~ **4 portes** 4-door model.

c (*interprétation*) [*incident, faits*] version. **donner sa ~ des faits** to give one's (own) version of the facts.

verso [vɛʀso] **nm** back. **au ~** on the back (of the page); **"voir au ~"** "see over(leaf)".

verste [vɛʀst] **nf** verst.

versus [vɛʀsys] **prép** versus.

vert, verte [vɛʀ, vɛʀt] 1 **adj** a (*couleur*) green. ~ **de peur** green with fear; *voir* **feu**[1], **haricot, numéro, tapis** *etc*.

b (*pas mûr*) *céréale, fruit* unripe, green; *vin* young; (*frais, non séché*) *foin, bois* green. **être au régime ~** to be on a green-vegetable diet *ou* a diet of green vegetables; (*fig: par dépit*) **ils sont trop ~s!** it's sour grapes; *voir* **cuir**.

c (*fig*) *vieillard* vigorous, sprightly, spry. **au temps de sa verte jeunesse** in the first bloom of his youth.

d (*†: sévère*) *réprimande* sharp, stiff.

e *propos, histoire* spicy, saucy. **elle en a vu des vertes et des pas mûres*** she has been through it, she has had a hard time (of it); **il en a dit des vertes (et des pas mûres)*** he said some pretty spicy *ou* saucy things; *voir* **langue**.

f (*Agr*) **tourisme ~** country holidays; **classe verte** school camp; **l'Europe verte** European agriculture; **avoir les pouces ~s** *ou* **la main verte** to have green fingers.

g (*écologiste*) green (*épith*). **le parti ~** the Green Party.

2 **nm** a (*couleur*) green; (*Golf*) green. ~ **olive/pistache/émeraude** olive/pistachio/emerald(-green); ~ **pomme/d'eau/bouteille** apple-/sea-/bottle-green; ~ **amande/mousse** almond/moss green; **mettre un cheval au ~** to put a horse out to grass *ou* to pasture; (*fig*) **se mettre au ~** [*vacancier*] to take a rest *ou* a refreshing break in the country; [*gangster*] to lie low *ou* hole up for a while in the country; (*Aut*) **passer au ~** to go through on the green light; *voir* **tendre**[2].

b (*Pol: écologistes*) **les V~s** the Greens.

3 **verte nf** (*†*: absinthe*) absinth(e).

4 **comp ►vert-de-gris nm inv** verdigris ◊ **adj inv** grey(ish)-green **►vert-de-grisé, e adj (mpl vert-de-grisés)** coated with verdigris; (*fig*) grey(ish)-green.

vertébral, e, mpl -aux [vɛʀtebʀal, o] **adj** vertebral; *voir* **colonne**.

vertèbre [vɛʀtɛbʀ] **nf** vertebra. **se déplacer une ~** to slip a disc, dislocate a vertebra (*SPÉC*).

vertébré, e [vɛʀtebʀe] **adj, nm** vertebrate.

vertement [vɛʀtəmɑ̃] **adv** *réprimander, répliquer* sharply, in no uncertain terms.

vertex [vɛʀtɛks] **nm** (*Anat*) vertex.

vertical, e, mpl -aux [vɛʀtikal, o] 1 **adj** (*gén*) *ligne, plan, éclairage* vertical; *position du corps, station* vertical, upright; *voir* **concentration**.

2 **verticale nf** a **la ~e** the vertical; *s'élever, tomber* **à la ~e** vertically; **falaise à la ~e** vertical *ou* sheer cliff; **écarté de la ~e** off the vertical. b (*ligne, Archit*) vertical line. 3 **nm** (*Astron*) vertical circle.

verticalement [vɛʀtikalmɑ̃] **adv** *monter* vertically, straight up; *descendre* vertically, straight down.

verticalité [vɛʀtikalite] **nf** verticalness, verticality.

vertige [vɛʀtiʒ] **nm** a (*peur du vide*) **le ~** vertigo; **avoir le ~** to suffer from vertigo, get dizzy *ou* giddy; **il eut soudain le ~** *ou* **fut pris soudain de ~** he was suddenly overcome by vertigo *ou* dizziness *ou* giddiness, he suddenly felt dizzy *ou* giddy, he had a sudden fit of vertigo *ou* dizziness *ou* giddiness; **un précipice à donner le ~** a precipice that would make you (feel) dizzy *ou* giddy; **cela me donne le ~** it makes me feel dizzy *ou* giddy, it gives me vertigo.

b (*étourdissement*) dizzy *ou* giddy spell, dizziness (*NonC*), giddiness (*NonC*). **avoir un ~** to have a dizzy *ou* giddy spell *ou* turn; **être pris de ~s** to get dizzy *ou* giddy turns *ou* spells.

c (*fig: égarement*) fever. **les spéculateurs étaient gagnés par ce ~** the speculators had caught this fever; **le ~ de la gloire** the intoxication of glory; **d'autres, gagnés eux aussi par le ~ de l'expansion** ... others, who had also been bitten by the expansion bug ... *ou* who had also caught the expansion fever ...; **le ~ de la violence** the heady lure of violence.

vertigineusement [vɛʀtiʒinøzmɑ̃] **adv: ~ haut** vertiginously *ou* breathtakingly high, of a dizzy height; **se lancer ~ dans la descente** to plunge into a vertiginous *ou* breathtaking descent; **les prix montent ~** prices are rising at a dizzy *ou* breathtaking rate, prices are rocketing *ou* are going sky-high*; **les cours se sont effondrés ~** stock market prices have dropped at a dizzy *ou* breathtaking rate.

vertigineux, -euse [vɛʀtiʒinø, øz] **adj** a *plongée, descente* vertiginous, breathtaking; *précipice* breathtakingly high; *vitesse, hauteur* breathtaking, dizzy (*épith*), giddy (*épith*). **nous descendions par un sentier ~** we came down by a vertiginous path. b (*fig: très rapide*) breathtaking. **une hausse/baisse de prix ~euse** a breathtaking rise/drop in price. c (*Méd*) vertiginous.

vertigo [vɛʀtigo] **nm** (*Vét*) (blind) staggers.

vertu [vɛʀty] **nf** a (*gén: morale*) virtue. **à la ~ farouche** of fierce virtue; (*fig: personne*) **ce n'est pas une ~** she's no saint *ou* angel, she's no paragon of virtue; **les ~s bourgeoises** the bourgeois virtues; **les (quatre) ~s cardinales** the (four) cardinal virtues; **~s théologales** theological virtues; *voir* **femme, nécessité, parer**[1], **prix**.

b (*littér*) (*pouvoir*) virtue (*†, littér*), power; (*courage*) courage, bravery. ~ **magique** magic power; ~ **curative** healing virtue.

c **en ~ de** in accordance with; **en ~ des pouvoirs qui me sont conférés** in accordance with *ou* by virtue of the powers conferred upon me; **en ~ de l'article 4 de la loi** in accordance *ou* compliance with article 4 of the law; **en ~ de quoi je déclare** in accordance with which I declare, by virtue of which I declare.

vertueusement [vɛʀtɥøzmɑ̃] **adv** virtuously.

vertueux, -euse [vɛʀtɥø, øz] **adj** virtuous.

vertugadin [vɛʀtygadɛ̃] **nm** (*Hist: vêtement*) farthingale.

verve [vɛʀv] **nf** a (*esprit, éloquence*) witty eloquence. **être en ~** to be in brilliant form. b (*littér: fougue, entrain*) verve, vigour, zest. **la ~ de son style** the verve *ou* vigour of his style.

verveine [vɛʀvɛn] **nf** (*plante*) vervain, verbena; (*tisane*) verbena tea; (*liqueur*) vervain liqueur.

vésical, e, mpl -aux [vezikal, o] **adj** vesical.

vésicant, e [vezikɑ̃, ɑ̃t] **adj** vesicant, vesicatory.

vésicatoire [vezikatwaʀ] 1 **adj** vesicatory. 2 **nm** (*Méd*) vesicatory.

vésiculaire [vezikylɛʀ] **adj** vesicular.

vésicule [vezikyl] **nf** vesicle. **la ~ (biliaire)** the gall-bladder.

vésiculeux, -euse [vezikylø, øz] **adj** = **vésiculaire**.

Vespa [vɛspa] **nf** ® Vespa ®.

vespasienne [vɛspazjɛn] **nf** urinal.

vespéral, e, mpl -aux [vɛspeʀal, o] 1 **adj** (*littér*) evening (*épith*). 2 **nm** (*Rel*) vesperal.

vesse [vɛs] **nf** (*Bot*) **~-de-loup** (**pl ~s-~-~**) puffball.

vessie [vesi] **nf** (*Anat*) bladder, vesica (*SPÉC*); (*animale: utilisée comme sac*) bladder. ~ **natatoire** swim bladder; **elle veut nous faire prendre des ~s pour des lanternes** she would have us believe that the moon is made of green cheese, she's trying to pull the wool over our eyes.

Vesta [vɛsta] **nf** Vesta.

vestale [vɛstal] **nf** (*Hist*) vestal; (*fig littér*) vestal, vestal virgin.

veste [vɛst] **nf** a jacket. ~ **droite/croisée** single-/double-breasted jacket; ~ **de pyjama** pyjama jacket *ou* top; ~ **d'intérieur** smoking jacket. b (**loc*) **retourner sa ~** to turn one's coat, change one's colours; **ramasser** *ou* **prendre une ~** (*gén*) to come a cropper* (*Brit*), fall flat on one's face; (*dans une élection etc*) to be beaten hollow; *voir* **tomber**.

vestiaire [vɛstjɛʀ] **nm** a [*théâtre, restaurant*] cloakroom; [*stade, piscine*] changing-room. **la dame du ~** the cloakroom attendant *ou* lady; **réclamer son ~** to get one's belongings out of *ou* collect one's belongings from the cloakroom; **au ~! au ~!*** get off! b (*meuble*) coat stand, hat stand. (*métallique*) **(armoire-)~** locker. c (*garde-robe*) wardrobe. **un ~ bien fourni** a well-stocked wardrobe.

vestibulaire [vɛstibylɛʀ] **adj** vestibular.

vestibule [vɛstibyl] nm a *[maison]* hall; *[hôtel]* hall, vestibule; *[église]* vestibule. b (*Anat*) vestibule.

vestige [vɛstiʒ] nm (*objet*) relic; (*fragment*) trace; *[coutume, splendeur, gloire]* vestige, remnant, relic. **~s** *[ville]* remains, vestiges; *[civilisation, passé]* vestiges, remnants, relics; **il avait gardé un ~ de son ancienne arrogance** he had retained a trace *ou* vestige of his former arrogance; **les ~s de leur armée décimée** the remnants of their decimated army; **les ~s de la guerre** the vestiges of war.

vestimentaire [vɛstimɑ̃tɛʀ] adj: **dépenses ~s** clothing expenditure, expenditure on clothing; **élégance ~** sartorial elegance; **ces fantaisies ~s n'étaient pas de son goût** these eccentricities of dress were not to his taste; **il se préoccupait beaucoup de détails ~s** he was very preoccupied with the details of his dress.

veston [vɛstɔ̃] nm jacket; *voir* **complet**.

Vésuve [vezyv] nm Vesuvius.

vêtement [vɛtmɑ̃] nm a (*article d'habillement*) garment, item *ou* article of clothing; (*ensemble, combinaison*) set of clothes, clothing (*NonC*), clothes (*pl*); (*frm: de dessus: manteau, veste*) coat. (*Comm: industrie*) **le ~** the clothing industry, the rag trade*, the garment industry (*US*); **c'est un ~ très pratique** it's a very practical garment *ou* item of clothing *ou* article of clothing; **le ~ anti-g des astronautes** astronauts' anti-gravity clothing *ou* clothes.
b **~s** clothes; **où ai-je mis mes ~s?** where did I put my clothes? *ou* things?*; **emporte des ~s chauds** take (some) warm clothes *ou* clothing; **porter des ~s de sport/de ville** to wear sports/town clothes *ou* sports/town gear*; **acheter des ~s de bébé** to buy baby garments *ou* clothes; **il portait des ~s de tous les jours** he was wearing ordinary *ou* everyday clothes; **~s sacerdotaux** pastoral robes; **~s de travail** working clothes; **~s de deuil** mourning clothes; **~s du dimanche** Sunday clothes, Sunday best (*parfois hum ou péj*).
c (*rayon de magasin*) **(rayon) ~s** clothing department; **~s pour hommes/dames/enfants** menswear (*NonC*)/ladies' wear (*NonC*)/children's wear (*NonC*); **~s de sport** sportswear (*NonC*); **~s de ski** skiwear (*NonC*); **~s de bébé** babywear (*NonC*).
d (*parure*) garment (*fig*). **le langage est le ~ de la pensée** language clothes thought.

vétéran [veteʀɑ̃] nm (*Mil*) veteran, old campaigner; (*fig*) veteran, old hand, old stager; (*sportif*) veteran. **un ~ de l'enseignement primaire** a veteran of *ou* an old hand* at primary teaching.

vétérinaire [veteʀinɛʀ] 1 nmf vet, veterinary surgeon (*Brit*), veterinarian (*US*). 2 adj veterinary. **école ~** veterinary college *ou* school.

vétille [vetij] nf trifle, triviality. **ergoter sur des ~s** to quibble over trifles *ou* trivia *ou* trivialities.

vétilleux, -euse [vetijø, øz] adj punctilious.

vêtir [vetiʀ] [20] 1 vt a (*habiller*) *enfant, miséreux* to clothe, dress (*de* in). b (*revêtir*) *uniforme* to don (*frm*), put on. 2 **se vêtir** vpr to dress (o.s.). **aider qn à se ~** to help sb (to) get dressed; (*littér*) **les monts se vêtaient de pourpre** the mountains were clothed *ou* clad in purple (*littér*).

vétiver [vetivɛʀ] nm vetiver.

veto [veto] nm (*Pol, gén*) veto. **opposer son ~ à qch** to veto sth; **droit de ~** right of veto; **je mets mon ~** I veto that.

véto* [veto] nmf (abrév de **vétérinaire**) vet (*Brit*), veterinarian (*US*).

vêtu, e [vety] (ptp de **vêtir**) adj dressed. **bien/mal ~** well-/badly-dressed; **court ~e** short-skirted; **à demi-~** half-dressed, half-clad; **~ de** dressed in, wearing; **~e d'une jupe** wearing a skirt, dressed *ou* clad in a skirt, with a skirt on; **~ de bleu** dressed in *ou* wearing blue; (*littér*) **colline ~e des ors de l'automne** hill clad *ou* clothed in the golden hues of autumn (*littér*).

vétuste [vetyst] adj dilapidated, ancient, timeworn.

vétusté [vetyste] nf *[objet]* dilapidation, (great) age. **clause de ~** obsolescence clause.

veuf, veuve [vœf, vœv] 1 adj a widowed. **il est deux fois ~** he has been twice widowed, he is a widower twice over; **rester ~/veuve de qn** to be left sb's widower/widow; (*fig*) **ce soir je suis ~/veuve** I'm a bachelor/grass widow tonight. b (*fig littér*) **~ de** bereft of. 2 nm widower. 3 **veuve** nf a (*gén*) widow. **défenseur de la veuve et de l'orphelin** defender of the weak and of the oppressed. b (*Orn*) whydah (bird), widow bird.

veule [vøl] adj *personne, air* spineless.

veulerie [vølʀi] nf spinelessness.

veuvage [vœvaʒ] nm *[femme]* widowhood; *[homme]* widowerhood.

veuve [vœv] *voir* **veuf**.

vexant, e [vɛksɑ̃, ɑ̃t] adj a (*contrariant*) annoying, vexing. **c'est ~ de ne pas pouvoir profiter de l'occasion** it's annoying *ou* vexing *ou* a nuisance not to be able to take advantage of the opportunity. b (*blessant*) *paroles* hurtful (*pour* to).

vexation [vɛksasjɔ̃] nf a (*humiliation*) (little) humiliation. **essuyer des ~s** to suffer (little) humiliations. b (*littér*, †: *exaction*) harassment.

vexatoire [vɛksatwaʀ] adj *procédés, attitude* persecutory, hurtful. **mesures ~s** harassment.

vexer [vɛkse] [1] 1 vt (*offenser*) to hurt, upset, offend. **être vexé par qch** to be hurt by sth, be upset *ou* offended at sth; **vexé comme un pou*** really livid* *ou* mad*. 2 **se vexer** vpr to be hurt (*de* by), be *ou* get upset *ou* offended (*de* at). **se ~ d'un rien** to be easily hurt *ou* upset *ou* offended.

VF [veɛf] nf (abrév de **version française**) *voir* **version**.

VHF [veaʃɛf] (abrév de **very high frequency**) VHF. **antenne ~** VHF aerial.

via [vja] prép via, by way of.

viabilisé, e [vjabilize] adj *terrain* with services (laid on), serviced. **entièrement ~** fully serviced.

viabiliser [vjabilize] [1] vt *terrain* to service.

viabilité [vjabilite] nf a *[chemin]* practicability. **avec/sans ~** *terrain* with/without services (laid on), serviced/unserviced. b *[organisme, entreprise]* viability.

viable [vjabl] adj *situation, enfant, compromis* viable.

viaduc [vjadyk] nm viaduct.

viager, -ère [vjaʒe, ɛʀ] 1 adj (*Jur*) *rente, revenus* life (*épith*), for life (*attrib*). **à titre ~** for as long as one lives, for the duration of one's life.
2 nm (*rente*) life annuity; (*bien*) *property mortgaged for a life annuity*. **mettre/acheter un bien en ~** *to sell/buy a property in return for a life annuity*.

viande [vjɑ̃d] nf a meat. **rouge/blanche** red/white meat; **~ de boucherie** fresh meat, (butcher's) meat; (*charcuterie*) **~s froides** cold meat(s); **~ hachée** minced meat (*Brit*), mince (*Brit*), ground meat (*US*), hamburger (*US*); *voir* **plat²**. b (‡) **montrer sa ~** to bare one's flesh; **amène ta ~!** shift your carcass *ou* butt (*US*) over here!‡; *voir* **sac**.

viander (se)* [vjɑ̃de] [1] vpr to smash o.s. up* *ou* get smashed up* in an accident.

viatique [vjatik] nm (*argent*) money (for the journey); (*provisions*) provisions (*pl*) (for the journey); (*Rel: communion*) viaticum; (*littér: soutien*) (precious) asset. **la culture est un ~** culture is a precious asset.

vibrant, e [vibʀɑ̃, ɑ̃t] 1 adj a (*lit*) *corde, membrane* vibrating. b *son, voix* vibrant, resonant; (*Phonétique*) *consonne* lateral, vibrant. **voix ~e d'émotion** voice vibrant *ou* resonant with emotion. c *discours* (powerfully) emotive; *nature* emotive. **~ d'émotion contenue** vibrant with suppressed emotion. 2 **vibrante** nf (*consonne*) vibrant.

vibraphone [vibʀafɔn] nm vibraphone, vibes (*pl*).

vibraphoniste [vibʀafɔnist] nmf vibraphone player, vibes player.

vibrateur [vibʀatœʀ] nm vibrator.

vibratile [vibʀatil] adj vibratile.

vibration [vibʀasjɔ̃] nf (*gén, Phys*) vibration. **la ~ de sa voix** the vibration *ou* resonance of his voice; **la ~ de l'air (due à la chaleur)** the quivering *ou* shimmering of the air (due to the heat).

vibrato [vibʀato] nm vibrato. **jouer qch avec ~** to play sth (with) vibrato.

vibratoire [vibʀatwaʀ] adj vibratory.

vibrer [vibʀe] [1] 1 vi a (*gén, Phys*) to vibrate. **faire ~ qch** to cause sth to vibrate, vibrate sth. b (*d'émotion*) *[voix]* to quiver, be vibrant *ou* resonant; *[passion]* to be stirred; *[personne, âme]* to thrill (*de* with). **~ en écoutant Beethoven** to be stirred when listening to a piece by Beethoven; **faire ~ qn/un auditoire** to stir *ou* thrill sb/an audience, send a thrill through sb/an audience; **~ d'enthousiasme** to be vibrant with enthusiasm; **des accents qui font ~ l'âme** accents which stir *ou* thrill the soul. 2 vt (*Tech*) *béton* to vibrate.

vibreur [vibʀœʀ] nm vibrator.

vibrion [vibʀijɔ̃] nm (*bacille*) vibrio; (*: *enfant*) fidget*.

vibromasseur [vibʀomasœʀ] nm vibrator.

vicaire [vikɛʀ] nm *[paroisse]* curate. *[évêque]* **grand ~, ~ général** vicar-general; *[pape]* **~ apostolique** vicar apostolic; **le ~ de Jésus-Christ** the vicar of Christ.

vicariat [vikaʀja] nm curacy.

vice [vis] nm a (*défaut moral, mauvais penchant*) vice. (*mal, débauche*) **le ~** vice; (*hum*) **le tabac est mon ~** tobacco is my vice (*hum*); **elle travaille quinze heures par jour: c'est du ~!*** it's perverted *ou* it's sheer perversion the way she works 15 hours a day like that!; **vivre dans le ~** to live a life of vice; *voir* **oisiveté, pauvreté**. b (*défectuosité*) fault, defect; (*Jur*) defect. **~ de prononciation** fault in pronunciation; **~ de conformation** congenital malformation; **~ de construction** construction fault *ou* defect, fault *ou* defect in construction; (*Jur*) **~ rédhibitoire** redhibitory defect; (*Jur*) **~ de forme** legal flaw *ou* irregularity; **~ caché** latent defect.

vice- [vis] 1 préf vice-. 2 comp ►**vice-amiral** nm (pl **vice-amiraux**) vice-admiral, rear admiral; **vice-amiral d'escadre** vice-admiral ►**vice-chancelier** nm (pl **vice-chanceliers**) vice-chancellor ►**vice-consul** nm (pl **vice-consuls**) vice-consul ►**vice-consulat** nm (pl **vice-consulats**) vice-consulate ►**vice-légat** nm (pl **vice-légats**) vice-legate ►**vice-légation** nf (pl **vice-légations**) vice-legateship ►**vice-présidence** nf (pl **vice-présidences**) vice-presidency, vice-chairmanship ►**vice-président, e** nm,f (mpl **vice-présidents**) vice-president, vice-chairman ►**vice-reine** nf (pl **vice-reines**) lady viceroy, vicereine ►**vice-roi** nm (pl **vice-rois**) viceroy ►**vice-royauté** nf (pl **vice-royautés**) viceroyalty.

vicelard, e‡ [vis(ə)laʀ, aʀd] adj, nm,f = **vicieux**.

vicennal, e, mpl **-aux** [visenal, o] adj vicennial.

vicésimal, e, mpl **-aux** [visezimal, o] adj vigesimal, vicenary.

vice versa [visevɛʀsa] adv vice versa.

vichy [viʃi] nm a (*Tex*) gingham. b (**eau de) V~** vichy *ou* Vichy water; ~ **fraise** strawberry syrup in vichy water; **carottes** ~ boiled carrots, carrots vichy; (*Pol*) **le gouvernement de V~** the Vichy government.

vichyssois, e [viʃiswa, waz] adj *gouvernement* Vichy (*épith*); *population* of Vichy.

viciation [visjasjɔ̃] nf (*voir* **vicier**) pollution; tainting; vitiation (*frm*); contamination.

vicié, e [visje] (ptp de **vicier**) adj (*voir* **vicier**) polluted; tainted; vitiated (*frm*); contaminated.

vicier [visje] 7 vt a *atmosphère* to pollute, taint, vitiate (*frm*); *sang* to contaminate, taint, vitiate (*frm*). b (*fig*) *rapports* to taint; *esprit, atmosphère* to taint, pollute. c (*Jur*) *élection* to invalidate; *acte juridique* to vitiate, invalidate.

vicieusement [visjøzmɑ̃] adv (*voir* **vicieux**) licentiously; lecherously; pervertedly; nastily*; incorrectly; wrongly.

vicieux, -ieuse [visjø, jøz] 1 adj a (*pervers*) *personne, penchant* licentious, dissolute, lecherous, perverted, depraved. **c'est un petit** ~ he's a little lecher. b (*littér: pourri de vices*) vicious (*littér*), depraved, vice-ridden. c (*rétif*) *cheval* restive, unruly. d (*trompeur, pas franc*) *attaque, balle* well-disguised, nasty*; *voir* **cercle**. e (*fautif*) *prononciation, expression* incorrect, wrong. 2 nm,f pervert.

vicinal, e, mpl **-aux** [visinal, o] adj (*Admin*) **chemin** ~ by-road, byway.

vicissitudes [visisityd] nfpl (*infortunes*) vicissitudes, tribulations, trials, trials and tribulations; (*littér: variations, événements*) vicissitudes, vagaries. **il a connu bien des** ~ he has had many ups and downs *ou* trials and tribulations.

vicomte [vikɔ̃t] nm viscount.

vicomté [vikɔ̃te] nf viscountcy, viscounty.

vicomtesse [vikɔ̃tɛs] nf viscountess.

victime [viktim] nf (*gén*) victim; *[accident, catastrophe]* casualty, victim; (*Jur*) aggrieved party, victim. **la** ~ **du sacrifice** the sacrificial victim; **entreprise** ~ **de la concurrence** business which was a victim of competition; **il a été** ~ **de son imprudence/imprévoyance** he was the victim of his own imprudence/lack of foresight; **être** ~ **de** *escroc, crise cardiaque, calomnie* to be the victim of; **l'incendie a fait de nombreuses** ~**s** the fire claimed many casualties *ou* victims.

victoire [viktwaʀ] nf (*gén*) victory; (*Sport*) win, victory. (*Boxe*) ~ **aux points** win on points; ~ **à la Pyrrhus** Pyrrhic victory; **crier** *ou* **chanter** ~ to crow (over one's victory); **ne criez pas** ~ **trop tôt** don't count your chickens before they're hatched.

Victor [viktɔʀ] nm Victor.

Victoria [viktɔʀja] 1 nf Victoria. **le lac** ~ Lake Victoria. 2 nm (*Géog*) Victoria.

victoria [viktɔʀja] nf (*Bot, Hist: voiture*) victoria.

victorien, -ienne [viktɔʀjɛ̃, jɛn] adj Victorian.

victorieusement [viktɔʀjøzmɑ̃] adv (*voir* **victorieux**) victoriously; triumphantly.

victorieux, -ieuse [viktɔʀjø, jøz] adj *général, campagne, armée* victorious; *équipe* winning (*épith*), victorious; *parti* victorious; *air, sourire* triumphant.

victuailles [viktɥɑj] nfpl provisions, victuals.

vidage [vidaʒ] nm a *[récipient]* emptying. b (*: *expulsion*) kicking out*, chucking out*.

vidame [vidam] nm (*Hist*) vidame.

vidange [vidɑ̃ʒ] nf a *[fosse, tonneau, réservoir, fosse d'aisance]* emptying; (*Aut*) oil change. **entreprise de** ~ sewage disposal business; (*Aut*) **faire la** ~ to change the oil, do an *ou* the oil change. b (*matières*) ~**s** sewage. c (*dispositif*) *[lavabo]* waste outlet.

vidanger [vidɑ̃ʒe] 3 vt a *réservoir, fosse d'aisance* to empty. b *huile, eau* to drain (off), empty out.

vidangeur [vidɑ̃ʒœʀ] nm cesspool emptier.

vide [vid] 1 adj a (*lit*) (*gén*) empty; (*disponible*) *appartement, siège* empty, vacant; (*Ling*) *élément* empty. **avoir l'estomac** *ou* **le ventre** ~ to have an empty stomach; **ne partez pas le ventre** ~ don't leave on an empty stomach; (*Comm*) **bouteilles/caisses** ~**s** empty bottles/cases, empties*; *voir* **case, ensemble, main.**

b (*fig*) (*sans intérêt, creux*) *journée, heures* empty; (*stérile*) *discussion, paroles, style* empty, vacuous. **sa vie était** ~ his life was empty *ou* a void; **passer une journée** ~ to spend a day with nothing to do, spend an empty day; *voir* **tête.**

c ~ **de** empty *ou* (de)void of; ~ **de sens** *mot, expression* meaningless, empty *ou* (de)void of (all) meaning; *paroles* meaningless, empty; **les rues** ~**s de voitures** the streets empty *ou* devoid of cars; **elle se sentait** ~ **de tout sentiment** she felt (de)void *ou* empty of all feeling.

2 nm a (*absence d'air*) vacuum. **le** ~ **absolu** an absolute vacuum; **pompe à** ~ vacuum pump; **faire le** ~ **dans un récipient** to create a vacuum in a container; **sous** ~ under vacuum; **emballé sous** ~ vacuum-packed; **emballage sous** ~ vacuum packing; *voir* **nature, tube.**

b (*trou*) (*entre objets*) gap, empty space; (*Archit*) void. (*Constr*) ~ **sanitaire** underfloor space.

c (*abîme*) drop. (*l'espace*) **le** ~ the void; **être au-dessus du** ~ to be over *ou* above a drop; **tomber dans le** ~ to fall into empty space *ou* into the void; **j'ai peur/je n'ai pas peur du** ~ I am/I am not afraid of heights, I have no head/I have a good head for heights.

d (*néant*) emptiness. **le** ~ **de l'existence** the emptiness of life; **ce lieu n'est que** ~ **et silence** this place is nothing but emptiness and silence; **regarder dans le** ~ to gaze *ou* stare into space *ou* emptiness.

e (*fig: manque*) **un** ~ **douloureux dans son cœur** an aching void in one's heart; **son départ/sa mort laisse un grand** ~ his departure/his death leaves a big empty space *ou* a great emptiness; ~ **juridique** gap in the law.

f (*loc*) **faire le** ~ **autour de soi** to isolate o.s., drive everyone away; **faire le** ~ **autour de qn** to isolate sb completely, leave sb on his own; **faire le** ~ **dans son esprit** to make one's mind a blank; **parler dans le** ~ (*sans objet*) to talk vacuously; (*personne n'écoute*) to talk to a brick wall, waste one's breath; *[camion]* **repartir à** ~ to go off again empty; *voir* **nettoyage, passage, tourner.**

vide- [vid] préf *voir* **vider.**

vidé, e [vide] (ptp de **vider**) adj (*) *personne* worn out, dead beat*, all in*.

vidéaste [videast] nmf video director.

vidéo [video] 1 adj inv video. **caméra/jeu/signal** ~ video camera/game/signal; **cassette** ~ video cassette. 2 nf video.

vidéocassette [videokasɛt] nf video cassette.

vidéoclip [videoklip] nm (*chanson*) video.

vidéoclub [videoklœb] nm videoclub.

vidéoconférence [videokɔ̃feʀɑ̃s] nf videoconference, teleconference.

vidéodisque [videodisk] nm videodisk.

vidéofréquence [videofʀekɑ̃s] nf video frequency.

vidéotex [videotɛks] adj inv, nm inv ® videotex ®.

vidéothèque [videotɛk] nf video library.

vider [vide] 1 1 vt a *récipient, réservoir, meuble, pièce* to empty; *étang, citerne* to empty, drain. ~ **un appartement de ses meubles** to empty *ou* clear a flat of its furniture; ~ **un étang de ses poissons** to empty *ou* clear a pond of fish; ~ **un tiroir sur la table/dans une corbeille** to empty a drawer (out) onto the table/into a wastebasket; (*en consommant*) **ils ont vidé 3 bouteilles** they emptied *ou* drained 3 bottles; **il vida son verre et partit** he emptied *ou* drained his glass and left; (*en emportant*) **ils ont vidé tous les tiroirs** they cleaned out *ou* emptied all the drawers.

b *contenu* to empty (out). ~ **l'eau d'un bassin** to empty the water out of a basin; **va** ~ **les ordures** go and empty (out) the rubbish; ~ **des déchets dans une poubelle** to empty waste into a dustbin.

c (*faire évacuer*) *lieu* to empty, clear. **la pluie a vidé les rues** the rain emptied *ou* cleared the streets.

d (*quitter*) *endroit, logement* to quit, vacate. ~ **les lieux** to quit *ou* vacate the premises.

e (*évider*) *poisson, poulet* to gut, clean out; *pomme* to core.

f (†: *régler*) *querelle, affaire* to settle.

g (*Équitation*) *cavalier* to throw. ~ **les arçons/les étriers** to leave the saddle/the stirrups.

h (*: *expulser*) *trouble-fête, indésirable* to throw out*, chuck out*. ~ **qn d'une réunion/d'un bistro** to throw *ou* chuck sb out of a meeting/café*.

i (*épuiser*) to wear out. **ce travail m'a vidé*** this piece of work has worn me out; **travail qui vous vide l'esprit** occupation that leaves you mentally drained *ou* exhausted.

j (*loc*) ~ **son sac*** to come out with it*; ~ **l'abcès** to root out the evil; ~ **son cœur** to pour out one's heart.

2 **se vider** vpr *[récipient, réservoir, bassin]* to empty. **les eaux sales se vident dans l'égout** the dirty water empties *ou* drains into the sewer; **ce réservoir se vide dans un canal** this reservoir empties into a canal; **en août, la ville se vide (de ses habitants)** in August, the town empties (of its inhabitants).

3 comp ▸**vide-ordures** nm inv rubbish chute (*Brit*), garbage chute (*US*) ▸**vide-poches** nm inv tidy; (*Aut*) glove compartment ▸**vide-pomme** nm (pl **vide-pommes**) apple-corer.

videur [vidœʀ] nm *[boîte de nuit]* bouncer*.

viduité [vidɥite] nf (*Jur*) *[femme]* widowhood, viduity (*SPÉC*); *[homme]* widowerhood, viduity (*SPÉC*). **délai de** ~ minimum legal period of widowhood (*ou* widowerhood).

vie [vi] nf a (*gén, Bio, fig*) life. **la** ~ life; (*Rel*) **la V~** the Life; **être en** ~ to be alive; **être bien en** ~ to be well and truly alive, be alive and kicking*; **donner la** ~ to give birth (*à* to); **donner/risquer sa** ~ **pour** to give/risk one's life for; **rappeler qn à/revenir à la** ~ to bring sb back/come back to life; **tôt/tard dans la** ~ early/late in life; **attends de connaître la** ~ **pour juger** wait until you know (something) about life before you pass judgment; ~ **intra-utérine** life in the womb, intra-uterine life (*SPÉC*); ~ **végétative** vegetable existence.

b (*animation*) life. **être plein de** ~ to be full of life; **donner de la** ~ **à, mettre de la** ~ **dans** to liven up, enliven, bring life to; **sa présence met de la** ~ **dans la maison** he brings some life *ou* a bit of life into the house, he livens the house up.

c (*activités*) life. **dans la** ~ **courante** in everyday life; **(mode de)** ~ way of life, life style; **avoir/mener une** ~ **facile/dure** to have/lead an easy/a hard life; **mener une** ~ **sédentaire** to have a sedentary way of life *ou* a sedentary life style, lead a sedentary life; **mener joyeuse ~** to have a happy life, lead a happy *ou* lively existence; **la ~ intellectuelle à Paris** the intellectual life of Paris, intellectual life in Paris; **~ sentimentale/conjugale/professionnelle** love/married/professional life; **~ de garçon** bachelor's life *ou* existence (*voir* **enterrer**); **la ~ militaire** life in the services; **la ~ d'un professeur n'est pas toujours drôle** a teacher's life *ou* the life of a teacher isn't always much fun; **la ~ des animaux/des plantes** animal/plant life; **il poursuivit sa petite ~** he carried on with his day-to-day existence *ou* his daily affairs; **la ~ (à l')américaine** the American way of life; **~ de bohème/de patachon*** bohemian/disorderly way of life *ou* life style; **mener la ~ de château** to live a life of luxury *ou* the life of Riley*; *voir* **certificat, vivre** *etc.*

d (*moyens matériels*) living. **(le coût de) la ~** the cost of living; **la ~ augmente** the cost of living is rising *ou* going up; **la ~ chère est la cause du mécontentement** the high cost of living is the cause of discontent; *voir* **coût, gagner, niveau.**

e (*durée*) life(time). **il a habité ici toute sa ~** he lived here all his life; **des habits qui durent une ~** clothes that last a lifetime; **faire qch une fois dans sa ~** to do sth once in one's life(time); **une telle occasion arrive une seule fois dans la ~** such an opportunity occurs *ou* happens only once in a lifetime.

f (*biographie*) life (story). **écrire/lire une ~ de qn** to write/read a life of sb; **j'ai lu la ~ de Hitler** I read Hitler's life story *ou* the story of Hitler's life; **elle m'a raconté toute sa ~** she told me her whole life story, she told me the story of her life.

g (*loc*) (*nommer qn etc*) **à ~** for life; **il est nommé à ~** he is appointed for life, he has a life appointment; **directeur nommé à ~** life director, director for life; **à la ~ à la mort** *amitié, fidélité* undying (*épith*); **amis à la ~ à la mort** friends for life; **entre nous, c'est à la ~ à la mort** we have sworn eternal friendship, we are friends for life; **rester fidèle à qn à la ~ à la mort** to remain faithful to sb to one's dying day; **il est infirme pour la ~** he is an invalid for life; **amis pour la ~** friends for life, lifelong friends; **passer de ~ à trépas** to pass on; **faire passer qn de ~ à trépas** to dispatch sb into the next world; **une question de ~ ou de mort** a matter of life and death; **de ma ~ je n'ai jamais vu de telles idioties** never (in my life) have I seen such stupidity, I have never (in my life) seen such stupidity; **c'était la belle ~!** those were the days!; **il a la belle ~** he has an easy *ou* a cushy* life; **c'est la belle ~!** this is the life!; **ce n'est pas une ~!** it's a rotten* *ou* hard life!; **~ de bâton de chaise** riotous *ou* wild existence; **c'est une ~ de chien!*** it's a rotten *ou* a dog's life!*; **c'est la ~!** that's life!; **la ~ est ainsi faite!** such is life!, that's life!; **jamais de la ~ je n'y retournerai** I shall never go back there in my life, I shall never go there again, I shall never ever go back there; **jamais de la ~!** never!, not on your life!; **être entre la ~ et la mort** to be at death's door; **avoir la ~ dure** *[personne, animal]* to have nine lives; *[superstitions]* to die hard; **mener la ~ dure à qn** to give sb a hard time of it, make life hard for sb; **sans ~** *personne* (*mort*) lifeless; (*évanoui*) insensible; (*amorphe*) lifeless, listless; *regard* lifeless, listless; **vivre sa ~** to live (one's life) as one pleases *ou* sees fit, live one's own life; **elle a refait sa ~ avec lui** she started *ou* made a new life with him; **faire la ~** (*se débaucher*) to live it up, lead a life of pleasure; (*: *faire une scène*) to kick up* a fuss *ou* a row, make a scene; **chaque fois [illegible]e me fait la ~** she goes on (and on) at me every time; **il en a fait une ~ lorsque ...** he kicked up a real row* *ou* fuss* *ou* made a real scene when ...; **faire une ~ impossible à qn** to make sb's life intolerable *ou* impossible (for him); **laisser la ~ sauve à qn** to spare sb's life; **il dut à sa franchise d'avoir la ~ sauve** he owed his life to his frankness, it was thanks to his frankness that his life was spared; **voir la ~ en rose** to see life through rose-tinted *ou* rose-coloured glasses, take a rosy view of life; **ce roman montre la ~ en rose** this novel gives a rosy picture *ou* view of life.

vieil [vjɛj] **adj m** *voir* **vieux.**

vieillard [vjɛjaʀ] **nm** old man, old timer*. **les ~s** the elderly, old people *ou* men; *voir* **asile, hospice.**

vieille[1] [vjɛj] *voir* **vieux.**

vieille[2] [vjɛj] **nf** (*poisson*) wrasse.

vieillerie [vjɛjʀi] **nf** a (*objet*) old-fashioned thing; (*idée*) old *ou* worn-out *ou* stale idea. **aimer les ~s** to like old *ou* old-fashioned things *ou* stuff. b (*littér: cachet suranné*) outdatedness, old-fashionedness.

vieillesse [vjɛjɛs] **nf** a (*période*) old age; (*fait d'être vieux*) (old) age. **mourir de ~** to die of old age; **dans sa ~** in his old age; *voir* **assurance, bâton.** b (*vieillards*) **la ~** the old, the elderly, the aged; **aide à la ~** help for the old *ou* the elderly *ou* the aged; *voir* **jeunesse.** c *[choses]* age, oldness.

vieilli, e [vjeji] (**ptp de vieillir**) **adj** (*marqué par l'âge*) aged, grown old (*attrib*); (*suranné*) dated. **vin ~ en cave** wine aged in the cellar; **~ dans la profession** grown old in the profession; **une ville ~e** a town which has aged *ou* grown old; **une population ~e** an ageing *ou* aged population.

vieillir [vjejiʀ] 2 1 **vi** a (*prendre de l'âge*) *[personne, maison, organe]* to grow *ou* get old; *[population]* to age. **~ dans un métier** to grow old in a job; **savoir ~** to grow old gracefully; **l'art de ~** the art of growing old gracefully; **il a bien/mal vieilli** *[personne]* he has/has not aged well; *[film]* it has/has not stood the test of time, it has not/has become dated.

b (*paraître plus vieux*) to age. **il a vieilli de 10 ans en quelques jours** he aged (by) 10 years in a few days; **je la trouve très vieillie** I find she has aged a lot; **il ne vieillit pas** he doesn't get any older.

c (*fig: passer de mode*) *[auteur, mot, doctrine]* to become (out)dated.

d (*Culin*) *[vin, fromage]* to age.

2 **vt** a *[coiffure, maladie]* to age, put years on. **cette coiffure vous vieillit** that hair style ages you *ou* puts years on you *ou* makes you look older.

b (*par fausse estimation*) **~ qn** to make sb older than he (really) is; **vous me vieillissez de 5 ans** you're making me 5 years older than I (really) am.

3 **se vieillir vpr** to make o.s. older. **il se vieillit à plaisir** he makes himself older when it suits him.

vieillissant, e [vjejisɑ̃, ɑ̃t] **adj** *personne* ageing, who is growing old; *œuvre* ageing, which is becoming (out)dated.

vieillissement [vjejismɑ̃] **nm** a *[personne, population, maison, institution]* ageing. **le ~ fait perdre à la peau son élasticité** ageing *ou* the ageing process makes the skin lose its elasticity. b *[mot, doctrine, œuvre]* becoming (out)dated. **le ~ prématuré d'un auteur** an author's becoming dated before his time. c *[vin, fromage]* ageing. **~ forcé** artificial ageing.

vieillot, -otte [vjɛjo, ɔt] **adj** a (*démodé*) antiquated, quaint. b (*vieux*) old-looking.

vielle [vjɛl] **nf** hurdy-gurdy (*kind of viol*).

Vienne [vjɛn] **n** (*en Autriche*) Vienna.

viennois, e [vjenwa, waz] 1 **adj** Viennese. **café/chocolat ~** coffee/hot chocolate with whipped cream; *voir* **pain.** 2 **nm,f: V~(e)** Viennese.

viennoiserie [vjenwazʀi] **nf** Viennese bread and buns.

Vientiane [vjɛntjan] **n** Vientiane.

vierge [vjɛʀʒ] 1 **nf** a (*pucelle*) virgin.

b (*Rel*) **la (Sainte) V~** the (Blessed) Virgin; **la V~ (Marie)** the Virgin (Mary); (*tableau, statue*) **une V~ romane/gothique** a Romanesque/Gothic (statue of the) Virgin; *voir* **fil.**

c (*Astron*) **la V~** Virgo, the Virgin; **être (de la) V~** to be (a) Virgo *ou* a Virgoan.

2 **adj** a *personne* virgin (*épith*). **rester/être ~** to remain/be a virgin.

b *ovule* unfertilized.

c (*fig*) *feuille de papier* blank, virgin (*épith*); *film* unexposed; *bande magnétique, disquette d'ordinateur* blank; *casier judiciaire* clean; *terre, neige* virgin (*épith*); (*Sport*) *sommet* unclimbed; *voir* **huile, laine, vigne** *etc.*

d (*littér: exempt*) **~ de** free from, unsullied by; **~ de tout reproche** free from (all) reproach.

Viêt-nam, Vietnam [vjɛtnam] **nm** Vietnam. **~ du Nord/du Sud** North/South Vietnam.

vietnamien, -ienne [vjɛtnamjɛ̃, jɛn] 1 **adj** Vietnamese. 2 **nm** (*Ling*) Vietnamese. 3 **nm,f: V~(ne)** Vietnamese; **V~(ne) du Nord/Sud** North/South Vietnamese.

vieux [vjø], **vieille[1]** [vjɛj], **vieil** [vjɛj] *devant nm commençant par une voyelle ou h muet*, **mpl vieux** [vjø] 1 **adj** a (*âgé*) old. **très ~** ancient, very old; **un vieil homme** an old man; **une vieille femme** an old woman; **c'est un homme déjà ~** he's already an old man; **les vieilles gens** old people, old folk, the aged *ou* elderly; **il est plus ~ que moi** he is older than I am; **~ comme Hérode** *ou* **comme le monde** as old as the hills; **histoire vieille de vingt ans** story which goes back twenty years; **il commence à se faire ~** he is getting on (in years), he's beginning to grow old *ou* to age; **il est ~ avant l'âge** he is old before his time; **sur ses ~ jours, il était devenu sourd** he had gone deaf in his old age; **un ~ retraité** an old pensioner; **il n'a pas fait de ~ os** he didn't last *ou* live long; **il n'a pas fait de ~ os dans cette entreprise** he didn't last long in that firm; *voir* **retraite, vivre.**

b (*ancien: idée de valeur*) *demeure, bijoux, meuble* old. **une belle vieille demeure** a fine old house; **un vin ~** an old wine; **vieilles danses** old dances; **~ français** Old French; **vieil anglais** Old English.

c (*expérimenté*) *marin, soldat, guide* old, seasoned. **un ~ renard** a sly old fox *ou* dog; **un ~ routier de la politique** a wily old politician, an old hand at politics; **un ~ loup de mer** an old sea dog.

d (*usé*) *objet, maison, habits* old. **ce pull est très ~** this sweater is ancient *ou* very old; **~ papiers** waste paper; **~ journaux** old (news)papers; **de vieilles nouvelles** old news.

e (*avant n: de longue date*) *ami, habitude, amitié* old, long-standing; (*passé*) *coutumes* old, ancient. **un vieil ami, un ami de vieille date** a long-standing friend, a friend of long standing; **de vieille race** *ou* **souche** of ancient lineage; **vieille famille** old *ou* ancient family; **connaître qn de vieille date** to have known sb for a very long time; **c'est une vieille histoire** it's an old story; **nous avons beaucoup de ~ souvenirs en commun** we have a lot of old memories in common; **c'est la vieille question/le ~ problème** it's the same old question/problem; **traîner un ~ rhume** to have a cold that is dragging on.

f (*avant n: de naguère*) old; (*précédent*) old, former, previous. **la vieille génération** the older generation; **mon vieil enthousiasme** my old *ou* former *ou* previous enthusiasm; **ma vieille voiture était plus rapide**

que la nouvelle my old *ou* former *ou* previous car was quicker than the new one; **le ~ Paris/Lyon** old Paris/Lyons; **dans le bon ~ temps** in the good old days *ou* times; **la vieille France/Angleterre** the France/England of bygone days; **il est de la vieille école** he belongs to *ou* is (one) of the old school; **ses vieilles craintes se réveillaient** his old fears were aroused once more.

g (*péj: intensif*) **vieille bique‡, vieille peau‡** old bag‡; **~ jeton*** *ou* **shnock‡** old misery*; **vieille noix*** (silly) old twit* *ou* fathead‡; **quel ~ chameau!*** what an old beast!* *ou* pig!‡; **espèce de ~ crétin*!** stupid twit!*; **c'est un ~ gâteux*** he's an old dodderer*; **n'importe quel ~ bout de papier fera l'affaire** any old bit of paper will do; *voir* **bon¹**.

2 **nm** a old man, old timer*. **les ~** the old *ou* aged *ou* elderly, old people, old folk; **un ~ de la vieille*** one of the old brigade; (*père*) **le ~‡** my *ou* the old man‡; (*parents*) **ses ~‡** his folks*, his old man and woman *ou* lady‡; **mon (petit) ~*, tu vas m'expliquer ça** listen you, you're going to give me an explanation; **alors, (mon) ~*, tu viens?** are you coming then, old man?* *ou* old chap?* (*Brit*) *ou* old boy?* (*Brit*) *ou* old buddy* (*US*); **comment ça va, mon ~?*** how are you, old boy?* (*Brit*) *ou* old buddy?* (*US*); **tu fais partie des ~ maintenant** you're one of the old folks* now; *voir* **petit**.

b **préférer le ~ au neuf** to prefer old things to new; **faire du neuf avec du ~** to turn old into new; *voir* **coup**.

3 **vieille nf** old woman. (*mère*) **la vieille‡** my *ou* the old woman‡ *ou* lady‡; **alors, ma vieille*, tu viens?** are you coming then, old girl?*; (*hum: à un homme*) are you coming then, old man?* *ou* old chap?* (*Brit*) *ou* old boy?* (*Brit*); **comment ça va, ma vieille?*** how are you, old girl?*; *voir* **petit**.

4 **adv** *vivre* to an old age, to a ripe old age; *s'habiller* old. **elle s'habille trop ~** she dresses too old (for herself); **ce manteau fait ~** this coat makes you (look) old.

5 **comp** ► **vieux beau** (*péj*) ageing beau ► **vieille branche** († *hum fig*) old fruit* (*Brit*) *ou* bean* (*hum*) ► **vieille fille** spinster, old maid; **elle est très vieille fille** she is very old-maidish ► **vieille France adj inv** *personne, politesse* old-world, old(e)-world(e) (*hum*) ► **vieux garçon** bachelor; **des habitudes de vieux garçon** bachelor ways ► **la vieille garde** the old guard ► **vieux jeu adj inv** *idées* old hat (*attrib*), outmoded; *personne* behind the times (*attrib*), old-fashioned, old hat (*attrib*); *vêtement* old-fashioned, out-of-date (*épith*), out of date (*attrib*) ► **vieilles lunes** olden days ► **le Vieux Monde** the Old World ► **vieil or n, adj inv** old gold ► **vieux rose adj inv** old rose.

vif, vive¹ [vif, viv] 1 **adj** a (*plein de vie*) *enfant, personne* lively, vivacious; *mouvement, rythme, style* lively, animated, brisk; (*alerte*) sharp, quick (*attrib*); *imagination* lively, keen; *intelligence* keen, quick. **il a l'œil** *ou* **le regard ~** he has a sharp *ou* keen eye; **à l'esprit ~** quick-witted; **eau vive** running water; *voir* **haie, mémoire¹**.

b (*brusque, emporté*) *personne* sharp, brusque, quick-tempered; *ton, propos, attitude* sharp, brusque, curt. **il s'est montré un peu ~ avec elle** he was rather sharp *ou* brusque *ou* curt *ou* quick-tempered with her; **le débat prit un tour assez ~** the discussion took on a rather acrimonious tone.

c (*profond*) *émotion* keen (*épith*), intense, strong; *souvenirs* vivid; *impression* vivid, intense; *plaisirs, désir* intense, keen (*épith*); *déception* acute, keen (*épith*), intense. **j'ai le sentiment très ~ de l'avoir vexé** I have the distinct feeling that I have offended him.

d (*fort, grand*) *goût* strong, distinct; *chagrin, regret, satisfaction* deep, great; *critiques, réprobation* strong, severe. **une vive satisfaction** a great *ou* deep feeling of satisfaction, deep *ou* great satisfaction; **une vive impatience** great impatience; **il lui fit de ~s reproches** he severely reprimanded him; **un ~ penchant pour ...** a strong liking *ou* inclination for ...; **à vive allure** at a brisk pace; (*formules de politesse*) **avec mes plus ~s remerciements** with my most profound thanks; **c'est avec un ~ plaisir que ...** it is with very great pleasure that ... .

e (*cru, aigu*) *lumière, éclat* bright, brilliant; *couleur* vivid, brilliant; *froid* biting, bitter, sharp; *douleur* sharp; *vent* keen, biting, bitter; *ongles, arête* sharp. **l'air ~ les revigorait** the sharp *ou* bracing air gave them new life; **rouge ~** vivid *ou* brilliant red; **il faisait un froid très ~** it was bitterly cold.

f (*à nu*) *pierre* bare; *joints* dry.

g (†: *vivant*) alive. **être brûlé/enterré ~** to be burnt/buried alive; **de vive voix** *renseigner, communiquer, remercier* personally, in person; **il vous le dira de vive voix** he'll tell you himself *ou* in person; *voir* **chaux, mort², œuvre** *etc.*

2 **nm** a (*loc*) **à ~** *chair* bared; *plaie* open; **avoir les nerfs à ~** to have frayed nerves, be on edge; **avoir la sensibilité à ~** to be highly strung *ou* very sensitive; **être atteint** *ou* **touché** *ou* **piqué au ~** to be cut *ou* hurt to the quick; **tailler** *ou* **couper** *ou* **trancher dans le ~** (*lit*) to cut into the living flesh; (*fig: prendre une décision*) to take strong *ou* firm action; **entrer dans le ~ du sujet** to get to the heart of the matter; **sur le ~** *peindre, décrire* from life; **prendre qn (en photo) sur le ~** to photograph sb in a real-life situation; **faire un reportage sur le ~** to do a live *ou* on-the-spot broadcast; **les réactions de qn sur le ~** sb's instant *ou* on-the-spot reactions.

b (*Pêche*) live bait (*NonC*). **pêcher au ~** to fish with live bait.

c (*Jur: personne vivante*) living person. **donation entre ~s** donation inter vivos; *voir* **mort²**.

3 **comp** ► **vif-argent** (*Chim* ††) **nm inv** quicksilver; (*fig*) **il a du vif-argent dans les veines, c'est du vif-argent** he is a real live wire*.

vigie [viʒi] **nf** a (*Naut*) (*matelot*) look-out, watch; (*poste*) *[mât]* look-out post, crow's-nest; *[proue]* look-out post. **être en ~** to be on watch. b (*Rail*) **~ de frein** brake cabin.

vigilance [viʒilɑ̃s] **nf** (*voir* **vigilant**) vigilance; watchfulness.

vigilant, e [viʒilɑ̃, ɑ̃t] **adj** *personne, œil* vigilant, watchful; *attention, soins* vigilant.

vigile¹ [viʒil] **nf** (*Rel*) vigil.

vigile² [viʒil] **nm** (*Hist*) watch; (*veilleur de nuit*) (night) watchman; *[police privée]* vigilante.

vigne [viɲ] 1 **nf** a (*plante*) vine. (†) **être dans les ~s du Seigneur** to be in one's cups†; *voir* **cep, feuille, pied.** b (*vignoble*) vineyard. **des champs de ~** vineyards; (*activité*) **la ~ rapporte peu** wine-growing is not profitable; **les produits de la ~** the produce of the vineyards; *voir* **pêche¹**. 2 **comp** ► **vigne vierge** Virginia creeper.

vigneau, pl ~x [viɲo] **nm** winkle.

vigneron, -onne [viɲ(ə)ʀɔ̃, ɔn] **nm,f** wine grower.

vignette [viɲɛt] **nf** a (*Art: motif*) vignette. b (†: *illustration*) illustration. c (*Comm: timbre*) (manufacturer's) label *ou* seal. (*Aut*) **la ~ (automobile)** ≃ the (road) tax disc (*Brit*), (annual) licence tag (*US*); **~ de la Sécurité sociale** *price label on medicines for reimbursement by Social Security.*

vignoble [viɲɔbl] **nm** vineyard. (*ensemble de vignobles*) **le ~ français/bordelais** the vineyards of France/Bordeaux.

vignot [viɲo] **nm** = **vigneau.**

vigogne [vigɔɲ] **nf** (*Zool*) vicuna; (*Tex*) vicuna (wool).

vigoureusement [viguʀøzmɑ̃] **adv** *taper, frotter* vigorously, energetically; *protester, résister* vigorously; *peindre, écrire* vigorously, with vigour. **plante qui pousse ~** plant that grows vigorously *ou* sturdily.

vigoureux, -euse [viguʀø, øz] **adj** a (*robuste*) *personne* sturdy, vigorous; *corps* robust, vigorous; *bras* sturdy, strong; *mains* strong, powerful; *santé* robust; *plante* vigorous, sturdy, robust. **manier la hache d'un bras ~** to wield the axe with vigour, wield the axe vigorously; **il est encore ~ pour son âge** he's still hale and hearty *ou* still vigorous for his age. b (*fig*) *esprit* vigorous; *style, dessin* vigorous, energetic; *sentiment, passion* strong; *résistance, protestations* vigorous, strenuous. **donner de ~ coups de poing à qch** to deal sth sturdy *ou* strong *ou* energetic blows.

vigueur [vigœʀ] **nf** a (*robustesse: voir* **vigoureux**) sturdiness; vigour; robustness; strength. **sans ~** without vigour; **dans toute la ~ de la jeunesse** in the full vigour of youth; **se débattre avec ~** to defend o.s. vigorously *ou* with vigour; **donner de la ~ à** to invigorate.

b (*spirituelle, morale*) vigour, strength; *[réaction, protestation]* vigour, vigorousness. **~ intellectuelle** intellectual vigour; **s'exprimer/protester avec ~** to express o.s./protest vigorously.

c (*fermeté*) *[coloris, style]* vigour, energy.

d **en ~** *loi, dispositions* in force; *terminologie, formule* current, in use; **entrer en ~** to come into force *ou* effect; **en ~ depuis hier** in force as of *ou* from yesterday; **faire entrer en ~** to bring into force *ou* effect *ou* operation; **cesser d'être en ~** to cease to apply.

Viking [vikiŋ] **nm** Viking.

vil, e [vil] **adj** a (*littér: méprisable*) vile, base. b (†: *non noble*) low(ly). c (†: *sans valeur*) *marchandises* worthless, cheap. **métaux ~s** base metals. d **à ~ prix** at a very low price.

vilain, e [vilɛ̃, ɛn] 1 **adj** a (*laid à voir*) *personne, visage* plain(-looking), ugly(-looking); *vêtement* ugly, unattractive; *couleur* nasty. **elle n'est pas ~e** she's not bad-looking, she's not unattractive; **le V~ petit canard** the Ugly Duckling; (*fig*) **1 000 F d'augmentation, ce n'est pas ~** 1,000 francs rise – that's not bad.

b (*mauvais*) *temps* nasty, bad, lousy*; *odeur* nasty, bad. **il a fait ~ toute la semaine*** it has been nasty *ou* lousy* (weather) all week.

c (*grave, dangereux*) *blessure, affaire* nasty, bad. **une ~e plaie** a nasty wound; *voir* **drap.**

d (*méchant*) *action, pensée* wicked; *enfant, conduite* naughty, bad. **~s mots** naughty *ou* wicked words; **c'est un ~ monsieur** *ou* **coco*** he's a nasty customer *ou* piece of work* (*Brit*); **il a été ~** he was a naughty *ou* bad boy (*avec* with); **il a été ~ au cinéma/avec sa grand-mère** he was naughty at the cinema/with his grandmother; **jouer un ~ tour à qn** to play a nasty *ou* naughty trick on sb.

2 **nm** a (*Hist*) villein, villain.

b (*méchant*) (*garçon*) naughty *ou* bad boy. **oh le (gros) ~!** what a naughty boy (you are)!

c (*: *loc*) **il va y avoir du ~, ça va tourner au ~, ça va faire du ~** it's going to turn nasty.

3 **vilaine nf** (*méchant*) naughty *ou* bad girl. **oh la (grosse) ~e!** what a naughty girl (you are)!

vilainement [vilɛnmɑ̃] **adv** wickedly.

vilebrequin [vilbʀəkɛ̃] **nm** (*outil*) (bit-)brace; (*Aut*) crankshaft.

vilement [vilmɑ̃] **adv** (*littér*) vilely, basely.

vilenie [vil(ə)ni] **nf** (*littér*) (*caractère*) vileness, baseness; (*acte*) villainy, vile *ou* base deed.

vilipender [vilipɑ̃de] 1 **vt** (*littér*) to revile, vilify, inveigh against.

villa [villa] **nf** a (*maison*) villa, (detached) house. (*Antiq*) **les ~s romaines** Roman villas. b (*impasse privée*) ≃ mews.

village [vilaʒ] **nm** (*bourg, habitants*) village. **~ de toile** tent village, holiday encampment (*Brit*); **~ de vacances** holiday (*Brit*) *ou* vacation (*US*) village; **~ club** holiday village; *voir* **idiot.**

villageois, e [vilaʒwa, waz] 1 **adj** *atmosphère, coutumes* village (*épith*), rustic (*épith*). **un air ~** a rustic air. 2 **nm** (*résident*) villager, village resident; (†: *campagnard*) countryman. 3 **villageoise nf** villager, village resident; countrywoman.

ville [vil] 1 **nf** a (*cité, habitants*) town; (*plus importante*) city. **en ~, à la ~** in town, in the city; **aller en ~** to go into town; **habiter la ~** to live in a town *ou* city; **sa ~ d'attache était Genève** the town he had most links with was Geneva, Geneva was his home-base; *voir* **centre, hôtel, opération, sergent**[1].
b (*quartier*) **~ basse/haute** lower/upper (part of the) town; **vieille ~** old (part of) town; **~ arabe/européenne** Arab/European quarter.
c (*municipalité*) ≃ local authority, town *ou* city council. **dépenses assumées par la ~** local authority spending *ou* expenditure.
d (*vie urbaine*) **la ~** town *ou* city life, the town *ou* city; **aimer la ~** to like town *ou* city life *ou* the town *ou* city; **les gens de la ~** towns-people, townsfolk, city folk; **vêtements de ~** town wear *ou* clothes.
2 **comp ►ville champignon** mushroom town **►ville d'eaux** spa (town) **►la Ville éternelle** the Eternal City **►ville forte** fortified town **►ville industrielle** industrial town *ou* city **►la Ville lumière** the City of Light, Paris **►ville nouvelle** new town **►ville ouverte** open city **►Ville sainte** Holy City **►ville satellite** satellite town **►ville universitaire** university town *ou* city.

villégiature [vi(l)leʒjatyʀ] **nf** a (*séjour*) holiday (*Brit*), vacation (*US*). **être en ~ quelque part** to be on holiday (*Brit*) *ou* vacation (*US*) *ou* to be holidaying (*Brit*) *ou* vacationing (*US*) somewhere; **aller en ~ dans sa maison de campagne** to go for a holiday (*Brit*) *ou* vacation (*US*) *ou* to holiday (*Brit*) *ou* vacation (*US*) in one's country cottage. b **(lieu de) ~** (holiday (*Brit*) *ou* vacation (*US*)) resort.

villeux, -euse [vilø, øz] **adj** villous.

villosité [vilozite] **nf** villosity.

Vilnius [vilnjys] **n** Vilnius.

vin [vɛ̃] **nm** a wine. **~ blanc/rouge/rosé** white/red/rosé wine; **~ mousseux/de liqueur/de coupage** sparkling/fortified/blended wine; **~ ordinaire** *ou* **de table/de messe** ordinary *ou* table/altar *ou* communion wine; **~ nouveau** new wine; **grand ~, ~ fin** vintage wine; **petit ~, ~ de pays** local wine; **~ chaud** mulled wine; **~ cuit** liqueur wine; *voir* **lie, quand** *etc.* b (*réunion*) **~ d'honneur** reception (*where wine is served*).
c (*liqueur*) **~ de palme/de canne** palm/cane wine. d (*loc*) **être entre deux ~s** to be tipsy; **avoir le ~ gai/triste/mauvais** to get happy/get depressed/turn nasty when one has had a drink *ou* after a few glasses (of wine *etc*).

vinaigre [vinɛgʀ] **nm** vinegar. **~ de vin/d'alcool** wine/spirit vinegar; (*fig*) **tourner au ~** to turn sour; (*fig*) **faire ~*** to hurry up, get a move on; *voir* **mère, mouche.**

vinaigrer [vinegʀe] 1 **vt** to season with vinegar. **salade trop vinaigrée** salad with too much vinegar (on it).

vinaigrerie [vinɛgʀəʀi] **nf** (*fabrication*) vinegar-making; (*usine*) vinegar factory.

vinaigrette [vinɛgʀɛt] **nf** French dressing, vinaigrette, oil and vinegar dressing. **tomates (en** *ou* **à la) ~** tomatoes in French dressing *ou* in oil and vinegar dressing, tomatoes (in) vinaigrette.

vinaigrier [vinɛgʀije] **nm** a (*fabricant*) vinegar-maker; (*commerçant*) vinegar dealer. b (*flacon*) vinegar cruet *ou* bottle.

vinasse [vinas] **nf** (*péj*) plonk* (*Brit péj*), cheap wine; (*Tech*) vinasse.

Vincent [vɛ̃sɑ̃] **nm** Vincent.

vindicatif, -ive [vɛ̃dikatif, iv] **adj** vindictive.

vindicte [vɛ̃dikt] **nf** (*Jur*) **~ publique** prosecution and conviction; **désigner qn à la ~ publique** to expose sb to public condemnation.

vineux, -euse [vinø, øz] **adj** a *couleur, odeur, goût* win(e)y, of wine; *pêche* wine-flavoured, that tastes win(e)y; *haleine* wine-laden (*épith*), that smells of wine; *teint* (cherry-)red. **d'une couleur ~euse** wine-coloured, win(e)y-coloured, the colour of wine; **rouge ~** wine-red, win(e)y red. b (*Tech*) full-bodied. c (†: *riche en vin*) **coteaux ~** vine-covered hills; **une région ~euse** a rich wine-growing area.

vingt [vɛ̃] ([vɛ̃t] *en liaison et dans les nombres de 22 à 29*) 1 **adj inv, nm inv** twenty. **je te l'ai dit ~ fois** I've told you a hundred times; **il n'avait plus son cœur/ses jambes de ~ ans** he no longer had the heart/legs of a young man *ou* of a twenty-year-old; **~ dieux!** ye gods!; **il mérite ~ sur ~** he deserves full marks; *pour autres loc voir* **six, soixante.**
2 **comp ►vingt-deux adj inv, nm inv** twenty-two; **vingt-deux!*** watch out!; **vingt-deux (voilà) les flics!‡** watch out! it's the fuzz!‡; (*carabine*) **22 Long Rifle** .22 rifle, point two two rifle **►vingt-quatre heures** twenty-four hours; **vingt-quatre heures sur vingt-quatre** round the clock, twenty-four hours a day **►vingt et un** (*nombre*) twenty-one; (*jeu*) **le vingt-et-un** blackjack, pontoon, vingt-et-un, twenty-one (*US*).

vingtaine [vɛ̃tɛn] **nf**: **une ~** about twenty, twenty or so, (about) a score; **une ~ de personnes** (about) a score of people, twenty people or so, about twenty people; **un jeune homme d'une ~ d'années** a young man of around *ou* about twenty *ou* of twenty or so.

vingtième [vɛ̃tjɛm] 1 **adj** twentieth. **la ~ partie** the twentieth part; **au ~ siècle** in the twentieth century. 2 **nm** twentieth, twentieth part.

vingtièmement [vɛ̃tjɛmmɑ̃] **adv** in the twentieth place.

vinicole [vinikɔl] **adj** *industrie* wine (*épith*); *région* wine-growing (*épith*), wine-producing; *établissement* wine-making (*épith*).

vinifère [vinifɛʀ] **adj** viniferous.

vinification [vinifikasjɔ̃] **nf** *[raisin]* wine-making (process), wine production; *[sucres]* vinification.

vinifier [vinifje] 7 **vt** *moût* to convert into wine.

vinyle [vinil] **nm** vinyl.

vinylique [vinilik] **adj** (*peinture*) vinyl (*épith*).

vioc‡ [vjɔk] **nmf** = **vioque‡**.

viol [vjɔl] **nm** *[femme]* rape; *[temple]* violation, desecration. **au ~!** rape!

violacé, e [vjɔlase] (**ptp de violacer**) 1 **adj** purplish, mauvish. 2 **violacée nf** (*Bot*) **les ~es** the violaceae.

violacer [vjɔlase] 3 1 **vt** to make *ou* turn purple *ou* mauve. 2 **se violacer vpr** to turn *ou* become purple *ou* mauve, take on a purple hue (*littér*).

violateur, -trice [vjɔlatœʀ, tʀis] **nm,f** a (*profanateur*) *[tombeau]* violator, desecrator; *[lois]* transgressor. b (††) *[femme]* ravisher (*littér*).

violation [vjɔlasjɔ̃] **nf** (*voir* **violer**) violation; breaking; transgression; infringement; desecration. (*Jur*) **~ de domicile** forcible entry (*into a person's home*); (*Jur*) **~ du secret professionnel** breach *ou* violation of professional secrecy; (*Jur*) **~ de sépulture** violation *ou* desecration of graves.

violâtre [vjɔlɑtʀ] **adj** purplish, mauvish.

viole [vjɔl] **nf** viol. **~ d'amour** viola d'amore; **~ de gambe** viola da gamba, bass viol.

violemment [vjɔlamɑ̃] **adv** violently.

violence [vjɔlɑ̃s] **nf** a (*caractère*: *voir* **violent**) violence; pungency; fierceness; strenuousness; drastic nature. b (*force brutale*) violence; (*acte*) violence (*NonC*), act of violence. **mouvement de ~** violent impulse; **répondre à la ~ par la ~** to meet violence with violence; **commettre des ~s contre qn** to commit acts of violence against sb; **inculpé de ~ à agent** found guilty of assaulting a police officer *ou* of an assault on a police officer; *voir* **non.** c (*contrainte*) **faire ~ à qn** to do violence to sb; **faire ~ à une femme†** to use a woman violently††; **se faire ~** to force o.s.; **faire ~ à** *texte, sentiments* to do violence to, savage, desecrate; *voir* **doux.**

violent, e [vjɔlɑ̃, ɑ̃t] **adj** a (*gén*) violent; *odeur* pungent; *orage, vent* violent, fierce; *exercice, effort* violent, strenuous; *remède* drastic. **c'est un ~** he is a violent man; **~ besoin de s'affirmer** intense *ou* urgent need to assert o.s.; **saisi d'une peur ~e** seized by a violent *ou* rabid fear; *voir* **mort**[1], **révolution.** b (*: *excessif*) **c'est un peu ~!** it's a bit much!*, that's going a bit far!*

violenter [vjɔlɑ̃te] 1 **vt** a *femme* to assault (sexually). **elle a été violentée** she has been sexually assaulted. b (*littér*) *texte, désir* to do violence to, desecrate, savage.

violer [vjɔle] 1 **vt** a *traité* to violate, break; *loi* to violate, transgress, break; *droit* to violate, infringe; *promesse* to break. b *sépulture, temple* to violate, desecrate; *frontières, territoire* to violate. **~ le domicile de qn** to force an entry into sb's home. c *consciences* to violate. d *femme* to rape, ravish (†, *littér*), violate (*littér*). **se faire ~** to be raped.

violet, -ette [vjɔlɛ, ɛt] 1 **adj** purple; (*pâle*) violet. 2 **nm** (*couleur*) purple; (*pâle*) violet. **le ~ lui va bien** purple suits him (well); **porter du ~** to wear purple; **peindre qch en ~** to paint sth purple; (*Peinture*) **un tube de ~** a tube of purple; **robe d'un ~ assez pâle** dress in a rather pale shade of purple *ou* violet, dress in (a) rather pale purple *ou* violet.
3 **violette nf** (*Bot*) violet. **~ette odorante** sweet violet; **~ette de Parme** Parma violet.

violeur [vjɔlœʀ] **nm** rapist.

violine [vjɔlin] **adj** dark purple, deep purple.

violon [vjɔlɔ̃] **nm** a (*instrument d'orchestre*) violin, fiddle*; (*de violoneux*) fiddle; *voir* **accorder.** b (*musicien d'orchestre*) violin, fiddle*. **premier ~** *[orchestre]* leader; *[quatuor]* first violin *ou* fiddle*; **second ~** second violin *ou* fiddle*; (*groupe*) **les premiers/seconds ~s** the first/second violins; *voir* **vite.** c (*: *prison*) cells (*pl*), jug‡, nick‡ (*Brit*). **au ~** in the cells *ou* the jug‡ *ou* the nick‡ (*Brit*). d **~ d'Ingres** (artistic) hobby.

violoncelle [vjɔlɔ̃sɛl] **nm** cello, violoncello (*SPÉC*).

violoncelliste [vjɔlɔ̃selist] **nmf** cellist, cello player, violoncellist (*SPÉC*).

violoneux [vjɔlɔnø] **nm** (*de village, péj*) fiddler.

violoniste [vjɔlɔnist] **nmf** violinist, violin player, fiddler*.

vioque‡ [vjɔk] **nmf** (*vieillard*) old person, old timer*. (*père, mère*) **le ~** my *ou* the old man‡; **la ~** my *ou* the old woman‡ *ou* lady‡; **mes ~s** my folks*.

viorne [vjɔʀn] **nf** (*Bot*) viburnum.

VIP [veipe] **nmf** (**abrév de Very Important Person**) VIP.

vipère [vipɛʀ] **nf** adder, viper. **~ aspic** asp; **cette femme est une ~** that woman is a (real) viper; **elle a une langue de ~** she's got a viper's tongue *ou* a poisonous *ou* venomous tongue; *voir* **nœud.**

vipereau, pl **~x** [vip(ə)ʀo] **nm** young viper.

vipérin, e [vipeʀɛ̃, in] 1 **adj** (*Zool*) viperine; (*fig*) *propos* vicious, poisonous. 2 **vipérine** nf a (*Bot*) viper's bugloss. b (*Zool*) **(couleuvre)** ~ viperine snake (*SPÉC*), grass snake.

virage [viʀaʒ] nm a (*action*) *[avion, véhicule, coureur, skieur]* turn. (*Aviat*) **faire un ~ sur l'aile** to bank; (*Aut*) **prendre un ~ sur les chapeaux de roues** to take a bend (*Brit*) *ou* curve (*US*) *ou* turn (*US*) on two wheels *ou* on one's hub caps; **prendre un ~ à la corde** to hug the bend *ou* turn; (*Ski*) ~ **parallèle** parallel turn.
b (*Aut: tournant*) bend (*Brit*), turn (*US*). ~ **en épingle à cheveux** hairpin bend *ou* turn; ~ **en S** S-bend, S-curve (*US*); **"~s sur 3 km"** "bends for 3 km"; ~ **relevé** banked corner; **voiture qui chasse dans les ~s** car which skids round bends *ou* turns; **cette voiture prend bien les ~s** this car corners well, this car takes bends *ou* corners well; **il a pris son ~ trop vite** he went into *ou* took the bend *ou* curve (*US*) too fast; **accélérer dans les ~s** to accelerate round the bends *ou* corners.
c (*fig*) change in policy *ou* of direction. **le ~ européen du gouvernement britannique** the British government's change of policy *ou* direction over Europe, the change in the British government's European policy; **amorcer un ~ à droite** to take a turn to the right; **un ~ à 180 degrés de la politique française** a U-turn in French politics; **savoir prendre le ~** to adapt to meet new circumstances.
d (*transformation*) (*Chim*) *[papier de tournesol]* change in colour. (*Phot*) ~ **à l'or/au cuivre** gold/copper toning; (*Méd*) ~ **d'une cuti-réaction** positive reaction of a skin test.

virago [viʀago] nf virago.

viral, e, mpl **-aux** [viʀal, o] adj viral.

vire [viʀ] nf ledge (*on slope, rock face*).

virée [viʀe] nf (*en voiture*) drive, run, trip, ride, spin; (*de plusieurs jours*) trip, tour; (*à pied*) walk; (*de plusieurs jours*) walking *ou* hiking tour; (*en vélo*) run, trip; (*de plusieurs jours*) trip; (*dans les cafés etc*) tour. **faire une ~** to go for a run (*ou* walk, drive *etc*); **faire une belle ~ (à vélo) dans la campagne** to go for a nice (bicycle) run in the country, go for a nice run *ou* trip in the country (on one's bicycle); **faire une ~ en voiture** to go for a drive, go for a run *ou* trip *ou* ride *ou* spin in the car; **on a fait une ~ en Espagne** we went on a trip *ou* tour round Spain; **cette ~ dans les cafés de la région s'est mal terminée** this tour of the cafés of the district had an unhappy ending.

virelai [viʀlɛ] nm (*Littérat*) virelay.

virement [viʀmɑ̃] nm a (*Fin*) ~ **(bancaire)** credit transfer; ~ **postal** ≃ (National) Giro transfer (*Brit*); **faire un ~ (d'un compte sur un autre)** to make a (credit) transfer (from one account to another); ~ **budgétaire** reallocation of funds. b (*Naut*) ~ **de bord** tacking.

virer [viʀe] 1 1 vi a (*changer de direction*) *[véhicule, avion, bateau]* to turn. (*Aviat*) ~ **sur l'aile** to bank.
b (*Naut*) ~ **de bord** to tack; ~ **vent devant** to go about; ~ **vent arrière** to wear; ~ **sur ses amarres** to turn at anchor; ~ **au cabestan** to heave at the capstan.
c (*changer de place*) to move (out of the way). (*littér*, †) ~ **à tout vent** to be as changeable as a weathercock.
d (*changer de couleur, d'aspect*) *[couleur]* to turn, change; (*Phot*) *[épreuves]* to tone; (*Méd*) *[cuti-réaction]* to come up positive. **bleu qui vire au violet** blue which is turning purple, blue which is changing to purple; ~ **à l'aigre** to turn sour; *[temps]* ~ **au froid/à la pluie/au beau** to turn cold/rainy/fine *ou* fair.
2 vt a (*Fin*) to transfer (*à un compte* (in) to an account).
b (*) (*expulser*) to kick out*, chuck out*; (*renvoyer*) to sack (*Brit*), kick out*, chuck out*. ~ **qn d'une réunion** to kick *ou* chuck sb out of a meeting*; **se faire ~** (*expulser*) to get o.s. kicked *ou* thrown out, get put out (*de* of); (*renvoyer*) to get (o.s.) kicked *ou* chucked out (of one's job)*, get the sack (*Brit*).
c (*) (*jeter*) to chuck out*, throw out, get rid of; (*changer de place*) to get rid of.
d (*Phot*) *épreuve* to tone. (*Méd*) **il a viré sa cuti(-réaction)*** he gave a positive skin test, his skin test came up positive; (*fig*) ~ **sa cuti*** to throw off the fetters (*fig*).

vireux, -euse [viʀø, øz] adj (*littér*) noxious. **amanite ~euse** amanita virosa.

virevoltant, e [viʀvɔltɑ̃, ɑ̃t] adj *danseuse* twirling, pirouetting; *cheval* pirouetting; *jupons* twirling.

virevolte [viʀvɔlt] nf *[danseuse]* twirl, pirouette; *[cheval]* demivolt, pirouette; (*fig: volte-face*) about-turn, volte-face. **les ~s élégantes de la danseuse** the elegant twirling of the dancer.

virevolter [viʀvɔlte] 1 vi *[danseuse]* to twirl around, pirouette; *[cheval]* to do a demivolt, pirouette.

Virgile [viʀʒil] nm Virgil.

virginal, e, mpl **-aux** [viʀʒinal, o] 1 adj (*littér*) virginal, maidenly (*littér*). **blanc ~** virgin white. 2 nm (*Mus*) virginal, virginals (*pl*).

Virginie [viʀʒini] nf a (*Géog*) Virginia. **~-Occidentale** West Virginia. b (*prénom*) Virginia.

virginité [viʀʒinite] nf a (*lit*) virginity, maidenhood (*littér*). (*hum*) **se refaire une ~** to restore one's image. b (*fig littér*) *[neige, aube, âme]* purity. **il voulait rendre à ce lieu sa ~** he wished to give back to this place its untouched *ou* virgin quality.

virgule [viʀgyl] nf a (*ponctuation*) comma. **mettre une ~** to put a comma; (*fig*) **sans y changer une ~** without changing a (single) thing, without touching a single comma; (*fig*) **moustaches en ~** curled moustache; *voir* **point¹**. b (*Math*) (decimal) point. **(arrondi à) 3 chiffres après la ~** (correct to) 3 decimal places; **5 ~ 2** 5 point 2; ~ **fixe/flottante** fixed/floating decimal (point).

viril, e [viʀil] adj *attributs, apparence, formes* male, masculine; *attitude, courage, langage, traits* manly, virile; *prouesses, amant* virile. **force ~e virile** *ou* manly strength; (*Sport*) **jeu ~** aggressive style; *voir* **âge, membre, toge.**

virilement [viʀilmɑ̃] adv in a manly *ou* virile way.

virilisant, e [viʀilizɑ̃, ɑ̃t] adj *médicament* that provokes male characteristics.

virilisation [viʀilizasjɔ̃] nf (*Méd*) virilism.

viriliser [viʀilize] 1 vt (*Bio*) to give male characteristics to; (*en apparence*) *femme* to make appear mannish *ou* masculine; *homme* to make (appear) more manly *ou* masculine.

virilisme [viʀilism] nm virility.

virilité [viʀilite] nf (*voir* **viril**) masculinity; manliness; virility.

virole [viʀɔl] nf a (*bague*) ferrule. b (*Tech: moule*) collar (*mould*).

viroler [viʀɔle] 1 vt a *couteau, parapluie* to ferrule, fit with a ferrule. b (*Tech*) to place in a collar.

virologie [viʀɔlɔʒi] nf virology.

virologique [viʀɔlɔʒik] adj virological.

virologiste [viʀɔlɔʒist] nmf, **virologue** [viʀɔlɔg] nmf virologist.

virose [viʀoz] nf viral infection.

virtualité [viʀtɥalite] nf (*voir* **virtuel**) potentiality; virtuality.

virtuel, -elle [viʀtɥɛl] adj (*gén*), *sens, revenu* potential; (*Philos, Phys*) virtual; *voir* **image.**

virtuellement [viʀtɥɛlmɑ̃] adv a (*littér: en puissance*) potentially. b (*pratiquement*) virtually, to all intents and purposes. **c'était ~ fini** it was virtually finished, to all intents and purposes it was finished, it was as good as finished.

virtuose [viʀtɥoz] 1 nmf (*Mus*) virtuoso; (*fig: artiste*) master, virtuoso. ~ **du violon** violin virtuoso; ~ **de la plume** master of the pen, virtuosic writer; ~ **du pinceau** master of the brush, virtuosic painter. 2 adj virtuoso.

virtuosité [viʀtɥozite] nf virtuosity. (*Mus*) **exercices de ~** exercises in virtuosity; (*péj*) **c'est de la ~ pure** it's technically brilliant (but lacking in feeling).

virulence [viʀylɑ̃s] nf virulence, viciousness, harshness. **critiquer avec ~** to criticize virulently *ou* viciously *ou* harshly.

virulent, e [viʀylɑ̃, ɑ̃t] adj virulent, vicious, harsh.

virus [viʀys] nm (*lit, Ordin*) virus. ~ **de la rage** rabies virus; (*fig*) **le ~ de la danse/du jeu** the dancing/gambling bug*; **attraper le ~ du jeu** to be bitten by the gambling bug*.

vis¹ [vis] 1 nf a (*à bois etc*) screw. ~ **à bois** wood screw; ~ **à métaux** metal screw; ~ **à tête plate/à tête ronde** flat-headed/round-headed screw; ~ **à ailettes** wing nut; ~ **cruciforme** Phillips screw ®; **il faudra donner un tour de ~** you'll have to give the screw a turn *ou* tighten the screw a little; *voir* **pas¹, serrer, tour².** b **escalier à ~, ~†** spiral staircase. 2 comp ► **vis d'Archimède** Archimedes' screw ► **vis sans fin** worm, endless screw ► **vis micrométrique** micrometer screw ► **vis platinées** (*Aut*) (contact) points ► **vis de pressoir** press screw ► **vis de serrage** binding *ou* clamping screw.

vis² [vi] *voir* **vivre, voir.**

visa [viza] nm (*gén*) stamp; *[passeport]* visa. ~ **de censure** (censor's) certificate; (*fig*) ~ **pour ...** passport to ...; (*Fin*) **carte ~** ® Visa ® card.

visage [vizaʒ] 1 nm a (*figure, fig: expression, personne, aspect*) face. **au ~ pâle/joufflu** pale-/chubby-faced; **un ~ connu/ami** a known/friendly face; **je lui trouve bon ~** (to me) he is looking well; **sans ~** faceless; **le vrai ~ de ...** the true face of ...; **un homme à deux ~s** a two-faced man; (*fig*) **donner un nouveau ~ à** *ville* to give au new look to; *entreprise, parti* to change the face of; **à ~ humain** *socialisme, entreprise* with a human face; *voir* **soin.**
b (*loc*) **agir/parler à ~ découvert** to act/speak openly; **elle changea de ~** her face *ou* expression changed; **faire bon ~** to put a good face on it; **faire bon ~ à qn** to put on a show of friendliness *ou* amiability (*frm*) for sb.
2 comp ► **Visage pâle** paleface.

visagiste [vizaʒist] nmf: **(coiffeur) ~** (hair) stylist; **(maquilleur) ~** cosmetician.

vis-à-vis [vizavi] 1 prép a (*en face de*) ~ **de la place** opposite *ou* vis-à-vis the square.
b (*comparé à*) ~ **de** beside, vis-à-vis, next to, against; **mon savoir est nul ~ du sien** my knowledge is nothing next to *ou* beside *ou* against *ou* vis-à-vis his.
c ~ **de** (*envers*) towards, vis-à-vis; (*à l'égard de*) as regards, with regard to, vis-à-vis; **être sincère ~ de soi-même** to be frank with oneself; **être méfiant ~ de la littérature** to be mistrustful towards literature; **j'en ai honte ~ de lui** I'm ashamed of it in front of *ou* before him.
2 adv (*face à face*) face to face. **leurs maisons se font ~** their houses are facing *ou* opposite each other.
3 nm inv a (*position*) **en ~** facing *ou* opposite each other; **des**

immeubles en ~ buildings facing *ou* opposite each other; **assis en ~** sitting facing *ou* opposite each other, sitting face to face.
b (*tête-à-tête*) encounter, meeting. **un ~ ennuyeux** a tiresome encounter *ou* meeting.
c (*personne faisant face*) person opposite; (*aux cartes: partenaire*) partner; (*homologue*) opposite number, counterpart.
d (*immeuble etc*) **immeuble sans ~** building with an open *ou* unimpeded outlook; **avoir une école pour ~** to have a school opposite, look out at *ou* on a school.
e (*canapé*) tête-à-tête.

viscéral, e, mpl -aux [viseʀal, o] **adj** a (*Anat*) visceral. b (*fig*) *haine, peur* visceral, deep-seated, deep-rooted.

viscéralement [viseʀalmɑ̃] **adv:** **détester ~ qch** to have a gut* *ou* visceral hatred of sth; **~ jaloux** pathologically jealous.

viscère [visɛʀ] **nm** (*gén pl*) **~s** intestines, entrails, viscera (*SPÉC*).

viscose [viskoz] **nf** viscose.

viscosité [viskozite] **nf** *[liquide]* viscosity; *[surface gluante]* stickiness, viscosity.

visée [vize] **nf** a (*avec une arme*) taking aim (*NonC*), aiming (*NonC*); (*Arpentage*) sighting. **pour faciliter la ~, ce fusil comporte un dispositif spécial** to help you to (take) aim *ou* to help your aim, this rifle comes equipped with a special device; *voir* **ligne**[1]. b (*gén pl: dessein*) aim, design. **avoir des ~s sur qn/qch** to have designs on sb/sth; **~s coupables** wicked designs.

viser[1] [vize] 1 1 **vt** a *objectif* to aim at *ou* for; *cible* to aim at.
b (*ambitionner*) *effet* to aim at; *carrière* to aim at, set one's sights on.
c (*concerner*) *[mesure]* to be aimed at, be directed at; *[remarque]* to be aimed *ou* directed at, be meant *ou* intended for. **cette mesure vise tout le monde** this measure applies to everyone, everyone is affected by this measure; **se sentir visé** to feel one is being got at*.
d (*‡: regarder*) to have a dekko‡ (*Brit*) at, take a look at. **vise un peu ça!** just have a dekko‡ (*Brit*) *ou* take a look at that!
2 **vi** a *[tireur]* to aim, take aim. **~ juste/trop haut/trop bas** to aim accurately/(too) high/(too) low; **~ à la tête/au cœur** to aim for the head/heart.
b (*fig: ambitionner*) **~ haut/plus haut** to set one's sights high/higher, aim high/higher.
3 **viser à vt indir** (*avoir pour but de*) **~ à qch/à faire** to aim at sth/at doing *ou* to do; **scène qui vise à provoquer le rire** scene which sets out to raise a laugh *ou* to make people laugh; **mesures qui visent à la réunification de la majorité** measures which are aimed at reuniting *ou* which aim *ou* are intended to reunite the majority.

viser[2] [vize] 1 **vt** (*Admin*) *passeport* to visa; *document* to stamp. **faire ~ un passeport** to have a passport visaed.

viseur [vizœʀ] **nm** a *[arme]* sights (*pl*); *[caméra, appareil photo]* viewfinder. (*Phot*) **~ à cadre lumineux** collimator viewfinder. b (*Astron: lunette*) telescopic sight.

Vishnou, Vishnu [viʃnu] **nm** Vishnu.

visibilité [vizibilite] **nf** (*gén, Sci*) visibility. **bonne/mauvaise ~** good/bad visibility; **~ nulle** nil *ou* zero visibility; **ce pare-brise permet une très bonne ~** this windscreen gives excellent visibility; *pilotage, virage* **sans ~** blind (*épith*).

visible [vizibl] **adj** a (*lit*) visible. **~ à l'œil nu/au microscope** visible to the naked eye/under a microscope.
b (*fig: évident, net*) *embarras, surprise* obvious, evident, visible; *amélioration, progrès* clear, visible, perceptible; *réparation, reprise* obvious. **son embarras était ~** his embarrassment was obvious *ou* evident *ou* visible, you could see his embarrassment *ou* that he was embarrassed; **il ne le veut pas, c'est ~** he doesn't want to, that's obvious *ou* apparent *ou* clear; **il est ~ que ...** it is obvious *ou* apparent *ou* clear that ... .
c (*en état de recevoir*) **Monsieur est-il ~?** is Mr X (*ou* Lord X *etc*) able to receive visitors?, is Mr X (*ou* Lord X *etc*) receiving visitors?; **elle n'est pas ~ le matin** she's not at home to visitors *ou* not in to visitors in the morning.

visiblement [vizibləmɑ̃] **adv** a (*manifestement*) visibly, obviously, clearly. **il était ~ inquiet** he was visibly *ou* obviously *ou* clearly worried; **~, c'est une erreur** obviously *ou* clearly it's a mistake. b (*de façon perceptible à l'œil*) visibly, perceptibly.

visière [vizjɛʀ] **nf** a *[casquette plate, képi etc]* peak; (*pour le soleil, en celluloïd*) eyeshade. **mettre sa main en ~** to shade one's eyes with one's hand. b *[armure]* visor; *voir* **rompre**.

vision [vizjɔ̃] **nf** a (*action de voir qch*) **la ~ de ce film l'avait bouleversé** seeing this film had really upset him.
b (*faculté*) (eye)sight, vision (*frm, SPÉC*); (*perception*) vision, sight. **une ~ défectueuse** defective (eye)sight *ou* vision; **le mécanisme de la ~** the mechanism of vision *ou* sight; **champ de ~** field of view *ou* vision; **pour faciliter la ~** to aid (eye)sight *ou* vision; **~ nette/floue** clear/hazy vision; **porter des lunettes pour la ~ de loin** to wear glasses for seeing distances *ou* for seeing at a distance.
c (*conception*) vision. **la ~ romantique de ce peintre** this painter's romantic vision.
d (*image, apparition, mirage*) vision. **tu as des ~s*** you're seeing things.

visionnaire [vizjɔnɛʀ] **adj, nmf** visionary.

visionner [vizjɔne] 1 **vt** to view.

visionneuse [vizjɔnøz] **nf** viewer (*for transparencies or film*).

visiophone [vizjɔfɔn] **nm** videophone, viewphone.

Visitation [vizitasjɔ̃] **nf** (*Rel*) **la ~** the Visitation.

visite [vizit] 1 **nf** a (*action: voir* **visiter**) visiting; going round; examination, inspection; going over, searching; going through; calling on. (*à la prison, l'hôpital*) **heures/jour de ~** *ou* **des ~s** visiting hours/day; **la ~ du château a duré 2 heures** it took 2 hours to go round (*Brit*) *ou* go through (*US*) the castle; *voir* **droit**[3].
b (*tournée, inspection*) visit; (*Méd*) *[médecin hospitalier avec ses étudiants]* ward round. **au programme il y a des ~s de musée** there are museum visits on the programme; **~ accompagnée** *ou* **guidée** guided tour; **ces ~s nocturnes au garde-manger** these nocturnal visits *ou* trips to the pantry; **il redoutait les ~s de l'inspecteur** he feared the inspector's visits.
c (*chez une connaissance etc*) visit. **une courte ~** a short visit, a call; **une ~ de politesse/de remerciements** a courtesy/thank you call *ou* visit; **être en ~ chez qn** to be paying sb a visit, be on a visit to sb; **rendre ~ à qn** to pay sb a visit, call on sb, visit sb; **je vais lui faire une petite ~, cela lui fera plaisir** I'm going to pay him a call *ou* a short visit *ou* I'm going to call on him — that will please him; **rendre à qn sa ~** to return sb's visit, pay sb a return visit; **avoir** *ou* **recevoir la ~ de qn** to have a visit from sb; *voir* **carte**.
d (*visiteur*) visitor. **nous avons des ~s** we've got visitors *ou* company *ou* guests; **j'ai une ~ dans le salon** I have a visitor *ou* I have company in the lounge; **nous attendons de la ~** *ou* **des ~s** we are expecting visitors *ou* company *ou* guests; (*hum*) **tiens, nous avons de la ~*** hey, we've got company *ou* guests.
e (*officielle*) *[chef d'État]* visit. **en ~ officielle au Japon** on an official visit to Japan.
f (*médicale*) **~ (à domicile)** (house)call, visit; **~ de contrôle** follow-up visit; **la ~** (*chez le médecin*) (medical) consultation; (*Mil*) (*quotidienne*) sick parade; (*d'entrée*) medical (*Brit*), medical examination (*Brit*), physical examination (*US*); **aller à la ~** to go to the surgery (for a consultation); *[recrue etc]* **passer à la ~ (médicale)** to have a medical (*Brit*) *ou* physical (*US*) examination; **l'heure de la ~ dans un service d'hôpital** the time when the doctor does his ward round(s) in hospital.
g (*Comm*) visit, call; (*d'expert*) inspection. **j'ai reçu la ~ d'un représentant** I received a visit *ou* call from a representative, a representative called (on me).
2 **comp ▸visite du diocèse** (*Rel*) = **visite épiscopale ▸visite domiciliaire** (*Jur*) house search **▸visite de douane** customs inspection *ou* examination **▸visite épiscopale** (*Rel*) pastoral visitation.

visiter [vizite] 1 **vt** a (*en touriste, curieux*) *pays, ville* to visit; *château, musée* to go round, visit. **~ une maison** (*à vendre*) to go over *ou* view a house, look a house over, look over a house; **il me fit ~ sa maison/son laboratoire** he showed me round (*Brit*) *ou* through (*US*) his house/his laboratory; **il nous a fait ~ la maison que nous envisagions d'acheter** he showed us round (*Brit*) *ou* through (*US*) *ou* over (*Brit*) the house we were thinking of buying.
b (*en cherchant qch*) *bagages* to examine, inspect; *boutiques* to go over, search; *recoins* to search (in), examine; *armoire* to go through, search (in); (*Admin*) *navire* to inspect; (*hum*) *coffre-fort* to visit (*hum*), pay a visit to (*hum*).
c (*par charité*) *malades, prisonniers* to visit.
d *[médecin, représentant, inspecteur]* to visit, call on.
e (*Rel*) to visit.
f (*fréquenter*) *voisins, connaissances* to visit, call on.

visiteur, -euse [vizitœʀ, øz] 1 **nm,f** (*gén: touriste, à l'hôpital*) visitor. (*représentant*) **~ en bonneterie/pharmacie** hosiery/pharmaceutical *ou* drugs representative *ou* rep*; *voir* **infirmière**. 2 **comp ▸visiteur des douanes** customs inspector **▸visiteur médical** medical representative *ou* rep*.

vison [vizɔ̃] **nm** (*animal, fourrure*) mink; (*manteau*) mink (coat).

visonnière [vizɔnjɛʀ] **nf** (*Can*) mink farm, minkery (*Can*).

visqueux, -euse [viskø, øz] **adj** a *liquide* viscous, thick; *pâte* sticky, viscous; (*péj*) *surface, objet* sticky, goo(e)y*, viscous. b (*fig péj*) *personne, manière* smarmy (*Brit*), slimy.

vissage [visaʒ] **nm** screwing (on *ou* down).

visser [vise] 1 **vt** a (*au moyen de vis*) *plaque, serrure* to screw on; *couvercle* to screw down *ou* on. **ce n'est pas bien vissé** it's not screwed down *ou* up properly; **~ un objet sur qch** to screw an object on to sth; (*fig*) **rester vissé sur sa chaise** to be *ou* sit rooted *ou* glued to one's chair; (*fig*) **rester vissé devant qn** to be rooted to the spot before sb; **le chapeau vissé sur la tête** with his hat jammed hard *ou* tight on his head.
b (*en tournant*) *couvercle, bouchon, écrou* to screw on. **ce couvercle se visse** this is a screw-on lid, this lid screws on; **ce n'est pas bien vissé** *[bouchon]* it's not screwed on *ou* down properly; *[écrou]* it's not screwed down *ou* up properly.
c (*Sport: donner de l'effet à*) *balle* to put (a) spin on.

d (*: *surveiller*) *élève, employé* to keep a tight rein on, crack down on*. **depuis la fugue du petit Marcel, ils les vissent** ever since little Marcel ran off they keep a tight rein on them *ou* they have really cracked down on them*.

Vistule [vistyl] **nf: la ~** the Vistula.

visu [vizy] **adv: de ~** with one's own eyes; **s'assurer de qch de ~** to check sth with one's own eyes *ou* for oneself.

visualisation [vizɥalizasjɔ̃] **nf** (*voir* **visualiser**) visualization; making visual; (*Ordin*) display; *voir* **console, écran.**

visualiser [vizɥalize] 1 **vt** (*Tech: par fluorescence etc*) *courant de particules etc* to make visible, visualize; (*audiovisuel*) *concept, idée* to make visual; (*Ordin*) to display.

visuel, -elle [vizɥɛl] 1 **adj** (*gén*) visual. **troubles ~s** eye trouble (*NonC*); **cet écrivain est un ~** visual images predominate in the writings of this author; *voir* **audio-, champ.** 2 **nm** (*Ordin*) visual display unit, VDU; (*Publicité*) visual. **~ graphique** graphical display unit.

visuellement [vizɥɛlmɑ̃] **adv** visually.

vit [vi] *voir* **vivre, voir.**

vital, e, mpl -aux [vital, o] **adj** (*Bio, gén*) vital; *voir* **centre, espace, minimum.**

vitalisme [vitalism] **nm** (*Philos*) vitalism.

vitalité [vitalite] **nf** *[personne]* energy, vitality; *[institution, terme]* vitality. **il est plein de ~** he's full of energy *ou* go *ou* vitality; **la ~ de ces enfants est incroyable** the energy of these children is unbelievable.

vitamine [vitamin] **nf** vitamin. **~ A/C/D** *etc* vitamin A/C/D *etc; voir* **carence.**

vitaminé, e [vitamine] **adj** with added vitamins.

vitaminique [vitaminik] **adj** vitamin (*épith*).

vite [vit] 1 **adv** a (*à vive allure*) *rouler, marcher* fast, quickly; *progresser, avancer* quickly, rapidly, swiftly.

b (*rapidement*) *travailler, se dérouler, se passer* quickly, fast; (*en hâte*) *faire un travail* quickly, in a rush *ou* hurry. **ça s'est passé si ~, je n'ai rien vu** it happened so quickly *ou* fast I didn't see a thing; **il travaille ~ et bien** he works quickly *ou* fast and well; **c'est trop ~ fait** it was done too quickly *ou* in too much of a rush *ou* hurry; **inutile d'essayer de faire cela ~: ce sera du mauvais travail** there's no point in trying to do that quickly *ou* in a hurry *ou* rush – it will just be a bad piece of work; **vous avez fait ~ pour venir** it didn't take you long to come, you were quick getting here; **ça ne va pas ~** it's slow work; **fais ~!** be quick about it!, look sharp!*; **le temps passe ~** time flies; (*fig*) **la police est allée ~ en besogne*** the police were quick off the mark *ou* worked fast *ou* didn't waste any time; **vous allez un peu ~ en besogne*** you're going too fast, you're a bit too quick off the mark; **aller plus ~ que les violons** *ou* **la musique** to jump the gun; **elle s'est tirée ~ fait*** she took off as quick as a flash*; **il l'a terminé ~ fait, bien fait** he finished it nice and quickly*; **il l'a peint ~ fait, bien fait** he gave it a quick coat of paint; **c'est du ~ fait, bien fait** it's a nice quick job; **c'est ~ dit*** it's easier said than done; *voir* **aller.**

c (*sous peu, tôt*) soon, in no time. **on a ~ fait de dire que ...** it's easy to say that ...; **il eut ~ fait de découvrir que ...** he soon *ou* quickly discovered that ..., in no time he discovered that ...; **ce sera ~ fait** it won't take long, it won't take a moment *ou* a second; **elle sera ~ arrivée/guérie** she'll soon be here/better, she'll be here/better in no time.

d (*sans délai, toute de suite*) quick. **lève-toi ~!** get up quick!; **va voir!** go and see quick!; **au plus ~** as quickly as possible; **il faut le prévenir au plus ~** he must be warned as quickly *ou* as soon as possible; **faites-moi ça, et ~!** do this for me and be quick about it!; **eh, pas si ~!** hey, not so fast!, hey, hold on (a minute)!; **~! un médecin** quick! a doctor; **et plus ~ que ça!** and get a move on!*, and be quick about it!; **là il (y) va un peu ~** he's being a bit hasty.

2 **adj** (*style journalistique: Sport*) fast.

vitellus [vitelys] **nm** (*Bio*) vitellin.

vitesse [vitɛs] 1 **nf** a (*promptitude, hâte*) speed, quickness, rapidity. **surpris de la ~ avec laquelle ils ont fait ce travail/répondu** surprised at the speed *ou* quickness *ou* rapidity with which they did this piece of work/replied; **en ~** (*rapidement*) quickly; (*en hâte*) in a hurry *ou* rush; **faites-moi ça en ~** do this for me quickly; **faites-moi ça, et en ~!** do this for me and be quick about it!; **on va prendre un verre en ~** we'll go for a quick drink; **écrire un petit mot en ~** to scribble a hasty note; **j'ai préparé le déjeuner/cette conférence un peu en ~** I prepared lunch/this lecture in a bit of a hurry *ou* rush; **à toute ~, en quatrième ~** at full *ou* top speed; **il faut toujours tout faire en quatrième ~** everything always has to be done at top speed *ou* in a great rush; **(à la nouvelle) il est arrivé en quatrième ~** *ou* **à toute ~** (on hearing the news) he came like a shot *ou* at the double.

b *[courant, processus]* speed; *[véhicule, projectile]* speed, velocity. **aimer la ~** to love speed; **à la ~ de 60 km/h** at (a speed of) 60 km/h; **à quelle ~ allait-il, quelle ~ faisait-il?** what speed was he going at? *ou* doing?; **faire de la ~** to go *ou* drive fast; **faire une ~ (moyenne) de 60** to do an average (speed) of 60; **prendre de la ~** to gather *ou* increase speed, pick up speed; **gagner** *ou* **prendre qn de ~** (*lit*) to beat sb, outstrip sb; (*fig*) to beat sb to it, pip sb at the post* (*Brit*), beat sb by a nose (*US*); **il est parti à la ~ grand V*** he went tearing off*, he left like a bullet from a gun; **entraîné par sa propre ~** carried along by his own momentum; **~ moyenne/maximale** average/maximum speed; **~ de propagation/de réaction/de rotation** speed of propagation/reaction/rotation; *voir* **course, deux, excès, perte.**

c (*Rail*) **grande/petite ~** fast/slow goods service; **expédier un colis en petite ~** to send a parcel by slow goods service; **expédier un colis en grande ~** to express (*Brit*) a parcel, send a parcel express *ou* by fast goods service.

d (*Aut*) gear. **changer de ~** to change gear; **2e/4e ~** 2nd/4th gear; **passer les ~s** to go *ou* run through the gears; *voir* **boîte.**

2 **comp** ►**vitesse acquise** momentum ►**vitesse de croisière** cruising speed ►**vitesse initiale** muzzle velocity ►**vitesse de libération** escape velocity *ou* speed ►**vitesse de pointe** maximum *ou* top speed ►**vitesse de sédimentation** sedimentation speed ►**vitesse du son** speed of sound ►**vitesse de sustentation** minimum flying speed.

viticole [vitikɔl] **adj** *industrie* wine (*épith*); *région* wine-growing (*épith*), wine-producing; *établissement* wine-producing, wine-making (*épith*). **culture ~** wine growing, viticulture (*SPÉC*).

viticulteur, -trice [vitikyltœʀ, tʀis] **nm,f** wine grower, viticulturist (*SPÉC*).

viticulture [vitikyltyʀ] **nf** wine growing, viticulture (*SPÉC*).

vitrage [vitʀaʒ] **nm** a (*action: voir* **vitrer**) glazing. b (*vitres*) windows (*pl*); (*cloison*) glass partition; (*toit*) glass roof. **double ~** double glazing. c (*rideau*) net curtain; (*tissu*) net curtaining.

vitrail, pl -aux [vitʀaj, o] **nm** stained-glass window, church window. **l'art du ~, le ~** the art of stained-glass window making.

vitre [vitʀ] **nf** a *[fenêtre, vitrine]* (window) pane, pane (of glass); *[voiture]* window. **poser/mastiquer une ~** to put in/putty a window pane *ou* a pane of glass; **verre à ~** window glass; **laver les ~s** to wash the windows; **appuyer son front à la ~** to press one's forehead against the window (pane); **les camions font trembler les ~s** the lorries make the window panes *ou* the windows rattle; **casser une ~** to break a window (pane); (*Aut*) **la ~ arrière** the rear window *ou* windscreen (*Brit*) *ou* windshield (*US*). b (*fenêtre*) **~s** windows; **fermer les ~s** to close the windows.

vitré, e [vitʀe] (**ptp de vitrer**) **adj** a *porte, cloison* glass (*épith*); *voir* **baie.** b (*Anat*) **corps ~** vitreous body; **humeur ~e** vitreous humour.

vitrer [vitʀe] 1 **vt** *fenêtre* to glaze, put glass in; *véranda, porte* to put windows in, put glass in.

vitrerie [vitʀəʀi] **nf** (*activité*) glaziery, glazing; (*marchandise*) glass.

vitreux, -euse [vitʀø, øz] **adj** a (*Anat*) *humeur* vitreous. b (*Géol*) vitreous; *voir* **porcelaine.** c (*péj: terne, glauque*) *yeux* glassy, dull; *regard* glassy, glazed, lacklustre (*épith*); *surface, eau* dull.

vitrier [vitʀije] **nm** glazier.

vitrification [vitʀifikasjɔ̃] **nf** (*voir* **vitrifier**) vitrification; glazing; sealing, varnishing.

vitrifier [vitʀifje] 7 1 **vt** (*par fusion*) to vitrify; (*par enduit*) to glaze, put a glaze on; *parquet* to seal, varnish. 2 **se vitrifier vpr** to vitrify.

vitrine [vitʀin] **nf** a (*devanture*) (shop) window. **en ~** in the window; **la ~ du boucher/de la pâtisserie** the butcher's/cake (*Brit*) *ou* pastry shop window; **faire les ~s** to dress the windows; **~ publicitaire** display case, showcase; (*fig*) **cette exposition est la ~ de l'Europe** this exhibition is Europe's shop window; *voir* **lécher.** b (*armoire*) (*chez soi*) display cabinet; (*au musée etc*) showcase, display cabinet.

vitriol [vitʀijɔl] **nm** (*Hist Chim*) vitriol. **huile de ~** oil of vitriol; (*fig*) **une critique/un style au ~** a vitriolic review/style; († *fig*) **un alcool au ~, du ~** firewater.

vitriolage [vitʀijɔlaʒ] **nm** (*Tech*) vitriolization.

vitrioler [vitʀijɔle] 1 **vt** a (*Tech*) to vitriolize, treat with vitriol *ou* (concentrated) sulphuric acid. b *victime d'agression* to throw acid *ou* vitriol at.

vitro [vitʀo] **adj, adv** *voir* **in vitro.**

vitrocéramique [vitʀoseʀamik] **nf** vitreous ceramic. **table de cuisson en ~** ceramic hob.

vitupération [vitypeʀasjɔ̃] **nf** (*propos*) **~s** rantings and ravings, vituperations (*frm*).

vitupérer [vitypeʀe] 6 1 **vi** to vituperate (*contre* against), rant and rave (*contre* about). **~ contre qn/qch** to rail against sb/sth, rant and rave about sb/sth. 2 **vt** (*littér*) to vituperate, revile, inveigh against.

vivable [vivabl] **adj** a (*) *personne* livable-with*. **il n'est pas ~** he's not livable-with*, he's impossible to live with; **ce n'est pas ~!** it's unbearable! *ou* intolerable! b *milieu, monde* fit to live in. **cette maison n'est pas ~** this house is not fit to live in.

vivace[1] [vivas] 1 **adj** a *arbre* hardy. **plante ~** (hardy) perennial. b *préjugé* inveterate, indestructible; *haine* indestructible, inveterate, undying; *souvenir* vivid; *foi* steadfast, undying. 2 **nf** (*plante*) perennial.

vivace[2] [vivatʃe] **adv, adj** (*Mus*) vivace.

vivacité [vivasite] **nf** a (*rapidité, vie*) *[personne]* liveliness, vivacity; *[mouvement]* liveliness, briskness; *[intelligence]* sharpness, quickness, keenness. **~ d'esprit** quick-wittedness; **avoir de la ~** to be lively *ou* vivacious. b (*brusquerie*) sharpness, brusqueness. c *[lumière, éclat]* brightness, brilliance; *[couleur]* vividness; *[froid]* bitterness; *[douleur]* sharpness; *[vent]* keenness. d (*intensité*) *[émotion, plaisir]* keenness, intensity; *[impression]* vividness.

vivandière [vivɑ̃djɛʀ] **nf** (*Hist*) vivandière.

vivant, e [vivɑ̃, ɑ̃t] 1 **adj** a (*en vie*) living, alive (*attrib*), live (*épith*). **né ~** born alive; **il est encore ~** he's still alive *ou* living; **il n'en sortira pas ~** he won't come out of it alive; **expériences sur des animaux ~s** experiments on live *ou* living animals, live animal experiments; (*fig*) **c'est un cadavre/squelette ~** he's a living corpse/skeleton.

b (*plein de vie*) *regard, visage, enfant* lively; *ville, quartier, rue* lively, full of life (*attrib*); *portrait* lifelike, true to life (*attrib*); *dialogue, récit, film* lively; (*fig*) *personnage* lifelike.

c (*doué de vie*) *matière, organisme* living; *voir* **être**.

d (*constitué par des êtres vivants*) *machine, témoignage, preuve* living. **c'est le portrait ~ de sa mère** he's the (living) image of his mother; *voir* **tableau**.

e (*en usage*) *expression, croyance, influence* living. **une expression encore très ~e** an expression which is still very much alive; *voir* **langue**.

f (*Rel*) **le pain ~** the bread of life; **le Dieu ~** the living God.

2 **nm** a (*personne*) (*Rel*) **les ~s** the living; **les ~s et les morts** (*gén*) the living and the dead; (*Bible*) the quick and the dead; **rayer qn du nombre des ~s** to strike sb's name from the number of the living; *voir* **bon**[1].

b (*vie*) **de son ~** in his lifetime, while he was alive; **du ~ de ma mère, mon père ne buvait pas beaucoup** in my mother's lifetime *ou* while my mother was alive, my father didn't drink much.

vivarium [vivaʀjɔm] **nm** vivarium.

vivat [viva] **nm** (*gén pl*) **~s** cheers.

vive[2] [viv] 1 *voir* **vif, vivre.** 2 **excl: ~ le roi/la France/l'amour!** long live the king/France/love!; **vivent les vacances!** three cheers for *ou* hurrah for the holidays!

vive[3] [viv] **nf** weever.

vivement [vivmɑ̃] **adv** a (*avec brusquerie*) sharply, brusquely. b (*beaucoup*) *regretter* deeply, greatly; *désirer* keenly, greatly; *affecter, ressentir, intéresser* deeply, keenly. **s'intéresser ~ à** to take a keen *ou* deep interest in, be keenly *ou* deeply interested in. c (*avec éclat*) *colorer* brilliantly, vividly; *briller* brightly, brilliantly. d (*littér: rapidement*) *agir, se mouvoir* in a lively manner. e (*marque un souhait*) **~ les vacances!** I can't wait for the holidays!, if only the vacation were here! (*US*), roll on the holidays!* (*Brit*); **~ que ce soit fini!** I'll be glad when it's all over!, roll on the end!* (*Brit*).

viveur [vivœʀ] **nm** high liver, reveller, roisterer.

vivier [vivje] **nm** (*étang*) fishpond; (*réservoir*) fish-tank; (*fig*) breeding ground.

vivifiant, e [vivifjɑ̃, jɑ̃t] **adj** *air, brise* invigorating, enlivening, bracing; *joie, ambiance* invigorating, enlivening, vivifying; *voir* **grâce**.

vivifier [vivifje] [7] **vt** a *personne* to invigorate, enliven; *sang, plante* to invigorate; (*fig littér*) *âme* to vitalize, quicken (*littér*); *race* to vitalize, give life to. b (*Rel, littér*) *[foi, force]* to give life, quicken (*littér*). **l'esprit vivifie** the spirit gives life.

vivipare [vivipaʀ] 1 **adj** viviparous. 2 **nm** viviparous animal. **~s** vivipara.

viviparité [viviparite] **nf** viviparity.

vivisection [vivisɛksjɔ̃] **nf** vivisection.

vivo [vivo] **adj, adv** *voir* **in vivo**.

vivoter [vivɔte] [1] **vi** *[personne]* to rub *ou* get along (somehow), live from hand to mouth; *[entreprise]* to struggle along.

vivre [vivʀ] [46] 1 **vi** a (*être vivant*) to live, be alive. **il n'a vécu que quelques jours** he only lived a few days; **je ne savais pas qu'il vivait encore** I did not know he was still alive *ou* living; **quand l'ambulance est arrivée, il vivait encore** he was still alive when the ambulance arrived; **quand elle arriva, il avait cessé de ~** he was dead when she arrived; **~ vieux** to live to a ripe old age, live to a great age; **il vivra centenaire** he'll live to be a hundred; **le peu de temps qu'il lui reste à ~** the little time he has left (to live); **le colonialisme a vécu** colonialism is a thing of the past, colonialism has had its day; **ce manteau a vécu*** this coat is finished *ou* has had its day; **il fait bon ~** it's good to be alive, it's a good life; *voir* **âme, qui.**

b (*habiter*) to live. **~ à Londres/en France** to live in London/in France; **~ avec qn** to live with sb; **ils vivent ensemble/comme mari et femme** they live together/as husband and wife; **~ dans le passé/dans ses livres/dans la crainte** to live in the past/in one's books/in fear.

c (*exister, se comporter*) to live. **~ saintement** to lead a saintly life, live like a saint; **~ en paix (avec soi-même)** to be at peace (with oneself); **~ dangereusement** to live dangerously; **se laisser ~** to live for the day, take life *ou* each day as it comes; **être facile/difficile à ~** to be easy/difficult to live with *ou* to get on with; **ces gens-là savent ~** those people (really) know how to live; *voir* **apprendre**.

d (*exister*) to live. **on vit bien en France** life is good in France; **c'est un homme qui a beaucoup vécu** he's a man who has seen a lot of life; (*fig*) **elle ne vit plus depuis que son fils est pilote** she lives on her nerves since her son became a pilot; **il ne vit que pour sa famille** he lives only for his family; *voir* **art, joie, savoir**.

e (*subsister*) to live (*de* on). **~ de laitages/de son traitement/de rentes** to live on dairy produce/one's salary/one's (private) income; (*Bible*) **l'homme ne vit pas seulement de pain** man shall not live by bread alone; **~ au jour le jour** to live from day to day *ou* from hand to mouth; **~ largement** *ou* **bien** to live well; **avoir (juste) de quoi ~** to have (just) enough to live on; **il vit de sa peinture/musique** he earns his living by painting/with his music; **travailler/écrire pour ~** to work/write for a living; **il faut bien ~!** a man (*ou* woman) has got to live!, you have to live!; **faire ~ qn** to provide (a living) for sb, support sb; **~ de l'air du temps** to live on air; **~ d'amour et d'eau fraîche** to live on love alone; **~ sur sa réputation** to get by on the strength of one's reputation; *voir* **crochet.**

f (*fig*) *[portrait, idée, rue, paysage]* to be alive. **un portrait qui vit** a lively *ou* lifelike portrait, a portrait which seems alive; **sa gloire vivra longtemps** his glory will live on *ou* will endure; **les plantes et les roches vivent comme les hommes** plants and rocks are alive *ou* have a life of their own just like men.

2 **vt** a (*passer*) to live, spend. **~ des jours heureux/des heures joyeuses** to live through *ou* spend happy days/hours; **il vivait un beau roman d'amour** his life was a love story come true; **la vie ne vaut pas la peine d'être vécue** life is not worth living.

b (*être mêlé à*) *événement, guerre* to live through. **nous vivons des temps troublés** we are living in *ou* through troubled times; **le pays vit une période de crise** the country is going through a period of crisis.

c (*éprouver intensément*) **~ sa vie** to live one's own life, live as one pleases *ou* sees fit; **~ sa foi/son art** to live out one's faith/one's art; **~ l'instant/le présent** to live for the moment/the present; **~ son époque intensément** to be intensely involved in the period one lives in; **il a mal vécu son divorce/son adolescence/la mort de sa mère** he had a hard time of it when he got divorced/as an adolescent/when his mother died.

3 **nm** (*littér*) **le ~ et le couvert** bed and board; **le ~ et le logement** board and lodging.

4 **nmpl: les ~s** supplies, provisions; *voir* **couper**.

vivrier, -ière [vivʀije, ijɛʀ] **adj** food-producing (*épith*).

vizir [viziʀ] **nm** vizier.

v'là [vla] **prép** (**abrév de voilà**) **~ le facteur** here's the postman (*Brit*) *ou* mailman (*US*).

vlan, v'lan [vlɑ̃] **excl** wham!, bang! **et ~!** **dans la figure** smack *ou* slap-bang in the face; **et ~! il est parti en claquant la porte** wham! *ou* bang! he slammed the door and left.

VO [veo] **nf** (**abrév de version originale**) **film en ~** film in the original version *ou* language; **en ~ sous-titrée** in the original version with subtitles.

vocable [vɔkabl] **nm** a (*mot*) term. b (*Rel*) **église sous le ~ de saint Pierre** church dedicated to St Peter.

vocabulaire [vɔkabylɛʀ] **nm** a (*dictionnaire*) vocabulary, word list. **~ français-anglais** French-English vocabulary; **~ de la photographie** dictionary *ou* lexicon of photographic terms. b (*d'un individu, d'un groupe; terminologie*) vocabulary. **~ actif/passif** active/passive vocabulary; **enrichir son ~** to enrich one's vocabulary; **il avait un ~ exact** he had a very precise vocabulary; **quel ~!** what language!; **~ technique/médical** technical/medical vocabulary.

vocal, e, **mpl -aux** [vɔkal, o] **adj** *organe, musique* vocal. **synthèse ~e** voice *ou* speech synthesis; *voir* **corde**.

vocalement [vɔkalmɑ̃] **adv** vocally.

vocalique [vɔkalik] **adj** vowel (*épith*), vocalic. **système ~** vowel system.

vocalisation [vɔkalizasjɔ̃] **nf** (*Ling*) vocalization; (*Mus*) singing exercise.

vocalise [vɔkaliz] **nf** singing exercise. **faire des ~s** to practise (one's) singing exercises.

vocaliser [vɔkalize] [1] 1 **vt** (*Ling*) to vocalize. 2 **vi** (*Mus*) to practise (one's) singing exercises. 3 **se vocaliser vpr** (*Ling*) to become vocalized.

vocalisme [vɔkalism] **nm** (*Ling*) (*théorie*) vocalism; (*système vocalique*) vowel system; *[mot]* vowel pattern.

vocatif [vɔkatif] **nm** vocative (case).

vocation [vɔkasjɔ̃] **nf** a (*Rel, pour un métier, une activité*) vocation, calling. **~ contrariée** frustrated vocation; **avoir/ne pas avoir la ~** to have/lack a vocation; **avoir la ~ de l'enseignement/du théâtre** to be cut out to be a teacher *ou* for teaching/for acting *ou* the theatre; **~ artistique** artistic calling; **rater sa ~** to miss one's vocation; (*hum*) **il a la ~** it's a real vocation for him. b (*destin*) vocation, calling. **la ~ maternelle de la femme** woman's maternal vocation *ou* calling; **la ~ industrielle du Japon** the industrial calling of Japan. c (*Admin*) **avoir ~ à *ou* pour** to have authority to.

vociférateur, -trice [vɔsifeʀatœʀ, tʀis] 1 **adj** vociferous. 2 **nm,f** vociferator.

vocifération [vɔsifeʀasjɔ̃] **nf** cry of rage, vociferation.

vociférer [vɔsifeʀe] [6] 1 **vi** to utter cries of rage, vociferate. **~ contre qn** to shout angrily at sb, scream at sb. 2 **vt** *insulte, ordre* to shout (out), scream. **~ des injures** to hurl abuse, shout (out) *ou* scream insults.

vodka [vɔdka] **nf** vodka.

vœu, **pl ~x** [vø] **nm** a (*promesse*) vow. **faire (le) ~ de faire** to vow to do, make a vow to do; **~x de religion** religious vows; **~x de célibat** vows of celibacy; (*Rel*) **prononcer ses ~x** to take one's vows; **~ de**

chasteté vow of chastity; faire ~ de pauvreté to take a vow of poverty.
b (*souhait*) wish. faire un ~ to make a wish; nous formons des ~x pour votre santé we send our good wishes for your recovery *ou* health; tous nos ~x de prompt rétablissement our best wishes for a speedy recovery; l'assemblée a émis le ~ que ... the assembly expressed the wish *ou* its desire that ...; je fais le ~ qu'il me pardonne I pray (that) he may forgive me; tous nos ~x (de bonheur) all good wishes *ou* every good wish for your happiness; tous nos ~x vous accompagnent our very best wishes go with you; ~ pieux pious hope.
c (*au jour de l'an*) les ~x télévisés du président de la République the President of the Republic's televised New Year speech *ou* address; il a reçu les ~x du corps diplomatique he received New Year's greetings from the diplomatic corps; tous nos (meilleurs *ou* bons) ~x de bonne et heureuse année, meilleurs ~x best wishes for the New Year, happy New Year; (*sur une carte*) "Season's Greetings".

vogue [vɔg] nf a (*popularité*) fashion, vogue. connaître une ~ extraordinaire to be extremely fashionable *ou* popular, be tremendously in vogue; être en ~ to be in fashion *ou* vogue, be fashionable; la ~ de la mini-jupe est en baisse miniskirts are going out of fashion, the fashion *ou* vogue for miniskirts is on the way out; c'est la grande ~ maintenant it's all the rage now. b (*dial: foire*) fair.

voguer [vɔge] 1 vi (*littér*) [*embarcation, vaisseau spatial*] to sail; (*fig*) [*pensées*] to drift, wander. nous voguions vers l'Amérique we were sailing towards America; l'embarcation voguait au fil de l'eau the boat was drifting *ou* floating along on *ou* with the current; (*fig*) nous voguons, frêles esquifs, au gré du hasard we drift (along), frail vessels on the waters of fate (*littér*); (*hum*) vogue la galère! come what may!

voici [vwasi] prép a (*pour désigner: opposé à voilà*) here is, here are, this is, these are. ~ mon bureau et voilà le vôtre here is *ou* this is my office and there is *ou* that is yours; ~ mon frère et voilà sa femme this is *ou* here is my brother and there is *ou* that is his wife; ~ mes parents here are *ou* these are my parents.
b (*pour désigner: même valeur que voilà*) here is, here are, this is, these are. ~ mon frère this is my brother; ~ le livre que vous cherchiez here's the book you were looking for; l'homme/la maison que ~ this (particular) man/house; M. Dupont, que ~ Mr Dupont here; il m'a raconté l'histoire que ~ he told me the following story.
c (*pour annoncer, introduire*) here is, here are, this is, these are. ~ le printemps/la pluie here comes spring/the rain; ~ la fin de l'hiver the end of winter is here; me/nous/le *etc* ~ here I am/we are/he is *etc*; les ~ prêts à partir they're ready to leave, that's them ready to leave*; nous ~ arrivés here we are, we've arrived; le ~ qui se plaint encore there he goes, complaining again, that's him complaining again*; me ~ à me ronger les sangs pendant que lui ... (*au présent*) here am I *ou* here's me* in a terrible state while he ...; (*au passé*) there was I *ou* there was me* in a terrible state while he ...; vous voulez des preuves, en ~ you want proof, well here you are then; nous y ~ (*lieu*) here we are; (*question délicate etc*) now we're getting there *ou* near it; ~ qui va vous surprendre here's something that'll surprise you; ~ qu'il se met à pleuvoir maintenant and now it's starting to rain; ~ ce que je compte faire this is what I'm hoping to do; ~ ce qu'il m'a dit/ce dont il s'agit this is what he told me/what it's all about; ~ comment il faut faire this is the way to do it, this is how it's done; ~ pourquoi je l'ai fait this *ou* that was why I did it; ~ pourquoi je l'avais supprimé that was why I'd eliminated it; ~ que tombe la nuit night is falling, it is getting dark.
d (*il y a*) ~ 5 ans que je ne l'ai pas vu it's 5 years (now) since I last saw him, I haven't seen him for the past 5 years; il est parti ~ une heure he left an hour ago, it's an hour since he left; ~ bientôt 20 ans que nous sommes mariés it'll soon be 20 years since we got married, we'll have been married 20 years soon.

voie [vwa] 1 nf a (*chemin*) way; (*Admin: route, rue*) road; (*itinéraire*) route. (*Hist*) ~ romaine/sacrée Roman/sacred way; par la ~ des airs by air; emprunter la ~ maritime to go by sea, use the sea route; ~s de communication communication routes; ~ sans issue no through road, cul-de-sac; ~ privée private road; ~ à double sens two-way road; ~ à sens unique one-way road.
b (*partie d'une route*) lane. "travaux — passage à ~ unique" "roadworks — single-lane traffic"; route à ~ unique single-lane road, single-track road; route à 3/4 ~s 3-/4-lane road; ~ réservée aux autobus bus lane; ~ à contresens contraflow lane; une ~ de circulation a été mise en sens inverse sur ... there is a contraflow system in operation on ... .
c (*Rail*) track, (railway) line. ligne à ~ unique/à 2 ~s single-/double-track line; ligne à ~ étroite narrow-gauge line; on répare les ~s the line *ou* track is under repair; ~ montante/descendante up/down line; le train est annoncé sur la ~ 2 the train will arrive at platform 2.
d (*Anat*) ~s digestives/respiratoires/urinaires digestive/respiratory/urinary tract; par ~ buccale *ou* orale orally; évacuer qch par les ~s naturelles to get rid of sth by the natural routes *ou* naturally.
e (*fig*) way. la ~ du bien/mal the path of good/evil; la ~ de l'honneur the honourable course; rester dans la ~ du devoir to keep to the line *ou* path of duty; entrer dans la ~ des aveux to make a confession; ouvrir/tracer/montrer la ~ to open up/mark out/show the way; préparer la ~ à qn/qch to prepare *ou* pave the way for sb/sth; continuez sur cette ~ continue in this way; il est sur la bonne ~ he's on the right track; l'affaire est en bonne ~ the matter is shaping *ou* going well; mettre qn sur la ~ to put sb on the right track; trouver sa ~ to find one's way (in life); la ~ est libre the way is clear *ou* open.
f (*filière, moyen*) par des ~s détournées by devious *ou* roundabout means; par la ~ hiérarchique/diplomatique through official/diplomatic channels; par ~ de conséquence in consequence, as a result.
g en ~ de: en ~ de réorganisation in the process of reorganization, undergoing reorganization; en ~ d'exécution in (the) process of being carried out, being carried out; pays en ~ de développement developing country; en ~ de guérison getting better, regaining one's health, on the road to recovery; en ~ de cicatrisation (well) on the way to healing over; en ~ d'achèvement (well) on the way to completion, nearing completion, being completed; elle est en ~ de réussir she's on the way *ou* road to success; il est en ~ de perdre sa situation he is on the way to losing his job, he's heading for dismissal.
2 comp ►**voie d'accès** access road ►**voie Appienne** Appian Way ►**voie de dégagement urbain** urban relief road ►**les voies de Dieu, les voies divines** the ways of God *ou* Providence; les voies de Dieu sont impénétrables *ou* insondables the ways of God are unfathomable ►**voie d'eau** leak ►**voie express** motorway (*Brit*), freeway (*US*), express way ►**voie de fait** (*Jur*) assault (and battery) (*NonC*); voie de fait simple common assault; se livrer à des voies de fait sur qn to assault sb, commit an assault on sb ►**voie ferrée** (*Rail*) railway (*Brit*) *ou* railroad (*US*) line ►**voie de garage** (*Rail*) siding; (*fig*) mettre sur une voie de garage *affaire* to shelve; *personne* to shunt to one side; (*Téléc*) on m'a mis sur une voie de garage they put my call on hold, they didn't put my call through ►**la voie lactée** the Milky Way ►**voies navigables** waterways ►**voie de passage** major route ►**les voies de la Providence** = les voies de Dieu ►**la voie publique** (*Admin*) the public highway ►**voie de raccordement** slip road ►**voie rapide** = voie express ►**les voies du Seigneur** = les voies de Dieu ►**voie vicinale** (*Admin*) local road.

voilà [vwala] 1 prép a (*pour désigner: opposé à voici*) there is, there are, that is, those are; (*même sens que voici*) here is, here are, this is, these are. voici mon bureau et ~ le vôtre here's *ou* this is my office and there's *ou* and that's yours; voici mon frère et ~ sa femme this is *ou* here is my brother and that is *ou* there is his wife; ~ mon frère this is *ou* here is my brother; ~ le livre que vous cherchiez there's *ou* here's the book you were looking for; l'homme/la maison que ~ that man/house (there); M. Dupont que ~ Mr Dupont there; il m'a raconté l'histoire que ~ he told me the following story.
b (*pour annoncer, introduire*) there is, there are, that is, those are. ~ le printemps/la pluie here comes spring/the rain; ~ la fin de l'hiver the end of winter is here; le ~, c'est lui there he is, that's him; le ~ prêt à partir he's ready to leave, that's him ready to leave*; le ~ qui se plaint encore there he goes, complaining again, that's him complaining again*; me ~ à me ronger les sangs pendant que lui ... (*au présent*) there am I *ou* there's me* in a terrible state while he ...; (*au passé*) there was I *ou* there was me* in a terrible state while he ...; ~ ce que je compte faire this is what I'm hoping to do; ~ ce qu'il m'a dit/ce dont il s'agit that's *ou* this is what he told me/what it's all about; ~ comment il faut faire that's how it's done; ~ pourquoi je l'ai fait that's why I did it; ~ que tombe la nuit night is falling, it's getting dark; ~ qu'il se met à pleuvoir maintenant now it's starting to rain, here comes the rain now; ~ où je veux en venir that's what I'm getting at, that's my point; nous y ~ (*lieu*) here we are; (*question délicate etc*) now we're getting there *ou* near it.
c (*pour résumer*) ... et ~ pourquoi je n'ai pas pu le faire ... and that's why *ou* that's the reason I wasn't able to do it; ~ ce qui fait que c'est impossible that's what makes it impossible; ~ qui est louche that's a bit odd *ou* suspicious; ~ qui s'appelle parler that's what I call talking, that's something like talking*; ~ ce que c'est (que) de ne pas obéir that's what comes of not doing what you're told, that's what happens when you don't do what you're told.
d (*il y a*) ~ une heure que je l'attends I've been waiting for him for an hour now, that's a whole hour I've been waiting for him now; ~ 5 ans que je ne l'ai pas vu it's 5 years since I last saw him, I haven't seen him for the past 5 years; il est parti ~ une heure he left an hour ago, it's an hour since he left; ~ bientôt 20 ans que nous sommes mariés it'll soon be 20 years since we got married, we'll have been married 20 years soon.
e (*loc*) en ~ une histoire/blague! what a story/joke!, that's some story/joke!; en ~ un imbécile! there's an idiot for you!, what a fool!; en ~ assez! that's enough!, that'll do!; veux-tu de l'argent? — en ~ do you want some money? — here's some *ou* here you are; vous voulez des preuves, en ~ you want proof, well here you are then; ~ le hic that's the snag *ou* catch, there's *ou* that's the hitch; ~ tout that's all; et ~ tout and that's all there is to it *ou* all there is to say, and that's the top and bottom of it* (*Brit*); ~ bien les Français! how like the French!, isn't that just like the French!, that's the French all over!*; (et) ne ~-t-il pas qu'il s'avise de se déshabiller lo and behold, he suddenly decides to get undressed!, I'm blest if he doesn't suddenly decide to get undressed!; nous ~ frais! now we're in a mess! *ou* a nice pickle!*, that's a fine mess *ou* pickle we're in!*; *voir* vouloir.

2 excl: ~! j'arrive! here I come!, there – I'm coming!; ah! ~! je comprends! oh, (so) that's it, I understand!, oh, I see!; ~ autre chose! (*incident*) that's all I need(ed)!; (*impertinence*) what a cheek!, the cheek of it!; je n'ai pas pu le faire, et ~! I couldn't do it and that's all there was to it! *ou* so there!*; ~, je m'appelle M. Dupont et je suis votre nouvel instituteur right (then), my name is Mr Dupont and I'm your new teacher; ~, tu l'as cassé! there you are, you've broken it!

voilage [vwalaʒ] nm (*rideau*) net curtain; (*tissu*) net (*NonC*), netting (*NonC*), veiling (*NonC*); *[chapeau, vêtement]* gauze (*NonC*), veiling (*NonC*).

voile[1] [vwal] nf a *[bateau]* sail. ~ carrée/latine square/lateen sail; faire ~ vers to sail towards; mettre à la ~ to make way under sail; (*lit*) mettre toutes ~s dehors to crowd *ou* cram on all sail; se rapprocher toutes ~s dehors to draw near with full sail on; (* *fig*) mettre les ~s to clear off‡, push off‡; *[bisexuel]* marcher à la ~ et à la vapeur* to be AC/DC‡ *ou* bi‡, swing both ways‡; *voir* planche, vent, vol[1] *etc.* b (*gén littér: embarcation*) sail (*inv: littér*), vessel. c (*navigation, sport*) sailing, yachting. faire de la ~ to sail, go sailing *ou* yachting; demain on va faire de la ~ we're going sailing *ou* yachting tomorrow.

voile[2] [vwal] nm a (*gén: coiffure, vêtement*) veil. ~ de deuil (mourning) veil; les musulmanes portent le ~ Moslem women wear the veil; (*Rel*) prendre le ~ to take the veil.

b *[statue, plaque commémorative]* veil.

c (*tissu*) net (*NonC*), netting (*NonC*). ~ de coton/de tergal ® cotton/Terylene ® net *ou* netting.

d (*fig: qui cache*) veil. le ~ de l'oubli the veil of oblivion; sous le ~ de la franchise under the veil *ou* a pretence of candour; jeter/tirer un ~ sur qch to cast/draw a veil over sth; lever le ~ de to unveil, lift the veil from; soulever un coin du ~ to lift a corner of the veil.

e (*fig: qui rend flou*) ~ de brume veil of mist, veiling mist; avoir un ~ devant les yeux to have a film before one's eyes.

f (*Phot*) fog (*NonC*). un ~ sur la photo a shadow on the photo.

g (*Méd*) ~ au poumon shadow on the lung; le ~ noir/gris/rouge des aviateurs blackout/greyout/redout.

h (*Anat*) ~ du palais soft palate, velum.

i (*Bot*) *[champignon]* veil.

j (*enregistrement du son*) warp.

voilé, e[1] [vwale] (ptp de voiler[1]) adj a *femme, statue* veiled. b *termes, allusion, sens* veiled. accusation à peine ~e thinly disguised accusation; il fit une allusion peu ~e à he made a broad hint at *ou* a thinly veiled reference to. c (*flou*) *lumière, ciel, soleil* hazy; *éclat* dimmed; *regard* misty; *contour* hazy, misty; *photo* fogged. les yeux ~s de larmes his eyes misty *ou* misted (over) *ou* blurred with tears; sa voix était un peu ~e his voice was slightly husky.

voilé, e[2] [vwale] (ptp de voiler[2]) adj (*tordu*) *roue* buckled; *planche* warped.

voilement [vwalmɑ̃] nm (*Tech*) *[roue]* buckle; *[planche]* warp.

voiler[1] [vwale] [1] 1 vt (*lit, fig: littér*) to veil. les larmes voilaient ses yeux tears dimmed his eyes, his eyes were misty with tears; un brouillard voilait les sommets the peaks were veiled in *ou* by *ou* shrouded in fog; (*fig*) je préfère lui ~ la vérité I prefer to shield him from the truth *ou* to conceal the truth from him. 2 se voiler vpr a se ~ le visage *[musulmane]* to wear a veil; (*fig*) se ~ la face to hide one's face, look away, avert one's gaze. b (*devenir flou*) *[horizon, soleil]* to mist over; *[ciel]* to grow hazy *ou* misty; *[regard, yeux]* to mist over, become glazed; *[voix]* to become husky.

voiler[2] [vwale] [1] 1 se voiler vpr *[roue]* to buckle; *[planche]* to warp. 2 vt to buckle; to warp.

voilerie [vwalʀi] nf sail-loft.

voilette [vwalɛt] nf (hat) veil.

voilier [vwalje] nm a (*navire à voiles*) sailing ship; (*de plaisance*) sailing dinghy *ou* boat, yacht. b (*fabricant de voiles*) sail maker. c (*Zool*) long-flight bird.

voilure[1] [vwalyʀ] nf a *[bateau]* sails. réduire la ~ to shorten sail; une ~ de 1 000 m² 1,000 m² of sail. b *[planeur]* aerofoils. c *[parachute]* canopy.

voilure[2] [vwalyʀ] nf = voilement.

voir [vwaʀ] [30] 1 vt a to see. je l'ai vu de mes (propres) yeux, je l'ai vu, de mes yeux vu I saw it with my own eyes; est-ce que tu le vois? can you see it?; je vois deux arbres I (can) see two trees; on n'y voit rien you can't see a thing; c'est un film à ~ it's a film worth seeing; aller ~ un film/une exposition to go to (see) a film/an exhibition; il a vu du pays he has been around a bit *ou* seen the world; nous les avons vus sauter we saw them jump; on a vu le voleur entrer the thief was seen entering; j'ai vu bâtir ces maisons I saw these houses being built; il faut le ~ pour le croire it has to be seen to be believed; as-tu jamais vu pareille impolitesse? have you ever seen *ou* did you ever see such rudeness?; je voudrais la ~ travailler avec plus d'enthousiasme I'd like to see her work more enthusiastically; je voudrais t'y ~ ~! I'd like to see how you'd do it!, I'd like to see you try!; (*fig*) je l'ai vu naître! I've known him since he was born *ou* since he was a baby; le pays qui l'a vu naître the land of his birth, his native country; il a vu deux guerres he has lived through *ou* seen two wars; cette maison a vu bien des drames this house has known *ou* seen many a drama; à le ~ si joyeux/triste seeing him look so happy/sad; vous m'en voyez ravi/navré I'm delighted/terribly sorry about that, that's wonderful/dreadful (news)!; (*fig*) on commence à y ~ plus clair the smoke is beginning to clear, things are beginning to come clear; ~ Naples et mourir see Naples and die.

b (*imaginer, se représenter*) to see, imagine. je ne le vois pas *ou* je le vois mal habitant la banlieue I (somehow) can't see *ou* imagine him living in the suburbs; nous ne voyons pas qu'il ait de quoi s'inquiéter we can't see that he has any reason for worrying; ne ~ que par qn to see only *ou* see everything through sb's eyes; je le verrais bien dans ce rôle I could just see him in this role; voyez-vous une solution? can you see a solution?; ~ la vie en rose to look at life through rose-coloured glasses, take a rosy view of life; ~ les choses en noir to take a black view of things; ~ loin to see ahead; ~ le problème sous un autre jour to see *ou* view the problem in a different light; je ne vois pas comment ils auraient pu gagner I can't *ou* don't see how they could have won; je n'y vois pas d'inconvénient I can't see any drawback; on n'en voit pas le bout *ou* la fin there seems to be no end to it.

c (*examiner, étudier*) *problème, dossier* to look at; *leçon* to look *ou* go over; *circulaire* to see, read. il faudra ~ la question de plus près we'll have to look at *ou* into the question more closely, the question requires closer examination; il faut *ou* il faudra ~ we'll have to see; je verrai (ce que je dois faire) I'll have to see, I'll think about it *ou* think what to do; il a encore 3 malades à ~ he still has 3 patients to see.

d (*juger, concevoir*) to see. c'est à vous de ~ s'il est compétent it's up to you to see *ou* decide whether he is competent; voici comment on peut ~ les choses you can look at things this way; se faire mal ~ (de qn) to be frowned on (by sb); se faire bien ~ (de qn) to (try to) make o.s. popular (with sb), be well viewed (by sb); nous ne voyons pas le problème de la même façon we don't see *ou* view the problem in the same way, we don't take the same view of the problem; façon de ~ view of things, outlook; il a vu petit/grand he planned things on a small/grand *ou* big scale, he thought small/big; ne ~ aucun mal à to see no harm in; ~ qch d'un bon/mauvais œil to look on sth *ou* view sth with approval/disapproval; ~ qn comme un ami to look upon *ou* regard sb as a friend, consider sb a friend; ne ~ que son intérêt to consider only one's own interest; à ~ son train de vie, elle doit être très riche if her lifestyle is anything to go by she must be very rich.

e (*découvrir, constater*) to see, find (out). aller ~ s'il y a quelqu'un to go and see *ou* go and find out if there is anybody there; vous verrez que ce n'est pas leur faute you will see *ou* find that they are not to blame *ou* that it's not their fault; il ne fera plus cette erreur – c'est à ~ he won't make the same mistake again – that remains to be seen *ou* – we shall see; nous allons bien ~! we'll soon find out!, we'll see soon enough!; (attendons) on verra bien let's wait and see; voyez si elle accepte see if she'll agree; des meubles comme on en voit dans tous les appartements bourgeois the sort of furniture you find in any middle-class home.

f (*recevoir, rendre visite à*) *médecin, avocat* to see. il voit le directeur ce soir he is seeing the manager tonight; on ne vous voit plus we never see you these days, you've become quite a stranger; le ministre doit ~ les délégués the minister is to see *ou* meet the delegates; il la voit beaucoup he sees a lot of her; passez me ~ quand vous serez à Paris look me up *ou* call in and see me (*Brit*) when you're in Paris; aller ~ *docteur, avocat* to go and see; *connaissance* to go and see, call on, visit; aller ~ qn à l'hôpital to visit sb *ou* go and see sb in hospital; je l'ai assez vu* I've had (quite) enough of him*.

g (*faire l'expérience de*) il en a vu (de dures *ou* de toutes les couleurs *ou* des vertes et des pas mûres*) he has been through the mill *ou* through some hard times, he has taken some hard knocks; en faire ~ (de dures *ou* de toutes les couleurs) à qn to give sb a hard time, lead sb a merry dance; j'en ai vu d'autres! I've been through *ou* seen worse!; a-t-on jamais vu ça?, on n'a jamais vu ça! did you ever see *ou* hear the like?; on aura tout vu! we've seen everything now!, that beats all!; vous n'avez encore rien vu! you haven't seen anything yet!

h (*comprendre*) to see. il ne voit pas ce que vous voulez dire he doesn't see *ou* grasp what you mean; elle ne voyait pas le côté drôle de l'aventure she could not see *ou* appreciate the funny side of what had happened; vous aurez du mal à lui faire ~ que ... you will find it difficult to make him see *ou* realize that ...; je ne vois pas comment il a pu oublier I don't see how he could forget; ~ clair dans un problème/une affaire to have a clear understanding of a problem/matter, grasp a problem/matter clearly.

i (*avec faire, laisser, pouvoir*) laisser ~ (*révéler*) to show, reveal; il a bien laissé ~ sa déception he couldn't help showing his disappointment *ou* making his disappointment plain; faire ~ (*montrer*) to show; fais ~! show me!, let me have a look!; faites-moi ~ ce dessin let me see *ou* show me this picture; elle ne peut pas le ~ (en peinture)* she can't stand (the sight of) him; va te faire ~ (ailleurs)!‡ nothing doing!*, get lost!*, no way!*; qu'il aille se faire ~ (chez les Grecs)!‡ he can go to hell!‡

j ~ venir to wait and see; ~ venir (les événements) to wait and see (what happens); on t'a vu venir* they saw you coming!*; je te vois venir* I can see what you're leading up to *ou* getting at.

k (*avec vb à l'infinitif: constater*) to see. ce journal a vu son tirage augmenter this newspaper has seen an increase in its circulation; un pays qui voit renaître le fascisme a country which is witnessing *ou* seeing the rebirth *ou* re-emergence of fascism.

l (*loc*) tu vois, vois-tu, voyez-vous you see; voyons let's see now; tu vois ça d'ici you can just imagine it; un peu de charité, voyons! come (on) now, let's be charitable; mais voyons, il n'a jamais dit cela! come, come, *ou* come now, he never said that; dites ~, vous connaissez la nouvelle? tell me, have you heard the news?; dis-moi ~ tell me; voyons ~!* let's see now!; essaie ~!* just try it and see!, just you try it!; c'est ce que nous verrons we'll see about that; regarde ~ ce qu'il a fait* just look what he has done!; histoire de ~, pour ~ just to see; (*menace*) essaie un peu, pour ~!, faudrait ~ à ~!* just you try!; son travail est fait (il) faut ~ (comme)!‡ you should just see the state of the work he has done!; c'est tout vu it's a foregone conclusion; il ferait beau ~ qu'il ... it would be a fine thing if he ...; va ~ ailleurs si j'y suis‡ get lost‡; allez donc ~ si c'est vrai! just try and find out if it's true!; je n'ai rien à ~ dans cette affaire this matter has nothing to do with me *ou* is no concern of mine; cela n'a rien/a quelque chose à ~ avec ... this has got nothing/something to do with ...; n'y ~ que du feu to be completely hoodwinked *ou* taken in; (*être ivre*) ~ double to see double; ~ trente-six chandelles to see stars; ne pas ~ plus loin que le bout de son nez to see no further than the end of one's nose; je l'ai vu comme je vous vois I saw him as plainly as I see you now.

2 vi to be able to see. ~ clair to see clearly; (*fig*) je vois clair dans son jeu I can see what his game is, I know exactly what he's up to*; (*fig*) reprenons tous ces arguments pour y ~ plus clair let's go over all the arguments again so we can sort our ideas out; ~ mal to have trouble seeing; on voit mal ici you can't see very well here; ~ trouble to have blurred vision.

3 voir à vt indir (*littér: veiller à*) to make sure that, see (to it) that. nous verrons à vous contenter we shall do our best *ou* our utmost to please you; il faudra ~ à ce qu'il obéisse we must see *ou* make sure that he obeys; voyez à être à l'heure see that *ou* make sure that you are on time *ou* are prompt; (*menace*) il faudrait ~ à ne pas nous ennuyer you had better make sure not to cause us any trouble, you had better not cause us any trouble.

4 se voir vpr a (*sens réfléchi*) se ~ dans une glace to see oneself in a mirror; il ne s'est pas vu mourir death took him unawares; elle se voyait déjà célèbre she pictured herself famous already; je me vois mal habiter *ou* habitant là I can't see myself living there somehow.

b (*sens réciproque*) to see each other. ils se voient beaucoup they see a lot of each other; ils ne peuvent pas se ~* they can't stand the sight of each other*; nous essayerons de nous ~ à Londres we shall try to see each other *ou* to meet (up) in London.

c (*se trouver*) se ~ forcé de to find o.s. forced to; je me vois dans la triste obligation de sadly, I find myself obliged to; se ~ soudain dans la misère to find o.s. suddenly in poverty.

d (*être visible, évident*) [*tache, couleur, sentiments*] to show. cette reprise/tache ne se voit pas this alteration/stain doesn't show; cela se voit! that's obvious!; cela se voit comme le nez au milieu du visage *ou* de la figure it's as plain as the nose on your face* *ou* as a pikestaff.

e (*se produire*) cela se voit tous les jours it happens every day, it's an every day occurrence; ça ne se voit pas tous les jours it's not something you see every day, it's quite a rare event; cela ne s'est jamais vu! it's unheard of!; une attitude qui ne se voit que trop fréquemment an all-too-common attitude; des attitudes/préjugés qui se voient encore chez ... attitudes/prejudices which are still commonplace *ou* encountered in ... .

f (*fonction passive*) ils se sont vu interdire l'accès du musée they found themselves refused admission *ou* they were refused admission to the museum; ces outils se sont vus relégués au grenier these tools have been put away in the attic; je me suis vu répondre que c'etait trop tard I was told (that) it was too late.

voire [vwaʀ] adv a (*frm: et même*) indeed, nay (†, *littér*). il faudrait attendre une semaine, ~ un mois you would have to wait a week or (perhaps) even a month; c'est révoltant, ~ même criminel it's disgusting, indeed even criminal. b (†, *hum: j'en doute*) indeed? (†, *hum*).

voirie [vwaʀi] nf a (*enlèvement des ordures*) refuse collection; (*dépotoir*) refuse dump. b (*entretien des routes etc*) highway maintenance; (*service administratif*) highways department; (*voie publique*) (public) highways.

voisé, e [vwaze] adj (*Phonétique*) voiced.

voisement [vwazmɑ̃] nm (*Phonétique*) voicing.

voisin, e [vwazɛ̃, in] 1 adj a (*proche*) neighbouring; (*adjacent*) next. les maisons/rues ~es the neighbouring houses/streets; il habite la maison/rue ~e he lives in the next house/street; 2 maisons ~es (l'une de l'autre) 2 adjoining houses, 2 houses next to each other; une maison ~e de l'église a house next to *ou* adjoining the church; les pays ~s de la Suisse the countries bordering on *ou* adjoining Switzerland; les années ~es de 1870 the years around 1870.

b (*fig*) *idées, espèces, cas* connected. ~ de akin to, related to; un animal ~ du chat an animal akin to *ou* related to the cat; dans un état ~ de la folie in a state bordering on *ou* akin to madness.

2 nm,f a (*gén*) neighbour. nos ~s d'à côté our next-door neighbours, the people next door; nos ~s de palier our neighbours across the landing; un de mes ~s de table one of the people next to me at table, one of my neighbours at table; je demandai à mon ~ de me passer le sel I asked the person (sitting) next to me *ou* my neighbour to pass me the salt; (*en classe*) qui est ta ~e cette année? who is sitting next to you this year?; mon ~ de dortoir/de salle the person in the next bed to mine (in the dormitory/ward); (*pays*) notre ~ allemand our neighbour, Germany, our German neighbours.

b (*fig: prochain*) fellow.

voisinage [vwazinaʒ] nm a (*voisins*) neighbourhood. ameuter tout le ~ to rouse the whole neighbourhood; être connu de tout le ~ to be known throughout the neighbourhood.

b (*relations*) être en bon ~ avec qn, entretenir des relations de bon ~ avec qn to be on neighbourly terms with sb.

c (*environs*) vicinity. les villages du ~ the villages in the vicinity, the villages round about; se trouver dans le ~ to be in the vicinity.

d (*proximité*) proximity, closeness. le ~ de la montagne the proximity *ou* closeness of the mountains; il n'était pas enchanté du ~ de cette usine he wasn't very happy at having the factory so close *ou* on his doorstep.

e (*Math*) [*point*] neighbourhood.

voisiner [vwazine] 1 vi (*être près de*) ~ avec qch to be (placed) side by side with sth.

voiture [vwatyʀ] nf a (*automobile*) car, motor car (*Brit*), automobile (*US*). ~-balai (*Tour de France*) broom wagon; (*métro*) last train; ~ cellulaire prison *ou* police van (*Brit*), patrol *ou* police wagon (*US*); ~ de compétition competition car; ~ de course racing car; ~ décapotable convertible; ~-école driving-school car; ~ de fonction company car; ~ de formule un Formula-One car; (*Admin*) ~ de grande remise hired limousine (with chauffeur); ~ de location hire car (*Brit*), hired (*Brit*) *ou* rented car; ~ de maître chauffeur-driven car; ~ particulière private car; ~ pie† ≃ panda car (*Brit*), police (patrol) car; ~ piégée car bomb, booby-trapped car; (*Admin*) ~ de place taxi cab, hackney carriage (*Brit*); ~ de pompiers fire engine; (*Tour de France*) ~ publicitaire promoter's *ou* sponsor's back-up vehicle; ~-radio radio car; ~ sans chauffeur self-drive hire car; ~, de service, ~ de société company car; ~ de sport sportscar; ~ de tourisme saloon (*Brit*), sedan (*US*); ~-ventouse illegally parked car (*exceeding the time limit for parking*).

b (*wagon*) carriage, coach (*Brit*), car (*US*). ~ de tête/queue front/back carriage *ou* coach (*Brit*) *ou* car (*US*); ~-bar buffet car; ~-couchette couchette; ~-lit sleeper (*Brit*), Pullman (*US*); ~-restaurant dining car; en ~! all aboard!

c (*véhicule attelé, poussé*) (*pour marchandises*) cart; (*pour voyageurs*) carriage, coach. ~ à bras handcart; ~ à cheval horse-drawn carriage; ~ d'enfant pram (*Brit*), baby carriage (*US*), perambulator (*Brit frm*); ~ d'infirme wheelchair, invalid carriage (*Brit*); ~ de poste mailcoach, stagecoach; ~ des quatre saisons costermonger's (*Brit*) *ou* greengrocer's (*Brit*) barrow, sidewalk vegetable barrow (*US*); voir petit.

voiturée† [vwatyʀe] nf [*choses*] cartload; [*personnes*] carriageful, coachload.

voiturer [vwatyʀe] 1 vt (†, *hum*) (*sur un chariot*) to wheel in; (**: en voiture*) to take in the car.

voiturette [vwatyʀɛt] nf (*d'infirme*) carriage; (*petite auto*) little *ou* small car.

voiturier [vwatyʀje] nm (†, *Jur*) carrier, carter; [*hôtel, casino*] doorman (*responsible for parking clients' cars*).

voix [vwɑ] nf a voice. à ~ basse/haute in a low *ou* hushed/loud voice; ils parlaient à ~ basse they were talking in hushed *ou* low voices *ou* in undertones; ~ de crécelle/de fausset/de gorge rasping/falsetto/throaty voice; d'une ~ blanche in a toneless *ou* flat voice; à haute et intelligible ~ loud and clear; avoir de la ~ to have a good (singing) voice; être *ou* rester sans ~ to be speechless (*devant* before, at); de la ~ et du geste by word and gesture, with words and gestures; une ~ lui cria de monter a voice shouted to him to come up; donner de la ~ (*aboyer*) to bay, give tongue; (**: crier*) to bawl; la ~ des violons the voice of the violins; voir élever, gros, portée[2] etc.

b (*conseil, avertissement*) ~ de la conscience/raison voice of conscience/reason; se fier à la ~ d'un ami to rely on *ou* trust to a friend's advice; la ~ du sang the ties of blood, the call of the blood; c'est la ~ du sang qui parle he must heed the call of his blood.

c (*opinion*) voice; (*Pol: suffrage*) vote. la ~ du peuple the voice of the people, vox populi; mettre qch aux ~ to put sth to the vote; la proposition a recueilli 30 ~ the proposal received *ou* got 30 votes; demander la mise aux ~ d'une proposition to ask for a vote on a proposal, ask for a proposal to be put to the vote; avoir ~ consultative to have consultative powers *ou* a consultative voice; avoir ~ prépondérante to have a casting vote; gagner des ~ to win votes; donner sa ~ à un candidat to give a candidate one's vote, vote for a candidate; le parti obtiendra peu de/beaucoup de ~ en Écosse the party will poll badly/heavily in Scotland; avoir ~ au chapitre to have a say in the matter.

d (*Mus*) voice. chanter à 2/3 ~ to sing in 2/3 parts; fugue à 3 ~

fugue in 3 voices; ~ **de basse/de ténor** bass/tenor (voice); **chanter d'une ~ fausse/juste** to sing out of tune/in tune; ~ **de tête/de poitrine** head/chest voice; **être/ne pas être en** ~ to be/not to be in good voice; **la ~ humaine/céleste de l'orgue** the vox humana/voix céleste on the organ.

e (*Ling*) voice. ~ **active/passive** active/passive voice.

vol¹ [vɔl] 1 nm a *[oiseau, avion]* (*gén*) flight. (*Zool*) ~ **ramé/plané** flapping/gliding flight; **faire un ~ plané** *[oiseau]* to glide through the air; (*fig: tomber*) to fall flat on one's face; (*Aviat*) ~ **d'essai/de nuit** trial/night flight; ~ **régulier** scheduled flight; **il y a 8 heures de ~ entre ...** it's an 8-hour flight between ...; **le ~ Paris-Londres** The Paris-London flight; **heures/conditions de ~** flying hours/conditions; *voir* **haut, ravitaillement.**

b (*Zool: formation*) flock, flight. **un ~ de perdrix** a covey *ou* flock of partridges; **un ~ de canards sauvages** a flight of wild ducks; **un ~ de moucherons** a cloud of gnats.

c (*loc*) **en (plein)** ~ in (full) flight; **prendre son ~** (*lit*) to take wing, fly off *ou* away; (*fig*) to take off; **attraper au ~** *autobus* to leap onto as it moves off; *ballon, objet lancé* to catch as it flies past, catch in mid-air; **saisir une occasion au ~** to leap at *ou* seize an opportunity; **saisir** *ou* **cueillir une remarque/une impression au ~** to catch a chance *ou* passing remark/impression; **à ~ d'oiseau** as the crow flies; **tirer un oiseau au ~** to shoot (at) a bird on the wing.

2 comp ► **vol libre** hang-gliding; **pratiquer le vol libre** to hang-glide, go hang-gliding ► **vol à voile** gliding.

vol² [vɔl] 1 nm (*délit*) theft. (*Jur*) ~ **simple/qualifié** common/aggravated *ou* compound theft; **~s de voiture** car thefts; (*fig*) **c'est du ~!** it's daylight robbery!, it's a rip-off!‡; (*fig*) **c'est du ~ organisé** it's a racket. 2 comp ► **vol à l'arraché** bagsnatching ► **vol domestique** *theft committed by an employee* ► **vol avec effraction** robbery *ou* theft with breaking and entering ► **vol à l'étalage** shoplifting (*NonC*) ► **vol à main armée** armed robbery ► **vol à la roulotte** car theft, theft of objects from cars ► **vol à la tire** pickpocketing (*NonC*).

volage [vɔlaʒ] adj *époux, cœur* flighty, fickle, inconstant.

volaille [vɔlɑj] nf (*Culin, Zool*) **une ~** a fowl; **la ~** (*lit*) poultry; (‡: *les flics*) the cops‡ (*Brit*), the fuzz‡; (‡: *les femmes*) the birds‡ (*Brit*), the chicks‡ (*US*); **les ~s cancanaient dans la basse-cour** the poultry *ou* fowls were cackling in the farmyard; ~ **rôtie** roast poultry (*NonC*) *ou* fowl.

volailler, -ère [vɔlɑje, ɛʀ] nm,f poulterer.

volant¹ [vɔlɑ̃] 1 nm a (*Aut*) steering wheel. **être au ~** to be at *ou* behind the wheel; **la femme au ~** the woman driver, women drivers; **prendre le ~, se mettre au ~** to take the wheel; **un brusque coup de ~** a sharp turn of the wheel; **as du ~** crack *ou* ace driver. b (*Tech: roue*) (*régulateur*) flywheel; (*de commande*) (hand)wheel. c *[rideau, robe]* flounce. **jupe à ~s** flounced skirt, skirt with flounces. d (*balle de badminton*) shuttlecock; (*jeu*) badminton, battledore and shuttlecock††. e *[carnet à souches]* tear-off portion. 2 comp ► **volant magnétique** magneto ► **volant de sécurité** reserve, margin, safeguard ► **volant de trésorerie** cash reserve.

volant², e [vɔlɑ̃, ɑ̃t] adj a (*gén, Aviat: qui vole*) flying. (*Aviat*) **le personnel ~, les ~s** the flight *ou* flying staff; *voir* **poisson, soucoupe, tapis** *etc.* b (*littér: fugace*) *ombre, forme* fleeting. c (*mobile, transportable*) *pont, camp, personnel* flying. (*Police*) **(brigade) ~e** flying squad; *voir* **feuille.**

volapük [vɔlapyk] nm Volapuk.

volatil, e¹ [vɔlatil] adj (*Chim*) volatile; (*littér: éphémère*) evanescent, ephemeral; *voir* **alcali.**

volatile² [vɔlatil] nm (*gén hum*) (*volaille*) fowl; (*tout oiseau*) winged *ou* feathered creature.

volatilisable [vɔlatilizabl] adj volatilizable.

volatilisation [vɔlatilizasjɔ̃] nf (*voir* **volatiliser**) volatilization; extinguishing; obliteration.

volatiliser [vɔlatilize] 1 1 vt (*Chim*) to volatilize; (*fig*) to extinguish, obliterate. 2 **se volatiliser** vpr (*Chim*) to volatilize; (*fig*) to vanish (into thin air).

volatilité [vɔlatilite] nf volatility.

vol-au-vent [vɔlovɑ̃] nm inv vol-au-vent.

volcan [vɔlkɑ̃] nm a (*Géog*) volcano. ~ **en activité/éteint** active/extinct volcano. b (*fig*) (*personne*) spitfire; (*situation*) powder keg, volcano. **nous sommes assis sur un ~** we are sitting on a powder keg *ou* a volcano.

volcanique [vɔlkanik] adj (*lit, fig*) volcanic.

volcanisme [vɔlkanism] nm volcanism.

volcanologie [vɔlkanɔlɔʒi] nf vulcanology.

volcanologue [vɔlkanɔlɔg] nmf vulcanologist.

volée [vɔle] nf a *[oiseaux]* (*envol, distance*) flight. (*groupe*) **une ~ de moineaux/corbeaux** a flock *ou* flight of sparrows/crows; (*fig*) **une ~ d'enfants** a swarm of children; **prendre sa ~** (*lit*) to take wing, fly off *ou* away; (*fig: s'affranchir*) to spread one's wings; *voir* **haut.**

b (*décharge, tir*) ~ **de flèches** flight *ou* volley of arrows; ~ **d'obus** volley of shells.

c (*suite de coups*) volley. **une ~ de coups** a volley of blows; **une ~ de coups de bâton** a volley *ou* flurry of blows; **une ~ de bois vert** (†: *coups*) a volley *ou* flurry of blows; (*réprimande*) a volley of reproaches; **administrer/recevoir une bonne ~** to give/get a sound thrashing *ou* beating.

d (*Ftbl, Tennis*) volley. **de ~** on the volley; (*Tennis*) ~ **croisée/de face** cross/forehand volley; ~ **coupée** *ou* **arrêtée** chop; *voir* **demi-.**

e ~ **d'escalier** flight of stairs.

f (*loc*) **à la ~: jeter qch à la ~** to fling sth about; **semer à la ~** to sow broadcast, broadcast; **attraper la balle à la ~** to catch the ball in midair; **saisir une allusion à la ~** to pick up a passing allusion; **à la ~, à toute ~** *gifler, lancer* vigorously, with full force; **les cloches sonnaient à toute ~** the bells were pealing out; **il referma la porte/fenêtre à la ~** *ou* **à toute ~** he slammed the door/window shut.

voler¹ [vɔle] 1 vi a *[oiseau, avion, pilote]* to fly. **vouloir ~ avant d'avoir des ailes** to want to run before one can walk; ~ **de ses propres ailes** to stand on one's own two feet, fend for o.s.; *voir* **entendre.**

b (*fig*) *[flèche, pierres, insultes]* to fly. ~ **en éclats** to fly *ou* smash into pieces; *[neige, voile, feuille]* ~ **au vent** to fly in the wind, float on the wind; *[nouvelles]* ~ **de bouche en bouche** to fly from mouth to mouth, spread like wildfire; **plaisanterie/discussion qui vole bas** feeble joke/low-level discussion.

c (*s'élancer*) ~ **vers qn/dans les bras de qn** to fly to sb/into sb's arms; ~ **au secours de qn** to fly to sb's assistance; **il lui a volé dans les plumes*** (*physiquement*) he flew at him, he attacked him, he went for him; (*verbalement*) he flew off the handle at him; **se ~ dans les plumes*** to go for each other, fly at each other.

d (*littér: passer, aller très vite*) *[temps]* to fly; *[embarcation, véhicule]* to fly (along). **son cheval volait/semblait ~** his horse flew (along)/seemed to fly (along).

voler² [vɔle] 1 vt a ~ **de l'argent/une idée/un baiser** *etc* **à qn** to steal money/an idea/a kiss *etc* from sb; ~ **par nécessité** to steal out of necessity; **se faire ~ ses bagages** to have one's luggage stolen; (*fig*) **il ne l'a pas volé!** he asked for it!; *voir* **qui.**

b ~ **qn** (*dérober son argent*) to rob sb; ~ **les clients** to rob *ou* cheat customers; ~ **les clients sur le poids/la quantité** to cheat customers over (the) weight/quantity, give customers short measure; ~ **qn lors d'un partage** to cheat sb when sharing out; **se sentir volé** (*spectacle interrompu etc*) to feel cheated *ou* robbed; **on n'est pas volé*** you get your money's worth all right*, it's good value for money; **le boucher ne t'a pas volé sur le poids** the butcher gave you good weight.

volet [vɔlɛ] nm a *[fenêtre, hublot]* shutter. b (*Aviat*) flap. ~ **d'intrados/de freinage** split/brake flap; ~ **de courbure** *[parachute]* flap. c (*Aut: panneau articulé*) bonnet flap; (*Tech*) *[roue à aube]* paddle. ~ **de carburateur** throttle valve, butterfly valve. d *[triptyque]* volet, wing; *[feuillet, carte]* section; *voir* **trier.** e *[émission, plan d'action]* part.

voleter [vɔl(ə)te] 4 vi *[oiseau]* to flutter about, flit about; *[rubans, flocons]* to flutter.

voleur, -euse [vɔlœʀ, øz] 1 adj: **être ~** (*gén*) to be light-fingered, be a (bit of a) thief; *[commerçant]* to be a cheat *ou* swindler, be dishonest; *[animal]* to be a thief; ~ **comme une pie** thievish as a magpie. 2 nm,f (*malfaiteur*) thief; (*escroc, commerçant*) swindler. ~ **de grand chemin** highwayman; ~ **à l'étalage** shoplifter; ~ **à la tire**† pickpocket; ~ **d'enfants**† kidnapper; **au ~!** stop thief!; ~ **de voitures** car thief; **se sauver comme un ~** to run off *ou* take to one's heels like a thief.

Volga [vɔlga] nf Volga.

volière [vɔljɛʀ] nf (*cage*) aviary. (*fig*) **ce bureau est une ~** this office is a proper henhouse* (*hum*).

volige [vɔliʒ] nf *[toit]* lath.

volitif, -ive [vɔlitif, iv] adj volitional, volitive.

volition [vɔlisjɔ̃] nf volition.

volley [vɔlɛ] nm, **volley-ball** [vɔlɛbol] nm volleyball.

volleyer [vɔleje] 8 vi (*Tennis*) to volley.

volleyeur, -euse [vɔlɛjœʀ, øz] nm,f (*Volley-ball*) volleyball player; (*Tennis*) volleyer.

volontaire [vɔlɔ̃tɛʀ] 1 adj a (*voulu*) *acte, enrôlement, prisonnier* voluntary; *oubli* intentional; *voir* **engagé.** b (*décidé*) *personne* self-willed, wilful, headstrong; *expression, menton* determined. 2 nmf (*Mil, gén*) volunteer.

volontairement [vɔlɔ̃tɛʀmɑ̃] adv a (*de son plein gré*) voluntarily, of one's own free will; (*Jur: facultativement*) voluntarily. b (*exprès*) intentionally, deliberately. **il a dit ça ~** he said it on purpose *ou* deliberately. c (*d'une manière décidée*) determinedly.

volontariat [vɔlɔ̃taʀja] nm (*gén*) voluntary participation; (*Mil*) voluntary service.

volontarisme [vɔlɔ̃taʀism] nm voluntarism.

volontariste [vɔlɔ̃taʀist] adj, nmf voluntarist.

volonté [vɔlɔ̃te] nf a (*faculté*) will; (*souhait, intention*) wish, will (*frm*). **manifester sa ~ de faire qch** to show one's intention of doing sth; **accomplir/respecter la ~ de qn** to carry out/respect sb's wishes; **la ~ nationale** the will of the nation; **la ~ générale** the general will; ~ **de puissance** will for power; ~ **de guérir/réussir** will to recover/succeed; (*Rel*) **que ta** *ou* **votre ~ soit faite** Thy will be done; *voir* **dernier, indépendant, quatre.**

b (*disposition*) **bonne ~** goodwill, willingness; **mauvaise ~** lack of goodwill, unwillingness; **il a beaucoup de bonne ~ mais peu d'aptitude** he has a lot of goodwill but not much aptitude, he shows great willingness but not much aptitude; **il met de la bonne/mauvaise ~ à faire son**

travail he goes about his work with goodwill/grudgingly, he does his work willingly/unwillingly *ou* with a good/bad grace; **il fait preuve de bonne/mauvaise ~** his attitude is positive/negative; **paix sur la terre, aux hommes de bonne ~** peace on earth (and) goodwill to all men; **faire appel aux bonnes ~s pour construire qch** to appeal to volunteers to construct sth; **avec la meilleure ~ du monde** with the best will in the world.
c (*caractère, énergie*) willpower, will. **faire un effort de ~** to make an effort of will(power); **avoir de la ~** to have willpower; **cet homme a une ~ de fer** this man has an iron will *ou* a will of iron; **réussir à force de ~** to succeed through sheer will(power) *ou* determination; **échouer par manque de ~** to fail through lack of will(power) *ou* determination; **faire preuve de ~** to display willpower.
d (*loc*) **servez-vous de pain à ~** take as much bread as you like; **"sucrer à ~"** "sweeten to taste"; **vous pouvez le prendre ou le laisser à ~** you can take it or leave it as you wish *ou* just as you like; **nous avons de l'eau à ~** we have as much water as we want, we have plenty of water; **vin à ~ pendant le repas** as much wine as one wants *ou* unlimited wine with the meal; (*Comm*) **billet payable à ~** promissory note payable on demand; **il en fait toujours à sa ~** he always does things his own way, he always does as he pleases *ou* likes, he always suits himself; *voir* **feu**[1].

volontiers [vɔlɔ̃tje] **adv** a (*de bonne grâce*) with pleasure, gladly, willingly. **je l'aiderais ~** I would gladly *ou* willingly help him; **voulez-vous dîner chez nous? — ~** would you like to eat with us? — I'd love to *ou* with pleasure. b (*naturellement*) readily, willingly. **il lit ~ pendant des heures** he will happily *ou* willingly read for hours on end; **on croit ~ que ...** people readily believe that ..., people are apt *ou* quite ready to believe that ...; **il est ~ pessimiste** he is given to pessimism, he is pessimistic by nature.

volt [vɔlt] **nm** volt.

voltage [vɔltaʒ] **nm** voltage.

voltaïque [vɔltaik] **adj** voltaic, galvanic.

voltaire [vɔltɛʀ] **nm** Voltaire chair.

voltairien, -ienne [vɔltɛʀjɛ̃, jɛn] **adj** Voltairian, Voltairean.

volte [vɔlt] **nf** (*Équitation*) volte.

volte-face [vɔltəfas] **nf inv** a (*lit*) **faire ~** to turn round. b (*fig*) volte-face, about-turn. **faire une ~** to make a volte-face, do *ou* make an about-turn.

volter [vɔlte] [1] **vi** (*Équitation*) **faire ~ un cheval** to make a horse circle.

voltige [vɔltiʒ] **nf** (*Équitation*) trick riding. (*Aviat*) **~ (aérienne)** aerobatics (*pl*); (*Gym*) **(haute) ~** acrobatics; (*Gym*) **faire de la ~** to do acrobatics; **c'est de la (haute) ~ intellectuelle** it's mental gymnastics.

voltiger [vɔltiʒe] [3] **vi** *[oiseaux]* to flit about, flutter about; *[objet léger]* to flutter about.

voltigeur [vɔltiʒœʀ] **nm** a (*acrobate*) acrobat. b (*Hist Mil*) light infantryman.

voltmètre [vɔltmɛtʀ] **nm** voltmeter.

volubile [vɔlybil] **adj** a *personne, éloquence* voluble. b (*Bot*) voluble.

volubilis [vɔlybilis] **nm** convolvulus, morning glory.

volubilité [vɔlybilite] **nf** volubility.

volucompteur [vɔlykɔ̃tœʀ] **nm** ® (volume) indicator.

volume [vɔlym] **nm** a (*livre, tome*) volume. b (*gén, Art, Géom, Sci: espace, quantité*) volume. **~ moléculaire/atomique** molecular/atomic volume; **~ d'eau d'un fleuve** volume of water in a river; **eau oxygénée à 20 ~s** 20-volume hydrogen peroxide; **le ~ des importations** the volume of imports; (*Bourse*) **~ des transactions** volume of transactions; *[gros objets]* **faire du ~** to be bulky, take up space. c (*intensité*) *[son]* volume. **~ de la voix/la radio** volume of the voice/radio; **~ sonore** sound volume.

volumétrique [vɔlymetʀik] **adj** volumetric.

volumineux, -euse [vɔlyminø, øz] **adj** voluminous, bulky.

volumique [vɔlymik] **adj: masse ~ d'un corps** voluminal mass of a body.

volupté [vɔlypte] **nf** (*sensuelle*) sensual delight, sensual *ou* voluptuous pleasure; (*morale, intellectuelle*) exquisite delight *ou* pleasure.

voluptueusement [vɔlyptɥøzmɑ̃] **adv** voluptuously.

voluptueux, -euse [vɔlyptɥø, øz] **adj** voluptuous.

volute [vɔlyt] **nf** a *[colonne, grille, escalier]* volute, scroll; *[fumée]* curl, wreath; *[vague]* curl. **en ~** voluted, scrolled. b (*Zool*) volute.

volve [vɔlv] **nf** volva.

vomi [vɔmi] **nm** vomit.

vomique [vɔmik] **adj f** *voir* **noix.**

vomiquier [vɔmikje] **nm** nux vomica (*tree*).

vomir [vɔmiʀ] [2] **vt** a *aliments* to vomit, bring up; *sang* to spit, bring up. b (*emploi absolu*) to be sick, vomit. **il a vomi partout** he was sick everywhere; **ça te fera ~** it'll make you vomit *ou* be sick; **avoir envie de ~** to want to be sick; (*fig*) **cela donne envie de ~, c'est à ~** it makes you *ou* it's enough to make you sick, it's nauseating. c (*fig*) *lave, flammes* to belch forth, spew forth; *injures, haine* to spew out. d (*fig: détester*) to loathe, abhor. **il vomit les intellectuels** he has a loathing for *ou* loathes intellectuals.

vomissement [vɔmismɑ̃] **nm** a (*action*) vomiting (*NonC*). **il fut pris de ~s** he (suddenly) started vomiting. b (*matières*) vomit (*NonC*).

vomissure [vɔmisyʀ] **nf** vomit (*NonC*).

vomitif, -ive [vɔmitif, iv] **adj, nm** (*Pharm*) emetic, vomitory.

vorace [vɔʀas] **adj** *animal, personne, curiosité* voracious. **appétit ~** voracious *ou* ravenous appetite; **plantes ~s** plants which deplete the soil.

voracement [vɔʀasmɑ̃] **adv** voraciously.

voracité [vɔʀasite] **nf** voracity, voraciousness.

vortex [vɔʀtɛks] **nm** (*littér*) vortex.

vos [vo] **adj poss** *voir* **votre.**

Vosges [voʒ] **nfpl: les ~** the Vosges.

vosgien, -ienne [voʒjɛ̃, jɛn] 1 **adj** Vosges (*épith*), of *ou* from the Vosges. 2 **nm,f: V~(ne)** inhabitant *ou* native of the Vosges.

VOST (**abrév de version originale sous-titrée**) *voir* **version.**

votant, e [vɔtɑ̃, ɑ̃t] **nm,f** voter.

votation [vɔtasjɔ̃] **nf** (*Suisse*) voting.

vote [vɔt] **nm** a *[projet de loi]* vote (*de* for); *[loi, réforme]* passing; *[crédits]* voting. b (*suffrage, acte, opération*) vote; (*ensemble des votants*) voters. **le ~ socialiste** Socialist voters, the Socialist vote; **~ de confiance** vote of confidence; **~ à main levée** vote by a show of hands; **~ à bulletin secret/par correspondance** secret/postal vote *ou* ballot; **~ par procuration** proxy vote; **~ direct/indirect** direct/indirect vote; **procéder au ~** to proceed to a vote, take a vote; *voir* **bulletin, bureau, droit**[3].

voter [vɔte] [1] 1 **vi** to vote. **~ à main levée** to vote by a show of hands; **~ à droite/pour X** to vote for the Right/for X; **~ utile** to vote tactically; **~ pour/contre qch** to vote for/against sth; **j'ai voté contre** I voted against it; **~ sur une motion** to vote on a motion. 2 **vt** (*adopter*) *projet de loi* to vote for; *loi, réforme* to pass; *crédits* to vote. **~ la censure** to pass a vote of censure; **ne pas ~** *amendement* to vote out; **~ libéral** to vote Liberal.

votif, -ive [vɔtif, iv] **adj** votive.

votre [vɔtʀ], **pl vos** [vo] **adj poss** your; (*emphatique*) your own; (†, *Rel*) thy. **laissez ~ manteau et vos gants au vestiaire** (*à une personne*) leave your coat and gloves in the cloakroom; (*à plusieurs personnes*) leave your coats and gloves in the cloakroom; (†, *Rel*) **que ~ volonté soit faite** Thy will be done (†); **V~ Excellence/Majesté** Your Excellency/Majesty; *pour autres loc voir* **son**[1], **ton**[1].

vôtre [votʀ] 1 **pron poss: le ~, la ~, les ~s** yours, your own; **ce sac n'est pas le ~** this bag is not yours, this is not your bag; **nos enfants sont sortis avec les ~s** our children are out with yours *ou* your own; **à la (bonne) ~!** your (good) health!, cheers!; (*fig*) **vous voulez y aller quand même — à la (bonne) ~!** you still want to go? — rather you than me!; *pour autres loc voir* **sien.**
2 **nmf** a **j'espère que vous y mettrez du ~** I hope you'll pull your weight *ou* do your bit*; *voir aussi* **sien.**
b **les ~s** your family, your (own) folks*; **vous et tous les ~s** you and all those like you, you and your ilk (*péj*); **bonne année à vous et à tous les ~s** Happy New Year to you and yours; **nous pourrons être des ~s ce soir** we shall be able to join your party *ou* join you tonight; *voir* **sien.**
3 **adj poss** (*littér*) yours. **son cœur est ~ depuis toujours** his (*ou* her) heart has always been yours; *voir* **sien.**

vouer [vwe] [1] **vt** a (*Rel*) **~ qn à Dieu/à la Vierge** to dedicate sb to God/to the Virgin Mary; *voir* **savoir.** b (*promettre*) to vow. **il lui a voué un amour éternel** he vowed his undying love to her. c (*consacrer*) to devote. **~ son temps à ses études** to devote one's time to one's studies; **se ~ à une cause** to dedicate o.s. *ou* devote o.s. to a cause. d (*gén ptp: condamner*) to doom. **projet voué à l'échec** plan doomed to *ou* destined for failure; **famille vouée à la misère** family doomed to poverty.

vouloir [vulwaʀ] [31] 1 **vt** a (*sens fort: exiger*) *objet, augmentation, changement* to want. **~ faire** to want to do; **je veux que tu viennes tout de suite** I want you to come at once; **~ que qn fasse/qch se fasse** to want sb to do/sth to be done; **il veut absolument ce jouet/venir/qu'elle parte** he is set on this toy/coming/her leaving, he is determined to have this toy/to come/(that) she should leave; **il ne veut pas y aller/qu'elle y aille** he doesn't want to go/her to go; (*Prov*) **~, c'est pouvoir** where there's a will there's a way (*Prov*); **qu'est-ce qu'ils veulent maintenant?** what do they want now?; **il sait ce qu'il veut** he knows what he wants.
b (*sens affaibli: désirer, souhaiter*) **voulez-vous à boire/manger?** would you like something to drink/eat?; **tu veux** (*ou* **vous voulez**) **quelque chose à boire?*** would you like *ou* do you want something to drink?; **comment voulez-vous votre poisson, frit ou poché?** how would you like your fish — fried or poached?; **je ne veux pas qu'il se croie obligé de ...** I shouldn't like *ou* I don't want him to feel obliged to ...; **je voulais vous dire** I meant to tell you; **il voulait partir hier mais ...** he meant *ou* intended to leave yesterday but ...; **il ne voulait pas vous blesser** he didn't want *ou* mean to hurt you; **ça va comme tu veux** (*ou* **vous voulez**)?* is everything going all right *ou* O.K. (for you)?*; **veux-tu que je te dise *ou* raconte pourquoi ...?** shall I tell you why ...?; **~ du bien/mal à qn** to wish sb well/ill *ou* harm, be well-/ill-disposed towards sb; **je ne lui veux pas de mal** I don't wish him any harm; (*iro*) **un ami qui vous veut du bien** a well-wisher (*iro*); **que lui voulez-vous?** what do you want with him?
c (*avec le conditionnel*) **je voudrais ceci/faire ceci/qu'il fasse cela** I would like this/to do this/him to do this; **je voudrais une livre de beurre** I

would like a pound of butter; **il aurait voulu être médecin mais ...** he would have liked to be a doctor *ou* he'd like to have been a doctor but ...; **je voudrais/j'aurais voulu que vous voyiez sa tête!** I wish you could see/could have seen his face!; **je voudrais qu'il soit plus énergique,** (*frm*) **je lui voudrais plus d'énergie** I wish he showed *ou* would show more energy.

d (*avec si, comme*) **si tu veux (*ou* vous voulez)** if you like; **s'il voulait, il pourrait être ministre** if he wanted (to), he could be a minister, he could be a minister if he so desired; **s'il voulait (bien) nous aider, cela gagnerait du temps** if he'd help us *ou* if he felt like helping us, it would save time; **comme tu veux (*ou* vous voulez)** as you like *ou* wish *ou* please; **bon, comme tu voudras** all right, have it your own way *ou* as you like *ou* suit yourself*; **comme vous voulez, moi ça m'est égal** just as you like *ou* please *ou* wish, it makes no difference to me; **oui, si on veut** (*dans un sens, d'un côté*) yes, if you like; **s'ils veulent garder leur avance, ils ne peuvent se permettre de relâcher leur effort** if they want *ou* are *ou* intend to keep their lead they can't afford to reduce their efforts.

e (*escompter, demander*) ~ **qch de qn** to want sth from sb; **je veux de vous plus de fermeté/une promesse** I want more firmness/a promise from you; ~ **un certain prix de qch** to want a certain price for sth; **j'en veux 1 000 F** I want 1,000 francs for it.

f **bien** ~: **je veux bien le faire/qu'il vienne** (*très volontiers*) I'm happy *ou* I'll be happy to do it/for him to come; (*il n'y a pas d'inconvénient*) I'm quite happy to do it/for him to come; (*s'il le faut vraiment*) I don't mind doing it/if he comes; **moi je veux bien le croire mais ...** I'll take his word for it but ..., I'm quite willing *ou* prepared to believe him but ...; **je voudrais bien y aller** I'd really like *ou* I'd love to go; **si tu voulais bien le faire, ça nous rendrait service** if you'd care *ou* be willing to do it *ou* if you'd be kind enough to do it, you'd be doing us a favour; **moi je veux bien, mais ...** fair enough*, but ... .

g (*consentir*) **ils ne voulurent pas nous recevoir** they wouldn't see us, they weren't willing to see us; **le moteur ne veut pas partir** the engine won't start; **le feu n'a pas voulu prendre** the fire wouldn't light *ou* catch; **il joue bien quand il veut** he plays well when he wants to *ou* has a mind (to) *ou* when he puts his mind to it.

h *[choses]* (*requérir*) to want, require. **ces plantes veulent de l'eau** these plants want *ou* need water; **l'usage veut que ...** custom requires that ... .

i (*ordre*) **veux-tu (bien) te taire!, voulez-vous (bien) vous taire!** will you be quiet!; **veuillez quitter la pièce immédiatement** please leave the room at once; **veux-tu bien arrêter!** will you please stop it!, stop it will you *ou* please!

j *[destin, sort etc]* **le hasard voulut que ...** chance decreed that ..., as fate would have it ... .

k (*chercher à, essayer*) to try. **elle voulut se lever mais elle retomba** she tried to get up but she fell back; **il veut se faire remarquer** he wants to make himself noticed, he's out to be noticed.

l (*s'attendre à*) to expect. **comment voulez-vous que je sache?** how do you expect me to know?, how should I know?; **il a tout, pourquoi voudriez-vous qu'il réclame?** he has everything so why should he complain?; **qu'est-ce que vous voulez que j'y fasse?** what do you expect *ou* want me to do about it?; **et dans ces conditions, vous voudriez que nous acceptions?** and under these conditions you expect us to agree? *ou* you would have us agree?

m (*formules de politesse*) **voulez-vous bien leur dire que ...** would you please tell them that ...; **voudriez-vous avoir l'obligeance** *ou* **l'amabilité de** would you be so kind as to; **veuillez croire à toute ma sympathie** please accept my deepest sympathy; **voulez-vous me prêter ce livre?** will you lend me this book?; **voudriez-vous fermer la fenêtre?** would you mind closing the window?; *voir* **agréer**.

n (*prétendre*) to claim. **une philosophie qui veut que l'homme soit ...** a philosophy which claims that man is ...; **il veut que les hommes soient égaux: je ne suis pas d'accord avec lui** he'd have it that *ou* he makes out that men are equal but I don't agree with him.

o **en ~ à: en ~ à qn** to have sth against sb, have a grudge against sb; **en ~ à qn de qch** to hold sth against sb; **il m'en veut beaucoup d'avoir fait cela** he holds a tremendous grudge against me for having done that; **il m'en veut d'avoir fait rater ce projet** he holds it against me that I made the plan fail, he has a grudge against me for making the plan fail; **il m'en veut de mon incompréhension** he holds my lack of understanding against me, he resents my failure to understand; **je m'en veux d'avoir accepté** I could kick myself *ou* I'm so annoyed with myself for accepting; **ne m'en voulez pas,** (*frm*) **ne m'en veuillez pas** don't hold it against me; **tu ne m'en veux pas?** no hard feelings?; **en ~ à qch** to be after sth; **il en veut à son argent** he is after her money.

p ~ **dire** (*signifier*) to mean; **qu'est-ce que cela veut dire?** *[mot etc]* what does that mean?; *[attitude de qn]* what does that imply? *ou* mean?; **je veux dire qu'il a raison** I mean (to say) he's right, what I mean is he's right.

q (*loc*) **que voulez-vous! (*ou* que veux-tu!), qu'est-ce que vous voulez!** what can we do?, what can *ou* do you expect!; **je voudrais bien vous y voir!** I'd like to see how you'd do it! *ou* you doing it!; **je veux être pendu si ...** I'll be hanged *ou* damned if ...; **qu'est-ce que vous voulez qu'on y fasse?** what can anyone do about it?, what can be done about it?, what do you expect us (*ou* them *etc*) to do?; **sans le** ~ unintentionally, involuntarily, inadvertently; **tu l'as voulu** you asked for it; **tu l'auras voulu** it'll have been your own fault, you'll have brought it on yourself; **qu'il le veuille ou non** whether he likes it or not; **il veut sans** ~ he only half wants to; **il y a eu des discours en veux-tu en voilà** there were speeches galore; **elle fait de lui ce qu'elle veut** she does what she likes with him, she twists him round her little finger; **ça te dirait d'aller à la mer? — je veux!*** how would you like to go to the seaside? — that would be great!* *ou* you bet!* *ou* I'd love to!; **tu vas lui demander? — je veux!*** are you going to ask him? — you bet (I am)!*

2 **vouloir de** vt indir (*gén nég, interrog*) ~ **de qn/qch** to want sb/sth; **on ne veut plus de lui au bureau** they don't want him *ou* won't have him in the office any more; **je ne veux pas de lui comme chauffeur** I don't want him *ou* won't have him as a driver; **voudront-ils de moi dans leur nouvelle maison?** will they want me in their new house?; **elle ne veut plus de ce chapeau** she doesn't want this hat any more; *[gâteau]* **est-ce que tu en veux?** do you want some?, would you like some?; **il en veut** (*lit*) (*gâteau*) he wants some; (*fig: il veut réussir*) he's dead keen*, he wants to win; **l'équipe de France en veut ce soir** the French team is raring to go* *ou* is out to win tonight.

3 **se vouloir** vpr (*vouloir être, prétendre être*) **journal qui se veut objectif** newspaper that likes to think it's objective; **peinture qui se veut réaliste** painting which is supposed to be realistic.

4 nm **a** (*littér: volonté*) will.

b **bon** ~ goodwill; **mauvais** ~ ill will, reluctance; **selon le bon ~ de** according to the pleasure of; **avec un mauvais ~ évident** with obvious ill will; **attendre le bon ~ de qn** to wait on sb's pleasure; **cette décision dépend du bon ~ du ministre** this decision depends on the minister's good will.

voulu, e [vuly] (ptp de **vouloir**) adj **a** (*requis*) required, requisite. **il n'avait pas l'argent** ~ he didn't have the required *ou* requisite money *ou* the money required; **le temps** ~ the time required. **b** (*volontaire*) deliberate, intentional. **c'est ~*** it's done on purpose, it's intentional *ou* deliberate.

vous [vu] **1** pron pers **a** (*sujet, objet*) you; (*sg: tu, toi*) you. (*valeur indéfinie*) **les gens qui viennent ~ poser des questions** people who come asking questions *ou* who come and ask you questions; ~ **avez bien répondu tous les deux** you both answered well, the two of you answered well; **vous et lui, ~ êtes aussi têtus l'un que l'autre** you and he are as stubborn (the) one as the other, you are both equally stubborn; **si j'étais ~, j'accepterais** if I were you *ou* in your shoes I'd accept; **eux ont accepté, ~ pas** *ou* **pas ~** they accepted but you didn't, they accepted but not you; ~ **parti(s), je pourrai travailler** once you've gone *ou* with you out of the way, I'll be able to work; **c'est enfin ~, ~ voilà enfin** here you are at last; **qui l'a vu?, ~?** who saw him?, (did) you? *ou* was it you?; **je ~ ai demandé de m'aider** I asked you to help me; **elle n'obéit qu'à** ~ you're the only one *ou* ones she obeys.

b (*emphatique: insistance, apostrophe*) (*sujet*) you, you yourself (*sg*), you yourselves (*pl*); (*objet*) you. ~ **tous écoutez-moi** listen to me all of you *ou* the lot of you*; ~, **vous n'avez pas à vous plaindre** you have no cause to complain; **vous ne le connaissez pas** ~ you don't know him; **pourquoi ne le ferais-je pas: vous l'avez bien fait, ~!** why shouldn't I do it — you did (it)! *ou* you yourself *ou* you yourselves did it!; ~ **mentir?, ce n'est pas possible** you tell a lie?, I can't believe it; **alors ~ vous ne partez pas?** so what about you — aren't you going?; ~ **aidez-moi!** you (there) *ou* hey you, give me a hand!; **je vous demande à ~ parce que je vous connais** I'm asking you because I know you; **je vous connais ~!** I know you; ~ **vous m'agacez!, vous m'agacez ~!** (oh) you're getting on my nerves!; ~ **je vois que vous n'êtes pas bien** it's obvious to me that you are not well.

c (*emphatique avec qui, que*) **c'est ~ qui avez raison** it's you who is *ou* are right; ~ **tous qui m'écoutez** all of you listening to me; **et ~ qui détestiez le cinéma, vous avez bien changé** and (to think) you were the one who hated the cinema *ou* you used to say you hated the cinema — well you've changed a lot!

d (*avec prép*) you. **à ~ 4 vous pourrez le porter** with 4 of you *ou* between (the) 4 of you you'll be able to carry it; **cette maison est-elle à ~?** does this house belong to you?, is this house yours? *ou* your own?; **vous n'avez même pas une chambre à ~ tout seul/tout seuls?** you don't even have a room of your own? *ou* a room to yourself/yourselves?; **c'est à ~ de décider** (*sg*) it's up to you *ou* to yourself to decide; (*pl*) it's up to you *ou* to yourselves to decide; **l'un de ~** *ou* **d'entre ~ doit le savoir** one of you must know; **de ~ à moi** between you and me; **vous ne pensez qu'à** ~ you think only of yourself *ou* yourselves.

e (*dans comparaisons*) you. **il me connaît mieux que** ~ (*mieux qu'il ne vous connaît*) he knows me better than (he knows) you; (*mieux que vous ne me connaissez*) he knows me better than you do; **il est plus/moins fort que** ~ he is stronger than you/not as strong as you (are); **il a fait comme** ~ he did as *ou* what you did, he did like you* *ou* the same as you.

f (*avec vpr: souvent non traduit*) ~ **êtes-vous bien amusé(s)?** did you have a good time?; **je crois que vous ~ connaissez** I believe you know each other; **servez-~ donc** do help yourself *ou* yourselves; **ne** ~

disputez pas don't fight; **asseyez-~ donc** do sit down.
2 nm: **dire ~ à qn** to call sb "vous"; **le ~ est de moins en moins employé** (the form of address) "vous" *ou* the "vous" form is used less and less frequently.

vous-même, pl **vous-mêmes** [vumɛm] pron *voir* **même**.

vousseau [vuso] nm, **voussoir** [vuswaʀ] nm voussoir.

voussoyer [vuswaje] 8 vt = **vouvoyer**.

voussure [vusyʀ] nf (*courbure*) arching; (*partie cintrée*) arch; (*Archit: archivolte*) archivolt.

voûte [vut] 1 nf (*Archit*) vault; (*porche*) archway. **~ en plein cintre/d'arête** semi-circular/groined vault; **~ en ogive/en berceau** ribbed/barrel vault; **~ en éventail** fan-vaulting (*NonC*); **en ~** vaulted; (*fig*) **la ~ d'une caverne** the vault of a cave; (*fig*) **une ~ d'arbres** an archway of trees; *voir* **clef**. 2 comp ►**la voûte céleste** the vault *ou* canopy of heaven ►**voûte crânienne** dome of the skull, vault of the cranium (*SPÉC*) ►**la voûte étoilée** the starry vault *ou* dome ►**voûte du palais** *ou* **palatine** roof of the mouth, hard palate ►**voûte plantaire** arch (of the foot).

voûté, e [vute] (ptp de **voûter**) adj a *cave, plafond* vaulted, arched. b *dos* bent; *personne* stooped. **être ~, avoir le dos ~** to be stooped, have a stoop.

voûter [vute] 1 vt a (*Archit*) to arch, vault. b *personne, dos* to make stooped. **la vieillesse l'a voûté** age has given him a stoop; **il s'est voûté avec l'âge** he has become stooped with age.

vouvoiement [vuvwamɑ̃] nm addressing sb as "vous", using the "vous" form.

vouvoyer [vuvwaje] 8 vt: **~ qn** to address sb as "vous", use the "vous" form to sb.

vox populi [vɔkspɔpyli] nf vox populi, voice of the people.

voyage [vwajaʒ] nm a journey, trip. **le ~, les ~s** travelling; **il aime les ~s** he likes travel *ou* travelling; **le ~ le fatigue** travelling tires him; **le ~ l'a fatigué** the journey tired him; **j'ai fait un beau ~** I had a very nice trip; **les ~s de Christophe Colomb** the voyages *ou* journeys of Christopher Columbus; **les V~s de Gulliver** Gulliver's Travels; **il revient de ~** he's just come back from a journey *ou* a trip; **les fatigues du ~** the strain of the journey; **il est en ~** he's away; **il est absent — il est parti en ~** he's away — he has gone off on a trip *ou* a journey; **au moment de partir en ~** just as he (*ou* I *etc*) was setting off on his (*ou* my *etc*) journey *ou* travels; **il reste 3 jours de ~** there are still 3 days' travelling left, the journey will take another 3 days (to do); **lors de notre ~ en Espagne** on our trip to Spain, during *ou* on our travels in Spain; **frais/souvenirs de ~** travel expenses/souvenirs; **~ d'affaires/d'agrément/d'études** business/pleasure/study *ou* field trip; **~ d'information** fact-finding trip; **~ de noces** honeymoon; **~ organisé** *ou* **à forfait** package tour *ou* holiday (*Brit*); (*Prov*) **les ~s forment la jeunesse** travel broadens the mind; *voir* **agence, bon**[1], **sac**[1] *etc*.
b (*course*) trip, journey. **faire 2 ~s pour transporter qch** to make 2 trips *ou* journeys to transport sth; **j'ai dû faire le ~ de Grenoble une seconde fois** I had to make the trip *ou* journey to Grenoble a second time; **un ~ de charbon devrait suffire** one load of coal should be enough.
c (*Drogue*) trip.

voyager [vwajaʒe] 3 vi a (*faire des voyages*) to travel. **comment as-tu voyagé?** how did you travel?; **j'ai voyagé en avion/par mer/en 1ère classe** I travelled by air/by sea/1st class; **aimer ~** to be fond of travelling; **il a beaucoup voyagé** he has travelled widely *ou* a great deal, he has done a lot of travelling.
b (*Comm*) to travel. **~ pour un quotidien parisien** to travel for a Paris daily paper.
c *[chose]* to travel. **cette malle a beaucoup voyagé** this trunk has travelled a great deal *ou* has done a lot of travelling; **ces vins/ces denrées voyagent mal/bien** these wines/goods travel badly/well; **ce paquet s'est abîmé en voyageant** this package has been damaged in transit.

voyageur, -euse [vwajaʒœʀ, øz] 1 adj (*littér*) *humeur, tempérament* wayfaring (*littér*); *voir* **commis, pigeon**. 2 nm,f (*explorateur, Comm*) traveller; (*passager*) traveller, passenger. **~ de commerce,** (*Admin*) **~, représentant, placier** commercial traveller, sales representative.

voyagiste [vwajaʒist] nm tour operator.

voyance [vwajɑ̃s] nf clairvoyance.

voyant, e [vwajɑ̃, ɑ̃t] 1 adj *couleurs* loud, gaudy, garish. 2 nm,f (*illuminé*) visionary, seer; (*personne qui voit*) sighted person. 3 **voyante** nf (*cartomancienne etc*) **~e (extra-lucide)** clairvoyant. 4 nm a (*signal*) **~ (lumineux)** (warning) light; **~ d'essence/d'huile** petrol/oil warning light. b (*de l'arpenteur*) levelling rod *ou* staff.

voyelle [vwajɛl] nf vowel. **~ orale/nasale/cardinale/centrale** oral/nasal/cardinal/central vowel.

voyeur, -euse [vwajœʀ, øz] nm,f (*f rare*) voyeur; (*qui se cache*) Peeping Tom.

voyeurisme [vwajœʀism] nm voyeurism.

voyou [vwaju] 1 nm a (*délinquant*) lout, hoodlum, hooligan, yobbo‡ (*Brit*). b (*garnement, enfant*) street urchin, guttersnipe. **espèce de petit ~!** you little rascal! 2 adj (*gén inv, f rare:* **voyoute**) loutish. **un air ~** a loutish manner.

VPC [vepese] nf (abrév de **vente par correspondance**) *voir* **vente**.

vrac [vʀak] adv: **en ~** (*au poids, sans emballage*) (*au détail*) loose; (*en gros*) in bulk *ou* quantity; (*fig: en désordre*) in a jumble, higgledy-piggledy; **acheter du vin en ~** to buy wine in bulk for bottling o.s.; **il a tout mis en ~ dans la valise** he jumbled everything into the case, he filled the case any old how; **il a cité en ~ Hugo, Balzac et Baudelaire** he quoted Hugo, Balzac and Baudelaire at random, he jumbled together quotes from Hugo, Balzac and Baudelaire.

vrai, vraie [vʀɛ] 1 adj a (*après n: exact*) *récit, fait* true; (*Art, Littérat*) *couleurs, personnage* true. **ce que tu dis est ~** what you say is true *ou* right; **c'est dangereux, c'est** *ou* (*frm*) **il est ~, mais ...** it's dangerous, it's true *ou* certainly, but ...; **le tableau, tristement ~, que cet auteur peint de notre société** the picture, sadly only too true (to life), which this author paints of our society; **pas ~?*** right?*, aren't (*ou* won't *etc*) we (*ou* you *etc*)?; **c'est pas ~!*** oh no!; **il n'en est pas moins ~ que** it's nonetheless *ou* nevertheless true that; **ce n'est que trop ~** it's only too true; **cela est si ~ que** it's absolutely true that; *voir* **trop, vérité**.
b (*gén avant n: réel*) real. **ce sont ses ~s cheveux** that's his real *ou* own hair; **une vraie blonde** a real *ou* genuine blonde; **un ~ Picasso** a real *ou* genuine Picasso; **son ~ nom c'est Charles** his real *ou* true name is Charles; **des bijoux en or ~** jewellery in real gold; **lui c'est un cheik, un ~ de ~*** he's a sheik — the real thing *ou* the genuine article; **un ~ socialiste** a true socialist.
c (*avant n: intensif*) real. **c'est un ~ fou!** he's really mad!, he's downright mad!; **c'est un ~ mendiant!** he's a real beggar!; **c'est une vraie mère pour moi** she's a real mother to me; **un ~ chef-d'œuvre/héros** a real masterpiece/hero.
d (*avant n: bon*) real. **c'est le ~ moyen de le faire** that's the real way to do it.
e (*Sci*) **le temps solaire ~** true solar time; **le jour ~** true time.
2 nm a (*la vérité*) **le ~** the truth; **il y a du ~ dans ce qu'il dit** there's some truth *ou* there's an element of truth in what he says; **distinguer le ~ du faux** to distinguish truth from falsehood *ou* the true from the false; **être dans le ~** to be right; *voir* **plaider**.
b (*loc*) **il dit ~** he's right (in what he says), it's true what he says; **à dire ~, à ~ dire, à dire le ~** to tell (you) the truth, in (actual) fact; (*gén langage enfantin*) **pour de ~*** for real*, really, seriously; **c'est pour de ~?*** is it for real?*, do you (*ou* they *etc*) really mean it?; **au ~†, de ~†** in (actual) fact.
3 adv: **faire ~** *[décor, perruque]* to look real *ou* like the real thing; *[peintre, artiste]* to strive for realism, paint (*ou* draw *etc*) realistically; **~†, quelle honte!** oh really, how shameful!

vraiment [vʀɛmɑ̃] adv a (*véritablement*) really. **s'aiment-ils ~?** do they really (and truly) love each other?; **nous voulons ~ la paix** we really (and truly) want peace. b (*intensif*) really. **il est ~ idiot** he's a real idiot; **~, il exagère!** really, he's going too far!; **je ne sais ~ pas quoi faire** I really *ou* honestly don't know what to do; **oui ~, c'est dommage** yes, it's a real shame; **vous trouvez? — ah oui, ~!** do you think so? — oh yes, definitely! c (*de doute*) **— ~?** really?, is that so? **il est parti — ~?** he has gone — (has he) really?

vraisemblable [vʀɛsɑ̃blabl] adj *hypothèse, interprétation* likely; *situation, intrigue* plausible, convincing. *excuse, histoire* **peu ~** improbable, unlikely; **il est (très) ~ que** it's (highly *ou* very) likely *ou* probable that.

vraisemblablement [vʀɛsɑ̃blabləmɑ̃] adv probably, in all likelihood *ou* probability, very likely. **viendra-t-il? — ~/~ pas** will he come? — probably/probably not; **la fin, ~ proche, des hostilités** the likelihood of an imminent end to the hostilities.

vraisemblance [vʀɛsɑ̃blɑ̃s] nf *[hypothèse, interprétation]* likelihood; *[situation romanesque]* plausibility, verisimilitude. **selon toute ~** in all likelihood, in all probability.

vraquier [vʀakje] nm bulk carrier.

V/Réf (abrév de **votre référence**) your ref.

vrille [vʀij] nf a (*Bot*) tendril. b (*Tech*) gimlet. c (*spirale*) spiral; (*Aviat*) spin, tailspin. **escalier en ~** spiral staircase; (*Aviat*) **descente en ~** spiral dive; (*Aviat*) **descendre en ~** to spiral downwards, come down in a spin; (*Aviat*) **se mettre en ~** to go into a tailspin.

vrillé, e [vʀije] (ptp de **vriller**) adj *tige* tendrilled; *fil* twisted.

vriller [vʀije] 1 1 vt to bore into, pierce. 2 vi (*Aviat*) to spiral, spin; *[fil]* to become twisted.

vrombir [vʀɔ̃biʀ] 2 vi *[moteur]* to roar, hum. **faire ~ son moteur** to rev one's engine.

vrombissement [vʀɔ̃bismɑ̃] nm humming (*NonC*).

vroum [vʀum] excl brum! brum!

VRP [veɛʀpe] nm (abrév de **voyageur, représentant, placier**) sales rep*; *voir aussi* **voyageur**.

VS (abrév de **versus**) vs, v.

V.S.O.P. [veɛsɔpe] adj abrév de **very superior old pale**.

VTT [vetete] nm (abrév de **vélo tout terrain**) *voir* **vélo**.

vu[1], **vue**[1] [vy] (ptp de **voir**) 1 adj a (*: *compris*) **c'est ~?** all right?, got it?*, understood?; **c'est bien ~?** all clear?*, is that quite clear?; **~?** O.K.?*, right?*; **c'est tout ~** it's a foregone conclusion; *voir* **ni**. b (*jugé*) **une balle/passe/remarque bien vue** a well-judged ball/pass/remark. c (*considéré*) **bien ~** *personne* well thought of, highly regarded; *chose* good form (*attrib*); **mal ~** *personne* poorly thought of; *chose* bad form (*attrib*); **il est mal ~ du patron** the boss thinks poorly of him *ou* has a poor opinion of him; **ici c'est bien ~ de porter une cravate** it's good form *ou* the done thing here to wear a tie. 2 **nm: au ~ et au su de tous** openly and publicly; *voir* **déjà**.

vu² [vy] 1 **prép** (*gén, Jur*) in view of. **~ la situation, cela valait mieux** it was better, in view of *ou* considering *ou* given the situation. 2 **conj** (*) **~ que** in view of the fact that, seeing *ou* considering that; **~ qu'il était tard, nous avons abandonné la partie** seeing *ou* considering how late it was, we abandoned the game.

vue² [vy] **nf** a (*sens*) sight, eyesight. **perdre la ~** to lose one's (eye)sight; **troubles de la ~** sight trouble, disorders of vision (*frm*); **il a la ~ basse** *ou* **courte** he is short-sighted (*Brit*) *ou* near-sighted (*US*); **don de seconde** *ou* **double ~** gift of second sight.

b (*regard*) **détourner la ~** to look away, avert one's gaze; (*littér*) **porter la ~ sur qn/qch** to cast one's eyes over sb/sth, look in sb's direction/in the direction of sth; **s'offrir à la ~ de tous** to present o.s. for all to see; **il l'a fait à la ~ de tous** he did it in full view of everybody; (*lit, fig*) **perdre de ~** to lose sight of; **il lui en a mis plein la ~*** he put on quite a show for her; **il a essayé de m'en mettre plein la ~*** he tried to impress me.

c (*panorama*) view. **de cette colline, on a une très belle ~ de la ville** there's a very fine view *ou* you get a very good *ou* fine view of the town from this hill; **avec ~ imprenable** with an open *ou* unobstructed view *ou* outlook (*no future building plans*); **ces immeubles nous bouchent la ~** those buildings block our view; **cette pièce a ~ sur la mer** this room looks out onto the sea; **de là, on avait une ~ de profil de la cathédrale** from there you had a side view of the cathedral; *voir* **perte, point¹**.

d (*spectacle*) sight. **la ~ du sang l'a fait s'évanouir** the sight of the blood made him faint; **à sa ~ elle s'est mise à rougir** when she saw him she began to blush.

e (*image*) view. **des ~s de Paris** views of Paris; **un film de 36 ~s** a 36-exposure film; **~ photographique** photographic view, shot; **ils nous ont montré des ~s prises lors de leurs vacances** they showed us some photos they'd taken on their holidays; **~ de la ville sous la neige** view of the town in the snow; *voir* **pris**.

f (*opinion*) **~s** views; **présenter ses ~s sur un sujet** to present one's views on a subject; **de courtes ~s** short-sighted views; *voir* **échange**.

g (*conception*) view. **il a une ~ pessimiste de la situation** he has a pessimistic view of the situation; **donner une ~ d'ensemble** to give an overall view *ou* an overview; **c'est une ~ de l'esprit** that's a purely theoretical view; *voir* **point¹**.

h (*projet*) **~s** plans; (*sur qn ou ses biens*) designs; **il a des ~s sur la fortune de cette femme** he has designs on *ou* he has his eye on that woman's fortune; **elle a des ~s sur lui** (*pour un projet, pour l'épouser*) she has her eye on him.

i (*Jur: fenêtre*) window.

j (*loc*) **de ~** by sight; **je le connais de ~** I know him by sight; **à ~** *payable etc* at sight; (*Aviat*) *piloter, atterrir* visually; *atterrissage* visual; **à ~ d'œil** (*rapidement*) before one's very eyes; (*par une estimation rapide*) at a quick glance; **il maigrit à ~ d'œil** he seems to be getting thinner before our very eyes *ou* by the minute*; **à ~ de nez*** roughly*, at a rough guess; **en ~** (*lit, fig: proche*) in sight; (*en évidence*) **(bien) en ~** conspicuous; (*célèbre*) **très/assez en ~** very much/much in the public eye; **il a mis sa pancarte bien en ~** he put his placard in a prominent *ou* a conspicuous position *ou* where everyone could see it; **c'est un des politiciens les plus en ~** he's one of the most prominent *ou* best-known men in politics; **avoir un poste en ~** to have one's sights on a job; **avoir un collaborateur en ~** to have an associate in mind; **avoir en ~ de faire** to have it in mind to do, plan to do; **il a acheté une maison en ~ de son mariage** he has bought a house with his marriage in mind; **il s'entraîne en ~ de la course de dimanche/de devenir champion du monde** he's training with a view to the race on Sunday/ becoming world champion; **il a dit cela en ~ de le décourager** he said that with the idea of *ou* with a view to discouraging him; *voir* **changement, garder, tirer**.

Vulcain [vylkɛ̃] **nm** Vulcan.

vulcain [vylkɛ̃] **nm** (*papillon*) red admiral.

vulcanisation [vylkanizasjɔ̃] **nf** vulcanization.

vulcaniser [vylkanize] 1 **vt** to vulcanize.

vulcanologie [vylkanɔlɔʒi] **nf** vulcanology.

vulcanologue [vylkanɔlɔg] **nmf** vulcanologist.

vulgaire [vylgɛʀ] 1 **adj** a (*grossier*) *langage, personne* vulgar, coarse; *genre, décor* vulgar, crude. b (*prosaïque*) *réalités, problèmes* commonplace, everyday (*épith*), mundane. c (*usuel, banal*) common, popular. **nom ~** common *ou* popular name; **langues ~s** common languages; *voir* **latin**. d (*littér,†: du peuple*) common. **esprit ~** common mind; **l'opinion ~** the common opinion. e (*avant n: quelconque*) common, ordinary. **~ escroc** common swindler; **de la ~ matière plastique** ordinary plastic, common or garden plastic (*Brit*). 2 **nm** (†, *hum: peuple*) **le ~** the common herd; (*la vulgarité*) **tomber dans le ~** to lapse into vulgarity.

vulgairement [vylgɛʀmɑ̃] **adv** a (*grossièrement*) vulgarly, coarsely. b (*couramment*) *dénommer* popularly, commonly. **le fruit de l'églantier, ~ appelé** *ou* **que l'on appelle ~ gratte-cul** the fruit of the wild rose, commonly known as *ou* called haws.

vulgarisateur, -trice [vylgaʀizatœʀ, tʀis] **nm,f** popularizer.

vulgarisation [vylgaʀizasjɔ̃] **nf** popularization. **~ scientifique** scientific popularization; **ouvrage de ~** popularizing work; **ouvrage de ~ scientifique** popular scientific work.

vulgariser [vylgaʀize] 1 **vt** a *ouvrage* to popularize. b (*littér: rendre vulgaire*) to coarsen. **cet accent la vulgarise** this accent makes her sound coarse.

vulgarisme [vylgaʀism] **nm** vulgarism.

vulgarité [vylgaʀite] **nf** a (*grossièreté*) vulgarity, coarseness (*NonC*). **des ~s** vulgarities. b (*littér: terre à terre*) commonplaceness, ordinariness.

vulgate [vylgat] **nf** vulgate.

vulgum pecus* [vylgɔmpekys] **nm** (*hum*) **le ~** the common herd.

vulnérabilité [vylneʀabilite] **nf** vulnerability.

vulnérable [vylneʀabl] **adj** (*gén, Cartes*) vulnerable.

vulvaire [vylvɛʀ] 1 **adj** (*Anat*) vulvar. 2 **nf** (*Bot*) stinking goosefoot.

vulve [vylv] **nf** vulva.

vulvite [vylvit] **nf** vulvitis.

vumètre [vymɛtʀ] **nm** recording level gauge.

Vve **abrév de veuve**.

W

W[1], **w** [dubləve] nm (*lettre*) W, w.
W[2] (abrév de **Watt**) W.
wagnérien, -ienne [vagneʀjɛ̃, jɛn] 1 adj Wagnerian. 2 nm,f Wagnerian, Wagnerite.
wagon [vagɔ̃] 1 nm a (*Rail: véhicule*) (*de marchandises*) truck, wagon, freight car (*US*); (*de voyageurs*) carriage, car (*US*). b (*contenu*) truckload, wagonload. **un plein ~ de marchandises** a truckful *ou* truckload of goods; **il y en a tout un ~*** there are stacks of them*, there's a whole pile of them*.
2 comp ▸**wagon à bestiaux** cattle truck *ou* wagon ▸**wagon-citerne** nm (pl **wagons-citernes**) tanker, tank wagon ▸**wagon-couchettes** nm (pl **wagons-couchettes**) couchette car *ou* carriage, ≃ sleeping car ▸**wagon-foudre** nm (pl **wagons-foudres**) (wine) tanker *ou* tank wagon ▸**wagon frigorifique** refrigerated van ▸**wagon-lit** nm (pl **wagons-lits**) sleeper (*Brit*), Pullman (*US*) ▸**wagon de marchandises** goods truck, freight car (*US*) ▸**wagon-poste** nm (pl **wagons-postes**) mail van ▸**wagon-réservoir** nm (pl **wagons-réservoirs**) = **wagon-citerne** ▸**wagon-restaurant** nm (pl **wagons-restaurants**) restaurant *ou* dining car ▸**wagon de voyageurs** passenger carriage *ou* car (*US*).
wagonnet [vagɔnɛ] nm small truck.
Walhalla [valala] nm Valhalla.
Walkman [wɔkman] nm ® Walkman ®, personal stereo.
walkyrie [valkiʀi] nf Valkyrie.
wallaby, pl **wallabies** [walabi] nm wallaby.
Wallis-et-Futuna [walisefutuna] n Wallis and Futuna Islands.
wallon, -onne [walɔ̃, ɔn] 1 adj Walloon. 2 nm (*Ling*) Walloon. 3 nm,f: **W~(ne)** Walloon.
Wallonie [walɔni] nf French-speaking part of Belgium.
wapiti [wapiti] nm wapiti.
Washington [waʃiŋtɔn] 1 n (*ville*) Washington D.C. 2 nm a (*personne*) Washington. b (*État*) Washington (State).
wassingue [vasɛ̃g] nf floorcloth.
water-closet(s) [watɛʀklozɛt] nmpl = **waters.**
Waterloo [watɛʀlo] n Waterloo. **la bataille de ~** the Battle of Waterloo.
water-polo [watɛʀpɔlo] nm water polo.
waters [watɛʀ] nmpl toilet, lavatory, loo* (*Brit*). **où sont les ~?** where is the toilet?
watt [wat] nm watt.
wattheure [watœʀ] nm watt hour.
wattman† [watman] nm tram driver.
W.-C. [(dubl(ə)vese] nmpl (abrév de **water-closet(s)**) = **waters.**
weber [vebɛʀ] nm weber.
week-end, pl **week-ends** [wikɛnd] nm weekend. **partir en ~** to go away for the weekend; **partir en ~ prolongé** to go away on *ou* for a long weekend.
Weimar [vajmaʀ] n Weimar. **la république de ~** the Weimar Republic.
Wellington [wɛliŋtɔn] nWellington.
welter [wɛltɛʀ] nm *voir* **poids.**
western [wɛstɛʀn] nm western. **~-spaghetti** *ou* **italien** spaghetti western.
Westphalie [vɛsfali] nf Westphalia.
whisky, pl **whiskies** [wiski] nm whisky; (*irlandais*) whiskey. **~ américain** bourbon; **~ soda** whisky and soda.
whist [wist] nm whist.
white-spirit [wajtspiʀit] nm white-spirit.
Wight [wait] n *voir* **île.**
wigwam [wigwam] nm wigwam.
winch [win(t)ʃ] nm (*Naut*) winch.
Winchester [winʃɛstɛʀ] 1 nf: **(carabine) ~** Winchester (rifle). 2 nm (*Ordin*) **(disque) ~** Winchester disk.
Windhoek [windøk] n Windhoek.
Wisconsin [viskɔnsin] nm Wisconsin.
wishbone [wiʃbon] nm (*Naut*) wishbone.
wisigoth, e [vizigo, ɔt] 1 adj Visigothic. 2 nm,f: **W~(e)** Visigoth.
wisigothique [vizigɔtik] adj Visigothic.
wolfram [vɔlfʀam] nm wolfram.
woofer [wufœʀ] nm woofer.
Wyoming [wajɔmiŋ] nm Wyoming.

X, x [iks] **nm** a (*lettre*) X, x; (*Math*) x. (*Bio*) **chromosome X** X-chromosome; (*Math*) **l'axe des x** the x axis; **croisés en X** forming an x; **ça fait x temps que je ne l'ai pas vu*** I haven't seen him for n months*, it's months since I (last) saw him; **je te l'ai dit x fois** I've told you umpteen times *ou* innumerable times; (*Jur*) **plainte contre X** action against person or persons unknown; **Monsieur X** Mr X; **film classé X** X film†, 18 film; *voir* **rayon.** b (*arg Univ*) **l'X** the École Polytechnique; **un X** a student of the École Polytechnique.

Xavier [gzavje] **nm** Xavier.

xénon [gzenɔ̃] **nm** xenon.

xénophobe [gzenɔfɔb] 1 **adj** xenophobic. 2 **nmf** xenophobe.

xénophobie [gzenɔfɔbi] **nf** xenophobia.

Xénophon [gzenɔfɔ̃] **nm** Xenophon.

xérès [gzeʀɛs] 1 **nm** (*vin*) sherry. 2 **n: X~** (*ville*) Jerez.

Xerxès [gzɛʀsɛs] **nm** Xerxes.

xylographe [gzilɔgʀaf] **nm** xylographer.

xylographie [gzilɔgʀafi] **nf** (*technique*) xylography; (*gravure*) xylograph.

xylographique [gzilɔgʀafik] **adj** xylographic.

xylophène [gzilɔfɛn] **nm** ® woodworm and pesticide fluid.

xylophone [gzilɔfɔn] **nm** xylophone.

Y

Y, y[1] [igʀɛk] **nm** (*lettre*) Y, y. (*Bio*) **chromosome Y** Y-chromosome; (*Math*) **l'axe des y** the y axis.

y[2] [i] 1 **adv** (*indiquant le lieu*) there. **restez-~** stay there; **nous ~ avons passé 2 jours** we spent 2 days there; **il avait une feuille de papier et il ~ dessinait un bateau** he had a sheet of paper and he was drawing a ship on it; **avez-vous vu le film? — j'~ vais demain** have you seen the film? – I'm going (to see it) tomorrow; **les maisons étaient neuves, personne n'~ avait habité** the houses were new and nobody had lived in them; **la pièce est sombre, quand on ~ entre, on n'~ voit rien** the room is dark and when you go in you can't see a thing; **j'~ suis, j'~ reste** here I am and here I stay; (*fig*) **ah! j'~ suis!** (*comprendre*) oh, I understand!; (*se rappeler*) oh, I remember!; **vous ~ allez, à ce dîner?*** are you going to this dinner then?; **je suis passé le voir mais il n'~ était pas** I called in (*Brit*) *ou* I stopped by to see him but he wasn't there.

2 **pron pers** a (*gén se rapportant à des choses*) it. **vous serez là? — n'~ comptez pas** you'll be there? – it's highly unlikely *ou* I don't suppose so *ou* I doubt it; **n'~ pensez plus** forget (about) it, don't think about it; **à votre place, je ne m'~ fierais pas** if I were you I wouldn't trust it; **il a plu alors que personne ne s'~ attendait** it rained when no one was expecting it (to); **il ~ trouve du plaisir** he finds pleasure in it, he gets enjoyment out of it.

b (*loc*) **elle s'~ connaît** she knows all about it, she's an expert; **il faudra vous ~ faire** you'll just have to get used to it; **je n'~ suis pour rien** it is nothing to do with me, I had no part in it; **je n'~ suis pour personne** I'm not in to anyone; **ça ~ est! c'est fait!** that's it, it's done!; **ça ~ est, il a cassé le verre** there you are, he's broken the glass; **ça ~ est, il a signé le contrat** that's it *ou* that's settled, he's signed the contract; **ça ~ est oui!, je peux parler?** is that it then? *ou* have you finished then? can I talk now?; **ça ~ est, tu es prêt? — non ça n'~ est pas** is that it then, are you ready? – no I'm not; **ça ~ est pour quelque chose** it has something to do with it; *voir* **avoir, comprendre, voir** *etc.*

c (*: *il*) (*aussi iro*) **c'est-~ pas gentil?** isn't it nice?; **~ en a qui exagèrent** some people *ou* folk go too far; **du pain? ~ en a pas** bread? there's none *ou* there isn't any.

yacht ['jɔt] **nm** yacht. **~-club** yacht club.

yachting† ['jɔtiŋ] **nm** yachting. **faire du ~** to go out on one's yacht, go yachting.

yacht(s)man† ['jɔtman], **pl yacht(s)men** ['jɔtmɛn] **nm** yacht owner, yacht(s)man.

yack, yak ['jak] **nm** yak.

Yahvé ['jave] **nm** Yahveh.

Yalta ['jalta] **nm** Yalta. **la conférence de ~** the Yalta conference.

Yamoussoukro ['jamusukʀo] **n** Yamoussoukro.

yang ['jɑ̃g] **nm** yang.

Yang-Tsê Kiang ['jɑ̃gtsekjɑ̃g] **nm** Yangtze (Kiang).

yankee ['jɑ̃ki] **adj, nmf** Yankee.

Yaoundé ['jaunde] **n** Yaoundé.

yaourt ['jauʀt] **nm** yog(h)urt.

yaourtière ['jauʀtjɛʀ] **nf** yoghurt-maker.

yard ['jaʀd] **nm** yard.

yatagan ['jatagɑ̃] **nm** yataghan.

yearling ['jœʀliŋ] **nm** (*cheval*) yearling.

Yémen ['jemɛn] **nm: le ~** the Yemen; **Nord-/Sud-~** North/South Yemen.

yéménite ['jemenit] 1 **adj** Yemeni. 2 **nmf: Y~** Yemeni.

yen ['jɛn] **nm** (*Fin*) yen.

yeti ['jeti] **nm** yeti.

yeuse ['jøz] **nf** holm oak, ilex.

yeux ['jø] **nmpl de œil.**

yé-yé*, yé-yés ['jeje] 1 **adj inv: musique ~** pop music (*of the early 1960s*); (*fig*) **il veut faire ~** he wants to look with-it*. 2 **nmf inv** *pop singer or teenage fan of the early 1960s.*

yiddish ['jidiʃ] **adj, nm** Yiddish.

Yi king ['jikiŋ] **nm** I Ching.

yin ['jin] **nm** yin.

ylang-ylang [ilɑ̃ilɑ̃] **nm** ylang-ylang, ilang-ilang.

yod ['jɔd] **nm** yod.

yoga ['jɔga] **nm** yoga. **faire du ~** to do yoga.

yoghourt ['jɔguʀt] **nm** = **yaourt.**

yogi ['jɔgi] **nm** yogi.

yole ['jɔl] **nf** skiff.

Yom Kippur ['jɔmkipuʀ] **nm** Yom Kippur.

yougoslave ['jugɔslav] 1 **adj** Yugoslav, Yugoslavian. 2 **nmf: Y~** Yugoslav, Yugoslavian.

Yougoslavie† ['jugɔslavi] **nf** Yugoslavia†.

youp ['jup] **excl** hup! **allez ~ dégagez!** come on, get a move on!

youpi ['jupi] **excl** yippee.

youpin, e** ['jupɛ̃, in] **nm,f** Yid**.

yourte ['juʀt] **nf** yurt.

youyou ['juju] **nm** (*Naut*) dinghy.

Yo-Yo ['jojo] **nm inv** ® yo-yo.

ypérite [ipeʀit] **nf** mustard gas, yperite (*SPÉC*).

ytterbium [itɛʀbjɔm] **nm** ytterbium.

yttrium [itʀijɔm] **nm** yttrium.

yucca ['juka] **nm** yucca.

Yukon ['jykɔ̃] **nm** Yukon. **le (territoire du) ~** the Yukon (Territory).

Z

Z, z [zɛd] nm (*lettre*) Z, z; *voir* **A**.
ZAC [zak] nf (**abrév de zone d'aménagement concerté**) *voir* **zone**.
Zacharie [zakaʀi] nm Zechariah.
ZAD [zad] nf (**abrév de zone d'aménagement différé**) *voir* **zone**.
Zagreb [ʒagʀɛb] n Zagreb.
Zaïre [zaiʀ] nm Zaire.
zaïrois, -oise [zaiʀwa, waz] 1 adj Zairian. 2 nm,f: **Z~(e)** Zairian.
zakouski [zakuski] nmpl zakuski, zakouski.
Zambèze [zɑ̃bɛz] nm: **le ~** the Zambezi.
Zambie [zɑ̃bi] nf Zambia.
zambien, -ienne [zɑ̃bjɛ̃, jɛn] 1 adj Zambian. 2 nm,f: **Z~(ne)** Zambian.
zanzi [zɑ̃zi] nm dice game.
Zanzibar [zɑ̃zibaʀ] n Zanzibar.
zapper [zape] 1 vi to zap.
Zarathoustra [zaʀatustʀa] nm Zarathustra.
zazou [zazu] nmf (*parfois péj*) ≃ hepcat*.
zébi [zebi] nm *voir* **peau**.
zèbre [zɛbʀ] nm (*Zool*) zebra; (**: individu*) bloke* (*Brit*), guy*. **un drôle de ~** a queer fish*, an odd bod* (*Brit*); **filer** *ou* **courir comme un ~** to run like a hare *ou* the wind.
zébrer [zebʀe] 6 vt to stripe, streak (*de* with).
zébrure [zebʀyʀ] nf (*rayure*) stripe, streak; [*coup de fouet*] weal, welt.
zébu [zeby] nm zebu.
Zélande [zelɑ̃d] nf Zealand; *voir* **nouveau**.
zélateur, -trice [zelatœʀ, tʀis] nm,f (*gén*) champion, partisan (*péj*), zealot (*péj*); (*Rel*) Zealot.
zèle [zɛl] nm zeal. **avec ~** zealously, with zeal; (*péj*) **faire du ~** to be over-zealous, overdo it; **pas de ~!** don't overdo it!; *voir* **grève**.
zélé, e [zele] adj zealous.
zélote [zelɔt] nm (*Hist*) Zealot.
zen [zɛn] nm, adj inv Zen.
zénana [zenana] nm *voir* **peau**.
zénith [zenit] nm (*lit, fig*) zenith. **le soleil est au ~** *ou* **à son ~** the sun is at its zenith *ou* height; **au ~ de la gloire** at the zenith *ou* peak of glory.
zénithal, e, mpl **-aux** [zenital, o] adj zenithal.
Zénon [zenɔ̃] nm Zeno.
ZEP [zɛp] nf a (**abrév de zone d'éducation prioritaire**) *voir* **zone**. b (**abrév de zone d'environnement protégé**) *voir* **zone**.
zéphyr [zefiʀ] nm (*vent*) zephyr. (*Myth*) **Z~** Zephyr(us).
zéphyrien, -ienne [zefiʀjɛ̃, jɛn] adj (*littér*) zephyr-like (*littér*).
zeppelin [zɛplɛ̃] nm zeppelin.
zéro [zeʀo] 1 nm a (*gén, Math*) zero, nought (*Brit*); (*compte à rebours*) zero; (*dans un numéro de téléphone*) 0 (*Brit*), zero (*US*). **remettre un compteur à ~** to reset a meter at *ou* to zero; **tout ça, pour moi, c'est ~, je veux des preuves*** as far as I'm concerned that's worthless *ou* a waste of time — I want some proof; **les avoir à ~**‡ to be scared out of one's wits*, be scared stiff*; **repartir de ~, recommencer à ~** to start from scratch *ou* rock-bottom again, go back to square one; **taux de croissance ~** zero growth; (*Mil*) **l'option ~** the zero option; *voir* **moral, partir[1], réduire**.
b (*température*) freezing (point), zero (*Centigrade*). **3 degrés au-dessus de ~** 3 degrees above freezing (point) *ou* above zero; **3 degrés au-dessous de ~** 3 degrees below freezing (point) *ou* below zero, 3 degrees below*, minus 3 (degrees Centigrade); **~ absolu** absolute zero.
c (*Rugby, Ftbl*) nil (*Brit*), zero, nothing (*US*); (*Tennis*) love. (*Tennis*) **mener par 2 jeux/sets à ~** to lead (by) 2 games/sets to love; **~ à ~** *ou* **~ partout à la mi-temps** no score at half time; **gagner par 2 (buts) à ~** to win 2 nil (*Brit*), win by 2 goals to nil (*Brit*) *ou* zero; **la France avait ~ à la mi-temps** France hadn't scored *ou* had no score by half time.
d (*Scol*) zero, nought. **~ de conduite** bad mark for behaviour *ou* conduct; **~ pointé** (*Scol*) nought (*Brit*), nothing (*counted in the final average mark*); (*fig*) **le gouvernement mérite un ~ pointé** the government deserves nothing out of 20; (*fig*) **mais en cuisine, ~ (pour la question)*** but as far as cooking goes he's (*ou* she's) useless *ou* a dead loss*.
e (**: personne*) nonentity, dead loss*, washout*.
2 adj: **~ heure** (*gén*) midnight; (*heure GMT*) zero hour; **~ heure trente** (*gén*) half-past midnight; (*heure GMT*) zero thirty hours; **il a fait ~ faute** he didn't make any mistakes, he didn't make a single mistake; **j'ai eu ~ point** I got no marks (*Brit*) *ou* points (*US*) (at all), I got zero; **ça m'a coûté ~ franc ~ centime*** I got it for precisely *ou* exactly nothing.
zeste [zɛst] nm [*citron, orange*] peel (*NonC*); (*en cuisine*) zest (*NonC*), peel (*NonC*). **avec un ~ de citron** with a piece of lemon peel; (*fig*) **un ~ de folie/d'humour** a touch *ou* spark of madness/humour.
zêta [dzɛta] nm zeta.
zeugma [zøgma] nm zeugma.
Zeus [zøs] nm Zeus.
zézaiement [zezɛmɑ̃] nm lisp.
zézayer [zezeje] 8 vi to lisp.
ZI [ʒɛdi] nf (**abrév de zone industrielle**) *voir* **zone**.
zibeline [ziblin] nf sable.
zieuter‡ [zjøte] 1 vt (*longuement*) to eye; (*rapidement*) to have a dekko at‡ (*Brit*), have a squint at*.
zig*† [zig] nm, **zigomar***† [zigɔmaʀ] nm, **zigoto***† [zigɔto] nm guy*, bloke* (*Brit*), chap* (*Brit*), geezer*†. **c'est un drôle de ~** he's a queer fish*, he's a strange geezer*†; **faire le ~** to muck about *ou* around.
ziggourat [ziguʀat] nf ziggurat, zik(k)urat.
zigouiller* [ziguje] 1 vt to do in*.
zigue*† [zig] nm = **zig***†.
zigzag [zigzag] nm zigzag. **route en ~** windy *ou* winding *ou* zigzagging road; **faire des ~s** [*route*] to zigzag; [*personne*] to zigzag along; (*fig*) **avoir fait** *ou* **eu une carrière en ~** to have a chequered career (*péj*), have a varied career.
zigzaguer [zigzage] 1 vi to zigzag (along).
Zimbabwe [zimbabwe] nm Zimbabwe.
zimbabwéen, -enne [zimbabweɛ̃, ɛn] 1 adj Zimbabwean. 2 nm,f: **Z~(ne)** Zimbabwean.
zinc [zɛ̃g] nm a (*métal*) zinc. b (**: avion*) plane. c (**: comptoir*) bar, counter. **boire un coup sur le ~** to have a drink (up) at the bar *ou* counter.
zinguer [zɛ̃ge] 1 vt *toiture* to cover with zinc; *acier* to coat with zinc.
zingueur [zɛ̃gœʀ] nm zinc worker.
zinnia [zinja] nm zinnia.
zinzin* [zɛ̃zɛ̃] 1 adj cracked*, nuts*, barmy*. 2 nm thingummy(jig)* (*Brit*), thingamajig (*US*), what's-it*.
zip [zip] nm ® zip.
zippé, e [zipe] (ptp de **zipper**) adj zip-up (*épith*), with a zip.
zipper [zipe] 1 vt to zip up.
zircon [ziʀkɔ̃] nm zircon.
zirconium [ziʀkɔnjɔm] nm zirkonium.
zizanie [zizani] nf ill-feeling. **mettre** *ou* **semer la ~ dans une famille** to set a family at loggerheads, stir up ill-feeling in a family.
zizi* [zizi] nm (*hum, langage enfantin: pénis*) willy* (*Brit hum*), peter* (*US hum*).
zob** [zɔb] nm (*pénis*) dick**, prick**, cock**.
Zodiac [zɔdjak] nm ® rubber dinghy.
zodiacal, e, mpl **-aux** [zɔdjakal, o] adj *constellation, signe* of the zodiac; *lumière* zodiacal.
zodiaque [zɔdjak] nm zodiac. *voir* **signe**.
zombi [zɔ̃bi] nm zombie.
zona [zona] nm shingles (*sg*), herpes zoster (SPÉC).
zonage [zonaʒ] nm (*Urbanisme*) zoning.
zonard‡ [zonaʀ] nm (*marginal*) dropout*.
zone [zon] 1 nf a (*gén, Sci*) zone, area. (*Agr*) **~ d'élevage** *etc* cattle-breeding *etc* area; **~ d'influence (d'un pays)** sphere *ou* zone of influence

(of a country); ~ **franc/sterling** franc/sterling area; (*fig*) **de deuxième/troisième** ~ second-/third-rate.
b (*bidonville*) **la** ~ the slum belt.
2 **comp** ▸**zone d'activités** business park, enterprise zone ▸**zone d'aménagement concerté** urban development zone ▸**zone d'aménagement différé** future development zone ▸**la zone des armées** the war zone ▸**zone artisanale** industrial estate (*Brit*) *ou* park (*US*) for small businesses ▸**zone bleue** ≃ restricted parking zone *ou* area ▸**zone dangereuse** danger zone ▸**zone de dépression** (*Mét*) trough of low pressure ▸**zone d'éducation prioritaire** *area targeted for special help in education* ▸**zone d'environnement protégé** environmentally protected zone, ≃ SSSI (*Brit*) ▸**zone érogène** erogenous zone ▸**zone franche** free zone ▸**zone industrielle** industrial estate (*Brit*) *ou* park (*US*) ▸**zone libre** (*Hist France*) French zone ▸**zone occupée** (*Hist France*) occupied zone ▸**zone piétonnière** pedestrian precinct ▸**zone de salaires** salary weighting ▸**zone à urbaniser en priorité**† (*Admin*) urban development zone.
zoner [zone] 1 1 **vt** to zone. 2 **vi** (‡) *[marginal]* to bum around‡.
zoo [zo(o)] **nm** zoo.
zoologie [zɔɔlɔʒi] **nf** zoology.
zoologique [zɔɔlɔʒik] **adj** zoological.
zoologiste [zɔɔlɔʒist] **nmf**, **zoologue** [zɔɔlɔg] **nmf** zoologist.
zoom [zum] **nm** (*objectif*) zoom lens; (*effet*) zoom.
zoomer [zume] 1 **vi** to zoom in (*sur* on).
zoomorphe [zoomɔʀf] **adj** zoomorphic.
zootechnicien, -ienne [zooteknisjɛ̃, jɛn] **nmf** zootechnician.
zootechnique [zooteknik] **adj** zootechnic.
Zoroastre [zɔʀɔastʀ] **nm** Zoroaster, Zarathustra.
zoroastrisme [zɔʀɔastʀism] **nm** Zoroastrianism.
zou [zu] **excl**: **(allez)** ~! (*partez*) off with you!, shoo!*; (*dépêchez-vous*) get a move on!*; **et** ~, **les voilà partis!** zoom, off they go!*
zouave [zwav] **nm** Zouave, zouave. **faire le** ~* to play the fool, fool around.
Zoulou [zulu] **nm** Zulu.
Zoulouland [zululɑ̃d] **nm** Zululand.
zozo*† [zozo] **nm** nit(wit)*, ninny*.
zozoter [zɔzɔte] 1 **vi** to lisp.
ZUP [zyp] **nf** (**abrév de zone à urbaniser en priorité**) *voir* **zone**.
Zurich [zyʀik] **n** Zurich. **le lac de** ~ Lake Zurich.
zut* [zyt] **excl** (*c'est embêtant*) dash (it)!* (*Brit*), darn (it)!*, drat (it)!*; (*tais-toi*) (do) shut up!*
zygomatique [zigɔmatik] 1 **adj** zygomatic. **os/arcade** ~ zygomatic bone/arch. 2 **nm** zygomatic major (muscle) (*SPÉC*).
zygote [zigɔt] **nm** zygote.
zymase [zimɑz] **nf** zymase.

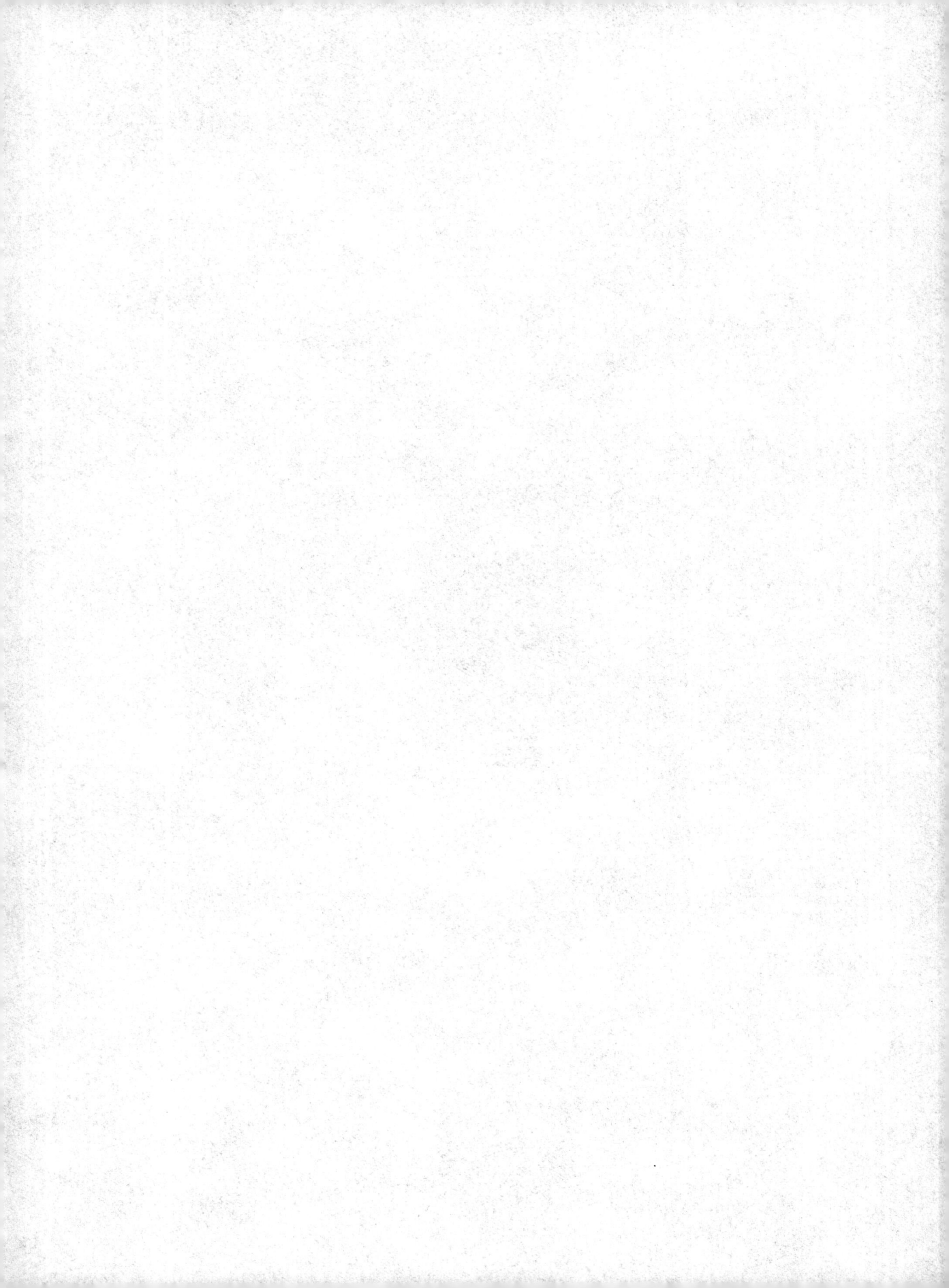

LANGUAGE IN USE

GRAMMAIRE ACTIVE

Beryl T. Atkins and Hélène M. A. Lewis

INTRODUCTION

One need which cannot be supplied within the word-based format of the conventional bilingual dictionary is that experienced by people trying to set down their own thoughts in a foreign language. They may not know even in their own language exactly how these thoughts might best be expressed, and indeed many language teachers rightly object to the framing of the thought in the native language before the expression process begins, maintaining that this leads to a distortion both of the thought itself and of its eventual expression in the other language. Non-native speakers, even the most competent, often have difficulty in expressing their thoughts in a sufficiently sensitive, varied and sophisticated way. It is to meet the needs of these people that we have designed this new section in our bilingual dictionary.

This section contains thousands of phrases and expressions grouped according to the **function** that is being performed when they are used in communication. A glance at the Contents Table on p.72 will show the themes that have been included. Some of the most notorious areas of difficulty are addressed in this section, for example the concepts of possibility, obligation and so on, often expressed in English by modal verbs, where the difficulty for the non-native speaker is as much syntactical as lexical.

Each function presents an individual set of problems and challenges for the user. For example, the needs of someone attempting to express tactful advice or contradiction are quite different from those of someone drawing up a job application, and these varied needs are met in correspondingly varied ways within this section.

The **design** of this section is entirely different from that of the dictionary proper, in that the approach is monolingual rather than bilingual. There is no question of any attempt to make the parallel columns into sets of equivalents, but simply to construct useful bridges across the language barrier.

Like the rest of this dictionary, this section has been designed as a **tool** for non-native speakers: it will serve particularly those skilled in the other language and able to recognise what they are looking for when they see it. It is not, and could not be, a comprehensive listing of the immense riches that each language offers in any area of thought. It is, rather, a selection, we hope a useful one, made to provide a channel between the user's passive and active knowledge of the foreign language. In controlled situations, such as the classroom, this section of the dictionary will also, we trust, provide a valuable teaching aid in language learning.

The authors

L'un des besoins auxquels le dictionnaire bilingue traditionnel, limité par la classification alphabétique, ne peut répondre de façon entièrement satisfaisante est celui de l'usager qui, au lieu de traduire, essaie d'exprimer ses propres idées dans une langue étrangère. À ce stade de la réflexion, celui-ci ne sait peut-être même pas comment formuler exactement sa pensée dans sa propre langue, et d'ailleurs, de nombreux professeurs s'opposent à ce que le message soit préalablement énoncé dans la langue maternelle, affirmant à juste titre qu'une telle démarche déforme à la fois la pensée elle-même et son expression finale dans la langue d'arrivée. Quelle que soit sa compétence, la personne cherchant à communiquer dans une langue qui n'est pas la sienne éprouve souvent des difficultés à atteindre un niveau d'expression qui soit riche, précis et élégant. C'est pour suppléer cette lacune que nous avons conçu cette nouvelle section de notre dictionnaire.

Ces pages contiennent plusieurs milliers d'expressions et locutions regroupées selon la **fonction** qu'elles accomplissent dans la communication. Il suffit de se reporter à la Table des matières (p.72) pour voir les thèmes qui ont été inclus. On trouvera dans cette section certains points traditionnellement considérés comme particulièrement complexes, tels que par exemple les concepts de possibilité et d'obligation, souvent traduits en anglais par les verbes modaux, qui présentent à l'usager étranger des difficultés syntactiques autant que lexicales.

Pour l'usager, chaque fonction présente des difficultés et des nuances spécifiques. Par exemple, le vocabulaire d'appoint nécessaire est différent selon qu'on fait une demande d'emploi ou qu'on cherche à exprimer avec politesse son désaccord. Par conséquent, la présentation varie suivant les besoins pratiques de chaque page.

La **conception** de cette section diffère totalement de celle du reste du dictionnaire, dans la mesure où la méthode de présentation est monolingue plutôt que bilingue. Les expressions des deux colonnes ne cherchent en aucun cas à être des traductions ou des équivalences présentées en miroir, mais sont incorporées en guise de passerelles entre deux systèmes linguistiques.

Cette section est avant tout un **outil** de travail destiné à l'usager cherchant à s'exprimer dans une langue étrangère, et qui, possédant des connaissances avancées, reconnaîtra en la voyant l'expression dont il a besoin et qui lui échappe. Ces pages ne sauraient être un catalogue exhaustif des richesses dont chaque langue dispose pour exprimer des idées. Elles constituent une sélection qui devra permettre au lecteur d'utiliser ses connaissances passives pour enrichir ses connaissances actives de la langue. Dans des situations dirigées telles que le cours de langue, cette section du dictionnaire devrait aussi constituer un support pédagogique facilitant l'acquisition de la langue étrangère.

Les auteurs

See CONTENTS page 72

Voir TABLE des MATIÈRES page 72

SUGGESTIONS

GIVING SUGGESTIONS

Je suggère que *or* **Je propose que** vous lui en parliez bientôt. — *I suggest that*

N'oubliez surtout pas de mentionner votre situation de famille. — *you mustn't forget to ...*

On pourrait adopter une autre méthode. — *we could*

Que diriez-vous si on partait pour Londres à la fin de la semaine? — *what would you say if*

Avez-vous pensé à *or* **Avez-vous songé à** reprendre vos études? — *have you (ever) thought of*

Vous pourriez remettre cela à plus tard. — *you could*

Pourquoi ne pas faire un peu de sport l'hiver prochain? — *why don't you*

Est-ce que cela ne vous tente pas d'aller en Grèce? — *doesn't the idea of ... tempt you?*

Voici mes suggestions: tout d'abord nous faisons une étude de marché, puis ... — *here are my suggestions:*

Vous auriez intérêt à changer de situation bientôt. — *you'd be as well to ...*

Vous feriez bien de *or* **Vous feriez mieux de** prendre vos vacances au mois de septembre. — *you'd be as well to ...*

Vous devriez l'envoyer par exprès puisque c'est tellement important. — *you ought to ...*

À votre place *or* **Si j'étais vous** *or* **Personnellement,** je demanderais des renseignements. — *if I were you*

À mon avis, tu ne devrais pas refuser. — *in my view*

Je vous conseille de prendre des précautions. — *I advise you to ...*

Si vous le permettez, je viendrai vous chercher demain. — *if you agree, I shall ...*

(Et) si on allait à l'île de Ré cet été? — *what if we were to ...*

(more tentatively)

Ce ne serait pas une mauvaise idée de lui demander son avis là-dessus. — *it might not be a bad idea to ...*

On pourrait envisager une révision des programmes. — *we could think of doing*

Il serait bon de *or* **Il serait recommandé de** lui envoyer le dossier aussitôt que possible. — *it would be as well to ...*

Il conviendrait de contacter l'entreprise sans plus attendre. — *the correct thing to do would be to ...*

Ce serait une excellente idée de visiter l'exposition de sculpture moderne. — *it would be an excellent idea to ...*

J'aimerais vous suggérer une solution possible. — *I'd like to suggest*

Puis-je faire une suggestion *or* **Puis-je émettre un avis?** Il me semble que ... — *may I make a suggestion?*

Si je peux me permettre une suggestion, je crois qu'il vaudrait mieux inclure une carte de la région. — *if I might suggest something*

Nous aimerions vous soumettre quelques propositions. — *we should like to put to you*

Rien ne vous empêche de demander une augmentation ... — *there is nothing to prevent you from*

Puis-je vous rappeler que le directeur attend votre réponse? — *may I remind you that*

Il serait souhaitable de *or* **Il serait préférable de** fournir à chacun un exemplaire de ce document. — *it would be advisable to ...*

Il vaudrait peut-être mieux en informer ses parents. — *it might be better to ...*

Peut-être faudrait-il envisager une refonte radicale du projet? — *perhaps one should*

Il suffirait de le prévenir à temps. — *you only need to ...*

Dans l'état actuel des choses, **il n'y a qu'à** attendre. — *we can only*

Est-ce que cela vous ennuierait beaucoup de me renvoyer sa lettre? — *would you mind very much*

Je serais très heureux de vous faire visiter le château. — *I'd be very happy to ...*

ASKING FOR SUGGESTIONS

Que ferais-tu **à ma place?** — *what would you do if you were me?*

Que fait-on en pareil cas? — *what can you do?*

Peut-être avez-vous une meilleure proposition en ce qui concerne le financement? — *perhaps you have a better suggestion*

AND, ACCORDING TO CONTEXT:

prenez soin de ne pas / pourquoi ne pas / voulez-vous, je vous prie, / je vous conseille vivement de / il est indispensable de / je souhaiterais pouvoir / essayez quand même de / je me demande si vous ne feriez pas mieux de / permettez-moi de vous proposer / si vous n'y voyez pas d'inconvénient / cela pourrait être une façon indirecte de / supposons qu'il s'agisse de / il n'est pas impossible que ce soit / on ne peut qu'émettre des conjectures en ce qui concerne / ceci expliquerait

ADVICE

ASKING FOR ADVICE

Je voudrais vous demander conseil *or* **J'aimerais quelques conseils** au sujet de la carrière que je souhaite entreprendre.	*I'd like some advice*
J'ai besoin d'un conseil: vaut-il mieux acheter une voiture neuve ou une voiture d'occasion?	*I need some advice:*
Vu les circonstances, **que me conseillez-vous de faire** *or* **que dois-je faire?**	*what would you advise me to do?*
À ma place, que feriez-vous?	*what would you do in my place?*
Je vous serais très reconnaissant de bien vouloir me conseiller sur la marche à suivre.	*I should be very grateful if you would advise me about*
Je voudrais que vous me donniez votre avis sur cette question.	*I'd like your opinion on*

GIVING ADVICE

Personnellement, je trouve que tu devrais *or* **Moi, je trouve que tu devrais** passer ton permis de conduire.	*personally, I think you should*
Mon conseil serait de rompre tout contact avec eux.	*my advice would be to ...*
Il est déconseillé de prendre trop de médicaments en même temps.	*it is inadvisable to ...*
Si j'ai un conseil à vous donner, c'est de ne pas vous mêler de cette affaire.	*if I can offer you a piece of advice*
Il serait judicieux d'obtenir son autorisation avant d'aller plus loin.	*it would be wise to ...*
Je ne saurais trop vous recommander d'être discret à ce sujet.	*I urge you to ...*
Je vous déconseille (vivement) d'y aller en train.	*I (strongly) advise you not to ...*
À votre place *or* **Si j'étais vous,** je démissionnerais tout de suite.	*if I were you*
À mon avis, tu devrais faire appel à un spécialiste pour un travail de ce genre.	*in my opinion, you should*
Surtout, ne croyez pas tout ce qu'on raconte!	*whatever you do*
Pars en vacances — **c'est ce que tu as de mieux à faire!**	*it's the best thing you can do*
Tu as (tout) intérêt à le faire aussitôt que possible.	*you would be best to ...*
Tu aurais tort de ne pas demander à être payé pour tes heures supplémentaires.	*you'd be wrong not to ...*
Vous auriez tort de lui confier une tâche aussi délicate.	*you'd be wrong to ...*

(more tentatively)

Il n'y a pas de raison que tu te prives *(subj)* pour eux.	*there's no reason why you should*
Puis-je me permettre de suggérer que vous alliez à Oslo?	*might I suggest that*
Est-ce que tu as pensé à la possibilité d'un cours de recyclage?	*have you ever thought of*
Il serait peut-être bon de le prévenir en premier.	*it might be a good idea to ...*
Ce ne serait pas une mauvaise idée d'en acheter deux douzaines.	*it wouldn't be a bad idea to ...*
Il nous semble peu prudent d'engager des fonds aussi importants dans cette affaire.	*it seems to us rash to ...*
Vous pourriez peut-être le lui expliquer vous-même?	*perhaps you could*
Je me demande si vous ne devriez pas attendre encore quelques jours?	*I wonder if you shouldn't*

WARNING SOMEONE ABOUT SOMETHING

Vous feriez mieux de lui en envoyer une copie, **sinon** il va se plaindre qu'on l'oublie.	*you'd be as well to ... or else he will*
Méfiez-vous des soi-disant vendeurs qui font du porte-à-porte.	*beware of*
Ce serait de la folie de partir le 14 juillet.	*it would be madness to ...*
Je vous préviens que si vous n'avez pas terminé à temps, je ne pourrai pas vous payer.	*I warn you that*
Vous courez le risque de perdre toutes vos économies.	*you're running the risk of*
Tu auras des ennuis si tu continues à ne pas travailler.	*you'll be in trouble if*
Un conseil *or* **Un avertissement:** ne cherchez pas à savoir pourquoi il est parti.	*a word of warning:*
Je vous avertis que je commence à en avoir assez de vos absences répetées.	*I'm warning you that*
Ne venez pas vous plaindre que votre nom ne figure pas sur la liste.	*don't come to me complaining that*

AND, ACCORDING TO CONTEXT:

que fait-on dans ces cas-là? / il faut que vous m'aidiez à prendre une décision / je ne sais comment m'y prendre / est-ce que tu crois que / quelle serait votre réaction si / je me demande ce que je dois faire / si vous alliez le voir / essayez donc de / je trouve que vous devriez / n'hésitez pas à / il est dans votre intérêt de / moi, j'éviterais de / n'oubliez pas de / je ne sais pas ce que vous penseriez de / pourquoi ne pas / vous voilà prévenu / tant pis pour toi si

OFFERS

Puis-je vous faire visiter Paris? — *may I*

Est-ce que je peux faire quelque chose pour vous aider? — *can I*

Je peux vous trouver quelqu'un pour vous aider au bureau, **si vous voulez**. — *I can ... if you like*

Me permettriez-vous de vous faire visiter Paris? — *would you allow me to ...*

Voulez-vous que je vous aide *(subj)* à classer les documents? — *would you like me to ...*

Voudriez-vous que nous organisions le voyage ensemble? — *would you like us to ...*

Aimeriez-vous que j'essaie *(subj)* de louer un chalet pour les vacances? — *would you like me to ...*

Laissez-moi au moins payer les fleurs et le gâteau! — *at least allow me to ...*

J'irais **volontiers** tenir compagnie à votre grand-mère le dimanche, si elle se sent seule. — *I would willingly*

Nous aimerions vous offrir le poste de secrétaire adjoint. — *we should like to offer you*

Si vous avez besoin d'aide au moment des fêtes, **n'hésitez pas à me le demander**. — *don't hesitate to ask me*

Je veux bien m'en charger, puisque personne ne s'est porté volontaire. — *I'll look after that*

Si vous le souhaitez, **je suis prêt à** m'occuper de la préparation des repas. — *I'm ready to ...*

Si cela vous arrange, **je serais très heureux de** mettre mon appartement **à** votre disposition. — *I would be happy to ...*

Et si je venais garder les enfants ce soir-là? — *what if I were to ...*

(more indirectly)

Cela me ferait très plaisir de vous faire visiter Saint-Martin. — *it would be a great pleasure to ...*

Pourquoi n'irais-je **pas** le chercher à la gare? — *why shouldn't I*

Que diriez-vous si j'essayais d'organiser une réunion des anciens élèves? — *what would you say if*

Je ne demande pas mieux que de chercher de nouveaux volontaires pour votre projet. — *I should really like to ...*

Nous pourrions peut-être y aller ensemble, si cela ne vous ennuie pas? — *we might perhaps*

REQUESTS

Pourriez-vous *or* **Vous serait-il possible de** me louer une voiture sans chauffeur pour qu'elle soit disponible dès mon arrivée? — *could you*

Puis-je vous demander de bien vouloir vous occuper des réservations? — *may I ask you to ...*

Nous aimerions *or* **Nous souhaiterions** savoir si l'établissement reste ouvert après 22 heures. — *we should like to ...*

Nous comptons sur vous pour nous faire parvenir un règlement par chèque dans les plus brefs délais. — *we are counting on you to ...*

Je dois vous demander de ne pas retenir le personnel après 18 heures. — *I must ask you not to ...*

J'insiste pour que dorénavant vous vous adressiez à notre président. — *I must insist that*

Je préférerais que vous ne lui rapportiez pas ce que j'ai dit. — *I would rather you ...*

(more indirectly)

Cela vous dérangerait-il beaucoup *or* **Cela vous ennuierait-il beaucoup** de m'en prêter un exemplaire? — *would you mind (doing)*

Cela me rendrait service *or* **Cela m'arrangerait** si vous vouliez bien me remplacer la semaine prochaine. — *it would be very helpful if you*

(more formally)

Je vous prie de bien vouloir me confirmer la date et l'heure de votre arrivée. — *would you please be kind enough to ...*

Vous êtes prié de nous rendre immédiatement les ouvrages empruntés dans le courant de l'année. — *you are requested to ...*

Auriez-vous l'amabilité de me faire savoir s'il vous en reste encore? — *would you very kindly*

Veuillez avoir l'obligeance de me faire parvenir deux exemplaires de cet ouvrage. — *would you kindly*

Je vous serais reconnaissant de bien vouloir me réserver une chambre avec salle de bains du 5 au 15 juillet inclus. — *I should be grateful if you would*

Je vous saurais gré d'observer la plus grande discrétion dans cette affaire. — *I should be most grateful if you will*

Nous vous serions obligés de bien vouloir régler cette facture. — *we should be grateful if you would*

AND, ACCORDING TO CONTEXT:

si cela ne vous gêne pas trop / j'espère que vous ne m'en voudrez pas, mais / j'ose à peine vous demander de / j'espérais que vous / je voudrais vous demander un service / je vous demanderai de bien vouloir / en espérant que ceci ne causera pas trop de / n'oubliez surtout pas de / nous nous permettons de vous rappeler

COMPARISONS

Par comparaison avec les supermarchés *or* **En comparaison des** supermarchés, les magasins de quartier sont souvent chers. — *in comparison with*

Oui, peut-être, mais **comparé à** son premier roman *or* **si vous le comparez à** son premier roman, celui-ci est beaucoup moins bon. — *compared with*

Si on le compare à Londres, on se rend compte que Paris est en fait plus petit. — *if you compare it with*

On l'a souvent comparé à Tolstoï. // On a souvent **établi une comparaison** *or* **fait un rapprochement entre** lui et Tolstoï. — *often compared him to*

Pour une location, c'est **comparativement** cher pour le mois de juillet. — *comparatively*

Les statistiques de cette année sont **(bien) plus** intéressantes **que** celles de l'an dernier. — *(much) more ... than ...*

Les ventes ont considérablement augmenté **par rapport à** celles de l'année dernière. — *in comparison with*

Il devient **de plus en plus** difficile de trouver un studio à Paris. // Il devient **de moins en moins** facile de trouver un studio. — *more and more // less and less*

C'est **par contraste avec** la chaleur de l'air que l'eau semble froide. — *in contrast with*

Sa nouvelle maison **ressemble à** l'ancienne, **mais en moins** grand. // Cela **fait penser à** un écran de télévision, **mais en plus** petit. — *is like ... but bigger (or smaller, etc)*

La forme de la lampe **rappelle** celle d'un champignon. — *is reminiscent of*

Leurs façons de procéder **ne se ressemblent vraiment en rien.** — *are not at all alike*

Dans les deux romans, l'action se passe dans la Sicile du 19ème siècle, mais **la ressemblance s'arrête là.** — *there the likeness ends*

Cette maison-ci a un joli jardin, **alors que** *or* **tandis que** l'autre n'a qu'une cour. — *whereas*

Ils se ressemblent, à cette différence près que le premier est un peu plus grand. — *they are like each other, but ...*

Ce qui le différencie de *or* **Ce qui le distingue de** ses contemporains, c'est son sens du progrès. — *what differentiates him from*

(comparing favourably)

Ce vin est **de très loin supérieur à** l'autre. // Il est **de beaucoup supérieur** à l'autre. — *far superior to*

Sans comparaison possible, c'est lui le plus sympathique de tous. — *there's no comparison: he ...*

Pour ce qui est du climat, **je préfère** le Midi. — *I prefer*

(comparing unfavourably)

le film **est loin d'être aussi intéressant que** le livre dont on l'a tiré. — *is far less interesting than*

Ce tissu **est certainement inférieur en qualité à** celui que nous avions auparavant. — *is certainly inferior in quality to*

Sa dernière pièce **ne mérite pas d'être comparée à** *or* **ne supporte pas la comparaison avec** celle qu'il avait écrite il y a deux ans. — *does not bear comparison with*

Ses poèmes **sont loin de valoir** ses romans. — *are not nearly as good as*

Il n'arrive pas à la cheville de son frère. — *he can't hold a candle to*

(great similarity)

Les deux maisons **sont comparables**: en effet, elles ont toutes les deux cinq chambres. — *are quite comparable*

C'est **l'équivalent de** six semaines de travail. // Cela **représente** six semaines de travail. // Cela **correspond à** six semaines de travail. — *is the equivalent of*

Les deux tableaux **sont d'égale valeur** *or* **valent le même prix.** — *are equal in value*

Je n'arrive pas à trouver de différence *or* **Je n'arrive pas à faire la différence entre** les deux méthodes. — *I cannot distinguish between*

Les compagnies connaissent actuellement des difficultés financières, et **il en est de même pour** les ouvriers, qui voient leur niveau de vie baisser. — *the same is true of*

(great difference)

Il n'y a vraiment aucune comparaison possible entre les deux candidats. — *there is simply no comparison between*

Il serait certainement difficile d'**établir une comparaison entre** les deux. — *to draw a comparison between*

On ne saurait comparer deux œuvres aussi différentes. — *one cannot compare*

Les deux procédés **n'ont rien de comparable**: le premier est chimique et le second mécanique. — *there are no points of comparison between*

AND, ACCORDING TO CONTEXT:

tout bien considéré / dans l'ensemble / en gros / en fin de compte / il faut reconnaître que / on est obligé d'admettre / personnellement je préfère / c'est à peu près la même chose / ils se ressemblent jusqu'à un certain point mais / c'est un peu comme si / le premier ... le second / ils est impossible de substituer A à B

OPINIONS

ASKING FOR SOMEBODY'S OPINION

Que pensez-vous de sa façon d'agir?	*what do you think of*
Pourriez-vous me donner votre avis *or* **votre opinion là-dessus?**	*can you give me your opinion*
À votre avis *or* **Selon vous,** faut-il donner plus de liberté aux jeunes?	*in your opinion, should one ...*
Avez-vous une opinion *or* **Quelle est votre opinion en ce qui concerne** la télévision privée?	*what is your attitude to*
Pourriez-vous me dire ce que vous pensez personnellement de ce changement?	*can you tell me what your own feelings are about*
J'aimerais savoir votre avis *or* **votre opinion sur** le programme du festival.	*I'd like to know what you think of*
J'ai appris que le projet a été annulé et **je voudrais savoir comment vous accueillez cette décision.**	*... I would like to know your reaction to the decision*

EXPRESSING YOUR OPINION

Je pense/crois/estime que nous avons maintenant tous les renseignements nécessaires.	*I think/believe/reckon that*
Je présume/suppose/imagine qu'elle sait ce qui l'attend.	*I presume/suppose/imagine that*
Je crois savoir que leur proposition a été accueillie favorablement.	*I believe that*
Je trouve qu'on ne fait pas suffisamment appel à l'imagination des enfants.	*my feeling is that*
À mon avis, c'était ce qui pouvait lui arriver de mieux.	*to my mind*
Selon moi *or* **D'après moi** *or* **Pour moi,** on ne devrait pas la laisser toute seule.	*in my opinion*
Personnellement *or* **En ce qui me concerne,** je crois que nous avons déjà trop tardé.	*personally, I think that*
À mon point de vue, le gouvernement n'a pas agi assez vite.	*my own point of view is that ...*
À ce qu'il me semble, il serait préférable de rassembler tout le matériel en un seul endroit.	*I have an idea that ...*
J'ai l'impression que ses parents ne la comprennent pas.	*I have the impression that*
À la réflexion, il me semble que nous ferions bien d'en commander plusieurs.	*on second thoughts, we'd better ...*
Je suis persuadé qu'il finira par nous accorder son soutien.	*I am convinced that*
Je suis convaincu que c'est vraiment la seule solution.	*it is my belief that*
Je considère qu'il doit nous demander notre autorisation.	*I feel that*
Je dois dire que les résultats me semblent très décevants.	*I must say that*
Je crains qu'il ne soit trop tard maintenant.	*I fear it may be ...*
Si vous voulez mon opinion là-dessus, il est fou de prendre de telles responsabilités.	*if you want my opinion, ...*
Je ne peux pas m'empêcher de penser que c'est délibéré.	*I can't help thinking that*
La sélection à l'entrée de l'université finira par devenir indispensable. **C'est du moins mon opinion.**	*at least, this is what I feel*
Sans vouloir vous contredire, il me semble que cette solution n'est pas satisfaisante.	*with due respect, I feel that*
Si je puis me permettre d'exprimer une opinion, la prison crée plus de problèmes qu'elle n'en résout.	*if I may express an opinion, ...*

REPLYING WITHOUT GIVING AN OPINION

Il est difficile de prévoir combien il en faudra exactement.	*it is difficult to tell ...*
Je préférerais ne pas avoir à me prononcer là-dessus.	*I'd rather not commit myself*
Il me semble difficile de donner un avis définitif sur la question.	*it is difficult to give a final opinion*
Je dois reconnaître que je n'ai pas d'opinion bien précise là-dessus.	*I have no particular views*
Vous me prenez au dépourvu: **je n'y ai jamais vraiment réfléchi** *or* **je ne me suis jamais vraiment posé la question.**	*... I've never really thought about it*
Je ne suis pas à même de dire s'il a eu raison de le faire, car je n'ai pas lu son rapport.	*I'm not in a position to say*
Tout dépend de ce que vous voulez dire par 'études de langues'.	*it all depends on what you mean by ...*

AND, ACCORDING TO CONTEXT:

je ne suis pas au courant de / je ne connais pas très bien / ce n'est qu'une supposition de ma part / pour le moment on peut dire que / j'ignore tout de / c'est une question de point de vue / vous en savez autant que moi là-dessus

LIKES, DISLIKES AND PREFERENCES

ASKING ABOUT THESE

Est-ce que vous aimeriez vous remettre à jouer au tennis? — *would you like to ...*

Est-ce que cela vous plaît de travailler avec lui? — *do you like*

Est-ce que cela vous plairait *or* **Est-ce que cela vous ferait plaisir de** visiter le Louvre quand vous viendrez à Paris? — *would you like to ...*

Qu'est-ce que vous préférez *or* **Qu'est-ce que vous aimez le plus** — le piano ou le violon? — *which do you prefer*

Pouvez-vous m'indiquer vos préférences, pour que je commence à faire une sélection? — *could you let me know what (or which ones) you prefer*

Je serais heureux d'avoir votre opinion sur le choix des matériaux. — *I'd be happy to have your opinion*

SAYING WHAT YOU LIKE

La visite de la cathédrale **m'a beaucoup plu** *or* **m'a beaucoup intéressé.** — *I liked ... a lot*

Je trouve beaucoup de plaisir *or* **Je trouve beaucoup de satisfaction** à tous les travaux manuels. — *I really enjoy*

L'un de mes plus grands plaisirs, c'est la randonnée en montagne. — *one of my greatest pleasures is*

J'aime que les gens soient à l'heure. — *I like people to ...*

Son interprétation de Hamlet **ne me déplaît pas.** — *I quite like*

Ce que j'aime par-dessus tout, c'est *or* **Ce que je préfère à tout, c'est** une soirée passée au coin du feu. — *what I like better than anything else is*

Pour moi, rien n'est comparable à *or* **Pour moi rien ne vaut** un prélude de Debussy. — *for me, there's nothing to compare with*

SAYING WHAT YOU DISLIKE

Ce que je déteste (le plus), c'est attendre l'autobus sous la pluie. — *what I hate (most) is*

J'ai horreur des gens qui se croient importants. — *I really hate*

Sa façon d'agir **ne me plaît pas du tout.** — *I don't like ... at all*

Je n'ai aucun plaisir à travailler dans de telles conditions. — *I don't enjoy*

Il m'est pénible de prendre la parole en public. — *I find it hard to ...*

Je ne peux pas supporter que les gens soient en retard. — *I can't bear*

Je l'ai pris en aversion dès que je l'ai vu. — *I took a dislike to him*

Je ne comprends pas que tout le monde s'extasie devant cela: **ça n'a rien d'extraordinaire.** — *it's nothing special*

SAYING WHAT YOU PREFER

Je préfère les pêches **aux** abricots. **Je préfère** prendre l'avion plutôt **que d**'aller en voiture. — *I prefer X to Y*

La lecture est certainement une de mes occupations **préférées** *or* **favorites.** — *favourite*

Si cela ne vous ennuie pas, **je préférerais** prendre le plus grand. — *I would prefer to ...*

J'aimerais mieux que vous partiez tout de suite. — *I should prefer you to ...*

J'en voudrais des vertes **de préférence** *or* **J'en prendrais plutôt** des vertes. — *I'd rather have*

Il vaudrait mieux en acheter *or* **Il me paraît préférable d'**en acheter un tout petit. — *it would be better to ...*

Cela m'arrangerait mieux vendredi. Vendredi **me conviendrait mieux.** — *... would suit me better*

J'aime autant ne pas vous dire son nom. — *I'd as soon not*

Ils ont **une préférence marquée** *or* **une prédilection pour** les petits restaurants de campagne. — *they have a marked preference for*

EXPRESSING INDIFFERENCE

Croyez-moi, **il m'est complètement égal qu'**il vienne ou non. — *it's all the same to me whether*

Très honnêtement *or* Sans façons, **je n'ai aucune préférence là-dessus.** — *I have no particular preference*

C'est comme vous voulez: elles me plaisent toutes les deux. — *it's as you please:*

Il faut reconnaître que **cela n'a aucune espèce d'importance** *or* **n'a pas la moindre importance.** — *it's of no importance whatsoever*

Le genre de livres qu'il lit **ne m'intéresse absolument pas** *or* **me laisse froid.** — *... doesn't interest me in the slightest*

AND, ACCORDING TO CONTEXT:

peu importe / bof! à vous de décider / avez-vous envie de / je n'arrive pas à me décider / ça ne m'emballe pas / dans l'ensemble c'est bien / cela dépend de / j'admire la façon dont / j'en ai vraiment assez de

INTENTIONS AND DESIRES

ASKING WHAT SOMEONE INTENDS OR WANTS

Que comptez-vous faire? // Qu'envisagez-vous de faire? — *what do you intend to do?*

Il nous serait utile de connaître vos intentions à cet égard. — *it would be useful to know what your intentions are*

Pourquoi *or* **Dans quel but** suivez-vous des cours d'art dramatique? — *why*

Je n'arrive pas à comprendre ce que **vous comptez** obtenir en agissant ainsi. — *what you are hoping to ...*

Il serait souhaitable que vous **fassiez part de vos intentions aux** membres de l'association. — *better if you were to communicate your intentions to the ...*

Nous cherchons à découvrir ce que nos clients **souhaitent** trouver à leur disposition. — *want to know what our clients expect to find*

SAYING WHAT YOU INTEND

Un jour, j'achèterai une petite maison à la campagne. **Je vais** y aller demain. — *(use of future tense) I'm going to ...*

Je voulais lui en parler *or* **J'avais l'intention de lui en parler,** mais j'ai oublié. — *I was going to speak to him about it*

Je n'ai pas la moindre intention *or* **Il n'est pas dans mes intentions de** lui communiquer mes conclusions à ce sujet. — *I have no intention of*

Ce que je cherchais, c'était *or* **Ce que je voulais, c'était** lui faire prendre conscience de ses responsabilités. — *what I wanted to do was to ...*

Il a emprunté des livres à la bibliothèque **pour** *or* **dans le but de** *or* **dans l'intention de** se renseigner sur les coléoptères. — *with the aim of*

J'envisage de faire agrandir la cuisine l'année prochaine. — *I intend to ...*

Il avait **formé le projet de** restaurer un vieux château. — *was planning to ...*

Nous nous proposons de nommer un expert qui sera responsable de cette partie du programme. — *we propose to ...*

Il a prévu de partir en voyage d'affaires le mois prochain. — *he planned to ...*

SAYING WHAT YOU WANT TO DO OR NOT DO

Je veux maigrir de quatre kilos. — *I want to ...*

Je veux que l'entrée soit repeinte avant Noël. — *I want*

Je voudrais m'entretenir avec lui aussi rapidement que possible. — *I'd like to ...*

Je désire que ce rapport soit expédié à tous les membres du comité. // **Je désire** leur faire parvenir ce rapport. — *I want*

Il faut que toutes les dispositions soient prises avant l'automne. — *it's essential that*

J'ai décidé d'inviter toute la famille à la maison pour Noël. — *I have decided to ...*

Il est résolu à *or* **Il est bien décidé à** faire le tour du monde en bateau. — *he is determined to ...*

Elle a pris la résolution de faire 5 heures de travail bénévole par semaine. — *she resolved to ...*

Je tiens à ce que tout le monde soit prévenu des modifications dès demain. — *I want everyone to be ...*

Il n'est pas question de vendre la voiture. — *there is no question of*

Je m'oppose formellement à ce qu'on lui accorde *(subj)* un délai supplémentaire. — *I am absolutely against*

SAYING WHAT YOU WOULD LIKE

Je voudrais *or* **J'aimerais** deux places pour demain soir, mais je crains que ce ne soit complet. — *I'd like (to have)*

j'ai envie d'aller au cinéma. — *I'd like to ...*

Je voudrais exprimer ma reconnaissance à tous ceux qui m'ont aidé dans cette tâche difficile. — *I'd like to ...*

J'aurais aimé pouvoir le féliciter moi-même. — *I should have liked to be able to ...*

Si seulement j'avais un peu plus de temps libre! // **J'aimerais tellement** avoir un peu plus de temps libre! — *if only I had*

Il faut espérer que tout se déroulera comme prévu. — *it is to be hoped that*

Il est à souhaiter que *or* **Il serait souhaitable que** les pays occidentaux prennent conscience de leurs responsabilités dans ce domaine. — *it is to be hoped that*

Je forme le souhait que *or* **Je fais le vœu que** les liens entre nos deux associations se développent. — *what I wish is that*

AND, ACCORDING TO CONTEXT:

j'aimerais savoir ce que vous en pensez / nous aimerions prendre connaissance des objectifs ... / je pense avoir fini d'ici la fin de l'année / je voudrais qu'on + *subj* / il songe à écrire un roman / il nous a fait part de son désir de / il veut à tout prix le faire / on exige actuellement / il a refusé de le faire / elle rêve de faire du cinéma

PERMISSION

ASKING FOR PERMISSION

Puis-je *or* **Pourrais-je** être transféré dans un autre groupe?	*may I*
Me serait-il possible d'avoir un radiateur supplémentaire dans ma chambre?	*would it be possible for me to ...*
J'espère que cela ne vous ennuiera pas si je change quelques détails au dernier moment.	*I hope it won't bother you if*
J'aimerais bien participer au stage, **si cela ne vous dérange pas.**	*I'd like to ... if it is no trouble*
Me permettez-vous de *or* **M'autorisez-vous à** me servir de votre ordinateur?	*would you allow me to ...*
Voyez-vous un inconvénient à ce que *or* **Avez-vous une objection à ce que** j'annule *(subj)* les réservations?	*would you have any objection to my ...*
Auriez-vous la gentillesse de me prêter votre voiture?	*would you be kind enough to ...*
Est-il permis d'emprunter *or* **Nous est-il permis d'**emprunter des dictionnaires à la bibliothèque?	*are people allowed to ...*

GIVING PERMISSION

Vous pouvez en acheter un neuf, si vous voulez.	*you may*
Je vous en prie, faites ce que vous jugez nécessaire en pareilles circonstances.	*by all means, do ...*
Je consens avec plaisir **à ce que** vous partiez au Canada en voyage d'études.	*I agree willingly that you should ...*
Je vous permets de terminer votre rapport la semaine prochaine.	*I give you my permission to ...*
Je vous autorise bien volontiers à lui en parler. // Naturellement, **vous êtes autorisé à** lui en parler.	*I certainly authorise you to ...*

REFUSING PERMISSION

Vous ne pouvez pas vous inscrire à plus de cinq cours par semaine.	*you can't*
Je ne vous permets pas de *or* **Je ne vous autorise pas à** lui envoyer ces photographies.	*I will not allow you to ...*
Je regrette de ne pouvoir consentir à votre projet.	*I am sorry I cannot agree to*
Je crains d'être dans l'obligation de vous décevoir en ce qui concerne votre demande.	*I am afraid I must disappoint you*
Je préférerais que vous n'y alliez **pas** pour le moment.	*I'd rather you didn't ...*
Je refuse absolument que *or* **Je m'oppose absolument à ce que** tu abandonnes *(subj)* tes études!	*I absolutely refuse to allow you to ...*
Je vous interdis formellement de communiquer avec nos concurrents.	*I categorically forbid you to ...*

HAVING PERMISSION OR NOT HAVING IT

Il m'est interdit *or* **Il m'est défendu de** fumer.	*I have been forbidden to ...*
Mon médecin m'**interdit** l'alcool.	*my doctor has banned*
Il s'oppose catégoriquement à ce que je demande *(subj)* une entrevue avec le directeur.	*he is totally against my ...*
Il est défendu de consulter le grand catalogue.	*it is against the rules to ...*
Il est formellement interdit de rouler à bicyclette sur les trottoirs.	*it is strictly prohibited to ...*
On m'a permis de payer le solde en plusieurs versements.	*I have been allowed to ...*
Il m'a dit que **je pouvais** m'absenter une heure ou deux si j'en avais envie.	*he said I could ... if I wanted to*
Nous ne sommes pas tenus de *or* **obligés de** soumettre un rapport chaque semaine.	*we don't have to ...*
Je suis autorisé à signer les bons de commande à sa place.	*I am authorised to ...*
Vous n'êtes pas censé déjeuner à la cantine si vous ne faites pas partie du personnel.	*you are not supposed to ...*
Ils le laissent boire du café bien qu'il n'ait que trois ans.	*they let him*
Ces formalités **peuvent effectivement** être accomplies par les parents de l'intéressé.	*may indeed be carried out by*
Pour ce type de calcul, **on permet** *or* **on autorise** 3% d'erreur dans les deux sens.	*3% error is allowable*

AND, ACCORDING TO CONTEXT:

je voulais vous demander si on peut / si vous êtes d'accord / je crains de ne pouvoir / accepteriez-vous que je ... / si c'est possible, je préférerais / il me serait très difficile de / tenez-vous vraiment à ce que / je suppose que oui / si c'est absolument nécessaire / si vous ne pouvez vraiment pas faire autrement / à la rigueur / je n'y vois pas d'inconvénient / cela m'est égal / faites comme vous voudrez / ce n'est pas possible / je regrette / vous ne devez en aucun cas / il n'en est pas question / je n'ai eu aucune difficulté à obtenir son accord / on m'a donné carte blanche / il s'est résigné à me laisser / il n'a pas formulé d'objections

OBLIGATION

SAYING WHAT SOMEONE MUST DO

Vous devez absolument faire preuve de plus de tolérance, sinon la situation deviendra impossible.	*you really must*
Toute commande de plus de **1000 F doit** être contresignée par le directeur.	*... must be ...*
J'ai le devoir de vous informer que votre demande a été rejetée.	*it is my duty to ...*
Il faut absolument lui présenter vos excuses. // **Il faut absolument que** vous lui présentiez vos excuses.	*you absolutely must*
On ne peut entrer à l'université **si on n'a pas** le baccalauréat.	*you cannot ... without ...*
Cette grève **m'oblige** *or* **me force à** reporter mon départ à demain.	*the strike forces me to ...*
Vous êtes obligé de prendre un avocat pour vous défendre.	*you have got to ...*
Elle s'est trouvée obligée de rester deux heures de plus.	*she found herself having to ...*
Il s'est vu contraint de demander au directeur d'intervenir.	*he found himself forced to ...*
Il est obligatoire de payer la somme entière au 1er janvier.	*it is compulsory to ...*
Ce n'est pas que j'aie envie de le faire, mais **on m'y force** *or* **j'y suis forcé.**	*I find myself forced to*
Encore une fois, **je me vois dans l'obligation de** solliciter un prêt.	*I find myself forced to ...*
Il est indispensable de le signaler *or* **Il est indispensable que** ce soit signalé dans les 24 heures qui suivent l'accident.	*it is essential to ...*
Vous prendrez deux de ces comprimés chaque matin.	*(use of future tense in orders)*
Pour obtenir ce document, **on ne peut** s'adresser **qu'au** consulat.	*in order to ... you have to ...*
Je ne peux faire autrement que d'accepter.	*I cannot do other than accept*
On m'a chargé d'organiser le programme du séminaire.	*I have been given the task of*
On exige que les candidats aient de solides connaissances en algèbre.	*candidates must have*
Il est spécifié que *or* **Il est stipulé que** le mode d'emploi doit aussi figurer sur le paquet.	*it is laid down that*

(enquiring if one is obliged to do something)

Est-il nécessaire d'avoir une carte d'entrée? // **Faut-il** *or* **Doit-on** avoir une carte d'entrée?	*is it necessary to ...*
Faut-il vraiment prendre *or* **Faut-il vraiment que** je prenne un parapluie? // **Est-ce que j'ai vraiment besoin de** prendre un parapluie?	*must I really*

SAYING WHAT SOMEONE IS NOT OBLIGED TO DO

On n'a pas besoin de les prévenir si longtemps à l'avance.	*there is no need to ...*
Vous n'êtes pas obligé *or* **Vous n'êtes pas forcé de** déjeuner à la cantine.	*you don't have to ...*
Je ne vous oblige pas à me dire de qui il s'agit.	*I am not forcing you to ...*
Il n'est pas obligatoire d'avoir ses papiers d'identité sur soi.	*... is not compulsory*
Il n'est pas nécessaire *or* **Il n'est pas indispensable de** téléphoner pour confirmer.	*it is not necessary to ...*
Ce n'était pas la peine de traduire tout le premier chapitre.	*it wasn't worthwhile*
Il n'est pas utile de lui demander son avis.	*there's no point in*
Vous n'avez pas à lui dire ce qu'il doit faire.	*you don't have to ...*
Il s'est cru obligé de démissionner.	*he thought he had to ...*

SAYING WHAT SOMEONE MUST NOT DO

On n'a pas le droit de se présenter plus de trois fois à l'examen.	*one is not allowed to ...*
Il est interdit *or* **Il est défendu de** garer sa voiture sur un passage protégé.	*it is forbidden to ...*
Il ne faut pas empêcher un enfant de se faire des amis.	*one must not*
Vous ne pouvez pas vous absenter plus de trois jours par mois.	*you must not*
On ne peut pas demander de carte de séjour **tant qu'on n'a pas** *or* **si on n'a pas** de domicile fixe.	*you cannot ... unless you ...*
Je ne vous permets pas de me parler sur ce ton.	*I will not allow you to ...*
Je vous interdis *or* **Je ne vous permets pas** d'y aller seul.	*I forbid you to ...*
Nous ne pouvons tolérer un tel manque de soin.	*we cannot allow*
Surtout ne lui en parlez pas.	*whatever you do, don't ...*

AND, ACCORDING TO CONTEXT:

il est de mon devoir de / je suis dans la nécessité de / il vous appartient de / il est indispensable de / bon gré mal gré / il est extrêmement important de / on est censé connaître / je n'ai pas le choix / il m'est impossible de faire autrement / je n'ai pas pu m'empêcher de / on n'y peut rien / pour des raisons indépendantes de ma volonté / au pis-aller on pourrait / si c'est une question de vie ou de mort / je ne veux pas vous y contraindre / ne vous sentez pas obligé de / je ne vous impose pas de ...

AGREEMENT

AGREEING WITH A STATEMENT

Nous sommes du même avis que vous sur ce point. // **Nous sommes entièrement de votre avis** *or* **Nous partageons votre avis** *or* **Nous partageons vos sentiments** sur ce point.	*we agree with you*
Je suis entièrement d'accord avec ce que vous avez dit à ce sujet.	*I entirely agree with*
Comme vous, je suis d'avis que nous remettions la décision à plus tard.	*like you, I believe that*
Vous avez bien raison *or* **Vous avez entièrement raison** de vouloir clarifier la situation dès maintenant.	*you are quite right to ...*
Comme vous l'avez fait remarquer, **il est vrai que** *or* **il est juste que** nous ne disposons pas encore de toutes les données nécessaires.	*it is true that*
Je reconnais que *or* **J'admets que** Richard ne manque pas d'intelligence.	*I admit that*
Je conviens que le problème est délicat.	*I agree that*
Je comprends très bien que vous hésitiez à laisser votre mère toute seule pendant si longtemps.	*I fully understand that*
Je vous accorde que j'ai peut-être manqué de tact.	*I grant you that*
Sans doute avez-vous raison quand vous affirmez que c'est plus facile, mais ...	*you are probably right when you say*

AGREEING TO A PROPOSAL

Je suis d'accord pour que vous repreniez contact avec eux dès la première occasion.	*I agree that you should*
Nous avons pris connaissance de votre projet et **nous nous empressons de donner notre accord.**	*we hasten to give our agreement*
Nous donnons notre accord à la réfection des locaux.	*we agree to ...*
Je suis en accord avec ce que vous proposez.	*I agree with what ...*
J'accepte vos propositions **dans les grandes lignes.**	*I am broadly in agreement with*
J'accepte de consulter un expert sur ce point, comme vous me le suggérez.	*I agree we should*
Je suis heureux d'apporter mon soutien à cette proposition. // **Je suis heureux de donner mon assentiment à** ce plan.	*I am happy to support*
Je ne manquerai pas d'appuyer votre demande au cours de la prochaine réunion du comité.	*I shall certainly support*
Après la lecture des modalités de vente, **nous souscrivons à** toutes vos propositions.	*we agree to*
Je trouve que tu as raison de suggérer le mois de septembre pour partir en vacances.	*I think you are right to ...*
J'ai appris que vous aviez retiré votre candidature, et **je ne peux que vous donner raison.**	*I can only agree with you*
Il est entendu que vous n'en parlez à personne.	*it is agreed that*
À première vue, **cela semble exactement ce dont nous avons besoin, mais** je crains que ce ne soit très cher.	*it seems just what we need, but ...*

AGREEING TO A REQUEST

J'accepte avec grand plaisir votre aimable invitation. // **C'est avec grand plaisir que j'accepte** votre aimable invitation.	*I have much pleasure in accepting*
Je quitterai donc l'appartement le 22 septembre, **ainsi que vous me l'avez demandé** *or* **comme vous me l'avez demandé.**	*as you asked me to*
Je tiens à vous assurer que **je suivrai vos instructions à la lettre.**	*I shall follow your instructions to the letter*
Je ne manquerai pas de tenir compte de vos observations en ce qui concerne la préparation du programme.	*I shall certainly follow your advice about*
Nous essayerons naturellement **de nous conformer à vos désirs** dans le choix des matériaux.	*we shall try to meet your preferences*
Je serai enchanté *or* **Je serai ravi d'**aller chercher votre tante à la gare.	*I shall be delighted to ...*
Nous prenons bonne note de votre commande, que nous honorerons dans les plus brefs délais.	*we have noted*
La date qui a été retenue **me convient parfaitement.**	*... suits me perfectly*

AND, ACCORDING TO CONTEXT:

c'est une bonne idée / cela me semble convenir / cela me plaît beaucoup / je suis prêt à / il est évident que / je suis enclin à penser que / il est difficile de trouver à y redire / je m'associe à tout ce qui a été dit / il est absolument exact que / il est indéniable que / j'en suis convaincu / il n'est pas faux de dire

DISAGREEMENT

DISAGREEING WITH WHAT SOMEONE HAS SAID

Il est faux de dire *or* **Il n'est pas juste de dire que** le travail a été fait sans soin.	*it is wrong to say*
Il est faux que vous m'ayez vu au restaurant, je n'y étais pas.	*it is untrue that*
Je ne suis pas d'accord avec vous *or* **Je suis en désaccord avec vous sur** ce point.	*I don't agree with you*
Vous vous trompez si vous croyez que j'ai envie d'y aller.	*you're wrong*
Je lui accorde que la présentation n'est pas très claire, mais **il s'agit néanmoins d'une erreur.**	*there has still been a mistake*
Vous avez tort de croire que notre oubli était volontaire.	*you are wrong to ...*
Je vous donne tort de lui avoir répondu sur ce ton.	*I think you were wrong to ...*
Je ne partage pas votre point de vue là-dessus.	*I don't share your opinion*
Je rejette les arguments que vous avancez.	*I reject*
Je suis catégoriquement opposé à la vivisection. // **Je suis absolument contre** la vivisection.	*I am absolutely opposed to*
Il m'est impossible d'accepter votre point de vue là-dessus.	*I cannot accept*
Je nie catégoriquement être intervenu auprès du directeur.	*I flatly deny*
Je ne comprends pas que vous puissiez partir en vacances dans des circonstances pareilles.	*I can't understand how*
Sans vouloir vous vexer, **je vois la chose tout à fait différemment.**	*I see it quite differently*
Je suis désolé de devoir vous contredire *or* **Je suis navré de devoir vous contredire,** mais je l'ai vu moi-même.	*I am sorry to have to contradict you, but ...*

DISAGREEING WITH WHAT SOMEONE PROPOSES

Il ne vous est plus possible *or* **Il vous est impossible de** changer le programme maintenant.	*it's impossible to ...*
Je ne suis pas d'accord pour qu'on annule *(subj)* la réunion.	*I don't agree one should*
Nous nous opposons catégoriquement à la construction d'un supermarché dans le village.	*we are totally opposed to*
Je refuse de vous laisser changer l'emploi du temps.	*I refuse to ...*
Puisque vous pensez à donner votre démission, je vous préviens que **j'y mettrai mon veto.**	*I shall veto it*
Je crains fort de ne pouvoir approuver votre démarche.	*I'm afraid I can't approve*
Je suis au regret de ne pouvoir appuyer votre demande.	*I am sorry I cannot support*
C'est très gentil à vous d'offrir de m'aider, **mais je crois que je vais y arriver tout seul.**	*I think I can manage*
Je regrette sincèrement de ne pas être en mesure d'accepter votre aimable proposition.	*I am sorry I cannot accept your kind offer*

REFUSING A REQUEST

Il m'est vraiment impossible de le faire avant samedi.	*I cannot possibly do it*
Je ne pourrai malheureusement pas rencontrer votre représentant, comme vous l'aviez demandé.	*unfortunately I cannot*
En raison du nombre de dossiers en attente, **il m'est difficile de** donner suite à votre demande.	*it is difficult for me to ...*
Je ne suis pas en mesure de répondre à une telle question, car ce sujet est très délicat.	*I am not in a position to ...*
Nous regrettons de ne pouvoir donner suite à vos propositions.	*we are sorry we cannot go ahead with*
Il est hors de question que je m'en occupe *(subj)* en ce moment.	*it is out of the question for me to ...*
Je refuse absolument d'exécuter un plan qui a été conçu à la hâte.	*I totally refuse to ...*
Jamais je n'accepterai de travailler avec lui.	*I will never agree to ...*
Bien que je sois très sensible à l'honneur que vous me faites, **je dois malheureusement décliner** votre invitation.	*I am unfortunately unable to accept*
Nous sommes au regret de vous faire savoir que nous ne pourrons pas exécuter votre commande dans les délais habituels.	*we regret to have to inform you that we cannot*

AND, ACCORDING TO CONTEXT:

votre interprétation est tendancieuse / je n'admets pas / comment osez-vous dire / de quel droit vous permettez-vous de critiquer / je rejette votre insinuation / je me demande si vous y avez bien réfléchi / peut-être n'êtes-vous pas au courante de / permettez-moi de vous faire remarquer que / en théorie ... mais en réalité ... / il est déplorable que / il est vraiment fort regrettable que / je doute fort que / il est inexact de dire / les faits sont en contradiction avec / c'est loin de la vérité / il me serait très difficile de me libérer / je voudrais pouvoir vous aider, mais ...

APPROVAL

Quelle excellente idée!	*what an excellent idea!*
Vous avez bien fait de le prévenir aussitôt.	*you did right to ...*
Je trouve que vous avez raison *or* **Je trouve que vous n'avez pas tort de** vouloir chercher de nouveaux débouchés aux États-Unis.	*I think you are right to ...*
Nous vous approuvons dans votre décision de remettre *or* **Nous vous approuvons d'avoir décidé de** remettre la réunion à la semaine prochaine.	*we agree with your decision to ...*
Nous sommes en faveur de *or* **Nous sommes favorable à** ce changement d'attitude.	*we are in favour of*
Je trouve bon qu'il approfondisse ainsi sa culture générale.	*I approve of his ...*
J'ai beaucoup apprécié la gentillesse avec laquelle il nous a offert ses services.	*I greatly appreciated*
J'ai bien aimé la mise en scène. // La mise en scène **m'a beaucoup plu.**	*I liked very much*
Le grand mérite de ce projet, c'est qu'il peut être réalisé très rapidement.	*the great merit of this project is that*

(more formally)

Nous acceptons vos propositions dans les grandes lignes, mais souhaitons recevoir de plus amples détails.	*we accept*
Ce livre **est le bienvenu** car il apporte un nouvel éclairage sur la question.	*... is very welcome*
L'auteur souligne ce détail **à juste titre** *or* **avec raison.**	*... rightly emphasises ...*
On ne peut qu'admirer la clarté avec laquelle il présente les faits.	*one can but admire*
Nous approuvons sans réserve toute initiative de votre part.	*we approve*
Nous accueillons avec enthousiasme le projet de restauration des remparts.	*we welcome wholeheartedly*
En définitive, **nous portons un jugement favorable sur** ce qui a été fait jusqu'à présent.	*we are favourably impressed by*
Nous apportons par avance notre soutien à *or* **Nous accordons par avance notre soutien à** tous ceux qui prennent la défense de ces victimes.	*we declare our support for*

AND, ACCORDING TO CONTEXT:

c'est exactement ce que j'espérais / nous sommes entièrement d'accord / on comprend fort bien que / cela vaut la peine de / il était grand temps que / cet exemple mérite d'être suivi / il serait effectivement souhaitable que

DISAPPROVAL

Je désapprouve toute démarche visant à supprimer cette partie du programme.	*I disapprove of*
Je vous reproche de ne pas avoir terminé à temps.	*I blame you for not ...*
Il n'aurait pas dû présenter la chose sous cet angle-là.	*he shouldn't have*
Vous auriez plutôt dû *or* **Vous auriez mieux fait de** lui suggérer de partir le premier.	*you would have been better to ...*
Je trouve qu'il a eu tort de procéder ainsi.	*I think he was wrong to ...*
Je n'ai guère apprécié la façon dont le débat a été mené.	*I didn't think much of*
Cette idée **me déplaît profondément.**	*I am profoundly unhappy about*
Il est regrettable que *or* **Il est (fort) dommage que** la commande ait été exécutée avec tant de retard.	*it is a (great) pity that*
Je ne peux que regretter l'absence de conclusions dans un rapport par ailleurs excellent.	*I can only regret*
Je condamne l'intransigeance dont vous avez fait preuve dans cette affaire.	*I condemn*
Je me sens tenu d'exprimer ma désapprobation devant le coût astronomique de cette réalisation.	*I feel bound to express my disapproval of*
Je ne puis admettre *or* **Je ne puis tolérer** *or* **Je ne supporte pas** un tel manque de franchise.	*I cannot tolerate*
Je ne comprends pas comment on peut négliger un tel problème. // **Il me semble incompréhensible qu'**on puisse négliger un tel problème.	*I can't understand how*
Je suis profondément déçu par les résultats du deuxième trimestre.	*I am profoundly disappointed by*
Je suis farouchement opposé à la vivisection.	*I am fiercely opposed to*
Je proteste contre *or* **Je m'élève contre** la sévérité avec laquelle il a été traité.	*I protest against*
De quel droit se permet-on de changer des dispositions aussi importantes sans prévenir?	*what right has anyone to ...*

AND, ACCORDING TO CONTEXT:

je suis consterné de / cela laisse à désirer / il n'y a vraiment pas de quoi être fier / cela ne me dit rien qui vaille / je n'aime pas sa façon de / cela pourrait être désastreux / je répugne à / je déplore / c'est absolument scandaleux / je commence à en avoir assez de / je ne veux pas en entrendre parler

CERTAINTY, POSSIBILITY AND CAPABILITY

EXPRESSING CERTAINTY

Je suis sûr que *or* **Je suis certain que** j'ai expédié ces documents hier. // **Je suis sûr d'**avoir *or* **certain d'**avoir expédié ces documents hier.	*I am sure that*
Nous sommes convaincus *or* **Nous sommes persuadés** qu'un tel projet permettrait de redonner vie au village.	*we are convinced that*
Il ne fait aucun doute que la proposition sera rejetée. // **Sans aucun doute,** la proposition sera rejetée.	*there is no doubt that*
Il est certain que *or* **Il est évident que** le nouveau règlement va compliquer les choses.	*it is clear that*
Il est incontestable que *or* **Il est indéniable que** leur situation financière est bien plus saine que l'an dernier.	*it is indisputable that*
Il est hors de doute que le nouveau centre culturel attirera un public de jeunes. // **Nul doute que** le nouveau centre n'attire *(subj)* un public de jeunes.	*there is no doubt that*
Il va sans dire que cette commande sera suivie de beaucoup d'autres.	*it goes without saying that*
Il faut bien reconnaître que *or* **Il faut bien admettre que** les désavantages sont considérables.	*it must be recognised that*
De toute évidence, le nouveau système est très coûteux. // **Il faut se rendre à l'évidence**: le nouveau système est très coûteux.	*from the evidence it is clear that*
Qu'il soit intelligent, **personne ne peut le nier.**	*no one can deny that*
Le doute n'est plus permis quant à son rôle dans cette affaire.	*there can be no more doubt about*
J'ai la conviction qu'il *or* **J'ai la certitude qu'**il nous a menti.	*I am convinced that*
Nous ne manquerons pas de vous communiquer les résultats de l'enquête.	*we shall not fail to ...*
Tout me porte à croire qu'il faut se mettre en rapport avec eux immédiatement.	*everything leads me to believe that*

EXPRESSING PROBABILITY

Il est probable que le comité se réunira le mois prochain. // Le comité se réunira **probablement** le mois prochain.	*it is probable that*
Il doit lui être arrivé un accident. // **Il a dû avoir** un accident. // **Il a sans doute eu** un accident.	*he has doubtless had ...*
Le chèque que je vous ai envoyé **devrait** vous parvenir avant la fin de la semaine.	*... should reach you ...*
On dirait que le temps va changer.	*it looks as though*
Vous avez dû en être informé par vos collègues.	*you must have been told*
Cela ne m'étonnerait pas qu'il n'ait pas l'argent nécessaire.	*I would not be surprised if*
Je pense m'absenter pour affaires la semaine prochaine.	*I am thinking of*
Je crois que la nouvelle machine sera installée bientôt.	*I think that*
Il y a de fortes chances que le projet ne soit pas mis à exécution.	*there is a strong chance that*
Il est bien possible qu'il n'en ait pas été informé.	*it is very possible that*
Il semble bien que votre demande n'ait pas été considerérée avec les autres.	*it seems likely that*
Il se pourrait bien qu'il y ait des retards à cause de la grève.	*it is quite possible that*
Sans doute a-t-il été obligé de modifier le programme.	*doubtless he has had to ...*
Tout semble indiquer qu'il y a eu un accident.	*everything seems to point to the fact that*

EXPRESSING POSSIBILITY

Il s'agit **peut-être** du nouvel élève.	*perhaps*
Peut-être est-il déjà trop tard pour s'inscrire. // **Peut-être qu'**il est déjà trop tard pour s'inscrire. // Il est **peut-être** déjà trop tard pour s'inscrire.	*perhaps it is*
La situation **peut** changer du jour au lendemain.	*... could change ...*
Il est possible que la baisse du prix du pétrole ait un effet néfaste sur l'économie.	*it is possible that*
Est-il possible que l'on ne nous ait pas dit toute la vérité?	*is it possible that*
Il n'est pas impossible que sa demande soit acceptée.	*it is not impossible that*
Ils pourraient déjà avoir passé un accord avec une compagnie rivale.	*they could already have ...*
Il se peut que je sois de passage à Paris la semaine prochaine.	*it may be that*
Il se pourrait que le conseil municipal en décide autrement.	*it could be that*
Il me semble que les conditions de travail sont en train de s'améliorer. // Les conditions de travail s'améliorent, **semble-t-il.**	*it seems that*
Il arrive qu'on découvre encore des chefs-d'œuvre inconnus.	*it happens that*
À ce qu'il paraît, des progrès considérables ont été accomplis.	*as far as one can make out*

EXPRESSING DOUBT

Je doute fort qu'elle puisse venir demain. — *I doubt if*

Il est douteux qu'elle puisse arriver avant la fin de la semaine. — *it is doubtful whether*

Je doute d'avoir jamais fait une telle proposition. — *I doubt if I ever . . .*

Le doute subsiste quant au nombre exact des victimes. — *there is still some doubt about*

D'après ce qu'on dit, **il n'est pas sûr** *or* **il n'est pas certain qu'**elle soit malade. — *it is not certain that*

Elle n'est **pas forcément** malade. — *she's not necessarily ill*

Je ne suis pas sûr *or* **Je ne suis pas certain** *or* **Je ne suis pas convaincu de** pouvoir vous en donner une explication satisfaisante. — *I am not sure I can . . .*

Il serait étonnant que *or* **Cela m'étonnerait que** des fonds suffisants aient été réunis. — *I'd be surprised if*

Nous sommes encore incertains quant au choix des matériaux. — *we are still unsure about*

Nous sommes encore dans l'incertitude en ce qui concerne le sort des victimes. — *we are still in the dark about*

Rien ne permet de penser que la nouvelle méthode soit plus économique. — *nothing leads us to believe that*

On ne sait pas encore exactement *or* **On ne sait pas encore au juste ce que** le président va proposer. — *as yet no one knows exactly what*

Nous nous demandons si nous devons accepter leurs propositions. — *we are wondering whether*

EXPRESSING IMPROBABILITY

Il est peu probable que *or* **Il n'est guère probable que** la réforme soit acceptée. — *it is very improbable that*

Il risque d'y avoir un retard dans la livraison. // Les marchandises **risquent de** ne pas arriver à temps. — *there could be a delay*

Vous n'en avez **probablement pas** encore entendu parler. — *you probably haven't*

Cela m'étonnerait vraiment qu'il soit reçu à son permis de conduire. — *I'd be amazed if*

Il ne semble pas qu'elle soit malade. — *it doesn't seem as if she's ill*

Il y a peu de chances qu'on puisse enrayer l'épidémie. — *there is not much chance that*

Il est douteux que le nouveau système soit réellement supérieur. — *it is doubtful whether*

Je crains fort que nous n'arrivions pas à nous entendre sur ce point. — *I doubt very much whether we shall ever*

EXPRESSING IMPOSSIBILITY

Il n'est pas possible que *or* **Il est impossible que** les marchandises aient été endommagées en transit. — *it is not possible that*

Il ne peut s'agir de la même personne. — *it can't . . .*

Il m'est matériellement impossible de m'absenter la semaine prochaine. — *it is totally impossible for me to . . .*

Il n'y a aucune chance que nous terminions cette traduction à temps. // **Nous n'avons aucune chance de** terminer cette traduction à temps. — *there's no chance that*

Il est absolument exclu que nous leur soumettions les plans à l'avance. — *it is out of the question for us to . . .*

Je suis malheureusement dans l'impossibilité d'accepter votre aimable offre. — *unfortunately it is impossible for me to . . .*

Toute collaboration avec eux **est hors de question. // Il est hors de question que** nous collaborions avec eux. — *is out of the question*

Le changement de gouvernement **a rendu impossible** toute négociation à ce sujet. — *has ruled out*

EXPRESSING WHAT SOMEONE IS ABLE OR UNABLE TO DO

Les candidats doivent **être capables de** traduire des textes scientifiques. — *must be able to . . .*

Savez-vous vous servir de la nouvelle machine? — *do you know how to . . .*

Il sait faire du ski/nager. — *he can . . .*

Je comprends le français. — *I can understand French*

Je vois la maison sur la colline. // **J'arrive tout juste** *or* **Je peux tout juste** en distinguer les contours. — *I can see // I can just see*

Il est incapable de prendre une décision. // **Il ne sait pas** prendre une décision. — *he is quite unable to . . .*

Je ne sais pas comment vous l'expliquer, mais si vous le comparez à l'autre, il est . . . — *I don't know how to explain it to you*

Il n'a pas l'aptitude nécessaire pour le travail. — *he hasn't the aptitude for*

Je peux me libérer pour 17 heures. // **Il m'est possible de** me libérer pour 17 heures. — *it's possible for me to . . .*

Je peux vous prêter 5000 F. // **Je suis en mesure de** vous prêter 5000 F. — *I am able to . . .*

Je suis dans l'impossibilité de me rendre à Paris pour cette conférence. — *it is impossible for me to . . .*

Nous sommes à même de vous proposer les conditions suivantes. — *we are in a position to . . .*

EXPLANATIONS

PREPOSITIONS

Il n'a pas pu accepter le poste **à cause de** sa situation de famille.	*because of*
Il a refusé, **pour raisons de** santé.	*for ... reasons*
Elle a obtenu de l'avancement **grâce au** tact dont elle a fait preuve.	*thanks to*
Il n'a pas terminé sa dissertation, **faute de** temps.	*for lack of*
Le vol AF232 a été retardé **en raison des** conditions météorologiques.	*owing to*
Avec tout ce qui se passe en ce moment, les gens n'osent plus sortir le soir.	*with*
Bien des gens ont annulé leurs projets de vacances **par suite de** *or* **à la suite de** la hausse du prix du pétrole.	*as a result of*
En échange de leur collaboration, nous leur avons permis d'utiliser nos archives.	*in return for*

CONJUNCTIONS

On lui a donné le poste d'inspecteur **parce qu'**il avait obtenu d'excellents résultats.	*because*
Les négociations sont dans l'impasse **car** les syndicats rejettent les nouvelles propositions.	*for*
Comme il se faisait tard, elle a pris un taxi.	*as*
Essayez de vous coucher tôt, **puisque** vous êtes si fatigué.	*since*
Il m'est difficile de m'absenter en ce moment; je ne peux **donc** pas envisager un séjour à l'étranger.	*therefore*
Si elle les a convoqués, **c'est qu'**elle veut leur parler.	*since she ... she must ...*
Étant donné que *or* **Puisque** vous serez absent, il faudra bien qu'elle s'en occupe à votre place.	*since, as*
Il refuse de partir en vacances, **de crainte d'**être cambriolé *or* **de crainte qu'**on ne le cambriole *(subj)*.	*for fear of/that*
Vous vous croyez dispensé du moindre effort **sous prétexte que** vous n'y comprenez rien.	*on the grounds that*
Vu *or* **Étant donné** la situation économique actuelle, on ne peut espérer de reprise avant 1995.	*in view of*
On ne peut pas se fier à ces chiffres, **attendu que** *or* **vu que** les calculs sont approximatifs.	*in view of the fact that*
La tension sociale existera **tant que** le taux du chômage augmentera.	*as long as*
Ils ont considérablement développé leur réseau, **si bien qu'**ils ont maintenant des succursales dans la plupart des régions.	*with the result that*

OTHER USEFUL VOCABULARY

À Glins, les ouvriers sont en grève: **en effet,** la direction envisage de supprimer un certain nombre d'emplois.	*(juxtaposition of effect and cause, + 'en effet')*
La crue de la Moselle **a causé** des dégâts importants.	*caused*
Voilà de quoi il s'agit: je voudrais faire restaurer une partie de la maison.	*it's like this:*
Tout ceci **est dû à** *or* **provient de** la pénurie de matières premières.	*is due to / comes from*
Cela **tient à** *or* **résulte de** son attitude initiale.	*arises from*
Cette erreur **vient de ce que** nous ne disposions pas des renseignements nécessaires.	*comes from the fact that*
C'est la hausse du dollar qui **a provoqué** cette crise.	*provoked*
Tout ceci **remonte à** la décision de vendre le terrain.	*goes back to*
Son refus **est lié à** des problèmes personnels.	*is to do with*
Par la suite **il s'est avéré que** les fonds étaient insuffisants.	*it transpired that*
Personnellement, je l'**attribue à** une erreur de sa part.	*attribute ... to*
Les causes en sont difficiles à établir.	*the causes are*
La raison pour laquelle ils sont absents est qu'ils nous gardent rancune du malentendu.	*the reason (that or why) ...*
C'est pour cette raison que j'ai accepté d'y aller.	*it was for that very reason that ...*
Il s'était trompé: **voilà pourquoi** il a dû demander un nouveau crédit.	*that's why*
Ils ne vont pas souvent en ville: **c'est que** l'autocar ne passe qu'une fois par jour.	*the thing is ...*
La situation étant très grave, une intervention immédiate est nécessaire.	*(use of present participle)*

AND ACCORDING TO CONTEXT:

ainsi / d'ailleurs / autrement dit / pour ne prendre qu'un seul exemple / c'est-à-dire que / il ne faut pas oublier que / il va sans dire que / il est clair que / il faut également tenir compte du fait que / comme chacun le sait / il est possible que ce soit / à ce qu'il me semble /d'une part ... d'autre part / non seulement ... mais aussi / il s'ensuit que / il en résulte que

APOLOGIES

Excusez-moi d'avoir oublié de vous téléphoner la semaine dernière.	*I am sorry I ...*
Veuillez m'excuser de ne pas vous avoir mis au courant plus tôt.	*please accept my apologies for*
Je suis vraiment désolé de ne pas vous avoir prévenu à temps. // Je suis **désolé qu'**on vous ait dérangé ainsi.	*I am very sorry indeed for // that*
Je suis vraiment navré de ce malentendu.	*I am very sorry about*
Pardonnez-moi de ne pas vous avoir demandé la permission.	*do forgive me for*
Je suis impardonnable!	*it's unforgivable of me*
Il est vraiment regrettable que vous ne puissiez venir.	*it is indeed a pity that*
Je regrette infiniment, mais je ne peux pas me libérer vendredi prochain.	*I am very sorry but*
Malheureusement, il m'est impossible d'accepter votre aimable invitation.	*unfortunately I cannot*
C'est moi le fautif *or* **C'est moi le coupable** — je n'avais pas compris ce qu'il fallait faire.	*it's my fault*

(more formally)

Je ne peux que vous **renouveler mes excuses** pour ce malencontreux incident.	*I can only say once again how sorry I am*
Nous tenons à vous présenter nos excuses pour les difficultés qui en ont résulté.	*we must apologise for*
Je vous prie d'excuser le retard que j'ai mis à vous répondre.	*I must ask you to forgive*
Nous regrettons de ne pouvoir publier votre article.	*we are sorry not to ...*
Nous regrettons vivement les complications que cela a causées.	*we greatly regret*
Je suis au regret de vous informer que votre demande est arrivée trop tard.	*I must regretfully inform you that*
Je regrette de devoir vous annoncer que votre candidature n'a pas été retenue.	*I must regretfully inform you that*
J'ai le regret de ne pouvoir me rendre à ce séminaire, car j'ai un autre engagement.	*I regret that I cannot*

(more tentatively, or suggesting explanation)

Je me rends bien compte maintenant que **je n'aurais jamais dû** dire ça.	*I should never have*
Je reconnais que j'ai eu tort de lui donner votre numéro de téléphone.	*I realise I was wrong*
Si seulement je n'en avais pas parlé!	*if only*
Vous comprendrez, j'espère, que je ne suis pas personnellement responsable de ce retard, qui est dû à la grève des postes.	*you will understand I hope that*
C'est à cause d'une erreur de notre part que cela est arrivé.	*it is because of a mistake on our part*
Je suis sûr que vous comprendrez les raisons qui m'ont poussé à agir ainsi.	*I am sure you will understand*
Hélas, j'avais complètement oublié ce détail.	*unfortunately*
C'est moi qui suis responsable de ce malentendu.	*it's I who am responsible for*
J'avoue *or* **Je reconnais** avoir pensé que cela faciliterait les choses.	*I admit that I ...*
J'accepte l'entière responsabilité de cette affaire.	*I accept full responsibility for*
Je vous jure que **je n'ai pas fait exprès** de casser le vase.	*I didn't do it on purpose*
Je ne voulais pas vous ennuyer avec tous ces détails.	*I didn't want to worry you with*
Je n'avais pas l'intention d'y aller, mais on m'y a forcé.	*I didn't mean to ...*
Je sais bien que ce n'est pas la meilleure solution, mais **j'ai dû** prendre une décision sur le champ.	*I had to ...*
J'avais cru bien faire en lui disant qu'il vous reverrait bientôt.	*I thought I was doing right*
Que voulez-vous, **je ne pouvais pas faire autrement.**	*I couldn't do anything else*
Je sais que les apparences sont contre moi, mais je vous assure que **je n'y suis pour rien.**	*I had nothing to do with it*
J'espère que vous me croyez quand je dis que **nous avons été obligés d'**accepter leurs conditions.	*we were obliged to*
Nous avions cru comprendre que les crédits avaient été accordés.	*we believed that*

AND, ACCORDING TO CONTEXT:

permettez-moi au moins de vous expliquer / je ne peux pas m'empêcher d'y penser / j'aurais dû vous écrire plus tôt / j'essayais simplement de vous éviter ... / nous espérons que vous ne nous tiendrez pas rigueur de / soyez assuré que cela ne se reproduira pas / nous ferons tout notre possible pour / c'est une véritable catastrophe / je me sens très coupable d'avoir ... / il faut que vous sachiez combien je regrette / ce que j'avais voulu dire, c'est que

HÉLÈNE MOLVAU
6 AVENUE DU GRAND PRÉ
17028 LA ROCHELLE

Société Intervins[1]
Service du personnel
18 avenue de la Libération
33000 Bordeaux

La Rochelle, le 4 juin 1993

Objet: demande d'emploi
d'attaché(e) de direction

Messieurs,

En réponse à votre annonce parue cette semaine dans Commerce et Industrie, je me permets de poser ma candidature au poste d'attachée de direction dans votre compagnie.

Je vous prie de bien vouloir trouver ci-joint mon curriculum vitae, et me tiens à votre disposition pour vous communiquer tout complément d'information que vous pourriez souhaiter.

Dans l'espoir que vous voudrez bien considérer favorablement ma demande et dans l'attente de votre réponse, je vous prie de croire, Messieurs, à l'assurance de mes sentiments respectueux.

Hélène Molvau

CURRICULUM VITAE

NOM	MOLVAU
PRÉNOMS	Hélène Marthe Alice
ADRESSE	6 avenue du Grand Pré, 17028 La Rochelle.
TÉLÉPHONE	56 02 71 38
DATE DE NAISSANCE	15.11.1966
LIEU DE NAISSANCE	Paris, XVe.
SITUATION DE FAMILLE	Célibataire.
NATIONALITÉ	Française.
DIPLÔMES[2]	Baccalauréat (Langues) - 1984 - Mention Assez bien. Licence de langues étrangères appliquées (anglais et russe) - Université de Poitiers, 1988 - plusieurs mentions. Diplôme de secrétaire bilingue - 1989 - délivré par l'École de commerce de Poitiers.
POSTES OCCUPÉS	Du 8.10.89 au 30.1.91, secrétaire de direction, France-Exportations, Cognac. Du 10.3.91 à ce jour, adjointe du directeur à l'exportation, Agriventes, La Rochelle.
AUTRES RENSEIGNEMENTS	Bonnes connaissances d'allemand. Permis de conduire. Stage d'informatique dans le cadre de la formation continue, 1991. Nombreux voyages en Europe et aux États-Unis.

[1] This address is appropriate if you are writing to a firm or to an institution. However, if you are writing to the holder of a particular post, you should write thus:

Monsieur le Directeur du personnel,
Société Intervins,
18 avenue de la Libération,
33000 Bordeaux.

In this case, you should begin your letter with "Monsieur le Directeur du personnel, ...", and repeat this in the closing formula.

If the actual name of the person is known to you, you should write:

Monsieur Joël Rivedoux,
OR
Madame Marguerite Fabien,
Directeur du personnel,
Société Intervins etc.

Your letter should then begin: "Monsieur, ..." or "Madame, ...".

More information about letter-writing is to be found on pages 20 and 22.

[2] People with British or American etc qualifications applying for jobs in a French-speaking country might use some form of wording such as "équivalence baccalauréat (3 A-levels)", "équivalence licence de lettres (B.A. Hons.)" etc.

USEFUL VOCABULARY

Me référant à votre annonce parue aujourd'hui dans le *Quotidien du Midi,* je vous serais reconnaissant de bien vouloir m'envoyer des renseignements plus complets sur ce poste, ainsi qu'un dossier de candidature.

In reply to your advertisement in today's 'Quotidien du Midi', I should be grateful if you would please send me further details of this post, together with an application form.

Par votre annonce insérée dans l'édition d'hier de *Voyages et Transports*, j'ai appris que vous cherchez un correspondant bilingue et j'ai l'honneur de solliciter cet emploi.

I wish to apply for the post of bilingual correspondent which you advertise in yesterday's 'Voyages et Transports'.

Je souhaite vivement travailler en France pendant les vacances universitaires et vous serais très reconnaissant de me faire savoir s'il me serait possible d'obtenir un emploi dans votre compagnie.

I am anxious to find a job in France during my summer vacation from University, and wonder whether you are able to offer me work in any capacity.

J'ai travaillé pendant trois ans comme employé de bureau et sais utiliser un système de traitement de textes.

I have three years' experience of office work, and have used a word-processor.

Bien que je n'aie pas d'expérience personnelle de ce type de travail, j'ai eu d'autres emplois intérimaires au cours des étés précédents et puis vous fournir, si vous le désirez, des attestations de mes anciens employeurs.

Although I have not got any previous experience of this type of work, I have had other holiday jobs, and can supply references from my employers, if you would like them.

Mon salaire actuel est de ... par an et j'ai quatre semaines de congés payés.

My present salary is ... per annum, and I have four weeks holiday per year with pay.

Ce poste m'intéresse tout particulièrement, car je souhaite vivement travailler dans l'édition.

I am particularly interested in this job, as I am very anxious to work in publishing.

Je suis désireux de travailler en France afin de perfectionner mes connaissances de français et d'acquérir une certaine expérience de l'hôtellerie.

I wish to work in France in order to improve my French and to gain experience of hotel work.

Je parle couramment l'anglais, j'ai de bonnes connaissances d'allemand, et je lis le suédois.

As well as speaking fluent English, I have a working knowledge of German and a reading knowledge of Swedish.

Je serai disponible à partir de la fin du mois d'avril.

I shall be available from the end of April.

Je vous remercie de votre lettre du 19 mars et serai très heureux de me rendre à vos bureaux, avenue Parmentier, pour une entrevue le 12 novembre à 15 heures.

Thank you for your letter of 19th March. I shall be delighted to attend for interview at your offices in avenue Parmentier on 12th November at 3 p.m.

Dans mon dossier de candidature pour le poste, je dois donner les noms de deux personnes voulant bien me recommander, et je vous serais très reconnaissant de me permettre de donner le vôtre comme référence.

I have to give names of two referees with my application for this job, and I am writing to ask if you would be kind enough to allow me to put your name forward.

J'ai sollicité pour cet été un emploi de serveuse à l'hôtel Bel Air, à Sainte-Marie, et le directeur me demande une attestation. Je vous serais très reconnaissante si vous pouviez avoir l'amabilité de m'en fournir une.

I have applied for the job of waitress for the summer in the Hotel Bel Air, in Sainte-Marie, and they have asked me to supply a reference. I wonder if you would be kind enough to give me one? I should be most grateful if you would agree to do this.

Monsieur Jean Legrand sollicite une place de réceptionniste dans notre hôtel, et il a donné votre nom comme référence. Nous vous serions reconnaissants de bien vouloir nous dire si vous avez été satisfait de ses services.

Mr. Jean Legrand has applied for the post of hotel receptionist with us, and has given your name as a reference. I should be grateful if you would kindly let me know whether in your opinion he is suitable for this post.

Votre réponse sera considérée comme strictement confidentielle.

Your answer will be treated in strict confidence.

Auriez-vous l'obligeance de nous dire depuis combien de temps et à quel titre vous connaissez Mademoiselle Claude Bernard, et si vous la recommandez pour un emploi de ce type?

Would you be kind enough to mention in your reply how long you have known Miss Claude Bernard, in what capacity, and whether you can recommend her for this type of employment.

C'est avec grand plaisir que je vous recommande Madame Marion Lebrun pour le poste de responsable du logement. Je connais Madame Lebrun depuis plus de dix ans. Elle est d'un caractère agréable, pleine de bonne volonté et digne de confiance.

It is with pleasure that I write to recommend Mrs. Marion Lebrun for the post of housing officer: I have known her for over ten years, during which time I have found her friendly, helpful and reliable at all times.

Monsieur Renaud travaille pour nous depuis onze ans. Il est méthodique, ponctuel et extrêmement consciencieux dans son travail. Nous n'avons aucune hésitation à recommander quelqu'un d'aussi sérieux.

Mr. Renaud has worked for me for the past eleven years, and during that time I have been impressed by his careful approach to his work, his punctuality and his sense of responsibility: he is a thoroughly reliable worker.

LA MAISON RUSTIQUE
FABRICATION DE MOBILIER
ZONE INDUSTRIELLE DE DAMPIERRE
B.P. 531 – 17015 DAMPIERRE CEDEX
TÉL: 06 28 42 37

Vos réf: HL/SA 50746
Nos réf: MB/AL 16064
Objet: envoi de documentation

Cuisines d'hier et d'aujourd'hui
3 place du Petit marché
16042 Nimeuil

Dampierre, le 3 novembre 1992

Messieurs

Nous vous remercions de votre lettre du 30 octobre, ainsi que de votre demande de renseignements concernant notre gamme de sièges de cuisine. Nous vous prions de trouver ci-joint une documentation complète, accompagnée de notre liste de prix. Toutefois, nous nous permettons d'attirer votre attention sur nos nouveaux modèles 'Saintonge', qui semblent convenir particulièrement à vos besoins. Ces modèles sont actuellement offerts à des prix très avantageux.
Nous nous tenons à votre entière disposition pour toute demande de renseignements supplémentaires et vous prions d'agréer, Messieurs, l'assurance de nos sentiments dévoués.

Le Directeur commercial

Jean Leclerc

Jean Leclerc

PJ: 1 documentation complète

Maison Duquesnois
Porcelaine et Orfèvrerie
14 rue Montpensier–84000 Poitiers

Madame Marianne Legrand
3 chemin des Princesses
16010 Granbourg

Poitiers, 27 mai 1993

Madame

Nous vous remercions de votre lettre du 21 mai, qui a retenu notre meilleure attention. Malheureusement, nous ne suivons plus le modèle qui vous intéresse, et sommes donc au regret de ne pouvoir vous satisfaire.

Nous vous prions d'agréer, Madame, l'assurance de nos sentiments respectueux.

Le Directeur

Gérard Marquet

Gérard Marquet

ENQUIRIES

Nous voyons d'après votre annonce parue dans le dernier numéro de *l'Industrie des Loisirs* que vous offrez une gamme d'articles pour les sports de plein air.

We see from your advertisement in the latest edition of 'Industrie des Loisirs' that you are offering a range of outdoor sports equipment.

Nous vous serions reconnaissants de nous envoyer une documentation complète concernant ces articles, et de nous faire connaître vos prix courants, les remises consenties et les délais de livraison.

We should be grateful if you would send us full details of these goods, including your prices, discounts offered, and delivery times.

... AND REPLIES

Par suite à votre lettre, nous vous prions de trouver ci-joint une documentation concernant la gamme actuelle de nos produits, ainsi que notre liste de prix (ceux-ci étant fermes jusqu'au 31 mars).	*In response to your enquiry, we enclose details of our current range of goods, and our price list, which is valid until 31 March.*
Nous vous remercions de votre lettre du 16 juin ainsi que de votre demande de renseignements concernant nos marchandises, et avons le plaisir de vous faire l'offre suivante: ...	*We thank you for your enquiry of 16th June, and are pleased to submit the following quotation: ...*
Cette offre est valable sous réserve d'acceptation avant le 31 janvier prochain.	*This offer is subject to your firm acceptance by 31 January next.*

ORDERS

Veuillez nous envoyer immédiatement les articles suivants, dans les tailles et quantités spécifiées ci-dessous: ...	*Please send us immediately the following items, in the sizes and quantities specified: ...*
Cet ordre est basé sur vos prix catalogue et tient compte de la remise de 10% que vous consentez sur les commandes en gros.	*This order is based on your current price list, assuming your usual discount of 10% on bulk orders.*

... AND REPLIES

Nous vous remercions de votre commande *or* de votre ordre en date du 16 mai que nous exécuterons dans les plus brefs délais.	*We thank you for your order of 16 May, and shall execute it as soon as possible.*
L'exécution de votre ordre demandera un délai de trois semaines environ.	*We shall require approximately three weeks to complete this order.*
En raison d'une pénurie de matières premières, nous regrettons de ne pouvoir commencer la fabrication avant le 1er avril.	*Unfortunately, because of a shortage of raw materials, we cannot start manufacture until April 1st.*

DELIVERIES

Nos délais de livraison sont de deux mois à dater de la réception de votre ordre.	*Our delivery time is two months from receipt of firm order.*
Nous attendons vos instructions concernant la livraison.	*We await your instructions with regard to delivery.*
Ces marchandises vous ont été expédiées par chemin de fer le 4 juillet.	*These goods were sent to you by rail on 4th July.*
Nous n'avons pas encore reçu les articles commandés le 26 août (voir bon de commande no. 6496).	*We have not yet received the items ordered on 26 August (our order no. 6496 refers).*
Nous accusons réception de vos deux expéditions du 3 mars.	*We acknowledge receipt of the two consignments shipped by you on 3rd March.*
Nous tenons à vous signaler une erreur dans l'expédition que nous avons reçue le 3 février.	*We wish to draw your attention to an error in the consignment received on 3 February.*
Malheureusement, les marchandises ont été endommagées en transit.	*Unfortunately, the goods were damaged in transit.*
Nous sommes désolés d'apprendre que vous n'êtes pas satisfaits de l'expédition et sommes prêts à remplacer les marchandises en question.	*We regret that the consignment was unsatisfactory, and agree to replace these goods.*
Nous ne pouvons accepter aucune responsabilité pour les dommages.	*We cannot accept responsibility for this damage.*

PAYMENT

Nous vous prions de trouver ci-joint notre facture No. 64321.	*Please find enclosed our invoice no. 64321.*
Le montant total à régler s'élève à ...	*The total amount payable is ...*
Veuillez donner votre attention immédiate à cette facture.	*We would be grateful if you would attend to this account immediately.*
Nous vous remettons sous ce pli notre chèque d'un montant de ... pour solde de *or* en règlement de votre facture No. 678B/31.	*We have pleasure in enclosing our cheque for ... in settlement of your invoice no. 678B/31.*
Nous regrettons de devoir vous signaler une erreur qui s'est glissée dans votre facture et vous serions reconnaissants de bien vouloir la rectifier.	*We must point out an error in your account ... and would be grateful if you would adjust your invoice accordingly.*
Il s'agit effectivement d'une regrettable erreur de comptabilité et nous vous prions de trouver ci-joint un bon de crédit pour la somme correspondante.	*This mistake was due to a book-keeping error, and we enclose a credit note for the sum involved.*
Nous vous remercions de votre chèque de ... en règlement de notre relevé et espérons rester en relations avec vous.	*Thank you for your cheque for ... in settlement of our statement: we look forward to doing further business with you in the near future.*

Saint-Pierre, le 10 mars 1993

Chers Francine et Roger,

Comme cela fait bien longtemps que nous ne nous sommes pas vus, je vous écris pour vous demander si vous aimeriez venir passer deux ou trois jours chez nous. Nous pourrions vous faire visiter un peu les environs et je suis sûre que nous aurions beaucoup de choses à nous raconter. J'ai pensé que les vacances de Pâques approchant, il vous serait peut-être plus facile de vous libérer. Le week-end du 27 mars vous conviendrait-il? Sinon, dites-nous quand vous seriez disponibles. Naturellement, nous serions ravis d'accueillir les enfants!

Dans l'espoir de vous revoir bientôt, je vous envoie à tous deux mes plus affectueuses pensées.

Hélène Morvan

MARIANNE LEGRAND
3 chemin des Princesses,
16010 Granbourg

Maison Duquesnois
14 rue Montpensier
84000 Poitiers.

Granbourg le 16 février 1993

Messieurs,

Il y a quelques années, j'avais acheté chez vous un service à café en porcelaine de Limoges, modèle "Trianon". Ayant malheureusement cassé deux des tasses, je souhaite remplacer les pièces manquantes et voudrais donc savoir si vous suivez ce modèle. Si tel est le cas, je vous serais reconnaissante de bien vouloir m'envoyer votre liste de prix, et de m'indiquer les délais de livraison.

Veuillez accepter, Messieurs, l'expression de mes sentiments distingués.

Marianne Legrand

Marianne Legrand

STANDARD OPENING AND CLOSING FORMULAE

Used when the person is not personally known to you		
Monsieur, Madame,	Je vous prie de croire, [...], à l'assurance de mes salutations distinguées.	
Mademoiselle,	Veuillez agréer, [...], l'expression de mes sentiments les meilleurs.[1]	[1] *used by a man only*
	Je vous prie d'accepter, [...], l'expression de mes respectueux hommages.[2]	[2] *man to woman only*
Used only if the person is known to you personally		
Cher Monsieur, Chère Madame, Chère Mademoiselle,	As above plus: Croyez, [...], à l'expression de mes sentiments les meilleurs.	

TO ACQUAINTANCES AND FRIENDS

Still fairly formal		
Cher Monsieur, Chère Madame, Chère Mademoiselle, Cher Monsieur, chère Madame, Chers amis,	Recevez, je vous prie, mes meilleures amitiés. Je vous envoie mes bien amicales pensées. Je vous adresse à tous deux mon très amical souvenir.	
Fairly informal: 'Tu' or 'Vous' forms could be used		
Cher Patrick, Chère Sylvie, Chers Chantal et Jean-Claude,	Bien amicalement Cordialement Amitiés	

TO CLOSE FRIENDS AND FAMILY

Cher Franck, Chère tante Jacqueline, Mon cher Jean, Ma très chère Ingrid, Chers grands-parents, Mon cher cousin,	Je t'embrasse bien affectueusement Bien des choses à tous Bons baisers Bien à toi À bientôt Salut!	*'tu' or 'vous' can be used, though 'tu' is more likely in all these expressions*

WRITING TO A FIRM OR AN INSTITUTION (see also page 20)

Messieurs,[1]	Je vous prie d'agréer, [...], l'assurance de mes sentiments distingués.	[1] *to a firm*
Monsieur,[2]	Veuillez accepter, [...], l'expression de mes sentiments distingués.	[2] *to a man*
Madame,[3]		[3] *to a woman*

TO A PERSON IN AN IMPORTANT POSITION

Very formal		
Monsieur le Directeur (*or* le Maire *etc*), Madame le Professeur (*or* le Consul *etc*),	Je vous prie d'agréer, [...], l'assurance de ma considération distinguée (*or* de mes sentiments respectueux[1] *or* de mes sentiments dévoués[1]).	[1] *used by a man only*
Used only if the person is well known to you		
Cher Monsieur, Chère Madame,	Je vous prie d'accepter, [...], l'expression de mes salutations distinguées (*or* de mes sentiments distingués[1]). Veuillez croire, [...], à l'assurance de mes sentiments les meilleurs.	
Cher Collègue,[2] Chère Collègue,[2]	Croyez, [...], à l'assurance de mes sentiments les meilleurs[1].	[2] *to someone in the same profession*

STARTING A LETTER

Je te remercie de ta lettre, qui est arrivée hier.
Thank you for your letter, which came yesterday.

J'ai été très content d'avoir de vos nouvelles.
It was good to hear from you.

Je suis vraiment désolé de ne pas vous avoir écrit depuis si longtemps et espère que vous voudrez bien me pardonner: il se trouve que j'ai beaucoup de travail ces temps-ci, et que ...
I am very sorry I haven't written for so long, and hope you will forgive me — I've had a lot of work recently, and ...

Voici bien longtemps que je ne vous ai pas donné de nouvelles. C'est pourquoi je vous envoie ce petit mot rapide ...
It's such a long time since we had any contact, that I felt I must write a few lines just to say hallo ...

Je ne sais par où commencer cette lettre et j'espère que vous comprendrez mon embarras.
This is a difficult letter for me to write, and I hope you will understand how I feel.

Je vous serais reconnaissant de me faire savoir si vous avez en librairie un ouvrage intitulé ...
I am writing to ask whether you have in stock a book entitled ...

Je vous prie de m'envoyer ... Je joins à cette lettre un chèque au montant de 35 F.
Would you please send me ... I enclose my cheque for £3.50.

Ayant effectué un séjour d'une semaine dans votre hôtel, je crains d'avoir oublié dans ma chambre un imperméable beige. Je vous serais obligé de bien vouloir me dire si un tel vêtement a été retrouvé après mon départ.
When I left your hotel after spending a week there, I think I may have left a beige raincoat in my room. Would you kindly let me know whether this has been found.

Ayant appris que vous organisez des cours internationaux d'été, je vous serais reconnaissant de me faire savoir s'il vous reste des places pour ...
I have seen the details of your summer courses, and wish to know whether you still have any vacancies on the ...

ENDING A LETTER

Pierre se joint à moi pour vous envoyer nos meilleurs vœux.
Pierre joins me in sending very best wishes to you all.

Transmettez, s'il vous plaît, mes amitiés à Denis.
Do give my kindest regards to Denis.

Jeanne vous envoie ses amitiés (*or* vous embrasse).
Jeanne sends her kindest regards (ou her love).

Catherine me charge de vous transmettre ses amitiés.
Catherine asks me to give you her best wishes.

Veuillez transmettre mon meilleur souvenir à votre mère.
Please remember me to your mother.

Embrasse Olivier et Marion pour moi, et dis-leur bien combien ils me manquent.
Give my love to Olivier and Marion, and tell them how much I miss them.

Marie vous embrasse tous les deux.
Marie sends her love to you both.

Dis bonjour à Sandrine pour moi.
Say hullo to Sandrine for me.

N'hésitez pas à m'écrire si je puis vous être utile.
If there is anything else I can do, please do not hesitate to get in touch again.

Écris-moi si tu as une petite minute de libre.
Do write when you have a minute.

N'oublie pas de nous donner de tes nouvelles de temps en temps.
Let us have your news from time to time.

J'attends avec impatience une lettre de vous.
I look forward to hearing from you.

TRAVEL PLANS

Je vous serais reconnaissant de bien vouloir me communiquer vos tarifs.
Please give me details of your prices.

Je voudrais retenir une chambre avec petit déjeuner.
I would like to book bed-and-breakfast accommodation with you.

Je voudrais retenir une chambre avec un grand lit pour ma femme et moi-même, ainsi qu'une chambre à lits jumeaux pour nos deux fils, tous deux âgés de moins de 12 ans.
I wish to book one double room for my wife and myself, and one twin-bedded room for our sons, who are both under 12 years of age.

Veuillez me faire savoir, par retour du courrier, si vous avez une chambre pour une personne, avec douche et en pension complète, pour la semaine du 24 juin.
Please let me know by return of post if you have one single room with shower, full board, for the week beginning June 24th.

Veuillez m'indiquer le montant des arrhes que je dois verser pour la réservation.
Would you please let me know what deposit you require on this booking.

Je confirme ainsi ma réservation et vous prie de me garder la chambre, jusqu'à une heure tardive si besoin est.
Please consider this a firm booking, and hold the room until I arrive, however late in the evening.

Sauf imprévu, nous arriverons en début de soirée.
We expect to arrive in the early evening, unless something unforeseen prevents us.

Je me vois obligé de vous demander de reporter ma réservation du 25 août au 3 septembre.
I am afraid I must ask you to alter my booking from 25 August to 3 September.

Pour des raisons indépendantes de ma volonté, je suis contraint d'annuler la réservation que j'avais faite pour la semaine du 5 septembre.
Owing to unforeseen circumstances, I am afraid that I must cancel the booking made with you for the week beginning 5 September.

Je voudrais retenir un emplacement pour une caravane et une tente (2 adultes et 2 enfants) du 15 juin au 7 juillet inclus.
I wish to reserve a site for a caravan and a tent (2 adults and 2 children) from 15 June to 7 July inclusive.

THANKS AND BEST WISHES

EXPRESSING THANKS

Jean et moi **te remercions de** ton aimable attention. — *... thank you for your kind thought.*

Je vous écris pour vous remercier de tout cœur des magnifiques fleurs qui ont été livrées aujourd'hui. — *I am writing to thank you most warmly for*

Je ne sais comment vous remercier de votre aide. — *I don't know how to thank you for*

C'est vraiment très gentil de votre part de m'avoir écrit à la suite de mon accident. — *it is really very kind of you to have ...*

Remercie-le de ma part pour tout ce qu'il a fait. — *give him my thanks for*

Merci de m'avoir prévenu de votre changement d'adresse. — *thank you for having told me about*

Je vous remercie d'y avoir consacré tant de temps. — *thank you for*

Mon mari et moi **vous sommes extrêmement reconnaissants des** précieux conseils que vous avez bien voulu nous donner. — *... are exceedingly grateful to you for*

Transmettez, je vous prie, mes remerciements à vos collègues. — *please give my warmest thanks to your colleagues*

Au nom du comité, je tiens à vous exprimer notre gratitude pour le soutien que vous nous avez apporté au cours de ces derniers mois. — *I am writing on behalf of ... to express our gratitude to you for ...*

Acceptez, je vous prie, mes très sincères remerciements pour votre généreuse contribution à notre fonds de secours. — *I would ask you to accept my most sincere thanks for*

BEST WISHES

Meilleurs vœux [...] de la part de *(+ signature). [...] will be expressions like 'de bonheur', 'pour le succès de la réunion', 'à l'occasion de votre départ en retraite', 'de prompt rétablissement' etc.* — *(formula for a card) with all good wishes for ... from ...*

Tous nos meilleurs vœux. // Amicalement. — *All good wishes // Love ...*

Paul et moi vous adressons tous nos meilleurs vœux [...] — *we send you our best wishes for ...*

Veuillez trouver ici l'expression de nos vœux les plus sincères à l'occasion de ... — *(more formally) please accept our best wishes for ...*

Transmettez, je vous prie, mes meilleurs vœux à Louis (pour ...) — *please give him my best wishes (for ...)*

Je vous souhaite de passer d'excellentes vacances. // J'espère que vous ferez bon voyage. — *(standard phrases in a letter) I send you my best wishes for ...*

(Season's greetings)

(NB: In France cards are usually sent for New Year rather than Christmas, and may be written in the first few weeks of January)

Joyeux Noël! Bonne et heureuse année! *(+ signature)* — *Merry Christmas and a Happy New Year from ...*

Bonnes fêtes de fin d'année et meilleurs vœux pour 1994 *(+ signature)* — *Season's greetings from ...*

Au seuil de la Nouvelle Année, je viens vous présenter mes vœux les plus sincères pour vous et votre famille. Que 1994 vous apporte, ainsi qu'aux vôtres, de nombreuses joies! — *(more formal) I send you and your family all my best wishes for health and happiness in the New Year.*

Pierre Vernon vous présente ses meilleurs vœux à l'occasion du Nouvel An. — *(formal: on a correspondence card) ... sends you his best wishes for the New Year.*

(birthday greetings)

Joyeux anniversaire! Tous nos vœux de bonheur et de bonne santé. *(+ signature)* — *(on card) Many happy returns of the day, and best wishes from ...*

Je vous souhaite un très heureux anniversaire et vous présente tous mes vœux de bonheur et de santé. — *I send you my best wishes for health and happiness on your birthday.*

(get well wishes)

J'ai été désolé d'apprendre que vous êtes souffrant, et vous adresse tous mes vœux de prompte guérison. — *I was very sorry to hear you were ill, and send you my best wishes for a speedy recovery.*

(wishing someone success)

Je vous écris pour vous présenter tous mes vœux de succès dans votre nouvelle entreprise. — *I am writing to wish you every success in your new undertaking.*

Je vous souhaite tout le succès que vous méritez dans votre nouvelle carrière. — *I wish you every success in your new career.*

Je t'écris pour te souhaiter bonne chance, de notre part à tous, pour tes examens. Je suis sûr que tout se passera bien. — *I'm writing to wish you the best of luck from all of us for your exams. I'm sure everything will go well.*

(sending congratulations)

Je tiens à vous féliciter de votre succès au baccalauréat/d'avoir passé votre permis de conduire/de votre avancement. — *(usual formula) congratulations on ...*

Permettez-moi de vous offrir mes félicitations les plus sincères pour cette belle réussite. — *(more formal) allow me to congratulate you on ...*

Je t'écris pour te dire combien je suis heureux que tu aies enfin obtenu le poste que tu désirais. Tu le mérites bien! — *... how happy I am that you have ...*

ANNOUNCEMENTS, INVITATIONS AND RESPONSES

ANNOUNCEMENTS

(announcing a birth)

Maurice et Renée Gillot ont la grande joie de vous faire part de la naissance de leur fille Christine, le 16 juin 1993, à Paris.

Formal announcement (newspaper or printed card): 'are happy to announce the birth of'

J'ai le plaisir de t'annoncer que Hélène et Martyn ont eu un petit garçon le 27 octobre dernier. Ils l'ont appelé James. Tout s'est très bien passé et les heureux parents sont ravis.

Letter to friend: 'I'm happy to tell you that they've had a little boy'

(... and responding)

Nous vous félicitons de l'heureuse arrivée de Christine et souhaitons au bébé santé et prospérité.

Fairly formal letter: 'we send you our warmest congratulations on'

Roger et moi sommes très heureux d'apprendre la naissance de James et espérons faire bientôt sa connaissance. En attendant, nous envoyons tous nos vœux de santé et de prospérité au bébé et à ses heureux parents.

Informal letter to friend: 'are delighted to learn of the birth of'

(announcing an engagement)

Monsieur et Madame Pierre Lepetit sont heureux d'annoncer les fiançailles de leur fille Jacqueline avec M. Jacques Martin.

Formal announcement (newspaper or printed card): 'are happy to announce the engagement of'

Laure et Guy viennent d'annoncer leurs fiançailles. Ils n'ont pas encore fixé la date du mariage, mais nous nous réjouissons tous de leur bonheur.

Informal letter: 'have got engaged ... we are all very happy for them'

(... and responding)

C'est avec beaucoup de joie que j'ai appris vos fiançailles avec Jacques. Je vous adresse à tous deux mes vœux de bonheur les plus sincères.

Fairly formal letter: 'I send you both my very best wishes for happiness'

Nous nous réjouissons avec vous des fiançailles de Laure et de Guy. Transmettez tous nos vœux de bonheur aux jeunes fiancés.

Fairly informal letter: 'we are glad to hear of ... send them our best wishes for their future happiness'

(announcing a marriage)

Monsieur et Madame Olivier Laplace ont l'honneur de vous faire part du prochain mariage de leur fille Catherine avec M. Paul Lenoir, et vous prient d'assister à la messe qui sera célébrée le 7 avril prochain en l'église Saint-Jean à La Roche.

Formal invitation: 'request the pleasure of your company at the wedding of' (this by itself is not an invitation to reception.)

Le Docteur et Madame Albert Cognac sont heureux de vous faire part du mariage de leur fille Joséphine avec M. Bernard Lefèvre, qui a été célébré dans l'intimité familiale le 8 mai 1993.

Formal announcement of wedding: 'are happy to announce the marriage of ... which took place ...'

J'ai le bonheur de t'annoncer que Richard et Marguerite se sont mariés samedi dernier. La cérémonie a eu lieu à l'église de Saint-Martin, et ...

Informal letter: 'Some good news ... got married last ...'

(... and responding)

Monsieur et Madame Michel Wolff félicitent Monsieur et madame Olivier Laplace à l'occasion du prochain mariage de leur fille Catherine, et acceptent avec plaisir leur aimable invitation/mais regrettent de ne pouvoir se joindre à eux en cette journée.

Formal reply to invitation: 'and have much pleasure in accepting/but regret they are unable to accept'

Monsieur et Madame André Bureau adressent leurs sincères félicitations aux parents de Joséphine et tous leurs vœux de bonheur aux futurs époux.

Formal congratulations, written on card: 'send their congratulations and best wishes on the engagement of ...

Pour Catherine et Paul, avec toutes mes félicitations pour votre mariage et tous mes vœux de bonheur.

Card with gift: 'With congratulations and best wishes'

C'est avec une grande joie que nous avons appris le mariage de votre fille avec Bernard Lefèvre. Nous vous présentons toutes nos félicitations et souhaitons aux jeunes mariés beaucoup de bonheur et de prospérité.

Fairly formal letter: 'send you our congratulations and best wishes on'

J'ai été très heureux d'apprendre par ta lettre le mariage de Richard et de Marguerite. Tu sais que je leur souhaite tout le bonheur possible.

Informal letter: 'I was delighted to hear of'

(announcing a change of address)

Nous vous prions de bien vouloir noter notre nouvelle adresse, qui sera, à partir du 1er novembre 1993: 26 Avenue de Rome, 92000 Boulogne.

Formal private or business letter

(announcing a death)

Monsieur et Madame Jacques Bonnard et leurs enfants ont la douleur de vous faire part de la mort soudaine de M. Henri Bonnard, leur père et grand-père, survenue le 3 avril 1993. La cérémonie religieuse aura lieu le 7 avril en l'église St. Thomas et sera suivie de l'inhumation au cimetière de Clamart.

Formal announcement: 'announce with deep sorrow and regret the death of'

Nous avons la très grande peine de vous faire part de la perte cruelle que nous venons d'éprouver en la personne de notre mère, décédée le 2 janvier après une brève maladie. Le service religieux et l'inhumation ont eu lieu dans la plus stricte intimité.

Formal letter: 'it is with deepest sorrow that we have to inform you of our sad loss ...'

C'est avec beaucoup de peine que je t'écris pour t'annoncer que mon père est décédé la semaine dernière.

Informal letter: 'I am writing to tell you the sad news that my father died last week'

(... and responding)

Monsieur et Madame Paul Lambert vous prient d'accepter l'expression de leur profonde sympathie et vous adressent leurs plus sincères condoléances à l'occasion du deuil qui vient de vous frapper.
Formal, on card: 'send their deepest sympathy on the occasion of'

C'est avec une profonde tristesse que nous avons appris la disparition de votre frère. Croyez que nous prenons part à votre peine et soyez assurés de notre sincère sympathie.
Formal letter: 'it is with the greatest sorrow that we learnt of'

J'ai été bouleversé d'apprendre la disparition de ta sœur. Je tiens à te dire combien je pense à toi en ces moments douloureux.
Informal letter to friend: 'I was terribly upset to learn of the death of ...'

INVITATIONS

(formal invitations)

See p.26, **'announcing a marriage'**.

Madame Paul Ambre et Madame Michel Potet recevront après la cérémonie religieuse au Relais des Glycines, route de Marleroy, Fontanes. R.S.V.P.
'request the pleasure of your company afterwards at ... ' (On card inside wedding invitation.)

Les éditions Roget ont le plaisir de vous inviter à un cocktail à l'occasion de la sortie du premier livre de la collection Espoir le lundi 9 août 1993 à partir de 18 h 30.
'have pleasure in inviting you to ...'

Monsieur et Madame André Bureau prient Madame Labadie de leur faire le plaisir de venir dîner le mercredi 27 octobre à 20 heures.
'request the pleasure of your company at dinner on ...'

(... and replies)

See p.26, **'announcing a marriage ... and responding'**.

Mademoiselle Charlotte Leblanc accepte avec grand plaisir de se rendre au cocktail organisé le 9 août par les éditions Roget/regrette profondément de ne pouvoir se rendre au cocktail *etc.*
'thanks ... and accepts with pleasure/ but regrets that she cannot accept'

Madame Jeanne Labadie remercie Monsieur et Madame André Bureau de leur aimable invitation à dîner qu'elle accepte avec le plus grand plaisir/ qu'elle regrette de ne pouvoir accepter en raison d'un autre engagement.
'thanks ... which she is happy to accept/which she regrets that she cannot accept owing to a previous engagement

(informal invitations)

Pour fêter les fiançailles de Geneviève et de Xavier, nous organisons une réception à l'Hôtel de France, à Saint Martin, le 2 septembre à 20 heures et serions très heureux si vous pouviez vous joindre à nous.
'we are having a party to celebrate their engagement ... and hope you will be able to join us there'

Michèle et Philippe doivent venir déjeuner dimanche prochain et nous espérons que vous pourrez être des nôtres.
'are coming to lunch ... and we hope you will be able to join us'

Est-ce que cela te dirait d'aller passer la journée à La Rochelle?
'would you like to spend the day ...'

Lors de votre passage à Lyon, vous nous feriez très plaisir si vous pouviez nous consacrer une soirée pour que nous dînions ensemble.
'when you are in ... lovely if you would spend an evening with us ... have dinner together'

Nous projetons de passer le mois de juillet à l'île de Ré et serions très heureux de vous y accueillir quelques jours.
'we are planning to spend July ... and would be happy to welcome you ...'

(... and replies)

Je vous remercie de votre aimable invitation et me fais une joie de venir.
'thank you for your very kind invitation ... I am looking forward to it'

C'est très gentil de votre part de m'inviter et je me réjouis d'être des vôtres.
'very kind of you to invite me ... looking forward very much to being with you'

Nous pensons passer le week-end de Pentecôte à Lyon et vous téléphonerons dès notre arrivée pour arranger une rencontre.
'we are thinking of spending Whit weekend in ... and shall telephone you to arrange a meeting'

Votre invitation pour l'île de Ré nous a fait grand plaisir et nous espérons passer un week-end chez vous vers le 14 juillet.
'thank you very much for your invitation ... we hope to come for a weekend about ...'

C'est avec le plus grand plaisir que je vous accompagnerai à l'Opéra. Merci d'avoir pensé à moi.
'I am free that evening ... and will gladly go with you to ... thank you for thinking of me'

C'est vraiment très aimable à vous de m'inviter pour votre soirée de samedi, mais je me vois malheureusement contraint de refuser, car j'ai déjà accepté une invitation pour ce soir-là.
'It was so kind of you to invite me ... unfortunately I have to refuse ... already accepted another invitation for that evening'

J'aimerais beaucoup passer un week-end chez vous, mais malheureusement, aucune des dates que vous proposez ne me convient.
'I should like very much to spend a weekend with you ... unfortunately none of the dates is any good to me'

Malheureusement, je ne peux pas me libérer le mois prochain. Peut-être pourrons-nous arranger une rencontre en octobre?
'unfortunately I can't get away then ... perhaps we can arrange a meeting in ...'

ESSAY WRITING

THE BROAD OUTLINE OF THE ESSAY

Introductory remarks

Dans son journal, Gide écrit: C'est avec les beaux sentiments qu'on fait de la mauvaise littérature'. **Ce jugement** peut paraître tranchant, mais il **soulève néanmoins une question essentielle** — celle des rapports de l'art et de la morale. — *this assertion ... raises a fundamental question ...*

Aujourd'hui tout le monde s'accorde à dire que le chômage menace la structure même de la société telle que nous la connaissons. **Cependant,** certaines des mesures actuellement suggérées pour lutter contre ce problème **impliquent,** elles aussi, des changements fondamentaux, et **ceci nous amène à nous demander si,** dans certains cas, le remède ne serait pas pire que le mal. — *it is generally agreed today that ... however ... imply ... this leads us to wonder whether ...*

'La voiture est un luxe indispensable'. **Voici une remarque fréquemment entendue** qui illustre les problèmes de notre société de consommation moderne. **Il convient donc d'examiner** le rôle actuel de l'automobile. — *such a remark is often heard ... let us therefore take a closer look at ...*

Depuis quelque temps, les problèmes de la sidérurgie sont à la une de l'actualité et nous avons tous présentes à l'esprit les images des manifestations violentes qui ont eu lieu la semaine dernière dans l'Est. **La question est** donc de savoir si l'on doit sacrifier une communauté entière au nom de l'intérêt économique? — *once more the question arises*

Presque chaque semaine on trouve dans la presse des articles portant sur les problèmes démographiques en France. **Tantôt** on s'inquiète du vieillissement de la population, **tantôt** on affirme que nous sommes trop ou trop peu nombreux. — *hardly a week goes by without ... sometimes ..., sometimes ...*

Ces attitudes contradictoires montrent à quel point la place de la famille est actuellement **remise en question.** — *this clash of opinions ... called into question*

Un problème dont il est souvent question aujourd'hui est celui de la faim dans le Tiers Monde. — *one recurring problem today is*

On ne peut nier le fait que la télévision influence profondément la façon dont nous percevons la vie politique. — *it cannot be denied that*

Il serait naïf de croire que les hommes politiques agissent *(subj)* toujours pour des motifs désintéressés. — *it would be naïve to consider that*

On exagérerait à peine en disant que ce sont les accidents de la route qui grèvent le budget de la Sécurité sociale. — *it would hardly be an exaggeration to state that*

Nous vivons dans un monde où la paix est constamment menacée. — *we live in a world where*

L'histoire nous fournit de nombreux exemples de génies incompris à leur époque et reconnus par les générations suivantes. — *history offers us numerous examples of*

Il n'est guère possible d'ouvrir le journal sans y découvrir un nouvel exemple de violence. — *it is scarcely possible to open a newspaper without finding some new example of*

Le problème se résume donc à ceci: Sartre peut-il être à la fois romancier et philosophe? — *the problem may be summarised thus: ...*

Une telle attitude mérite d'être examinée de plus près et il serait donc utile de la replacer dans son contexte historique. — *such an attitude deserves closer attention*

Developing the argument

La première constatation qui s'impose, c'est que le sujet traité par l'auteur est mal connu du grand public. — *the first thing that must be said is that*

Prenons comme point de départ le rôle que le gouvernement a joué dans l'élaboration de ce programme. — *let us begin with*

Il serait utile d'examiner la façon dont l'auteur définit ses personnages dans le premier chapitre. — *it would be useful to consider*

En premier lieu il convient d'examiner *or* **En premier lieu examinons** l'attitude selon laquelle le sport est un devoir. — *let us first of all look at*

Selon l'auteur, la province serait une prison empêchant le héros de s'épanouir, et **il revient sur cette idée** à plusieurs reprises. — *the author would have us believe that ... he comes back to this idea*

En cherchant à analyser les causes de ce malaise, **il faut tout d'abord reconnaître que** les enseignants en ont assez des réformes incessantes. — *in an attempt to analyse ... it must first be recognised that*

Le premier argument que l'on puisse faire valoir, c'est que les jeunes ne savent plus s'amuser. — *the first telling argument is that*

Rappelons les faits: les pluies acides détruisent chaque année une fraction croissante de la forêt européenne. — *let us state the facts once more:*

La première question qui se pose, c'est de savoir quel est le motif qui peut pousser l'héroïne à agir ainsi. — *the first question that arises is ...*

The other side of the argument

Après avoir étudié la progression de l'action, **considérons maintenant** le style *or* **il faut maintenant parler du** style.	*let us now consider*
Puisque l'étude de l'environnement ne nous apporte pas de réponse satisfaisante sur ce point, **cherchons d'autres facteurs** susceptibles de contribuer à cette détérioration.	*let us look for other factors*
L'auteur **a beau** insister sur l'importance des rapports entre le maître et le valet, il n'arrive pas toujours à les rendre convaincants. Pourquoi?	*however hard the author tries to ...*
Il est maintenant nécessaire d'aborder la question de la censure à la télévision.	*we must now consider*
Venons-en maintenant à l'analyse des personnages.	*now we come to ...*
Est-ce vraiment là une raison suffisante pour réclamer le rétablissement de la peine de mort?	*is this really a good reason for*
Tournons-nous maintenant vers *or* **Passons maintenant à** un autre aspect du problème — celui des conséquences de cette mesure sur l'emploi des femmes.	*let us now turn our attention to*
Puisqu'il a été établi que le héros n'est pas poussé par le désir du gain, **examinons de plus près** la scène où il se trouve en présence de son père.	*let us take a closer look at*
Il serait intéressant de voir si le même phénomène se produit dans d'autres pays.	*it would be interesting to see whether*
Il est raisonnable de penser que l'auteur exprime ses vues avec sincérité.	*it is reasonable to believe that*
On peut également aborder le problème sous un angle différent et considérer la portée politique de ces mesures.	*the problem could also be approached from another angle, by ...*
Pour l'auteur, la forme est plus importante que le fond, **mais il se peut, bien sûr, que le contraire soit vrai.**	*for the author ... but of course the opposite may very well be true*
Est-on pour autant autorisé à dire que les défenseurs des droits des animaux sont les prophètes d'une nouvelle moralité?	*is it reasonable to claim that*
Un deuxième argument qui est loin d'être négligeable consiste à dire que les plus jeunes, tout comme les plus vieux, sont particulièrement défavorisés dans notre société.	*there is a second argument which cannot be ignored, namely that*

The balanced view

Au terme de cette analyse on doit cependant faire remarquer que la rapidité du changement est peut-être le facteur le plus important.	*at the end of the day, it must however be pointed out that*
Il faut néanmoins reconnaître que l'action individuelle et l'éducation ne suffisent pas: des mesures doivent être prises à l'échelon gouvernemental.	*it must however be recognised that*
Cependant, **il faut envisager un troisième facteur.**	*we must allow for a third factor*
Enfin, nous devons nous demander si le véritable intérêt de l'ouvrage ne réside pas dans l'étude des mœurs de l'époque.	*finally, we must ask ourselves if*
La position de l'auteur est **encore plus nuancée** qu'on ne le pense.	*is still more complex ...*
Peut-être faudrait-il étendre un peu le problème et se demander si la corruption du pouvoir ne forme pas le sujet essentiel de la pièce.	*we should perhaps go further, and ask whether*

In conclusion

Quelles conclusions tirer de *or* **Quelles conclusions déduire de** cette analyse?	*what conclusions may be drawn from*
Les différents accidents **dont il a été question ci-dessus prouvent** *or* **démontrent que** les normes de sécurité ne sont pas respectées.	*which have been discussed earlier ... prove that*
Il semble donc que dans son roman, l'auteur n'accorde d'importance particulière ni au cadre, ni à l'action. **En fait,** toute son attention est concentrée sur l'analyse psychologique.	*it would seem clear that ... in point of fact*
Il résulte de tout ceci que la prison peut transformer un délinquant en criminel.	*all this goes to show that*
Est-on en mesure de **dresser le bilan de** ces premiers mois de gouvernement?	*... assess the performance of*
D'après ce qui précède, il semble que *or* **D'après ce qui vient d'être dit, il semble que** l'auteur se cache soigneusement derrière ses personnages.	*from this, it would seem that*
En définitive *or* **De toute façon,** le plus grand problème actuel, c'est notre manque d'imagination en ce que concerne l'avenir.	*all in all*
Ainsi, il apparaît que l'opinion publique est de plus en plus consciente des dangers du nucléaire.	*it would appear then that*
Tels seraient donc les principaux moyens d'expression utilisés par l'auteur.	*these then are ...*

CONSTRUCTING A PARAGRAPH

Ordering various elements within it

On peut invoquer ici plusieurs arguments différents.
at this point, several arguments could be mentioned

Plusieurs facteurs ont contribué au succès du produit: **tout d'abord,** le directeur a obtenu une licence de fabrication du Japon, **ensuite** il a organisé une grande campagne de publicité, **et enfin,** il a lancé une gamme de dérivés ... (*or* **en premier/deuxième** *etc*/**dernier lieu)**
several factors contributed to ... first ... then ... and lastly ...

Qui sont les pauvres aujourd'hui? Eh bien, **d'une part,** il y a ceux qui naissent pauvres, **et d'autre part,** ceux qui le deviennent (*or* **d'un côté ... de l'autre).**
on the one hand ... and on the other

Les premiers connaissent des problèmes de travail et de logement, **les seconds** sont pris en charge par l'aide sociale (*or* **Ceux-là ... ceux-ci ...**).
the first ... the second ... (the former ... the latter)

Ceci est dû essentiellement à trois facteurs: **premièrement** ... *etc.*
this is basically due to three factors first ... etc

L'éducation nationale fait l'objet de critiques continuelles et **il en va de même** pour la sécurité sociale.
and so also does ...

De même que les étudiants se demandent à quoi leurs études vont leur servir, **de même** les professeurs s'interrogent sur leur rôle.
as students ... so also teachers ...

D'ailleurs *or* **De toute façon,** le président n'a pas le choix.
in any case

À cet égard *or* **À ce propos,** il faut noter une détérioration dans la qualité de l'enseignement.
in this connection

Bref *or* **En un mot,** il refuse.
in a word

On peut noter en passant que *or* **On peut mentionner en passant que** l'auteur n'y fait jamais allusion.
one may point out in passing that

Avant d'aborder la question du style, **mentionnons brièvement** le choix des métaphores.
let us make brief mention of

Sans nous appesantir sur les détails *or* **Sans nous attarder sur les détails,** notons toutefois que le rôle du conseil de l'ordre a été déterminant.
without going into too much detail, we should ...

Comme nous le verrons plus en détail par la suite, ce sont surtout les personnages secondaires qui font progresser l'action.
as we shall see in greater detail later

Nous ne pouvons dissocier ce facteur de la décision mentionnée plus haut.
this factor cannot be dissociated from

Nous reprenons ainsi une idée suggérée antérieurement.
here we touch again on an idea

Nous reviendrons plus loin sur cette question, **mais** signalons déjà l'absence totale d'émotion dans ce passage.
we shall return to this later, but ...

Mais pour en revenir au sujet qui nous intéresse, la cuisine française est en train de changer du tout au tout.
but to return to the topic which interests us most, ...

Adding, enumerating etc

De plus *or* **Par ailleurs,** il s'agit là d'un progrès tout à fait remarquable.
moreover

En outre, il faut noter que *or* **Il faut également noter que** les employés sont mal payés.
we must also remember that

Il examine les origines du problème, **ainsi que** certaines des solutions suggérées.
as well as, in addition to

Différentes formules sont offertes au client — voyage à forfait, **ou bien** hébergement chez l'habitant, **ou encore** demi-pension, **ou enfin** camping dans un village de vacances.
or else ... or alternatively ... or finally

Faut-il inclure dans les statistiques les handicapés et les personnes âgées? **Ou bien** doit-on exclure les jeunes et les travailleurs temporaires? **Ou encore** est-il nécessaire d'analyser le mode de vie en plus des revenus?
or else ... or yet again ...

Plusieurs catégories professionnelles ont été oubliées, **notamment** *or* **parmi lesquelles** les employés de bureau et les réceptionnistes.
in particular

Ils connaissent **des problèmes de** scolarité, de travail et d'hébergement, **problèmes qui** sont tous exacerbés dans le cas des groupes ethniques minoritaires.
they have problems of schooling, of ... etc, problems which are ...

Du parti communiste **à** l'extrême-droite, **tous** sont d'accord pour condamner cet acte de terrorisme.
from the X on the one hand, to the Y on the other, all are agreed ...

Médecins, chirurgiens, anesthésistes et infirmiers, **tous** sont surmenés.
doctors, surgeons etc — all are ...

Ajoutons à cela *or* **Il faut ajouter à cela** *or* **À cela s'ajoute** un sens remarquable du détail.
added to that, ...

Pour ce qui est des personnages secondaires, ils sont, eux aussi, remarquablement vivants.
as far as the ... are concerned

En ce qui concerne la pollution chimique, il faut reconnaître qu'elle constitue aussi un grave danger.
as far as ... is concerned, as for the matter of ...

Quant aux émissions sportives, elles suivent toujours le même modèle précis.
as for the ...

De même, on pourrait suggérer que le style de l'auteur manque d'originalité.
similarly

Introducing one's own point of view

À mon avis *or* **Selon moi** *or* **D'après moi,** ce chapitre est le meilleur du livre.	*in my view, as far as I am concerned*
En ce qui me concerne *or* **Pour ma part,** je déplore l'évolution actuelle de l'enseignement supérieur.	*as far as I am concerned, for my part*
Personnellement, ce qui me frappe le plus dans cette affaire, **c'est** le ton de la déclaration du juge.	*from my own point of view, what I find most striking is*
Si je puis me permettre d'exprimer une opinion personnelle, il me semble que l'auteur s'aventure sur un terrain dangereux.	*if I may be permitted to give a personal opinion ...*
Je soutiens que *or* **Je suis de l'opinion que** la télévision a un effet néfaste sur l'éducation des enfants.	*I maintain that ..., it is my view that ...*
L'auteur affirme, **à juste titre selon moi,** que cette attitude est défaitiste.	*... and rightly, in my opinion ...*

Introducing someone else's point of view

Selon l'auteur *or* **D'après l'auteur** *or* **Suivant l'auteur,** le motif principal du crime est la jalousie.	*according to the author*
Comme le soulignent (*or* **le laissent entendre** *etc*) **les experts,** l'important est d'inventer des solutions nouvelles.	*as the experts emphasize (or imply etc)*
Le budget du ministère est, **dit-il** (*or* **affirme-t-il** *etc*), dans les normes de la CEE.	*... he says (or he declares etc)*
Il dit/pense/croit/affirme/déclare que ce système présente de nombreux avantages.	*he says/thinks/believes/states/declares that*
L'auteur **attire notre attention sur/nous rappelle/nous signale** l'ampleur de ce changement.	*the author draws our attention to/ reminds us of/points out*
Il insiste sur le fait que/Il maintient que/Il soutient que ces rivalités internes sont la véritable faiblesse du mouvement.	*he emphasizes/maintains/claims that*
Un soi-disant expert **prétend qu'**il est possible/**voudrait nous faire croire qu'**il est possible d'apprendre les langues vivantes sans effort.	*claims that/wants to convince us that*
Selon la version officielle des faits, ceci ne pourrait avoir de conséquences néfastes pour la population.	*according to the official version of the facts*

Introducing an example

Prenons le cas de Louis dans le Nœud de Vipères.	*consider the case of*
Il suffit de donner comme exemple les documentaires à valeur éducative.	*one has only to instance*
Un seul exemple suffit à montrer l'importance de cette réorganisation.	*one single example is enough to show*
L'un des exemples les plus frappants se trouve au deuxième chapitre.	*one of the most striking examples*
Mille travailleurs, **dont** 10% de femmes, risquent de perdre leur emploi.	*10% of whom are*

Introducing a quotation or source

Suivant *or* **Selon** *or* **D'après** les auteurs du rapport, 'l'important n'est pas de nourrir l'Afrique, mais de la faire reverdir'.	*according to*
'La raison du plus fort est toujours la meilleure', **constate/affirme/observe** La Fontaine.	*concludes/declares/observes*
Comme l'a fait remarquer le président, 'la croissance économique dépend du taux d'investissement'.	*as the president points out*
Chénier avait écrit 'l'art ne fait que des vers, le cœur seul est poète', et **Musset reprend la même idée** 'Ah, frappe-toi le cœur, c'est là qu'est le génie'.	*Chénier had written ... and Musset takes up the same theme ...*
Selon les paroles de Duhamel, 'le romancier est l'historien du présent'.	*in the words of Duhamel ...*
Dans sa remarquable étude sur le folklore vendéen, Jean Thomas **observe** ...	*in his remarkable study of ... he observes ...*
Dans un article récemment publié dans le journal *Le Temps*, nous trouvons cette remarque **sous la plume de** Jean Lefèvre: '...	*in a recent article in ... from the pen of*

THE MECHANICS OF THE ARGUMENT

Introducing a fact

Il est exact que les travaux ont commencé.	*it is true that*
On constate *or* **On observe** un progrès soutenu.	*... is noticeable*
On peut noter que la **CEE** n'a pas donné son accord.	*one should note that*
Il s'agit d'une histoire toute simple.	*it is a ...*
Le nouveau programme **fait l'objet de** violentes critiques.	*has been a target for*
Rappelons les faits: la pollution du Rhin devient inquiétante et ...	*we must not lose sight of the facts:*
À mesure qu'on avance dans la lecture de l'ouvrage, on découvre des perspectives nouvelles.	*as the reader progresses, new perspectives open up*
L'auteur rapporte que de nombreuses superstitions concernent les plantes et les animaux.	*the author reports that*

Indicating a supposition

On est en droit de supposer que cette solution sera adoptée.	*one might justifiably suppose that*
Il est probable que leur réaction sera connue sous peu.	*it is probable that*
On évoque ici la possibilité d'une nouvelle réunion au sommet.	*the possibility of ... is mentioned*
Il pourrait y avoir une autre explication.	*there could be*
Supposons que l'essence sans plomb devienne obligatoire: l'automobiliste devra l'accepter, et ...	*let us suppose that*
Le refus du comité **laisse supposer** *or* **permet de penser** que les fonds nécessaires n'ont pas été réunis à temps.	*leads one to believe that*
Il n'est pas impossible qu'il y ait eu une explosion.	*it is not impossible that*
Ceci expliquerait la baisse des ventes en février.	*this would explain*
On peut supposer que l'auteur est au courant des faits.	*one may suppose that*

Expressing a certainty

Il est certain que *or* **Il est évident que** cette découverte constitue un grand pas en avant.	*it is clear that*
Son deuxième roman est **incontestablement** *or* **indéniablement** supérieur au premier.	*... is indisputably or undeniably ...*
Tout pousse à croire que *or* **Tout permet de penser que** son rival l'emportera.	*everything leads one to the conclusion that*
Qu'il ait du talent **ne fait aucun doute. // Sans aucun doute** il a du talent.	*there can be no doubt that*
Tout le monde s'accorde pour critiquer les méthodes qu'il emploie.	*everyone agrees in criticising ...*
Il est clair que les événements prennent une tournure tragique.	*it is clear that*
Comme chacun le sait, la camomille est un remède souverain contre l'insomnie.	*as everyone knows*

Indicating doubt or uncertainty

Il semble qu'elle ait essayé de prendre contact avec eux.	*it would seem that*
Il est possible que *or* **Il se peut que** l'héroïne n'en ait pas conscience.	*it is possible that*
Peut-être préfère-t-on aujourd'hui voir des films plus gais.	*perhaps people prefer ...*
Sans doute est-il préférable d'économiser dès maintenant certains des minerais les plus rares.	*perhaps it is preferable to ...*
Il pourrait s'agir d'un nouveau virus.	*it could be*
Ceci pourrait expliquer le retard avec lequel la nouvelle lui est parvenue.	*this could explain*
Ceci remet en question la validité de ces statistiques.	*this calls into question again ...*
On hésite à croire qu'une telle décision ait été prise.	*it is difficult to believe that*

Conceding a point

Nous savons réduire les effets de la pollution, et **pourtant** *or* **toutefois** *or* **cependant** *or* **néanmoins,** nous hésitons souvent à le faire à cause du coût.	*however*
Bien que *or* **Quoique** les personnages soient étudiés avec soin, ils manquent de vie.	*although*
Le style est intéressant, **quoique** *or* **bien que** *or* **encore que** lent parfois.	*albeit*
Ils ont raison **jusqu'à un certain point, mais** certains de leurs idées prendraient trop longtemps à réaliser.	*up to a certain point they are right, but ...*
Je suis d'accord avec l'auteur sur bien des points, **mais** je dois néanmoins formuler quelques réserves.	*I agree with him on many points, but ...*
Bien sûr, la limitation de vitesse réduirait le nombre des accidents, **mais** elle créerait aussi d'autres problèmes.	*of course ... but ...*
Selon elle, le plus gros du travail est fait. **Toujours est-il qu'**il reste encore de nombreux détails à mettre au point.	*the fact still remains that*
Quel que soit le talent du metteur en scène, il n'arrive pas à rendre plausible une histoire aussi rocambolesque.	*however great the talent ...*
On ne peut nier que *or* **Il est indéniable que** la robotique conduit *or* conduise à des suppressions d'emploi, mais ...	*it cannot be denied that*
Certes, les spots publicitaires font vendre, mais il coûtent aussi très cher.	*undoubtedly*
Sans aller jusqu'à dire que la femme est exploitée, **il faut cependant reconnaître qu'**elle rencontre des difficultés particulières dans le monde du travail.	*it must be recognised that*
Tout en reconnaissant que les grands ensembles ont permis de loger des milliers de sans-abri, **il faut néanmoins accepter que** les conditions y sont souvent déplorables.	*while recognising ... one must also agree that*
Sans doute la solitude est-elle un fléau moderne, **mais** c'est souvent à l'individu de lutter contre elle.	*doubtless ... but ...*
Le moins que l'on puisse dire, c'est que le personnage est fascinant.	*the least one can say is that*

Emphasizing particular points

Pour souligner la complexité du problème, l'auteur nous décrit les effets secondaires de ces produits.	*in order to emphasize*
Il faut bien préciser qu'il *or* **Précisons bien qu'**il s'agit là d'une méthode couramment employée.	*let us make it quite clear that*
Cette décision **met en lumière** l'ignorance et les préjugés de celui qui l'a prise.	*... highlights ...*
N'oublions pas que les femmes vivent dans l'ensemble plus longtemps que les hommes.	*let us not forget that*
Il faut insister sur le fait que personne n'était au courant de ces tentatives.	*we must make it absolutely clear that*
C'est cet incident **qui** est à l'origine de la réforme des prisons. **C'est** dans les lycées **que** le mécontentement est le plus évident.	*it is this ... which ...*
Si elle ne s'en est pas encore occupée, **c'est** par indifférence, **et non pas** par manque de temps.	*it is indifference, not lack of time, that has prevented her from ...*
Non seulement il s'est opposé à la réduction du budget, **mais** il a demandé de nouveaux crédits.	*not only did he ... but ...*
Cela ne veut pas dire que la pièce est *or* soit mauvaise, **mais plutôt que** l'auteur manque encore d'expérience.	*this does not mean that ..., but rather that ...*
L'ambition — **voilà** ce qui différencie le héros des autres personnages.	*that is what ...*
Bien loin de nous transformer en imbéciles, la télévision nous instruit et nous divertit tout à la fois.	*far from changing us into ...*
Non pas qu'il *or* **Ce n'est pas qu'**il condamne *(subj)* cette attitude, **mais** il craint qu'elle soit incomprise.	*it is not that ... but rather that ...*
Le chômage va encore augmenter, **d'autant plus que** le gouvernement refuse d'aider les industries en difficulté.	*and all the more so because ...*
J'irais même jusqu'à dire qu'il a tort.	*I would even go so far as to say that*
La pièce comporte de nombreuses inexactitudes historiques, **et qui plus est,** la chronologie est déformée.	*and what is more serious ..., and more than that ...*
Cette loi a toujours été injuste, **à plus forte raison maintenant que** l'opinion publique a évolué.	*and more than ever now that*

Moderating a statement

Sans vouloir critiquer cette façon de procéder, il semble cependant qu'une autre méthode pourrait avoir de meilleurs résultats.	*without wishing to criticize*
L'auteur a certainement raison **dans l'ensemble,** mais certains détails mériteraient d'être revus.	*by and large*
Une mise au point serait souhaitable.	*one might offer a slight clarification here*
Sans attacher trop d'importance à des détails, il semble pourtant qu'une révision s'impose.	*without laying too much emphasis on details*
Il serait injuste de reprocher à l'auteur son manque d'expérience.	*it would be unfair to ...*
Il serait mal venu de demander plus de détails.	*it would be churlish to ...*

Indicating agreement

Beaucoup de gens trouvent les grands ensembles très laids, et **en effet** *or* **effectivement,** ils sont souvent hideux.	*and indeed*
Il faut reconnaître que les résultats sont décevants.	*one must admit that*
Sa description de l'événement est **exacte en tous points.**	*is correct in every detail*
L'explication qu'il en donne est **tout à fait convaincante.**	*is wholly convincing*
Nous ne pouvons que nous incliner devant ces conclusions.	*we can only bow to these conclusions*
Comme le suggère l'auteur, il semble indispensable de pousser plus loin les recherches.	*as the author suggests*
Tout semble effectivement indiquer qu'il y a eu un accident d'une gravité exceptionnelle.	*everything certainly seems to point to*
Il est évident que cette méthode est efficace.	*it is clear that*
Rien n'est plus vrai que cette description de l'exil.	*nothing is more true than*

Indicating disagreement

Il est impossible d'accepter le point de vue de l'auteur sur ce point.	*it is impossible to accept*
Cette explication **ne mérite pas d'être retenue.**	*is not worthy of our attention*
Les habitants de l'île **protestent contre** la construction du pont.	*protest against*
Ces faits **sont en contradiction avec** la version officielle.	*these facts contradict*
Il ne saurait être question de procéder à de nouvelles élections.	*there can be no question of*
Je me sens tenu de **formuler quelques réserves/de soulever quelques objections.**	*... to make some reservations/to raise some objections*
Le professeur Durand **réfute l'argument selon lequel** la médecine préventive est plus économique que la médecine curative.	*refutes the claim that*
À tous ceux qui critiquent la publicité, **on peut répondre que** *or* **on peut répliquer que** c'est un nouveau genre artistique.	*one can reply that*
Cette affirmation **me semble contestable.**	*... seems to me to be questionable*
L'auteur commet une grave erreur en laissant entendre qu'un accord avait été conclu.	*the author makes a grave mistake in*
Bien que son raisonnement soit intéressant, **je ne partage pas le point de vue de l'auteur.**	*... I do not share the author's point of view*
Quand bien même il aurait raison sur ce point, cela ne résout pas le problème dans son ensemble.	*even if he is right*
Quand on dit que la catastrophe a fait 2 000 victimes, **on est très loin de la vérité.**	*this is far from the truth*
Il faut s'élever contre cette vue pessimiste de l'existence.	*one cannot let this pass without comment*

Indicating approval

Heureusement, l'auteur nous précise plus tard que ce n'est pas le cas.	*fortunately*
On comprend fort bien que cette attitude plaise.	*one can well understand how ...*
La meilleure solution serait effectivement de restaurer le bâtiment.	*the best solution would certainly be to ...*
Il suffit de lire ces lignes pour se croire transporté au XVIIIe siècle.	*you have only to read these lines to be ...*
Les responsables de l'enquête **ont raison d'**inclure les moins de 15 ans.	*... were right to ...*
L'auteur souligne ce détail **à juste titre** *or* **avec raison.**	*... rightly emphasizes*
Il était grand temps que quelqu'un prenne la défense des personnes âgées.	*it was certainly time that*
Enfin un ouvrage qui traite vraiment des problèmes des femmes qui travaillent!	*at last, a work which really ...*
Ce livre est le bienvenu car il apporte un nouvel éclairage sur la question.	*this book is welcome because*

Indicating disapproval

Il est regrettable que l'auteur n'ait pas apporté le même soin à la présentation de son ouvrage.	*it is a pity that*
Il serait vraiment dommage qu'une découverte aussi importante ne soit pas reconnue à sa juste valeur.	*it would be a pity if*
Malheureusement, cette étude est très inégale.	*unfortunately*
On peut s'étonner de la rapidité avec laquelle la réforme a été appiquée.	*one may well be surprised at*
On voit mal comment les élèves pourraient bénéficier de cette mesure.	*it is difficult to see how*
Les habitants **condamnent** *or* **critiquent** le projet d'autoroute, qui va détruire la tranquillité du village.	*condemn*
Ils **reprochent aux** autorités *or* ils **accusent** les autorités **de** ne pas les avoir consultés à temps.	*they complain that the authorities ...*

Making a correction

En réalité *or* **En fait,** il ne s'agit pas du tout de cela.	*in (actual) fact*
Il ne s'agit pas à proprement parler de commerce, **mais plutôt de** troc.	*it is not a question of X, but rather of Y*
Son récit est **très loin de la vérité: en fait ...**	*... is very far from the truth: in fact ...*
Ces critiques **ne semblent pas justifiées.**	*... do not seem to be justified*
Ces craintes **sont** absolument **sans fondement.**	*are quite without foundation*
Pour rétablir les faits, je dirai que ...	*to re-establish the facts, I shall ...*

Indicating the reason for something

Ceci tient à *or* **Ceci résulte d'**un malentendu.	*this arises from*
C'est pour cette raison que tout retour en arrière est impossible.	*it is for this reason that*
Le vieux château sera réparé: **en effet,** il constitue un des meilleurs exemples de l'architecture du XVIIe siècle.	*indeed, it constitutes ...*
On ne peut se fier à ces chiffres, **attendu que** *or* **vu que** les calculs sont approximatifs.	*given that*
S'il a accepté, **c'est certainement qu'**on a fait pression sur lui.	*it is certainly because ...*
Ceci expliquerait la baisse des ventes en février.	*this would explain*
L'auteur **laisse entendre que** *or* **suggère que** l'explication est ailleurs.	*suggests that*

Setting out the consequences of something

Cette décision **a eu d'heureuses conséquences/a eu des conséquences néfastes.**	*had happy/fatal consequences*
Sa nomination **a eu pour conséquence de** créer un mécontentement considérable au sein de l'organisation.	*had the effect of*
On peut donc en déduire que *or* **On en arrive à la conclusion que** l'auteur désapprouve cette conception de l'autorité.	*one is led to the conclusion that*
Il était très mécontent des conditions qui lui étaient offertes, **aussi** a-t-il donné sa démission.	*which is why*
Voilà pourquoi *or* **C'est pourquoi** la famille occupe une place de choix dans ses romans.	*and that is why*
La fermeture de l'usine **aura pour conséquence** *or* **aura comme résultat** *or* **mènera à** la disparition du village.	*will result in*
Les compagnies aériennes ont augmenté leurs tarifs, **d'où** une réduction du nombre des passagers.	*leading to*
Le nombre de postes sera réduit à trois, **ce qui implique** *or* **ce qui signifie** le départ de quatre employés.	*which means*
Le héros n'apparaissant pas dans ce chapitre, **il s'ensuit que** *or* **il en résulte que** les personnages secondaires occupent le premier plan.	*it follows from this that*
Il s'est refusé à tout commentaire, **ce qui tend à prouver qu'**il avait menti.	*which seems to confirm that*
Ainsi, la personnalité du héros se révèle être beaucoup plus complexe qu'elle ne le semblait au premier abord.	*thus*

Contrasting or comparing

Certains disent que la production d'énergie est essentielle à notre avenir, **d'autres affirment** que nous en produisons déjà trop.	*some say ... others declare ...*
Certains parlent aujourd'hui de la faillite de l'école. **Inversement, d'autres** proclament les progrès de l'éducation.	*some people ... conversely, others ...*
Il dépasse de loin son rival. // **Il n'arrive pas à la cheville de** son rival.	*he is far better than // not nearly as good as*
Comparé à son premier roman, celui-ci a plus de finesse.	*compared with*
Il n'y a pas de comparaison possible **entre** les deux.	*there is no comparison possible between the two*

LE TÉLÉPHONE

THE TELEPHONE

POUR OBTENIR UN NUMÉRO

Could you get me Newhaven 465786 please.
(four-six-five-seven-eight-six)
You'll have to look up the number in the directory.
You should get the number from International Directory Enquiries.
Would you give me Directory Enquiries please.

Can you give me the number of the Decapex company, of 54 Broad Street, Newham.
It's not in the book.
They're ex-directory *(Brit)*. // They're unlisted *(US)*.
What is the code for Exeter?
Can I dial direct to Colombia?
You omit the '0' when dialling England from France.

How do I make an outside call? // What do I dial for an outside line?

GETTING A NUMBER

Je voudrais le 46 09 37 12, s'il vous plaît.
(quarante-six zéro-neuf trente-sept douze)
Vous devez consulter l'annuaire.
Vous pourrez obtenir le numéro par les renseignements internationaux.
Pourriez-vous me passer les renseignements, s'il vous plaît?
Je voudrais le numéro de la société Decapex, 20 rue de la Marelle, à Pierrefitte.
Je n'ai pas trouvé le numéro dans l'annuaire.
Désolé, leur numéro est sur la liste rouge.
Quel est l'indicatif pour Briançon?
Est-ce que je peux appeler la Colombie par l'automatique?
Si vous téléphonez de France en Angleterre, ne faites pas le zéro.
Comment est-ce que je peux téléphoner à l'extérieur?

LES DIFFÉRENTS TYPES DE COMMUNICATIONS

It's a local call.
This is a long-distance call from Worthing.

I want to make an international call.
I want to make a reverse charge call *ou* a transferred charge call to a London number *(Brit)*. // I want to call a London number collect *(US)*.
I'd like to make a personal call *(Brit) ou* a person-to-person call *(US)* to Joseph Broadway on Jamestown 123456.
I want an ADC call to Bournemouth.

I'd like a credit card call to Berlin.

What do I dial to get the speaking clock?
I'd like an alarm call for 7.30 tomorrow morning.

DIFFERENT TYPES OF TELEPHONE CALL

C'est une communication locale.
C'est une communication interurbaine en provenance de Lille.
Je voudrais une communication pour l'étranger.
Je voudrais appeler Londres en PCV. (N.B.: system no longer exists in France.)

Je voudrais une communication avec préavis à l'intention de M. Gérard Leblanc au 26 85 77 08.
Je voudrais une communication avec indication de durée pour Bourges.
Je voudrais une communication payable avec carte de crédit pour Berlin.
Quel numéro dois-je faire pour l'horloge parlante?
Je voudrais être réveillé à 7.30 demain.

LE STANDARDISTE PARLE

Number, please.
What number do you want? // What number are you calling? // What number are you dialling?
Where are you calling from?
Would you repeat the number please.
You can dial the number direct.
Replace the receiver and dial again.

There's a Mr Sandy Campbell calling you from Canberra and wishes you to pay for the call. Will you accept it?
Can Mr Williams take a personal call *(Brit)*? // Can Mr Williams take a person-to-person call *(US)*?
Go ahead, caller.
(Directory Enquiries) There's no listing under that name.
There's no reply from 45 77 57 84.
I'll try to reconnect you.

Hold the line, caller.
All lines to Bristol are engaged — please try later.

It's a card phone.
I'm trying it for you now.

It's ringing. // Ringing for you now.
The line is engaged *(Brit)*. // The line is busy *(US)*.

THE OPERATOR SPEAKS

Quel numéro voulez-vous?
Quel numéro demandez-vous?

D'où appelez-vous?
Pourriez-vous répéter le numéro, s'il vous plaît?
Vous pouvez obtenir ce numéro par l'automatique.
Raccrochez et renouvelez votre appel. // Raccrochez et recomposez le numéro.
M. Ladret vous appelle en PCV d'Amsterdam. Est-ce que vous acceptez la communication?
Il y a un appel avec préavis pour M. Williams — est-ce qu'il est là?
C'est à vous. // Vous êtes en ligne.
(aux Renseignements) Il n'y a pas d'abonné à ce nom.
Le 45 77 57 84 ne répond pas.
J'essaie de rétablir la communication. // Je vais essayer de refaire le numéro.
Ne quittez pas.
Par suite de l'encombrement des lignes, votre appel ne peut aboutir. Veuillez rappeler ultérieurement.
C'est un téléphone à carte.
J'essaie de vous mettre en ligne. // J'essaie d'obtenir la communication.
Ça sonne.
La ligne est occupée.

QUAND L'ABONNÉ RÉPOND

Could I have extension 516? // Can you give me extension 516?
Is that Mr Lambert's phone?
Could I speak to Mr Swinton please? // I'd like to speak to Mr Swinton, please. // Is Mr Swinton there?
Could you put me through to Dr Henderson, please?
Who's speaking?
I'll try again later.
I'll call back in half an hour.
Could I leave my number for her to call me back?
I'm ringing from a callbox *(Brit).* // I'm calling from a pay station *(US)*.
I'm phoning from England.
Would you ask him to ring me when he gets back.

Could you ring that number for me?

WHEN YOUR NUMBER ANSWERS

Pourriez-vous me passer le poste 516, s'il vous plaît?

Je suis bien chez M. Lambert?
Je voudrais parler à M. Wolff, s'il vous plaît?. // Pourrais-je parler à M. Wolff, s'il vous plaît?
Pourriez-vous me passer le docteur Dupont, s'il vous plaît?
Qui est à l'appareil?
Je rappellerai plus tard.
Je rappellerai dans une demi-heure.
Pourrais-je laisser mon numéro pour qu'elle me rappelle?
Je vous appelle d'une cabine téléphonique. // Je téléphone d'une cabine.
J'appelle d'Angleterre. // Je téléphone d'Angleterre.
Pourriez-vous lui demander de me rappeler quand il rentrera?
Voulez-vous appeler ce numéro pour moi?

LE STANDARD DE L'ABONNÉ PARLE

Queen's Hotel, can I help you?

Who is calling, please?
Who shall I say is calling?
Do you know his extension number?
I am connecting you now. // I'm putting you through now.
I'm putting you through now to Mrs Thomas.
I have a call from Tokyo for Mrs Thomas.
I've got Miss Martin on the line for you.
Miss Paxton is calling you from Paris.
Dr Craig is talking on the other line.
Sorry to keep you waiting.
There's no reply.
You're through to our Sales Department.

THE SWITCHBOARD OPERATOR SPEAKS

Allô — Hôtel des Glycines, j'écoute. // Allô — Hôtel des Glycines, à votre service.
Qui est à l'appareil?
C'est de la part de qui?
Est-ce que vous connaissez le numéro du poste?
Je vous le passe.
Je vous passe Mme Thomas.
Quelqu'un en ligne de Tokyo demande Mme Thomas.
J'ai Mlle Martin à l'appareil.
Mme Dupuis vous appelle de Paris.
M. Potain est sur l'autre ligne.
Ne quittez pas.
Ça ne répond pas.
Vous avez le service des ventes en ligne.

POUR RÉPONDRE AU TÉLÉPHONE

Hullo, this is Anne speaking.
(Is that Anne?) Speaking.
Would you like to leave a message?
Can I take a message for him?
Don't hang up yet.
Put the phone down and I'll call you back.
This is a recorded message.

Please speak after the tone.

ANSWERING THE TELEPHONE

Allô, c'est Anne à l'appareil.
(C'est Anne à l'appareil?) Elle-même.
Voulez-vous laisser un message?
Voulez-vous que je lui fasse une commission?
Ne quittez pas. // Ne raccrochez pas.
Raccrochez et je vous rappelle.
Vous êtes en communication avec un répondeur automatique.
Au bip sonore, veuillez laisser votre message.

EN CAS DE DIFFICULTÉ

I can't get through (at all).
The number is not ringing.
I'm getting 'number unobtainable'. // I'm getting the 'number unobtainable' signal.

Their phone is out of order.
We were cut off.
I must have dialled the wrong number.
We've got a crossed line.
I've called them several times with no reply.
You gave me a wrong number.
I got the wrong extension.

This is a very bad line.

WHEN IN TROUBLE

Je n'arrive pas à avoir le numéro.
Ça ne sonne pas.
Tout ce que j'obtiens, c'est 'il n'y a pas d'abonné au numéro que vous demandez'. // Tout ce que j'obtiens, c'est 'le numéro que vous demandez n'est pas attribué'.
Leur téléphone est en dérangement.
On nous a coupés. // La communication a été coupée.
J'ai dû faire un faux numéro.
Il y a quelqu'un d'autre sur la ligne.
J'ai appelé plusieurs fois, mais ça ne répond pas.
Vous m'avez donné un faux numéro.
On ne m'a pas donné le bon poste. // On s'est trompé de poste.
La ligne est très mauvaise.

LA SUGGESTION

We could stop off in Barcelona for a day or two, if you would like to.	*nous pourrions*
How do you fancy a couple of days at the sea?	*as-tu envie de*
What would you say to a morning on Grand Canal?	*que diriez-vous de*
Would you like to visit the castle while you are here?	*aimeriez-vous*
I suggest *ou* **I would suggest** *ou* **I'd like to suggest that** we offer him the job.	*je suggère que*
What if we were to arrange a meeting for the end of May?	*et si on organisait*
Perhaps we should ask him if he would like to come with us?	*peut-être devrions-nous*
Why not go round to see him yourself?	*pourquoi ne pas*
Suppose *ou* **Supposing** you were to rent a house in Sicily?	*supposons que*
Perhaps you might care to add your name to this list?	*voudriez-vous*
You could *ou* **You might** buy the tickets for both of us, if you agree.	*vous pourriez peut-être*
You might like to write to him and explain what happened.	*vous pourriez toujours*
In your place *ou* **If I were you,** I'd be very careful.	*à votre place*
What do you think about trying to set up such a meeting?	*que pensez-vous de*
Have you ever thought of applying for the job?	*avez-vous jamais pensé à*
I've got an idea — let's invite him over here.	*j'ai une idée — invitons-le . . .*
If I may make a suggestion, why not discuss it with him?	*si je puis faire une suggestion*
If I might be permitted to suggest something: would you take her on in your department for a while?	*si je puis me permettre de suggérer quelque chose*
We propose that half the fee be paid in advance, and half on completion of the contract.	*nous proposons que*

(avec une certaine hésitation)

It is quite important that you should wait till he returns.	*il est important que*
I am convinced that this would be a dangerous step to take.	*je suis convaincu que*
I was thinking of going there next month — how about it?	*je pensais*
There would be a lot to be said for acting at once.	*il y aurait un gros avantage à*
Might I be allowed to offer a little advice? — talk it over with your parents first.	*puis-je offrir un conseil?*
If you want my advice, I'd steer well clear of them.	*à mon avis, vous feriez bien de*
In these circumstances, **it might be better to** wait.	*il vaudrait peut-être mieux*
It might be a good thing *ou* **It might be a good idea** to warn her about this.	*il serait bon de*
If you were to give me the negative, **I could** get copies made.	*si vous me donniez . . . je pourrais*
Would it matter if you didn't hand in the essay on time?	*est-ce que cela serait grave si*
Say you were to change the date of your holiday?	*et si vous changiez . . .*
Some people might prefer to wait until they are sure of the money before acting.	*il y a des gens qui préféreraient*
Perhaps it might be as well to ask her permission first?	*peut-être serait-il préférable de*
I'd be very careful not to commit myself.	*je ferais très attention à ne pas*

DEMANDANT DES SUGGESTIONS

What would you do in my place *ou* **What would you do if you were me?**	*que feriez-vous à ma place?*
Have you any idea what the best way to go about it is?	*savez-vous . . .*
I wonder if you have any suggestion to offer on where we might go for a few days?	*je me demande si vous pouvez suggérer*
I'm a bit doubtful about where to start.	*je ne sais pas exactement*

ET, SELON LE CONTEXTE:

if you don't object / I'd like to ask you a favour / I would advise you to . . . / take care not to . . . / I would recommend / whatever you do, don't . . . / perhaps you would kindly / I cannot put it too strongly / my idea was to . . . / how do you feel about this? / I should be grateful if you would / it could be in your interest to . . . / it occurred to me that / I would be delighted to . . . / I hope you will not be offended if / if I were to make an informed guess, I'd say / it might have something to do with / if you ask me, you'd better / it would certainly be advisable to . . .

LE CONSEIL

POUR DEMANDER UN CONSEIL

I'd like your advice about *ou* **I'd appreciate your advice about** where to go in Italy.	*je voudrais vous demander votre avis sur*
What would you advise me to do in the circumstances?	*que me conseilleriez-vous de faire*
Would you advise me to do as they ask?	*à votre avis, dois-je ...*
How would you go about it, in my place? // **What would you do,** if you were me?	*que feriez-vous*
Do you think I ought to sell it to him?	*pensez-vous que je devrais*
What would you recommend in these circumstances?	*que recommandez-vous*

POUR DONNER UN CONSEIL

If you want my advice, I'd steer well clear of them.	*si vous voulez mon avis, vous feriez bien de*
Take my advice and don't rush into anything.	*suivez mon conseil*
My advice would be to have nothing to do with this affair.	*je vous conseillerais de*
I would strongly advise you to reconsider this decision.	*je vous conseille vivement de*
I would advise against any such course of action.	*je déconseillerais*
It would certainly be advisable *ou* **You would be well advised to** get his permission before going any further in this matter.	*il serait recommandé de*
In your place I would *ou* **If I were you I would** clear it with her headmaster first.	*à votre place, je ...*
I think you should send *ou* **I think you ought to** send it by express post, as time is so important.	*à mon avis, vous devriez*
Why don't you explain to her exactly what happened?	*pourquoi ne pas*
If you want my opinion, I'd go by air to save time.	*je trouve que tu devrais*
You'd be as well to think it over carefully, before taking any decision.	*tu ferais bien de*
Would you allow me to suggest something? You could go there direct from London.	*me permettez-vous une suggestion?*
If you ask me, you'd better find another travel agency.	*à mon avis, vous feriez mieux de*
Do be sure you read the small print before you sign anything.	*prenez soin de*
Try to avoid a quarrel with him, for my sake.	*essaie de*
Whatever you do, don't drink the local brandy.	*quoi qu'il arrive*
We believe that **you would be ill-advised to** have any dealings with this firm.	*vous auriez tort de*
Please believe me when I say **it is in your interest to** act promptly now.	*il est dans votre intérêt de*

(de façon moins directe)

It might be wise *ou* **It might be a good thing to** go and see your doctor about this.	*il serait peut-être prudent de*
In view of the present situation, **it might be better to** think it over for a while before acting.	*il serait peut-être préférable de*
I'd be very careful not to commit myself.	*je ferais très attention de ne pas*
You might like *ou* **You might care to** write to him and explain what happened.	*vous pourriez peut-être*
There would be something to be said for acting at once.	*il y a quelques avantages à*
I wonder if it might be as well to wait for another few days?	*peut-être serait-il souhaitable de*

POUR LANCER UN AVERTISSEMENT

Take care not to spend too much money.	*faites attention de ne pas*
Be careful not to believe everything they tell you.	*veillez à ne pas*
Make sure you don't *ou* **Mind you don't** sign anything.	*surtout, ne signez rien*
I'd think twice about going on holiday with her.	*j'hésiterais à*
It would be sensible to consult someone who knows the country before making detailed plans.	*il serait bon de*
It would be sheer madness to marry him when you feel that way about him.	*ce serait de la folie de*
You're risking a long delay in Cairo, if you decide to come back by that route.	*vous risquez*

ET, SELON LE CONTEXTE:

what would you do in my position? / can you help me to ... / I should be grateful if you could / what would your reaction be if / might I be allowed to offer some advice? / we would urge you to ... / things being what they are / in your shoes, I would / my view of the matter is / it's really none of my business but ... / a word of caution ... / it would seem a good idea to ... / I hope you don't think I'm interfering but ... / it occurred to me that you might / don't be offended if I suggest / if I might be permitted to ... / I should warn you that / instinct tells me that

L'OFFRE

May I show you the city when you are here?	*puis-je*
Would you like me to find out more about it for you?	*voudriez-vous que je*
Is there anything I can do about your accommodation?	*puis-je vous aider*
We would like to offer you the post of assistant manager.	*nous voudrions vous offrir*
I might perhaps *ou* **I could perhaps** give you a hand with the painting?	*je pourrais peut-être*
Shall I collect the documents for you on my way there?	*voulez-vous que je*
How about letting me find some help for you in the house?	*et si je ...*

(de façon plus indirecte)

Say I were to lend you the money till your bursary comes through?	*mettons que je ...*
Would you allow me to contribute towards the cost?	*me permettriez-vous de*
I would be delighted to help, if I may.	*je serais enchanté de*
I hope you will not be offended if I offer a contribution towards the expense you are incurring.	*j'espère que vous ne serez pas vexé si*
It would give me great pleasure to welcome you to my home.	*je serais très heureux de*
I'd like to pay my share, **if it's all the same to you.**	*si cela vous est égal*
If you don't mind, I'll buy my own tickets.	*si cela ne vous ennuie pas*
Do let me know if I can help you on anything else.	*prévenez-moi si*
If I can be of any assistance, please **do not hesitate to** write to me.	*n'hésitez pas à*
What if I were to call for you in the car?	*et si je ...*
It occurred to me that I might go with you as far as the border at least?	*j'ai pensé que je pourrais peut-être*

LA REQUÊTE

Would you please *ou* **Will you please** call in and see her if you have time when you are in Rome.	*voudriez-vous avoir la gentillesse de*
Would you please *ou* **Would you kindly** reserve one single room for those nights.	*veuillez avoir l'obligeance de*
Could you arrange *ou* **Would it be possible for you to** arrange for a car to come to the airport for me?	*pourriez-vous*
Would you mind letting me have a copy of your letter to him?	*est-ce que cela vous ennuierait de*
Might I ask you to *ou* **Could I ask you to** let me have a note of his address some time?	*puis-je vous demander de*

(dans une langue plus soutenue)

I should be grateful if you would let me know which you have in stock.	*je vous serais reconnaissant de bien vouloir*
I would ask you *ou* **I must ask you** not to use the telephone for long-distance calls.	*je dois vous demander de ne pas*
We should be glad to receive your cheque for this amount by return of post.	*nous vous serons obligés de nous envoyer*
You are requested to return the books to us at once.	*vous êtes prié de*
Kindly inform us when your account will be in credit.	*veuillez ...*

(de façon plus indirecte)

I would rather you didn't tell him what I said.	*je préférerais que vous ne ...*
It would be very helpful *ou* **It would be very useful if** you could find me a room there.	*cela me rendrait service si ...*
I was hoping that you might find time to go and see her.	*j'espérais que*
I wonder whether you might not ask her for it?	*pourquoi ne pas*
I would appreciate it if you could let me have copies of the best photographs.	*je vous serais reconnaissant de*

ET, SELON LE CONTEXTE:

I apologize for troubling you with such a request / I hope this will not take up too much of your time / if it is not too much trouble / if I am not disturbing you / I hope you don't mind about this / don't forget to ... / for heaven's sake don't / may I remind you to ... / we look forward to receiving from you / if you do not ... we shall

LA COMPARAISON

This year's sales figures are very high **in comparison with** *ou* **compared with** *ou* **when compared with** those of our competitors.	*en comparaison de*
By comparison, this one is much more expensive.	*par comparaison*
If you compare New York and Washington, you realise how pleasant the latter is to live in.	*si l'on compare*
If we set the overall cost **against** our estimate, we can see how inaccurate it was.	*si nous comparons*
This house has a lovely garden, **whereas** *ou* **whilst** the other has only a small yard.	*tandis que*
The quality of the paintings is very disappointing **beside** that of the sculpture section in the exhibition.	*comparé à*
In contrast to Joan's, Anne's career has flourished since she left university.	*par contraste avec*
As opposed to John's *ou* **Unlike** John's, Peter's work is careful and thorough.	*par opposition à*
This is **nowhere near as** large **as** the other one.	*loin d'être aussi ... que*
Let us compare and contrast the two approaches.	*comparons et contrastons*
We must now attempt to **note the similarities and the differences.**	*noter les ressemblances et les différences*
There is no comparison between them *ou* **You cannot compare them at all** *ou* **They are simply not comparable** — the first scheme is clearly much more ambitious than the second.	*ils ne sont pas comparables*
The former looks good, but **the latter** is more effective.	*le premier ... le second*
There is some (*ou* **no** *ou* **a certain** *etc***) resemblance between** the two photographs. // **There is** some (*ou* **no** *etc)* **similarity between** them.	*il y a une certaine* etc *resemblance entre*
There is some (*ou* **no** *etc)* **difference between** them.	*il y a une certaine* etc *différence entre*
It's swings and roundabouts — what you gain on one, you lose on the other.	*c'est du pareil au même*
It is something like a television screen, **but** much smaller. // **He's like** his brother, **only** fairer.	*ressemble à ... mais en plus ...*
What differentiates him from similar writers is his grasp of social truths.	*ce qui le distingue de*

(comparaisons favorables)

It is greatly superior to that restaurant we went to last time we were in Rome.	*c'est infiniment supérieur à*
The imported version just **can't compete with** the one we make ourselves.	*ne peut se comparer à*
I think James **has the edge over** Paul in maths.	*est légèrement supérieur à*
The little chest of drawers is really **in a class of its own.**	*unique en son genre*

(comparaisons défavorables)

It is **much inferior to** the sample they sent us.	*est très inférieur à*
His book **is not worthy of comparison with** *ou* **does not bear comparison with** the writings of the experts in the field.	*n'est pas comparable à*
I'm afraid her work simply **does not measure up to** that of her classmates.	*n'est pas aussi bon que*
The English forwards **were no match for** the French, who scored three goals in the first half.	*étaient très inférieurs aux*
As far as brains go, **he is not in the same class as** *ou* **he is not a patch on** his father.	*il est loin d'être aussi bien que*

(ce qui est semblable)

It is really **much the same as** the other. // **There's not much difference between** them. // **There's not much to choose between** them.	*il n'y a pas grande différence entre*
These rings are about **equal in** value. // They are **of equal** value.	*sont de valeur égale*
The value of this house **is equivalent to** *ou* **corresponds to** that of the one you own.	*correspond à*
It has been likened to *or* **It has been compared to** one of Wordworth's later poems.	*on l'a comparé à*
His exam results **are on a par with** those of his brother.	*valent ceux de*

(ce qui ne peut pas se comparer)

They are simply not comparable *ou* **You just can't compare them at all** — they are so different in their approach.	*on ne peut pas les comparer*
There is little correlation between one set of results and the other.	*il n'y a pas vraiment de corrélation entre*
They have so little in common that it is a waste of time trying to assess their respective merits.	*ils se ressemblent si peu*

L'OPINION

POUR S'ENQUÉRIR DE L'OPINION DE QUELQU'UN

What do you think of *ou* **What is your opinion on** the way he has behaved over this?	*que pensez-vous de*
If I may ask your opinion, **how do you see** the traffic developing in this part of the town?	*à votre avis, comment est-ce que*
I'd be interested to know what your reaction is to the latest report on food additives.	*j'aimerais savoir ce que vous pensez de*
Can you tell me **what your own feelings are about** the way the house was sold?	*pouvez-vous me dire ce que vous pensez personnellement de*
What are your thoughts on the subject of how to earn more money?	*avez-vous une opinion en ce que concerne*
I have been asked to find out **what your attitude is to** this problem.	*quelle est votre attitude en ce qui concerne*
Have you come to any conclusions about how we should plan the next stage?	*est-ce que vous avez décidé de ce que*

POUR EXPRIMER SON OPINION

In my opinion *ou* **As I see it,** that was the best thing that could have happened to them.	*à mon avis*
I feel children shouldn't be ordered around too much.	*je trouve que*
Personally, I believe her sister should have invited her to stay.	*personnellement, je trouve que*
When I think about it, **it seems to me that** there are too many people chasing too few jobs.	*il me semble bien que*
I have the impression that there has been enough money spent on this project already.	*j'ai l'impression que*
I have an idea *ou* **a hunch** he might be coming back before the end of the summer.	*j'ai comme une idée que*
I daresay he'll apologise if you give him time.	*j'imagine que*
To my mind, he's the wrong man for the job.	*à mon avis*
From my point of view *ou* **As far as I am concerned,** television is a complete waste of time.	*en ce qui me concerne*
My own view of the matter is that the government will have to act quickly.	*pour ma part, je pense que*
My own point of view is that *ou* **it's my belief that** people are best left to sort out their own lives.	*personnellement je trouve que*
It's my opinion that *ou* **I am of the opinion that** such people should not be allowed to get access to public funds.	*je considère que*
I am convinced that they did it in order to make things difficult for us.	*je suis convaincu que*
From where I stand, it looks as though the school will have to close.	*de mon point de vue, il semble que*
If you ask me *ou* **If you want to know what I think** *ou* **if you want my opinion,** he should have been sent to hospital right away.	*si vous me demandez mon avis, je trouve que*

POUR RÉPONDRE SANS EXPRIMER D'OPINION

I should prefer not to comment on that statement at the moment.	*je préférerais ne pas donner mon avis sur*
I would rather not commit myself at this stage.	*je préférerais ne pas m'engager*
I don't know what to think about *ou* **I don't know what to say about** the new scheme to brighten up to town.	*je ne sais que penser de*
This is not something I have given a lot of thought to.	*je n'y ai pas vraiment réfléchi*
I have no particular views on this subject. // **I haven't any strong feelings** about it.	*je n'ai pas d'opinion particulière sur*
I am not in a position to say much about what is going on at these talks, as I have been abroad for some time.	*je ne suis pas à même de dire*
I haven't any idea *ou* **I haven't the slightest notion** what we ought to do now.	*je n'ai pas la moindre idée de ce que*
I'm afraid **I am totally ignorant about** *ou* **I know nothing at all about** the internal combustion engine.	*j'ignore tout de*
It all depends on what you mean by …	*tout dépend de ce que vous voulez dire par …*
It depends on your point of view.	*c'est une question de point de vue*
It is difficult to say who is right about this.	*il est difficile de dire*
Your guess is as good as mine.	*vous en savez autant que moi*
It doesn't much matter to me, whether or not he decides to go.	*cela m'est égal …*
I wouldn't like to give an opinion on that.	*je n'aimerais pas me prononcer là-dessus*

LES GOÛTS ET PRÉFÉRENCES

POUR S'ENQUÉRIR DE CE QU'ON AIME OU PRÉFÈRE

Would you like to visit the castle, while you are here? — *aimeriez-vous*

How do you feel about going to a cricket match when you're in England? — *avez-vous envie de*

What do you like doing best, when you are on holiday? — *que préférez-vous faire*

What's your favourite way to spend an evening? — *quelle est votre occupation favorite*

Which of the two do you prefer? — *lequel des deux préférez-vous?*

We could either go to Ottawa or stay in New York — **which would you rather do?** — *que préférez-vous*

POUR DIRE CE QU'ON AIME

I greatly enjoy going to the cinema, especially to see a good French film. — *j'aime beaucoup*

I'm very keen on gardening. — *j'aime énormément*

As for seaside towns, **I'm very fond of** Brighton. — *j'aime particulièrement*

What I like better than anything else is *ou* **There's nothing I like more than** a quiet evening by the fire with a book. — *ce que j'aime le mieux, c'est*

For me, there's nothing to compare with the Italian Renaissance painters. — *pour moi, rien ne vaut ...*

I must admit to a certain **affection for** *ou* **fondness for** *ou* **weakness for** Victorian houses. — *un penchant pour*

I have **a soft spot for** labradors. — *un faible pour*

I like people **to be** on time for their appointments. — *j'aime qu'on soit*

POUR DIRE CE QU'ON N'AIME PAS

I very much dislike that sort of holiday. — *je n'aime pas du tout*

I can't stand *ou* **I can't bear** books that other people have written on. — *je déteste*

I'm not too keen on seaside holidays. — *je n'aime pas trop*

I can't say writing essays **appeals to me very much.** — *je ne peux pas dire que j'aime*

It's not my kind of book *(ou* film *ou* place *etc).* — *ce n'est pas mon genre de*

I'm fed up with snooker on television. — *j'en ai assez de*

Cowboy films **aren't my favourite** form of entertainment. — *ne sont pas ce que je préfère*

I'm not too wild about *ou* **I can't get up any enthusiasm for** hill-walking. — *je ne suis pas emballé par*

Knitting **isn't really my thing,** I'm afraid. — *n'est pas qch que j'aime*

I've gone off the idea of cycling round Holland. — *je n'ai plus envie de*

There's nothing I like less *ou* **There's nothing I dislike more** than having to get up at dawn. — *il n'y a rien qui me déplaise plus que*

I don't much like the fact that he is always late on Monday mornings. — *je n'aime pas beaucoup le fait que*

I took a dislike to him the moment I saw him. — *il m'a déplu*

What I hate most is waiting in queues for buses. — *ce que je déteste le plus*

I find it intolerable that there should be no public transport here on Sundays. — *il est intolérable que*

I have a particular aversion to *ou* **I have a particular dislike of** people who think like that. — *je ne peux pas supporter*

POUR DIRE CE QU'ON PRÉFÈRE

I should prefer to *ou* **I would rather** wait until we have enough money to go by air. — *je préférerais*

I'd prefer not to *ou* **I'd rather not** go and see her until I have found the book she lent me. — *je préférerais ne pas*

I'd prefer you not to *ou* **I'd rather you didn't** invite him. — *je préférerais que vous ne ... pas*

We should prefer you to put any comments in writing, and send them to our Service Manager. — *nous préférerions que vous*

I like the blue curtains **better than** the red ones. // **I prefer** the blue curtains **to** the red ones. — *j'aime mieux les ... que les ...*

POUR EXPRIMER L'INDIFFÉRENCE

I have no particular preference. — *je n'ai aucune préference*

I don't mind at all — let's do whichever is easiest. — *ça m'est complètement égal*

I really don't care what you tell her. — *peu importe*

It's all the same to me whether he comes with us or not: I suggest you decide. — *ça n'a pas d'importance si*

I don't feel strongly about what sort of transport we choose — why don't you make that decision? — *je n'ai pas de préférence marquée*

It makes no odds, one way or the other. — *ça ne change rien*

L'INTENTION ET LA VOLONTÉ

POUR S'ENQUÉRIR DE CE QUE QUELQU'UN COMPTE FAIRE

Will you take the job? // **Do you intend to** *ou* **Do you mean to** take the job?	*avez-vous l'intention de*
What flight **do you mean** *ou* **do you intend to** take to New York?	*pensez-vous prendre*
What do you propose to do with the money you have inherited?	*que comptez-vous faire*
It would be useful to know **what your intentions are** *ou* **what you intend to do.**	*ce que vous comptez faire*
What had you in mind for the rest of the programme?	*qu'envisagiez-vous*
Did you mean to tell him how much you had paid for the house, or did the figure just slip out?	*aviez-vous l'intention de*

POUR EXPRIMER SES INTENTIONS

I am going *ou* **I intend** *ou* **I mean** *ou* **My intention is to** sell the car as soon as I can.	*j'ai l'intention de*
They **intended him to** go to university, but he did not pass his exams.	*ils voulaient qu'il aille*
I have made up my mind *ou* **I have decided** to go to university.	*j'ai décidé*
I am thinking of going to live in the country when I retire.	*je fais le projet de*
I am hoping to go and see her when I am in the States.	*j'espère*
They have every intention of returning next year.	*ils sont bien décidés à*
I went to London, **intending to** visit her *ou* **with the intention of** visiting her, but she was away on business.	*dans l'intention de*
What I have in mind is to start a small hardware business.	*mon intention est de*
I aim to reach Africa in three months.	*mon but est de*
He resolved *ou* **He made a resolution to** devote his life to the welfare of the underprivileged.	*il a résolu de*
Our aim *ou* **Our object** in buying the company is to provide work for the people of the village.	*notre intention*
My whole point in complaining **was to** get something done about the state of the roads.	*c'était afin de*
We plan to move *ou* **We are planning on** moving into the European market next year.	*nous comptons*
They bought the land **in order to** farm it *ou* **for the purpose of** farming it.	*dans le but de*
He studied history, **with a view to** becoming a politician when he left college.	*afin de*

POUR EXPRIMER CE QU'ON N'A PAS L'INTENTION DE FAIRE

I didn't mean *ou* **I didn't intend to** offend her, but she made me very angry.	*je ne voulais pas*
I intend not to pay *ou* **I don't intend to pay** unless he completes the work.	*j'ai l'intention de ne pas payer*
His parents **didn't intend him to** be a lion-tamer, but it was the only work he could find.	*n'avaient pas voulu en faire*
He had no intention of accepting the post even it it were offered to him.	*il n'avait nullement l'intention de*
We are not thinking of advertising this post at the moment.	*nous n'envisageons pas de*

POUR EXPRIMER CE QU'ON DÉSIRE FAIRE

I should like to see the Sistine Chapel.	*je voudrais*
Her father **wanted her to** be a teacher.	*voulait qu'elle soit*
Robert **wished** to work abroad but could not get a work permit.	*désirait*
I am very keen to see more students take up engineering.	*je voudrais bien voir*
I'm longing *ou* **I'm dying to** go to Australia, but I can't afford it yet.	*je meurs d'envie de*
I insist that you inform me as soon as you hear from them.	*j'insiste pour que*

POUR EXPRIMER CE QU'ON NE VEUT PAS FAIRE

I don't want *ou* **I have no wish** *ou* **I haven't any desire** to take the credit for something I did not do.	*je n'ai pas l'intention de*
I wouldn't want you to change your plans for my sake.	*je ne veux pas que*
I refuse to tell you where I put the documents.	*je refuse de*
I should prefer you not to speak to her about this.	*je préférerais que vous ne ... pas*

ET, SELON LE CONTEXTE:

what have you in view for / have you anyone in mind for / I am trying to discover your exact aims / did you do it intentionally? / I did it on purpose / it was by design / it was quite deliberate / it was not intentional / I went into this with my eyes open / he contrived to ... / we were figuring on / we were reckoning on / they do not envisage / her dearest wish was to ... / he had set his sights on / his ambition is / I did not bargain for

LA PERMISSION

POUR DEMANDER LA PERMISSION

May I *ou* **Might I** *ou* **Can I** *ou* **Could I** tell her about this?	*puis-je*
Would you let me *ou* **Would you allow me to** be present at the interview?	*me permettriez-vous*
Would it be possible for us to leave the car in your garage for a week?	*nous serait-il possible de*
Is there any chance of borrowing your boat while we are at the lake?	*y a-t-il un petit espoir de*
Do you mind if I come to the meeting next week?	*cela vous ennuierait-il si*
Would it be all right if I arrived on Monday instead of Tuesday?	*cela vous dérangerait-il si*
Would it bother you if I invited him? // **Would you have anything against my** inviting him?	*cela vous ennuierait-il si*
Would you have any objection *ou* **Would there be any objection to** my bringing a friend with me?	*est-ce que vous avez une objection à ce que*
Would you be kind enough to allow me *ou* **I should be grateful if you would allow me to** travel with your group as far as the border.	*je vous serais reconnaissant de bien vouloir me permettre de*
May I be permitted *ou* **May I be allowed to** leave early on these three days?	*me serait-il permis de*
Are we allowed *ou* **Are we permitted** *ou* **Is it allowed** *ou* **Is it permitted to** visit the Cathedral? // **Is** visiting the Cathedral **permitted?**	*est-ce qu'il nous est permis de*
Is it permissible to take photographs inside the gallery?	*est-il permis de*

POUR DONNER LA PERMISSION

You can *ou* **You may** have the car if you promise to drive carefully.	*tu peux*
Of course you must borrow our boat — we are always glad when friends use it. // **By all means,** borrow our boat ...	*je vous en prie*
I should be delighted if you gave my name as a reference for this job.	*je vous permets volontiers de*
It's all right by me *ou* **I'm quite happy** if you want to skip the Cathedral visit.	*je ne vois pas d'inconvénient*
Of course I don't mind if you prefer to stay in Italy for another week.	*bien sûr que cela m'est égal*
I have no objection at all to your quoting me in your article. // **I have nothing against** your quoting me.	*je n'ai pas d'objection à ce que*
You have my permission to be absent for that week.	*je vous permets de*
We should be happy to allow you to inspect the papers here.	*nous vous donnons volontiers l'autorisation de*
You are allowed to visit the Museum, as long as you apply in writing to the Curator first.	*vous avez le droit de*
We have been given permission *ou* **We have been authorised to** hold the meeting in the town hall.	*on nous a donné l'autorisation de*
The manager **is quite agreeable to** *or* **has agreed to** our using his premises.	*veut bien que*

POUR REFUSER LA PERMISSION

You can't *ou* **You mustn't** go anywhere near the research lab.	*vous ne devez pas*
I should prefer you not to *ou* **I wouldn't want you to** *ou* **I'd rather you didn't** give them my name.	*je préférerais que vous ne ... pas*
We regret that it is not possible for you to visit the castle at the moment, owing to the building works.	*il est malheureusement impossible de*
I cannot allow this *ou* **I cannot permit this** for the time being.	*je ne peux le permettre*
I couldn't possibly allow you to show the photographs to a publisher.	*je ne peux en aucun cas vous autoriser à*
I'm not allowed to visit such places alone.	*je n'ai pas le droit de*
I forbid you to approach him on my behalf. // **You must not** approach him.	*je vous interdis de*
You must not *ou* **You are forbidden to** enter the premises without authority from the owners.	*il vous est interdit de*
I've been forbidden to swim for the moment.	*on m'a interdit de*
My doctor **forbids me** any alcohol. // **I've been forbidden** alcohol by my doctor.	*m'interdit*
It is strictly forbidden to carry weapons in this country. // Carrying weapons **is strictly prohibited.**	*il est strictement interdit de*

ET, SELON LE CONTEXTE:

I wanted to ask you if I might / I wonder if I might / if it's all right by you, I ... / can I have the go-ahead to ... / with your permission, I should like to ... / if you agree / that's OK by me / permission is granted / I'm sorry, there's no chance of this / I'm sorry to have to say no, but ... / we are obliged to withhold permission / I am afraid we must reject this request / he has no objection to our ... / they won't object / I managed to get him to agree to ... / he wouldn't hear of it / he refused point-blank

L'OBLIGATION

POUR EXPRIMER CE QU'ON EST OBLIGÉ DE FAIRE

You must *or* **You have got to** *ou* **You have to** be back before midnight.	*vous devez*
You must not fail to pay the amount owing, or you will become liable to prosecution.	*il est indispensable que*
You will go directly to the headmaster's office, and wait for me there.	*(emploi du futur pour marquer l'obligation)*
They could not get into the country **without** a visa. // **They had to have a** visa **to** get into the country.	*il leur fallait . . . pour*
She was obliged to give up her room in the hostel.	*elle a dû*
He was forced to *ou* **obliged to ask** his family for a loan. // He was **driven to** asking his family for a loan.	*il a été contraint de*
You need to *ou* **You must** *ou* **You have to** have an address in Rome before you can apply for the job.	*vous êtes obligé de*
Three passport photos **are required.**	*. . . sont requises*
It is essential *ou* **It is of the utmost importance to** know what the career options are like, before choosing a course of study.	*il est extrêmement important de*
Go and see Pompeii — **it's a must!**	*il faut l'avoir vu*
You really must *ou* **You really should** *ou* **You really ought to** be more careful with your things.	*tu devrais vraiment*
You certainly ought to visit the Colosseum.	*vous devriez en tout cas*
A clean driving licence **is indispensable** *ou* **necessary** *ou* **essential** *ou* **compulsory** for the job. // It is **a requirement of** the job.	*. . . est indispensable*
I must now offer my resignation: in the circumstances, **I cannot do otherwise** *ou* **I have no alternative.**	*je n'ai pas le choix*
You have to come with me — **there's no two ways about it,** since I don't speak the language at all.	*tu devras . . . il n'y a pas d'autre possibilité*

(pour savoir si l'on est obligé de faire quelque chose)

Do I need to *ou* **Must I** *ou* **Do I have to** *ou* **Have I got to** have a work permit?	*dois-je*
Ought I to *ou* **Should I** take some reading matter?	*devrais-je*
Is it necessary to *ou* **Must one** *ou* **Does one need to** *ou* **Does one have to** *ou* **Has one got to** own a pair of skis?	*est-il nécessaire de*
Am I meant *ou* **Am I expected** *ou* **Am I supposed to** fill in this bit of the form too?	*est-ce que je suis censé*

POUR EXPRIMER CE QU'ON N'EST PAS OBLIGÉ DE FAIRE

You needn't *ou* **You don't have to** *ou* **You haven't got to** go there if you don't want to.	*vous n'êtes pas obligé de*
I haven't got to apply before September, but I'd like to do so before I leave on holiday.	*il n'est pas nécessaire que*
It is not necessary *ou* **There's no need** *ou* **It is not compulsory** *ou* **It is not obligatory to** have a letter of acceptance in advance, but it does help.	*il n'est pas obligatoire de*
You are not obliged *ou* **You are under no obligation to** invite him, but it would be a kindness to do so.	*vous n'êtes pas obligé de*
Surely I needn't *ou* **Surely I haven't got to** give him all the details immediately?	*je ne dois quand même pas*

POUR EXPRIMER CE QU'ON NE DOIT PAS FAIRE

You must not *ou* **You are not allowed to** sit the exam more than three times.	*vous n'avez pas le droit de*
You must not *ou* **On no account must you** show this document to any unauthorised person.	*vous ne devez pas*
It is forbidden *ou* **It is not allowed to** bring cameras into the gallery without prior permission from the owners.	*il est interdit de*
I forbid you to return there. // **You are forbidden to** return there.	*je vous défends de*
Smoking **is forbidden** *ou* **is prohibited** in the dining room. // Smoking is **not allowed** *ou* **is not permitted** in the dining room.	*il est interdit de*
You're not supposed to *ou* **You're not meant to** use this room unless you are a club member.	*en principe vous ne devez pas*
You cannot be out of the country for longer than three months **without** losing your right to this grant.	*vous devez rentrer . . . sinon vous perdrez . . .*

ET, SELON LE CONTEXTE:

he had to go, willy-nilly / it was obligatory / they had made it compulsory / it's vital that / it is necessary / it is quite indispensable / it is a prerequisite of / it is my duty to . . . / I'm duty bound to . . . / the onus is on you to . . . / we could not but agree / he was compelled to . . .

L'ACCORD

POUR EXPRIMER L'ACCORD AVEC CE QUI EST DIT

I fully agree with you *ou* **I totally agree with you** on this point. // **We are in complete agreement** on this.	*je suis entièrement d'accord avec vous*
You're quite right *ou* **You are quite correct** when you say the fault lies with the government policy here.	*vous avez raison de dire que*
I share your opinion that this was extremely badly arranged. // **I share** your concern about this matter. // **I share** your views about this.	*je partage*
I think **we see eye to eye** on the question of who should pay for these.	*nous sommes d'accord sur*
We are of the same mind, certainly, **when it comes to** allocating responsibility within the department.	*nous sommes d'accord quand il s'agit de*
We have been thinking along the same lines, that is quite clear.	*nos vues convergent*
We are broadly in agreement with you on the way to approach this problem.	*dans l'ensemble nous sommes d'accord sur*
There are several points of contact between us.	*nous sommes d'accord sur plusieurs points*
My own experience certainly **bears out** *ou* **confirms** what you say.	*confirme ce que vous dites*
Our conclusions **are entirely consistent with** your findings.	*correspondent tout à fait à*
My own independent statistics **corroborate** those of your researcher.	*corroborent . . .*
We must endorse, with some hesitation, your conclusions on this matter.	*nous adhérons à vos conclusions*
Our opinion coincides with yours on all the important points.	*notre opinion coïncide avec la vôtre*
We applaud the group's decision to stand firm on this point.	*nous approuvons le groupe d'avoir décidé*
I take your point about the increased transport costs.	*je reconnais*
I am prepared to **concede that** a trip to Australia is justified.	*je vous accorde que*
It's true that you had the original idea, **but** many other people worked on it.	*il est vrai que . . . mais*
I have no objection to this being done. // **I do not object to** your doing this.	*je n'ai pas d'objection à*

POUR EXPRIMER L'ACCORD AVEC CE QUI EST PROPOSÉ

This solution is most **acceptable to** us.	*est tout à fait acceptable*
We will readily fall in with these proposals.	*nous accepterons volontiers*
I like the sound of what you say about *ou* **I do like your idea of** limiting sightseeing to mornings only.	*j'approuve ce que vous dites à propos de*
This certainly **seems the right way to go about it.**	*. . . semble être la bonne façon de procéder*
As for the idea of your speaking to him about it, **I should certainly welcome this.**	*j'y serai certainement favorable*
The proposed scheme **meets with our approval.**	*nous approuvons*
This is a proposal **which deserves our wholehearted support.**	*qui mérite tout notre soutien*
I will certainly **give my backing to** such a scheme.	*j'apporterai mon soutien à*
We assent to *ou* **We give our assent to** your plan to develop this site commercially.	*nous donnons notre accord à*

POUR EXPRIMER L'ACCORD AVEC CE QUI EST DEMANDÉ

Of course **I shall be happy to** get the tickets.	*je serai heureux de*
I'll do as you suggest and send him the documents.	*je suivrai votre conseil*
There is no problem about getting tickets for him, and I shall do it at the end of the week.	*il n'y a pas de problème pour*
We should be delighted to cooperate with you in this enterprise.	*nous serions enchantés de*
We shall comply with your request at once.	*nous ferons ce que vous demandez*

ET, SELON LE CONTEXTE:

I think the same as you do / as you have quite rightly pointed out / I'll go along with that / it makes sense to do this / I am fully in accord with / I am prepared to give the go-ahead to / I am certainly in favour of / I can see no reason to oppose this / this is quite satisfactory / I am quite ready to . . . / we shall sanction the use of / if you insist, I shall . . . / there can be no doubt about / I cannot dispute the facts given in / there's no denying that / I hasten to agree with / this is just what I had hoped for / after thinking this over / I hoped you would say this / I would urge you to do so / I have taken this on board, and shall . . . / I note your suggestion about / it is eminently sensible to . . . / this is justified by / I have given it some thought / I agree in theory, but in practice . . . / I can't help thinking that / I agree up to a point

LE DÉSACCORD

POUR EXPRIMER LE DÉSACCORD AVEC CE QUI EST DIT

I cannot agree with what you say about this. // **I absolutely disagree** *ou* **I totally disagree** with you on this.	*je ne suis absolument pas d'accord*
You are quite wrong when you suggest that it was his fault.	*vous vous trompez*
There must be some mistake — the ferry could not cost as much as that.	*il doit s'agir d'une erreur*
This cannot be the case. // I am obliged to point out that **this is not the case.**	*ce n'est pas le cas*
You are wrong *ou* **You are mistaken** in believing that my son was involved.	*vous avez tort*
This is your view of the events: **it is certainly not mine.**	*il n'en est pas de même pour moi*
Surely you cannot believe all this?	*j'espère que vous n'y croyez pas*
I can't share your point of view on this. // This is your opinion: I am afraid **I cannot share it.** // **I cannot share** your concern for this section of the group.	*je ne partage pas*
I cannot accept this interpretation of the events.	*je ne peux accepter*
I entirely reject all you say about this.	*je rejette absolument*
We explicitly reject the implication in your letter.	*nous rejetons catégoriquement*
We must agree to differ on this one.	*il faut se résigner à ne pas être d'accord*
I think it might be better if you **thought it over** again.	*il vaudrait mieux y réfléchir un peu plus*
I cannot support you on this matter.	*je ne peux pas vous apporter mon soutien*
I am afraid that **I'm not altogether with you** on this.	*je ne suis pas tout à fait d'accord avec vous*
I can't go along with all you say about them.	*je ne suis pas d'accord avec*
I have discussed this matter with my colleagues, and **we cannot accept your version of the events.**	*nous ne pouvons accepter votre version des événements*
The facts do not bear out this assertion.	*les faits sont en contradiction avec*
This report **diverges from the facts** as I know them.	*ne correspond pas aux faits*
I am afraid I think **the whole thing sounds rather unlikely.**	*c'est peu probable*
I take great exception to this statement.	*je suis indigné de*

POUR EXPRIMER LE DÉSACCORD AVEC CE QUI EST PROPOSÉ

I am not too keen on this idea. // **I don't think much of** this idea.	*je ne crois pas que ce soit une bonne idée*
I am afraid it seems to me to be **the wrong sort of approach to** such a problem.	*ce n'est pas la meilleure façon d'aborder . . .*
This does not seem to be the right way of dealing with the problem.	*ce n'est probablement pas la meilleure façon de . . .*
While we are grateful for the suggestion, **we are unfortunately unable to** implement this change.	*il nous est malheureusement impossible de*
It is not feasible to change the schedule at this late stage.	*il n'est plus possible de*
This is **not a viable** alternative.	*ce n'est pas faisable*
I'd dead against this idea.	*je m'y oppose catégoriquement*
I will not hear of such a thing.	*je ne veux pas en entendre parler*
I regret that I am not in a position to accept your kind offer, but it is much appreciated nonetheless.	*je ne suis pas malheureusement en mesure d'accepter*

POUR EXPRIMER LE DÉSACCORD AVEC CE QUI EST DEMANDÉ

I am afraid **I must refuse.** // **I can't do it,** I'm sorry to say.	*je crains de devoir refuser*
I won't agree *ou* **I can't agree** to do that.	*je refuse*
I cannot in all conscience do what you request.	*je ne peux pas en mon âme et conscience . . .*
I hope you are not too upset, but **I just can't manage it.**	*je ne vais pas y arriver*
I cannot possibly comply with this request.	*je ne peux pas faire ce que vous demandez*
I wouldn't dream of doing a thing like that.	*je ne ferais jamais cela*
I refuse point blank to have anything to do with this affair.	*je refuse catégoriquement*
It would not be possible for me to do this.	*il ne me serait pas possible de*
This is quite **out of the question** for the time being.	*il n'en est pas question*
It is unfortunately impracticable for us to commit ourselves at this stage.	*il nous serait malheureusement difficile de . . .*
In view of the proposed timescale, **I must reluctantly decline to** take part.	*je regrette de ne pouvoir*

L'APPROBATION

You are quite right to wait before making such an important decision. — *vous avez tout à fait raison de*

I entirely approve of the idea of meeting you all in Geneva. — *j'approuve entièrement*

I have a very high opinion of *ou* **I have a very high regard for** *ou* **I think very highly of** the school, and of its headmistress. — *je pense le plus grand bien de*

We are all very enthusiastic about *ou* **We are all very keen on** his proposals for a new sports centre here. — *nous accueillons avec enthousiasme*

It's just the sort of arrangement *(etc)* **I wanted.** — *c'est exactement ce que je voulais*

I certainly go along with that! — *entièrement d'accord!*

I am very much in favour of that sort of thing. — *je suis tout à fait en faveur de*

This project is **worthy of our admiration,** in that it attempts to alleviate poverty and hunger. — *... est admirable*

I greatly appreciated the comfort and cleanliness of the hotel. — *j'ai beaucoup apprécié*

I certainly admire his courage in attempting such a daunting task. — *en tout cas j'admire*

I applaud your honesty in admitting all that. — *j'applaudis*

I shall certainly give it my backing, as it seems the best hope the company has of surviving this very difficult period. — *j'apporterai mon soutien*

Thank you for sending the draft programme: **I like the look of it very much indeed.** — *il me plaît beaucoup*

I must congratulate you on the careful way you approached this problem. — *je vous félicite de*

There are considerable advantages in such a method, not only from the point of view of cost effectiveness, but also ... — *... présente des avantages considérables*

I can thoroughly recommend this plan of action, which has clearly been carefully thought out. — *je recommande vivement*

This plan **deserves our total support** *ou* **our wholehearted approval.** — *... mérite notre soutien*

We are pleased to recognize the merits of this scheme. — *nous sommes heureux de reconnaître les avantages de*

We view this proposal **favourably,** not least because it is based on a clear perception of the needs of the situation. — *nous portons un jugement favorable sur*

We endorse completely all that is proposed for this region. — *nous appuyons tout à fait*

ET, SELON LE CONTEXTE:

that's the way it should be / it's exactly what I had in mind / it's just the job / we should do all we can to see that this is a success / you have a real gift for ... / I couldn't have put it better myself / it is worth the effort / I fully agree with what is being done / he rightly suggests / what a splendid thing to do / an excellent idea

LA DÉSAPPROBATION

I strongly disapprove of *ou* **I heartily disapprove of** such behaviour. — *je désapprouve complètement*

I cannot support *ou* **I cannot approve of** any sort of testing of the drug on live animals. — *je suis opposé à*

We are opposed to *ou* **We condemn** all forms of professional malpractice. — *nous condamnons*

I write to complain of what is being done in the name of progress. — *j'écris pour protester contre*

I must object to this attempt to damage our hospital service. — *je dois m'élever contre*

I can't say I'm pleased about what has happened. — *je ne peux pas dire que je sois content de*

I don't think much of what this government has done so far. — *je n'aime pas beaucoup*

I take a dim view of *ou* **I take a poor view of** students who do not do enough work. — *je critique*

I have a poor opinion of *ou* **I have a low opinion of** people like him. — *je n'ai pas une bien haute opinion de*

I'm fed up with having to wait so long for a passport. — *j'en ai assez de*

I've had about enough of this sort of insinuation. — *je commence à en avoir assez de*

I can't bear *ou* **I can't stand** people who smoke between courses in a restaurant. — *je ne supporte pas*

I am very unhappy about your idea of going off to Turkey on your own. — *je suis contre*

He was quite wrong to tell her what I said about her. — *il a eu tort de*

They should not have refused to give her the money. — *ils n'auraient pas dû*

How dare he say that such people do not matter! — *comment ose-t-il ...*

ET, SELON LE CONTEXTE:

it is really necessary to ... / this does not seem to be the right way of going about it / it seems to be the wrong approach / I greatly dislike / I write to protest against / this is a dreadful nuisance / with considerable dissatisfaction / I reproach him with / I am sorry to learn that / it is a disgrace / it is a scandal

LA CERTITUDE, LA POSSIBILITÉ ET LA CAPACITÉ

POUR EXPRIMER LA CERTITUDE

I am sure *ou* **I am certain** *ou* **I am positive** *ou* **I am convinced that** he will keep his word to us.	*je suis convaincu que*
We now know for certain *ou* **We now know for sure that** the exam papers were seen by several students before the day of the exam.	*nous savons maintenant avec certitude que*
It is certain *ou* **It is indisputable** *ou* **It is undeniable that** the two men met last Friday in London.	*il est certain que*
There is no doubt *ou* **There can be no doubt** that the goods arrived in Liverpool on May 9th.	*il ne fait aucun doute*
It has been established beyond all possible doubt *ou* **It has been established once and for all** that he was working for a foreign power during the time he was in Cairo.	*c'est un fait établi*
From all the evidence it is clear that they were planning to gain control of the company.	*les faits montrent clairement que*
It is beyond all doubt *ou* **It is beyond dispute** *ou* **It is beyond question** that their country is rich enough to support such research.	*il est incontestable que*
The facts are these: we cannot sell the goods without their marketing resources.	*voilà les faits:*
No one can deny that the weather there is better for skiing.	*il est indéniable que*
We shall not fail to let you have the papers as soon as we have processed them.	*nous ne manquerons pas de*
It is inevitable that they will get to know of our meeting.	*il est inévitable que*
You have my absolute assurance that this is the case.	*je peux vous garantir que*
Make no mistake about it — I shall return when I have proof of your involvement.	*soyez certain que*
I can assure you that I have had nothing to do with any dishonest trading.	*je peux vous assurer que*
She was bound to discover that you and I had talked.	*il était inévitable qu'elle ...*
I made sure that *ou* **I made certain that** no one was listening to our conversation.	*j'ai veillé à ce que*

POUR EXPRIMER LA PROBABILITÉ

It is highly probable *ou* **quite likely that** they will come to the airport to meet you. // They will **very probably** come to meet you.	*il est très probable que*
He must know what we want of him.	*il doit savoir ce que*
The cheque **should** reach you in Saturday's post.	*devrait*
It wouldn't surprise me to learn that he was working for the Americans.	*cela ne m'étonnerait pas d'apprendre que*
There is a strong chance that *ou* **It seems highly likely that** they will agree to the deal.	*il y a de fortes chances que*
It could very well turn out to be the case that they had run out of funds.	*il se pourrait bien après tout que*
The probability is *ou* **The likelihood is that** we shall have to pay more for it if we buy it from them. // **In all probability** *ou* **In all likelihood** we shall have to pay more.	*il est très probable que*
It is reasonable to think that he will agree to join us.	*il est légitime de penser que*
It would appear *ou* **It would seem that** he knew James Joyce in Ireland.	*il semblerait que*
The chances are that *ou* **The odds are that** *ou* **There is a good chance that** you are right.	*il y de fortes chances que*
It stands to reason that he had seen the book before.	*il est logique de penser que*

POUR EXPRIMER LA POSSIBILITÉ

The situation **could** *ou* **might** change from day to day.	*pourrait*
Perhaps he has already arrived.	*peut-être est-il ...*
It would appear *ou* **It would seem that** the grey car had been in an accident.	*il semblerait que*
It is possible that *ou* **It is conceivable that** they had met before.	*il est possible que*
It may be that I shall come to the States in the autumn.	*il se peut que*
It may be the case that they got your name from your former department.	*il se peut que*
It is within the bounds of possibility that he will know the man you speak of.	*il est possible que*
There is reason to believe that the books were stolen from the library.	*il y a de bonnes raisons de penser que*
There are grounds for believing *ou* **There are grounds for the belief that** they knew what we were doing as early as 1970.	*on a de bonnes raisons de croire que*
I venture to suggest that he could be the man we need.	*je me permets de suggérer que*
There is the outside chance that the hotel isn't yet full.	*il est tout juste possible que*

POUR EXPRIMER LE DOUTE OU L'INCERTITUDE

I doubt if he knows where it came from. // **It is doubtful whether** he knows where it came from. — *je doute que*

There is still some doubt surrounding his exact whereabouts. — *le doute subsiste quant à*

It isn't certain *ou* **It isn't known for sure** where she is. — *on ne sait pas exactement*

It is not necessarily the case. — *ce n'est pas forcément*

I am not sure *ou* **I am not certain** *ou* **I am not convinced** *ou* **I cannot say definitely** that these goods will sell. — *je ne suis pas certain*

We are still in the dark about where the letter came from. — *nous ne savons pas encore*

I am wondering if I should offer to help them out? — *je me demande si je devrais*

There is no proof *ou* **There is no evidence that** what he says is correct. — *rien ne prouve que*

It is touch-and-go whether they can save the company. — *il n'est pas sûr que*

It's all still up in the air — we shan't know for certain until the end of next week. — *rien n'est encore décidé*

It is debatable whether there is any value in interviewing him so long after the event. — *il n'est pas sûr que*

It's anyone's guess who will be chosen. — *personne ne peut prévoir*

I have my doubts about the value of the experiment. — *j'ai des doutes en ce qui concerne*

POUR EXPRIMER L'IMPROBABILITÉ

It is highly improbable that there could be any saving in the original budget. — *il est tout à fait improbable que*

You probably have not yet seen the document I am referring to. — *vous n'avez probablement pas vu*

It is very doubtful now whether the expedition will reach the summit. — *il est très peu probable que*

In the unlikely event that she should get in touch with you, please let me know immediately. — *si jamais elle ...*

There is but a small chance that anyone survived such a horrendous accident. — *il y a très peu de chances que*

It is scarcely to be expected that the university will contribute towards the cost. — *on ne peut guère s'attendre à ce que*

POUR EXPRIMER L'IMPOSSIBILITÉ

Such a thing **cannot** happen. — *cela ne peut pas*

It cannot be the case that they want to return to the East. — *il est impossible que*

It is quite impossible that *ou* **It is out of the question that** *ou* **It is unthinkable that** such a thing should happen. — *il est vraiment impossible que*

They **couldn't possibly have** arrived already. — *il n'est pas possible que*

This rules out any possibility of their working with us again. — *ceci exclut la possibilité que*

There is not (even) the remotest chance that *ou* **There is absolutely no chance that** he will succeed. — *il est absolument impossible que*

There is no question of our giving them a contribution to this fund. — *il est hors de question que*

There can be no return to earlier standards. — *il n'est pas possible de ...*

POUR EXPRIMER CE QU'ON EST CAPABLE OU INCAPABLE DE FAIRE

I can drive a car. // **I am able to** drive a car. // **I know how to** drive a car. — *je sais conduire*

I can't drive a car, I'm afraid. **I don't know how to** drive a car. — *je ne sais pas conduire*

Applicants **must be able to** use a word processor. — *doivent être capables de*

Can you speak French? // **Do you speak** French? — *parlez-vous français?*

I can *ou* **I am able to** lend him the money. — *je suis en mesure de*

He is quite incapable of telling a lie. // **He is quite unable to** tell a lie. // **He cannot** tell a lie. — *il est incapable de*

He was quite **incapable of** passing that examination. // He was quite **unable to** pass it. — *il était incapable de*

It is quite impossible for me to be in Paris next week. // **I cannot** be in Paris next week. — *il m'est impossible de*

We are not in a position to give any sort of decision yet. — *nous ne sommes pas à même de*

He has been ill, and is still not **up to** *ou* **equal to** any heavy work. — *n'est pas en état de*

I'm quite hopeless at *ou* **I am no good at** decorating and practical things. — *je suis incapable de*

I'm afraid the task proved quite **beyond his powers** *ou* **beyond his capabilities** *ou* **beyond his abilities.** // It proved quite **beyond him.** — *a été trop difficile pour lui*

He simply could not cope with the stresses of family life. — *il ne pouvait faire face à*

He is qualified to teach physics. — *il a les diplômes requis pour*

L'EXPLICATION

PRÉPOSITIONS

He had to refuse promotion, **because of** *ou* **on account of** his wife's health.	*à cause de*
He behaved like that **out of** *ou* **through** *ou* **from** sheer embarrassment.	*par*
Owing to lack of time, we have been unable to complete the job.	*par suite de*
We have been forced to reduce our staff **as a result of** the economic crisis.	*par suite de*
I have succeeded in proving my innocence, **thanks to** your timely help.	*grâce à*
By virtue of his connection with the family, he was allowed to enter the building.	*en vertu de*
The government financed this **by means of** massive tax increases.	*au moyen de*
In exchange for *ou* **In return for** financial aid, we gave them a lot of publicity.	*en échange de*
Following this incident, all trade between the two countries was stopped.	*à la suite de*
We gave them the contract **on the strength of** these promises.	*sur la foi de*
In view of their poor production record, we have decided not to renew their contract.	*étant donné*
In the light of what has happened so far, we have decided not to renew their licence.	*étant donné*
The Government extended police powers **in the face of** the renewed outbursts of violence.	*devant*
He hid the wallet, **for fear of** their anger/being accused of having stolen it.	*de crainte de*
We cannot do this **for lack of** *ou* **for want of** funds.	*faute de*
With so many people there, it was difficult to find him.	*avec*

CONJONCTIONS

They won't come, **because** they can't afford it.	*parce que*
They won't come, **for the simple reason that** they can't afford it.	*tout simplement parce que*
As we have none in stock at the moment, we are forced to delay this shipment.	*comme*
Given that inflation is still rising, house prices are unlikely to remain stable.	*étant donné que*
Since for the moment these are out of stock, we cannot dispatch your order.	*puisque*
Seeing that *ou* **In view of the fact that** there is no money left, we cannot do what we planned.	*vu que*
This will have no immediate effect, **for** some delay is inevitable.	*car*
They can't afford it, **so** they won't come.	*donc*
We have to re-order the parts: **therefore** there will be a delay of several weeks.	*donc*
He refused, **on the grounds that** he had so little time at his disposal.	*sous prétexte que*
Now (that) beef is so expensive, more people are buying pork.	*maintenant que*

AUTRE VOCABULAIRE UTILE

I attribute this to lack of foresight on the part of the committee.	*attribue*
The change in his attitude was **caused by** *ou* **brought about by** their rejection of his proposals.	*a été causé par*
The situation **goes back to** *ou* **dates from** his decision not to contest the seat.	*remonte à*
This situation is **due to** an unfortunate miscalculation on our part.	*dû à*
He was retired early, **on** health **grounds** *ou* **for** health **reasons.**	*pour raisons de*
It was like this: she had been ill for several weeks and hadn't heard the news.	*voilà de quoi il s'agit:*
This alteration to the programme **gave rise to** *ou* **provoked** *ou* **produced** a lot of comment.	*a donné lieu à*
The reason that they withdrew was that the scheme cost too much.	*la raison pour laquelle*
It was her stupidity that **led to** *ou* **caused** the accident.	*a causé*
The thing is that her French isn't good enough.	*c'est que*

ET, SELON LE CONTEXTE:

it is obvious why / for a start / for one thing ... for another / to be precise, we ... / this brings me to / to give only one example / I would point out that / it is true to say that / it is based on / this had the effect of / this has something to do with / consequently / as a result / that's why

L'EXCUSE

I'm really very sorry — I can't come on Sunday after all, as I have to go and visit my sister. — *je suis vraiment désolé*

I'm sorry to disturb you. // **I'm sorry that** you have been troubled. — *je suis désolé de/que*

I can't tell you how sorry I am about this unfortunate incident. — *je suis vraiment navré*

Please forgive me for not asking your permission before approaching him. — *je vous prie de me pardonner*

Do forgive me — I should have checked with your office first. — *pardonnez-moi*

I must apologise for all the inconvenience you have been caused. — *je dois vous prier de m'excuser de*

I am sorry to have to tell you that your application arrived too late. — *je regrette de devoir vous dire*

(dans une langue plus soutenue)

I would ask you to excuse this misunderstanding on our part. — *je vous prie d'excuser*

I can only apologize once again, on behalf of the Committee, for the disturbances at your lecture. — *je ne peux que renouveler mes excuses*

I am writing to ask you to forgive our apparent rudeness in not replying to your original letter. — *je vous écris pour vous demander de nous excuser*

We send you our most sincere apologies for all the difficulties that have occurred in this matter. — *nous vous présentons toutes nos excuses pour*

(pour exprimer le regret)

I am very upset about the whole affair, which should never have happened. — *je suis très contrarié de*

I am really ashamed of what happened last week. — *j'ai vraiment honte de*

I wish I hadn't mentioned it at all, although at the time it didn't seem important. — *si seulement je n'avais pas ...*

I should never have said a thing like that. — *je n'aurais jamais dû*

To my great regret, we have been unable to dissuade him. — *à mon grand regret*

Unfortunately, it is not possible for me to do any more to help you in this matter. — *malheureusement, il m'est impossible de*

I am entirely to blame for all this — I should have phoned the travel agency myself. — *tout ceci est de ma faute*

It is my fault that this misunderstanding happened, and I have written to the head of department explaining the circumstances. — *c'est moi qui suis responsable du fait que*

I have absolutely no excuse for this error on my part. — *mon erreur est absolument inexcusable*

I am afraid I quite forgot about it until the office had closed. — *je crains d'avoir*

I admit I gave him the papers, and should not have done so. — *je reconnais avoir*

It was an accident — I can assure you **I didn't mean to** break the clock. — *c'était accidentel ... je n'ai pas fait exprès de ...*

I really didn't do it on purpose — I had not realised that the handle had already been damaged. — *je ne l'ai pas fait exprès*

It is exceedingly unfortunate that the tickets were mislaid. — *il est extrêmement regrettable que*

We regret to inform you that *ou* **We must regretfully inform you that** this title is now out of print. — *nous sommes au regret de vous informer que*

We very much regret that we cannot publish this work. — *nous regrettons infiniment de ne pas pouvoir*

(pour suggérer une explication)

I was simply trying to give you less work. — *j'essayais simplement de*

You may find this difficult to believe, but **I thought I was doing the right thing.** — *je croyais bien faire*

There has obviously been an error in our accounting procedure, possibly owing to our recent change in computing facilities. — *manifestement il y a eu une erreur*

I was anxious not to upset him any more, as he was clearly very worried by what happened. — *je voulais éviter de*

I was acting in good faith when I showed them the documents. — *j'étais de bonne foi quand*

We were obliged to accept their conditions. — *nous avons été obligés de*

We were under the impression that these figures had been passed by the Accounts Office. — *nous croyions que*

We had unfortunately no choice in the matter. — *nous n'avions malheureusement pas le choix*

I can assure you that **I had nothing to do with** the arrangements. — *je n'y étais pour rien*

We had no alternative but to terminate his contract at once. — *nous ne pouvions rien faire d'autre que de*

ET, SELON LE CONTEXTE:

I feel sure you will understand why / I can promise you it won't happen again / you can be sure that we shall be more careful in future / I assure you that this cannot now happen / I shall do all in my power to see that ... / we shall do all we can to improve ... / I undertake to do all that is necessary in this respect.

11 North Street
Barnton
BN7 2BT

19th August 1993

The Personnel Director,
Messrs. J. M. Kenyon Ltd.,
Firebrick House,
Clifton,
MC45 6RB

Dear Sir or Madam,[1]

With reference to your advertisement in today's Guardian, I wish to apply for the post of systems analyst.

I enclose my curriculum vitae. Please do not hesitate to contact me if you require any further details.

Yours faithfully,

Rosalind A Williamson

CURRICULUM VITAE

Name:	Rosalind Anna WILLIAMSON
Address:	11 North Street, Barnton, BN7 2BT, England
Telephone:	Barnton (0294) 476230
Date of Birth:	6.5.1968
Marital Status:	Single
Nationality:	British
Qualifications:[2]	B.A. 2nd class Honours degree in Italian with French, University of Newby, England (June 1990) A-levels: Italian (A), French (B), English (D) (1986) O-Levels in 9 subjects. (1984)
Present Post:	Assistant Personnel Officer, Metal Company plc, Barnton (since January 1992)
Previous Employment	Nov. 1990 - Jan. 1991: Personnel trainee Metal Company plc. Oct. 1986 - June 1990: Student, University of Newby

Skills, Interests and Experience: fluent Italian & French; adequate German; som[e] Russian; car owner and driver (clean licence); riding & sailing.

The following have agreed to provide references:

Ms. Alice Bluegown, Personnel Manager, Metal Company plc, Barnton, NB4 [...]
Dr. I.O. Sono, Department of Italian, University of Newby, Newby, SR13 2RR

[1] Quand on ne sait pas si la personne à qui on s'adresse est un homme ou une femme, il convient d'utiliser la présentation ci-dessus. Toutefois, si l'on connaît le nom de la personne, la présentation suivante est préférable:

Mr. Derek Balder,
OU
Mrs. Una Claridge,
Personnel Director,
Messrs. J.M. Kenyon Ltd. etc.

Pour commencer votre lettre, la formule à employer est la suivante: "Dear Sir ou "Dear Madam ...".

Toute lettre commençant ainsi doit se terminer par la formule "Yours faithfully" suivie de la signature. Pour plus de détails, voir pages 56 et 58.

[2] Si l'on pose sa candidature à un poste à l'étranger, l'emploi de formules telles que "French equivalent of A-levels (Baccalauréat Langues)" est conseillé.

EXPRESSIONS UTILES

In reply to your advertisement for a trainee manager in today's *Daily News,* I should be grateful if you would please send me further details of this post, together with an application form.	*Me référant à votre annonce parue aujourd'hui dans le 'Daily News', je vous serais reconnaissant de bien vouloir m'envoyer des renseignements plus complets sur ce poste, ainsi qu'un dossier de candidature.*
I wish to apply for the post of bilingual correspondent which you advertise in yesterday's *Travel Agency News.*	*Par votre annonce insérée dans l'édition d'hier de 'Travel Agency News', j'ai appris que vous cherchez un correspondant bilingue et j'ai l'honneur de solliciter cet emploi.*
I am anxious to find a job in Britain during my summer vacation from University, and wonder whether you are able to offer me work in any capacity?	*Je souhaite vivement travailler en Angleterre pendant les vacances universitaires et vous serais très reconnaissant de me faire savoir s'il me serait possible d'obtenir un emploi dans votre compagnie.*
I have three years' experience of office work, and have used a word-processor.	*J'ai travaillé pendant trois ans comme employé de bureau et sais utiliser un système de traitement de textes.*
Although I have not got any previous experience of this type of work, I have had other holiday jobs, and can supply references from my employers, if you would like them.	*Bien que je n'aie pas d'expérience personnelle de ce type de travail, j'ai eu d'autres emplois intérimaires au cours des étés précédents et puis vous fournir, si vous le désirez, des attestations de mes anciens employeurs.*
My present salary is ... per annum, and I have four weeks holiday per year with pay.	*Mon salaire actuel est de ... par an et j'ai quatre semaines de congés payés.*
I am particularly interested in this job, as I am very anxious to work in publishing.	*Ce poste m'intéresse tout particulièrement, car je souhaite vivement travailler dans l'édition.*
I wish to work in England in order to improve my English and to gain experience of hotel work.	*Je suis désireux de travailler en Angleterre afin de perfectionner mes connaissances d'anglais et d'acquérir une certaine expérience de l'hôtellerie.*
As well as speaking fluent English, I have a working knowledge of German and a reading knowlege of Swedish.	*Je parle couramment l'anglais, j'ai de bonnes connaissances d'allemand, et je lis le suédois.*
I shall be available from the end of April.	*Je serai disponible à partir de la fin du mois d'avril.*
I enclose a stamped addressed envelope for your reply.	*Je vous prie de trouver ci-joint pour votre réponse une enveloppe timbrée à mes nom et adresse.*
Thank you for your letter of 19th June. I shall be pleased to attend for interview at your offices in Park Lane on Thursday, 24th June, at 10.30 a.m.	*Je vous remercie de votre lettre du 19 juin et serai très heureux de me rendre à vos bureaux, Park Lane, pour une entrevue jeudi le 24 juin à 10.30 heures.*
I have to give names of two referees with my application for this job, and I am writing to ask if you would be kind enough to allow me to put your name forward.	*Dans mon dossier de candidature pour le poste, je dois donner les noms de deux personnes voulant bien me recommander, et je vous serais très reconnaissant de me permettre de donner le vôtre comme référence.*
I have applied for the job of waitress for the summer in the Hotel Beaufort, in Furness, and they have asked me to supply a reference. I wonder if you would be kind enough to give me one? I should be most grateful if you would agree to do this.	*J'ai sollicité pour cet été un emploi de serveuse à l'hôtel Beaufort, à Furness et le directeur me demande une attestation. Je vous serais très reconnaissante si vous pouviez avoir l'amabilité de m'en fournir une.*
Mr. John Addams has applied for the post of hotel receptionist with us, and has given your name as a reference. I should be grateful if you would kindly let me know whether in your opinion he is suitable for this post.	*Monsieur John Addams sollicite une place de réceptionniste dans notre hôtel, et il a donné votre nom comme référence. Nous vous serions reconnaissants de bien vouloir nous dire si vous avez été satisfait de ses services.*
Your answer will be treated in confidence.	*Votre réponse sera considérée comme strictement confidentielle.*
Would you be kind enough to mention in your reply how long you have known Miss Jones, in what capacity, and whether you can recommend her for this type of employment.	*Auriez-vous l'obligeance de nous dire depuis combien de temps et à quel titre vous connaissez Mademoiselle Jones, et si vous la recommandez pour un emploi de ce type?*
It is with pleasure that I write to recommend Mrs. Amy Whitehead for the post of housing officer: I have known her for over ten years, during which time I have found her cheerful, friendly and helpful at all times.	*C'est avec grand plaisir que je vous recommande Madame Amy Whitehead pour le poste de responsable du logement. Je connais Madame Whitehead depuis plus de dix ans. Elle est d'un caractère agréable, pleine de bonne volonté et digne de confiance.*
Mr. Partridge has worked for me for the past eleven years, and during that time I have been impressed by his careful approach to his work, his punctuality and his sense of responsibility: he is a thoroughly reliable worker.	*Monsieur Partridge travaille pour nous depuis onze ans. Il est méthodique, ponctuel et extrêmement consciencieux dans son travail. Nous n'avons aucune hésitation à recommander quelqu'un d'aussi sérieux.*

James & Hedgehopper Limited
MASTER CUTLERS
Railway Arcade, Harley SG16 4BD
Tel: Harley (0123) 99876

29th January, 1993

Dr. T. Armitage
65 Middlewich Street,
Addenborough,
AG3 9LL

Dear Sir,

Thank you for your letter of 22nd January. We still stock the type of knife that you are looking for, and are pleased to enclose our catalogue and price list. We would draw your attention to the discount prices which are operative until 12th March on this range of goods.

Yours faithfully
for JAMES & HEDGEHOPPER LTD

William Osgood

William Osgood
Managing Director

Smith, Jones & Robertson Limited
RAINWEAR MANUFACTURERS
Block 39, Newtown Industrial Estate, Newtown SV7 3QS Tel: 0965 477366

Our ref: SAL/35/IM
Your Ref: JCB/JO

12th August 1992

Messrs. Kidsfunwear Ltd.,
3 High Street,
Barnton, BN17 2EJ

For the attention of Mr. J. Brown

Dear Sir,

Thank you for your enquiry about our children's rainwear. We have pleasure in enclosing our latest catalogue and current price list, and would draw your attention particularly to our SUNFLOWER range. We are prepared to offer the usual discount on these items, and we look forward to receiving your order.

Yours faithfully

Ian MacIntosh

Ian MacIntosh
Sales Department

DEMANDES DE RENSEIGNEMENTS

We see from your advertisement in the latest edition of *International Toy Manufacturing* that you are offering a range of outdoor sports equipment.

We should be grateful if you would send us full details of these goods, including your prices, discounts offered, and delivery times.

Nous voyons d'après votre annonce parue dans le dernier numéro de 'International Toy Manufacturing' que vous offrez une gamme d'articles pour les sports de plein air.

Nous vous serions reconnaissants de nous envoyer une documentation complète concernant ces articles, et de nous faire connaître vos prix courants, les remises consenties et les délais de livraison.

... ET COMMENT RÉPONDRE

In response to your enquiry, we enclose our details of our current range of goods, and our price list, which is valid until 31 March.

Par suite à votre lettre, nous vous prions de trouver ci-joint une documentation concernant la gamme actuelle de nos produits, ainsi que notre liste de prix (ceux-ci étant fermes jusqu'au 31 mars).

We thank you for your enquiry of 16th June, and are pleased to submit the following quotation ...

Nous vous remercions de votre lettre du 16 juin, et avons le plaisir de vous faire l'offre suivante: ...

This offer is subject to your firm acceptance by 31 January next.

Cette offre est valable sous réserve d'acceptation avant le 31 janvier prochain.

COMMANDES

Please send us immediately the following items, in the sizes and quantities specified: ...

Veuillez nous envoyer immédiatement les articles suivants, dans les tailles et quantités spécifiées ci-dessous: ...

This order is based on your current price list, assuming our usual discount of 10% on bulk orders.

Cet ordre est basé sur vos prix catalogue et tient compte de la remise de 10% que vous consentez sur les commandes en gros.

... ET COMMENT RÉPONDRE

We thank you for your order of 16 May, and shall execute it as soon as possible.

Nous vous remercions de votre ordre en date du 16 mai que nous exécuterons dans les plus brefs délais.

We shall require approximately three weeks to complete this order.

L'exécution de votre ordre demandera un délai de trois semaines environ.

Unfortunately, because of a shortage of raw materials, we cannot start manufacture until April 1st.

En raison d'une pénurie de matières premières, nous regrettons de ne pouvoir commencer la fabrication avant le 1er avril.

LIVRAISONS

Our delivery time is two months from receipt of firm order.

Nos délais de livraison sont de deux mois à dater de la réception de votre ordre.

We await your instructions with regard to delivery.

Nous attendons vos instructions concernant la livraison.

These goods were sent to you by rail on 4th July.

Ces marchandises vous ont été expédiées par chemin de fer le 4 juillet.

We have not yet received the items ordered on 26 August (our order no. 6496 refers).

Nous n'avons pas encore reçu les articles commandés le 26 août (voir bon de commande no. 6496).

We acknowledge receipt of the two consignments shipped by you on 3rd March.

Nous accusons réception de vos deux expéditions du 3 mars.

We wish to draw your attention to an error in the consignment received on 3rd February.

Nous tenons à vous signaler une erreur dans l'expédition que nous avons reçue le 3 février.

Unfortunately, the goods were damaged in transit.

Malheureusement, les marchandises ont été endommagées en transit.

We regret that the consignment was unsatisfactory, and agree to replace these goods.

Nous sommes désolés d'apprendre que vous n'êtes pas satisfaits de l'expédition et sommes prêts à remplacer les marchandises en question.

We cannot accept responsibility for this damage.

Nous ne pouvons accepter aucune responsabilité pour les dommages.

RÈGLEMENT

Please find enclosed our invoice no. 64321.

Nous vous prions de trouver ci-joint notre facture No. 64321.

The total amount payable is ...

Le montant total à régler s'élève à ...

We would be grateful if you would attend to this account immediately.

Veuillez donner votre attention immédiate à cette facture.

We have pleasure in enclosing our cheque for ... in settlement of your invoice no. 678B/31.

Nous vous remettons sous ce pli notre chèque d'un montant de ... pour solde de votre facture No. 678B/31.

We must point out an error in your account ... and would be grateful if you would adjust your invoice accordingly.

Nous regrettons de devoir vous signaler une erreur qui s'est glissée dans votre facture et vous serions reconnaissants de bien vouloir la rectifier.

This mistake was due to a book-keeping error, and we enclose a credit note for the sum involved.

Il s'agit effectivement d'une regrettable erreur de comptabilité et nous vous prions de trouver ci-joint un bon de crédit pour la somme correspondante.

Thank you for your cheque for ... in settlement of our statement: we look forward to doing further business with you in the near future.

Nous vous remercions de votre chèque de ... en règlement de notre relevé et espérons rester en relations avec vous.

11 South Street
BARCOMBE
BN7 2BT

14th March 1993

Dear Betty,

It seems such a long time since we last met and caught up with each other's news. However, I'm writing to say that Peter and I plan to take our holiday this summer in the Lake District, and we'll be driving past Preston on the M.6 some time during the morning of Friday, July 23rd. Will you be at home then? Perhaps we could call in? It would be lovely to see you and Alan again and to get news of Janie and Mark. Do let me know whether Friday, 23rd is convenient. We would expect to arrive at your place around 11 a.m. or so, and hope very much to see you then.

With love from

Susan.

65 Middlewich Street
ADDENBOROUGH
AG3 9LL

23rd January, 1993

Mr. J. Hedgehopper,
Hedgehoppers Knives Ltd.,
Railway Arcade
HARLEY

Dear Mr. Hedgehopper,

Some years ago I bought a SHARPCUTTER penknife from you, and, as you know, it has been invaluable to me. Unfortunately, however, I have now lost it, and wonder if you still stock this range? If so, I should be grateful if you would let me have details of the various types of knife you make, and of their prices.

Yours sincerely,

Thomas Armitage

Thomas Armitage

Le schéma ci-dessous donne des exemples de formules couramment employées en début et fin de lettres. Les permutations sont possible à l'intérieur de chaque section:

À QUELQU'UN QU'ON CONNAÎT PERSONNELLEMENT

Dear Mr. Brown,		
Dear Mrs. Drake,		
Dear Mr. & Mrs. Charlton,	Yours sincerely	
Dear Miss Baker,		
Dear Ms. Black,		
Dear Dr. Armstrong,	With all good wishes, Yours sincerely	*plus amical*
Dear Professor Lyons,		
Dear Sir Gerald,	With kindest regards, Yours sincerely	
Dear Lady McLeod,		
Dear Andrew,		
Dear Margaret,		

À UN(E) AMI(E) PROCHE, À UN(E) PARENT(E)

Dear Victoria,	With love from	
My dear Albert,	Love from	
Dear Aunt Eleanor,		
Dear Granny and Grandad,	Love to all	
Dear Mum and Dad,	Love from us all	*plus familier*
My dear Elizabeth,	Yours	
Dearest Norman,	All the best	
My dearest Mother,		
My dearest Dorinda,	With much love from	
My darling Augustus,	Lots of love from	*plus affectueusement*
	Much love, as always	
	All my love	

LETTRES COMMERCIALES (voir aussi page 56)

Dear Sirs,[1]		[1] *Pour s'adresser à une compagnie*
Dear Sir,[2]		[2] *Pour s'adresser à un homme*
Dear Madam,[3]	Yours faithfully	[3] *Pour s'adresser à une femme*
Dear Sir or Madam,[4]		[4] *Quand on ne sait pas si la personne à qui l'on s'adresse est un homme ou une femme*

À UNE CONNAISSANCE OU À UN(E) AMI(E)

Conviennent en toutes circonstances		
Dear Alison,	Yours sincerely	
Dear Annie and George,		
Dear Uncle Eric,	With best wishes, Yours sincerely	
Dear Mrs. Newman,		
Dear Mr. and Mrs. Jones,	With kindest regards, Yours sincerely	*plus amical*
My dear Miss Armitage,	All good wishes, Yours sincerely	
	With best wishes, *(etc)* Yours ever	*plus familier*
	Kindest regards,	
	Best wishes	
	With best wishes, As always	

POUR COMMENCER UNE LETTRE

Thank you for your letter, which came yesterday.
Je te remercie de ta lettre, qui est arrivée hier.

It was good to hear from you.
J'ai été très content d'avoir de vos nouvelles.

I am very sorry I haven't written for so long, and hope you will forgive me — I've had a lot of work recently and ...
Je suis vraiment désolé de ne pas vous avoir écrit depuis si longtemps et espère que vous voudrez bien me pardonner: il se trouve que j'ai beaucoup de travail ces temps-ci, et que ...

It's such a long time since we had any contact, that I felt I must write a few lines just to say hallo ...
Voici bien longtemps que je ne vous ai pas donné de nouvelles. C'est pourquoi je vous envoie ce petit mot rapide ...

This is a difficult letter for me to write, and I hope you will understand how I feel.
Je ne sais par où commencer cette lettre et j'espère que vous comprendrez mon embarras.

I am writing to ask whether you have in stock a book entitled ...
Je vous serais reconnaissant de me faire savoir si vous avez en librairie un ouvrage intitulé ...

Would you please send me ... I enclose my cheque for £3.50.
Je vous prie de m'envoyer ... je joins à cette lettre un chèque au montant de 35 F.

When I left your hotel after spending a week there, I think I may have left a beige raincoat in my room. Would you kindly let me know whether this has been found.
Ayant effectué un séjour d'une semaine dans votre hôtel, je crains d'avoir oublié dans ma chambre un imperméable beige. Je vous serais obligé de bien vouloir me dire si un tel vêtement a été retrouvé après mon départ.

I have seen the details of your summer courses, and wish to know whether you still have any vacancies on the ...
Ayant appris que vous organisez des cours internationaux d'été, je vous serais reconnaissant de me faire savoir s'il vous reste des places pour ...

POUR TERMINER UNE LETTRE

Pierre joins me in sending very best wishes to you all.
Pierre se joint à moi pour vous envoyer nos meilleurs vœux.

Do give my kindest regards to Denis.
Transmettez, s'il vous plaît, mes amitiés à Denis.

Jeanne sends her kindest regards (*ou* her love).
*Jeanne vous envoie ses amitiés (*or *vous embrasse).*

Catherine asks me to give you her best wishes.
Catherine me charge de vous transmettre ses amitiés.

Please remember me to your mother — I hope she is well.
Veuillez transmettre mon meilleur souvenir à votre mère.

Give my love to Olivier and Marion, and tell them how much I miss them.
Embrasse Olivier et Marion pour moi, et dis-leur bien combien ils me manquent.

Mary sends her love to you both.
Mary vous embrasse tous les deux.

Say hullo to Jimmy for me.
Dis bonjour à Jimmy pour moi.

If there is anything else I can do, please do not hesitate to get in touch again.
N'hésitez pas à m'écrire si je puis vous être utile.

Do write when you have a minute.
Écris-moi si tu as une petite minute de libre.

Do let us have your news from time to time.
N'oublie pas de nous donner de tes nouvelles de temps en temps.

I look forward to hearing from you.
J'attends avec impatience une lettre de vous.

Hoping to hear from you before too long.
À bientôt une lettre de toi, j'espère.

L'ORGANISATION DES VOYAGES

Please give me details of your prices.
Je vous serais reconnaissant de bien vouloir me communiquer vos tarifs.

I would like to book bed-and-breakfast accommodation with you.
Je voudrais retenir une chambre avec petit déjeuner.

I wish to book one double room for my wife and myself, and one twin-bedded room for our sons, who are both under 12 years of age.
Je voudrais retenir une chambre avec un grand lit pour ma femme et moi-même, ainsi qu'une chambre à lits jumeaux pour nos deux fils, tous deux âgés de moins de 12 ans.

Please let me know by return of post if you have one single room with shower, full board, for the week beginning May 24th.
Veuillez me faire savoir, par retour du courrier, si vous avez une chambre pour une personne, avec douche et en pension complète, pour la semaine du 24 mai.

Please consider this a firm booking, and hold the room until I arrive, however late in the evening.
Je confirme ainsi ma réservation et vous prie de me garder la chambre, jusqu'à une heure tardive si besoin est.

We expect to arrive in the early evening, unless something unforeseen prevents us.
Sauf imprévu, nous arriverons en début de soirée.

I am afraid I must ask you to alter my booking from 25 August to 3 September.
Je me vois obligé de vous demander de reporter ma réservation du 25 août au 3 septembre.

Owing to unforeseen circumstances, I am afraid that I must cancel the booking made with you for the week beginning 5 September.
Pour des raisons indépendantes de ma volonté, je suis contraint d'annuler la réservation que j'avais faite pour la semaine du 5 septembre.

LES REMERCIEMENTS ET VŒUX

LES REMERCIEMENTS

Thank you very much (indeed) for remembering my birthday. — *merci beaucoup de*

I am writing to say thank you *ou* **Just a line to say thank you** for the lovely book which arrived today. — *je vous écris pour vous remercier*

Would you please thank him from me. — *remerciez-le de ma part*

We all send you our warmest thanks for a wonderful evening. — *nous vous envoyons tous nos vifs remerciements pour*

I cannot thank you enough for all you did for Amanda. — *je ne sais comment vous remercier pour*

We greatly appreciate the time and trouble you took for us. — *nous vous sommes très reconnaissants de*

I have been asked to thank you on behalf of the club for the excellent talk you gave us yesterday. — *je dois vous remercier, au nom de ...*

We would ask you to accept our most grateful thanks for all that you have done. — *nous vous adressons tous nos remerciements pour*

Would you please give our most sincere thanks to your colleagues. — *transmettez nos remerciements à vos collègues*

POUR FORMULER DES VŒUX

NB: Dans la section suivante, [...] pourrait être 'a Merry Christmas and a Happy New Year', 'a happy birthday', 'a speedy recovery', 'your new job', etc.

With all good wishes for [...] from *(+ signature)* — *(formule couramment employée sur une carte, souvent pour accompagner un cadeau) tous mes vœux de ...*

With love and best wishes for [...] — *tous nos meilleurs vœux de/pour*

Do give my best wishes to your mother for [...] — *transmettez mes meilleurs vœux de/pour ... à*

Roger joins me in sending you all our very best wishes for [...] — *... se joint à moi pour vous envoyer nos meilleurs vœux de/pour*

I hope you have a lovely holiday/a pleasant journey *etc.* — *j'espère que vous ...*

(à l'occasion de Noël et du Nouvel An)

NB: en G.B., aux U.S.A. etc, il est traditionnel d'envoyer des cartes de vœux pour Noël et le Nouvel An, avant le 25 décembre.

With season's greetings, and very best wishes from *(+ signature)* — *(formule couramment employée) bonnes fêtes de fin d'année ...*

A Merry Christmas to you all, and best wishes for health, happiness and prosperity in the New Year. — *Joyeux Noël, Bonne Année à tous*

Mary and I send you all our very best wishes for 1994. — *nous vous envoyons nos meilleurs vœux pour 1994*

(à l'occasion d'un anniversaire)

I am writing to wish you many happy returns of the day. — *je vous souhaite un très heureux anniversaire*

This is to send you our fondest love and very best wishes on your eighteenth birthday — Many Happy Returns from us all. — *tous nos vœux les plus affectueux pour ton anniversaire*

I'd like to wish you a happy birthday for next Saturday. — *je vous souhaite un heureux anniversaire samedi*

(pour envoyer des vœux de rétablissement)

I was very sorry to learn that you were not well, and send you my best wishes for a speedy recovery. — *tous mes vœux de prompt rétablissement*

Sorry you're ill — get well soon! — *... j'espère que tu seras bientôt rétabli*

(pour souhaiter bonne chance à quelqu'un)

NB: Dans la section suivante, [...] pourrait être 'interview', 'driving test', 'exam', 'new job', etc.

I am writing to send you best wishes for your [...] — *je vous écris pour vous souhaiter bonne chance pour*

Good luck for your [...] — I hope things go well for you on Friday. — *bonne chance pour*

(pour féliciter quelqu'un)

This is to send you our warmest congratulations and best wishes on [...] — *nous vous adressons toutes nos félicitations pour*

Allow me to offer you my heartiest congratulations on [...] — *permettez-moi de vous féliciter de ...*

We all send you our love and congratulations on such an excellent result. — *... toutes nos félicitations — bravo!*

LES FAIRE-PART, INVITATIONS ET RÉPONSES

COMMENT ANNONCER UNE NAISSANCE

Mr. and Mrs. Peter Thomson are happy to announce the birth of their daughter, Stephanie Jane, in Cambridge, on 31 July 1993.

Faire-part: convient en toutes circonstances: 'ont la joie d'annoncer'

I am very glad to say that Helen and Martyn had a son, Alexander Edward John, on 22 July, and that mother and child are both well.

Lettre à un ami ou à une connaissance: 'J'ai le plaisir de vous annoncer que'

... ET COMMENT RÉPONDRE

With warmest congratulations to you both on the birth of your son, and best wishes to Alexander for good health and happiness throughout his life.

Carte accompagnant un cadeau: 'Toutes nos félicitations et nos vœux les meilleurs'

We were delighted to learn of the birth of Stephanie, and send our most sincere congratulations to you both, and our very best wishes to the baby for health, happiness and prosperity throughout her life.

Lettre à des amis ou à des connaissances: 'Nous vous félicitons pour'

COMMENT ANNONCER DES FIANÇAILLES

Mr. and Mrs. Robert Jamieson are pleased to announce the engagement of their daughter Fiona to Mr. Joseph Bloggs.

Faire-part: convient en toutes circonstances: 'sont heureux d'annoncer'

Polly and Richard have got engaged — you can imagine how delighted we all are about this.

Lettre à un ami ou à une connaissance: 'ont annoncé leurs fiançailles ... vous imaginez comme nous en sommes heureux'

... ET COMMENT RÉPONDRE

Fiona and Joseph: with our warmest congratulations on your engagement, and our best wishes for a long and happy life together.

Carte accompagnant un cadeau: 'Toutes nos félicitations et nos vœux de bonheur'

I was very glad to learn of your engagement to Richard, and send you both my congratulations and very best wishes for your future happiness.

Lettre à un ami ou à une connaissance: 'J'ai été ravi d'apprendre vos fiançailles'

COMMENT ANNONCER UN MARIAGE

Mr. and Mrs. William Morris are happy to announce the marriage of their daughter Sarah to Mr. Jack Bond, in St. Francis Church, Newtown, on 27 October 1993.

Faire-part: pourrait convenir en toutes circonstances: 'ont l'honneur de vous faire part du mariage de'

Stephen and Amanda were married here, in the registry office, last Saturday.

Lettre à un ami ou à une connaissance: 'se sont mariés samedi dernier'

... ET COMMENT RÉPONDRE

With congratulations on your marriage and all good wishes to you both for your future happiness.

Carte accompagnant un cadeau: 'Toutes nos félicitations et nos vœux de bonheur'

We were delighted to learn of your daughter's marriage to Jack Bond, and send you our best wishes on this happy occasion.

Dans la langue soignée, à une connaissance: 'C'est avec joie que nous avons appris'

I was so glad to hear that you and Robin were getting married, and send you both my most sincere congratulations and best wishes for your future happiness.

Lettre à des amis: 'C'est avec une grande joie que j'ai appris'

COMMENT ANNONCER UN DEUIL

Mrs. Mary Smith announces with deep sorrow the death of her husband, John R. Smith, at Sheffield, on 8th March 1993, after a long illness. The funeral took place privately.

Faire-part: 'ont la douleur de vous faire part de': en cas de mention 'No letters please', il convient de ne pas écrire

It is with the deepest sorrow that I have to tell you that Joe's father passed away three weeks ago.

Lettre à une connaissance: 'C'est avec beaucoup de peine que'

I lost my dear wife a little over a month ago.

Lettre à un ami: 'J'ai eu le malheur de perdre ma femme ...'

... ET COMMENT RÉPONDRE

My husband and I were greatly saddened to learn of the passing of Dr. Smith, and send you and your family our most sincere condolences in your very sad loss.

Lettre à une connaissance: 'Nous prenons part à votre peine'

I was terribly upset to hear of Jim's death, and I am writing to send you all my warmest love and deepest sympathy in your tragic loss.

Lettre à un ami: 'J'ai été bouleversé d'apprendre la disparition de ... et tiens à vous exprimer ma profonde sympathie'

LES INVITATIONS OFFICIELLES

Mr. and Mrs. Mark Green request the pleasure of the company of Mr. James Brown at the marriage of their daughter Annabel to Mr. Paul Piper, in St. Peter's Church, Newtown, on Saturday, 20th November 1993 at 3 p.m., and afterwards at the Grand Hotel, Newtown. *'vous prient d'assister au mariage de ...'*

The Chairman and Governors of Trentbury College request the pleasure of the company of Miss Charlotte Young at a dinner to mark the fiftieth anniversary of the founding of the college. *'prient Mlle Charlotte Young de venir au dîner'*

Peter and Susan Atkins request the pleasure of your company at a reception *(or* dinner *etc)* to celebrate their Silver Wedding, on Saturday, 10 July 1993, at 8 p.m. at the Bows Hotel. *'ont le plaisir de vous inviter à une réception ...'*

... ET COMMENT RÉPONDRE

Mr. James Brown thanks Mr. and Mrs. Green for their kind invitation to the marriage of their daughter Annabel on 20th November, and accepts with pleasure/but regrets that he is unable to accept. *'remercie ... accepte avec plaisir/ regrette de ne pouvoir accepter'*

Miss Charlotte Young wishes to thank the Chairman and Governors of Trentbury College for their kind invitation to dinner and has much pleasure in accepting/but regrets that she is unable to accept. *'remercie ... accepte avec plaisir/ regrette de ne pouvoir accepter'*

LES INVITATIONS PLUS LIBRES

We are celebrating Rosemary's engagement to David by holding a dinner and dance at the Central Hotel on Friday, 21st May, and very much hope that you will be able to join us then. *'espérons que vous viendrez à une réception pour fêter les fiançailles de ...'*

We are giving a small dinner party on Saturday next for Lorna and Ian, who are home from Canada for a few weeks, and hope you will be able to come. *'nous organisons un dîner en l'honneur de ... et espérons que vous pourrez venir'*

We should be very pleased if you and Letitia could dine with us on the Sunday evening, if you have arrived in town by then. *'nous serions très heureux si vous pouviez venir dîner ...'*

Our Managing Director, James Glasgow, will be in Edinburgh on Friday 19 November, and we are holding a small dinner party for him on that day at 8 p.m. here. We hope that you and Margery will be able to join us then. *'nous organisons un dîner en son honneur ... et nous espérons que vous vous joindrez à nous'*

Would you be free for lunch one day next week? Any day but Thursday would suit me. *'pourrions-nous déjeuner ensemble'*

We are planning a trip to Norway, probably in June for two weeks, and wonder if you would like to join us. *'nous nous demandons si vous auriez envie de vous joindre à nous'*

Would you be interested in coming with us to the Lake District? *'est-ce que cela te dirait de venir avec nous'*

It would give us great pleasure to welcome you and your family to our home. *'nous serions très heureux de vous accueillir'*

Why don't you come over for a weekend and let us show you Sussex? *'pourquoi ne pas venir passer un week-end ...'*

... ET COMMENT RÉPONDRE

It was so kind of you to invite me to meet James Glasgow and I shall be happy to come to dinner that evening/but I am afraid that I cannot accept your invitation to dinner. *'je vous remercie de ... je suis heureux d'accepter/regrette de ne pouvoir accepter'*

Thank you for inviting me — I accept with the greatest of pleasure. *'merci ... j'accepte avec grand plaisir'*

Thank you for your kind invitation to dinner — I shall be very pleased to come. *'merci ... je suis très heureux d'accepter'*

It is very kind of you to invite me, and I shall be very happy to join you. *'c'est très aimable à vous de m'inviter — je serais heureux d'accepter'*

How kind of you to ask me to go with you — I shall look forward to that very much. *'comme c'est gentil à vous de m'inviter à ... je m'en réjouis d'avance'*

Thank you so much for your kind invitation to dinner on Saturday — unfortunately George and I will be out of town that weekend, and so I am afraid we have to refuse. *'merci ... nous ne serons pas là ... nous ne pouvons pas accepter'*

I am terribly sorry, but I shan't be able to come on Saturday. *'je regrette beaucoup, mais je ne pourrai pas venir'*

I'm afraid I couldn't possibly accept. *'je suis dans l'impossibilité d'accepter'*

ET, SELON LE CONTEXTE:

it's just what I've always wanted to do / I've been longing to do something like that for ages / it will be such fun / I cannot make any definite plans until ... / I'd rather not commit myself yet / it's unfortunately out of the question for the moment / I doubt if we could / it's somewhat difficult to explain, but / because of pressure of work / I am afraid I have already promised to ... / I wish I could, but ... / unfortunately ... / much to our regret, we cannot ...

LA DISSERTATION

LES GRANDES LIGNES DE L'ARGUMENT

Pour introduire un sujet

It is often said *ou* **It is often asserted** *ou* **It is often claimed that the** youth of today doesn't care for anything but pleasure.	*on dit souvent que*
It would be universally acknowledged that unemployment is the greatest scourge of our days.	*il est généralement reconnu que*
It is a truism *ou* **It is a commonplace that** nothing of value is achieved without dedication.	*il est banal de dire que*
It is undeniably true that war springs from greed.	*on ne peut nier le fait que*
It is a well-known fact that children up to the age of three have no concept of extension in time.	*tout le monde sait que*
For the great majority of people, literature is a subject that is studied in school but which has no relevance to life as they know it.	*pour la plupart des gens*
It is sometimes forgotten that investment is essential for economic growth.	*on oublie parfois que*
It would be naïve to suppose that all politicians act in the public interest all of the time.	*il serait naïf de croire que*
It would hardly be an exaggeration to say that carelessness is the reason for all road accidents.	*on exagérerait à peine en disant que*
There are several aspects to the problem of understanding Shakespearean comedy.	*le problème de ... comporte différents aspects*
A problem that is often debated nowadays is that of world famine and how to deal with it.	*un problème dont il est souvent question aujourd'hui est celui de*
The question of whether Hamlet was really mad has occupied critics for generations.	*la question de savoir si ...*
The concept of existentialism **is not an easy one to grasp.**	*le concept de ... est difficile à saisir*
The idea of getting rich without too much effort **has universal appeal.**	*l'idée de ... plaît toujours*
We live in a world in which capitalism seems triumphant.	*nous vivons dans un monde où ...*
One of the most striking features of this problem (*ou* **issue** *ou* **topic** *ou* **question)** is the way it arouses strong emotions. // **One of the most striking aspects of ...**	*l'un des aspects le plus frappants de ce problème est ...*
A number of key issues arise from this statement.	*... soulève quelques questions fondamentales*
History provides numerous instances of misguided national heroes who eventually did more harm than good.	*l'histoire nous fournit de nombreux exemples de*
It is hard to open a newspaper nowadays without being faced (*ou* **confronted) with** some new example of mindless violence.	*il n'est guère possible d'ouvrir le journal sans y découvrir ...*
What this question boils down to is: was Eliot at heart more of a philosopher than a poet?	*la question se résume à ceci: ...*
What can we make of a somewhat sweeping assertion like this? It would be dangerous to reject it in its entirety without ...	*que faire d'une telle généralisation?*
First of all, let us try to understand what the writer really means.	*tout d'abord, essayons de comprendre ...*
It is easy enough to make broad generalisations about the evils of alcohol, **but in reality the issue is an extremely complex one.**	*il est facile de généraliser ... mais en réalité, il s'agit là d'un problème très complexe*
This statement **merits closer examination.** We might ask ourselves why ...	*mérite d'être examiné de plus près*
The public in general tends to believe that all education is a good thing, without regard to the quality of that education.	*le public a tendance à croire que*
What we are mainly concerned with here is the conflict between what the hero says and what he does.	*ce qui nous préoccupe ici, c'est ...*
It is often the case that truth is stranger than fiction, and never more so than in this instance.	*il est souvent vrai que*
By way of introduction, let us give a brief review of the background to this question.	*en guise d'introduction*
We commonly think of people **as** isolated individuals, but in fact few of us ever spend more than an hour or two of our waking hours alone.	*généralement nous pensons à ... comme à ...*
It is surprising that faith survives at all, far less that it should flourish, **in an industrialised society like ours.**	*... dans une société industrielle comme la nôtre*

Pour commencer un développement, présenter une thèse

The first thing that needs to be said is that the author is presenting a one-sided, even bigoted, view.
il convient tout d'abord de signaler que

What should be established at the very outset is that we are dealing here with a practical rather than a philosophical issue.
la première constatation qui s'impose est que

First of all, let us consider the advantages of urban life.
considérons tout d'abord

Let us begin with *ou* **I propose to consider first** the social aspects of this question.
commençons par examiner

Let us see if there is any real substance in this claim (*ou* **assertion** *ou* **statement).**
voyons d'abord si cette affirmation est justifiée

Was Othello a naïve man or not? **This is a question at which we must take a careful (***ou* **close) look,** before we ...
une question qui doit retenir notre attention

An argument in support of this approach is that it does in fact produce practical results.
un argument en faveur de cette méthode, c'est qu'elle ...

We are often faced in daily life with the choice between our sense of duty and our own personal inclinations.
dans la vie courante, nous devons souvent choisir entre ...

Even the most superficial look at this issue raises fundamental questions about the nature and purpose of human existence.
un coup d'œil rapide suffit à découvrir des questions d'une importance fondamentale concernant

We must distinguish carefully between the two possible interpretations of this statement.
il faut établir une distinction précise entre

This brings us to the question of whether the language used is appropriate to the task the author sets himself.
ceci nous amène à nous demander si ...

It is interesting to consider how far this is true of other nations.
il est intéressant de voir si ...

One might mention, **in support of the above thesis,** the striking speech of Frederick in Act III.
... pour appuyer cette hypothèse ...

The second reason for advocating this course of action is that it benefits the community at large.
la deuxième raison pour

Another telling argument in support of this viewpoint **is that** it makes sense economically.
un autre argument de poids ... est que

An important aspect of Milton's imagery **is** the play of light and shade.
un aspect important de ... est ...

It would be reasonable to assume that the writer is sincere in his praise of such behaviour.
il est raisonnable de penser que

The fundamental reason for believing this assumption to be true is that subsequent events seem to prove it.
la raison principale pour laquelle on peut y croire est que

We need not concern ourselves here with the author's intentions in disclosing these facts so early in the book.
ce qui nous intéresse ici, ce n'est pas ...

It is now time to discuss the character of Sir James, and how this develops during the course of the first act.
il faut en venir maintenant au caractère de ...

When we speak of culture, **we have in mind** the development of the human spirit and its expression in various ways.
quand nous parlons de ... nous pensons à ...

I will confine myself to a brief outline of the problem, looking more particularly at how it affects the poorer countries of Africa.
je me contenterai d'esquisser ...

I am not here concerned with the undoubted difficulties and pitfalls inherent in the introduction of a new form of examination in secondary education.
mon propos ici n'est pas d'examiner ...

It is worth stating at this point that the position is exactly the same in most other countries.
il faudrait remarquer à ce stade que

Finally, there is the related problem of how to explain the concept of original sin.
enfin, il y a un problème annexe

Pour présenter un point de vue différent, une antithèse

On the other hand, it is observable that people do not normally behave like this in practice.	*d'un autre côté, on remarque que*
It may be asserted, however, that this is a superficial point of view.	*on peut cependant affirmer que*
The other side of the coin is, however, that free enterprise may create economic chaos in certain circumstances.	*mais il y a le revers de la médaille: ...*
Another way of looking at this question is to consider its social implications.	*on peut aussi aborder le problème sous un angle différent en considérant ...*
The snag about this argument is that it undermines the principles of free speech.	*l'inconvénient de cet argument est que*
The author says it is style that matters. **The very opposite may be true.**	*il se peut que le contraire soit vrai*
The claim she makes **has much to recommend it, but** it goes too far.	*... est tout à fait valable, mais ...*
It is difficult to share the writer's belief (*ou* **view** *ou* **opinion) that** with a little goodwill everything comes right in the end.	*il est difficile de suivre l'auteur quand il dit que*
To say that Parker's death was fortuitous **is,** however, **a totally unjustified assumption.**	*... est une supposition totalement injustifiée*
In actual fact it would be more accurate to say that the fault lies in the monetary system itself.	*en fait, il serait plus juste de dire que*
All this may well be true enough, but we should not forget the victim herself.	*tout ceci a beau être vrai, mais ...*
If you consider the author's real intentions, **this argument is an extremely weak one.**	*cet argument manque de solidité*
Hackneyed arguments of this kind are scarcely convincing even in the popular press, far less in a work which claims to have been seriously researched.	*des arguments rebattus comme celui-ci*
Paradoxical though it may seem, we must look for good in evil itself, for without that evil, how may good be identified?	*aussi paradoxal que cela puisse paraître*
It will be objected that punctuality, or at least a semblance of it, is necessary for civilized life.	*on objectera que*
The difficulty about supporting this statement **is that** the facts appear to contradict it.	*il est difficile de ... parce que ...*

Pour présenter une solution, une synthèse

The fact of the matter is surely that *ou* **The truth of the matter is surely that** television presentation does influence voting patterns.	*la vérité est que*
We have now established certain principles, but **when all is said and done it must be acknowledged that** a purely theoretical approach to social issues is sterile.	*en fin de compte, il faut reconnaître que*
How can we reconcile these two apparently contradictory viewpoints?	*comment réconcilier ...*
Of all these attempts to explain the playwright's intentions, **the last seems to offer the most convincing explanation.**	*la dernière explication semble être la plus convaincante*
There is much to be said on both sides of this question. On balance (*ou* **On reflection), however,** the arguments for the local rather than the national approach **have most to recommend them.**	*après avoir soigneusement pesé le pour et le contre, on peut conclure en faveur de ...*
If one weighs the pros and cons (of the case), the argument for freedom of speech in these circumstances is hard to sustain.	*si l'on pèse le pour et le contre*
One might be tempted to think that better technology is the solution, **but in actual fact** human attitudes are the vital element.	*... en réalité ...*
It is easy to believe that this could never happen in a civilized society, **but the truth is that** it happens everywhere, and it happens more and more often.	*... mais la vérité est que*
From all this it follows that these claims are false.	*il s'ensuit de tout cela que*
The key to this whole problem must surely be the development of heavy industries in that part of the country.	*la solution de ce problème réside sûrement dans ...*
The social and economic **consequences of the facts we have mentioned above** are too important to ignore.	*les conséquences ... de ce que nous venons de mentionner*
These two points of view, **while distinct, are not mutually exclusive.**	*... bien que distincts, ne s'excluent pas l'un l'autre*
In the final analysis, the themes of the novel are confused.	*en dernière analyse*
To recap *ou* **To sum up,** the cost of raw materials is falling faster than was ever expected in the early 1990s.	*récapitulons: ...*

Pour conclure

What conclusions can be drawn from all this?	*quelles conclusions pouvons-nous tirer de*
The most sensible (*ou* **satisfactory** *ou* **convincing) conclusion we can come to** is that the author has not succeeded in putting his message across.	*la conclusion la plus satisfaisante est que*
All this goes to show that it is unwise to make generalisations about human beings.	*tout ceci prouve bien que*
Surely the lesson to be learned from what has happened in Europe is that minorities should be respected.	*le leçon qu'il convient de tirer de ... est que*
The inescapable conclusion which emerges from what I have said is that health is too important to leave to the doctors.	*la conclusion inéluctable de ce que je viens de dire est que*
The problem we have considered **clearly does not admit of an easy solution, but** it is to be hoped that governments will take steps to ameliorate its worst effects.	*il est manifestement difficile de trouver une solution à ce problème, mais ...*
This brief account of the origin of the play is necessarily limited in scope.	*ce rapide récit de*
The relations between the hero and heroine appear complex, but **to put the whole matter in a nutshell,** they are both more interested in power than in love.	*... pour les résumer en un mot ...*
Ultimately, then, these two approaches are impossible to reconcile.	*en définitive*
All in all, we must acknowledge that the main interest of the book lies in its treatment of jealousy.	*au fond*
The play no doubt has an important message: nevertheless, **at the end of the day, it must be acknowledged that** it is a very bad play.	*en fin de compte il faut reconnaître que*
The best way of summing up the arguments I have put forward for equality of opportunity is that human rights have precedence over social inhibitions.	*la meilleure façon de résumer*
It would appear, then, that in a sane society nobody would be a social outcast.	*il semblerait donc que*
I have demonstrated that Cox's claims are based on a false assumption.	*j'ai démontré que*
To sum up, I believe that urgent action is needed.	*en résumé*

POUR RÉDIGER UN PARAGRAPHE

Pour ajouter, comparer, relier etc

This brings us to the question of whether we can believe in a benevolent deity.	*ceci nous amène à la question suivante: pouvons-nous ...*
On the one hand, wealth corrupts: **on the other,** it can achieve great things.	*d'une part ... d'autre part ...*
As for the theory of value, it counts for nothing in this connection.	*quant à*
Compared with the heroine, Alison is an insipid character.	*comparée à*
In the first (*ou* second *ou* third *etc*) place, let us consider the style of the novel.	*en premier* (etc) *lieu*
First of all, I will outline the benefits of the system: **next,** I propose to examine its disadvantages: **finally,** we will consider the views of the recipients.	*tout d'abord ... puis ... enfin*
The arguments in favour of this theory **fall into two groups: first,** those which rely on statistics, and **secondly,** those based on principle.	*... se divisent en deux catégories: premièrement ... deuxièmement ...*
Incidentally, we must not forget the contribution of Horatio to this scene.	*notons au passage*
As far as his character **is concerned,** we can only admire his persistence.	*en ce qui concerne*
Over and above all these considerations, there is the question of whether the country can afford such luxuries.	*enfin, ...*
Added to that, there is his remarkable sense of detail.	*ajoutons à cela*
Similarly, a good historian will never be obsessed with dates.	*de même*
There is a fundamental difference between people who act from the heart and those who act from the head.	*il y a une différence fondamentale entre*
There are important differences between these two approaches — differences which we ignore at our peril.	*il y a des différences considérables entre*
In the field of education it is clear that we have not learned by our mistakes.	*dans le domaine de l'éducation*
From the earliest days of nuclear development, it was plain that the potential danger of the process was perhaps the most important single aspect.	*dès le début de*
Once, **many decades ago,** a foreign observer commented that English people were incapable of discussing principles.	*il y a de nombreuses années*
The alternative is to accept the world as it is, and concentrate one's efforts on one's own spiritual development.	*l'autre solution est de*
A further complication is that the characters on stage at this point include the music master himself.	*une complication supplémentaire est que*
He considers the effect of this on the lives of the people, **as well as** on the economy of the country.	*ainsi que*
Also, there is the question of how this may be validated.	*de plus, il y a*
The book has considerable depth: **equally,** it has style.	*de même*
As regards *ou* **As for** the habits of foreigners, **one may observe that** they are very like our own.	*en ce qui concerne ... on peut remarquer que*
In order to clear the ground, I will give a brief account of Mason's theory.	*pour déblayer le terrain*
The problem is how to explain why people behave as they do.	*le problème est de savoir pourquoi*

Pour exprimer un point de vue personnel

My own view of this is that the writer is quite wrong in this assertion.	*je trouve que*
That is the popular viewpoint, **but speaking personally** I cannot see its logic.	*mais en ce qui me concerne, ...*
Jennings is, **it seems to me,** over-optimistic in his claim that no one is ever hurt by such wheeling and dealing.	*à ce qu'il me semble*
My personal opinion of this argument is that it lacks depth.	*personnellement, je trouve que*
The author argues for patriotism, but **I feel strongly that** this is a delusion.	*je suis convaincu que*
In my opinion, nearly everybody overestimates the size of the problem.	*à mon avis*
For my part, I cannot discount what their spokesman said.	*personnellement*
I maintain that no one has the right to deprive these people of their home.	*je maintiens que*

Pour introduire le point de vue d'autrui

The writer asserts (*ou* claims *ou* maintains *ou* states) that intelligence is conditioned by upbringing.	*l'auteur affirme que*
They would have us believe that the market is fair.	*ou voudrait nous faire croire que*
The official view is that this cannot affect the population adversely.	*selon l'opinion officielle*
The author gives us to understand that his main aim is merely to please.	*l'auteur nous fait comprendre que*
The position was put, with commendable clarity, by James Armitage, in a classic essay on this subject some years ago.	*cette position a été exprimée, avec une remarquable simplicité*
When one considers the man's achievements, **the portrait of him painted in this volume** amounts to little more than a calumny.	*la façon dont il est représenté dans cet ouvrage*
The writer **puts the case for** restrictions on the freedom of speech very persuasively.	*présente les arguments en faveur de*
The House of Commons, **it has been said,** is like an elephant's trunk: it can fell an oak or pick up a pin.	*on a constaté que*
This line of thinking leads the author into the dangerous territory of feminist polemics.	*cette démarche ...*
The animals are perhaps more attractive — **which brings us to another side of the question**: can the human race survive?	*ce qui nous amène à un autre aspect de la question: ...*
The writer here **is clearly concerned to** convey her conviction that life is seldom worth living, and never worth living to the full.	*souhaite particulièrement ...*
The author **draws our attention to the fact that** nowhere in the world is the soil so poor.	*attire notre attention sur le fait que*
What this character **is really saying is that** he disagrees with the foundations of religious belief.	*ce que le personnage veut dire, c'est qu'il ...*
According to the writer, these figures are inaccurate	*selon l'auteur*
The speaker is claiming, **if I understand her rightly,** that people do not really care about politics.	*si je ne me trompe*

Pour introduire un exemple, une citation

We should consider, **for example** *ou* **for instance,** the problems faced by tourists in a strange land.	*par exemple*
Take the case of Heathcote in 'Lost Masters'.	*prenons le cas de*
To illustrate the truth of this, one has only to mention the tragic death of Ophelia.	*pour illustrer ceci*
A single, but striking, example of this tendency is the way people dress for parties.	*un exemple frappant de*
One instance is enough to show how powerful a device this is.	*un seul exemple suffit à montrer*
As Chesterton **remarked,** there is a purpose to everything.	*comme l'a remarqué ...*
A recent newspaper article claimed that inflation was now beaten.	*dans un récent article, on affirmait que*
Wordsworth **observed with much truth** that daffodils are impressive in large numbers.	*a remarqué avec justesse*
According to the Prime Minister, our foreign policy is benevolent.	*selon*
The writer **makes this point graphically,** by instancing the plight of those whose beliefs clash with the society they belong to.	*illustre ceci de façon frappante*
Writing in 1932, Professor Armour-Jenkins said that unemployment had destroyed the minds of one generation, and the bodies of the next.	*en 1932, ... a écrit que*
This passage **serves to illustrate** the way in which the writer, more than any other Irish writer of his time, looks sympathetically at the problems of the English middle classes.	*illustre bien*
Take another example: many thousands of people have been and still are condemned to a life of sickness and pain because the hospital service cannot cope with the demand for its services.	*prenons un autre exemple*

LES MÉCANISMES DE LA DISCUSSION

Pour souligner un argument

It is obvious to everyone that Freud is right.	*il est manifeste que*
What is quite certain is that justice will triumph.	*ce qui est sûr c'est que*
The writer **clearly** does not understand the issue.	*il est clair que*
The fact of the matter is that nuclear waste is and always will be harmful.	*la vérité est que*
It is easy to concentrate on this aspect of the problem, but **the real question at issue** is different.	*le vrai problème*
The facts speak for themselves: James is guilty.	*les faits se passent de commentaires: ...*
Politicians make much of education aims, but **what we are concerned with here is** the financial resources to achieve these.	*ce qui nous préoccupe ici, c'est ...*
It should be stressed that this is only a preliminary assumption.	*il faut souligner le fait que*
It would be ridiculous to assert that any one political doctrine holds the answer to our quest for Utopia.	*il serait ridicule d'affirmer que*
Few will dispute the claim that the microchip has changed our lives, although many will wish to take issue with the statement that it has changed them for the better.	*on ne peut nier que*
It is undoubtedly true that time is money.	*il est vrai sans aucun doute que*

Pour atténuer un argument

The new law **could have far-reaching implications for** patterns of crime.	*... pourrait avoir des consequences d'une grande portée sur ...*
There might well be an explanation which we have overlooked.	*il pourrait y avoir*
Such a response **suggests that** *ou* **might be taken to mean that** the group lacked enthusiasm for the project.	*... laisse supposer que*
Let us assume (*ou* **suppose** *ou* **conjecture) that** Mary does love Worthington.	*supposons que*
There is a strong possibility that *ou* **There is strong probability that** Worthington loves Mary.	*il est fort possible que*
One might reasonably suppose *ou* **One might justifiably assume that** such behaviour would be frowned upon in any civilised society.	*on est en droit de supposer que*

Pour exprimer le doute

It is questionable whether the author intended this.	*il n'est pas sûr que*
The government's present attitude **raises the whole question of** whether local government can survive in its present form.	*... soulève la question de savoir si ...*
This line of reasoning **sets a serious question mark against** the future of education.	*met en doute*
It remains to be seen (however) whether new techniques can be found in time.	*il reste à savoir si*
It is to be doubted whether the book is intended to convey a real message.	*il n'est pas certain que*
It may well be that Johnson is serious in this, but his motives are certainly **questionable.**	*il se peut que ... mais on peut mettre en doute*
Few people would deny the benefits of such a scheme. **But, it may be urged,** few people would identify the need for it in the first place.	*mais on pourrait répliquer que*
It is certainly true that moral factors are important in this area, **but I wonder whether** the economic background is not more crucial.	*il est certain que ... mais je me demande cependant si ...*
We can believe the author **up to a point, but** it is hard to be sure that he is right all the time.	*jusqu'à un certain point, mais ...*
In spite of the known facts, there must be serious doubts about the validity of this approach.	*malgré les faits*
It is certainly possible that *ou* **It cannot be ruled out that** the author wished us to believe this.	*il se peut bien que*
It may be conceded that in this play Hector is a type rather than a person.	*on est obligé d'admettre que*
Of course, one could reduce the number of accidents by such a method, **but** we must ask ourselves whether the price is not too high.	*bien sûr ... mais*
Undoubtedly this has improved life for a large section of our society, **but** we must consider carefully the implications of this fact.	*certes ... mais*
It cannot be denied that the buildings are unusual, **but** whether they are beautiful is quite another matter.	*on ne peut nier que ... mais*
He has begun well. **It remains to be seen whether** he will continue as impressively.	*reste à savoir si*

Pour marquer l'accord

Nothing could be more true than this portrayal of the pangs of youthful love. — *rien n'est plus vrai que*

We must acknowledge the validity of the point made by Bevin. — *nous devons accepter*

In a minor sense, however, one is forced to admit that **these criticisms have some validity.** — *ces critiques sont justifées jusqu'à un certain point*

It is, **as the writer says,** a totally unexpected event. — *comme dit l'auteur*

Their opponents **are to be congratulated on** the accuracy of their predictions. — *on doit féliciter ...*

He says, **rightly in my view,** that there is no meaning in this statement. — *et à juste titre selon moi*

In Act II, the hero makes **an extremely perspicacious remark** about John's intentions. — *dit quelque chose de très perspicace à propos de*

Pour marquer le désaccord

It is hard to agree with the popular view that religious belief is out-of-date. — *il est difficile d'être d'accord avec*

This statement **is totally inaccurate** *ou* **is very far from the truth** in many respects. — *... est très loin de la vérité*

Unfortunately, **there is not the slighest evidence to justify such a claim.** — *rien ne prouve que cette affirmation soit vraie*

This argument **offers no solution to** the problems which have beset the artist from time immemorial. — *n'offre pas de solution à*

This is clearly a false view of the poet's intentions. — *il s'agit là d'une déformation de*

The pessimistic view of life **should not go unchallenged.** — *il faut s'élever contre ...*

This simplistic notion of Shakespeare's aim **is quite unconvincing.** — *cette interprétation simpliste de ... n'est pas convaincante*

I find it impossible to accept the philosophical argument for this. — *il m'est impossible d'accepter*

Pour mettre un détail en valeur

Let us be clear that the essential question is not one of money. — *il est clair que*

It should never be forgotten that the writer belongs to his own times. — *n'oublions pas que*

It is hard to overemphasize the importance of keeping an open mind. — *on ne peut sous-estimer l'importance de*

This disaster **underlines the importance of** good safety measures. — *... souligne l'importance de*

Most important of all, we must understand the feelings of the victims. — *le plus important est de*

The reasoning behind this conclusion **deserves especial consideration.** — *... doit être examiné avec une attention toute particulière*

Not only does this passage enlighten us, **but it also** inspires us. — *non seulement ... mais aussi ...*

It is well worth noting the background to this argument. — *il faut noter*

It is essential to realise that the problem will not be solved by more spending. — *il importe de comprendre que*

This scene is a difficult one, **especially in view of** the unlikely background events. — *surtout si l'on considère ...*

Next **I wish to focus our attention on** the use of dramatic irony. — *je tiens à attirer l'attention sur ...*

What is more, the argument lacks conviction. — *de plus*

It is no coincidence that law comes before order in the popular mind. — *ce n'est pas un hasard que*

Another argument supports this thesis: without the contribution which the working married woman makes to the economy, taxes would rise immediately. — *il y a un autre argument en faveur de cette thèse: ...*

The chief feature of this scheme is its emphasis on equality of opportunity rather than material goods. — *la principale caractéristique*

Let us remember that any chain is only as strong as its weakest link. — *n'oublions pas que*

Moreover, it was significant that the Conference rejected the call for peace at any price. — *de plus, il était révélateur que*

Virginia Woolf's attitude to this, as to many things, **is particularly interesting in that** it reflects the artist's sense of isolation. — *... est particulièrement intéressante dans la mesure où*

LANGUAGE IN USE

CONTENTS

(French-English section)

GRAMMAIRE ACTIVE

TABLE DES MATIÈRES

(Section anglais-français)

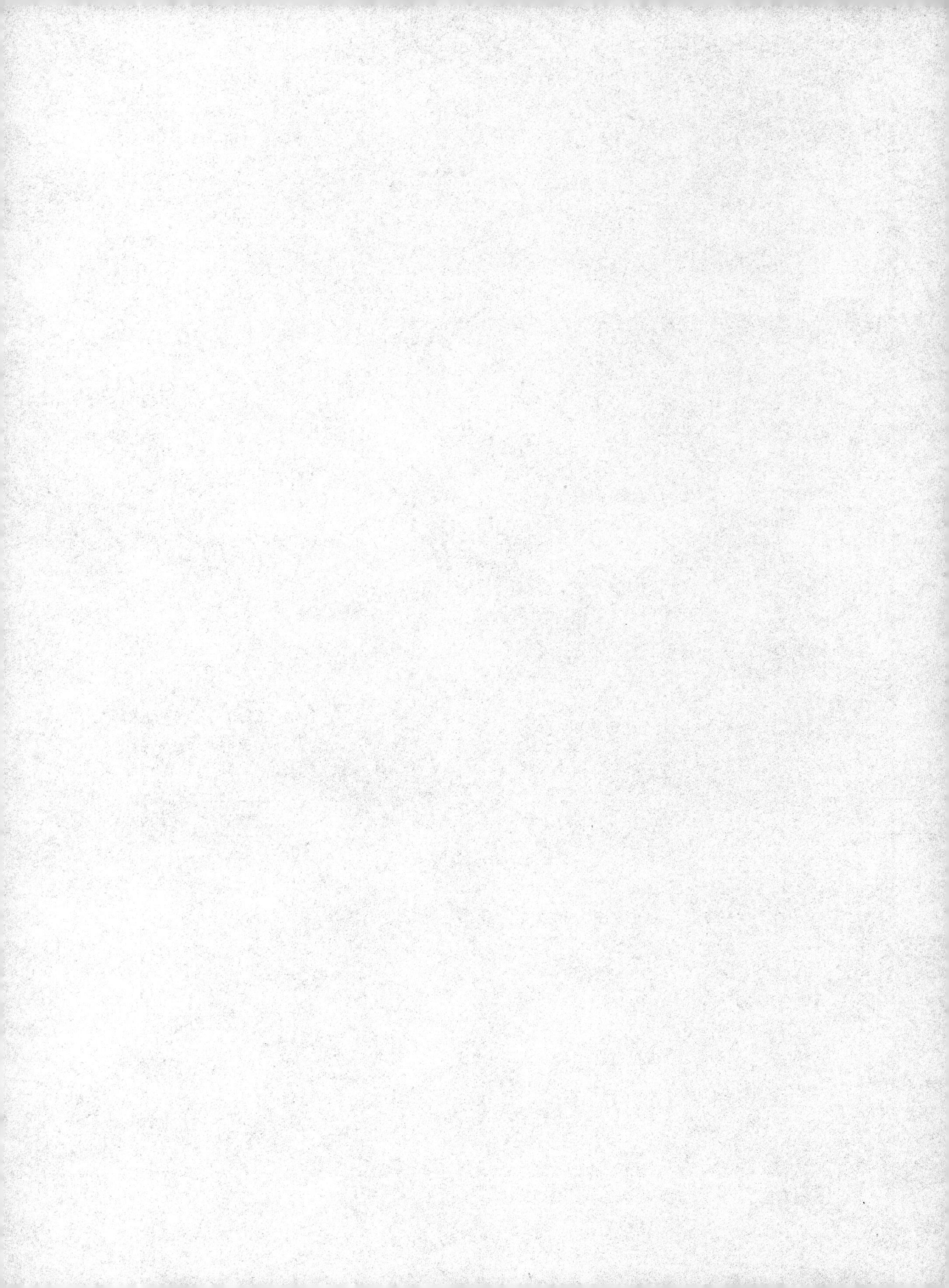

ENGLISH-FRENCH DICTIONARY

DICTIONNAIRE FRANÇAIS-ANGLAIS

A, a[1] [eɪ] 1 n a (*letter*) A, a *m*. **A for Able** A comme Anatole; **to know sth from A to Z** connaître qch de A (jusqu')à Z; **he doesn't know A from B** il est ignare; (*in house numbers*) **24a** le 24 bis; **to get from A to B** aller d'un endroit à un autre; (*Brit Aut*) **on the A4** sur la (route) A4, ≃ sur la RN4 *or* la nationale 4.

b (*Mus*) la *m*; *see* **key**.

c (*Scol*) excellent (*de 15 à 20 sur 20*).

d (*Elec*) (**abbr of ampere(s)**) A.

2 **comp** ►**A-1** parfait, champion* ►**A3/A4 (paper)** (papier *m*) A3/ A4 *m* ►**ABC** *see* **ABC** ►**A-bomb** bombe *f* A *or* atomique ►**A levels** (*Brit Scol*) ≃ baccalauréat *m*; (*Brit Scol*) **to do an A level in geography** passer l'épreuve de géographie au bac ►**A-line dress** robe *f* trapèze *inv* ►**A and M college** (*US*) ≃ école supérieure d'agriculture ►**A number 1** (*US*) = **A-1** ►**A-OK*** = **A-1** ►**A-side** *[record]* face *f* A ►**A-test** essai *m* de la bombe A.

a[2] [eɪ, ə] **indef art** (*before vowel or mute h:* **an**) a un, une. **~ tree** un arbre; **an apple** une pomme; **such ~ hat** un tel *or* pareil chapeau; **so large ~ country** un si grand pays.

b (*def art in French*) le, la, les. **he smokes ~ pipe** il fume la pipe; **to set an example** donner l'exemple; **I have read ~ third of the book** j'ai lu le tiers du livre; **we haven't ~ penny** nous n'avons pas le sou; **~ woman hates violence** les femmes détestent la violence.

c (*absent in French*) **she was ~ doctor** elle était médecin; **as ~ soldier** en tant que soldat; **my uncle, ~ sailor** mon oncle, qui est marin; **what ~ pleasure!** quel plaisir!; **to make ~ fortune** faire fortune.

d un(e) certain(e). **I have heard of ~ Mr X** j'ai entendu parler d'un certain M. X.

e le *or* la même. **they are much of an age** ils sont du même âge; **they are of ~ size** ils sont de la même grandeur.

f (*a single*) un(e) seul(e). **to empty a glass at ~ draught** vider un verre d'un trait; **at ~ blow** d'un seul coup.

g (*with abstract nouns*) du, de la, des. **to make ~ noise/~ fuss** faire du bruit/des histoires.

h **~ few survivors** quelques survivants; **~ lot of** *or* **~ great many flowers** beaucoup de fleurs.

i (*distributive use*) **£4 ~ person/head** 4 livres par personne/par tête; **3 francs ~ kilo** 3 F le kilo; **twice ~ month** deux fois par mois; **twice ~ year** deux fois l'an *or* par an; **80 km an hour** 80 km/h, 80 kilomètres-heure, 80 kilomètres à l'heure.

AA [eɪ'eɪ] **n** a (*Brit*) (**abbr of Automobile Association**) ≃ Touring Club *m* de France. b (**abbr of Alcoholics Anonymous**) *see* **alcoholic**. c (*US Univ*) (**abbr of Associate in Arts**) ≃ DEUG *m* de Lettres.

AAA [ˌeɪeɪ'eɪ] **n** a (*Brit*) **abbr of Amateur Athletics Association.** b (*US*) ['trɪplˌeɪ] (**abbr of American Automobile Association**) ≃ Touring Club *m* de France.

Aachen ['ɑːxən] **n** Aix-la-Chapelle.

Aaron ['ɛərən] **n** Aaron *m*.

A.A.U. [ˌeɪeɪ'juː] **n** (*US*) **abbr of Amateur Athletic Union.**

A.A.U.P. [ˌeɪeɪjuː'piː] **n** (*US*) **abbr of American Association of University Professors.**

A.B. [eɪ'biː] **n abbr of able-bodied seaman.**

A.B.A. [ˌeɪbiː'eɪ] **n abbr of Amateur Boxing Association.**

aback [ə'bæk] **adv**: **to be taken ~** être interloqué *or* décontenancé, en rester tout interdit *or* déconcerté.

abacus ['æbəkəs] **n, pl ~es** *or* **abaci** ['æbəsaɪ] a boulier *m* (compteur), abaque *m*. b (*Archit*) abaque *m*.

Abadan [ˌæbə'dæn] **n** Abadan.

abaft [ə'bɑːft] (*Naut*) 1 **adv** sur *or* vers l'arrière. 2 **prep** en arrière de, sur l'arrière de.

abalone [ˌæbə'ləʊnɪ] **n** (*US*) ormeau *m*, haliotide *f*.

abandon [ə'bændən] 1 **vt** a (*forsake*) *person* abandonner; *wife, child* abandonner, délaisser; *car* abandonner, laisser. (*fig*) **to ~ o.s. to** se livrer à, s'abandonner à, se laisser aller à. b *property, right, project* renoncer à; *action* se désister de. **to ~ the attempt to do sth** renoncer à faire qch; (*Sport*) **play was ~ed** la partie a été interrompue. c (*Jur*) *cargo* faire (acte de) délaissement de. (*Naut*) **to ~ ship** abandonner le navire; (*Jur*) **to ~ any claim** renoncer à toute prétension. 2 **n** (*NonC*) laisser-aller *m*, abandon *m*, relâchement *m*. **with (gay) ~** avec (une belle) désinvolture.

abandoned [ə'bændənd] **adj** a (*forsaken*) *person* abandonné, délaissé; *place* abandonné. b (*dissolute*) débauché. c *dancing* frénétique; *emotion* éperdu.

abandonment [ə'bændənmənt] **n** (*lit, fig*) abandon *m*; (*Jur*) *[action]* désistement *m*; *[property, right]* cession *f*; *[cargo]* délaissement *m*.

abase [ə'beɪs] **vt** (*humiliate*) *person* mortifier, humilier; (*degrade*) *person* abaisser, avilir; *person's qualities, actions* rabaisser, ravaler. **to ~ o.s. so far as to do** s'abaisser *or* s'humilier jusqu'à faire.

abasement [ə'beɪsmənt] **n** (*NonC*) (*moral decay*) dégradation *f*, avilissement *m*; (*humiliation*) humiliation *f*, mortification *f*.

abashed [ə'bæʃt] **adj** confus.

abate [ə'beɪt] 1 **vi** *[storm, emotions, pain]* s'apaiser, se calmer; *[noise, flood]* baisser; *[fever]* baisser, décroître; *[wind]* se modérer; (*Naut*) mollir; *[courage]* faiblir, s'affaiblir, diminuer; *[rent]* baisser. 2 **vt** *tax* baisser; (*Jur*) *writ* annuler; *sentence* remettre.

abatement [ə'beɪtmənt] **n** (*NonC*) (*gen*) réduction *f*. (*Fin*) **~ of the levy** abattement *m* sur le prélèvement; *see* **noise.**

abattoir ['æbətwɑːr] **n** abattoir *m*.

abbess ['æbɪs] **n** abbesse *f*.

abbey ['æbɪ] **n** abbaye *f*. **Westminster A~** l'Abbaye de Westminster.

abbot ['æbət] **n** abbé *m*, (Père *m*) supérieur *m*.

abbreviate [ə'briːvɪeɪt] **vt** abréger (*to* en), raccourcir.

abbreviation [əˌbriːvɪ'eɪʃən] **n** abréviation *f*.

ABC [ˌeɪbiː'siː] **n** a abc *m*, alphabet *m*. (*Brit Rail*) **the ~ (guide)** l'indicateur *m* des chemins de fer; **it's as easy** *or* **simple as ~*** c'est simple comme bonjour, rien de plus simple. b **abbr of Associated British Cinemas.** c **abbr of Australian Broadcasting Commission.** d (**abbr of American Broadcasting Corporation**) ABC.

abdicate ['æbdɪkeɪt] 1 **vt** *right* renoncer à, abdiquer; *post, responsibility* se démettre de. **to ~ the throne** renoncer à la couronne, abdiquer. 2 **vi** abdiquer.

abdication [ˌæbdɪ'keɪʃən] **n** *[king]* abdication *f*, renonciation *f*; *[mandate etc]* démission *f* (*of* de); *[right]* renonciation (*of* à), désistement *m* (*of* de).

abdomen ['æbdəmən], (*Med*) [æb'dəʊmen] **n** abdomen *m*.

abdominal [æb'dɒmɪnl] **adj** abdominal.

abduct [æb'dʌkt] **vt** enlever, kidnapper.

abduction [æb'dʌkʃən] **n** enlèvement *m*, rapt *m*; *see* **child.**

abductor [æb'dʌktər] **n** a (*person*) ravisseur *m*, -euse *f*. b (*Anat*) abducteur *m*.

abed† [ə'bed] **adv** (*liter*) au lit, couché. **to lie ~** rester couché.

Abel ['eɪbl] **n** Abel *m*.

Aberdonian [ˌæbə'dəʊnɪən] 1 **n** habitant(e) *m(f)* *or* natif *m*, -ive *f* d'Aberdeen. 2 **adj** d'Aberdeen.

aberrant [ə'berənt] **adj** (*Bio, fig*) aberrant, anormal.

aberration [ˌæbə'reɪʃən] **n** (*lit, fig*) aberration *f*.

abet [ə'bet] **vt** encourager, soutenir. **to ~ sb in a crime** aider qn à commettre un crime; *see* **aid 3.**

abetter, abettor [ə'betər] **n** complice *mf*.

abeyance [ə'beɪəns] **n** (*NonC*) *[law, custom]* **to be in ~** ne pas être en vigueur; **to fall into ~** tomber en désuétude; **the question is in ~** la question reste en suspens.

abhor [əb'hɔːr] **vt** abhorrer, avoir en horreur, exécrer; *see* **nature.**

abhorrence [əb'hɒrəns] **n** horreur *f*, aversion *f* (*of* de), répulsion *f*. **to hold in ~** avoir horreur de, avoir en horreur.

abhorrent [əb'hɒrənt] **adj** odieux, exécrable, répugnant (*to* à).

abide [ə'baɪd] 1 **vt** a (*neg only: tolerate*) **I can't ~ her** je ne peux pas la supporter *or* la souffrir; **I can't ~ living here** je ne supporte pas de vivre ici. b (*liter: await*) attendre. 2 **vi** (†: *endure*) subsister, durer, se maintenir; (*live*) demeurer, habiter.

▸**abide by** vt fus *rule, decision* se soumettre à, se conformer à, respecter; *consequences* accepter, supporter; *promise* rester *or* demeurer fidèle à; *resolve* maintenir, s'en tenir à. **I abide by what I said** je maintiens ce que j'ai dit.

abiding [ə'baɪdɪŋ] adj (*liter*) constant, éternel; *see* **law** *etc.*

ability [ə'bɪlɪtɪ] n a (*NonC: power, proficiency*) aptitude *f* (*to do* à faire), capacité *f* (*to do* pour faire), compétence *f* (*in* en, *to do* pour faire). **to the best of one's ~** *or* **abilities** de son mieux; (*Fin, Jur*) **~ to pay** solvabilité *f*; (*Fin, Jur*) **~ to pay tax** capacité *or* faculté contributive. b (*NonC: cleverness*) habileté *f*, talent *m*. **a person of great ~** une personne de grand talent; **he has a certain artistic ~** il a un certain don *or* talent artistique. c (*mental powers*) **abilities** talents *mpl*, dons intellectuels; (*Scol etc*) compétences *fpl*.

abject ['æbdʒekt] adj *person, action* abject, vil, méprisable; *state, condition* misérable, pitoyable; *apology* servile. **in ~ poverty** dans la misère noire.

abjectly ['æbdʒektlɪ] adv *apologize etc* avec servilité.

abjure [əb'dʒʊəʳ] vt *one's rights* renoncer (publiquement *or* par serment) à. **to ~ one's religion** abjurer sa religion, apostasier.

ablative ['æblətɪv] 1 n ablatif *m*. **in the ~** à l'ablatif; **~ absolute** ablatif absolu. 2 adj ablatif.

ablaze [ə'bleɪz] adv, adj (*lit*) en feu, en flammes. **to set ~** embraser (*liter*); **to be ~** flamber; (*fig*) **~ with anger** enflammé de colère; (*fig*) **~ with light** resplendissant de lumière.

able ['eɪbl] 1 adj a (*"to be ~" sert d'infinitif à l'auxiliaire de mode "can/could" dans quelques-uns des sens de cet auxiliaire*) **to be ~ to do** (*have means or opportunity*) pouvoir faire; (*know how to*) savoir faire; (*be capable of*) être à même de *or* en mesure de faire; **I ran fast and so was ~ to catch the bus** en courant vite j'ai réussi à attraper l'autobus (*NB "could" ne peut être employé dans ce contexte*).

b (*having power, means, opportunity*) capable, en état (*to do* de faire), apte, propre (*to do* à faire). **~ to pay** en mesure de payer; **you are better ~ to do it than he is** (*it's easier for you*) vous êtes mieux à même de le faire *or* plus en état de le faire que lui; (*you're better qualified*) vous êtes plus propre à le faire *or* mieux désigné pour le faire que lui.

c (*clever*) capable, compétent, de talent. **an ~ man** un homme de talent.

d (*Med: healthy*) sain. (*Jur*) **~ in body and mind** sain de corps et d'esprit.

2 comp ▸**able-bodied** robuste, fort, solide; (*Mil*) *recruit* bon pour le service ▸**able-minded** intelligent ▸**able rating** (*Brit Naut*) matelot breveté ▸**able seaman** (*Naut*) matelot breveté *or* de deuxième classe.

ablution [ə'blu:ʃən] n (*Rel*) ablution *f*.

ably ['eɪblɪ] adv de façon très compétente, habilement.

ABM [ˌeɪbi:'em] n abbr of **anti-ballistic missile**.

abnegate ['æbnɪgeɪt] vt *responsibility* renier, répudier, rejeter; *one's rights* renoncer à; *one's religion* abjurer.

abnegation [ˌæbnɪ'geɪʃən] n (*denial*) reniement *m*, désaveu *m*; (*renunciation*) renoncement *m*. **self-~** abnégation *f*.

abnormal [æb'nɔ:məl] adj anormal.

abnormality [ˌæbnɔ:'mælɪtɪ] n a (*NonC*) caractère anormal *or* exceptionnel. b (*instance of this, also Bio, Psych*) anomalie *f*; (*Med*) difformité *f*, malformation *f*.

abnormally [æb'nɔ:məlɪ] adv anormalement.

aboard [ə'bɔ:d] 1 adv a (*Aviat, Naut*) à bord. **to go ~** (s')embarquer, monter à bord; **to take ~** embarquer; **all ~!** (*Rail*) en voiture!; (*Naut*) tout le monde à bord! b (*Naut*) le long du bord. **close ~** bord à bord. 2 prep (*Aviat, Naut*) à bord de. **~ the train/bus** dans le train/le bus; **~ ship** à bord.

abode [ə'bəʊd] n (*liter*) demeure *f*. (*Jur*) **place of ~** domicile *m*; (*Jur*) **right of ~** droit *m* de résidence; **to take up one's ~** élire domicile; *see* **fixed**.

abolish [ə'bɒlɪʃ] vt *practice, custom* supprimer; *death penalty* abolir; *law* abroger, abolir.

abolishment [ə'bɒlɪʃmənt] n, **abolition** [ˌæbəʊ'lɪʃən] n (*see* **abolish**) suppression *f*; abolition *f*; abrogation *f*.

abolitionist [ˌæbəʊ'lɪʃənɪst] n (*Hist*) abolitionniste *mf*, antiesclavagiste *mf*.

abominable [ə'bɒmɪnəbl] adj (*hateful*) abominable, odieux, détestable; (*unpleasant*) abominable, affreux, horrible. **the ~ snowman** l'abominable homme *m* des neiges.

abominably [ə'bɒmɪnəblɪ] adv a abominablement, odieusement. b **it's ~ cold** il fait un froid abominable.

abominate [ə'bɒmɪneɪt] vt abhorrer, exécrer, abominer.

abomination [əˌbɒmɪ'neɪʃən] n a (*NonC*) abomination *f*. **I hold him in ~** je l'ai en abomination *or* en horreur, il me remplit d'horreur. b (*loathsome thing, act*) abomination *f*, objet *m* d'horreur, acte *m* abominable. **this coffee is an ~*** ce café est abominable *or* est une abomination*.

aboriginal [ˌæbə'rɪdʒənl] adj, n *person* autochtone *(mf)*, aborigène *(mf)*; *plant, animal* aborigène; (*Austral*) aborigène d'Australie.

aborigine [ˌæbə'rɪdʒɪnɪ] n aborigène *mf*; (*Austral*) aborigène d'Australie.

abort [ə'bɔ:t] 1 vi (*Med, fig*) avorter; (*Mil, Space*) échouer; (*Comput*) abandonner. 2 vt (*Med, fig*) faire avorter; (*Comput*) abandonner; (*Space*) *mission, operation* abandonner *or* interrompre (pour raison de sécurité); (* *fig*) *deal, agreement* faire capoter. 3 n (*Comput*) abandon *m*.

abortion [ə'bɔ:ʃən] n a (*Med*) avortement *m*, interruption *f* (volontaire) de grossesse. **spontaneous ~** avortement spontané, interruption de grossesse; **to have an ~** se faire avorter; **~ law reform** réforme *f* de la loi sur l'avortement. b (*fig*) *[plans etc]* avortement *m*.

abortionist [ə'bɔ:ʃənɪst] n avorteur *m*, -euse *f*. **backstreet ~** faiseuse *f* d'anges.

abortive [ə'bɔ:tɪv] adj a (*unsuccessful*) *plan* manqué, raté, qui a échoué. **it was an ~ effort** c'était un coup manqué *or* raté; **he made an ~ attempt to speak** il a fait une tentative infructueuse pour parler. b (*Med*) *method, medicine* abortif.

abortively [ə'bɔ:tɪvlɪ] adv en vain.

abound [ə'baʊnd] vi *[fish, resources etc]* abonder; *[river, town, area etc]* abonder (*in* en), regorger (*in* de).

about [ə'baʊt] (*phr vb elem*) 1 adv a (*approximately*) vers, à peu près, environ. **~ 11 o'clock** vers 11 heures, sur les 11 heures; **it's ~ 11 o'clock** il est environ *or* à peu près 11 heures; (*emphatic*) **it's ~ time!** il est (bien) temps!; **it's ~ time to go** il est presque temps de partir; **there were ~ 25 and now there are ~ 30** il y en avait environ 25 *or* dans les 25 et à présent il y en a une trentaine; **she's ~ as old as you** elle est à peu près de votre âge; **that's ~ it** *or* **all** c'est à peu près tout; **I've had ~ enough!*** je commence à en avoir marre!* *or* en avoir jusque là!* *or* en avoir ras le bol!⁑

b (*here and there*) çà *or* ici et là, de tous côtés. **shoes lying ~** des chaussures dans tous les coins *or* traînant çà et là; **to throw one's arms ~** gesticuler, agiter les bras en tous sens.

c (*near*) près, par ici, par là. **is anyone ~?** y a quelqu'un?; **there was nobody ~** il n'y avait personne; **there is a rumour ~ that ...** le bruit court que ..., on dit que ...; **he's somewhere ~** il n'est pas loin, il est par ici quelque part, il est (quelque part) dans les parages; **there's a lot of flu ~** il y a beaucoup de cas de grippe en ce moment.

d (*all round*) autour, à la ronde. **all ~** tout autour; **to glance ~** jeter un coup d'œil autour de soi.

e (*opposite direction*) à l'envers. (*fig*) **it's the other way ~** c'est tout le contraire; (*Mil*) **~ turn!, ~ face!** demi-tour, marche!; (*Naut*) **to go** *or* **put ~** virer de bord; *see* **ready, right**.

f (*in phrases*) **to be ~ to do** être sur le point de faire, aller faire; **she's up and ~ again** elle est de nouveau sur pied; **you should be out and ~!** ne restez donc pas enfermé!; *see* **bring about, come about, turn about** *etc*.

2 prep a (*concerning*) au sujet de, concernant, à propos de. **~ it** en (*before vb*); **I heard nothing ~ it** je n'en ai pas entendu parler; **what is it ~?** de quoi s'agit-il?; **I know what it's all ~** je sais de quoi il retourne; **to speak ~ sth** parler de qch; **well, what ~ it?*** (*does it matter?*) et alors?*; (*what do you think?*) alors qu'est-ce que tu en penses?; **what ~ me?** et moi alors?*; **how ~** *or* **what ~ going to the pictures?*** si on allait au cinéma?; **what ~ a coffee?*** si on prenait un café?, est-ce que tu veux un café?

b (*near to*) vers, dans le voisinage de; (*somewhere in*) en, dans. **I dropped it ~ here** je l'ai laissé tomber par ici *or* près d'ici; **round ~ the Arctic Circle** près du Cercle polaire; **~ the house** quelque part dans la maison; **to wander ~ the town/the streets** errer dans la ville/par les rues.

c (*occupied with*) occupé à. **what are you ~?** que faites-vous?, qu'est-ce que vous fabriquez là?*; **while we're ~ it** pendant que nous y sommes; **I don't know what he's ~** je ne sais pas ce qu'il fabrique*; **mind what you're ~!** faites (un peu) attention!; **how does one go ~ it?** comment est-ce qu'on s'y prend?; **to go ~ one's business** s'occuper de ses (propres) affaires; **to send sb ~ his business** envoyer promener* qn.

d (*with, on*) **I've got it ~ me somewhere** je l'ai quelque part sur moi; **there is something horrible ~ him** il y a quelque chose d'horrible en lui; **there is something interesting ~ him** il a un côté intéressant; **there is something charming ~ him** il a un certain charme.

e (*round*) autour de. **the trees (round) ~ the pond** les arbres qui entourent l'étang; **the countryside (round) ~ Edinburgh** la campagne autour d'Édimbourg.

about-face [ə'baʊt'feɪs], **about-turn** [ə'baʊt'tɜ:n] 1 vi (*Mil*) faire un demi-tour; (*fig*) faire volte-face. 2 n (*Mil*) demi-tour *m*; (*fig*) volte-face *f*. **to do an ~** faire un demi-tour; (*fig*) faire volte-face.

above [ə'bʌv] (*phr vb elem*) 1 adv a (*overhead, higher up*) au-dessus, en haut. **from ~** d'en haut; **view from ~** vue plongeante; **the flat ~** l'appartement au-dessus *or* du dessus; **the powers ~** (*of higher rank*) les autorités supérieures; (*in heaven*) les puissances célestes; (*fig*) **a warning from ~** un avertissement (venu) d'en haut.

b (*more*) **boys of 16 and ~** les garçons à partir de 16 ans; **seats at 10 francs and ~** places à partir de 10 F; *see* **over**.

c (*earlier: in book etc*) ci-dessus, plus haut. **as ~** comme ci-dessus, comme plus haut; **the address as ~** l'adresse ci-dessus.

d (*upstream*) en amont, plus haut.

2 prep a (*higher than, superior to*) au-dessus de, plus haut que. ~ **it** plus haut; ~ **the horizon** au-dessus de l'horizon; ~ **average** au-dessus de la moyenne, supérieur à la moyenne; ~ **all (else)** par-dessus tout, surtout.

b (*more than*) plus de. **children ~ 7 years of age** les enfants de plus de 7 ans *or* au-dessus de 7 ans; **it will cost ~ £10** ça coûtera plus de 10 livres; **over and ~ (the cost of)** ... en plus de (ce que coûte) ... .

c (*beyond*) au-delà de. **to get ~ o.s.** avoir des idées de grandeur; **to live ~ one's means** vivre au-delà de *or* au-dessus de ses moyens; **that is quite ~ me*** ceci me dépasse; **this book is ~ me*** ce livre est trop compliqué pour moi; *see* **head.**

d (*too proud, honest etc for*) **he is ~ such behaviour** il est au-dessus d'une pareille conduite; **he's not ~ stealing/theft** il irait jusqu'à voler/ jusqu'au vol; **he's not ~ playing with the children** il ne dédaigne pas de jouer avec les enfants.

e (*upstream from*) en amont de, plus haut que.

f (*north of*) au nord de, au-dessus de.

3 adj ci-dessus mentionné, précité. **the ~ decree** le décret précité.

4 n: **the ~ is a photo of** ... ci-dessus nous avons une photo de ...; **please translate the ~** veuillez traduire ce qui se trouve au-dessus.

5 comp ►**aboveboard** adj *person, action* régulier, correct ◊ adv cartes sur table ►**aboveground** (*lit*) au-dessus du sol, à la surface; (*Tech*) extérieur; (* *US fig*) déclaré ►**above-mentioned** mentionné ci-dessus, susmentionné, précité ►**above-named** susnommé.

abracadabra [ˌæbrəkəˈdæbrə] excl abracadabra!

abrade [əˈbreɪd] vt user en frottant *or* par le frottement; *skin etc* écorcher, érafler; (*Geol*) éroder.

Abraham [ˈeɪbrəhæm] n Abraham *m*.

abrasion [əˈbreɪʒən] n (*see* **abrade**) frottement *m*; (*Med*) écorchure *f*; érosion *f*; (*Tech*) abrasion *f*.

abrasive [əˈbreɪsɪv] 1 adj abrasif; (*fig*) *voice* caustique; *wit* corrosif. 2 n abrasif *m*.

abreaction [ˌæbrɪˈækʃən] n abréaction *f*.

abreast [əˈbrest] adv a *[horses, vehicles, ships]* de front; *[persons]* de front, l'un(e) à côté de l'autre, côte à côte. **to walk 3 ~** marcher 3 de front; (*Naut*) **(in) line ~** en ligne de front. b **~ of** à la hauteur de, parallèlement à, en ligne avec; (*Naut*) **to be ~ of a ship** être à la hauteur *or* par le travers d'un navire; (*fig*) **to be ~ of the times** marcher avec son temps; (*fig*) **to keep ~ of** (suivre (les progrès de), se maintenir *or* se tenir au courant de.

abridge [əˈbrɪdʒ] vt *book* abréger; *article, speech* raccourcir, abréger; *interview* écourter; *text* réduire.

abridgement [əˈbrɪdʒmənt] n a (*shortened version*) résumé *m*, abrégé *m*. b (*NonC*) diminution *f*, réduction *f*.

abroad [əˈbrɔːd] adv a (*in foreign land*) à l'étranger. **to go/be ~** aller/être à l'étranger; **news from ~** nouvelles de l'étranger; *see* **home.** b (*far and wide*) au loin; (*in all directions*) de tous côtés, dans toutes les directions. **scattered ~** éparpillé de tous côtés *or* aux quatre vents; **there is a rumour ~ that** ... le bruit circule *or* court que ...; *see* **noise.** c (†: *out of doors*) (au) dehors, hors de chez soi.

abrogate [ˈæbrəʊgeɪt] vt abroger, abolir.

abrogation [ˌæbrəʊˈgeɪʃən] n abrogation *f*.

abrupt [əˈbrʌpt] adj *turn* soudain; *question, dismissal* brusque; *departure* précipité; *person, conduct* bourru, brusque; *style, speech* heurté; *slope* abrupt, raide.

abruptly [əˈbrʌptlɪ] adv *turn, move* brusquement, tout à coup; *speak, behave* avec brusquerie, sans cérémonie, abruptement; *rise* en pente raide, à pic.

abruptness [əˈbrʌptnɪs] n (*suddenness*) soudaineté *f*; (*haste*) précipitation *f*; *[style]* décousu *m*; *[person, behaviour]* brusquerie *f*, rudesse *f*; (*steepness*) raideur *f*.

ABS [eɪbiːˈes] n (abbr of **anti-lock braking system**) ABS *m*. **~ brakes** freins ABS.

abscess [ˈæbses] n abcès *m*.

abscond [əbˈskɒnd] vi s'enfuir, prendre la fuite (*from* de).

absconder [əbˈskɒndəʳ] n fugitif *m*, -ive *f*; (*from prison*) évadé(e) *m(f)*.

absconding [əbˈskɒndɪŋ] 1 adj en fuite. 2 n fuite *f*; *[prisoner]* évasion *f*.

abseil [ˈæbseɪl] 1 vi descendre en rappel. 2 n (descente *f* en) rappel *m*. **~ device** descendeur *m*.

abseiling [ˈæbseɪlɪŋ] n (descente *f* en) rappel *m*.

absence [ˈæbsəns] n a (*NonC*) (*being away*) absence *f*, éloignement *m*; (*Jur*) non-comparution *f*, défaut *m*. **in** *or* **during the ~ of sb** pendant *or* en l'absence de qn; (*Jur*) **sentenced in his ~** condamné par contumace; **~ makes the heart grow fonder** l'éloignement renforce les sentiments; *see* **leave, unauthorized.** b (*instance of this*) absence *f*. **an ~ of 3 months** une absence de 3 mois. c (*NonC: lack*) manque *m*, défaut *m*. **in the ~ of information** faute de renseignements. d **~ of mind** distraction *f*, absence *f*.

absent [ˈæbsənt] 1 adj a (*away*) absent (*from* de). **to be** *or* **go ~ without leave** (*Mil*) être absent sans permission; (*: *gen*) être sorti sans permission; **to ~ friends!** à nos amis absents! b (*absent-minded*) distrait. c (*lacking*) absent. **sympathy was noticeably ~ from his manner** son attitude révélait clairement un manque de sympathie. 2 comp ►**absent-minded** *person* distrait; *air, manner* absent, distrait ►**absent-mindedly** distraitement, d'un air distrait *or* absent ►**absent-mindedness** distraction *f*, absence *f*. 3 [æbˈsent] vt: **to ~ o.s.** s'absenter (*from* de).

absentee [ˌæbsənˈtiː] 1 n absent(e) *m(f)*, manquant(e) *m(f)*; (*habitual*) absentéiste *mf*. 2 comp ►**absentee ballot** (*US Pol*) vote *m* par correspondance ►**absentee landlord** propriétaire *mf* absentéiste *mf* ►**absentee rate** (*Ind, Scol*) taux *m* d'absentéisme ►**absentee voter** électeur *m*, -trice *f* par correspondance.

absenteeism [ˌæbsənˈtiːɪzəm] n absentéisme *m*.

absently [ˈæbsəntlɪ] adv distraitement.

absinth(e) [ˈæbsɪnθ] n absinthe *f*.

absolute [ˈæbsəluːt] 1 adj a (*whole, undeniable*) absolu, total, complet (*f* -ète); (*Chem*) *alcohol* absolu, anhydre. (*Jur*) **the divorce was made ~** le (jugement en) divorce a été prononcé; **it's an ~ scandal*** c'est un véritable scandale; **~ idiot*** parfait crétin*; **it's an ~ fact that** ... c'est un fait indiscutable que ... . b (*unlimited*) *power* absolu, souverain; *monarch* absolu. c (*unqualified*) *refusal, command, majority* absolu; (*Jur*) *proof* irréfutable, formel. **~ veto** véto formel; (*Fin, Jur*) **~ liability** responsabilité objective; *see* **ablative.** d (*Mus*) **to have ~ pitch** avoir l'oreille absolue. e (*Math, Phys*) *value, temperature, zero* absolu. 2 n absolu *m*.

absolutely [ˌæbsəˈluːtlɪ] adv a (*completely*) absolument, complètement, tout à fait. b (*unconditionally*) *refuse* absolument, formellement. c (*certainly*) absolument. **oh ~!** mais bien sûr!; **~ not!** absolument pas! d [ˈæbsəluːtlɪ] (*Gram*) **verb used ~** verbe employé absolument *or* dans un sens absolu.

absolution [ˌæbsəˈluːʃən] n absolution *f*, remise *f* des péchés. (*in liturgy*) **the A~** l'absoute *f*.

absolutism [ˈæbsəluːtɪzəm] n (*Pol*) absolutisme *m*; (*Rel*) prédestination *f*.

absolve [əbˈzɒlv] vt (*from sin, of crime*) absoudre (*from, of* de); (*Jur*) acquitter (*of* de); (*from obligation, oath*) décharger, délier (*from* de).

absorb [əbˈsɔːb] vt a (*lit, fig*) absorber; *sound, shock* amortir. **to ~ surplus stocks** absorber les surplus. b (*gen pass*) **to become ~ed in one's work/in a book** s'absorber dans son travail/dans la lecture d'un livre; **to be ~ed in a book** être plongé dans un livre; **to be completely ~ed in one's work** être tout entier à son travail.

absorbency [əbˈsɔːbənsɪ] n pouvoir absorbant; (*Chem, Phys*) absorptivité *f*.

absorbent [əbˈsɔːbənt] 1 adj absorbant. (*US*) **~ cotton** coton *m* hydrophile. 2 n absorbant *m*.

absorbing [əbˈsɔːbɪŋ] adj (*lit*) absorbant; (*fig*) *book, film* passionnant, captivant; *work* absorbant.

absorption [əbˈsɔːpʃən] n a (*Phys, Physiol*) absorption *f*; (*Aut*) *[shocks]* amortissement *m*; (*fig*) *[person into group etc]* absorption, intégration *f*. b (*fig*) concentration *f* (d'esprit). **his ~ in his studies prevented him from** ... ses études l'absorbaient à tel point qu'elles l'empêchaient de ... .

absquatulate* [æbˈskwɒtʃəleɪt] vi se tirer‡, mettre les voiles‡.

abstain [əbˈsteɪn] vi a s'abstenir (*from* de, *from doing* de faire). b (*be teetotaller*) s'abstenir complètement (de l'usage) des boissons alcoolisées.

abstainer [əbˈsteɪnəʳ] n a (*also* **total ~**) personne *f* qui s'abstient de toute boisson alcoolisée. b (*Pol*) abstentionniste *mf*.

abstemious [əbˈstiːmɪəs] adj *person* sobre, frugal; *meal* frugal.

abstemiousness [əbˈstiːmɪəsnɪs] n (*see* **abstemious**) sobriété *f*; frugalité *f*.

abstention [əbˈstenʃən] n (*from voting*) abstention *f*; (*from drinking*) abstinence *f*. (*Parl etc*) **400 votes with 3 ~s** 400 voix et 3 abstentions.

abstinence [ˈæbstɪnəns] n (*also Rel*) abstinence *f* (*from* de). **(total) ~** abstention *f* de toute boisson alcoolisée.

abstinent [ˈæbstɪnənt] adj sobre, tempérant; (*Rel*) abstinent.

abstract [ˈæbstrækt] 1 adj *idea, number, noun, art, artist* abstrait. **~ expressionism** lyrisme abstrait. 2 n a (*Philos*) abstrait *m*; (*idea*) abstraction *f*. **in the ~** dans l'abstrait. b (*summary*) résumé *m*, abrégé *m*. (*Fin*) **~ of accounts** extrait *m* de compte. c (*work of art*) œuvre abstraite. 3 [æbˈstrækt] vt a (*also Chem: remove*) extraire (*from* de). b (*steal*) soustraire (*sth from sb* qch à qn), dérober. c (*summarize*) *book* résumer.

abstracted [æbˈstræktɪd] adj *person* (*absent-minded*) distrait; (*preoccupied*) préoccupé, absorbé.

abstractedly [æbˈstræktɪdlɪ] adv distraitement.

abstraction [æbˈstrækʃən] n a (*act of removing*) extraction *f*; (*: *stealing*) appropriation *f*. b (*absent-mindedness*) distraction *f*. **with an air of ~** d'un air distrait *or* préoccupé. c (*concept*) idée abstraite, abstraction *f*.

abstruse [æbˈstruːs] adj abstrus.

abstruseness [æbˈstruːsnɪs] n complexité *f*, caractère abstrus.

absurd [əbˈsɜːd] 1 adj déraisonnable, absurde. **it's ~!** c'est idiot!, c'est insensé!, c'est absurde! 2 n (*Philos*) absurde *m*.

absurdity [əbˈsɜːdɪtɪ] n absurdité *f*.

absurdly [əb'sɜːdlɪ] adv absurdement, ridiculement.

ABTA ['æbtə] n abbr of **Association of British Travel Agents.**

Abu Dhabi [ˌæbu'dɑːbɪ] n Abou Dhabî.

abundance [ə'bʌndəns] n (*NonC*) a (*plenty*) abondance *f*, profusion *f*. **in ~** en abondance, à foison, à profusion. b (*wealth*) abondance *f*, aisance *f*. **to live in ~** vivre dans l'abondance.

abundant [ə'bʌndənt] adj riche (*in* en), abondant. **there is ~ proof that he is guilty** les preuves de sa culpabilité abondent.

abundantly [ə'bʌndəntlɪ] adv abondamment, copieusement. **to grow ~** pousser à foison; **it was ~ clear that ...** il était tout à fait clair que ...; **he made it ~ clear to me that ...** il m'a bien fait comprendre *or* m'a bien précisé que ... .

abuse [ə'bjuːz] 1 vt a (*misuse*) *privilege* abuser de. b *person* (*insult*) injurier, insulter; (*ill-treat*) maltraiter, malmener. 2 [ə'bjuːs] n a *[power, authority]* abus *m*. b (*unjust practice*) abus *m*. **to remedy ~s** réprimer les abus. c (*NonC: curses, insults*) insultes *fpl*, injures *fpl*; (*ill treatment*) mauvais traitements *mpl* (*of* infligés à). **child ~** mauvais traitements infligés aux enfants.

Abu Simbel [ˌæbu'sɪmbl] n Abou Simbel.

abusive [əb'juːsɪv] adj a (*offensive*) *speech, words* injurieux, offensant, grossier. **to use ~ language to sb** injurier qn; **he was very ~** il s'est montré très grossier, ce qu'il a dit était très offensant. b (*wrongly used*) abusif, mauvais.

abut [ə'bʌt] vi: **to ~ on** confiner à, être contigu (*f* -guë) à.

abutment [ə'bʌtmənt] n (*Archit*) contrefort *m*, piédroit *m*; (*esp on bridge*) butée *f*.

abuzz [ə'bʌz] adj: **the office was ~ with the news** la nouvelle courait dans tout le bureau.

abysmal [ə'bɪzməl] adj *taste, quality* épouvantable, catastrophique*. **~ ignorance** ignorance crasse *or* sans bornes; **his work was quite ~** son travail était tout à fait exécrable.

abysmally [ə'bɪzməlɪ] adv abominablement, atrocement. **~ ignorant** d'une ignorance crasse *or* sans bornes; **his work is ~ bad** son travail est atrocement *or* abominablement mauvais.

abyss [ə'bɪs] n (*lit, fig*) abîme *m*, gouffre *m*; (*in sea*) abysse *m*.

Abyssinia [ˌæbɪ'sɪnɪə] n Abyssinie *f*.

Abyssinian [ˌæbɪ'sɪnɪən] 1 adj abyssinien, abyssin (*rare*). 2 n Abyssinien(ne) *m(f)*, Abyssin(e) *m(f)* (*rare*). **the ~ Empire** l'empire *m* d'Éthiopie.

AC [ˌeɪ'siː] n abbr of **alternating current.**

a/c n (abbr of **account**) C, compte.

acacia [ə'keɪʃə] n acacia *m*.

Acad. abbr of **academy** *and* **academic.**

academic [ˌækə'demɪk] 1 adj a (*of studying, colleges*) universitaire, scolaire, *failure, progress* scolaire. **~ dress** toge *f* et mortier *m* (noirs); **~ gown** toge *f* de professeur *or* d'étudiant; **~ freedom** liberté *f* de l'enseignement; **~ year** année *f* universitaire; **~ standards** niveaux *mpl* scolaires; (*US*) **~ dean** ≃ président(e) *m(f)* de faculté; (*US*) **~ advisor** directeur *m*, -trice *f* des études; (*US*) **~ officers** personnel enseignant et cadres administratifs; (*US*) **~ rank** grade *m*.

b (*theoretical*) théorique, spéculatif. **~ debate** discussion sans portée pratique *or* toute théorique.

c (*scholarly*) *style, approach* intellectuel.

d (*of no practical use*) **that's all quite ~, it's an ~ question** ça n'a aucun intérêt pratique; **out of purely ~ interest** par simple curiosité.

e *art, portrait* académique.

2 n (*university teacher*) universitaire *mf*.

academically [ˌækə'demɪkəlɪ] adv *gifted, competent* sur le plan scolaire; *sound* intellectuellement. **~ qualified** possédant des diplômes universitaires.

academicals [ˌækə'demɪkəlz] npl toge *f*, (épitoge *f*) et bonnet *m* universitaires.

academician [əˌkædə'mɪʃən] n académicien(ne) *m(f)*.

academy [ə'kædəmɪ] n a (*private college*) école privée, collège *m*, pensionnat *m*. **military/naval ~** école militaire/navale; (*Brit*) **~ of music** conservatoire *m*; *see* **police.** b (*society*) académie *f*, société *f*. **the (Royal) A~** l'Académie Royale (*de Londres*); **A~ Award** Oscar *m*; *see* **French.**

acanthus [ə'kænθəs] n, pl **~es** *or* **acanthi** [ə'kænθaɪ] acanthe *f*.

ACAS, Acas ['eɪkæs] n abbr of **Advisory, Conciliation and Arbitration Service.**

accede [æk'siːd] vi a **to ~ to** *request* agréer, donner suite à; *suggestion* agréer, accepter. b (*gain position*) entrer en possession (*to an office* d'une charge). **to ~ to the throne** monter sur le trône. c (*join*) adhérer, se joindre (*to a party* à un parti).

accelerate [æk'seləreɪt] 1 vt *movement* accélérer; *work* activer; *events* précipiter, hâter. (*Econ*) **~d** *depreciation, increments etc* accéléré; (*US Univ*) **~d program** cursus intensif. 2 vi (*esp Aut*) accélérer.

acceleration [ækˌselə'reɪʃən] n accélération *f*. (*Fin*) **~ clause** clause *f* d'accélération; (*Fin*) **repayment by ~** remboursement *m* par déchéance du terme.

accelerator [æk'seləreɪtəʳ] n (*Brit Aut*) accélérateur *m*. **to step on the ~** appuyer sur l'accélérateur *or* le champignon*.

accelerometer [ækˌselə'rɒmɪtəʳ] n accéléromètre *m*.

accent ['æksənt] 1 n a (*stress on part of word*) accent *m* (tonique). b (*intonation, pronunciation*) accent *m*. **to speak French without an ~** parler français sans accent. c (*written mark*) accent *m*; *see* **acute** *etc* d (*liter: way of speaking*) **~s** accents *mpl*, paroles *fpl*; **in ~s of rage** avec des accents de rage (dans la voix). 2 [æk'sent] vt a (*emphasize*) *word* accentuer, mettre l'accent sur; *syllable* accentuer. b (*fig: make prominent*) accentuer, mettre en valeur.

accentuate [æk'sentjʊeɪt] vt (*emphasize*) accentuer, faire ressortir, souligner; (*draw attention to*) attirer l'attention sur.

accentuation [ækˌsentjʊ'eɪʃən] n accentuation *f*.

accept [ək'sept] vt a *gift, invitation, apology* accepter; *goods* prendre livraison de; *excuse, fact, report, findings* admettre, accepter; *one's duty* se soumettre à; *one's fate* accepter, se résigner à; *task* se charger de, accepter; (*Comm*) *bill* accepter. **I ~ that ...** je conviens que ... . b (*allow*) *action, behaviour* admettre, accepter.

acceptability [əkˌseptə'bɪlɪtɪ] n (*Ling*) acceptabilité *f*.

acceptable [ək'septəbl] adj a (*worth accepting*) *offer, suggestion* acceptable (*also Ling*). **I hope you will find this ~** j'espère que cela vous conviendra; (*frm*) **if this offer is ~ to you** si la présente offre est à votre convenance. b (*welcome*) bienvenu, opportun; *gift* qui fait plaisir. **the money was most ~** l'argent était vraiment le bienvenu.

acceptance [ək'septəns] n a *[invitation, gift]* acceptation *f*; *[proposal]* consentement *m* (*of* à); (*Comm*) *[bill]* acceptation; (*Comm, Jur: of delivered goods*) réception *f*. **~ house** banque *f* d'acceptation. b (*approval*) réception *f* favorable, approbation *f*. **the idea met with general ~** l'idée a reçu l'approbation générale.

acceptation [ˌæksep'teɪʃən] n a (*meaning*) acception *f*, signification *f*. b (*approval*) approbation *f*.

accepted [ək'septɪd] adj accepté; *fact* reconnu; *idea* répandu; *behaviour, pronunciation* admis. **in the ~ sense of the word** dans le sens usuel *or* courant du mot.

acceptor [ək'septəʳ] n (*Comm*) accepteur *m*.

access ['ækses] 1 n a (*NonC: way of approach*) accès *m*, abord *m*; (*Jur*) (*through lane etc*) droit *m* de passage; (*into property*) droit *m* d'accès. **easy of ~** d'accès facile, facilement accessible; **~ to his room is by a staircase** on accède à sa chambre par un escalier; *[road]* **to give ~ to** donner accès à.

b (*way of entry*) **there is another ~ to this room** cette pièce a une autre ouverture.

c (*NonC: permission to see, use*) accès *m*; (*Jur: in divorce*) droit *m* de visite. **to have ~ to sb** avoir accès auprès de qn, avoir ses entrées chez qn; **to have (right of) ~ to papers** avoir accès à des documents.

d (*Comput*) **~ port/time** port *m*/temps *m* d'accès; *see* **random.**

e (*sudden outburst*) *[anger, remorse]* accès *m*; *[generosity]* élan *m*; *[illness]* accès, attaque *f*, crise *f*.

2 comp ▸**access road** route *f* d'accès; *[motorway]* bretelle *f* d'accès *or* de raccordement; (*to motorway*) **there is an access road for Melun** Melun est raccordé (à l'autoroute).

3 vt (*Comput*) *file etc* accéder à.

accessary [æk'sesərɪ] (*Jur*) 1 n complice *mf*. **~ before the fact/after the fact** complice par instigation/par assistance. 2 adj complice (*to* de).

accessibility [ækˌsesɪ'bɪlɪtɪ] n accessibilité *f*.

accessible [æk'sesəbl] adj a *place* accessible, d'accès facile; *knowledge* à la portée de tous, accessible; *person* accessible, approchable, d'un abord facile. b (*able to be influenced*) ouvert, accessible (*to* à).

accession [æk'seʃən] 1 n a (*gaining of position*) accession *f* (*to* à); (*to fortune, property*) accession (*to* à), entrée *f* en possession (*to* de). **~ (to the throne)** avènement *m*. b (*addition, increase*) accroissement *m*, augmentation *f*. **the ~ of new members to the party** l'adhésion *f* de membres nouveaux au parti. c (*consent*) accord *m*, assentiment *m*; (*Jur, Pol: to a treaty etc*) adhésion *f*. d (*in library, museum*) nouvelle acquisition. 2 vt *library book etc* mettre au catalogue.

accessory [æk'sesərɪ] 1 adj a (*additional*) accessoire, auxiliaire. b (*Jur*) = **accessary 2.** 2 n a (*gen pl: Dress, Theat etc*) accessoire(s) *m(pl)*; (*Comm, Tech*) accessoire. **car accessories** accessoires d'automobile; **toilet accessories** objets *mpl* de toilette. b (*Jur*) = **accessary 1.**

accidence ['æksɪdəns] n (*Ling*) morphologie flexionnelle; (*Philos*) accident *m*.

accident ['æksɪdənt] 1 n a (*mishap, disaster*) accident *m*, malheur *m*. **to meet with** *or* **have an ~** avoir un accident; **road ~** accident de la route *or* de la circulation; **~s in the home** accidents domestiques.

b (*unforeseen event*) événement fortuit, accident *m*; (*chance*) hasard *m*, chance *f*. **by ~** *injure, break* accidentellement; *meet, find* par hasard.

c (*Philos*) accident *m*.

2 comp ▸**(road) accident figures/statistics** chiffres *mpl*/statistiques *fpl* des accidents de la route ▸**accident insurance** assurance *f* (contre les) accidents ▸**accident prevention** (*Aut*) prévention *or* sécurité routière; (*in home, factory*) prévention *f* des accidents ▸**accident-prone: to be accident-prone** être prédisposé(e) *or* sujet(te) aux accidents, attirer les accidents ▸**accident protection**

(*Aut*) protection routière ►**Accident (and Emergency) Unit** (service *m* des) urgences *fpl*.

accidental [ˌæksɪˈdentl] 1 **adj** a (*happening by chance*) death accidentel; *meeting* fortuit. b (*of secondary importance*) *effect, benefit* secondaire, accessoire. c (*Mus, Philos*) accidentel. 2 **n** (*Mus*) accident *m*.

accidentally [ˌæksɪˈdentəlɪ] **adv** (*by chance*) par hasard; (*not deliberately*) accidentellement. **it was done quite ~** on ne l'a pas fait exprès.

acclaim [əˈkleɪm] 1 **vt** (*applaud*) acclamer. **to ~ sb king** proclamer qn roi. 2 **n** acclamations *fpl*. **it met with great public/critical ~** cela a été salué unanimement par le public/les critiques.

acclamation [ˌækləˈmeɪʃən] **n** acclamation *f*.

acclimate [əˈklaɪmət] **vt** (*US*) = **acclimatize**.

acclimatization [əˌklaɪmətaɪˈzeɪʃən] **n**, (*US*) **acclimation** [ˌæklaɪˈmeɪʃən] **n** (*lit*) acclimatation *f*; (*fig: to new situation etc*) accoutumance *f* (*to* à).

acclimatize [əˈklaɪmətaɪz], (*US*) **acclimate** [əˈklaɪmət] 1 **vt** (*lit, fig*) acclimater (*to* à). 2 **vi** (*also* **become ~d**) (*lit*) s'acclimater (*to* à); (*fig*) s'accoutumer (*to* à).

acclivity [əˈklɪvɪtɪ] **n** montée *f*.

accolade [ˈækəʊleɪd] **n** accolade *f*; (*fig*) marque *f* d'approbation.

accommodate [əˈkɒmədeɪt] **vt** a (*provide lodging or housing for*) loger; (*contain*) *[car]* contenir; *[house]* contenir, recevoir. **the hotel can ~ 60 people** l'hôtel peut recevoir *or* accueillir 60 personnes. b (*supply*) équiper (*sb with sth* qn de qch), fournir (*sb with sth* qch à qn); (*satisfy*) *demand etc* accéder à. **to ~ sb with a loan** consentir un prêt à qn; **I think we can ~ you** je crois que nous pouvons satisfaire à votre demande. c (*adapt*) *plans, wishes* accommoder, adapter (*to* à). **to ~ o.s. to** s'adapter à, s'accommoder à.

accommodating [əˈkɒmədeɪtɪŋ] **adj** (*obliging*) obligeant; (*easy to deal with*) accommodant, conciliant.

accommodation [əˌkɒməˈdeɪʃən] 1 **n** a *[person]* logement *m*. (*US*) **~s** logement *m*; **"~ (to let)"** "appartements *mpl or* chambres *fpl* à louer"; **we have no ~ (available)** nous n'avons pas de place, c'est complet; **there is no ~ for children** on n'accepte pas les enfants; **"office ~ (to let)"** "bureaux (à louer)"; *see* **seating**.

b (*compromise*) compromis *m*.

c (*Anat, Psych*) accommodation *f*.

d (*Fin*) prêt *m*, crédit *m*. **to take ~** contracter un emprunt, faire un prêt.

2 **comp** ►**accommodation address** adresse *f* (*utilisée simplement pour la correspondance*) ►**accommodation bill** (*Comm*) billet *m or* effet *m* de complaisance ►**accommodation bureau** agence *f* de logement ►**accommodation ladder** (*Naut*) échelle *f* de coupée ►**accommodation officer** responsable *mf* de l'hébergement ►**accommodation road** route *f* à usage restreint ►**accommodation train** (*US Rail*) (train *m*) omnibus *m*.

accompaniment [əˈkʌmpənɪmənt] **n** accompagnement *m*, complément *m*; (*Mus*) accompagnement; (*Culin*) accompagnement, garniture *f*.

accompanist [əˈkʌmpənɪst] **n** (*Mus*) accompagnateur *m*, -trice *f*.

accompany [əˈkʌmpənɪ] **vt** a (*escort*) accompagner, suivre. **accompanied by** accompagné de *or* par. b (*fig*) accompagner. **cold accompanied by shivering** rhume accompagné de frissons. c (*Mus*) accompagner (*on* à).

accomplice [əˈkʌmplɪs] **n** complice *mf*. **to be an ~ to** *or* **in a crime** tremper dans un crime, être complice d'un crime.

accomplish [əˈkʌmplɪʃ] **vt** accomplir, exécuter; *task* accomplir, achever; *desire* réaliser; *journey* effectuer. **to ~ one's object** arriver à ses fins.

accomplished [əˈkʌmplɪʃt] **adj** *person* doué, accompli, qui possède tous les talents; *performance* accompli, parfait.

accomplishment [əˈkʌmplɪʃmənt] **n** a (*achievement*) œuvre accomplie, projet réalisé. b (*skill: gen pl*) **~s** talents *mpl*. c (*NonC: completion*) réalisation *f*, accomplissement *m*.

accord [əˈkɔːd] 1 **vt** *favour* accorder, concéder (*to* à). 2 **vi** s'accorder, concorder (*with* avec). 3 **n** a (*NonC: agreement*) consentement *m*, accord *m*. **of his own ~** de son plein gré, de lui-même, de son propre chef; **with one ~** d'un commun accord; **to be in ~ with** être d'accord avec. b (*treaty*) traité *m*, pacte *m*.

accordance [əˈkɔːdəns] **n** accord *m* (*with* avec), conformité (*with* à). **in ~ with** conformément à, suivant, en accord avec; **to be in ~ with** être conforme à, correspondre à.

according [əˈkɔːdɪŋ] **adv** a **~ to** (*gen*) selon, suivant; **classified ~ to size** classés par ordre de grandeur; **everything went ~ to plan** tout s'est passé comme prévu *or* sans anicroches; **~ to what he says** d'après ce qu'il dit, à en juger par ce qu'il dit; **~ to him they've gone** selon lui *or* d'après lui ils sont partis; **to act ~ to the law** agir conformément à la loi. b **~ as** dans la mesure où, selon que, suivant que + *indic*.

accordingly [əˈkɔːdɪŋlɪ] **adv** a (*therefore*) en conséquence, par conséquent. b (*in accordance with circumstances*) en conséquence. **and he acted ~** et il a fait le nécessaire.

accordion [əˈkɔːdɪən] **n** accordéon *m*. **~ pleat** pli *m* (en) accordéon.

accordionist [əˈkɔːdɪənɪst] **n** accordéoniste *mf*.

accost [əˈkɒst] **vt** accoster, aborder; (*Jur*) accoster.

account [əˈkaʊnt] 1 **n** a (*Comm, Fin*) compte *m*. **to open an ~** ouvrir un compte; **put it on my ~** (*in shop*) vous le mettrez à *or* sur mon compte; (*in hotel*) vous le mettrez sur mon compte *or* sur ma note; (*Bank*) **to pay a sum into one's ~** verser une somme à son compte; (*shop*) **I have an ~ with them** ils me font crédit; **in ~ with** en compte avec; **~s payable** comptes clients, comptes créditeurs; **to ~ rendered** facture non payée; **~s receivable** comptes fournisseurs, effets *mpl* à recevoir; **on ~** à compte; **payment on ~** acompte *m*, à-valoir *m*, paiement *m* à compte; **to pay £50 on ~** verser un acompte de 50 livres; (*in shop*) **cash or ~?** vous payez comptant ou je le mets sur votre compte?; (*Advertising*) **they have the Michelin ~** ce sont eux qui détiennent le budget *or* la publicité (de) Michelin; *see* **bank**[2], **current**, **settle**[2] *etc*

b **~s** (*calculation*) comptabilité *f*, comptes *mpl*; (*department*) (service *m*) comptabilité *f*; **to do/keep the ~s** faire/tenir la comptabilité *or* les comptes.

c (*NonC: benefit*) profit *m*, avantage *m*. **to turn** *or* **put sth to (good) ~** mettre qch à profit, tirer parti de qch.

d (*explanation*) compte rendu, explication *f*. **to call sb to ~ for having done** demander des comptes à qn pour avoir fait; **to be held to ~ for sth** devoir rendre des comptes pour qch; **he gave a good ~ of himself** il s'en est bien tiré, il a fait bonne impression; (*fig*) **to settle** *or* **square ~s with sb** régler son compte à qn.

e (*report*) compte rendu, exposé *m*, récit *m*. **by all ~s** d'après l'opinion générale, au dire de tous; **to give an ~ of** faire le compte rendu de *or* un exposé sur; **by her own ~** d'après ce qu'elle dit, d'après ses dires.

f (*NonC: importance, consideration*) importance *f*, valeur *f*. **man of no ~** homme sans importance; **your statement is of no ~ to them** ils n'attachent aucune importance *or* valeur à votre déclaration; **to take ~ of sth/sb, to take sth/sb into ~** tenir compte de qch/qn; **these facts must be taken into ~** ces faits doivent entrer en ligne de compte; **to leave sth out of ~, to take no ~ of sth** ne pas tenir compte de qch; **to take little ~ of** faire peu de cas de; **that is of little ~ to them** ils ne s'en soucient guère, cela leur importe peu.

g **on ~ of** à cause de; **on no ~, not on any ~** en aucun cas, sous aucun prétexte; **on her ~** à cause d'elle; **on this** *or* **that ~** pour cette raison.

2 **comp** ►**account book** livre *m* de comptes ►**account day** (*Comm, Fin*) terme *m*, jour *m* de liquidation ►**account executive** (*Advertising*) responsable *mf* de budget ►**accounts department** (service *m* de) comptabilité *f*.

3 **vt** estimer, juger. **to ~ o.s. lucky** s'estimer heureux; **to ~ sb (to be) innocent** considérer qn comme innocent.

►**account for** **vt fus** a (*explain, justify*) *expenses* rendre compte de, justifier de; *one's conduct* justifier; *circumstances* expliquer. **there's no accounting for tastes** des goûts et des couleurs on ne dispute pas (*Prov*), chacun son goût; **everyone is accounted for** on n'a oublié personne; (*after accident etc*) **3 people have not yet been accounted for** 3 personnes n'ont pas encore été retrouvées.

b (*represent*) représenter. **this ~s for 10% of the total** ceci représente 10% du chiffre total; **the Greens account for 10% of the vote** les Verts totalisent *or* représentent 10% des voix; **this area ~s for most of the country's mineral wealth** cette région produit *or* possède la plus grande partie des ressources minières du pays; **the rise in the birthrate ~s for the increase in population** la hausse du taux de la natalité est responsable de la croissance de la population.

c (*kill, destroy*) (*shooting etc*) tuer; (*Fishing: catch*) attraper. **he ~ed for 4 enemy planes** il a abattu 4 avions ennemis.

accountability [əˌkaʊntəˈbɪlɪtɪ] **n** responsabilité *f*; (*financial*) responsabilité financière.

accountable [əˈkaʊntəbl] **adj** responsable (*for* de). **to be ~ to sb for sth** être responsable de qch *or* répondre de qch devant qn; **he is not ~ for his actions** (*need not account for*) il n'a pas à répondre de ses actes; (*is not responsible for*) il n'est pas responsable de ses actes.

accountancy [əˈkaʊntənsɪ] **n** (*subject*) comptabilité *f*; (*profession*) profession *f* de comptable. **to study ~** faire des études de comptable *or* de comptabilité.

accountant [əˈkaʊntənt] **n** comptable *mf*. **~'s office** agence *f* comptable.

accounting [əˈkaʊntɪŋ] **n** comptabilité *f*. **~ practices/policy** pratique *f*/ politique *f* comptable; **~ period**, **~ year** exercice *m* comptable.

accoutred [əˈkuːtəd] **adj** (*esp Mil*) équipé (*with* de).

accoutrements [əˈkuːtrəmənts], (*US*) **accouterments** [əˈkuːtərmənts] **npl** (*Mil*) équipement *m*; (*gen*) attirail *m*.

accredit [əˈkredɪt] **vt** a (*credit*) *rumour* accréditer. **to ~ sth to sb** attribuer qch à qn; **to be ~ed with having done** être censé avoir fait. b *representative, ambassador* accréditer (*to* auprès de). c (*Univ, Scol*) **~ed institution** *école/université etc dont les diplômes sont reconnus par l'État*.

accreditation [əˌkredɪˈteɪʃn] **n** (*US Scol, Univ*) habilitation *f*. (*US Scol*) **~ officer** inspecteur *m* d'académie.

accredited [əˈkredɪtɪd] **adj** *person* accrédité, autorisé; *opinion, belief*

admis, accepté; *agent* accrédité. ~ **representative** représentant accrédité (*to* auprès de).
accretion [əˈkriːʃən] n a (*increase, growth*) accroissement *m* (organique). b (*result of growth: Geol etc*) concrétion *f*, addition *f*; *[wealth etc]* accroissement *m*, accumulation *f*.
accruals [əˈkruːəlz] (*Fin*) compte *m* de régularisation (du passif).
accrue [əˈkruː] vi a *[money, advantages]* revenir (*to* à). b (*Fin*) *[interest]* courir, s'accroître, s'accumuler. ~**d interest** intérêt couru; ~**d income** recettes échues; (*Fin*) ~**d expenses/charges** frais *mpl*/charges *fpl* à payer; (*Jur*) ~**d alimony** pension *f* alimentaire due.
accumulate [əˈkjuːmjʊleɪt] 1 vt accumuler. 2 vi s'accumuler. **to allow interest to** ~ laisser courir les intérêts.
accumulation [əˌkjuːmjʊˈleɪʃən] n a (*NonC*) accumulation *f*; (*Fin*) *[capital]* accroissement *m*; *[interest]* accumulation. b (*objects accumulated*) amas *m*, tas *m*, monceau *m*.
accumulative [əˈkjuːmjʊlətɪv] adj qui s'accumule; (*Fin*) cumulatif.
accumulator [əˈkjuːmjʊleɪtəʳ] n (*Elec*) accumulateur *m*, accus* *mpl*.
accuracy [ˈækjʊrəsɪ] n *[figures, clock]* exactitude *f*; *[aim, shot, story, report]* précision *f*; *[translation]* exactitude, fidélité *f*; *[judgment, assessment]* justesse *f*.
accurate [ˈækjʊrɪt] adj (*see* **accuracy**) exact; précis; juste; *memory, translation* fidèle. **to take** ~ **aim** viser juste, bien viser.
accurately [ˈækjʊrɪtlɪ] adv (*see* **accuracy**) avec précision; fidèlement; exactement.
accursed, accurst [əˈkɜːst] adj (*liter*) (*damned*) maudit; (*hateful*) détestable, exécrable.
accusal [əˈkjuːzl] n accusation *f*.
accusation [ˌækjʊˈzeɪʃən] n accusation *f*; (*Jur*) accusation, plainte *f*. (*Jur*) **to bring an** ~ **against sb** porter plainte *or* déposer (une) plainte contre qn.
accusative [əˈkjuːzətɪv] 1 n accusatif *m*. **in the** ~ à l'accusatif. 2 adj accusatif.
accuse [əˈkjuːz] vt accuser (*sb of sth* qn de qch, *sb of doing* qn de faire). (*Jur*) **they stand** ~**d of murder** ils sont accusés de meurtre.
accused [əˈkjuːzd] n, pl ~ (*Jur*) accusé(e) *m(f)*, inculpé(e) *m(f)*.
accuser [əˈkjuːzəʳ] n accusateur *m*, -trice *f*.
accusing [əˈkjuːzɪŋ] adj accusateur (*f* -trice).
accusingly [əˈkjuːzɪŋlɪ] adv d'une manière accusatrice.
accustom [əˈkʌstəm] vt habituer, accoutumer (*sb to sth* qn à qch, *sb to doing* qn à faire). **to** ~ **o.s. to** s'habituer à, s'accoutumer à.
accustomed [əˈkʌstəmd] adj a (*used*) habitué, accoutumé (*to* à, *to do, to doing* à faire). **to become** *or* **get** ~ **to sth/to doing** s'habituer *or* s'accoutumer à qch/à faire; **I am not** ~ **to such treatment** je n'ai pas l'habitude qu'on me traite (*subj*) de cette façon. b (*usual*) habituel, coutumier, familier.
AC/DC [ˈeɪsiːˈdiːsiː] 1 n abbr of **alternating current/direct current.** 2 adj: **he's** ~‡ il marche à la voile et à la vapeur‡.
ace [eɪs] 1 n a (*Cards, Dice, Dominoes*) as *m*; (*Tennis: shot*) ace *m*. ~ **of diamonds** as de carreau; (*fig*) **to have** *or* **keep an** ~ **up one's sleeve,** (*US*) **to have an** ~ **in the hole*** avoir une carte maîtresse *or* un atout en réserve; (*fig*) **to play one's** ~ jouer sa meilleure carte; (*fig*) **to hold all the** ~**s** avoir tous les atouts en main; (*fig*) **within an** ~ **of sth** à deux doigts de qch; (*US*) **A**~ ® **bandage** bande *f* Velpeau ®; *see* **clean.** b (*pilot, racing driver etc*) as *m*. (*US fig*) **he's** ~**s*** il est super*. 2 adj super*. **an** ~ **driver** un as du volant.
acerbity [əˈsɜːbɪtɪ] n âpreté *f*, aigreur *f*.
acetate [ˈæsɪteɪt] n acétate *m*.
acetic [əˈsiːtɪk] adj acétique. ~ **acid** acide *m* acétique.
acetone [ˈæsɪtəʊn] n acétone *f*.
acetylene [əˈsetɪliːn] 1 n acétylène *m*. 2 comp ▸**acetylene burner** chalumeau *m* à acétylène ▸**acetylene lamp** lampe *f* à acétylène ▸**acetylene torch** = **acetylene burner** ▸**acetylene welding** soudure *f* acétylène.
ache [eɪk] 1 vi faire mal, être douloureux. **my head** ~**s** j'ai mal à la tête; **to be aching all over** (*after exercise*) être courbaturé; (*from illness*) avoir mal partout; **it makes my heart** ~ cela me brise *or* me fend le cœur; **her heart** ~**d for them** elle souffrait pour eux; (*fig*) **to be aching** *or* **to** ~ **to do** mourir d'envie de faire, brûler de faire. 2 n a (*physical*) douleur *f*, souffrance *f*. **all his** ~**s and pains** toutes ses douleurs, tous ses maux; **he's always complaining of** ~**s and pains** il se plaint toujours d'avoir mal partout; *see* **tooth** *etc* b (*fig*) peine *f*; *see* **heart.**
achieve [əˈtʃiːv] 1 vt (*gen*) accomplir, réaliser; *aim, standard* atteindre, arriver à; *success* obtenir; *fame* parvenir à; *victory* remporter. **what they have** ~**d** ce qu'ils ont accompli *or* réalisé; **how did you** ~ **that?** comment est-ce que vous avez réussi à faire ça?; **to** ~ **something in life** arriver à quelque chose dans la vie; **I feel I've really** ~**d something today** j'ai l'impression d'avoir fait quelque chose de valable aujourd'hui; *see* **under.** 2 vi (*be successful*) réussir.
achievement [əˈtʃiːvmənt] n a (*success, feat*) exploit *m*, réussite *f*, haut fait. b (*Scol*) **the level of** ~ le niveau des élèves; (*Brit Scol*) ~ **test** test *m* de niveau (*fait dans les écoles primaires*). c (*NonC: completion*) exécution *f*, accomplissement *m*, réalisation *f*.
achiever [əˈtʃiːvəʳ] n (*successful person*) gagneur *m*, -euse *f*. **high-/low-**~ sujet *m* doué/peu doué.
Achilles [əˈkɪliːz] n Achille *m*. (*fig*) ~**' heel** talon *m* d'Achille; (*Anat*) ~**' tendon** tendon *m* d'Achille.
aching [ˈeɪkɪŋ] adj douloureux, endolori. (*fig*) **to have an** ~ **heart** avoir le cœur gros.
achromatic [ˌeɪkrəʊˈmætɪk] adj achromatique.
acid [ˈæsɪd] 1 n a acide *m*. b (*Drugs sl*) acide‡ *m*. 2 comp ▸**acid head** (*Drugs sl*) drogué(e) *m(f)* au LSD ▸**Acid (house)** acid music *f* ▸**Acid house party** acid party *f* ▸**acid-proof** résistant aux acides ▸**acid rain** pluies *fpl* acides ▸**acid test** (*fig*) épreuve décisive; (*fig*) **to stand the acid test** être à toute épreuve. 3 adj a (*sour*) acide. (*Brit*) ~ **drops** bonbons acidulés. b (*fig: sharp*) *person* revêche; *voice* aigre; *remark* mordant, acide.
acidic [əˈsɪdɪk] adj acide.
acidify [əˈsɪdɪfaɪ] vt acidifier.
acidity [əˈsɪdɪtɪ] n (*Chem, fig*) acidité *f*.
acidly [ˈæsɪdlɪ] adv acidement, d'un ton acide.
acidulous [əˈsɪdjʊləs] adj acidulé.
ack-ack [ˈækˈæk] n défense *f* contre avions, D.C.A. *f*. ~ **fire** tir *m* de D.C.A.; ~ **guns** canons antiaériens *or* de D.C.A.
acknowledge [əkˈnɒlɪdʒ] vt a (*admit*) avouer, admettre; *error* reconnaître, avouer, confesser. **to** ~ **sb as leader** reconnaître qn pour chef; **to** ~ **o.s. beaten** s'avouer battu.
b (*confirm receipt of*) *greeting* répondre à; (*also* ~ **receipt of**) *letter, parcel* accuser réception de. **to** ~ **a gift from sb** remercier qn pour *or* d'un cadeau.
c (*express thanks for*) *person's action, services, help* manifester sa gratitude pour, se montrer reconnaissant de; *applause, cheers* saluer pour répondre à.
d (*indicate recognition of*) faire attention à. **I smiled at him but he didn't even** ~ **me** je lui ai souri mais il n'a même pas fait mine d'y répondre *or* mais il a fait comme s'il ne me voyait pas; **he didn't even** ~ **my presence** il a fait comme si je n'étais pas là; (*Jur*) **to** ~ **a child** reconnaître un enfant.
acknowledged [əkˈnɒlɪdʒd] adj *leader, expert etc* reconnu (de tous); *child* reconnu; *letter* dont on a accusé réception.
acknowledgement [əkˈnɒlɪdʒmənt] n a (*NonC*) reconnaissance *f*; *[one's error etc]* aveu *m*. **in** ~ **of your help** en reconnaissance *or* en remerciement de votre aide. b *[money]* reçu *m*, récépissé *m*, quittance *f*; *[letter]* accusé *m* de réception. (*in preface etc*) ~**s** remerciements *mpl*; **to quote without** ~ faire une citation sans mentionner la source.
A.C.L.U. [ˌeɪsiːelˈjuː] n (*US*) (abbr of **American Civil Liberties Union**) Ligue *f* des Droits de l'Homme.
acme [ˈækmɪ] n point culminant, faîte *m*, apogée *m*.
acne [ˈæknɪ] n acné *f*.
acolyte [ˈækəʊlaɪt] n acolyte *m*.
aconite [ˈækənaɪt] n aconit *m*.
acorn [ˈeɪkɔːn] n (*Bot*) gland *m*. ~ **cup** cupule *f*.
acoustic [əˈkuːstɪk] adj acoustique. (*Phon*) ~ **feature** trait *m* distinctif acoustique; (*Phon*) ~ **phonetics** phonétique *f* acoustique; ~ **guitar** guitare *f* acoustique; (*Audio Recording*) ~ **feedback** *or* **regeneration** effet *m* Larsen, réaction *f* acoustique; (*Comput*) ~ **hood** capot *m* insonorisant; (*in office*) ~ **screen** cloison *f* insonorisante; *see* **coupler.**
acoustics [əˈkuːstɪks] n a (*Phys: + sg vb*) acoustique *f*. b *[room etc]* (*+ pl vb*) acoustique *f*.
ACPO [ˈækpəʊ] n abbr of **Association of Chief Police Officers.**
acquaint [əˈkweɪnt] vt a (*inform*) aviser, avertir, instruire (*sb with sth* qn de qch), renseigner (*sb with sth* qn sur qch). **to** ~ **sb with the situation** mettre qn au courant *or* au fait de la situation. b **to be** ~**ed with** *person, subject* connaître; *fact* savoir, être au courant de; **to become** *or* **get** ~**ed with sb** faire la connaissance de qn; **to become** ~**ed with the facts** prendre connaissance des faits; **to get** ~**ed** faire connaissance.
acquaintance [əˈkweɪntəns] n a (*NonC*) connaissance *f*. **to make sb's** ~ faire la connaissance de qn, faire connaissance avec qn; **to improve upon** ~ gagner à être connu; **to have some** ~ **with French** avoir une certaine connaissance du français, savoir un peu le français; **a person of my** ~ une connaissance; *see* **claim.** b (*person*) relation *f*, connaissance *f*. **to have a wide circle of** ~**s** avoir des relations très étendues; **she's an** ~ **of mine** je la connais un peu, c'est une de mes relations; **old** ~**s** de vieilles connaissances.
acquaintanceship [əˈkweɪntənsʃɪp] n relations *fpl*, cercle *m* de connaissances. **a wide** ~ de nombreuses relations.
acquiesce [ˌækwɪˈes] vi acquiescer, consentir. **to** ~ **in an opinion** se ranger à une opinion *or* à un avis; **to** ~ **in a proposal** donner son accord *or* son assentiment à une proposition.
acquiescence [ˌækwɪˈesns] n consentement *m*, assentiment *m*.
acquiescent [ˌækwɪˈesnt] adj consentant.
acquire [əˈkwaɪəʳ] vt *house, car, knowledge, money, fame, experience* acquérir; *language* apprendre; *habit* prendre, contracter; *reputation* se faire. **to** ~ **a taste for** prendre goût à; (*hum*) **she has** ~**d a new husband** elle s'est dotée d'un nouveau mari.
acquired [əˈkwaɪəd] adj acquis. ~ **characteristic** caractère acquis; **it's an** ~ **taste** on finit par aimer ça, c'est un goût qui s'acquiert; ~

immune deficiency syndrome syndrome *m* immuno-déficitaire acquis.

acquirement [ə'kwaɪəmənt] n (*NonC*) acquisition *f* (*of* de).

acquisition [ˌækwɪ'zɪʃən] n acquisition *f* (*also Ling*); (*: *person*) recrue *f* (*to* pour). (*Fin*) ~ **of holdings** prise *f* de participations.

acquisitive [ə'kwɪzɪtɪv] adj (*for money*) âpre au gain, thésauriseur (*liter*); (*greedy*) avide (*of* de). ~ **instinct** instinct *m* de possession; **to have an ~ nature** avoir l'instinct de possession très développé.

acquisitiveness [ə'kwɪzɪtɪvnɪs] n instinct *m* de possession, goût *m* de la propriété.

acquit [ə'kwɪt] vt a (*Jur*) acquitter, décharger (*of* de). b **to ~ o.s. well in battle** bien se conduire *or* se comporter au combat; **it was a difficult job but he ~ted himself well** c'était une tâche difficile mais il s'en est bien tiré. c *debt* régler, s'acquitter de.

acquittal [ə'kwɪtl] n a (*Jur*) acquittement *m*. b *[duty]* accomplissement *m*. c *[debt]* acquittement *m*.

acre ['eɪkə^r] n ≃ demi-hectare *m*, arpent† *m*, acre *f*. **he owns a few ~s in Sussex** il possède quelques hectares dans le Sussex; (*fig*) **the rolling ~s of the estate** la vaste étendue du domaine; (*fig*) **~s of*** des kilomètres et des kilomètres de; *see* **god**.

acreage ['eɪkərɪdʒ] n aire *f*, superficie *f*. **what ~ have you?** combien avez-vous d'hectares?; **to farm a large ~** cultiver *or* exploiter de grandes superficies.

acrid ['ækrɪd] adj (*lit*) âcre; (*fig*) *remark, style* acerbe, mordant.

Acrilan ['ækrɪlæn] n ® Acrilan *m* ®.

acrimonious [ˌækrɪ'məʊnɪəs] adj acrimonieux, aigre.

acrimony ['ækrɪmənɪ] n acrimonie *f*, aigreur *f*.

acrobat ['ækrəbæt] n acrobate *mf*.

acrobatic [ˌækrəʊ'bætɪk] adj acrobatique.

acrobatics [ˌækrəʊ'bætɪks] npl acrobatie *f*. **to do ~** faire des acrobaties *or* de l'acrobatie.

acronym ['ækrənɪm] n acronyme *m*.

Acropolis [ə'krɒpəlɪs] n Acropole *f*.

across [ə'krɒs] (*phr vb elem*) 1 prep a (*from one side to other of*) d'un côté à l'autre de. ~ **it** d'un côté à l'autre; **bridge ~ the river** pont *m* sur le fleuve; **to walk ~ the road** traverser la route.

b (*on other side of*) de l'autre côté de. ~ **it** de l'autre côté; **he lives ~ the street (from me/him)** il habite en face (de chez moi/lui); **the shop ~ the road** le magasin d'en face, le magasin de l'autre côté de la rue; **lands ~ the sea** terres *fpl* d'outre-mer; **from ~ the Channel** de l'autre côté de la Manche, d'outre-Manche.

c (*crosswise over*) en travers de, à travers. ~ **it** en travers; **to go ~ the fields** *or* **~ country** aller *or* prendre à travers champs; **plank ~ a door** planche *f* en travers d'une porte; **with his arms folded ~ his chest** les bras croisés sur la poitrine.

2 adv (*from one side to other*) **the river is 5 km ~** le fleuve a 5 km de large; **to help sb ~** aider qn à traverser; (*fig*) **to get sth ~** faire comprendre *or* apprécier qch (*to sb* à qn), faire passer la rampe à qch; ~ **from** en face de.

acrostic [ə'krɒstɪk] n acrostiche *m*.

acrylic [ə'krɪlɪk] adj, n acrylique (*m*).

act [ækt] 1 n a (*deed*) acte *m*. **in the ~ of doing** en train de faire; **caught in the ~** pris sur le fait *or* en flagrant délit; ~ **of God** désastre naturel; ~ **of faith** acte de foi; (*Rel*) **A~s of the Apostles** Actes des Apôtres.

b (*Jur*) loi *f*. **A~ of Parliament/Congress** loi (*adoptée par le Parlement/Congrès*).

c *[play]* acte *m*; (*in circus etc*) numéro *m*. (*Theat*) **they're a brilliant ~** ils font un numéro superbe; (*fig*) **he's just putting on an ~** il joue la comédie; (*fig*) **it's just an ~** c'est du cinéma; (*fig*) **to get in on the ~*** s'imposer; (*fig*) **to get one's ~ together*** se reprendre en main.

2 vi a (*do sth*) agir. **the government must ~ now** le gouvernement doit agir immédiatement *or* prendre des mesures immédiates; **you have ~ed very generously** vous avez été très généreux; **to ~ for the best** faire pour le mieux; **to ~ on sb's behalf, ~ for sb** agir au nom de qn, représenter qn; (*Admin*) **the Board, ~ing by a majority** le conseil statuant à la majorité; (*Admin*) **~ing on a proposal from the Commission** sur proposition de la Commission.

b (*behave*) agir, se comporter, se conduire. **to ~ like a fool** agir *or* se comporter comme un imbécile.

c (*Theat*) jouer. **have you ever ~ed before?** avez-vous déjà fait du théâtre (*or* du cinéma)?; **she's not crying, she's only ~ing** elle ne pleure pas, elle fait seulement semblant *or* elle joue la comédie.

d (*serve*) servir, faire office (*as* de). **the table ~s as a desk** la table sert de bureau; **she ~s as his assistant** elle lui sert d'assistante.

e *[medicine, chemical]* (*have an effect*) agir (*on* sur).

3 vt (*Theat*) *part* jouer, tenir. **to ~ Hamlet** jouer *or* tenir le rôle d'Hamlet, incarner Hamlet; (*Theat, fig*) **to ~ the part of** tenir le rôle de; (*fig*) **to ~ the fool*** *or* **~ stupid*** faire l'idiot(e).

▸**act out** vt sep *event* faire un récit mimé de; *fantasies* vivre; *emotions* exprimer, mimer.

▸**act up** vi a (*) *[person]* se conduire mal. **the car has started acting up** la voiture s'est mise à faire des caprices. b **to act up to one's principles** mettre ses principes en pratique.

▸**act (up)on** vt fus *advice, suggestion* suivre, se conformer à; *order* exécuter. **I acted (up)on your letter at once** j'ai fait le nécessaire dès que j'ai reçu votre lettre.

acting ['æktɪŋ] 1 adj suppléant, provisoire, par intérim. ~ **headmaster** directeur suppléant; ~ **president/head of department/police superintendent** *etc* président *m*/chef *m* de section/commissaire *m* par intérim. 2 n (*Cine, Theat: performance*) jeu *m*, interprétation *f*. **his ~ is very good** il joue très bien; **I like his ~** j'aime son jeu; **he has done some ~** il a fait du théâtre (*or* du cinéma).

actinic [æk'tɪnɪk] adj actinique.

actinium [æk'tɪnɪəm] n actinium *m*.

action ['ækʃən] 1 n a (*NonC*) action *f*, effet *m*. **to put into ~** *plan* mettre à exécution; *one's principles, a suggestion* mettre en action *or* en pratique; *machine* mettre en marche; **the time has come for ~** il est temps d'agir; **they want a piece of the ~*** *or* **their share of the ~*** ils veulent être dans le coup*; **let's go where the ~ is*** allons où ça bouge vraiment* *or* où il se passe quelque chose; **to take ~** agir, prendre des mesures; **to go into ~** entrer en action, passer à l'action *or* à l'acte (*see* **1f**); **he needs prodding into ~** il faut vraiment le pousser pour qu'il agisse *or* qu'il passe à l'action; **telephone out of ~** appareil *m* en dérangement; (*lit, fig*) **to put sth out of ~** mettre qch hors d'usage *or* hors de service; **machine out of ~** machine hors d'usage *or* détraquée; **his illness put him out of ~ for 6 weeks** sa maladie l'a mis hors de combat pendant 6 semaines; **through** *or* **by volcanic** *etc* **~** sous l'action des volcans *etc*

b (*deed*) acte *m*, action *f*. **to judge sb by his ~s** juger qn sur ses actes; **to suit the ~ to the word** joindre le geste à la parole; **~s speak louder than words** les actes sont plus éloquents que les paroles.

c (*Theat*) *[play]* intrigue *f*, action *f*. (*Cine*) **~!** moteur!; **the ~ (of the play) takes place in Greece** l'action (de la pièce) se passe en Grèce; **there's not enough ~ in the play** la pièce manque d'action *or* n'avance pas.

d (*Jur*) procès *m*, action *f* en justice. **~ for damages/libel** procès *m* *or* action *f* en dommages-intérêts/en diffamation; **to bring an ~ against sb** intenter une action *or* un procès contre qn, poursuivre qn en justice, actionner qn.

e (*Tech*) mécanisme *m*, marche *f*; *[piano]* action *f*, mécanique *f*; *[clock etc]* mécanique *f*.

f (*Mil*) combat *m*, engagement *m*, action *f*. **to go into ~** *[unit, person]* aller *or* marcher au combat; *[army]* engager le combat; **killed in ~** tué à l'ennemi *or* au combat, tombé au champ d'honneur (*frm*); **he saw (some) ~ in North Africa** il a combattu *or* il a vu le feu en Afrique du Nord; *see* **enemy**.

2 comp ▸**action committee/group** comité *m*/groupe *m* d'action ▸**action-packed** *film* plein d'action; *week-end* bien rempli ▸**action painting** tachisme *m* ▸**action replay** (*Brit: TV Sport*) *répétition immédiate d'une séquence*; (*slow-motion*) ralenti *m* ▸**action stations** (*Mil*) postes *mpl* de combat; (*Mil, fig*) **action stations!** à vos postes!

3 vt (*Admin*) exécuter.

actionable ['ækʃnəbl] adj *claim* recevable; *person* passible de poursuites.

activate ['æktɪveɪt] vt (*also Chem, Tech*) activer; (*Phys*) rendre radioactif. **~d sludge** boues *fpl* activées.

active ['æktɪv] adj a *person* actif, leste, agile; *life, population* actif; *mind, imagination* vif, actif; *file, case* en cours. ~ **volcano** volcan *m* en activité; **to take an ~ part in** prendre une part active à, avoir un rôle positif dans; **to be an ~ member of** *or* **be ~ in an organization** être un membre actif d'une organisation; **to give ~ consideration to sth** soumettre qch à une étude attentive; **we're giving ~ consideration to the idea of doing** nous examinons sérieusement la possibilité *or* le projet de faire; **in ~ employment** en activité; (*Med*) **~ childbirth** accouchement sauvage *or* accroupi.

b (*Mil*) **on ~ service** en campagne; **he saw ~ service in Italy and Germany** il a fait campagne *or* il a servi en Italie et en Allemagne; **the ~ list** l'armée active; **to be on the ~ list** être en activité (de service).

c (*Gram*) **~ voice** voix active, actif *m*; **in the ~ (voice)** à l'actif.

d (*Comm*) **~ assets** capital *m* productif; **~ money** monnaie *f* *or* argent *m* en circulation; **partner** partenaire *m* actif; **Germany has an ~ trade balance** l'Allemagne a une balance commerciale excédentaire.

actively ['æktɪvlɪ] adv activement.

activism ['æktɪvɪzəm] n activisme *m*.

activist ['æktɪvɪst] n militant(e) *m(f)*, activiste *mf*.

activity [æk'tɪvɪtɪ] 1 n a (*NonC*) *[person]* activité *f*; *[town, port]* mouvement *m*. b **activities** activités *fpl*, occupations *fpl*; **business activities** activités professionnelles. 2 comp ▸**activity holiday** vacances actives, vacances à thème ▸**activity method** (*Scol*) méthode active.

actor ['æktə^r] n acteur *m*, comédien *m*.

actress ['æktrɪs] n actrice *f*, comédienne *f*.

A.C.T.T.† [ˌeɪsiːtiː'tiː] n abbr of **Association of Cinematographic, Television and Allied Technicians**.

actual ['æktjʊəl] adj (*real*) réel, véritable; (*factual*) concret, positif. **the ~ figures** les chiffres exacts; **its ~ value** sa valeur réelle; **this is the ~ house** voici la maison elle-même *or* en question; **and this is the ~ house**

they bought et vous voyez ici la maison qu'ils ont acheté; **there is no ~ contract** il n'y a pas vraiment *or* à proprement parler de contrat; **the ~ result** le résultat même *or* véritable; **to take an ~ example** prendre un exemple concret; **an ~ fact** un fait positif *or* réel; **in ~ fact** en fait; **his ~ words were ...** il a dit très exactement ...; (*Insurance*) **~ total loss** perte *f* totale absolue; (*Fin*) **~s** chiffres *mpl* réels.

actuality [ˌæktjʊ'ælɪtɪ] **n** a (*NonC*) réalité *f*. **in ~** en réalité. b **actualities** réalités *fpl*, conditions réelles *or* actuelles.

actualize ['æktjʊəlaɪz] **vt** réaliser; (*Philos*) actualiser.

actually ['æktjʊəlɪ] **adv** a (*gen*) en fait; (*truth to tell*) en fait, à vrai dire. **~ I don't know him at all** en fait *or* à vrai dire je ne le connais pas du tout; **his name is Smith, ~** en fait, il s'appelle Smith; **the person ~ in charge is ...** la personne véritablement responsable *or* la personne responsable en fait, c'est ...; **~ you were quite right** en fait *or* au fond vous aviez entièrement raison; **I don't ~ feel like going** au fond je n'ai pas envie d'y aller, je n'ai pas vraiment envie d'y aller; **I bet you've never done that! — ~ I have** je parie que tu n'as jamais fait ça! – si, en fait.
b (*truly, even: often showing surprise*) vraiment. **are you ~ going to buy it?** est-ce que tu vas vraiment l'acheter?; **if you ~ own a house ...** si vous êtes vraiment *or* bel et bien propriétaire d'une maison ...; **what did he ~ say?** qu'est-ce qu'il a dit exactement? *or* au juste?; **did it ~ happen?** est-ce que ça s'est vraiment *or* réellement passé?; **it's ~ taking place right now** ça se produit en ce moment même.

actuarial [ˌæktjʊ'ɛərɪəl] **adj** actuariel. **~ expectation** espérance *f* mathématique; **~ tables** tableaux *mpl* d'espérance de vie.

actuary ['æktjʊərɪ] **n** actuaire *mf*.

actuate ['æktjʊeɪt] **vt** *person* faire agir, inciter, pousser.

acuity [ə'kjuːɪtɪ] **n** acuité *f*.

acumen ['ækjʊmen] **n** flair *m*, perspicacité *f*. **business ~** sens aigu des affaires.

acupressure ['ækjʊpreʃəʳ] **n** shiatsu *m*.

acupuncture ['ækjʊpʌŋktʃəʳ] **n** acupuncture *f*, acuponcture *f*.

acupuncturist [ˌækjʊ'pʌŋktʃərɪst] **n** acupuncteur *m*, acuponcteur *m*.

acute [ə'kjuːt] **adj** a *person, mind* pénétrant, perspicace, avisé; *intelligence* aigu (*f* -guë). **to have an ~ sense of smell/~ hearing** avoir l'odorat fin/l'oreille fine. b (*Med*) aigu (*f* -guë); (*fig*) *remorse, anxiety* vif; *pain* aigu, vif; *situation* critique, grave. **an ~ scarcity** un manque aigu, une grave pénurie; (*Med*) **~ respiratory disease** maladie aigüe de l'appareil respiratoire. c (*Math*) **~ angle** angle aigu; **~-angled** acutangle. d (*Gram*) **~ accent** accent aigu; **e ~** e accent aigu.

acutely [ə'kjuːtlɪ] **adv** a (*intensely*) *suffer* vivement, intensément. **I am ~ aware that** je suis profondément conscient du fait que. b (*shrewdly*) *observe* avec perspicacité.

acuteness [ə'kjuːtnɪs] **n** a (*Med*) violence *f*. b *[person]* perspicacité *f*, finesse *f*, pénétration *f*; *[senses]* finesse.

A.D. [eɪ'diː] **n** a (**abbr of Anno Domini**) ap J.-C. b (*US Mil*) (**abbr of active duty**) service actif.

A/D [eɪ'diː] (**abbr of analogue-digital**) *see* **analogue**.

ad* [æd] **n** (**abbr of advertisement**) (*announcement*) annonce *f*; (*Comm*) pub* *f*; *see* **small**.

adage ['ædɪdʒ] **n** adage *m*.

Adam ['ædəm] **n** Adam *m*. **~'s apple** pomme *f* d'Adam; (*fig*) **I don't know him from ~*** je ne le connais ni d'Ève ni d'Adam.

adamant ['ædəmənt] **adj** inflexible. **to be ~ that ...** maintenir catégoriquement que ...

adamantly ['ædəməntlɪ] **adv** *say, refuse* catégoriquement; *opposed* résolument.

adapt [ə'dæpt] 1 **vt** adapter, approprier, ajuster (*sth to sth* qch à qch). **to ~ o.s.** s'adapter, s'accommoder, se faire (*to* à); **to ~ a novel for television** adapter un roman pour la télévision. 2 **vi** s'adapter. **he ~s easily** il s'adapte bien *or* à tout; **she's very willing to ~** elle est très accommodante *or* très conciliante.

adaptability [əˌdæptə'bɪlɪtɪ] **n** *[person]* faculté *f* d'adaptation. **~ of a play to television** possibilité *f* qu'il y a d'adapter une pièce pour la télévision.

adaptable [ə'dæptəbl] **adj** adaptable.

adaptation [ˌædæp'teɪʃən] **n** adaptation *f* (*of* de, *to* à).

adapted [ə'dæptɪd] **adv** adapté (*for, to* à; *from* de).

adapter, adaptor [ə'dæptəʳ] **n** a (*person*) adaptateur *m*, -trice *f*. b (*device*) adaptateur *m*; (*Brit Elec*) prise *f* multiple. (*Phot*) **~ ring** bague *f* intermédiaire.

ADC [ˌeɪdɪ'siː] **n** a **abbr of aide-de-camp.** b (**abbr of analogue-digital converter**) *see* **analogue**.

add [æd] **vt** a ajouter (*to* à). **~ some more pepper** ajoutez encore *or* rajoutez un peu de poivre; **to ~ insult to injury** (et) pour comble; **that would be ~ing insult to injury** ce serait vraiment dépasser la mesure *or* aller trop loin; **~ed to which** *or* **this ...** ajoutez à cela que ...; *see also* **added.** b (*Math*) *figures* additionner; *column of figures* totaliser. c (*say besides*) ajouter (*that* que). **there is nothing to ~** c'est tout dire, il n'y a rien à ajouter.

►**add in** **vt sep** *details* inclure, ajouter; *considerations* faire entrer en ligne de compte.

►**add on** **vt sep** rajouter; *see* **add-on**.

►**add to** **vt fus** (*amount, numbers*) augmenter; (*anxiety, danger*) accroître, ajouter à.

►**add together** **vt sep** *figures, advantages, drawbacks* additionner.

►**add up** 1 **vi** *[figures, results]* se recouper. (*Math*) **these figures don't add up (right)** *or* **won't add up** ces chiffres ne font pas le compte (exact); (*fig*) **it all adds up*** tout cela concorde, tout s'explique; (*fig*) **it doesn't add up*** cela ne rime à rien, il y a quelque chose qui cloche. 2 **vt sep** a *figures* additionner. **to add up a column of figures** totaliser une colonne de chiffres. b (*fig*) *advantages, reasons* faire la somme de.

►**add up to** **vt fus** *[figures]* s'élever à, se monter à; (* *fig: mean*) signifier, se résumer à.

added ['ædɪd] **adj** *advantage, benefit* supplémentaire. (*on packets*) **"no ~ colouring/salt"** "sans adjonction de colorants/de sel".

addendum [ə'dendəm] **n, pl addenda** [ə'dendə] addendum *m*.

adder ['ædəʳ] **n** a (*snake*) vipère *f*. b (*machine*) additionneur *m*.

addict ['ædɪkt] 1 **n** (*Med*) intoxiqué(e) *m(f)*; (*fig*) fanatique *mf*. **he's an ~ now** il ne peut plus s'en passer; **he's a yoga ~*** c'est un fanatique *or* un mordu* *or* un fana* du yoga; *see* **drug, heroin** *etc* 2 [ə'dɪkt] **vt: to ~ o.s. to** s'adonner à.

addicted [ə'dɪktɪd] **adj** adonné (*to* à). **to become ~ to** s'adonner à; **~ to drink/drugs** adonné à la boisson/aux stupéfiants; **he's ~ to drugs** c'est un drogué *or* toxicomane; **he's ~ to cigarettes** c'est un fumeur invétéré; (*fig*) **to be ~ to football*** se passionner pour le football, être un mordu* *or* un fana* du football.

addiction [ə'dɪkʃən] **n** penchant *or* goût très fort (*to* pour); (*Med*) dépendance *f* (*to* à). **this drug produces ~** cette drogue crée une dépendance; *see* **drug.**

addictive [ə'dɪktɪv] **adj** (*lit*) qui crée une dépendance; (*fig*) *crosswords, computer games* prenant. (*fig*) **these biscuits are very ~** on devient vite accro* de ces biscuits.

adding ['ædɪŋ] **n** (*NonC*) = **addition a. ~ machine** machine *f* à calculer.

Addis Ababa ['ædɪs'æbəbə] **n** Addis-Ababa, Addis-Abeba.

addition [ə'dɪʃən] **n** a (*Math etc*) addition *f*. b (*increase*) augmentation *f* (*to* de); (*to tax, income, profit*) surcroît *m* (*to* de); (*fact of adding*) adjonction *f*. **in ~** de plus, de surcroît, en sus; **in ~ to** en plus de, en sus de; **there's been an ~ to the family** la famille s'est agrandie; **he is a welcome ~ to our team** son arrivée enrichit notre équipe; **this is a welcome ~ to the series/collection** *etc* ceci enrichit la série/la collection *etc*.

additional [ə'dɪʃənl] **adj** additionnel; (*extra*) supplémentaire, de plus. (*Fin*) **~ benefits** avantages *mpl* accessoires; (*Fin*) **~ charge** supplément *m* de prix; (*Jur*) **~ agreement** accord *m* complémentaire.

additionally [ə'dɪʃənəlɪ] **adv** de plus, en outre, en sus.

additive ['ædɪtɪv] **adj, n** additif (*m*). **~-free** sans additifs.

addled ['ædld] **adj** (*fig*) *brain* fumeux, brouillon; (*lit*) *egg* pourri.

addle-headed ['ædl'hedɪd] **adj** écervelé, brouillon.

add-on ['ædɒn] 1 **n** a (*Comput*) accessoire *m*. b (*Telec*) conférence *f* à trois. 2 **adj** a (*Comput*) *component, equipment, memory* complémentaire. b (*Aviat*) **~ fare** tarif *m* complémentaire.

address [ə'dres] 1 **n** a *[person]* (*on letter etc*) adresse *f*. **~ book** carnet *m* d'adresses; **to change one's ~** changer d'adresse *or* de domicile; **he has left this ~** il n'est plus à cette adresse; *see* **name.**
b (*Comput, Ling*) adresse *f*.
c (*talk*) discours *m*, allocution *f*; *see* **public.**
d (*way of speaking*) conversation *f*; (*way of behaving*) abord *m*.
e **form** *or* **manner of ~** titre *m* (*à employer en s'adressant à qn*).
f (†, *liter*) **~es** cour *f*, galanterie *f*; **to pay one's ~es to a lady** faire la cour à une dame.
2 **vt** a (*put address on*) *envelope, parcel* adresser (*to sb* à qn), mettre *or* écrire l'adresse sur; (*direct*) *speech, writing, complaints* adresser (*to* à). **this is ~ed to you** *[letter etc]* ceci vous est adressé; *[words, comments]* ceci s'adresse à vous; **to ~ o.s. to a task** s'attaquer *or* se mettre à une tâche; **to ~ (o.s. to) an issue** aborder un problème.
b (*speak to*) s'adresser à; *crowd* haranguer; (*write to*) adresser un écrit à. **he ~ed the meeting** il a pris la parole devant l'assistance; **don't ~ me as "Colonel"** ne m'appelez pas "Colonel"; *see* **chair.**

addressee [ˌædre'siː] **n** destinataire *mf*; (*Ling*) allocutaire *mf*.

addresser, addressor [ə'dresəʳ] **n** expéditeur *m*, -trice *f*.

addressing [ə'dresɪŋ] **n** (*Comput*) adressage *m*.

adduce [ə'djuːs] **vt** *proof, reason* apporter, fournir; *authority* invoquer, citer.

adductor [ə'dʌktəʳ] **n** (*Anat*) adducteur *m*.

Adelaide ['ædəleɪd] **n** Adelaïde.

Aden ['eɪdn] **n** Aden. **Gulf of ~** golfe *m* Saint Vincent.

adenoidal ['ædɪnɔɪdl] **adj** adénoïde. **in an ~ voice** en parlant du nez.

adenoids ['ædɪnɔɪdz] **npl** végétations *fpl* (adénoïdes).

adept ['ædept] 1 **n** expert *m* (*in, at* en). 2 [ə'dept] **adj** expert (*in, at* à, en, dans, *at doing* à faire), compétent (*in* en). **he's ~ with numbers** il manie bien les chiffres.

adequacy ['ædɪkwəsɪ] **n** *[reward, punishment, amount]* fait *m* d'être suffisant; *[description]* à-propos *m*; *[person]* compétence *f*, capacité *f*; (*Ling*) adéquation *f*.

adequate ['ædɪkwɪt] **adj** *amount, supply* suffisant, adéquat (*for sth* pour

qch, *to do* pour faire); *tool etc* adapté, qui convient (*to* à); *essay, performance* satisfaisant, acceptable; (*Ling*) adéquat. **to feel ~ to the task** se sentir à la hauteur de la tâche.
adequately ['ædɪkwɪtlɪ] adv *prepared, equipped* suffisamment, convenablement. **he behaved ~** il s'est conduit convenablement.
adhere [əd'hɪəʳ] vi **a** (*stick*) adhérer, coller (*to* à). **b** (*be faithful to*) **to ~ to** *party* adhérer à, donner son adhésion à; *rule* obéir à; *resolve* persister dans, maintenir; **the plan must be ~d to** il faut se conformer au plan.
adherence [əd'hɪərəns] n adhésion *f* (*to* à).
adherent [əd'hɪərənt] n (*gen*) adhérent(e) *m(f)*, partisan *m*; *[religion, doctrine]* adepte *mf*.
adhesion [əd'hi:ʒən] n (*lit, Med, Tech*) adhérence *f*; (*fig: support*) adhésion *f*.
adhesive [əd'hi:zɪv] **1** adj *paper etc* adhésif, collant; *envelope* gommé. **~ plaster** pansement adhésif; **~ tape** (*Med*) sparadrap *m*; (*stationery*) ruban adhésif, Scotch *m* ®. **2** n adhésif *m*.
ad hoc [,æd'hɒk] **1** adj *decision, solution* ad hoc, adapté aux circonstances, improvisé. **~ committee** commission *f* temporaire; **on an ~ basis** de façon ad hoc. **2** adv de façon ad hoc.
adieu [ə'dju:] n, excl adieu *m*. (†, *frm*) **to bid sb ~** faire ses adieux à qn.
ad infinitum [,ædɪnfɪ'naɪtəm] adv à l'infini.
ad interim ['æd'ɪntərɪm] **1** adv par intérim. **2** adj (*Jur*) *judgment* provisoire.
adipose ['ædɪpəʊs] adj adipeux.
adiposity [,ædɪ'pɒsɪtɪ] n adiposité *f*.
adjacent [ə'dʒeɪsənt] adj (*Math*) *angle* adjacent; *street* adjacent (*to* à); *room, house* voisin (*to* de), contigu (*f* -guë) (*to* à); *building* qui jouxte, jouxtant; *territory* limitrophe.
adjectival [,ædʒek'taɪvəl] adj adjectif, adjectival.
adjectivally [,ædʒek'taɪvəlɪ] adv *use* adjectivalement.
adjective ['ædʒektɪv] n adjectif *m*.
adjoin [ə'dʒɔɪn] **1** vt être contigu (*f* -guë) à, toucher à. **2** vi se toucher, être contigu.
adjoining [ə'dʒɔɪnɪŋ] adj voisin, attenant. **the room ~ the kitchen** la pièce à côté de *or* attenant à la cuisine; **in the ~ room** dans la pièce voisine *or* à côté.
adjourn [ə'dʒɜ:n] **1** vt ajourner, renvoyer, remettre, reporter (*to, for, until* à). **to ~ sth until the next day** ajourner *or* renvoyer *or* remettre *or* reporter qch au lendemain; **to ~ sth for a week** remettre *or* renvoyer qch à huitaine; **to ~ a meeting** (*break off*) suspendre la séance; (*close*) lever la séance.
2 vi **a** (*break off*) suspendre la séance; (*close*) lever la séance. **the meeting ~ed** on a suspendu *or* levé la séance; **Parliament ~ed** (*concluded debate*) la séance de la Chambre a été levée; (*interrupted debate*) la Chambre a suspendu *or* interrompu la séance; (*recess*) la Chambre s'est ajournée jusqu'à la rentrée.
b (*move*) se retirer (*to* dans, à), passer (*to* à). **to ~ to the drawing room** passer au salon.
adjournment [ə'dʒɜ:nmənt] n *[meeting]* suspension *f*, ajournement *m*; (*Jur*) *[case]* remise *f*, renvoi *m*. (*Parl*) **to move the ~** demander la clôture; (*Parl*) **~ debate** ≃ débat *m* de clôture.
adjudge [ə'dʒʌdʒ] vt **a** (*pronounce, declare*) déclarer. **he was ~d the winner** il a été déclaré gagnant. **b** (*Jur*) (*pronounce*) prononcer, déclarer; (*decree*) décider; (*award*) *costs, damages* adjuger, accorder (*to sb* à qn). **to ~ sb bankrupt** déclarer qn en faillite; **the court ~d that ...** le tribunal a décidé que ...; **the court shall ~ costs** le tribunal statue sur les frais.
adjudicate [ə'dʒu:dɪkeɪt] **1** vt *competition* juger; *claim* décider. **2** vi (*frm*) se prononcer (*upon* sur).
adjudication [ə,dʒu:dɪ'keɪʃən] n **a** jugement *m*, arrêt *m*, décision *f* (*du juge etc*). **b** (*Jur*) **~ of bankruptcy** déclaration *f* de faillite.
adjudicator [ə'dʒu:dɪkeɪtəʳ] n juge *m* (*d'une compétition etc*).
adjunct ['ædʒʌŋkt] **1** n **a** (*thing*) accessoire *m*; (*person*) adjoint(e) *m(f)*, auxiliaire *mf*. **b** (*Gram*) adjuvant *m*. **2** adj **a** (*added, connected*) accessoire, complémentaire. **b** (*subordinate*) *person* subordonné, auxiliaire, subalterne.
adjure [ə'dʒʊəʳ] vt adjurer, supplier (*sb to do* qn de faire).
adjust [ə'dʒʌst] **1** vt **a** *height, speed, flow, tool* ajuster, régler; *knob, lever, length of clothes* ajuster; *machine, engine, brakes* régler, mettre au point; *formula, plan, production, terms* ajuster, adapter (*to* à), mettre au point; (*Admin*) *salaries, wages, prices* rajuster; (*correct*) *figures etc* rectifier; *differences* régler; *hat, tie, clothes* rajuster. **you can ~ the record player to 3 different speeds** on peut régler *or* mettre l'électrophone sur 3 vitesses différentes; (*TV*) **do not ~ your set** ne changez pas le réglage de votre appareil; **to ~ sth to meet requirements** adapter qch pour satisfaire aux conditions requises; **the terms have been ~ed in your favour** on a ajusté les conditions en votre faveur; **we have ~ed all salaries upwards/downwards** nous avons relevé/abaissé tous les salaires; **figures ~ed for seasonal variation(s)** en données corrigées des variations saisonnières; **to ~ o.s. to a new situation** s'adapter à une situation nouvelle; **to ~ o.s. to new demands** faire face à de nouvelles exigences.
b (*Insurance*) **to ~ a claim** régler une demande d'indemnité.
2 vi **a** *[person]* (*to new country, circumstances*) s'adapter (*to* à); (*to new requirements, demands*) faire face (*to* à).
b *[device, machine]* se régler, s'ajuster. **the seat ~s to various heights** on peut régler *or* ajuster le siège à différentes hauteurs.
adjustability [ə,dʒʌstə'bɪlɪtɪ] n (*NonC: see* **adjustable**) possibilité *f* de réglage *or* d'ajustement; adaptabilité *f*.
adjustable [ə'dʒʌstəbl] adj **a** *height, angle, tool etc* ajustable, réglable; *shape* ajustable, adaptable; *rate of production, repayment rate, dates, hours* flexible. **~ spanner** clef *f* à ouverture variable, clé universelle; (*Scol, Univ*) **~ timetable** horaire aménagé. **b** *person, animal* adaptable, qui sait s'adapter.
adjusted [ə'dʒʌstɪd] adj (*Psych*) **badly/well/normally ~** mal/bien/normalement adapté.
adjustment [ə'dʒʌstmənt] n (*to height, speed etc*) ajustage *m* (*to* à), réglage *m*; (*to knob, lever, clothes*) ajustage; (*to machine, engine*) réglage, mise *f* au point; (*to plan, terms etc*) ajustement *m* (*to* à), mise au point; (*to wages, prices etc*) rajustement *m* (*to* à). **the text needs a lot of ~** ce texte a vraiment besoin d'une mise au point; **to make ~s** (*psychologically, socially*) s'adapter (*to* à); **"exchange flat for house — cash ~"** "échangerais appartement contre maison: règlement de la différence comptant".
adjutant ['ædʒətənt] n **a** (*Mil*) adjudant-major *m*. **b** (*also* **~ bird**) marabout *m*.
Adlerian [æd'lɪərɪən] adj de Adler.
ad lib [æd'lɪb] **1** adv *continue* à volonté; (*Mus*) ad libitum. **2** n **ad-lib** (*Theat*) improvisation(s) *f(pl)*, paroles improvisées; (*witticism*) mot *m* d'esprit impromptu. **3** adj *speech, performance* improvisé, spontané, impromptu. **4** vi (*Theat etc*) improviser. **5** vt (**: gen, also Theat*) *speech, joke* improviser.
Adm. **a** (abbr of **Admiral**) Am. **b** abbr of **Admiralty**.
adman* ['ædmæn] n publicitaire *m*, spécialiste *m* de la publicité.
admass ['ædmæs] **1** n masse(s) *f(pl)*. **2** comp *culture, life* de masse, de grande consommation.
admin* ['ædmɪn] n (*Brit*) abbr of **administration a**.
administer [əd'mɪnɪstəʳ] **1** vt **a** (*manage*) *business, company* gérer, administrer; *sb's affairs, funds* gérer; *property* régir; *public affairs, a department, a country* administrer. **b** (*dispense etc*) *alms* distribuer (*to* à); *justice* rendre, dispenser; *punishment, sacraments, medicine, drug, relief* administrer (*to* à). **to ~ the law** appliquer la loi; **to ~ an oath to sb** faire prêter serment à qn; **the oath has been ~ed to the witness** le témoin a prêté serment; (*US*) **~ed price** prix imposé (par le fabricant). **2** vi: **to ~ to sb's needs** subvenir *or* pourvoir aux besoins de qn.
administrate [əd'mɪnɪ,streɪt] vt gérer, administrer.
administration [əd,mɪnɪ'streɪʃən] n **a** (*NonC: management*) *[business, company etc]* administration *f*, gestion *f*, direction *f*; *[funds]* gestion; *[public affairs, department, country]* administration; (*paperwork*) administration; (*Jur*) *[estate, inheritance]* curatelle *f*. (*Jur*) **~ order** *ordonnance instituant l'administrateur judiciaire d'une succession ab intestat*; **his new job contains a lot of ~** son nouveau poste est en grande partie administratif. **b** (*Pol*) (*government*) gouvernement *m*; (*ministry*) ministère *m*. **under previous ~s** sous des gouvernements précédents. **c** (*NonC*) *[justice, remedy, sacrament]* administration *f*; *[oath]* prestation *f*.
administrative [əd'mɪnɪstrətɪv] adj administratif. (*US Jur*) **~ court** tribunal administratif; **~ machinery** rouages administratifs.
administratively [əd'mɪnɪstrətɪvlɪ] adv administrativement.
administrator [əd'mɪnɪstreɪtəʳ] n *[business, public affairs etc]* administrateur *m*, -trice *f*; (*Jur*) *[estate, inheritance]* curateur *m*, -trice *f*.
admirable ['ædmərəbl] adj admirable, excellent.
admirably ['ædmərəblɪ] adv admirablement.
admiral ['ædmərəl] n **a** (*Naut*) amiral *m* (d'escadre). **A~ of the Fleet** ≃ Amiral *m* de France. **b** (*butterfly*) vanesse *f*, paon-de-jour *m*; *see* **red**.
admiralty ['ædmərəltɪ] n: **A~** (*Brit: since 1964* **~ Board**) ≃ ministère *m* de la Marine; (*US Jur*) **~ court** tribunal *m* maritime.
admiration [,ædmə'reɪʃən] n admiration *f* (*of, for* pour). **to be the ~ of** faire l'admiration de.
admire [əd'maɪəʳ] vt admirer.
admirer [əd'maɪərəʳ] n **a** admirateur *m*, -trice *f*. **b** (†: *suitor*) soupirant† *m*.
admiring [əd'maɪərɪŋ] adj admiratif.
admiringly [əd'maɪərɪŋlɪ] adv avec admiration.
admissibility [əd,mɪsə'bɪlɪtɪ] n admissibilité *f*; (*Jur, Fin*) recevabilité *f*.
admissible [əd'mɪsəbl] adj *idea, plan* acceptable, admissible; (*Jur*) *appeal, evidence, witness* recevable; *document* valable.
admission [əd'mɪʃən] n **a** (*entry*) admission *f*, entrée *f*, accès *m* (*to* à). **~ free** entrée gratuite; **no ~ to minors** entrée interdite aux mineurs; **a visa is necessary for ~ to this country** il faut un visa pour entrer dans ce pays; **~ to a school** admission à une école; **to gain ~ to sb** trouver accès auprès de qn; **to gain ~ to a school/club** être admis dans une école/un club; **to grant sb ~ to a society** admettre qn dans

une association; ~ **fee** droits *mpl* d'admission; (*US Univ*) **~s office** service *m* des inscriptions; (*US Univ*) **~s form** dossier *m* d'inscription.
b (*person admitted*) entrée *f*.
c (*Jur*) *[evidence etc]* acceptation *f*, admission *f*.
d (*confession*) aveu *m*. **by** *or* **on one's own** ~ de son propre aveu; **it's an ~ of guilt** en fait, c'est un aveu.

admit [əd'mɪt] **vt** a (*let in*) *person* laisser entrer, faire entrer; *light, air* laisser passer, laisser entrer. **children not ~ted** entrée interdite aux enfants; **this ticket ~s 2** ce billet est valable pour 2 personnes; (*US Med*) **~ting office** service *m* d'admissions.
b (*have space for*) *[halls, harbours etc]* contenir, (pouvoir) recevoir.
c (*acknowledge, recognize*) reconnaître, admettre (*that* que). **to ~ the truth of sth** reconnaître *or* admettre que qch est vrai; **he ~ted that this was the case** il a reconnu *or* admis que tel était le cas; **I must ~ that** je le reconnais, je l'admets, j'en conviens; **I must ~ I was wrong, I was wrong I ~** je reconnais que j'ai eu tort, j'ai eu tort, j'en conviens.
d *[criminal, wrongdoer]* avouer (*that* que); *crime, murder etc* reconnaître avoir commis. **he ~ted stealing the books** il a reconnu avoir volé les livres; **you'll never get him to ~ it** vous ne le lui ferez jamais avouer *or* reconnaître; **to ~ one's guilt** reconnaître sa culpabilité, s'avouer coupable.
e *claim* faire droit à. (*Jur*) **to ~ sb's evidence** admettre comme valable le témoignage de qn, prendre en considération les preuves fournies par qn.

▶**admit of** **vt fus** admettre, permettre. **it admits of no delay** cela n'admet *or* ne peut souffrir aucun retard; *see* **excuse**.

▶**admit to** **vt fus** reconnaître; *crime* reconnaître avoir commis. **to admit to a feeling of ...** avouer avoir un sentiment de ... .

admittance [əd'mɪtəns] **n** droit *m* d'entrée, admission *f* (*to sth* à qch), accès *m* (*to sth* à qch; *to sb* auprès de qn). **I gained ~ to the hall** on m'a laissé entrer dans la salle; **I was denied** *or* **refused ~** on m'a refusé l'entrée; **~: £5** droit d'entrée: 5 livres; **no ~** accès interdit au public; **no ~ except on business** accès interdit à toute personne étrangère au service.

admittedly [əd'mɪtɪdlɪ] **adv** de l'aveu général, de l'aveu de tous. **~ this is true** il faut reconnaître *or* convenir que c'est vrai.

admixture [əd'mɪkstʃə^r] **n** mélange *m*, incorporation *f*. **X with an ~ of Y** X additionné de Y.

admonish [əd'mɒnɪʃ] **vt** a (*reprove*) admonester, réprimander (*for doing* pour avoir fait; *about, for* pour, à propos de). b (*warn*) avertir, prévenir (*against doing* de ne pas faire), mettre en garde (*against* contre); (*Jur*) avertir. c (*exhort*) exhorter, engager (*to do* à faire). d (†, *liter: remind*) **to ~ sb of a duty** rappeler qn à un devoir.

admonition [,ædməʊ'nɪʃən] **n** a (*rebuke*) remontrance *f*, réprimande *f*, admonestation *f*. b (*warning*) avertissement *m*, admonition *f*; (*Jur*) avertissement.

ad nauseam [,æd'nɔːsɪæm] **adv** *repeat* à satiété; *do* jusqu'à saturation, à satiété. **to talk ~ about sth** raconter des histoires à n'en plus finir sur qch.

adnominal [,æd'nɒmɪnl] **adj, n** (*Ling*) adnominal (*m*).

ado [ə'duː] **n** agitation *f*, embarras *m*, affairement *m*. **much ~ about nothing** beaucoup de bruit pour rien; **without more ~** sans plus de cérémonie *or* d'histoires*.

adobe [ə'dəʊbɪ] **n** pisé *m*. **~ wall** mur *m* d'adobe.

adolescence [,ædəʊ'lesns] **n** adolescence *f*.

adolescent [,ædəʊ'lesnt] **adj, n** adolescent(e) *m(f)*.

Adonis [ə'dəʊnɪs] **n** (*Myth, fig*) Adonis *m*.

adopt [ə'dɒpt] **vt** a *child* adopter. b *idea, method* adopter, choisir, suivre; *career* choisir; (*Pol*) *motion* adopter; *candidate* choisir; (*Jur, Admin*) *wording* retenir.

adopted [ə'dɒptɪd] **adj** *child* adopté; *country* d'adoption, adoptif. **~ son** fils adoptif; **~ daughter** fille adoptive.

adoption [ə'dɒpʃən] **n** *[child, country, law]* adoption *f*; *[career, idea, method]* choix *m*. **a Londoner by ~** un Londonien d'adoption.

adoptive [ə'dɒptɪv] **adj** *parent, child* adoptif; *country* d'adoption.

adorable [ə'dɔːrəbl] **adj** adorable.

adoration [,ædə'reɪʃən] **n** adoration *f*.

adore [ə'dɔː^r] **vt** adorer.

adoring [ə'dɔːrɪŋ] **adj** *expression* d'adoration; *eyes* remplis d'adoration. **his ~ wife** sa femme qui est en adoration devant lui.

adoringly [ə'dɔːrɪŋlɪ] **adv** avec adoration.

adorn [ə'dɔːn] **vt** *room* orner (*with* de); *dress* orner, parer (*with* de). **to ~ o.s.** se parer.

adornment [ə'dɔːnmənt] **n** a (*in room*) ornement *m*; (*on dress*) parure *f*. b (*NonC*) décoration *f*.

A.D.P. [,eɪdiː'piː] **n abbr of automatic data processing.**

adrate* ['ædreɪt] **n** tarif *m* publicitaire *or* des annonces.

adrenal [ə'driːnl] 1 **adj** surrénal. 2 **n** (*also* **~ gland**) surrénale *f*.

adrenalin [ə'drenəlɪn] **n** (*Brit*) adrénaline *f*. (*fig*) **he felt the ~ rising** il a senti son pouls s'emballer.

Adriatic [,eɪdrɪ'ætɪk] **adj** *coast* adriatique. **~ (Sea)** (mer *f*) Adriatique *f*.

adrift [ə'drɪft] **adv, adj** (*Naut*) à la dérive; (*fig*) à l'abandon. *[ship]* **to go ~** aller à la dérive; (*fig*) **to be (all) ~** divaguer; (*fig*) **to turn sb ~** laisser qn se débrouiller tout seul; (*fig*) **to come ~*** *[wire etc]* se détacher; *[plans]* tomber à l'eau.

adroit [ə'drɔɪt] **adj** adroit, habile.

adroitly [ə'drɔɪtlɪ] **adv** adroitement, habilement.

adroitness [ə'drɔɪtnɪs] **n** adresse *f*, dextérité *f*.

adspeak* ['ædspiːk] **n** style *m* *or* jargon *m* de publicité.

ADT [eɪdiː'tiː] **n** (*US, Can*) **abbr of Atlantic Daylight Time.**

adulate ['ædjʊleɪt] **vt** aduler, flagorner.

adulation [,ædjʊ'leɪʃən] **n** adulation *f*, flagornerie *f*.

adult ['ædʌlt] 1 **n** adulte *mf*. (*Cine etc*) **~s only** interdit aux moins de 18 ans. 2 **adj** a *person, animal* adulte. b *film, book* pour adultes. **~ classes** cours *mpl* pour *or* d'adultes; **~ education** enseignement *m* pour adultes (*donné généralement en cours de soir*); **~ literacy** alphabétisation *f* des adultes; *see* **literacy.**

adulterate [ə'dʌltəreɪt] 1 **vt** frelater, falsifier. **~d milk** lait falsifié. 2 **adj** *goods, wine* falsifié, frelaté.

adulteration [ə,dʌltə'reɪʃən] **n** frelatage *m*, falsification *f*.

adulterer [ə'dʌltərə^r] **n** adultère *m* (*personne*).

adulteress [ə'dʌltərɪs] **n** adultère *f*.

adulterous [ə'dʌltərəs] **adj** adultère.

adultery [ə'dʌltərɪ] **n** adultère *m*.

adulthood ['ædʌlthʊd] **n** âge *m* adulte.

adumbrate ['ædʌmbreɪt] **vt** esquisser, ébaucher; *event* faire pressentir, préfigurer.

ad val ['æd'væl] **adj, adv** (*Comm*) **abbr of ad valorem.**

ad valorem [ædvə'lɔːrəm] **adj, adv** (*Comm*) ad valorem, sur la valeur.

advance [əd'vɑːns] 1 **n** a (*progress, movement forward*) avance *f*, marche *f* en avant; *[science, ideas]* progrès *mpl*; (*Mil*) avance, progression *f*. **with the ~ of (old) age** avec l'âge; **to make ~s in technology** faire des progrès en technologie.
b (*NonC*) **in ~** *book, warn, prepare, announce* à l'avance; *thank, pay, decide* à l'avance, d'avance; **to send sb on in ~** envoyer qn en avant; **£10 in ~** 10 livres d'avance; **he arrived in ~ of the others** il est arrivé en avance sur les autres; **to be in ~ of one's time** être en avance sur *or* devancer son époque; **a week in ~** une semaine à l'avance; (*Rail*) **luggage in ~** bagages enregistrés.
c (*in prices, wages*) hausse *f*, augmentation *f* (*in* de).
d (*sum of money*) avance *f* (*on* sur). **an ~ against security** une avance sur nantissement.
e (*overtures of friendship*) **~s** avances *fpl*; **to make ~s to sb** faire des avances à qn.
2 **comp** ▸ **advance booking:** **"advance booking advisable"** "il est conseillé de louer les places à l'avance"; **advance booking (office)** (guichet *m* de) location *f* ▸ **advance copy** *[book]* exemplaire *m* de lancement; *[speech]* texte distribué à l'avance (*à la presse*) ▸ **advance deposit** dépôt *m* préalable ▸ **advance factory** usine-pilote *f* ▸ **advance guard** (*Mil*) avant-garde *f* ▸ **advance man** (*US Pol*) organisateur *m* de la publicité (*pour une campagne publicitaire*) ▸ **advance notice** préavis *m*, avertissement *m* ▸ **advance party** (*Mil*) pointe *f* d'avant-garde ▸ **advance payment** (*Fin*) paiement anticipé *or* par anticipation ▸ **advance post** (*Mil*) poste avancé ▸ **advance publicity** publicité *f* d'amorçage ▸ **advance warning** = **advance notice.**
3 **vt** a (*move forward*) *date, time* avancer; (*Mil*) *troops* avancer; *work, knowledge, project* faire progresser *or* avancer; *interest, growth* développer; *cause* promouvoir; (*promote*) *person* élever, promouvoir (*to* à).
b (*suggest, propose*) *reason, explanation* avancer; *opinion* avancer, émettre.
c (*pay on account*) avancer, faire une avance de; (*lend*) prêter.
d (*raise*) *prices* augmenter, faire monter, hausser.
e (*US Pol*) *campaign* organiser.
4 **vi** a (*go forward*) avancer, s'avancer, marcher (*on, towards* vers); *[army]* avancer (*on* sur); (*during a battle*) *[troops]* se porter en avant. **he ~d upon me** il est venu vers *or* a marché sur moi; **the advancing army** l'armée en marche.
b (*progress*) *[work, civilization, mankind]* progresser, faire des progrès; *[person]* (*in rank*) recevoir de l'avancement; (*Mil*) monter en grade.
c (*rise*) *[prices]* monter, augmenter, être en hausse.

advanced [əd'vɑːnst] **adj** *ideas, age, pupil, child* avancé; *studies, class* supérieur; *work* poussé; *equipment etc* de pointe. **~ mathematics** hautes études mathématiques; **~ technology** technologie avancée *or* de pointe; **the season is well ~** la saison est bien avancée; **~ in years** d'un âge avancé; (*Brit Scol*) **~ level** = **A level** (*see* **A**); to receive ~ standing être admis par équivalence.

advancement [əd'vɑːnsmənt] **n** a (*improvement*) progrès *m*, avancement *m*. b (*promotion*) avancement *m*, promotion *f*.

advantage [əd'vɑːntɪdʒ] 1 **n** a avantage *m*. **to have an ~ over sb, to have the ~ of sb** avoir un avantage sur qn; **that gives you an ~ over me** cela vous donne un avantage sur moi; **to get the ~ of sb** prendre l'avantage sur qn (*by doing* en faisant); **to have the ~ of numbers** avoir l'avantage du nombre (*over* sur); **to take ~ of sb** profiter de qn; *[employer etc]* exploiter qn; (*sexually*) abuser de qn; **I took ~ of the opportunity** j'ai profité de l'occasion; **to turn sth to (one's) ~** tirer parti de qch, tourner qch à son avantage; **I find it to my ~** j'y trouve mon compte; **it is to his ~ to do it** cela l'arrange *or* c'est son intérêt de le faire; **to the best ~** le plus avantageusement possible; **this dress shows her off to ~** cette robe l'avantage.

b (*Tennis*) avantage *m*. (*Rugby*) **to play the ~ rule** laisser jouer la règle de l'avantage.

2 **vt** avantager. (*wealthy*) **~d** privilégié.

advantageous [ˌædvənˈteɪdʒəs] **adj** avantageux (*to* pour).

advent [ˈædvənt] **n** a venue *f*, avènement *m*. b (*Rel*) **A~** l'Avent *m*; **A~ Calendar** calendrier *m* de l'Avent; **A~ Sunday** dimanche *m* de l'Avent.

Adventist [ˈædventɪst] **n** adventiste *mf*.

adventitious [ˌædvenˈtɪʃəs] **adj** fortuit, accidentel; (*Bot, Med*) adventice.

adventure [ədˈventʃəʳ] 1 **n** aventure *f*. **to have an ~** avoir une aventure. 2 **vt** aventurer, risquer, hasarder. 3 **vi** s'aventurer, se risquer (*on* dans). 4 **comp** *story, film* d'aventures ▸**adventure playground** aire *f* de jeux.

adventurer [ədˈventʃərəʳ] **n** aventurier *m*.

adventuress [ədˈventʃərɪs] **n** aventurière *f*.

adventurous [ədˈventʃərəs] **adj** *person* aventureux, audacieux; *journey* aventureux, hasardeux.

adventurously [ədˈventʃərəsˌlɪ] **adv** audacieusement.

adverb [ˈædvɜːb] **n** adverbe *m*.

adverbial [ədˈvɜːbɪəl] **adj** adverbial.

adverbially [ədˈvɜːbɪəlɪ] **adv** adverbialement.

adversarial [ˌædvəˈsɛərɪəl] **adj** *politics* de confrontation. **the ~ system** le système de débat contradictoire.

adversary [ˈædvəsərɪ] **n** adversaire *mf*.

adverse [ˈædvɜːs] **adj** *factor, report, opinion* défavorable, hostile; *circumstances* défavorable; *wind* contraire, debout. **~ to** hostile à, contraire à.

adversity [ədˈvɜːsɪtɪ] **n** a (*NonC*) adversité *f*. **in ~** dans l'adversité. b (*event*) malheur *m*.

advert[1] [ədˈvɜːt] **vi** se reporter, faire allusion, se référer (*to* à).

advert[2]* [ˈædvɜːt] **n** (*Brit*) (**abbr of advertisement**) (*announcement*) annonce *f* (publicitaire); (*Comm*) publicité *f*, pub* *f*.

advertise [ˈædvətaɪz] 1 **vt** a (*Comm etc*) *goods* faire de la publicité pour. **I've seen that soap ~d on television** j'ai vu une publicité pour ce savon à la télévision.

b (*in newspaper etc*) **to ~ a flat (for sale)** mettre *or* insérer une annonce pour vendre un appartement. **I saw it ~d in a shop window** j'ai vu une annonce là-dessus dans une vitrine.

c (*draw attention to*) afficher. **don't ~ your ignorance!** inutile d'afficher votre ignorance!; **don't ~ the fact that ...** essaie de ne pas trop laisser voir que ..., ne va pas crier sur les toits que ... .

2 **vi** a (*Comm*) faire de la publicité *or* de la réclame. **it pays to ~** la publicité paie.

b chercher par voie d'annonce. **to ~ for a flat/a secretary** faire paraître une annonce pour trouver un appartement/une secrétaire.

advertisement [ədˈvɜːtɪsmənt] **n** a (*Comm*) réclame *f*, publicité *f*; (*TV*) spot *m* publicitaire. (*Cine, Press, Rad, TV*) **~s** publicité; **I saw an ~ for that soap in the papers** j'ai vu une réclame *or* une publicité pour ce savon dans les journaux; **I made tea during the ~s** j'ai fait le thé pendant que passait la publicité; **he's not a good ~ *or* an ~ for his school** il ne constitue pas une bonne réclame pour son école.

b (*private: in newspaper etc*) annonce *f*. **~ column** petites annonces; **to put an ~ in a paper** mettre une annonce dans un journal; **I got it through an ~** je l'ai eu par *or* grâce à une annonce; *see* **classified, small.**

c (*NonC*) réclame *f*, publicité *f*. (*fig*) **his arrival received no ~** son arrivée n'a pas été annoncée; *see* **self.**

advertiser [ˈædvətaɪzəʳ] **n** annonceur *m* (publicitaire).

advertising [ˈædvətaɪzɪŋ] 1 **n** (*activity*) publicité *f*; (*advertisements*) réclames *fpl*. **a career in ~** une carrière dans la publicité. 2 **comp** *firm, work* publicitaire ▸**advertising agency** agence *f* de publicité ▸**advertising campaign** campagne *f* publicitaire ▸**advertising manager** directeur *m*, -trice *f* de la publicité ▸**advertising medium** organe *m* de publicité ▸**advertising rates** tarifs *mpl* publicitaires ▸**advertising revenues** recettes *fpl* publicitaires ▸**Advertising Standards Authority** (*Brit*) ≃ Bureau *m* de vérification de la publicité; *see* **jingle.**

advertorial [ˌædvəˈtɔːrɪəl] 1 **n** publireportage *m*. 2 **adj** de publireportage.

advice [ədˈvaɪs] **n** a (*NonC*) conseils *mpl*, avis *m*. **a piece of ~** un avis, un conseil; **to seek ~ from sb** demander conseil à qn; **to take medical/legal ~** consulter un médecin/un avocat; **to take *or* follow sb's ~** suivre le(s) conseil(s) de qn; (*US Press*) **~ column** courrier *m* du cœur. b (*Comm: notification*) avis *m*. **as per ~ of *or* from** suivant avis de; **~ note** avis; **~ of dispatch** avis d'expédition.

advisability [ədˌvaɪzəˈbɪlɪtɪ] **n** opportunité *f* (*of sth* de qch, *of doing* de faire).

advisable [ədˈvaɪzəbl] **adj** conseillé, recommandé. **it is ~ to be vaccinated** il est conseillé de se faire vacciner; **I do not think it ~ for you to come** je ne vous conseille pas de venir.

advise [ədˈvaɪz] **vt** a (*give advice to*) conseiller, donner des conseils à (*sb on/about sth* qn sur/à propos de qch). **to ~ sb to do** conseiller à qn de faire, recommander à qn de faire, engager qn à faire; **to ~ sb against sth** déconseiller qch à qn; **to ~ sb against doing** conseiller à qn de ne pas faire.

b (*recommend*) *course of action* recommander. **I shouldn't ~ your going to see him** je ne vous conseillerais *or* recommanderais pas d'aller le voir; **you would be well/ill ~d to wait** vous feriez bien/vous auriez tort d'attendre.

c (*inform*) **to ~ sb of sth** aviser *or* informer qn de qch, faire part à qn de qch; (*Fin*) **advising bank** banque notificatrice.

advisedly [ədˈvaɪzɪdlɪ] **adv** délibérément, en (toute) connaissance de cause, après mûre réflexion.

adviser, advisor [ədˈvaɪzəʳ] **n** conseiller *m*, -ère *f*. (*Brit: Scol Admin*) **French/maths ~** conseiller *m*, -ère *f* pédagogique de français/de maths; *see* **educational, legal, spiritual.**

advisory [ədˈvaɪzərɪ] **adj** consultatif. **~ board** conseil consultatif; **in an ~ capacity** à titre consultatif; **~ service** (*for students etc*) service *m* de renseignements; (*US Pol*) **~ committee** comité consultatif; (*US Jur*) **~ opinion** avis consultatif de la cour.

advocacy [ˈædvəkəsɪ] **n** *[cause etc]* plaidoyer *m* (*of* en faveur de).

advocate [ˈædvəkɪt] 1 **n** a (*upholder*) *[cause etc]* défenseur *m*, avocat(e) *m(f)*. **to be an ~ of** être partisan(e) de; **to become the ~ of** se faire le champion (*or* la championne) de; *see* **devil.** b (*Scot Jur*) avocat *m* (plaidant); *see* **lord.** 2 [ˈædvəkeɪt] **vt** recommander, préconiser, prôner.

advt. (**abbr of advertisement**) publicité *f*.

adz(e) [ædz] **n** herminette *f*, doloire *f*.

A & E [ˌeɪanˈdiː] **n abbr of Accident and Emergency.**

A.E.A. [ˌeiːiːˈeɪ] **n** (*Brit*) (**abbr of Atomic Energy Authority**) ≃ C.E.A. *m*.

A.E.C. [ˌeiːiːˈsiː] **n** (*US*) (**abbr of Atomic Energy Commission**) ≃ C.E.A. *m*.

Aegean [iːˈdʒiːən] **adj** égéen. **~ (Sea)** (mer *f*) Égée *f*; **~ Islands** îles *fpl* de la mer Égée.

Aegeus [iːˈdʒiːəs] **n** Égée *m*.

aegis [ˈiːdʒɪs] **n** égide *f*. **under the ~ of** sous l'égide de.

aegrotat [ˈaɪgrəʊˌtæt] **n** (*Brit Univ*) équivalence *f* d'obtention d'un examen (*accordée à un bon étudiant malade*).

Aeneas [ɪˈniːəs] **n** Énée *m*.

Aeneid [ɪˈniːɪd] **n** Énéide *f*.

aeolian [iːˈəʊlɪən] **adj** éolien. **~ harp** harpe éolienne.

Aeolus [ˈiːələs] **n** Éole *m*.

aeon [ˈiːən] **n** temps infini, période *f* incommensurable. **through ~s of time** à travers des éternités.

aerate [ˈɛəreɪt] **vt** *liquid* gazéifier; *blood* oxygéner; *soil* retourner. **~d water** eau gazeuse.

aerial [ˈɛərɪəl] 1 **adj** a (*in the air*) aérien. **~ cableway** téléphérique *m*; **~ camera** appareil *m* de photo pour prises de vues aériennes; (*US*) **~ ladder** échelle pivotante; **~ photograph** photographie aérienne; **~ railway** téléphérique; **~ survey** levé aérien. b (*immaterial*) irréel, imaginaire. 2 **n** (*esp Brit: Telec etc*) antenne *f*; *see* **indoor.** 3 **comp** ▸**aerial input** puissance reçue par l'antenne ▸**aerial mast** mât *m* d'antenne ▸**aerial tanker** ravitailleur *m* en vol.

aerie [ˈɛərɪ] **n** (*esp US*) aire *f* (*d'aigle etc*).

aero... [ˈɛərəʊ] **pref** aéro... .

aerobatics [ˈɛərəʊˈbætɪks] **npl** acrobatie(s) aérienne(s).

aerobic [ɛəˈrəʊbɪk] **adj** (*Chem*) aérobic; *exercises* d'aérobic.

aerobics [ɛəˈrəʊbɪks] **n** (*NonC*) aérobic *f or m*. **to do ~** faire de l'aérobic.

aerodrome [ˈɛərədrəʊm] **n** (*Brit*) aérodrome *m*.

aerodynamic [ˈɛərəʊdaɪˈnæmɪk] **adj** aérodynamique.

aerodynamics [ˈɛərəʊdaɪˈnæmɪks] **n** (*NonC*) aérodynamique *f*.

aero-engine [ˈɛərəʊˌendʒɪn] **n** aéromoteur *m*.

aerogram [ˈɛərəʊgræm] **n** a (*air letter*) aérogramme *m*. b (*radio telegram*) radiotélégramme *m*.

aerograph [ˈɛərəʊgræf] **n** météorographe *m*.

aerolite [ˈɛərəlaɪt] **n** aérolithe *m*.

aeromodelling [ˈɛərəʊˈmɒdlɪŋ] **n** aéromodélisme *m*.

aeronaut [ˈɛərənɔːt] **n** aéronaute *mf*.

aeronautic(al) [ˌɛərəˈnɔːtɪk(əl)] **adj** aéronautique. **~ engineering** aéronautique *f*.

aeronautics [ˌɛərəˈnɔːtɪks] **n** (*NonC*) aéronautique *f*.

aeroplane [ˈɛərəpleɪn] **n** (*Brit*) avion *m*, aéroplane† *m*.

aerosol [ˈɛərəsɒl] 1 **n** a (*system*) aérosol *m*. b (*container, contents*) bombe *f*. 2 **comp** *insecticide, paint* en aérosol, en bombe; *perfume* en atomiseur.

aerospace [ˈɛərəʊspeɪs] **adj** *industry, project* aérospatial.

Aeschylus [ˈiːskələs] **n** Eschyle *m*.

Aesculapius [ˌiːskjʊˈleɪpɪəs] **n** Esculape *m*.

Aesop [ˈiːsɒp] **n** Ésope *m*. **~'s Fables** les fables *fpl* d'Ésope.

aesthete, (*US*) **esthete** [ˈiːsθiːt] **n** esthète *mf*.

aesthetic(al), (*US*) **esthetic(al)** [iːsˈθetɪk(əl)] **adj** esthétique.

aesthetically, (*US*) **esthetically** [iːsˈθetɪkəlɪ] **adv** esthétiquement.

aestheticism, (*US*) **estheticism** [iːsˈθetɪsɪzəm] **n** esthétisme *m*.

aesthetics, (*US*) **esthetics** [iːsˈθetɪks] **n** (*NonC*) esthétique *f*.

aether [ˈiːθəʳ] **n** = **ether.**

A.E.U. [ˌeɪiː'juː] n (*Brit*) (abbr of **Amalgamated Engineering Union**) *syndicat*.
a.f. [ˌeɪ'ef] n (abbr of **audiofrequency**) audiofréquence *f*.
A.F.A. [ˌeɪef'eɪ] n (*Brit*) abbr of **Amateur Football Association**.
afar [ə'fɑːʳ] adv au loin, à distance. **from ~** de loin.
AFB [ˌeɪef'biː] n (*US Mil*) abbr of **Air Force Base**.
AFC [ˌeɪeʃ'siː] n a (abbr of **Association Football Club**) AFC. b abbr of **automatic frequency control**.
AFDC [ˌeɪefdiː'siː] n (*US Admin*) abbr of **Aid to Families with Dependent Children**.
affability [ˌæfə'bɪlɪtɪ] n affabilité *f*, amabilité *f*.
affable ['æfəbl] adj affable, aimable.
affably ['æfəblɪ] adv avec affabilité, affablement.
affair [ə'fɛəʳ] n a (*event*) affaire *f*. **it was a scandalous ~** ce fut un scandale; **it was an odd ~ altogether** c'était vraiment (une histoire *or* une affaire) bizarre; **~ of honour** affaire d'honneur; **the Suez ~** l'affaire de Suez.
b (*concern*) affaire *f*. **this is not her ~** ce n'est pas son affaire, cela ne la regarde pas; **that's my ~** c'est mon affaire, ça ne regarde que moi; **it's not your ~ what I do in the evenings** ce que je fais le soir ne te regarde pas.
c (*business of any kind*) **~s** affaires *fpl*; **in the present state of ~s** les choses étant ce qu'elles sont, étant donné les circonstances actuelles; **it was a dreadful state of ~s** la situation était épouvantable; **~s of state** affaires d'État; **to put one's ~s in order** (*business*) mettre de l'ordre dans ses affaires; (*belongings*) mettre ses affaires en ordre; **your private ~s don't concern me** votre vie privée ne m'intéresse pas; **she never interferes with his business ~s** elle n'intervient jamais dans ses activités professionnelles *or* dans ses affaires; *see* **current, foreign**.
d (*love ~*) liaison *f*, affaire *f* de cœur, aventure *f* (amoureuse). **to have an ~ with sb** avoir une liaison avec qn.
e (**: material object*) affaire *f*, chose *f*.
affect [ə'fekt] 1 vt a (*have effect on*) *result, experiment, numbers* avoir un effet *or* des conséquences sur, modifier; *decision, career, the future* influer sur; (*Jur*) avoir une incidence sur; (*have detrimental effect on*) *person* atteindre, toucher; *conditions, substance, health* détériorer. **this will certainly ~ the way we approach the problem** cela va certainement influer sur la façon dont nous aborderons le problème; **you mustn't let it ~ you** ne te laisse pas décourager *or* abattre par ça.
b (*concern*) concerner, toucher. **this decision ~s all of us** cette décision nous concerne tous; **it does not ~ me personally** cela ne me touche pas personnellement.
c (*emotionally: move*) émouvoir, affecter; (*sadden*) affecter, toucher, frapper. **she was deeply ~ed by the news** elle a été très affectée *or* touchée par la nouvelle.
d *[disease] organ, powers of recuperation* attaquer, atteindre; *[drug]* agir sur.
e (*feign*) *ignorance, surprise* affecter, feindre.
f (*† or frm: have liking for*) affectionner. **she ~s bright colours** elle a une prédilection pour *or* elle affectionne les couleurs vives.
2 n ['æfekt] (*Psych*) affect *m*.
affectation [ˌæfek'teɪʃən] n a (*pretence*) affectation *f*, simulation *f*. **an ~ of interest/indifference** une affectation d'intérêt/d'indifférence. b (*artificiality*) affectation *f*, manque *m* de naturel. **her ~s annoy me** ses manières affectées *or* ses poses *fpl* m'agacent.
affected [ə'fektɪd] adj (*insincere*) *person, behaviour* affecté, maniéré; *accent, clothes* affecté. *[person]* **to be ~** poser.
affectedly [ə'fektɪdlɪ] adv avec affectation, d'une manière affectée.
affecting [ə'fektɪŋ] adj touchant, émouvant.
affection [ə'fekʃən] n a (*NonC: fondness*) affection *f*, tendresse *f* (*for, towards* pour). **to win sb's ~(s)** se faire aimer de qn, gagner l'affection *or* le cœur de qn; **I have a great ~ for her** j'ai beaucoup d'affection pour elle. b (*Med*) affection *f*, maladie *f*.
affectionate [ə'fekʃənɪt] adj *person* affectueux, tendre, aimant; *tone* tendre, affectueux; *memories* tendre. (*letter-ending*) **your ~ daughter** votre fille affectionnée.
affectionately [ə'fekʃənɪtlɪ] adv affectueusement. (*letter-ending*) **yours ~** (bien) affectueusement (à vous).
affective [ə'fektɪv] adj affectif (*also Ling*).
affidavit [ˌæfɪ'deɪvɪt] n (*Jur*) déclaration écrite sous serment. **to swear an ~ (to the effect that)** déclarer par écrit sous serment (que).
affiliate [ə'fɪlɪeɪt] 1 vt affilier (*to, with* à). **to ~ o.s., to be ~d** s'affilier (*to, with* à); (*Comm*) **~d company** (*gen*) filiale *f*; (*on balance sheet*) société *f* liée *or* apparentée. 2 [ə'fɪlɪət] n membre *m* affilié.
affiliation [əˌfɪlɪ'eɪʃən] n a (*Comm etc*) affiliation *f*. b (*Jur*) attribution *f* de paternité. **~ order** jugement *m* en constatation de paternité; **~ proceedings** action *f* en recherche de paternité. c (*connection*) affiliation *f*, attaches *fpl*.
affinity [ə'fɪnɪtɪ] n a (*gen, Bio, Chem, Ling, Math, Philos*) affinité *f* (*with, to* avec, *between* entre); (*connection, resemblance*) ressemblance *f*, rapport *m*. **the ~ of one thing to another** la ressemblance d'une chose avec une autre. b (*Jur: relationship*) affinité *f* (*to, with* avec). c (*liking*) attrait *m*, attraction *f* (*with, for* pour). **there is a certain ~ between them** ils ont des affinités.
affirm [ə'fɜːm] vt affirmer, soutenir (*that* que).
affirmation [ˌæfə'meɪʃən] n affirmation *f*, assertion *f*.
affirmative [ə'fɜːmətɪv] 1 n (*Ling*) affirmatif *m*. **in the ~** à l'affirmatif; (*gen*) **to answer in the ~** répondre affirmativement *or* par l'affirmative, répondre que oui. 2 adj affirmatif. **if the answer is ~** si la réponse est affirmative, si la réponse est oui *or* dans l'affirmative; (*US: Pol, Ind*) **~ action** mesures *fpl* anti-discriminatoires en faveur des minorités.
affirmatively [ə'fɜːmətɪvlɪ] adv affirmativement.
affix [ə'fɪks] 1 vt *seal, signature* apposer, ajouter (*to* à); *stamp* coller (*to* à). 2 ['æfɪks] n (*Gram*) affixe *m*.
afflict [ə'flɪkt] vt affliger. **to be ~ed by** *or* **with gout** être affligé *or* souffrir de la goutte.
affliction [ə'flɪkʃən] n a (*NonC*) affliction *f*, détresse *f*. **people in ~** les gens dans la détresse. b **the ~s of old age** les misères *fpl or* les calamités *fpl* de la vieillesse.
affluence ['æflʊəns] n (*plenty*) abondance *f*; (*wealth*) richesse *f*. **to rise to ~** parvenir à la fortune.
affluent ['æflʊənt] 1 adj (*plentiful*) abondant; (*wealthy*) riche. **to be ~** vivre dans l'aisance; **the ~ society** la société d'abondance. 2 n (*Geog*) affluent *m*.
afflux ['æflʌks] n a (*Med*) afflux *m*. b *[people etc]* affluence *f*, afflux *m*.
afford [ə'fɔːd] vt a (*following can, could, be able to*) **to be able to ~ to buy sth** avoir les moyens d'acheter qch; **I can't ~ a new hat** je ne peux pas m'offrir *or* me payer* un nouveau chapeau; **he can well ~ a new car** il a tout à fait les moyens de s'acheter une nouvelle voiture; (*fig*) **he can't ~ (to make) a mistake** il ne peut pas se permettre (de faire) une erreur; **I can't ~ the time to do it** je n'ai pas le temps de le faire; *see* **ill**. b (*provide*) fournir, offrir, procurer. **to ~ sb great pleasure** procurer un grand plaisir à qn; **this will ~ me an opportunity to say** ceci me fournira l'occasion de dire.
affordable [ə'fɔːdəbl] adj abordable. **easily ~** très abordable.
afforest [æ'fɒrɪst] vt reboiser.
afforestation [æˌfɒrɪs'teɪʃən] n boisement *m*. **~ policy** politique *f* de boisement.
affranchise [æ'frænʧaɪz] vt affranchir.
affray [ə'freɪ] n bagarre *f*, échauffourée *f*, rixe *f*.
affricate ['æfrɪˌkɪt] n (*Phon*) affriquée *f*.
affright [ə'fraɪt] (*†, liter*) 1 vt effrayer, terrifier. 2 n effroi *m*, épouvante *f*, terreur *f*.
affront [ə'frʌnt] 1 vt a (*insult*) insulter, faire un affront à, offenser. b (*face*) affronter, braver. 2 n affront *m*, insulte *f*.
Afghan ['æfgæn] 1 n a Afghan(e) *m(f)*. b (*Ling*) afghan *m*. c (*also ~* **hound**) lévrier afghan. 2 adj afghan.
Afghanistan [æf'gænɪstæn] n Afghanistan *m*.
aficionado [əˌfɪʃjə'nɑːdəʊ] n: **he's an ~ of jazz** *or* **a jazz ~** c'est un fana* *or* un mordu* du jazz.
afield [ə'fiːld] adv: **far ~** *be* au loin; *go* loin; **countries further ~** pays plus lointains; **very far ~** très loin; **too far ~** trop loin; **to explore farther ~** pousser plus loin l'exploration; (*fig*) **to go farther ~ for help/support** chercher plus loin de l'aide/un soutien.
afire [ə'faɪəʳ] adj, adv (*liter*) (*lit*) en feu, embrasé (*liter*); (*fig*) enflammé (*with* de).
aflame [ə'fleɪm] adj, adv en flammes, en feu, embrasé (*liter*). (*fig*) **to be ~ with colour** briller de vives couleurs, rutiler; (*fig*) **~ with anger** enflammé de colère.
AFL-CIO [ˌeɪef'elˌsiːaɪ'əʊ] (abbr of **American Federation of Labor and Congress of Industrial Organizations**) *fédération des syndicats indépendants américains*.
afloat [ə'fləʊt] 1 adv a (*on water*) à flot, sur l'eau. **to set a boat ~** mettre un bateau à l'eau *or* à flot; **to stay ~** *[person]* garder la tête hors de l'eau, surnager; *[thing]* flotter, surnager; (*fig: stay solvent*) se maintenir à flot; **to get** *or* **set a business ~** lancer une affaire; **to keep a business ~** maintenir une affaire à flot; **to keep bills ~** faire circuler des effets. b (*Naut: on board ship*) en mer, à la mer. **service ~** service *m* à bord; **to serve ~** servir en mer. c (*fig: of rumour etc*) en circulation, qui court *or* se répand. 2 adj (*Commodity Exchange*) **~ price** prix *m* à flot *or* à bord.
afocal ['eɪˌfəʊkəl] adj (*Phot*) afocal.
afoot [ə'fʊt] adv a (*in progress*) **there is something ~** il se prépare quelque chose; **there is a plan ~ to do** on a formé le projet *or* on envisage de faire. b (*†, liter*) *go, come* à pied. **to be ~** être sur pied.
aforementioned [əˌfɔː'menʃənd] adj, **aforenamed** [ə'fɔːneɪmd] adj, **aforesaid** [ə'fɔːsed] adj (*Jur etc*) susdit, susmentionné, précité.
aforethought [ə'fɔːθɔːt] adj prémédité; *see* **malice**.
afoul [ə'faʊl] adv (*esp US*) **to run ~ of sb** se mettre qn à dos, s'attirer le mécontentement de qn; **to run ~ of a ship** entrer en collision avec un bateau.
afp [ˌeɪef'piː] n (abbr of **alpha-fetoprotein**) alpha F.P.
afraid [ə'freɪd] adj a (*frightened*) **to be ~** avoir peur; **to be ~ of sb/sth** avoir peur de qn/qch, craindre qn/qch; **don't be ~!** n'ayez pas peur!, ne craignez rien!; **I am ~ of hurting him** *or* **that I might hurt him** j'ai peur *or* je crains de lui faire mal; **I am ~ he will** *or* **might hurt me**, (*liter*) **I**

am ~ lest he (might) hurt me je crains *or* j'ai peur qu'il (ne) me fasse mal; **I am ~ to go** *or* **of going** je n'ose pas y aller, j'ai peur d'y aller; **he is ~ of work** il n'aime pas beaucoup travailler; **he is not ~ of work** le travail ne lui fait pas peur *or* ne le rebute pas.

b (*expressing polite regret*) **I'm ~ I can't do it** je regrette *or* je suis désolé, (mais) je ne pourrai pas le faire; **I'm ~ that ...** je regrette de vous dire que ...; **I am ~ I shall not be able to come** je suis désolé de ne pouvoir venir, je crains de ne pas pouvoir venir; **are you going? — I'm ~ not/I'm ~ so** vous y allez? — hélas non/hélas oui; **there are too many people, I'm ~** je regrette, mais il y a trop de monde.

afresh [ə'freʃ] adv de nouveau. **to start ~** recommencer.

Africa ['æfrɪkə] n Afrique *f*; *see* **south**.

African ['æfrɪkən] 1 n Africain(e) *m(f)*. 2 adj africain. **~ elephant** éléphant *m* d'Afrique; **~ National Congress** African National Congress *m*; **~ violet** saintpaulia *f*; *see* **south**.

Afrikaans [ˌæfrɪ'kɑːns] 1 n (*Ling*) afrikaans *m*. 2 adj afrikaans.

Afrikaner [ˌæfrɪ'kɑːnəʳ] 1 n Afrikaner *mf*. 2 adj afrikaner.

afro ['æfrəʊ] adj, pref: **to go ~*** s'africaniser; **~ hair style** coiffure *f* afro*; **A~-American** afro-américain; **A~-Asian** afro-asiatique.

aft [ɑːft] adv (*Naut*) sur *or* à *or* vers l'arrière. **wind dead ~** vent en poupe, vent arrière.

after ['ɑːftəʳ] (*phr vb elem*) 1 prep a (*time*) après. **~ that** après cela, après ça; **~ dinner** après le dîner (*see also* **6**); **the day ~ tomorrow** après-demain *m*; **~ this date** passé cette date; **shortly ~ 10 o'clock** peu après 10 heures; **it was ~ 2 o'clock** il était plus de 2 heures; (*US*) **it was 20 ~ 3** il était 3 heures 20; **~ hours*** après la fermeture, après le travail; **~ seeing her** après l'avoir vue; **~ which he sat down** après quoi il s'est assis; **~ what has happened** après ce qui s'est passé.

b (*order*) après. **the noun comes ~ the verb** le substantif vient après le verbe; **~ you, sir** après vous, Monsieur; **~ you with the salt*** passez-moi le sel s'il vous plaît (quand vous aurez fini).

c (*place*) après. **to run ~ sb** courir après qn; **he shut the door ~ her** il a refermé la porte sur elle; **come in and shut the door ~ you** entrez et (re)fermez la porte (derrière vous); **to shout ~ sb** crier à qn.

d **~ all** après tout; **to succeed ~ all** réussir malgré *or* après tout; **~ all, no one made him go** après tout, personne ne l'a obligé à y aller; **~ all, you'd expect her to say that** évidemment, il n'est pas étonnant qu'elle dise ça; **it's only 2 days, ~ all** après tout *or* au fond, ça fait seulement 2 jours.

e (*often expressing surprise*) après. **~ all I said to him** après tout ce que je lui ai dit; **~ all I've done for you!** après tout ce que j'ai fait pour toi!, quand je pense à tout ce que j'ai fait pour toi!; **~ all that happened, it's not surprising** avec tout ce qui est arrivé *or* quand on pense à tout ce qui est arrivé, ça n'a rien d'étonnant.

f (*succession*) **day ~ day** jour après jour, tous les jours; **(for) kilometre ~ kilometre** sur des kilomètres et des kilomètres; **kilometre ~ kilometre of forest** des kilomètres et des kilomètres de forêt; **you tell me lie ~ lie** tu me racontes mensonge sur mensonge; **she gave one excuse ~ another** elle a avancé une excuse après l'autre; **time ~ time** maintes (et maintes) fois; **they went out one ~ the other** (*individually*) ils sont sortis les uns après les autres; (*in a line*) ils sont sortis à la file.

g (*manner: according to*) **~ El Greco** d'après Le Gréco; **~ the old style** à la vieille mode, à l'ancienne; **she takes ~ her mother** elle tient de sa mère; **a young man ~ your own heart** un jeune homme comme tu les aimes; **to name a child ~ sb** donner à un enfant le nom de qn.

h (*pursuit, inquiry*) **to be ~ sb/sth** chercher qn/qch; (*after loss, disappearance etc*) rechercher qn/qch; **the police are ~ him for this robbery** il est recherché par la police *or* la police est à ses trousses pour ce vol; **she's ~ a green hat** elle cherche *or* voudrait un chapeau vert; **what are you ~?** (*want*) qu'est-ce que vous voulez? *or* désirez?; (*have in mind*) qu'avez-vous en tête?; **I see what he's ~** je vois où il veut en venir; (*fig: nagging*) **she's always ~ her children*** elle est toujours après ses enfants*; **she inquired ~ you** elle a demandé de vos nouvelles.

2 adv (*place, order, time*) après, ensuite. **for years ~** pendant des années après cela; **soon ~** bientôt après; **the week ~** la semaine d'après, la semaine suivante; **what comes ~?** qu'est-ce qui vient ensuite?, et ensuite?

3 conj après (que). **~ he had closed the door, she spoke** après qu'il eut fermé la porte, elle parla; **~ he had closed the door, he spoke** après avoir fermé la porte, il a parlé.

4 adj: **in ~life** *or* **~ years** *or* **~ days** plus tard (dans la vie), par *or* dans la suite.

5 npl (*Brit: dessert*) **~s*** le dessert.

6 comp ►**afterbirth** (*Med*) placenta *m* ►**afterburner, afterburning** postcombustion *f* ►**aftercare** *[convalescent]* post-cure *f*; *[appliance, product]* entretien *m*; **(prisoner) aftercare** assistance *f* (aux anciens détenus) ►**afterdeck** (*Naut*) arrière-pont *m*, pont *m* arrière ►**after-dinner drink** digestif *m* ►**after-dinner speaker** orateur *m* (de fin de repas); **he's a good after-dinner speaker** il fait de très bonnes allocutions *or* de très bons discours (de fin de repas) ►**aftereffect** *[events etc]* suite *f*, répercussion *f*; *[treatment]* réaction *f*; *[illness]* séquelle *f*; (*Psych*) after-effect *m* ►**afterglow** *[setting sun]* dernières lueurs, derniers reflets; *[person]* (*after exercise*) réaction *f* agréable ►**after-hours** *see* **hour c** ►**after-hours drinking** consommation *f* de boissons après la fermeture des pubs (*or* du pub) ►**afterlife** vie future (*see* **4**) ►**after-lunch: to have an after-lunch nap** faire la sieste ►**aftermath** suites *fpl*, conséquences *fpl*, séquelles *fpl*; **the aftermath of war** le contrecoup *or* les conséquences de la guerre ►**afternoon** *see* **afternoon** ►**afterpains** douleurs *fpl* suivant un (*or* l')accouchement ►**after-sales service** (*Comm*) service *m* après-vente ►**after-school** *activities etc* extra-scolaire; (*US Scol*) **after-school center,** (*Brit Scol*) **after-school club** garderie *f* ►**aftershave** lotion *f* après-rasage, after-shave *m* ►**aftertaste** (*lit, fig*) arrière-goût *m* ►**after-tax** après impôts ►**afterthought** *see* **afterthought** ►**after-treatment** (*Med etc*) soins *mpl*; (*Tex*) apprêt *m*, fixage *m* ►**afterwards** *see* **afterwards**.

afternoon ['ɑːftə'nuːn] 1 n après-midi *m or f*. **in the ~, ~s*** l'après-midi; **at 3 o'clock in the ~** à 3 heures de l'après-midi; **on Sunday ~(s)** le dimanche après-midi; **every ~** l'après-midi, chaque après-midi; **on the ~ of December 2nd** l'après-midi du 2 décembre, le 2 décembre dans l'après-midi; **he will go this ~** il ira cet après-midi; **good ~!** (*on meeting sb*) bonjour!; (*on leaving sb*) au revoir!; **have a nice ~!** bon après-midi!; **in the early ~** tôt dans l'après-midi; **this ~** cet après-midi; **tomorrow/yesterday ~** demain/hier après-midi; **the next** *or* **following ~** l'après-midi suivant; **the ~ before** l'après-midi précédant; **every Sunday ~** le dimanche après-midi; **one summer ~** (par) un après-midi d'été.

2 comp *lecture, class, train, meeting etc* (de) l'après-midi ►**afternoon performance** matinée *f* ►**afternoon tea** thé *m* (de cinq heures).

afterthought ['ɑːftəθɔːt] n pensée *f* après coup. **I had an ~** cela m'est venu après coup; **I had ~s** *or* **an ~ about my decision** j'ai eu après coup des doutes sur ma décision; **the window was added as an ~** la fenêtre a été ajoutée après coup.

afterward(s) ['ɑːftəwəd(z)] adv après, ensuite, plus tard, par la suite.

A.G. [eɪ'dʒiː] n a abbr of **Adjutant General.** b abbr of **Attorney General.**

again [ə'gen] (*phr vb elem*) adv a (*once more*) de nouveau, encore une fois, une fois de plus. **here we are ~!** nous revoilà!; **it's him ~!** c'est encore lui!; **~ and ~, time and ~** à plusieurs reprises, maintes et maintes fois; **I've told you ~ and ~** je te l'ai dit et répété (je ne sais combien de fois); **he was soon well ~** il s'est vite remis; **she is home ~** elle est rentrée chez elle, elle est de retour chez elle; **what's his name ~?** comment s'appelle-t-il déjà?; **to begin ~** recommencer; **to see ~** revoir; *see* **now**.

b (*with neg*) **not ... ~** ne ... plus; **I won't do it ~** je ne le ferai plus; **never ~** jamais plus, plus jamais; **I won't do it ever ~** je ne le ferai plus jamais; (*excl*) **never ~!** c'est bien la dernière fois!; (*iro*) **not ~!** encore!

c **as much ~** deux fois autant; **he is as old ~ as Mary** il a deux fois l'âge de Marie.

d (*emphatic: besides, moreover*) de plus, d'ailleurs, en outre. **then ~, and ~** d'autre part, d'un autre côté; **~, it is not certain that ...** et d'ailleurs *or* et encore il n'est pas sûr que ... .

against [ə'genst] (*phr vb elem*) prep a (*indicating opposition, protest*) contre, en opposition à, à l'encontre de. **~ the law** (adj) contraire à la loi; (adv) contrairement à la loi; (*lit, fig*) **there's no law ~ it** il n'y a pas de loi qui s'y oppose, il n'y a pas de loi contre*; **I've got nothing ~ him/it** je n'ai rien contre lui/rien contre (cela); **conditions are ~ us** les conditions nous sont défavorables *or* sont contre nous; **to be ~ capital punishment** être contre la peine de mort; **I'm ~ helping him at all** je ne suis pas d'avis qu'on l'aide (*subj*); **I'm ~ it** je suis contre (cela); **to be dead ~ sth** s'opposer absolument à qch; (*Pol*) **to run ~ sb** se présenter contre qn; **~ all comers** envers et contre tous; **now we're up ~ it!** nous voici au pied du mur!, c'est maintenant qu'on va s'amuser!*; **~ my will** (*despite myself*) malgré moi, à contre-cœur; (*despite my opposition*) malgré moi, contre ma volonté; **to work ~ time** *or* **the clock** travailler contre la montre, faire la course contre la montre (*fig*); *see* **grain, hair, odds**.

b (*indicating collision, impact*) contre, sur. **to hit one's head ~ the mantelpiece** se cogner la tête contre la cheminée; **the truck ran ~ a tree** le camion s'est jeté sur *or* a percuté un arbre.

c (*indicating support*) contre. **to lean ~ a wall** s'appuyer contre un mur *or* au mur; **push the chairs right back ~ the wall** repoussez les chaises tout contre le mur; **he leaned ~ it** il s'y est appuyé, il s'est appuyé contre*; *see* **up 1h**.

d (*in contrast to*) contre, sur. **~ the light** à contre-jour; **the trees stood out ~ the sunset** les arbres se détachaient sur le (soleil) couchant.

e (*in preparation for*) en vue de, en prévision de, pour. **preparations ~ sb's return** préparatifs pour le retour *or* en prévision du retour de qn; **to have the roof repaired ~ the rainy season** faire réparer le toit en vue de la saison des pluies.

f (*indicating comparison*) **(as) ~** contre, en comparaison de; **my rights as ~ his** mes droits comparés aux siens; **the strength of the pound (as) ~ the dollar** la fermeté de la livre par rapport au dollar; **~ that, it might be said ...** en revanche *or* par contre, on pourrait dire ...; *see* **over, word**.

g **numbered tickets are available ~ this voucher** on peut obtenir des billets numérotés contre remise de ce bon; **~ presentation of docu-**

ments sur présentation des pièces justificatives.

Agamemnon [ˌæɡəˈmemnən] n Agamemnon *m*.

agape [əˈɡeɪp] adj, adv bouche bée.

agar(-agar) [ˌeɪɡəˈeɪɡəʳ] n agar-agar *m*, gélose *f*.

agaric [əˈɡærɪk] n agaric *m*.

agate [ˈæɡət] n agate *f*.

agave [əˈɡeɪvɪ] n agavé *m*.

age [eɪdʒ] 1 n a (*length of life*) âge *m*. **what's her ~?, what ~ is she?** quel âge a-t-elle?; **when I was your ~** quand j'avais votre âge; **I have a daughter your ~ or the same ~ as you** j'ai une fille de votre âge; **be or act your ~!** allons, sois raisonnable!; **he is 10 years of ~** il a 10 ans; **you don't look your ~** vous ne faites pas votre âge; **he's twice your ~** il a le double de votre âge; **we are of an ~** nous sommes du même âge; (*Jur etc*) **to be under ~** être mineur; **to come of ~** atteindre sa majorité; **to be of ~** être majeur; (*Jur*) **~ of consent** âge de consentement; *see* **middle** *etc*.

b (*latter part of life*) vieillesse *f*, âge *m*. **the infirmities of ~** les infirmités de la vieillesse *or* de l'âge; *see* **old**.

c (*Geol etc*) âge *m*; (*Hist, Literat*) époque *f*, siècle *m*; *see* **enlightenment, stone** *etc*.

d (*: *gen pl: long time*) **I haven't seen him for ~s** il y a un siècle que je ne le vois plus, il y a une éternité que je ne l'ai vu; **she stayed for ~s or for an ~** elle est restée (là) pendant une éternité *or* un temps fou.

2 vi vieillir, prendre de l'âge. **she had ~d beyond her years** elle paraissait *or* faisait maintenant plus que son âge; **to ~ well** *[wine]* s'améliorer en vieillissant; *[person]* vieillir bien; **he has ~d a lot** il a beaucoup vieilli, il a pris un coup de vieux.

3 vt a vieillir. **this dress ~s you** cette robe vous vieillit.

b *wine etc* laisser vieillir.

c *accounts* classer par antériorité *or* par ancienneté. **to ~ inventories** classer *or* analyser le stock par date d'entrée.

4 comp d'âge ►**age allowance** (*Brit Tax*) abattement *m* vieillesse ►**age bracket** = **age group** ►**age discrimination** (*US*) discrimination *f* pour raisons d'âge, âgisme *m* ►**age group** tranche *f* d'âge; **the 40-50 age group** la tranche d'âge de 40 à 50 ans, les 40 à 50 ans ►**age limit** limite *f* d'âge ►**age-old** séculaire, antique ►**age range: children in the age range 12-14** les enfants (qui sont) âgés de 12 à 14 ans.

aged [eɪdʒd] 1 adj a âgé de. **a boy ~ 10** un garçon (âgé) de 10 ans. b [ˈeɪdʒɪd] (*old*) âgé, vieux (*f* vieille). 2 npl: **the ~** les personnes âgées; **the ~ and infirm** les gens âgés et infirmes.

ageing [ˈeɪdʒɪŋ] 1 adj *person* vieillissant, qui se fait vieux (*f* vieille); *hairstyle etc* qui fait paraître plus vieux (*f* vieille). 2 n vieillissement *m*.

ageism [ˈeɪdʒɪzəm] n âgisme *m*.

ageist [ˈeɪdʒɪst] 1 adj faisant preuve d'âgisme. 2 n personne *f* faisant preuve d'âgisme.

ageless [ˈeɪdʒlɪs] adj *person* sans âge; *beauty* toujours jeune.

agency [ˈeɪdʒənsɪ] n a (*Comm*) agence *f*, bureau *m*; (*Govt*) organisme *m*. **this garage has the Citroën ~** ce garage est le concessionnaire Citroën; **he has the sole ~ for ...** il a l'exclusivité de ...; **~ agreement** contrat *m* de représentation; *see* **advertising, news, tourist** *etc*. b (*means*) action *f*, intermédiaire *m*, entremise *f*. **through or by the ~ of friends** par l'intermédiaire *or* l'entremise d'amis, grâce à des amis; **through the ~ of water** par l'action de l'eau.

agenda [əˈdʒendə] n ordre *m* du jour, programme *m*. **on the ~** à l'ordre du jour.

agent [ˈeɪdʒənt] n a (*Comm*) (*person*) agent(e) *m(f)*, représentant(e) *m(f)* (*of, for* de); (*firm*) concessionnaire *m*; *see* **foreign, free, law, special** *etc*. b (*thing, person, also Ling*) agent *m*; *see* **chemical, principal** *etc*.

agentive [ˈeɪdʒəntɪv] n (*Ling*) agentif *m*.

agglomerate [əˈɡlɒməreɪt] 1 vt agglomérer. 2 vi s'agglomérer. 3 adj aggloméré.

agglomeration [əˌɡlɒməˈreɪʃən] n agglomération *f*.

agglutinate [əˈɡluːtɪneɪt] 1 vt agglutiner. (*Ling*) **agglutinating language** langue agglutinante. 2 vi s'agglutiner. 3 adj agglutiné; (*Ling*) agglutinant.

agglutination [əˌɡluːtɪˈneɪʃən] n agglutination *f*.

agglutinative [əˈɡluːtɪnətɪv] adj *substance, language* agglutinant.

aggrandize [əˈɡrændaɪz] vt agrandir, grandir.

aggrandizement [əˈɡrændɪzmənt] n agrandissement *m*; *[influence]* accroissement *m*.

aggravate [ˈæɡrəveɪt] vt a *illness* aggraver, (faire) empirer; *quarrel, situation* envenimer; *pain* augmenter. (*Jur*) **~d assault** coups *mpl* et blessures. b (*annoy*) exaspérer, agacer, porter *or* taper sur les nerfs de*.

aggravating [ˈæɡrəveɪtɪŋ] adj a (*worsening*) *circumstances* aggravant. b (*annoying*) exaspérant, agaçant.

aggravation [ˌæɡrəˈveɪʃən] n (*see* **aggravate**) aggravation *f*; envenimement *m*; exaspération *f*, agacement *m*, irritation *f*.

aggregate [ˈæɡrɪɡɪt] 1 n a ensemble *m*, total *m*. **in the ~** dans l'ensemble, en somme; **on ~** ≃ au total des points (*dans le groupe de sélection*). b (*Constr, Geol*) agrégat *m*. 2 adj collectif, global, total. **~ value** valeur collective. 3 [ˈæɡrɪɡeɪt] vt a (*gather together*) agréger, rassembler. b (*amount to*) s'élever à, former un total de. 4 vi s'agréger, s'unir en un tout.

aggression [əˈɡreʃən] n (*also Psych*) agression *f*; (*aggressiveness*) agressivité *f*; *see* **non-aggression**.

aggressive [əˈɡresɪv] adj *person, behaviour, speech* agressif; *salesman, ad etc* accrocheur; (*Mil etc*) *tactics, action* offensif; (*Psych*) agressif.

aggressively [əˈɡresɪvlɪ] adv agressivement.

aggressiveness [əˈɡresɪvnɪs] n agressivité *f*.

aggressor [əˈɡresəʳ] n agresseur *m*.

aggrieved [əˈɡriːvd] adj chagriné, blessé, affligé (*at, by* par); *see* **party**.

aggro* [ˈæɡrəʊ] n (*Brit*) (abbr of **aggravation**) (*emotion*) agressivité *f*; (*physical violence*) grabuge* *m*; (*hassle*) embêtements *mpl*.

aghast [əˈɡɑːst] adj atterré (*at* de), frappé d'horreur.

agile [ˈædʒaɪl] adj agile, leste.

agility [əˈdʒɪlɪtɪ] n agilité *f*, souplesse *f*.

Agincourt [ˈædʒɪnˌkɔːt] n Azincourt.

aging [ˈeɪdʒɪŋ] = **ageing**.

agio [ˈædʒɪəʊ] n agio *m*.

agiotage [ˈædʒətɪdʒ] n agiotage *m*.

agism [ˈeɪdʒɪzəm] = **ageism**.

agist [ˈeɪdʒɪst] = **ageist**.

agitate [ˈædʒɪteɪt] 1 vt a *liquid* agiter, remuer. b (*excite, upset*) agiter, émouvoir, troubler. 2 vi: **to ~ for/against sth** faire campagne *or* mener une campagne en faveur de/contre qch.

agitated [ˈædʒɪteɪtɪd] adj inquiet (*f* -ète), agité. **to be very ~** être dans tous ses états.

agitatedly [ˈædʒɪteɪtɪdlɪ] adv avec agitation.

agitation [ˌædʒɪˈteɪʃən] n a *[mind]* émotion *f*, trouble *m*, agitation *f*. **in a state of ~** agité. b (*social unrest*) agitation *f*, troubles *mpl*; (*deliberate stirring up*) campagne *f* (*for* pour, *against* contre). c *[liquid]* agitation *f*, mouvement *m*.

agitator [ˈædʒɪteɪtəʳ] n a (*person*) agitateur *m*, -trice *f*, fauteur *m* (de troubles), trublion *m*. b (*device*) agitateur *m*.

agitprop [ˈædʒɪtˌprɒp] 1 n agit-prop *f inv*. 2 comp agit-prop *inv*.

aglow [əˈɡləʊ] adj *sky* embrasé (*liter*); *fire* rougeoyant, incandescent. **the sun sets the mountain ~** le soleil embrase la montagne; (*fig*) **~ with pleasure/health** rayonnant de plaisir/de santé.

A.G.M. [ˌeɪdʒiːˈem] n (abbr of **annual general meeting**) AG *f*, assemblée générale.

Agnes [ˈæɡnɪs] n Agnès *f*.

agnostic [æɡˈnɒstɪk] adj, n agnostique (*mf*).

agnosticism [æɡˈnɒstɪsɪzəm] n agnosticisme *m*.

ago [əˈɡəʊ] adv il y a. **a week ~** il y a huit jours; **how long ~?** il y a combien de temps (de cela)?; **a little while ~** il y a peu de temps; **he left 10 minutes ~** il est sorti il y a 10 minutes *or* depuis 10 minutes; **as long ~ as 1950** déjà en 1950, dès 1950; **no longer ~ than yesterday** pas plus tard qu'hier; *see* **long**.

agog [əˈɡɒɡ] adj en émoi. **to be (all) ~ (with excitement) about sth** être en émoi à cause de qch; **to set ~** mettre en émoi; **to be ~ to do** griller d'envie *or* être impatient de faire, brûler de faire; **~ for news** impatient d'avoir des nouvelles.

agonize [ˈæɡənaɪz] vi: **to ~ over or about sth** se tourmenter à propos de qch; **to ~ over how to do sth** se ronger les sangs pour savoir comment faire qch.

agonized [ˈæɡənaɪzd] adj atroce, d'angoisse.

agonizing [ˈæɡənaɪzɪŋ] adj *situation* angoissant; *cry* déchirant. **~ reappraisal** réévaluation *or* révision déchirante.

agony [ˈæɡənɪ] 1 n (*mental pain*) angoisse *f*, supplice *m*; (*physical pain*) douleur *f* atroce. **it was ~** la douleur était atroce; **death ~** agonie *f*; **to suffer agonies** souffrir le martyre *or* mille morts; **to be in an ~* of impatience** se mourir d'impatience; **to be in ~** souffrir le martyre; *see* **pile on, prolong**. 2 comp ►**agony aunt*** (*Brit Press*) *journaliste qui tient la rubrique du courrier du cœur* ►**agony column** courrier *m* du cœur.

agoraphobia [ˌæɡərəˈfəʊbɪə] n agoraphobie *f*.

agoraphobic [ˌæɡərəˈfəʊbɪk] adj agoraphobique.

AGR [ˌeɪdʒiːˈɑːʳ] abbr of **advanced gas-cooled reactor**.

agrammatical [ˌeɪɡrəˈmætɪkəl] adj agrammatical.

agraphia [ˌeɪˈɡræfɪə] n agraphie *f*.

agrarian [əˈɡreərɪən] 1 adj *reform, laws* agraire. **A~ Revolution** réforme(s) *f(pl)* agraire(s). 2 n (*Pol Hist*) agrarien(ne) *m(f)*.

agree [əˈɡriː] 1 vt a (*consent*) consentir (*to do* à faire), accepter (*to do* de faire); *statement, report* accepter *or* reconnaître la véracité de. **he ~d to do it** il a consenti à *or* accepté de le faire, il a bien voulu le faire.

b (*admit*) reconnaître, admettre (*that* que). **I ~ (that) I was wrong** je reconnais *or* conviens que je me suis trompé.

c (*come to an agreement*) convenir (*to do* de faire), se mettre d'accord (*to do* pour faire); *time, price* se mettre d'accord sur, convenir de; (*be of same opinion*) être d'accord (*with* avec; *that* que). **everyone ~s that we should stay** tout le monde s'accorde à reconnaître que *or* tout le monde est unanime pour reconnaître que nous devrions rester, de l'avis de tous nous devrions rester; **they ~d (amongst**

themselves) to do it ils ont convenu de le faire, ils se sont mis d'accord *or* se sont accordés pour le faire; **it was ~d** c'était convenu; **to ~ to differ** rester sur ses positions, garder chacun son opinion; **I ~ that it's difficult** je suis d'accord que c'est difficile; **the delivery was later than ~d** la livraison a été effectuée après la date convenue; (*Jur*) **unless otherwise ~d** sauf accord contraire, sauf convention contraire.

2 **vi** a (*hold same opinion*) être d'accord (*with* avec), être du même avis (*with* que). **I (quite) ~** je suis (tout à fait) d'accord; **I don't ~ (at all)** je ne suis pas (du tout) d'accord; **I ~ about trying again tomorrow** je suis d'accord avec l'idée de ressayer demain; **they all ~d in finding the play dull** tous ont été d'accord pour trouver la pièce ennuyeuse, tous ont été d'avis que la pièce était ennuyeuse; **she ~s with me that it is unfair** elle est d'accord avec moi pour dire *or* elle trouve comme moi que c'est injuste; **he entirely ~s with me** il est tout à fait d'accord *or* en plein accord avec moi; **I can't ~ with you there** je ne suis absolument pas d'accord avec vous sur ce point; **I don't ~ with children smoking** je n'admets pas que les enfants fument (*subj*).

b (*come to terms*) se mettre d'accord (*with* avec); (*get on well*) s'entendre (bien), s'accorder (bien). **to ~ about** *or* **on sth** se mettre d'accord sur qch, convenir de qch; **we haven't ~d about the price/about where to go** nous ne nous sommes pas mis d'accord sur le prix/sur l'endroit où aller, nous n'avons pas convenu du prix/de l'endroit où aller; **they ~d as to** *or* **on how to do it/as to what it should cost** ils sont tombés *or* se sont mis d'accord sur la manière de le faire/sur le prix que cela devrait coûter; *see* **agreed**.

c **to ~ to a proposal** accepter une proposition, donner son consentement *or* son adhésion à une proposition; **he won't ~ to that** il ne sera jamais d'accord, il n'acceptera pas; **I ~ to your marriage/your marrying her** je consens à votre mariage/à ce que vous l'épousiez; **he ~d to the project** il a donné son adhésion au projet.

d *[ideas, stories, assessments]* concorder, coïncider (*with* avec). **his explanation ~s with what I know** son explication correspond à ce que je sais; **these statements do not ~ with each other** ces affirmations ne concordent pas.

e (*Gram*) s'accorder (*with* avec; *in* en).

f (*suit the health of*) **sea air ~s with invalids** l'air marin est bon pour les malades *or* réussit aux malades; **the heat does not ~ with her** la chaleur l'incommode; **onions don't ~ with me** les oignons ne me réussissent pas.

agreeable [ə'griːəbl] **adj** a (*pleasant*) agréable. b (*willing*) consentant. **to be ~ to (doing) sth** consentir volontiers à (faire) qch; **I am quite ~** volontiers, je veux bien; **I am quite ~ to doing it** je ne demande pas mieux que de le faire.

agreeably [ə'griːəblɪ] **adv** agréablement.

agreed [ə'griːd] **adj** a d'accord. **we are ~** nous sommes d'accord (*about* au sujet de, à propos de, *on* sur); **the ministers were ~** les ministres sont tombés d'accord. b *time, place, amount* convenu. **it's all ~** c'est tout décidé *or* convenu; **as ~** comme convenu; **it's ~ that** il est convenu que + *indic*; **(is that) ~?** entendu?, d'accord?; **~!** entendu!, d'accord!

agreement [ə'griːmənt] **n** a (*mutual understanding*) accord *m*, harmonie *f*. **to be in ~ on a subject** être d'accord sur un sujet; **by (mutual) ~** (*both thinking same*) d'un commun accord; (*without quarrelling*) à l'amiable. b (*arrangement, contract*) accord *m*, accommodement *m*; (*Pol, frm*) pacte *m*. **to come to an ~** parvenir à une entente *or* un accommodement, tomber d'accord; **to sign an ~** signer un accord; **the Helsinki ~** les accords *mpl* d'Helsinki; *see* **gentleman.** c (*Gram*) accord *m*.

agribusiness ['ægrɪ,bɪznɪs] **n** agro-industries *fpl*.

agricultural [,ægrɪ'kʌltʃərəl] **adj** *worker, produce, country* agricole; *tool* aratoire, agricole. **~ engineer** ingénieur *m* agronome; **~ expert** expert *m* agronome; **~ college** école *f* d'agriculture; **~ show** exposition *f* agricole, salon *m* de l'agriculture; (*local*) comice *m* agricole.

agriculture ['ægrɪkʌltʃəʳ] **n** agriculture *f*. (*Brit*) **Minister/Ministry of A~**, (*US*) **Secretary/Department of A~** ministre *m*/ministère *m* de l'Agriculture.

agricultur(al)ist [,ægrɪ'kʌltʃər(əl)ɪst] **n** agronome *mf*; (*farmer*) agriculteur *m*.

agrifoodstuffs ['ægrɪ'fuːdstʌfz] **npl** agro-alimentaire *m*.

agrobiology [,ægrəʊbaɪ'ɒlədʒɪ] **n** agrologie *f*.

agrochemical [,ægrəʊ'kemɪkəl] 1 **adj** agrochimique. 2 **n** substance *f* agrochimique. (*industry*) **~s** agrochimie *f*.

agronomist [ə'grɒnəmɪst] **n** agronome *mf*.

agronomy [ə'grɒnəmɪ] **n** agronomie *f*.

aground [ə'graʊnd] **adv, adj** *ship* échoué. **to be ~** toucher le fond; **to be fast ~** être bien échoué; **to run ~** s'échouer.

ague†† ['eɪgjuː] **n** (*Med*) fièvre *f*.

ah [ɑː] **excl** ah!

aha [ɑː'hɑː] **excl** ah, ah!

Ahasuerus [ə,hæzjʊ'ɪərəs] **n** Assuérus *m*.

ahead [ə'hed] (*phr vb elem*) **adv** a (*in space*) en avant, devant. **to draw ~** gagner de l'avant; **stay here, I'll go on ~** restez ici, moi je vais en avant; (*lit, fig*) **to get ~** prendre de l'avance; (*Naut, also fig*) **full speed ~!** en avant toute!; *see* **fire ahead, go ahead** *etc*.

b (*in classification, sport etc*) en tête. **to be 5 points** *etc* **~** être en tête de *or* avoir une avance de 5 points *etc*.

c (*in time*) *book, plan* à l'avance. **~ of time** *decide, announce* d'avance; *arrive, be ready* avant l'heure, en avance; **~ of the meeting** avant la réunion; **2 hours ~ of the next car** en avance de 2 heures sur la voiture suivante; **he's 2 hours ~ of you** il a 2 heures d'avance sur vous; **clocks here are 2 hours ~ of clocks over there** les pendules d'ici ont 2 heures d'avance sur celles de là-bas *or* avancent de 2 heures sur celles de là-bas; **the months ~** les mois à venir *or* en perspective; **looking** *or* **thinking ~ 5 years, what ...** essayez d'imaginer la situation dans 5 ans d'ici – qu'est-ce que ...; (*fig*) **to be ~ of one's time** être en avance sur son époque; **to plan ~** faire des projets à l'avance; **to think ~** prévoir, penser à l'avenir, anticiper; **what is** *or* **lies ~** ce qui reste à venir.

ahoy [ə'hɔɪ] **excl** (*Naut*) ohé!, holà! **ship ~!** ohé du navire!

A.I. [,eɪ'aɪ] **n** a (**abbr of artificial intelligence**) IA *f*, intelligence artificielle. b (**abbr of artificial insemination**) IA *f*, insémination artificielle. c **abbr of Amnesty International.**

aid [eɪd] 1 **n** a (*NonC*) (*help*) aide *f*, assistance *f*, secours *m*; (*international*) aide. **by** *or* **with the ~ of sb** avec l'aide de qn; **by** *or* **with the ~ of sth** à l'aide de qch; **sale in ~ of the blind** vente *f* (de charité) au profit des aveugles; (*Brit fig*) **what is the meeting in ~ of?*** c'est dans quel but *or* en quel honneur* cette réunion?, à quoi rime cette réunion? (*pej*); **Marshall A~** le plan Marshall; *see* **first aid, mutual.**

b (*helper*) aide *mf*, assistant(e) *m(f)*; (*gen pl: equipment, apparatus*) aide *f*. **audio-visual ~s** support audio-visuel, moyens audio-visuels; **teaching ~s** outils *mpl or* matériel *m* pédagogique(s); *see* **deaf.**

2 **comp ▸aid agency** organisation *f* humanitaire **▸aid climbing** (*Climbing*) escalade artificielle.

3 **vt** *person* aider, assister, secourir, venir en aide à; *progress, recovery* contribuer à. **to ~ one another** s'entraider, s'aider les uns les autres; **to ~ sb to do** aider qn à faire; (*Jur*) **to ~ and abet (sb)** être complice (de qn).

A.I.D. [,eɪaɪ'diː] a (**abbr of artificial insemination by donor**) *see* **artificial.** b (*US*) **abbr of Agency for International Development.** c (*US Admin*) **abbr of Aid to Families with Dependent Children.**

aide [eɪd] 1 **n** aide *mf*, assistant(e) *m(f)*. 2 **comp ▸ ~-de-camp (pl ~s-~-~)** aide *m* de camp **▸ ~-mémoire (pl ~s-~)** mémorandum *m*.

AIDS, Aids, aids [eɪdz] **n** (**abbr of acquired immune deficiency syndrome**) SIDA *m*. **~ victim** sidatique *mf*, sidéen(ne) *m(f)*; *see* **sufferer.**

aigrette [e'gret] **n** (*Bot, Zool*) aigrette *f*.

aikido ['aɪkɪdəʊ] **n** aïkido *m*.

ail [eɪl] 1 **vt: what ~s you?** qu'avez-vous?; **what's ~ing them?** quelle mouche les a piqués? 2 **vi** souffrir, être souffrant.

aileron ['eɪlərɒn] **n** (*Aviat*) aileron *m*.

ailing ['eɪlɪŋ] **adj** en mauvaise santé, souffrant. **she is always ~** elle est de santé fragile, elle a une petite santé; **an ~ company** une compagnie qui périclite.

ailment ['eɪlmənt] **n** affection *f*. **all his (little) ~s** tous ses maux.

aim [eɪm] 1 **n** a **to miss one's ~** manquer son coup *or* son but; **to take ~** viser; **to take ~ at sb/sth** viser qn/qch; **his ~ is bad** il vise mal.

b (*fig: purpose*) but *m*, objet *m*, visées *fpl*. **with the ~ of doing** dans le but de faire; **her ~ is to do** elle a pour but de faire, elle vise à faire; **the ~ of this policy is to ...** cette politique vise à ...; **the ~ of this government is to ...** le but que s'est fixé ce gouvernement est de ...; **his ~s are open to suspicion** ses visées ambitieuses *or* ses ambitions sont suspectes; **political ~s** finalités *fpl or* buts *mpl* politiques.

2 **vt** a (*direct*) *gun* braquer (*at* sur); *missile* pointer (*at* sur); *blow* allonger, décocher (*at* à); *remark* diriger (*at* contre). **to ~ a gun at sb** braquer un revolver sur qn, viser qn avec un revolver; **to ~ a stone at sb** lancer une pierre sur *or* à qn; (*fig*) **his remarks are ~ed at his father** ses remarques visent son père.

b (*intend*) viser, aspirer (*to do, at doing* à faire).

3 **vi** viser. **to ~ at** (*lit*) viser; (*fig*) viser, aspirer à; *see* **high.**

aimless ['eɪmlɪs] **adj** *person, way of life* sans but, désœuvré; *pursuit* sans objet, qui ne mène à rien, futile.

aimlessly ['eɪmlɪslɪ] **adv** *wander* sans but; *stand around* sans trop savoir que faire; *chat, kick ball about* pour passer le temps.

ain't‡ [eɪnt] = **am not, is not, are not, has not, have not;** *see* **be, have.**

air [ɛəʳ] 1 **n** a air *m*. **in the open ~** en plein air; **a change of ~** un changement d'air; **I need some ~!** j'ai besoin d'air!; **to go out for a breath of (fresh) ~** sortir prendre l'air *or* le frais; **to take the ~†** prendre le frais; **to transport by ~** transporter par avion; **to go by ~** aller en *or* voyager par avion; **to throw sth (up) into the ~** jeter qch en l'air; **the balloon rose up into the ~** le ballon s'est élevé (dans les airs); **(seen) from the ~** vu d'en haut.

b (*fig phrases*) **there's sth in the ~** il se prépare qch, il se trame qch; **it's still all in the ~** ce ne sont encore que des projets en l'air *or* de vagues projets; **all her plans were up in the ~** (*vague*) tous ses projets étaient vagues *or* flous; **all her plans have gone up in the ~** (*destroyed*) tous ses projets sont tombés à l'eau; **there's a rumour in the ~ that ...** le bruit court que ...; **he went up in the ~* when he heard the news** (*in anger*) il a bondi en apprenant la nouvelle; (*in excitement*) il a sauté d'enthousiasme en apprenant la nouvelle; **to be up in the ~ about*** (*an-*

gry) être très monté *or* très en colère à l'idée de; (*excited*) être tout en émoi *or* très excité à l'idée de; **I can't live on ~** je ne peux pas vivre de l'air du temps; **to be walking** *or* **treading on ~** être aux anges, ne pas se sentir de joie; (*US*) **to give sb the ~*** *[employer]* virer* *or* renvoyer qn; *[girlfriend etc]* plaquer‡ qn; *see* **castle, hot, mid**[1], **thin.**

c **on the ~** (*Rad*) à la radio, sur les ondes, à l'antenne; (*TV*) à l'antenne; **you're on the ~** vous êtes à *or* avez l'antenne; **he's on the ~ every day** il parle à la radio tous les jours; **the station is on the ~** la station émet; **the programme goes** *or* **is put on the ~ every week** l'émission passe (sur l'antenne) *or* est diffusée toutes les semaines; **to go off the ~** quitter l'antenne.

d (†: *breeze*) brise *f*, léger souffle.

e (*manner*) aspect *m*, mine *f*, air *m*. **with an ~ of bewilderment** d'un air perplexe; **with a proud ~** d'un air fier, avec une mine hautaine; **she has an ~ about her** elle a de l'allure, elle a un certain chic; **to put on ~s, to give o.s. ~s** se donner de grands airs; **~s and graces** minauderies *fpl*; **to put on ~s and graces** minauder.

f (*Mus*) air *m*.

2 **vt** a *clothes, room, bed* aérer.

b *anger* exhaler; *opinions* faire connaître; *idea, proposal* mettre sur le tapis.

c (* *US: broadcast*) diffuser.

3 **comp** ▸ **air alert** alerte aérienne ▸ **air bag** (*Aut*) sac *m* gonflable (*en cas de collision*) ▸ **air base** base aérienne ▸ **air bed** (*Brit*) matelas *m* pneumatique ▸ **airborne** *troops* aéroporté; **the plane was airborne** l'avion avait décollé ▸ **air brake** (*on truck*) frein *m* à air comprimé; (*Aviat*) frein aérodynamique, aérofrein *m* ▸ **air brick** (*Constr*) brique évidée *or* creuse ▸ **air bridge** pont aérien ▸ **air brush** aérographe ® *m* ▸ **air bubble** (*in liquids*) bulle *f* d'air; (*in glass, metal*) soufflure *f* ▸ **air burst** explosion aérienne ▸ **air chamber** (*Aut, Physiol*) chambre *f* à air ▸ **air chief marshal** (*Brit*) général *m* d'armée aérienne ▸ **air commodore** (*Brit*) général *m* de brigade aérienne ▸ **air-conditioned** climatisé ▸ **air conditioner** climatiseur *m* ▸ **air conditioning** climatisation *f* ▸ **air-cooled** *engine* à refroidissement par air; (*US* *) *room* climatisé ▸ **air corridor** couloir aérien ▸ **air cover** couverture aérienne ▸ **aircraft pl inv** avion *m* ▸ **aircraft carrier** porte-avions *m inv* ▸ **aircraft(s)man** (*Brit*) soldat *m* de deuxième classe (de l'armée de l'air) ▸ **aircrew** équipage *m* (*d'un avion*) ▸ **air current** courant *m* atmosphérique ▸ **air cushion** coussin *m* pneumatique; (*Tech*) matelas *m or* coussin d'air ▸ **air cylinder** cylindre *m* à air comprimé ▸ **air disaster** catastrophe aérienne ▸ **air display** fête *f* aéronautique, meeting *m* d'aviation ▸ **airdrome** (*US*) aérodrome *m* ▸ **airdrop vt** parachuter ◊ **n** parachutage *m* ▸ **air-dry** sécher à l'air ▸ **air duct** (*Tech*) conduit *m* d'air *or* d'aération ▸ **air express** (*US*) cargo aérien ▸ **airfare** prix *m* d'un (*or* du) billet d'avion ▸ **air ferry** avion transbordeur ▸ **airfield** terrain *m* d'aviation, (petit) aérodrome *m* ▸ **air filter** filtre *m* à air ▸ **air flow** courant *m* atmosphérique; (*in wind tunnel*) écoulement *m* d'air ▸ **air force** armée *f* de l'air, aviation *f* militaire ▸ **Air Force One** (*US*) l'avion présidentiel ▸ **air-force blue** bleu pétrole *inv* ▸ **airframe** cellule *f* (d'avion) ▸ **airframe industry** industrie *f* de la construction des cellules aéronautiques ▸ **air freight** (*goods*) fret aérien; (*method*) transport aérien; **to send by air freight** expédier par voie aérienne ▸ **air guitar** (*hum*) *guitare imaginaire que l'on fait semblant de jouer en écoutant de la musique* ▸ **airgun** fusil *m or* carabine *f* à air comprimé ▸ **air hole** trou *m* d'aération ▸ **air hostess** hôtesse *f* de l'air ▸ **air intake** entrée *f* d'air, prise *f* d'air ▸ **air lane** couloir aérien *or* de navigation aérienne ▸ **air letter** aérogramme *m* ▸ **airlift n** pont aérien ◊ **vt** évacuer (*or* amener *etc*) par pont aérien ▸ **airline** (*Aviat*) ligne aérienne, compagnie *f* d'aviation; (*diver's*) voie *f* d'air ▸ **airliner** avion *m* de ligne, (avion) long-courrier *m or* moyen-courrier *m* ▸ **airlock** (*in spacecraft, caisson etc*) sas *m*; (*in pipe*) bouchon *m or* bulle *f* d'air ▸ **airmail** *see* **airmail** ▸ **airman** aviateur *m*; (*Brit Aviat*) soldat *m* (de l'armée de l'air); (*US Aviat*) soldat *m* de première classe ▸ **airman first class** (*US*) caporal *m* ▸ **air marshal** général *m* de corps aérien ▸ **air mass** (*Met*) masse *f* d'air ▸ **air mattress** matelas *m* pneumatique ▸ **air miss** quasi-collision *f* ▸ **airmobile** (*US Mil*) aéroporté ▸ **airplane** (*US*) avion *m* ▸ **airplay** (*Rad*) temps *m* de passage à l'antenne; **to get a lot of airplay** passer souvent à l'antenne ▸ **air pocket** trou *m or* poche *f* d'air ▸ **airport** aéroport *m* ▸ **airport lounge** salon *m* d'aéroport ▸ **airport tax(es)** taxes *fpl* d'aéroport ▸ **air power** puissance aérienne ▸ **air pressure** pression *f* atmosphérique ▸ **air pump** compresseur *m*, machine *f* pneumatique ▸ **air purifier** purificateur *m* d'air ▸ **air raid** attaque aérienne, raid aérien ▸ **air-raid precautions** défense passive ▸ **air-raid shelter** abri antiaérien ▸ **air-raid warden** préposé(e) *m(f)* à la défense passive ▸ **air-raid warning** alerte *f* (aérienne) ▸ **air rifle** carabine *f* à air comprimé ▸ **airscrew** (*Brit*) hélice *f* (*d'avion*) ▸ **air-sea base** base aéronavale ▸ **air-sea rescue** sauvetage *m* en mer (*par hélicoptère etc*) ▸ **air shaft** (*Min*) puits *m* d'aérage; (*Naut*) manche *f* à vent ▸ **airshed** hangar *m* (d'aviation) ▸ **airship** (ballon *m*) dirigeable *m* ▸ **air show** (*trade exhibition*) salon *m* de l'aéronautique; (*flying display*) meeting *m or* rallye *m* d'aviation ▸ **air shuttle** navette aérienne ▸ **airsick: to be airsick** avoir le mal de l'air ▸ **airsickness** mal *m* de l'air ▸ **air sock** manche *f* à air ▸ **air space** espace aérien; **French air space** l'espace aérien français ▸ **airspeed** (*Aviat*) vitesse relative ▸ **airspeed indicator** badin *m* ▸ **air stream** courant *m* atmosphérique; (*Ling*) colonne *f* d'air ▸ **airstrip** piste *f* d'atterrissage ▸ **air superiority** supériorité aérienne ▸ **air suspension** (*Aut*) suspension *f* pneumatique ▸ **air terminal** aérogare *f* ▸ **airtight** hermétique, étanche (à l'air) ▸ **air time** temps *m* d'antenne ▸ **air-to-air** (*Mil*) air-air *inv*, avion-avion *inv* ▸ **air-to-ground, air-to-surface** (*Mil*) air-sol *inv* ▸ **air-to-sea** air-mer *inv* ▸ **air traffic control** contrôle *m* du trafic aérien ▸ **air traffic controller** contrôleur *m*, -euse *f* de la navigation aérienne, aiguilleur *m* du ciel ▸ **airtrap*: to airtrap from coast to coast*** traverser le continent en faisant de nombreuses escales ▸ **air valve** soupape *f* ▸ **air vent** prise *f* d'air ▸ **air vice marshal** (*Brit*) général *m* de division aérienne ▸ **air waves** ondes *fpl* (hertziennes); **on the air waves** (*on radio*) sur les ondes ▸ **airway** (*route*) voie aérienne; (*airline company*) compagnie *f* d'aviation; (*ventilator shaft*) conduit *m* d'air ▸ **airwoman** aviatrice *f*; (*in Air Force*) (femme *f*) auxiliaire *f* (de l'armée de l'air) ▸ **airworthiness** navigabilité *f* (*see* **certificate a**) ▸ **airworthy** en état de navigation.

Airedale ['ɛədeɪl] **n** airedale *m*.

airily ['ɛərɪlɪ] **adv** légèrement, d'un ton dégagé, avec désinvolture *or* insouciance.

airiness ['ɛərɪnɪs] **n** *[room]* aération *f*, (bonne) ventilation *f*; (*fig*) *[manner]* désinvolture *f*, insouciance *f*.

airing ['ɛərɪŋ] 1 **n** *[linen]* aération *f*. (*fig*) **to go for** *or* **take an ~*** (aller) prendre l'air, faire un petit tour; (*fig*) **to give an idea an ~** mettre une idée en discussion *or* sur le tapis. 2 **comp** ▸ **airing cupboard** (*Brit*) placard-séchoir *m*.

airless ['ɛəlɪs] **adj** a *room* privé d'air. **it is ~ in here** il n'y a pas d'air ici, cela sent le renfermé ici. b *weather* lourd.

airmail ['ɛəmeɪl] 1 **n** poste aérienne. **by ~** par avion. 2 **vt** *letter, parcel* expédier par avion. 3 **comp** ▸ **airmail edition** édition *f* par avion ▸ **airmail letter** lettre *f* par avion ▸ **airmail paper** papier *m* pelure ▸ **airmail stamp, airmail sticker** étiquette *f* "par avion".

airy ['ɛərɪ] 1 **adj** a *room* clair. b (*immaterial*) léger, impalpable, éthéré. c (*casual*) *manner* léger, désinvolte, dégagé. **~ promises** promesses *fpl* en l'air *or* vaines. 2 **comp** ▸ **airy-fairy*** (*Brit*) *idea, person* farfelu.

aisle [aɪl] **n** a *[church]* bas-côté *m*, nef latérale; (*between pews*) allée centrale. **to take a girl up the ~** mener une jeune fille à l'autel; (*after wedding*) **when they were walking down the ~** alors qu'ils sortaient de l'église. b *[theatre, cinema]* allée *f*; *[plane, train, coach]* couloir *m* (central). (*on plane etc*) **~ seat** place *f* côté couloir.

aitch [eɪtʃ] **n** (*letter*) H, h *m or f*. (*Culin*) **~ bone** culotte *f* (de bœuf); *see* **drop.**

Ajaccio [ə'ʒæsjəʊ] **n** Ajaccio.

ajar [ə'dʒɑːʳ] **adj, adv** entrouvert, entrebâillé.

Ajax ['eɪdʒæks] **n** Ajax *m*.

AK. (*US*) **abbr of Alaska.**

a.k.a., AKA **abbr of also known as.**

akimbo [ə'kɪmbəʊ] **adj: with arms ~** les poings sur les hanches.

akin [ə'kɪn] **adj: ~ to** (*similar*) qui tient de, qui ressemble à, analogue à; (*of same family as*) parent de, apparenté à.

AL, Al(a). (*US*) **abbr of Alabama.**

Alabama [ˌælə'bæmə] **n** Alabama *m*. **in ~** dans l'Alabama.

alabaster ['æləbɑːstəʳ] 1 **n** albâtre *m*. 2 **comp** (*lit, fig*) d'albâtre.

alacrity [ə'lækrɪtɪ] **n** empressement *m*, promptitude *f*, alacrité *f*.

Aladdin [ə'lædɪn] **n** Aladin *m*.

Alan ['ælən] **n** Alain *m*.

alarm [ə'lɑːm] 1 **n** a (*warning*) alarme *f*, alerte *f*. **to raise the ~** donner l'alarme *or* l'éveil; **~s and excursions** (*Theat*) bruits *mpl* de bataille en coulisse; (*fig*) branle-bas *m* de combat; *see* **burglar, false.**

b (*NonC: fear*) inquiétude *f*, alarme *f*. **to cause sb ~** mettre qn dans l'inquiétude, alarmer qn.

c = **~ clock;** *see* **3.**

2 **vt** a (*frighten*) *person* alarmer, éveiller des craintes chez; *animal, bird* effaroucher, faire peur à. **to become ~ed** *[person]* prendre peur, s'alarmer; *[animal]* prendre peur, s'effaroucher.

b (*warn*) alerter, alarmer.

3 **comp** ▸ **alarm bell** sonnerie *f* d'alarme ▸ **alarm call** appel *m* du service réveil; **I'd like an alarm call (for ...)** je voudrais être réveillé (à ...) ▸ **alarm clock** réveil *m*, réveille-matin *m inv* ▸ **alarm signal** signal *m* d'alarme ▸ **alarm system** système *m* d'alarme.

alarming [ə'lɑːmɪŋ] **adj** alarmant.

alarmingly [ə'lɑːmɪŋlɪ] **adv** d'une manière alarmante.

alarmist [ə'lɑːmɪst] **adj, n** alarmiste *(mf)*.

Alas. (*US*) **abbr of Alaska.**

alas [ə'læs] **excl** hélas!

Alaska [ə'læskə] **n** Alaska *m*. **in ~** en Alaska; **~ Highway** route *f* de l'Alaska; **~ Range** chaîne *f* de l'Alaska; *see* **bake.**

Alaskan [ə'læskən] 1 **n** habitant(e) *m(f)* de l'Alaska. 2 **adj** de l'Alaska.

alb [ælb] **n** aube *f* (*d'un prêtre*).

Albania [æl'beɪnɪə] **n** Albanie *f*.

Albanian [æl'beɪnɪən] 1 adj albanais. 2 n a Albanais(e) *m(f)*. b (*Ling*) albanais *m*.
albatross ['ælbətrɒs] n albatros *m* (*also Brit Golf*).
albeit [ɔːl'biːɪt] conj (*liter*) encore que + *subj*, bien que + *subj*.
Albert ['ælbɜːt] n Albert *m*.
Alberta [æl'bɜːtə] n (*Geog*) Alberta *f*.
Albigensian [ˌælbɪ'dʒensɪən] 1 n Albigeois(e) *m(f)*. 2 adj albigeois.
albinism ['ælbɪnɪzəm] n albinisme *m*.
albino [æl'biːnəʊ] n albinos *mf*. ~ **rabbit** lapin *m* albinos.
Albion ['ælbɪən] n Albion *f*.
album ['ælbəm] n (*book, long-playing record*) album *m*.
albumen, albumin ['ælbjʊmɪn] n (*egg white*) albumen *m*, blanc *m* de l'œuf; (*Bot*) albumen; (*Physiol*) albumine *f*.
albuminous [æl'bjuːmɪnəs] adj albumineux.
Alcestis [æl'sestɪs] n Alceste *f*.
alchemist ['ælkɪmɪst] n alchimiste *m*.
alchemy ['ælkɪmɪ] n (*lit, fig*) alchimie *f*.
alcohol ['ælkəhɒl] n alcool *m*. ~ **abuse** abus *m* d'alcool; *[drink]* ~ **content** teneur *f* en alcool.
alcoholic [ˌælkə'hɒlɪk] 1 adj *person* alcoolique; *drink* alcoolisé, alcoolique. 2 n alcoolique *mf*. **A~s Anonymous** Alcooliques *mpl* anonymes.
alcoholism ['ælkəhɒlɪzəm] n alcoolisme *m*.
alcove ['ælkəʊv] n (*in room*) alcôve *f*; (*in wall*) niche *f*; (*in garden*) tonnelle *f*, berceau *m*.
alder ['ɔːldəʳ] n aulne *m* or aune *m*.
alderman ['ɔːldəmən] n alderman *m*, conseiller *m*, -ère *f* municipal(e); (*Hist*) échevin *m*.
ale [eɪl] n bière *f*, ale *f*; *see* **brown, light², pale¹**.
aleatoric [ˌælɪə'tɒrɪk] adj (*Mus*) aléatoire.
Alec ['ælɪk] n (**dim of Alexander**) Alex *m*; *see* **smart**.
Aleppo [ə'lepəʊ] n Alep.
alert [ə'lɜːt] 1 n alerte *f*. **to give the** ~ donner l'alerte; **on the** ~ (*gen*) sur le qui-vive; (*Mil*) en état d'alerte. 2 adj (*watchful*) vigilant; (*bright*) alerte, vif; *child* éveillé. 3 vt alerter; (*fig*) éveiller l'attention de (*to* sur). **we are now ~ed to the dangers** notre attention est maintenant éveillée sur les dangers, nous sommes maintenant sensibilisés aux dangers.
alertness [ə'lɜːtnɪs] n (*see* **alert 2**) vigilance *f*; vivacité *f*; esprit éveillé.
Aleutian [ə'luːʃən] adj: ~ **Islands**, ~**s** (îles *fpl*) Aléoutiennes *fpl*.
alevin ['ælɪvɪn] n alevin *m*.
alewife ['ælwaɪf] n (sorte *f* d')alose *f*.
Alexander [ˌælɪg'zɑːndəʳ] n Alexandre *m*.
Alexandria [ˌælɪg'zɑːndrɪə] n Alexandrie.
alexandrine [ˌælɪg'zændraɪn] adj, n alexandrin (*m*).
alfalfa [æl'fælfə] n luzerne *f*.
Alfonso [ˌæl'fɒnsəʊ] n Alphonse *m*.
Alfred ['ælfrɪd] n Alfred *m*.
alfresco [æl'freskəʊ] adj, adv en plein air.
alga ['ælgə] n, pl **algae** ['ældʒiː] (*gen pl*) algue(s) *f(pl)*.
algebra ['ældʒɪbrə] n algèbre *f*.
algebraic [ˌældʒɪ'breɪɪk] adj algébrique.
Algeria [æl'dʒɪərɪə] n Algérie *f*.
Algerian [æl'dʒɪərɪən] 1 n Algérien(ne) *m(f)*. 2 adj algérien.
Algiers [æl'dʒɪəz] n Alger.
ALGOL ['ælgɒl] n (*Comput*) ALGOL *m*.
Algonquian [ˌæl'gɒŋkwɪən], **Algonquin** [æl'gɒŋkwɪn] adj algonquin, algonkin.
algorithm ['ælgəˌrɪðəm] n (*Comput, Ling*) algorithme *m*.
algorithmic [ˌælgə'rɪ'ðmɪk] adj algorithmique.
Alhambra [ˌæl'hæmbrə] n Alhambra *m*.
alias ['eɪlɪæs] 1 adv alias. 2 n faux nom, nom d'emprunt; *[writer]* pseudonyme *m*.
Ali Baba ['ælɪ'bɑːbə] n Ali Baba *m*.
alibi ['ælɪbaɪ] 1 n (*Police*) alibi *m*; (*: *gen*) excuse *f*, alibi (*hum*). 2 vi (* *US*) trouver des excuses (*for sth* pour expliquer qch; *for doing sth* pour avoir fait qch). 3 vt (* *US*) **to** ~ **sb** trouver des excuses à qn.
Alice ['ælɪs] n Alice *f*. ~ **band** bandeau *m* (*pour les cheveux*); ~ **in Wonderland** Alice au pays des merveilles.
alien ['eɪlɪən] 1 n (*from abroad*) étranger *m*, -ère *f*; (*from outer space*) extra-terrestre *mf*. 2 adj a (*foreign*) étranger; (*from outer space*) extra-terrestre. b (*different*) ~ **to sth** contraire à qch, opposé à qch; **cruelty is** ~ **to him** la cruauté lui est étrangère, il ne sait pas ce que c'est que la cruauté *or* que d'être cruel.
alienate ['eɪlɪəneɪt] vt (*also Jur*) aliéner. **this has ~d all his friends** ceci (lui) a aliéné tous ses amis; **she has ~d all her friends** elle s'est aliéné tous ses amis (*by doing* en faisant).
alienated ['eɪlɪəneɪtɪd] adj (*estranged*) étranger (*from* à); (*Psych*) aliéné. **to become** ~ **from** se détacher de.
alienation [ˌeɪlɪə'neɪʃən] n a (*estrangement*) désaffection *f*, éloignement *m* (*from* de). b (*Jur, Psych*) aliénation *f*.
alienist ['eɪlɪənɪst] n aliéniste *mf*.
alight¹ [ə'laɪt] vi *[person]* descendre (*from* de), mettre pied à terre; *[bird]* se poser (*on* sur).
►**alight on** vt fus *fact* apprendre par hasard; *idea* tomber sur.
alight² [ə'laɪt] adj *fire* allumé; *building* en feu. **keep the fire** ~ ne laissez pas éteindre le feu; **to set sth** ~ mettre le feu à qch; (*fig*) **her face was** ~ **with pleasure** son visage rayonnait de joie.
align [ə'laɪn] 1 vt a aligner, mettre en ligne; (*Tech*) dégauchir. b (*Fin, Pol*) aligner (*on, with* sur). **to** ~ **o.s. with sb** s'aligner sur qn; **the non-~ed countries** les pays non-alignés *or* neutralistes. 2 vi *[persons]* s'aligner (*with* sur); *[objects]* être alignés.
alignment [ə'laɪnmənt] n (*lit, fig*) alignement *m*; (*Aut*) parallélisme *m*; *see* **non-alignment**.
alike [ə'laɪk] 1 adj semblable, pareil, égal. *[people]* **to be** ~ se ressembler, être semblables; **it's all** ~ **to me** cela m'est tout à fait égal, je n'ai pas de préférence. 2 adv *treat, speak* de la même façon. **winter and summer** ~ été comme hiver; **they always think** ~ ils sont toujours du même avis; **to dress** ~ s'habiller de la même façon.
alimentary [ˌælɪ'mentərɪ] adj alimentaire. ~ **canal** tube digestif.
alimony ['ælɪmənɪ] n (*Jur*) pension *f* alimentaire.
aliterate [eɪ'lɪtərət] 1 n ennemi(e) *m(f)* de la lecture. 2 adj antilecture.
alive [ə'laɪv] adj a (*living*) vivant, en vie, vif; (*in existence*) au monde. **to burn** ~ brûler vif; **to bury sb** ~ enterrer qn vivant; **while** ~, **he was always** ... de son vivant, il était toujours ...; **it's good to be** ~ il fait bon vivre; **no man** ~ personne au monde; **to do sth as well as anyone** ~ faire qch aussi bien que n'importe qui; **to keep** ~ (*lit*) *person* maintenir en vie; **to stay** ~ rester en vie, survivre.
b (*fig: lively*) **to bring** ~ *meeting etc* animer; *past* faire revivre; **to keep** ~ *tradition* préserver; *memory* garder; **to come** ~ s'animer.
c ~ **to** sensible à; **I am very** ~ **to the honour you do me** je suis très sensible à l'honneur que vous me faites; **to be** ~ **to one's interests** veiller à ses intérêts; **to be** ~ **to a danger** être conscient d'un danger.
d (*alert*) alerte, vif; (*active*) actif, plein de vie. **to be** ~ **and kicking*** (*living*) être bien en vie; (*full of energy*) être plein de vie; **look** ~!* allons, remuez-vous!*
e ~ **with insects** grouillant d'insectes.
alkali ['ælkəlaɪ] n, pl ~**s** *or* ~**es** alcali *m*.
alkaline ['ælkəlaɪn] adj alcalin.
alkalinity [ˌælkə'lɪnɪtɪ] n alcalinité *f*.
alkaloid ['ælkəlɔɪd] n alcaloïde *m*.
all [ɔːl] 1 adj a (*every one of, the whole*) tout (le), toute (la), tous (les), toutes (les). ~ **the country** tout le pays, le pays tout entier; ~ **my life** toute ma vie; **people of** ~ **countries** les gens de tous les pays; ~ **the others** tous (*or* toutes) les autres; ~ **you boys** vous (tous) les garçons; ~ **three** tous (*or* toutes) les trois; ~ **three men** les trois hommes; ~ **three said the same** tous les trois ont dit la même chose; ~ **(the) day** toute la journée; **to dislike** ~ **sport** détester le sport *or* tout (genre de) sport; ~ **that** tout cela; **and** ~ **that (kind of thing)** et tout ça, et que sais-je (encore); **it's not as bad as** ~ **that** ce n'est pas (vraiment) si mal que ça; **for** ~ **that** malgré tout, en dépit de tout cela; ~ **kinds of,** ~ **sorts of,** ~ **manner of** toutes sortes de; **it is beyond** ~ **doubt** c'est indéniable *or* incontestable; **why ask me of** ~ **people?** pourquoi me le demander à moi?; ~ **things considered** à tout prendre.
b (*the utmost*) tout, le plus possible. **with** ~ **haste** en toute hâte; **with** ~ **(possible) care** avec tout le soin possible.
2 pron a (*the whole amount, everything*) tout *m*. ~ **is well** tout va bien; **that is** ~ c'est tout, voilà tout; **if that's** ~ **then it's not important** s'il n'y a que cela *or* si ce n'est que cela alors ce n'est pas important; ~ **in good time** chaque chose en son temps; **when** ~ **is said and done** somme toute, en fin de compte, tout compte fait; **and I don't know what** ~* et je ne sais quoi encore; **what with the snow and** ~* **we didn't go** avec la neige et (tout) le reste* nous n'y sommes pas allés; ~ **of the house** toute la maison; ~ **of it was lost** (le) tout a été perdu; **he drank** ~ **of it** il a tout bu, il l'a bu en entier; ~ **of Paris** Paris tout entier; ~ **or nothing** tout ou rien; **that is** ~ **he said** c'est tout ce qu'il a dit; ~ **I want is to sleep** tout ce que je veux c'est dormir; **he saw** ~ **there was to see** il a vu tout ce qu'il y avait à voir; ~ **that is in the box is yours** tout ce qui est dans la boîte est à vous; **bring it** ~ apportez le tout.
b (*pl*) tous *mpl*, toutes *fpl*. **we** ~ **sat down** nous nous sommes tous assis (*or* toutes assises); **the girls** ~ **knew that** ... les jeunes filles savaient toutes que ...; ~ **of them failed** ils ont tous échoué, tous ont échoué; ~ **of the boys came** tous les garçons sont venus, les garçons sont tous venus; **they were** ~ **broken** ils étaient tous cassés; **one and** ~ tous sans exception; ~ **who knew him loved him** tous ceux qui l'ont connu l'ont aimé; ~ **(whom) I saw said that** ... tous ceux que j'ai vus ont dit que ...; **evening,** ~!* bonsoir, tout le monde!; **the score was two** ~ (*Tennis*) le score était deux partout; (*other sports*) le score était deux à deux; *see* **each, sundry**.
c (*in phrases*) **if she comes at** ~ si tant est qu'elle vienne; **do you think she will come at** ~**?** croyez-vous seulement qu'elle vienne?; **very rarely if at** ~ très rarement si tant est, très rarement et encore; **I don't know at** ~ je n'en sais rien (du tout); **if you study this author at** ~ pour peu que vous étudiiez cet auteur; **if there is any water at** ~ si seulement il y a de l'eau; **if at** ~ **possible** dans la mesure du possible;

are you going? — **not at ~** vous y allez? — pas du tout; **thank you!** — **not at ~!** merci! — je vous en prie! *or* (il n'y a) pas de quoi! *or* de rien!*; **it was ~ I could do to stop him from leaving** c'est à peine *or* tout juste si j'ai pu l'empêcher de s'en aller; **it was ~ I could do not to laugh** c'est à peine *or* tout juste si j'ai pu m'empêcher de rire, j'ai eu toutes les peines du monde à m'empêcher de rire; **it isn't ~ that expensive!*** ce n'est pas si cher que ça!; **that's ~ very well but** ... tout cela est bien beau *or* joli mais ...; **~ in ~** ... (*adding everything*) en tout; (*all things considered*) l'un dans l'autre; **taking it ~ in ~** à tout prendre; **she is ~ in ~ to him** elle est tout pour lui; **~ but** presque, à peu de choses près; **~ but finished/dead** *etc* pratiquement fini/mort *etc;* **he ~ but lost it** c'est tout juste s'il ne l'a pas perdu, il a bien failli le perdre; **the film was ~ but over** le film touchait à sa fin; **for ~ I know** autant que je sache; **for ~ his wealth he was unhappy** toute sa fortune ne l'empêchait pas d'être malheureux; **for ~ he may say** quoi qu'il en dise; **once and for ~** une fois pour toutes; **most of ~** surtout; **it would be best of ~ if he resigned, the best of ~ would be for him to resign** le mieux serait qu'il donne (*subj*) sa démission.

3 **adv** a (*quite, entirely*) tout, tout à fait, complètement. **~ of a sudden** tout à coup, tout d'un coup, soudain, subitement; **~ too soon it was time to go** malheureusement il a bientôt fallu partir; **the evening passed ~ too quickly** la soirée n'est passée que trop rapidement; **dressed ~ in white** habillé tout en blanc, tout habillé de blanc; **she was ~ ears** elle était tout oreilles; **~ along the road** tout le long de la route; **I feared that ~ along** je l'ai craint depuis le début; **he won the race ~ the same** il a néanmoins *or* tout de même gagné la course; **it's ~ the same to me** cela m'est tout à fait égal, peu m'importe; **it's ~ one to them** cela leur est entièrement égal; **~ over** (*everywhere*) partout, d'un bout à l'autre; (*finished*) fini; **covered ~ over with dust** tout couvert de poussière; **the match was ~ over before** ... le match était fini *or* terminé avant ...; **to be ~ over sb*** *see* **over 2e; suddenly he was ~ over me** tout à coup il s'est jeté sur moi; **to be ~ for sth*** être tout à fait en faveur de qch; **I'm ~ for it*** je suis tout à fait pour*; **to be ~ for doing*** ne demander qu'à faire, vouloir à toute force faire; **~ in one piece** tout d'une pièce; **to be ~ in*** être éreinté, n'en pouvoir plus, être à bout*; **to be ~ there*** être sain d'esprit, avoir toute sa tête; **she's not quite ~ there*** il lui manque une case*; **it is ~ up with him*** il est fichu*; **~ at one go** d'un seul coup; *see* **all right, over 1c, over 2e, square.**

b (*with comps*) **~ the better!** tant mieux!; **~ the more ... as** d'autant plus ... que; **~ the more so since** ... d'autant plus que ... .

4 **n: I would give my ~ to see him** je donnerais tout ce que j'ai pour le voir; **to stake one's ~** risquer le tout pour le tout; **she had staked her ~ on his coming** elle avait tout misé sur sa venue.

5 **comp ▸all-American** cent pour cent américain **▸all-around** (*US*) *see* **all-round ▸all clear: all clear!** fin d'alerte!; **all clear (signal)** (*lit*) (signal *m* de) fin *f* d'alerte; (*fig*) **to give sb the all clear** (*gen*) donner le feu vert à qn; (*doctor to patient*) dire à qn que tout va bien **▸all-day** qui dure toute la journée **▸all-embracing** qui embrasse tout, compréhensif **▸all-fired*** (*US*) rudement* **▸All Fools' Day** le premier avril **▸all found** logé et nourri **▸all fours: on all fours** à quatre pattes **▸all get-out**‡: (*US*) **angry** *etc* **as all get-out** vachement* en colère **▸All Hallows** la Toussaint **▸all-important** de la plus haute importance, capital **▸all in** *see* **all 3a ▸all-in** (*Brit*) *price* net, tout compris; *insurance policy* tous risques; (*Comm*) *tariff* inclusif; (*Brit*) **the holiday cost £80 all-in** les vacances ont coûté 80 livres tout compris **▸all-in wrestling** lutte *f* libre, catch *m* **▸all-inclusive** *price, rate* tout compris, net; *policy* tous risques **▸all-metal body** (*Aut*) carrosserie toute en tôle **▸all-nighter** *film, concert etc qui dure toute la nuit* **▸all-night pass** (*Mil*) permission *f* de nuit **▸all-night service** (*Comm etc*) permanence *f* de nuit, service *m* de nuit **▸all-night showing** (*Cine*) spectacle *m* de nuit **▸all out: to go all out** (*gen*) faire tout son possible; (*physically*) y mettre toutes ses forces **▸all-out effort** effort *m* maximum **▸all-out strike** grève totale **▸all-out war** guerre totale **▸allover** (qui est) sur toute la surface **▸allover pattern** dessin *m or m* qui recouvre toute une surface **▸all-points bulletin** (*US*) message *m* à toutes les patrouilles (*on* à propos de) **▸all-powerful** tout-puissant **▸all-purpose** qui répond à tous les besoins; *knife, spanner* universel **▸all-right** *see* **all-right ▸all-round** *sportsman* complet (*f* -ète); *improvement* général, sur toute la ligne **▸all-risks insurance** assurance *f* tous risques **▸all-rounder: to be a good all-rounder** être solide en tout *or* bon en tout **▸All Saints' Day** (le jour de) la Toussaint **▸All Souls' Day** le jour *or* la fête des Morts **▸allspice** quatre-épices *m inv* **▸all-star:** (*Theat*) **all-star performance, show with an all-star cast** plateau *m* de vedettes **▸all-terrain vehicle** véhicule *m* tout-terrain **▸all-time** *see* **all-time ▸all told** en tout **▸all-weather** de toute saison, tous temps **▸all-weather court** (terrain *m* en) quick *m* ® **▸all-wheel-drive** quatre (*or* six *etc*) roues motrices **▸all-the-year-round** *sport* que l'on pratique toute l'année; *resort* ouvert toute l'année.

Allah ['ælə] **n** Allah *m.*

allay [ə'leɪ] **vt** *fears* modérer, apaiser; *pain, thirst* soulager, apaiser. **to ~ suspicion** dissiper les soupçons.

allegation [ˌælɪ'geɪʃən] **n** allégation *f.*

allege [ə'ledʒ] **vt** alléguer, prétendre (*that* que). **to ~ illness** prétexter *or* alléguer une maladie; **he is ~d to have said that** ... il aurait dit que ..., on prétend qu'il a dit que ... .

alleged [ə'ledʒd] **adj** *reason* allégué, prétendu; *thief, author* présumé.

allegedly [ə'ledʒɪdlɪ] **adv** à ce que l'on prétend, paraît-il.

allegiance [ə'liːdʒəns] **n** allégeance *f* (*to* à). (*Brit*) **the oath of ~** le serment d'allégeance.

allegoric(al) [ˌælɪ'gɒrɪk(əl)] **adj** allégorique.

allegorically [ˌælɪ'gɒrɪkəlɪ] **adv** sous forme d'allégorie, allégoriquement.

allegory ['ælɪgərɪ] **n** allégorie *f.*

alleluia [ˌælɪ'luːjə] **excl** alléluia!

allergen ['ælədʒen] **n** allergène *m.*

allergenic [ˌælə'dʒenɪk] **adj** allergène.

allergic [ə'lɜːdʒɪk] **adj** (*Med,* * *fig*) allergique (*to* à).

allergist ['ælədʒɪst] **n** allergologiste *mf*, allergologue *mf.*

allergy ['ælədʒɪ] **n** allergie *f* (*to* à).

alleviate [ə'liːvɪeɪt] **vt** *pain* alléger, soulager, calmer; *sorrow* adoucir; *thirst* apaiser, calmer.

alleviation [əˌliːvɪ'eɪʃən] **n** (*see* **alleviate**) allègement *m*, soulagement *m*; adoucissement *m*; apaisement *m.*

alley[1] ['ælɪ] 1 **n** (*between buildings*) ruelle *f*; (*in garden*) allée *f*; (*US: between counters*) passage *m.* (*fig*) **this is right up my ~*** c'est tout à fait mon rayon; *see* **blind, bowling.** 2 **comp ▸alley cat** chat *m* de gouttière; **she's got the morals of an alley cat**‡ elle couche à droite et à gauche* **▸alleyway** ruelle *f.*

alley[2] ['ælɪ] **n** (*Sport*) (grosse) bille *f*, callot *m.*

alliance [ə'laɪəns] **n** *[states]* alliance *f*, pacte *m*, union *f*; *[persons]* alliance. **to enter into an ~ with** s'allier avec.

allied ['ælaɪd] **adj** a allié, apparenté (*to* à, *with* avec). **~ nations** nations alliées *or* coalisées; (*Jur*) **~ products** produits assimilés; (*US*) **~ health professional** ≃ auxiliaire *mf* médical(e). b (*Bio*) de la même famille *or* espèce. (*fig*) **history and ~ subjects** l'histoire et sujets connexes *or* apparentés.

alligator ['ælɪgeɪtə^r] **n** alligator *m.* **~(-skin) bag** sac *m* en alligator.

alliteration [əˌlɪtə'reɪʃən] **n** allitération *f.*

alliterative [ə'lɪtərətɪv] **adj** allitératif.

allocate ['æləʊkeɪt] **vt** a (*allot*) *money, task* allouer, attribuer (*to sb* à qn); *money* affecter (*to a certain use* à un certain usage). b (*apportion*) répartir, distribuer (*among* parmi). c (*Jur, Fin*) ventiler.

allocation [ˌæləʊ'keɪʃən] **n** a (*allotting*) affectation *f*, allocation *f*; (*to individual*) attribution *f.* b (*apportioning*) répartition *f.* c (*money allocated*) part *f*, allocation *f.* d (*Jur, Fin*) ventilation *f.*

allograph ['æləˌgrɑːf] **n** (*Ling*) allographe *m.*

allomorph ['æləˌmɔːf] **n** (*Ling*) allomorphe *m.*

allopathic [ˌælə'pæθɪk] **adj** allopathique.

allopathy [ə'lɒpəθɪ] **n** (*NonC*) allopathie *f.*

allophone ['æləˌfəʊn] **n** (*Ling*) allophone *m.*

allot [ə'lɒt] **vt** a attribuer, assigner (*sth to sb* qch à qn). **everyone was ~ted a piece of land** chacun a reçu un terrain en lot; **to do sth in the time ~ted (to one)** faire qch dans le temps qui (vous) est imparti *or* assigné; **to ~ sth to a certain use** affecter *or* destiner qch à un certain usage. b (*share among group*) répartir, distribuer.

allotment [ə'lɒtmənt] **n** a (*Brit: ground for cultivation*) parcelle *f or* lopin *m* de terre (*loué pour la culture*), lotissement *m.* b (*division of shares*) partage *m*, lotissement *m*; (*distribution of shares*) distribution *f*, part *f.*

allotrope ['æləˌtrəʊp] **n** variété *f* allotropique.

allottee [əlɒ'tiː] **n** (*St Ex*) attributaire *mf.*

allow [ə'laʊ] **vt** a (*permit*) permettre, autoriser; (*tolerate*) tolérer, souffrir. **to ~ sb sth** permettre qch à qn; **to ~ sb to do** permettre à qn de faire, autoriser qn à faire; **to ~ sb in/out/past** *etc* permettre à qn d'entrer/de sortir/de passer *etc;* **to ~ sth to happen** laisser se produire qch; **to ~ o.s. to be persuaded** se laisser persuader; **~ us to help you** permettez que nous vous aidions, permettez-nous de vous aider; **we are not ~ed much freedom** on nous accorde peu de liberté; **smoking is not ~ed** il est interdit *or* défendu de fumer; **no children/dogs ~ed** interdit aux enfants/chiens; **I will not ~ such behaviour** je ne tolérerai *or* souffrirai pas une telle conduite.

b (*grant*) *money* accorder, allouer. **to ~ sb £30 a month** allouer *or* accorder à qn 30 livres par mois; (*Jur*) **to ~ sb a thousand pounds damages** accorder à qn mille livres de dommages et intérêts; **to ~ space for** prévoir *or* ménager de la place pour; (*Comm*) **to ~ sb a discount** faire bénéficier qn d'une remise, consentir une remise à qn; **~ (yourself) an hour to cross the city** comptez une heure pour traverser la ville; **~ 5 cm for shrinkage** prévoyez 5 cm (de plus) pour le cas où le tissu rétrécirait.

c (*agree as possible*) *claim* admettre.

d (*concede*) admettre, reconnaître, convenir (*that* que). **~ing that** ... en admettant que ... + *subj.*

▸allow for vt fus tenir compte de; *money spent, funds allocated* (*by deduction*) déduire pour; (*by addition*) ajouter pour. **allowing for the circumstances** compte tenu des circonstances; **after allowing for his expenses** déduction faite de *or* en tenant compte de ses dépenses; **we must allow for the cost of the wood** il faut compter (avec) le prix du bois; **allowing for the shrinking of the material** en tenant compte du rétrécissement du tissu *or* du fait que le tissu rétrécit; **to allow for all possibilities** parer à toute éventualité.

▶**allow of** vt fus admettre, souffrir.

allowable [ə'laʊəbl] adj permis, admissible, légitime; (*Tax*) déductible. ~ **against tax** déductible des impôts.

allowance [ə'laʊəns] n a (*money given to sb*) allocation *f*, rente *f*, pension *f*; (*for lodgings, food etc*) indemnité *f*; (*from separated husband*) pension *f* alimentaire; (*salary*) appointements *mpl*; (*food*) ration *f*; (*esp US: pocket money*) argent *m* de poche. **he makes his mother an** ~ il verse une rente *or* une pension à sa mère; **his father gives him an** ~ **of £100 per month** son père lui alloue 100 livres par mois *or* lui verse une mensualité de 100 livres; **rent** ~ allocation de logement; **London** ~ indemnité de vie chère pour poste basé à Londres; ~ **in kind** prestation *f* en nature; (*Mil*) ~ **for quarters** indemnité de logement; *see* **car, clothing, family** *etc*.
b (*Comm, Fin: discount*) réduction *f*, rabais *m*, concession *f*; (*: for damaged or lost goods*) réfaction *f*. **tax ~s** sommes *fpl* déductibles.
c **you must learn to make ~s** tu dois apprendre à faire la part des choses; **to make ~(s) for sb** (*excuse*) se montrer indulgent envers qn, essayer de comprendre qn; (*allow for*) **to make ~(s) for sth** tenir compte de qch, prendre qch en considération.

alloy ['ælɔɪ] 1 n alliage *m*; *[gold]* carature *f*. ~ **steel** acier allié *or* spécial; (*Aut*) ~ **wheels** roues *fpl* en alliage léger. 2 [ə'lɔɪ] vt (*Metal*) allier, faire un alliage de.

all right ['ɔːl'raɪt] 1 adj a (*satisfactory*) bien. **he's** ~ (*doubtfully*) il est correct; (*approvingly*) il est bien; **it's** ~ ça va*; (*don't worry*) ce n'est pas grave; **is it** ~ **if ...?** ça (ne) vous dérange (pas) si ...?; **that's** ~ (*don't worry*) ce n'est pas grave; **it's** *or* **that's** ~ **by me** ça me va*, ça me convient; **see you later,** ~ je te verrai plus tard, d'accord?
b (*safe, well*) **to be** ~ (*healthy*) aller bien, être en bonne santé; (*safe*) être sain et sauf.
c (*well-provided*) **to be** ~ **for money/paper** *etc* avoir assez d'argent/de papier *etc*; **we're** ~ **for the rest of our lives** nous sommes tranquilles *or* nous avons tout ce qu'il nous faut pour le restant de nos jours; **I'm** ~ **Jack*** moi, je suis peinard*.
2 excl (*in approval*) ça y est!, ça va!*; (*in agreement*) entendu!, c'est ça!; (*in exasperation*) ça va!*; **you say I was wrong. A~ but ...** vous dites que j'avais tort. D'accord *or* Admettons, mais ... .
3 adv a (*without difficulty*) sans problème. **he's getting on** ~ il se débrouille bien; **I managed that ~, but I couldn't ...** j'ai réussi à faire ça sans problème, mais je n'ai pas pu ...; **he's doing** ~ **for himself** il se débrouille bien.
b (*certainly*) **he's at home** ~ **but he's not answering the phone** il est chez lui c'est sûr, c'est simplement qu'il ne répond pas au téléphone.

all-right* ['ɔːl'raɪt] adj (*US*) **an** ~ **guy** un type sûr *or* réglo.

all-time ['ɔːl'taɪm] adj sans précédent, inouï, de tous les temps. ~ **record** record *m* sans précédent; **an** ~ **low*** un record de médiocrité; **the pound has reached an** ~ **low** la livre a atteint son niveau le plus bas.

allude [ə'luːd] vi: **to** ~ **to** *[person]* faire allusion à; *[letter etc]* avoir trait à, se rapporter à.

allure [ə'ljʊəʳ] 1 vt (*attract*) attirer; (*entice*) séduire. 2 n attirance *f*, charme *m*, attrait *m*.

alluring [ə'ljʊərɪŋ] adj attrayant, séduisant.

allusion [ə'luːʒən] n allusion *f*.

allusive [ə'luːsɪv] adj allusif, qui contient une allusion.

allusively [ə'luːsɪvlɪ] adv par allusion.

alluvial [ə'luːvɪəl] adj *ground* alluvial; *deposit* alluvionnaire.

alluvium [ə'luːvɪəm] n, pl **~s** *or* **alluvia** [ə'luːvɪə] alluvion *f*.

ally¹ [ə'laɪ] 1 vt allier, unir (*with* avec). **to** ~ **o.s. with** s'allier avec. 2 ['ælaɪ] n (*gen*) allié(e) *m(f)*; (*Pol*) allié(e), coalisé(e) *m(f)*. **the Allies** les Alliés.

ally² ['ælɪ] n = **alley²**.

alma ['ælmə] : ~ **mater** n *lycée ou université dont on est issu.*

almanac ['ɔːlmənæk] n almanach *m*, annuaire *m*; *see* **nautical.**

almighty [ɔːl'maɪtɪ] 1 adj a tout-puissant, omnipotent. **A~ God** Dieu Tout-Puissant; **the** ~ **dollar** le dollar tout-puissant. b (*) *row, scandal* formidable, fantastique. **an** ~ **din** un vacarme de tous les diables. 2 n: **the A~** le Tout-Puissant. 3 adv (*) extrêmement, énormément.

almond ['ɑːmənd] 1 n amande *f*; (*also* ~ **tree**) amandier *m*. **split ~s** amandes effilées; *see* **burnt, sugar** *etc*. 2 comp *oil, paste* d'amande ▶**almond-eyed** aux yeux en amande ▶**almond-shaped** en amande.

almoner† ['ɑːmənəʳ] n (*Brit*) **(lady)** ~ assistante sociale (*attachée à un hôpital*).

almost ['ɔːlməʊst] adv presque. **it is** ~ **midnight** il est presque *or* bientôt minuit; ~ **always** presque toujours; **he** ~ **fell** il a failli tomber; **you are** ~ **there** vous y êtes presque; **I can** ~ **do it** j'arrive presque à le faire; ~ **finished/cooked/cold** *etc* presque *or* à peu près terminé/cuit/froid *etc*.

alms [ɑːmz] n aumône *f*. **to give** ~ faire l'aumône *or* la charité; ~ **box** tronc *m* des *or* pour les pauvres; (*Hist*) ~ **house** hospice *m*.

aloe ['æləʊ] n aloès *m*; *see* **bitter.**

aloft [ə'lɒft] adv (*also* **up** ~) en haut, en l'air; (*Naut*) dans la mâture; (*hum*) au ciel.

Aloha [ə'ləʊə] nf: (*US*) **the** ~ **State** Hawaï.

alone [ə'ləʊn] adj, adv a (*by o.s.*) seul. **all** ~ tout(e) seul(e); **quite** ~ tout à fait seul(e); **you can't do it** ~ vous ne pouvez pas le faire seul; **leave them** ~ **together** laissez-les seuls ensemble; *see* **get j.**
b (*the only one*) seul. **he** ~ **could tell you** lui seul pourrait vous le dire; **you** ~ **can do it** vous êtes le seul à pouvoir le faire; **we are not** ~ **in thinking** nous ne sommes pas les seuls à penser, il n'y a pas que nous à penser *or* qui pensions; **he lives on bread** ~ il ne vit que de pain, il vit uniquement de pain; **this book is mine** ~ ce livre est à moi seul; **that charm which is hers** ~ ce charme qui lui est propre *or* qui n'appartient qu'à elle.
c (*fig*) **to let** *or* **leave sb** ~ laisser qn tranquille, laisser la paix à qn; **leave** *or* **let me** ~! laisse-moi tranquille!, fiche-moi la paix!*; **leave** *or* **let him** ~ **to do it** laisse-le faire tout seul; **leave** *or* **let the book** ~! ne touche pas au livre!, laisse le livre tranquille!*; **I advise you to leave the whole business** ~ je vous conseille de ne pas vous mêler de l'affaire; (*Prov*) **let well** ~ le mieux est l'ennemi du bien (*Prov*).
d (*as conj*) **let** ~ sans parler de; **he can't read, let** ~ **write** il ne sait pas lire, encore moins écrire; **he can't afford food, let** ~ **clothes** il n'a pas de quoi s'acheter de la nourriture, sans parler de vêtements *or* encore moins des vêtements.

along [ə'lɒŋ] (*phr vb elem*) 1 adv a en avant. **come** ~! allez venez!, venez donc!; **to go** *or* **move** ~ avancer; **to run/roll** ~ avancer en courant/en roulant; **I'll be** ~ **in a moment** j'arrive tout de suite; **she'll be** ~ **tomorrow** elle viendra demain; **how is he getting** ~**?** (*in health*) comment va-t-il?; (*in business etc*) comment vont ses affaires?; (*Scol*) comment vont ses études?; *see* **move along** *etc*.
b **come** ~ **with me** venez avec moi; **he came** ~ **with 6 others** il est venu accompagné de 6 autres; **bring your friend** ~ amène ton camarade (avec toi); ~ **here** dans cette direction-ci, par là, de ce côté-ci; (*fig*) **get** ~ **with you!*** (*go away*) fiche le camp!*, décampe!‡; (*you can't mean it*) allons donc!, sans blague!*
c **all** ~ (*space*) d'un bout à l'autre; (*time*) depuis le début; **I could see all** ~ **that he would refuse** je voyais depuis le début qu'il allait refuser.
2 prep le long de. **to walk** ~ **the beach** se promener le long de la plage; **the railway runs** ~ **the beach** la ligne de chemin de fer longe la plage; **the trees** ~ **the road** les arbres qui sont au bord de la route *or* qui bordent la route; **all** ~ **the street** tout le long de *or* d'un bout à l'autre de la rue; **somewhere** ~ **the way he lost a glove** quelque part en chemin il a perdu un gant; (*fig*) **somewhere** ~ **the way** *or* **somewhere** ~ **the line* someone made a mistake** à un moment donné quelqu'un a fait une erreur; **to proceed** ~ **the lines suggested** agir *or* procéder conformément à la ligne d'action proposée.

alongside [ə'lɒŋ'saɪd] 1 prep (*along: also Naut*) le long de; (*beside*) à côté de, près de. **to work** ~ **sb** travailler aux côtés de qn; (*Naut*) **to come** ~ **the quay** accoster le quai; **the road runs** ~ **the beach** la route longe la plage; *[vehicle]* **to stop** ~ **the kerb** s'arrêter le long du trottoir; **the car drew up** ~ **me** la voiture s'est arrêtée à côté de moi *or* à ma hauteur. 2 adv a (*Naut*) *[ships]* (*beside one another*) bord à bord, à couple. **to come** ~ accoster; **to make fast** ~ (*quayside*) s'amarrer à *or* au quai; (*another vessel*) s'amarrer bord à bord, s'amarrer à *or* en couple; **to pass** ~ **of a ship** longer un navire. b *[people]* (*side by side*) côte à côte.

aloof [ə'luːf] 1 adj *person, character* distant. **he was very** ~ **with me** il s'est montré très distant à mon égard; **she kept very (much)** ~ elle s'est montrée très distante, elle a gardé *or* conservé ses distances. 2 adv à distance, à l'écart. **to remain** *or* **stay** *or* **stand** *or* **keep** ~ **from a group** se tenir à l'écart *or* à distance d'un groupe; **to remain** *or* **stay** *or* **stand** *or* **keep** ~ **from arguments** ne pas se mêler aux discussions, ne jamais se mêler à la discussion.

aloofness [ə'luːfnɪs] n réserve *f*, attitude distante.

alopecia [ˌæləʊ'piːʃə] n alopécie *f*.

aloud [ə'laʊd] adv *read* à haute voix, à voix haute, tout haut; *laugh, think, wonder* tout haut.

alp [ælp] n (*peak*) pic *m*; (*mountain*) montagne *f*; (*pasture*) alpe *f*. **the A~s** les Alpes.

alpaca [æl'pækə] n alpaga *m*.

alpenhorn ['ælpɪnˌhɔːn] n cor *m* des Alpes.

alpenstock ['ælpɪnstɒk] n alpenstock *m*.

alpha ['ælfə] n a (*letter*) alpha *m*. ~ **particle** particule *f* alpha; **~-fetoprotein** alpha-fœto-protéine *f*. b (*Brit: Scol, Univ*) ≃ très bonne note. ~ **plus** ≃ excellente note.

alphabet ['ælfəbet] n alphabet *m*. ~ **soup** (*Culin*) potage *m* aux pâtes (en forme de lettres); (* *fig pej*) salade *f* de sigles; *see* **deaf, finger.**

alphabetic(al) [ˌælfə'betɪk(əl)] adj alphabétique. **in alphabetical order** par ordre alphabétique, dans l'ordre alphabétique.

alphabetically [ˌælfə'betɪkəlɪ] adv alphabétiquement, par ordre alphabétique.

alphabetize ['ælfəbətaɪz] vt classer par ordre alphabétique.

alphanumeric [ˌælfənjuː'merɪk] adj alphanumérique.

alpine ['ælpaɪn] adj des Alpes; *climate, scenery* alpestre; *club, skiing, troops* alpin. ~ **hut** (chalet-)refuge *m*; ~ **range** chaîne alpine; ~ **plants** (*on lower slopes*) plantes *fpl* alpestres, (*on higher slopes*) plantes alpines.

alpinist [ˈælpɪnɪst] n alpiniste *mf*.

already [ɔːlˈredɪ] adv déjà. (*US* ‡: *expressing impatience*) **that's enough ~!**‡ ça va comme ça!*

alright [ˌɔːlˈraɪt] = **all right**.

Alsace [ˈælsæs] n Alsace *f*.

Alsace-Lorraine [ˈælsæsləˈreɪn] n Alsace-Lorraine *f*.

Alsatian [ælˈseɪʃən] 1 n a Alsacien(ne) *m(f)*. b (*Brit: also* ~ **dog**) chien *m* loup, berger allemand. 2 adj alsacien, d'Alsace; *wine* d'Alsace.

also [ˈɔːlsəʊ] 1 adv a (*too*) aussi, également. **her cousin ~ came** son cousin aussi est venu *or* est venu également. b (*moreover*) de plus, en outre, également. **~ I must explain that ...** de plus *or* en outre, je dois expliquer que ..., je dois également expliquer que ... . 2 comp ▸**also-ran** (*Sport*) autre concurrent *m* (*n'ayant pas pu se classer*); (*Horse-racing*) cheval non classé; (*: *person*) perdant(e) *m(f)*.

Altamira [ˌæltəˈmiːrə] n: **the ~ caves** les grottes *fpl* d'Altamira.

altar [ˈɒltəʳ] 1 n (*Rel*) autel *m*. **high ~** maître-autel *m*; (*fig*) **he was sacrificed on the ~ of productivity** il a été immolé sur l'autel de la productivité. 2 comp ▸**altar boy** enfant *m* de chœur ▸**altar cloth** nappe *f* d'autel ▸**altar piece** retable *m* ▸**altar rail(s)** clôture *f or* balustre *m* (du chœur); (*Rel*) table *f* de communion.

alter [ˈɒltəʳ] 1 vt a (*gen*) changer, modifier, (*stronger*) transformer; (*adapt*) adapter, ajuster; *painting, poem, speech etc* retoucher, (*stronger*) remanier; *garment* retoucher, (*stronger*) transformer. **to ~ one's plans** modifier *or* transformer ses projets; **to ~ one's attitude** changer d'attitude (*to* envers); **that ~s the case** voilà qui est différent *or* qui change tout; (*Naut*) **to ~ course** changer de cap *or* de route; **to ~ sth for the better** changer qch en mieux, améliorer qch; **to ~ sth for the worse** changer qch en mal, altérer qch.
b (*falsify*) *date, evidence* falsifier, fausser; *text* altérer.
c (*US: castrate*) châtrer, castrer.
2 vi changer. **to ~ for the better** *[circumstances]* s'améliorer; *[person, character]* changer en mieux; **to ~ for the worse** *[circumstances]* empirer, s'aggraver; *[person, character]* changer en mal.

alteration [ˌɒltəˈreɪʃən] n a (*NonC: see* **alter**: *act of altering*) changement *m*, modification *f*; transformation *f*; retouchage *m*, remaniement *m*. **programme/timetable subject to ~** programme/horaire sujet à des changements *or* modifications.
b (*to plan, rules etc*) modification *f*, changement *m* (*to, in* apporté à); (*to painting, poem, essay etc*) retouche *f*, (*major*) remaniement *m*; (*to garment*) retouche, (*major*) transformation *f*. (*Archit*) **~s** transformations *fpl* (*to* apportées à); **they're having ~s made to their house** ils font des travaux dans leur maison; **he made several ~s to his canvas/manuscript** en peignant/en écrivant il a eu plusieurs repentirs; (*Naut*) **~ of route** (*deliberate*) changement de route; (*involuntary*) déroutement *m*.

altercation [ˌɒltəˈkeɪʃən] n altercation *f*. **to have an ~** se disputer, avoir une altercation.

alter ego [ˈæltərˈiːgəʊ] n alter ego *m*. **he is my ~** c'est un autre moi-même, c'est mon alter ego.

alternate [ɒlˈtɜːnɪt] 1 adj a (*by turns*) alterné; (*Bot, Math*) *leaves, angle* alterne. **~ action of tranquillizers and stimulants** action alternée des tranquillisants et des stimulants; **a week of ~ rain and sunshine** une semaine de pluie et de beau temps en alternance; (*Poetry*) **~ rhymes** rimes croisées *or* alternées.
b (*every second*) tous les deux. **on ~ days** tous les deux jours, un jour sur deux; **they work on ~ days** ils travaillent un jour sur deux à tour de rôle, l'un travaille un jour et l'autre le lendemain.
c (*US*) = **alternative 1**.
2 n (*US*) remplaçant(e) *m(f)*, suppléant(e) *m(f)*.
3 [ˈɒltɜːneɪt] vt faire alterner, employer alternativement *or* tour à tour. **to ~ crops** alterner les cultures, pratiquer l'assolement.
4 vi a (*occur etc in turns*) alterner (*with* avec), se succéder (tour à tour).
b **to ~ between one thing and another** aller *or* passer d'une chose à une autre.
c (*interchange regularly*) se relayer, travailler (*or* jouer *etc*) en alternance.
d (*Elec*) changer de sens de façon périodique.

alternately [ɒlˈtɜːnɪtlɪ] adv alternativement, tour à tour, à tour de rôle. **~ with** en alternance avec.

alternating [ˈɒltɜːneɪtɪŋ] adj alternant, en alternance; *movement* alternatif. (*Math*) **~ series** série alternée; (*Elec*) **~ current** courant alternatif.

alternation [ˌɒltɜːˈneɪʃən] n alternance *f*; *[emotions etc]* alternatives *fpl*.

alternative [ɒlˈtɜːnətɪv] 1 adj a *possibility, answer* autre; (*Philos*) *proposition* alternatif; (*Mil*) *position* de repli; (*Tech*) de rechange. **~ proposal** contre-proposition *f*; **the only ~ method** la seule autre méthode, la seule méthode de rechange; (*Aut*) **~ route** itinéraire *m* de délestage; **A~ Vote** vote *m* alternatif.
b (*non-traditional*) *society, medicine etc* parallèle, alternatif; *lifestyle* alternatif, différent. **~ technology** les technologies douces; (*US*) **~ school** *école privée adoptant des méthodes nouvelles;* (*US*) **~ education** *enseignement privé basé sur des méthodes nouvelles;* **~ comedian** nouveau comique *m*; **~ comedy** nouvelle comédie *f*; **~ (sources of) energy** (sources *fpl* d')énergie *f* de substitution.
2 n (*choice*) (*between two*) alternative *f*, choix *m*; (*among several*) choix; (*solution*) (*only one*) alternative, seule autre solution, solution unique de rechange; (*one of several*) autre solution, solution de rechange; (*Philos*) terme *m* d'une alternative *or* d'un dilemme. **she had no ~ but to accept** elle n'avait pas d'autre solution que d'accepter, force lui a été d'accepter; **there's no ~** il n'y a pas le choix.

alternatively [ɒlˈtɜːnətɪvlɪ] adv comme alternative, sinon. **(or) ~** ou bien.

alternator [ˈɒltɜːneɪtəʳ] n (*Brit Elec*) alternateur *m*.

although [ɔːlˈðəʊ] conj bien que + *subj*, quoique + *subj*, malgré le fait que + *subj*, encore que + *subj*. **~ it's raining there are 20 people here already** bien qu'il pleuve *or* malgré la pluie il y a déjà 20 personnes; **I'll do it ~ I don't want to** je le ferai bien que *or* quoique *or* encore que je n'en aie pas envie; **~ poor they were honest** ils étaient honnêtes bien que *or* quoique *or* encore que pauvres; **~ young he knew that ...** bien qu'il *or* quoiqu'il *or* encore qu'il fût jeune, il savait que ..., malgré sa jeunesse il savait que ...; **~ he might agree to go** quand bien même il accepterait d'y aller; (*liter*) **I will do it ~ I (should) die in the attempt** je le ferai dussé-je y laisser la vie.

altimeter [ˈæltɪmiːtəʳ] n altimètre *m*.

altitude [ˈæltɪtjuːd] n (*height above sea level*) altitude *f*; *[building]* hauteur *f*. (*gen pl: high place*) **~s** hauteur(s), altitude; **it is difficult to breathe at these ~s** *or* **at this ~** il est difficile de respirer à cette altitude; **~ sickness** mal *m* d'altitude *or* des montagnes.

alto [ˈæltəʊ] 1 n a (*female voice*) contralto *m*; (*male voice*) haute-contre *f*. b (*instrument*) alto *m*. 2 adj *part, voice* de contralto; de haute-contre; d'alto. **~ clef** clef *f* d'ut; **~ saxophone/flute** saxophone *m*/flûte *f* alto.

altogether [ˌɔːltəˈgeðəʳ] 1 adv a (*wholly*) entièrement, tout à fait, complètement. **it is ~ out of the question** il n'en est absolument pas question. b (*on the whole*) somme toute, tout compte fait, au total. **~ it wasn't very pleasant** somme toute ce n'était pas très agréable. c (*with everything included*) en tout. **what do I owe you ~?** je vous dois combien en tout?, combien vous dois-je au total?; **taken ~** à tout prendre. 2 n (*hum*) **in the ~*** tout nu, en costume d'Adam (*or* d'Ève)*.

altruism [ˈæltrʊɪzəm] n altruisme *m*.

altruist [ˈæltrʊɪst] n altruiste *mf*.

altruistic [ˌæltrʊˈɪstɪk] adj altruiste.

ALU [ˌeɪelˈjuː] n (*Comput*) (**abbr of arithmetical logic unit**) UAL *f*.

alum [ˈæləm] n alun *m*.

alumina [əˈluːmɪnə] n alumine *f*.

aluminium [ˌæljʊˈmɪnɪəm] (*Brit*), (*US*), **aluminum** [əˈluːmɪnəm] 1 n aluminium *m*. 2 comp *pot, pan etc* en *or* d'aluminium ▸**aluminium bronze** bronze *m* d'aluminium ▸**aluminium foil** papier *m* aluminium ▸**aluminium oxide** oxyde *m* d'aluminium.

alumna [əˈlʌmnə] n, pl **alumnae** [əˈlʌmniː] (*US*) (*Scol*) ancienne élève *f*; (*Univ*) ancienne étudiante *f*.

alumnus [əˈlʌmnəs] n, pl **alumni** [əˈlʌmnaɪ] (*US*) (*Scol*) ancien élève *m*; (*Univ*) ancien étudiant *m*.

alveolar [ælˈvɪələʳ] adj alvéolaire. **~ ridge** alvéoles *fpl* dentaires.

alveolus [ælˈvɪələs] n, pl **alveoli** [ælvɪəˈlaɪ] alvéole *f*.

always [ˈɔːlweɪz] adv toujours. **as/for/nearly ~** comme/pour/presque toujours; **office ~ open** (bureau *m* ouvert en) permanence *f*; *see* **excepting**.

Alzheimer's disease [ˈælts,haɪmez dɪˈziːz] n maladie *f* d'Alzheimer.

AM [ˌeɪˈem] (**abbr of amplitude modulation**) AM; *see* **modulation**.

am [æm] *see* **be**.

a.m. [eɪˈem] adv (**abbr of ante meridiem**) du matin.

A.M.A. [ˌeɪemˈeɪ] n **abbr of American Medical Association**.

amalgam [əˈmælgəm] n amalgame *m*.

amalgamate [əˈmælgəmeɪt] 1 vt *metals* amalgamer; *companies, shares* (faire) fusionner, unifier. 2 vi *[metals]* s'amalgamer; *[companies]* fusionner, s'unifier; *[ethnic groups]* se mélanger.

amalgamation [əˌmælgəˈmeɪʃən] n (*see* **amalgamate**) amalgamation *f*; fusion *f*, fusionnement *m*, unification *f*; *[ethnic groups]* mélange *m*.

amanuensis [əˌmænjʊˈensɪs] n, pl **amanuenses** [əˌmænjʊˈensiːz] (*secretary, assistant*) secrétaire *mf*; (*copyist*) copiste *mf*.

amaryllis [ˌæməˈrɪlɪs] n amaryllis *f*.

amass [əˈmæs] vt *objects* amasser, accumuler, amonceler; *fortune* amasser, réunir.

amateur [ˈæmətəʳ] 1 n (*also Sport*) amateur *m*. 2 comp *painter, sports, player* amateur *inv*; *photography etc* d'amateur ▸**amateur dramatics** théâtre *m* amateur ▸**amateur interest: to have an amateur interest in sth** s'intéresser à qch en amateur ▸**amateur status** statut *m* d'amateur ▸**amateur work** (*pej*) travail *m* d'amateur *or* de dilettante (*gen pej*).

amateurish [ˈæmətərɪʃ] adj (*pej*) d'amateur, de dilettante. **~ efforts/work** efforts/travail peu sérieux.

amateurism [ˈæmətərɪzəm] n amateurisme *m* (*also pej*), dilettantisme *m*.

amatory [ˈæmətərɪ] adj (*frm, liter*) *feelings* amoureux; *poetry* galant;

letter d'amour.

amaze [ə'meɪz] **vt** stupéfier, frapper de stupeur, ébahir. (*iro*) **you ~ me!** pas possible!, c'est pas vrai!* (*iro*).

amazed [ə'meɪzd] **adj** *glance, expression* ébahi, plein de stupeur; *person* ébahi, frappé de stupeur. **to be ~ at (seeing) sth** être stupéfait de (voir) qch.

amazement [ə'meɪzmənt] **n** stupéfaction *f*, stupeur *f*, ébahissement *m*. **she listened in ~** elle écoutait, complètement stupéfaite *or* ébahie.

amazing [ə'meɪzɪŋ] **adj** stupéfiant, ahurissant, renversant*. **it's ~!** c'est ahurissant!, je n'en reviens pas!; (*Comm*) "**~ new offer**" "offre sensationnelle".

amazingly [ə'meɪzɪŋlɪ] **adv** étonnamment. **~ (enough), he got it right first time** chose étonnante, il a réussi du premier coup; **~, he survived** par miracle il en a réchappé; **she is ~ courageous** elle est d'un courage extraordinaire *or* étonnant.

Amazon ['æməzən] **n** **a** (*river*) Amazone *f*. **the ~ Basin** le bassin amazonien *or* de l'Amazone; **the ~ jungle/rainforest** la jungle/la forêt tropicale amazonienne. **b** (*Myth*) Amazone *f*. (*US pej*) **a~** virago *f*, grande bonne femme; (*fig*) **she's a real ~** c'est une véritable athlète.

Amazonia [,æmə'zəʊnɪə] **n** (*Geog*) Amazonie *f*.

Amazonian [æmə'zəʊnɪən] **adj** (*Geog*) amazonien.

ambassador [æm'bæsədə^r] **n** (*lit, fig*) ambassadeur *m* (*to France* en France). **French ~** ambassadeur de France; **~-at-large** ambassadeur extraordinaire *or* chargé de mission(s).

ambassadorial [æm,bæsə'dɔːrɪəl] **adj** d'ambassadeur.

ambassadorship [æm'bæsədəʃɪp] **n** fonction *f* d'ambassadeur, ambassade *f*.

ambassadress [æm'bæsɪdrɪs] **n** (*lit, fig*) ambassadrice *f*.

amber ['æmbə^r] **1** **n** ambre *m*. (*Brit Aut*) **~ gambler*** chauffard* *m* qui fonce à l'orange. **2** **adj** *jewellery* d'ambre. **~-coloured** ambré; (*Brit Aut*) **~ light** feu *m* orange; **the lights are at ~** les feux sont à l'orange.

ambergris ['æmbəgriːs] **n** ambre gris.

ambi... ['æmbɪ] **pref** ambi... .

ambiance ['æmbɪəns] = **ambience**.

ambidextrous [,æmbɪ'dekstrəs] **adj** ambidextre.

ambience ['æmbɪəns] **n** ambiance *f*, atmosphère *f*.

ambient ['æmbɪənt] **1** **adj** ambiant. **2** **n** (*Phot*) lumière *f* d'ambiance.

ambiguity [,æmbɪ'gjʊɪtɪ] **n** **a** (*NonC*) *[word, phrase]* ambiguïté *f* (*also Ling*), équivoque *f*; (*in thought, speech: lack of clarity*) ambiguïté, obscurité *f*. **b** (*ambiguous phrase etc*) ambiguïté *f*, expression ambiguë.

ambiguous [æm'bɪgjʊəs] **adj** *word, phrase* ambigu (*f* -guë) (*also Ling*), équivoque; *thought* obscur; *past* douteux, équivoque.

ambiguously [æm'bɪgjʊəslɪ] **adv** de façon ambiguë.

ambit ['æmbɪt] **n** *[person]* sphère *f* d'attributions, compétence *f*; *[authority etc]* étendue *f*, portée *f*.

ambition [æm'bɪʃən] **n** ambition *f*. **it is my ~ to do** mon ambition est de faire, j'ai l'ambition de faire.

ambitious [æm'bɪʃəs] **adj** *person, plan* ambitieux. **to be ~ to do** ambitionner de faire; **to be ~ of** *or* **for fame** briguer la gloire.

ambitiously [æm'bɪʃəslɪ] **adv** ambitieusement.

ambivalence [æm'bɪvələns] **n** ambivalence *f*.

ambivalent [æm'bɪvələnt] **adj** ambivalent.

amble ['æmbl] **1** **vi** *[horse]* aller l'amble, ambler; *[person]* aller *or* marcher d'un pas tranquille. **to ~ in/out** *etc* entrer/sortir *etc* d'un pas tranquille; *[person]* **to ~ along** se promener *or* aller sans se presser; **he ~d up to me** il s'est avancé vers moi sans se presser; **the train ~s through the valley** le train traverse lentement la vallée. **2** **n** *[horse]* amble *m*; *[person]* pas *m or* allure *f* tranquille.

ambrosia [æm'brəʊzɪə] **n** ambroisie *f*.

ambrosial [æm'brəʊzɪəl] **adj** (au parfum *or* au goût) d'ambroisie.

ambulance ['æmbjʊləns] **1** **n** ambulance *f*; *see* **flying**. **2** **comp** ▸**ambulance chaser*** (*US pej*) avocat *m* marron (*qui encourage les victimes d'accident à le consulter*) ▸**ambulance driver** ambulancier *m*, -ière *f* ▸**ambulance man** (*driver*) ambulancier *m*; (*inside*) infirmier *m* (d'ambulance); (*carrying stretcher*) brancardier *m* ▸**ambulance nurse** infirmière *f* (d'ambulance) ▸**ambulance train** train *m* sanitaire.

ambulatory [,æmbjʊ'leɪtərɪ] **adj** (*US Med*) ambulatoire. **~ patient/care** malade *mf*/traitement *m* ambulatoire.

ambush ['æmbʊʃ] **1** **n** embuscade *f*, guet-apens *m*. **troops in ~** troupes embusquées; **to be** *or* **lie in ~** se tenir en embuscade; **to be** *or* **lie in ~ for sb** tendre une embuscade à qn; *see* **fall**. **2** **vt** (*wait for*) tendre une embuscade à; (*attack*) faire tomber dans une embuscade.

ameba [ə'miːbə] **n** = **amoeba**.

ameliorate [ə'miːlɪəreɪt] **1** **vt** améliorer. **2** **vi** s'améliorer.

amelioration [ə,miːlɪə'reɪʃən] **n** amélioration *f*.

amen ['ɑː'men] **1** **excl** (*Rel*) amen, ainsi soit-il. **2** **n** amen *m inv*. (*Rel, fig*) **to say ~ to, to give one's ~ to** dire amen à.

amenable [ə'miːnəbl] **adj** **a** (*answerable*) *person* responsable (*to sb* envers qn, *for sth* de qch). **~ to the law** responsable devant la loi. **b** (*tractable, responsive*) *person* maniable, souple. **he is ~ to argument** c'est un homme qui est prêt à se laisser convaincre; **~ to discipline** disciplinable; **~ to kindness** sensible à la douceur; **~ to reason** raisonnable, disposé à entendre raison. **c** (*within the scope of*) **~ to** qui relève de, du ressort de.

amend [ə'mend] **1** **vt** *rule* amender, modifier; (*Parl*) amender; *wording* modifier; *mistake* rectifier, corriger; *habits* réformer. **2** **vi** s'amender.

amendment [ə'mendmənt] **n** (*see* **amend**) amendement *m*; modification *f*; rectification *f*; (*Parl*) amendement; (*Fin: to contract*) avenant *m* (*to* à). (*Jur*) **proposals for the ~ of this treaty** projet *m* tendant à la révision du présent traité.

amends [ə'mendz] **npl** compensation *f*, réparation *f*, dédommagement *m*. **to make ~** (*apologize*) faire amende honorable; (*by doing sth*) se racheter; **to make ~ to sb for sth** dédommager qn de qch, faire réparation à qn de qch; **to make ~ for an injury** (*with money*) compenser un dommage; (*with kindness*) réparer un tort; **I'll try to make ~** j'essaierai de réparer mes torts *or* de me racheter.

amenity [ə'miːnɪtɪ] **1** **n** **a** (*NonC: pleasantness*) *[district, climate, situation]* charme *m*, agrément *m*. **b** (*gen pl*) **amenities** (*pleasant features*) agréments *mpl*; (*facilities*) aménagements *mpl*, équipements *mpl* (locaux); (*Jur*) **public amenities** équipements collectifs. **c** († *pl: courtesies*) **amenities** civilités *fpl*, politesses *fpl*. **2** **comp** ▸**amenity bed** (*Brit Med*) lit "privé" (dans un hôpital) ▸**amenity society** association *f* pour la sauvegarde de l'environnement.

amenorrhoea, (*US*) **amenorrhea** ['eɪmenə'rɪə] **n** (*Med*) aménorrhée *f*.

Amerasia [,æmə'reɪʒə] **n** Amérique *f* jaune, Asie américaine.

Amerasian [,æmə'reɪʒən] **1** **adj** amérasien. **2** **n** Amérasien(ne) *m(f)*.

America [ə'merɪkə] **n** Amérique *f*; *see* **north, united** *etc*.

American [ə'merɪkən] **1** **adj** (*of America*) américain, d'Amérique; (*of USA*) américain, des États-Unis. (*US*) **~ cheese** cheddar américain; **~ Civil War** guerre *f* de Sécession; **the ~ Dream** le rêve américain; **~ Eagle** aigle *m* d'Amérique; **~ embassy** ambassade *f* des États-Unis; **~ English** anglais américain; **~ Indian** (**n**) Indien(ne) *m(f)* d'Amérique; (**adj**) des Indiens d'Amérique; (*US: in hotels*) **~ plan** (chambre *f* avec) pension complète. **2** **n** **a** Américain(e) *m(f)*. **b** (*Ling*) américain *m*.

Americana [ə,merɪ'kɑːnə] **n** (*US*) *objets ou documents appartenant à l'héritage culturel américain*.

americanism [ə'merɪkənɪzəm] **n** américanisme *m*.

americanize [ə'merɪkənaɪz] **vt** américaniser.

americium [,æmə'rɪsɪəm] **n** (*Chem*) américium *m*.

Amerind ['æmərɪnd] **n** **a** Indien(ne) *m(f)* d'Amérique. **b** (*Ling*) langue amérindienne.

Amerindian [æmə'rɪndɪən] **1** **n** = **Amerind**. **2** **adj** amérindien.

amethyst ['æmɪθɪst] **1** **n** améthyste *f*. **2** **comp** *jewellery* d'améthyste; *colour* violet d'améthyste *inv*.

amiability [,eɪmɪə'bɪlɪtɪ] **n** amabilité *f*, gentillesse *f* (*to, towards* envers).

amiable ['eɪmɪəbl] **adj** aimable, gentil.

amiably ['eɪmɪəblɪ] **adv** aimablement, avec amabilité, avec gentillesse.

amicable ['æmɪkəbl] **adj** *feeling* amical; *relationship* amical, d'amitié. (*Jur*) **~ settlement** arrangement *m* à l'amiable.

amicably ['æmɪkəblɪ] **adv** amicalement; (*Jur*) à l'amiable.

amidships [ə'mɪdʃɪps] **adv** (*Naut*) au milieu *or* par le milieu du navire.

amid(st) [ə'mɪd(st)] **prep** parmi, au milieu de.

amino acid [ə'miːnəʊ'æsɪd] **n** acide aminé, aminoacide *m*.

amiss [ə'mɪs] **1** **adv** (*wrongly*) mal, de travers; (*at wrong place, time etc*) mal à propos. **to take sth ~** prendre qch de travers *or* en mauvaise part; **don't take it ~** ne le prenez pas mal, ne vous en offensez pas; **to speak ~ of** parler mal de; **nothing comes ~ to him** il tire parti de tout, il s'arrange de tout; **a drink wouldn't come ~*** je ne refuserais pas un verre; **a little courtesy on his part wouldn't come ~** un peu de politesse ne lui ferait pas de mal. **2** **adj** (*wrongly worded, timed etc*) mal à propos. **something is ~ in your calculations** il y a quelque chose qui ne va pas *or* qui cloche* dans tes calculs; **what's ~ with you?** qu'est-ce qui ne va pas?, qu'est-ce qui te tracasse?; **there's something ~** il y a quelque chose qui ne va pas *or* qui cloche*; **to say something ~** dire quelque chose mal à propos.

amity ['æmɪtɪ] **n** amitié *f*, bonne intelligence; (*between two countries*) concorde *f*, bons rapports, bonnes relations.

Amman [ə'mɑːn] **n** Amman.

ammeter ['æmɪtə^r] **n** ampèremètre *m*.

ammo ['æməʊ] **n** (*Mil sl*) (**abbr of ammunition**) munitions *fpl*.

ammonia [ə'məʊnɪə] **n** (gaz *m*) ammoniac *m*; (*liquid*) ammoniaque *f*; *see* **household, liquid**.

ammonium [ə'məʊnɪəm] **n** ammonium *m*. **~ chloride** chlorure *m* d'ammonium.

ammunition [,æmjʊ'nɪʃən] **1** **n** munitions *fpl*. **2** **comp** ▸**ammunition belt** ceinturon *m* ▸**ammunition dump** dépôt *m or* parc *m* de munitions ▸**ammunition pouch** cartouchière *f*.

amnesia [æm'niːzɪə] **n** amnésie *f*.

amnesiac [,æm'niːzɪæk] **adj** amnésique.

amnesty ['æmnɪstɪ] **1** **n** amnistie *f*. **under an ~** en vertu d'une amnistie; **A~ International** Amnesty International. **2** **vt** amnistier.

amniocentesis [,æmnɪəʊsən'tiːsɪs] **n**, **pl** **amniocenteses** [,æmnɪəʊsən'tiːsiːz] amniocentèse *f*.

amnion ['æmnɪən] n, pl ~s *or* **amnia** ['æmnɪə] (*Anat*) amnios *m*.
amniotic [ˌæmnɪ'ɒtɪk] adj (*Anat*) amniotique. ~ **fluid/cavity** liquide *m*/cavité *f* amniotique; ~ **sac** poche *f* des eaux.
amoeba [ə'miːbə] n, pl ~s, **amœbæ** [ə'miːbiː] amibe *f*.
amoebic [ə'miːbɪk] adj amibien. ~ **dysentery** dysenterie amibienne.
amok [ə'mɒk] adv: **to run** ~ (*lit*) être pris d'un accès *or* d'une crise de folie meurtrière *or* furieuse; (*in Far East*) s'abandonner à l'amok; (*fig*) *[person]* perdre tout contrôle de soi-même; *[crowd]* se déchaîner.
among(st) [ə'mʌŋ(st)] prep parmi, entre. ~ **the crowd** parmi la foule; **divide the chocolates** ~ **you** partagez-vous les chocolats; ~ **the lambs is one black one** un des agneaux est noir, parmi les agneaux il y en a un noir; **this is** ~ **the things we must do** ceci fait partie des choses que nous avons à faire; **settle it** ~ **yourselves** arrangez cela entre vous; **don't quarrel** ~ **yourselves** ne vous disputez pas, pas de disputes entre vous; **he is** ~ **those who know** il est de ces gens qui savent, il fait partie de ceux qui savent; ~ **others,** ~ **other things** entre autres (choses); ~ **the French** chez les Français; **to count sb** ~ **one's friends** compter qn parmi *or* au nombre de ses amis; **to be** ~ **friends** être entre amis; ~ **tonight's programmes** au programme de ce soir; **one** ~ **a thousand** un entre mille; **to be sitting** ~ **the audience** être assis au milieu des *or* parmi les spectateurs.
amoral [eɪ'mɒrəl] adj amoral.
amorality [eɪmə'rælɪtɪ] n amoralité *f*.
amorous ['æmərəs] adj amoureux. **to make** ~ **advances to** faire des avances à (*connotations sexuelles*).
amorously ['æmərəslɪ] adv amoureusement.
amorphous [ə'mɔːfəs] adj (*also Miner*) amorphe; (*fig*) *personality* amorphe; *style, ideas* informe, sans forme.
amortization [əˌmɔːtaɪ'zeɪʃən] n amortissement *m*.
amortize [ə'mɔːtaɪz] vt *debt* amortir. ~**d mortgage loan** prêt *m* hypothécaire à remboursements périodiques.
amortizement [ə'mɔːtɪzmənt] n = **amortization**.
amount [ə'maʊnt] n **a** (*total*) montant *m*, total *m*; (*sum of money*) somme *f*. **the** ~ **of a bill** le montant d'une facture; **debts to the** ~ **of £20** dettes qui se montent à 20 livres; **there is a small** ~ **still to pay** il reste une petite somme à payer; (*Fin, Comm*) **to the** ~ **of** à concurrence de; (*US*) **check in the** ~ **of $50** chèque de 50 dollars; (*Fin*) ~ **allotted to** dotation accordée à.
b (*quantity*) quantité *f*. **I have an enormous** ~ **of work** j'ai énormément de travail; **quite an** ~ **of** beaucoup de; **any** ~ **of** quantité de, énormément de; **she's got any** ~ **of friends** elle a énormément *or* des quantités d'amis; **I've got any** ~ **of time** j'ai tout le temps qu'il (me) faut, j'ai tout mon temps.
c (*NonC: value, importance*) importance *f*, signification *f*. **the information is of little** ~ ce renseignement n'a pas grande importance.
►**amount to** vt fus **a** (*Math etc*) *[sums, figures, debts]* s'élever à, se monter à, se chiffrer à. **b** (*be equivalent to*) équivaloir à, se ramener à, se réduire à. **it amounts to the same thing** cela revient au même; **it amounts to stealing** cela revient *or* équivaut à du vol; **it amounts to a change in policy** cela représente un changement de politique; **this amounts to very little** cela ne représente pas grand-chose; **he will never amount to much** il ne fera jamais grand-chose; **one day he will amount to something** un jour il sera quelqu'un.
amour [ə'mʊəʳ] **1** n intrigue amoureuse, liaison *f*. **2** comp ►**amour-propre** amour-propre *m*.
amp* [æmp] n (abbr of **amplifier**) ampli* *m*.
amp(ère) ['æmp(ɛəʳ)] **1** n ampère *m*. **2** comp ►**ampère-hour** ampère-heure *m* ► **a 13-amp plug** une prise de 13 ampères.
ampersand ['æmpəsænd] n esperluète *f*.
amphetamine [æm'fetəmiːn] n amphétamine *f*.
amphibia [æm'fɪbɪə] npl batraciens *mpl*, amphibiens *mpl*.
amphibian [æm'fɪbɪən] **1** adj *animal, vehicle, tank* amphibie. **2** n (*Zool*) amphibie *m*; (*car*) voiture *f* amphibie; (*aircraft*) avion *m* amphibie; (*tank*) char *m* amphibie.
amphibious [æm'fɪbɪəs] adj amphibie.
amphitheatre, (*US*) **amphitheater** ['æmfɪˌθɪətəʳ] n (*Hist, Theat, gen*) amphithéâtre *m*; (*in mountains*) cirque *m*.
amphora ['æmfərə] n, pl **amphorae** ['æmfəˌriː] *or* ~**s** amphore *f*.
ample ['æmpl] adj **a** (*more than enough of*) *money etc* bien *or* largement assez de; *reason, motive* solide; *resources* gros, abondant. ~ **grounds for divorce** de solides motifs de divorce; **to have** ~ **means** avoir de gros moyens *or* une grosse fortune; **to have** ~ **reason to believe that** ... avoir de fortes *or* de solides raisons de croire que ...; **there is** ~ **room for** il y a largement la place pour; (*fig*) **there is** ~ **room for improvement** il y a encore bien du chemin *or* bien des progrès à faire; **to have** ~ **time** avoir grandement *or* largement le temps (*to do* de *or* pour faire). **b** (*large*) *garment* ample.
amplification [æmplɪfɪ'keɪʃən] n amplification *f*. (*Jur*) ~ **of previous evidence** amplification des offres de preuve.
amplifier ['æmplɪfaɪəʳ] n amplificateur *m*, ampli* *m*.
amplify ['æmplɪfaɪ] vt *sound* amplifier; *instrument* amplifier le son de; *statement, idea* développer; *story* amplifier.
amplitude ['æmplɪtjuːd] n (*Astron, Phys*) amplitude *f*; *[style, thought]* ampleur *f*; *see* **modulation**.
amply ['æmplɪ] adv amplement, grandement, largement.
ampoule, (*US*) **ampule** ['æmpuːl] n ampoule *f* (*pour seringue*).
ampulla [æm'pʊlə] n, pl **ampullae** [æm'pʊliː] (*Anat*) ampoule *f*.
amputate ['æmpjʊteɪt] vt amputer. **to** ~ **sb's leg** amputer qn de la jambe.
amputation [ˌæmpjʊ'teɪʃən] n amputation *f*. **to carry out the** ~ **of a limb** pratiquer l'amputation d'un membre.
amputee [ˌæmpjʊ'tiː] n amputé(e) *m(f)*.
Amsterdam ['æmstədæm] n Amsterdam.
Amtrak ['æmtræk] n (*US*) *société mixte de transports ferroviaires interurbains pour voyageurs*.
amuck [ə'mʌk] adv = **amok**.
amulet ['æmjʊlɪt] n amulette *f*.
amuse [ə'mjuːz] vt **a** (*cause mirth to*) amuser, divertir, faire rire. **it** ~**d us** cela nous a fait rire; **to be** ~**d at** *or* **by** s'amuser de; **he was not** ~**d** il n'a pas trouvé ça drôle; **an** ~**d expression** un air amusé. **b** (*entertain*) distraire, divertir, amuser. **to** ~ **o.s. by doing** s'amuser à faire; **to** ~ **o.s. with sth/sb** s'amuser avec qch/aux dépens de qn; **you'll have to** ~ **yourselves** il va vous falloir trouver de quoi vous distraire *or* de quoi vous occuper; **to keep oneself** ~**d** se distraire.
amusedly [ə'mjuːzɪdlɪ] adv avec amusement, d'un air amusé.
amusement [ə'mjuːzmənt] **1** n **a** (*NonC*) amusement *m*, divertissement *m*. **look of** ~ regard amusé; **to hide one's** ~ dissimuler son envie de rire; **to do sth for** ~ faire qch pour se distraire; **(much) to my** ~ à mon grand amusement; **there was general** ~ **at this** ceci a fait rire tout le monde. **b** (*diversion, pastime*) distraction *f*, jeu *m*, amusement *m*. (*Brit: in arcade*) ~**s** jeux *mpl* d'arcade; **a town with plenty of** ~**s** une ville qui offre beaucoup de distractions. **2** comp ►**amusement arcade** (*Brit*) galerie *f* de jeux *or* d'attractions ►**amusement park** (*fairground*) parc *m* d'attractions; (*playground*) parc.
amusing [ə'mjuːzɪŋ] adj amusant, drôle, divertissant. **highly** ~ divertissant au possible, très drôle.
amusingly [ə'mjuːzɪŋlɪ] adv d'une manière amusante, drôlement.
amyl ['æmɪl] n: ~ **alcohol** alcool *m* amylique; ~ **nitrite** nitrite *m* amylique.
amylase ['æmɪleɪz] n (*Physiol*) amylase *f*.
an [æn, ən, n] **1** indef art *see* **a²**. **2** conj (††) si.
Anabaptist [ˌænə'bæptɪst] n, adj anabaptiste *(mf)*.
anabolic [ˌænə'bɒlɪk] adj anabolique. ~ **steroid** stéroïde *m* anabolisant.
anachronism [ə'nækrənɪzəm] n anachronisme *m*.
anachronistic [əˌnækrə'nɪstɪk] adj anachronique.
anacoluthon [ˌænəkə'luːθɒn] n, pl **anacolutha** [ˌænəkə'luːθə] anacoluthe *f*.
anaconda [ˌænə'kɒndə] n eunecte *m*, anaconda *m*.
Anacreon [ə'nækrɪɒn] n Anacréon *m*.
anacreontic [əˌnækrɪ'ɒntɪk] **1** adj anacréontique. **2** n poème *m* anacréontique.
anaemia [ə'niːmɪə] n anémie *f*; *see* **pernicious**.
anaemic [ə'niːmɪk] adj (*Med, fig*) anémique. **to become** ~ s'anémier.
anaerobic [ˌæneə'rəʊbɪk] adj anaérobic.
anaesthesia [ˌænɪs'θiːzɪə] n anesthésie *f*.
anaesthetic [ˌænɪs'θetɪk] **1** n anesthésique *m*. **under the** ~ sous anesthésie; **to give sb an** ~ anesthésier qn. **2** adj anesthésique.
anaesthetist [æ'niːsθɪtɪst] n (médecin *m*) anesthésiste *mf*.
anaesthetize [æ'niːsθɪtaɪz] vt (*by anaesthetic*) anesthésier; (*by other methods*) insensibiliser.
anaglyph ['ænəglɪf] n (*Art*) anaglyphe *m*.
Anaglypta [ˌænə'glɪptə] n ® ≃ papier *m* gaufré.
anagram ['ænəgræm] n anagramme *f*.
anal ['eɪnəl] adj anal. (*Psych*) ~ **retentive** souffrant de rétention anale.
analgesia [ˌænæl'dʒiːzɪə] n analgésie *f*.
analgesic [ˌænæl'dʒiːsɪk] adj, n analgésique *(m)*.
analog ['ænəlɒg] n (*US*) = **analogue**. ~ **computer** calculateur *m* analogique; ~ **data** données *fpl* analogiques.
analogic(al) [ˌænə'lɒdʒɪk(əl)] adj analogique.
analogous [ə'næləgəs] adj analogue (*to, with* à).
analogue ['ænəlɒg] n analogue *m*. ~ **device** unité *f* analogique; ~-**digital converter** convertisseur *m* analogique-numérique; ~ **watch** montre *f* à lecture analogique.
analogy [ə'nælədʒɪ] n analogie *f* (*between* entre; *with* avec). **to argue from** ~ raisonner par analogie; **by** ~ par analogie (*with* avec).
analysand [ə'nælɪˌsænd] n (*Psych*) sujet *m* en analyse.
analyse, (*US*) **analyze** ['ænəlaɪz] vt **a** analyser, faire l'analyse de; (*Gram*) *sentence* faire l'analyse logique de. **b** (*Psych*) psychanalyser.
analysis [ə'næləsɪs] n, pl **analyses** [ə'nælɪsiːz] **a** analyse *f*; (*Gram*) *[sentence]* analyse logique. (*fig*) **in the ultimate** *or* **last** *or* **final** ~ en dernière analyse, finalement. **b** (*Psych*) psychanalyse *f*. **to be in** ~ poursuivre une analyse, être en cours d'analyse.
analyst ['ænəlɪst] n **a** (*Chem etc*) analyste *m*. **b** (*Psych*) (psych)analyste *mf*; *see* **news**.
analytic(al) [ˌænə'lɪtɪk(əl)] adj analytique. ~ **mind** esprit *m* analytique; ~ **psychology** psychologie *f* analytique *or* des profondeurs; (*Comput*) ~ **engine** machine *f* de Babbage.

analyze ['ænəlaɪz] vt (*US*) = **analyse**.
anamorphosis [ˌænə'mɔːfəsɪs] n, pl **anamorphoses** [ˌænə'mɔːfəˌsiːz] anamorphose *f*.
anapaest, (*US*) **anapest** ['ænəpiːst] n anapeste *m*.
anaphoric [ˌænə'fɒrɪk] adj (*Ling*) anaphorique.
anarchic(al) [æ'nɑːkɪk(əl)] adj anarchique.
anarchism ['ænəkɪzəm] n anarchisme *m*.
anarchist ['ænəkɪst] n, adj anarchiste *(mf)*.
anarchy ['ænəkɪ] n anarchie *f*.
anastigmatic [ˌænəstɪg'mætɪk] adj (*Phot*) anastigmate.
anathema [ə'næθɪmə] n (*Rel, fig*) anathème *m*. (*fig*) **the whole idea of exploiting people was ~ to him** il avait en abomination l'idée d'exploiter les gens.
anathematize [ə'næθɪmətaɪz] vt frapper d'anathème.
Anatolia [ˌænə'təʊlɪə] n Anatolie *f*.
Anatolian [ˌænə'təʊlɪən] adj anatolien.
anatomical [ˌænə'tɒmɪkəl] adj anatomique.
anatomist [ə'nætəmɪst] n anatomiste *mf*.
anatomize [ə'nætəmaɪz] vt disséquer.
anatomy [ə'nætəmɪ] n (*Med, Sci*) anatomie *f*; (*fig*) *[country etc]* structure *f*. **he had spots all over his ~** il avait des boutons partout, il était couvert de boutons.
ANC [ˌeɪen'siː] n (abbr of **African National Congress**) ANC *m*.
ancestor ['ænsɪstəʳ] n (*lit*) ancêtre *m*, aïeul *m*; (*fig*) ancêtre.
ancestral [æn'sestrəl] adj ancestral. **~ home** château ancestral.
ancestress ['ænsɪstrɪs] n aïeule *f*.
ancestry ['ænsɪstrɪ] n **a** (*lineage*) ascendance *f*. **b** (*collective n*) ancêtres *mpl*, aïeux *mpl*, ascendants *mpl*.
anchor ['æŋkəʳ] **1** n ancre *f*; (*fig*) point *m* d'ancrage. **to be at ~** être à l'ancre; **to come to ~** jeter l'ancre, mouiller; *see* **cast, ride, up 6, weigh** *etc*. **2** vt (*Naut*) mettre à l'ancre; (*fig*) ancrer, enraciner. **3** vi (*Naut*) mouiller, jeter l'ancre, se mettre à l'ancre. **4** comp ▸**anchor ice** glaces *fpl* de fond ▸**anchorman/anchorwoman** (*Rad, TV*) présentateur-réalisateur *m*/présentatrice-réalisatrice *f*; (*in team, organization*) pilier *m*, pivot *m*.
anchorage ['æŋkərɪdʒ] n (*Naut*) mouillage *m*, ancrage *m*. **~ dues** droits *mpl* de mouillage *or* d'ancrage; (*Aut*) **~ point** point *m* d'ancrage.
anchorite ['æŋkəraɪt] n anachorète *m*.
anchovy ['æntʃəvɪ] n anchois *m*. **~ paste** pâte *f* d'anchois (*vendue toute préparée*); **~ sauce** sauce *f* aux anchois.
ancient ['eɪnʃənt] **1** adj **a** *world, painting* antique; *document, custom* ancien. **in ~ days** dans les temps anciens; **~ history** histoire ancienne; **it's ~ history*** c'est de l'histoire ancienne; (*Brit*) **(scheduled as an) ~ monument** (classé) monument *m* historique; **~ Rome** la Rome antique; **~ rocks** de vieilles roches. **b** (**: gen hum*) *person* très vieux (*f* vieille); *clothes, object* antique, antédiluvien*. **this is positively ~** cela remonte à Mathusalem *or* au déluge; **a really ~ car** une antique guimbarde*; **he's getting pretty ~** il se fait vieux, il prend de la bouteille*. **2** n **a** (*people of long ago*) **the ~s** les anciens *mpl*. **b** (*hum*) vieillard *m*, patriarche *m*.
ancillary [æn'sɪlərɪ] adj *service, help, forces* auxiliaire. **~ to** subordonné à; **(hospital) ~ workers** personnel *m* des services auxiliaires (des hôpitaux), agents *mpl* des hôpitaux; (*Brit Scol*) **~ staff** agents *mpl* (d'un établissement scolaire); (*Fin, Comm*) **~ costs** frais *mpl* accessoires *or* annexes.
and [ænd, ənd, nd, ən] conj **a** et. **a man ~ a woman** un homme et une femme; **his table ~ chair** sa table et sa chaise; **~ how!*** et comment!*; **~?** et alors?; **on Saturday ~/or Sunday** (*Admin*) samedi et/ou dimanche; (*gen*) samedi ou dimanche ou les deux.
b (*in numbers*) **three hundred ~ ten** trois cent dix; **two thousand ~ eight** deux mille huit; **two pounds ~ six pence** deux livres (et) six pence; **an hour ~ twenty minutes** une heure vingt (minutes); **five ~ three quarters** cinq trois quarts.
c (*+ infin vb*) **try ~ come** tâchez de venir; **wait ~ see** on verra bien, attendez voir.
d (*repetition, continuation*) **better ~ better** de mieux en mieux; **now ~ then** de temps en temps; **for hours ~ hours** pendant des heures et des heures; **I rang ~ rang** j'ai sonné et resonné; **he talked ~ talked/waited ~ waited** il a parlé/attendu pendant des heures; **~ so on, ~ so forth** et ainsi de suite; **he goes on ~ on*** quand il commence il n'y a plus moyen de l'arrêter.
e (*with compar adj*) **uglier ~ uglier** de plus en plus laid; **more ~ more difficult** de plus en plus difficile.
f (*with neg or implied neg*) ni. **to go out without a hat ~ coat** sortir sans chapeau ni manteau; **you can't buy ~ sell here** on ne peut ni acheter ni vendre ici.
g (*phrases*) **eggs ~ bacon** œufs au bacon; **summer ~ winter (alike)** été comme hiver; **a carriage ~ pair** une voiture à deux chevaux.
h (*implying cond*) **flee ~ you are lost** fuyez et vous êtes perdu, si vous fuyez vous êtes perdu.
Andalucia, Andalusia [ˌændəlʊ'siːə] n Andalousie *f*.
Andalucian, Andalusian [ˌændəlʊ'siːən] adj andalou (*f* -ouse).
Andean ['ændɪən] adj des Andes, andin.
Andes ['ændiːz] n Andes *fpl*.
andiron ['ændaɪən] n chenet *m*.
Andorra [ˌæn'dɔːrə] n (la république d')Andorre *f*.
Andorran [ˌæn'dɔːrən] **1** adj andorran. **2** n Andorran(e) *m(f)*.
Andrew ['ændruː] n André *m*.
androgen ['ændrədʒən] n (*Physiol*) androgène *m*.
android ['ændrɔɪd] adj, n androïde *m*.
Andromache [æn'drɒməkɪ] n Andromaque *f*.
Andromeda [æn'drɒmɪdə] n Andromède *f*.
androsterone [æn'drɒstəˌrəʊn] n androstérone *f*.
anecdotal [ˌænɪk'dəʊtəl] adj anecdotique. **his lecture was very ~** sa conférence faisait une large part à l'anecdote.
anecdote ['ænɪkdəʊt] n anecdote *f*.
anemia [ə'niːmɪə] n = **anaemia**.
anemic [ə'niːmɪk] adj = **anaemic**.
anemometer [ˌænɪ'mɒmɪtəʳ] n anémomètre *m*.
anemone [ə'nemənɪ] n anémone *f*; *see* **sea**.
anent [ə'nent] prep (*Scot*) concernant, à propos de.
aneroid ['ænərɔɪd] adj anéroïde. **~ (barometer)** baromètre *m* anéroïde.
anesthesia [ˌænɪs'θiːzɪə] n = **anaesthesia**.
anesthesiologist [ˌænɪsθiːzɪ'ɒlədʒɪst] n (*US*) (médecin *m*) anesthésiste *mf*.
anesthetic [ˌænɪs'θetɪk] n, adj = **anaesthetic**.
anesthetist [æ'niːsθɪtɪst] n = **anaesthetist**.
anesthetize [æ'niːsθɪtaɪz] vt = **anaesthetize**.
aneurism, aneurysm ['ænjʊrɪzəm] n anévrisme *m*.
anew [ə'njuː] adv (*again*) de nouveau, encore; (*in a new way*) à nouveau. **to begin ~** recommencer.
angel ['eɪndʒəl] **1** n ange *m*; (**: person*) ange, amour *m*; (*Theat* ‡) commanditaire *mf*. **~ of Darkness** ange des Ténèbres; **be an ~ and fetch me my gloves** apporte-moi mes gants, tu seras un ange; **speak** *or* **talk of ~s!*** quand on parle du loup (on en voit la queue)!; (*fig*) **to go where ~s fear to tread** s'aventurer en terrain dangereux; *see* **guardian**. **2** comp ▸**angel cake** ≃ gâteau *m* de Savoie ▸**angelfish** scalaire *m*; (*shark*) ange *m* de mer ▸**angel food cake** (*US*) = **angel cake** ▸**angel shark** ange *m* de mer.
Angeleno [ˌændʒə'liːnəʊ] n (*US*) habitant(e) *m(f)* de Los Angeles.
angelic [æn'dʒelɪk] adj angélique.
angelica [æn'dʒelɪkə] n angélique *f*.
angelical [æn'dʒelɪkəl] adj angélique.
Angelino [ˌændʒe'liːnəʊ] n = **Angeleno**.
angelus ['ændʒɪləs] n (*prayer, bell*) angélus *m*.
anger ['æŋgəʳ] **1** n colère *f*; (*violent*) fureur *f*, courroux *m* (*liter*). **to act in ~** agir sous l'empire *or* sous le coup de la colère, agir avec emportement; **words spoken in ~** mots prononcés sous l'empire *or* sous le coup de la colère; **to move sb to ~** mettre qn en colère; **his ~ knew no bounds** sa colère *or* son emportement ne connut plus de bornes; **in great ~** furieux, courroucé (*liter*). **2** vt mettre en colère, irriter; (*greatly*) courroucer (*liter*). **to be easily ~ed** se mettre facilement en colère, s'emporter facilement.
angina [æn'dʒaɪnə] n angine *f*. **~ (pectoris)** angine de poitrine; **to have ~** avoir une angine.
angle¹ ['æŋgl] **1** n **a** (*also Math*) angle *m*. **at an ~ of** formant un angle de; **at an ~** en biais (*to* par rapport à); **cut at an ~** *pipe, edge* coupé en biseau; **the building stands at an ~ to the street** le bâtiment fait angle avec la rue; (*Aviat*) **~ of climb** angle d'ascension; (*Constr*) **~ iron** fer *m*, équerre *f*; *see* **acute, right**.
b (*fig: aspect, point of view*) angle *m*, aspect *m*. **the various ~s of a topic** les divers aspects d'un sujet; **to study a topic from every ~** étudier un sujet sous toutes ses faces *or* sous tous les angles; **this article gives a new ~ on the question** cet article apporte un éclairage original sur la question; **from the parents' ~** du point de vue des parents; **let's have your ~ on it*** dites-nous votre point de vue là-dessus, dites-nous comment vous voyez ça*.
2 vt **a** (***) *information, report* présenter sous un certain angle. **he ~d his article towards middle-class readers** il a rédigé son article à l'intention des classes moyennes *or* de façon à plaire au lecteur bourgeois.
b (*Tennis*) **to ~ a shot** croiser sa balle, jouer la diagonale.
c *lamp etc* régler à l'angle voulu. **she ~d the lamp towards her desk** elle a dirigé la lumière (de la lampe) sur son bureau.
angle² ['æŋgl] vi **a** (*lit*) pêcher à la ligne. **to ~ for trout** pêcher la truite. **b** (*fig*) **to ~ for sb's attention** chercher à attirer l'attention de qn; **to ~ for compliments** chercher *or* quêter des compliments; **to ~ for a rise in salary/for an invitation** chercher à se faire augmenter/à se faire inviter; **she's angling for a husband** elle fait la chasse au mari.
Anglepoise ['æŋglˌpɔɪz] n ®: **~ lamp** lampe *f* d'architecte.
angler ['æŋgləʳ] n pêcheur *m*, -euse *f* (à la ligne). **~ (fish)** lotte *f* de mer.
Angles ['æŋglz] npl (*Hist*) Angles *mpl*.
Anglican ['æŋglɪkən] adj, n anglican(e) *m(f)*. **the ~ Communion** la communion *or* la communauté anglicane.
Anglicanism ['æŋglɪkənɪzəm] n anglicanisme *m*.
anglicism ['æŋglɪsɪzəm] n anglicisme *m*.
anglicist ['æŋglɪsɪst] n angliciste *mf*.

anglicize ['æŋglɪsaɪz] vt angliciser.

angling ['æŋglɪŋ] n pêche *f* (à la ligne).

Anglo*‡* ['æŋgləʊ] n Américain blanc, Américaine blanche (d'origine non hispanique).

Anglo- ['æŋgləʊ] pref anglo-.

Anglo-American ['æŋgləʊə'merɪkən] 1 adj anglo-américain. 2 n (*US*) Anglo-américain(e) *m(f)*.

Anglo-Catholic ['æŋgləʊ'kæθəlɪk] adj, n anglo-catholique *(mf)*.

Anglo-Catholicism ['æŋgləʊkə'θɒlɪsɪzəm] n anglo-catholicisme *m*.

Anglo-French ['æŋgləʊ'frentʃ] 1 adj anglo-français, franco-britannique, franco-anglais. 2 n (*Ling*) anglo-normand *m*.

Anglo-Indian ['æŋgləʊ'ɪndɪən] n (*English person in India*) Anglais(e) *m(f)* des Indes; (*person of English and Indian descent*) métis(se) *m(f)* d'Anglais(e) et d'Indien(ne).

anglophile ['æŋgləʊfaɪl] adj, n anglophile *(mf)*.

anglophobe ['æŋgləʊfəʊb] adj, n anglophobe *(mf)*.

Anglo-Saxon ['æŋgləʊ'sæksən] 1 adj anglo-saxon. 2 n a Anglo-Saxon(ne) *m(f)*. b (*Ling*) anglo-saxon *m*.

Angola [æŋ'gəʊlə] n Angola *m*.

Angolan [æŋ'gəʊlən] 1 adj angolais. 2 n Angolais(e) *m(f)*.

angora [æŋ'gɔːrə] 1 n a (*cat/rabbit*) (chat *m*/lapin *m*) angora *m*; (*goat*) chèvre *f* angora. b (*wool*) laine *f* angora, angora *m*. 2 adj *cat, rabbit etc* angora *inv*; *sweater* (en) angora.

angostura [æŋgə'stjʊərə] n angusture *f*. ® ~ **bitters** bitter *m* à base d'angusture.

angrily ['æŋgrɪlɪ] adv *leave* en colère; *talk* avec colère, avec emportement.

angry ['æŋgrɪ] adj a *person* en colère, fâché (*with sb* contre qn, *at sth* à cause de qch, *about sth* à propos de qch); (*furious*) furieux (*with sb* contre qn, *at sth* de qch, *about sth* à cause de qch); (*annoyed*) irrité (*with sb* contre qn, *at sth* de qch, *about sth* à cause de qch); *look* irrité, furieux, courroucé (*liter*); *reply* plein *or* vibrant de colère; (*fig*) *sea* mauvais, démonté. **to get** ~ se fâcher, se mettre en colère; **to make sb** ~ mettre qn en colère; **he was** ~ **at being dismissed** il était furieux d'avoir été renvoyé *or* qu'on l'ait renvoyé; **in an** ~ **voice** sur le ton de la colère; **you won't be** ~ **if I tell you?** vous n'allez pas vous fâcher si je vous le dis?; **this sort of thing makes me** ~ ce genre de chose me met hors de moi; **there were** ~ **scenes when it was announced that ...** des incidents violents ont éclatés quand on a annoncé que ...; (*Brit Literat*) ~ **young man** jeune homme *m* en colère.
b (*inflamed*) *wound* enflammé, irrité; (*painful*) douloureux. **the blow left an** ~ **mark on his forehead** le coup lui a laissé une vilaine meurtrissure au front.

angstrom ['æŋstrəm] n angström *m*, angstroem *m*.

Anguilla [æŋ'gwɪlə] n Anguilla.

anguish ['æŋgwɪʃ] n (*mental*) angoisse *f*, anxiété *f*; (*physical*) supplice *m*. **to be in** ~ (*mentally*) être dans l'angoisse *or* angoissé; (*physically*) être au supplice, souffrir le martyre.

anguished ['æŋgwɪʃt] adj (*mentally*) angoissé; (*physically*) plein de souffrance.

angular ['æŋgjʊlə^r] adj anguleux; *face* anguleux, osseux, maigre; *features* anguleux; *movement* dégingandé, saccadé.

aniline ['ænɪliːn] n aniline *f*. ~ **dyes** colorants *mpl* à base d'aniline.

anima ['ænɪmə] n (*Psych*) anima *f*.

animal ['ænɪməl] 1 n (*lit*) animal *m*; (* *pej: person*) brute *f*. **I like** ~**s** j'aime les animaux *or* les bêtes; **man is a social** ~ l'homme est un animal sociable; (*pej*) **the** ~ **in him** la bête en lui, son côté bestial; **he's nothing but an** ~ ce n'est qu'une petite brute; (*fig*) **there's no such** ~ ça n'existe pas; (*fig*) **they're two different** ~**s** ce sont deux choses complètement différentes.
2 adj *fats, oil, instinct* animal. ~ **experiment** expérience *f* sur un animal (*or* les animaux); ~ **experimentation** expérimentation animale *or* sur les animaux; ~ **husbandry** élevage *m*; ~ **kingdom** règne animal; ~ **lover** personne *f* qui aime les animaux; ~ **rights** les droits *mpl* des animaux; ~ **rights campaigner** défenseur *m* des droits des animaux; ~ **spirits** entrain *m*, vivacité *f*; **full of** ~ **spirits** plein d'entrain *or* de vivacité *or* de vie.

animate ['ænɪmɪt] 1 adj (*living*) vivant, animé; (*Ling*) animé. 2 ['ænɪmeɪt] vt a (*lit*) animer, vivifier (*liter*). b (*fig*) *discussion* animer, rendre vivant, aviver.

animated ['ænɪmeɪtɪd] adj animé. **to become** ~ s'animer; **the talk was growing** ~ la conversation s'animait *or* s'échauffait; (*Cine*) (~) **cartoon** dessin(s) animé(s), film *m* d'animation.

animatedly ['ænɪmeɪtɪdlɪ] adv *talk* d'un ton animé, avec animation; *behave* avec entrain, avec vivacité.

animation [ˌænɪ'meɪʃən] n *[person]* vivacité *f*, entrain *m*; *[face]* animation *f*; *[scene, street etc]* activité *f*, animation; (*Cine*) animation; *see* **suspend**.

animator ['ænɪmeɪtə^r] n (*Cine*) animateur *m*, -trice *f*.

animism ['ænɪmɪzəm] n animisme *m*.

animist ['ænɪmɪst] adj, n animiste *(mf)*.

animosity [ˌænɪ'mɒsɪtɪ] n animosité *f* (*against, towards* contre), hostilité *f* (*against, towards* envers), antipathie *f* (*against, towards* pour).

animus ['ænɪməs] n a (*NonC*) = **animosity**. b (*Psych*) animus *m*.

anise ['ænɪs] n anis *m*.

aniseed ['ænɪsiːd] 1 n graine *f* d'anis. 2 comp *flavoured* à l'anis ►**aniseed ball** bonbon *m* à l'anis.

anisette [ˌænɪ'zet] n anisette *f*.

Anjou [ɑ̃'ʒuː] n Anjou *m*.

Ankara ['æŋkərə] n Ankara.

ankle ['æŋkl] 1 n cheville *f*. 2 comp ►**anklebone** astragale *m* ►**ankle-deep: he was ankle-deep in water** l'eau lui montait *or* il avait de l'eau (jusqu')à la cheville; **the water is ankle-deep** l'eau monte *or* vient (jusqu')à la cheville ►**ankle joint** articulation *f* de la cheville ►**ankle sock** (*Brit*) socquette *f* ►**ankle strap** bride *f*.

anklet ['æŋklɪt] n bracelet *m or* anneau *m* de cheville; (*US*) socquette *f*.

ankylosis [ˌæŋkɪ'ləʊsɪs] n ankylose *f*.

Ann [æn] n Anne *f*.

annalist ['ænəlɪst] n annaliste *m*.

annals ['ænəlz] npl annales *fpl*.

Annam [æ'næm] n Annam *m*.

Annapurna [ˌænə'pʊənə] n Annâpurnâ *m*.

Anne [æn] n Anne *f*; *see* **queen**.

anneal [ə'niːl] vt *glass, metal* recuire.

annex [ə'neks] 1 vt annexer. 2 ['æneks] n (*building, document*) annexe *f*.

annexation [ˌænek'seɪʃən] n (*act*) annexion *f* (*of* de); (*territory*) territoire *m* annexe.

annexe ['æneks] n = **annex 2**.

Annie Oakley*‡* [ˌænɪ'əʊklɪ] n (*US*) billet *m* de faveur.

annihilate [ə'naɪəleɪt] vt *army, fleet* anéantir; *space, time* annihiler, supprimer; *effect* annihiler.

annihilation [əˌnaɪə'leɪʃən] n (*Mil*) anéantissement *m*; (*fig*) suppression *f*.

anniversary [ˌænɪ'vɜːsərɪ] 1 n anniversaire *m* (*d'une date, d'un événement*); *see* **wedding**. 2 comp ►**anniversary dinner** dîner commémoratif *or* anniversaire.

Anno Domini ['ænəʊ'dɒmɪnaɪ] n a l'an *m* de notre ère, après Jésus-Christ, ap. J.-C., l'an de grâce (*liter*). **in 53** ~ en 53 après Jésus-Christ *or* ap. J.-C., en l'an 53 de notre ère; **the 2nd century** ~ le 2e siècle de notre ère. b (*) vieillesse *f*, le poids des ans (*hum*). **he is showing signs of** ~ il commence à prendre de l'âge *or* à se faire vieux.

annotate ['ænəʊteɪt] vt annoter.

annotation [ˌænəʊ'teɪʃən] n annotation *f*, note *f*.

announce [ə'naʊns] vt annoncer. **to** ~ **the birth/death of** faire part de la naissance de/du décès de; **"I won't" he** ~**d** "je ne le ferai pas" annonça-t-il; **it is** ~**d from London** on apprend de Londres.

announcement [ə'naʊnsmənt] n (*gen*) annonce *f*; (*esp Admin*) avis *m*; *[birth, marriage, death]* avis; (*privately inserted or circulated*) faire-part *m inv*.

announcer [ə'naʊnsə^r] n (*Rad, TV*) (*linking programmes*) speaker(ine) *m(f)*, annonceur *m*, -euse *f*; (*within a programme*) présentateur *m*, -trice *f*; (*newsreader*) journaliste *mf*; (*at airport, station*) annonceur *m*, -euse *f*.

annoy [ə'nɔɪ] vt (*vex*) ennuyer, agacer, contrarier; (*deliberately irritate*) *person, animal* agacer, énerver, embêter*; (*inconvenience*) importuner, ennuyer. **to be/get** ~**ed with sb** être/se mettre en colère contre qn; **to be** ~**ed about** *or* **over an event** être contrarié par un événement; **to be** ~**ed about** *or* **over a decision** être mécontent d'une décision; **to be** ~**ed with sb about sth** être mécontent de qn à propos de qch, savoir mauvais gré à qn de qch (*frm*); **to get** ~**ed with a machine** se mettre en colère *or* s'énerver contre une machine; **don't get** ~**ed!** ne vous fâchez pas!; **I am very** ~**ed that he hasn't come** je suis très ennuyé *or* contrarié qu'il ne soit pas venu; **I am very** ~**ed with him for not coming** je suis très mécontent qu'il ne soit pas venu.

annoyance [ə'nɔɪəns] n a (*displeasure*) mécontentement *m*, déplaisir *m*, contrariété *f*. **with a look of** ~ d'un air contrarié *or* ennuyé; **he found to his great** ~ **that ...** il s'est aperçu à son grand mécontentement *or* déplaisir que ... . b (*cause of* ~) tracas *m*, ennui *m*, désagrément *m*.

annoying [ə'nɔɪɪŋ] adj (*slightly irritating*) agaçant, énervant, embêtant*; (*very irritating*) ennuyeux, fâcheux. **the** ~ **thing about it is that ...** ce qui est agaçant *or* ennuyeux dans cette histoire c'est que ...; **how** ~! que c'est agaçant! *or* ennuyeux!

annoyingly [ə'nɔɪɪŋlɪ] adv d'une façon agaçante. **the sound was** ~ **loud** le son était si fort que ç'en était gênant.

annual ['ænjʊəl] 1 adj annuel. (*Comm etc*) ~ **general meeting** assemblée générale annuelle. 2 n a (*Bot*) plante annuelle; ~ **ring** anneau *m* de croissance; *see* **hardy**. b (*book*) publication annuelle; (*children's*) album *m*.

annualize ['ænjʊəlaɪz] vt annualiser.

annually ['ænjʊəlɪ] adv annuellement, tous les ans. **£5,000** ~ 5.000 livres par an.

annuity [ə'njuːɪtɪ] n (*regular income*) rente *f*; (*for life*) rente viagère, viager *m*; (*investment*) viager. **to invest money in an** ~ placer de l'argent en viager; ~ **bond** titre *m* de rente; *see* **defer[1]**, **life**.

annul [ə'nʌl] vt *law* abroger, abolir; *decision, judgment* casser, annuler,

infirmer; *marriage* annuler.
annulment [ə'nʌlmənt] **n** (*see* **annul**) abrogation *f*, abolition *f*, cassation *f*, annulation *f*, infirmation *f*.
Annunciation [ə,nʌnsɪ'eɪʃən] **n** Annonciation *f*.
anode ['ænəʊd] **n** anode *f*.
anodize ['ænədaɪz] **vt** anodiser.
anodyne ['ænəʊdaɪn] **1 n** (*Med*) analgésique *m*, calmant *m*; (*fig liter*) baume *m*. **2 adj** (*Med*) antalgique, analgésique, calmant; (*fig liter*) apaisant.
anoint [ə'nɔɪnt] **vt** oindre (*with* de), consacrer *or* bénir par l'onction. **to ~ sb king** sacrer qn, faire qn roi par la cérémonie du sacre; **the ~ed King** le roi consacré; (*fig: lucky*) **to be ~ed*** avoir une veine de pendu*.
anointing [ə'nɔɪntɪŋ] **n** (*Rel*) **~ of the sick** onction *f* des malades.
anomalous [ə'nɒmələs] **adj** (*Med*) anormal, irrégulier; (*Gram*) anomal; (*fig*) anormal.
anomaly [ə'nɒməlɪ] **n** anomalie *f*.
anomie, anomy ['ænəʊmɪ] **n** (*NonC*) anomie *f*.
anon[1] [ə'nɒn] **adv** († *or hum*) tout à l'heure, sous peu; *see* **ever**.
anon[2] [ə'nɒn] **adj** (**abbr of anonymous**) anonyme. (*at end of text*) **"A~"** "anonyme", "auteur inconnu".
anonymity [,ænə'nɪmɪtɪ] **n** anonymat *m*.
anonymous [ə'nɒnɪməs] **adj** anonyme. **to remain ~** garder l'anonymat.
anonymously [ə'nɒnɪməslɪ] **adv** *publish* anonymement, sans nom d'auteur; *donate* anonymement, en gardant l'anonymat.
anorak ['ænəræk] **n** anorak *m*.
anorexia [ænə'reksɪə] **n** anorexie *f*. **~ nervosa** anorexie mentale.
anorexic [ænə'reksɪk] **adj, n** anorexique *(mf)*.
another [ə'nʌðəʳ] **1 adj a** (*one more*) un ... de plus, encore un. **take ~ 10** prenez-en encore 10; **to wait ~ hour** attendre une heure de plus *or* encore une heure; **I shan't wait ~ minute!** je n'attendrai pas une minute de plus!; **without ~ word** sans ajouter un mot, sans un mot de plus; **~ glass?** vous reprendrez bien un verre?; **in ~ 20 years** dans 20 ans d'ici; (*what's more*) **and ~ thing** et de plus, et d'ailleurs.
b (*similar*) un autre, un second. **there is not ~ book like it, there is not ~ such book** il n'y a pas d'autre livre qui lui ressemble (*subj*), ce livre est unique dans son genre; **he will be ~ Hitler** ce sera un second *or* nouvel Hitler.
c (*different*) un autre. **that's quite ~ matter** c'est une tout autre question, c'est tout autre chose; **do it ~ time** remettez cela à plus tard, vous le ferez une autre fois.
2 pron a un(e) autre, encore un(e). **in one form or ~** sous une forme ou une autre; **he was opening bottles one after ~** il ouvrait des bouteilles les unes après les autres; **between** *or* **what with one thing and ~** en fin de compte; *see also* **after f, thing c**.
b one ~ = each other; *see* **each**.
anoxia [ə'nɒksɪə] **n** anoxie *f*.
anoxic [ə'nɒksɪk] **adj** anoxique.
ANSI [,eɪenes'aɪ] **n** (*US*) (**abbr of American National Standards Institute**) ANSI *m*, institut *m* américain de normalisation.
answer ['ɑːnsəʳ] **1 n a** réponse *f*; (*sharp*) réplique *f*, riposte *f*; (*to criticism, objection*) réponse, réfutation *f*. **to get an ~** obtenir une réponse; **to write sb an ~** répondre à qn (par écrit); **his only ~ was to shrug his shoulders** pour toute réponse il a haussé les épaules, il a répondu par un haussement d'épaules; (*Telec*) **there's no ~** ça ne répond pas; **I knocked but there was no ~** j'ai frappé mais sans réponse *or* mais on ne m'a pas répondu; (*Comm*) **in ~ to your letter** suite à *or* en réponse à votre lettre; **I could find no ~** je n'ai rien trouvé à répondre; **she's always got an ~** elle a réponse à tout; (*Jur*) **~ to a charge** réponse à une accusation; (*Rel*) **the ~ to my prayer** l'exaucement *m* de ma prière; (*hum*) **it's the ~ to a maiden's prayer*** c'est ce dont j'ai toujours rêvé; (*hum*) **for her he was the ~ to a maiden's prayer*** c'était l'homme de ses rêves; **there is no ~ to that** que voulez-vous répondre à ça?; **it's the poor man's ~ to caviar** c'est le caviar du pauvre; *see* **know**.
b (*solution to problem*) solution *f*. **~ to the riddle** mot *m* de l'énigme; (*fig*) **there is no easy ~** c'est un problème difficile à résoudre; **there must be an ~** il doit y avoir une explication *or* une solution, cela doit pouvoir s'expliquer.
2 comp ►answer-back (code) indicatif *m*.
3 vt a *letter, question* répondre à; *criticism* répondre à, (*sharply*) répliquer à. **~ me** répondez-moi; **to ~ the bell** *or* **door** aller *or* venir ouvrir (la porte), aller voir qui est à la porte *or* qui est là; *[servant summoned]* **to ~ the bell** répondre au coup de sonnette; **to ~ the phone** répondre (au téléphone); **I didn't ~ a word** je n'ai rien répondu, je n'ai pas soufflé mot; **~ing machine** répondeur *m* téléphonique; **~ing service** permanence *f* téléphonique.
b (*fulfil, solve*) *description* répondre à, correspondre à; *prayer* exaucer; *problem* résoudre; *need* répondre à, satisfaire. **it ~s the purpose** cela fait l'affaire; **this machine ~s several purposes** cet appareil a plusieurs utilisations.
c (*Jur*) **to ~ a charge** répondre à *or* réfuter une accusation.
d (*Naut*) **to ~ the helm** obéir à la barre.
4 vi a (*say, write in reply*) répondre, donner une réponse.
b (*succeed*) *[plan etc]* faire l'affaire, réussir.
c he ~s to the name of il répond au nom de, il s'appelle; **he ~s to that description** il répond à cette description.
►answer back 1 vi, vt sep répondre (avec impertinence) (*sb, to sb* à qn). **don't answer back!** ne réponds pas! **2 answer-back n** *see* **answer 2**.
►answer for vt fus *sb's safety etc* répondre de, se porter garant de, être responsable de. **to answer for the truth of sth** garantir l'exactitude de qch; **he has a lot to answer for** il a bien des comptes à rendre, il a une lourde responsabilité.
answerable ['ɑːnsərəbl] **adj a** *question* susceptible de réponse, qui admet une réponse; *charge, argument* réfutable; *problem* soluble. **b** (*responsible*) responsable (*to sb* devant qn, *for sth* de qch), garant (*to sb* envers qn, *for sth* de qch), comptable (*to sb* à qn, *for sth* de qch). **I am ~ to no one** je n'ai de comptes à rendre à personne.
ant [ænt] **n** fourmi *f*. **~eater** fourmilier *m*; **~-heap, ~hill** fourmilière *f*; (*fig*) **to have ~s in one's pants*** ne pas tenir en place.
antacid ['ænt'æsɪd] **1 adj** alcalin, antiacide. **2 n** (médicament *m*) alcalin *m*, antiacide *m*.
antagonism [æn'tægənɪzəm] **n** antagonisme *m* (*between* entre), opposition *f* (*to* à). **to show ~ to an idea** se montrer hostile à une idée.
antagonist [æn'tægənɪst] **n** antagoniste *mf*, adversaire *mf*.
antagonistic [æn,tægə'nɪstɪk] **adj** *force, interest* opposé,contraire. **to be ~ to sth** être opposé *or* hostile à qch; **to be ~ to sb** être en opposition avec qn; **two ~ ideas/decisions** deux idées/décisions antagonistes *or* opposées.
antagonize [æn'tægənaɪz] **vt** *person* éveiller l'hostilité de, contrarier. **I don't want to ~ him** je ne veux pas le contrarier *or* me le mettre à dos.
Antarctic [ænt'ɑːktɪk] **1 n** régions antarctiques *or* australes, Antarctique *m*. **2 adj** antarctique, austral. **~ Circle** cercle *m* Antarctique; **~ (Ocean)** océan *m* Antarctique *or* Austral.
Antarctica [ænt'ɑːktɪkə] **n** Antarctique *m*, continent *m* antarctique, Antarctide *f*.
ante ['æntɪ] **1 n** (*Cards: in poker*) première mise; (*fig*) **to raise the ~*** placer plus haut la barre (*fig*). **2 vi** (*Cards*) faire une première mise; (*US *: pay*) casquer*.
►ante up vi (*Cards*) augmenter l'enjeu; (*US *: pay*) casquer*.
ante... ['æntɪ] **pref** anté..., anti... .
antebellum [,æntɪ'beləm] **adj** (*US Hist*) d'avant la guerre de Sécession.
antecedent [,æntɪ'siːdənt] **1 adj** antérieur (*to* à), précédent. **2 n a** (*Gram, Math, Philos*) antécédent *m*. **b the ~s of sb** les antécédents *or* le passé de qn.
antechamber ['æntɪ,tʃeɪmbəʳ] **n** antichambre *f*.
antedate ['æntɪ'deɪt] **vt a** (*give earlier date to*) *document* antidater. **b** (*come before*) *event* précéder, dater d'avant.
antediluvian ['æntɪdɪ'luːvɪən] **adj** antédiluvien; (* *hum*) *person, hat* antédiluvien* (*hum*).
antelope ['æntɪləʊp] **n, pl ~** *or* **~s** antilope *f*.
antenatal ['æntɪ'neɪtl] **1 n** (*examination*) examen *m* prénatal. **2 adj** prénatal. **~ clinic** service *m* de consultation prénatale; **to attend an ~ clinic** aller à la consultation prénatale; **~ ward** salle *f* de surveillance prénatale.
antenna [æn'tenə] **n, pl ~s** *or* **antennae** [æn'teniː] (*Rad, Telec, TV, Zool*) antenne *f*.
antepenult [,ætɪpɪ'nʌlt] **n** (*Ling*) antépénultième *f*.
antepenultimate ['æntɪpɪ'nʌltɪmɪt] **adj** antépénultième.
anterior [æn'tɪərɪəʳ] **adj** antérieur (*to* à).
anteroom ['æntɪrʊm] **n** antichambre *f*, vestibule *m*.
anthem ['ænθəm] **n** motet *m*; *see* **national**.
anther ['ænθəʳ] **n** anthère *f*.
anthologist [æn'θɒlədʒɪst] **n** anthologiste *mf*.
anthologize [æn'θɒlə,dʒaɪz] **vt** faire une anthologie de.
anthology [æn'θɒlədʒɪ] **n** anthologie *f*.
Anthony ['æntənɪ] **n** Antoine *m*.
anthracite ['ænθrəsaɪt] **1 n** anthracite *m*. **2 adj: ~ (grey)** (gris) anthracite *inv*.
anthrax ['ænθræks] **n, pl anthraces** ['ænθrə,siːz] (*Med, Vet: disease*) charbon *m*; (*Med: boil*) anthrax *m*.
anthropo... ['ænθrəʊpɒ] **pref** anthropo... .
anthropoid ['ænθrəʊpɔɪd] **adj, n** anthropoïde *(m)*.
anthropological [,ænθrəpə'lɒdʒɪkəl] **adj** anthropologique.
anthropologist [,ænθrə'pɒlədʒɪst] **n** anthropologiste *mf*, anthropologue *mf*.
anthropology [,ænθrə'pɒlədʒɪ] **n** anthropologie *f*.
anthropometry [,ænθrə'pɒmɪtrɪ] **n** anthropométrie *f*.
anthropomorphic [,ænθrəpəʊ'mɔːfɪk] **adj** anthropomorphiste, anthropomorphique.
anthropomorphism [,ænθrəʊpə'mɔːfɪzəm] **n** anthropomorphisme *m*.
anthropomorphist [,ænθrəpəʊ'mɔːfɪst] **adj, n** anthropomorphiste *(mf)*.
anthropomorphous [,ænθrəʊpə'mɔːfəs] **adj** anthropomorphe.
anthropophagi [,ænθrəʊ'pɒfəgaɪ] **npl** anthropophages *mpl*, cannibales *mpl*.
anthropophagous [,ænθrəʊ'pɒfəgəs] **adj** anthropophage, cannibale.

anthropophagy [ˌænθrəʊˈpɒfədʒɪ] n anthropophagie *f*, cannibalisme *m*.
anthroposophical [ˌænθrəpəʊˈsɒfɪkəl] adj anthroposophique.
anthroposophy [ˌænθrəˈpɒsəfɪ] n anthroposophie *f*.
anti* [ˈæntɪ] 1 adj: **he's rather ~** il est plutôt contre*. 2 n: **the ~s** ceux qui sont contre*. 3 prep: **to be ~ sth** être contre qch.
anti... [ˈæntɪ] pref anti..., contre... .
antiabortion [ˈæntɪəˈbɔːʃən] n: **~ campaign** campagne *f* contre l'avortement.
antiabortionist [ˌæntɪəˈbɔːʃənɪst] n adversaire *m* de l'avortement.
anti-aircraft [ˈæntɪˈɛəkrɑːft] adj *gun, missile* antiaérien. **~ defence** défense *f* contre avions, D.C.A. *f*.
anti-apartheid [ˈæntɪəˈpɑːteɪt, ˈæntɪəˈpɑːtaɪd] adj anti-apartheid.
antiauthority [ˈæntɪɔːˈθɒrɪtɪ] adj contestataire.
antibacterial [ˈæntɪbækˈtɪərɪəl] adj antibactérie.
antiballistic [ˈæntɪbəˈlɪstɪk] adj *missile* antibalistique.
antibiotic [ˈæntɪbaɪˈɒtɪk] adj, n antibiotique *(m)*.
antibody [ˈæntɪˌbɒdɪ] n anticorps *m*.
antic [ˈæntɪk] n *(gen pl) [child, animal]* cabriole *f*, gambade *f*; *[clown]* bouffonnerie *f*, singerie *f*. *(pej: behaviour)* **all his ~s** tout le cinéma* *or* le cirque‡ qu'il a fait; **he's up to his ~s again** il fait de nouveau des siennes*.
Antichrist [ˈæntɪkraɪst] n Antéchrist *m*.
anticipate [ænˈtɪsɪpeɪt] vt a *(expect, foresee)* prévoir, s'attendre à. **we don't ~ any trouble** nous ne prévoyons pas d'ennuis; **I ~ that he will come** je m'attends à ce qu'il vienne; **do you ~ that it will be easy?** pensez-vous que ce sera facile?; **they ~d great pleasure from this visit** ils se sont promis beaucoup de joie de cette visite; **I ~ seeing him tomorrow** je pense le voir demain; **the attendance is larger than I ~d** je ne m'attendais pas à ce que l'assistance soit aussi nombreuse; **as ~d** comme prévu.
b *(use, deal with or get before due time) pleasure* savourer à l'avance; *grief, pain* souffrir à l'avance; *success* escompter; *wishes, objections, command, request* aller au devant de, prévenir, devancer; *needs* aller au devant de; *blow, attack, events* anticiper sur. **to ~ one's income/profits** anticiper sur son revenu/sur ses bénéfices.
c *(forestall)* **to ~ sb's doing sth** faire qch avant qn; **they ~d Columbus' discovery of America** *or* **~d Columbus in discovering America** ils ont découvert l'Amérique avant Christophe Colomb.
anticipation [ænˌtɪsɪˈpeɪʃən] n a *(expectation, foreseeing)* attente *f*. b *(experiencing etc in advance) [pleasure]* attente *f*; *[grief, pain]* appréhension *f*; *[profits, income]* jouissance anticipée. **~ of sb's wishes** *etc* empressement *m* à aller au-devant des désirs *etc* de qn. c **in ~** par anticipation, à l'avance; *(Comm)* **thanking you in ~** en vous remerciant d'avance, avec mes remerciements anticipés; **in ~ of a fine week** en prévision d'une semaine de beau temps; **we wait with growing ~** nous attendons avec une impatience grandissante.
anticipatory [ænˈtɪsɪpeɪtərɪ] adj *(Phon)* régressif.
anticlerical [ˈæntɪˈklerɪkl] adj, n anticlérical(e) *m(f)*.
anticlericalism [ˈæntɪˈklerɪkəlɪzəm] n anticléricalisme *m*.
anticlimax [ˈæntɪˈklaɪmæks] n *[style, thought]* chute *f* (dans le trivial). **the ceremony was an ~** la cérémonie a été une déception par contraste à l'attente *or* n'a pas répondu à l'attente; **what an ~!** quelle retombée!, quelle douche froide!
anticline [ˈæntɪklaɪn] n anticlinal *m*.
anticlockwise [ˈæntɪˈklɒkwaɪz] adv *(Brit)* dans le sens inverse des aiguilles d'une montre.
anticoagulant [ˈæntɪkəʊˈægjʊlənt] adj, n anticoagulant *(m)*.
anticorrosive [ˈæntɪkəˈrəʊsɪv] adj, n anticorrosif *(m)*.
anticyclone [ˈæntɪˈsaɪkləʊn] n anticyclone *m*.
antidandruff [ˌæntɪˈdændrʌf] adj anti-pelliculaire.
anti-dazzle [ˈæntɪˈdæzl] adj antiaveuglant. *(Aut)* **~ headlights** phares anti-éblouissants.
antidepressant [ˈæntɪdɪˈpresənt] n antidépresseur *m*.
antidotal [ˈæntɪdəʊtəl] adj antivénéneux.
antidote [ˈæntɪdəʊt] n *(Med, fig)* antidote *m* *(for, to* à, contre), contrepoison *m* *(for, to* de).
anti-dumping [ˌæntɪˈdʌmpɪŋ] n anti-dumping *m*. **~ agreement** convention *f* anti-dumping.
antiestablishment [ˈæntɪɪˈstæblɪʃmənt] adj contestataire.
antifog [ˌæntɪˈfɒg] adj: *(US)* **~ spray** bombe *f* antibuée.
antifreeze [ˈæntɪˈfriːz] n antigel *m*.
anti-friction [ˈæntɪˈfrɪkʃən] adj antifriction *inv*.
antigen [ˈæntɪdʒən] n antigène *m*.
anti-glare [ˈæntɪˈglɛəʳ] adj = **anti-dazzle**.
Antigone [ænˈtɪgənɪ] n Antigone *f*.
Antigua [ænˈtɪgjʊə] n: **~ and Barbuda** Antigua-et-Barbuda.
antihero [ˈæntɪˌhɪərəʊ] n, pl **~es** antihéros *m*.
antiheroine [ˈæntɪˈherəʊɪn] n antihéroïne *f*.
antihistamine [ˌæntɪˈhɪstəmɪn] n (produit *m*) antihistaminique *m*.
anti-inflammatory [ˈæntɪɪnˈflæmət(ə)rɪ] adj *(Med)* anti-inflammatoire.
anti-inflationary [ˌæntɪɪnˈfleɪʃənərɪ] adj anti-inflationniste.
anti-interference [ˈæntɪɪntəˈfɪərəns] adj antiparasite.
anti-knock [ˈæntɪˈnɒk] n antidétonant *m*.
Antilles [ænˈtɪliːz] n: **the ~** les Antilles *fpl*; **the Greater/the Lesser ~** les Grandes/Petites Antilles.
anti-lock [ˈæntɪˈlɒk] adj *(Aut)* **~ braking system** système *m* anti-blocage *or* ABS; **~ device** dispositif *m* anti-blocage.
antilogarithm [ˌæntɪˈlɒgərɪθəm] n antilogarithme *m*.
antimacassar [ˈæntɪməˈkæsəʳ] n têtière *f*, appui-tête *m*.
antimagnetic [ˈæntɪmægˈnetɪk] adj antimagnétique.
anti-marketeer [ˈæntɪmɑːkəˈtɪəʳ] n *(Brit Pol)* adversaire *m* du Marché commun.
antimatter [ˈæntɪˌmætəʳ] n antimatière *f*.
antimissile [ˈæntɪˈmɪsaɪl] adj antimissile.
antimony [ˈæntɪmənɪ] n antimoine *m*.
anti-motion-sickness [ˈæntɪˈməʊʃənˈsɪknɪs] adj: **~ tablets** comprimés *mpl* contre le mal des transports.
antinuclear [ˈæntɪˈnjuːklɪəʳ] adj antinucléaire.
antinuke* [ˌæntɪˈnjuːk] adj antinucléaire.
Antioch [ˈæntɪɒk] n Antioche.
antipathetic [ˌæntɪpəˈθetɪk] adj antipathique *(to* à).
antipathy [ænˈtɪpəθɪ] n antipathie *f*, aversion *f* *(against, to* pour).
antipersonnel [ˈæntɪpɜːsəˈnel] adj *(Mil)* antipersonnel *inv*.
antiperspirant [ˈæntɪˈpɜːspɪrənt] 1 n déodorant *m* anti-transpiration. 2 adj anti-transpiration.
antiphony [ænˈtɪfənɪ] n *(Mus)* antienne *f*.
antipodean [ænˌtɪpəˈdɪən] adj des antipodes.
antipodes [ænˈtɪpədiːz] npl antipodes *mpl*.
antiquarian [ˌæntɪˈkwɛərɪən] 1 adj d'antiquaire. **~ bookseller** libraire *mf* spécialisé(e) dans le livre ancien; **~ collection** collection *f* d'antiquités. 2 n a amateur *m* d'antiquités. b *(Comm)* antiquaire *mf*. **~'s shop** magasin *m* d'antiquités.
antiquary [ˈæntɪkwərɪ] n *(collector)* collectionneur *m*, -euse *f* d'antiquités; *(student)* archéologue *mf*; *(Comm)* antiquaire *mf*.
antiquated [ˈæntɪkweɪtɪd] adj vieilli, vieillot *(f* -otte); *ideas, manners* vieillot, suranné; *person* vieux jeu *inv*; *building* vétuste.
antique [ænˈtiːk] 1 adj *(very old)* ancien; *(pre-medieval)* antique; *(* hum)* antédiluvien*. **~ furniture** meubles anciens. 2 n *(sculpture, ornament etc)* objet *m* d'art (ancien); *(furniture)* meuble ancien. **it's a genuine ~** c'est un objet (*or* un meuble) d'époque. 3 comp ▶**antique dealer** antiquaire *mf* ▶**antique shop** magasin *m* d'antiquités.
antiquity [ænˈtɪkwɪtɪ] n a *(NonC: old times)* antiquité *f*. b **antiquities** *(buildings)* monuments *mpl* antiques; *(works of art)* objets *mpl* d'art antiques, antiquités *fpl*.
antiracism [ˈæntɪˈreɪsɪzəm] n antiracisme *m*.
antiracist [ˈæntɪˈreɪsɪst] adj antiraciste, contre le racisme.
antireligious [ˈæntɪrɪˈlɪdʒəs] adj antireligieux.
anti-riot [ˈæntɪˈraɪət] adj: **~ police** ≃ garde *f* mobile; *(Police)* **~ squad** brigade *f* anti-émeute.
anti-roll bar [ˈæntɪˈrəʊlbɑːʳ] n *(Brit)* barre *f* anti-roulis, stabilisateur *m*.
antirrhinum [ˌæntɪˈraɪnəm] n muflier *m*, gueule-de-loup *f*.
anti-rust [ˈæntɪˈrʌst] adj antirouille *inv*.
antisegregationist [ˈæntɪsegrəˈgeɪʃənɪst] adj antiségrégationniste.
anti-Semite [ˈæntɪˈsiːmaɪt] n antisémite *mf*.
anti-Semitic [ˈæntɪsɪˈmɪtɪk] adj antisémite, antisémitique.
anti-Semitism [ˈæntɪˈsemɪtɪzəm] n antisémitisme *m*.
antisepsis [ˌæntɪˈsepsɪs] n antisepsie *f*.
antiseptic [ˌæntɪˈseptɪk] adj, n antiseptique *(m)*.
anti-skid [ˈæntɪˈskɪd] adj antidérapant.
antislavery [ˈæntɪˈsleɪvərɪ] adj antiesclavagiste.
anti-smoking [ˈæntɪˈsməʊkɪŋ] adj anti-tabac.
antisocial [ˈæntɪˈsəʊʃəl] adj *tendency, behaviour* antisocial. **don't be ~*, come and join us** ne sois pas si sauvage, viens nous rejoindre.
antispasmodic [ˈæntɪspæzˈmɒdɪk] adj, n antispasmodique *(m)*.
antistatic [ˈæntɪˈstætɪk] adj antistatique.
anti-strike [ˈæntɪˈstraɪk] adj antigrève.
anti-submarine [ˈæntɪsʌbməˈriːn] adj anti-sous-marin.
anti-tank [ˈæntɪˈtæŋk] adj antichar. **~ mines** mines *fpl* antichars.
anti-terrorist [ˈæntɪˈterərɪst] adj antiterroriste. **~ squad** brigade *f* antigang.
anti-theft [ˈæntɪˈθeft] adj: **~ device** *(Aut)* antivol *m*; *(gen)* dispositif *m* contre le vol, dispositif antivol.
antithesis [ænˈtɪθɪsɪs] n, pl **antitheses** [ænˈtɪθɪsiːz] a *(direct opposite)* opposé *m*, contraire *m* *(to, of* de). b *(contrast) [ideas etc]* antithèse *f* *(between* entre, *of one thing to another* d'une chose avec une autre), contraste *m*, opposition *f* *(between* entre). c *(Literat)* antithèse *f*.
antithetic(al) [ˌæntɪˈθetɪk(əl)] adj antithétique.
antithetically [ˌæntɪˈθetɪkəlɪ] adv par antithèse.
antitoxic [ˈæntɪˈtɒksɪk] adj antitoxique.
antitoxin [ˈæntɪˈtɒksɪn] n antitoxine *f*.
antitrust [ˈæntɪˈtrʌst] adj *(US)* **~ commission** commission *f* antimonopole; *(esp US)* **~ law** loi *f* antitrust *inv*.
antivivisection [ˈæntɪˌvɪvɪˈsekʃən] n antivivisection *f*, antivivisectionnisme *m*.
antivivisectionist [ˈæntɪˌvɪvɪˈsekʃənɪst] n adversaire *mf* de la

vivisection.

anti-wrinkle ['æntɪ'rɪŋkl] adj antirides *inv.*

antler ['æntləʳ] n merrain *m.* **the ~s** les bois *mpl*, la ramure (*NonC*).

Antony ['æntənɪ] n Antoine *m.*

antonym ['æntənɪm] n antonyme *m.*

antonymous [æn'tɒnɪməs] adj antonymique.

antonymy [æn'tɒnɪmɪ] n antonymie *f.*

antsy* ['æntsɪ] adj (*US*) nerveux, agité.

Antwerp ['æntwɜːp] n Anvers.

anus ['eɪnəs] n anus *m.*

anvil ['ænvɪl] n enclume *f.*

anxiety [æŋ'zaɪətɪ] n a (*concern*) anxiété *f*, grande inquiétude, appréhension *f*; (*Psych*) anxiété. **deep ~** angoisse *f*; **this is a great ~ to me** ceci m'inquiète énormément, ceci me donne énormément de soucis; (*Psych*) **~ neurosis** anxiété névrotique. b (*keen desire*) grand désir, désir ardent, fièvre *f.* **~ to do well** grand désir de réussir; **in his ~ to be gone he left his pen behind** il était si préoccupé de partir qu'il en a oublié son stylo, dans son souci de partir au plus vite il a oublié son stylo.

anxious ['æŋkʃəs] adj a (*troubled*) anxieux, angoissé, (très) inquiet (*f* -ète). **very ~ about** très inquiet de; **with an ~ glance** jetant un regard anxieux *or* angoissé; **to be over-~** être d'une anxiété maladive; **she is ~ about my health** mon état de santé la préoccupe *or* l'inquiète beaucoup.

b (*causing anxiety*) *news* inquiétant, alarmant, angoissant. **an ~ moment** un moment d'anxiété *or* de grande inquiétude; **~ hours** des heures sombres.

c (*strongly desirous*) anxieux, impatient, très désireux (*for* de). **~ for praise** avide de louanges; **~ to start** pressé *or* impatient de partir; **he is ~ to see you before you go** il tient beaucoup à *or* désirerait beaucoup vous voir avant votre départ; **I am ~ that he should do it** je tiens beaucoup à ce qu'il le fasse; **I am ~ for her return** *or* **for her to come back** il me tarde qu'elle revienne, j'attends son retour avec impatience; **not to be very ~ to do** avoir peu envie de faire.

anxiously ['æŋkʃəslɪ] adv a (*with concern*) avec inquiétude, anxieusement. b (*eagerly*) avec impatience.

anxiousness ['æŋksəsnɪs] n = **anxiety.**

any ['enɪ] 1 adj a (*with neg and implied neg = some*) **I haven't ~ money/books** je n'ai pas d'argent/de livres; **you haven't ~ excuse** vous n'avez aucune excuse; **this pan hasn't ~ lid** cette casserole n'a pas de couvercle; **there isn't ~ sign of life** il n'y a pas le moindre signe de vie; **without ~ difficulty** sans la moindre difficulté; **the impossibility of giving them ~ money/advice** l'impossibilité de leur donner de l'argent/aucun conseil; **I have hardly ~ money left** il ne me reste presque plus d'argent.

b (*in interrog sentences, clauses of cond and hypotheses = some*) **have you ~ butter?** avez-vous du beurre?; **can you see ~ birds in this tree?** voyez-vous des oiseaux dans cet arbre?; **are there ~ others?** y en a-t-il d'autres?; **is it ~ use trying?** est-ce que cela vaut la peine d'essayer?; **have you ~ complaints?** avez-vous quelque sujet de vous plaindre?, avez-vous à vous plaindre de quelque chose?; **is there ~ man who will help me?** y a-t-il quelqu'un qui pourrait m'aider?; **he can do it if ~ man can** si quelqu'un peut le faire c'est bien lui; **if it is in ~ way inconvenient to you** si cela vous cause un dérangement quel qu'il soit, si cela vous cause le moindre dérangement; **if you see ~ children** si vous voyez des enfants; **if you have ~ money** si vous avez de l'argent.

c (*no matter which*) n'importe quel, quelconque; (*each and every*) tout. **take ~ two points** prenez deux points quelconques; **take ~ dress you like** prenez n'importe quelle robe, prenez la robe que vous voulez, prenez n'importe laquelle de ces robes; **come at ~ time** venez à n'importe quelle heure; **at ~ hour of the day (or night)** à toute heure du jour (ou de la nuit); **~ number of** n'importe quelle quantité de; **~ person who breaks the rules will be punished** toute personne qui enfreindra le règlement sera punie; **he's not just ~ (old) footballer** ce n'est pas n'importe quel footballeur; *see* **day, minute** *etc.*

d (*phrases*) **in ~ case** de toute façon; **at ~ rate** en tout cas; **we have ~ amount of time/money** nous avons tout le temps/tout l'argent qu'il nous faut; **there are ~ number of ways to do it** il y a des quantités de façons *or* il y a mille façons de le faire.

2 pron a (*with neg and implied neg*) **she has 2 brothers and I haven't ~** elle a 2 frères alors que moi je n'en ai pas (un seul); **I don't believe ~ of them has done it** je ne crois pas qu'aucun d'eux l'ait fait; **I have hardly ~ left** il ne m'en reste presque plus; **I haven't any gloves and I can't go out without ~** je ne peux pas sortir sans gants et je n'en ai pas, je n'ai pas de gants et je ne peux pas sortir sans*.

b (*in interrog, cond, hypothetical constructions*) **have you got ~?** en avez-vous?; **if ~ of you can sing** si l'un (quelconque) d'entre vous *or* si quelqu'un parmi vous sait chanter; **if ~ of them come out** si quelques uns d'entre eux sortent, s'il y en a parmi eux qui sortent; **if ~ of them comes out** si l'un (quelconque) d'entre eux sort; **few, if ~, will come** il viendra peu de gens — si tant est qu'il en vienne, il viendra peu de gens et peut-être même personne.

c (*in affirmative sentences*) **~ of those books will do** n'importe lequel de ces livres fera l'affaire; **~ but him would have been afraid** tout autre que lui aurait eu peur.

3 adv a (*in neg sentences, gen with comps*) nullement, en aucune façon, aucunement. **she is not ~ more intelligent than her sister** elle n'est nullement *or* aucunement plus intelligente que sa sœur; **I can't hear him ~ more** je ne l'entends plus; **don't do it ~ more!** ne recommence pas!; **we can't go ~ further** nous ne pouvons pas aller plus loin; **I shan't wait ~ longer** je n'attendrai pas plus longtemps; **they didn't behave ~ too well** ils ne se sont pas tellement bien conduits; **without ~ more discussion they left** ils sont partis sans ajouter un mot.

b (*in interrog, cond and hypothetical constructions, gen with comps*) un peu, si peu que ce soit. **are you feeling ~ better?** vous sentez-vous un peu mieux?; **do you want ~ more soup?** voulez-vous encore de la soupe? *or* encore un peu de soupe?; **if you see ~ more beautiful flower than this** si vous voyez jamais plus belle fleur que celle-ci; **I couldn't do that ~ more than I could fly** je ne serais pas plus capable de faire cela que de voler.

c **(*) the rope didn't help them ~** la corde ne leur a pas servi à grand-chose *or* ne leur a servi à rien du tout.

anybody ['enɪbɒdɪ] pron a (*with neg and implied neg = somebody*) **I can't see ~** je ne vois personne; **there is hardly ~ there** il n'y a presque personne là; **without ~ seeing him** sans que personne le voie; **it's impossible for ~ to see him today** personne ne peut le voir aujourd'hui.

b (*in interrog, cond and hypothetical constructions = somebody*) quelqu'un. **was there ~ there?** est-ce qu'il y avait quelqu'un (là)?; **did ~ see you?** est-ce que quelqu'un t'a vu?, est-ce qu'on t'a vu?; **~ want my sandwich?*** quelqu'un veut mon sandwich?*; **if ~ touches that** si quelqu'un touche à cela; **if ~ can do it, he can** si quelqu'un peut le faire c'est bien lui.

c (*in affirmative sentences: no matter who*) **~ who wants to do it should say so now** si quelqu'un veut le faire qu'il le dise tout de suite; **~ could tell you** n'importe qui pourrait vous le dire; **~ would have thought he had lost** on aurait pu croire *or* on aurait cru qu'il avait perdu; **bring ~ you like** amenez qui vous voudrez; **~ who had heard him speak would agree** quiconque l'a entendu parler serait d'accord; **~ with any sense would know that!** le premier venu saurait cela pourvu qu'il ait un minimum de bon sens!; **~ but Robert** n'importe qui d'autre que *or* tout autre que Robert; **~ else** n'importe qui d'autre, toute autre personne; **~ else would have cried but not him** un autre aurait pleuré, lui non; **bring ~ else you like** amenez n'importe qui d'autre; **is there ~ else I can talk to?** est-ce qu'il y a quelqu'un d'autre à qui je puisse parler?; **bring somebody to help us, ~ will do** amenez quelqu'un pour nous aider, n'importe qui *or* le premier venu fera l'affaire.

d (*person of importance*) quelqu'un (d'important *or* de bien *or* de connu); (*person of no importance*) n'importe qui. **work harder if you want to be ~** il faut travailler plus si vous voulez devenir quelqu'un; **he's not just ~, he's the boss** ce n'est pas n'importe qui, c'est le patron.

anyhow ['enɪhaʊ] adv a (*in any way whatever*) **do it ~ you like** faites-le comme vous voulez; **the house was closed and I couldn't get in ~** la maison était fermée et je n'avais aucun moyen d'entrer; **~ I do it, it always fails** de quelque façon que je m'y prenne ça ne réussit jamais.

b (*carelessly, haphazardly: also* **any old how***) n'importe comment. **I came in late and finished my essay ~*** je suis rentré tard et j'ai fini ma dissertation n'importe comment *or* à la va-vite*; **the books were all ~* on the floor** les livres étaient tous en désordre *or* en vrac *or* n'importe comment par terre.

c (*in any case, at all events*) en tout cas, dans tous les cas, de toute façon. **whatever you say, they'll do it ~** vous pouvez dire ce que vous voulez, ils le feront de toute façon *or* quand même; **~ he eventually did it** toujours est-il qu'il a fini par le faire, il a quand même fini par le faire; **you can try ~** vous pouvez toujours essayer.

anyone ['enɪwʌn] pron = **anybody.**

anyplace* ['enɪpleɪs] adv (*US*) = **anywhere.**

anyroad* ['enɪrəʊd] adv (*Brit*) = **anyhow c.**

anything ['enɪθɪŋ] pron a (*with neg and implied neg = something*) **there wasn't ~ to be done** il n'y avait rien à faire; **there isn't ~ in the box** il n'y a rien dans la boîte; **we haven't seen ~** nous n'avons rien vu; **he won't eat meat** *or* **cheese** *or* **~*** il ne veut manger ni viande ni fromage ni rien*; **hardly ~** presque rien; **without ~ happening** sans qu'il se passe (*subj*) rien; **this is ~ but pleasant** ceci n'a vraiment rien d'agréable; (*reply to question*) **~ but!** pas du tout!, pas le moins du monde!, tout *or* bien au contraire!

b (*in interrog, cond and hypothetical constructions = something*) **was there ~ in the room?** est-ce qu'il y avait quelque chose dans la pièce?; **did you see ~?** avez-vous vu quelque chose?; **are you doing ~ tonight?** faites-vous *or* vous faites* quelque chose ce soir?, avez-vous quelque chose de prévu pour ce soir?; **is there ~ in this idea?** peut-on tirer quoi que ce soit de cette idée?; **can ~ be done?** y a-t-il quelque chose à faire?, peut-on faire quelque chose?; **can't ~ be done?** n'y a-t-il rien à faire?, ne peut-on faire quelque chose?; **~ else?** (*Comm*) et avec ça?*, c'est tout ce qu'il vous faut?, ce sera tout?; (*have you anything more to tell me, give me etc*) c'est tout?, il y a quelque chose d'autre?; **have you heard ~ of her?** avez-vous de ses nouvelles?; **if ~ should happen to me** s'il m'arrivait quelque chose *or* quoi que ce soit; **if I see ~ I'll tell you** si je vois quelque chose je te le dirai; **he must have ~**

between 15 and 20 apple trees il doit avoir quelque chose comme 15 ou 20 pommiers; **if ~ it's an improvement** ce serait plutôt une amélioration; **it is, if ~, even smaller** c'est peut-être encore plus petit.

c (*with adj*) **I didn't see ~ interesting** je n'ai rien vu d'intéressant; **did you see ~ interesting?** tu as vu quelque chose d'intéressant? **is there ~ more tiring than ...?** y a-t-il rien de plus fatigant que ...?

d (*no matter what*) **say ~ (at all)** dites n'importe quoi; **take ~ you like** prenez ce que vous voudrez; **~ else would disappoint her** s'il en était autrement elle serait déçue; **~ else is impossible** il n'y a pas d'autre possibilité; **I'll try ~ else** j'essaierai n'importe quoi d'autre; **I'd give ~ to know the secret** je donnerais n'importe quoi pour connaître le secret; **this isn't just ~** ce n'est pas n'importe quoi; **they eat ~** (*they're not fussy*) ils mangent de tout; (*also* **they eat any old thing***) ils mangent n'importe quoi.

e (**: intensive adv phrases*) **he ran like ~** il s'est mis à courir comme un dératé* *or* un fou; **she cried like ~** elle a pleuré comme une Madeleine*; **we laughed like ~** on a ri comme des fous, ce qu'on a pu rire!; **they worked like ~** ils ont travaillé d'arrache-pied *or* comme des dingues‡; **it's raining like ~** ce qu'il peut pleuvoir!, il pleut *or* tombe des cordes*; **it's as big as ~** c'est très très grand; **it was as silly as ~** c'était idiot comme tout*.

anytime ['enɪtaɪm] adv = **any time**; *see* **time**.

anyway ['enɪweɪ] adv = **anyhow c**.

anywhere ['enɪwɛəʳ] adv a (*in affirmative sentences*) n'importe où, partout. **I'd live ~ in France** j'habiterais n'importe où en France; **put it down ~** pose-le n'importe où; **you can find that soap ~** ce savon se trouve partout; **go ~ you like** va où tu veux; **~ you go it's the same** où que vous alliez c'est la même chose, c'est partout pareil; **~ else** partout ailleurs; **miles from ~** loin de tout; **~ between 200 and 300** quelque chose entre 200 et 300; **the books were all ~* on the shelves** les livres étaient rangés *or* placés n'importe comment sur les rayons.

b (*in neg sentences*) nulle part, en aucun endroit, en aucun lieu. **they didn't go ~** ils ne sont allés nulle part; **not ~ else** nulle part ailleurs; **not ~ special** nulle part en particulier; **we aren't ~ near Paris** nous sommes loin de Paris; **the house isn't ~ near big enough** la maison est loin d'être assez grande; (*fig: in guessing etc*) **you aren't ~ near it!** vous n'y êtes pas du tout!; (*fig*) **it won't get you ~** cela ne vous mènera à rien; (*Sport etc*) **he came first and the rest didn't come ~*** il est arrivé très loin en tête des autres.

c (*in interrog sentences*) quelque part. **have you seen it ~?** l'avez-vous vu quelque part?; **~ else?** ailleurs?

Anzac ['ænzæk] n (*abbr of* **Australia-New Zealand Army Corps**) *soldat australien ou néo-zélandais*.

AOB, a.o.b. [ˌeɪəʊ'biː] *see* **A.O.C.B.**

A.O.C.B. [ˌeɪəʊsiː'biː] (*abbr of* **any other (competent) business**) autres matières *fpl* à l'ordre du jour.

aorist ['eərɪst] n aoriste *m*.

aorta [eɪ'ɔːtə] n, pl **~s** *or* **aortae** [eɪ'ɔːtiː] aorte *f*.

aortic [eɪ'ɔːtɪk] adj (*Anat*) aortique.

Aosta [æ'ɒstə] n Aoste.

A.P. [ˌeɪ'piː] (*abbr of* **Associated Press**) *agence de presse*.

apace [ə'peɪs] adv rapidement, vite.

Apache [ə'pætʃɪ] n Apache *mf*.

apart [ə'pɑːt] (*phr vb elem*) adv a (*separated*) **houses a long way ~** maisons (fort) éloignées l'une de l'autre *or* à une grande distance l'une de l'autre; **set equally ~** espacés à intervalles réguliers; **their birthdays were 2 days ~** leurs anniversaires étaient à 2 jours d'intervalle; **to stand with one's feet ~** se tenir les jambes écartées; *see* **class, world**.

b (*on one side*) à part, de côté, à l'écart. **to hold o.s. ~** se tenir à l'écart (*from* de); **joking ~** plaisanterie à part; **that ~** à part cela, cela mis à part; **~ from these difficulties** en dehors de *or* à part ces difficultés, ces difficultés mises à part; **~ from the fact that** outre que, hormis que.

c (*separately, distinctly*) séparément. **they are living ~ now** ils sont séparés maintenant; **he lives ~ from his wife** il est séparé de sa femme, il n'habite plus avec sa femme; **you can't tell the twins ~** on ne peut distinguer les jumeaux l'un de l'autre; **we'll have to keep those boys ~** il va falloir séparer ces garçons.

d (*into pieces*) en pièces, en morceaux. **to take ~** démonter, désassembler; *see* **come, fall apart, tear apart** *etc*.

apartheid [ə'pɑːteɪt, ə'pɑːtaɪd] n apartheid *m*. **the ~ laws** la législation permettant l'apartheid.

apartment [ə'pɑːtmənt] n a (*Brit*) (*room*) pièce *f*; (*bedroom*) chambre *f*. **a 5-~ house** une maison de 5 pièces; (*notice*) **"~s"** "chambres à louer"; **furnished ~s** meublé *m*. b (*US*) appartement *m*, logement *m*. **~ building, ~ house** (*block*) immeuble *m* (*de résidence*); (*divided house*) maison *f* (divisée en appartements).

apathetic [ˌæpə'θetɪk] adj apathique, indifférent, sans réaction.

apathy ['æpəθɪ] n apathie *f*, indifférence *f*.

APB [ˌeɪpiː'biː] n (*US*) (*abbr of* **all-points bulletin**) message *m* à toutes les patrouilles (*on* à propos de). **to put out an ~** envoyer un message à toutes les patrouilles.

ape [eɪp] 1 n (*Zool*) (grand) singe *m*, anthropoïde *m*. (*pej: person*) **big ~*** grande brute; (*US*) **to go ~‡** s'emballer* (*over* pour). 2 vt singer.

Apennines ['æpənaɪnz] npl Apennin *m*.

aperient [ə'pɪərɪənt] adj, n laxatif (*m*).

aperitif [əˌperɪ'tiːf] n apéritif *m*.

aperture ['æpətʃjʊəʳ] n (*hole*) orifice *m*, trou *m*, ouverture *f*; (*gap*) brèche *f*, trouée *f*; (*Phot*) ouverture (du diaphragme).

apex ['eɪpeks] n, pl **~es** *or* **apices** ['eɪpɪsiːz] (*Geom, Med*) sommet *m*; [*tongue*] apex *m*, pointe *f*; (*fig*) sommet, point culminant.

APEX ['eɪpeks] n a (*abbr of* **Association of Professional, Executive, Clerical and Computer Staff**) *syndicat*. b (*also* **apex**) (*abbr of* **advance purchase excursion**) **~ fare/ticket** prix *m*/billet *m* APEX.

aphasia [æ'feɪzɪə] n aphasie *f*.

aphasic [æ'feɪzɪk] adj aphasique.

aphid ['eɪfɪd] n puceron *m* (des plantes).

aphis ['eɪfɪs] n, pl **aphides** ['eɪfɪdiːz] aphidé *m*.

aphonic [ˌeɪ'fɒnɪk] adj aphonique.

aphorism ['æfərɪzəm] n aphorisme *m*.

aphrodisiac [ˌæfrəʊ'dɪzɪæk] adj, n aphrodisiaque (*m*).

Aphrodite [ˌæfrə'daɪtɪ] n Aphrodite *f*.

apiarist ['eɪpɪərɪst] n apiculteur *m*, -trice *f*.

apiary ['eɪpɪərɪ] n rucher *m*.

apiece [ə'piːs] adv (*each person*) chacun(e), par personne, par tête; (*each thing*) chacun(e), (la) pièce.

aplenty [ə'plentɪ] adv (*liter*) en abondance.

aplomb [ə'plɒm] n sang-froid *m*, assurance *f*, aplomb *m* (*pej*).

Apocalypse [ə'pɒkəlɪps] n Apocalypse *f* (*also fig*).

apocalyptic [əˌpɒkə'lɪptɪk] adj apocalyptique.

apocopate [ə'pɒkəpeɪt] vt raccourcir par apocope.

apocope [ə'pɒkəpɪ] n apocope *f*.

Apocrypha [ə'pɒkrɪfə] npl apocryphes *mpl*.

apocryphal [ə'pɒkrɪfəl] adj apocryphe.

apogee ['æpəʊdʒiː] n apogée *m*.

apolitical [ˌeɪpə'lɪtɪkəl] adj apolitique.

Apollo [ə'pɒləʊ] n (*Myth*) Apollon *m*; (*Space*) Apollo *m*.

apologetic [əˌpɒlə'dʒetɪk] adj *smile, look, gesture* d'excuse. **an ~ air** un air de s'excuser; **he was very ~ for not coming** il s'est confondu *or* s'est répandu en excuses de n'être pas venu; **she was very ~ about her mistake** elle s'est beaucoup excusée de son erreur.

apologetically [əˌpɒlə'dʒetɪkəlɪ] adv en s'excusant, pour s'excuser.

apologetics [əˌpɒlə'dʒetɪks] n (*NonC*) apologétique *f*.

apologize [ə'pɒlədʒaɪz] vi s'excuser. **to ~ to sb for sth** s'excuser de qch auprès de qn, faire *or* présenter des excuses à qn pour qch; **she ~d to them for her son** elle leur a demandé d'excuser la conduite de son fils; **to ~ profusely** se confondre *or* se répandre en excuses.

apologue ['æpəlɒg] n apologue *m*.

apology [ə'pɒlədʒɪ] n a (*expression of regret*) excuses *fpl*. **a letter of ~** une lettre d'excuses; **to make an ~ for sth/for having done** s'excuser de qch/d'avoir fait, faire *or* présenter ses excuses pour qch/pour avoir fait; (*for absence at meeting*) **there are apologies from X** X vous prie d'excuser son absence; **to send one's apologies** envoyer une lettre d'excuse; (*more informally*) envoyer un mot d'excuse.

b (*defence: for beliefs etc*) apologie *f*, justification *f* (*for* de).

c (*pej*) **it was an ~ for a bed/speech** en fait de *or* comme lit/discours c'était plutôt minable*; **he gave me an ~ for a smile** il m'a gratifié d'une sorte de grimace qui se voulait être un sourire; **we were given an ~ for a lunch** on nous a servi un casse-croûte minable pompeusement appelé déjeuner, on nous a servi un déjeuner absolument minable*.

apoplectic [ˌæpə'plektɪk] 1 adj apoplectique. (*Med, fig*) **~ fit** attaque *f* d'apoplexie. 2 n apoplectique *mf*.

apoplexy ['æpəpleksɪ] n apoplexie *f*.

apostasy [ə'pɒstəsɪ] n apostasie *f*.

apostate [ə'pɒstɪt] adj, n apostat(e) *m(f)*.

apostatize [ə'pɒstətaɪz] vi apostasier.

a posteriori ['eɪpɒsˌterɪ'ɔːraɪ, 'eɪpɒsˌterɪ'ɔːrɪ] adj, adv a postériori.

apostle [ə'pɒsl] n apôtre *m*. **A~s' Creed** symbole *m* des apôtres, Credo *m*; **to say the A~s' Creed** dire le Credo; **~ spoon** *petite cuiller décorée d'une figure d'apôtre*.

apostolate [ə'pɒstəleɪt] n apostolat *m*.

apostolic [ˌæpəs'tɒlɪk] adj apostolique.

apostrophe [ə'pɒstrəfɪ] n (*Gram, Literat*) apostrophe *f*.

apostrophize [ə'pɒstrəfaɪz] vt apostropher.

apothecary†† [ə'pɒθɪkərɪ] n apothicaire†† *m*.

apotheosis [əˌpɒθɪ'əʊsɪs] n, pl **apotheoses** [əˌpɒθɪ'əʊsiːz] apothéose *f*.

appal, (US) appall [ə'pɔːl] vt consterner; (*frighten*) épouvanter. **I am ~led at your behaviour** ta conduite me consterne.

Appalachian [ˌæpə'leɪʃən] adj, n: **the ~ Mountains, the ~s** les (monts *mpl*) Appalaches *mpl*.

appalling [ə'pɔːlɪŋ] adj *destruction* épouvantable, effroyable; *ignorance* consternant, navrant.

appallingly [ə'pɔːlɪŋlɪ] adv épouvantablement, effroyablement.

apparatchik [ˌæpə'rætʃiːk] n apparatchik *m*.

apparatus [ˌæpə'reɪtəs] n, pl **~** *or* **~es** (*for heating etc: also Anat*) appareil *m*; (*for filming, camping etc*) équipement *m*; (*in laboratory etc*) instruments *mpl*; (*in gym*) agrès *mpl*; (*device: for explosives etc*) dispositif *m*, mécanisme *m*; (*fig: of government*) machine *f*. **camping ~** équipement *m* de camping; **heating ~** appareil de chauffage; (*in gym*) **~ work** exercises *mpl* aux agrès; (*Literat*) **critical ~** appareil *m or* apparat *m* critique.

apparel† [ə'pærəl] (*liter*) 1 n (*NonC*) habillement *m*. 2 vt vêtir.

apparent [ə'pærənt] adj a (*obvious*) évident, apparent, manifeste. **a shape became ~** une forme est devenue visible *or* est apparue; **her incompetence is becoming more and more ~** son incompétence devient de plus en plus évidente; *see* **heir.** b (*not real*) apparent, de surface. **in spite of his ~ weakness** malgré son air de faiblesse; **more ~ than real** plus apparent que réel.

apparently [ə'pærəntlɪ] adv apparemment, en apparence; (*according to rumour*) à ce qu'il paraît. **this is ~ the case** il semble que ce soit le cas, c'est paraît-il *or* apparemment le cas.

apparition [ˌæpə'rɪʃən] n (*spirit, appearance*) apparition *f*.

appeal [ə'piːl] 1 vi a (*request publicly*) lancer un appel (*on behalf of* en faveur de, *for sth* pour obtenir qch). **to ~ for the blind** lancer un appel au profit des *or* pour les aveugles; **to ~ for calm** faire un appel au calme; (*Fin*) **to ~ for funds** faire un appel de fonds; **he ~ed for silence** il a demandé le silence; **he ~ed for tolerance** il a demandé à ses auditeurs d'être tolérants; (*Pol*) **to ~ to the country** en appeler au pays.

b (*beg*) faire appel (*to* à). **she ~ed to his generosity** elle a fait appel à sa générosité; **to ~ to sb for money/help** demander de l'argent/des secours à qn; **I ~ to you!** je vous le demande instamment!, je vous en supplie!; *see* **better.**

c (*Jur*) interjeter appel, se pourvoir en appel. **to ~ to the supreme court** se pourvoir en cassation; **to ~ against a judgment** appeler d'un jugement; **to ~ against a decision** faire opposition à une décision.

d (*attract*) **to ~ to** *[object, idea]* plaire à; attirer, tenter; *[person]* plaire à; **it doesn't ~ to me** cela ne m'intéresse pas, cela ne me dit rien*; **the idea ~ed to him** l'idée l'a séduit; **it ~s to the imagination** cela parle à l'imagination.

2 n a (*public call*) appel *m*. **~ to arms** appel aux armes; (*Comm, Fin*) **~ for funds** appel de fonds; **he made a public ~ for the blind** il a lancé un appel au profit des aveugles.

b (*by individual: for help etc*) appel *m* (*for* à); (*for money*) demande *f* (*for* de); (*supplication*) prière *f*, supplication *f*. **with a look of ~** d'un air suppliant *or* implorant; **~ for help** appel au secours.

c (*Jur*) appel *m*, pourvoi *m*. **notice of ~** infirmation *f*; **act of ~** acte *m* d'appel; **with no right of ~** sans appel; **acquitted on ~** acquitté en seconde instance; *see* **enter, lodge, lord.**

d (*attraction*) *[person, object]* attrait *m*, charme *m*; *[plan, idea]* intérêt *m*.

3 comp ▸**Appeal Court** (*Jur*) cour *f* d'appel.

appealing [ə'piːlɪŋ] adj (*moving*) émouvant, attendrissant; *look* pathétique; (*begging*) suppliant, implorant; (*attractive*) attirant, attachant.

appealingly [ə'piːlɪŋlɪ] adv (*see* **appealing**) de façon émouvante; d'un air suppliant; (*charmingly*) avec beaucoup de charme.

appear [ə'pɪəʳ] vi a (*become visible*) *[person, sun etc]* apparaître, se montrer; *[ghost, vision]* apparaître, se manifester (*to sb* à qn).

b (*arrive*) arriver, se présenter, faire son apparition (*hum*). **he ~ed from nowhere** il est apparu comme par miracle *or* comme par un coup de baguette magique; **where did you ~ from?** d'où est-ce que tu sors?

c (*Jur etc*) comparaître. **to ~ before a court** comparaître devant un tribunal; **to ~ on a charge of** être jugé pour; **to ~ for sb** plaider pour qn, représenter qn; **to ~ for the defence/for the accused** plaider pour la défense/pour l'accusé; *see* **fail, failure.**

d (*Theat*) **to ~ in "Hamlet"** jouer dans "Hamlet"; **to ~ as Hamlet** jouer Hamlet; **to ~ on TV** passer à la télévision.

e *[publication]* paraître, sortir, être publié.

f (*seem: physical aspect*) paraître, avoir l'air. **they ~ (to be) ill** ils ont l'air malades.

g (*seem: on evidence*) paraître (*that* que + *indic*). **he came then? — so it ~s *or* so it would ~** il est donc venu? — il paraît que oui; **it ~s that he did say that** il paraît qu'il a bien dit cela (*see also* **h**); **he got the job *or* so it ~s *or* so it would ~** il a eu le poste à ce qu'il paraît, il paraît qu'il a eu le poste; **as will presently ~** comme il paraîtra par la suite, comme on verra bientôt; **it's raining! — (*iro*) so it ~s!** il pleut! — on dirait! (*iro*).

h (*seem: by surmise*) sembler (*that* que *gen* + *subj*), sembler bien (*that* que + *indic*), sembler à qn (*that* que + *indic*). **there ~s to be a mistake** il semble qu'il y ait une erreur; **it ~s he did say that** il semble avoir bien dit cela, il semble bien qu'il a dit cela; **it ~s to me they are mistaken** il me semble qu'ils ont tort; **how does it ~ to you?** qu'en pensez-vous?, que vous en semble-t-il?

appearance [ə'pɪərəns] n a (*act*) apparition *f*, arrivée *f*, entrée *f*. **to make an ~** faire son apparition, se montrer, se présenter; **to make a personal ~** apparaître en personne; **to put in an ~** faire acte de présence; **~ money** cachet *m*.

b (*Jur*) **~ before a court** comparution *f* devant un tribunal.

c (*Theat*) **since his ~ in "Hamlet"** depuis qu'il a joué dans "Hamlet"; **in order of ~** par ordre d'entrée en scène; **his ~ on TV** son passage à la télévision.

d (*publication*) parution *f*.

e (*look, aspect*) apparence *f*, aspect *m*. **to have a good ~** *[object, house]* avoir bon air; *[person]* faire bonne figure; **at first ~** au premier abord, à première vue; **the ~ of the houses** l'aspect des maisons; **it had all the ~s of a murder** cela avait tout l'air d'un meurtre, cela ressemblait fort à un meurtre; **his ~ worried us** la mine qu'il avait nous a inquiétés; **~s are deceptive *or* deceiving** il ne faut pas se fier aux apparences, les apparences peuvent être trompeuses; **you shouldn't go by ~s** il ne faut pas se fier aux apparences; **for ~s' sake, (in order) to keep up ~s** pour sauver les apparences, pour la forme; **to *or* by all ~s** selon toute apparence; **contrary to *or* against all ~s** contrairement aux apparences, contre toute apparence.

appease [ə'piːz] vt apaiser, calmer.

appeasement [ə'piːzmənt] n apaisement *m*; (*Pol*) apaisement, conciliation *f*.

appellant [ə'pelənt] 1 n partie appelante, appelant(e) *m(f)*. 2 adj appelant.

appellate [ə'pelɪt] adj (*US Jur*) **~ court** cour *f* d'appel; **~ jurisdiction** juridiction *f* d'appel.

appellation [ˌæpe'leɪʃən] n appellation *f*, désignation *f*.

append [ə'pend] vt *notes* joindre, ajouter; *document* joindre, annexer; *signature* apposer; (*Comput*) ajouter (*à la fin d'un fichier*).

appendage [ə'pendɪdʒ] n appendice *m*.

appendectomy [ˌæpen'dektəmɪ] n, **appendicectomy** [ˌæpendɪ'sektəmɪ] n appendicectomie *f*.

appendicitis [əˌpendɪ'saɪtɪs] n appendicite *f*. **to have ~** avoir une (crise d')appendicite; **was it ~?** c'était une appendicite?

appendix [ə'pendɪks] n, pl **~es** *or* **appendices** [ə'pendɪsiːz] a (*Anat*) appendice *m*. **to have one's ~ out** se faire opérer de l'appendicite. b *[book]* appendice *m*; *[document]* annexe *f*.

apperception [ˌæpə'sepʃən] n aperception *f*.

appertain [ˌæpə'teɪn] vi (*belong*) appartenir (*to* à); (*form part*) faire partie (*to* de); (*relate*) se rapporter (*to* à), relever (*to* de).

appetite ['æpɪtaɪt] 1 n appétit *m*. **he has no ~** il n'a pas d'appétit; **to have a good ~** avoir bon appétit; **to eat with (an) ~** manger de bon appétit; **skiing gives one an ~** le ski ouvre l'appétit; (*fig*) **I have no ~ for this sort of book** je n'ai pas de goût pour ce genre de livre; *see* **spoil.** 2 comp ▸**appetite depressant** coupe-faim *m inv*.

appetizer ['æpɪtaɪzəʳ] n (*drink*) apéritif *m*; (*food*) amuse-gueule *m inv*.

appetizing ['æpɪtaɪzɪŋ] adj (*lit, fig*) appétissant.

appetizingly ['æpɪtaɪzɪŋlɪ] adv de manière appétissante.

Appian ['æpɪən] adj: **~ Way** voie Appienne.

applaud [ə'plɔːd] vt *person, thing* applaudir; (*fig*) *decision, efforts* applaudir à, approuver.

applause [ə'plɔːz] n (*NonC*) applaudissements *mpl*, acclamation *f*. **to win the ~ of** être applaudi *or* acclamé par; **there was loud ~** les applaudissements ont crépité.

apple ['æpl] 1 n pomme *f*; (*also* **~ tree**) pommier *m*. **he's/it's the ~ of my eye** je tiens à lui/j'y tiens comme à la prunelle de mes yeux; **~ of discord** pomme de discorde; (*US*) **the (Big) A~*** New York; *see* **Adam, cooking, eating.**

2 comp ▸**apple blossom** fleur *f* de pommier ▸**apple brandy** eau-de-vie *f* de pommes ▸**applecart** *see* **upset 1a** ▸**applecore** trognon *m* de pomme ▸**apple dumpling** pomme *f* au four (*enrobée de pâte brisée*) ▸**apple fritter** beignet *m* aux pommes ▸**apple green** vert pomme ▸**applejack** (*US*) = **apple brandy** ▸**apple orchard** champ *m* de pommiers, pommeraie *f* ▸**apple pie** tourte *f* aux pommes (*recouverte de pâte*) ▸**apple-pie bed** (*Brit*) lit *m* en portefeuille ▸**in apple-pie order** en ordre parfait ▸**apple sauce** (*Culin*) compote *f* de pommes; (*US * fig*) bobards* *mpl* ▸**apple tart** tarte *f* aux pommes; (*individual*) tartelette *f* aux pommes ▸**apple turnover** chausson *m* aux pommes.

appliance [ə'plaɪəns] n a appareil *m*; (*smaller*) dispositif *m*, instrument *m*. **electrical/domestic ~s** appareils électriques/ménagers. b (*Brit: fire engine*) autopompe *f*.

applicability [ˌæplɪkə'bɪlɪtɪ] n applicabilité *f*.

applicable [ə'plɪkəbl] adj applicable (*to* à).

applicant ['æplɪkənt] n (*for job*) candidat(e) *m(f)* (*for a post* à un poste), postulant(e) *m(f)*; (*Jur*) requérant(e) *m(f)*; (*Admin: for money, assistance etc*) demandeur *m*, -euse *f*.

application [ˌæplɪ'keɪʃən] 1 n a (*request*) demande *f* (*for* de). **~ for a job** demande d'emploi, candidature *f* à un poste; **~ for membership** demande d'adhésion; **on ~** sur demande; **to make ~ to sb for sth** s'adresser à qn pour obtenir qch; **to submit an ~** faire une demande; **details may be had on ~ to X** s'adresser à X pour tous renseignements.

b (*act of applying*) application *f* (*of sth to sth* de qch à qch). (*Pharm*) **for external ~ only** réservé à l'usage externe.

c (*diligence*) application *f*, attention *f*.

d (*relevancy*) portée *f*, pertinence *f*. **his arguments have no ~ to the present case** ses arguments ne s'appliquent pas au cas présent.

e (*Comput*) application *f*; *see also* **2.**

2 comp ▶**application form** (*gen: for benefits etc*) formulaire *m* de demande; (*for job*) formulaire de demande d'emploi; (*for more important post*) dossier *m* de candidature; (*Univ*) dossier d'inscription ▶**application package** (*Comput*) progiciel *m* d'application ▶**application software** logiciels *mpl* d'application.

applicator ['æplɪkeɪtəʳ] n applicateur *m*.

applied [ə'plaɪd] adj (*gen, Ling, Math, Sci etc*) appliqué. ~ **arts** arts décoratifs; ~ **sciences** sciences appliquées.

appliqué [æ'pli:keɪ] 1 vt coudre (en application). 2 n (*ornament*) application *f*; (*end product: also* ~ **work**) travail *m* d'application.

apply [ə'plaɪ] 1 vt a *paint, ointment, dressing* appliquer, mettre (*to* sur). **to ~ heat to sth** (*Tech*) exposer qch à la chaleur; (*Med*) traiter qch par la thermothérapie; **to ~ a match to sth** mettre le feu à qch avec une allumette, allumer qch avec une allumette.

b *theory* appliquer (*to* à), mettre en pratique *or* en application; *rule, law* appliquer (*to* à). **we can't ~ this rule to you** nous ne pouvons pas appliquer cette règle à votre cas.

c **to ~ pressure on sth** exercer une pression sur qch; **to ~ pressure on sb** faire pression sur qn; (*Aut, Tech*) **to ~ the brakes** actionner les freins, freiner.

d **to ~ one's mind** *or* **o.s. to (doing) sth** s'appliquer à (faire) qch; **to ~ one's attention to** porter *or* fixer son attention sur.

2 vi s'adresser, avoir recours (*to sb for sth* à qn pour obtenir qch). ~ **at the office/to the manager** adressez-vous au bureau/au directeur; (*on notice*) s'adresser au bureau/au directeur; (*Jur*) **right to ~ to the courts against decisions by ...** possibilité *f* de recours juridictionnel à l'encontre des décisions de ... .

▶**apply for** vt fus *scholarship, grant, money, assistance* demander. **to apply for a job** faire une demande d'emploi (*to sb* auprès de qn), poser sa candidature pour *or* être candidat à un poste; (*Jur*) **to apply for a divorce** formuler une demande en divorce; *see* **apply 2, patent.**

▶**apply to** vt fus (*gen*) s'appliquer à; *[remarks]* s'appliquer à, se rapporter à. **this does not apply to you** ceci ne s'applique pas à vous, ceci ne vous concerne pas; *see* **apply 2.**

appoggiatura [ə,pɒdʒə'tʊərə] n, pl ~s *or* **appoggiature** [ə,pɒdʒə'tʊəre] appoggiature *f*.

appoint [ə'pɔɪnt] vt a (*fix, decide*) *date, place* fixer, désigner. **at the ~ed time** à l'heure dite *or* convenue; **~ed agent** agent attitré. b (*nominate*) nommer, désigner (*sb to a post* qn à un poste). **to ~ sb manager** nommer qn directeur; **to ~ a new secretary** engager une nouvelle secrétaire. c (†: *ordain*) prescrire, ordonner (*that* que + *subj*), décider (*that* que + *indic*). d **a well-~ed house** une maison bien aménagée *or* installée.

appointee [əpɔɪn'ti:] n candidat retenu, titulaire *mf* du poste; (*esp US*) délégué *m* (*or* ambassadeur *m etc*) nommé pour des raisons politiques.

appointive [ə'pɔɪntɪv] adj (*US*) *position* pourvu par nomination.

appointment [ə'pɔɪntmənt] n a (*arrangement to meet*) rendez-vous *m*; (*meeting*) entrevue *f*. **to make an ~ with sb** donner rendez-vous à qn, prendre rendez-vous avec qn; *[2 people]* **to make an ~** se donner rendez-vous; **to keep an ~** aller à un rendez-vous; **I have an ~ at 10 o'clock** j'ai (un) rendez-vous à 10 heures; (*to caller*) **have you an ~?** avez-vous pris rendez-vous?; **I have an ~ to see Mr X** j'ai rendez-vous avec M. X; **to meet sb by ~** rencontrer qn sur rendez-vous; *see* **break.**

b (*selection, nomination*) nomination *f*, désignation *f* (*to a post* à un emploi); (*office assigned*) poste *m*; (*posting*) affectation *f*. **there are still several ~s to be made** il y a encore plusieurs postes à pourvoir; (*Comm*) **"By ~ to Her Majesty the Queen"** "fournisseur *m* de S.M. la Reine"; (*Press*) **"~s (vacant)"** "offres *fpl* d'emploi"; **~s bureau** *or* **office** agence *f or* bureau *m* de placement.

apportion [ə'pɔ:ʃən] vt *money* répartir, partager; *land, property* lotir; *blame* répartir. **to ~ sth to sb** assigner qch à qn.

apportionment [ə'pɔ:ʃənmənt] n (*US Pol*) répartition *f* des sièges (par districts).

apposite ['æpəzɪt] adj juste, à propos, pertinent.

apposition [,æpə'zɪʃən] n apposition *f*. **in ~** en apposition.

appositional [,æpə'zɪʃənl] adj en apposition.

appraisal [ə'preɪzəl] n évaluation *f*, estimation *f*, appréciation *f*.

appraise [ə'preɪz] vt *property, jewellery* évaluer, apprécier, estimer (la valeur *or* le coût de); *importance* évaluer, estimer, apprécier; *worth* estimer, apprécier.

appraiser [ə'preɪzəʳ] n *[property, value, asset]* expert *m*.

appreciable [ə'pri:ʃəbl] adj appréciable, sensible.

appreciably [ə'pri:ʃəblɪ] adv sensiblement, de façon appréciable.

appreciate [ə'pri:ʃɪeɪt] 1 vt a (*assess, be aware of*) *fact, difficulty, sb's attitude* se rendre compte de, être conscient de. **to ~ sth at its true value** estimer qch à sa juste valeur; **yes, I ~ that** oui, je sais bien *or* je comprends bien *or* je m'en rends bien compte; **I fully ~ the fact that** je me rends parfaitement compte du fait que; **they did not ~ the danger** ils ne se sont pas rendu compte du danger.

b (*value, esteem, like*) *help* apprécier; *music, painting, books* apprécier, goûter; *person* apprécier (à sa juste valeur), faire (grand) cas de.

c (*be grateful for*) être sensible à, être reconnaissant de. **we do ~ your kindness/your work/what you have done** nous vous sommes très reconnaissants de votre gentillesse/du travail que vous avez fait/de ce que vous avez fait; (*Comm: in letter*) **we should ~ an early reply, an early reply would be ~d** nous vous serions obligés de bien vouloir nous répondre dans les plus brefs délais; **we deeply ~ this honour** nous sommes profondément sensibles à cet honneur; **he felt that nobody ~d him** il ne se sentait pas apprécié à sa juste valeur, il avait le sentiment que personne ne l'appréciait à sa juste valeur.

d (*raise in value*) hausser la valeur de.

2 vi (*Fin etc*) *[currency]* monter; *[object, property]* prendre de la valeur.

appreciation [ə,pri:ʃɪ'eɪʃən] n a (*judgment, estimation*) appréciation *f*, évaluation *f*, estimation *f*; (*Art, Literat, Mus*) critique *f*. b (*gratitude*) reconnaissance *f*. **she smiled her ~** elle a remercié d'un sourire; **in ~ of ...** en remerciement de ... . c (*Fin*) hausse *f*, augmentation *f*, valorisation *f*.

appreciative [ə'pri:ʃɪətɪv] adj *person* sensible (*of* à); (*admiring*) appréciatif, admiratif; (*grateful*) reconnaissant; *comment* élogieux. **to be ~ of good food** apprécier la bonne cuisine.

appreciatively [ə'pri:ʃɪətɪvlɪ] adv (*with pleasure*) avec plaisir; (*gratefully*) avec reconnaissance.

apprehend [,æprɪ'hend] vt a (*arrest*) appréhender, arrêter. b (*fear*) redouter, appréhender.

apprehension [,æprɪ'henʃən] n a (*fear*) appréhension *f*, inquiétude *f*, crainte *f*. b (*arrest*) arrestation *f*.

apprehensive [,æprɪ'hensɪv] adj inquiet (*f* -ète), appréhensif, craintif. **to be ~ for sb's safety** craindre pour la sécurité de qn; **to be ~ of danger** appréhender *or* craindre *or* redouter le danger.

apprehensively [,æprɪ'hensɪvlɪ] adv avec appréhension, craintivement.

apprentice [ə'prentɪs] 1 n apprenti(e) *m(f)*; (*Archit, Mus etc*) élève *mf*. **to place sb as an ~ to** mettre qn en apprentissage chez; **plumber's/joiner's ~** apprenti plombier/menuisier. 2 vt mettre *or* placer en apprentissage (*to* chez), placer comme élève (*to* chez). **he is ~d to a joiner** il est en apprentissage chez un menuisier; **he is ~d to an architect** c'est l'élève d'un architecte. 3 comp ▶**apprentice plumber** apprenti *m* plombier.

apprenticeship [ə'prentɪʃɪp] n apprentissage *m*.

apprise [ə'praɪz] vt informer, instruire, prévenir (*sb of sth* qn de qch), apprendre (*sb of sth* qch à qn). **to be ~d of sth** prendre connaissance de qch.

appro* ['æprəʊ] n (*Comm*) (abbr of **approval**) **on ~** à *or* sous condition, à l'essai.

approach [ə'prəʊtʃ] 1 vi *[person, vehicle]* (s')approcher; *[date, season, death, war]* approcher, être proche.

2 vt a *place, person* s'approcher de, s'avancer vers. **I saw him ~ing me** je l'ai vu qui venait vers moi.

b (*tackle*) *problem, subject, task* aborder. **it all depends on how one ~es it** tout dépend de la façon dont on s'y prend.

c (*speak to*) **to ~ sb about sth** s'adresser à qn à propos de qch, parler de qch à qn; **have you ~ed him already?** est-ce que vous lui avez déjà parlé?; **a man ~ed me in the street** un homme m'a abordé dans la rue; (*fig*) **he is easy/difficult to ~** il est d'un abord facile/difficile.

d (*get near to*) approcher de. **we are ~ing the time when ...** le jour approche où ...; **she is ~ing 30** elle approche de la trentaine, elle va sur ses 30 ans; **it was ~ing midnight** il était près de *or* presque minuit; **a colour ~ing red** une couleur qui touche au rouge *or* voisine du rouge.

3 n a *[person, vehicle]* approche *f*, arrivée *f*. **the cat fled at his ~** le chat s'est enfui à son approche; **we watched his ~** nous l'avons regardé arriver.

b *[date, season, death etc]* approche(s) *f(pl)*. **at the ~ of Easter** à l'approche *or* aux approches de Pâques.

c (*fig*) **his ~ to the problem** sa façon d'aborder le problème; **I like his ~ (to it)** j'aime sa façon de s'y prendre; **a new ~ to teaching French** une nouvelle façon d'enseigner le français; **to make ~es to sb** (*Comm etc, gen*) faire des avances *fpl or* des ouvertures *fpl* à qn, faire des démarches *fpl* auprès de qn; (*amorous*) faire des avances à qn; (*Comm, gen*) **to make an ~ to sb** faire une proposition à qn; **he is easy/not easy of ~** il est d'un abord facile/difficile; *see also* **3d.**

d (*access route: to town*) approche *f*, abord *m*, voie *f* d'accès; (*Climbing*) marche *f* d'approche. **a town easy/not easy of ~** une ville d'accès facile/difficile; **the ~ to the top of the hill** le chemin qui mène au sommet de la colline; **the station ~** les abords de la gare.

e (*approximation*) ressemblance *f* (*to* à), apparence *f* (*to* de). **some ~ to gaiety** une certaine apparence de gaieté.

4 comp ▶**approach light** (*Aviat*) balise *f* ▶**approach lights** (*Aviat*) balisage *m* ▶**approach march** (*Climbing*) marche *f* d'approche ▶**approach road** (*gen*) route *f* d'accès; (*to motorway*) voie *f* de raccordement, bretelle *f* ▶**approach shot** (*Golf*) approche *f* ▶**approach stage** (*Aviat*) phase *f* d'approche.

approachable [ə'prəʊtʃəbl] adj *place* accessible, approchable; *person* abordable, approchable, accessible.

approaching [ə'prəʊtʃɪŋ] adj *date, event* prochain, qui (s')approche. **the ~ vehicle** le véhicule venant en sens inverse.

approbation [ˌæprəˈbeɪʃən] n approbation *f.* **a nod of ~** un signe de tête approbateur.

appropriate [əˈprəʊprɪɪt] 1 adj *moment, decision, ruling* opportun; *remark* bien venu, opportun, juste; *word* juste, propre; *name* bien choisi; *authority, department* compétent. **~ for** *or* **to** propre à, approprié à; **words/behaviour/a speech ~ to the occasion** paroles/conduite/un discours de circonstance; **it would not be ~ for me to comment** ce n'est pas à moi de faire des commentaires; **he is the ~ person to ask** c'est à lui qu'il faut le demander. 2 [əˈprəʊprɪeɪt] vt a (*take for one's own use*) s'approprier, s'attribuer, s'emparer de. b (*set aside for special use*) *funds* affecter (*to, for* à).

appropriately [əˈprəʊprɪɪtlɪ] adv *speak, comment* avec à-propos, pertinemment; *decide* à juste titre; *design* convenablement. **~ situated** situé au bon endroit, situé où il faut; **~ named** bien nommé, au nom bien choisi.

appropriateness [əˈprəʊprɪɪtnɪs] n *[moment, decision]* opportunité *f*; *[remark, word]* justesse *f.*

appropriation [əˌprəʊprɪˈeɪʃən] n (*act: also Jur*) appropriation *f*; (*funds assigned*) dotation *f*; (*US Pol*) crédit *m* budgétaire. (*US Pol*) **~ bill** projet *m* de loi de finances; (*US Pol*) **A~s Committee** *commission des finances de la Chambre des Représentants (examinant les dépenses)*.

approval [əˈpruːvəl] n approbation *f*, assentiment *m.* (*Comm*) **on ~** à *or* sous condition, à l'essai; **a nod of ~** un signe de tête approbateur; **does it meet with your ~?, has it got your ~?** l'approuvez-vous?, y consentez-vous?, cela a-t-il votre approbation?

approve [əˈpruːv] vt *action, publication, medicine, drug* approuver; *decision* ratifier, homologuer; *request* agréer. **to be ~d by** recueillir *or* avoir l'approbation de; **read and ~d** lu et approuvé; (*Brit* †) **~d school** maison *f* de correction†.

►**approve of** vt fus *behaviour, idea* approuver, être partisan de; *person* avoir bonne opinion de. **I don't approve of his conduct** je n'approuve pas sa conduite; **I don't approve of your decision** je ne peux pas approuver *or* je désapprouve la décision que vous avez prise; **she doesn't approve of smoking/drinking** elle n'approuve pas qu'on fume (*subj*)/boive; **he doesn't approve of me** il n'a pas bonne opinion de moi, il n'approuve pas *or* il désapprouve ma façon d'être; **we approve of our new neighbours** nos nouveaux voisins nous plaisent.

approving [əˈpruːvɪŋ] adj approbateur (*f* -trice), approbatif.

approvingly [əˈpruːvɪŋlɪ] adv d'un air *or* d'un ton approbateur.

approx abbr of **approximately**.

approximate [əˈprɒksɪmɪt] 1 adj *time, date, heat, amount, calculation* approximatif. **a sum ~ to what is needed** une somme voisine *or* proche de celle qui est requise; **figures ~ to the nearest franc** chiffres arrondis au franc près. 2 [əˈprɒksɪmeɪt] vi être proche, se rapprocher (*to* de).

approximately [əˈprɒksɪmətlɪ] adv approximativement, à peu près, environ.

approximation [əˌprɒksɪˈmeɪʃən] n approximation *f.*

appurtenance [əˈpɜːtɪnəns] n (*gen pl*) **~s** installations *fpl*, accessoires *mpl*; **the house and its ~s** (*outhouses etc*) l'immeuble avec ses dépendances *fpl*; (*Jur: rights, privileges etc*) l'immeuble avec ses circonstances et dépendances *or* ses appartenances.

APR [ˌeɪpiːˈɑːʳ] n (abbr of **annual(ized) percentage rate**) taux annuel.

après-ski [ˌæpreɪˈskiː] 1 n après-ski *m* (*période*). 2 comp d'après-ski.

apricot [ˈeɪprɪkɒt] 1 n abricot *m*; (*also* **~ tree**) abricotier *m.* 2 comp ►**apricot jam** confiture *f* d'abricots ►**apricot tart** tarte *f* aux abricots.

April [ˈeɪprəl] 1 n avril *m*; *for phrases see* **September**. 2 comp ►**April fool** (*person*) victime *f* d'un poisson d'avril; (*joke*) poisson d'avril; **to make an April fool of sb** faire un poisson d'avril à qn ►**April Fools' Day** le premier avril ►**April showers** ≃ giboulées *fpl* de mars.

a priori [eɪpraɪˈɔːraɪ, ɑːprɪˈɔːrɪ] adj, adv a priori.

apron [ˈeɪprən] n a (*garment*) tablier *m.* (*fig*) **tied to his mother's ~ strings** pendu aux jupes de sa mère. b (*Aviat*) aire *f* de stationnement. c (*Tech*) tablier *m.* d (*Theat: also* **~ stage**) avant-scène *f.* e (*Phot*) bande gaufrée.

apropos [ˌæprəˈpəʊ] 1 adv à propos, opportunément. **~ of** à propos de. 2 adj opportun, (fait) à propos.

apse [æps] n abside *f.*

apt [æpt] adj a (*inclined, tending*) *thing* susceptible (*to do* de faire), sujet; *person* enclin, porté, disposé (*to sth* à qch, *to do* à faire). **he is ~ to be late** il a tendance à être en retard; **one is ~ to believe that ...** on croit volontiers que ..., on a tendance à croire que ... . b (*likely*) **am I ~ to find him in at this time?** ai-je une chance de le trouver chez lui à cette heure-ci?; **he's ~ to be out in the afternoons** il a tendance à ne pas être chez lui l'après-midi, il lui arrive souvent d'être sorti l'après-midi. c (*appropriate*) *remark, comment, reply* approprié, juste, pertinent. d (*gifted*) *pupil* doué, intelligent.

apt. (abbr of **apartment**) appt.

APT [ˌeɪpiːˈtiː] n (abbr of **Advanced Passenger Train**) ≃ T.G.V. *m*, train *m* à grande vitesse.

aptitude [ˈæptɪtjuːd] n aptitude *f* (*for* à), disposition *f* (*for* pour). **to have an ~ for learning** avoir des dispositions pour l'étude; **he shows great ~** il promet beaucoup; **~ test** test *m* d'aptitude.

aptly [ˈæptlɪ] adv *answer* pertinemment, avec justesse; *behave* avec propos, à propos. **~ enough, he arrived just then** il est arrivé, fort à propos, juste à ce moment-là; (*iro*) comme par hasard, il est arrivé juste à ce moment-là (*iro*); **it's ~ named** c'est bien nommé, ça porte bien son nom.

aptness [ˈæptnɪs] n a (*suitability*) *[remark etc]* à-propos *m*, justesse *f.* b (*giftedness*) = **aptitude**.

Apulia [əˈpjuːljə] n Pouilles *fpl.*

aquaculture [ˈækwəˌkʌltʃəʳ] n = **aquafarming**.

aquafarming [ˈækwəfɑːmɪŋ] n aquaculture *f.*

aqualung [ˈækwəlʌŋ] n scaphandre *m* autonome.

aquamarine [ˌækwəməˈriːn] 1 n (*stone*) aigue-marine *f*; (*colour*) bleu vert *m inv*. 2 adj bleu-vert *inv*.

aquanaut [ˈækwənɔːt] n scaphandrier *m*, plongeur *m.*

aquaplane [ˈækwəpleɪn] 1 n aquaplane *m.* 2 vi a (*Sport*) faire de l'aquaplane. b (*Aut*) faire de l'aquaplaning *m.*

Aquarian [əˈkwɛərɪən] n (personne née sous le signe du) Verseau *m.*

aquarium [əˈkwɛərɪəm] n, pl **~s** *or* **aquaria** [əˈkwɛərɪə] aquarium *m.*

Aquarius [əˈkwɛərɪəs] n (*Astron*) le Verseau. **I'm (an) ~** je suis (du) Verseau.

aquatic [əˈkwætɪk] adj *animal, plant* aquatique; *sport* nautique.

aquatint [ˈækwətɪnt] n aquatinte *f.*

aqueduct [ˈækwɪdʌkt] n aqueduc *m.*

aqueous [ˈeɪkwɪəs] adj aqueux. **~ humour** humeur aqueuse.

aquiculture [ˈækwɪˌkʌltʃəʳ, ˈeɪkwɪˌkʌltʃəʳ] n = **aquafarming**.

aquiline [ˈækwɪlaɪn] adj *nose* aquilin, en bec d'aigle; *profile* aquilin.

Aquinas [əˈkwaɪnəs] n: **St Thomas ~** saint Thomas d'Aquin.

AR (*US*) abbr of **Arkansas**.

Arab [ˈærəb] 1 n a Arabe *mf*; *see* **street**. b (*horse*) (cheval *m*) arabe *m.* 2 adj arabe. **the ~ States** les États *mpl* arabes; **the United ~ Emirates** les Émirats arabes unis; **the ~-Israeli Wars** le conflit israélo-arabe.

arabesque [ˌærəˈbesk] n arabesque *f.*

Arabia [əˈreɪbɪə] n Arabie *f.*

Arabian [əˈreɪbɪən] adj arabe, d'Arabie. **~ Desert** désert *m* d'Arabie; **~ Gulf** golfe *m* Arabique; **the ~ Nights** les Mille et Une Nuits; **~ Sea** mer *f* d'Arabie.

Arabic [ˈærəbɪk] 1 n (*Ling*) arabe *m.* **written ~** l'arabe littéral. 2 adj arabe. **~ numerals** chiffres *mpl* arabes; *see* **gum²**.

Arabist [ˈærəbɪst] n (*scholar*) arabisant(e) *m(f)*; (*politician*) pro-Arabe *mf.*

arabization [ˌærəbaɪˈzeɪʃən] n arabisation *f.*

arabize [ˈærəbaɪz] vt arabiser.

arable [ˈærəbl] adj arable, cultivable. **~ farming** culture *f.*

arachnid [əˈræknɪd] n: **~s** arachnides *mpl.*

Aramaic [ˌærəˈmeɪɪk] n araméen *m.*

Aran [ˈærən] n: **the ~ Islands** les îles *fpl* Ar(r)an.

arbiter [ˈɑːbɪtəʳ] n arbitre *m*, médiateur *m*, -trice *f.*

arbitrage [ˈɑːbɪtrɪdʒ] n (*Fin, St Ex*) arbitrage *m*, opération *f* d'arbitrage.

arbitrager, arbitrageur [ˈɑːbɪtræˈʒɜːʳ] n arbitragiste *m.*

arbitrarily [ˈɑːbɪtrərəlɪ] adv arbitrairement.

arbitrary [ˈɑːbɪtrərɪ] adj arbitraire.

arbitrate [ˈɑːbɪtreɪt] 1 vt arbitrer, juger, trancher. 2 vi décider en qualité d'arbitre, arbitrer.

arbitration [ˌɑːbɪˈtreɪʃən] n (*also Ind*) arbitrage *m.* **to go to ~** recourir à l'arbitrage; **~ tribunal** instance chargée d'arbitrer les conflits sociaux; **~ clause** clause *f* compromissoire; *see* **refer**.

arbitrator [ˈɑːbɪtreɪtəʳ] n arbitre *m*, médiateur *m*, -trice *f.*

arboreal [ɑːˈbɔːrɪəl] adj *shape* arborescent; *animal, technique* arboricole.

arboretum [ˌɑːbəˈriːtəm] n, pl **arboreta** [ˌɑːbəˈriːtə] *or* **~s** arboretum *m*, collection *f* d'arbres.

arbour, (*US*) **arbor** [ˈɑːbəʳ] n tonnelle *f*, charmille† *f.*

arbutus [ɑːˈbjuːtəs] n arbousier *m.*

arc [ɑːk] 1 n arc *m.* 2 comp ►**arc lamp, arc light** lampe *f* à arc; (*Cine, TV*) sunlight *m* ►**arc welding** soudure *f* à l'arc voltaïque. 3 vi a décrire un arc (de cercle). **the rocket ~ed down into the sea** la fusée a décrit un arc avant de retomber dans la mer. b (*Elec*) former un arc (électrique).

A.R.C. [ˌeɪɑːˈsiː] n a (abbr of **AIDS-related complex**) ARC. b (abbr of **American Red Cross**) Croix-Rouge américaine.

arcade [ɑːˈkeɪd] n (*series of arches*) arcade *f*, galerie *f*; (*shopping precinct*) passage *m*, galerie marchande; (*Brit: also:* **amusement ~**) galerie *f* de jeux *or* d'attractions. (*Brit*) **~ game** jeu *m* vidéo (*dans une galerie de jeux*).

Arcadia [ɑːˈkeɪdɪə] n Arcadie *f.*

Arcadian [ɑːˈkeɪdɪən] 1 adj arcadien, d'Arcadie. 2 n Arcadien(ne) *m(f).*

Arcady [ˈɑːkədɪ] n (*Poet, Liter*) Arcadie *f.*

arcane [ɑːˈkeɪn] adj esotérique, obscur.

arch¹ [ɑːtʃ] 1 n a (*Archit*) (*in church etc*) arc *m*, cintre *m*, voûte *f*; *[bridge etc]* arche *f.* **~way** voûte (d'entrée), porche *m*, (*longer*) passage voûté. b *[eyebrow]* arcade *f*; *[foot]* cambrure *f*, voûte *f* plantaire. ~ **support** semelle *f* orthopédique; *see* **fallen.** 2 **vi** former voûte, être en forme d'arche, s'arquer. 3 **vt** arquer, cambrer. **the cat ~es his back** le chat fait le gros dos.

arch² [ɑːtʃ] **adj** a (*cunning*) *glance, person* malicieux. b (*superior*) *look, remark* condescendant.

arch³ [ɑːtʃ] 1 **adj** (*gen*) grand, par excellence. **an ~ traitor** un grand traître, le traître par excellence; **an ~ villain** un grand *or* parfait scélérat, un scélérat achevé; **the ~ villain** le principal scélérat. 2 **pref** arch(i).

archaeological, (*US*) **archeological** [ˌɑːkɪəˈlɒdʒɪkəl] **adj** archéologique.

archaeologist, (*US*) **archeologist** [ˌɑːkɪˈɒlədʒɪst] **n** archéologue *mf*.

archaeology, (*US*) **archeology** [ˌɑːkɪˈɒlədʒɪ] **n** archéologie *f*.

archaic [ɑːˈkeɪɪk] **adj** archaïque.

archaism [ˈɑːkeɪɪzəm] **n** archaïsme *m*.

archangel [ˈɑːkˌeɪndʒəl] **n** archange *m*. **the A~ Michael** l'archange Michel, saint Michel archange.

archbishop [ˈɑːtʃˈbɪʃəp] **n** archevêque *m*.

archbishopric [ɑːtʃˈbɪʃəprɪk] **n** archevêché *m*.

archdeacon [ˈɑːtʃˈdiːkən] **n** archidiacre *m*.

archdiocese [ˈɑːtʃˈdaɪəsɪs] **n** archidiocèse *m*.

archduchess [ˈɑːtʃˈdʌtʃɪs] **n** archiduchesse *f*.

archduchy [ˈɑːtʃˈdʌtʃɪ] **n** archiduché *m*.

archduke [ˈɑːtʃˈdjuːk] **n** archiduc *m*.

arched [ɑːtʃt] **adj** *back etc* cambré; *eyebrows* arqué; *window* cintré.

arch-enemy [ˈɑːtʃˈenɪmɪ] **n** ennemi *m* par excellence. (*Rel*) **the A~** Satan *m*.

archeology [ˌɑːkɪˈɒlədʒɪ] *etc* (*US*) = **archaeology** *etc*.

archer [ˈɑːtʃəʳ] **n** archer *m*.

archery [ˈɑːtʃərɪ] **n** tir *m* à l'arc.

archetypal [ˈɑːkɪtaɪpəl] **adj** archétype.

archetypally [ˌɑːkɪˈtaɪpəlɪ] **adv** exemplairement.

archetype [ˈɑːkɪtaɪp] **n** archétype *m*.

Archimedes [ˌɑːkɪˈmiːdiːz] **n** Archimède *m*.

archipelago [ˌɑːkɪˈpelɪgəʊ] **n, pl ~s** *or* **~es** archipel *m*.

archiphoneme [ˌɑːkɪˈfəʊniːm] **n** archiphonème *m*.

architect [ˈɑːkɪtekt] **n** architecte *m*; (*fig*) architecte, artisan *m*; *see* **naval.**

architectonic [ˌɑːkɪtekˈtɒnɪk] **adj** (*Art*) architectonique.

architectural [ˌɑːkɪˈtektʃərəl] **adj** architectural.

architecturally [ˌɑːkɪˈtektʃərəlɪ] **adv** architecturalement.

architecture [ˈɑːkɪtektʃəʳ] **n** architecture *f*.

architrave [ˈɑːkɪtreɪv] **n** (*Archit*) architrave *f*; *[door, window]* encadrement *m*.

archive [ˈɑːkaɪv] 1 **n** (*also* **~s**) archives *fpl*. (*Comput*) ~ **file** fichier *m* d'archives. 2 **vt** archiver.

archivist [ˈɑːkɪvɪst] **n** archiviste *mf*.

archly [ˈɑːtʃlɪ] **adv** a (*cunningly*) malicieusement. b (*in a superior way*) avec condescendance.

archness [ˈɑːtʃnɪs] **n** malice *f*.

archpriest [ˈɑːtʃˈpriːst] **n** archiprêtre *m*.

Arctic [ˈɑːktɪk] 1 **adj** (*Geog*) arctique. (*fig: very cold*) **a~** glacial. 2 **n: the ~ (regions)** les régions *fpl* arctiques, l'Arctique *m*. 3 **comp** ▸**Arctic Circle** cercle *m* polaire arctique ▸**Arctic Ocean** océan *m* Arctique ▸**Arctic skua** (*Orn*) labbe *m* parasite ▸**Arctic tern** (*Orn*) sterne *f* arctique.

ARD [ˌeɪɑːˈdiː] (**abbr of acute respiratory disease**) *see* **acute.**

ardent [ˈɑːdənt] **adj** ardent, passionné, fervent. **to be an ~ admirer of** être un fervent admirateur de.

ardently [ˈɑːdəntlɪ] **adv** ardemment, avec ardeur.

ardour, (*US*) **ardor** [ˈɑːdəʳ] **n** ardeur *f*, ferveur *f*.

arduous [ˈɑːdjʊəs] **adj** *work* ardu, difficile, laborieux; *road* ardu, raide; *hill* raide, escarpé.

arduously [ˈɑːdjʊəslɪ] **adv** péniblement, laborieusement.

arduousness [ˈɑːdjʊəsnɪs] **n** difficulté *f*, dureté *f*.

are [ɑːʳ, əʳ] *see* **be.**

area [ˈɛərɪə] 1 **n** a (*surface measure*) aire *f*, superficie *f*. **this field has an ~ of 800 m²** ce champ a une superficie de 800 m² *or* a 800 m² de superficie, l'aire de ce champ est de 800 m².

b (*region*) région *f*; (*Mil, Pol*) (*large*) territoire *m*; (*smaller*) secteur *m*, zone *f*. **the London ~** la région londonienne *or* de Londres; **in the whole ~** dans toute l'étendue du pays *or* de la région; **~ of outstanding natural beauty** site naturel; *see* **sterling.**

c (*fig*) *[knowledge, enquiry]* domaine *m*, champ *m*. **the ~s of disagreement** les zones *fpl* de désaccord; **in this ~** à ce propos.

d (*Brit: courtyard*) courette *f* en contre-bas (*sur la rue*).

e (*place with specified function*) (*part of room*) **dining ~** coin *m* salle-à-manger; **sleeping ~** coin chambre; (*part of building, housing estate etc*) **play/parking ~** aire *f* de jeux/de stationnement.

2 **comp** ▸**area code** (*Brit Post*) code postal; (*US Telec*) indicatif *m* de zone ▸**area manager** directeur régional ▸**area office** agence régionale ▸**areaway** (*US*) = **area d.**

arena [əˈriːnə] **n** arène *f*. (*fig*) **to enter the ~** descendre dans l'arène, entrer en lice; (*fig*) **the political ~** l'arène politique.

aren't [ɑːnt] = **are not, am not;** *see* **be.**

areola [əˈrɪələ] **n, pl ~s** *or* **areolae** [əˈrɪəˌliː] (*Anat*) aréole *f*.

Argentina [ˌɑːdʒənˈtiːnə] **n** Argentine *f*.

Argentine [ˈɑːdʒəntaɪn] 1 **n** a (*Geog*) **the ~** l'Argentine *f*; **in the ~** en Argentine. b = **Argentinian.** 2 **adj** argentin.

Argentinean [ˌɑːdʒənˈtɪnɪən] **adj** (*US*) = **Argentinian.**

Argentinian [ˌɑːdʒənˈtɪnɪən] 1 **n** Argentin(e) *m(f)*. 2 **adj** argentin.

argon [ˈɑːgɒn] **n** argon *m*.

Argonaut [ˈɑːgənɔːt] **n** Argonaute *m*.

Argos [ˈɑːgɒs] **n** Argos.

argosy [ˈɑːgəsɪ] **n** (*liter*) galion *m* (*de commerce*).

arguable [ˈɑːgjʊəbl] **adj** discutable, contestable. **it is ~ that** on peut soutenir que.

arguably [ˈɑːgjʊəblɪ] **adv: he is ~ the worst president ever known** on peut soutenir que *or* on pourrait dire que c'est le pire président qu'on ait jamais vu.

argue [ˈɑːgjuː] 1 **vi** a (*dispute, quarrel*) se disputer (*with sb* avec qn; *about sth* au sujet *or* à propos de qch). **they are always arguing** ils se disputent tout le temps; **don't ~!** pas de discussion!; (*to others arguing*) **stop arguing!** arrêtez de vous disputer!

b (*debate*) argumenter (*frm*) (*against sb* contre qn; *about sth* sur qch). **he ~d against going** il a donné les raisons qu'il avait de ne pas vouloir y aller; **they ~d (about it) for hours** ils ont discuté (là-dessus) pendant des heures; **to ~ from sth** tirer argument de qch.

c (*Jur etc*) *[fact, evidence]* témoigner (*against* contre; *in favour of* en faveur de). **it ~s well for him** cela parle en sa faveur.

2 **vt** a **to ~ sb into/out of doing** persuader/dissuader qn de faire; **to ~ sb into/out of a scheme** persuader/dissuader qn d'adopter un projet; **they ~d me into believing it** à force d'arguments ils sont arrivés à me le faire croire.

b (*debate*) *case* discuter, débattre. **a well-~d case** un cas étayé de bons arguments; **to ~ one's way out of a situation** se sortir d'une situation à force d'argumentation *or* d'arguments; **to ~ the toss*** discuter le coup*.

c (*show evidence of*) dénoter, indiquer. **it ~s a certain lack of feeling** cela dénote *or* indique une certaine insensibilité.

d (*maintain*) soutenir, affirmer (*that* que).

▸**argue out vt sep** *problem* discuter *or* débattre (à fond).

argument [ˈɑːgjʊmənt] **n** a (*debate*) discussion *f*, controverse *f*, débat *m*. **it is beyond ~** c'est indiscutable; **you've only heard one side of the ~** tu n'as entendu qu'une seule version de l'affaire *or* de l'histoire; **for ~'s sake** à titre d'exemple; **he is open to ~** il est prêt à écouter les arguments; **it is open to ~ that** on peut soutenir que.

b (*dispute*) dispute *f*, discussion *f*. **to have an ~** se disputer (*with sb* avec qn); (*hum*) **he has had an ~ with a tree** il s'est bagarré* avec un arbre (*hum*).

c (*reasons advanced*) argument *m*. **his ~ is that ...** il soutient que ..., son argument est que ...; **there is a strong ~ in favour of** *or* **for doing** il y a de bonnes raisons pour faire; **there is a strong ~ in favour of his resignation** il y a de bonnes raisons pour qu'il démissionne (*subj*); **the ~ that the EC needs Britain** le raisonnement selon lequel la CE a besoin de la Grande Bretagne; *see* **line¹.**

d (*synopsis*) sommaire *m*, argument *m*.

argumentation [ˌɑːgjʊmənˈteɪʃən] **n** argumentation *f*.

argumentative [ˌɑːgjʊˈmentətɪv] **adj** ergoteur, raisonneur.

argy-bargy* [ˈɑːdʒɪˈbɑːdʒɪ] **n** (*Brit*) discutailleries* *fpl*. **to get caught up in an ~** se laisser entraîner dans des discussions sans fin.

aria [ˈɑːrɪə] **n** aria *f*.

Ariadne [ˌærɪˈædnɪ] **n** Ariane *f*.

Arian [ˈɛərɪən] 1 **n** Arien(ne) *m(f)*. 2 **adj** arien.

Arianism [ˈɛərɪənɪzəm] **n** arianisme *m*.

ARIBA [əˈriːbə] (**abbr of Associate of the Royal Institute of British Architects**) *membre de l'institut des architectes.*

arid [ˈærɪd] **adj** (*lit*) aride, desséché; (*fig*) aride, ingrat.

aridity [əˈrɪdɪtɪ] **n** (*lit, fig*) aridité *f*.

Aries [ˈɛəriːz] **n** (*Astron*) le Bélier. **I'm (an) ~** je suis (du) Bélier.

aright [əˈraɪt] **adv** bien, correctement, juste. **to set things ~** mettre bon ordre à l'affaire.

arise [əˈraɪz] **pret arose** [əˈrəʊz], **ptp arisen** [əˈrɪzn] **vi** a *[difficulty]* survenir, surgir; *[question]* se présenter, se poser; *[cry]* s'élever. **if the question ~s** le cas échéant; **should the need ~** en cas de besoin, si le besoin s'en fait sentir; **should the occasion ~** si l'occasion se présente; **a doubt arose** un doute s'est fait jour. b (*result*) résulter, provenir (*from* de). c (†, *liter*) *[person]* se lever; *[sun]* se lever, paraître, poindre (*liter*).

aristo [ˈærɪstəʊ] **n** (**abbr of aristocrat**) aristo* *mf*.

aristocracy [ˌærɪsˈtɒkrəsɪ] **n** aristocratie *f*.

aristocrat [ˈærɪstəkræt] **n** aristocrate *mf*.

aristocratic [ˌærɪstəˈkrætɪk] **adj** aristocratique.

Aristophanes [ˌærɪsˈtɒfəniːz] **n** Aristophane *m*.

Aristotelian [ˌærɪstəˈtiːlɪən] **adj** aristotélicien.

Aristotelianism [ˌærɪstəˈtiːlɪənɪzəm] **n** aristotélisme *m*.

Aristotle [ˈærɪstɒtl] n Aristote *m*.

arithmetic [əˈrɪθmətɪk] 1 n arithmétique *f*. 2 [ˌærɪθˈmetɪk] adj arithmétique. (*Comput*) ~ **logic unit** unité *f* arithmétique et logique; ~ **mean** moyenne *f* arithmétique.

arithmetical [ˌærɪθˈmetɪkəl] adj arithmétique.

arithmetician [əˌrɪθməˈtɪʃən] n arithméticien(ne) *m(f)*.

Ariz. (*US*) abbr of **Arizona**.

Arizona [ˌærɪˈzəʊnə] n Arizona *m*.

Ark. (*US*) abbr of **Arkansas**.

ark [ɑːk] n (*Hist*) arche *f*. (*Rel*) **A~ of the Covenant** arche d'alliance; (*fig*) **it's out of the ~*** c'est vieux comme Hérode, c'est antédiluvien*; *see* **Noah**.

Arkansas [ˈɑːkənsɔː] n Arkansas *m*.

arm[1] [ɑːm] 1 n a (*Anat*) bras *m*. **to hold sth/sb in one's ~s** tenir qch/qn dans ses bras; **he had a coat over his ~** il avait un manteau sur le bras; **take my ~** prenez mon bras; **to give one's ~ to sb** donner *or* offrir le bras à qn; (†, *liter*) **to have sb on one's ~** avoir qn à son bras; **on her husband's ~** au bras de son mari; **to take sb in one's ~s** prendre qn dans ses bras; **to put one's ~ round sb** passer son bras autour des épaules de qn; ~ **in** ~ bras dessus bras dessous; **with ~s wide apart** les bras écartés *or* en croix; **within ~'s reach** à portée de la main; **with folded ~s** les bras croisés; **at ~'s length** à bout de bras; (*fig*) **to keep sb at ~'s length** tenir qn à distance (*see also* **2**); **with open ~s** à bras ouverts; (*liter*) **in the ~s of Morpheus** dans les bras de Morphée; **the (long) ~ of the law** le bras de la justice; **a list as long as your ~*** une liste qui n'en finit (*or* finissait) pas *or* longue comme ça*; (*fig*) **to have a long ~** avoir le bras long; (*US*) **to put the ~ on sb*** (*gen*) forcer la main à qn (*to do* pour qu'il fasse); (*make him pay up*) faire cracher‡ qn; **I'd give my right ~** *or* **I'd give an ~ and a leg* for that/to do that** je donnerais n'importe quoi pour avoir ça/pour faire ça; **they must have paid an ~ and a leg for that, that must have cost them an ~ and a leg** ça a dû leur coûter les yeux de la tête*; *see* **babe, chance, open**.

b [*river, crane, pick-up*] bras *m*; [*spectacle frames*] branche *f* (de monture); [*coat etc*] manche *f*; [*armchair*] bras, accoudoir *m*. ~ **of the sea** bras de mer.

2 comp ▸**armband** brassard *m*; (*mourning*) brassard de deuil, crêpe *m* ▸**armchair** fauteuil *m*; **armchair general** *etc* (*fig*) général *m etc* en chambre ▸**armhole** emmanchure *f* ▸**armlet** *see* **armlet** ▸**armpit** aisselle *f* ▸**armrest** accoudoir *m* ▸**arm's length: arm's length agreement** (*Jur*) contrat conclu dans les conditions normales du commerce; **arm's length price** (*Fin*) prix fixé dans les conditions normales de la concurrence ▸**arm-twisting*** pressions *fpl* directes; **I don't like his arm-twisting* techniques** je n'aime pas ses façons de faire pression sur les gens ▸**arm-wrestle: to arm-wrestle with sb** faire une partie de bras de fer avec qn ▸**arm-wrestling** bras *m* de fer.

arm[2] [ɑːm] 1 n a (*weapon*) arme *f*. **under ~s** sous les armes; **in ~s** armé; **to ~s!** aux armes!; (*lit, fig*) **to take up ~s against sb/sth** s'insurger contre qn/qch (*lit, fig*); (*fig*) **to be up in ~s against sb/the authorities** être en rébellion ouverte contre qn/les autorités; **to be up in ~s against a decision/the cost of living** *etc* s'élever contre *or* partir en guerre contre une décision/le coût de la vie *etc*; **she was up in ~s about it** cela la mettait hors d'elle-même; **no need to get up in ~s over such a small thing!** pas la peine de te monter *or* t'emballer pour si peu!; *see* **man**.

b (*branch of military service*) arme *f*; *see* **fleet**[1].

c (*Her*) ~**s** armes *fpl*, armoiries *fpl*; *see* **coat**.

2 comp ▸**arms control** contrôle *m* des armements ▸**arms factory** fabrique *f* d'armes ▸**arms limitation** = **arms control** ▸**arms manufacturer** (*Comm*) fabricant *m* d'armes, armurier *m* ▸**arms race** course *f* aux armements.

3 vt a *person, nation* armer. (*fig*) **to ~ o.s. with patience** s'armer de patience. b *missile* munir d'une (tête d')ogive.

4 vi (s')armer, prendre les armes (*against* contre).

Armada [ɑːˈmɑːdə] n Armada *f*.

armadillo [ˌɑːməˈdɪləʊ] n tatou *m*.

Armageddon [ˌɑːməˈgedn] n (*lit*) Armageddon *m*; (*fig*) Armageddon, la lutte suprême.

armament [ˈɑːməmənt] n a (*gen pl: fighting strength*) force *f* de frappe. b (*weapons*) ~**s** armement *m*, matériel *m* de guerre. c (*NonC: preparation for war*) armement *m*.

armature [ˈɑːmətjʊəʳ] n (*gen, also Elec, Phys*) armature *f*; (*Zool*) carapace *f*.

armed [ɑːmd] adj (*lit, fig*) armé (*with* de); *missile* muni d'une (tête d')ogive. ~ **to the teeth** armé jusqu'aux dents; ~ **conflict/struggle** conflit *m* armé/lutte *f* armée; **the ~ forces** les (forces) armées *fpl*; ~ **neutrality** neutralité armée; ~ **robbery** vol *m or* attaque *f* à main armée.

-armed [ɑːmd] adj ending in comps: **long-/short-armed** aux bras longs/courts.

Armenia [ɑːˈmiːnɪə] n Arménie *f*.

Armenian [ɑːˈmiːnɪən] 1 adj arménien. 2 n a Arménien(ne) *m(f)*. b (*Ling*) arménien *m*.

armful [ˈɑːmfʊl] n brassée *f*. **in ~s** à pleins bras; **to have ~s of** avoir plein les bras de.

armistice [ˈɑːmɪstɪs] n armistice *m*. **A~ Day** le onze novembre (*anniversaire de l'armistice*).

armlet [ˈɑːmlɪt] n (*armband*) brassard *m*; (*bracelet*) bracelet *m*.

armorial [ɑːˈmɔːrɪəl] 1 adj armorial. ~ **bearings** armoiries *fpl*. 2 n armorial *m*.

armour, (*US*) **armor** [ˈɑːməʳ] 1 n a (*NonC*) [*knight*] armure *f*. **in full ~** armé de pied en cap; *see* **suit**. b (*Mil*) (*NonC: ~-plating*) blindage *m*; (*collectively*) (*vehicles*) blindés *mpl*; (*forces*) forces blindées. 2 comp ▸**armour-clad** (*Mil*) blindé; (*Naut*) cuirassé, blindé ▸**armoured car** voiture *f* blindée ▸**armoured personnel carrier** véhicule blindé de transport de troupes ▸**armour-piercing** (*Mil*) *mine, gun* antichar; *shell, bullet* perforant ▸**armour-plate, armour-plating** (*Mil*) blindage *m*; (*Naut*) cuirasse *f* ▸**armour-plated** = **armour-clad**.

armourer, (*US*) **armorer** [ˈɑːmərəʳ] n armurier *m*.

armoury, (*US*) **armory** [ˈɑːmərɪ] n dépôt *m* d'armes, arsenal *m*; (*US: arms factory*) fabrique *f* d'armes, armurerie *f*.

army [ˈɑːmɪ] 1 n a armée *f* (de terre). **to be in the ~** être dans l'armée, être militaire; **to join the ~** s'engager; **to go into the ~** [*professional*] devenir militaire *m* (de carrière); [*conscript*] partir au service; *see* **occupation, territorial**. b (*fig*) foule *f*, multitude *f*, armée *f*. 2 comp *life, nurse, uniform* militaire; *family* de militaires ▸**army corps** corps *m* d'armée ▸**Army List** annuaire *m* militaire, annuaire des officiers de carrière (*armée de terre*) ▸**army officer** officier *m* (de l'armée de terre).

Arno [ˈɑːnəʊ] n Arno *m*.

aroma [əˈrəʊmə] n arôme *m*.

aromatherapy [əˌrəʊməˈθerəpɪ] n aromathérapie *f*.

aromatic [ˌærəʊˈmætɪk] 1 adj aromatique. 2 n aromate *m*.

arose [əˈrəʊz] pret of **arise**.

around [əˈraʊnd] (*phr vb elem*) 1 adv a autour. **all ~** tout autour, de tous côtés; **for miles ~** sur *or* dans un rayon de plusieurs kilomètres.

b (*nearby*) dans les parages. **he is somewhere ~** il est dans les parages; **to stroll ~** se promener (quelque part) par là; **she'll be ~ soon** elle sera bientôt là *or* ici; **is he ~?*** (est-ce qu')il est là?; **there's a lot of flu ~** il y a beaucoup de cas de grippe en ce moment; **he's been ~*** (*travelled*) il a pas mal roulé sa bosse*; (*experienced*) il n'est pas né d'hier *or* de la dernière pluie; **it's been ~* for more than 20 years** ça existe depuis plus de 20 ans.

2 prep (*esp US*) a (*round*) autour de. ~ **the fire** autour du feu; ~ **it** autour; **to go ~ an obstacle** faire le tour d'un *or* contourner un obstacle; **the country ~ the town** les environs *mpl or* alentours *mpl* de la ville; **the first building ~ the corner** le premier immeuble après le coin; **it's just ~ the corner** (*lit*) c'est juste après le coin; (*fig: very near*) c'est à deux pas (d'ici); (*in time*) c'est pour demain (*fig*).

b (*about*) **to wander ~ the city** errer dans *or* par toute la ville; **they are somewhere ~ the house** ils sont quelque part dans la maison.

c (*approximately*) environ, à peu près. ~ **2 kilos** environ *or* à peu près 2 kilos, 2 kilos environ; ~ **1800** vers *or* aux alentours de 1800; ~ **10 o'clock** vers 10 heures, vers *or* sur les 10 heures.

arousal [əˈraʊzəl] n (*sexual*) excitation (sexuelle); [*emotions*] éveil *m*.

arouse [əˈraʊz] vt a (*awaken*) *person* réveiller, éveiller. **to ~ sb from his sleep** tirer qn du sommeil. b (*cause*) *suspicion, curiosity etc* éveiller, susciter; *anger* exciter, provoquer; *contempt* susciter, provoquer. c (*stimulate*) stimuler, réveiller*; (*stir to action*) pousser à agir, secouer. **that ~d him to protest** cela l'a poussé à protester; **to ~ sb to an effort** obtenir un effort de qn.

arpeggio [ɑːˈpedʒɪəʊ] n arpège *m*.

arraign [əˈreɪn] vt (*Jur*) traduire en justice; (*fig*) accuser, mettre en cause.

arraignment [əˈreɪnmənt] n (*Jur*) ≃ lecture *f* de l'acte d'accusation.

Arran [ˈærən] n île *f* d'Arran (*dans l'estuaire de la Clyde*).

arrange [əˈreɪndʒ] 1 vt a (*put in order*) *room, clothing* arranger; *books, objects* ranger, mettre en ordre; *flowers* arranger, disposer. **to ~ one's hair** arranger sa coiffure; **flower arranging** *or* **arrangement** art *m* de faire des bouquets, décoration florale; **room ~d as a waiting room** pièce aménagée en salon d'attente.

b (*decide on*) *meeting* arranger, organiser, fixer; *date* fixer; *plans, programme* arrêter, convenir de, s'entendre sur; *marriage* arranger. **it was ~d that ...** il a été arrangé *or* décidé *or* convenu que ... + *cond*; **I have something ~d for tonight** j'ai quelque chose de prévu pour ce soir.

c (†: *settle*) *dispute* régler, arranger.

d (*Mus*) arranger, adapter. **to ~ sth for violin and piano** arranger qch pour violon et piano.

2 vi (*fix details*) s'arranger (*to do* pour faire; *with sb about sth* avec qn au sujet de qch), prendre des *or* ses dispositions (*for sb to do* pour que qn fasse). **we have ~d for the goods to be dispatched** nous avons fait le nécessaire pour que les marchandises soient expédiées; **to ~ for sb's luggage to be sent up** faire monter les bagages de qn; **to ~ with sb to do** décider avec qn de faire, s'entendre avec qn pour faire.

arrangement [əˈreɪndʒmənt] n a [*room*] aménagement *m*; [*furniture*] arrangement *m*, disposition *f*; [*flowers, hair, clothing*] arrangement; *see* **flower**.

b (*agreement*) règlement *m*, arrangement *m*. **to do sth by ~ with sb** s'entendre *or* s'arranger avec qn pour faire qch; **larger sizes by ~** tailles supérieures sur demande; **price by ~** prix *m* à débattre; **to come** to an ~ with sb arriver à un arrangement avec qn, s'arranger *or* s'entendre avec qn (*to do* pour faire); by ~ with Covent Garden avec l'autorisation *f* de Covent Garden; *see* exceptional.

c (*sth decided*) décision *f*, arrangement *m*. (*plans, preparations*) ~s mesures *fpl*, dispositions *fpl*, préparatifs *mpl*; this ~ suited everyone cette décision *or* cet arrangement convenait à tous; I want to change the ~s we made je veux changer les dispositions que nous avons prises *or* l'arrangement auquel nous étions arrivés; the ~ whereby he should visit her monthly l'arrangement selon lequel il doit aller la voir une fois par mois; I write to confirm these ~s je vous écris pour confirmer ces dispositions; to make ~s for a holiday faire des préparatifs pour des vacances, organiser des vacances (à l'avance); to make ~s for sth to be done prendre des mesures *or* dispositions pour faire faire qch; can you make ~s to come tomorrow? pouvez-vous vous arranger pour venir demain?

d (*Mus*) adaptation *f*, arrangement *m*.

arrant ['ærənt] adj *fool* fini; *liar* fieffé.

array [ə'reɪ] 1 vt a (*Mil*) *troops* déployer, ranger, disposer. b (*liter: clothe*) *person* revêtir (*in* de). 2 n a (*Mil*) rang *m*, ordre *m*. in battle ~ en ordre de bataille. b *[objects]* ensemble impressionnant, collection *f*, étalage *m*; *[people]* assemblée *f*. an ~ of satellites une batterie de satellites. c (*Math etc: also Comput*) tableau *m*. ~ of figures tableau de nombres. d (*ceremonial dress*) habit *m* d'apparat; (*fine clothes*) parure *f*, atours *mpl* (*iro*).

arrears [ə'rɪəz] npl arriéré *m*, arrérages *mpl*. rent in ~ (loyer) arriéré; to get into ~ s'arriérer; she is 3 months in ~ with her rent, her rent is 3 months in ~ elle doit 3 mois de loyer; to be/get in ~ with one's correspondence avoir/prendre du retard dans sa correspondance; ~ of work accumulation *f* de travail en retard.

arrest [ə'rest] 1 vt a *[police etc] suspect* arrêter, appréhender.

b *person's attention, interest* retenir, attirer.

c *growth, development, progress* (*stop*) arrêter; (*hinder*) entraver; (*retard*) retarder. measures to ~ inflation des mesures pour arrêter l'inflation; (*Med*) to ~ (the course of) a disease enrayer une maladie; ~ed development (*Med*) arrêt *m* de croissance; (*Psych*) atrophie *f* de la personnalité.

2 n a *[person]* arrestation *f*. under ~ en état d'arrestation; (*Mil*) aux arrêts; to put sb under ~ arrêter qn; (*Mil*) mettre qn aux arrêts; to make an ~ procéder à une arrestation; (*Mil*) open/close ~ ≃ arrêts *mpl* simples/de rigueur.

b (*Jur*) ~ of judgment suspension *f* d'exécution d'un jugement.

arresting [ə'restɪŋ] adj frappant, saisissant.

arrhythmia [ə'rɪðmɪə] n (*NonC*) arythmie *f*.

arrival [ə'raɪvəl] n a (*NonC*) *[person, vehicle, letter, parcel]* arrivée *f*; (*Comm*) *[goods in bulk]* arrivage *m*. on ~ à l'arrivée; (*Rail etc*) ~s and departures arrivées et départs; ~ platform quai *m* d'arrivée; ~s board, (*US*) ~ board tableau *m* des arrivées; ~s lounge salon *m* d'arrivée. b (*consignment*) an ~ of un arrivage de; (*person*) who was the first ~? qui est arrivé le premier?; a new ~ un nouveau venu, une nouvelle venue; (*: *baby*) un(e) nouveau-né(e); the latest ~ le dernier arrivé.

arrive [ə'raɪv] vi a *[person, vehicle, letter, goods]* arriver. to ~ at a town arriver à *or* atteindre une ville; as soon as he ~s dès qu'il arrivera, dès son arrivée; (*on timetable etc*) arriving Paris (at) 14.43 arrivée *f* à Paris (à) 14h.43; to ~ (up)on the scene survenir; the moment has ~d when we must go le moment est venu pour nous de partir. b (*succeed in business etc*) arriver, réussir.

►arrive at vt fus *decision, solution* aboutir à, parvenir à; *perfection* atteindre. to arrive at a price *[one person]* fixer un prix; *[2 people]* se mettre d'accord sur un prix; they finally arrived at the idea of doing ils en sont finalement venus à l'idée de faire.

arrogance ['ærəgəns] n arrogance *f*, morgue *f*.

arrogant ['ærəgənt] adj arrogant, plein de morgue.

arrogate ['ærəʊgeɪt] vt a (*claim unjustly*) *authority, right* revendiquer à tort, s'arroger; *victory* s'attribuer. b (*attribute unjustly*) attribuer injustement (*to sb* à qn).

arrow ['ærəʊ] 1 n (*weapon, directional sign*) flèche *f*. to fire *or* shoot *or* loose an ~ décocher une flèche. 2 vt *item on list etc* cocher; *route, direction* flécher. (*insert*) to ~ sth in indiquer l'emplacement de qch. 3 comp **►arrowhead** fer *m*, pointe *f* (de flèche) **►arrowroot** (*Culin*) arrow-root *m*; (*Bot*) marante *f*.

arse** [ɑːs] n (*esp Brit*) cul** *m*. shift *or* move your ~! (*move over*) bouge ton cul**!; (*hurry up*) magne-toi le cul**!; get (up) off your ~ (*stand up*) lève ton cul de là**; (*fig*) bouge-toi le cul**; (*fig*) he doesn't know his ~ from his elbow il comprend rien à rien*; *see* ass[2], pain.

►arse about**, **arse around**** vi déconner**.

arsehole** ['ɑːshəʊl] n (*lit, also fig: idiot*) trou *m* du cul**.

arsenal ['ɑːsɪnl] n arsenal *m*.

arsenic ['ɑːsnɪk] n arsenic *m*. ~ poisoning empoisonnement *m* à l'arsenic.

arsenical [ɑː'senɪkəl] adj *substance* arsenical. ~ poisoning empoisonnement *m* à l'arsenic.

arson ['ɑːsn] n incendie volontaire *or* criminel.

arsonist ['ɑːsənɪst] n (*gen*) incendiaire *mf*; (*maniac*) pyromane *mf*.

art[1] [ɑːt] 1 n a (*NonC*) art *m*. ~ for ~'s sake l'art pour l'art; to study ~ (*gen*) faire des études d'art; (*Univ*) faire les beaux-arts; the ~s les arts; *see* work.

b (*human skill*) art *m*, habileté *f*. the ~ of embroidering/embroidery l'art de broder/de la broderie; to do sth with ~ faire qch avec art *or* habileté; ~s and crafts artisanat *m* (d'art); *see* black, fine[1], state *etc*.

c (*Univ*) A~s lettres *fpl*; Faculty of A~s faculté *f* des Lettres (et Sciences Humaines); he's doing A~s il fait des (études de) lettres; *see* bachelor, master.

d (*cunning*) artifice *m*, ruse *f*; (*trick*) stratagème *m*, artifice, ruse. to use every ~ in order to do user de tous les artifices pour faire.

2 comp **►art collection** collection *f* de tableaux **►art college** ≃ école *f* des beaux-arts **►art deco** art *m* déco **►art exhibition** exposition *f* (de peinture *or* de sculpture) **►art form** moyen *m* d'expression artistique **►art gallery** (*museum*) musée *m* d'art; (*shop*) galerie *f* (de tableaux *or* d'art) **►art nouveau** Modern Style *m* **►art paper** papier couché **►art school** ≃ école *f* des beaux-arts **►Arts Council** (*Brit*) *organisme autonome d'encouragement aux activités culturelles* **►Arts degree** (*Univ*) licence *f* ès lettres **►art student** étudiant(e) *m(f)* des *or* en beaux-arts **►Arts student** étudiant(e) *m(f)* de *or* en lettres (et sciences humaines) **►artwork** maquette *f* (*prête pour la photogravure*).

art[2] [ɑːt] (††, *liter*) thou ~ = you are; *see* be.

artefact ['ɑːtɪfækt] n objet *m* (fabriqué), artefact *m*.

Artemis ['ɑːtɪmɪs] n Artémis *f*.

arterial [ɑː'tɪərɪəl] adj a (*Anat*) artériel. b (*Rail*) ~ line grande ligne; (*Aut*) ~ road route *f or* voie *f* à grande circulation, (grande) artère *f*.

arteriole [ɑː'tɪərɪəʊl] n (*Anat*) artériole *f*.

arteriosclerosis [ɑː'tɪərɪəʊsklɪ'rəʊsɪs] n artériosclérose *f*.

artery ['ɑːtərɪ] n (*Anat*) artère *f*; (*fig: road*) artère, route *f or* voie *f* à grande circulation.

artesian [ɑː'tiːzɪən] adj: ~ well puits artésien.

artful ['ɑːtfʊl] adj rusé, malin (*f* -igne), astucieux. he's an ~ one* c'est un petit malin*; ~ dodger roublard(e)* *m(f)*.

artfully ['ɑːtfəlɪ] adv (*cunningly*) astucieusement, avec astuce; (*skilfully*) avec adresse, habilement.

artfulness ['ɑːtfʊlnɪs] n (*cunning*) astuce *f*, ruse *f*; (*skill*) adresse *f*, habileté *f*.

arthritic [ɑː'θrɪtɪk] adj, n arthritique (*mf*).

arthritis [ɑː'θraɪtɪs] n arthrite *f*; *see* rheumatoid.

arthropod ['ɑːθrəpɒd] n arthropode *m*.

Arthurian [ɑː'θjʊərɪən] adj du roi Arthur, d'Arthur.

artichoke ['ɑːtɪtʃəʊk] n artichaut *m*; *see* globe, Jerusalem.

article ['ɑːtɪkl] 1 n a (*object*) objet *m*; (*Comm*) article *m*, marchandise *f*. ~ of clothing pièce *f* d'habillement; ~s of clothing vêtements *mpl*; ~ of food produit *m or* denrée *f* alimentaire; ~s of value objets de valeur. b (*Press*) article *m*; *see* leading. c (*Jur etc*) *[treaty, document]* article *m*. ~s of apprenticeship contrat *m* d'apprentissage; ~ of faith article de foi; (*Rel*) the Thirty-Nine A~s *les trente-neuf articles de foi de l'Église anglicane;* (*US Mil*) ~s of war code *m* de justice militaire. d (*Gram*) article *m*; *see* definite, indefinite.

2 vt a *apprentice* (*to trade*) mettre en apprentissage (*to* chez); (*to profession*) mettre en stage (*to* chez, auprès de). b (*Jur*) stipuler.

articulate [ɑː'tɪkjʊlɪt] 1 adj a *speech* bien articulé, net, distinct; *thought* clair, net; *person* qui s'exprime bien, qui sait s'exprimer. b (*Anat, Bot*) articulé. 2 [ɑː'tɪkjʊleɪt] vt a *word, sentence* articuler; (*fig*) *plan, goal* exprimer clairement. b (*Anat, Bot*) articuler. (*Brit*) ~d lorry semi-remorque *m*. 3 vi articuler.

articulately [ɑː'tɪkjʊlɪtlɪ] adv avec facilité, avec aisance.

articulation [ɑːˌtɪkjʊ'leɪʃən] n (*also Ling*) articulation *f*.

articulatory [ɑːˌtɪkjʊ'leɪtərɪ] adj: ~ phonetics phonétique *f* articulatoire.

artifact ['ɑːtɪfækt] n = artefact.

artifice ['ɑːtɪfɪs] n a (*will, stratagem*) artifice *m*, ruse *f*, stratagème *m*. b (*NonC: cunning*) adresse *f*, art *m*. c (†: *contrivance*) stratagème *m*.

artificial [ˌɑːtɪ'fɪʃəl] adj a (*synthetic*) *light, flowers* artificiel; (*Comm*) *leather, jewel* synthétique, artificiel. ~ climbing escalade artificielle; ~ hair cheveux *mpl* postiches; ~ insemination (by donor) insémination artificielle (par un donneur); ~ intelligence intelligence artificielle; ~ leg jambe artificielle; ~ limb prothèse *f*, membre artificiel; ~ manure engrais *mpl* chimiques; ~ respiration respiration artificielle; ~ silk rayonne *f*, soie artificielle; ~ teeth fausses dents, prothèse *f* dentaire.

b (*affected*) *manner* factice, étudié, artificiel; *tears* feint, factice; *smile* forcé; *person* affecté. it was a very ~ situation la situation manquait de spontanéité *or* de naturel.

artificiality [ˌɑːtɪfɪʃɪ'ælɪtɪ] n manque *m* de naturel.

artificially [ˌɑːtɪ'fɪʃəlɪ] adv artificiellement.

artillery [ɑː'tɪlərɪ] n artillerie *f*. ~man artilleur *m*.

artisan ['ɑːtɪzæn] n artisan *m*. (*collectively*) the ~s l'artisanat *m*.

artist ['ɑːtɪst] n a (*Art etc, also fig*) artiste *mf*. b = artiste. c (**) con *etc* ~ spécialiste *mf* de l'escroquerie *etc*.

artiste [ɑːˈtiːst] n (*Cine, Theat, TV*) artiste *mf*; *see* **variety**.
artistic [ɑːˈtɪstɪk] adj *arrangement, activity, sense* artistique; *temperament* artiste. **she is very ~** elle a un sens artistique très développé.
artistically [ɑːˈtɪstɪkəlɪ] adv artistiquement, avec art.
artistry [ˈɑːtɪstrɪ] n (*NonC*) art *m*, talent *m* artistique.
artless [ˈɑːtlɪs] adj a (*without guile*) *person* naturel, ingénu. **~ beauty** beauté naturelle; **~ charm** charme ingénu. b (*slightly pej: crude*) *object* grossier; *translation* mal fait, lourd.
artlessly [ˈɑːtlɪslɪ] adv ingénument.
artlessness [ˈɑːtlɪsnɪs] n (*see* **artless**) ingénuité *f*; naturel *m*.
arty* [ˈɑːtɪ] adj *person* qui a le genre artiste *or* bohème; *clothes* de style bohème; *decoration, style* (d'un art) apprêté.
arty-crafty* [ˈɑːtɪˈkrɑːftɪ] adj, (*US*) **artsy-craftsy*** [ˈɑːtsɪˈkrɑːftsɪ] adj (*pej*) *object, style* (exagérément) artisanal; *person* qui affiche un genre artiste *or* bohème.
ARV [ˌeɪɑːˈviː] (*US Bible*) (abbr of **American Revised Version**) *traduction américaine de la Bible*.
arvee* [ɑːˈviː] n (*US*) (abbr of **recreational vehicle**) *see* **recreational**.
Aryan [ˈɛərɪən] 1 n Aryen(ne) *m(f)*. 2 adj aryen.
as [æz, əz] 1 conj a (*when, while*) comme, alors que, tandis que, pendant que. **~ she was resting she heard it** tandis qu'elle *or* comme elle se reposait elle l'entendit; **I saw him ~ he came out** je l'ai vu au moment où *or* comme il sortait; **~ a child, she was obedient** (étant) enfant, elle était obéissante; **he got deafer ~ he got older** il devenait plus sourd à mesure qu'il vieillissait *or* en vieillissant.
b (*since*) puisque, étant donné que, comme. **~ he has not come, we cannot leave** puisqu'il *or* comme il *or* étant donné qu'il n'est pas arrivé, nous ne pouvons pas partir.
c (*in comparisons of equality*) **as ... ~** aussi ... que; **not as** *or* **not so ... ~** pas aussi *or* si ... que; **I am as tall ~ you** je suis aussi grand que vous; **I am not so** *or* **not as tall ~ you** je ne suis pas aussi *or* pas si grand que vous; **is it as difficult ~ that?** est-ce si *or* aussi difficile que ça?; **it's not so** *or* **not as good ~ all that** ce n'est pas si bon que cela; **you hate it as much ~ I do** vous en avez autant horreur que moi; **she is twice as rich ~ her sister** elle est deux fois plus riche que sa sœur; **it was one-third ~ expensive** cela coûtait trois fois moins; **by day (as well) ~ by night** de jour comme de nuit, le jour comme la nuit; (*frm*) **be so good/kind ~ to help me** soyez assez bon/assez gentil pour m'aider, ayez la bonté/la gentillesse de m'aider; *see* **far, long[1]** *etc*.
d (*concessive*) **big ~ the box is, it won't hold them all** si grande que soit la boîte elle ne pourra pas les contenir tous; **important ~ the president is ...** pour *or* si important que soit le président ...; **try ~ he would, he couldn't do it** il a eu beau essayer, il n'y est pas arrivé; **be that ~ it may** quoi qu'il en soit.
e (*manner*) comme, de même que, ainsi (que). **do ~ you like** faites comme vous voudrez; **a woman dressed ~ a man** une femme vêtue comme un homme *or* habillée en homme; **disguised ~ a woman** déguisé en femme; **m ~ in Marcel** m comme Marcel; **she left ~ (she had) promised** elle est partie comme (elle l'avait) promis; **he came ~ (had been) agreed** il est venu comme (cela avait été) entendu *or* prévu; **~ (is) usual** comme d'habitude, comme à l'ordinaire; **"My Autobiography", by X ~ told to John Smith** "Ma vie", par X, propos recueillis par John Smith; **~ often happens** comme il arrive souvent; **the village, nestling ~ it does in the valley** le village, ainsi blotti dans la vallée; (*liter*) **~ the father does, so will the son do** de même que fait le père ainsi fera le fils (*liter*); **knowing him ~ I do** le connaissant comme je le connais; **she is very gifted, ~ is her brother** elle est très douée, comme son frère *or* ainsi que son frère *or* de même que son frère; **France, ~ you know, is ...** la France, comme *or* ainsi que vous le savez, est ...; **~ it were** pour ainsi dire; **~ you were!** (*Mil*) repos!; (*: *in discussion etc*) au temps pour moi!; **~ it is, I can't come** les choses étant ce qu'elles sont, je ne peux pas venir; **leave it ~ it is** laisse ça tel quel *or* tel que*; **to buy sth ~ is** acheter qch en l'état.
f (*in rel clauses following "same" and "such"*) **such people ~ knew him** les gens qui le connaissaient; **such a book ~ you gave him** un livre comme celui que tu lui as donné; **the same day ~ last year** le même jour que l'année dernière; **the same woman ~ spoke to me** la femme *or* celle qui m'a parlé; **the same girl ~ I saw yesterday** la même fille que j'ai vue hier; **such a man ~ he is, a man such ~ he is** un homme tel que lui, un homme comme lui; **animals such ~ cats, such animals ~ cats** les animaux tels que les chats, les animaux comme (par exemple) les chats.
g **~ if, ~ though** comme si, comme; **he walks ~ if he's been drinking** il marche comme s'il avait bu *or* comme quelqu'un qui aurait bu; **he rose ~ if to go out** il s'est levé comme pour sortir; **it was ~ if** *or* **though he had not died** c'était comme s'il n'était pas mort; **why does she like him? it's not ~ if** *or* **though he's intelligent** pourquoi l'aime-t-elle? il n'est pourtant pas intelligent.
h **~ for, ~ to, ~ regards** quant à; **~ for her mother ...** quant à sa mère ...; **to question sb ~ to his intentions** interroger qn sur ses intentions.
i **so ~ to** + *infin* pour, de façon à, afin de + *infin*; **he stood up so ~ to see better** il s'est levé pour mieux voir; **she put it down gently so ~ not to break it** elle l'a posé doucement pour ne pas le casser.
j **~ from** *or* **~ of last Tuesday** depuis mardi dernier; **~ from** *or* **~ of today/next Tuesday** à partir d'aujourd'hui/de mardi prochain.
2 prep a (*in the capacity of*) en tant que, en qualité de, comme. **sold ~ a slave** vendu comme esclave; **~ a bachelor he cannot comment** étant donné qu'il est *or* en tant que célibataire il ne peut rien dire là-dessus; (*Theat*) **Olivier ~ Hamlet** Olivier dans le rôle de Hamlet; **Napoleon, ~ a statesman but not ~ a soldier, decided ...** Napoléon, en homme d'État mais pas en soldat, décida ...; **~ such** (*in that capacity*) à ce titre, comme tel (*f* telle), en tant que tel; (*in itself*) en soi; **the soldier, ~ such, deserves respect** tout soldat, comme tel, mérite le respect; **the work ~ such is boring but the pay is good** le travail en soi est ennuyeux mais le salaire est bon.
b (*after certain vbs*) **to treat sb ~ a child** traiter qn comme un enfant *or* en enfant; **to acknowledge sb ~ leader** reconnaître qn pour chef; **think of her ~ a teacher** considère-la comme un professeur; *see* **dress, regard, represent** *etc*.
3 adv aussi, si. **I am ~ tall as you** je suis aussi grand que vous; **I am not ~ tall as you** je ne suis pas si *or* pas aussi grand que vous; **~ distinct from** contrairement à; *see* **yet**.
A.S. [eɪˈes] a abbr of **American Samoa**. b (*US*) (abbr of **Associate in Sciences**) ≈ *titulaire du DEUG des Sciences*.
A.S.A. [ˌeɪesˈeɪ] a (*Brit*) (abbr of **Advertising Standards Authority**) *see* **advertising**. b (*Brit*) (abbr of **Amateur Swimming Association**) *fédération de natation*. c (*US*) abbr of **American Standards Association. 100/200 ASA** 100/200 ASA.
ASA/BS [ˌeɪesˌeɪbiːˈes] abbr of **American Standards Association/British Standard.**
a.s.a.p. [ˌeɪeseɪˈpiː] (abbr of **as soon as possible**) aussitôt que possible.
asbestos [æzˈbestəs] n amiante *f*, asbeste *m*. **~ mat** plaque *f* d'amiante.
asbestosis [ˌæzbesˈtəʊsɪs] n asbestose *f*.
ascend [əˈsend] 1 vi monter, s'élever (*to* à, jusqu'à); (*in time*) remonter (*to* à). **in ~ing order** en ordre croissant; (*Mus*) **~ing scale** gamme ascendante *or* montante. 2 vt *ladder* monter à; *mountain* gravir, faire l'ascension de; *river* remonter; *staircase* monter. **to ~ the throne** monter sur le trône.
ascendancy [əˈsendənsɪ] n (*influence*) ascendant *m*, empire *m* (*over* sur); (*rise to power etc*) montée *f*, ascension *f*.
ascendant [əˈsendənt] 1 n (*Astrol, fig*) ascendant *m*. (*Astrol*) **to be in the ~** être à l'ascendant; (*fig*) **his fortunes are in the ~** tout lui sourit. 2 adj (*gen*) dominant; (*Astrol*) ascendant.
ascension [əˈsenʃən] n ascension *f*. (*Rel*) **the A~** l'Ascension; **A~ Day** (jour *m or* fête *f* de) l'Ascension; **A~ Island** île *f* de l'Ascension.
ascensionist [əˈsenʃənɪst] n ascensionniste *mf*.
ascent [əˈsent] n [*mountain etc*] ascension *f*; (*fig: in time*) retour *m*; (*in rank*) montée *f*, avancement *m*.
ascertain [ˌæsəˈteɪn] vt (*gen*) établir; *person's age, name, address etc* vérifier. **to ~ that sth is true** s'assurer *or* vérifier que qch est vrai; **when the facts were ~ed** quand les faits ont été vérifiés *or* avérés.
ascertainable [ˌæsəˈteɪnəbl] adj vérifiable.
ascertainment [ˌæsəˈteɪnmənt] n constatation *f*, vérification *f*.
ascetic [əˈsetɪk] 1 adj ascétique. 2 n ascète *mf*.
asceticism [əˈsetɪsɪzəm] n ascétisme *m*.
ASCII [ˈæskiː] n (abbr of **American Standard Code for Information Interchange**) ASCII *m*. **~ file** fichier ASCII.
ascorbic acid [əˈskɔːbɪkˈæsɪd] n acide *m* ascorbique.
ascribable [əˈskraɪbəbl] adj (*see* **ascribe**) attribuable, imputable (*to* à).
ascribe [əˈskraɪb] vt *virtue, piece of work* attribuer (*to* à); *fault, blame* imputer (*to* à).
ascription [əˈskrɪpʃən] n (*see* **ascribe**) attribution *f*; imputation *f*.
asdic [ˈæzdɪk] n (*Brit Mil*) asdic *m*.
ASEAN [ˌeɪesˈiːeɪˈen] (abbr of **Association of South-East Asian Nations**) Association *f* des Nations de l'Asie du Sud-Est.
asemantic [eɪsɪˈmæntɪk] adj asémantique.
aseptic [eɪˈseptɪk] adj aseptique. (*Space*) **~ tank** cuve *f* W.-C.
asexual [eɪˈseksjʊəl] adj asexué.
ASH [ˈæʃ] (abbr of **Action on Smoking and Health**) *comité contre le tabagisme*.
ash[1] [æʃ] n (*Bot: also* **~ tree**) frêne *m*; *see* **mountain** *etc*.
ash[2] [æʃ] 1 n [*fire, coal, cigarette*] cendre *f*. (*of the dead*) **~es** cendres; **to reduce sth to ~es** mettre *or* réduire qch en cendres; (*Rel*) **~es to ~es, dust to dust** tu es poussière et tu retourneras en poussière; (*Cricket*) **the A~es** *trophée des matches Australie-Angleterre*; *see* **sack[2]**. 2 comp ► **ash-bin** (*for ashes*) cendrier *m* (*d'un four etc*); (*for rubbish*) boîte *f* à ordures, poubelle *f* ► **ash blond(e)** blond cendré *inv* ► **ashcan** (*US*) poubelle *f* ► **ash-coloured** gris cendré *inv* ► **ashman** (*US*) éboueur *m* ► **ash pan** cendrier *m* (*de poêle etc*) ► **ashtray** cendrier *m* ► **Ash Wednesday** (*Rel*) mercredi *m* des Cendres.
ashamed [əˈʃeɪmd] adj honteux, confus. **to be** *or* **feel ~, to be ~ of o.s.** avoir honte; **to be ~ of** avoir honte de, rougir de; **I am ~ of her** j'ai honte d'elle, elle me fait honte; **you ought to be ~ (of yourself)** vous devriez avoir honte; **I am ~ to say that** à ma honte je dois dire que; **he was ~ to ask for money** il était embarrassé d'avoir à demander de l'argent.

ashen ['æʃn] adj a (*pale*) *face* terreux, cendreux, plombé; (*greyish*) cendré, couleur de cendre. b (*of ashwood*) en (bois de) frêne.

ashlar ['æʃləʳ] n pierre *f* de taille (*équarrie*).

ashore [ə'ʃɔːʳ] adv (*on land*) à terre; (*to the shore*) vers la rive, vers le rivage. **to go ~** débarquer, descendre à terre; **to set** *or* **put sb ~** débarquer qn; **to swim ~** rejoindre la rive à la nage.

ashram ['æʃrəm] n ashram *m*.

ashy ['æʃɪ] adj a (*ash-coloured*) cendré, couleur de cendre; (*pale*) terreux, cendreux, plombé. b (*covered with ashes*) couvert de cendres.

Asia ['eɪʃə] n Asie *f*. **~ Minor** Asie Mineure.

Asian ['eɪʃn] 1 adj asiatique. (*Med*) **Asian flu** grippe *f* asiatique. 2 n Asiatique *mf*.

Asiatic [ˌeɪsɪ'ætɪk] 1 adj = **Asian 1.** 2 n (*offensive usage*) = **Asian 2.**

aside [ə'saɪd] (*phr vb elem*) 1 adv de côté, à l'écart, à part. **to put sth ~** mettre qch de côté; **can you put it ~ for me?** pouvez-vous me le réserver? *or* me le mettre de côté?; **to turn ~** se détourner (*from* de); **to stand ~, to step ~** s'écarter, faire un pas de côté; **to take sb ~** prendre qn à part; (*Jur*) **to set ~ a verdict** casser un jugement; **joking ~** plaisanterie *or* blague* à part; **~ from** à part. 2 n (*esp Theat*) aparté *m*. **to say sth in an ~** dire qch en aparté.

asinine ['æsɪnaɪn] adj sot (*f* sotte), stupide, idiot.

ask [ɑːsk] 1 vt a (*inquire*) demander. **to ~ sb sth** demander qch à qn; **to ~ sb about sth** interroger qn *or* questionner qn *or* poser des questions à qn au sujet de qch; **to ~ (sb) a question** poser une question (à qn); **I don't know, ~ your father** je ne sais pas, demande(-le) à ton père; **~ him if he has seen her** demande-lui s'il l'a vue; **~ed whether this was true, he replied ...** quand on lui a demandé si c'était vrai, il a répondu ...; **don't ~ me!*** allez savoir!*, est-ce que je sais (moi)!*; (*in exasperation*) **I ~ you!*** je vous demande un peu!*; (*keep quiet*) **I'm not ~ing you!*** je ne te demande rien (à toi)!*

b (*request*) demander, solliciter; (*Comm*) *price* demander. **to ~ sb to do** demander à qn de faire, prier qn de faire; **to ~ that sth be done** demander que qch soit fait; **to ~ sb for sth** demander qch à qn; **he ~ed to go on the picnic** il a demandé à se joindre *or* s'il pouvait se joindre au pique-nique; **I don't ~ much from you** je ne t'en demande pas beaucoup; **that's ~ing a lot/too much!** c'est beaucoup/trop (en) demander!; **that's ~ing the impossible** c'est demander l'impossible; (*Comm*) **how much are they ~ing for it?** ils en demandent *or* veulent combien?; (*Comm*) **he is ~ing £80,000 for the house** il demande 80.000 livres *or* veut 80.000 livres pour la maison; (*Comm*) **~ing price** prix *m* de départ, prix demandé au départ.

c (*invite*) inviter. **to ~ sb to (go to) the theatre** inviter qn (à aller) au théâtre; **to ~ sb to lunch** inviter qn à déjeuner; **I was ~ed into the drawing room** on m'a prié d'entrer au salon; **how about ~ing him?** et si on l'invitait?, et si on lui demandait de venir?; **to ~ sb in/out/up** *etc* demander à qn *or* prier qn d'entrer/de sortir/de monter *etc*.

2 vi demander. **to ~ about sth** s'informer de qch, se renseigner sur qch; (*Make enquiries*) **to ~ around** demander autour de soi; **it's there for the ~ing** il suffit de le demander (pour l'obtenir), on l'a comme on veut; **now you're ~ing!*** est-ce que je sais (moi)!*.

▸**ask after** vt fus *person* demander des nouvelles de. **to ask after sb's health** s'informer de la santé de qn.

▸**ask along** vt sep inviter; (*to one's home*) inviter (à la maison).

▸**ask back** vt sep a (*for a second visit*) réinviter. b (*on a reciprocal visit*) **to ask sb back** rendre son invitation à qn.

▸**ask for** vt fus *help, permission, money* demander; *person* demander à voir. **he asked for his pen back** il a demandé qu'on lui rende son stylo; **to ask for the moon** demander la lune; **they are asking for trouble*** ils cherchent les ennuis *or* les embêtements*; **she was asking for it!*** elle l'a bien cherché!*, elle ne l'a pas volé!*

▸**ask in** vt sep inviter à entrer. **to ask sb in for a drink** inviter qn à (entrer) prendre un verre.

▸**ask out** vt sep inviter à sortir. **he asked her out to dinner/to see a film** il l'a invitée (à dîner) au restaurant/au cinéma.

▸**ask round** vt sep inviter (à la maison).

askance [ə'skɑːns] adv: **to look ~ at** (*sideways*) regarder de côté; (*suspiciously/disapprovingly*) regarder d'un air soupçonneux/d'un œil désapprobateur; **to look ~ at a suggestion** se formaliser d'une suggestion.

askew [ə'skjuː] adj, adv de travers, de guingois*. (*US fig*) **something is ~** il y a quelque chose qui ne tourne pas rond*.

aslant [ə'slɑːnt] 1 adv de travers, de *or* en biais, obliquement. 2 prep en travers de.

asleep [ə'sliːp] 1 adj a (*sleeping*) endormi. **to be ~** dormir, être endormi; **to be fast** *or* **sound ~** dormir profondément *or* d'un sommeil profond *or* à poings fermés. b (*numb*) *finger etc* engourdi. 2 adv: **to fall ~** s'endormir.

ASLEF, Aslef ['æzlef] n (*Brit*) (abbr of **Associated Society of Locomotive Engineers and Firemen**) *syndicat de cheminots*.

asocial [eɪ'səʊʃəl] adj asocial.

asp¹ [æsp] n (*Zool*) aspic *m*.

asp² [æsp] n (*Bot*) = **aspen.**

asparagus [ə'spærəgəs] n (*NonC*) asperge *f*. **to eat ~** manger des asperges; **~ tips** pointes *fpl* d'asperges; **~ fern** asparagus *m*.

aspartame [ə'spɑːˌteɪm] n aspartam(e) *m*.

A.S.P.C.A. [ˌeɪespiːsiː'eɪ] (*US*) (abbr of **American Society for the Prevention of Cruelty to Animals**) *S.P.A. américaine*.

aspect ['æspekt] n a (*appearance*) aspect *m*, air *m*, mine *f*. **of fierce ~** à la mine *or* à l'aspect féroce. b *[question, subject etc]* aspect *m*, angle *m*, face *f*. **to study every ~ of a question** étudier une question sous toutes ses faces *or* tous ses aspects; **seen from this ~** vu sous cet angle. c *[building etc]* exposition *f*, orientation *f*. **the house has a southerly ~** la maison est exposée *or* orientée au midi. d (*Gram*) aspect *m*.

aspen ['æspən] n (*Bot*) tremble *m*. **to shake** *or* **tremble like an ~** trembler comme une feuille.

asperity [æs'perɪtɪ] n a (*NonC*) *[manner, style, voice]* aspérité *f*; *[person]* rudesse *f*. b (*gen pl*) *[climate, weather]* rigueur(s) *f(pl)*.

aspersion [əs'pɜːʃən] n (*untruthful*) calomnie *f*; (*truthful*) médisance *f*; *see* **cast.**

asphalt ['æsfælt] 1 n asphalte *m*. 2 vt asphalter. 3 comp *road* asphalté ▸**asphalt jungle** jungle *f* des rues.

asphyxia [æs'fɪksɪə] n asphyxie *f*.

asphyxiate [æs'fɪksɪeɪt] 1 vt asphyxier. 2 vi s'asphyxier.

asphyxiation [æsˌfɪksɪ'eɪʃən] n asphyxie *f*.

aspic ['æspɪk] n (*Culin*) gelée *f* (*pour hors d'œuvre*). **chicken in ~** aspic *m* de volaille.

aspidistra [ˌæspɪ'dɪstrə] n aspidistra *m*.

aspirant ['æspɪrənt] n aspirant(e) *m(f)*, candidat(e) *m(f)* (*to, after* à).

aspirate ['æspərɪt] 1 n aspirée *f*. 2 adj aspiré. **~ h** h aspiré(e). 3 ['æspəreɪt] vt aspirer.

aspiration [ˌæspə'reɪʃən] n (*also Ling*) aspiration *f*.

aspirator ['æspəˌreɪtəʳ] n aspirateur *m*.

aspire [əs'paɪəʳ] vi: **to ~ after** *or* **to sth** aspirer *or* viser à qch, ambitionner qch; **to ~ to do** aspirer à faire; **to ~ to fame** briguer la célébrité; **to ~ to a second car** ambitionner (d'avoir) une deuxième voiture; **we can't ~ to that** nos prétentions ne vont pas jusque-là.

aspirin ['æsprɪn] n, pl **~** *or* **~s** (*substance*) aspirine *f*; (*tablet*) (comprimé *m* d')aspirine.

aspiring [əs'paɪərɪŋ] adj *artist, poet, writer* en herbe; *manager, officer* potentiel.

ass¹ [æs] n a âne *m*. **she-~** ânesse *f*; **~'s foal** ânon *m*. b (* *pej*) idiot(e) *m(f)*, imbécile *mf*. **he is a perfect ~** il est bête comme ses pieds*; **to make an ~ of o.s.** se rendre ridicule, se conduire comme un idiot *or* imbécile; **don't be an ~!** (*action*) ne fais pas l'imbécile!; (*speech*) ne dis pas de sottises!

ass²** [æs] (*US*) 1 n cul** *m*. **my ~!** mon cul!**; **stick it** *or* **shove it up your ~!** tu peux te le foutre au cul!**; **to have one's ~ in a sling** être dans la merde*; **to get one's ~ in gear** se remuer le cul**; **a piece of ~** (*act*) une baise**; (*girl*) une fille bonne à baiser**; *see* **bust.** 2 comp ▸**asshole**** (*lit*) trou *m* du cul**; (*person*) sale con** ▸**ass kisser**** lèche-cul** *mf inv m*▸**ass-wipe**** papier-cul** *m*.

assail [ə'seɪl] vt (*lit*) attaquer, assaillir; (*fig: with questions etc*) assaillir, accabler, harceler (*with* de); (*gen pass*) *[doubts etc]* assaillir.

assailant [ə'seɪlənt] n agresseur *m*, assaillant(e) *m(f)*.

Assam [æ'sæm] n Assam *m*.

assassin [ə'sæsɪn] n (*Pol*) assassin *m*.

assassinate [ə'sæsɪneɪt] vt (*Pol*) assassiner.

assassination [əˌsæsɪ'neɪʃən] n (*Pol*) assassinat *m*.

assault [ə'sɔːlt] 1 n a (*Mil, Climbing*) assaut *m* (*on* de). **taken by ~** emporté *or* pris d'assaut; **to make an ~ on** donner l'assaut à, aller *or* monter à l'assaut de. b (*Jur*) agression *f*. **~ and battery** coups *mpl* et blessures *fpl*, voies *fpl* de fait; **the ~ on the old lady** l'agression dont a été victime la vieille dame; (*fig*) **~ on sb's good name** atteinte *f* à la réputation de qn; *see* **aggravate, common, indecent.** 2 vt agresser; (*Jur: attack*) se livrer à des voies de fait sur; (*attack sexually*) se livrer à des violences sexuelles sur, violenter. (*fig*) **to ~ people's sensibilities** blesser la sensibilité des gens. 3 comp ▸**assault course** (*Mil*) parcours *m* du combattant.

assay [ə'seɪ] 1 n essai *m* (*d'un métal précieux etc*). (*US*) **~ office** laboratoire *m* d'essais (*d'un hôtel des monnaies*). 2 vt a *mineral, ore* essayer. b (††: *try*) essayer, tenter (*to do* de faire).

assemblage [ə'semblɪdʒ] n a (*Tech: putting together*) assemblage *m*, montage *m*. b (*collection*) *[things]* collection *f*, ensemble *m*; *[people]* assemblée *f*.

assemble [ə'sembl] 1 vt *objects, ideas* assembler; *people* rassembler, réunir; (*Tech*) *device, machine* monter, assembler. 2 vi s'assembler, se réunir, se rassembler.

assembler [ə'sembləʳ] n (*Comput*) assembleur *m*.

assembly [ə'semblɪ] 1 n a (*meeting*) assemblée *f*, réunion *f*; (*Brit Scol*) réunion *f* de tous les élèves de l'établissement (*pour la prière etc*). **in open ~** en séance publique; *see* **unlawful.** b (*Tech: assembling of framework, machine*) assemblage *m*, montage *m*; (*whole unit*) assemblage. **the engine ~** le bloc moteur; *see* **tail.** c (*Mil: call*) rassemblement *m* (*sonnerie*). d (*Pol*) assemblée *f*. e (*Comput*) assemblage *m*. 2 comp ▸**assembly language** (*Comput*) langage *m* d'assemblage ▸**assembly line** chaîne *f* de montage ▸**assemblyman** (*US*) membre *m* d'une assemblée législative ▸**assembly room(s)**

salle *f* de réunion; *[town hall]* salle des fêtes ►**assembly shop** atelier *m* de montage.

assent [ə'sent] 1 **n** assentiment *m*, consentement *m*, acquiescement *m*. **with one ~** (*two people*) d'un commun accord; (*more than two people*) à l'unanimité; *see* **nod, royal.** 2 **vi** consentir, donner son assentiment, acquiescer (*to* à).

assert [ə'sɜːt] **vt** a (*declare*) affirmer, soutenir; *one's innocence* protester de. b (*maintain*) *claim* défendre; *one's due* revendiquer; *one's authority* faire respecter. **to ~ o.s.** *or* **one's rights** faire valoir ses droits.

assertion [ə'sɜːʃən] **n** a (*statement*) affirmation *f*, assertion *f*; *see* **self.** b *[one's rights]* revendication *f*.

assertive [ə'sɜːtɪv] **adj** *tone, manner* assuré; (*pej*) péremptoire.

assertiveness [ə'sɜːtɪvnɪs] **n** assurance *f*. **~ training** ≃ séminaire *m* de motivation, stage *m* de mise en confiance.

assess [ə'ses] **vt** a (*estimate*) estimer, évaluer. b *payment* fixer *or* déterminer le montant de; *income tax* établir; *rateable property* calculer la valeur imposable de; *damages* fixer. **~ed income** revenu *m* imposable; *see* **basis.** c (*fig: evaluate*) *situation* évaluer; *time, amount* estimer, évaluer; *candidate* juger (la valeur de).

assessable [ə'sesəbl] **adj** imposable. (*Fin*) **~ income** (*or* **profits** *etc*) assiette *f* de l'impôt.

assessment [ə'sesmənt] **n** (*see* **assess**) a estimation *f*, évaluation *f*. b détermination *f* (du montant); établissement *m* (de l'impôt); calcul *m* (de la valeur imposable). c (*fig*) évaluation *f*; estimation *f*; *[candidate]* jugement *m* (*of* sur), opinion *f* qu'on se fait (*of* de). **what is his ~ of the situation?** comment voit-il *or* juge-t-il la situation? d (*Educ*) contrôle *m* de connaissances; (*on pupil's report*) appréciation *f* des professeurs. **methods of ~** modalités *fpl* de contrôle; *see* **continuous.**

assessor [ə'sesəʳ] **n** a (*Jur*) (juge *m*) assesseur *m*. b *[property]* expert *m*. (*US*) **~ of taxes** contrôleur *m*, -euse *f* des contributions directes.

asset ['æset] 1 **n** a **~s** biens *mpl*, avoir *m*, capital *m*; (*Comm, Fin, Jur*) actif *m*; **~s and liabilities** actif et passif *m*; **their ~s amount to £1M** ils ont un million de livres à leur actif, leur actif est d'un million de livres; *see* **liquid.** b (*advantage*) avantage *m*, atout *m*. **he is one of our greatest ~s** sa collaboration (*or* sa présence *etc*) constitue un de nos meilleurs atouts. 2 **comp** ►**asset-stripper** (*Fin*) récupérateur *m* d'entreprises (en faillite) ►**asset-stripping** (*Fin*) récupération *m* d'entreprises (en faillite).

asseverate [ə'sevəreɪt] **vt** affirmer solennellement; *one's innocence, loyalty* protester de.

asseveration [əˌsevə'reɪʃən] **n** (*see* **asseverate**) affirmation *f* (solennelle); protestation *f*.

assiduity [ˌæsɪ'djuːɪtɪ] **n** assiduité *f*, zèle *m*.

assiduous [ə'sɪdjʊəs] **adj** assidu.

assiduously [ə'sɪdjʊəslɪ] **adv** assidûment.

assign [ə'saɪn] **vt** a (*allot*) *task, office* assigner; *date* assigner, fixer; *room* attribuer (*to sb* à qn), affecter (*to a purpose* à un usage); *meaning* donner, attribuer, attacher (*to* à). **to ~ a reason for sth** donner la raison de qch; **the event is ~ed to the year 1600** on fait remonter cet événement à 1600. b (*appoint*) *person* nommer, affecter, désigner (*to* à). c (*Jur*) *property, right* céder, faire cession de (*to sb* à qn), transférer (*to sb* au nom de qn).

assignation [ˌæsɪg'neɪʃən] **n** a (*appointment*) rendez-vous *m* (*souvent galant*). b (*allocation*) attribution *f*; *[money]* allocation *f*; *[person, room]* affectation *f*. c (*Jur*) cession *f*, transfert *m* (de biens).

assignee [ˌæsaɪ'niː] **n** (*Jur*) cessionnaire *mf*.

assignment [ə'saɪnmənt] **n** a (*task*) mission *f*; (*Scol*) devoir *m*; (*Univ*) devoir, (*essay*) dissertation *f*. b (*NonC*) (*allocation*) attribution *f*; *[money]* allocation *f*; *[person, room]* affectation *f*. c (*Jur*) **~ of contract** cession *f* des droits et obligations découlant d'un *or* du contrat.

assignor [ˌæsɪ'nɔːʳ] **n** (*Jur*) cédant *m*.

assimilate [ə'sɪmɪleɪt] 1 **vt** a (*absorb*) *food, knowledge* assimiler. b (*compare*) comparer, assimiler (*to* à), rapprocher (*to* de). 2 **vi** s'assimiler, être assimilé.

assimilation [əˌsɪmɪ'leɪʃən] **n** (*absorption*) assimilation *f*; (*comparison*) assimilation (*to* à), comparaison *f*, rapprochement *m* (*to* avec); (*Phon*) assimilation.

Assisi [ə'siːzɪ] **n** Assise.

assist [ə'sɪst] 1 **vt** aider, assister (*to do, in doing* à faire), prêter son assistance à (*to do, in doing* pour faire). **to ~ sb in/out** *etc* aider qn à entrer/sortir *etc*; **to ~ one another** s'entr'aider; **~ed by** avec le concours de; (*Travel*) **~ed passage** billet subventionné. 2 **vi** a (*help*) aider, prêter secours. **to ~ in (doing) sth** aider à (faire) qch. b (*frm: be present*) assister (*at* à).

assistance [ə'sɪstəns] **n** aide *f*, secours *m*, assistance *f*. **to give ~ to sb** prêter secours à qn; **to come to sb's ~** venir à l'aide *or* au secours de qn, secourir qn; **can I be of ~?** puis-je vous aider?, puis-je vous être utile?

assistant [ə'sɪstənt] 1 **n** aide *mf*, auxiliaire *mf*. **(foreign language) ~** (*Scol*) assistant(e) *m(f)*; (*Univ*) lecteur *m*, -trice *f*; *see* **shop** *etc*. 2 **comp** adjoint, sous- ►**assistant judge** (*US Jur*) juge adjoint ►**assistant librarian** bibliothécaire *mf* adjoint(e) ►**assistant manager** sous-directeur *m*, directeur adjoint ►**assistant master, assistant mistress** (*Scol*) professeur *m* (qui n'a pas la responsabilité d'une section) ►**assistant priest** vicaire *m* ►**assistant principal** (*Scol*) directeur *m*, -trice *f* adjoint(e), (*in lycée*) censeur *m* ►**assistant professor** (*US Univ*) ≃ maître assistant ►**assistant secretary** secrétaire *mf* adjoint(e), sous-secrétaire *mf* ►**assistant teacher** (*primary*) instituteur *m*, -trice *f*, (*secondary*) professeur *m* (qui n'a pas la responsabilité d'une section).

assistantship [ə'sɪstəntʃɪp] **n** (*US Univ*) poste *m* d'étudiant(e) chargé(e) de travaux dirigés.

assizes [ə'saɪzɪz] **npl** (*Brit Jur*) assises *fpl*.

assn. **abbr of association.**

assoc. 1 **abbr of association.** 2 **abbr of associated.**

associate [ə'səʊʃɪɪt] 1 **adj** uni, associé, allié. (*Jur*) **~ judge** juge *m* assesseur; (*US Jur*) **A~ Justice** juge *m* de la Cour suprême; (*US Univ*) **~ professor** ≃ maître *m* de conférences.

2 **n** a (*fellow worker*) associé(e) *m(f)*, collègue *mf*; (*Jur: also* **~ in crime**) complice *mf*. **to be ~s in an undertaking** participer conjointement à une entreprise; *see* **business.**

b *[a society]* membre *m*, associé *m*; *[learned body]* (membre) correspondant *m*; (*US Univ*) **~'s degree** ≃ D.E.U.G. *m*.

3 [ə'səʊʃɪeɪt] **vt** a *ideas, things* associer (*one thing with another* une chose à *or* avec une autre).

b **to be ~d with sth** être associé à qch; **to ~ o.s.** *or* **be ~d with sb in an undertaking** s'associer à *or* avec qn dans une entreprise; **to be ~d with a plot** tremper dans un complot; **I should like to ~ myself with what has been said** je voudrais me faire l'écho de cette opinion; **I don't wish to be ~d with it** je préfère que mon nom ne soit pas mêlé à ceci.

4 **vi: to ~ with sb** fréquenter qn, être en relations avec qn.

association [əˌsəʊsɪ'eɪʃən] 1 **n** a (*NonC*) association *f* (*with* avec), fréquentation *f* (*with* de). **in ~ with** en association avec. b (*organization*) association *f*, union *f*, société *f*, club *m*. **to form an ~** constituer une société; *see* **freedom.** c (*connection*) *[ideas]* association *f*. **by ~ of ideas** par (une) association d'idées; **full of historic ~s** riche en souvenirs historiques; **this word has nasty ~s** ce mot a des connotations *fpl* désagréables. 2 **comp** ►**association football** (*Brit*) football *m* (association).

associative [ə'səʊʃɪətɪv] **adj** (*Comput*) **~ storage** mémoire associative.

assonance ['æsənəns] **n** assonance *f*.

assort [ə'sɔːt] 1 **vt** ranger, classer, classifier. 2 **vi** *[colours etc]* s'assortir, aller bien (*with* avec).

assorted [ə'sɔːtɪd] **adj** assorti. **well-/ill-~** bien/mal assortis; (*Comm*) **in ~ sizes** dans toutes les tailles.

assortment [ə'sɔːtmənt] **n** *[objects]* collection *f*, assortiment *m*; *[people]* mélange *m*. **this shop has a good ~** ce magasin a un grand choix *or* a une bonne sélection; **an ~ of people/guests** des gens/des invités (très) divers.

asst **abbr of assistant.**

assuage [ə'sweɪdʒ] **vt** *hunger, desire, thirst* assouvir; *anger, pain* soulager, apaiser; *person* apaiser, calmer.

assume [ə'sjuːm] **vt** a (*accept, presume, suppose*) supposer, présumer, admettre. **assuming this to be true** en admettant *or* supposant que ceci est *or* soit vrai; **~d innocent** présumé innocent; **let us ~ that** admettons *or* supposons que + *subj*; **you resigned, I ~** vous avez démissionné, je suppose *or* présume; **you are assuming a lot** vous faites bien des suppositions.

b (*take upon o.s.*) *responsibility, burden* assumer, endosser; *power, importance, possession* prendre; *title, right, authority* s'arroger, s'approprier, s'attribuer; *name* adopter, prendre; *air, attitude* adopter, se donner. **to ~ control of** prendre en main la direction de; **to ~ the role of arbiter** assumer le rôle d'arbitre; **to ~ a look of innocence** affecter un air d'innocence; **to go under an ~d name** se servir d'un nom d'emprunt *or* d'un pseudonyme.

assumption [ə'sʌmpʃən] **n** a (*supposition*) supposition *f*, hypothèse *f*. **on the ~ that** en supposant que + *subj*; **to go on the ~ that** présumer que. b *[power etc]* appropriation *f*; *[indifference]* affectation *f*. c (*Rel*) **the A~** l'Assomption *f*; **A~ Day** (jour *m* *or* fête *f* de) l'Assomption; (*public holiday*) le 15 août.

assurance [ə'ʃʊərəns] **n** a (*certainty*) assurance *f*, conviction *f*. **in the ~ that** avec la conviction *or* l'assurance que. b (*self-confidence*) confiance *f* en soi, assurance *f*; (*overconfidence*) audace *f*. c (*promise*) garantie *f*, promesse formelle, assurance *f* ferme. **you have my ~ that** je vous promets formellement que. d (*Brit: insurance*) assurance *f*; *see* **life.**

assure [ə'ʃʊəʳ] **vt** a (*state positively*) affirmer, assurer, certifier; (*convince, reassure*) convaincre, assurer (*sb of sth* qn de qch). **it is so, I (can) ~ you** c'est vrai, je vous assure; *see* **rest.** b (*make certain*) *happiness, success* garantir, assurer. c (*Brit: insure*) assurer.

assured [ə'ʃʊəd] **adj, n** assuré(e) *m(f)* (*of* de). **will you be ~ of a good salary?** aurez-vous la garantie d'un bon salaire?

assuredly [ə'ʃʊərɪdlɪ] **adv** assurément, certainement, sans aucun *or* le moindre doute.

Assyria [əˈsɪrɪə] n Assyrie *f*.
Assyrian [əˈsɪrɪən] 1 n Assyrien(ne) *m(f)*. 2 adj assyrien.
A.S.T. [eɪesˈtiː] (*US, Can*) (abbr of **Atlantic Standard Time**) *see* **Atlantic**.
astatine [ˈæstətiːn] n astate *m*.
aster [ˈæstəʳ] n aster *m*.
asterisk [ˈæstərɪsk] 1 n astérisque *m*. 2 vt marquer d'un astérisque.
astern [əˈstɜːn] adv (*Naut*) à *or* sur l'arrière, en poupe. **to go** *or* **come** ~ faire machine arrière, battre en arrière, culer; ~ **of** à *or* sur l'arrière de.
asteroid [ˈæstərɔɪd] n astéroïde *m*.
asthma [ˈæsmə] n asthme *m*. ~ **sufferer** asthmatique *mf*.
asthmatic [æsˈmætɪk] adj, n asthmatique *(mf)*.
astigmatic [ˌæstɪgˈmætɪk] adj, n astigmate *(mf)*.
astigmatism [æsˈtɪgmətɪzəm] n astigmatisme *m*.
astir [əˈstɜːʳ] adj, adv (*excited*) agité, en émoi; (*out of bed*) debout *inv*, levé.
A.S.T.M.S. [ˌeɪestiːemˈes] (abbr of **Association of Scientific, Technical and Managerial Staffs**) *syndicat*.
astonish [əˈstɒnɪʃ] vt étonner; (*stronger*) ahurir, ébahir, stupéfier. (*iro*) **you** ~ **me!** non! pas possible!, ce n'est pas vrai! (*iro*).
astonished [əˈstɒnɪʃt] adj étonné, stupéfait. **I am** ~ **that** cela m'étonne *or* m'ahurit que + *subj*.
astonishing [əˈstɒnɪʃɪŋ] adj étonnant; (*stronger*) ahurissant, stupéfiant. **that is** ~, **coming from them** venant d'eux, c'est ahurissant *or* étonnant; **with an** ~ **lack of discretion** avec un incroyable manque de discrétion.
astonishingly [əˈstɒnɪʃɪŋlɪ] adv incroyablement. ~ **enough** pour étonnant *or* stupéfiant que cela paraisse.
astonishment [əˈstɒnɪʃmənt] n étonnement *m*, surprise *f*; (*stronger*) ahurissement *m*, stupéfaction *f*. **look of** ~ regard stupéfait; **to my** ~ à mon grand étonnement, à ma stupéfaction; *see* **stare**.
astound [əˈstaʊnd] vt stupéfier, confondre, abasourdir, ébahir.
astounded [əˈstaʊndɪd] adj abasourdi, ébahi. **I am** ~ j'en reste abasourdi, je n'en crois pas mes yeux *or* mes oreilles.
astounding [əˈstaʊndɪŋ] adj stupéfiant, ahurissant, époustouflant*.
astrakhan [ˌæstrəˈkæn] 1 n astrakan *m*. 2 comp *coat* d'astrakan.
astral [ˈæstrəl] adj astral.
astray [əˈstreɪ] adv (*lit, fig*) **to go** ~ s'égarer; *see* **lead¹**.
astride [əˈstraɪd] 1 adj, adv à califourchon, à cheval. **to ride** ~ monter à califourchon. 2 prep à califourchon sur, à cheval sur, chevauchant.
astringent [əsˈtrɪndʒənt] 1 adj (*Med*) astringent; (*fig*) dur, sévère. ~ **lotion** lotion astringente. 2 n (*Med*) astringent *m*.
astro... [ˈæstrəʊ] pref astro... .
astrologer [əsˈtrɒlədʒəʳ] n astrologue *mf*.
astrological [ˌæstrəˈlɒdʒɪkəl] adj astrologique.
astrologist [əsˈtrɒlədʒɪst] n astrologue *mf*.
astrology [əsˈtrɒlədʒɪ] n astrologie *f*.
astronaut [ˈæstrənɔːt] n astronaute *mf*.
astronautic(al) [ˌæstrəʊˈnɔːtɪk(əl)] adj astronautique.
astronautics [ˌæstrəʊˈnɔːtɪks] n (*NonC*) astronautique *f*.
astronomer [əsˈtrɒnəməʳ] n astronome *mf*.
astronomic(al) [ˌæstrəˈnɒmɪk(əl)] adj (*lit, fig*) astronomique.
astronomically [ˌæstrəˈnɒmɪkəlɪ] adv astronomiquement. ~ **expensive** hors de prix.
astronomy [əsˈtrɒnəmɪ] n astronomie *f*.
astrophysicist [ˌæstrəʊˈfɪzɪsɪst] n astrophysicien(ne) *m(f)*.
astrophysics [ˌæstrəʊˈfɪzɪks] n (*NonC*) astrophysique *f*.
Astroturf [ˈæstrəʊtɜːf] n ® gazon artificiel.
Asturias [æˈstʊərɪæs] n Asturies *fpl*.
astute [əsˈtjuːt] adj fin, astucieux, malin (*f* -igne), rusé (*pej*). **how very** ~ **of you!** quelle finesse! (*also iro*).
astutely [əsˈtjuːtlɪ] adv avec finesse, astucieusement.
astuteness [əsˈtjuːtnɪs] n (*NonC*) finesse *f*, sagacité *f*, astuce *f*.
asunder [əˈsʌndəʳ] adv (*liter*) (*apart*) écartés, éloignés (l'un de l'autre); (*in pieces*) en morceaux.
Aswan [æsˈwɑːn] n Assouan. ~ **High Dam** haut barrage d'Assouan.
asylum [əˈsaɪləm] n a (*NonC*) asile *m*, refuge *m*. **political** ~ asile politique. b (†: *also* **lunatic** ~) asile *m* (d'aliénés)†.
asymmetric(al) [ˌeɪsɪˈmetrɪk(əl)] adj asymétrique. (*Sport*) ~ **bars** barres *fpl* asymétriques.
asymptomatic [ˌeɪsɪmptəˈmætɪk] adj asymptomatique.
asynchronous [æˈsɪŋkrənəs] adj (*Comput*) asynchrone.
at [æt] (*phr vb elem*) 1 prep a (*place, position*) à. ~ **the table** à la table; ~ **my brother's** chez mon frère; ~ **home** à la maison, chez soi; **to dry o.s.** ~ **the fire** se sécher devant le feu; **to stand** ~ **the window** se tenir à *or* devant la fenêtre; ~ **her heels** sur ses talons; **to come in** ~ **the door** entrer par la porte; **to find a gap to go in** ~ trouver une brèche par où passer *or* entrer; *see* **hand, sea** *etc*.
b (*direction*) vers, dans la direction de, sur. **look** ~ **them** regardez-les; **to aim** ~ **sb** viser qn; **an attempt** ~ **escape** une tentative d'évasion; *see* **jump at, laugh at** *etc*.
c (*arrival*) à. **to arrive** ~ **the house** arriver à la maison; (*fig*) **to get** ~ **the truth** parvenir à la vérité.
d (*time, frequency, order*) à. ~ **10 o'clock** à 10 heures; ~ **night** la nuit; **3** ~ **a time** 3 par 3, 3 à la fois, (*stairs, steps*) 3 à 3; ~ **times** de temps en temps, parfois; ~ **once** (*immediately*) immédiatement, tout de suite; (*at the same time*) en même temps, à la fois; ~ **a time like this** à un moment pareil; ~ **my time of life** à mon âge.
e (*activity*) en train de, occupé à. **to play** ~ **football** jouer au football; **pupils** ~ **play** élèves en récréation; **while we are** ~ **it*** pendant que nous y sommes *or* qu'on y est*; **let me see you** ~ **it again!*** que je t'y reprenne!*; **they are** ~ **it again!*** les voilà qui recommencent!, voilà qu'ils remettent ça!*; **they are** ~ **it all day*** ils font ça toute la journée.
f (*state, condition*) en. **good** ~ **languages** bon en langues; ~ **war** en guerre.
g (*manner*) ~ **full speed** à toute allure; ~ **80 km/h** à 80 km/h; **he drove** ~ **80 km/h** il faisait du 80 (à l'heure).
h (*cause*) (à cause) de, à propos de. **to be surprised** ~ **sth** être étonné de qch; **annoyed** ~ contrarié par; **angry** ~ en colère contre; ~ **the request of** à *or* sur la demande *or* la requête de.
i (*rate, value, degree*) à, dans, en. ~ **best** au mieux; ~ **best I cannot arrive before ten** c'est tout au plus si je pourrai arriver à dix heures; ~ **first** d'abord; **nothing** ~ **all** rien du tout; ~ **all costs** à tout prix; **he sells them** ~ **12 francs a kilo** il les vend 12 F le kilo; **let's leave it** ~ **that** restons-en là!; **he's only a teacher and a poor one** ~ **that** ce n'est qu'un professeur et encore assez piètre.
j (**: nagging*) **she's been** ~ **me the whole day** elle m'a harcelé *or* tanné* toute la journée; **she was (on)** ~ **her husband to buy a new car** elle a harcelé son mari pour qu'il achète (*subj*) une nouvelle voiture; **he's always (on)** ~ **me*** il est toujours après moi*.
k (**: stage in progress etc*) **where are we** ~? où en sommes-nous?
l (**: fashionable*) **this is where it's** ~ c'est là que ça se passe*.
2 comp ▸**at-home** réception *f* (*chez soi*).
AT [eɪˈtiː] (abbr of **alternative technology**) *see* **alternative**.
atavism [ˈætəvɪzəm] n atavisme *m*.
atavistic [ˌætəˈvɪstɪk] adj atavique.
ataxia [əˈtæksɪə] n ataxie *f*.
ataxic [əˈtæksɪk] adj ataxique.
A.T.C. [eɪtiːˈsiː] (abbr of **Air Training Corps**) *préparation à l'école de l'air*.
ate [et, eɪt] pret of **eat**.
Athalia [əˈθeɪlɪə] n Athalie *f*.
Athanasian [ˌæθəˈneɪʃən] adj: ~ **Creed** symbole *m* de saint Athanase.
Athanasius [ˌæθəˈneɪʃəs] n Athanase *m*.
atheism [ˈeɪθɪɪzəm] n athéisme *m*.
atheist [ˈeɪθɪɪst] n athée *mf*.
atheistic(al) [ˌeɪθɪˈɪstɪk(əl)] adj athée.
Athena [əˈθiːnə], **Athene** [əˈθiːnɪ] n Athéna *f*.
athenaeum [ˌæθɪˈniːəm] n association *f* littéraire (*or* culturelle).
Athenian [əˈθiːnɪən] 1 n Athénien(ne) *m(f)*. 2 adj athénien.
Athens [ˈæθɪnz] n Athènes.
athirst [əˈθɜːst] adj (*liter: lit, fig*) altéré, assoiffé (*for* de).
athlete [ˈæθliːt] n (*in competitions*) athlète *mf*. (*gen*) **he's a fine** ~ il est très sportif, c'est un sportif; (*Med*) ~**'s foot** mycose *f*.
athletic [æθˈletɪk] adj *activity* athlétique; *meeting* sportif, d'athlétisme; (*gen*) *person* (*sporty*) sportif, (*muscular*) athlétique. (*US Scol, Univ*) ~ **coach** entraîneur *m* (sportif); ~ **sports** athlétisme *m*; ~ **support(er)** suspensoir *m*.
athletics [æθˈletɪks] n (*NonC*) (*Brit*) athlétisme *m*; (*US*) sport *m*.
Athos [ˈæθɒs] n: **Mount** ~ le mont Athos.
athwart [əˈθwɔːt] 1 adv en travers; (*Naut*) par le travers. 2 prep en travers de; (*Naut*) par le travers de.
Atlantic [ətˈlæntɪk] adj *coast, current* atlantique; *winds, island* de l'Atlantique. **the** ~ **(Ocean)** l'Atlantique *m*, l'océan Atlantique; ~ **Charter** Pacte *m* atlantique; ~ **liner** transatlantique *m*; (*Can*) **the** ~ **Provinces** les Provinces *fpl* atlantiques; ~ **Standard Time** l'heure normale de l'Atlantique; *see* **north** *etc*.
Atlanticism [ətˈlæntɪsɪzəm] n (*Pol*) atlantisme *m*.
Atlanticist [ətˈlæntɪsɪst] adj, n atlantiste *(mf)*.
Atlantis [ətˈlæntɪs] n Atlantide *f*.
atlas [ˈætləs] n a atlas *m*. b (*Myth*) **A**~ Atlas *m*; **A**~ **Mountains** (monts *mpl* de l')Atlas *m*.
atmosphere [ˈætməsfɪəʳ] n (*lit, Phys*) atmosphère *f*; (*fig*) atmosphère, ambiance *f*. (*fig*) **I can't stand** ~**s** je ne peux pas supporter une ambiance hostile.
atmospheric [ˌætməsˈferɪk] adj atmosphérique; *film, music* d'ambiance.
atmospherics [ˌætməsˈferɪks] n (*NonC: Rad, Telec*) parasites *mpl*.
atoll [ˈætɒl] n atoll *m*.
atom [ˈætəm] 1 n atome *m*; (*fig*) atome, grain *m*, brin *m*, parcelle *f*. **smashed to** ~**s** réduit en miettes; **not an** ~ **of truth** pas l'ombre *f* de la vérité, pas un brin *or* pas un grain de vérité; **if you had an** ~ **of sense** si tu avais une parcelle *or* un grain *or* un atome de bon sens. 2 comp ▸**atom bomb** bombe *f* atomique.
atomic [əˈtɒmɪk] 1 adj atomique.
2 comp ▸**atomic age** ère *f* atomique ▸**atomic bomb** bombe *f* atomique ▸**atomic clock** horloge *f* atomique ▸**atomic energy**

énergie *f* atomique *or* nucléaire ▸**Atomic Energy Authority** (*Brit*) *or* **Commission** (*US*) ≃ Commissariat *m* à l'Énergie atomique ▸**atomic number** nombre *m or* numéro *m* atomique ▸**atomic physicist/physics** physicien(ne) *m(f)*/physique *f* atomique ▸**atomic pile** pile *f* atomique ▸**atomic-powered** (fonctionnant à l'énergie) atomique ▸**atomic power station** centrale *f* nucléaire ▸**atomic reactor** réacteur *m* atomique ▸**atomic structure** structure *f* atomique ▸**atomic theory** théorie *f* atomique ▸**atomic warfare** guerre *f* nucléaire *or* atomique ▸**atomic weight** poids *m or* masse *f* atomique.

atomize ['ætəmaɪz] vt pulvériser, atomiser.

atomizer ['ætəmaɪzəʳ] n atomiseur *m*.

atonal [æ'təʊnl] adj atonal.

atonality [ˌeɪtəʊ'nælɪtɪ] n atonalité *f*.

atone [ə'təʊn] vi: **to ~ for** *sin* expier; *mistake* racheter, réparer.

atonement [ə'təʊnmənt] n (*see* **atone**) expiation *f*; réparation *f*. **to make ~ for a sin** expier un péché; **to make ~ for a mistake** réparer une erreur.

atonic [æ'tɒnɪk] adj *syllable* atone; *muscle* atonique.

atop [ə'tɒp] 1 adv en haut, au sommet. 2 prep en haut de, au sommet de.

ATP [ˌeɪtiː'piː] n (abbr of **adenosine triphosphate**) ATP *m*.

Atreus ['eɪtrɪəs] n Atrée *m*.

atria ['eɪtrɪə] npl of **atrium**.

Atridae ['ætrɪdeɪ] npl Atrides *mpl*.

atrium ['eɪtrɪəm] n, pl **atria** (*Anat*) orifice *m* de l'oreillette.

atrocious [ə'trəʊʃəs] adj *crime* atroce; (**: very bad*) affreux, horrible, atroce.

atrociously [ə'trəʊʃəslɪ] adv affreusement, horriblement.

atrocity [ə'trɒsɪtɪ] n atrocité *f*.

atrophy ['ætrəfɪ] 1 n atrophie *f*. 2 vt atrophier. 3 vi s'atrophier.

att. a (*Comm*) abbr of **attached**. b abbr of **attorney**.

attaboy* ['ætəbɔɪ] excl bravo! vas-y! mon gars *or* allez-y les gars!

attach [ə'tætʃ] 1 vt a (*join*) attacher, lier, joindre (*to* à). **document ~ed to a letter** document joint à une lettre; **the ~ed letter** la lettre ci-jointe; (*in letter*) **I ~ a report from ...** je joins à cette lettre un rapport de ...; **to ~ o.s. to a group** se joindre à un groupe, entrer dans un groupe; (*fig: fond of*) **to be ~ed to sb/sth** être attaché à qn/qch; **he's ~ed*** (*married etc*) il n'est pas libre.

b (*attribute*) *value* attacher, attribuer (*to* à). **to ~ credence to** ajouter foi à; *see* **importance**.

c (*Jur*) *person* arrêter, appréhender; *goods, salary* saisir.

d *employee, troops* affecter (*to* à). **he is ~ed to the Foreign Office** il est attaché au ministère des Affaires étrangères.

2 vi (*rare, frm*) être attribué, être imputé (*to* à). **no blame ~es to you** le blâme ne repose nullement sur vous; **salary ~ing to a post** salaire afférent à un emploi (*frm*).

attaché [ə'tæʃeɪ] n attaché(e) *m(f)*. **~ case** mallette *f*, attaché-case *m*.

attachment [ə'tætʃmənt] n a (*NonC*) fixation *f*. b (*for tool etc: accessory*) accessoire *m*. c (*fig: affection*) attachement *m* (*to* à), affection *f* (*to* pour). d (*Jur*) (*on person*) arrestation *f*; (*on goods, salary*) saisie *f* (*on* de). e (*period of practical work, temporary transfer*) stage *m*. **to be on ~** faire un stage (*to* à, auprès de, chez).

attack [ə'tæk] 1 n a (*gen, Mil, Sport*) attaque *f* (*on* contre). **to return to the ~** revenir à la charge; **~ on sb's life** attentat *m* contre qn; (*Jur*) attentat à la vie de qn; (*fig*) **to leave o.s. open to ~** prêter le flanc à la critique; **~ is the best form of defence** le meilleur moyen de défense c'est l'attaque; **to be under ~** (*Mil*) être attaqué (*from* par); (*fig*) être en butte aux attaques (*from* de); (*Psych*) **to feel under ~** se sentir agressé.

b (*Med etc*) crise *f*. **~ of fever** accès *m* de fièvre; **~ of nerves** crise de nerfs; *see* **heart**.

2 vt a (*lit, fig*) *person* attaquer; (*Mil*) *enemy* attaquer, assaillir. (*fig*) **to be ~ed by doubts** être assailli par des doutes.

b *task, problem* s'attaquer à; *poverty etc* combattre.

c (*Chem*) *metal* attaquer, corroder, ronger. (*fig*) **this idea ~s the whole structure of society** cette idée menace toute la structure de la société.

3 vi attaquer.

attackable [ə'tækəbl] adj attaquable.

attacker [ə'tækəʳ] n attaquant(e) *m(f)*, agresseur *m*.

attain [ə'teɪn] 1 vt *aim, rank, age* atteindre, parvenir à, arriver à; *knowledge* acquérir; *happiness* atteindre à; *one's hopes* réaliser. 2 vi (*to perfection etc*) atteindre, toucher (*to* à); (*to power, prosperity*) parvenir (*to* à).

attainable [ə'teɪnəbl] adj accessible (*by* à), à la portée (*by* de).

attainder [ə'teɪndəʳ] n (*Jur*) mort civile; *see* **bill**.

attainment [ə'teɪnmənt] n a (*NonC*) [*knowledge*] acquisition *f*; [*happiness*] conquête *f*; [*one's hopes*] réalisation *f*. b (*gen pl: achievement*) travail *m*, résultats *mpl* (obtenus).

attempt [ə'tempt] 1 vt essayer, tenter (*to do* de faire); *task* entreprendre, s'attaquer à. **~ed escape/murder/theft** *etc* tentative *f* d'évasion/de meurtre/de vol *etc*; **to ~ suicide** essayer *or* tenter de se suicider.

2 n a tentative *f*, entreprise *f*, effort *m*; (*unsuccessful*) essai *m*. **an ~ at escape** une tentative d'évasion; **to make one's first ~** faire son coup d'essai, essayer pour la première fois; **to make an ~ at doing** essayer de faire, s'essayer à faire; **to be successful at the first ~** réussir du premier coup; **he failed at the first ~** la première fois, il a échoué; **he had to give up the ~** il lui a fallu (y) renoncer; **he made no ~ to help us** il n'a rien fait pour nous aider, il n'a pas essayé de nous aider; **to make an ~ on the record** essayer de battre le record; **he made two ~s at it** il a essayé par deux fois de le faire; **it was a good ~ on his part but ...** il a vraiment essayé mais ... .

b (*attack*) attentat *m* (*upon sb's life* contre qn).

attend [ə'tend] 1 vt a *meeting, lecture* assister à, être à; *classes, course of studies* suivre; *church, school* aller à. **the meeting was well ~ed** il y avait beaucoup de monde à la réunion; *see also* **well 6**. b (*serve, accompany*) servir, être au service de. [*doctor*] **to ~ a patient** soigner un malade; **~ed by a maid** servi par une *or* accompagné d'une femme de chambre; (*fig*) **method ~ed by great risks** méthode qui comporte de grands risques. 2 vi a (*pay attention*) faire attention (*to* à). b (*be present*) être présent *or* là. **will you ~?** est-ce que vous y serez?

▸**attend to** vt fus (*pay attention to*) *lesson, speech* faire attention à; *advice* prêter attention à; (*deal with, take care of*) s'occuper de. **to attend to a customer** s'occuper d'un client, servir un client; (*in shop*) **are you being attended to?** est-ce qu'on s'occupe de vous?

▸**attend (up)on**† vt fus *person* être au service de.

attendance [ə'tendəns] 1 n a service *m*. **he was in ~ on the queen** il escortait la reine; **to be in ~** être de service; (*Med*) **~ on a patient** visites *fpl* à un malade; *see* **dance**.

b (*being present*) présence *f*. **regular ~ at** assiduité *f* à; **is my ~ necessary?** est-il nécessaire que je sois présent? *or* là?

c (*number of people present*) assistance *f*. **a large ~** une nombreuse assistance; **what was the ~ at the meeting?** combien de gens y avait-il à la réunion?

2 comp ▸**attendance centre** (*Brit Jur*) prison *f* de week-end ▸**attendance officer** (*Scol*) ≃ inspecteur *m* (chargé de faire respecter l'obligation scolaire) ▸**attendance order** (*Brit*) *injonction exigeant des parents l'assiduité scolaire de leur enfant* ▸**attendance record, attendance register** (*book*) registre *m* de(s) présence(s); **his attendance record is bad** il est souvent absent ▸**attendance sheet** feuille *f* d'appel.

attendant [ə'tendənt] 1 n a (*servant*) serviteur† *m*, domestique *mf*; [*museum etc*] gardien(ne) *m(f)*; [*petrol station*] pompiste *mf*. b (*US: in hospital*) garçon *m* de salle; (†: *doctor*) médecin *m* (de famille). c (*gen pl: companions, escort*) **~s** membres *mpl* de la suite (*on* de); **the prince and his ~s** le prince et sa suite. 2 adj a (*accompanying*) qui accompagne. **the ~ crowd** la foule qui était présente; **the ~ circumstances** les circonstances concomitantes; **the ~ rise in prices** la hausse des prix correspondante; **old age and its ~ ills** la vieillesse et les infirmités qui l'accompagnent. b (*serving*) au service (*on sb* de qn).

attention [ə'tenʃən] 1 n a (*NonC: consideration, notice, observation*) attention *f*. **may I have your ~?** puis-je avoir votre attention?; **give me your ~ for a moment** accordez-moi votre attention un instant; **to pay ~ to** faire *or* prêter attention à; **to pay little/no ~ to** prêter peu d'attention/ne prêter aucune attention à; **to pay special ~ to** faire tout particulièrement attention à, prêter une attention toute particulière à; **no ~ has been paid to my advice** on n'a fait aucun cas de *or* tenu aucun compte de *or* prêté aucune attention à mes conseils; **it has come to my ~ that** j'ai appris que; **for the ~ of X** à l'attention de X; **it needs daily ~** il faut s'en occuper tous les jours; (*Comm etc*) **it shall have my earliest ~** je m'en occuperai dès que possible; **I was all ~*** j'étais tout oreilles; *see* **attract, call, catch, hold**.

b (*kindnesses*) **~s** attentions *fpl*, soins *mpl*, prévenances *fpl*; **to show ~s to** avoir des égards pour; **to pay one's ~s to a woman** faire la cour à *or* courtiser une femme.

c (*Mil*) garde-à-vous *m*. **to stand at/come** *or* **stand to ~** être/se mettre au garde-à-vous; **~!** garde-à-vous!

2 comp ▸**attention-seeking** adj cherchant à se faire remarquer ◊ n désir *m* de se faire remarquer ▸**attention span**: **his attention span is too short** il ne peut pas se concentrer assez longtemps.

attentive [ə'tentɪv] adj a prévenant (*to sb* envers qn), empressé (*to sb* auprès de qn). **~ to sb's interests** soucieux des intérêts de qn; **~ to detail** soucieux du détail, méticuleux. b *audience, spectator* attentif (*to* à).

attentively [ə'tentɪvlɪ] adv attentivement, avec attention. **to listen ~** écouter de toutes ses oreilles *or* attentivement.

attentiveness [ə'tentɪvnɪs] n attention *f*, prévenance *f*.

attenuate [ə'tenjʊeɪt] 1 vt *statement* atténuer, modérer; *gas* raréfier; *thread, line* affiner, amincir. **attenuating circumstances** circonstances atténuantes. 2 vi s'atténuer, diminuer. 3 adj (*also* **~d**) atténué, diminué; (*fig: refined*) adouci, émoussé.

attenuation [əˌtenjʊ'eɪʃən] n atténuation *f*, diminution *f*.

attest [ə'test] 1 vt a (*certify*) attester (*that* que); (*under oath*) affirmer sous serment (*that* que); (*prove*) démontrer, témoigner de, prouver; (*Jur*) *signature* légaliser. (*Brit Agr*) **~ed herd** cheptel certifié (*comme ayant été tuberculinisé*); (*Ling*) **~ed form** forme attestée. b (*put on oath*) faire prêter serment à. 2 vi prêter serment. **to ~ to sth** se porter garant de qch, témoigner de qch.

attestation [ˌætesˈteɪʃən] n attestation *f* (*that* que); (*Jur*) attestation, témoignage *m*; *[signature]* légalisation *f*; (*taking oath*) assermentation *f*, prestation *f* de serment.

attic [ˈætɪk] n grenier *m*. **~ room** mansarde *f*.

Attica [ˈætɪkə] n Attique *f*.

Attila [əˈtɪlə] n Attila *m*.

attire [əˈtaɪəʳ] 1 vt (*frm*) vêtir, parer (*in* de). **to ~ o.s. in** se parer de; **elegantly ~d** vêtu avec élégance. 2 n (*NonC, frm*) vêtements *mpl*, habits *mpl*; (*ceremonial*) tenue *f*; (*hum*) atours *mpl* (*hum*). **in formal ~** en tenue de cérémonie.

attitude [ˈætɪtjuːd] n a (*way of standing*) attitude *f*, position *f*. **to strike an ~** poser, prendre une pose affectée *or* théâtrale. b (*way of thinking*) disposition *f*, attitude *f*. **~ of mind** état *m or* disposition d'esprit; **his ~ towards me** son attitude envers moi *or* à mon égard; **I don't like your ~** je n'aime pas l'attitude que vous prenez; **if that's your ~** si c'est ainsi *or* si c'est comme ça* que tu le prends.

attitudinize [ˌætɪˈtjuːdɪnaɪz] vi se donner des attitudes, poser, prendre un air *or* un style affecté.

attorney [əˈtɜːnɪ] n a (*Comm, Jur*) mandataire *m*, représentant *m*; *see* **power**. b (*US: also* **~-at-law**) avoué *m*; *see* **district**. c **A~ General** (*Brit*) ≃ Procureur Général; (*US*) ≃ Garde *m* des Sceaux, Ministre *m* de la Justice.

attract [əˈtrækt] vt a *[magnet etc]* attirer. (*fig*) **to ~ sb's interest/attention** susciter *or* éveiller *or* attirer l'intérêt/l'attention de qn. b (*charm, interest*) *[person, subject, quality]* attirer, séduire, exercer une attraction sur. **I am not ~ed to her** elle ne me plaît pas, elle ne m'attire pas.

attraction [əˈtrækʃən] n a (*NonC: Phys, fig*) attraction *f*. **~ of gravity** attraction universelle. b (*often pl: pleasant things*) attrait(s) *m(pl)*, séductions *fpl*. **the chief ~ of this plan** l'attrait principal de ce projet; **the chief ~ of the party** (*star turn*) le clou de la fête; **one of the ~s of family life** un des charmes de la vie de famille.

attractive [əˈtræktɪv] adj a *person, manner* attrayant, séduisant, attirant; *price, sum, idea, plan* intéressant; *prospect, offer* attrayant, intéressant. **a most ~ old house** une très belle vieille maison. b (*Phys*) attractif.

attractively [əˈtræktɪvlɪ] adv d'une manière attrayante *or* séduisante. **~ designed garden** jardin agréablement dessiné; **~ dressed woman** femme élégamment habillée.

attributable [əˈtrɪbjʊtəbl] adj attribuable, imputable (*to* à).

attribute [əˈtrɪbjuːt] 1 vt attribuer (*sth to sb* qch à qn); *feelings, words* prêter, attribuer (*to sb* à qn); *crime, fault* imputer (*to sb* à qn). **they ~ his failure to his laziness** ils attribuent son échec à sa paresse, ils mettent son échec sur le compte de sa paresse. 2 [ˈætrɪbjuːt] n a attribut *m*. b (*Gram*) attribut *m*.

attribution [ˌætrɪˈbjuːʃən] n (*gen*) attribution *f*. **~ of sth to a purpose** affectation *f* de qch à un but.

attributive [əˈtrɪbjʊtɪv] 1 adj attributif; (*Gram*) attributif. 2 n attribut *m*; (*Gram*) attribut *m*.

attributively [əˈtrɪbjʊtɪvlɪ] adv (*Gram*) comme attribut.

attrition [əˈtrɪʃən] n a usure *f* (*par frottement*). b (*Comm*) **~ rate** *[customers]* pourcentage *m* de clients perdus; *[subscribers]* taux *m* de désabonnement; *see* **war**.

attune [əˈtjuːn] vt (*lit, fig*) harmoniser, mettre à l'unisson, accorder (*to* avec). **tastes ~d to mine** des goûts en accord avec les miens; **to ~ o.s. to (doing) sth** s'habituer à (faire) qch.

A.T.V. [eɪtiːˈviː] n a (*Brit*) (**abbr of Associated Television**) *société de télévision*. b (*US*) (**abbr of all terrain vehicle**) *see* **all 5**.

atypical [ˌeɪˈtɪpɪkəl] adj atypique.

aubergine [ˈəʊbəʒiːn] n (*esp Brit*) aubergine *f*.

auburn [ˈɔːbən] adj auburn *inv*.

auction [ˈɔːkʃən] 1 n (vente *f* aux) enchères *fpl*, (vente à la) criée *f*. **to sell by ~** vendre aux enchères *or* à la criée; **to put sth up for ~** mettre qch dans une vente aux enchères; *see* **Dutch**. 2 vt (*also* **~ off**) vendre aux enchères *or* à la criée. 3 comp ▸**auction bridge** bridge *m* aux enchères ▸**auction room** salle *f* des ventes ▸**auction sale** (vente *f* aux) enchères *fpl*, vente à la criée.

auctioneer [ˌɔːkʃəˈnɪəʳ] n commissaire-priseur *m*.

audacious [ɔːˈdeɪʃəs] adj (*bold*) audacieux, hardi, intrépide; (*impudent*) effronté, insolent, impudent.

audaciously [ɔːˈdeɪʃəslɪ] adv (*see* **audacious**) audacieusement, hardiment, effrontément, insolemment, impudemment.

audacity [ɔːˈdæsɪtɪ] n (*see* **audacious**) audace *f*, hardiesse *f*, intrépidité *f*; effronterie *f*, insolence *f*, impudence *f*. **to have the ~ to say** avoir l'effronterie *or* l'audace de dire.

audibility [ˌɔːdɪˈbɪlɪtɪ] n audibilité *f*.

audible [ˈɔːdɪbl] adj (*gen*) audible, perceptible; *words* intelligible, distinct. **she was hardly ~** on l'entendait à peine; **there was ~ laughter** des rires se firent entendre.

audibly [ˈɔːdɪblɪ] adv distinctement.

audience [ˈɔːdɪəns] 1 n a (*NonC*) (*Theat*) spectateurs *mpl*, public *m*; (*of speaker*) auditoire *m*, assistance *f*; (*Mus, Rad*) auditeurs *mpl*; (*TV*) téléspectateurs *mpl*. (*Theat*) **the whole ~ applauded** toute la salle a applaudi; **those in the ~** les gens dans la salle, les membres de l'assistance *or* du public; **there was a big ~** les spectateurs étaient nombreux.
b (*formal interview*) audience *f*. **to grant an ~ to** donner *or* accorder audience à.
2 comp ▸**audience appeal: it's got audience appeal** cela plaît au public ▸**audience chamber** salle *f* d'audience ▸**audience participation** participation *f* de l'assistance (*à ce qui se passe sur scène*) ▸**audience rating** (*Rad, TV*) indice *m* d'écoute ▸**audience research** (*Rad, TV*) études *fpl* d'opinion.

audio [ˈɔːdɪəʊ] 1 adj acoustique. **~ equipment** équipement *m* acoustique; **~ frequency** audiofréquence *f*; **~ recording** enregistrement *m* sonore; **~ system** système *m* audio. 2 n (*) partie *f* son. **the ~'s on the blink*** il n'y a plus de son.

audio- [ˈɔːdɪəʊ] pref audio-.

audio-cassette [ˌɔːdɪəʊkəˈset] n cassette *f* audio.

audiometer [ˌɔːdɪˈɒmɪtəʳ] n audiomètre *m*.

audiotronic [ˌɔːdɪəʊˈtrɒnɪk] adj audio-électronique.

audiotyping [ˈɔːdɪəʊtaɪpɪŋ] n audiotypie *f*.

audiotypist [ˈɔːdɪəʊtaɪpɪst] n audiotypiste *mf*.

audio-visual [ˌɔːdɪəʊˈvɪzjʊəl] adj audio-visuel. **~ aids** supports *or* moyens audio-visuels; **~ methods** l'audio-visuel *m*, méthodes audio-visuelles.

audit [ˈɔːdɪt] 1 n vérification *f* des comptes, audit *m*. 2 vt a *accounts* vérifier, apurer. **~ed statement of accounts** état vérifié des comptes. b (*US Univ*) **to ~ a lecture course** assister (à un cours) comme auditeur libre.

auditing [ˈɔːdɪtɪŋ] n (*Fin*) **~ of accounts** audit *m or* vérification *f* des comptes.

audition [ɔːˈdɪʃən] 1 n a (*Theat etc*) audition *f*; (*Cine, TV*) (séance *f* d')essai *m*. **to give sb an ~** (*Theat*) auditionner qn; (*Cine*) faire faire un essai à qn. b (*NonC: power of hearing*) ouïe *f*, audition *f*. 2 vt auditionner. **he was ~ed for the part** on lui a fait passer une audition *or* fait faire un essai pour le rôle. 3 vi (*Theat*) auditionner. **he ~ed for (the part of) Hamlet** (*Theat*) il a auditionné pour le rôle de Hamlet; (*Cine, TV*) on lui a fait faire un essai pour le rôle de Hamlet.

auditor [ˈɔːdɪtəʳ] n a (*listener*) auditeur *m*, -trice *f*. b (*Comm*) expert-comptable *m*, vérificateur *m* (de comptes); *see* **internal**. c (*US Univ*) auditeur *m* libre.

auditorium [ˌɔːdɪˈtɔːrɪəm] n, pl **~s** *or* **auditoria** [ˌɔːdɪˈtɔːrɪə] salle *f*.

auditory [ˈɔːdɪtərɪ] adj (*Physiol etc*) auditif. **~ phonetics** phonétique *f* auditoire.

Audubon [ˈɔːdəbɒn] n (*US*) **~ Society** société *f* de protection de la nature.

A.U.E.W. [ˌeɪjuːiːˈdʌbljʊ] n (*Brit*) (**abbr of Amalgamated Union of Engineering Workers**) *syndicat*.

au fait [əʊfeɪ] adj au courant, au fait (*with* de).

Augean [ɔːˈdʒiːən] adj: **the ~ Stables** les écuries *fpl* d'Augias.

auger [ˈɔːgəʳ] n (*Carpentry*) vrille *f*; (*Tech*) foreuse *f*.

aught [ɔːt] n (††, *liter*) = **anything**. **for ~ I know** (pour) autant que je sache; **for ~ I care** pour ce que cela me fait.

augment [ɔːgˈment] 1 vt augmenter (*with, by* de), accroître; (*Mus*) augmenter. (*Mus*) **~ed sixth/third** sixte/tierce augmentée. 2 vi augmenter, s'accroître, grandir.

augmentation [ˌɔːgmenˈteɪʃən] n augmentation *f*, accroissement *m*.

augmentative [ɔːgˈmentətɪv] adj augmentatif.

augur [ˈɔːgəʳ] 1 n augure *m*. 2 vi: **to ~ well/ill** être de bon/de mauvais augure (*for* pour). 3 vt (*foretell*) prédire, prévoir; (*be an omen of*) présager. **it ~s no good** cela ne présage *or* n'annonce rien de bon.

augury [ˈɔːgjʊrɪ] n (*omen, sign*) augure *m*, présage *m*; (*forecast*) prédiction *f*. **to take the auguries** consulter les augures.

August [ˈɔːgəst] n août *m*; *for phrases see* **September**.

august [ɔːˈgʌst] adj auguste, imposant, majestueux.

Augustan [ɔːˈgʌstən] adj a d'Auguste. **the ~ Age** (*Latin Literat*) le siècle d'Auguste; (*English Literat*) l'époque *f* néoclassique. b **~ Confession** Confession *f* d'Augsbourg.

Augustine [ɔːˈgʌstɪn] n Augustin *m*.

Augustinian [ˌɔːgəsˈtɪnɪən] 1 adj augustinien, de (l'ordre de) saint Augustin. 2 n augustin(e) *m(f)*.

Augustus [ɔːˈgʌstəs] n: **(Caesar) ~** (César) Auguste *m*.

auk [ɔːk] n pingouin *m*.

aunt [ɑːnt] n tante *f*. **yes ~** oui ma tante; (*Brit*) **A~ Sally** (*game*) jeu *m* de massacre; (*fig: person*) tête *f* de Turc.

auntie*, aunty* [ˈɑːntɪ] n tantine* *f*, tata* *f*. **~ Mary** tante Marie; (*Brit hum*) **A~** la B.B.C.

au pair [ˈəʊˈpɛə] 1 adj: **~ girl** jeune fille *f* au pair. 2 n, pl **au pairs** jeune fille *f* au pair. 3 adv au pair.

aura [ˈɔːrə] n, pl **~s** *or* **aurae** [ˈɔːriː] (*emanating from a person*) aura *f*, émanation *f*; (*surrounding a place*) atmosphère *f*, ambiance *f*.

aural [ˈɔːrəl] adj a (*Anat*) auriculaire (*des oreilles*). b (*Educ*) **~ comprehension (work)** compréhension *f* (orale); **~ comprehension (test)** exercice *m* de compréhension (orale); (*Mus*) **~ training** dictée

musicale.
aureole ['ɔːrɪəʊl] n (*Art, Astron*) auréole *f*.
auricle ['ɔːrɪkl] n (*Med*) *[ear]* pavillon *m* auriculaire, oreille *f* externe; *[heart]* oreillette *f*.
aurochs ['ɔːrɒks] n, pl ~ aurochs *m*.
aurora [ɔː'rɔːrə] n, pl ~s *or* **aurorae** [ɔː'rɔːriː] :~ **borealis/australis** aurore boréale/australe.
auscultate ['ɔːskəlteɪt] vt ausculter.
auscultation [ˌɔːskəl'teɪʃən] n auscultation *f*.
auspices ['ɔːspɪsɪz] npl (*all senses*) auspices *mpl*. **under the ~ of** sous les auspices de.
auspicious [ɔːs'pɪʃəs] adj *sign* de bon augure; *occasion, wind* propice, favorable. **to make an ~ start** prendre un bon départ.
auspiciously [ɔːs'pɪʃəslɪ] adv favorablement, sous d'heureux auspices. **to start ~** prendre un bon départ.
Aussie* ['ɒzɪ] = **Australian**.
austere [ɒs'tɪəʳ] adj austère, sévère.
austerely [ɒs'tɪəlɪ] adv avec austérité, austèrement.
austerity [ɒs'terɪtɪ] n austérité *f*. **days** *or* **years of ~** période *f* d'austérité, temps *m* de restrictions.
Australasia [ˌɔːstrə'leɪzɪə] n Australasie *f*.
Australasian [ˌɔːstrə'leɪzɪən] 1 n habitant(e) *m(f)* *or* natif *m*, -ive *f* d'Australasie. 2 adj d'Australasie.
Australia [ɒs'treɪlɪə] n: **(the Commonwealth of) ~** l'Australie *f*.
Australian [ɒs'treɪlɪən] 1 n a Australien(ne) *m(f)*. b (*Ling*) australien *m*. 2 adj australien. ~ **Alps** Alpes australiennes; ~ **Antarctic Territory** Antarctide australienne; ~ **Capital Territory** Territoire fédéral de Canberra.
Austria ['ɒstrɪə] n Autriche *f*.
Austrian ['ɒstrɪən] 1 n Autrichien(ne) *m(f)*. 2 adj autrichien.
Austro- ['ɒstrəʊ] pref austro-. **~Hungarian** austro-hongrois.
A.U.T. [eɪjuː'tiː] n (*Brit*) (abbr of **Association of University Teachers**) *syndicat*.
autarchy ['ɔːtɑːkɪ] n autocratie *f*.
authentic [ɔː'θentɪk] adj authentique. (*Jur*) **both texts shall be deemed ~** les deux textes feront foi.
authentically [ɔː'θentɪkəlɪ] adv authentiquement.
authenticate [ɔː'θentɪkeɪt] vt *document* authentifier; *report* établir l'authenticité de; *signature* légaliser.
authentication [ɔːˌθentɪ'keɪʃən] n *[documents]* authentification *f*; *[report]* confirmation *f* (de l'authenticité de).
authenticity [ˌɔːθen'tɪsɪtɪ] n authenticité *f*.
author ['ɔːθəʳ] 1 n a (*writer*) écrivain *m*, auteur *m*. **~'s copy** manuscrit *m* de l'auteur. b *[any work of art]* auteur *m*, créateur *m*; *[plan, trouble etc]* auteur. 2 vt (*US*, † *Brit: be author of*) être l'auteur de.
authoress ['ɔːθərɪs] n femme *f* auteur *or* écrivain, auteur *m*, écrivain *m*.
authoritarian [ˌɔːθɒrɪ'tɛərɪən] 1 adj autoritaire. 2 n partisan(e) *m(f)* de l'autorité.
authoritative [ɔː'θɒrɪtətɪv] adj *opinion, source* autorisé; *person* autoritaire; *treatise, edition* qui fait autorité.
authoritatively [ɔː'θɒrɪtətɪvlɪ] adv (*see* **authoritative**) de façon autorisée; autoritairement.
authority [ɔː'θɒrɪtɪ] n a (*power to give orders*) autorité *f*, pouvoir *m*. **I'm in ~ here** c'est moi qui commande ici; **to be in ~ over sb** avoir autorité sur qn; **those in ~** ceux qui nous gouvernent.
b (*permission, right*) autorisation *f* (formelle), mandat *m*, pouvoir *m*. **to give sb ~ to do** autoriser qn à faire; **to do sth without ~** faire qch sans autorisation; **she had no ~ to do it** elle n'avait pas qualité pour le faire; **on her own ~** de son propre chef, de sa propre autorité; **on whose ~?** avec l'autorisation de qui?; **to speak with ~** parler avec compétence *or* autorité; **to carry ~** faire autorité; **I have it on good ~ that ...** je tiens *or* sais de source sûre *or* de bonne source que ...; **what is your ~?** sur quoi vous appuyez-vous (pour dire cela)?; **to say sth on the ~ of Plato** dire qch en invoquant l'autorité de Platon.
c (*gen pl: person or group*) **authorities** autorités *fpl*, corps constitués, administration *f*; **apply to the proper authorities** adressez-vous à qui de droit *or* aux autorités compétentes; **the health authorities** les services *mpl* de la santé publique; **the public/local/district authorities** les autorités publiques/locales/régionales.
d (*person with special knowledge*) autorité *f* (*on* en matière de), expert *m* (*on* en); (*book*) autorité, source *f* (autorisée). *[person, book]* **to be an ~** faire autorité (*on* en matière de); **to consult an ~** consulter un avis autorisé.
authorization [ˌɔːθəraɪ'zeɪʃən] n a (*giving of authority*) autorisation *f* (*of, for* pour, *to do* de faire). b (*legal right*) pouvoir *m*, mandat *m* (*to do* de faire).
authorize ['ɔːθəraɪz] vt autoriser (*sb to do* qn à faire). **to be ~d to do** avoir qualité pour faire, être autorisé à faire; **~d by custom** sanctionné par l'usage; **~d bank** banque agréée; (*Fin*) **~d capital** ≃ capital *m* social; (*Comm*) **~d dealer** distributeur agréé; (*Jur, Fin*) **duly ~d officer** représentant *m* dûment habilité; (*Jur, Fin*) **~d signature** signature sociale; (*Rel*) **the A~d Version** la Bible de 1611.
authorship ['ɔːθəʃɪp] n *[book, idea etc]* paternité *f*. **to establish the ~ of a book** identifier l'auteur d'un livre, établir la paternité littéraire d'un livre.
autism ['ɔːtɪzəm] n autisme *m*.
autistic [ɔː'tɪstɪk] adj autistique.
auto ['ɔːtəʊ] (*US*) 1 n voiture *f*, auto *f*. 2 comp ▸**Auto show** Salon *m* de l'Auto ▸**auto worker** ouvrier *m* de l'industrie automobile.
auto- ['ɔːtəʊ] pref auto-.
autobank ['ɔːtəʊbæŋk] n distributeur *m* automatique de billets (de banque).
autobiographic(al) ['ɔːtəʊˌbaɪəʊ'græfɪk(əl)] adj autobiographique.
autobiography [ˌɔːtəʊbaɪ'ɒgrəfɪ] n autobiographie *f*.
autocade ['ɔːtəʊkeɪd] n (*US*) cortège *m* d'automobiles.
autocracy [ɔː'tɒkrəsɪ] n autocratie *f*.
autocrat ['ɔːtəʊkræt] n autocrate *m*.
autocratic [ˌɔːtəʊ'krætɪk] adj autocratique.
autocross ['ɔːtəʊkrɒs] n auto-cross *m*.
Autocue ['ɔːtəʊkjuː] n (*Brit TV*) ® téléprompteur *m*.
autocycle ['ɔːtəʊsaɪkl] n (*small*) cyclomoteur *m*; (*more powerful*) vélomoteur *m*.
auto-da-fe ['ɔːtəʊdɑː'feɪ] n, pl **autos-da-fe** autodafé *m*.
autodrome ['ɔːtəʊdrəʊm] n autodrome *m*.
autogenic [ˌɔːtəʊ'dʒenɪk] adj: ~ **training** training *m* autogène, autorelaxation *f*.
autogiro ['ɔːtəʊ'dʒaɪərəʊ] n autogire *m*.
autograph ['ɔːtəgrɑːf] 1 n autographe *m*. ~ **album** livre *m* *or* album *m* d'autographes; ~ **hunter** collectionneur *m*, -euse *f* d'autographes. 2 vt *book* dédicacer; *other object* signer.
autohypnosis [ˌɔːtəʊhɪp'nəʊsɪs] n autohypnose *f*.
autoimmune [ˌɔːtəʊɪ'mjuːn] adj *disease* auto-immune.
autoloading ['ɔːtəʊləʊdɪŋ] adj semi-automatique.
automata [ɔː'tɒmətə] npl of **automaton**.
automat ['ɔːtəmæt] n cafétéria *f* automatique (*munie exclusivement de distributeurs*).
automate ['ɔːtəmeɪt] vt automatiser. **~d teller** distributeur *m* automatique de billets.
automatic [ˌɔːtə'mætɪk] 1 adj (*lit, fig*) automatique. (*Comput*) ~ **data processing** traitement *m* automatique de l'information; (*Phot*) ~ **exposure** exposition *f* automatique; ~ **vending machine** distributeur *m* automatique; (*Aviat*) **on ~ pilot** en pilotage *or* sur pilote automatique; (*fig*) **to work/drive on ~ pilot*** travailler/conduire comme un automate. 2 n (*gun, washing machine*) automatique *m*; (*Brit Aut*) voiture *f* à boîte *or* à transmission automatique. (*Aut*) **a Citroën ~** une Citroën à boîte *or* transmission automatique.
automatically [ˌɔːtə'mætɪkəlɪ] adv (*lit, fig*) automatiquement. (*Jur*) ~ **void** nul de plein droit.
automation [ˌɔːtə'meɪʃən] n (*technique, system, action*) automatisation *f*; (*state of being automated*) automation *f*. **industrial ~** productique *f*.
automaton [ɔː'tɒmətən] n, pl ~s *or* **automata** automate *m*.
automobile ['ɔːtəməbiːl] n automobile *f*, auto *f*.
automobilia [ˌɔːtəməʊ'biːlɪə] npl accessoires *mpl* auto.
automotive [ˌɔːtə'məʊtɪv] adj a (*Aut*) *industry, design* (de l')automobile. b (*self-propelled*) automoteur.
autonomous [ɔː'tɒnəməs] adj autonome.
autonomy [ɔː'tɒnəmɪ] n autonomie *f*.
autonymous [ɔː'tɒnɪməs] adj (*Ling*) autonyme.
autopilot ['ɔːtəʊpaɪlət] n pilote *m* automatique. **on ~** sur pilote automatique.
autopsy ['ɔːtɒpsɪ] n autopsie *f*.
autosuggestion ['ɔːtəʊsə'dʒestʃən] n autosuggestion *f*.
auto-teller ['ɔːtəʊteləʳ] n (*Banking*) distributeur *m* automatique de billets.
autotimer ['ɔːtəʊtaɪməʳ] n *[oven]* programmateur *m* (de four).
autumn ['ɔːtəm] 1 n automne *m*. **in ~** en automne. 2 comp d'automne, automnal (*liter*) ▸**autumn leaves** (*dead*) feuilles mortes; (*on tree*) feuilles d'automne.
autumnal [ɔː'tʌmnəl] adj d'automne, automnal (*liter*).
auxiliary [ɔːg'zɪlɪərɪ] 1 adj subsidiaire (*to* à), auxiliaire. (*US*) ~ **police** corps *m* de policiers auxiliaires volontaires; (*Brit Scol*) ~ **staff** personnel *m* auxiliaire non enseignant; (*Aviat*) ~ **tank** réservoir *m* supplémentaire; ~ **verb** verbe *m* auxiliaire. 2 n a auxiliaire *mf*. **nursing ~** infirmier *m*, -ière *f* auxiliaire, aide-soignant(e) *m(f)*; (*Mil*) **auxiliaries** auxiliaires *mpl*. b (*Gram*) (verbe *m*) auxiliaire *m*.
AV [eɪ'viː] abbr of **audio-visual**.
a.v., A/V abbr of **ad valorem**.
avail [ə'veɪl] 1 vt: **to ~ o.s. of** *opportunity* saisir, profiter de; *right* user de, valoir de; *service* utiliser. (*Jur*) **to ~ o.s. of the rules of jurisdiction** invoquer les règles de compétence. 2 vi († *liter*) être efficace, servir. **nought ~ed** rien n'y faisait; **it ~ed him nothing** cela ne lui a servi à rien. 3 n: **to no ~** sans résultat; **your advice was of no ~** vos conseils n'ont eu aucun effet; **it is of no ~ to complain** il ne sert à rien de protester; **to little ~** sans grand effet; **it is of** *or* **to little ~** cela ne sert pas à grand-chose.

availability [əˌveɪlə'bɪlɪtɪ] n **a** *[material, people]* disponibilité *f*. **b** (*US: validity*) validité *f*.

available [ə'veɪləbl] adj **a** *personnel* disponible; *thing* disponible, utilisable. **the next ~ flight** le prochain vol (*avec des places disponibles*); **to make sth ~ to sb** mettre qch à la disposition de qn; (*Comm*) **other sizes/colours ~** existe également en d'autres tailles/couleurs; **to try every ~ means** essayer (par) tous les moyens (possibles); **he is not ~ just now** il n'est pas libre en ce moment; (*Press*) **he is not ~ for comment** il se refuse à toute déclaration. **b** (*US: valid*) valable, valide (*for* pour).

avalanche ['ævəlɑːnʃ] **1** n (*lit, fig*) avalanche *f*. **2** comp ▸**avalanche precautions** mesures *fpl* de sécurité anti-avalanche ▸**avalanche warning** alerte *f* aux avalanches; (*on sign*) "attention (aux) avalanches". **3** vi tomber en avalanche.

avalement [ɑvɑl'mɑ̃] n (*Ski*) avalement *m*.

avant-garde ['ævɑ̃ŋgɑːd] **1** n (*Mil, fig*) avant-garde *f*. **2** comp (*fig*) *dress, style* d'avant-garde, ultramoderne.

avarice ['ævərɪs] n avarice *f*, cupidité *f*.

avaricious [ˌævə'rɪʃəs] adj avare, cupide (*liter*).

Av., Ave n (**abbr of Avenue**) av.

avdp n **abbr of avoirdupois.**

Ave Maria ['ɑːveɪmə'rɪə] n avé Maria *m inv*.

avenge [ə'vendʒ] vt *person, thing* venger. **to ~ o.s.** se venger, prendre sa revanche (*on sb* sur qn).

avenger [ə'vendʒə^r] n vengeur *m*, -eresse *f*.

avenging [ə'vendʒɪŋ] adj vengeur (*f* -eresse) (*liter*).

avenue ['ævənjuː] n (*private road with trees*) avenue *f*, allée bordée d'arbres; (*wide road in town*) avenue, boulevard *m*; (*fig*) route *f*.

aver [ə'vɜː^r] vt affirmer, déclarer.

average ['ævərɪdʒ] **1** n **a** moyenne *f*. **on ~** en moyenne; **a rough ~** une moyenne approximative; **to take an ~ of results** prendre la moyenne des résultats; **above/below ~** au-dessus/en-dessous de la moyenne; **to do an ~ of 70 km/h** rouler à *or* faire une moyenne de 70 km/h, faire du 70 de moyenne*.

b (*Marine Insurance*) avarie *f*. **to adjust the ~** répartir les avaries.

2 adj (*lit, fig*) moyen. **an ~ pupil** un élève moyen.

3 vt **a** (*find the ~ of*) établir *or* faire la moyenne de.

b (*reach an ~ of*) atteindre la moyenne de. **we ~ 8 hours' work a day** nous travaillons en moyenne 8 heures par jour; **the sales ~ 200 copies a month** la vente moyenne est de 200 exemplaires par mois; (*Aut*) **we ~d 50 the whole way** nous avons fait (du) 50 de moyenne pendant tout le trajet.

▸**average out** **1** vi: **it'll average out in the end** en fin de compte ça va s'égaliser; **our working hours average out at 8 per day** nous travaillons en moyenne 8 heures par jour. **2** vt sep faire la moyenne de.

averager ['ævərɪdʒə^r] n (*Marine Insurance*) répartiteur *m* d'avaries, dispacheur *m*.

averse [ə'vɜːs] adj ennemi (*to* de), peu disposé (*to* à). **to be ~ to doing** répugner à faire; **he is ~ to getting up early** il a horreur de se lever tôt; **I am not ~ to an occasional drink** je ne suis pas opposé à un petit verre de temps à autre.

aversion [ə'vɜːʃən] n **a** (*NonC: strong dislike*) aversion *f*, dégoût *m*, répugnance *f*. **he has a strong ~ to work** il a horreur de travailler; **I have an ~ to garlic** une chose que je déteste, c'est l'ail; **he has a strong ~ to me** il ne peut pas me souffrir; **I took an ~ to it** je me suis mis à détester cela; **I have an ~ to him** il m'est antipathique. **b** (*object of ~*) objet *m* d'aversion. **my greatest ~ is ...** ce que je déteste le plus, c'est ...; *see* **pet[1]**.

avert [ə'vɜːt] vt *danger, accident* prévenir, éviter; *blow* détourner, parer; *suspicion* écarter; *one's eyes, one's thoughts* détourner (*from* de).

aviary ['eɪvɪərɪ] n volière *f*.

aviation [ˌeɪvɪ'eɪʃən] n aviation *f*. **~ fuel** kérosène *m*; **~ industry** aéronautique *f*.

aviator ['eɪvɪeɪtə^r] n aviateur *m*, -trice *f*. **~ glasses** lunettes *fpl* sport.

avid ['ævɪd] adj avide (*for* de).

avidity [ə'vɪdɪtɪ] n avidité *f* (*for* de).

avidly ['ævɪdlɪ] adv avidement, avec avidité.

Avila ['ævɪlə] n Avila.

avocado [ˌævə'kɑːdəʊ] n (*Brit also* **~ pear**) avocat *m*; (*tree*) avocatier *m*.

avocation [ˌævəʊ'keɪʃən] n **a** (*employment*) métier *m*, profession *f*. **b** (*minor occupation*) activité *f* de loisir, passe-temps *m inv* (habituel), violon *m* d'Ingres.

avocet ['ævəset] n avocette *f*.

avoid [ə'vɔɪd] vt *person, obstacle* éviter; *danger* échapper à, éviter. esquiver. **to ~ tax** (*legally*) se soustraire à l'impôt; (*illegally*) frauder le fisc; **to ~ doing** éviter de faire; **~ being seen** évitez qu'on ne vous voie; **to ~ sb's eye** fuir le regard de qn; **to ~ notice** échapper aux regards; **I can't ~ going now** je ne peux plus faire autrement que d'y aller, je ne peux plus me dispenser d'y aller; **this way we ~ London** en passant par ici nous évitons Londres; **it is to be ~ed like the plague** il faut fuir cela comme la peste; *see* **plague**.

avoidable [ə'vɔɪdəbl] adj évitable.

avoidance [ə'vɔɪdəns] n: **his ~ of me** le soin qu'il met à m'éviter; **his ~ of his duty** ses manquements *mpl* au devoir; **tax ~** évasion fiscale.

avoirdupois [ˌævədə'pɔɪz] **1** n **a** (*lit*) système *m* des poids commerciaux (*système britannique des poids et mesures*). **b** (*: *overweight*) embonpoint *m*. **2** comp *conforme aux poids et mesures officiellement établis* ▸**avoirdupois pound** livre *f* (*453,6 grammes*).

avow [ə'vaʊ] vt avouer, confesser, admettre. **to ~ o.s. defeated** s'avouer *or* se déclarer battu.

avowal [ə'vaʊəl] n aveu *m*.

avowed [ə'vaʊd] adj *enemy, opponent, supporter* déclaré. **he is an ~ atheist** il avoue *or* reconnaît être athée.

avowedly [ə'vaʊɪdlɪ] adv de son propre aveu.

avuncular [ə'vʌŋkjʊlə^r] adj avunculaire.

AWACS ['eɪwæks] n **abbr of Airborne Warning and Control System. ~ plane** (avion *m*) AWACS *m*.

await [ə'weɪt] vt **a** (*wait for*) *object, event* attendre, être dans l'attente de; *person* attendre. **parcels ~ing delivery** colis en souffrance; **long-~ed event** événement longtemps attendu. **b** (*be in store for*) être réservé à, être préparé pour, attendre. **the fate that ~s us** le sort qui nous attend *or* qui nous est réservé.

awake [ə'weɪk] pret **awoke** *or* **awaked**†, ptp **awoken** *or* **awaked**† **1** vi s'éveiller, se réveiller. **to ~ from sleep** sortir du sommeil, s'éveiller, se réveiller; (*fig*) **to ~ to one's responsibilities** s'éveiller à *or* prendre conscience de *or* se rendre compte de ses responsabilités; (*fig*) **to ~ to the fact that** s'apercevoir du fait que; (*fig*) **to ~ from one's illusions** revenir de ses illusions.

2 vt **a** (*wake*) *person* éveiller, réveiller.

b (*fig: arouse*) *suspicion* éveiller; *hope, curiosity* éveiller, faire naître; *memories* réveiller.

3 adj **a** (*not asleep*) éveillé, réveillé. **he was ~** il était réveillé, il ne dormait pas; **he was still ~** il ne s'était pas encore endormi; **to lie ~** être au lit sans (pouvoir) dormir; **to stay ~ all night** (*deliberately*) veiller toute la nuit; (*involuntarily*) passer une nuit blanche; **I couldn't stay** *or* **keep ~** je n'arrivais pas à rester éveillé; **it kept me ~** cela m'a empêché de dormir.

b (*alert*) en éveil, vigilant. **to be ~ to** être conscient de.

awaken [ə'weɪkən] vti = **awake 1, 2**.

awakening [ə'weɪknɪŋ] **1** n (*lit, fig*) réveil *m*. (*lit, fig*) **a rude ~** un réveil brutal. **2** adj *interest, passion* naissant.

award [ə'wɔːd] **1** vt *prize etc* décerner, attribuer (*to* à); *sum of money* allouer, attribuer (*to* à); *dignity, honour* conférer (*to* à); *damages* accorder (*to* à). **2** n **a** (*prize*) prix *m*; (*for bravery etc*) récompense *f*, décoration *f*; (*scholarship*) bourse *f*. **b** (*Jur: judgment*) décision *f*, sentence arbitrale; (*sum of money*) montant *m* (*or* dommages-intérêts *mpl*) accordé(s) par le juge. **3** comp ▸**award-winner** (*person*) lauréat(e) *m(f)*; (*book etc*) livre *etc* primé ▸**award-winning** *person, book, film* primé.

aware [ə'wɛə^r] adj **a** (*conscious*) conscient (*of* de); (*informed*) au courant, averti (*of* de). **to become ~ of sth/that sth is happening** prendre conscience *or* se rendre compte de qch/que qch se passe; **to be ~ of sth** être conscient de qch, avoir conscience de qch; **to be ~ that something is happening** être conscient *or* avoir conscience que quelque chose se passe; **I am quite ~ of it** je le sais, je ne l'ignore pas, je m'en rends bien compte; **as far as I am ~** autant que je sache; **not that I am ~ of** pas que je sache; **to make sb ~ of sth** rendre qn conscient de qch.

b (*knowledgeable*) informé, avisé. **politically ~** politisé; **socially ~** au courant des problèmes sociaux.

awareness [ə'wɛənɪs] n (*NonC*) conscience *f* (*of* de). **~ programme** programme *m* de sensibilisation.

awash [ə'wɒʃ] adj (*Naut*) à fleur d'eau, qui affleure; (*flooded*) inondé (*with* de).

away [ə'weɪ] (*phr vb elem*) **1** adv **a** (*to or at a distance*) au loin, loin. **far ~** au loin, très loin; **the lake is 3 km ~** le lac est à 3 km de distance *or* à une distance de 3 km; **~ back in the distance** très loin derrière (dans le lointain); **~ back in prehistoric times** dans les temps reculés de la préhistoire; **~ back in 1600** il y a bien longtemps en 1600; **~ back in the 40s** il y a longtemps déjà dans les années 40; **keep the child ~ from the fire** tenez l'enfant loin *or* éloigné du feu; **~ over there** là-bas au loin *or* dans le lointain, loin là-bas.

b (*absent*) **~!** hors d'ici!; **~ with you!** allez-vous-en!; **he's ~ today** (*gen*) il est absent *or* il n'est pas là aujourd'hui; *[businessman etc]* il est en déplacement aujourd'hui; **he is ~ in London** il est (parti) à Londres; **when I have to be ~** lorsque je dois m'absenter; **she was ~ before I could speak** elle était partie avant que j'aie pu parler; *see* **brush away, go away** *etc*.

c (*Sport*) **they're playing ~ this week** ils jouent à l'extérieur cette semaine; **Chelsea are ~ to Everton on Saturday** Chelsea se déplace à Everton samedi.

d (*continuously*) sans arrêt *or* interruption, continuellement. **to be talking/working ~** parler/travailler sans arrêt.

e (*expressing loss, lessening, exhaustion*) **to die ~** s'éteindre, s'évanouir, se dissiper; **to gamble ~ one's money** perdre son argent au jeu; **the snow has melted ~** la neige a fondu complètement; *see* **boil away, get away**.

f (*phrases*) **now she's ~ with the idea that*** ... la voilà partie avec l'idée que ...; *see* **far, out, right** *etc.*

2 adj (*Sport*) **~ match** match *m* à l'extérieur; **~ team** (équipe *f* des) visiteurs *mpl*, équipe jouant à l'extérieur.

awe [ɔː] 1 n crainte révérentielle, effroi mêlé de respect *or* d'admiration. **to be** *or* **stand in ~ of sb** être intimidé par qn, être rempli du plus grand respect pour qn. 2 vt inspirer un respect mêlé de crainte à. **in an ~d voice** d'une voix (à la fois) respectueuse et intimidée. 3 comp ▸**awe-inspiring, awesome** (*impressive*) impressionnant, imposant; (*frightening*) terrifiant ▸**awe-struck** (*frightened*) frappé de terreur; (*astounded*) stupéfait.

awful ['ɔːfəl] adj a affreux, terrible, atroce. **he's an ~ bore** il est assommant*; **what ~ weather!** quel temps affreux! *or* de chien!*; **he's got an ~ cheek!** il a un de ces culots!* *or* un fameux culot!*; **how ~!** comme c'est affreux!, quelle chose affreuse!; **it was simply ~** c'était affreux vous ne pouvez pas savoir*; **his English is ~** il parle anglais comme une vache espagnole; **an ~ lot of** un nombre incroyable de. b (*dreadful*) épouvantable, terrifiant, effrayant.

awfully ['ɔːflɪ] adv vraiment, très, terriblement. **he is ~ nice** il est absolument charmant *or* gentil comme tout*; **thanks ~** merci infiniment; **I am ~ glad** je suis rudement* content; **I am ~ sorry** je suis vraiment désolé; **an ~ big house** une très grande maison.

awfulness ['ɔːfʊlnɪs] n *[situation etc]* horreur *f*. **the ~ of it** ce qu'il y a d'affreux *or* de terrible dans cette affaire, ce que cette affaire a d'affreux *or* de terrible.

awhile [ə'waɪl] adv un instant, un moment, (pendant) quelque temps. **wait ~** attendez un peu; **not yet ~** pas de sitôt.

awkward ['ɔːkwəd] adj a (*inconvenient, difficult etc*) *tool* peu commode, peu maniable, mal conçu; *path* difficile, malaisé; (*Aut*) *bend* difficile *or* malaisé à négocier; *problem, task* délicat; *question* gênant, embarrassant; *silence* gêné, embarrassé; *situation* délicat, gênant. **at an ~ time** au mauvais moment; **an ~ moment** (*inconvenient*) un moment inopportun *or* mal à propos; (*embarrassing*) un moment gênant; **he's an ~ customer*** c'est un type pas commode *or* pas facile*; **an ~ shape** une forme malcommode; **can you come tomorrow? — it's a bit ~** pouvez-vous venir demain? — ce n'est pas très commode; **it's ~ for me** cela m'est assez difficile, cela ne m'est pas très facile; **he's being ~ about it** il ne se montre pas très coopératif à ce sujet; **it's all a bit ~** tout ceci est un peu ennuyeux *or* gênant; **to make things ~ for sb** rendre les choses difficiles pour qn.

b (*clumsy*) *person* gauche, maladroit, empoté*; *movement, gesture* maladroit, peu élégant; *style* gauche, lourd, peu élégant. **the ~ age** l'âge ingrat.

awkwardly ['ɔːkwədlɪ] adv a *speak* d'un ton embarrassé *or* gêné. b *behave, handle* gauchement, maladroitement; *move, walk* maladroitement, peu élégamment. **~ placed** placé à un endroit difficile *or* gênant; **~ expressed** gauchement exprimé, mal dit.

awkwardness ['ɔːkwədnɪs] n a (*clumsiness*) gaucherie *f*, maladresse *f*. b *[situation]* côté gênant *or* embarrassant. c (*discomfort*) embarras *m*, gêne *f*.

awl [ɔːl] n alêne *f*, poinçon *m*.

awning ['ɔːnɪŋ] n (*Naut*) taud *m or* taude *f*, tente *f*; *[shop]* banne *f*, store *m*; *[hotel door]* marquise *f*; *[tent]* auvent *m*; (*in garden*) vélum *m*.

awoke [ə'wəʊk] pret of **awake**.

awoken [ə'wəʊkən] ptp of **awake**.

AWOL ['eɪwɒl] (*Mil*) (abbr of **absent without leave**) *see* **absent**.

awry [ə'raɪ] adj, adv a (*askew*) de travers, de guingois*. b (*wrong*) de travers. **to go ~** *[plan etc]* s'en aller à vau-l'eau; *[undertaking]* mal tourner.

axe, (US) ax [æks] 1 n hache *f*; (*fig: in expenditure etc*) coupe *f* sombre; (*Mus sl: guitare*) guitare *f*. (*fig*) **to have an ~ to grind** prêcher pour son saint (*fig*); (*fig*) **I've no ~ to grind** ce n'est pas mon intérêt personnel que j'ai en vue, je ne prêche pas pour mon saint; (*fig*) **when the ~ fell** quand le couperet est tombé. 2 vt (*fig*) *scheme, project* annuler, abandonner; *jobs* supprimer; *employees* licencier. **to ~ expenditure** réduire les dépenses, faire *or* opérer des coupes sombres dans le budget. 3 comp ▸**axeman** (*Mus sl: guitarist*) guitariste *m*; **(mad) axeman*** tueur *m* fou (*qui se sert d'une hache*).

axial ['æksɪəl] adj axial.

axiom ['æksɪəm] n axiome *m*.

axiomatic [,æksɪəʊ'mætɪk] adj axiomatique; (*clear*) évident.

axis ['æksɪs] n, pl **axes** ['æksiːz] axe *m*. (*Hist*) **the A~ (Powers)** les puissances *fpl* de l'Axe.

axle ['æksl] n *[wheel]* axe *m*; (*Aut*: **~-tree**) essieu *m*. **front/rear axle** essieu avant/arrière. 2 comp ▸**axle-box** (*Rail*) boîte *f* d'essieu ▸**axle cap** chapeau *m* de roue *or* de moyeu ▸**axle grease** graisse *f* à essieux ▸**axle-pin** esse *f*, clavette *f* d'essieu.

ayatollah [,aɪə'tɒlə] n ayatollah *m*.

ay(e) [aɪ] 1 particle (*esp Scot, N Engl*) oui. (*Naut*) **~, ~ sir!** oui, commandant (*or* capitaine *etc*). 2 n oui *m*. (*in voting*) **the ~s and noes** les voix *fpl* pour et contre; **90 ~s and 2 noes** 90 pour et 2 contre; **the ~s have it** les oui l'emportent.

aye† [eɪ] adv (*Scot*) toujours.

AYH [,eɪwaɪ'eɪtʃ] n (*US*) abbr of **American Youth Hostels**.

AZ (*US*) abbr of **Arizona**.

azalea [ə'zeɪlɪə] n azalée *f*.

Azerbaijan [,æzəbaɪ'dʒɑːn] n Azerbaïdjan *m*.

Azerbaijani [,æzəbaɪ'dʒɑːnɪ] 1 adj azerbaïdjanais. 2 n a Azerbaïdjanais(e) *m(f)*. b (*Ling*) Azerbaïdjanais *m*.

AZERTY, azerty [ə'zɜːtɪ] adj: **~ keyboard** clavier *m* azerty.

Azores [ə'zɔːz] npl Açores *fpl*.

AZT [eɪzed'tiː] (abbr of **azidothymidine**) AZT *f*.

Aztec ['æztek] 1 n Aztèque*mf*. 2 adj aztèque.

azure ['eɪʒə^r] 1 n azur *m*. 2 adj azuré, d'azur, bleu ciel *inv*.

B

B, b [biː] n a (*letter*) B, b *m*. **B for Baker** B comme Berthe; (*in house numbers*) **number 7b** numéro *m* 7 ter; (*US*) **B-girl*** entraîneuse *f* (de bar). b (*Mus*) si *m*; *see* **key.** c (*Scol*) bien (≃ *14 sur 20*). d (*Cine*) ~ **movie** *or* **picture** *or* **film** film *m* de série B. e *[record]* **B side** face *f* B.

B.A. [biː'eɪː] n (*Univ*) (**abbr of Bachelor of Arts**) **to have a ~ in French** avoir une licence de français; *see* **bachelor.**

BAA [biːeiˈeiː] n (**abbr of British Airports Authority**) *see* **British.**

baa [bɑː] 1 n bêlement *m*. ~! bê!; ~**-lamb** (*mot enfantin désignant un*) petit agneau. 2 vi bêler.

babble ['bæbl] 1 n *[voices]* rumeur *f*; *[baby]* babil *m*, babillage *m*; *[stream]* gazouillement *m*. 2 vi (*hastily, indistinctly*) bredouiller, bafouiller*; (*foolishly*) bavarder; *[baby]* gazouiller, babiller; *[stream]* jaser, gazouiller. 3 vt (*also* ~ **out**) (*hastily, indistinctly*) bredouiller; (*foolishly*) raconter. **to ~ (out) a secret** laisser échapper un secret.

▸**babble away, babble on** vi babiller *or* jaser sans arrêt.

babbler ['bæbləʳ] n bavard(e) *m(f)*.

babbling ['bæblɪŋ] 1 adj *person, baby, stream* babillard. 2 n = **babble 1.**

babe [beɪb] n a (*liter*) bébé *m*, enfant *mf* (en bas âge), petit(e) enfant. ~ **in arms** enfant au berceau *or* qui vient de naître. b (*: *inexperienced person*) naïf *m*, naïve *f*, innocent(e) *m(f)*. c (*US* ‡: *girl*) pépée‡ *f*, minette* *f*, nana‡ *f*. **come on ~!** viens ma belle!

babel ['beɪbəl] n (*noise*) brouhaha *m*; (*confusion*) tohu-bohu *m*; *see* **tower.**

baboon [bə'buːn] n babouin *m*.

baby ['beɪbɪ] 1 n a bébé *m*. **the ~ of the family** le petit dernier, la petite dernière, le benjamin, la benjamine; **I have known him since he was a ~** je l'ai connu tout petit *or* tout bébé; (*pej*) **don't be such a ~ (about it)!** ne fais pas l'enfant!; (*fig*) **he was left holding the ~*** tout lui est retombé dessus, il est resté avec l'affaire sur les bras*; (*fig*) **to throw out the ~ with the bathwater** jeter le bébé avec l'eau du bain, pécher par excès de zèle; *see* **have.**

b (*US* ‡) (*girlfriend*) copine* *f*, petite amie, nana‡ *f*; (*man, person*) mec‡ *m*. **come on ~!** (*to woman*) viens ma belle!; (*to man*) viens mon gars!*

c (*: *special responsibility*) **the new system is his ~** le nouveau système est son affaire, il est le père du nouveau système; **that's not my ~** je n'ai rien à voir là-dedans.

d (*esp US* ‡: *thing*) petite merveille.

2 vt (*) *person* dorloter, cajoler.

3 comp *clothes etc* de bébé; *rabbit etc* bébé- ▸**baby-batterer** bourreau *m* d'enfants ▸**baby-battering** mauvais traitements infligés aux enfants ▸**baby boom** baby boom *m* ▸**baby boomer** enfant *mf* du baby boom ▸**Baby-bouncer** ® Baby Bouncer *m* ® ▸**baby boy** petit garçon ▸**baby-buggy** ® (*Brit*)poussette *f* ▸**baby carriage** (*US*) voiture *f* d'enfant ▸**baby-doll pyjamas** baby-doll *m* ▸**baby elephant** éléphanteau *m* ▸**baby face** visage poupin ▸**baby food(s)** aliments *mpl* infantiles ▸**baby girl** petite fille ▸**baby grand (piano)** (piano *m*) demi-queue *m* ▸**Baby-gro** ® babygro *m* ® ▸**baby linen** layette *f* ▸**baby-minder** nourrice *f* (*qui garde les enfants pendant que leurs mères travaillent*) ▸**baby-scales** pèse-bébé *m* ▸**baby seat** siège *m* pour bébés ▸**baby-sit** garder les bébés *or* les enfants ▸**baby-sitter** baby-sitter *mf* ▸**baby-sitting** garde *f* d'enfants, baby-sitting *m*; **to go baby-sitting** faire du baby-sitting ▸**baby snatcher** ravisseur *m*, -euse *f* d'enfant; (*fig*) **he/she is a baby snatcher!*** il/elle les prend au berceau!* ▸**baby talk** langage enfantin *or* de bébé ▸**baby tooth*** dent *f* de lait ▸**baby-walker** trotte-bébé *m nv* ▸**baby wipe** lingette *f* (*pour bébé*).

babyhood ['beɪbɪhʊd] n petite enfance.

babyish ['beɪbɪɪʃ] adj puéril, enfantin.

Babylon ['bæbɪlən] n (*Geog, fig*) Babylone.

Babylonian [ˌbæbɪ'ləʊnɪən] 1 adj babylonien. 2 n Babylonien(ne) *m(f)*.

baccalaureate [ˌbækə'lɔːrɪɪt] n (*frm*) licence *f*.

baccara(t) ['bækərɑː] n baccara *m*.

bacchanal ['bækənæl] 1 adj bachique. 2 n (*worshipper*) adorateur *m*, -trice *f* de Bacchus; (*reveller*) noceur* *m*, -euse* *f*; (*orgy*) orgie *f*.

bacchanalia [ˌbækə'neɪlɪə] n (*festival*) bacchanales *fpl*; (*orgy*) orgie *f*.

bacchanalian [ˌbækə'neɪlɪən] adj, **bacchic** ['bækɪk] adj bachique.

Bacchus ['bækəs] n Bacchus *m*.

baccy‡ ['bækɪ] n (**abbr of tobacco**) tabac *m*.

bachelor ['bætʃələʳ] 1 n a (*unmarried man*) célibataire *m*; *see* **confirmed.** b (*Univ*) **B~ of Arts/of Science/of Law** licencié(e) *m(f)* ès lettres/ès sciences/en droit; **B~ of Education/Engineering** licencié(e) d'enseignement/d'ingénierie; **~'s degree** ≃ licence *f*. c (*Hist*) bachelier *m*. 2 adj *uncle etc* célibataire; *life, habits* de célibataire. ~ **flat** garçonnière *f*, studio *m*; ~ **girl** célibataire *f*.

bachelorhood ['bætʃələhʊd] n vie *f* de garçon, célibat *m* (*hommes seulement*).

bacillary [bə'sɪlərɪ] adj bacillaire.

bacillus [bə'sɪləs] n, pl **bacilli** [bə'sɪlaɪ] bacille *m*.

back [bæk] (*phr vb elem*) 1 n a *[person, animal]* dos *m*. **to be on one's ~** (*lit*) être (étendu) sur le dos; (*: *be ill*) être au lit; **to fall on one's ~** tomber à la renverse; **to carry sb/sth on one's ~** porter qn/qch sur son dos; (*fig*) **behind sb's ~** derrière le dos de qn, en cachette de qn; (*fig*) **he went behind the teacher's ~ to the headmaster** il est allé voir le directeur derrière le dos du professeur *or* en cachette du professeur; (*lit, fig*) **~ to ~** dos à dos (*see also* **4**); **with one's ~ to the light** le dos à la lumière; **he had his ~ to the houses** il tournait le dos aux maisons; **to stand** *or* **sit with one's ~ to sb/sth** tourner le dos à qn/qch; **he stood with his ~ (up) against the wall** il était adossé au mur; (*fig*) **to have one's ~ to the wall** être au pied du mur (*fig*); (*fig*) **to live off the ~ of sb/sth** vivre sur le dos de qn/qch; **to put one's ~ into doing sth** mettre toute son énergie à faire qch; (*fig*) **put your ~ into it!*** allons, un peu de nerf!*; **to put** *or* **get sb's ~ up** braquer qn; **to get off sb's ~** laisser qn en paix, cesser de harceler qn; (*fig*) **I was glad to see the ~ of him*** j'étais content de le voir partir; (*fig*) **he's at the ~ of* all this trouble** il est à l'origine de tous ces ennuis; *see* **break, see[1]** *etc.*

b *[chair]* dossier *m*; *[book]* dos *m*. **the ship broke its ~** le navire s'est cassé en deux; *see* **hard** *etc.*

c (*as opposed to front*) (*gen*) dos *m*, derrière *m*; *[hand, hill, medal]* revers *m*; *[record]* deuxième face *f*; *[dress]* dos; *[head, house]* derrière; *[page, cheque]* verso *m*; *[material]* envers *m*. **you've got it on ~ to front** tu l'as mis devant derrière; **at the ~ (of)** à l'arrière (de); **at the ~ of the book** à la fin du livre; **to sit in the ~ (of a car)** être à l'arrière (d'une voiture); (*US*) **in ~ of the house** derrière la maison; (*behind a building*) **out the ~** à l'arrière, derrière; **round the ~** à l'arrière, derrière; **I know Paris like the ~ of my hand** je connais Paris comme ma poche; *see* **mind 1b.**

d (*furthest from the front*) *[cupboard, garden, hall, stage]* fond *m*. **at the very ~** tout au fond; (*fig*) **in** *or* **at the ~ of beyond*** au diable (vert*), en pleine cambrousse*.

e (*Ftbl etc*) arrière *m*. **right/left ~** arrière droit/gauche.

2 adj a (*not front*) *wheel* arrière *inv*; *door* de derrière. (*fig*) **to enter a profession through the ~ door** entrer dans une profession par la petite porte; (*Brit*) ~ **garden** jardin *m* de derrière; *[animal]* ~ **legs** pattes *fpl* arrières; (*Ftbl*) ~ **pass** passe *f* en retrait; ~ **room** chambre *f* sur le derrière *or* du fond (*see also* **4**); ~ **seat** siège *m* de derrière, siège *or* banquette *f* arrière; (*fig*) **to take a ~ seat*** passer au second plan; (*fig*) **he's a ~seat driver*** il est toujours à donner des conseils (au conducteur); (*Aut*) **in the ~ seat** sur le siège arrière; (*Sport*) ~ **straight** ligne droite opposée; ~ **street** rue écartée; (*pej*) rue mal fréquentée *or* mal famée; **he grew up in the ~ streets of Leeds** il a grandi dans les quartiers pauvres de Leeds; ~ **tooth** molaire *f*; (*Ling*) ~ **vowel** voyelle postérieure; ~ **wheel** roue *f* arrière.

b (*overdue*) *taxes* arriéré. **to make up ~ payments** solder l'arriéré; ~ **interest** intérêts courus; **to owe ~ rent** devoir un arriéré de loyer.

3 adv a (*to the rear*) en arrière, à *or* vers l'arrière. **(stand) ~!**

rangez-vous!, reculez!; **far ~** loin derrière; **the house stands ~ from the road** la maison est en retrait par rapport à la route; **to go ~ and forth, to go ~ and forward** *[person]* faire des allées et venues; *[pendulum]* osciller; *[piston]* faire un mouvement de va-et-vient; *see* **keep back, look back, pull back** *etc.*

b (*in return*) **to give ~** rendre; *see* **answer back, pay back** *etc.*

c (*again: often re- + vb in French*) **to come ~** revenir; **to go ~** retourner; **to go ~ home** rentrer (chez soi); **to be ~** être de retour, être rentré; **he's not ~ yet** il n'est pas encore rentré *or* revenu; **I'll be ~ at 6** je serai de retour *or* je rentrerai à 6 heures; **as soon as I'm ~** dès mon retour; **he went to Lyons and then ~ to Paris** il est allé à Lyon et puis est rentré à Paris; **he went to Paris and ~** il a fait le voyage de Paris aller et retour, il a fait Paris et retour*; **the journey there and ~** le trajet aller et retour; **you can go there and ~ in a day** tu peux faire l'aller et retour en une journée.

d (*in time phrases*) **as far ~ as 1800** dès 1800, en 1800 déjà; **far ~ in the past** à une époque reculée; **a week ~*** il y a une semaine.

4 **comp** ►**backache** mal *m* de reins; **I've got (a) backache** j'ai mal aux reins ►**backbench** (*Brit Parl*) banc *m* des membres sans portefeuille (*de la majorité ou de l'opposition*) ►**backbencher** membre *m* du Parlement sans portefeuille (*dans la majorité comme dans l'opposition*), ≃ député *m*; **the backbenchers** le gros des députés ►**backbite** médire de, débiner* ►**backbiting** médisance *f* ►**backboard** (*US Sport*) panneau *m* ►**back boiler** (*Brit*) (petite) chaudière *f* (*à l'arrière d'une cheminée*) ►**backbone** *see* **backbone** ►**backbreaking: back-breaking work** travail *m* à vous casser les reins ►**back burner: to put sth on the back burner** mettre qch en veilleuse *or* en attente ◊ **adj a back burner issue** (*postponed*) une question mise en attente; (*to be postponed*) une question à mettre en attente ►**backchat** (* *NonC*) impertinence *f* ►**back-cloth** (*Brit: Theat*) = **backdrop** ►**back-comb** (*Brit*) *hair* crêper ►**backdate** *cheque* antidater; **increase backdated to January** augmentation *f* avec rappel *or* avec effet rétroactif à compter de janvier ►**backdoor** *loan, attempt etc* déguisé; *methods* détourné ►**backdrop** (*Theat, fig*) toile *f* de fond ►**back-end** *[bus, train]* arrière *m*; (*Brit*) **back-end of the year** arrière-saison *f* ►**backfire** *see* **backfire** ►**back-formation** (*Ling*) dérivation régressive ►**backgammon** trictrac *m*, jacquet *m* ►**background** *see* **background** ►**backhand adj** *blow* en revers; *writing* penché à gauche ◊ **n** (*Tennis*) revers *m*; **backhand drive** coup *m* droit de dos; **backhand volley** volée *f* de revers ►**backhanded** *shot, blow* donné du revers de la main; *action* déloyal; *compliment* équivoque ►**backhander** (*Brit*) (*blow*) revers *m*; (**: reproof*) réprimande *f*, semonce *f*; (**: bribe*) pot-de-vin *m* ►**back interest** (*Fin*) arriérés *mpl* d'intérêts ►**back issue** *[magazine]* vieux numéro *m* ►**back-kitchen** arrière-cuisine *f* ►**backlash** (*Tech*) secousse *f*, saccade *f*; *[explosion]* contre-coup *m*, répercussion *f*; (*Pol, fig*) réaction brutale, répercussions *fpl*, choc *m* en retour; (*fig*) **there will be a white backlash** il y aura un choc en retour chez les Blancs ►**backless** *dress etc* dos nu ►**back-line player** (*US Sport*) arrière *m* ►**back-lit adj** *picture, stage* éclairé de derrière *or* par l'arrière; (*Comput*) *screen* rétro-éclairé ►**backlog** (*of rent etc*) arriéré *m* (de loyers); (*of work*) arriéré de travail, accumulation *f* de travail (en retard); (*Comm*) **backlog of orders** commandes *fpl* en carnet, commandes inexécutées; (*Fin*) **backlog of accumulated arrears** accumulation *f* d'arriérés de paiement ►**back matter** *[book]* appendice(s) *m(pl)* ►**back number** *[newspaper etc]* vieux numéro; *[person]* **to be a back number** ne plus être dans le coup* ►**back-pack** (*Space*) appareil dorsal de survie; (*Sport*) sac *m* à dos *or* de montagne ►**back-packer** randonneur *m*, -euse *f* ►**back-packing: to go back-packing** faire de la randonnée (*sac au dos*) ►**back pain** (*Med*) mal *m* *or* maux *mpl* de dos ►**back passage** (*Anat*) rectum *m* ►**back pay** rappel *m* de salaire *or* de traitement; (*Mil, Naut*) rappel *or* arriéré *m* de solde ►**back-pedal** rétropédaler, pédaler en arrière; (*fig: retreat*) faire marche arrière ►**back-pedalling** (*lit*) rétropédalage *m*; (*fig*) reculade *f* ►**back projection** (*Cine*) transparence *f* ►**backrest** dossier *m* ►**backroom:** (*fig*) **the backroom boys*** (*gen*) ceux qui restent dans la coulisse; (*experts, scientists*) les chercheurs *mpl* anonymes *or* qui travaillent dans l'anonymat ►**backshift** (*period*) poste *m* du soir; (*workers*) équipe *f* du soir; **to be on the backshift** faire le (poste du) soir ►**back-shop** arrière-boutique *f* ►**backside** (*back part*) arrière *m*; (**: buttocks*) derrière *m*, postérieur* *m*; (*fig*) **to sit on one's backside*** rester le derrière sur sa chaise* ►**back sight** *[rifle]* cran *m* de mire; (*Surv*) rétrovisée *f* ►**backslapping*** (*fig*) (grandes) démonstrations *fpl* d'amitié ►**backslider** (*ex-prisoner*) récidiviste *mf* ►**backsliding** (*gen*) récidive *f* ►**backspace** (*Typ*) rappeler le chariot ►**backspace key, backspacer** (*Typ*) rappel *m* de chariot, rappel arrière ►**backspin** (*Tennis etc*) coupé *m*; **to give a ball backspin, put backspin on a ball** couper une balle ►**backstage adv** derrière la scène, dans la *or* les coulisse(s) ◊ **n** coulisse(s) *f(pl)*; **to go backstage** aller dans la coulisse ►**backstair(s)** *see* **backstair(s)** ►**backstitch** point *m* arrière ►**backstreet abortion** avortement *m* clandestin ►**backstreet abortionist** faiseuse *f* d'anges, avorteuse *f* ►**backstroke** (*Swimming*) dos crawlé ►**back talk** (*US *: NonC*) = **backchat** ►**back-to-back** dos à dos; (*Brit*) **a row of back-to-back houses** une rangée de maisons adossées les unes aux autres ►**back-to-the-office report** compte rendu de mission ►**backtrack** faire marche arrière *or* machine arrière (*fig*); **to backtrack on a promise** revenir sur une promesse; (*US*) **to backtrack home*** retourner chez soi ►**backup** *see* **backup** ►**backward** *see* **backward** ►**backwash** (*Naut, fig*) remous *m* (*from* provoqué par) ►**backwater** (*pool*) eau stagnante; *[river]* bras mort; (*fig: backward place*) trou *m* perdu; (*fig: peaceful spot*) (petit) coin *m* tranquille; **to live in a backwater** habiter un petit coin tranquille; (*pej*) habiter en plein bled* (*pej*) ►**backwoods** région (forestière) inexploitée; (*fig pej*) **to live in the backwoods** vivre en plein bled* (*pej*) ►**backwoodsman** pionnier *m*; (*fig pej*) rustre *m* ►**backyard** (*Brit*) arrière-cour *f*; (*US*) jardin *m* (de derrière).

5 **vt** a (*strengthen, support*) *wall, map* renforcer; *book* endosser; *picture* maroufler; (*fig*) *singer* accompagner; (*encourage, support*) *person* soutenir, appuyer; *candidate* pistonner*; (*finance*) *person, enterprise* financer, commanditer; *loan* garantir. (*Fin*) **to ~ a bill** endosser *or* avaliser un effet; *see* **hilt.**

b (*bet on*) *horse* parier sur, miser sur, jouer. **the horse was heavily ~ed** le cheval était bien coté; **to ~ a horse each way** jouer un cheval gagnant et placé; (*lit, fig*) **to ~ the wrong horse** miser sur le mauvais cheval; **to ~ a loser** (*Sport*) parier *or* miser sur un (cheval) perdant; (*Comm*) mal placer son argent; (*fig*) soutenir une cause perdue d'avance.

c (*reverse*) *car, horse, cart* faire reculer; *train* refouler. **to ~ the car in/out** *etc* entrer/sortir *etc* en marche arrière; (*Naut*) **to ~ water** *or* **the oars** nager à culer.

6 **vi** a (*move backwards*) *[person, animal]* reculer; *[vehicle]* faire marche arrière. **to ~ in/out** *etc [vehicle]* entrer/sortir *etc* en marche arrière; *[person]* entrer/sortir *etc* à reculons.

b *[wind]* tourner en sens inverse des aiguilles d'une montre.

►**back away vi** (se) reculer. **to back away from** *problem etc* prendre ses distances par rapport à.

►**back down vi** (*lit*) descendre à reculons; (*fig*) se dérober, se dégonfler*.

►**back off vi** ne pas insister; (*US: withdraw*) tirer son épingle du jeu.

►**back on to vt fus** *[house etc]* donner par derrière sur.

►**back out** 1 **vi** (*lit*) *[person]* sortir à reculons; *[car etc]* sortir en marche arrière (*of* de); (*fig*) (*of problem, deal*) se dégager (*of* de); (*of argument, duty*) se soustraire (*of* à), se dérober (*of* de). **at the last minute he backed out (of the outing)** à la dernière minute il a décidé de ne pas venir. 2 **vt sep** *vehicle* sortir en marche arrière.

►**back up** 1 **vi** a (*Aut*) faire marche arrière. b *[water]* refouler. c (*Comput*) *file* sauvegarder. 2 **vt sep** a (*support*) appuyer, soutenir, épauler. b (*reverse*) *vehicle* faire reculer. 3 **backup** *see* **backup.**

backbone ['bækbəʊn] **n** a *[person, animal]* épine dorsale, colonne vertébrale; *[fish]* arête centrale. **English to the ~** anglais jusqu'à la moelle (des os). b (*fig: main part, axis*) point *m* d'appui, pivot *m*. **to be the ~ of an organization** être *or* former le pivot d'une organisation. c (*fig: strength of character*) énergie *f*, fermeté *f*, caractère *m*. **he's got no ~** c'est un mou* *or* un invertébré*.

-backed [bækt] **adj ending in comps** a à dossier. **low-backed chair** chaise *f* à dossier bas. b doublé de. **rubber-backed carpet** tapis doublé de caoutchouc. c (*supported by*) soutenu (*by* par). **American-backed** soutenu par les américains.

backer ['bækəʳ] **n** (*supporter*) partisan(e) *m(f)*; (*Betting*) parieur *m*, -euse *f*; (*Fin*) *[bill]* avaliseur *m*; *[firm, play, film]* commanditaire *m*.

backfire ['bæk'faɪəʳ] 1 **n** (*Aut*) (*explosion*) raté *m* (d'allumage); (*noise*) pétarade *f*; (*US: for halting a fire*) contre-feu *m*. 2 **vi** (*Aut*) pétarader, avoir un raté (d'allumage); (*miscarry*) *[plan etc]* échouer, foirer‡; (*US: halt a fire*) allumer un contre-feu. (*fig*) **his attacks on his opponent seemed to ~** ses attaques contre son adversaire se sont retournées contre lui.

background ['bækgraʊnd] 1 **n** a (*Theat, Cine*) découverte *f*; *[design, fabric, picture, photo]* fond *m*. **in the ~** dans le fond, à l'arrière-plan (*see also* **b**); **on a blue ~** sur fond bleu.

b (*fig*) arrière-plan *m*, second plan. **to remain in the ~** s'effacer, rester dans l'ombre; **to keep sb in the ~** tenir qn à l'écart.

c (*circumstances etc*) antécédents *mpl*; (*Soc*) milieu socio-culturel, cadre *m* de vie; (*Pol*) climat *m* politique; (*basic knowledge*) données *fpl* *or* éléments *mpl* de base; (*experience*) fonds *m*, acquis *m*, formation *f*. **he has a good professional ~** il a de l'acquis *or* une bonne formation; **family/working-class ~** milieu familial/ouvrier; **what is his ~?** (*social*) de quel milieu est-il?; (*professional*) qu'est-ce qu'il a comme formation?; (*fig*) **from diverse ~s** venant d'horizons différents; **what is the ~ to these events?** quel est le contexte de ces événements?; **this decision was taken against a ~ of violence** cette décision a été prise dans un contexte de violence.

d (*relevant information*) documentation *f*. **to fill in the ~** compléter la documentation.

2 **comp** ►**background music** (*Rad, Theat, TV etc*) musique *f* de fond; **to play sth as background music** passer qch en fond sonore ►**background noise** bruit *m* de fond ►**background paper** documents *m* de référence *or* d'information ►**background reading** lectures générales (autour du sujet) ►**background story** (*Press*) papier *m* d'ambiance ►**background studies** (études *fpl* de) culture

générale.

backing ['bækɪŋ] 1 n a (*lit*) renforcement *m*, support *m*; *[book]* endossure *f*; *[picture]* entoilage *m*; (*fig*) (*Fin, Pol*) soutien *m*; (*Mus*) accompagnement *m*. b (*Betting*) paris *mpl*. c (*movement*) *[horse, cart etc]* recul *m*; *[boat]* nage *f* à culer; *[wind]* changement *m* de direction en sens inverse des aiguilles d'une montre. 2 comp ▸**backing singer** (*Mus*) choriste *mf* ▸**backing store** (*Comput*) mémoire *f* auxiliaire ▸**backing vocals** (*Mus*) chœurs *mpl*.

backstair(s) ['bæk'stɛə(z)] 1 n escalier *m* de service; (*secret*) escalier dérobé. (*fig*) ~ **gossip** propos *mpl* d'antichambre; (*fig*) ~ **intrigue** menées *fpl*, manigances *fpl*. 2 adj, adv (*in servants' quarter*) du côté des domestiques; (*fig*) *rumour, gossip* de couloirs.

backup ['bækʌp] 1 n (*support*) appui *m*, soutien *m* (*from sb* de qn); (*reserves*) réserves *fpl*, *[personnel]* remplaçants *mpl* (éventuels). 2 adj a *vehicles, supplies, weapons* supplémentaire, de réserve; *pilot, personnel etc* remplaçant. b (*Comput*) de secours. ~ **copy/disk** copie *f*/disque *m* sauvegarde; ~ **store** mémoire *f* auxiliaire; ~ **file** sauvegarde *f*.

backward ['bækwəd] 1 adj a (*to the rear*) *look, step* en arrière; (*fig*) *step, move* rétrograde, en arrière. ~ **and forward movement** mouvement *m* de va-et-vient; ~ **flow** contre-courant *m*. b (*retarded*) *district, nation, culture* arriéré, peu avancé; (*Med*) *child* retardé. c (*reluctant*) lent, peu disposé (*in doing* à faire), hésitant. **he was not ~ in taking the money** il ne s'est pas fait prier pour prendre l'argent. 2 adv = **backwards**. 3 comp ▸**backwardation** (*St Ex*) report *m* ▸**backward-looking** *project, attitude* rétrograde.

backwardness ['bækwədnɪs] n (*Psych*) retard mental; (*Econ*) état arriéré; (*reluctance, shyness*) manque *m* d'empressement, lenteur *f* (*in doing* à faire). **industrial ~** retard industriel.

backwards ['bækwədz] (phr vb elem) adv a (*towards the back*) en arrière. **to fall ~** tomber à la renverse; **to flow ~** aller *or* couler à contre-courant; **to walk ~ and forwards** marcher de long en large, aller et venir; **to go ~ and forwards between two places** aller et venir *or* faire la navette entre deux endroits; *see* **lean over**.

b (*back foremost*) à rebours. **to go/walk ~** aller/marcher à reculons *or* à rebours; **the car moved ~ a little** la voiture a reculé un peu.

c (*in reverse of usual way*) à l'envers, en commençant par la fin. **I know the poem ~*** je sais le poème sur le bout des doigts; **I know this road ~*** je connais cette route comme ma poche; (*fig: misunderstood*) **he's got it ~*** il a tout compris de travers.

d (*fig: in time*) en arrière, vers le passé. **to look ~** jeter un regard en arrière, remonter dans le passé; **to reckon ~ to a date** remonter jusqu'à une date.

e (*retrogressively*) en rétrogradant.

bacon ['beɪkən] n lard *m* (*gén. en tranches*). ~ **fat/rind** gras *m*/couenne *f* de lard; ~ **and eggs** œufs *mpl* au lard; **a ~ rasher** une tranche de lard; **~-slicer** coupe-jambon *m inv*; (*fig*) **to bring home the ~*** (*achieve goal*) décrocher la timbale*; (*be breadwinner*) faire bouillir la marmite*; *see* **boil¹, save¹, streaky**.

Baconian [beɪ'kəʊnɪən] adj baconien.

bacteria [bæk'tɪərɪə] npl of **bacterium**.

bacterial [bæk'tɪərɪəl] adj bactérien.

bacteriological [bæk,tɪərɪə'lɒdʒɪkəl] adj bactériologique.

bacteriologist [bæk,tɪərɪ'ɒlədʒɪst] n bactériologiste *mf*.

bacteriology [bæk,tɪərɪ'ɒlədʒɪ] n bactériologie *f*.

bacterium [bæk'tɪərɪəm] n, pl **bacteria** bactérie *f*.

bad [bæd] 1 adj, compar **worse**, superl **worst** a (*wicked*) *action, habit* mauvais; *person* méchant; *behaviour* mauvais, détestable. ~ **language** grossièretés *fpl*, gros mots; **he's a ~ lot** *or* **sort** *or* **type** c'est un mauvais sujet *or* un sale type*; **it was a ~ thing to do/to say** ce n'était pas bien de faire cela/de dire cela; **it was very ~ of him to frighten the children** ce n'était vraiment pas bien de sa part de faire peur aux enfants; **you ~ boy!** vilain!, méchant!; ~ **dog!** vilain chien!; *see* **blood 1a**.

b (*inferior*) *workmanship* mauvais, de mauvaise qualité; (*decayed*) *food* mauvais, gâté; *tooth* carié; (*false*) *coin, money* faux (*f* fausse); (*unfavourable*) *report* mauvais; *opinion* mauvais, triste; *result* mauvais, malheureux; (*unpleasant*) *news, weather, smell* mauvais; (*serious*) *mistake, accident* grave. **it is not so ~** ce n'est pas si mal; **it is not ~ at all** ce n'est pas mal du tout; **(that's) too ~!** (*indignant*) c'est un peu fort!; (*sympathetic*) quel dommage!; **it's too ~ of you** ce n'est vraiment pas bien de votre part; **she's ill? that's very ~** elle est malade? c'est bien ennuyeux; **how is he? — (he's) not so ~** comment va-t-il? — (il ne va) pas trop mal; **I did not know she was so ~** je ne la savais pas si malade; **that is ~ for the health/the eyes** cela ne vaut rien *or* c'est mauvais pour la santé/les yeux; **this is ~ for you** cela ne vous vaut rien; **it's ~ for him to eat fatty foods** les aliments gras sont mauvais pour lui; **to feel ~** se sentir mal; (*fig*) **I feel ~ about it*** je suis ennuyé; **things are going from ~ to worse** tout va *or* les choses vont de mal en pis; **business is ~** les affaires vont mal; **she speaks ~ English** elle parle un mauvais anglais; ~ **at English/spelling** mauvais en anglais/en orthographe; **I'm ~ at languages/remembering birthdays** je ne suis pas doué pour les langues/pour me rappeler des anniversaires; **to go ~** *[food]* se gâter, pourrir; *[milk]* tourner; *[bread etc]* moisir; *[teeth]* se gâter, se carier; **it's a ~ business** (*sad*) c'est une triste affaire; (*unpleasant*) c'est une mauvaise histoire; (*Insurance*) ~ **claim** réclamation mal fondée; ~ **debt** créance douteuse *or* irrécouvrable; **to come to a ~ end** mal finir; **a ~ error of judgment** une grossière erreur de jugement; **in ~ faith** de mauvaise foi; **it is ~ form to do** il est de mauvais ton de faire; **to be in a ~ mood** *or* **temper** être de mauvaise humeur; **to have a ~ name** avoir (une) mauvaise réputation; ~ **quality food/material** *etc* aliments *mpl*/tissu *m etc* de qualité inférieure *or* de mauvaise qualité; (*Ling*) **in a ~ sense** dans un sens péjoratif; **there is a ~ smell in this room** ça sent mauvais dans cette pièce; **it wouldn't be a ~ thing (to do)** ça ne ferait pas de mal (de faire), ce ne serait pas une mauvaise idée (de faire); *see* **news, penny, shot** *etc*.

c *accident, illness* grave; *sprain, wound* sérieux. ~ **cold** mauvais *or* gros *or* sale* rhume; ~ **back** dos *m* en mauvais état; ~ **headache** violent mal de tête; **to have a ~ head*** avoir mal à la tête; **his ~ leg** sa mauvaise jambe, sa jambe malade; **a ~ case of chickenpox/flu** une mauvaise varicelle/grippe.

2 n (*NonC*) mauvais *m*. **to take the good with the ~** prendre le bon avec le mauvais; **he's gone to the ~*** il a mal tourné; **I am 50p to the ~*** j'en suis de 50 pence*; (*US*) **I'm in ~ with him** je ne suis pas dans ses petits papiers, je suis mal vu de lui.

3 adv (*is obsessed by*) **he's got it ~*** (*about hobby etc*) c'est une marotte chez lui; (*about person*) il l'a dans la peau‡.

4 comp ▸**badlands** (*US*) bad-lands *mpl* ▸**badman*** (*US*) bandit *m* ▸**bad-mannered** mal élevé ▸**bad-mouth*** (*US*) débiner* ▸**bad-tempered** *person* qui a mauvais caractère, (*on one occasion*) de mauvaise humeur; *look, answer* désagréable.

baddie‡ ['bædɪ] n méchant *m*.

baddish ['bædɪʃ] adj pas fameux, pas brillant.

bade [bæd, beɪd] pret of **bid**.

badge [bædʒ] n *[team, association]* insigne *m*; *[an order, police]* plaque *f*; (*Mil*) insigne; (*sew-on, stick-on: for jeans etc*) badge *m*; (*Scouting*) badge; (*fig: symbol*) symbole *m*, signe *m* (distinctif). **his ~ of office** l'insigne de sa fonction.

badger ['bædʒəʳ] 1 n (*animal, brush*) blaireau *m*. (*US*) **the B~ State** le Wisconsin *m*. 2 vt harceler, importuner (*with* de). **to ~ sb to do sth** harceler qn jusqu'à ce qu'il fasse qch; **to ~ sth out of sb** soutirer qch à qn à force de le harceler.

badly ['bædlɪ] adv, compar **worse**, superl **worst** a mal. ~ **dressed** mal habillé; (*in interview, exam etc*) **he did ~** il a mal réussi, ça a mal marché (pour lui); **you did ~ (out of it), you came off ~** tu n'as pas été gâté; **I came off ~ in that transaction** c'est moi qui ai fait les frais de cette transaction; (*Comm, Fin*) **to be doing ~** faire de mauvaises affaires; **things are going ~** les choses vont *or* tournent mal; **he took it very ~** il a très mal pris la chose; **to speak ~ of sb** critiquer qn; *[machine etc]* **to work ~** mal fonctionner; **to be ~ off** être dans la gêne; **to be ~ off for sth** manquer de qch.

b (*seriously*) *wound, injure* grièvement, gravement; *disrupt, affect* sérieusement, gravement. **they were ~ defeated (by)** ils se sont vu infliger une sévère défaite (par), ils ont subi une sévère défaite; **he was ~ beaten** (*physically*) il a reçu des coups violents, on l'a violemment frappé; **the ~ disabled** les grands infirmes, les grands invalides.

c (*very much*) **to want sth ~** avoir grande envie de qch; **I need it ~** j'en ai absolument besoin, il me le faut absolument; **he ~ needs a beating*** il a sérieusement besoin d'une correction.

badminton ['bædmɪntən] n badminton *m*.

badness ['bædnɪs] n (*NonC*) a (*poor quality*) mauvaise qualité, mauvais état. b (*wickedness*) méchanceté *f*.

Baffin ['bæfɪn] n: ~ **Bay** mer *f or* baie *f* de Baffin; ~ **Island** terre *f* de Baffin.

baffle ['bæfl] 1 vt *person* déconcerter, dérouter; *pursuers* semer; *plot* déjouer; *hope, expectation* décevoir, tromper; *description, explanation* échapper à, défier. 2 n (*Tech*) déflecteur *m*; (*Acoustics*) baffle *m*. 3 comp ▸**baffle-board** écran *m* ▸**baffle-plate** (*Tech*) déflecteur *m*; (*Acoustics*) baffle *m*.

baffling ['bæflɪŋ] adj déconcertant, déroutant.

BAFTA ['bæftə] n (abbr of **British Academy of Film and Television Arts**) *Académie britannique chargée de promouvoir le cinéma et la télévision*.

bag [bæg] 1 n sac *m*; (*luggage*) valise *f*; (*Zool*) sac, poche *f*. **a ~ of sweets/apples** *etc* un sac de bonbons/pommes *etc*; (*Brit*) **a ~ of chips** un cornet de frites; (*fig*) **a ~ of bones** un sac d'os*; **~s** (*luggage*) bagages *mpl*, valises *fpl*; (*Brit* ‡*: trousers*) falzar‡ *m*, pantalon *m*; (*Brit*) **~s of*** des masses de*; **paper ~** sac en papier; **she's got ~s under the eyes*** elle a des poches sous les yeux; **with ~ and baggage** avec armes et bagages; **to pack up ~ and baggage** plier bagage, prendre ses cliques et ses claques*; **the whole ~ of tricks** tout le bataclan*, tout le fourbi*; **tea/coffee ~** sachet *m* de thé/café; (*Hunting*) **to get a good ~** faire bonne chasse, faire un beau tableau; **it's in the ~‡** c'est dans le sac* *or* dans la poche*; (*US*) **to be left holding the ~*** payer les pots cassés*; (*pej*) **she's an old ~‡** c'est une vieille teigne; **you stupid (old) ~!‡** espèce *f* de vieille croûte!‡; *see* **cat, money** *etc*.

2 vt a (**: get possession of*) empocher, mettre le grappin sur*;

(*: *steal*) faucher*, piquer*. (*Brit*) **~s I, I ~s (that)!*** moi, je le prends!; (*claim in advance*) **Anne has already ~ged that seat** Anne s'est déjà réservé cette place.

b (*Hunting: kill*) tuer.

c (*also* **~ up**) *flour, goods* mettre en sac, ensacher.

3 **vi** (*also* **~ out**) *[garment]* goder.

4 **comp** ▶**bag lady*** clocharde *f* ▶**bagpiper** joueur *m* de cornemuse, joueur de biniou ▶**bagpipe(s)** *[Scotland]* cornemuse *f*; *[Brittany]* biniou *m*, cornemuse ▶**bag-snatching** vol *m* à l'arraché.

bagatelle [ˌbægəˈtel] **n** (*trifle*) bagatelle *f*; (*Mus*) divertissement *m*; (*board game*) *sorte de flipper;* (*Billiards*) billard anglais, billard à blouses.

bagel [ˈbeɪgl] **n** (*Culin*) *petit pain en croissant ou en couronne.*

bagful [ˈbægfʊl] **n** sac *m* plein, plein sac.

baggage [ˈbægɪdʒ] 1 **n** a (*NonC: luggage*) bagages *mpl*; (*Mil*) équipement *m*; *see* **bag.** b (*†) (*pert girl*) coquine† *f*. 2 **comp** ▶**baggage car** (*esp US*) fourgon *m* ▶**baggage check** (*US: receipt*) bulletin *m* de consigne; (*security check*) contrôle *m* des bagages ▶**baggage checkroom** (*US*) consigne *f* ▶**baggage elastic** pieuvre *f* ▶**baggage hall** = **baggage reclaim (area)** ▶**baggage handler** bagagiste *m* ▶**baggage locker** (casier *m* de) consigne *f* automatique ▶**baggage reclaim (area)** *[airport]* livraison *f* des bagages ▶**baggage room** consigne *f* ▶**baggage train** (*Mil*) train *m* des équipages ▶**baggage wagon** = **baggage car.**

bagging [ˈbægɪŋ] **n** (*Tex*) toile *f* à sac.

baggy [ˈbægɪ] **adj** a (*puffy*) gonflé, bouffant. b *jacket, coat* trop ample, flottant; (*fashionably*) ample. **trousers ~ at the knees** pantalon *m* qui fait des poches aux genoux.

Baghdad [bægˈdæd] **n** Baghdâd, Bagdad.

Bahama [bəˈhɑːmə] **adj, n: the ~ Islands, the ~s** les Bahamas *fpl*.

Bahamian [bəˈheɪmɪən] 1 **n** bahamien(ne) *m(f)*. 2 **adj** bahamien.

Bahrain [bɑːˈreɪn] **n** Bahrein *m*.

Bahraini [bɑːˈreɪnɪ] 1 **n** bahreinite *mf*. 2 **adj** bahreinite.

Bahrein [bɑːˈreɪn] **n** Bahrein *m*.

Baikal [baɪˈkɑːl] **n: Lake ~** le lac Baïkal.

bail[1] [beɪl] 1 **n** (*Jur*) mise *f* en liberté sous caution; (*sum*) caution *f*; (*person*) caution, répondant *m*. **on ~** sous caution; **to free sb on ~** mettre qn en liberté provisoire sous caution; **to go** *or* **stand ~ for sb** se porter *or* se rendre garant de qn; **to find ~ for sb** fournir une caution pour qn (*pour sa mise en liberté provisoire*); **to ask for/grant/refuse ~** demander/accorder/refuser la mise en liberté sous caution; **to put up ~ for sb** payer la caution de qn; *see* **jump, remand.** 2 **vt** a (*Jur*) (*also* **~ out**) faire mettre en liberté provisoire sous caution. b *goods* mettre en dépôt.

▶**bail out vt sep** a = **bail**[1] **2a.** b (*fig*) sortir d'affaire.

bail[2] [beɪl] **n** (*Cricket*) **~s** bâtonnets *mpl* (*qui couronnent le guichet*).

bail[3] [beɪl] 1 **vt** *boat* écoper; *water* vider. 2 **n** écope *f*.

▶**bail out** 1 **vi** (*Aviat*) sauter (en parachute). 2 **vt sep** *boat* écoper; *water* vider; *person, firm* renflouer, tirer d'affaire; *project* renflouer. (*fig*) **to bail o.s. out** s'en sortir. 3 **n bailout** *see* **bailout.**

bailee [beɪˈliː] **n** (*Jur*) dépositaire *m*.

bailey [ˈbeɪlɪ] **n** (*wall*) mur *m* d'enceinte; (*courtyard*) cour intérieure. **B~ bridge** pont *m* Bailey; *see* **old.**

bailiff [ˈbeɪlɪf] **n** (*Jur*) huissier *m*; (*Brit*) *[estate, lands]* régisseur *m*, intendant *m*; (*Hist*) bailli *m*, gouverneur *m*.

bailor [ˈbeɪləʳ] **n** (*Jur*) déposant *m*.

bailout [ˈbeɪlaʊt] **n** *[company]* sauvetage *m*, renflouement *m*.

bain-marie [ˌbeɪnməˈriː, bɛ̃mɑri] **n** bain-marie *m*.

bairn [bɛən] **n** (*Scot, N Engl*) enfant *mf*.

bait [beɪt] 1 **n** (*Fishing, Hunting*) amorce *f*, appât *m*; (*fig*) appât, leurre *m*. (*lit, fig*) **to rise to** *or* **take** *or* **swallow the ~** mordre à l'hameçon. 2 **vt** a *hook, trap* amorcer, appâter, garnir. b (*torment*) tourmenter; *see* **bear**[2].

baize [beɪz] **n** serge *f*, reps *m*; (*Snooker*) tapis *m*. **(green) ~ door** porte matelassée.

bake [beɪk] 1 **vt** a (*Culin*) faire cuire au four. **she ~s her own bread** elle fait son pain elle-même; **to ~ a cake** faire (cuire) un gâteau; **~d apples/potatoes** pommes *fpl*/pommes de terre au four; **~d Alaska** omelette norvégienne; **~d beans** haricots blancs à la sauce tomate; *see* **half.**

b *pottery, bricks* cuire (au four). **earth ~d by the sun** sol desséché *or* cuit par le soleil.

2 **vi** a *[bread, cakes]* cuire (au four).

b **she ~s every Tuesday** (*makes bread*) elle fait du pain le mardi; (*bakes cakes*) elle fait de la pâtisserie tous les mardis.

c *[pottery etc]* cuire. (*fig*) **we are baking in this heat*** on cuit* *or* on grille* par cette chaleur; **it's baking (hot) today!*** il fait une de ces chaleurs aujourd'hui!

3 **comp** ▶**bakehouse** boulangerie *f* (*lieu de fabrique*).

Bakelite [ˈbeɪkəlaɪt] **n** ® Bakélite *f* ®.

baker [ˈbeɪkəʳ] **n** boulanger *m*, -ère *f*. **~'s shop** boulangerie *f*; (*fig*) **~'s dozen** treize à la douzaine.

bakery [ˈbeɪkərɪ] **n** boulangerie(-pâtisserie) *f*.

Bakewell tart [ˈbeɪkwelˈtɑːt] **n** tourte *f* de Bakewell.

baking [ˈbeɪkɪŋ] 1 **n** a (*NonC*) cuisson *f*. **the bread is our own ~** nous faisons le pain nous-mêmes. b *[bread]* fournée *f*; *[bricks etc]* cuisson *f*. 2 **comp** ▶**baking dish** plat *m* allant au four ▶**baking powder** levure *f* (chimique) ▶**baking sheet** = **baking tray** ▶**baking soda** bicarbonate *m* de soude ▶**baking tin** *[cakes]* moule *m* (à gâteaux); *[tarts]* tourtière *f* ▶**baking tray** plaque *f* à gâteaux *or* de four.

baksheesh [ˈbækʃiːʃ] **n** bakchich *m*.

Balaclava, Balaklava [ˌbæləˈklɑːvə] **n** (*Geog*) Balaklava. (*Brit*) **b~ (helmet)** passe-montagne *m*.

balalaika [ˌbæləˈlaɪkə] **n** balalaïka *f*.

balance [ˈbæləns] 1 **n** a (*scales*) balance *f*. (*fig*) **to be** *or* **hang in the ~** être en balance; (*fig*) **to hold the ~** faire pencher la balance; *see* **spring.**

b (*NonC: equilibrium*) équilibre *m*, aplomb *m*. (*lit, fig*) **to keep/lose one's ~** garder/perdre son équilibre; (*lit, fig*) **off ~** mal équilibré; **to throw sb off ~** (*lit*) faire perdre l'équilibre à qn; (*fig*) couper le souffle à qn; **the ~ of nature** l'équilibre *m* de la nature; (*Jur*) **when the ~ of his mind was disturbed** alors qu'il n'était pas responsable de ses actes; (*fig*) **to strike a ~** trouver le juste milieu; **he has no sense of ~** il n'a aucun sens des proportions *or* de la mesure; **a nice ~ of humour and pathos**un délicat dosage d'humour et de pathétique.

c (*Comm, Fin*) solde *m*; (*also* **bank ~**) solde *m* (d'un compte). (*in bank*) **what's my ~ ?** quelle est la position de mon compte?; **credit/debit ~** solde créditeur/débiteur; **~ in hand** solde créditeur; **~ carried forward** (*gen*) solde à reporter; (*on balance sheet*) report *m* à nouveau; **~ due** solde débiteur; **to pay off the ~ of an account** solder un compte; **sterling ~s** balances sterling; (*fig*) **on ~** à tout prendre, tout compte fait.

d (*remainder*) reste *m*.

e *[clock, watch]* régulateur *m*, balancier *m*.

2 **comp** ▶**balance of payments** balance *f* des paiements; **balance of payments surplus** excédent *m* de la balance des paiements; **balance of payments deficit** déficit *m* de la balance des paiements ▶**balance of power** balance *or* équilibre *m* des forces; **the European balance of power** l'équilibre européen ▶**balance of terror** équilibre de la terreur ▶**balance of trade** (*Econ*) balance *f* commerciale ▶**balance sheet** bilan *m* ▶**balance weight** contrepoids *m*.

3 **vt** a (*maintain equilibrium of*) tenir en équilibre; (*place in equilibrium*) mettre *or* poser en équilibre; *wheels* équilibrer; (*fig*) équilibrer, compenser. **I ~d the glass on top of the books** je plaçai en équilibre le verre sur les livres; **the seal ~d the ball on its nose** le phoque posa le ballon en équilibre sur son nez.

b (*compare etc*) balancer, peser; *two arguments, two solutions* comparer. **this must be ~d against that** il faut peser le pour et le contre.

c (*counterbalance*) (*in weighing, symmetrical display etc*) équilibrer; (*in value, amount*) compenser, contrebalancer. *[2 objects]* **they ~ each other** (*in weighing*) ils se font contrepoids; (*in symmetrical display*) ils s'équilibrent.

d (*Comm, Fin*) **to ~ an account** arrêter un compte; **to ~ the budget** équilibrer le budget; **to ~ the books** arrêter les comptes, dresser le bilan; **to ~ the cash** faire la caisse.

4 **vi** a *[2 objects]* se faire contrepoids; *[acrobat etc]* se maintenir en équilibre; *[scales]* être en équilibre. **to ~ on one foot** se tenir en équilibre sur un (seul) pied.

b (*Comm, Fin*) *[accounts]* s'équilibrer, être en équilibre.

▶**balance out vt sep** (*fig*) contrebalancer, compenser.

balanced [ˈbælənst] **adj** (*gen*) équilibré. **~ views** vues *fpl* sensées *or* mesurées.

balancing [ˈbælənsɪŋ] **n** a (*equilibrium*) mise *f* en équilibre, stabilisation *f*. **to do a ~ act** (*Theat*) faire de l'équilibrisme; (*fig*) jongler. b (*Comm, Fin*) **~ of accounts** règlement *m* *or* solde *m* des comptes; (*Comm, Fin*) **~ of the books** balances *fpl* (mensuelles).

balcony [ˈbælkənɪ] **n** a balcon *m*. b (*Theat*) fauteuils *mpl* *or* stalles *fpl* de deuxième balcon.

bald [bɔːld] 1 **adj** a (*gen*) chauve; *tyre* lisse. **~ as a coot*** *or* **an egg*** chauve comme une boule de billard* *or* comme un œuf*; **to be going ~** perdre ses cheveux, devenir chauve, se déplumer*; **~ patch** *[person]* (petite) tonsure *f*; *[animal]* place dépourvue de poils; *[carpet etc]* coin *m* dégarni *or* pelé. b *style* plat, sec. **a ~ statement** une simple exposition de faits; **a ~ lie** un mensonge flagrant *or* non déguisé. 2 **comp** ▶**bald eagle** aigle *m* impérial ▶**bald-headed** chauve, à (la) tête chauve; (*fig*) **he went bald-headed at it*** il s'y est pris brutalement.

baldachin [ˈbɔːldəkən] **n, baldachino** [ˌbældəˈkiːnəʊ] **n** baldaquin *m*.

balderdash [ˈbɔːldədæʃ] **n** bêtises *fpl*, balivernes *fpl*.

balding [ˈbɔːldɪŋ] **adj** qui devient chauve, atteint de calvitie naissante.

baldly [ˈbɔːldlɪ] **adv** *say, state* abruptement.

baldness [ˈbɔːldnɪs] **n** (*see* **bald**) *[person]* calvitie *f*; *[tyre]* état *m* lisse; *[mountains etc]* nudité *f*; *[style]* platitude *f*, pauvreté *f*.

bale[1] [beɪl] 1 **n** *[cotton, hay]* balle *f*. 2 **vt** (*also* **~ up**) emballoter; emballer.

bale[2] [beɪl] **vt** (*Naut*) = **bail**[3] **1.**

▶**bale out** = **bail out;** *see* **bail**[3].

Balearic [ˌbælɪˈærɪk] adj, n: **the ~ Islands, the ~s** les (îles *fpl*) Baléares *fpl*.

baleful [ˈbeɪlfʊl] adj sinistre, funeste, maléfique. **to give sb/sth a ~ look** regarder qn/qch d'un œil torve.

balefully [ˈbeɪlfəlɪ] adv *look* d'un œil torve; *say* d'un ton menaçant.

balk [bɔːk] 1 n (*Agr*) terre *f* non labourée; (*Constr*) (*on ceiling*) solive *f*; (*building timber*) bille *f*. 2 vt contrecarrer. 3 vi *[person]* s'arrêter, reculer, hésiter (*at* devant), regimber (*at* contre); *[horse]* se dérober (*at* devant).

Balkan [ˈbɔːlkən] adj, n: **the ~s** les Balkans *mpl*; **the ~ States** les États *mpl* balkaniques; **the ~ Peninsula** la péninsule Balkanique.

balkanization [ˈbɔːlkənaɪˈzeɪʃən] n balkanisation *f*.

ball[1] [bɔːl] 1 n a (*gen, Cricket, Golf, Hockey, Tennis*) balle *f*; (*inflated: Ftbl etc*) ballon *m*; (*Billiards*) bille *f*, boule *f*; (*Croquet*) boule. **as round as a ~** rond comme une boule *or* bille; (*US fig*) **behind the eight ~*** dans le pétrin*; **cat curled up in a ~** chat couché en rond *or* pelotonné (en boule); **tennis/golf** *etc* **~** balle de tennis/de golf *etc*; **croquet ~** boule de croquet; (*US fig*) **that's the way the ~ bounces!*** c'est la vie!; (*US*) **to have sth/a lot on the ~*** en avoir là-dedans* *or* dans le ciboulot‡; (*fig: esp US*) **take the ~ and run with it!** vas-y fonce!*, saisis ta chance!; (*fig*) **to keep the ~ rolling** (*maintain conversation*) continuer *or* soutenir la conversation; (*maintain activity*) continuer à faire marcher la machine*, assurer la continuité; (*maintain interest*) soutenir l'intérêt; (*fig*) **to start** *or* **set the ~ rolling*** faire démarrer une affaire (*or* la conversation *etc*); (*fig*) **he's got the ~ at his feet** c'est à lui de saisir cette chance; (*Brit fig*) **the ~ is with you** *or* **in your court** (c'est) à vous de jouer; (*fig*) **to be on the ~*** (*competent*) être à la hauteur (de la situation *or* des circonstances); (*alert*) ouvrir l'œil et le bon*; (*Met*) **~ of fire, ~ lightning** globe *m* de feu, éclair *m* en boule; (*fig*) **he's a real ~ of fire*** il est débordant d'activité; *see* **eye, play, tennis** *etc*.

b *[rifle etc]* balle *f*. (*lit, fig*) **~ and chain** boulet *m*; *see* **cannon**.

c *[wool, string]* pelote *f*, peloton *m*. **to wind up into a ~** mettre en pelote.

d (*Culin*) *[meat, fish]* boulette *f*; *[potato]* croquette *f*.

e (*Tech*) bille *f* (de roulement).

f (*Anat*) **~ of the foot** (partie *f* antérieure de la) plante *f* du pied; **~ of the thumb** (partie charnue du) pouce *m*; *see* **eye**.

g **~s**** (*Anat*) couilles** *fpl*; (*Brit: nonsense*) conneries** *fpl*, couillonnades** *fpl*; (*Brit: courage*) **to have ~s**** avoir des couilles**; (*excl*) **~s!**** quelles conneries!**

2 comp ▸**ball-and-socket joint** (joint *m* à) rotule *f* ▸**ball bearings** roulement *m* à billes ▸**ballboy** (*Tennis*) ramasseur *m* de balles ▸**ball-breaker*** (femme *f*) dominatrice *f* ▸**ball cartridge** cartouche *f* à balle ▸**ballcock** robinet *m* à flotteur ▸**ball game** jeu *m* de balle (*or* ballon); (*US*) match *m* de base-ball; (*fig*) **it's a whole new ball game*, it's not the same ball game*** c'est une tout autre histoire ▸**ballpark** (*US*) stade *m* de base-ball; (*fig*) **in the ballpark*** dans cet ordre de grandeur; **in the ballpark of*** aux alentours de, environ; **we're in the same ballpark*** on arrive à peu près à la même somme, on n'est pas très éloignés l'un de l'autre; **ballpark figure*** chiffre approximatif ▸**ball-point (pen)** stylo *m* (à) bille, (pointe *f*) Bic *m* ® ▸**ball-shaped** sphérique ▸**balls-up****: (*Brit*) **he made a balls-up of the job** il a salopé le boulot‡; (*Brit*) **the meeting was a balls-up** la réunion a été bordélique‡ *or* un vrai bordel‡ ▸**ball-up**** (*US*) = **balls-up****.

3 vt *wool etc* mettre en pelote, pelotonner.

4 vi s'agglomérer.

▸**ball up** 1 vi (*Ski etc*) botter. 2 vt sep (**) = **balls up****.

▸**balls up**** 1 vt sep semer la pagaïe dans*, foutre la merde dans**. **to be/get ballsed up‡** être/se retrouver en pleine pagaïe* *or* dans la merde jusqu'au cou‡. 2 **balls-up**** n *see* **ball[1] 2**.

ball[2] [bɔːl] 1 n (*dance*) bal *m*. (*lit, fig*) **to open the ~** ouvrir le bal; **to have a ~*** s'amuser comme des fous, se marrer*; *see* **fancy** *etc*. 2 comp ▸**ballroom** *[hotel]* salle *f* de danse; *[mansion]* salle de bal; **ballroom dancing** (*NonC*) danse *f* de bal.

ballad [ˈbæləd] n (*Mus*) romance *f*; (*Literat*) ballade *f*.

ballast [ˈbæləst] 1 n (*NonC*) a (*Aviat, Naut*) lest *m*. **ship in ~** vaisseau *m* en lest; **to sail in ~** être sur lest. b (*stone, clinker*) pierraille *f*; (*Rail*) ballast *m*. 2 vt a (*Aviat, Naut*) lester. b (*Tech*) empierrer, caillouter; (*Rail*) ballaster.

ballerina [ˌbæləˈriːnə] n ballerine *f*.

ballet [ˈbæleɪ] 1 n a (*show, work of art*) ballet *m*. b (*type of dancing*) danse *f* classique. 2 comp ▸**ballet dancer** danseur *m*, -euse *f* de ballet ▸**ballet lesson** cours *m* de danse (classique) ▸**ballet school** école *f* de danse (classique) ▸**ballet shoe** chausson *m* de danse ▸**ballet skirt** tutu *m*.

ballistic [bəˈlɪstɪk] adj balistique. **~ missile** engin *m* balistique.

ballistics [bəˈlɪstɪks] n (*NonC*) balistique *f*.

balloon [bəˈluːn] 1 n a (*Aviat*) ballon *m*, aérostat *m*. **navigable/captive ~** ballon dirigeable/captif; **to go up in a ~** monter en ballon; (*fig*) **the ~ went up*** l'affaire a éclaté; **(meteorological** *or* **weather) ~** ballon-sonde *m*; *see* **barrage** *etc*. b (*toy*) ballon *m*. c (*for brandy: also* **~ glass**) verre *m* ballon *inv*; (*Chem: also* **~ flask**) ballon *m*. d (*in drawings, comics: for speech etc*) bulle *f*. 2 vi a **to go ~ing** faire une (*or* des) ascension(s) en ballon. b (*swell out*) gonfler, être ballonné. 3 comp ▸**balloon tyre** pneu *m* ballon.

balloonist [bəˈluːnɪst] n aéronaute *mf*.

ballot [ˈbælət] 1 n a (*Pol etc*) (*paper*) bulletin *m* de vote; (*method of voting*) scrutin *m*; (*round of voting*) (tour *m* de) scrutin. **to vote by ~** voter par scrutin; **first/second ~** premier/second tour de scrutin; **to take a ~** procéder à un scrutin *or* à un vote. b (*drawing of lots*) tirage *m* au sort. 2 vi a (*Pol etc*) voter au scrutin secret. b (*draw lots*) tirer au sort. **to ~ for a place** tirer au sort pour avoir une place. 3 comp ▸**ballot box** urne *f* (électorale); (*US Pol*) **ballot-box stuffing** fraude *f* électorale ▸**ballot paper** bulletin *m* de vote ▸**ballot rigging** (*Brit*) fraude *f* électorale.

balloting [ˈbælətɪŋ] n (*US Pol*) scrutin *m*.

bally*† [ˈbælɪ] adj (*before noun*) (*Brit*) sacré*, satané.

ballyhoo* [ˌbælɪˈhuː] n (*pej*) (*publicity*) battage* *m*, bourrage *m* de crâne*; (*nonsense*) balivernes *fpl*.

balm [bɑːm] n a (*lit, fig*) baume *m*. b (*Bot*) mélisse *f* officinale; (*lemon ~*) citronnelle *f*.

balmy [ˈbɑːmɪ] adj a (*liter*) (*fragrant*) embaumé, parfumé; (*mild*) doux (*f* douce), adoucissant. b (*Bot*) balsamique. c (*Brit* *†) timbré*, maboul‡.

baloney* [bəˈləʊnɪ] n (*NonC*) idiotie(s) *f(pl)*, balivernes *fpl*.

balsa [ˈbɔːlsə] n (*also* **~ wood**) balsa *m*.

balsam [ˈbɔːlsəm] n a (*substance*) baume *m*. **~ fir** sapin *m* baumier. b (*plant*) balsamine *f*. c (*Chem*) oléorésine *f*.

Baltic [ˈbɔːltɪk] 1 n: **the ~ (Sea)** la (mer) Baltique. 2 adj *trade, port* de la Baltique. **the ~ States** les pays *mpl* baltes.

baluster [ˈbæləstəʳ] n balustre *m*. **~s** = **bannisters**.

balustrade [ˌbæləsˈtreɪd] n balustrade *f*.

bamboo [bæmˈbuː] 1 n bambou *m*. 2 comp *chair, fence* de *or* en bambou ▸**Bamboo Curtain** (*Pol*) rideau *m* de bambou ▸**bamboo shoots** pousses *fpl* de bambou

bamboozle* [bæmˈbuːzl] vt a (*deceive*) avoir*, mettre dedans*, embobiner*. **he was ~d into writing the letter** en l'embobinant on est parvenu à lui faire écrire la lettre. b (*perplex*) déboussoler*. **she was quite ~d** elle ne savait plus où elle en était, elle était complètement perdue *or* déboussolée*.

ban [bæn] 1 n interdit *m*; (*Comm*) embargo *m*. **to put a ~ on sth/sb's doing** interdire qch/à qn de faire. 2 vt (*gen*) interdire (*sth* qch; *sb from doing* à qn de faire); (*exclude*) *person* exclure (*from* de); (*South Africa*) *person* proscrire. **B~ the Bomb Campaign** campagne *f* contre la bombe atomique.

banal [bəˈnɑːl] adj banal, ordinaire.

banality [bəˈnælɪtɪ] n banalité *f*.

banana [bəˈnɑːnə] 1 n (*fruit*) banane *f*; (*tree*) bananier *m*. 2 comp ▸**banana-boat** bananier *m* (*cargo*) ▸**banana republic** (*pej*) république *f* bananière ▸**banana skin** peau *f* de banane. 3 adj: **to go ~s‡** devenir dingue*; (*get angry*) piquer une crise*.

band[1] [bænd] 1 n (*gen, Comm*) bande *f*; (*narrow*) bandelette *f*; *[barrel]* cercle *m*; *[metal wheel]* bandage *m*; (*leather*) lanière *f*; *[cigar]* bague *f*; *[hat]* ruban *m*; (*Rad*) bande; (*magnetic tape*) bande (magnétique); *[gramophone record]* plage *f*; (*Tech*) bande *or* courroie *f* de transmission; (*Educ*) tranche *f*. (*Opt*) **~s of the spectrum** bandes du spectre; **metal ~** bande métallique; **elastic** *or* **rubber ~** élastique *m*; *[figures, prices etc]* **to vary within a narrow ~** varier à l'intérieur d'une fourchette étroite; *see* **frequency, waist, wave** *etc*. 2 comp ▸**band-saw** (*Tech*) scie *f* à ruban ▸**bandwidth** (*Comput*) largeur *f* de bande.

band[2] [bænd] 1 n a (*group*) bande *f*, troupe *f*. b (*Mus*) orchestre *m*; (*Mil etc*) clique *f*, fanfare *f*, musique *f*. **members of the ~** musiciens *mpl*; *see* **brass, one-man** *etc*. 2 comp ▸**bandmaster** chef *m* d'orchestre, (*Mil etc*) chef de musique *or* de fanfare ▸**bandsman** musicien *m* ▸**bandstand** kiosque *m* (à musique) ▸**bandwagon**: (*fig*) **to jump** *or* **climb on the bandwagon** suivre le mouvement, prendre le train en marche*

▸**band together** vi se grouper; (*form a gang*) former une bande.

bandage [ˈbændɪdʒ] 1 n (*for wound*) bande *f*; (*Med: prepared dressing*) bandage *m*, pansement *m*; *[blindfolding]* bandeau *m*. **head swathed in ~s** tête enveloppée de pansements *or* de bandages; *see* **crêpe**. 2 vt (*also* **~ up**) *broken limb* bander; *wound* mettre un pansement *or* un bandage sur; *person* mettre un pansement *or* un bandage à.

Band-Aid [ˈbændeɪd] n ® pansement *m* adhésif; (*US fig:* *) *measures* de fortune. **a ~ approach** une méthode qui tient du rafistolage.

bandan(n)a [bænˈdænə] n foulard *m* (*à pois*).

B & B [ˌbiːənd'biː] n (*Brit*) (**abbr of bed and breakfast**) *see* **bed**.

bandbox [ˈbænd̩bɒks] n (*Brit*) carton *m* à chapeau(x). (*fig*) **to look as if you had just stepped out of a ~** avoir l'air de sortir d'une boîte.

bandeau [ˈbændəʊ] n, pl **bandeaux** [ˈbændəʊz] bandeau *m*.

banderol(e) [ˈbændərəl] n (*Archit, Her, Naut*) banderole *f*.

banding [ˈbændɪŋ] n (*Brit Scol*) répartition *f* en classes de niveaux (*dans le primaire*).

bandit [ˈbændɪt] n (*lit, fig*) bandit *m*; *see* **one**.

banditry [ˈbændɪtrɪ] n (*NonC*) banditisme *m*.

bandolier [ˌbændəˈlɪəʳ] n cartouchière *f*.

bandy[1] [ˈbændɪ] vt *ball, reproaches* se renvoyer; *jokes* échanger. **to ~**

blows (with sb) échanger des coups (avec qn); **to ~ words** discuter, avoir des mots* (avec qn).

►**bandy about** vt sep *story, report* faire circuler. **to bandy sb's name about** parler de qn; **to have one's name bandied about** faire parler de soi.

bandy[2] [ˈbændɪ] adj **a** *leg* arqué, bancal. **b** (*also* **~-legged**) *person* bancal; *horse* arqué. **to be ~-legged** avoir les jambes arquées.

bane [beɪn] n **a** fléau *m*, peste *f*. **he's/it's the ~ of my life*** il/cela m'empoisonne la vie, il est/c'est le fléau de mon existence. **b** (*poison*) poison *m*.

baneful [ˈbeɪnfʊl] adj funeste, fatal; *poison* mortel.

banefully [ˈbeɪnfəlɪ] adv funestement.

bang[1] [bæŋ] **1** n **a** (*noise*) *[gun, explosives]* détonation *f*, fracas *m*; (*Aviat*) bang *m* (supersonique); *[door]* claquement *m*. **the door closed with a ~** la porte a claqué; **to go off with a ~** *[fireworks]* détoner, éclater; (‡: *succeed*) être une réussite sensationnelle *or* du tonnerre*.
b (*blow*) coup *m* (violent).
2 adv (*) **to go ~** éclater; **~ in the middle** au beau milieu, en plein milieu; **~ against the wall** tout contre le mur; **I ran ~ into the worst traffic** je suis tombé en plein dans le pire embouteillage; **he came ~ up against fierce opposition** il s'est brusquement trouvé face à une opposition farouche; (*Brit*) **to hit the target ~ on** frapper en plein dans la cible *or* le mille; (*Brit*) **his answer was ~ on*** sa réponse est tombée pile; (*Brit*) **she came ~ on time*** elle est arrivée à l'heure pile; **~ went a £10 note!*** et pan, voilà un billet de 10 livres de parti!*
3 excl pan!, vlan!, boum!
4 vt **a** frapper violemment. **to ~ one's fist on the table** taper du poing sur la table, frapper la table du poing; **to ~ one's head against** *or* **on sth** se cogner la tête contre *or* à qch; (*fig*) **you're ~ing your head against a brick wall when you argue with him*** autant cracher en l'air* que d'essayer de discuter avec lui; **to ~ the door** (faire) claquer la porte; **he ~ed the window shut** il a claqué la fenêtre.
b (**‡: *have sex with*) *woman* baiser**‡.
5 vi **a** *[door]* claquer, (*repeatedly*) battre; *[fireworks]* éclater; *[gun]* détoner.
b **to ~ on** *or* **at the door** donner de grands coups dans la porte; **to ~ on the table** taper du poing sur la table.

►**bang about***, **bang around*** **1** vi faire du bruit *or* du potin*. **2** vt sep *books, boxes, chairs* cogner les uns contre les autres.

►**bang away** vi *[guns]* tonner; *[person]* (*keep firing*) tirer sans arrêt (*at* sur); *[workman etc]* faire du vacarme. **to bang away at** taper sans arrêt sur.

►**bang down** vt sep poser *or* jeter brusquement. **to bang down the lid** rabattre violemment le couvercle; (*Telec*) **to bang down the receiver** raccrocher brutalement.

►**bang into** vt fus **a** (*collide with*) se cogner contre, heurter. **the car banged into a tree** la voiture a heurté un arbre *or* est rentrée* dans un arbre. **b** (‡: *meet*) tomber sur, se trouver nez à nez avec.

►**bang out** vt sep *tune etc* taper.

►**bang to** vi *[door etc]* se fermer en claquant.

►**bang together** vt sep *objects* cogner l'un(e) contre l'autre. **I could have banged their heads together!*** j'en aurais pris un pour taper sur l'autre!

►**bang up against** vt fus = **bang into**.

bang[2] [bæŋ] n *[hair]* (*also US* **bangs**) frange *f* (droite).

banger [ˈbæŋəʳ] n (*Brit*) **a** (*) (*sausage*) saucisse *f*. **~s and mash** saucisses à la purée. **b** (*) (*old car*) (vieux) tacot* *m*, (vieille) guimbarde *f*. **c** (*firework*) pétard *m*.

Bangkok [bæŋˈkɒk] n Bangkok.

Bangladesh [ˌbæŋgləˈdeʃ] n Bangladesh *m*.

Bangladeshi [ˌbæŋgləˈdeʃɪ] **1** n habitant(e) *m(f)* *or* natif *m* (*f* native) du Bangladesh. **2** adj du Bangladesh.

bangle [ˈbæŋgl] n *[arm, ankle]* bracelet *m*, (*rigid*) jonc *m*.

bang-up‡ [ˈbæŋʌp] adj (*US*) formidable, impec*.

banish [ˈbænɪʃ] vt *person* exiler (*from* de, *to* en, à), bannir (*from* de); *cares, fear* bannir, chasser.

banishment [ˈbænɪʃmənt] n bannissement *m*, exil *m*.

banister [ˈbænɪstəʳ] n = **bannister**.

banjax‡ [ˈbændʒæks] vt (*US*) assommer.

banjo [ˈbændʒəʊ] n, pl **~s** *or* **~es** banjo *m*.

bank[1] [bæŋk] **1** n **a** (*mound: of earth, snow, flowers*) talus *m*; (*Rail: embankment*) remblai *m*; (*on road, racetrack*) bord relevé; (*in horseracing*) banquette *f* irlandaise; (*Min: coal face*) front *m* de taille; (*pithead*) carreau *m*; *[sand, sea, river]* banc *m*. **a ~ of clouds** un amoncellement de nuages.
b (*edge*) *[river, lake]* bord *m*, rive *f*; (*above water level*) berge *f*; *[canal]* bord, berge. *[river, lake]* **the ~s** le rivage; *[Paris]* **the left/right ~** la Rive gauche/droite.
c (*Aviat*) virage *m* incliné *or* sur l'aile.
2 vt **a** (*also* **~ up**) *road* relever (*dans un virage*); *river* endiguer; *earth* amonceler. **to ~ the fire** couvrir le feu.
b **to ~ an aircraft** faire faire à un avion un virage sur l'aile.
3 vi **a** *[snow, clouds etc]* s'entasser, s'accumuler, s'amonceler.
b *[pilot, aircraft]* virer (sur l'aile).

bank[2] [bæŋk] **1** n **a** (*institution*) banque *f*; (*office*) agence *f* (bancaire), (bureau *m* de) banque. **~ of issue** banque *f* d'émission; **the B~ of France** la Banque de France; **the B~ of England** la Banque d'Angleterre; (*fig*) **it is as safe as the B~ of England** ça ne court aucun risque, c'est de tout repos, c'est de l'or en barre; *see* **saving**.
b (*Betting*) banque *f*. **to break the ~** faire sauter la banque.
c (*Med*) banque *f*; *see* **blood, eye** *etc*.
2 comp *cheque, credit, employee, staff* bancaire ►**bank acceptance** acceptation *f* bancaire ►**bank account** compte *m* en banque, compte bancaire ►**bank balance** soldes *mpl* bancaires ►**bank bill** (*US*) billet *m* de banque; (*Brit*) effet *m* bancaire ►**bank-book** livret *m* *or* carnet *m* de banque ►**bank card** carte *f* d'identité bancaire ►**bank charges** (*Brit*) frais *mpl* bancaires ►**bank clerk** (*Brit*) employé(e) *m(f)* de banque ►**bank draft** traite *f* bancaire ►**Bank Giro** (*Brit*) (paiement *m* par) virement *m* bancaire ►**bank holiday** (*Brit*) jour férié ►**bank loan** crédit *m* bancaire ►**bank manager** directeur *m* d'agence (bancaire); **my bank manager** le directeur de l'agence où j'ai mon compte (bancaire); (*hum*) **I'll have to speak to my bank manager** il faudra que j'en parle à mon banquier ►**banknote** (*Brit*) billet *m* de banque ►**bank rate** taux *m* d'escompte ►**bankroll*** (*US*) n fonds *mpl*, finances *fpl* ◊ vt financer ►**bank statement** relevé *m* de compte ►**bank transfer**: **by bank transfer** par virement *m* bancaire.
3 vt *money* mettre *or* déposer en banque; (*Med*) *blood* entreposer, conserver.
4 vi: **to ~ with Lloyds** avoir un compte à la Lloyds; **where do you ~?** quelle est votre banque?

►**bank on** vt fus (*fig*) compter sur. **you mustn't** *or* **I wouldn't bank on it** il ne faut pas compter là-dessus.

bank[3] [bæŋk] **1** n **a** (*row, tier*) *[organ]* clavier *m*; *[type-writer]* rang *m*; (*Elec*) *[switches]* rangée *f*. **~ of oars** rangée d'avirons. **b** (*rowers' bench*) banc *m* (de rameurs). **2** vt (*Sport*) **double/single ~ed rowing** nage *f* à couple/en pointe.

►**bank up** vt sep **a** (*arrange in tiers*) étager, disposer par étages. **b** *see* **bank**[1] **2a**.

bankable [ˈbæŋkəbl] adj bancable, négociable en banque.

banker [ˈbæŋkəʳ] n (*Betting, Fin*) banquier *m*. **~'s card** carte *f* d'identité bancaire; **~'s draft** traite *f* bancaire; (*Brit*) **~'s order** prélèvement *m* bancaire (*pour paiements réguliers*); **~'s reference** références *fpl* bancaires.

banking[1] [ˈbæŋkɪŋ] n (*Aviat*) virage *m* sur l'aile.

banking[2] [ˈbæŋkɪŋ] **1** n (*Fin*) (*transaction*) opérations *fpl* de banque *or* bancaires; (*profession*) profession *f* de banquier, la banque. **to study ~** faire des études bancaires. **2** comp ►**banking account** compte *m* en banque, compte bancaire ►**banking charges** frais *mpl* bancaires ►**banking hours** heures *fpl* d'ouverture des banques ►**banking house** banque *f*, établissement *m* bancaire; **the big banking houses** la haute banque, les grandes banques ►**banking industry** secteur *m* bancaire

bankrupt [ˈbæŋkrʌpt] **1** n (*Jur*) failli(e) *m(f)*; (* *fig: penniless person*) fauché(e)* *m(f)*. **~'s certificate** concordat *m*; **~'s estate** actif *m* de la faillite. **2** adj (*Jur*) failli; (* *fig: penniless*) fauché*. (*fig*) **~ of ideas** *etc* dépourvu *or* dénué d'idées *etc*; (*fig*) **spiritually/morally** *etc* **~** dépourvu *or* dénué de spiritualité/de moralité; *[person, business]* **to go ~** faire faillite; *[person]* **to be ~** être en faillite; **to be declared ~** être déclaré *or* mis en faillite. **3** vt *person* mettre en faillite; (*: *fig*) ruiner.

bankruptcy [ˈbæŋkrəptsɪ] n (*Jur*) faillite *f*; (* *fig: pennilessness*) ruine *f*. (*Brit*) **B~ Court** ≃ tribunal *m* de commerce; **~ estate** masse *f* *or* actif *m* de la faillite; **~ proceedings** procédure *f* de faillite; (*fig*) **spiritual/moral** *etc* **~**manque *m* de spiritualité/de moralité *etc*.

banner [ˈbænəʳ] n bannière *f*, étendard *m*; (*Rel, fig*) bannière. (*Press*) **~ headlines** gros titres; **in ~ headlines** en gros titres, sur cinq colonnes à la une.

banning [ˈbænɪŋ] n (*see* **ban 2**) interdiction *f*, exclusion *f*, proscription *f*.

bannister [ˈbænɪstəʳ] n rampe *f* (d'escalier). **to slide down the ~(s)** descendre sur la rampe.

banns [bænz] npl bans *mpl* (*de mariage*).

banquet [ˈbæŋkwɪt] **1** n (*ceremonial dinner*) banquet *m*; (*lavish meal*) festin *m*. **2** vt (*ceremoniously*) offrir un banquet à; (*more lavishly*) offrir un festin à, régaler. **3** vi faire un banquet, festoyer. **4** comp ►**banquet(ing) hall** salle *f* de(s) banquet(s).

banshee [bænˈʃiː] n (*Ir Myth*) fée *f* (*dont les cris présagent la mort*).

bantam [ˈbæntəm] n coq nain, poule naine (*de Bantam*). (*Boxing*) **~-weight** poids *m* coq.

banter [ˈbæntəʳ] **1** n badinage *m*, plaisanterie *f*. **2** vi badiner, plaisanter.

bantering [ˈbæntərɪŋ] adj plaisantin, badin.

Bantu [ˈbæntuː] **1** adj bantou. **2** n **a** (*Ling*) Bantou *m*. **b** (*people*) **~(s)** Bantous *mpl*.

banyan [ˈbænɪən] n banian *m*.

B.A.O.R. [ˌbiːeɪəʊˈɑːʳ] n (abbr of **British Army of the Rhine**) *troupes britanniques stationnées en RFA*.

baptism [ˈbæptɪzəm] n baptême *m*. (*fig*) **~ of fire** baptême du feu.

baptismal [bæp'tɪzməl] adj de baptême, baptismal. ~ **font** fonts baptismaux; ~ **name** nom *m* de baptême; ~ **vows** vœux *mpl* du baptême.

baptist ['bæptɪst] 1 n a baptiste *m*. **(Saint) John the B~** saint Jean-Baptiste. b (*Rel*) **B~** baptiste *mf*; **the B~ Church** l'Église *f* baptiste. 2 adj (*Rel*) **B~** baptiste.

baptize [bæp'taɪz] vt (*Rel, fig*) baptiser.

bar¹ [bɑːʳ] 1 n a (*slab*) *[metal]* barre *f*; *[wood]* planche *f*; *[gold]* lingot *m*; *[chocolate]* tablette *f*. ~ **of soap** savonnette *f*, pain *m* de savon; ~ **of gold** lingot (d'or).

b (*rod*) *[window, cage]* barreau *m*; *[grate]* barre *f*; *[door]* barre, bâcle *f*; (*Sport*) barre; *[ski-lift]* perche *f*. **to be/put sb behind (prison) ~s** être/mettre qn sous les verrous; (*Aut*) **anti-roll** ~ barre *f* anti-roulis; *see* **parallel** *etc*.

c *[river, harbour]* barre *f*.

d (*fig: obstacle*) obstacle *m*. **to be a ~ to progress** *etc* faire obstacle au progrès *etc*; *see* **colour**.

e *[light]* raie *f*; *[colour]* bande *f*.

f (*NonC: Jur*) (*profession*) barreau *m*; (*in court*) barre *f*. (*Brit*) **to call to the ~**, (*US*) **to admit to the ~** inscrire au barreau; (*Brit*) **to be called** *or* (*US*) **admitted to the ~** s'inscrire au barreau; **to read for the ~** préparer le barreau; **the prisoner at the ~** l'accusé(e) *m(f)*.

g (*public house*) café *m*, bar *m*, bistro(t)* *m*; *[hotel, theatre]* bar; *[station]* café, bar; (*at open-air shows etc*) buvette *f*; *see* **coffee, public**.

h (*counter*) (*for drinks*) comptoir *m*. **to have a drink at the ~** prendre un verre au comptoir *or* sur le zinc*; (*Comm*) **stocking/hat ~** rayon *m* des bas/des chapeaux; **heel ~** talons-minute *m*.

i (*Mus*) mesure *f*; (*also* ~ **line**) barre *f* de mesure. **the opening ~s** les premières mesures; *see* **double**.

j (*Brit Mil*) barrette *f* (*portée sur le ruban d'une médaille*), ≃ palme *f*; (*US Mil*) galon *m*.

k (*Her*) burelle *f*. ~ **sinister** barre *f* de bâtardise.

l (*Met*) bar *m*.

2 comp ▸**barbell** (*US Sport*) barre *f* à disques ▸**bar chart** = **bar graph** ▸**bar code** (*Comm*) code *m* barres; **bar-code reader** lecteur *m* de code barres ▸**bar-coded** avec code barres ▸**barfly*** (*US*) pilier *m* de bistro ▸**bar girl*** (*US*) entraîneuse *f* de bar ▸**bar graph** graphique *m* en barres *or* en tuyaux d'orgue ▸**barmaid** serveuse *f* (*de bar*), barmaid *f* ▸**barkeeper** (*US*), **barman** (*Brit*) barman *m* ▸**barroom** (*US*) salle *f* de bar ▸**bartender** (*US*) barman *m*.

3 vt a (*obstruct*) *road* barrer. **to ~ sb's way** *or* **path** barrer le passage à qn, couper la route à qn; **to ~ the way to progress** faire obstacle au progrès.

b (*put bars on*) *window* munir de barreaux. **to ~ the door** mettre la barre à la porte; (*lit, fig*) **to ~ the door against sb** barrer la porte à qn.

c (*exclude, prohibit*) *person* exclure (*from* de); *action, thing* défendre. **to ~ sb from doing** interdire à qn de faire; **to ~ sb from a career** barrer une carrière à qn; **she ~s smoking in her house** elle défend qu'on fume (*subj*) chez elle; (*Jur*) *[contract provisions]* **to be ~red** se prescrire; *see* **hold**.

d (*stripe*) rayer, barrer.

bar² [bɑːʳ] prep excepté, sauf, à l'exception de, à part. ~ **accidents** sauf accident, à moins d'accident(s), sauf imprévu; ~ **none** sans exception; ~ **one** sauf un(e); *see also* **shouting**.

Barabbas [bə'ræbəs] n Barabbas *m*.

barb¹ [bɑːb] 1 n a *[fish hook]* barbillon *m*; *[arrow]* barbelure *f*; *[feather]* barbe *f*; (*fig*) *[wit etc]* trait *m*. **the ~s of criticism** les traits acérés de la critique; ~ **wire** = **barbed wire**; *see* **barbed 2**. b (*Dress*) barbette *f*. 2 vt *arrow* garnir de barbelures, barbeler; *fish hook* garnir de barbillons.

barb² [bɑːb] n (*horse*) (cheval *m*) barbe *m*.

Barbadian [bɑː'beɪdɪən] 1 n Barbadien(ne) *m(f)*. 2 adj barbadien.

Barbados [bɑː'beɪdɒs] n Barbade *f*. **in ~** à la Barbade.

barbarian [bɑː'bɛərɪən] adj, n (*Hist, fig*) barbare *(mf)*.

barbaric [bɑː'bærɪk] adj (*Hist, fig*) barbare, de barbare.

barbarism ['bɑːbərɪzəm] n a (*NonC*) barbarie *f*. b (*Ling*) barbarisme *m*.

barbarity [bɑː'bærɪtɪ] n barbarie *f*, cruauté *f*, inhumanité *f*. **the barbarities of modern warfare** la barbarie *or* les atrocités *fpl* de la guerre moderne.

barbarize ['bɑːbəraɪz] vt a *people* ramener à l'état barbare. b *language* corrompre.

Barbarossa [ˌbɑːbə'rɒsə] n Barberousse *m*.

barbarous ['bɑːbərəs] adj (*Hist, Ling, fig*) barbare.

barbarously ['bɑːbərəslɪ] adv cruellement, inhumainement.

Barbary ['bɑːbərɪ] 1 n Barbarie *f*, États *mpl* barbaresques. 2 comp ▸**Barbary ape** magot *m* ▸**Barbary Coast** Barbarie *f* ▸**Barbary duck** canard *m* de Barbarie ▸**Barbary horse** (cheval *m*) barbe *m*.

barbecue ['bɑːbɪkjuː] (vb: prp **barbecuing**) 1 n (*grid, occasion*) barbecue *m*. **to have a ~** faire *or* organiser un barbecue. 2 vt *steak etc* griller au charbon de bois; *animal* rôtir tout entier. 3 comp ▸**barbecue sauce** sauce *f* barbecue.

barbed [bɑːbd] 1 adj *arrow* barbelé; (*fig*) *words, wit* acéré. 2 comp ▸**barbed wire** fil *m* de fer barbelé; **barbed-wire entanglements** (réseau *m* de) barbelés *mpl*; **barbed-wire fence** haie *f* barbelée, haie de barbelés.

barbel ['bɑːbəl] n (*fish*) barbeau *m*, (*smaller*) barbillon *m*; (*filament*) barbillon.

barber ['bɑːbəʳ] 1 n coiffeur *m* (pour hommes). **~'s pole** enseigne *f* de coiffeur. 2 comp ▸**barbershop** (*US*) (*lit*) boutique *f* de coiffeur (pour hommes); (*Mus*) mélodies *fpl* sentimentales (*chantées en harmonie étroite*); **barbershop quartet** *groupe de 4 hommes chantant en harmonie étroite*.

barbican ['bɑːbɪkən] n barbacane *f*.

Barbie ['bɑːbɪ] n: ~ **doll** ® poupée *f* Barbie ®.

barbitone ['bɑːbɪtəʊn] n véronal *m*.

barbiturate [bɑː'bɪtjʊrɪt] n barbiturique *m*. ~ **poisoning** le barbiturisme.

barbituric [ˌbɑːbɪ'tjʊərɪk] adj barbiturique.

barbs* [bɑːbz] npl (*US*) barbis* *fpl*, barbituriques *mpl*.

barcarol(l)e [ˌbɑːkə'rəʊl] n barcarolle *f*.

Barcelona [ˌbɑːsɪ'ləʊnə] n Barcelone.

bard¹ [bɑːd] n (*minstrel*) (*esp Celtic*) barde *m*; *[Ancient Greece]* aède *m*; (*Poetry, also hum: poet*) poète *m*. **the B~ of Avon** le chantre d'Avon (*Shakespeare*).

bard² [bɑːd] (*Culin*) 1 n barde *f* (de lard). 2 vt barder.

bardic ['bɑːdɪk] adj (*esp Celtic*) *poetry etc* du barde, des bardes.

bare [bɛəʳ] 1 adj a (*naked, uncovered*) *person, skin, sword, floor etc* nu; *hill, summit* pelé; *countryside, tree* dénudé, dépouillé; (*Elec*) *wire* dénudé, à nu. ~ **to the waist** nu jusqu'à la ceinture; **in his ~ skin** tout nu; **he killed the wolf with his ~ hands** il a tué le loup à mains nues; (*Boxing*) **to fight with ~ hands** boxer à main nue; ~ **patch** place dénudée *or* pelée; **the dog had a few ~ patches on his back** le chien avait la peau du dos pelée par endroits; **with his head ~** nu-tête *inv*; **to sleep on ~ boards** coucher sur la dure; **to lay ~ one's heart** mettre son cœur à nu; **to lay ~ a secret** révéler *or* dévoiler un secret; (*fig*) **the ~ bones** l'essentiel *m*, les grandes lignes *fpl*, les lignes *fpl* essentielles; (*fig*) **to strip sth down to the ~ bones** réduire qch à l'essentiel *or* à sa plus simple expression (*see also* **3**); (*Cards*) **ace/king ~** as/roi sec.

b (*empty, unadorned*) *garden* dépouillé de sa végétation; *wall* nu; *style* dépouillé. **room ~ of furniture** pièce *f* vide; ~ **cupboard** placard *m* vide *or* dégarni; ~ **statement of facts** simple énoncé *m* des faits.

c (*just enough*) **the ~ necessities (of life)** le strict nécessaire; **to earn a ~ living** gagner tout juste *or* à peine de quoi vivre; ~ **majority** faible majorité *f*; **the ~ minimum** le plus strict minimum; **it's a ~ possibility** c'est tout juste possible; **a ~ thank you** un merci tout sec.

2 vt mettre à nu, découvrir; *sword* dégainer, mettre à nu, tirer du fourreau; (*Elec*) *wire* dénuder, mettre à nu. *[person, animal]* **to ~ one's teeth** montrer les dents (*at* à); **he ~d his teeth in a smile** il a grimacé un sourire; **to ~ one's head** se découvrir (la tête); **to ~ one's soul (to sb)** mettre son cœur à nu (à qn).

3 comp ▸**bareback** adv à nu, à cru; **bareback rider** cavalier *m*, -ière *f* qui monte à cru ▸**bare-bones** (*US*) réduit à l'essentiel *or* à sa plus simple expression ▸**barefaced** *lie, liar* éhonté, impudent, effronté; **it is barefaced robbery** c'est un *or* du vol manifeste ▸**barefoot(ed)** adv nu-pieds, (les) pieds nus ◊ adj aux pieds nus ▸**bareheaded** adv nu-tête *inv*, (la) tête nue ◊ adj nu-tête *inv*; *woman* en cheveux ▸**barelegged** adv nu-jambes, (les) jambes nues ◊ adj aux jambes nues ▸**bare owner** nu-propriétaire *mf* ▸**bare ownership** *or* **property** nue-propriété *f*.

barely ['bɛəlɪ] adv a (*scarcely*) à peine, tout juste. **he can ~ read** c'est tout juste *or* à peine s'il sait lire, il sait tout juste *or* à peine lire. b **a ~ furnished room** une pièce pauvrement meublée. c (*plainly*) sans détails. **to state a fact ~** donner un fait sans détails *or* tout sec.

bareness ['bɛənɪs] n *[person]* nudité *f*; *[room]* dénuement *m*; *[furniture]* pauvreté *f*; *[style]* (*poverty*) sécheresse *f*, pauvreté; (*simplicity*) dépouillé *m*.

Barents Sea ['bærənts'siː] n mer *f* de Barents.

barf* [bɑːf] vi (*US*) dégueuler*, vomir.

bargain ['bɑːgɪn] 1 n a (*transaction*) marché *m*, affaire *f*. **to make** *or* **strike** *or* **drive a ~** conclure un marché (*with* avec); **it's a ~!*** c'est convenu! *or* entendu!; **a bad/good ~** une mauvaise/bonne affaire, une affaire désavantageuse/avantageuse; **a ~'s a ~** marché conclu reste conclu; (*fig*) **into the ~** par-dessus le marché, par surcroît, en plus; *see* **best, drive** *etc*.

b (*good buy*) occasion *f*. **it's a (real) ~!** c'est une véritable occasion! *or* affaire!

2 comp ▸**bargain basement** coin *m* des (bonnes) affaires ▸**bargain-hunter** chercheur *m*, -euse *f* d'occasions ▸**bargain-hunting** chasse *f* aux (bonnes) occasions ▸**bargain offer** (*Comm*) offre exceptionnelle; **this week's bargain offer** la promotion de la semaine ▸**bargain price** prix avantageux ▸**bargain sale** soldes *mpl*.

3 vi a (*haggle*) **to ~ with sb** marchander avec qn; **to ~ over an article** marchander un article.

b (*negotiate*) négocier, entrer en négociation (*with* avec). **to ~ with sb for sth** négocier qch avec qn.

c (*fig*) **to ~ for sth** s'attendre à qch; **I did not ~ for that** je ne m'attendais pas à cela; **I got more than I ~ed for** je ne m'attendais pas à un coup pareil, j'ai eu du fil à retordre; **to ~ on sth** compter sur qch.

bargaining ['bɑːgənɪŋ] n marchandage *m*. **that gives us more ~ power** ceci nous donne une position de force *or* plus d'atouts dans les négociations; *see* **collective**.

barge [bɑːdʒ] 1 n (*on river, canal*) chaland *m*; (*large*) péniche *f*; (*with sail*) barge *f*. **the admiral's ~** la vedette de l'amiral; **motor ~** chaland *m* automoteur, péniche *f* automotrice; **state ~** barque *f* de cérémonie. 2 comp ►**bargeman** batelier *m*, marinier *m* ►**barge pole** gaffe *f*; (*Brit*) **I wouldn't touch it with a barge pole*** (*revolting*) je n'y toucherais pas avec des pincettes; (*risky*) je ne m'y frotterais pas. 3 vi: **to ~ into a room** faire irruption dans une pièce, entrer sans façons dans une pièce; **he ~d through the crowd** il bousculait les gens pour passer.

►**barge about, barge around** vi aller et venir comme un troupeau d'éléphants*.

►**barge in** vi (*enter*) faire irruption; (*interrupt*) interrompre la conversation; (*interfere*) se mêler de ce qui ne vous regarde pas.

►**barge into** vt fus (*knock against*) *person* rentrer dans*; *thing* donner *or* se cogner contre; (*interfere in*) *discussion, affair* intervenir mal à propos dans, se mêler de, mettre son nez dans.

►**barge through** vi traverser comme un ouragan.

bargee [bɑː'dʒiː] n (*Brit*) batelier *m*, marinier *m*. **to swear like a ~** jurer comme un charretier.

baritone ['bærɪtəʊn] 1 n (*voice, singer, instrument*) baryton *m*. 2 comp *voice, part* de baryton.

barium ['bɛərɪəm] n baryum *m*. (*Med*) **~ enema** lavement *m* baryté; (*Med*) **~ meal** (bouillie *f* de) sulfate *m* de baryum.

bark¹ [bɑːk] 1 n [*tree*] écorce *f*. **to strip the ~ off a tree** écorcer un arbre. 2 vt *tree* écorcer. **to ~ one's shins** s'écorcher *or* s'égratigner les jambes.

bark² [bɑːk] 1 n [*dog*] aboiement *m*, aboi *m*; [*fox*] glapissement *m*; (**: cough*) toux *f* sèche. **the ~ of a gun** un coup de canon; **to let out a ~** (*lit*) aboyer, pousser un aboiement; (*cough*) tousser; **his ~ is worse than his bite** il fait plus de bruit que de mal, tous les chiens qui aboient ne mordent pas (*Prov*). 2 vi [*dog*] aboyer (*at* après); [*fox*] glapir; [*gun*] aboyer; (*speak sharply*) crier, vociférer, aboyer; (*cough*) tousser. **to ~ at sb** aboyer après qn; (*fig*) **to ~ up the wrong tree** faire fausse route, se tromper d'adresse.

►**bark out** vt sep *order* glapir.

bark³ [bɑːk] n (*liter*) barque *f*; (*Naut*) trois-mâts *m inv or* quatre-mâts *m inv* carré.

barker ['bɑːkəʳ] n [*fairground*] bonimenteur *m*, aboyeur† *m*.

barking ['bɑːkɪŋ] 1 n [*dog*] aboiement *m*; [*fox*] glapissement *m*. 2 adv (*Brit*) **~ mad*** complètement cinglé* *or* frappé‡.

barley ['bɑːlɪ] 1 n orge *f*. **pearl ~** orge *m* perlé (*note gender*); **Scotch ~** orge *m* mondé (*note gender*). 2 comp ►**barley beer** cervoise *f* ►**barleycorn** grain *m* d'orge ►**barley field** champ *m* d'orge ►**barley sugar** sucre *m* d'orge ►**barley water** (*esp Brit*) boisson orgée, orgeat *m* ►**barley wine** *sorte de bière très forte et sucrée*. 3 excl (*N Engl, Scot: in games*) pouce!

barm [bɑːm] n levure *f* (de bière).

bar mitzvah, Bar Mitzvah [bɑː'mɪtsvə] n bar-mitzva *f*.

barmy*† ['bɑːmɪ] adj (*Brit*) timbré*, maboul‡.

barn [bɑːn] 1 n a grange *f*. **it's a great ~ of a house*** c'est une énorme bâtisse. b (*US*) [*horses*] écurie *f*; [*cattle*] étable *f*. 2 comp ►**barn dance** soirée *f* de danse campagnarde *or* paysanne ►**barn dancing** danse campagnarde *or* paysanne ►**barn door: it's as big as a barn door** c'est gros comme une maison ►**barn owl** chouette-effraie *f*, chat-huant *m* ►**barnstorm** (*Theat*) jouer sur les tréteaux; (*US Pol*) faire une tournée électorale (dans les circonscriptions rurales) ►**barnstormer** (*Theat*) acteur ambulant; (*US Pol*) orateur *m* électoral ►**barnstorming** (*Theat*) ≃ tournée *f* théâtrale; (*US Pol*) tournée *f or* campagne *f* électorale ►**barnyard** basse-cour *f*; **barnyard fowls** volaille *f*.

barnacle ['bɑːnəkl] n a (*shellfish*) bernache *f*, anatife *m*; (*pej: person*) crampon* *m*; (*‡: old sailor*) vieux loup de mer* *m*. b (*Orn: also* **~ goose**) bernache (nonnette) *f*, bernacle *f*.

barney* ['bɑːnɪ] n (*Brit: quarrel*) prise *f* de bec*.

barogram ['bærəʊgræm] n barogramme *m*.

barograph ['bærəʊgrɑːf] n barographe *m*.

barometer [bə'rɒmɪtəʳ] n (*lit, fig*) baromètre *m*. **the ~ is showing set fair** le baromètre est au beau fixe; *see* **aneroid** *etc*.

barometric [ˌbærəʊ'metrɪk] adj barométrique.

baron ['bærən] n a baron *m*. (*fig*) **cattle ~** magnat *m or* gros industriel *m* du bétail; **drug(s) ~** baron de la drogue; **industrial ~** magnat de l'industrie, gros industriel. b **~ of beef** double aloyau *m* de bœuf.

baroness ['bærənɪs] n baronne *f*.

baronet ['bærənɪt] n baronnet *m*.

baronetcy ['bærənɪtsɪ] n dignité *f* de baronnet.

baronial [bə'rəʊnɪəl] adj (*lit, fig*) baronnial, de baron, seigneurial. **~ hall** demeure *f* seigneuriale.

barony ['bærənɪ] n baronnie *f*.

baroque [bə'rɒk] adj, n (*Archit, Art, Mus*) baroque (*m*).

barque† [bɑːk] n = **bark³**.

barrack¹ ['bærək] 1 n: **~s** (*often with sg vb*) (*Mil*) caserne *f*, quartier *m*; **cavalry ~** quartier de cavalerie; **in ~s** à la caserne, au quartier; (*Brit*) **it's a (great) ~(s) of a place*** c'est une (vraie) caserne*; *see* **confine, naval** *etc*. 2 comp ►**barrack life** vie *f* de caserne ►**barrack room** chambrée *f*; **barrack-room joke/language** plaisanterie *f*/propos *mpl* de caserne *or* de corps de garde; (*fig*) **to be a barrack-room lawyer** se promener toujours avec le code sous le bras ►**barracks bag** (*US*) sac *m* (*de soldat*) ►**barrack square** cour *f* (de caserne).

barrack² ['bærək] vt chahuter.

barracuda [ˌbærə'kjuːdə] n, pl **~** *or* **~s** barracuda *m*.

barrage ['bærɑːʒ] n a [*river*] barrage *m*. b (*Mil*) tir *m* de barrage; (*fig*) [*questions, reproaches*] pluie *f*; [*words*] flot *m*, déluge *m*. **~ balloon** ballon *m* de barrage *or* de D.C.A.

barratry ['bærətrɪ] n (*Maritime Insurance*) baraterie *f*.

barred [bɑːd] adj *window etc* muni de barreaux.

-barred [bɑːd] adj ending in comps: **five-barred gate** barrière *f* à cinq barreaux.

barrel ['bærəl] 1 n a (*cask*) [*wine*] tonneau *m*, barrique *f*, fût *m*; [*cider*] futaille *f*; [*beer*] tonneau; [*herring*] caque *f*; [*oil*] baril *m*; [*tar*] gonne *f*; (*small*) baril. (*fig*) **to have (got) sb over a ~*** tenir qn à sa merci; *see* **biscuit, scrape**.

b [*firearm*] canon *m*; [*fountain pen*] corps *m*; [*key*] canon; [*lock, clock*] barillet *m*. (*fig*) **to give sb both ~s*** lâcher ses deux coups sur qn*.

2 vt *wine etc* mettre en fût *etc*.

3 vi (*US **) foncer*, aller à toute pompe*.

4 comp ►**barrel-chested** au torse *m* puissant ►**barrel-house jazz** (*US*) jazz *m* de bastringue ►**barrel organ** orgue *m* de Barbarie ►**barrel-shaped** en forme de barrique *or* de tonneau; *person* gros comme une barrique ►**barrel vault** voûte *f* en berceau.

barren ['bærən] 1 adj *land* stérile, improductif; (*dry*) aride; *tree, plant, woman* stérile; (*fig*) (*lacking content*) stérile; (*lacking interest*) ingrat, aride; *discussion* stérile; *style* aride, sec (*f* sèche). **B~ Lands** *or* **Grounds** toundra canadienne. 2 n (*esp US: gen pl*) **~(s)** lande(s) *f(pl)*.

barrenness ['bærənnɪs] n (*see* **barren**) stérilité *f*; aridité *f*; sécheresse *f*.

barrette [bə'ret] n (*US*) barrette *f*.

barricade [ˌbærɪ'keɪd] 1 n barricade *f*; (*fig*) barrière *f*. 2 vt *street* barricader; (*also* **~ in**) *person* barricader. **to ~ o.s. (in)** se barricader.

barrier ['bærɪəʳ] n barrière *f*; (*Rail: also* **ticket ~**) portillon *m* (d'accès); (*fig*) obstacle *m* (*to* à). **~ cream** crème isolante *or* protectrice; **~ reef** barrière *f or* récif *m* de corail; **the Great B~ Reef** la Grande Barrière (de corail *or* d'Australie); *see* **sound¹** *etc*.

barring ['bɑːrɪŋ] prep excepté, sauf. **~ accidents** sauf accident, à moins d'accident(s); **~ the unforeseen** sauf imprévu.

barrio ['bærɪəʊ] n (*US*) quartier *m* latino-américain.

barrister ['bærɪstəʳ] n (*Brit: also* **~-at-law**) avocat *m*.

barrow¹ ['bærəʊ] 1 n (*also* **wheel~**) brouette *f*; (*also* **coster's ~**) voiture *f* des quatre saisons; (*Rail: also* **luggage ~**) diable *m*; (*also* **hand ~**) civière *f*, (*without wheels*) brancard *m*; (*Min*) wagonnet *m*. **to wheel sth in a ~** brouetter qch. 2 comp ►**barrow-boy** marchand *m* des quatre saisons.

barrow² ['bærəʊ] n (*Archeol*) tumulus *m*.

Bart [bɑːt] n (*Brit*) abbr of **baronet**.

barter ['bɑːtəʳ] 1 n échange *m*, troc *m*. 2 vt échanger, troquer (*for* contre). 3 vi faire un échange *or* un troc.

►**barter away** vt *rights, liberty* vendre (*for* pour); *one's honour* faire trafic de.

Bartholomew [bɑː'θɒləmjuː] n Barthélemy *m*. (*Hist*) **the Massacre of St ~** (le massacre de) la Saint-Barthélemy.

barytone ['bærɪtəʊn] n (*Mus*) baryton *m* (*instrument*).

basal ['beɪsl] adj (*lit, fig*) fondamental; (*Physiol*) basal.

basalt ['bæsɔːlt] n basalte *m*.

bascule ['bæskjuːl] n bascule *f*. **~ bridge** pont *m* à bascule.

base¹ [beɪs] 1 n a (*main ingredient*) base *f*; (*starting point*) base, point *m* de départ; (*Chem, Math, Ling*) base; (*lowest part*) base, partie inférieure; [*column*] base, pied *m*; [*building*] soubassement *m*; [*cartridge, electric bulb*] culot *m*; [*tree*] pied. (*Comput*) **~ 2/10** *etc* base 2/10 *etc*.

b (*Mil etc*) base *f*; *see* **air** *etc*.

c (*Baseball*) base *f*. (*US fig*) **he's way off ~*** il n'y est pas du tout; (*US fig*) **to touch ~ with sb*** prendre les nouvelles de qn (*au téléphone*); **we'll touch ~ this afternoon*** on se tient au courant *or* on s'appelle cet après-midi; **I'll touch ~ with you about the schedule*** je t'appellerai pour discuter le programme.

2 vt (*fig*) *reasoning, belief, opinion* baser, fonder (*on* sur). (*Mil etc*) **to be ~d in** *or* **on York** être basé à York; **the post will be ~d in** *or* **on London but will involve considerable travel** le poste sera centré sur Londres mais il exigera de nombreux déplacements; **I am ~d in** *or* **on Glasgow now** j'opère maintenant à partir de Glasgow; **the company is ~d in Glasgow** l'entreprise a son siège à Glasgow.

3 comp ►**baseball** base-ball *m* ►**baseboard** (*US Constr*) plinthe *f* ►**base camp** (*Climbing*) camp *m* de base ►**base coat** [*paint*] première couche ►**base form** (*Ling*) forme *f* de base ►**base lending rate** (*Fin*) taux *m* de base bancaire ►**base line** (*Baseball*) ligne *f* des bases; (*Surv*) base *f*; [*diagram*] ligne zéro; (*Tennis*) ligne de fond;

(*Art*) ligne de fuite; (*Fin*) **baseline costs** coûts *mpl* de base ►**baseman** (*Baseball*) gardien *m* de base ►**base period** (*Statistics*) période *f* de référence *or* de base ►**base rate** (*Fin*) = **base lending rate** ►**base year** (*Fin*) année *f* de référence.

base[2] [beɪs] **adj** a *action, motive, thoughts* bas (*f* basse), abject, indigne; *behaviour* ignoble; *ingratitude, mind* bas; *birth, descent* bas; (*before n*) *task* bas, servile; *coin* faux (*f* fausse). ~ **metal** métal vil. b (*US*) = **bass**[1] **2**.

-based [beɪst] **adj ending in comps: London-based** *firm* dont le centre d'opérations est Londres; *person* qui opère à partir de Londres; **oil-based economy** économie basée sur le pétrole; **sea-/land-based missile** missile *m* marin/terrestre.

Basel ['bɑːzəl] **n** Bâle.

baseless ['beɪslɪs] **adj** *accusation etc* sans fondement; *suspicion* sans fondement, injustifié.

basely ['beɪslɪ] **adv** bassement, vilement, lâchement.

basement ['beɪsmənt] **n** sous-sol *m*. **in the** ~ au sous-sol; ~ **flat** appartement *m* en sous-sol.

baseness ['beɪsnɪs] **n** (*see* **base**[2]) bassesse *f*, indignité *f*; ignominie *f*.

bases[1] ['beɪsiːz] **npl of basis**.

bases[2] ['beɪsɪz] **npl of base**[1].

bash* [bæʃ] 1 **n** a coup *m*, coup de poing. **to give sb a ~ on the nose** donner un coup de poing sur le nez de qn; **the car bumper has had a** ~ le pare-choc est cabossé *or* bosselé; **to have a ~ at sth/at doing*** s'essayer à qch/à faire; **I'll have a ~ (at it)*, I'll give it a ~*** je vais essayer un coup*; **have a ~!*** vas-y, essaie toujours! b (*party*) surboum* *f*. 2 **vt** frapper, cogner. (*lit, fig*) **to ~ one's head against a wall** se cogner la tête contre le mur; **to ~ sb on the head** assommer qn.

►**bash about*, bash around*** **vt sep** *person* (*hit*), flanquer* des coups à; (*ill-treat*) *person* maltraiter, rudoyer; *object* malmener.

►**bash in*** **vt sep** *door* enfoncer; *hat, car* cabosser, défoncer; *lid, cover* défoncer. **to bash sb's head in*** défoncer le crâne de qn*.

►**bash on*** **vi** continuer (*with sth* avec qch).

►**bash up*** **vt sep** *car* bousiller*; (*Brit*) *person* tabasser‡.

basher* ['bæʃəʳ] 1 **n** cogneur* *m*. 2 **n ending in comps: he's a queer-basher‡** il déblatère toujours contre les pédés‡.

bashful ['bæʃfʊl] **adj** (*shy*) timide, intimidé; (*modest*) pudique; (*shamefaced*) honteux.

bashfully ['bæʃfəlɪ] **adv** (*see* **bashful**) timidement, avec timidité; pudiquement; avec honte.

bashfulness ['bæʃfʊlnɪs] **n** (*see* **bashful**) timidité *f*; modestie *f*, pudeur *f*; honte *f*.

bashing‡ ['bæʃɪŋ] 1 **n** rossée* *f*, raclée* *f*. **to take a** ~ *[team, regiment]* prendre une raclée* *or* une dérouillée‡; *[car, carpet etc]* en prendre un (vieux *or* sacré) coup*. 2 **n ending in comps: union-bashing** dénigrement *m* systématique à l'encontre des syndicats; *see* **Paki, queer**.

BASIC, Basic ['beɪsɪk] **n** (*Comput*) basic *m*.

basic ['beɪsɪk] 1 **adj** a (*fundamental*) *difficulty, principle, problem, essentials* fondamental; (*elementary*) *rule* élémentaire. (*Math*) **the four ~ operations** les quatre opérations fondamentales; ~ **French** le français fondamental *or* de base; **a ~ knowledge of Russian** une connaissance de base du russe; ~ **research** recherche *f* fondamentale; ~ **vocabulary** vocabulaire *m* de base; **B~ English** l'anglais fondamental; ~ **needs** besoins *mpl* essentiels.

b (*forming starting point*) *salary, working hours* de base. **a ~ suit to which one can add accessories** un petit tailleur neutre auquel on peut ajouter des accessoires; **a ~ black dress** une petite robe noire.

c (*Chem*) basique. ~ **salt** sel *m* basique; ~ **slag** scorie *f* de déphosphoration.

2 **n: the ~s** l'essentiel *m*; **to get down to the ~s** en venir à l'essentiel.

3 **comp** ►**basic account** compte *m* de base ►**basic airman** (*US*) soldat *m* de deuxième classe ►**basic overhead expenditure** (*Fin*) frais généraux essentiels ►**basic rate** (*Fin, Comm*) taux *m* de référence; **basic rate of tax** première tranche *f* d'imposition ►**basic training**: (*Mil*) **to do one's basic training** faire ses classes ►**basic turn** (*Ski*) stem *m* ►**basic wage** salaire *m* de base.

basically ['beɪsɪklɪ] **adv** au fond. **it's ~ simple** au fond, c'est simple; **it's ~ the same** c'est pratiquement la même chose; **he's ~ lazy** au fond, il est paresseux, il est avant tout *or* fondamentalement paresseux; **well, ~, all I have to do is ...** eh bien, en fait, je n'ai qu'à ...; ~ **we agree** en principe *or* dans l'ensemble, nous sommes d'accord.

basil ['bæzl] **n** (*Bot*) basilic *m*.

basilica [bə'zɪlɪkə] **n** basilique *f*.

basilisk ['bæzɪlɪsk] **n** (*Myth, Zool*) basilic *m*.

basin ['beɪsn] **n** a (*gen*) cuvette *f*, bassine *f*; (*for food*) bol *m*; (*wide: for cream etc*) jatte *f*; (*also* **wash~, wash-hand** ~) cuvette; (*plumbed in*) lavabo *m*; *[lavatory]* cuvette; *[fountain]* vasque *f*; *see* **sugar** *etc*. b (*Geog*) *[river]* bassin *m*; (*valley*) cuvette *f*; (*harbour*) bassin; *see* **catchment, tidal** *etc*.

basinful ['beɪsnfʊl] **n** *[milk]* bolée *f*; *[water]* pleine cuvette *f*. **I've had a ~‡** j'en ai par-dessus la tête* *or* ras le bol* (*of* de).

basis ['beɪsɪs] **n, pl bases** (*lit, fig*) base *f*. **on an ad hoc** ~ de façon ad hoc, en fonction des circonstances; **paid on a daily/day-to-day/regular** ~ payé à la journée/au jour le jour/régulièrement; **on a mileage** ~ en fonction du kilométrage; **open on a 24-hour** ~ ouvert 24 heures sur 24; **payments are calculated on a family** ~ les paiements sont calculés en prenant pour base la famille; **on that** ~ dans ces conditions; **on the ~ of what you've told me** par suite de ce que vous m'avez dit, en me basant sur ce que vous m'avez dit; (*Fin*) ~ **for assessing VAT** assiette *f* de la TVA.

bask [bɑːsk] **vi: to ~ in the sun** se dorer au soleil; **to ~ in sb's favour** jouir de la faveur de qn; **~ing shark** (requin *m*) pèlerin *m*.

basket ['bɑːskɪt] 1 **n** (*gen*) corbeille *f*; (*shopping* ~) (*one-handled*) panier *m*; (*deeper, two-handled*) cabas *m*; (*clothes* ~) corbeille *or* panier à linge (sale); (*wastepaper* ~) corbeille (à papier); (*on person's back*) hotte *f*; (*on donkey*) panier; (*for game, fish, oysters*) bourriche *f*; (*Basketball*) panier; (*on ski stick*) rondelle *f* (de ski). (*Econ*) **a ~ of currencies/products** un panier de devises/produits; **a ~(ful) of eggs** un panier d'œufs; (*Basketball*) **to make a** ~ marquer un panier; *see* **laundry, luncheon, picnic, work** *etc*.

2 **comp** *handle etc* de panier ►**basketball** basket(-ball) *m*; **basketball player** basketteur *m*, -euse *f* ►**basket case** (*US‡*) grand(e) invalide *m(f)*; (*US* ‡) **he's a basket case‡** (*inadequate*) c'est un paumé*, (*nervous*) c'est un paquet de nerfs* ►**basket chair** chaise *f* en osier ►**basket maker** vannier *m* ►**basketweave** (*cloth*) tissage *m*; (*cane*) tressage *m* ►**basketwork** vannerie *f*.

Basle [bɑːl] **n** Bâle.

basmati [bəz'mætɪ] **n** (*also* ~ **rice**) (riz *m*) basmati *m*.

Basque [bæsk] 1 **n** a Basque *m*, Basque *f or* Basquaise *f*. b (*Ling*) basque *m*. 2 **adj** basque. **a ~ woman** une Basque, une Basquaise; ~ **Country** Pays *m* basque; ~ **Provinces** provinces *fpl* basques.

bas-relief ['bæsrɪ,liːf] **n** bas-relief *m*.

Bass [bæs] **n:** ~ **Strait** détroit *m* de Bass.

bass[1] [beɪs] (*Mus*) 1 **n** (*part, singer, guitar*) basse *f*; (*double bass*) contrebasse *f*; *see* **double** *etc*. 2 **adj** *voice, note* bas (*f* basse), de basse; (*low-sounding*) bas, grave. ~ **tones** sons *mpl* graves. 3 **comp** ►**bass-baritone** baryton-basse *m* ►**bass clarinet** clarinette *f* basse ►**bass clef** clef *f* de fa ►**bass drum** grosse caisse ►**bass flute** flûte *f* basse ►**bass guitar** guitare *f* basse ►**bass guitarist** bassiste *mf* ►**bass horn** serpent *m* ►**bassline** (ligne *f* de) basse *f* ►**bass-relief** = **bas-relief** ►**bass strings** basses *fpl* ►**bass trombone** trombone *m* basse ►**bass tuba** tuba *m* d'orchestre ►**bass viol** viole *f* de gambe.

bass[2] [bæs] **n** (*fish*) (*freshwater*) perche *f*; (*sea*) bar *m*, loup *m*.

basset ['bæsɪt] **n** a (*also* ~ **hound**) (chien *m*) basset *m*. b (*Mus*) ~ **horn** cor *m* de basset.

bassi ['bæsɪ] **npl of basso**.

bassist ['beɪsɪst] **n** bassiste *mf*.

basso ['bæsəʊ] **n, pl ~s** *or* **bassi** (*Mus*) ~ **continuo** basse *f* continue; ~ **profundo** basse profonde.

bassoon [bə'suːn] **n** basson *m*; *see* **double**.

bastard ['bɑːstəd] 1 **n** a (*lit*) bâtard(e) *m(f)*, enfant naturel(le) *m(f)*. b (‡ *pej: unpleasant person*) salaud‡ *m*, saligaud‡ *m*. c (‡) **he's a lucky ~!** c'est un drôle de veinard!*; **you old ~!** sacré vieux!*; **poor** ~ pauvre type*; **silly ~!** quel corniaud!‡ 2 **adj** *child* naturel, bâtard; *language, dialect* corrompu, abâtardi; (*Typ*) *character* d'un autre œil. ~ **title** faux-titre *m*.

bastardized ['bɑːstədaɪzd] **adj** *language* corrompu, abâtardi.

bastardy ['bɑːstədɪ] **n** bâtardise *f*.

baste[1] [beɪst] **vt** (*Sewing*) bâtir, faufiler.

baste[2] [beɪst] **vt** (*Culin*) arroser.

bastion ['bæstɪən] **n** bastion *m*.

Basutoland [bə'suːtəʊlænd] **n** Bas(o)utoland *m*.

bat[1] [bæt] **n** (*Zool*) chauve-souris *f*. (*fig*) **an old ~*** une vieille bique*; (*fig*) **to have ~s in the belfry*** avoir une araignée au plafond*; **to flee like a ~ out of hell*** s'enfuir comme si l'on avait le diable à ses trousses; *see* **blind**.

bat[2] [bæt] (*Sport etc*) 1 **n** a (*Baseball, Cricket*) batte *f*; (*Table Tennis*) raquette *f*. (*fig*) **off one's own** ~ de sa propre initiative, de son propre chef; (*US*) **right off the** ~ sur-le-champ; (*Sport*) **he's a good** ~ il manie bien la batte. b (*blow*) coup *m*. 2 **vi** (*Baseball, Cricket*) manier la batte. **he ~ted yesterday** il était à la batte hier; (*US fig: support*) **to go to ~ for sb*** intervenir en faveur de qn. 3 **vt** a *ball* frapper (*avec une batte, raquette etc*). b (*: *hit*) cogner*, flanquer un coup à*. (*US fig: discuss*) **to ~ sth around*** discuter de qch (à bâtons rompus); (*US fig*) **to ~ sth out*** faire qch en vitesse.

bat[3] [bæt] **vt: he didn't ~ an eyelid** (*Brit*) *or* **an eye** (*US*) il n'a pas sourcillé *or* bronché; **without ~ting an eyelid** (*Brit*) *or* **an eye** (*US*) sans sourciller *or* broncher.

bat[4]‡ [bæt] **n** a (*Brit: speed*) allure *f*. b (*US: spree*) fête *f*, bombe* *f*, bringue‡ *f*. **to go off on a** ~ (aller) faire la fête *or* la bombe* *or* la bringue‡.

batch [bætʃ] 1 **n** *[loaves]* fournée *f*; *[people]* groupe *m*; *[prisoners]* convoi *m*; *[recruits]* contingent *m*, fournée; *[letters]* paquet *m*, liasse *f*, tas *m*; (*Comm*) *[goods]* lot *m*; *[concrete]* gâchée *f*. 2 **comp** ►**batch mode**: (*Comput*) **in batch mode** en temps différé ►**batch-process** **vt** traiter par lots ►**batch processing** traitement *m* par lots.

bated ['beɪtɪd] adj: **with ~ breath** en retenant son souffle.

bath [bɑːθ] 1 n, pl **~s** [bɑːðz] a bain *m*; (~ *tub*) baignoire *f*. **to take** *or* **have a ~** prendre un bain; **to give sb a ~** baigner qn, donner un bain à qn; **while I was in my** *or* **the ~** pendant que j'étais dans *or* que je prenais mon bain; *[hotel]* **room with (private) ~** chambre *f* avec salle de bains (particulière); *see* **blood, eye, Turkish** *etc*.
b **~s** (*washing*) (établissement *m* de) bains(-douches) *mpl*; (*swimming*) piscine *f*; (*Hist*) thermes *mpl*.
c (*Chem, Phot, Tech*) bain *m*; (*Phot: container*) cuvette *f*.
2 vt (*Brit*) baigner, donner un bain à.
3 vi (*Brit*) prendre un bain.
4 comp ►**Bath bun** (*Brit*) pain *m* aux raisins ►**bathchair** fauteuil *m* roulant, voiture *f* de malade ►**bath cube** cube soluble parfumé pour le bain ►**bathhouse** bains *mpl* publics ►**bathmat** tapis *m* de bain ►**bath oil** huile *f* pour le bain ►**bath pearl** perle *f* pour le bain ►**bathrobe** peignoir *m* de bain ►**bathroom** *see* **bathroom** ►**bath salts** sels *mpl* de bain ►**bath sheet/towel** drap *m*/serviette *f* de bain ►**bathtub** baignoire *f*; (*round*) tub *m* ►**bathwater** eau *f* du bain.

bathe [beɪð] 1 vt (*gen, also fig*) baigner; *wound* laver. **to ~ one's eyes** se baigner *or* se bassiner les yeux; **to ~ one's feet** prendre un bain de pieds; **~d in tears** baigné de larmes; **to be ~d in sweat** être en nage, ruisseler (de sueur); (*US*) **to ~ the baby** baigner l'enfant; (*fig*) **~d in light** baigné *or* inondé de lumière. 2 vi se baigner, prendre un bain (*de mer, de rivière*); (*US*) prendre un bain (*dans une baignoire*). 3 n bain *m* (*de mer, de rivière*). **an enjoyable ~** une baignade agréable; **to take** *or* **have a ~** se baigner; **let's go for a ~** allons nous baigner.

bather ['beɪðəʳ] n baigneur *m*, -euse *f*.

bathing ['beɪðɪŋ] 1 n bains *mpl*, baignade(s) *f(pl)*. **~ prohibited** défense de se baigner, baignade interdite; **safe ~** baignade sans (aucun) danger; *see* **sea**. 2 comp ►**bathing beauty** belle *f* baigneuse ►**bathing cap** bonnet *m* de bain ►**bathing costume** (*Brit*) maillot *m* (de bain) ►**bathing hut** cabine *f* (de bains) ►**bathing machine** cabine de bains roulante ►**bathing suit** = **bathing costume** ►**bathing trunks** (*Brit*) maillot *m or* slip *m* de bain, caleçon *m* de bain ►**bathing wrap** peignoir *m or* sortie *f* de bain.

bathos ['beɪθɒs] n (*Literat*) chute *f* du sublime au ridicule.

bathroom ['bɑːθrʊm] 1 n salle *f* de bains. **to go to** *or* **use the ~** aller aux toilettes. 2 comp ►**bathroom cabinet** armoire *f* de toilette ►**bathroom fittings** (*main fixtures*) appareils *mpl or* installations *fpl* sanitaires; (*accessories*) accessoires *mpl* (de salle de bains) ►**bathroom scales** balance *f*, pèse-personne *m inv*.

bathysphere ['bæθɪsfɪəʳ] n bathysphère *f*.

batik [bə'tiːk] n batik *m*.

batiste [bæ'tiːst] n batiste *f*.

batman ['bætmæn] n (*Brit Mil*) ordonnance *f*.

baton ['bætən] n (*Mil, Mus*) bâton *m*, baguette *f*; (*Brit*) *[policeman]* matraque *f*; *[French traffic policeman]* bâton; *[relay race]* témoin *m*. **~ charge** charge *f* (*de police etc*) à la matraque; (*Mil*) **~ round** balle *f* en plastique.

bats‡ [bæts] adj toqué*, timbré*.

batsman ['bætsmən] n (*Cricket*) batteur *m*.

battalion [bə'tælɪən] n (*Mil, fig*) bataillon *m*.

batten¹ ['bætn] 1 n (*Carpentry*) latte *f*; *[roofing]* volige *f*; *[flooring]* latte, planche *f* (de parquet); (*Naut*) latte (de voile); (*Theat*) herse *f*. 2 vt latter; *roof* voliger; *floor* planchéier.

►**batten down** vt sep (*Naut*) **to batten down the hatches** fermer les écoutilles, condamner les panneaux.

batten² ['bætn] vi (*prosper illegitimately*) s'engraisser (*on sb* aux dépens de qn, *on sth* de qch); (*feed greedily*) se gorger, se gaver, se bourrer (*on* de).

batter¹ ['bætəʳ] n (*Culin*) (*for frying*) pâte *f* à frire; (*for pancakes*) pâte à crêpes. **fried fish in ~** poisson frit (enrobé de pâte à frire).

batter² ['bætəʳ] 1 vt a (*strike repeatedly*) battre, frapper; *baby* maltraiter, martyriser. **ship ~ed by the waves** navire battu par les vagues; **town ~ed by bombing** ville ravagée *or* éventrée par les bombardements. b (*Typ*) *type* endommager. 2 vi: **to ~ at the door** cogner *or* frapper à la porte à coups redoublés. 3 n (*US Sport*) batteur *m*.

►**batter about** vt sep *person:* rouer de coups, rosser.

►**batter down** vt sep *wall* démolir, abattre; (*Mil*) battre en brèche.

►**batter in** vt sep *door* enfoncer, défoncer; *skull* défoncer.

battered ['bætəd] adj *hat, pan* cabossé, bosselé; *face* (*lit*) meurtri; (*fig*) buriné; *furniture, house* délabré. (*Med*) **~ babies** *or* **children** enfants martyrs; (*Med*) **~ child syndrome** syndrome *m* de l'enfant martyr; **~ wife** *or* **woman** femme *f* battue; **a ~ old car** un vieux tacot cabossé*.

battering ['bætərɪŋ] n: **the town took a dreadful ~ during the war** la ville a été terriblement éprouvée pendant la guerre; **he got such a ~** on l'a roué de coups, on l'a rossé; (*Mil*) **~ ram** bélier *m*; *see* **baby**.

battery ['bætərɪ] 1 n a (*guns*) batterie *f*. b (*Elec*) *[torch, radio]* pile *f*; *[vehicle]* batterie *f*, accumulateurs *mpl*, accus* *mpl*. c (*number of similar objects*) batterie *f*. (*fig*) **a ~ of questions** une pluie de questions. d (*Agr*) éleveuse *f*. e (*Jur*) voie *f* de fait; *see* **assault**. 2 comp ►**battery charger** (*Elec*) chargeur *m* ►**battery farming** (*Agr*) élevage intensif *or* en batterie ►**battery fire** (*Mil*) tir *m* par salves ►**battery hen** (*Agr*) poule *f* de batterie ►**battery lead connection** (*Aut*) cosse *f* de batterie ►**battery-operated, battery-powered** à pile(s) ►**battery set** (*Rad*) poste *m* à piles.

battle ['bætl] 1 n (*lit, fig*) bataille *f*, combat *m*. **to fight a ~** se battre, lutter (*against* contre); **the B~ of Britain** la bataille d'Angleterre; (*Mil*) **killed in ~** tué à l'ennemi; **to have a ~ of wits** jouer au plus fin; **life is a continual ~** la vie est un combat perpétuel *or* une lutte perpétuelle; (*fig*) **to do ~ for/against** lutter pour/contre; (*fig*) **to fight sb's ~s** se battre à la place de qn; (*fig*) **we are fighting the same ~** nous nous battons pour la même cause; (*fig*) **that's half the ~*** c'est déjà pas mal*; (*fig*) **~ for control of sth/to control sth** lutte *or* combat pour obtenir le contrôle de qch/pour contrôler qch; *see* **join, losing, Nile** *etc*.
2 comp ►**battle array: in battle array** en bataille ►**battle-axe** (*weapon*) hache *f* d'armes; (* *pej: woman*) virago *f* ►**battle cruiser** croiseur *m* cuirassé ►**battle cry** cri *m* de guerre ►**battle dress** (*Mil*) tenue *f* de campagne *or* de combat ►**battle fatigue** *troubles mentaux causés par la tension éprouvée dans une situation de guerre* ►**battlefield, battleground** (*Mil, fig*) champ *m* de bataille ►**battle order: in battle order** = **in battle array** ►**battle royal** (*quarrel*) bataille *f* en règle ►**battle-scarred** (*lit*) *troops, country* marqué par les combats; (*fig*) *person* marqué par la vie; (* *hum*) *furniture* endommagé, abîmé ►**battleship** cuirassé *m* ►**battle zone** zone *f* de combat.
3 vi (*lit, fig*) se battre, lutter (*against* contre, *to do* pour faire), batailler (*to do* pour faire). (*fig*) **to ~ for breath** haleter.

battledore ['bætldɔːʳ] n (*Sport*) raquette *f*. **~ and shuttlecock** (jeu *m* de) volant *m*.

battlements ['bætlmənts] npl (*wall*) remparts *mpl*; (*crenellation*) créneaux *mpl*.

batty‡ ['bætɪ] adj = **bats‡**.

bauble ['bɔːbl] n babiole *f*, colifichet *m*; *[jester]* marotte *f*.

baud [bɔːd] n (*Comput*) baud *m*. **~ rate** vitesse *f* en bauds.

baulk [bɔːlk] = **balk**.

bauxite ['bɔːksaɪt] n bauxite *f*.

Bavaria [bə'vɛərɪə] n Bavière *f*.

Bavarian [bə'vɛərɪən] 1 n Bavarois(e) *m(f)*. 2 adj bavarois. **~ Alps** Alpes *fpl* bavaroises; (*Culin*) **~ cream** bavaroise *f*.

bawbee† [bɔː'biː] n (*Scot*) sou† *m*.

bawd†† [bɔːd] n (*prostitute*) catin† *f*.

bawdiness ['bɔːdɪnɪs] n paillardise *f*.

bawdy ['bɔːdɪ] adj paillard. **~house†** maison *f* close.

bawl [bɔːl] 1 vi a brailler, gueuler‡, beugler* (*at* contre). b (‡: *weep*) brailler, beugler*. 2 vt brailler, hurler, beugler*.

►**bawl out** vt sep a = **bawl 2**. b (‡: *scold*) engueuler‡.

bay¹ [beɪ] n (*Geog*) baie *f*, (*small*) anse *f*. **the B~ of Biscay** le golfe de Gascogne; (*US*) **the B~ State** le Massachusetts.

bay² [beɪ] 1 n (*Bot: also* **~ tree, sweet ~**) laurier(-sauce) *m*. (*fig*) **~ wreath, ~s** couronne *f* de laurier. 2 comp ►**bay leaf** feuille *f* de laurier ►**bay rum** lotion *f* capillaire.

bay³ [beɪ] n a (*Archit*) travée *f*; *[window]* baie *f*. **~ window** (*lit*) fenêtre *f* en saillie; (*US fig* *) grosse bedaine* *f*. b (*Rail*) voie *f* d'arrêt, quai *m* subsidiaire; *see* **bomb, loading, parking, sick** *etc*.

bay⁴ [beɪ] 1 n (*Hunting, fig*) **to be at ~** être aux abois; (*Hunting, fig*) **to bring to ~** acculer; (*fig*) **to keep** *or* **hold at ~** tenir à distance *or* en échec. 2 vi aboyer (*at* à, après), donner de la voix. **to ~ (at) the moon** aboyer *or* hurler à la lune.

bay⁵ [beɪ] 1 adj *horse* bai. 2 n cheval *m* bai. (*horse*) **red ~** alezan *m*.

Baykal [baɪ'kɑːl] n: **Lake ~** le lac Baïkal.

bayonet ['beɪənɪt] 1 n baïonnette *f*; *see* **fix** *etc*. 2 vt passer à la baïonnette. 3 comp ►**bayonet charge** charge *f* à la baïonnette ►**bayonet point: at bayonet point** à (la pointe de) la baïonnette ►**bayonet practice** exercices *mpl* de baïonnette ►**bayonet socket** (*Elec*) douille *f* à baïonnette.

bayou ['baɪjuː] n (*US*) bayou *m*, marécages *mpl*.

bazaar [bə'zɑːʳ] n (*in East*) bazar *m*; (*large shop*) bazar; (*sale of work*) vente *f* de charité.

bazoo‡ [bə'zuː] n (*US*) gueule‡ *f*, bouche *f*.

bazooka [bə'zuːkə] n bazooka *m*.

B.B. [biː'biː] n a (**abbr of Boys' Brigade**) *patronage pour garçons*. b (*US*) **~ gun** carabine *f* à air comprimé.

B.B.C. [biːbiː'siː] n (**abbr of British Broadcasting Corporation**) B.B.C. *f*.

B.C. [biː'siː] a (**abbr of Before Christ**) av. J.-C. b **abbr of British Columbia**.

BCD [biːsiː'diː] n (*Comput*) (**abbr of binary-coded decimal**) DCB *f*.

BCG [biːsiː'dʒiː] n (**abbr of bacille Calmette-Guérin**) B.C.G. *m*.

B.D. [biː'diː] n (*Univ*) (**abbr of Bachelor of Divinity**) *licence de théologie*.

B.D.S. [biːdiː'es] n (*Univ*) (**abbr of Bachelor of Dental Surgery**) *diplôme de chirurgie dentaire*.

be [biː] pres **am, is, are**, pret **was, were, wast†, wert†**, ptp **been** 1 copulative vb a (*joining subject and predicate*) être. **the sky is blue** le ciel est bleu; **~ good!** sois sage!; **my coffee is cold** mon café est froid; **he is lucky** il a de la chance; **he is a soldier** il est soldat; **he wants to ~ a doctor** il veut être médecin; **she is an Englishwoman** c'est une Anglaise; **who is that? — it's me!** qui est-ce? — c'est moi!
b (*health*) aller, se porter. **how are you?** comment allez-vous?,

comment vous portez-vous? (*frm*); **I am better now** je vais mieux maintenant; **she is none too well** elle ne va pas trop *or* très bien.

c (*physical or mental state*) **to ~ cold/hot/hungry/thirsty/ashamed/right/wrong** avoir froid/chaud/faim/soif/honte/raison/tort; **my feet are cold** j'ai froid aux pieds; **my hands are frozen** j'ai les mains gelées; **I am worried** je suis inquiet.

d (*age*) **how old is he?** quel âge a-t-il?; **he will ~ 3 next week** il aura 3 ans la semaine prochaine.

e (*measurement*) être. **the road is 1 km from the house** la route est à 1 km de la maison; **how far is London from here?** Londres est à quelle distance d'ici?, combien y a-t-il d'ici à Londres?; **the door is 3 metres high** la porte a 3 mètres de haut; **how tall are you?** combien mesurez-vous?

f (*cost*) coûter. **how much is it?** combien cela coûte-t-il?; **the book is 10 francs** le livre coûte 10 F; **it is cheap at the price** c'est bon marché à ce prix-là.

g (*Math*) faire. **2 and 2 are 4** 2 et 2 font 4; **3 times 2 is 6** 3 fois 2 font 6.

h (+ *poss pron*) être, appartenir. **that book is mine** ce livre m'appartient *or* est à moi; **it's his** c'est à lui, c'est le sien.

2 **aux vb** a (+ *prp* = *continuous tense*) être en train de + *infin*. **what are you doing? — I am reading a book** qu'est-ce que vous faites? — je lis *or* je suis en train de lire un livre; **what have you been doing this week?** qu'avez-vous fait cette semaine?; **I have just been packing my case** je viens de faire ma valise; **I have been waiting for you for an hour** je vous attends depuis une heure; **the bus is stopping** l'autobus s'arrête; **so you aren't coming with us? — but I AM coming!** alors, vous ne venez pas avec nous? — mais si, je viens avec vous!; **she is always complaining** elle se plaint toujours, elle est toujours en train de se plaindre; **will you ~ seeing her tomorrow?** est-ce que vous allez la voir demain?, comptez-vous la voir demain?; **what's been keeping you?** qu'est-ce qui t'a retenu?

b (+ *ptp* = *passive*) être. **he was killed** il a été tué; **the door was shut in his face** on lui a fermé la porte au nez; **there is nothing left** il ne reste plus rien; **he is to ~ pitied** il est à plaindre; **the car is to ~ sold** la voiture doit être vendue; **peaches are sold by the kilo** les pêches se vendent au kilo; **let it ~ done at once** qu'on le fasse tout de suite; **it is said that** on dit que; **not to ~ confused with** à ne pas confondre avec; **is it to ~ wondered at if ...?** faut-il s'étonner si ...?

c (*in tag questions, short answers*) **he's always late, isn't he? — yes, he is** il est toujours en retard, n'est-ce pas? — oui, toujours; **she is pretty — no, she isn't** elle est jolie — non, elle n'est pas jolie; **you are not ill, are you?** tu n'es pas malade j'espère?; **it's all done, is it?** tout est fait, alors?; **was he pleased to hear it!*** il a été rudement* content de l'apprendre!; **but wasn't she glad when*** ... mais n'empêche qu'elle a été contente quand* ... .

d (+ *to* + *infin*) **he is to do it** (*from duty, destiny, prearrangement*) il doit le faire; (*intention*) il va le faire; **I am to look after my mother** je dois m'occuper de ma mère; **they are shortly to ~ married** ils vont bientôt se marier; **she was never to return** elle ne devait jamais revenir; **the telegram was to warn us of the delay** le télégramme était pour nous avertir du retard.

e (+ *neg* + *infin* = *prohibition*) **you are not to touch that** tu ne dois pas y toucher; **I am not to speak to him** on m'a défendu de lui parler; **I wasn't to tell you his name** je ne devais pas vous dire son nom; **this door is not to ~ opened** il est interdit *or* défendu d'ouvrir cette porte.

f (*modal "were": possibility, supposition*) **if we were** *or* (*frm*) **were we in London now** si nous étions à Londres maintenant; **if I were** *or* (*frm*) **were I to tell him, what could he do?** et à supposer même que je le lui dise *or* et quand bien même je le lui dirais, que pourrait-il faire?; **if I were you I should refuse** à votre place *or* si j'étais vous je refuserais.

3 **vi** a (*exist, live, occur, remain, be situated*) être, exister. **to ~ or not to ~** être ou ne pas être; **the best artist that ever was** le meilleur peintre qui ait jamais existé *or* qui fût jamais; **that may ~** cela se peut, peut-être; **~ that as it may** quoi qu'il en soit; **how is it that ...?** comment se fait-il que ...? + *indic or subj*; **let me ~** laissez-moi tranquille; **leave it as it is** laissez-le tel quel; **don't ~ too long in coming** ne tardez pas trop à venir; **I won't ~ long** je n'en ai pas pour longtemps; **to ~ in danger** être *or* se trouver en danger; **Christmas Day is on a Monday this year** Noël tombe un lundi cette année; **the match is tomorrow** le match a lieu demain; **he is there just now but he won't ~ (there) much longer** il est là en ce moment mais il ne va plus y être (pour) très longtemps.

b **there is, there are** il y a, il est (*liter*); **there is a mouse in the room** il y a une souris dans la pièce; **there was once a castle here** il y avait autrefois un château ici; **there will ~ dancing** on dansera; **there were three of us** nous étions trois; **there is nothing more beautiful** il n'y a *or* il n'est rien de plus beau; **there is no knowing what may happen** il est impossible de savoir ce qui va se passer; **he's a rogue if ever there was one** voilà un filou si jamais il en fut; **let there ~ light and there was light** que la lumière soit et la lumière fut; **there ~ing no alternative solution** comme il n'y a aucune autre solution.

c (*presenting, pointing out*) **here is a book** voici un livre; **here are 2 books** voici 2 livres; **there is the church** voilà l'église; **there are the 2 churches** voilà les 2 églises; **here you are!** (*I've found you*) ah vous voici!; (*take this*) tenez!; **there he was, sitting at the table** il était là, assis à la table.

d (*come, go: esp in perfect tense*) aller, venir, être. **I have been to see my aunt** je suis allé voir ma tante; **I have already been to Paris** j'ai déjà été *or* je suis déjà allé à Paris; **the postman has already been** le facteur est déjà passé; **has anyone been while I was out?** il est venu quelqu'un pendant que je n'étais pas là?; **he has been and gone** il est venu et reparti; **now you've been and done it!**‡ eh bien, tu as fait du joli! (*iro*); **I've just been and broken it!**‡ (ça y est) voilà que je l'ai cassé!; **that dog of yours has been and dug up all my daffodils!**‡ ton sale chien est allé déterrer toutes mes jonquilles!*

e **the bride-/mother-to-~** la future mariée/maman.

4 **impers vb** a (*weather etc*) faire. **it is fine/cold/dark** il fait beau/froid/nuit; **it is windy/foggy** il fait du vent/du brouillard.

b (*time*) être. **it is morning** c'est le matin; **it is 6 o'clock** il est 6 heures; **tomorrow is Friday** demain c'est vendredi; **it is the 14th June today** nous sommes (aujourd'hui) *or* c'est aujourd'hui le 14 juin; **it is a long time since I last saw you** il y a longtemps que je ne vous ai vu.

c (*distance*) **it is 5 km to the nearest town** la ville la plus proche est à 5 km.

d (*emphatic*) **it is he who did it** c'est lui qui l'a fait; **it is they who are responsible** ce sont eux les responsables; **it is us who found it** c'est nous qui l'avons trouvé.

e (*supposition, probability*) **were it not that** si ce n'était que; **were it not for my friendship for him** si ce n'était mon amitié pour lui; **had it not been for him we should all be dead** sans lui nous serions tous morts; **as it were** pour ainsi dire; **and even if it were so** et quand bien même ce serait vrai.

5 **comp** ►**the be-all and end-all** le but suprême (*of* de), la fin des fins.

B.E. [biː'iː] **n** (*Comm*) (**abbr of bill of exchange**) *see* **bill**.

beach [biːtʃ] 1 **n** *[sea]* plage *f*; (*shore*) grève *f*; *[lake]* rivage *m*. **private/sandy ~** plage privée/de sable. 2 **vt** *boat* échouer. 3 **comp** ►**beach ball** ballon *m* de plage ►**beach buggy** buggy *m* ►**beachcomber** (*person*) (*lit*) ramasseur *m* d'épaves; (*fig: idler*) propre *mf* à rien; (*wave*) vague *f* déferlante ►**beachhead** tête *f* de pont ►**beach hut** cabine *f* de bain *or* de plage ►**beach umbrella** parasol *m* ►**beachwear** tenue *f* de plage.

beacon ['biːkən] 1 **n** a (*danger signal*) phare *m*, signal *m* lumineux; (*lantern itself*) fanal *m*; (*Naut*) balise *f*; (*Aviat*) balise, phare; (*fig*) phare, guide *m*, flambeau *m*; *see* **Belisha beacon, radio.** b (*Hist: on hills*) feu *m* (d'alarme). c (*hill: gen in place-names*) colline *f*. 2 **comp** ►**beacon light** balise *f* lumineuse.

bead [biːd] **n** a (*of glass, coral, amber etc*) perle *f*; *[rosary]* grain *m*. **(string of) ~s** collier *m*; *see* **tell** *etc*. b (*drop*) *[dew]* perle *f*; *[sweat]* goutte *f*; (*bubble*) bulle *f*. **his forehead was covered in ~s of sweat** la sueur lui perlait au front. c *[gun]* guidon *m*. **to draw a ~ on** ajuster, viser.

beaded ['biːdəd] **adj** *fabric, dress* perlé, orné de perles. (*fig*) **his forehead was ~ with sweat** la sueur perlait à son front.

beading ['biːdɪŋ] **n** (*Carpentry*) baguette *f*; (*Archit*) chapelet *m*; (*Dress*) broderie *f* perlée, garniture *f* de perles.

beadle ['biːdl] **n** (*Brit Univ*) appariteur *m*, huissier *m*; (*Rel*) bedeau *m*.

beady ['biːdɪ] **adj**: **to watch sth with ~ eyes** regarder qch avec des yeux de fouine; **~-eyed** (*glittering*) aux yeux en boutons de bottines; (*pej*) aux yeux de fouine.

beagle ['biːgl] 1 **n** beagle *m*. 2 **vi** chasser avec des beagles.

beak [biːk] **n** a *[bird, turtle etc]* bec *m*; (‡: *also* **~ed nose**) nez crochu. b (*Brit* ‡: *judge etc*) juge *m*; († *Brit Scol sl: headmaster*) protal *m* (*sl*).

beaker ['biːkəʳ] **n** gobelet *m*; (*wide*) coupe *f*; (*Chem etc*) vase *m* à bec.

beam [biːm] 1 **n** a (*Archit*) poutre *f*, solive *f*; (*thick*) madrier *m*; (*small*) poutrelle *f*, soliveau *m*; (*Sport: in gym*) poutre; *see* **cross** *etc*.

b (*Naut*) (*transverse member*) barrot *m*; (*greatest width*) largeur *f*. **on the ~** par le travers; (*Naut*) **on the port ~** à bâbord; **on the starboard ~** à tribord; *see* **broad** *etc*.

c (*Tech*) *[scales]* fléau *m*; *[engine]* balancier *m*; *[plough]* age *m*; *[loom]* rouleau *m*.

d *[light, sunlight]* rayon *m*, trait *m*; *[lighthouse, headlight, searchlight]* faisceau *m* (lumineux); (*Phys*) faisceau; (*Aviat, Naut*) chenal *m* de radio-guidage. **to be on/be off (the) ~** être/ne pas être dans le chenal de radio-guidage; (*fig*) **to be on (the) ~*** être sur la bonne voie; (*fig*) (*Brit*) **to be off (the) ~***, (*US*) **to be off the ~*** dérailler*; *see* **electron** *etc*.

e (*smile*) sourire *m* épanoui.

2 **vi** a *[sun]* rayonner, darder ses rayons. **to ~ forth** apparaître.

b **she ~ed** son visage s'est épanoui en un large sourire; **at the sight of the money she ~ed at me** elle a levé vers moi un visage épanoui *or* rayonnant en voyant l'argent; **her face was ~ing with joy** son visage rayonnait de joie.

3 **vt** (*Rad, Telec*) *message* transmettre par émission dirigée. **to ~ a programme to the Arab-speaking countries** diffuser un programme à l'intention des pays de langue arabe.

4 comp (*Naut*) *sea, wind* de travers ►**beam balance** balance *f* à fléau ►**beam compass** compas *m* à verge ►**beam-ends:** (*Naut*) **on her beam-ends** couché sur le côté *or* le flanc; (*fig*) **to be on one's beam-ends*** être dans la dèche‡ *or* dans la gêne.

beaming ['bi:mɪŋ] adj *sun* radieux, resplendissant; *smile, face* rayonnant, radieux, épanoui.

bean [bi:n] 1 n (*Bot, Culin*) haricot *m*; (*green* ~) haricot vert; (*broad* ~) fève *f*; *[coffee]* grain *m*; (*US* *) (*head*) tête *f*, tronche‡ *f*; (*brain*) cervelle *f*. (*Brit*) **to be full of ~s*** être en pleine forme, péter le feu*; (*US*) **he doesn't know ~s about it*** il n'en sait trois fois rien; **it isn't worth a ~*** ça ne vaut pas un clou*; (*Brit*) **he hasn't a ~‡** il n'a pas le sou *or* un radis‡; **hullo, old ~!‡†** salut mon pote!‡; *see* **bake, kidney, spill[1]** *etc*.

2 comp ►**beanbag** (*for throwing*) balle *f* lestée; (*chair*) sacco *m* ►**bean curd** fromage *m* de soja ►**beanfeast*** (*Brit*), **beano*†** (*Brit*) (*meal*) gueuleton‡ *m*; (*spree*) bombe* *f*, nouba* *f* ►**beanpole** (*lit, fig*) perche *f* ►**beanshoots, beansprouts** (*Culin*) germes *mpl* de soja ►**beanstalk** tige *f* de haricot.

3 vt frapper à la tête.

bear[1] [bɛəʳ] pret **bore**, ptp **borne** 1 vt a (*carry*) *burden, arms, message* porter. **music borne on the wind** musique portée par le vent; **to ~ away** emporter; **to ~ back** rapporter; *see* **mind**.

b (*show*) *inscription, mark, traces, signature* porter. **to ~ some resemblance to** ressembler à, offrir une ressemblance avec; **to ~ no relation to** être sans rapport avec, n'avoir aucun rapport avec.

c (*be known by*) *name* porter.

d **he bore himself like a soldier** (*carried himself*) il avait une allure militaire *or* de soldat; (*conducted himself*) il se comportait en soldat.

e (*feel*) avoir en soi, porter. **the love/hatred he bore her** l'amour/la haine qu'il lui portait *or* qu'il avait à son égard; **to ~ sb ill will** en avoir contre qn; *see* **grudge**.

f (*bring, provide*) apporter, fournir. **to ~ witness to sth** *[thing, result etc]* témoigner de qch; *[person]* attester qch; **to ~ false witness** porter un faux témoignage; **to ~ sb company†** tenir compagnie à qn.

g (*sustain, support*) supporter. **to ~ the weight of** supporter le poids de; **to ~ comparison with** soutenir la comparaison avec; **to ~ the expense of sth** prendre les frais de qch à sa charge; **to ~ the responsibility for sth** assumer la responsabilité de qch.

h (*endure*) supporter, tolérer, souffrir. **I cannot ~ (the sight of) that man** je ne peux pas souffrir *or* voir cet homme; **he can't ~ the smell of cooking** il ne peut pas supporter les odeurs de cuisine; **she cannot ~ being laughed at** elle ne supporte pas qu'on se moque (*subj*) d'elle; **his language will not ~ repeating** ses propos sont trop grossiers pour être rapportés; *see* **brunt, grin**.

i (*produce, yield*) porter, produire, rapporter. (*lit, fig*) **to ~ fruit** porter des fruits; (*Fin*) **investment which ~s 5%** placement *m* qui rapporte 5%; (*Fin*) **to ~ interest at 5%** produire *or* rapporter un intérêt de 5%.

j (*give birth to*) donner naissance à, mettre au monde. **she has borne him 3 daughters** elle lui a donné 3 filles; *see* **born**.

k (*push, press*) entraîner, pousser, porter. **he was borne along by the crowd** il s'est trouvé entraîné *or* emporté par la foule.

2 vi a (*move*) se diriger. **to ~ right/left** prendre sur la droite/la gauche *or* à droite/à gauche; **~ towards the church** allez vers l'église; **~ north at the windmill** prenez la direction nord au moulin; (*Naut*) **to ~ off** virer (de bord).

b *[ice etc]* porter, supporter.

c *[fruit tree etc]* donner, produire.

d (*lean, press*) porter, appuyer (*on* sur). **he bore heavily on his stick** il s'appuyait lourdement sur sa canne; (*fig*) **these taxes ~ most heavily on the poor** ces impôts pèsent le plus lourdement sur les pauvres.

e (*phrases with "bring"*) **to bring one's energies to ~ on sth** consacrer *or* mettre toute son énergie à qch; **to bring one's mind to ~ on sth** porter son attention sur qch; **to bring pressure to ~ on sth** exercer une pression sur qch; (*fig*) **to bring pressure to ~ on sb** faire pression sur qn; **to bring a telescope to ~ on** braquer une lunette sur; **to bring a gun to ~ on a target** pointer un canon sur un objectif.

►**bear down** 1 vi a (*approach*) **to bear down on** *[ship]* venir sur; *[person]* foncer sur. b (*press*) appuyer fermement, peser (*on* sur). c *[woman in labour]* pousser. 2 vt sep (*liter*) abattre, vaincre. **borne down by adversity** abattu par l'adversité.

►**bear in (up)on** vt fus (*pass only*) **it was gradually borne in upon me that** la conviction s'est faite peu à peu en moi que, il est apparu de plus en plus évident à mes yeux que.

►**bear on** vt fus = **bear upon**.

►**bear out** vt sep confirmer, corroborer. **to bear sb out, to bear out what sb says** corroborer les dires de qn, corroborer ce que qn dit; **the result bears out our suspicions** le résultat confirme nos soupçons; **you will bear me out that ...** vous serez d'accord avec moi (pour dire) que ... .

►**bear up** vi ne pas se laisser abattre *or* décourager, tenir le coup*. **he bore up well under** *or* **against the death of his father** il a supporté courageusement la mort de son père; **bear up!** courage!; **how are you? — bearing up!*** comment ça va? — ça se maintient* *or* on tient le coup* *or* on fait aller*; *see* **bear[1] 2a**.

►**bear upon** vt fus (*be relevant to*) se rapporter à, être relatif à, avoir trait à; (*concern*) intéresser, concerner.

►**bear with** vt fus *person, sb's moods etc* supporter patiemment. **bear with me a little longer** je vous demande encore un peu de patience.

bear[2] [bɛəʳ] 1 n a ours(e) *m(f)*. (*fig*) **he's like a ~ with a sore head*** il est d'une humeur massacrante *or* de dogue, il n'est pas à prendre avec des pincettes; (*Astron*) **the Great/the Little B~** la Grande/la Petite Ourse; *see* **grizzly, koala, polar** *etc*.

b (*pej: person*) ours *m* (*pej*).

c (*St Ex*) baissier *m*.

2 vt (*St Ex*) chercher à faire baisser.

3 vi (*St Ex*) jouer à la baisse.

4 comp ►**bear-baiting** combat *m* d'ours et de chiens ►**bear cub** ourson *m* ►**bear garden** (*fig*) pétaudière *f* ►**bear hug: he gave me a big bear hug** il m'a serré très fort dans ses bras ►**bear market** (*St Ex*) marché *m* (orienté) à la baisse, marché baissier ►**bear pit** fosse *f* aux ours ►**bearskin** (*Mil Dress*) bonnet *m* à poil ►**the Bear State** (*US*) l'Arkansas *m*.

bearable ['bɛərəbl] adj supportable, tolérable.

beard [bɪəd] 1 n a barbe *f*; (*small, pointed*) barbiche *f*, bouc *m*. **to have a ~** porter la barbe; **to wear a full ~** porter sa barbe entière; **a man with a ~** un homme barbu *or* à barbe, un barbu; **a week's (growth of) ~** une barbe de huit jours. b *[fish, oyster]* barbe *f*; *[goat]* barbiche *f*; *[grain]* barbe, arête *f*; *[hook etc]* barbe, barbelure *f*; (*Typ*) talus *m*. 2 vt (*face up to*) affronter, braver. (*fig*) **to ~ the lion in his den** aller braver le lion dans sa tanière.

bearded ['bɪədɪd] adj (*gen*) barbu. **a ~ man** un barbu; **the ~ lady** la femme à barbe.

beardless ['bɪədlɪs] adj imberbe, sans barbe. (*fig*) **~ youth** (petit) jeunet *m*.

bearer ['bɛərəʳ] 1 n a *[letter, news, burden]* porteur *m*,-euse *f*; (*at funeral*) porteur; (*servant*) serviteur *m*. b *[cheque, name, title]* porteur *m*; *[passport]* titulaire *mf*. c (*Bot*) **a good ~** un arbre qui donne bien. d (*Constr, Tech*) support *m*. 2 comp ►**bearer bond** titre *m* au porteur ►**bearer cheque** chèque *m* au porteur.

bearing ['bɛərɪŋ] 1 n a (*posture, behaviour*) maintien *m*, port *m*, allure *f*. **soldierly ~** allure martiale; **noble ~** maintien noble; **queenly ~** port de reine.

b (*relation, aspect*) relation *f*, rapport *m*. **to have a** *or* **some ~ on sth** influer sur qch; **to have no ~ on the subject** n'avoir aucun rapport avec le sujet.

c **it is beyond (all) ~** c'est absolument insupportable.

d (*Naut: direction*) position *f*. **to take a compass ~** prendre un relèvement au compas; **to take a ship's ~s** faire le point; **to take** *or* **get one's ~s** s'orienter, se repérer; (*fig*) **to lose one's ~s** être désorienté, perdre le nord.

e (*Tech*) palier *m*; *see* **ball[1], main** *etc*.

f (*Her*) *see* **armorial**.

2 n ending in comps: **carbon-/oxygen-bearing** *etc* contenant du carbone/de l'oxygène *etc*.

bearish ['bɛərɪʃ] adj (*St Ex*) ~ **tendency** tendance *f* à la baisse, tendance baissière.

beast [bi:st] n a bête *f*, animal *m*. (*Rel*) **the B~** l'Antéchrist *m*, la grande Bête de l'Apocalypse; **the king of the ~s** le roi des animaux; **~ of burden** bête de somme *or* de charge; **~ of prey** prédateur *m*; (*Agr*) **~s** bétail *m*, bestiaux *mpl*; *see* **brute, wild**. b (*pej: person*) (*cruel*) brute *f*; (**: disagreeable*) vache* *f*, chameau* *m*. *[greedy person]* **to make a ~ of o.s.** se goinfrer*.

beastliness ['bi:stlɪnɪs] n (*NonC*) (*act, quality*) bestialité *f*; *[language]* obscénité *f*; (**: unpleasantness*) caractère *m* infect; *[person]* méchanceté *f*, rosserie* *f*.

beastly ['bi:stlɪ] 1 adj *person, conduct* bestial, brutal; *language* obscène; *food, sight* dégoûtant, répugnant; (**: less strong*) abominable, infect*; *child, trick* sale, vilain (*both bef n*). **what ~ weather!*** quel temps infect!*, quel sale temps!; **it's a ~ business*** c'est une sale affaire; **to be ~ to sb*** être infect* avec qn, se conduire de façon abominable avec qn. 2 adv (*Brit* *) terriblement, vachement‡.

beat [bi:t] (vb: pret **beat**, ptp **beaten**) 1 n a *[heart, pulse]* battement *m*, pulsation *f*; *[drums]* battement, roulement *m*; (*Acoustics*) battement. **to march to the ~ of the drum** marcher au (son du) tambour; *see also* **drum**.

b (*Mus*) temps *m*; *[conductor's baton]* battement *m* (de la mesure); (*Jazz*) rythme *m*. **strong/weak ~** temps fort/faible.

c *[policeman]* ronde *f*, secteur *m*; *[sentry]* ronde. **the policeman on the ~ noticed it** l'agent l'a remarqué pendant qu'il effectuait sa ronde; **the system of the policeman on the ~** le système des agents affectés à la surveillance d'un quartier, ≃ l'îlotage *m*; **policeman on the ~** ≃ îlotier *m*; (*fig*) **that's off my ~** cela n'est pas de mon domaine *or* de mon rayon*; *see* **off**.

d (*Hunting*) battue *f*.

e (‡) = **beatnik**.

2 adj a (**: also* **dead-~**) éreinté, claqué*, crevé*.

b (‡) beatnik *inv*.

3 comp ►**beaten-up*** déglingué‡, bousillé* ►**Beat Generation** Beat Generation *f* ►**beat-up** = **beaten-up**.

4 vt a (*strike*) *person, animal* battre, frapper; *carpet* battre; *eggs, cream* fouetter, battre; *metal* battre. **to ~ sth flat** aplatir qch; **to ~ sb with a stick** donner des coups de bâton à qn; **to ~ sb black and blue** rouer qn de coups, battre qn comme plâtre; **to ~ a drum** battre du tambour; (*US fig: publicize*) **to ~ a drum for sth*** faire du battage* autour de qch; (*Mil*) **to ~ the retreat** battre la retraite; (*Mil, fig*) **to ~ a retreat** battre en retraite; **~ it!‡** fiche le camp!*, fous le camp!‡, file!*; (*liter*) **to ~ one's breast** se frapper la poitrine; **to ~ a way through sth** se frayer un passage *or* un chemin à travers qch; (*Hunting*) **to ~ the forest/the moors** battre les bois/les landes; **~ing the air with its wings** battant l'air de ses ailes; **the bird ~s its wings** l'oiseau bat des ailes; **to ~ time** battre la mesure; (*Brit Hist*) **to ~ the bounds** *marquer les limites d'une paroisse (au cours d'une procession)*; *see* **dead, tattoo**.

b (*defeat*) vaincre, battre, triompher de. **the army was ~en** l'armée a été battue; **to ~ sb to the top of a hill** arriver au sommet d'une colline avant qn; (*fig*) **to ~ sb to it*** couper l'herbe sous le pied à qn, devancer qn; **to ~ sb at chess** battre qn aux échecs; **to ~ sb hollow** (*Brit*) *or* **hands down** *or* **into a cocked hat** battre qn à plate(s) couture(s); **to ~ the record** battre le record; **to ~ the system** trouver le joint (*fig*); (*US*) *[accused person]* **to ~ the charge*** échapper à l'accusation; (*US*) **to ~ the rap‡** échapper à la taule; **coffee ~s tea any day*** le café vaut tout le thé du monde; **the police confess themselves ~en** la police s'avoue vaincue; **the problem has got me ~en** *or* **~*** le problème me dépasse complètement; (*fig*) **that ~s everything!*, that takes some ~ing!*** ça, c'est le bouquet!*, faut le faire!*; (*fig*) **his behaviour takes some ~ing*** sa conduite dépasse tout; (*admiring*) **that will take some ~ing!*** pour faire mieux, il faudra se lever de bonne heure!*; (*fig*) **that ~s me*** cela me dépasse; (*fig*) **it ~s me how you can speak to her*** je ne comprends pas *or* ça me dépasse* que tu lui adresses (*subj*) la parole; **can you ~ that** *or* **it!*** tu as déjà vu ça, toi!*, faut le faire!*

5 vi a *[rain, wind]* battre; *[sun]* (*also* **~ down**) taper*, darder ses rayons. **to ~ at the door** cogner à la porte; **the rain was ~ing against the window** la pluie battait contre la vitre; **the waves ~ against the cliff** les vagues battent la falaise; (*fig*) **he doesn't ~ about the bush** il n'y va pas par quatre chemins, il ne tourne pas autour du pot; **well, not to ~ about the bush, he ...** bref, il ... .

b *[heart, pulse, drum]* battre. **her heart was ~ing with joy** son cœur battait *or* palpitait de joie; **with ~ing heart** le cœur battant; **his pulse began to ~ quicker** son pouls s'est mis à battre plus fort; **they heard the drums ~ing** ils entendaient le roulement des tambours.

c (*Naut*) **to ~ (to windward)** louvoyer au plus près.

►**beat back** vt sep *enemy, flames* repousser.

►**beat down** 1 vi: **the rain was beating down** il pleuvait à verse *or* à seaux *or* à torrents; *see also* **beat 5a**. 2 vt sep a (*reduce*) rabattre, baisser, faire baisser; *prices* faire baisser; *person* faire baisser ses prix à. **I beat him down to £2** je l'ai fait descendre à 2 livres. b **the rain has beaten down the wheat** la pluie a couché les blés.

►**beat in** vt sep *door* défoncer. **to beat sb's brains in*** défoncer le crâne à qn.

►**beat off** vt sep *attack, attacker, competition* repousser.

►**beat out** vt sep a *fire* étouffer. b *metal* marteler, étaler *or* amincir au marteau. (*US fig*) **to beat one's brains out*** se creuser la cervelle. c **to beat out the rhythm** marquer le rythme, battre la mesure.

►**beat up** 1 vt sep a *eggs, cream* fouetter, battre; (* *fig*) *person* passer à tabac, tabasser*. (*fig*) **to beat it up‡** faire la bombe*. b *recruits, volunteers, customers* racoler, recruter. **he beat up all the help he could** il a battu le rappel. 2 **beat-up*** adj *see* **beat 3**. 3 **beating-up** n *see* **beating 2**.

beaten ['biːtn] 1 ptp of **beat**. 2 adj a *metal* battu, martelé; *earth, path* battu. **~ track** chemin *m or* sentier *m* battu; (*lit, fig*) **off the ~ track** hors des sentiers battus. b (*defeated*) battu, vaincu. c (*exhausted*) éreinté, claqué*, crevé*.

beater ['biːtəʳ] n a (*gadget*) *[carpet]* tapette *f*; *[eggs]* (*whisk*) fouet *m*; (*rotary*) batteur *m*; (*Tex*) peigne *m*. b (*Shooting*) rabatteur *m*.

beatific [ˌbiːə'tɪfɪk] adj béatifique. **to wear a ~ smile** sourire aux anges, arborer un sourire béat.

beatification [biːˌætɪfɪ'keɪʃən] n béatification *f*.

beatify [biː'ætɪfaɪ] vt béatifier.

beating ['biːtɪŋ] 1 n a (*series of blows*) correction *f*, raclée* *f*. **to give sb a ~** flanquer une correction *or* une raclée* à qn; **to get a ~** recevoir une correction *or* une raclée*. b (*NonC*) *[metal]* batte *f*; *[drums]* battement *m*, roulement *m*; *[carpet]* battage *m*. c (*defeat*) défaite *f*. (*Sport, also* *) **to take a ~** se faire battre à plate(s) couture(s), se faire piler*; **the car takes a ~ on that road*** la voiture en voit de dures sur cette route; *see* **beat 4b**. d *[wings, heart etc]* battement *m*. e (*Shooting*) battue *f*. 2 comp ►**beating-up*** passage *m* à tabac, raclée* *f*.

beatitude [biː'ætɪtjuːd] n béatitude *f*. **the B~s** les béatitudes.

beatnik ['biːtnɪk] n, adj beatnik (*mf*).

beau [bəʊ] n, pl **~s** *or* **~x** [bəʊz] (*dandy*) élégant *m*, dandy *m*; (*suitor*) galant *m*; (*US: boyfriend*) petit ami*.

Beaufort ['bəʊfət] n: **~ scale** échelle *f* de Beaufort.

beaut* [bjuːt] n: **what a ~!** quelle merveille!*

beauteous ['bjuːtɪəs] adj (*liter*) = **beautiful 1**.

beautician [bjuː'tɪʃən] n esthéticien(ne) *m(f)*, visagiste *mf*.

beautiful ['bjuːtɪfʊl] 1 adj *person, music, picture, clothes* beau (*before vowel* bel; *f* belle); *weather* superbe, splendide, magnifique; *dinner* magnifique. **really ~** de toute beauté. 2 n: **the ~** le beau.

beautifully ['bjuːtɪflɪ] adv *sew, drive etc* admirablement, à la perfection, on ne peut mieux; *quiet, empty* merveilleusement. **that will do ~** cela convient parfaitement, c'est tout à fait ce qu'il faut.

beautify ['bjuːtɪfaɪ] vt embellir, orner. **to ~ o.s.** se faire une beauté.

beauty ['bjuːtɪ] 1 n a (*NonC*) beauté *f*. **to mar** *or* **spoil** *or* **ruin the ~ of sth** déparer qch; (*Prov*) **~ is only skin-deep** la beauté n'est pas tout; (*Prov*) **~ is in the eye of the beholder** il n'y a pas de laides amours; (*fig*) **the ~ of it is that*** ... le plus beau, c'est que ...; (*fig*) **that's the ~ of it** c'est ça qui est formidable*.

b beauté *f*. **she is a ~** elle est d'une grande beauté, c'est une beauté; **she is no ~*** ce n'est pas une beauté; **B~ and the Beast** la Belle et la Bête; **isn't this car/this apple** *etc* **a ~!*** quelle merveille que cette voiture/cette pomme! *etc*.

2 comp ►**beauty competition, beauty contest** concours *m* de beauté ►**beauty cream** crème *f* de beauté ►**beauty editor** rédacteur *m*, -trice *f* de la rubrique beauté ►**beauty parlour** institut *m or* salon *m* de beauté ►**beauty preparations** produits *mpl* de beauté ►**beauty queen** reine *f* de beauté ►**beauty salon** = **beauty parlour** ►**beauty sleep: off you go to bed now, you need your beauty sleep** va te coucher maintenant pour être tout frais demain matin ►**beauty specialist** esthéticien(ne) *m(f)*, visagiste *mf* ►**beauty spot** *[skin]* (*natural*) grain *m* de beauté; (*applied*) mouche *f*; (*in countryside*) site *m* superbe; (*in tourist guide etc*) site touristique ►**beauty treatment** soins *mpl* de beauté.

beaver ['biːvəʳ] 1 n a (*Zool*) castor *m*; (*fur*) (fourrure *f* de) castor; (*hat*) (chapeau *m* de) castor. **to work like a ~** travailler d'arrache-pied; *see* **eager**. b (*US* **‡**) foufoune*‡ *f*, chagatte*‡ *f*. 2 comp *coat, hat* (en poil) de castor ►**Beaverboard** ® (*Constr*) aggloméré *m* (*bois*) ►**the Beaver State** (*US*) l'Oregon *m*. 3 vi (*Brit fig*) **to ~ away* at sth** travailler d'arrache-pied à qch.

becalm [bɪ'kɑːm] vt (*gen pass*) **to be ~ed** être encalminé.

became [bɪ'keɪm] pret of **become**.

because [bɪ'kɒz] 1 conj parce que. **I did it ~ you asked me to** je l'ai fait parce que tu me l'as demandé; **I shan't go out ~ it's raining** je ne sortirai pas à cause de la pluie; **it is the more surprising ~ we were not expecting it** c'est d'autant plus surprenant que nous ne nous y attendions pas; **if I did it, it was ~ it had to be done** je l'ai fait parce qu'il fallait bien le faire; **~ he lied, he was punished** il a été puni pour avoir menti *or* parce qu'il avait menti; **we are annoyed ~ the weather is bad** nous sommes contrariés parce qu'il fait mauvais *or* de ce qu'il fait mauvais; **not ~ he was offended but ~ he was angry** non qu'il fût offusqué mais parce qu'il était furieux; **~ he was leaving** à cause de son départ.

2 prep: **~ of** à cause de, en raison de, vu; **~ of his age** en raison de son âge, vu son âge.

bechamel [ˌbeɪʃə'mɛl] adj: **~ sauce** (sauce *f*) béchamel *f*.

beck[1] [bek] n: **to be at sb's ~ and call** être à l'entière disposition de qn, être constamment à la disposition de qn; **to have sb at one's ~ and call** faire marcher qn à la baguette *or* au doigt et à l'œil.

beck[2] [bek] n (*N Engl*) ruisseau *m*, ru *m*.

beckon ['bekən] vti faire signe (*to sb* à qn). **he ~ed (to) her to follow him** il lui a fait signe de le suivre; **he ~ed me in/back/over** *etc* il m'a fait signe d'entrer/de revenir/d'approcher *etc*.

become [bɪ'kʌm] pret **became**, ptp **become** 1 vi a (*grow to be*) devenir, se faire. **to ~ famous** *etc* devenir célèbre *etc*; **to ~ old** vieillir, se faire vieux; **to ~ thin** maigrir; **to ~ fat** grossir; **to ~ accustomed to** s'accoutumer à, s'habituer à; **to ~ interested in** commencer à s'intéresser à; *[person]* **to ~ known** commencer à être connu, se faire connaître; **we are fast becoming a nation of cynics** nous nous transformons rapidement en une nation de cyniques.

b (*acquire position of*) devenir. **to ~ king** devenir roi; **to ~ a doctor** devenir *or* se faire médecin.

2 impers vb: **what has ~ of him?** qu'est-il devenu?; **I don't know what will ~ of her** je ne sais pas ce qu'elle va devenir.

3 vt (*liter, frm*) a (*suit*) aller à. **her hat does not ~ her** son chapeau ne lui va pas *or* ne lui sied pas (*frm*).

b (*befit*) convenir à, être digne de. **it does not ~ him to speak thus** il lui sied mal de parler ainsi.

becoming [bɪ'kʌmɪŋ] adj *behaviour, speech* convenable, bienséant; *clothes, hair style* seyant, qui va bien. **her hat is not ~** son chapeau ne lui va pas *or* n'est pas seyant.

becquerel [ˌbekə'rel] n becquerel *m*.

bed [bed] 1 n a (*furniture*) lit *m*. **room with 2 ~s** chambre *f* à 2 lits; **to go to ~** se coucher; (*euph*) **to go to ~ with sb*** coucher avec qn*; **to get into ~** se coucher, se mettre au lit; **to get out of ~** se lever; (*fig*) **to get out of ~ on the wrong side**, (*US*) **to get up on the wrong**

side of the ~* se lever du pied gauche*; **to get sb to ~** réussir à coucher qn; **to put sb to ~** coucher qn; **to make the ~** faire le lit; **to turn down the ~** préparer le lit (*en repliant le haut des draps*), faire la couverture; **to be in ~** être couché; (*through illness*) être alité, garder le lit; **to go home to ~** rentrer se coucher; **to sleep in separate ~s** faire lit à part; **before ~** avant de se coucher; (*frm, hum*) **~ of sickness** lit de douleur; (*Brit*) **"~ and breakfast"** "chambres" (*avec petit déjeuner*); (*Brit*) **to book in (at a hotel) for ~ and breakfast** prendre une chambre avec le petit déjeuner (à l'hôtel); (*Brit*) **we stayed at ~-and-breakfast places** nous avons pris pension *or* pris une chambre chez des particuliers; **~ and board** le gîte *or* le vivre et le couvert; *[hotel etc]* pension *f* complète; (*Prov*) **as you make your ~ so you must lie on it** comme on fait son lit on se couche; (*fig*) **life is not a ~ of roses** la vie n'est pas une partie de plaisir; (*fig*) **my job isn't exactly a ~ of roses*** mon travail n'est pas exactement une sinécure; († *liter*) **she was brought to ~ of a boy** elle accoucha d'un garçon; (*Press*) **to put a paper to ~*** mettre un journal sous presse; (*Press*) **the paper has gone to ~*** le journal est sous presse; *see* **camp¹, death, feather** *etc.*

b (*layer*) (*Geol*) *[coal]* couche *f*, gisement *m*; *[clay]* couche, lit *m*; *[coral]* banc *m*; *[ore]* gisement; (*Constr*) *[mortar]* bain *m* (de mortier); (*Zool*) *[oysters]* banc.

c (*base*) (*Tech*) *[engine]* berceau *m*; *[lathe]* banc *m*; *[machine]* base *f*, bâti *m*; *[truck]* plateau *m*; (*Archit*) *[building]* assises *fpl*. (*Culin*) **on a ~ of lettuce/rice** sur un lit de laitue/riz.

d (*bottom*) *[sea]* fond *m*; *[river]* lit *m*.

e (*Horticulture*) *[vegetables]* planche *f*, (*square*) carré *m*; *[flowers]* parterre *m*, massif *m*, (*strip*) plate-bande *f*, (*oval, circular*) corbeille *f*.

2 **comp** ▸**bed bath** (grande) toilette *f* (*d'un malade*) ▸**bedbug** punaise *f* ▸**bedclothes** couvertures *fpl* et draps *mpl* (de lit) ▸**bedcover** couvre-lit *m*, dessus-de-lit *m inv* ▸**bedfellows**: (*lit*) **they were bedfellows for a night** ils ont partagé le même lit une nuit; (*fig*) **they are strange bedfellows** ils forment une drôle de paire *or* un drôle de couple ▸**bedhead** tête *f* de lit, chevet *m* ▸**bed jacket** liseuse *f* ▸**bed linen** draps *mpl* de lit (et taies *fpl* d'oreillers) ▸**bedmate*** (*US*) partenaire *mf*, concubin(e) *m(f)* ▸**bed of nails** (*lit*) lit *m* à clous; (*Brit fig*) **it's a bed of nails** c'est extrêmement pénible ▸**bed pad** (*waterproof*) alaise *f*, (*for extra comfort*) molleton *m* ▸**bedpan** bassin *m* (hygiénique) ▸**bedpost** colonne *f* de lit ▸**bedridden** alité, cloué au lit, (*permanently*) grabataire ▸**bedrock** (*Geol*) soubassement *m*; (*fig*) base *f* ▸**bedroll** tapis *m* de couchage ▸**bedroom** *see* **bedroom** ▸**bedsettee** canapé-lit *m* ▸**bedside** *see* **bedside** ▸**bed-sitter** (*Brit*), **bedsitting room** (*Brit*), **bedsit‡** (*Brit*) chambre meublée, studio *m* ▸**bedsocks** chaussettes *fpl* (de lit) ▸**bedsore** escarre *f* ▸**bedspread** dessus-de-lit *m inv*, couvre-lit *m* ▸**bedspring** (*framework: US*) sommier *m* à ressorts; (*single spring*) ressort *m* de sommier ▸**bedstead** châlit *m*, bois *m* de lit ▸**bedstraw** (*Bot*) gaillet *m* ▸**bedtime** *see* **bedtime** ▸**bedwetting** (*Med*) incontinence *f* nocturne.

3 **vt** a (*Horticulture*) **to ~ (out) plants** repiquer des plantes.

b (*Tech*) *foundations* asseoir. **to ~ stones in mortar** cimenter *or* sceller des pierres.

c (‡) *woman* coucher avec*.

▸**bed down** 1 **vi** (*go to bed*) (aller) se coucher; (*spend night*) coucher. 2 **vt** (*children etc*) coucher.

B.Ed. [biːˈed] **n** (**abbr of Bachelor of Education**) *see* **bachelor.**

bedaub [bɪˈdɔːb] **vt** barbouiller (*with* de).

-bedded [ˈbedɪd] **adj ending in comps: twin-bedded room** chambre *f* à deux lits.

bedding [ˈbedɪŋ] **n** a literie *f*; (*Mil*) matériel *m* de couchage; *[animals]* litière *f*. b (*Horticulture*) **~ out** repiquage *m*; **~ (-out) plants** plantes *fpl* à repiquer.

bedeck [bɪˈdek] **vt** parer, orner (*with* de); (*slightly pej*) attifer* (*with* de).

bedevil [bɪˈdevl] **vt** (*confuse*) *issue, person* embrouiller; (*torment*) *person* tourmenter, harceler. **to be ~led by** *[person, project]* souffrir de.

bedevilment [bɪˈdevlmənt] **n** (*confusion*) confusion *f*; (*torment*) tourment *m*, harcèlement *m*.

bedlam [ˈbedləm] **n** a (*uproar*) chahut* *m*, chambard‡ *m*. **the class was a regular ~** la classe faisait un chahut terrible*. b (*Hist*) maison *f* de fous.

Bedouin [ˈbedʊɪn] 1 **n, pl ~** *or* **~s** Bédouin(e) *m(f)*. 2 **adj** bédouin.

bedraggled [bɪˈdrægld] **adj** *clothes, person* débraillé; *hair* embroussaillé; (*wet*) trempé.

bedroom [ˈbedrʊm] 1 **n** chambre *f* (à coucher); *see* **spare.** 2 **comp** ▸**bedroom farce** (*Theat*) comédie *f* de boulevard ▸**bedroom scene** ≃ scène *f* d'amour ▸**bedroom slipper** pantoufle *f* ▸**bedroom suburb*** (*US fig*) banlieue-dortoir *f* ▸**bedroom suite** chambre *f* à coucher (*mobilier*).

-bedroomed [ˈbedrʊmd] **adj ending in comps: a two-/four-bedroomed house** une maison avec deux/quatre chambres; **a one-bedroomed flat** un (appartement) deux-pièces.

Beds. [bedz] **n abbr of Bedfordshire.**

bedside [ˈbedsaɪd] 1 **n** chevet *m*. **at his ~** à son chevet. 2 **comp** *book, lamp* de chevet ▸**bedside manner** *[doctor]* comportement *m* envers les malades; **he has a good bedside manner** il sait parler à ses malades ▸**bedside rug** descente *f* de lit ▸**bedside table** table *f* de chevet *or* de nuit.

bedtime [ˈbedtaɪm] 1 **n** heure *f* du coucher. **it is ~** il est l'heure d'aller se coucher *or* d'aller au lit; **his ~ is 7 o'clock** il se couche à 7 heures; **it's past your ~** tu devrais être déjà couché. 2 **comp** ▸**bedtime drink** boisson chaude (avant de se coucher) ▸**bedtime reading** ≃ lecture *f* de plage ▸**bedtime story: to tell a child a bedtime story** raconter une histoire à un enfant avant qu'il s'endorme.

bee [biː] 1 **n** a abeille *f*. (*fig*) **to have a ~ in one's bonnet*** avoir une idée fixe (*about* en ce qui concerne), avoir une marotte; **they crowded round him like ~s round a honeypot** ils se pressaient autour de lui comme des mouches sur un pot de confiture; **it is the ~'s knees*** c'est extra* *or* super*; **he thinks he is the ~'s knees*** il se croit sorti de la cuisse de Jupiter*; *see* **bumblebee, busy, queen** *etc.*

b (*esp US: meeting*) réunion *f* de voisins pour une tâche commune. **they have a sewing ~ on Thursdays** elles se réunissent pour coudre le jeudi; *see* **spelling.**

2 **comp** ▸**bee eater** (*Orn*) guêpier *m* ▸**beehive** (*lit, fig*) ruche *f*; **beehive hair style** coiffure *f* en casque de Minerve *or* toute en hauteur; (*US*) **the Beehive State** l'Utah *m* ▸**beekeeper** apiculteur *m*, -trice *f* ▸**beeline: in a beeline** à vol d'oiseau, en ligne droite; **to make a beeline for** (*go straight to*) se diriger tout droit *or* en droite ligne vers; (*rush towards*) se ruer sur, filer droit sur ▸**beeswax n** cire *f* d'abeille ◊ **vt** *floor etc* cirer, encaustiquer.

Beeb* [biːb] **n** (*Brit*) **the ~** la B.B.C.

beech [biːtʃ] 1 **n** (*also* **~ tree**) hêtre *m*; (*wood*) (bois *m* de) hêtre; *see* **copper.** 2 **comp** *hedge, chair* de hêtre ▸**beech grove** hêtraie *f* ▸**beechmast** faînes *fpl* (tombées) ▸**beechnut** faîne *f* ▸**beechwood** (*material*) (bois *m* de) hêtre *m*; (*group of trees*) bois *m* de hêtres.

beef [biːf] 1 **n** a (*NonC*) bœuf *m*. **roast ~** rôti *m* de bœuf, rosbif *m*; **there's too much ~ on him‡** il a trop de viande‡, il est trop gros; *see* **bully, corned** *etc.* b (*US ‡: complaint*) **what's your ~?** qu'est-ce que tu as à râler?* 2 **comp** ▸**beefburger** ≃ hamburger *m* ▸**beefcake*** (*hum*) monsieur-muscles* *m* ▸**beef cattle** bœufs *mpl* de boucherie ▸**beefeater** (*Brit*) hallebardier *m* (*de la Tour de Londres*) ▸**beef olive** paupiette *f* de bœuf ▸**beef sausage** ≃ saucisse *f* de Strasbourg ▸**beefsteak** bifteck *m*, steak *m* ▸**beef tea** bouillon *m* (de viande). 3 **vi** (‡*: complain*) rouspéter*, râler* (*about* contre).

▸**beef up‡ vt sep** *speech, essay* étoffer; *team* renforcer.

beefy* [ˈbiːfɪ] **adj** (*pej*) (*strong*) costaud* (*f inv*); (*fat*) bien en chair; *flavour* de bœuf.

been [biːn] **ptp of be.**

beep [biːp] 1 **n** *[watch]* bip *m*. 2 **vi** faire bip.

beeper [ˈbiːpəʳ] **n = bleeper.**

beer [bɪəʳ] 1 **n** bière *f*. (*Brit*) **life's not all ~ and skittles** tout n'est pas qu'une partie de rigolade* en ce monde; *see* **ginger** *etc.* 2 **comp** ▸**beer barrel** tonneau *m* à bière ▸**beer belly*** bedaine* *f* (de buveur de bière) ▸**beer bottle** canette *f* ▸**beer can** boîte *f* de bière (vide) ▸**beer drinker** buveur *m*, -euse *f* de bière ▸**beer engine** pompe *f* à bière ▸**beerfest** (*US*) fête *f* de la bière ▸**beer glass** bock *m* ▸**beer gut* = beer belly*** ▸**beer pump = beer engine.**

beery [ˈbɪərɪ] **adj** *atmosphere, room* qui sent la bière; *party* où la bière coule à flots; *person* un peu éméché*, parti*. **~ face** trogne *f* d'ivrogne*.

beet [biːt] 1 **n** betterave *f*. (*US*) **red ~** betterave (potagère); *see* **sugar** *etc.* 2 **comp** ▸**beetroot** (*Brit*) betterave *f* (potagère); **to go beetroot*** devenir rouge comme une tomate, devenir cramoisi; **beetroot salad** salade *f* de betterave(s) ▸**beet sugar** sucre *m* de betterave.

beetle¹ [ˈbiːtl] 1 **n** (*gen*) scarabée *m*; (*Zool*) coléoptère *m*; *see* **black, Colorado, death, stag** *etc.* 2 **vi** (‡) **to ~ in/through** *etc* entrer/traverser *etc* en vitesse.

▸**beetle off‡ vi** décamper, ficher le camp*.

beetle² [ˈbiːtl] **comp** ▸**beetle-browed** (*bushy eyebrows*) aux sourcils broussailleux; (*sullen*) renfrogné.

beetle³ [ˈbiːtl] **n** (*mallet*) mailloche *f*; (*heavier*) mouton *m*.

beetling [ˈbiːtlɪŋ] **adj: ~ brow** front *m* proéminent; **~ cliffs** falaises *fpl* surplombantes.

beetroot [ˈbiːtruːt] **n** *see* **beet 2.**

befall [bɪˈfɔːl] **pret befell, ptp befallen** (*liter: only infin and 3rd person*) 1 **vi** arriver, advenir, survenir. **whatever may ~** quoi qu'il puisse arriver, quoi qu'il advienne. 2 **vt** arriver à, échoir à. **a misfortune befell him** il lui arriva un malheur.

befit [bɪˈfɪt] **vt** (*frm: only infin and 3rd person*) convenir à. **it ill ~s him to speak thus** il lui convient *or* il lui sied (*frm*) mal de parler ainsi.

befitting [bɪˈfɪtɪŋ] **adj** convenable, seyant. **with ~ humility** avec l'humilité qui convient *or* qui sied (*frm*).

befog [bɪˈfɒg] **vt** (*puzzle*) brouiller, embrouiller; (*obscure*) *origin, meaning* obscurcir. **she was quite ~ged** elle était dans le brouillard (le plus complet).

before [bɪˈfɔːʳ] (*phr vb elem*) 1 **prep** a (*time*) avant. **~ Christ** avant Jésus-Christ; **the day ~ yesterday** avant-hier *m*; **he came the year ~ last** il est venu il y a deux ans; **the year ~ last was his centenary** son centenaire a eu lieu il y a deux ans; **the programme ~ last** l'avant-dernier programme; **the day ~ their departure** la veille de leur départ;

two days ~ Christmas l'avant-veille *f* de Noël; **I got there ~ you** je suis arrivé avant vous, je vous ai devancé; **that was ~ my time** (*before I was here*) je n'étais pas encore là; (*before I was born*) je n'étais pas encore né; **I cannot do it ~ next week** je ne peux pas le faire avant la semaine prochaine; **~ it, ~ now, ~ then** avant (cela *or* ça), auparavant; **you should have done it ~ now** vous devriez l'avoir déjà fait; **~ long** avant peu, sous peu, d'ici peu, bientôt; **~ doing** avant de faire.

b (*order, rank*) avant. **ladies ~ gentlemen** les dames avant les messieurs; **~ everything** avant tout; **to come ~ sb/sth** précéder qn/qch.

c (*place, position*) devant. **he stood ~ me** il était (là) devant moi; **~ my (very) eyes** sous mes (propres) yeux; **the question ~ us** la question qui nous occupe; **the task ~ him** la tâche qu'il a devant lui *or* qui l'attend; **he fled ~ the enemy** il s'est enfui à l'approche de *or* devant l'ennemi; (*Naut*) **to sail ~ the mast** servir comme simple matelot; (*Naut*) **to run ~ the wind** aller *or* avoir vent arrière; *see* **carry**.

d (*in presence of*) devant, en présence de. **he said it ~ us all** il l'a dit en notre présence *or* devant nous tous; **~ a lawyer** par-devant notaire; **to appear/go ~ a court/a judge** comparaître/passer devant un tribunal/un juge; **he brought the case ~ the court** il a saisi le tribunal de l'affaire.

e (*rather than*) plutôt que. **to put death ~ dishonour** préférer la mort au déshonneur; **he would die ~ betraying his country** il mourrait plutôt que de trahir sa patrie.

2 **adv** a (*time*) avant, auparavant. **the day ~** la veille; **the evening ~** la veille au soir; **the week/year ~** la semaine/l'année d'avant *or* précédente; **two days ~** l'avant-veille, deux jours avant *or* auparavant; **I have read that book ~** j'ai déjà lu ce livre; **I had read it ~** je l'avais déjà lu, je l'avais lu auparavant; **I said ~ that ...** j'ai déjà dit que ...; **she has never met him ~** c'est la première fois qu'elle le rencontre, elle ne l'a jamais encore rencontré; **it has never happened ~** c'est la première fois que cela arrive; **long ~** longtemps auparavant; **to continue as ~** faire comme par le passé; **he should have told me ~** il aurait dû me le dire avant *or* plus tôt *or* auparavant.

b (*place*) en avant, devant.

c (*order*) avant. **that chapter and the one ~** ce chapitre et le précédent *or* et celui d'avant.

3 **conj** a (*time*) avant de + *infin*, avant que (+ ne) + *subj*. **I did it ~ going out** je l'ai fait avant de sortir; **go and see him ~ he goes** allez le voir avant son départ *or* avant qu'il (ne) parte; **~ I come/go/return** avant mon arrivée/mon départ/mon retour; **we will need a year ~ it is finished** il nous faudra un an pour l'achever; **it will be a long time ~ he comes again** il ne reviendra pas de *or* d'ici longtemps; **it will be 6 weeks ~ the boat returns** le bateau ne reviendra pas avant 6 semaines; (*fig*) **~ you could say Jack Robinson** en moins de rien, en moins de deux, en moins de temps qu'il n'en faut pour le dire; **~ I forget, your mother phoned** avant que je n'oublie (*subj*), votre mère a téléphoné.

b (*rather than*) plutôt que de + *infin*. **he will die ~ he surrenders** il mourra plutôt que de se rendre.

4 **comp ▸before-and-after test** test *m* "avant-après" **▸beforehand** *see* **beforehand ▸before-tax** *income* brut; *profit* avant impôts.

beforehand [bɪ'fɔːhænd] **adv** d'avance, à l'avance, avant, au préalable. **you must tell me ~** il faut me le dire à l'avance, il faut me prévenir avant *or* au préalable; **to make preparations well ~** faire des préparatifs bien à l'avance.

befoul [bɪ'faʊl] **vt** (*liter: lit, fig*) souiller (*liter*), salir.

befriend [bɪ'frend] **vt** (*help*) venir en aide à, aider; (*be friend to*) traiter en ami, donner son amitié à.

befuddle [bɪ'fʌdl] **vt** (*confuse*) brouiller l'esprit *or* les idées de; (*make tipsy*) griser, émécher. **~d with drink** éméché.

beg [beg] 1 **vt** a *money, alms, food* mendier.

b *favour* solliciter, quémander. **to ~ sb's pardon** demander pardon à qn; **(I) ~ your pardon** (*apologizing*) je vous demande pardon; (*not having heard*) pardon?, vous disiez?; **to ~ (sb's) forgiveness (for sth)** implorer le pardon (de qn) (pour avoir fait qch); (*frm*) **I ~ to state that** je me permets de (vous) faire remarquer que, qu'il me soit permis de faire remarquer que; **I ~ to differ** permettez-moi d'être d'un autre avis, je me permets de ne pas partager cet avis; (*frm*) **I ~ to inform you that** je tiens à *or* j'ai l'honneur (*frm*) de vous faire savoir que; (*frm*) **to ~ leave to do** solliciter l'autorisation de faire.

c (*entreat*) supplier. **to ~ (of) sb to do** supplier qn de faire; **I ~ (of) you!** je vous en supplie!, de grâce!

d **to ~ the question** (*evade the issue*) éluder la question; (*assume sth already proved*) présumer la question résolue.

2 **vi** a mendier, demander la charité. **to ~ for money** mendier; **to ~ for food** mendier de la nourriture; *[dog]* **to sit up and ~** faire le beau; (*fig*) **I'll have that sausage if it's going ~ging*** donne-moi cette saucisse s'il n'y a pas d'amateurs.

b (*entreat*) supplier. **to ~ for mercy/help** demander grâce/de l'aide; *see also* **1c**.

▸beg off* (*US*) **vi** se faire excuser (*from* de).

began [bɪ'gæn] **pret of begin**.

beget [bɪ'get] **pret begot, ptp begotten vt** (*lit:* ††) engendrer; (*fig*) engendrer, causer. **the only begotten Son of the Father** le Fils unique engendré par le Père.

beggar ['begəʳ] 1 **n** a (*also* **~ man, ~ woman**) mendiant(e) *m(f)*, mendigot(e)* *m(f)*; (*fig: very poor person*) indigent(e) *m(f)*, pauvre(sse) *m(f)*. (*Prov*) **~s can't be choosers** nécessité fait loi (*Prov*); **~'s opera** opéra *m* de quat' sous. b (**: fellow*) **poor ~!** pauvre diable!*; **a lucky ~** un veinard*; **a queer little ~** un drôle de petit bonhomme. 2 **vt** (*lit*) réduire à la mendicité; (*fig: ruin*) mettre sur la paille, ruiner. (*fig*) **to ~ description** défier toute description. 3 **comp ▸beggar-my-neighbour** (*Cards*) bataille *f*; (*Econ*) **beggar-my-neighbour policy** politique *f* protectionniste.

beggarly ['begəlɪ] **adj** *amount* piètre, misérable; *existence* misérable, sordide; *meal* maigre, piètre, pauvre; *wage* dérisoire, de famine.

beggary ['begərɪ] **n** mendicité *f*.

begging ['begɪŋ] 1 **n** mendicité *f*. **to live by ~** vivre de charité *or* d'aumône; *see also* **beg 2a**. 2 **adj**: **~ letter** lettre *f* quémandant de l'argent.

begin [bɪ'gɪn] **pret began, ptp begun** 1 **vt** a (*start*) commencer (*to do, doing* à faire, de faire), se mettre (*to do, doing* à faire); *work* commencer, se mettre à; *task* entreprendre; *song* commencer (à chanter), entonner; *attack* déclencher; *bottle, packet, cheese etc* commencer, entamer, déboucher; *book, letter [writer]* commencer (à écrire); *[reader]* commencer (à lire). **to ~ a cheque book/a page** commencer *or* prendre un nouveau carnet de chèques/une nouvelle page; **to ~ a journey** partir en voyage; **he began the day with a glass of milk** il a bu un verre de lait pour bien commencer la journée; **to ~ the day right** bien commencer la journée, se lever du pied droit; **to ~ life as** débuter dans la vie comme; **that doesn't (even) ~ to compare with ...** cela est loin d'être comparable à ..., cela n'a rien de comparable avec ...; **it soon began to rain** il n'a pas tardé à pleuvoir; **I'd begun to think you were not coming** je commençais à croire que tu ne viendrais pas; **to ~ again** *or* **afresh** recommencer (*to do* à faire), recommencer à zéro; **"it's late" he began** "il est tard" commença-t-il.

b (*originate, initiate*) *discussion* commencer, ouvrir; *conversation* amorcer, engager; *quarrel, argument, dispute* faire naître; *reform, movement, series of events* déclencher; *fashion* lancer; *custom, policy* inaugurer; *war* causer; *rumour* faire naître.

2 **vi** a *[person]* commencer, s'y mettre; *[speech, programme, meeting, ceremony]* commencer (*with* par). **let's ~!** commençons!, allons-y!, on s'y met!*; **we must ~ at once** il faut commencer *or* nous y mettre immédiatement; **well, to ~ at the beginning** eh bien! pour commencer par le commencement; **it's ~ning rather well/badly** cela s'annonce plutôt bien/mal; **to ~ in business** se lancer dans les affaires; **just where the hair ~s** à la naissance des cheveux; **before October ~s** avant le début d'octobre; **to ~ again** *or* **afresh** recommencer (à zéro); **classes ~ on Monday** les cours commencent *or* reprennent lundi; **the classes ~ again soon** les cours reprennent bientôt, c'est bientôt la rentrée; **~ning from Monday** à partir de lundi; **he began in the sales department/as a clerk** il a débuté dans le service des ventes/comme employé; **he began as a Marxist** il a commencé par être marxiste, au début *or* au départ il a été marxiste; **he began with the intention of writing a thesis** au début son intention était *or* il avait l'intention d'écrire une thèse; **to ~ by doing** commencer par faire; **~ by putting everything away** commence par tout ranger; **to ~ with sth** commencer *or* débuter par qch; **~ with me!** commencez par moi!; **to ~ with, there were only 3 of them but later ...** (tout) d'abord ils n'étaient que 3, mais plus tard ...; **this is false to ~ with** pour commencer *or* d'abord c'est faux; **we only had 100 francs to ~ with** nous n'avions que 100 F pour commencer *or* au début; **~ on a new page** prenez une nouvelle page.

b (*broach*) **to ~ on** *book* commencer (à écrire *or* à lire); *course of study* commencer, entreprendre; *bottle, packet, cheese etc* commencer, entamer. **I began on the job last week** j'ai commencé à travailler *or* j'ai débuté dans mon travail la semaine dernière.

c *[music, noise, guns]* commencer, retentir; *[fire]* commencer, prendre; *[river]* prendre sa source; *[road]* partir (*at* de); *[political party, movement, custom]* commencer, naître. **that's when the trouble ~s** c'est alors *or* là que les ennuis commencent; **it all began when he refused to pay** toute cette histoire a commencé *or* tout a commencé quand il a refusé de payer; **since the world began** depuis le commencement du monde, depuis que le monde est monde.

beginner [bɪ'gɪnəʳ] **n** a (*novice*) débutant(e) *m(f)*, novice *mf*. **it's just ~'s luck** aux innocents les mains pleines (*Prov*). b (*originator*) auteur *m*, cause *f*.

beginning [bɪ'gɪnɪŋ] **n** a *[speech, book, film, career etc]* commencement *m*, début *m*. **to make a ~** commencer, débuter; **the ~ of the academic year** la rentrée (universitaire *or* scolaire); **the ~ of the world** le commencement *or* l'origine *f* du monde; **in the ~** au commencement, au début; **from the ~** dès le début, dès le commencement; **since the ~ of time** depuis le commencement du monde, depuis que le monde est monde; **from ~ to end** du début *or* du commencement à la fin, de bout en bout, d'un bout à l'autre; **to start again at** *or* **from the ~** recommencer au commencement; **the ~ of negotiations** l'amorce *f or* l'ouverture *f* des négociations; **it was the ~ of the end for him** pour lui ce fut le commencement de la fin; **they taught him the ~s of science** ils lui ont enseigné les rudiments *mpl* de la science.

b (*origin*) origine *f*, commencement *m*. **the shooting was the ~ of the rebellion** la fusillade a été à l'origine de la révolte; **fascism had its ~s in Italy** le fascisme prit naissance en Italie.

begone [bɪ'gɒn] excl (*liter* ††) partez!, hors d'ici! (*liter*).

begonia [bɪ'gəʊnɪə] n bégonia *m*.

begot [bɪ'gɒt] pret of **beget**.

begotten [bɪ'gɒtn] ptp of **beget**.

begrimed [bɪ'graɪmd] adj noirci, sale.

begrudge [bɪ'grʌdʒ] vt = **grudge 1**.

beguile [bɪ'gaɪl] vt a tromper, duper. **to ~ sb with promises** bercer qn de promesses, endormir qn avec des promesses; **to ~ sb into doing sth** amener *or* entraîner qn par supercherie à faire qch; **to ~ the time (doing)** faire passer le temps (en faisant). b (*charm*) séduire captiver; (*amuse*) distraire.

beguiling [bɪ'gaɪlɪŋ] adj *woman, charm* captivant, séduisant; *ideas, theory* séduisant; *story* captivant.

begum ['beɪgəm] n bégum *f*.

begun [bɪ'gʌn] ptp of **begin**.

behalf [bɪ'hɑːf] n: **on ~ of** (*as representing*) de la part de, au nom de, pour; (*in the interest of*) en faveur de, dans l'intérêt de, pour; **to come on sb's ~** venir de la part de qn; **to act on sb's ~** agir pour qn *or* pour le compte de qn; **he spoke on my ~** il a parlé pour moi *or* en mon nom; **to plead on sb's ~** plaider en faveur de qn; **he was worried on my ~** il s'inquiétait pour moi *or* à mon sujet.

behave [bɪ'heɪv] vi (*also* **~ o.s.**) a (*conduct o.s.*) se conduire, se comporter. **to ~ (o.s.) well/badly** se conduire *or* se comporter bien/mal; **to ~ well towards sb** se comporter bien à l'égard de *or* envers qn, bien agir envers qn; **to ~ wisely** agir sagement; **to ~ like an honest man** se comporter *or* se conduire en honnête homme. b (*conduct o.s. well*) bien se tenir; *[child]* être sage. **he knows how to ~ in society** il sait se tenir dans le monde; **~ yourself!** sois sage!, tiens-toi bien! c *[machines etc]* marcher, fonctionner. **the ship ~s well at sea** le navire tient bien la mer.

behaviour, (*US*) **behavior** [bɪ'heɪvjəʳ] n a (*manner, bearing*) conduite *f*, comportement *m*. **to be on one's best ~** se conduire de son mieux; *[child]* se montrer d'une sagesse exemplaire; **~ modification** modification *f* du comportement; **~ therapy** thérapie *f* de comportement. b (*conduct towards others*) conduite *f*, comportement *m*, façon *f* d'agir *or* de se comporter (*to sb, towards sb* envers qn, à l'égard de qn). c *[machines]* fonctionnement *m*.

behavioural, (*US*) **behavioral** [bɪ'heɪvjərəl] adj a *sciences, studies* behavioriste. b *pattern* de comportement. **~ problems** troubles *mpl* du comportement.

behaviourism, (*US*) **behaviorism** [bɪ'heɪvjərɪzəm] n behaviorisme *m*.

behaviourist, (*US*) **behaviorist** [bɪ'heɪvjərɪst] adj, n behavioriste (*mf*).

behead [bɪ'hed] vt décapiter.

beheld [bɪ'held] pret, ptp of **behold**.

behest [bɪ'hest] n (*liter*) commandement *m*, ordre *m*. **at the ~ of** sur l'ordre de.

behind [bɪ'haɪnd] (*phr vb elem*) 1 adv a (*in or at the rear*) derrière, par derrière, en arrière. **to stay ~** rester derrière les autres *or* en arrière; **to look ~** regarder en arrière; (*lit, fig*) **to leave ~** laisser derrière soi; **to come ~** suivre, venir derrière; **to follow a long way ~** *or* **far ~/not far ~** suivre de loin/d'assez près; *see* **fall behind** *etc*.

b (*late*) en retard. **to be ~ with one's studies/payments** être en retard dans ses études/ses paiements; **to be ~ with one's work** avoir du travail en retard, être en retard dans son travail; **I'm too far ~ to catch up now** j'ai pris trop de retard pour me rattraper maintenant.

2 prep a (*lit, fig: at the back of*) derrière. **~ the table** derrière la table; **come out from ~ the door** sortez de derrière la porte; **walk close ~ me** suivez-moi de près; **~ my back** (*lit*) derrière mon dos; (*fig*) derrière mon dos, à mon insu; (*fig*) **to put sth ~ one** oublier qch, refuser de penser à qch; (*Theat, fig*) **~ the scenes** dans les coulisses; (*fig*) **he has the Communists ~ him** il a les communistes derrière lui; (*fig*) **SHE'S the one ~ this scheme** c'est elle qui est à l'origine de ce projet; (*fig*) **what is ~ this?** qu'y a-t-il là-dessous?

b (*more backward than*) en arrière de, en retard sur. **her son is ~ the other pupils** son fils est en retard sur les autres élèves.

c (*time*) **~ time** en retard; (*fig*) **to be ~ the times** être en retard sur son temps, ne pas être de son époque; **their youth is far ~ them** leur jeunesse est loin derrière eux.

3 n (**: buttocks*) derrière *m*, postérieur* *m*.

behindhand [bɪ'haɪndhænd] adv en retard (*with* dans).

behold [bɪ'həʊld] pret, ptp **beheld** vt (*liter*) voir, apercevoir. **~!** voici!, tenez!, regardez!; **~ thy servant** voici ton serviteur; **and ~ I am with you** et voici que je suis avec vous; *see* **lo**.

beholden [bɪ'həʊldən] adj (*frm*) **to be ~** être redevable (*to sb for sth* à qn de qch).

behove [bɪ'həʊv], (*US*) **behoove** [bɪ'huːv] impers vt (*frm*) incomber, appartenir (*sb to do* à qn de faire), être du devoir *or* de l'intérêt (*sb to do* de qn de faire).

beige [beɪʒ] adj, n beige (*m*).

Beijing ['beɪ'dʒɪŋ] n Beijing.

being ['biːɪŋ] n a (*NonC: existence*) existence *f*. **to come into ~** prendre naissance; **the world came into ~** le monde fut créé; **to bring** *or* **call into ~** faire naître, susciter; **to bring a plan into ~** exécuter *or* réaliser un plan; **then in ~** qui existait alors. b être *m*, créature *f*. **human ~s** êtres humains; *see* **supreme**. c (*essential nature*) être *m*, essence *f*. **all my ~ revolts at the idea** tout mon être se révolte à cette idée.

Beirut [beɪ'ruːt] n Beyrouth.

bejewelled, (*US*) **bejeweled** [bɪ'dʒuːəld] adj *person* paré de bijoux; *thing* incrusté de joyaux; (*fig*) *grass* émaillé (*with* de).

belabour, (*US*) **belabor** [bɪ'leɪbəʳ] vt rouer de coups; (*fig: with words*) invectiver.

belated [bɪ'leɪtɪd] adj *apology, greetings, measures* tardif.

belatedly [bɪ'leɪtɪdlɪ] adv tardivement.

belay [bɪ'leɪ] 1 vt a (*Naut*) amarrer. **~ing pin** cabillot *m* (d'amarrage). b (*Climbing*) assurer. 2 vi assurer. 3 n assurage *m*, assurance *f*.

belch [beltʃ] 1 vi *[person]* faire un renvoi, roter*. 2 vt (*also* **~ forth** *or* **out**) *[volcano, gun] smoke, flames* vomir, cracher. 3 n renvoi *m*, rot* *m*.

beleaguered [bɪ'liːgəd] adj *city* assiégé, investi; *army* cerné.

Belfast ['belfɑːst] n Belfast.

belfry ['belfrɪ] n beffroi *m*; *[church]* clocher *m*, beffroi; *see* **bat¹**.

Belgian ['beldʒən] 1 n Belge *mf*. 2 adj belge, de Belgique.

Belgium ['beldʒəm] n Belgique *f*.

Belgrade [bel'greɪd] n Belgrade.

belie [bɪ'laɪ] vt (*fail to justify*) *hopes* démentir, tromper; (*prove false*) *words* donner le démenti à, démentir; *proverb* faire mentir; (*misrepresent*) *facts* donner une fausse impression *or* idée de.

belief [bɪ'liːf] n a (*NonC: acceptance as true*) croyance *f* (*in* en, à). **~ in ghosts** croyance aux revenants; **~ in God** croyance en Dieu; **he has lost his ~ in God** il ne croit plus en Dieu, il a perdu la foi (en Dieu); **worthy of ~** digne de foi; **it is beyond** *or* **past (all) ~** c'est incroyable, c'est à ne pas (y) croire; **wealthy beyond ~** incroyablement riche.

b (*Rel*) (*faith*) foi *f*; (*doctrine*) credo *m*.

c (*conviction*) opinion *f*, conviction *f*. **in the ~ that** persuadé que, convaincu que; **it is my ~ that** je suis convaincu *or* persuadé que; **to the best of my ~** autant que je sache; **to entertain the ~ that** être convaincu que, croire que; *see* **strong**.

d (*NonC: trust*) confiance *f*, foi *f* (*in* en). **he has no ~ in doctors** il n'a aucune confiance dans les médecins; **he has no ~ in the future** il ne fait pas confiance à l'avenir.

believable [bɪ'liːvəbl] adj croyable.

believe [bɪ'liːv] 1 vt a (*accept truth of*) *statement, account, evidence* croire, donner *or* ajouter foi à; *person* croire. **to ~ what sb says** croire ce que dit qn; **I don't ~ a word of it** je n'en crois rien *or* pas un mot; (*in exasperation*) **I don't ~ it!** non mais ce n'est pas vrai!; **don't you ~ it!*** ne va pas croire ça!*, crois-le et bois de l'eau (fraîche)*; **he could hardly ~ his eyes/ears** il en croyait à peine ses yeux/ses oreilles; **if he is to be ~d** à l'en croire, s'il faut l'en croire; **~ it or not, he ...** c'est incroyable, mais il ...; **~ me** crois-moi, tu peux me croire; **~ you me** tu peux m'en croire; **I ~ you, thousands wouldn't*** moi, je te crois, mais je dois être le seul!

b (*think*) croire, estimer. **I ~ I'm right** je crois avoir raison; **I don't ~ he will come** je ne crois pas qu'il viendra *or* qu'il vienne; **he is ~d to be ill** on le croit malade; **he is ~d to have a chance of succeeding** on lui donne des chances de succès; **that is ~d to be true** cela passe pour vrai; **I have every reason to ~ that ...** j'ai tout lieu de croire que ...; **I ~ so** je crois que oui, je le crois; **I ~ not** je crois que non, je ne (le) crois pas; **I don't know what to ~** je ne sais que croire *or* à quoi m'en tenir; *see* **make**.

2 vi croire; (*Rel*) croire, avoir la foi. **to ~ in** *God* croire en; *ghosts, promises, antibiotics etc* croire à; **to ~ in sb** croire en qn, avoir confiance en qn; **to ~ in a method** être partisan d'une méthode; **I don't ~ in doctors** je n'ai pas confiance dans les médecins, je ne crois pas aux médecins; **I don't ~ in letting children do what they want** je ne suis pas d'avis qu'il faille laisser les enfants faire ce qu'ils veulent.

believer [bɪ'liːvəʳ] n a partisan(e) *m(f)*, adepte *mf*. **~ in capital punishment** partisan de la peine capitale; **he is a great ~ in** il est très partisan de. b (*Rel*) croyant(e) *m(f)*. **to be a ~** être croyant, avoir la foi; **to be a ~ in ghosts/in astrology** croire aux revenants/à l'astrologie.

Belisha beacon [bɪ'liːʃə'biːkən] n lampadaire *m* (*à globe orange marquant un passage clouté*).

belittle [bɪ'lɪtl] vt *person, action, object* déprécier, rabaisser. **to ~ o.s.** se déprécier.

Belize [be'liːz] n Bélize *m*. **in ~** à Bélize.

Belizean [be'liːzɪən] 1 n Bélizien(ne) *m(f)*. 2 adj bélizien.

bell¹ [bel] 1 n a *[church, school]* cloche *f*; (*hand~*) clochette *f*; *[toys, cat's collar etc]* grelot *m*; *[cows]* cloche, clarine *f*; *[goats, sheep]* clochette; *[door]* sonnette *f*; (*electric*) sonnerie *f*; *[cycle, typewriter]* timbre *m*; *[telephone]* sonnerie. **great ~** bourdon *m*, grosse cloche; **the first ~ for mass was ringing** le premier coup de la messe sonnait; (*Brit: phone sb*) **to give sb a ~*** donner un coup de fil *or* bigophone à qn*; **there's**

the ~! *[door]* on sonne!, ça sonne!*; *[telephone]* le téléphone (sonne)!; (*Naut*) ~**s** coups *mpl* de cloche; **eight ~s** huit coups piqués; **to sound four/six/eight ~s** piquer quatre/six/huit (coups); *see* **answer, chime, ring²** *etc.*

b *[flower]* calice *m*, clochette *f*; *[trumpet]* pavillon *m*.

2 vt mettre une cloche à. (*fig*) **to ~ the cat** attacher le grelot (*fig*).

3 comp ►**bell-bottomed trousers, bell-bottoms** (pantalon *m* à) pattes *fpl* d'éléphant; (*Naut*) pantalon de marine ►**bellboy** groom *m*, chasseur *m* ►**bell buoy** bouée *f* à cloche ►**bell glass** cloche *f* (en verre) ►**bell heather** bruyère cendrée ►**bellhop** (*US*) = **bellboy** ►**bell jar** cloche *f* en verre ►**bell pull** *[door]* poignée *f* de sonnette; *[room]* cordon *m* de sonnette ►**bell push** bouton *m* de sonnette ►**bell ringer** sonneur *m*, carillonneur *m* ►**bell rope** *[belfry]* corde *f* de cloche; *[room]* cordon *m* de sonnette ►**bell-shaped** en forme de cloche *or* de clochette ►**bell tent** tente *f* conique ►**bell tower** clocher *m*.

bell² [bel] 1 n *[stag]* bramement *m*. 2 vi bramer.

belladonna [ˌbeləˈdɒnə] n (*Bot, Med*) belladone *f*.

belle [bel] n beauté *f*, belle *f*. **the ~ of the ball** la reine du bal.

bellicose [ˈbelɪkəʊs] adj belliqueux, guerrier.

bellicosity [ˌbelɪˈkɒsɪtɪ] n caractère belliqueux.

-bellied [ˈbelɪd] adj ending in comps: **big-** *or* **fat-bellied** avec un gros ventre; **flat-bellied** au ventre plat.

belligerence [bɪˈlɪdʒərəns] n, **belligerency** [bɪˈlɪdʒərənsɪ] n belligérance *f*.

belligerent [bɪˈlɪdʒərənt] adj, n belligérant(e) *m(f)*.

bellow [ˈbeləʊ] 1 vi *[animals]* mugir; *[esp cow, bull]* beugler, meugler; *[person]* brailler, beugler* (*with* de); *[wind, ocean]* mugir. 2 vt (*also* **~ out**) *song, order* brailler, beugler*, hurler; *blasphemies* vociférer. 3 n *[animal]* mugissement *m*; *[esp cow, bull]* beuglement *m*, meuglement *m*; *[person]* hurlement *m*, beuglement*; *[storm, ocean]* mugissement.

bellows [ˈbeləʊz] npl *[forge, organ]* soufflerie *f*; *[fire]* soufflet *m*. **a pair of ~** un soufflet.

belly [ˈbelɪ] 1 n a (**: abdomen*) ventre *m*; (*big*) panse* *f*, bedaine* *f*. **his eyes were bigger than his ~** il a eu les yeux plus grands que le ventre.

b *[pregnant woman]* ventre *m*.

c *[container]* panse *f*, ventre *m*; *[stone]* renflement *m*; *[violin]* table *f* harmonique; *[guitar]* table harmonique, ventre; *[ship]* ventre; *[sail]* creux *m*.

d (*Culin*) **~ of pork** poitrine *f* de porc.

2 vt *[wind]* gonfler, enfler.

3 vi (*also* **~ out**) se gonfler, s'enfler.

4 comp ►**bellyache** n mal *m* de *or* au ventre ◊ vi (‡) ronchonner*, bougonner*; **to have a bellyache** avoir mal au ventre ►**bellyaching‡** ronchonnement* *m*, bougonnement* *m* ►**bellyband** sous-ventrière *f* ►**belly button*** nombril *m* ►**belly dance** danse *f* du ventre ►**belly dancer** danseuse orientale ►**bellyflop**: (*Swimming*) **to do a bellyflop** faire un plat ►**belly-landing** (*Aviat*) atterrissage *m* sur le ventre; (*Aviat*) **to make a belly-landing** atterrir *or* se poser sur le ventre ►**belly laugh** gros rire (gras) ►**belly tank** (*Aviat*) réservoir *m* de secours.

bellyful [ˈbelɪfʊl] n *[food]* ventre plein. (*fig*) **he had had a ~‡** il en avait plein le dos*, il en avait ras le bol*.

belong [bɪˈlɒŋ] vi a (*be the property*) appartenir, être (*to* à). **this book ~s to me** ce livre m'appartient, ce livre est à moi; **lands which ~ to the Crown** terres qui appartiennent à la Couronne; **the lid ~s to this box** le couvercle va avec cette boîte, c'est le couvercle de cette boîte.

b (*be member, inhabitant etc*) **to ~ to a society** faire partie *or* être membre d'une société; **to ~ to a town** *[native]* être originaire *or* natif d'une ville; *[inhabitant]* habiter une ville.

c (*be in right place*) être à sa place. **to feel that one doesn't ~** se sentir étranger; **to ~ together** aller ensemble; **stockings that don't ~ (together)** des bas qui ne font pas la paire; **the book ~s on this shelf** le livre va sur ce rayon; **put it back where it ~s** remets-le à sa place; **murder ~s under the heading of capital crimes** le meurtre rentre dans la catégorie des crimes capitaux.

d (*be the concern*) appartenir (*to* à), relever, être l'affaire, dépendre (*to* de). **that does not ~ to my duties** cela ne relève pas de mes fonctions; (*Jur*) **this case ~ed to the Appeal Court** ce procès ressortissait à la cour d'appel.

belongings [bɪˈlɒŋɪŋz] npl affaires *fpl*, possessions *fpl*. **personal ~** objets *or* effets personnels.

Belorussia [ˌbeləʊˈrʌʃə] n = **Byelorussia**.

Belorussian [ˌbeləʊˈrʌʃən] adj, n = **Byelorussian**.

beloved [bɪˈlʌvɪd, bɪˈlʌvd] 1 adj bien-aimé, chéri. **~ by all** aimé de tous; **dearly ~ brethren** mes bien chers frères. 2 n bien-aimé(e) *m(f)*.

below [bɪˈləʊ] (*phr vb elem*) 1 prep a (*under*) sous; (*lower than*) au-dessous de. **~ the bed** sous le lit; **on the bed and ~ it** sur le lit et en dessous; **her skirt is well ~ her knees** sa jupe est bien au-dessous du genou; **~ average/sea level** au-dessous de la moyenne/du niveau de la mer; **~ freezing point** au-dessous de zéro; **~ the horizon** au-dessous de l'horizon; **~ the surface** sous la surface; **to be ~ sb in rank** occuper un rang inférieur à qn, être au-dessous de qn.

b *[river]* en aval de. **the Thames ~ Oxford** la Tamise en aval de Oxford.

c (*unworthy of*) **it would be ~ my dignity to speak to him** je m'abaisserais en lui parlant.

2 adv a (*lower down*) en bas, en dessous, plus bas; (*Naut*) en bas. **the tenants ~** les locataires du dessous *or* d'en dessous; **they live 2 floors ~** ils habitent 2 étages en dessous; **~, we could see the valley** en bas *or* plus bas *or* en dessous nous apercevions la vallée; **voices from ~** des voix venant d'en bas; **the road ~** la route en contre-bas; (*on earth*) **here ~** ici-bas; (*in hell*) **down ~** en enfer; *see* **go below** *etc.*

b *[documents]* **see ~** voir plus bas *or* ci-dessous; **as stated ~** comme indiqué ci-dessous.

belt [belt] 1 n a (*Dress, Judo, fig*) ceinture *f*; (*Mil etc*) ceinturon *m*, ceinture; (*corset*) gaine *f*. **(shoulder) ~** baudrier *m*; (*fig*) **he has 10 years' experience under his ~** il a 10 années d'expérience à son actif *or* à son acquis; (*Boxing, also fig*) **blow below the ~** coup bas; **to hit below the ~** porter un coup bas; (*fig*) **that was below the ~!** c'était un coup bas! *or* un coup en traître!; (*fig*) **to pull in** *or* **tighten one's ~** se mettre *or* se serrer la ceinture*; (*Judo*) **to be a Black B~** être ceinture noire; (*Scot Scol* †) **to give sb the ~** punir qn à coups d'étrivière; *see* **safety** *etc.*

b (*tract of land*) région *f*. **industrial ~** région industrielle; **the cotton ~** la région de culture du coton; *see* **green**.

c (*Tech*) courroie *f*. **~ pulley** poulie *f* de courroie; *see* **conveyor** *etc.*

d (*US: road*) route *f* de ceinture.

2 comp ►**belt-and-braces:** (*fig*) **it was a belt-and-braces job*** on a fait ça pour se donner une marge de sécurité *or* être vraiment tranquille ►**beltway** (*US*) route *f* de ceinture; (*motorway-type*) périphérique *m*.

3 vt a (*thrash*) administrer une correction à, donner une raclée* à; (‡: *hit*) flanquer *or* coller un gnon‡ à. **she ~ed him (one) in the eye‡** elle lui a flanqué *or* collé un gnon‡ dans l'œil.

b (*US*) = **belt out**.

4 vi (‡: *rush*) **to ~ in/out/across** *etc* entrer/sortir/traverser *etc* à toutes jambes *or* à toute blinde‡; **he ~ed down the street** il a descendu *or* dévalé la rue à fond de train.

►**belt down‡** vt sep (*US*) *drink* descendre‡, se taper‡.

►**belt out*** vt sep: **to belt out a song** chanter une chanson de tout son cœur *or* à pleins poumons.

►**belt up** vi a (*put on seat belt*) attacher sa ceinture. b (*Brit* ‡: *be quiet*) la boucler‡, la fermer‡. **belt up!** la ferme!‡, boucle-la!‡

belting* [ˈbeltɪŋ] n (*beating*) raclée* *f*, dérouillée‡ *f*. **to give sb a good ~** donner *or* filer* une bonne raclée *or* dérouillée à qn.

belvedere [ˌbelvɪˈdɪəʳ] n belvédère *m*.

bemoan [bɪˈməʊn] vt pleurer, déplorer.

bemuse [bɪˈmjuːz] vt stupéfier.

ben [ben] n (*Scot*) mont *m*, sommet *m*. **B~ Nevis** Ben Nevis *m*.

bench [bentʃ] 1 n a (*seat*) (*gen, Parl*) banc *m*; (*in tiers*) gradin *m*; (*padded*) banquette *f*; *see* **back, opposition** *etc.*

b (*Jur*) **the B~** (*court*) la cour, le tribunal; (*judges collectively*) les magistrats *mpl*; **to be raised to the ~** être nommé juge; **to be on the ~** (*permanent office*) être juge (*or* magistrat); (*when in court*) siéger au tribunal; **to appear before the ~** comparaître devant le tribunal; **the B~ has ruled that** la cour a décrété que; *see* **king**.

c (*also* **work~**) *[laboratory, factory, workshop]* établi *m*; *see* **test**.

2 comp ►**bench lathe** tour *m* à banc ►**bench mark** (*Surv*) repère *m* de nivellement; (*fig: reference point*) point *m* de référence, repère; (*Comput*) jeu *m* d'essai; (*Statistics*) **the 1984 bench mark** l'année *f* de référence 1984; (*Econ, Comm*) **benchmark price** prix *m* de base *or* de référence; **benchmark tests** (*Comput*) tests *mpl* d'évaluation de performance ►**bench-press** (*Weightlifting*) soulever ►**bench scientist** expérimentateur *m*, -trice *f* ►**bench seat** banquette *f* ►**bench study** étude-pilote *f* ►**bench vice** étau *m* d'établi ►**benchwarmer*** (*US Sport*) joueur *m* (médiocre) en réserve.

3 vt (*US Sport **) *player* exclure du jeu (*souvent comme pénalisation*).

bencher [ˈbentʃəʳ] n (*Brit Jur*) ≃ membre *m* de l'ordre des avocats; *see* **back**.

bend [bend] (vb: pret, ptp **bent**) 1 n *[river]* coude *m*, détour *m*; *[tube, pipe]* coude; *[arm]* pli *m*, saignée *f*; *[knee]* pli; *[road]* courbe *f*, coude, virage *m*; (*Naut: knot*) nœud *m* de jonction. **there is a ~ in the road** la route fait un coude *or* un virage; (*Aut*) **~s for 8 km** virages sur 8 km; *[car]* **to take a ~** prendre un virage *or* un tournant; (*Brit*) **round the ~‡** tombé sur la tête*, cinglé‡; (*Med*) **the ~s*** la maladie des caissons; (*Her*) **~ sinister** barre *f* de bâtardise; *see* **double, hair** *etc.*

2 vt a *back, body* courber; *leg, arm* plier; *knee, leg* fléchir, plier; *head* baisser, pencher, courber; *branch* courber, faire ployer; *light ray* réfracter; *rail, pipe, rod, beam* tordre, courber; *bow* bander; (*Naut*) *cable* étalinguer; *sail* enverguer; (*fig **) *rule, one's principles* faire une entorse à. **to ~ lightly** infléchir, arquer; **to ~ at right angles** couder; **to ~ out of shape** fausser, gauchir; **with head bent over a book** la tête penchée *or* courbée sur un livre; **on ~ed knee(s)** à genoux; **to go down on ~ed knee** s'agenouiller, se mettre à genoux; (*fig: drink*) **to ~ the elbow*** lever le coude*; (*fig*) **to ~ o.s. to sb's will** se plier à la volonté de qn; (*fig*) **to ~ sb to one's will** mettre qn sous son joug; (*fig*) **to ~ sb's ear** accaparer (l'attention de) qn; *see also* **bent¹**.

b (*direct*) **to ~ one's steps towards** se diriger vers, porter ses pas vers; **all eyes were bent on him** tous les yeux *or* les regards étaient fixés *or* braqués sur lui; **to ~ one's efforts towards changing sth** diriger ses efforts vers la transformation de qch.

c (*pass only*) **to be bent on doing** être résolu *or* décidé à faire, vouloir absolument faire; **he is bent on seeing me** il veut absolument me voir; **he is bent on pleasure** il ne recherche que son plaisir.

3 **vi** *[person]* se courber; *[branch, instrument etc]* être courbé, plier; *[river, road]* faire un coude, tourner; (*fig: submit*) se soumettre, céder (*to* à). **to ~ under a burden** ployer sous un fardeau; **to ~ backward/forward** se pencher en arrière/en avant; *see* **catch.**

►**bend back** 1 **vi** *[wire etc]* se recourber; *[person]* se pencher en arrière. 2 **vt sep** replier, recourber.

►**bend down** 1 **vi** *[person]* se courber, se baisser; *[tree, branch]* ployer, plier, se courber. 2 **vt sep** *wire* replier, recourber; *branch* faire ployer.

►**bend over** 1 **vi** *[person]* se pencher. (*fig*) **to bend over backwards to help sb*** se mettre en quatre pour aider qn. 2 **vt sep** replier.

bender ['bendəʳ] **n** a (*Tech*) cintreuse *f*. b **to go on a ~‡** aller se cuiter*.

beneath [bɪ'ni:θ] 1 **prep** a (*under*) sous. **~ the table** sous la table; **to bend ~ a burden** ployer sous un fardeau. b (*lower than*) au-dessous de, sous. **town ~ the castle** ville (située) au-dessous du château. c (*unworthy of*) indigne de. **it is ~ my notice** cela ne mérite pas mon attention *or* que je m'y arrête (*subj*); **it is ~ her to interfere** il est indigne d'elle d'intervenir; **to marry ~ one** faire une mésalliance. 2 **adv** dessous, au-dessous, en bas. **the flat ~** l'appartement au-dessous *or* du dessous.

Benedict ['benɪdɪkt] **n** Benoît *m*.

Benedictine [ˌbenɪ'dɪktɪn] 1 **n** a (*Rel*) bénédictin(e) *m(f)*. b **b~** [ˌbenɪ'dɪkti:n] (*liqueur*) Bénédictine *f*. 2 **adj** bénédictin.

benediction [ˌbenɪ'dɪkʃən] **n** (*blessing*) bénédiction *f*; (*at table*) bénédicité *m*; (*Rel: office*) salut *m*.

benefaction [ˌbenɪ'fækʃən] **n** (*good deed*) bienfait *m*; (*gift*) donation *f*, don *m*.

benefactor ['benɪfæktəʳ] **n** bienfaiteur *m*.

benefactress ['benɪfæktrɪs] **n** bienfaitrice *f*.

benefice ['benɪfɪs] **n** bénéfice *m* (*Rel*).

beneficence [bɪ'nefɪsəns] **n** a (*NonC*) bienfaisance *f*. b (*act*) acte *m or* œuvre *f* de bienfaisance.

beneficent [bɪ'nefɪsənt] **adj** *person* bienfaisant; *thing* salutaire.

beneficial [ˌbenɪ'fɪʃəl] **adj** salutaire, avantageux (*to* pour), favorable (*to* à). **~ to the health** bon pour la santé; **the change will be ~ to you** le changement vous fera du bien *or* vous sera salutaire; (*Jur*) **~ owner** usufruitier *m*, -ière *f*.

beneficially [ˌbenɪ'fɪʃəlɪ] **adv** avantageusement.

beneficiary [ˌbenɪ'fɪʃərɪ] **n** *[will etc]* bénéficiaire *mf*, légataire *mf*; *[person]* ayant droit *m*; (*Rel*) bénéficier *m*.

benefit ['benɪfɪt] 1 **n** a (*gen*) avantage *m*. **for the ~ of your health** dans l'intérêt de votre santé; **it's to your ~** c'est dans votre intérêt; **the book was not (of) much ~ to me, I didn't get much ~ from the book** le livre ne m'a pas beaucoup aidé *or* ne m'a pas été très utile; **did he get much ~ from his holiday?** est-ce que ses vacances lui ont profité? *or* lui ont fait du bien?; **he's beginning to feel the ~ of his stay in the country** il commence à ressentir les bienfaits de son séjour à la campagne; **he had the ~ of the work I had put in** il a profité de mon travail; **a concert for the ~ of the refugees** un concert au profit des réfugiés; **we're doing all this for his ~** c'est pour lui que nous faisons tout cela; (*fig*) **he's not really hurt, he's just crying for your ~*** il ne s'est pas vraiment fait mal, il pleure pour se faire remarquer (par vous); **to give sb/get the ~ of the doubt** laisser à qn/avoir le bénéfice du doute; **the ~s of a good education** les bienfaits *mpl or* les avantages *mpl* d'une bonne éducation.

b (*Admin: money*) allocation *f*, prestation *f*. **unemployment ~** allocation (de) chômage; *see* **sickness.**

c **~ of clergy** (*privileges*) privilège *m* du clergé; (*rites*) rites *mpl* de l'Église, rites religieux; **marriage without ~ of clergy** mariage non béni par l'Église.

2 **vt** faire du bien à; (*financially*) profiter à.

3 **vi** *[person]* se trouver bien (*from, by* de); (*financially*) gagner (*from, by doing* à faire); *[work, situation]* être avantagé (*from* par). **he will ~ from a holiday** des vacances lui feront du bien.

4 **comp** ►**benefit association** (*US*) = **benefit society** ►**benefit club** assurance mutuelle, caisse *f* de secours mutuel ►**benefit match** (*Sport*) match *m* au profit d'un joueur ►**benefit performance** représentation *f* de bienfaisance ►**benefit society** (*US*) société *f* de prévoyance, (société) mutuelle *f*.

Benelux ['benɪlʌks] **n** Bénélux *m*. **the ~ countries** les pays du Bénélux.

benevolence [bɪ'nevələns] **n** a (*NonC*) (*kindness*) bienveillance *f*; (*generosity*) bienfaisance *f*, générosité *f*. b (*gift, act*) bienfait *m*. c (*Hist*) don forcé (*au souverain*).

benevolent [bɪ'nevələnt] **adj** a (*kind*) bienveillant (*to* envers). **~ smile** sourire bienveillant *or* plein de bonté. b (*charitable*) *organization, society* de bienfaisance. **~ fund** fonds *m* de secours.

benevolently [bɪ'nevələntlɪ] **adv** avec bienveillance *or* bonté.

B.Eng. **n** (**abbr of Bachelor of Engineering**) *see* **bachelor.**

Bengal [beŋ'gɔ:l] 1 **n** Bengale *m*. **Bay of ~** golfe *m* du Bengale. 2 **comp** ►**Bengal light** feu *m* de Bengale ►**Bengal tiger** tigre *m* du Bengale.

Bengali [beŋ'gɔ:lɪ] 1 **n** a Bengali *mf*. b (*Ling*) bengali *m*. 2 **adj** bengali (*f inv*).

benighted [bɪ'naɪtɪd] **adj** a (*fig*) *person* plongé dans (les ténèbres de) l'ignorance; *policy etc* à courte vue, aveugle. b († *lit*) surpris par la nuit.

benign [bɪ'naɪn] **adj, benignant** [bɪ'nɪgnənt] **adj** a (*kindly*) bienveillant, affable; (*beneficial*) bienfaisant, salutaire; *climate* doux (*f* douce). b (*Med*) *tumour* bénin (*f* -igne).

benignly [bɪ'naɪnlɪ] **adv** avec bienveillance.

Benin [be'ni:n] **n** Bénin *m*.

Beninese [ˌbenɪ'ni:z] 1 **npl** Béninois *mpl*. 2 **adj** béninois.

benison ['benɪzn] **n** bénédiction *f*.

Benjamin ['bendʒəmɪn] **n** Benjamin *m*.

benny ['benɪ] **n** (*Drugs sl*) (comprimé *m* de) benzédrine *f*.

bent¹ [bent] 1 **pret, ptp of bend.** 2 **adj** *wire, pipe* tordu; (‡: *dishonest*) véreux; (‡: *homosexual*) homosexuel; *see* **bend.**

bent² [bent] **n** a (*aptitude*) dispositions *fpl*, aptitudes *fpl* (*for* pour). **to have a ~ for languages** avoir des dispositions pour les langues. b (*liking*) penchant *m*, goût *m*. **to have a ~ for** *or* **towards sth** avoir du goût *or* un penchant pour qch; **to follow one's ~** suivre son inclination *f*; **of literary ~** tourné vers les lettres.

bent³ [bent] **n** (*grass, rushes*) agrostide *f*; (*land*) lande *f*.

bentwood ['bentwʊd] **adj** *furniture* en bois courbé.

benumb [bɪ'nʌm] **vt** *limb* engourdir, endormir.

benumbed [bɪ'nʌmd] **adj** (*cold*) *person* transi (de froid); *fingers* engourdi par le froid; (*frightened*) transi de peur; (*shocked*) paralysé.

Benzedrine ['benzɪdri:n] **n** ® benzédrine *f*.

benzene ['benzi:n] **n** benzène *m*.

benzine ['benzi:n] **n** benzine *f*.

benzoin¹ ['benzəʊɪn] **n** (*resin*) benjoin *m*; (*shrub*) styrax *m* (benjoin).

benzoin² ['benzəʊɪn] **n** (*Chem*) benzoïne *f*.

bequeath [bɪ'kwi:ð] **vt** (*in will*) léguer (*to* à); (*fig*) *tradition* transmettre, léguer (*to* à).

bequest [bɪ'kwest] **n** legs *m*.

berate [bɪ'reɪt] **vt** admonester (*liter*), réprimander.

Berber ['bɜ:bəʳ] 1 **n** a Berbère *mf*. b (*Ling*) berbère *m*. 2 **adj** berbère.

bereave [bɪ'ri:v] **vt** a **pret, ptp bereft** (*deprive*) priver, dépouiller, déposséder (*of* de); *see also* **bereft.** b **pret, ptp** *gen* **bereaved** (*by death*) ravir (*sb of sb* qn à qn).

bereaved [bɪ'ri:vd] 1 **adj** endeuillé, affligé. 2 **npl: the ~** la famille du disparu.

bereavement [bɪ'ri:vmənt] **n** (*loss*) perte *f*; (*state*) deuil *m*. **a sad ~** une perte cruelle; **in his ~** dans son deuil; **owing to a recent ~** en raison d'un deuil récent.

bereft [bɪ'reft] 1 **pret, ptp of bereave a.** 2 **adj: ~ of** privé *or* démuni de; **~ of hope** désespéré; **he is ~ of reason** il a perdu la raison.

beret ['bereɪ] **n** béret *m*.

berg* [bɜ:g] **n abbr of iceberg.**

bergamot ['bɜ:gəmɒt] **n** bergamote *f*.

bergschrund ['berkʃrʊnt] **n** (*Climbing*) rimaye *f*.

beriberi ['berɪ'berɪ] **n** béribéri *m*.

Bering ['beɪrɪŋ] **adj: ~ Sea/Strait** mer *f*/détroit *m* de Béring *or* Behring.

berk‡ [bɜ:k] **n** connard‡ *m*, connasse‡ *f*.

berkelium [bɜ:'ki:lɪəm] **n** berkélium *m*.

Berks [bɑ:ks] **n abbr of Berkshire.**

Berlin [bɜ:'lɪn] 1 **n** a (*Geog*) Berlin. **East/West ~†** Berlin Est/Ouest†. b (*carriage*) **b~** berline *f*. 2 **comp** ►**the Berlin Wall** le mur de Berlin ►**Berlin wool** laine *f* à broder.

Berliner [bɜ:'lɪnəʳ] **n** Berlinois(e) *m(f)*.

berm [bɜ:m] **n** (*US Aut*) accotement *m*, bas-côté *m*.

Bermuda [bɜ:'mju:də] 1 **n** Bermudes *fpl*. 2 **comp** ►**Bermuda shorts** bermuda *m* ►**the Bermuda Triangle** le triangle des Bermudes.

Bern [bɜ:n] **n** Berne.

Bernard ['bɜ:nəd] **n** Bernard *m*.

Bernese ['bɜ:ni:z] 1 **adj** bernois. **~ Alps** *or* **Oberland** Oberland *m* bernois. 2 **n** Bernois(e) *m(f)*.

berry ['berɪ] 1 **n** baie *f*; *see* **brown.** 2 **vi: to go ~ing** aller cueillir des baies.

berserk [bə'sɜ:k] **adj** fou furieux (*f* folle furieuse). **to go ~** devenir fou furieux, se déchaîner.

berth [bɜ:θ] 1 **n** a *[plane, train, ship]* couchette *f*. (*easy job*) **to find a soft ~‡** trouver une bonne planque‡. b (*Naut: place for ship*) mouillage *m*, poste *m* d'amarrage. **to give a wide ~ to a ship** passer au large d'un navire; (*fig*) **to give sb a wide ~** éviter qn, se tenir à une distance respectueuse de qn; (*fig*) **you should give him a wide ~** vous devriez l'éviter à tout prix. 2 **vi** (*at anchor*) mouiller; (*alongside*) venir à quai, accoster. 3 **vt** *ship* (*assign place*) donner *or* assigner un poste d'amarrage à; (*perform action*) amarrer, faire accoster.

beryl ['berɪl] **n** béryl *m*.

beryllium [be'rɪljəm] **n** béryllium *m.*

beseech [bɪ'siːtʃ] **pret, ptp besought** *or* **beseeched vt** (*liter*) **a** (*ask for*) *permission* demander instamment, solliciter; *pardon* implorer. **b** (*entreat*) supplier, implorer, conjurer (*sb to do* qn de faire).

beseeching [bɪ'siːtʃɪŋ] **1 adj** *voice, look* suppliant, implorant. **2 n** supplications *fpl.*

beseechingly [bɪ'siːtʃɪŋlɪ] **adv** d'un air *or* d'un ton suppliant *or* implorant.

beset [bɪ'set] **pret, ptp beset vt** *[dangers, fears]* assaillir; *[temptations]* entourer. **path ~ with obstacles** chemin semé d'obstacles; **~ with difficulties** *enterprise, journey* hérissé de difficultés; **he is ~ with difficulties** les difficultés l'assaillent (de toutes parts); **~ with** *or* **by doubts** rongé *or* assailli par le doute.

besetting [bɪ'setɪŋ] **adj: his ~ sin** son grand défaut.

beside [bɪ'saɪd] **prep a** (*at the side of*) à côté de, auprès de. **she sat down ~ him** elle s'est assise à côté de lui; **~ it** à côté. **b** (*compared with*) en comparaison de, auprès de, à côté de, comparé à, par rapport à. **c** (*phrases*) **that's ~ the point** *or* **the mark** cela n'a rien à voir; **it's quite ~ the point to suggest that ...** il est tout à fait inutile de suggérer que ...; **this is ~ the question** ceci n'a rien à voir avec la question; **to be ~ o.s. (with anger)** être hors de soi; **he was quite ~ himself (with excitement)** il ne se possédait plus; **he is ~ himself with joy** il est fou *or* transporté de joie, il ne se sent pas de joie.

besides [bɪ'saɪdz] **1 adv a** (*in addition*) en outre, en plus, de plus. **many more ~** bien d'autres encore; **he wrote a novel and several short stories ~** il a écrit un roman et aussi plusieurs nouvelles.

b (*else*) de plus, d'autre. **there is nothing ~** il n'y a rien de plus *or* d'autre.

c (*moreover*) d'ailleurs, du reste, en outre.

2 prep a (*in addition to*) en plus de, en dehors de, outre. **others ~ ourselves** d'autres que nous; **there were 3 of us ~ Mary** nous étions 3 sans compter Marie; **~ this book I bought others** outre ce livre, j'en ai acheté d'autres; **~ which he was unwell** sans compter qu'il était souffrant, et par-dessus le marché il était souffrant.

b (*except*) excepté, hormis, en dehors de. **no one ~ you** personne en dehors de vous *or* excepté vous, personne d'autre que vous; **who ~ them** qui si ce n'est eux, qui à part eux *or* hormis eux.

besiege [bɪ'siːdʒ] **vt a** *town* assiéger, mettre le siège devant. **b** (*fig: surround*) assaillir, entourer, se presser autour de. **~d by journalists** assailli par des journalistes. **c** (*fig: pester*) assaillir, harceler (*with* de). **~d with questions** assailli de questions.

besmear [bɪ'smɪəʳ] **vt** (*lit*) barbouiller (*with* de); (*fig*) salir, souiller (*liter*).

besmirch [bɪ'smɜːtʃ] **vt** ternir, entacher.

besom ['biːzəm] **n** balai *m* de bouleau.

besotted [bɪ'sɒtɪd] **adj a** (*drunk*) abruti, hébété (*with* de). **b** (*infatuated*) entiché, fou (*f* folle) (*with* de). **c** (*foolish*) idiot, imbécile.

besought [bɪ'sɔːt] **pret, ptp of beseech.**

bespatter [bɪ'spætəʳ] **vt** éclabousser (*with* de).

bespeak [bɪ'spiːk] **pret bespoke, ptp bespoken** *or* **bespoke vt a** (*order*) *goods* commander; *room, place* retenir, réserver. **b** (*indicate*) annoncer, témoigner de, prouver; *weakness, fault* accuser.

bespectacled [bɪ'spektɪkld] **adj** à lunettes.

bespoke [bɪ'spəʊk] **1 pret, ptp of bespeak. 2 adj** (*Brit*) *goods* fait sur commande; *garments* fait sur mesure; *tailor etc* à façon. (*Comput*) **~ software** logiciel *m* sur mesure.

bespoken [bɪ'spəʊkən] **ptp of bespeak.**

besprinkle [bɪ'sprɪŋkl] **vt** (*with liquid*) arroser, asperger (*with* de); (*with powder*) saupoudrer (*with* de); (*dot with*) parsemer (*with* de).

Bess [bes] **n** (**dim of Elizabeth**) Lisette *f*, Babette *f.* (*Brit Hist*) **Good Queen ~** la bonne reine Élisabeth (1ère).

Bessarabia [ˌbesə'reɪbɪə] **n** Bessarabie *f.*

best [best] **1 adj** (**superl of good**) le meilleur, la meilleure. **the ~ pupil in the class** le meilleur élève de la classe; **the ~ novel he's written** le meilleur roman qu'il ait écrit; **the ~ route to Paris** la route la meilleure *or* la plus directe pour Paris; **the ~ thing about her is ...** ce qu'il y a de meilleur chez elle c'est ...; **the ~ thing to do is to wait** le mieux c'est d'attendre; **the ~ years of one's life** les plus belles années de sa vie; **in one's ~ clothes** vêtu de ses plus beaux vêtements, sur son trente et un; **may the ~ man win!** que le meilleur gagne!; **to put one's ~ foot** *or* **leg forward** (*in walking*) allonger le pas; (*do one's best*) faire de son mieux; (*Cards*) **to have the ~ diamond** être maître à carreau; **she is her ~ friend** c'est sa meilleure amie; **she's his ~ girl*** c'est sa petite amie *or* sa nana‡; (*fig*) **the ~ part of** la plus grande partie de; **for the ~ part of an hour/month** pendant près d'une heure/d'un mois; (*Comm: on product*) **~ before ...** à consommer de préférence avant ... (*see also* **5**); *see* **behaviour, second-best, wish** *etc.*

2 n: the ~ le mieux, le meilleur; **all the ~*** (*goodbye*) salut*; (*end of letter*) amicalement, amitiés; **all the ~ to your sister** mes amitiés à ta sœur; **all the ~ for your exam** bonne chance pour ton examen; **to do one's (level) ~ (to win)** faire de son mieux (pour gagner), faire tout son possible (pour gagner); **do the ~ you can!** faites de votre mieux!, faites pour le mieux!; **it's the ~ I can do** je ne peux pas faire mieux; **to get the ~ out of sb/sth** tirer le maximum de qn/qch; **to get the ~ of the bargain** *or* **of it** l'emporter, avoir le dessus; **he wants the ~ of both worlds** il veut gagner sur les deux tableaux, il veut tout avoir; **the ~ there is** ce qu'il y a de mieux; **to make the ~ of sth** s'accommoder de qch (du mieux que l'on peut); **to make the ~ of a bad job** *or* **a bad business** *or* **a bad bargain** faire contre mauvaise fortune bon cœur; **to make the ~ of one's opportunities** profiter au maximum des occasions qui se présentent; **the ~ of it** *or* **the ~ of the matter is that ...** le plus beau de l'affaire c'est que ...; **to be the ~ of friends** être les meilleurs amis (du monde); **it's all for the ~** c'est pour le mieux; **to do sth for the ~** faire qch dans les meilleures intentions; **to the ~ of my ability/knowledge/recollection** *etc* autant que je puisse/que je sache/que je me souvienne *etc*; **in one's (Sunday) ~*** endimanché, sur son trente et un; **to look one's ~** être resplendissant; *[woman]* être en beauté; **she looks her ~ when she's in blue** c'est le bleu qui l'avantage le plus; (*on form*) **to be at one's ~** être en pleine forme* *or* en train; **the roses are at their ~ just now** les roses sont de toute beauté en ce moment; **that is Racine at his ~** voilà du meilleur Racine; **even at the ~ of times** même dans les circonstances les plus favorables; **even at the ~ of times he's not very patient but ...** il n'est jamais particulièrement patient mais ...; **at ~** au mieux; **even the ~ of us can make mistakes** tout le monde peut se tromper; **the ~ of plans can go astray** les meilleurs projets peuvent échouer; **he can sing with the ~ of them** il sait chanter comme pas un*.

3 adv (**superl of well**) le mieux, le plus. **the ~ dressed man in Paris** l'homme le mieux habillé de Paris; **the ~ loved actor** l'acteur le plus aimé; **I like apples ~** ce que je préfère, ce sont les pommes; **I like strawberries ~ of all** je préfère les fraises à n'importe quoi *or* à tout; **that is the hat which suits her ~** voilà le chapeau qui lui va le mieux; **I helped him as ~ I could** je l'ai aidé de mon mieux *or* du mieux que j'ai pu; **he thought it ~ to accept** il a trouvé *or* jugé préférable d'accepter; **do as you think ~** faites à votre idée, faites pour le mieux; **you know ~** vous savez mieux que personne, c'est vous le mieux placé pour en juger, vous êtes (le) meilleur juge en la matière; **you had ~ go at once** tu ferais mieux de t'en aller tout de suite.

4 vt (*defeat, win over*) battre, l'emporter sur.

5 comp ▸best-before date (*Comm*) date *f* limite d'utilisation optimale **▸best man** *[wedding]* garçon *m* d'honneur, témoin *m* **▸bestseller** (*book*) best-seller *m*, livre *m* à succès, succès *m* de librairie; (*Comm: other article*) article *m* de grosse vente, best-seller; (*author*) auteur *m* à succès **▸best-selling** *book, writer* à succès; *disk* qui remporte un grand succès.

bestial ['bestɪəl] **adj** (*lit, fig*) bestial.

bestiality [ˌbestɪ'ælɪtɪ] **n a** (*NonC*) bestialité *f.* **b** (*act*) acte bestial.

bestiary ['bestɪərɪ] **n** bestiaire *m* (*recueil*).

bestir [bɪ'stɜːʳ] **vt: to ~ o.s.** se remuer, se démener, s'activer.

bestow [bɪ'stəʊ] **vt a** (*grant*) *favour, sb's hand* accorder (*on, upon* à); *title* conférer (*on, upon* à). **b** (*devote*) *energy* consacrer, employer (*upon* à); *admiration* accorder. **to ~ friendship on sb** prendre qn en amitié; **the attention ~ed on this boy** l'attention dont ce garçon est l'objet.

bestowal [bɪ'stəʊəl] **n** (*NonC*) octroi *m.*

bestraddle [bɪ'strædl] **vt** *horse, bicycle* enfourcher; *wall* chevaucher; *chair* se mettre à califourchon sur.

bestrew [bɪ'struː] **pret bestrewed, ptp bestrewed** *or* **bestrewn vt** (*liter*) parsemer, joncher (*with* de).

bestride [bɪ'straɪd] **pret bestrode** [bɪ'strəʊd], **ptp bestridden** [bɪ'strɪdn] **vt a** *chair* être à cheval *or* à califourchon sur; *horse, bicycle* enfourcher. **b** *brook, ditch* enjamber.

bet [bet] **pret, ptp bet** *or* **betted 1 vi** parier, miser (*against* contre, *on* sur, *with* avec). **to ~ 10 to 1** parier *or* miser à 10 contre 1; **to ~ on horses** parier *or* jouer aux courses; **to ~ on a horse** jouer un cheval, miser sur un cheval.

2 vt: to ~ £10 on a horse parier *or* miser 10 livres sur un cheval; **she ~ me £10 he would refuse** elle m'a parié 10 livres qu'il refuserait; (*fig*) **I ~ he'll come!** je te parie qu'il vient!* *or* qu'il viendra!; **I'll ~ you anything (you like)** je te parie tout ce que tu veux; **~ you won't do it*** (je te parie que) t'es pas capable de le faire‡; **you ~!*** un peu!*, tu parles!*; **~ you can't!*** chiche!*; **you can ~ your boots*** *or* **your bottom dollar*** *or* **your life* that ...** tu peux parier tout ce que tu veux *or* parier ta chemise que ...; **don't ~ on it, I wouldn't ~ on it** ne compte pas trop dessus.

3 n pari *m.* **to make** *or* **lay a ~ (on)** parier (sur), faire un pari (sur); **to accept** *or* **take (on) a ~** accepter un pari; **to win a ~** gagner un pari; (*fig*) **this is your best ~** c'est ce que vous avez de mieux à faire; (*fig*) **it's a good** *or* **safe ~ that she'll turn up** il est à peu près certain qu'elle viendra; *see* **hedge, lay**[1].

beta ['biːtə] **n** bêta *m.* (*Med, Pharm*) **~ blocker** bêta-bloquant *m*; **~-blocking** bêta-bloquant.

betake [bɪ'teɪk] **pret betook, ptp betaken** [bɪ'teɪkən] **vt: to ~ o.s. to** (s'en) aller à, se rendre à.

betcha‡ ['betʃə] **excl: (you) ~!** un peu!*, tu parles!*

betel ['biːtəl] **n** bétel *m.* **~ nut** noix *f* de bétel.

Bethany ['beθənɪ] **n** Béthanie.

bethink [bɪ'θɪŋk] **pret, ptp bethought vt: to ~ o.s.** réfléchir, considérer;

to ~ o.s. of sth/to do/that ... s'aviser de qch/de faire/que ... .

Bethlehem ['beθlɪhem] **n** Bethléem.

bethought [bɪ'θɔːt] **pret, ptp of bethink.**

betide [bɪ'taɪd] **vti: whatever (may) ~** quoi qu'il advienne *or* arrive (*subj*); *see* **woe.**

betimes [bɪ'taɪmz] **adv** (*liter*) (*early*) de bonne heure, tôt; (*quickly*) promptement, vite; (*in good time*) à temps, assez tôt.

betoken [bɪ'təʊkən] **vt** (*forecast*) présager, annoncer; (*indicate*) dénoter, être signe de.

betook [bɪ'tʊk] **pret of betake.**

betray [bɪ'treɪ] **vt** a (*be disloyal to*) *one's country* trahir, être traître à; *friends* trahir; *woman* tromper, trahir; (*fig*) *hope etc* trahir, tromper, décevoir. **he has ~ed our trust** il a trahi notre confiance, il a commis un abus de confiance. b (*give up treacherously*) *person, secret* livrer (*to* à), trahir. **to ~ sb into enemy hands** livrer qn à l'ennemi *or* aux mains de l'ennemi. c (*disclose*) *age, fears, intentions, facts, truth* trahir, révéler. **to ~ o.s.** se trahir; **his speech ~ed the fact that he had been drinking** on devinait à l'écouter qu'il avait bu.

betrayal [bɪ'treɪəl] **n** (*see* **betray**) a (*NonC*) *[country, ally etc]* trahison *f*; *[age, secret, plan]* divulgation *f*; *[fears, intentions]* manifestation *f* (involontaire); *[facts, truth]* révélation *f*. **~ of trust** abus *m* de confiance. b (*deed*) (acte *m* de) trahison *f*. **the ~ of Christ** la trahison envers le Christ.

betrayer [bɪ'treɪər] **n** *[country]* traître(sse) *m(f)* (*of* à, envers); *[friend]* dénonciateur *m*, -trice *f* (*of* de). **she killed her ~** elle a tué celui qui l'avait trahie.

betroth [bɪ'trəʊð] **vt** (*liter*, ††) fiancer (*to* à, avec), promettre en mariage (*to* à).

betrothal [bɪ'trəʊðəl] **n** (*liter*) fiançailles *fpl* (*to* avec).

betrothed [bɪ'trəʊðd] **adj, n, pl inv** (*liter or hum*) fiancé(e) *m(f)*.

better[1] ['betər] 1 **adj** (**compar of good**) meilleur. **that book is ~ than this one** ce livre-là est meilleur que celui-ci; **she is a ~ dancer than her sister, she is ~ at dancing than her sister** elle danse mieux que sa sœur; **she is ~ at dancing than at singing** elle danse mieux qu'elle ne chante; **he's a ~ man than his brother** il est mieux que son frère; (*hum*) **you're a ~ man than I am!** tu as plus de courage que moi!; **he's no ~ than a thief** c'est un voleur ni plus ni moins; **she's no ~ than she should be!** (*slightly dishonest*) ce n'est pas l'honnêteté qui l'étouffe!*; (*sexually*) elle n'est pas d'une vertu farouche!; (*Med*) **he is much ~ now** il va *or* se porte bien mieux maintenant; (*Med*) **how are you? — much ~** comment allez-vous? — bien mieux; (*Med*) **he got ~ very quickly after his illness** il s'est très vite remis de sa maladie; **the weather is getting ~** le temps s'améliore; **this book gets ~ towards the end** ce livre s'améliore vers la fin; **his technique got ~ as he grew older** sa technique s'est affirmée avec l'âge; **his writing is ~ since he got a new pen** son écriture est meilleure depuis qu'il a un nouveau stylo; **(it's getting) ~ and ~!** (ça va) de mieux en mieux!; **that's ~!** voilà qui est mieux!; **it couldn't be ~, nothing could be ~!** ça ne pourrait pas mieux tomber! *or* mieux se trouver!; **it would be ~ to stay at home** il vaudrait mieux rester à la maison; **wouldn't it be ~ to refuse?** ne vaudrait-il pas mieux refuser?; **it is ~ not to promise anything than to let him down** il vaut mieux ne rien promettre que de le décevoir; **a ~ class of hotel** un hôtel de catégorie supérieure; **he has seen ~ days** il a connu des jours meilleurs; **this hat has seen ~ days** ce chapeau n'est plus de la première fraîcheur; (*hum*) **his ~ half*** sa moitié* (*hum*); **his ~ nature stopped him from ...** ses bons sentiments, reprenant le dessus, l'ont empêché de ...; **to appeal to sb's ~ nature** faire appel au bon cœur de qn; **to go one ~ than sb** damer le pion à qn; **the ~ part of a year/of 200 km** *etc* près d'un an/de 200 km *etc*; **to hope for ~ things** espérer mieux.

2 **adv** (**compar of well**) mieux. **he sings ~ than you** il chante mieux que toi; **he sings ~ than he dances** il chante mieux qu'il ne danse; **the ~ I know him the more I admire him** mieux je le connais plus je l'admire; **I like it ~ than I used to** je l'aime mieux qu'autrefois *or* que je ne l'aimais autrefois; **all the ~, so much the ~** tant mieux (*for* pour); (*in order to*) **the ~ to see/hear** pour mieux voir/entendre; **he was all the ~ for it** il s'en est trouvé mieux; **it would be all the ~ for a drop of paint** un petit coup de peinture ne lui ferait pas de mal; **they are ~ off than we are** (*richer*) ils ont plus d'argent que nous; (*more fortunate*) ils sont dans une meilleure position que nous; **he is ~ off at his sister's than living alone** il est mieux chez sa sœur que s'il vivait tout seul; **I had ~ do it** (*must do it*) il faut que je le fasse; (*would be preferable to do it*) il vaut mieux que je le fasse; **hadn't you ~ speak to him?** ne vaudrait-il pas mieux que tu lui parles? (*subj*); **write to her, or ~ still go and see her** écris-lui, ou mieux encore va la voir; **~ dressed** mieux habillé; **~ known** plus *or* mieux connu; (*Prov*) **~ late than never** mieux vaut tard que jamais (*Prov*); *see* **know, think** *etc.*

3 **n** a mieux *m*. **it's a change for the ~** c'est une amélioration, c'est un changement en mieux; **for ~ or (for) worse** pour le meilleur ou pour le pire; **to get the ~ of sb** triompher de qn; **to get the ~ of sth** venir à bout de qch.

b **one's ~s** ses supérieurs *mpl*.

4 **vt** *sb's achievements* dépasser; *record, score* améliorer. **to ~ o.s.** améliorer sa condition.

better[2] ['betər] **n** parieur *m*, -euse *f*; (*at races*) turfiste *mf* (*qui parie sur les chevaux*).

betterment ['betəmənt] **n** amélioration *f*; (*Jur*) *[property]* plus-value *f*. (*Jur*) **~ tax** impôt *m* sur les plus-values.

betting ['betɪŋ] 1 **n** pari(s) *m(pl)*. **the ~ was brisk** les paris allaient bon train; **the ~ was 2 to 1 on ...** la cote était 2 contre 1 sur ..., on pariait à 2 contre 1 sur ...; **what is the ~ on his horse?** quelle cote fait son cheval?; (*fig*) **the ~ is he won't succeed** il y a peu de chances (pour) qu'il réussisse. 2 **comp ►betting man: if I were a betting man I'd say that ...** si j'avais l'habitude de faire des paris je dirais que ... **►betting news** résultats *mpl* des courses **►betting shop** (*Brit*) bureau *m* de paris (*appartenant à un bookmaker*), ≈ bureau *m* de P.M.U **►betting slip** (*Brit*) bulletin *m* de pari individuel (≈ P.M.U.).

bettor ['betər] **n** = **better**[2].

Betty ['betɪ] **n** (**dim of Elizabeth**) Lisette *f*, Babette *f*, Betty *f*.

between [bɪ'twiːn] (*phr vb elem*) 1 **prep** a (*of place*) entre. **sit ~ those two boys** asseyez-vous entre ces deux garçons.

b (*of order, rank*) entre. **F comes ~ E and G** (la lettre) F se trouve *or* vient entre E et G; **a captain comes ~ a lieutenant and a major** un capitaine a un rang intermédiaire entre un lieutenant et un commandant.

c (*of time*) entre. **~ 5 and 6 o'clock** entre 5 et 6 heures.

d (*of distance, amount*) entre. **~ 6 and 7 km/litres** *etc* entre 6 et 7 km/litres *etc*; **she is ~ 25 and 30** elle a entre 25 et 30 ans.

e (*to and from*) entre. **the ferry goes ~ Dover and Calais** le ferry fait la navette entre Douvres et Calais.

f (*from one to other*) entre. **you will have time to rest ~ planes** vous aurez le temps de vous reposer entre les deux avions; **~ London and Birmingham there are several large towns** entre Londres et Birmingham il y a plusieurs grandes villes; **the train does not stop ~ here and London** le train est direct d'ici (à) Londres; **~ now and next week we must ...** d'ici la semaine prochaine nous devons ... .

g (*connection, relationship*) entre. **the friendship ~ Paul and Robert** l'amitié entre Paul et Robert; **after all there has been ~ us** après tout ce qu'il y a eu entre nous; **no one can come ~ us** personne ne peut nous séparer; **to choose ~ 2 hats** choisir entre 2 chapeaux; **the difference ~ them** la différence entre eux; **the match ~ A and B** le match qui oppose (*or* opposait *etc*) A à B; **the war ~ the 2 countries** la guerre entre les 2 pays; **a comparison ~ the 2 books** une comparaison entre les 2 livres, une comparaison des 2 livres; **the distance ~ them** la distance qui les sépare (l'un de l'autre), la distance entre eux.

h (*sharing*) entre. **divide the sweets ~ the 2 children** partagez les bonbons entre les 2 enfants; **the 4 boys have 5 oranges ~ them** les 4 garçons ont 5 oranges en tout *or* à eux tous; **~ ourselves** *or* **~ you and me, he is not very clever** entre nous, il n'est pas très intelligent.

i (*combination, cooperation*) **the boys managed to lift the box ~ (the two of) them** à eux deux les garçons sont arrivés à soulever la caisse; **we got the letter written ~ us** à nous tous nous avons réussi à écrire la lettre.

j (*combined effect*) entre. **~ housework and study I have no time for going out** entre le ménage et mes études je n'ai pas le temps de sortir; **~ rage and alarm she could hardly think properly** prise entre la colère et l'inquiétude elle avait du mal à mettre de l'ordre dans ses pensées.

2 **adv** au milieu, dans l'intervalle. **her visits are few and far ~** ses visites sont très espacées *or* très rares; **rows of trees with grass in ~** des rangées d'arbres séparées par de l'herbe.

betweentimes [bɪ'twiːnˌtaɪmz] **adv** dans l'intervalle, entre-temps.

betwixt [bɪ'twɪkst] 1 **prep** (††, *liter, dial*) = **between 1.** 2 **adv: ~ and between** entre les deux, ni l'un ni l'autre.

bevel ['bevəl] 1 **n** (*surface*) surface *f* oblique; (*also* **~ edge**) biseau *m*; (*tool: also* **~ square**) fausse équerre. 2 **comp** en biseau **►bevel gear** engrenage *m* conique **►bevel wheel** roue dentée conique. 3 **vt** biseauter, tailler de biais *or* en biseau. **~led edge** bord biseauté; **~led mirror** glace biseautée.

beverage ['bevərɪdʒ] **n** boisson *f*; (*liter, hum*) breuvage *m*.

bevy ['bevɪ] **n** (*gen*) bande *f*, troupe *f*; *[girls, beauties]* essaim *m*; *[larks, quails]* volée *f*; *[roe deer]* harde *f*.

bewail [bɪ'weɪl] **vt** *one's lot* se lamenter sur, déplorer; *sb's death* pleurer.

beware [bɪ'wɛər] **vti** (*ne s'emploie qu'à l'impératif et à l'infinitif*) **to ~** prendre garde (*of sb/sth* à qn/à qch; *of doing* de faire), se méfier (*of sth* de qch); **~ of falling** prenez garde de tomber; **~ of being deceived,** (*frm*) **~ lest you are** *or* **lest you be deceived** prenez garde qu'on ne vous trompe (*subj*); **~ of listening to him** gardez-vous de l'écouter; **~ (of) how you speak** faites attention à ce que vous dites, surveillez vos paroles; **"~ of the dog!"** "(attention) chien méchant"; **"~ of pickpockets!"** "attention aux pickpockets!"; **"trespassers ~!"** "défense d'entrer!"; (*Comm*) **"~ of imitations"** "se méfier des contrefaçons".

bewhiskered [bɪ'wɪskəd] **adj** (*liter*) barbu (*or* moustachu).

bewilder [bɪ'wɪldər] **vt** dérouter; (*stronger*) abasourdir.

bewildered [bɪ'wɪldəd] **adj** *person, look* perplexe.

bewildering [bɪ'wɪldərɪŋ] **adj** déroutant, déconcertant; (*stronger*) ahurissant.

bewilderingly [bɪˈwɪldərɪŋlɪ] adv d'une façon déroutante *or* déconcertante *or* (*stronger*) ahurissante. **it is ~ complicated** c'est d'un compliqué déconcertant.
bewilderment [bɪˈwɪldəmənt] n confusion *f*, perplexité *f*; (*stronger*) ahurissement *m*.
bewitch [bɪˈwɪtʃ] vt ensorceler, enchanter; (*fig*) charmer, enchanter.
bewitching [bɪˈwɪtʃɪŋ] adj *look, smile* enchanteur (*f* -teresse), charmant, charmeur; *face, person* séduisant, charmant.
bewitchingly [bɪˈwɪtʃɪŋlɪ] adv d'une façon séduisante *or* enchanteresse. **~ beautiful** belle à ravir.
bey [beɪ] n bey *m*.
beyond [bɪˈjɒnd] (*phr vb elem*) 1 prep a (*place*) au-delà de, de l'autre côté de. **~ the Pyrenees** au-delà des Pyrénées; **you can't go ~ the barrier** vous ne pouvez pas aller au-delà de la barrière, vous ne pouvez pas dépasser la barrière; **~ the convent walls** en dehors des *or* par-delà les murs du couvent; **the countries ~ the sea** les pays au-delà des mers, les pays d'outre-mer.
b (*in time*) plus de. **she won't stay much ~ a month** elle ne restera pas beaucoup plus d'un mois; **~ next week/June** au-delà de *or* après la semaine prochaine/juin; **it was ~ the middle of June** on avait dépassé la mi-juin; **~ bedtime** passé l'heure du coucher.
c (*surpassing, exceeding*) au-dessus de. **a task ~ her abilities** une tâche au-dessus de ses capacités; **this work is quite ~ him** ce travail le dépasse complètement; **it was ~ her to pass the exam** réussir à l'examen était au-dessus de ses forces; **maths is quite ~ me** les maths, ça me dépasse*; **it's ~ me why he hasn't left her*** je ne comprends pas *or* ça me dépasse* qu'il ne l'ait pas quittée; **~ my reach** hors de ma portée; **~ doubt** (**adj**) hors de doute, indubitable; (**adv**) à n'en pas douter, indubitablement; **that is ~ human understanding** cela dépasse l'entendement humain; **he is ~ caring** il ne s'en fait plus du tout; **~ repair** irréparable; **~ his means** au-dessus de ses moyens; *see* **compare, grave**[1], **help** *etc*.
d (*with neg or interrog*) sauf, excepté. **he gave her no answer ~ a grunt** il ne lui a répondu que par un grognement, pour toute réponse il a émis un grognement.
2 adv au-delà, plus loin, là-bas. **the 90s and ~** les années 90 et au-delà; **the room ~** la pièce d'après; **the lands ~** les terres lointaines.
3 n au-delà *m*. **the great B~** l'au-delà; *see* **back**.
bezant [ˈbezənt] n besant *m*.
bezel [ˈbezl] 1 n [*chisel*] biseau *m*; [*gem*] facette *f*; (*holding gem*) chaton *m*; (*holding watch glass*) portée *f*. 2 vt tailler en biseau.
bezique [bɪˈziːk] n bésigue *m*.
B.F.P.O. [biːefpiːˈəʊ] n (*Brit Mil*) abbr of **British Forces Post Office**.
bhaji [ˈbɑːdʒɪ] n bhaji *m* (*beignet indien à base de légumes et d'épices*).
Bhutan [buːˈtɑːn] n Bhoutan *m*, Bhutân *m*.
bi... [baɪ] pref bi... .
Biafra [bɪˈæfrə] n Biafra *m*.
Biafran [bɪˈæfrən] 1 n Biafrais(e) *m(f)*. 2 adj biafrais.
biannual [baɪˈænjʊəl] adj semestriel.
bias [ˈbaɪəs] 1 n a (*inclination*) tendance *f*, inclination *f* (*towards* à), penchant *m* (*towards* pour); (*prejudice*) préjugé *m*, parti pris (*towards* pour, *against* contre), prévention *f* (*towards* en faveur de, *against* contre); (*Jur*) distorsion *f*. **strong ~ towards** penchant marqué pour; **he is without ~** il n'a aucun parti pris, il est sans préjugés. b (*Sewing*) biais *m*. **cut on the ~** coupé dans le biais; **~ binding** biais (*ruban*). c (*Sport*) [*bowls*] (*weight*) *poids placé à l'intérieur d'une boule*; (*swerve*) déviation *f*. 2 vt (*give inclination*) influencer (*towards* en faveur de, *against* contre); (*prejudice*) prévenir (*towards* en faveur de, *against* contre).
bias(s)ed [ˈbaɪəst] adj *person, jury* qui n'est pas impartial; *judgment* qui n'est pas objectif; *report* déformé, tendancieux.
bib [bɪb] n a [*child*] bavoir *m*. b [*apron*] bavette *f*. (*fig*) **in her best ~ and tucker*** sur son trente et un.
Bible [ˈbaɪbl] 1 n (*lit*) Bible *f*; (*fig*) bible, évangile *m*; *see* **holy**.
2 comp ►**Bible-basher*** prédicateur *m*, -trice *f* frénétique* ►**Bible-bashing***: **he really likes Bible-bashing** il brandit sa Bible à tout va*; **a Bible-bashing preacher** un prêcheur qui brandit sa Bible à tout va* ►**the Bible Belt** (*US*) *les États du Sud profondément protestants* ►**Bible class** (*Scol*) classe *f* d'instruction religieuse; (*Rel*) catéchisme *m* ►**Bible college** université *f* de théologie ►**Bible oath** serment *m* (prêté) sur la Bible ►**Bible school** (*US*) cours *m* d'été d'instruction religieuse ►**Bible stories** histoires tirées de la Bible ►**Bible study** étude *f* de la Bible; (*in group*) lecture commentée de la Bible ►**Bible-thumper*** (*pej*) = **Bible-basher*** ►**Bible-thumping*** = **Bible-bashing***.
biblical [ˈbɪblɪkəl] adj biblique.
biblio... [ˈbɪblɪəʊ] pref biblio... .
bibliographer [ˌbɪblɪˈɒgrəfəʳ] n bibliographe *mf*.
bibliographic(al) [ˌbɪblɪəʊˈgræfɪk(əl)] adj bibliographique.
bibliography [ˌbɪblɪˈɒgrəfɪ] n bibliographie *f*.
bibliomania [ˌbɪblɪəʊˈmeɪnɪə] n bibliomanie *f*.
bibliomaniac [ˌbɪblɪəʊˈmeɪnɪæk] n bibliomane *mf*.
bibliophile [ˈbɪblɪəʊfaɪl] n bibliophile *mf*.
bibulous [ˈbɪbjʊləs] adj adonné à la boisson; *look* aviné; *evening, party* bien arrosé.
bicameral [baɪˈkæmərəl] adj bicaméral. **~ system** bicamérisme *m*.
bicarbonate [baɪˈkɑːbənɪt] n bicarbonate *m*. **~ of soda** bicarbonate de soude.
bicentenary [ˌbaɪsenˈtiːnərɪ] adj, n bicentenaire *(m)*.
bicentennial [ˌbaɪsenˈtenɪəl] adj, n (*US*) bicentenaire *(m)*.
bicephalous [baɪˈsefələs] adj bicéphale.
biceps [ˈbaɪseps] npl inv biceps *m*.
bichloride [ˈbaɪˈklɔːraɪd] n bichlorure *m*.
bichromate [ˈbaɪˈkrəʊmɪt] n bichromate *m*.
bicker [ˈbɪkəʳ] vi a (*quarrel*) se chamailler. **they are always ~ing** ils sont toujours à se chamailler *or* toujours en bisbille*. b [*stream*] murmurer; [*flame*] trembloter, vaciller.
bickering [ˈbɪkərɪŋ] 1 n chamailleries *fpl*. 2 adj a *person* querelleur. b *stream* murmurant; *flame* tremblotant, vacillant.
bicuspid [baɪˈkʌspɪd] 1 adj bicuspidé. 2 n (dent *f*) prémolaire *f*.
bicycle [ˈbaɪsɪkl] 1 n bicyclette *f*, vélo *m*. **to ride a ~** faire de la bicyclette *or* du vélo; *see* **racing** *etc*. 2 vi faire de la bicyclette *or* du vélo, aller à *or* en* bicyclette. 3 comp *lamp, chain, wheel* de bicyclette, de vélo ►**bicycle bell** sonnette *f or* timbre *m* de bicyclette ►**bicycle clip** pince *f* de cycliste ►**bicycle kick** (*Ftbl*) coup *m* de pied retourné ►**bicycle pump** pompe *f* à bicyclette ►**bicycle rack** râtelier *m* à bicyclettes; (*on car roof*) porte-vélos *m inv* ►**bicycle rickshaw** vélo-pousse *m* ►**bicycle shed** abri *m* à bicyclettes ►**bicycle touring** (*Sport*) cyclo-tourisme *m* ►**bicycle track** piste *f* cyclable.
bid [bɪd] pret **bade** *or* **bid**, ptp **bidden** *or* **bid** 1 vt a (*command*) ordonner, commander, enjoindre (*sb to do* à qn de faire). **he was ~den to come** on lui a ordonné de venir; **do what I ~ you** fais ce que je te dis *or* t'ordonne.
b (*say*) dire. **to ~ sb good morning** dire bonjour à qn; **to ~ sb farewell** dire au revoir à qn; **to ~ sb welcome** souhaiter la bienvenue à qn.
c (*††: invite*) inviter, convier.
d (*offer*) *amount* offrir, faire une offre de; (*at auction*) faire une enchère de. **he is ~ding 2,000 francs for the painting** il fait une offre *or* une enchère de 2 000 F pour le tableau; **I did not ~ (high) enough** je n'ai pas offert assez; **the one that ~s most** le plus offrant.
e (*Cards*) demander. **he ~ 3 spades** il a demandé 3 piques.
2 vi a (*make an offer*) faire une offre, offrir, proposer un prix (*for* pour). **to ~ for sth** faire une offre pour qch; (*at auction*) faire une enchère pour qch; **to ~ against sb** renchérir sur qn; (*US Comm*) **to ~ on** *contract etc* soumissionner.
b (*phrases*) **to ~ for power/fame** viser *or* ambitionner le pouvoir/la gloire; **to ~ fair to do** sembler devoir faire, promettre de faire; **everything ~s fair to be successful** tout semble annoncer *or* promettre le succès.
3 n a (*Comm*) offre *f*; (*at auction*) enchère *f*. **to make a ~ for** faire une offre pour; (*at auction*) faire une enchère pour; **a high ~** une forte enchère; **a higher ~** une surenchère; **to make a higher ~** surenchérir.
b (*Cards*) demande *f*, annonce *f*. **to raise the ~** monter; (*Bridge*) **to make no ~** passer parole; **"no ~"** "parole", "passe".
c (*attempt*) tentative *f*. **suicide ~** tentative de suicide; **to make a ~ for power** tenter de s'emparer du pouvoir; **to make a ~ for freedom** tenter de s'évader; **to make a ~ to do** tenter de faire.
4 comp ►**bid bond** caution *f* de soumission.
biddable [ˈbɪdəbl] adj a *child* docile, obéissant. b (*Cards*) **~ suit** couleur *f* demandable.
bidden [ˈbɪdn] ptp of **bid**.
bidder [ˈbɪdəʳ] n (*at sale*) enchérisseur *m*, offrant *m*; (*Fin*) soumissionnaire *m*. **the highest ~** (*at sale*) le plus offrant; (*Fin*) le soumissionnaire le plus offrant; **the lowest ~** (*at sale*) le moins offrant; (*Fin*) le soumissionnaire le moins disant; **successful ~** adjudicataire *mf*; **there were no ~s** personne n'a fait d'offre.
bidding [ˈbɪdɪŋ] n a (*at sale*) enchère(s) *f(pl)*. **~ up** surenchères *fpl*; **~ was brisk** les enchères étaient vives; **the ~ is closed** l'enchère est faite, c'est adjugé; (*at sale*) **to raise the ~** surenchérir. b (*Cards*) enchères *fpl*. c (*order*) ordre *m*, commandement *m*. **at whose ~?** sur l'ordre de qui?; **I did his ~** j'ai fait ce qu'il m'a ordonné *or* demandé; **at sb's ~** sur l'ordre *or* l'injonction de qn; **he needed no second ~** il ne se l'est pas fait dire deux fois.
biddy [ˈbɪdɪ] n († *or dial*) **old ~** vieille bonne femme.
bide [baɪd] (†, *liter, dial*) 1 vi = **abide 2**. 2 vt a (*still used*) **to ~ one's time** se réserver, attendre son heure *or* le bon moment, attendre le moment d'agir. b = **abide 1**.
bidet [ˈbiːdeɪ] n bidet *m*.
bidirectional [baɪdɪˈrekʃənl] adj (*Comput*) bidirectionnel.
biennial [baɪˈenɪəl] 1 adj a (*happening every two years*) biennal, bisannuel. b (*lasting two years*) biennal. 2 n (*Bot*) **~ (plant)** (plante *f*) bisannuelle *f*.
bier [bɪəʳ] n (*for coffin*) brancards *mpl* (de cercueil); (*for corpse*) bière *f*.
biff* [bɪf] 1 n coup *m* de poing, baffe‡ *f*. 2 excl vlan!, pan! 3 vt cogner sur, flanquer une baffe à‡. **to ~ sb on the nose** flanquer* son

poing dans *or* sur la figure de qn.

bifocal [ˈbaɪˈfəʊkəl] 1 adj bifocal, à double foyer. 2 npl: ~s verres *mpl* à double foyer, lunettes bifocales.

bifurcate [ˈbaɪfɜːkeɪt] 1 vi bifurquer. 2 adj à deux branches.

bifurcation [ˌbaɪfɜːˈkeɪʃən] n bifurcation *f*, embranchement *m*.

big [bɪg] 1 adj a (*in height*) *person, building, tree* grand. **a ~ fellow** un grand gaillard; **a ~ man** un homme grand et fort; **to grow ~** *or* **~ger** grandir; *see also* **1b**.

b (*in bulk, amount*) *person, fruit, parcel, book* gros (*f* grosse). (*US: $1000*) **a ~ one**‡ (un billet de) mille dollars; **to grow ~** *or* **~ger** grossir; **a ~ stick** un gros bâton (*see also* **stick**); **~ toe** gros orteil; **~ with child** grosse, enceinte; *see* **drum, money** *etc*.

c (*in age*) grand, aîné. **a ~ boy/girl** un grand garçon/une grande fille; **my ~ brother** mon grand frère, mon frère aîné; **to be a ~ brother to sb** servir de conseiller à qn (*see also* **3**); **I am ~ enough to know** je suis assez grand pour savoir.

d (*important*) grand, important, marquant, remarquable. **a ~ man** un grand homme, un homme marquant *or* remarquable *or* important; **to look ~** faire l'important; **~ bug**‡, (*Brit*) **~ noise***, **~ shot*** huile‡ *f*, grosse légume‡; **~ business** les grandes entreprises, les grandes firmes; (*fig: fashionable*) **boots are ~ this year*** les bottes sont in‡ cette année; **a ~ event** un événement marquant; **to have ~ ideas** voir grand; **a ~ lie** un gros mensonge; (*person*) **he's a ~ name in politics** c'est un grand nom de la politique; **the ~ger they are, the harder they fall** plus haut ils sont arrivés, plus dure sera la chute; **to do things in a ~ way** faire les choses en grand; **a tragedy? that's rather a ~ word** une tragédie? c'est un bien grand mot; **to make the ~ time*** arriver, réussir (*see also* **3**).

e (*conceited*) *person* prétentieux; *words* ambitieux. **~ talk** fanfaronnades *fpl*, grands discours; **he's too ~ for his boots*** il a des prétentions; **he's got a ~ head*** il est crâneur*, il a la grosse tête*; **he's got a ~ mouth*** il ne sait pas se taire *or* la boucler*; **why can't you keep your ~ mouth shut!*** pas moyen que tu te taises!*, tu aurais mieux fait de la boucler!‡; *see also* **3**.

f (*generous*) grand, généreux. **a heart as ~ as yours** un cœur aussi grand *or* aussi généreux que le vôtre; (*iro*) **that's ~ of you!*** quelle générosité! (*iro*); **to be ~ on**‡ *person* adorer, être un fan* de; *thing* être grand amateur *or* un fana* de.

2 adv: **to talk ~*** fanfaronner, se faire mousser*; **to go over ~**‡ avoir un succès fou *or* monstre*; **to make it ~*** avoir un succès fou*; **his speech went down ~ with his audience**‡ ses auditeurs ont été emballés* par son discours.

3 comp ▸**big band** (*Mus*) grand orchestre (*années 40-50*) ▸**big bang** (*Phys*) big-bang *m*; (*Brit St Ex*) **the Big Bang** le Big Bang (*informatisation de la Bourse de Londres*) ▸**Big Ben** (*Brit*) Big Ben *m* ▸**big-boned** bien *or* fortement charpenté ▸**Big Brother** (*Pol etc*) l'État omniprésent; **Big Brother is watching you** l'État vous a à l'œil ▸**big cat** fauve *m*, grand félin *m* ▸**the big city** la grande agglomération ▸**the Big Dipper** (*US Astron*) la Grande Ourse ▸**big dipper** *[fairground]* montagnes *fpl* russes ▸**the Big Eight/Ten** (*US Univ*) les huit/dix grandes universités du Centre-Ouest ▸**big end** (*Aut*) tête *f* de bielle ▸**the Big Four** (*Pol*) les Quatre (Grands) ▸**big game** (*Brit*) gros gibier; **big game hunter** chasseur *m* de gros gibier; **big game hunting** chasse *f* au gros gibier ▸**bighead*** crâneur* *m*, -euse* *f* ▸**bigheaded*** crâneur* ▸**big-hearted** au grand cœur; **to be big-hearted** avoir bon cœur, avoir du cœur; **a big-hearted fellow** un homme de cœur ▸**bigmouth*** gueulard(e)‡ *m(f)*, hâbleur *m*, -euse *f*; **he is just a bigmouth** il ne sait jamais la boucler‡ ▸**big-mouthed*** fort en gueule*; **to be big-mouthed*** avoir une grande gueule* ▸**big-sounding** *idea, plan etc* prétentieux; *name* ronflant, pompeux ▸**the Big Ten** *see* **the Big Eight** ▸**big time***: **to make the big time** faire sa percée ▸**big-time*** adj *politician, industrialist* de première catégorie; *part, role* de premier plan; *farming* sur une grande échelle; **big-time gambler** flambeur‡ *m* ▸**big top** (*circus*) cirque *m*; (*main tent of it*) grand chapiteau ▸**bigwig**‡ grosse légume‡, huile‡ *f*; *see* **apple 1, deal**.

bigamist [ˈbɪgəmɪst] n bigame *mf*.

bigamous [ˈbɪgəməs] adj bigame.

bigamy [ˈbɪgəmɪ] n bigamie *f*.

biggish [ˈbɪgɪʃ] adj (*see* **big**) assez *or* relativement grand/gros/important *etc*.

bight [baɪt] n a (*Geog*) baie *f*, anse *f*; (*larger*) golfe *m*. b *[rope]* boucle *f*.

bigot [ˈbɪgət] n (*Philos, Pol, Rel*) fanatique *mf*, sectaire *mf*. **(religious) ~** bigot(e) *m(f)*.

bigoted [ˈbɪgətɪd] adj (*Rel*) bigot; (*Pol etc*) *person* fanatique, sectaire; *attitude, devotion* fanatique.

bigotry [ˈbɪgətrɪ] n (*NonC*) (*Rel*) bigoterie *f*; (*Philos, Pol etc*) fanatisme *m*, sectarisme *m*.

Bihar [bɪˈhɑːʳ] n Bihâr *m*.

bijou [ˈbiːʒuː] adj (*Brit*) "**~ residence for sale**" "maison à vendre, véritable petit bijou".

bike [baɪk] 1 n (*) vélo *m*, bécane* *f*; (**abbr of motorbike**) moto *f*. (*Brit*) **on your ~ !*** (*go away!*) dégage!*; (*no way!*) tu plaisantes!* 2 vi (‡) aller *or* venir à vélo. 3 comp ▸**bike shed** abri *m* à bicyclettes ▸**bikeway** piste *f* cyclable.

biker* [baɪkəʳ] n motard(e) *m(f)*.

bikini [bɪˈkiːnɪ] n bikini *m*. **(pair of) ~ pants** slip *m* mini.

bilabial [baɪˈleɪbjəl] 1 adj bilabial. 2 n bilabiale *f*.

bilateral [baɪˈlætərəl] adj bilatéral.

bilberry [ˈbɪlbərɪ] n myrtille *f*, airelle *f*.

bile [baɪl] n a (*Anat*) bile *f*. **~ duct** canal *m* biliaire; **~ stone** calcul *m* biliaire. b (*fig: anger*) mauvaise humeur. c (*Hist: choler*) bile *f*.

bilevel [baɪˈlevl] adj sur *or* à deux niveaux.

bilge [bɪldʒ] n a (*Naut*) (*rounded part of hull*) bouchain *m*, renflement *m*; (*bottom of hold*) fond *m* de cale, sentine *f*; (*also* **~ water**) eau *f* de cale *or* de sentine. b (‡: *nonsense*) idioties *fpl*, foutaises‡ *fpl*.

bilharzia [bɪlˈhɑːzɪə] n, **bilharziasis** [ˌbɪlhɑːˈzaɪəsɪs] n bilharziose *f*.

bilingual [baɪˈlɪŋgwəl] adj bilingue.

bilingualism [baɪˈlɪŋgwəlɪzəm] n bilinguisme *m*.

bilious [ˈbɪlɪəs] adj a (*Med*) bilieux. **~ attack** crise *f* de foie. b (*fig*) maussade, irritable.

biliousness [ˈbɪlɪəsnɪs] n (*NonC*) (*Med*) affection *f* hépatique.

bilk [bɪlk] vt *creditor* filouter, blouser*. **to ~ sb's efforts** mettre des bâtons dans les roues à qn.

Bill [bɪl] (**dim of William**) Guillaume *m*.

bill[1] [bɪl] 1 n a (*for product, work done*) facture *f*; (*for gas etc*) note *f*; (*esp Brit*) *[restaurant]* addition *f*; *[hotel]* note. **have you paid the milk ~?** as-tu payé le lait?; **a pile of ~s in the post** une pile de factures dans le courrier; **may I have the ~ please** l'addition (*or* la note) s'il vous plaît; **put it on my ~ please** mettez-le sur ma note, s'il vous plaît; **the factory has a high wages ~** l'usine a d'importantes sorties en salaires, le poste salaires est élevé dans l'entreprise; *see* **foot, pay, settle**[2] *etc*.

b (*written statement*) état *m*, liste *f*. **~ of fare** menu *m*, carte *f* (du jour); **~ of costs** état des frais; (*Customs*) **~ of entry** déclaration *f* d'entrée en douane; (*Naut*) **~ of health** patente *f* (de santé) (*see* **clean**); (*Comm*) **~ of lading** connaissement *m*; (*Constr*) **~ of quantities** métré *m* (*devis*); (*Hist*) **B~ of Rights** déclaration *f* des droits; (*fig*) **~ of rights** déclaration des droits (*d'un peuple*); (*US*) **to sell sb a ~ of goods**‡ rouler‡ *or* posséder‡ qn.

c (*Comm, Fin etc*) effet *m*, traite *f*. **to meet a ~** faire honneur à un effet; **to draw a ~ on** tirer une traite sur, faire traite sur; (*Fin*) **~s receivable** effets à recevoir; **~ of exchange** lettre *f or* effet de change; **~ of sale** acte *m or* contrat *m* de vente; **exchequer ~** bon *m* du Trésor; **foreign ~** devise étrangère; *see* **endorse** *etc*.

d (*US: banknote*) billet *m* (de banque). **5-dollar ~** billet de 5 dollars.

e (*Parl*) projet *m* de loi. **to propose/pass/throw out a ~** présenter/voter/rejeter un projet de loi; (*Brit*) **the ~ passed the Commons** le projet de loi a été voté par la Chambre des Communes.

f (*Jur*) plainte *f*, requête *f*. **~ of indictment** acte *m* d'accusation; **~ of attainder** décret *m* de confiscation de biens et de mort civile.

g (*poster, advertisement*) (*Theat etc*) affiche *f*; *[house for sale]* écriteau *m*; (*public notice*) placard *m*. **to head** *or* **top the ~** être en vedette, être en tête d'affiche; *see* **fill, hand, stick** *etc*.

2 vt a *goods* facturer. **to ~ sb for sth** envoyer la facture de qch à qn.

b *play* mettre à l'affiche, annoncer. **he is ~ed to play Hamlet** il est à l'affiche dans le rôle de Hamlet.

3 comp ▸**billboard** panneau *m* d'affichage ▸**billfold** (*US*) portefeuille *m* ▸**billposter, billsticker** colleur *m* d'affiches, afficheur *m*.

bill[2] [bɪl] 1 n a *[bird]* bec *m*. **long-~ed bird** oiseau *m* à long bec; *see* **scissor** *etc*. b (*Geog*) promontoire *m*, cap *m*, bec *m*. **Portland B~** le Bec de Portland. 2 vi *[birds]* se becqueter. (*lit, fig*) **to ~ and coo** roucouler.

bill[3] [bɪl] n a (*tool*) serpe *f*. **~hook** serpette *f*. b (*Hist: weapon*) hache *f* d'armes.

billet[1] [ˈbɪlɪt] 1 n (*Mil*) (*document*) billet *m* de logement; (*accommodation*) cantonnement *m* (chez l'habitant). (*fig*) **a cushy ~**‡ un fromage*, une planque*. 2 vt (*Mil*) *soldier* loger, cantonner (*on sb* chez qn; *on a town* dans une ville).

billet[2] [ˈbɪlɪt] n *[wood etc]* billette *f* (*also Archit*).

billeting [ˈbɪlɪtɪŋ] n (*Mil*) cantonnement *m*. **~ officer** chef *m* de cantonnement.

billiard [ˈbɪljəd] 1 n (*NonC*) **~s** (jeu *m* de) billard *m*; **to have a game of ~s** faire une partie de billard. 2 comp ▸**billiard ball** boule *f* de billard ▸**billiard cue** queue *f* de billard ▸**billiard(s) saloon** (*Brit*) (salle *f* de *or* café-)billard *m* ▸**billiard table** (table *f* de) billard *m*.

billing[1] [ˈbɪlɪŋ] n (*Theat*) **to get top/second ~** figurer en tête d'affiche/en deuxième place à l'affiche.

billing[2] [ˈbɪlɪŋ] n (*lit, fig*) **~ and cooing** roucoulements *mpl*.

billing[3] [ˈbɪlɪŋ] n (*Comm*) facturation *f*.

Billingsgate [ˈbɪlɪŋzgeɪt] n *marché au poisson de Londres*. (*foul language*) **to talk ~** *[man]* parler comme un charretier; *[woman]* parler comme une poissonnière.

billion [ˈbɪljən] n, pl **~** *or* **~s** milliard *m*; (*Brit* †) billion *m*.

billionaire [ˌbɪljəˈnɛəʳ] n milliardaire *mf*.

billow [ˈbɪləʊ] 1 n (*liter*) **the ~s** les flots *mpl* (*liter*). 2 vi *[sail]* se gonfler; *[cloth]* onduler; *[smoke]* s'élever en tourbillons *or* en volutes,

tournoyer.
▸**billow out** vi *[sail etc]* se gonfler.
billowy [ˈbɪləʊɪ] adj *sea* houleux, agité; *waves* gros (*f* grosse); *sail* gonflé (par le vent); *smoke* en (grosses) volutes.
billy¹ [ˈbɪlɪ] n (*US: club*) matraque *f*.
billy² [ˈbɪlɪ] n (*also* ~ **can**) gamelle *f*.
billy goat [ˈbɪlɪgəʊt] n bouc *m*. **~-goat beard** bouc *m* (*barbe*).
billy-ho*, billy-o* [ˈbɪlɪhəʊ] n: **like ~** *laugh* à gorge déployée; *run* à toutes jambes.
bimbo* [ˈbɪmbəʊ] n, pl **~s** *or* **~es** (*pej*) ravissante idiote, potiche *f*. **he's out with his ~** il est sorti avec sa minette*.
bimetallic [ˌbaɪmɪˈtælɪk] adj bimétallique.
bimetallism [baɪˈmetəlɪzəm] n bimétallisme *m*.
bimonthly [ˈbaɪˈmʌnθlɪ] 1 adj (*twice a month*) bimensuel; (*every two months*) bimestriel. 2 adv deux fois par mois; tous les deux mois.
bin [bɪn] 1 n a *[coal, corn]* coffre *m*; *[bread]* boîte *f*, (*larger*) huche *f*. b (*Brit*) *[wine]* casier *m* (à bouteilles). **~ end** fin *f* de série. c (*Brit: also* **dust~, rubbish ~**) boîte *f* à ordures, poubelle *f*. **~ bag** (grand) sac *m* poubelle; **~ liner** sac *m* poubelle; (*dustmen*) **~men*** boueux* *mpl*. 2 vt *coal, corn* mettre dans un coffre; (*throw away*) mettre *or* jeter à la poubelle.
binary [ˈbaɪnərɪ] adj binaire. (*Comput*) **~ code** code *m* binaire; (*Comput*) **~ compatible** compatible binaire; (*Mus*) **~ form** forme *f* binaire; (*Math*) **~ notation/number/system** numération *f*/nombre *m*/système *m* binaire.
bind [baɪnd] pret, ptp **bound** 1 vt a (*fasten*) *thing* attacher; *2 or more things* attacher, lier; *person, animal* lier, attacher (*to* à); *prisoner* ligoter. **he bound the sticks (together) with string** il a attaché *or* lié les baguettes avec une ficelle; **bound hand and foot** pieds et poings liés; (*fig*) **bound by gratitude to sb** attaché à qn par la reconnaissance; *[people, ideas]* **to be bound together** être liés.
b (*encircle*) entourer (*with* de), ceindre (*with* de) (*liter*); (*Med*) *artery* ligaturer; *wound* bander.
c (*secure edge of*) *material, hem* border (*with* de).
d *book* relier. **bound in calf** relié (en) veau.
e (*oblige, pledge*) obliger, contraindre (*sb to do* qn à faire). **to ~ o.s. to sth/to do sth** s'engager à qch/à faire qch; **to ~ sb to a promise** astreindre qn à tenir une promesse; **to ~ by an oath** lier par (un) serment; **to ~ sb as an apprentice (to)** mettre qn en apprentissage (chez); *see* **bound³ 2c**.
f (*stick together*) lier, cimenter, donner de la cohésion à; (*Med*) *bowels* resserrer. (*Culin*) **~ the mixture with an egg** lier la préparation avec un œuf.
2 vi *[rule]* être obligatoire; *[agreement]* engager; *[machinery]* se coincer, (se) gripper.
3 n a (*Mus*) liaison *f*.
b (*Brit* ‡*: nuisance*) (*person*) crampon* *m*, casse-pieds* *mf inv*, scie* *f*; (*thing*) scie*. **what a ~ you've got to go** quelle barbe* que tu aies à partir; **that meeting is a terrible ~** cette réunion me casse les pieds* *or* me barbe*; **to be in a ~** être dans le pétrin‡, être coincé.
4 comp ▸**bindweed** liseron *m*.
▸**bind down** vt sep (*fig*) obliger, contraindre, astreindre (*sb to do* qn à faire). **to be bound down (to do)** être obligé *or* contraint (de faire), être astreint (à faire).
▸**bind on** 1 vt sep attacher (*avec une corde etc*). 2 vi (*) rouspéter*, geindre* (*about* à propos de).
▸**bind over** vt sep (*Jur*) mettre en liberté conditionnelle. **to bind sb over to keep the peace** relaxer qn sous condition qu'il ne trouble (*subj*) pas l'ordre public; **he was bound over for six months** on l'a relaxé sous peine de comparaître en cas de récidive dans les six mois.
▸**bind together** vt sep (*lit*) *sticks* lier; (*fig*) *people* unir.
▸**bind up** vt sep *wound* panser, bander; (*fig*) lier, attacher. **your life is bound up in hers** votre existence est étroitement liée à la sienne; **to be totally bound up with sb** se dévouer entièrement à qn; **to be totally bound up with one's work** se donner corps et âme à son travail; **question closely bound up with another** question étroitement liée à une autre; **it's all bound up with whether he comes or not** tout dépend s'il va venir ou pas*.
binder [ˈbaɪndəʳ] n a (*Agr*) (*machine*) lieuse *f*; (*person*) lieur *m*, -euse *f*; *see* **book**. b (*for papers*) classeur *m*; *see* **spring**. c (*Med etc*) bandage *m*. d (*Constr*) (*cement, mortar*) liant *m*, agglomérant *m*; (*joist*) entrait *m*. e (*US: agreement in deal*) engagement *m*, option *f* d'achat.
bindery [ˈbaɪndərɪ] n atelier *m* de reliure.
binding [ˈbaɪndɪŋ] 1 n a *[book]* reliure *f*; *see* **cloth, half**. b (*tape*) extra-fort *m*; *see* **bias**. c *[skis]* fixation *f*. 2 adj a *rule* obligatoire; *agreement, promise* qui lie, qui engage; *price* ferme. **to be ~ on sb** être obligatoire pour qn, lier qn, engager qn; **a promise is ~** on est lié par une promesse; (*Jur: of agreement*) **~ effect** force *f* obligatoire; (*Jur*) **measure ~ on each contracting party** mesure *f* exécutoire pour chaque partie contractante; (*US Pol*) **~ primary** *élection primaire dont le résultat lie le vote des délégués à la convention du parti*. b (*Med*) *food etc* constipant; (*Constr*) agglomérant.
binge‡ [bɪndʒ] n bringue‡ *f*. **to go on a ~, to have a ~** aller faire la bombe* *or* la bringue‡.
bingo [ˈbɪŋgəʊ] 1 n (jeu *m* de) loto *m* (*joué collectivement en public pour de l'argent*). 2 excl: **~!*** Eurêka!*
binnacle [ˈbɪnəkl] n (*Naut*) habitacle *m*.
binocular [bɪˈnɒkjʊləʳ] 1 adj binoculaire. 2 npl: **~s** jumelle(s) *f(pl)*.
binomial [baɪˈnəʊmɪəl] adj, n (*Math*) binôme (*m*). **~ distribution** distribution binomiale; **the ~ theorem** le théorème (de binôme) de Newton.
bint‡ [bɪnt] n nana‡ *f*.
binuclear [baɪˈnjuːklɪəʳ] adj binucléaire.
bio... [ˈbaɪəʊ] pref bio... .
biochemical [ˈbaɪəʊˈkemɪkəl] adj biochimique.
biochemist [ˈbaɪəʊˈkemɪst] n biochimiste *mf*.
biochemistry [ˈbaɪəʊˈkemɪstrɪ] n biochimie *f*.
biodegradable [ˈbaɪəʊdɪˈgreɪdəbl] adj biodégradable.
biodiversity [ˌbaɪəʊdaɪˈvɜːsətɪ] n biodiversité *f*.
bioengineering [ˌbaɪəʊˌendʒɪˈnɪərɪŋ] n bioingénierie *f*.
biofeedback [ˌbaɪəʊˈfiːdbæk] n biofeedback *m*.
biofuel [ˈbaɪəʊfjʊəl] n combustible *m* organique.
biogenesis [ˈbaɪəʊˈdʒenɪsɪs] n biogénèse *f*.
biographer [baɪˈɒgrəfəʳ] n biographe *mf*.
biographic(al) [ˌbaɪəʊˈgræfɪk(əl)] adj biographique.
biography [baɪˈɒgrəfɪ] n biographie *f*.
biological [ˌbaɪəˈlɒdʒɪkəl] adj biologique. **~ clock** horloge *f* physiologique; **~ soap powder** lessive *f* aux enzymes; **~ warfare** guerre *f* biologique.
biologically [ˌbaɪəʊˈlɒdʒɪkəlɪ] adv biologiquement.
biologist [baɪˈɒlədʒɪst] n biologiste *mf*.
biology [baɪˈɒlədʒɪ] n biologie *f*.
biomass [ˈbaɪəʊmæs] n biomasse *f*.
biome [ˈbaɪəʊm] n biome *m*.
biometrics [baɪəˈmetrɪks] n (*NonC*), **biometry** [baɪˈɒmɪtrɪ] n (*NonC*) biométrie *f*.
bionic [baɪˈɒnɪk] adj bionique.
bionics [baɪˈɒnɪks] n (*NonC*) bionique *f*.
biophysical [ˌbaɪəʊˈfɪzɪkəl] adj biophysique.
biophysicist [ˌbaɪəʊˈfɪzɪsɪst] n biophysicien(ne) *m(f)*.
biophysics [ˌbaɪəʊˈfɪzɪks] n (*NonC*) biophysique *f*.
biopic* [ˈbaɪəʊˌpɪk] n film *m* biographique.
biopsy [ˈbaɪɒpsɪ] n biopsie *f*.
biorhythm [ˈbaɪəʊrɪðəm] n biorythme *m*.
biosphere [ˈbaɪəsfɪəʳ] n biosphère *f*.
biosynthesis [ˌbaɪəʊˈsɪnθɪsɪs] n biosynthèse *f*, anabolisme *m*.
biosynthetic [ˌbaɪəʊˌsɪnˈθetɪk] adj biosynthétique.
biota [baɪˈəʊtə] n biote *m*.
biotechnology [ˌbaɪəʊtekˈnɒlədʒɪ] n biotechnologie *f*.
biotic [baɪˈɒtɪk] adj biotique.
biowarfare [ˈbaɪəʊˈwɔːfɛəʳ] n guerre *f* biologique.
bipartisan [ˌbaɪˈpɑːtɪzæn] adj biparti *or* bipartite. **~ politics** politique *f* qui fait l'unanimité.
bipartite [baɪˈpɑːtaɪt] adj (*Bio, Pol*) biparti *or* bipartite; (*Jur*) *document* rédigé en double.
biped [ˈbaɪped] adj, n bipède (*m*).
biplane [ˈbaɪpleɪn] n (avion *m*) biplan *m*.
bipolar [baɪˈpəʊləʳ] adj bipolaire.
bipolarization [baɪˌpəʊləraɪˈzeɪʃən] n bipolarisation *f*.
bipolarize [baɪˈpəʊləraɪz] vt bipolariser.
birch [bɜːtʃ] 1 n (*also* **~ tree**) bouleau *m*; (*also* **~ wood**) (bois *m* de) bouleau; (*for whipping*) verge *f*, fouet *m*. (*Jur*) **the ~** la peine du fouet (avec les verges); *see* **silver**. 2 vt fouetter. 3 comp de bouleau ▸**birch plantation** boulaie *f*, plantation *f* de bouleaux.
birching [ˈbɜːtʃɪŋ] n peine *f* du fouet (avec les verges).
bird [bɜːd] 1 n a oiseau *m*; (*game*) gibier *m* (à plume); (*Culin*) volaille *f*. **they shot six ~s** ils ont abattu six pièces de gibier; **young** *or* **little ~** petit oiseau, oisillon *m*; (*liter*) **~ of ill omen** oiseau de mauvais augure *or* de malheur; (*lit, fig*) **~ of passage** oiseau de passage; **~ of prey** oiseau de proie; **~ of paradise** oiseau de paradis; (*Prov*) **a ~ in the hand is worth two in the bush** un tiens vaut mieux que deux tu l'auras (*Prov*); (*Prov*) **~s of a feather flock together** qui se ressemble s'assemble (*Prov*); **they're ~s of a feather** ils sont à mettre dans le même sac; **a little ~ told me*** mon petit doigt me l'a dit; (*fig*) **the ~ has flown** l'oiseau s'est envolé; (*fig*) **to give sb the ~‡** envoyer paître* *or* bouler* qn; (*Theat sl*) huer *or* siffler qn; (*Theat sl*) **to get the ~** se faire siffler *or* huer; **that's strictly for the ~s‡** ça c'est bon pour les imbéciles; (*hum*) **he'll have to be told about the ~s and the bees** il va falloir lui expliquer comment font les petits oiseaux *or* que les bébés ne naissent pas dans les choux; *see* **early, jail, kill** *etc*.
b (‡) (*fellow*) individu *m*, type* *m*; (*girl*) fille *f*, nana‡ *f*, pépée‡ *f*. **he's a queer ~** c'est un drôle d'oiseau *or* de numéro*; **he's a cunning old ~** c'est un vieux singe *or* rusé.
c (‡) (*term in prison*) **5 years ~** 5 ans de *or* en taule‡; **to do ~‡** faire de la taule‡.
2 comp ▸**bird bath** vasque *f* pour les oiseaux ▸**bird brain*** (*pej*) étourneau *m*, tête *f* de linotte ▸**bird-brained*** (*pej*) qui a une cervelle

d'oiseau, écervelé ▸**birdcage** cage *f* à oiseaux; (*large*) volière *f* ▸**bird call** cri *m* d'oiseau ▸**bird dog** (*US*) chien *m* pour le gibier à plume ▸**bird fancier** aviculteur *m*, -trice *f* ▸**bird feeder** mangeoire *f*, trémie *f* ▸**bird-like** *eyes, features* d'oiseau ▸**birdlime** glu *f* ▸**bird nesting**: **to go bird nesting** aller dénicher les oiseaux ▸**bird sanctuary** refuge *m* d'oiseaux, réserve *f* d'oiseaux ▸**birdseed** millet *m*, graine *f* pour les oiseaux ▸**birds' eggs** œufs *mpl* d'oiseaux ▸**bird's eye** (*Bot*) petit chêne; (*lit*) **a bird's-eye view of Paris** Paris vu d'avion; (*fig*) **bird's-eye view** vue *f* d'ensemble, vue générale ▸**bird's foot** (*Bot*) pied-de-poule *m* ▸**bird's nest** nid *m* d'oiseau(x); (*Culin*) **bird's nest soup** soupe *f* aux nids d'hirondelles ▸**bird table** (*in garden*) mangeoire *f* ▸**bird-watcher** ornithologue *mf* amateur ▸**bird-watching** ornithologie *f*; **to go bird-watching** aller observer les oiseaux; *see* **paradise**.

birdie ['bɜːdɪ] **n** a (*baby talk*) (gentil) petit oiseau. (*for photo*) **"watch the ~!"*** "le petit oiseau va sortir!" b (*Golf*) birdie *m*.

biretta [bɪ'retə] **n** barrette *f*.

birling ['bɜːlɪŋ] **n** (*US*) *sport de bûcheron, consistant à faire tourner avec les pieds, sans tomber, un tronc d'arbre flottant*.

Biro ['baɪərəʊ] **n** ® (*Brit*) stylo *m* (à) bille, (pointe *f*) Bic *m* ®.

birth [bɜːθ] 1 **n** a (*being born*) naissance *f*; (*childbirth*) accouchement *m*, couches *fpl*; *[animal]* mise *f* bas. **during the ~** pendant l'accouchement; **to give ~ to** *[woman]* donner naissance à; *[animal]* mettre bas; **blind/orphan from ~** aveugle/orphelin de naissance; **the village/country of one's ~** son village/pays natal; *see* **child, place, premature**.

b (*parentage*) naissance *f*, extraction *f*. **Scottish by ~** écossais de naissance; **of good ~** bien né, de bonne famille; **of humble ~** de basse extraction.

c (*fig*) *[movement, idea]* naissance *f*, éclosion *f*; *[new era]* naissance, commencement *m*; *[trend, project]* naissance, lancement *m*; *[phenomenon]* apparition *f*.

2 **comp** ▸**birth certificate** (*original*) acte *m* de naissance; (*copy*) extrait *m* de naissance ▸**birth control** régulation *f or* limitation *f* des naissances; **birth control pill** = **birth pill** ▸**birthday** *see* **birthday** ▸**birth defect** défaut *m* de naissance ▸**birthmark** tache *f* de vin, nævus *m*, angiome *m* ▸**birth pill** (*Med*) pilule *f* (anticonceptionnelle) ▸**birthplace** (*gen, Admin*) lieu *m* de naissance; (*house*) maison natale; **the birthplace of civilization** le berceau de la civilisation ▸**birth rate** (taux *m* de) natalité *f* ▸**birthright**: **it is the birthright of every Englishman** c'est un droit que chaque Anglais a *or* acquiert en naissant ▸**birthstone** pierre *f* porte-bonheur (*selon le jour de naissance*).

birthday ['bɜːθdeɪ] 1 **n** anniversaire *m*. **what did you get for your ~?** qu'est-ce que tu as eu pour ton anniversaire?; *see* **happy**. 2 **comp** ▸**birthday cake** gâteau *m* d'anniversaire ▸**birthday card** carte *f* d'anniversaire ▸**Birthday Honours** (*Brit*) *see* **honour 2** ▸**birthday party**: **she is having a birthday party** on a organisé une petite fête *or* une soirée pour son anniversaire ▸**birthday present** cadeau *m* d'anniversaire ▸**birthday suit***: (*hum*) **in one's birthday suit** dans le costume d'Adam (*or* d'Ève)*, dans le plus simple appareil (*hum*).

biscuit ['bɪskɪt] 1 **n** a (*Brit*) petit gâteau sec, biscuit *m*. **that takes the ~!**‡ ça c'est le bouquet!*; **he takes the ~!**‡ il est marrant ce gars-là!‡; *see* **digestive, ship, water** *etc*. b (*US*) biscuit *m* sec. 2 **comp** ▸**biscuit barrel** boîte *f* à biscuits ▸**biscuit-firing** (*Pottery*) dégourdi *m* ▸**biscuit ware** (*Pottery*) biscuit *m*. 3 **adj** (*also* **~-coloured**) (couleur) biscuit *inv*, beige.

bisect [baɪ'sekt] 1 **vt** couper *or* diviser en deux; (*Math*) couper en deux parties égales. 2 **vi** *[road etc]* bifurquer.

bisection [baɪ'sekʃən] **n** (*Math*) division *f* en deux parties égales; *[angle]* bissection *f*.

bisector [baɪ'sektəʳ] **n** (*Math*) bissectrice *f*.

bisexual ['baɪ'seksjʊəl] **adj** (*Bio, Zool*) bis(s)exué; (*Psych*) (sexuellement) ambivalent, bis(s)exuel.

bishop ['bɪʃəp] **n** (*Rel*) évêque *m*; (*Chess*) fou *m*.

bishopric ['bɪʃəprɪk] **n** (*diocese*) évêché *m*; (*function*) épiscopat *m*.

bismuth ['bɪzməθ] **n** bismuth *m*.

bison ['baɪsn] **n, pl inv** bison *m*.

bisque [bɪsk] **n** (*Culin, Sport*) bisque *f*; (*Pottery*) biscuit *m*.

bissextile [bɪ'sekstaɪl] 1 **n** année *f* bissextile. 2 **adj** bissextile.

bistable [baɪ'steɪbl] **adj** (*Comput*) bistable.

bistoury ['bɪstʊrɪ] **n** bistouri *m*.

bistre ['bɪstəʳ] **adj, n** bistre (*m*).

bistro ['biːstrəʊ] **n** petit restaurant *m* (*style bistrot*).

bit[1] [bɪt] **n** a *[horse]* mors *m*. (*lit, fig*) **to get** *or* **take the ~ between one's teeth** prendre le mors aux dents; *see* **champ**[1]. b (*tool*) mèche *f*; *see* **brace, centre**.

bit[2] [bɪt] 1 **n** a (*piece*) *[bread]* morceau *m*; *[paper, string]* bout *m*; *[book, talk etc]* passage *m*; (*tiny amount*) peu *m*. **a ~ of garden** un bout de jardin, un tout petit jardin; **a tiny little ~** un tout petit peu; **there's a ~ of the soldier in him** il y a un peu du soldat en lui; **a ~ of advice** un petit conseil; **a ~ of news** une nouvelle; **a ~ of luck** une chance; **what a ~ of luck!*** quelle chance! *or* veine!*; (*euph*) **he's got a ~ on the side**‡ il a une poule* quelque part.

b (*phrases*) **a ~** un peu; **a ~ of money** un peu d'argent; **it is** *or* **that is a ~ much** (*expensive*) c'est un peu exagéré!; (*unfair*) c'est un peu fort*!; **a good ~ of** *or* **quite a ~ of money** pas mal d'argent; **he paid a good ~ for it** ça lui a coûté assez cher (*lit*); **I'm a ~/a little ~/a good ~ late** je suis un peu/un petit peu/très en retard; **it's a good ~ further than we thought** c'est bien *or* beaucoup plus loin que nous ne pensions; **a good ~ bigger** bien *or* beaucoup plus grand; **every ~ as good as** tout aussi bon que; **every ~ of the wall** le mur tout entier; **he's every ~ a soldier** il est militaire jusqu'à la moelle; **I'm a ~ of a socialist*** je suis un peu socialiste sur les bords*; **she's a ~ of a liar** elle est un brin *or* un tantinet menteuse; **it was a ~ of a shock** ça (nous) a plutôt fait un choc; **that's a ~ of all right**‡ c'est terrible‡ *or* chouette*; **that's a ~ thick!*** ça c'est un peu fort* *or* violent*; **not a ~** pas du tout; **not a ~ of it!** pas du tout!, pas le moins du monde!; **don't believe a (single) ~ of it** n'en croyez pas un mot; **it's not a ~ of use** cela ne sert strictement *or* absolument à rien; **he wasn't a ~ the wiser** *or* **the better for it** il n'en était pas plus avancé; **in ~s and pieces** (*broken*) en morceaux, en miettes; (*dismantled*) en pièces détachées; (*fig*) *plan, scheme* en ruines; **bring all your ~s and pieces** apporte toutes tes petites affaires; **~s and bobs*** petits trucs*, petites affaires; **to come to ~s** (*break*) s'en aller *or* tomber en morceaux; (*dismantle*) se démonter; **he went to ~s*** il a craqué*; **~ by ~** petit à petit; **and a ~ over** et même un peu plus; **to do one's ~** fournir sa part d'effort; **when it comes to the ~*** en fin de compte, quand tout est dit; *see* **much 1a**.

c (*of time*) **after a ~** après un bout de temps; **a good** *or* **quite a ~** un bon bout de temps*; **wait a ~** attendez un instant *or* un peu.

d (*coin: gen*) pièce *f*; *see* **threepenny, two**.

e (*Comput*) bit *m*.

2 **adj** (*Theat*) **~ part** petit rôle, panne *f* (*Theat sl*).

bit[3] [bɪt] **pret of bite**.

bitch [bɪtʃ] 1 **n** a *[dog]* chienne *f*; *[canines generally]* femelle *f*; *[fox]* renarde *f*; *[wolf]* louve *f*. **terrier ~** terrier *m* femelle. b (‡ *pej: woman*) garce‡ *f*. **she's a ~** elle est rosse*, c'est une garce‡; **that ~ of a car**‡ cette garce de bagnole‡; **that ~ of a job**‡ cette saloperie de boulot‡. c (*esp US: complaint*) **what's your ~?**‡ qu'est-ce que tu as à râler?‡ 2 **vi** (‡*: complain*) rouspéter*, râler* (*about* contre).

bitchy‡ ['bɪtʃɪ] **adj** rosse*, vache‡. **to be ~ to/about sb** être vache‡ avec/en ce qui concerne qn; **he was ~ about it** il a été vache‡ à ce sujet; **that was a ~ thing to do** c'était (un coup) vache‡.

bite [baɪt] (**vb: pret bit, ptp bitten**) 1 **n** a *[dog etc]* morsure *f*; *[snake, insect]* piqûre *f*. **face covered in (insect) ~s** visage couvert de piqûres d'insectes; (*US fig*) **to put the ~ on sb**‡ essayer de taper qn‡; *see* **bark**[2], **flea** *etc*.

b (*piece bitten off*) bouchée *f*; (*something to eat*) morceau *m*, quelque chose (à manger). **a ~ (to eat)** un casse-graine; **in two ~s** en deux bouchées; **chew each ~ carefully** mâchez bien chaque bouchée; **she grudged him every ~** elle lui reprochait chaque bouchée; **I'll get a ~ on the train** je mangerai un morceau dans le train; **there's not a ~ to eat** il n'y a rien à manger, il n'y a rien à se mettre sous la dent; **come and have a ~*** venez manger un morceau; (*fig*) **to have two ~s** *or* **another** *or* **a second ~ at the cherry** s'y reprendre à deux fois.

c (*Fishing*) touche *f*. **I haven't had a ~ all day** je n'ai pas eu une seule touche aujourd'hui; **got a ~?*** ça a mordu?

d *[sauce etc]* piquant *m*. (*fig*) **there's a ~ in the air** l'air est piquant; **his speech hadn't much ~** son discours manquait de mordant.

2 **vt** a *[person, animal]* mordre. **to ~ one's nails** se ronger les ongles; **to ~ one's lips/fingers** se mordre les lèvres/les doigts; (*lit, fig*) **to ~ one's tongue** se mordre la langue; (*hum*) **it won't ~ (you)!*** ça ne mord pas!*; **to ~ in two** couper en deux d'un coup de dents; **to ~ the bullet*** serrer les dents (*fig*); (*lit, fig*) **to ~ the dust** mordre la poussière; (*fig*) **to ~ the hand that feeds you** être d'une ingratitude monstrueuse; (*Prov*) **once bitten twice shy** chat échaudé craint l'eau froide (*Prov*); **to be bitten with* the desire to do** mourir d'envie de faire; (*be cheated*) **to get bitten**‡ se faire avoir*, se faire rouler*; **I've been bitten!**‡ j'ai été fait (comme un rat); *see* **biter**.

b *[snake, insect]* piquer, mordre. (*fig*) **what's biting you?**‡ qu'est-ce que tu as à râler?*

3 **vi** *[dog]* mordre; *[fish]* mordre (à l'hameçon); *[insect]* piquer; *[cold, frost, wind]* mordre, piquer, pincer; *[cogs]* s'engrener; *[anchor, screw]* mordre. **to ~ into sth** *[person]* mordre (dans) qch; *[acid]* mordre sur qch.

▸**bite back** **vt sep** *words* ravaler.

▸**bite off** **vt sep** arracher d'un coup de dent(s). **she bit off a piece of apple** elle a mordu dans la pomme; (*fig*) **he has bitten off more than he can chew** il a eu les yeux plus grands que le ventre, il a visé trop haut; (*fig*) **to bite sb's head off*** rembarrer qn (brutalement).

▸**bite on** **vt fus** mordre, trouver prise sur.

▸**bite through** **vt fus** *tongue, lip* mordre (de part en part); *string, thread* couper *or* casser avec les dents.

biter ['baɪtəʳ] **n** (*loc*) **the ~ bit** tel est pris qui croyait prendre (*Prov*).

biting ['baɪtɪŋ] **adj** *cold* âpre, perçant, mordant; *winter* dur, rude; *wind* piquant, cinglant; (*fig*) *style, wit, remarks* mordant, caustique, cinglant. **~ irony** ironie mordante *or* cinglante; **~ sarcasm** sarcasme acerbe *or* mordant; **~ insects** insectes piqueurs *or* voraces.

bitingly ['baɪtɪŋlɪ] **adv** *speak* d'un ton mordant *or* caustique.

bitten ['bɪtn] **ptp of bite**.

bitter ['bɪtəʳ] 1 adj a *taste* amer, âpre. (*fig*) **it was a ~ pill to swallow** la pilule était amère.
b *cold, weather* glacial; *wind* glacial, cinglant; *winter* rude, rigoureux.
c *person* amer; *critic, criticism* acerbe; *disappointment, reproach, tears* amer; *fate, sorrow* pénible, cruel; *hatred* acharné, profond; *opposition, protest* violent; *remorse* cuisant; *sight, look* amer, plein d'amertume; *suffering* âpre, cruel; *tone* âpre, amer, dur. (*fig*) **to the ~ end** jusqu'au bout; **his ~ enemy** son ennemi acharné; **he was always a ~ enemy of corruption** il a toujours été un adversaire acharné de la corruption; **I feel (very) ~ about the whole business** toute cette histoire m'a rempli d'amertume.
2 n a (*Brit: beer*) bière anglaise (*pression*).
b (*Pharm*) amer *m*. (*drink*) **~s** bitter *m*, amer *m*; **gin and ~s** cocktail *m* au gin et au bitter.
3 comp ▸**bitter aloes** aloès *m* (médicinal) ▸**bitter lemon** Schweppes *m* ® au citron ▸**bitter orange** orange amère, bigarade *f* ▸**bittersweet** adj (*lit, fig*) aigre-doux (*f* -douce) ◊ n (*Bot*) douce-amère *f*; (*fig*) amère douceur.

bitterly ['bɪtəlɪ] adv a *speak, complain* amèrement, avec amertume; *criticize, reproach* âprement; *weep* amèrement; *oppose, resist* avec acharnement. b *disappointed* cruellement; *jealous* profondément, horriblement. (*Met*) **it was ~ cold** il faisait un froid sibérien *or* de loup.

bittern ['bɪtɜːn] n butor *m* (*oiseau*).

bitterness ['bɪtənɪs] n (*NonC*) (*gen*) amertume *f*; [*opposition etc*] violence *f*.

bitty* ['bɪtɪ] adj (*Brit*) décousu.

bitumen ['bɪtjʊmɪn] n bitume *m*.

bituminous [bɪ'tjuːmɪnəs] adj bitumineux.

bivalent ['baɪ'veɪlənt] adj (*Bio, Chem*) bivalent.

bivalve ['baɪvælv] adj, n bivalve (*m*).

bivouac ['bɪvʊæk] 1 n bivouac *m*. 2 vi bivouaquer.

bi-weekly ['baɪ'wiːklɪ] 1 adj (*twice in a week*) bihebdomadaire; (*fortnightly*) bimensuel. 2 adv (*twice a week*) deux fois par semaine; (*fortnightly*) tous les quinze jours.

biz‡ [bɪz] n (abbr of **business**) *see* **show 2**.

bizarre [bɪ'zɑːʳ] adj bizarre.

bk a abbr of **book**. b abbr of **bank**.

B.L. [biː'el] a (abbr of **Bachelor of Law**) *see* **bachelor**. b abbr of **British Leyland**.

blab [blæb] 1 vi a (*tell secret*) manger le morceau‡. b (*chatter*) jaser. 2 vt (*also* **~ out**) *secret* laisser échapper, aller raconter.

blabber* ['blæbəʳ] vi (*also* **~ on**) = **blab 1a**.

blabbermouth* ['blæbə,maʊθ] n (*pej*) grande bouche* *f*, grande gueule‡ *f*.

black [blæk] 1 adj a *hair, bread, clouds, coffee etc* noir. **eyes as ~ as sloes** des yeux noirs comme (du) jais, des yeux de jais; (*fig*) **~ and blue** couvert de bleus; **to beat sb ~ and blue** battre qn comme plâtre, rouer qn de coups; **~ bread** pain *m* de seigle; **~ gold** l'or noir; (*on invitation*) "**~ tie**" "smoking", "cravate noire"; *see also* **3** *and* **belt, coal, jet²**, **pot** *etc*.
b *race, skin* noir. **~ man** Noir *m*; **~ woman** Noire *f*; **the ~ Americans** les Américains noirs; **~ art** art *m* nègre; "**~ is beautiful**" ≃ nous sommes fiers d'être noirs; (*US Univ*) **~ college** université noire; **~ consciousness** conscience *f* de la négritude; **B~ English** anglais *m* des Noirs américains; (*US*) **B~ Nationalism** mouvement nationaliste noir; **B~ Studies** études afro-américaines; *see also* **3**.
c (*dark*) obscur, noir, sans lumière. **it is as ~ as pitch** il fait nuit noire, il fait noir comme dans un four.
d (*dirty*) noir, sale. **his hands were ~** il avait les mains noires; **he was as ~ as a sweep** il était noir de la tête aux pieds.
e (*fig*) (*wicked*) *crime, action* noir; *thought* mauvais; (*gloomy*) *thoughts, prospects* noir; *grief* intense, violent; *rage* noir; *despair* sombre; (*angry*) furieux, menaçant. **he looked as ~ as thunder** il avait l'air furibond; **to look ~** avoir l'air hors de soi; **to give sb a ~ look** jeter un regard noir à qn; **none of your ~ looks at me!** inutile de me lancer ces regards noirs! *or* meurtriers!; (*fig*) **~ in the face** noir de fureur; **you can scream till you're ~ in the face but ...** tu peux toujours t'égosiller *or* t'époumoner mais ...; **a ~ deed** un crime, un forfait (*liter*); **he painted their conduct in the ~est colours** il a présenté leur conduite sous les couleurs les plus noires; **he's not as ~ as he's painted** il n'est pas aussi mauvais qu'on le dit; **it's a ~ outlook, things are looking ~** les choses se présentent très mal; **it's a ~ outlook** *or* **things are looking ~ for him** ses affaires se présentent très mal; **a ~ day on the roads** une sombre journée sur les routes; **it's a ~ day for England** c'est un jour (bien) triste pour l'Angleterre, (*stronger*) c'est un jour de deuil pour l'Angleterre; (*Brit Ind: during strike*) **to declare a cargo** *etc* **~** boycotter une cargaison *etc*; (*Ind*) **~ goods** marchandises boycottées; **~ economy** économie parallèle *or* souterraine.
2 n a (*colour*) noir *m*, couleur noire; (*mourning*) noir, deuil *m*; (*Roulette etc*) noir. **dressed in ~** habillé de noir; **to wear ~ for sb** porter le deuil de qn; **there it is in ~ and white** c'est écrit noir sur blanc; (*Art*) **~ and white** dessin *m* en noir et blanc; **~ and white artist** artiste *m* qui travaille en noir et blanc; (*fig*) **two ~s don't make a white** la faute de l'un n'excuse pas (celle de) l'autre; **to swear that ~ is white** [*obstinate person*] se refuser à l'évidence, nier l'évidence; [*liar*] mentir effrontément; (*fig*) **to be in the ~*** être créditeur; *see* **lamp**.
b (*person*) Noir(e) *m(f)*.
c (*darkness*) ténèbres *fpl*, obscurité *f*; (*outdoors only*) nuit noire.
3 comp ▸**black art(s)** magie noire, sciences *fpl* occultes ▸**blackball** n vote *m* contraire ◊ vt blackbouler ▸**black bass** achigan *m* ▸**black beetle** cafard *m*, cancrelat *m* ▸**blackberry** mûre *f*; **blackberry bush** mûrier *m*, ronce *f* (des haies) ▸**blackberrying: to go blackberrying** aller cueillir les *or* des mûres ▸**blackbird** merle *m* ▸**blackboard** tableau *m* (noir); **blackboard duster** chiffon *m*; **the blackboard jungle** la loi de la jungle (dans les classes); **blackboard rubber** frottoir *m* ▸**black books: she was in his black books** elle n'était pas dans ses petits papiers*, elle était mal vue (de lui) ▸**black box** (*Aviat*) boîte noire *or* enregistreuse ▸**black cap** (*Orn*) fauvette *f* à tête noire; (*Brit Hist Jur*) bonnet noir (*que mettait un juge avant de prononcer la peine de mort*) ▸**black-coated worker** (*fig*) (*in office*) employé(e) *m(f)* de bureau; (*in shop*) commis *m*, employé de magasin ▸**blackcock** coq *m* de bruyère (*petit*), tétras-lyre *m* ▸**black comedy** comédie noire ▸**Black Country** Pays Noir (*de l'Angleterre*) ▸**blackcurrant** (*fruit, bush*) cassis *m* ▸**Black Death** (*Hist*) peste noire ▸**black eye** œil poché *or* au beurre noir*; **to give sb a black eye** pocher l'œil à qn ▸**blackface:** (*US Theat*) **in blackface** déguisé en nègre ▸**Black Forest** Forêt-Noire *f*; **Black Forest gateau** gâteau *m* Forêt-Noire ▸**Black Friar** frère *m* prêcheur ▸**black frost** gel *m* ▸**black grouse** = **blackcock** ▸**blackguard** *see* **blackguard** ▸**blackhead** point noir ▸**black-headed gull** mouette rieuse ▸**black-hearted** mauvais, malfaisant ▸**black hole** (*Astron*) trou noir; (*Brit Hist*) **the Black Hole of Calcutta** le cachot de Calcutta ▸**black humour** humour noir ▸**black ice** verglas *m* ▸**blackjack** n (*flag*) pavillon noir (*des pirates*); (*drinking vessel*) pichet *m*; (*Min*) blende *f*; (*US: weapon*) matraque *f*; (*Cards*) vingt-et-un *m* ◊ vt (*beat*) matraquer; (*coerce*) contraindre sous la menace (*sb into doing* qn à faire) ▸**black knight** (*Comm*) *personne ou société entreprenant une OPA hostile* ▸**blacklead** n mine *f* de plomb, graphite *m* ◊ vt *stove* frotter à la mine de plomb ▸**blackleg** *see* **blackleg** ▸**blacklist** n liste noire ◊ vt *person* mettre sur la liste noire; *book* mettre à l'index ▸**black magic** magie noire ▸**black mark:** (*fig*) **that gets a black mark** c'est zéro; **that's a black mark for** *or* **against him** c'est un mauvais point pour lui ▸**blackmail** *see* **blackmail** ▸**Black Maria*** (*Brit*) panier *m* à salade* ▸**black market** marché noir; **on the black market** au marché noir ▸**black marketeer** profiteur *m*, -euse *f* (*vendant au marché noir*) ▸**black mass** messe noire ▸**Black Muslim** Musulman(e) Noir(e) *m(f)*, Black Muslim *mf* ▸**blackout** *see* **blackout** ▸**Black Panthers** (*Pol*) Panthères Noires ▸**Black Papers** (*Brit Scol*) *livres blancs sur le système éducatif* ▸**black pepper** poivre noir ▸**Black Power (movement)** Black Power *m*, Pouvoir Noir ▸**the Black Prince** (*Brit Hist*) le Prince Noir ▸**black pudding** (*Brit*) boudin *m* ▸**Black Rod** (*Brit Parl*) Huissier *m* à verge noire (*de la chambre des Lords*) ▸**Black Sea** mer Noire ▸**Black September** (*Pol*) Septembre noir ▸**black sheep (of the family)** (*fig*) brebis galeuse (de la famille) ▸**blackshirt** (*Pol*) chemise noire (*fasciste*) ▸**blacksmith** (*shoes horses*) maréchal-ferrant *m*; (*forges iron*) forgeron *m* ▸**black spot** (*also* **accident black spot**) (*Brit*) point noir ▸**blackthorn** (*Bot*) épine noire, prunellier *m* ▸**black-tie** *dinner, function* habillé, en smoking (*see also* **1a**) ▸**black velvet** *cocktail de champagne et de stout* ▸**Black Watch** (*Brit Mil*) Black Watch *mpl* (*régiment écossais*) ▸**blackwater fever** fièvre bilieuse hémoglobinurique.
4 vt a noircir; *shoes* cirer. **to ~ one's face** se noircir le visage; **to ~ sb's eye (for him)** pocher l'œil à qn.
b (*Brit Ind*) *cargo, firm, goods* boycotter.

▸**black out** 1 vi (*faint*) s'évanouir, tomber dans les pommes*, tourner de l'œil*. 2 vt sep (*in wartime*) *town, building* faire le black-out dans. (*in peacetime*) **a power cut blacked out the building** une panne d'électricité a plongé l'immeuble dans l'obscurité (totale); (*Theat*) **to black out the stage** faire l'obscurité sur scène. 3 **blackout** n *see* **blackout**.

blackamoor†† ['blækəmʊəʳ] n nègre *m*.

blacken ['blækən] 1 vt a (*with dirt, soot, dust*) noircir, salir. **hands ~ed with filth** des mains noires de crasse. b (*with paint, cosmetics etc*) noircir, barbouiller de noir. c (*with smoke, by fire*) noircir. **~ed remains** restes calcinés; **there were ~ed pots on the open fire** il y avait dans la cheminée des marmites noircies. d (*fig: discredit*) salir, noircir, ternir. 2 vi [*sky*] noircir, s'assombrir; [*furniture*] noircir, devenir noir.

blackguard† ['blægɑːd] n canaille *f*, fripouille *f*.

blackguardly ['blægɑːdlɪ] adj *deed, person* infâme, ignoble.

blacking ['blækɪŋ] n [*shoes*] cirage *m* (noir); [*stoves*] pâte *f* à noircir; [*goods, cargo*] boycottage *m*.

blackish ['blækɪʃ] adj tirant sur le noir, noirâtre (*pej*).

blackleg ['blækleg] (*Brit Ind*) 1 n jaune *m*, briseur *m* de grève. 2 vi briser la grève.

blackmail ['blækmeɪl] 1 n chantage *m*. **emotional ~** chantage *m* émotionnel. 2 vt faire chanter, faire du chantage auprès de. **to ~ sb into doing** forcer qn par le chantage à faire.

blackmailer ['blækmeɪləʳ] n maître-chanteur *m*.

blackness ['blæknɪs] n *[colour, substance]* couleur *or* teinte noire, noir *m*; *[night]* obscurité *f*, ténèbres *fpl*; *[hands, face]* saleté *f*, crasse *f*; *[crime etc]* atrocité *f*, noirceur *f* (*liter*).

blackout ['blækaʊt] n a (*amnesia*) trou *m* de mémoire; (*fainting*) étourdissement *m*, évanouissement *m*. **to have a ~** avoir un étourdissement, s'évanouir. b *[lights]* panne *f* d'électricité; (*during war*) black-out *m*; (*Theat*) obscurcissement *m* de la scène; *see* **news 2**.

bladder ['blædəʳ] 1 n (*Anat*) vessie *f*; (*Bot*) vésicule *f*; (*Ftbl etc*) vessie (*de ballon*); *see* **gall¹**. 2 comp ▸**bladder kelp** fucus vésiculeux ▸**bladderwort** utriculaire *f* ▸**bladderwrack** = **bladder kelp**.

blade [bleɪd] n a *[knife, tool, weapon, razor]* lame *f*; *[chopper, guillotine]* couperet *m*; *[tongue]* dos *m*; *[oar]* plat *m*, pale *f*; *[spade]* fer *m*; *[turbine motor]* aube *f*; *[propeller]* pale, aile *f*; *[windscreen wiper]* caoutchouc *m*, balai *m*; *[grass, mace]* brin *m*; *[cereal]* pousse *f*; *[leaf]* limbe *m*. **wheat in the ~** blé *m* en herbe; *see* **shoulder**. b (*liter: sword*) lame *f*. c (†: *gallant*) gaillard *m*.

-bladed ['bleɪdɪd] adj ending in comps: **two-bladed knife** canif *m* à deux lames.

blaeberry ['bleɪbərɪ] n myrtille *f*, airelle *f*.

blah* [blɑː] 1 n boniment *m*, blablabla* *m*. **~, ~, ~** bla, bla, bla*; (*US*) **the ~s** le cafard‡. 2 adj (*US*) barbant‡, peu attrayant.

blamable ['bleɪməbl] adj blâmable.

blame [bleɪm] 1 vt a (*fix responsibility on*) **to ~ sb for sth, to ~ sth on sb*** rejeter la responsabilité de qch sur qn, mettre qch sur le dos de qn*; **I'm not to ~** ce n'est pas ma faute; **you have only yourself to ~** tu ne peux t'en prendre qu'à toi-même, tu l'as bien cherché!; **whom/what are we to ~ for this accident?** à qui/à quoi attribuer cet accident?; *see* **workman**.

b (*censure*) condamner, blâmer. **to ~ sb for doing** reprocher à qn de faire; **to ~ sb for sth** reprocher qch à qn; **to ~ o.s. for sth/for having done** se reprocher qch/d'avoir fait; **he was greatly to ~ for doing that** il a eu grand tort de faire cela; **you can't ~ him for wanting to leave** vous ne pouvez lui reprocher de vouloir s'en aller; **he's leaving — you can't ~ him!** il part — tu ne peux pas lui en vouloir!

2 n a (*responsibility*) faute *f*, responsabilité *f*. **to put** *or* **lay** *or* **place** *or* **throw the ~ for sth on sb** rejeter la responsabilité de qch sur qn; **to bear the ~** supporter la responsabilité.

b (*censure*) blâme *m*, reproches *mpl*. **without ~** exempt de blâme, irréprochable.

blameless ['bleɪmlɪs] adj irréprochable, sans reproche, exempt de blâme.

blamelessly ['bleɪmlɪslɪ] adv d'une manière irréprochable, irréprochablement.

blameworthy ['bleɪmwɜːðɪ] adj *action* répréhensible; *person* blâmable.

blanch [blɑːntʃ] 1 vt (*gen, Agr, Culin*) blanchir. **~ed almonds** amandes (é)mondées *or* épluchées. 2 vi *[person]* blêmir.

blancmange [blə'mɒnʒ] n blanc-manger *m*.

bland [blænd] adj *taste, food* fade; *book, film* fade, terne; *person, character* terne, falot; *smile, expression* terne.

blandish ['blændɪʃ] vt flatter, cajoler.

blandishment ['blændɪʃmənt] n (*gen pl*) flatterie(s) *f(pl)*.

blandly ['blændlɪ] adv (*see* **bland**) avec affabilité, affablement; aimablement; d'un air mielleux; d'un air un peu narquois, d'un ton légèrement moqueur *or* narquois.

blank [blæŋk] 1 adj a *paper* blanc (*f* blanche); *page* blanc, vierge; *map* muet; *cheque* en blanc. (*fig*) **to give sb a ~ cheque (to do)** donner à qn carte blanche (pour faire); **~ cartridge** cartouche *f* à blanc; **~ space** blanc *m*, (espace *m*) vide *m*; **~ form** formulaire *m*, imprimé *m* (à remplir); (*on form*) **please leave ~** laisser en blanc s.v.p.

b (*unrelieved*) *wall* aveugle; *silence, darkness* profond; *refusal, denial* absolu, net; (*empty*) *life etc* dépourvu d'intérêt, vide; (*expressionless*) *face* sans expression; *look* sans expression, vide; (*puzzled*) déconcerté, dérouté. **to look ~** (*expressionless*) être sans expression; (*puzzled*) avoir l'air interdit; **a look of ~ astonishment** un regard ébahi; **his mind went ~** il a eu un passage à vide *or* un trou.

c (*Poetry*) **~ verse** vers blancs *or* non rimés.

2 n a (*void*) blanc *m*, (espace *m*) vide *m*; (*fig: gap*) lacune *f*, trou *m*. **she left several ~s in her answers** elle a laissé plusieurs de ses réponses en blanc; **your departure has left a ~** votre départ a laissé un vide; **my mind was a ~** j'avais la tête vide, j'ai eu un passage à vide.

b (*form*) formulaire *m*, imprimé *m*, fiche *f*. **telegraph ~** formule *f* de télégramme.

c *[target]* but *m*; (*Dominoes*) blanc *m*; *[coin, medal, record]* flan *m*; *[key]* ébauche *f*; (*cartridge*) cartouche *f* à blanc. (*fig*) **to draw a ~** (*fail in search etc*) échouer, faire chou blanc; (*mentally*) avoir un trou; (*Dominoes*) **double ~** double blanc.

blanket ['blæŋkɪt] 1 n couverture *f*; *[snow etc]* couche *f*; *[fog]* manteau *m*, nappe *f*; *[smoke]* nuage *m*. **born on the wrong side of the ~** (de naissance) illégitime, adultérin; *see* **electric, wet**.

2 comp *alteration, condemnation etc* général, global ▸**blanket bath** toilette *f* (*de malade alité*); **to give sb a blanket bath** faire la toilette de qn dans son lit ▸**blanket cover: this insurance policy gives blanket cover** cette police d'assurances couvre tous les risques *or* est tous risques ▸**blanket finish** arrivée très serrée *or* dans un mouchoir ▸**blanket stitch** point *m* de feston ▸**blanket-stitch** border au point de feston.

3 vt a *[snow]* recouvrir; *[smoke]* recouvrir, envelopper.

b *sounds* étouffer, assourdir.

c (*Naut*) déventer.

▸**blanket out** vt noyer.

blankety-blank* ['blæŋkɪtɪ'blæŋk] adj (*euph*) = **blinking 1**.

blankly ['blæŋklɪ] adv *look* (*expressionlessly*) avec des yeux vides; (*puzzledly*) d'un air interdit *or* ébahi; *say, announce* positivement, carrément. **to look ~ at sb/sth** (*expressionlessly*) jeter sur qn/qch un regard dénué de toute expression; (*without understanding*) regarder qn/qch sans comprendre.

blankness ['blæŋknɪs] n (*NonC*) (*in eyes, face*) air mort, absence *f* d'expression; *[life]* vide *m*.

blare [blɛəʳ] 1 n (*gen*) vacarme *m*; *[hooter, car horn]* bruit *m* strident; *[radio, music]* beuglement *m*; *[trumpet]* sonnerie *f*. 2 vi (*also* **~ out**) *[music, horn etc]* retentir; *[loud voice]* trompeter, claironner; *[radio]* beugler. 3 vt (*also* **~ out**) *music* faire retentir.

blarney* ['blɑːnɪ] 1 n boniment* *m*, bobards* *mpl*. (*loc*) **he's kissed the B~ stone** il sait faire du boniment*. 2 vt *person* enjôler, embobeliner*. 3 vi manier la flatterie.

blasé ['blɑːzeɪ] adj blasé.

blaspheme [blæs'fiːm] vti blasphémer (*against* contre).

blasphemer [blæs'fiːməʳ] n blasphémateur *m*, -trice *f*.

blasphemous ['blæsfɪməs] adj *person* blasphémateur (*f* -trice); *words* blasphématoire.

blasphemously ['blæsfɪməslɪ] adv d'une façon impie, avec impiété. **to speak ~** blasphémer.

blasphemy ['blæsfɪmɪ] n blasphème *m*. **to utter ~** blasphémer, dire des blasphèmes; **it is ~ to say that** c'est blasphémer que de dire cela.

blast [blɑːst] 1 n a (*sound*) *[bomb]* explosion *f*; *[space rocket]* grondement *m*, rugissement *m*; *[trumpets etc]* fanfare *f*, sonnerie *f*; *[whistle, car horn]* coup *m* strident. **~ on the siren** coup de sirène; **to blow a ~ on the bugle** donner un coup de clairon; **the radio was going (at) full ~** la radio marchait à plein.

b (*explosion*) explosion *f*; (*shock wave*) *[bomb etc]* souffle *m*; (*gust*) *[furnace]* souffle (d'air chaud). **~ victims** victimes *fpl* de l'explosion; (*lit, fig*) **at full ~** à plein; **~ of air/steam** jet *m* d'air/de vapeur; **~ of wind** coup *m* de vent, rafale *f*.

c (*liter: wind*) **the icy ~** le souffle glacé (du vent).

d (*US *: party etc*) fête *f*, foire *f*. **to have a ~** faire la foire; **to get a ~ out of sth** trouver qch marrant*.

2 comp ▸**blast effect** effet *m* de souffle ▸**blast furnace** haut fourneau ▸**blast-off** (*Space*) lancement *m*, mise *f* à feu (*d'une fusée spatiale*).

3 vt *[lightning] tree* foudroyer; (*with powder*) *rocks* faire sauter; (*blight*) *plant* détruire; (*fig*) *reputation, hopes, future* anéantir, détruire, briser; (*verbally*) attaquer à boulets rouges *or* violemment.

4 excl (*Brit* *) la barbe!* **~ him!** il est embêtant!* *or* empoisonnant!*

▸**blast away** vi *[music, band]* brailler; *[gun]* retentir. **to blast away with a rifle/shotgun** *etc* tirer continuellement avec un fusil/fusil de chasse *etc*.

▸**blast off** 1 vi *[rocket etc]* être mis à feu; (*US fig* ‡) partir. 2 **blast-off** n *see* **blast 2**.

▸**blast out** 1 vi *[music, radio]* brailler. 2 vt sep *song, tune* brailler.

blasted ['blɑːstɪd] adj a *heath* désolé, desséché; *tree* foudroyé, frappé par la foudre; (*fig*) *hopes* anéanti. b (*: *annoying*) fichu* (*before noun*). **he's a ~ nuisance** c'est un enquiquineur*, il nous enquiquine*.

blasting ['blɑːstɪŋ] n (*Tech*) minage *m*. **"~ in progress"** "attention, tir de mines"; **to give sb a ~ for sth/for having done** attaquer violemment qn pour qch/pour avoir fait.

blastoderm ['blæstəʊdɜːm] n blastoderme *m*.

blatancy ['bleɪtənsɪ] n (*flagrance*) caractère flagrant, évidence *f*; (*showiness*) aspect criard *or* voyant.

blatant ['bleɪtənt] adj *injustice, lie etc* criant, flagrant; *bully, social climber* éhonté; *coward, thief* fieffé. **a ~ liar** un menteur éhonté, un fieffé menteur.

blatantly ['bleɪtəntlɪ] adv d'une manière flagrante.

blather ['blæðəʳ] 1 vi raconter *or* débiter des bêtises, parler à tort et à travers; (*Scot *: chat*) bavarder. 2 n a bêtises *fpl*, fadaises *fpl*, blablabla* *m*; (*Scot *: chat*) causette *f*. (*Scot* *) **to have a ~** bavarder, causer. b (*: *person*) **she's a ~** elle dit n'importe quoi, elle dit tout ce qui lui passe par la tête. 3 comp ▸**blatherskite**‡ (*Scot: chatterbox*) moulin *m* à paroles; (*NonC: US: nonsense*) fadaises *fpl*.

blaze¹ [bleɪz] 1 n a (*fire*) feu *m*, flamme *f*, flambée *f*; (*conflagration*) incendie *m*, brasier *m*; (*light from fire*) lueur *f* des flammes *or* du brasier. **forest ~** incendie de forêt; **all in a ~** en flammes.

b *[gems, beauty etc]* éclat *m*, splendeur *f*. **~ of day** éclat du jour; **~ of light** torrent *m* de lumière; **~ of colour** flamboiement *m* de couleur(s).

c *[rage]* explosion *f*. **in a ~ of anger he killed her** dans le feu de la colère *or* dans une explosion de colère il l'a tuée.

d (*) **go to ~s!** va te faire voir!*; **what the ~s!** qu'est-ce que ça peut bien fiche!*; **how the ~s!** comment diable!; **what the ~s have you done now?** qu'est-ce que tu as encore fichu?*; **like ~s** comme un fou *or* dingue*, furieusement; **he ran like ~s** il a filé comme un zèbre; **he worked like ~s** il a travaillé comme une brute *or* un dingue*.

2 **vi** a *[fire]* flamber; *[sun]* flamboyer, darder ses rayons.

b *[colour]* flamboyer; *[jewel, light]* resplendir, jeter un vif éclat; *[anger]* éclater; (*fig*) resplendir (*with* de). **garden blazing with colour** jardin resplendissant de couleur.

▶**blaze abroad** **vt sep** (*liter*) *news etc* crier sur tous les toits.

▶**blaze away** **vi** *[fire etc]* flamber (toujours); *[soldiers, guns]* maintenir un feu nourri (*at* contre).

▶**blaze down** **vi** *[sun]* flamboyer, darder ses rayons.

▶**blaze forth** **vi** (*liter*) *[sun]* apparaître soudain (dans tout son éclat); *[anger]* éclater.

▶**blaze out** **vi** *[fire]* se déclencher, s'embraser, éclater; *[sun]* apparaître soudain; *[light]* ruisseler; *[anger, hatred]* éclater.

▶**blaze up** **vi** *[fire]* s'enflammer, s'embraser (*liter*); (*fig*) *[person]* éclater, s'emporter; *[anger]* éclater.

blaze[2] [bleɪz] 1 **n** (*mark*) *[horse etc]* étoile *f*; *[tree]* marque *f*, encoche *f*. 2 **vt** *tree* marquer. **to ~ a trail** (*lit*) frayer un *or* le chemin; (*fig*) montrer la voie, faire un travail de pionnier(s).

blazer ['bleɪzəʳ] **n** blazer *m*.

blazing ['bleɪzɪŋ] **adj** a *building etc* en feu, en flammes, embrasé; *torch* enflammé; *sun* éclatant, ardent; (*fig*) *eyes* flamboyant, qui jette des éclairs; *jewel* étincelant; *colour* très vif. b (*: *also* **~ angry**) furibond, furibard*.

blazon ['bleɪzn] 1 **n** (*Her*) blason *m*. 2 **vt** (*Her*) blasonner; (*fig: also* **~ abroad, ~ forth**) *virtues, story* proclamer, claironner.

bleach [bliːtʃ] 1 **n** décolorant *m*; (*liquid*) eau oxygénée. **(household) ~** eau de Javel. 2 **vt** a *linen, bones etc* blanchir. **~ing agent** produit *m* à blanchir, décolorant *m*; **~ing powder** (chlorure *m*) décolorant. b *hair* décolorer, oxygéner. **to ~ one's hair** se décolorer (les cheveux); **~ed hair** cheveux décolorés *or* oxygénés. c (*Phot*) *image* blanchir. 3 **vi** blanchir.

▶**bleach out** **vt sep** *colour* enlever.

bleachers ['bliːtʃəz] **n** (*US*) gradins *mpl* (*de stade en plein soleil*).

bleak[1] [bliːk] **n** (*fish*) ablette *f*.

bleak[2] [bliːk] **adj** *country, landscape* exposé au vent, morne, désolé; *room* nu, austère; *weather, wind* froid, glacial; (*fig*) *existence* sombre, désolé; *prospect* triste, morne, lugubre; *smile* pâle; *voice, tone* monocorde, morne. **it looks** *or* **things look rather ~ for him** les choses se présentent plutôt mal pour lui.

bleakly ['bliːklɪ] **adv** *look* d'un air désolé, sombrement; *speak* d'un ton morne, sombrement.

bleakness ['bliːknɪs] **n** *[landscape]* aspect morne *or* désolé; *[room, furnishings]* austérité *f*; *[weather]* froid *m*, rigueurs *fpl*; *[prospects, future]* aspect sombre *or* décourageant.

blearily ['blɪərɪlɪ] **adv** *look* avec un regard trouble.

bleary ['blɪərɪ] **adj** a *eyes* (*from sleep, fatigue*) trouble, voilé; (*from illness*) chassieux; (*from tears, wind etc*) larmoyant. **~-eyed** aux yeux troubles (*or* chassieux *or* larmoyants). b *outline* indécis, vague.

bleat [bliːt] 1 **vi** a *[sheep]* bêler; *[goat]* bêler, chevroter. b *[person, voice]* bêler, chevroter; (*: *talk nonsense*) débiter des idioties, débloquer‡; (‡: *complain*) se plaindre (*about* de), bêler*. **what are you ~ing about?‡** qu'est-ce que tu as à te lamenter? 2 **vt** (*also* **~ out**) dire d'une voix bêlante, chevroter. 3 **n** a *[sheep]* bêlement *m*; *[voice, goat]* bêlement, chevrotement *m*. b (‡: *complaint*) lamentation *f*, jérémiade* *f*.

bleb [bleb] **n** *[skin]* cloque *f*, ampoule *f*; *[glass, water]* bulle *f*.

bled [bled] **pret, ptp of bleed.**

bleed [bliːd] **pret, ptp bled** 1 **vi** a saigner, perdre du sang. **his nose is ~ing** il saigne du nez; **he is ~ing to death** il perd tout son sang; **the wound bled profusely** la plaie saignait copieusement; (*liter*) **his heart is ~ing** son cœur saigne; (*gen iro*) **my heart ~s for you** tu me fends le cœur (*iro*), tu vas me faire pleurer (*iro*). b *[plant]* pleurer, perdre sa sève. 2 **vt** a (*Med*) *person* saigner, faire une saignée à; *brakes, radiator* purger. b (*fig *: get money from*) tirer de l'argent à, faire casquer‡. **to ~ sb dry** *or* **white** saigner qn à blanc. 3 **n** saignement *m*; *see* **nose.**

bleeder ['bliːdəʳ] **n** a (*Med **) hémophile *mf*. b (*Brit* **‡*) salaud‡ *m*, saligaud‡ *m*.

bleeding ['bliːdɪŋ] 1 **n** a (*taking blood from*) saignée *f*; (*losing blood*) saignement *m*; (*more serious*) hémorragie *f*. **~ from the nose** saignement de nez; **to stop the ~** arrêter l'hémorragie. b *[plant]* écoulement *m* de sève. 2 **adj** a *wound* saignant; *person* qui saigne, ensanglanté; (*fig*) *heart* blessé, brisé. (*US: fig, pej*) **~-heart Liberal** libéral(e) *m(f)* au grand cœur. b (**‡*: *bloody*) foutu‡ (*before noun*), maudit (*before noun*). 3 **adv** (**‡*: *bloody*) vachement‡, foutrement**‡*.

bleep [bliːp] 1 **n** (*Rad, TV*) top *m*; (*pocket device*) bip *m*. 2 **vi** *[transmitter]* émettre des signaux. 3 **vt** (*in hospital etc*) biper.

bleeper ['bliːpəʳ] **n** (*pocket device*) bip *m*.

blemish ['blemɪʃ] 1 **n** (*defect*) défaut *m*, imperfection *f*; (*on fruit*) tache *f*; (*fig*) (*moral*) souillure *f* (*liter*), tare *f*; (*inborn*) défaut. **there's a ~ in this cup** cette tasse a un défaut; **to find a ~ in sth** trouver à redire à qch; **a ~ on his reputation** une tache *or* une souillure (*liter*) à sa réputation; **without (a) ~** (*lit*) sans imperfection; (*fig*) sans tache, sans souillure (*liter*). 2 **vt** *beauty etc* gâter; *reputation, honour* ternir, flétrir. **~ed** *fruit* talé, meurtri, abîmé; *skin* abîmé.

blench [blentʃ] **vi** a (*flinch*) sursauter. **without ~ing** sans sourciller, sans broncher. b (*turn pale*) pâlir *or* blêmir (de peur).

blend [blend] 1 **n** (*mixture*) *[tea, paint, whisky etc]* mélange *m*; *[qualities]* alliance *f*, mélange, fusion *f*. **excellent ~ of tea** thé *m* d'excellente qualité; *[coffee]* **Brazilian ~** café *m* du Brésil; **"our own ~"** "mélange (spécial de la) maison".

2 **vt** (*also* **~ in**) mélanger, mêler (*with* à, avec), faire un mélange (*sth with sth* de qch avec qch); *teas, coffees etc* mélanger, faire un mélange de; *wines* couper, mélanger; *qualities* joindre, unir (*with* à); *ideas, people* fusionner; *colours, styles* fondre, mêler. **~ed** *whisky* mélangé; *wine* de coupage; *tea* mélangé.

3 **vi** (*also* **~ in**) se mêler, se mélanger (*with* à, avec), former un mélange (*with* avec), se confondre (*into* en); *[voices, perfumes]* se confondre, se mêler, se mélanger; *[styles]* se marier, s'allier; *[ideas, political parties, races]* fusionner; *[colours]* (*shade into one another*) se fondre; (*go well together*) aller bien ensemble. **the colours ~ (in) well** les couleurs vont bien ensemble.

blender ['blendəʳ] **n** (*machine*) (*Tech*) malaxeur *m*; (*Culin*) mixer *m*.

blenny ['blenɪ] **n** (*fish*) blennie *f*.

bless [bles] **pret, ptp blest** *or* **blessed** [blest] **vt** *[God, priest, person, fate]* bénir. **God ~ the king!** Dieu bénisse le roi!; **to be ~ed with** avoir le bonheur de posséder; **God did not ~ them with ...** Dieu ne leur accorda pas le bonheur d'avoir ...; **Nature ~ed him with ...** la Nature l'a doué de ...; **I was never ~ed with children** je n'ai jamais connu le bonheur d'avoir des enfants; (*iro*) **she'll ~ you for this!** elle va te bénir!*; **~ you!** mille fois merci!, vous êtes un ange!; (*sneezing*) à vos souhaits!; **and Paul, ~ his heart, had no idea that ...** et ce brave Paul (dans son innocence) ne savait pas que ...; **~ his little heart!** qu'il est mignon!; **~ my soul!*†** Mon Dieu!, Seigneur!†; **well, I'm blest!*** par exemple!, ça alors!*; **I'm** *or* **I'll be blest if I remember!*** c'est bien le diable* si je m'en souviens.

blessed ['blesɪd] 1 **adj** a (*Rel*) (*holy*) béni, saint, sanctifié; (*beatified*) bienheureux. **B~ Virgin** Sainte Vierge; **B~ Sacrament** Saint Sacrement; **~ be God!** (que) Dieu soit béni!; **the B~ John X** le bienheureux Jean X.

b (*Rel, liter: happy*) bienheureux, heureux. **~ are the pure in heart** bienheureux *or* heureux ceux qui ont le cœur pur; **of ~ memory** d'heureuse mémoire.

c (*liter: giving joy*) *thing* béni; *person* cher.

d (* *euph: cursed*) sacré* (*before noun*), fichu* (*before noun*), satané (*before noun*). **that child is a ~ nuisance!** cet enfant, quelle peste! *or* quel poison!*; **the whole ~ day** toute la sainte journée; **every ~ evening** tous les soirs que le bon Dieu fait*.

2 **npl: the B~** les bienheureux *mpl*.

blessedly ['blesɪdlɪ] **adv** merveilleusement.

blessedness ['blesɪdnɪs] **n** (*Rel*) béatitude *f*; (*happiness*) bonheur *m*, félicité *f*.

blessing ['blesɪŋ] **n** a (*divine favour*) grâce *f*, faveur *f*; (*prayer*) bénédiction *f*; (*at meal*) bénédicité *m*. **with God's ~ we shall succeed** nous réussirons par la grâce de Dieu; **the priest pronounced the ~** le prêtre a donné la bénédiction; (*at meal*) **to ask a** *or* **the ~** dire le bénédicité; (*fig*) **the plan had his ~*** il avait donné sa bénédiction à ce projet*.

b (*benefit*) bien *m*, bienfait *m*. **the ~s of civilization** les bienfaits *or* les avantages *mpl* de la civilisation; **what a ~ that ...!** quelle chance que ...! + *subj*, heureusement que ...; **this rain has been a real ~*** cette pluie a été une vraie bénédiction*; **it was a ~ in disguise** c'était malgré les apparences un bien, à quelque chose malheur est bon (*Prov*); *see* **count[1]**.

blest [blest] (*liter*) 1 **pret, ptp of bless.** 2 **adj** heureux.

blether ['bleðəʳ] = **blather.**

blew [bluː] **pret of blow[1].**

blight [blaɪt] 1 **n** *[cereals]* rouille *f*, nielle *f*, charbon *m*; *[potato]* mildiou *m*; *[rose]* rouille; *[fruit trees]* cloque *f*. **this marriage was a ~ on his happiness** ce mariage a terni son bonheur; **she's been a ~ on his life** elle a gâché son existence; **what a ~ that woman is!‡** cette femme est un vrai fléau! *or* une véritable plaie!*; **urban ~** dégradation urbaine. 2 **vt** *[disease] plants* rouiller; *wheat etc* nieller; *[wind]* saccager; (*fig*) *hopes* anéantir, ruiner, détruire; *career, life* gâcher, briser; *future* gâcher.

blighter* ['blaɪtəʳ] **n** (*Brit*) type* *m*, bonne femme. **a funny ~** un drôle de numéro*; **silly ~** crétin(e)* *m(f)*, imbécile *mf*; **lucky ~!** quel(le) veinard(e)*!; **you ~!** espèce de chameau!*

Blighty ['blaɪtɪ] **n** (*Brit Mil sl:†*) l'Angleterre *f*, "le pays".

blimey‡ ['blaɪmɪ] **excl** (*Brit*) mince alors!*, merde alors!‡

blimp [blɪmp] **n** a (*Brit*) **a (Colonel) B~*** une (vieille) culotte de peau (*pej*). b (*Aviat*) petit dirigeable *m* de reconnaissance.

blind [blaɪnd] 1 **adj** a *person, passion, obedience* aveugle. **a ~ man/woman** un/une aveugle; **a ~ boy** un jeune aveugle; **~ from birth** aveugle de naissance; **~ in one eye** borgne; **she is as ~ as a bat** elle est myope comme une taupe; ~ **spot** (*Med*) point *m* aveugle; (*Aut, Aviat*) angle *m* mort; (*fig*) **that was his ~ spot** sur ce point il avait un bandeau sur les yeux *or* il refusait d'y voir clair; (*Aut, Aviat*) **it was approaching on his ~ side** cela approchait dans son angle mort; **she was ~ to his faults** elle ne voyait pas ses défauts; **I am not ~ to that consideration** cette considération ne m'échappe pas; (*fig*) **to turn a ~ eye to** fermer les yeux sur; ~ **with passion** aveuglé par la passion; *see* **colour, love 1a**.

b (*fig*) *corner, flying, landing* sans visibilité; *passage* sans issue; *door, window* aveugle, faux (*f* fausse). (*lit, fig*) ~ **alley** impasse *f*, cul-de-sac *m*; (*fig*) **a ~-alley job** une situation sans avenir; ~ **date** (*meeting*) rendez-vous *m* (avec quelqu'un qu'on ne connaît pas), rencontre arrangée; (*person*) inconnu(e) *m(f)* (avec qui on a rendez-vous); **not a ~ bit of use**‡ qui ne sert strictement à rien; **she didn't take a ~ bit of notice of it** elle n'y a prêté strictement aucune attention.

2 **vt** aveugler, rendre aveugle; *[sun, light]* aveugler, éblouir; (*fig*) aveugler, empêcher de voir. **the war ~ed** les aveugles *mpl* de guerre; **her love ~ed her to his faults** son amour l'aveuglait sur ses défauts; *see* **science**.

3 **n** a *[window]* store *m*, jalousie† *f*; *see* **Venetian**.

b (*pretence*) feinte *f*, faux prétexte, masque *m*. **this action is only a ~** cette action n'est qu'une feinte *or* qu'un masque.

c **to go on a ~**‡ (aller) se soûler la gueule‡.

d (*Hunting*) affût *m*.

4 **npl**: **the ~** les aveugles *mpl*; (*fig*) **it's the ~ leading the ~** c'est comme l'aveugle qui conduit l'aveugle.

5 **adv** (*Aviat*) **to fly ~** voler sans visibilité; **to swear ~ that** jurer ses grands dieux que; ~ **drunk**‡ bourré‡, bituré‡, (complètement) rond‡.

6 **comp** ▸**blind man's buff** colin-maillard *m* ▸**blind-stitch n** point perdu ◊ **vi** coudre à points perdus ▸**blind test** (*Marketing*) test *m* (en) aveugle, blind-test *m* ▸**blindworm** orvet *m*.

blinder ['blaɪndəʳ] **n** (*US*) œillère *f*.

blindfold ['blaɪndfəʊld] 1 **vt** bander les yeux à *or* de. 2 **n** bandeau *m*. 3 **adj** (*also* **~ed**) aux yeux bandés. 4 **adv** (*also* **~ed**) les yeux bandés. **it's so easy I could do it ~** (c'est si facile que) je le ferais les yeux bandés.

blinding ['blaɪndɪŋ] **adj** aveuglant.

blindingly ['blaɪndɪŋlɪ] **adv**: **it is ~ obvious** c'est d'une évidence flagrante, ça saute aux yeux.

blindly ['blaɪndlɪ] **adv** (*lit*) en aveugle, comme un aveugle; (*fig*) *obey, follow* aveuglément, à l'aveuglette.

blindness ['blaɪndnɪs] **n** cécité *f*; (*fig*) aveuglement *m* (*to* devant, à l'égard de). ~ **to the truth** refus *m* de voir la vérité; *see* **colour**.

blini(s) ['blɪnɪ(z)] **n** blinis *m*.

blink [blɪŋk] 1 **n** *[eyes]* clignotement *m* (des yeux), battement *m* des paupières; *[sun]* (petit) rayon *m*; *[hope]* lueur *f*; (*glimpse*) coup *m* d'œil. (*fig*) **in the ~ of an eye** en un clin d'œil; **my telly's on the ~*** ma télé est détraquée. 2 **vi** a cligner des yeux; (*half-close eyes*) plisser les yeux. b *[light]* vaciller. 3 **vt**: **to ~ one's eyes** cligner des yeux; **to ~ back the tears** refouler les larmes (d'un battement de paupières).

blinker ['blɪŋkəʳ] **n** a (*Brit*) **~s** œillères *fpl*; (*Aut*) feux *mpl* de détresse, clignotants *mpl*; (*fig*) **to wear ~s** avoir des œillères. b (*also* **~ light**) (feu *m*) clignotant *m*.

blinkered ['blɪŋkəd] **adj** (*lit, fig*) **to be ~** avoir des œillères; (*fig*) **to have a ~ view of sth** *or* **approach to sth** voir qch avec des œillères; ~ **self-interest** intérêt personnel aveugle.

blinking ['blɪŋkɪŋ] 1 **adj** (*) sacré* (*before noun*), fichu* (*before noun*), satané (*before noun*). ~ **idiot** espèce *f* d'idiot. 2 **n** *[eyes]* clignement *m* (d'yeux); *[light]* vacillement *m*.

blip [blɪp] **n** a (*Radar etc*) spot *m*; (*beep*) bip *m*. b (*on graph*) petite déviation *f*; (*fig: aberration*) petite anomalie *f* (passagère).

bliss [blɪs] **n** a (*Rel*) béatitude *f*; (*gen*) félicité *f*, bonheur suprême *or* absolu. b (*fig* *) **what ~ to collapse into a chair!** quelle volupté de se laisser tomber dans un fauteuil!; **the concert was ~** le concert était divin; **isn't he ~!** c'est un ange!; **it's ~!** c'est merveilleux!, c'est divin!

▸**bliss out**‡ **vi** (*US*) être au septième ciel*.

blissful ['blɪsfʊl] **adj** (*Rel, gen*) bienheureux; (*: *wonderful*) divin, merveilleux.

blissfully ['blɪsfəlɪ] **adv** *smile* d'un air heureux *or* béat. ~ **happy** merveilleusement heureux; (*iro*) ~ **unaware that ...** parfaitement inconscient du *or* dans l'ignorance béate du fait que ... .

blister ['blɪstəʳ] 1 **n** *[skin]* ampoule *f*, cloque *f*; *[paintwork]* cloque; *[metal, glass]* soufflure *f*; *[glass]* bulle *f*; (‡ *pej: person*) fléau *m*, poison* *m*, plaie* *f*. 2 **comp** ▸**blister-pack** (*for pills etc*) plaquette *f*; (*for pens, plugs etc*) emballage *m* pellicule ▸**blister-packed** *pills etc* en plaquette; *pens, plugs etc* sous emballage pelliculé. 3 **vi** *[skin]* cloquer; (*more widespread*) se couvrir d'ampoules; *[paintwork]* cloquer; *[metal, glass]* former des soufflures. 4 **vt** *paint* faire cloquer. **~ed** *paint* cloqué; *skin, hand, feet etc* cloqué; (*more widespread*) couvert d'ampoules.

blistering ['blɪstərɪŋ] 1 **n** *[skin]* formation *f* d'ampoules; *[paint]* boursouflage *m*. 2 **adj** *heat* étouffant; *sun* brûlant; (*fig*) *attack, condemnation* cinglant, virulent, impitoyable. **a ~ day** un jour de canicule.

blithe [blaɪð] **adj** (*liter*) joyeux, gai, allègre.

blithely ['blaɪðlɪ] **adv** (*gaily*) gaiement, joyeusement, avec allégresse; (*unthinkingly*) avec insouciance.

blithering* ['blɪðərɪŋ] **adj**: ~ **idiot** crétin fini*; (*excl*) **you ~ idiot!** espèce d'idiot!

blithesome ['blaɪðsəm] **adj** = **blithe**.

B.Litt. [biː'lɪt] **abbr of Bachelor of Literature**.

blitz [blɪts] 1 **n** (*Mil*) attaque *f* éclair *inv*; (*Aviat*) bombardement *m* (aérien). **the B~** le Blitz; (*fig*) **to have a ~ on sth** s'attaquer à qch. 2 **comp** ▸**blitzkrieg** guerre-éclair *f*. 3 **vt** bombarder. **~ed houses** maisons bombardées *or* sinistrées (*par un bombardement*); (*fig: drunk*) **~ed**‡ bourré‡, rond*.

blizzard ['blɪzəd] **n** tempête *f* de neige; (*in Arctic*) blizzard *m*.

bloated ['bləʊtɪd] **adj** gonflé, boursouflé, bouffi; *face* bouffi, boursouflé; *stomach* gonflé, ballonné; (*fig: with pride etc*) bouffi, gonflé (*with* de); *style* bouffi.

bloater ['bləʊtəʳ] **n** hareng saur *or* fumé.

blob [blɒb] **n** (*drop: gen*) (grosse) goutte *f*; *[ink]* pâté *m*, tache *f*; (*stain*) tache.

bloc [blɒk] **n** a (*Pol*) bloc *m*. b **en ~** en bloc, en gros.

block [blɒk] 1 **n** a *[stone]* bloc *m*; *[wood]* bille *f*; *[blacksmith, butcher, executioner]* billot *m*; *[chocolate]* tablette *f*. (*toys*) **~s** (jeu *m* de) cubes *mpl*, jeu de construction; **a ~ of ice cream** un litre (*or* demi-litre *etc*) de glace; **butcher's ~** billot de boucher; (*US*) **on the ~** *buy* aux enchères; *pay* rubis sur l'ongle; **to die on the ~** périr sur le billot *or* l'échafaud; *see* **chip**.

b *[buildings]* pâté *m* (de maisons). (*Brit*) **a ~ of flats** un immeuble; **to take a stroll round the ~** faire le tour du pâté de maisons, faire un tour dans le coin; (*US*) **she lived 3 ~s away** elle habitait 3 rues plus loin.

c (*part of prison, hospital etc*) quartier *m*, pavillon *m*; *[factory etc]* bâtiment *m*. **H B~** bâtiment *m* *or* bloc *m* H.

d (*obstruction*) *[traffic]* embouteillage *m*, encombrement *m*; *[pipe]* obstruction *f*; (*Med, Psych*) blocage *m*. (*fig*) **I've got a (mental) ~ about that whole period** j'ai un trou (de mémoire), je ne me souviens d'absolument rien au sujet de cette période; (*fig: frightened etc*) **I couldn't do it — I had a mental ~ about it** je n'ai pas pu le faire, c'est plus fort que moi; *[writer]* **he's/I've got a ~** c'est le vide *or* blocage total; *see* **road**.

e *[tickets]* série *f*; *[shares]* tranche *f*; *[seats]* groupe *m*.

f (*Brit Typ*) cliché *m* (*plaque*).

g (*also* **~ and tackle**) palan *m*, moufles *mpl*.

h (‡: *head*) caboche* *f*, ciboulot‡ *m*; *see* **knock**.

i (*Brit: writing pad*) bloc *m*.

j (*Comput*) bloc *m*.

k (*Fin*) *[shares]* paquet *m*; (*larger*) bloc *m*.

2 **comp** ▸**block association** association *f* de copropriétaires (*d'un immeuble*) ▸**block booking** réservation *f* de groupe ▸**blockbuster*** (*bomb*) bombe *f* de gros calibre; (*film*) film *m* à grand succès; (*book*) roman *m* à grand succès; (*argument*) argument *m* massue *inv*; **he's a real blockbuster*** il est d'une efficacité à tout casser ▸**block capitals**: **in block capitals = in block letters** ▸**block diagram** (*Comput, Geog*) bloc-diagramme *m*; (*Elec*) schéma *m* (de principe) ▸**block grant** (*Brit Admin*) dotation *ou* enveloppe gouvernementale (*accordée aux autorités escales*) ▸**blockhead*** (*pej*) imbécile *mf*, crétin(e)* *m(f)* ▸**blockhouse** (*Mil*) casemate *f*, blockhaus *m* ▸**block letters**: **in block letters** en (caractères) majuscules d'imprimerie ▸**block release** (*Brit Educ*) système de stages de formation alternant avec l'activité professionnelle ▸**block system** (*Rail*) bloc-système *m*, bloc *m* automatique à signaux lumineux ▸**block vote** (*Pol, Ind*) vote groupé ▸**blockvoting** (*Pol, Ind*) la pratique du vote groupé.

3 **vt** a *pipe etc* boucher, bloquer, obstruer; *road* bloquer, barrer; *harbour, wheel* bloquer; *progress, traffic* entraver, gêner; (*Ftbl*) *opponent* gêner; *transaction, credit, negotiations* bloquer; (*Med*) *pain* anesthésier, neutraliser. **the leaves ~ed the drain** les feuilles mortes ont bouché *or* bloqué le puisard; **to ~ sb's way** barrer le chemin à qn; (*Ftbl etc*) **to ~ the ball** bloquer (la balle).

b *title, design* graver au fer.

4 **vi** *[wheel]* (se) bloquer.

▸**block off vt sep** *part of road etc* interdire, condamner; (*accidentally*) obstruer.

▸**block out vt sep** a (*obscure*) *view* boucher; *light* empêcher de passer. b (*from mind*) *thoughts, idea* refouler, repousser. c (*sketch*) *scheme, design* ébaucher.

▸**block up vt sep** *gangway* encombrer; *pipe etc* bloquer, boucher; *window, entrance* murer, condamner; *hole* boucher, bloquer.

blockade [blɒ'keɪd] 1 **n** (*Mil*) blocus *m*; (*fig*) barrage *m*. **under ~** en état de blocus; **to break/raise the ~** forcer/lever le blocus. 2 **comp** ▸**blockade runner** briseur *m* de blocus. 3 **vt** a (*Mil*) *town, port* bloquer, faire le blocus de; (*fig*) bloquer, obstruer. b (*US*) *traffic* bloquer; *street* encombrer.

blockage ['blɒkɪdʒ] **n** (*gen*) obstruction *f*; (*Med*) obstruction, blocage *m*; (*intestinal*) occlusion *f*; (*mental*) blocage; (*fig*) bouchon *m*.

bloke* [bləʊk] **n** (*Brit*) type* *m*, mec‡ *m*.

blond(e) [blɒnd] adj, n blond(e) *(m(f))*; *see* **ash², platinum.**

blood [blʌd] 1 n a *(NonC)* sang *m*. **till the ~ comes** jusqu'au sang; **it's like trying to get ~ out of a stone** c'est comme si on parlait à un mur; **to give** *or* **donate ~** donner son sang; **bad ~** animosité *f*; **there is bad ~ between them** le torchon brûle (entre eux); *(liter)* **his ~ will be on your head** vous aurez sa mort sur la conscience; *(fig)* **there is ~ on his hands** il a la mort de quelqu'un sur la conscience, il a du sang sur les mains; **the ~ rushed to his face** le sang lui est monté au visage; **it makes my ~ boil** cela me fait bouillir; **my ~ was boiling** je bouillais (de rage); **his ~ is up** il est très monté; **he's out for ~*** il cherche quelqu'un sur qui passer sa colère; **she is out for his ~*** elle veut sa peau*; **you make my ~ run cold** vous me donnez le frisson; **his ~ ran cold** son sang s'est figé *or* s'est glacé dans ses veines; **the ties of ~** les liens du sang; *(Prov)* **~ is thicker than water** la voix du sang est la plus forte; **it's in his ~** il a cela dans le sang; **of Irish ~** de sang irlandais; *(fig)* **this firm needs new** *or* **fresh** *or* **young ~** cette maison a besoin d'un *or* de sang nouveau; *see* **blue, cold, flesh** *etc.*

b (†: *dashing young man*) petit-maître† *m*.

c *(US ‡)* (abbr of **blood brother**) frère *m*.

2 vt *(Hunting) hounds* acharner, donner le goût du sang à; *(fig) troops* donner le baptême du feu à.

3 comp ▸**blood-and-thunder: a blood-and-thunder film** (*or* **play**) un sombre mélodrame; **blood-and-thunder novel** roman *m* à sensation ▸**blood bank** *(Med)* banque *f* du sang ▸**blood bath** *(fig)* bain *m* de sang, massacre *m* ▸**blood blister** pinçon *m* ▸**blood brother** frère *m* de sang ▸**blood cell** cellule sanguine; **red/white blood cell** globule *m* rouge/blanc ▸**blood corpuscle** globule sanguin ▸**blood count** *(Med)* numération *f* globulaire ▸**bloodcurdling** à (vous) figer *or* tourner* le sang, qui (vous) fige le sang ▸**blood donor** donneur *m*, -euse *f* de sang ▸**blood doping** dopage *m* par autotransfusion ▸**blood feud** vendetta *f* ▸**blood group** *(Med)* groupe sanguin ▸**blood grouping** *(Med)* recherche *f* du groupe sanguin ▸**blood heat** température *f* du sang ▸**bloodhound** *(dog)* limier *m*; (*: *detective*) détective *m*, limier ▸**bloodletting** *(Med)* saignée *f* ▸**bloodline** lignée *f* ▸**blood lust** soif *f* de sang ▸**bloodmobile** *(US)* centre *m* mobile de collecte du sang ▸**blood money** prix *m* du sang ▸**blood orange** (orange *f*) sanguine *f* ▸**blood plasma** plasma sanguin ▸**blood poisoning** empoisonnement *m* du sang ▸**blood pressure** *see* **blood pressure** ▸**blood pudding** *(US)* boudin *m* ▸**blood-red** rouge *(m)* sang *inv* ▸**blood relation** parent(e) *m(f)* par le sang ▸**blood sausage** *(US)* = **blood pudding** ▸**bloodshed** effusion *f* de sang, carnage *m*; **without bloodshed** sans verser de sang, sans effusion de sang ▸**bloodshot** *eyes* injecté (de sang); **to become bloodshot** s'injecter ▸**blood sports** sports *mpl* sanguinaires ▸**bloodstain** tache *f* de sang ▸**bloodstained** taché de sang, souillé *(liter)* de sang, ensanglanté ▸**bloodstock** bêtes *fpl* de race (pure) *or* de sang ▸**bloodstone** héliotrope *m* *(pierre)* ▸**bloodstream** sang *m*, système sanguin ▸**bloodsucker** *(Zool, also *pej)* sangsue *f* ▸**blood sugar** sucre *m* dans le sang; **blood sugar level** taux *m* de sucre dans le sang ▸**blood test** *(Med)* analyse *f* de sang, examen *m* du sang ▸**bloodthirstiness** *[person, animal]* soif *f* de sang; *[book, story]* cruauté *f*, caractère *m* sanguinaire ▸**bloodthirsty** *person, animal* altéré *or* assoiffé de sang, sanguinaire; *disposition, tale* sanguinaire ▸**blood transfusion** transfusion sanguine *or* de sang ▸**blood type** = **blood group** ▸**blood vessel** vaisseau sanguin; *see* **burst.**

bloodied ['blʌdɪd] adj sanglant, ensanglanté. *(loc fig)* **~ but unbowed** vaincu mais sa fierté intacte.

bloodiness ['blʌdɪnɪs] n *(lit)* état sanglant.

bloodless ['blʌdlɪs] adj *(without blood)* exsangue; *complexion* anémié, pâle; *victory* sans effusion de sang, pacifique. *(Brit Hist)* **the B~ Revolution** la révolution en Angleterre (1688-89).

bloodlessly ['blʌdlɪslɪ] adv sans effusion de sang, pacifiquement.

blood pressure ['blʌdpreʃəʳ] n tension *f* (artérielle). **to have high/low ~** faire de l'hypertension/hypotension; **to take sb's ~** prendre la tension de qn; *(Med)* **his ~ went up/down** sa tension a monté/a baissé; *(fig)* **his ~ rose at the news** il a failli avoir une attaque en apprenant la nouvelle.

bloody ['blʌdɪ] 1 adj a *(lit)* sanglant, taché de sang, ensanglanté; *battle* sanglant, sanguinaire; *(blood-coloured)* rouge, rouge sang *inv*. **a ~ nose** un nez en sang; **with ~ hands** les mains couvertes de sang *or* ensanglantées; **a ~ sun** un soleil rouge sang; **~ mary** vodka *f* (au) jus de tomate, bloody mary *m*.

b *(Brit **)* foutu‡ *(before noun)*, sacré* *(before noun)*. **this ~ machine won't start!** cette bon Dieu‡ de machine *or* cette foutue‡ machine ne veut pas démarrer!; **shut the ~ door!** (mais) nom de Dieu** veux-tu fermer la porte!; **it's a ~ nuisance** ce que c'est emmerdant‡; **you ~ fool!** espèce de con!**; **you've got a ~ cheek!** *or* **nerve!** tu charries!‡; **those ~ doctors!** ces bon Dieu‡ de médecins, ces foutus‡ médecins; **~ hell!** merde alors!‡; **it's a ~ miracle he wasn't killed!** c'est un sacré* miracle qu'il n'ait pas été tué; **we had a perfectly ~ evening with them** ils nous ont fait passer une soirée (drôlement) emmerdante‡.

2 adv *(Brit **)* vachement‡. **not ~ likely!** tu te fous de moi!‡, tu te fous de ma gueule!‡; **I've ~ (well) lost it!** je l'ai perdu nom de Dieu!‡

3 comp ▸**bloody-minded‡** *(Brit) person* qui fait toujours des difficultés; *attitude* buté; **he's being bloody-minded‡** il le fait pour emmerder le monde‡ ▸**bloody-mindedness‡: out of sheer bloody-mindedness** (rien que) pour emmerder le monde‡.

4 vt ensanglanter, souiller de sang *(liter)*.

bloom [bluːm] 1 n a fleur *f*. b *(NonC) [flower, plant]* floraison *f*; *(fig)* épanouissement *m*, floraison. **in ~** *tree* en fleurs; *flower* éclos; **in full ~** *tree* en pleine floraison; *flower* épanoui; **to burst** *or* **come into ~** fleurir, s'épanouir; *(fig)* **in the ~ of her youth** dans la fleur de sa jeunesse, en pleine jeunesse. c *[fruit, skin]* velouté *m*. **the ~ had gone from her cheek** ses joues avaient perdu leurs fraîches couleurs. 2 vi *[flower]* éclore; *[tree]* fleurir; *[person]* être florissant. **~ing with health** resplendissant de santé.

bloomer ['bluːməʳ] n a (‡) bévue *f*, gaffe *f*. **to make a ~** faire une gaffe, se foutre dedans‡, mettre les pieds dans le plat. b *(Dress)* **~s** culotte bouffante.

blooming ['bluːmɪŋ] adj a *tree* en fleur, fleuri; *looks, health* florissant. b (*) = **blinking 1.**

blooper‡ ['bluːpəʳ] n *(US)* gaffe *f*.

blossom ['blɒsəm] 1 n a *(NonC)* floraison *f*, fleur(s) *f(pl)*. **a spray of ~** une petite branche fleurie, un rameau en fleur(s); **tree in ~** arbre *m* en fleur(s); **pear trees in full ~** poiriers *mpl* en pleine floraison; **to come into ~** fleurir, s'épanouir; **peach ~** fleur de pêcher; *see* **orange.** b *(flower)* fleur *f*. 2 vi fleurir, être en fleur(s), se couvrir de fleurs; *[person]* s'épanouir. *(fig)* **to ~ (out) into** devenir.

blot [blɒt] 1 n *[ink]* tache *f*, pâté *m*; *(fig)* tache, souillure *f* *(liter)*. **a ~ on his character** *or* **on his escutcheon** une tache à sa réputation; **to be a ~ on the landscape** déparer le paysage *(also fig hum)*. 2 vt a *(spot with ink)* tacher, faire des pâtés sur, barbouiller. *(Brit fig)* **you've really ~ted your copybook** ta réputation en a pris un coup*. b *(dry) ink, page* sécher. 3 vi *[blotting paper]* boire (l'encre).

▸**blot out** vt sep a *words* biffer, rayer; *memories* effacer; *[fog etc] view* voiler, masquer. b *(destroy) nation* exterminer, liquider*; *city* annihiler, rayer de la carte.

blotch [blɒtʃ] 1 n a *(on skin)* *(mark)* tache *f*, marbrure *f*; *(spot)* bouton *m*. b *[ink, colour]* tache *f*. 2 vt *paper, written work* tacher, barbouiller, faire des taches sur. **~ed with** taché de, couvert de taches de.

blotchy ['blɒtʃɪ] adj *skin, complexion* marbré, couvert de taches *or* de marbrures; *drawing, written work* couvert de taches, barbouillé.

blotter ['blɒtəʳ] n a *(block)* (bloc *m*) buvard *m*; *(sheet)* buvard; *(hand ~)* tampon *m* buvard; *(desk pad)* sous-main *m inv*. b *(US: notebook)* registre *m*.

blotting ['blɒtɪŋ] comp ▸**blotting pad** (bloc *m*) buvard *m* ▸**blotting paper** (papier *m*) buvard *m*.

blotto‡ ['blɒtəʊ] adj bourré‡, bituré‡, rond comme une barrique‡.

blouse [blaʊz] n *[woman]* corsage *m*, chemisier *m*; *[workman, artist, peasant]* blouse *f*, sarrau *m*; *(US Mil)* vareuse *f*.

blouson ['bluːzɒn] n blouson *m*.

blow¹ [bləʊ] (vb: pret **blew**, ptp **blown**) 1 n a **to give a ~** *(through mouth)* souffler; *(through nose)* se moucher.

b *(wind)* coup *m* de vent, bourrasque *f*. **to go out for a ~** sortir prendre l'air *or* le frais.

2 comp ▸**blow drier, blow dryer** sèche-cheveux *m inv* ▸**blow-dry** n brushing *m* ◊ vt **to blow-dry sb's hair** faire un brushing à qn ▸**blowfly** mouche *f* à viande ▸**blowgun** sarbacane *f* ▸**blowhard*** *(US)* vantard *m* ▸**blowhole** *[whale]* évent *m*; *(Tech)* évent, bouche *f* d'aération; *(Metal)* **blowholes** soufflures *fpl* ▸**blow job****: **to give sb a blow job** tailler une pipe à qn** ▸**blowlamp** *(Brit)* lampe *f* à souder, chalumeau *m* ▸**blow-out** *see* **blow-out** ▸**blowpipe** *(weapon)* sarbacane *f*; *(Chem, Ind)* chalumeau *m*; *(Glass-making)* canne *f* (de souffleur), fêle *f* ▸**blowtorch** lampe *f* à souder, chalumeau *m* ▸**blow-up** explosion *f*; (‡: *quarrel*) engueulade‡ *f*, prise *f* de bec*, dispute *f*; *(Phot *)* agrandissement *m*.

3 vt a *[wind] ship* pousser; *leaves* chasser, faire voler. **the wind blew the ship off course** le vent a fait dévier le navire (de sa route) *or* a dérouté le navire; **a gust of wind blew her hat off** un coup de vent a fait s'envoler son chapeau; **the wind blew the chimney down** le vent a fait tomber *or* a renversé la cheminée; **the wind blew away the clouds** le vent a chassé *or* dispersé les nuages; **the wind blew the door open/shut** un coup de vent a ouvert/fermé la porte; *see* **ill.**

b *(drive air into) fire* souffler sur; *bellows* faire marcher. **to ~ one's nose** se moucher; **to ~ an egg** vider un œuf *(en soufflant dedans)*.

c *(make by blowing) bubbles* faire; *glass* souffler. **to ~ a kiss** envoyer un baiser.

d *trumpet, horn* jouer de, souffler dans. **the referee blew his whistle** l'arbitre a sifflé *(see also* **whistle**); *(fig)* **to ~ one's own trumpet** chanter ses propres louanges, se faire mousser*; **he blew the dust off the record** il a enlevé la poussière du disque en soufflant dessus; *(fig)* **that blew the lid off the whole business*** c'est cela qui a fait découvrir le pot aux roses.

e *(Drugs sl)* **to ~ grass** fumer de l'herbe *(sl)*.

f *(destroy) fuse, safe* faire sauter. *(Aut)* **to ~ a gasket** griller* *or* faire sauter un joint de culasse; *(fig)* **to ~ a gasket*** *or* *(US)* **one's**

cork* *or* (*US*) **one's stack*** *or* **one's top*** piquer une crise, exploser de rage; (*fig*) **the whole plan has been ~n sky-high** tout le projet a sauté.

g (‡: *spend extravagantly*) *wages, money* claquer‡, bouffer‡. **I blew £20 on a new hat** j'ai claqué (un billet de) 20 livres pour un nouveau chapeau.

h (*: *spoil, fail*) rater, gâcher; **he blew it*** il l'a loupé*, il a tout raté; **to ~ one's lines** mal dire son texte, se tromper dans son texte.

i (*phrases*) **to ~ one's mind‡** prendre son pied‡, flipper‡; **to ~ sb's mind‡** faire prendre son pied à qn‡; **to ~ the gaff‡** vendre la mèche; **to ~ the gaff on sb‡** dénoncer *or* vendre qn; (*kill*) **to ~ sb away*** descendre* *or* flinguer* qn; **he realized he was ~n‡** il a compris qu'il était brûlé*; **~ the expense!*** tant pis pour la dépense!, au diable la dépense!; **well, I'm ~ed!*** ça alors!*, par exemple!; **I'll be ~ed if I'll do it!*** pas question que je le fasse!, je veux être pendu si je le fais!*; **~ it!*** la barbe!*, zut!*

4 vi a *[wind]* souffler. **the wind was ~ing hard** le vent soufflait très fort, il faisait grand vent; **it was ~ing a gale** le vent soufflait en tempête; **it's ~ing great guns*** il fait un vent à décorner les bœufs*; **the wind was ~ing from the south** le vent soufflait du sud; (*fig*) **to see which way the wind ~s** regarder *or* voir de quel côté souffle le vent; **she ~s hot and cold with me** avec moi elle souffle le chaud et le froid; **her enthusiasm ~s hot and cold** son enthousiasme a des hauts et des bas.

b (*move with wind*) **the door blew open/shut** un coup de vent a ouvert/a fermé la porte; **his hat blew out of the window** son chapeau s'est envolé par la fenêtre.

c *[trumpet]* sonner; *[whistle]* retentir; *[foghorn]* mugir. **when the whistle ~s** au coup de sifflet.

d (*breathe out hard*) souffler; (*breathe hard*) *[person]* souffler, être à bout de souffle; *[animal]* souffler. **to ~ on one's fingers** souffler dans ses doigts; **to ~ on one's soup** souffler sur sa soupe; *see* **puff**.

e *[whale]* souffler (par les évents). **there she ~s!** elle souffle!

f *[fuse, light bulb]* sauter, griller*; *[tyre]* éclater.

g (‡: *leave*) filer*.

5 excl (*) la barbe!*, zut!*

▶**blow down** 1 vi *[tree etc]* être abattu par le vent, se renverser, tomber. 2 vt sep *[wind]* faire tomber; *[person]* faire tomber (en soufflant), abattre (en soufflant).

▶**blow in** 1 vi (*) s'amener*, débarquer*; (*unexpectedly*) arriver *or* débarquer* à l'improviste. 2 vt sep *door, window* enfoncer. **look what the wind's blown in!*** regardez qui s'amène!*

▶**blow off** 1 vi a *[hat]* s'envoler. b (*Brit* ‡) lâcher un pet, péter. 2 vt sep a *hat* emporter. b *air* laisser échapper, lâcher. (*fig*) **to blow off steam*** se défouler*, dire ce qu'on a sur le cœur (*about* au sujet de).

▶**blow out** 1 vi *[light]* s'éteindre; *[tyre]* éclater; *[fuse]* sauter. 2 vt sep a *light* éteindre; *candle* souffler. **the storm blew itself out** la tempête finit par s'apaiser. b (*puff out*) *one's cheeks* gonfler. c **to blow one's brains out** se faire sauter *or* se brûler la cervelle. 3 **blow-out** n *see* **blow-out**.

▶**blow over** 1 vi *[storm, dispute]* se calmer, s'apaiser, passer. 2 vt sep *tree* renverser, abattre.

▶**blow up** 1 vi a *[bomb]* exploser, sauter. (*fig*) **the whole thing has blown up** tout a été fichu en l'air*. b *[wind]* se lever; *[storm]* se préparer. c (*) (*with anger, indignation*) sauter au plafond*. d (*start up*) *[affair, crisis]* se déclencher. 2 vt sep a *mine* (faire) exploser, faire sauter; *building, bridge* faire sauter. b *tyre* gonfler. (*fig*) **blown up with pride** gonflé *or* bouffi d'orgueil. c *photo* agrandir; *event* exagérer. d (‡: *reprimand*) *person* passer un (bon) savon à*. 3 **blow-up** n *see* **blow**[1] **2**.

blow[2] [bləʊ] n a (*lit*) coup *m*; (*with fist*) coup de poing. **to come to ~s** en venir aux mains; **at one ~** du premier coup; (*fig*) **to cushion** *or* **soften the ~** amortir le choc; (*fig*) **he gave me a ~-by-~ account** il ne m'a fait grâce d'aucun détail; *see* **strike** *etc*. b (*fig: sudden misfortune*) coup *m*, malheur *m*. **it was a terrible ~ for them** cela a été un coup terrible pour eux.

blow[3] [bləʊ] vi (††, *liter*) *[flowers]* fleurir, s'épanouir.

blower ['bləʊəʳ] n *[grate]* tablier *m or* rideau *m* de cheminée; *[ventilation]* ventilateur *m* (soufflant), machine *f* à vent; (*Min*) jet *m* de grisou; (*whale*) baleine *f*; (‡: *loudspeaker*) haut-parleur *m*; (*Brit* ‡: *telephone*) bigophone* *m*. **to get on the ~‡ to sb** passer un coup de bigophone‡ à qn; *see* **glass**.

-blown [bləʊn] adj ending in comps *see* **fly**[1], **wind**[1].

blow-out ['bləʊaʊt] n a *[tyre]* éclatement *m*. **he had a ~** il a eu un pneu qui a éclaté. b (*Elec*) **there's been a ~** les plombs *mpl* ont sauté. c *[gaswell, oilwell]* jaillissement *m*. d (‡: *meal*) gueuleton‡ *m*. **to have a ~** faire un gueuleton‡, faire une grande bouffe‡.

blowy ['bləʊɪ] adj venté, venteux.

blowzed ['blaʊzd] adj, **blowzy** ['blaʊzɪ] adj *hair* mal peigné; *woman* débraillé.

blub [blʌb] vi (*cry*) pleurer comme un veau.

blubber ['blʌbəʳ] 1 n a *[whale]* blanc *m* de baleine. **~-lipped** lippu. b **to have a ~** pleurer *or* chialer‡ un (bon) coup. 2 vi (*cry*) pleurer comme un veau.

blubbery ['blʌbərɪ] adj (*fat*) plein de graisse. **~ lips** grosses lèvres molles.

bludgeon ['blʌdʒən] 1 n gourdin *m*, matraque *f*. 2 vt matraquer, assener un coup de gourdin *or* de matraque à. (*fig*) **he ~ed me into doing it** il m'a forcé la main (pour que je le fasse).

blue [bluː] 1 adj a bleu. **~ with cold** violet *or* bleu de froid; (*lit*) **to be ~ in the face** avoir le visage cyanosé; **you may talk till you are ~ in the face*** tu peux toujours parler; **I've told you till I'm ~ in the face*** je me tue à te le dire; **once in a ~ moon** tous les trente-six du mois; **like a ~ streak*** *run, go* comme une flèche, au triple galop; **to have a ~ fit‡** piquer une crise*; *see also* **4** *and* **black, murder, true**.

b (*: *miserable*) cafardeux*, triste. **to feel ~** broyer du noir‡, avoir le cafard*; **to be in a ~ funk** avoir la frousse* *or* la trouille‡.

c (*fig: obscene*) *talk* grivois, gaulois, salé; *book, film* porno* *inv*.

2 n a (*colour*) bleu *m*, azur *m*; *see* **navy, Prussian, sky** *etc*.

b (*sky*) azur *m* (*liter*), ciel *m*. (*fig*) **to come out of the ~** (*gen*) être complètement inattendu; *[pleasant thing]* tomber du ciel; **to go off into the ~** (*into the unknown*) partir à l'aventure; (*out of touch*) disparaître de la circulation*; *see* **bolt**.

c (*liter: sea*) **the ~** la mer, les flots *mpl*.

d (*: *depression*) **the ~s** le cafard*; **to have the ~s** broyer du noir, avoir le cafard*, avoir des idées noires; (*Mus*) **the ~s** le blues.

e (*Brit Univ*) **Dark/Light B~s** équipe *f* d'Oxford/de Cambridge; **he's got his ~ for rugby, he is a rugby ~** il a représenté son université au rugby (*gén Oxford ou Cambridge*).

f (*in washing*) bleu *m*.

3 vt (*Brit* ‡: *squander*) *inheritance, fortune* manger, gaspiller; *money* claquer‡. **to ~ money on sth** gaspiller de l'argent pour qch.

4 comp ▶**blue baby** enfant bleu ▶**Bluebeard** Barbe-bleue *m* ▶**bluebell** jacinthe *f* des bois; (*Scot: harebell*) campanule *f* ▶**blueberry** myrtille *f*, airelle *f* ▶**bluebird** (*Orn*) oiseau bleu; (*fig*) oiseau bleu (du bonheur) ▶**blue-black** noir bleuté ▶**blue blood** sang bleu *or* noble ▶**blue-blooded** de sang noble, aristocratique ▶**blue book** (*Brit Parl*) livre bleu; (*US Scol etc*) cahier *m* d'examen ▶**bluebottle** mouche bleue *or* de la viande; (*Bot*) bleuet *m*; (‡†: *policeman*) poulet* *m*, flic* *m* ▶**blue cheese** (fromage *m*) bleu *m* ▶**blue chips, blue-chip securities** valeurs *fpl* de premier ordre, placements *mpl* de tout repos *or* de père de famille ▶**blue collar worker** col bleu ▶**blue-eyed** aux yeux bleus; (*Brit fig*) **the blue-eyed boy** le chouchou*, le chéri ▶**blue fin tuna, blue fin tunny** thon *m* rouge ▶**blue grass** (*US*) pâturin *m* des champs; (*US*) **the Blue Grass State** le Kentucky; (*US*) **blue grass music** musique *f* bluegrass ▶**the Blue Hen State** (*US*) le Delaware ▶**blue jeans** blue-jean(s) *m(pl)* ▶**blue law*** (*US*) *loi limitant les activités publiques le dimanche* ▶**blue pencil** vt (*US*) corriger ▶**Blue Peter** (*Naut*) pavillon *m* de partance ▶**blueprint** (*print, process*) bleu *m* (*tirage*); (*fig*) plan *m*, projet *m*, schéma directeur (*for* de) ▶**the blue riband** *or* (*US*) **ribbon** (*Sport*) le Ruban Bleu ▶**blue rinse** rinçage *m* bleuté ▶**blue-rinsed** *hair* aux reflets bleutés; *woman* à la chevelure bleutée ▶**blue shark** requin bleu ▶**blue-sky** (*US*) *stock, bond* douteux; (*US*) **blue-sky laws** *lois protégeant le public contre les titres douteux* ▶**bluestocking** (*fig*) bas-bleu *m* ▶**blue tit** mésange bleue ▶**blue whale** baleine bleue.

blueness ['bluːnɪs] n bleu *m*.

bluey ['bluːɪ] adj bleuté. **~ green** vert bleuâtre *or* bleuté; **~ grey** gris bleu.

bluff[1] [blʌf] 1 adj a *person* carré, direct. b *cliff, coast* à pic, escarpé. 2 n (*headland*) falaise avancée, cap *m*, promontoire *m*.

bluff[2] [blʌf] 1 vi (*also Cards*) bluffer*. 2 vt a *person* bluffer*, donner le change à. **we ~ed him into believing ...** nous l'avons si bien bluffé* qu'il a cru ... . b (*Cards*) *opponent* bluffer*. 3 n (*esp Cards*) bluff *m*; *see* **call**.

bluffer ['blʌfəʳ] n bluffeur *m*, -euse *f*.

bluish ['bluːɪʃ] adj tirant sur le bleu; (*pej*) bleuâtre. **~ grey** gris bleuté; **~ white** blanc bleuté *or* aux reflets bleus.

blunder ['blʌndəʳ] 1 n (*gaffe*) bévue *f*, impair *m*, gaffe *f*; (*error*) faute *f*, bourde *f*. **to make a ~** faire une gaffe *or* une bévue *or* un impair; **social ~** impair. 2 vi a (*make mistake*) faire une bévue *or* une gaffe. **we ~ed through to victory** de bévue en bévue nous sommes parvenus à la victoire. b (*move clumsily*) avancer à l'aveuglette, tâtonner. **to ~ in/out** *etc* entrer/sortir *etc* à l'aveuglette; **to ~ against** *or* **into sth** buter *or* se cogner contre qch. 3 vt *affair, business* gâcher, saboter.

blunderbuss ['blʌndəbʌs] n tromblon *m*, espingole *f*.

blunderer ['blʌndərəʳ] n gaffeur *m*, -euse *f*.

blundering ['blʌndərɪŋ] 1 adj *person* gaffeur*, maladroit; *words, act* maladroit, malavisé. 2 n maladresse *f*.

blunt [blʌnt] 1 adj a *blade, knife* émoussé, qui ne coupe plus, peu tranchant; *pencil* mal taillé, épointé; *point, needle* émoussé, épointé. (*Jur, Police*) **with a ~ instrument** avec un instrument contondant. b (*fig: outspoken*) *person, speech* brusque, carré; *fact* brutal. **he was very ~** il n'a pas mâché ses mots. 2 vt *blade, knife, point, sword* émousser; *pencil, needle* épointer; (*fig*) *palate, feelings* blaser, lasser.

bluntly ['blʌntlɪ] adv *speak* carrément, sans ménagements, sans mettre de gants.

bluntness ['blʌntnɪs] n (*see* **blunt**) manque *m* de tranchant, état émoussé; absence *f* de pointe; (*outspokenness*) brusquerie *f*. ~ **of speech** franc-parler *m*.

blur [blɜːʳ] 1 n a (*smear, blot*) tache *f*; *[ink]* pâté *m*, bavure *f*. b (*vague form*) masse confuse, tache floue *or* indistincte. c (*mist: on mirror etc*) buée *f*. 2 vt a *shining surface* embuer, troubler; *writing, inscription* estomper, effacer; *view, outline* estomper. b *sight, judgment* troubler, brouiller. **eyes ~red with tears** yeux voilés de larmes.

blurb [blɜːb] n notice *f* publicitaire; *[book]* (texte *m* de) présentation *f*, texte de couverture (*or* au volet de jaquette).

blurred [blɜːd] adj, **blurry** ['blɜːrɪ] adj *photo, image* flou; *eyesight* troublé. *[outline, inscription]* **to become ~** s'estomper.

blurt [blɜːt] vt (*also* ~ **out**) *word* lâcher, jeter; *information, secrets* laisser échapper, lâcher étourdiment *or* à l'étourdie.

blush [blʌʃ] 1 vi a rougir, devenir rouge (*with* de). **to ~ deeply** rougir très fort, devenir tout rouge, piquer un fard*; **to ~ up to the ears** rougir jusqu'aux oreilles. b (*fig: be ashamed*) rougir, avoir honte. **I ~ for him** j'ai honte pour lui; **I ~ to say so** je rougis de le dire. 2 n rougeur *f*. **with a ~** en rougissant; **without a ~** sans rougir; (*liter*) **the first ~ of dawn** les premières rougeurs de l'aube; (*liter*) **the ~ of the rose** l'incarnat *m* de la rose (*liter*); **at the first ~** au premier aspect, de prime abord; *see* **spare**.

blusher ['blʌʃəʳ] n fard *m* à joues.

blushing ['blʌʃɪŋ] adj (*with shame*) le rouge au front; (*from embarrassment*) le rouge aux joues. (*hum*) **the ~ bride** la mariée rougissante.

bluster ['blʌstəʳ] 1 vi a *[wind]* faire rage, souffler violemment *or* en rafales; *[storm]* faire rage, se déchaîner. b (*rage*) tempêter, fulminer (*at sb* contre qn); *[boast]* fanfaronner. 2 n (*boasting*) air *m* bravache, fanfaronnade(s) *f(pl)*.

blusterer ['blʌstərəʳ] n fanfaron(ne) *m(f)*, bravache *m*.

blustering ['blʌstərɪŋ] 1 adj fanfaron. 2 n fanfaronnades *fpl*.

blustery ['blʌstərɪ] adj *wind* de tempête, qui souffle en rafales; *weather, day* venteux, à bourrasques.

B.M. [biː'em] abbr of **British Museum**.

B.M.A. [biːem'eɪ] (abbr of **British Medical Association**) ≃ ordre *m* des Médecins.

B. Mus. (abbr of **Bachelor of Music**) diplômé(e) *m(f)* des études musicales.

B.O. [biː'əʊ] a (abbr of **body odour**) odeur *f* corporelle. **he's got ~** il dégage des odeurs corporelles. b (*US*) abbr of **box office**.

boa ['bəʊə] n (*snake; fur or feather wrap*) boa *m*. ~ **constrictor** (boa) constricteur *m*.

Boadicea [ˌbəʊædɪ'siːə] n Boadicée *f*.

boar [bɔːʳ] 1 n (*wild*) sanglier *m*; (*male pig*) verrat *m*. **young (wild) ~** marcassin *m*; (*Culin*) **~'s head** hure *f* (de sanglier). 2 comp ▸**boarhound** vautre *m*; **pack of boarhounds** vautrait *m* ▸**boar-hunting** chasse *f* au sanglier.

board [bɔːd] 1 n a (*piece of wood*) planche *f*; († *or hum: table*) table *f*. (*Theat*) **the ~s** les planches, les tréteaux *mpl*, la scène; (*fig*) **it is all quite above ~** c'est tout ce qu'il y a de plus régulier, c'est tout à fait dans les règles; (*fig*) **across the ~** (adv) systématiquement; (adj) général, de portée générale; *see* **bread, chess, diving** *etc*.
b (*NonC: provision of meals*) pension *f*. (*Brit*) **~ and lodging** (chambre *f* avec) pension; (*Brit*) **full ~** pension complète; *see* **bed, half**.
c (*group of officials, council*) conseil *m*, comité *m*, commission *f*. **~ of directors** conseil d'administration; (*Fin, Ind*) **he is on the ~, he has a seat on the ~** il siège au conseil d'administration; (*Brit*) **B~ of Trade** ministère *m* du Commerce; (*US*) **~ of trade** chambre *f* de commerce; (*US Jur*) **~ of pardons** commission de remises des peines; (*US Jur*) **~ of parole** commission de remise en liberté surveillée; **medical ~** commission médicale; (*US*) **~ of health** service municipal d'hygiène; (*Mil*) conseil de révision; **~ of inquiry** commission d'enquête; (*Scol, Univ*) **~ of examiners** jury *m* d'examen; (*Brit Scol*) **~ of governors** ≃ conseil d'établissement (*d'un lycée ou d'un IUT*); (*Brit Scol*) **~ of managers** ≃ conseil d'établissement (*d'une école primaire*); (*US Univ*) **~ of trustees** *or* **regents** ≃ conseil d'université; (*US Scol*) **~ of education** ≃ conseil d'établissement.
d (*NonC: Aviat, Naut*) bord *m*. **to go on ~** monter à bord, (s')embarquer; **to take goods on ~** embarquer des marchandises; **on ~ the Queen Elizabeth** à bord du Queen Elizabeth; **on ~ (ship)** à bord; (*fig*) **to go by the ~** *[plan, attempt]* échouer; *[principles, hopes, dreams]* être abandonné; *[business, firm]* aller à vau-l'eau; **to take sth on ~** (*take note of*) prendre note de qch; (*undertake, accept responsibility for*) prendre qch sur soi, assumer qch.
e (*NonC: cardboard*) carton *m* (*NonC*); (*for games*) tableau *m*.
2 comp (*Ind, Comm*) *decision etc* du conseil d'administration ▸**board game** jeu *m* de société (*se jouant sur un tableau*) ▸**board meeting** (*Ind, Comm*) réunion *f* du conseil d'administration ▸**board room** salle *f* de conférence; (*in large organization*) salle *f* du conseil ▸**Board school** (*Hist*) école communale ▸**boardwalk** (*US*) passage *m* en bois, trottoir *m* en planches; (*on beach*) promenade *f* (en planches).
3 vt a (*go on to*) *ship, plane* monter à bord de; (*Naut*) (*in attack*) monter à l'abordage de, prendre à l'abordage; (*for inspection*) arraisonner; *train, bus* monter dans.
b (*cover with boards*) couvrir *or* garnir de planches, planchéier.
c (*feed, lodge*) prendre en pension *or* comme pensionnaire.
4 vi a (*lodge*) **to ~ with sb** être en pension chez qn.
b *[passengers]* embarquer. **your flight is now ~ing** l'embarquement *m* a commencé; **"flight A123 is now ~ing at gate 3"** "vol A123: embarquement immédiat porte 3".

▸**board out** vt sep *person* mettre en pension (*with* chez).

▸**board up** vt sep *door, window* boucher, clouer des planches en travers de.

boarder ['bɔːdəʳ] n a pensionnaire *mf*. **to take in ~s** prendre des pensionnaires. b (*Brit Scol*) interne *mf*, pensionnaire *mf*; *see* **day**.

boarding ['bɔːdɪŋ] 1 n a *[floor]* planchéiage *m*; *[fence]* planches *fpl*. b *[ship, plane]* embarquement *m*; (*Naut*) (*in attack*) abordage *m*; (*for inspection*) arraisonnement *m*.
2 comp ▸**boarding card** (*Brit: Aviat, Naut*) carte *f* d'embarquement ▸**boarding house** pension *f* (de famille); (*Scol*) internat *m*; **to live at a boarding house** vivre dans une *or* en pension ▸**boarding officer** officier chargé de l'arraisonnement ▸**boarding party** (*Naut*) section *f* d'abordage ▸**boarding pass** = **boarding card** ▸**boarding school** pension *f*, pensionnat *m*, internat *m*; **to send a child to boarding school** mettre un enfant en pension, mettre un enfant comme interne *or* pensionnaire (au lycée *etc*); **to be at boarding school** être interne.

boast [bəʊst] 1 n rodomontade *f*, fanfaronnade *f*. **it is their ~ that they succeeded** ils se vantent *or* ils s'enorgueillissent d'avoir réussi; **it is their ~ that no one went hungry** ils se vantent que personne n'ait eu faim. 2 vi se vanter (*about, of* de). **without ~ing** *or* **without wishing to ~, I may say ...** sans (vouloir) me vanter, je peux dire ...; **that's nothing to ~ about** il n'y a pas de quoi se vanter. 3 vt être fier de posséder, se glorifier d'avoir. **the church ~s a fine organ** l'église est fière de posséder un bel orgue.

boaster ['bəʊstəʳ] n vantard(e) *m(f)*, fanfaron(ne) *m(f)*.

boastful ['bəʊstfʊl] adj *person, words* fanfaron, vantard.

boastfully ['bəʊstfəlɪ] adv en se vantant, avec forfanterie.

boasting ['bəʊstɪŋ] n vantardise *f*, fanfaronnade(s) *f(pl)*.

boat [bəʊt] 1 n (*gen*) bateau *m*; (*small light ~*) embarcation *f*; (*ship*) navire *m*, bâtiment *m*; (*vessel*) vaisseau *m*; (*liner*) paquebot *m*; (*rowing ~*) barque *f*, canot *m*; (*ship's ~*) canot, chaloupe *f*; (*sailing ~*) voilier *m*; (*barge*) chaland *m*, péniche *f*. **to go by ~** prendre le bateau; **to cross the ocean by ~** traverser l'océan en bateau *or* en paquebot; **to take the ~ at Dover** s'embarquer à *or* prendre le bateau à Douvres; (*fig*) **we're all in the same ~** nous sommes tous logés à la même enseigne, nous sommes tous dans la même galère; *see* **burn[1], life, miss[1]** *etc*.
2 vi: **to go ~ing** aller faire une partie de canot; **to ~ up/down the river** remonter/descendre la rivière en bateau.
3 comp ▸**boatbuilder** constructeur *m* de bateaux ▸**boatbuilding** construction *f* de bateaux ▸**boat deck** pont *m* des embarcations ▸**boat hook** gaffe *f* ▸**boathouse** hangar *m* *or* abri *m* à bateaux ▸**boatload** *[goods etc]* cargaison *f*; *[people]* plein bateau, cargaison (*hum*) ▸**boatman** (*boat-hire proprietor*) loueur *m* de canots; (*actually rowing*) passeur *m* ▸**boat people** boat people *mpl* ▸**boat race** course *f* d'aviron, régates *fpl*; **the Boat Race** la course d'aviron (*entre les Universités d'Oxford et de Cambridge*) ▸**boat-shaped** en forme de bateau ▸**boat train** train *m* (qui assure la correspondance avec le ferry) ▸**boatyard** chantier *m* de construction de bateaux.

boater ['bəʊtəʳ] n (*hat*) canotier *m*.

boatful ['bəʊtfʊl] n *[goods]* cargaison *f*; *[people]* plein bateau, cargaison (*hum*).

boating ['bəʊtɪŋ] 1 n canotage *m*. 2 comp *club, accident* de canotage ▸**boating holiday/trip** vacances *fpl*/excursion *f* en bateau.

boatswain ['bəʊsn] n maître *m* d'équipage. **~'s chair** sellette *f*; **~'s mate** second maître; **~'s pipe** sifflet *m*.

Bob [bɒb] n (dim of **Robert**) Bob *m*. (*Brit*) **~'s your uncle!*** ce n'est pas plus difficile que cela!, c'est simple comme bonjour!

bob[1] [bɒb] 1 vi a **to ~ (up and down)** (*in the air*) pendiller; (*in water*) danser sur l'eau; **to ~ for apples** *essayer d'attraper avec les dents des pommes flottant sur l'eau*. b (*curtsy*) faire une (petite) révérence. 2 n a (*curtsy*) (petite) révérence *f*; (*nod*) (bref) salut *m* de tête; (*jerky movement*) petite secousse, petit coup. b (*weight*) *[pendulum]* poids *m*; *[plumbline]* plomb *m*; (*float*) bouchon *m*; (*bait*) paquet *m* de vers. 3 vi (*Fishing*) pêcher à la ligne flottante.

▸**bob down** vi a (*duck*) baisser la tête; (*straight*) se baisser subitement. b (*‡: be quiet*) la fermer‡.

▸**bob up** vi remonter brusquement.

bob[2]*† [bɒb] n, pl inv (*Brit*) shilling *m*.

bob[3] [bɒb] 1 n (*curl*) boucle *f*, mèche courte; (*gen: short haircut*) coiffure courte; (*haircut: chin-length all round*) coiffure au carré, coiffure à la Jeanne d'Arc; (*horse's tail*) queue écourtée. 2 vt *hair* (*see* 1) couper court *or* au carré *or* à la Jeanne d'Arc; *horse's tail* écourter. 3 comp ▸**bobcat** (*US*) lynx *m* ▸**bobtail** (*tail*) queue écourtée (*see* **rag[1]**); (*horse/dog*) cheval/chien écourté ▸**bobtailed** à (la) queue écourtée.

bob[4] [bɒb] n (*sleigh: also* **~sled, ~sleigh**) bobsleigh *m*, bob *m*; (*runner*) patin *m*.

bobbin ['bɒbɪn] n *[thread, wire]* bobine *f*; *[sewing machine]* bobine;

[lace] fuseau *m*. ~ **lace** dentelle *f* aux fuseaux.

bobble ['bɒbl] 1 n a (*pompom*) pompon *m*. b (*US *: mistake etc*) cafouillage* *m*. 2 vt (*US *: handle ineptly*) cafouiller*.

Bobby ['bɒbɪ] n (**dim of Robert**) Bob *m*.

bobby* ['bɒbɪ] n (*policeman*) flic* *m*.

bobby pin ['bɒbɪpɪn] n (*esp US*) pince *f* à cheveux.

bobbysocks* ['bɒbɪsɒks] npl (*US*) socquettes *fpl* (*de filles*).

bobbysoxer* ['bɒbɪsɒksəʳ] n (*US*) minette* *f* (des années 40).

Boche* [bɒʃ] (*pej*) 1 n Boche* *m* (*pej*). 2 adj boche* (*pej*).

bock [bɒk] n (*US*: ~ **beer**) a (*NonC*) bière *f* bock. b (*glass of beer*) bock *m*.

bod‡ [bɒd] n (*Brit*) type* *m*; (*US*) physique *m*, corps *m*; *see* **odd**.

bode [bəʊd] 1 vi: **to ~ well** être de bon augure (*for* pour); **it ~s ill (for)** cela est de mauvais augure (pour), cela ne présage rien de bon (pour). 2 vt présager, annoncer, augurer.

bodega [bəʊ'di:gə] n (*US*) épicerie portoricaine.

bodge* [bɒdʒ] (*Brit*) = **botch**.

bodice ['bɒdɪs] n a *[dress]* corsage *m*; *[peasant's dress]* corselet *m*. b (*undergarment*) cache-corset *m*.

-bodied ['bɒdɪd] adj **ending in comps** *see* **able, full** *etc*.

bodily ['bɒdɪlɪ] 1 adv *lift* à bras-le-corps; *carry* dans ses *etc* bras. 2 adj *need, comfort* matériel; *pain* physique. ~ **illness** troubles *mpl* physiques; ~ **harm** blessure *f*; *see* **grievous**.

bodkin ['bɒdkɪn] n (*big darning needle*) aiguille *f* à repriser; (*for threading tape*) passe-lacet *m*; (*for leather*) alêne *f*; (††: *hairpin*) épingle *f* à cheveux.

body ['bɒdɪ] 1 n a *[man, animal]* corps *m*. **just enough to keep ~ and soul together** juste assez pour subsister; **to belong to sb ~ and soul** appartenir à qn corps et âme; *see* **sound²**.

b (*corpse*) cadavre *m*, corps *m*.

c (*main part of structure*) *[dress]* corsage *m*, corps *m* (de robe); *[car]* carrosserie *f*; *[plane]* fuselage *m*; *[ship]* coque *f*; *[church]* nef *f*; *[camera]* boîtier *m*; *[speech, document]* fond *m*, corps. **in the ~ of the hall** au centre de la salle.

d (*group, mass*) masse *f*, ensemble *m*, corps *m*. ~ **of troops** corps de troupes; **the main ~ of the army** le gros de l'armée; **the great ~ of readers** la masse des lecteurs; **a large ~ of people** une masse de gens, une foule nombreuse; **in a ~** en masse; **taken in a ~** pris ensemble, dans leur ensemble; **the ~ politic** le corps politique; **legislative ~** corps législatif; **a large ~ of water** une grande masse d'eau; **a strong ~ of evidence** une forte accumulation de preuves; **a strong ~ of opinion was against it** une grande partie de l'opinion était contre.

e (*) (*man*) bonhomme* *m*; (*woman*) bonne femme*. **an inquisitive old ~** une vieille fouine; **a pleasant little ~** une gentille petite dame.

f (*Phys etc: piece of matter*) corps *m*. **heavenly ~** corps céleste; *see* **foreign**.

g (*NonC*) *[wine, paper]* corps *m*. **this wine has not enough ~** ce vin n'a pas assez de corps; **to give one's hair ~** donner du volume à ses cheveux.

h (*also* ~ **stocking**) body *m*.

2 comp ▸**bodybag** (*esp Mil*) *sac dans lequel on transporte les cadavres* ▸**bodybuilder** (*Aut*) carrossier *m*; (*food*) aliment *m* énergétique; (*person*) culturiste *m*; (*apparatus*) extenseur *m* ▸**body building** culturisme *m*; **body-building exercises** exercices *mpl* de culturisme *or* de musculation ▸**body corporate** (*Jur*) personne morale ▸**body count:** (*US*) **to do a body count** compter le nombre des personnes; (*after battle*) compter le nombre des morts ▸**bodyguard** (*person*) garde *m* du corps, (*group*) gardes *mpl* du corps ▸**body language** langage *m* du corps ▸**body lotion** lait *m* pour le corps ▸**body mike** micro *m* (*porté autour du cou*) ▸**body odour** odeur *f* corporelle ▸**body repair shop** (*Aut*) = **body shop** ▸**body repairs** (*Aut*) travaux *mpl* de carrosserie ▸**body scanner** scanner *m*, scanographe *m* ▸**body shop** (*Aut*) atelier *m* de carrosserie ▸**body snatcher** (*Hist*) déterreur *m* de cadavres ▸**body stocking** body *m* ▸**body swerve** (*Sport*) écart *m* ▸**body warmer** gilet matelassé ▸**body-waste disposal** (*Space*) évacuation *f* des matières organiques ▸**bodywork** (*Aut*) carrosserie *f*.

Boeotia [bɪ'əʊʃɪə] n Béotie *f*.

Boeotian [bɪ'əʊʃɪən] adj béotien.

Boer ['bəʊəʳ] 1 n Boer *mf*. **the ~ War** la guerre des Boers. 2 adj boer (*f inv*).

boffin* ['bɒfɪn] n (*Brit*) chercheur *m* (*scientifique ou technique*).

boffo‡ ['bɒfəʊ] adj (*US*) sensationnel.

bog [bɒg] 1 n a marais *m*, marécage *m*; *[peat]* tourbière *f*. b (*Brit ‡: lavatory*) goguenot‡ *m*. 2 vt (*also* ~ **down**: *gen pass*) *cart etc* embourber, enliser. (*lit, fig*) **to be** *or* **get ~ged down** s'embourber, s'enliser (*in* dans). 3 comp ▸**bog oak** chêne *m* des marais ▸**bog paper‡** (*Brit*) PQ‡ *m* ▸**bog roll‡** (*Brit*) rouleau *m* de PQ‡; **there's no bog roll** il n'y a pas de PQ‡.

bogey¹ ['bəʊgɪ] n (*frightening*) épouvantail *m*, démon *m*; (*bugbear*) bête noire. **~man** croque-mitaine *m*, père fouettard; (*fig*) **this is a ~ for them** c'est leur bête noire.

bogey² ['bəʊgɪ] n (*Golf*) bogey *m*, bogée *m*.

bogey³‡ ['bəʊgɪ] n crotte *f* de nez.

boggle ['bɒgl] 1 vi a (*be alarmed, amazed*) être ahuri. **the mind ~s!** on croit rêver!; **his mind ~d when he heard the news** la nouvelle l'a plongé dans l'ahurissement. b (*hesitate*) hésiter (*at* à), reculer (*at* devant). 2 vt (*US*) **to ~ sb's mind** époustoufler qn.

boggy ['bɒgɪ] adj *ground* marécageux, bourbeux, tourbeux.

bogie¹ ['bəʊgɪ] n = **bogey², bogey³**.

bogie² ['bəʊgɪ] n (*Rail*) bogie *m*; (*esp Brit: trolley*) diable *m*.

Bogotá [ˌbɒgə'tɑ:] n Bogotá.

bogus ['bəʊgəs] adj faux (*f* fausse), bidon‡ *inv*, simulé. ~ **transaction** transaction *f or* affaire *f* bidon‡ *inv or* à la gomme‡.

bogy ['bəʊgɪ] n = **bogey**.

Bohemia [bəʊ'hi:mɪə] n Bohême *f*.

Bohemian [bəʊ'hi:mɪən] 1 n (*Geog*) Bohémien(ne) *m(f)*; (*gipsy*) bohémien(ne); (*artist, writer etc*) bohème *mf*. 2 adj (*Geog*) bohémien; (*gipsy*) bohémien; *artist, surroundings* bohème. ~ **life** (vie *f* de) bohème *f*.

bohemianism [bəʊ'hi:mɪənɪzəm] n (vie *f* de) bohème *f*.

boil¹ [bɔɪl] 1 vi a *[water etc]* bouillir. **the kettle is ~ing** l'eau bout (dans la bouilloire); **to begin to ~** se mettre à bouillir, entrer en ébullition; **to ~ fast/gently** bouillir à gros bouillons/à petits bouillons; **to let the kettle/the vegetables ~ dry** laisser s'évaporer complètement l'eau de la bouilloire/des légumes; (*Culin*) **the potatoes were ~ing** les pommes de terre bouillaient; *see* **pot**.

b *[sea]* bouillonner; (*fig*) *[person]* bouillir (*with* de). **he was ~ing with rage** il bouillait (de rage); *see* **blood, boiling**.

2 vt a *water* faire bouillir, amener à ébullition.

b *food* (faire) cuire à l'eau, (faire) bouillir. **~ed bacon** lard bouilli; **~ed beef** bœuf bouilli, pot-au-feu *m*; **~ed egg** œuf *m* à la coque; **~ed ham** jambon cuit (à l'eau); **~ed peas** pois cuits à l'eau; **~ed potatoes** pommes *fpl* à l'anglaise *or* à l'eau; (*Brit*) **~ed sweet** bonbon *m* à sucer; **~-in-the-bag** que l'on cuit dans le sachet, ≃ prêt-à-cuire; *see* **hard, soft**.

c (*wash*) **to ~ the whites** faire bouillir le (linge) blanc; **~ed shirt*** chemise empesée.

3 n: **on the ~** (*lit*) bouillant, qui bout; (*fig*) *situation, project* en ébullition; **off the ~** (*lit*) qui ne bout plus; (*fig*) *situation* en voie d'apaisement; *project* au ralenti; **to bring to the** (*Brit*) *or* **a** (*US*) **~** faire bouillir; **to come to the** (*Brit*) *or* **a** (*US*) **~** venir à ébullition; **to go off the ~** (*lit*) cesser de bouillir; (*fig*) *[person]* baisser; (*fig*) **to bring a situation to the ~** amener une situation au point critique.

▸**boil away** vi a (*go on boiling*) bouillir très fort. b (*evaporate completely*) s'évaporer, se réduire (par ébullition).

▸**boil down** 1 vi *[jam etc]* se réduire; (*fig*) se ramener, revenir (*to* à). **all the arguments boil down to this** tous les arguments se résument *or* reviennent *or* se ramènent à ceci; **it all boils down to the same thing** tout cela revient absolument au même. 2 vt sep *sauce etc* faire réduire (par ébullition); (*fig*) *text* réduire (*to* à), abréger.

▸**boil over** vi a *[water]* déborder; *[milk]* se sauver, déborder. **the kettle boiled over** (l'eau dans) la bouilloire a débordé. b (*with rage*) bouillir (*with* de). (*fig*) **their anger boiled over into violence** leur colère a débouché sur la violence.

▸**boil up** vi (*lit*) *[milk]* monter. (*fig*) **anger was boiling up in him** la moutarde lui montait au nez; **they are boiling up* for a real row!** le torchon brûle!

boil² [bɔɪl] n (*Med*) furoncle *m*, clou *m*.

boiler ['bɔɪləʳ] 1 n a (*for hot water, steam*) chaudière *f*; (*Brit: for washing clothes*) lessiveuse *f*; (*pan*) casserole *f*; *see* **double, pot**. b (*fowl*) poule *f* à faire au pot. 2 comp ▸**boiler house** bâtiment *m* des chaudières ▸**boilermaker** chaudronnier *m* ▸**boilermaking** grosse chaudronnerie ▸**boilerman** (*Tech*) chauffeur *m* ▸**boiler room** (*gen*) salle *f* des chaudières; (*Naut*) chaufferie *f*, chambre *f* de chauffe ▸**boiler suit** (*Brit*) bleu(s) *m(pl)* (de travail *or* de chauffe).

boiling ['bɔɪlɪŋ] 1 n *[water etc]* ébullition *f*, bouillonnement *m*. 2 adj a *water, oil* bouillant. (*Brit fig*) **the whole ~‡ lot** tout le bataclan*, tout le bazar*; **it's ~ (hot) today** il fait une chaleur terrible aujourd'hui; **I'm ~ (hot)*** je meurs de chaleur! b (* *fig: angry*) bouillant de colère, en rage. **he is ~** il bout de colère. c (*Culin*) *beef* pour pot-au-feu. ~ **fowl** poule *f* à faire au pot. 3 adv: ~ **hot** (*lit*) tout bouillant; (*fig*) *see* **2**. 4 comp ▸**boiling point** point *m* d'ébullition; (*fig*) **at boiling point** à ébullition.

boisterous ['bɔɪstərəs] adj a (*rough*) *sea* tumultueux, houleux, agité; *wind* furieux, violent. b (*exuberant*) *person* tapageur, bruyant, turbulent; *meeting* houleux. ~ **spirits** gaieté bruyante *or* débordante.

boisterously ['bɔɪstərəslɪ] adv tumultueusement, bruyamment, impétueusement.

bold [bəʊld] 1 adj a (*brave*) *person, action* hardi, audacieux, intrépide. **to grow ~** s'enhardir; **a ~ step** une démarche osée *or* audacieuse; **a ~ stroke** un coup d'audace; *see* **face**.

b *person, look* (*forward*) hardi, effronté (*pej*); (*not shy*) assuré. **to be** *or* **make so ~ as to do** avoir l'audace de faire, oser faire; **to make ~ with sth** prendre la liberté de se servir de qch; **if I may make so ~ ...** si je peux me permettre de faire remarquer ...; **as ~ as brass** d'une impudence peu commune, culotté*.

c (*Art, Literat: striking*) hardi, vigoureux. **to bring out in ~ relief**

faire ressortir vigoureusement; **to paint in ~ strokes** avoir une touche puissante.
d (*Typ*) en grasse, gras.
e *cliff, coastline* escarpé, abrupt.
2 n (*NonC: Typ*) caractères *mpl* gras.

boldly ['bəʊldlɪ] adv (*see* **bold**) hardiment, audacieusement, avec audace; effrontément, avec impudence; avec vigueur, vigoureusement.

boldness ['bəʊldnɪs] n (*see* **bold**) hardiesse *f*, audace *f*, intrépidité *f*; impudence *f*, effronterie *f*; vigueur *f*, hardiesse; escarpement *m*.

bole [bəʊl] n fût *m*, tronc *m* (d'arbre).

bolero [bə'lɛərəʊ] n a (*music, dance*) boléro *m*. b ['bɒlərəʊ] (*jacket*) boléro *m*.

boletus [bəʊ'li:təs] n, pl **~s** *or* **boleti** [bəʊ'li:,taɪ] bolet *m*.

bolide ['bəʊlaɪd] n (*Astron*) bolide *m*.

Bolivia [bə'lɪvɪə] n Bolivie *f*.

Bolivian [bə'lɪvɪən] 1 n Bolivien(ne) *m(f)*. 2 adj bolivien.

boll [bəʊl] n graine *f* (*du cotonnier, du lin*). **~ weevil** anthonome *m* (*du cotonnier*).

bollard ['bɒləd] n *[quay]* bollard *m*; (*Brit*) *[road]* borne *f*.

bollix‡ ['bɒlɪks] vt (*US: also* **~ up**) = **ball(s) up 1**.

bollocking*‡ ['bɒləkɪŋ] n engueulade‡ *f*. **to give sb a ~** engueuler qn‡; **I got a real ~ from him** il m'a bien engueulé‡.

bollocks*‡ ['bɒləks] n (*Brit*) = **balls***‡; *see* **ball[1] 1h**.

Bologna [bə'ləʊnjə] n Bologne.

bolognese [bɒlə'njeɪz] adj: **~ sauce** sauce bolognaise.

boloney‡ [bə'ləʊnɪ] n (*US: sausage*) *sorte de saucisson;* (*nonsense*) idioties *fpl*, foutaises‡ *fpl*.

Bolshevik ['bɒlʃəvɪk] 1 n Bolchevik *mf*. 2 adj bolchevique.

Bolshevism ['bɒlʃəvɪzəm] n bolchevisme *m*.

Bolshevist ['bɒlʃəvɪst] n, adj bolcheviste *(mf)*.

bolshie*, **bolshy*** ['bɒlʃɪ] (*pej*) 1 n (*Pol*) rouge *mf*. 2 adj (*Pol*) rouge. (*fig*) **he's rather ~** il ne pense qu'à enquiquiner le monde*, c'est un mauvais coucheur; **he turned ~** il a commencé à râler*.

bolster ['bəʊlstəʳ] 1 n a *[bed]* traversin *m*. b (*Constr*) racinal *m*, sous-poutre *f*. 2 vt (*also* **~ up**) *person, morale* soutenir (*with* par).

bolt [bəʊlt] 1 n a *[door, window]* verrou *m*; *[lock]* pêne *m*; (*Tech: for nut*) boulon *m*; *[crossbow]* carreau *m*; *[rifle]* culasse *f* mobile; (*Climbing: also* **expansion ~**) piton *m* à expansion; *[cloth]* rouleau *m*; (*lightning*) éclair *m*. (*fig*) **a ~ from the blue** un coup de tonnerre dans un ciel bleu; *see* **shoot**.
b (*dash*) fuite soudaine, départ *m* brusque. **he made a ~ for the door** il a fait un bond *or* a bondi vers la porte; **to make a ~ for it*** filer* *or* se sauver à toutes jambes.
2 adv: **~ upright** droit comme un piquet *or* comme un i.
3 comp ▶**bolt cutters** pince *f* coupante ▶**bolt-hole** *[animal]* terrier *m*, trou *m*; *[person]* abri *m*, refuge *m*.
4 vi a (*run away*) *[horse]* s'emballer; *[person]* filer*, se sauver.
b (*move quickly*) se précipiter, foncer*. **he ~ed along the corridor** il a enfilé le couloir à toutes jambes.
c *[plant]* monter.
5 vt a *food* engouffrer, engloutir.
b *door, window* verrouiller, fermer au verrou. **~ the door!** mettez *or* poussez le(s) verrou(s)!
c (*Tech*) *beams* boulonner.
d (*US *: stop*) abandonner, laisser tomber.

▶**bolt in** 1 vi (*rush in*) entrer comme un ouragan. 2 vt sep (*lock in*) enfermer au verrou.

▶**bolt on** vt sep (*Tech*) boulonner.

▶**bolt out** vi (*rush out*) sortir comme un ouragan.

bolus ['bəʊləs] n, pl **~es** (*Med*) bol *m*.

bomb [bɒm] 1 n bombe *f*; (*US *: film etc*) fiasco *m*, bide* *m*. **letter/parcel ~** lettre *f*/paquet *m* piégé(e); **the B~** la bombe atomique; (*Brit fig*) **his party went like a ~*** sa réception a été (un succès) du tonnerre*; (*Brit fig*) **this car goes like a ~**‡ elle file, cette bagnole*; (*Brit fig*) **the car cost a ~**‡ la bagnole* a coûté les yeux de la tête; *see* **A, car, H** *etc*.
2 comp ▶**bomb aimer** (*Aviat*) bombardier *m* (*aviateur*) ▶**bomb attack** attentat *m* à la bombe ▶**bomb bay** soute *f* à bombes ▶**bomb crater** entonnoir *m* ▶**bomb disposal** déminage *m*; **bomb disposal expert** artificier *m*; **bomb disposal squad** *or* **unit** équipe *f* de déminage ▶**bombproof** blindé ▶**bomb scare** alerte *f* à la bombe ▶**bombshell** *see* **bombshell** ▶**bomb shelter** abri *m* (anti-aérien) ▶**bombsight** viseur *m* de bombardement ▶**bomb site** lieu bombardé.
3 vt *town* bombarder; *see* **dive**.
4 vi a (*US *: fail*) être un fiasco *or* un bide*.
b (**: go quickly*) **to ~ along** foncer, bomber*; **we ~ed down the road** nous avons foncé le long de la rue; **we ~ed down to London** nous avons bombé* jusqu'à Londres.

▶**bomb out** vt sep a *house* détruire par un bombardement. **the family was bombed out** la famille a dû abandonner sa maison bombardée; **bombed out families** familles sinistrées (*par bombardement*). b (* *fig: crowded*) **~ed out** bondé, plein à craquer*.

bombard [bɒm'bɑ:d] vt (*Mil, Phys, fig*) bombarder (*with* de).

bombardier [,bɒmbə'dɪəʳ] n (*Mil*) caporal *m* d'artillerie; (*Aviat*) bombardier *m* (*aviateur*).

bombardment [bɒm'bɑ:dmənt] n bombardement *m*.

bombast ['bɒmbæst] n grandiloquence *f*, boursouflure *f*.

bombastic [bɒm'bæstɪk] adj *style* ampoulé, grandiloquent, pompeux; *person* grandiloquent, pompeux.

bombastically [bɒm'bæstɪkəlɪ] adv *speak* avec grandiloquence, avec emphase; *write* dans un style ampoulé.

Bombay [bɒm'beɪ] n Bombay. (*Culin*) **~ duck** poisson salé (*pour accompagner un curry*).

bombazine ['bɒmbəzi:n] n bombasin *m*.

bomber ['bɒməʳ] 1 n (*aircraft*) bombardier *m*; (*terrorist*) plastiqueur *m*. 2 comp ▶**bomber command** aviation *f* de bombardement ▶**bomber jacket** blouson *m* d'aviateur ▶**bomber pilot** pilote *m* de bombardier.

bombing ['bɒmɪŋ] 1 n (*Aviat*) bombardement *m*; (*by terrorist*) attentat *m* à la bombe; *see* **dive**. 2 adj *raid, mission, plane* de bombardement.

bombshell ['bɒmʃel] n a (*Mil*) obus *m*. (*fig*) **to come like a ~** éclater comme une bombe, faire l'effet d'une bombe; **this news was a ~ to them** cette nouvelle leur est tombée dessus comme une bombe. b (*fig*) **she's a real ~!*** c'est une fille sensass!*

bona fide ['bəʊnə'faɪdɪ] adj *traveller* véritable; *offer* sérieux.

bona fides ['bəʊnə'faɪdɪz] n bonne foi.

bonanza [bə'nænzə] n (*fig*) aubaine *f*, filon *m*, mine *f* d'or; (*US Min*) riche filon. **~ year** année exceptionnelle; (*US*) **the B~ State** le Montana; **the North Sea oil ~** la manne pétrolière de la mer du Nord.

Bonaparte ['bəʊnəpɑ:t] n Bonaparte *m*.

bond [bɒnd] 1 n a (*agreement*) engagement *m*, obligation *f*, contrat *m*. **to enter into a ~** s'engager (*to do* à faire).
b (*link*) lien(s) *m(pl)*, attachement *m*. **to break a ~ with the past** rompre les liens avec le passé; **~s** (*chains*) fers *mpl*, chaînes *fpl*; (*fig: ties*) liens; **marriage ~s** liens conjugaux; *see* **pair**.
c (*Comm, Fin*) bon *m*, titre *m*.
d (*NonC: Comm: custody of goods*) entreposage *m* (*en attendant le paiement de la taxe*). **to put sth into ~** entreposer qch en douane; **to take goods out of ~** dédouaner des marchandises.
e (*adhesion between surfaces*) adhérence *f*.
f (*Constr*) appareil *m*.
g (*Chem*) liaison *f*.
h (*also* **~ paper**) papier *m* à lettres de luxe.
2 vt a (*Comm*) *goods* entreposer. **~ed warehouse** entrepôt *m* des douanes.
b (*stick*) coller; *bricks* liaisonner.
c (*Fin*) lier (par une garantie financière).
d (*place under bond*) placer sous caution; (*put up bond for*) se porter caution pour.
3 vi (*stick together*) coller.
4 comp ▶**bondholder** (*Fin*) porteur *m* d'obligations *or* de bons ▶**bond market** (*Fin*) marché *m* obligataire ▶**bondsman** (*Hist*) serf *m*, esclave *m*; (*Jur*) garant *m*, caution *f*.

bondage ['bɒndɪdʒ] n a (*lit*) esclavage *m*, servage *m*. (*Hist*) **to be in ~ to** être le serf de. b (*fig*) esclavage *m*, asservissement *m*.

bonding ['bɒndɪŋ] n (*Constr*) liaison *f*; *[wood, plastic etc]* collage *m* (*à la résine synthétique*); (*Elec*) système *or* circuit régulateur de tension; (*Psych*) liens affectifs (*entre parents et enfants*).

bone [bəʊn] 1 n a os *m*; *[fish]* arête *f*. **~s** *[the dead]* ossements *mpl*, os *mpl*, restes *mpl*; (*Mus*) castagnettes *fpl*; (‡*: dice*) dés *mpl* (à jouer); **chilled to the ~** transi de froid, glacé jusqu'à la moelle (des os); (*hum*) **my old ~s** mes vieux os, ma vieille carcasse*; (*fig*) **I feel it in my ~s** j'en ai le pressentiment, quelque chose me le dit; **~ of contention** pomme *f* de discorde; (*fig*) **to have a ~ to pick with sb** avoir un compte à régler avec qn; **he made no ~s about saying what he thought** il n'a pas hésité à dire ce qu'il pensait; **he made no ~s about it** il n'y est pas allé avec le dos de la cuiller* *or* par quatre chemins, il y est allé carrément; **there are no ~s broken** (*lit*) il n'y a rien de cassé; (*fig*) il y a plus de peur que de mal, il n'y a rien de grave; (*fig*) **he won't make old ~s** il ne fera pas de vieux os*; *see* **ankle, bag 1, skin, work** *etc*.
b (*NonC: substance*) os *m*. **~ handle, handle (made) of ~** manche *m* en os.
c *[corset]* baleine *f*.
2 comp *buttons etc* en os ▶**bone china** porcelaine *f* tendre ▶**bone-dry** absolument sec (*f* sèche) ▶**bonehead**‡ crétin(e)* *m(f)*, abruti(e)* *m(f)* ▶**boneheaded**‡ idiot ▶**bone-idle***, **bone-lazy*** fainéant *or* paresseux comme un loir *or* comme une couleuvre ▶**bone meal** engrais *m* (de cendres d'os) ▶**bone-shaker**‡ (*car*) vieille guimbarde, tacot* *m*; (†*: cycle*) vélocipède† *m* (*sans pneus*) ▶**boneyard*** (*US*) cimetière *m*.
3 vt a *meat, fowl* désosser; *fish* ôter les arêtes de.
b (‡*: steal*) piquer*, barboter*.

▶**bone up**‡ vt sep, **bone up on**‡ vt fus *subject* bûcher*, potasser*, bosser‡.

boned [bəʊnd] adj a *meat* désossé; *fish* sans arêtes. b *corset* baleiné.

boneless ['bəʊnlɪs] adj *meat* désossé, sans os; *fish* sans arêtes.

boner‡ ['bəʊnəʳ] n (*US*) gaffe *f*, bourde *f*. **to pull a ~** faire une gaffe*, mettre les pieds dans le plat.
bonfire ['bɒnfaɪəʳ] n feu *m* (de joie); (*for rubbish*) feu (de jardin). (*Brit*) **B~ Night** le 5 novembre (*commémoration de la tentative infructueuse de Guy Fawkes en 1605 de faire sauter le Parlement anglais*).
bong [bɒŋ] n bong *m*.
bongo (drum) ['bɒŋgəʊ(drʌm)] n (tambour *m*) bongo *m*.
bonhomie ['bɒnɒmi:] n bonhomie *f*.
bonk [bɒŋk] 1 n a (**: hit*) coup *m*; (*with hand*) beigne‡ *f*, pain* *m*. b (*sex*) **to have a ~‡** s'envoyer en l'air‡. 2 vi (*‡: have sex*) s'envoyer en l'air‡. 3 vt a (**: hit*) frapper, filer un coup à*; (*with hand also*) filer une beigne‡ *or* un pain* à. b (*‡: have sex with*) s'envoyer‡, sauter‡. 4 excl bang.
bonkers‡ ['bɒŋkəz] adj (*Brit*) cinglé*, dingue*.
bonking‡ ['bɒŋkɪŋ] n partie *f* de jambe en l'air‡.
Bonn [bɒn] n Bonn.
bonnet ['bɒnɪt] n a (*hat*) *[woman]* capote *f*, bonnet *m*, chapeau *m* à brides; *[child]* béguin *m*, bonnet; (*Scot dial*) *[man]* béret *m*, bonnet; *see* **bee, sun** *etc*. b (*Brit Aut*) capot *m*. c (*Archit*) auvent *m*; *[chimney]* capuchon *m*. d (*Naut*) bonnette *f*.
bonny ['bɒnɪ] adj (*esp Scot*) joli, beau (*f* belle).
bonsai ['bɒnsaɪ] n, pl inv bonsai *m*.
bonus ['bəʊnəs] n gratification *f*, prime *f*; (*Comm*) prime; (*Brit Fin*) dividende exceptionnel; (*Educ, Cycling*) bonification *f*. **~ of 500 francs** 500 F de prime; (*fig*) **as a ~** en prime; (*Fin*) **~ issue** émission *f* d'actions gratuites; **~ share** action gratuite; *see* **incentive, no** *etc*.
bony ['bəʊnɪ] adj a (*Anat*) *tissue* osseux; (*fig*) *knee, person* anguleux, maigre, décharné. b *fish* plein d'arêtes; *meat* plein d'os.
boo [bu:] 1 excl hou!, peuh! **he wouldn't say ~ to a goose*** il n'ose jamais ouvrir le bec*. 2 vt *actor, play* huer, siffler, conspuer. **to be ~ed off the stage** sortir de scène sous les huées *or* les sifflets. 3 vi huer. 4 n huée *f*.
boob‡ [bu:b] 1 n a (*Brit: mistake*) gaffe *f*; (*silly person*) ballot* *m*, nigaud(e) *m(f)*. b (*breast*) sein *m*, nichon‡ *m*. 2 vi (*Brit*) gaffer. 3 comp ▸**boobtube** (*US: TV set*) télé *f*; (*Dress: sun top*) bain *m* de soleil.
boo-boo‡ ['bu:'bu:] n boulette‡ *f*, bourde *f*.
booby ['bu:bɪ] 1 n nigaud(e) *m(f)*, bêta(sse)* *m(f)*. 2 comp ▸**booby hatch** (*Naut*) écoutillon *m*; (*US pej ‡: mental hospital*) cabanon‡ *m* ▸**booby prize** prix *m* de consolation (*décerné au dernier*) ▸**booby trap** traquenard *m*; (*Mil*) objet piégé ▸**booby-trapped** *car, door etc* piégé.
boodle‡† ['bu:dl] n (*money*) oseille‡ *f*, pèze‡ *m*; (*US: bribe*) pot-de-vin *m*. (*US*) **the whole ~** le tout, tous les trucs*.
booger‡ [bu:gəʳ] n (*US*) crotte *f* de nez.
boogie* ['bu:gɪ] 1 n (*dance*) **to have a ~** guincher*; **to go for a ~** aller guincher* *or* se trémousser*. 2 vi guincher*.
boogie-woogie ['bu:gɪ,wu:gɪ] n boogie-woogie *m*.
boohoo* [,bu:'hu:] 1 vi pleurnicher, brailler*. 2 excl ouin! ouin!
booing ['bu:ɪŋ] n huées *fpl*.
book [bʊk] 1 n a livre *m*, bouquin* *m*. **the (Good) B~** la Bible; *see* **bank², telephone, text** *etc*.
b (*division*) *[Bible etc]* livre *m*; *[poem]* chant *m*. (*Bible*) **the B~ of Job/Kings** *etc* le livre de Job/des Rois *etc*.
c (*also* **exercise ~**) cahier *m*; *see* **note**.
d *[tickets, stamps, cheques etc]* carnet *m*. **~ of matches** pochette *f* d'allumettes; *see* **cheque, pass**.
e (*Comm, Fin*) **(account)** **~s** livre *m* de comptes; **to keep the ~s of a firm** tenir les livres *or* la comptabilité *or* les comptes *mpl* d'une firme; **the ~s and records** la comptabilité.
f *[club, society]* registre *m*. **to be on the ~s of an organization** être inscrit à une organisation; **to take one's name off the ~s** donner sa démission.
g (*Betting*) **to keep a ~ on sth** prendre les paris sur qch; **to make a ~** (*take bets*) inscrire les paris; (*bet*) parier; **to open** *or* **start a ~ (on sth)** ouvrir les paris sur qch.
h (*libretto*) *[opera etc]* livret *m*.
i (*Comm*) **~ of samples** album *m or* jeu *m* d'échantillons.
j (*phrases*) **to bring sb to ~** obliger qn à rendre des comptes; **by the ~** selon les règles; **to go by the ~, to stick to the ~** appliquer strictement le règlement; **I am in his good ~s** je suis dans ses petits papiers*, il m'a à la bonne‡; **to be in sb's bad** *or* **black ~s** être mal vu de qn; (*fig*) **in my ~* he's unreliable** à mon avis *or* d'après moi on ne peut pas se fier à lui; **he knew the district like a ~** il connaissait la région comme sa poche; **that's one for the ~!*** c'est à marquer d'une pierre blanche!, il faut faire une croix à la cheminée!; **already on the ~s** *[regulation etc]* qui figure déja dans les textes; *[member etc]* déjà inscrit au registre; **to go on the ~s** entrer en vigueur; *see* **suit, throw**.
2 comp ▸**bookbinder** relieur *m*, -euse *f* ▸**bookbinding** reliure *f* (*NonC*) ▸**bookcase** bibliothèque *f* (*meuble*) ▸**book club** cercle *m* de lecture, club *m* du livre ▸**book ends** serre-livres *m inv*, presse-livres *m inv* ▸**book fair** salon *m* du livre ▸**book jacket** jaquette *f* ▸**bookkeeper** comptable *mf* ▸**book-keeping** comptabilité *f* ▸**book knowledge, book learning** connaissances *fpl* livresques ▸**book lover** bibliophile *mf* ▸**bookmaker** bookmaker *m* ▸**bookmark** marque *f*, signet *m* ▸**bookmobile** (*US*) bibliobus *m* ▸**bookplate** ex-libris *m inv* ▸**book post** tarif *m* livres *inv* ▸**bookrest** support *m* à livres ▸**bookseller** libraire *mf* (*see* **secondhand**) ▸**bookshelf** rayon *m* (de bibliothèque), étagère *f* (à livres) ▸**bookshop** librairie *f*; **secondhand bookshop** boutique *f* de livres d'occasion ▸**bookstall** (*Brit*) *[station etc]* kiosque *m* à journaux; *[secondhand books]* étalage *m* de bouquiniste ▸**bookstore** librairie *f* ▸**book token** (*Brit*) bon-cadeau *m* (*négociable en librairie*), chèque-livre *m* ▸**bookworm** (*fig*) rat *m* de bibliothèque.
3 vt a *seat* louer; *room, sleeper* retenir, réserver; (*Brit*) *ticket* prendre. **to ~ one's seat in advance** louer sa place à l'avance *or* d'avance; (*Theat*) **tonight's performance is ~ed up** *or* **fully ~ed** on joue à bureaux fermés *or* à guichets fermés ce soir; **the hotel is ~ed up** *or* **fully ~ed** l'hôtel est complet; **I'm ~ed for tomorrow lunch** je suis pris demain à déjeuner; **~ed solid** *[hotel, film etc]* archi-complet; *[person]* complètement pris; (*Rail*) **to ~ sb through to Birmingham** assurer à qn une réservation jusqu'à Birmingham; **I've ~ed (up) my holiday** j'ai fait les réservations pour mes vacances.
b (*Comm, Fin*) *order* inscrire, enregistrer. **to ~ goods to sb's account** inscrire des marchandises au compte de qn.
c (*Police*) *driver etc* donner *or* mettre un procès-verbal *or* P.-V.* à; (*Ftbl*) *player* montrer un carton jaune à. **to be ~ed for speeding** attraper une contravention *or* une contredanse* pour excès de vitesse; (*Ftbl*) **to be ~ed** recevoir un carton jaune.
4 vi réserver. **to ~ into a hotel** réserver une chambre dans un hôtel.
▸**book in** 1 vi (*at hotel etc*) prendre une chambre. 2 vt sep *person* réserver une chambre à.
▸**book up** 1 vi réserver. 2 vt sep retenir, réserver. **the school booked up all the seats on the coach** l'école a réservé toutes les places dans le car; **the tour is booked up** on ne prend plus d'inscriptions pour l'excursion; **the hotel is booked up** *or* **fully booked until September** l'hôtel est complet jusqu'en septembre; **I'm very booked up** je suis très pris; *see also* **book 3a**.
bookable ['bʊkəbl] adj *seat etc* qu'on peut retenir *or* réserver *or* louer. **seats ~ in advance** on peut retenir ses places (à l'avance); **seats ~ from 6th June** location (des places) ouverte dès le 6 juin.
bookie* ['bʊkɪ] n book‡ *m*, bookmaker *m*.
booking ['bʊkɪŋ] 1 n a (*esp Brit*) réservation *f*. **to make a ~** louer, réserver, faire une réservation. b (*Ftbl*) **there were 3 ~s at the game** l'arbitre a dû prendre le nom de 3 joueurs durant le match. 2 comp ▸**booking clerk** (*Brit: Rail etc*) préposé(e) *m(f)* aux réservations ▸**booking office** (*Brit: Rail, Theat*) (bureau *m* de) location *f*.
bookish ['bʊkɪʃ] adj qui aime les livres *or* la lecture, studieux; *word, phrase* livresque.
booklet ['bʊklɪt] n petit livre, brochure *f*, plaquette *f*.
Boolean ['bu:lɪən] adj booléen.
boom¹ [bu:m] n a (*barrier: across river etc*) barrage *m* (*de radeaux, de chaînes etc*), bôme *f*. b *[boat]* gui *m*; (*Tech: also* **derrick ~**) bras *m*; *[crane]* flèche *f*; *[microphone, camera]* perche *f*, girafe *f*.
boom² [bu:m] 1 n (*sound*) *[sea, waves]* grondement *m*, mugissement *m*; *[wind]* mugissement, hurlements *mpl*; *[guns, thunder]* grondement; *[storm]* rugissement *m*; *[organ]* ronflement *m*; *[voices]* rugissement, grondement. (*Aviat*) **sonic ~** bang *m* supersonique. 2 vi a *[sea]* gronder, mugir; *[wind]* hurler, mugir (sourdement); *[thunder]* gronder, rouler. b (*also* **~ out**) *[organ]* ronfler; *[guns]* tonner, gronder; *[voice]* retentir, résonner, tonner; *[person]* tonner, tonitruer. 3 vt **"never!" he ~ed** "jamais", dit-il d'une voix tonitruante.
boom³ [bu:m] 1 vi a (*Comm*) *[trade]* être en expansion *or* en hausse, prospérer. **business is ~ing** le commerce marche très bien *or* est en plein essor; **his books are ~ing** ses livres marchent très bien *or* se vendent comme des petits pains.
b (*Comm, Fin, St Ex*) *[prices]* monter en flèche.
2 vt (*US **) *market, sales* développer; (*publicize*) *person, place* promouvoir.
3 n (*Comm*) *[business, transactions]* montée *f* en flèche, forte hausse; *[firm]* forte progression; *[product]* popularité *f*, vogue *f*, boom *m*; *[sales]* progression *f*, accroissement *m*; (*Comm, Fin, St Ex*) *[prices, shares]* brusque *or* très forte hausse; (*Econ: period of economic growth*) (vague *f* de) prospérité *f*, boom.
4 comp ▸**boom baby** bébé *m* du baby boom ▸**boom town** ville *f* en plein développement, ville champignon *inv*.
boomerang ['bu:məræŋ] 1 n (*lit, fig*) boomerang *m*. 2 vi (*fig*) *[words, actions]* faire boomerang.
booming ['bu:mɪŋ] adj *sound* retentissant; *voice* tonitruant.
boomlet ['bu:mlɪt] n (*Econ*) expansion *f* de faible amplitude.
boon [bu:n] 1 n a (*blessing*) bénédiction* *f*, aubaine *f*. **it would be a ~ if he went** quelle aubaine s'il s'en allait; **this new machine is a great ~** cette nouvelle machine est une bénédiction*; **it is a ~ to me** cela m'est très précieuse. b (*††: favour*) faveur *f*. 2 comp ▸**boon companion** joyeux compère, compagnon *m* de virée.
boondocks* ['bu:ndɒks] npl (*Mil sl*) brousse *f*, bled *m*. (*US*) **the ~** le bled* (*pej*).

boondoggle⁑ ['buːndɒgl] **vi** (*US*) a (*work uselessly*) passer son temps à des tâches secondaires. b (*esp Pol*) créer des emplois bidon*.

boonies⁑ ['buːnɪz] **npl** = **boondocks***.

boor [bʊəʳ] **n** (*coarse*) rustre *m*; (*ill-mannered*) malotru(e) *m(f)*, butor *m*.

boorish ['bʊərɪʃ] **adj** rustre, grossier, malappris.

boorishly ['bʊərɪʃlɪ] **adv** (*see* **boor**) *behave* en rustre; *speak* grossièrement.

boorishness ['bʊərɪʃnɪs] **n** rudesse *f*, manque *m* d'éducation *or* de savoir-vivre, goujaterie *f*.

boost [buːst] 1 **n**: **to give sb a ~ (up)** (*lit*) soulever qn par derrière *or* par en dessous; (*fig: also* **give a ~ to sb's morale**) remonter le moral à qn; (*do publicity for*) **to give sb/a product a ~** faire du battage* pour qn/un produit.

2 **vt** a (*Elec*) survolter; (*Aut*) *engine* suralimenter. **the rockets ~ed the spacecraft** les fusées ont propulsé le vaisseau spatial. b (*Comm, Ind etc: increase*) *price* hausser, faire monter; *output, productivity* accroître, développer; *sales, product* promouvoir, faire monter en flèche; *confidence etc* renforcer. (*Econ*) **to ~ the economy** donner du tonus à l'économie. c (*do publicity for*) *person, product* faire de la réclame *or* du battage* pour.

booster ['buːstəʳ] **n** (*Elec*) (*device*) survolteur *m*; (*charge*) charge *f* d'appoint; (*Rad*) amplificateur *m*; (*Rail*) booster *m*; (*Space: also* **~ rocket**) fusée *f* de lancement, booster; (*Med: also* **~ shot, ~ dose**) (piqûre *f* de) rappel *m*; (*US* *: *supporter*) supporter actif *or* enthousiaste.

boot¹ [buːt] 1 **n** a (*gen*) botte *f*; (*ankle ~*) bottillon *m*; (*men's fashion*) boot *m*; (*wellington ~*) botte (en caoutchouc); (*lady's button ~*) bottine *f*; (*jack~, riding ~*) botte à l'écuyère; *[soldier]* brodequin *m*; *[workman etc]* grosse chaussure (montante), brodequin. (*Brit fig*) **the ~ is on the other foot** les rôles sont renversés; (*fig*) **to give sb (the order of) the ~⁑** flanquer* qn à la porte, sacquer* qn; **to get** *or* **be given the ~⁑** être flanqué* à la porte, être sacqué*; (*Brit*) **B~s** garçon *m* d'hôtel; *see* **bet, big, die¹, lick** *etc*.

b (*Brit*) *[car etc]* coffre *m*, malle *f* (arrière).

c (*Hist: for torture*) brodequin *m*.

2 **vt** donner *or* flanquer* des coups de pied à; (*Comput: also* **~ up**) amorcer. (*lit, fig* *) **to ~ sb out** flanquer* qn à la porte.

3 **comp** ►**bootblack** cireur *m* (de chaussures) ►**booting up** (*Comput*) remise *f* à zéro; **booting up switch** commande *f* de remise à zéro ►**bootlace** lacet *m* (de chaussure) ►**bootleg*** (*US*) **vi** faire la contrebande de l'alcool *or* des boissons alcooliques ◊ **vt** vendre *or* importer en contrebande, fabriquer illicitement ◊ **adj** *spirits* de contrebande ►**bootlegger⁑** (*US*) bootlegger *m* ►**bootlicker** lécheur* *m*, -euse* *f*, lèche-bottes* *mf inv* ►**bootmaker** bottier *m* ►**boot-polish** cirage *m* ►**boot sale** = **car boot sale** *see* **car 2** ►**boot scraper** décrottoir *m* ►**bootstrap** (*lit*) tirant *m* de botte; (*Comput*) programme *m* amorce, amorce *f*; **to pull o.s. up by one's (own) bootstraps** se faire tout seul.

boot² [buːt] **n**: **to ~** par-dessus le marché, en plus, de plus, par surcroît; **and his insolence to ~** sans parler de son insolence.

bootee [buː'tiː] **n** *[baby]* petit chausson (*tricoté*); *[woman]* bottillon *m*.

booth [buːð] **n** *[fair]* baraque *f* (foraine); *[cinema, language laboratory, telephone etc]* cabine *f*; (*voting ~*) isoloir *m*.

bootless ['buːtlɪs] **adj** a (*without boots*) sans bottes. b (*liter: to no avail*) infructueux.

booty ['buːtɪ] **n** butin *m*.

booze* [buːz] 1 **n** (*NonC*) boisson(s) *f(pl)* alcoolisée(s). **bring the ~** apporte à boire; **I'm going to buy some ~** je vais acheter à boire; **to go on the ~** picoler⁑; **he's on the ~ just now** il picole⁑ *or* biberonne* pas mal ces temps-ci; **he's off the ~** il ne boit plus. 2 **vi** biberonner*, lever le coude*. 3 **comp** ►**booze-up⁑** (*Brit*) beuverie *f*, partie *f* de soûlographie*.

boozed⁑ [buːzd] **adj** bourré⁑, bituré⁑.

boozer⁑ ['buːzəʳ] **n** a (*drunkard*) pochard(e)⁑ *m(f)*, poivrot(e)⁑ *m(f)*, soûlard(e)⁑ *m(f)*. b (*Brit: pub*) bistro* *m*.

boozy⁑ ['buːzɪ] **adj** *person* qui a la dalle en pente⁑, pochard⁑, soûlard⁑. **~ party** (partie *f* de) soûlographie* *f*.

bop¹ [bɒp] 1 **n** a (*Mus*) bop *m*. b (*: *dance*) **to have a ~** guincher*. 2 **vi** guincher*.

bop²⁑ [bɒp] **vt** (*hit*) cogner⁑, taper.

►**bop off** **vi** (*US*) filer.

bo-peep [bəʊ'piːp] **n** cache-cache *m*. **Little Bo-Peep** la petite bergère (*chanson enfantine*).

boraces ['bɔːrəˌsiːz] **npl of borax**.

boracic [bə'ræsɪk] **adj** borique.

borage ['bɒrɪdʒ] **n** bourrache *f*.

borax ['bɔːræks] **n, pl ~es** *or* **boraces** borax *m*.

Bordeaux [bɔː'dəʊ] **n** a (*Geog*) Bordeaux. **native of ~** Bordelais(e) *m(f)*. b (*wine*) bordeaux *m*.

bordello [bɔː'deləʊ] **n** maison *f* de tolérance.

border ['bɔːdəʳ] 1 **n** a (*edge, side*) *[lake]* bord *m*, rive *f*; *[woods, field]* lisière *f*, limite *f*, bordure *f*.

b (*boundary, frontier*) frontière *f*, limite *f*. **within the ~s of** dans les limites *or* frontières de, à l'intérieur des frontières de; **to escape over the ~** s'enfuir en passant la frontière; **on the ~s of France** aux frontières françaises; (*Brit Geog*) **the B~s** la région frontière du sud-est de l'Écosse.

c *[garden]* bordure *f*, plate-bande *f*; *see* **herbaceous**.

d (*edging*) *[carpet, dress]* bord *m*; *[picture]* bordure *f*, encadrement *m*, cadre *m*. *[notepaper]* **black ~** liseré noir.

2 **comp** *state, post* frontière *inv*; *zone, town* frontière *inv*, frontalier; *search, taxes* à la frontière ►**Border** (*Brit Geog*) **adj** du sud-est de l'Écosse ►**border dispute** différend *m* sur une question de frontière(s) ►**border incident** incident *m* de frontière ►**borderland** pays *m* frontière, région *f* limitrophe; (*fig*) **on the borderland of sleep** aux frontières du sommeil et de la veille ►**borderline** ligne *f* de démarcation; **borderline case** cas *m* limite ►**border patrol** (*US Police*) patrouille frontalière ►**border police** police *f* de l'air et des frontières ►**border raid** incursion *f*.

3 **vt** a *[trees etc]* (*line edges of*) border; (*surround*) entourer, encadrer.

b **France ~s Germany** la France touche à l'Allemagne, la France et l'Allemagne ont une frontière commune; **~ing countries** pays avoisinants *or* limitrophes.

►**border (up)on** **vt fus** a *[esp country]* être limitrophe de, avoisiner. **the two countries border (up)on one another** les deux pays ont une frontière commune *or* se touchent; **his estate borders (up)on mine** sa propriété et la mienne se touchent. b (*fig: come near to being*) être voisin *or* proche de, frôler. **to border (up)on insanity** être voisin de *or* frôler la folie; **it borders (up)on fanaticism** cela touche au fanatisme, cela frise le fanatisme; **with a boldness bordering (up)on insolence** avec une hardiesse qui frisait l'insolence.

borderer ['bɔːdərəʳ] **n** frontalier *m*, -ière *f*; (*Brit*) Écossais(e) *m(f)* *or* Anglais(e) *m(f)* frontalier (*f* -ière).

bore¹ [bɔːʳ] 1 **vt** a *hole* percer; *well* forer, creuser; *tunnel* creuser, percer. b *rock* forer. **to ~ one's way through** se frayer un chemin en creusant *or* en forant à travers. 2 **vi** forer, sonder. **to ~ for oil** forer (le sous-sol) pour extraire du pétrole, rechercher du pétrole par sondage *or* forage. 3 **n** a (*also* **~hole**) trou *m* de sonde. b *[tube, pipe, shot, gun, musical instrument]* calibre *m*. **a 12-~ shotgun** un fusil de (calibre) 12.

bore² [bɔːʳ] 1 **n** (*person*) raseur* *m*, -euse* *f*, casse-pieds* *mf inv*, importun(e) *m(f)*; (*event, situation*) ennui *m*, corvée *f*, scie* *f*. **what a ~ he is!** ce qu'il peut être ennuyeux! *or* raseur!* *or* casse-pieds!*; **it's a frightful ~ to have to do that** quel ennui *or* quelle barbe* *or* quelle scie* d'avoir à faire cela; **what a ~ this meeting is!** quelle corvée cette réunion! 2 **vt** ennuyer, assommer, raser*, casser les pieds* à. **to ~ sb stiff*** *or* **to death*** *or* **to tears*, to ~ the pants off sb⁑** ennuyer qn à mourir *or* mortellement.

bore³ [bɔːʳ] **pret of bear¹**.

bore⁴ [bɔːʳ] **n** (*tidal wave*) mascaret *m*.

bored [bɔːd] **adj** *person* qui s'ennuie; *look* de quelqu'un qui s'ennuie. **to be ~ rigid*** *or* **stiff*** *or* **to death*** *or* **to tears*** s'ennuyer ferme *or* à mourir, se casser les pieds*; **to be ~ (with doing)** s'ennuyer (à faire); **I am ~ with this work/this book/this film** ce travail/ce livre/ce film m'ennuie *or* m'assomme *or* me rase*; **he was ~ with reading** il en avait assez de lire.

boredom ['bɔːdəm] **n** ennui *m*. **his ~ with the whole proceedings** l'ennui que lui inspirait toute cette cérémonie.

borer ['bɔːrəʳ] **n** a (*Tech: tool*) (*for wood*) vrille *f*, perforatrice *f*, foret *m*; (*for metal cylinders*) alésoir *m*; (*for a well, mine*) foret, sonde *f*; (*person*) foreur *m*, perceur *m*. b (*Zool: insect*) insecte térébrant.

boric ['bɔːrɪk] **adj** borique.

boring¹ ['bɔːrɪŋ] (*Tech*) 1 **n** (*see* **borer a**) perforation *f*, forage *m*; alésage *m*; sondage *m*. 2 **adj**: **~ machine** (*gen*) perforatrice *f*; (*for metal cylinders*) alésoir *m*.

boring² ['bɔːrɪŋ] **adj** (*tedious*) ennuyeux, assommant, rasant*.

born [bɔːn] 1 **adj** a né. **to be ~** naître; **to be ~ again** renaître (*see also* **2**); **~ in Paris** né à Paris; **the town where he was ~** la ville où il est né, sa ville natale; **Napoleon was ~ in 1769** Napoléon naquit en 1769; **3 sons ~ to her** 3 fils nés d'elle; **every baby ~ into the world** tout enfant qui vient au monde; **when he was ~** quand il est né; **~ and bred** né et élevé; **a Parisian ~ and bred** un Parisien de souche; (*fig*) **he wasn't ~ yesterday*** il n'est pas né d'hier *or* de la dernière pluie; **in all my ~ days*** de toute ma vie; **high/low~** de haute/de basse extraction; **~ of poor parents** né de parents pauvres; **people ~ to riches** ceux qui naissent riches; **poets are ~, not made** on naît poète, on ne le devient pas; **qualities ~ in him** qualités innées (en lui); (*fig*) **misfortunes ~ of war** malheurs dûs à la guerre; **anger ~ of frustration** colère *f* issue de la frustration; **there's one ~ every minute*** je (*or* il *etc*) tombe toujours dans le panneau*; *see* **first, new, silver, still²** *etc*.

b (*innate*) **a ~ poet** un poète-né; **~ fool** parfait idiot; *see* **loser**.

2 **comp** ►**born-again** (*fig*) régénéré; **born-again Christian** évangéliste *m*.

-born [bɔːn] **adj ending in comps** natif de + *n*, originaire de + *n*, d'origine + *adj*. **Chicago-born** natif *or* originaire de Chicago, né à Chicago;

Australian-born d'origine australienne.
borne [bɔːn] ptp of **bear**[1].
...borne [bɔːn] adj ending in comps: **airborne** *assault, troops* aérien; *supplies* transporté par air; **seaborne** *assault, troops, traffic* maritime; *supplies* transporté par mer; **waterborne** *disease* véhiculé par l'eau.
Borneo ['bɔːnɪəʊ] n Bornéo *m*.
boron ['bɔːrɒn] n bore *m*.
borough ['bʌrə] n municipalité *f*; (*in London*) arrondissement *m*; (*Brit Parl*) circonscription électorale urbaine.
borrow ['bɒrəʊ] vt *money, word, book* emprunter (*from* à); (*fig*) *idea etc* emprunter (*from* à), adapter (*from* de). **a ~ed word** un mot d'emprunt; (*US*) **to ~ trouble** voir toujours tout en noir; (*Math: in subtraction*) **~ 10** ≃ j'ajoute 10.
borrower ['bɒrəʊəʳ] n emprunteur *m*, -euse *f*.
borrowing ['bɒrəʊɪŋ] n (*Fin, Ling*) emprunt *m*. (*Econ, Fin*) **~ rate** taux *m* d'intérêt des emprunts.
Borstal ['bɔːstl] n (*Brit Jur* †) ≃ maison *f* de redressement†. **~ boy** jeune délinquant (*qui est ou a été en maison de redressement*).
borzoi ['bɔːzɔɪ] n (lévrier *m*) barzoï *m*.
bosh†* [bɒʃ] n blague(s)* *f(pl)*, bêtises *fpl*, foutaises‡ *fpl*.
bosk [bɒsk] n, **bosket** ['bɒskət] n (*plantation*) bosquet *m*; (*thicket*) fourré *m*.
bos'n ['bəʊsn] n = **boatswain**.
Bosnia ['bɒznɪə] n Bosnie *f*. **~-Herzegovina** Bosnie-Herzégovine *f*.
Bosnian ['bɒznɪən] 1 adj bosnien, bosniaque. 2 n Bosnien(ne) *m(f)*, Bosniaque *mf*.
bosom ['bʊzəm] n *[person]* poitrine *f*, seins *mpl*; *[dress]* corsage *m*; (*fig*) sein, milieu *m*, fond *m*. **in the ~ of the family** au sein de la famille; (*liter*) **the ~ of the earth** les entrailles *fpl* (*liter*) de la terre; **~ friend** ami(e) *m(f)* intime *or* de cœur.
bosomy ['bʊzəmɪ] adj à la poitrine généreuse.
Bosphorus ['bɒsfərəs] n, **Bosporus** ['bɒspərəs] n: **the ~** le Bosphore.
bosquet ['bɒskɪt] n = **bosk**.
BOSS [bɒs] (*South Africa*) abbr of **Bureau of State Security**.
boss[1]* [bɒs] 1 n patron(ne) *m(f)*, chef *m*; *[gang etc]* caïd‡ *m*; (*US Pol*) chef (du parti). **to be one's own ~** être son propre patron; **we'll have to show him who's ~** il va falloir lui montrer qui commande ici; **who's the ~ round here?** qui est le chef ici?; **it's his wife who is the ~** c'est sa femme qui porte la culotte*. 2 vt *person* mener, régenter; *organization* mener, diriger, faire marcher. 3 adj (*US* ‡: *terrific*) formidable, terrible*.
►**boss about*, boss around*** vt sep *person* mener à la baguette, régenter.
boss[2] [bɒs] 1 n (*knob*) *[shield]* ombon *m*; (*Archit*) bossage *m*; (*Tech*) mamelon *m*, bossage; *[propeller]* moyeu *m*. 2 comp ►**boss-eyed***: **to be boss-eyed** loucher.
bossy* ['bɒsɪ] adj autoritaire, tyrannique. **she's very ~** elle aime mener tout le monde à la baguette, c'est un vrai gendarme*.
Boston ['bɒstən] n Boston. (*US*) **~ ivy** vigne *f* vierge.
Bostonian [bɒs'təʊnɪən] n Bostonien(ne) *m(f)*.
bosun ['bəʊsn] n = **boatswain**.
botanic(al) [bə'tænɪk(əl)] adj botanique. **~ garden** jardin *m* botanique.
botanist ['bɒtənɪst] n botaniste *mf*.
botanize ['bɒtənaɪz] vi herboriser.
botany ['bɒtənɪ] n (*NonC*) botanique *f*. **~ wool** laine *f* mérinos.
botch [bɒtʃ] 1 vt (*also* **~ up**) (*repair*) rafistoler*; (*bungle*) saboter, bousiller*, cochonner‡. 2 n (*also* **~-up**): **to make a ~ of sth** bousiller* *or* saboter qch; **a ~ job*** un travail bâclé *or* de cochon‡ *or* de sagouin‡.
both [bəʊθ] 1 adj les deux, l'un(e) et l'autre. **~ books are his** les deux livres sont à lui, les livres sont à lui tous les deux; **on ~ sides** des deux côtés, de part et d'autre; **to hold sth in ~ hands** tenir qch à *or* des deux mains; (*fig*) **you can't have it ~ ways*** il faut choisir.
2 pron tous (les) deux *m*, toutes (les) deux *f*, l'un(e) et l'autre *m(f)*. **~ (of them) were there, they were ~ there** ils étaient là tous les deux; **from ~ of us** de nous deux; **~ of us agree** nous sommes d'accord tous les deux; **~ alike** l'un comme l'autre.
3 adv: **~ this and that** non seulement ceci mais aussi cela, aussi bien ceci que cela; **~ you and I saw him** nous l'avons vu vous et moi, vous et moi (nous) l'avons vu; **~ Paul and I came** Paul et moi sommes venus tous les deux; **she was ~ laughing and crying** elle riait et pleurait à la fois; **he can ~ read and write** il sait et lire et écrire.
bother ['bɒðəʳ] 1 vt (*annoy*) ennuyer, raser*, embêter*; (*pester*) harceler; (*worry*) inquiéter, ennuyer. **don't ~ me!** laisse-moi tranquille!, fiche-moi la paix!*, ne viens pas m'embêter!*; **don't ~ him with your problems** ne l'embête pas* *or* ne l'ennuie pas avec tes problèmes; **I'm sorry to ~ you** je m'excuse de vous déranger; **does it ~ you if I smoke?** ça vous ennuie *or* dérange que je fume? (*subj*) *or* si je fume?; **to ~ o.s. about sth** se tracasser au sujet de qch, se mettre martel en tête au sujet de qch; **to be ~ed about sb/sth** se faire du souci *or* s'inquiéter au sujet de qn/qch; **which do you prefer? — I'm not ~ed** lequel tu préfères? — ça m'est égal; **to get (all hot and) ~ed*** se mettre dans tous ses états (*about* au sujet de); **I can't be ~ed going out** *or* **to go out** je n'ai pas le courage de sortir; **are you going? — I can't be ~ed** tu y vas? — non, je n'en ai pas envie *or* non, ça me casse les pieds*; **his leg ~s him a lot** sa jambe le fait pas mal souffrir.
2 vi se donner la peine (*to do* de faire). **please don't ~ to get up!** ne vous donnez pas la peine de vous lever!; **you needn't ~ to come** ce n'est pas la peine de venir; **don't ~ about me/about my lunch** ne vous occupez pas de moi/de mon déjeuner, ne vous tracassez pas pour moi/pour mon déjeuner; **I'll do it — please don't ~** je vais le faire — non ce n'est pas la peine *or* ne vous donnez pas cette peine; **why ~?** à quoi bon?
3 n a (*nuisance*) ennui *m*, barbe* *f*, scie* *f*. **what a ~ it all is!** quel ennui *or* quelle barbe* que tout cela!
b (*NonC*) (*problems*) ennui *m*, embêtement* *m*. **she's having** *or* **she's in a spot of ~** elle a des ennuis *or* des embêtements* en ce moment; **we had a spot** *or* **bit of ~ with the car** on a eu un petit embêtement* avec la voiture.
c (*effort*) mal *m*. **to go to (all) the ~ of doing sth** se donner beaucoup de mal pour faire qch; **it is no ~ (at all)** il n'y a pas de problème; **he found it without any ~** il l'a trouvé sans aucune difficulté; **he is no ~ to look after** il est facile à garder.
4 excl (*: *esp Brit*) zut!*, flûte!*, la barbe!* **~ that child!** quelle barbe ce gosse!*
botheration†* [ˌbɒðə'reɪʃən] excl zut!*, flûte!*, la barbe!*
bothersome ['bɒðəsəm] adj ennuyeux, gênant.
Bothnia ['bɒθnɪə] n: **Gulf of ~** golfe *m* de Botnie.
Botswana [ˌbɒt'swɑːnə] n Botswana *m*.
bottle ['bɒtl] 1 n a (*container, contents*) bouteille *f*; (*perfume ~*) flacon *m*; (*medicine ~*) flacon, fiole *f*; (*wide-mouthed*) bocal *m*; (*goatskin*) outre *f*; (*of stone*) cruche *f*, cruchon *m*; (*for beer*) canette *f*; (*baby's ~*) biberon *m*. **wine ~** bouteille à vin; **to drink a ~ of wine** boire une bouteille de vin; **we'll discuss it over a ~** nous en discuterons en prenant un verre; **he is too fond of the ~*** il aime trop la bouteille*; **to take to the ~*** se mettre à boire *or* picoler‡; **her husband's on the ~‡** son mari lève le coude*; **child brought up on the ~** enfant élevé *or* nourri au biberon; *see* **hot, ink** *etc*.
b (*fig* *) **he's got a lot of ~** il a un drôle de cran*; **to lose one's ~** perdre courage.
2 comp ►**bottle bank** conteneur *m* de collecte du verre usagé ►**bottle blonde** (*pej*) fausse blonde *f* ►**bottlebrush** rince-bouteilles *m inv* ►**bottle feed** vt allaiter au biberon ►**bottle glass** verre *m* à bouteilles ►**bottle-green** vert (*m*) bouteille *inv* ►**bottleneck** (*lit*) goulot *m*; (*fig*) *[road]* rétrécissement *m* de la chaussée; *[traffic]* embouteillage *m*, bouchon *m*; *[production etc]* goulet *m* d'étranglement ►**bottle-opener** décapsuleur *m*, ouvre-bouteille(s) *m* ►**bottle party** surprise-party *f* (*où chacun apporte une bouteille*) ►**bottle rack** porte-bouteilles *m inv*, casier *m* à bouteilles ►**bottlewasher** laveur *m*, -euse *f* de bouteilles, plongeur *m*, -euse *f* (*see* **cook**).
3 vt *wine* mettre en bouteille(s); *fruit* mettre en bocal *or* en conserve. **~d beer** bière *f* en canette; **~d wine** vin *m* en bouteille(s); **~d fruit** fruits *mpl* en bocal *or* en conserve.
►**bottle out*** vi se dégonfler*.
►**bottle up** vt sep (*fig*) *feelings etc* contenir, ravaler, refouler.
bottom ['bɒtəm] 1 n *[box]* (*outside*) bas *m*, (*inside*) fond *m*; *[glass, well]* fond; *[dress, heap, page]* bas; *[tree, hill]* pied *m*; *[sea, lake, river]* fond; *[garden]* fond, bas; *[chair]* siège *m*, fond; *[ship]* carène *f*; (*buttocks*) derrière *m*, postérieur* *m*; (*fig: origin, foundation*) base *f*, origine *f*, fondement *m*. (*on label*) "~" "dessous", "fond", "bas"; **at the ~ of page 10** en *or* au bas de la page 10; **at the ~ of the hill** au pied *or* au bas de la colline; **the name at the ~ of the list** le nom en bas de la liste; (*fig*) **he's at the ~ of the list** il est en queue de liste; (*fig*) **to be at the ~ of the heap** *or* **pile** être en bas de l'échelle; **to be (at the) ~ of the class** être le dernier de la classe; **~s up!‡** cul sec!; **from the ~ of my heart** du fond de mon cœur; **at ~** au fond; **to knock the ~ out of an argument** démolir un argument; (*Fin*) **the ~ has fallen out of the market** le marché s'est effondré; **the ~ fell out of his world*** son monde s'est effondré *or* a basculé (sous ses pieds); **at the ~ of the table** en bout de table, au bout de la table; **the ship went to the ~** le navire a coulé; **the ship touched the ~** le navire a touché le fond; **the ship was floating ~ up** le navire flottait la quille en l'air; **to be at the ~ of sth** être à l'origine de qch; **to get to the ~ of a mystery** aller jusqu'au fond d'un mystère; **we can't get to the ~ of it** impossible de découvrir le fin fond de cette histoire *or* affaire.
2 adj *shelf* du bas, inférieur; *step, rung etc* premier; *price* le plus bas; *part of garden etc* du fond. **~ dollar** dernier dollar (*see* **bet**); (*Brit*) **to put sth away in one's ~ drawer** mettre qch de côté pour son trousseau; *[building]* **~ floor** rez-de-chaussée *m*; (*Aut*) **~ gear** première *f* (vitesse); **~ half** *[box]* partie inférieure; *[class, list]* deuxième moitié *f*; (*US*) **~ land** terre alluviale; (*US*) **~ lands** plaine alluviale; **the ~ line** (*Fin*) le résultat financier; (*fig*) l'essentiel *m*; **the ~ right-hand corner** le coin en bas à droite; (*US Culin*) **~ round** gîte *m* à la noix; *see* **rock-bottom**.
3 comp ►**bottomless** *pit, well* sans fond, insondable; *supply* inépuisable ►**bottommost** le plus bas ►**bottom-up**: **bottom-up design/information** conception *f*/information *f* ascendante; **bottom-up planning** planification *f* de bas en haut *or* de la base au sommet, planification pyramidale.

►**bottom out*** vi *[figures, sales]* atteindre son niveau plancher; *[recession]* atteindre son plus bas niveau.

bottomry ['bɒtəmrɪ] n (*Marketing*) hypothèque *f* à la grosse aventure.

botulism ['bɒtjʊlɪzəm] n botulisme *m*.

bouclé [buː'kleɪ] 1 n (laine *f or* tissu *m*) bouclette *f*. 2 adj en laine *or* en tissu bouclette.

boudoir ['buːdwɑːʳ] n boudoir *m*.

bouffant ['buːfɒŋ] 1 n (*hairdo*) coiffure *f* bouffante. 2 adj *hairdo* bouffant.

bougainvill(a)ea [ˌbuːgən'vɪlɪə] n bougainvillée *f*, bougainvillier *m*.

bough [baʊ] n (*liter*) rameau *m*, branche *f*.

bought [bɔːt] pret, ptp of **buy**.

bouillon ['buːjɒn] n bouillon *m*, consommé *m*. ~ **cube** bouillon cube *m*.

boulder ['bəʊldəʳ] n rocher *m* (rond), grosse pierre; (*smaller*) (gros) galet *m*. (*Geol*) ~ **clay** dépôt *m* (argileux) erratique.

boulevard ['buːləvɑːʳ] n boulevard *m*.

bounce [baʊns] 1 vi a *[ball]* rebondir; *[person]* bondir, sauter, se précipiter (*into* dans, *out of* hors de). *[person]* **to ~ in/out** *etc* entrer/sortir *etc* d'un bond; **the child ~d up and down on the bed** l'enfant faisait des bonds sur le lit; **the car ~d along the bad road** la voiture faisait des bonds sur la route défoncée; **the ball ~d down the stairs** la balle a rebondi de marche en marche.
b (*) *[cheque]* être sans provision, être refusé pour non-provision.
2 vt a *ball* faire rebondir.
b (‡: *eject*) *person* vider‡, flanquer* à la porte (*out of* de).
c (*) *cheque* refuser.
3 n a (*rebound*) *[ball]* bond *m*, rebond *m*.
b (*NonC*) **this ball hasn't much ~ left** cette balle ne rebondit plus beaucoup; **to give your hair ~** pour donner du volume à vos cheveux; (*fig*) **he's got plenty of ~*** il a beaucoup d'allant, il est très dynamique.
c **to get the ~‡** se faire virer*; **to give sb the ~‡** virer qn*.

►**bounce back** vi se remettre très vite.

bouncer‡ ['baʊnsəʳ] n (*at pub, dance hall etc*) videur‡ *m*.

bouncing ['baʊnsɪŋ] adj rebondi, dodu, potelé. ~ **baby** beau bébé (florissant de santé).

bouncy ['baʊnsɪ] adj *ball, mattress* élastique; *hair* vigoureux; *person* dynamique, plein d'allant.

bound¹ [baʊnd] 1 n (*lit, fig*) **~s** limite(s) *f(pl)*, bornes *fpl*; **his ambition knows no ~s** son ambition est sans bornes; **to keep within ~s** (*fig*) rester dans la juste mesure, user de modération; (*lit*) rester dans les limites; **within the ~s of probability** dans les limites du probable; **within the ~s of possibility** dans la limite du possible; **to go over** *or* **pass over the ~s** dépasser les bornes; **out of ~s** *place etc* dont l'accès est interdit; (*Scol*) interdit aux élèves; (*Sport*) hors du terrain, sorti; **it's out of ~s to soldiers** c'est interdit *or* consigné aux soldats; *see* **break**. 2 vt (*gen pass*) *country* borner. **~ed by** borné *or* limité par.

bound² [baʊnd] 1 n bond *m*, saut *m*. **at a ~** d'un saut, d'un bond; *see* **leap**. 2 vi *[person]* bondir, sauter; *[horse]* bondir, faire un bond *or* des bonds. **to ~ in/away/back** *etc* entrer/partir/revenir *etc* en bondissant *or* d'un bond; **the horse ~ed over the fence** le cheval sauta la barrière (d'un bond).

bound³ [baʊnd] 1 pret, ptp of **bind**.
2 adj a lié, attaché; (*Ling*) *morpheme* lié. ~ **hand and foot** pieds et poings liés; *see* **earth, ice, spell¹** *etc*.
b *book etc* relié. ~ **in boards** cartonné.
c (*fig*) (*obliged*) obligé, tenu; (*sure*) sûr, certain. **you are not ~ to do it** vous n'êtes pas obligé de le faire; **to be ~ by law/an oath** *etc* **to do sth** être tenu par la loi/un serment à faire qch; **I am ~ to confess** je suis forcé d'avouer; **to feel ~ to do sth** se sentir obligé de faire qch; **you're ~ to do it** (*obliged to*) vous êtes tenu *or* obligé de le faire; (*sure to*) vous le ferez sûrement; **he's ~ to say so** (*obliged to*) il est de son devoir de le dire, il doit le dire; (*sure to*) il le dira sûrement, il ne manquera pas de le dire; **it is ~ to rain** il va sûrement pleuvoir, il ne peut pas manquer de pleuvoir; **it was ~ to happen** cela devait arriver, c'était à prévoir; *see* **duty, honour** *etc*.
d (*destined*) ~ **for** *person* en route pour; *parcel* à destination de; *train* en direction de, à destination de; *ship, plane* à destination de, en route pour; (*about to leave*) en partance pour; **where are you ~ for?** où allez-vous?

-bound [baʊnd] adj ending in comps: **Australia-bound** à destination de l'Australie; **Paris-bound traffic** la circulation dans le sens province-Paris; *see* **north, outward** *etc*.

boundary ['baʊndərɪ] 1 n limite *f*, frontière *f*. (*Cricket*) **to score a ~** envoyer une balle jusqu'aux limites du terrain. 2 comp ►**boundary changes**: (*Brit Pol*) **to make boundary changes** effectuer un redécoupage électoral ►**boundary line** ligne *f* frontière *inv or* de démarcation; (*Sport: gen*) limites *fpl* du terrain; (*Basketball*) ligne *f* de touche ►**boundary-stone** borne *f*, pierre *f* de bornage.

bounden ['baʊndən] adj: ~ **duty** devoir impérieux.

bounder†* ['baʊndəʳ] n (*esp Brit*) butor *m*, goujat *m*.

boundless ['baʊndlɪs] adj *space* infini; *trust* illimité; *ambition, devotion* sans bornes.

bounteous ['baʊntɪəs] adj, **bountiful** ['baʊntɪfʊl] adj *harvest* abondant; *rain* bienfaisant; *person* généreux, libéral, prodigue; *see* **lady**.

bounty ['baʊntɪ] n a (*NonC: generosity*) générosité *f*, libéralité *f*. b (*gift*) don *m*; (*reward*) prime *f*. **~-fed farmers** agriculteurs *mpl* qui ne vivent que de subventions; ~ **hunter†** chasseur *m* de primes.

bouquet ['bʊkeɪ] 1 n a *[flowers]* bouquet *m*. b *[wine]* bouquet *m*. 2 comp ►**bouquet garni** (*Culin*) (pl **~s ~s**) bouquet garni *m*.

Bourbon ['bʊəbən] n a (*Hist*) Bourbon. b ['bɜːbən] (*US*) **b~** (whisky) bourbon *m*.

bourgeois ['bʊəʒwɑː] 1 adj bourgeois. 2 n, pl inv bourgeois(e) *m(f)*.

bourgeoisie [ˌbʊəʒwɑː'ziː] n bourgeoisie *f*.

bout [baʊt] n a (*period*) période *f*; *[malaria etc]* attaque *f*, accès *m*. ~ **of rheumatism** crise *f* de rhumatisme; ~ **of fever** accès de fièvre; **a ~ of bronchitis** une bronchite; **a ~ of flu** une grippe; **he's had several ~s of illness** il a été malade plusieurs fois; **a ~ of work(ing)** une période de travail intensif; **drinking ~** beuverie *f*. b (*Boxing, Wrestling*) combat *m*; (*Fencing*) assaut *m*.

boutique [buː'tiːk] n (*shop*) boutique *f* (*de mode ou d'objets branchés*); (*within a store*) **hat/teenage ~** rayon *m* des chapeaux/des jeunes.

bovine ['bəʊvaɪn] adj (*lit, fig*) bovin. ~ **spongiform encephalopathy** encéphalopathie *f* spongiforme bovine.

bovver boots‡ ['bɒvəˌbuːts] npl (*Brit*) brodequins *mpl*.

bow¹ [bəʊ] 1 n a (*weapon etc*) arc *m*. **to draw the ~** tirer à l'arc; *see* **cross, long¹, string** *etc*. b (*Mus*) archet *m*. c (*curve*) *[rainbow etc]* arc *m*; *see* **saddle**. d (*knot*) *[ribbon etc]* nœud *m* (à boucles), rosette *f*. 2 vi (*Mus*) manier l'archet. 3 comp ►**bow and arrow** arc *m* et des flèches, jeu *m* de tir à l'arc ►**bow compass** compas *m* à balustre ►**bow-legged** aux jambes arquées ►**bowlegs** jambes arquées ►**bowman** (*Archery*) archer *m* ►**bowstring** (*Archery, Mus*) corde *f* ►**bow tie** nœud *m* papillon ►**bow window** fenêtre *f* en saillie, bow-window *m*.

bow² [baʊ] 1 n (*with head*) salut *m*; (*with body*) révérence *f*. **to make a (deep) ~** saluer (bas); **to give sb a gracious ~** adresser un gracieux salut à qn; (*fig*) **to make one's ~ (as a pianist** *etc*) faire ses débuts (de pianiste *etc*); **to take a ~** saluer.
2 vi a (*in greeting*) saluer, incliner la tête. **to ~ to sb** saluer qn; **to ~ and scrape** faire des courbettes; **~ing and scraping** salamalecs *mpl*, courbettes *fpl*.
b (*bend*) *[branch etc]* (*in wind*) fléchir, se courber, (*under weight*) ployer; *[person]* se courber.
c (*fig: submit*) s'incliner (*before, to* devant, *under* sous), se soumettre (*before, to* à, *under* sous). **to ~ before the storm** laisser passer l'orage; **we must ~ to your greater knowledge** nous devons nous incliner devant vos très grandes connaissances; **to ~ to sb's opinion** se soumettre à l'opinion de qn; **to ~ to the inevitable** s'incliner devant les faits *or* devant l'inévitable; **to ~ to the majority** s'incliner devant la majorité.
3 vt courber. **to ~ one's back** courber le dos; **to ~ one's knee** fléchir le genou; **to ~ one's head** pencher *or* courber la tête; **his head was ~ed in thought** il méditait la tête penchée; **to ~ one's consent** signifier son consentement par une inclination de tête; **to ~ sb in/out** faire entrer/faire sortir qn en saluant; **to ~ o.s. out** saluer pour prendre congé.

►**bow down** 1 vi (*lit, fig*) s'incliner (*to sb* devant qn). 2 vt sep (*lit*) faire plier, courber; (*fig*) écraser, briser.

►**bow out** vi (*fig*) tirer sa révérence (*fig*); *see also* **bow² 3**.

bow³ [baʊ] 1 n a (*often pl*) *[ship]* avant *m*, proue *f*. **in the ~s** à l'avant, en proue; **on the port ~** par bâbord devant; **on the starboard ~** par tribord devant. b (*oarsman*) nageur *m* de l'avant. 2 comp ►**bowsprit** beaupré *m*.

Bow bells ['bəʊ'belz] npl les cloches *fpl* de l'église de St-Mary-le-Bow (*à Londres*). **born within the sound of ~** né en plein cœur de Londres.

bowdlerization [ˌbaʊdləraɪ'zeɪʃən] n expurgation *f*.

bowdlerize ['baʊdləraɪz] vt *book* expurger.

bowel ['baʊəl] n (*Anat: gen pl*) *[person]* intestin(s) *m(pl)*; *[animal]* boyau(x) *m(pl)*, intestin(s). ~ **cancer** cancer *m* des intestins; ~ **complaint** dérangement intestinal; **to empty** *or* **relieve one's ~s** déféquer; (*fig*) **~s** entrailles *fpl*; **~s of the earth** entrailles de la terre; (*liter*) **~s of compassion** tendresse *f*, pitié *f*; *see* **move 2b, movement e**.

bower ['baʊəʳ] n (*arbour*) berceau *m* de verdure, tonnelle *f*, retraite ombragée; (††, *liter: cottage*) chaumière *f*, petite maison (à la campagne); *[lady]* boudoir *m*.

bowing¹ ['bəʊɪŋ] n (*Mus*) technique *f* d'archet; (*marked on score*) indications *fpl* d'archet. **his ~ was sensitive** il avait un coup d'archet délicat; **to mark the ~** indiquer *or* introduire les coups d'archet.

bowing² ['baʊɪŋ] n *see* **bow² 2a**.

bowl¹ [bəʊl] n a (*container: gen*) bol *m*; (*larger*) saladier *m*, jatte *f*; (*for water*) cuvette *f*; (*for fruit*) coupe *f*; *[beggar]* sébile *f*; (*US Sport*) championnat *m*, coupe *f*. **a ~ of milk** un bol de lait; **a ~ of water** une cuvette d'eau; **a ~ of punch** un bol de punch; *see* **finger, salad, sugar** *etc*. b *[wineglass]* coupe *f*; *[pipe]* fourneau *m*; *[spoon]* creux *m*; *[lamp]* globe *m*; *[lavatory, sink]* cuvette *f*. c (*Geog*) bassin *m*, cuvette *f*.

bowl² [bəʊl] 1 n (*Sport*) boule *f*. **(game of) ~s** (*Brit*) (jeu *m* de) boules; (*in Provence*) pétanque *f*, boules; (*US: skittles*) bowling *m*. 2 vi a (*Brit*) jouer aux boules; (*US*) jouer au bowling; (*Provence*) jouer à la pétanque; (*Cricket*) lancer (la balle) (*to* à). **b** *[person, car]* **to ~ down the street** descendre la rue à bonne allure; *[car]* **to ~ along, to go ~ing along** rouler bon train. **3** **vt** **a** (*Sport*) *bowl, hoop* faire rouler; *ball* lancer. **b** (*Cricket*) *ball* servir; *batsman* (*also* **~ out**) éliminer (*en lançant la balle contre les guichets*).

►bowl down* **vt sep** renverser.

►bowl out **vt sep** *see* **bowl² 3b.**

►bowl over **vt sep** **a** *ninepins* renverser, faire tomber. **b** (*fig*) stupéfier, renverser, sidérer*. **to be bowled over (by)** (*surprise*) rester stupéfait *or* abasourdi *or* sidéré* (devant); (*emotion*) être bouleversé (par); (*impressed*) **she was bowled over by him** il l'a éblouie.

bowler¹ ['bəʊləʳ] **n** (*Brit*) joueur *m*, -euse *f* de boules; (*US*) joueur de bowling; (*Provence*) joueur de pétanque, bouliste *mf*, pétanquiste *mf*; (*Cricket*) lanceur *m*, -euse *f* (de la balle).

bowler² ['bəʊləʳ] **n** (*Brit: also* **~ hat**) (chapeau *m*) melon *m*.

bowline ['bəʊlɪn] **n** (*knot*) nœud *m* de chaise; (*rope*) bouline *f*.

bowling ['bəʊlɪŋ] **1** **n** (*Brit*) jeu *m* de boules; (*US*) bowling *m*; (*Provence*) pétanque *f*. **2** **comp** ►**bowling alley** bowling *m* ►**bowling green** terrain *m* de boules (*sur gazon*) ►**bowling match** (*Brit*) concours *m* de boules; (*US*) concours de bowling; (*Provence*) concours de pétanque.

bow-wow ['baʊwaʊ] (*baby talk*) **1** **n** toutou *m*. **2** ['baʊ'waʊ] **excl** oua, oua!

box¹ [bɒks] **1** **n** **a** boîte *f*; (*crate*) caisse *f*; (*cardboard ~*) (boîte en) carton *m*; (*casket*) coffret *m*; (*†: trunk*) malle *f*. **a ~ of matches/chocolates** une boîte d'allumettes/de chocolats; (*Brit: television*) **(on) the ~*** (à) la télé*; *see* **ice, letter, tool** *etc*.

b (*money*) caisse *f*; (*in church*) tronc *m*; *see* **strong** *etc*.

c (*Aut, Tech*) *[axle, steering]* carter *m*; *see* **axle, gear** *etc*.

d (*Theat*) loge *f*; *[coachman]* siège *m* (du cocher); (*Jur*) *[jury, press]* banc *m*; *[witness]* barre *f*; *[stable]* box *m*; *see* **horse, sentry, signal** *etc*.

e (*Sport: protection*) coquille *f*.

f (*Brit: road junction*) zone *f* (de carrefour) d'accès réglementé.

2 **comp** ►**boxboard** carton compact ►**box calf** box(-calf) *m* ►**box camera** appareil *m* (photographique) (du modèle le plus rudimentaire) ►**boxcar** (*Rail*) wagon *m* (de marchandises) couvert ►**box file** boîte *f* à archives ►**box girder** (*Constr*) poutre-caisson *f* ►**box junction** (*Brit*) = **box¹ 1f** ►**box kite** cerf-volant *m* cellulaire ►**box number** (*Post*) (*in newspaper*) numéro *m* d'annonce (*see also* **post³**) ►**box office** *see* **box office** ►**box pleat** (*Sewing*) pli creux ►**boxroom** (*Brit*) (cabinet *m* de) débarras *m* ►**box spring** sommier *m* à ressorts ►**box stall** (*US*) box *m*.

3 **vt** **a** mettre en boîte *or* en caisse *etc*. **~ed set** coffret *m*.

b (*Naut*) **to ~ the compass** réciter les aires du vent.

►box in **vt sep** *bath, sink* encastrer. (*fig*) **to feel boxed in** se sentir confiné *or* à l'étroit; **house boxed in by tall buildings** maison coincée entre de grands immeubles.

►box off **vt sep** compartimenter.

►box up **vt sep** mettre en boîte; (*fig*) enfermer.

box² [bɒks] **1** **vi** (*Sport*) boxer, faire de la boxe. **2** **vt** **a** (*Sport*) boxer avec, boxer*. **b** **to ~ sb's ears** chauffer les oreilles à qn, gifler *or* claquer qn, flanquer* une claque *or* une gifle à qn. **3** **n: a ~ on the ear** une claque, une gifle.

box³ [bɒks] **1** **n** (*Bot*) buis *m*. **2** **comp** en *or* de buis ►**boxwood** buis *m*.

boxer¹ ['bɒksəʳ] **n** (*Sport*) boxeur *m*. **~ shorts** boxer-short *m*.

boxer² ['bɒksəʳ] **n** (*dog*) boxer *m*.

boxing ['bɒksɪŋ] **1** **n** boxe *f*. **2** **comp** *gloves, match* de boxe ►**boxing ring** ring *m*.

Boxing Day ['bɒksɪŋdeɪ] **n** (*Brit*) le lendemain de Noël.

box office ['bɒksɒfɪs] (*Theat*) **1** **n** (*office*) bureau *m* de location; (*window*) guichet *m* (de location). **this show will be good ~** ce spectacle fera recette. **2** **comp** ►**box-office attraction** spectacle *m* à (grand) succès ►**box-office receipts** recette *f* ►**box-office success** pièce *f etc* qui fait courir les foules *or* qui fait recette.

boy [bɔɪ] **1** **n** **a** (*child*) garçon *m*, enfant *m*; (*young man*) jeune *m* (homme *m*), garçon; (*son*) fils *m*, garçon; (*Scol*) élève *m*, garçon. **little ~** petit garçon, garçonnet *m*; **beggar ~** petit mendiant; **English ~** petit *or* jeune Anglais; **come here, my ~** viens ici mon petit *or* mon grand; **bad ~!, naughty ~!** vilain!; **the Jones ~** le petit Jones; **I lived here as a ~** j'habitais ici quand j'étais petit *or* enfant; **he knew me from a ~** il me connaissait depuis mon (*or* son) enfance, il me connaissait depuis tout petit; **~s will be ~s!** les garçons, on ne les changera jamais!; **he was as much a ~ as ever** il était toujours aussi gamin; (*Brit Scol*) **an old ~** un ancien élève; (*Scol*) **sit down, ~s** (*to small boys*) asseyez-vous mes enfants; (*to sixth formers etc*) asseyez-vous messieurs *or* mes amis; *see* **choir, day, page²** *etc*.

b (**: fellow*) **my dear ~** mon cher (ami); **old ~** mon vieux; **the old ~** (*boss*) le patron; (*father*) le paternel*; **a night out with the ~s** une sortie avec les copains; *see* **wide**.

c (*native servant*) boy *m*.

2 **comp** ►**boyfriend** petit ami ►**the boys in blue** (*Brit **) les défenseurs *mpl* de l'ordre ►**boy-meets-girl story** (*film, novel etc*) histoire romantique conventionnelle ►**boy scout†** (*Catholic*) scout *m*; (*non-Catholic*) éclaireur *m* ►**boy soprano** soprano *m*.

3 **excl** (*) bigre!

boycott ['bɔɪkɒt] **1** **vt** *person, product, place* boycotter. **2** **n** boycottage *m*.

boyhood ['bɔɪhʊd] **n** enfance *f*, adolescence *f*.

boyish ['bɔɪɪʃ] **adj** *male's behaviour* d'enfant, de garçon; *smile* gamin; (*pej*) enfantin, puéril; (*tomboyish*) *girl* garçonnier; *behaviour* garçonnier, de garçon. **he looks very ~** il fait très gamin; **his ~ good looks** son air de beau garçon.

boyishly ['bɔɪɪʃlɪ] **adv** comme un garçon. **~ cut hair** cheveux *mpl* coupés à la garçonne.

boysenberry ['bɔɪzənbərɪ] **n** boysenberry *f* (*variété de mûre*).

bozo‡ ['bəʊzəʊ] **n** (*US*) bozo* *m*, drôle de type‡ *m*.

Bp **abbr of Bishop**.

bpi [biːpiː'aɪ] **n** (*Comput*) (**abbr of bits per inch**) bits *mpl* par pouce.

bps [biːpiː'es] **n** (*Comput*) (**abbr of bits per second**) bits *mpl* par seconde.

B.R. [biː'ɑːʳ] **n** (**abbr of British Rail**) *compagnie ferroviaire britannique*.

bra [brɑː] **n** (**abbr of brassière**) soutien-gorge *m*. **half-cup ~** soutien-gorge pigeonnant.

Brabant [brə'bænt] **n** Brabant *m*.

brace [breɪs] **1** **n** **a** attache *f*, agrafe *f*; (*Med*) appareil *m* orthopédique; (*Constr*) entretoise *f*, étrésillon *m*; (*US Mil sl*) garde-à-vous *m* rigide. (*Brit Dress*) **~s** bretelles *fpl*; (*for teeth*) **~(s)** appareil *m* dentaire *or* orthodontique; (*Tech*) **~ (and bit)** vilebrequin *m* (*à main*).

b (**pl inv**) (*pair*) *[animals, pistols]* paire *f*.

c (*Mus, Typ: also* **~ bracket**) accolade *f*.

2 **vt** **a** (*support, strengthen*) soutenir, consolider; *structure* entretoiser, étrésillonner; *beam* armer (*with* de), soutenir.

b **to ~ o.s.** (*lit*) s'arc-bouter; (*fig*) rassembler ses forces (*to do* à faire), fortifier son âme (*to do* pour faire); **he ~d his leg against the door** il bloqua la porte avec sa jambe; **~ yourself for the news!** tenez-vous bien que je vous raconte (*subj*) la nouvelle *or* que je vous en dise une bien bonne*.

c *[climate etc]* fortifier, tonifier.

►brace up **1** **vt sep** *person* retremper, revigorer, remonter. **to brace o.s. up** rassembler ses forces (*to do* pour faire); (*by having a drink*) reprendre des forces (*hum*). **2** **excl: brace up!** du courage!

bracelet ['breɪslɪt] **n** **a** bracelet *m*. **b** (*handcuffs*) **~s‡** menottes *fpl*, bracelets *mpl* (*hum*).

bracer‡ ['breɪsəʳ] **n** (*drink*) remontant *m*.

bracing ['breɪsɪŋ] **adj** *air, climate* fortifiant, tonifiant. **a ~ wind** un vent vivifiant.

bracken ['brækən] **n** (*NonC*) fougère *f*.

bracket ['brækɪt] **1** **n** **a** (*angled support*) support *m*; *[shelf]* tasseau *m*, gousset *m*, potence *f*; (*Archit*) support, console *f*, corbeau *m*.

b *[lamp]* fixation *f*. **~ lamp** applique *f*.

c (*small shelf*) rayon *m*, étagère *f*.

d (*Typ*) (*round*) parenthèse *f*; (*square*) crochet *m*; (*Mus, Typ: also* **brace**) accolade *f*. **in ~s** entre parenthèses.

e (*fig: group*) classe *f*, groupe *m*, tranche *f*. **the lower/upper income ~** la tranche des petits/des gros revenus; **he's in the £30,000 a year ~** il est dans la tranche (de revenus) des 30 000 livres par an; **price ~** fourchette *f* de prix; **tax ~** tranche *f* d'imposition.

2 **vt** **a** (*Typ*) *sentence etc* mettre entre parenthèses *or* entre crochets.

b (*join by brackets*) réunir par une accolade; (*fig: also* **~ together**) *names, persons* mettre dans le même groupe *or* dans la même catégorie; *candidates etc* mettre ex aequo, accoler; (*fig: link in one's mind*) mettre dans le même sac. (*Scol, Sport etc*) **~ed first** premiers ex aequo.

c (*Mil*) *target* encadrer.

bracketing ['brækətɪŋ] **n** (*Gram*) parenthétisation *f*.

brackish ['brækɪʃ] **adj** *water, taste* saumâtre.

brad [bræd] **n** semence *f*, clou *m* de tapissier. **~ awl** poinçon *m*.

brae [breɪ] **n** (*Scot*) pente *f*, côte *f*.

brag [bræg] **1** **vi** se vanter, se glorifier, se targuer (*about, of* de, *about or of doing* de faire). **2** **vt: to ~ that one has done sth** se vanter d'avoir fait qch. **3** **n** **a** (*boast*) vantardise *f*, fanfaronnades *fpl*. **b** = **braggart**. **c** (*Cards*) *jeu de cartes semblable au poker*.

braggart ['brægət] **n** vantard(e) *m(f)*, fanfaron(ne) *m(f)*.

bragging ['brægɪŋ] **n** vantardise *f* (*about* à propos de).

Brahma ['brɑːmə] **n** **a** (*god*) Brahma *m*. **b** (*US Zool*) zébu américain.

Brahman ['brɑːmən] **n, pl ~s** **a** (*person*) brahmane *m*. **b** = **Brahma b.**

Brahmaputra [ˌbrɑːmə'puːtrə] **n** Brahmapoutre *m*, Brahmaputra *m*.

Brahmin ['brɑːmɪn] **n, pl ~** *or* **~s** = **Brahman a.**

braid [breɪd] **1** **vt** **a** (*plait*) tresser, natter; (*interweave*) entrelacer (*with* avec). **b** (*trim with ~*) *clothing, material* soutacher, galonner, passementer. **~ed** galonné. **2** **n** **a** (*US, Brit †: plait of hair*) tresse *f*, natte *f*. **b** (*NonC: trimming*) soutache *f*, ganse *f*, galon *m*; (*Mil*) galon. **gold ~** galon d'or *or* doré.

Braille [breɪl] **1** **n** braille *m*. **2** **adj** braille *inv*.

brain [breɪn] **1** **n** **a** (*Anat*) cerveau *m*; (*fig*) cerveau, tête *f*. (*Anat,*

Culin) ~s cervelle *f*; (*fig*) **he's got that on the ~*** il ne pense qu'à ça!, ça le tient!*; (*fig*) **he's got politics on the ~*** il n'a que la politique en tête; **his ~ reeled** la tête lui a tourné; **to beat sb's ~s out*** estourbir qn*; **to blow sb's ~s out*** brûler la cervelle à qn; (*Culin*) **calves' ~** cervelle de veau; *see* **pick, rack²** *etc.*

b (*fig: gen pl: intelligence*) ~s intelligence *f*; **he's got ~s** il est intelligent; **he's the ~s of the family** c'est lui le cerveau de la famille.

2 vt (‡: *knock out*) *person* assommer.

3 comp (*Med*) *disease, operation* cérébral ►**brain-box*** tête* *f*, cerveau *m* ►**brain-child** idée personnelle, invention personnelle; **it's his brain-child** c'est lui qui l'a inventé ►**brain damage** lésions cérébrales ►**brain dead** (*Med*) dans un coma dépassé; (*: *stupid*) balourd* ►**brain death** (*Med*) mort cérébrale ►**brain drain** exode *m* des cerveaux ►**brain fever** fièvre cérébrale ►**brain pan** boîte crânienne ►**brain scan** scanographie *f* du cerveau ►**brain scanner** scanner *m* ►**brainstorm** (*Med*) congestion cérébrale; (*Brit fig: sudden aberration*) moment *m* d'aberration; (*brilliant idea*) idée géniale ►**brainstorming** remue méninges *m* (*hum*), brain-storming *m* ►**brains trust** (*panel of experts*) groupe *m* d'experts *or* de spécialistes; (*US: advisory experts: also* **brain trust**) brain-trust *m* ►**brainwash** faire un lavage de cerveau à; **he was brainwashed into believing that ...** on a réussi à lui faire croire *or* à lui mettre dans la tête que ... ►**brainwashing** *[prisoners etc]* lavage *m* de cerveau; (*) *[the public etc]* bourrage* *m* de crâne, intox* *f* ►**brainwave** idée géniale, inspiration *f* ►**brainwork** travail intellectuel.

brainless ['breɪnlɪs] adj *person* sans cervelle, stupide; *idea* stupide. *[person]* **to be ~** n'avoir rien dans la tête.

brainy* ['breɪnɪ] adj intelligent, doué.

braise [breɪz] vt (*Culin*) braiser.

brake¹ [breɪk] n (*Bot*) (*bracken*) fougère *f*; (*thicket*) fourré *m*.

brake² [breɪk] n (*vehicle*) break *m*.

brake³ [breɪk] 1 n (*Aut etc*) frein *m*. **to put on** *or* **apply the ~s** freiner; (*fig*) **to act as a ~ on sb's activities** mettre un frein aux activités de qn; *see* **hand, slam on** *etc.* 2 vi freiner. 3 comp ►**brake band** ruban *m* de frein ►**brake block** sabot *m or* patin *m* de frein ►**brake drum** tambour *m* de frein ►**brake fluid** liquide *m* de freins, lockheed *m* ® ►**brake horse power** puissance *f* au frein ►**brake lever** frein *m* à main ►**brake light** feu *m* de stop ►**brake lining** garniture *f* de frein ►**brakeman** (*US Rail*) chef *m* de train ►**brake pad** plaquette *f* de frein ►**brake pedal** pédale *f* de frein ►**brake shoe** mâchoire *f* de frein ►**brake-van** (*Brit Rail*) fourgon *m* à frein.

braking ['breɪkɪŋ] 1 n freinage *m*. 2 comp ►**braking distance** distance *f* de freinage ►**braking power** puissance *f* de freinage.

bramble ['bræmbl] n a (*thorny shrub*) roncier *m*, roncière *f*. b (*blackberry*) (*bush*) ronce *f* des haies, mûrier *m* sauvage; (*berry*) mûre *f* (sauvage).

brambling ['bræmblɪŋ] n (*bird*) pinson *m* du nord.

bran [bræn] n son *m* (*de blé*). **~ loaf** pain *m* au son; **~ mash** bran *or* son mouillé; (*Brit*) **~ tub** pêche miraculeuse (*jeu*).

branch [brɑːntʃ] 1 n a *[tree, candelabra]* branche *f*; *[river]* bras *m*, branche; *[mountain chain]* ramification *f*; *[road]* embranchement *m*; *[railway]* bifurcation *f*, raccordement *m*; *[pipe]* branchement *m*; *[family, race]* ramification, branche; (*Ling*) rameau *m*; *[subject, science etc]* branche; (*Admin*) division *f*, section *f*. (*Mil*) **he did not belong to their ~ of the service** il n'appartenait pas à leur arme; *see* **olive, root** *etc.*

b (*Comm*) *[store]* succursale *f*; *[company]* succursale, branche *f*; *[bank]* agence *f*, succursale; *[police force]* antenne *f*.

c (*Comput*) branchement *m*.

d (*US: stream*) ruisseau *m*.

2 comp ►**branch depot** (*Comm*) dépôt *m* auxiliaire ►**branch line** (*Rail*) ligne *f* secondaire ►**branch manager** (*gen*) directeur *m* de succursale (*etc*); *[bank]* directeur d'agence ►**branch office** succursale *f* (locale); *[bank]* agence *f*, succursale ►**branch water*** (*US*) eau plate.

3 vi a *[tree]* se ramifier.

b *[road]* bifurquer; *[river]* (*divide into two*) bifurquer; (*into more than two*) se ramifier. **the road ~es off the main road at ...** la route quitte la grand-route à ... .

►**branch off** vi *[road]* bifurquer.

►**branch out** vi *[person, company]* étendre ses activités. **the firm is branching out into the publishing business** la compagnie étend la sphère de ses activités à *or* se lance dans l'édition.

branching ['brɑːnʃɪŋ] n (*Gram*) branchement *m*, arborescence *f*. **~ rules** règle *f* de formation d'arbre.

brand [brænd] 1 n a (*Comm: trademark: also* **~ name**) marque *f* (de fabrique). **that rum is an excellent ~** c'est une excellente marque de rhum, ce rhum est de très bonne marque.

b (*mark*) *[cattle, property]* marque *f*; *[prisoner]* flétrissure *f*; (*fig: stigma*) marque, stigmate *m*.

c (*also* **~ing-iron**) fer *m* à marquer.

d (*burning wood*) tison *m*, brandon *m*, flambeau *m* (*liter*); *see* **fire**.

e (*liter*, †: *sword*) glaive *m* (*liter*), épée *f*.

2 vt *cattle, property* marquer (au fer rouge); (*fig*) *person* étiqueter (*as* comme), stigmatiser. (*fig*) **he was ~ed (as) a traitor** on lui a donné l'étiquette infamante de traître; **to ~ sth on sb's memory** graver qch dans la mémoire de qn; (*Comm*) **~ed goods** produits *mpl* de marque.

3 comp ►**brand acceptance** (*Comm*) accueil réservé à une marque ►**brand awareness** (*Comm*) notoriété *f* de marque (*chez le consommateur*) ►**brand image** (*Comm*) image *f* de marque ►**branding-iron** fer *m* à marquer ►**brand-new** tout neuf (*f* toute neuve), flambant neuf (*f* flambant neuve).

brandish ['brændɪʃ] vt brandir.

brandy ['brændɪ] n cognac *m*. **~ and soda** fine à l'eau; **plum ~** eau-de-vie *f* de prune *or* de quetsche; **~ butter** *beurre sucré et aromatisé au cognac*; (*Culin*) **~ snap** cornet croquant.

brash [bræʃ] adj (*reckless*) impétueux, fougueux; (*impudent*) impertinent, effronté; *colour* criard.

brashly ['bræʃlɪ] adv (*see* **brash**) impétueusement, fougueusement; avec impertinence, effrontément.

brashness ['bræʃnɪs] n (*see* **brash**) impétuosité *f*, fougue *f*; impertinence *f*, effronterie *f*; *[colour]* caractère criard.

Brasilia [brəˈzɪljə] n Brasilia.

brass [brɑːs] 1 n a (*NonC*) cuivre *m* (jaune), laiton *m*; *see* **bold**.

b (*tablet*) plaque *f* mortuaire (en cuivre).

c (*object/ornament of ~*) objet *m*/ornement *m* en cuivre. **to do/clean the ~(es)** faire/astiquer les cuivres; (*Mus*) **the ~** les cuivres *mpl*; (*Mil sl*) **the (top) ~** les huiles‡ *fpl*.

d (‡: *NonC*) (*impudence*) toupet* *m*, culot* *m*; (*Brit: money*) pognon‡ *m*.

2 comp *ornament etc* en *or* de cuivre ►**brass band** fanfare *f*, orchestre *m* de cuivres ►**brass farthing***: **it's not worth a brass farthing** cela ne vaut pas un clou *or* un pet de lapin‡ (*see* **care**) ►**brass foundry** fonderie *f* de cuivre ►**brass hat** (*Mil sl*) huile* *f* ►**brass knuckles** coup de poing américain ►**brass monkey‡**: (*Brit*) **it is brass monkey weather** *or* **brass monkeys** il fait un froid de canard* ►**brass neck‡**: **he's got a brass neck** il a du toupet* *or* du culot* ►**brass plate** plaque *f* de cuivre; *[church]* plaque mortuaire *or* commémorative ►**brass rubbing** (*action*) décalquage *m* par frottement; (*object*) décalque *m* ►**brass tacks:*** **to get down to brass tacks** en venir aux faits *or* aux choses sérieuses ►**brassware** chaudronnerie *f* d'art, dinanderie *f*.

brasserie ['brɑːsərɪ] n brasserie *f*.

brassie ['brɑːsɪ] n (*Golf*) = **brassy 2**.

brassière† ['bræsɪəʳ] n soutien-gorge *m*.

brassy ['brɑːsɪ] 1 adj *colour etc* cuivré; *sound* cuivré, claironnant; (*: *impudent*) *person* culotté*. 2 n (*Golf*) brassie *m*.

brat [bræt] n (*pej*) moutard* *m*, môme* *mf*, gosse* *mf*. **all these ~s** toute cette marmaille*; **one of his ~s** un de ses lardons‡; **~pack** jeunes loups *mpl*.

bravado [brəˈvɑːdəʊ] n, pl ~s *or* ~es bravade *f*.

brave [breɪv] 1 adj a *person* courageux, brave, vaillant; *smile, attempt, action* courageux, brave. **to be as ~ as a lion** être courageux comme un lion, être intrépide; **be ~!** du courage!; **be ~ and tell her** prends ton courage à deux mains et va lui dire; *see* **face.** b (*liter: fine*) beau (*f* belle), élégant. (*iro*) **it's a ~ new world!** on n'arrête pas le progrès! (*iro*). 2 n a **the ~st of the ~** le brave des braves. b (*Indian warrior*) guerrier indien, brave *m*. 3 vt *danger, person, sb's anger* braver, affronter.

►**brave out** vt sep: **to brave it out** faire face à la situation.

bravely ['breɪvlɪ] adv *fight, answer* bravement, courageusement, vaillamment. **the flag was flying ~** le drapeau flottait splendidement.

bravery ['breɪvərɪ] n (*NonC*) courage *m*, vaillance *f*, bravoure *f*.

bravo ['brɑːˈvəʊ] excl, n, pl ~es *or* ~s bravo (*m*).

bravura [brəˈvʊərə] n (*also Mus*) bravoure *f*.

brawl [brɔːl] 1 vi se bagarrer*, se quereller. 2 n rixe *f*, bagarre *f*. **drunken ~** querelle *f* d'ivrognes.

brawling ['brɔːlɪŋ] 1 adj bagarreur*, querelleur. 2 n rixe *f*, bagarre *f*.

brawn [brɔːn] n a (*Brit Culin*) fromage *m* de tête. b (*muscle*) muscle(s) *m(pl)*; (*strength*) muscle. **to have plenty of ~** être bien musclé, avoir du muscle; (*hum*) **he is all ~ and no brain** il est tout en muscles et sans cervelle.

brawny ['brɔːnɪ] adj *arm* musculeux, fort; *person* musclé, vigoureux, costaud*.

bray [breɪ] 1 n *[ass]* braiement *m*; *[trumpet]* fanfare *f*, son éclatant. 2 vi *[ass]* braire; *[trumpet]* résonner, éclater.

braze [breɪz] vt souder (au laiton).

brazen ['breɪzn] 1 adj (*brass*) de cuivre (jaune), de laiton; *sound* cuivré; (*fig: also* **~-faced**) impudent, effronté. **~ lie** mensonge effronté. 2 vt: **to ~ it out** payer d'effronterie, crâner*.

brazenly ['breɪznlɪ] adv impudemment, effrontément.

brazier¹ ['breɪzɪəʳ] n *[fire]* brasero *m*.

brazier² ['breɪzɪəʳ] n (*craftsman*) chaudronnier *m*.

Brazil [brəˈzɪl] n Brésil *m*. **~ nut** noix *f* du Brésil.

Brazilian [brəˈzɪlɪən] 1 n Brésilien(ne) *m(f)*. 2 adj brésilien, du Brésil.

BRCS [ˌbiːɑːsiːˈes] n (abbr of **British Red Cross Society**) *see* **British**.

breach [briːtʃ] 1 n a (*Jur etc: violation*) infraction *f* (*of* à), manquement *m* (*of* à, aux devoirs de); *[rules, order, discipline]* infraction; *[friendship, good manners]* manquement (*of* à); *[law]* violation *f* (*of* de). ~ **of contract** rupture *f* de contrat; **a** ~ **of decorum** une inconvenance; ~ **of faith** déloyauté *f*; ~ **of the peace** attentat *m* à l'ordre public; (*US Pol*) ~ **of privilege** atteinte portée aux prérogatives parlementaires; ~ **of promise** violation de promesse de mariage; **action for** ~ **of promise** ≃ action *f* en dommages-intérêts (*pour promesse de mariage*); ~ **of professional secrecy** violation du secret professionnel; ~ **of trust** abus *m* de confiance.

b (*estrangement*) brouille *f*, désaccord *m*.

c (*gap: in wall etc*) brèche *f*, trou *m*. (*Mil*) **to make a** ~ **in the enemy's lines** percer les lignes ennemies; (*fig*) **to step into the** ~ prendre la place.

2 **vt** *wall* ouvrir une brèche dans, faire une trouée dans; (*Mil*) *enemy lines, defences* percer.

3 **vi** *[whale]* sauter hors de l'eau.

bread [bred] 1 **n** a pain *m*. **loaf of** ~ pain, miche *f*; **new** ~ pain frais; ~ **fresh from the oven** du pain sortant du four; **an invalid on a diet of** ~ **and milk** un malade qui se nourrit de pain trempé dans du lait; ~ **and butter** tartine *f* (beurrée *or* de beurre) (*see also* **2**); (*fig*) **writing is his** ~ **and butter** sa plume est son gagne-pain, il vit de sa plume; **to earn one's** ~ gagner son pain *or* sa vie; **to take the** ~ **out of sb's mouth** retirer à qn le pain de la bouche; **to put sb on (dry)** ~ **and water** mettre qn au pain (sec) et à l'eau; (*fig*) **he knows which side his** ~ **is buttered** il sait où est son intérêt; (*fig*) **to throw** *or* **cast one's** ~ **upon the water(s)** agir de façon désintéressée; (*Rel*) **the** ~ **and wine** les (deux) espèces *fpl*; (*Rel*) **to break** ~ *[congregation]* recevoir la communion; *[priest]* administrer la communion; *see* **brown, ginger, sliced 2** *etc*.

b (*‡: money*) fric‡ *m*, oseille‡ *f*.

2 **comp** ►**bread-and-butter** (*fig*) *job etc* qui assure le nécessaire; (*reliable*) *player etc* sur qui l'on peut compter; **bread-and-butter letter** lettre *f* de château, lettre de remerciements (*pour hospitalité reçue*); **bread-and-butter pudding** pudding *m* de pain ►**breadbasket n** corbeille *f* à pain; (*‡: stomach*) estomac *m* ◊ **adj** (*Econ etc*) fondamental ►**breadbin** boîte *f* à pain; (*larger*) huche *f* à pain ►**breadboard** planche *f* à pain; (*Comput, Elec*) montage *m* expérimental ►**breadbox** (*US*) = **breadbin** ►**breadcrumb** miette *f* de pain ►**breadcrumbs** (*Culin*) chapelure *f*; **fried in breadcrumbs** pané; **with breadcrumbs** gratiné (*à la chapelure*) ►**breadfruit** (**pl** ~ *or* ~**s**) (*tree*) arbre *m* à pain; (*fruit*) fruit *m* de l'arbre à pain ►**breadknife** couteau *m* à pain ►**bread line** (*US*) *queue de gens qui attendent pour toucher des vivres;* (*Brit*) **to be on the bread line*** être sans le sou *or* dans la purée* ►**bread poultice** cataplasme *m* à la mie de pain ►**bread pudding** gâteau *m* à la mie de pain ►**bread sauce** sauce *f* à la mie de pain ►**breadwinner** soutien *m* (de famille).

breaded ['bredɪd] **adj** *cutlet, fillet* pané.

breadth [bretθ] 1 **n** a (*width*) largeur *f*. **this field is 100 metres in** ~ ce champ a 100 mètres de large; *see* **hairbreadth** *etc*. b (*fig*) *[mind, thought]* largeur *f*; (*style*) ampleur *f*; (*Art*) largeur d'exécution; (*Mus*) jeu *m* large. (*Mus*) ~ **of tone** ampleur du son. 2 **comp** ►**breadthwise** en largeur, dans la largeur.

break [breɪk] (**vb: pret broke, ptp broken**) 1 **n** a (*fracture*) (*lit*) cassure *f*, rupture *f*; (*fig*) *[relationship]* rupture, brouille *f*.

b (*gap*) *[wall]* trouée *f*, brèche *f*; *[rock]* faille *f*; *[line]* interruption *f*, rupture *f*.

c (*interruption, interval*) *[conversation]* interruption *f*, pause *f*; *[TV programme etc]* interruption; *[journey]* arrêt *m*; (*Brit Scol*) récréation *f*; (*Gram, Typ*) points *mpl* de suspension. **I need a** ~ (*few minutes*) il faut que je m'arrête (*subj*) cinq minutes; (*holiday*) j'ai besoin de vacances; (*change*) j'ai besoin de me changer les idées; **to take a** ~ s'arrêter cinq minutes; prendre des vacances; se changer les idées; **6 hours without a** ~ 6 heures de suite, 6 heures sans discontinuer; (*Rad*) ~ **in transmission** interruption (due à un incident technique); (*Rad, TV: advertisements*) **after the** ~ après l'intermède *m* de publicité; (*Elec*) ~ **in circuit** rupture *f* de circuit; **a** ~ **in the clouds** une éclaircie; **a** ~ **in the weather** un changement de temps; **with a** ~ **in her voice** d'une voix entrecoupée.

d (*liter*) **at** ~ **of day** au point du jour, à l'aube.

e (**: escape: also* ~**out**) évasion *f*, fuite *f*, cavale‡ *f*. **to make a** ~ **for it** prendre la fuite; **he made a** ~ **for the door** il s'est élancé vers la porte.

f (**: luck, opportunity*) chance *f*, veine* *f*. **to have a good/bad** ~ avoir une période de veine/déveine*; **he's had all the** ~**s** il a eu toutes les veines*; **give him a** ~! (*give him a chance*) donnez-lui une chance!; (*leave him alone*) fichez-lui la paix!*

g (*Snooker*) série *f*.

h (*vehicle*) break *m*.

2 **comp** ►**breakaway n** (*separating*) *[people]* séparation *f*; *[group, movement]* rupture *f*; (*Sport*) échappée *f*; (*Boxing*) dégagement *m*; (*Cine*) accessoire *m* cassable ◊ **adj** *group, movement* séparatiste, dissident; (*Pol*) **breakaway state** état dissident ►**break bulk agent** dégroupeur *m* ►**break dancer** smurfer *m* ►**break dancing** le smurf ►**breakdown** *see* **breakdown** ►**break-even point** (*Comm*) seuil *m* de rentabilité ►**break-in** cambriolage *m* ►**breakneck: at breakneck speed** (*run*) à une allure folle, à fond de train; (*drive*) à une allure folle, à tombeau ouvert ►**breakout** évasion *f* (*de prison*) ►**break point** (*Tennis*) point *m* d'avantage; (*Comput*) point de rupture ►**breakthrough** (*Mil*) percée *f*; *[research etc]* découverte capitale ►**break-up** *[ship]* dislocation *f*; *[ice]* débâcle *f*; *[friendship]* rupture *f*; *[empire]* démembrement *m*; *[political party]* débâcle *f* ►**breakwater** brise-lames *m inv*, digue *f*.

3 **vt** a (*smash, fracture, tear*) *cup, chair* casser, briser; *shoelace* casser; *stick* casser, briser, rompre; *bone* casser, fracturer; *skin* entamer, écorcher. **to** ~ **sth in two** casser qch en deux; **the child has broken all his toys** l'enfant a cassé *or* brisé *or* démoli tous ses jouets; **to** ~ **one's neck** se rompre *or* se casser le cou (*see also* **2**); (*fig*) **I'll** ~ **his neck* if I catch him doing that again** si je l'y reprends je lui tords le cou*; **to** ~ **one's leg** se casser *or* se fracturer la jambe; (*Theat*) ~ **a leg!*** bonne chance!, merde!‡; **the bone is not broken** il n'y a pas de fracture; **his skin is not broken** il ne s'est pas écorché; **to** ~ **open** *door* enfoncer, forcer; *packet* ouvrir; *lock, safe* fracturer, forcer; (*fig*) **to** ~ **new** *or* **fresh ground** innover, faire œuvre de pionnier; (*Aviat*) **to** ~ **the sound barrier** franchir le mur du son; (*Sport etc*) **to** ~ **a record** battre un record; **to** ~ **one's back** se casser la colonne vertébrale; **he almost broke his back trying to lift the stone** il s'est donné un tour de reins en essayant de soulever la pierre; (*Brit fig*) **to** ~ **the back of a task** faire le plus dur *or* le plus gros d'une tâche; **to** ~ **one's heart over sth** avoir le cœur brisé par qch; **to** ~ **sb's heart** briser le cœur à *or* de qn; **to** ~ **the ice** (*lit, also in conversation etc*) briser *or* rompre la glace; (*broach tricky matter*) entamer le sujet délicat; **to** ~ **surface** *[submarine]* faire surface; *[diver]* réapparaître; **to** ~ **wind** lâcher un vent; *see* **bone, bread**.

b (*fig: fail to observe*) *promise* manquer à, violer; *treaty* violer; *commandment* désobéir à. (*Mil*) **to** ~ **bounds** violer la consigne; **to** ~ **faith with sb** manquer de parole à qn; **to** ~ **the law** violer la loi; **to** ~ **the sabbath** violer le sabbat; **to** ~ **a vow** rompre un serment, transgresser un vœu; **to** ~ **an appointment with sb** faire faux bond à qn; *see* **parole**.

c (*weaken, vanquish*) *health* abîmer, détériorer; *strike* briser; *rebellion* mater; *courage, spirit* abattre, briser; *horse* dresser; (*Mil*) *officer* casser. **to** ~ **sb** (*morally*) causer la perte de qn; (*financially*) ruiner qn; **this will make or** ~ **him** (*financially*) cela fera sa fortune ou sa ruine; (*morally*) cela sera son salut ou sa perte; **to** ~ **sb of a habit** faire perdre une habitude à qn; **to** ~ **a habit** se débarrasser *or* se défaire d'une habitude; (*Betting*) **to** ~ **the bank** faire sauter la banque; (*fig*) **it won't** ~ **the bank*** cela ne va pas te (*or* nous *or* vous *or* les *etc*) ruiner.

d (*interrupt*) *silence, spell, fast* rompre; (*Elec*) *current, circuit* couper. (*Tennis*) **to** ~ **sb's service** prendre le service de qn; **to** ~ **one's journey** faire une étape (*or* des étapes); **to** ~ **the thread of a story** couper le fil d'un récit.

e (*leave*) **to** ~ **jail** s'évader (de prison); **to** ~ **cover** *[fox, hare]* débusquer; *[stag]* débucher; *[hunted person]* sortir à découvert; **to** ~ **ranks** *[soldiers]* rompre les rangs; (*fig*) *[splinter group]* décider de faire bande à part; **to** ~ **camp** lever le camp.

f (*soften*) *fall, blow* amortir, adoucir. **the wall** ~**s the force of the wind** le mur coupe le vent.

g *news* révéler, annoncer. **try to** ~ **it to her gently** essayez de le lui annoncer avec ménagements.

h (*Naut*) *flag, signal* déferler.

4 **vi** a (*fracture, fall apart*) (*gen*) (se) casser, se briser; *[stick, rope]* se casser, se rompre; *[bone]* se casser, se fracturer; *[wave]* déferler; *[clouds]* se disperser, se dissiper; *[troops]* rompre les rangs; *[ranks]* se rompre; (*fig*) *[heart]* se briser. **to** ~ **in two** se casser en deux; (*Med*) **her waters broke** elle a perdu ses eaux.

b (*escape*) se libérer (*from* de). **to** ~ **free** se libérer, se dégager; **to** ~ **loose** *[person, animal]* s'échapper (*from* de); *[ship]* rompre ses amarres, partir à la dérive.

c *[news, story]* éclater, se répandre; *[storm]* éclater, se déchaîner.

d (*weaken, change*) *[health]* s'altérer, se détériorer; *[voice]* (*boy's*) muer; (*in emotion*) s'altérer, se briser, s'étrangler (*with* de); *[weather]* se gâter, s'altérer. **the heatwave was** ~**ing** la vague de chaleur touchait à sa fin; **he broke under torture** il a craqué sous la torture; **his courage** *or* **spirit broke** son courage l'a abandonné.

e (*Boxing*) se dégager. (*fig*) **to** ~ **with a friend** rompre avec un ami.

f *[dawn]* poindre; *[day]* se lever, poindre.

g **to** ~ **even** *[individual]* s'y retrouver, s'en tirer sans gains ni pertes; *[shop, company]* atteindre l'équilibre financier.

h (*fig: pause*) **we broke for lunch** nous nous sommes arrêtés *or* nous avons fait une pause pour le déjeuner.

i (*Ling*) *[vowel]* se diphtonguer.

j (*Sport*) *[ball]* dévier.

►**break away** 1 **vi** a *[piece of cliff, railway coach]* se détacher (*from* de); *[boat]* rompre ses amarres, partir à la dérive. **to break away from a group** (*lit*) se détacher d'un groupe; (*fig*) se séparer d'un groupe; **to break away from routine** sortir de la routine. b (*Ftbl*) s'échapper; (*Racing*) s'échapper, se détacher du peloton. 2 **vt sep** (*lit, fig*) détacher (*from* de). 3 **breakaway** adj, n *see* **break 2**.

▸**break down** 1 vi a (*fail, cease to function*) *[vehicle, machine]* tomber en panne; *[health]* se détériorer; *[argument]* s'effondrer; *[resistance]* céder; *[negotiations, plan]* échouer. **after negotiations broke down** après l'échec *m or* la rupture des négociations. b (*weep*) fondre en larmes, éclater en sanglots. 2 vt sep a (*demolish*) démolir, mettre en morceaux; *door* enfoncer; (*fig*) *opposition* briser. b (*analyse*) *accounts* analyser, détailler; *reasons* décomposer (*into* en); *sales figures, costs* ventiler; (*Chem*) *substance* décomposer. **he broke down his argument into 3 points** il a décomposé son raisonnement en 3 points. 3 **breakdown** n, comp *see* **breakdown**.

▸**break forth** vi (*liter*) *[light, water]* jaillir; *[storm]* éclater. **to break forth into song** se mettre à chanter, entonner un chant.

▸**break in** 1 vi a (*interrupt, intrude*) interrompre. **to break in (up)on sb/sth** interrompre qn/qch. b (*enter illegally*) entrer par effraction. 2 vt sep a *door* enfoncer; *cask* défoncer. b (*tame, train*) *horse* dresser; (*US*) *engine, car* roder. **it will take you 6 months before you're broken in* (to the job)** vous mettrez 6 mois à vous faire au métier *or* à vous roder*. 3 **break-in** n *see* **break 2**.

▸**break into** vt fus a (*enter illegally*) *house* entrer par effraction dans. **to break into a safe** fracturer *or* forcer un coffre-fort; **to break into the cashbox** forcer la caisse. b (*use part of*) *savings* entamer. **to break into a new box of sth** entamer une nouvelle boîte de qch. c (*Comm*) **to break into a new market** percer sur un nouveau marché. d (*begin suddenly*) commencer à, se mettre à. **to break into song** se mettre à chanter; **he broke into a long explanation** il s'est lancé dans une longue explication; **to break into a trot** *[horse]* prendre le trot; *[person]* se mettre à trotter.

▸**break off** 1 vi a *[piece, twig]* se détacher net, se casser net. b (*stop*) s'arrêter (*doing* de faire). **to break off from work** prendre un moment de répit *or* de récréation, interrompre le travail, faire la pause. c (*end relationship*) rompre (*with sb* avec qn). d (*Snooker*) commencer la partie. 2 vt sep a *piece of rock, chocolate etc* casser, détacher. b (*end, interrupt*) *engagement, negotiations* rompre; *habit* rompre avec, se défaire de; *work* interrompre, cesser.

▸**break out** 1 vi a *[epidemic, fire]* éclater, se déclarer; *[storm, war, argument]* éclater. **to break out in(to) spots** se couvrir de boutons; **to break out into a sweat** prendre une suée*, (*from fear etc*) commencer à avoir des sueurs froides; **he broke out into a stream of insults** il a sorti un chapelet d'injures. b (*escape*) s'échapper, s'évader (*of* de). 2 vt sep *champagne etc* sortir. 3 **breakout** n *see* **break 2**.

▸**break through** 1 vi (*Mil*) faire une percée; *[sun]* percer (les nuages). 2 vt *fus defences, obstacles* enfoncer, percer. **to break through sb's reserve** percer la réserve de qn; **to break through the crowd** se frayer un passage à travers la foule; (*Aviat*) **to break through the sound barrier** franchir le mur du son. 3 **breakthrough** n *see* **break 2**.

▸**break up** 1 vi a *[ice]* craquer, se fêler; *[road]* être défoncé; *[ship in storm]* se disloquer; *[partnership]* cesser, prendre fin; *[health]* se détériorer, se délabrer. **the weather is breaking up** le temps se gâte; **their marriage is breaking up** leur mariage est en train de se briser *or* est à vau-l'eau.

b (*disperse*) *[clouds, crowd]* se disperser; *[group]* se disperser, se séparer; *[meeting]* se disperser; *[friends]* se quitter, se séparer; (*Brit*) *[school, college]* entrer en vacances. **the schools break up tomorrow** les vacances (scolaires) commencent demain.

c (*US* ‡: *laugh*) avoir le fou rire.

2 vt sep a (*lit*) mettre en morceaux, morceler; *house* démolir; *ground* ameublir; *road* défoncer. **to break sth up into 3 pieces** mettre *or* casser qch en 3 morceaux.

b (*fig*) *coalition* briser, rompre; *empire* démembrer. **to break up a marriage/a home** désunir un ménage/une famille; **to do sth to break up one's day** faire qch pour faire paraître la journée moins longue.

c (*disperse*) *crowd, meeting* disperser; **break it up!** séparez-vous!; (*said by policeman*) circulez!

d (*US* ‡: *make laugh*) donner le fou rire à.

3 **break-up** n, **breaking-up** n *see* **breaking 2**.

breakable ['breɪkəbl] 1 adj cassable, fragile. 2 n: **~s** objets *mpl* fragiles.

breakage ['breɪkɪdʒ] n (*in chain*) rupture *f*; *[glass, china]* casse *f*, bris *m*. **to pay for ~s** payer la casse.

breakdown ['breɪkdaʊn] 1 n a *[machine, vehicle, electricity supply]* panne *f*. b *[communications etc]* rupture *f*; *[railway system etc]* interruption *f* (subite) de service; (*fig*) *[moral values etc]* érosion *f*, dégradation *f*. c (*Med*) (*mental*) dépression nerveuse; (*physical*) effondrement *m*. d (*analysis*) analyse *f*; (*into categories*) décomposition *f* (*into* en); *[sales figures, costs etc]* ventilation *f*. **give me a ~ of these results** faites-moi l'analyse de ces résultats. 2 comp *gang, service* de dépannage ▸**breakdown van** *or* **truck** (*Brit Aut*) dépanneuse *f*.

breaker ['breɪkəʳ] n a (*wave*) brisant *m*. b (*person*) briseur *m*, casseur *m*. **to send to the ~'s** *ship* envoyer à la démolition; *car* envoyer à la casse; *see* **house, law** *etc*. c (*machine*) concasseur *m*, broyeur *m*; *see* **ice** *etc*. d (*CB user*) cibiste *mf*.

breakfast ['brekfəst] 1 n petit déjeuner *m*. **to have ~** déjeuner, prendre le (petit) déjeuner; *see* **wedding** *etc*. 2 vi déjeuner (*off, on* de). 3 comp ▸**breakfast cereals** céréales *fpl* (*flocons d'avoine, de maïs etc*) ▸**breakfast cloth** nappe *f* (ordinaire) ▸**breakfast cup** déjeuner *m* (*tasse*) ▸**breakfast meeting** (*Comm*) petit déjeuner *m* d'affaires ▸**breakfast room** petite salle à manger ▸**breakfast set** service *m* à petit déjeuner ▸**breakfast table: they were still sitting at the breakfast table** ils étaient encore assis à la table du petit déjeuner ▸**breakfast TV** la télévision du matin *or* du petit déjeuner.

breaking ['breɪkɪŋ] 1 n *[cup, chair]* bris *m*; *[bone, limb]* fracture *f*; (*Jur*) *[window, seals]* bris; *[promise]* manquement *m* (*of* à), violation *f* (*of* de); *[treaty, law]* violation (*of* de); *[commandment]* désobéissance *f* (*of* à); *[silence, spell]* rupture *f*; *[journey]* interruption *f* (*of* de).

2 comp ▸**breaking and entering** (*Jur*) effraction *f* ▸**breaking-point** (*Tech*) point *m* de rupture; **to try sb's patience to breaking-point** pousser à bout la patience de qn; **she has reached breaking-point** elle est à bout, elle n'en peut plus; (*Pol etc*) **the situation has reached breaking-point** on est au point de rupture ▸**breaking strain** (*Tech*) point *m* de rupture ▸**breaking strength** module *m* de résistance ▸**breaking stress** = **breaking strain** ▸**breaking-up** *[school, college]* début *m* des vacances, fin *f* des classes; *[meeting etc]* clôture *f*, levée *f*.

bream [briːm] n, pl inv brème *f*.

breast [brest] 1 n a (*chest*) *[man, woman]* poitrine *f*; *[animal]* poitrine, poitrail *m*; (*Culin*) *[chicken etc]* blanc *m*; *see* **beat, clean**.

b *[woman]* sein *m*, mamelle *f* (†, *liter*); *[man]* sein. **baby at the ~** enfant *mf* au sein.

c (*Min*) front *m* de taille; *see* **chimney**.

2 vt a (*face*) *waves, storm, danger* affronter.

b *hill* atteindre le sommet de. (*Sport*) **to ~ the tape** franchir la ligne d'arrivée (le premier).

3 comp ▸**breastbone** sternum *m*; *[bird]* bréchet *m* ▸**breast cancer** cancer *m* du sein ▸**breast-fed** nourri au sein ▸**breast-feed** vt allaiter, donner le sein à ◊ vi allaiter ▸**breast-feeding** allaitement maternel *or* au sein ▸**breastplate** *[priest]* pectoral *m*; *[armour]* plastron *m* (de cuirasse) ▸**breast-pocket** poche *f* de poitrine ▸**breast-stroke** brasse *f*; **to swim breast-stroke** nager la brasse ▸**breastwork** (*Mil*) parapet *m*; (*Naut*) rambarde *f*.

breath [breθ] 1 n a haleine *f*, souffle *m*, respiration *f*. **bad ~** mauvaise haleine; **to have bad ~** avoir (une) mauvaise haleine; **to get one's ~ back** reprendre haleine, retrouver son souffle; **out of ~** à bout de souffle, essoufflé, hors d'haleine; **to take ~** respirer, reprendre haleine; **to take a deep ~** respirer à fond; (*fig*) **take a deep ~!** accroche-toi bien!*; (*fig*) **to take sb's ~ away** couper le souffle à qn; **save your ~!** inutile de gaspiller ta salive!; **to be short of ~** avoir le souffle court; **to gasp for ~** haleter; **to stop for ~** s'arrêter pour reprendre haleine; **below** *or* **beneath** *or* **under one's ~** (*gen*) à voix basse, tout bas; **to laugh under one's ~** rire sous cape; **she contradicted herself in the same ~** elle s'est contredite dans la même seconde; **to say sth (all) in one ~** dire qch tout d'un trait; (*fig*) **it was the ~ of life to him** c'était (toute) sa vie, cela lui était aussi précieux que la vie même; **his last** *or* **dying ~** son dernier soupir; **with one's dying ~** en mourant; (*liter*) **to draw one's last ~** rendre l'âme, rendre le dernier soupir; *see* **catch, hold, waste** *etc*.

b (*air in movement*) souffle *m*. **there wasn't a ~ of air** il n'y avait pas un souffle d'air; **to go out for a ~ of (fresh) air** sortir prendre l'air; (*fig*) **a ~ of fresh air** une bouffée d'air frais; **a little ~ of wind** un (léger) souffle d'air; (*fig*) **not a ~ of scandal** pas le moindre soupçon de scandale.

2 comp ▸**breath test** (*Aut*) Alcootest ® *m* ▸**breath-test** vt faire subir l'Alcootest ® à.

breathable ['briːðəbl] adj *air, atmosphere* respirable.

breathalyse, (*US*) **breathalyze** ['breθəlaɪz] vt faire subir l'Alcootest ® à.

Breathalyser, (*US*) **Breathalyzer** ['breθəlaɪzəʳ] n ® Alcootest *m* ®.

breathe [briːð] 1 vi respirer. **to ~ deeply, to ~ heavily** (*after running etc*) haleter, souffler (fort); (*in illness*) respirer péniblement; **to ~ hard** souffler (fort), haleter; (*fig*) **to ~ freely** *or* **again** *or* **more easily** (pouvoir) respirer; (*be alive*) **she is still breathing** elle vit encore, elle est toujours en vie; (*fig*) **to ~ down sb's neck** harceler qn, talonner qn.

2 vt a *air* respirer. **to ~ one's last (breath)** rendre le dernier soupir; **to ~ air into sth** insuffler de l'air *or* souffler dans qch; **to ~ new life into sb** redonner goût à la vie *or* du courage à qn.

b (*utter*) *sigh* exhaler, laisser échapper, pousser; *prayer* murmurer. **to ~ a sigh of relief** pousser un soupir de soulagement; **don't ~ a word (about it)!** n'en dis rien à personne!, motus!

c (*Ling*) aspirer.

▸**breathe in** vi, vt sep aspirer, inspirer.

▸**breathe out** vi, vt sep expirer.

breather* ['briːðəʳ] n a (*short rest*) moment *m* de repos *or* répit. **to give sb a ~** laisser souffler qn. b (*fresh air*) **let's go (out) for a ~** sortons prendre l'air.

breathing ['briːðɪŋ] 1 n a respiration *f*, souffle *m*; *[singer, flautist etc]* respiration *f*. **heavy ~** respiration bruyante. b (*Ling*) aspiration *f*. (*Greek Gram*) **rough/smooth ~** esprit rude/doux. 2 comp ▸**breathing apparatus** appareil *m* respiratoire ▸**a breathing space** (*fig*) le temps de souffler, un moment de répit.

breathless ['breθlɪs] adj (*from exertion*) hors d'haleine, haletant; (*through illness*) oppressé, qui a de la peine à respirer. ~ **with excitement** le souffle coupé par l'émotion; **a ~ silence** un silence ému; **in ~ terror** le souffle coupé par la terreur.
breathlessly ['breθlɪslɪ] adv (en) haletant; (*fig*) en grande hâte.
breathlessness ['breθlɪsnɪs] n difficulté *f* respiratoire.
breathtaking ['breθteɪkɪŋ] adj stupéfiant, à vous couper le souffle.
breathtakingly ['breθteɪkɪŋlɪ] adv: ~ **beautiful** beau à vous couper le souffle, d'une beauté stupéfiante.
breathy ['breθɪ] adj *voice* voilé.
bred [bred] 1 pret, ptp of **breed**. 2 adj ending in comps: **well-bred** bien élevé; *see* **country, ill.**
breech [briːtʃ] 1 n a [*gun*] culasse *f*. b (*Med*) ~ **(birth** *or* **delivery)** (accouchement *m* par le) siège *m*; **he** *or* **she was a ~*** c'était un siège. 2 vt *gun* munir d'une culasse. 3 comp ►**breechblock** bloc *m* de culasse ►**breechcloth** (*US*) pagne *m* (*d'étoffe*) ►**breechloader** (*Mil*) arme *f* qui se charge par la culasse.
breeches ['brɪtʃɪz] 1 npl: **(pair of)** ~ (*knee* ~) haut-de-chausses *m*; (*riding* ~) culotte *f* (de cheval); **his wife wears the ~** c'est sa femme qui porte la culotte. 2 ['briːtʃɪz] comp ►**breeches buoy** (*Naut*) bouée-culotte *f*.
breed [briːd] pret, ptp **bred** 1 vt *animals* élever, faire l'élevage de; (††) *children* élever; (*fig: give rise to*) faire naître, donner naissance à, engendrer. **he ~s horses** il fait l'élevage des chevaux; **to ~ in/out a characteristic** faire acquérir/faire perdre une caractéristique (*par la sélection*); **to be bred for sth/to do sth** [*animals*] être élevé pour qch/pour faire qch; [*people*] être conditionné pour qch/pour faire qch. *see* **born, cross, familiarity.**
2 vi [*animals*] se reproduire, se multiplier. **they ~ like rabbits** ils se multiplient comme des lapins.
3 n (*Zool*) (*race*) race *f*, espèce *f*; (*within race*) type *m*; (*Bot*) espèce; (*fig*) sorte *f*, espèce; *see* **cross, half.**
breeder ['briːdəʳ] n a (*Phys: also* ~ **reactor**) sur(ré)générateur *m*. b (*Agr etc: person*) éleveur *m*, -euse *f*; *see* **cattle, plant, stock** *etc*.
breeding ['briːdɪŋ] n a (*reproduction*) reproduction *f*, procréation *f*. ~ **ground** (*lit*) zone *f* de reproduction; (*fig*) ~ **ground for revolution/germs** terrain *m* propice à la révolution/aux microbes; (*fig*) ~ **ground for talent/revolutionaries** pépinière *f* de talents/de révolutionnaires; ~ **season** [*animals*] saison *f* des accouplements; [*birds*] saison des nids. b (*Agr: raising*) élevage *m*; *see* **cattle** *etc*. c (*upbringing*) **(good)** ~ (bonne) éducation *f*, bonnes manières, savoir-vivre *m*; **to lack** ~ manquer de savoir-vivre. d (*Phys*) surrégénération *f*.
breeks [briːks] npl (*Scot*) pantalon *m*.
breeze[1] [briːz] 1 n a (*wind*) brise *f*. **gentle ~** petite brise, souffle *m* de vent; **stiff ~** vent frais; **there is quite a ~** cela souffle; *see* **sea** *etc*. b (*US **) **it's a ~** c'est facile comme tout; **to do sth in a ~** faire qch les doigts dans le nez*. 2 vi: **to ~ in/out** *etc* (*jauntily*) entrer/sortir *etc* d'un air dégagé; (*briskly*) entrer/sortir *etc* en coup de vent; (*US*) **to ~ through sth*** faire qch les doigts dans le nez*.
breeze[2] [briːz] n (*cinders*) cendres *fpl* (de charbon). (*Brit*) ~ **block** parpaing *m*.
breezily ['briːzɪlɪ] adv jovialement.
breezy ['briːzɪ] adj *weather, day* frais (*f* fraîche); *corner, spot* éventé; (*fig*) *person* jovial.
Bren [bren] n (*Mil*) ~ **gun** fusil-mitrailleur; ~ **(gun) carrier** chenillette *f* (pour fusil-mitrailleur).
brent [brent] adj: ~ **goose** bernache cravant *m*.
brethren ['breðrɪn] npl a (††, *Rel*) frères *mpl*. b (*fellow members*) [*trade union etc*] camarades *mpl*.
Breton ['bretən] 1 adj breton. 2 n a Breton(ne) *m(f)*. b (*Ling*) breton *m*.
breve [briːv] n (*Typ*) brève *f*; (*Mus*) double ronde *f*.
brevet ['brevɪt] n (*esp Mil*) brevet *m*.
breviary ['briːvɪərɪ] n bréviaire *m*.
brevity ['brevɪtɪ] n (*shortness*) brièveté *f*; (*conciseness*) concision *f*; (*abruptness*) [*reply*] laconisme *m*; [*manner*] brusquerie *f*. (*Prov*) ~ **is the soul of wit** les plaisanteries les plus courtes sont les meilleures.
brew [bruː] 1 n a [*beer*] brassage *m*; (*amount brewed*) brassin *m*; *see* **home.**
b [*tea*] infusion *f*; [*herbs*] tisane *f*. **witch's ~** brouet *m* de sorcière (†, *hum*); (*hum*) **what's this ~* in the jug?** qu'est-ce que c'est que ce liquide *or* cette mixture dans la cruche?
2 comp ►**brew-up***: (*Brit*) **let's have a brew-up** on va se faire du thé.
3 vt *beer* brasser; *tea* faire infuser, préparer; *punch* préparer, mélanger; (*fig*) *scheme, mischief, plot* préparer, tramer, mijoter*.
4 vi a (*make beer*) brasser, faire de la bière.
b [*beer*] fermenter; [*tea*] infuser; (*fig*) [*storm*] couver, se préparer; [*plot*] se tramer, (se) mijoter*. **there's trouble ~ing** il y a de l'orage dans l'air, ça va barder‡, il va y avoir du grabuge*; **something's ~ing** il se trame quelque chose.
►**brew up** 1 vi a (*: *make tea*) faire du thé. b [*storm, dispute*] se préparer. 2 **brew-up*** n *see* **brew 2.**
brewer ['bruːəʳ] n brasseur *m*.
brewery ['bruːərɪ] n brasserie *f* (*fabrique*).
briar ['braɪəʳ] n = **brier.**
bribe [braɪb] 1 n pot-de-vin *m*. **to take a ~** se laisser corrompre *or* acheter, accepter un pot-de-vin; **to offer a ~** faire une tentative de corruption, offrir un pot-de-vin; **I'll give the child a sweet as a ~ to be good** je donnerai un bonbon à l'enfant pour qu'il se tienne tranquille.
2 vt suborner, acheter (la conscience de), soudoyer; *witness* suborner. **to ~ sb into silence** acheter le silence de qn; **to ~ sb to do sth** soudoyer *or* corrompre qn pour qu'il fasse qch; **to let o.s. be ~d** se laisser soudoyer.
bribery ['braɪbərɪ] n corruption *f*; (*Jur*) [*witness*] subornation *f*; (*Pol*) corruption électorale. (*Jur*) ~ **and corruption** corruption; **open to ~** corruptible.
bric-à-brac ['brɪkəbræk] n (*NonC*) bric-à-brac *m*. ~ **dealer** brocanteur *m*.
brick [brɪk] 1 n a (*Constr*) brique *f*. **made of ~** en brique(s); **it has not damaged the ~s and mortar** ça n'a pas endommagé les murs; (*fig*) **to put one's money into ~s and mortar** investir dans la pierre *or* l'immobilier; (*Prov*) **you can't make ~s without straw** à l'impossible nul n'est tenu (*Prov*); (*fig*) **he came down on me like a ton of ~s*** il m'a passé un de ces savons!*; (*fig*) **you might as well talk to a ~ wall*** autant (vaut) parler à un mur, autant cracher en l'air*; (*fig*) **to run one's head against** *or* **come up against a ~ wall** se heurter à un mur; *see* **cat, drop.**
b (*Brit: toy*) cube *m* (*de construction*). **box of ~s** jeu *m* *or* boîte *f* de construction.
c **a ~ of ice cream** une glace (*empaquetée*).
d (*†: *person*) type *m* sympa*, fille *f* sympa*. **be a ~!** sois sympa!* *or* chic!
2 comp *house* en brique(s) ►**brickbat** (*lit*) morceau *m* de brique; (* *fig*) critique *f* ►**brick-built** en brique(s) ►**brick-kiln** four *m* à briques ►**bricklayer** maçon *m* ►**brick red** (rouge) brique *inv* ►**brickwork** briquetage *m*, brique *f* ►**brickworks, brickyard** briqueterie *f*.
►**brick in** vt sep = **brick up.**
►**brick off** vt sep *area* (em)murer.
►**brick up** vt sep *door, window* murer.
brickie* ['brɪkɪ] n (*Brit*) (abbr of **bricklayer**) maçon *m*.
bridal ['braɪdl] adj *feast* de noce; *bed, chamber, procession* nuptial; *veil, gown* de mariée. ~ **suite** suite *f* réservée aux jeunes mariés.
bride [braɪd] 1 n (jeune) mariée *f*; (*before wedding*) (future) mariée. **the ~ and (~)groom** les (jeunes) mariés; (*Rel*) **the ~ of Christ** l'épouse *f* du Christ. 2 comp ►**bridegroom** (*just married*) (jeune) marié *m*; (*about to be married*) (futur) marié ►**bridesmaid** demoiselle *f* d'honneur ►**bride-to-be** future mariée; **his bride-to-be** sa future femme, sa promise (*hum*).
bridge[1] [brɪdʒ] 1 n a pont *m*. **to build/throw a ~ across a river** construire/jeter un pont sur un fleuve; *see* **burn, cross, draw, foot** *etc*. b (*Naut*) passerelle *f* (de commandement). c [*nose*] arête *f*, dos *m*; [*spectacles*] arcade *f*; [*violin*] chevalet *m*. d (*Dentistry*) bridge *m*. 2 vt *river* construire *or* jeter un pont sur. (*fig*) **to ~ a gap** (*between people*) établir un rapprochement (*between* entre); (*in knowledge, facts*) combler une lacune (*in* dans); (*in budget*) combler un trou (*in* dans). 3 comp ►**bridgebuilder** (*fig*) médiateur *m*, -trice *f* ►**bridge-building** (*Mil*) pontage *m*; (*fig*) efforts *mpl* de rapprochement ►**bridgehead** (*Mil*) tête *f* de pont.
bridge[2] [brɪdʒ] 1 n (*Cards*) bridge *m*. **to play ~** bridger, jouer au bridge; *see* **auction, contract**[1]. 2 comp ►**bridge party** soirée *f* *or* réunion *f* de bridge ►**bridge player** bridgeur *m*, -euse *f* ►**bridge roll** petit pain (brioché).
bridging ['brɪdʒɪŋ] 1 n (*Climbing*) opposition *f*. 2 comp ►**bridging loan** (*Brit Fin*) prêt relais *m*.
bridle ['braɪdl] 1 n [*horse*] bride *f*; (*fig*) frein *m*, contrainte *f*. ~ **path** sentier *m*, piste cavalière. 2 vt *horse* brider; *one's emotions* refréner, mettre la bride à. **to ~ one's tongue** se taire, tenir sa langue. 3 vi (*in anger*) regimber, se rebiffer; (*in scorn*) lever le menton (*de mépris*).
brief [briːf] 1 adj a (*short*) *life, meeting* bref; *stay* court, de courte durée, passager. **for a ~ period** pendant un temps très court; ~ **interval** court intervalle.
b (*concise*) *speech etc* bref, concis. ~ **account** exposé *m* sommaire; **in ~** en deux mots, en résumé; **to be ~, he didn't come** bref *or* pour vous dire la chose en deux mots, il n'est pas venu.
c (*curt, abrupt*) *speech, reply* laconique; *manner* brusque.
2 n a (*Jur*) dossier *m*, cause *f*, affaire *f*. (*Jur*) **to hold a ~ for sb** représenter qn en justice; (*fig*) **I hold no ~ for those who ...** je ne me fais pas l'avocat *or* le défenseur de ceux qui ...; (*fig*) **I hold no ~ for him** je ne prends pas sa défense; **to have a watching ~ for** veiller (en justice) aux intérêts de; (*Jur*) **to take a ~** accepter de plaider une cause.
b (*Mil: instructions*) briefing *m*. (*fig*) **his ~ is to ...** la tâche qui lui a été assignée consiste à ... .
c (*Dress*) ~**s** slip *m*.
3 vt a (*Jur*) *barrister* confier une cause à.
b (*Mil*) *pilots, soldiers* donner des instructions à; (*gen*) *person* (*give order to*) donner des instructions à; (*bring up to date*) mettre au

courant (*on sth* de qch). (*Mil*) **the pilots were ~ed** les pilotes ont reçu leurs (dernières) instructions.

c (*Comm*) *salesman* donner des instructions à. **we ~ our salesmen once a week** nous faisons un briefing hebdomadaire à l'intention de nos vendeurs.

4 **comp** ▸ **briefcase** serviette *f*, (*handleless*) porte-documents *m inv*.

briefing ['bri:fɪŋ] **n** (*Aviat, Mil*) instructions *fpl*; (*gen*) briefing *m*; (*notes*) notes *fpl*.

briefly ['bri:flɪ] **adv** *visit* en coup de vent; *reply* laconiquement, en peu de mots; *speak* brièvement.

briefness ['bri:fnɪs] **n** (*see* **brief**) brièveté *f*; courte durée; concision *f*; laconisme *m*; brusquerie *f*.

brier ['braɪəʳ] **n** a (*wood*) (racine *f* de) bruyère *f*; (*also* **~ pipe**) pipe *f* de bruyère. b (*wild rose*) églantier *m*; (*thorny bush*) ronces *fpl*; (*thorn*) épine *f*. **~ rose** églantine *f*.

brig [brɪg] **n** (*Naut*) brick *m*.

Brig. **abbr of brigadier. ~ A. Robert** le général A. Robert.

brigade [brɪ'geɪd] **n** (*Mil, fig*) brigade *f*. (*fig*) **one of the old ~** un vétéran, un vieux de la vieille; *see* **fire**.

brigadier [ˌbrɪgə'dɪəʳ] 1 **n** (*Brit*) général *m* de brigade. 2 **comp** ▸ **brigadier general** (*US*) (**pl ~ ~s**) (*Mil*) général *m* de brigade; (*Aviat*) général de brigade aérienne.

brigand ['brɪgənd] **n** brigand *m*, bandit *m*.

brigandage ['brɪgəndɪdʒ] **n** brigandage *m*.

Bright [braɪt] **n**: **~'s disease** mal *m* de Bright, néphrite *f* chronique.

bright [braɪt] **adj** a (*shining*) *eyes* brillant, vif; *star, gem* brillant; *light* vif; *fire* vif, clair; *weather* clair, radieux; *sunshine* éclatant; *day, room* clair; *colour* vif, éclatant, lumineux; *metal* poli, luisant. **~-eyed** aux yeux brillants; (*fig*) **~-eyed and bushy-tailed*** frais (*f* fraîche) comme la rosée; (*Met*) **to become ~er** s'éclaircir; (*Met*) **~ intervals** *or* **periods** éclaircies *fpl*; **the outlook is ~er** (*Met*) on prévoit une amélioration (du temps); (*fig*) l'avenir se présente mieux *or* sous des couleurs plus favorables; (*fig*) **the ~ lights*** la vie à la ville.

b (*cheerful*) gai, joyeux; (*vivacious*) vif, animé; *face, smile, expression* rayonnant, radieux (*with* de); *look* radieux, brillant (*with* de); *prospects, future* brillant, splendide; *example, period of history* glorieux. **~er days** des jours plus heureux; **as ~ as a button** gai comme un pinson; **~ and early** de bon matin; (*fig*) **we must look on the ~ side** nous devons essayer d'être optimistes.

c (*intelligent*) *person* intelligent, doué, brillant; *child* éveillé. **he's a ~ spark*** il est vraiment futé*, il est plein d'idées.

brighten ['braɪtn] (*also* **~ up**) 1 **vt** a (*make cheerful*) *room, spirits, person* égayer; *conversation* égayer, animer; *prospects, situation, future* améliorer. b (*make shine*) faire briller, rendre (plus) brillant; *metal* faire reluire; *colour* aviver. 2 **vi** a *[weather, sky]* s'éclaircir, se dégager. b *[eyes]* s'éclairer, s'allumer; *[expression]* s'éclairer, s'épanouir; *[person]* s'égayer, s'animer; *[prospects, future]* s'améliorer, se présenter sous un meilleur jour. 3 **comp** ▸ **brightening agent** *[washing powder]* agent *m* blanchissant.

brightly ['braɪtlɪ] **adv** (*see* **bright**) a avec éclat, brillamment. **the sun shone ~** le soleil brillait d'un vif éclat, le soleil flamboyait; **the fire burnt ~** un feu clair flambait. b *say, answer* gaiement, joyeusement; *smile, look* d'un air radieux.

brightness ['braɪtnɪs] **n** (*see* **bright**) a éclat *m*, brillant *m*; *[light]* intensité *f*. *[TV, computer screen]* **~ (control)** (bouton *m* de) luminosité *f*. b gaieté *f* *or* gaîté *f*, joie *f*; vivacité *f*. c intelligence *f*.

brill¹ [brɪl] **n, pl ~** *or* **~s** barbue *f*.

brill²* [brɪl] **adj** (**abbr of brilliant**) sensass* *inv*, super* *inv*.

brilliance ['brɪljəns] **n**, **brilliancy** ['brɪljənsɪ] **n** a (*splendour: lit, fig*) éclat *m*, brillant *m*. b (*great intelligence*) intelligence supérieure.

brilliant ['brɪljənt] **adj** a *sunshine, light* éclatant. b (*very clever*) *person, book, style, wit* brillant. c (*: *excellent*) super* *inv*.

brilliantine ['brɪljənˌti:n] **n** brillantine *f*.

brilliantly ['brɪljəntlɪ] **adv** (*shine*) avec éclat; *suggest, devise* brillamment. **~ lit** fortement éclairé; **~ coloured** aux couleurs *fpl* éclatantes; **he did ~ in his exam** il a brillamment réussi son examen; **she played/drove ~*** elle a super bien joué/conduit *etc**.

Brillo ['brɪləʊ] **adj** ®: **~ pad** tampon *m* Jex ®.

brim [brɪm] 1 **n** *[cup, hat, lake]* bord *m*. 2 **vi** (être plein à) déborder (*with* de). (*fig*) **~ming with** débordant de.

▸**brim over** **vi** (*lit, fig*) déborder (*with* de).

brimful ['brɪm'fʊl] **adj** (*lit*) plein à déborder; (*fig*) débordant (*with* de).

brimstone ['brɪmstəʊn] **n** soufre *m*; *see* **fire**.

brindle(d) ['brɪndl(d)] **adj** moucheté, tavelé.

brine [braɪn] **n** a (*salt water*) eau salée; (*Culin*) saumure *f*. b (*liter*) (*sea*) mer *f*, océan *m*; (*sea water*) eau *f* de mer.

bring [brɪŋ] **pret, ptp brought** 1 **vt** a *person, animal, vehicle* amener; *object, news, information* apporter. **to ~ sb up/down/across** *etc* faire monter/faire descendre/faire traverser *etc* qn (avec soi); **to ~ sth up/down** monter/descendre qch; **I brought him up his breakfast** je lui ai monté son petit déjeuner; *see* **bacon, bed**.

b (*cause*) amener, entraîner, causer; (*produce*) produire. **his books brought him a good income** ses livres lui rapportaient bien *or* lui étaient d'un bon rapport; **the hot weather ~s storms** le temps chaud provoque *or* amène des orages; **to ~ good/bad luck** porter bonheur/malheur; **to ~ a blush to sb's cheeks** faire rougir qn, faire monter le rouge aux joues de qn; **to ~ tears to sb's eyes** faire venir les larmes aux yeux de qn; **that brought him to the verge of insanity** cela l'a mené *or* amené au bord de la folie; **to ~ sth (up)on o.s.** s'attirer qch; **to ~ sb to book** faire rendre des comptes à qn; **to ~ sth to a close** *or* **an end** faire aboutir qch, mettre fin à qch; **to ~ sb to his feet** faire lever qn; **to ~ sb to justice** traduire qn en justice; (*fig*) **to ~ sth to light** mettre qch en lumière; **to ~ sb low** abaisser qn; **to ~ sth to sb's knowledge** signaler qch à qn, porter qch à la connaissance de qn (*frm*); **to ~ sth to mind** rappeler qch, évoquer qch; **to ~ sth into question** (*throw doubt on*) remettre qch en question; (*make one think about*) faire s'interroger sur; **to ~ to nothing** faire échouer, faire avorter; (*liter*) **to ~ sth to pass** causer qch; **to ~ to perfection** porter à la perfection; **to ~ sth into play** *or* **line** faire jouer *or* agir qch; **to ~ sb to his senses** ramener qn à la raison; **to ~ into the world** mettre au monde; *see* **bear¹, head**.

c (+ *infin: persuade*) amener, pousser, persuader (*sb to do* qn à faire). **he brought him to understand that ...** il l'a amené à comprendre que ...; **I cannot ~ myself to speak to him** je ne peux me résoudre à lui parler.

d (*Jur*) **to ~ an action against sb** intenter un procès à qn; **to ~ a charge against sb** porter une accusation contre qn; **the case was brought before Lord X** la cause fut entendue par Lord X; **to ~ evidence** avancer *or* fournir des preuves.

2 **comp** ▸ **bring-and-buy sale** (*Brit*) vente *f* de charité *or* de bienfaisance.

▸**bring about** **vt sep** a *reforms, review* amener, provoquer; *war* causer, provoquer; *accident* provoquer, occasionner, faire arriver; *sb's ruin* entraîner, amener. b *boat* faire virer de bord.

▸**bring along** **vt sep**: **to bring sth along (with one)** apporter qch (avec soi); **to bring sb along (with one)** amener qn (avec soi); **may I bring along a friend?** puis-je amener un ami?

▸**bring back** **vt sep** a *person* ramener; *object* rapporter. **to bring a spacecraft back to earth** récupérer un vaisseau spatial; **her holiday brought back her health** ses vacances lui ont rendu la santé; **a rest will bring him back to normal** du repos le remettra d'aplomb. b (*call to mind*) rappeler (à la mémoire).

▸**bring down** **vt sep** a *kite etc* ramener au sol; (*Hunting*) *animal, bird* descendre; *plane* faire atterrir; (*Mil*) *enemy plane* abattre, descendre; *tree, one's enemy* abattre. b *dictator, government* faire tomber; *temperature, prices, cost of living* faire baisser; *swelling* réduire; (*Math*) *figure* abaisser. **his action brought down everyone's wrath upon him** son action lui a attiré *or* lui a valu la colère de tout le monde; **the play brought the house down*** la pièce a fait crouler la salle sous les applaudissements.

▸**bring forth** **vt sep** (*liter*) *fruit* produire; *child* mettre au monde; *animal* mettre bas; (*fig*) *protests, criticism* provoquer.

▸**bring forward** **vt sep** a *person* faire avancer; *chair etc* avancer; *witness* produire; *evidence, proof, argument* avancer. b (*advance time of*) *meeting* avancer. c (*Book-keeping*) *figure, amount* reporter.

▸**bring in** **vt sep** a *person* faire entrer; *object* rentrer. b (*introduce*) *fashion* lancer; *custom, legislation* introduire. **to bring in the police/the troops** faire intervenir la police/l'armée; (*Parl*) **to bring in a bill** présenter *or* déposer un projet de loi. c (*Fin*) *income* rapporter. **to bring in interest** rapporter des intérêts. d (*Jur*) *[jury]* **to bring in a verdict** rendre un verdict; **to bring in a verdict of guilty** déclarer qn coupable.

▸**bring off** **vt sep** a *people from wreck* sauver. b *plan, aim* réaliser; *deal* mener à bien, conclure; *attack, hoax* réussir. **he didn't manage to bring it off** il n'a pas réussi son coup.

▸**bring on** **vt sep** a (*cause*) *illness, quarrel* provoquer, causer. **to bring on sb's cold** enrhumer qn. b (*Agr etc*) *crops, flowers* faire pousser. c (*Theat*) *person* amener; *thing* apporter sur (la) scène.

▸**bring out** **vt sep** a *person* faire sortir; *object* sortir; (*fig*) *meaning* faire ressortir, mettre en évidence; *colour* faire ressortir; *qualities* faire valoir, mettre en valeur. **it brings out the best in him** c'est dans des cas comme celui-là qu'il se montre sous son meilleur jour. b *book* publier, faire paraître; *actress, new product* lancer.

▸**bring over** **vt sep** a *person* amener; *object* apporter. b (*convert*) *person* convertir, gagner (*to* à).

▸**bring round** **vt sep** a (*to one's house etc*) *person* amener, faire venir; *object* apporter. (*fig*) **to bring the conversation round to football** ramener la conversation sur le football. b *unconscious person* ranimer. c (*convert*) *person* convertir, gagner (*to* à).

▸**bring through** **vt sep** *sick person* sauver.

▸**bring to** **vt sep** a (*Naut*) mettre en panne. b *unconscious person* ranimer.

▸**bring together** **vt sep** a (*put in touch*) *people* mettre en contact, faire se rencontrer. b (*end quarrel between*) réconcilier. c *facts etc* rassembler.

▸**bring under** **vt sep** (*fig*) assujettir, soumettre.

▸**bring up** **vt sep** a *person* faire monter; *object* monter.

b *child, animal* élever. **well/badly brought-up child** enfant bien/mal élevé.

c (*vomit*) vomir, rendre.

d (*call attention to*) *fact, allegation, problem* mentionner; *question* soulever. **we shan't bring it up again** nous n'en reparlerons plus.

e (*stop*) *person, vehicle* (faire) arrêter. **the question brought him up short** la question l'a arrêté net.

f (*Jur*) **to bring sb up before a court** citer *or* faire comparaître qn devant un tribunal.

g **to bring up to date** *accounts, correspondence etc* mettre qch à jour; *method etc* moderniser; **to bring sb up to date on sth** mettre qn au courant (des derniers développements) de qch.

brink [brɪŋk] **n** (*lit, fig*) bord *m*. **on the ~ of sth** à deux doigts de qch, au bord de qch; **on the ~ of doing** à deux doigts de faire, sur le point de faire.

brinkmanship* ['brɪŋkmənʃɪp] **n** stratégie *f* de la corde raide.

briny ['braɪnɪ] 1 **adj** saumâtre, salé. 2 **n** (†, *hum*) **the ~** la grande bleue (†, *hum*).

briquet(te) [brɪ'ket] **n** briquette *f*, aggloméré *m*.

brisk [brɪsk] **adj** a *person* (*lively*) vif, animé; (*abrupt in manner*) brusque. b *movement* vif, rapide. **~ pace** allure (très) vive; **to take a ~ walk** marcher *or* se promener d'un bon pas; **at a ~ trot** au grand trot; *see* **start**. c *attack* vigoureux, vivement mené; *trade* actif, florissant; *demand* important. **business is ~** les affaires marchent (bien); (*St Ex*) **trading was ~** le marché était actif; **the betting was ~** les paris allaient bon train. d *beer* mousseux; *champagne, cider* pétillant. e *air, weather* vivifiant, vif, frais (*f* fraîche); *day* frais.

brisket ['brɪskɪt] **n** poitrine *f* de bœuf.

briskly ['brɪsklɪ] **adv** *move* vivement; *walk* d'un bon pas; *speak* brusquement; *act* sans tarder. (*Comm etc*) **these goods are selling ~** ces articles se vendent (très) bien.

briskness ['brɪsknɪs] **n** (*see* **brisk**) *[person]* vivacité *f*, animation *f*; brusquerie *f*; *[movement]* rapidité *f*; *[trade]* activité *f*; *[air]* fraîcheur *f*.

brisling ['brɪzlɪŋ] **n** sprat *m*.

bristle ['brɪsl] 1 **n** *[beard, brush]* poil *m*; *[boar etc]* soie *f*; *[plant]* poil, soie. **brush with nylon ~s** brosse en nylon. 2 **comp ▸ bristle brush** (*also* **pure bristle brush**) (*Comm*) brosse *f* pur sanglier *inv*. 3 **vi** a *[animal hair]* se hérisser. (*fig*) **shirt bristling with pins** chemise hérissée d'épingles; **bristling with difficulties** hérissé de difficultés; **town bristling with police** ville grouillante de policiers. b (*fig*) *[person]* s'irriter (*at* de), se hérisser. **he ~d at the suggestion** il s'est hérissé à cette suggestion.

bristly ['brɪslɪ] **adj** *animal* au(x) poil(s) raide(s) *or* dur(s); *chin* mal rasé; *hair, beard, moustache* hérissé.

Bristol ['brɪstəl] **n** a **~ Channel** canal *m* de Bristol; (*Art, Comm*) **~ board** bristol *m*; *see* **shipshape**. b **b~s**‡ roberts‡ *mpl*, seins *mpl*.

Brit* [brɪt] **n** (**abbr of British (subject)**) Britannique *mf*, Anglais(e) *m(f)* (*surtout à l'étranger*).

Britain ['brɪtən] **n** (*also* **Great ~**) Grande-Bretagne *f*.

Britannia [brɪ'tænɪə] **n** Britannia *f*. **~ metal** métal anglais.

Britannic [brɪ'tænɪk] **adj: His** *or* **Her ~ Majesty** sa Majesté britannique.

Briticism ['brɪtɪsɪzəm] **n** anglicisme *m* (*par opposition à américanisme*).

British ['brɪtɪʃ] 1 **adj** britannique, anglais. **~ ambassador/embassy** ambassadeur *m*/ambassade *f* de Grande-Bretagne; **~ Antarctic Territory** Territoire *m* britannique de l'Antarctique; **~ Airports Authority** administration *f* des aéroports britanniques; **~ Columbia** Colombie *f* britannique; **~ Columbian** (**adj**) de la Colombie britannique; (**n**) habitant(e) *m(f)* de la Colombie britannique; **the ~ Broadcasting Corporation** la BBC; **the ~ Commonwealth** le Commonwealth; (*US*) **~ English** l'anglais *m* d'Angleterre; **~ Honduras** Honduras *m* britannique; **~ Isles** îles *fpl* Britanniques; **the ~ nation** la nation britannique; **~ Rail** British Rail *f*; **~ Red Cross Society** Croix *f* Rouge britannique.

2 **npl: the ~** les Britanniques *mpl*, les Anglais *mpl*.

Britisher ['brɪtɪʃəʳ] **n** (*US*) Britannique *mf*, Anglais(e) *m(f)*.

Briton ['brɪtən] **n** a Britannique *mf*, Anglais(e) *m(f)*. b (*Hist*) Breton(ne) *m(f)* (d'Angleterre).

Brittany ['brɪtənɪ] **n** Bretagne *f*.

brittle ['brɪtl] **adj** cassant, fragile; (*Culin*) friable. (*fig*) **in a ~ voice** d'une voix crispée.

Bro. (*Rel*) **abbr of Brother**.

broach [brəʊtʃ] 1 **vt** *barrel* mettre en perce; *box, supplies* entamer; *subject, topic* entamer, aborder. 2 **n** (*Culin*) broche *f*; (*tool*) perçoir *m*, foret *m*.

broad [brɔːd] 1 **adj** a (*wide*) *road, smile* large; (*extensive*) *ocean, estates* vaste, immense. **to grow ~er** s'élargir; **to make ~er** élargir; **to be ~ in the shoulder** être large d'épaules; (*fig*) **he's got a ~ back** il a bon dos; **the lake is 200 metres ~** le lac a 200 mètres de largeur *or* de large; (*fig*) **it's as ~ as it is long** c'est du pareil au même*, c'est bonnet blanc et blanc bonnet; **~ in the beam** *ship* ventru; (* *pej*) *person* fort de l'arrière-train*; **in ~ daylight** (*lit*) en plein jour, au grand jour; (*fig*) au vu et au su de tous; **it was ~ daylight** il faisait grand jour; **~ hint** allusion transparente *or* à peine voilée; *see* **gauge**.

b (*not detailed*) grand, général. **these are the ~ outlines** voilà les grandes lignes *or* les données générales; **as a ~ rule** en règle générale; **in the ~est sense** au sens le plus large; (*Ling*) **~ transcription** notation *f* large; (*US Jur*) **~ construction** interprétation *f* large.

c (*liberal*) *mind, ideas* large, libéral. **B~ Church** groupe libéral au sein de l'Église anglicane.

d (*strongly marked*) *accent* prononcé. **he speaks ~ Scots** il parle avec un accent écossais à couper au couteau*.

e (*coarse*) grossier, vulgaire. **~ humour** humour grivois, gauloiserie *f*; **~ joke** plaisanterie grasse.

2 **n** a (*widest part*) **the ~ of the back** le milieu du dos; (*Geog*) **the (Norfolk) B~s** les Broads *or* les lacs *mpl* et estuaires *mpl* du Norfolk.

b (*US* ‡: *pej*) (*woman*) nana‡ *f*; (*prostitute*) putain‡ *f*.

3 **comp ▸ broad bean** fève *f* **▸ broad-brimmed** *hat* à larges bords **▸ broadbrush** (*fig*) *analysis, report* schématique, sommaire **▸ broadcast** *see* **broadcast ▸ broadcloth** drap fin (*en grande largeur*) **▸ broad jump** (*US Sport*) saut *m* en longueur **▸ broadleaved (tree)** feuillu (*m*) **▸ broadline supplier** (*Comm*) *fournisseur offrant une large gamme de produits* **▸ broadloom** *carpet* en grande largeur **▸ broad-minded: he is broad-minded** il a les idées (très) larges **▸ broad-mindedness** largeur *f* d'esprit, tolérance *f* **▸ broadsheet** (*Hist, Typ*) placard *m*; (*Press*) journal *m* plein format **▸ broad-shouldered** large d'épaules **▸ broadside** *see* **broadside ▸ broadsword** épée *f* à deux tranchants, glaive†† *m* **▸ broadways, broadwise** en largeur, dans le sens de la largeur.

broadcast ['brɔːdkɑːst] **pret, ptp broadcast** 1 **vt** a *news, speech, programme* (*Rad*) (radio)diffuser, émettre; (*TV*) téléviser, émettre; (*fig*) *news, rumour etc* diffuser, répandre, raconter partout. (*fig*) **don't ~ it!*** ne va pas le crier sur les toits!

b (*Agr*) *seed* semer (à la volée).

2 **vi** (*Rad, TV*) *[station]* émettre; *[actor, interviewee]* participer à une émission; *[interviewer]* faire une émission. **X ~s by permission of ...** X participe à cette émission avec l'accord de ... .

3 **n** (*Rad, TV*) émission *f*. **live/recorded ~** émission en direct/en différé; **repeat ~** reprise *f*, rediffusion *f*.

4 **adj** (*Rad*) (radio)diffusé; (*TV*) télévisé. **~ account of a match** (*Rad*) reportage radiodiffusé d'un match; (*TV*) reportage télévisé d'un match; **~ journalism** reportage télévisé (*or* radiodiffusé); **~ satellite** satellite *m* de radiodiffusion.

5 **adv** *sow* à la volée.

broadcaster ['brɔːdkɑːstəʳ] **n** (*Rad, TV*) personnalité *f* de la radio *or* de la télévision.

broadcasting ['brɔːdkɑːstɪŋ] 1 **n** (*Rad*) radiodiffusion *f*; (*TV*) télévision *f*. **that is the end of ~ for tonight** ainsi prennent fin nos émissions de la journée; **~ was interrupted** les émissions ont été interrompues; **a career in ~** une carrière à la radio (*or* à la télévision).

2 **comp ▸ broadcasting station** station *f* de radio, poste émetteur; *see* **British**.

broaden ['brɔːdn] (*also* **~ out**: *lit, fig*) 1 **vt** élargir. **to ~ one's outlook** élargir ses horizons. 2 **vi** s'élargir.

broadly ['brɔːdlɪ] **adv** (*fig*) dans les grandes lignes, en gros, généralement. **~-based** large; **~ speaking** en gros, généralement parlant.

broadness ['brɔːdnɪs] **n** *[road]* largeur *f*; *[joke, story]* grossièreté *f*, vulgarité *f*; *[accent]* caractère prononcé.

broadside ['brɔːdsaɪd] 1 **n** a (*Naut*) *[ship]* flanc *m*. (*Naut*) **~ on** (se présentant) par le travers; **he** *or* **his car hit me ~ on** il m'est rentré dans le flanc, il m'a heurté par le travers. b (*Naut*) bordée *f*; (*fig: verbal*) attaque cinglante; (*insults*) bordée d'injures *or* d'invectives. (*Naut*) **to fire a ~** lâcher une bordée; (*fig*) **he let him have a ~** il l'a incendié*, il l'a descendu en flammes*. 2 **adv** (*sideways*) par le travers.

brocade [brəʊ'keɪd] 1 **n** brocart *m*. 2 **comp** de brocart.

broccoli ['brɒkəlɪ] **n** brocoli *m*.

brochure ['brəʊʃjʊəʳ] **n** *[college, vacation course]* prospectus *m*; *[hotel, travel agent]* brochure *f*, dépliant *m* (touristique).

brock [brɒk] **n** (*Brit: Zool, rare*) blaireau *m*.

brogue¹ [brəʊg] **n** (*shoe*) chaussure *f* de marche, richelieu *m*.

brogue² [brəʊg] **n** (*accent*) (*Irish*) accent irlandais; (*gen*) accent du terroir.

broil [brɔɪl] 1 **vt** (*US Culin*) griller, faire cuire sur le gril; (*fig*) griller*. **~ing sun** soleil brûlant. 2 **vi** (*also fig*) griller.

broiler ['brɔɪləʳ] **n** a (*fowl*) poulet *m* (à rôtir). **~ house** éleveuse *f*. b (*US: grill*) rôtisserie *f*, gril *m*.

broke [brəʊk] 1 **pret of break**. 2 **adj** (*) à sec*, fauché*. **to be dead** *or* **stony ~** être fauché (comme les blés)*, être (complètement) à sec*; **to go ~** faire faillite; **to go for ~*** jouer le tout pour le tout.

broken ['brəʊkən] 1 **ptp of break**.

2 **adj** a (*lit*) cassé, brisé; *window* cassé; *neck, leg* fracturé, cassé; *rib* cassé, enfoncé; *walnuts, biscuits etc* brisé; (*fig*) *promise* rompu, violé; *appointment* manqué; (*Ling*) *vowel* diphtongué. **~ bones** fractures *fpl* (d'os); (*Mus*) **~ chord** arpège *m*; **~ heart** cœur brisé; **she died of a ~ heart** elle est morte de chagrin *or* morte le cœur brisé; **~ home** foyer brisé; (*Comm*) **~ lots** articles dépareillés; **~ marriage** mariage brisé, ménage désuni; (*Math*) **~ numbers** fractions *fpl*; **he is a ~ reed** on ne peut jamais compter sur lui; **a spell of ~ weather** un

temps variable.
b (*uneven*) *ground* accidenté; *road* défoncé; *surface* raboteux; *line* brisé; *coastline* dentelé; *see* **check³**.
c (*interrupted*) *journey* interrompu; *sleep* (*disturbed*) interrompu, (*restless*) agité; *sounds, gestures* incohérent; *voice* entrecoupé, brisé; *words* haché. **to speak ~ English** parler un mauvais anglais, baragouiner* l'anglais; **in ~ English** en mauvais anglais; **I've had several ~ nights** j'ai eu plusieurs mauvaises nuits.
d (*spoilt, ruined*) *health* délabré, affaibli; *spirit* abattu. **he is a ~ man** (*no spirit left*) il est brisé; (*financially*) il est ruiné; (*reputation-wise*) il est perdu de réputation.
3 **comp** ▸**broken-down** *car* en panne; *machine* détraqué; *house* délabré; (*fig : old, worn-out*) fini, à bout ▸**broken-hearted** au cœur brisé ▸**broken-winded** poussif.

brokenly [ˈbrəʊkənlɪ] **adv** *say* d'une voix entrecoupée; *sob* par à-coups.

broker [ˈbrəʊkəʳ] **n** a (*St Ex*) ≈ courtier *m* (en bourse), agent *m* de change. b (*Comm*) courtier *m*; (*Naut*) courtier maritime. **wine ~** courtier en vins. c (*secondhand dealer*) brocanteur *m*; *see* **pawn²** *etc.*

brokerage [ˈbrəʊkərɪdʒ] **n**, **broking** [ˈbrəʊkɪŋ] **n** (*trade, commission*) courtage *m*.

brolly* [ˈbrɒlɪ] **n** (*Brit*) pépin* *m*, parapluie *m*.

bromide [ˈbrəʊmaɪd] **n** a (*Chem, Typ*) bromure *m*; (*Med* *) bromure (de potassium). **~ paper** papier *m* au (gélatino-)bromure d'argent. b (*fig*) banalité *or* platitude euphorisante.

bromine [ˈbrəʊmiːn] **n** brome *m*.

bronchi [ˈbrɒŋkaɪ] **npl of bronchus**.

bronchial [ˈbrɒŋkɪəl] **adj** *infection* des bronches, bronchique. **~ tubes** bronches *fpl*.

bronchiole [ˈbrɒŋkɪəʊl] **n** bronchiole *f*.

bronchitis [brɒŋˈkaɪtɪs] **n** (*NonC*) bronchite *f*. **to get** *or* **have ~** avoir *or* faire une bronchite.

bronchopneumonia [ˌbrɒŋkəʊnjuːˈməʊnɪə] **n** (*NonC*) broncho-pneumonie *f*.

bronchus [ˈbrɒŋkəs] **n**, **pl bronchi** bronche *f*.

bronco [ˈbrɒŋkəʊ] **n** cheval *m* semi-sauvage (de l'Ouest américain). (*US*) **~buster**‡ cowboy *m* (*qui dompte les chevaux sauvages*).

brontosaurus [ˌbrɒntəˈsɔːrəs] **n**, **pl ~s** *or* **brontosauri** [ˌbrɒntəˈsɔːraɪ] brontosaure *m*.

Bronx [brɒŋks] **n**: **the ~** le Bronx; (*US fig*) **~ cheer** bruit *m* de dérision.

bronze [brɒnz] 1 **n** (*metal, colour, work of art*) bronze *m*. 2 **vi** se bronzer, brunir. 3 **vt** *metal* bronzer; *skin* brunir, faire bronzer. 4 **comp** en bronze; (*colour*) (couleur *f* de) bronze *inv* ▸**Bronze Age** âge *m* du bronze ▸**bronze medal** médaille *f* de bronze.

bronzed [brɒnzd] **adj** *skin, person* bronzé, basané.

brooch [brəʊtʃ] **n** broche *f* (*bijou*).

brood [bruːd] 1 **n** [*birds*] couvée *f*, nichée *f*; [*mice*] nichée; [*children*] progéniture *f*, nichée (*hum*); [*vipers, scoundrels*] engeance *f*. **she has a great ~ of children** elle a une nombreuse progéniture; **I'm going to take my ~ home*** je vais remmener ma progéniture *or* ma nichée à la maison. 2 **comp** ▸**brood hen** couveuse *f* ▸**brood mare** (jument *f*) poulinière *f*. 3 **vi** [*bird*] couver; [*storm, danger*] couver, menacer; [*person*] broyer du noir, ruminer. [*person*] **to ~ on** *misfortune* remâcher; *plan* ruminer; *the past* ressasser; **to ~ over sth** [*night etc*] planer sur qch; [*storm*] couver sur qch, (*oppressively*) peser sur qch.

brooding [ˈbruːdɪŋ] 1 **adj** a (*disturbing*) troublant. b (*reflective*) rêveur, songeur; (*gloomy*) maussade, soucieux. 2 **n** rumination *f*.

broody [ˈbruːdɪ] **adj** a **~ hen** (poule *f*) couveuse *f*; (* *hum*) **to be feeling ~** être en mal d'enfant. b (*) *person* rêveur, distrait; (*gloomy*) cafardeux*.

brook¹ [brʊk] **n** ruisseau *m*.

brook² [brʊk] **vt** (*liter*) *contradiction* souffrir, supporter, tolérer; *delay, reply* admettre, souffrir.

brooklet [ˈbrʊklɪt] **n** ruisselet *m*, petit ruisseau.

broom [brʊm] **n** a (*Bot*) genêt *m*. b (*brush*) balai *m*. (*Prov*) **a new ~ sweeps clean** tout nouveau, tout beau (*Prov*); **this firm needs a new ~** cette compagnie a besoin d'un bon coup de balai *or* a besoin de sang nouveau; **~stick** manche *m* à balai.

Bros. [brɒs] (*Comm*) (**abbr of Brothers**) Frères *mpl*.

broth [brɒθ] **n** bouillon *m* de viande et de légumes.

brothel [ˈbrɒθl] **n** bordel‡ *m*, maison *f* de tolérance.

brother [ˈbrʌðəʳ] 1 **n** a (*gen, Rel*) frère *m*. **older/younger ~** frère aîné/cadet; **B~ Francis** Frère François; *see* **lay⁴**. b (*in trade unions etc*) camarade *m*; (*US: also* **soul ~**) frère *m* (de couleur). 2 **adj**: **his ~ prisoners** *etc* ceux qui sont (*or* étaient *etc*) prisonniers *etc* comme lui, les autres prisonniers *etc*; **his ~ officers** ses compagnons *mpl* d'armes. 3 **comp** ▸**brother-in-law** (**pl ~s-~-~**) beau-frère *m*.

brotherhood [ˈbrʌðəhʊd] **n** a (*NonC: lit*) fraternité *f*; (*fig*) fraternité, confraternité *f*. **~ of man** fraternité des hommes. b (*association: esp Rel*) confrérie *f*; (*US*) corporation *f*. (*Freemasonry*) **the B~** la franc-maçonnerie.

brotherly [ˈbrʌðəlɪ] **adj** fraternel. **~ love** l'amour fraternel.

brougham [ˈbruːəm] **n** coupé *m* de ville.

brought [brɔːt] **pret, ptp of bring**.

brouhaha* [ˈbruːhɑːhɑː] **n** histoires* *fpl*.

brow [braʊ] **n** a (*forehead*) front *m*; (*arch above eye*) arcade sourcilière; (*eyebrow*) sourcil *m*; *see* **beetle², high, knit, sweat** *etc.* b [*hill*] sommet *m*; [*cliff*] bord *m*; (*Min*) tour *f* d'extraction.

browbeat [ˈbraʊbiːt] **pret browbeat, ptp browbeaten vt** intimider, rudoyer, brusquer. **to ~ sb into doing sth** forcer qn à faire qch par l'intimidation.

browbeaten [ˈbraʊbiːtən] 1 **ptp of browbeat.** 2 **adj** avili.

brown [braʊn] 1 **adj** a brun, marron *inv*; *hair* châtain; *boots, shoes, leather* marron. (*Judo*) **~ belt** ceinture *f* marron; **~ bread** pain *m* bis; **~ flour** farine complète; **light ~ hair** cheveux *mpl* châtain clair *inv*; **light ~ material** étoffe *f* marron clair; **~ ale** bière brune; **~ bear** ours brun; **~ owl** (*Orn*) chat-huant *m*; [*Brownie Guides*] cheftaine *f*; **~ paper** papier *m* d'emballage; **~ rice** riz complet; (*fig*) **in a ~ study** plongé dans ses pensées *or* méditations; **~ sugar** cassonade *f*, sucre brun; **to go ~** [*leaves*] roussir; *see* **nut**.
b (*tanned*) *person, skin* bronzé, bruni, hâlé. **to go ~** brunir; **as ~ as a berry** tout bronzé.
c (*dusky-skinned*) brun de peau.
d (*US fig*) **to do sth up ~**‡ soigner qch dans les moindres détails.
2 **n** brun *m*, marron *m*. **her hair was a rich, deep ~** ses cheveux étaient d'un beau brun foncé.
3 **comp** ▸**brownbag***: (*US*) **to brownbag it** apporter son repas (dans un sac en papier) ▸**brown-nose**‡ **n** lèche-cul *m inv*, lèche-bottes* *mf inv* ◊ **vt** lécher le cul à *or* de, lécher les bottes* de ▸**brown-out** (*US*) (*Mil*) camouflage partiel des lumières; (*Elec*) panne partielle ▸**brownstone** (*US*) (*material*) grès brun; (*house*) bâtiment *m* de grès brun.
4 **vt** a [*sun*] *skin, person* bronzer, brunir, hâler.
b (*Culin*) *meat, fish, potatoes* faire dorer; *sauce* faire roussir.
c (*Brit*) **he is ~ed off**‡ il en a marre* *or* ras le bol‡, il n'a plus le moral*.
5 **vi** a [*leaves*] roussir.
b [*person, skin*] brunir.
c (*Culin*) dorer.

brownie [ˈbraʊnɪ] **n** a (*fairy*) lutin *m*, farfadet *m*. b **B~ (Guide)** jeannette *f*; **to win** *or* **get** *or* **earn B~ points** ≈ gagner des bons points. c ® (*camera*) brownie *m* kodak ®. d (*US: cake*) *gâteau au chocolat et aux noix*.

browning [ˈbraʊnɪŋ] **n** (*Brit Culin*) *produit préparé pour roux brun*.

brownish [ˈbraʊnɪʃ] **adj** tirant sur le brun, brunâtre (*slightly pej*).

browse [braʊz] 1 **vi** a (*in bookshop, library*) feuilleter les livres; (*in other shops*) regarder sans acheter. (*fig*) **to ~ through a book** feuilleter *or* parcourir un livre; (*in shop*) **I'm only browsing** je regarde seulement, merci. b [*animal*] brouter, paître. 2 **vt** *animals* brouter, paître. 3 **n**: **to have a browse = to browse**; *see* **browse 1a**.

BRS [ˈbiːɑːrˈes] **n** (*Brit*) (**abbr of British Road Services**) *société nationale de transports routiers*.

brucellosis [ˌbruːsəˈləʊsɪs] **n** brucellose *f*.

bruise [bruːz] 1 **vt** a *person, part of body* faire un bleu à, contusionner; *finger* faire un pinçon à; *fruit* abîmer, taler; *lettuce* froisser. **to ~ one's foot** se faire un bleu au pied; **to be ~d all over** avoir le corps *or* être couvert de bleus, être tout contusionné.
b (*crush*) écraser, piler. (*liter*) **~d heart** cœur meurtri *or* blessé; (*liter*) **~d spirit** esprit meurtri; **to feel ~d** se sentir secoué.
2 **vi** [*fruit*] se taler, s'abîmer. **peaches ~ easily** les pêches se talent facilement; **he ~s easily** il se fait facilement des bleus.
3 **n** [*person*] bleu *m*, contusion *f*, ecchymose *f*, meurtrissure *f*; [*fruit*] meurtrissure, talure *f*. **body covered with ~s** corps couvert d'ecchymoses *or* de meurtrissures.

bruiser* [ˈbruːzəʳ] **n** malabar* *m*, cogneur* *m*.

bruising [ˈbruːzɪŋ] 1 **n** bleus *mpl*, contusions *fpl*. **light** *or* **minor/heavy** *or* **severe ~** contusions légères/graves. 2 **adj** éprouvant.

Brum* [brʌm] **n** (*Brit*) (**abbr of Brummagem**) Birmingham.

brum* [brʊm] **excl** (*baby talk*) [*car etc*] ~, ~! broum, broum!

Brummie* [ˈbrʌmɪ] **n** (*Brit*) habitant(e) *m(f)* *or* natif *m*, -ive *f* de Birmingham.

brunch [brʌntʃ] **n** brunch *m*.

brunette [bruːˈnet] 1 **n** (femme *f*) brune *f*, brunette *f*. 2 **adj** *person, skin* brun; *eyes* marron *inv*; *hair* châtain.

brunt [brʌnt] **n**: **the ~** [*attack, blow*] le (plus gros du) choc; [*argument, displeasure*] le poids; **to bear the ~ of the assault** soutenir *or* essuyer le plus fort de l'attaque; **to bear the ~ of the work** faire le (plus) gros du travail; **to bear the ~ of the expense** payer le (plus) gros des frais; **he bore the ~ of it all** c'est lui qui a porté le poids de l'affaire.

brush [brʌʃ] 1 **n** a brosse *f*; (*paint ~*) pinceau *m*, brosse; (*broom*) balai *m*; (*short-handled: hearth ~ etc*) balayette *f*; (*scrubbing ~*) brosse (dure); (*bottle ~*) goupillon *m*, rince-bouteilles *m inv*; (*shaving ~*) blaireau *m*. **hair/nail/shoe/tooth~** brosse à cheveux/à ongles/à chaussures/à dents; **clothes/hat ~** brosse à habits/à chapeau; *see* **pastry, tar¹** *etc.*
b coup *m* de brosse. **give your coat a ~** donne un coup de brosse à ton manteau.
c (*light touch*) effleurement *m*.
d [*fox*] queue *f*.

e (*NonC: undergrowth*) broussailles *fpl*, taillis *m*.

f (*skirmish*) accrochage *m*, escarmouche *f*. **to have a ~ with the law** avoir des démêlés *mpl* avec la justice, avoir maille à partir avec la justice; (*quarrel*) **to have a ~ with sb** avoir un accrochage *or* une prise de bec* avec qn.

g (*Elec*) *[commutator]* balai *m*; *[dynamo]* frottoir *m*; (*discharge*) décharge *f*.

2 **comp** ►**brush maker** (*manufacturer*) fabricant *m* de brosses; (*employee*) brossier *m*, -ière *f* ►**brush-off***: **to give sb the brush-off** envoyer promener *or* bouler* *or* balader* qn; **to get the brush-off** se faire envoyer sur les roses* *or* balader* *or* bouler* ►**brush-stroke** coup *m or* trait *m* de pinceau ►**brush-up** coup *m* de brosse (*see* **wash**); **to give one's English a brush-up*** rafraîchir ses notions d'anglais ►**brushwood** (*undergrowth*) broussailles *fpl*, taillis *m*; (*cuttings*) menu bois, brindilles *fpl* ►**brushwork** (*Art*) facture *f*.

3 **vt** a *carpet* balayer; *clothes, hair etc* brosser, donner un coup de brosse à. **to ~ one's teeth** se brosser *or* se laver les dents; **to ~ one's hair** se brosser les cheveux; **hair ~ed back** cheveux ramenés *or* rejetés en arrière; **he ~ed the chalk off his coat** il a enlevé (à la main *or* à la brosse) les traces de craie qui étaient sur son manteau.

b (*touch lightly*) frôler, effleurer; *the ground* raser.

c (*Tech*) *wool* gratter. (*Tex*) **~ed cotton** pilou *m*, finette *f*; **~ed nylon** nylon gratté.

4 **vi**: **to ~ against sb/sth** effleurer *or* frôler qn/qch; **to ~ past sb/sth** frôler qn/qch en passant.

►**brush aside** **vt sep** *argument, objections* balayer (d'un geste); *protester, objector* repousser.

►**brush away** **vt sep** *tears* essuyer; *mud, dust* (*on clothes*) enlever à la brosse *or* à la main; (*on floor*) balayer; *insects* chasser.

►**brush down** **vt sep** *person, garment* donner un coup de brosse à; *horse* brosser.

►**brush off** 1 **vi**: **the mud brushes off easily** avec un coup de brosse la boue s'enlève facilement. 2 **vt sep** *mud, snow* enlever (à la brosse *or* à coups de balai); *insect* balayer, écarter d'un geste; *fluff on coat* enlever à la brosse *or* à la main. 3 **brush-off*** **n** *see* **brush 2**.

►**brush up** 1 **vt sep** a *crumbs, dirt* ramasser avec une brosse *or* à la balayette. b *wool* gratter. c (*: *revise, improve*) se remettre à, revoir, réviser. **to brush up (on) one's English** se remettre à l'anglais. 2 **brush-up** **n** *see* **brush 2**, *also* **wash**.

brusque [bruːsk] **adj** *person, tone, manner* brusque, bourru, brutal.

brusquely ['bruːsklɪ] **adv** *behave, speak* avec brusquerie, avec rudesse.

brusqueness ['bruːsknɪs] **n** brusquerie *f*, rudesse *f*.

Brussels ['brʌslz] 1 **n** Bruxelles. 2 **comp** *lace* de Bruxelles ►**Brussels sprouts** choux *mpl* de Bruxelles.

brutal ['bruːtl] **adj** a *person, behaviour, reply* brutal, cruel. b (*lit*) brutal; *instincts* animal, de brute.

brutality [bruː'tælɪtɪ] **n** brutalité *f*, sauvagerie *f*.

brutalize ['bruːtəlaɪz] **vt** a (*ill-treat*) brutaliser. b (*make brutal*) rendre brutal.

brutally ['bruːtəlɪ] **adv** *hit, attack* brutalement, sauvagement; *say, reply* brutalement, cruellement. **~ assaulted** sauvagement attaqué.

brute [bruːt] 1 **n** (*animal*) brute *f*, bête *f*; (*person*) (*cruel*) brute, brutal *m*; (*coarse*) brute (épaisse). **this machine is a ~!*** quelle vache que cette machine!‡ 2 **adj** a (*animal-like*) de brute, animal, bestial. **the ~ beast** la brute. b *strength, passion* brutal; *matter* brut. **by (sheer) ~ force** par la force.

brutish ['bruːtɪʃ] **adj** (*animal-like*) de brute, animal, bestial; (*unfeeling*) grossier, brutal; (*uncultured*) inculte, ignare.

BS [biː'es] **abbr of British Standard**.

B.S.A. [ˌbiːes'eɪ] **n** (*US*) (**abbr of Boy Scouts of America**) *scouts américains*.

BSC [ˌbiːes'siː] **n** (*Brit*) (**abbr of Broasdcasting Standards Council**) ≃ CSA *m*.

B.Sc. [ˌbiːes'siː] **n** (*Univ*) (**abbr of Bachelor of Science**) **to have a ~ in biology** avoir une licence de biologie; *see* **bachelor 1b**.

BSE [ˌbiːes'iː] (**abbr of bovine spongiform encephalopathy**) ESB *f*.

BSI [ˌbiːes'aɪ] **n** (*Brit*) (**abbr of British Standards Institution**) ≃ AFNOR *f*.

B.S.T. [ˌbiːes'tiː] **n** (*Brit*) (**abbr of British Summer Time**) heure *f* d'été.

Bt **abbr of Baronet**.

btu [ˌbiːtiː'juː] **n** (**abbr of British thermal unit**) *see* **thermal**.

bubble ['bʌbl] 1 **n** a (*gen: also* **air ~**) bulle *f*; (*in liquid*) bouillon *m*; (*in glass*) bulle, soufflure *f*; (*in paint*) boursouflure *f*; (*in metal*) soufflure, boursouflement *m*. **to blow ~s** faire des bulles; **soap ~** bulle de savon; (*fig*) **the ~ burst** (*gen*) le rêve s'est envolé; (*Econ*) la chance a tourné.

b (*fig*) chimère *f*; (*Comm*) affaire pourrie.

c (*sound*) glouglou *m*.

2 **comp** ►**bubble and squeak** (*Brit*) *purée aux choux et à la viande hachée* ►**bubble bath** bain moussant ►**bubble-car** (*Brit*) petite voiture (*à toit transparent*) ►**bubble company** (*Comm, Fin*) compagnie véreuse ►**bubblegum** bubble-gum *m* ►**bubble memory** (*Comput*) mémoire *f* à bulles ►**bubble pack, bubble package** (*for pills etc*) plaquette *f*; (*in supermarket: for pens, plugs etc*) emballage pelliculé ►**bubble wrap** ® papier *m* bulle, Bullpack ®.

3 **vi** a *[liquid]* bouillonner, dégager des bulles; *[champagne]* pétiller; *[gas]* barboter; (*gurgle*) faire glouglou, glouglouter.

b (*: *cry*) chialer‡, pleurer.

►**bubble out** **vi** *[liquid]* sortir à gros bouillons.

►**bubble over** **vi** (*lit, fig*) déborder. **to bubble over with joy** déborder de joie.

►**bubble up** **vi** *[liquid]* monter en bouillonnant; *[excitement etc]* monter.

bubbly ['bʌblɪ] 1 **adj** *drink* pétillant, plein de bulles; *person, character* d'une vitalité pétillante. 2 **n** (‡: *NonC*) champagne *m*.

bubonic [bjuː'bɒnɪk] **adj** bubonique. **~ plague** peste *f* bubonique.

buccaneer [ˌbʌkə'nɪəʳ] **n** (*Hist*) boucanier *m*; (*fig*) flibustier *m*, pirate *m*.

buccaneering [ˌbʌkə'nɪərɪŋ] **adj** (*pej, fig*) aventurier, intrigant.

Bucharest [ˌbuːkə'rest] **n** Bucarest.

buck [bʌk] 1 **n** a (*male of deer, rabbit, hare etc*) mâle *m*.

b (†: *dandy*) élégant *m*, dandy *m*.

c (*US* *: *dollar*) dollar *m*. **to be down to one's last ~** être sur la paille; **to make a few ~s on the side** se faire un peu de pognon‡ à côté, se faire un petit à-côté*; (*at sb's expense*) se sucrer en douce*; **to make a fast** *or* **quick ~** gagner du fric‡ facile.

d **to pass the ~** refiler* la responsabilité aux autres; **the ~ stops here*** la responsabilité commence ici.

e (*sawhorse*) chevalet *m*, baudet *m*; (*Gymnastics*) cheval *m* d'arçons.

f **the horse gave a ~** le cheval a lancé une ruade.

2 **comp** ►**the Buckeye State** (*US*) l'Ohio *m* ►**buck private** (*US Mil*) deuxième classe *m inv* ►**buck rabbit** lapin *m* mâle ►**bucksaw** scie *f* à bois (montée dans un cadre) ►**buck sergeant** (*US Mil*) simple sergent *m* ►**buck's fizz** *cocktail de champagne et de jus d'orange* ►**buckshot** chevrotine(s) *f(pl)* ►**buckskin** peau *f* de daim ►**buck teeth** dents proéminentes; **to have buck teeth, to be buck-toothed** avoir des dents de lapin ►**buck-toothed** *see* **buck teeth** ►**buckthorn** nerprun *m*, bourdaine *f* ►**buckwheat** sarrasin *m*, blé noir.

3 **vi** a *[horse]* lancer *or* décocher une ruade.

b (*object to*) **to ~ at sth‡** regimber devant qch.

c (*US*) **to ~ for sth*** rechercher qch.

4 **vt** (*US*) **to ~ the system*** lutter contre l'ordre établi.

►**buck up*** 1 **vi** a (*hurry up*) se grouiller*, se magner‡; (*exert o.s.*) se remuer*, se magner‡. **buck up!** remue-toi!*, grouille-toi!*, active un peu!* b (*cheer up*) se secouer*. 2 **vt sep** *person* remonter le moral de, ravigoter*. **you'll need to buck up your ideas** il va falloir que tu te remues un peu*.

bucked‡ [bʌkt] **adj** tout content.

bucket ['bʌkɪt] 1 **n** a seau *m*. **~ of water** seau d'eau; **to weep ~s*** pleurer toutes les larmes de son corps; **chain of ~s** chaîne *f* de seaux; **they made a chain of ~s to fight the fire** ils ont fait la chaîne pour combattre l'incendie; *see* **kick, rain**. b (*Tech*) *[dredger, grain elevator]* godet *m*; *[pump]* piston *m*; *[wheel]* auget *m*. 2 **vi**: **it's ~ing*, the rain is ~ing (down)*** il pleut à seaux *or* comme vache qui pisse‡, il tombe des cordes*. 3 **comp** ►**bucket elevator** (*Tech*) noria *f* ►**bucket seat** (siège-)baquet *m* ►**bucket shop** (*Fin*) bureau *m or* maison *f* de contrepartie, bureau de courtier marron; (*for air tickets*) organisme *m* de vente de billets d'avion à prix réduit.

bucketful ['bʌkɪtfʊl] **n** plein seau. **I've had a ~‡ of him/his nonsense** j'en ai ras le bol‡ *or* par-dessus la tête de lui/de ses idioties.

buckle ['bʌkl] 1 **n** a *[shoe, belt]* boucle *f*. b (*distortion*) *[wheel]* voilure *f*; *[metal]* gauchissement *m*, flambage *m*. 2 **vt** a *belt, shoe etc* boucler, attacher. b *wheel* voiler; *metal* gauchir, fausser. 3 **vi** a *[belt, shoe]* se boucler, s'attacher. b *[metal]* gauchir, se déformer; *[wheel]* se voiler.

►**buckle down*** **vi** se coller au boulot*. **to buckle down to a job** s'atteler à un boulot*; **buckle down to it!** au boulot!*

►**buckle in** **vt sep** (*into seat*) attacher.

►**buckle on** **vt sep** *armour* revêtir, endosser; *sword* ceindre.

►**buckle to*** **vi** s'y mettre, s'y coller*.

buckra* ['bʌkrə] **n** (*US pej*) Blanc *m*.

buckram ['bʌkrəm] **n** bougran *m*.

Bucks [bʌks] **n abbr of Buckinghamshire**.

bucksheе‡ [bʌk'ʃiː] **adj, adv** (*Brit*) gratis *inv*, à l'œil*.

bucolic [bjuː'kɒlɪk] 1 **adj** bucolique, pastoral. 2 **n** (*Literat*) **the B~s** les Bucoliques *fpl*.

bud¹ [bʌd] 1 **n** a *[tree, plant]* bourgeon *m*, œil *m*; *[grafting]* écusson *m*. **to be in ~** bourgeonner; (*fig*) **poet** *etc* **in the ~** poète *m etc* en herbe; *see* **nip** *etc*. b *[flower]* bouton *m*. **in ~** en bouton; *see* **rose²**. c (*Anat*) papille *f*; *see* **taste**. 2 **vi** *[tree, plant]* bourgeonner, se couvrir de bourgeons; *[flower]* former des boutons; *[horns]* (commencer à) poindre *or* percer; *[talent etc]* (commencer à) percer. 3 **vt** (*Horticulture*) *tree* greffer, écussonner.

bud²* [bʌd] **n** (*US*) = **buddy***.

Budapest [ˌbjuːdə'pest] **n** Budapest.

Buddha ['bʊdə] **n** Bouddha *m*.

Buddhism ['bʊdɪzəm] **n** bouddhisme *m*.

Buddhist ['bʊdɪst] 1 **n** Bouddhiste *mf*. 2 **adj** *monk, nation* bouddhiste; *religion, art, dogma* bouddhique.

budding ['bʌdɪŋ] adj *plant* bourgeonnant; *flower* en bouton; (*fig*) *poet etc* en herbe; *passion* naissant.

buddleia ['bʌdlɪə] n buddleia *m*, lilas *m* de Chine.

buddy* ['bʌdɪ] n (*US*) copain *m*, pote‡ *m*. **hi there, ~!** salut, mon pote!‡; **~ movie** *or* **film** *film qui raconte l'histoire de deux amis;* **they use the ~ system** ils travaillent en équipe de deux.

budge [bʌdʒ] 1 vi (*move*) bouger; (*fig*) changer d'avis. **I will not ~ an inch** (*lit*) je ne bougerai pas d'ici; (*fig*) rien ne me fera changer d'avis. 2 vt faire bouger. (*fig*) **you can't ~ him** il reste inébranlable, vous ne le ferez pas changer d'avis.

►**budge over***, **budge up*** vi se pousser.

budgerigar ['bʌdʒərɪgɑːʳ] n perruche *f*.

budget ['bʌdʒɪt] 1 n (*gen, Fin*) budget *m*; (*Parl*) budget, loi *f* des finances. **my ~ won't run to steak nowadays** mon budget ne me permet plus d'acheter de bifteck; **to be on a tight ~** disposer d'un budget modeste.

2 adj a (*Econ, Fin*) *spending, credit* budgétaire. (*Comm*) **~ account** compte-crédit *m*; (*Econ*) **~ cuts** compressions *fpl* budgétaires; (*Parl*) **~ day** jour *m* de la présentation du budget; (*Econ*) **~ deficit** découvert *m* budgétaire; (*Econ, Comm*) **~ heading** poste *m* budgétaire; (*US Comm*) **~ plan** système *m* de crédit; (*Parl*) **~ speech** discours *m* de présentation du budget; (*Econ*) **~ surplus** excédent *m* budgétaire.

b (*cut-price*) *tour, holiday, price* pour petits budgets, économique.

3 vi dresser *or* préparer un budget. **to ~ for sth** (*Econ*) inscrire *or* porter qch au budget, budgétiser qch; (*gen*) inscrire qch à son budget, prévoir des frais de qch.

4 vt budgétiser, budgéter. **to ~ one's time** planifier son temps; **~ed balance sheet** bilan *m* provisionnel; **a ~ed expense** une dépense budgétée.

budgetary ['bʌdʒɪtrɪ] adj budgétaire. **~ year** exercice *m* budgétaire.

budgeting ['bʌdʒɪtɪŋ] n *[company, institution]* prévisions *fpl* budgétaires. **with careful ~ ...** si l'on équilibre soigneusement le budget ... .

budgie* ['bʌdʒɪ] n abbr of **budgerigar**.

Buenos Aires ['bweɪnɒs'aɪrɪz] n Buenos Aires.

buff[1] [bʌf] 1 n a (*leather*) (peau *f* de) buffle *m*; (*colour*) (couleur *f*) chamois *m*. **in the ~**‡ à poil‡. b (*polishing disc*) polissoir *m*. 2 adj a (en peau) de buffle, en buffle. b (*also* **~-coloured**) (couleur) chamois *inv*. **~ envelope** enveloppe *f* (en papier) bulle. 3 vt *metal* polir.

buff[2] [bʌf] n (*: *enthusiast*) mordu(e)* *m(f)*. **a film ~** un(e) mordu(e)* du cinéma.

buffalo ['bʌfələʊ] n, pl **~** *or* **~es** (*wild ox*) buffle *m*, bufflesse *f*; (*esp in US*) bison *m*; *see* **water**.

buffer[1] ['bʌfəʳ] 1 n (*lit, fig*) tampon *m*; (*Rail*) (*on train*) tampon; (*at terminus*) butoir *m*; (*US Aut*) pare-chocs *m inv*; (*Comput*) mémoire *f* tampon. 2 comp ►**buffer fund** (*Fin, Econ*) fonds régulateur ►**buffer memory** (*Comput*) mémoire *f* tampon ►**buffer solution** (*Chem*) solution *f* tampon ►**buffer state** (*Pol*) état *m* tampon ►**buffer stock** (*Comm*) stock *m* de sécurité *or* de régularisation. 3 vt (*Chem*) tamponner; (*fig*) *shocks* amortir.

buffer[2] ['bʌfəʳ] n (*for polishing*) polissoir *m*.

buffer[3]‡ ['bʌfəʳ] n (*Brit*) vieux fossile*.

buffet[1] ['bʌfɪt] 1 n (*blow*) (*with hand*) gifle *f*, soufflet *m*; (*with fist*) coup *m* de poing. (*fig*) **the ~s of fate** les coups du sort. 2 vt (*with hand*) frapper, souffleter; (*with fist*) donner un coup de poing à. **~ed by the waves** battu *or* ballotté par les vagues; **~ed by the wind** secoué par le vent; (*fig*) **~ed by events** secoué par les événements.

buffet[2] ['bʊfeɪ] 1 n (*refreshment bar, sideboard*) buffet *m*. (*in menu*) **cold ~** viandes froides. 2 comp ►**buffet car** (*Brit Rail*) voiture-buffet *f*, buffet *m* ►**buffet lunch** lunch *m* ►**buffet supper** (souper-)buffet *m*.

buffeting ['bʌfɪtɪŋ] 1 n *[person, object]* bourrades *fpl*, coups *mpl*; *[wind, rain etc]* assaut *m*. **to get a ~ from the waves** être ballotté (de tous côtés) par les vagues. 2 adj *wind* violent.

buffing ['bʌfɪŋ] n polissage *m*.

buffoon [bə'fuːn] n bouffon *m*, pitre *m*, clown *m*.

buffoonery [bə'fuːnərɪ] n bouffonnerie(s) *f(pl)*.

bug [bʌg] 1 n a (*bedbug etc*) punaise *f*; (*: *any insect*) insecte *m*, bestiole* *f*. (*important person*) **big ~**‡ grosse légume*, huile* *f*; *see* **fire**.

b (*: *germ*) microbe *m*. **he picked up a ~ on holiday** il a attrapé un microbe pendant ses vacances; **the flu ~** le virus de la grippe.

c (*defect, snag*) défaut *m*, inconvénient *m*; (*Comput*) erreur *f*.

d (*: *hidden microphone*) micro *m* (caché).

e (*US *: car*) petite voiture, coccinelle* *f*.

f (*: *enthusiasm*) **to be bitten by** *or* **get the jogging ~** attraper le virus du jogging.

g (*US* ‡: *enthusiast*) **a basketball ~** un(e) mordu(e)* du basket.

2 vt a (*) *phone etc* brancher sur table d'écoute; *room etc* poser *or* installer des micros (cachés) dans.

b (*: *annoy*) embêter*, casser les pieds à*.

3 comp ►**bugbear** épouvantail *m* (*fig*), cauchemar *m* ►**bug-eyed**‡ aux yeux à fleur de tête ►**bughouse**‡ (*US: asylum*) cabanon* *m*, maison *f* de dingues‡; (*Brit: cinema*) cinoche‡ *m* ►**bug-hunter**‡ entomologiste *mf*, chasseur *m* de petites bestioles* ►**bug-ridden** infesté de punaises.

►**bug out**‡ vi (*US*) foutre le camp‡.

bugaboo ['bʌgəbuː] n croque-mitaine *m*, loup-garou *m*.

bugger ['bʌgəʳ] 1 n a (*Jur*) pédéraste *m*. b (*Brit* ‡‡: *sod*) con‡‡ *m*, couillon‡‡ *m*, salaud‡ *m*. **silly ~** pauvre con‡‡; **to play silly ~s** déconner‡; **lucky ~** veinard‡ *m*; **poor little ~** pauvre petit bonhomme*. c (*Brit* ‡‡: *difficulty, annoyance*) **it is a ~** c'est casse-couilles‡‡ *mf inv* *or* casse-pieds* *mf inv*. 2 excl: **~ (it)!**‡‡ merde alors!‡ 3 vt a (*Jur*) se livrer à la pédérastie avec. b (*Brit* ‡‡) **well, I'm ~ed!** merde alors!‡; **I'll be** *or* **I'm ~ed if I'm going to do that!** je préfère plutôt crever (que de faire ça)!‡; **~ all** que dalle‡; **~ him!** il peut aller se faire foutre!‡‡; **~ the consequences** je me fous des conséquences‡; **convenience be ~ed!** je me fous de la commodité!‡

►**bugger about**‡‡, **bugger around**‡‡ (*Brit*) 1 vi glandouiller‡. (*play around with*) **to bugger around with sth** faire le con avec qch‡‡ 2 vt sep emmerder‡, faire chier‡‡.

►**bugger off**‡‡ vi (*Brit*) foutre le camp‡. **bugger off!** va te faire foutre!‡‡

►**bugger up**‡‡ vt sep (*Brit*) foutre en l'air‡.

buggered‡‡ ['bʌgəd] (*Brit*) 1 pret, ptp of **bugger**. 2 adj (*ruined*) foutu‡; (*exhausted*) crevé‡, défoncé*.

buggery ['bʌgərɪ] n sodomie *f*.

bugging ['bʌgɪŋ] n utilisation *f* d'appareils d'écoute. **~ device** appareil *m* d'écoute (*clandestine*).

buggy ['bʌgɪ] n (*horse-drawn*) boghei *m*; (*for beach*) buggy *m*; (*for moon*) jeep *f* lunaire; (‡: *car*) bagnole* *f*. **(baby) ~** (*Brit: pushchair*) poussette-canne *f*; (*US: pram*) voiture *f* d'enfant.

bugle ['bjuːgl] n clairon *m*. **~ call** sonnerie *f* de clairon.

bugler ['bjuːgləʳ] n (joueur *m* de) clairon *m*.

bugs‡ [bʌgz] adj (*US*) cinglé*, dingue*.

build [bɪld] (vb: pret, ptp **built**) 1 n carrure *f*, charpente *f*. **man of strong ~** homme solidement bâti *or* charpenté; **of medium ~** de corpulence moyenne; **of slim ~** fluet; **he's got the ~ of a wrestler** il a une carrure de catcheur, il est bâti comme un catcheur; **of the same ~ as ...** de même carrure que ... .

2 vt *house, town* bâtir, construire; *bridge, ship, machine* construire; *temple* bâtir, édifier; *nest* faire, bâtir; (*fig*) *theory, plan* bâtir, construire, édifier; *empire, company* fonder, bâtir; (*Games*) *words, sequence* former. **the house is being built** la maison se bâtit; **the architect who built the palace** l'architecte qui a bâti *or* qui a fait bâtir le palais; **the car was not built for speed** la voiture n'était pas conçue pour la vitesse; (*fig*) **to ~ castles in the air** faire des châteaux en Espagne; **to ~ a mirror into a wall** encastrer un miroir dans un mur; **house built into the hillside** maison *f* bâtie à flanc de colline; (*fig*) **his theory is not built on facts** sa théorie n'est pas basée *or* construite sur des faits.

3 vi bâtir; *[edifice]* se bâtir. **to ~ (up)on a piece of land** bâtir sur un terrain; (*lit, fig*) **to ~ upon sand** bâtir sur le sable; (*fig*) **it's a good start — something to ~ on** c'est une base solide sur laquelle on peut bâtir; (*frm*, †) **to ~ upon sb/a promise** faire fond sur qn/une promesse.

►**build in** 1 vt sep (*lit*) *wardrobe etc* encastrer (*into* dans); (*fig*) *safeguards* intégrer (*into* à); *see also* **build 2**. 2 **built-in** adj *see* **built 3**.

►**build on** vt sep *room, annex* ajouter (*to* à).

►**build up** 1 vi *[business connection etc]* se développer; *[pressure]* s'accumuler; *[tension, excitement]* monter, augmenter. 2 vt sep a (*establish*) *reputation* édifier, bâtir; *business* créer, monter; *theory* échafauder; (*increase*) *production, forces* accroître, augmenter; *pressure* accumuler; *tension, excitement* augmenter, faire monter. **to build up one's strength** prendre des forces. b (*cover with houses*) *area, land* urbaniser. c (*fig: publicize*) *person, reputation* faire de la publicité pour, faire du battage* autour de. 3 **build-up** n *see* **build-up**. 4 **built-up** adj *see* **built 3**.

builder ['bɪldəʳ] n a *[houses etc]* (*owner of firm*) entrepreneur *m*; (*worker*) maçon *m*; *[ships, machines]* constructeur *m*. **~'s labourer** ouvrier *m* du bâtiment; *see* **organ**. b (*fig*) fondateur *m*, -trice *f*, créateur *m*, -trice *f*; *see* **empire**.

building ['bɪldɪŋ] 1 n a bâtiment *m*, construction *f*; (*imposing*) édifice *m*; (*habitation or offices*) immeuble *m*; (*Jur, Insurance: in contract etc*) immeuble; *see* **public**.

b (*NonC*) construction *f*. **the ~ of the church took 7 years** la construction de l'église a demandé 7 ans, il a fallu 7 ans pour construire *or* édifier l'église; *see* **body, empire**.

2 comp ►**building block** (*toy*) cube *m*; (*fig*) composante *f* ►**building contractor** entrepreneur *m* (de bâtiment *or* de construction) ►**building industry** (industrie *f* du) bâtiment *m* ►**building labourer** ouvrier *m* du bâtiment ►**building land** terrain *m* à bâtir ►**building materials** matériaux *mpl* de construction ►**building permit** permis *m* de construire ►**building plot** (petit) terrain *m* à bâtir ►**building site** chantier *m* (de construction) ►**building society** (*Brit*) ≃ société *f* de crédit immobilier ►**building trade** = **building industry**; **the building trades** les métiers du bâtiment ►**building workers** ouvriers *mpl* du bâtiment.

build-up ['bɪldʌp] n a (*increase*) *[pressure]* intensification *f*; *[gas]* accumulation *f*; (*Mil*) *[troops]* rassemblement *m*; *[production]* accroissement *m*; (*Comm*) *[stock etc]* accumulation; *[tension, excitement]* montée *f*. (*Mil*) **arms ~** accumulation des armements. b (*fig*) présentation *f* publicitaire, battage* *m*. **to give sb/sth a good ~** faire une bonne publicité pour qn/qch, faire beaucoup de battage* autour de qn/qch.

built [bɪlt] 1 **pret, ptp of build.** 2 **adj** *house* bâti, construit (*of* de, en). *[person]* **to be solidly/slightly ~** avoir la charpente solide, être puissamment charpenté/être fluet *or* de petite constitution; *see* **well**². 3 **comp ▸built-in** *oven, wardrobe, mirror, beam* encastré; (*fig*) *desire etc* inné, ancré (*see also* **obsolescence**); **built-in cupboard** placard *m* (encastré) **▸built-up** (*Dress*) *shoulders* rehaussé; *shoes* à semelle compensée; **built-up area** agglomération *f* (urbaine).

-built [bɪlt] **adj ending in comps: pine-built house** maison *f* (construite) en bois de pin; **French-built ship** navire *m* de construction française.

bulb [bʌlb] **n** a *[plant]* bulbe *m*, oignon *m*. **~ of garlic** tête *f* d'ail; **tulip ~** bulbe *or* oignon de tulipe; **~ fibre** terreau enrichi (pour bulbes). b (*Elec*) ampoule *f*. c (*Chem*) ballon *m*; *[thermometer]* cuvette *f*.

bulbous ['bʌlbəs] **adj** *plant* bulbeux; *nose* gros (*f* grosse), bulbeux.

Bulgaria [bʌl'gɛərɪə] **n** Bulgarie *f*.

Bulgarian [bʌl'gɛərɪən] 1 **adj** bulgare. 2 **n** a Bulgare *mf*. b (*Ling*) bulgare *m*.

bulge [bʌldʒ] 1 **n** a *[surface, metal]* bombement *m*; *[cheek]* gonflement *m*; *[column]* renflement *m*; *[jug, bottle]* panse *f*, ventre *m*; *[plaster]* bosse *f*; *[tyre]* soufflure *f*, hernie *f*; *[pocket, jacket]* renflement; (*Brit Mil*) saillant *m*. (*Hist*) **the Battle of the B~** la contre-offensive *or* la bataille des Ardennes (*1944*). b (*increase*) *[numbers]* augmentation *f* temporaire; *[sales, prices, profits]* hausse *f*, poussée *f*; *[birth rate]* poussée. **the postwar ~** l'explosion *f* démographique de l'après-guerre.

2 **vi** (*also* **~ out**) (*swell*) se renfler, bomber; (*stick out*) faire *or* former saillie; *[plaster]* être bosselé; *[pocket, sack, cheek]* être gonflé (*with* de).

bulging ['bʌldʒɪŋ] **adj** *forehead, wall* bombé; *stomach* ballonné, protubérant; *furniture* pansu, ventru; *eyes* protubérant, globuleux, exorbité; *pockets, suitcase* bourré, plein à craquer.

bulgur ['bʌlgəʳ] **n** boulgour *m*.

bulimia [bə'lɪmɪə] **n** (*also* **~ nervosa**) boulimie *f*.

bulk [bʌlk] 1 **n** a (*great size*) *[thing]* grosseur *f*, grandeur *f*; *[person]* corpulence *f*; (*large volume*) masse *f*, volume *m*. **a ship of great ~** un navire de fort tonnage.

b (*main part*) **the ~** la majeure partie, la plus grande partie, le (plus) gros (*of* de); **the ~ of the working community** la plus grande partie *or* l'ensemble *m* de la population ouvrière; **the ~ of the work is done** le plus gros du travail est fait.

c (*Comm*) **in ~** (*in large quantities*) en gros; (*not prepacked*) en vrac.

d (*in food*) fibre *f* (végétale).

e (*Naut*) cargaison *f* (en cale).

2 **comp ▸bulk-buy** *[trader]* acheter en gros; *[individual]* acheter par *or* en grosses quantités **▸bulk-buying** *[trader]* achat *m* en gros; *[individual]* achat *m* par *or* en grosses quantités **▸bulk carrier** transporteur *m* de vrac **▸bulkhead** (*Brit Naut*) cloison *f* **▸bulk transport** transport *m* en vrac.

3 **adj** *order, supplies etc* en gros. **~ mailing** mailing *m* à grande diffusion; **~ mail** lettres *fpl or* envois *mpl* en nombre.

4 **vi: to ~ large** occuper une large place *or* une place importante (*in sb's eyes* aux yeux de qn, *in sb's thoughts* dans la pensée *or* l'esprit de qn).

5 **vt** (*Customs*) estimer. **to ~ a container** estimer le contenu d'un conteneur.

bulkiness ['bʌlkɪnɪs] **n** *[parcel, luggage]* grosseur *f*, volume *m*; *[person]* corpulence *f*.

bulky ['bʌlkɪ] **adj** *parcel, suitcase* volumineux, encombrant; *book* épais (*f* -aisse); *person* gros (*f* grosse), corpulent.

bull¹ [bʊl] 1 **n** a taureau *m*. (*fig*) **to take *or* seize *or* grasp the ~ by the horns** prendre *or* saisir le taureau par les cornes; **like a ~ in a china shop** comme un éléphant dans un magasin de porcelaine; **to him this word is like a red rag to a ~** c'est un mot qui lui fait monter la moutarde au nez; **to go at it like a ~ at a gate*** foncer tête baissée; (*Astron*) **the B~** le Taureau; *see* **bull's-eye, cock, John.**

b (*male of elephant, whale etc*) mâle *m*.

c (*St Ex*) haussier *m*. **the market is all ~s** le marché est orienté à la hausse.

d (*Mil sl: cleaning, polishing*) fourbissage *m*.

e (*‡: claptrap*) = **bullshit*‡ 1.**

2 **comp** *elephant etc* mâle; (*St Ex*) à la hausse **▸bull calf** jeune taureau *m*, taurillon *m* **▸bulldog** *see* **bulldog ▸bulldoze** *see* **bulldoze ▸bull's-eye** *see* **bull's-eye ▸bullfight** course *f* de taureaux, corrida *f* **▸bullfighter** matador *m*, torero *m*, toréador *m* **▸bullfighting** courses *fpl* de taureaux; (*art*) tauromachie *f* **▸bullfinch** bouvreuil *m* **▸bullfrog** grosse grenouille (d'Amérique) **▸bull neck** cou *m* de taureau **▸bull-necked** au cou de taureau, épais d'encolure **▸bullring** arène *f* (*pour courses de taureaux*) **▸bull session*** (*US*) discussion *f* entre hommes **▸bullshit*‡** *see* **bullshit*‡ ▸bull terrier** bull-terrier *m*.

3 **vt** (*St Ex*) *stocks, shares* pousser à la hausse. **to ~ the market** pousser les cours à la hausse.

bull² [bʊl] **n** (*Rel*) bulle *f*. **papal ~** bulle papale.

bulldog ['bʊldɒg] 1 **n** bouledogue *m*. 2 **comp** *tenacity etc* acharné **▸bulldog breed:** (*fig*) **he is one of the bulldog breed** il est d'une ténacité à toute épreuve **▸bulldog clip** (*Brit*) pince *f* à dessin.

bulldoze ['bʊldəʊz] **vt** (*Constr*) passer au bulldozer. (*fig*) **to ~ sb into doing sth*** employer les grands moyens pour faire faire qch à qn; **he ~d his way into the meeting*** (*forced his way in*) il a réussi à pénétrer dans la salle où avait lieu la réunion; (*managed to contribute*) il a réussi à participer à cette réunion à la force du poignet.

bulldozer ['bʊldəʊzəʳ] **n** bulldozer *m*.

bullet ['bʊlɪt] 1 **n** balle *f* (*projectile*). 2 **comp ▸bullet-headed** à (la) tête ronde **▸bullet hole** trou *m* de balle **▸bulletproof adj** *garment etc* pare-balles *inv*; *car etc* blindé ◊ **vt** blinder **▸bullet train** train *m* à grande vitesse (*japonais*) **▸bullet wound** blessure *f* par balle.

bulletin ['bʊlɪtɪn] **n** bulletin *m*, communiqué *m*. **health ~** bulletin de santé; (*gen, Comput*) **~ board** tableau *m* d'affichage; *see* **news.**

bullhorn ['bʊlhɔːn] **n** (*US*) porte-voix *m inv*, mégaphone *m*.

bullion¹ ['bʊljən] **n** (*NonC*) encaisse-or *f*; (*gold ~*) or *m* en barre *or* en lingot(s); (*silver ~*) argent *m* en lingot(s).

bullion² ['bʊljən] **n** (*fringe*) frange *f* de cannetille.

bullish ['bʊlɪʃ] **adj** (*St Ex*) haussier.

bullock ['bʊlək] **n** bœuf *m*; (*young*) bouvillon *m*. **~ cart** char *m* à bœufs.

bull's-eye ['bʊlzaɪ] **n** a *[target]* centre *m*, noir *m* (de la cible), mille *m*. (*lit, fig*) **to get a ~, to hit the ~** faire mouche, tirer *or* mettre dans le mille. b (*sweet*) gros bonbon à la menthe. c (*window*) œil-de-bœuf *m*, oculus *m*; (*in glass*) boudine *f*.

bullshit*‡ ['bʊl,ʃɪt] 1 **n** foutaise(s)‡ *f(pl)*, connerie(s)‡ *f(pl)*. **(that's) ~!** c'est de la foutaise!‡ 2 **vi** déconner‡, dire des conneries‡. 3 **vt** raconter des conneries à‡.

bully¹ ['bʊlɪ] 1 **n** a tyran *m*; (*esp Scol*) petit(e) dur(e) *m(f)*, (petite) brute *f*. b (*Brit Hockey: also* **~-off**) engagement *m* (du jeu). 2 **comp ▸bully boy*** dur *m*, brute *f*. 3 **vt** (*persecute*) tyranniser, persécuter; (*treat cruelly*) malmener, brutaliser; (*frighten*) intimider; (*Scol*) brutaliser, brimer. **to ~ sb into doing sth** contraindre qn par la menace à faire qch. 4 **vi** être une brute.

▸bully off vi (*Brit*) mettre la balle en jeu, engager (le jeu).

bully²‡ ['bʊlɪ] 1 **adj** (†) épatant†. 2 **excl: ~ for you!** t'es un chef!‡

bully³* ['bʊlɪ] **n** (*Mil: also* **~ beef**) corned-beef *m*, singe‡ *m*.

bullying ['bʊlɪɪŋ] 1 **adj** *person, manner* tyrannique, brutal. 2 **n** brimade(s) *f(pl)*, brutalité(s) *f(pl)*.

bulrush ['bʊlrʌʃ] **n** jonc *m*.

bulwark ['bʊlwək] **n** (*rampart*) rempart *m*, fortification *f*; (*breakwater*) brise-lames *m inv*; (*fig: defence*) rempart; (*Naut*) bastingage *m*.

bum¹* [bʌm] (*esp US*) 1 **n** (*vagrant*) clochard *m*, clodo‡ *m*; (*good-for-nothing*) bon à rien *m*. **to give sb the ~'s rush‡** vider qn par la peau des fesses‡; **to live on the ~*** vivre en clochard. 2 **adj** (*bad*) moche*, minable*, de camelote*; (*false*) faux (*f* fausse). **a ~ rap‡** une accusation montée de toutes pièces; **a ~ steer*** un mauvais tuyau*, un tuyau percé*. 3 **vi** a (*scrounge*) taper* les autres. b (*loaf: also* **~ about** *or* **around**) fainéanter, être clochard *or* clodo‡. 4 **vt** *money, food* écornifler*. **to ~ a meal off sb** taper qn d'un repas*.

bum²‡ [bʌm] 1 **n** (*Brit: bottom*) derrière *m*, arrière-train* *m*. 2 **comp ▸bumbag** (*Ski*) banane *f* **▸bumfreezer*** pet-en-l'air *m*.

bumbershoot* ['bʌmbəʃuːt] **n** (*US* †) pépin* *m*, parapluie *m*.

bumble ['bʌmbl] **vi** a (*walk*) marcher en titubant *or* d'un pas chancelant. **to ~ about *or* around (a place)** s'affairer (dans un endroit) sans rien faire de valable. b (*speak*) bafouiller. **to ~ on about sth** bafouiller *or* rabâcher qch.

bumblebee ['bʌmblbiː] **n** (*Zool*) bourdon *m*.

bumbling ['bʌmblɪŋ] **adj** (*inept*) empoté; (*muttering*) rabâcheur.

bumboat ['bʌmbəʊt] **n** canot *m* d'approvisionnement.

bumf* [bʌmf] **n** (*Brit*) (*pej: forms etc*) paperasses *fpl*, paperasserie *f*; (*toilet paper*) papier *m* de cabinets*.

bummer‡ ['bʌməʳ] **n** (*disappointment*) douche* *f*, déception *f*; (*flop*) fiasco *m*; (*Drugs sl*) mauvais trip*. (*what a pity*) **what a ~!** oh merde!‡

bump [bʌmp] 1 **n** a (*blow*) choc *m*, heurt *m*, coup *m*; (*jolt*) cahot *m*, secousse *f*; (*Boat-racing*) heurt.

b (*lump: on head, in road, Ski*) bosse *f*. **~ of locality*** sens *m* de l'orientation.

c (*Aviat: rising air current*) (soudain) courant ascendant.

2 **vt** *[car]* *another car* heurter, tamponner; *boat* heurter. **to ~ one's head/knee** se cogner la tête/le genou (*against* contre); *[fairground]* **~ing cars** autos tamponneuses.

3 **vi: to ~ along** cahoter, bringuebaler; **to ~ down** (*sit*) s'asseoir brusquement.

4 **comp ▸bump-start vt** *car* démarrer en poussant; **to give a car a bump-start** démarrer une voiture en la poussant.

5 **adv: the car ran ~ into a tree** la voiture est entrée de plein fouet *or* en plein dans un arbre.

6 **excl** boum!, pan!

▸bump into vt fus a *[person]* butter contre, se cogner contre; *[vehicle]*

entrer en collision avec, tamponner, rentrer dans*. b (*: *meet*) rencontrer par hasard, tomber sur*.

►**bump off**‡ vt sep liquider*, supprimer; (*with gun*) descendre‡.

►**bump up** 1 vi: **the car bumped up onto the pavement** la voiture a grimpé sur le trottoir. 2 vt sep (*: *increase sharply*) *prices, sales, statistics* faire grimper*.

►**bump up against** vt fus = **bump into**.

bumper [ˈbʌmpəʳ] 1 n a *[car]* pare-chocs *m inv*. b (*full glass*) rasade *f*, plein verre. 2 adj *crop, issue* exceptionnel, sensationnel. ~ **sticker** *or* **strip** autocollant *m* (*pour voiture*); **to be ~-to-~** être pare-chocs contre pare-chocs, être à touche-touche*.

bumph* [bʌmf] n = **bumf***.

bumpkin [ˈbʌmpkɪn] n (*also* **country ~**) rustre *m*, péquenaud‡ *m*, paysan *m* (*pej*).

bumptious [ˈbʌmpʃəs] adj suffisant, prétentieux.

bumpy [ˈbʌmpɪ] adj *road* inégal, bosselé; *forehead* couvert de bosses; *ride* cahoteux; *crossing* agité. **we had a ~ flight/drive/crossing** nous avons été très secoués *or* chahutés* pendant le vol/sur la route/pendant la traversée.

bun [bʌn] 1 n a (*Culin*) petit pain au lait. **to have a ~ in the oven**‡ avoir un polichinelle dans le tiroir‡. b *[hair]* chignon *m*. c (*US* ‡: *get drunk*) **to get a ~ on** prendre une biture‡; **he had a ~ on** il tenait une de ces bitures!‡. 2 comp ►**bun-fight*** thé *m* (*servi pour un grand nombre de gens*).

bunch [bʌntʃ] 1 n a *[roses, tulips]* botte *f*, (*for presentation*) bouquet *m*; *[feathers]* touffe *f*; *[hair]* touffe, houppe *f*; *[bananas]* régime *m*; *[radishes, asparagus]* botte *f*; *[twigs]* poignée *f*, paquet *m*; *[keys]* trousseau *m*; *[ribbons]* nœud *m*, flot *m*. ~ **of flowers** bouquet (de fleurs); ~ **of grapes** grappe *f* de raisins; (*Brit*) **to wear one's hair in ~es** porter des couettes; (*fig*) **the pick of the ~** le dessus du panier.

b *[people]* groupe *m*, bande *f*, équipe* *f*; (*Sport*) *[runners, cyclists]* peloton *m*. **the best of the ~** le meilleur de la bande *or* de l'équipe*; **the best of a bad ~*** le *or* les moins médiocre(s); **what a ~!** quelle équipe!*

2 vt *flowers* mettre en bouquets; *vegetables, straw* botteler, mettre en bottes.

►**bunch together** 1 vi se serrer (en foule), se grouper. 2 vt sep *people, things* grouper, concentrer.

►**bunch up** 1 vi **don't bunch up so much, space out!** ne vous entassez pas les uns sur les autres, desserrez-vous! 2 vt sep a *dress, skirt* retrousser, trousser. b **they sat bunched up on the bench** ils étaient (assis) serrés sur le banc.

bunco* [ˈbʊŋkəʊ] (*US*) 1 n (*swindle*) arnaque‡ *m*, escroquerie *f*. 2 vt arnaquer‡, escroquer. 3 comp ►**bunco squad** ≃ brigade *f* de la répression des fraudes.

buncombe‡ [ˈbʌŋkəm] n (*US*) = **bunkum**‡.

bundle [ˈbʌndl] 1 n a *[clothes]* paquet *m*, ballot *m*, balluchon* *m*; *[goods]* paquet, ballot; *[hay]* botte *f*; *[letters, papers]* liasse *f*; *[linen]* paquet; *[firewood]* fagot *m*; *[rods, sticks]* faisceau *m*, poignée *f*, paquet. **he is a ~ of nerves** c'est un paquet de nerfs; **he is a ~ of laughs*** *or* **fun*** c'est un marrant*; (*: *baby*) **~ (of joy)** (petit) bout *m* de chou*; **that child is a ~ of mischief*** cet enfant est un sac à malices.

b (‡: *money*) **a ~** beaucoup d'argent, un magot*, un matelas‡; **to make a ~** faire son beurre*.

c (*Comput*) lot *m*.

2 vt a (*also* **~ up**) empaqueter, mettre en paquet; *clothes* faire un ballot de; *hay* botteler; *papers, banknotes* mettre en liasse; *letters* mettre en paquet; *sticks* mettre en faisceau.

b (*put hastily*) **to ~ sth into a corner** fourrer* *or* entasser qch dans un coin; **to ~ sb into the house** pousser *or* faire entrer qn dans la maison à la hâte *or* sans cérémonie.

►**bundle off** vt sep *person* faire sortir (en toute hâte), pousser dehors (sans façons). **he was bundled off to Australia** on l'a expédié en Australie.

►**bundle out** vt sep pousser dehors (sans façons), faire sortir (en toute hâte).

►**bundle up** vt sep a = **bundle 2a**. b emmitoufler.

bung [bʌŋ] 1 n *[cask]* bondon *m*, bonde *f*. **~hole** bonde. 2 vt a (*also* **~ up**) *cask* boucher; *pipe etc* boucher, obstruer. **his eyes were/his nose was ~ed up*** il avait les yeux tout bouffis/le nez bouché *or* pris; **I'm all ~ed up*** j'ai un gros rhume (de cerveau). b (*Brit* ‡: *throw*) envoyer*, balancer*.

►**bung in**‡ vt sep (*include*) rajouter (par-dessus le marché).

►**bung out**‡ vt sep flanquer* à la porte; *rubbish* jeter.

►**bung up** vt sep *see* **bung 2a**.

bungaloid [ˈbʌŋgəlɔɪd] adj (*pej*) de bungalow, genre *or* style bungalow. **~ growth** extension *f* pavillonnaire.

bungalow [ˈbʌŋgələʊ] n (petit) pavillon *m* (*en rez-de-chaussée*); (*in East*) bungalow *m*.

bungee [ˈbʌndʒiː] n: **~ jumping** saut *m* à l'élastique.

bungle [ˈbʌŋgl] 1 vt *attempt, robbery* rater; *piece of work* gâcher, bousiller*. **he ~d it** il s'y est mal pris, il a tout bousillé*; **it was a ~d job** c'était fait n'importe comment. 2 vi s'y prendre mal, faire les choses n'importe comment.

bungler [ˈbʌŋgləʳ] n bousilleur* *m*, -euse *f*. **he is a ~** il bousille* tout, il est incompétent.

bungling [ˈbʌŋglɪŋ] 1 adj *person* maladroit, incompétent; *attempt* maladroit, gauche. 2 n (*NonC*) gâchis *m*, bousillage* *m*.

bunion [ˈbʌnjən] n (*Med*) oignon *m*.

bunk [bʌŋk] 1 n a (*Naut, Rail etc: bed*) couchette *f*. b (*Brit*) **to do a ~**‡ mettre les bouts‡ *or* les voiles*. c (‡) abbr of **bunkum**. 2 vi a (*: *also* **~ down**) coucher, camper (*dans un lit de fortune*). b (‡: *also* **~ off**) mettre les bouts‡ *or* les voiles*. 3 comp ►**bunk beds** lits superposés ►**bunkhouse** (*esp US*) bâtiment-dortoir *m* ►**bunk-up***: **to give sb a bunk-up** soulever qn par derrière *or* par en dessous.

bunker [ˈbʌŋkəʳ] 1 n a *[coal]* coffre *m*; (*Naut*) soute *f* (à charbon *or* à mazout). b (*Golf*) bunker *m*; (*fig*) obstacle *m*. c (*Mil*) blockhaus *m*, bunker *m*. **(nuclear) ~** bunker *or* abri *m* anti-nucléaire. 2 vt a (*Naut*) *coal, oil* mettre en soute. (*Naut*) **to ~ a ship** mettre du charbon *or* du mazout en soute. b **to be ~ed** (*Golf*) se trouver dans un bunker; (‡ *fig*) se trouver face à un obstacle, se trouver dans une impasse. 3 vi (*Naut*) charbonner, mazouter.

bunkum‡ [ˈbʌŋkəm] n blague(s)* *f(pl)*, foutaise(s)‡ *f(pl)*, histoires *fpl*. **to talk ~** dire *or* débiter des balivernes *or* des foutaises‡; **that's all ~** tout ça c'est de la blague!*

bunny [ˈbʌnɪ] n a (*also* **~ rabbit**) Jeannot *m* lapin. b (*US* *: *pretty girl*) pépée* *f*, jolie fille; (*also* **~ girl**) hôtesse *f* (*du Club Playboy*); *see* **ski, snow**.

Bunsen [ˈbʌnsn] n: **~ burner** bec *m* Bunsen.

bunting[1] [ˈbʌntɪŋ] n (*Orn*) bruant *m*; *see* **reed** *etc*.

bunting[2] [ˈbʌntɪŋ] n (*NonC*) (*material*) étamine *f* (à pavillon); (*flags etc*) drapeaux *mpl*, banderoles *fpl*, pavoisement *m*.

buoy [bɔɪ] 1 n bouée *f*, balise flottante. **to put down a ~** mouiller une bouée; **~ rope** orin *m*; *see* **life, mooring** *etc*. 2 vt *waterway* baliser; *net* liéger.

►**buoy up** vt sep (*lit*) faire flotter, maintenir à flot; (*fig*) soutenir.

buoyancy [ˈbɔɪənsɪ] n a *[ship, object]* flottabilité *f*; *[liquid]* poussée *f*. **~ aid** gilet *m* de sauvetage; (*Naut*) **~ chamber** *or* **tank** caisson *m* étanche. b (*lightheartedness*) gaieté *f*, entrain *m*. c (*Fin*) fermeté *f*, tendance *f* à la hausse.

buoyant [ˈbɔɪənt] adj a *ship, object* capable de flotter, flottable; *liquid* dans lequel les objets flottent. **fresh water is not so ~ as salt water** l'eau douce ne porte pas si bien que l'eau salée. b (*lighthearted*) *person* enjoué, plein d'entrain *or* d'allant; *mood* gai, optimiste; *step* léger, élastique. c (*Fin*) *market* soutenu, ferme, actif.

buoyantly [ˈbɔɪəntlɪ] adv *walk, float* légèrement; (*fig*) gaiement *or* gaîment, avec entrain, avec optimisme.

bur[1] [bɜːʳ] n (*Bot*) bardane *f*; (‡ *pej: person*) crampon* *m* (*pej*). **chestnut ~** bogue *f*.

bur[2] [bɜːʳ] 1 n (*Ling*) grasseyement *m*. **to speak with a ~** grasseyer. 2 vti: **to ~ (one's Rs)** prononcer les R grasseyés.

burble [ˈbɜːbl] 1 vi *[stream]* murmurer; *[person]* marmonner. **what's he burbling (on) about?** qu'est-ce qu'il marmonne (dans sa barbe)? 2 n *[stream]* murmure *m*.

burbling [ˈbɜːblɪŋ] 1 n (*NonC*) *[stream]* murmure *m*; *[person]* jacassements *mpl*. 2 adj *person* qui n'arrête pas de jacasser.

burbot [ˈbɜːbət] n, pl **~** *or* **~s** lotte *f* (de rivière).

burden [ˈbɜːdn] 1 n a (*lit*) fardeau *m*, charge *f*, faix *m*; *see* **beast**.

b (*fig*) fardeau *m*, charge *f*; *[taxes, years]* poids *m*; *[debts]* fardeau; (*Fin, Jur: debt weighing on company's balance sheet or on an estate*) encombrement *m*. **to be a ~ to** être un fardeau pour; **to make sb's life a ~** rendre la vie intenable à qn; **the ~ of the expense** les frais *mpl* à charge; (*Jur*) **~ of proof** charge *or* fardeau de la preuve; **the ~ of proof lies** *or* **rests with him** la charge de la preuve lui incombe, il lui incombe d'en fournir la preuve.

c (*Naut*) port *m*, tonnage *m*. **ship of 4,000 tons' ~** navire *m* qui jauge 4 000 tonneaux.

d (*chorus*) refrain *m*.

e (*chief theme*) substance *f*, fond *m*, essentiel *m*. **the ~ of their complaint** leur principal grief *or* sujet de plainte.

2 vt (*place ~ on*) charger (*with* de); (*oppress*) accabler (*with* de). **to ~ the people with taxes** grever le peuple d'impôts; **to ~ one's memory with facts** se (sur)charger la mémoire de faits.

burdensome [ˈbɜːdnsəm] adj *load* lourd, pesant, écrasant; *task, restriction* pénible.

burdock [ˈbɜːdɒk] n bardane *f*.

bureau [ˈbjʊərəʊ] n, pl **~s** *or* **~x** a (*esp Brit: writing desk*) bureau *m*, secrétaire *m*. b (*US: chest of drawers*) commode *f* (*souvent à miroir*). c (*office*) bureau *m*; *see* **information, travel** *etc*. d (*esp US: government department*) service *m* (gouvernemental). (*US*) **federal ~** bureau fédéral; (*US*) **B~ of Prisons** administration *f* pénitentiaire.

bureaucracy [bjʊəˈrɒkrəsɪ] n bureaucratie *f*.

bureaucrat [ˈbjʊərəʊkræt] n bureaucrate *mf*.

bureaucratese* [ˌbjʊərəʊkræˈtiːz] n jargon administratif.

bureaucratic [ˌbjʊərəʊˈkrætɪk] adj bureaucratique.

bureaux [ˈbjʊərəʊz] npl of **bureau**.

burette [bjʊəˈret] n éprouvette graduée.

burg* [bɜːg] n (*US pej: town*) bled* *m*, patelin* *m*.

burgeon ['bɜːdʒən] **vi** (*liter*) *[flower]* (commencer à) éclore; *[plant]* bourgeonner, se couvrir de bourgeons; *[talent]* naître; *[population]* être en pleine croissance; *[trade, industry]* être en pleine expansion.

burger ['bɜːgəʳ] **n** hamburger *m*.

burgess ['bɜːdʒɪs] **n a** (*Brit Hist*) (*citizen*) bourgeois *m*, citoyen *m*; (*Parl*) député *m*, représentant *m* (au Parlement) d'un bourg *or* d'une circonscription universitaire. **b** (*US Hist*) député *m*.

burgh ['bʌrə] **n** (*Scot*) ville *f* (*possédant une charte*).

burgher ['bɜːgəʳ] **n** († *or liter*) citoyen *m*.

burglar ['bɜːgləʳ] **1 n** cambrioleur *m*, -euse *f*; *see* **cat. 2 comp** ▸**burglar alarm** sonnerie *f* d'alarme ▸**burglar-proof** *house* muni d'une sonnerie d'alarme; *lock* incrochetable.

burglarize ['bɜːgləraɪz] **vt** (*US*) cambrioler.

burglary ['bɜːglərɪ] **n** cambriolage *m*.

burgle ['bɜːgl] **1 vt** cambrioler, dévaliser. **2 vi** cambrioler.

burgomaster ['bɜːgəˌmɑːstəʳ] **n** bourgmestre *m*.

Burgundian [bɜːˈgʌndɪən] **1 adj** bourguignon, de Bourgogne. **2 n** Bourguignon(ne) *m(f)*.

Burgundy ['bɜːgəndɪ] **n** (*Geog*) Bourgogne *f*. (*wine*) **b~** le bourgogne, le vin de Bourgogne.

burial ['berɪəl] **1 n** (*interment*) enterrement *m*, inhumation *f*, ensevelissement *m* (*liter*); (*religious*) sépulture *f*; (*ceremony*) funérailles *fpl*, obsèques *fpl*; *[hopes etc]* mort *f*, fin *f*. **Christian ~** sépulture ecclésiastique *or* chrétienne. **2 comp** ▸**burial ground** cimetière *m* ▸**burial mound** tumulus *m* ▸**burial place** lieu *m* de sépulture ▸**burial service** office *m* des morts, service *m* funèbre ▸**burial vault** tombeau *m*.

burin ['bjʊərɪn] **n** burin *m* (à graver).

burke [bɜːk] **vt** (*suppress*) *scandal* étouffer; (*shelve*) *question* escamoter.

Burkina-Faso [bɜːˈkiːnəˈfæsəʊ] **n** Burkina-Faso *m*.

burlap ['bɜːlæp] **n** toile *f* d'emballage, toile à sac.

burlesque [bɜːˈlesk] **1 n a** (*parody*) *[book, poem etc]* parodie *f*; *[society, way of life]* caricature *f*. **b** (*NonC: Literat*) (genre *m*) burlesque *m*. **c** (*US: striptease*) revue déshabillée (*souvent vulgaire*). **2 adj** *poem etc* burlesque; *description* caricatural. **3 vt** (*make ridiculous*) tourner en ridicule; (*parody*) *book, author* parodier.

burly ['bɜːlɪ] **adj** de forte carrure, solidement charpenté. **a big ~ fellow** un grand costaud*; **a ~ policeman** un grand gaillard d'agent.

Burma ['bɜːmə] **n** Birmanie *f*.

Burmese [bɜːˈmiːz] **1 adj** birman, de Birmanie. **the ~ Empire** l'Empire birman; **~ cat** chat(te) *m(f)* de Birmanie. **2 n a (pl inv)** Birman(e) *m(f)*. **b** (*Ling*) birman *m*.

burn¹ [bɜːn] **(vb: pret, ptp burned or** (*Brit*) **burnt) 1 n a** (*also Med*) brûlure *f*. **cigarette ~** brûlure de cigarette; *see* **degree**.

b (*Space*) *[rocket]* (durée *f* de) combustion *f*.

2 comp ▸**burnout:** (*Elec*) **there's been a burnout** les circuits sont grillés.

3 vt a (*gen*) brûler; *town, building* incendier, mettre le feu à, faire brûler. **to ~ to a cinder** carboniser, calciner; **to be ~t to death** être brûlé vif, mourir carbonisé; **to be ~t alive** *or* **at the stake** être brûlé vif; **to ~ o.s.** se brûler; **to ~ one's finger** se brûler le doigt; **he ~t a hole in his coat with a cigarette** il a fait un trou à son manteau avec une cigarette; (*fig*) **you could ~ your fingers over this** vous risquez de vous brûler les doigts dans cette affaire; (*fig*) **money ~s a hole in my pocket** l'argent me fond dans les mains; (*fig*) **to ~ one's boats/one's bridges** brûler ses vaisseaux/les ponts; (*fig*) **to ~ the candle at both ends** brûler la chandelle par les deux bouts; *see* **midnight** *etc*.

b (*Culin*) *meat, toast, cakes* laisser brûler; *sauce, milk* laisser attacher.

c *[acid]* brûler, ronger; *[sun] person, skin* brûler. **his skin was ~t black by the sun** il était noir d'avoir été brûlé par le soleil.

4 vi a *[wood, meat, cakes etc]* brûler; *[milk, sauce]* attacher. **you left all the lights ~ing** vous avez laissé toutes les lumières allumées; **her skin ~s easily** elle a la peau facilement brûlée par le soleil, elle attrape facilement des coups de soleil; **my head is ~ing** j'ai la tête brûlante; **the wound was ~ing** la blessure cuisait.

b *[person]* (*lit*) être brûlé vif; (*fig*) brûler (*with* de). **he was ~ing to get his revenge** *or* **~ing for revenge** il brûlait (du désir) de se venger.

c acid ~s into metal l'acide ronge le métal; (*fig*) **the date ~ed into his memory** la date se grava dans sa mémoire.

d (*Space*) *[rocket]* brûler.

▸**burn away 1 vi a** (*go on burning*) **the fire was burning away** le feu flambait *or* brûlait bien. **b** (*be consumed*) se consumer. **2 vt sep** détruire (par le feu); *paint* brûler (au chalumeau).

▸**burn down 1 vi a** *[house etc]* brûler complètement, être réduit en cendres. **b** *[fire, candle]* baisser. **2 vt sep** *building* incendier. **the house was burnt down** la maison a été réduite en cendres *or* calcinée.

▸**burn off vt sep** *paint etc* brûler (au chalumeau).

▸**burn out 1 vi** *[fire, candle]* s'éteindre; *[light bulb]* griller, sauter. **2 vt sep a** *candle* laisser brûler jusqu'au bout; *lamp* griller. **the candle burnt itself out** la bougie est morte; (*fig*) **he burnt himself out** il s'est usé (à force de travail). **b** (*force out by fire*) *enemy troops etc* forcer à sortir en mettant le feu. **they were burnt out of house and home** un incendie a détruit leur maison avec tout ce qu'ils possédaient. **3 n burnout** *see* **burn¹ 2**.

▸**burn up 1 vi a** *[fire etc]* flamber, monter. **b** *[rocket etc in atmosphere]* se volatiliser, se désintégrer. **2 vt sep a** *rubbish* brûler. **b burned up with envy** dévoré d'envie. **c** (*US *: make angry*) foutre en rogne‡.

burn² [bɜːn] **n** (*Scot*) ruisseau *m*.

burner ['bɜːnəʳ] **n** *[gas cooker]* brûleur *m*; *[lamp]* bec *m* (de gaz); *see* **back, Bunsen, charcoal, front** *etc*.

Burnham ['bɜːnəm] **n** (*Brit Scol Admin*) **~ scale** *grille indiciaire des enseignants*.

burning ['bɜːnɪŋ] **1 adj a** (*on fire*) *town, forest* en flammes, embrasé (*liter*), incendié; *fire, candle* allumé; *coals* ardent; *feeling* cuisant. **the ~ bush** le buisson ardent; **with a ~ face** (*shame*) le rouge au front; (*embarrassment*) le rouge aux joues.

b (*fig*) *thirst, fever* brûlant; *faith* ardent, intense; *indignation* violent; *words* véhément, passionné; *topic* brûlant, passionnant. **a ~ question** une question brûlante; **it's a ~* shame that ...** c'est une honte *or* un scandale que ... (+ *subj*).

2 n a there is a smell of ~ ça sent le brûlé *or* le roussi; **I could smell ~** je sentais une odeur de brûlé.

b (*setting on fire*) incendie *m*, embrasement *m*. **they ordered the ~ of the town** ils ont ordonné l'incendie de la ville, ils ont ordonné qu'on mette le feu à la ville.

burnish ['bɜːnɪʃ] **vt** *metal* brunir, polir. **~ed hair/skin/leaves** (beaux) cheveux *mpl* brillants/(belle) peau *f* luisante/feuilles *fpl* aux reflets dorés.

burnisher ['bɜːnɪʃəʳ] **n** (*person*) brunisseur *m*, -euse *f*; (*tool*) brunissoir *m*.

burnous(e), (*US*) **burnoos** [bɜːˈnuːs] **n** burnous *m*.

burnt [bɜːnt] **1 pret, ptp of burn¹**. **2 adj** brûlé, carbonisé. (*Prov*) **a ~ child dreads the fire** chat échaudé craint l'eau froide (*Prov*); **~ almond** amande grillée, praline *f*; **~ lime** chaux vive; **~ offering, ~ sacrifice** holocauste *m*; **~ orange** orange foncé *inv*; **~ sienna, ~ umber** terre *f* de sienne *or* d'ombre brûlée; **~ smell/taste** odeur *f*/goût *m* de brûlé; **~ sugar** caramel *m*.

burp* [bɜːp] **1 vi** roter*, faire un renvoi. **2 vt: to ~ a baby** faire faire son rot* *or* son renvoi à un bébé. **3 n** rot* *m*, renvoi *m*.

burr [bɜːʳ] **n = bur**.

burrow ['bʌrəʊ] **1 n** terrier *m*. **2 vi** *[rabbits etc]* creuser un terrier; *[dog]* creuser (la terre). *[person]* **to ~ under** (*in earth*) se creuser un chemin sous; (*under blanket*) se réfugier sous; (*feel around in*) fouiller sous; (*fig*) **to ~ into the past** fouiller dans le passé. **3 vt** creuser. **to ~ one's way underground** (se) creuser (un chemin) sous terre.

bursa ['bɜːsə] **n, pl ~s** *or* **bursae** ['bɜːsiː] (*Anat*) bourse *f*.

bursar ['bɜːsəʳ] **n a** (*administrator: gen*) intendant(e) *m(f)*; (*in private school, hospital*) économe *mf*. **b** (*Brit: student*) (élève *mf*) boursier *m*, -ière *f*.

bursary ['bɜːsərɪ] **n** bourse *f* (d'études).

bursitis [bɜːˈsaɪtɪs] **n** hygroma *m*.

burst [bɜːst] **(vb: pret, ptp burst) 1 n** *[shell etc]* explosion *f*, éclatement *m*; *[anger, indignation]* explosion; *[anger, laughter]* éclat *m*; *[affection, eloquence]* élan *m*, transport *m*; *[activity]* vague *f*; *[enthusiasm]* accès *m*, montée *f*; *[thunder]* coup *m*; *[applause]* salve *f*; *[flames]* jaillissement *m*, jet *m*. **~ of rain** averse *f*; **to put on a ~ of speed** faire une pointe de vitesse; **~ of gunfire** rafale *f* (de tir); **~ of weeping** crise *f* de larmes; (*Comm*) **~ advertising** matraquage *m* publicitaire.

2 adj (*Med*) **~ blood vessel** vaisseau *m* éclaté; (*Plumbing*) **~ pipe** tuyau *m* éclaté.

3 vi a *[bomb, shell]* éclater, faire explosion; *[boiler, pipe]* éclater, sauter; *[bubble, balloon, abscess]* crever; *[tyre]* (*blow out*) éclater; (*puncture*) crever; *[bud]* éclore. **to ~ open** *[door]* s'ouvrir violemment; *[container]* s'éventrer.

b *[sack etc]* **to be ~ing (at the seams)** être plein à craquer (*with* de); **to fill a sack to ~ing point** remplir un sac à craquer; (*fig*) **to be ~ing with health** déborder de santé; **to be ~ing with impatience** brûler d'impatience; **to be ~ing with pride** éclater d'orgueil; **to be ~ing with joy** déborder de joie; **I was ~ing to tell you*** je mourais d'envie de vous le dire; **to be ~ing*** avoir très envie d'aller aux toilettes.

c (*move etc suddenly*) se précipiter, se jeter (*into* dans, *out of* hors de).

d (*begin etc suddenly*) **the horse ~ into a gallop** le cheval a pris le galop; **he suddenly ~ into speech/song** il s'est mis tout d'un coup à parler/chanter; **the truth ~ (in) upon him** la vérité lui a soudain sauté aux yeux; **the applause ~ upon our ears** les applaudissements ont éclaté à nos oreilles; **to ~ into tears** fondre en larmes; *[flower]* **to ~ into bloom** s'épanouir (soudain); **to ~ into flames** prendre feu (soudain); **the sun ~ through the clouds** le soleil a percé les nuages; **the oil ~ from the well** le pétrole a jailli du puits.

4 vt *balloon, bubble* crever; *tyre* (*blow out*) faire éclater; (*puncture*) crever; *boiler, pipe* faire sauter. **to ~ open** *door* ouvrir violemment; *container* éventrer; **the river has ~ its banks** le fleuve a rompu ses digues; **to ~ one's sides with laughter*** se tordre de rire; (*Med*) **to ~ a blood vessel** (se) faire éclater une veine, (se) rompre un vaisseau; (*with anger etc*) **he almost ~ a blood vessel*** il a failli (en) prendre un coup de sang* *or* (en) avoir une attaque*.

▶**burst forth** vi (*liter*) *[person]* sortir précipitamment; *[sun]* surgir.

▶**burst in** 1 vi entrer en trombe *or* en coup de vent, faire irruption. **he burst in (on us/them** *etc*) il a fait irruption (chez nous/eux *etc*); **to burst in on a conversation** interrompre brutalement une conversation. 2 vt sep *door* enfoncer.

▶**burst out** vi a **to burst out of a room** se précipiter hors d'une pièce, sortir d'une pièce en trombe. b **she's bursting out of that dress** elle éclate de partout *or* elle est très boudinée* dans cette robe. c (*in speech*) s'exclamer, s'écrier. **to burst out into explanations/threats** *etc* se répandre en explications/menaces *etc.* d **to burst out laughing** éclater de rire; **to burst out crying** fondre en larmes; **to burst out singing** se mettre tout d'un coup à chanter.

bursting ['bɜːstɪŋ] n (*Comput*) déliassage *m*.

burthen†† ['bɜːðən] = **burden**.

burton ['bɜːtn] n: (*Brit*) **he's gone for a ~**‡ il a eu son compte*, il est fichu* *or* foutu‡; **it's gone for a ~*** (*broken etc*) c'est fichu* *or* foutu‡; (*lost*) ça a disparu.

Burundi [bə'rʊndɪ] n Burundi *m*.

bury ['berɪ] vt a (*gen*) enterrer; (*at funeral*) enterrer, ensevelir, inhumer. **to ~ sb alive** enterrer qn vivant; **he was buried at sea** son corps fut immergé (en haute mer); **buried by an avalanche** enseveli par une avalanche; *see* **dead**.
b *treasure* enterrer, enfouir; (*fig*) *quarrel* enterrer, oublier. **the dog buried a bone** le chien a enterré un os; (*fig*) **to ~ one's head in the sand** pratiquer la politique de l'autruche; (*fig*) **to ~ the hatchet** *or* (*US*) **the tomahawk** enterrer la hache de guerre.
c (*conceal*) enfouir, cacher. **to ~ o.s. under the blankets** s'enfouir sous les couvertures; **to ~ one's face in one's hands** se couvrir *or* se cacher la figure de ses mains; **the bullet was buried deep in the woodwork** la balle était fichée profondément dans le bois; **a village buried in the country** un village enfoui *or* caché *or* perdu en pleine campagne; **she buried herself in the country** elle est allée s'enterrer à la campagne.
d (*engross: gen ptp*) plonger. **to ~ one's head** *or* **o.s. in a book** se plonger dans un livre; **to ~ o.s. in one's studies** se plonger dans ses études; **buried in one's work** plongé *or* absorbé dans son travail; **buried in thought** plongé dans une rêverie *or* dans ses pensées.
e (*plunge*) *hands, knife* enfoncer, plonger (*in* dans).

▶**bury away** vt sep: **to be buried away** être enterré (*fig*).

bus [bʌs] 1 n, pl **~es**, (*US*) **~es** *or* **~ses** a bus *m*, autobus *m*; (*long-distance*) autocar *m*, car *m*. **all ~es stop here** arrêt *m* fixe *or* obligatoire; *see* **double, miss**[1], **trolley** *etc*.
b (‡) (*car*) bagnole* *f*; (*plane*) (vieux) coucou* *m*.
c (*Comput*) bus *m*.
2 vi a (*: *go by* ~) prendre l'autobus (*or* le car).
b (*US *: in café*) travailler comme aide-serveur, desservir.
3 vt (*esp US*) **to ~ children to school** transporter des enfants à l'école en car (*see* **bussing**).
4 comp ▶**busbar** (*Comput*) bus *m* ▶**busboy** (*US*) aide-serveur *m* ▶**bus conductor/conductress** receveur *m*, -euse *f* d'autobus ▶**bus depot** dépôt *m* d'autobus ▶**bus driver** conducteur *m* d'autobus ▶**bus lane** (*Brit*) voie réservée aux autobus ▶**busload: a busload of children** un autobus *or* un autocar plein d'enfants; **they came by the busload** *or* **in busloads** ils sont venus par cars entiers ▶**busman** (*driver*) conducteur *m* d'autobus; (*conductor*) receveur *m*; (*fig*) **to take a busman's holiday** passer ses vacances à travailler; **the busmen's strike** la grève des employés des autobus ▶**bus route: the house is/is not on a bus route** la maison est/n'est pas sur un trajet d'autobus ▶**bus service** réseau *m* *or* service *m* d'autobus ▶**bus shelter** abribus *m* ▶**bus station** gare *f* d'autobus; *[coaches]* gare routière *or* des cars ▶**bus stop** arrêt *m* d'autobus ▶**bus ticket** ticket *m* d'autobus.

busby ['bʌzbɪ] n (*Brit*) bonnet *m* à poil (*de soldat*).

bush[1] [bʊʃ] 1 n a (*shrub*) buisson *m*. (*fig*) **he had a great ~ of hair** il avait une épaisse tignasse; *see* **beat, burning, rose**[2] *etc*.
b (*thicket*) taillis *m*, fourré *m*; (*NonC: brushwood*) broussailles *fpl*. *[Africa, Australia]* **the ~** la brousse; **to take to the ~** partir *or* se réfugier dans la brousse; *[Corsica]* prendre le maquis.
2 comp ▶**bush baby** (*Zool*) galago *m* ▶**bushfighting** guérilla *f* ▶**bushfire** feu *m* de brousse ▶**bush jacket** saharienne *f* ▶**bush-league*** (*US Baseball*) de catégorie médiocre ▶**bush leaguer*** (*US*) (*Baseball*) joueur *m* de catégorie médiocre; (*fig*) minus *m* ▶**Bushman** *[South Africa]* Boschiman *m* ▶**bushman** *[Australia]* broussard* *m* ▶**bushranger** *[Australia]* forçat réfugié dans la brousse, broussard* *m*; *[Canada, US]* trappeur *m* ▶**bush telegraph** (*lit*) téléphone *m* de brousse; (* *fig*) téléphone arabe ▶**bushwhack** (*US*) vi se frayer un chemin à travers la brousse ◊ vt (*ambush*) tendre une embuscade à ▶**bushwhacker** (*frontiersman*) colon *m* de la brousse; (*guerilla soldier*) guérillero *m*; (*bandit*) bandit *m* de la brousse; *[Australia]* (*lumberjack*) bûcheron *m* ▶**bushwhacking** (*US*) = **bushfighting**.

bush[2] [bʊʃ] n (*Tech*) bague *f*.

bushed [bʊʃt] adj a (‡) (*puzzled*) ahuri; (*exhausted*) flapi*, claqué*. b (*Austral*) perdu en brousse.

bushel ['bʊʃl] n (*Brit: measure*) boisseau *m*; *see* **hide**[1].

bushing ['bʊʃɪŋ] n (*Tech: esp US*) bague *f*.

bushy ['bʊʃɪ] adj *land, ground* broussailleux, couvert de buissons; *shrub* épais (*f* -aisse); *tree* touffu; *beard, eyebrows, hair* touffu, broussailleux.

busily ['bɪzɪlɪ] adv (*actively, eagerly*) activement; (*pej: officiously*) avec trop de zèle. **to be ~ engaged in sth/in doing** être très occupé *or* activement occupé à qch/à faire.

business ['bɪznɪs] 1 n a (*NonC: commerce*) affaires *fpl*. **big ~** les grandes entreprises, les grandes firmes; **it's good for ~** ça fait marcher les affaires; **to be in ~** être dans les affaires; **to be in the grocery ~** être dans l'épicerie *or* l'alimentation; **to be in ~ for o.s.** travailler pour son propre compte, être à son compte; **to set up in ~ as a butcher** *etc* s'établir boucher *etc;* **to go out of ~** *[businessman]* fermer; *[company]* cesser ses activités, fermer; **to put out of ~** *company, businessman* faire fermer; **to do ~ with sb** faire des affaires avec qn, travailler avec qn, traiter avec qn (*frm*); **~ is looking up** les affaires reprennent; **~ is ~** les affaires sont les affaires; **to go to Paris on ~** aller à Paris pour affaires; **to be away on ~** être en déplacement pour affaires; **his ~ is cattle rearing** il a une affaire d'élevage de bestiaux; **his line of ~** sa partie; **what's his line of ~?*** qu'est-ce qu'il fait (dans la vie)?; **to know one's ~** connaître son affaire, s'y connaître; (*fig*) **to get down to ~** passer aux choses sérieuses; (*fig*) **now we're in ~!*** tout devient possible!; **he means ~*** il ne plaisante pas; **to mix ~ with pleasure** joindre l'utile à l'agréable.
b (*NonC: volume of trade*) **our ~ has doubled in the last year** notre chiffre d'affaires a doublé par rapport à l'année dernière, nous travaillons deux fois plus que l'année dernière; **most of the shop's ~ comes from women** la clientèle de la boutique est essentiellement féminine; **he gets a lot of ~ from the Americans** il travaille beaucoup avec les Américains; **during the 10 days of the fair ~ was excellent** pendant les 10 jours de la foire, le courant d'affaires fut excellent; **~ is good** les affaires marchent bien; **to lose ~** perdre des clients.
c (*commercial enterprise*) commerce *m*. **he has a little ~ in the country** il tient un petit commerce *or* il a une petite affaire à la campagne; **he owns a grocery ~** il a un commerce d'alimentation.
d (*task, duty*) affaire *f*, devoir *m*. **the ~ of the day** les affaires courantes; **it's all part of the day's ~** cela fait partie de la routine journalière; (*Admin etc*) **the ~ before the meeting** l'ordre *m* du jour de l'assemblée; **we're not in the ~ of misleading the public** notre propos *m* n'est pas de tromper le public; **to make it one's ~ to do sth** se charger de faire qch; **that's none of his ~** ce n'est pas son affaire, cela ne le regarde pas; **it's your ~ to do it** c'est à vous de le faire; **you've no ~ to do that** ce n'est pas à vous de faire cela; **that's my ~ and none of yours** c'est mon affaire et non la vôtre; **mind your own ~** mêlez-vous de vos affaires *or* de ce qui vous regarde; **I know my own ~** je ne veux pas me mêler de ce qui ne me regarde pas; **to go about one's ~** s'occuper de ses propres affaires; **to send sb about his ~** envoyer promener* qn.
e (*difficult job*) **finding a flat is quite a ~** c'est toute une affaire de trouver un appartement; **she made a (terrible) ~ of helping him** elle a fait toute une histoire* pour l'aider.
f (*pej*) affaire *f*, histoire *f*. **it's a bad ~** c'est une sale affaire *or* histoire; (*pej*) **I am tired of this protest ~** j'en ai assez de cette histoire de contestation; **there's some funny ~ going on** il se passe quelque chose de louche *or* de pas catholique*.
g (*) *[dog etc]* **to do its ~** faire ses besoins.
2 comp *lunch, meeting* d'affaires ▶**business accounting** comptabilité *f* d'entreprise ▶**business activity** activité industrielle et commerciale ▶**business address: his business address** l'adresse *f* de son travail *or* de son bureau ▶**business associate** collègue *mf*; **Jones & Co are business associates of ours** nous sommes en relations commerciales avec Jones & Cie ▶**business card** carte *f* de visite (professionnelle) ▶**business centre** centre *m* des affaires ▶**business college** école *f* de commerce ▶**business contact** relation *f* de travail ▶**business cycle** cycle *m* économique ▶**business day** jour *m* ouvrable ▶**business deal** affaire *f* ▶**business district** centre *m* commercial ▶**business end:** (*fig*) **the business end of a knife** le côté opérant *or* la partie coupante d'un couteau ▶**business expenses** frais généraux ▶**business girl** jeune femme *f* d'affaires ▶**business hours** heures *fpl* ouvrables ▶**business letter** lettre *f* commerciale ▶**businessman** homme *m* d'affaires; **big businessman** brasseur *m* d'affaires; **he's a good businessman** il a le sens des affaires ▶**business manager** (*Comm, Ind*) directeur commercial; (*Sport*) manager *m*; (*Theat*) directeur *m* ▶**business park** parc *m* d'activités ▶**business plan**plan *m* d'activité ▶**business proposition**proposition *f* ▶**business reply service** service-lecteurs *m* ▶**business school** = **business college** ▶**business sense: to have business sense** avoir du flair pour les affaires ▶**business studies** (*Univ etc*) études commerciales *or* de commerce ▶**business suit** complet *m* (veston) ▶**business trip** voyage *m* d'affaires ▶**businesswoman** femme *f* d'affaires.

businesslike ['bɪznɪslaɪk] adj *person* pratique, méthodique, efficace; *firm, transaction* sérieux, régulier; *manner* sérieux, carré; *method* pratique, efficace; *style* net, précis; *appearance* sérieux. **this is a very ~ knife!*** ça c'est un couteau (sérieux)!*

busing ['bʌsɪŋ] n = **bussing**.

busk [bʌsk] vi (*Brit*) jouer (*or* chanter) dans la rue.
busker ['bʌskəʳ] n (*Brit*) musicien ambulant *or* des rues.
bussing ['bʌsɪŋ] n ramassage *m* scolaire (*surtout aux U.S.A. comme mesure de déségrégation*).
bust¹ [bʌst] n a (*Sculp*) buste *m*. b (*Anat*) buste *m*, poitrine *f*. **~ measurement** tour *m* de poitrine.
bust² [bʌst] 1 adj a (*: *broken*) fichu*, foutu*.
b (*: *bankrupt*) **to go ~** faire faillite; **to be ~** être fauché*, être à sec*.
2 n a (*: *spree*) bombe* *f*, bringue* *f*. **to go on the ~, to have a ~** faire la bombe* *or* la bringue*.
b (*US* *: *failure*) fiasco *m*.
3 comp ▶**bust-up*** engueulade* *f*; **to have a bust-up with sb** s'engueuler avec qn* (*et rompre*).
4 vt a (*) = **burst 3. to ~ a gut*** (*lit*) attraper une hernie; (*fig*) se donner un mal de chien* (*to do* pour faire); (*US*) **to ~ one's ass*** s'éreinter*, se crever le cul* (*to do* pour faire).
b (*) (*of police: break up*) *crime ring etc* démanteler; (*arrest*) *person* choper*, arrêter; (*raid*) *place* perquisitionner; (*esp US*) (*demote*) *police officer* rétrograder.
c (*US* *) *horse* dresser.
5 vi (*) = **burst 2. New York or ~!** New York ou la mort!
▶**bust out*** vi (*escape*) **he bust out (of jail)** il s'est fait la malle (de la prison)*.
▶**bust up*** 1 vi *[friends]* se brouiller, rompre après une engueulade*. 2 vt sep (*fig*) *marriage, friendship* flanquer en l'air*. 3 **bust-up*** n *see* **bust² 3.**
bustard ['bʌstəd] n outarde *f*.
buster* ['bʌstəʳ] n: **hi, ~!** salut mon pote!*
bustier [buːstɪeɪ] n bustier *m*.
bustle¹ ['bʌsl] 1 vi s'affairer, se démener, s'agiter. **to ~ about** s'affairer; **to ~ in/out** *etc* entrer/sortir *etc* d'un air affairé; (*fig*) *[place, streets etc]* **to be bustling with** grouiller de; *see also* **bustling.** 2 n affairement *m*, remue-ménage *m*.
bustle² ['bʌsl] n (*Dress*) tournure *f*.
bustling ['bʌslɪŋ] 1 adj *person* actif, empressé, affairé; *place* bruyant, agité. **~ with life** plein de vie, plein d'animation, trépidant. 2 n = **bustle¹ 2.**
busty* ['bʌstɪ] adj *woman* à la poitrine plantureuse. **she's rather ~** il y a du monde au balcon*, elle a une poitrine de nourrice*.
busy ['bɪzɪ] 1 adj a *person* (*occupied*) occupé (*doing* à faire, *with sth* à qch); (*active*) énergique. **she's ~ cooking** elle est en train de faire la cuisine; **he's ~ playing with the children** il est occupé à jouer avec les enfants; **too ~ to do sth** trop occupé pour faire qch; **he was ~ at his work** il était tout entier à *or* absorbé dans son travail; **she's always ~** (*active*) elle n'arrête pas; (*not free*) elle est toujours prise *or* occupée; **as ~ as a bee** très occupé; **she's a real ~ bee*** elle est toujours à s'activer, elle est débordante d'activité; **to keep o.s. ~** trouver à s'occuper; **to get ~** s'y mettre.
b *day* chargé; *period* de grande activité; *place* plein de mouvement *or* d'animation; *street* passant, animé; *town* animé, grouillant d'activité. **a ~ time** une période de grande activité; **to keep a factory ~** fournir du travail à une usine; **the shop is at its busiest in summer** c'est en été qu'il y a le plus d'affluence dans le magasin.
c (*esp US*) *telephone line, room etc* occupé. (*US*) **~ signal** tonalité *f* occupé *inv*.
2 vt: **to ~ o.s.** s'appliquer, s'occuper (*doing* à faire, *with sth* à qch).
3 n (*: *detective*) flic* *m*.
4 comp ▶**busybody**: **to be a busybody** faire la mouche du coche ▶**busy Lizzie** impatiente *f*, impatiens *f*.
but [bʌt] 1 conj a (*coordinating*) mais. **I should like to do it ~ I have no money** j'aimerais le faire, mais je n'ai pas d'argent; **she was poor ~ she was honest** elle était pauvre, mais honnête.
b (*contradicting*) mais. **he's not English ~ Irish** il n'est pas anglais, mais irlandais; **he wasn't singing, ~ he was shouting** il ne chantait pas, plutôt il criait.
c (*subordinating*) **I never eat asparagus ~ I remember that evening** je ne mange jamais d'asperges sans me souvenir de cette soirée; **never a week passes ~ she is ill** il ne se passe jamais une semaine qu'elle ne soit malade; (*fig*) **it never rains ~ it pours** un malheur n'arrive jamais seul.
2 adv seulement, ne ... que. (*liter*) **she's ~ a child** ce n'est qu'une enfant; **I cannot (help) ~ think** je suis bien obligé de penser, je ne peux m'empêcher de penser; **you can ~ try** (*to sb trying sth*) vous pouvez toujours essayer; (*after sth has gone wrong*) ça valait quand même la peine d'essayer; (*liter*) **if I could ~ tell you why** si je pouvais seulement vous dire pourquoi; (*liter*) **she left ~ a few minutes ago** il n'y a que quelques minutes qu'elle est partie.
3 prep sauf, excepté; sinon. **no one ~ me could do it** personne sauf moi ne pourrait le faire, je suis le seul à pouvoir *or* qui puisse le faire; **they've all gone ~ me** ils sont tous partis sauf *or* excepté moi; **who could do it ~ me?** qui pourrait le faire sinon moi?; **no one ~ him** personne d'autre que lui; **anything ~ that** tout mais pas ça; **there was nothing for it ~ to jump** il n'y avait plus qu'à sauter; **the last house ~ one** l'avant-dernière maison; **the next house ~ one** la seconde maison à partir d'ici; **~ for you/~ for that I would be dead** sans vous/sans cela je serais mort.
4 n: **no ~s about it!** il n'y a pas de mais (qui tienne)!; *see* **if.**
butane ['bjuːteɪn] n butane *m*; (*US: for camping*) butagaz *m* ®. **~ gas** gaz *m* butane, butagaz *m*.
butch* [bʊtʃ] 1 adj (*gen*) hommasse; (*homosexual*) de gouine* (*hommasse*). 2 n gouine* *f* (*hommasse*).
butcher ['bʊtʃəʳ] 1 n a (*for meat*) boucher *m*. **at the ~'s** chez le boucher; **~'s boy** garçon *m* boucher, livreur *m* (*du boucher*); **~ meat** viande *f* de boucherie; **~'s shop** boucherie *f* (*magasin*); **~'s wife** bouchère *f*; (*Brit*) **to have a ~'s (hook)*** regarder, zieuter*; *see* **pork** *etc*. b (*US: candy etc seller*) vendeur ambulant. 2 vt *animal* tuer, abattre; *person* égorger, massacrer; (*fig*) massacrer.
butchery ['bʊtʃərɪ] n a (*NonC*) (*lit*) abattage *m*; (*fig*) boucherie *f*, massacre *m*, carnage *m*. b (*slaughterhouse*) abattoir *m*.
butler ['bʌtləʳ] n maître *m* d'hôtel, majordome *m*. **~'s pantry** office *f*; **~'s tray** (petit) plateau *m* (*de service*).
butt¹ [bʌt] n *[wine, rainwater etc]* (gros) tonneau *m*.
butt² [bʌt] n (*end*) (gros) bout *m*; *[rifle]* crosse *f*; *[cigarette]* mégot *m*; (*US* *: *cigarette*) clope* *f*; (*US* *: *bottom*) cul** *m*, arrière-train* *m*.
butt³ [bʌt] n (*target*) cible *f*; (*earth mound*) butte *f* (de tir). **the ~s** le champ de tir, le polygone (de tir); (*fig*) **to be a ~ for ridicule** être un objet de risée, être en butte au ridicule; **the ~ of a practical joker** la victime d'un farceur.
butt⁴ [bʌt] 1 n coup *m* de tête; *[goat etc]* coup de corne. 2 vt a *[goat]* donner un coup de corne à; *[person]* donner un coup de tête à. b (*Tech*) abouter.
▶**butt in** vi (*fig*) s'immiscer dans les affaires des autres, intervenir; (*speaking*) dire son mot, mettre son grain de sel*. **I don't want to butt in** je ne veux pas m'immiscer dans la conversation *or* déranger.
▶**butt into** vt fus *meeting, conversation* intervenir dans, s'immiscer dans.
▶**butt out*** vi (*US*) **to butt out of sth** ne pas se mêler de qch; **butt out!** mêle-toi de ce qui te regarde!*
butter ['bʌtəʳ] 1 n beurre *m*. **he looks as if ~ wouldn't melt in his mouth** on lui donnerait le bon Dieu sans confession; *see* **bread, peanut** *etc*.
2 comp ▶**butterball*** (*US*) patapouf* *m*, rondouillard(e) *m(f)* ▶**butter bean** (*Brit*) (gros) haricot blanc ▶**butter cloth** mousseline *f* à beurre, étamine *f* ▶**butter cooler** pot *m* à (rafraîchir le) beurre ▶**buttercup** (*Bot*) bouton *m* d'or, renoncule *f* des champs ▶**butter dish** beurrier *m* ▶**butter-fingered**: **he is butter-fingered, he's a butterfingers** tout lui glisse des mains *or* des doigts ▶**butterfingers** maladroit(e) *m(f)*, empoté(e)* *m(f)*; (*excl*) **butterfingers!** espèce d'empoté!* (*see also* **butter-fingered**) ▶**butterfly** *see* **butterfly** ▶**butter icing** glaçage *m* au beurre ▶**butter knife** couteau *m* à beurre ▶**buttermilk** babeurre *m* ▶**butter muslin** mousseline *f* à beurre, étamine *f*; (*dress material*) mousseline ▶**butter paper** papier *m* à beurre, papier sulfurisé ▶**butterscotch** caramel dur (au beurre).
3 vt *bread etc* beurrer; *vegetables* mettre du beurre sur. **~ed** *peas, potatoes* au beurre.
▶**butter up*** vt sep (*Brit fig*) passer de la pommade* à.
butterfly ['bʌtəflaɪ] 1 n (*Zool, also fig*) papillon *m*. **to have butterflies in the stomach*** avoir le trac*. 2 comp ▶**butterfly bush** buddleia *m* ▶**butterfly knot** nœud *m* papillon ▶**butterfly net** filet *m* à papillons ▶**butterfly nut** papillon *m*, écrou *m* à ailettes ▶**butterfly stroke** brasse *f* papillon *inv*.
buttery ['bʌtərɪ] 1 adj *taste* de beurre; (*spread with butter*) *bread, paper* beurré; *fingers* couvert de beurre. 2 n *[college, school]* dépense *f*, office *f*.
buttock ['bʌtək] n fesse *f*. **~s** *[person]* fesses; *[animal]* croupe *f*.
button ['bʌtn] 1 n a *[garment, door, bell, lamp, fencing foil]* bouton *m*. **chocolate ~s** pastilles *fpl* de chocolat; (*esp Brit*) *[hotel]* **B~s*** groom *m*, chasseur *m*; (*fig*) **on the ~*** absolument exact. b (*Bot*) bouton *m*. c (*US* *: *tip of chin*) pointe *f* de menton. 2 vt a (*also* **~ up**) *garment* boutonner. b **to ~ one's lip*** la fermer*; **~ your lip!** boucle-la!*, la ferme!*. 3 vi *[garment]* se boutonner. 4 comp ▶**button-down** (*lit*) *collar* boutonné; (*fig: square*) conformiste ▶**buttonhook** tire-bouton *m* ▶**button lift** (*Ski*) téléski *m* à perche ▶**button mushroom** (petit) champignon *m* de couche *or* de Paris ▶**button-through dress** robe *f* chemisier.
buttonhole ['bʌtnhəʊl] 1 n a *[garment]* boutonnière *f*. **~ stitch** point *m* de boutonnière. b (*Brit: flower*) fleur *f* (*portée à la boutonnière*). **to wear a ~** avoir *or* porter une fleur à sa boutonnière. 2 vt a (*fig*) *person* accrocher*. b (*Sewing*) faire du point de boutonnière sur.
buttress ['bʌtrɪs] 1 n (*Archit*) contrefort *m*, éperon *m*; (*flying ~*) arc-boutant *m*; (*fig*) pilier *m*, soutien *m*, appui *m*. 2 vt (*Archit*) arc-bouter, soutenir, étayer; (*fig*) *argument* étayer, soutenir.
butty ['bʌtɪ] n (*dial*) sandwich *m*.
buxom ['bʌksəm] adj bien en chair, aux formes généreuses.
buy [baɪ] pret, ptp **bought** 1 vt a (*purchase*) acheter (*sth from sb* qch à qn, *sth for sb* qch pour *or* à qn). **to ~ o.s. sth** s'acheter qch; **the**

things that money cannot ~ les choses qui ne s'achètent pas; **to ~ petrol** prendre de l'essence; **to ~ a train ticket** prendre un billet de chemin de fer; **to ~ a theatre ticket** louer *or* retenir *or* prendre une place de théâtre; **to ~ and sell goods** acheter et revendre des marchandises; **to ~ a pig in a poke*** acheter chat en poche; **to ~ sth cheap** acheter qch bon marché *or* pour une bouchée de pain; (*Comm*) **to ~ (one's way) into a company** prendre une participation dans une entreprise; (*fig*) **the victory was dearly bought** la victoire fut chèrement payée.

b (*bribe*) *person* acheter, corrompre. **to ~ one's way into a business** avoir recours à la corruption pour entrer dans une affaire.

c (*: *believe*) croire. **he won't ~ that explanation** il n'est pas question qu'il avale* (*subj*) cette explication; **they bought the whole story** ils ont avalé* *or* gobé* toute l'histoire; **all right, I'll ~ it** (bon,) d'accord *or* je marche*.

d (‡: *die*) **he's bought it** il y est resté*.

2 n affaire *f*. **that house is a good/bad ~** cette maison est une bonne/mauvaise affaire.

3 comp ▸**buy-back** *price, clause* de rachat; **buy-back option** option *f* *or* possibilité *f* de rachat ▸**buyout** rachat *m* (d'entreprise); **leveraged buyout** rachat *m* d'entreprise financé par l'endettement (*see also* **management**.)

▸**buy back** 1 vt sep racheter. 2 **buy-back** adj *see* **buy 3**.

▸**buy in** vt sep (*Brit*) *goods* s'approvisionner en, stocker; (*St Ex*) acquérir, acheter.

▸**buy off** vt sep (*bribe*) *person, group* acheter (le silence de).

▸**buy out** 1 vt sep (*Fin*) *business partner* désintéresser, racheter la part de. (*Mil*) **to buy o.s. out** se racheter (*d'un engagement dans l'armée*).

2 **buyout** n *see* **buy 3**.

▸**buy over** vt sep (*bribe*) corrompre, acheter.

▸**buy up** vt sep acheter tout ce qu'il y a de, rafler*.

buyer [ˈbaɪəʳ] n a (*gen*) acheteur *m*, -euse *f*, acquéreur *m*. **~'s market** marché acheteur *or* à la hausse; **house-/car-~s** les gens *mpl* qui achètent un logement/une voiture.

b (*for business, firm, shop etc*) acheteur *m*, -euse *f* (professionnel(le)).

buying [ˈbaɪɪŋ] n achat *m*. **~ group** centrale *f* d'achat; **~ power** pouvoir *m* d'achat.

buzz [bʌz] 1 n a *[insect]* bourdonnement *m*, vrombissement *m*.

b *[conversation]* bourdonnement *m*, brouhaha *m*. **~ of approval** murmure *m* d'approbation.

c (*: *telephone call*) coup *m* de fil*. **to give sb a ~** donner *or* passer un coup de fil* à qn.

d (*Rad, Telec etc: extraneous noise*) friture *f*.

e (*: *sensation*) **driving fast gives me a ~, I get a ~ from driving fast** je prends mon pied quand je conduis vite‡; *[drug]* **it gives you a ~, you get a ~ from it** tu t'éclates quand tu prends ça‡.

2 comp ▸**buzz bomb** V1 *m* ▸**buzz saw** scie *f* mécanique *or* circulaire ▸**buzz word*** mot *m* à la mode.

3 vi a *[insect]* bourdonner, vrombir.

b *[ears]* tinter, bourdonner. **my head is ~ing** j'ai des bourdonnements (dans la tête).

c *[hall, town]* être (tout) bourdonnant (*with* de).

4 vt a (*call by buzzer*) *person* appeler (par interphone); (*US* *: *telephone*) donner *or* passer un coup de fil* à.

b (*Aviat*) *building* raser; *plane* frôler.

▸**buzz about*, buzz around*** vi s'affairer, s'agiter, s'activer.

▸**buzz off‡** vi (*Brit*) filer*, décamper*, foutre le camp‡.

buzzard [ˈbʌzəd] n (*falcon*) buse *f*; (*vulture*) urubu *m*.

buzzer [ˈbʌzəʳ] n a (*intercom*) interphone *m*.

b (*factory hooter*) sirène *f*, sifflet *m*.

c (*electronic: on cooker, timer etc*) sonnerie *f*.

buzzing [ˈbʌzɪŋ] 1 n a = **buzz 1a, 1b**. b (*in ears*) tintement *m*, bourdonnement *m*. 2 adj *insect* bourdonnant, vrombissant; *sound* confus, sourd.

BVDs [ˌbiːviːˈdiːz] npl ® (*US*) sous-vêtements *mpl* (d'homme).

by [baɪ] (*phr vb elem*) 1 adv a (*near*) près. **close** *or* **hard ~** tout près; *see* **stand by** *etc*.

b (*past*) **to go** *or* **pass ~** passer; **time goes ~** le temps passe; **he'll be ~ any minute** il sera là dans un instant; **it'll be difficult but we'll get ~** cela sera difficile mais on y arrivera; *see* **come by** *etc*.

c (*in reserve*) **to put** *or* **lay ~** mettre de côté; **I had £10 ~ for a rainy day** j'avais mis 10 livres de côté pour les mauvais jours.

d (*phrases*) **~ and ~** bientôt, (un peu) plus tard (*see also* **3**); **~ and large** généralement parlant; **taking it ~ and large** à tout prendre.

2 prep a (*close to*) à côté de, près de. **sitting ~ the fire** assis près du feu; **sitting ~ it** assis à côté *or* tout près; **the house ~ the church** la maison à côté de l'église; **a holiday ~ the sea** des vacances au bord de la mer; **I've got it ~ me** je l'ai sous la main; **he is all ~ himself** il est (tout) seul; **he did it ~ himself** il l'a fait tout seul.

b (*direction: through, across, along*) par. **to come ~ the forest path** venir par le chemin de la forêt; **I went ~ Dover** j'y suis allé par Douvres; **he came in ~ the window** il est entré par la fenêtre; **to meet sb ~ the way** rencontrer qn en route; (*fig*) **~ the way, ~ the by(e)** à propos, au fait, soit dit en passant; (*Mil*) **"~ the right, march!"** "à droite, droite!"

c (*direction: past*) le long de, à côté de, devant. **I go ~ the church every day** je passe devant l'église tous les jours; **I go ~ it every day** je passe devant *or* à côté tous les jours; **he rushed ~ me without seeing me** dans sa précipitation il est passé à côté de moi sans me voir.

d (*time: during*) **~ day** le jour, de jour; **~ night** la nuit, de nuit.

e (*time: not later than*) avant, pas plus tard que. **can you do it ~ tomorrow?** pouvez-vous le faire avant demain?; **I'll be back ~ midnight** je rentrerai avant minuit *or* pas plus tard que minuit; **~ tomorrow I'll be in France** d'ici demain je serai en France; **~ 1990** d'ici à 1990; **~ the time I got there he had gone** lorsque je suis arrivé *or* le temps que j'arrive (*subj*) il était parti; **~ 30th September we had paid out £500** au 30 septembre nous avions payé 500 livres; **~ yesterday I had realized that** dès hier je m'étais rendu compte que; **he ought to be here ~ now** il devrait être déjà ici; **~ then I knew he wasn't coming** à ce moment-là je savais déjà qu'il ne viendrait pas.

f (*amount*) à. **to sell ~ the metre/the kilo** vendre au mètre/au kilo; **to pay ~ the hour** payer à l'heure; **to rent a house ~ the month** louer une maison au mois; **to count ~ tens** compter par dix *or* par dizaines; **~ degrees** par degrés, graduellement; **one ~ one** un à un; **little ~ little** petit à petit, peu à peu.

g (*agent, cause*) par, de. **he was killed ~ lightning** il a été tué par la foudre; **he was killed ~ it** ça l'a tué; **he was warned ~ his neighbour** il a été prévenu par son voisin; **a painting ~ Van Gogh** un tableau de Van Gogh; **surrounded ~ soldiers** entouré de soldats.

h (*method, means, manner*) par. **~ land and (~) sea** par terre et par mer; **~ bus/car** en autobus/voiture; **~ bicycle** à bicyclette; **~ rail, ~ train** par le train, en train; **~ moonlight** au clair de lune; **~ electric light** à la lumière électrique; **~ return of post** par retour du courrier; **to know ~ heart** savoir par cœur; **to know sb ~ name/~ sight** connaître qn de nom/de vue; **he goes ~ the name of** il est connu sous le nom de; **~ chance** par hasard; **~ mistake** par (suite d'une) erreur; **made ~ hand/~ machine** fait à la main/à la machine; **to lead ~ the hand** conduire par la main; **to pay ~ cheque** payer par chèque; **he had a daughter ~ his first wife** il a eu une fille de sa première femme; **~ means of** au moyen de, par; **~ leaving early he missed the rush** en partant de bonne heure il a évité la foule; **~ saving hard he managed to buy it** en économisant *or* à force d'économiser *or* à force d'économies il est arrivé à l'acheter; **~ nature** par nature; **~ birth** de naissance; **French ~ birth** français de naissance.

i (*according to*) d'après, suivant, selon. **~ what he says** d'après *or* selon ce qu'il dit; **if we can go ~ what he says** si nous pouvons tabler sur ce qu'il dit; **to judge ~ appearances** juger sur les *or* d'après les apparences; **~ right** de droit; **~ rights** en toute *or* bonne justice; **~ my watch it is 9 o'clock** il est 9 heures à ma montre *or* d'après ma montre; **~ the rule** selon les règles; **to do one's duty ~ sb** remplir son devoir envers qn; **~ your leave** avec votre permission (*see also* **3**); **~ the terms of Article 1** aux termes de l'article 1; **to call sth ~ its proper name** appeler qch de son vrai nom; **it's all right ~ me*** je veux bien, je n'ai rien contre*.

j (*measuring difference*) de. **broader ~ a metre** plus large d'un mètre; **to win ~ a head** gagner d'une tête; **it missed me ~ 10 centimetres** cela m'a manqué de 10 centimètres, c'est passé à 10 centimètres de moi; **he's too clever ~ half*** il est beaucoup trop malin; **better ~ far** (adv) beaucoup mieux; (adj) bien meilleur; **~ far the best/dearest** de loin le meilleur/le plus cher.

k (*Math, Measure*) **to divide ~** diviser par; **a room 3 metres ~ 4** une pièce de 3 mètres sur 4.

l (*points of compass*) **south ~ south west** sud quart sud-ouest; **south-west ~ south** sud-ouest quart sud.

m (*in oaths*) par. **I swear ~ all I hold sacred** je jure par tout ce que j'ai de plus sacré; (*Jur*) **"I swear ~ Almighty God"** ≃ "je le jure"; **~ God‡ I'll get you for this!** nom d'un chien‡ *or* nom de Dieu*‡ je te le ferai payer!; **he swears ~ this remedy*** il ne jure que par ce remède.

3 comp ▸**by-and-by***: (*hum*) **in the sweet by-and-by** un de ces jours ▸**by-election** élection (législative) partielle ▸**bygone** *see* **bygone** ▸**by-law** (*Brit*) arrêté *m* (municipal) ▸**by-line** (*Press*) signature *f* (*en tête d'un article*) ▸**bypass** *see* **bypass** ▸**by-play** (*Theat*) jeu *m* de scène secondaire ▸**by-product** (*Ind etc*) sous-produit *m*, dérivé *m*; (*fig*) conséquence *f* (secondaire) ▸**by-road** chemin détourné, chemin de traverse ▸**bystander** spectateur *m*, -trice *f* ▸**byway** chemin *m* (écarté); (*fig*) *[subject]* à-côté *m* (*see* **highway**) ▸**byword**: (*Brit*) **he** *or* **his name was a byword for meanness** son nom était devenu synonyme d'avarice ▸**by-your-leave: without so much as a by-your-leave** sans même demander la permission.

bye[1] [baɪ] 1 n: **by the ~** à propos, au fait, soit dit en passant. 2 comp ▸**bye-election** = **by-election** ▸**bye-law** = **by-law**.

bye[2]* [baɪ] excl (abbr of **goodbye**) au revoir!, salut!*, tchao!* **~ for now!** à tout à l'heure!

bye-bye* [ˈbaɪˈbaɪ] 1 excl au revoir!, salut!*, tchao!*

2 n (*baby talk*) **to go to ~s** aller au dodo*, aller faire dodo*.

Byelorussia [ˌbjeləʊ'rʌʃə] **n** Biélorussie *f*.
Byelorussian [ˌbjeləʊ'rʌʃən] 1 **adj** biélorusse.
2 **n** Biélorusse *mf*.
bygone ['baɪgɒn] 1 **adj** passé, d'autrefois. **in ~ days** dans l'ancien temps, jadis. 2 **n** (*loc*) **let ~s be ~s** oublions le passé, passons l'éponge (là-dessus).
bypass ['baɪpɑːs] 1 **n** a (*road*) route *f or* bretelle *f* de contournement *m*. **the Carlisle ~** la route qui contourne Carlisle.
b (*Tech: pipe etc*) conduit *m* de dérivation, by-pass *m inv*.
c (*Elec*) dérivation *f*, by-pass *m inv*.
d (*Med*) pontage *m*.
2 **vt** a *town, village* contourner, éviter.
b *source of supply, material* éviter d'utiliser, se passer de; *part of programme, method* omettre; *regulations* contourner. (*fig*) **he ~ed his foreman and went straight to see the manager** il est allé trouver le directeur sans passer par le contremaître.
3 **comp ►bypass operation** (*Med*) pontage *m* **►bypass surgery** (*NonC*) = **bypass operation**.
byre ['baɪəʳ] **n** (*Brit*) étable *f* (à vaches).
byte [baɪt] **n** (*Comput*) octet *m*, multiplet *m*.
Byzantine [baɪ'zæntaɪn] **adj** byzantin, de Byzance.
Byzantium [baɪ'zæntɪəm] **n** Byzance.

C

C, c [siː] 1 n a (*letter*) C, c *m*. **C for Charlie** C comme Célestin. b (*Mus*) do *m*, ut *m*; *see* **key, middle.** c (*Comput*) C *m*. d (*Scol: mark*) assez bien (≃ *12 sur 20*). 2 a (**abbr of Celsius, Centigrade**) C. b (*US etc*) **abbr of cent.** c **abbr of century.** d (**abbr of circa**) vers. e **abbr of centime.** f **abbr of cubic.**
CA (*US*) **abbr of California.**
C.A. [ˌsiːˈeɪ] n a (**abbr of chartered accountant**) *see* **chartered.** b (**abbr of Central America**) *see* **central.**
C/A (*Fin*) a (**abbr of capital account**) *see* **capital.** b (**abbr of current account**) *see* **current.** c (**abbr of credit account**) *see* **credit.**
C.A.A. [ˌsiːeɪˈeɪ] a (*Brit*) **abbr of Civil Aviation Authority.** b (*US*) **abbr of Civil Aeronautics Authority.**
C.A.B. [ˌsiːeɪˈbiː] (*Brit*) (**abbr of Citizens' Advice Bureau**) ≃ INC.
cab [kæb] 1 n a (*taxi*) taxi *m*; (*horse-drawn*) fiacre *m*. **by ~** en taxi, en fiacre. b (*Aut, Rail: driver's ~*) cabine *f*. 2 **comp** ▸ **cabdriver, cabman** = **cabby*** ▸ **cab rank, cab stand** station *f* de taxis.
cabal [kəˈbæl] n (*intrigue*) cabale *f*, intrigue *f*; (*group*) cabale, clique *f*.
cabana [kəˈbɑːnə] n (*US*) cabine *f* (de plage).
cabaret [ˈkæbəreɪ] n cabaret *m*; (*Brit: floor show*) spectacle *m* (de cabaret).
cabbage [ˈkæbɪdʒ] 1 n chou *m*. (*fig pej*) **she's just a ~*** elle végète. 2 **comp** ▸ **cabbage lettuce** laitue pommée ▸ **cabbage rose** rose *f* cent-feuilles ▸ **cabbage tree** palmiste *m* ▸ **cabbage white (butterfly)** piéride *f* du chou.
cab(b)ala [kəˈbɑːlə] n cabale *f* (*juive*).
cab(b)alistic [ˌkæbəˈlɪstɪk] adj cabalistique.
cabbie*, cabby* [ˈkæbɪ] n *[taxi]* chauffeur *m* (de taxi), taxi* *m*; *[horse-drawn cab]* cocher *m* (de fiacre).
caber [ˈkeɪbəʳ] n (*Sport*) tronc *m*. **to toss the ~** lancer le tronc; **tossing the ~** le lancement du tronc.
cabin [ˈkæbɪn] 1 n (*hut*) cabane *f*, hutte *f*; (*Naut*) cabine *f*; (*Rail: signal box*) cabine d'aiguillage; (*Aut, Rail: driver's ~*) cabine; *see* **log¹**. 2 **comp** ▸ **cabin boy** (*Naut*) mousse *m* ▸ **cabin class** deuxième classe *f* ▸ **cabin crew** (*Aviat*) équipage *m* ▸ **cabin cruiser** cruiser *m* ▸ **cabin trunk** malle-cabine *f*.
cabinet [ˈkæbɪnɪt] 1 n a (*furniture*) meuble *m* (de rangement); (*glass-fronted*) vitrine *f*; (*filing ~*) classeur *m*; *see* **medicine.** b (*Parl*) cabinet *m*, ≃ Conseil *m* des ministres. **to form a ~** former un gouvernement. 2 **comp** (*Parl*) *crisis, decision, post* ministériel ▸ **cabinetmaker** ébéniste *m* ▸ **cabinetmaking** ébénisterie *f* ▸ **Cabinet meeting** (*Parl*) réunion *f* du cabinet *or* du Conseil des ministres ▸ **Cabinet minister** ministre *m* siégeant au Cabinet; *see* **reshuffle.**
cable [ˈkeɪbl] 1 n (*Elec, Telec, gen*) câble *m*; (*Naut: measure*) encablure *f*. (*Telec*) **by ~** par câble; *see* **overhead.** 2 vt câbler, télégraphier (*sth to sb* qch à qn). 3 **comp** ▸ **cablecar** téléphérique *m*; (*on rail*) funiculaire *m* ▸ **cablecast** (*TV*) n émission *f* de télévision par câble ◊ vt transmettre par câble ▸ **cablegram** câblogramme *m* ▸ **cable-laying** pose *f* de câbles; **cable(-laying) ship** câblier *m* ▸ **cable railway** funiculaire *m* ▸ **cable release** (*Phot*) déclencheur *m* souple ▸ **cable stitch** (*Knitting*) point *m* de torsade ▸ **cable television, cablevision** télévision câblée *or* par câble ▸ **cableway** benne suspendue.
caboodle‡ [kəˈbuːdl] n: **the whole ~** tout le bataclan*, tout le fourbi*.
caboose [kəˈbuːs] n (*Brit Naut*) coquerie *f*; (*US Rail*) fourgon *m* de queue.
cabotage [ˌkæbəˈtɑːʒ] n *fait de réserver aux transporteurs d'un pays le trafic intérieur.*
ca'canny* [ˈkɔːˈkænɪ] excl (*Scot*) doucement!
cacao [kəˈkɑːəʊ] n (*bean*) cacao *m*; (*tree*) cacaoyer *m*.
cache [kæʃ] 1 n (*place*) cachette *f*. **a ~ of guns** des fusils cachés. 2 vt mettre dans une cachette.
cachepot [ˈkæʃˌpɒt, kæʃˈpəʊ] n cache-pot *m*.
cachet [ˈkæʃeɪ] n (*all senses*) cachet *m*.
cack-handed* [ˈkækˈhændɪd] adj (*Brit*) maladroit.
cackle [ˈkækl] 1 n *[hen]* caquet *m*; *[people]* (*laugh*) gloussement *m*; (*talking*) caquetage *m*, jacasserie *f*; *see* **cut.** 2 vi *[hens]* caqueter; *[people]* (*laugh*) glousser; (*talk*) caqueter, jacasser.
cacophonous [kæˈkɒfənəs] adj cacophonique, discordant.
cacophony [kæˈkɒfənɪ] n cacophonie *f*.
cactus [ˈkæktəs] n, pl **cacti** [ˈkæktaɪ] *or* **~es** cactus *m*.
CAD [kæd] (**abbr of computer-aided design**) CAO *f*.
cad*† [kæd] n (*Brit*) goujat *m*, malotru *m*, mufle *m*.
cadaver [kəˈdeɪvəʳ, kəˈdɑːvəʳ] n cadavre *m*.
cadaverous [kəˈdævərəs] adj (*lit, fig*) *complexion* cadavéreux; *appearance* cadavérique.
CADCAM [ˈkædˌkæm] (**abbr of computer-aided design and manufacture**) CFAO *f*.
caddie [ˈkædɪ] (*Golf*) 1 n caddie *m*, caddy *m*. 2 vi: **to ~ for sb** être le caddie de qn.
caddish*† [ˈkædɪʃ] adj *person* grossier, mufle. **a ~ thing to do** une muflerie.
caddy¹ [ˈkædɪ] n a (*also* **tea ~**) boîte *f* à thé. b (*US: shopping trolley*) chariot *m*, caddie *m*.
caddy² [ˈkædɪ] = **caddie.**
cadence [ˈkeɪdəns] n (*intonation*) modulation *f* (de la voix); (*rhythm*) cadence *f*, rythme *m*; (*Mus*) cadence.
cadenza [kəˈdenzə] n (*Mus*) cadence *f*.
cadet [kəˈdet] 1 n a (*Mil etc*) élève *m* officier (*d'une école militaire ou navale*); (*Brit Police*) élève *mf* agent de police; (*Scol*) *collégien qui poursuit une préparation militaire.* b (*younger son*) cadet *m*. 2 adj cadet. 3 **comp** ▸ **cadet corps** (*Brit*) (*in school*) peloton *m* de préparation militaire; (*Police*) corps *m* d'élèves policiers (*de moins de 18 ans*) ▸ **cadet school** école *f* militaire.
cadge [kædʒ] vt (*Brit*) **to ~ 10 francs from** *or* **off sb** taper* qn de 10 F; **to ~ a meal from** *or* **off sb** se faire inviter par qn, se faire payer* à manger par qn; **to ~ a lift from** *or* **off sb** se faire emmener en voiture par qn; **he's always cadging** il est toujours à quémander quelque chose *or* à mendier.
cadger [ˈkædʒəʳ] n (*Brit*) parasite *m*; *[money]* tapeur* *m*, -euse* *f*; *[meals]* pique-assiette *mf inv*.
Cadiz [kəˈdɪz] n Cadix.
cadmium [ˈkædmɪəm] n cadmium *m*.
cadre [ˈkædrɪ] n (*Mil, fig*) cadre *m*.
CAE [ˌsiːeɪˈiː] n (**abbr of computer-aided engineering**) IAO *f*.
caecum, (*US*) **cecum** [ˈsiːkəm] n, pl **caeca,** (*US*) **ceca** [ˈsiːkə] caecum *m*.
Caesar [ˈsiːzəʳ] n César *m*. **Julius ~** Jules César.
Caesarea [ˌsiːzəˈrɪə] n Caesarée.
Caesarean, Caesarian [siːˈzɛərɪən] adj césarien. (*Med*) **~ (operation** *or* **section)** césarienne *f*.
caesium, (*US*) **cesium** [ˈsiːzɪəm] n caesium *m*.
caesura [sɪˈzjʊərə] n, pl **~s** *or* **caesurae** [sɪˈzjʊəriː] césure *f*.
C.A.F. [ˌsiːeɪˈef] (**abbr of cost and freight**) *see* **cost 3.**
café [ˈkæfeɪ] n (*Brit*) snack(-bar) *m*.
cafeteria [ˌkæfɪˈtɪərɪə] n (*gen*) cafétéria *f*; (*US Scol*) cantine *f*; (*US Univ*) restaurant *m* universitaire.
caff‡ [kæf] n = **café.**
caffein(e) [ˈkæfiːn] n caféine *f*. **~-free** décaféiné.
caftan [ˈkæftæn] n caftan *m*.
cage [keɪdʒ] 1 n cage *f*; *[elevator]* cabine *f*; (*Min*) cage; (*fig*) prison *f* (*fig*). **~ bird** oiseau *m* de volière *or* d'appartement. 2 vt (*also* **~ up**) mettre en cage, encager. **~d bird** oiseau *m* en cage.
cagey* [ˈkeɪdʒɪ] adj réticent; (*suspicious*) méfiant. **she is ~ about her age** elle n'aime pas avouer son âge.
cagily* [ˈkeɪdʒəlɪ] adv prudemment.
cagoule [kəˈguːl] n anorak *m* (long).
cahoot(s)* [kəˈhuːt(s)] n: **to be in ~ (with)** être de mèche (avec)*.
CAI [ˌsiːeɪˈaɪ] n (**abbr of computer-aided instruction**) EAO *m*.

caiman ['keɪmən] n, pl ~s caïman *m*.

Cain [keɪn] n Caïn *m*. **to raise ~*** (*noise*) faire un boucan de tous les diables*; (*fuss*) faire tout un scandale (*about* à propos de).

cairn [kɛən] n a (*pile of stones*) cairn *m*. b ~ **(terrier)** cairn *m*.

cairngorm ['kɛəngɔːm] n a (*stone*) quartz fumé. b **C~ Mountains, C~s** monts *mpl* Cairngorm.

Cairo ['kaɪərəʊ] n Le Caire.

caisson ['keɪsən] n (*Mil, Naut*) caisson *m*.

cajole [kə'dʒəʊl] vt cajoler. **to ~ sb into doing sth** faire faire qch à qn à force de cajoleries.

cajolery [kə'dʒəʊlərɪ] n cajoleries *fpl*.

Cajun ['keɪdʒən] (*US*) 1 n Acadien(ne) *m(f)*. 2 adj acadien.

cake [keɪk] 1 n a (*large*) gâteau *m*; (*small*) pâtisserie *f*, gâteau; (*fruit ~ etc*) cake *m*; (*sponge ~ etc*) génoise *f*, gâteau de Savoie. (*fig*) **~s and ale** plaisirs *mpl*; **it's selling** *or* **going like hot ~s*** cela se vend comme des petits pains; **it's a piece of ~*** c'est du gâteau*, c'est de la tarte*; **he takes the ~*** à lui le pompon*; **that takes the ~!*** ça, c'est le bouquet!* *or* le comble!; **they want a slice of the ~, they want a fair(er) share of the ~** ils veulent leur part du gâteau (*fig*); (*fig*) **you can't have your ~ and eat it** on ne peut pas tout avoir, il faut choisir; *see* **Christmas, fish** *etc*.

b [*chocolate*] tablette *f*; [*wax, tobacco*] pain *m*. **~ of soap** savonnette *f*, (pain de) savon *m*.

2 comp ▸ **cake mix** préparation instantanée pour gâteaux ▸ **cake shop** pâtisserie *f* (*magasin*) ▸ **cake stand** assiette montée *or* à pied, (*tiered*) serviteur *m*; (*in shop*) présentoir *m* (à gâteaux) ▸ **cake tin** (*for storing*) boîte *f* à gâteaux; (*Brit*) (*for baking*) moule *m* à gâteaux ▸ **cakewalk** (*Mus*) cake-walk *m*.

3 vt: **~d** *blood* coagulé; *mud* séché; **his clothes were ~d with mud/blood** ses vêtements étaient raidis par la boue/le sang.

4 vi [*mud*] durcir, faire croûte; [*blood*] se coaguler.

CAL [ˌsiːeɪ'el] n (abbr of **computer-aided learning**) EAO *m*.

Cal. (*US*) abbr of **California**.

calabash ['kæləbæʃ] n (*fruit*) calebasse *f*, gourde *f*; (*tree*) calebassier *m*; (*Mus*) calebasse (*utilisée comme bongo ou maraca*).

calaboose* ['kæləbuːs] n (*US*) taule‡ *f*.

calabrese [ˌkælə'breɪzɪ] n brocoli *m*.

Calabria [kə'læbrɪə] n Calabre *f*.

Calabrian [kə'læbrɪən] adj calabrais.

calamine ['kæləmaɪn] n calamine *f*. **~ lotion** lotion calmante à la calamine.

calamitous [kə'læmɪtəs] adj *event, decision* catastrophique, désastreux; *person* infortuné.

calamity [kə'læmɪtɪ] n calamité *f*, désastre *m*.

calcareous [kæl'kɛərɪəs] adj calcaire. **~ clay** marne *f*.

calcification [ˌkælsɪfɪ'keɪʃən] n calcification *f*.

calcify ['kælsɪfaɪ] 1 vt calcifier. 2 vi se calcifier.

calcination [ˌkælsɪ'neɪʃən] n calcination *f*.

calcine ['kælsaɪn] 1 vt (*Ind*) calciner. 2 vi (*Ind*) se calciner.

calcium ['kælsɪəm] 1 n calcium *m*. 2 comp ▸ **calcium chloride/oxyde** *etc* chlorure *m*/oxyde *m etc* de calcium.

calculable ['kælkjʊləbl] adj calculable.

calculate ['kælkjʊleɪt] 1 vt a *speed, weight, distance, numbers etc* calculer (*also Math*); (*reckon, judge*) *probability, consequence, risk etc* évaluer; (*US: suppose*) supposer, estimer. **to ~ the cost of** calculer le prix de; **to ~ one's chances of escape** évaluer les chances qu'on a de s'évader; **he ~d that he would have enough money to do it** il a estimé *or* calculé qu'il aurait assez d'argent pour le faire.

b (*fig*) **it is ~d to do** (*intended*) c'est conçu *or* calculé pour faire; **this was not ~d to reassure me** (*didn't have the effect of*) cela n'était pas fait pour me rassurer.

2 vi (*Math*) calculer, faire des calculs. (*fig*) **to ~ for sth** prévoir qch; (*fig*) **to ~ (on) doing** avoir l'intention de faire.

▸**calculate (up)on** vt fus compter sur. **to calculate (up)on having good weather** compter sur le beau temps.

calculated ['kælkjʊleɪtɪd] adj *action, decision* délibéré, réfléchi; *insult* délibéré, prémédité; *gamble, risk* pris en toute connaissance de cause. **~ indiscretion** indiscrétion voulue *or* délibérée; *see* **calculate 1**.

calculating ['kælkjʊleɪtɪŋ] adj a (*scheming, unemotional*) calculateur (*f* -trice), intéressé; (*cautious*) prudent, prévoyant. b **~ machine** = **calculator a**.

calculation [ˌkælkjʊ'leɪʃən] n (*Math, fig*) calcul *m*. **to make a ~** faire *or* effectuer un calcul; **by my ~s** d'après mes calculs; **after much ~ they decided** après avoir fait beaucoup de calculs ils ont décidé; **it upset his ~s** cela a perturbé ses calculs.

calculator ['kælkjʊleɪtəʳ] n a (*machine*) machine *f* à calculer, calculatrice *f*; (*pocket*) calculatrice de poche, calculette *f*. b (*table of figures*) table *f*.

calculus ['kælkjʊləs] n, pl ~es (*Math, Med*) calcul *m*; *see* **differential, integral**.

Calcutta [kæl'kʌtə] n Calcutta.

caldron ['kɔːldrən] n = **cauldron**.

Caledonia [ˌkælɪ'dəʊnɪə] n Calédonie *f*.

Caledonian [ˌkælɪ'dəʊnɪən] 1 n (*liter*) Calédonien(ne) *m(f)*. 2 adj calédonien.

calendar ['kæləndəʳ] 1 n a calendrier *m*. b (*directory*) annuaire *m*. (*Brit*) **university ~** ≃ livret *m* de l'étudiant. c (*Jur*) rôle *m*. 2 comp ▸ **calendar month** mois *m* (de calendrier) ▸ **calendar year** année civile. 3 vt (*index*) classer (*par ordre de date*); (*record*) inscrire sur un calendrier.

calends ['kæləndz] npl calendes *fpl*. (*fig*) **at the Greek ~** aux calendes grecques.

calf[1] [kɑːf] 1 n, pl **calves** a (*young cow or bull*) veau *m*. **a cow in** *or* **with ~** une vache pleine; *see* **fat**. b (*also* **~skin**) (cuir *m* de) veau *m*, vachette *f*; (*for shoes, bags*) box(-calf) *m*. c [*elephant*] éléphanteau *m*; [*deer*] faon *m*; [*whale*] baleineau *m*; [*buffalo*] bufflетin *m*. 2 comp ▸ **calf love** (*fig*) amour *m* juvénile.

calf[2] [kɑːf] n, pl **calves** (*Anat*) mollet *m*.

caliber ['kælɪbəʳ] n (*US*) = **calibre**.

calibrate ['kælɪbreɪt] vt étalonner, calibrer.

calibration [ˌkælɪ'breɪʃən] n étalonnage *m*, calibrage *m*.

calibre, (*US*) **caliber** ['kælɪbəʳ] n (*lit, fig*) calibre *m*. **a man of his ~** un homme de son envergure *or* de son calibre.

calico ['kælɪkəʊ] n, pl ~es *or* ~s calicot *m*; (*US*) indienne *f*.

Calif. abbr of **California**.

California [ˌkælɪ'fɔːnɪə] n Californie *f*.

Californian [ˌkælɪ'fɔːnɪən] 1 n Californien(ne) *m(f)*. 2 adj californien.

californium [ˌkælɪ'fɔːnɪəm] n californium *m*.

calipers ['kælɪpəz] npl (*US*) = **callipers**.

caliph ['keɪlɪf] n calife *m*.

calisthenics [ˌkælɪs'θenɪks] n (*NonC*) gymnastique *f* suédoise.

calk[1] [kɔːk] 1 vt *shoe, horseshoe* munir de crampons. 2 n [*shoe, horseshoe*] crampon *m*.

calk[2] [kɔːk] vt *drawing, design* décalquer, calquer.

call [kɔːl] 1 n a (*shout*) appel *m*, cri *m*. **within ~** à portée de (la) voix; **a ~ for help** un appel au secours; *see* **roll**.

b [*bird*] cri *m*; [*bugle, trumpet*] sonnerie *f*; [*drum*] batterie *f*.

c (*also* **telephone ~**) coup *m* de téléphone, coup de fil*. **to make a ~** téléphoner, donner *or* passer un coup de fil*; **there's a ~ for you** on te demande au téléphone, il y a un coup de téléphone *or* un coup de fil* pour toi; [*operator*] **I have a ~ for you from London** on vous appelle de Londres, j'ai un appel pour vous de Londres; [*operator*] **I'm putting your ~ through** je vous mets en communication; **I want to pay for the 3 ~s I made** je voudrais régler mes 3 communications (téléphoniques); *see* **local, long**[1]**, trunk**.

d (*summons, invitation: gen, also Comput*) appel *m*; [*justice*] exigence *f*; [*conscience*] voix *f*; (*Theat*) (*actor's reminder*) appel; (*curtain call*) rappel *m*; (*vocation*) vocation *f*; (*Rel: in Presbyterian church*) nomination *f* (de pasteur). (*Rel*) **to have** *or* **receive a ~ to** être nommé pasteur à; **to give sb an early morning ~** réveiller qn de bonne heure; **I'd like a ~ at 7 a.m.** j'aimerais qu'on me réveille (*subj*) à 7 heures; (*Telec, Rad etc*) **they put out a ~ for him** on l'a fait appeler, on a lancé un appel à son intention; [*doctor etc*] **to be on ~** être de garde; **the ~ of the unknown** l'attrait *m* de l'inconnu; **the ~ of the sea** l'appel du large; **the ~ of duty** l'appel du devoir; (*euph*) **a ~ of nature** un besoin naturel; (*Fin*) **~ for capital** appel de fonds.

e (*short visit: also Med*) visite *f*. **to make** *or* **pay a ~ on sb** rendre visite à qn, aller voir qn; **I have several ~s to make** j'ai plusieurs visites à faire; (*Naut*) **place** *or* **port of ~** (port *m* d')escale *f*; *see also* **pay**.

f (*phrases*) (*Comm*) **there's not much ~ for these articles** ces articles ne sont pas très demandés; (*Fin*) **money repayable at** *or* **on ~/at 3 months' ~** argent remboursable sur demande/à 3 mois; **I have many ~s on my time** je suis très pris *or* très occupé; **to have first ~ on sb's time** avoir la priorité dans l'emploi du temps de qn; **I have many ~s on my purse** j'ai beaucoup de dépenses *or* de frais; **there is no ~ for you to worry** vous n'avez pas besoin de *or* il n'y a pas lieu de vous inquiéter; **there was** *or* **you had no ~ to say that** vous n'aviez aucune raison de dire cela, vous n'aviez pas à dire cela.

g (*Bridge*) annonce *f*; (*Solo Whist*) demande *f*. **whose ~ is it?** à qui de parler? *or* d'annoncer?

2 comp ▸ **callback** (*Comm*) [*defective product*] rappel *m* (*de marchandises défectueuses*) ▸ **callbox** (*Brit*) cabine *f* (téléphonique); (*US*) téléphone *m* de police-secours ▸ **callboy** (*Theat*) avertisseur *m*; [*hotel*] chasseur *m*, groom *m* ▸ **call girl** prostituée *f* (*qu'on appelle par téléphone*), call-girl *f* ▸ **call-in (program)** (*US Rad*) programme *m* à ligne ouverte ▸ **call letters** (*US Telec*) indicatif *m* (d'appel) ▸ **call loan** (*Fin*) prêt *m* exigible ▸ **call money** (*Fin*) taux *m* de l'argent au jour le jour ▸ **call number** (*US*) [*library book*] cote *f* ▸ **call option** (*St Ex*) option *f* d'achat ▸ **call-over** appel nominal; (*Mil*) appel ▸ **call sign, call signal** (*Telec*) indicatif *m* (d'appel) ▸ **call slip** (*in library*) fiche *f* de prêt ▸ **call-up** (*Mil*) (*military service*) appel *m* (sous les drapeaux), convocation *f*; [*reservists*] rappel *m*; (*in wartime*) **general call-up** mobilisation générale, levée *f* en masse; **call-up papers** feuille *f* de route.

3 vt a *person* appeler, (*from afar*) héler; *sb's name* appeler, crier. **to ~ sb in/out/up** *etc* crier à qn d'entrer/de sortir/de monter *etc*; **"hullo"**

he ~ed "ohé" cria-t-il; (*US fig*) **to ~ the shots*** mener la barque*; *see* **tune**.

b (*give name to*) appeler. **to be ~ed** s'appeler; **what are you ~ed?** comment vous appelez-vous?; **he is ~ed after his father** on lui a donné *or* il porte le nom de son père; **he ~s himself a colonel** il se prétend colonel; (*fig*) **to ~ a spade a spade** appeler un chat un chat, ne pas avoir peur des mots; **are you ~ing me a liar?** dites tout de suite que je suis un menteur; **he ~ed her a liar** il l'a traitée de menteuse; *see* **name, so**.

c (*consider*) trouver, considérer. **would you ~ French a difficult language?** diriez-vous que le français est difficile?; **I ~ that a shame** j'estime que c'est une honte; (*agreeing on price*) **shall we ~ it £1?** disons une livre?

d (*summon*) appeler, convoquer; (*waken*) réveiller. **to ~ a doctor** appeler *or* faire venir un médecin; **~ me at eight** réveillez-moi à huit heures; (*Rad*) **London ~ing** ici Londres; **the fire brigade was ~ed** on a appelé les pompiers; **~ me a taxi!** appelez-moi *or* faites venir un taxi!; **duty ~s (me)** le devoir m'appelle; **to ~ a meeting** convoquer une assemblée; (*Rel*) **to feel** *or* **be ~ed to (do) sth** se sentir *or* être appelé (par Dieu) à (faire) qch; (*Jur*) **his case was ~ed today** son affaire est venue aujourd'hui devant le tribunal; **to ~ sb as a witness** (*Jur*) citer qn comme témoin; (*fig*) prendre qn à témoin (*to* de).

e (*telephone*) appeler. **who's ~ing?** c'est de la part de qui?; **don't ~ us — we'll ~ you** (ce n'est pas la peine de nous appeler) on vous rappellera.

f (*Bridge*) **to ~ 3 spades** annoncer *or* demander 3 piques; **to ~ game** demander la sortie.

g (*US Sport*) *game* arrêter, suspendre.

h (*phrases*) **to ~ sb to account** demander des comptes à qn; (*Parl*) **to ~ a division** passer au vote; (*Mil*) **to ~ to arms** *[rebel leader]* appeler aux armes; *[government]* appeler sous les drapeaux; **to ~ (sb's) attention to sth** attirer l'attention (de qn) sur qch; (*Rel*) **to ~ the banns** publier les bans; (*Brit Jur*) **to be ~ed to the bar** être inscrit au barreau; **to ~ sth into being** faire naître qch, créer qch; **he ~ed my bluff** il a prouvé que je bluffais*, il m'a coincé*; **let's ~ his bluff** on va essayer de prouver qu'il bluffe*, on va le mettre au pied du mur; **let's ~ it a day!*** ça suffira pour aujourd'hui!; **we ~ed it a day* at 3 o'clock** à 3 heures on a décidé de s'en tenir là; **to ~ a halt to sth** mettre fin à qch; **I haven't a minute to ~ my own*** je n'ai pas une minute à moi; (*fig*) **to ~ sth into play** mettre qch en jeu; **to ~ sth into question** remettre qch en question; **to ~ the roll** faire l'appel; **to ~ a strike** lancer un ordre de grève; **to ~ a truce** conclure *or* établir une trêve; *see* **mind** *etc*.

4 **vi** a *[person]* appeler, crier; *[birds]* pousser un cri. **I have been ~ing for 5 minutes** cela fait 5 minutes que j'appelle; **to ~ (out) to sb** appeler qn, (*from afar*) héler qn.

b (*visit: also* **~ in**) passer. **she ~ed (in) to see her mother** elle est passée voir sa mère; **he was out when I ~ed (in)** il n'était pas là quand je suis passé chez lui; **will you ~ (in) at the grocer's?** voulez-vous passer *or* vous arrêter chez l'épicier?; (*Naut*) **to ~ (in) at a port/at Dover** faire escale dans un port/à Douvres.

►**call aside** **vt sep** *person* prendre à part, tirer à l'écart.

►**call away** **vt sep**: **to be called away on business** être obligé de s'absenter pour affaires; **to be called away from a meeting** devoir quitter une réunion (*pour affaires plus pressantes*).

►**call back** (*Telec*) 1 **vi** rappeler. 2 **vt sep** rappeler.

►**call down** **vt sep** a *curses* appeler (*on sb* sur la tête de qn). b (*US *: scold*) enguirlander*, attraper.

►**call for** **vt fus** a (*summon*) *person* appeler; *food, drink* demander, commander; (*fig*) *courage* demander, exiger, nécessiter. **to call for measures against** demander que des mesures soient prises contre; **the situation calls for a new approach** il est nécessaire d'envisager la situation d'une autre manière; **this contract calls for the development of ...** ce contrat prévoit le développement de ...; **strict measures are called for** des mesures strictes sont nécessaires, il est nécessaire de prendre des mesures strictes; **such rudeness was not called for** une telle grossièreté n'était pas justifiée.

b (*collect*) **I'll call for you at 6 o'clock** je passerai vous prendre à 6 heures; **he called for the books** il est passé chercher les livres.

►**call forth** **vt sep** (*liter*) *protest* soulever, provoquer; *remark* provoquer.

►**call in** 1 **vi** = **call 4b**. 2 **vt sep** a *doctor* faire venir, appeler; *police* appeler. **he was called in to arbitrate** on a fait appel à lui pour arbitrer. b *money, library books* faire rentrer; *banknotes* retirer de la circulation; *faulty machines etc* rappeler. **the bank called in his overdraft** la banque l'a obligé à combler son découvert *or* à approvisionner son compte.

►**call off** 1 **vi** se décommander. 2 **vt sep** a *appointment* annuler; *agreement* rompre, résilier; *match* (*cancel*) annuler; (*cut short*) interrompre. **to call off a deal** résilier *or* annuler un marché; **to call off a strike** annuler un ordre de grève. b *dog* rappeler.

►**call on** **vt fus** a (*visit*) *person* rendre visite à, aller *or* passer voir. (*Comm*) **our representative will call on you** notre représentant passera vous voir. b (*also*: **call upon**) **to call (up)on sb to do** (*invite*) inviter qn à faire, prier qn de faire, mettre qn en demeure de faire; **I now call (up)on Mr X to speak** je laisse maintenant la parole à M. X; **to call (up)on sb for sth** demander *or* réclamer qch à qn; **to call (up)on God** invoquer le nom de Dieu.

►**call out** 1 **vi** pousser un *or* des cri(s). **to call out for sth** demander qch à haute voix; **to call out to sb** héler qn, interpeller qn. 2 **vt sep** a *doctor* appeler; *troops, fire brigade, police* faire appel à. **to call workers out (on strike)** donner la consigne de grève. b (*for duel*) appeler sur le terrain.

►**call over** 1 **vt sep** a *list of names* faire l'appel de. b **he called me over to see the book** il m'a appelé pour que je vienne voir le livre. 2 **call-over** **n** *see* **call 2**.

►**call round** **vi**: **to call round to see sb** passer voir qn; **I'll call round in the morning** je passerai dans la matinée.

►**call up** 1 **vt sep** a (*Mil*) *reinforcements, troops* appeler, mobiliser; *reservists* rappeler. b (*esp US: Telec*) appeler (au téléphone), téléphoner à. c (*recall*) *memories* évoquer. d (*Comput*) **to call up a file** rappeler un texte à l'écran. 2 **call-up** **n, adj** *see* **call 2**.

Callanetics [ˌkælə'netɪks] **n** ® (*NonC*) *gymnastique douce (caractérisée par la répétition fréquente de légers exercices musculaires)*.

caller ['kɔːləʳ] **n** (*visitor*) visiteur *m*, -euse *f*; (*Brit Telec*) demandeur *m*, -euse *f*.

calligramme, (*US*) **calligram** ['kælɪgræm] **n** calligramme *m*.

calligraphic [ˌkælɪ'græfɪk] **adj** calligraphique.

calligraphy [kə'lɪgrəfɪ] **n** calligraphie *f*.

calling ['kɔːlɪŋ] 1 **n** a (*occupation*) métier *m*, état† *m*; (*vocation*) vocation *f*. **by ~** de son état. b (*NonC*) *[meeting etc]* convocation *f*. 2 **comp** ► **calling card** (*US*) carte *f* de visite.

calliope [kə'laɪəpɪ] **n** (*US*) orgue *m* à vapeur.

callipers ['kælɪpəz] **npl** (*Brit*) a (*Math*) compas *m*. b (*Med*) (*for limb*) gouttière *f*; (*for foot*) étrier *m*; (*leg-irons*) appareil *m* orthopédique.

callisthenics [ˌkælɪs'θenɪks] **n** (*NonC*) = **calisthenics**.

callosity [kæ'lɒsɪtɪ] **n** callosité *f*.

callous ['kæləs] **adj** a (*fig*) dur, sans cœur, sans pitié. **~ to** insensible à. b (*Med*) calleux.

callously ['kæləslɪ] **adv** *act* sans pitié, durement; *speak* avec dureté, durement; *decide, suggest* cyniquement.

callousness ['kæləsnɪs] **n** (*see* **callous**) dureté *f*, manque *m* de cœur *or* de pitié, insensibilité *f*.

callow ['kæləʊ] **adj** inexpérimenté, novice. **a ~ youth** un blanc-bec*; **~ youth** la folle jeunesse.

callus ['kæləs] **n, pl ~es** cal *m*, durillon *m*.

calm [kɑːm] 1 **adj** *day* calme, paisible, tranquille; *person, sea* calme; *attitude, behaviour* calme, tranquille. **the sea was dead ~** la mer était d'huile *or* était plate; **the weather is ~** le temps est au calme; **keep ~!** du calme!, calmez-vous!; **to grow ~** se calmer; (*fig*) **~ and collected** maître (*f* maîtresse) de soi. 2 **n** a (**~ period**) période *f* de calme *or* de tranquillité; (*after movement, agitation*) accalmie *f*. (*Naut*) **a dead ~** un calme plat; (*lit, fig*) **the ~ before the storm** le calme qui précède la tempête. b (*calmness*) calme *m*; (*under stress*) calme, sang-froid *m*. **I admire his ~** j'admire le calme *or* le sang-froid dont il fait preuve. 3 **vt** calmer, apaiser.

►**calm down** 1 **vi** se calmer, s'apaiser. **calm down!** du calme!, ne t'énerve pas! 2 **vt sep** *person* calmer, apaiser.

calming ['kɑːmɪŋ] **adj** calmant, apaisant.

calmly ['kɑːmlɪ] **adv** *speak, act* calmement, avec calme. **she ~ told me that she wouldn't help me** elle m'a dit sans sourciller qu'elle ne m'aiderait pas.

calmness ['kɑːmnɪs] **n** *[person]* calme *m*; (*under stress*) sang-froid *m*; *[sea, elements]* calme.

Calor ['kæləʳ] **n** ® (*Brit*) **~ gas** butane *m*, Butagaz *m* ®.

caloric ['kælərɪk] 1 **adj** thermique. **~ energy** énergie *f* thermique. 2 **n** chaleur *f*.

calorie ['kælərɪ] **n** calorie *f*. **she's too ~-conscious*** elle a trop la hantise des calories *or* de sa ligne; **~-controlled diet** régime *m* à faible teneur en calories; *see* **low¹**.

calorific [ˌkælə'rɪfɪk] **adj** calorifique. **~ value** valeur *f* énergétique.

calque [kælk] **n** (*also Ling*) calque *m* (*on* de).

calumniate [kə'lʌmnɪeɪt] **vt** calomnier.

calumny ['kæləmnɪ] **n** calomnie *f*; (*Jur*) diffamation *f*.

calvary ['kælvərɪ] **n** (*monument*) calvaire *m*. **C~** le Calvaire.

calve [kɑːv] **vi** vêler, mettre bas.

Calvinism ['kælvɪnɪzəm] **n** calvinisme *m*.

Calvinist ['kælvɪnɪst] **adj, n** calviniste (*mf*).

Calvinistic [ˌkælvɪ'nɪstɪk] **adj** calviniste.

calypso [kə'lɪpsəʊ] **n** calypso *m*.

calyx ['keɪlɪks] **n, pl ~es** *or* **calyces** ['keɪlɪsiːz] (*Bot*) calice *m*.

calzone [kæl'tsəʊnɪ] **n** calzone *f or* pizza *f* soufflée.

CAM [kæm] (**abbr of computer-aided manufacture**) FAO *f*.

cam [kæm] **n** came *f*. (*Aut*) **~shaft** arbre *m* à cames.

camaraderie [ˌkæmə'rɑːdərɪ] **n** camaraderie *f*.

camber ['kæmbəʳ] 1 **n** *[road]* bombement *m*; (*Archit*) cambre *f*, cambrure *f*, courbure *f*; (*Aviat*) courbure; (*Naut*) *[deck]* tonture *f*. 2 **vt** *road* bomber; *beam* cambrer; (*Naut*) *deck* donner une tonture à. 3 **vi** *[beam]* être cambré; *[road]* bomber, être bombé.

Cambodia [kæm'bəʊdɪə] n Cambodge *m.*

Cambodian [kæm'bəʊdɪən] 1 adj cambodgien. 2 n a Cambodgien(ne) *m(f).* b (*Ling*) cambodgien *m.*

Cambrian ['kæmbrɪən] adj (*Geol*) *period* cambrien. ~ **Mountains** monts *mpl* Cambriens.

cambric ['keɪmbrɪk] n, (*US*) **chambray** n batiste *f.*

Cambs. abbr of **Cambridgeshire.**

camcorder ['kæm,kɔːdəʳ] n caméscope *m.*

came [keɪm] pret of **come.**

camel ['kæməl] 1 n (*gen*) chameau *m*; (*she-*~) chamelle *f*; (*dromedary*) dromadaire *m*; (*racing* ~) méhari *m*; see **straw.** 2 comp (*colour*) *coat* (de couleur) fauve *inv* ►**the Camel Corps** (*Mil*) les méharistes *mpl* ►**camel hair, camel's hair** n poil *m* de chameau ◊ adj *brush, coat* en poil de chameau ►**camel train** caravane *f* de chameaux.

camellia [kə'miːlɪə] n camélia *m.*

cameo ['kæmɪəʊ] n a camée *m.* b (*Cine*) ~ **(part** *or* **appearance)** brève apparition (d'une grande vedette).

camera ['kæmərə] 1 n a appareil *m* (photographique), appareil-photo *m*; (*movie* ~) caméra *f*; **on** ~ filmé, enregistré; see **aerial, colour, film, capture 1.** b (*Jur*) **in** ~ à huis clos, en privé. 2 comp ►**cameraman** (pl **-men**) (*Cine, TV*) cameraman *m*, cadreur *m*; (*on credits*) "prise *f* de vue(s)" ►**camera obscura** chambre noire (*appareil*) ►**camera-ready copy** (*Typ*) copie *f* prête à la reproduction ►**camera-shy** qui déteste être pris en photo ►**camerawork** (*Cine*) prise *f* de vue(s).

Cameroon [,kæmə'ruːn] n: **(République of)** ~ (République *f* du) Cameroun *m.*

Cameroonian [,kæmə'ruːnɪən] 1 n Camerounais(e) *m(f).* 2 adj camerounais.

camiknickers ['kæmɪ,nɪkəz] npl chemise-culotte *f*; (*modern*) teddy *m.*

camisole ['kæmɪsəʊl] n camisole *f.*

camomile ['kæməʊmaɪl] n camomille *f.* ~ **shampoo** *etc* shampoing *etc* à la camomille; ~ **tea** (infusion *f* de) camomille.

camouflage ['kæməflɑːʒ] (*Mil, fig*) 1 n camouflage *m.* 2 vt camoufler.

camp¹ [kæmp] 1 n camp *m*, (*less permanent*) campement *m*; (*fig*) camp, parti *m.* **to be in** ~ camper; **to go to** ~ partir camper; (*fig*) **in the same** ~ du même bord; **to have a foot in both** ~**s** avoir un pied dans chaque camp; **to set up** ~ installer son camp; (*fig*) s'installer; see **break 3e, concentration, holiday, pitch¹** *etc.*

2 comp ►**campbed** (*Brit*) lit *m* de camp ►**camp counsellor** (*US Scol*) animateur *m*, -trice *f* (*de camp de vacances*) ►**campfire** feu *m* de camp ►**camp follower** (*fig*) sympathisant(e) *m(f)*; (*Mil* †: *prostitute*) prostituée *f*; (*Mil* †: *civilian worker*) civil *m* accompagnant une armée ►**camp(ing) chair** chaise pliante (de camping) ►**camping gas** ® (*Brit: gas*) butane *m*; (*US: stove*) camping-gaz *m inv* ►**camp(ing) ground, camp(ing) site** (*commercialized*) (terrain *m* de) camping *m*; (*clearing etc*) endroit *m* où camper, emplacement *m* de camping; (*with tent on it*) camp *m* ►**camp(ing) stool** pliant *m* ►**camp(ing) stove** réchaud *m* de camping ►**camping van** camping-car *m.*

3 vi camper. **to go** ~**ing** (aller) faire du camping.

►**camp out** vi camper, vivre sous la tente. (*fig*) **we'll have to camp out in the kitchen*** il va falloir que nous campions (*subj*) dans la cuisine.

camp²* [kæmp] 1 adj a (*affected*) *person, behaviour, talk etc* affecté, maniéré; (*over-dramatic*) *person* cabotin; *gestures etc* théâtral; (*affecting delight in bad taste*) qui aime le kitsch, qui fait parade de mauvais goût; (*fashionable because of poor taste*) kitsch *inv.* b (*effeminate*) efféminé; (*homosexual*) *man* (qui fait) pédé⁑ *or* tapette⁑; *manners, clothes* de pédé⁑, de tapette⁑. 2 n (*also* **high** ~) *[manners]* affectation *f*, cabotinage *m*; (*effeminate*) manières efféminées. 3 vt: **to** ~ **it up** cabotiner.

campaign [kæm'peɪn] 1 n (*Mil, fig*) campagne *f.* **to lead** *or* **conduct** *or* **run a** ~ **for/against** mener une campagne *or* faire campagne pour/contre; see **advertising, election, publicity.** 2 vi (*Mil*) faire campagne; (*fig*) mener une *or* faire campagne (*for* pour, *against* contre). 3 comp ►**campaign worker** (*Pol*) membre *m* de l'état-major (*d'un candidat*).

campaigner [kæm'peɪnəʳ] n (*Mil*) **old** ~ vétéran *m*; (*fig*) **a** ~ **for/against apartheid** un(e) militant(e) *m(f)* pour/contre l'apartheid; (*Pol*) **his qualities as a** ~ ses qualités en tant que candidat en campagne (électorale).

Campania [kæm'peɪnɪə] n Campanie *f.*

campanile [,kæmpə'niːlɪ] n campanile *m.*

camper ['kæmpəʳ] n (*person*) campeur *m*, -euse *f*; (*van*) camping-car *m*; (*US*) caravane pliante.

camphor ['kæmfəʳ] n camphre *m.*

camphorated ['kæmfəreɪtɪd] adj camphré. ~ **oil** huile camphrée.

camping ['kæmpɪŋ] 1 n camping *m* (*activité*). 2 comp see **camp¹ 2.**

campion ['kæmpɪən] n (*Bot*) lychnis *m.*

campus ['kæmpəs] 1 n, pl ~**es** (*Univ: gen*) campus *m*; (*building complex*) campus, complexe *m* universitaire (*terrain, unités d'enseignement, résidence*); (*fig*) monde *m* universitaire; see **off, on.** 2 comp ►**campus police** (*US Univ*) vigiles *mpl.*

campy⁑ ['kæmpɪ] adj = **camp² 1.**

CAMRA ['kæmrə] (*Brit*) (abbr of **Campaign for Real Ale**) *association qui cherche à améliorer la qualité de la bière.*

can¹ [kæn] 1 modal aux vb: neg **cannot**; cond and pret **could.** a (*indicating possibility; in neg improbability*) **the situation can change from day to day** la situation peut changer d'un jour à l'autre; **it could be true** cela pourrait être vrai, il se peut que cela soit vrai; **she could still decide to go** elle pourrait encore décider d'y aller; **you could be making a big mistake** tu fais peut-être *or* tu es peut-être en train de faire une grosse erreur; **can he have done it already?** est-il possible qu'il l'ait déjà fait?; **could he have done it without being seen?** est-ce qu'il aurait pu le faire *or* lui aurait-il été possible de le faire sans être vu?; **can** *or* **could you be hiding something from us?** est-il possible *or* se peut-il que vous nous cachiez (*subj*) quelque chose?; **he could have changed his mind without telling you** il aurait pu changer d'avis sans vous le dire; **(perhaps) he could have forgotten** il a peut-être oublié; **it could have been you who got hurt** cela aurait aussi bien pu être vous le blessé; **you can't be serious!** (ce n'est pas possible,) vous ne parlez pas sérieusement!; **he can't have known about it until you told him** (il est) impossible qu'il l'ait su avant que vous (ne) lui en ayez parlé; **she can't be very clever if she failed this exam** elle ne doit pas être très intelligente pour avoir été refusée; **things can't be as bad as you say they are** la situation n'est sûrement pas aussi mauvaise que tu le dis; **that cannot be!**† c'est impossible!; (*stressed, expressing astonishment*) **he CAN'T be dead!** ce n'est pas possible, il n'est pas mort!; **how CAN you say that?** comment pouvez-vous *or* osez-vous dire ça?; **where CAN he be?** où peut-il bien être?; **what CAN it be?** qu'est-ce que cela peut bien être?; **what COULD she have done with it?** qu'est-ce qu'elle a bien pu en faire?; (*phrases*) **as big/pretty** *etc* **as can** *or* **could be** aussi grand/joli *etc* que possible; **as soon as can** *or* **could be** aussitôt *or* dès que possible, le plus vite possible.

b (*am etc able to*) (je) peux *etc.* **he can lift the suitcase if he tries hard** il peut soulever la valise s'il fait l'effort nécessaire; **help me if you can** aidez-moi si vous (le) pouvez; **more cake? — no, I really couldn't** encore du gâteau? — non, je n'ai vraiment plus faim; **he will do what he can** il fera ce qu'il pourra, il fera son possible; **he will help you all he can** il vous aidera de son mieux; **can you come tomorrow?** pouvez-vous venir demain?; **he couldn't speak because he had a bad cold** il ne pouvait pas parler parce qu'il était très enrhumé; **I could have done that 20 years ago but can't now** il y a 20 ans j'aurais pu le faire mais (je ne peux) plus maintenant; **he could have helped us if he'd wanted to** il aurait pu nous aider s'il l'avait voulu; **he could have described it but he refused to do so** il aurait pu *or* su le décrire mais il a refusé (de le faire).

c (*know how to*) (je) sais *etc.* **he can read and write** il sait lire et écrire; **he can speak Italian** il parle italien, il sait parler (l')italien; **she could not swim** elle ne savait pas nager.

d (*with verbs of perception*) **I can see you** je vous vois; **they could hear him speak** ils l'entendaient parler; **can you smell it?** tu le sens?; **I could see them coming in** je les voyais entrer *or* qui entraient; **he could hear her shouting** il l'entendait crier.

e (*have the right to, have permission to*) (je) peux *etc.* **you can go** vous pouvez partir; **can I have some milk? — yes, you can** puis-je avoir du lait? — (mais oui,) bien sûr; **could I have a word with you? — yes, you could** est-ce que je pourrais vous parler un instant (s'il vous plaît)? — oui bien sûr *or* certainement *or* mais naturellement; **I could have left earlier but decided to stay** j'aurais pu partir plus tôt, mais j'ai décidé de rester; **I can't go out** je n'ai pas le droit de sortir; **I couldn't leave until the meeting ended** il m'était impossible de partir *or* je ne pouvais pas partir avant la fin de la réunion.

f (*indicating suggestion*) **you could try telephoning him** tu pourrais (toujours) lui téléphoner; (*indicating reproach*) **you could have been a little more polite** tu aurais pu être un peu plus poli; **you could have told me before** tu aurais pu me le dire avant *or* plus tôt.

g (*be occasionally capable of*) **she can be very unpleasant** elle peut *or* sait (parfois) être très désagréable; **it can be very cold here** il arrive qu'il fasse très froid ici.

h (*: **could** = *want to*) **I could smack him!** je le giflerais!, je pourrais le gifler!; **I could have smacked him** je l'aurais giflé; **I could have wept** j'en aurais pleuré.

2 comp ►**can-do*** (*US*) *person, organization* dynamique.

can² [kæn] 1 n a *[milk, oil, water, petrol]* bidon *m*; *[garbage]* boîte *f* à ordures, poubelle *f*; see **carry.**

b *[preserved food]* boîte *f* (de conserve). **a** ~ **of fruit** une boîte de fruits (en conserve); **a** ~ **of beer** une boîte de bière; **meat in** ~**s** de la viande en boîte *or* en conserve.

c (*Cine*) *[film]* boîte *f.* (*fig*) **it's in the** ~* c'est prêt.

d (*US* ⁑) (*lavatory*) waters *mpl*, chiottes*⁑ *fpl*; (*buttocks*) postérieur* *m.*

e (*US* ⁑: *jail*) taule⁑ *f*, prison *f.*

2 comp ►**can opener** ouvre-boîtes *m inv.*

3 vt a *food* mettre en boîte(s) *or* en conserve. ~**ned fruit/salmon** fruits *mpl*/saumon *m* en boîte *or* en conserve; ~**ned food,** ~**ned goods** conserves *fpl*; (*US*) ~**ned heat** méta *m* ®; (*fig*) ~**ned music*** musique *f*

en conserve* *or* enregistrée; (*Rad etc*) **~ned laughter** rires *mpl* préenregistrés; (*fig: drunk*) **to be ~ned⁑** être rétamé⁑ *or* rond⁑; (*US*) **~ it!⁑** ferme-la!⁑, la ferme!⁑ b (*US *: dismiss from job*) virer*, renvoyer.

Canaan ['keɪnən] **n** terre *f or* pays *m* de C(h)anaan.

Canaanite ['keɪnənaɪt] **n** C(h)ananéen(ne) *m(f)*.

Canada ['kænədə] **n** Canada *m*.

Canadian [kə'neɪdɪən] 1 **adj** (*gen*) canadien; *government, embassy etc* du Canada, canadien. (*Ling*) **~ English** anglo-canadien *m*, anglais *m* du Canada; **~ French** franco-canadien *m*, français *m* du Canada; **~ elk** orignal *m*. 2 **n** Canadien(ne) *m(f)*; *see* **French**.

canal [kə'næl] 1 **n** a canal *m*. b (*Anat*) conduit *m*, canal *m*; *see* **alimentary.** 2 **comp** ▸**canal barge, canal boat** chaland *m*, péniche *f* ▸**the Canal Zone** (*Geog*) (*Brit: Suez*) la zone du canal de Suez; (*US: Panama*) la zone du canal de Panama.

canalization [ˌkænəlaɪ'zeɪʃən] **n** canalisation *f*.

canalize ['kænəlaɪz] **vt** canaliser.

canapé ['kænəpeɪ] **n** (*Culin*) canapé *m*.

canard [kæ'nɑːd] **n** canard* *m*, bobard* *m*.

canary [kə'nɛərɪ] 1 **n** a (*bird*) canari *m*, serin *m*. b (*wine*) vin *m* des Canaries. 2 **comp** (*also* **canary yellow**) (de couleur) jaune serin *inv*, jaune canari *inv* ▸**canary grass** (*Bot*) alpiste *m* ▸**Canary Islands** *or* **Isles, Canaries** (*Geog*) (îles *fpl*) Canaries *fpl* ▸**canary seed** (*Bot*) millet *m*.

canasta [kə'næstə] **n** canasta *f*.

Canberra ['kænbərə] **n** Canberra.

cancan ['kænkæn] **n** (*also* **French ~**) cancan *m*.

cancel ['kænsəl] 1 **vt** a *reservation, room booked, travel tickets, plans* annuler; (*annul, revoke*) *agreement, contract* résilier, annuler; *order, arrangement, meeting, performance, debt* annuler; *cheque* faire opposition à; *taxi, coach or car ordered, appointment, party* décommander, annuler; *stamp* oblitérer; *mortgage* lever; *decree, will* révoquer; *application* retirer; *ticket* (*punch*) poinçonner; (*stamp*) oblitérer. b *flight, train etc* annuler; (*withdraw permanently*) supprimer. c (*Math*) *figures, amounts* éliminer. d (*cross out, delete*) barrer, rayer, biffer. 2 **vi** [*tourist etc*] se décommander.

▸**cancel out** **vt sep** (*Math*) *noughts* barrer; *amounts etc* annuler, éliminer; (*fig*) neutraliser. **they cancel each other out** (*Math*) ils s'annulent, ils s'éliminent; (*fig*) ils se neutralisent.

cancellation [ˌkænsə'leɪʃən] **n** (*see* **cancel**) annulation *f*; résiliation *f*; opposition *f*; oblitération *f*; levée *f*; révocation *f*; biffage *m*; suppression *f*; retrait *m*; (*Math*) élimination *f*. **~ fee** taxe *f* d'annulation; **~s will not be accepted after ...** (*travel, hotel*) les réservations ne peuvent être annulées après ...; (*Theat*) les locations ne peuvent être annulées après ...; **I have 2 ~s for tomorrow** j'ai 2 personnes qui se sont décommandées pour demain, j'ai 2 réservations qui ont été annulées pour demain.

cancer ['kænsəʳ] 1 **n** a (*Med*) cancer *m*. **she has ~** elle a un cancer; **lung** *etc* **~** cancer du poumon *etc*. b (*Astron, Geog*) **C~** le Cancer; **I'm (a) C~** je suis (du) Cancer; *see* **tropic.** 2 **comp** ▸**cancer-causing** cancérigène ▸**cancer patient** cancéreux *m*, -euse *f* ▸**cancer-producing** = **cancer-causing** ▸**cancer research** cancérologie *f*, (*in appeals, funds, charities*) la lutte contre le cancer ▸**cancer specialist** cancérologue *mf* ▸**cancer stick⁑** (*Brit pej*) cigarette *f*.

Cancerian [kæn'sɪərɪən] **n: to be a ~** être (du) Cancer.

cancerous ['kænsərəs] **adj** cancéreux.

candelabra [ˌkændɪ'lɑːbrə] **n, pl ~** *or* **~s** candélabre *m*.

candelabrum [ˌkændɪ'lɑːbrəm] **n, pl ~s** *or* **candelabra** = **candelabra.**

candid ['kændɪd] **adj** *person, smile, criticism* franc (*f* franche), sincère; *report, biography* qui ne cache rien. **he gave me his ~ opinion of it** il m'a dit franchement ce qu'il en pensait; **~ camera** (*Phot*) appareil *m* photo à instantanés; (*TV game*) la Caméra invisible; (*Phot*) **a ~ camera shot** un instantané.

candida ['kændɪdə] **n** (*Med*) candidose *f*.

candidacy ['kændɪdəsɪ] **n** (*esp US*) candidature *f*.

candidate ['kændɪdeɪt] **n** candidat(e) *m(f)*. **to stand as/be a ~** se porter/être candidat.

candidature ['kændɪdətʃəʳ] **n** (*Brit*) candidature *f*.

candidly ['kændɪdlɪ] **adv** franchement, sincèrement.

candidness ['kændɪdnɪs] **n** franchise *f*, sincérité *f*.

candied ['kændɪd] **adj** (*Culin*) *whole fruit* glacé, confit; *cherries, angelica etc* confit. **~ peel** écorce d'orange *or* de citron *etc* confite.

candle ['kændl] 1 **n** a (*wax: household, on cakes etc*) bougie *f*; (*tallow: tall, decorative*) chandelle *f*; [*church*] cierge *m*. **the game is not worth the ~** le jeu n'en vaut pas la chandelle; *see* **burn¹, hold, Roman.** b = **candle-power;** *see* **2.**
2 **comp** ▸**candle grease** (*from household candle*) suif *m*; (*from others*) cire *f* ▸**candlelight: by candlelight** à la lueur d'une bougie (*or* de chandelles *etc*) ▸**candlelight dinner** dîner *m* aux chandelles ▸**candlelit** *room, restaurant* éclairé à la bougie *or* aux chandelles ▸**candle pin** (*US*) quille *f* ▸**candle pins** (*US: game*) jeu *m* de quilles ▸**candle-power:** (*Elec*) **a 20 candle-power lamp** une (lampe de) 20 bougies ▸**candlestick** (*flat*) bougeoir *m*; (*tall*) chandelier *m* ▸**candlewick bedspread** dessus-de-lit *m* en chenille (de coton).

Candlemas ['kændlmæs] **n** la Chandeleur.

candour, (US) candor ['kændəʳ] **n** franchise *f*, sincérité *f*.

candy ['kændɪ] 1 **n** sucre candi; (*US*) bonbon(s) *m(pl)*. 2 **vt** *sugar* faire candir; *fruit* glacer, confire. 3 **vi** se candir, se cristalliser. 4 **comp** ▸**candy-floss** (*Brit*) barbe *f* à papa ▸**candy store** (*US*) confiserie *f* (*souvent avec papeterie, journaux et tabac*) ▸**candy-striped** à rayures multicolores ▸**candy striper** (*US*) *jeune fille s'occupant d'œuvres de bienfaisance dans un hôpital.*

cane [keɪn] 1 **n** a [*bamboo etc*] canne *f*; (*in basket- and furniture-making*) rotin *m*, jonc *m*; *see* **sugar.** b (*walking stick*) canne *f*; [*officer, rider*] badine *f*, jonc *m*; [*punishment*] trique *f*, bâton *m*; (*Scol*) verge *f*, baguette *f*. **the schoolboy got the ~** l'écolier a été fouetté *or* a reçu le fouet. 2 **vt** administrer *or* donner des coups de trique *or* de bâton à; (*Scol*) fouetter; (*fig **) administrer une bonne volée à. 3 **comp** canné ▸**cane chair/furniture** chaise *f*/meubles *mpl* en rotin ▸**cane sugar** sucre *m* de canne.

canine ['kænaɪn] **adj** canin. (*Anat*) **~ (tooth)** canine *f*; (*US Police*) **~ corps** corps *m* des maîtres-chiens.

caning ['keɪnɪŋ] **n: to get a ~** (*lit*) recevoir la trique; (*Scol*) recevoir le fouet, être fouetté; (*fig **) recevoir une bonne volée; **to give sb a ~** = **to cane sb;** *see* **cane.**

canister ['kænɪstəʳ] **n** boîte *f* (*gén en métal*). **a ~ of teargas** une bombe lacrymogène.

canker ['kæŋkəʳ] 1 **n** (*Med*) ulcère *m*, (*gen syphilitic*) chancre *m*; (*Bot, fig*) chancre. **~-worm** ver *m*.
2 **vt** (*Med*) ronger.

cankerous ['kæŋkərəs] **adj** *sore* rongeur; *tissue* chancreux.

cannabis ['kænəbɪs] **n** a (*plant*) chanvre indien. b (*resin*) cannabine *f*. c (*drug*) cannabis *m*.

cannel(l)oni [ˌkænɪ'ləʊnɪ] **n** (*NonC*) cannelloni *mpl*.

cannery ['kænərɪ] **n** (*US*) fabrique *f* de conserves, conserverie *f*.

cannibal ['kænɪbəl] **adj, n** cannibale *(mf)*, anthropophage *(mf)*.

cannibalism ['kænɪbəlɪzəm] **n** cannibalisme *m*, anthropophagie *f*.

cannibalization [ˌkænɪbəlaɪ'zeɪʃən] **n** [*machine, product*] cannibalisation *f*.

cannibalize ['kænɪbəlaɪz] **vt** (*Tech*) *machine, car* démonter pour en réutiliser les pièces. **~d parts** pièces récupérées.

canning ['kænɪŋ] **n** mise *f* en conserve *or* en boîte. **~ factory** fabrique *f* de conserves, conserverie *f*; **~ industry** industrie *f* de la conserve, conserverie.

cannon ['kænən] 1 **n** a (*Mil: pl* **~** *or* **~s**) canon *m*; *see* **water.** b (*Tech*) canon *m*. c (*Brit Billiards*) carambolage *m*. 2 **comp** ▸**cannonball** boulet *m* de canon ▸**cannonball serve** (*Tennis*) service *m* en boulet de canon ▸**cannon fodder** (*fig*) chair *f* à canon* ▸**cannon-shot: within cannon-shot** à portée de canon. 3 **vi** (*Brit Billiards*) caramboler. **to ~ off the red** caramboler la rouge; (*fig*) **to ~ into** *or* **against sth** percuter qch; (*fig*) **to ~ into** *or* **against sb** se heurter contre qn.

cannonade [ˌkænə'neɪd] **n** canonnade *f*.

cannot ['kænɒt] **neg of can¹.**

canny ['kænɪ] **adj** (*cautious*) prudent, circonspect; (*shrewd*) malin (*f* -igne), rusé, futé; (*careful with money*) regardant* (*pej*), économe. **~ answer** réponse *f* de Normand; *see* **ca'canny.**

canoe [kə'nuː] 1 **n** canoë *m*; (*African*) pirogue *f*; (*single-seated river* ~) canoë monoplace; (*Sport*) kayac *m*; *see* **paddle.** 2 **vi** (*see* **1**) faire du canoë; (*Sport*) faire du kayac; aller en pirogue.

canoeing [kə'nuːɪŋ] **n** (*Sport*) canoë-kayac *m*.

canoeist [kə'nuːɪst] **n** canoéiste *mf*.

canon ['kænən] **n** a (*Mus, Rel, Tech*) canon *m*; (*fig*) canon, critère *m*. (*Rel*) **~ of the mass** canon de la messe; (*Rel*) **~ law** droit *m* canon. b (*Rel: chapter member*) chanoine *m*.

cañon ['kænjən] **n** (*US*) = **canyon.**

canonical [kə'nɒnɪkəl] **adj** (*Rel*) canonique, conforme aux canons de l'église; (*Mus*) en canon; (*fig*) autorisé, qui fait autorité. (*Rel*) **~ dress, ~s** vêtements sacerdotaux.

canonization [ˌkænənaɪ'zeɪʃən] **n** (*Rel*) canonisation *f*.

canonize ['kænənaɪz] **vt** (*Rel, fig*) canoniser.

canoodle⁑ † [kə'nuːdl] **vi** se faire des mamours*.

canopied ['kænəpɪd] **adj** *bed* à baldaquin.

canopy ['kænəpɪ] **n** [*bed*] baldaquin *m*, ciel *m* de lit; [*throne etc*] dais *m*; [*tent etc*] marquise *f*; (*Archit*) baldaquin; (*Aviat*) [*parachute*] voilure *f*; [*cockpit*] verrière *f*; (*fig*) [*sky, heavens, foliage*] voûte *f*.

cant¹ [kænt] 1 **n** a (*insincere talk*) paroles *fpl* hypocrites; (*stock phrases*) phrases toutes faites, clichés *mpl*, expressions stéréotypées. b (*jargon*) jargon *m*, argot *m* de métier. **lawyers' ~** jargon juridique; *see* **thief.** 2 **vi** parler avec hypocrisie *or* affectation.

cant² [kænt] 1 **n** a (*slope, steepness*) pente *f*, déclivité *f*; (*sloping surface*) plan incliné, surface *f* oblique. **this wall has a definite ~** ce mur penche très nettement. b (*jolt*) secousse *f*, cahot *m*, à-coup *m*. 2 **vi** (*tilt*) pencher, s'incliner; (*Naut: change direction*) prendre une direction oblique. 3 **vt** (*tilt*) incliner, pencher; (*overturn*) renverser *or* retourner d'une saccade, retourner d'un coup sec.

can't [kɑːnt] (**abbr of cannot**) *see* **can¹.**

Cantab. (**abbr of Cantabrigiensis**) de Cambridge.

Cantabrian [kæn'teɪbrɪən] n, adj: **the ~s, the ~ Mountains** les (monts *mpl*) Cantabriques *mpl*.

cantaloup(e) ['kæntəluːp] n cantaloup *m*.

cantankerous [kæn'tæŋkərəs] adj (*ill-tempered*) acariâtre, revêche; (*aggressive*) hargneux; (*quarrelsome*) querelleur.

cantata [kæn'tɑːtə] n cantate *f*.

canteen [kæn'tiːn] n **a** (*restaurant*) cantine *f*. **b** (*Mil*) (*flask*) bidon *m*; (*mess tin*) gamelle *f*. **c a ~ of cutlery** une ménagère (*couverts de table*).

canter ['kæntəʳ] **1** n petit galop (*très rassemblé*). **to go for a ~** aller faire une promenade à cheval (*au petit galop*); (*Brit fig*) **to win in** *or* **at a ~*** gagner haut la main, arriver dans un fauteuil*. **2** vi aller au petit galop. **3** vt mener *or* faire aller au petit galop.

Canterbury ['kæntəbərɪ] n Cantorbéry. (*Bot*) **~ bell** campanule *f*; (*Literat*) **~ Tales** les Contes *mpl* de Cantorbéry.

cantharides [kæn'θærɪdiːz] npl cantharides *fpl*.

canticle ['kæntɪkl] n cantique *m*, hymne *m*. **the C~s** le cantique des cantiques.

cantilever ['kæntɪliːvəʳ] **1** n (*Tech*) cantilever *m*; (*Archit*) corbeau *m*, console *f*.
2 comp ▸ **cantilever beam** poutre *f* en console ▸ **cantilever bridge** pont *m* cantilever *inv*.

canting ['kæntɪŋ] adj (*whining*) pleurnicheur, pleurard; (*hypocritical*) hypocrite, tartufe.

cantle ['kæntl] n troussequin *m*.

canto ['kæntəʊ] n chant *m* (*d'un poème*).

canton ['kæntɒn] **1** n (*Admin*) canton *m*. **2** vt **a** *land* diviser en cantons. **b** (*Mil*) *soldiers* cantonner.

cantonal ['kæntənl] adj cantonal.

Cantonese [ˌkæntə'niːz] **1** adj cantonais. **2** n **a** (pl inv) Cantonais(e) *m(f)*. **b** (*Ling*) cantonais *m*.

cantonment [kən'tuːnmənt] n cantonnement *m*.

cantor ['kæntɔːʳ] n (*Rel*) chantre *m*.

Cantuar. (*Brit Rel*) (abbr of **Cantuariensis**) de Cantorbéry.

Canuck* [kə'nʊk] n (*sometimes pej*) Canadien(ne) français(e) *m(f)*.

Canute [kə'njuːt] n Canut *m*.

canvas¹ ['kænvəs] **1** n **a** (*NonC*) (*Art, Naut, also of tent*) toile *f*; (*Tapestry*) canevas *m*. **under ~** (*in a tent*) sous la tente; (*Naut*) sous voiles. **b** (*painting*) toile *f*, tableau *m*. **2** comp en *or* de toile ▸ **canvas chair** chaise pliante (*de toile*) ▸ **canvas shoes** (*rope-soled*) espadrilles *fpl*; (*gen*) chaussures *fpl* de toile.

canvas² ['kænvəs] = **canvass**.

canvass ['kænvəs] **1** vt **a** (*Pol*) *district* faire du démarchage électoral dans; *person* solliciter la voix *or* le suffrage de; (*US: scrutinize votes*) pointer.
b (*Comm*) *customers* solliciter des commandes de; *district* prospecter.
c (*seek support of*) *influential person* solliciter le soutien de. **candidates must not ~ committee members** les candidats doivent s'abstenir de toute démarche personnelle auprès des membres du comité.
d (*seek opinion of*) *person* sonder (*on* à propos de). **to ~ opinions on sth** sonder l'opinion à propos de qch.
e (*discuss*) *matter, question* débattre, examiner à fond.
2 vi **a** (*Pol*) *[candidate]* solliciter des suffrages *or* des voix. **to ~ for sb** (*Pol*) solliciter des voix pour qn; (*gen*) faire campagne pour qn.
b (*Comm*) visiter la clientèle, faire la place; (*door to door*) faire du démarchage.
3 n = **canvassing**.

canvasser, (*also US*) **canvaser** ['kænvəsəʳ] n **a** (*Pol: esp Brit: for support*) agent électoral (*qui sollicite les voix des électeurs*); (*US: checking votes*) scrutateur *m*, -trice *f*. **b** (*Comm*) placier *m*; (*door to door*) démarcheur *m*. **"no ~s"** "accès interdit aux colporteurs".

canvassing ['kænvəsɪŋ] n (*Pol*) démarchage électoral (*pour solliciter les suffrages*); (*when applying for job, membership etc*) visites *fpl* de candidature; (*US: inspection of votes*) vérification *f* des votes. (*to job applicants etc*) **no ~ allowed** ≃ s'abstenir de toute démarche personnelle.

canyon ['kænjən] n cañon *m*, gorge *f*.

CAP [ˌsiːeɪ'piː] n (*Pol*) (abbr of **Common Agricultural Policy**) PAC *f*.

cap [kæp] **1** n **a** (*headgear*) *[man, woman, boy, jockey]* casquette *f*; (*for women: regional*) coiffe *f*; *[judge]* toque *f*; *[baby, sailor]* bonnet *m*; *[officer]* képi *m*; *[soldier]* calot *m*; (*skull~*) calotte *f*; *[cardinal]* barrette *f*. (*Univ*) **~ and gown** costume *m* universitaire; (*fig*) **~ in hand** chapeau bas, humblement; (*fig*) **if the ~ fits, wear it** qui se sent morveux (qu'il) se mouche; *[woman]* **to set one's ~ at**† jeter son dévolu sur; **~ and bells** marotte *f* (de bouffon); (*Brit Sport*) **he's got his ~ for England, he's an England ~** il a été sélectionné pour l'équipe d'Angleterre, il joue pour l'Angleterre; *see* **black, feather, night, thinking**.
b (*lid, cover*) *[bottle]* capsule *f*; *[fountain pen]* capuchon *m*; (*Mil: on shell*) fusée *f*; (*Aut: of radiator, tyre-valve*) bouchon *m*; (*Med: contraceptive*) diaphragme *m*; (*Naut: of mast*) chouque *m or* chouquet *m*; (*Archit*) chapiteau *m*, couronnement *m*; *[mushroom]* chapeau *m*; *see* **axle, knee, toe** *etc*.
c (*percussion ~*) capsule fulminante; (*for toy gun*) amorce *f*.
2 vt **a** (*see* **1b**: *put cover on*) (*gen*) couvrir d'une capsule, d'un capuchon *etc*; *bottle etc* capsuler; (*Mil*) *shell* visser la fusée de; *see* **snow**.
b *person* coiffer; (*Univ*) conférer un grade universitaire à. (*Sport*) **he was ~ped 4 times for England** il a joué 4 fois dans l'équipe d'Angleterre.
c (*surpass, improve on*) *sb's words* renchérir sur; *achievements* surpasser. **he ~ped this story/quotation** il a trouvé une histoire/une citation encore meilleure que celle-ci; **to ~ it all** pour couronner le tout, pour comble; **that ~s it all!** ça, c'est le bouquet!* *or* le comble!
d (*limit*) *spending etc* restreindre; *see also* **rate, charge 2**.

cap.* [kæp] n abbr of **capital letter**.

capability [ˌkeɪpə'bɪlɪtɪ] n **a** (*NonC*) aptitude *f* (*to do, of doing* à faire), capacité *f* (*to do, for doing* de faire). **he has the ~ to do it** il est capable de le faire, il en a la capacité, il a l'aptitude nécessaire. **b capabilities** moyens *mpl*; **this child has capabilities** cet enfant a des moyens *or* est assez doué. **c** *[machine]* potentiel *m*; (*Mil: range of weapons etc*) capacité *f*.

capable ['keɪpəbl] adj **a** *person* capable; *event, situation* susceptible (*of* de). **he is ~ of great anger/of getting angry very quickly** il est capable de se mettre très en colère/de s'emporter très vite; **the situation is ~ of review** *or* **of being reviewed** la situation est susceptible d'être reconsidérée. **b** (*competent*) *child* capable; *worker* capable, compétent.

capably ['keɪpəblɪ] adv habilement, avec compétence.

capacious [kə'peɪʃəs] adj *hall, hotel* vaste, d'une grande capacité; *container* d'une grande contenance *or* capacité.

capacitance [kə'pæsɪtəns] n (*Elec*) capacitance *f*.

capacitor [kə'pæsɪtəʳ] n (*Elec*) condensateur *m*.

capacity [kə'pæsɪtɪ] **1** n **a** (*ability to hold, cubic content etc*) *[container]* contenance *f*, capacité *f*; *[hall, hotel]* capacité. **filled to ~** *jug* plein; *box, suitcase* plein, bourré; *hall, bus etc* plein, comble *inv*, bondé; **the hall has a seating ~ of 400** la salle peut contenir 400 personnes, la salle a 400 places assises; **the tank has a ~ of 100 litres** le réservoir a une capacité *or* une contenance de 100 litres.
b (*Elec, Phys*) capacité *f*.
c (*Ind*) (*production potential*) moyens *mpl* de production; (*output, production*) rendement *m*. **to work at (full) ~** produire à plein rendement; **we are increasing (our) ~** nous augmentons nos moyens de production; **we haven't yet reached ~** nous n'avons pas encore atteint notre rendement maximum.
d (*mental ability: also* **capacities**) aptitude *f*, capacité(s) *f(pl)*, moyens *mpl*. **~ to do sth** aptitude à faire qch; **to the extent of my ~** dans la mesure de mes moyens; **this book is within the ~ of children** ce livre est à la portée des enfants; **he had lost all ~ for happiness** il avait perdu toute aptitude au bonheur *or* à être heureux; **his ~ for hard work** sa grande aptitude au travail.
e (*position, status*) qualité *f*, titre *m*. **in my ~ as a doctor** en ma qualité de médecin; **in his official ~** dans l'exercice de ses fonctions; **in an advisory ~** à titre consultatif; **we must not employ him in any ~ whatsoever** il ne faut pas l'employer à quelque titre que ce soit.
f (*legal power*) pouvoir légal (*to do* de faire). **to have the ~ to do** avoir qualité pour faire.
2 comp ▸ **capacity attendance: there was a capacity attendance** c'était plein *or* bondé ▸ **capacity audience: they were hoping for a capacity audience** ils espéraient faire salle comble ▸ **capacity booking: there was capacity booking** toutes les places étaient louées *or* retenues, on jouait à guichets fermés ▸ **capacity crowd: there was a capacity crowd** il n'y avait plus une place (de) libre; (*Sport*) le stade était comble.

caparison [kə'pærɪsn] (*liter*) **1** n caparaçon *m*. **2** vt *horse* caparaçonner.

cape¹ [keɪp] n (*full length*) cape *f*; (*half length*) pèlerine *f*; (*policeman's, cyclist's*) pèlerine.

cape² [keɪp] **1** n (*Geog*) cap *m*; (*high ~*) promontoire *m*. **2** comp ▸ **Cape Canaveral** le cap Canaveral ▸ **Cape Coloureds** (*in South Africa*) métis sud-africains ▸ **Cape Horn** le cap Horn ▸ **Cape of Good Hope** le cap de Bonne-Espérance ▸ **Cape Province** province *f* du Cap ▸ **Cape Town** Le Cap ▸ **Cape Verde Islands** îles *fpl* du Cap-Vert.

caper¹ ['keɪpəʳ] **1** vi *[child, elf]* (*also* **~ about**) gambader, faire des gambades *or* des cabrioles. (*fool around*) **to ~ about*** faire l'idiot. **2** n **a** (*leap, jump*) cabriole *f*, gambade *f*. (*fig, gen pl: pranks*) **~s** farces *fpl*. **b** (**: fun*) **that was quite a ~** ça a été une vraie rigolade*; **how did your French ~ go?** comment s'est passée votre petite virée* en France? **c** (**: slightly pej: hassle*) **what a ~!** quelle affaire!; **how did the Golden Wedding ~ go?** votre bamboula*, pour les noces d'or, comment ça s'est passé?

caper² ['keɪpəʳ] n (*Culin*) câpre *f*; (*shrub*) câprier *m*. **~ sauce** sauce *f* aux câpres.

capercaillie, capercailzie [ˌkæpə'keɪlɪ] n grand tétras, grand coq de bruyère.

Capernaum [kə'pɜːnɪəm] n Capharnaüm.

capeskin ['keɪpskɪn] n (*US*) peau *f* souple pour ganterie.
capful ['kæpfʊl] n (*measure of liquid*) **one ~ to 4 litres of water** une capsule (pleine) pour 4 litres d'eau.
capillary [kə'pɪlərɪ] adj, n (*Bio, Bot*) capillaire (*m*).
capital ['kæpɪtl] 1 adj a (*Jur*) capital. **~ offence** crime capital; **~ punishment** peine capitale, peine de mort; **~ sentence** condamnation *f* à mort.
b (*essential, important*) capital, fondamental, essentiel. **of ~ importance** d'une importance capitale.
c (*chief, principal*) capital, principal. **~ city** *see* **2a**; (*Naut*) **~ ship** grosse unité de guerre.
d **~ letter** majuscule *f*, capitale *f*; **~ A, B** *etc* A, B *etc* majuscule; **Art/Life with a ~ A/L** l'Art/la Vie avec un grand A/V.
e (*†: *splendid*) épatant*, fameux*.
2 n a (*also* **~ city**) capitale *f*.
b (*Typ: ~ letter*) majuscule *f*, capitale *f*.
c (*NonC: Comm, Fin*) (*money and property*) capital *m* (en espèces et en nature); (*money only*) capital, capitaux *mpl*, fonds *mpl*. **~ invested** mise *f* de fonds; **~ and labour** le capital et la main d'œuvre; (*fig*) **to make ~ out of** tirer parti *or* profit de; *see* **working**.
d (*Archit*) chapiteau *m*.
3 comp ► **capital account** (*Fin, Econ etc*) compte capital ► **capital allowances** amortissements *mpl* admis par le fisc ► **capital assets** biens *mpl* de capital ► **capital cost** coût *m* d'investissement ► **capital equipment** biens *mpl* d'équipement *or* de capital ► **capital expenditure** dépense *f* d'investissement ► **capital gains** augmentation *f* de capital, plus-values *fpl* (en capital); **capital gains tax** impôt *m* sur les plus-values (en capital) ► **capital goods** biens *mpl* d'équipement ► **capital intensive** *industry etc* à forte intensité de capital ► **capital levy** prélèvement *m or* impôt *m* sur le capital ► **capital reserves** réserves *fpl* et provisions *fpl* ► **capital stock** capital *m* social ► **capital sum** capital *m* ► **capital transactions** transactions *fpl* en capital ► **capital transfer tax** impôt *m* sur le transfert de capitaux.
capitalism ['kæpɪtəlɪzəm] n capitalisme *m*.
capitalist ['kæpɪtəlɪst] adj, n capitaliste (*mf*).
capitalistic [ˌkæpɪtə'lɪstɪk] adj capitaliste.
capitalization [kəˌpɪtəlaɪ'zeɪʃən] n capitalisation *f*.
capitalize [kə'pɪtəlaɪz] 1 vt a (*Fin*) *property, plant* capitaliser; *company* constituer le capital social de (*par émission d'actions*); (*fig*) tirer profit *or* parti de. (*Fin*) **over-/under-~d** sur-/sous-capitalisé. b (*Typ*) *word* mettre une majuscule à; *letter(s)* mettre en majuscule(s). 2 vi (*fig*) **to ~ on** *circumstances, information* exploiter, tirer profit *or* parti de; *talents* tirer parti de; (*financially*) monnayer.
capitation [ˌkæpɪ'teɪʃən] n (*Fin: also* **~ tax**) capitation *f*. (*Brit Scol Admin*) **~ allowance** dotation *f* forfaitaire par élève (*accordée à un établissement*).
Capitol ['kæpɪtl] n: **the ~** (*US*) le Capitole (*siège du Congrès américain*); (*Roman Hist*) le Capitole.
capitulate [kə'pɪtjʊleɪt] vi (*Mil, fig*) capituler.
capitulation [kəˌpɪtjʊ'leɪʃən] n a (*Mil, fig*) capitulation *f*. b (*summary*) récapitulation *f*, sommaire *m*. c (*Jur*) **~s** capitulation *f*.
capo ['kæpəʊ] n (*US*) chef *m* de mafia.
capon ['keɪpən] n chapon *m*.
cappuccino [ˌkæpʊ'tʃiːnəʊ] n cappuccino *m*.
Capri [kə'priː] n Capri. **in ~** à Capri.
caprice [kə'priːs] n a (*change of mood*) saute *f* d'humeur; (*whim*) caprice *m*. b (*Mus*) capriccio *m*.
capricious [kə'prɪʃəs] adj capricieux, fantasque.
capriciously [kə'prɪʃəslɪ] adv capricieusement.
Capricorn ['kæprɪkɔːn] n (*Astron, Geog*) le Capricorne. **I'm (a) ~** je suis (du) Capricorne; *see* **tropic**.
caps [kæps] npl (*abbr of* **capital letters**) *see* **capital**.
capsicum ['kæpsɪkəm] n (*plant, fruit*) (*sweet*) piment doux, poivron *m*; (*hot*) piment.
capsize [kæp'saɪz] 1 vi se renverser; (*Naut*) chavirer. 2 vt renverser; (*Naut*) faire chavirer.
capstan ['kæpstən] n (*Naut*) cabestan *m*. (*Brit*) **~ lathe** tour *m* revolver.
capsule ['kæpsjuːl] 1 n (*all senses*) capsule *f*. 2 adj *description, résumé* succint.
Capt. n (*Mil*) (*abbr of* **Captain**) (*on envelope*) **~ P. Martin** Le capitaine P. Martin.
captain ['kæptɪn] 1 n (*Army, US Aviat*) capitaine *m*; (*Navy*) capitaine (de vaisseau); (*Merchant Navy*) capitaine; (*Sport*) capitaine (d'équipe); (*US Police: also* **precinct ~**) ≈ commissaire *m* (de police) de quartier. (*Brit*) **(school) ~** *élève (des classes terminales) chargé(e) d'un certain nombre de responsabilités;* **~ of industry** capitaine d'industrie. 2 vt (*Sport*) *team* être le capitaine de; (*Mil, Naut*) commander; (*fig*) diriger.
captaincy ['kæptənsɪ] n (*Mil*) grade *m* de capitaine; (*Sport*) poste *m* de capitaine. (*Mil*) **to get one's ~** être promu *or* passer capitaine; (*Sport*) **during his ~** quand il était capitaine (de l'équipe).
caption ['kæpʃən] 1 n a (*Press*) (*heading*) sous-titre *m*; (*under illustration*) légende *f*. b (*Cine*) sous-titre *m*. 2 vt *illustration* mettre une légende à; (*Cine*) sous-titrer.
captious ['kæpʃəs] adj *person* chicanier, vétilleux, qui trouve toujours à redire; *remark* critique.
captivate ['kæptɪveɪt] vt captiver, fasciner, tenir sous le charme.
captivating ['kæptɪveɪtɪŋ] adj captivant.
captive ['kæptɪv] 1 n captif *m*, -ive *f*. **to take sb ~** faire qn prisonnier; **to hold sb ~** garder qn en captivité; (*fig*) captiver qn, tenir qn sous le charme. 2 adj *person* captif, prisonnier; *balloon* captif. **she had a ~ audience** son auditoire était bien obligé de l'écouter; (*Comm*) **~ market** marché *m* captif.
captivity [kæp'tɪvɪtɪ] n captivité *f*. **in ~** en captivité.
captor ['kæptə^r] n (*unlawful*) ravisseur *m*; (*lawful*) personne *f* qui capture.
capture ['kæptʃə^r] 1 vt *animal, soldier* prendre, capturer; *escapee* reprendre; *city* prendre, s'emparer de; (*fig*) *attention* capter, captiver; *interest* gagner; (*Art*) reproduire, rendre. **they have ~d a large part of that market** ils ont conquis une grande partie de ce marché; **to ~ sth on camera/film** saisir qch en photo/sur son film. 2 n *[town, treasure, escapee]* capture *f*.
capuchin ['kæpjʊʃɪn] n a cape *f* (*avec capuchon*). b (*Rel*) **C~** capucin(e) *m(f)*.
car [kɑː^r] 1 n a (*Aut*) voiture *f*, automobile *f*, auto *f*; *see* **racing, saloon, sport** *etc*.
b (*US Rail*) wagon *m*, voiture *f*; *see* **dining car, freight** *etc*.
c (*tramcar*) (voiture *f* de) tramway *m*, tram *m*.
d *[lift, elevator]* cabine *f* (d'ascenseur).
e (*Aviat*) nacelle *f* (*de dirigeable*).
2 comp *wheel etc* de voiture; *travel etc* en voiture ► **car allowance** indemnité *f* de déplacements (en voiture) ► **car bomb** *or* **bombing** voiture piégée ► **car-boot sale** (*Brit*) vente *f* sauvage (*d'objets usagés etc par des particuliers*) ► **carborne** (*US*) transporté en voiture ► **car chase** course-poursuite *f* ► **car coat** autocoat *m*, manteau *m* trois-quarts ► **car expenses** frais *mpl* de déplacements (en voiture) ► **car-fare** (*US*) prix *m* du trajet ► **car-ferry** *[sea]* ferry(-boat) *m*; *[river, small channel]* bac *m* (pour voitures) ► **car hire** location *f* de voitures; **car hire company** société *f* de location de voitures ► **carhop** (*US*) (*serving food*) serveur *m*, -euse *f* (*qui apporte à manger aux automobilistes dans leur voiture*); (*parking cars*) gardien *m* de parking (*qui gare les voitures*) ► **car industry** industrie *f* automobile ► **car journey** voyage *m* en voiture; (*shorter*) trajet *m* en voiture ► **car licence** vignette *f* (de l'impôt) ► **carload** voiture *f* entière; **a carload of people** une voiture remplie de gens ► **car number** (*Brit*) numéro *m* d'immatriculation ► **car park** (*Brit*) parking *m*, parc *m* de stationnement ► **car phone** téléphone *m* de voiture ► **car-pool** (*US*) pool *m* de transport (*grâce auquel plusieurs personnes se servent d'une même voiture pour se rendre à leur travail*) (*see also* **pool**) ► **carport** auvent *m* (pour voiture(s)) ► **car radio** autoradio *m* ► **car rental** location *f* de voitures ► **car sick: to be car sick** être malade en voiture, avoir le mal de la route ► **car sickness** mal *m* de la route ► **car sleeper** (*Rail*) train *m* auto-couchettes ► **car transporter** (*Aut*) camion *m or* (*Rail*) wagon *m* pour transport d'automobiles ► **car wash** (*action*) lavage *m* de voitures; (*place*) portique *m* de lavage automatique ► **car-worker** (*Ind*) ouvrier *m*, -ière *f* de l'industrie automobile.
Caracas [kə'rækəs] n Caracas.
carafe [kə'ræf] n carafe *f*; (*small*) carafon *m*.
caramel ['kærəməl] n caramel *m*. **~ custard** *or* **cream** crème *f* (au) caramel.
caramelize ['kærəməlaɪz] 1 vt caraméliser. 2 vi se caraméliser.
carapace ['kærəpeɪs] n carapace *f*.
carat ['kærət] n carat *m*. **22 ~ gold** or *m* à 22 carats.
caravan ['kærəvæn] 1 n (*Brit Aut*) caravane *f*; *[gipsy]* roulotte *f*; (*group: in desert etc*) caravane. **~ site** *[tourists]* camping *m* pour caravanes; *[gipsies]* campement *m*. 2 vi: **to go ~ning** faire du caravaning.
caravanette [ˌkærəvə'net] n (*Brit*) auto-camping *f*, voiture-camping *f*.
caravel [kærə'vel] n (*Naut*) caravelle *f*.
caraway ['kærəweɪ] n cumin *m*, carvi *m*. **~ seeds** (graines *fpl* de) cumin, (graines de) carvi.
carbide ['kɑːbaɪd] n carbure *m*.
carbine ['kɑːbaɪn] n carabine *f*.
carbohydrate ['kɑːbəʊ'haɪdreɪt] n hydrate *m* de carbone. (*in diets etc*) **~s** farineux *mpl*, féculents *mpl*.
carbolic [kɑː'bɒlɪk] adj phéniqué. **~ acid** phénol *m*.
carbon ['kɑːbən] 1 n (*Chem*) carbone *m*; (*Art, Elec*) charbon *m*; (*paper, copy*) carbone. 2 comp ► **carbon copy** n *[typing etc]* carbone *m*; (*fig*) réplique *f* ◊ adj (*fig*) identique ► **carbon-date** vt (*Archeol*) analyser le carbone 14 de ► **carbon(-14) dating** datation *f* à l'analyse du carbone 14 ► **carbon dioxide** gaz *m* carbonique ► **carbon fibre** fibre *f* de carbone ► **carbon microphone** microphone *m* à charbon ► **carbon monoxide** oxyde *m* de carbone ► **carbon paper** (*Typ*) (papier *m*) carbone *m* ► **carbon ribbon** (*Typ*) ruban *m* de machine à écrire ► **carbon tissue** (*Phot*) = **carbon paper**.

carbonaceous [ˌkɑːbəˈneɪʃəs] adj charbonneux; (*Chem*) carboné.
carbonate [ˈkɑːbənɪt] n carbonate *m*.
carbonated [ˈkɑːbəneɪtɪd] adj *water, drink* gazeux.
carbonic [kɑːˈbɒnɪk] adj carbonique.
carboniferous [ˌkɑːbəˈnɪfərəs] adj carbonifère.
carbonization [ˌkɑːbənaɪˈzeɪʃən] n carbonisation *f*.
carbonize [ˈkɑːbənaɪz] vt carboniser.
carbonless [ˈkɑːbənlɪs] adj: ~ **paper** papier autocopiant.
Carborundum [ˌkɑːbəˈrʌndəm] n ® Carborundum *m* ®, siliciure *m* de carbone.
carboy [ˈkɑːbɔɪ] n bonbonne *f*.
carbuncle [ˈkɑːbʌŋkl] n a (*jewel*) escarboucle *f*. b (*Med*) furoncle *m*.
carburation [ˌkɑːbjʊˈreɪʃən] n carburation *f*.
carburettor, (*US*) **carburetor** [ˌkɑːbjʊˈretəʳ] n carburateur *m*.
carcass [ˈkɑːkəs] n a *[animal]* carcasse *f*, cadavre *m*; (*Butchery*) carcasse; (*human corpse*) cadavre; (*‡: hum, iro: body*) carcasse. (*Culin*) **chicken** ~ os *mpl or* carcasse de poulet. b (*Aut, Naut, Tech*) charpente *f*, carcasse *f*. c (*Brit*) ~ **trade‡** commerce *m* de fausses antiquités.
carcinogen [kɑːˈsɪnədʒen] n substance *f* cancérigène *or* cancérogène.
carcinogenic [ˌkɑːsɪnəˈdʒenɪk] 1 n = **carcinogen**. 2 adj cancérigène *or* cancérogène.
carcinoma [ˌkɑːsɪˈnəʊmə] n, pl ~**s** *or* **carcinomata** [ˌkɑːsɪˈnəʊmətə] carcinome *m*.
card¹ [kɑːd] 1 n a (*gen*) carte *f*; (*playing* ~) carte; (*visiting* ~) carte (de visite); (*invitation* ~) carton *m or* carte d'invitation; (*post*~) carte (postale); (*index* ~) fiche *f*; (*member's* ~) carte de membre *or* d'adhérent; (*press* ~) carte de presse; (*library* ~) carte (d'abonnement); (*at dance, races*) programme *m*; (*piece of cardboard*) (morceau *m* de) carton *m*. **identity** ~ carte d'identité; **game of** ~**s** partie *f* de cartes; **to play** ~**s** jouer aux cartes; **high/low** ~ haute/basse carte; *see* **court, face, score, trump** *etc*.
b (*fig phrases*) **to play one's** ~**s well** bien mener son jeu *or* sa barque; **if you play your** ~**s right** si vous manœuvrez habilement; **to play one's best/last** ~ jouer sa meilleure/dernière carte; **to hold all the** ~**s** avoir tous les atouts (dans son jeu *or* en main); **to put** *or* **lay one's** ~**s on the table** jouer cartes sur table; **to have a** ~ **up one's sleeve** avoir un atout dans sa manche; **to throw in the** ~**s** abandonner la partie (*fig*); **it's on the** ~**s*** *or* (*US*) **in the** ~**s* that** ... il y a de grandes chances (pour) que ... + *subj*; (*Brit Ind etc*) **to get one's** ~**s** être mis à la porte, être licencié; (*Brit Ind etc*) **to ask for one's** ~**s** plaquer* *or* quitter son travail; **he's (quite) a** ~**!*†** c'est un rigolo!*
2 comp ▸ **cardboard** n carton *m* (*NonC*) ◊ adj *bookcover* cartonné; *doll* de *or* en carton; **cardboard box** (boîte *f* en) carton *m*; **cardboard cutout** (*lit*) figurine *f* de carton à découper; (*fig*) homme *m* de paille; **cardboard city*** *endroit de la ville où dorment les sans-abris*; **he sleeps in cardboard city*** ≃ il dort sous les ponts ▸ **card-carrying member** membre *m*, adhérent(e) *m(f)* ▸ **card catalogue** catalogue *m*, fichier *m* (*de bibliothèque etc*) ▸ **card game** (*e.g. bridge, whist etc*) jeu *m* de cartes; (*game of cards*) partie *f* de cartes ▸ **card-holder** *[political party, organization etc]* membre *m*, adhérent(e) *m(f)*; *[library]* abonné(e) *m(f)*; *[restaurant etc]* habitué(e) *m(f)*; *[credit cards]* titulaire *mf* d'une carte (*or* de cartes) de crédit ▸ **card hopper** (*Comput*) magasin *m* d'alimentation ▸ **card index** n fichier *m* ▸ **card-index** vt ficher, mettre sur fiches ▸ **cardphone** (*Brit Telec*) téléphone *m* à carte (magnétique) ▸ **card punch** perforatrice *f* de cartes ▸ **card reader** (*Comput*) lecteur *m* de cartes perforées ▸ **cardsharp(er)** tricheur *m*, -euse *f* (*professionnel*) ▸ **card stacker** (*Comput*) case *f* de réception ▸ **card table** table *f* de jeu *or* à jouer ▸ **card trick** tour *m* de cartes ▸ **card vote** (*Ind*) vote *m* sur carte (*même nombre de voix que d'adhérents représentés*).
3 vt a (*put on cards*) ficher, mettre sur fiches.
b (*US: check sb's identity*) **to** ~ **sb*** demander à voir les pièces d'identité de qn.
card² [kɑːd] (*Tech*) 1 n carde *f*. 2 vt *wool, cotton* carder.
cardamom [ˈkɑːdəməm] n cardamome *f*.
carder [ˈkɑːdəʳ] n (*Tech*) cardeuse *f*.
cardiac [ˈkɑːdɪæk] adj cardiaque. ~ **arrest** arrêt *m* du cœur.
cardie* [ˈkɑːdɪ] n (**dim of cardigan**).
cardigan [ˈkɑːdɪgən] n cardigan *m*, gilet *m* (de laine).
cardinal [ˈkɑːdɪnl] 1 adj *number, point,* (*Ling*) *vowel* cardinal. ~ **sin** (*Rel*) péché *m* capital; (*fig: serious mistake*) gros péché *m*, grande faute *f*; **the four** ~ **virtues** les quatre vertus cardinales; **of** ~ **importance/significance** d'une importance/portée capitale. 2 n (*Rel*) cardinal *m*. ~ **red** rouge cardinal *inv*, pourpre; *see* **college**.
cardio... [ˈkɑːdɪəʊ] pref cardio-. ~**vascular** cardio-vasculaire.
cardiogram [ˈkɑːdɪəgræm] n cardiogramme *m*.
cardiograph [ˈkɑːdɪəgræf] n cardiographe *m*.
cardiography [ˌkɑːdɪˈɒgrəfɪ] n cardiographie *f*.
cardiological [ˌkɑːdɪəˈlɒdʒɪkəl] adj cardiologique.
cardiologist [ˌkɑːdɪˈɒlɪdʒɪst] n cardiologue *mf*.
cardiology [ˌkɑːdɪˈɒlədʒɪ] n cardiologie *f*.
cardy [ˈkɑːdɪ] n (**dim of cardigan**).

care [kɛəʳ] 1 n a (*NonC: attention, heed*) attention *f*, soin *m*; (*charge, responsibility*) soins *mpl*, charge *f*, garde *f*. **with the greatest** ~ avec le plus grand soin; (*on parcels*) **"with ~"** "fragile"; **to take** ~ faire attention; **it got broken despite all our** ~ ça s'est cassé bien que nous y ayons fait très attention; **take** ~ **not to catch cold** *or* **that you don't catch cold** faites attention de *or* à ne pas prendre froid; **take** ~ (fais) attention; (*as good wishes*) fais bien attention (à toi); **have a** ~**!†** prenez garde!; **you should take more** ~ **with** *or* **give more** ~ **to your work** vous devriez apporter plus d'attention *or* plus de soin à votre travail; **you should take more** ~ **of yourself** tu devrais faire plus attention (à ta santé); **he took** ~ **to explain why** ... il a pris soin d'expliquer pourquoi ...; **to take** ~ **of** *book, details, arrangements* s'occuper de, se charger de; *valuables* garder; *person, animal* prendre soin de, s'occuper de; **to take good** ~ **of sb** bien s'occuper de qn; **to take good** ~ **of sth** prendre grand soin de qch; (*threateningly*) **I'll take** ~ **of him!** je vais m'occuper de lui!; **I'll take** ~ **of that** je vais m'en occuper; **he can take** ~ **of himself** il peut *or* sait se débrouiller* tout seul; **that can take** ~ **of itself** cela s'arrangera tout seul; **let the car take** ~ **of itself for a moment!*** laisse la voiture tranquille cinq minutes!; (*Jur*) **convicted of driving without due** ~ **and attention** condamné pour conduite négligente; **I leave** *or* **put it in your** ~ je le confie à vos soins, je vous le confie; (*on letters*) ~ **of** (*abbr* **c/o**) aux bons soins de, chez; **he was left in his aunt's** ~ on l'a laissé à la garde de sa tante; (*frm*) **to be in** ~ **of sb** être sous la garde *or* la surveillance de qn; **he is in the** ~ **of Dr X** c'est le docteur X qui le soigne.
b (*anxiety*) souci *m*. **he hasn't a** ~ **in the world** il n'a pas le moindre souci; **full of** ~**s** accablé de soucis; **the** ~**s of State** les responsabilités *fpl* de l'État.
c (*Admin, Soc*) **to put a child in** *or* **take a child into** ~ retirer un enfant à la garde de ses parents; **he's been in** ~ **since the age of 3** on l'a retiré à la garde de ses parents quand il avait 3 ans.
2 comp ▸ **carefree** sans souci, insouciant ▸ **careful** *etc see* **careful** *etc* ▸ **care label** (*on garment*) instructions *fpl* de lavage (*étiquette*) ▸ **careless** *etc see* **careless** *etc* ▸ **caretaker** (*Brit*) gardien(ne) *m(f)* (d'immeuble), concierge *mf*; (*Pol*) **caretaker government** gouvernement *m* intérimaire ▸ **careworn** rongé par les soucis.
3 vi a (*feel interest, anxiety, sorrow*) se soucier (*about* de), s'intéresser (*about* à). **money is all he** ~**s about** il n'y a que l'argent qui l'intéresse (*subj*); **to** ~ **deeply about sth** être profondément concerné par qch; **to** ~ **deeply about sb** être profondément attaché à qn; **not to** ~ **about** se soucier peu de, se moquer de, se ficher de*; **he really** ~**s (about this)** c'est vraiment important pour lui; **I don't** ~**!, as if I** ~**d!** ça m'est égal!, je m'en moque!, je m'en fiche!*; **what do I** ~**?** qu'est-ce que cela me fait? *or* peut me faire?; **for all I** ~ pour ce que cela me fait; **I couldn't** ~ **less* what people say** je me fiche pas mal* de ce que les gens peuvent dire; **shall we go to the pictures or not? — I don't** ~ **either way*** on va au cinéma ou non? — (l'un ou l'autre,) ça m'est égal; **he doesn't** ~ **a (brass) farthing*** *or* **a hang*** *or* **two hoots*** *or* **a damn‡** il s'en fiche* comme de l'an quarante *or* de sa première chemise; **who** ~**s!** qu'est-ce que cela peut bien faire!, on s'en moque!, on s'en fiche!*; *see* **naught**.
b (*like*) aimer. **would you** ~ **to take off your coat?** voulez-vous vous débarrasser de votre manteau?; **I shouldn't** ~ **to meet him** je n'aimerais pas le rencontrer, ça ne me dirait rien de le rencontrer; **I don't much** ~ **for it** cela ne me dit pas grand-chose; **I don't** ~ **for him** il ne me plaît pas tellement *or* beaucoup; **would you** ~ **for a cup of tea?** voulez-vous (prendre) une tasse de thé?; **would you** ~ **for a walk?** voulez-vous faire une promenade?
▸**care for** vt fus *invalid* soigner; *child* s'occuper de. **well-cared for** *invalid* qu'on soigne bien; *child* dont on s'occupe bien; *hands, hair* soigné; *garden* bien entretenu; *house* bien tenu.
careen [kəˈriːn] 1 vt (*Naut*) *ship* caréner, mettre *or* abattre en carène. 2 vi (*Naut*) donner de la bande (*de façon dangereuse*).
career [kəˈrɪəʳ] 1 n a (*profession, occupation*) carrière *f*, profession *f*. **journalism is his** ~ il fait carrière dans le journalisme; **he is making a** ~ **(for himself) in advertising** il est en train de faire carrière dans la publicité.
b (*life, development, progress*) vie *f*, carrière *f*. **he studied the** ~**s of the great** il a étudié la vie des grands hommes.
c (*movement*) **in full** ~ en pleine course.
2 comp *soldier, diplomat* de carrière ▸ **career girl** jeune fille *f* qui s'intéresse avant tout à sa carrière; **she's a career girl** elle s'intéresse avant tout à sa carrière, elle est très ambitieuse ▸ **career move** changement *m* d'emploi pour favoriser le développement de sa carrière ▸ **career prospects** possibilités *fpl* d'avancement ▸ **careers advisor** (*Brit*), **careers counselor** (*US*) conseiller *m*, -ère *f* d'orientation professionnelle ▸ **careers guidance** (*Brit*) orientation professionnelle ▸ **careers office** centre *m* d'orientation (professionnelle) ▸ **careers officer** (*Brit*), **careers teacher** (*Brit Scol*) = **careers advisor**.
3 vi (*also* ~ **along**) aller à toute vitesse *or* à toute allure. **to** ~ **up/down** *etc* monter/descendre *etc* à toute allure.
careerism [kəˈrɪərɪzəm] n carriérisme *m*.
careerist [kəˈrɪərɪst] n (*pej*) carriériste *mf* (*pej*).

careful ['kɛəfʊl] adj a (*painstaking*) *writer, worker* consciencieux, soigneux; *work* soigné. ~ **over detail** attentif aux détails.
b (*cautious*) prudent; (*acting with care*) soigneux. **(be) ~!** (fais) attention!; **be ~ with the glasses** fais attention aux verres; **be ~ to shut the door** n'oubliez pas de fermer la porte; **be ~ not to let it fall, be ~ (that) you don't let it fall** faites attention à ne pas le laisser tomber; **be ~ of the dog** (faites) attention au chien; **be ~ what you do** faites attention à ce que vous faites; **be ~ (that) he doesn't hear you** faites attention à ce qu'il ne vous entende pas, prenez garde qu'il ne vous entende; **he was ~ to point out that** il a pris soin de faire remarquer que; **he was ~ not to offend them** il était soucieux de ne pas les offenser; **you can't be too ~** (*gen*) on n'est jamais trop prudent, prudence est mère de sûreté (*Prov*); (*when double-checking sth*) deux précautions valent mieux qu'une.
c (*rather miserly*) parcimonieux; (* *pej*) regardant. **he is very ~ with (his) money** il regarde à la dépense, il est très regardant.
carefully ['kɛəfəlɪ] adv a (*painstakingly*) soigneusement, avec soin. b (*cautiously*) prudemment, avec précaution. (*fig*) **we must go ~ here** il faut nous montrer prudents là-dessus; **he replied ~** il a répondu avec circonspection.
carefulness ['kɛəfʊlnɪs] n soin *m*, attention *f*.
careless ['kɛəlɪs] adj a (*taking little care*) négligent, qui manque de soin; (*unconcerned*) inattentif (*of* à), insouciant (*of* de); (*done without care*) *action* inconsidéré, irréfléchi; *work* peu soigné. ~ **driver** conducteur négligent; **convicted of ~ driving** condamné pour conduite négligente; ~ **mistake** faute *f* d'inattention; **this work is too ~** ce travail n'est pas assez soigné. b (*carefree*) sans souci, insouciant.
carelessly ['kɛəlɪslɪ] adv a (*inattentively, thoughtlessly*) négligemment, sans faire attention. b (*in carefree way*) avec insouciance.
carelessness ['kɛəlɪsnɪs] n (*see* **careless**) négligence *f*, manque *m* de soin; manque d'attention, insouciance *f*. **the ~ of his work** le peu de soin qu'il apporte à son travail.
carer ['kɛərəʳ] n (*professional*) travailleur *m* social; (*relative, friend*) *personne qui s'occupe d'un proche qui est malade*.
caress [kə'res] 1 n caresse *f*. 2 vt (*fondle*) caresser; (*kiss*) embrasser.
caret ['kærət] n (*Typ*) lambda *m* (*signe d'insertion*).
cargo ['kɑːgəʊ] n, pl ~**es** *or* ~**s** cargaison *f*, chargement *m*. ~ **boat** cargo *m*; ~ **plane** avion-cargo *m*.
Caribbean [ˌkærɪ'biːən], *esp* (*US*) [kə'rɪbɪən] adj caraïbe, des Caraïbes. **the ~ (Sea)** la mer des Antilles *or* des Caraïbes; ~ **Islands** petites Antilles.
caribou ['kærɪbuː] n, pl ~**s** *or* ~ caribou *m*.
caricature ['kærɪkətjʊəʳ] 1 n a (*Art, fig*) caricature *f*. b (*NonC*) art *m* de la caricature. 2 vt (*Art, fig*) caricaturer.
caricaturist [ˌkærɪkə'tjʊərɪst] n caricaturiste *mf*.
Caricom ['kærɪˌkɒm] n abbr of **Carribbean Community**.
caries ['kɛərɪiːz] n, pl inv carie *f*.
carillon [kə'rɪljən] n carillon *m*.
caring ['kɛərɪŋ] adj *parent* aimant; *teacher* bienveillant. **a ~ society** une société humanitaire; **the ~ professions** les professions à vocation sociale; **a child needs a ~ environment** un enfant a besoin d'être entouré d'affection.
carious ['kɛərɪəs] adj carié, gâté.
Carmelite ['kɑːməlaɪt] adj, n carmélite (*f*).
carminative ['kɑːmɪnətɪv] adj (*Med*) carminatif.
carmine ['kɑːmaɪn] adj, n carmin (*m*).
carnage ['kɑːnɪdʒ] n carnage *m*.
carnal ['kɑːnl] adj (*of the flesh*) charnel; (*sensual*) sensuel; (*worldly*) *pleasure* matériel; *person* matérialiste; (*sexual*) sexuel. (*Jur*) **to have ~ knowledge of sb** avoir des relations sexuelles avec qn.
carnation [kɑː'neɪʃən] 1 n (*Bot*) œillet *m*. 2 adj (*pink*) rose; (*red*) incarnat.
carnet ['kɑːneɪ] n (*Jur, Comm*) passavant *m*.
carnival ['kɑːnɪvəl] 1 n carnaval *m*; (*US: fair*) fête foraine. 2 comp *hat, procession* de carnaval.
carnivora [kɑː'nɪvərə] npl (*Zool*) carnivores *mpl*.
carnivore ['kɑːnɪvɔːʳ] n carnivore *m*, carnassier *m*.
carnivorous [kɑː'nɪvərəs] adj carnivore, carnassier.
carny‡ ['kɑːnɪ] n (*US*) (*carnival*) foire *f*, fête foraine; (*person*) forain *m*.
carob ['kærəb] n: ~ **(powder)** (poudre *f* de) caroube *f*; ~ **tree** caroubier *m*.
carol ['kærəl] 1 n a (*song*) chant joyeux. **(Christmas) ~** chant de Noël; ~**-singers** *groupe de gens qui chantent des chants de Noël*. b [*birds*] ramage *m*; [*small birds*] gazouillis *m*. 2 vi chanter joyeusement; [*birds*] chanter; [*small birds*] gazouiller. 3 vt chanter, célébrer (par des chants).
caroller ['kærələʳ] n chanteur *m*, -euse *f*.
carom ['kærəm] (*Billiards*) 1 n carambolage *m*. 2 vi caramboler.
carotene ['kærətiːn] n carotène *m*.
carotid [kə'rɒtɪd] 1 n carotide *f*. 2 adj carotidien. ~ **artery** carotide *f*.
carousal [kə'raʊzəl] n beuverie *f*, ribote† *f*.
carouse [kə'raʊz] vi faire ribote†.
carousel [ˌkæruː'sel] n a (*merry-go-round*) manège *m* (*de chevaux de bois etc*). b (*Phot: for slides*) magasin *m or* panier *m* circulaire (pour diapositives). c (*at airport: for luggage*) carrousel *m*, tapis roulant à bagages.
carp¹ [kɑːp] n, pl ~ *or* ~**s** (*fish*) carpe *f*.
carp² [kɑːp] vi critiquer. **to ~ at** *person* critiquer, blâmer; *thing, action* trouver à redire à.
carpal ['kɑːpl] adj (*Anat*) carpien.
Carpathians [kɑː'peɪθɪənz] npl: **the ~** les Carpates *fpl*.
carpel ['kɑːpl] n (*Bot*) carpelle *m*.
Carpentaria [ˌkɑːpən'tɛərɪə] n: **Gulf of ~** golfe *m* de Carpentarie.
carpenter ['kɑːpɪntəʳ] 1 n charpentier *m*; (*joiner*) menuisier *m*. 2 vi faire de la charpenterie, faire de la menuiserie.
carpentry ['kɑːpɪntrɪ] n (*see* **carpenter 1**) charpenterie *f*; menuiserie *f*.
carpet ['kɑːpɪt] 1 n tapis *m*; (*fitted*) moquette *f*. (*fig*) **to be on the ~*** [*subject*] être sur le tapis; [*person scolded*] être sur la sellette; *see* **fitted, red, sweep**.
2 vt a *floor* recouvrir d'un tapis; (*with fitted carpet*) recouvrir d'une moquette, moquetter. (*fig*) **garden ~ed with flowers** jardin tapissé de fleurs.
b (* †: *scold*) *person* houspiller.
3 comp ►**carpetbagger*** (*US*) profiteur *m*, -euse *f* (*qui s'installe quelque part pour y faire fortune*); (*Hist*) *profiteur nordiste installé dans le sud des États-Unis après la guerre de Sécession* ►**carpet bombing** (*Mil*) bombardement *m* intensif ►**carpet slippers** pantoufles *fpl* ►**carpet sweeper** (*mechanical*) balai *m* mécanique; (*vacuum cleaner*) aspirateur *m* ►**carpet tile** dalle *f* de moquette.
carpeting ['kɑːpɪtɪŋ] n (*NonC*) moquette *f*; *see* **wall**.
carping ['kɑːpɪŋ] 1 adj *person* chicanier, qui trouve à redire à tout; *manner* chicanier; *criticism* mesquin; *voice* malveillant. 2 n chicanerie *f*, critique *f* (malveillante).
carpus ['kɑːpəs] n, pl **carpi** ['kɑːpaɪ] (*Anat*) carpe *m*.
carriage ['kærɪdʒ] 1 n a (*horse-drawn*) voiture *f* (de maître), équipage *m*. ~ **and pair/and four** voiture *or* équipage *or* attelage *m* à deux chevaux/à quatre chevaux.
b (*Brit Rail*) voiture *f*, wagon *m* (de voyageurs).
c (*NonC: Brit Comm: conveyance of goods*) transport *m*, factage *m*. ~ **forward** (en) port dû; ~ **free** franco de port; ~ **paid** (en) port payé.
d [*typewriter*] chariot *m*; [*printing press*] train *m*; (*Mil: also* **gun-~**) affût *m*.
e [*person*] (*bearing*) maintien *m*, port *m*.
2 comp ►**carriage clock** réveil *m* officier ►**carriage drive** allée *f* (pour voitures), grande allée ►**carriage return** (*Typ*) retour *m* (du) chariot ►**carriage trade** (*Comm*) clientèle *f* riche, grosse clientèle ►**carriageway** (*Brit*) chaussée *f*; *see* **dual**.
carrier ['kærɪəʳ] 1 n a (*Comm*) (*company*) entreprise *f* de transports; (*truck owner etc*) entrepreneur *m* de transports, transporteur *m*, camionneur *m*. **by ~** (*Aut*) par la route, par camion; (*Rail*) par chemin de fer; **express ~** messageries *fpl*. b (*for luggage: on car, cycle etc*) porte-bagages *m inv*; (*bag*) sac *m* (en plastique). c (*Med*) porteur *m*, -euse *f*. d (*aircraft ~*) porte-avions *m inv*; (*troop ~*) (*plane*) appareil *m* transporteur (de troupes); (*ship*) transport *m*. 2 comp ►**carrier-bag** (*Brit*) sac *m* (en plastique) ►**carrier-pigeon** pigeon voyageur.
carrion ['kærɪən] 1 n (*NonC*) charogne *f*. 2 comp ►**carrion crow** corneille noire ►**carrion feeder** (*vulture*) charognard *m*; (*other*) *animal qui se nourrit de charognes* ►**carrion flesh** charogne *f*.
carrot ['kærət] n (*lit, fig*) carotte *f*.
carroty ['kærətɪ] adj *hair* carotte *inv*, roux (*f* rousse). **to have ~ hair** être rouquin* *or* poil-de-carotte *inv*.
carrousel [ˌkærə'sel] n (*US*) = **carousel**.
carry ['kærɪ] 1 vt a (*bear, transport*) [*person*] porter; [*vehicle*] transporter; *goods, heavy loads* transporter; *message, news* porter. **she was ~ing the child in her arms** elle portait l'enfant dans ses bras; **this ship carries coal/passengers** ce bateau transporte du charbon/des passagers; **this coach carries 30 people** ce car contient 30 personnes; **they carried enormous sacks of apples all day** ils ont transporté d'énormes sacs de pommes toute la journée; **as fast as his legs could ~ him** à toutes jambes; **the sea carried the boat westward** la mer a emporté le bateau vers l'ouest; **to ~ in one's head** retenir dans sa tête; (*fig*) **he carried his audience with him** il a enthousiasmé son auditoire, il a emporté la conviction de son auditoire; (*fig*) **to ~ coals to Newcastle** porter de l'eau à la rivière; (*Brit fig*) **(to be left) to ~ the can*** (devoir) payer les pots cassés; **he carries his life in his hands** il risque sa vie; **£5 won't ~ you far these days** de nos jours on ne va pas loin avec 5 livres; **enough food to ~ us through the winter** assez de provisions pour nous durer *or* nous faire* tout l'hiver; **he's had one or two drinks more than he can ~*** il a bu un ou deux verres de trop; *see* **torch**.
b (*have on one's person*) *identity card, documents* porter *or* avoir (sur soi); *matches, cigarettes, money* avoir (sur soi); *umbrella, gun, sword* porter.
c (*have, be provided with*) *label, tag* porter, être muni de; *warning, notice* comporter. (*Comm*) **it carries a 5-year guarantee** c'est garanti

pour 5 ans.

d (*involve, lead to, entail*) avoir comme conséquence(s), produire; *consequences* entraîner. **to ~ conviction** être convaincant; (*Fin*) **to ~ interest** rapporter *or* produire des intérêts; **to ~ a mortgage** être grevé d'une hypothèque; **this job carries a lot of responsibility** ce travail implique *or* comporte de grandes responsabilités; **it also carries extra pay** cela comporte aussi un salaire supplémentaire; **this offence carries a penalty of £100** ce délit est passible d'une amende de 100 livres; **to ~ a crop** donner *or* produire une récolte; (*fig*) **to ~ authority** faire autorité; *see* **weight** *etc.*

e (*support*) *[pillar etc]* supporter, soutenir, porter. **the ship was ~ing too much canvas** *or* **sail** le navire portait trop de toile.

f (*Comm*) *goods, stock* stocker, vendre. **we don't ~ that article** nous ne faisons pas cet article.

g (*Tech*) *[pipe] water, oil* amener; *[wire] sound* conduire.

h (*extend*) faire passer. **they carried the pipes under the street** ils ont fait passer les tuyaux sous la rue; (*fig*) **to ~ sth too far** *or* **to excess** pousser qch trop loin; **this basic theme is carried through the book** ce thème fondamental se retrouve tout au long du livre.

i (*win*) gagner, remporter; *fortress* enlever; *enemy's position* emporter d'assaut. **to ~ the day** (*fig*) gagner (la partie), l'emporter; (*Mil*) être vainqueur; **to ~ all** *or* **everything before one** marcher en vainqueur, l'emporter sur tous les tableaux; **he carried his point** il a eu gain de cause; **the motion/bill was carried** la motion/le projet de loi a été voté(e); (*US Pol*) *[presidential candidate]* **he will ~ Ohio** il va l'emporter dans l'Ohio.

j **to ~ o.s.** se tenir, se comporter, se conduire; **she carries herself very well** elle se tient très droite; **he carries himself like a soldier** il a le port d'un militaire; **he carries himself with dignity** (*stands, walks*) il a un maintien fort digne; (*frm: behave*) il se comporte avec dignité; **he carried his head erect** il tenait la tête bien droite.

k *[newspaper etc] story, details* rapporter. **all the papers carried (the story of) the murder** l'histoire du meurtre était dans tous les journaux, tous les journaux ont parlé du meurtre.

l (*Math*) retenir. **... and ~ three** ... et je retiens trois.

m (*Med*) *child* attendre. **when she was ~ing her third son** quand elle était enceinte de *or* quand elle attendait son troisième fils.

2 vi *[voice, sound]* porter.

3 comp ►**carryall** (*US*) fourre-tout *m inv* (*sac*) ►**carrycot** (*Brit*) (*gen*) porte-bébé *m*; (*wicker*) moise *m* ►**carry-on*** (*pej*) histoires* *fpl*; **what a carry-on about nothing!*** que d'histoires pour rien!* ►**carry-out** (*Scot*) adj *meal etc* à emporter ◊ n snack *m* à emporter; (*drink*) boisson *f* à emporter.

►**carry away** vt sep a (*lit*) *person* emporter; *thing* emporter, enlever; *[tide, wind]* emporter. b (*fig*) transporter. **he was carried away by his friend's enthusiasm** il a été transporté par l'enthousiasme de son ami; **to get carried away by sth*** s'emballer* *or* s'enthousiasmer pour qch; **don't get carried away!*** ne t'emballe pas!*, du calme!; **I got carried away*** (*with excitement etc*) je me suis laissé entraîner (*by* par), je n'ai pas su me retenir; (*with enthusiasm: forgetting time*) je n'ai pas vu l'heure passer, j'étais complètement absorbé.

►**carry back** vt sep (*lit*) *things* rapporter; *person* ramener; (*fig*) reporter; (*Fin*) reporter (*sur comptes antérieurs*). (*fig*) **the music carried me back to my youth** la musique m'a reporté à l'époque de ma jeunesse.

►**carry forward** vt sep (*Book-keeping, gen*) reporter (*to* à). **carried forward** à reporter.

►**carry off** vt sep a (*lit*) *thing* emporter, enlever; (*kidnap*) enlever, ravir. b (*fig*) *prizes, honours* remporter. **to carry it off well** s'en tirer à son honneur; **to carry it off*** réussir (son coup). c (*euph: kill*) emporter. **he was carried off by pneumonia** il a été emporté par une pneumonie.

►**carry on** 1 vi a continuer (*doing* à *or* de faire). **carry on!** continuez!; **carry on with your work!** continuez votre travail!; **if you carry on like that** si tu continues comme ça.

b (**: make a scene*) faire une scène, faire des histoires. **you do carry on!** tu en fais des histoires!*; **don't carry on so!** ne fais (donc) pas tant d'histoires!* *or* toute une scène!

c (**: have an affair*) **to carry on with sb** avoir une liaison avec qn.

2 vt sep a (*conduct*) *business, trade* faire marcher, diriger; *correspondence* entretenir; *conversation* soutenir; *negotiations* mener.

b (*continue*) *business, conversation* continuer, poursuivre; *tradition* poursuivre, entretenir, continuer.

3 **carry-on*** n *see* **carry 3**.

4 **carrying-on** n *see* **carrying-on**.

►**carry out** vt sep a (*lit*) *thing, person,* (*Scot*) *meal* emporter. b (*fig: put into action*) *plan* exécuter, mener à bonne fin, réaliser; *order* exécuter; *idea* mettre à exécution, donner suite à; *obligation* s'acquitter de; *experiment* se livrer à, effectuer; *search, investigation, inquiry* mener, procéder à, conduire; *reform* effectuer, opérer; *the law, regulations* appliquer. **to carry out one's duty** faire son devoir; **to carry out one's duties** s'acquitter de ses fonctions; **to carry out a promise** respecter *or* tenir une promesse.

►**carry over** vt sep a (*lit*) faire passer du côté opposé, faire traverser. b (*from one page to the other*) reporter (d'une page à l'autre); (*Book-keeping, St Ex*) reporter. (*Comm*) **to carry over stock from one season to the next** stocker des marchandises d'une saison à l'autre.

►**carry through** vt sep *plan* mener à bonne fin, exécuter, réaliser; *person* soutenir dans l'épreuve. **his courage carried him through** son courage lui a permis de surmonter l'épreuve.

►**carry up** vt sep monter.

carrying-on ['kærɪɪŋ'ɒn] n a (*NonC*) *[work, business etc]* continuation *f*. b (** pej: often pl*) **carryings-on** façons *fpl* de se conduire *or* de faire.

cart [kɑːt] 1 n (*horse-drawn*) charrette *f*; (*tip-~*) tombereau *m*; (*hand ~*) voiture *f* à bras; (*US: for luggage, shopping*) chariot *m*. (*fig*) **to put the ~ before the horse** mettre la charrue devant *or* avant les bœufs; (*fig*) **to be in the ~*** être dans le pétrin; *see* **dog.** 2 comp ►**cart horse** cheval *m* de trait ►**cartload** (*see* **1**) charretée *f*, tombereau *m*, voiturée *f* ►**cart track** chemin rural *or* de terre ►**cartwheel** (*lit*) roue *f* de charrette; (*fig*) **to do** *or* **turn a cartwheel** faire la roue (*en gymnastique etc*) ►**cartwright** charron *m*. 3 vt *goods* (*in van, truck*) transporter (par camion), camionner; (*in cart*) charroyer, charrier; (**: also* **~ about, ~ around**) *shopping, books* trimballer*, coltiner.

►**cart away** vt sep *goods* emporter; *garbage* ramasser.

cartage ['kɑːtɪdʒ] n (*in van, truck*) camionnage *m*, transport *m*; (*in cart*) charroi *m*.

cartel [kɑː'tel] n (*Comm*) cartel *m*.

carter ['kɑːtəʳ] n (*with lorry*) camionneur *m*; (*with cart*) charretier *m*.

Cartesian [kɑː'tiːzɪən] adj, n cartésien(ne) *m(f)*.

Cartesianism [kɑː'tiːzɪənɪzəm] n cartésianisme *m*.

Carthage ['kɑːθɪdʒ] n Carthage.

Carthaginian [ˌkɑːθə'dʒɪnɪən] 1 n: **the ~s** les Carthaginois *mpl*. 2 adj carthaginois.

Carthusian [kɑː'θjuːzɪən] 1 adj de(s) chartreux. **a ~ monk** un chartreux. 2 n chartreux *m*, -euse *f*.

cartilage ['kɑːtɪlɪdʒ] n cartilage *m*.

cartographer [kɑː'tɒgrəfəʳ] n cartographe *mf*.

cartography [kɑː'tɒgrəfɪ] n cartographie *f*.

cartomancy ['kɑːtəmænsɪ] n cartomancie *f*.

carton ['kɑːtən] n (*for yogurt, cream*) pot *m* (en carton); (*for milk, squash*) carton *m*, brick *m*; (*for ice cream*) boîte *f* (*en carton*); (*for cigarettes*) cartouche *f*.

cartoon [kɑː'tuːn] 1 n *[newspaper etc]* dessin *m* (humoristique); (*Cine, TV*) dessin animé; (*Art: sketch*) carton *m*. 2 vt caricaturer, ridiculiser (*par un dessin humoristique*).

cartoonist [ˌkɑː'tuːnɪst] n *[newspaper etc]* caricaturiste *mf*, dessinateur *m*, -trice *f* humoristique; (*Cine, TV*) dessinateur, -trice de dessins animés, animateur *m*, -trice *f*.

cartridge ['kɑːtrɪdʒ] 1 n *[rifle etc]* cartouche *f*; *[cannon]* gargousse *f*; *[stylus]* cellule *f*; *[recording tape, typewriter or printer ribbon, pen]* cartouche; *[camera]* chargeur *m*; (*Comput*) chargeur *m*, cartouche *f*. 2 comp ►**cartridge belt** (*belt*) (ceinture-)cartouchière *f*; (*strip*) bande *f* (de mitrailleuse) ►**cartridge case** *[rifle]* douille *f*, étui *m* (de cartouche); *[cannon]* douille ►**cartridge clip** chargeur *m* (d'arme à feu) ►**cartridge paper** papier *m* à cartouche, papier fort ►**cartridge player** lecteur *m* de cartouche.

carve [kɑːv] 1 vt tailler (*in, out of* dans); (*sculpt*) sculpter (*in, out of* dans); (*chisel*) ciseler (*in, out of* dans); (*Culin*) découper. **to ~ one's initials on** graver ses initiales sur *or* dans; **to ~ one's way through sth** se frayer un chemin à travers qch à coups de hache (*or* d'épée *etc*). 2 comp ►**carve-up*** (*fig*) *[inheritance]* partage *m*; *[estate, country]* morcellement *m*.

►**carve out** vt sep *piece of wood* découper (*from* dans); *piece of land* prendre (*from* à); *statue, figure* sculpter, tailler (*of* dans); *tool* tailler. (*fig*) **to carve out a career for o.s.** faire carrière, se tailler une carrière.

►**carve up** 1 vt sep a *meat* découper; (*fig*) *country* morceler; (**: disfigure*) *person* amocher‡ à coups de couteau; (***) *sb's face* taillader, balafrer. b (‡ *fig*) *play, performer* massacrer*, éreinter; *candidate, opponent* massacrer*. 2 **carve-up*** n *see* **carve 2**.

carver ['kɑːvəʳ] n a (*Culin: knife*) couteau *m* à découper. **~s** service *m* à découper. b (*person*) personne *f* qui découpe. c (*Brit: chair*) chaise *f* de salle à manger avec accoudoirs.

carvery ['kɑːvərɪ] n ≃ grill *m* (*où l'on sert la viande rôtie*).

carving ['kɑːvɪŋ] n a (*Art*) sculpture *f*. b (*NonC: Culin*) découpage *m*. **~ knife** couteau *m* à découper.

caryatid [ˌkærɪ'ætɪd] n, pl **~s** *or* **~es** [ˌkærɪ'ætɪˌdiːz] cariatide *f*.

Casablanca [ˌkæsə'blæŋkə] n Casablanca.

cascade [kæs'keɪd] 1 n cascade *f*; (*fig*) *[ribbons, silks, lace]* flot *m*; *[sparks]* pluie *f*. 2 vi tomber en cascade.

cascara [kæs'kɑːrə] n (*Pharm*) cascara sagrada *f*.

case[1] [keɪs] 1 n a cas *m*. **is it the ~ that ...?** est-il vrai que ...?; **that's not the ~** ce n'est pas le cas, il n'en est pas ainsi; **if that's the ~** en ce cas, dans ce cas-là; **as is the ~ here** comme c'est le cas ici; **such being the ~, in such a ~** en tel cas, en pareil cas; **if such is the ~** (*now*) si tel est le cas; (*if it happens*) le cas échéant, en tel *or* pareil cas; **put the ~ that ...** admettons que ... + *subj*; **as the ~ may be** selon le cas; **it's a clear ~ of lying** c'est un exemple manifeste de mensonge;

in ~ he comes au cas où *or* pour le cas où il viendrait; **in ~ of** en cas de; **(just) in ~** à tout hasard, pour le cas où*; **in any ~** en tout cas; **in this ~** dans *or* en ce cas; **in that ~** dans ce cas-là; **in no ~** en aucun cas; **in the present ~** dans le cas présent; **as in the ~ of** comme dans le cas de; **in the ~ in point** en l'occurrence; **here is a ~ in point** en voici un bon exemple, en voici un exemple typique; **in your ~** dans votre cas; **in most ~s** dans la plupart des cas; **in nine ~s out of ten** neuf fois sur dix; **that alters the (whole) ~** cela change tout; **a difficult ~** un cas difficile.

b (*Med*) cas *m*; (*Soc*) cas social. **6 ~s of pneumonia** 6 cas de pneumonie; **the most serious ~s were sent to hospital** les cas les plus graves *or* les malades les plus atteints ont été envoyés à l'hôpital; (*fig: person*) **he's a hard ~** c'est un dur*; **she's a real ~!*** c'est un cas* *or* un numéro* (celle-là)!

c (*Jur*) affaire *f*, procès *m*, cause *f*. **to try a ~** juger une affaire; **to win one's ~** (*Jur*) gagner son procès; (*fig*) avoir gain de cause; **the ~ for the defendant** les arguments *mpl* en faveur de l'accusé; **there is no ~ against ...** il n'y a pas lieu à poursuites contre ...; **he's working on the Smith ~** il s'occupe de l'affaire Smith; **~ before the Court** affaire portée devant le tribunal.

d (*argument, reasoning*) arguments *mpl*. **to make out one's ~** expliquer ses raisons, présenter ses arguments, établir le bien-fondé de ce qu'on avance; **to make out a good ~ for sth** réunir *or* présenter de bons arguments en faveur de qch; **to make out a good ~ for doing** bien expliquer pourquoi il faudrait faire; **there is a strong ~ for/against compulsory vaccination** il y a *or* aurait beaucoup à dire en faveur de la/contre la vaccination obligatoire; **that is my ~** voilà mes arguments; **a ~ of conscience** un cas de conscience; **to have a good/strong ~** avoir de bons/solides arguments.

e (*Gram*) cas *m*.

2 **comp ▸ casebook** (*Soc*) comptes rendus *mpl or* rapports *mpl* de cas sociaux (*réunis dans un registre*) **▸ case file** (*Jur, Med, Soc*) dossier *m* **▸ case grammar** (*Gram*) grammaire *f* des cas **▸ case history** (*Soc*) évolution *f* du cas social; (*Med*) (*past facts*) antécédents médicaux; (*past and present development*) évolution *f* de la maladie **▸ case law** (*Jur*) droit jurisprudentiel **▸ case load** (*Soc*) dossiers sociaux (*confiés à un(e) assistant(e) social(e)*); **to have a heavy case load** avoir beaucoup de dossiers (sur les bras) **▸ case notes** (*Jur, Med, Soc*) (notes *fpl* pour l'établissement d'un) dossier *m* **▸ case papers** (*Jur, Med, Soc*) pièces *fpl* de dossier **▸ case study** étude *f* de cas; (*US Univ*) **case study method** méthode *f* d'études de cas **▸ case system** (*Gram*) système casuel **▸ case work** (*Soc*) travail *m* avec des cas (sociaux) individuels **▸ case worker** (*Soc*) ≃ assistant(e) social(e).

case² [keɪs] 1 **n** a (*Brit: suitcase*) valise *f*; (*packing ~*) caisse *f*; (*crate: for bottles etc*) caisse; (*for peaches, lettuce, oysters etc*) cageot *m*; (*box*) boîte *f*; (*chest*) coffre *m*; (*for goods on display*) vitrine *f*; (*for jewels*) coffret *m*; (*for watch, pen, necklace etc*) écrin *m*; (*for camera, binoculars etc*) étui *m*; (*covering*) enveloppe *f*; (*Bookbinding*) couverture *f*; (*Tech*) boîte; (*Aut*) carter *m*. **violin/umbrella** *etc* **~** étui à violon/parapluie *etc; see* **book, pillow** *etc.*

b (*Typ*) casse *f*; *see* **lower¹, upper.**

2 **vt** a (*see* **1a**) mettre dans une caisse *or* un cageot *etc;* mettre en boîte. **~d edition** (*of book*) édition cartonnée.

b [*burglars etc*] **to ~ the joint‡** surveiller la maison *etc* (*avant un mauvais coup*).

3 **comp ▸ caseharden** (*Metal*) cémenter; (*fig*) endurcir **▸ case knife** (*US*) couteau *m* à gaine.

casement ['keɪsmənt] **n** (*window*) fenêtre *f* (à battants), croisée *f*; (*frame*) battant *m* de fenêtre; (*liter*) fenêtre *f*.

cash [kæʃ] 1 **n** (*NonC*) a (*notes and coins*) espèces *fpl*, argent *m*. **how much ~ is there in the till?** combien d'argent y a-t-il dans la caisse?; **I want to be paid in ~ and not by cheque** je veux être payé en espèces et non pas par chèque; **to pay in ~** payer en argent comptant *or* en espèces; **to take the ~ to the bank** porter l'argent à la banque; **ready ~** (argent *m*) liquide *m*; **how much do you have in (ready) ~?** combien avez-vous en liquide?; *see* **hard, petty, spot.**

b (*immediate payment*) **~ down** argent comptant; **to pay ~ (down)** payer comptant *or* cash*; **discount for ~** escompte *m or* remise *f* au comptant; **~ with order** payable à la commande; **~ on delivery** paiement *m* à la livraison, livraison contre espèces *or* contre remboursement; **~ on shipment** comptant *m* à l'expédition.

c (**: money in general*) argent *m*, sous* *mpl*. **how much ~ have you got?** combien d'argent as-tu?, qu'est-ce que tu as comme argent *or* comme sous?*; **I have no ~** je n'ai pas un sou *or* un rond*; **to be short of ~** être à court (d'argent); **I am out of ~** je suis à sec*, je suis sans le rond*.

2 **comp** (*gen*) *problems, calculations etc* d'argent **▸ cash account** compte *m* de caisse **▸ cash advance** (*Fin*) crédit *m* de caisse **▸ cash-and-carry n** libre-service *m* de gros, cash and carry *m inv* ◊ **adj** *goods, business* de gros, de cash and carry **▸ cash bar** (*US*) bar payant (*à une réception*) **▸ cashbook** livre *m* de caisse **▸ cashbox** caisse *f* **▸ cash card** carte *f* de crédit (*utilisable dans les distributeurs automatiques*), carte *f* de retrait bancaire **▸ cash cow*** (*Comm*) mine *f* d'or **▸ cash crop** culture *f* de rapport *or* commerciale **▸ cash dealings** transactions immédiates **▸ cash deficit** déficit *m or* découvert *m* de trésorerie **▸ cashdesk** [*shop, restaurant*] caisse *f*; [*cinema, theatre*] guichet *m* **▸ cash discount** escompte *m or* remise *f* au comptant **▸ cash dispenser** (*Brit*) distributeur *m* automatique de billets **▸ cash economy** économie *f* monétaire **▸ cash flow** marge brute d'autofinancement, cash-flow *m*; **cash flow problems** difficultés *fpl* de trésorerie **▸ cash holdings** avoirs *mpl* en caisse *or* en numéraire **▸ cash income** revenu *m* monétaire **▸ cash in hand** espèces *fpl* en caisse, encaisse *f* **▸ cash machine** (*US*) = **cash dispenser ▸ cash offer** offre *f* d'achat avec paiement comptant; **he made me a cash offer** il m'a proposé de payer comptant **▸ cash payment** paiement *m* comptant, versement *m* en espèces **▸ cash point** (*in shop*) caisse *f*; (*cash dispenser*) distributeur *m* automatique de billets **▸ cash price** prix *m* (au) comptant **▸ cash prize** prix *m* en espèces **▸ cash receipts** recettes *fpl* de caisse **▸ cash reduction** = **cash discount ▸ cash register** caisse *f* (enregistreuse) **▸ cash sale** vente *f* (au) comptant **▸ cash reserves** réserves *fpl* de caisse **▸ cash squeeze** (*Econ*) restrictions *fpl* de crédit **▸ cash terms** conditions *fpl* au comptant **▸ cash transaction** affaire *f or* opération *f* au comptant.

3 **vt** *cheque* encaisser, toucher; *banknote* changer, faire la monnaie de. **to ~ sb a cheque** donner à qn de l'argent contre un chèque; [*bank*] payer un chèque à qn; **to ~ a bill** encaisser une facture.

▸cash in vt sep *bonds, savings certificates* réaliser, se faire rembourser.

▸cash in on* vt fus tirer profit de.

▸cash up vi (*Brit*) faire sa caisse.

cashew [kæ'ʃuː] **n** anacardier *m*; (*also* **~ nut**) noix *f* de cajou.

cashier¹ [kæ'ʃɪəʳ] **n** (*Comm, Banking*) caissier *m*, -ière *f*.

cashier² [kæ'ʃɪəʳ] **vt** (*Mil*) casser; (*gen*) renvoyer, congédier.

cashless ['kæʃlɪs] **adj: the ~ society** la société sans argent (*où l'on ne paie plus qu'en argent électronique*).

cashmere [kæʃ'mɪəʳ] 1 **n** (*Tex*) cachemire *m*. 2 **comp** de *or* en cachemire.

casing ['keɪsɪŋ] **n** (*gen*) revêtement *m*, enveloppe *f*; [*door, window*] chambranle *m*; [*tyre*] enveloppe extérieure; [*oil well*] cuvelage *m*.

casino [kə'siːnəʊ] **n** casino *m*.

cask [kɑːsk] **n** (*gen*) tonneau *m*, fût *m*; (*large*) pièce *f*, barrique *f*; (*small*) baril *m*. **wine in ~** vin *m* en fût.

casket ['kɑːskɪt] **n** [*jewels etc*] coffret *m*, boîte *f*; (*esp US: coffin*) cercueil *m*.

Caspian ['kæspɪən] **adj: the ~ Sea** la mer Caspienne.

Cassandra [kə'sændrə] **n** (*Myth*) Cassandre *f*; (*fig*) oiseau *m* de malheur.

cassava [kə'sɑːvə] **n** (*Bot*) manioc *m*; (*Culin*) farine *f* de manioc.

casserole ['kæsərəʊl] 1 **n** (*Brit Culin: utensil*) cocotte *f*; (*food*) ragoût *m* en cocotte. 2 **vt** *meat* (faire) cuire en *or* à la cocotte.

cassette [kæ'set] 1 **n** (*Sound Recording*) cassette *f*; (*Phot*) recharge *f*. 2 **comp ▸ cassette deck** platine *f* à cassettes **▸ cassette player** lecteur *m* de cassettes **▸ cassette recorder** magnétophone *m* à cassettes.

cassis [kæ'siːs] **n** cassis *m*.

cassock ['kæsək] **n** soutane *f*.

cassowary ['kæsəwεərɪ] **n** casoar *m*.

cast [kɑːst] (**vb: pret, ptp cast**) 1 **n** a (*throw*) [*dice, net*] coup *m*; (*Fishing*) lancer *m*.

b (*Art, Tech*) (*act of ~ing metal*) coulage *m*, coulée *f*.

c (*mould*) moule *m*; (*in plaster, metal etc*) moulage *m*; [*medallion etc*] empreinte *f*. (*Med*) **to have one's leg in a ~** avoir une jambe dans le plâtre; (*fig*) **~ of features** traits *mpl* (du visage); **~ of mind** mentalité *f*, tournure *f* d'esprit; **a man of quite a different ~** un homme d'un tout autre genre; *see* **plaster** *etc.*

d (*Theat*) (*actors*) acteurs *mpl*; (*list on programme etc*) distribution *f*. (*Cine, TV*) **~ (and credits)** générique *m*; (*Theat etc*) **~ list** distribution; **he was in the ~ of Evita** il a joué dans Evita.

e [*snake*] dépouille *f*; [*worm*] déjections *fpl*.

f (*Med: squint*) strabisme *m*. **to have a ~ in one eye** avoir un œil qui louche, loucher d'un œil.

2 **comp ▸ castaway** naufragé(e) *m(f)*; (*fig: from society etc*) réprouvé(e) *m(f)* **▸ cast-iron n** fonte *f* ◊ **adj** de *or* en fonte; (*fig*) *will, constitution* de fer; *excuse, alibi* inattaquable, irréfutable; *case* solide **▸ cast-off clothes, cast-offs** vêtements *mpl* dont on ne veut plus, (*pej*) vieilles nippes* *or* frusques*; (*fig*) **the cast-offs from society** les laissés *mpl* pour compte (de la société).

3 **vt** a (*throw*) *dice* jeter; *net, fishing line, stone* lancer, jeter. (*Naut*) **to ~ anchor** jeter l'ancre, mouiller (l'ancre); **to ~ into jail** jeter en prison; **to ~ sb's horoscope** tirer l'horoscope de qn; (*liter*) **to ~ o.s. on sb's mercy** s'en remettre à la clémence de qn (*liter*), remettre son sort entre les mains de qn; **to ~ a vote** voter; **to ~ aspersions on sth/sb** dénigrer qch/qn; **to ~ the blame on sb** rejeter le blâme sur qn; **to ~ doubt on** émettre des doutes sur; **to ~ a look at** jeter un regard sur; **to ~ a shadow on** (*lit*) projeter une ombre sur; (*fig*) jeter une ombre sur; **to ~ one's eye(s) round a room** promener ses regards *or* ses yeux sur une pièce, balayer une pièce du regard; **to ~ one's eye(s) in the direction of** porter ses regards du côté de; *see* **die², light, lot, spell¹** *etc.*

b (*shed*) se dépouiller de, se débarrasser de, perdre. *[snake]* **to ~ its skin** muer; *[horse]* **to ~ a shoe** perdre un fer; *[animal]* **to ~ its young** mettre bas (un petit) avant terme.

c (*Art, Tech*) *plaster* couler; *metal* couler, fondre; *statue* mouler; *see* **mould**[1].

d (*Theat*) *play* distribuer les rôles de. **he was ~ as Hamlet** *or* **for the part of Hamlet** on lui a donné le rôle de Hamlet.

►**cast about, cast around** **vi: to cast about for sth** chercher qch; **to cast about for how to do/how to reply** chercher le moyen de faire/la façon de répondre.

►**cast aside** **vt sep** rejeter, mettre de côté; (*fig*) rejeter, abandonner, se défaire de.

►**cast away** 1 **vt sep** rejeter; (*fig*) se défaire de. (*Naut*) **to be cast away** être naufragé. 2 **castaway** **n** *see* **cast 2**.

►**cast back** 1 **vi** (*fig, liter*) revenir (*to* à). 2 **vt sep: to cast one's thoughts back** se reporter en arrière.

►**cast down** **vt sep** *object* jeter par terre, jeter vers le bas; *eyes* baisser; *weapons* déposer, mettre bas. (*fig, liter*) **to be cast down** être abattu *or* découragé *or* démoralisé.

►**cast in** **vi, vt sep: to cast in (one's lot) with sb** partager le sort de qn.

►**cast off** 1 **vi** (*Naut*) larguer les amarres, appareiller; (*Knitting*) arrêter (les mailles). 2 **vt sep** (*Naut*) larguer *or* lâcher les amarres de; (*Knitting*) arrêter; *bonds, chains* (*lit*) se défaire de, se libérer de; (*fig*) s'affranchir de. 3 **cast-off** **n, adj** *see* **cast 2**.

►**cast on** (*Knitting*) 1 **vi** monter les mailles. 2 **vt sep** *stitch, sleeve* monter.

►**cast out** **vt sep** (*liter*) renvoyer, chasser, expulser.

►**cast up** **vt sep** a (*lit*) lancer en l'air. (*fig*) **to cast one's eyes up** lever les yeux au ciel. b (*Math*) calculer. c (*fig: reproach*) **to cast sth up to** *or* **at sb** reprocher qch à qn.

castanets [ˌkæstəˈnets] **npl** castagnettes *fpl*.

caste [kɑːst] 1 **n** caste *f*, classe sociale. **to lose ~** déroger, déchoir. 2 **comp** ►**caste mark** (*in India*) signe *m* de (la) caste; (*fig*) signe distinctif (d'un groupe) ►**caste system** système *m* de caste(s).

castellated [ˈkæstəleɪtɪd] **adj** (*Archit*) crénelé, de style féodal. (*Tech*) **~ nut** écrou crénelé.

caster [ˈkɑːstəʳ] **n** a (*sifter*) saupoudroir *m*. (*Brit*) **~ sugar** sucre *m* en poudre. b (*wheel*) roulette *f*. (*Aut*) **~ angle** angle *m* de chasse.

castigate [ˈkæstɪgeɪt] **vt** *person* châtier (*liter*), corriger, punir; *book etc* critiquer sévèrement; *theory, vice* fustiger (*liter*).

castigation [ˌkæstɪˈgeɪʃən] **n** *[person]* châtiment *m*, correction *f*, punition *f*; *[book]* critique *f* sévère.

Castile [kæˈstiːl] **n** Castille *f*.

Castilian [kæsˈtɪlɪən] 1 **adj** castillan. 2 **n** a Castillan(e) *m(f)*. b (*Ling*) espagnol *m*, castillan *m*.

casting [ˈkɑːstɪŋ] 1 **n** (*NonC: act of throwing*) jet *m*, lancer *m*, lancement *m*; (*Tech*) (*act*) fonte *f*, coulée *f*; (*object*) pièce fondue; (*Art*) moulage *m*; (*Theat*) distribution *f*; (*Cine*) casting. 2 **comp** ►**casting couch: she got the role on the casting couch** elle a dû coucher avec le directeur pour avoir ce rôle ►**casting director** (*Theat*) directeur *m* de la distribution; (*Cine*) directeur *m* du casting ►**casting vote** voix prépondérante; **to have a** *or* **the casting vote** avoir voix prépondérante.

castle [ˈkɑːsl] 1 **n** a château *m* (fort). (*fig*) **~s in the air** châteaux en Espagne. b (*Chess*) tour *f*. 2 **vi** (*Chess*) roquer.

castling [ˈkɑːslɪŋ] **n** (*Chess*) roque *f*.

castor[1] [ˈkɑːstəʳ] **n = caster.**

castor[2] [ˈkɑːstəʳ] **n** a (*beaver*) castor *m*. b (*Med*) castoréum *m*. **~ oil** huile *f* de ricin; **~ oil plant** ricin *m*.

castrate [kæsˈtreɪt] **vt** *animal, man* châtrer, castrer, émasculer; (*fig*) *personality* émasculer; *text, film, book* expurger.

castration [kæsˈtreɪʃən] **n** castration *f*.

castrato [kæsˈtrɑːtəʊ] **n, pl ~** *or* **castrati** [kæsˈtrɑːtɪ] castrat *m*.

Castroism [ˈkæstrəʊɪzəm] **n** (*Pol*) castrisme *m*.

Castroist [ˈkæstrəʊɪst] **adj,n** (*Pol*) castriste *(mf)*.

casual [ˈkæʒjʊl] 1 **adj** a (*happening by chance*) *error etc* fortuit, fait par hasard; *fall, spark* accidentel; *meeting* de hasard; *walk, stroll* sans but précis; *caller* venu par hasard; *remark* fait au hasard *or* en passant. **a ~ acquaintance (of mine)** quelqu'un que je connais un peu; **~ glance** coup *m* d'œil (jeté) au hasard; **a ~ (love) affair** une passade, une aventure; **to have ~ sex** faire l'amour au hasard d'une rencontre; **I don't approve of ~ sex** je n'approuve pas les rapports sexuels de rencontre.

b (*informal*) *person, manners* sans-gêne *inv*, désinvolte; *tone, voice* désinvolte; *clothes* sport *inv*. **he tried to sound ~** il a essayé de parler avec désinvolture; **he was very ~ about it** il ne semblait pas y attacher beaucoup d'importance; **she was very ~ about the whole business** elle a pris tout ça avec beaucoup de désinvolture.

c *work* intermittent; *worker* temporaire. **~ conversation** conversation *f* à bâtons rompus; **~ labourer** (*on building sites*) ouvrier *m* sans travail fixe; (*on a farm*) journalier *m*, -ière *f*.

2 **n** a **~s** (*shoes*) chaussures *fpl* de sport; (*clothes*) vêtements *mpl* sport *inv*.

b (*worker*) (*in office*) employé(e) *m(f)* temporaire; (*in factory*) ouvrier *m*, -ière *f* temporaire.

c (*Brit: type of football hooligan*) hooligan *m* (*portant des vêtements chics et chers*).

casually [ˈkæʒjʊlɪ] **adv** (*by chance*) par hasard, fortuitement; (*informally, carelessly*) avec sans-gêne, avec désinvolture. **he said it (quite) ~** il l'a dit sans insister *or* en passant.

casualty [ˈkæʒjʊltɪ] 1 **n** a (*Mil*) (*dead*) mort(e) *m(f)*; (*wounded*) blessé(e) *m(f)*. **casualties** les morts *mpl* et blessés *mpl*; (*dead*) les pertes *fpl*. b (*accident victim*) accidenté(e) *m(f)*, victime *f*; (*accident*) accident *m*. 2 **comp** ►**casualty department** service *m* des urgences ►**casualty list** (*Mil*) état *m* des pertes; (*Aviat, gen*) liste *f* des victimes ►**casualty ward** salle *f* de traumatologie *or* des accidentés.

casuist [ˈkæzjʊɪst] **n** casuiste *mf*.

casuistry [ˈkæzjʊɪstrɪ] **n** (*NonC*) casuistique *f*; (*instance of this*) arguments *mpl* de casuiste.

CAT [ˈsiːˈeɪˈtiː] **n** (**abbr of computer-aided teaching**) EAO *m*.

cat [kæt] 1 **n** a chat(te) *m(f)*; (*species*) félin *m*; (* *pej: woman*) rosse* *f*. (*Zool*) **the big ~s** les fauves *mpl*; *see* **tabby, tom.**

b = **cat-o'nine-tails;** *see* **2.**

c (*phrases*) **to let the ~ out of the bag** vendre la mèche; **the ~'s out of the bag** ce n'est plus un secret maintenant; **to wait for the ~ to jump, to wait to see which way the ~ jumps** attendre pour voir la tournure prise par les événements *or* voir d'où vient le vent; **has the ~ got your tongue?** tu as perdu ta langue?; **to fight like ~ and dog** (*lit*) se battre comme des chiffonniers; (*fig*) être *or* s'entendre *or* vivre comme chien et chat; **to lead a ~ and dog life** être *or* s'entendre *or* vivre comme chien et chat; (*Prov*) **a ~ may look at a king** un chien regarde bien un évêque; **to be** *or* **jump around like a ~ on hot bricks** être sur des charbons ardents; (*Prov*) **when the ~'s away the mice will play** quand le chat n'est pas là les souris dansent; **that set the ~ among the pigeons** ça a été le pavé dans la mare; **he thinks he's the ~'s whiskers*** il se prend pour le nombril du monde* (*see also* **2**); (*pej*) **look what the ~ dragged in** *or* **brought in** regarde donc un peu qui pointe son nez; (*pej*) **you look like something the ~ dragged in** *or* **brought in** non mais regarde à quoi tu ressembles!; *see* **bell**[1]**, grin, rain, room, skin 3a.**

d (*US*) (*man*) mec‡ *m*; (*woman*) gonzesse‡ *f*.

e **~s and dogs** (*St Ex*) actions *fpl* et obligations *fpl* de valeur douteuse; (*Comm*) articles *mpl* peu demandés.

f (*: *catalytic converter*) pot *m* catalytique.

2 **comp** ►**cat-and-mouse:** (*fig*) **to play (at) cat-and-mouse with sb, to play a cat-and-mouse game with sb** jouer au chat et à la souris avec qn ►**cat-basket** (*for carrying*) panier *m* pour chat; (*for sleeping*) corbeille *f* de chat ►**catbird:** (*US*) **to be in the catbird seat*** trôner en sécurité ►**cat burglar** monte-en-l'air* *m inv* ►**catcall** (*Theat*) **n** sifflet *m* ◊ **vi** siffler ►**cat door** porte *f* va-et-vient (*pour animal familier*) ►**catfish** poisson-chat *m* ►**cat flap** = **cat door** ►**catfood** nourriture *f* pour chats ►**catgut** (*Mus, Sport*) boyau *m* (de chat); (*Med*) catgut *m* ►**cathouse‡** (*US*) bordel‡ *m* ►**cat-lick*** toilette *f* de chat, brin *m* de toilette; **to give o.s. a cat-lick** faire une toilette de chat *or* un brin de toilette ►**catlike** **adj** félin ◊ **adv** comme un chat ►**cat litter** litière *f* (pour chats) ►**catmint** herbe *f* aux chats ►**catnap** **vi** sommeiller, faire un (petit) somme ◊ **n** (petit) somme *m*; **to take a catnap** sommeiller, faire un (petit) somme ►**catnip** (*US*) = **catmint** ►**cat-o'nine-tails** **pl inv** martinet *m*, chat-à-neuf-queues *m* ►**cat's-cradle** (jeu *m* des) figures *fpl* (*que l'on forme entre ses doigts avec de la ficelle*) ►**cat's-eye** (*gemstone*) œil-de-chat *m*; (*Brit Aut*) clou *m* à catadioptre, catadioptre *m*, cataphote *m* ►**cat's-paw** dupe *f* (*qui tire les marrons du feu*) ►**catsuit** combinaison-pantalon *f* ►**cat's-whisker** (*Rad*) chercheur *m* (de détecteur à galène) ►**catwalk** (*Constr, Theat*) passerelle *f* (*gén courant le long d'une construction*).

cataclysm [ˈkætəklɪzəm] **n** cataclysme *m*.

cataclysmic [ˌkætəˈklɪzmɪk] **adj** cataclysmique.

catacombs [ˈkætəkuːmz] **npl** catacombes *fpl*.

catafalque [ˈkætəfælk] **n** catafalque *m*.

Catalan [ˈkætəˌlæn] 1 **n** Catalan(e) *m(f)*; (*Ling*) catalan *m*. 2 **adj** catalan.

catalepsy [ˈkætəlepsɪ] **n** catalepsie *f*.

cataleptic [ˌkætəˈleptɪk] **adj** cataleptique.

catalogue, (*US*) **catalog** [ˈkætəlɒg] 1 **n** (*gen*) catalogue *m*; (*in library*) fichier *m*; (*US Univ etc: brochure*) brochure *f* (*d'un établissement d'enseignement supérieur*). 2 **vt** cataloguer.

Catalonia [ˌkætəˈləʊnɪə] **n** Catalogne *f*.

catalysis [kəˈtæləsɪs] **n, pl catalyses** [kəˈtæləˌsiːz] catalyse *f*.

catalyst [ˈkætəlɪst] **n** catalyseur *m*.

catalytic [ˌkætəˈlɪtɪk] **adj** catalytique. (*Aut*) **~ converter** pot *m* catalytique.

catamaran [ˌkætəməˈræn] **n** catamaran *m*.

cataphoric [ˌkætəˈfɒrɪk] **adj** (*Ling*) cataphorique.

catapult [ˈkætəpʌlt] 1 **n** (*slingshot*) lance-pierre(s) *m inv*; (*Aviat, Mil*) catapulte *f*. (*Aviat*) **~-launched** catapulté; (*Aviat*) **~ launching** catapultage *m*. 2 **vt** (*gen, Aviat, fig*) catapulter.

cataract [ˈkætərækt] **n** a (*waterfall*) cataracte *f*. **~ of words** déluge *m* de paroles. b (*Med*) cataracte *f*.

catarrh [kə'tɑːʳ] n rhume *m* (chronique), catarrhe *m*.
catarrhal [kə'tɑːrəl] adj catarrheux.
catastrophe [kə'tæstrəfɪ] n catastrophe *f*.
catastrophic [ˌkætə'strɒfɪk] adj catastrophique (*lit, fig* *).
catatonic [ˌkætə'tɒnɪk] adj catatonique.
catch [kætʃ] (vb: pret, ptp **caught**) 1 n a (*act, thing caught*) prise *f*, capture *f*; (*person caught*) capture; (*Fishing*) pêche *f*, prise. (*Sport*) **good ~!** bien rattrapé!; **the fisherman lost his whole ~** le pêcheur a perdu toute sa pêche *or* prise; (*as husband*) **he's a good ~*** c'est un beau parti.
b (*concealed drawback*) attrape *f*, entourloupette* *f*. **there must be a ~ in it somewhere** il doit y avoir une entourloupette* *or* attrape là-dessous; **where's the ~?** qu'est-ce qui se cache là-dessous?
c *[buckle]* ardillon *m*; (*Brit: on door*) loquet *m*; *[latch]* mentonnet *m*; *[wheel]* cliquet *m*; (*Brit: on window*) loqueteau *m*.
d (*fig*) **with a ~ in one's voice** d'une voix entrecoupée.
e (*Mus*) canon *m*.
f (*game*) jeu *m* de balle.
2 comp ▸ **catch 22***: **it's a catch 22 situation** il n'y a pas moyen de s'en sortir, de toute façon on perd ▸ **catch-all** n fourre-tout *m inv* (*fig*) ◊ adj *regulation, clause etc* général, fourre-tout *inv*; **catch-all phrase** expression *f* passe-partout *inv* ▸ **catch-as-catch-can** catch *m* ▸ **catch phrase** (*constantly repeated*) rengaine *f*, scie *f*; (*vivid, striking phrase*) slogan accrocheur ▸ **catch question** colle* *f* ▸ **catchup** (*US*) = **ketchup** ▸ **catchword** (*slogan*) slogan *m*; (*Pol*) mot *m* d'ordre, slogan; (*Printing*) *[foot of page]* réclame *f*; *[top of page]* mot-vedette *m*; (*Theat: cue*) réplique *f*.
3 vt a *ball* attraper; *object* attraper, saisir, prendre; *fish, mice, thief* prendre, attraper. **to ~ sb by the arm** prendre *or* saisir qn par le bras; **you can usually ~ me (in) around noon*** en général on peut m'avoir* *or* me trouver vers midi; (*Rowing*) **to ~ a crab** plonger la rame trop profond; *see* **sun 2**.
b (*take by surprise*) surprendre, prendre, attraper. **to ~ sb doing sth** surprendre qn à faire qch; **she caught herself dreaming of Spain** elle se surprit à rêver de l'Espagne; **if I ~ them at it!*** si je les y prends!; **if I ~ you at it again!*** que je t'y reprenne!; **(you won't) ~ me doing that again!*** (il n'y a) pas de danger que je recommence! (*subj*), c'est bien la dernière fois que je le fais!; **to catch sb in the act** prendre qn sur le fait *or* en flagrant délit; (*US*) **to ~ sb dead to rights** prendre qn sur le fait *or* en flagrant délit; **we were caught in a storm** nous avons été pris dans *or* surpris par un orage; **to get caught by sb** se faire *or* se laisser attraper par qn.
c (*be in time for*) prendre, ne pas manquer. **I've got to ~ the train** il ne faut pas que je manque (*subj*) le train; **he didn't ~ his train** il a manqué son train; **to ~ the post** arriver à temps pour la levée.
d (*manage to see/hear etc*) *film, radio programme etc* réussir à voir/à entendre *etc*.
e (*become entangled etc*) **the branch caught my skirt, I caught my skirt on the branch** ma jupe s'est accrochée à la branche; **the door caught my skirt, I caught my skirt on the door** ma jupe s'est prise dans la porte; **the top of the lorry caught the bridge** le haut du camion a accroché le pont; **to ~ one's foot in** se prendre le pied dans.
f (*understand, hear*) saisir, comprendre. **to ~ the meaning of** saisir le sens de; **I didn't ~ what he said** je n'ai pas saisi *or* compris ce qu'il a dit.
g *flavour* sentir, discerner; *tune* attraper. **to ~ the sound of sth** percevoir le bruit de qch.
h (*Med*) *disease* attraper. **to ~ a cold** attraper un rhume; **to ~ cold** attraper *or* prendre froid; **to ~ one's death of cold*, to ~ one's death**‡ attraper la crève‡, prendre la mort*.
i (*phrases*) **to ~ sb's attention** attirer l'attention de qn; **to ~ sb's eye** attirer l'attention de qn; **to ~ the chairman's eye**, (*Brit Parl*) **to ~ the Speaker's eye** obtenir *or* se faire accorder *or* se faire donner la parole; **to ~ sb a blow** donner un coup à qn; **she caught him one on the nose*** elle lui a flanqué* un (bon) coup sur le nez; **to ~ one's breath** retenir son souffle (un instant); **to ~ fire** prendre feu; **her dress caught fire** le feu a pris à sa robe, sa robe s'est enflammée *or* a pris feu; (*Art, Phot*) **to ~ a likeness** saisir une ressemblance; **to ~ sight of sb/sth** apercevoir qn/qch; **you'll ~ it!*** tu vas écoper!*, tu vas prendre quelque chose!*; **he caught it all right!*** qu'est-ce qu'il a pris!*; **to ~ sb on the wrong foot, to ~ sb off balance** (*lit*) prendre qn à contre-pied; (*fig*) prendre qn au dépourvu; **to ~ sb napping** *or* **bending** prendre qn en défaut.
4 vi a *[fire, wood, ice]* prendre; (*Culin*) attacher.
b *[lock]* fermer; *[key]* mordre.
c **her dress caught in the door/on a nail** sa robe s'est prise dans la porte/s'est accrochée à un clou.
▸**catch at** vt fus *object* (essayer d')attraper. **to catch at an opportunity** sauter sur une occasion.
▸**catch on** vi a (*become popular*) *[fashion]* prendre; *[song]* devenir populaire, marcher. b (*understand*) saisir, comprendre, piger‡ (*to sth* qch).
▸**catch out** vt sep (*esp Brit*) (*catch napping*) prendre en défaut; (*catch in the act*) prendre sur le fait. **to catch sb out in a lie** surprendre qn en train de mentir, prendre qn à mentir; **to be caught out (by sth)** être pris par surprise (par qch); **he'll get caught out some day** un beau jour il se fera prendre.
▸**catch up** 1 vi a se rattraper, combler son retard; (*with studies*) se rattraper, se remettre au niveau; (*with news, gossip*) se remettre au courant. **to catch up on** *or* **with one's work** se (re)mettre à jour dans son travail; **to catch up on one's sleep** rattraper *or* combler son retard de sommeil; **to catch up on** *or* **with sb** (*going in the same direction*) rattraper qn, rejoindre qn; (*in work etc*) rattraper qn; **the police caught up with him in Vienna** la police l'a attrapé à Vienne; **the truth/illness has finally caught up with him** la vérité/maladie a fini par le rattraper.
b **to be** *or* **get caught up in sth** (*in net etc*) être pris dans qch; (*fig*) (*in activity, campaign etc*) être pris dans *or* mêlé à qch; (*in sb's enthusiasm etc*) être gagné par qch; (*in sb's ideas etc*) être emballé par qch; (*in circumstances etc*) être prisonnier de qch.
2 vt sep a *person* rattraper.
b (*interrupt*) *person* interrompre, couper la parole à.
c (*pick up quickly*) ramasser vivement.
d *hair* relever; *curtain* retenir.
catcher ['kætʃəʳ] n a (*Baseball*) attrapeur *m*. **~'s mitt** gant *m* de baseball. b *see* **mole¹, rat** *etc*.
catching ['kætʃɪŋ] adj (*Med*) contagieux; (* *fig*) *laughter, enthusiasm* contagieux, communicatif; *habit, mannerism* contagieux.
catchment ['kætʃmənt] n captage *m*. **~ area** (*Geog: also* **~ basin**) bassin *m* hydrographique; *[hospital]* circonscription hospitalière; *[school]* secteur *m* de recrutement scolaire.
catchpenny ['kætʃˌpenɪ] (*pej*) 1 adj clinquant, accrocheur. 2 n: **it's a ~** c'est de la pacotille.
catchy ['kætʃɪ] adj *tune* facile à retenir, entraînant.
catechism ['kætɪkɪzəm] n catéchisme *m*.
catechist ['kætɪkɪst] n catéchiste *mf*.
catechize ['kætɪkaɪz] vt (*Rel*) catéchiser; (*fig*) (*teach*) instruire (*par questions et réponses*); (*examine*) interroger, questionner.
categoric(al) [ˌkætɪ'gɒrɪk(əl)] adj catégorique.
categorically [ˌkætɪ'gɒrɪkəlɪ] adv catégoriquement.
categorization [ˌkætɪgəraɪ'zeɪʃən] n catégorisation *f*.
categorize ['kætɪgəraɪz] vt classer par catégories.
category ['kætɪgərɪ] n catégorie *f*.
cater ['keɪtəʳ] vi (*provide food*) s'occuper de la nourriture, préparer un *or* des repas (*for* pour). (*fig*) **to ~ for** *sb's needs* pourvoir à; *sb's tastes* satisfaire; **this magazine ~s for all ages** ce magazine s'adresse à tous les âges; (*expect*) **I didn't ~ for that*** je n'avais pas prévu cela.
cater-cornered ['keɪtə'kɔːnəd] adj (*US*) diagonal.
caterer ['keɪtərəʳ] n (*providing meals*) traiteur *m*; (*providing supplies*) fournisseur *m* (*en alimentation*).
catering ['keɪtərɪŋ] 1 n (*providing meals*) restauration *f*; (*providing supplies*) approvisionnement *m*, ravitaillement *m*. **the ~ for our reception was done by X** le buffet de notre réception a été confié à X *or* aux soins de X, le traiteur pour notre réception était X. 2 comp ▸ **catering industry** industrie *f* de la restauration ▸ **catering manager** intendant(e) *m(f)* ▸ **catering trade** restauration *f*.
caterpillar ['kætəpɪləʳ] 1 n (*Tech, Zool*) chenille *f*. 2 comp *vehicle, wheel* à chenilles ▸ **Caterpillar track** ® (*Tech*) chenille *f* ▸ **Caterpillar tractor** ® autochenille *f*.
caterwaul ['kætəwɔːl] 1 vi *[cat]* miauler; (*) *[person]* brailler, pousser des braillements. 2 n *[cat]* miaulement *m*.
caterwauling ['kætəwɔːlɪŋ] n *[cat]* miaulement *m*; *[music]* cacophonie *f*; *[person]* braillements *mpl*, hurlements *mpl*.
Cath a abbr of **Cathedral**. b abbr of **Catholic**.
Cathar ['kæθəʳ] 1 n, pl **~s** *or* **Cathari** ['kæθərɪ] Cathare *mf*. 2 adj cathare.
catharsis [kə'θɑːsɪs] n, pl **catharses** [kə'θɑːsiːz] (*Literat, Psych*) catharsis *f*.
cathartic [kə'θɑːtɪk] 1 adj (*Literat, Med, Psych*) cathartique. 2 n (*Med*) purgatif *m*, cathartique *m*.
Cathay [kæ'θeɪ] n Cathay *m*.
cathedral [kə'θiːdrəl] 1 n cathédrale *f*. 2 comp ▸ **cathedral church** cathédrale *f* ▸ **cathedral city** évêché *m*, ville épiscopale.
Catherine ['kæθərɪn] n Catherine *f*. (*Hist*) **~ the Great** la Grande Catherine, Catherine la Grande; (*firework*) **~ wheel** soleil *m*.
catheter ['kæθɪtəʳ] n cathéter *m*; (*for extracting fluid*) sonde creuse.
catheterize ['kæθɪtəˌraɪz] vt *bladder, person* sonder.
cathiodermie [ˌkæθɪəʊ'dɜːmɪ] n ionophorèse *f*.
cathode ['kæθəʊd] 1 n cathode *f*. 2 comp *ray* cathodique ▸ **cathode ray tube** tube *m* cathodique.
catholic ['kæθəlɪk] 1 adj a (*Rel*) **C~** catholique; **the C~ Church** l'Église *f* catholique; **C~ school** école *f* catholique. b (*varied, all-embracing*) *taste(s), person* éclectique; (*universal*) universel; (*broad-minded*) *views, person* libéral. **to be ~ in one's tastes** avoir des goûts éclectiques; **to be ~ in one's views** avoir des opinions libérales. 2 n: **C~** catholique *mf*.
Catholicism [kə'θɒlɪsɪzəm] n catholicisme *m*.
cation ['kætaɪən] n (*Chem*) cation *m*.
catkin ['kætkɪn] n (*Bot*) chaton *m*.

Cato ['keɪtəʊ] n Caton *m*.
catsup ['kætsəp] n (*US*) = **ketchup**.
cattery ['kætərɪ] n pension *f* pour chats.
cattiness* ['kætɪnɪs] n méchanceté *f*, rosserie* *f*.
cattle ['kætl] 1 collective n bovins *mpl*, bétail *m*, bestiaux *mpl*. **the prisoners were herded like ~** les prisonniers étaient parqués comme du bétail; **"~ crossing"** "passage *m* de troupeaux"; *see* **head**.
2 comp ▸ **cattle breeder** éleveur *m* (de bestiaux) ▸ **cattle breeding** élevage *m* (du bétail) ▸ **cattle drive** (*US*) rassemblement *m* de bétail ▸ **cattle grid** (*Brit*) *grille à même la route permettant aux voitures mais non au bétail de passer* ▸ **cattleman** vacher *m*, bouvier *m* ▸ **cattle market** (*lit, fig*) foire *f or* marché *m* aux bestiaux ▸ **cattle plague** peste bovine ▸ **cattle raising** = **cattle breeding** ▸ **cattle shed** étable *f* ▸ **cattle show** concours *m* agricole (où l'on présente du bétail) ▸ **cattle truck** (*Aut*) fourgon *m* à bestiaux; (*Brit Rail*) fourgon *or* wagon *m* à bestiaux.
catty* ['kætɪ] adj (*pej*) *person, gossip, criticism* méchant, rosse*, vache*. ~ **remark** rosserie* *f*, vacherie* *f*; **to be ~ about sb/sth** dire des rosseries* *or* vacheries* de qn/qch.
Catullus [kə'tʌləs] n Catulle *m*.
CATV (abbr of **community antenna television**) *see* **community 2**.
Caucasia [kɔː'keɪzɪə] n Caucase *m* (*région*).
Caucasian [kɔː'keɪzɪən] 1 adj (*Geog*) caucasien; (*Ethnology*) de race blanche *or* caucasique. 2 n (*Geog*) Caucasien(ne) *m(f)*; (*Ethnology*) Blanc *m*, Blanche *f*.
caucasoid ['kɔːkəsɔɪd] 1 adj de race blanche *or* caucasique. 2 n Blanc *m*, Blanche *f*.
Caucasus ['kɔːkəsəs] n Caucase *m* (*montagnes*).
caucus ['kɔːkəs] n, pl **~es** (*US*) (*committee*) comité électoral; (*meeting*) réunion *f* du comité électoral; (*Brit pej*) coterie *f* politique.
caudal ['kɔːdl] adj caudal.
caught [kɔːt] pret, ptp of **catch**.
caul [kɔːl] n (*Anat*) coiffe *f*.
cauldron ['kɔːldrən] n chaudron *m*.
cauliflower ['kɒlɪflaʊə^r] 1 n chou-fleur *m*. 2 comp ▸ **cauliflower cheese** (*Culin*) chou-fleur *m* au gratin ▸ **cauliflower ear** (*fig*) oreille *f* en chou-fleur *or* en feuille de chou.
caulk [kɔːk] vt (*Naut*) calfater.
causal ['kɔːzəl] adj causal; (*Gram*) causal, causatif.
causality [kɔː'zælɪtɪ] n causalité *f*.
causation [kɔː'zeɪʃən] n (*causing*) causalité *f*; (*cause-effect relation*) relation *f* de cause à effet.
causative ['kɔːzətɪv] 1 adj causal; (*Gram*) causal, causatif. (*frm*) **~ of** (qui est) cause de. 2 n (*Gram*) mot causal *or* causatif.
cause [kɔːz] 1 n a (*gen, also Philos*) cause *f*; (*reason*) cause, raison *f*, motif *m*. **~ and effect** la cause et l'effet *m*; **the relation of ~ and effect** la relation de cause à effet; **the ~ of his failure** la cause de son échec; **to be the ~ of** être cause de, causer; **the ~ is ...** la cause en est ...; (*Jur*) **~ of action** fondement *m* (d'une action en justice); (*Jur*) **~ of loss** fait générateur du sinistre; **she has no ~ to be angry** elle n'a aucune raison de se fâcher; **there's no ~ for anxiety** il n'y a pas lieu de s'inquiéter *or* de raison de s'inquiéter *or* de quoi s'inquiéter; **with (good) ~** à juste titre, de façon très justifiée; **without ~** sans cause *or* raison *or* motif; **without good ~** sans raison *or* cause *or* motif valable; **~ for complaint** sujet *m* de plainte.
b (*purpose*) cause *f*, parti *m*. **to make common ~ with** faire cause commune avec; **in the ~ of justice** pour (la cause de) la justice; **to work in a good ~** travailler pour la *or* une bonne cause; **it's all in a good ~*** c'est pour le bien de la communauté (*hum*); *see* **lost**.
c (*Jur*) cause *f*. **to plead sb's ~** plaider la cause de qn; **~ list** rôle *m* des audiences.
2 vt causer, occasionner, produire. **to ~ damage/an accident** causer des dégâts/un accident; **to ~ grief to sb** causer du chagrin à qn; **to ~ trouble** semer la perturbation; **to ~ trouble to sb** créer des ennuis à qn; **I don't want to ~ you any trouble** je ne veux en rien vous déranger; **to ~ sb to do sth** faire faire qch à qn; **to ~ sth to be done** faire faire qch.
causeway ['kɔːzweɪ] n chaussée *f*.
caustic ['kɔːstɪk] 1 adj (*Chem, fig*) caustique. **~ soda** soude *f* caustique; **~ remark** remarque *f* caustique. 2 n substance *f* caustique, caustique *m*.
cauterize ['kɔːtəraɪz] vt cautériser.
cautery ['kɔːtərɪ] n cautère *m*.
caution ['kɔːʃən] 1 n a (*NonC: circumspection*) prudence *f*, circonspection *f*. **proceed with ~** (*gen*) agissez avec prudence *or* circonspection; (*Aut*) avancez lentement. b (*warning*) avertissement *m*; (*rebuke*) réprimande *f*. (*on label*) **"~"** "attention"; **he got off with a ~** il s'en est tiré avec une réprimande; (*Jur*) **~ money** cautionnement *m*. c (*†: rascal*) numéro* *m*, phénomène* *m*. 2 vt avertir, donner un avertissement à; (*Police: on charging suspect*) informer qn de ses droits. **to ~ sb against sth** mettre qn en garde contre qch; **to ~ sb against doing sth** prévenir qn de ce qui se passera s'il fait qch, déconseiller à qn de faire qch.
cautionary ['kɔːʃənərɪ] adj (servant) d'avertissement; (*Jur*) donné en garantie. **a ~ tale** un récit édifiant.
cautious ['kɔːʃəs] adj prudent, circonspect. **to be ~ about doing sth** longuement réfléchir avant de faire qch.
cautiously ['kɔːʃəslɪ] adv prudemment, avec prudence *or* circonspection.
cautiousness ['kɔːʃəsnɪs] n prudence *f*, circonspection *f*.
cavalcade [ˌkævəl'keɪd] n cavalcade *f*.
cavalier [ˌkævə'lɪə^r] 1 n (*gen, Mil*) cavalier *m*; (*Brit Hist*) royaliste *m* (*partisan de Charles Ier et de Charles II*). 2 adj a (*Brit Hist*) royaliste. b (*slightly pej*) *person, manners* (*free and easy*) cavalier, désinvolte; (*supercilious*) arrogant, orgueilleux.
cavalierly [ˌkævə'lɪəlɪ] adv cavalièrement.
cavalry ['kævəlrɪ] 1 n cavalerie *f*; *see* **household**. 2 comp ▸ **cavalry charge** charge *f* de cavalerie ▸ **cavalryman** cavalier *m* (*soldat*) ▸ **cavalry officer** officier *m* de cavalerie ▸ **cavalry twill** (*Tex*) drap *m* sergé pour culotte de cheval, tricotine *f*.
cave[1] [keɪv] 1 n caverne *f*, grotte *f*. 2 comp ▸ **cave dweller** (*Hist*) (*in prehistory*) homme *m* des cavernes; *[primitive tribes]* troglodyte *mf* ▸ **cave-in** *[floor, building]* effondrement *m*, affaissement *m*; (**: defeat, surrender*) effondrement, dégonflage* *m* ▸ **caveman** (*Hist*) homme *m* des cavernes ▸ **cave painting** peinture *f* rupestre ▸ **caving-in** = **cave-in**. 3 vi: **to go caving** faire de la spéléologie.
▸ **cave in** 1 vi a *[floor, building]* s'effondrer, s'affaisser; *[wall, beam]* céder. b (**: yield*) se dégonfler*, caner*. 2 **cave-in, caving-in** n *see* **cave**[1] **2**.
cave[2] ['keɪvɪ] excl (*Brit Scol sl †*) ~! pet pet!*, vingt-deux!‡; **to keep ~** faire le guet.
caveat ['kævɪæt] n (*gen*) avertissement *m*; (*Jur*) notification *f* d'opposition. **~ emptor** sans garantie du fournisseur, aux risques de l'acheteur.
cavern ['kævən] n caverne *f*.
cavernous ['kævənəs] adj a (*fig*) **~ darkness** ténèbres épaisses; **~ eyes** yeux *mpl* caves; **~ voice** voix caverneuse; **~ yawn** bâillement profond. b *mountain* plein de cavernes.
caviar(e) ['kævɪɑː^r] n caviar *m*.
cavil ['kævɪl] vi ergoter, chicaner (*about, at* sur).
caving ['keɪvɪŋ] n spéléologie *f*.
cavity ['kævɪtɪ] 1 n *[wood, metal, earth]* cavité *f*, creux *m*; *[bone, tooth]* cavité; (*Phon*) orifice *m*. 2 comp ▸ **cavity wall** mur *m* avec vide d'air; **cavity wall insulation** isolation *f* des murs creux.
cavort* [kə'vɔːt] vi (*jump about*) cabrioler, faire des cabrioles *or* des gambades. (*fig*) **while you were ~ing (around) in Paris ...** pendant que tu te donnais du bon temps* à Paris ... .
cavy ['keɪvɪ] n (*Zool*) cobaye *m*, cochon *m* d'Inde.
caw [kɔː] 1 vi croasser. 2 n croassement *m*.
cawing ['kɔːɪŋ] n (*NonC*) croassement *m*.
cay [keɪ] n (*sandbank*) banc *m* de sable; (*coral reef*) récif *m or* banc de corail.
Cayenne ['keɪen] n (*also* **C~ pepper**) (poivre *m* de) Cayenne *m*.
cayman ['keɪmən] n, pl **~s** a caïman *m*. b **the C~ Islands** les îles *fpl* Caïmans.
CB ['siː'biː] a (abbr of **Citizens' Band Radio**) C.B. *f*. **~ fan** *or* **user** cibiste *mf*. b (*Mil*) (abbr of **confined to barracks**) *see* **confined**.
C.B. ['siː'biː] n (abbr of **Companion (of the Order) of the Bath**) *titre honorifique*.
C.B.E. ['siː'biː'iː] n (abbr of **Companion (of the Order) of the British Empire**) *titre honorifique*.
C.B.I. ['siː'biː'aɪ] n (abbr of **Confederation of British Industry**) *conseil du patronat*.
C.B.S. ['siː'biː'es] n abbr of **Columbia Broadcasting System**.
cc ['siː'siː] a (abbr of **cubic centimetre(s)**) cm^3. b abbr of **carbon copy, carbon copies**.
C.C. ['siː'siː] (abbr of **County Council**) *conseil général du Comté*.
CCTV ['siː'siː'tiː'viː] n (abbr of **closed circuit television**) *see* **closed**.
CD ['siː'diː] n (abbr of **compact disc**) CD *m*. **~ player** platine *f* laser.
C.D. ['siː'diː] a (abbr of **Corps Diplomatique**) CD *m*. b (abbr of **Civil Defence**) *see* **civil**. c (*US*) (abbr of **Congressional District**) *see* **congressional**.
CDI ['siː'diː'aɪ] n (abbr of **compact disc interactive**) CD-I *m*, disque *m* compact interactif.
Cdr. (*Mil*) abbr of **Commander**. (*on envelope*) **~ J. Thomas** Le commandant J. Thomas.
CD-ROM ['siː'diː'rɒm] n (abbr of **compact disc read only memory**) CD-ROM *m*.
CDT ['siː'diː'tiː] (*US*) (abbr of **Central Daylight Time**) *see* **central 1**.
CDV ['siː'diː'viː] n, **CD-video** [ˌsiːdiː'vɪdɪəʊ] n (abbr of **compact-disc video**) CD-V *m*, vidéodisque *m* compact.
CE, C of E ['siː'iː, 'siːə'viː] n (abbr of **Church of England**) *see* **church 1d**.
cease [siːs] 1 vi *[activity, noise etc]* cesser, s'arrêter. (*†, liter*) **to ~ from work** cesser le travail; (*†, liter*) **to ~ from doing** cesser *or* s'arrêter de faire. 2 vt *work, activity* cesser, arrêter. **to ~ doing** cesser *or* arrêter de faire; (*Mil*) **to ~ fire** cesser le feu; (*Comm*) **to ~ trading** fermer, cesser ses activités. 3 n: **without ~** sans cesse. 4 comp ▸ **ceasefire** (*Mil*) cessez-le-feu *m inv*.

ceaseless [ˈsiːslɪs] adj incessant, continuel.
ceaselessly [ˈsiːslɪslɪ] adv sans cesse, sans arrêt, continuellement.
cecum [ˈsiːkəm] n (*US*) = **caecum.**
cedar [ˈsiːdəʳ] 1 n cèdre *m*. ~ **of Lebanon** cèdre du Liban. 2 comp de *or* en cèdre ▸ **cedar wood** (bois *m* de) cèdre *m*.
cede [siːd] vt céder.
cedilla [sɪˈdɪlə] n cédille *f*.
ceilidh [ˈkeɪlɪ] n (*Scot etc*) bal *m* folklorique écossais *etc*.
ceiling [ˈsiːlɪŋ] 1 n (*gen, Aviat, fig*) plafond *m*. **to fix a** ~ **for** *or* **put a** ~ **on prices/wages** fixer un plafond pour les prix/salaires; **to hit the** ~ (*: *get angry*) sortir de ses gonds, piquer une crise*; *[prices]* crever le plafond; **prices have reached their** ~ **at X** les prix plafonnent à X. 2 comp *lamp, covering* de plafond; (*fig*) *rate, charge* plafond *inv* ▸ **ceiling decoration** décoration *f* de plafond ▸ **ceiling price** prix *m* plafond *inv*.
celadon [ˈseləˌdɒn] n (*porcelain*) céladon.
celandine [ˈseləndaɪn] n chélidoine *f*.
celebrant [ˈselɪbrənt] n célébrant *m*, officiant *m*.
celebrate [ˈselɪbreɪt] 1 vt *person* célébrer, glorifier; *event* célébrer, fêter. **to** ~ **the anniversary of sth** commémorer qch; (*Rel*) **to** ~ **mass** célébrer la messe. 2 vi a (*Rel*) célébrer (l'office). b (*) **let's** ~! il faut fêter ça!; (*with drink*) il faut arroser ça!*
celebrated [ˈselɪbreɪtɪd] adj célèbre.
celebration [ˌselɪˈbreɪʃən] 1 n a (*often* ~**s**) fête(s) *f(pl)*; (*at Christmas, for family event etc*) fête, festivités *fpl*; (*public event*) cérémonies *fpl*, fête(s). **we must have a** ~ il faut fêter ça!; **to join in the** ~**s** participer à la fête *or* aux festivités; **the victory** ~**s** les cérémonies marquant la victoire. b (*NonC: act of celebrating*) *[event]* (*also Rel*) célébration *f*; *[past event]* commémoration *f*; *[sb's virtues etc]* éloge *m*, louange *f*. **in** ~ **of** ... *victory etc* pour fêter *or* célébrer ...; *past victory etc* pour commémorer ...; *sb's achievements* pour célébrer ... . 2 comp *dinner, outing etc* de fête; (*for past event*) commémoratif.
celebratory [ˌselɪˈbreɪtərɪ] adj de célébration.
celebrity [sɪˈlebrɪtɪ] n (*fame; person*) célébrité *f*.
celeriac [səˈlerɪæk] n céleri(-rave) *m*.
celerity [sɪˈlerɪtɪ] n célérité *f*, rapidité *f*, promptitude *f*.
celery [ˈselərɪ] 1 n céleri *m* (ordinaire *or* à côtes). **a bunch** *or* **head of** ~ un pied de céleri; **a stick of** ~ une côte de céleri. 2 comp *seeds, salt* de céleri.
celesta [sɪˈlestə] n célesta *m*.
celestial [sɪˈlestɪəl] adj (*lit, fig*) céleste.
celiac [ˈsiːlɪˌæk] adj (*esp US*) = **coeliac.**
celibacy [ˈselɪbəsɪ] n célibat *m*.
celibate [ˈselɪbɪt] adj, n célibataire *(mf)*.
cell [sel] n a (*gen: also Bio, Bot, Phot*) cellule *f*; (*Elec*) élément *m* (*de pile*). (*Pol*) **to form a** ~ créer une cellule. b (*Police etc*) cellule *f*. **he spent the night in the** ~**s** il a passé la nuit au poste *or* en cellule; *see* **condemn, death** *etc*.
cellar [ˈseləʳ] n *[wine, coal]* cave *f*; *[food etc]* cellier *m*. **he keeps an excellent** ~ il a une excellente cave; *see* **coal** *etc*.
cellist [ˈtʃelɪst] n violoncelliste *mf*.
cello [ˈtʃeləʊ] n violoncelle *m*.
Cellophane [ˈseləfeɪn] n ® Cellophane *f* ®.
cellphone [ˈselfəʊn] n (abbr of **cellular (tele)phone**) *see* **cellular c.**
cellular [ˈseljʊləʳ] adj a (*Anat, Bio etc*) cellulaire. b (*Tex*) *blanket* en cellular. c (*Rad*) ~ **radio** radio *f* cellulaire; ~ **(tele)phone** téléphone *m* cellulaire.
cellulite [ˈseljʊˌlaɪt] n cellulite *f* (*gonflement*).
cellulitis [ˌseljʊˈlaɪtɪs] n cellulite *f* (*inflammation*).
Celluloid [ˈseljʊlɔɪd] 1 n ® Celluloïd *m* ®. 2 comp en celluloïd.
cellulose [ˈseljʊləʊs] 1 n cellulose *f*. 2 adj cellulosique, en *or* de cellulose. ~ **acetate** acétate *m* de cellulose; ~ **varnish** vernis *m* cellulosique.
Celsius [ˈselsɪəs] adj Celsius *inv*. **degrees** ~ degrés *mpl* Celsius.
Celt [kelt, selt] n Celte *mf*.
Celtic [ˈkeltɪk, ˈseltɪk] 1 adj celtique, celte. 2 n (*Ling*) celtique *m*.
cembalo [ˈtʃembələʊ] n, pl ~**s** *or* **cembali** [ˈtʃembəlɪ] (*Mus*) clavecin *m*.
cement [səˈment] 1 n a (*Constr, fig*) ciment *m*. b (*Chem, Dentistry*) amalgame *m*. c = **cementum.** 2 vt (*Constr, fig*) cimenter; (*Chem*) cémenter; (*Dentistry*) obturer. 3 comp ▸ **cement mixer** bétonnière *f*.
cementation [ˌsiːmenˈteɪʃən] n (*Constr, fig*) cimentation *f*; (*Tech*) cémentation *f*.
cementum [sɪˈmentəm] n (*Anat*) cément *m*.
cemetery [ˈsemɪtrɪ] n cimetière *m*.
cenotaph [ˈsenətɑːf] n cénotaphe *m*.
censer [ˈsensəʳ] n encensoir *m*.
censor [ˈsensəʳ] 1 n censeur *m*. 2 vt censurer.
censorious [senˈsɔːrɪəs] adj *person, comments* hypercritique, sévère.
censorship [ˈsensəʃɪp] n (*NonC*) (*censoring*) censure *f*; (*function of censor*) censorat *m*.
censurable [ˈsenʃərəbl] adj blâmable, critiquable.
censure [ˈsenʃəʳ] 1 vt blâmer, critiquer. 2 n critique *f*, blâme *m*; *see* **vote.**
census [ˈsensəs] n, pl ~**es** recensement *m*. **to take a** ~ **of the population** faire le recensement de la population; **the increase between** ~**es** l'augmentation *f* intercensitaire; (*Brit*) ~ **enumerator,** (*US*) ~ **taker** agent *m* recenseur.
cent [sent] n a **per** ~ pour cent. b (*Can, US: coin*) cent *m*. **I haven't a** ~* je n'ai pas un sou *or* rond*.
cent. a abbr of **centigrade.** b abbr of **central.** c abbr of **century.**
centaur [ˈsentɔːʳ] n centaure *m*.
centenarian [ˌsentɪˈnɛərɪən] adj, n centenaire *(mf)*.
centenary [senˈtiːnərɪ] 1 adj centenaire. ~ **celebrations** fêtes *fpl* du centenaire. 2 n (*anniversary*) centenaire *m*; (*century*) siècle *m*. **he has just passed his** ~ il vient de fêter son centième anniversaire *or* son centenaire.
centennial [senˈtenɪəl] 1 adj (*100 years old*) centenaire, séculaire; (*every 100 years*) séculaire (*frm*). 2 n centenaire *m*, centième anniversaire *m*. (*US*) **The C~ State** le Colorado.
center [ˈsentəʳ] n (*US*) = **centre.**
centesimal [senˈtesɪməl] adj centésimal.
cent(i)... [ˈsent(ɪ)] pref centi... .
centigrade [ˈsentɪgreɪd] adj *thermometer, scale* centigrade; *degree* centigrade, Celsius *inv*.
centigramme, (*US*) **centigram** [ˈsentɪgræm] n centigramme *m*.
centilitre, (*US*) **centiliter** [ˈsentɪˌliːtəʳ] n centilitre *m*.
centimetre, (*US*) **centimeter** [ˈsentɪˌmiːtəʳ] n centimètre *m*.
centipede [ˈsentɪpiːd] n mille-pattes *m inv*.
CENTO [ˈsentəʊ] (*Pol*) (abbr of **Central Treaty Organization**) C.E.N.T.O. *m*.
central [ˈsentrəl] 1 adj central. **C~ African Republic** (n) République centrafricaine; (adj) centrafricain; **C~ America** Amérique centrale; **C~ American** (adj) de l'Amérique centrale; (n) habitant(e) *m(f)* de l'Amérique centrale; **C~ Asia** Asie centrale; ~ **bank** banque *f* centrale; (*US*) **C~ Daylight Time** heure *f* d'été du Centre; (*Aut*) ~ **(door) locking device** condamnation *f* électromagnétique des serrures; (*Aut*) ~ **(door) locking** verrouillage *m* central (des portes); **C~ Europe** Europe centrale; **C~ European** (adj) de l'Europe centrale; (n) habitant(e) *m(f)* de l'Europe centrale; **C~ European Time** heure *f* de l'Europe centrale; **C~ Government** le gouvernement central; ~ **heating** chauffage central; (*Physiol*) ~ **nervous system** système nerveux central; (*Comput*) ~ **processing unit** unité centrale, UC *f*; (*Brit Aut*) ~ **reservation** terre-plein *m* (*sur chaussée*); (*Can, US*) ~ **standard time** heure normale du Centre.
2 n (*US*) central *m* téléphonique.
centralism [ˈsentrəlɪzəm] n (*Pol*) centralisme *m*.
centralist [ˈsentrəlɪst] adj, n (*Pol*) centraliste *(mf)*.
centralization [ˌsentrəlaɪˈzeɪʃən] n centralisation *f*.
centralize [ˈsentrəlaɪz] 1 vt centraliser. 2 vi se centraliser, être centralisé.
centrally [ˈsentrəlɪ] adv *organize etc* de façon centralisée. ~**-based** centralisé; ~**-heated** doté du chauffage central; ~ **planned economy** économie *f* dirigée.
centre, (*US*) **center** [ˈsentəʳ] 1 n a (*gen, Comput*) centre *m*. **the** ~ **of the target** le centre de la cible, le mille; **in the** ~ au centre; ~ **of gravity** centre de gravité; ~ **of attraction** (*lit*) centre d'attraction; (*fig*) point *m* de mire; **city** ~ centre de la ville; ~ **of commerce** centre commercial (*ville*); *see* **nerve** *etc*.
b (*place for specific activity*) centre *m*. **adult education** ~ centre d'enseignement post-scolaire; **law/business consultancy** ~ boutique *f* de droit/de gestion; *see* **civic, community, job.**
2 comp *row etc* central ▸ **centre armrest** (*Aut*) accoudoir central ▸ **centre bit** (*Tech*) mèche *f* (*d'une vrille*), foret *m*, mèche anglaise ▸ **centreboard** (*Naut*) dérive *f* (*d'un bateau*) ▸ **centre court** (*Tennis*) court central ▸ **centre fold** (*Press*) double page *f* (détachable); (*pinup picture*) photo *f* de pin up (*au milieu d'un magazine*) ▸ **centre-forward** (*Sport*) avant-centre *m* ▸ **centre-half** (*Sport*) demi-centre *m* ▸ **centre parties** (*Pol*) partis *mpl* du centre ▸ **centre-piece** *[table]* milieu *m* de table ▸ **centre spread** (*Advertising*) pages *fpl* centrales ▸ **centre three-quarter** (*Sport*) trois-quarts *m* centre ▸ **centre vowel** (*Phon*) voyelle centrale.
3 vt (*gen, Comput*) centrer. (*Ftbl*) **to** ~ **the ball** centrer.
4 vi a *[thoughts, hatred]* se concentrer (*on, in* sur); *[problem, talk etc]* tourner (*on* autour de).
b (*Archery*) frapper au centre.
-centred [ˈsentəd] adj ending in comps: basé sur.
centrifugal [senˈtrɪfjʊgəl] adj centrifuge. ~ **force** force *f* centrifuge.
centrifuge [ˈsentrɪfjuːʒ] n (*Tech*) centrifugeur *m*, centrifugeuse *f*.
centripetal [senˈtrɪpɪtl] adj centripète. ~ **force** force *f* centripète.
centrism [ˈsentrɪzəm] n (*Pol*) centrisme *m*.
centrist [ˈsentrɪst] adj, n (*Pol*) centriste *(mf)*.
centurion [senˈtjʊərɪən] n centurion *m*.
century [ˈsentjʊrɪ] 1 n a siècle *m*. **several centuries ago** il y a plusieurs siècles; **in the twentieth** ~ au vingtième siècle. b (*Mil Hist*) centurie *f*. c (*Sport*) centaine *de points*. 2 comp ▸ **centuries-old** séculaire, vieux (*f* vieille) de plusieurs siècles, plusieurs fois centenaire ▸ **century note*** (*US*) billet *m* de cent dollars.
CEO [ˈsiːˈiːˈəʊ] (*US*) (abbr of **chief executive officer**) *see* **chief.**

cephalic [sɪ'fælɪk] adj céphalique.
ceramic [sɪ'ræmɪk] 1 adj *art* céramique; *cup, vase* en céramique. ~ **hob** table *f* de cuisson en vitrocéramique. 2 n a (*NonC*) ~s la céramique. b (objet *m* en) céramique *f*.
Cerberus ['sɜːbərəs] n Cerbère *m*.
cereal ['sɪərɪəl] 1 n (*plant*) céréale *f*; (*grain*) grain *m* (*de céréale*). **baby** ~ Blédine *f* ®; **breakfast** ~ céréale *f*.
2 adj de céréale(s).
cerebellum [ˌserɪ'beləm] n, pl ~s *or* **cerebella** [ˌserɪ'belə] cervelet *m*.
cerebral ['serɪbrəl] adj cérébral. ~ **death** mort cérébrale; ~ **palsy** paralysie cérébrale.
cerebration [ˌserɪ'breɪʃən] n cogitation *f*, méditation *f*; (*: *hard thinking*) cogitation (*iro*).
cerebrum ['serɪbrəm] n, pl ~s *or* **cerebra** ['serɪbrə] (*Anat*) cerveau *m*.
ceremonial [ˌserɪ'məʊnɪəl] 1 adj *rite* cérémoniel; *dress* de cérémonie; (*US*) *office, post* honorifique. 2 n cérémonial *m* (*NonC*); (*Rel*) cérémonial, rituel *m*.
ceremonially [ˌserɪ'məʊnɪəlɪ] adv selon le cérémonial d'usage.
ceremonious [ˌserɪ'məʊnɪəs] adj solennel; (*slightly pej*) cérémonieux.
ceremoniously [ˌserɪ'məʊnɪəslɪ] adv solennellement, avec cérémonie; (*slightly pej*) cérémonieusement.
ceremony ['serɪmənɪ] n a (*event*) cérémonie *f*; *see* **master**. b (*NonC*) cérémonies *fpl*, façons *fpl*. **to stand on** ~ faire des cérémonies, faire des façons; **with** ~ cérémonieusement; **without** ~ sans cérémonie(s).
cerise [sə'riːz] adj (de) couleur cerise, cerise *inv*.
cerium ['sɪərɪəm] n cérium *m*.
cert‡ [sɜːt] n (*Brit*) certitude *f*. **it's a dead** ~ ça ne fait pas un pli*, c'est couru*; **he's a** ~ **for the job** il est sûr et certain de décrocher le poste*.
cert. a abbr of **certificate.** b abbr of **certified.**
certain ['sɜːtən] 1 adj a (*definite, indisputable*) certain, sûr, indiscutable; *death, success* certain, inévitable; *remedy, cure* infaillible. **he is** ~ **to come** il viendra sans aucun doute; **it is** ~ **that he will go** il est certain qu'il ira; **that's for** ~* c'est sûr et certain*, il n'y a pas de doute; **he'll do it for** ~ il est certain qu'il le fera; **I cannot say for** ~ **that** ... je ne peux pas affirmer que ...; **I don't know for** ~ je n'en suis pas sûr.
b (*sure*) *person* certain, convaincu, sûr. **I am** ~ **he didn't do it** je suis certain qu'il n'a pas fait cela; **are you** ~ **of** *or* **about that?** en êtes-vous sûr *or* certain?; **be** ~ **to go** allez-y sans faute, ne manquez pas d'y aller; **you can be** ~ **of success** vous êtes sûr *or* assuré de réussir; **you don't sound very** ~ tu n'as pas l'air très convaincu *or* sûr; **to make** ~ **of sth** (*get facts about*) s'assurer de qch; (*be sure of getting*) s'assurer qch; **you should make** ~ **of your facts** vous devriez vérifier les faits que vous avancez; **I must make** ~ **of a seat** il faut que je m'assure (*subj*) d'avoir une place; **to make** ~ **that** s'assurer que.
c (*particular*) certain (*before n*), particulier; (*specific*) certain (*before n*), déterminé, précis. **a** ~ **gentleman** un certain monsieur; **on a** ~ **day in spring** un certain jour de printemps; **at a** ~ **hour** à une heure bien précise *or* déterminée; **there is a** ~ **way of doing it** il existe une façon particulière de le faire; **in** ~ **countries** dans certains pays.
d (*some*) certain (*before n*), quelque. **he had a** ~ **courage all the same** il avait tout de même un certain *or* du courage; **a** ~ **difficulty** une certaine difficulté, quelque difficulté; **to a** ~ **extent** dans une certaine mesure.
2 pron certains. ~ **of our members have not paid** certains *or* quelques uns de nos membres n'ont pas payé.
certainly ['sɜːtənlɪ] adv certainement, assurément, sans aucun doute. **will you do this?** — ~! voulez-vous faire cela? — bien sûr! *or* volontiers!; ~ **not!** certainement pas!, sûrement pas!; **this meat is** ~ **tough** il n'y a pas de doute, cette viande est dure; **it is** ~ **true that** on ne peut pas nier que + *subj or indic*; **I shall** ~ **be there** j'y serai sans faute, je ne manquerai pas d'y être; **you may** ~ **leave tomorrow** vous pouvez partir demain bien sûr; ~, **madam!** (mais) certainement *or* tout de suite, madame!
certainty ['sɜːtəntɪ] n a (*fact, quality*) certitude *f*, fait *or* événement certain. **for a** ~ à coup sûr, sans aucun doute; **to a** ~ certainement; **to be on a** ~ parier à coup sûr; **his success is a** ~ son succès est certain *or* ne fait aucun doute; **it is a moral** ~ c'est une certitude morale; **faced with the** ~ **of disaster** voyant le désastre inévitable. b (*NonC: conviction*) certitude *f*, conviction *f*.
certifiable [ˌsɜːtɪ'faɪəbl] adj a *fact, statement* qu'on peut certifier. b (*: *mad*) bon à enfermer.
certificate [sə'tɪfɪkɪt] n a (*legal document*) certificat *m*, acte *m*. ~ **of airworthiness** *or* **seaworthiness** certificat de navigabilité; (*Comm*) ~ **of origin/value** certificat d'origine/de valeur; ~ **of posting** récépissé *m*; ~ **of baptism** extrait *m* de baptême; **birth** ~ acte *or* extrait de naissance; *see* **death, marriage.** b (*academic document*) diplôme *m*; (*for skilled or semi-skilled work*) qualification professionnelle. (*Brit Scol*) **C~ of Secondary Education** ≃ brevet *m* (d'études du premier cycle) (*dans une seule matière*); *see* **teacher.**
certificated [sə'tɪfɪkeɪtɪd] adj diplômé.
certification [ˌsɜːtɪfɪ'keɪʃən] n a (*NonC*) certification *f*, authentification *f*. b (*document*) certificat *m*.
certify ['sɜːtɪfaɪ] 1 vt a certifier, assurer, attester (*that* que). (*Jur*) **certified as a true copy** certifié conforme; (*Psych*) **to** ~ **sb (insane)** déclarer qn atteint d'aliénation mentale; (*US*) **certified public accountant** expert-comptable *m*, comptable agréé (*Can*); (*US Scol*) **certified teacher** (*state school*) professeur diplômé; (*private school*) professeur habilité. b (*Fin*) *cheque* certifier. **certified cheque** chèque certifié. c (*Comm*) *goods* garantir. (*US Post*) **to send by certified mail** ≃ envoyer avec accusé de réception; (*US*) **certified milk** *lait soumis aux contrôles d'hygiène réglementaires.* 2 vi: **to** ~ **to sth** attester qch.
certitude ['sɜːtɪtjuːd] n certitude *f*, conviction absolue.
cerulean [sɪ'ruːlɪən] adj (*liter*) bleu ciel *inv*, azuré.
cerumen [sɪ'ruːmen] n cérumen *m*.
ceruminous [sɪ'ruːmɪnəs] adj cérumineux.
cervical ['sɜːvɪkəl] adj cervical. ~ **cancer** cancer *m* du col de l'utérus; ~ **smear** frottis (cervico-)vaginal.
cervix ['sɜːvɪks] n, pl ~es *or* **cervices** [sə'vaɪsiːz] col *m* de l'utérus.
cesium ['siːzɪəm] n (*esp US*) = **caesium.**
cessation [se'seɪʃən] n cessation *f*, arrêt *m*, interruption *f*, suspension *f*. ~ **of hostilities** cessation des hostilités.
cession ['seʃən] n cession *f*. **act of** ~ acte *m* de cession.
cesspit ['sespɪt] n fosse *f* d'aisance; (*fig*) cloaque *m*.
cesspool ['sespuːl] n = **cesspit.**
C.E.T. ['siː'iː'tiː] (abbr of **Central European Time**) *see* **central 1.**
cetacean [sɪ'teɪʃɪən] adj, n cétacé (*m*).
Ceylon [sɪ'lɒn] n Ceylan *m*.
Ceylonese [sɪlɒ'niːz] 1 adj cingalais, ceylanais. 2 n a Cingalais(e) *m(f)*, Ceylanais(e) *m(f)*. b (*Ling*) cingalais *m*.
cf. (abbr of **confer**) cf.
c/f (*Fin*) (abbr of **carried forward**) *see* **carry forward.**
CFC ['siː'ef'siː] n (abbr of **chlorofluorocarbon**) C.F.C. *m*.
cg (abbr of **centigram(me)(s)**) cg.
C.G. ['siː'dʒiː] (abbr of **Coast Guard**) *see* **coast 3.**
CGA [ˌsiːdʒiː'eɪ] n (*Comput*) (abbr of **colour graphics adaptor**) adaptateur *m* de graphique couleur.
C.H. (abbr of **Companion of Honour**) *titre honorifique*.
Ch. abbr of **chapter.**
c.h. (abbr of **central heating**) *see* **central.**
Chad [tʃæd] 1 n Tchad *m*. **Lake** ~ le lac Tchad. 2 adj tchadien.
chafe [tʃeɪf] 1 vt a (*rub*) frotter, frictionner. **she** ~**d the child's hands to warm them** elle a frictionné les mains de l'enfant pour les réchauffer. b (*rub against, irritate*) frotter contre, irriter. **his shirt** ~**d his neck** sa chemise frottait contre son cou *or* lui irritait le cou; **his neck was** ~**d** il avait le cou irrité. c (*wear*) *collar, cuffs, rope* user (en frottant); (*Naut*) raguer. 2 vi s'user; [*rope*] raguer; (*fig*) s'impatienter, s'irriter (*at* de). **he** ~**d against these restrictions** ces restrictions l'irritaient; (*liter*) **they** ~**d under the yoke of tyranny** ils rongeaient leur frein sous la tyrannie.
chaff[1] [tʃɑːf] 1 n (*NonC: Agr*) [*grain*] balle *f*; (*cut straw*) menue paille; *see* **wheat.** 2 vt *straw* hacher.
chaff[2] [tʃɑːf] 1 n (*NonC: banter*) taquinerie *f*. 2 vt taquiner, blaguer*.
chaffinch ['tʃæfɪntʃ] n pinson *m*.
chafing dish ['tʃeɪfɪŋdɪʃ] n poêlon *m* (de table).
chagrin ['ʃægrɪn] 1 n contrariété *f*, (vive) déception *f*, (vif) dépit *m*. **much to my** ~ à mon vif dépit. 2 vt contrarier, décevoir.
chain [tʃeɪn] 1 n a (*gen, also ornamental*) chaîne *f*. (*fetters*) ~s chaînes, entraves *fpl*, fers *mpl*; [*mayor*] ~ **of office** chaîne (*insigne de la fonction de maire*); **to keep a dog on a** ~ tenir un chien à l'attache; **in** ~**s** enchaîné; (*Aut*) **(snow)** ~**s** chaînes (à neige); [*lavatory*] **to pull the** ~ tirer la chasse (d'eau); *see* **ball, bicycle** *etc*.
b [*mountains, atoms etc*] chaîne *f*; (*fig*) [*ideas*] enchaînement *m*; [*events*] série *f*, suite *f*. (*Comm*) ~ **of shops** chaîne de magasins; [*people*] **to make a** ~ faire la chaîne; *see* **bucket.**
c (*Tech*) (*for measuring*) chaîne *f* d'arpenteur; (*measure*) chaînée *f*.
2 comp ►**chain gang** chaîne *f* de forçats ►**chain letter** lettre *f* faisant partie d'une chaîne; **chain letters** chaîne *f* (de lettres) ►**chain lightning** éclairs *mpl* en zigzag ►**chain mail** (*NonC*) cotte *f* de mailles ►**chain reaction**: (*Phys, fig*) **to set up a chain reaction** provoquer une réaction en chaîne ►**chain saw** tronçonneuse *f* ►**chain smoke** fumer cigarette sur cigarette, fumer comme un sapeur *or* un pompier ►**chain smoker** fumeur *m*, -euse *f* invétéré(e) (*qui fume sans discontinuer*) ►**chain stitch** (*Sewing*) point *m* de chaînette ►**chain store** grand magasin (à succursales multiples).
3 vt (*lit, fig*) enchaîner; *door* mettre la chaîne à. **he was** ~**ed to the wall** il était enchaîné au mur.
►**chain down** vt sep enchaîner.
►**chain up** vt sep *animal* mettre à l'attache.
chair [tʃɛəʳ] 1 n a chaise *f*; (*armchair*) fauteuil *m*; (*seat*) siège *m*; (*Univ*) chaire *f*; (*sedan* ~) chaise à porteurs; (*wheel* ~) fauteuil roulant; (*US: electric* ~) chaise électrique. **to take a** ~ s'asseoir; **dentist's** ~ fauteuil de dentiste; (*Univ*) **to hold the** ~ **of French** être titulaire de *or* avoir la chaire de français; (*US*) **to go to the** ~ passer

à la chaise électrique; *see* **deck, easy, high** *etc.*
b (*Admin etc: function*) fauteuil présidentiel, présidence *f.* **to take the ~, to be in the ~** prendre la présidence, présider; **to address the ~** s'adresser au président; ~! ~! à l'ordre!
c (*Admin*) = **chairman.**
2 **comp** ►**chair back** dossier *m* (de chaise) ►**chairlift** télésiège *m* ►**chairman** *see* **chairman** ►**chairperson*** président *m* ►**chairwarmer*** (*US*) rond-de-cuir *m* (paresseux) ►**chairwoman** présidente *f.*
3 **vt** a (*Admin*) *meeting* présider.
b *hero* porter en triomphe.

chairman ['tʃɛəmən] **n** président *m* (*d'un comité etc*). **Mr C~** Monsieur le Président; **Madam C~** Madame la Présidente; (*US*) **~ and chief executive officer** président-directeur général, P.D.G. *m*; **C~ Mao** le président Mao.

chairmanship ['tʃɛəmənʃɪp] **n** présidence *f* (*d'un comité etc*). **under the ~ of** sous la présidence de.

chaise [ʃeɪz] **n** cabriolet *m.*

chaise longue ['ʃeɪz'lɒŋ] **n** méridienne *f.*

chalet ['ʃæleɪ] **n** (*gen*) chalet *m*; *[motel]* bungalow *m.*

chalice ['tʃælɪs] **n** (*Rel*) calice *m*; (*liter: wine cup*) coupe *f.*

chalk [tʃɔːk] 1 **n** (*NonC*) craie *f.* **a (piece of) ~** une craie, un morceau de craie; (*Brit*) **they're as different as ~ from cheese** (*persons*) ils sont comme le jour et la nuit; (*things*) ce sont deux choses qui n'ont rien en commun, c'est le jour et la nuit; (*Brit fig*) **by a long ~** de beaucoup, de loin; **did he win? — not by a long ~** est-ce qu'il a gagné? — non, loin de là *or* il s'en faut de beaucoup; *see* **French.**
2 **comp** ►**chalk board** (*US*) tableau *m* (noir) ►**chalkpit** carrière *f* de craie ►**chalk talk** (*US*) conférence illustrée au tableau noir.
3 **vt** (*write with ~*) écrire à la craie; (*rub with ~*) frotter de craie; *billiard cue* enduire de craie; *luggage* marquer à la craie.

►**chalk out** **vt sep** (*lit*) *pattern* esquisser, tracer (à la craie); (*fig*) *project* esquisser; *plan of action* tracer.

►**chalk up** **vt sep** a **chalk it up** mettez-le sur mon compte; **he chalked it up to experience** il l'a mis au compte de l'expérience. b *achievement, victory* remporter.

chalky ['tʃɔːkɪ] **adj** *soil* crayeux, calcaire; *water* calcaire; *complexion* crayeux, blafard.

challenge ['tʃælɪndʒ] 1 **n** a défi *m.* **to issue** *or* **put out a ~** lancer un défi; **to rise to the ~** se montrer à la hauteur; **to take up the ~** relever le défi; (*fig*) **the ~ of new ideas** la stimulation qu'offrent de nouvelles idées; **the ~ of the 20th century** le défi du 20e siècle; **Smith's ~ for leadership** la tentative qu'a faite Smith pour s'emparer du pouvoir; **this is a ~ to us all** c'est un défi qui s'adresse à nous tous; **the job was a great ~ to him** cette tâche constituait pour lui une gageure; **action that is a ~ to authority** action qui défie l'autorité; **it was a ~ to his skill** c'était un défi à son savoir-faire.
b (*Mil: by sentry*) sommation *f.*
c (*Jur: of juror, jury*) récusation *f.*
2 **vt** a (*summon, call*) défier (*sb to do* qn de faire); (*Sport*) inviter (*sb to a game* qn à faire une partie). **to ~ sb to a duel** provoquer qn en duel.
b (*call into question*) *statement* mettre en question, contester, révoquer en doute (*frm*). **to ~ sb's authority to do** contester à qn le droit de faire; **to ~ the wisdom of a plan** mettre en question la sagesse d'un projet; (*Jur*) **to ~ a measure** attaquer une mesure.
c (*Mil*) *[sentry]* faire une sommation à.
d (*Jur*) *juror, jury* récuser.

challenger ['tʃælɪndʒəʳ] **n** provocateur *m*, -trice *f*; (*Sport, also fig: Pol*) challenger *m.*

challenging ['tʃælɪndʒɪŋ] **adj** *remark, speech* provocateur *m* (*f* -trice); *look, tone* de défi; *book* stimulant. **he found himself in a ~ situation** il s'est trouvé là devant une gageure; **this is a very ~ situation** cette situation est une véritable gageure.

chamber ['tʃeɪmbəʳ] 1 **n** a (†, *frm*) (*room*) salle *f*, pièce *f*; (*also* **bed~**) chambre *f.*
b (*Brit*) (*lodgings*) **~s** logement *m*, appartement *m*; *[bachelor]* garçonnière *f*; *[barrister, judge, magistrate]* cabinet *m*; *[solicitor]* étude *f.* (*Jur*) **to hear a case in ~s** ≃ juger un cas en référé.
c (*hall*) chambre *f.* **C~ of Commerce** Chambre *f* de commerce; **C~ of Trade** Chambre *f* des métiers; **the C~ of Deputies** la Chambre des députés; (*Parl*) **the Upper/Lower C~** la Chambre haute/basse; **the C~ of Horrors** la Chambre d'épouvante; *see* **audience, second¹.**
d *[revolver]* chambre *f*; (*Anat*) cavité *f.* **the ~s of the eye** les chambres de l'œil.
e (†, *) = **chamber pot**; *see* **2.**
2 **comp** ►**chamber concert** concert *m* de musique de chambre ►**chambermaid** femme *f* de chambre (*dans un hôtel*) ►**chamber music** musique *f* de chambre ►**chamber orchestra** orchestre *m* de chambre ►**chamberpot** pot *m* de chambre, vase *m* de nuit†.

chamberlain ['tʃeɪmbəlɪn] **n** chambellan *m*; *see* **lord 3.**

chambray ['tʃæmbreɪ] **n** (*US*) = **cambric.**

chameleon [kə'miːlɪən] **n** (*Zool, fig*) caméléon *m.*

chamfer ['tʃæmfəʳ] (*Tech*) 1 **n** (*bevel*) chanfrein *m*; (*groove*) cannelure *f.* 2 **vt** chanfreiner; canneler.

chammy* ['ʃæmɪ] **n** = **chamois (cloth)**; *see* **chamois b.**

chamois ['ʃæmwɑː] **n, pl inv** a (*Zool*) chamois *m.* b ['ʃæmɪ] (*also* **~ cloth**) chamois *m.* **~ leather** peau *f* de chamois.

chamomile ['kæməʊmaɪl] **n** = **camomile.**

champ¹ [tʃæmp] 1 **vi** mâchonner. (*lit, fig*) **to ~ at the bit** ronger son frein. 2 **vt** mâchonner.

champ²* [tʃæmp] **n abbr of champion 1b.**

champagne [ʃæm'peɪn] 1 **n** (*wine*) champagne *m.* (*Geog*) **C~** Champagne *f.* 2 **comp** (*also* **champagne-coloured**) champagne *inv* ►**champagne cup** cocktail *m* au champagne ►**champagne glass** verre *m* à champagne; (*wide*) coupe *f* à champagne; (*tall and narrow*) flûte *f* à champagne ►**champagne lifestyle** grand train *m* de vie ►**champagne socialist** gauche *mf* caviar.

champion ['tʃæmpjən] 1 **n** a champion(ne) *m(f).* **the ~ of free speech** le champion de la liberté d'expression. b (*Sport: person, animal*) champion(ne) *m(f).* **world ~** champion(ne) du monde; **boxing ~** champion de boxe; **skiing ~** champion(ne) de ski. 2 **adj** a *show animal* champion. **~ swimmer/skier** *etc* champion(ne) *m(f)* de natation/de ski *etc.* b (*best*) sans rival, de première classe; (*: excellent*) *meal, holiday, film* du tonnerre*. **that's ~!** bravo!, chapeau!*, c'est champion!* 3 **vt** *person* prendre fait et cause pour; *action, cause, sb's decision* se faire le champion de, défendre.

championship ['tʃæmpjənʃɪp] **n** a (*Sport*) championnat *m.* **world ~** championnat du monde; **boxing ~** championnat de boxe; **world boxing ~** championnat du monde de boxe. b (*NonC*) *[cause etc]* défense *f.*

chance [tʃɑːns] 1 **n** a (*luck*) hasard *m.* **totally by ~, by sheer ~** tout à fait par hasard, par pur hasard; (*fortunately*) par pure chance, par un coup de chance; **have you a pen on you by (any) ~?** auriez-vous par hasard un stylo sur vous?; **it was not ~ that he came** s'il est venu ce n'est pas par hasard, ce n'est pas par hasard qu'il est venu; **to trust to ~** s'en remettre au hasard; **a game of ~** un jeu de hasard; **to leave things to ~** laisser faire le hasard; **he left nothing to ~** il n'a rien laissé au hasard.
b (*possibility*) chance(s) *f(pl)*, possibilité *f.* **to stand a good** *or* **fair ~** avoir des chances de réussir; **he hasn't much ~ of winning** il n'a pas beaucoup de chances de gagner; **he's still in with a ~** il a encore une petite chance; **on the ~ of your returning** dans le cas où vous reviendriez; **I went there on the ~ of seeing him** j'y suis allé dans l'espoir de le voir; **the ~s are that** il y a de grandes chances que + *subj*, il est très possible que + *subj*; **the ~s are against that happening** il y a peu de chances pour que cela arrive (*subj*); **the ~s are against him** il y a peu de chances pour qu'il réussisse; **there is little ~ of his coming** il est peu probable qu'il vienne; **you'll have to take a ~ on his coming** tu verras bien s'il vient ou non; **he's taking no ~s** il ne veut rien laisser au hasard, il ne veut prendre aucun risque; **that's a ~ we'll have to take** c'est un risque que nous allons devoir prendre *or* que nous avons à courir; **no ~!*, not a ~!*** pas de danger!*, jamais!; *see* **long¹, off.**
c (*opportunity*) occasion *f*, chance *f.* **I had the ~ to go** *or* **of going** j'ai eu l'occasion d'y aller, l'occasion m'a été donnée d'y aller; **if there's a ~ of buying it** s'il y a une possibilité d'achat; **to lose a ~** laisser passer une occasion; **she was waiting for her ~** elle attendait son heure; **she was waiting for her ~ to speak** elle attendait *or* guettait l'occasion de parler; **now's your ~!** (*in conversation, traffic etc*) vas-y!; (*in career etc*) saute sur l'occasion!, à toi de jouer!; **this is his big ~** c'est le grand moment pour lui; **give him another ~** laisse-lui encore sa chance; **he has had every ~** il a eu toutes les chances; **he never had a ~ in life** il n'a jamais eu sa chance dans la vie; **give me a ~ to show you what I can do** donnez-moi la possibilité de vous montrer ce que je sais faire; **you'll have your ~** (*your turn will come*) votre tour viendra; *see* **eye.**
2 **adj** fortuit, de hasard, accidentel. **a ~ companion** un compagnon rencontré par hasard; **a ~ discovery** une découverte accidentelle; **~ meeting** rencontre fortuite *or* de hasard.
3 **vt** a (*happen*) **to ~ to do** faire par hasard, venir à faire (*frm*); **I ~d to hear his name** j'ai entendu son nom par hasard, il s'est trouvé que j'ai entendu son nom; **it ~d that I was there** il s'est trouvé que j'étais là.
b (*risk*) *rejection, fine* risquer, courir le risque de. **to ~ doing** se risquer à faire, prendre le risque de faire; **I'll go round without phoning and ~ finding him there** je vais passer chez lui sans téléphoner en espérant l'y trouver *or* avec l'espoir de l'y trouver; **I want to see her alone and I'll have to ~ finding her husband there** je voudrais la voir seule, mais il faut que je prenne le risque d'y trouver son mari; **I'll ~ it!** je vais risquer le coup!; **to ~ one's arm*** risquer le tout (pour le tout); **to ~ one's luck** tenter *or* courir sa chance.

►**chance upon** **vt fus** (*frm*) *person* rencontrer par hasard; *thing* trouver par hasard.

chancel ['tʃɑːnsəl] **n** chœur *m* (*d'une église*). **~ screen** clôture *f* du chœur, jubé *m.*

chancellery ['tʃɑːnsələrɪ] **n** chancellerie *f.*

chancellor ['tʃɑːnsələʳ] **n** (*Hist, Jur, Pol*) chancelier *m*; (*Brit Univ*) président(e) *m(f)* honoraire; (*US Univ*) président(e) *m(f)* d'université. (*Brit*) **C~ of the Exchequer** Chancelier *m* de l'Échiquier, ≃ ministre *m* des Finances; *see* **lord.**

chancellorship ['tʃɑːnsələʃɪp] **n** fonctions *fpl* de chancelier.

chancer* ['tʃɑːnsəʳ] **n** arnaqueur* *m*, -euse *f*; (*child*) loustic* *m*.

chancery ['tʃɑːnsərɪ] **n** **a** (*Brit, Jur*) cour *f* de la chancellerie (*une des 5 divisions de la Haute Cour de justice anglaise*). **ward in ~** pupille *mf* (*sous tutelle judiciaire*). **b** (*US*) = **chancellery.** **c** (*US: also* **court of ~**) ≃ cour *f* d'équité *or* de la chancellerie.

chancre ['ʃæŋkəʳ] **n** (*Med*) chancre *m*.

chancy* ['tʃɑːnsɪ] **adj** (*risky*) risqué, hasardeux; (*doubtful*) aléatoire, problématique.

chandelier [ˌʃændə'lɪəʳ] **n** lustre *m*.

chandler ['tʃɑːndləʳ] **n: (ship's) ~** shipchandler *m*, marchand de fournitures pour bateaux.

change [tʃeɪndʒ] **1 n a** (*alteration*) changement *m* (*from, in* de, *into* en); (*slight*) modification *f*. **a ~ for the better** un changement en mieux, une amélioration; **a ~ for the worse** un changement en pire *or* en plus mal; **~ in the weather** changement de temps; **~ in public opinion** revirement *m* de l'opinion publique; **~ in attitudes** changement d'attitudes, évolution *f* des attitudes; **(just) for a ~** pour changer un peu; **by way of a ~** histoire de changer*; **to make a ~ in sth** changer qch, modifier qch; (*fig*) **to make a ~ of direction** changer son fusil d'épaule (*fig*); (*fig*) **to have a ~ of heart** changer d'avis; **it makes a ~** ça change un peu; **it will be a nice ~** cela nous fera un changement, voilà qui nous changera agréablement!; (*iro*) ça nous changera! (*iro*); **a picnic will be** *or* **make a nice ~ from being stuck indoors** un pique-nique nous changera de rester toujours enfermé à l'intérieur; **the ~ of life** le retour d'âge.
b (*substitution*) changement *m*, substitution *f*. **~ of address** changement d'adresse; **~ of air** changement d'air; **he brought a ~ of clothes** il a apporté des vêtements de rechange; **I need a ~ of clothes** il faut que je me change (*subj*); **~ of scene** (*Theat*) changement de décor; (*fig*) changement d'air; **~ of horses** relais *m*; **~ of job** changement de travail *or* de poste.
c (*NonC*) changement *m*, variété *f*. **she likes ~** elle aime le changement *or* la variété.
d (*NonC: money*) monnaie *f*. **small ~** petite monnaie; **can you give me ~ for this note/of £1?** pouvez-vous me faire la monnaie de ce billet/d'une livre?; **keep the ~** gardez la monnaie; (*notice*) **"no ~ given"** "on est tenu de faire l'appoint"; **you don't get much ~ from a fiver these days** aujourd'hui il ne reste jamais grand-chose d'un billet de cinq livres; **you won't get much ~ out of him*** tu perds ton temps avec lui.
e (*St Ex*) **the C~** la Bourse; **on the C~** en Bourse.
2 comp ▸ change machine distributeur *m* de monnaie **▸ changeover** changement *m*, passage *m* (*from one thing to another* d'une chose à une autre); (*NonC: Mil*) [*guard*] relève *f* **▸ change purse** (*US*) porte-monnaie *m inv*.
3 vt a (*by substitution*) changer de. **to ~ (one's) clothes** changer de vêtements, se changer; **to ~ one's shirt/skirt** *etc* changer sa *or* de chemise/jupe *etc*; **to ~ one's address** changer d'adresse; **to ~ the baby/his nappy** changer le bébé/ses couches; **to ~ colour** changer de couleur; **to ~ hands** (*one's grip*) changer de main; [*goods, property*] changer de main *or* de propriétaire; [*money*] (*between several people*) circuler de main en main; (*from one person to another*) être échangé; (*Mil*) **to ~ (the) guard** faire la relève de la garde; (*Theat*) **to ~ the scene** changer le décor; **let's ~ the subject** changeons de sujet, parlons d'autre chose; **to ~ one's tune** changer de ton; **to ~ trains/stations/buses** changer de train/de gare/d'autobus; **to ~ one's name/seat** changer de nom/place; **to ~ one's opinion** *or* **mind** changer d'avis; **to ~ sb's mind (about sth)** faire changer qn d'avis (à propos de qch); (*Aut*) **to ~ gear** changer de vitesse; (*Aut*) **to ~ a wheel** changer une roue; (*fig*) **to ~ tracks** changer d'angle *or* de perspective.
b (*exchange*) échanger, troquer (*sth for sth else* qch contre qch d'autre). (*lit*) **to ~ places (with sb)** changer de place (avec qn); (*fig*) **I wouldn't like to ~ places with you** je n'aimerais pas être à votre place; **to ~ sides** *or* **ends** (*Tennis*) changer de côté; (*Ftbl etc*) changer de camp; (*fig: in argument etc*) **to ~ sides** changer de camp; **they ~d hats (with one another)** ils ont échangé leurs chapeaux.
c *banknote, coin* faire la monnaie de, changer; *foreign currency* changer, convertir (*into* en).
d (*alter, modify, transform*) changer, modifier, transformer (*sth into sth else* qch en qch d'autre). **the witch ~d him into a cat** la sorcière l'a changé en chat; **his wife's death ~d him suddenly from a young man into an old one** la mort de sa femme a fait du jeune homme qu'il était un vieillard, il a vieilli tout d'un coup après la mort de sa femme; **this has ~d my ideas** ceci a modifié mes idées; **success has greatly ~d her** la réussite l'a complètement transformée.
4 vi a (*become different*) changer, se transformer. **you've ~d a lot!** tu as beaucoup changé!; **he will never ~** il ne changera jamais, on ne le changera pas; **the prince ~d into a swan** le prince s'est changé en cygne.
b (*~ clothes*) se changer. **I must ~ at once** je dois me changer tout de suite; **she ~d into an old skirt** elle s'est changée et a mis une vieille jupe.
c (*Rail etc*) changer. **you must ~ at Edinburgh** vous devez changer à Édimbourg; **all ~!** tout le monde descend!
d [*moon*] entrer dans une nouvelle phase.
▸change down vi (*Aut*) rétrograder.
▸change over 1 vi (*gen*) passer (*from* de, *to* à); [*two people*] faire l'échange; (*Sport: change ends*) changer de côté. **2 changeover n** *see* **change 2.**
▸change up vi (*Aut*) monter les vitesses.

changeability [ˌtʃeɪndʒə'bɪlɪtɪ] **n** [*circumstances, weather*] variabilité *f*.

changeable ['tʃeɪndʒəbl] **adj** *person* changeant, inconstant; *character* versatile, changeant; *colour* changeant; *weather, wind, circumstances* variable.

changeless ['tʃeɪndʒlɪs] **adj** *rite* immuable, invariable; *person* constant; *character* inaltérable.

changeling ['tʃeɪndʒlɪŋ] **n** enfant *mf* changé(e) (*substitué à un enfant volé*).

changing ['tʃeɪndʒɪŋ] **1 adj** *wind, prices, interest rates* variable, changeant; *expression* mobile; *social attitudes, principles* qui change, qui évolue. **a ~ society** une société en mutation. **2 n** (*NonC*) acte *m* de (se) changer, changement *m*. **the ~ of the guard** la relève de la garde; (*Brit Sport*) **~-room** vestiaire *m*.

channel ['tʃænl] **1 n a** (*bed of river etc*) lit *m*; (*navigable passage*) chenal *m*; (*between two land masses*) bras *m* de mer; [*irrigation*] (*small*) rigole *f*, (*wider*) canal *m*; (*in street*) caniveau *m*; (*duct*) conduit *m*. (*Geog*) **the (English) C~** la Manche.
b (*groove in surface*) rainure *f*; (*Archit*) cannelure *f*.
c (*TV*) chaîne *f*.
d (*Customs*) **red/green ~** file *f* marchandises à déclarer/rien à déclarer.
e (*fig*) direction *f*. **he directed the conversation into a new ~** il a fait prendre à la conversation une nouvelle direction; **~ of communication** voie *f* de communication; (*Admin*) **to go through the usual ~s** suivre la filière (habituelle).
f (*Comput*) canal *m*.
2 comp ▸ the Channel Isles *or* **Islands** (*Geog*) les îles anglo-normandes, les îles de la Manche **▸ the Channel tunnel** le tunnel sous la Manche.
3 vt a (*see* **1a**) (*make ~s in*) creuser des rigoles *or* des canaux dans; *street* pourvoir d'un *or* de caniveau(x). **the river ~led its way towards ...** la rivière a creusé son lit vers ... .
b (*fig*) *crowd* canaliser (*into* vers); *energies, efforts, resources* canaliser, diriger, orienter (*towards, into* vers); *information* canaliser (*into, towards* vers), concentrer (*into, towards* dans).
c (*Archit*) canneler.
▸channel off vt sep (*lit*) *water* capter; (*fig*) *energy, resources* canaliser.

chant [tʃɑːnt] **1 n** (*Mus*) chant *m* (lent), mélopée *f*; (*Rel Mus*) psalmodie *f*; [*crowd, demonstrators, audience etc*] chant scandé. **2 vt** (*sing*) chanter lentement; (*recite*) réciter; (*Rel*) psalmodier; [*crowd, demonstrators etc*] scander, crier sur l'air des lampions. **3 vi** chanter; (*Rel*) psalmodier; [*crowd, demonstrators etc*] scander des slogans.

chantey ['ʃæntɪ] **n** (*US*) chanson *f* de marin.

chaos ['keɪɒs] **n** (*lit, fig*) chaos *m*. **the ~ theory** la théorie du chaos.

chaotic [keɪ'ɒtɪk] **adj** chaotique.

chap¹ [tʃæp] **1 n** (*Med*) gerçure *f*, crevasse *f*. **C~ Stick ®** pommade *f* rosat *or* pour les lèvres. **2 vi** se gercer, se crevasser. **3 vt** gercer, crevasser.

chap² [tʃæp] **n** = **chop².**

chap³* [tʃæp] **n** (*man*) type* *m*. (*term of address*) **old ~** mon vieux*; **he was a young ~** c'était un jeune homme; **a nice ~** un chic type*; **the poor old ~** le pauvre vieux*; **poor little ~** pauvre petit, pauvre bonhomme; **he's very deaf, poor ~** pauvre garçon *or* pauvre vieux*, il est très sourd; **be a good ~ and say nothing** sois gentil (et) ne dis rien.

chapat(t)i [tʃə'pætɪ, tʃə'pɑːtɪ] **n, pl ~** *or* **~s** *or* **~es** pain indien.

chapel ['tʃæpəl] **n a** [*church, school, castle etc*] chapelle *f*; [*house*] oratoire *m*. **~ of ease** (église *f*) succursale *f*; **~ of rest** chapelle ardente; *see* **lady. b** (*nonconformist church*) église *f*, temple *m*. **a ~ family** une famille non-conformiste. **c** (*Ind*) [*printers etc*] association *f*.

chaperon(e) ['ʃæpərəʊn] **1 n** chaperon *m*. **she was the ~** elle faisait office de chaperon.
2 vt chaperonner.

chaplain ['tʃæplɪn] **n** [*armed forces, prison, school, hospital etc*] aumônier *m*; (*to nobleman etc*) chapelain *m*.

chaplaincy ['tʃæplənsɪ] **n** (*see* **chaplain**) aumônerie *f*; chapellenie *f*.

chaplet ['tʃæplɪt] **n** [*flowers etc*] guirlande *f*; (*Archit, Rel*) chapelet *m*.

chappy* ['tʃæpɪ] **n** = **chap³.**

chaps [tʃæps] **npl** (*US*) jambières *fpl* de cuir (*portées par les cowboys*).

chapter ['tʃæptəʳ] **1 n a** [*book*] chapitre *m*. **in ~ 4** au chapitre 4; (*fig*) **to give** *or* **quote ~ and verse** citer ses références *or* ses autorités. **b** (*Rel*) chapitre *m*. **c** (*fig: period*) chapitre *m*, épisode *m*. **a ~ of accidents** une succession de mésaventures, une kyrielle de malheurs; **this ~ is now closed** en voilà assez sur ce chapitre. **d** (*branch of society, club, organization etc*) branche *f*, section *f*. **2 comp ▸ chapterhouse** (*Rel*) chapitre *m* (*lieu*) **▸ chapter room** (*Rel*) salle *f* du chapitre *or* capitulaire.

char¹ [tʃɑːʳ] 1 vt (*burn black*) carboniser. 2 vi être carbonisé.
char²* [tʃɑːʳ] (*Brit*) 1 n (*charwoman*) femme *f* de ménage. 2 vi (*also* **go out ~ring**) faire des ménages.
char³* [tʃɑːʳ] n (*Brit: tea*) thé *m*.
char-à-banc† [ˈʃærəbæŋ] n (auto)car *m* (*décapotable*).
character [ˈkærɪktəʳ] 1 n a (*temperament, disposition*) *[person]* caractère *m*, tempérament *m*. **he has the same ~ as his brother** il a le même caractère que son frère; **it's very much in ~ (for him)** c'est bien de lui, cela lui ressemble tout à fait; **that was not in ~ (for him)** cela ne lui ressemble pas, ce n'est pas dans son caractère.
b (*NonC*) *[country, village]* caractère *m*; *[book, film]* caractère, nature *f*.
c (*NonC: strength, energy, determination etc*) caractère *m*, détermination *f*, volonté *f*. **it takes ~ to say such a thing** il faut avoir du caractère pour dire une chose pareille.
d (*outstanding individual*) personnage *m*; (*: *original person*) numéro* *m*, phénomène* *m*. **he's quite a ~!*** c'est un numéro!* *or* un phénomène!*; **he's a queer** *or* **an odd ~** c'est un type* curieux *or* un curieux personnage.
e réputation *f*. **of good/bad ~** qui a une bonne/qui a mauvaise réputation; (*Jur*) **evidence of good ~** preuve *f* d'honorabilité.
f (*testimonial*) références *fpl*.
g (*Literat*) personnage *m*; (*Theat*) personnage, rôle *m*. **one of Shakespeare's ~s** un des personnages de Shakespeare; **he played the ~ of Hamlet** il a joué (le rôle de) Hamlet.
h (*Typ*) caractère *m*, signe *m* (typographique). **Gothic ~s** caractères gothiques.
i (*Comput*) caractère *m*. **~ set** répertoire *m* de caractères; **~s per inch** caractères par pouce; **~s per second** caractères/seconde *mpl*.
2 comp ▸ **character actor/actress** (*Theat*) acteur *m*/actrice *f* de genre ▸ **character assassination** diffamation *f* (*destinée à ruiner la réputation de qn*) ▸ **character-building** qui forme le caractère ▸ **character comedy** comédie *f* de caractère ▸ **character part** rôle *m* de composition ▸ **character sketch** portrait *m or* description *f* rapide ▸ **character space** (*Typ*) espace *m* ▸ **character string** (*Comput*) chaîne *f* de caractères.
characteristic [ˌkærɪktəˈrɪstɪk] 1 adj caractéristique, typique. **with (his) ~ enthusiasm** avec l'enthousiasme qui le caractérise. 2 n caractéristique *f*, trait distinctif; (*Math*) caractéristique.
characteristically [ˌkærɪktəˈrɪstɪkəlɪ] adv (*gen*) d'une façon caractéristique, typiquement. **~, he refused** comme on pouvait s'y attendre, il a refusé, il a refusé, ce qui était bien dans son caractère.
characterization [ˌkærɪktəraɪˈzeɪʃən] n (*gen*) caractérisation *f*; (*by playwright*) représentation *f* (des caractères); (*by novelist etc*) peinture *f* des caractères; (*by actor*) interprétation *f*. **~ in Dickens** la peinture des caractères chez Dickens, l'art du portrait chez Dickens.
characterize [ˈkærɪktəraɪz] vt caractériser, être caractéristique de; (*Literat*) caractériser, décrire *or* peindre le caractère de.
characterless [ˈkærɪktəlɪs] adj sans caractère, fade.
charade [ʃəˈrɑːd] n charade *f*. (*game*) **~s** charades *fpl*.
charcoal [ˈtʃɑːkəʊl] 1 n charbon *m* de bois. 2 comp *drawing, sketch* au charbon; (*colour: also* **charcoal-grey**) gris foncé *inv*, (gris) anthracite *inv* ▸ **charcoal burner** (*person*) charbonnier *m*; (*stove*) réchaud *m* à charbon de bois.
chard [tʃɑːd] n (*also* **swiss ~**) bettes *fpl*.
charge [tʃɑːdʒ] 1 n a (*Jur*) inculpation *f*, chef *m* d'accusation. **what is the ~?** quelle est l'inculpation?, de quoi est-il (*or* suis-je *etc*) inculpé?; **the ~ was murder** il était (*or* j'étais *etc*) inculpé de meurtre; **to be on a murder ~** être inculpé de meurtre; **the ~ was read** on a lu l'acte *m* d'accusation; **no ~ was brought (against him)** il n'y a pas eu de poursuites (judiciaires), il n'a pas été poursuivi *or* inculpé; **the ~ was dropped** l'inculpation a été retirée, il y a eu cessation de poursuites; **to press ~s (against sb)** engager des poursuites (contre qn); **to bring** *or* **lay a ~ against sb** porter plainte *or* déposer une plainte contre qn; **to give sb in ~** remettre qn à la police; **he was arrested on a ~ of murder** il a été arrêté sous l'inculpation de meurtre; **they were convicted on all three ~s** ils ont été reconnus coupables aux trois chefs d'accusation; *[soldier]* **to be on a ~** être aux arrêts.
b (*gen: accusation*) accusation *f* (*of* de). **he denied these ~s** il a nié, il a repoussé ces accusations; **there were many ~s of cruelty** on les *etc* a fréquemment accusés de cruauté; **the ~s made against him** les accusations *or* les charges portées contre lui; **~s that he had betrayed his friends** des accusations comme quoi il avait trahi ses amis; **to repudiate a ~** repousser une accusation.
c (*esp Mil: attack*) charge *f*, attaque *f*; *[police, bull]* charge. **the police made three ~s into the crowd** la police a chargé trois fois la foule; (*Mil*) **to sound the ~** sonner la charge; *see* **baton, bayonet**.
d (*fee*) prix *m*. **what's the ~?** ça coûte combien?, ça revient à combien?; **what is his ~?** combien prend-il?; **is there a ~?** faut-il payer?, y a-t-il quelque chose à payer?; **there's no ~ for this, no ~ is made for this** c'est gratuit; **free of ~** gratuit; **at a ~ of ...** pour ..., moyennant ...; **there is an extra** *or* **additional ~ for ...** il y a un supplément (à payer) pour ...; **to make a ~ for sth** faire payer qch; **he made no ~ for mending it** il n'a pas fait payer la réparation, il n'a rien pris pour la réparation; **he made a ~ of £5 for doing it** il a pris 5 livres pour le faire; **~ for admission** droit *m* d'entrée; **"no ~ for admission"** "entrée libre"; (*Comm*) **the ~ for delivery, the delivery ~** les frais *mpl* de port; **for a small ~, we can supply ...** pour un prix modique, nous pouvons fournir ...; *see* **bank, reverse** *etc*.
e (*control*) **who's in ~ here?** qui est le *or* la responsable?; **look, I'm in ~ here!** c'est moi qui commande ici!; **the person in ~** le *or* la responsable; **to be in ~ of** *firm, department* diriger, être à la tête de; *ship, plane* commander; *operation, project* diriger, être responsable de; *children, animals* s'occuper de, avoir la charge de; **a few months later, he was in ~ of the shop** au bout de quelques mois, il dirigeait le magasin; **he's in ~ of the shop when I'm out** c'est lui qui s'occupe du magasin *or* qui surveille le magasin quand je m'absente; (*fml*) **while in ~ of a car, he ...** alors qu'il était au volant d'un véhicule, il ...; **to put sb in ~ of** *firm, department* confier à qn la direction de; *ship, plane* confier à qn le commandement de; *operation, project* confier à qn; *children, animals* confier aux soins *or* à la garde de qn; **to put sb in ~ of doing sth** charger qn de faire qch; **to take ~** (*in firm etc*) prendre *or* assurer la direction (*of* de); (*in project*) devenir responsable (*of* de); (*in ship, plane*) prendre *or* assurer le commandement (*of* de); **he took ~ of the situation at once** il a immédiatement pris la situation en main; **will you take ~ of the children while I'm away?** est-ce que tu veux bien te charger des enfants pendant mon absence?; **the patients in** *or* **under her ~** les malades dont elle a la charge; **I left him in ~** je lui ai laissé la charge de tout.
f (*person/thing cared for*) personne *f*/chose *f* confiée à la garde *or* à la charge (*de qn*); (*priest's parish*) cure *f*. **the priest's ~s** (*his parishioners*) les ouailles *fpl* du curé; **she took her ~s for a walk** elle a fait faire une promenade aux malades (*or* aux enfants *or* aux élèves *etc*) confiés à sa garde *or* dont elle avait la charge.
g (*financial burden*) charge *f*, fardeau *m* (*on* pour). **to be a ~ on** constituer une charge *or* un fardeau pour.
h (*instructions*) recommandation *f*, instruction *f*. **to have strict ~ to do** avoir reçu l'ordre formel de faire; (*Jur*) **the judge's ~ to the jury** les recommandations données aux jurés par le juge.
i (*Elec, Phys*) charge *f*. **to put a battery on ~** mettre une batterie en charge; **there is no ~ left in the battery** la batterie est déchargée *or* à plat.
j *[firearm]* charge *f*; *[rocket]* charge *f*; *see* **depth**.
k (*Her*) meuble *m*.
2 comp ▸ **charge account** (*Comm*) compte *m* ▸ **charge-capping** (*Brit*) plafonnement *m* des impôts locaux ▸ **charge card** (*Comm*) carte *f* de clientèle ▸ **charge hand** (*Brit*) sous-chef *m* d'équipe ▸ **charge nurse** (*Brit*) infirmier *m* en chef ▸ **charge sheet** (*Police*) ≃ procès-verbal *m*.
3 vt a (*accuse: gen*) accuser (*sb with sth* qn de qch, *sb with doing/having done* qn de faire/d'avoir fait); (*Jur*) inculper (*sb with sth* qn de qch). (*Jur*) **he was ~d with murder/with having stolen a car** il a été inculpé de meurtre/de vol de voiture; (*US*) **he ~d that some companies had infringed the regulations** il a allégué que certaines compagnies avaient enfreint le règlement.
b (*attack*) *[troops]* charger, attaquer; *[police, bull etc]* charger.
c (*in payment*) *person* faire payer; *amount* prendre, demander (*for* pour). **to ~ a commission** prélever une commission *or* un pourcentage; **I ~d him £2 for this table** je lui ai fait payer cette table 2 livres; **how much do you ~ for mending shoes?** combien prenez-vous pour réparer des chaussures?; **to ~ sb too much for sth** compter *or* faire payer qch trop cher à qn; **I won't ~ you for that** je ne vous compterai *or* prendrai rien pour cela.
d (*record as debt: also* **~ up**) mettre sur le compte, porter au compte *or* au débit (*to sb* de qn). **~ all these purchases (up) to my account** mettez tous ces achats sur mon compte; (*in shop*) **cash or ~?** vous payez comptant ou vous voulez que je le mette sur votre compte?; **I can ~ it to the company** je peux le faire payer *or* rembourser par la compagnie; (*US: in library*) **to ~ a book** inscrire un livre au registre du prêt.
e *firearm, battery* charger (*also Phys*). (*fig*) **~d with emotion, emotionally ~** plein d'émotion; **a highly ~d atmosphere** une atmosphère très tendue.
f (*command etc*) **to ~ sb to do** ordonner *or* commander *or* enjoindre (*liter*) à qn de faire, sommer qn de faire; **to ~ sb with sth** confier qch à qn.
4 vi a (*rush*) se précipiter, foncer*. **to ~ in/out** entrer/sortir en coup de vent; **to ~ up/down** grimper/descendre à toute vitesse; **to ~ through** foncer à travers*.
b (*Mil*) **to ~ (down) on the enemy** fondre *or* foncer* sur l'ennemi.
c *[battery]* se (re)charger, être en charge.
▸**charge down** vt sep (*Rugby*) **to charge a kick down** contrer un coup de pied, faire un contre; *see also* **charge 4**.
▸**charge off** vt sep (*Comm*) *machine* amortir. **they charged off drilling costs as business expenses** ils ont imputés les coûts de forage à l'exploitation; **to charge off an expense** passer une dépense en charge.
▸**charge up** vt sep a = **charge 3d**. b *battery* charger.
chargé d'affaires [ˈʃɑːʒeɪ dæˈfeə] n, pl **chargés d'affaires** chargé *m*

d'affaires.

chargeable ['tʃɑːdʒəbl] adj a (*Jur*) *person* ~ **with** passible de poursuites pour. b ~ **to** à mettre aux frais de, à porter au compte de; (*Fin*) ~ **event** fait *m* générateur de la taxe.

charger ['tʃɑːdʒəʳ] n a *[battery, firearm]* chargeur *m*. b (*Mil: horse*) cheval *m* (de bataille).

charily ['tʃɛərɪlɪ] adv prudemment, avec prudence *or* circonspection.

chariot ['tʃærɪət] n char *m*.

charioteer [ˌtʃærɪə'tɪəʳ] n conducteur *m* de char, aurige *m*.

charisma [kæ'rɪzmə] n (*Rel*) charisme *m*; (*fig*) charisme, rayonnement *m*, magnétisme *m*.

charismatic [ˌkærɪz'mætɪk] adj (*Rel*) charismatique; (*fig*) charismatique, plein de magnétisme.

charitable ['tʃærɪtəbl] adj *person, thought* charitable, généreux; *deed* de charité, charitable. ~ **foundation** *or* **institution** fondation *f* charitable; ~ **organization** organisme *m* caritatif, œuvre *f* de bienfaisance.

charitably ['tʃærɪtəblɪ] adv charitablement.

charity ['tʃærɪtɪ] 1 n a (*NonC*) (*Christian virtue*) charité *f*; (*kindness*) charité, amour *m* du prochain. **for ~'s sake, out of** ~ par (pure) charité; (*Prov*) ~ **begins at home** charité bien ordonnée commence par soi-même (*Prov*); (*Rel*) **sister of C~** sœur *f* de charité; *see* **cold, faith.**
b (*charitable action*) acte *m* de charité, action *f* charitable.
c (*NonC: alms*) charité *f*, aumône *f*. **to live on** ~ vivre d'aumônes; **to collect for** ~ faire une collecte pour une œuvre (charitable); **the proceeds go to** ~ les fonds recueillis sont versés à des œuvres.
d (*charitable society*) fondation *f or* institution *f* charitable, œuvre *f* de bienfaisance.
2 comp ▸ **charity sale** vente *f* de charité *or* de bienfaisance ▸ **charity toss** (*Basketball*) lancer *m* franc.

charlady ['tʃɑːleɪdɪ] n (*Brit*) femme *f* de ménage.

charlatan ['ʃɑːlətən] 1 n charlatan *m*. 2 adj charlatanesque.

Charlemagne ['ʃɑːləmeɪn] n Charlemagne *m*.

Charles [tʃɑːlz] n Charles *m*.

charleston ['tʃɑːlstən] n charleston *m*.

charley horse* ['tʃɑːlɪhɔːs] n (*US*) crampe *f*, spasme *m*.

Charlie ['tʃɑːlɪ] n Charlot *m*. (*Brit*) **he must have looked a proper ~!**‡ il a dû avoir l'air fin! *or* malin!*; (*Brit*) **I felt a right ~!**‡ j'ai vraiment eu l'air idiot!

charlotte ['ʃɑːlət] n (*Culin*) charlotte *f*. **apple** ~ charlotte aux pommes.

charm [tʃɑːm] 1 n a (*attractiveness*) charme *m*, attrait *m*. **a lady's ~s** les charmes d'une dame; **to have a lot of** ~ avoir beaucoup de charme; **to fall victim to the ~s of** se rendre aux charmes de.
b (*spell*) charme *m*, enchantement *m*, sortilège *m*. **to hold sb under a** ~ tenir qn sous le charme; **it works like a** ~ ça marche à merveille.
c (*amulet*) charme *m*, fétiche *m*, amulette *f*; (*trinket*) breloque *f*.
2 comp ▸ **charm bracelet** bracelet *m* à breloques ▸ **charm price** prix *m* psychologique ▸ **charm school** cours *m* de maintien.
3 vt (*attract, please*) charmer, enchanter; (*cast spell on*) enchanter, ensorceler; *snakes* charmer. **to have** *or* **lead a ~ed life** être béni des dieux; **to ~ sth out of sb** obtenir qch de qn par le charme *or* en lui faisant du charme.

▸**charm away** vt sep faire disparaître comme par enchantement *or* par magie. **to charm away sb's cares** dissiper les soucis de qn comme par enchantement *or* par magie.

charmer ['tʃɑːməʳ] n charmeur *m*, -euse *f*; *see* **snake.**

charming ['tʃɑːmɪŋ] adj charmant.

charmingly ['tʃɑːmɪŋlɪ] adv d'une façon charmante, avec (beaucoup de) charme. **a ~ simple dress** une robe d'une simplicité charmante.

charnel-house ['tʃɑːnlhaʊs] n ossuaire *m*, charnier *m*.

charr [tʃɑːʳ] n = **char³**.

chart [tʃɑːt] 1 n a (*map*) carte *f* (marine).
b (*graphs etc*) graphique *m*, diagramme *m*, tableau *m*; (*Med*) courbe *f*. **temperature** ~ (*sheet*) feuille *f* de température; (*line*) courbe *f* de température.
c (*Mus*) **the ~s** le Top 50, le hit-parade, le palmarès de la chanson; **in the ~s** au Top 50 *or* au hit-parade; **to reach the ~s** figurer au Top 50 *or* au hit-parade; **to top the ~s** être en tête des meilleures ventes *or* du Top 50 *or* du hit-parade.
2 vt a (*draw on map*) *route, journey* porter sur la carte.
b (*on graph*) *sales, profits, results* faire le graphique *or* la courbe de. **this graph ~s the progress made last year** ce graphique montre les progrès accomplis l'an dernier.
c (*fig: plan*) organiser, planifier.
3 comp ▸ **chart topper** (*Mus*) numéro 1 du Top 50 ▸ **chart-topping** qui vient en tête des meilleures ventes *or* du Top 50.

charter ['tʃɑːtəʳ] 1 n a (*document*) charte *f*; *[society, organization]* statuts *mpl*, acte constitutif. **the C~ of the United Nations** la Charte des Nations Unies. b (*NonC*) *[boat, plane, coach, train etc]* affrètement *m*. **on** ~ sous contrat d'affrètement. c (*also* ~ **flight**) (vol) charter *m*. 2 comp ▸ **charter flight** (vol *m*) charter *m*; **to take a charter flight to Rome** aller à Rome en charter ▸ **charter member** (*US*) membre fondateur ▸ **charter party** (*Jur*) charte-partie *f* ▸ **charter plane** charter *m* ▸ **charter train** train *m* charter. 3 vt a accorder une charte à, accorder un privilège (par une charte) à. b *plane etc* affréter.

chartered ['tʃɑːtəd] adj (*Brit, Can*) ~ **accountant** expert-comptable *m*, comptable agréé (*Can*); ~ **company** société privilégiée; ~ **society** compagnie *f* à charte; ~ **surveyor** expert immobilier.

charterer ['tʃɑːtərəʳ] n affréteur *m*.

Chartist ['tʃɑːtɪst] n (*Hist*) **the ~s** les chartistes *mpl*.

charwoman ['tʃɑːˌwʊmən] n femme *f* de ménage.

chary ['tʃɛərɪ] adj a (*cautious*) prudent, circonspect, avisé. **to be ~ of doing** hésiter à faire. b (*stingy*) économe, avare, peu prodigue (*of* de). **he is ~ of praise** il est avare de compliments.

chase¹ [tʃeɪs] 1 n a (*action*) chasse *f*, poursuite *f*. **to give ~ to** faire *or* donner la chasse à, poursuivre; **in ~ of** à la poursuite de; **the ~** (*Sport*) la chasse (à courre); (*huntsmen*) la chasse, les chasseurs *mpl*; *see* **paper, steeple, wild** *etc*. b (*game*) gibier *m*; (*enemy hunted*) ennemi *m* (poursuivi). 2 vt poursuivre, faire *or* donner la chasse à; *success, women etc* courir après. **he ~d him down the hill** il l'a poursuivi jusqu'au bas de la colline; **go and ~ yourself!**‡ va te faire voir!‡; (*Drugs sl*) **to ~ the dragon** chasser le dragon. 3 vi a (*lit, fig*) **to ~ after sb** courir après qn. b (*rush*) **to ~ up/down/out** *etc* monter/descendre/sortir *etc* au grand galop; (*Brit*) **to ~ about, to ~ here and there** galoper*, courir à droite et à gauche.

▸**chase away, chase off** 1 vi (*) filer*, se trotter‡. 2 vt sep *person, animal* chasser, faire partir.

▸**chase up** vt sep *information* rechercher; *sth already asked for* réclamer. **to chase sb up for sth** rappeler à qn de faire (*or* donner *etc*) qch; **I'll chase it** (*or* **him** *etc*) **up for you** je vais essayer d'activer les choses.

chase² [tʃeɪs] vt (*Tech*) *diamond* enchâsser (*in* dans); *silver* ciseler; *metal* repousser; *screw* fileter.

chaser ['tʃeɪsəʳ] n a *[person, ship, plane]* chasseur *m*. b (*Tech*) graveur *m* sur métaux; *[screw]* peigne *m* (à fileter). c (*: *drink*) verre pris pour en faire descendre un autre.

chasm ['kæzəm] n (*lit, fig*) gouffre *m*, abîme *m*.

chassis ['ʃæsɪ] n, pl **chassis** ['ʃæsɪz] (*Aut*) châssis *m*; (*Aviat*) train *m* d'atterrissage; (*US* ‡: *body*) châssis‡.

chaste [tʃeɪst] adj *person* chaste, pur; *style* sobre, simple, pur.

chastely ['tʃeɪstlɪ] adv *behave* chastement; *dress* avec sobriété, simplement.

chasten ['tʃeɪsn] vt (*punish*) châtier, corriger; (*subdue*) assagir, calmer; *style* châtier, épurer, corriger.

chastened ['tʃeɪsnd] adj *person* assagi, calmé; *style* châtié.

chasteness ['tʃeɪstnɪs] n (*see* **chaste**) chasteté *f*, pureté *f*; sobriété *f*, simplicité *f*.

chastening ['tʃeɪsnɪŋ] adj *thought* qui fait réfléchir (à deux fois). **the accident had a very ~ effect on him** l'accident l'a fait réfléchir *or* l'a assagi.

chastise [tʃæs'taɪz] vt (*scold*) réprimander; (*punish*) punir, châtier; (*beat*) battre, corriger.

chastisement ['tʃæstɪzmənt] n (*see* **chastise**) punition *f*, châtiment *m*; correction *f*.

chastity ['tʃæstɪtɪ] n chasteté *f*, pudeur *f*. ~ **belt** ceinture *f* de chasteté.

chasuble ['tʃæzjʊbl] n chasuble *f*.

chat [tʃæt] 1 n (*NonC*) bavardage *m*; (*conversation*) causette *f*, brin *m* de conversation. **to have a** ~ bavarder, causer; **they were having a ~ in the corridor** ils bavardaient *or* causaient dans le couloir; **I must have a ~ with him about this** il faut que je lui en parle. 2 comp ▸ **chatline** ≃ conversation *f* à trois ▸ **chat show** (*Brit TV*) causerie télévisée. 3 vi bavarder, causer (*with, to* avec).

▸**chat up*** vt sep (*Brit*) baratiner*; (*from sexual motive*) baratiner*, faire du plat* à.

chattel ['tʃætl] 1 npl: **~s** (*gen*) biens *mpl*, possessions *fpl*; (*Jur*) biens meubles. **with all his goods and** ~ avec tout ce qu'il possède (*or* possédait *etc*). 2 comp ▸ **chattel mortgage** (*Jur, Fin*) nantissement *m* de biens meubles.

chatter ['tʃætəʳ] 1 vi a (*gen*) bavarder, jacasser (*pej*); *[children, monkeys]* jacasser; *[birds]* jacasser, jaser. b *[engines]* cogner; *[tools]* brouter. **his teeth were ~ing** il claquait des dents. 2 n *[person]* bavardage *m*; *[birds, children, monkeys]* jacassement *m*; *[engines]* cognement *m*; *[tools]* broutement *m*; *[teeth]* claquement *m*. 3 comp ▸ **chatterbox** moulin *m* à paroles*, bavard(e) *m(f)*; **to be a chatterbox** avoir la langue bien pendue, être bavard comme une pie.

chatterer ['tʃætərəʳ] n = **chatterbox**; *see* **chatter 3.**

chattering ['tʃætərɪŋ] 1 n bavardage m. 2 comp ▸ **the ~ classes*** (*Brit pej*) les intellos* *mpl*.

chatty* ['tʃætɪ] adj *person* bavard; *style* familier, qui reste au niveau du bavardage; *letter* plein de bavardages.

Chaucerian [tʃɔː'sɪərɪən] adj de Chaucer, chaucérien.

chauffeur ['ʃəʊfəʳ] 1 n chauffeur *m* (de maître). 2 vt: **to ~ sb around** *or* **about** servir de chauffeur à qn. 3 comp ▸ **chauffeur-driven car** voiture *f* avec chauffeur.

chauvinism ['ʃəʊvɪnɪzəm] n (*gen*) chauvinisme *m*; (*male* ~) machisme *m*, phallocratie *f*.

chauvinist ['ʃəʊvɪnɪst] 1 n (*gen*) chauvin(e) *m(f)*; (*male* ~) macho *m*, phallocrate *m*. 2 adj (*gen*) chauvin; (*male* ~) macho* *inv*, machiste, de phallocrate. **male ~ pig** phallocrate *m*.

chauvinistic [ˌʃəʊvɪˈnɪstɪk] **adj** (*gen*) chauvin; (*male ~*) macho* *inv*, machiste, de phallocrate.

chaw [tʃɔː] (*dial*) = **chew**.

C.H.E. [ˈsiːˈeɪtʃˈiː] (**abbr of Campaign for Homosexual Equality**) campagne *f* pour l'égalité des homosexuels.

cheap [tʃiːp] **1 adj a** (*inexpensive*) bon marché *inv*, peu cher (*f* peu chère); *tickets* à prix réduit; *fare* réduit; (*Econ*) *money* bon marché. **on the ~** *buy, decorate* à bon marché, pour pas cher; (*pej: too cheaply*) au rabais, en faisant un minimum de dépenses; (*Comm*) **to come** *or* **be ~er** revenir *or* coûter moins cher; **it's ~ at the price** (*Comm*) c'est une occasion à ce prix-là; (*fig*) les choses auraient pu être pires; **a ~er coat** un manteau meilleur marché *or* moins cher; **the ~est coat** le manteau le meilleur marché *or* le moins cher; (*Printing*) **~ edition** édition *f* populaire *or* bon marché; **~ and cheerful** sans prétentions; **~ labour** main d'œuvre pas chère; *see* **dirt**.
b (*pej: of poor quality*) de mauvaise qualité, de pacotille. **this stuff is ~ and nasty** c'est de la camelote*.
c (*fig pej: worthless*) *success, joke* facile. **his behaviour was very ~** il s'est très mal conduit; *[woman]* **to make o.s. ~** être facile; **to feel ~** avoir honte (*about* de); **human life is ~** la vie humaine n'a pas grande importance *or* ne compte pas beaucoup.
2 adv (*not expensive*) bon marché; (*cut-price*) au rabais.
3 comp ▸ cheapjack adj de camelote **▸ cheapshot*** (*US*) **vt** débiner*, dénigrer.

cheapen [ˈtʃiːpən] **1 vt** baisser le prix de; (*fig*) déprécier. **to ~ o.s.** *[woman]* être facile; (*gen*) se déconsidérer. **2 vi** baisser, devenir moins cher.

cheapie‡ [ˈtʃiːpɪ] **1 adj** pas cher. **2 n** (*ticket/meal etc*) billet/repas *etc* pas cher.

cheaply [ˈtʃiːplɪ] **adv** à bon marché, à bas prix, pour pas cher. (*fig*) **to get off ~*** s'en tirer à bon compte.

cheapness [ˈtʃiːpnɪs] **n** (*lit*) bas prix *m*.

cheapo* [ˈtʃiːpəʊ] **adj** bon marché.

cheapskate* [ˈtʃiːpskeɪt] **n** grigou* *m*, radin *mf*, avare *mf*.

cheat [tʃiːt] **1 vt** (*deceive*) tromper, duper; (*defraud*) frauder; (*swindle*) escroquer; (*fig*) *time etc* tromper. **to ~ sb at cards** tromper qn aux cartes; **to ~ sb out of sth** escroquer qch à qn; **to ~ sb into doing sth** faire faire qch à qn en le trompant; **to feel ~ed** se sentir floué; (*betrayed*) se sentir trahi. **2 vi** (*at cards, games*) tricher (*at* à); (*defraud*) frauder. (*US: be unfaithful to*) **to ~ on sb*** tromper qn, être infidèle à qn. **3 n** (*person*) tricheur *m*, -euse *f*; (*deception*) escroquerie. **it's a bit of a ~ to use ready-prepared meals** c'est un peu de la triche d'utiliser des plats tout prêts.

cheating [ˈtʃiːtɪŋ] **1 n** (*at cards, games*) tricherie *f*; (*deceitful act*) tromperie *f*; (*fraud*) fraude *f*; (*swindle*) escroquerie *f*. **2 adj** tricheur.

check¹ [tʃek] **1 n** = **cheque**. **2 comp ▸ checkbook** carnet *m* de chèques, chéquier *m*.

check² [tʃek] **1 n a** (*setback*) *[movement]* arrêt *m* brusque; *[plans etc]* empêchement *m*; (*Mil*) échec *m*, revers *m*; (*pause, restraint*) arrêt momentané, pause *f*, interruption *f*. **to hold** *or* **keep in ~** (*gen*) *emotions etc* contenir, maîtriser; (*Mil*) tenir en échec; **to put a ~ on** mettre un frein à; **to act as a ~ upon** freiner; (*US Pol*) **~s and balances** équilibre *m* des pouvoirs, mécanisme *m* d'équilibre.
b (*examination*) *[papers, passport, ticket]* contrôle *m*; *[luggage]* vérification *f*; (*at factory door*) pointage *m*; (*mark*) marque *f* de contrôle. **to make a ~ on** contrôler, vérifier, pointer; **to keep a ~ on** surveiller; (*US*) **~!*** d'accord!, OK!*
c (*Chess*) échec *m*. **in ~** en échec; (*excl*) **~!** échec au roi!
d *[left luggage]* bulletin *m* de consigne; (*Theat*) contremarque *f*; *[restaurant]* addition *f*. (*US fig*) **to cash in one's ~s**‡ passer l'arme à gauche‡, mourir.
2 comp ▸ check-in (*at airport*) enregistrement *m* (des bagages); **your check-in time is half-an-hour before departure** présentez-vous à l'enregistrement des bagages une demi-heure avant le départ **▸ check-list** (*gen*) liste *f* de contrôle; (*Aviat*) check-list *f*, (liste de) contrôle *m* **▸ checkmate n** (*Chess*) échec et mat *m*; (*fig*) échec total, fiasco *m* ◊ **vt** (*Chess*) faire échec et mat à; (*fig*) *person* coincer*, mettre en déconfiture*; *plans etc* déjouer **▸ check-out** (*Comm*) caisse *f* (*dans un libre-service*); (*in hotel*) **check-out time** heure *f* limite d'occupation **▸ checkpoint** (*Aut, Mil, Sport*) contrôle *m* (*poste*); (*Mil*) **Checkpoint Charlie** checkpoint *m* Charlie **▸ checkroom** (*US: cloakroom*) vestiaire *m* **▸ checkup** (*gen*) contrôle *m*, vérification *f*; (*Med*) examen *m* médical, bilan *m* de santé, check-up *m*; (*Med*) **to go for** *or* **have a checkup** se faire faire un bilan (de santé).
3 vt a (*also ~ out*) (*examine, verify*) *accounts, figures, statement, quality etc* vérifier; *tickets, passports* contrôler; (*mark off*) pointer, faire le pointage de; (*tick off*) cocher. **to ~ a copy against the original** vérifier une copie en se référant à l'original, collationner une copie avec l'original; **is it there? — hold on, I'll just ~** ça y est? — attends, je vais vérifier.
b (**: also ~ out: look at*) regarder, viser*. **~ out his shoes** vise un peu ses chaussures.
c (*stop*) *enemy* arrêter; *advance* enrayer; (*restrain*) *excitement* refréner, contenir; *anger* maîtriser, réprimer. **he was going to protest, but she ~ed him** il allait protester, mais elle l'a retenu; **to ~ o.s.** se contrôler, se retenir.
d (*rebuke*) réprimander.
e (*Chess*) faire échec à.
f (*US*) *coats* (*in cloakroom*) mettre au vestiaire; (*Rail*) *luggage* (*register*) faire enregistrer; (*left luggage*) mettre à la consigne.
4 vi a (*pause*) s'arrêter (*momentanément*).
b (*also ~ out: confirm each other*) *[figures, stories]* correspondre, s'accorder.

▸check in 1 vi (*in hotel*) (*arrive*) arriver; (*register*) remplir une fiche (d'hôtel); (*at airport*) se présenter à l'enregistrement. **2 vt sep** faire remplir une fiche (d'hôtel) à; (*at airport*) enregistrer. **3 check-in n, adj** *see* **check² 2**.

▸check off vt sep pointer, cocher.

▸check on vt fus *information, time etc* vérifier. **to check on sb** voir ce que fait qn; **just go and check on the baby** va jeter un coup d'œil sur le bébé.

▸check out 1 vi a (*from hotel*) régler sa note. **b** *see* **check² 4b**. **c** (‡ *euph: die*) passer l'arme à gauche‡, mourir. **2 vt sep a** *see* **check² 3a, 3b**. **b** (**: look at*) jeter un œil à*. **c** *luggage* retirer; *person* contrôler la sortie de; *hotel guest* faire payer sa note à. **3 check-out n, adj** *see* **check² 2**.

▸check over vt sep examiner, vérifier.

▸check up 1 vi se renseigner, vérifier. **to check up on sth** vérifier qch; **to check up on sb** se renseigner sur qn. **2 checkup n** *see* **check² 2**.

check³ [tʃek] **1 n** (*gen pl*) **~s** (*pattern*) carreaux *mpl*, damier *m*; (*cloth*) tissu *m* à carreaux; **broken ~** pied-de-poule *m*. **2 comp** = **checked**.

checked [tʃekt] **adj a** *tablecloth, suit, pattern* à carreaux. **b** (*Phon*) **~ vowel** voyelle entravée.

checker [ˈtʃekəʳ] **n** (*see* **check² 3a**) vérificateur *m*, -trice *f*; contrôleur *m*, -euse *f*; (*US: in supermarket*) caissier *m*, -ière *f*; (*US: in cloakroom*) préposé(e) *m(f)* au vestiaire.

checkerboard [ˈtʃekəbɔːd] **n** (*US*) (*Chess*) échiquier *m*; (*Checkers*) damier *m*. **~ pattern** motif *m* à damiers.

checkered [ˈtʃekəd] **adj** (*US*) = **chequered**.

checkers [ˈtʃekəz] **npl** (*US*) jeu *m* de dames.

checking [ˈtʃekɪŋ] **1 n** (*see* **check² 3a**) vérification *f* (*of, on* de); contrôle *m* (*of, on* de). **2 comp ▸ checking account** (*US Fin*) compte courant **▸ checking deposit** dépôt *m* à vue.

cheddar [ˈtʃedəʳ] **n** (fromage *m* de) cheddar *m*.

cheek [tʃiːk] **1 n a** (*Anat*) joue *f*. **~ by jowl** côte à côte; **~ by jowl with** tout près de; **to dance ~ to ~** danser joue contre joue; **~bone** pommette *f*; *see* **tongue, turn**. **b** (**: buttock*) fesse *f*. **c** (**: impudence*) toupet* *m*, culot* *m*. **to have the ~ to do** avoir le toupet* *or* le culot* de faire; **what (a) ~!, of all the ~!** quel culot!*, quel toupet!* **2 vt** (*Brit *: also ~ up*) *person* être insolent avec, narguer.

cheekily [ˈtʃiːkɪlɪ] **adv** effrontément, avec insolence.

cheekiness [ˈtʃiːkɪnɪs] **n** effronterie *f*, toupet* *m*, culot* *m*.

cheeky [ˈtʃiːkɪ] **adj** *child* effronté, insolent, culotté*; *remark* impertinent. **~ child** petit(e) effronté(e) *m(f)*; **you ~ monkey!*, you ~ thing!*** quel toupet!*

cheep [tʃiːp] **1 n** *[bird]* piaulement *m*; *[mouse]* couinement *m*. **2 vi** *[bird]* piauler; *[mouse]* couiner. **3 vt** *[person]* couiner*.

cheer [tʃɪəʳ] **1 n a ~s** acclamations *fpl*, applaudissements *mpl*, hourras *mpl*, bravos *mpl*; **to give three ~s for** acclamer; **three ~s for ...!** un ban pour ...!, hourra pour ...!; **three ~s!** hourra!; **the children gave a loud ~** les enfants ont poussé des acclamations; (*esp Brit*) **~s!*** (*your health!*) à la vôtre!* (*or* à la tienne!*); (*goodbye*) au revoir!, tchao!*; (*thanks*) merci!
b (*†: cheerfulness*) gaieté *f*, joie *f*. **words of ~** paroles *fpl* d'encouragement; **be of good ~!** prenez courage!
c (*†: food etc*) chère *f*. **good ~** bonne chère.
2 comp ▸ cheerleader (*Sport*) meneur *m* (qui rythme les cris des supporters).
3 vt a (*also ~ up*) *person* remonter le moral à, réconforter; *room* égayer.
b (*applaud*) acclamer, applaudir.
4 vi applaudir, pousser des vivats *or* des hourras.

▸cheer on vt sep *person, team* encourager (*par des cris, des applaudissements*).

▸cheer up 1 vi (*be gladdened*) s'égayer, se dérider; (*be comforted*) prendre courage, prendre espoir. **cheer up!** courage! **2 vt sep** = **cheer 3a**.

cheerful [ˈtʃɪəfʊl] **adj** *person, smile, conversation* joyeux, gai, enjoué, plein d'entrain; *place, appearance, colour* gai, riant; *prospect* attrayant; *news* réconfortant, réjouissant, qui réjouit le cœur. (*iro*) **that's ~!** c'est réjouissant! (*iro*); *see* **cheap**.

cheerfully [ˈtʃɪəfəlɪ] **adv** gaiement, joyeusement, avec entrain.

cheerfulness [ˈtʃɪəfʊlnɪs] **n** *[person]* bonne humeur *f*, gaieté *f*, entrain *m*; *[smile, conversation]* gaieté; *[place]* gaieté, aspect riant *or* réjouissant.

cheerily [ˈtʃɪərɪlɪ] **adv** gaiement, joyeusement, avec entrain.

cheering [ˈtʃɪərɪŋ] 1 n (*NonC*) applaudissements *mpl*, acclamations *fpl*, hourras *mpl*. 2 adj *news, sight* réconfortant, réjouissant, qui remonte le moral.
cheerio* [ˈtʃɪərɪˈəʊ] excl (*esp Brit*) a (*goodbye*) au revoir!, salut!*, tchao!* b (*your health*) à la vôtre! (*or* à la tienne!)
cheerless [ˈtʃɪəlɪs] adj *person, thing* morne, sombre, triste.
cheery [ˈtʃɪərɪ] adj gai, joyeux.
cheese [tʃiːz] 1 n fromage *m*. **Dutch ~** fromage de Hollande; (*for photograph*) **"say ~"** "un petit sourire"; *see* **cottage, cream, lemon.**
2 vt a (*Brit*) **to be ~d (off)**‡ en avoir marre*; **to be ~d off with sth**‡ en avoir marre de qch*.
b (*US*) **~ it!**‡ (*look out*) vingt-deux!‡; (*run away*) tire-toi!‡
3 comp *sandwich* au fromage ▸ **cheese and wine (party)** ≃ buffet *m* campagnard ▸ **cheeseboard** (*dish*) plateau *m* à fromage(s); (*with cheeses on it*) plateau de fromages ▸ **cheeseburger** hamburger *m* au fromage ▸ **cheesecake** (*NonC*) (*Culin*) flan *m* au fromage blanc; (*: *fig*) photo *f* (de fille) déshabillée ▸ **cheesecloth** (*for cheese*) étamine *f*, mousseline *f* à fromage; (*for clothes*) toile *f* à beurre ▸ **cheese dip** dip *m* au fromage ▸ **cheese dish** = **cheese board** ▸ **cheeseparing** n économie(s) *f(pl)* de bouts de chandelles ◊ adj *person* pingre, qui fait des économies de bouts de chandelles; *attitude, action* (de) rapiat*, pingre.
cheesy [ˈtʃiːzɪ] n a (*lit*) qui a un goût de fromage, qui sent le fromage. b (*US* ‡: *pej*) moche*. c (*broad*) *grin* figé.
cheetah [ˈtʃiːtə] n guépard *m*.
chef [ʃef] n chef *m* (de cuisine).
chef d'œuvre [ʃedʒːvrə] n, pl **chefs d'œuvre** chef-d'œuvre *m*.
cheiromancer [ˈkaɪərəmænsəʳ] n = **chiromancer.**
cheiromancy [ˈkaɪərəmænsɪ] n = **chiromancy.**
Chekhov [ˈtʃekɒf] n Tchekhov *m*.
chemical [ˈkemɪkəl] 1 adj chimique. **~ agent** agent *m* chimique; **~ engineer** ingénieur *m* chimiste; **~ engineering** génie *m* chimique; **~ warfare** guerre *f* chimique; **~ weapons** armes *fpl* chimiques. 2 n (*gen pl*) produit *m* chimique.
chemically [ˈkemɪkəlɪ] adv chimiquement.
chemise [ʃəˈmiːz] n (††: *undergarment*) chemise *f* (*de femme*); (*dress*) robe-chemisier *f*.
chemist [ˈkemɪst] n a (*researcher etc*) chimiste *mf*. b (*Brit: pharmacist*) pharmacien(ne) *m(f)*. **~'s (shop)** pharmacie *f*.
chemistry [ˈkemɪstrɪ] 1 n chimie *f*. (*fig*) **they work so well together because the ~ is right** ils travaillent très bien ensemble parce que le courant passe. 2 comp ▸ **chemistry set** panoplie *f* de chimiste.
chemotherapy [ˌkeməʊˈθerəpɪ] n chimiothérapie *f*.
chenille [ʃəˈniːl] n (*Tex*) chenille *f*.
cheque, (*US*) **check** [tʃek] 1 n chèque *m*. **~ for £10** chèque de 10 livres; **~ in the amount of $10** chèque de 10 dollars; **to pay by ~** payer par chèque; **bad** *or* **dud ~** chèque sans provision *or* en bois*. 2 comp ▸ **cheque account** compte-chèques *m* ▸ **chequebook** carnet *m* de chèques, chéquier *m* ▸ **chequebook journalism** *pratique qui consiste à payer des sommes considérables pour obtenir les confidences exclusives de personnes impliquées dans une affaire* ▸ **cheque card** (*Brit*) carte *f* d'identité bancaire; *see* **traveller** *etc*.
chequered, (*US*) **checkered** [ˈtʃekəd] adj (*lit*) à carreaux, à damier; (*fig*) varié. **he had a ~ career** sa carrière a connu des hauts et des bas.
chequers [ˈtʃekəz] n jeu *m* de dames.
cherish [ˈtʃerɪʃ] vt *person* chérir, aimer; *feelings, opinion* entretenir; *hope, illusions* nourrir, caresser; *memory* chérir. **one of his ~ed dreams** l'un de ses rêves les plus chers.
cheroot [ʃəˈruːt] n petit cigare (*à bouts coupés*), cigarillo *m*.
cherry [ˈtʃerɪ] 1 n (*fruit*) cerise *f*; (*also* **~ tree**) cerisier *m*. **wild ~** (*fruit*) merise *f*; (*tree*) merisier *m*; *see* **bite.** 2 comp (*colour*) (rouge) cerise *inv*; (*liter*) *lips* vermeil; (*Culin*) *pie, tart* aux cerises ▸ **cherry brandy** cherry-brandy *m* ▸ **cherry orchard** cerisaie *f* ▸ **cherry-red** (rouge) cerise *inv* ▸ **cherry tomato** tomate-cerise *f*.
cherub [ˈtʃerəb] n a *pl* **~s** chérubin *m*, petit amour, petit ange. b (*Rel*) *pl* **~im** chérubin *m*.
cherubic [tʃeˈruːbɪk] adj *face* de chérubin; *child, smile* angélique.
chervil [ˈtʃɜːvɪl] n cerfeuil *m*.
Ches. abbr of **Cheshire.**
chess [tʃes] 1 n échecs *mpl*. 2 comp ▸ **chessboard** échiquier *m* ▸ **chessman** pièce *f* (de jeu d'échecs) ▸ **chessplayer** joueur *m*, -euse *f* d'échecs.
chest[1] [tʃest] 1 n (*box*) coffre *m*, caisse *f*; (*tea ~*) caisse *f*. 2 comp ▸ **chest freezer** congélateur-bahut *m* ▸ **chest of drawers** commode *f*; *see* **medicine, tool** *etc*.
chest[2] [tʃest] 1 n (*Anat*) poitrine *f*, cage *f* thoracique (*Med frm*). **to have a weak ~** être faible des bronches; **to get something off one's ~*** déballer* ce qu'on a sur le cœur. 2 comp ▸ **chest cold** rhume *m* de poitrine ▸ **chest expander** extenseur *m* (*pour développer les pectoraux*) ▸ **chest infection** infection *f* des voies respiratoires ▸ **chest pain** (*NonC*), **chest pains** douleurs *fpl* de poitrine ▸ **chest specialist** spécialiste *mf* des voies respiratoires.
chesterfield [ˈtʃestəfiːld] n canapé *m*, chesterfield *m*.
chestnut [ˈtʃesnʌt] 1 n a châtaigne *f*; (*Culin*) châtaigne, marron *m*. (*fig*) **to pull sb's ~s out of the fire** tirer les marrons du feu pour qn; *see* **horse, Spanish, sweet.** b (*also* **~ tree**) châtaignier *m*, marronnier *m*. c (*horse*) alezan *m*. d (* *pej: story*) **(old) ~** vieille histoire rabâchée, vieille blague* usée. 2 adj: **~-brown** châtain; **~ hair** cheveux châtains; **~ horse** (cheval *m*) alezan *m*.
chesty [ˈtʃestɪ] adj (*Brit*) *person* fragile de la poitrine; *cough* de poitrine.
cheval glass [ʃəˈvælglɑːs] n psyché *f* (*glace*).
chevron [ˈʃevrən] n chevron *m*.
chew [tʃuː] 1 vt mâcher, mastiquer. **to ~ tobacco** chiquer; (*lit, fig*) **to ~ the cud** ruminer; **to ~ the fat**‡ *or* **the rag**‡ tailler une bavette*. 2 n mâchement *m*, mastication *f*; [*tobacco*] chique *f*. 3 comp ▸ **chewing gum** chewing-gum *m*.
▸**chew on** vt fus (*fig*) *facts, problem* tourner et retourner.
▸**chew out** vt sep engueuler.
▸**chew over** vt sep *problem etc* (*think over*) tourner et retourner; (*discuss*) discuter de.
▸**chew up** vt sep mâchonner, mâchouiller*.
chewy [ˈtʃuːɪ] adj (*pej*) difficile à mâcher. **~ toffee** caramel mou.
chiaroscuro [kɪˌɑːrəsˈkʊərəʊ] n clair-obscur *m*.
chiasma [kaɪˈæzmə] n, pl **~s** *or* **chiasmata** [kaɪˈæzmətə] (*Anat*) chiasma *m*, chiasme *m*.
chic [ʃiːk] 1 adj chic *inv*, élégant. 2 n chic *m*, élégance *f*.
chicanery [ʃɪˈkeɪnərɪ] n (*legal trickery*) chicane *f*; (*false argument*) chicane, chicanerie *f*.
Chicano [tʃɪˈkɑːnəʊ] n (*US*) Mexicain(e)-Américain(e) *m(f)*, Chicano *mf*.
chichi* [ˈʃiːˌʃiː] adj (*too stylish*) trop recherché.
chick [tʃɪk] 1 n a (*chicken*) poussin *m*; (*nestling*) oisillon *m* (*qui vient d'éclore*); *see* **day.** b (‡: *child*) poulet* *m*, coco* *m*. **come here ~!** viens ici mon coco! *or* mon petit poulet! c (*US* *: *girl*) pépée‡ *f*, poulette‡ *f*. 2 comp ▸ **chickpea** pois *m* chiche ▸ **chickweed** mouron blanc *or* des oiseaux.
chickadee [ˈtʃɪkəˌdiː] n mésange *f* à tête noire.
chicken [ˈtʃɪkɪn] 1 n poulet(te) *m(f)*; (*very young*) poussin *m*; (*Culin*) poulet. (*pej*) **she's no (spring) ~!*** elle n'est plus toute jeune *or* de la première jeunesse; (*fig*) **which came first, the ~ or the egg?** quelle est la cause et quel est l'effet? allez savoir!; **it's a ~ and egg situation** c'est comme l'histoire de la poule et de l'œuf; *see* **count**[1].
2 adj (* *pej: cowardly*) froussard*. **to play ~** jouer au premier qui se dégonfle*.
3 comp ▸ **chicken farmer** éleveur *m* avicole *or* de volailles, volailleur *m* ▸ **chicken farming** élevage *m* avicole *or* de volailles ▸ **chickenfeed** (*lit*) nourriture *f* pour volaille; (* *pej: insignificant sum*) somme *f* dérisoire, bagatelle *f* ▸ **chicken-hearted** peureux ▸ **chicken liver** foie(s) *m(pl)* de volaille ▸ **chickenpox** varicelle *f* ▸ **chicken run** poulailler *m* ▸ **chicken wire** grillage *m*.
▸**chicken out**‡ vi se dégonfler*. **he chickened out of his exams** au moment de ses examens, il s'est dégonflé*.
chicory [ˈtʃɪkərɪ] n [*coffee*] chicorée *f*; [*salads*] endive *f*.
chide [tʃaɪd] pret **chid** [tʃɪd] *or* **chided**, ptp **chidden** [ˈtʃɪdn] *or* **chided** vt gronder, réprimander.
chief [tʃiːf] 1 n a (*gen, Her*) chef *m*. (*principally*) **in ~** principalement, surtout; **~ of police** ≃ préfet *m* (de police); (*Mil*) **~ of staff** chef d'état-major; (*US*) **(White House) C~ of Staff** secrétaire *m* général (de la Maison Blanche); **~ of state** chef d'État; (*fig*) **too many ~s and not enough Indians** trop de chefs et pas assez d'exécutants; *see* **commander, lord.**
b (*: *boss*) patron *m*. **yes, ~!** oui, chef! *or* patron!
2 adj principal, en chef. **~ assistant** premier assistant; (*Brit Police*) **~ constable** ≃ directeur *m* (de police); (*Scol*) **~ education officer** ≃ recteur *m* d'académie; (*Naut*) **~ engineer** ingénieur *m* en chef; **C~ Executive** (*Brit: local government*) directeur *m*; (*US Pol*) chef *m* de l'Exécutif, président *m* des États-Unis; (*US Ind, Comm*) **~ executive officer** directeur général; **~ inspector** (*gen*) inspecteur principal *or* en chef; (*Brit Police*) commandant *m* (des gardiens de la paix); (*Brit Scol*) **~ inspector of schools** ≃ inspecteur général; (*US Aviat*) **~ master sergeant** major *m*; (*Naut*) **~ petty officer** ≃ maître *m*; **~ priest** archiprêtre *m*; **~ rabbi** grand rabbin; (*US Scol*) **~ state school officer** ≃ recteur *m* d'académie; (*Brit Police*) **~ superintendent** ≃ commissaire *m* divisionnaire; **~ technician** technicien *m* en chef; **~ town** chef-lieu *m*; (*Mil*) **~ warrant officer** adjudant *m* chef; *see* **lord.**
chiefly [ˈtʃiːflɪ] adv principalement, surtout.
chieftain [ˈtʃiːftən] n chef *m* (*de clan, de tribu*).
chiffchaff [ˈtʃɪfˌtʃæf] n pouillot *m* véloce.
chiffon [ˈʃɪfɒn] 1 n mousseline *f* de soie. 2 adj *dress* en mousseline (de soie).
chignon [ˈʃiːnjɔ̃ːŋ] n chignon *m*.
chihuahua [tʃɪˈwɑːwɑː] n chihuahua *m*.
chilblain [ˈtʃɪlbleɪn] n engelure *f*.
child [tʃaɪld], pl **children** 1 n a enfant *mf*. **when still a ~, he ...** tout enfant, il ...; **don't be such a ~** ne fais pas l'enfant; **she has 3 children** elle a 3 enfants; **to be with ~**† être enceinte.

b (*fig*) produit *m*, fruit *m*. **the ~ of his imagination** le produit *or* le fruit de son imagination; *see* **brain.**

2 **comp** *labour* des enfants; *psychology, psychiatry* de l'enfant, infantile; *psychologist, psychiatrist* pour enfants ► **child abduction** (*Jur*) enlèvement *m* d'enfant ► **child abuse** *or* **battering** mauvais traitements à enfant ► **childbearing** (*NonC*) maternité *f*; **constant childbearing** accouchements répétés, grossesses répétées; **of childbearing age** en âge d'avoir des enfants ► **childbed**†: **in childbed** en couches ► **child benefit** (*Brit*) ≃ allocations *fpl* familiales ► **childbirth** accouchement *m*; **in childbirth** en couches ► **child care** protection *f* infantile *or* de l'enfance, assistance *f* à l'enfance; (*US*) **child care center** crèche *f*, garderie *f* ► **child guidance** hygiène sociale de l'enfance; **child guidance centre** *or* **clinic** centre *m* psychopédagogique ► **childlike** d'enfant, innocent, pur ► **child lock** *[door]* serrure *f* de sécurité enfants ► **childminder** (*Brit*) gardienne *f* d'enfants (en bas âge) ► **childminding** (*Brit*) garde *f* d'enfants (en bas âge) ► **child molester** violeur *m* d'enfants ► **child prodigy** enfant *mf* prodige ► **childproof** *door etc* sans danger pour les enfants; **childproof (door) lock** serrure *f* de sécurité enfants; **the house is childproof** (*safe*) la maison est sans danger pour les enfants; (*cannot be damaged*) les enfants ne peuvent rien abîmer dans la maison ► **child's play**: (*fig*) **it's child's play** c'est enfantin, c'est un jeu d'enfant (*to sb* pour qn) ► **child-resistant** sécurité enfants ► **child welfare** protection *f* de l'enfance; **Child Welfare Centre** centre *m or* service *m* de protection de l'enfance.

childhood ['tʃaɪldhʊd] **n** enfance *f*. **in his ~ he ...** tout enfant il ...; *see* **second.**

childish ['tʃaɪldɪʃ] **adj** a (*slightly pej*) *behaviour* puéril (*pej*), d'enfant, enfantin. **~ reaction** réaction puérile; **don't be so ~** ne fais pas l'enfant; **he was very ~ about it** il s'est montré très puéril à ce sujet. b *ailment, disease* infantile. **~ games** jeux *mpl* d'enfant.

childishly ['tʃaɪldɪʃlɪ] **adv** *think, say* comme un enfant, puérilement; *behave* en enfant, comme un enfant.

childishness ['tʃaɪldɪʃnɪs] **n** (*slightly pej*) puérilité *f*, enfantillage *m*.

childless ['tʃaɪldlɪs] **adj** sans enfants.

children ['tʃɪldrən] **npl of child**; *see* **home 1c.**

Chile ['tʃɪlɪ] **n** Chili *m*.

Chilean ['tʃɪlɪən] 1 **adj** chilien. 2 **n** Chilien(ne) *m(f)*.

chili ['tʃɪlɪ] **n** (*Brit*) piment *m* (rouge). **~ con carne** chili con carne; **~ powder** piment *m* (rouge) en poudre, poudre *m* de piment (rouge).

chill [tʃɪl] 1 **n** a fraîcheur *f*, froid *m*. **there's a ~ in the air** il fait assez frais *or* un peu froid; **to take the ~ off** *wine* chambrer; *water* dégourdir; *room* réchauffer un peu.

b (*fig*) froid *m*, froideur *f*. **to cast a ~ over** jeter un froid sur; **there was a certain ~ in the way she looked at me** il y avait une certaine froideur dans sa façon de me regarder; **it sent a ~ down my spine** j'en ai eu un frisson dans le dos; **he felt a certain ~ as he remembered ...** il a eu un *or* le frisson en se rappelant ... .

c (*Med*) refroidissement *m*, coup *m* de froid. **to catch a ~** prendre froid, prendre un refroidissement.

2 **adj** frais (*f* fraîche), froid; (*fig*) froid, glacial, glacé.

3 **vt** a (*lit*) *person* faire frissonner, donner froid à; *wine, melon* (faire) rafraîchir; *champagne* frapper; *meat* frigorifier, réfrigérer; *dessert* mettre au frais; *plant* geler; (*Tech*) tremper en coquille. **to be ~ed to the bone** *or* **marrow** être transi jusqu'aux os *or* jusqu'à la moelle.

b (*fig*) *enthusiasm* refroidir. **to ~ sb's blood** glacer le sang de qn; *see* **spine.**

4 **vi** *[wine]* rafraîchir.

►**chill out*** **vi** (*esp US*) se relaxer, décompresser*. **chill out** relax!*

chilli ['tʃɪlɪ] **n = chili.**

chill(i)ness ['tʃɪl(ɪ)nɪs] **n** (*cold*) froid *m*; (*coolness*) fraîcheur *f*; (*fig*) froideur *f*.

chilling ['tʃɪlɪŋ] **adj** *wind* frais, froid; *look* froid, glacial, glacé; *thought* qui donne le frisson.

chilly ['tʃɪlɪ] **adj** *person* frileux; *weather, wind* froid, très frais (*f* fraîche); *manner, look, smile* glacé, froid. *[person]* **to feel ~** avoir froid; **it's rather ~** il fait frais *or* frisquet*.

chime [tʃaɪm] 1 **n** carillon *m*. **to ring the ~s** carillonner; **a ~ of bells** un carillon; **(door) ~s** carillon *m* de porte. 2 **vi** *[bells, voices]* carillonner; *[clock]* sonner. 3 **vt** *bells, hours* sonner.

►**chime in vi** (*fig*) *[person]* faire chorus. **he chimed in with another complaint** il a fait chorus pour se plaindre à son tour.

chimera [kaɪ'mɪərə] **n** chimère *f*.

chimerical [kaɪ'merɪkəl] **adj** chimérique.

chimney ['tʃɪmnɪ] 1 **n** (*Archit, Geog, Naut, Sport*) cheminée *f*; *[lamp]* verre *m*. 2 **comp** ► **chimney breast** manteau *m* de (la) cheminée ► **chimney-climbing** (*Climbing*) ramonage *m* ► **chimney corner** coin *m* du feu ► **chimneypiece** (dessus *m or* tablette *f* de) cheminée *f* ► **chimney pot** tuyau *m* de cheminée ► **chimney-pot hat*** tuyau *m* de poêle* ► **chimney stack** (*group of chimneys*) souche *f* de cheminée; *[factory]* tuyau *m* de cheminée (d'usine) ► **chimney sweep** ramoneur *m*.

chimp* [tʃɪmp] **n = chimpanzee.**

chimpanzee [ˌtʃɪmpæn'ziː] **n** chimpanzé *m*.

chin [tʃɪn] 1 **n** menton *m*. **to keep one's ~ up*** tenir bon, tenir le coup*; **(keep your) ~ up!*** courage!, du cran!*; (*fig*) **to take it on the ~*** encaisser*; *see* **double.** 2 **comp** ► **chin-chin!*** tchin-tchin!* ► **chinstrap** jugulaire *f* (*de casque etc*) ► **chin-up:** (*Sport*) **to do chin-ups** faire des tractions à la barre fixe ► **chinwag**‡ causerie *f*; **to have a chinwag**‡ tailler une bavette*, papoter. 3 **vi** (* *US*) bavarder.

China ['tʃaɪnə] 1 **n** Chine *f*. 2 **comp** ► **Chinaman** (*pej*) Chinois *m*, Chin(e)toque‡ *m* (*pej*) ► **China Sea** mer *f* de Chine ► **China tea** thé *m* de Chine ► **Chinatown** le quartier chinois (*d'une ville*).

china ['tʃaɪnə] 1 **n** (*NonC: material, dishes*) porcelaine *f*. **a piece of ~** une porcelaine; *see* **bone.** 2 **comp** *cup, figure* de *or* en porcelaine ► **china cabinet** dressoir *m* ► **china clay** kaolin *m* ► **china industry** industrie *f* de la porcelaine ► **chinaware** (*NonC*) (objets *mpl* de) porcelaine *f*.

chinchilla [tʃɪn'tʃɪlə] **n** chinchilla *m*. **~ coat** manteau *m* de chinchilla.

Chinese [tʃaɪ'niːz] 1 **adj** chinois. **~ checkers** (*US*) *or* **chequers** (*Brit*) solitaire *m*; **~ lantern** lanterne vénitienne; **~ gooseberry** kiwi *m* (*fruit*); **~ leaves** bette *f*; **~ puzzle** casse-tête *m inv* chinois; **~ white** blanc *m* de zinc. 2 **n** a (**pl inv**) Chinois(e) *m(f)*. b (*Ling*) chinois *m*. c (*: *also* **~ meal**) (repas *m*) chinois *m*; (*: *also* **~ restaurant**) (restaurant *m*) chinois *m*.

chink[1] [tʃɪŋk] **n** (*slit, hole*) *[wall]* fente *f*, fissure *f*; *[door]* entrebâillement *m*. (*fig*) **the ~ in the armour** le défaut de la cuirasse, le point faible *or* sensible.

chink[2] [tʃɪŋk] 1 **n** (*sound*) tintement *m* (*de verres, de pièces de monnaie*). 2 **vt** faire tinter. 3 **vi** tinter.

Chink‡ [tʃɪŋk] **n** (*pej*) Chin(e)toque‡ *mf* (*pej*).

chinning ['tʃɪnɪŋ] **adj** (*Sport*) **~ bar** barre *f* fixe.

chinos ['tʃiːnəʊz] **npl** chinos *mpl*.

chintz [tʃɪnts] **n** (*Tex*) chintz *m*. **~ curtains** rideaux *mpl* de chintz.

chintzy ['tʃɪntsɪ] **adj** a *style* rustique. b (‡ *US: mean*) moche*, mesquin.

chip [tʃɪp] 1 **n** a (*gen*) fragment *m*; *[wood]* copeau *m*, éclat *m*; *[glass, stone]* éclat; (*Electronics*) microplaquette *f*. **he's a ~ off the old block*** c'est bien le fils de son père; **to have a ~ on one's shoulder** être aigri; **to have a ~ on one's shoulder because ...** n'avoir jamais digéré le fait que* ...; (*Naut sl*) **C~s** charpentier *m*; *see* **polystyrene.**

b (*Culin*) **~s** (*Brit*) (pommes *fpl* de terre) frites *fpl*; (*US*) chips *mpl*.

c (*Comput*) puce *f*, pastille *f*.

d (*break*) *[stone, crockery, glass]* ébréchure *f*; *[furniture]* écornure *f*. **this cup has a ~** cette tasse est ébréchée.

e (*Poker etc*) jeton *m*, fiche *f*. (*fig*) **to pass in** *or* **hand in** *or* **cash in one's ~s*** passer l'arme à gauche*; **he's had his ~s**‡ il est cuit* *or* fichu*; **when the ~s are down*** dans les moments cruciaux; (*US*) **in the ~s**‡ plein aux as‡.

f (*Golf*) coup coché.

2 **comp** ► **chip basket** (*Brit*) panier *m* à frites ► **chipboard** (*US*) carton *m*; (*Brit*) panneau *m* de particules ► **chip shop** (*Brit*) friterie *f*.

3 **vt** a (*damage*) *cup, plate* ébrécher; *furniture* écorner; *varnish, paint* écailler; *stone* écorner, enlever un éclat de. **to ~ wood** faire des copeaux; **the chicken ~ped the shell open** le poussin a cassé sa coquille.

b (*Brit*) *vegetables* couper en lamelles. **~ped potatoes** (pommes *fpl* de terre) frites *fpl*.

c (*cut deliberately*) tailler.

d (*Golf*) **to ~ the ball** cocher.

4 **vi** (*see* **3a**) s'ébrécher; s'écorner; s'écailler.

►**chip at vt fus** a *stone etc* enlever des éclats de. b (*: *make fun of*) se ficher de*.

►**chip away** 1 **vi** *[paint etc]* s'écailler. (*fig*) **to chip away at** *sb's authority, lands* réduire petit à petit; *law, decision* réduire petit à petit la portée de. 2 **vt sep** *paint etc* enlever *or* décaper petit à petit (*au couteau etc*).

►**chip in vi** a (*: *interrupt*) dire son mot, mettre son grain de sel*. b (*: *contribute*) contribuer, souscrire (*à une collecte etc*). **he chipped in with 10 francs** il y est allé de (ses) 10 F*.

►**chip off = chip away.**

chipmunk ['tʃɪpmʌŋk] **n** tamia *m*, suisse *m* (*Can*).

chipolata [tʃɪpə'lɑːtə] **n** (*Brit*) chipolata *f*.

chippings ['tʃɪpɪŋz] **npl** gravillons *mpl*. **"loose ~"** "attention gravillons".

chippy* ['tʃɪpɪ] **n** (*Brit*) friterie *f*.

chiromancer ['kaɪərəmænsə^r] **n** chiromancien(ne) *m(f)*.

chiromancy ['kaɪərəmænsɪ] **n** chiromancie *f*.

chiropodist [kɪ'rɒpədɪst] **n** (*Brit*) pédicure *mf*.

chiropody [kɪ'rɒpədɪ] **n** (*Brit*) (*science*) podologie *f*; (*treatment*) soins *mpl* du pied, traitement *m* des maladies des pieds.

chiropractic ['kaɪərəpræktɪk] **n** (*NonC*) chiropraxie *f*, chiropractie *f*.

chiropractor ['kaɪərəpræktə^r] **n** chiropracteur *m*.

chirp [tʃɜːp] 1 **vi** a *[birds]* pépier, gazouiller; *[crickets]* chanter, striduler (*liter*). b (*: *slightly pej*) *[person]* pépier, couiner* (*pej*). 2 **n** *[birds]* pépiement *m*, gazouillis *m*; *[crickets]* chant *m*, stridulation *f*;

[person] murmure *m*. **not a ~ from you!*** je ne veux pas t'entendre!, je ne veux pas entendre un seul murmure!

chirpy* ['tʃɜːpɪ] **adj** *person* gai, de bonne humeur; *voice, mood* gai.

chirrup ['tʃɪrəp] = **chirp**.

chisel ['tʃɪzl] 1 **n** *[carpenter, sculptor, silversmith]* ciseau *m*; *[stonemason]* burin *m*; (*blunt ~*) matoir *m*; (*hollow ~*) gouge *f*; (*mortise ~*) bédane *m*; (*roughing-out ~*) ébauchoir *m*; *see* **cold**.
2 **vt** a ciseler; (*Engraving*) buriner. **~led features** traits burinés; **finely ~led features** traits finement ciselés.
b (*: *swindle*) *thing* resquiller; *person* rouler*, posséder*. **to ~ sb out of sth** carotter* qch à qn.

chiseller*, (*US*) **chiseler*** ['tʃɪzləʳ] **n** (*crook*) escroc *m*, filou *m*; (*scrounger*) resquilleur *m*, -euse *f*.

chit[1] [tʃɪt] **n**: **she's a mere ~ of a girl** ce n'est qu'une gosse* *or* une gamine* *or* une mioche*.

chit[2] [tʃɪt] **n** (*gen*) bulletin *m* de livraison; (*receipt*) reçu *m*; (*note*) note *f*.

chitchat ['tʃɪttʃæt] **n** bavardage *m*.

chitterlings ['tʃɪtəlɪŋz] **npl** tripes *fpl* (de porc).

chitty ['tʃɪtɪ] **n** = **chit**[2].

chiv* [tʃɪv] **n** surin* *m*, couteau *m*.

chivalresque [ʃɪvəl'resk] **adj**, **chivalric** [ʃɪ'vælrɪk] **adj** chevaleresque.

chivalrous ['ʃɪvəlrəs] **adj** (*courteous*) chevaleresque; (*gallant*) galant.

chivalrously ['ʃɪvəlrəslɪ] **adv** (*see* **chivalrous**) de façon chevaleresque; galamment.

chivalry ['ʃɪvəlrɪ] **n** a chevalerie *f*. **the rules/the age of ~** les règles *fpl*/l'âge *m* de la chevalerie; (*hum*) **the age of ~ is not dead** on sait encore être galant aujourd'hui. b (*quality*) qualités *fpl* chevaleresques; (*gallantry*) galanterie *f*. c (*collective: Hist: knights*) chevalerie *f*.

chive [tʃaɪv] **n** (*gen pl*) ciboulette *f*, civette *f*.

chivvy* ['tʃɪvɪ] **vt** (*Brit*) a (*also ~* **along**) *person, animal* chasser, pourchasser. b (*pester*) ne pas laisser la paix à. **she chivvied him into writing the letter** elle l'a harcelé jusqu'à ce qu'il écrive la lettre.

►**chivvy about*** **vt sep** (*Brit*) *person* harceler, tarabuster.

►**chivvy up*** **vt sep** *person* faire activer.

chlamydia [klə'mɪdɪə] **n** (*Med*) chlamydia *f*.

chloral ['klɔːrəl] **n** chloral *m*.

chlorate ['klɔːreɪt] **n** chlorate *m*.

chloric ['klɔːrɪk] **adj** chlorique. **~ acid** acide *m* chlorique.

chloride ['klɔːraɪd] **n** chlorure *m*. **~ of lime** chlorure de chaux.

chlorinate ['klɒrɪneɪt] **vt** *water* chlorer; (*Chem*) chlorurer.

chlorination [klɒrɪ'neɪʃən] **n** *[water]* javellisation *f*.

chlorine ['klɔːriːn] **n** chlore *m*.

chlorofluorocarbon [ˌklɔːrəˌflʊərəʊ'kɑːbən] **n** (*Chem*) chlorofluorocarbone *m*.

chloroform ['klɒrəfɔːm] 1 **n** chloroforme *m*. 2 **vt** chloroformer.

chlorophyll ['klɒrəfɪl] **n** chlorophylle *f*.

chloroplast ['klɔːrəʊˌplæst] **n** chloroplaste *m*.

choc* [tʃɒk] **n** (**abbr of chocolate**) choco* *m*. **~-ice** esquimau *m*.

chocaholic [ˌtʃɒkə'hɒlɪk] **n** accro* *mf* du chocolat.

chock [tʃɒk] 1 **n** *[wheel]* cale *f*; *[barrel]* cale, chantier *m*; (*Naut*) chantier, cale.
2 **vt** *wheel* caler; (*Naut*) mettre sur le chantier *or* sur cales.
3 **comp** ► **chock-a-block, chock-full** *basket, pan, box* plein à déborder (*with, of* de); *room* plein à craquer (*with, of* de), comble.

chocolate ['tʃɒklɪt] 1 **n** chocolat *m*. (**drinking**) **~** chocolat; **a ~** un chocolat, une crotte au chocolat; *see* **dessert, milk, plain** *etc*. 2 **comp** (*made of ~*) en chocolat; (*with ~ in it, flavoured with ~*) (au) chocolat, chocolaté; (*colour: also ~* **brown**) chocolat *inv* ► **chocolat bar** barre *f* de *or* au chocolat ► **chocolate biscuit** biscuit *or* petit gâteau au chocolat ► **chocolate-box adj** trop joli *or* mignon ► **chocolate chip cookie** biscuit *m* aux perles de chocolat ► **chocolate eclair** éclair *m* au chocolat.

choice [tʃɔɪs] 1 **n** a (*act or possibility of choosing*) choix *m*. **to make a ~** faire un choix, choisir; **to take one's ~** faire son choix; **to have no ~** ne pas avoir le choix; **be careful in your ~** faites attention en choisissant; **he didn't have a free ~** il n'a pas été libre de choisir; **to have a very wide ~** avoir l'embarras du choix; **he had no ~ but to obey** il ne pouvait qu'obéir; **it's Hobson's ~** c'est à prendre ou à laisser; **from** *or* **for ~** de *or* par préférence; **he did it from ~** il l'a fait de son propre choix, il a choisi de le faire; **the house/girl of his (own) ~** la maison/fille de son (propre) choix; **it's your ~!*** c'est ton problème!*
b (*thing or person chosen*) choix *m*. **this book would be my ~** c'est ce livre que je choisirais.
c (*Comm etc: variety to choose from*) choix *m*, variété *f*. **a wide ~ of dresses** un grand choix de robes.
2 **adj** a (*Comm*) *goods, fruit* de choix. **~st** de premier choix.
b *word, phrase* bien choisi, approprié.

choir ['kwaɪəʳ] 1 **n** a (*Mus*) chœur *m*, chorale *f*; (*Rel*) chœur, maîtrise *f*. **to sing in the ~** faire partie du chœur *or* de la chorale, chanter dans la maîtrise. b (*Archit, Rel*) chœur *m*. 2 **vti** chanter en chœur. 3 **comp** ► **choirboy** jeune choriste *m*, petit chanteur ► **choirmaster** (*Mus*) chef *m* de(s) chœur(s); (*Rel*) maître *m* de chapelle ► **choir organ** petit orgue; (*keyboard*) positif *m* ► **choir practice**: **to go to choir practice** aller à la chorale ► **choir school** maîtrise *f*, manécanterie *f* (*rattachée à une cathédrale*) ► **choir-stall** stalle *f* (du chœur).

choke [tʃəʊk] 1 **vt** a *person, voice, breathing* étrangler. **to ~ the life out of sb** étrangler qn; **in a voice ~d with sobs** d'une voix étranglée par les sanglots. b (*fig*) *fire* étouffer; *pipe, tube* boucher, obstruer, engorger. **flowers ~d by weeds** fleurs étouffées par les mauvaises herbes; **street ~d with traffic** rue engorgée *or* embouteillée. 2 **vi** étouffer, s'étrangler. **she ~d with anger** la rage l'étouffait, elle étouffait de rage; **he was choking with laughter** il s'étranglait de rire. 3 **n** (*Aut*) starter *m*; (*Rad*) bobine *f* de réactance, inductance *f* de protection. 4 **comp** ► **choke chain** collier *m* étrangleur.

►**choke back vt sep** *feelings* réprimer, étouffer, contenir; *tears* refouler; *words* contenir.

►**choke down vt sep** *rage* contenir; *sobs* ravaler, étouffer.

►**choke off*** **vt sep** (*fig*) *suggestions etc* étouffer (dans l'œuf); *discussion* empêcher; *person* envoyer promener*.

►**choke up** 1 **vi** s'engorger, se boucher. 2 **vt sep** *pipe, drain* engorger, obstruer, boucher.

choked [tʃəʊkt] **adj** (*: *Brit*) (*upset*) estomaqué*. **in a ~ voice** d'une voix étranglée.

choker ['tʃəʊkəʳ] **n** a (*scarf*) foulard *m*, écharpe *f*; (*necktie*) cravate *f*; (*collar*) col droit; (*necklace*) collier *m* (de chien). b (*) argument *m* massue. **that's a ~!** ça vous la boucle!*

choking ['tʃəʊkɪŋ] **n** (*Med*) suffocation *f*.

cholera ['kɒlərə] **n** choléra *m*.

choleric ['kɒlərɪk] **adj** colérique, coléreux.

cholesterol [kə'lestəˌrɒl] **n** cholestérol *m*.

chomp* [tʃɒmp] **vti** mâcher bruyamment. **to ~ (away) on** *or* **at sth** dévorer qch à belles dents.

Chomskyan ['tʃɒmskɪən] **adj** chomskyen, de Chomsky.

choose [tʃuːz] **pret chose, ptp chosen** 1 **vt** a (*select*) choisir, faire choix de; (*elect*) élire. **which will you ~?** lequel choisirez-vous?; **they chose a president** ils ont élu un président; **he was chosen leader** ils l'ont pris pour chef; **the Chosen (People)** les Élus; **the chosen (few)** les (quelques) élus *mpl*; **there is little** *or* **not much to ~ between them** il n'y a guère de différence entre eux; **there is nothing to ~ between them** ils se valent; (*pej*) ils ne valent pas mieux l'un que l'autre; **in a few (well-)chosen words** en quelques mots choisis.
b décider, juger bon (*to do* de faire), vouloir (*to do* faire). **he chose not to speak** il a jugé bon de se taire, il a préféré se taire; **I didn't ~ to do so** (*decided not to*) j'ai décidé de ne pas le faire; (*did it unwillingly*) je ne l'ai pas fait de mon propre choix.
2 **vi** choisir. **as you ~** comme vous voulez *or* l'entendez, à votre gré; **if you ~** si cela vous dit; **he'll do it when he ~s** il le fera quand il voudra *or* quand ça lui plaira; **to ~ between/among** faire un choix entre/parmi; **there's not much to ~ from** il n'y a pas tellement de choix.

choos(e)y* ['tʃuːzɪ] **adj** *person* difficile (à satisfaire). **I'm not ~** ça m'est égal; **you can't be ~ in your position** votre situation ne vous permet pas de faire le difficile; **I'm ~ about the people I go out with** je ne sors pas avec n'importe qui.

chop[1] [tʃɒp] 1 **n** a (*Culin*) côtelette *f*. **mutton/pork ~** côtelette de mouton/de porc; *see* **loin**.
b (*blow*) coup *m* (de hache *etc*). **you're the next for the ~*** tu es le prochain à y passer*; **to get the ~*** *[employee]* se faire sacquer* *or* virer*; *[project]* être annulé.
c (*Tennis*) volée coupée *or* arrêtée.
2 **comp** ► **chop-chop*** **adv** en moins de deux* ◊ **excl** au trot!*, et que ça saute!* ► **chophouse** (petit) restaurant *m*, gargote *f* (*pej*) ► **chopping block** billot *m* ► **chopping board** planche *f* à hacher ► **chopping knife** hachoir *m* (*couteau*) ► **chopsticks** baguettes *fpl* (*pour manger*).
3 **vt** a trancher, couper (*à la hache*). **to ~ wood** couper *or* casser du bois (*à la hache*); **to ~ one's way through** se frayer un chemin à coups de hache à travers; (*fig *: cancel*) **to ~ a project** annuler un projet; (*fig *: reduce*) *costs, bills* faire des coupes sombres dans, sabrer dans.
b (*Culin*) *meat, vegetables* hacher.
c (*Sport*) *ball* couper.

►**chop at vt fus** *person etc* essayer de frapper; (*with axe*) *wood* taillader (*à la hache*).

►**chop down vt sep** *tree* abattre.

►**chop off vt sep** trancher, couper. **they chopped off his head** on lui a tranché la tête.

►**chop up vt sep** hacher, couper en morceaux; (*Culin*) hacher menu.

chop[2] [tʃɒp] **n** (*Culin*) *[pork]* joue *f*. **~s** (*jaws of animals*) mâchoires *fpl*; (*cheeks*) joues; *[animals]* bajoues *fpl*; (*Tech*) *[vice]* mâchoires; **to lick one's ~s** se lécher *or* se pourlécher les babines.

chop[3] [tʃɒp] 1 **vi** a (*Naut*) *[wind]* varier; *[waves]* clapoter. b (*fig*) **to ~ and change** changer constamment d'avis; **he's always ~ping and changing** c'est une vraie girouette, il ne sait pas ce qu'il veut. 2 **vt** (*pej*) **to ~ logic** ergoter, discutailler.

chop[4]* [tʃɒp] **n** nourriture *f*, bouffe* *f*.

chopper [ˈtʃɒpəʳ] 1 n a (*for cutting*) couperet *m*, hachoir *m*; (*Agr*) coupe-racines *m inv*. b (**: helicopter*) hélicoptère *m*, hélico* *m*, banane‡ *f*; (** US: motorcycle*) chopper *m*; (*Brit: cycle*) vélo *m* à haut guidon. 2 vi (‡ *US: go by helicopter*) se rendre en hélicoptère (*to* à).

choppy [ˈtʃɒpɪ] adj *lake* clapoteux; *sea* un peu agité; *wind* variable.

chop suey [tʃɒpˈsuːɪ] n chop suey *m*, (*sorte de ragoût en cuisine sino-américaine*).

choral [ˈkɔːrəl] adj choral, chanté en chœur. ~ **society** chorale *f*.

chorale [kɒˈrɑːl] n choral *m*.

chord [kɔːd] n (*Anat, Geom: also of harp etc*) corde *f*; (*Mus*) accord *m*. ~ **change** changement *m* d'accord; ~ **progression** suite *f* d'accords; (*fig*) **to strike** *or* **touch a ~, to touch the right ~** toucher la corde sensible; *see* **vocal**.

chore [tʃɔːʳ] n (*everyday*) travail *m* de routine; (*unpleasant*) corvée *f*. **the ~s** les travaux du ménage; **to do the ~s** faire le ménage.

choreograph [ˈkɒrɪəˌgrɑːf] vt a composer la chorégraphie. b (*fig: stage*) monter, mettre en scène (*fig*).

choreographer [ˌkɒrɪˈɒgrəfəʳ] n chorégraphe *mf*.

choreographic [ˌkɒrɪəʊˈgræfɪk] adj chorégraphique.

choreography [ˌkɒrɪˈɒgrəfɪ] n chorégraphie *f*.

chorister [ˈkɒrɪstəʳ] n (*Rel*) choriste *mf*.

chortle [ˈtʃɔːtl] 1 vi rire (*about, at, over* de), glousser. **he was chortling over the newspaper** la lecture du journal le faisait glousser. 2 n gloussement *m*.

chorus [ˈkɔːrəs] 1 n, pl **~es** a (*Mus, Theat: song, singers, speakers*) chœur *m*. **in ~** en chœur; **she's in the ~** (*at concert*) elle chante dans les chœurs; (*Theat*) elle fait partie de la troupe; (*Theat*) **~ girl** girl *f*; (*fig*) **a ~ of praise/objections** un concert de louanges/protestations. b (*part of song*) refrain *m*. **to join in the ~** *[one person]* reprendre le refrain; *[several people]* reprendre le refrain en chœur. 2 vt *song* chanter *or* réciter en chœur; *verse* réciter en chœur. **"yes" they ~sed** "oui" répondirent-ils en chœur.

chose [tʃəʊz] pret of **choose**.

chosen [ˈtʃəʊzn] ptp of **choose**; *see* **choose 1a**.

chough [tʃʌf] n crave *m* à bec rouge.

choux [ʃuː] n (*Culin*) ~ **pastry** pâte *f* à choux.

chow[1] [tʃaʊ] n (*dog*) chow-chow *m*.

chow[2]‡ [tʃaʊ] n (*food*) bouffe‡ *f*, boustifaille‡ *f*.

chowder [ˈtʃaʊdəʳ] n (*US*) soupe épaisse de palourdes; *see* **clam**.

Christ [kraɪst] 1 n le Christ, Jésus-Christ. 2 excl: **~!*‡** merde (alors)!‡, Bon Dieu (de Bon Dieu)!‡; **~ (only) knows!*‡** Dieu seul le sait*. 3 comp ▸ **the Christ Child** l'enfant Jésus ▸ **Christlike** qui ressemble *or* semblable au Christ; **he had a Christlike forbearance** il avait la patience du Christ.

Christadelphian [ˌkrɪstəˈdelfɪən] adj, n christadelphe (*mf*).

christen [ˈkrɪsn] vt (*Rel, also Naut*) baptiser; (*gen: name*) appeler, nommer; (*nickname*) surnommer; (*use for first time*) étrenner. **to ~ sb after** donner à qn le nom de; **he was ~ed Robert but everyone calls him Bob** son nom de baptême est Robert mais tout le monde l'appelle Bob.

Christendom [ˈkrɪsndəm] n chrétienté *f*.

christening [ˈkrɪsnɪŋ] n baptême *m*. ~ **robe** robe *f* de baptême.

Christian [ˈkrɪstɪən] 1 adj (*lit*) chrétien; (*fig*) charitable, compatissant. **the ~ era** l'ère chrétienne; **early ~** paléochrétien; **~ name** prénom *m*, nom *m* de baptême; **my ~ name is Mary** je m'appelle Marie, mon prénom est Marie; **~ Science** science chrétienne; **~ scientist** scientiste *mf* chrétien(ne). 2 n chrétien(ne) *m(f)*. **to become a ~** se faire chrétien.

christiania [ˌkrɪstɪˈɑːnɪə] n (*Ski*) christiania *m*.

Christianity [ˌkrɪstɪˈænɪtɪ] n (*faith, religion*) christianisme *m*; (*character*) caractère *m or* qualité *f* du chrétien. **his ~ did not prevent him from ...** le fait d'être chrétien ne l'a pas empêché de ... .

Christianize [ˈkrɪstɪənaɪz] vt christianiser.

christie [ˈkrɪstɪ] n (*Ski*) christiania *m*.

Christmas [ˈkrɪsməs] 1 n Noël *m*. **at ~** à Noël; **the week before ~** la semaine précédant Noël; **for ~** pour Noël; **she spent ~ with us** elle a passé (la) Noël chez nous; *see* **father, happy, merry**.

2 comp *visit, gift* de Noël ▸ **Christmas box** (*Brit*) étrennes *fpl* (*offertes à Noël*) ▸ **Christmas cake** gâteau *m* de Noël, *gros cake décoré au sucre glace* ▸ **Christmas card** carte *f* de Noël ▸ **Christmas carol** chant *m* de Noël, noël *m*; (*Rel*) cantique *m* de Noël ▸ **Christmas Day** le jour de Noël ▸ **Christmas Eve** la veille de Noël ▸ **Christmas Island** île *f* Christmas ▸ **Christmas party** fête *f or* arbre *m* de Noël ▸ **Christmas present** cadeau *m* de Noël ▸ **Christmas pudding** (plum-)pudding *m* (*gâteau traditionnel de Noël*) ▸ **Christmas rose** rose *f* de Noël ▸ **Christmas stocking: I got it in my Christmas stocking** ≃ je l'ai trouvé dans mon soulier *or* dans la cheminée *or* sous l'arbre (de Noël) ▸ **Christmas time** la période de Noël *or* des fêtes; **at Christmas time** à Noël ▸ **Christmas tree** arbre *m* de Noël.

Christopher [ˈkrɪstəfəʳ] n Christophe *m*.

christy [ˈkrɪstɪ] n (*Ski*) = **christie**.

chromatic [krəˈmætɪk] adj (*Art, Mus*) chromatique. ~ **printing** impression *f* polychrome; **~ scale** gamme *f* chromatique.

chromatics [krəˈmætɪks] n (*NonC*) science *f* des couleurs.

chromatography [ˌkrəʊməˈtɒgrəfɪ] n chromatographie *f*.

chrome [krəʊm] 1 n chrome *m*. 2 comp *fittings etc* chromé ▸ **chrome dioxide** dioxyde *m* de chrome ▸ **chrome lacquer** laque *f or* peinture laquée (à base de chrome) ▸ **chrome steel** acier chromé ▸ **chrome yellow** jaune *m* de chrome.

chromium [ˈkrəʊmɪəm] 1 n chrome *m*. 2 comp ▸ **chromium-plated** chromé ▸ **chromium-plating** chromage *m*.

chromosome [ˈkrəʊməsəʊm] n chromosome *m*.

chronic [ˈkrɒnɪk] adj (*Med*) *disease, state* chronique; (*fig*) *liar, smoker etc* invétéré; *shortages, problems* persistant; (**: dreadful*) affreux, atroce*. **what ~ weather!*** quel temps affreux! *or* atroce!*; **he's ~!*** il est imbuvable!*

chronically [ˈkrɒnɪkəlɪ] adv chroniquement.

chronicle [ˈkrɒnɪkl] 1 n chronique *f*. (*Bible*) **(the Book of) C~s** le livre des Chroniques; (*fig*) **a ~ of disasters** une succession de catastrophes. 2 vt faire la chronique de, enregistrer au jour le jour.

chronicler [ˈkrɒnɪkləʳ] n chroniqueur *m*.

chronological [ˌkrɒnəˈlɒdʒɪkəl] adj chronologique. ~ **age** âge *m* réel; **in ~ order** par ordre chronologique.

chronologically [ˌkrɒnəˈlɒdʒɪkəlɪ] adv chronologiquement.

chronology [krəˈnɒlədʒɪ] n chronologie *f*.

chronometer [krəˈnɒmɪtəʳ] n chronomètre *m*.

chrysalis [ˈkrɪsəlɪs] n, pl **chrysalises** [ˈkrɪsəlɪsɪz] chrysalide *f*.

chrysanthemum [krɪˈsænθəməm] n *also abbr* **chrysanth*** [krɪˈsænθ] chrysanthème *m*.

chub [tʃʌb] n, pl ~ *or* **~s** chevesne *m*, chevaine *m*.

chubby [ˈtʃʌbɪ] adj *person, arm* potelé. **~-cheeked, ~-faced** joufflu.

chuck[1] [tʃʌk] 1 vt a (**: throw*) lancer, jeter, envoyer. b (*‡: give up*) *job, hobby* lâcher, laisser tomber*; *girlfriend* plaquer‡, laisser tomber*. **~ it!** assez!, ça va!*, laisse tomber!* c **he ~ed her under the chin** il lui a pris *or* caressé le menton. 2 n a **to give sb a ~ under the chin** prendre *or* caresser le menton à qn. b **to give sb the ~‡** balancer qn*; **he got the ~‡** il s'est fait balancer* *or* vider*.

▸**chuck away*** vt sep (*throw out*) *old clothes, books* balancer*; (*waste*) *money* jeter par les fenêtres; *opportunity* laisser passer.

▸**chuck in‡** vt sep = **chuck up a**.

▸**chuck out*** vt sep *useless article* balancer*; *person* vider*, sortir*.

▸**chuck up‡** vt sep a *job, hobby* lâcher, laisser tomber*. b (‡ *US: vomit*) dégueuler‡, vomir.

chuck[2] [tʃʌk] 1 n (*Tech*) mandrin *m*. 2 vt (*Tech*) fixer sur un mandrin.

chuck[3] [tʃʌk] n a (*also* ~ **steak**) morceau *m* dans le paleron. b (*US* ‡) bouffe‡ *f*, graille‡ *f*. ~ **wagon** cantine ambulante (*de l'Ouest américain*).

chucker-out‡ [ˈtʃʌkərˈaʊt] n (*Brit*) videur* *m*.

chuckle [ˈtʃʌkl] 1 n gloussement *m*, petit rire. **we had a good ~ over it** ça nous a bien fait rire. 2 vi rire (*over, at* de), glousser.

chuffed‡ [tʃʌft] adj (*Brit*) vachement‡ content (*about* de). **he was quite ~ about it** il était vachement‡ content.

chug [tʃʌg] 1 n *[machine]* souffle *m*; *[car, railway engine]* teuf-teuf *m*. 2 vi *[machine]* souffler; *[car]* haleter, faire teuf-teuf.

▸**chug along** vi *[car, train]* avancer en haletant *or* en faisant teuf-teuf.

chug-a-lug‡ [ˈtʃʌgəlʌg] vt (*US*) boire d'un trait.

chum* [tʃʌm] (*slightly* †) 1 n copain* *m*, copine* *f*. 2 vi (*share lodgings*) crécher ensemble‡.

▸**chum up*** vi fraterniser (*with* avec).

chummy* [ˈtʃʌmɪ] adj sociable, (très) liant. **she is very ~ with him** elle est très copine avec lui*.

chump [tʃʌmp] n a (*) ballot* *m*, crétin(e)* *m(f)*. b (*‡: head*) boule* *f*, caboche* *f*. **he's off his ~** il est timbré* *or* toqué*, il a perdu la boule*. c (*Culin*) ~ **chop** côte *f* de mouton.

chunk [tʃʌŋk] n *[wood, metal, dough]* gros morceau; *[bread]* quignon *m*.

chunky [ˈtʃʌŋkɪ] adj *person* trapu; *knitwear* de grosse laine.

Chunnel* [ˈtʃʌnəl] n (abbr of **Channel Tunnel**) tunnel *m* sous la Manche.

church [tʃɜːtʃ] 1 n a (*building*) église *f*; *[French Protestants]* église, temple *m*. **he is inside the ~ now** il est maintenant dans l'église *or* dans le temple.

b (*NonC*) **to go to ~** (*to church service: gen*) aller à l'église *f*; *[Catholics]* aller à la messe; **he doesn't go to ~ any more** il n'est plus pratiquant, il ne va plus à l'église *or* à la messe; **to be in ~** être à l'église; *[Catholics]* être à la messe; **after ~** après l'office; (*for Catholics*) après la messe.

c (*whole body of Christians*) **the C~** l'Église *f*; **the C~ Militant** l'Église militante.

d (*denomination*) **the C~ of England** l'Église anglicane; **the C~ of Rome** l'Église catholique; **the C~ of Scotland/Ireland** l'Église d'Écosse/d'Irlande; *see* **high** *etc*.

e (*religious orders*) **C~** ordres *mpl*; **he has gone into the C~** il est entré dans les ordres.

2 comp ▸ **Church Fathers** Pères *mpl* de l'Église ▸ **churchgoer** pratiquant(e) *m(f)* ▸ **church hall** salle paroissiale ▸ **churchman** (*clergy*) ecclésiastique *m*; **he is/is not a good churchman** il est/n'est pas pratiquant ▸ **church owl** chouette *f* des clochers, effraie *f* ▸ **churchwarden** (*person*) bedeau *m*, marguillier *m*; (*pipe*) longue pipe (en terre) ▸ **churchyard** cimetière *m* (*autour d'une église*).

3 vt (*Rel*) faire assister à une messe.
Churchillian [tʃəˈtʃɪlɪən] adj churchillien.
churching [ˈtʃɜːtʃɪŋ] n (*Rel*) **the ~ of women** la messe de relevailles.
churchy* [ˈtʃɜːtʃɪ] adj (*pej*) *person* bigot, calotin* (*pej*). **a ~ person** une grenouille de bénitier* (*pej*).
churl [tʃɜːl] n a (*ill-mannered person*) rustre *m*, malotru *m*; (*bad-tempered person*) ronchon *m*, personne *f* revêche. b (*Hist*) manant† *m*.
churlish [ˈtʃɜːlɪʃ] adj (*ill-mannered*) fruste, grossier; (*bad-tempered*) hargneux, revêche. **it would be ~ not to thank him** il serait grossier *or* impoli de ne pas le remercier.
churlishly [ˈtʃɜːlɪʃlɪ] adv (*see* **churlish**) grossièrement; avec hargne.
churlishness [ˈtʃɜːlɪʃnɪs] n (*bad manners*) grossièreté *f*; (*bad temper*) mauvaise humeur *f*.
churn [tʃɜːn] 1 n baratte *f*; (*Brit: milk can*) bidon *m*. 2 vt a (*Culin*) *butter* baratter. b (*also* **~ up**) *water* battre, fouetter, faire bouillonner. (*fig*) **to ~ sb up*** retourner* qn. c (*Aut*) *engine* faire tourner. 3 vi [*sea etc*] bouillonner; [*stomach*] se soulever.
►**churn out** vt sep *objects* débiter; *essays, letters, books* produire à la chaîne, pondre en série*.
►**churn up** vt sep = **churn 2b**.
chute [ʃuːt] n a glissière *f*; *see* **coal, refuse**[2]. b (*in river*) rapide *m*. c (*) = **parachute**. d (*Sport, for toboggans*) piste *f*; (*Brit: children's slide*) toboggan *m*.
chutney [ˈtʃʌtnɪ] n condiment *m* (*à base de fruits*). **apple/tomato ~** condiment à la pomme/à la tomate.
chutzpa(h)* [ˈxʊtspə] n (*US*) culot* *m*.
chyme [kaɪm] n chyme *m*.
C.I. (abbr of **Channel Islands**) *see* **channel 2**.
C.I.A. [ˌsiːaɪˈeɪ] (*US*) (abbr of **Central Intelligence Agency**) *surveillance du territoire*.
ciao [tʃaʊ] interj salut!*, tchao!
cicada [sɪˈkɑːdə] n, pl **~s** *or* **cicadae** [sɪˈkɑːdiː] cigale *f*.
cicatrice [ˈsɪkətrɪs] n cicatrice *f*.
cicatrize [ˈsɪkəˌtraɪz] vi (*Med*) (se) cicatriser.
Cicero [ˈsɪsərəʊ] n Cicéron *m*.
cicerone [ˌtʃɪtʃəˈrəʊnɪ] n, pl **~s** *or* **ciceroni** [ˌtʃɪtʃəˈrəʊnɪ] cicérone *m*.
Ciceronian [ˌsɪsəˈrəʊnɪən] adj cicéronien.
C.I.D. [ˌsiːaɪˈdiː] 1 (*Brit*) abbr of **Criminal Investigation Department**. 2 n ≃ P.J. *f*, police *f* judiciaire. 3 comp *operation, team etc* de la P.J. ► **C.I.D. man** *or* **officer** inspecteur *m* de police judiciaire *or* de la P.J.
cider [ˈsaɪdəʳ] 1 n cidre *m*. 2 comp ► **cider-apple** pomme *f* à cidre ► **cider-press** pressoir *m* à cidre ► **cider vinegar** vinaigre *m* de cidre.
c.i.f., CIF [ˌsiːaɪˈef] (abbr of **cost, insurance, freight**) CAF.
cig* [sɪg] n (*Brit*) = **ciggy***.
cigar [sɪˈgɑːʳ] 1 n cigare *m*. 2 comp *box etc* à cigares ► **cigar case** étui *m* à cigares, porte-cigares *m inv* ► **cigar holder** fume-cigare *m inv* ► **cigar lighter** (*in car*) allume-cigare *m inv* ► **cigar-shaped** en forme de cigare.
cigarette [ˌsɪgəˈret] 1 n cigarette *f*. 2 comp *box etc* à cigarettes ► **cigarette ash** cendre *f* de cigarette ► **cigarette card** *carte avec des publicités ou des jeux dans les paquets de cigarettes* ► **cigarette case** étui *m* à cigarettes, porte-cigarettes *m inv* ► **cigarette end** mégot *m* ► **cigarette holder** fume-cigarette *m inv* ► **cigarette lighter** briquet *m* ► **cigarette paper** papier *m* à cigarettes.
ciggy* [ˈsɪgɪ] n (*Brit*) clope* *m*, tige* *f*.
ciliary [ˈsɪlɪərɪ] adj ciliaire.
CIM [ˌsiːaɪˈem] n (*Comput*) (abbr of **computer-integrated manufacturing**) FIO *f*.
C.-in-C. (abbr of **Commander-in-Chief**) *see* **commander**.
cinch [sɪntʃ] 1 n a (*US: saddle girth*) sous-ventrière *f*, sangle *f* (de selle). b **it's a ~*** (*certain*) c'est du tout cuit*, c'est du gâteau*; (*easy*) c'est l'enfance de l'art. 2 vt a *horse* sangler; *saddle* attacher par une sangle (de selle). b (*fig*) *success* rendre sûr, assurer.
cinder [ˈsɪndəʳ] 1 n cendre *f*. **~s** (*burnt coal*) cendres *fpl* (de charbon); [*furnace, volcano*] scories *fpl*; **to rake out the ~s** racler les cendres (du foyer); **burnt to a ~** réduit en cendres. 2 comp ► **cinder block** (*US*) parpaing *m* ► **cinder track** (piste *f*) cendrée *f*.
Cinderella [ˌsɪndəˈrelə] n Cendrillon *f*.
cine-camera [ˈsɪnɪˈkæmərə] n (*Brit*) caméra *f*.
cine-film [ˈsɪnɪfɪlm] n (*Brit*) film *m*.
cinema [ˈsɪnəmə] 1 n cinéma *m*. **to go to the ~** aller au cinéma. 2 comp ► **cinema complex** multisalle *f* ► **cinema-going** n fréquentation *f* des cinémas; **the cinema-going public** le public qui fréquente les cinémas.
Cinemascope [ˈsɪnəməskəʊp] n ® Cinémascope *m* ®.
cinematic [ˌsɪnɪˈmætɪk] adj filmique.
cinematograph [ˌsɪnɪˈmætəgrɑːf] n (*Brit*) cinématographe *m*.
cinematographer [ˌsɪnɪməˈtɒgrəfəʳ] n (*US*) directeur *m* de la photo.
cinematography [ˌsɪnɪməˈtɒgrəfɪ] n cinématographie *f*.
cine-projector [ˌsɪnɪprəˈdʒektəʳ] n (*Brit*) projecteur *m* de cinéma.
Cinerama [ˌsɪnəˈrɑːmə] n ® Cinérama *m* ®.
cinerary [ˈsɪnərərɪ] adj cinéraire.
cinnabar [ˈsɪnəbɑːʳ] n cinabre *m*.
cinnamon [ˈsɪnəmən] 1 n cannelle *f*. 2 comp *cake, biscuit* à la cannelle; (*colour*) cannelle *inv*.
Cinque [sɪŋk] adj (*Brit Hist*) **the ~ Ports** les Cinq Ports *mpl*, *ancienne confédération des cinq ports du Kent et du Sussex*.
cipher [ˈsaɪfəʳ] 1 n a (*Arabic numeral*) chiffre *m* (*arabe*); (*zero*) zéro *m*. (*fig*) **he's a mere ~** c'est un zéro *or* une nullité. b (*secret writing*) chiffre *m*, code secret. **in ~** en chiffre, en code. c (*message*) message chiffré *or* codé. d (*monogram*) chiffre *m*, monogramme *m*. 2 vt *calculations, communications* chiffrer.
circa [ˈsɜːkə] prep circa, environ.
circadian [sɜːˈkeɪdɪən] adj circadien.
circle [ˈsɜːkl] 1 n cercle *m*; [*hills, houses, vehicles*] cercle; [*mountains*] cirque *m*; (*round eyes*) cerne *m*; (*Gymnastics*) soleil *m*; (*Astron: orbit*) orbite *f*; (*Brit: Theat*) balcon *m*; [*knowledge*] cercle, sphère *f*; (*group of persons*) cercle, groupe *m*; [*underground railway*] ligne *f* de ceinture. **to stand in a ~** faire (un) cercle, se tenir en cercle; **to draw a ~** tracer un cercle; (*Math*) tracer une circonférence *or* un cercle; **an inner ~ of advisers** un groupe de proches conseillers; **in political ~s** dans les milieux *mpl* politiques; **to come full ~** revenir à son point de départ; (*fig*) **they were going** *or* **running round in ~s** ils tournaient en rond.
2 vt a (*go round outside of sth*) contourner, faire un circuit autour de; (*keep moving round sth*) tourner autour de; (*liter: encircle*) entourer, encercler.
b (*draw ~ round*) entourer d'un cercle.
3 vi [*birds*] faire *or* décrire des cercles; [*aircraft*] tourner (en rond). **the cyclists ~d round him** les cyclistes ont tourné autour de lui.
►**circle about, circle around, circle round** vi faire *or* décrire des cercles, tourner.
circlet [ˈsɜːklɪt] n petit cercle *m*; [*hair*] bandeau *m*; [*arm*] brassard *m*; [*finger*] anneau *m*.
circuit [ˈsɜːkɪt] 1 n a (*journey around*) tour *m*, circuit *m*. **to make a ~ of** faire le tour de; **to make a wide ~ round a town** faire un grand détour *or* circuit autour d'une ville.
b (*Brit Jur*) (*journey*) tournée *f* (*des juges d'assises*); (*district*) circonscription *f* (judiciaire). **he is on the eastern ~** il fait la tournée de l'est.
c (*Cine, Theat: houses visited by same company*) tournée *f*; (*houses owned by same owner*) groupe *m*.
d (*Sport: series of races, matches etc*) circuit *m*. (*Tourism*) **the Scottish cathedrals ~** le circuit des cathédrales d'Écosse.
e (*Elec*) circuit *m*; *see* **closed, short**.
f (*Sport: track*) circuit *m*, parcours *m*.
2 comp ► **circuit board** (*Comput*) plaquette *f* ► **circuit-breaker** (*Elec*) disjoncteur *m*.
circuitous [sɜːˈkjʊɪtəs] adj *road, route* indirect, qui fait un détour; (*fig*) *means* détourné; *method* indirect.
circuitously [sɜːˈkjʊɪtəslɪ] adv (*lit*) *reach* en faisant un détour; (*fig*) *allude* de façon détournée *or* indirecte, indirectement.
circuitry [ˈsɜːkɪtrɪ] n (*Elec*) circuit *m*.
circular [ˈsɜːkjʊləʳ] 1 adj *outline, saw, ticket* circulaire. **~ letter** circulaire *f*; **~ tour** voyage *m* circulaire, circuit *m*. 2 n (*letter*) circulaire *f*; (*printed advertisement etc*) prospectus *m*.
circularity [ˌsɜːkjʊˈlærɪtɪ] n circularité *f*.
circularize [ˈsɜːkjʊləraɪz] vt *person, firm* envoyer des circulaires *or* des prospectus à.
circulate [ˈsɜːkjʊleɪt] 1 vi (*all senses*) circuler. 2 vt *object, bottle* faire circuler; *news, rumour* propager; *document* (*from person to person*) faire circuler; (*send out*) diffuser. (*Math*) **circulating decimal** fraction *f* périodique; **circulating library** bibliothèque *f* de prêt; (*Fin*) **circulating medium** monnaie *f* d'échange.
circulation [ˌsɜːkjʊˈleɪʃən] 1 n (*NonC*) (*Anat, Bot, Fin, Med*) circulation *f*; [*news, rumour*] propagation *f*; [*newspaper etc*] tirage *m*. **a magazine with a ~ of 10,000** un magazine qui tire à 10 000; (*Med*) **he has poor ~** il a une mauvaise circulation; (*Fin*) **to put into ~** mettre en circulation; (*Fin*) **to take out of** *or* **withdraw from ~** retirer de la circulation; (*Fin*) **in ~** en circulation; **he's now back in ~*** il est à nouveau dans le circuit*; *see* **drop out**. 2 comp ► **circulation manager** (*Press*) directeur *m* du service de la diffusion.
circulatory [ˌsɜːkjʊˈleɪtərɪ] adj circulatoire.
circum... [ˈsɜːkəm] pref circon... .
circumcise [ˈsɜːkəmsaɪz] vt (*Med*) circoncire; (*fig*) purifier.
circumcision [ˌsɜːkəmˈsɪʒən] n circoncision *f*. (*Rel*) **the C~** (la fête de) la Circoncision.
circumference [səˈkʌmfərəns] n circonférence *f*.
circumflex [ˈsɜːkəmfleks] 1 adj circonflexe. 2 n accent *m* circonflexe.
circumlocution [ˌsɜːkəmləˈkjuːʃən] n circonlocution *f*.
circumlunar [ˌsɜːkəmˈluːnəʳ] adj autour de la lune. **~ flight** vol *m* autour de la lune.
circumnavigate [ˌsɜːkəmˈnævɪgeɪt] vt *cape* doubler,contourner. **to ~ the globe** faire le tour du monde en bateau, naviguer tout autour du globe.
circumnavigation [ˈsɜːkəmˌnævɪˈgeɪʃən] n circumnavigation *f*.
circumscribe [ˈsɜːkəmskraɪb] vt (*gen*) circonscrire; *powers* limiter.
circumspect [ˈsɜːkəmspekt] adj circonspect.
circumspection [ˌsɜːkəmˈspekʃən] n circonspection *f*.

circumspectly ['sɜːkəmspektlɪ] adv avec circonspection, de façon circonspecte.

circumstance ['sɜːkəmstəns] n a (*gen pl*) circonstance *f*, état *m* de choses; (*fact, detail*) circonstance, détail *m*. **in** *or* **under the present ~s** dans les circonstances actuelles, vu l'état des choses; **in** *or* **under no ~s** en aucun cas; **under similar ~s** en pareil cas; **to take the ~s into account** tenir compte des *or* faire la part des circonstances; (*fig*) **a victim of ~** une victime des circonstances; *see* **attenuate, extenuate, pomp.**

b (*financial condition*) **~s** situation financière *or* pécuniaire; **in easy ~s** dans l'aisance, à l'aise; **in poor ~s** gêné, dans la gêne; **what are his ~s?** quelle est sa situation financière *or* pécuniaire?; **if our ~s allow it** si nos moyens nous le permettent.

circumstantial [ˌsɜːkəm'stænʃəl] adj a (*detailed*) *report, statement* circonstancié, détaillé. b (*indirect*) *knowledge* indirect. (*Jur*) **~ evidence** preuve indirecte. c (*not essential*) accessoire, subsidiaire.

circumstantiate [ˌsɜːkəm'stænʃɪeɪt] vt *evidence* confirmer en donnant des détails sur; *event* donner des détails circonstanciés sur.

circumvent [ˌsɜːkəm'vent] vt *person* circonvenir; *law, regulations, rule* tourner; *sb's plan, project* faire échouer.

circumvention [ˌsɜːkəm'venʃən] n [*plan, project*] mise *f* en échec. **the ~ of the guard/rule proved easy** circonvenir le garde/tourner le règlement s'avéra facile.

circus ['sɜːkəs] 1 n, pl **~es** (*Hist, Theat*) cirque *m*; (*in town*) rond-point *m*. 2 comp *animal, clown* de cirque.

cirrhosis [sɪ'rəʊsɪs] n cirrhose *f*.

cirrus ['sɪrəs] n, pl **cirri** ['sɪraɪ] a (*cloud*) cirrus *m*. b (*Bot*) vrille *f*.

CIS [ˌsiːaɪ'es] (abbr of **Commonwealth of Independent States**) CEI *f*.

cissy ['sɪsɪ] n = **sissy**.

Cistercian [sɪs'tɜːʃən] 1 n cistercien(ne) *m(f)*. 2 adj cistercien. **~ Order** ordre *m* de Cîteaux; **a ~ monk** un cistercien.

cistern ['sɪstən] n citerne *f*; [*WC*] réservoir *m* de la chasse d'eau; [*barometer*] cuvette *f*.

citadel ['sɪtədl] n citadelle *f*.

citation [saɪ'teɪʃən] n (*gen, Jur, Mil*) citation *f*.

cite [saɪt] vt (*gen, Jur, Mil*) citer. **to ~ as an example** citer en exemple; (*Jur*) **to ~ sb to appear** citer qn; *see* **dispatch.**

citified ['sɪtɪˌfaɪd] adj (*pej*) qui a pris les manières de la ville.

citizen ['sɪtɪzn] n [*town*] habitant(e) *m(f)*; [*state*] citoyen(ne) *m(f)*; (*Admin*) ressortissant(e) *m(f)*; (*Hist*) bourgeois(e) *m(f)*; (*townsman*) citadin(e) *m(f)*. **the ~s of Paris** les habitants de Paris, les Parisiens *mpl*; **French ~** ressortissant français; **~ of the world** citoyen du monde; **Citizens' Advice Bureau** ≃ Bureau *m* d'aide sociale; **Citizen's Band Radio** *fréquence réservée au public*; *see* **fellow.**

citizenry ['sɪtɪznrɪ] n: **the ~** l'ensemble *m* des habitants.

citizenship ['sɪtɪznʃɪp] n citoyenneté *f*. (*US*) **~ papers** déclaration *f* de naturalisation.

citrate ['sɪtreɪt] n citrate *m*.

citric ['sɪtrɪk] adj citrique. **~ acid** acide *m* citrique.

citron ['sɪtrən] n (*fruit*) cédrat *m*; (*tree*) cédratier *m*.

citronella [ˌsɪtrə'nelə] n (*grass*) citronnelle *f*; (*oil*) (huile *f* de) citronnelle.

citrus ['sɪtrəs] n, pl **~es** citrus *mpl*. **~ fruits** agrumes *mpl*.

city ['sɪtɪ] 1 n a (*gen*) (grande) ville *f*. (*people*) **the ~** la ville; **large cities like Leeds** les grandes villes comme Leeds; **life in the modern ~** la vie dans la cité *or* la ville moderne.

b (*Brit*) **the C~** la Cité (de Londres) (*centre des affaires*); **he's (something) in the C~*** il est dans les affaires, il travaille dans la Cité (de Londres).

2 comp *streets etc* de la ville; *offices, authorities etc* municipal; (*Brit Press*) *editor, page, news* financier ► **City and Guilds (examination)** (*Brit*) ≃ C.A.P. *m*, certificat *m* d'aptitude professionnelle ► **city centre** centre *m* (de la) ville ► **city college** (*US Univ*) université *f* (*financée par la ville*) ► **city councilman** (*US*) conseiller municipal ► **city desk** (*Brit*) antenne *f* financière; (*US*) antenne *f* locale ► **city dweller** citadin(e) *m(f)* ► **city editor** (*US*) rédacteur en chef (pour les nouvelles locales) ► **city fathers** édiles *mpl* ► **city hall** (*lit*) mairie *f*; (*in large towns*) hôtel *m* de ville; (*US fig: city authorities*) administration *f* ► **city manager** (*US*) administrateur communal (*payé par une municipalité et faisant fonction de maire*) ► **city planner** (*US*) urbaniste *mf* ► **city planning** (*US*) urbanisme *m* ► **city police** (*US*) police municipale ► **city slicker*** (*pej*) citadin mielleux et habile ► **city state** cité *f* ► **city technology college** (*Brit*) établissement *m* d'enseignement technologique.

cityfied ['sɪtɪˌfaɪd] adj (*pej*) = **citified.**

cityscape ['sɪtɪskeɪp] n (*US*) paysage *m or* panorama *m* urbain.

civet ['sɪvɪt] n (*cat, substance*) civette *f*.

civic ['sɪvɪk] adj *rights, virtues* civique; *guard, authorities* municipal. (*Brit*) **~ centre** centre administratif (municipal); **~ event** cérémonie officielle locale; **~ restaurant** restaurant *m* communautaire.

civics ['sɪvɪks] n instruction *f* civique.

civies* ['sɪvɪz] npl (*US*) = **civvies;** *see* **civvy 2.**

civil ['sɪvl] adj a (*of a community; also non-military*) civil. **C~ Aviation Authority** ≃ Direction *f* Générale de l'Aviation Civile; **~ commotion** émeute *f*; **~ defence** défense passive; **~ disobedience** résistance passive (à la loi); **~ disobedience campaign** campagne *f* de résistance passive; **~ divorce** *divorce non reconnu par l'église*; **~ engineer** ingénieur *m* des travaux publics; **~ engineering** génie civil; **~ law** (*system*) code civil; (*study*) droit civil; **~ liberties** libertés *fpl* civiques; (*Brit*) **~ list** liste civile (*allouée à la famille royale*); **~ marriage** mariage *m* civil; **~ rights** droits civils; **~ rights campaign, ~ rights movement** campagne *f* pour les droits civils; **~ servant** fonctionnaire *mf*; **~ service** fonction publique, administration *f*; **Civil Service Commission** commission *f* de recrutement dans la fonction publique; **~ service examination** concours *m* d'entrée dans la fonction publique; **~ service recruitment** recrutement *m* de(s) fonctionnaires; **~ war** guerre civile; **(American) Civil War** guerre *f* de Sécession; **~ wedding** mariage civil; **to have a ~ wedding** se marier civilement.

b (*polite*) civil, poli. **that's very ~ of you** vous êtes bien aimable; *see* **tongue.**

civilian [sɪ'vɪlɪən] 1 n civil(e) *m(f)* (*opposé à militaire*). 2 adj civil.

civility [sɪ'vɪlɪtɪ] n politesse *f*, courtoisie *f*, civilité *f*. **civilities** civilités.

civilization [ˌsɪvɪlaɪ'zeɪʃən] n civilisation *f*.

civilize ['sɪvɪlaɪz] vt civiliser.

civilized ['sɪvɪlaɪzd] adj civilisé. **to become ~** se civiliser.

civilizing ['sɪvɪlaɪzɪŋ] adj civilisateur *m*, -trice *f*.

civilly ['sɪvɪlɪ] adv poliment.

civism ['sɪvɪzəm] n civisme *m*.

civvy* ['sɪvɪ] (abbr of **civilian**) 1 adj (*Brit*) **~ street** vie civile; **to be in ~ street** être civil *or* pékin*. 2 npl: **civvies** vêtements civils; **in civvies** (habillé) en civil *or* en bourgeois*.

cl (abbr of **centilitre(s)**) cl.

clack [klæk] 1 n claquement *m*; [*pump etc*] clapet *m*; (*fig: talk*) jacasserie *f*, caquet *m*. 2 vi claquer; (*fig*) jacasser. **this will set tongues ~ing** cela va faire jaser (les gens).

clad [klæd] adj habillé, vêtu (*in* de).

cladding ['klædɪŋ] n [*building*] revêtement *m*.

claim [kleɪm] 1 vt a (*demand as one's due*) revendiquer, réclamer (*from sb* à qn); *property, prize, right* revendiquer. **to ~ diplomatic immunity** réclamer l'immunité diplomatique; **to ~ the right to decide** revendiquer le droit de décider; **the group which ~ed responsibility for the attack** le groupe qui a revendiqué l'attentat; **no one has yet ~ed responsibility for the explosion** l'explosion n'a pas encore été revendiquée; **to ~ damages** réclamer des dommages et intérêts; (*fig*) **the epidemic has ~ed 100 victims** l'épidémie a fait 100 victimes; *see* **credit.**

b (*profess, contend, maintain*) prétendre, déclarer. **to ~ acquaintance with sb** prétendre connaître qn; **he ~s to have seen you** il prétend *or* déclare vous avoir vu, il déclare qu'il vous a vu; **both armies ~ed the victory** les deux armées ont revendiqué la victoire.

c (*demand*) *sb's attention* demander, solliciter; *sb's sympathy* solliciter.

2 n a (*act of claiming, instance of this*) revendication *f*, réclamation *f*; (*Insurance*) ≃ déclaration *f* de sinistre, demande *f* d'indemnité. **to lay ~ to** prétendre à, avoir des prétentions à; **there are many ~s on my time** mon temps est très pris; **there are many ~s on my purse** j'ai beaucoup de frais, on fait beaucoup appel à ma bourse; **that's a big ~ to make!** la *or* cette prétention est de taille!; **his ~ that he acted legally** son affirmation d'avoir agi d'une manière licite; **to put in a ~** (*gen*) faire une réclamation; (*Insurance*) faire une déclaration de sinistre *or* une demande d'indemnité; (*Ind*) **they put in a ~ for £1 per hour more** ils ont demandé une augmentation de 1 livre de l'heure; (*Insurance*) **the ~s were all paid** les dommages ont été intégralement payés *or* réglés; (*Ind*) **a ~ for an extra £5 per week** une demande d'augmentation de 5 livres par semaine; *see* **outstanding.**

b (*right*) droit *m*, titre *m*. **~ to ownership** droit à la propriété; **~ to the throne** titre à la couronne; **~s to sb's friendship** droits à l'amitié de qn.

c (*Min etc*) concession *f*; *see* **stake.**

3 comp ► **claim form** (*Admin*) (*for benefit*) (formulaire *m* de) demande *f*; (*for expenses*) (feuille *f* pour) note *f* de frais ► **claims adjuster** (*Insurance*) agent général d'assurances.

claimant ['kleɪmənt] n [*throne*] prétendant(e) *m(f)* (*to* à); [*social benefits*] demandeur *m*, -eresse *f*; (*Jur*) requérant(e) *m(f)*.

clairvoyance [kleə'vɔɪəns] n voyance *f*, (don *m* de) seconde vue.

clairvoyant(e) [kleə'vɔɪənt] 1 n voyant(e) *m(f)*, extra-lucide *mf*. 2 adj doué de seconde vue.

clam [klæm] 1 n a (*Zool*) palourde *f*, clam *m*. b (*‡ US*) dollar *m*. 2 comp ► **clambake** (*US Culin*) *pique-nique où l'on cuisine des fruits de mer*; (*party*) réunion *f* à la bonne franquette ► **clam chowder** (*US Culin*) soupe épaisse de palourdes.

►**clam up*** vi la boucler‡, la fermer‡. **to be clammed up like an oyster** être muet comme une carpe *or* comme la tombe; **he clammed up on me** il l'a bouclée‡, il ne m'a plus dit un mot là-dessus.

clamber ['klæmbəʳ] 1 vi grimper (*en s'aidant des mains ou en rampant*), se hisser (avec difficulté). **to ~ up a hill** gravir péniblement une colline; **to ~ over a wall** escalader un mur. 2 n escalade *f*.

clammy ['klæmɪ] adj *hand, touch* moite (et froid); *wall* suintant; *weath-*

er humide, lourd.

clamorous ['klæmərəs] adj *crowd* vociférant, bruyant; (*fig*) *demand* impérieux, criant.

clamour, (*US*) **clamor** ['klæməʳ] 1 n (*shouts*) clameur *f*, vociférations *fpl*, cris *mpl*; (*demands*) revendications *or* réclamations bruyantes. 2 vi vociférer, pousser des cris. **to ~ against sth/sb** vociférer contre qch/qn; **to ~ for sth/sb** (*lit: shout*) demander qch/qn à grands cris; (*fig: demand*), réclamer qch/qn à cor et à cri.

clamp[1] [klæmp] 1 n (*gen*) attache *f*, pince *f*; (*bigger*) crampon *m*; (*Med*) clamp *m*; (*also* **ring ~**) collier *m* de serrage; (*Carpentry*) valet *m* (d'établi); (*Archit*) agrafe *f*; *[china]* agrafe; (*Elec*) serre-fils *m inv*; (*Naut*) serre-cables *m inv*.

2 comp ▸ **clampdown** (*gen*) répression *f* (*on sth* de qch, *on sb* contre qn); **a clampdown on terrorists** la répression *or* des mesures répressives contre les terroristes; **a clampdown on arms sales** un renforcement des restrictions sur la vente d'armes.

3 vt a (*put ~ on*) serrer, cramponner; *stones, china* agrafer; *car wheels* mettre un sabot à. **to ~ sth to sth** fixer qch à qch.

b **to ~ shut** *or* **together** *teeth* serrer.

c (* *US*) *embargo, curfew* imposer (*on* sur).

▸**clamp down on*** 1 vt fus *person* serrer la vis à, prendre des mesures autoritaires contre; *inflation, expenditure* mettre un frein à; *information* supprimer, censurer; *the press, the opposition* bâillonner. 2 **clampdown** n *see* **clamp**[1] **2.**

▸**clamp together** vt sep serrer ensemble.

clamp[2] [klæmp] 1 n *[bricks]* tas *m*, pile *f* (*de briques séchées*); *[potatoes]* silo *m* (*de pommes de terre sous paille etc*). 2 vt entasser.

clamp[3] [klæmp] (*thump*) 1 n pas lourd *or* pesant. 2 vi marcher d'un pas pesant.

clan [klæn] 1 n clan *m* (écossais); (*fig*) famille *f*. 2 comp ▸ **clansman, clanswoman** membre *m* d'un clan (écossais).

clandestine [klæn'destɪn] adj clandestin.

clang [klæŋ] 1 n (*also* **~ing noise**) bruit *m or* son *m* métallique; (*louder*) fracas *m* métallique. 2 vi émettre un son métallique. **the gate ~ed shut** la grille s'est refermée bruyamment *or* avec un bruit métallique.

clanger*⁑ ['klæŋəʳ] n (*Brit*) gaffe *f*. **to drop a ~** faire une gaffe, gaffer lourdement.

clangorous ['klæŋgərəs] adj *noise* métallique.

clangour, (*US*) **clangor** ['klæŋgəʳ] n son *m or* bruit *m or* fracas *m* métallique.

clank ['klæŋk] 1 n cliquetis *m*, bruit *m* métallique (*de chaînes etc*). 2 vi cliqueter, émettre un son métallique. 3 vt faire cliqueter.

clankpin ['klæŋkpɪn] n (*Aut*) maneton *m*.

clannish ['klænɪʃ] adj (*slightly pej: exclusive, unwelcoming*) *group* fermé; *person* qui a l'esprit de clan *or* de clique.

clap[1] [klæp] 1 n (*sound*) claquement *m*, bruit sec; *[hands]* battement *m*; (*action*) tape *f*; (*applause*) applaudissements *mpl*. **a ~ on the back** une tape dans le dos; **to give the dog a ~** donner une tape amicale au chien; **a ~ of thunder** un coup de tonnerre; **he got a good ~** il a été très applaudi.

2 comp ▸ **clapboard** bardeau *m* ▸ **claptrap*** boniment* *m*, baratin* *m*.

3 vt a battre, frapper, taper; (*applaud*) applaudir. **to ~ one's hands** battre des mains; **to ~ sb on the back** donner à qn une tape dans le dos; **to ~ a dog** donner des tapes amicales à un chien; **he ~ped his hand over my mouth** il a mis *or* collé* sa main sur ma bouche.

b flanquer*, fourrer*. **to ~ sb in irons** jeter qn aux fers; **to ~ sb into prison** jeter qn en prison; **to ~ eyes on** voir; **to ~ hands on sb** prendre qn sur le fait.

4 vi taper *or* frapper dans ses mains; (*applaud*) applaudir.

▸**clap on** vt sep: **to clap on one's hat** enfoncer son chapeau sur sa tête; (*Naut*) **to clap on sail** mettre toutes voiles dehors; (*Aut*) **to clap on the brakes** freiner brusquement, donner un coup de frein brutal.

▸**clap to** vti claquer.

clap[2]⁑ [klæp] n (*disease*) chaude-pisse⁑ *f*.

clapped-out* ['klæptaʊt] adj *person* crevé*, flapi*; *horse* fourbu; *car* crevé*.

clapper ['klæpəʳ] n *[bell]* battant *m*. (*Brit*) **to go like the ~s⁑** aller à toute blinde⁑.

clapperboard ['klæpəˌbɔːd] n clap *m*, claquette *f*.

clapping ['klæpɪŋ] n applaudissements *mpl*.

claque [klæk] n (*Theat*) claque *f*.

Clare [klɛəʳ] n Claire *f*. (*Rel*) **the Poor ~s** clarisses *fpl*, Pauvres Dames *fpl*.

claret ['klærət] 1 n (vin *m* de) bordeaux *m* (rouge). 2 adj (*also* **~-coloured**) bordeaux *inv*.

clarification [ˌklærɪfɪ'keɪʃən] n (*gen*) clarification *f*, éclaircissement *m*; *[wine]* collage *m*. (*Jur*) **request for ~** demande *f* d'éclaircissement.

clarify ['klærɪfaɪ] 1 vt *sugar, butter* clarifier; *wine* coller; (*fig*) *situation* éclaircir, clarifier. 2 vi se clarifier; (*fig*) s'éclaircir.

clarinet [ˌklærɪ'net] n clarinette *f*.

clarinettist [ˌklærɪ'netɪst] n clarinettiste *mf*.

clarion ['klærɪən] (*liter*) 1 n clairon *m*. (*lit, fig*) **a ~ call** un appel de clairon. 2 vt: **to ~ (forth)** claironner.

clarity ['klærɪtɪ] n clarté *f*, précision *f*.

clash [klæʃ] 1 vi a (*bang noisily*) *[swords, metallic objects]* s'entrechoquer; *[cymbals]* résonner.

b (*be in dispute*) *[armies]* se heurter. **the 2 parties ~ over the question of ...** les 2 partis sont en désaccord total en ce qui concerne ... .

c (*conflict*) *[interests]* se heurter, être incompatible *or* en contradiction (*with* avec); *[personalities]* être incompatible (*with* avec); *[colours]* jurer, détonner (*with* avec).

d (*coincide*) *[two events, invitations etc]* tomber en même temps (*or* le même jour *etc*). **the dates ~** les deux événements (*or* rencontres *etc*) tombent le même jour.

2 vt *metallic objects* heurter *or* choquer *or* entrechoquer bruyamment; *cymbals* faire résonner. (*Aut*) **to ~ the gears** faire grincer les vitesses.

3 n a (*sound*) choc *m or* fracas *m* métallique.

b *[armies, weapons]* choc *m*, heurt *m*; (*between people, parties*) accrochage* *m*; (*with police, troops*) affrontement *m*, accrochage, échauffourée *f*. **during a ~ with the police** au cours d'un affrontement *or* d'une échauffourée avec la police; **I don't want a ~ with him about it** je ne veux pas me disputer avec lui à ce sujet; **to have a (verbal) ~ with sb** avoir un accrochage* *or* une algarade avec qn.

c *[interests]* conflit *m*. **a ~ of personalities** une incompatibilité de caractères.

d *[colours]* discordance *f*, heurt *m*.

e *[dates, events, invitations]* coïncidence fâcheuse.

clasp [klɑːsp] 1 n a *[brooch, necklace, purse]* fermoir *m*; *[belt]* boucle *f*. b (*NonC: in one's arms, of a hand*) étreinte *f*. 2 comp ▸ **clasp knife** grand couteau pliant, eustache*† *m*. 3 vt étreindre, serrer. **to ~ sb's hand** serrer la main de qn; **to ~ one's hands (together)** joindre les mains; **with ~ed hands** les mains jointes; **to ~ sb in one's arms/to one's heart** serrer qn dans ses bras/sur son cœur. 4 vi s'agrafer, s'attacher, se fermer.

class [klɑːs] 1 n a (*group, division*) classe *f*, catégorie *f*; (*Bot, Ling, Mil, Soc, Zool etc*) classe; (*Naut: of ship*) type *m*; (*in Lloyd's Register*) cote *f*. (*fig*) **he's not in the same ~ as his brother** il n'arrive pas à la cheville de son frère; **these books are just not in the same ~** il n'y a pas de comparaison (possible) entre ces livres; **in a ~ by itself, in a ~ of its own** hors concours, unique; **they are in a ~ apart** ils sont tout à fait à part; **a good ~ (of) hotel** un très bon hôtel, un hôtel de très bonne classe; **the ruling ~** la classe dirigeante; (*Brit Univ*) **what ~ of degree did he get?** quelle mention a-t-il eue (à sa licence)?; **first ~ honours in history** ≃ licence *f* d'histoire avec mention très bien; *see* **middle, working** *etc*.

b (*Scol, Univ, gen*) (*lesson*) classe *f*, cours *m*; (*students*) classe; (*US: year*) promotion *f* scolaire. **to give** *or* **take a ~** faire un cours; **to attend a ~** suivre un cours; **the French ~** la classe *or* le cours de français; **an evening ~** un cours du soir; (*US*) **the ~ of 1970** la promotion *or* la promo* de 1970.

c (* *NonC*) classe *f*, distinction *f*. **to have ~** avoir de la classe.

2 vt classer, classifier; (*Naut Insurance*) coter. **he was ~ed with the servants** il était assimilé aux domestiques.

3 comp ▸ **class action:** (*Jur*) **class actions** actions *fpl* de groupe; **class action suit** (*Jur*) recours collectif en justice ▸ **class bias** (*Soc*) préjugés *mpl* de classe ▸ **class-conscious** *person* conscient des distinctions sociales; (*pej: snobbish*) *person, attitude* snob *inv* ▸ **class consciousness** conscience *f* de classe *or* des distinctions sociales ▸ **class distinction** distinction sociale ▸ **class list** (*Scol*) liste nominative des élèves ▸ **classmate** (*Brit*) camarade *mf* de classe; (*US*) camarade de promotion (*or* de classe) ▸ **class number** (*Brit: in library*) cote *f* (*d'un livre en bibliothèque*) ▸ **class president** (*US*) ≃ chef *m* de classe ▸ **class rank** (*US Scol, Univ*) numéro *m* de sortie ▸ **class roll** = **class list** ▸ **classroom** (salle *f* de) classe *f* ▸ **class society** (*Pol*) société *f* de classes ▸ **class struggle** lutte *f* des classes ▸ **class teacher** (*Brit Scol*) professeur principal ▸ **class war(fare)** = **class struggle.**

classic ['klæsɪk] 1 adj (*lit, fig*) classique. **it was ~!*** c'était le coup classique!* 2 n (*author, work*) classique *m*; (*Racing*) classique *f*. **to study (C)~s** étudier les humanités; (*fig*) **it is a ~ of its kind** c'est un classique du genre.

classical ['klæsɪkəl] adj classique. **~ Latin** latin *m* classique; **~ scholar** humaniste *mf*.

classically ['klæsɪkəlɪ] adv classiquement.

classicism ['klæsɪsɪzəm] n classicisme *m*.

classicist ['klæsɪsɪst] n spécialiste *mf* de lettres classiques.

classifiable ['klæsɪfaɪəbl] adj qu'on peut classifier.

classification [ˌklæsɪfɪ'keɪʃən] n classification *f*.

classified ['klæsɪfaɪd] adj a classifié. (*Press*) **~ advertisement** petite annonce. b (*Admin: secret etc*) *document* classé secret (*f* classée secrète). **~ information** renseignements (classés) secrets.

classify ['klæsɪfaɪ] vt a classer, classifier. b (*Admin: restrict circulation*) classer secret.

classless ['klæslɪs] adj *society* sans classe; *person* qui n'appartient à aucune classe; *accent* standard.

classy* ['klɑːsɪ] adj *car, apartment, hotel* chic *inv*, de luxe; *person* chic *inv*, qui a de l'allure. ~ **clothes** des vêtements tout ce qu'il y a de chic.

clatter ['klætəʳ] 1 n (*noise*) cliquetis *m*, (*louder*) fracas *m*. **the ~ of cutlery** le bruit *or* cliquetis de couverts entrechoqués. 2 vi (*rattle*) [*heels, keys, typewriter, chains*] cliqueter; (*bang*) [*large falling object, cymbals*] résonner. **to ~ in/out/away** *etc* entrer/sortir/partir *etc* bruyamment. 3 vt choquer *or* entrechoquer bruyamment.

clause [klɔːz] n a (*Gram*) membre *m* de phrase, proposition *f*. **principal/subordinate ~** proposition principale/subordonnée. b (*Jur*) [*contract, law, treaty*] clause *f*; [*will*] disposition *f*; *see* **saving**.

claustrophobia [ˌklɔːstrə'fəʊbɪə] n claustrophobie *f*.

claustrophobic [ˌklɔːstrə'fəʊbɪk] 1 adj *person* claustrophobe; *feeling* de claustrophobie; *situation, atmosphere* claustrophobique. 2 n claustrophobe *mf*.

clavichord ['klævɪkɔːd] n clavicorde *m*.

clavicle ['klævɪkl] n clavicule *f*.

claw [klɔː] 1 n a [*cat, lion, small bird etc*] griffe *f*; [*bird of prey*] serre *f*; [*lobster etc*] pince *f*; (*‡: hand*) patte* *f*. **to get one's ~s into sb*** tenir qn entre ses griffes; **to get one's ~s on*** mettre le grappin sur*; **get your ~s off (that)!‡** bas les pattes!* b (*Tech*) [*bench*] valet *m*; [*hammer*] pied-de-biche *m*. 2 comp ▸ **clawback** (*Econ*) récupération *f* ▸ **claw-hammer** marteau fendu, marteau à pied-de-biche. 3 vt (*scratch*) griffer; (*rip*) déchirer *or* labourer avec ses griffes *or* ses serres; (*clutch*) agripper, serrer. (*fig*) **to ~ one's way to the top** se hisser en haut de l'échelle.

▸**claw at** vt fus *object* essayer de s'agripper à; *person* essayer de griffer.

▸**claw back** 1 vt sep (*Econ*) récupérer. 2 **clawback** n *see* **claw 2**.

clay [kleɪ] 1 n argile *f*, (terre *f*) glaise *f*; (*Tennis*) terre *f* battue. **potter's ~** argile (à potier); (*Tennis*) **to play on ~** *or* **on a ~ court** jouer sur terre battue *or* sur un court de terre battue; *see* **china**. 2 comp ▸ **clay court** (*Tennis*) court *m* de terre battue ▸ **clay pigeon** pigeon *m* d'argile *or* de ball-trap; (*US fig*) victime *f or* cible *f* facile; **clay pigeon shooting** ball-trap *m* ▸ **clay pipe** pipe *f* en terre ▸ **clay pit** argilière *f*, glaisière *f* ▸ **clay-with-flints** (*Geol*) argile *f* à silex.

clayey ['kleɪɪ] adj argileux, glaiseux.

clean [kliːn] 1 adj a (*not dirty*) *clothes, plates, hands, house, car* propre, net; (*having clean habits*) *person, animal* propre. **to have ~ hands** avoir les mains propres; (*fig*) avoir les mains nettes *or* la conscience nette, n'avoir été mêlé à rien; **a ~ piece of paper** une feuille blanche; (*fig*) **a ~ bomb** une bombe propre *or* sans retombées (radio-actives); **to wipe sth ~** essuyer qch; **keep it ~** ne le salissez pas, tenez-le propre; **as ~ as a new pin** propre comme un sou neuf; (*fig*) **to make a ~ breast of it** décharger sa conscience, dire ce qu'on a sur la conscience; **to make a ~ sweep** faire table rase (*of* de).

b (*pure etc*) *reputation* net, sans tache; *joke, story* qui n'a rien de choquant; *contest, game* loyal; *smell, air, taste, sound* pur. **~ living** une *or* la vie saine; (*Jur*) **a ~ record** *or* **sheet** un casier (judiciaire) vierge; **a ~ driving licence** un permis de conduire où n'est portée aucune contravention; (*fig*) **let's keep the party ~!*** pas d'inconvenances!, pas de grossièretés!; **~ player** joueur *m*, -euse *f* fair-play *inv*; **the doctor gave him a ~ bill of health** le médecin l'a trouvé en parfait état de santé; (*Comm*) **~ bill of lading** connaissement net *or* sans réserves.

c (*elegant etc*) *shape* fin, net, bien proportionné; *line, stroke* net; *profile* pur. **~ outlines** des contours nets *or* dégagés; **a ~ ship** un navire aux lignes élégantes; **this car has very ~ lines** cette voiture a une belle ligne; **a ~ cut** une coupure nette *or* franche; **~ leap** saut *m* sans toucher (l'obstacle); (*Tennis*) **a ~ ace** un as.

d (‡) **he's ~** (*unarmed*) il n'est pas armé, il n'a rien sur lui; (*innocent*) il n'a rien fait; (*no incriminating material in it*) **his room was quite ~** il n'y avait rien dans sa chambre, on n'a rien trouvé dans sa chambre.

e (*in nuclear processes etc*) propre.

2 adv entièrement, complètement, tout à fait. **I ~ forgot** j'ai complètement oublié; **he got ~ away** il a décampé sans laisser de traces; **to cut ~ through sth** couper qch de part en part; **he jumped ~ over the fence** il a sauté la barrière sans la toucher; **the car went ~ through the hedge** la voiture est carrément passée à travers la haie; **the fish jumped ~ out of the net** le poisson a sauté carrément hors du filet; **to break off ~** casser net; (*fig*) **to come ~‡** se mettre à table‡; **to come ~ about sth‡** révéler qch, tout dire sur qch.

3 n: **to give sth a good ~(up)** bien nettoyer qch.

4 comp ▸ **clean-and-jerk** (*Weightlifting*) épaulé-jeté *m* ▸ **clean-cut** bien délimité, net, clair; *person* aux traits nets ▸ **clean-limbed** bien proportionné, bien découplé ▸ **clean-living** décent, honnête ▸ **clean-out** nettoyage *m* à fond ▸ **clean-shaven** *face* rasé de près, glabre; *head* rasé; **to be clean-shaven** n'avoir ni barbe ni moustache, être glabre ▸ **cleanup** *see* **cleanup**.

5 vt *clothes, room, fish* nettoyer; *vegetables* laver; *blackboard* essuyer. **to ~ one's teeth** se laver les dents; **to ~ one's nails** se nettoyer les ongles; **to ~ one's face** se débarbouiller, se laver la figure; **to ~ the windows** faire les vitres; *see* **dry**.

6 vi a (*do housework*) faire le ménage.

b (*be cleaned*) se nettoyer. **that floor ~s easily** ce plancher se nettoie facilement *or* est facile à nettoyer.

▸**clean off** vt sep *writing* (*on blackboard*) essuyer; (*on wall*) enlever.

▸**clean out** 1 vt sep *drawer, box* nettoyer à fond; *cupboard, room* nettoyer *or* faire à fond; (** fig: leave penniless etc*) *person* nettoyer*. **the hotel bill cleaned me out*** la note de l'hôtel m'a nettoyé* *or* m'a mis à sec*; **he was cleaned out*** il était fauché *or* à sec*; **the burglars had cleaned out the whole house*** les cambrioleurs avaient complètement vidé la maison. 2 **clean-out** n *see* **clean 4**.

▸**clean up** 1 vi a tout nettoyer, mettre de l'ordre. **she had to clean up after the children's visit** elle a dû tout remettre en ordre après la visite des enfants; **to clean up after sb** nettoyer après qn.

b (** fig: make profit*) faire son beurre*. **he cleaned up on that sale*** cette vente lui a rapporté gros, il a touché un joli paquet* sur cette vente.

2 vt a *room, mess, person* nettoyer. **to clean o.s. up** se laver, se débarbouiller.

b (*fig*) (re)mettre de l'ordre dans (les affaires de), épurer. **the new mayor cleaned up the city** le nouveau maire a épuré la ville *or* a remis de l'ordre dans la ville; **they are trying to clean up television** ils essaient d'épurer la télévision.

3 **cleanup** n *see* **cleanup**.

cleaner ['kliːnəʳ] n a (*woman*) (*in home*) femme *f* de ménage; (*in office, school*) femme de service; (*in hospital*) fille *f* de salle; (*man*) agent *m* de service, ouvrier *m* nettoyeur. b (*Comm*) teinturier *m*, -ière *f*; (*device*) appareil *m* de nettoyage; (*household ~*) produit *m* d'entretien; (*stain-remover*) détachant *m*. **the ~'s shop** la teinturerie; **he took his coat to the ~'s** il a donné son pardessus à nettoyer *or* au teinturier; (*fig*) **to take sb to the ~'s‡** nettoyer* qn, soutirer le maximum à qn; *see* **dry, vacuum** *etc*.

cleaning ['kliːnɪŋ] 1 n nettoyage *m*; (*housework*) ménage *m*; *see* **spring**. 2 comp ▸ **cleaning fluid** (*for stains*) détachant *m* ▸ **cleaning lady** *or* **woman** femme *f* de ménage.

cleanliness ['klenlɪnɪs] n propreté *f*, habitude *f* de la propreté. (*Prov*) **~ is next to godliness** la propreté du corps est parente de la propreté de l'âme.

cleanly¹ ['kliːnlɪ] adv proprement, nettement.

cleanly² ['klenlɪ] adj *person, animal* propre.

cleanness ['kliːnnɪs] n propreté *f*.

cleanse [klenz] vt nettoyer; *ditch, drain etc* curer; (*Bible: cure*) guérir; (*fig*) *person* laver (*of* de); (*Rel*) *soul etc* purifier. (*Med*) **to ~ the blood** dépurer le sang.

cleanser ['klenzəʳ] n (*detergent*) détersif *m*, détergent *m*; (*for complexion*) démaquillant *m*.

cleansing ['klenzɪŋ] 1 adj (*for complexion*) démaquillant; (*fig*) purifiant. **~ cream/lotion** crème/lotion démaquillante; **~ department** service *m* de voirie. 2 n nettoyage *m*.

cleanup ['kliːnʌp] n a [*room*] nettoyage *m*; [*person*] débarbouillage *m*; (*fig*) épuration *f*, assainissement *m*. **to give o.s. a ~** se laver, se débarbouiller; *see also* **clean 3**. b (** fig*) profit *m*. **he made a good ~ from that business** il a fait son beurre dans cette affaire*, cette affaire lui a rapporté gros.

clear [klɪəʳ] 1 adj a (*not opaque, cloudy, indistinct*) *piece of glass, plastic* transparent; *water* clair, limpide, transparent; *lake, stream* limpide, transparent; *sky* clair, sans nuages; *weather* clair, serein; *photograph* net; *outline* clair, net, distinct; *complexion* clair, lumineux, transparent. **on a ~ day** par temps clair; **~ honey** miel *m* liquide; **~ red** (n) rouge *m* vif; (adj) rouge vif *inv*; **~ soup** bouillon *m*; (*made with meat*) bouillon (gras), consommé *m*; **my conscience is ~** j'ai la conscience tranquille; **he left with a ~ conscience** il est parti la conscience tranquille.

b (*easily heard*) *sound* clair, distinct, qui s'entend nettement. **his words were quite ~** ses paroles étaient tout à fait distinctes *or* s'entendaient très nettement; **you're not very ~** je ne vous entends pas bien.

c (*keen, discerning, lucid*) *explanation, account* clair, intelligible; *reasoning* clair, lucide; *intelligence* clair, pénétrant; *style* clair, net. **~ mind** *or* **thinker** esprit *m* lucide; **I want to be quite ~ on this point** (*understand clearly*) je veux savoir exactement ce qu'il en est; (*explain unambiguously*) je veux bien me faire comprendre; **he is not quite ~ about what he must do** il n'a pas bien compris *or* saisi ce qu'il doit faire; **to be quite ~ about sth, to get sth ~** bien comprendre qch.

d (*obvious, indisputable*) *proof, sign, consequence* évident, clair, manifeste; *motive* clair, évident. **~ indication** signe manifeste *or* certain; **it was a ~ case of murder** c'était un cas d'assassinat manifeste, il s'agissait manifestement d'un assassinat; **to make o.s.** *or* **one's meaning ~** se faire bien comprendre, bien préciser ce que l'on veut dire; **is that ~?, do I make myself quite ~?** est-ce que c'est bien clair?, vous me comprenez?; **to make it ~ to sb that** faire comprendre à qn que; **I wish to make it ~ that** je tiens à préciser que; **as ~ as day** clair comme le jour *or* comme de l'eau de roche; (*iro*) **as ~ as mud‡** clair comme de l'encre; **it is ~ that he knows about such things** il est clair *or* évident qu'il s'y connaît; **it is ~ to me that** il me paraît hors de doute que; *see* **crystal**.

e (*free of obstacles etc*) *road, path etc* libre, dégagé; *route* sans obstacles, sans dangers. **the road is ~** la route est dégagée *or* libre;

Thursday morning/next week is ~, I'm ~ Thursday morning/next week je suis libre jeudi matin/la semaine prochaine; **~ space** espace *m* libre; **all ~!** (*you can go through*) la voie est libre; (*the alert is over*) l'alerte est passée; (*Mil*) fin d'alerte!; **we had a ~ view** rien ne gênait la vue; **after this traffic holdup we had a ~ run home** une fois ce bouchon passé la route était dégagée jusqu'à la maison; **we were ~ of the town** nous étions hors de *or* sortis de l'agglomération; **~ of** (*free of*) débarrassé de, libre de, libéré de; **~ of debts** libre de dettes; **a ~ profit** un bénéfice net; **a ~ loss** une perte sèche; **a ~ majority** une nette majorité; **3 ~ days** 3 jours pleins *or* entiers; *see* **coast**.

f (*Phon*) *vowel* clair.

2 **n: to send a message in ~** envoyer un message en clair; **to be in the ~*** (*above suspicion*) être au-dessus de tout soupçon; (*no longer suspected*) n'être plus soupçonné, être blanchi de tout soupçon; (*out of debt*) être libre de toutes dettes; (*out of danger*) être hors de danger.

3 **adv** a distinctement, nettement. **loud and ~** très distinctement.

b entièrement, complètement. **the thief got ~ away** le voleur a disparu sans laisser de traces, on n'a jamais revu le voleur.

c **~ of** à l'écart de, à distance de; (*Naut*) **to steer ~ of** passer au large de; **to steer** *or* **keep** *or* **stay ~ of sth/sb** éviter qch/qn; **to stand ~** s'écarter, se tenir à distance; **stand ~ of the doors!** dégagez les portes!; **to get ~ of** (*go away from*) s'éloigner *or* s'écarter de; (*rid o.s. of*) se débarrasser de; **it will be easier once we get ~ of winter** cela sera plus facile une fois l'hiver passé.

d (*net*) **he'll get £250 ~** il aura 250 livres net.

4 **comp ► clear-cut** *outline, shape* net, précis, nettement défini; *attitude, proposal, situation* précis, clair; *problem, division* précis; **clear-cut features** traits nets *or* bien dessinés **► clear-headed** lucide, perspicace **► clear-headedness** perspicacité *f*, lucidité *f* **► clear-out** rangement *m* complet **► clear-sighted** *person* clairvoyant, qui voit juste; *plan* réaliste, lucide **► clear-sightedness** *[person]* clairvoyance *f*; *[plan]* réalisme *m* **► clearway** (*Brit*) route *f* à stationnement interdit.

5 **vt** a (*clarify*) *liquid* clarifier; *wine* coller, clarifier; *skin* purifier; *complexion* éclaircir; (*Med*) *blood* dépurer, purifier; *bowels* purger, dégager; (*fig*) *situation, account* éclaircir, clarifier. **to ~ the air** aérer; (*fig*) détendre l'atmosphère; **to ~ one's throat** s'éclaircir la voix; **to ~ one's head** (*from fuzziness, hangover etc*) se dégager le cerveau; (*clear one's ideas*) se remettre les idées en place.

b (*remove obstacles etc from*) *canal, path, road, railway line* débarrasser, dégager, déblayer; *pipe* déboucher; *land* défricher; (*Comput*) *screen, memory* effacer. **to ~ the table** débarrasser la table, desservir; **to ~ the decks (for action)** se mettre en branle-bas (de combat); (*fig*) tout déblayer; **to ~ sth of rubbish** déblayer qch; (*lit*) **to ~ the way for** faire place à, libérer le passage pour; (*fig*) **to ~ the way for further discussions** préparer le terrain pour *or* ouvrir la voie à des négociations ultérieures; **~ the way!** circulez!, dégagez!*; **to ~ a way** *or* **a path through** (se) frayer un passage à travers; **to ~ a room** (*of people*) faire évacuer une salle; (*of things*) débarrasser une salle; (*Jur*) **to ~ the court** faire évacuer la salle; (*fig*) **to ~ the ground** déblayer le terrain; (*Post*) **the box is ~ed twice a day** la levée a lieu deux fois par jour; (*Ftbl*) **to ~ the ball** dégager le ballon.

c (*find innocent, acceptable etc*) *person* innocenter, disculper (*of* de). **he was ~ed of the murder charge** il a été disculpé de l'accusation d'assassinat; **he will easily ~ himself** il se disculpera facilement, il prouvera facilement son innocence; **to ~ sb of suspicion** laver qn de tout soupçon; **you will have to be ~ed by our security department** il faudra que nos services de sécurité donnent (*subj*) le feu vert en ce qui vous concerne; **we've ~ed it with him before beginning** nous avons obtenu son accord avant de commencer; **you must ~ the project with the manager** il faut que le directeur donne (*subj*) le feu vert à votre projet.

d (*get past or over*) sauter, franchir, sauter *or* passer par-dessus (sans toucher); *obstacle* éviter; (*Naut*) *rocks* éviter; *harbour* quitter. **the horse ~ed the gate by 10 cm** le cheval a sauté *or* a franchi la barrière avec 10 cm de reste *or* de marge; **the car ~ed the lamppost** la voiture a évité le réverbère de justesse; **raise the car till the wheel ~s the ground** soulevez la voiture jusqu'à ce que la roue ne touche (*subj*) plus le sol; **the boat just ~ed the bottom** le bateau a réussi à passer sans toucher le fond.

e *cheque* compenser; *account* solder, liquider; *debt* s'acquitter de; *profit* gagner net; (*Comm*) *goods* liquider; (*Customs*) *goods* dédouaner; *port dues* acquitter; *ship* expédier; (*fig*) *one's conscience* décharger; *doubts* dissiper. (*Comm*) **"half price to ~"** "solde à moitié prix pour liquider"; **you must ~ your homework before you go out** il faut que tu te débarrasses (*subj*) de *or* que tu finisses tes devoirs avant de sortir; **I've ~ed £100 on this business** cette affaire me rapporte 100 livres net *or* tous frais payés; **I didn't even ~ my expenses** je ne suis même pas rentré dans mes frais.

6 **vi** *[weather]* s'éclaircir; *[sky]* se dégager; *[fog]* se dissiper; *[face, expression]* s'éclairer; (*Naut*) *[ship]* prendre la mer; *[complexion]* s'éclaircir; *[skin]* devenir plus sain. **his brow ~ed** son visage s'est éclairé.

►clear away 1 **vi** a *[mist etc]* se dissiper. b (*clear the table*) desservir. 2 **vt sep** enlever, emporter, ôter. **to clear away the dishes** desservir, débarrasser (la table).

►clear off 1 **vi** (*) filer*, décamper. **clear off!** fichez le camp!*, filez!* 2 **vt sep** a (*get rid of*) se débarrasser de; *debts* s'acquitter de; (*Comm*) *stock* liquider; *goods* solder. **to clear off arrears of work** rattraper le retard dans son travail. b (*remove*) *things on table etc* enlever.

►clear out 1 **vi** (*) = **clear off 1.** 2 **vt sep** *cupboard* vider; *room* nettoyer, débarrasser; *unwanted objects* enlever, jeter. **he cleared everyone out of the room** il a fait évacuer la pièce; **he cleared everything out of the room** il a débarrassé la pièce, il a fait le vide dans la pièce. 3 **clear-up n** *see* **clear 4**.

►clear up 1 **vi** a *[weather]* s'éclaircir, se lever. **I think it will clear up** je pense que ça va se lever. b *[illness, spots]* disparaître. **his face/skin has cleared up** il n'a plus de boutons. c (*tidy*) ranger, faire des rangements. 2 **vt sep** a *mystery* éclaircir, résoudre; *matter, subject* éclaircir, tirer au clair. b (*tidy*) *room* ranger, mettre en ordre; *books, toys* ranger.

clearance ['klɪərəns] 1 **n** a (*NonC*) *[road, path]* déblaiement *m*, dégagement *m*; *[land, bombsite]* déblaiement; *[room, court]* évacuation *f*; *[litter, objects, rubbish]* enlèvement *m*; (*Comm*) soldes *mpl*, liquidation *f* (du stock).

b *[boat, car etc]* dégagement *m*, espace *m* libre. **2 metre ~** espace de 2 mètres; **how much ~ is there between my car and yours?** je suis à combien de votre voiture?

c *[cheque]* compensation *f*; (*Customs*) dédouanement *m*; (*permission etc*) autorisation *f*, permis *m* (*de publier etc*). (*Naut*) **~ outwards/inwards** permis de sortie/d'entrée; **the despatch was sent to the Foreign Office for ~** la dépêche a été soumise au ministère des Affaires étrangères pour contrôle; (*Aviat*) **to give (sb) ~ for takeoff** donner (à qn) l'autorisation de décoller.

d (*Ftbl*) dégagement *m*.

2 **comp ► clearance certificate** (*Naut*) congé *m* de navigation, lettre *f* de mer **► clearance sale** (*Comm*) soldes *mpl*.

clearing ['klɪərɪŋ] 1 **n** a (*in forest*) clairière *f*.

b (*NonC*) *[liquid]* clarification *f*; *[wine]* collage *m*; (*Med*) *[bowels]* purge *f*; *[blood]* dépuration *f*.

c (*NonC: tidying, unblocking*) *[room, cupboard, passage]* dégagement *m*, désencombrement *m*; *[rubbish]* ramassage *m*, déblaiement *m*; *[objects]* enlèvement *m*; *[land]* défrichement *m*; *[pipe etc]* débouchage *m*; *[road]* dégagement, déblaiement; *[room, court]* évacuation *f*.

d (*Jur*) *[accused]* disculpation *f*.

e (*Fin*) *[cheque]* compensation *f*; *[account]* liquidation *f*; *[debt]* acquittement *m*.

2 **comp ► clearing bank** (*Brit*) banque *f* (appartenant à une chambre de compensation) **► clearing house** (*Banking*) chambre *f* de compensation; (*fig: for documents etc*) bureau central.

clearly ['klɪəlɪ] **adv** a (*distinctly*) *see, state* clairement, nettement; *hear* distinctement, nettement; *understand* bien, clairement. **~ visible** bien visible. b (*obviously*) manifestement, évidemment.

clearness ['klɪənɪs] **n** a *[air, liquid]* transparence *f*, limpidité *f*; *[glass]* transparence. b *[sound, sight, print, thought etc]* clarté *f*, netteté *f*.

cleat [kliːt] **n** (*Carpentry*) tasseau *m*; (*Naut*) taquet *m*; (*on shoe*) clou *m*.

cleavage ['kliːvɪdʒ] **n** (*lit*) (*Chem, Geol*) clivage *m*; (*Bio*) *[cell]* division *f*; (*fig*) *[opinion]* division, clivage. **a dress which showed her ~*** une robe qui laissait voir la naissance des seins.

cleave[1] [kliːv] **pret cleft** *or* **clove, ptp cleft** *or* **cloven** 1 **vt** (*gen liter*) fendre; (*Chem, Geol*) cliver; (*Bio*) diviser; (*fig*) diviser, séparer, désunir. 2 **vi** se fendre; (*Chem, Geol*) se cliver; (*Bio*) se diviser. **to ~ through the waves** fendre les vagues.

cleave[2] [kliːv] **pret, ptp cleaved vi** (*liter*) (*stick*) coller, adhérer (*to* à); (*fig*) s'attacher, rester attaché *or* fidèle (*to* à).

cleaver ['kliːvəʳ] **n** fendoir *m*, couperet *m*.

clef [klef] **n** (*Mus*) clef *f* *or* clé *f* (*signe*); *see* **bass[1]**, **treble** *etc.*

cleft [kleft] 1 **pret, ptp of cleave[1]**. 2 **adj** fendu; *stick* fourchu. (*fig*) **to be in a ~ stick** se trouver *or* être dans une impasse; (*Anat*) **~ palate** palais fendu; (*Gram*) **~ sentence** phrase clivée. 3 **n** (*in rock*) crevasse *f*, fissure *f*.

cleg [kleg] **n** taon *m*.

clematis ['klemətɪs] **n** clématite *f*.

clemency ['klemənsɪ] **n** *[person]* clémence *f* (*towards* envers); *[weather etc]* douceur *f*, clémence.

clement ['klemənt] **adj** *person* clément (*towards* envers); *weather* doux (*f* douce), clément.

clementine ['kleməntaɪn] **n** clémentine *f*.

clench [klentʃ] 1 **vt** a **to ~ sth (in one's hands)** empoigner *or* serrer qch dans ses mains; **to ~ one's fists/teeth** serrer les poings/les dents. b = **clinch 1.** 2 **n** = **clinch 3a.**

Cleopatra [ˌkliːəˈpætrə] **n** Cléopâtre *f*. **~'s needle** l'obélisque *m* de Cléopâtre.

clerestory ['klɪəstɔːrɪ] **n** (*Archit*) claire-voie *f*, clair-étage *m*.

clergy ['klɜːdʒɪ] **collective n** (membres *mpl* du) clergé *m*. **~man** ecclésiastique *m*; (*Protestant*) pasteur *m*; (*Roman Catholic*) prêtre *m*, curé *m*.

cleric ['klerɪk] n ecclésiastique *m*.

clerical ['klerɪkəl] adj a (*Rel*) clérical, du clergé; *collar* de pasteur. b (*Comm, Fin, Jur*) *job, position* de commis, d'employé; *work, worker, staff* de bureau. ~ **error** (*in book-keeping*) erreur *f* d'écriture (commise par un employé); (*in manuscripts*) faute *f* de copiste.

clericalism ['klerɪkəlɪzəm] n cléricalisme *m*.

clerihew ['klerɪhju:] n petit poème humoristique (*pseudo-biographique*).

clerk [klɑ:k], (*US*) [klɜ:rk] 1 n a (*in office*) employé(e) *m(f)* (*de bureau, de commerce*), commis *m*; (*Jur*) clerc *m*. **bank** ~ employé(e) de banque; (*in hotel*) **desk** ~ réceptionniste *mf*; (*Jur*) **C~ of the Court** greffier *m* (du tribunal); *see* **head, town.** b (††) (*Rel*) ecclésiastique *m*; (*scholar*) clerc†† *m*, savant *m*. c (*US: shop assistant*) vendeur *m*, -euse *f*. d (*Brit Constr*) ~ **of works** conducteur *m* de travaux. 2 vi a (*US Jur*) **to ~ for a judge** être assistant(e) *m(f)* stagiaire d'un juge. b (*US Comm*) travailler comme vendeur/vendeuse.

clerkship ['klɑ:kʃɪp], (*US*) ['klɜ:rkʃɪp] n fonctions *fpl* d'employé de bureau, emploi *m* de commis; (*Med*) stage *m*.

clever ['klevəʳ] 1 adj a (*intelligent*) *person* intelligent, à l'esprit éveillé, astucieux; *book* intelligemment écrit, ingénieux; *play, film* intelligemment *or* bien fait, intelligent; *machine, invention, explanation* ingénieux; *idea* astucieux, intelligent; *joke* fin, astucieux; *story* bien conduit, astucieux. ~ **pupil** élève doué; **to be ~ at French** être fort en français.

b (*skilful*) *person* habile, adroit; *piece of work etc* bien fait. **a ~ workman** un ouvrier habile; **to be ~ at doing sth** être habile à faire qch; **to be ~ with one's hands** être adroit de ses mains; **he's very ~ with cars** il s'y connaît en voitures.

c (*smart*) *person* astucieux, malin (*f* -igne); *action* ingénieux, astucieux. **a ~ trick** un tour ingénieux *or* astucieux; **he was too ~ for me** il m'a roulé*, il m'a eu*; (*pej*) ~ **Dick** petit *or* gros malin; *see* **half.**

2 comp ► **clever-clever*** (*pej*) un peu trop futé.

cleverly ['klevəlɪ] adv (*see* **clever**) intelligemment; astucieusement; ingénieusement; habilement, adroitement.

cleverness ['klevənɪs] n (*see* **clever**) intelligence *f*; astuce *f*, ingéniosité *f*; habileté *f*, adresse *f* (*at* à).

clew [klu:] n (*US*) = **clue.**

cliché ['kli:ʃeɪ] n cliché *m*, expression *or* phrase toute faite. ~**d** rebattu, galvaudé.

click [klɪk] 1 n déclic *m*, petit bruit sec; *[tongue]* claquement *m*; *[wheel]* cliquet *m*; (*Phon*) clic *m*.

2 vi a faire un bruit sec, cliqueter. **the door ~ed shut** la porte s'est refermée avec un déclic; **the part ~ed into place** la pièce s'est mise en place *or* s'est enclenchée avec un déclic; (*fig*) **suddenly it ~ed*** j'ai (*or* il a *etc*) pigé‡ tout à coup; (*fig*) **to ~ with sb*** se découvrir des atomes crochus* avec qn; (*sexually*) taper dans l'œil à qn*.

b (*: *be successful*) *[product, invention]* bien marcher.

3 vt: **to ~ one's heels** claquer des talons; **to ~ one's tongue** faire claquer sa langue, clapper de la langue; **she ~ed the shelf back into place** elle a remis l'étagère en place avec un déclic.

►**click on** vt fus (*Comput*) cliquer.

clicking ['klɪkɪŋ] n cliquetis *m*.

client ['klaɪənt] n client(e) *m(f)*.

clientele [,kli:ɑ̃:n'tel] n (*Comm*) clientèle *f*; (*Theat*) habitués *mpl*.

cliff [klɪf] 1 n *[seashore]* falaise *f*; *[mountains]* escarpement *m*; (*Climbing*) à-pic *m*. 2 comp ► **cliff-dweller** (*lit*) troglodyte *mf*; (*US*) habitant(e) *m(f)* de gratte-ciel ► **cliff-hanger*** récit *m* (*or* situation *f etc*) à suspense; (*moment of suspense*) moment *m* d'angoisse ► **cliff-hanging*** tendu, à suspense; **cliff-hanging vote*** vote *m* à suspense.

climacteric [klaɪ'mæktərɪk] 1 n climatère *m*; (*Med, esp US*) ménopause *f*. 2 adj climatérique; (*fig*) crucial, dangereux.

climactic [klaɪ'mæktɪk] adj à son *or* au point culminant, à son apogée.

climate ['klaɪmɪt] n (*Met, fig*) climat *m*. **the ~ of opinion** (les courants *mpl* de) l'opinion *f*.

climatic [klaɪ'mætɪk] adj climatique.

climatology [,klaɪmə'tɒlədʒɪ] n climatologie *f*.

climax ['klaɪmæks] 1 n point culminant, apogée *m*; (*sexual*) orgasme *m*; (*Rhetoric*) gradation *f*. **the ~ of his political career** l'apogée de sa vie politique; **this brought matters to a ~** cela a porté l'affaire à son point culminant; (*fig*) **to come to a ~** atteindre son point culminant; (*fig*) **to work up to a ~** *[story, events]* tendre vers son point culminant, s'intensifier; *[speaker]* amener le point culminant. 2 vt amener *or* porter à son point culminant *or* au point culminant. 3 vi atteindre son *or* le point culminant; (*sexually*) jouir.

climb [klaɪm] 1 vt (*also* ~ **up**) *stairs, steps, slope* monter, grimper; *hill* grimper, escalader; *tree, ladder* grimper *or* monter sur *or* à; *rope* monter à; *cliff, wall* escalader; *mountain* gravir, faire l'ascension de; (*fig*) **the record ~ed 3 places** le disque a gagné 3 places (au hit-parade); (*St Ex*) **shares ~ed 3 points** les actions ont augmenté de 3 points; (*fig*) **to be ~ing the wall** être dingue.

2 vi a (*lit, fig: also* ~ **up**) monter, grimper; *[aircraft, rocket]* monter, prendre de l'altitude; *[sun]* monter; *[prices, shares, costs]* augmenter; (*Sport*) escalader, grimper; (*also* **rock-~**) varapper.

b **to ~ down a tree** descendre d'un arbre; **to ~ down a mountain** descendre d'une montagne, effectuer la descente d'une montagne; **to ~ over a wall/an obstacle** escalader un mur/un obstacle; **to ~ into an aircraft/a boat** monter *or* grimper à bord d'un avion/bateau; **to ~ out of a hole** se hisser hors d'un trou; (*Sport*) **to go ~ing** faire de l'alpinisme; (*fig*) **to ~ to power** s'élever (jusqu')au pouvoir.

3 n *[hill]* montée *f*, côte *f*; (*Climbing*) ascension *f*; *[aircraft]* montée, ascension.

4 comp ► **climb-down*** reculade *f*, dérobade *f*.

►**climb down** 1 vi a (*lit*) (*from tree, wall*) descendre; (*Climbing*) descendre, effectuer une descente. b (*: *abandon one's position*) en rabattre. 2 **climb-down*** n *see* **climb 4.**

►**climb up** *see* **climb 1, 2a.**

climber ['klaɪməʳ] n (*person*) grimpeur *m*, -euse *f*; (*mountaineer*) alpiniste *mf*, ascensionniste *mf*; (*fig pej*) arriviste *mf* (*pej*); (*plant*) plante grimpante; (*bird*) grimpeur *m*; (*also* **rock-~**) varappeur *m*.

climbing ['klaɪmɪŋ] 1 adj *person, bird* grimpeur; (*Bot*) grimpant; (*Astron, Aviat*) ascendant. 2 n montée *f*, escalade *f*; (*Sport*) alpinisme *m*; (*also* **rock-~**) varappe *f*; (*fig*) arrivisme *m* (*pej*). 3 comp ► **climbing frame** cage *f* à poules ► **climbing irons** crampons *mpl* ► **climbing speed** (*Aviat*) vitesse ascensionnelle.

clinch [klɪntʃ] 1 vt (*also* **clench**) (*Tech*) *nail, rivet* river; (*Naut*) étalinguer; (*fig*) *argument* consolider, confirmer; *bargain* conclure. **to ~ the deal** conclure l'affaire; **to ~ an agreement** sceller un pacte; **that ~es it** comme ça c'est réglé, ça coupe court à tout*. 2 vi (*Boxing*) combattre corps à corps. 3 n a (*also* **clench**) (*Tech*) rivetage *m*; (*Naut*) étalingure *f*. b (*Boxing*) corps-à-corps *m*. **to get into a ~** lutter corps à corps. c (‡: *embrace*) étreinte *f*, enlacement *m*. **in a ~** enlacés.

clincher* ['klɪntʃəʳ] adj argument *m* décisif.

clinching ['klɪntʃɪŋ] adj convaincant, concluant.

cline [klaɪn] n cline *m*.

cling [klɪŋ] pret, ptp **clung** 1 vi a (*hold tight*) se cramponner, s'accrocher (*to* à). **to ~ together, to ~ to one another** se tenir étroitement enlacés, se cramponner l'un à l'autre; (*fig*) **despite the opposition of all he clung to his opinion** il s'est cramponné à *or* a maintenu son opinion envers et contre tous; (*fig*) **to ~ to a belief** se raccrocher à une croyance; **to ~ to the belief that** se raccrocher à la notion que. b (*stick*) adhérer, (se) coller, s'attacher (*to* à); *[clothes]* coller. **to ~ together, to ~ to one another** rester *or* être collés l'un à l'autre. 2 comp ► **clingfilm** ®, **clingwrap** film alimentaire transparent, Scellofrais ® *m*.

clinging ['klɪŋɪŋ] adj *garment* collant, qui moule le corps; *odour* tenace; (*pej*) *person* crampon* *inv*, collant*. (*US fig*) ~ **vine** pot-de-colle* *m*, personne collante.

clinic ['klɪnɪk] n (*private nursing home, consultant's teaching session*) clinique *f*; (*health centre*) centre médico-social *or* d'hygiène sociale; (*also* **outpatients'** ~) service *m* de consultation (externe), dispensaire *m* (municipal).

clinical ['klɪnɪkəl] adj a (*Med*) *conditions, lecture* clinique; *tests* en laboratoire. ~ **thermometer** thermomètre médical. b (*fig*) *attitude, approach* objectif, impartial; *tone* détaché; *decor, style* austère, froid.

clinically ['klɪnɪkəlɪ] adv (*lit*) *test* en laboratoire; (*fig*) *say* sur un ton détaché.

clink¹ [klɪŋk] 1 vt faire tinter *or* résonner *or* sonner. **to ~ glasses with sb** trinquer avec qn. 2 vi tinter, résonner. 3 n tintement *m* (*de verres etc*).

clink² [klɪŋk] n (‡) taule‡ *f or* tôle‡ *f*, bloc* *m*.

clinker ['klɪŋkəʳ] 1 n a (*burnt out coal*) mâchefer *m*, scories *fpl*. b (*paving material*) brique vitrifiée. c (*US* ‡: *mistake*) (*Mus*) pavé *m*; (*gen*) couac *m*; (*failed film, play etc*) four* *m*, bide* *m*. 2 comp ► **clinker-built** (*Naut*) (bordé) à clins.

clip¹ [klɪp] 1 n (*for papers*) attache *f*, trombone *m*; (*for tube*) collier *m*, bague *f*; (*also* **cartridge** ~) chargeur *m*; (*brooch*) clip *m*. 2 vt a *papers* attacher (avec un trombone). **to ~ a brooch on one's dress** fixer une broche sur sa robe. b (*US fig*) **to ~* the customers** estamper* les clients. 3 comp ► **clipboard** (*gen*) écritoire *f* à pince, clipboard *m*; (*Comput*) bloc-notes *m*.

►**clip on** 1 vt sep *brooch* fixer; *document etc* attacher (avec un trombone). 2 **clip-on** *see* **clip² 3.**

►**clip together** vt sep attacher.

clip² [klɪp] 1 vt a (*cut, snip*) couper (avec des ciseaux); *hedge* tailler; *sheep, dog* tondre; *ticket* poinçonner; *article from newspaper* découper; *hair* couper; *wings* rogner, couper. (*fig*) **to ~ sb's wings** rogner les ailes à qn; (*fig*) **he has a ~ped way of speaking** il avale ses mots *or* les syllabes (en parlant); (*fig*) **in a ~ped voice** d'un ton sec.

b (*: *hit*) flanquer une taloche à*. **I ~ped him on the jaw*** je lui ai flanqué un marron‡ à travers la figure.

c (*reduce time*) **to ~ a few seconds off a record** améliorer un record de quelques secondes.

2 n a **to give sth a ~ = to clip sth**; *see* **1a.**

b (*Cine, Rad*) court extrait; (*TV*) clip *m*.

c (*: *blow*) taloche* *f*, marron‡ *m*. **he gave him a ~ on the head** *or* **round the ear** il lui a flanqué une bonne taloche*.

d (*US*) **at a ~** à toute vitesse.

3 comp ► **clip joint**‡ (*pej*) boîte *f* où l'on se fait tondre *or* fusiller*; **that's a real clip joint** c'est vraiment le coup de fusil dans cette boîte* ► **clip-on** avec clip.

clipper ['klɪpəʳ] n a (*Aviat, Naut*) clipper *m*. b **~s** (*tool*) tondeuse *f*; *see* **hair, hedge, nail**.

clippie‡ ['klɪpɪ] n (*Brit: conductress*) receveuse *f*.

clipping ['klɪpɪŋ] n a [*newspaper etc*] coupure *f* de presse *or* de journal. b **~s** [*grass, hedge*] déchets *mpl*; [*nails*] bouts *mpl* d'ongles (qu'on a coupés).

clique [kli:k] n (*slightly pej*) clique *f*, coterie *f*, chapelle *f*.

cliquey ['kli:kɪ] adj, **cliquish** ['kli:kɪʃ] adj (*slightly pej*) exclusif, qui a l'esprit de clique *or* de (petite) chapelle.

cliquishness ['kli:kɪʃnɪs] n (*slightly pej*) esprit *m* de clique *or* de chapelle.

clitoral ['klɪtərəl] adj clitoridien.

clitoris ['klɪtərɪs] n clitoris *m*.

Cllr n abbr of **Councillor**.

cloak [kləʊk] 1 n grande cape; [*shepherd etc*] houppelande *f*; (*fig*) manteau *m*, voile *m*. (*fig*) **as a ~ for sth** pour cacher *or* masquer qch; **under the ~ of darkness** sous le manteau *or* le voile de la nuit. 2 vt (*fig*) masquer, déguiser, cacher; (*dress*) revêtir d'un manteau. (*fig*) **~ed with respectability/mystery** empreint de respectabilité/de mystère. 3 comp ► **cloak-and-dagger** clandestin; **the cloak-and-dagger boys*** les membres *mpl* du service secret, les barbouzes‡ *fpl*; **a cloak-and-dagger story** un roman d'espionnage.

cloakroom ['kləʊkrʊm] n a [*coats etc*] vestiaire *m*; (*Brit: left luggage*) consigne *f*. **to put** *or* **leave in the ~** *clothes* mettre *or* déposer au vestiaire; *luggage* mettre à la consigne; **~ attendant** (*in theatre*) préposé(e) *m(f)* au vestiaire; (*Brit: in toilets*) préposé(e) *m(f)* aux toilettes; **~ ticket** [*clothes*] numéro *m* de vestiaire; [*luggage*] bulletin *m* de consigne. b (*Brit euph: toilet*) (*public*) toilettes *fpl*; (*in house*) cabinets *mpl*.

clobber* ['klɒbəʳ] 1 n (*NonC: Brit: belongings*) barda* *m*. 2 vt (*hit*) tabasser‡; (*fig*) mettre à plat*, démolir*.

cloche [klɒʃ] n (*Agr, Dress*) cloche *f*.

clock [klɒk] 1 n a (*large*) horloge *f*; (*smaller*) pendule *f*. **it's midday by the church ~** il est midi à l'horloge de *or* au clocher de l'église; **it lasted 2 hours by the ~** cela a duré 2 heures d'horloge; **to keep one's eyes on the ~, to watch the ~** surveiller l'heure; **they're watching the premises round the ~** ils surveillent les locaux vingt-quatre heures sur vingt-quatre; **to work round the ~** travailler vingt-quatre heures d'affilée; (*fig*) travailler sans relâche; **to work against the ~** travailler contre la montre; **to do sth by the ~** *or* **according to the ~** faire qch en respectant l'horaire; **to put the ~ back/forward** retarder/avancer l'horloge; (*fig*) **to put** *or* **set** *or* **turn the ~ back** revenir en arrière (*fig*); (*fig*) **you can't put the ~ back** ce qui est fait est fait; **this decision will put the ~ back 50 years** cette décision va nous ramener 50 ans en arrière; *see* **grand, o'clock, sleep** *etc*.

b [*taxi*] compteur *m*, taximètre *m*; (*Aut *: milometer*) ≃ compteur (kilométrique). (*Aut*) **there were 50,000 miles on the ~** la voiture avait 50 000 milles au compteur.

c (*Comput*) horloge *f*, base *f* de temps.

2 comp ► **clock card** (*Ind*) carte *f* de pointage ► **clock-golf** jeu *m* de l'horloge ► **clockmaker** horloger *m*, -ère *f* ► **clock-radio** radio-réveil *m* ► **clock repairer** horloger réparateur ► **clock-tower** clocher *m* ► **clock-watcher**: (*pej*) **he's a terrible clock-watcher** il ne fait que guetter l'heure de sortie, il a les yeux fixés sur la pendule ► **clock-watching**: **to be guilty of clock-watching** passer son temps à surveiller les aiguilles de la pendule.

3 vt a (*Sport*) *runner* chronométrer. **he ~ed 4 minutes for the mile** il a fait le mille en 4 minutes.

b (*Brit* ‡: *hit*) **he ~ed him one** il lui a flanqué un ramponneau‡ *or* un marron‡.

c (*Brit *: notice*) voir.

d (*Aut sl*) **to ~ a car** trafiquer* le compteur d'une voiture.

►**clock in** 1 vi (*Ind*) pointer (à l'arrivée). 2 vt sep: **he clocked in 3 hours' work** il a fait 3 heures de travail.

►**clock off** vi (*Ind*) pointer (à la sortie).

►**clock on** = **clock in 1**.

►**clock out** = **clock off**.

►**clock up** vt sep a = **clock in 2**. b (*Aut*) **he clocked up 250 miles** il a fait 250 milles au compteur.

clockwise ['klɒkwaɪz] adv, adj dans le sens des aiguilles d'une montre.

clockwork ['klɒkwɜ:k] 1 n (*mechanism*) [*clock*] mouvement *m* (d'horloge); [*toy etc*] mécanisme *m*, rouages *mpl*. (*fig*) **to go like ~** aller comme sur des roulettes; *see* **regular**. 2 comp *toy, train, car* mécanique; (*fig*) précis, régulier ► **clockwork precision**: **with clockwork precision** avec la précision d'une horloge.

clod [klɒd] 1 n a [*earth etc*] motte *f* (de terre *etc*). b (* *pej*) balourd(e)* *m(f)*. 2 comp ► **clodhopper**‡ (*pej*) (*person*) lourdaud *m*, balourd *m*; (*shoe*) godillot‡ *m*.

clog [klɒg] 1 n (*shoe*) (*wooden*) sabot *m*; (*with wooden soles*) socque *m*, galoche† *f*. 2 vt (*also* **~ up**) *pipe* boucher, encrasser; *wheel* bloquer; *passage* boucher, bloquer, obstruer; (*fig*) entraver, gêner. 3 vi (*also* **~ up**) [*pipe etc*] se boucher, s'encrasser.

cloister ['klɔɪstəʳ] 1 n (*Archit, Rel*) cloître *m*. 2 vt (*Rel*) cloîtrer. (*fig*) **to lead a ~ed life** mener une vie monacale *or* de cloîtré.

clone [kləʊn] 1 n clone *m*. 2 vt cloner.

cloning ['kləʊnɪŋ] n clonage *m*.

clonk [klɒnk] 1 n (*sound*) bruit *m* sourd. 2 vi (*make sound*) émettre un bruit sourd.

close[1] [kləʊs] 1 adj a (*near*) proche (*to* de), voisin (*to* de); (*fig*) proche, intime. **the house is ~ to the shops** la maison est près *or* proche des magasins; **sit here ~ to me** asseyez-vous ici près de moi; **his birthday is ~ to mine** son anniversaire est proche du mien; **to be ~ to tears** être au bord des larmes; **in ~ proximity to** dans le voisinage immédiat de, tout près de; **at ~ quarters** *or* **range** (*gen*) tout près (*to* de); (*Mil: hand to hand*) corps à corps; **~ connection between** rapport étroit entre; **~ contact** contact direct; **a ~ friendship** une amitié intime; **a ~ relative** un parent proche; **~ resemblance** ressemblance exacte *or* fidèle; **to bear a ~ resemblance to** ressembler beaucoup à; (*lit*) **to have a ~ shave** se (faire) raser de près; (*fig*) **to have a ~ call*** *or* **shave*** l'échapper belle, y échapper de justesse; **that was a ~ call!*** *or* **shave!*** il était moins une!*, on l'a échappé belle!; **she was very ~ to her brother** (*in age*) son frère et elle étaient d'âges très rapprochés *or* se suivaient de près; (*in friendship*) elle était très proche de son frère; **they were very ~ (friends)** ils étaient intimes; **a ~ circle of friends** un petit cercle d'amis intimes; *see* **bone, comfort, home**.

b (*compact*) *handwriting, texture, rain, order, rank* serré; *grain* fin, dense; *account* près *or* proche de la vérité; *argument* concis, précis; *reasoning* serré. (*Aviat, Mil*) **in ~ formation** *or* **order** en ordre serré.

c (*strict*) *control, surveillance* étroit, qui ne se relâche pas; (*thorough*) *questioning, checking* serré, minutieux, attentif; *examination, study* attentif, rigoureux; *attention* soutenu; *translation* serré, fidèle; *silence* impénétrable; *investigation, enquiry* minutieux, détaillé. **to keep a ~ watch on sb/sth** surveiller qn/qch de près; **in ~ confinement** en détention surveillée.

d (*airless*) *room* mal aéré, qui manque de ventilation *or* d'air; *atmosphere* lourd, étouffant; *air* (*in a room*) renfermé. **it's very ~ in here** on ne respire pas ici, il n'y a pas d'air ici; **a ~ smell** une odeur de renfermé; **~ weather** temps lourd *or* étouffant; (*Met*) **it's ~ today** il fait lourd aujourd'hui.

e (*almost equal*) serré. **~ contest** lutte très serrée; **~ finish** arrivée serrée; **~ election** élection extrêmement serrée; **the two candidates were very ~** les deux candidats étaient presque à égalité.

f (*like*) **~ to** proche de; **it was something ~ to obsession** c'était quelque chose qui s'approchait de l'obsession.

g (*Ling*) *vowel* fermé.

h (*secretive*) *person* renfermé, secret, peu communicatif.

i (*Sport*) **~ season** fermeture *f* de la chasse (*or* de la pêche).

2 adv étroitement, de près. **to hold sb ~** serrer qn dans ses bras, tenir qn tout contre soi; **to look at sth ~ up** *or* **to** regarder qch de très près; **~ by** tout près; **~ by** *or* **to the bridge** (tout) près du pont; **~ to the surface of the water** à fleur d'eau; **~ to the ground** au ras du sol; **~ by us** tout à côté de nous; **~ at** *or* **to hand** tout près; **~ (up)on** tout près de; **he is ~ on 60** il a près de 60 ans, il frise la soixantaine; **it's ~ on midnight** il est près de minuit; **he followed ~ behind me** il me suivait de près, il m'emboîtait le pas; **~ against the wall** tout contre le mur; **~ together** serrés les uns contre les autres; **to come ~r together** se rapprocher; **shut ~, ~ shut** hermétiquement fermé *or* clos.

3 comp ► **close combat** corps à corps *m* ► **close-cropped** *hair* (coupé) ras; *grass* ras ► **close company** (*Brit Fin*) *société dont les actionnaires sont limités en nombre* ► **close-fisted** avare, grippe-sou *inv*, pingre ► **close-fitting** *clothes* ajusté, près du corps ► **close-grained** *wood* au grain serré ► **close-harmony singing** chant *m* dans une tessiture restreinte *or* rapprochée *or* réduite ► **close-knit** (*fig*) très uni ► **close-mouthed** (*fig*) taciturne, peu bavard ► **close-run**: **close-run race** course très serrée; (*fig*) **it was a close-run thing** ils sont arrivés dans un mouchoir ► **close-set eyes** yeux rapprochés ► **close-shaven** rasé de près ► **close-up** (*Cine, TV*) (*photo, shot*) gros plan *m*; **in close-up** en gros plan ► **close-up lens** bonnette *f*.

4 n (*enclosure*) clos *m*; [*cathedral*] enceinte *f*; (*Scot: alleyway*) passage *m*, couloir *m*.

close[2] [kləʊz] 1 n (*end*) fin *f*, conclusion *f*. **to come to a ~** arriver à sa fin, se terminer, prendre fin; **to draw to a ~** tirer à sa fin, approcher de sa conclusion; **to draw sth** *or* **bring sth to a ~** mettre fin à qch; (*liter*) **the ~ of (the) day** la tombée *or* la chute du jour; **towards the ~ of the century** vers la fin du siècle.

2 comp ► **close-down** [*shop, business etc*] fermeture *f* (définitive); (*Brit: Rad, TV*) fin *f* des émissions ► **close-out sale, closing-out sale** (*US*) liquidation *f* avant fermeture.

3 vt a (*shut*) fermer, clore; *eyes, door, factory, shop* fermer; *pipe, tube, opening* boucher; *road* barrer. **road ~d to traffic** route interdite à la circulation; **the shop is ~d** le magasin est fermé; **the shop is ~d on Sundays** le magasin ferme le dimanche; (*fig*) **to ~ one's mind to new ideas** fermer son esprit à toute idée nouvelle; *see* **ear**[1], **eye** *etc*.

b (*bring to an end*) *proceedings, discussion* achever, terminer, mettre fin à, clore; (*Fin*) *account* arrêter, clore; *bargain* conclure. **to ~ the**

meeting lever la séance.

c (*bring together*) serrer, rapprocher. **to ~ a gap between 2 objects** réduire l'intervalle qui sépare 2 objets; (*Mil, also fig*) **to ~ ranks** serrer les rangs.

d (*Elec*) *circuit* fermer.

4 vi a *[door, box, lid, drawer]* fermer, se fermer; *[museum, theatre, shop]* fermer. **the door ~d** la porte s'est fermée; **the door/box ~s badly** la porte/la boîte ferme mal; **the shop ~s on Sundays/at 6 o'clock** le magasin ferme le dimanche/à 6 heures; **his eyes ~d** ses yeux se fermèrent; **his fingers ~d around the pencil** ses doigts se sont refermés sur le crayon.

b (*end*) *[session]* se terminer, prendre fin; *[speaker]* terminer, finir. **the meeting ~d abruptly** la séance a pris fin *or* s'est terminée brusquement; **he ~d with an appeal to their generosity** il a terminé par un appel à leur générosité; (*St Ex*) **shares ~d at 120p** les actions étaient cotées à *or* valaient 120 pence en clôture.

►**close down** 1 vi *[business, shop]* fermer (définitivement); (*Brit: Rad, TV*) terminer les émissions. 2 vt sep *shop, business* fermer (définitivement). 3 **close-down** n *see* **close[2] 2.**

►**close in** 1 vi *[hunters etc]* se rapprocher, approcher; *[evening, night]* approcher, descendre, tomber; *[darkness, fog]* descendre. **the days are closing in** les jours raccourcissent (de plus en plus); **to close in on sb** (*approach*) s'approcher *or* se rapprocher de qn; (*encircle*) cerner qn de près. 2 vt sep clôturer, enclore.

►**close off** vt sep *room* condamner; *road etc* bloquer.

►**close on** vt fus a (*get nearer to: in race, achievement etc*) rattraper. b (*US*) = **close in on**; *see* **close in 1.**

►**close out** vt sep (*US Comm*) *stock* liquider (avant fermeture).

►**close up** 1 vi *[people in line etc]* se rapprocher, se serrer; (*Mil*) serrer les rangs; *[wound]* se refermer. 2 vt sep *house, shop* fermer (complètement); *pipe, tube, opening* fermer, obturer, boucher; *wound* refermer, recoudre.

►**close with** vt fus a (*strike bargain with*) conclure un marché avec, tomber d'accord avec. b (*agree to*) *offer, conditions* accepter. c (*grapple with*) se prendre corps à corps avec.

closed [kləʊzd] adj *door, eyes* fermé, clos; *road* barré; *pipe, opening etc* bouché, obturé; *class, economy* fermé; (*Ling*) *syllable* couvert. (*notice*) **"~"** (*gen*) "fermé"; (*Theat*) "relâche"; (*lit, fig*) **to find the door ~** trouver porte close; **to have a ~ mind** avoir l'esprit étroit, être fermé à de nouvelles idées; (*Jur*) **~ session** huis clos; **maths are a ~ book to me*** je suis complètement rebelle aux maths *or* bouché* en maths; (*fig*) **behind ~ doors** à l'abri des indiscrets; **~-circuit television** télévision *f* en circuit fermé; (*US Pol*) **~ primary** *élection primaire réservée aux membres d'un parti;* (*Sport*) **~ season** fermeture *f* de la chasse (*or* de la pêche); (*Ind*) **~ shop** atelier *m or* organisation *f* qui n'admet que des travailleurs syndiqués; (*Ind*) **the unions insisted on a ~-shop policy** les syndicats ont exigé l'exclusion des travailleurs non syndiqués; (*Brit Fin*) **~ company** *société dont le nombre d'actionnaires est limité;* (*US*) **~ staff hospital** *hôpital où des médecins agréés peuvent traiter leurs propres malades.*

closely [ˈkləʊslɪ] adv *guard* étroitement; *grasp* en serrant fort; *watch, follow* de près; *resemble* beaucoup; *study* de près, minutieusement, attentivement; *listen* attentivement. **he held her ~ to him** il la serrait *or* la tenait serrée (tout) contre lui; **a ~ contested match** un match très serré *or* disputé; **they are ~ related** ils sont proches parents; **a matter ~ connected with ...** une affaire en relation directe avec *or* étroitement liée à ... .

closeness [ˈkləʊsnɪs] n a *[cloth, weave]* texture *or* contexture serrée; *[friendship]* intimité *f*; *[resemblance, translation, reproduction]* fidélité *f*; *[examination, interrogation, study]* minutie *f*, rigueur *f*; *[reasoning]* logique *f*; *[pursuit]* vigueur *f*; *[pursuers]* proximité *f*. **~ of blood relationship** proche degré *m* de parenté. b (*proximity*) proximité *f*. c *[weather, atmosphere]* lourdeur *f*; *[room]* manque *m* d'air. d (*stinginess*) avarice *f*.

closet [ˈklɒzɪt] 1 n a (*cupboard*) armoire *f*, placard *m*; (*for hanging clothes*) penderie *f*.

b (*small room*) cabinet *m* (de travail), (petit) bureau *m*.

c (*also* **water ~**) cabinets *mpl*, waters *mpl*.

d (*fig*) **to come out of the ~*** sortir de l'anonymat; **many bisexuals are coming out of the ~*** beaucoup de gens n'essaient plus de cacher leur bisexualité; **it was something that few people brought out of the ~*** c'était quelque chose dont peu de gens consentaient à parler.

2 comp (* *fig: secret*) honteux, qui n'ose pas s'avouer ► **closet fascist*: he's a closet fascist** il n'ose pas avouer qu'il est fasciste.

3 vt (*gen pass*) enfermer (*dans un cabinet de travail etc*). **he was ~ed with his father for several hours** son père et lui sont restés plusieurs heures enfermés à discuter; **she ~ed herself (away) in her bedroom** elle s'est cloîtrée dans sa chambre.

closing [ˈkləʊzɪŋ] 1 n (*NonC*) *[factory, house, shop]* fermeture *f*; *[meeting]* clôture *f*; (*Fin*) clôture. 2 adj a final, dernier. **~ remarks** observations finales; **~ speech** discours *m* de clôture. b de fermeture. **~ date** (*for applications*) date *f* limite de dépôt; (*Fin, Jur*) date de réalisation (d'une opération); (*Brit*) **~ time** heure *f* de fermeture (*d'un magasin, d'un café etc*); **when is ~ time?** à quelle heure fermez-vous?; **"~ time!"** "on ferme!"; (*St Ex*) **~ price** cours *m* en clôture; *see* **early.**

closure [ˈkləʊʒəʳ] n (*NonC: act, condition*) *[factory, business]* fermeture *f*; (*Parl*) clôture *f*. (*Parl*) **to move the ~** demander la clôture; (*US Pol*) **~ rule** règlement *m* limitant le temps de parole; *see* **lane.**

clot [klɒt] 1 n a *[blood, milk]* caillot *m*. **a ~ in the lung/on the brain** une embolie pulmonaire/cérébrale; **a ~ in the leg** une thrombose. b (*Brit ‡ pej: person*) ballot* *m*, balourd *m*, gourde* *f*. 2 vt *blood* coaguler. (*Brit*) **~ted cream** crème *f* en grumeaux. 3 vi *[blood]* (se) coaguler.

cloth [klɒθ] 1 n a (*NonC*) tissu *m*, étoffe *f*; *[linen, cotton]* toile *f*; *[wool]* drap *m*; (*Bookbinding*) toile; (*Naut*) toile, voile *f*. **book bound in ~** livre relié toile; **~ of gold** drap d'or; *see* **oil.** b (*tablecloth*) nappe *f*; (*duster*) chiffon *m*, linge *m*; *see* **dish, tea** *etc.* c (*Rel*) (*collective*) **the ~** le clergé; **out of respect for his ~** par respect pour son sacerdoce. 2 comp (*made of ~*) de *or* en tissu, de *or* en étoffe ► **cloth-binding** *[books]* reliure *f* en toile ► **cloth-bound book** livre relié toile ► **cloth cap** (*Brit*) casquette *f* (d'ouvrier) ► **cloth-eared‡** (*deaf*) sourdingue‡, dur de la feuille‡ ► **cloth ears‡: wake up cloth ears!** hé! tu es sourd ou quoi?*

clothe [kləʊð] vt habiller, vêtir (*in, with* de); (*fig*) revêtir, couvrir (*in, with* de).

clothes [kləʊðz] 1 npl a vêtements *mpl*, habits *mpl*. **with one's ~ on** (tout) habillé; **with one's ~ off** déshabillé, (tout) nu; **to put on one's ~** s'habiller; **to take off one's ~** se déshabiller; *[baby]* **in long ~** au *or* en maillot; *see* **plain.**

b (*also* **bed~**) draps *mpl* et couvertures *fpl*.

2 comp ► **clothes basket** panier *m* à linge ► **clothes brush** brosse *f* à habits ► **clothes drier** *or* **dryer** séchoir *m* (à linge), sèche-linge *m* ► **clothes hanger** cintre *m* ► **clothes horse** séchoir *m* (à linge); (*fig*) mannequin *m*; (*US: clothes-conscious*) **she's just a clothes horse*** elle ne pense qu'à ses toilettes ► **clothes line** corde *f* (à linge) ► **clothes moth** mite *f* ► **clothes peg** (*Brit*), **clothespin** (*US, Scot*) pince *f* à linge ► **clothespole, clothes prop** perche *f or* support *m* pour corde à linge ► **clothes rack** (*in shop*) portant *m* de vêtements ► **clothes rope** = **clothes line** ► **clothes shop** magasin *m* de confection ► **clothes tree** (*US*) portemanteau *m*.

clothier [ˈkləʊðɪəʳ] n (*clothes seller*) marchand *m* (de vêtements) de confection; (*cloth dealer, maker*) drapier *m*.

clothing [ˈkləʊðɪŋ] n (*NonC*) a (*clothes*) vêtements *mpl*. **an article of ~** un vêtement, une pièce d'habillement; **~ allowance** indemnité *f* vestimentaire. b (*act of ~*) habillage *m*; *[monks, nuns]* prise *f* d'habit; (*providing with clothes*) habillement *m*.

cloture [ˈkləʊtʃəʳ] n (*US Pol*) clôture *f*. **~ rule** règlement *m* limitant le temps de parole.

cloud [klaʊd] 1 n a (*Met*) nuage *m*, nuée *f* (*liter*); *[smoke, dust etc]* nuage; *[insects, arrows etc]* nuée; *[gas]* nappe *f*. **to have one's head in the ~s** être dans les nuages *or* dans la lune; **to be on ~ nine‡** être aux anges *or* au septième ciel*; (*Prov*) **every ~ has a silver lining** à quelque chose malheur est bon; (*fig*) **under a ~** (*under suspicion*) en butte aux soupçons; (*in disgrace*) en disgrâce; *see* **silver.**

b (*cloudiness*) *[liquid]* nuage *m*; *[mirror]* buée *f*; *[marble]* tache noire.

2 vt *liquid* rendre trouble; *mirror* embuer; *prospects, career* assombrir; *reputation* ternir. **a ~ed sky** un ciel couvert *or* nuageux; **a ~ed expression** *or* **face** un air sombre *or* attristé; **a ~ed mind** un esprit obscurci; **to ~ the issue** brouiller les cartes (*fig*).

3 vi (*also* **~ over**) *[sky]* se couvrir (de nuages), s'obscurcir; (*fig*) *[face, expression]* s'assombrir, se rembrunir.

4 comp ► **cloudberry** (*berry*) (variété *f* de) framboise *f*; (*bush*) (variété de) framboisier *m* ► **cloudburst** trombe(s) *f(pl)* (d'eau), grosse averse ► **cloud-capped** (*liter*) couronné de nuages (*liter*) ► **cloud cover** couche *f* de nuages ► **cloud-cuckoo land: she lives in cloud-cuckoo land** elle plane complètement, elle n'a pas les pieds sur terre.

cloudiness [ˈklaʊdɪnɪs] n *[sky]* état *or* aspect nuageux; *[liquid]* aspect trouble; *[mirror]* buée *f*.

cloudless [ˈklaʊdlɪs] adj (*lit, fig*) sans nuages.

cloudy [ˈklaʊdɪ] adj *sky* nuageux, couvert; *liquid* trouble; *diamond etc* taché, nuageux; *fabric* chiné, moiré; *leather* marbré; (*fig*) *ideas* nébuleux, embrumé (*fig*). (*Met*) **it was ~** le temps était couvert.

clout [klaʊt] 1 n a (*blow*) coup *m* de poing (*or* de canne *etc*). b (* *fig: influence*) influence *f*, poids *m*. **he's got** *or* **he carries** *or* **he wields a lot of ~*** il a le bras long. c (*dial*) (*cloth*) chiffon *m*; (*garment*) vêtement *m*. 2 vt *object* frapper; *person* donner un coup de poing (*or* de canne *etc*) à.

clove[1] [kləʊv] n clou *m* de girofle. **oil of ~s** essence *f* de girofle; **~ of garlic** gousse *f* d'ail.

clove[2] [kləʊv] 1 pret of **cleave[1]**. 2 comp ► **clove hitch** (*knot*) demi-clef *f*.

cloven [ˈkləʊvn] 1 ptp of **cleave[1]**. 2 comp ► **clovenfooted** *animal* aux sabots fendus; *devil* aux pieds fourchus ► **cloven hoof** *[animal]* sabot fendu; *[devil]* pied fourchu.

clover [ˈkləʊvəʳ] n trèfle *m*. (*fig*) **to be in ~*** être *or* vivre comme un coq en pâte; **~leaf** (*Bot*) feuille *f* de trèfle; (*road intersection*) (croisement *m* en) trèfle; *see* **four**.

clown [klaʊn] 1 **n** *[circus etc]* clown *m*; (†, *Theat*) bouffon *m*, paillasse *m*; (*fig*) (*funny person*) clown, pitre *m*; (*idiot*) imbécile *m*. 2 **vi** (*fig: also* (*Brit*) **~ about, ~ around**) faire le clown *or* le pitre *or* le singe.

clowning ['klaʊnɪŋ] **n** (*NonC*) pitreries *fpl*, singeries *fpl*.

cloy [klɔɪ] 1 **vt** rassasier (*with* de), écœurer. 2 **vi** perdre son charme.

cloying ['klɔɪɪŋ] **adj** (*lit, fig*) écœurant.

cloze test ['kləʊz ˌtest] **n** texte *m* à trous *or* blancs.

club [klʌb] 1 **n** a (*weapon*) massue *f*, matraque *f*, gourdin *m*; (*also* **golf ~**) club *m*; *see* **Indian**.

b (*Cards*) **~s** trèfles *mpl*; **the ace of ~s** l'as *m* de trèfle; **the six of ~s** le six de trèfle; **one ~** un trèfle; **he played a ~** il a joué (un *or* du) trèfle; **~s are trumps** atout trèfle; **a low/high ~** un petit/gros trèfle; **have you any ~s?** avez-vous du trèfle?; **I haven't any ~s** je n'ai pas de trèfle; **3 tricks in ~s** 3 levées à trèfle.

c (*circle, society*) club *m*, cercle *m*. **tennis ~** club de tennis; **he is dining at his ~** il dîne à son club *or* à son cercle; (*fig*) **join the ~!*** tu n'es pas le *or* la seul(e)!; *see* **benefit, youth** *etc*.

d (*Brit: pregnant*) **to be in the ~**‡ être en cloque‡.

2 **vt** *person* matraquer, frapper avec un gourdin *or* une massue. **to ~ sb with a rifle** assommer qn d'un coup de crosse.

3 **comp** *premises, secretary etc* du club ► **club car** (*US Rail*) wagon-restaurant *m* ► **club chair** fauteuil *m* club *inv* ► **club class** classe *f* club ► **club-foot** pied-bot *m* ► **club-footed** pied-bot *inv* ► **clubhouse** (*Sport*) pavillon *m* ► **clubman** membre *m* d'un club; (*man about town*) homme *m* du monde, mondain *m*; **he is not a clubman** il n'est pas homme à fréquenter les clubs *or* les cercles ► **club member: he is a club member** il est membre du club ► **clubroom** salle *f* de club *or* de réunion ► **club sandwich** sandwich *m* mixte (à 2 étages) ► **club soda** (*US*) eau *f* de seltz ► **club steak** (*US*) (bifteck pris dans la) queue *f* de filet ► **club subscription** cotisation *f*.

►**club together** **vi** se cotiser (*to buy* pour acheter).

clubbable* ['klʌbəbl] **adj** sociable.

clubber* ['klʌbəʳ] **n** (*Brit*) *personne qui sort en boîte de nuit*.

clubbing* ['klʌbɪŋ] **n** (*Brit*) sortir en boîte de nuit.

cluck [klʌk] 1 **vi** *[hens, people]* glousser. 2 **n** gloussement *m*.

clue, (*US*) **clew** [kluː] **n** indice *m*, indication *f*, fil directeur; *[crosswords]* définition *f*. **to find the ~ to sth** découvrir *or* trouver la clef de qch; (*lit*) **to have a ~** être sur une piste; (*fig*) **I haven't a ~!*** je n'en ai pas la moindre idée!, aucune idée!*

►**clue in**‡ **vt sep** mettre au courant *or* au parfum* (*on, about sth* à propos de qch).

►**clue up**‡ **vt sep** (*gen pass*) renseigner (*on* sur), mettre au courant (*on* de), affranchir‡. **to get clued up about** *or* **on sth** se faire renseigner sur qch; **he's very clued up on politics** il est très calé* en politique.

clueless* ['kluːlɪs] **adj** (*Brit*) sans *or* qui n'a pas la moindre idée, qui ne sait rien de rien*.

clump[1] [klʌmp] 1 **n** *[shrubs]* massif *m*; *[trees]* bouquet *m*; *[flowers]* touffe *f*, (*larger*) massif; *[grass]* touffe. 2 **vt ~ (together)** rassembler.

clump[2] [klʌmp] 1 **n** (*noise*) bruit *m* de pas lourd(s) *or* pesant(s). 2 **vi** (*also* **~ about**) marcher d'un pas lourd *or* pesant.

clumsily ['klʌmzɪlɪ] **adv** (*inelegantly*) gauchement, maladroitement; (*tactlessly*) sans tact.

clumsiness ['klʌmzɪnɪs] **n** *[person, action]* gaucherie *f*, maladresse *f*; *[tool etc]* incommodité *f*, caractère *m* peu pratique; *[shape, form]* lourdeur *f*; (*fig: tactlessness*) *[person,remark]* gaucherie, manque *m* de tact *or* de discrétion.

clumsy ['klʌmzɪ] **adj** *person, action* gauche, maladroit; *tool etc* malcommode, peu maniable, peu pratique; *shape, form* lourd, disgracieux; *painting, forgery* maladroit; (*fig: tactless*) *person, remark* gauche, maladroit, sans tact; *apology, style* gauche, lourd, inélégant.

clung [klʌŋ] **pret, ptp of cling.**

Cluniac ['kluːnɪæk] **adj, n** clunisien *(m)*.

clunk [klʌŋk] 1 **n** a (*sound*) bruit sourd. b (*US* ‡: *stupid person*) pauvre imbécile *mf*. 2 **vi** (*make sound*) faire un bruit sourd.

clunker‡ ['klʌŋkəʳ] **n** (*US: old car*) guimbarde* *f*.

cluster ['klʌstəʳ] 1 **n** *[flowers, blossom, fruit]* grappe *f*; *[bananas]* régime *m*; *[trees]* bouquet *m*; *[bees]* essaim *m*; *[persons]* (petit) groupe *m*, rassemblement *m*; (*Ling*) groupe *m*, agglomérat *m*; *[houses, islands]* groupe; *[stars]* amas *m*; *[diamonds]* entourage *m*. 2 **comp** ► **cluster bomb** bombe *f* à fragmentation ► **cluster pack** (*Comm*) emballage *m* groupé, pack *m*. 3 **vi** *[people]* se rassembler, se grouper (*around* autour de); *[things]* (*see* **1**) former un groupe *or* une grappe *or* un bouquet *etc* (*around* autour de).

clutch [klʌtʃ] 1 **n** a (*action*) étreinte *f*, prise *f*.

b (*Aut*) embrayage *m*; (*also* **~ pedal**) pédale *f* d'embrayage. **to let in the ~** embrayer; **to let out the ~** débrayer; **~ linkage play, ~ pedal play** garde *f* d'embrayage; **~ plate** disque *m* d'embrayage.

c *[chickens, eggs]* couvée *f*. (*fig*) **a ~ of** *prizes etc* un petit groupe de.

d (*fig*) **to fall into sb's/sth's ~es** tomber sous les griffes *fpl or* sous la patte* de qn/qch; **to get out of sb's/sth's ~es** se tirer des griffes de qn/qch.

e (*US* ‡: *crisis*) crise *f*.

2 **comp** ► **clutch bag** pochette *f*.

3 **vt** (*grasp*) empoigner, se saisir de, saisir, agripper; (*hold tightly*) étreindre, serrer fort; (*hold on to*) se cramponner à.

4 **vi: to ~ at** (*lit*) se cramponner à, s'agripper à; (*fig*) se cramponner à, se raccrocher à; (*fig*) **to ~ at a straw** *or* **at straws** se raccrocher à n'importe quoi.

clutter ['klʌtəʳ] 1 **n** a (*NonC: disorder, confusion*) désordre *m*, pagaïe* *f*. **in a ~** en désordre, en pagaïe*. b (*objects lying about*) désordre *m*, fouillis *m*. 2 **vt** (*also* **~ up**) (*lit*) mettre en désordre, mettre le désordre dans (*à force de laisser traîner des objets divers*); (*lit, fig*) encombrer (*with* de).

Clytemnestra [ˌklaɪtɪm'nestrə] **n** Clytemnestre *f*.

cm **abbr of centimetre(s).**

Cmdr **n** (*Mil*) **abbr of Commander.**

CNAA [ˌsiːenerˈeɪ] (*Brit Educ*) (**abbr of Council for National Academic Awards**) *organisme qui valide les diplômes de l'enseignement supérieur décernés en dehors des universités*.

C.N.D. [siːen'diː] (**abbr of Campaign for Nuclear Disarmament**) *mouvement pour le désarmement nucléaire*.

CO (*US*) **abbr of Colorado.**

C.O. [siː'əʊ] a (*Mil*) (**abbr of Commanding Officer**) *see* **commanding.** b (*Brit Admin*) (**abbr of Commonwealth Office**) *see* **commonwealth.** c (**abbr of conscientious objector**) *see* **conscientious.** d (*US Post*) **abbr of Colorado.**

Co. a (*Comm*) (**abbr of company**) Cie. **Joe and Co. are coming** Joe et compagnie *or* et sa bande* vont venir. b **abbr of County.**

c/o ['keərəv] (**abbr of care of**) chez, aux bons soins de.

co..., co- [kəʊ] **pref** co..., co-. **co-organizer** co-organisateur *m*; *see also* **co-driver, co(-)partner** *etc*.

coach [kəʊtʃ] 1 **n** a (*Rail*) voiture *f*, wagon *m*; (*motor* **~**) car *m*, autocar *m*; (*horse-drawn*) carrosse *m*; (*stagecoach*) diligence *f*, coche *m*. **~ and four** carrosse à quatre chevaux.

b (*tutor*) répétiteur *m*, -trice *f*; (*Sport: gen*) entraîneur *m*; (*Ski*) moniteur *m*, -trice *f*.

2 **vt** donner des leçons particulières à; (*Sport*) entraîner. **to ~ sb for an exam** préparer qn à un examen; **he had been ~ed in what to say** on lui avait fait répéter ce qu'il aurait à dire.

3 **comp** ► **coachbuilder** (*Brit Aut*) carrossier *m* ► **coach building** (*Brit*) carrosserie *f* (*construction*) ► **coach driver** chauffeur *m* d'autocar ► **coachload: a coachload of tourists** un car entier *or* plein de touristes ► **coachman** cocher *m* ► **coach operator** compagnie *f* de cars ► **coach park** (*Brit*) parking *m* des bus ► **coach trip** excursion *f* en car ► **coachwork** (*Brit Aut*) carrosserie *f* (*caisse d'une automobile*).

coaching ['kəʊtʃɪŋ] **n** (*esp Sport*) entraînement *m*; (*Scol*) soutien *m*.

coadjutant [kəʊ'ædʒʊtənt] **n** assistant(e) *m(f)*, aide *mf*.

coagulant [kəʊ'ægjʊlənt] **n** coagulant *m*.

coagulate [kəʊ'ægjʊleɪt] 1 **vt** coaguler. 2 **vi** se coaguler.

coagulation [kəʊˌægjʊ'leɪʃən] **n** coagulation *f*.

coal [kəʊl] 1 **n** charbon *m*; (*Ind*) houille *f*. **piece of ~** morceau *m* de charbon; **soft ~** houille grasse; (*fig*) **to be on hot ~s** être sur des charbons ardents; *see* **carry, heap.**

2 **vt** fournir *or* ravitailler en charbon. (*Naut*) **to ~ ship** charbonner.

3 **vi** (*Naut*) charbonner.

4 **comp** *fire* de charbon; *box, shed* à charbon ► **coal basin** bassin houiller ► **coal-black** noir comme du charbon ► **Coal Board** (*Brit*) ≃ Charbonnages *mpl* ► **coal-burning** à charbon, qui marche au charbon ► **coal cellar** cave *f* à charbon ► **coal chute** glissière *f* à charbon ► **coal cutter** haveur *m* ► **coal depot** dépôt *m* de charbon ► **coaldust** poussier *m*, poussière *f* de charbon ► **coal face** front *m* de taille ► **coalfield** bassin houiller, gisement *m* de houille ► **coal fire** feu *m* de cheminée ► **coal-fired power station** centrale *f* thermique au charbon ► **coalfish** lieu noir *m*, colin *m* ► **coal gas** gaz *m* (de houille) ► **coal hod** seau *m* à charbon ► **coal hole** petite cave à charbon ► **coal industry** industrie houillère, charbonnages *mpl* ► **coaling station** dépôt *m* de charbon ► **coalman** charbonnier *m*, marchand *m* de charbon; (*delivery man*) charbonnier ► **coal measures** (*Geol*) gisements houillers ► **coal merchant** = **coalman** ► **coalmine** houillère *f*, mine *f* de charbon ► **coalminer** mineur *m*; **coalminer's lung*** anthracose *f* pulmonaire, pneumoconiose *f* ► **coalmining** charbonnage *m* ► **coal oil** (*US*) pétrole lampant, kérosène *m* ► **coalpit** = **coalmine** ► **coal scuttle** seau *m* à charbon ► **coal strike** (*Ind*) grève *f* des mineurs ► **coal tar** coaltar *m*, goudron *m* de houille ► **coal tit** (*Orn*) mésange noire ► **coal yard** dépôt *m* de charbon.

coalesce [ˌkəʊə'les] **vi** (*lit, fig*) s'unir (*en une masse, en un groupe etc*), se fondre (ensemble), se grouper.

coalescence [ˌkəʊə'lesəns] **n** (*lit, fig*) fusion *f*, combinaison *f*, union *f*.

coalition [ˌkəʊə'lɪʃən] **n** coalition *f*. (*Pol*) **~ government** gouvernement *m* de coalition.

coarse [kɔːs] 1 **adj** a (*in texture*) *material* rude, grossier. **~ cloth** drap grossier; **~ linen** grosse toile; **~ salt** gros sel; **~ sand** sable *m* à gros grains, gros sable; **~ sandpaper** papier *m* de verre à gros grain; **~ skin** peau *f* rude; **~ weave** texture grossière. b (*common*) commun, ordinaire, grossier. ~ **food** nourriture *f* fruste; ~ **red wine** gros rouge. c (*pej*) (*uncouth*) *manners* grossier, vulgaire; (*indecent*) *language, joke* grossier, indécent, cru; *laugh* gros, gras; *accent* commun, vulgaire. 2 comp ▸ **coarse fishing** pêche *f* à la ligne (*de poissons autres que le saumon et la truite*) ▸ **coarse-grained** à gros grain.

coarsely ['kɔːslɪ] adv (*see* **coarse**) grossièrement, vulgairement; indécemment, crûment; grassement. ~ **woven cloth** tissu *m* de texture grossière.

coarsen ['kɔːsn] (*see* **coarse**) 1 vt rendre grossier *or* vulgaire *etc.* 2 vi devenir rude *or* grossier *or* vulgaire *etc.*

coarseness ['kɔːsnɪs] n (*see* **coarse**) rudesse *f*; caractère *m* vulgaire *or* grossier; vulgarité *f*, grossièreté *f*.

coast [kəʊst] 1 n côte *f*; (*also* ~**line**) littoral *m*. **from** ~ **to** ~ du nord au sud; (*fig*) **the** ~ **is clear** la voie *or* le champ est libre.
2 vi a (*Aut, Cycling*) **to** ~ **along/down** avancer/descendre en roue libre; (*fig*) **to** ~ **along** avancer (sans problèmes); (*fig*) **to** ~ **through** passer sans difficulté. b (*Naut*) caboter.
3 comp ▸ **coastguard** *see* **coastguard**.

coastal ['kəʊstəl] adj *defence, state* côtier. ~ **navigation** navigation côtière; ~ **traffic** navigation côtière, cabotage *m*.

coaster ['kəʊstəʳ] 1 n a (*Naut*) caboteur *m*. b (*drip mat*) dessous *m* de verre *or* de bouteille; (*wine tray*) présentoir *m* à bouteilles (*parfois roulant*). c **roller** ~ *see* **roller**. 2 comp ▸ **coaster brake** (*US*) [*cycle*] frein *m* à rétropédalage.

coastguard ['kəʊst,gɑːd] 1 n a (*service*) ≃ gendarmerie *f* maritime. b (*person*) membre *m* de la gendarmerie maritime; (*Hist*) garde-côte *m*. 2 comp ▸ **coastguard(s)man** (*esp US*) = **coastguard 1b** ▸ **coastguard station** (bureau *m* de la) gendarmerie *f* maritime ▸ **coastguard vessel** (vedette *f*) garde-côte *m*.

coat [kəʊt] 1 n a [*man, woman*] manteau *m*; [*man*] (*also* **over**~, **top**~) pardessus *m*. (*fig*) **to turn one's** ~ retourner sa veste*; **a** ~ **and dress** un ensemble manteau et robe coordonnés; (*Her*) ~ **of arms** blason *m*, armoiries *fpl*, écu *m*; ~ **of mail** cotte *f* de maille; *see* **house, morning, sport** *etc.*
b [*animal*] pelage *m*, poil *m*; [*horse*] robe *f*.
c (*covering*) [*paint, tar etc*] couche *f*; [*plastic*] enveloppe *f*; *see* **base¹**, **top** *etc.*
2 vt enduire, couvrir, revêtir (*with* de); (*Elec*) armer; (*Culin*) (*with chocolate or breadcrumbs etc*) enrober; (*with egg*) dorer. **to** ~ **the wall with paint** passer une couche de peinture sur le mur; (*Med*) **his tongue was** ~**ed** il avait la langue chargée; (*fig*) **(in order) to** ~ **the pill** (pour) dorer la pilule; (*Phot*) ~**ed lens** objectif traité.
3 comp ▸ **coat hanger** cintre *m* ▸ **coat rack, coatstand** portemanteau *m* ▸ **coattails** queue *f* de pie (*habit*); (*fig*) **to be hanging on sb's coattails** être pendu aux basques de qn; (*US Pol*) **to ride on sb's coattails** se faire élire dans le sillage *or* à la traîne (*pej*) de qn.

-coated ['kəʊtɪd] adj **ending in comps** recouvert de. **chocolate-coated** enrobé de chocolat.

coating ['kəʊtɪŋ] n (*gen*) couche *f*; (*on saucepan etc*) revêtement *m*.

co-author ['kəʊ,ɔːθəʳ] n co-auteur *m*.

coax [kəʊks] vt cajoler, câliner (*pour amadouer*). **to** ~ **sb into doing** amener qn à force de cajoleries *or* de câlineries à faire; **to** ~ **sth out of sb** obtenir *or* tirer qch de qn par des cajoleries *or* des câlineries.

coaxial [kəʊ'æksɪəl] adj (*gen, Geom, Elec*) coaxial. (*Comput*) ~ **cable** câble coaxial.

coaxing ['kəʊksɪŋ] 1 n câlineries *fpl*, cajolerie(s) *f(pl)*. 2 adj enjôleur, câlin.

coaxingly ['kəʊksɪŋlɪ] adv *speak, ask* d'une manière câline, d'un ton enjôleur; *look* d'un air câlin *or* enjôleur.

cob [kɒb] n (*swan*) cygne *m* mâle; (*horse*) cob *m*; (*also* ~**-nut**) grosse noisette; (*Brit: also* ~ **loaf**) miche *f* (de pain); [*maize*] épi *m* (de maïs); *see* **corn¹**.

cobalt ['kəʊbɒlt] n cobalt *m*. ~ **60** cobalt 60, cobalt radioactif; ~ **blue** bleu *m* de cobalt; ~ **bomb** bombe *f* au cobalt.

cobber⁑ ['kɒbəʳ] n (*Australian*) pote⁑ *m*.

cobble ['kɒbl] 1 vt: **to** ~ **together** *object, figures* bricoler*; *solution, agreement* bricoler*, concocter*. 2 n = **cobblestone**.

cobbled ['kɒbld] adj: ~ **street** rue pavée (*de pavés ronds*).

cobbler ['kɒbləʳ] n a cordonnier *m*. ~**'s wax** poix *f* de cordonnier. b (*US Culin*) tourte *f* aux fruits. c (*US: drink*) (sorte *f* de) punch *m* (glacé). d (*Brit: nonsense*) **that's a load of** ~**s!**⁑ c'est de la connerie!⁑

cobblestone ['kɒblstəʊn] n pavé rond.

COBOL, Cobol ['kəʊbɔːl] n (*Comput*) COBOL *m*.

cobra ['kəʊbrə] n cobra *m*.

cobweb ['kɒbweb] n toile *f* d'araignée. (*fig*) **to blow** *or* **clear away the** ~**s** remettre les idées en place.

cocaine [kə'keɪn] n cocaïne *f*. ~ **addict** cocaïnomane *mf*; ~ **addiction** cocaïnomanie *f*.

coccus ['kɒkəs] n, pl **cocci** ['kɒksaɪ] coccidie *f*.

coccyx ['kɒksɪks] n, pl **coccyges** [kɒk'saɪdʒiːz] coccyx *m*.

co-chairman ['kəʊ,tʃɛəmən] n co-président(e) *m(f)*.

co-chairmanship [kəʊ'tʃɛəmən,ʃɪp] n co-présidence *f*.

Cochin-China [,kəʊtʃɪn'tʃaɪnə] n Cochinchine *f*.

cochineal ['kɒtʃɪniːl] n (*insect*) cochenille *f*; (*colouring*) colorant *m* rouge.

cochlea ['kɒklɪə] n, pl **cochleae** ['kɒklɪ,iː] (*Anat*) limaçon *m*.

cock [kɒk] 1 n a (*rooster*) coq *m*; (*male bird*) (oiseau *m*) mâle *m*. (*fig*) **the** ~ **of the walk** le roi (*fig*); *see* **fighting, game, weather** *etc.*
b (*tap*) robinet *m*.
c [*rifle*] chien *m*. **at full** ~ armé; **at half** ~ au cran de repos.
d [*hay*] meulon *m*; [*corn, oats*] moyette *f*.
e (⁂) bitte⁂ *f*.
2 vt a *gun* armer.
b **to** ~ **one's ears** (*lit*) dresser les oreilles; (*fig*) dresser l'oreille; **to** ~ **one's eye at** glisser un coup d'œil à; (*lit*) **to** ~ **a snook (at)*** faire un pied de nez (à); (*fig*) **to** ~ **a snook at*** faire la nique à.
3 comp *bird* mâle ▸ **cock-a-doodle-doo** cocorico *m* ▸ **cock-a-hoop** adj fier comme Artaban ◊ adv d'un air de triomphe ▸ **cock-a-leekie** *or* **cockieleekie soup** (*Scot*) *potage à la volaille et aux poireaux* ▸ **cock-and-bull story** (*pej*) histoire *f* à dormir debout ▸ **cockchafer** hanneton *m* ▸ **cockcrow**: **at cockcrow** au premier chant du coq, à l'aube ▸ **cock-eyed** (*: *cross-eyed*) qui louche; (*: *crooked*) de travers, de traviole*; (*: *mad, absurd*) absurde, qui ne tient pas debout, dingue⁑; (⁑: *drunk*) soûl*, schlass⁑ *inv* ▸ **cockfight** combat *m* de coqs ▸ **cockfighting** combats *mpl* de coqs ▸ **cock lobster** homard *m* (mâle) ▸ **cockpit** [*aircraft*] poste *m* de pilotage, cockpit *m*; [*yacht*] cockpit; [*racing car*] poste du pilote; (*Cockfighting*) arène *f* (*pour combats de coqs*); (*fig*) arènes ▸ **cockroach** cafard *m*, blatte *f*, cancrelat *m* ▸ **cockscomb** (*Orn*) crête *f* (*de coq*); (*Bot*) crête-de-coq *f* (*see* **coxcomb**) ▸ **cock sparrow** moineau *m* (mâle) ▸ **cocksure** (*pej*) (trop) sûr de soi, outrecuidant ▸ **cocktail** *see* **cocktail** ▸ **cock-teaser**⁂ n allumeuse⁑ *f* ▸ **cock-up**⁑: **he made a cock-up of the job** il a salopé le boulot⁑; **the meeting was a cock-up** la réunion a été bordélique⁑ *or* un vrai bordel⁑.

▸**cock up**⁑ 1 vt sep saloper⁑; *exam* foirer⁑. 2 vi tout saloper⁑; foirer⁑. 3 *see* **cock 3**.

cockade [kɒ'keɪd] n cocarde *f*.

Cockaigne [kɒ'keɪn] n: **(land of)** ~ pays *m* de Cocagne.

cockamamie* [,kɒkə'meɪmɪ] adj (*US*) farfelu.

cockatoo [,kɒkə'tuː] n cacatoès *m*.

cocked [kɒkt] adj: ~ **hat** chapeau *m* à cornes; (*two points*) bicorne *m*; (*three points*) tricorne *m*; **to knock sb into a** ~ **hat*** battre qn à plate(s) couture(s).

cocker ['kɒkəʳ] n (*also* ~ **spaniel**) cocker *m*.

cockerel ['kɒkərəl] n jeune coq *m*.

cockily ['kɒkɪlɪ] adv avec suffisance.

cockiness ['kɒkɪnɪs] n suffisance *f*.

cockle ['kɒkl] 1 n a (*shellfish*) coque *f*. (*fig*) **it warmed the** ~**s of his heart** cela lui a réchauffé *or* réjoui le cœur. b (*wrinkle*) [*paper*] froissure *f*, pliure *f*; [*cloth*] faux pli. 2 comp ▸ **cockle shell** (*Zool*) (coquille *f* de) coque *f*; (*boat*) petit canot, coquille de noix. 3 vt (*wrinkle*) *paper* froisser; *cloth* chiffonner. 4 vi [*paper*] se froisser; [*cloth*] se chiffonner.

cockney ['kɒknɪ] 1 n a (*person*) Cockney *mf* (*personne née dans l'"East End" de Londres*). b (*Ling*) cockney *m*. 2 adj cockney, londonien.

cocktail ['kɒkteɪl] 1 n (*lit, fig*) cocktail *m* (*boisson*). **fruit** ~ salade *f* de fruits; (*Brit*) **prawn** ~, (*US*) **shrimp** ~ coupe *f or* cocktail de crevettes; *see* **Molotov.** 2 comp ▸ **cocktail bar** bar *m* (*dans un hôtel*) ▸ **cocktail cabinet** bar *m* (*meuble*) ▸ **cocktail dress** robe *f* de cocktail ▸ **cocktail lounge** bar *m* (*de luxe, dans un hôtel*) ▸ **cocktail onion** petit oignon (à apéritif) ▸ **cocktail party** cocktail *m* (*réunion*) ▸ **cocktail sausage** petite saucisse (à apéritif) ▸ **cocktail shaker** shaker *m*.

cocky ['kɒkɪ] adj (*pej*) suffisant, trop sûr de soi.

cocoa ['kəʊkəʊ] n (*drink, powder*) cacao *m*. ~ **bean** graine *f* de cacao; ~ **butter** beurre *m* de cacao.

coconut ['kəʊkənʌt] 1 n noix *f* de coco. 2 comp ▸ **coconut matting** tapis *m* de fibre (*de noix de coco*) ▸ **coconut oil** huile *f* de coco ▸ **coconut palm** cocotier *m* ▸ **coconut shy** jeu *m* de massacre ▸ **coconut tree** cocotier *m*.

cocoon [kə'kuːn] 1 n cocon *m*. (*fig*) **wrapped in a** ~ **of blankets** emmitouflé dans des couvertures.
2 vt (*fig*) *object* envelopper avec soin; *child* couver. (*fig*) ~**ed from** à l'abri de; ~**ed in the bosom of one's family** bien à l'abri au sein de sa famille.

cod [kɒd] 1 n, pl ~ *or* ~**s** (*Zool*) morue *f*; (*Culin*) (*also* **fresh** ~) morue fraîche, cabillaud *m*. **dried** ~ merluche *f*. 2 comp ▸ **codfish** inv morue *f* ▸ **cod-liver oil** huile *f* de foie de morue ▸ **the Cod War** (*Brit*) la guerre de la morue.

C.O.D. [,siːəʊ'diː] a (*Brit*) (**abbr of cash on delivery**) *see* **cash.** b (*US*) (**abbr of collect on delivery**) *see* **collect.**

coda ['kəʊdə] n coda *f*.

coddle ['kɒdl] vt a *child, invalid* dorloter, choyer. b (*Culin*) *eggs* (faire) cuire à feu doux.

code [kəʊd] 1 n a (*Admin, Comput, Jur, Ling, fig*) code *m*. ~ **of behaviour/of honour** code de conduite/de l'honneur; ~ **of ethics** (*gen*) sens *m* des valeurs morales, moralité *f*; [*profession etc*] déontologie *f*; ~

of practice (*gen*) déontologie *f*; (*set of rules*) règlements et usages *mpl*; *see* **highway, penal.**
b (*cipher*) code *m*, chiffre *m*; (*Bio, Comput, Post etc*) code. **in ~** en code, chiffré; *see* **Morse, zip.**
2 vt *letter, despatch* chiffrer, coder; (*Comput*) programmer. (*fig: veiled*) **~d** *threat, criticism* voilé, masqué.
3 comp ► **code dating** (*Comm*) inscription *f* de date codée (*sur denrées périssables*) ► **code letter** chiffre *m* ► **code name** nom codé ► **code-named** qui a pour nom codé *or* de code ► **code number** (*Tax*) ≃ indice *m* des déductions fiscales ► **code word** (*lit*) mot *m* de passe; (*fig: Pol*) mot codé.
codeine [ˈkəʊdiːn] n codéine *f*.
codex [ˈkəʊdeks] n, pl **codices** [ˈkɒdɪsiːz] manuscrit *m* (ancien).
codger* [ˈkɒdʒəʳ] n drôle de vieux bonhomme *m*.
codicil [ˈkɒdɪsɪl] n codicille *m*.
codify [ˈkəʊdɪfaɪ] vt codifier.
coding [ˈkəʊdɪŋ] 1 n (*NonC*) *[telegram, message]* mise *f* en code, chiffrage *m*, codification *f*; (*Comput*) codage *m*; *see* **tax.** 2 comp ► **coding sheet** (*Comput*) feuille *f* de programmation.
codpiece [ˈkɒd,piːs] n braguette *f* (*portée aux 15e et 16e siècles*).
co-driver [ˈkəʊdraɪvəʳ] n (*in race*) copilote *m*; *[lorry, bus]* deuxième chauffeur *m*.
codswallop* [ˈkɒdzwɒləp] n (*NonC: Brit*) bobards* *mpl*, foutaises* *fpl*.
coed* [ˈkəʊˈed] 1 adj abbr of **coeducational.** 2 n (*US*) étudiante *f* (*dans un établissement mixte*).
co-edition [,kəʊɪˈdɪʃən] n co-édition *f*.
coeducation [ˈkəʊ,edjʊˈkeɪʃən] n éducation *f* mixte.
coeducational [ˈkəʊ,edjʊˈkeɪʃənl] adj *school, teaching* mixte.
coefficient [,kəʊɪˈfɪʃənt] n coefficient *m*.
coeliac [ˈsiːlɪ,æk] adj cœliaque. **~ disease** cœlialgie *f*.
coequal [,kəʊˈiːkwəl] adj, n égal(e) *m(f)*.
coerce [kəʊˈɜːs] vt contraindre. **to ~ sb into obedience/into obeying** contraindre qn à l'obéissance/à obéir.
coercion [kəʊˈɜːʃən] n contrainte *f*, coercition *f*.
coercive [kəʊˈɜːsɪv] adj coercitif.
coeval [kəʊˈiːvəl] 1 adj contemporain (*with* de), du même âge (*with* que). 2 n contemporain(e) *m(f)*.
coexist [ˈkəʊɪgˈzɪst] vi coexister (*with* avec).
coexistence [ˈkəʊɪgˈzɪstəns] n coexistence *f*; *see* **peaceful.**
coexistent [ˈkəʊɪgˈzɪstənt] adj coexistant (*with* avec).
coextensive [ˈkəʊɪkˈstensɪv] adv: **~ with** (*in space*) de même étendue que; (*in time*) de même durée que.
C. of C. [,siːɒvˈsiː] (abbr of **Chamber of Commerce**) *see* **chamber.**
C. of E. [,siːɒvˈiː] (*Brit*) (abbr of **Church of England**) *see* **church.**
coffee [ˈkɒfɪ] 1 n café *m* (*grain, boisson*). **a cup of ~** une tasse de café; **one** *or* **a ~** un café; **black ~** café noir *or* nature; (*Brit*) **white ~,** (*US*) **~ with milk** (*gen*) café au lait; (*in café: when ordering*) **a white ~, a ~ with milk** un (café-)crème.
2 comp (**~** *flavoured*) au café; (**~** *coloured*) couleur café ► **coffee bar** (*Brit*) café *m*, cafétéria *f* ► **coffee bean** grain *m* de café ► **coffee break** pause(-)café *f* ► **coffee cake** (*Brit: coffee-flavoured*) moka *m* (*au café*); (*US: served with coffee*) gâteau *m* (*que l'on sert avec le café*) ► **coffee-coloured** (couleur) café au lait *inv* ► **coffee cup** tasse *f* à café, (*smaller*) tasse à moka ► **coffee filter** filtre *m* à café ► **coffee grounds** marc *m* de café ► **coffee house** (*Hist*) café *m* (*au 18e siècle*) ► **coffee machine** (*in café etc*) percolateur *m*; (*vending machine*) machine *f* à café ► **coffee-maker** (*electric*) cafetière *f* électrique; (*non-electric*) cafetière *f* ► **coffee mill** moulin *m* à café ► **coffee morning** vente *f* de charité (*où l'on sert le café*) ► **coffee percolator** = **coffee-maker** ► **coffeepot** cafetière *f* ► **coffee service, coffee set** service *m* à café ► **coffee shop** (*restaurant*) cafétéria *f*; (*shop*) brûlerie *f* ► **coffee spoon** cuiller *f* à café *or* à moka ► **coffee table** (petite) table basse; **a coffee table book** un beau livre grand format (*pour faire de l'effet*) ► **coffee tree** caféier *m* ► **coffee whitener** succédané *m* de lait.
coffer [ˈkɒfəʳ] n a coffre *m*, caisse *f*. (*fig*) (*funds*) **~s** coffres; **the ~s (of State)** les coffres de l'État. b (*Hydraulics*) caisson *m*. c (*also* **~dam**) batardeau *m*.
coffin [ˈkɒfɪn] n cercueil *m*, bière *f*. (*cigarette*) **~ nail***† sèche* *f*.
C. of I. [,siːɒvˈaɪ] (*Brit*) abbr of **Church of Ireland.**
C. of S. [,siːɒvˈes] a (*Brit*) abbr of **Church of Scotland.** b (*Mil*) (abbr of **Chief of Staff**) *see* **chief.**
cog [kɒg] n (*Tech*) dent *f* (*d'engrenage*). (*fig*) **he's only a ~ in the wheel** *or* **machine** il n'est qu'un simple rouage (de *or* dans la machine); **~ wheel** roue dentée.
cogency [ˈkəʊdʒənsɪ] n *[argument etc]* puissance *f*, force *f*.
cogent [ˈkəʊdʒənt] adj (*compelling*) irrésistible; (*convincing*) puissant, convaincant; (*relevant*) pertinent, (fait) à-propos.
cogently [ˈkəʊdʒəntlɪ] adv (*see* **cogent**) irrésistiblement; puissamment; pertinemment, (avec) à-propos.
cogitate [ˈkɒdʒɪteɪt] 1 vi méditer, réfléchir ((*up*)*on* sur). 2 vt *scheme* méditer.
cogitation [,kɒdʒɪˈteɪʃən] n (*NonC*) réflexion *f*; (*liter, iro*) cogitations *fpl* (*liter, iro*).
cognac [ˈkɒnjæk] n cognac *m*.
cognate [ˈkɒgneɪt] 1 adj apparenté, analogue (*with* à), de même origine *or* source (*with* que); (*Ling*) *word, language* apparenté; (*Jur*) parent. 2 n (*Ling*) mot apparenté; (*Jur*) cognat *m*, parent *m* proche.
cognition [kɒgˈnɪʃən] n (*NonC*) connaissance *f*; (*Philos*) cognition *f*.
cognitive [ˈkɒgnɪtɪv] adj cognitif. (*Ling*) **~ meaning** sens cognitif; **~ psychology/therapy** psychologie *f*/thérapie *f* cognitive.
cognizance [ˈkɒgnɪzəns] n a (*Jur, gen: frm*) connaissance *f*. **to take/have ~ of** prendre/avoir connaissance de; **this is outside his ~** ceci n'est pas de sa compétence; (*Jur*) **this case falls within the ~ of the court** cette affaire est de la compétence du tribunal. b (*Her*) emblème *m*.
cognizant [ˈkɒgnɪzənt] adj (*frm*) instruit, ayant connaissance (*of* de); (*Jur*) compétent (*of* pour).
cognomen [kɒgˈnəʊmen] n, pl **~s** *or* **cognomina** [kɒgˈnɒmɪnə] (*surname*) nom *m* de famille; (*nickname*) surnom *m*.
cognoscenti [,kɒgnəˈʃentɪ, kɒnjəʊˈʃentɪ] npl: **the ~** les spécialistes, les connaisseurs.
cohabit [kəʊˈhæbɪt] vi cohabiter (*with* avec).
cohabitant [kəʊˈhæbɪtənt] n, **cohabiter** [kəʊˈhæbɪtəʳ] n = **cohabitee.**
cohabitation [,kəʊhæbɪˈteɪʃən] n cohabitation *f*.
cohabitee [,kəʊhæbɪˈtiː] n (*Admin*) concubin(e) *m(f)*.
coheir [ˈkəʊˈɛəʳ] n cohéritier *m*.
coheiress [ˈkəʊˈɛərɪs] n cohéritière *f*.
cohere [kəʊˈhɪəʳ] vi (*fig*) *[argument]* (se) tenir; *[reasoning]* se suivre logiquement; *[style]* être cohérent; (*lit: stick*) adhérer.
coherence [kəʊˈhɪərəns] n (*fig*) cohérence *f*; (*lit*) adhérence *f*.
coherent [kəʊˈhɪərənt] adj (*fig*) *person, words, behaviour* cohérent, logique; *account, story, speech* facile à comprendre *or* à suivre; (*lit*) adhérent.
coherently [kəʊˈhɪərəntlɪ] adv (*fig*) avec cohérence, d'une façon cohérente.
cohesion [kəʊˈhiːʒən] n cohésion *f*.
cohesive [kəʊˈhiːsɪv] adj cohésif.
cohort [ˈkəʊhɔːt] n (*Mil*) cohorte *f*.
COHSE [ˈkəʊzɪ] (*Brit*) (abbr of **Confederation of Health Service Employees**) *syndicat*.
C.O.I. [,siːəʊˈaɪ] (*Brit*) (abbr of **Central Office of Information**) *service d'information gouvernemental*.
coif [kɔɪf] n (*headdress*) coiffe *f*; (*skullcap*) calotte *f*.
coiffure [kwɒˈfjʊəʳ] n coiffure *f* (*arrangement des cheveux*).
coil [kɔɪl] 1 vt *rope* enrouler; *hair* enrouler, torsader; (*Elec*) *wire* bobiner; (*Naut*) gléner. **the snake ~ed itself (up)** le serpent s'est lové.
2 vi *[river]* onduler, serpenter; *[rope]* s'enrouler (*round, about* autour de); *[snake]* se lover. 3 n a (*loops, roll*) *[rope, wire etc]* rouleau *m*; (*Naut*) glène *f*; *[hair]* rouleau; (*at back of head*) chignon *m*; (*over ears*) macaron *m*. b (*one loop*) spire *f*; *[cable]* tour *m*, plet *m* (*rare*); *[hair]* boucle *f*; *[snake, smoke]* anneau *m*. c (*Elec*) bobine *f*; (*one loop*) spire *f*. d (*Med *: contraceptive*) **the ~** le stérilet. 4 comp ► **coil spring** ressort hélicoïdal.
coin [kɔɪn] 1 n a pièce *f* de monnaie. **a 10p ~** une pièce de 10 pence; *see* **toss** *etc.* b (*NonC*) monnaie *f*. **current ~** monnaie courante; **in (the) ~ of the realm** en espèces (sonnantes et trébuchantes); (*fig*) **to pay sb back in his own ~** rendre à qn la monnaie de sa pièce. 2 comp ► **coin box** (*Telec*) cabine *f* téléphonique ► **coin-operated** automatique; **coin-operated laundry** (*abbr* **coin-op***) laverie *f* automatique (*à libre-service*). 3 vt a *money, medal* frapper. (*fig*) **he is ~ing money** il fait des affaires d'or. b (*fig*) *word, phrase* inventer, fabriquer. (*hum, iro*) **to ~ a phrase** si je peux m'exprimer ainsi.
coinage [ˈkɔɪnɪdʒ] n (*NonC*) a (*coins*) monnaie *f*; (*system*) système *m* monétaire. b (*act*) *[money]* frappe *f*; (*fig*) *[word etc]* création *f*, invention *f*.
coincide [,kəʊɪnˈsaɪd] vi coïncider (*with* avec).
coincidence [kəʊˈɪnsɪdəns] n coïncidence *f*.
coincident [kəʊˈɪnsɪdənt] adj (*frm*) identique (*with* à).
coincidental [kəʊ,ɪnsɪˈdentl] adj de coïncidence. **it's entirely ~** c'est une pure coïncidence.
coincidentally [kəʊ,ɪnsɪˈdentlɪ] adv tout-à-fait par hasard. **not ~, we ...** ce n'est pas un hasard si nous ... .
coinsurance [,kəʊɪnˈʃʊərəns] n (*US Med*) *assurance dont les cotisations sont payées pour moitié par l'entreprise*.
coir [kɔɪəʳ] n coco *m*, coir *m*. **~ matting** tapis *m* de coco.
coitus [ˈkɔɪtəs] n coït *m*. **~ interruptus** rapport *m* interrompu; **to practise ~ interruptus** pratiquer le retirer.
coke¹ [kəʊk] n coke *m*. **~ oven** four *m* à coke.
coke² [kəʊk] n (*Drugs sl*) coco *f*, cocaïne *f*, neige *f*.
Coke [kəʊk] n ® Coca *m* ®.
col. a abbr of **column.** b abbr of **colour.**
Col. (*Mil*) abbr of **Colonel.** (*on envelope*) **Col. T. Richard** le Colonel T. Richard.
cola [ˈkəʊlə] n cola *f*. **~ nut** noix *f* de cola.
colander [ˈkʌləndəʳ] n passoire *f*.
cold [kəʊld] 1 adj a *day, drink, meal, meat, metal, water* froid. **to be as**

~ as ice *[object]* être froid comme de la glace; *[room]* être glacial; *[person]* être glacé jusqu'aux os; (*Met*) **it's as ~ as charity** il fait un froid de canard* *or* un froid sibérien; **it's a ~ morning/day** il fait froid ce matin/aujourd'hui; **I am ~** j'ai froid; **my feet are ~** j'ai froid aux pieds; (*fig*) **to have** *or* **get ~ feet** avoir la frousse* *or* la trouille*; **to get ~** *[weather, room]* se refroidir; *[food]* refroidir; *[person]* commencer à avoir froid, (*catch a chill*) attraper froid; (*in guessing etc games*) **you're getting ~(er)!** tu refroidis!; (*Met*) **~ front** front froid; (*Met*) **~ snap** courte offensive du froid; **~ wave** (*Met*) vague *f* de froid; (*Hairdressing*) minivague *f*; (*Aut*) (*Brit*) **~ start**, (*US*) **~ starting** démarrage *m* à froid; **a ~ colour** une couleur froide; **~ steel** arme blanche; **the scent is ~** la voie est froide, la piste a disparu (*also fig*); **that's ~ comfort** ce n'est pas tellement réconfortant *or* rassurant, c'est une maigre consolation; **to be in a ~ sweat (about)*** avoir des sueurs froides (au sujet de); **that brought him out in a ~ sweat** cela lui a donné des sueurs froides; (*fig*) **to throw ~ water on** *plans* démolir; *sb's enthusiasm* doucher; *see also* **2** *and* **blow**[1], **icy** *etc.*

b (*fig*) (*unfriendly*) froid, manquant de *or* sans cordialité; (*indifferent*) froid, indifférent; (*dispassionate*) froid, calme, objectif. **a ~ reception** un accueil froid; **to be ~ to sb** se montrer froid envers qn; **that leaves me ~*** ça ne me fait ni chaud ni froid, cela me laisse froid; **in ~ blood** de sang-froid; **he is a ~ fish*** qu'est-ce qu'il est froid!

c (*: *unconscious*) sans connaissance. **he was out ~** il était sans connaissance *or* dans les pommes*; (*lit, fig*) **it knocked him ~** ça l'a mis K.O.

2 **comp** ▸ **cold-blooded** (*Zool*) à sang froid; (*fig*) *person* insensible, sans pitié; *murder, attack* commis de sang-froid; (*fig*) **to be cold-blooded about sth** faire qch sans aucune pitié ▸ **cold-bloodedly** de sang-froid ▸ **cold chisel** ciseau *m* à froid ▸ **cold cream** crème *f* de beauté, cold-cream *m* ▸ **cold cuts** (*Culin*) assiette anglaise ▸ **cold frame** (*Agr*) châssis *m* de couches ▸ **cold-hearted** impitoyable, sans pitié ▸ **cold room** chambre froide *or* frigorifique ▸ **cold shoulder***: (*fig*) **to give sb the cold shoulder**, (*US*) **to turn a cold shoulder on** *or* **to sb, to cold-shoulder sb** battre froid à qn, se montrer froid envers qn ▸ **cold sore** (*Med*) bouton *m* de fièvre ▸ **cold storage** conservation *f* par le froid; **to put into cold storage** *food* mettre en chambre froide *or* frigorifique; *fur coat* mettre en garde; (*fig*) *idea, book, scheme* mettre de côté *or* en attente ▸ **cold store** entrepôt *m* frigorifique ▸ **cold turkey** (*Drugs sl*) manque *m* ▸ **the cold war** (*Pol*) la guerre froide.

3 **n** a (*Met etc*) froid *m*. **I am beginning to feel the ~** je commence à avoir froid, je n'ai plus très chaud; **I never feel the ~** je ne crains pas le froid, je ne suis pas frileux; **don't go out in this ~!** ne sors pas par ce froid!; **to come in out of** *or* **from the ~** se mettre à l'abri; (*fig*) rentrer en grâce; (*fig*) **to be left out in the ~** rester en plan*.

b (*Med*) rhume *m*. **~ in the head/on the chest** rhume de cerveau/de poitrine; **a heavy** *or* **bad ~** un gros *or* sale* rhume; **to have a ~** être enrhumé; **to get a ~** s'enrhumer, attraper un rhume; *see* **catch, head.**

4 **adv** (*US* *) (*completely*) absolument; (*unexpectedly*) de façon totalement inattendue. **to know sth ~** connaître qch à fond *or* sur le bout du doigt.

coldly ['kəʊldlɪ] **adv** *look, say* froidement; *behave* avec froideur.

coldness ['kəʊldnɪs] **n** (*lit, fig*) froideur *f*.

coleslaw ['kəʊlslɔː] **n** salade *f* de chou cru.

coley ['kəʊlɪ] **n** lieu noir *m*, colin *m*.

colic ['kɒlɪk] **n** coliques *fpl*.

colicky ['kɒlɪkɪ] **adj** *baby* qui souffre de coliques; *pain* dû à des coliques; (*fig*) *disposition* grincheux.

Coliseum [ˌkɒlɪ'siːəm] **n** Colisée *m*.

colitis [kɒ'laɪtɪs] **n** colite *f*.

collaborate [kə'læbəreɪt] **vi** (*also pej*) collaborer. **to ~ with sb on** *or* **in sth** collaborer avec qn à qch.

collaboration [kəˌlæbə'reɪʃən] **n** (*also pej*) collaboration *f* (*in* à).

collaborative [kə'læbərətɪv] **adj** fait en collaboration, commun.

collaborator [kə'læbəreɪtə^r] **n** (*gen*) collaborateur *m*, -trice *f*; (*pej: World War II*) collaborateur, -trice, collaborationniste *mf*, collabo* *mf*.

collage [kɒ'lɑːʒ] **n** (*Art*) collage *m*.

collapsar [kə'læpsə^r] **n** (*Astron*) trou *m* noir.

collapse [kə'læps] 1 **vi** a *[person, building, roof, floor]* s'écrouler, s'effondrer, s'affaisser; *[balloon]* se dégonfler; *[beam]* fléchir; (*fig*) *[one's health]* se délabrer, flancher*; *[government]* tomber, faire la culbute*; *[prices, defences]* s'effondrer; *[civilization, society, institution]* s'effondrer, s'écrouler; *[plan, scheme]* s'écrouler, tomber à l'eau; (*: *with laughter*) être plié en deux, se tordre (de rire). **he ~d at work and was taken to hospital** il a eu un grave malaise à son travail et on l'a emmené à l'hôpital; (*Med*) **his lung ~d** il a fait un collapsus pulmonaire; (*Med*) **~d lung** collapsus *m* pulmonaire.

b (*lit: fold for storage etc*) *[table, chairs]* se plier.

2 **vt** *table, chair* plier; (*fig*) *paragraphs, items* réduire, comprimer.

3 **n** *[person, building, roof]* écroulement *m*, effondrement *m*; *[lung etc]* collapsus *m*; *[beam]* fléchissement *m*; *[health]* délabrement *m*; *[government]* chute *f*; *[prices, defences]* effondrement; *[civilization, plan, scheme]* effondrement, écroulement.

collapsible [kə'læpsəbl] **adj** *table, chair, umbrella* pliant.

collar ['kɒlə^r] 1 **n** (*attached: on garment*) col *m*; (*separate*) (*for men*) faux-col *m*; (*for women*) col, collerette *f*; (*for dogs, horses etc*) collier *m*; (*part of animal's neck*) collier; (*Culin*) *[beef]* collier; *[mutton etc]* collet *m*; (*Tech: on pipe etc*) bague *f*. **to get hold of sb by the ~** saisir qn au collet; *see* **white** *etc.* 2 **vt** a (*) *person* (*lit*) prendre *or* saisir au collet, colleter; (*fig*) accrocher, intercepter*; *book, object* faire main basse sur. b (*Tech*) baguer. 3 **comp** ▸ **collarbone** clavicule *f* ▸ **collar button** (*US*), **collarstud** (*Brit*) bouton *m* de col.

collate [kɒ'leɪt] **vt** a collationner (*with* avec). b (*Rel*) nommer (*to* à).

collateral [kɒ'lætərəl] 1 **adj** a (*parallel*) parallèle; *fact, phenomenon* concomitant; (*Jur*) *relationship,* (*Med*) *artery* collatéral. b (*subordinate*) secondaire, accessoire; (*Fin*) subsidiaire. (*Fin*) **~ security** nantissement *m*. c (*Mil*) **~ damage** dommages *mpl* de guerre. 2 **n** a (*Fin*) nantissement *m*. **securities lodged as ~** titres remis en nantissement. b (*Jur*) collatéral(e) *m(f)*.

collateralize [kɒ'lætərəlaɪz] **vt** garantir par nantissement.

collation [kə'leɪʃən] **n** collation *f*.

colleague ['kɒliːg] **n** collègue *mf*, confrère *m*, consœur *f* (*rare*).

collect[1] ['kɒlekt] **n** (*Rel*) collecte *f* (*prière*).

collect[2] [kə'lekt] 1 **vt** a (*gather together, assemble*) *valuables, wealth* accumuler, amasser; *facts, information* rassembler, recueillir; *documents* recueillir, rassembler, grouper; *evidence, proof* rassembler. **the ~ed works of Shakespeare** les œuvres complètes de Shakespeare; **she ~ed (together) a group of volunteers** elle a rassemblé *or* réuni un groupe de volontaires; **the dam ~s the water from the mountains** le barrage accumule *or* retient l'eau des montagnes; (*fig*) **to ~ one's wits** rassembler ses esprits; (*fig*) **to ~ o.s.** (*regain control of o.s.*) se reprendre; (*reflect quietly*) se recueillir; (*fig*) **to ~ one's thoughts** se recueillir, se concentrer.

b (*pick up*) *seashells etc* ramasser; *eggs* lever, ramasser. **the children ~ed (up) the books for the teacher** les enfants ont ramassé les livres pour l'instituteur; **these vases ~ the dust** ces vases prennent *or* ramassent* la poussière.

c (*obtain*) *money, subscriptions* recueillir; *taxes, dues, fines* percevoir; *rents* encaisser, toucher. (*US*) **~ on delivery** paiement *m* à la livraison, livraison *f* contre remboursement.

d (*take official possession of*) *[bus or railway company] luggage etc* prendre à domicile; *[ticket collector] tickets* ramasser. (*Brit Post*) **to ~ letters** faire la levée du courrier; **the rubbish is ~ed twice a week** les ordures sont enlevées *or* ramassées deux fois par semaine; **the firm ~s the empty bottles** la compagnie récupère les bouteilles vides; (*Comm*) **to ~ goods/an order** retirer des marchandises/une commande.

e (*as hobby*) *stamps, antiques, coins* collectionner, faire collection de. (*pej*) **she ~s* poets/lame ducks** *etc* elle collectionne* les poètes/canards boiteux *etc.*

f (*call for*) *person* aller chercher, (passer) prendre. **I'll ~ you in the car/at 8 o'clock** j'irai vous chercher *or* je passerai vous prendre en voiture/à 8 heures; **to ~ one's mail/one's keys** *etc* (passer) prendre son courrier/ses clefs *etc*; **I'll come and ~ the book this evening** je passerai prendre le livre ce soir; **the bus ~s the children each morning** l'autobus ramasse les enfants tous les matins.

2 **vi** a *[people]* se rassembler, se réunir, se grouper; *[things]* s'amasser, s'entasser; *[dust, water]* s'amasser, s'accumuler.

b **to ~ for the injured** faire la quête *or* quêter pour les blessés.

3 **adv** (*US Telec*) **to call ~** téléphoner en PCV.

4 **comp** ▸ **collect call** (*US Telec*) communication *f* en PCV.

collected [kə'lektɪd] **adj** serein.

collection [kə'lekʃən] 1 **n** a (*act of collecting: see* **collect**[2]) *[wealth, valuables]* accumulation *f*; *[facts]* rassemblement *m*; *[seashells, eggs]* ramassage *m*; *[taxes]* perception *f*; *[rents]* encaissement *m*; *[luggage]* livraison *f*. (*at meetings, for charity etc*) **the ~ of money** la collecte; **your order is now awaiting ~** votre commande est prête.

b (*Rel etc: money*) collecte *f*, quête *f*; (*Brit Post*) *[mail]* levée *f*. **a ~ was made for the blind** on a fait une quête *or* collecte pour les aveugles; **there were several ~s for charity in the course of the evening** on a fait plusieurs quêtes *or* on a quêté pour plusieurs œuvres au cours de la soirée; (*Post*) **there are 5 ~s daily** il y a 5 levées par jour.

c (*set of things*) collection *f*. **the spring ~** la collection de printemps; **his ~ of stamps** sa collection de timbres; (*fig: a lot of*) **there was a ~ of books on the table** il y avait un tas de livres sur la table.

2 **comp** ▸ **collection charges** (*Fin, Comm*) frais *mpl* d'encaissement ▸ **collection box** tronc *m* ▸ **collection plate** (*Rel*) ≃ sébile *f* ▸ **collection tin** = **collection box.**

collective [kə'lektɪv] 1 **adj** (*gen, Jur, Psych*) *responsibility, farm, ownership, ticket, security* collectif. **~ bargaining** (négociations *fpl* pour une) convention collective de travail; (*Ling*) **~ noun** collectif *m*. 2 **n** association collective.

collectively [kə'lektɪvlɪ] **adv** collectivement.

collectivism [kə'lektɪvɪzəm] **n** collectivisme *m*.

collectivist [kə'lektɪvɪst] **adj, n** collectiviste (*mf*).

collectivize [kə'lektɪvaɪz] **vt** collectiviser.

collector [kə'lektə^r] **n** *[taxes]* percepteur *m*; *[dues]* receveur *m*; *[rent, cash]* encaisseur *m*; *[stamps, coins etc]* collectionneur *m*, -euse *f*; (*also* **ticket ~**) contrôleur *m*, -euse *f*. **~'s item** pièce *f* de collection.

colleen [ˈkɒliːn] n jeune Irlandaise; (*in Ireland*) jeune fille *f*.

college [ˈkɒlɪdʒ] 1 n a (*institution for higher education*) collège *m*, établissement *m* d'enseignement supérieur; (*for professional training*) école professionnelle, collège technique. (*Brit*) **C~ of Advanced Technology** ≃ IUT *m*, Institut *m* universitaire de technologie; **~ of agriculture** institut *m* agronomique; **~ of art** école des beaux-arts; **~ of domestic science** école *or* centre *m* d'enseignement ménager; (*Brit*) **C~ of Education** (*for primary teachers*) ≃ école normale primaire; (*for secondary*) ≃ centre pédagogique régional de formation des maîtres; (*Brit*) **C~ of Further Education** ≃ institut *m* d'éducation permanente; **~ of music** conservatoire *m* de musique; (*Brit*) **to go to ~*** faire des études supérieures; (*US Univ*) **~ catalog(ue)** livret *m* de l'étudiant; **~ staff** corps enseignant; *see* **naval, teacher** *etc*.
b (*within a university*) collège *m*.
c (*institution*) collège *m*, société *f*, académie *f*. **C~ of Physicians/Surgeons** Académie de médecine/de chirurgie; **the C~ of Cardinals** le Sacré Collège; *see* **electoral**.
2 comp ▸ **college-bound**: (*US Scol*) **college-bound student** élève *mf* qui se destine aux études universitaires; (*US Scol*) **college-bound program** programme *m* de préparation aux études universitaires.

collegiate [kəˈliːdʒɪɪt] adj *life* de collège; (*Can*) *studies* secondaire. **~ church** collégiale *f*.

collide [kəˈlaɪd] vi a (*lit*) entrer en collision, se heurter, se tamponner. **to ~ with** entrer en collision avec, heurter, tamponner; (*Naut*) aborder. b (*fig*) se heurter (*with* à), entrer en conflit (*with* avec).

collie [ˈkɒlɪ] n colley *m*.

collier [ˈkɒlɪəʳ] n (*miner*) mineur *m*; (*ship*) charbonnier *m*.

colliery [ˈkɒlɪərɪ] n houillère *f*, mine *f* (de charbon).

collimator [ˈkɒlɪˌmeɪtəʳ] n collimateur *m*. (*Phot*) **~ viewfinder** viseur *m* à cadre lumineux.

collision [kəˈlɪʒən] 1 n a (*lit*) collision *f*, heurt *m*, choc *m*; (*Rail*) collision, tamponnement *m*; (*Naut*) abordage *m*. **to come into ~ with** *[car]* entrer en collision avec; *[train]* entrer en collision avec, tamponner; *[boat]* aborder. b (*fig*) conflit *m*, opposition *f*. 2 comp ▸ **collision course: to be on a collision course** (*Naut etc*) être sur une route de collision; (*fig*) aller au-devant de l'affrontement (*with* avec).

collocate [ˈkɒləˌkeɪt] (*Ling*) 1 n cooccurrent *m*. 2 vi *[words]* être cooccurrents. **to ~ with** être cooccurrent de.

collocation [ˌkɒləˈkeɪʃən] n (*Ling*) collocation *f*.

colloquial [kəˈləʊkwɪəl] adj (*language*) familier, parlé, de la conversation; *style* familier.

colloquialism [kəˈləʊkwɪəlɪzəm] n (*Ling*) expression familière.

colloquially [kəˈləʊkwɪəlɪ] adv familièrement, dans le langage de la conversation, dans la langue parlée.

colloquium [kəˈləʊkwɪəm] n, pl **~s** *or* **colloquia** [kəˈləʊkwɪə] colloque *m*.

colloquy [ˈkɒləkwɪ] n colloque *m*, conversation *f*.

collude [kəˈluːd] vi s'associer (*dans une affaire louche*).

collusion [kəˈluːʒən] n collusion *f*. **in ~ with** de complicité avec, de connivence avec.

collywobbles* [ˈkɒlɪˌwɒblz] npl: **to have the ~** (*be scared*) avoir la frousse* *or* la trouille*; (*have stomach trouble*) avoir des coliques.

Colo. (*US*) abbr of **Colorado**.

Cologne [kəˈləʊn] n a Cologne. b **(eau de) ~** eau *f* de Cologne.

Colombia [kəˈlɒmbɪə] n Colombie *f*.

Colombian [kəˈlɒmbɪən] 1 n Colombien(ne) *m(f)*. 2 adj colombien.

colon¹ [ˈkəʊlən] n, pl **~s** *or* **cola** [ˈkəʊlə] (*Anat*) côlon *m*.

colon² [ˈkəʊlən] n, pl **~s** (*Gram*) deux-points *m inv*.

colonel [ˈkɜːnl] n colonel *m*. **C~ Smith** le colonel Smith; (*on envelope*) le Colonel Smith.

colonial [kəˈləʊnɪəl] 1 adj a colonial. **C~ Office** ministère *m* des Colonies. b (*US*) *house* en style du 18e siècle. 2 n colonial(e) *m(f)*.

colonialism [kəˈləʊnɪəlɪzəm] n colonialisme *m*.

colonialist [kəˈləʊnɪəlɪst] adj, n colonialiste (*mf*).

colonic [kəʊˈlɒnɪk] adj du côlon. **~ irrigation** lavement *m*.

colonist [ˈkɒlənɪst] n colon *m*, (*habitant etc d'une colonie*).

colonization [ˌkɒlənaɪˈzeɪʃən] n colonisation *f*.

colonize [ˈkɒlənaɪz] vt coloniser.

colonnade [ˌkɒləˈneɪd] n colonnade *f*.

colony [ˈkɒlənɪ] n (*all senses*) colonie *f*; *see* **leper**.

colophon [ˈkɒləfən] n (*emblem*) logotype *m*, colophon *m*; (*end text in book*) achevé *m* d'imprimer; (*end text in manuscript*) colophon.

color [ˈkʌləʳ] *etc* (*US*) = **colour** *etc*.

Colorado [ˌkɒləˈrɑːdəʊ] n (*state, river*) Colorado *m*. **in ~** *be, go* au Colorado; *live* dans le Colorado; **~ beetle** doryphore *m*.

colorant [ˈkʌlərənt] n colorant *m*.

coloration [ˌkʌləˈreɪʃən] n coloration *f*, coloris *m*; *see* **protective**.

coloratura [ˌkɒlərəˈtʊərə] 1 n colorature *f*. 2 adj *voice, part* de colorature.

colorcast [ˈkʌləkɑːst] 1 n émission *f* en couleurs. 2 vt retransmettre en couleurs.

colossal [kəˈlɒsl] adj (*lit, also fig*) colossal.

colossi [kəˈlɒsaɪ] npl of **colossus**.

Colossians [kəˈlɒʃənz] n Colossiens *mpl*.

colossus [kəˈlɒsəs] n, pl **colossi** [kəˈlɒsaɪ] *or* **~es** colosse *m*.

colostomy [kəˈlɒstəmɪ] n colostomie *f*.

colostrum [kəˈlɒstrəm] n colostrum *m*.

colour, (*US*) **color** [ˈkʌləʳ] 1 n a (*hue*) couleur *f*, teinte *f*. **what ~ is it?** de quelle couleur est-ce?; **there is not enough ~ in it** cela manque de couleur; **to take the ~ out of sth** décolorer qch; (*fig*) **the ~ of a newspaper** la couleur *or* les opinions *fpl* d'un journal; (*fig*) **let's see the ~ of your money*** fais voir la couleur de ton fric*; (*fig*) **a symphony/a poem full of ~** une symphonie pleine/un poème plein de couleur; (*fig*) **to give** *or* **lend ~ to a tale** colorer un récit; (*fig*) **to give a false ~ to sth** présenter qch sous un faux jour, dénaturer qch; (*fig*) **under (the) ~ of** sous prétexte *or* couleur de; *see* **primary**.
b (*complexion*) teint *m*, couleur *f* (*du visage*). **to change ~** changer de couleur *or* de visage; **to lose (one's) ~** pâlir, perdre ses couleurs; **to get one's ~ back** reprendre des couleurs; **he looks an unhealthy ~** il a très mauvaise mine; **to have a high ~** être haut en couleur; *see* **off**.
c (*Art*) (*pigment*) matière colorante, couleur *f*; (*paint*) peinture *f*; (*dye*) teinture *f*; (*shades, tones*) coloris *m*, couleur, ton *m*. **to paint sth in bright/dark ~s** (*lit*) peindre qch de couleurs vives/sombres; (*fig*) peindre qch sous de belles couleurs/sous des couleurs sombres; (*fig*) **to see sth in its true ~s** voir qch sous son vrai jour (*see also* **d**); *see* **local, water** *etc*.
d (*symbol of allegiance*) **~s** couleurs *fpl* (*d'un club, d'un parti etc*); (*Mil*) couleurs, drapeau *m*; (*Naut*) couleurs, pavillon *m*; (*Sport*) **to get** *or* **win one's ~s** être sélectionné pour (faire partie de) l'équipe; **to salute the ~s** saluer le drapeau; **to fight with the ~s** combattre sous les drapeaux; (*fig*) **to stick to one's ~s** rester fidèle à ses principes *or* à ce qu'on a dit; (*fig*) **he showed his true ~s when he said ...** il s'est révélé tel qu'il est vraiment quand il a dit ...; *see* **flying, nail, troop**.
e (*Pol*) *[race]* couleur *f*. **his ~ counted against him** sa couleur jouait contre lui; **it is not a question of ~** ce n'est pas une question de race.
2 comp ▸ **colour bar** (*Brit*) discrimination raciale ▸ **colour-blind** daltonien ▸ **colour blindness** daltonisme *m*, achromatopsie *f* ▸ **colour camera** (*TV*) caméra *f* couleur *inv* ▸ **colour code** code *m* couleurs ▸ **colour-code** codifier par couleurs ▸ **colourfast** grand teint *inv* ▸ **colour film** (*for camera*) pellicule *f* (en) couleurs; (*for movie camera; in cinema*) film *m* en couleurs ▸ **colour filter** (*Phot*) filtre coloré ▸ **colour graphics adaptor** (*Comput*) adaptateur *m* de graphique couleur ▸ **color line** (*US*) = **colour bar** ▸ **colour photograph** photographie *f* en couleurs ▸ **colour photography** photographie *f* en couleurs ▸ **colour problem** problème racial *or* du racisme ▸ **colour scheme** combinaison *f* de(s) couleurs; **to choose a colour scheme** assortir les couleurs *or* les tons ▸ **colour sergeant** (*Brit Mil*) ≃ sergent-chef *m* ▸ **colour slide** diapositive *f* en couleurs ▸ **colour supplement** (*Brit Press*) supplément illustré ▸ **colour television** télévision *f* en couleurs ▸ **colourway** (*Brit*) coloris *m*.
3 vt a (*lit*) (*give ~ to*) colorer, donner de la couleur à; (*with paint*) peindre; (*with crayons etc*) colorier; (*dye*) teindre; (*tint*) teinter. **to ~ sth red** colorer (*or* colorier *etc*) qch en rouge; **to ~ (in) a picture** colorier une image; *[children]* **a ~ing book** un album à colorier.
b (*fig*) *story, description* colorer; *facts* (*misrepresent*) fausser; (*exaggerate*) exagérer.
4 vi *[things]* se colorer; *[persons]* (*also* **~ up**) rougir.

coloured, (*US*) **colored** [ˈkʌləd] 1 adj a *liquid, complexion* coloré; *drawing* colorié; *pencil* de couleur; *picture, photograph, slide, television* en couleur. (*fig*) **a highly ~ tale** un récit très coloré. b **(adj ending in comps) -coloured** (de) couleur. **a straw-coloured hat** un chapeau couleur paille; **muddy-coloured** couleur de boue. c *person, race* de couleur. 2 n: **~s** (*US, Brit*) personnes *fpl* de couleur; (*in South Africa*) métis *mpl*; *see* **cape²**.

colourful, (*US*) **colorful** [ˈkʌləfʊl] adj (*lit*) coloré, vif, éclatant; (*fig*) *personality* pittoresque, original; *account* coloré.

colourfully [ˈkʌləfʊlɪ] adv avec beaucoup de couleurs.

colouring, (*US*) **coloring** [ˈkʌlərɪŋ] n a (*complexion*) teint *m*. **high ~** teint coloré. b (*NonC*) coloration *f*; *[drawings etc]* coloriage *m*; (*fig*) *[news, facts etc]* travestissement *m*, dénaturation *f*. **~ book** album *m* à colorier. c (*hue*) coloris *m*, coloration *f*. d (*in food*) colorant *m* (alimentaire).

colourless, (*US*) **colorless** [ˈkʌləlɪs] adj (*lit*) sans couleur, incolore; (*fig*) incolore, terne, fade.

colt [kəʊlt] 1 n a (*Zool*) poulain *m*; (*fig: a youth*) petit jeune (*pej*), novice *m*. b ® (*pistol*) colt *m*, pistolet *m* (automatique). 2 comp ▸ **coltsfoot** (*Bot*) (pl **~s**) pas-d'âne *m inv*, tussilage *m*.

coltish [ˈkɒltɪʃ] adj (*frisky*) guilleret, folâtre; (*inexperienced*) jeunet, inexpérimenté.

Columbia [kəˈlʌmbɪə] n (*US*) **(District of) ~** district fédéral de Columbia; *see* **British**.

columbine [ˈkɒləmbaɪn] n ancolie *f*.

Columbine [ˈkɒləmbaɪn] n (*Theat*) Colombine *f*.

Columbus [kəˈlʌmbəs] n: **(Christopher) ~** Christophe Colomb *m*.

column [ˈkɒləm] n (*all senses*) colonne *f*. **~ inch** *dans un journal, espace de 2,5 centimètres sur la largeur d'une colonne; see* **fifth** *etc*.

columnist [ˈkɒləmnɪst] n (*Press*) chroniqueur *m*, échotier *m*, -ière *f*.

coma ['kəʊmə] n coma *m*. **in a ~** dans le coma.
comatose ['kəʊmətəʊs] adj comateux.
comb [kəʊm] 1 n a peigne *m*; (*large-toothed*) démêloir *m*. **to run a ~ through one's hair, to give one's hair a ~** se donner un coup de peigne, se peigner; *see* **tooth.** b (*for horse*) étrille *f*; (*Tech: for wool etc*) peigne *m*, carde *f*; (*Elec*) balai *m*. c *[fowl]* crête *f*; *[helmet]* cimier *m*. d (*honeycomb*) rayon *m* de miel. 2 vt a peigner; (*Tech*) peigner, carder; *horse* étriller. **to ~ one's hair** se peigner; **to ~ sb's hair** peigner qn. b (*fig: search*) *area, hills, town* fouiller, ratisser. **he ~ed (through) the papers looking for evidence** il a dépouillé le dossier à la recherche d'une preuve.
►**comb out** vt sep *hair* peigner, démêler. **they combed out the useless members of the staff** on a passé le personnel au peigne fin et éliminé les incapables.
combat ['kɒmbæt] 1 n combat *m*; *see* **close¹, unarmed** *etc*. 2 comp ► **combat duty: on combat duty** en service commandé ► **combat car** (véhicule *m*) blindé *m* léger de campagne ► **combat fatigue** *trouble mental causé par la tension éprouvée dans une situation de guerre* ► **combat jacket** veste *f* de treillis ► **combat troops** troupes *fpl* de combat ► **combat zone** zone *f* de combat. 3 vt (*lit, fig*) combattre, lutter contre. 4 vi combattre, lutter (*for* pour, *with, against* contre).
combatant ['kɒmbətənt] adj, n combattant(e) *m(f)*.
combative ['kɒmbətɪv] adj combatif.
combe [kuːm] = **coomb.**
combination [,kɒmbɪ'neɪʃən] 1 n (*gen, Chem, Math: also of lock*) combinaison *f*; *[people]* association *f*, coalition *f*; *[events]* concours *m*; *[interests]* coalition. (*undergarment*) **~s** combinaison-culotte *f* (de femme); (*Brit Aut*) **(motorcycle) ~** side-car *m*. 2 comp ► **combination lock** serrure *f* à combinaison.
combine [kəm'baɪn] 1 vt combiner (*with* avec), joindre (*with* à); (*Chem*) combiner. **he ~d generosity with discretion** il alliait la générosité à la discrétion; **they ~d forces/efforts** ils ont uni *or* joint leurs forces/efforts; **to ~ business with pleasure** joindre l'utile à l'agréable; **~d clock and radio** combiné *m* radio-réveil; **their ~d wealth was not enough** leurs richesses réunies n'ont pas suffi; **a ~d effort** un effort conjugué; (*Mil*) **~d forces** forces alliées; (*Mil*) **~d operation** (*by several nations*) opération alliée; (*by the different forces of the same nation*) opération interarmes *inv*; (*fig*) entreprise réalisée en commun.
2 vi s'unir, s'associer; *[parties]* fusionner; *[workers]* se syndiquer; (*Chem*) se combiner; (*fig*) se liguer (*against* contre); *[events]* concourir (*to do* à faire). (*Ling*) **combining form** élément *m* de mot.
3 ['kɒmbaɪn] n a association *f*; (*Comm, Fin*) trust *m*, cartel *m*; (*Jur*) corporation *f*.
b (*also* **~ harvester**) moissonneuse-batteuse *f*.
combo‡ ['kɒmbəʊ] n (*Mus*) petite formation musicale.
combustible [kəm'bʌstɪbl] adj combustible.
combustion [kəm'bʌstʃən] n combustion *f*. (*Aut*) **~ chamber** chambre *f* d'explosion; *see* **internal, spontaneous.**
come [kʌm] pret **came,** ptp **come** 1 vi a (*move*) venir; (*arrive*) venir, arriver. **~ here** venez ici; **~ with me** venez avec moi; **~ and see me soon,** (*US*) **~ see me soon** venez me voir bientôt; **he has ~ to mend the television** il est venu réparer la télévision; **he has ~ from Edinburgh** il est venu d'Édimbourg; **he has just ~ from Edinburgh** il arrive d'Édimbourg; (*fig: originate from*) **to ~ from** *[person]* venir de, être originaire *or* natif de; *[object, commodity]* provenir *or* venir de; **he ~s of a very poor family** il vient *or* est d'une famille très pauvre; **he has ~ a long way** (*lit*) il est venu de loin; (*fig: made much progress*) il a fait du chemin; **to ~ and go** aller et venir; **they were coming and going all day** ils n'ont fait qu'aller et venir toute la journée; **the pain ~s and goes** la douleur est intermittente; (*fig*) **I don't know whether I'm coming or going** je ne sais plus où donner de la tête; **to ~ running/shouting** *etc* arriver en courant/en criant *etc*; **to ~ hurrying** arriver en toute hâte; **to ~ home** rentrer (chez soi *or* à la maison); **to ~ for sb/sth** venir chercher *or* venir prendre qn/qch; **you go on, I'll ~ after (you)** allez-y, je vous suis; **coming!** j'arrive!; (*excl*) **~, ~!, ~ now!** allons!, voyons!; **when did he ~?** quand est-il arrivé?; **no one has ~** personne n'est venu; **they came to a town** ils sont arrivés à une ville, ils ont atteint *or* gagné une ville; **the rain came closely after the thunderclap** la pluie a suivi de près le coup de tonnerre; **help came in time** les secours sont arrivés à temps; **it came into my head that** il m'est venu à l'esprit que; **it came as a shock to him** cela lui a fait un choc; **it came as a surprise to him** cela l'a (beaucoup) surpris; **when your turn ~s, when it ~s your turn** quand ce sera (à) votre tour, quand votre tour viendra; **when it ~s to mathematics, no one can beat him** pour ce qui est des mathématiques, personne ne peut le battre; **when it ~s to choosing** quand il faut choisir; (*fig*) **he will never ~ to much** il ne sera *or* fera jamais grand-chose; **the time will ~ when ...** un jour viendra où ..., il viendra un temps où ...; (*Jur*) **to ~ before a judge** *[accused]* comparaître devant un juge; *[case]* être entendu par un juge.
b (*have its place*) venir, se trouver, être placé. **May ~s before June** mai vient avant *or* précède juin; **July ~s after June** juillet vient après *or* suit juin; **this passage ~s on page 10** ce passage se trouve à la page 10; **the adjective must ~ before the noun** l'adjectif doit être placé devant *or* précéder le substantif; **a princess ~s before a duchess** une princesse prend le pas *or* a la préséance sur une duchesse; *see* **first.**
c (*happen*) arriver, advenir (*to* à), se produire. **no harm will ~ to him** il ne lui arrivera rien de mal; **~ what may** quoi qu'il arrive (*subj*) *or* advienne, advienne que pourra; **recovery came slowly** la guérison a été lente; **nothing came of it** il n'en est rien résulté; **that's what ~s of disobeying!** voilà ce que c'est que de désobéir!, voilà ce qui arrive quand on désobéit; **no good will ~ of it** ça ne mènera à rien de bon, il n'en sortira rien de bon; **how do you ~ to be so late?** comment se fait-il que vous soyez si en retard?
d (*+ to + n*) **to ~ to a decision** parvenir à *or* prendre une décision; **to ~ to an end** toucher à sa fin; **to ~ to the throne** monter sur le trône; *see* **agreement, blow², grief** *etc*.
e (*+ into + n*) **to ~ into sight** apparaître, devenir visible; *see* **bloom, blossom, effect** *etc*.
f (*+ adj, adv etc = be, become*) devenir, se trouver. **his dreams came true** ses rêves se sont réalisés; **the handle has ~ loose** le manche s'est desserré; **it ~s less expensive to shop in town** cela revient moins cher de faire ses achats en ville; **swimming/reading ~s naturally** *or* **natural* to him** il est doué pour la natation/la lecture; **everything came right in the end** tout s'est arrangé à la fin; **this dress ~s in 3 sizes** cette robe existe *or* se fait en 3 tailles; **to ~ undone** se défaire, se dénouer; **to ~ apart** (*come off*) se détacher; (*come unstuck*) se décoller; (*fall to pieces*) tomber en morceaux; **it came apart in my hands** ça s'est cassé tout seul.
g (*+ infin = be finally in a position to*) en venir à, finir par. **I have ~ to believe him** j'en suis venu à le croire; **he came to admit he was wrong** il a fini par reconnaître qu'il avait tort; **now I ~ to think of it** réflexion faite, quand j'y songe; (*frm, liter*) **it came to pass that** il advint que (*liter*).
h (*phrases*) **the life to ~** la vie future; **the years to ~** les années à venir; **in time to ~** à l'avenir; **if it ~s to that, you shouldn't have done it either** à ce compte-là *or* à ce moment-là* tu n'aurais pas dû le faire non plus; **I've known him for 3 years ~ January** cela fera 3 ans en janvier que je le connais; **she will be 6 ~ August** elle aura 6 ans au mois d'août *or* en août; **she is coming* 6** elle va sur ses 6 ans, elle va avoir 6 ans; **a week ~ Monday** il y aura huit jours lundi; **she had it coming to her*** elle l'a *or* l'avait (bien) cherché; **he got what was coming to him** il n'a eu que ce qu'il méritait; (*fig: cause trouble*) **to ~ between two people** (venir) se mettre entre deux personnes; **she's as clever as they ~*** elle est futée comme pas une*; **how do you like your tea? — as it ~s** comment voulez-vous votre thé? — peu importe *or* ça m'est égal; **you could see that coming*** on voyait venir ça de loin, c'était gros comme le nez au milieu de sa figure; **~ again?**‡ comment?, pardon?; **how ~?*** comment ça se fait?*; **how ~ you can't find it?*** comment se fait-il que tu n'arrives (*subj*) pas à le trouver?; **he tried to ~ the innocent with me**‡ il a essayé de jouer aux innocents avec moi; **that's coming it a bit strong!**‡ tu y vas un peu fort!*, tu pousses!*, tu charries!‡; (*Brit*) **don't ~ that game with me** ne jouez pas ce petit jeu-là avec moi; *see* **clean.**
i (‡: *reach orgasm*) jouir, partir‡.
2 comp ► **come-at-able*** accessible ► **comeback** (*Theat etc*) retour *m*, rentrée *f*; (*US: response*) réplique *f*; **to make** *or* **stage a comeback** (*Theat*) faire une rentrée; (*fig*) faire un comeback ► **comedown** dégringolade* *f*, déchéance *f*; **it was rather a comedown for him to have to work*** c'était assez humiliant pour lui d'avoir à travailler ► **come-hither*: she gave him a come-hither look** elle lui a lancé un regard aguichant ► **come-on*** (*gen: lure*) attrape-nigaud *m*, truc* *m*; (*sexual*) **to give sb the come-on** provoquer qn, allumer* qn ► **come-to-bed eyes*: she has come-to-bed eyes** elle a un regard provocant *or* aguicheur ► **comeuppance*** *see* **comeuppance*.**
►**come about** vi a (*impers: happen*) se faire (*impers*) + *que* + *subj*, arriver, se produire. **how does it come about that you are here?** comment se fait-il que vous soyez ici?; **this is why it came about** voilà pourquoi c'est arrivé *or* cela s'est produit. b (*Naut*) *[wind]* tourner, changer de direction.
►**come across** 1 vi a (*cross*) traverser.
b **he comes across as an honest man** il donne l'impression d'être un homme honnête; **his speech came across very well** son discours a fait beaucoup d'effet; **his speech came across very badly** son discours n'a pas fait d'effet *or* n'a pas passé la rampe; **despite his attempts to hide them, his true feelings came across quite clearly** malgré ses efforts pour les cacher, ses vrais sentiments se faisaient sentir clairement.
c (*US *: keep promise etc*) s'exécuter, tenir parole.
2 vt fus (*find or meet by chance*) *thing* trouver par hasard, tomber sur; *person* rencontrer par hasard, tomber sur. **if you come across my watch** si vous tombez sur ma montre.
►**come across with*** vt fus *money* se fendre de*, y aller de; *information* donner, vendre. **he came across with £10** il s'est fendu* de 10 livres; **the criminal came across with the names of his accomplices** le criminel a donné* ses complices.
►**come along** vi a (*imper only*) **come along!** (*impatiently*) (allons *or* voyons), dépêchez-vous!; (*in friendly tone*) (allez,) venez!
b (*accompany*) venir, suivre. **may my sister come along as well?** est-ce que ma sœur peut venir aussi?; **why don't you come along?**

pourquoi ne viendrais-tu pas?; **come along with me** suivez-moi, accompagnez-moi, venez avec moi.

c (*progress*) avancer, faire des progrès; *[plants, children]* pousser; *[plans]* avancer. **he's coming along in French** il fait des progrès en français; **how is your broken arm? — it's coming along quite well** comment va votre bras cassé? — il *or* ça se remet bien; **my book isn't coming along at all well** mon livre n'avance pas bien.

►**come around** vi = **come round.**

►**come at** vt fus a (*reach, get hold of*) (*lit*) saisir, mettre la main sur; (*fig*) découvrir, déterminer. **we could not come at the documents** nous n'avons pas pu mettre la main sur les documents; **it was difficult to come at the exact facts/what exactly had happened** il était difficile de déterminer les faits exacts/ce qui s'était passé exactement. b (*attack*) attaquer. **he came at me with an axe** il s'est jeté sur moi en brandissant une hache.

►**come away** vi a (*leave*) partir, s'en aller. **she had to come away before the end** elle a dû partir avant la fin; **come away from there!** sors de là!, écarte-toi de là! b (*become detached*) *[button etc]* se détacher, partir. **it came away in my hands** cela m'est resté dans les mains.

►**come back** 1 vi *[person etc]* revenir; *[fashion etc]* revenir en vogue *or* à la mode. **he came back 2 hours later** il est revenu 2 heures plus tard; (*Sport*) **he came back strongly into the game** il est revenu en force dans le jeu; **I asked her to come back with me** je lui ai demandé de me raccompagner; **to come back to what I was saying** pour en revenir à ce que je disais; **I'll come back to you on that one*** nous en reparlerons (plus tard); (*fig*) **his face/name is coming back to me** son visage/son nom me revient (à la mémoire *or* à l'esprit). 2 **comeback** n *see* **come 2.**

►**come back with** vt fus répondre par. **when accused, he came back with a counter-accusation** quand on l'a accusé il a répondu par une contre-accusation.

►**come by** 1 vi passer (par là). **he came by yesterday and told us** il est venu *or* passé (par là) hier et nous l'a raconté. 2 vt fus (*obtain*) *object* obtenir, se procurer; *idea, opinion* se faire. **how did you come by that book?** comment vous êtes-vous procuré ce livre?, comment avez-vous déniché ce livre?

►**come down** 1 vi a (*from ladder, stairs*) descendre (*from* de); (*from mountain*) descendre, faire la descente (*from* de); *[aircraft]* descendre. **come down from there at once!** descends de là tout de suite!; (*fig*) **to come down in the world** descendre dans l'échelle sociale, déchoir; (*fig*) **she had come down to begging** elle en était réduite à mendier *or* à la mendicité; **her hair comes down to her shoulders** ses cheveux lui descendent jusqu'aux épaules *or* lui tombent sur les épaules; (*fig*) **to come down (strongly) for** *or* **in favour of sth** prendre (fermement) position en faveur de qch.

b *[buildings etc]* (*be demolished*) être démoli, être abattu; (*fall down*) s'écrouler.

c (*drop*) *[prices]* baisser.

d (*be transmitted*) *[traditions etc]* être transmis (de père en fils).

2 **comedown*** n *see* **come 2.**

►**come down (up)on** vt fus a (*punish*) punir; (*rebuke*) s'en prendre à. **he came down on me like a ton of bricks*** il m'est tombé dessus à bras raccourcis. b **they came down on me* for a subscription** ils m'ont mis le grappin dessus* pour que je souscrive.

►**come down with** vt fus a (*become ill from*) attraper. **to come down with flu** attraper une grippe. b (**: pay out*) allonger‡.

►**come forward** vi se présenter (*as* comme). **who will come forward as a candidate?** qui va se présenter comme candidat? *or* se porter candidat?; **after the burglary, her neighbours came forward with help/money** après le cambriolage, ses voisins ont offert de l'aider/lui ont offert de l'argent; **to come forward with a suggestion** offrir une suggestion; **to come forward with an answer** suggérer une réponse.

►**come in** vi a *[person]* entrer; *[trains etc]* arriver; *[tide]* monter. (*fig*) **when** *or* **where do I come in?** quand est-ce que j'entre en jeu, moi?; (*fig*) **where does your brother come in?** (*how is he involved?*) qu'est-ce que ton frère a à voir là-dedans?; (*what's to be done with him?*) qu'est-ce qu'on fait de ton frère là-dedans?, qu'est-ce que ton frère devient là-dedans?; (*fig*) **this is where we came in!** nous sommes revenus à la case départ!

b *[fashion]* faire son entrée *or* apparition dans la mode. **when do strawberries come in?** quand commence la saison des fraises?

c (*in a race*) arriver. **he came in fourth** il est arrivé quatrième; (*Scol*) **he came in first in geography** il a eu la meilleure note en géographie, il a été premier en géographie.

d (*Pol: be elected to power*) être élu, arriver au pouvoir. **the socialists came in at the last election** les socialistes sont arrivés au pouvoir aux dernières élections.

e **he has £10,000 coming in every year** il touche *or* encaisse 10 000 livres chaque année; **there is at least £200 coming in each week to that household** c'est au moins 200 livres par semaine qui entrent dans ce ménage; **if I'm not working my pay won't be coming in** si je ne travaille pas ma paye ne tombera pas.

f **to come in handy** *or* **useful** avoir son utilité, venir à propos; **to come in handy** *or* **useful for sth** servir à qch, être commode pour qch.

►**come in for** vt fus (*receive*) *criticism* être l'objet de, subir, être en butte à; *reproach* subir; *praise* recevoir.

►**come into** vt fus (*inherit*) hériter de, entrer en possession de. **to come into some money** (*gen*) recevoir une somme d'argent; (*by inheritance*) hériter (d'une somme d'argent); (*fig*) **to come into one's own** se réaliser, trouver sa voie.

►**come near to** vt fus: **to come near to doing** faillir faire, être près de faire, être à deux doigts de faire; **I came near to telling her everything** pour un peu je lui aurais tout dit, j'étais à deux doigts de tout lui dire; **he came near to (committing) suicide** il a failli se suicider.

►**come off** 1 vi a *[button]* se détacher, se découdre; *[stains, marks]* s'enlever, partir.

b (*take place*) avoir lieu, se produire. **her wedding did not come off after all** son mariage n'a finalement pas eu lieu.

c (*succeed*) *[plans etc]* se réaliser; *[attempts, experiments]* réussir.

d (*acquit o.s.*) se tirer d'affaire, s'en tirer, s'en sortir. **he came off well by comparison with his brother** il s'en est très bien tiré en comparaison de son frère; **to come off best** gagner.

e (*Theat*) *[actor]* sortir de scène; *[play]* s'arrêter, cesser d'être donné.

f (*‡: reach orgasm*) partir‡.

2 vt fus a **a button came off his coat** un bouton s'est détaché *or* décousu de son manteau; **he came off his bike** il est tombé de son vélo; (*Fin*) **to come off the gold standard** abandonner l'étalon-or.

b *drugs, medication* arrêter.

c **come off it!*** et puis quoi encore?, à d'autres!

►**come on** 1 vi a (*follow*) suivre; (*continue to advance*) continuer de venir *or* d'avancer.

b (*imper only*) **come on, try again!** allons *or* voyons *or* allez, encore un effort!

c (*progress, develop*) faire des progrès, avancer, venir bien. **how are your lettuces/plans/children coming on?** où en sont vos laitues/vos projets/vos enfants?; **my lettuces are coming on nicely** mes laitues viennent bien; **my plans are coming on nicely** mes plans avancent; **how are the children? — they're coming on** comment vont les enfants? — ils poussent bien *or* ça pousse!*

d (*start*) *[night]* tomber; *[illness]* se déclarer; *[storm]* survenir, éclater; *[seasons]* arriver. **it came on to rain, the rain came on** il s'est mis à pleuvoir; **I feel a cold coming on** je sens que je m'enrhume.

e (*arise for discussion or judgment*) *[subjects]* être soulevé, être mis *or* venir sur le tapis; *[questions]* être posé. (*Jur*) **his case comes on this afternoon** son affaire viendra devant le juge cet après-midi.

f (*Theat*) *[actor]* entrer en scène; *[play]* être joué *or* représenté *or* donné. **"Hamlet" is coming on next week** on donne "Hamlet" la semaine prochaine.

g (*US fig*) **he came on quite sincere** il a donné l'impression d'être tout à fait sincère; **he came on as a fine man** il a fait l'effet d'être un homme bien.

2 vt fus = **come upon.**

3 **come-on** n *see* **come 2.**

►**come on to** vt fus *question, topic, issue* aborder. **I'll come on to that in a moment** j'aborderai cela dans un moment.

►**come out** vi a (*gen*) sortir (*of* de); *[sun, stars]* paraître, se montrer; *[flowers]* pousser, sortir, venir; *[spots, rash]* sortir; *[secret, news]* être divulgué *or* révélé; *[truth]* se faire jour; *[books, magazines]* paraître, sortir, être publié; *[films]* paraître, sortir; (*Brit Ind: also* **to come out on strike**) se mettre en grève, faire grève; (*go into society*) faire ses débuts dans le monde; *[homosexual]* (*also* **to come out of the closet**) se montrer au grand jour; (*Scol etc: in exams*) se classer; *[qualities]* se manifester, se révéler, se faire remarquer; *[stains]* s'enlever, s'en aller, partir; *[dyes, colours]* (*run*) déteindre; (*fade*) passer, se faner; (*Math*) *[problems]* se résoudre; *[division etc]* tomber juste. **this photo didn't come out well** cette photo n'a rien donné *or* est très mal venue; **the photo came out well** la photo a réussi *or* est très bonne; **you always come out well in photos** tu es toujours très bien sur les photos, tu es très photogénique; **the total comes out at** *or* **to 500** le total s'élève à 500; **he came out third in French** il s'est classé *or* il est troisième en français; (*Med*) **to come out in a rash** avoir une poussée de boutons, avoir une éruption; (*fig*) **to come out for/against sth** se déclarer ouvertement pour/contre qch, prendre position pour/contre qch; (*fig*) **to come out of o.s.** *or* **one's shell** sortir de sa coquille *or* réserve (*fig*).

b (*result from*) **come out of** être né de.

►**come out with*** vt fus (*say*) dire, sortir*, accoucher de‡. **you never know what she's going to come out with next** on ne sait jamais ce qu'elle va sortir*; **come out with it!** dis ce que tu as à dire!, accouche!‡

►**come over** 1 vi a (*lit*) venir. **he came over to England for a few months** il est venu passer quelques mois en Angleterre; **his family came over with the Normans** sa famille s'est installée ici du temps des Normands; (*fig*) **he came over to our side** il est passé de notre côté; **he came over to our way of thinking** il s'est rangé à notre avis.

b (**: feel suddenly*) **to come over queer** *or* **giddy** *or* **funny** se sentir mal tout d'un coup, se sentir tout chose*; **she came over faint** elle a failli s'évanouir *or* tourner de l'œil‡.

c (*make impression*) **he came over well in his speech** son discours l'a bien mis en valeur; **his speech came over well** son discours a fait bonne impression; **he came over as a fine politician** il a donné l'impression d'être un bon homme politique.

2 **vt fus** *[influences, feelings] person* affecter, saisir, s'emparer de. **a feeling of shyness came over her** la timidité la saisit, elle fut saisie de timidité; **I don't know what came over her to speak like that!** je ne sais pas ce qui lui a pris de parler comme cela!; **what's come over you?** qu'est-ce qui vous prend?

►**come round** **vi** a faire le tour *or* un détour. **the road was blocked and we had to come round by the farm** la route était bloquée et nous avons dû faire un détour par la ferme.

b venir, passer. **do come round and see me one evening** passez me voir un de ces soirs.

c (*recur regularly*) revenir périodiquement. **your birthday will soon come round again** ce sera bientôt à nouveau ton anniversaire.

d (*change one's mind*) changer d'avis. **perhaps in time she will come round** peut-être qu'elle changera d'avis avec le temps; **he came round to our way of thinking in the end** il a fini par se ranger à notre avis.

e (*regain consciousness*) revenir à soi, reprendre connaissance; (*get better*) se rétablir, se remettre (*after* de).

f (*throw off bad mood etc*) se radoucir, redevenir aimable. **leave her alone, she'll soon come round** laissez-la tranquille, elle reviendra bientôt à d'autres sentiments.

g *[boat]* venir au vent.

►**come through** 1 **vi** a (*survive*) s'en tirer. b (*Telec*) **the call came through** on a reçu *or* eu la communication. 2 **vt fus** (*survive*) *illness* survivre à; *danger, war* se tirer indemne de.

►**come through with** **vt fus** (*US*) = **come up with**.

►**come to** 1 **vi** a (*regain consciousness*) revenir à soi, reprendre connaissance. b (*Naut: stop*) s'arrêter. 2 **vt fus** (*Comm etc*) revenir à, se monter à. **how much does it come to?** cela fait combien?, cela se monte à combien?; **it comes to much less per metre if you buy a lot** cela revient beaucoup moins cher le mètre si vous en achetez beaucoup.

►**come together** **vi** (*assemble*) se rassembler; (*meet*) se rencontrer. (*fig*) **to come together again** se réconcilier.

►**come under** **vt fus** a (*be subjected to*) *sb's influence, domination* tomber sous, subir, être soumis à; *attack, criticism* être soumis à, être l'objet de. b (*be classified under*) être classé sous. **that comes under "towns"** c'est classé *or* cela se trouve sous la rubrique "villes"; (*Admin etc*) **this comes under another department** c'est du ressort *or* de la compétence d'un autre service.

►**come up** **vi** a (*lit*) monter. (*fig*) **do you come up to town often?** est-ce que vous êtes souvent en ville?; **he came up to me with a smile** il m'a abordé en souriant; (*Brit*) **he came up to Oxford last year** il est entré à (l'université d')Oxford l'année dernière; (*in restaurant*) **"coming up!"** "ça marche!"; (*fig*) **he has come up in the world** il a grimpé les échelons.

b (*Jur*) *[accused]* comparaître (*before* devant); *[case]* être entendu (*before* par).

c *[plants]* sortir, germer, pointer. **the tulips haven't come up yet** les tulipes ne sont pas encore sorties.

d *[sun]* se lever.

e (*fig*) *[matters for discussion]* être soulevé, être mis *or* venir sur le tapis; *[questions]* se poser, être soulevé. **the question of a subsidy came up** la question d'une subvention s'est posée *or* a été soulevée; **I'm afraid something's come up** malheureusement j'ai eu un empêchement.

f *[job, vacancy]* se présenter.

►**come up against** **vt fus** se heurter (*fig*) à *or* contre. **he came up against total opposition to his plans** il s'est heurté à une opposition radicale à ses projets; **to come up against sb** entrer en conflit avec qn.

►**come upon** **vt fus** a (*attack by surprise*) tomber sur, fondre sur, surprendre. b (*find or meet by chance*) *object* trouver par hasard, tomber sur; *person* rencontrer par hasard, tomber sur.

►**come up to** **vt fus** a (*reach up to*) s'élever jusqu'à, arriver à. **the water came up to his knees** l'eau lui montait *or* venait *or* arrivait jusqu'aux genoux; **my son comes up to my shoulder** mon fils m'arrive à l'épaule. b (*equal*) répondre à. **to come up to sb's hopes** réaliser les *or* répondre aux espoirs de qn; **his work has not come up to our expectation** son travail n'a pas répondu à notre attente.

►**come up with** **vt fus** *object, money, funds* fournir; *idea, plan* proposer, suggérer, sortir*. **he comes up with some good ideas** il sort* de bonnes idées.

Comecon† ['kɒmɪˌkɒn] **n** (**abbr of Council for Mutual Economic Aid**) COMECON *m*.

comedian [kəˈmiːdɪən] **n** a (*Theat*) *[variety]* comique *m*; *[plays]* comédien *m*; (*fig*) comique, pitre *m*, clown *m*. b (††: *author*) auteur *m* de comédies.

comedienne [kəˌmiːdɪˈen] **n** (*Theat*) *[variety]* actrice *f* comique; *[plays]* comédienne *f*.

comedy ['kɒmɪdɪ] **n** (*play: also fig*) comédie *f*; (*NonC: style of play*) la comédie, le genre comique. **C~ of Errors** Comédie des Méprises; **~ of manners** comédie de mœurs; **high ~** haute comédie; **low ~** farce *f*; (*fig*) **cut (out) the ~!**‡ pas de comédie!; *see* **musical.**

comeliness ['kʌmlɪnɪs] **n** (*see* **comely**) (*liter*) beauté *f*, charme *m*, grâce *f*; (††) bienséance *f*.

comely ['kʌmlɪ] **adj** (*liter: beautiful*) beau (*f* belle), charmant, gracieux; (††: *proper*) bienséant.

comer ['kʌmə^r] **n** (**gen in comps**) arrivant(e) *m(f)*. **open to all ~s** ouvert à tout venant *or* à tous; **the first ~** le premier venu, le premier arrivant; *see* **late, new** *etc*.

comestible† [kəˈmestɪbl] 1 **adj** comestible. 2 **n** (*gen pl*) **~s** denrées *fpl* comestibles, comestibles *mpl*.

comet ['kɒmɪt] **n** comète *f*.

comeuppance* [ˌkʌmˈʌpəns] **n**: **to get one's ~*** recevoir ce qu'on mérite; **he got his ~*** il a échoué (*or* perdu *etc*) et il ne l'a pas volé* *or* et il l'a bien cherché.

comfit ['kʌmfɪt] **n** dragée *f*.

comfort ['kʌmfət] 1 **n** a (*well-being: NonC*) confort *m*, bien-être *m*. (*material goods*) **~s** aises *fpl*, commodités *fpl* (de la vie); **he has always been used to ~** il a toujours eu tout le *or* son confort; **to live in ~** vivre dans l'aisance *or* à l'aise; **every (modern) ~** tout le confort moderne; **he likes his ~s** il aime ses aises; **he has never lacked ~s** il n'a jamais manqué des choses matérielles.

b (*consolation*) consolation *f*, réconfort *m*, soulagement *m*. **to take ~ from sth** trouver du réconfort *or* une consolation à *or* dans qch; **your presence is/you are a great ~ to me** votre présence est/vous êtes pour moi d'un grand réconfort; **if it's any ~ to you** si ça peut te consoler; **it is a ~ to know that ...** c'est un soulagement *or* c'est consolant de savoir que ...; **to take ~ from the fact that/from the knowledge that** trouver rassurant le fait que/de savoir que; *see* **cold.**

c (*peace of mind*) **the fighting was too close for (my) ~** les combats étaient trop près pour ma tranquillité (d'esprit) *or* mon goût.

2 **comp** ► **comfort station** (*US euph*) toilette(s) *f(pl)*.

3 **vt** (*console*) consoler; (*bring relief to*) soulager; (††: *hearten*) réconforter, encourager.

comfortable ['kʌmfətəbl] **adj** *armchair, bed, journey, hotel* confortable; *temperature* agréable; *person* à l'aise; *thought, idea, news* rassurant, réconfortant; *win, majority* confortable. **I am quite ~ here** je me trouve très bien ici; **to make o.s. ~** (*in armchair etc*) s'installer confortablement; (*make o.s. at home*) se mettre à son aise, faire comme chez soi; **to have a ~ income** avoir un revenu très suffisant; **he is in ~ circumstances** il mène une vie aisée *or* large; (*Sport etc*) **we've got a ~ lead** nous avons une bonne avance; (*fig*) **I am not very ~ about it** cela m'inquiète un peu.

comfortably ['kʌmfətəblɪ] **adv** (*see* **comfortable**) confortablement; agréablement; à son aise, à l'aise; *live* à l'aise, dans l'aisance. **they are ~ off** ils sont à l'aise.

comforter ['kʌmfətə^r] **n** (*person*) consolateur *m*, -trice *f* (*liter*); (*scarf*) cache-nez *m inv*; (*dummy-teat*) tétine *f*, sucette *f*; (*US: quilt*) édredon *m*.

comforting ['kʌmfətɪŋ] **adj** (*see* **comfort 3**) consolant; soulageant; réconfortant, encourageant. **it is ~ to think that ...** il est réconfortant de penser que ... .

comfortless ['kʌmfətlɪs] **adj** *room* sans confort; *person* désolé, triste; *thought, prospect* désolant, peu rassurant, triste.

comfy* ['kʌmfɪ] **adj** *chair, room etc* confortable, agréable. **are you ~?** êtes-vous bien?

comic ['kɒmɪk] 1 **adj** comique, amusant; (*Theat*) comique, de la comédie. **~ opera** opéra *m* comique; **~ relief** (*Theat*) intervalle *m* comique; (*fig*) moment *m* de détente (comique); **~ verse** poésie *f* humoristique. 2 **n** a (*person*) (acteur *m*) comique *m*, actrice *f* comique. b (*magazine*) comic *m*. (*within newspaper etc*) **the ~s** les bandes dessinées. 3 **comp** ► **comic book** magazine *m* de bandes dessinées ► **comic strip** bande dessinée.

comical ['kɒmɪkəl] **adj** drôle, cocasse, comique.

comically ['kɒmɪkəlɪ] **adv** drôlement, comiquement.

coming ['kʌmɪŋ] 1 **n** a arrivée *f*, venue *f*. **~ and going** va-et-vient *m*; **~s and goings** allées *fpl* et venues; **~ away/back/down/in/out** *etc* départ *m*/retour *m*/descente *f*/entrée *f*/sortie *f etc*. b (*Rel*) avènement *m*; *see* **second**[1]. c **~ of age** passage *m* à l'âge adulte. 2 **adj** a (*future*) à venir, futur; (*in the near future*) prochain. **the ~ year** l'année à venir, l'année prochaine; **~ generations** les générations à venir *or* futures. b (*promising*) qui promet, d'avenir. **a ~ politician** un homme politique d'avenir; **it's the ~ thing*** c'est le truc* à la mode; *see* **up.**

Comintern† ['kɒmɪnˌtɜːn] **n** Komintern *m*.

comity ['kɒmɪtɪ] **n** courtoisie *f*. (*Jur*) **~ of nations** courtoisie internationale.

comm. a **abbr of commerce.** b **abbr of commercial.** c **abbr of committee.**

comma ['kɒmə] **n** a (*Gram*) virgule *f*; *see* **invert.** b (*Mus*) comma *m*.

command [kəˈmɑːnd] 1 **vt** a (*order*) ordonner, commander, donner l'ordre (*sb to do* à qn de faire). **to ~ that ...** ordonner *or* commander que ... + *subj*; **to ~ sth to be done** donner l'ordre de (faire) faire qch.

b (*be in control of*) *army, ship* commander; *passions, instincts* maîtriser, dominer.

c (*be in position to use*) *money, services, resources* disposer de, avoir à sa disposition.

d (*deserve and get*) *respect etc* imposer, exiger. **that ~s a high price** cela se vend très cher.

e *[places, building]* (*overlook*) avoir vue sur, donner sur; (*overlook and control*) commander, dominer.

2 **vi** (*be in* ~) (*Mil, Naut*) commander, avoir le commandement; (*gen*) commander; (*order*) commander, donner un ordre.

3 **n** a (*order*) ordre *m*; (*Mil*) commandement *m*; (*Comput*) commande *f*. **at** *or* **by the ~ of** sur l'ordre de; **at the word of ~** au commandement.

b (*NonC: Mil: power, authority*) commandement *m*. **to be in ~ of** être à la tête de, avoir sous ses ordres; **to have/take ~ of** avoir/prendre le commandement de; **under the ~ of** sous le commandement *or* les ordres de; (*gen*) **who's in ~ here?** qui est-ce qui commande ici?; *see* **second**[1].

c (*Mil*) (*troops*) troupes *fpl*; (*district*) région *f* militaire; (*military authority*) commandement *m*; *see* **high** *etc*.

d (*fig: possession, mastery*) maîtrise *f*, possession *f*. **~ of the seas** maîtrise des mers; **he has a ~ of 3 foreign languages** il possède 3 langues étrangères; **his ~ of English** sa maîtrise de l'anglais; **to have at one's ~** avoir à sa disposition; **all the money at my ~** tout l'argent à ma disposition *or* dont je peux disposer; **to be at sb's ~** être à la disposition de qn, être prêt à obéir à qn **to be in full ~ of one's faculties** être en pleine possession de ses moyens.

4 **comp** ▸ **command economy** économie *f* planifiée ▸ **command key** (*Comput*) touche *f* de commande ▸ **command language** (*Comput*) ordres *mpl* de gestion ▸ **command line** (*Comput*) ligne *f* de commande ▸ **command module** (*Space*) module *m* de commande ▸ **command performance** (*Brit Theat*) ≃ représentation *f* de gala (*à la requête du souverain*) ▸ **command post** (*Mil*) poste *m* de commandement.

commandant [ˈkɒmənˌdænt] **n** (*Mil*) commandant *m* (*d'un camp militaire, d'une place forte etc*).

commandeer [ˌkɒmənˈdɪəʳ] **vt** réquisitionner.

commander [kəˈmɑːndəʳ] **n** a (*gen*) chef *m*; (*Mil*) commandant *m*; (*Naut*) capitaine *m* de frégate; (*Brit Police*) ≃ commissaire *m* (de police) divisionnaire, divisionnaire *m*. (*Mil*) **~ in chief** (**~s ~ ~**) commandant *m* en chef, généralissime *m*; *see* **lieutenant, wing.** b *[order of chivalry]* commandeur *m*.

commanding [kəˈmɑːndɪŋ] 1 **adj** a *look* impérieux; *air* imposant; *voice, tone* impérieux, de commandement. b *position* (*overlooking*) élevé; (*overlooking and controlling*) dominant. (*lit, fig*) **to be in a ~ position** avoir une position dominante. 2 **comp** ▸ **commanding officer** (*Mil*) commandant *m*.

commandment [kəˈmɑːndmənt] **n** commandement *m* (*de Dieu ou de l'Église*). **the Ten C~s** les dix commandements, le décalogue (*frm*).

commando [kəˈmɑːndəʊ] **n, pl ~s** *or* **~es** (*all senses*) commando *m*.

commemorate [kəˈmeməreɪt] **vt** commémorer.

commemoration [kəˌmeməˈreɪʃən] **n** commémoration *f*; (*Rel*) commémoraison *f*.

commemorative [kəˈmemərətɪv] **adj** commémoratif.

commence [kəˈmens] **vti** commencer (*sth* qch, *to do, doing* à faire). (*Jur*) **to ~ proceedings against** former un recours contre (*devant une juridiction*).

commencement [kəˈmensmənt] **n** a commencement *m*, début *m*; *[law]* date *f* d'entrée en vigueur. b (*Univ: Cambridge, Dublin, US*) remise *f* des diplômes.

commend [kəˈmend] **vt** (*praise*) louer, faire l'éloge de; (*recommend*) recommander, conseiller; (*entrust*) confier (*to* à), remettre (*to* aux soins de). **to ~ o.s. to** *[person]* se recommander à; *[idea, project]* être du goût de; **his scheme did not ~ itself to the public** son projet n'a pas été du goût du public; **his scheme has little to ~ it** son projet n'a pas grand-chose qui le fasse recommander; (†, *frm*) **~ me to Mr X** présentez mes devoirs à M. X (*frm*), rappelez-moi au bon souvenir de M. X; **to ~ one's soul to God** recommander son âme à Dieu.

commendable [kəˈmendəbl] **adj** louable.

commendably [kəˈmendəblɪ] **adv** *behave etc* d'une façon louable. **that was ~ short** cela avait le mérite de la brièveté.

commendation [ˌkɒmenˈdeɪʃən] **n** a (*see* **commend**) louange *f*, éloge *m*; recommandation *f*. b (*NonC*) remise *f* (*to* à, aux soins de).

commensurable [kəˈmenʃərəbl] **adj** commensurable (*with, to* avec).

commensurate [kəˈmenʃərɪt] **adj** (*of equal extent*) de même mesure (*with* que); (*Math*) coétendu (*with* à), de même mesure (*with* que); (*proportionate*) proportionné (*with, to* à).

comment [ˈkɒment] 1 **n** (*spoken, written*) commentaire *m* (*bref*), observation *f*, remarque *f*; (*written*) annotation *f*; (*critical*) critique *f*. **his action went** *or* **passed without ~** son action n'a donné lieu à aucun commentaire; **he let it pass without ~** il ne l'a pas relevé; (*Press*) **"no ~"** "je n'ai rien à dire"; **he passed a sarcastic ~** il a fait une observation *or* une remarque sarcastique; **put your ~s in the margin** inscrivez vos commentaires dans la marge; (*Scol: on report*) **teacher's ~s** appréciations *fpl* du professeur.

2 **vt** *text* commenter. **he ~ed that ...** il a remarqué que ..., il a fait la remarque que ... .

3 **vi** faire des remarques *or* des observations *or* des commentaires. **to ~ on sth** commenter qch, faire des remarques *or* des observations sur qch.

commentary [ˈkɒməntərɪ] **n** (*remarks*) commentaire *m*, observation *f*; (*Rad, TV: on news, events*) commentaire; (*Sport*) reportage *m*; *see* **running.**

commentate [ˈkɒmenteɪt] 1 **vi** (*Rad, TV*) faire un reportage (*on* sur). 2 **vt** (*Rad, TV*) *match* commenter.

commentator [ˈkɒmenteɪtəʳ] **n** a (*Rad, TV*) reporter *m*; *see* **sport.** b (*on texts etc*) commentateur *m*, -trice *f*.

commerce [ˈkɒmɜːs] **n** a (*Comm*) commerce *m* (*généralement en gros ou international*), affaires *fpl*. **he is in ~** il est dans le commerce *or* dans les affaires; (*US*) **Secretary/Department of C~** ≃ ministre *m*/ministère *m* du Commerce; *see* **chamber.** b (*fig: intercourse, dealings*) relations *fpl*, rapports *mpl*.

commercial [kəˈmɜːʃəl] 1 **adj** (*Admin, Comm, Fin, Jur*) *dealings, art, attaché, radio, TV* commercial; *world* du commerce; *value* marchand, commercial; *district* commerçant. **~ artist** dessinateur *m* de publicité, créateur *m*, -trice *f* publicitaire, graphiste *mf*; **~ bank** banque commerciale *or* de commerce; (*TV, Rad*) **~ break** page *f* de publicité; **~ college** école *f* de commerce; **~ law** droit *m* commercial; **~ traveller** voyageur *m or* représentant *m* de commerce, commis-voyageur† *m*; **~ vehicle** véhicule *m* utilitaire; *see* **establishment.** 2 **n** (*Rad, TV*) annonce *f* publicitaire, publicité *f*, spot *m*.

commercialese [kəˌmɜːʃəˈliːz] **n** jargon *m* commercial.

commercialism [kəˈmɜːʃəlɪzəm] **n** (*NonC*) (*attitude*) mercantilisme *m* (*pej*), esprit commerçant; (*on large scale*) affairisme *m* (*pej*); (*business practice*) (pratique *f* du) commerce *m*, (pratique des) affaires *fpl*.

commercialization [kəˌmɜːʃəlaɪˈzeɪʃən] **n** commercialisation *f*.

commercialize [kəˈmɜːʃəlaɪz] **vt** commercialiser.

commercialized [kəˈmɜːʃəlaɪzd] **adj** (*pej*) commercial.

commercially [kəˈmɜːʃəlɪ] **adv** commercialement.

commie* [ˈkɒmɪ] **adj, n** (**abbr of communist**) coco‡ (*mf*) (*pej*).

commiserate [kəˈmɪzəreɪt] **vi** (*show commiseration*) témoigner de la sympathie (*with* à); (*feel commiseration*) éprouver de la commisération (*with* pour). **I do ~ with you** je compatis; **I went to ~ with him on his exam results** je suis allé m'apitoyer avec lui sur ses résultats d'examen.

commiseration [kəˌmɪzəˈreɪʃən] **n** commisération *f*.

commissar† [ˈkɒmɪsɑːʳ] **n** commissaire *m* du peuple (*en URSS etc*).

commissariat [ˌkɒmɪˈsɛərɪət] **n** (*Mil*) intendance *f*; (*Admin, Pol*) commissariat *m*; (*food supply*) ravitaillement *m*.

commissary [ˈkɒmɪsərɪ] **n** a (*US Mil etc: shop*) intendance *f*. b (*US Mil: officer*) intendant *m*. c (*US Cine*) restaurant *m* du studio. d (*representative*) représentant *m*; (*Rel: of bishop*) délégué *m* (*d'un évêque*).

commission [kəˈmɪʃən] 1 **n** a (*gen*) ordres *mpl*, instructions *fpl*; (*to artist etc*) commande *f*. **he gave the artist a ~** il a passé une commande à l'artiste.

b (*Comm*) commission *f*, courtage *m*. **on a ~ basis** à la commission; **he gets 10 % ~** il reçoit une commission de 10 %.

c (*errand*) commission *f*.

d (*NonC*) *[crime etc]* perpétration *f* (*Jur, liter*).

e (*official warrant*) pouvoir *m*, mandat *m*; (*Mil*) brevet *m*. **to get one's ~** être nommé officier; **to give up one's ~** démissionner.

f (*NonC: delegation of authority etc*) délégation *f* de pouvoir *or* d'autorité, mandat *m*.

g (*body of people*) commission *f*, comité *m*. **~ of inquiry** commission d'enquête; (*Brit*) **C~ for Racial Equality** *commission pour l'égalité des races; see* **royal.**

h (*NonC: Naut*) armement *m* (*d'un navire*). **to put in ~** armer; **to take out of ~** désarmer; **in ~** en armement, en service; **out of ~** (*Naut*) hors de service; (*Naut: in reserve*) en réserve; (*gen: not in working order*) hors service.

2 **comp** ▸ **commission agent** (*bookmaker*) bookmaker *m*; (*Comm*) courtier *m*.

3 **vt** a donner pouvoir *or* mission à, déléguer. **he was ~ed to inquire into ...** il reçut mission de faire une enquête sur ...; **I have been ~ed to say** j'ai été chargé de dire.

b *artist* passer une commande à; *book, painting, article* commander. **this work was ~ed by the town council** cette œuvre a été commandée par le conseil municipal.

c (*Mil etc*) *officer* nommer à un commandement. **~ed officer** officier *m*; **he was ~ed in 1970** il a été nommé officier en 1970; **he was ~ed sub-lieutenant** il a été nommé *or* promu au grade de sous-lieutenant.

d (*Naut*) *ship* mettre en service, armer.

commissionaire [kəˌmɪʃəˈnɛəʳ] **n** (*Brit, Can*) commissionnaire *m* (*d'un hôtel etc*), chasseur *m*, coursier *m*.

commissioner [kəˈmɪʃənəʳ] **n** membre *m* d'une commission, commissaire *m*; (*Brit Police*) ≃ préfet *m* de police; (*US Police*) (commissaire *m*) divisionnaire *m*. (*US Scol, Univ*) **~ of education** ≃

recteur *m*, doyen *m*; (*Jur*) ~ **for oaths** *officier ayant qualité pour recevoir les déclarations sous serment;* (*Can*) **C~ of Official Languages** Commissaire *m* aux langues officielles; *see* **high, lord.**

commit [kəˈmɪt] **vt** a *crime, sacrilege* commettre; *mistake* commettre, faire. **to ~ hara-kiri** faire hara-kiri; **to ~ perjury** se parjurer, (*Jur*) faire un faux serment; **to ~ suicide** se suicider.

b (*consign*) *letter etc* confier (*to* à), remettre (*to* à la garde de, aux soins de); *person* confier (*to* à). **to ~ sb to sb's care** confier qn à la garde de qn; (*Jur*) **to ~ sb (to prison)** faire incarcérer qn; **to ~ sb to a mental hospital** interner qn; (*Jur*) **to ~ sb for trial** mettre qn en accusation; **to ~ to writing** *or* **to paper** consigner *or* coucher par écrit; (*liter*) **to ~ to the flames** livrer aux flammes; **to ~ to memory** apprendre par cœur; (*US Jur*) **~ting magistrate** juge *m* d'instruction.

c (*Parl*) *bill* renvoyer à une commission.

d **to ~ o.s.** s'engager (*to sth* à qch, *to doing* à faire); **to be ~ted to a policy** s'être engagé à poursuivre une politique; **I'm afraid I'm ~ted** je regrette, je me suis déjà engagé.

commitment [kəˈmɪtmənt] **n** a (*gen*) engagement *m*; (*responsibility, obligation*) charges *fpl*, responsabilité(s) *f(pl)*; (*Comm, Fin*) engagement financier. (*Comm*) **"without ~"** "sans obligation"; (*Fin*) **~ fee** commission *f* d'engagement; **teaching ~s** (heures *fpl* d')enseignement *m*; **he has heavy teaching ~s** il a un enseignement chargé; (*Comm etc*) **to have a ~ to another firm** avoir des obligations envers une autre société. b (*Jur: also* **~ order**) mandat *m* de dépôt. c (*Parl*) *[bill]* renvoi *m* à une commission.

committal [kəˈmɪtl] **n** a (*NonC*) remise *f* (*to* à, aux soins de); (*to prison*) incarcération *f*, emprisonnement *m*; (*to mental hospital*) internement *m*; (*burial*) mise *f* en terre. **~ for trial** mise en accusation; (*Jur*) **~ order** mandat *m* de dépôt; **~ proceedings** ≈ mise *f* en accusation. b (*NonC*) *[crime etc]* perpétration *f* (*Jur, liter*). c (*Parl*) = **commitment c.**

committed [kəˈmɪtɪd] **adj** *writer etc* engagé; *Christian etc* convaincu; *parent etc* dévoué, attentif. **a ~ supporter** un supporter ardent.

committee [kəˈmɪtɪ] 1 **n** commission *f*, comité *m*; (*Parl*) commission. **to be** *or* **sit on a ~** faire partie d'une commission *or* d'un comité; (*Parl*) **~ of inquiry** commission d'enquête; (*US Pol*) **C~ of the Whole** *séance de commission étendue à la chambre entière; see* **management, organize.** 2 **comp** ▸ **committee meeting** réunion *f* de commission *or* de comité ▸ **committee member** membre *m* d'une commission *or* d'un comité.

commode [kəˈməʊd] **n** a (*chest of drawers*) commode *f*. b (*also* **night-~**) chaise percée.

commodious [kəˈməʊdɪəs] **adj** spacieux, vaste.

commodity [kəˈmɒdɪtɪ] 1 **n** produit *m* de base, matière première; (*consumer goods*) produit *m*, article *m*; (*food*) denrée *f*. **staple commodities** produits de base; **household commodities** articles de ménage; **dollar commodities** matières premières négociées en dollars. 2 **comp** ▸ **commodity exchange** bourse *f* du commerce *or* des marchandises ▸ **commodity loan** financement *m* de marchandises gagées ▸ **commodity markets** bourse *f* de marchandises ▸ **commodity-producing countries** pays *mpl* de production primaire ▸ **commodity trade** négoce *m* de matières premières.

commodore [ˈkɒmədɔːʳ] **n** (*Mil*) contre-amiral *m*; (*Naut*) commodore *m*; *[yacht club]* président *m*; *[shipping line]* doyen *m* (*des capitaines*).

common [ˈkɒmən] 1 **adj** a (*used by or affecting many*) *interest, cause, language* commun. **to make ~ cause with sb** faire cause commune avec qn; **by ~ consent** d'un commun accord; (*fig*) **~ ground** point commun, terrain *m* d'entente; **there is no ~ ground for negotiations** il n'y a aucun terrain d'entente pour (entreprendre) des négociations; **it's ~ knowledge** *or* **property that ...** chacun sait que ..., il est de notoriété publique que ...; **~ land** terrain communal *or* banal; **~ lodging house** hospice *m*, asile *m* de nuit; **the C~ Market** le Marché commun; **C~ Agricultural Policy** politique *f* agricole commune; **~ ownership** copropriété *f*; (*Admin, Jur*) **~ prostitute** prostituée *f*; **~ wall** mur mitoyen; (*Jur*) **~ assault** voie *f* de fait simple; *see* **talk.**

b (*usual, ordinary*) commun, ordinaire; *plant* commun; (*universal*) général, universel; (*not outstanding*) moyen, ordinaire. **it's quite ~** c'est très courant, ça n'a rien d'extraordinaire, c'est tout à fait banal (*pej*); **~ belief** croyance universelle; (*Med*) **the ~ cold** le rhume de cerveau; **it's a ~ experience** cela arrive à tout le monde, c'est une chose qui arrive à tout le monde; **it is only ~ courtesy to apologise** la politesse la plus élémentaire veut qu'on s'excuse (*subj*); (*pej*) **the ~ herd** la plèbe, la populace (*pej*); **~ honesty** la simple honnêteté; **the ~ man** l'homme du commun *or* du peuple; **the ~ people** le peuple, les gens du commun (*pej*); **a ~ occurrence** une chose fréquente *or* répandue; **in ~ parlance** dans le langage courant; (*Rel*) **the Book of C~ Prayer** *le livre du rituel anglican;* **the ~ run of mankind** le commun des hommes *or* des mortels; **out of the ~ run** hors du commun, exceptionnel; **~ salt** sel *m* (ordinaire); **~ gull** goéland cendré; **a ~ sight** un spectacle familier; **a ~ soldier** un simple soldat; **~ or garden (adj)** *plant* commun; (*hum*) **he's just a ~ or garden office boy** il n'est qu'un vulgaire *or* simple garçon de bureau; (*hum*) **the ~ or garden variety** le modèle standard *or* ordinaire.

c (*vulgar*) *accent, clothes, person* commun, vulgaire.

d (*Math*) commun. **~ denominator/factor** dénominateur/facteur commun; **~ multiple** commun multiple; *see also* **low 1c.**

e (*Gram*) *gender* non marqué; *noun* commun.

f (*Mus*) **~ time** *or* **measure** (*duple*) mesure *f* à deux temps; (*quadruple*) mesure à quatre temps **~ chord** accord *m* parfait.

2 **n** a (*land*) terrain communal. (*Jur*) **right of ~** *[land]* communauté *f* de jouissance; *[property]* droit *m* de servitude.

b **in ~** en commun; **to hold in ~** partager; (*fig*) **they have nothing in ~** ils n'ont rien de commun; **in ~ with** en commun avec; (*by agreement with*) en accord avec.

3 **comp** ▸ **common area charges** (*US*) charges locatives ▸ **common carrier** transporteur *m* (public), entreprise *f* de transport public ▸ **common core, common-core syllabus** (*Educ*) tronc *m* commun ▸ **common crab** dormeur *m*, tourteau *m* ▸ **Common Entrance** (*Brit Scol*) *examen d'entrée dans l'enseignement privé* ▸ **common law** le droit coutumier; **common-law wife** concubine *f*; **common-law marriage** concubinage *m* ▸ **commonplace adj** banal, commun, ordinaire ◊ **n** lieu commun, platitude *f*, banalité *f*; **such things are commonplace** de telles choses sont courantes *or* sont monnaie courante ▸ **common room** salle commune; (*staffroom*) salle des professeurs ▸ **commonsense** sens commun, bon sens; **commonsense attitude** attitude sensée *or* pleine de bon sens ▸ **common stock** (*US St Ex*) actions cotées en Bourse.

commonality [ˌkɒməˈnælɪtɪ] **n** (*Ind*) standardisation *f*. **we are looking for commonalities** nous cherchons à utiliser des composants communs à plusieurs produits.

commoner [ˈkɒmənəʳ] **n** (*not noble*) roturier *m*, -ière *f*; (*at Univ Oxford etc*) étudiant(e) *m(f)* non boursier (-ière); (*Brit Jur: with common land rights*) personne *f* qui a droit de vaine pâture.

commonly [ˈkɒmənlɪ] **adv** a (*usually*) communément, ordinairement, généralement. b (*vulgarly*) vulgairement, d'une façon vulgaire *or* commune.

commonness [ˈkɒmənnɪs] **n** (*NonC*) (*frequency*) fréquence *f*; (*ordinariness*) caractère commun *or* ordinaire, banalité *f* (*pej*); (*universality*) généralité *f*, universalité *f*, caractère général *or* universel; (*vulgarity*) vulgarité *f*.

commons [ˈkɒmənz] **npl** a **the ~** le peuple, le tiers état; (*Parl*) **the C~** les Communes *fpl*; *see* **house.** b (*food*) nourriture *f* (*partagée en commun*). **to be on short ~** faire maigre chère, être réduit à la portion congrue.

commonweal [ˈkɒmənˌwiːl] **n** (*general good*) bien public; (*the people*) l'État *m*.

commonwealth [ˈkɒmənwelθ] **n** a **the (British) C~ (of Nations)** le Commonwealth; (*Brit*) **Minister of** *or* **Secretary of State for Commonwealth Affairs** ministre *m* du Commonwealth. b (*Brit Hist*) **the C~** la république de Cromwell. c (††) = **commonweal.** d **the C~ of Australia/Puerto Rico** *etc* le Commonwealth d'Australie/de Porto-Rico *etc;* **C~ of Independent States** Communauté *f* des États Indépendants.

commotion [kəˈməʊʃən] **n** a (*noise*) **to make a ~** faire du tapage; **what a ~!** quel brouhaha *or* vacarme! b (*upheaval*) **to cause a ~** semer la perturbation; **what a ~!** quel cirque!; **to be in a (state of) ~** *[person]* être bouleversé *or* vivement ému; *[crowd]* être agité; *[town]* être en émoi. c (*Pol: uprising*) insurrection *f*, révolte *f*, troubles *mpl*; *see* **civil.**

communal [ˈkɒmjuːnl] **adj** (*of whole community*) *profit, good* communautaire, de la communauté; (*owned etc in common*) commun. **a ~ bathroom** une salle de bains commune; **~ life** la vie collective.

communally [ˈkɒmjuːnəlɪ] **adv** en commun, collectivement.

commune [kəˈmjuːn] 1 **vi** a converser intimement, avoir un entretien à cœur ouvert (*with* avec). **to ~ with nature** communier avec la nature. b (*US Rel*) communier. 2 [ˈkɒmjuːn] **n** a (*group of people living together*) communauté *f*. **to live in a ~** vivre en communauté. b (*administrative division*) commune *f*. c (*French Hist*) **the C~** la Commune.

communicable [kəˈmjuːnɪkəbl] **adj** communicable; (*Med*) transmissible.

communicant [kəˈmjuːnɪkənt] 1 **n** a (*Rel*) communiant(e) *m(f)*. b (*informant*) informateur *m*, -trice *f*. 2 **adj** a qui communique (avec), communicant. b (*Rel*) **~ member** fidèle *mf*, pratiquant(e) *m(f)*.

communicate [kəˈmjuːnɪkeɪt] 1 **vt** a *news etc* communiquer, transmettre, faire parvenir *or* connaître; *illness* transmettre (*to* à); *feelings, enthusiasm etc* communiquer, faire partager. b (*Rel*) donner la communion à. 2 **vi** a communiquer, se mettre en rapport, entrer en contact *or* relations (*with* avec). **to ~ with sb by letter/by telephone** communiquer avec qn par lettre/par téléphone; **I no longer ~ with him** je n'ai plus aucun contact avec lui. b *[rooms]* communiquer. **communicating rooms** des chambres qui communiquent *or* communicantes. c (*Rel*) communier, recevoir la communion.

communication [kəˌmjuːnɪˈkeɪʃən] 1 **n** a (*NonC*) communication *f*. **to be in ~ with sb** être en contact *or* rapport *or* relations avec qn, avoir des communications avec qn; **to be in radio ~ with sb** communiquer avec qn par radio; **to get into ~ with sb** se mettre *or* entrer en contact *or* rapport *or* relations avec qn; **there is/has been no ~ between them** il n'y a/n'y a eu aucun contact entre eux.

b (*message transmitted*) communication *f*, message *m*, information *f*, renseignement *m*.

c (*roads, railways, telegraph lines etc*) ~**s** communications *fpl*; (*Mil*) liaison *f*, communications.

2 comp ▸ **communication cord** (*Brit Rail*) sonnette *f* d'alarme ▸ **communication gap** manque *m or* absence *f* de communication ▸ **communication line** (*Mil etc*) ligne *f* de communication ▸ **communications satellite** satellite *m* de communication ▸ **communication science** sciences *fpl* de la communication ▸ **communication skills** techniques *fpl* de communication ▸ **communications zone** (zone *f* des) arrières *mpl*.

communicative [kə'mju:nɪkətɪv] adj a (*talkative*) communicatif, expansif, bavard. b *difficulties etc* de communication. ~ **competence** compétence *f* à la communication.

communion [kə'mju:nɪən] 1 n (*gen*) communion *f*; (*Rel*) (*religious group*) communion; (*denomination*) confession *f*; (*also* **Holy C~**) communion. **a ~ of interests** des intérêts *mpl* en commun; **to make one's ~** communier; **to make one's Easter ~** faire ses pâques; **to take ~** recevoir la communion. 2 comp ▸ **communion rail** (*Rel*) table *f* de communion, balustre *m* du chœur ▸ **communion service** office *m* de communion (*protestant*) ▸ **communion table** sainte table.

communiqué [kə'mju:nɪkeɪ] n communiqué *m*; *see* **joint**.

communism ['kɒmjʊnɪzəm] n communisme *m*.

communist ['kɒmjʊnɪst] adj, n communiste (*mf*). **the C~ Manifesto** le Manifeste communiste.

communistic [ˌkɒmjʊ'nɪstɪk] adj communisant.

community [kə'mju:nɪtɪ] 1 n a (*group of people*) communauté *f*, groupement *m*; *[monks, nuns]* communauté. **the French ~ in Edinburgh** la colonie française d'Édimbourg; **the student ~** les étudiants *mpl*, le monde étudiant; **to belong to the same ~** appartenir à la même communauté; **the ~** le public, la communauté; **for the good of the ~** pour le bien de la communauté.

b (*common ownership*) propriété collective; (*Jur*) communauté *f*. **~ of goods/interests** communauté de biens/d'intérêts.

c (*Pol: EEC*) **the C~** la Communauté.

2 comp ▸ **community antenna distribution** câblodistribution *f* ▸ **Community antenna television** télévision *f* à émission régionale ▸ **Community bodies/budget** (*Pol*) instances *fpl*/budget *m* communautaire(s) ▸ **community centre** foyer municipal ▸ **community charge** (*Brit Pol*) capitation *f* ▸ **community chest** (*US*) fonds commun ▸ **community college** (*US Univ*) centre *m* universitaire (de premier cycle) ▸ **community correctional center** (*US*) centre *m* de détention ▸ **community education** (*Brit*) cours *mpl* organisés par les municipalités ▸ **community health centre** centre médico-social ▸ **community home** (*Brit*) centre *m* d'éducation surveillée ▸ **community hospital** (*US Med*) hôpital communal ▸ **community life** (*Soc*) la vie associative ▸ **community medicine** médecine générale ▸ **community policeman** (*Brit*) ≃ îlotier *m* ▸ **community policing** ≃ îlotage *m* ▸ **community property** (*US Jur*) communauté *f* des biens entre époux ▸ **Community regulations** (*Pol*) règlements *mpl* communautaires ▸ **community school** (*Brit*) école servant de maison de la culture ▸ **community service** (*Jur*) travaux *mpl* d'intérêt général ▸ **community singing** chants *mpl* en chœur (*improvisés*) ▸ **community spirit** sens *m or* esprit *m* communautaire, sens de la solidarité ▸ **community worker** animateur *m*, -trice *f* socio(-)culturel(le).

communize ['kɒmju:naɪz] vt a *people, countries* (*convert to communism*) convertir au communisme; (*impose communism on*) imposer le régime communiste à. b *land, factories* collectiviser.

commutability [kəˌmju:tə'bɪlɪtɪ] n interchangeabilité *f*, permutabilité *f*; (*Jur*) commuabilité *f*.

commutable [kə'mju:təbl] adj interchangeable, permutable; (*Jur*) commuable (*to* en).

commutation [ˌkɒmjʊ'teɪʃən] n a échange *m*, substitution *f*; (*Fin*) échange; (*Elec, Jur*) commutation *f*. (*Jur*) **~ of punishment** commutation de peine. b (*US*) trajet journalier. ~ **ticket** carte *f* d'abonnement.

commutative [kə'mju:tətɪv] adj (*Math*) ~ **laws** lois commutatives.

commutator ['kɒmjʊˌteɪtə] n commutateur *m*.

commute [kə'mju:t] 1 vt substituer (*into* à); interchanger, échanger (*for, into* pour, contre, avec); (*Elec*) commuer; (*Jur*) commuer (*into* en). (*Jur*) **~d sentence** sentence commuée. 2 vi faire un *or* le trajet régulier, faire la navette (*between* entre, *from* de).

commuter [kə'mju:təʳ] n banlieusard(e) *m(f)* (*qui fait un trajet régulier pour se rendre à son travail*). (*Brit*) **I work in London but I'm a ~** je travaille à Londres mais je fais la navette; (*Brit*) **the ~ belt** la grande banlieue; **~ train** train *m* de banlieue.

commuting [kə'mju:tɪŋ] n (*NonC*) migrations quotidiennes, trajets réguliers. **~ every day is hell!** venir de la banlieue tous les jours, c'est l'enfer!

Comoro ['kɒməˌrəʊ] n: **the ~ Islands, the ~s** les Comores *fpl*.

compact [kəm'pækt] 1 adj (*lit*) compact, dense, serré; (*fig*) *style* concis, condensé. **~ disc** disque compact; **~ disc player** lecteur *m* de disques compacts; **~ video disc** compact disc *m* vidéo; **a ~ mass** une masse compacte; **the house is very ~** la maison n'a pas de place perdue. 2 vt (*gen pass*) (*lit*) rendre compact, resserrer; (*fig*) condenser. (††) **~ed of** composé de. 3 ['kɒmpækt] n a (*agreement*) contrat *m*, convention *f*; (*informal*) entente *f*. b (*also* **powder ~**) poudrier *m*. c (*US: also* **~ car**) (voiture *f*) compacte *f*, voiture *f* de faible encombrement. d (*also* **compact camera**) (appareil-photo *m*) compact *m*.

compactly [kəm'pæktlɪ] adv (*see* **compact 1**) d'une manière *or* de façon compacte; (*fig*) dans un style concis, d'une manière concise. **~ built/designed** construit/conçu sans perte de place *or* sans espace perdu.

compactness [kəm'pæktnɪs] n (*see* **compact 1**) compacité *f*, densité *f*; (*fig*) concision *f*. **the ~ of the kitchen** l'économie *f* d'espace dans la cuisine.

companion [kəm'pænjən] 1 n a compagnon *m*, compagne *f*; (*also* **lady ~**) dame *f* de compagnie; (*in order of knighthood*) compagnon. **travelling ~s** compagnons de voyage; **~s in arms/in misfortune** compagnons d'armes/d'infortune. b (*one of pair of objects*) pendant *m*. c (*handbook*) manuel *m*. 2 comp ▸ **companion ladder** (*Naut*) (*Navy*) échelle *f*; (*Merchant Navy*) escalier *m* ▸ **companion volume** volume *m* qui va de pair (*to* avec) ▸ **companionway** (*Naut*) escalier *m* des cabines; *[small vessel]* montée *f*, descente *f*; (*in yacht: also* **companion hatch**) capot *m* (d'escalier).

companionable [kəm'pænjənəbl] adj *person* sociable, d'une société agréable; *presence* sympathique.

companionship [kəm'pænjənʃɪp] n (*NonC*) a (*friendliness*) **I enjoy the ~ at the club** j'apprécie la camaraderie *or* l'esprit cordial du cercle. b (*company*) compagnie *f*. **she keeps a cat for ~** elle a un chat, ça lui fait une compagnie.

company ['kʌmpənɪ] 1 n a compagnie *f*. **to keep sb ~** tenir compagnie à qn; **to keep ~ with** fréquenter; **to part ~ with** se séparer de; **in ~** en public *or* société; **in ~ with** en compagnie de; **he is good ~** on ne s'ennuie pas avec lui; **he's bad ~** il n'est pas d'une compagnie très agréable; **she keeps a cat, it's ~ for her** elle a un chat, ça lui fait une compagnie *or* ça lui tient compagnie; *see* **two**.

b (*guests*) assemblée *f*, compagnie *f*, société *f*. **we are expecting ~** nous attendons des visites *or* des invités; **we've got ~** nous avons de la visite*; (*lit, fig*) **to be in good ~** être en bonne compagnie; *see* **present**.

c (*companions*) compagnie *f*, fréquentation *f*. **to keep** *or* **get into good/bad ~** avoir de bonnes/mauvaises fréquentations; **she is no(t) fit ~ for your sister** ce n'est pas une compagnie *or* une fréquentation pour votre sœur; (*Prov*) **a man is known by the ~ he keeps** dis-moi qui tu hantes, je te dirai qui tu es (*Prov*).

d (*Comm, Fin*) société *f*, compagnie *f*, firme *f*. **Smith & C~** Smith et Compagnie; **shipping ~** compagnie de navigation; (*US: CIA*) **the C~*** la CIA; (* *also pej*) **... and ~** ... et compagnie; *see* **affiliate, holding** *etc*.

e (*group*) compagnie *f*; *[actors]* troupe *f*, compagnie. **National Theatre C~** la troupe du Théâtre National; (*Naut*) **ship's ~** équipage *m*.

f (*Mil*) compagnie *f*.

2 comp ▸ **Companies Act** (*Jur*) loi *f* sur les sociétés ▸ **company car** (*Brit*) voiture *f* de fonction ▸ **company commander** (*Mil*) capitaine *m* (de compagnie) ▸ **company doctor** médecin *m* du travail ▸ **company director** directeur *m* général ▸ **company law** le droit des affaires ▸ **company lawyer** (*Brit Jur*) avocat *m* d'entreprise; (*working within company*) juriste *m* ▸ **company man** employé dévoué; **he's a real company man** il a vraiment l'esprit maison ▸ **company manners*** (*Brit*) belles manières ▸ **company policy** politique *f* de l'entreprise ▸ **company secretary** (*Brit Comm*) secrétaire général (*d'une société*) ▸ **company sergeant-major** (*Mil*) adjudant *m* ▸ **company time** heures *fpl* de bureau ▸ **company union** (*US*) syndicat-maison *m or* syndicat *m* groupant les employés d'une même société.

comparability [ˌkɒmpərə'bɪlətɪ] n comparabilité *f*. **pay ~** alignement *m* des salaires (*sur ceux d'autres secteurs industriels*).

comparable ['kɒmpərəbl] adj comparable (*with, to* à). **the two things are not ~** il n'y a pas de comparaison possible entre les *or* ces deux choses.

comparative [kəm'pærətɪv] 1 adj a *method* comparatif; *literature etc* comparé; (*Gram*) comparatif. **~ linguistics/law** linguistique comparée/droit comparé. b (*relative*) *cost, freedom* relatif; **to live in ~ luxury** vivre dans un luxe relatif; **he's a ~ stranger** je le connais relativement peu. 2 n (*Gram*) comparatif *m*. **in the ~** au comparatif.

comparatively [kəm'pærətɪvlɪ] adv comparativement; (*relatively*) relativement.

compare [kəm'pɛəʳ] 1 vt a comparer (*with* à, avec), mettre en comparaison *or* dans la balance (*with* avec). **~ the first letter with the second** comparez la première lettre à *or* avec la seconde; **~d to** *or* **with** en comparaison de, par comparaison avec; (*fig*) **to ~ notes with sb** échanger ses impressions *or* ses vues avec qn.

b comparer, assimiler (*to* à). **the poet ~d her eyes to stars** le poète compara ses yeux à des étoiles.

c (*Gram*) *adjective, adverb* former les degrés de comparaison de.

2 vi être comparable (*with* à). **how do the cars ~ for speed?** quelles sont les vitesses respectives des voitures?; **how do the prices ~?** est-ce que les prix sont comparables?; **it doesn't** *or* **can't ~ with the**

previous one il n'y a aucune comparaison avec le précédent; **he can't ~ with you** il n'y a pas de comparaison (possible) entre vous et lui; **it ~s very favourably** cela soutient la comparaison.
3 **n: beyond** *or* **without** *or* **past ~** (adv) incomparablement; (adj) sans comparaison possible.

comparison [kəm'pærɪsn] **n** a comparaison *f*. **in ~ with** en comparaison de; **by ~ (with)** par comparaison (avec); **to stand** *or* **bear ~ (with)** soutenir la comparaison (avec); **there's no ~** il n'y a pas de comparaison (possible); **~ test** essai comparatif. b (*Gram*) comparaison *f*. **degrees of ~** degrés *mpl* de comparaison.

compartment [kəm'pɑːtmənt] **n** compartiment *m*, subdivision *f*; (*Naut, Rail*) compartiment; *see* **water**.

compartmentalize [ˌkɒmpɑːt'mentəlaɪz] **vt** compartimenter.

compass ['kʌmpəs] 1 **n** a boussole *f*; (*Naut*) compas *m*; *see* **box¹**, **point** *etc.* b (*Math*) **~es** (*also* **a pair of ~es**) compas *m*. c (*fig*) (*extent*) étendue *f*; (*reach*) portée *f*; (*scope*) rayon *m*, champ *m*; (*Mus*) *[voice]* étendue, portée. **within the ~ of education/religion** dans les limites de l'enseignement/la religion; **within the ~ of this committee** pour ce qui est du ressort de ce comité; *see* **narrow**. 2 **comp** ► **compass card** (*Naut*) rose *f* des vents ► **compass course** route *f* magnétique ► **compass rose** = **compass card**. 3 **vt** (*go round*) faire le tour de; (*surround*) encercler, entourer.

compassion [kəm'pæʃən] **n** compassion *f*.

compassionate [kəm'pæʃənət] **adj** compatissant. **on ~ grounds** pour raisons de convenance personnelle *or* de famille; (*Mil*) **~ leave** permission exceptionnelle (*pour raisons de famille*).

compassionately [kəm'pæʃənətlɪ] **adv** avec compassion.

compatibility [kəmˌpætə'bɪlɪtɪ] **n** compatibilité *f* (*with* avec).

compatible [kəm'pætɪbl] 1 **adj** compatible (*with* avec). 2 **n** (*Comput*) compatible *m*. **an IBM-~** un compatible IBM.

compatibly [kəm'pætɪblɪ] **adv** d'une manière compatible.

compatriot [kəm'pætrɪət] **n** compatriote *mf*.

compel [kəm'pel] **vt** a contraindre, obliger, forcer (*sb to do* qn à faire). **to be ~led to do** être contraint *or* obligé *or* forcé de faire. b *admiration etc* imposer, forcer. **to ~ obedience/respect from sb** forcer *or* contraindre qn à obéir/à manifester du respect.

compelling [kəm'pelɪŋ] **adj** irrésistible.

compellingly [kəm'pelɪŋlɪ] **adv** irrésistiblement, d'une façon irrésistible.

compendious [kəm'pendɪəs] **adj** compendieux, concis.

compendium [kəm'pendɪəm] **n**, **pl ~s** *or* **compendia** [kəm'pendɪə] a (*summary*) abrégé *m*, condensé *m*, compendium *m*. b (*Brit*) **~ of games** boîte *f* de jeux.

compensate ['kɒmpənseɪt] 1 **vt** (*indemnify*) dédommager, indemniser (*for* de); (*pay*) rémunérer (*for* pour); (*in weight, strength*) compenser, contrebalancer; (*Tech*) compenser, neutraliser. 2 **vi** être *or* constituer une compensation (*for* de), compenser; (*in money*) indemniser, dédommager (*for* pour).

compensation [ˌkɒmpən'seɪʃən] **n** (*indemnity*) compensation *f*, dédommagement *m*, indemnité *f*; (*payment*) rémunération *f*; (*in weight etc*) contrepoids *m*; (*Tech*) compensation, neutralisation *f*. **in ~** en compensation; **as a ~ (for)** à titre de compensation (de); (*St Ex*) **C~ Fund** caisse *f* de garantie.

compensatory [ˌkɒmpən'seɪtərɪ] **adj** (*gen*) compensateur (*f* -trice). (*EEC Econ*) **~ levy** prélèvement *m* compensatoire.

compère ['kɒmpɛəʳ] (*Brit: Rad, Theat, TV*) 1 **n** animateur *m*, -trice *f*, meneur *m*, -euse *f* de jeu. 2 **vt** *show* animer, présenter.

compete [kəm'piːt] **vi** a (*gen*) rivaliser (*with sb* avec qn, *for sth* pour obtenir qch, *to do* pour faire). **there were 10 students competing for 6 places on the course** 10 étudiants se disputaient les 6 places disponibles pour cette option, il y avait 10 concurrents pour les 6 places disponibles de l'option; **there were only 4 people competing** il n'y avait que 4 concurrents; **they are competing for the history prize** ils se disputent le prix d'histoire, ils sont rivaux pour le prix d'histoire; **to ~ with sb for a prize** disputer un prix à qn; (*fig*) **his poetry can't ~ with Eliot's** sa poésie n'a rien de comparable avec celle d'Eliot, sa poésie ne peut pas rivaliser avec celle d'Eliot; (*fig*) **we can't ~ with their financial resources** vu leurs ressources financières, il nous est impossible de rivaliser avec eux; (*fig*) **he can't ~ any more** il est à bout de course maintenant.
b (*Comm*) faire concurrence (*with sb* à qn, *for sth* pour (obtenir) qch.) **there are 6 firms competing for a share in the market** 6 entreprises se font concurrence pour une part du marché; **they are forced to ~ with the multinationals** ils sont obligés d'entrer en concurrence *or* en compétition avec les multinationales.
c (*Sport*) concourir (*against sb* avec qn, *for sth* pour (obtenir) qch, *to do* pour faire). **to ~ in a race** participer à une course; **he's competing against world-class athletes** il concourt avec *or* il est en compétition avec des athlètes de réputation mondiale; **the teams are competing to be the first to do ...** les équipes sont en compétition pour être la première à faire ...; **there were only 4 horses/teams/runners competing** il n'y avait que 4 chevaux/équipes/coureurs sur les rangs.

competence ['kɒmpɪtəns] **n** a compétence *f* (*for* pour, *in* en), capacité *f* (*for* pour, *in* en), aptitude *f* (*for* à, *in* en); (*Ling*) compétence. b (*Jur*) compétence *f*. **within the ~ of the court** de la compétence du tribunal.

competency ['kɒmpɪtənsɪ] **n** a = **competence**. b (*money, means*) aisance *f*, moyens *mpl*.

competent ['kɒmpɪtənt] **adj** a (*capable*) compétent, capable; (*qualified*) qualifié (*for* pour), compétent (*for* pour). **he is a very ~ teacher** c'est un professeur très compétent *or* capable; **he is not ~ to teach English** il n'est pas compétent *or* qualifié pour enseigner l'anglais. b (*adequate*) *qualities* suffisant, satisfaisant, honorable. **a ~ knowledge of the language** une connaissance suffisante de la langue. c (*Jur*) *court* compétent; *evidence* admissible, recevable; *person* habile; *see* **court**.

competently ['kɒmpɪtəntlɪ] **adv** (*see* **competent**) avec compétence, d'une façon compétente; suffisamment.

competing [kəm'piːtɪŋ] **adj** concurrent.

competition [ˌkɒmpɪ'tɪʃən] 1 **n** a (*NonC*) compétition *f*, concurrence *f*, rivalité *f* (*for* pour); (*Comm*) concurrence. **unfair ~** concurrence *or* compétition déloyale; **there was keen ~ for it** on se l'est âprement disputé, il y a eu beaucoup de concurrence pour l'avoir; **in ~ with** en concurrence avec.
b concours *m* (*for* pour); (*Sport*) compétition *f*; (*Aut*) course *f*. **to choose by ~** choisir au concours; **to go in for a ~** se présenter à un concours; **beauty/swimming ~** concours de beauté/de natation; **I won it in a newspaper ~** je l'ai gagné en faisant un concours dans le journal.
c (*other competitors*) **he was waiting to see what the ~ would be like** il attendait de voir qui lui ferait concurrence *or* qui seraient ses rivaux.
2 **comp** ► **competition car** voiture *f* de compétition.

competitive [kəm'petɪtɪv] **adj** a *entry, selection* par concours, déterminé par un concours. **~ examination** concours *m*. b *person* qui a l'esprit de compétition; *price, market* concurrentiel, compétitif; *goods* à prix concurrentiel *or* compétitif. **~ bidding** appel *m* d'offres.

competitiveness [kəm'petətɪvnɪs] **n** compétitivité *f*.

competitor [kəm'petɪtəʳ] **n** (*also Comm*) concurrent(e) *m(f)*.

compilation [ˌkɒmpɪ'leɪʃən] **n** compilation *f*.

compile [kəm'paɪl] **vt** (*gen, Comput*) compiler; *dictionary* composer (par compilation); *list, catalogue, inventory* dresser.

compiler [kəm'paɪləʳ] **n** (*gen*) compilateur *m*, -trice *f*; *[dictionary]* rédacteur *m*, -trice *f*; (*Comput*) compilateur *m*.

complacence [kəm'pleɪsəns] **n**, **complacency** [kəm'pleɪsnsɪ] **n** contentement *m* de soi, suffisance *f*.

complacent [kəm'pleɪsənt] **adj** content *or* satisfait de soi, suffisant.

complacently [kəm'pleɪsəntlɪ] **adv** d'un air *or* ton suffisant, avec suffisance.

complain [kəm'pleɪn] **vi** a se plaindre (*of, about* de). **to ~ that** se plaindre que + *subj or indic or* de ce que + *indic;* **how are you? — I can't ~*** comment vas-tu? — je ne peux pas me plaindre. b (*make a complaint*) formuler une plainte *or* une réclamation (*against* contre), se plaindre. **you should ~ to the manager** vous devriez vous plaindre au directeur; (*Jur*) **to ~ to the court of justice** saisir la Cour de justice.

complainant [kəm'pleɪnənt] **n** (*Jur*) demandeur *m*, -deresse *f*.

complaint [kəm'pleɪnt] **n** a (*expression of discontent*) plainte *f*, récrimination *f*, doléances *fpl*; (*reason for ~*) grief *m*, sujet *m* de plainte; (*Jur*) plainte; (*Comm*) réclamation *f*. (*Comm*) **~s department** service *m* des réclamations; **don't listen to his ~s** n'écoutez pas ses doléances *or* ses récriminations; **I have no ~(s)**, **I have no cause for ~** je n'ai aucun sujet *or* motif de plainte, je n'ai pas lieu de me plaindre; (*Comm*) **to make a ~** se plaindre (*about* de), faire une réclamation; (*Jur*) **to lodge** *or* **lay a ~ against** porter plainte contre; *see* **police**.
b (*Med*) maladie *f*, affection *f*. **what is his ~?** de quoi souffre-t-il?, de quoi se plaint-il?; **a heart ~** une maladie de cœur; **bowel ~** affection intestinale.

complaisance [kəm'pleɪzəns] **n** complaisance *f*, obligeance *f*.

complaisant [kəm'pleɪzənt] **adj** complaisant, obligeant, aimable.

complected [kəm'plektɪd] **adj** (*US*) **dark/light-~** au teint foncé/clair.

complement ['kɒmplɪmənt] 1 **n** (*gen, Gram, Math*) complément *m*; *[staff etc]* personnel tout entier, effectif complet. **with full ~** au grand complet. 2 ['kɒmplɪment] **vt** compléter, être le complément de.

complementary [ˌkɒmplɪ'mentərɪ] **adj** (*gen, Math*) complémentaire.

complete [kəm'pliːt] 1 **adj** a (*having all necessary parts*) complet (*f* -ète); (*finished*) achevé, terminé, fini. (*Literat*) **the ~ works** les œuvres complètes; **the celebrations weren't ~ without him** les festivités n'étaient pas complètes sans lui; **at last her happiness was ~** enfin son bonheur était total; **the ~ man** l'homme complet.
b **~ with** doté de, pourvu de; **a house ~ with furniture** une maison meublée.
c (*thorough, absolute*) *surprise, victory, failure* complet (*f* -ète), total; *satisfaction, approval* complet, entier, total. **he's a ~ idiot** il est complètement idiot; **it was a ~ disaster** ça a été un désastre sur toute la ligne* *or* un désastre complet.
2 **vt** a *collection* compléter; *misfortune, happiness* mettre le comble à; *piece of work* achever, finir, terminer; *form, questionnaire* remplir. **and to ~ his happiness** et pour comble de bonheur; **and just to ~ things** et pour couronner le tout; **to ~ an order** exécuter une commande.

b (*fill in*) *form, questionnaire* remplir.
completely [kəm'pliːtlɪ] adv complètement.
completeness [kəm'pliːtnɪs] n état complet.
completion [kəm'pliːʃən] 1 n *[work]* achèvement *m*; *[happiness, misfortune]* comble *m*; (*Jur*) *[contract, sale]* exécution *f*. **near ~** près d'être achevé; **payment on ~ of contract** paiement *m* à la signature du contrat. 2 comp ▸ **completion date** (*Jur*) (*for work*) date *f* d'achèvement (des travaux); (*in house-buying*) date d'exécution du contrat.
complex ['kɒmpleks] 1 adj (*all senses*) complexe. 2 n a complexe *m*, ensemble *m*, tout *m*. **industrial/mining ~** complexe industriel/minier; **housing ~** (ensemble de) résidences *fpl*, (*high rise*) grand ensemble; *see* **cinema**. b (*Psych*) complexe *m*. **he's got a ~ about it** ça lui a donné un complexe, il en fait (tout) un complexe; *see* **guilt, inferiority** *etc*.
complexion [kəm'plekʃən] n *[face]* teint *m*; (*fig*) caractère *m*, aspect *m*. **that puts a new ~ on the whole affair** l'affaire se présente maintenant sous un tout autre aspect *or* jour.
-complexioned [kəm'plekʃənd] adj ending in comps, e.g. **dark-complexioned** de *or* au teint mat, mat de teint; **fair-complexioned** de *or* au teint clair, clair de teint.
complexity [kəm'pleksɪtɪ] n complexité *f*.
compliance [kəm'plaɪəns] n (*NonC*) a (*acceptance*) acquiescement *m* (*with* à); (*conformity*) conformité *f* (*with* avec). **in ~ with** conformément à, en accord avec; **~ officer** *or* **lawyer** conseiller *m* fiscal. b (*submission*) basse complaisance, servilité *f*.
compliant [kəm'plaɪənt] adj accommodant, docile.
complicate ['kɒmplɪkeɪt] vt compliquer (*with* de); (*muddle*) embrouiller. **that ~s matters** cela complique les choses; **she always ~s things** elle complique toujours tout, elle se crée des problèmes.
complicated ['kɒmplɪkeɪtɪd] adj (*involved*) compliqué, complexe; (*muddled*) embrouillé.
complication [ˌkɒmplɪ'keɪʃən] n (*gen, Med*) complication *f*.
complicity [kəm'plɪsɪtɪ] n complicité *f* (*in* dans).
compliment ['kɒmplɪmənt] 1 n a compliment *m*. **to pay sb a ~** faire *or* adresser un compliment à qn; (*fig*) **to return the ~** retourner le compliment, renvoyer l'ascenseur. b (*frm*) **~s** compliments *mpl*, respects *mpl*, hommages *mpl* (*frm*); **give him my ~s** faites-lui mes compliments; **(I wish you) the ~s of the season** (je vous présente) tous les vœux d'usage *or* tous mes vœux; **"with the ~s of Mr X"** "avec les hommages *or* les bons compliments de M. X"; **"with ~s"** "avec nos compliments"; (*Comm*) **~s slip** ≃ papillon *m* (avec les bons compliments de l'expéditeur). 2 ['kɒmplɪment] vt complimenter, féliciter (*on* de), faire des compliments à (*on* de, sur).
complimentary [ˌkɒmplɪ'mentərɪ] adj a (*praising*) flatteur. b (*gratis*) gracieux, à titre gracieux. **~ copy** exemplaire offert en hommage; **~ ticket** billet *m* de faveur.
complin(e) ['kɒmplɪn] n (*Rel*) complies *fpl*.
comply [kəm'plaɪ] vi a *[person]* se soumettre (*with* à). **to ~ with the rules** observer *or* respecter le règlement; **to ~ with sb's wishes** se conformer aux désirs de qn; **to ~ with a request** faire droit à une requête, accéder à une demande; (*Admin, Jur*) **to ~ with a clause** observer *or* respecter une disposition. b *[equipment, object]* (*to specifications etc*) être conforme (*with* à).
component [kəm'pəʊnənt] 1 adj composant, constituant. **the ~ parts** les parties constituantes. 2 n (*gen, also Econ*) élément *m*; (*Chem*) composant *m*; (*Aut, Tech*) pièce *f*. **~s factory** usine *f* de pièces détachées.
componential [ˌkɒmpə'nenʃəl] adj componentiel. (*Ling*) **~ analysis** analyse componentielle.
comport [kəm'pɔːt] 1 vt: **to ~ o.s.** se comporter, se conduire. 2 vi convenir (*with* à), s'accorder (*with* avec).
comportment [kəm'pɔːtmənt] n comportement *m*, conduite *f*.
compose [kəm'pəʊz] vt (*Literat, Mus, Typ*) composer; (*gen, Chem, Tech*) composer, constituer. **to be ~d of** se composer de; **to ~ o.s.** se calmer; **to ~ one's features** composer son visage; **to ~ one's thoughts** mettre de l'ordre dans ses pensées.
composed [kəm'pəʊzd] adj calme, tranquille, posé.
composedly [kəm'pəʊzɪdlɪ] adv avec calme, posément, tranquillement.
composer [kəm'pəʊzəʳ] n (*Mus*) compositeur *m*, -trice *f*.
composite ['kɒmpəzɪt] 1 adj (*gen, Archit, Phot*) composite; (*Bot, Math*) composé. (*Can*) **~ school** école polyvalente; **~ vote** vote *m* groupé. 2 n (*Archit*) (ordre *m*) composite *m*; (*Bot*) composée *f*, composacée *f*.
composition [ˌkɒmpə'zɪʃən] 1 n a (*NonC: gen, Art, Mus, Typ*) composition *f*. **music/verse of his own ~** de la musique/des vers de sa composition.
b (*thing composed*) composition *f*, œuvre *f*; (*Scol: essay*) rédaction *f*. **one of his most famous ~s** une de ses œuvres les plus célèbres.
c (*gen, Chem, Tech: parts composing whole*) composition *f*, constitution *f*; (*mixture of substances*) mélange *m*, composition, composé *m* (*of* de); (*Archit*) stuc *m*. **to study the ~ of a substance** étudier la constitution d'une substance.
d (*Gram*) *[sentence]* construction *f*; *[word]* composition *f*.
e (*temperament, make-up*) nature *f*, constitution intellectuelle *or* morale.
f (*Jur*) accommodement *m*, compromis *m*, arrangement *m* (*avec un créancier*). (*frm*) **to come to a ~** venir à composition (*frm*), arriver à une entente *or* un accord.
2 comp *substance* synthétique ▸ **composition rubber** caoutchouc *m* synthétique.
compositor [kəm'pɒzɪtəʳ] n (*Typ*) compositeur *m*, -trice *f*.
compos mentis ['kɒmpɒs'mentɪs] adj sain d'esprit.
compost ['kɒmpɒst] 1 n compost *m*. **~ heap** tas *m* de compost. 2 vt composter.
composure [kəm'pəʊʒəʳ] n calme *m*, sang-froid *m*, maîtrise *f* de soi.
compote ['kɒmpəʊt] n compote *f*; (*US: dish*) compotier *m*.
compound ['kɒmpaʊnd] 1 n a (*Chem*) composé *m* (*of* de); (*Gram*) (mot *m*) composé; (*Tech*) compound *f*.
b (*enclosed area*) enclos *m*, enceinte *f*.
2 adj (*Chem*) composé, combiné; (*Math*) *number* complexe; *interest* composé; (*Med*) *fracture* compliqué; (*Tech*) *engine* compound *inv*; (*Gram*) *tense, word* composé; *sentence* complexe. (*Mus*) **~ time** la mesure composée.
3 [kəm'paʊnd] vt a (*Chem, Pharm*) *mixture* composer (*of* de); *ingredients* combiner, mêler, mélanger; (*fig*) *problem, difficulties* aggraver.
b (*Jur etc*) *debt, quarrel* régler à l'amiable, arranger par des concessions mutuelles. **to ~ a felony** composer *or* pactiser (avec un criminel).
4 [kəm'paʊnd] vi (*Jur etc*) composer, transiger (*with* avec, *for* au sujet de, pour), s'arranger à l'amiable (*with* avec, *for* au sujet de). **to ~ with one's creditors** s'arranger à l'amiable *or* composer avec ses créanciers.
compounding ['kɒmpaʊndɪŋ] n (*Ling*) composition *f*.
comprehend [ˌkɒmprɪ'hend] 1 vt a (*understand*) comprendre, saisir. b (*include*) comprendre, englober, embrasser. 2 vi comprendre.
comprehending [ˌkɒmprɪ'hendɪŋ] adj compréhensif.
comprehensibility [ˌkɒmprɪhensə'bɪlətɪ] n intelligibilité *f*.
comprehensible [ˌkɒmprɪ'hensəbl] adj compréhensible, intelligible.
comprehensibly [kɒmprɪ'hensəblɪ] adv de façon compréhensible *or* intelligible.
comprehension [ˌkɒmprɪ'henʃn] n a (*understanding*) compréhension *f*, entendement *m*, intelligence *f*. **that is beyond my ~** cela dépasse ma compréhension *or* mon entendement. b (*Scol*) exercice *m* de compréhension. c (*inclusion*) inclusion *f*.
comprehensive [ˌkɒmprɪ'hensɪv] 1 adj a *description, report, review, survey* détaillé, complet (*f* -ète); *knowledge* vaste, étendu; *planning* global; *label, rule* compréhensif. **~ measures** mesures *fpl* d'ensemble; (*Insurance*) **~ insurance (policy)** assurance *f* tous-risques. b (*Brit Scol*) *education, system* polyvalent. **~ school** établissement secondaire polyvalent; **he is against ~ schools** il est pour les critères sélectifs d'entrée (*dans le secondaire*); **to go ~** abandonner les critères sélectifs d'entrée. 2 n = **~ school**; *see* **1**.
compress [kəm'pres] 1 vt *substance* comprimer; *essay, facts* condenser, concentrer, réduire; (*Comput*) *data* compresser. **~ed air** air comprimé. 2 vi se comprimer; se condenser, se réduire. 3 ['kɒmpres] n compresse *f*.
compression [kəm'preʃən] n compression *f*; (*fig*) condensation *f*, concentration *f*, réduction *f*. **~ pistol** ensemble *m* pistolet compresseur; (*Aut*) **~ ratio** taux *m* de compression.
compressor [kəm'presəʳ] n compresseur *m*. (*Comput*) **~ program** programme *m* de compression; **~ unit** groupe *m* compresseur.
comprise [kəm'praɪz] vt comprendre, être composé de, consister en.
compromise ['kɒmprəmaɪz] 1 n compromis *m*, transaction *f*. **to come to *or* reach a ~** aboutir à un compromis, transiger; **to agree to a ~** accepter un compromis. 2 vi transiger (*over* sur), aboutir à *or* accepter un compromis. 3 vt a *reputation etc* compromettre. **to ~ o.s.** se compromettre. b (*imperil*) mettre en péril, risquer. 4 comp ▸ **compromise decision** décision *f* de compromis ▸ **compromise solution** solution *f* de compromis.
compromising ['kɒmprəmaɪzɪŋ] adj compromettant.
comptometer [kɒmp'tɒmɪtəʳ] n ® machine *f* comptable. **~ operator** (opérateur *m*, -trice *f*) mécanographe *mf*.
comptroller [kən'trəʊləʳ] n (*Admin*) économe *mf*, intendant(e) *m(f)*, administrateur *m*, -trice *f*; (*Fin*) contrôleur *m*, -euse *f*. (*US Jur, Pol*) **C~ General** ≃ président *m* de la Cour des comptes.
compulsion [kəm'pʌlʃən] n contrainte *f*, force *f*, coercition *f*. **under ~** de force, sous la contrainte; **you are under no ~** vous n'êtes nullement obligé, rien ne vous force.
compulsive [kəm'pʌlsɪv] adj *reason, demand* coercitif; (*Psych*) *desire, behaviour* compulsif. **he's a ~ smoker** c'est un fumeur invétéré, il ne peut pas s'empêcher de fumer; **she's a ~ talker** parler est un besoin chez elle; **she's a ~ cleaner** c'est une maniaque de la propreté.
compulsively [kəm'pʌlsɪvlɪ] adv (*Psych*) *drink, smoke, talk* d'une façon compulsive, sans pouvoir s'en empêcher. **she doodled ~** elle griffonnait

machinalement *or* sans pouvoir s'en empêcher.

compulsorily [kəm'pʌlsərɪlɪ] adv *purchased, retired* d'office.

compulsory [kəm'pʌlsərɪ] 1 adj a *action, military service* obligatoire; *loan* forcé. ~ **education** instruction *f* obligatoire; (*Brit*) ~ **purchase (order)** (ordre *m* d')expropriation *f* pour cause d'utilité publique; (*Fin*) ~ **liquidation** liquidation forcée; ~ **retirement** mise *f* à la retraite d'office. b (*compelling*) *powers* coercitif, contraignant; *regulations* obligatoire. 2 n (*Skating*) **the compulsories** les figures imposées.

compunction [kəm'pʌŋkʃən] n remords *m*, scrupule *m*; (*Rel*) componction *f*. **without the slightest** ~ sans le moindre scrupule *or* remords; **he had no** ~ **about doing it** il n'a eu aucun scrupule à le faire.

computation [ˌkɒmpjʊ'teɪʃən] n a (*gen*) calcul *m*, computation *f*. b (*NonC*) estimation *f*, évaluation *f* (*of* de).

computational [ˌkɒmpjʊ'teɪʃənl] adj (*gen*) statistique, quantitatif. ~ **linguistics** linguistique computationelle.

compute [kəm'pjuːt] vt calculer. **to** ~ **sth at** évaluer *or* estimer qch à.

computer [kəm'pjuːtə^r] 1 n a (*electronic*) ordinateur *m*; (*mechanical*) calculatrice *f*. **he is in** ~**s** il est dans l'informatique; **on** ~ sur ordinateur; **to do sth by** ~ faire qch sur ordinateur; *see* **analog, digital, personal.**

b (*person*) calculateur *m*, -trice *f*.

2 comp ▸ **the computer age** l'ère *f* de l'ordinateur *or* de l'informatique ▸ **computer agency** bureau *m* d'informatique ▸ **computer-aided, computer-assisted** assisté par ordinateur ▸ **computer-dating (service)** club *m* de rencontres sélectionnées par ordinateur ▸ **computer game** jeu *m* électronique ▸ **computer graphics** (*field*) infographie *f*; (*pictures*) images *fpl* de synthèse ▸ **computer-integrated manufacturing** fabrication *f* intégrée par ordinateur ▸ **computer language** langage *m* de programmation, langage *m* machine ▸ **computer literacy** degré *m* d'initiation à l'informatique ▸ **computer literate** initié à l'informatique ▸ **computer model** modèle calculé par ordinateur ▸ **computer operator** opérateur *m*, -trice *f* ▸ **computer peripheral** périphérique *m* d'ordinateur ▸ **computer printout** listage *m* d'ordinateur ▸ **computer program** programme *m* informatique ▸ **computer programmer** programmeur *m*, -euse *f* ▸ **computer programming** programmation *f* ▸ **computer science** informatique *f* ▸ **computer scientist** informaticien(ne) *m(f)* ▸ **the computer society** la société à l'heure de l'informatique ▸ **computer studies** l'informatique *f* ▸ **computer system** système *m* informatique ▸ **computer typesetting** composition *f* informatique ▸ **computer virus** virus *m* informatique.

computerate* [kəm'pjuːtərɪt] adj = **computer literate;** *see* **computer 2.**

computerese* [kəmˌpjuːtə'riːz] n jargon *m* informatique.

computerist [kəm'pjuːtərɪst] n (*US*) informaticien(ne) *m(f)*.

computerization [kəmˌpjuːtəraɪ'zeɪʃən] n a *[information etc]* traitement *m* (électronique). b *[system, process]* automatisation *f or* automation *f* électronique; *[records, accounts]* mise *f* sur ordinateur.

computerize [kəm'pjuːtəraɪz] vt traiter *or* gérer par ordinateur, informatiser; *records, accounts* mettre sur ordinateur.

computing [kəm'pjuːtɪŋ] 1 n informatique *f*. 2 comp *service, facility, problem* informatique; *course, department* d'informatique.

comrade ['kɒmreɪd] n camarade *mf*. ~**-in-arms** compagnon *m* d'armes.

comradeship ['kɒmreɪdʃɪp] n camaraderie *f*.

comsat ['kɒmsæt] n (*US*) (abbr of **communications satellite**) *see* **communication 2.**

con¹ [kɒn] vt a (†: *study*) étudier soigneusement, apprendre par cœur. b (*Naut*) gouverner; (*US Naut*) piloter.

con² [kɒn] prep, n contre (*m*); *see* **pro¹**.

con³* [kɒn] 1 vt escroquer, duper. **to** ~ **sb into doing** amener qn à faire en l'abusant *or* en le dupant; **I've been** ~**ned!** on m'a eu!*, je me suis fait avoir!*; **he** ~**ned his way into the building** il est entré dans l'immeuble par ruse. 2 n a **it was all a big** ~ (*empty boasting etc*) tout ça c'était de la frime*; (*swindle*) c'était une vaste escroquerie. b (‡) (abbr of **convict**) taulard‡ *m*. 3 comp ▸ **con artist*** arnaqueur* *m* ▸ **con game** escroquerie *f* ▸ **con man** escroc *m*.

Con. n abbr of **constable.**

concatenate [kɒn'kætɪˌneɪt] vt enchaîner.

concatenation [kɒnˌkætɪ'neɪʃən] n *[circumstances]* enchaînement *m*; (*series*) série *f*, chaîne *f*; (*Ling, Comput*) concaténation *f*.

concave ['kɒn'keɪv] adj concave.

concavity [kɒn'kævɪtɪ] n concavité *f*.

conceal [kən'siːl] vt (*hide*) *object* cacher, dissimuler; (*keep secret*) *news, event* garder *or* tenir secret; *emotions, thoughts* dissimuler. **to** ~ **sth from sb** cacher qch à qn; **to** ~ **the fact that** dissimuler le fait que; ~**ed lighting** éclairage indirect; (*Aut*) ~**ed turning** *or* **road** intersection cachée.

concealment [kən'siːlmənt] n (*NonC*) dissimulation *f*; (*Jur*) *[criminal]* recel *m*; *[facts]* non-divulgation *f*; (*place of* ~) cachette *f*.

concede [kən'siːd] 1 vt *privilege* concéder, accorder; *point* concéder; (*Sport*) *match* concéder. **to** ~ **that** concéder *or* admettre *or* reconnaître que; **to** ~ **victory** s'avouer vaincu. 2 vi céder.

conceit [kən'siːt] n (*pride: NonC*) vanité *f*, suffisance *f*, prétention *f*; (*witty expression*) trait *m* d'esprit, expression brillante. (*liter*) **he is wise in his own** ~ il se croit très sage; (*Literat*) ~**s** concetti *mpl*.

conceited [kən'siːtɪd] adj vaniteux, suffisant, prétentieux.

conceitedly [kən'siːtɪdlɪ] adv avec vanité, avec suffisance, prétentieusement.

conceivable [kən'siːvəbl] adj concevable, imaginable. **it is hardly** ~ **that** il est à peine concevable que + *subj*.

conceivably [kən'siːvəblɪ] adv de façon concevable, en théorie. **she may** ~ **be right** il est concevable *or* il se peut bien qu'elle ait raison.

conceive [kən'siːv] 1 vt *child, idea, plan* concevoir. **to** ~ **a hatred/love for sb/sth** concevoir de la haine/de l'amour pour qn/qch; **I cannot** ~ **why he wants to do it** je ne comprends vraiment pas pourquoi il veut le faire. 2 vi: *[femme]* **unable to** ~ qui ne peut pas avoir d'enfants; **to** ~ **of** concevoir, avoir le concept de; **I cannot** ~ **of anything better** je ne conçois rien de mieux; **I cannot** ~ **of a better way to do it** je ne conçois pas de meilleur moyen de le faire.

concelebrant [kən'selɪˌbrənt] n (*Rel*) concélébrant *m*.

concentrate ['kɒnsəntreɪt] 1 vt *attention* concentrer (*on* sur); *hopes* reporter (*on* sur); *supplies* concentrer, rassembler; (*Chem, Mil*) concentrer. **it** ~**s the mind** cela fait réfléchir.

2 vi a (*converge*) *[troops, people]* se concentrer, converger. **the crowds began to** ~ **round the palace** la foule a commencé à se concentrer *or* à se rassembler autour du palais; **they** ~**d in the square** ils ont convergé vers la place.

b (*direct thoughts, efforts etc*) se concentrer, concentrer *or* fixer son attention (*on* sur). **to** ~ **on doing** s'appliquer à faire; **I just can't** ~**!** je n'arrive pas à me concentrer!; **try to** ~ **a little more** essaie de te concentrer un peu plus *or* de faire un peu plus attention; ~ **on getting yourself a job** essaie avant tout de *or* occupe-toi d'abord de te trouver du travail; **the terrorists** ~**d on the outlying farms** les terroristes ont concentré leurs attaques sur les fermes isolées; ~ **on getting well** occupe-toi d'abord de ta santé; *[speaker]* **today I shall** ~ **on the 16th century** aujourd'hui je traiterai en particulier le 16e siècle *or* m'occuperai en particulier du 16e siècle.

3 adj, n (*Chem*) concentré (*m*).

concentration [ˌkɒnsən'treɪʃən] n concentration *f*. ~ **camp** camp *m* de concentration.

concentric [kən'sentrɪk] adj concentrique.

concept ['kɒnsept] n concept *m*.

conception [kən'sepʃən] n (*gen, Med*) conception *f*; *see* **immaculate.**

conceptual [kən'septjʊəl] adj conceptuel.

conceptualize [kən'septjʊəˌlaɪz] vt concevoir, conceptualiser.

concern [kən'sɜːn] 1 vt a (*affect*) concerner, toucher, affecter; (*be of importance to*) concerner, intéresser, importer à; (*be the business of*) regarder, être l'affaire de; (*be about*) *[report etc]* se rapporter à. **that doesn't** ~ **you** cela ne vous regarde pas, ce n'est pas votre affaire; (*frm*) **to whom it may** ~ à qui de droit; **as** ~**s** en ce qui concerne, à propos de; **as far as** *or* **so far as he is** ~**ed** en ce qui le concerne, quant à lui; **where we are** ~**ed** en ce qui nous concerne; **the persons** ~**ed** les intéressés; **the department** ~**ed** (*under discussion*) le service en question *or* dont il s'agit; (*relevant*) le service compétent; **my brother is the most closely** ~**ed** le premier intéressé c'est mon frère; **to be** ~**ed in** avoir un intérêt dans; **to** ~ **o.s. in** *or* **with** se mêler de, s'occuper de, s'intéresser à; **we are** ~**ed only with facts** nous ne nous occupons que des faits.

b (*trouble: gen pass*) inquiéter. **to be** ~**ed by** *or* **for** *or* **about** *or* **at** s'inquiéter de, être inquiet (*f* -ète) de; **I am** ~**ed about him** je m'inquiète à son sujet, je me fais du souci à son sujet; **I am** ~**ed to hear that ...** j'apprends avec peine *or* inquiétude que ... .

2 n a (*relation, connexion*) rapport *m* (*with* avec), relation *f* (*with* avec). **to have no** ~ **with** n'avoir rien à voir avec, être sans rapport avec.

b (*interest, business*) affaire *f*; (*responsibility*) responsabilité *f*. **it's no** ~ **of his, it's none of his** ~ ce n'est pas son affaire, cela ne le regarde pas; **it is of no** ~ **to him** cela n'a aucun intérêt pour lui; **what** ~ **is it of yours?** en quoi est-ce que cela vous regarde?

c (*Comm: also* **business** ~) entreprise *f*, affaire *f*, firme *f*, maison *f* (de commerce); *see* **going.**

d (*interest, share*) intérêt(s) *m(pl)* (*in* dans). **he has a** ~ **in the business** il a des intérêts dans l'affaire.

e (*anxiety*) inquiétude *f*, souci *m*; (*stronger*) anxiété *f*. **he was filled with** ~ il était très soucieux *or* inquiet; **a look of** ~ un regard inquiet; **it is of great** ~ **to us (that ...)** c'est un grand souci pour nous (que ...); **this is a matter of great** ~ **to us** c'est un sujet de grande inquiétude pour nous.

f (*: *object, contrivance*) truc* *m*, bidule‡ *m*.

concerned [kən'sɜːnd] adj (*worried*) inquiet (*f* -ète), soucieux (*about, at, for* de); (*affected*) affecté (*by* par).

concerning [kən'sɜːnɪŋ] prep en ce qui concerne, au sujet de, à propos de, concernant.

concert ['kɒnsət] 1 n a (*Mus*) concert *m*. **in** ~ en concert.

b *[voices etc]* unisson *m*, chœur *m*. **in** ~ à l'unisson, en chœur.

c (*fig*) accord *m*, harmonie *f*, entente *f*. **in** ~ **with** de concert avec.

2 **comp** *ticket, hall* de concert ▸ **concertgoer** habitué(e) *m(f)* des concerts, amateur *m* de concerts ▸ **concert grand** piano *m* de concert ▸ **concertmaster** (*US*) premier violon *m* ▸ **concert party** (*Mus*) soirée *m* musicale (*chez un particulier*) ▸ **concert performer** concertiste *mf* ▸ **concert pianist** pianiste *mf* de concert ▸ **concert pitch** (*Mus*) le diapason (de concert); (*fig: on top form*) **at concert pitch** au maximum *or* à l'apogée de la forme ▸ **concert tour** tournée *f* de concerts.

3 [kən'sɜːt] **vt** concerter, arranger (ensemble).

concerted [kən'sɜːtɪd] **adj** concerté.

concertina [,kɒnsə'tiːnə] 1 **n** concertina *m*. (*Aut*) ~ **crash** carambolage *m*. 2 **vi: the vehicles ~ed into each other** les véhicules se sont emboutis *or* télescopés (les uns les autres).

concerto [kən'tʃɛətəʊ] **n, pl ~s** *or* **concerti** [kən'tʃɛətiː] concerto *m* (*for* pour).

concession [kən'seʃən] **n** (*gen, Jur*) concession *f*; (*Comm*) réduction *f*.

concessionaire [kən,seʃə'nɛər] **n** concessionnaire *mf*.

concessionary [kən'seʃənərɪ] 1 **adj** (*Fin, Jur etc*) concessionnaire; (*Comm*) *ticket, fare* à prix réduit. ~ **aid** aide libérale. 2 **n** concessionnaire *mf*.

conch [kɒntʃ] **n, pl ~s** [kɒŋks] *or* **~es** ['kɒntʃɪz] (*shell, Anat*) conque *f*; (*Archit*) voûte *f* semi-circulaire, (voûte d')abside *f*.

concha ['kɒŋkə] **n, pl conchae** ['kɒŋkiː] (*Anat*) conque *f*.

conchology [kɒŋ'kɒlədʒɪ] **n** conchyliologie *f*.

conciliate [kən'sɪlɪeɪt] **vt** a (*placate*) apaiser; (*win over*) se concilier (l'appui de). b (*reconcile*) *opposing views, extremes* concilier.

conciliation [kən,sɪlɪ'eɪʃən] **n** (*see* **conciliate**) apaisement *m*; conciliation *f*. (*Ind*) ~ **board** conseil *m* d'arbitrage; ~ **service** (*gen*) service *m* de conciliation; (*Ind*) service de règlement amiable.

conciliator [kən'sɪlɪ,eɪtər] **n** conciliateur *m*, -trice *f*; (*Ind*) médiateur *m*.

conciliatory [kən'sɪlɪətərɪ] **adj** *person* conciliateur (*f* -trice), conciliant; *speech, words, manner* conciliant; *spirit* de conciliation; (*Jur, Pol*) *procedure* conciliatoire.

concise [kən'saɪs] **adj** (*short*) concis; (*shortened*) abrégé.

concisely [kən'saɪslɪ] **adv** avec concision.

conciseness [kən'saɪsnɪs] **n, concision** [kən'sɪʒən] **n** concision *f*.

conclave ['kɒnkleɪv] **n** (*Rel*) conclave *m*; (*fig*) assemblée *f* (secrète), réunion *f* (privée). (*fig*) **in** ~ en réunion privée.

conclude [kən'kluːd] 1 **vt** a (*end*) *business, agenda* conclure, achever, finir, terminer. **"to be ~d"** "suite et fin au prochain numéro". b (*arrange*) *treaty* conclure, aboutir à. c (*infer*) conclure, déduire, inférer (*from* de, *that* que). d (*US: decide*) décider (*to do* de faire). 2 **vi** (*end*) *[things, events]* se terminer, s'achever (*with* par, sur); *[persons]* conclure. **to ~ I must say ...** pour conclure *or* en conclusion je dois dire ... .

concluding [kən'kluːdɪŋ] **adj** final.

conclusion [kən'kluːʒən] **n** a (*end*) conclusion *f*, fin *f*, terme *m*. **in ~** pour conclure, finalement, en conclusion; **to bring to a ~** mener à sa conclusion *or* à terme. b (*settling*) *[treaty etc]* conclusion *f*. c (*opinion, decision*) conclusion *f*, déduction *f*. **to come to the ~ that** conclure que; **to draw a ~ from** tirer une conclusion de; **this leads (one) to the ~ that** ... ceci amène à conclure que ...; *see* **foregone, jump.** d (*Philos*) conclusion *f*. e **to try ~s with sb** se mesurer avec *or* contre qn.

conclusive [kən'kluːsɪv] **adj** concluant, définitif.

conclusively [kən'kluːsɪvlɪ] **adv** de façon concluante, définitivement.

concoct [kən'kɒkt] **vt** (*Culin etc*) confectionner, composer; (*fig*) *scheme, excuse* fabriquer, inventer, combiner.

concoction [kən'kɒkʃən] **n** a (*Culin etc*) (*action*) confection *f*, préparation *f*; (*product*) mélange *m*, mixture *f* (*pej*). b (*NonC: fig*) *[scheme, excuse]* combinaison *f*, élaboration *f*.

concomitant [kən'kɒmɪtənt] 1 **adj** concomitant. 2 **n** événement concomitant.

concord ['kɒŋkɔːd] **n** a concorde *f*, harmonie *f*, entente *f*. **in complete ~** en parfaite harmonie. b (*Gram*) accord *m*. **to be in ~ with** s'accorder avec. c (*Mus*) accord *m*.

concordance [kən'kɔːdəns] **n** a (*agreement*) accord *m*. b (*index*) index *m*; *[Bible etc]* concordance *f*.

concordant [kən'kɔːdənt] **adj** concordant, s'accordant (*with* avec).

concordat [kɒn'kɔːdæt] **n** concordat *m*.

Concorde ['kɒnkɔːd] **n** (*Aviat*) Concorde *f*. **in ~** en Concorde.

concourse ['kɒŋkɔːs] **n** *[circumstances]* concours *m*; *[people, vehicles]* multitude *f*, affluence *f*, concours; (*crowd*) foule *f*; (*place*) lieu *m* de rassemblement; (*in pedestrian precinct*) parvis *m*, piazza *f*; (*US: in a park*) carrefour *m*; (*in building, station*) hall *m*; (*US: street*) cours *m*, boulevard *m*.

concrete ['kɒnkriːt] 1 **adj** a (*Philos*) concret (*f* -ète), réel, matériel; (*Gram, Liter, Math, Mus*) concret; (*fig*) *proof, advantage* concret, matériel; *offer* concret, précis. b (*Constr*) en béton. ~ **mixer** bétonnière *f*; (*fig*) **the ~ jungle** la jungle des villes; (*fig*) **they live in one of those ~ jungles** ils habitent dans une de ces jungles urbaines. 2 **n** a (*NonC: Constr*) béton *m*; *see* **prestressed, reinforce.** b (*Philos*) **the ~** le concret. 3 **vt** (*Constr*) bétonner.

concretion [kən'kriːʃən] **n** concrétion *f*.

concubine ['kɒŋkjʊbaɪn] **n** concubine *f*.

concupiscence [kən'kjuːpɪsəns] **n** concupiscence *f*.

concupiscent [kən'kjuːpɪsənt] **adj** concupiscent.

concur [kən'kɜːr] **vi** a (*agree*) *[person]* être d'accord, s'entendre (*with sb* avec qn, *in sth* sur *or* au sujet de qch); *[opinions]* converger. b (*happen together*) coïncider, arriver en même temps; (*contribute*) concourir (*to* à). **everything ~red to bring about this result** tout a concouru à produire ce résultat.

concurrent [kən'kʌrənt] **adj** a (*occurring at same time*) concomitant, coïncident, simultané. b (*acting together*) concerté. c (*in agreement*) concordant, d'accord. d (*Math, Tech*) concourant.

concurrently [kən'kʌrəntlɪ] **adv** simultanément.

concuss [kən'kʌs] **vt** a (*Med: gen pass*) commotionner. **to be ~ed** être commotionné, être sous l'effet d'un choc. b (*shake*) secouer violemment, ébranler.

concussion [kən'kʌʃən] **n** a (*Med*) commotion *f* (cérébrale). b (*shaking*) ébranlement *m*, secousse *f*.

condemn [kən'dem] **vt** a (*gen, Jur, Med, fig*) condamner (*to* à). (*Jur*) **to ~ to death** condamner à mort; **the ~ed man** le condamné; **the ~ed cell** la cellule des condamnés. b (*Tech*) *building* déclarer inhabitable, condamner; (*Mil, Tech*) *materials* réformer, déclarer inutilisable.

condemnation [,kɒndem'neɪʃən] **n** (*gen, Jur, fig*) condamnation *f*; (*US Jur: of property*) expropriation *f* pour cause d'utilité publique.

condemnatory [kəndem'neɪtərɪ] **adj** réprobateur, -trice.

condensation [,kɒnden'seɪʃən] **n** condensation *f*; (*on glass*) buée *f*, condensation.

condense [kən'dens] 1 **vt** condenser, concentrer; (*Phys*) *gas* condenser; *rays* concentrer; (*fig*) condenser, résumer. **~d milk** lait concentré; **~d book** livre condensé. 2 **vi** se condenser, se concentrer.

condenser [kən'densər] **n** (*Elec, Tech*) condensateur *m*; (*Phys*) *[gas]* condenseur *m*; *[light]* condensateur.

condescend [,kɒndɪ'send] **vi** a condescendre (*to do* à faire), daigner (*to do* faire). **to ~ to sb** se montrer condescendant envers *or* à l'égard de qn. b (†: *stoop to*) s'abaisser (*to* à), descendre (*to* à, jusqu'à).

condescending [,kɒndɪ'sendɪŋ] **adj** condescendant.

condescendingly [,kɒndɪ'sendɪŋlɪ] **adv** avec condescendance.

condescension [,kɒndɪ'senʃən] **n** condescendance *f*.

condign [kən'daɪn] **adj** (*fitting*) adéquat, proportionné; (*deserved*) mérité.

condiment ['kɒndɪmənt] **n** condiment *m*.

condition [kən'dɪʃən] 1 **n** a (*determining factor*) condition *f*. **on ~ that,** (*US*) **on the ~ that** à condition que + *fut indic or subj*, à condition de + *infin*; **on this ~** à cette condition; (*Comm*) **~ of sale** condition de vente; (*Jur*) **~ of a contract** condition d'un contrat; **he made the ~ that no one should accompany him** il a stipulé que personne ne devait l'accompagner; *see* **term.**

b (*circumstances*) **~s** conditions *fpl*, circonstances *fpl*; **under** *or* **in the present ~s** dans les conditions actuelles; **working/living ~s** conditions de travail/de vie; **weather ~s** conditions météorologiques.

c (*NonC: state, nature*) état *m*, condition *f*. **physical/mental ~** état physique/mental; **in ~** *thing* en bon état; *person* en forme, en bonne condition physique; (*Comm etc*) **in good ~** en bon état; **it's out of ~** c'est en mauvais état; **he's out of ~** il n'est pas en forme; **she was not in a ~** *or* **in any ~ to go out** elle n'était pas en état de sortir; (*euph*) **she is in an interesting ~*** elle est dans un état *or* une position intéressant(e) (*euph hum*).

d (*NonC: social position*) condition *f*, position *f*, situation *f*.

2 **vt** a (*determine*) déterminer, conditionner, être la condition de. **his standard of living is ~ed by his income** son niveau de vie dépend de ses revenus.

b (*bring into good ~*) *animals* mettre en forme; *things* remettre en bon état; *hair, skin* traiter; *see* **air.**

c (*Psych, fig*) *person, animal* provoquer un réflexe conditionné chez, conditionner; (*by propaganda*) *person* conditionner (*into believing* à croire), mettre en condition. **~ed reflex** réflexe conditionné; **~ed response** réaction conditionnée; **the nation has been ~ed into believing that the government is right** on a conditionné la nation à croire que le gouvernement a raison.

conditional [kən'dɪʃənl] 1 **adj** a *promise, agreement, offer* conditionnel. (*Jur*) ~ **clause** clause conditionnelle. b **to be ~ (up)on** dépendre de; **his appointment is ~ (up)on his passing his exams** sa nomination dépend de son succès aux examens, pour être nommé il faut qu'il soit reçu à ses examens. c (*Gram*) *mood, clause* conditionnel. d (*TV*) ~ **access** accès *m* limité aux abonnés. 2 **n** (*Gram*) conditionnel *m*. **in the ~** au conditionnel.

conditionally [kən'dɪʃnəlɪ] **adv** conditionnellement.

conditioner [kən'dɪʃənər] **n** (*for hair*) baume démêlant; (*for skin*) crème traitante *or* équilibrante; *see* **fabric.**

conditioning [kən'dɪʃənɪŋ] 1 **n** (*Psych*) conditionnement *m*; *[hair]* traitement *m*. 2 **adj** traitant.

condo ['kɒn,dəʊ] **n** (*US*) **abbr of condominium unit.**

condole [kən'dəʊl] **vi** exprimer *or* offrir ses condoléances, exprimer sa

sympathie (*with sb* à qn).
condolences [kən'dəʊlənsɪz] npl condoléances *fpl*.
condom ['kɒndəm] n préservatif *m*.
condominium [ˌkɒndə'mɪnɪəm] n, pl ~s **a** condominium *m*. **b** (*US*) (*ownership*) copropriété *f*; (*building*) immeuble *m* (en copropriété); (*rooms*) appartement *m* (dans un immeuble en copropriété). ~ **unit** appartement en copropriété.
condonation [ˌkɒndəʊ'neɪʃən] n (*Fin*) remise *f* d'une dette.
condone [kən'dəʊn] vt (*overlook*) fermer les yeux sur; (*forgive*) pardonner. (*Jur*) **to ~ adultery** ≈ pardonner un adultère; (*Educ*) **to ~ a student** repêcher un étudiant; **to ~ a student's exam results** remonter les notes d'un étudiant.
condonement [kən'dəʊnmənt] n *[student]* repêchage *m*.
condor ['kɒndɔːʳ] n condor *m*.
conduce [kən'djuːs] vi: **to ~ to** conduire à, provoquer.
conducive [kən'djuːsɪv] adj contribuant (*to* à). **to be ~ to** conduire à, provoquer, mener à.
conduct ['kɒndʌkt] **1** n **a** (*behaviour*) conduite *f*, tenue *f*, comportement *m*. **good/bad ~** bonne/mauvaise conduite *or* tenue; **his ~ towards me** sa conduite *or* son comportement à mon égard *or* envers moi; *see* **disorderly**.
b (*leading*) conduite *f*; *see* **safe**.
2 comp ► **conduct mark** (*Scol*) avertissement *m* ► **conduct report** (*Scol*) rapport *m* (*sur la conduite d'un élève*) ► **conduct sheet** (*Mil*) feuille *f or* certificat *m* de conduite; (*Naut*) cahier *m* des punis.
3 [kən'dʌkt] vt **a** (*lead*) conduire, mener. **he ~ed me round the gardens** il m'a fait faire le tour des jardins; **~ed visit** visite guidée; (*Brit*) **~ed tour** excursion accompagnée, voyage organisé; *[building]* visite guidée.
b (*direct, manage*) diriger. **to ~ one's business** diriger ses affaires; **to ~ an orchestra** diriger un orchestre; (*Jur*) **to ~ an inquiry** conduire *or* mener une enquête; (*Jur*) **to ~ sb's case** assurer la défense de qn.
c **to ~ o.s.** se conduire, se comporter.
d (*Elec, Phys*) *heat etc* conduire, être conducteur *m*, -trice *f* de.
conductance [kən'dʌktəns] n (*Elec, Phys*) conductance *f*.
conduction [kən'dʌkʃən] n (*Elec, Phys*) conduction *f*.
conductive [kən'dʌktɪv] adj (*Elec, Phys*) conducteur (*f* -trice).
conductivity [ˌkɒndʌk'tɪvɪtɪ] n (*Elec, Phys*) conductivité *f*.
conductor [kən'dʌktəʳ] n **a** (*leader*) conducteur *m*, chef *m*; (*Mus*) chef d'orchestre. **b** *[bus]* receveur *m*; (*US Rail*) chef *m* de train. **c** (*Phys*) (corps *m*) conducteur *m*; *see* **lightning**.
conductress [kən'dʌktrɪs] n receveuse *f*.
conduit ['kɒndɪt] n conduit *m*, tuyau *m*, canalisation *f*; (*Elec*) tube *m*.
condyle ['kɒndɪl] n (*Anat*) condyle *m*.
cone [kəʊn] n (*Astron, Geol, Math, Mil, Naut, Opt, Rad, Tech*) cône *m*; (*Aut*) cône *m* de signalisation; (*Bot*) *[pine etc]* cône, pomme *f*; (*Culin*) *[ice cream]* cornet *m*.
►**cone off** vt sep (*Aut*) placer des cônes de signalisation sur.
coney ['kəʊnɪ] = **cony**.
confab‡ ['kɒnfæb] n (brin *m* de) causette* *f*.
confabulate [kən'fæbjʊleɪt] vi converser, bavarder, causer (*with* avec).
confabulation [kənˌfæbjʊ'leɪʃən] n conciliabule *m*, conversation *f*.
confection [kən'fekʃən] n **a** (*Culin*) (*sweet*) sucrerie *f*, friandise *f*; (*cake*) gâteau *m*, pâtisserie *f*; (*dessert*) dessert *m* (sucré); (*Dress*) vêtement *m* de confection. **b** (*NonC*) confection *f*.
confectioner [kən'fekʃənəʳ] n (*sweet-maker*) confiseur *m*, -euse *f*; (*cakemaker*) pâtissier *m*, -ière *f*. **~'s (shop)** confiserie *f* (-pâtisserie *f*); (*US*) **~'s sugar** sucre *m* glace.
confectionery [kən'fekʃənərɪ] n confiserie *f*; (*Brit: cakes etc*) pâtisserie *f*. (*US*) **~ sugar** sucre *m* glace.
confederacy [kən'fedərəsɪ] n **a** (*Pol: group of states*) confédération *f*. (*US Hist*) **the C~** les États Confédérés. **b** (*conspiracy*) conspiration *f*.
confederate [kən'fedərɪt] **1** adj **a** confédéré. **b** (*US Hist*) **C~** Confédéré. **2** n **a** confédéré(e) *m(f)*; (*in criminal act*) complice *mf*. **b** (*US Hist*) **C~** Confédéré *m*. **3** [kən'fedəreɪt] vt confédérer. **4** vi se confédérer.
confederation [kənˌfedə'reɪʃən] n confédération *f*.
confer [kən'fɜːʳ] **1** vt conférer, accorder (*on* à). **to ~ a title** conférer un titre; (*at ceremony*) **to ~ a degree** remettre un diplôme. **2** vi conférer, s'entretenir (*with sb* avec qn, *on, about sth* de qch).
conferee [ˌkɒnfɜː'riː] n (*at congress*) congressiste *mf*.
conference ['kɒnfərəns] **1** n (*meeting, Pol*) conférence *f*, congrès *m*, assemblée *f*; (*especially academic*) congrès, colloque *m* (*on* sur); (*discussion*) conférence, consultation *f*. **to be in ~** être en conférence; **(the) ~ decided** ... les participants à la conférence *or* les congressistes ont décidé ...; *see* **press**.
2 comp ► **conference call** (*Telec*) audioconférence *f*, conférence *f* par téléphone ► **conference centre** (*town*) ville *f* de congrès; (*building*) palais *m* des congrès; (*in institution*) centre *m* de conférences ► **conference committee** (*US Pol*) *commission interparlementaire de compromis sur les projets de loi* ► **conference member** congressiste *mf* ► **conference room** salle *f* de conférences ► **conference table** (*lit, fig*) table *f* de conférence.
conferencing ['kɒnfərənsɪŋ] n (*Telec*) ~ **(facility)** possibilité *f* de réunion-téléphone.
conferment [kən'fɜːmənt] n action *f* de conférer; (*Univ*) *[degree]* remise *f* (de diplômes); *[title, favour]* octroi *m*.
confess [kən'fes] **1** vt **a** *crime* avouer, confesser; *mistake* reconnaître, avouer. **he ~ed that he had stolen the money/to having stolen the money** il a avoué *or* reconnu *or* confessé qu'il avait volé l'argent/avoir volé l'argent; **to ~ (to) a liking for sth** reconnaître qu'on aime qch; **she ~ed herself guilty/ignorant of** elle a confessé qu'elle était coupable/ignorante de. **b** (*Rel*) *faith* confesser, proclamer; *sins* confesser, se confesser de; *penitent* confesser. **2** vi **a** avouer, passer aux aveux. **to ~ to** *crime* avouer, confesser; *mistake* reconnaître, avouer; **to ~ to having done** avouer *or* reconnaître *or* confesser avoir fait; *see also* **1**. **b** (*Rel*) se confesser.
confessedly [kən'fesɪdlɪ] adv (*generally admitted*) de l'aveu de tous; (*on one's own admission*) de son propre aveu.
confession [kən'feʃən] n (*see* **confess**) **a** aveu *m*, confession *f* (*of* de). (*Jur*) **to make a full ~** faire des aveux complets. **b** (*Rel*) confession *f*. **to hear sb's ~** confesser qn; **to go to ~** aller se confesser; **to make one's ~** se confesser; **~ of faith** confession de foi; **general ~** confession générale; (*sects*) **~s** confessions.
confessional [kən'feʃənl] (*Rel*) **1** n confessionnal *m*. **under the seal of the ~** sous le secret de la confession. **2** adj confessionnel.
confessor [kən'fesəʳ] n confesseur *m*.
confetti [kən'fetiː] n confettis *mpl*.
confidant [ˌkɒnfɪ'dænt] n confident *m*.
confidante [ˌkɒnfɪ'dænt] n confidente *f*.
confide [kən'faɪd] vt **a** *object, person, job, secret* confier (*to sb* à qn). **to ~ sth to sb's care** confier qch à la garde *or* aux soins de qn; **to ~ secrets to sb** confier des secrets à qn. **b** avouer en confidence. **she ~d to me that** ... elle m'a avoué en confidence que ..., elle m'a confié que ... .
►**confide in** vt fus **a** (*have confidence in*) *sb's ability* se fier à, avoir confiance en. **you can confide in me** vous pouvez me faire confiance. **b** (*tell secrets to*) s'ouvrir à, se confier à. **to confide in sb about sth** confier qch à qn; **to confide in sb about what one is going to do** révéler à qn ce qu'on va faire.
confidence ['kɒnfɪdəns] **1** n **a** (*trust, hope*) confiance *f*. **to have ~ in sb/sth** avoir confiance en qn/qch, faire confiance à qn/qch; **to put one's ~ in sb/sth** mettre sa confiance en qn/qch; **to have every ~ in sb/sth** faire totalement confiance à qn/qch, avoir pleine confiance en qn/en *or* dans qch; **to have ~ in the future** faire confiance à l'avenir; **I have every ~ that he will come back** je suis sûr *or* certain qu'il reviendra; (*Pol etc*) **motion of no ~** motion *f* de censure; *see* **vote**.
b (*self-~*) confiance *f* en soi, assurance *f*. **he lacks ~** il manque d'assurance.
c (*NonC*) confidence *f*. **to take sb into one's ~** faire des confidences à qn, se confier à qn; **he told me that in ~** il me l'a dit en confidence *or* confidentiellement; **this is in strict ~** c'est strictement confidentiel; **"write in strict ~ to X"** "écrire à X: discrétion garantie".
d (*private communication*) confidence *f*. **they exchanged ~s** ils ont échangé des confidences.
2 comp ► **confidence game** abus *m* de confiance, escroquerie *f* ► **confidence man** escroc *m* ► **confidence trick** = **confidence game** ► **confidence trickster** = **confidence man**.
confident ['kɒnfɪdənt] adj **a** (*sure*) assuré, sûr, persuadé (*of* de). **to be ~ of success** *or* **of succeeding** être sûr de réussir; **I am ~ that he will succeed** je suis sûr *or* persuadé qu'il réussira. **b** (*self-~*) sûr de soi, assuré.
confidential [ˌkɒnfɪ'denʃəl] adj *letter, remark, information* confidentiel; *servant* de confiance. **~ clerk** homme *m* de confiance; **~ secretary** secrétaire *mf* particulier (-ière); **in a ~ tone of voice** sur le ton de la confidence.
confidentiality [ˌkɒnfɪˌdenʃɪ'ælɪtɪ] n confidentialité *f*.
confidentially [ˌkɒnfɪ'dənʃəlɪ] adv confidentiellement, en confidence.
confidently ['kɒnfɪdəntlɪ] adv avec confiance; *predict, state* avec assurance; *expect* avec optimisme.
confiding [kən'faɪdɪŋ] adj confiant, sans méfiance.
configuration [kənˌfɪgjʊ'reɪʃən] n configuration *f* (*also Ling, Comput*).
confine [kən'faɪn] **1** vt **a** (*imprison*) emprisonner, enfermer; (*shut up*) confiner, enfermer (*in* dans). **to ~ a bird in a cage** enfermer un oiseau dans une cage; **to be ~d to the house/to one's room/to bed** être obligé de rester chez soi/de garder la chambre/de garder le lit; (*Mil*) **to ~ sb to barracks** consigner qn.
b (*limit*) *remarks, opinions* limiter, borner, restreindre. **to ~ o.s. to doing** se borner à faire; **to ~ o.s. to generalities** s'en tenir à des généralités; **the damage is ~d to the back of the car** seul l'arrière de la voiture est endommagé.
2 **~s** ['kɒnfaɪnz] npl (*lit, fig*) confins *mpl*, bornes *fpl*, limites *fpl*; **within the ~s of** dans les limites de.
confined [kən'faɪnd] adj *atmosphere, air* confiné. **in a ~ space** dans un espace restreint *or* réduit; (*Mil*) **~ to barracks/base** consigné; (*in childbirth*) **to be ~** accoucher, être en couches.

confinement [kən'faɪnmənt] n (*Med*) couches *fpl*; (*imprisonment*) emprisonnement *m*, détention *f*, réclusion *f* (*Jur, liter*); (*Mil: also* ~ **to barracks**) consigne *f* (au quartier). (*Mil*) **to get 10 days' ~ to barracks** attraper 10 jours de consigne; ~ **to bed** alitement *m*; ~ **to one's room/the house** obligation *f* de garder la chambre/de rester chez soi; *see* **close**[1].

confirm [kən'fɜːm] vt *statement, report, news, suspicions* confirmer, corroborer; *arrangement, reservation* confirmer (*with sb* auprès de qn); *authority* (r)affermir, consolider; *one's resolve* fortifier, raffermir; *treaty, appointment* ratifier; (*Rel*) confirmer; (*Jur*) *decision* entériner, homologuer; *election* valider. **to ~ sth to sb** confirmer qch à qn; **to ~ sb in an opinion** confirmer *or* fortifier qn dans une opinion; **to be ~ed in one's opinion** voir son opinion confirmée; **we ~ receipt of your letter** nous avons bien reçu votre lettre, nous accusons réception de votre lettre.

confirmation [ˌkɒnfə'meɪʃən] n (*see* **confirm**) confirmation *f*; corroboration *f*; raffermissement *m*, consolidation *f*; ratification *f*; (*Rel*) confirmation; (*Jur*) entérinement *m*.

confirmed [kən'fɜːmd] adj *smoker, drunkard, liar* invétéré; *bachelor, sinner* endurci; *habit* incorrigible, invétéré; *booking, reservation* confirmé. **I am a ~ admirer of ...** je suis un fervent admirateur de ...; ~ **credit** crédit *m* confirmé; ~ **letter of credit** lettre *f* de crédit confirmée.

confiscate ['kɒnfɪskeɪt] vt confisquer (*sth from sb* qch à qn).

confiscation [ˌkɒnfɪs'keɪʃən] n confiscation *f*.

conflagration [ˌkɒnflə'greɪʃən] n incendie *m*, sinistre *m*; (*fig*) conflagration *f*.

conflate [kən'fleɪt] vt assembler, réunir.

conflation [kən'fleɪʃən] n assemblage *m*, réunion *f*.

conflict ['kɒnflɪkt] **1** n conflit *m*, lutte *f*; (*quarrel*) dispute *f*; (*Mil*) conflit, combat *m*; (*Jur*) conflit; (*fig*) *[interests, ideas, opinions]* conflit. (*Mil*) **armed ~** conflit armé; **to be in ~ (with)** être en conflit (avec); **to come into ~ with** entrer en conflit *or* en lutte avec; **a great deal of ~** un conflit considérable. **2** [kən'flɪkt] vi **a** être *or* entrer en conflit *or* en lutte (*with* avec). **b** *[opinions, ideas]* s'opposer, se heurter; *[dates]* coïncider. **that ~s with what he told me** ceci est en contradiction avec *or* contredit ce qu'il m'a raconté.

conflicting [kən'flɪktɪŋ] adj *views, opinions* incompatible, discordant; *reports, evidence* contradictoire.

confluence ['kɒnfluəns] n *[rivers]* (*place*) confluent *m*; (*act*) confluence *f*; (*fig: crowd*) foule *f*, assemblée *f*.

conform [kən'fɔːm] **1** vt *one's life, actions, methods* conformer, adapter, rendre conforme (*to* à). **2** vi **a** se conformer, s'adapter (*to, with* à); *[actions, sayings]* être en conformité (*to* avec). **b** (*gen, Rel*) être conformiste *mf*.

conformable [kən'fɔːməbl] adj **a** conforme (*to* à). **b** (*in agreement with*) adapté (*to* à), compatible, en accord (*to* avec). **c** (*submissive*) docile, accommodant.

conformation [ˌkɒnfə'meɪʃən] n conformation *f*, structure *f*.

conformist [kən'fɔːmɪst] adj, n (*gen, Rel*) conformiste (*mf*).

conformity [kən'fɔːmɪtɪ] n (*likeness*) conformité *f*, ressemblance *f*; (*agreement*) conformité, accord *m*; (*submission*) conformité, soumission *f*; (*Rel*) *adhésion f à la religion conformiste*. **in ~ with your wishes** en accord avec vos désirs, conformément à vos désirs.

confound [kən'faʊnd] vt (*perplex*) déconcerter; (*frm: defeat*) *enemy, plans* confondre (*frm*); (*mix up*) confondre (*sth with sth* qch avec qch), prendre (*sth with sth* qch pour qch). **~ it!*** la barbe!*; **~ him!*** qu'il aille au diable!, (que) le diable l'emporte!†; **it's a ~ed nuisance!*** c'est la barbe!*, quelle barbe!*

confront [kən'frʌnt] vt **a** (*bring face to face*) confronter (*with* avec), mettre en présence (*with* de). **the police ~ed the accused with the witnesses** la police a confronté l'accusé avec les témoins; **the police ~ed the accused with the evidence** la police a mis l'accusé en présence des témoignages; **to ~ two witnesses** confronter deux témoins (entre eux). **b** *enemy, danger* affronter, faire face à; (*defy*) affronter, défier. **the problems which ~ us** les problèmes auxquels nous devons faire face.

confrontation [ˌkɒnfrən'teɪʃən] n **a** (*military*) affrontement *m*; (*in human relationships*) conflit *m*, affrontement. **b** (*act of confronting*) confrontation *f* (*of sb with sth* de qn à *or* avec qch).

confrontational [ˌkɒnfrən'teɪʃənəl] adj conflictuel.

Confucian [kən'fjuːʃən] **1** adj confucéen. **2** n Confucianiste *mf*.

Confucianism [kən'fjuːʃənɪzəm] n Confucianisme *m*.

Confucius [kən'fjuːʃəs] n Confucius *m*.

confuse [kən'fjuːz] vt **a** (*throw into disorder*) *opponent* confondre; *plans* semer le désordre dans, bouleverser; (*perplex*) jeter dans la perplexité; (*embarras*) embarrasser; (*disconcert*) troubler; (*mix up*) *persons* embrouiller; *ideas* embrouiller, brouiller; *memory* brouiller. **you are just confusing me** tu ne fais que m'embrouiller (les idées); **to ~ the issue** compliquer *or* embrouiller les choses. **b to ~ sth with sth** confondre qch avec qch, prendre qch pour qch; **to ~ two problems** confondre deux problèmes.

confused [kən'fjuːzd] adj *person* (*muddled*) désorienté; (*perplexed*) déconcerté; (*embarrassed*) confus, embarrassé; *opponent* confondu; *mind* embrouillé, confus; *sounds, voices* confus, indistinct; *memories* confus, brouillé, vague; *ideas, situation* confus, embrouillé. **to have a ~ idea** avoir une vague idée; **to get ~** (*muddled up*) ne plus savoir où on en est, s'y perdre; (*embarrassed*) se troubler.

confusedly [kən'fjuːzɪdlɪ] adv confusément.

confusing [kən'fjuːzɪŋ] adj déroutant. **it's all very ~** on ne s'y retrouve plus, on s'y perd.

confusion [kən'fjuːʒən] n (*disorder, muddle*) confusion *f*, désordre *m*; (*embarrassment*) confusion, trouble *m*; (*mixing up*) confusion (*of sth with sth else* de qch avec qch d'autre). **he was in a state of ~** la confusion régnait dans son esprit, il avait l'esprit troublé; **the books lay about in ~** les livres étaient en désordre *or* pêle-mêle; *see* **throw**.

confute [kən'fjuːt] vt *person* prouver *or* démontrer l'erreur de, réfuter les arguments de; *argument* réfuter.

congeal [kən'dʒiːl] **1** vi *[oil]* (se) figer; *[milk]* (se) cailler; *[blood]* se coaguler; *[paint]* sécher. **2** vt *oil* faire figer; *milk* faire cailler; *blood* coaguler.

congenial [kən'dʒiːnɪəl] adj *person, atmosphere, surroundings* sympathique, agréable. **he found few people ~ to him** il y avait peu de gens qu'il trouvait sympathiques *or* avec lesquels il se trouvait en sympathie.

congenital [kən'dʒenɪtl] adj (*Med*) congénital; (*hum*) *liar* de naissance, né; *dislike* congénital.

congenitally [kən'dʒenɪtəlɪ] adv congénitalement; (*hum*) de naissance.

conger ['kɒŋgəʳ] n: ~ **eel** congre *m*, anguille *f* de roche.

congested [kən'dʒestɪd] adj *town, countryside* surpeuplé; *street* encombré, embouteillé; *corridors, pavement* encombré; *telephone lines* embouteillé; (*Med*) congestionné. ~ **traffic** embouteillage(s) *m(pl)*, encombrement(s) *m(pl)*.

congestion [kən'dʒestʃən] n *[town, countryside]* surpeuplement *m*; *[street, traffic]* encombrement *m*, embouteillage *m*; (*Med*) congestion *f*.

conglomerate [kən'glɒməreɪt] **1** vt conglomérer (*frm*), agglomérer. **2** vi s'agglomérer. **3** [kən'glɒmərɪt] adj congloméré (*also Geol*), aggloméré. **4** n (*gen, Econ, Geol*) conglomérat *m*.

conglomeration [kənˌglɒmə'reɪʃən] n **a** (*NonC: act, state*) conglomération *f* (*frm*), agglomération *f*. **b** (*group*) *[objects]* groupement *m*, rassemblement *m*; *[houses]* agglomération *f*.

Congo ['kɒŋgəʊ] n (*river, state*) Congo *m*.

Congolese [ˌkɒŋgəʊ'liːz] **1** adj congolais. **2** n, pl inv Congolais(e) *m(f)*.

congratulate [kən'grætjʊleɪt] vt féliciter, complimenter (*sb on sth* qn de qch, *sb on doing* qn d'avoir fait *or* (*future action*) de faire). **to ~ o.s. on sth/on doing sth** se féliciter de qch/d'avoir fait qch; **we would like to ~ you on your engagement** nous vous présentons toutes nos félicitations à l'occasion de vos fiançailles.

congratulations [kənˌgrætjʊ'leɪʃənz] npl félicitations *fpl*, compliments *mpl*. **~!** toutes mes félicitations!; **~ on your success/engagement** (toutes mes) félicitations pour votre succès/à l'occasion de vos fiançailles.

congratulatory [kən'grætjʊlətərɪ] adj de félicitations.

congregate ['kɒŋgrɪgeɪt] **1** vi se rassembler, s'assembler, se réunir (*round* autour de, *at* à). **2** vt rassembler, réunir, assembler.

congregation [ˌkɒŋgrɪ'geɪʃən] n rassemblement *m*, assemblée *f*; (*Rel*) *[worshippers]* assemblée (des fidèles), assistance *f*; *[cardinals, monks etc]* congrégation *f*; (*Univ*) *[professors]* assemblée générale.

congregational [ˌkɒŋgrɪ'geɪʃnl] adj (*see* **congregation**) de l'assemblée des fidèles, en assemblée; de congrégation, d'une congrégation. **the C~ Church** l'Église *f* congrégationaliste.

Congregationalist [ˌkɒŋgrɪ'geɪʃənəˌlɪst] adj,n congrégationaliste *(mf)*.

congress ['kɒŋgres] **1** n **a** congrès *m*. **education ~** congrès de l'enseignement; *see* **trade**. **b** (*US Pol*) **C~** Congrès *m*; (*session*) session *f* du Congrès. **2** comp ► **congressman** (*US Pol*) membre *m* du Congrès, ≃ député *m*; (*US*) **congressman-at-large** *représentant non attaché à une circonscription électorale;* **Congressman J. Smith said that ...** Monsieur le Député J. Smith a dit que ... ► **congress member** congressiste *mf* ► **congressperson** (*US*) membre *m* du Congrès ► **congresswoman** membre *m* du Congrès, ≃ député *m*.

congressional [kɒŋ'greʃənl] adj **a** d'un congrès. **b** (*US Pol*) **C~** du Congrès; **C~ Directory** annuaire *m* du Congrès; **C~ district** circonscription *f* d'un Représentant; **C~ Record** Journal Officiel du Congrès.

congruent ['kɒŋgrʊənt] adj d'accord, en harmonie (*with* avec), conforme (*with* à); (*suitable*) convenable (*with* à); (*Math*) *number* congru (*with* à); *triangle* congruent.

congruity [kɒŋ'gruːɪtɪ] n convenance *f*, congruité *f*.

congruous ['kɒŋgrʊəs] adj qui convient, convenable (*to, with* à), approprié (*to, with* à), qui s'accorde (*to, with* avec); (*Rel*) congru.

conic(al) ['kɒnɪk(əl)] adj (de forme) conique.

conifer ['kɒnɪfəʳ] n conifère *m*.

coniferous [kə'nɪfərəs] adj *tree* conifère; *forest* de conifères.

conjectural [kən'dʒektʃərəl] adj conjectural.

conjecture [kən'dʒektʃəʳ] **1** vt conjecturer, supposer. **2** vi conjecturer, faire des conjectures. **3** n conjecture *f*.

conjoin [kən'dʒɔɪn] **1** vt adjoindre, unir. **2** vi s'unir.

conjoint ['kɒn'dʒɔɪnt] adj joint, uni, associé.
conjointly ['kɒn'dʒɔɪntlɪ] adv conjointement.
conjugal ['kɒndʒʊgəl] adj *state, rights, happiness* conjugal.
conjugate ['kɒndʒʊgeɪt] (*Bio, Gram*) 1 vt conjuguer. 2 vi se conjuguer.
conjugation [ˌkɒndʒʊ'geɪʃən] n conjugaison *f.*
conjunct [kən'dʒʌŋkt] adj conjoint.
conjunction [kən'dʒʌŋkʃən] n (*Astron, Gram*) conjonction *f;* (*NonC*) conjonction, connexion *f,* jonction *f,* union *f.* **in ~ with** conjointement avec.
conjunctiva [ˌkɒndʒʌŋk'taɪvə] n, pl **~s** *or* **conjunctivae** [ˌkɒndʒʌŋk'taɪviː] (*Anat*) conjonctive *f.*
conjunctive [kən'dʒʌŋktɪv] adj (*Anat, Gram*) conjonctif.
conjunctivitis [kənˌdʒʌŋktɪ'vaɪtɪs] n conjonctivite *f.* **to have ~** avoir de la conjonctivite.
conjuncture [kən'dʒʌŋktʃər] n (*combination of circumstances*) conjoncture *f,* circonstance(s) *f(pl);* (*crisis*) moment *m* critique.
conjure [kən'dʒʊər] 1 vt a (*appeal to*) conjurer, prier, supplier (*sb to do* qn de faire). b ['kʌndʒər] faire apparaître (*par la prestidigitation*). **he ~d a rabbit from his hat** il a fait sortir un lapin de son chapeau. 2 ['kʌndʒər] vi faire des tours de passe-passe; (*juggle*) jongler (*with* avec); (*fig*) jongler (*with* avec). (*fig*) **a name to ~ with** un nom prestigieux.
►**conjure away** vt sep faire disparaître (comme par magie).
►**conjure up** vt sep *ghosts, spirits* faire apparaître; *memories* évoquer, rappeler. **to conjure up visions of ...** évoquer ... .
conjurer ['kʌndʒərər] n prestidigitateur *m,* -trice *f,* illusionniste *mf.*
conjuring ['kʌndʒərɪŋ] n prestidigitation *f,* illusionnisme *m.* **~ trick** tour *m* de passe-passe *or* de prestidigitation.
conjuror ['kʌndʒərər] = **conjurer.**
conk‡ [kɒŋk] 1 n (*Brit: nose*) pif‡ *m,* blair‡ *m;* (*US: head*) caboche‡ *f.* 2 vi *[engine, machine]* tomber *or* rester en panne. 3 vt (*US*) frapper sur la caboche‡. 4 comp ► **conk-out‡** (*US*) panne mécanique.
►**conk out*** 1 vi *[person]* crever‡, clamecer‡; *[engine, machine]* tomber *or* rester en panne. **her car conked out** sa voiture est restée en carafe*. 2 **conk-out‡** adj *see* **conk 4.**
conker* ['kɒŋkər] n (*Brit*) marron *m.*
Conn. (*US*) abbr of **Connecticut.**
connect [kə'nekt] 1 vt a (*join: gen*) *[person]* joindre, relier, rattacher (*with, to* à); (*Tech*) *pinions* embrayer; *wheels* engrener; *pipes, drains* raccorder (*to* à); *shafts etc* articuler, conjuguer; (*Elec*) *two objects* raccorder, connecter. (*Elec*) **to ~ to the mains** brancher sur le secteur; (*Elec*) **to ~ to earth** mettre à la masse; (*to water, electricity etc services*) **we haven't been ~ed yet** nous ne sommes pas encore reliés *or* branchés, nous n'avons pas encore l'eau *etc.*
b (*Telec*) *caller* mettre en communication (*with sb* avec qn); *telephone* brancher. **we're trying to ~ you** nous essayons d'obtenir votre communication; **I'm ~ing you now** vous êtes en ligne, vous avez votre communication; **~ed by telephone** *person, place* relié par téléphone (*to, with* à).
c (*associate*) associer (*with, to* à). **I always ~ Paris with springtime** j'associe toujours Paris au printemps; **I'd never have ~ed them** je n'aurais jamais fait le rapport entre eux; *see also* **connected.**
d (*form link between*) *[road, railway]* relier (*with, to* à); *[rope etc]* relier, rattacher (*with, to* à). **the city is ~ed to the sea by a canal** la ville est reliée à la mer par un canal.
2 vi a (*be joined*) *[two rooms]* être relié, communiquer; *[two parts, wires etc]* être connectés *or* raccordés.
b *[coach, train, plane]* assurer la correspondance (*with* avec). **this train ~s with the Rome express** ce train assure la correspondance avec l'express de Rome.
c (*: *hit etc*) *[golf club etc]* **to ~ with the ball** frapper la balle; **my fist ~ed with his jaw*** je l'ai touché à la mâchoire, mon poing l'a cueilli à la mâchoire.
connected [kə'nektɪd] adj a *languages* affin (*frm*), connexe; (*Bot, Jur*) connexe; (*fig*) *argument* logique; *talk, oration* suivi. **(closely) ~ professions** des professions *fpl* connexes; **a (properly) ~ sentence** une phrase correctement construite; (*Ling*) **~ speech** la chaîne parlée.
b **these matters are not ~ at all** ces affaires n'ont aucun lien *or* rapport entre elles; **these two things are ~ in my mind** les deux sont liés dans mon esprit; **to be ~ with** (*be related to*) être allié à, être parent de; (*have dealings with*) avoir des rapports *or* des contacts *or* des relations avec; (*have a bearing on*) se rattacher à, avoir rapport à; **people ~ with education** ceux qui ont quelque chose à voir avec le monde de l'éducation; **he is ~ with many big firms** il a des rapports *or* des contacts *or* des relations avec beaucoup de firmes importantes, il est en relations avec beaucoup de firmes importantes; **his departure is not ~ with the murder** son départ n'a aucun rapport *or* n'a rien à voir avec le meurtre; **he's very well ~** (*of good family*) il est de très bonne famille, il est très bien apparenté; (*of influential family*) sa famille a des relations; *see also* **connect.**
Connecticut [kə'netɪkət] n Connecticut. **in ~** dans le Connecticut.
connecting [kə'nektɪŋ] 1 adj *rooms etc* communicant; *parts, wires* raccordé, connecté. **bedroom with ~ bathroom** chambre avec salle de bains attenante. 2 comp ► **connecting flight** (vol *m* de) correspondance *f* ► **connecting rod** (*US Aut*) bielle *f.*
connection, connexion [kə'nekʃən] n a (*see* **connect**) jonction *f,* liaison *f;* (*Elec*) prise *f,* contact *m,* connexion *f;* (*Tech*) embrayage *m,* engrenage *m;* raccord *m,* raccordement *m;* articulation *f;* (*Telec*) communication *f* (téléphonique); (*act of connecting*) connexion. (*Telec*) **wrong ~** faux numéro, fausse communication.
b (*fig*) rapport *m* (*with* avec), lien *m* (*between* entre), relation *f,* liaison *f;* (*relationship*) rapports, relations. **this has no ~ with what he did** ceci n'a aucun rapport avec ce qu'il a fait; **in this** *or* **that ~** à ce sujet, à ce propos, dans cet ordre d'idées; **in ~ with** à propos de, relativement à; **in another ~** dans un autre ordre d'idées; **to form a ~ with sb** établir des relations *or* des rapports avec qn; **to break off a ~ (with sb)** rompre les relations (avec qn); **to build up a ~ with a firm** établir des relations d'affaires avec une firme; **to have no further ~ with** rompre tout contact avec; (*Comm*) **we have no ~ with any other firm** toute ressemblance avec une autre compagnie est purement fortuite; **to have important ~s** avoir des relations (importantes).
c (*clientele, business contacts*) clientèle *f,* relations *fpl* d'affaires. **this grocer has a very good ~** cet épicier a une très bonne clientèle.
d *[family]* (*kinship*) parenté *f;* (*relative*) parent(e) *m(f).* **~s** famille *f;* **there is some family ~ between them** ils ont un lien de parenté; **he is a distant ~** c'est un parent éloigné; **she is a ~ of mine** c'est une de mes parentes.
e (*Jur*) **criminal ~** liaison criminelle *or* adultérine; **sexual ~** rapports sexuels.
f (*Rail*) correspondance *f* (*with* avec). **to miss one's ~** manquer la correspondance.
g (*Drugs sl*) filière *f.*
h (*Rel*) secte *f* (religieuse).
connective [kə'nektɪv] 1 adj (*gen, Gram, Anat*) conjonctif. 2 n (*Gram, Logic*) conjonction *f.*
conning tower ['kɒnɪŋˌtaʊər] n *[submarine]* kiosque *m; [warship]* centre opérationnel.
conniption* [kə'nɪpʃən] n (*US: also* **~s**) crise *f* de colère *or* de rage.
connivance [kə'naɪvəns] n connivence *f,* accord *m* tacite. **this was done with her ~/in ~ with her** cela s'est fait avec sa connivence *or* son accord tacite/de connivence avec elle.
connive [kə'naɪv] vi: **to ~ at** (*pretend not to notice*) fermer les yeux sur; (*aid and abet*) être de connivence dans, être complice de; **to ~ (with sb) in sth/in doing** être de connivence (avec qn) dans qch/pour faire.
conniving [kə'naɪvɪŋ] 1 adj (*pej*) intrigant. 2 n (*NonC*) machinations *fpl,* intrigues *fpl.*
connoisseur [ˌkɒnə'sɜːr] n connaisseur *m,* -euse *f* (*of* de, en).
connotation [ˌkɒnəʊ'teɪʃən] n (*Ling*) connotation *f;* (*Philos*) connotation, compréhension *f;* (*Logic*) implication *f.*
connotative ['kɒnəˌteɪtɪv] adj (*meaning*) connotatif.
connote [kɒ'nəʊt] vt impliquer, suggérer, comporter l'idée de; (*Ling, Philos*) connoter; (*: *signify*) signifier.
connubial [kə'njuːbɪəl] adj conjugal.
conquer ['kɒŋkər] vt (*lit*) *person, enemy* vaincre, battre; *nation, country* conquérir, subjuguer; *castle* conquérir; (*fig*) *feelings, habits* surmonter, vaincre; *sb's heart, one's freedom* conquérir; *one's audience* subjuguer.
conquering ['kɒŋkərɪŋ] adj victorieux.
conqueror ['kɒŋkərər] n (*Mil*) conquérant *m;* (*of mountain etc*) vainqueur *m; see* **William.**
conquest ['kɒŋkwest] n conquête *f.* **to make a ~*** faire une conquête; **she's his latest ~*** c'est sa dernière conquête*.
consanguinity [ˌkɒnsæŋ'gwɪnɪtɪ] n consanguinité *f.*
conscience ['kɒnʃəns] 1 n conscience *f.* **to have a clear** *or* **an easy ~** avoir bonne conscience, avoir la conscience tranquille; **he left with a clear ~** il est parti la conscience tranquille; **he has a bad** *or* **guilty ~** il a mauvaise conscience, il n'a pas la conscience tranquille; **to have sth on one's ~** avoir qch sur la conscience; **in (all) ~** en conscience; **for ~' sake** par acquit de conscience; **upon my ~, I swear ...** en mon âme et conscience, je jure ...; **to make sth a matter of ~** faire de qch un cas de conscience.
2 comp ► **conscience clause** (*Jur*) clause *f or* article *m* qui sauvegarde la liberté de conscience ► **conscience money** argent restitué (*généralement au Trésor par scrupule de conscience*) ► **conscience-stricken** pris de remords.
conscientious [ˌkɒnʃɪ'enʃəs] adj a *person, worker, piece of work* consciencieux. b *scruple, objection* de conscience. **~ objector** objecteur *m* de conscience.
conscientiously [ˌkɒnʃɪ'enʃəslɪ] adv consciencieusement, avec conscience.
conscientiousness [ˌkɒnʃɪ'enʃəsnɪs] n conscience *f.*
conscious ['kɒnʃəs] 1 adj a conscient, ayant conscience (*of* de). **to be ~ of one's responsibilities** être conscient de ses responsabilités; **to be ~ of doing** avoir conscience de faire; **to become ~ of sth** prendre conscience de qch, s'apercevoir de qch. b (*Med*) conscient. **to become ~** revenir à soi, reprendre connaissance. c (*clearly felt*) *guilt*

conscient, dont on a conscience, ressenti clairement. **with ~ superiority** avec une supériorité consciente de soi, avec la nette conscience de sa (*or* leur *etc*) supériorité. d (*deliberate*) *insult* conscient, intentionnel, délibéré. **~ humour** humour voulu. e (*Philos*) conscient. 2 **n** (*Psych*) conscient *m*.

consciously [ˈkɒnʃəslɪ] **adv** consciemment; (*deliberately*) sciemment, intentionnellement.

consciousness [ˈkɒnʃəsnɪs] 1 **n** a (*Med*) connaissance *f*. **to lose ~** perdre connaissance; **to regain ~** revenir à soi, reprendre connaissance. b (*Philos*) conscience *f*. c (*awareness*) conscience *f* (*of* de), sentiment *m* (*of* de). **the ~ that he was being watched prevented him from ...** le sentiment qu'on le regardait l'empêchait de ... . 2 **comp** ▸ **consciousness-raising** (*Psych*) prise *f* de conscience (personnelle); **consciousness-raising is a priority** il nous faut d'abord faire prendre conscience aux gens.

conscript [kənˈskrɪpt] 1 **vt** *troops* enrôler, recruter (par conscription), appeler sous les drapeaux. (*fig*) **we were ~ed to help with the dishes** nous avons été embauchés pour aider à faire la vaisselle; **~ed men** *or* **labourers** forçats *mpl*. 2 [ˈkɒnskrɪpt] **n** conscrit *m*, appelé *m*. 3 **adj** conscrit.

conscription [kənˈskrɪpʃən] **n** conscription *f*.

consecrate [ˈkɒnsɪkreɪt] **vt** *church etc* consacrer; *bishop* consacrer, sacrer; (*fig*) *custom, one's life* consacrer (*to* à). **he was ~d bishop** il a été sacré *or* consacré évêque.

consecration [ˌkɒnsɪˈkreɪʃən] **n** (*see* **consecrate**) consécration *f*; sacre *m*.

consecutive [kənˈsekjʊtɪv] **adj** a consécutif. **on 4 ~ days** pendant 4 jours consécutifs *or* de suite. b (*Gram*) *clause* consécutif.

consecutively [kənˈsekjʊtɪvlɪ] **adv** consécutivement. **he won 2 prizes ~** il a gagné consécutivement *or* coup sur coup 2 prix; (*Jur*) **... the sentences to be served ~** ... avec cumul *m* de peines.

consensus [kənˈsensəs] 1 **n** consensus *m*, accord général. **~ of opinion** consensus d'opinion; **what is the ~?** quelle est l'opinion générale? 2 **adj** *decision, view* collectif.

consent [kənˈsent] 1 **vi** consentir (*to sth* à qch, *to do* à faire); (*to request*) accéder (*to sth* à qch). (*Jur*) **between ~ing adults** entre adultes consentants. 2 **n** consentement *m*, assentiment *m*. **to refuse one's ~ to** refuser son consentement *or* assentiment à; **by common ~** de l'aveu de tous *or* de tout le monde, de l'opinion de tous; **by mutual ~** (*general agreement*) d'un commun accord; (*private arrangement*) de gré à gré, à l'amiable; **divorce by (mutual) ~** divorce *m* par consentement mutuel; (*Jur*) **age of ~** âge *m* nubile (légal); *see* **silence**.

consentient [kənˈsenʃɪənt] **adj** d'accord, en accord (*with* avec).

consequence [ˈkɒnsɪkwəns] **n** a (*result, effect*) conséquence *f*, suites *fpl*. **in ~** par conséquent; **in ~ of which** par suite de quoi; **as a ~ of sth** en conséquence de qch; **to take** *or* **face the ~s** accepter *or* supporter les conséquences (*of* de). b (*NonC: importance*) importance *f*, conséquence *f*. **it's of no ~** cela ne tire pas à conséquence, cela n'a aucune importance; **a man of no ~** un homme de peu d'importance *or* de peu de poids; **he's of no ~** lui, il ne compte pas.

consequent [ˈkɒnsɪkwənt] **adj** (*following*) consécutif (*on* à); (*resulting*) résultant (*on* de). **the loss of harvest ~ upon the flooding** la perte de la moisson résultant des *or* causée par les inondations.

consequential [ˌkɒnsɪˈkwenʃəl] **adj** a consécutif, conséquent (*to* à). (*Jur*) **~ damages** dommages-intérêts indirects. b (*pej*) *person* suffisant, arrogant.

consequently [ˈkɒnsɪkwəntlɪ] **adv** par conséquent, donc, en conséquence.

conservancy [kənˈsɜːvənsɪ] **n** a (*Brit: commission controlling forests, ports etc*) ≃ Office *m* des eaux et forêts. b = **conservation**.

conservation [ˌkɒnsəˈveɪʃən] 1 **n** préservation *f*; *[nature]* défense *f* de l'environnement; (*Phys*) conservation *f*. 2 **comp** ▸ **conservation area** (*Brit*) secteur sauvegardé.

conservationist [ˌkɒnsəˈveɪʃənɪst] **n** défenseur *m* de l'environnement.

conservatism [kənˈsɜːvətɪzəm] **n** conservatisme *m*.

conservative [kənˈsɜːvətɪv] 1 **adj** a conservateur (*f* -trice). (*Pol*) **the C~ Party** le parti conservateur; **C~ and Unionist Party** parti conservateur et unioniste. b *assessment* modeste; *style, behaviour* traditionnel. **at a ~ estimate** au bas mot. 2 **n** (*Pol*) conservateur *m*, -trice *f*.

conservatoire [kənˈsɜːvətwɑːʳ] **n** (*Mus*) conservatoire *m*.

conservator [ˈkɒnsəˌveɪtəʳ] **n** (*gen*) gardien(ne) *m(f)*; (*US Jur*) tuteur *m* (*d'un incapable*).

conservatorship [ˈkɒnsəveɪtəˌʃɪp] **n** (*US Jur*) tutelle *f*.

conservatory [kənˈsɜːvətrɪ] **n** a (*greenhouse*) serre *f* (*attenante à une maison*). b (*Art, Mus, Theat*) conservatoire *m*.

conserve [kənˈsɜːv] 1 **vt** conserver, préserver; *one's resources, one's strength* ménager; *energy, electricity, supplies* économiser. 2 **n** (*Culin*) **~s** confitures *fpl*, conserves *fpl* (de fruits).

consider [kənˈsɪdəʳ] **vt** a (*think about*) *problem, possibility* considérer, examiner; *question, matter, subject* réfléchir à. **I had not ~ed taking it with me** je n'avais pas envisagé de l'emporter; **everything** *or* **all things ~ed** tout bien considéré, toute réflexion faite, tout compte fait; **it is my ~ed opinion that ...** après avoir mûrement réfléchi je pense que ...; **he is being ~ed for the post** on songe à lui pour le poste. b (*take into account*) *facts* prendre en considération; *person's feelings* avoir égard à, ménager; *cost, difficulties, dangers* tenir compte de, considérer, regarder à. **when one ~s that ...** quand on considère *or* pense que ... . c (*be of the opinion*) considérer, tenir. **she ~s him very mean** elle le considère comme très avare, elle le tient pour très avare; **to ~ o.s. happy** s'estimer heureux; **~ yourself lucky*** estimez-vous heureux; **~ yourself dismissed** considérez-vous comme renvoyé; **I ~ that we should have done it** je considère que *or* à mon avis nous aurions dû le faire; **to ~ sth as done** tenir qch pour fait; **I ~ it an honour to help you** je m'estime honoré de (pouvoir) vous aider.

considerable [kənˈsɪdərəbl] **adj** *number, size* considérable; *sum of money* considérable, important. **there was a ~ number of ...** il y avait un nombre considérable de ...; **to a ~ extent** dans une large mesure; **we had ~ difficulty in finding you** nous avons eu beaucoup de mal à vous trouver.

considerably [kənˈsɪdərəblɪ] **adv** considérablement.

considerate [kənˈsɪdərɪt] **adj** prévenant (*towards* envers), plein d'égards (*towards* pour, envers).

considerately [kənˈsɪdərɪtlɪ] **adv** *act* avec prévenance, avec égards.

consideration [kənˌsɪdəˈreɪʃən] **n** a (*NonC: thoughtfulness*) considération *f*, estime *f*, égard *m*. **out of ~ for** par égard pour; **to show ~ for sb's feelings** ménager les susceptibilités de qn. b (*NonC: careful thought*) considération *f*. **to take sth into ~** prendre qch en considération, tenir compte de qch; **taking everything into ~** tout bien considéré *or* pesé; **he left it out of ~** il n'en a pas tenu compte, il n'a pas pris cela en considération; **the matter is under ~** l'affaire est à l'examen *or* à l'étude; **in ~ of** en considération de, eu égard à; **after due ~** après mûre réflexion; **please give my suggestion your careful ~** je vous prie d'apporter toute votre attention à ma suggestion. c (*fact etc to be taken into account*) préoccupation *f*, considération *f*; (*motive*) motif *m*. **money is the first ~** il faut considérer d'abord *or* en premier lieu la question d'argent; **many ~s have made me act thus** plusieurs considérations *or* motifs m'ont amené à agir ainsi; **on no ~** à aucun prix, en aucun cas; **it's of no ~** cela n'a aucune importance; **money is no ~** l'argent n'entre pas en ligne de compte; **his age was an important ~** son âge constituait un facteur important. d (*reward, payment*) rétribution *f*, rémunération *f*. **to do sth for a ~** faire qch moyennant finance *or* contre espèces; (*Jur, Fin*) **for a good and valuable ~** ≃ moyennant contrepartie valable. e (*reason*) **on no ~** sous aucun prétexte.

considering [kənˈsɪdərɪŋ] 1 **prep** vu, étant donné. **~ the circumstances** vu *or* étant donné les circonstances. 2 **conj** vu que, étant donné que. **~ she has no money** vu que *or* étant donné qu'elle n'a pas d'argent. 3 **adv** tout compte fait, en fin de compte. **he played very well, ~** il a très bien joué, tout compte fait *or* en fin de compte.

consign [kənˈsaɪn] **vt** a (*send*) *goods* expédier (*to sb* à qn, à l'adresse de qn). b (*hand over*) *person, thing* confier, remettre. **to ~ a child to the care of** confier *or* remettre un enfant aux soins de.

consignee [ˌkɒnsaɪˈniː] **n** consignataire *mf*.

consigner [kənˈsaɪnəʳ] **n** = **consignor**.

consignment [kənˈsaɪnmənt] **n** a (*NonC*) envoi *m*, expédition *f*. **goods for ~ abroad** marchandises *fpl* à destination de l'étranger; (*Brit*) **~ note** (*Comm*) lettre *f* de voiture. b (*quantity of goods*) (*incoming*) arrivage *m*, (*outgoing*) envoi *m*.

consignor [kənˈsaɪnəʳ] **n** expéditeur *m*, -trice *f* (*de marchandises*), consignateur *m*, -trice *f*.

consist [kənˈsɪst] **vi** a (*be composed*) consister (*of* en). **what does the house ~ of?** en quoi consiste la maison?, de quoi la maison est-elle composée? b (*have as its essence*) consister (*in doing* à faire, *in sth* dans qch). **his happiness ~s in helping others** son bonheur consiste à aider autrui.

consistency [kənˈsɪstənsɪ] **n** *[liquids etc]* consistance *f*; (*fig*) *[actions, argument, behaviour]* cohérence *f*, uniformité *f*. (*fig*) **to lack ~** manquer de logique.

consistent [kənˈsɪstənt] **adj** *person, behaviour* conséquent, logique. **his arguments are not ~** ses arguments ne se tiennent pas; **~ with** compatible avec, en accord avec.

consistently [kənˈsɪstəntlɪ] **adv** a (*logically*) avec esprit de suite, avec logique. b (*unfailingly*) régulièrement, sans exception, immanquablement. c (*in agreement*) conformément (*with* à).

consolation [ˌkɒnsəˈleɪʃən] 1 **n** consolation *f*, réconfort *m*. 2 **comp** *prize* de consolation.

consolatory [kənˈsɒlətərɪ] **adj** consolant, consolateur (*f* -trice), réconfortant.

console¹ [kənˈsəʊl] **vt** consoler (*sb for sth* qn de qch).

console² [ˈkɒnsəʊl] **n** a *[organ, language lab]* console *f*; (*Comput*) console, pupitre *m*; *[aircraft]* tableau *m* de bord, commandes *fpl*. b (*radio cabinet*) meuble *m* de radio. c (*Archit*) console *f*.

consolidate [kənˈsɒlɪdeɪt] 1 **vt** a (*make strong*) *one's position* consolider, raffermir. b (*Comm, Fin: unite*) *businesses* réunir; *loan, funds, annuities* consolider. **~d balance sheet** bilan *m* consolidé; **~d**

deliveries livraisons *fpl* groupées; ~**d fund** ≃ fonds consolidés; (*Jur*) ~**d laws** codification *f* (des lois); (*US Scol*) ~**d school district** secteur scolaire élargi. 2 **vi** se consolider, s'affermir.
consolidation [kən,sɒlɪ'deɪʃən] **n** (*see* **consolidate**) a consolidation *f*, affermissement *m*. b (*Comm, Fin*) unification *f*, consolidation *f*; *[companies]* fusion *f*; *[balance sheet]* consolidation. (*Jur*) **C~ Act** codification *f*.
consoling [kən'səʊlɪŋ] **adj** consolant, consolateur (*f* -trice).
consols ['kɒnsɒlz] **npl** (*Brit Fin*) fonds consolidés.
consonance ['kɒnsənəns] **n** *[sounds]* consonance *f*, accord *m*; *[ideas]* accord, communion *f*.
consonant ['kɒnsənənt] 1 **n** (*Ling*) consonne *f*. ~ **cluster** groupe *m* consonantique; ~ **shift** mutation *f* consonantique. 2 **adj** en accord (*with* avec). **behaviour ~ with one's beliefs** comportement qui s'accorde avec ses croyances.
consonantal [,kɒnsə'næntl] **adj** consonantique.
consort ['kɒnsɔːt] 1 **n** a (*spouse*) époux *m*, épouse *f*; (*also* **prince** ~) (prince *m*) consort *m*. b (*Naut*) conserve *f*. **in ~** de conserve. 2 [kən'sɔːt] **vi** a (*associate*) **to ~ with sb** fréquenter qn, frayer avec qn. b (*be consistent*) *[behaviour]* s'accorder (*with* avec).
consortium [kən'sɔːtɪəm] **n, pl consortia** [kən'sɔːtɪə] consortium *m*, comptoir *m*.
conspectus [kən'spektəs] **n** vue générale.
conspicuous [kən'spɪkjʊəs] **adj** *person, behaviour, clothes* voyant, qui attire la vue; *bravery* insigne; *difference, fact* notable, remarquable, manifeste. **the poster was ~** l'affiche attirait les regards, on ne pouvait pas manquer de voir l'affiche; **there was a ~ lack of ...** il y avait un manque manifeste *or* une absence manifeste de ...; **he was in a ~ position** (*lit*) il était bien en évidence; (*fig*) il occupait une situation très en vue; **to make o.s. ~** se faire remarquer, se singulariser; **to be ~ by one's absence** briller par son absence; (*Econ etc*) ~ **consumption** consommation *f* ostentatoire.
conspicuously [kən'spɪkjʊəslɪ] **adv** *behave* d'une manière à se faire remarquer; *opposed, angry* visiblement, manifestement. **he was ~ absent** son absence se remarquait, il brillait par son absence.
conspiracy [kən'spɪrəsɪ] **n** a (*plot*) conspiration *f*, complot *m*, conjuration *f*. **a ~ of silence** une conspiration du silence (*on the part of sb* de la part de qn). b (*NonC: Jur*) (*also* **criminal ~**) ≃ association *f* de malfaiteurs. ~ **to defraud** *etc* complot *m* d'escroquerie *etc*.
conspirator [kən'spɪrətə^r] **n** conspirateur *m*, -trice *f*, conjuré(e) *m(f)*.
conspiratorial [kən,spɪrə'tɔːrɪəl] **adj** de conspirateur.
conspire [kən'spaɪə^r] 1 **vi** a *[people]* conspirer (*against* contre). **to ~ to do** comploter de *or* se mettre d'accord pour faire. b *[events]* conspirer, concourir (*to do* à faire). 2 **vt** (†) comploter, méditer.
constable ['kʌnstəbl] **n** (*Brit: also* **police ~**) (*in town*) agent *m* de police, gardien *m* de la paix; (*in country*) gendarme *m*. **"yes, C~"** "oui, monsieur l'agent (*or* monsieur le gendarme)"; *see* **chief, special**.
constabulary [kən'stæbjʊlərɪ] **collective n** (*Brit*) (*in town*) (la) police en uniforme; (*in country*) (la) gendarmerie; *see* **royal**.
Constance ['kɒnstəns] **n**: **Lake ~** le lac de Constance.
constancy ['kɒnstənsɪ] **n** (*firmness*) constance *f*, fermeté *f*; *[feelings, affection]* fidélité *f*, constance; *[temperature etc]* invariabilité *f*, constance.
constant ['kɒnstənt] 1 **adj** a (*occurring often*) *quarrels, interruptions* incessant, continuel, perpétuel. b (*unchanging*) *affection* inaltérable, constant; *friend* fidèle, loyal. 2 **n** (*Math, Phys*) constante *f*. (*US Scol*) ~**s** matières *fpl* obligatoires.
Constantine ['kɒnstən,taɪn] **n** Constantin *m*.
Constantinople [,kɒnstæntɪ'nəʊpl] **n** Constantinople.
constantly ['kɒnstəntlɪ] **adv** constamment, continuellement, sans cesse.
constellation [,kɒnstə'leɪʃən] **n** constellation *f*.
consternation [,kɒnstə'neɪʃən] **n** consternation *f*. **filled with ~** frappé de consternation, consterné, accablé; **there was general ~** la consternation était générale.
constipate ['kɒnstɪpeɪt] **vt** constiper.
constipated ['kɒnstɪpeɪtɪd] **adj** (*lit, fig*) constipé.
constipation [,kɒnstɪ'peɪʃən] **n** constipation *f*.
constituency [kən'stɪtjʊənsɪ] **n** (*Pol*) (*place*) circonscription électorale; (*people*) électeurs *mpl* (d'une circonscription). ~ **party** section locale (du parti).
constituent [kən'stɪtjʊənt] 1 **adj** *part, element* constituant, composant, constitutif. (*Pol*) ~ **assembly** assemblée constituante; ~ **power** pouvoir constituant. 2 **n** a (*Pol*) électeur *m*, -trice *f* (*de la circonscription d'un député*). **one of my ~s wrote to me ...** quelqu'un dans ma circonscription m'a écrit ...; **he was talking to one of his ~s** il parlait à un habitant *or* un électeur de sa circonscription. b (*part, element*) élément constitutif; (*Ling*) constituant *m*. (*Ling*) ~ **analysis** analyse *f* en constituants immédiats.
constitute ['kɒnstɪtjuːt] **vt** a (*appoint*) constituer, instituer, désigner. **to ~ sb leader of the group** désigner qn (comme) chef du groupe. b (*establish*) *organization* monter, établir; *committee* constituer. c (*amount to, make up*) faire, constituer. **these parts ~ a whole** toutes ces parties font *or* constituent un tout; **that ~s a lie** cela constitue un mensonge; **it ~s a threat to our sales** ceci représente une menace pour nos ventes; **so ~d that ...** fait de telle façon que ..., ainsi fait que ... .
constitution [,kɒnstɪ'tjuːʃən] **n** a (*Pol*) constitution *f*. **under the French ~** selon *or* d'après la constitution française; **the C~ State** le Connecticut. b *[person]* constitution *f*. **to have a strong/weak *or* poor ~** avoir une robuste/chétive constitution; **iron ~** santé *f* de fer. c (*structure*) composition *f*, constitution *f* (*of* de).
constitutional [,kɒnstɪ'tjuːʃənl] 1 **adj** a (*also Pol*) *government, reform, vote* constitutionnel, de constitution. (*Univ etc*) ~ **law** le droit constitutionnel. b (*Med*) *weakness, tendency* constitutionnel, diathésique. 2 **n** (* *hum*) **to go for a ~** faire sa petite promenade *or* son petit tour.
constitutionally [,kɒnstɪ'tjuːʃənəlɪ] **adv** a (*Pol etc*) constitutionnellement, conformément à la constitution. b de nature, par nature.
constitutive ['kɒnstɪtjuːtɪv] **adj** constitutif.
constrain [kən'streɪn] **vt** a (*force*) contraindre, forcer, obliger (*sb to do* qn à faire). **I find myself ~ed to write to you** je me vois dans la nécessité de vous écrire; **to be/feel ~ed to do** être/se sentir contraint *or* forcé *or* obligé de faire. b (*restrict*) *liberty, person* contraindre.
constrained [kən'streɪnd] **adj** *atmosphere* de gêne; *voice, manner, smile* contraint.
constraint [kən'streɪnt] **n** a (*compulsion*) contrainte *f*. **to act under ~** agir sous la contrainte. b (*restriction*) contrainte *f* (*upon* qui s'exerce sur), retenue *f*, gêne *f*; (*Ling*) contrainte. **to speak freely and without ~** parler librement et sans contrainte; **the ~s placed upon us** les contraintes auxquelles nous sommes soumis.
constrict [kən'strɪkt] **vt** (*gen*) resserrer; (*tighten*) *muscle etc* serrer; (*hamper*) *movements* gêner.
constricted [kən'strɪktɪd] **adj** a *space* réduit, restreint; *freedom* restreint; *movement* limité. (*fig*) **a ~ view of events** une vue bornée des événements; **to feel ~** (*by clothes etc*) se sentir à l'étroit; (*fig*) **I feel ~ by these regulations** le règlement me pèse. b (*Phon*) constrictif.
constricting [kən'strɪktɪŋ] **adj** *garment* gênant, étriqué; *ideology* étroit.
constriction [kən'strɪkʃən] **n** (*esp Med*) constriction *f*, resserrement *m*, étranglement *m*.
construct [kən'strʌkt] 1 **vt** *building* construire, bâtir; *novel, play* construire, composer; *theory, one's defence* bâtir; (*Ling*) construire. 2 ['kɒnstrʌkt] **n** (*Philos, Psych*) construction mentale; (*machine etc*) construction *f*.
construction [kən'strʌkʃən] 1 **n** a *[roads, buildings]* construction *f*, édification *f*. **in course of ~, under ~** en construction. b *[building, structure]* construction *f*, édifice *m*, bâtiment *m*. c (*interpretation*) interprétation *f*. **to put a wrong ~ on sb's words** mal interpréter *or* interpréter à contresens les paroles de qn. d (*Gram*) construction *f*. 2 **comp** ► **construction engineer** ingénieur *m* des travaux publics et des bâtiments.
constructional [kən'strʌkʃənl] **adj** de construction. ~ **engineering** construction *f* mécanique.
constructive [kən'strʌktɪv] **adj** constructif.
constructively [kən'strʌktɪvlɪ] **adv** d'une manière constructive.
constructivism [kən'strʌktɪvɪzəm] **n** constructivisme *m*.
constructivist [kən'strʌktɪvɪst] 1 **adj** constructiviste. 2 **n** constructiviste *mf*.
constructor [kən'strʌktə^r] **n** constructeur *m*, -trice *f*; (*Naut*) ingénieur *m* des constructions navales.
construe [kən'struː] 1 **vt** a (*gen: interpret meaning of*) interpréter. **you can ~ that in different ways** vous pouvez interpréter cela de différentes manières; **her silence was ~d as consent** son silence a été interprété comme *or* pris pour un assentiment; **this was ~d as a progress in the negotiations** cela a été interprété comme un progrès dans les négociations; **his words were wrongly ~d** ses paroles ont été mal comprises, on a interprété ses paroles à contresens.
b (*Gram: parse etc*) *sentence* analyser, décomposer; *Latin etc text* analyser.
c (*explain*) *poem, passage* expliquer.
2 **vi** (*Gram*) s'analyser grammaticalement. **the sentence will not ~** la phrase n'a pas de construction.
consul ['kɒnsəl] 1 **n** consul *m*. 2 **comp** ► **consul general** (**pl ~s ~**) consul général.
consular ['kɒnsjʊlə^r] **adj** consulaire. ~ **section** service *m* consulaire.
consulate ['kɒnsjʊlɪt] **n** consulat *m*. ~ **general** consulat général.
consulship ['kɒnsəlʃɪp] **n** poste *m* *or* charge *f* de consul.
consult [kən'sʌlt] 1 **vt** a *book, person, doctor* consulter (*about* sur, au sujet de). b (*show consideration for*) *person's feelings* avoir égard à, prendre en considération; *one's own interests* consulter. 2 **vi** consulter, être en consultation (*with* avec). **to ~ together over sth** se consulter sur *or* au sujet de qch. 3 **comp** ► **consulting engineer** ingénieur-conseil *m*, ingénieur consultant ► **consulting hours** (*Brit Med*) heures *fpl* de consultation ► **consulting room** (*Brit esp Med*) cabinet *m* de consultation.
consultancy [kən'sʌltənsɪ] **n** (*company, group*) cabinet *m* d'expertise. ~ **(service)** service *m* d'expertise.
consultant [kən'sʌltənt] 1 **n** (*gen*) consultant *m*, expert-conseil *m*, conseiller *m*; (*Brit Med*) médecin consultant, spécialiste *m*. **he acts as**

~ **to the firm** il est expert-conseil auprès de la compagnie; *see* **management** *etc.* 2 **comp** ▸ **consultant engineer** ingénieur-conseil *m*, ingénieur consultant ▸ **consultant physician/psychiatrist** médecin/psychiatre consultant(e).

consultation [ˌkɒnsəlˈteɪʃən] **n** a (*NonC*) consultation *f*. **in ~ with** en consultation avec. b consultation *f*. **to hold a ~** conférer (*about* de), délibérer (*about* sur), tenir une délibération.

consultative [kənˈsʌltətɪv] **adj** consultatif. **in a ~ capacity** dans un rôle consultatif.

consumable [kənˈsjuːməbl] **adj** (*Econ etc*) de consommation. **~ goods** biens *mpl or* produits *mpl* de consommation.

consumables [kənˈsjuːməblz] **npl** (*Econ etc*) produits *mpl* de consommation; (*Comput*) consommables *mpl*.

consume [kənˈsjuːm] **vt** *food, drink* consommer; *supplies, resources* consommer, dissiper; *[engine] fuel* brûler, consommer; *[fire] buildings* consumer,dévorer. (*fig*) **to be ~d with grief** se consumer de chagrin; **to be ~d with desire** brûler de désir; **to be ~d with jealousy** être rongé par la jalousie.

consumer [kənˈsjuːməʳ] 1 **n** (*gen*) consommateur *m*, -trice *f*; (*user*) abonné(e) *m(f)*. **gas** *etc* **~** abonné(e) *m(f)* au gaz *etc*.

2 **comp** ▸ **consumer behaviour** comportement *m* du consommateur ▸ **consumer credit** crédit *m* à la consommation ▸ **consumer demand** demande *f* de consommation ▸ **consumer durables** biens *mpl* durables ▸ **consumer electronics** électronique *f* grand public ▸ **consumer goods** biens *mpl* de consommation ▸ **consumer price index** (*US*) indice *m* des prix à la consommation, indice *m* des prix de détail ▸ **consumer protection** défense *f* du consommateur; (*Brit*) **Secretary of State for** *or* **Minister of Consumer Protection** ministre *m* pour la défense des consommateurs, ≃ secrétaire *m* d'État à la Consommation; **Department** *or* **Ministry of Consumer Protection** ministère *m* pour la défense des consommateurs, ≃ secrétariat *m* d'État à la Consommation ▸ **consumer research** études *fpl* de marchés ▸ **consumer resistance** résistance *f* du consommateur ▸ **consumer sampling** enquête *f* auprès des consommateurs ▸ **consumer society** société *f* de consommation ▸ **consumer spending** dépenses *fpl* de consommation *or* des ménages.

consumerism [kənˈsjuːməˌrɪzəm] **n** a (*consumer protection*) défense *f* du consommateur, consumérisme *m*. b (*Econ: policy*) consumérisme *m*.

consumerist [kənˈsjuːməˌrɪst] **n** consumériste *mf*, défenseur *m* des consommateurs.

consuming [kənˈsjuːmɪŋ] **adj** *desire, passion* dévorant, brûlant.

consummate [kənˈsʌmɪt] 1 **adj** consommé, accompli, achevé. 2 [ˈkɒnsʌmeɪt] **vt** consommer.

consummation [ˌkɒnsʌˈmeɪʃən] **n** *[union esp marriage]* consommation *f*; *[art form]* perfection *f*; *[one's desires, ambitions]* couronnement *m*, apogée *m*.

consumption [kənˈsʌmpʃən] **n** (*NonC*) a *[food, fuel]* consommation *f*. **not fit for human ~** (*lit*) non-comestible; (* *pej*) pas mangeable, immangeable. b (*Med* †*: tuberculosis*) consomption *f* (pulmonaire)†, phtisie† *f*.

consumptive† [kənˈsʌmptɪv] **adj, n** phtisique† *(mf)*, tuberculeux *m*, -euse *f*.

cont. **abbr of continued**.

contact [ˈkɒntækt] 1 **n** a contact *m*. **point of ~** point *m* de contact *or* de tangence; **to be in/come into/get into ~ with sb** être/entrer/se mettre en contact *or* rapport avec qn; **to make ~ (with sb)** prendre contact (avec qn); **we've lost ~ (with him)** nous avons perdu contact (avec lui); **we have had no ~ with him for 6 months** nous sommes sans contact avec lui depuis 6 mois; **I seem to make no ~ with him** je n'arrive pas à communiquer avec lui; (*Volleyball*) **~ with the net** faute *f* de filet.

b (*Elec*) contact *m*. **to make/break the ~** établir/couper le contact; (*Aviat*) ~! contact!

c (*person*) (*in secret service etc*) agent *m* de liaison; (*acquaintance*) connaissance *f*, relation *f*. **he has some ~s in Paris** il a des relations à Paris, il connaît des gens *or* il est en relation avec des gens à Paris; **a business ~** une relation *f* de travail.

d (*Med*) contamineur *m* possible, contact *m*.

2 **vt** *person* se mettre en contact *or* en rapport avec, entrer en relations avec, contacter. **we'll ~ you soon** nous nous mettrons en rapport avec vous sous peu.

3 **comp** *adhesive etc* de contact ▸ **contact breaker** (*Elec*) interrupteur *m*, rupteur *m* ▸ **contact cement** ciment *m* de contact ▸ **contact lenses** verres *mpl* de contact, lentilles cornéennes ▸ **contact man** (*Comm*) agent *m* de liaison ▸ **contact print** (*Phot*) (épreuve *f* par) contact *m*.

contagion [kənˈteɪdʒən] **n** contagion *f*.

contagious [kənˈteɪdʒəs] **adj** (*Med*) *illness, person* contagieux; (*fig*) *laughter, emotion* contagieux, communicatif.

contain [kənˈteɪn] **vt** a (*hold*) *[box, bottle, envelope etc]* contenir; *[book, letter, newspaper]* contenir, renfermer. **sea water ~s a lot of salt** l'eau de mer contient beaucoup de sel *or* a une forte teneur en sel; **the room will ~ 70 people** la salle peut contenir 70 personnes; *see* **self**. b (*hold back, control*) *one's emotions, anger* contenir, refréner, maîtriser. **he couldn't ~ himself for joy** il ne se sentait pas de joie; (*Mil*) **to ~ the enemy forces** contenir les troupes ennemies. c (*Math*) être divisible par.

contained [kənˈteɪnd] **adj** (*emotionally*) réservé.

container [kənˈteɪnəʳ] 1 **n** a (*goods transport*) conteneur *m*. b (*jug, box etc*) récipient *m*; (*for plants*) godet *m*. (*for food*) **(foil) ~** barquette *f* (en alu(minium)). 2 **comp** *train, ship* porte-conteneurs *inv* ▸ **container dock** dock *m* pour la manutention de conteneurs ▸ **container line** (*Naut*) ligne *f* transconteneurs *inv* ▸ **container port** port *m* à conteneurs ▸ **container terminal** terminal *m* (à conteneurs) ▸ **container transport** transport *m* par conteneurs.

containerization [kənˌteɪnəraɪˈzeɪʃən] **n** conteneurisation *f*.

containerize [kənˈteɪnəraɪz] **vt** mettre en conteneurs, conteneuriser.

containment [kənˈteɪnmənt] **n** (*Pol*) endiguement *m*.

contaminant [kənˈtæmɪnənt] **n** polluant *m*.

contaminate [kənˈtæmɪneɪt] **vt** (*lit, fig*) contaminer, souiller; *[radioactivity]* contaminer. **~d air** air vicié *or* contaminé.

contamination [kənˌtæmɪˈneɪʃən] **n** (*see* **contaminate**) contamination *f*; souillure *f*.

contango [kənˈtæŋgəʊ] **n** (*Brit*) report *m*.

contd **abbr of continued**.

contemplate [ˈkɒntempleɪt] **vt** a (*look at*) contempler, considérer avec attention. b (*plan, consider*) *action, purchase* envisager. **to ~ doing** envisager de *or* songer à *or* se proposer de faire; **I don't ~ a refusal from him** je ne m'attends pas à *or* je n'envisage pas un refus de sa part.

contemplation [ˌkɒntemˈpleɪʃən] **n** (*NonC*) a (*act of looking*) contemplation *f*. b (*deep thought*) contemplation *f*, méditation *f*. **deep in ~** plongé dans de profondes méditations. c (*expectation*) prévision *f*. **in ~ of their arrival** en prévision de leur arrivée.

contemplative [kənˈtemplətɪv] 1 **adj** *mood* contemplatif, méditatif; *attitude* recueilli; (*Rel*) *prayer, order* contemplatif. 2 **n** (*Rel*) contemplatif *m*, -ive *f*.

contemporaneous [kənˌtempəˈreɪnɪəs] **adj** contemporain (*with* de).

contemporaneously [kənˌtempəˈreɪnɪəslɪ] **adv** à la même époque (*with* que).

contemporary [kənˈtempərərɪ] 1 **adj** (*of the same period*) contemporain (*with* de), de la même époque (*with* que); (*modern*) contemporain, moderne. **Dickens and ~ writers** Dickens et les écrivains contemporains *or* de son époque; **he's bought an 18th century house and is looking for ~ furniture** il a acheté une maison du 18e siècle et il cherche des meubles d'époque; **a ~ narrative** un récit de l'époque; **I like ~ art** j'aime l'art contemporain *or* moderne; **it's all very ~** c'est tout ce qu'il y a de plus moderne. 2 **n** contemporain(e) *m(f)*.

contempt [kənˈtempt] **n** mépris *m*. **to hold in ~** mépriser, avoir du mépris pour; **this will bring you into ~** ceci vous fera mépriser; **in ~ of danger** au mépris *or* en dépit du danger; **it's beneath ~** c'est tout ce qu'il y a de plus méprisable, c'est au-dessous de tout; (*Jur*) **~ of court** outrage *m* à la Cour.

contemptible [kənˈtemptəbl] **adj** méprisable, indigne, vil.

contemptuous [kənˈtemptjʊəs] **adj** *person* dédaigneux (*of* de); *manner etc* méprisant, altier, dédaigneux; *gesture* de mépris.

contemptuously [kənˈtemptjʊəslɪ] **adv** avec mépris, dédaigneusement.

contend [kənˈtend] 1 **vi** combattre, lutter (*with* contre). **to ~ with sb for sth** disputer qch à qn; **to ~ with sb over sth** se disputer *or* se battre avec qn au sujet de qch; **they had to ~ with very bad weather conditions** ils ont dû faire face à des conditions météorologiques déplorables; **we have many problems to ~ with** nous sommes aux prises avec de nombreux problèmes; **he has a lot to ~ with** il a pas mal de problèmes à résoudre; **I should not like to have to ~ with him** je ne voudrais pas avoir affaire à lui; **you'll have me to ~ with** vous aurez affaire à moi. 2 **vt** soutenir, prétendre (*that* que).

contender [kənˈtendəʳ] **n** prétendant(e) *m(f)* (*for* à); (*in contest, competition, race*) concurrent(e) *m(f)*; (*in election, for a job*) candidat *m*. **presidential ~** candidat à l'élection présidentielle.

contending [kənˈtendɪŋ] **adj** opposé, ennemi.

content¹ [kənˈtent] 1 **adj** content, satisfait. **to be ~ with sth** se contenter *or* s'accommoder de qch; **she is quite ~ to stay there** elle ne demande pas mieux que de rester là. 2 **n** contentement *m*, satisfaction *f*; *see* **heart**. 3 **vt** *person* contenter, satisfaire. **to ~ o.s. with doing** se contenter de *or* se borner à faire.

content² [ˈkɒntent] **n** a **~s** (*thing contained*) contenu *m*; (*amount contained*) contenu, contenance *f*; *[house etc]* (*gen*) contenu; (*Insurance*) biens *mpl* mobiliers; *[book]* **(table of) ~s** table *f* des matières. b (*NonC*) *[book, play, film]* contenu *m* (*also Ling*); *[official document]* teneur *f*; *[metal]* teneur, titre *m*. **what do you think of the ~ of the article?** que pensez-vous du contenu *or* du fond de l'article?; **oranges have a high vitamin C ~** les oranges sont riches en vitamine C; **gold ~** teneur en or; **the play lacks ~** la pièce est mince *or* manque de profondeur.

contented [kənˈtentɪd] **adj** content, satisfait (*with* de).

contentedly [kənˈtentɪdlɪ] **adv** avec contentement. **to smile ~** avoir un sourire de contentement.

contentedness [kən'tentɪdnɪs] **n** contentement *m*, satisfaction *f*.

contention [kən'tenʃən] **n** **a** (*dispute*) démêlé *m*, dispute *f*, contestation *f*; *see* **bone**. **b** (*argument, point argued*) assertion *f*, affirmation *f*. **it is my ~ that** je soutiens que.

contentious [kən'tenʃəs] **adj** *person* querelleur, chamailleur; *subject, issue* contesté, litigieux.

contentment [kən'tentmənt] **n** contentement *m*, satisfaction *f*.

conterminous [ˌkɒn'tɜːmɪnəs] **adj** **a** (*contiguous*) *county, country* limitrophe (*with, to* de); *estate, house, garden* adjacent, attenant (*with, to* à). **b** (*end to end*) bout à bout. **c** (*coextensive*) de même étendue (*with* que).

contest [kən'test] **1 vt** **a** (*argue, debate*) *question, matter, result* contester, discuter; (*Jur*) *judgment* attaquer. **to ~ sb's right to do** contester à qn le droit de faire; (*Jur*) **to ~ a will** attaquer *or* contester un testament. **b** (*compete for*) disputer. (*Parl*) **to ~ a seat** disputer un siège; (*Pol*) **to ~ an election** disputer une élection. **2 vi** se disputer (*with, against* avec), contester. **3** ['kɒntest] **n** (*struggle: lit, fig*) combat *m*, lutte *f* (*with* avec, contre, *between* entre); (*Sport*) lutte; (*Boxing, Wrestling*) combat, rencontre *f*; (*competition*) concours *m*. **beauty ~** concours de beauté; **~ of skill** lutte d'adresse; **the mayoral ~** (la lutte pour) l'élection du maire.

contestant [kən'testənt] **n** **a** (*for prize, reward*) concurrent(e) *m(f)*. **b** (*in fight*) adversaire *mf*.

contestation [ˌkɒntes'teɪʃən] **n** contestation *f*.

context ['kɒntekst] **n** contexte *m*. **in/out of ~** dans le/hors contexte; **to put sth in(to) ~** mettre qch en contexte; **to see sth in ~** regarder qch dans son contexte; (*Ling*) **~ of situation** situation *f* de discours.

contextual [kɒn'tekstjʊəl] **adj** contextuel, d'après le contexte.

contiguous [kən'tɪgjʊəs] **adj** contigu (*f* -guë). **~ to** contigu à *or* avec, attenant à; **the 2 fields are ~** les 2 champs se touchent *or* sont contigus.

continence ['kɒntɪnəns] **n** (*see* **continent**[1]) continence *f*; chasteté *f*.

continent[1] ['kɒntɪnənt] **adj** (*chaste*) chaste; (*self-controlled*) continent†; (*Med*) qui n'est pas incontinent.

continent[2] ['kɒntɪnənt] **n** (*Geog*) continent *m*. (*Brit*) **the C~** l'Europe continentale; (*Brit*) **on the C~** en Europe (*continentale*).

continental [ˌkɒntɪ'nentl] **1 adj** continental. **~ breakfast** petit déjeuner à la française, café (*or* thé) complet; **~ climate** climat *m* continental; **~ crust** croûte *f* continentale; **~ drift** dérive *f* des continents; (*Brit*) **~ quilt** couette *f*; **~ shelf** plate-forme continentale, plateau continental; **~ shields** aires continentales. **2 n** (*Brit*) Européen(ne) *m(f)* (continental(e)).

contingency [kən'tɪndʒənsɪ] **1 n** **a** éventualité *f*, événement imprévu *or* inattendu. **in a ~, should a ~ arise** en cas d'imprévu; **to provide for all contingencies** parer à toute éventualité. **b** (*Statistics*) contingence *f*. **2 comp** ▸ **contingency fund** caisse *f* de prévoyance ▸ **contingency planning** mise *f* sur pied de plans d'urgence ▸ **contingency plans** plans *mpl* d'urgence ▸ **contingency reserve** (*Fin*) fonds *mpl* de prévoyance ▸ **contingency sample** (*Space*) échantillon *m* lunaire (*prélevé dès l'alunissage*).

contingent [kən'tɪndʒənt] **1 adj** contingent. **to be ~ upon sth** dépendre de qch, être subordonné à qch. **2 n** (*gen, also Mil*) contingent *m*.

continua [kən'tɪnjʊə] **npl of continuum**.

continual [kən'tinjʊəl] **adj** continuel.

continually [kən'tɪnjʊəlɪ] **adv** continuellement, sans cesse.

continuance [kən'tɪnjʊəns] **n** (*duration*) durée *f*; (*continuation*) continuation *f*; *[human race etc]* perpétuation *f*, continuité *f*.

continuant [kən'tɪnjuənt] **n** (*Phon*) continue *f*.

continuation [kənˌtɪnjʊ'eɪʃən] **n** **a** (*no interruption*) continuation *f*. **b** (*after interruption*) reprise *f*. **the ~ of work after the holidays** la reprise du travail après les vacances. **c** *[serial story]* suite *f*.

continue [kən'tɪnjuː] **1 vt** continuer (*to do* à *or* de faire); *piece of work* continuer, poursuivre; *tradition* perpétuer, maintenir; *policy* maintenir; (*after interruption*) *conversation, work* reprendre. *[serial story etc]* **to be ~d** à suivre; **~d on page 10** suite page 10; **to ~ (on) one's way** continuer *or* poursuivre son chemin; (*after pause*) se remettre en marche; **"and so," he ~d** "et ainsi," reprit-il *or* poursuivit-il; **to ~ sb in a job** maintenir qn dans un poste.

2 vi **a** (*go on*) *[road, weather, celebrations]* continuer; (*after interruption*) reprendre. **the forest ~s to the sea** la forêt s'étend jusqu'à la mer; **his speech ~d until 3 a.m.** son discours s'est prolongé jusqu'à 3 heures du matin.

b (*remain*) rester. **to ~ in one's job** garder *or* conserver son poste; **he ~d with his voluntary work** il a poursuivi son travail bénévole; **she ~d as his secretary** elle est restée sa secrétaire.

continuing [kən'tɪnjʊɪŋ] **adj** *argument* ininterrompu; *correspondence* soutenu. **~ education** formation permanente *or* continue.

continuity [ˌkɒntɪn'juːɪtɪ] **n** (*gen, Cine, Rad*) continuité *f*. (*Cine, TV*) **~ girl** script-girl *f*, script *f*.

continuo [kən'tɪnjʊˌəʊ] **n** (*Mus*) basse continue.

continuous [kən'tɪnjʊəs] **adj** **a** continu. (*Scol, Univ*) **~ assessment** contrôle continu des connaissances; (*Cine*) **~ performance** spectacle permanent; (*Comput*) **~ paper** *or* **stationery** papier *m* en continu. **b** (*Gram*) *aspect* imperfectif; *tense* progressif. **in the present/past ~** à la forme progressive du présent/du passé.

continuously [kən'tɪnjʊəslɪ] **adv** (*uninterruptedly*) sans interruption, continûment; (*repeatedly*) continuellement, sans arrêt.

continuum [kən'tɪnjʊəm] **n, pl ~s** *or* **continua** continuum *m*.

contort [kən'tɔːt] **vt** **a** *one's features, limbs* tordre, contorsionner. **a face ~ed by pain** un visage tordu *or* contorsionné par la douleur. **b** (*fig*) *sb's words, story* déformer, fausser.

contortion [kən'tɔːʃən] **n** *[esp acrobat]* contorsion *f*; *[features]* torsion *f*, crispation *f*, convulsion *f*.

contortionist [kən'tɔːʃənɪst] **n** contorsionniste *mf*.

contour ['kɒntʊə[r]] **1 n** contour *m*, profil *m* (*d'un terrain*). **2 vt: to ~ a map** tracer les courbes de niveau sur une carte. **3 comp** ▸ **contour flying** vol *m* à très basse altitude (qui épouse le relief) ▸ **contour line** courbe *f* de niveau ▸ **contour map** carte *f* avec courbes de niveau.

contra ['kɒntrə] **n** (*Pol*) contra *f*.

contra... ['kɒntrə] **pref** contre-, contra... .

contraband ['kɒntrəbænd] **1 n** contrebande *f*. **2 comp** *goods* de contrebande.

contrabass [ˌkɒntrə'beɪs] **n** contrebasse *f*.

contrabassoon [ˌkɒntrəbə'suːn] **n** contrebasson *m*.

contraception [ˌkɒntrə'sepʃən] **n** contraception *f*.

contraceptive [ˌkɒntrə'septɪv] **1 n** contraceptif *m*. **2 adj** *device, measures* contraceptif, anticonceptionnel.

contract ['kɒntrækt] **1 n** **a** contrat *m*; (*US Comm: tender*) adjudication *f*. **marriage ~** contrat de mariage; **to enter into a ~ with sb for sth** passer un contrat avec qn pour qch; **to put work out to ~** mettre *or* donner du travail en adjudication *or* à l'entreprise; **by ~** par *or* sur contrat; **under ~ (to)** sous contrat (avec); (*Jur*) **~ for services** contrat de louage d'ouvrage; (*fig: by killer*) **there's a ~ out on** *or* **for him*** on a payé quelqu'un pour le descendre*; *see* **breach**.

b (*also* **~ bridge**) (bridge *m*) contrat *m*.

2 comp ▸ **contract bargaining** (*Jur*) négociations *fpl* salariales ▸ **contracting party** partie contractante ▸ **contracting parties** contractants *mpl* ▸ **contract killer** tueur *m* à gages ▸ **contract price** prix *m* forfaitaire ▸ **contract work** travail *m* à forfait *or* à l'entreprise.

3 [kən'trækt] **vt** **a** *debts, illness* contracter; *habits, vices* prendre, contracter.

b *alliance* contracter. **to ~ to do** s'engager (par contrat) à faire; **to ~ with sb to do** passer un contrat avec qn pour faire.

c *metal, muscle etc* contracter.

d (*Ling*) *word, phrase* contracter (*to* en). **~ed form** forme contractée.

4 [ˌkən'trækt] **vi** **a** *[metal, muscles]* se contracter.

b (*Comm*) s'engager (par contrat). **he has ~ed for the building of the motorway** il a un contrat pour la construction de l'autoroute.

▸**contract in vi** s'engager (par contrat).

▸**contract out 1 vi** se libérer, se dégager (*of* de), se soustraire (*of* à). **to contract out of a pension scheme** cesser de cotiser à une caisse de retraite. **2 vt sep** *work etc* sous-traiter (*to sb* à qn).

contractile [kən'træktaɪl] **adj** contractile.

contraction [kən'trækʃən] **n** **a** (*NonC*) *[metal etc]* contraction *f*. **b** (*Ling*) forme contractée, contraction *f*. **can't is a ~ of cannot** can't est une forme contractée *or* contraction de cannot. **c** (*acquiring: of habit etc*) acquisition *f*. **~ of debts** endettement *m*.

contractionary [kən'trækʃənərɪ] **adj** (*Econ*): **~ pressure** poussée *f* récessionniste; **~ policy** politique *f* d'austérité.

contractor [kən'træktə[r]] **n** **a** (*Comm*) entrepreneur *m*. **army ~** fournisseur *m* de l'armée; *see* **building**. **b** (*Jur*) partie contractante.

contractual [kən'træktʃʊəl] **adj** contractuel.

contractually [kən'træktʃʊəlɪ] **adv** par contrat. **~, we have to ...** d'après le contrat, nous devons ... .

contradict [ˌkɒntrə'dɪkt] **vt** **a** (*deny truth of*) *person, statement* contredire. **don't ~!** ne (me) contredites pas! **b** (*be contrary to*) *statement, event* contredire, démentir. **his actions ~ed his words** ses actions démentaient ses paroles.

contradiction [ˌkɒntrə'dɪkʃən] **n** contradiction *f*, démenti *m*. **to be in ~ with** être en contradiction avec, donner le démenti à; **a ~ in terms** une contradiction dans les termes.

contradictory [ˌkɒntrə'dɪktərɪ] **adj** contradictoire, opposé (*to* à).

contradistinction [ˌkɒntrədɪs'tɪŋkʃən] **n** contraste *m*, opposition *f*. **in ~ to** en contraste avec, par opposition à.

contraflow ['kɒntrəˌfləʊ] **adj** (*Aut*) **~ lane** voie *f* à contresens; **there is a ~ system in operation on ...** une voie a été mise en sens inverse sur ...; **~ (bus) lane** couloir *m* (d'autobus) à contre-courant.

contraindicated [ˌkɒntrə'ɪndɪˌkeɪtɪd] **adj** (*Med*) contre-indiqué.

contraindication [ˌkɒntrəˌɪndɪ'keɪʃən] **n** (*Med*) contre-indication *f*.

contralto [kən'træltəʊ] **1 n, pl ~s** *or* **contralti** [kən'træltɪ] (*voice, person*) contralto *m*. **2 adj** *voice, part* de contralto; *aria* pour contralto.

contraption* [kən'træpʃən] **n** machin* *m*, bidule‡ *m*, truc* *m*.

contrapuntal [ˌkɒntrə'pʌntl] **adj** en contrepoint, contrapuntique.

contrarily [kən'trɛərɪlɪ] **adv** contrairement.

contrariness [kən'trɛərɪnɪs] **n** esprit *m* de contradiction, esprit contrariant.

contrariwise ['kɒntrərɪ,waɪz] adv a (*on the contrary*) au contraire, par contre. b (*in opposite direction*) en sens opposé.

contrary ['kɒntrərɪ] 1 adj a (*opposite*) contraire, opposé (*to* à), en opposition (*to* avec); *statements, winds* contraire. **in a ~ direction** en sens inverse *or* opposé; **~ to nature** contre nature.
b [kən'trɛərɪ] (*self-willed*) *person, attitude* contrariant, entêté.
2 adv contrairement (*to* à), à l'encontre (*to* de). **~ to accepted ideas** à l'encontre des idées reçues; **~ to what I had thought** contrairement à ce que j'avais pensé.
3 n contraire *m*. **on the ~** au contraire; **quite the ~!** bien au contraire!; **come tomorrow unless you hear to the ~** venez demain sauf avis contraire *or* sauf contrordre; **I have nothing to say to the ~** je n'ai rien à dire contre *or* à redire, je n'ai pas d'objections (à faire); *[events]* **to go by contraries** se passer contrairement à ce à quoi on s'attendait.

contrast [kən'trɑːst] 1 vt mettre en contraste, contraster (*one thing with another* une chose avec une autre). 2 vi contraster, faire contraste (*with* avec). *[colour]* **to ~ strongly** trancher (*with* sur). 3 ['kɒntrɑːst] n (*gen, TV*) contraste *m* (*between* entre). **in ~** par contraste; **in ~ to** par opposition à, par contraste avec; **to stand out in ~** (*in landscapes, photographs*) se détacher (*to* de, sur), ressortir (*to* sur, contre); *[colours]* contraster (*to* avec), trancher (*to* sur).

contrasting [kən'trɑːstɪŋ] adj *colours* contrasté; *opinions* opposé.

contrastive [kən'trɑːstɪv] adj contrastif.

contravene [,kɒntrə'viːn] vt a *law* enfreindre, violer, contrevenir à (*frm*). b *statement* nier, opposer un démenti à.

contravention [,kɒntrə'venʃən] n infraction *f* (*of the law* à la loi). **in ~ of the rules** en violation des règles, en dérogation aux règles.

contribute [kən'trɪbjuːt] 1 vt *money* contribuer, cotiser. **he has ~d £5** il a offert *or* donné 5 livres; **to ~ an article to a newspaper** donner *or* envoyer un article à un journal; **his presence didn't ~ much to the success of the evening** sa présence n'a pas beaucoup contribué à faire de la soirée un succès. 2 vi: **to ~ to a charity** contribuer à une (bonne) œuvre; **he ~d to the success of the venture** il a contribué à assurer le succès de l'affaire; **to ~ to a discussion** prendre part *or* participer à une discussion; **to ~ to a newspaper** collaborer à un journal; **it all ~d to the muddle** tout cela a contribué au désordre.

contribution [,kɒntrɪ'bjuːʃən] n *[money, goods etc]* contribution *f*; (*Admin*) cotisation *f*; (*to publication*) article *m*.

contributor [kən'trɪbjʊtə^r] n (*to publication*) collaborateur *m*,-trice *f*; *[money, goods]* donateur *m*, -trice *f*.

contributory [kən'trɪbjʊtərɪ] adj a *cause* accessoire. **it was a ~ factor in his downfall** cela a contribué à sa ruine *or* a été un des facteurs de sa ruine; **~ negligence** faute *f* de la victime; (*Jur*) compensation *f* des fautes. b **~ pension scheme** caisse *f* de retraite (à laquelle cotisent les employés).

contrite ['kɒntraɪt] adj penaud, contrit.

contritely [kən'traɪtlɪ] adv d'un air penaud *or* contrit.

contrition [kən'trɪʃən] n contrition *f*.

contrivance [kən'traɪvəns] n (*tool, machine etc*) appareil *m*, machine *f*, dispositif *m*; (*scheme*) invention *f*, combinaison *f*. **it is beyond his ~** il n'en est pas capable.

contrive [kən'traɪv] vt a (*invent, design*) *plan, scheme* combiner, inventer. **to ~ a means of doing** trouver un moyen pour faire. b (*manage*) s'arranger (*to do* pour faire), trouver (le) moyen (*to do* de faire). **can you ~ to be here at 3 o'clock?** est-ce que vous pouvez vous arranger pour être ici à 3 heures?; **he ~d to make matters worse** il a trouvé moyen d'aggraver les choses.

contrived [kən'traɪvd] adj artificiel, forcé, qui manque de naturel.

control [kən'trəʊl] 1 n a (*NonC*) (*authority, power to restrain*) autorité *f*; (*regulating*) *[traffic]* réglementation *f*; *[aircraft]* contrôle *m*; *[pests]* élimination *f*, suppression *f*. **the ~ of disease/forest fire** la lutte contre la maladie/les incendies de forêt; (*Pol*) **~ of the seas** maîtrise *f* des mers; **he has no ~ over his children** il n'a aucune autorité sur ses enfants; **to keep a dog under ~** tenir un chien, se faire obéir d'un chien; **to have a horse under ~** (savoir) maîtriser un cheval; **to lose ~ (of o.s.)** perdre tout contrôle de soi; **to lose ~ of a vehicle/situation** perdre le contrôle d'un véhicule/d'une situation, ne plus être maître d'un véhicule/d'une situation; **to be in ~ of a vehicle/situation, to have a vehicle/situation under ~** être maître d'un véhicule/d'une situation; **to bring** *or* **get under ~** *fire* maîtriser; *situation* dominer; *gangsters, terrorists, children, dog* mater; *inflation* maîtriser, mettre un frein à; **the situation is under ~** on a *or* on tient la situation bien en main; **everything's under ~*** tout est en ordre; **his car got out of ~** il a perdu le contrôle *or* la maîtrise de sa voiture; **the children are quite out of ~** les enfants sont déchaînés; **under French ~** sous contrôle français; **under government ~** sous contrôle gouvernemental; **circumstances beyond our ~** circonstances indépendantes de notre volonté; **who is in ~ here?** qui *or* quel est le responsable ici?; (*Sport*) **his ~ of the ball is not very good** il ne contrôle pas très bien le ballon; *see* **birth, self** *etc*.
b **~s** *[train, car, ship, aircraft]* commandes *fpl*; *[radio, TV]* boutons *mpl* de commande; (*Rail etc*) **to be at the ~s** être aux commandes; (*Rad, TV*) **volume/tone ~** (bouton *m* de) réglage *m* de volume/de sonorité.
c **price ~s** le contrôle des prix.
d (*Phys, Psych etc: standard of comparison*) cas *m* témoin.
e (*Comput*) **~ key** touche *f* de commande; **~ unit** unité *f* de commande; **"~ W"** "contrôle W"; *see also* **3**.
2 vt (*regulate, restrain*) *emotions* maîtriser, dominer, réprimer; *child, animal* se faire obéir de; *car* avoir *or* garder la maîtrise de; *crowd* contenir; *organization, business* diriger, être à la tête de; *expenditure* régler; *prices, wages* mettre un frein à la hausse de; *immigration* contrôler; *inflation, unemployment* maîtriser, mettre un frein à; *a market* dominer. **to ~ o.s.** se contrôler, se maîtriser, rester maître de soi; **~ yourself!** calmez-vous!, maîtrisez-vous!; **she can't ~ the children** elle n'a aucune autorité sur les enfants; **to ~ traffic** régler la circulation; **to ~ a disease** enrayer une maladie; (*Sport*) **to ~ the ball** contrôler le ballon; *see also* **controlled**.
3 comp ► **control case** (*Med, Psych etc*) cas *m* témoin ► **control column** (*Aviat*) manche *m* à balai ► **control experiment** (*Sci, Med, Psych etc*) expérience *f* de contrôle ► **control group** (*Med, Psych etc*) groupe *m* témoin ► **control key** (*Comput*) touche *f* contrôle ► **control knob** bouton *m* de commande *or* de réglage ► **control panel** *[aircraft, ship]* tableau *m* de bord; *[TV, computer]* pupitre *m* de commande ► **control point** contrôle *m* ► **control room** (*Naut*) poste *m* de commande; (*Mil*) salle *f* de commande; (*Rad, TV*) régie *f* ► **control tower** (*Aviat*) tour *f* de contrôle ► **control unit** (*Comput*) unité *f* de commande.

controllable [kən'trəʊləbl] adj *child, animal* discipliné; *expenditure, inflation, imports, immigration* qui peut être freiné *or* restreint; *disease* qui peut être enrayé.

controlled [kən'trəʊld] adj *emotion* contenu. **he was very ~** il se dominait très bien; **... he said in a ~ voice** ... dit-il en se contrôlant *or* en se dominant; (*Econ*) **~ economy** économie dirigée *or* planifiée.

-controlled [kən,trəʊld] adj ending in comps, e.g. **a Labour-controlled council** un conseil municipal à majorité travailliste; **a government-controlled organisation** une organisation sous contrôle gouvernemental; **computer-controlled equipment** outillage commandé par ordinateur.

controller [kən'trəʊlə^r] n a *[accounts etc]* contrôleur *m*, vérificateur *m*. b (*Admin, Ind etc: manager*) contrôleur *m*. c (*Tech: device*) appareil *m* de contrôle.

controlling [kən'trəʊlɪŋ] adj *factor* déterminant. (*Fin*) **~ interest** participation *f* majoritaire.

controversial [,kɒntrə'vɜːʃəl] adj *speech, action, decision* discutable, sujet à controverse; *book, suggestion* controversé, discuté. **one of the most ~ figures of his time** l'un des personnages les plus discutés de son époque.

controversy [kən'trɒvəsɪ] n controverse *f*, polémique *f*; (*Jur, Fin*) différend *m*. **there was a lot of ~ about it** ça a provoqué *or* soulevé beaucoup de controverses, ça a été très contesté *or* discuté; **to cause ~** provoquer *or* soulever une controverse; **they were having a great ~** ils étaient au milieu d'une grande polémique.

controvert ['kɒntrəvɜːt] vt (*rare*) disputer, controverser.

contumacious [,kɒntjʊ'meɪʃəs] adj rebelle, insoumis, récalcitrant.

contumacy ['kɒntjʊməsɪ] n (*resistance*) résistance *f*, opposition *f*; (*rebelliousness*) désobéissance *f*, insoumission *f*; (*Jur*) contumace *f*.

contumelious [,kɒntjʊ'miːlɪəs] adj (*liter*) insolent, méprisant.

contumely ['kɒntju(ː)mlɪ] n (*liter*) mépris *m*.

contusion [kən'tjuːʒən] n contusion *f*.

conundrum [kə'nʌndrəm] n devinette *f*, énigme *f*; (*fig*) énigme.

conurbation [,kɒnɜː'beɪʃən] n conurbation *f*.

convalesce [,kɒnvə'les] vi relever de maladie, se remettre (d'une maladie). **to be convalescing** être en convalescence.

convalescence [,kɒnvə'lesəns] n convalescence *f*.

convalescent [,kɒnvə'lesənt] 1 n convalescent(e) *m(f)*. 2 adj convalescent. **~ home** maison *f* de convalescence *or* de repos.

convection [kən'vekʃən] 1 n convection *f*. 2 comp *heating* à convection.

convector [kən'vektə^r] n (*also* **~ heater**) radiateur *m* (à convection).

convene [kən'viːn] 1 vt convoquer. 2 vi se réunir, s'assembler; *see also* **convening**.

convener [kən'viːnə^r] n président(e) *m(f)* (*de commission etc*).

convenience [kən'viːnɪəns] 1 n a (*NonC*) (*suitability, comfort*) commodité *f*. **the ~ of a modern flat** la commodité *or* le confort d'un appartement moderne; **I doubt the ~ of an office in the suburbs** je ne suis pas sûr qu'un bureau en banlieue soit pratique; **for ~'(s) sake** par souci de commodité; (*Comm*) **at your earliest ~** dans les meilleurs délais; **to find sth to one's ~** trouver qch à sa convenance; **do it at your own ~** faites-le quand cela vous conviendra; *see* **marriage**.
b **~s** commodités *fpl*; **the house has all modern ~s** la maison a tout le confort moderne.
c (*Brit euph*) toilettes *fpl*, W.-C. *mpl*; *see* **public**.
2 comp ► **convenience foods** aliments tout préparés; (*complete dishes*) plats cuisinés ► **convenience goods** produits *mpl* de grande diffusion *or* d'achat courant ► **convenience market** *or* **store** (*US*) épicerie *f* de dépannage, commerce *m* de proximité.

convenient [kən'viːnɪənt] adj *tool, place* commode. **if it is ~ to you** si vous n'y voyez pas d'inconvénient, si cela ne vous dérange pas; **will it be ~ for you to come tomorrow?** est-ce que cela vous arrange *or* vous convient de venir demain?; **what would be a ~ time for you?** quelle heure vous conviendrait?; **is it ~ to see Mr X now?** peut-on voir M X tout de suite sans le déranger?; **it is not a very ~ time** le moment n'est pas très bien choisi; **we were looking for a ~ place to stop** nous cherchions un endroit convenable *or* un bon endroit où nous arrêter; **his cousin's death was very ~ for him** la mort de sa cousine est tombée au bon moment pour lui; **the house is ~ for** *or* (*US*) **to shops and buses** la maison est bien située pour les magasins et les autobus; **he put it down on a ~ chair** il l'a posé sur une chaise qui se trouvait (là) à portée.

conveniently [kən'vi:nɪəntlɪ] adv d'une manière commode. **~ situated for the shops** bien situé pour les magasins; **her aunt ~ lent her a house** sa tante lui a prêté une maison fort à propos; **very ~ he arrived late** il est arrivé en retard de façon fort opportune.

convening [kən'vi:nɪŋ] 1 adj: **~ authority** autorité habilitée à *or* chargée de convoquer; **~ country** pays *m* hôte. 2 n convocation *f*.

convenor [kən'vi:nə^r] n = **convener.**

convent ['kɒnvənt] 1 n couvent *m*. **to go into a ~** entrer au couvent. 2 comp ► **convent school** couvent *m*.

conventicle [kən'ventɪkl] n conventicule *m*.

convention [kən'venʃən] n (*meeting, agreement*) convention *f*; (*accepted behaviour*) usage *m*, convenances *fpl*; (*conference, fair*) salon *m*. **according to ~** selon l'usage, selon les convenances; **there is a ~ that ladies do not dine here** l'usage veut que les dames ne puissent pas dîner ici; **stamp collectors' ~** salon *m* de la philatélie.

conventional [kən'venʃənl] adj a *method* conventionnel, classique. **~ weapons** armes *fpl* conventionnelles; **~ wisdom** la croyance populaire. b (*slightly pej*) *person, clothes* conventionnel, conformiste; *behaviour, remarks* conventionnel, de convention, banal.

conventionality [kən,venʃə'nælɪtɪ] n *[methods]* caractère *m* conventionnel; *[person, clothes]* conformisme *m*; *[behaviour, remarks]* banalité *f*.

converge [kən'vɜ:dʒ] vi converger (*on* sur).

convergence [kən'vɜ:dʒəns] n convergence *f*.

convergent [kən'vɜ:dʒənt] adj, **converging** [kən'vɜ:dʒɪŋ] adj convergent. **~ thinking** raisonnement convergent.

conversant [kən'vɜ:sənt] adj: **to be ~ with** *car, machinery* s'y connaître en; *language, science, laws, customs* connaître; *facts* être au courant de; **I am ~ with what he said** je suis au courant de ce qu'il a dit; **I am not ~ with mathematics** je ne comprends rien aux mathématiques; **I am not ~ with sports cars** je ne m'y connais pas en voitures de sport.

conversation [,kɒnvə'seɪʃən] 1 n conversation *f*, entretien *m*. **to have a ~ with sb** avoir une conversation *or* un entretien avec qn, s'entretenir avec qn; **I have had several ~s with him** j'ai eu plusieurs entretiens *or* conversations avec lui; **to be in ~ with** s'entretenir avec, être en conversation avec; **they were deep in ~** ils étaient en grande conversation; **what was your ~ about?** de quoi parliez-vous?; **she has no ~** elle n'a aucune conversation; **to make ~** faire (la) conversation. 2 comp ► **conversation piece** (*Art*) tableau *m* de genre, scène *f* d'intérieur; **her hat was a real conversation piece*** son chapeau a fait beaucoup jaser ► **conversation stopper***: **that was a conversation stopper** cela a arrêté net la conversation, cela a jeté un froid sur la conversation.

conversational [,kɒnvə'seɪʃənl] adj a *voice, words* de la conversation; *person* qui a la conversation facile. **to speak in a ~ tone** parler sur le ton de la conversation. b (*Comput*) conversationnel.

conversationalist [,kɒnvə'seɪʃnəlɪst] n causeur *m*, -euse *f*. **she's a great ~** elle a de la conversation, elle brille dans la conversation.

conversationally [,kɒnvə'seɪʃnəlɪ] adv *speak* sur le ton de la conversation. **"nice day" she said ~** "il fait beau" dit-elle du ton de quelqu'un qui cherche à entamer une conversation.

converse¹ [kən'vɜ:s] vi converser. **to ~ with sb about sth** s'entretenir avec qn de qch.

converse² ['kɒnvɜ:s] 1 adj (*opposite, contrary*) *statement* contraire, inverse; (*Math, Philos*) inverse; *proposition* inverse, réciproque. 2 n *[statement]* contraire *m*, inverse *m*; (*Math, Philos*) inverse.

conversely [kɒn'vɜ:slɪ] adv inversement, réciproquement. **... and ~ ...** et vice versa.

conversion [kən'vɜ:ʃən] 1 n (*NonC: gen, Fin, Math, Philos, Rel*) conversion *f*; (*Rugby*) transformation *f*. **the ~ of salt water into drinking water** la conversion *or* la transformation d'eau salée en eau potable; **the ~ of an old house into flats** l'aménagement *m or* l'agencement *m* d'une vieille maison en appartements; **improper ~ of funds** détournement *m* de fonds, malversations *fpl*; **his ~ to Catholicism** sa conversion au catholicisme. 2 comp ► **conversion table** table *f* de conversion.

convert ['kɒnvɜ:t] 1 n converti(e) *m(f)*. **to become a ~ to** se convertir à. 2 [kən'vɜ:t] vt a convertir, transformer, changer (*into* en); (*Rel etc*) convertir (*to* à). **to ~ pounds into francs** (*on paper*) convertir des livres en francs; (*by exchanging them*) changer *or* convertir des livres en francs; (*Rugby*) **to ~ a try** transformer un essai; **he has ~ed me to his way of thinking** il m'a converti *or* amené à sa façon de penser. b (*alter*) *house* arranger, aménager, agencer (*into* en). **they have ~ed one of the rooms into a bathroom** ils ont aménagé une des pièces en salle de bains.

converter [kən'vɜ:tə^r] n (*Elec, Metal*) convertisseur *m*; (*Rad*) changeur *m* de fréquence.

convertibility [kən,vɜ:tə'bɪlɪtɪ] n convertibilité *f*.

convertible [kən'vɜ:təbl] 1 adj (*gen*) convertible (*into* en). (*room, building*) **~ into** aménageable en. 2 n (*US Aut*) (voiture *f*) décapotable *f*.

convertor [kən'vɜ:tə^r] n = **converter.**

convex ['kɒn'veks] adj convexe.

convexity [kɒn'veksɪtɪ] n convexité *f*.

convey [kən'veɪ] vt *goods, passengers* transporter; *[pipeline etc]* amener; *sound* transmettre; (*Jur*) *property* transférer, transmettre, céder (*to* à); *opinion, idea* communiquer (*to* à); *order, thanks* transmettre (*to* à). **to ~ to sb that ...** faire comprendre à qn que ...; **I couldn't ~ my meaning to him** je n'ai pas pu lui communiquer ma pensée *or* me faire comprendre de lui; **would you ~ my congratulations to him?** voudriez-vous lui transmettre mes félicitations?; **words cannot ~ how I feel** les paroles ne peuvent traduire ce que je ressens; **the name ~s nothing to me** le nom ne me dit rien; **what does this music ~ to you?** qu'est-ce que cette musique évoque pour vous?

conveyance [kən'veɪəns] n a (*NonC*) transport *m*. **~ of goods** transport de marchandises; **means of ~** moyens *mpl* de transport. b (*vehicle*) voiture *f*, véhicule *m*. c (*Jur*) *[property]* transmission *f*, transfert *m*, cession *f*; (*document*) acte translatif (*de propriété*), acte de cession.

conveyancer [kən'veɪənsə^r] n rédacteur *m* d'actes translatifs de propriété.

conveyancing [kən'veɪənsɪŋ] n (*Jur*) (*procedure*) procédure translative (de propriété); (*operation*) rédaction *f* d'actes translatifs.

conveyor [kən'veɪə^r] n transporteur *m*, convoyeur *m*. (*Tech*) **~ belt** convoyeur, tapis roulant.

convict ['kɒnvɪkt] 1 n prisonnier *m*, détenu *m*. 2 [kən'vɪkt] vt (*Jur*) *person* déclarer *or* reconnaître coupable (*sb of a crime* qn d'un crime). **he was ~ed** il a été déclaré *or* reconnu coupable; **he is a ~ed criminal/murderer** il a été jugé *or* reconnu (*frm*) coupable de crime/meurtre. 3 [kən'vɪkt] vi *[jury]* rendre un verdict de culpabilité.

conviction [kən'vɪkʃən] n a (*Jur*) condamnation *f*. **there were 12 ~s for drunkenness** 12 personnes ont été condamnées pour ivresse; *see* **previous, record.** b (*NonC*) persuasion *f*, conviction *f*. **to be open to ~** être ouvert à la persuasion; **to carry ~** être convaincant; **his explanation lacked ~** son explication manquait de conviction *or* n'était pas très convaincante. c (*belief*) conviction *f*. **the ~ that ...** la conviction selon laquelle ...; *see* **courage.**

convince [kən'vɪns] vt convaincre, persuader (*sb of sth* qn de qch). **he ~d her that she should leave** il l'a persuadée de partir, il l'a convaincue qu'elle devait partir; **I am ~d he won't do it** je suis persuadé *or* convaincu qu'il ne le fera pas; **a ~d Christian** un chrétien convaincu.

convincing [kən'vɪnsɪŋ] adj *speaker, argument, manner, words* persuasif, convaincant; *win, victory* décisif, éclatant.

convincingly [kən'vɪnsɪŋlɪ] adv *speak* d'un ton *or* d'une façon convaincant(e), avec conviction; *win* de façon décisive *or* éclatante.

convivial [kən'vɪvɪəl] adj *person* amateur de bonnes choses, bon vivant; *atmosphere, evening* joyeux, plein d'entrain.

conviviality [kən,vɪvɪ'ælɪtɪ] n jovialité *f*, gaieté *f*.

convocation [,kɒnvə'keɪʃən] n (*act*) convocation *f*; (*assembly*) assemblée *f*, réunion *f*; (*Rel*) assemblée, synode *m*; (*US Educ*) cérémonie *f* de remise des diplômes.

convoke [kən'vəʊk] vt convoquer.

convoluted ['kɒnvəlu:tɪd] adj *pattern, object* convoluté (*also Bot*); (*fig*) *argument, ideas, speech* compliqué; *style* contourné; *excuses* embarrassé.

convolution [,kɒnvə'lu:ʃən] n circonvolution *f*.

convolvulus [kən'vɒlvjʊləs] n, pl **~es** *or* **convolvuli** [kən'vɒlvjʊ,laɪ] (*flower*) volubilis *m*; (*weed*) liseron *m*.

convoy ['kɒnvɔɪ] 1 n *[ships, vehicles]* convoi *m*. **in ~** en convoi. 2 vt convoyer, escorter (*to* à).

convulse [kən'vʌls] vt ébranler, bouleverser. **a land ~d by war** un pays bouleversé par la guerre; **a land ~d by earthquakes** un pays ébranlé par des tremblements de terre; (*fig*) **to be ~d (with laughter)** se tordre de rire; **a face ~d with pain** un visage décomposé *or* contracté par la douleur.

convulsion [kən'vʌlʃən] n a (*Med*) convulsion *f*. **to have ~s** avoir des convulsions; (*fig*) **to go into ~s of laughter** se tordre de rire. b (*violent disturbance*) *[land]* convulsion *f*, bouleversement *m*, ébranlement *m*; *[sea]* violente agitation.

convulsive [kən'vʌlsɪv] adj *movement, laughter* convulsif.

cony ['kəʊnɪ] n (*US*) lapin *m*; (*also* **~ skin**) peau *f* de lapin.

coo¹ [ku:] 1 vti *[doves etc]* roucouler; *[baby]* gazouiller; *see* **bill².** 2 n roucoulement *m*, roucoulade *f*.

coo²* [ku:] excl (*Brit*) ça alors!*

co-occur [,kəʊə'kɜ:r] vi (*Ling*) figurer simultanément, être cooccurrent(s) (*with* avec).

co-occurrence [,kəʊə'kʌrəns] n (*Ling*) cooccurrence *f*.

cooing ['ku:ɪŋ] n roucoulement *m*, roucoulade *f*.

cook [kʊk] 1 n cuisinier *m*, -ière *f*. **she is a good ~** elle est bonne cuisinière, elle fait bien la cuisine; **to be head** *or* **chief ~ and bottle-washer*** (*in a household*) servir de bonne à tout faire; (*elsewhere*) être le factotum.

2 **comp** ► **cookbook** livre *m* de cuisine ► **cook-chill foods** plats *mpl* cuisinés ► **cookhouse** (*Mil, Naut*) cuisine *f* ► **cookout** (*US*) grillade *f* en plein air.

3 **vt** a *food* (faire) cuire. (*fig*) **to ~ sb's goose*** mettre qn dans le pétrin*; **~ed breakfast** petit-déjeuner *m* complet à l'anglaise; **~ed meat** viande *f* froide; (*Comm*) **~ed meat(s)** ≃ charcuterie *f*.

b (*Brit* *: *falsify*) *accounts* truquer, maquiller. **to ~ the books*** truquer les comptes.

4 **vi** *[food]* cuire; *[person]* faire la cuisine, cuisiner. **she ~s well** elle fait bien la cuisine, elle cuisine bien; (*fig*) **what's ~ing?*** qu'est-ce qui se mijote?*

►**cook up*** **vt sep** *story, excuse* inventer, fabriquer.

cooker ['kʊkəʳ] **n** a (*Brit*) cuisinière *f* (*fourneau*); *see* **gas.** b (*apple*) pomme *f* à cuire.

cookery ['kʊkərɪ] **n** (*gen, also school etc subject*) cuisine *f* (*activité*). **~ book** livre *m* de cuisine; **~ teacher** professeur *m* d'enseignement ménager.

cookie ['kʊkɪ] **n** a (*Culin*) (*US*) petit gâteau (sec); (*Brit*) cookie *m*. **that's the way the ~ crumbles*** c'est la vie! b (*: *person*) type* *m*; (*US*) (*girl*) jolie fille. **a smart ~** un petit malin; **tough ~** dur à cuire *m*.

cooking ['kʊkɪŋ] 1 **n** cuisine *f* (*activité*). **plain/French ~** cuisine bourgeoise/française. 2 **comp** *utensils* de cuisine; *apples, chocolate* à cuire ► **cooking film** film *m* alimentaire ► **cooking foil** papier-alu *m*, papier *m* d'alu(minium) ► **cooking salt** gros sel, sel de cuisine.

cool [ku:l] 1 **adj** a *weather, day, water, hands, colour* frais (*f* fraîche); *drink* frais, rafraîchissant; (*not hot enough*) *soup etc* qui n'est plus chaud; (*lightweight*) *dress etc* qui ne tient pas chaud, léger. **"keep in a ~ place"** "tenir au frais", "conserver dans un endroit frais"; **"serve ~, not cold"** "servir frais et non glacé"; *[air temperature]* **it's quite ~** il fait plutôt frais; **it's turning ~er** le temps fraîchit *or* vire à la fraîcheur; **I feel quite ~ now** j'ai bien moins chaud maintenant; **it helps you (to) keep ~** *[drink, cologne]* c'est très rafraîchissant; *[fan]* ça vous donne un peu de fraîcheur; **she's as ~ as a cucumber** elle n'a pas chaud du tout (*see also* **1b**); **his brow is much ~er now** il a le front bien moins chaud maintenant; **to slip into something ~** passer quelque chose de plus léger.

b (*calm, unperturbed*) *person, manner* calme; (*relaxed*) cool*, relaxe*, décontracté. **to keep ~** garder son sang-froid; **to keep a ~ head** ne pas perdre la tête; **keep ~!** du calme!; **play it ~!*** pas de panique!*, ne nous emballons pas!; **to be as ~ as a cucumber** garder son calme *or* son sang-froid *or* son flegme; **"I've lost it" he said as ~ as a cucumber** "je l'ai perdu" dit-il sans sourciller *or* sans s'émouvoir *or* en gardant tout son flegme; **she looked as ~ as a cucumber** elle affichait un calme imperturbable; (*loc*) **~, calm and collected** très posé: **to be ~ and calculating** être froid et calculateur.

c (*unenthusiastic, unfriendly*) *greeting, reception* frais (*f* fraîche), froid. **to be ~ towards sb** battre froid à qn, traiter qn avec froideur.

d (*: *impertinent*) *behaviour* effronté. **he's a ~ customer** il a du culot*, il n'a pas froid aux yeux; **he spoke to her as ~ as you please** il lui a parlé sans la moindre gêne; **that was very ~ of him** quel toupet (il a eu)!*

e (*: *emphatic*) **he earns a ~ £40,000 a year** il se fait la coquette somme de 40 000 livres par an.

f (*: *elegant, sophisticated*) **a ~ blonde** une blonde éthérée.

g (*: *excellent*) super *inv*, génial. **that's ~, man!** c'est super, mec!*

h (*Jazz*) cool *inv*.

2 **adv** (*fig*) **to play it ~** ne pas s'exciter *or* s'énerver.

3 **comp** ► **cool bag, cool box** glacière *f* ► **cool-headed** calme, imperturbable.

4 **n** a fraîcheur *f*, frais *m*. **in the ~ of the evening** dans la fraîcheur du soir; **to keep sth in the ~** tenir qch au frais.

b (*) **keep your ~!** t'énerve pas!*; **he lost his ~** (*panicked*) il a paniqué*; (*got angry*) il s'est fichu en rogne*.

5 **vt** a *air* rafraîchir, refroidir. (*fig*) **to ~ one's heels** faire le pied de grue; **to leave sb to ~ his heels** faire attendre qn, faire poireauter* qn.

b **~ it!*** t'énerve pas!*, panique pas!*

6 **vi** (*also* **~ down**) *[air, liquid]* (se) rafraîchir, refroidir.

►**cool down** 1 **vi** (*lit*) refroidir; (*fig*) *[anger]* se calmer, s'apaiser; *[critical situation]* se détendre; (*) *[person]* se calmer. **let the situation cool down!** attendez que la situation se détende! *or* que les choses se calment! (*subj*). 2 **vt sep** (*lit*) faire refroidir; (*fig*) calmer.

►**cool off** **vi** (*lose enthusiasm*) perdre son enthousiasme, se calmer; (*change one's affections*) se refroidir (*towards sb* à l'égard de qn, envers qn); (*become less angry*) se calmer, s'apaiser.

coolant ['ku:lənt] **n** liquide *m* de refroidissement.

cooler ['ku:ləʳ] **n** a (*for food*) glacière *f*. **in the ~** dans la glacière. b (*Prison sl*) taule* *f*. **in the ~** en taule*; **to get put in the ~** se faire mettre au frais* *or* à l'ombre*. c (*drink*) *boisson faite de vin, de jus de fruit et d'eau gazeuse*.

coolie ['ku:lɪ] **n** coolie *m*.

cooling ['ku:lɪŋ] 1 **adj** *drink, swim* rafraîchissant. 2 **n** (*Aut*) refroidissement *m*. 3 **comp** ► **cooling fan** (*Aut*) ventilateur *m* ► **cooling-off period** (*Comm, Ind*) délai *m* de réflexion ► **cooling system** circuit *m* de refroidissement ► **cooling tower** (*Tech*) refroidisseur *m*.

coolly ['ku:lɪ] **adv** (*calmly*) de sang-froid, calmement; (*unenthusiastically*) fraîchement, froidement, avec froideur; (*impertinently*) avec impertinence, sans la moindre gêne, avec (le plus grand) culot*.

coolness ['ku:lnɪs] **n** *[water, air, weather]* fraîcheur *f*; *[welcome]* froideur *f*; (*calmness*) sang-froid *m*, impassibilité *f*, flegme *m*; (*impudence*) toupet* *m*, culot* *m*.

coomb [ku:m] **n** petite vallée, combe *f*.

coon [ku:n] **n** a (*Zool*) (**abbr of raccoon**) raton-laveur *m*. b (** *pej: Negro*) nègre *m*, négresse *f*.

coop [ku:p] 1 **n** (*also* **hen ~**) poulailler *m*, cage *f* à poules. 2 **vt** *hens* enfermer dans un poulailler.

►**coop up** **vt sep** *person* claquemurer, cloîtrer, enfermer; *feelings* refouler.

co-op ['kəʊ'ɒp] **n** a (*Brit: shop*) (**abbr of cooperative**) coopérative *f*, coop* *f*. b (*US*) (**abbr of cooperative apartment**) appartement *m* en copropriété. c (*US Univ*) (**abbr of cooperative**) coopérative étudiante.

cooper ['ku:pəʳ] **n** tonnelier *m*.

cooperage ['ku:pərɪdʒ] **n** tonnellerie *f*.

cooperate [kəʊ'ɒpəreɪt] **vi** coopérer, collaborer (*with sb* avec qn, *in sth* à qch, *to do* pour faire). **I hope he'll ~** j'espère qu'il va se montrer coopératif.

cooperation [kəʊˌɒpə'reɪʃən] **n** coopération *f*, concours *m*. **in ~ with, with the ~ of** avec la coopération *or* le concours de; (*Jur*) **international judicial ~** entraide *f* judiciaire internationale.

cooperative [kəʊ'ɒpərətɪv] 1 **adj** *person, firm, attitude* coopératif. (*US*) **~ apartment** appartement *m* en copropriété; (*Comm etc*) **~ society** coopérative *f*, société coopérative *or* mutuelle; (*Can Pol*) **C~ Commonwealth Federation** parti *m* social démocratique (*Can*). 2 **n** coopérative *f*.

cooperatively [kəʊ'ɒpərətɪvlɪ] **adv** (*jointly*) en coopération; (*obligingly*) de façon coopérative.

coopt [kəʊ'ɒpt] **vt** coopter (*on to* à). **~ed member** membre coopté.

cooption [kəʊ'ɒpʃən] **n** cooptation *f*.

coordinate [kəʊ'ɔ:dnɪt] 1 **adj** (*gen, Gram, Math*) coordonné. **~ geometry** géométrie *f* analytique. 2 **n** a (*gen, Math, on map*) coordonnée *f*. b (*Dress*) **~s** ensemble *m* (coordonné), coordonnés *mpl*. 3 [kəʊ'ɔ:dɪneɪt] **vt** coordonner (*one thing with another* une chose avec une autre). **coordinating committee** comité *m* de coordination; (*Ling*) **coordinating conjunction** conjonction *f* de coordination.

coordination [kəʊˌɔ:dɪ'neɪʃən] **n** coordination *f*.

coordinator [kəʊ'ɔ:dɪneɪtəʳ] **n** coordinateur *m*, -trice *f*.

coot [ku:t] **n** a (*Orn*) foulque *f*; *see* **bald.** b (*: *fool*) tourte* *f*.

co-owner ['kəʊ'əʊnəʳ] **n** copropriétaire *mf*.

co-ownership [ˌkəʊ'əʊnəʃɪp] **n** copropriété *f*.

cop* [kɒp] 1 **n** a (*policeman*) flic* *m*, poulet *m*. **to play at ~s and robbers** jouer aux gendarmes et aux voleurs. b (*Brit*) **it's no great ~*, it's not much ~*** ça ne vaut pas grand-chose *or* tripette. 2 **comp** ► **cop-out*** échappatoire *f*, excuse *f* facile, dérobade *f* ► **cop-shop*** maison *f* Poulaga*, commissariat *m* (de police). 3 **vt** (*Brit: arrest, catch*) pincer*, piquer*; (*steal*) piquer*, faucher; (*obtain*) obtenir. (*Brit*) **to ~ hold of*** prendre; (*Brit*) **to ~ it*** écoper*, trinquer*; (*US*) **to ~ a plea*** plaider coupable (*pour une charge mineure, afin d'en éviter une plus grave*).

►**cop out*** 1 **vi** se défiler*. 2 **cop-out** *see* **cop 2.**

copacetic* [ˌkəʊpə'setɪk] **adj** (*US*) formidable.

copartner ['kəʊ'pɑ:tnəʳ] **n** coassocié(e) *m(f)*, coparticipant(e) *m(f)*.

copartnership ['kəʊ'pɑ:tnəʃɪp] **n** (*Fin*) société *f* en nom collectif; (*gen*) coassociation *f*, coparticipation *f*. **to go into ~ with** entrer en coassociation avec.

cope[1] [kəʊp] **n** (*Dress Rel*) chape *f*.

cope[2] [kəʊp] **vi** se débrouiller, s'en tirer. **can you ~?** ça ira?, vous y arriverez?, vous vous débrouillerez?; **leave it to me, I'll ~** laissez cela, je m'en charge *or* je m'en occupe; **how are you coping without a secretary?** vous arrivez à vous débrouiller sans secrétaire?; **he's coping pretty well** il s'en tire *or* se débrouille très bien; **I can ~ in Spanish** je me débrouille en espagnol; **she just can't ~ any more** (*she's overworked etc*) elle ne s'en sort plus; (*work is too difficult for her*) elle n'est plus du tout dans la course*, elle est complètement dépassée.

►**cope with** **vt fus** *task, difficult person* se charger de, s'occuper de; *situation* faire face à; *difficulties, problems* (*tackle*) affronter; (*solve*) venir à bout de. **they cope with 500 applications a day** 500 formulaires leur passent entre les mains chaque jour; **you get the tickets, I'll cope with the luggage** va chercher les billets, moi je m'occupe *or* je me charge des bagages; **I'll cope with him** je m'occupe *or* je me charge de lui; **he's got a lot to cope with** (*work*) il a du pain sur la planche; (*problems*) il a pas mal de problèmes à résoudre; **we can't cope with all this work** avec tout ce travail nous ne pouvons plus en sortir.

Copenhagen [ˌkəʊpn'heɪgən] **n** Copenhague.

Copernicus [kə'pɜ:nɪkəs] **n** Copernic *m*.

copestone ['kəʊpstəʊn] n (*Archit*) couronnement *m*; *[wall]* chaperon *m*; (*fig*) *[career etc]* couronnement, point culminant.
copier ['kɒpɪəʳ] n machine *f* à photocopier.
co-pilot ['kəʊ'paɪlət] n (*Aviat*) copilote *m*, pilote *m* auxiliaire.
coping ['kəʊpɪŋ] n chaperon *m*. ~ **stone** = **copestone**.
copious ['kəʊpɪəs] adj *food, notes* copieux; *amount* ample, abondant; *harvest* abondant; *writer* fécond; *letter* prolixe.
copiously ['kəʊpɪəslɪ] adv copieusement.
copper ['kɒpəʳ] 1 n a (*NonC*) cuivre *m*.
b (*money*) ~s la petite monnaie; **I gave the beggar a ~** j'ai donné une petite pièce au mendiant.
c (*St Ex*) ~s les cuprifères *mpl*.
d (*washtub*) lessiveuse *f*.
e (*: *policeman*) flic‡ *m*, poulet‡ *m*. ~**'s nark** indic* *m*, mouchard *m*.
2 comp *mine* de cuivre; *wire, bracelet* de *or* en cuivre ► **copper beech** hêtre *m* pourpre ► **copper-bottomed** *saucepan* avec un fond en cuivre; *investment* sûr, solide ► **copper-coloured** cuivré ► **copperhead** (*US: snake*) vipère cuivrée ► **copperplate** (*in engraving*) n planche *f* (de cuivre) gravée ◊ adj sur cuivre, en taille-douce; **copperplate handwriting** écriture moulée, belle ronde ► **coppersmith** chaudronnier *m* (en cuivre) ► **copper sulphate** sulfate *m* de cuivre.
coppery ['kɒpərɪ] adj cuivré.
coppice ['kɒpɪs] n taillis *m*, boqueteau *m*.
copra ['kɒprə] n copra *m*.
co-presidency [kəʊ'prezɪdənsɪ] n coprésidence *f*.
co-president [kəʊ'prezɪdənt] n coprésident(e) *m(f)*.
copse [kɒps] n = **coppice**.
Copt [kɒpt] n Copte *mf*.
'copter* ['kɒptəʳ] n (abbr of **helicopter**) hélico* *m*.
coptic ['kɒptɪk] adj copte. **the C~ Church** l'Église copte.
copula ['kɒpjʊlə] n, pl ~s *or* **copulae** ['kɒpjʊ,liː] (*Gram*) copule *f*.
copulate ['kɒpjʊleɪt] vi copuler.
copulation [,kɒpjʊ'leɪʃən] n copulation *f*.
copulative ['kɒpjʊlətɪv] adj (*Gram*) copulatif.
copy ['kɒpɪ] 1 n a *[painting etc]* copie *f*, reproduction *f*; *[letter, document, memo]* copie; (*Phot: print*) épreuve *f*. **to take** *or* **make a ~ of sth** faire une copie de qch; *see* **carbon, fair¹, rough** *etc*.
b *[book]* exemplaire *m*; *[magazine, newspaper]* exemplaire, numéro *m*; *see* **author, presentation**.
c (*NonC*) (*for newspaper etc*) copie *f*, sujet *m* d'article, matière *f* à reportage; (*for advertisement*) message *m*, texte *m*. **it gave him ~ for several articles** cela lui a fourni la matière de *or* un sujet pour *or* de la copie pour plusieurs articles; **that's always good ~** c'est un sujet qui rend toujours bien; **the murder will make good ~** le meurtre fera de l'excellente copie; **the journalist handed in his ~** le journaliste a remis son article *or* papier*; **they are short of ~** ils sont à court de copie.
d (*Comput*) copie *f*.
2 comp ► **copybook** n cahier *m* (*see* **blot**) ◊ adj (*trite*) banal; (*ideal, excellent*) modèle ► **copyboy** (*Press*) grouillot *m* de rédaction ► **copycat**‡ n copieur *m*, -ieuse *f* ◊ adj *crime* d'imitation ► **copy-edit** corriger ► **copy editor** (*Press*) secrétaire *mf* de rédaction ► **copying ink** encre *f* à copier ► **copy machine** machine *f* à photocopier ► **copy press** presse *f* à copier ► **copyreader** (*US Press*) correcteur-rédacteur *m*, correctrice-rédactrice *f* ► **copyright** *see* **copyright** ► **copywriter** rédacteur *m*, -trice *f* publicitaire.
3 vt a (*also* ~ **down** *or* **out**) *letter, passage from book* copier.
b (*imitate*) *person, gestures* copier, imiter.
c (*Scol etc*) *sb else's work* copier. **he copied in the exam** il a copié à l'examen.
d (*Comput, Ling*) copier. **to ~ sth to a disk**copier qch sur une disquette.
e (*Rad, Telec: sl*)copier.
f (*send a copy to*) envoyer une copie à.
copyist ['kɒpɪɪst] n copiste *mf*, scribe *m*.
copyright ['kɒpɪraɪt] 1 n droit *m* d'auteur, copyright *m*. ~ **reserved** tous droits (de reproduction) réservés; **out of ~** dans le domaine public. 2 vt *book* obtenir les droits exclusifs sur *or* le copyright de.
coquetry ['kɒkɪtrɪ] n coquetterie *f*.
coquette [kə'ket] n coquette *f*.
coquettish [kə'ketɪʃ] adj *person* coquet, provocant; *look* aguichant, provocant.
cor‡ [kɔːʳ] excl (*Brit: also* ~ **blimey**) mince alors!*
coracle ['kɒrəkl] n coracle *m*, canot *m* (d'osier).
coral ['kɒrəl] 1 n corail *m*. 2 comp *necklace* de corail; *island* corallien; (*also* **coral-coloured**) (couleur) corail *inv* ► **coral lips**: (*liter*) **her coral lips** ses lèvres de corail ► **coral reef** récif *m* de corail ► **Coral Sea** mer *f* de Corail.
cor anglais ['kɔːr'ɑːŋgleɪ] n, pl **cors anglais** ['kɔːz'ɑːŋgleɪ] cor anglais.
corbel ['kɔːbəl] n corbeau *m*.
cord [kɔːd] 1 n a *[curtains, pyjamas etc]* cordon *m*; *[windows]* corde *f*; *[parcel etc]* ficelle *f*; (*US Elec*) cordon *or* fil *m* électrique; (*Anat: also* **umbilical** ~) cordon ombilical; *see* **spinal, vocal.** b (*NonC: Tex*) = **corduroy.** c ~s* (npl) pantalon *m* en velours côtelé. 2 comp *trousers* en velours côtelé ► **cord carpet** tapis *m* de corde. 3 vt (*tie*) corder.
cordage ['kɔːdɪdʒ] n (*NonC*) cordages *mpl*.
corded ['kɔːdɪd] adj *fabric* côtelé.
cordial ['kɔːdɪəl] 1 adj *person, atmosphere* cordial; *welcome* chaleureux. 2 n cordial *m*.
cordiality [,kɔːdɪ'ælɪtɪ] n cordialité *f*.
cordially ['kɔːdɪəlɪ] adv cordialement. **I ~ detest him** je le déteste cordialement.
cordite ['kɔːdaɪt] n cordite *f*.
cordless ['kɔːdlɪs] adj à piles, fonctionnant sur piles. ~ **telephone** téléphone *m* sans fil.
cordon ['kɔːdn] 1 n (*all senses*) cordon *m*. ~ **bleu** cordon bleu. 2 vt (*also* ~ **off**) *crowd* tenir à l'écart (*au moyen d'un cordon de police etc*); *area* interdire l'accès à (*au moyen d'un cordon de police etc*).
corduroy ['kɔːdərɔɪ] 1 n (*Tex*) velours côtelé. ~**s** pantalon *m* en velours côtelé. 2 comp *trousers, jacket* en velours côtelé; (*US*) *road* de rondins.
CORE [kɔːʳ] n (*US*) (abbr of **Congress of Racial Equality**) *défense des droits des Noirs*.
core [kɔːʳ] 1 n *[fruit]* trognon *m*, cœur; *[magnet, earth]* noyau *m*; *[cable]* âme *f*, noyau; (*Chem: of atom*) noyau; *[nuclear reactor]* cœur *m*; (*Comput: also* ~ **memory**) mémoire *f* centrale; (*fig: of problem etc*) essentiel *m*. **apple ~** trognon de pomme; **the earth's ~** le noyau terrestre; (*Geol*) ~ **sample** carotte *f*; (*fig*) **he is rotten to the ~** il est pourri jusqu'à l'os; **English to the ~** anglais jusqu'à la moelle (des os); *see* **hard.** 2 comp *issue, assumption, subject* fondamental ► **core curriculum** tronc commun ► **core subject** matière fondamentale ► **core time** plage *f* fixe. 3 vt *fruit* enlever le trognon *or* le cœur de.
co-religionist ['kəʊrɪ'lɪdʒənɪst] n coreligionnaire *mf*.
corer ['kɔːrəʳ] n (*Culin*) vide-pomme *m*.
co-respondent ['kəʊrɪs'pɒndənt] n (*Jur*) co-défendeur *m*, -deresse *f* (*d'un adultère*).
Corfu [kɔː'fuː] n Corfou.
corgi ['kɔːgɪ] n corgi *m*.
coriander [,kɒrɪ'ændəʳ] n coriandre *f*.
Corinth ['kɒrɪnθ] n Corinthe. ~ **Canal** le canal de Corinthe.
Corinthian [kə'rɪnθɪən] 1 adj corinthien. 2 n Corinthien(ne) *m(f)*.
Coriolanus ['kɒrɪə'leɪnəs] n Coriolan *m*.
cork [kɔːk] 1 n a (*NonC*) liège *m*. b (*in bottle etc*) bouchon *m*. **to pull the ~ out of a bottle** déboucher une bouteille; (*Fishing: also* ~ **float**) flotteur *m*, bouchon. 2 vt (*also* ~ **up**) *bottle* boucher. 3 comp *mat, tiles, flooring* de liège ► **cork oak** = **cork tree** ► **corkscrew** tire-bouchon *m*; **corkscrew curls** frisettes *fpl* ► **cork-tipped** à bout de liège ► **cork tree** chêne-liège *m*.
corkage ['kɔːkɪdʒ] n droit *m* de bouchon (*payé par le client qui apporte dans un restaurant une bouteille achetée ailleurs*).
corked [kɔːkt] adj *wine* qui sent le bouchon.
corker‡ ['kɔːkəʳ] n (*lie*) mensonge *m* de taille, gros mensonge; (*story*) histoire fumante*; (*Sport: shot, stroke*) coup fumant*; (*player*) crack* *m*; (*girl*) beau morceau (de fille). **that's a ~!** ça vous en bouche un coin!*
corking*† ['kɔːkɪŋ] adj (*Brit* †) épatant*†, fameux*, fumant*.
corm [kɔːm] n bulbe *m* (*de crocus etc*).
cormorant ['kɔːmərənt] n cormoran *m*.
corn¹ [kɔːn] 1 n a (*seed*) grain *m* (*de céréale*).
b (*Brit*) blé *m*; (*US*) maïs *m*. ~ **on the cob** épi *m* de maïs.
c (*US: whiskey*) bourbon *m*.
d (*sentimentality*) sentimentalité vieillotte *or* bébête; (*humour*) humour *m* bébête.
2 comp ► **corn bread** (*US*) pain *m* de maïs ► **corncob** (*US*) épi *m* de maïs ► **the Corncracker State** le Kentucky ► **corncrake** (*Orn*) râle *m* des genêts ► **corn crops** céréales *fpl* ► **corn dolly** (*Brit*) bouquet *m* de moisson ► **corn exchange** halle *f* au blé ► **cornfield** (*Brit*) champ *m* de blé; (*US*) champ de maïs ► **cornflakes** céréales *fpl*, cornflakes *fpl* ► **cornflour** (*Brit*) farine *f* de maïs, maïzena *f* ® ► **cornflower** n bleuet *m*, barbeau *m* ◊ adj *also* **cornflower blue** bleu vif *inv*, bleu barbeau *inv* ► **corn liquor** (*US*) gnôle *f* à base de maïs (*fabrication artisanale*) ► **corn meal** farine *f* de maïs ► **corn oil** huile *f* de maïs ► **corn poppy** coquelicot *m* ► **corn salad** doucette *f* ► **cornstarch** (*US*) = **cornflour** ► **corn whiskey** (*US*) whisky *m* (de maïs), bourbon *m*.
corn² [kɔːn] n (*Med*) cor *m*. (*Brit fig*) **to tread on sb's ~s** toucher qn à l'endroit sensible, blesser qn dans son amour-propre; (*Med*) ~ **plaster** pansement *m* (*pour cors*).
cornea ['kɔːnɪə] n, pl ~s *or* **corneae** ['kɔːnɪ,iː] cornée *f*.
corneal ['kɔːnɪəl] adj cornéen.
corned beef ['kɔːnd'biːf] n (*Brit*) corned-beef *m*.
cornelian [kɔː'niːlɪən] n cornaline *f*.
corner ['kɔːnəʳ] 1 n *[page, field, eye, mouth]* coin *m*; *[street, box, table]* coin, angle *m*; *[room]* coin, encoignure *f*, angle; (*Aut*) tournant *m*, virage *m*; (*Climbing*) dièdre *m*; (*Ftbl*) corner *m*, coup *m* (de pied) de coin. **to put a child in the ~** mettre un enfant au coin; (*fig*) **to drive sb into a ~** mettre qn au pied du mur, coincer* qn; (*fig*) **to be in a (tight) ~** être dans le pétrin, être dans une situation difficile, être coincé*; **to**

look at sb out of the ~ of one's eye regarder qn du coin de l'œil; **it's just round the ~** (*lit*) c'est juste après le coin; (*very near*) c'est à deux pas d'ici; **Christmas is just around the ~** on est presque à Noël; **the domestic robot is just around the ~** le robot domestique, c'est pour demain; **you'll find the church round the ~** vous trouverez l'église juste après le coin; **the little shop around the ~** la petite boutique du coin; **to take a ~** (*Aut*) prendre un tournant; (*Ftbl*) faire un corner; **in every ~ of the garden** dans tout le jardin; **treasures hidden in odd ~s** des trésors cachés dans des recoins; **in every ~ of the house** dans tous les coins et recoins de la maison; (*fig*) **in every ~ of Europe** dans toute l'Europe; **in (all) the four ~s of the earth** aux quatre coins du monde *or* de la planète; (*Fin*) **to make a ~ in wheat** accaparer le marché du blé; *see* **cut, turn** *etc.*

2 **vt** *hunted animal* acculer; (*fig: catch to speak to etc*) coincer*. (*Comm*) **to ~ the market** accaparer le marché; **she ~ed me in the hall** elle m'a coincé* dans l'entrée; (*fig*) **he's got you ~ed** il t'a coincé*, il t'a mis au pied du mur.

3 **vi** (*Aut*) prendre un virage.

4 **comp** ► **corner cupboard** placard *m* de coin ► **corner flag** (*Ftbl*) piquet *m* de coin; (*flagstone in roadway*) dalle *f* de coin ► **the corner house** la maison du coin, la maison qui fait l'angle (de la rue) ► **corner kick** (*Ftbl*) corner *m*, coup *m* (de pied) de coin ► **corner seat** (*Rail*) (place *f* de) coin *m* ► **corner shop** boutique *f* du coin ► **corner situation: the house has a corner situation** la maison fait l'angle ► **cornerstone** (*lit, fig*) pierre *f* angulaire; (*foundation stone*) première pierre ► **cornerways fold** pli *m* en triangle.

cornering ['kɔːnərɪŋ] **n** (*Aut*) façon *f* de prendre les virages.

cornet ['kɔːnɪt] **n** a (*Mus*) cornet *m* (à pistons). **~ player** cornettiste *mf*. b (*Brit*) *[sweets etc]* cornet *m*; *[ice cream]* cornet (de glace).

cornice ['kɔːnɪs] **n** corniche *f*.

corniche ['kɔːniːʃ, kɔː'niːʃ] (*also* **~ road**) corniche *f*.

Cornish ['kɔːnɪʃ] **adj** de Cornouailles, cornouaillais.

cornucopia [kɔːnjʊ'kəʊpɪə] **n** corne *f* d'abondance.

Cornwall ['kɔːnwəl] **n** (comté *m* de) Cornouailles *f*.

corny* ['kɔːnɪ] **adj** bébête; *joke* bébête, rebattu; *story* à l'eau de rose, bébête.

corolla [kə'rɒlə] **n** corolle *f*.

corollary [kə'rɒlərɪ] **n** corollaire *m*.

corona [kə'rəʊnə] **n, pl ~s** *or* **coronae** [kə'rəʊniː] (*Anat, Astron*) couronne *f*; (*Elec*) couronne électrique; (*Archit*) larmier *m*.

coronary ['kɒrənərɪ] 1 **adj** (*Anat*) coronaire. **~ bypass** pontage *m* coronarien; **~ care unit** unité *f* de soins coronariens; **~ heart disease** maladie *f* coronarienne; **~ thrombosis** infarctus *m* du myocarde, thrombose *f* coronarienne. 2 **n** (*Med **) infarctus *m*.

coronation [ˌkɒrə'neɪʃən] 1 **n** (*ceremony*) couronnement *m*; (*actual crowning*) sacre *m*. 2 **comp** *ceremony, oath, robe* du sacre; *day* du couronnement.

coroner ['kɒrənəʳ] **n** coroner *m* (*officiel chargé de déterminer les causes d'un décès*). **~'s inquest** enquête *f* judiciaire (*menée par le coroner*); **~'s jury** jury *m* (*siégeant avec le coroner*).

coronet ['kɒrənɪt] **n** *[duke etc]* couronne *f*; *[lady]* diadème *m*.

Corp, corp **abbr of corporation.**

corpora ['kɔːpərə] **npl of corpus.**

corporal¹ ['kɔːpərəl] **n** (*infantry, RAF*) caporal-chef *m*; *[cavalry etc]* brigadier-chef *m*. (*on envelope etc*) **C~ Smith** le Caporal-Chef Smith.

corporal² ['kɔːpərəl] **adj** corporel. **~ punishment** châtiment corporel.

corporate ['kɔːpərɪt] **adj** a (*Comm: forming a corporation*) constitué (en corporation). **I meant "we" in the ~ sense** je voulais dire "nous" au sens de l'ensemble de la société; **~ body** *or* **institution** personne morale. b (*Comm: of a corporation*) *property* appartenant à l'entreprise; *growth, image, identity, liabilities, logo, planning* de l'entreprise. **~ car** voiture *f* de fonction; **~ law** droit *m* des entreprises *or* des sociétés; **~ name** raison sociale; **~ stock** actions *fpl*; **~ tax** impôt *m* sur les sociétés. c (*joint, of a group*) *action, ownership* en commun; *decision, responsibility* collectif.

corporation [ˌkɔːpə'reɪʃən] 1 **n** a (*Brit*) *[town]* conseil municipal. **the Mayor and C~** le corps municipal, la municipalité. b (*Comm, Fin*) société commerciale; (*US*) société à responsabilité limitée, compagnie commerciale. **~ lawyer** avocat *m* d'entreprise. c (*Brit **) bedaine* *f*, brioche* *f*. **to develop a ~** prendre de la bedaine* *or* de la brioche*.

2 **comp** (*Brit*) *school, property* de la ville, municipal ► **corporation tax** (*Brit*) impôt *m* sur les sociétés.

corporatism ['kɔːpərətɪzəm] **n** corporatisme *m*.

corporatist ['kɔːpərətɪst] **adj** corporatiste.

corporeal [kɔː'pɔːrɪəl] **adj** *need* corporel, physique; *property* matériel.

corps [kɔːʳ] **n, pl corps** [kɔːz] corps *m*. **~ de ballet** corps de ballet; *see* **army, diplomatic** *etc.*

corpse [kɔːps] **n** cadavre *m*, corps *m*.

corpulence ['kɔːpjʊləns] **n** corpulence *f*, embonpoint *m*.

corpulent ['kɔːpjʊlənt] **adj** corpulent.

corpus ['kɔːpəs] **n, pl corpuses** *or* **corpora** ['kɔːpərə] (*Literat*) corpus *m*, recueil *m*; (*Ling*) corpus; (*Fin*) capital *m*. (*Rel*) **C~ Christi** la Fête-Dieu.

corpuscle ['kɔːpʌsl] **n** a (*Anat, Bio*) corpuscule *m*. **(blood) ~** globule sanguin; **red/white ~s** globules rouges/blancs. b (*Phys*) électron *m*.

corral [kə'rɑːl] (*US*) 1 **n** corral *m*. 2 **vt** *cattle* enfermer dans un corral; (** fig*) *people, support* réunir.

correct [kə'rekt] 1 **adj** a (*right, exact*) *answer, amount* correct, exact, juste; *temperature* exact; *forecast, estimate* correct. **have you the ~ time?** avez-vous l'heure exacte?; (*in buses etc*) **"~ money** *or* **change only"** "on est tenu de faire l'appoint"; **the predictions proved ~** les prédictions se sont avérées justes; **am I ~ in thinking ...?** ai-je raison de penser ...?; **you are quite ~** vous avez parfaitement raison; **he was quite ~ to do it** il a eu tout à fait raison de le faire.

b (*seemly, suitable*) *person, behaviour, manners, language* correct, convenable; *dress* correct, bienséant. **~ dress must be worn** une tenue correcte est exigée; **it's the ~ thing** c'est l'usage, c'est ce qui se fait; **the ~ procedure** la procédure d'usage.

2 **vt** a *piece of work, text, manuscript* corriger; *error* rectifier, corriger; (*Typ*) *proofs* corriger. **to ~ sb's punctuation/spelling** corriger la ponctuation/l'orthographe de qn.

b (*put right*) *person* reprendre, corriger. **he ~ed me several times during the course of my speech** il m'a repris plusieurs fois pendant mon discours; **I stand ~ed** je reconnais mon erreur; **~ me if I'm wrong** corrigez-moi si je me trompe.

c (*††: punish*) réprimander, reprendre.

correction [kə'rekʃən] **n** a (*NonC*) *[proofs, essay]* correction *f*; *[error]* correction, rectification *f*. **I am open to ~, but ...** corrigez-moi si je me trompe, mais ... . b *[school work, proof]* correction *f*; *[text, manuscript]* correction, rectification *f*. **a page covered with ~s** une page couverte de corrections; **~ fluid** liquide correcteur; **~ tape** ruban *m* correcteur. c (*††: punishment*) correction *f*, châtiment *m*. **house of ~††** maison *f* de correction†.

corrective [kə'rektɪv] **adj** *action* rectificatif; (*Jur, Med*) *measures, training* de rééducation, correctif.

correctly [kə'rektlɪ] **adv** (*see* **correct**) correctement, d'une manière exacte, avec justesse; convenablement.

correctness [kə'rektnɪs] **n** (*see* **correct**) correction *f*, exactitude *f*, justesse *f*; bienséance *f*.

Correggio [kə'redʒəʊ] **n** le Corrège.

correlate ['kɒrɪleɪt] 1 **vi** correspondre (*with* à), être en corrélation (*with* avec). 2 **vt** mettre en corrélation, corréler (*with* avec).

correlation [ˌkɒrɪ'leɪʃən] **n** corrélation *f*.

correlative [kɒ'relətɪv] 1 **n** corrélatif *m*. 2 **adj** corrélatif.

correspond [ˌkɒrɪs'pɒnd] **vi** a (*agree*) correspondre (*with* à), s'accorder (*with* avec). **that does not ~ with what he said** cela ne correspond pas à ce qu'il a dit. b (*be similar, equivalent*) correspondre (*to* à), être l'équivalent (*to* de). **this ~s to what she was doing last year** ceci est semblable *or* correspond à ce qu'elle faisait l'année dernière; **his job ~s roughly to mine** son poste équivaut à peu près au mien *or* est à peu près l'équivalent du mien. c (*exchange letters*) correspondre (*with* avec). **they ~** ils s'écrivent, ils correspondent.

correspondence [ˌkɒrɪs'pɒndəns] 1 **n** a (*gen*) correspondance *f* (*between* entre, *with* avec). b (*letter-writing*) correspondance *f*. **to be in ~ with sb** entretenir une *or* être en correspondance avec qn; **to read one's ~** lire son courrier *or* sa correspondance. 2 **comp** ► **correspondence card** carte-lettre *f* ► **correspondence college** établissement *m* d'enseignement par correspondance ► **correspondence column** (*Press*) courrier *m* (des lecteurs) ► **correspondence course** cours *m* par correspondance.

correspondent [ˌkɒrɪs'pɒndənt] **n** (*gen, Comm, Press, Bank*) correspondant(e) *m(f)*. **foreign/sports ~** correspondant étranger/sportif; *see* **special.**

corresponding [ˌkɒrɪs'pɒndɪŋ] **adj** correspondant. **~ to** conforme à; **a ~ period** une période analogue; **the ~ period** la période correspondante.

correspondingly [ˌkɒrɪs'pɒndɪŋlɪ] **adv** (*as a result*) en conséquence; (*proportionately*) proportionnellement.

corridor ['kɒrɪdɔːʳ] **n** couloir *m*, corridor *m*. (*Brit*) **~ train** train *m* à couloir; (*fig*) **the ~s of power** les allées du pouvoir.

corroborate [kə'rɒbəreɪt] **vt** corroborer, confirmer.

corroboration [kəˌrɒbə'reɪʃən] **n** confirmation *f*, corroboration *f*. **in ~ of** à l'appui de, en confirmation de.

corroborative [kə'rɒbərətɪv] **adj** qui confirme *or* corrobore.

corrode [kə'rəʊd] 1 **vt** *metal* corroder, attaquer, ronger; (*fig*) attaquer, corroder. 2 **vi** *[metals]* se corroder.

corrosion [kə'rəʊʒən] **n** corrosion *f*.

corrosive [kə'rəʊzɪv] 1 **adj** corrosif. 2 **n** corrosif *m*.

corrugated ['kɒrəgeɪtɪd] **adj** ridé, plissé; *road, surface* ondulé. **~ cardboard/paper** carton/papier ondulé; **~ iron** tôle ondulée.

corrupt [kə'rʌpt] 1 **adj** a *person, action, behaviour* (*evil, immoral*) corrompu, dépravé; (*dishonest*) vénal. **~ practices** (*dishonesty*) tractations *fpl* malhonnêtes; (*Jur: bribery etc*) trafic *m* d'influence, malversations *fpl*; **a ~ society** une société corrompue *or* pourrie; **~ tastes** des goûts pervers. b (*decaying, putrid*) vicié, corrompu. c (*incorrect*) *text* altéré. d (*Comput*) altéré, dégradé. 2 **vt** *person, morals* corrompre, dépraver, pervertir; (*bribe*) corrompre, soudoyer; *text* (*Comput*) altérer.

corruption [kə'rʌpʃən] **n** (*see* **corrupt**) corruption *f*; dépravation *f*;

altération *f*.

corsage [kɔːˈsɑːʒ] n (*bodice*) corsage *m*; (*flowers*) petit bouquet (*de fleurs porté au corsage*).

corsair [ˈkɔːsɛəʳ] n (*ship, pirate*) corsaire *m*, pirate *m*.

cors anglais [ˈkɔːzˈɑːŋgleɪ] npl of **cor anglais**.

corset [ˈkɔːsɪt] n (*Dress: also* ~s) corset *m*; (*lightweight*) gaine *f*; (*Med*) corset.

Corsica [ˈkɔːsɪkə] n Corse *f*.

Corsican [ˈkɔːsɪkən] 1 adj corse. 2 n Corse *mf*.

cortège [kɔːˈtɛːʒ] n cortège *m*.

cortex [ˈkɔːteks] n, pl **cortices** [ˈkɔːtɪsiːz] (*Bot*) cortex *m*, écorce *f*; (*Anat*) cortex.

corticoids [ˈkɔːtɪkɔɪdz], **corticosteroids** [ˌkɔːtɪkəʊˈstɪərɔɪdz] npl corticoïdes *mpl*.

cortisone [ˈkɔːtɪzəʊn] n cortisone *f*.

corundum [kəˈrʌndəm] n corindon *m*.

coruscate [ˈkɒrəskeɪt] vi briller, scintiller.

coruscating [ˈkɒrəskeɪtɪŋ] adj (*fig*) *wit, humour* brillant, scintillant.

corvette [kɔːˈvet] n (*Naut*) corvette *f*.

COS [ˌsiːəʊˈes] (abbr of **cash on shipment**) *see* **cash 1b**.

cos[1] [kɒs] n (*Brit: also* ~ **lettuce**) (laitue *f*) romaine *f*.

cos[2] [kɒs] n abbr of **cosine**.

cos[3]‡ [kɒz] conj parce que.

cosh [kɒʃ] (*Brit*) 1 vt (*) taper sur, cogner* sur. 2 n gourdin *m*, matraque *f*.

cosignatory [ˈkəʊˈsɪgnətərɪ] n cosignataire *mf*.

cosily, (*US*) **cozily** [ˈkəʊzɪlɪ] adv *furnished* confortablement; *settled* douillettement.

cosine [ˈkəʊsaɪn] n cosinus *m*.

cosiness [ˈkəʊzɪnɪs] n (*see* **cosy**) atmosphère douillette, confort *m*.

cosmetic [kɒzˈmetɪk] 1 adj *surgery* plastique, esthétique; *preparation* cosmétique; (*fig*) superficiel, symbolique. 2 n cosmétique *m*, produit *m* de beauté.

cosmic [ˈkɒzmɪk] adj (*lit*) cosmique; (*fig*) immense, incommensurable. ~ **dust/rays** poussière *f*/rayons *mpl* cosmique(s).

cosmogony [kɒzˈmɒgənɪ] n cosmogonie *f*.

cosmographer [kɒzˈmɒgrəfəʳ] n cosmographe *mf*.

cosmography [kɒzˈmɒgrəfɪ] n cosmographie *f*.

cosmology [kɒzˈmɒlədʒɪ] n cosmologie *f*.

cosmonaut [ˈkɒzmənɔːt] n cosmonaute *mf*.

cosmopolitan [ˌkɒzməˈpɒlɪtən] adj, n cosmopolite *(mf)*.

cosmos [ˈkɒzmɒs] n cosmos *m*.

co-sponsor [ˈkəʊˈspɒnsəʳ] n (*Advertising*) commanditaire *m* associé.

Cossack [ˈkɒsæk] n cosaque *m*.

cosset [ˈkɒsɪt] vt dorloter, choyer.

cost [kɒst] 1 vt (pret, ptp **cost**) a (*lit, fig*) coûter. **how much** *or* **what does the dress** ~? combien coûte *or* vaut la robe?; **how much** *or* **what will it** ~ **to have it repaired?** combien est-ce que cela coûtera de le faire réparer?; **what does it** ~ **to get in?** quel est le prix d'entrée?; **it** ~ **him a lot of money** cela lui a coûté cher; **it** ~**s him £6 a week** cela lui revient à *or* lui coûte 6 livres par semaine, il en a pour 6 livres par semaine; **it** ~**s too much** cela coûte trop cher, c'est trop cher; **it** ~**s the earth*** cela coûte les yeux de la tête; **I know what it** ~ **him to apologize** je sais ce qu'il lui en a coûté de s'excuser; **it cost her dear** (*fig*)/**her job** cela lui a coûté cher/son emploi; **it** ~ **him a great effort** cela lui a coûté *or* demandé un gros effort; **it** ~ **him a lot of trouble** cela lui a causé beaucoup d'ennuis; **it will** ~ **you your life** il vous en coûtera la vie; **it'll** *or* **that'll** ~ **you!*** tu vas le sentir passer!; **it will** ~ **you a present!** vous en serez quitte pour lui (*or* me *etc*) faire un cadeau!; **politeness** ~**s very little** il ne coûte rien d'être poli; (*fig*) ~ **what it may, whatever it** ~**s** coûte que coûte.

b (pret, ptp **costed**) (*Comm*) *articles for sale* établir le prix de revient de; *piece of work* évaluer le coût de. **the job was** ~**ed at £2,000** le devis pour (l'exécution de) ces travaux s'est monté à 2 000 livres.

2 n coût *m*. ~ **insurance and freight** coût *m* assurance *f* et fret *m*; **the** ~ **of these apples** le coût *or* le prix de ces pommes; (*Fin*) **to cut the** ~ **of loans** réduire le loyer de l'argent; **to bear the** ~ **of** (*lit*) faire face aux frais *mpl or* aux dépenses *fpl* de; (*fig*) faire les frais de; (*lit, fig*) **at great** ~ à grands frais; **at little** ~ à peu de frais; (*fig*) **at little** ~ **to himself** sans que cela lui coûte (*subj*) beaucoup; **at** ~ **(price)** au prix coûtant; (*Jur*) ~**s** dépens *mpl*, frais *mpl* judiciaires; (*Jur*) **to be ordered to pay** ~**s** être condamné aux dépens; (*fig*) **at all** ~**s, at any** ~ coûte que coûte, à tout prix; **at the** ~ **of his life/health** au prix de sa vie/santé; (*fig*) **to my** ~ à mes dépens; *see* **count**[1].

3 comp ▸ **cost accountant** analyste *mf* de coûts ▸ **cost accounting** comptabilité *f* analytique *or* d'exploitation ▸ **cost analysis** analyse *f* des coûts ▸ **cost-benefit analysis** analyse *f* coûts-avantages ▸ **cost centre** centre *m* de coût(s) ▸ **cost conscious** soucieux de ses dépenses ▸ **cost control** contrôle *m* des dépenses ▸ **cost-cutting** compression *f or* réduction *f* des coûts; **cost-cutting plan** *etc* plan *m etc* de réduction des coûts ▸ **cost-effective** rentable, d'un bon rapport rendement-prix ▸ **cost-effectiveness** rentabilité *f*, efficacité-coût *f* ▸ **cost estimate** devis *m*, estimation *f* des coûts ▸ **cost-in-use** coûts *mpl* d'utilisation ▸ **cost of living** coût *m* de la vie; **cost-of-living allowance** indemnité *f* de vie chère; **cost-of-living increase** rattrapage *m* pour cherté de la vie; **cost-of-living index** index *m* du coût de la vie ▸ **cost plus** prix *m* de revient majoré du pourcentage contractuel; **on a cost-plus basis** à des coûts majorés ▸ **cost price** (*Brit*) prix coûtant *or* de revient.

▸**cost out** vt sep *project* évaluer le coût de.

co-star [ˈkəʊstɑːʳ] (*Cine, Theat*) 1 n partenaire *mf*. 2 vi partager l'affiche (*with* avec). "~**ring X**" "avec X".

Costa Rica [ˈkɒstəˈriːkə] n Costa Rica *m*.

Costa Rican [ˈkɒstəˈriːkən] 1 adj costaricien. 2 n Costaricien(ne) *m(f)*.

coster [ˈkɒstəʳ] n, **costermonger** [ˈkɒstəˌmʌŋgəʳ] n (*Brit*) marchand(e) *m(f)* des quatre saisons.

costing [ˈkɒstɪŋ] n estimation *f* du prix de revient.

costive [ˈkɒstɪv] adj constipé.

costliness [ˈkɒstlɪnɪs] n (*value*) (grande) valeur; (*high price*) cherté *f*.

costly [ˈkɒstlɪ] adj *furs, jewels* de grande valeur, précieux; *undertaking, trip* coûteux; *tastes, habits* dispendieux, de luxe (*hum*).

costume [ˈkɒstjuːm] 1 n a (*gen*) costume *m*. **national** ~ costume national; (*fancy dress*) **in** ~ déguisé. b (†: *lady's suit*) tailleur *m*. 2 comp ▸ **costume ball** bal masqué ▸ **costume jewellery** bijoux *mpl* (de) fantaisie ▸ **costume piece** *or* **play** (*Theat*) pièce *f* historique (*en costume d'époque*).

costumier [kɒsˈtjuːmɪəʳ] n, (*esp US*) **costumer** [kɒsˈtjuːməʳ] n costumier *m*, -ière *f*.

cosy, (*US*) **cozy** [ˈkəʊzɪ] 1 adj *room* douillet, confortable; *atmosphere* douillet. **we are very** ~ **here** nous sommes très bien ici; **it is** ~ **in here** il fait bon ici; **a** ~ **little corner** un petit coin intime. 2 adv (*fig*) **to play it** ~‡ y aller mollo‡. 3 n (*tea* ~) couvre-théière *m*; (*egg* ~) couvre-œuf *m*. 4 vi (*esp US*) **to** ~ **up to sb**‡ faire de la lèche à qn‡.

cot [kɒt] n (*Brit: child's*) lit *m* d'enfant, petit lit; (*US: folding bed*) lit *m* de camp. ~**-death** mort subite du nourrisson.

coterie [ˈkəʊtərɪ] n coterie *f*, cénacle *m*, cercle *m*.

cotillion [kəˈtɪljən] n cotillon *m*, quadrille *f*.

cottage [ˈkɒtɪdʒ] 1 n petite maison (à la campagne), cottage *m*; (*thatched*) chaumière *f*; (*in holiday village etc*) villa *f*. 2 comp ▸ **cottage cheese** fromage blanc (égoutté) ▸ **cottage flat** (*Brit*) *bâtisse regroupant quatre appartements en copropriété* ▸ **cottage hospital** (*Brit*) petit hôpital ▸ **cottage industry** (*working at home*) industrie familiale; (*informally organized industry*) industrie artisanale ▸ **cottage loaf** (*Brit*) miche *f*, pain *m* de ménage ▸ **cottage pie** (*Brit*) hachis *m* parmentier.

cottager [ˈkɒtɪdʒəʳ] n (*Brit*) paysan(ne) *m(f)*; (*US*) propriétaire *mf* de maison de vacances.

cottaging* [ˈkɒtɪdʒɪŋ] n *rencontres homosexuelles dans des toilettes publiques*.

cottar, cotter [ˈkɒtəʳ] n (*Scot*) paysan(ne) *m(f)*.

cotton [ˈkɒtn] 1 n (*NonC*) (*Bot, Tex*) coton *m*; (*Brit: sewing thread*) fil *m* (de coton); *see* **absorbent, gin**.

2 comp *shirt, dress* de coton ▸ **cotton batting** (*US*) = **cotton wool** ▸ **the cotton belt** (*Agr*) le Sud cotonnier (*Alabama, Géorgie, Mississippi*) ▸ **cotton cake** tourteau *m* de coton ▸ **cotton candy** (*US*) barbe à papa *f* ▸ **cotton goods** cotonnades *fpl* ▸ **cotton grass** linaigrette *f*, lin *m* des marais ▸ **cotton industry** industrie cotonnière *or* du coton ▸ **cotton lace** dentelle *f* de coton ▸ **cotton mill** filature *f* de coton ▸ **cotton-picking** adj (*US: pej*) sale* (*before n*), sacré (*before n*) ▸ **cottonseed oil** huile *f* de coton ▸ **the Cotton State** l'Alabama ▸ **cottontail** (*US*) lapin *m* ▸ **cotton waste** déchets *mpl* de coton, coton *m* d'essuyage ▸ **cotton wool** (*Brit*) ouate *f*; **absorbent cotton wool** ouate *f or* coton *m* hydrophile; (*fig*) **to bring up a child in cotton wool** élever un enfant dans du coton; **my legs felt like cotton wool*** j'avais les jambes en coton ▸ **cottonwood** (*US*) peuplier *m* de Virginie ▸ **cotton yarn** fil *m* de coton.

▸**cotton on*** vi piger*. **to cotton on to sth** piger* qch, saisir qch.

▸**cotton to**‡ vt fus *person* avoir à la bonne‡; *plan, suggestion* apprécier, approuver. **I don't cotton to it much** je ne suis pas tellement pour*, ça ne me botte pas tellement‡.

cotyledon [ˌkɒtɪˈliːdən] n cotylédon *m*.

couch [kaʊtʃ] 1 n a (*settee*) canapé *m*, divan *m*, sofa *m*; *[doctor]* lit *m*; *[psychoanalyst]* divan; (*liter: bed*) couche *f* (*liter*). ~ **potato*** mollasson *m* (*qui passe son temps devant la télé*); (*US fig*) **to be on the** ~* être en analyse. b (*Bot: also* ~ **grass**) chiendent *m*. 2 vt formuler, exprimer. **request** ~**ed in insolent language** requête formulée *or* exprimée en des termes insolents; **request** ~**ed in the following terms** demande ainsi rédigée. 3 vi *[animal]* (*lie asleep*) être allongé *or* couché; (*ready to spring*) s'embusquer.

couchette [kuːˈʃet] n (*Rail etc*) couchette *f*.

cougar [ˈkuːgəʳ] n couguar *m or* cougouar *m*.

cough [kɒf] 1 n toux *f*. **to give a warning** ~ tousser en guise d'avertissement; **he has a (bad)** ~ il a une mauvaise toux, il tousse beaucoup. 2 comp ▸ **cough drop** *or* **lozenge** pastille *f* pour la toux ▸ **cough mixture** *or* **syrup** sirop *m* pour la toux, (sirop) antitussif *m*. 3 vi tousser.

▸**cough up** vt sep a (*lit*) expectorer, cracher en toussant. b (*: *fig*)

money cracher*.
coughing ['kɒfɪŋ] n toux *f*. **to hear ~** entendre tousser; **~ fit** quinte *f* de toux.
could [kʊd] pret, cond of **can**[1].
couldn't ['kʊdnt] = **could not**; *see* **can**[1].
could've ['kʊdəv] = **could have**; *see* **can**[1].
coulee ['ku:leɪ] n (*US*) ravine *f*.
couloir ['ku:lwɑ:ʳ] n (*Climbing*) couloir *m*.
council ['kaʊnsl] 1 n conseil *m*, assemblée *f*. **~ of war** conseil de guerre; **city** *or* **town ~** conseil municipal; **they decided in ~ that ...** l'assemblée a décidé que ...; **C~ of Europe** Conseil *m* de l'Europe; **the Security C~ of the UN** le conseil de Sécurité des Nations Unies; (*US*) **the C~ of Economic Advisors** les Conseillers *mpl* Économiques (du Président); *see* **lord, parish, privy**.
2 comp ▸ **council chamber** (*Brit*) salle *f* du conseil municipal ▸ **council flat/house** appartement *m*/maison *f* loué(e) à la municipalité, ≃ habitation *f* à loyer modéré, H.L.M. *m or f* ▸ **council housing** (*Brit*) logements sociaux ▸ **council (housing) estate** *or* **scheme** (*Scot*) quartier *m* de logements sociaux; (*high rise*) ≃ grand ensemble ▸ **councilman** (*US*) membre *m* d'un conseil, conseiller municipal ▸ **council school** (*Brit*) école publique ▸ **council tax** (*Brit*) ≃ impôts *mpl* locaux (*qui remplace la capitation*).
councillor ['kaʊnsɪləʳ] n conseiller *m*, -ère *f*, membre *m* d'un conseil. (*form of address*) **C~ X** Monsieur le conseiller municipal X, Madame la conseillère municipale X; *see* **privy, town**.
counsel ['kaʊnsəl] 1 n a (*NonC*) consultation *f*, conseil *m*, délibération *f*. **to take ~ with sb** prendre conseil de qn, consulter qn; **to keep one's own ~** garder ses intentions (*or* ses projets *or* ses opinions) pour soi. b (pl inv) (*Jur*) avocat(e) *m(f)*. (*Brit*) **~ for the defence** (avocat de la) défense *f*; (*Brit*) **~ for the prosecution** avocat du ministère public; **King's** *or* **Queen's C~** avocat de la couronne (*qui peut néanmoins plaider pour des particuliers*); *see* **defending, prosecute**. 2 vt (*frm, liter*) recommander, conseiller (*sb to do* à qn de faire). **to ~ caution** recommander *or* conseiller la prudence.
counseling (*US*), **counselling** ['kaʊnsəlɪŋ] 1 n (*gen: advice*) conseils *mpl*; (*Psych, Soc*) assistance *f* socio-psychologique; (*Brit Scol*) aide *f* psychopédagogique.
2 comp ▸ **counseling service** (*US Univ*) service *m* d'orientation et d'assistance universitaire.
counsellor, (*US also*) **counselor** ['kaʊnsləʳ] n a (*gen*) conseiller *m*, -ère *f*; (*Psych, Soc*) conseiller *m*, -ère *f* socio-psychologique; (*US Educ*) conseiller d'orientation; *see* **student**. b (*Ir, US: also* **~-at-law**) avocat *m*.
count[1] [kaʊnt] 1 n a compte *m*, dénombrement *m*, calcul *m*; *[votes at election]* dépouillement *m*. **to make a ~** faire un compte; **at the last ~** (*gen*) la dernière fois qu'on a compté; (*Admin*) au dernier recensement; (*Boxing*) **to be out for the ~, to take the ~** être (mis) knock-out, aller au tapis pour le compte; **to be out for the ~*** être K.-O.*; **to keep (a) ~ of** tenir le compte de; (*fig*) **to take no ~ of** ne pas tenir compte de; **every time you interrupt you make me lose ~** chaque fois que tu m'interromps je perds le fil; **I've lost ~** je ne sais plus où j'en suis; **I've lost ~ of the number of times I've told you** je ne sais plus combien de fois je te l'ai dit; **he lost ~ of the tickets he had sold** il ne savait plus combien de billets il avait vendus.
b (*Jur*) chef *m* d'accusation. **guilty on 3 ~s** coupable à 3 chefs.
2 comp ▸ **countdown** compte *m* à rebours ▸ **count noun** nom *m* comptable.
3 vt a (*add up*) compter; *inhabitants, injured, causes* dénombrer; *one's change etc* compter, vérifier. **to ~ the eggs in the basket** compter les œufs dans le panier; (*Admin, Pol*) **to ~ the votes** dépouiller le scrutin; (*Prov*) **don't ~ your chickens (before they're hatched)** il ne faut pas vendre la peau de l'ours (avant de l'avoir tué) (*Prov*); (*US fig*) **to ~ noses*** compter les présents; (*fig*) **to ~ sheep** compter les moutons; **to ~ the cost** (*lit*) compter *or* calculer la dépense; (*fig*) faire le bilan; (*lit, fig*) **without ~ing the cost** sans compter; **(you must) ~ your blessings** estimez-vous heureux; *see* **stand**.
b (*include*) compter. **10 people not ~ing the children** 10 personnes sans compter les enfants; **three more ~ing him** trois de plus lui inclus *or* compris; **to ~ sb among one's friends** compter qn parmi ses amis; **do not ~ his youth against him** ne lui faites pas grief de sa jeunesse; **will you ~ it against me if I refuse?** m'en tiendrez-vous rigueur *or* m'en voudrez-vous si je refuse?
c (*consider*) tenir, estimer. **to ~ sb as dead** tenir qn pour mort; **we must ~ ourselves fortunate** nous devons nous estimer heureux; **I ~ it an honour to (be able to) help you** je m'estime honoré de pouvoir vous aider.
4 vi a compter. **can he ~?** est-ce qu'il sait compter?; **~ing from tonight** à compter de ce soir; **~ing from the left** à partir de la gauche.
b (*be considered*) compter. **you ~ among my best friends** vous comptez parmi *or* au nombre de mes meilleurs amis; **two children ~ as one adult** deux enfants comptent pour un adulte; **that doesn't ~** cela ne compte pas.
c (*have importance*) compter. **every minute ~s** chaque minute compte, il n'y a pas une minute à perdre; **his lack of experience ~s against him** son inexpérience est un désavantage *or* un handicap; **that ~s for nothing** cela ne compte pas, cela compte pour du beurre*; **he ~s for a lot in that firm** il joue un rôle important dans cette compagnie; **a university degree ~s for very little nowadays** de nos jours un diplôme universitaire n'a pas beaucoup de valeur *or* ne pèse pas lourd*.
▸**count down** 1 vi faire le compte à rebours. 2 **countdown** n *see* **count**[1] **2**.
▸**count in*** vt sep compter. **to count sb in on a plan** inclure qn dans un projet; **you can count me in!** je suis de la partie!
▸**count out** vt sep a (*Boxing*) **to be counted out** être mis knock-out, être envoyé *or* aller au tapis pour le compte. b *money* compter pièce par pièce; *small objects* compter, dénombrer. c **you can count me out of* this business** ne comptez pas sur moi dans cette affaire. d (*Parl etc*) **to count out a meeting** ajourner une séance (*le quorum n'étant pas atteint*); (*Brit*) **to count out the House** ajourner la séance (*du Parlement*).
▸**count towards** vt fus: **these contributions/translations will count towards your pension/final mark** ces cotisations/traductions compteront pour *or* seront prises en considération pour votre retraite/note finale.
▸**count up** vt sep faire le compte de, compter, additionner.
▸**count (up)on** vt fus compter (sur). **I'm counting (up)on you** je compte sur vous; **to count (up)on doing** compter faire.
count[2] [kaʊnt] n (*nobleman*) comte *m*.
countability [ˌkaʊntə'bɪlɪtɪ] n (*Ling: fact of being countable*) fait *m* d'être comptable. **the problem of ~** le problème de savoir si un (*or* le *etc*) substantif est comptable ou non.
countable ['kaʊntəbl] adj comptable, dénombrable, nombrable. (*Gram*) **~ noun** nom *m* comptable.
countenance ['kaʊntɪnəns] 1 n a (*liter: face*) (expression *f* du) visage *m*, figure *f*; (*expression*) mine *f*. **out of ~** décontenancé; **to keep one's ~** ne pas se laisser décontenancer. b (*frm: approval*) **to give ~ to** *person* encourager; *plan* favoriser; *rumour, piece of news* accréditer. 2 vt approuver, admettre (*sth* qch; *sb's doing* que qn fasse).
counter[1] ['kaʊntəʳ] 1 n a (*in shop, canteen*) comptoir *m*; (*position: in bank, post office etc*) guichet *m*; (*in pub*) comptoir *m*, zinc* *m*. **the girl behind the ~** (*in shop*) la vendeuse; (*in pub*) la serveuse; (*fig*) **to buy/sell under the ~** acheter/vendre clandestinement; **it was all very under the ~*** tout ceci se faisait sous le manteau *or* très en-dessous *or* très en sous-main. b (*disc*) jeton *m*, fiche *f*. c (*Tech*) compteur *m*; *see* **Geiger counter** *etc*. 2 comp ▸ **counter hand** (*in shop*) vendeur *m*, -euse *f*; (*in snack bar*) serveur *m*, -euse *f* ▸ **counterman** (*US*) serveur *m* ▸ **counter staff** *[bank]* caissiers *mpl*, -ières *fpl*; *[shop]* vendeurs *mpl*, -euses *fpl*.
counter[2] ['kaʊntəʳ] 1 adv: **~ to** à l'encontre de, à l'opposé de, contrairement à; **to go or run ~ to** aller à l'encontre de. 2 vt *decision, order* aller à l'encontre de, s'opposer à; *plans* contrecarrer, contrarier; *blow* parer. 3 vi (*fig*) contre-attaquer, riposter; (*Boxing, Fencing etc*) (parer un coup et) riposter. **he ~ed with a right** il a riposté par un droit.
counter... ['kaʊntəʳ] pref contre... .
counteract [ˌkaʊntər'ækt] vt neutraliser, contrebalancer.
counterattack ['kaʊntərəˌtæk] (*Mil, fig*) 1 n contre-attaque *f*. 2 vti contre-attaquer.
counterattraction ['kaʊntərəˌtrækʃən] n attraction rivale, spectacle rival.
counterbalance ['kaʊntəˌbæləns] 1 n contrepoids *m*. 2 vt contrebalancer, faire contrepoids à.
counterbid ['kaʊntəˌbɪd] n surenchère *f*, suroffre *f*.
counterblast ['kaʊntəblɑ:st] n réfutation *f or* démenti *m* énergique.
countercharge ['kaʊntətʃɑ:dʒ] n (*Jur*) contre-accusation *f*.
countercheck ['kaʊntətʃek] 1 n deuxième contrôle *m or* vérification *f*. 2 vt revérifier.
counterclaim ['kaʊntəkleɪm] n (*Jur*) demande reconventionnelle. **to bring a ~** introduire une demande reconventionnelle.
counterclockwise [ˌkaʊntə'klɒkˌwaɪz] adv, adj en sens inverse des aiguilles d'une montre.
counterespionage [ˌkaʊntər'espɪəˌnɑ:ʒ] n contre-espionnage *m*.
counterexample ['kaʊntərɪgˌzɑ:mpəl] n contre-exemple *m*.
counterfeit ['kaʊntəfi:t] 1 adj faux (*f* fausse). **~ coin/money** fausse pièce/monnaie. 2 n faux *m*, contrefaçon *f*. 3 vt *banknote, signature* contrefaire. **to ~ money** fabriquer de la fausse monnaie.
counterfoil ['kaʊntəfɔɪl] n (*Brit*) *[cheque etc]* talon *m*, souche *f*.
counter-gambit ['kaʊntəgæmbɪt] n contre-gambit *m*.
counterinsurgency [ˌkaʊntərɪn'sɜ:dʒənsɪ] n contre-insurrection *f*.
counterinsurgent [ˌkaʊntərɪn'sɜ:dʒənt] n contre-insurgé(e) *m(f)*.
counterintelligence [ˌkaʊntərɪn'telɪdʒəns] n contre-espionnage *m*.
counterintuitive [ˌkaʊntərɪn'tju:ɪtɪv] adj contraire à l'intuition.
counterirritant [ˌkaʊntər'ɪrɪtənt] n (*Med*) révulsif *m*.
countermand ['kaʊntəmɑ:nd] vt *order* annuler. **unless ~ed** sauf contrordre.
countermeasure ['kaʊntəmeʒəʳ] n mesure défensive, contre-mesure *f*.
countermove ['kaʊntəmu:v] n (*Mil*) mouvement *m* en contre-attaque, retour offensif.

counteroffensive ['kaʊntərəfensɪv] **n** (*Mil*) contre-offensive *f*.
counteroffer ['kaʊntər,ɒfəʳ] **n** contre-offre *f*, contreproposition *f*.
counter-order ['kaʊntə,rɔːdəʳ] **n** contrordre *m*.
counterpane ['kaʊntəpeɪn] **n** dessus-de-lit *m inv*, couvre-lit *m*; (*quilted*) courtepointe *f*.
counterpart ['kaʊntəpɑːt] **n** *[document etc]* (*duplicate*) double *m*, contrepartie *f*; (*equivalent*) équivalent *m*; *[person]* homologue *mf*.
counterplea ['kaʊntəpliː] **n** réplique *f*.
counterpoint ['kaʊntəpɔɪnt] **n** (*Mus*) contrepoint *m*.
counterpoise ['kaʊntəpɔɪz] **1 n** (*weight, force*) contrepoids *m*; (*equilibrium*) équilibre *m*. **in ~** en équilibre. **2 vt** contrebalancer, faire contrepoids à.
counterproductive [,kaʊntəprə'dʌktɪv] **adj** (*Comm, Ind*) qui entrave la productivité. (*fig*) **that is ~** ça va à l'encontre du but recherché.
counter-proposal [,kaʊntəprə'pəʊzəl] **n** contre-proposition *f*.
Counter-Reformation [,kaʊntə,refə'meɪʃən] **n** (*Hist*) Contre-Réforme *f*.
counter-revolution [,kaʊntə,revə'luːʃən] **n** contre-révolution *f*.
counter-revolutionary [,kaʊntə,revə'luːʃənrɪ] **adj, n** contre-révolutionnaire (*mf*).
counter-shot ['kaʊntəʃɒt] **n** (*Cine*) contrechamp *m*.
countersign ['kaʊntəsaɪn] **1 vt** contresigner. **2 n** mot *m* de passe *or* d'ordre.
countersink ['kaʊntəsɪŋk] **vt** *hole* fraiser; *screw* noyer.
counter-stroke ['kaʊntəstrəʊk] **n** (*lit, fig*) retour offensif.
countersunk ['kaʊntəsʌŋk] **adj** fraisé.
countertenor [,kaʊntə'tenəʳ] **n** (*Mus*) (*singer*) haute-contre *m*; (*voice*) haute-contre *f*.
counter-turn ['kaʊntətɜːn] **n** (*Ski*) contre-virage *m*.
countervailing ['kaʊntəveɪlɪŋ] **adj** (*Fin*) **~ duties** droits *mpl* compensatoires.
counterweight ['kaʊntəweɪt] **n** contrepoids *m*.
countess ['kaʊntɪs] **n** comtesse *f*.
counting ['kaʊntɪŋ] **1 n** (*school subject*) calcul *m*. **2 comp** ▸ **counting house** (*Brit* †) salle *f or* immeuble *m* des comptables.
countless ['kaʊntlɪs] **adj** innombrable, sans nombre. **on ~ occasions** je ne sais combien de fois.
countrified ['kʌntrɪfaɪd] **adj** rustique, campagnard.
country ['kʌntrɪ] **1 n a** pays *m*. **the different countries of the world** les divers pays du monde; **the ~ wants peace** le pays désire la paix; (*Brit Pol*) **to go to the ~** appeler le pays aux urnes.
b (*native land*) patrie *f*. **to die for one's ~** mourir pour la patrie; *see* **old**.
c (*NonC: as opposed to town*) campagne *f*. **in the ~** à la campagne; **the ~ round the town** les environs *mpl* de la ville; **the surrounding ~** la campagne environnante; **to live off the ~** (*gen*) vivre des produits de la terre; (*Mil*) vivre sur le pays.
d (*NonC: region*) pays *m*, région *f*. **there is some lovely ~ to the north** il y a de beaux paysages dans le nord; **mountainous ~** région montagneuse; **this is good fishing ~** c'est une bonne région pour la pêche; **this is unknown ~ to me** (*lit*) je ne connais pas la région; (*fig*) je suis en terrain inconnu; *see* **open**.
2 comp *life-style* campagnard, de (la) campagne ▸ **country-and-western** (*US Mus*) musique *f* country (and western) ▸ **country born** né à la campagne ▸ **country bred** élevé à la campagne ▸ **country bumpkin** (*pej*) péquenaud(e)* *m(f)* (*pej*), cul-terreux* *m* (*pej*) ▸ **country club** club *m* de loisirs (*à la campagne*) ▸ **country cottage** petite maison (à la campagne); *[weekenders]* maison de campagne ▸ **country cousin** (*fig*) cousin *m* de province ▸ **country dance**, (*NonC*) **country dancing** danse *f* folklorique; **to go country dancing** danser (des danses folkloriques) ▸ **country dweller** campagnard(e) *m(f)* ▸ **country folk** gens *mpl* de la campagne, campagnards *mpl*, ruraux *mpl* ▸ **country gentleman** gentilhomme campagnard ▸ **country house** manoir *m*, (petit) château *m* ▸ **country life** vie *f* de la *or* à la campagne, vie campagnarde ▸ **countryman** (*also* **fellow countryman**) compatriote *m*, concitoyen *m*; (*opposed to town dweller*) habitant *m* de la campagne, campagnard *m* ▸ **country music** la musique country ▸ **country park** (*Brit*) réserve *f* naturelle ▸ **country people** campagnards *mpl*, gens *mpl* de la campagne ▸ **country road** petite route (de campagne) ▸ **country seat** château *m* ▸ **the countryside** la campagne ▸ **country-wide** qui englobe *or* touche tout le pays ▸ **countrywoman** (*also* **fellow countrywoman**) compatriote *f*, concitoyenne *f*; (*opposed to town dweller*) habitante *f* de la campagne, campagnarde *f*.
county ['kaʊntɪ] **1 n a** comté *m* (*division administrative*), ≃ département *m*; *see* **home**.
b (*people*) habitants *mpl* d'un comté. (*Brit: nobility etc*) **the ~** l'aristocratie terrienne (*du comté*).
2 adj (*Brit*) *voice, accent* aristocratique. **he's very ~** il est *or* fait très hobereau; **she's very ~** elle est *or* fait très aristocratie terrienne.
3 comp ▸ **county agent** (*US*) ingénieur-agronome *m* ▸ **county clerk** (*US Admin*) ≃ sous-préfet *m* ▸ **county council** (*Brit* †) ≃ conseil *m* régional ▸ **county court** (*Brit*) tribunal civil ▸ **county cricket** (*Brit*) *le cricket disputé entre les comtés* ▸ **county family** (*Brit*) vieille famille ▸ **county jail** (*US*) *or* **prison** centrale *f* ▸ **county police** (*US*) police régionale, ≃ gendarmerie *f* ▸ **county seat** (*US*), **county town** (*esp Brit*) chef-lieu *m*.
coup [kuː] **n** (beau) coup *m* (*fig*); (*Pol*) coup d'État.
coupé ['kuːpeɪ] **n** (*Aut*) coupé *m*.
couple ['kʌpl] **1 n** couple *m*. **to hunt in ~s** aller par deux; **the young (married) ~** les jeunes mariés *or* époux, le jeune ménage, le jeune couple; **a ~ of** deux; **I've seen him a ~ of times** je l'ai vu deux ou trois fois; **I did it in a ~ of hours** je l'ai fait en deux heures environ; **we had a ~* in the bar** nous avons pris un verre ou deux au bar; **when he's had a ~* he begins to sing** quand il a un verre dans le nez* il se met à chanter; *see* **first**. **2 vt a** (*also* **~ up**) *railway carriages* atteler, (ac)coupler; *ideas, names* associer, accoupler. **b ~d with (prep)** ajouté à; **~d with the fact that** venant en plus du fait que. **3 vi** (*mate*) s'accoupler.
coupledom ['kʌpldəm] **n** la vie de couple.
coupler ['kʌpləʳ] **n** (*Comput*) coupleur *m*; (*US Rail*) attelage *m*. (*Comput*) **acoustic ~** coupleur acoustique.
couplet ['kʌplɪt] **n** distique *m*.
coupling ['kʌplɪŋ] **n a** (*NonC*) accouplement *m*, association *f*. **b** (*device*) (*Rail*) attelage *m*; (*Elec*) couplage *m*.
coupon ['kuːpɒn] **n** *[newspaper advertisements etc]* coupon *m* (*détachable*); *[cigarette packets etc]* bon *m*, prime *f*, vignette *f*; (*Comm: offering price reductions*) bon de réduction; (*rationing*) ticket *m*, bon; (*Fin*) coupon, bon; *see* **football, international**.
courage ['kʌrɪdʒ] **n** courage *m*. **I haven't the ~ to refuse** je n'ai pas le courage de refuser, je n'ose pas refuser; **to take/lose ~** prendre/perdre courage; **to take ~ from sth** être encouragé par qch; **to have the ~ of one's convictions** avoir le courage de ses opinions; **to take one's ~ in both hands** prendre son courage à deux mains; *see* **Dutch, pluck up**.
courageous [kə'reɪdʒəs] **adj** courageux.
courageously [kə'reɪdʒəslɪ] **adv** courageusement.
courgette [kʊə'ʒet] **n** (*Brit*) courgette *f*.
courier ['kʊrɪəʳ] **n** (*messenger*) courrier *m*, messager *m*; (*tourist guide*) guide *m*, cicérone *m*.
course [kɔːs] **1 n a of ~** bien sûr, naturellement; **did he do it? — of ~ !/of ~ not!** est-ce qu'il l'a fait? — bien entendu! *or* naturellement!/bien sûr que non!; **may I take it? — of ~!/of ~ not!** est-ce que je peux le prendre? — bien sûr! *or* mais oui!/certainement pas!; **of ~ I won't do it!** je ne vais évidemment pas faire ça!; **you'll come on Saturday of ~** il va sans dire que *or* bien entendu vous venez samedi.
b (*duration, process*) *[life, events, time, disease]* cours *m*. **in the ordinary ~ of things** *or* **events** normalement, en temps normal *or* ordinaire; **in the ~ of conversation** au cours *or* dans le courant de la conversation; **a house in (the) ~ of construction** une maison en cours de construction; **it is in (the) ~ of being investigated** c'est en cours d'investigation; **in the ~ of centuries** au cours des siècles; **in the ~ of the next few months** pendant les *or* au cours des prochains mois; **in the ~ of time** finalement, un beau jour; **in the ~ of the week** dans le courant de la semaine; *see* **due, matter**.
c (*direction, way, route*) *[river]* cours *m*, lit *m*; *[ship]* route *f*; *[planet]* cours. **to keep** *or* **hold one's ~** poursuivre sa route; (*Naut*) **to hold (one's) ~** suivre son chemin; *[rocket etc]* **on ~** sur la bonne trajectoire; **on ~ for** (*lit*) en route pour; (*fig*) sur la voie de; (*Naut*) **to set ~ for** mettre le cap sur; (*Naut*) **to change ~** changer de cap; (*Naut, fig*) **to go off ~** faire fausse route; **to take a certain ~ of action** adopter une certaine ligne de conduite; **we have no other ~ but to ...** nous n'avons d'autre moyen *or* ressource que de ..., aucune autre voie ne s'offre à nous que de ...; **there are several ~s open to us** plusieurs partis s'offrent à nous; **what ~ do you suggest?** quel parti (nous) conseillez-vous de prendre?; **let him take his own ~** laissez-le agir à sa guise *or* faire comme il veut; **the best ~ would be to leave at once** la meilleure chose *or* le mieux à faire serait de partir immédiatement; **to let sth take its ~** laisser qch suivre son cours, laisser qch prendre son cours naturel; **the affair/the illness has run its ~** l'affaire/la maladie a suivi son cours; *see* **middle**.
d (*Scol, Univ*) cours *m*. **to go to a French ~** suivre un cours *or* des cours de français; **he gave a ~ of lectures on Proust** il a donné une série de conférences sur Proust; **I have bought part two of the German ~** j'ai acheté la deuxième partie de la méthode *or* du cours d'allemand; **~ of study** (*Scol*) programme *m* scolaire; (*Univ*) cursus *m* universitaire; (*Med*) **~ of treatment** traitement *m*; (*Univ*) **~ work** travail *m* (*en rapport avec le cours*); *see* **correspondence**.
e (*Sport*) (*distance covered: Racing, for military training etc*) parcours *m*; (*ground on which sport takes place: Golf etc*) terrain *m*; *see* **golf, race¹, stay¹** *etc*.
f (*Culin*) plat *m*. **first ~** entrée *f*; **three-/four-** *etc* **~ meal** repas *m* de *or* à trois/quatre *etc* plats; *see* **main**.
g (*Constr*) assise *f* (*de briques etc*); *see* **damp**.
h (*Naut*) **~s** basses voiles.
2 vi a *[water etc]* couler à flots. **tears ~d down her cheeks** les larmes ruisselaient sur ses joues; **it sent the blood coursing through his veins** cela lui fouetta le sang.
b (*Sport*) chasser (le lièvre).

3 vt (*Sport*) *hare* courir, chasser.

courser ['kɔːsəʳ] n (*person*) chasseur *m* (*gén de lièvres*); (*dog*) chien courant; (*liter: horse*) coursier *m* (*liter*).

coursing ['kɔːsɪŋ] n (*Sport*) chasse *f* au lièvre.

court [kɔːt] 1 n a (*Jur*) cour *f*, tribunal *m*. (*Brit*) ~ **of appeal,** (*US*) ~ **of appeals** cour d'appel; (*US*) **C~ of Claims** *tribunal fédéral chargé de régler les réclamations contre l'État;* ~ **of competent jurisdiction** tribunal compétent; ~ **of inquiry** commission *f* d'enquête; (*US*) **C~ of International Trade** *tribunal de commerce international;* ~ **of justice** palais *m* de justice; (*US*) ~ **of last resort** tribunal jugeant en dernier ressort; (*Scot*) **C~ of Session** cour de cassation; **to settle a case out of** ~ arranger une affaire à l'amiable; **to rule sth out of** ~ déclarer qch inadmissible; **to take sb to** ~ **over** *or* **about sth** poursuivre *or* actionner qn en justice à propos de qch; **he was brought before the ~s several times** il est passé plusieurs fois en jugement; **to clear the** ~ faire évacuer la salle; *see* **high, law.**
b *[monarch]* cour *f* (royale). **the C~ of St James** la cour de Saint-James; **to be at** ~ (*for short time*) être à la cour; (*for long time*) faire partie de la cour; (*fig*) **to hold** ~être entouré de sa cour.
c **to pay** ~ **to a woman** faire sa *or* la cour à une femme.
d (*Tennis*) court *m*; (*Basketball*) terrain *m*. (*Tennis*) **they've been on** ~ **for 2 hours** cela fait 2 heures qu'ils jouent.
e (*also* **~yard**) cour *f* (de maison, de château); (*passage between houses*) ruelle *f*, venelle *f*.
2 comp ► **court card** (*esp Brit*) figure *f* (*de jeu de cartes*) ► **court circular** bulletin quotidien de la cour ► **courthouse** (*Jur*) palais *m* de justice, tribunal *m* ► **courting couple** couple *m* d'amoureux ► **court order** (*Jur*) décision *f* judiciaire ► **court record** (*US Jur*) compte rendu *m* d'audience ► **court room** (*Jur*) salle *f* de tribunal ► **court shoe** (*Brit*) escarpin *m* ► **courtyard** cour *f* (*de maison, de château*).
3 vt *woman* faire la *or* sa cour à, courtiser; *sb's favour* solliciter, rechercher; *danger, defeat* aller au-devant de, s'exposer à.
4 vi: **they are ~ing†** ils sortent ensemble; **are you ~ing?†** tu as un petit copain* (*or* une petite amie*)?

Courtelle [kɔː'tel] n ® Courtelle *m* ®.

courteous ['kɜːtɪəs] adj courtois, poli (*towards* envers).

courteously ['kɜːtɪəslɪ] adv d'une manière courtoise, courtoisement, poliment.

courtesan [ˌkɔːtɪ'zæn] n courtisane *f* (*liter*).

courtesy ['kɜːtɪsɪ] 1 n courtoisie *f*, politesse *f*. **you might have had the** ~ **to explain yourself** vous auriez pu avoir la politesse de vous expliquer; **will you do me the** ~ **of reading it?** auriez-vous l'obligeance de le lire?; **exchange of courtesies** échange *m* de politesses; **by** ~ **of** avec la permission de. 2 comp ► **courtesy bus** navette *f* gratuite ► **courtesy call** visite *f* de politesse ► **courtesy car** voiture gratuite ► **courtesy card** (*US*) carte *f* de priorité (*utilisable dans les hôtels, banques etc*) ► **courtesy coach** (*Brit*) = **courtesy bus** ► **courtesy light** (*Aut*) plafonnier *m* ► **courtesy title** titre *m* de courtoisie ► **courtesy visit** = **courtesy call.**

courtier ['kɔːtɪəʳ] n courtisan *m*, dame *f* de la cour.

courtly ['kɔːtlɪ] adj élégant, raffiné. (*Hist, Literat*) ~ **love** amour courtois.

court martial ['kɔːt'mɑːʃəl] 1 n, pl **courts martial** *or* **court martials** (*Mil*) cour *f* martiale. **to be tried by** ~ passer en cour *f* martiale. 2 vt **court-martial** traduire *or* faire passer en conseil de guerre.

courtship ['kɔːtʃɪp] n: **his** ~ **of her** la cour qu'il lui fait (*or* faisait *etc*); **during their** ~ au temps où ils sortaient ensemble; *[birds, animals]* ~ **display** parade *f* de séduction.

cousin ['kʌzn] n cousin(e) *m(f)*; *see* **country, first** *etc*.

couth* [kuːθ] 1 adj raffiné. 2 n bonnes manières.

couturier [kuː'tʊərɪeɪ] n grand couturier *m*.

cove¹ [kəʊv] n (*Geog*) crique *f*, anse *f*; (*cavern*) caverne naturelle; (*US*) vallon encaissé.

cove²‡ [kəʊv] n (*Brit: fellow*) mec‡ *m*.

covenant ['kʌvɪnənt] 1 n (*gen*) convention *f*, engagement formel; (*Brit Fin*) engagement contractuel, (*Jewish Hist*) alliance *f*. (*Scot Hist*) **the C~** le Covenant (*de 1638*); *see* **deed.** 2 vt s'engager (*to do* à faire), convenir (*to do* de faire). (*Fin*) **to** ~ **(to pay) £100 per annum to a charity** s'engager par obligation contractuelle à verser 100 livres par an à une œuvre. 3 vi convenir (*with sb for sth* de qch avec qn).

covenanter ['kʌvɪnəntəʳ] n (*Scot Hist*) covenantaire *mf* (*adhérent au Covenant de 1638*).

Coventry ['kɒvəntrɪ] n Coventry. (*Brit fig*) **to send sb to** ~ mettre qn en quarantaine, boycotter qn.

cover ['kʌvəʳ] 1 n a *[table]* nappe *f*; *[umbrella]* (*fabric*) étoffe *f*; (*case*) fourreau *m*; (*for folding type*) étui *m*; (*over furniture, typewriter*) housse *f*; (*over merchandise, vehicle etc*) bâche *f*; (*bed~*) dessus-de-lit *m inv*; *[lens]* bouchon *m*; *[book]* couverture *f*; (*envelope*) enveloppe *f*; *[parcel]* emballage *m*. (*bedclothes*) **the ~s** les couvertures *fpl*; **to read a book from** ~ **to** ~ lire un livre de la première à la dernière page; (*Comm*) **under separate** ~ sous pli séparé; *see* **first, loose, plain.**
b (*shelter*) abri *m*; (*Hunting: for game*) fourré *m*, couvert *m*, abri; (*Mil etc: covering fire*) feu *m* de couverture *or* de protection. (*Mil, gen*) **there was no** ~ **for miles around** il n'y avait pas d'abri à des kilomètres à la ronde; **he was looking for some** ~ il cherchait un abri; **the trees gave him** ~ (*hid*) les arbres le cachaient; (*sheltered*) les arbres l'abritaient; (*to soldier etc*) **give me** ~! couvrez-moi!; **to take** ~ (*hide*) se cacher; (*Mil*) s'embusquer; (*shelter*) s'abriter, se mettre à l'abri; **to take** ~ **from the rain/the bombing** se mettre à l'abri *or* s'abriter de la pluie/des bombes; (*Mil*) **to take** ~ **from enemy fire** se mettre à l'abri du feu ennemi; **under** ~ à l'abri, à couvert; **to get under** ~ se mettre à l'abri *or* à couvert; **under** ~ **of darkness** à la faveur de la nuit; **under** ~ **of friendship** sous le masque de l'amitié; *see* **break.**
c (*Fin*) couverture *f*, provision *f*. (*Fin*) **to operate without** ~ opérer à découvert.
d (*Brit Insurance: gen*) couverture *f*, garantie *f* (d'assurances) (*against* contre). ~ **for a building against fire** *etc* couverture *or* garantie d'un immeuble contre l'incendie *etc*; **full** ~ garantie totale *or* tous risques; **fire** ~ assurance-incendie *f*; **they've got no (insurance)** ~ **for** *or* **on this** ils ne sont pas assurés pour *or* contre cela; **we must extend our (insurance)** ~ nous devons augmenter le montant de notre garantie (d'assurances); **the (insurance)** ~ **ends on 5th July** le contrat d'assurances *or* la police d'assurances expire le 5 juillet.
e (*in espionage etc*) fausse identité. **what's your** ~**?** quelle est votre identité d'emprunt?
f (*at table*) couvert *m*. **~s laid for 6**une table de 6 couverts.
g = ~ **version;** *see* **2.**
2 comp ► **coveralls** (*Dress*) bleu(s) *m(pl)* de travail, combinaison *f* (*d'ouvrier etc*) ► **cover charge** *[restaurant]* couvert *m* ► **covered wagon** chariot couvert *or* bâché ► **covergirl** cover-girl *f* ► **cover note** (*Brit Insurance*) ≃ récépissé *m* (d'assurance) ► **cover price** (*Publishing*) prix *m* en couverture ► **cover story** (*Press*) article principal (*illustré en couverture*); (*in espionage etc*) couverture *f*; **our cover story this week** en couverture cette semaine ► **cover-up** tentatives faites pour étouffer l'affaire ► **cover version** (*Mus*) reprise *f*.
3 vt a (*gen*) *object, person* couvrir (*with* de); *book, chair* recouvrir, couvrir (*with* de). **snow ~s the ground** la neige recouvre le sol; **ground ~ed with leaves** sol couvert de feuilles; **he ~ed the paper with writing** il a couvert la page d'écriture; **the car ~ed us in mud** la voiture nous a couverts de boue; **to** ~ **one's eyes** (*when crying*) se couvrir les yeux; (*against sun etc*) se protéger les yeux; **to** ~ **one's face with one's hands** se couvrir le visage des mains; **~ed with confusion/ridicule** couvert de confusion/de ridicule; **to** ~ **o.s. with glory** se couvrir de gloire.
b (*hide*) *feelings, facts* dissimuler, cacher; *noise* couvrir.
c (*protect*) *person* couvrir, protéger. **the soldiers ~ed our retreat** les soldats ont couvert notre retraite; (*fig*) **he only said that to** ~ **himself** il n'a dit cela que pour se couvrir.
d (*Insurance*) couvrir. **it ~s the house against fire** *etc* l'immeuble est couvert contre l'incendie *etc;* **it doesn't** ~ **you for** *or* **against flood damage** vous n'êtes pas couvert contre les dégâts des eaux; **it ~s (for) fire only** cela ne couvre que l'incendie.
e (*point gun at*) *person* braquer un revolver sur. **to keep sb ~ed** tenir qn sous la menace du revolver; **I've got you ~ed!** ne bougez pas ou je tire!
f (*Sport*) *opponent* marquer.
g *distance* parcourir, couvrir. **we ~ed 8 km in 2 hours** nous avons parcouru *or* couvert 8 km en 2 heures; **to** ~ **a lot of ground** (*travelling*) faire beaucoup de chemin; (*deal with many subjects*) traiter un large éventail de questions; (*do large amount of work*) faire du bon travail.
h (*be sufficient for*) couvrir; (*take in, include*) englober, traiter, comprendre. **his work ~s many different fields** son travail englobe *or* embrasse plusieurs domaines différents; **goods ~ed by this invoice** les marchandises faisant l'objet de cette facture; **the book ~s the subject thoroughly** le livre traite le sujet à fond; **the article ~s the 18th century** l'article traite tout le 18e siècle; **his speech ~ed most of the points raised** dans son discours il a traité la plupart des points en question; **such factories will not be ~ed by this report** ce rapport ne traitera pas de ces usines; **in order to** ~ **all possibilities** pour parer à toute éventualité; **in order to** ~ **the monthly payments** pour faire face aux mensualités; **to** ~ **one's costs** *or* **expenses** rentrer dans ses frais; **£5 will** ~ **everything** 5 livres payeront tout *or* suffiront à couvrir toutes les dépenses; **to** ~ **a deficit/a loss** combler un déficit/une perte.
i (*Press etc*) *news, story, scandal* assurer la couverture de; *lawsuit* faire le compte rendu de. **he was sent to** ~ **the riots** on l'a envoyé assurer le reportage des émeutes.
j *[animal]* couvrir.
4 vi a (*US*) = **cover up 1b.**
b *see* **3d** *above*.
c (*stand in*): **to** ~ **for sb** remplacer qn.

►**cover in** vt sep *trench, grave* remplir.

►**cover over** vt sep recouvrir.

►**cover up** 1 vi a se couvrir. **it's cold, cover up warmly** il fait froid, couvre-toi chaudement. b **to cover up for sb** couvrir qn, protéger qn.
2 vt sep a *child, object* recouvrir, envelopper (*with* de). b (*hide*) *truth, facts* dissimuler, cacher, étouffer. **to cover up one's tracks** (*lit*) couvrir sa marche; (*fig*) couvrir sa marche, brouiller les pistes. 3

cover-up n *see* **cover 2.**
coverage ['kʌvərɪdʒ] n a (*Press, Rad, TV*) reportage *m.* **to give full ~ to an event** assurer la couverture complète d'un événement, traiter à fond un événement; **the match got nationwide ~** (*Rad*) le reportage du match a été diffusé sur l'ensemble du pays; (*TV*) le match a été retransmis *or* diffusé sur l'ensemble du pays; (*Press*) **it got full-page ~ in the main dailies** les principaux quotidiens y ont consacré une page entière. b (*Insurance*) couverture *f.*
covering ['kʌvərɪŋ] 1 n (*wrapping etc*) couverture *f*, enveloppe *f*; (*of snow, dust etc*) couche *f.* 2 adj: **~ letter** lettre explicative; (*Mil*) **~ fire** feu *m* de protection *or* de couverture.
coverlet ['kʌvəlɪt] n dessus-de-lit *m inv*, couvre-lit *m*; (*quilted*) courtepointe *f.*
covert ['kʌvət] 1 adj *threat* voilé, caché; *attack* indirect; *glance* furtif, dérobé. 2 n (*Hunting*) fourré *m*, couvert *m*; (*animal's hiding place*) gîte *m*, terrier *m.*
covet ['kʌvɪt] vt convoiter.
covetous ['kʌvɪtəs] adj *person, attitude, nature* avide; *look* de convoitise. **to cast ~ eyes on sth** regarder qch avec convoitise.
covetously ['kʌvɪtəslɪ] adv avec convoitise, avidement.
covetousness ['kʌvɪtəsnɪs] n convoitise *f*, avidité *f.*
covey ['kʌvɪ] n compagnie *f* (*de perdrix*).
cow¹ [kaʊ] 1 n a vache *f*; (*female of elephant etc*) femelle *f.* (*fig*) **till the ~s come home*** jusqu'à la Trinité (*fig*), jusqu'au jour où les poules auront des dents*; (*fig*) **to wait till the ~s come home*** attendre la semaine des quatre jeudis*.
b (⁑ *pej: woman*) rosse* *f*, vache* *f*, chameau* *m.* **silly** *or* **stupid ~!** pauvre conne!⁑
2 comp ▶ **cowbell** sonnaille *f*, clochette *f* (à bestiaux) ▶ **cow buffalo** *etc* buffle *m etc* femelle ▶ **cowcatcher** (*Rail*) chasse-pierres *m inv* ▶ **cow college*** (*US Scol*) (*provincial college*) boîte *f* dans le bled*; (*agricultural college*) école *f* d'agriculture ▶ **cowherd** vacher *m*, bouvier *m* ▶ **cowhide** n (*skin*) peau *f* de vache; (*US: whip*) fouet *m* (à lanière de cuir) ◊ vt (*US*) fouetter (avec une lanière de cuir) ▶ **cowlick** mèche *f* (sur le front) ▶ **cowman** (*Brit*) = **cowherd** ▶ **cow parsley** (*Bot*) cerfeuil *m* sauvage ▶ **cowpat** bouse *f* (de vache) ▶ **cowpea** (*US*) dolique *f* ▶ **cowpoke** (*US*) cowboy *m* ▶ **cowpox** variole *f* de la vache; **cowpox vaccine** vaccin *m* antivariolique ▶ **cowpuncher*** (*US*) = **cowboy** ▶ **cowshed** étable *f* ▶ **cowslip** (*Bot*) coucou *m*, primevère *f* ▶ **cowtown** (*US pej*) bled *m*, patelin *m.*
cow² [kaʊ] vt *person* effrayer, intimider. **a ~ed look** un air de chien battu.
coward ['kaʊəd] n lâche *mf*, poltron(ne) *m(f).*
cowardice ['kaʊədɪs] n, **cowardliness** ['kaʊədlɪnɪs] n lâcheté *f.*
cowardly ['kaʊədlɪ] adj *person* lâche, poltron; *action, words* lâche.
cowboy ['kaʊ,bɔɪ] 1 n cow-boy *m*; (* *pej*) fumiste *m.* **to play ~s and Indians** jouer aux cow-boys. 2 adj (* *pej*) pas sérieux, fumiste. 3 comp ▶ **cowboy boots** rangers *mpl* ▶ **cowboy hat** chapeau *m* de cow-boy, feutre *m* à larges bords.
cower ['kaʊəʳ] vi (*also* **~ down**) se tapir, se recroqueviller. (*fig*) **to ~ before sb** trembler devant qn.
cowl [kaʊl] n a (*hood*) capuchon *m* (*de moine*). **~ neck(line)** col *m* boule. b [*chimney*] capuchon *m.*
co-worker ['kəʊ'wɜːkəʳ] n collègue *mf*, camarade *mf* (de travail).
cowrie, cowry ['kaʊrɪ] n cauri *m.*
cox [kɒks] 1 n (*Rowing*) barreur *m.* 2 vt (*Rowing*) *boat* barrer, gouverner. **~ed four** quatre barré, quatre avec barreur. 3 vi (*Rowing*) barrer.
coxcomb† ['kɒkskəʊm] n fat *m*, poseur *m*, muscadin† *m.*
coxless ['kɒkslɪs] adj (*Rowing*) **~ four** quatre *m* sans barreur.
coxswain ['kɒksn] n (*Rowing*) barreur *m*; (*Naut*) patron *m.*
coy [kɔɪ] adj (*affectedly shy*) *person* qui joue à *or* fait l'effarouché(e), qui fait le *or* la timide; *smile* de sainte nitouche (*pej*); (*coquettish*) *woman* qui fait la coquette.
coyly ['kɔɪlɪ] adv (*see* **coy**) avec une timidité feinte; avec coquetterie.
coyness ['kɔɪnɪs] n (*see* **coy**) airs effarouchés, timidité affectée *or* feinte; coquetterie *f.*
coyote [kɔɪ'əʊtɪ] n coyote *m.* **the C~ State** le Dakota du Sud.
cozy ['kəʊzɪ], **cozily** ['kəʊzɪlɪ] (*US*) = **cosy, cosily.**
C.P. [siː'piː] n a abbr of **Cape Province.** b abbr of **Communist Party.**
c/p (abbr of **carriage paid**) *see* **carriage.**
cp abbr of **compare.**
C.P.A. [,siːpiː'eɪ] n (*US*) (abbr of **Certified Public Accountant**) *see* **certify.**
cpi [,siːpiː'aɪ] (*Comput*) (abbr of **characters per inch**) CCPP *mpl.*
C.P.I. [,siːpiː'aɪ] n (*US*) (abbr of **Consumer Price Index**) *see* **consumer.**
Cpl. (*Mil*) abbr of **corporal.**
CP/M [,siː'piː'em] (abbr of **Control Program for Microprocessors**) CP/M *m.*
C.P.O. [,siːpiː'əʊ] n (*Naut*) (abbr of **chief petty officer**) *see* **chief.**
cps [,siːpiː'es] (*Comput*) a (abbr of **characters per second**) caractères/seconde. b (abbr of **cycles per second**) cycles *mpl* par seconde.
CPU [,siːpiː'juː] n (*Comput*) (abbr of **central processing unit**) UC *f.*
CPVE [,siːpiːviː'iː] n (*Brit*) (abbr of **Certificate of Pre-vocational Education**) *brevet technique.*
cr. a abbr of **credit.** b abbr of **creditor.**

crab¹ [kræb] n a (*Zool*) crabe *m*; *see* **catch.** b (*Tech*) [*crane*] chariot *m.* c (*Med: also* **~ louse**) morpion *m.* d (*Climbing*) mousqueton *m.*
crab² [kræb] n (*also* **~apple**) pomme *f* sauvage; (*also* **~(apple) tree**) pommier *m* sauvage.
crab³ [kræb] 1 vt (*US* ⁑: *spoil*) gâcher. **to ~ sb's act** gâcher les effets de qn; **to ~ a deal** faire rater* une affaire. 2 vi (*US* ⁑: *complain*) rouspéter* (*about* à cause de).
crabbed ['kræbd] adj *person* revêche, hargneux, grincheux. **in a ~ hand, in ~ writing** en pattes de mouche.
crabby ['kræbɪ] adj *person* revêche, grincheux, grognon.
crabwise ['kræb,waɪz] adv en crabe.
crack [kræk] 1 n a (*split, slit*) fente *f*, fissure *f*; (*in glass, mirror, pottery, bone etc*) fêlure *f*; (*in wall*) fente, lézarde *f*, crevasse *f*; (*in ground*) crevasse; (*in skin*) (petite) crevasse; (*Climbing*) fissure. (*in paint, varnish*) **~s** craquelure(s) *f(pl)*; **through the ~ in the door** (*slight opening*) par l'entrebâillement de la porte; **leave the window open a ~** laissez la fenêtre entrouverte; **at the ~ of dawn** au point du jour, dès potron-minet*.
b (*noise*) [*twigs*] craquement *m*; [*whip*] claquement *m*; [*rifle*] coup *m* (sec), détonation *f.* **~ of thunder** coup de tonnerre; **the ~ of doom** la trompette du Jugement dernier.
c (*sharp blow*) **to give sb a ~ on the head** assener à qn un grand coup sur la tête.
d (*: *joke etc*) plaisanterie *f.* **that was a ~* at your brother** ça, c'était pour votre frère; **that was a dirty ~* he made** c'est une vacherie⁑ ce qu'il a dit là, c'était vache* *or* rosse* de dire ça.
e (*try*) **to have a ~ at doing*** essayer (un coup*) de faire; **to have a ~ at sth*** se lancer dans qch, tenter le coup sur qch; **I'll have a ~ at it*** je vais essayer (un coup*); *see* **fair.**
f (*drug*) crack *m.*
2 comp *sportsman, sportswoman* de première classe, fameux*; **a crack tennis player/skier** un as *or* un crack du tennis/du ski ▶ **crack-brained** (*pej*) *person* détraqué; *plan* cinglé*; (*pej*) **a crack-brained idea** une idée saugrenue *or* loufoque* ▶ **crackdown: crackdown on** mesures *fpl* énergiques contre; mesures de répression contre; tour *m* de vis à ▶ **crackhead**⁑ accro⁑ *mf* du crack ▶ **crack-jaw*** impossible à prononcer, imprononçable; **crack-jaw* name** nom *m* à coucher dehors* ▶ **crackpot*** (*pej*) n (*person*) tordu(e)* *m(f)*, cinglé(e)* *m(f)* ◊ adj *idea* tordu ▶ **crack shot** bon *or* excellent fusil; (*Mil, Police etc*) tireur *m* d'élite ▶ **cracksman** (*Prison sl: burglar*) cambrioleur *m*, casseur *m* (*sl*) ▶ **crack-up*** [*plan, organization*] effondrement *m*, écroulement *m*; [*person*] (*physical*) effondrement; (*mental*) dépression nerveuse; (*US: accident*) [*vehicle*] collision *f*, accident *m*; [*plane*] accident (d'avion).
3 vt a *pottery, glass, bone* fêler; *wall* lézarder, crevasser; *ground* crevasser; *nut etc* casser. **to ~ one's skull** se fendre le crâne; **to ~ sb over the head** assommer qn; (*fig*) **to ~ a crib**⁑ faire un casse⁑, faire un fric-frac⁑; **to ~ a safe*** faire⁑ *or* cambrioler un coffre-fort; (*US Comm*) **to ~ a market*** réussir à s'implanter sur un marché; **to ~ a bottle*** ouvrir *or* déboucher une bouteille; (*US*) **to ~ a book*** ouvrir un livre (pour l'étudier).
b *petroleum etc* craquer, traiter par craquage.
c *whip* faire claquer. **to ~ one's finger joints** faire craquer ses doigts; (*fig*) **to ~ jokes*** faire des astuces, sortir des blagues*.
d *code etc* déchiffrer; *spy network* démanteler. [*detective, police*] **to ~ a case (wide open)** (être sur le point de) résoudre une affaire.
4 vi a [*pottery, glass*] se fêler; [*ground*] se crevasser, se craqueler; [*wall*] se fendiller, se lézarder; [*skin*] se crevasser, (*from cold*) se gercer; [*ice*] se craqueler.
b [*whip*] claquer; [*dry wood*] craquer. **we heard the pistol ~** nous avons entendu partir le coup de pistolet.
c [*voice*] se casser; [*boy's voice*] muer.
d (* *Brit*) **to get ~ing** s'y mettre, se mettre au boulot*; **let's get ~ing** allons-y!, au boulot!*; **get ~ing!** magne-toi!⁑, grouille-toi!⁑
▶**crack down on** 1 vt fus *person* sévir contre, serrer la vis à; *expenditure, sb's actions* mettre le frein à. 2 **crackdown** n *see* **crack 2.**
▶**crack up*** 1 vi a (*physically*) ne pas tenir le coup; (*mentally*) être au bout de son rouleau, s'effondrer, flancher*. (*hum*) **I must be cracking up!** ça ne tourne plus rond chez moi!* b (*US*) [*vehicle*] s'écraser; [*plane*] s'écraser (au sol). c [*person*] (*with laughter*) se tordre *or* éclater de rire. 2 vt sep a (*praise etc*) *person, quality, action, thing* vanter, louer; *method* prôner. **he's not all he's cracked up to be*** il n'est pas aussi sensationnel qu'on le dit *or* prétend. b (*US: crash etc*) *vehicle* emboutir; *plane* faire s'écraser. 3 **crack-up** n *see* **crack 2.**
cracked [krækt] adj a *plate* fêlé, fendu; *wall* lézardé. b (*: *mad*) toqué*, timbré*, cinglé*.
cracker ['krækəʳ] 1 n a (*biscuit*) craquelin *m*, cracker *m*, biscuit *m* (salé). b (*firework*) pétard *m.* c (*Brit: at parties etc, also* **Christmas ~**) diablotin *m.* d **(nut)~s** casse-noisettes *m inv*, casse-noix *m inv.* e (*US*) pauvre blanc *m* (du Sud). 2 comp ▶ **the Cracker State** la Géorgie.
cracker-barrel ['krækə,bærəl] adj (*US*) ≃ du café du commerce.
crackers⁑ ['krækəz] adj (*Brit*) cinglé*, dingue⁑.
cracking ['krækɪŋ] 1 n (*NonC*) a [*petroleum*] craquage *m*, cracking

m. b (*cracks: in paint, varnish etc*) craquelure *f.* 2 adj a **at a ~ speed** *or* **pace** à toute vitesse. b (* *Brit: excellent*) de premier ordre, de première. 3 adv (* *Brit*) formidablement.

crackle ['krækl] 1 vi *[twigs burning]* pétiller, crépiter; *[sth frying]* grésiller. 2 n a (*noise*) *[wood]* crépitement *m*, craquement *m*; *[food]* grésillement *m*; (*on telephone etc*) crépitement(s), friture* *f.* b *[china, porcelain etc]* craquelure *f.* **~ china** porcelaine craquelée.

crackling ['kræklɪŋ] n a (*sound*) crépitement *m*; (*Rad*) friture* *f* (*NonC*). b (*Culin*) couenne rissolée (*de rôti de porc*).

cracknel ['kræknl] n (*biscuit*) craquelin *m*; (*toffee*) nougatine *f.*

cradle ['kreɪdl] 1 n a (*lit, fig*) berceau *m.* **from the ~ to the grave** du berceau à la tombe; **the ~ of civilization** le berceau de la civilisation; (*US fig*) **to rob the ~*** les prendre au berceau*.

b (*Naut: framework*) ber *m*; (*Constr*) nacelle *f*, pont volant; *[telephone]* support *m*; (*Med*) arceau *m.*

2 vt: **to ~ a child (in one's arms)** bercer un enfant (dans ses bras); **she ~d the vase in her hands** elle tenait délicatement le vase entre ses mains; **he ~d the telephone under his chin** il maintenait le téléphone sous son menton.

3 comp ► **cradle cap** (*Med*) croûte *f* de lait (*sur le crâne des nouveau-nés*) ► **cradle snatcher:** (*pej*) **she's a cradle snatcher*** elle les prend au berceau* ► **cradlesong** berceuse *f.*

craft [krɑːft] 1 n a (*skill*) art *m*, métier *m*; (*job, occupation*) métier, profession *f* (*généralement de type artisanal*); (*NonC: Scol: subject*) travaux manuels; *see* **art¹**, **needle** *etc.*

b (*tradesmen's guild*) corps *m* de métier, corporation *f.*

c (pl inv) (*boat*) embarcation *f*, barque *f*, petit bateau; (*plane*) appareil *m*; *see* **air**, **space** *etc.*

d (*NonC: cunning*) astuce *f*, ruse *f* (*pej*). **by ~** par ruse; **his ~ in doing that** l'astuce dont il a fait preuve en le faisant.

2 comp ► **craftsman** artisan *m*; (*fig: musician etc*) artiste *m* ► **craftsmanship** (*NonC*) connaissance *f* d'un métier; (*artistry*) art *m*; **what craftsmanship!** quel travail!; **a superb piece of craftsmanship** un *or* du travail superbe ► **craft union** fédération *f.*

3 vt: *[vase, poem]* **beautifully ~ed** réalisé avec art.

craftily ['krɑːftɪlɪ] adv astucieusement, avec ruse (*pej*).

craftiness ['krɑːftɪnɪs] n astuce *f*, finesse *f*, ruse *f* (*pej*).

crafty ['krɑːftɪ] adj malin (*f* -igne), astucieux, rusé (*pej*). **he's a ~ one*** c'est un malin; **a ~ little gadget*** un petit truc* astucieux; **that was a ~ move*** *or* **a ~ thing to do** c'était un coup très astucieux.

crag [kræg] n rocher escarpé *or* à pic; (*Climbing*) école *f* d'escalade.

craggy ['krægɪ] adj *rock* escarpé, à pic; *area* plein d'escarpements. **~ features/face** traits/visage taillé(s) à la serpe *or* à coups de hache.

cram [kræm] 1 vt a fourrer (*into* dans). **to ~ books into a case** fourrer des livres dans une valise, bourrer une valise de livres; **we can ~ in another book** nous pouvons encore faire place pour un autre livre *or* y faire tenir un autre livre; **to ~ food into one's mouth** enfourner* de la nourriture; **we can't ~ any more people into the hall/the bus** on n'a plus la place de faire entrer qui que ce soit dans la salle/l'autobus; **we were all ~med into one room** nous étions tous entassés *or* empilés dans une seule pièce; **he ~med his hat (down) over his eyes** il a enfoncé son chapeau sur ses yeux.

b bourrer (*with* de). **shop ~med with good things** magasin *m* qui regorge de bonnes choses; **drawer ~med with letters** tiroir bourré de lettres; **to ~ sb with food** bourrer *or* gaver qn de nourriture; **to ~ o.s. with food** se bourrer *or* se gaver de nourriture; (*fig*) **he has his head ~med with odd ideas** il a la tête bourrée *or* farcie d'idées bizarres.

c (*Scol*) *pupil* chauffer*, faire bachoter.

2 vi a *[people]* s'entasser, s'empiler. **they all ~med into the kitchen** tout le monde s'est entassé dans la cuisine.

b **to ~ for an exam** bachoter, préparer un examen.

3 comp ► **cram-full** *room, bus* bondé; *case* bourré (*of* de).

crammer ['kræməʳ] n (*slightly pej*) (*tutor*) répétiteur *m*, -trice *f* (*qui fait faire du bachotage*); (*student*) bachoteur *m*, -euse *f*; (*book*) précis *m*, aide-mémoire *m inv*; (*also* **~'s**: *school*) boîte *f* à bachot*.

cramp¹ [kræmp] 1 n (*Med*) crampe *f.* **to have ~ in one's leg** avoir une crampe à la jambe; *see* **writer.** 2 vt (*hinder*) *person* gêner, entraver. **to ~ sb's progress** gêner *or* entraver les progrès de qn; (*fig*) **to ~ sb's style** priver qn de ses moyens, enlever ses moyens à qn; (*fig*) **your presence is ~ing my style*** tu me fais perdre (tous) mes moyens.

cramp² [kræmp] 1 n (*Constr, Tech*) agrafe *f*, crampon *m*, happe *f.* 2 vt *stones* cramponner.

cramped [kræmpt] adj a *handwriting* en pattes de mouche. b *space* resserré, à l'étroit. **we were very ~ (for space)** on était à l'étroit, on n'avait pas la place de se retourner; **in a ~ position** dans une position inconfortable.

crampon ['kræmpən] n (*Climbing, Constr*) crampon *m.* (*Climbing*) **~ technique** cramponnage *m.*

cramponning ['kræmpənɪŋ] n (*Climbing*) cramponnage *m.*

cranberry ['krænbərɪ] n (*Bot*) canneberge *f.* **turkey with ~ sauce** dinde *f* aux canneberges.

crane [kreɪn] 1 n (*Orn, Tech*) grue *f.* 2 comp ► **crane driver** grutier *m* ► **cranefly** tipule *f* ► **crane operator** = **crane driver** ► **crane's-bill** (*Bot*) géranium *m.* 3 vt: **to ~ one's neck** tendre le cou.

►**crane forward** vi tendre le cou (*pour voir etc*).

crania ['kreɪnɪə] npl of **cranium.**

cranial ['kreɪnɪəl] adj crânien.

cranium ['kreɪnɪəm] n, pl **~s** *or* **crania** crâne *m*, boîte crânienne.

crank¹ [kræŋk] n (*Brit* *: *person*) excentrique *mf*, loufoque* *mf.* **a religious ~** un fanatique religieux.

crank² [kræŋk] 1 n (*Tech*) manivelle *f.*

2 comp ► **crankcase** (*Aut*) carter *m* ► **crankshaft** (*Aut*) vilebrequin *m.*

3 vt (*also* **~ up**) *car* faire partir à la manivelle; *cine-camera, gramophone etc* remonter (à la manivelle); *barrel organ* tourner la manivelle de.

►**crank out** vt (*US*) produire (avec effort).

cranky* ['kræŋkɪ] adj (*eccentric*) excentrique, loufoque*; (*bad-tempered*) revêche, grincheux.

cranny ['krænɪ] n (petite) faille *f*, fissure *f*, fente *f*; *see* **nook.**

crap‡‡ [kræp] 1 n (*excrement*) merde‡‡ *f*; (*nonsense*) conneries‡‡ *fpl*, couillonnades‡ *fpl*; (*junk*) merde‡‡, saloperie‡ *f.* **the film was ~** le film était merdique‡‡. 2 adj = **crappy.** 3 vi chier‡‡.

►**crap out**‡ vi (*US: chicken out*) se dégonfler*.

crape [kreɪp] n a = **crêpe.** b (*for mourning*) crêpe *m* (*de deuil*). **~ band** brassard *m* (de deuil); (*US*) **~hanger**‡ rabat-joie *m inv.*

crappy‡‡ ['kræpɪ] adj merdique‡‡.

craps [kræps] n (*US*) jeu *m* de dés (*sorte de zanzi ou de passe anglaise*). **to shoot ~** jouer aux dés.

crapulous ['kræpjʊləs] adj crapuleux.

crash¹ [kræʃ] 1 n a (*noise*) fracas *m.* **a ~ of thunder** un coup de tonnerre; **a sudden ~ of dishes** un soudain fracas d'assiettes cassées; **~, bang, wallop!*** badaboum!, patatras!

b (*accident*) *[car]* collision *f*, accident *m*; *[aeroplane]* accident (d'avion). **in a car/plane ~** dans un accident de voiture/d'avion; **we had a ~ on the way here** nous avons eu un accident en venant ici.

c (*Fin*) *[company, firm]* faillite *f*; (*St Ex*) krach *m.*

2 adv: **he went ~ into the tree** il est allé se jeter *or* se fracasser contre l'arbre.

3 comp ► **crash barrier** (*Brit*) glissière *f* (de sécurité) ► **crash course** cours intensif ► **crash diet** régime *m* accéléré ► **crash helmet** casque *m* (protecteur) ► **crash-land** (*Aviat*) atterrir *or* se poser en catastrophe ► **crash landing** atterrissage forcé *or* en catastrophe ► **crashpad**‡ piaule‡ *f* de dépannage ► **crash programme** programme intensif.

4 vi a *[aeroplane]* s'écraser au sol; *[vehicle]* s'écraser; *[two vehicles]* se percuter, se rentrer dedans*. **the cars ~ed at the junction** les voitures se sont percutées au croisement; **to ~ into sth** rentrer dans qch*, percuter qch, emboutir qch; **the plate ~ed to the ground** l'assiette s'est fracassée par terre; **the car ~ed through the gate** la voiture a enfoncé la barrière *or* s'est jetée à travers la barrière.

b (*Comm, Fin*) *[bank, firm]* faire faillite. **the stock market ~ed** les cours de la Bourse se sont effondrés.

c (‡: *sleep*) pieuter‡, crécher‡. **can I ~ in your room for a few days?** est-ce que je peux pieuter‡ chez toi pendant quelques jours?; **to ~ at sb's place** pieuter‡ *or* crécher‡ chez qn.

d (*Comput*) tomber en panne.

5 vt a *car* avoir une collision *or* un accident avec. **he ~ed the car through the barrier** il a enfoncé la barrière (avec la voiture); **he ~ed the car into a tree** il a percuté un arbre (avec la voiture); **he ~ed the plane** il s'est écrasé (au sol); **to ~ the gears** faire grincer le changement de vitesse.

b (*Brit* *) **to ~ a party** s'introduire dans une réception sans invitation, resquiller; (*US Comm* ‡) **to ~ a market** pénétrer en force sur un marché.

►**crash down, crash in** vi *[roof etc]* s'effondrer (avec fracas).

►**crash out**‡ 1 vi (*fall asleep etc*) tomber raide. 2 vt sep: **to be crashed out** être raide* *or* pété‡ *or* fait‡.

crash² [kræʃ] n (*Tex*) grosse toile.

crashing ['kræʃɪŋ] adj: **a ~ bore** un raseur de première.

crass [kræs] adj grossier, crasse. **~ ignorance/stupidity** ignorance *f*/bêtise *f* crasse.

crassly ['kræslɪ] adv grossièrement.

crate [kreɪt] 1 n a *[fruit]* cageot *m*; *[bottles]* caisse *f* (à claire-voie); (*esp Naut*) caisse. b (‡: *aeroplane*) zinc* *m*; (‡: *car*) bagnole* *f.* 2 vt (*also* **~ up**) *goods* mettre en cageot(s) *or* en caisse(s).

crater ['kreɪtəʳ] n *[volcano, moon]* cratère *m.* **bomb ~** entonnoir *m*; **shell ~** trou *m* d'obus, entonnoir.

cravat(e) [krə'væt] n cravate *f*, foulard *m* (*noué autour du cou*).

crave [kreɪv] vti a (*also* **~ for**) *drink, tobacco etc* avoir un besoin maladif *or* physiologique de; **to ~ (for) affection** avoir soif *or* avoir grand besoin d'affection. b (*frm*) *attention* solliciter. **to ~ permission** avoir l'honneur de solliciter l'autorisation; **he ~d permission to leave** il supplia qu'on lui accordât la permission de partir; **may I ~ leave to ...?** j'ai l'honneur de solliciter l'autorisation de ...; **to ~ sb's pardon** implorer le pardon de qn.

craven ['kreɪvən] adj, n (*liter*) lâche (*mf*), poltron(ne) (*m(f)*).

craving ['kreɪvɪŋ] n *[drink, drugs, tobacco]* besoin *m* (maladif *or* physiologique) (*for* de); *[affection]* grand besoin, soif *f* (*for* de); *[freedom]* désir *m* insatiable (*for* de).

craw [krɔː] n *[bird]* jabot *m*; *[animal]* estomac *m*. (*fig*) **it sticks in my ~** cela me reste en travers de la gorge.

crawfish ['krɔːfɪʃ] 1 n (*esp US*) = **crayfish**. 2 vi (*US fig* ‡) se défiler*, faire marche arrière.

crawl [krɔːl] 1 n a *[vehicles]* allure très ralentie, poussette* *f*. **we had to go at a ~ through the main streets** nous avons dû avancer au pas *or* faire la poussette* dans les rues principales. b (*Swimming*) crawl *m*. **to do the ~** nager *or* faire le crawl, crawler. 2 vi a *[animals]* ramper, se glisser; *[person]* se traîner, ramper. **to ~ in/out** *etc* entrer/sortir *etc* en rampant *or* à quatre pattes; **to ~ on one's hands and knees** aller à quatre pattes; **the child has begun to ~ (around)** l'enfant commence à se traîner à quatre pattes; (*fig*) **to ~ to sb** s'aplatir devant qn, lécher les bottes de *or* à qn; **the fly ~ed up the wall/along the table** la mouche a grimpé le long du mur/a avancé le long de la table; **to make sb's skin ~** rendre qn malade de dégoût, donner la chair de poule à qn; **to ~ with vermin** grouiller de vermine; (*pej*) **the street is ~ing* with policemen** la rue grouille d'agents de police. b *[vehicles]* avancer au pas, faire la poussette*.

crawler* ['krɔːləʳ] n (*person*) lécheur* *m*, -euse* *f*, lèche-bottes* *mf inv*; (*vehicle*) véhicule lent. (*Brit Aut*) **~ lane** file *f or* voie *f* pour véhicules lents.

crayfish ['kreɪfɪʃ] n (*freshwater*) écrevisse *f*; (*saltwater*) (*large*) langouste *f*; (*small*) langoustine *f*.

crayon ['kreɪən] 1 n (*coloured pencil*) crayon *m* (de couleur); (*Art: pencil, chalk etc*) pastel *m*; (*Art: drawing*) crayon, pastel. 2 vt crayonner, dessiner au crayon; (*Art*) colorier au crayon *or* au pastel.

craze [kreɪz] 1 n engouement *m* (*for* pour), manie *f* (*for* de). **it's all the ~*** cela fait fureur. 2 vt a (*make mad*) rendre fou (*f* folle). b *glaze, pottery* craqueler. 3 vi *[glaze, pottery]* craqueler; *[windscreen]* s'étoiler.

crazed [kreɪzd] adj a (*mad*) affolé, rendu fou (*f* folle) (*with* de). b *glaze, pottery* craquelé; *windscreen* étoilé.

crazily ['kreɪzɪlɪ] adv *behave* follement, d'une manière insensée; *lean, slant* dangereusement.

crazy ['kreɪzɪ] 1 adj a (*mad*) fou (*f* folle). **to go ~** devenir fou *or* cinglé* *or* dingue‡; **to be ~ with anxiety** être fou d'inquiétude; **it's enough to drive you ~** c'est à vous rendre fou *or* dingue‡; **it was a ~ idea** c'était une idée idiote; **you were ~ to want to go there** tu étais fou *or* dingue‡ de vouloir y aller, c'était de la folie de vouloir y aller.

b (*: *enthusiastic*) fou (*f* folle), fana* (*f inv*) (*about sb/sth* de qn/qch). **I am not ~ about it** ça ne m'emballe* pas; **he's ~ about her** il en est fou, il l'aime à la folie.

c (*fig*) *price, height etc* incroyable; (*US: excellent*) terrible*, formidable. **the tower leant at a ~ angle** la tour penchait d'une façon menaçante *or* inquiétante.

d **like ~*** = **like mad**; *see* **mad 1a**.

2 comp ▸ **crazy bone** (*US*) petit juif* (*partie du coude*) ▸ **crazy house**‡ (*US*) cabanon* *m*, asile *m* d'aliénés ▸ **crazy paving** dallage irrégulier (*en pierres plates*).

CRE [ˌsiːɑːr'iː] n (*Brit*) abbr of **Commission for Racial Equality**.

creak [kriːk] 1 vi *[door hinge]* grincer, crier; *[shoes]* craquer, grincer; *[floorboard, joints]* craquer. 2 n (*see* **1**) grincement *m*; craquement *m*.

creaky ['kriːkɪ] adj *stair, floorboard, joints, shoes* qui craque *or* crisse; *hinge* grinçant.

cream [kriːm] 1 n a crème *f*. (*Brit*) **single/double ~** crème fraîche liquide/épaisse; **to take the ~ off the milk** écrémer le lait; (*fig*) **the ~ of society** la crème *or* la fine fleur de la société; (*Confectionery*) **chocolate ~** chocolat fourré (à la crème); **vanilla ~** (*dessert*) crème à la vanille; (*biscuit*) biscuit fourré à la vanille; *see* **clot**.

b (*face ~, shoe ~*) crème *f*; *see* **cold, foundation** *etc*.

2 adj (*~-coloured*) crème *inv*; (*made with ~*) *cake* à la crème.

3 comp ▸ **cream cheese** fromage *m* à la crème, fromage blanc *or* frais ▸ **cream cracker** (*Brit*) (cream) cracker *m* ▸ **cream jug** (*Brit*) pot *m* à crème ▸ **cream of tartar** crème *f* de tartre ▸ **cream of tomato soup** crème *f* de tomates ▸ **cream puff** chou *m* à la crème ▸ **cream tea** (*Brit*) *goûter où l'on sert des "scones" avec de la crème en grumeaux*.

4 vt a *milk* écrémer.

b (*Culin*) *butter* battre. **to ~ (together) sugar and butter** travailler le beurre en crème avec le sucre; **~ed potatoes** purée *f* de pommes de terre.

c (*US* ‡ *fig*) *enemy, opposing team* rosser*, rétamer; *car* bousiller*.

▸**cream off** vt sep (*fig*) *best talents, part of profits* prélever, écrémer.

creamer ['kriːməʳ] n a (*to separate cream*) écrémeuse *f*. b (*milk substitute*) succédané *m* de lait. c (*US: pitcher*) pot *m* à crème.

creamery ['kriːmərɪ] n a (*on farm*) laiterie *f*; (*butter factory*) laiterie, coopérative laitière. b (*small shop*) crémerie *f*.

creamy ['kriːmɪ] adj crémeux; *complexion* crème *inv*, crémeux. **~ white/yellow** blanc *m*/jaune *m* crème.

crease [kriːs] 1 n *[material, paper]* pli *m*, pliure *f*; *[trouser legs, skirt etc]* pli; (*unwanted fold*) faux pli; (*on face*) ride *f*. **~-resistant** infroissable. 2 vt (*crumple*) froisser, chiffonner, plisser; (*press ~ in*) plisser. 3 vi se froisser, se chiffonner, prendre un faux pli. (*fig*) **his face ~d with laughter** le rire a plissé son visage.

▸**crease up** 1 vt sep a (*crumple*) froisser, chiffonner. b (*: *amuse*) faire mourir de rire. 2 vi a (*crumple*) se froisser, se chiffonner. b (*: *laugh*) être plié en quatre.

create [kriː'eɪt] 1 vt (*gen*) créer; *new fashion* lancer, créer; *work of art, character, role* créer; *impression* produire, faire; (*Comput*) *file* créer; *problem, difficulty* créer, susciter, provoquer; *noise, din* faire. **to ~ a sensation** faire sensation; **two posts have been ~d** il y a eu deux créations de poste, deux postes ont été créés; **he was ~d baron** il a été fait baron. 2 vi (*Brit* ‡: *fuss*) faire une scène, faire un foin‡.

creation [kriː'eɪʃən] n a (*NonC*) création *f*. **since the ~** depuis la création du monde. b (*Art, Dress*) création *f*. **the latest ~s from Paris** les toutes dernières créations de Paris.

creative [kriː'eɪtɪv] adj *mind, power* créateur (*f* -trice); *person, atmosphere, activity* créatif; *design* novateur. (*Educ*) **~ toys** jouets *mpl* créatifs *or* d'éveil; **~ writing** la création littéraire.

creativity [ˌkriːeɪ'tɪvɪtɪ] n imagination *f* créatrice, esprit *m* créateur, créativité *f*.

creator [kriː'eɪtəʳ] n créateur *m*, -trice *f*.

creature ['kriːtʃəʳ] 1 n (*gen, also fig*) créature *f*; (*animal*) bête *f*, animal *m*; (*human*) être *m*, créature. **dumb ~s** les bêtes; **the ~s of the deep** les animaux marins; **she's a poor/lovely ~** c'est une pauvre/ravissante créature; (*fig pej*) **they were all his ~s** tous étaient ses créatures; *see* **habit 1a**. 2 comp ▸ **creature comforts** confort matériel; **he likes his creature comforts** il aime son petit confort *or* ses aises.

crèche [kreɪʃ] n (*Brit*) pouponnière *f*, crèche *f*; (*daytime*) crèche, garderie *f*.

credence ['kriːdəns] n croyance *f*, foi *f*. **to give ~ to** ajouter foi à.

credentials [krɪ'denʃəlz] npl (*identifying papers*) pièce *f* d'identité; *[diplomat]* lettres *fpl* de créance; (*references*) références *fpl*, certificat *m*. **to have good ~** avoir de bonnes références.

credibility [ˌkredə'bɪlɪtɪ] 1 n crédibilité *f*. **to lose ~** perdre sa crédibilité. 2 comp ▸ **credibility gap** manque *m* de crédibilité, crise *f* de confiance ▸ **credibility rating**: **his credibility rating is not very high** sa (marge de) crédibilité est très entamée.

credible ['kredɪbl] adj *witness* digne de foi; *person* crédible; *statement* plausible. **it's hardly ~** c'est peu plausible.

credit ['kredɪt] 1 n a (*Banking, Comm, Fin*) crédit *m*; (*Book-keeping*) crédit, avoir *m*. **to give sb ~** faire crédit à qn; **"no ~"** "la maison ne fait pas (de) crédit"; **to buy/sell on ~** acheter/vendre à crédit; **you have £10 to your ~** vous avez un crédit de 10 livres; (*account*) **in ~** approvisionné; **am I in ~?** est-ce que mon compte est approvisionné?

b (*belief, acceptance*) **to give ~ to** *[person]* ajouter foi à; *[event]* donner foi à, accréditer; **I gave him ~ for more sense** je lui supposais *or* croyais plus de bon sens; **to gain ~ with** s'accréditer auprès de; **his ~ with the electorate** son crédit auprès des électeurs.

c honneur *m*. **to his ~ we must point out that ...** il faut faire remarquer à son honneur *or* à son crédit que ...; **he is a ~ to his family** il fait honneur à sa famille, il est l'honneur de sa famille; **the only people to emerge with any ~** les seuls à s'en sortir à leur honneur; **to give sb ~ for his generosity** *etc* reconnaître la générosité *etc* de qn; **to give sb ~ for doing sth** reconnaître que qn a fait qch; **to claim** *or* **take (the) ~ for sth** s'attribuer le mérite de qch; **it does you (great) ~** cela est tout à votre honneur, cela vous fait grand honneur; **~ where ~'s due** il faut rendre à César ce qui appartient à César.

d (*Scol*) unité *f* d'enseignement *or* de valeur, U.V. *f*.

e (*Cine*) **~s** générique *m*.

2 vt a (*believe*) *rumour, news* croire, ajouter foi à. **I could hardly ~ it** je n'arrivais pas à le croire; **you wouldn't ~ it** vous ne le croiriez pas.

b **to ~ sb/sth with (having) certain powers/qualities** (*gen*) reconnaître à qn/qch certains pouvoirs/certaines qualités; **to be ~ed with having done** passer pour avoir fait; **I ~ed him with more sense** je lui croyais *or* supposais plus de bon sens; **it is ~ed with (having) magic powers** on lui attribue des pouvoirs magiques.

c (*Banking*) **to ~ £5 to sb** *or* **to sb's account, to ~ sb** *or* **sb's account with £5** créditer (le compte de) qn de 5 livres, porter 5 livres au crédit de qn.

3 comp ▸ **credit account** compte créditeur ▸ **credit agency** établissement *m or* agence *f* de crédit ▸ **credit arrangements** accords *mpl* de crédit ▸ **credit balance** (*Banking*) solde créditeur ▸ **credit card** carte *f* de crédit ▸ **credit charges** coût *m* du crédit ▸ **credit control** (*action*) encadrement *m* du crédit; (*department*) (service *m* de l')encadrement du crédit ▸ **credit entry** (*Fin*) inscription *f or* écriture *f* au crédit ▸ **credit facilities** (*Banking*) ligne *f* de crédit; (*Comm: to buyer*) facilités *fpl* de paiement *or* de crédit ▸ **credit hour** (*US Scol, Univ*) ≈ unité *f* de valeur ▸ **credit limit** limite *f or* plafond *m* de crédit ▸ **credit line** (*Banking*) ligne *f* de crédit; (*Cine*) mention *f* au générique; (*in book*) mention de la source ▸ **credit note** (*Brit*) avoir *m* ▸ **credit rating** réputation *f* de solvabilité ▸ **credit reference** évaluation *f*, notation *f*, rating *m*; **credit reference agency** agence *f*

d'évaluation *or* de notation *or* de rating ► **credit sales** ventes *fpl* à crédit ► **credit side**: (*Book-keeping, also fig*) **on the credit side** à l'actif ► **credit squeeze** (*Econ*) restrictions *fpl* de crédit ► **credit terms** conditions *fpl* de crédit ► **credit titles** (*Cine*) générique *m* ► **credit transfer** transfert *m*, virement *m* ► **creditworthiness** solvabilité *f*, capacité *f* d'emprunt ► **creditworthy** solvable.

creditable ['kredɪtəbl] **adj** honorable, estimable.

creditably ['kredɪtəblɪ] **adv** honorablement, avec honneur.

creditor ['kredɪtəʳ] **n** créancier *m*, -ière *f*. (*Econ*) ~ **nation** nation *f* créditrice.

credo ['kreɪdəʊ] **n** credo *m*.

credulity [krɪ'djuːlɪtɪ] **n** crédulité *f*.

credulous ['kredjʊləs] **adj** crédule, naïf (*f* naïve).

credulously ['kredjʊləslɪ] **adv** avec crédulité, naïvement.

creed [kriːd] **n** credo *m*, principes *mpl*. (*Rel*) **the C~** le Credo, le symbole des Apôtres.

creek [kriːk] **n** a (*esp Brit: inlet*) crique *f*, anse *f*. **to be up the ~**‡ (*be wrong*) se fourrer le doigt dans l'œil (jusqu'au coude)*; (*be in trouble*) être dans le pétrin. b (*stream*) ruisseau *m*, petit cours d'eau.

creel [kriːl] **n** panier *m* de pêche (*en osier*).

creep [kriːp] **pret, ptp crept** 1 **vi** *[animal, person]* ramper; *[plants]* ramper, grimper; (*move silently*) se glisser. **to ~ between** se faufiler entre; **to ~ in/out/away** *etc* *[person]* entrer/sortir/s'éloigner *etc* à pas de loup; *[animal]* entrer/sortir/s'éloigner *etc* sans un bruit; **to ~ about/along on tiptoe** marcher/avancer sur la pointe des pieds; **to ~ up on sb** *[person]* surprendre qn, s'approcher de qn à pas de loup; *[old age etc]* prendre qn par surprise; **old age is ~ing on** on se fait vieux*; **the traffic crept along** les voitures avançaient au pas; (*fig*) **an error crept into it** une erreur s'y est glissée; **a feeling of peace crept over me** un sentiment de paix me gagnait peu à peu *or* commençait à me gagner; **it makes my flesh ~** cela me donne la chair de poule.
2 **n**: **it gives me the ~s*** cela me donne la chair de poule, cela me fait froid dans le dos; (*pej*) **he's a ~**‡ il vous dégoûte, c'est un saligaud‡.

creeper ['kriːpəʳ] **n** a (*Bot*) plante grimpante *or* rampante; *see* **Virginia**. b (*US*) **~s** barboteuse *f*. c (*: *person*) lécheur* *m*, -euse* *f*, lèche-bottes* *mf inv*.

creeping ['kriːpɪŋ] **adj** a *plant* grimpant, rampant; (*fig pej*) *person* lécheur. b (*gradual*) *change* larvé; *inflation* rampant. (*Med*) ~ **paralysis** paralysie progressive.

creepy ['kriːpɪ] 1 **adj** *story, place* qui donne la chair de poule, qui fait frissonner, terrifiant. 2 **comp** ► **creepy-crawly*** (*Brit*) **adj** qui fait frissonner, qui donne la chair de poule, horrifiant ◊ **n** petite bestiole; **I hate creepy-crawlies*** je déteste toutes les petites bestioles qui rampent.

cremate [krɪ'meɪt] **vt** incinérer (*un cadavre*).

cremation [krɪ'meɪʃən] **n** crémation *f*, incinération *f*.

crematorium [ˌkremə'tɔːrɪəm] **n, pl ~s** *or* **crematoria** [ˌkremə'tɔːrɪə] (*Brit*), **crematory** ['kreməˌtɔːrɪ] (*US*) **n** (*place*) crématorium *m*, crématoire *m*; (*furnace*) four *m* crématoire.

crenellated ['krenɪleɪtɪd] **adj** crénelé, à créneaux.

crenellations [ˌkrenɪ'leɪʃənz] **npl** créneaux *mpl*.

creole ['kriːəʊl] 1 **adj** créole. 2 **n**: **C~** Créole *mf*; **the C~ State** la Louisiane.

creosote ['krɪəsəʊt] 1 **n** créosote *f*. 2 **vt** créosoter.

crêpe [kreɪp] 1 **n** (*Tex*) crêpe *m*. 2 **comp** ► **crêpe bandage** bande *f* Velpeau ® ► **crêpe paper** papier *m* crépon ► **crêpe(-soled) shoes** chaussures *fpl* à semelles de crêpe.

crept [krept] **pret, ptp of creep**.

crepuscular [krɪ'pʌskjʊləʳ] **adj** crépusculaire.

crescendo [krɪ'ʃendəʊ] 1 **n, pl ~s** *or* **crescendi** [krɪ'ʃendɪ] (*Mus, fig*) crescendo *m inv*. 2 **vi** (*Mus*) faire un crescendo.

crescent ['kresnt] 1 **n** a croissant *m*. (*Islamic faith etc*) **the C~** le Croissant. b (*street*) rue *f* (*en arc de cercle*). 2 **comp** ► **crescent moon** croissant *m* de (la) lune ► **crescent roll** (*Culin*) croissant *m* ► **crescent-shaped** en (forme de) croissant.

cress [kres] **n** cresson *m*; *see* **mustard, water**.

crest [krest] 1 **n** *[bird, wave]* crête *f*; *[helmet]* cimier *m*; *[mountain]* crête, (*long ridge*) arête *f*; *[road]* haut *m* *or* sommet *m* de côte; (*above coat of arms, shield*) timbre *m*; (*on seal etc*) armoiries *fpl*. **the family ~** les armoiries familiales; (*fig*) **he is on the ~ of the wave** tout lui réussit en ce moment. 2 **vt** *wave, hill* franchir la crête de. **~ed notepaper** papier à lettres armorié; **~ed tit** mésange huppée.

crestfallen ['krestˌfɔːlən] **adj** *person* déçu, découragé, déconfit. **to look ~** avoir l'air penaud, avoir l'oreille basse.

cretaceous [krɪ'teɪʃəs] **adj** crétacé. (*Geol*) **the C~ (age)** le crétacé.

Cretan ['kriːtən] 1 **adj** crétois. 2 **n** Crétois(e) *m(f)*.

Crete [kriːt] **n** Crète *f*. **in ~** en Crète.

cretin ['kretɪn] **n** (*Med*) crétin(e) *m(f)*; (* *pej*) crétin(e), imbécile *mf*, idiot(e) *m(f)*.

cretinism ['kretɪnɪzəm] **n** (*Med*) crétinisme *m*.

cretinous ['kretɪnəs] **adj** (*Med, also * pej*) crétin.

cretonne [kre'tɒn] **n** cretonne *f*.

crevasse [krɪ'væs] **n** (*Geol, Climbing*) crevasse *f*.

crevice ['krevɪs] **n** fissure *f*, fente *f*, lézarde *f*.

crew[1] [kruː] 1 **n** (*Aviat, Naut*) équipage *m*; (*Cine, Rowing etc*) équipe *f*; (*group, gang*) bande *f*, équipe. (*pej*) **what a ~!*** tu parles d'une équipe!*, quelle engeance! 2 **vi** (*Sailing*) **to ~ for sb** être l'équipier de qn; **would you like me to ~ for you?** voulez-vous de moi comme équipier? 3 **vt** *yacht* armer. 4 **comp** ► **crew cut: to have a crew cut** avoir les cheveux en brosse ► **crewman** (*TV etc*) équipier *m* ► **crew-neck sweater** pull(-over) *m* ras du cou.

crew[2] [kruː] **pret of crow**[2] **2a**.

crewel ['kruːɪl] **n** (*yarn*) laine *f* à tapisserie; (*work*) tapisserie *f* sur canevas.

crib [krɪb] 1 **n** a (*Brit: for infant*) berceau *m*; (*US: for toddler*) lit *m* d'enfant; (*Rel*) crèche *f*. b (*manger*) mangeoire *f*, râtelier *m*, crèche *f*. c (*plagiarism*) plagiat *m*, copiage *m*; (*Brit Scol*) anti-sèche* *f*. 2 **comp** ► **crib death** (*US*) mort subite du nourrisson. 3 **vt** (*Brit Scol*) copier, pomper*. **to ~ sb's work** copier le travail de qn, copier *or* pomper* sur qn. 4 **vi** copier. **to ~ from a friend** copier sur un camarade; **he had ~bed from Shakespeare** il avait plagié Shakespeare.

cribbage ['krɪbɪdʒ] **n** *sorte de jeu de cartes*.

crick [krɪk] 1 **n** crampe *f*. **~ in the neck** torticolis *m*; **~ in the back** tour *m* de reins. 2 **vt**: **to ~ one's neck** attraper un torticolis; **to ~ one's back** se faire un tour de reins.

cricket[1] ['krɪkɪt] **n** (*insect*) grillon *m*, cri-cri* *m inv*.

cricket[2] ['krɪkɪt] 1 **n** (*Sport*) cricket *m*. (*fig*) **that's not ~** cela ne se fait pas, ce n'est pas fair-play. 2 **comp** ► **cricket ball/bat/match/pitch** balle *f*/batte *f*/match *m*/terrain *m* de cricket.

cricketer ['krɪkɪtəʳ] **n** joueur *m* de cricket.

crier ['kraɪəʳ] **n** crieur *m*; *[law courts]* huissier *m*; *see* **town**.

crikey‡ ['kraɪkɪ] **excl** (*Brit*) mince (alors)!

crime [kraɪm] 1 **n** (*gen*) crime *m*; (*Mil*) manquement *m* à la discipline, infraction *f*. **minor ~** délit *m*; **~ and punishment** le crime et le châtiment; **a life of ~** une vie de criminel *or* de crime; **~ is on the increase/decrease** il y a un accroissement/une régression de la criminalité; **~ doesn't pay** le crime ne paye pas; **it's a ~ to make him do it*** c'est un crime de le forcer à le faire; *see* **organize d**.
2 **comp** ► **crime car** voiture de police banalisée ► **crime prevention** la lutte contre le crime; **crime prevention officer** policier chargé de la lutte contre le crime ► **Crime Squad** brigade criminelle ► **crime wave** vague *f* de criminalité ► **crime writer** auteur *m* de romans policiers.

Crimea [kraɪ'mɪə] **n**: **the ~** la Crimée.

Crimean [kraɪ'mɪən] **adj, n**: **the ~ (War)** la guerre de Crimée.

criminal ['krɪmɪnl] 1 **n** criminel *m*, -elle *f*.
2 **adj** *action, motive, law* criminel. (*fig*) **it's ~* to stay indoors today** c'est un crime de rester enfermé aujourd'hui; (*Jur*) **~ assault** agression criminelle, voie *f* de fait; (*US Jur*) **~ conversation** adultère *m* (*de la femme*); **~ investigation** enquête criminelle; (*Brit*) **the C~ Investigation Department** la police judiciaire, la P.J.; **~ law** droit pénal *or* criminel; **~ lawyer** pénaliste *m*, avocat *m* au criminel; **~ offence** délit *m*; **it's a ~ offence to do that** c'est un crime puni par la loi de faire cela; (*Jur*) **to take ~ proceedings against sb** poursuivre qn au pénal; **~ record** casier *m* judiciaire; **he hasn't got a ~ record** il a un casier judiciaire vierge; (*Brit*) **the C~ Records Office** l'identité *f* judiciaire; *see* **conspiracy**.

criminality [krɪmɪ'nælɪtɪ] **n** criminalité *f*.

criminalization [ˌkrɪmɪnəlaɪ'zeɪʃən] **n** criminalisation *f*.

criminalize ['krɪmɪnəlaɪz] **vt** criminaliser.

criminally ['krɪmɪnəlɪ] **adv** (*Jur*) **~ insane** fou (*f* folle) meurtrier (*f* -ière); (*Jur*) **~ negligent** ayant fait preuve de négligence criminelle.

criminologist [ˌkrɪmɪ'nɒlədʒɪst] **n** criminologiste *mf*.

criminology [ˌkrɪmɪ'nɒlədʒɪ] **n** criminologie *f*.

crimp [krɪmp] 1 **vt** a *hair* crêper, friser, frisotter; *pastry* pincer. **~ed** *fabric etc* plissé, froncé; *hair* ondulé. b (*US: hinder*) gêner, entraver.
2 **n** (*US*) (*person*) raseur *m*, -euse *f*. **to put a ~ in** mettre obstacle à, mettre des bâtons dans les roues de.

Crimplene ['krɪmpliːn] **n** ® ≃ crêpe *m* polyester.

crimson ['krɪmzn] **adj, n** cramoisi (*m*).

cringe [krɪndʒ] **vi** (*shrink back*) avoir un mouvement de recul, reculer (*from* devant); (*fig: humble o.s.*) ramper, s'humilier (*before* devant). (*fig*) **the very thought of it makes me ~*** rien qu'à y penser j'ai envie de rentrer sous terre.

cringing ['krɪndʒɪŋ] **adj** *movement* craintif, timide; *attitude, behaviour* servile, bas (*f* basse).

crinkle ['krɪŋkl] 1 **vt** *paper* froisser, chiffonner. 2 **vi** se froisser. **~d leaves** feuilles froissées. 3 **n** fronce *f*, pli *m*. (*Brit*) **~-cut** *chips, crisps* dentelé.

crinkly ['krɪŋklɪ] **adj** *paper* gaufré; *hair* crépu, crêpelé.

crinoline ['krɪnəlɪn] **n** crinoline *f*.

cripple ['krɪpl] 1 **n** (*lame*) estropié(e) *m(f)*, boiteux *m*, -euse *f*; (*disabled*) infirme *mf*, invalide *mf*; (*from accident, war*) invalide; (*maimed*) mutilé(e) *m(f)*. 2 **vt** a estropier. b (*fig*) *ship, plane* désemparer; (*Ind*) *[strikes etc] production, exports etc* paralyser. **activities ~d by lack of funds** activités paralysées par le manque de fonds.

crippled [krɪpld] **adj** *person* estropié, handicapé; (*fig*) *plane, vehicle* accidenté; (*after bomb etc*) *factory* gravement endommagé. **~ with**

rheumatism perclus de rhumatismes.

crippling ['krɪplɪŋ] adj *tax* écrasant. ~ **disease** *maladie qui laisse la personne très diminuée.*

crisis ['kraɪsɪs] 1 n, pl **crises** ['kraɪsi:z] crise *f*. **to come to a** ~, **to reach a** ~ atteindre un point critique; **to solve a** ~ dénouer *or* résoudre une crise; **we've got a** ~ **on our hands** nous avons un problème urgent, nous sommes dans une situation critique; **the first oil** ~ le premier choc pétrolier. 2 comp ▸ **crisis centre** *or* (*US*) **center** (*for large-scale disaster*) cellule *f* de crise; (*for personal help*) centre *m* d'aide; (*for battered women*) association *f* d'aide d'urgence ▸ **crisis management** gestion *f* de crise.

crisp [krɪsp] 1 adj *biscuit* croquant, croustillant; *vegetables* croquant; *bread* croustillant; *snow* craquant; *paper* raide, craquant; *linen* apprêté; *dress etc* pimpant; *weather* vif (*f* vive), piquant; *reply, style* vif, précis, tranchant (*pej*), brusque (*pej*); *tone, voice* acerbe, cassant (*pej*); *design* épuré, dépouillé. 2 n (*Brit*) **(potato)** ~**s** (pommes) chips *fpl*; **packet of** ~**s** sachet *m or* paquet *m* de chips. 3 comp ▸ **crispbread** pain *m* scandinave. 4 vt (*Culin: also* ~ **up**) faire réchauffer (*pour rendre croustillant*).

crisper ['krɪspəʳ] n (*salad* ~) bac *m* à légumes.

Crispin ['krɪspɪn] n Crépin *m*.

crisply ['krɪsplɪ] adv *say etc* d'un ton acerbe *or* cassant (*pej*).

crispness ['krɪspnɪs] n *[biscuit etc]* craquant *m*; *[style]* précision *f*, tranchant *m*; *[air, weather]* fraîcheur *f*, piquant *m*; *[design]* épurement *m*. **this biscuit has lost its** ~ ce gâteau n'est plus aussi craquant.

crispy ['krɪspɪ] adj croquant, croustillant. ~ **noodles** nouilles sautées; ~ **pancakes** crêpes croustillantes.

criss-cross ['krɪskrɒs] 1 adj *lines* entrecroisés; (*in muddle*) enchevêtré. **in a** ~ **pattern** en croisillons. 2 n entrecroisement *m*; enchevêtrement *m*. 3 vt entrecroiser (*by* de). 4 vi *[lines]* s'entrecroiser. 5 adv formant (un) réseau.

crit* [krɪt] n *[play, book etc]* papier* *m*, critique *f*.

criterion [kraɪ'tɪərɪən] n, pl ~**s** *or* **criteria** [kraɪ'tɪərɪə] critère *m*.

critic ['krɪtɪk] n *[books, painting, music, films etc]* critique *m*; (*faultfinder*) critique, censeur *m* (*frm*), détracteur *m*, -trice *f*. (*Press*) **film** ~ critique de cinéma; **he is a constant** ~ **of the government** il ne cesse de critiquer le gouvernement; **his wife is his most severe** ~ sa femme est son plus sévère critique.

critical ['krɪtɪkəl] adj a (*Pol etc*) critique, crucial; *situation* critique; (*Med*) *condition, stage of illness* critique. **at a** ~ **moment** à un moment critique *or* crucial; (*Aviat, Opt*) ~ **angle** angle *m* critique; ~ **mass** masse *f* critique; (*gen, Comput*) ~ **path** chemin *m* critique; ~ **path analysis** analyse *f* du chemin critique; ~ **path method** méthode *f* du chemin critique; ~ **temperature** température *f* critique.
b (*Art, Literat*) *writings, essay* critique, de critique; *analysis, edition* critique; (*from the critics*) *praise etc* de la critique, des critiques. ~ **work on Chaucer** travail *m or* travaux *mpl* critique(s) sur Chaucer.
c (*faultfinding*) *person, attitude, approach* sévère, critique. **to be** ~ **of** critiquer, trouver à redire à.

critically ['krɪtɪkəlɪ] adv a (*discriminatingly*) *judge, consider, discuss* en critique, d'un œil critique. b (*adversely*) *review, report* sévèrement. c ~ **ill** dangereusement *or* gravement malade; **the** ~ **ill** les grands malades.

criticism ['krɪtɪsɪzəm] n critique *f*.

criticize ['krɪtɪsaɪz] vt a (*assess*) *book etc* critiquer, faire la critique de. b (*find fault with*) *behaviour, person* critiquer, réprouver, censurer (*frm*). **I don't want to** ~, **but** ... je ne veux pas avoir l'air de critiquer, mais ... .

critique [krɪ'ti:k] n critique *f*.

critter* ['krɪtəʳ] n (*US*) créature *f*; (*animal*) bête *f*, bestiole *f*.

croak [krəʊk] 1 vi a *[frog]* coasser; *[raven]* croasser; *[person]* parler d'une voix rauque; (*: *grumble*) maugréer, ronchonner. b (*: *die*) claquer*, crever*. 2 vt dire avec une *or* d'une voix rauque *or* sourde. **"help" he** ~**ed feebly** "au secours" appela-t-il d'une voix rauque *or* sourde. 3 n *[frog]* coassement *m*; *[raven]* croassement *m*. **his voice was a mere** ~ il ne proférait que des sons rauques.

croaker* ['krəʊkəʳ] n (*US*) toubib* *m*.

Croat ['krəʊæt] n Croate *mf*.

Croatia [krəʊ'eɪʃɪə] n Croatie *f*.

Croatian [krəʊ'eɪʃɪən] adj croate.

crochet ['krəʊʃeɪ] 1 n (*NonC: also* ~ **work**) (travail *m* au) crochet *m*. ~ **hook** crochet. 2 vt *garment* faire au crochet. 3 vi faire du crochet.

crock [krɒk] n a (*pot*) cruche *f*, pot *m* de terre. (*broken pieces*) ~**s** débris *mpl* de faïence; **the** ~**s*** la vaisselle. b (*) (*horse*) vieille rosse, cheval fourbu; (*esp Brit: car etc*) guimbarde *f*, vieille bagnole*, vieux clou*. **he's an old** ~ c'est un croulant*.

crockery ['krɒkərɪ] n (*NonC*) (*earthenware*) poterie *f*, faïence *f*; (*cups, saucers, plates*) vaisselle *f*.

crocodile ['krɒkədaɪl] 1 n a crocodile *m*. ~ **tears** larmes *fpl* de crocodile. b (*Brit Scol*) cortège *m* en rangs (par deux). **to walk in a** ~ aller deux par deux. 2 comp *shoes, handbag* en crocodile, en croco* ▸ **crocodile clip** pince *f* crocodile.

crocus ['krəʊkəs] n, pl ~**es** crocus *m*.

Croesus ['kri:səs] n Crésus *m*. **as rich as** ~ riche comme Crésus.

croft [krɒft] n (*Brit*) petite ferme.

crofter ['krɒftəʳ] n (*Brit*) petit fermier.

Cromwellian [krɒm'welɪən] adj de Cromwell.

crone [krəʊn] n vieille ratatinée*, vieille bique.

crony* ['krəʊnɪ] n copain* *m*, copine* *f*.

crook [krʊk] 1 n a *[shepherd]* houlette *f*; *[bishop]* crosse *f*; (*Mus*) *[brass instrument]* ton *m* de rechange. b *[road]* angle *m*; *[river]* angle, coude *m*, détour *m*. c (*: *thief*) escroc *m*, filou *m*. 2 vt *one's finger* courber, recourber; *one's arm* plier.

crooked ['krʊkɪd] 1 adj a *stick* courbé, crochu, tordu. **a** ~ **old man** un vieillard tout courbé; **a** ~ **path** un sentier tortueux; **she gave a** ~ **smile** elle a fait un pauvre sourire *or* un sourire contraint; **the picture is** ~ le tableau est de travers. b (*fig*) *person, action, method* malhonnête. 2 adv (*) de travers, de traviole*.

crookedness ['krʊkɪdnɪs] n (*lit*) courbure *f*; (*fig*) malhonnêteté *f*, fausseté *f*.

croon [kru:n] vti (*sing softly*) chantonner, fredonner; (*in show business*) chanter (*en crooner*).

crooner ['kru:nəʳ] n chanteur *m*, -euse *f* de charme.

crooning ['kru:nɪŋ] n (*NonC*) la chanson de charme.

crop [krɒp] 1 n a (*produce*) produit *m* agricole, culture *f*; (*amount produced*) récolte *f*, (*of fruit etc*) récolte, cueillette *f*, (*of cereals*) moisson *f*; (*fig: of problems, questions*) série *f*, quantité *f*, tas* *m*. (*at harvest time*) **the** ~**s** la récolte; **one of the basic** ~**s** l'une des cultures de base; **we had a good** ~ **of strawberries** la récolte *or* la cueillette des fraises a été bonne; **to get the** ~**s in** faire la récolte *or* la cueillette *or* la moisson, rentrer les récoltes *or* la moisson.
b *[bird]* jabot *m*.
c *[whip]* manche *m*; (*also* **riding** ~) cravache *f*.
d (*Hairdressing*) **to give sb a (close)** ~ couper ras les cheveux de qn; **Eton** ~ cheveux *mpl* à la garçonne.
2 comp ▸ **crop dusting** = **crop spraying** ▸ **crop rotation** rotation *f* des cultures ▸ **crop sprayer** (*device*) pulvérisateur *m*; (*plane*) avion-pulvérisateur *m* ▸ **crop spraying** pulvérisation *f* des cultures.
3 vt a *[animals]* *grass* brouter, paître.
b *tail* écourter; *hair* tondre. ~**ped hair** cheveux coupés ras.
c (*Phot*) recadrer.
4 vi *[land]* donner *or* fournir une récolte.
▸**crop out** vi (*Geol*) affleurer.
▸**crop up** vi a *[questions, problems]* surgir, survenir, se présenter. **the subject cropped up during the conversation** le sujet a été amené *or* mis sur le tapis au cours de la conversation; **something's cropped up and I can't come** il s'est passé *or* il est survenu quelque chose qui m'empêche de venir; **he was ready for anything that might crop up** il était prêt à toute éventualité. b (*Geol*) affleurer.

cropper* ['krɒpəʳ] n (*lit, fig*) **to come a** ~ (*fall*) se casser la figure*; (*fail in attempt*) se planter*; (*in exam*) se faire coller* *or* étendre.

cropping ['krɒpɪŋ] n (*Phot*) recadrage *m*.

croquet ['krəʊkeɪ] 1 n croquet *m*. 2 comp ▸ **croquet hoop/mallet** arceau *m*/maillet *m* de croquet.

croquette [krəʊ'ket] n croquette *f*. **potato** ~ croquette de pommes de terre.

crosier ['krəʊʒəʳ] n crosse *f* (*d'évêque*).

cross [krɒs] 1 n a (*mark, emblem*) croix *f*. **to mark/sign with a** ~ marquer/signer d'une croix; **the iron** ~ la croix de fer; (*Rel*) **the C**~ la Croix; (*fig*) **it is a** ~ **he has to bear** c'est sa croix, c'est la croix qu'il lui faut porter; **we each have our** ~ **to bear** chacun a *or* porte sa croix; *see* **market, red, sign** *etc*.
b (*Bio, Zool*) hybride *m*. ~ **between two different breeds** mélange *m or* croisement *m* de deux races différentes, hybride; (*fig*) **it's a** ~ **between a novel and a poem** cela tient du roman et du poème.
c (*NonC*) *[material]* biais *m*. (*Sewing*) **to cut material on the** ~ couper du tissu dans le biais; **a skirt cut on the** ~ une jupe en biais; **line drawn on the** ~ ligne tracée en biais *or* en diagonale.
2 adj a (*angry*) *person* de mauvaise humeur, en colère. **to be** ~ **with sb** être fâché *or* en colère contre qn; **it makes me** ~ **when** ... cela m'agace quand ...; **to get** ~ **with sb** se mettre en colère *or* se fâcher contre qn; **don't be** ~ **with me** ne m'en veuillez *or* voulez* pas; **they haven't had a** ~ **word in 10 years** ils ne se sont pas disputés une seule fois en 10 ans.
b (*traverse, diagonal*) transversal, diagonal.
3 comp ▸ **crossbar** (*Rugby etc*) barre transversale; *[bicycle]* barre ▸ **crossbeam** traverse *f*, sommier *m* ▸ **crossbencher** (*Parl*) député non inscrit ▸ **crossbill** (*Orn*) bec-croisé *m* ▸ **crossbones** *see* **skull** ▸ **crossbow** arbalète *f*; **crossbow archery** tir *m* à l'arbalète ▸ **crossbred** métis (*f* -isse) ▸ **crossbreed** n (*animal*) hybride *m*, métis(se) *m(f)*; (* *pej: person*) sang-mêlé *mf inv* ◊ vt (pret, ptp **crossbred**) croiser, métisser ▸ **cross-Channel ferry** ferry *m* qui traverse la Manche ▸ **cross-check** n contre-épreuve *f*, recoupement *m* ◊ vt *facts* vérifier par contre-épreuve, faire se recouper ◊ vi vérifier par recoupement ▸ **cross-compiler** (*Comput*) compilateur croisé ▸ **cross-country** adj à travers champs; **cross-country race** *or* **running** cross(-country) *m*; **cross-country skier** skieur *m* de randonnée; **cross-country skiing** ski *m* de randonnée ▸ **cross court drive** (*Tennis*) coup

droit croisé ▸ **cross-cultural** multiculturel ▸ **cross-current** contre-courant *m* ▸ **cross-curricular** *approach etc* pluridisciplinaire ▸ **cross-cut chisel** bédane *m* ▸ **cross-disciplinary** interdisciplinaire ▸ **cross-dresser** travesti(e) *m(f)* ▸ **cross-dressing** (*transvestism*) travestisme ▸ **cross-examination** (*esp Jur*) contre-interrogatoire *m* ▸ **cross-examine** (*Jur*) faire subir un contre-interrogatoire à; (*gen*) interroger *or* questionner (de façon serrée) ▸ **cross-eyed** qui louche, bigleux*; **to be cross-eyed** loucher, avoir un œil qui dit zut* *or* merde‡ à l'autre ▸ **cross-fertilize** (*Bot*) *species* croiser avec une autre; *plants* faire un croisement de ▸ **crossfire** (*Mil*) feux croisés; (*Mil*) **exposed to crossfire** pris entre deux feux; (*fig*) **caught in a crossfire of questions** pris dans un feu roulant de questions ▸ **cross-grained** *wood* à fibres irrégulières; *person* aigre, acariâtre, atrabilaire ▸ **crosshatch** hachurer en croisillons ▸ **crosshatching** hachures croisées ▸ **cross-legged** en tailleur ▸ **cross-match** *blood* tester pour contrôler la compatibilité ▸ **crossover** n *[roads]* (croisement *m* par) pont routier; (*Rail*) voie *f* de croisement; (*Dress*) **crossover bodice** corsage croisé ▸ **crosspatch*** grincheux *m*, -euse *f*, grognon(ne) *m(f)* ▸ **crosspiece** traverse *f* ▸ **cross-ply** adj (*Aut*) à carcasse diagonale ▸ **cross-pollination** pollinisation croisée ▸ **cross-purposes: to be at cross-purposes with sb** (*misunderstand*) comprendre qn de travers; (*disagree*) être en désaccord avec qn; **I think we are at cross-purposes** je crois qu'il y a malentendu, nous nous sommes mal compris; **we were talking at cross-purposes** notre conversation tournait autour d'un quiproquo ▸ **cross-question** faire subir un interrogatoire à ▸ **cross-refer** renvoyer (*to* à) ▸ **cross-reference** n renvoi *m*, référence *f* (*to* à) ◊ vt renvoyer ▸ **crossroads** (*Brit*) (*lit*) croisement *m*, carrefour *m*; (*fig*) carrefour ▸ **cross section** (*Bio etc*) coupe transversale; *[population etc]* échantillon *m* ▸ **cross-stitch** n point *m* de croix ◊ vt coudre *or* broder au point de croix ▸ **cross swell** houle traversière ▸ **crosstalk** (*Rad, Telec*) diaphonie *f*; (*Brit: conversation*) joutes *fpl* oratoires ▸ **crosstie** (*esp US*) traverse *f* (de voie ferrée) ▸ **cross volley** (*Tennis*) volée croisée ▸ **cross-vote** vi (*Pol*) voter contre son parti ▸ **crosswalk** (*US*) passage clouté ▸ **crossway** (*US*) croisement *m* ▸ **crosswind** vent *m* de travers ▸ **crosswise** (*in shape of cross*) en croix; (*across*) en travers; (*diagonally*) en diagonale; en travers; en croix ▸ **crossword (puzzle)** mots croisés.

4 vt a *room, street, sea, continent* traverser; *river, bridge* traverser, passer; *threshold, fence, ditch* franchir. **the bridge ~es the river here** c'est ici que le pont franchit *or* enjambe la rivière; **it ~ed my mind that** ... il m'est venu à l'esprit que ..., l'idée m'est venue (à l'esprit) que ...; (*Prov*) **don't ~ your bridges before you come to them** chaque chose en son temps (*Prov*); (*fig*) **let's ~ that bridge when we come to it** on s'occupera de ce problème-là en temps et lieu; (*Ind*) **to ~ the picket lines** traverser un piquet de grève; (*fig*) **to ~ sb's path** se trouver sur le chemin de qn; (*Parl*) **to ~ the floor (of the House)** ≃ s'inscrire à un parti opposé.

b (*Rel*) **to ~ o.s.** se signer, faire le signe de (la) croix; (*fig*) **~ my heart (and hope to die)!*** croix de bois croix de fer (si je mens je vais en enfer)!*; **to ~ a "t"** barrer un "t"; (*Brit*) **to ~ a cheque** barrer un chèque; **to ~ sb's palm with silver** donner la pièce à qn.

c **to ~ one's arms/legs** croiser les bras/les jambes; (*lit, fig*) **to ~ swords with sb** croiser le fer avec qn; (*fig*) **to ~ one's fingers*** faire une petite prière (*fig*); (*fig*) **keep your fingers ~ed for me*** fais une petite prière pour moi(, ça me portera bonheur); (*Brit Telec*) **the lines are ~ed, we've got a ~ed line** les lignes sont embrouillées; (*fig*) **they've got their lines ~ed*** il y a un malentendu quelque part.

d (*thwart*) *person* contrarier, contrecarrer; *plans* contrecarrer. **~ed in love** malheureux en amour.

e *animals, plants* croiser (*with* avec). **to ~ two animals/plants** croiser *or* métisser deux animaux/plantes.

5 vi a (*also* **~ over**) **he ~ed from one side of the room to the other to speak to me** il a traversé la pièce pour venir me parler; **to ~ from one place to another** passer d'un endroit à un autre; **to ~ from Newhaven to Dieppe** faire la traversée de Newhaven à Dieppe.

b *[roads, paths]* se croiser, se rencontrer; *[letters, people]* se croiser.

▸**cross off** vt sep *item on list* barrer, rayer, biffer; *person* radier (*from* de). **to cross sb off a list** radier qn d'une liste.

▸**cross out** vt sep *word* barrer, rayer, biffer.

▸**cross over** 1 vi traverser; *see also* **cross 5a**. 2 **crossover** n, adj *see* **cross 3**.

crosse [krɒs] n crosse *f* (*au jeu de lacrosse*).

crossing ['krɒsɪŋ] n a (*esp by sea*) traversée *f*. **the ~ of the line** le passage de l'équateur *or* de la ligne. b (*road junction*) croisement *m*, carrefour *m*; (*also* **pedestrian ~**) passage clouté; (*Rail: also* **level ~**) passage à niveau. (*Brit*) (**school**) **~ patrol**, (*US*) **~ guard** contractuel *m*, -elle *f* (*chargé(e) de faire traverser la rue aux enfants*); (*on road*) **cross at the ~** traversez sur le passage clouté *or* dans les clous*; *see* **zebra**.

crossly ['krɒslɪ] adv avec (mauvaise) humeur.

crotch [krɒtʃ] n *[body, tree]* fourche *f*; *[garment]* entre-jambes *m inv*. **a kick in the ~** un coup de pied entre les jambes.

crotchet ['krɒtʃɪt] n (*Brit Mus*) noire *f*.

crotchety ['krɒtʃɪtɪ] adj grognon, grincheux.

crouch [kraʊtʃ] 1 vi (*also* **~ down**) *[person, animal]* s'accroupir, se tapir; (*before springing*) se ramasser. 2 n accroupissement *m*; action *f* de se ramasser.

croup[1] [kru:p] n (*Med*) croup *m*.

croup[2] [kru:p] n *[horse]* croupe *f*.

croupier ['kru:pɪeɪ] n croupier *m*.

crow[1] [krəʊ] 1 n (*Orn*) corneille *f*; (*generic term*) corbeau *m*. **as the ~ flies** à vol d'oiseau, en ligne droite; (*US*) **to make sb eat ~*** faire rentrer les paroles dans la gorge à qn; (*US*) **to eat ~*** faire des excuses humiliantes; *see* **carrion** *etc*. 2 comp ▸ **crowbar** (pince *f* à) levier *m* ▸ **crowfoot** (pl **~s**) (*Bot*) renoncule *f*; (*Naut*) araignée *f*; (*Mil*) chausse-trappe *f* ▸ **Crow Jim**‡ racisme *m* contre les Blancs, racisme inversé ▸ **crow's feet** pattes *fpl* d'oie (*rides*) ▸ **crow's-nest** (*Naut*) nid *m* de pie.

crow[2] [krəʊ] 1 n *[cock]* chant *m* du coq, cocorico *m*; *[baby]* gazouillis *m*; (*fig*) cri *m* de triomphe. 2 vi a pret **crowed** *or* **crew**, ptp **crowed** *[cock]* chanter. b pret, ptp **crowed** *[baby]* gazouiller; *[victor]* chanter victoire. **he ~ed with delight** il poussait des cris de joie; **it's nothing to ~ about** il n'y a pas de quoi pavoiser.

▸**crow over** vt fus *person* se vanter d'avoir triomphé de, chanter sa victoire sur.

crowd [kraʊd] 1 n a foule *f*, multitude *f*, masse *f*; (*disorderly*) cohue *f*. **in ~s** en foule, en masse; **to get lost in the ~** se perdre dans la foule; **a large ~** *or* **large ~s had gathered** une foule immense s'était assemblée; **there was quite a ~** il y avait beaucoup de monde, il y avait foule; **how big was the ~?** est-ce qu'il y avait beaucoup de monde?; **there was quite a ~ at the concert** il y avait une bonne salle au concert; (*Cine, Theat: actors*) **the ~** les figurants *mpl*; (*fig*) **that would pass in a ~*** ça peut passer si on n'y regarde pas de trop près, en courant vite on n'y verrait que du feu*; **there were ~s of** *or* **there was a whole ~ of books/people** il y avait des masses* de livres/de gens.

b (*NonC: people in general*) **the ~** la foule, la masse du peuple; **to follow** *or* **go with the ~** suivre la foule *or* le mouvement.

c (**: group, circle*) bande *f*, clique *f*. **I don't like that ~ at all** je n'aime pas du tout cette bande; **he's one of our ~** il fait partie de notre groupe *or* bande.

2 comp ▸ **crowd-puller*** grosse attraction; **to be a real crowd-puller** attirer les foules ▸ **crowd scene** (*Cine, Theat*) scène *f* de foule.

3 vi: **they ~ed into the small room** ils se sont entassés dans la petite pièce; **don't all ~ together** ne vous serrez donc pas comme ça; **to ~ through the gates** passer en foule par le portail; **they ~ed round to see** ... ils ont fait cercle *or* se sont attroupés pour voir ...; **they ~ed round him** ils se pressaient autour de lui; **they ~ed (up) against him** ils l'ont bousculé; **to ~ down/in/up** *etc* descendre/entrer/monter *etc* en foule.

4 vt (*push*) *objects* entasser (*into* dans); (*jostle*) *person* bousculer; *car* serrer. **pedestrians ~ed the streets** les piétons se pressaient dans les rues; **he was ~ed off the pavement** la cohue l'a forcé à descendre du trottoir; **don't ~ me** ne poussez pas, arrêtez de me bousculer; **the houses are ~ed together** les maisons sont les unes sur les autres; **a room ~ed with children** une pièce pleine d'enfants; **house ~ed with furniture** maison encombrée de meubles; **a house ~ed with guests** une maison pleine d'invités; **a week ~ed with incidents** une semaine riche en incidents; **memory ~ed with facts** mémoire bourrée de faits; (*Naut*) **to ~ on sail** mettre toutes voiles dehors; *see* **crowded**.

▸**crowd out** vt sep: **we shall be crowded out** la cohue nous empêchera d'entrer; **this article was crowded out of yesterday's edition** cet article n'a pas pu être inséré dans l'édition d'hier faute de place; **he's really crowding me out*** il me colle aux fesses‡.

crowded ['kraʊdɪd] adj *room, hall, train, café* bondé, plein; *bus* bondé, plein à craquer; *town* encombré (de monde); *streets* plein (de monde). **the streets are ~** il y a foule dans les rues; **the shops are too ~ for my liking** il y a trop d'affluence *or* de monde pour mon goût dans les magasins; (*Theat*) **~ house** salle *f* comble; **a ~ day** une journée chargée; **it is a very ~ profession** c'est une profession très encombrée *or* bouchée.

crowing ['krəʊɪŋ] n *[cockerel]* chant *m* du coq, cocorico *m*; (*fig: boasting*) vantardise *f*.

crown [kraʊn] 1 n a couronne *f*; (*fig*) couronne, pouvoir royal, monarchie *f*. **~ of roses/thorns** couronne de roses/d'épines; (*fig*) **to wear the ~** régner, porter la couronne; **to succeed to the ~** monter sur le trône; (*Jur*) **the C~** la Couronne, ≃ le ministère public; **the law officers of the C~** les conseillers *mpl* juridiques de la Couronne.

b (*money*) couronne *f* (*ancienne pièce de la valeur de cinq shillings*).

c *[head]* sommet *m* de la tête; *[hat]* fond *m*; *[road]* milieu *m*; *[roof]* faîte *m*; *[arch]* clef *f* (*d'une voûte*); *[tooth]* couronne *f*; *[anchor]* diamant *m*; *[hill]* sommet, faîte; *[tree]* cime *f*; (*size of paper*) couronne (*format 0,37 sur 0,47 cm*); (*fig: climax, completion*) couronnement *m*.

2 vt couronner (*with* de); *[draughts]* damer; *tooth* couronner; (**: hit*) flanquer* un coup sur la tête à. **he was ~ed king** il fut couronné roi; (*fig*) **all the ~ed heads of Europe** toutes les têtes couronnées d'Europe; **work ~ed with success** travail couronné de succès; **the hill is ~ed with trees** la colline est couronnée d'arbres; (*fig*) **to ~ it all* it**

began to snow pour comble (de malheur) *or* pour couronner le tout il s'est mis à neiger; **that ~s it all!*** il ne manquait plus que ça!
3 comp ▸ **Crown** (*Brit Jur*) *witness, evidence etc* à charge ▸ **crown colony** (*Brit*) colonie *f* de la couronne ▸ **Crown court** (*Jur*) ≃ Cour *f* d'assises (*en Angleterre et au Pays de Galles*) ▸ **crown estate** domaine *m* de la couronne ▸ **crown jewels** joyaux *mpl* de la couronne ▸ **crown lands** terres domaniales ▸ **crown law** droit pénal ▸ **crown prince** prince *m* héritier ▸ **crown princess** (*heiress*) princesse *f* héritière ▸ **Crown Prosecution Service** (*Brit*) ≃ Ministère *m* public (*décide si les affaires doivent être portées devant les tribunaux*) ▸ **crown wheel** (*Brit Aut*) grande couronne; **crown wheel and pinion** couple *m* conique.

crowning ['kraʊnɪŋ] 1 n (*ceremony*) couronnement *m*. 2 adj *achievement, moment* suprême. **his ~ glory** son plus grand triomphe.

crucial ['kru:ʃəl] adj critique, crucial, décisif; (*Med*) crucial.

crucible ['kru:sɪbl] n creuset *m*; (*fig: test*) (dure) épreuve *f*.

crucifix ['kru:sɪfɪks] n crucifix *m*, christ *m*; *[roadside]* calvaire *m*.

crucifixion [ˌkru:sɪ'fɪkʃən] n crucifiement *m*. (*Rel*) **the C~** la crucifixion, la mise en croix.

cruciform ['kru:sɪfɔ:m] adj cruciforme.

crucify ['kru:sɪfaɪ] vt (*lit*) crucifier, mettre en croix; (*fig*) crucifier, mettre au pilori. (*Rel*) **to ~ the flesh** mortifier la chair.

crud [krʌd] n a (‡) (*filth*) saloperies‡ *fpl*, saletés *fpl*; (*person*) salaud‡ *m*, ordure‡ *f*. (*illness*) **the ~** la crève‡. b (*residue*) résidu *m*.

cruddy‡ ['krʌdɪ] adj dégueulasse‡.

crude [kru:d] 1 adj *materials* brut; *sugar* non raffiné; *drawing* rudimentaire, qui manque de fini; *piece of work* à peine ébauché, mal fini, sommaire; *object, tool* grossier, rudimentaire; *light, colour* cru, vif; *person, behaviour* grossier; *manners* fruste, de rustre. **~ oil** (pétrole *m*) brut *m*; **he managed to make a ~ hammer** il a réussi à fabriquer un marteau rudimentaire; **he made a ~ attempt at building a shelter** il a essayé tant bien que mal de construire un abri; **a ~ expression** *or* **word** une grossièreté. 2 n (*also* **~ oil**) brut *m*; *see* **heavy**.

crudely ['kru:dlɪ] adv (*make, fashion*) imparfaitement, sommairement; (*say, order, explain*) crûment, grossièrement, brutalement, sans ménagements. **to put it ~ I think he's mad** pour dire les choses crûment je pense qu'il est fou.

crudeness ['kru:dnɪs] n, **crudity** ['kru:dɪtɪ] n (*see* **crude**) état brut; grossièreté *f*; manque *m* de fini, caractère *m* rudimentaire.

cruel ['krʊəl] adj cruel (*to* envers).

cruelly ['krʊəlɪ] adv cruellement.

cruelty ['krʊəltɪ] 1 n a cruauté *f* (*to* envers); *see* **prevention**. b (*Jur*) sévices *mpl*. **prosecuted for ~ to his wife** poursuivi pour sévices sur sa femme; **divorce on the grounds of ~** divorce *m* pour sévices; **mental ~** cruauté mentale. 2 comp ▸ **cruelty-free** non testé sur les animaux.

cruet ['kru:ɪt] n a (*Brit: also* **~ set, ~ stand**) service *m* à condiments, garniture *f* de table (pour condiments). b (*US: small bottle*) petit flacon (*pour l'huile ou le vinaigre*). c (*Rel*) burette *f*.

cruise [kru:z] 1 vi a *[fleet, ship]* croiser. **they are cruising in the Pacific** (*Naut*) ils croisent dans le Pacifique; *[tourists]* ils sont en croisière dans le Pacifique; **cruising yacht** yacht *m* de croisière. b *[cars]* rouler; *[aircraft]* voler. **the car was cruising (along) at 80 km/h** la voiture faisait 80 km/h sans effort; **we were cruising along the road when suddenly ...** nous roulions tranquillement quand tout à coup ...; (*Aut, Aviat*) **cruising speed** vitesse *f or* régime *m* de croisière; (*Aviat*) **cruising range** autonomie *f* de vol. c *[taxi, patrol car]* marauder, faire la maraude. **a cruising taxi** un taxi en maraude. d (* *US: looking for pick-up*) draguer‡ en voiture. 2 n a (*Naut*) croisière *f*. **to go on** *or* **for a ~** partir en croisière, faire une croisière. b (*also* **~ missile**) missile *m* de croisière. **a campaign against ~** une campagne contre les missiles de croisière. c (*Aut*) **~ control** cruise control *m* (de vitesse).

cruiser ['kru:zəʳ] n (*warship*) croiseur *m*; (*cabin* **~**) yacht *m* de croisière. (*Boxing*) **~ weight** poids *m* mi-lourd; *see* **battle** *etc*.

cruller ['krʌləʳ] n (*US*) beignet *m*.

crumb [krʌm] n miette *f*; (*NonC: inside of loaf*) mie *f*; (*fig*) miette, brin *m*; *[information]* miettes, fragments *mpl*. **a ~ of comfort** un brin de réconfort; **~s!*** ça alors!, zut!*; **he's a ~*** c'est un pauvre type*; *see* **bread**.

crumble ['krʌmbl] 1 vt *bread* émietter; *plaster* effriter; *earth, rocks* (faire s')ébouler. 2 vi *[bread]* s'émietter; *[buildings etc]* tomber en ruines, se désagréger; *[plaster]* s'effriter; *[earth, rocks]* s'ébouler; (*fig*) *[hopes etc]* s'effondrer, s'écrouler. 3 n (*Brit Culin*) crumble *m*.

crumbly ['krʌmblɪ] adj friable.

crumby‡, crummy‡ ['krʌmɪ] adj minable*. **what a ~ thing to do!** c'est un coup minable!*, c'est vraiment mesquin de faire ça!

crump [krʌmp] n éclatement *m* (*d'un obus*); (*Mil sl: shell*) obus *m*.

crumpet ['krʌmpɪt] n (*Culin*) petite crêpe épaisse (*servie chaude et beurrée*). (*Brit fig*) **a bit of ~‡** une belle nana*.

crumple ['krʌmpl] 1 vt froisser, friper; (*also* **~ up**) chiffonner. **he ~d the paper (up) into a ball** il a fait une boule de la feuille de papier. 2 vi se froisser, se chiffonner, se friper. (*fig*) **her features ~d when she heard the bad news** son visage s'est décomposé quand elle a appris la mauvaise nouvelle.

crunch [krʌntʃ] 1 vt a (*with teeth*) croquer. **to ~ an apple/a biscuit** croquer une pomme/un biscuit. b (*underfoot*) écraser, faire craquer. 2 vi: **he ~ed across the gravel** il a traversé en faisant craquer le gravier sous ses pas. 3 n (*sound of teeth*) coup *m* de dents; (*of broken glass, gravel etc*) craquement *m*, crissement *m*. (*fig: moment of reckoning*) **the ~*** l'instant *m* critique; **here's the ~*** c'est le moment crucial; **when it comes to the ~* he ...** dans une situation critique *or* au moment crucial, il ... .

▸**crunch up** vt sep broyer.

crunchy ['krʌntʃɪ] adj croquant.

crupper ['krʌpəʳ] n *[harness]* croupière *f*; (*hindquarters*) croupe *f* (*de cheval*).

crusade [kru:'seɪd] 1 n (*Hist: also fig*) croisade *f*. 2 vi (*fig*) faire une croisade (*against* contre, *for* pour); (*Hist*) partir en croisade, être à la croisade.

crusader [kru:'seɪdəʳ] n (*Hist*) croisé *m*; (*fig*) champion *m* (*for* de, *against* en guerre contre), militant(e) *m(f)* (*for* en faveur de, *against* en guerre contre). **the ~s for peace/against the bomb** ceux qui militent pour la paix/contre la bombe.

crush [krʌʃ] 1 n a (*crowd*) foule *f*, cohue *f*. **there was a great ~ to get in** c'était la bousculade pour entrer; **there was a terrible ~ at the concert** il y avait une vraie cohue au concert; **he was lost in the ~** il était perdu dans la foule *or* la cohue.
b **to have a ~ on sb*** avoir le béguin* pour qn.
c (*Brit: drink*) jus *m* de fruit. **orange ~** orange pressée.
2 comp ▸ **crush bar** *[theatre]* bar *m* du foyer ▸ **crush barrier** (*Brit*) barrière *f* de sécurité ▸ **crush-resistant** infroissable.
3 vt a (*compress*) *stones, old cars* écraser, broyer; *ice* piler; *grapes* écraser, presser; *ore* bocarder. **to ~ to a pulp** réduire en pulpe.
b (*crumple*) *clothes* froisser. **~ed velvet** panne *f* de velours; **to ~ clothes into a bag** fourrer *or* bourrer des vêtements dans une valise; **to ~ objects into a suitcase** tasser *or* entasser des objets dans une valise; **we were very ~ed in the car** nous étions très tassés dans la voiture.
c (*overwhelm*) *enemy* écraser, accabler; *opponent in argument, country* écraser; *revolution* écraser, réprimer; *hope* détruire; (*snub*) remettre à sa place, rabrouer.
4 vi a s'écraser, se presser, se serrer. **they ~ed round him** ils se pressaient autour de lui; **they ~ed into the car** ils se sont entassés *or* tassés dans la voiture; **to ~ (one's way) into/through** *etc* se frayer un chemin dans/à travers *etc*.
b *[clothes]* se froisser.

▸**crush out** vt sep *juice etc* presser, exprimer; *cigarette end* écraser, éteindre; (*fig*) *revolt* écraser, réprimer.

crushing ['krʌʃɪŋ] adj *defeat* écrasant; *reply* percutant.

crust [krʌst] 1 n (*on bread, pie, snow*) croûte *f*; (*piece of* **~**) croûton *m*, croûte; (*Med: on wound, sore*) croûte, escarre *f*; *[wine]* dépôt *m* (*de tanin*). **there were only a few ~s to eat** pour toute nourriture il n'y avait que quelques croûtes de pain; **a thin ~ of ice** une fine couche de glace; (*Geol*) **the earth's ~** la croûte terrestre; *see* **earn, upper**. 2 vt: **frost ~ing the windscreen** le givre recouvrant le pare-brise; **~ed snow** neige croûtée; **~ed with mud** *etc* couvert d'une croûte de boue *etc*.

crustacean [krʌs'teɪʃən] adj, n crustacé *(m)*.

crusty ['krʌstɪ] adj *loaf* croustillant; (* *fig: irritable*) hargneux, bourru.

crutch [krʌtʃ] n a (*support*) soutien *m*, support *m*; (*Med*) béquille *f*; (*Archit*) étançon *m*; (*Naut*) support (de gui). **he gets about on ~es** il marche avec des béquilles; (*fig*) **alcohol is a ~ for him** l'alcool lui sert de soutien. b (*Anat: crotch*) fourche *f*; *[trousers etc]* entre-jambes *m inv*.

crux [krʌks] n, pl **~es** *or* **cruces** ['kru:si:z] a point crucial; *[problem]* cœur *m*, centre *m*. **the ~ of the matter** le nœud de l'affaire, le point capital dans l'affaire. b (*Climbing*) passage-clef *m*.

cry [kraɪ] 1 n a (*loud shout: also of sellers, paperboys etc*) cri *m*; *[hounds]* aboiements *mpl*, voix *f*. **to give a ~** pousser un cri; **he gave a ~ for help** il a crié *or* appelé au secours; **he heard a ~ for help** il a entendu crier au secours; **the cries of the victims** les cris des victimes; (*fig*) **there was a great ~ against the rise in prices** la hausse des prix a soulevé un tollé; *see* **far, full**.
b (*watchword*) slogan *m*. **"votes for women" was their ~** leur slogan était "le vote pour les femmes"; *see* **battle, war**.
c (*weep*) **she had a good ~*** elle a pleuré un bon coup*.
2 comp ▸ **crybaby** pleurnicheur *m*, -euse *f*.
3 vt a (*shout out*) crier. **"here I am" he cried** "me voici" s'écria-t-il *or* cria-t-il; **"go away" he cried to me** "allez-vous-en" me cria-t-il; **to ~ mercy** crier grâce; **to ~ shame** crier au scandale; **to ~ shame on sb/sth** crier haro sur qn/qch; (*fig*) **to ~ wolf** crier au loup; *see* **quits**.
b **to ~ o.s. to sleep** s'endormir à force de pleurer; **to ~ one's eyes** *or* **one's heart out** pleurer toutes les larmes de son corps.
4 vi a (*weep*) pleurer (*about, for, over* sur). **to ~ with rage** pleurer de rage; **to laugh till one cries** pleurer de rire, rire aux larmes; **to ~ for sth** pleurer pour avoir qch; (*fig*) **I'll give him sth to ~ for!*** je vais lui apprendre à pleurnicher!; (*Prov*) **it's no use ~ing over spilt milk** ce qui est fait est fait; *see* **shoulder**.
b (*call out*) *[person, animal, bird]* pousser un cri *or* des cris. **the baby cried at birth** l'enfant a poussé un cri *or* a crié en naissant; **he**

cried (out) with pain il a poussé un cri de douleur; **to ~ for help** appeler à l'aide, crier au secours; **to ~ for mercy** demander miséricorde, implorer la pitié; **the starving crowd cried for bread** la foule affamée réclama du pain; *see* **moon**.

c *[hunting dogs]* donner de la voix, aboyer.

▶**cry down*** vt sep (*decry*) décrier.

▶**cry off** 1 vi (*from meeting*) se décommander; (*from promise*) se dédire, se rétracter. **I'm crying off!** je ne veux plus rien savoir! 2 vt fus (*cancel*) *arrangement, deal* annuler; (*withdraw from*) *project* ne plus se mêler à, se retirer de, se désintéresser de; *meeting* décommander.

▶**cry out** vi (*inadvertently*) pousser un cri; (*deliberately*) s'écrier. **he cried out with joy** il a poussé un cri de joie; **to cry out to sb** appeler qn à haute voix, crier pour appeler qn; **to cry out for sth** demander *or* réclamer qch à grands cris; **for crying out loud!*** pour l'amour de Dieu!; (*fig*) **that floor is just crying out to be washed*** ce plancher a grandement besoin d'être lavé; (*fig*) **the door is crying out for a coat of paint*** la porte a bien besoin d'une couche de peinture.

▶**cry out against** vt fus protester contre.

▶**cry up*** vt sep (*praise*) vanter, exalter. **he's not all he's cried up to be** il n'est pas à la hauteur de sa réputation, il n'est pas aussi formidable* qu'on le dit.

crying [ˈkraɪɪŋ] 1 adj (*lit*) pleurant, qui pleure; (*fig*) criant, flagrant. **~ injustice** injustice criante *or* flagrante; **~ need for sth** besoin pressant *or* urgent de qch; **it's a ~ shame** c'est une honte, c'est honteux. 2 n (*shouts*) cris *mpl*; (*weeping*) larmes *fpl*, pleurs *mpl*.

cryobiology [ˌkraɪəʊbaɪˈɒlədʒɪ] n cryobiologie *f*.

cryogenics [ˌkraɪəˈdʒenɪks] n (*NonC*) cryogénie *f*.

cryonics [kraɪˈɒnɪks] n (*NonC*) cryogénisation *f*.

cryosurgery [ˌkraɪəʊˈsɜːdʒərɪ] n cryochirurgie *f*.

crypt [krɪpt] n crypte *f*.

cryptic(al) [ˈkrɪptɪk(əl)] adj (*secret*) secret (*f* -ète); (*mysterious*) sibyllin, énigmatique; (*terse*) laconique.

cryptically [ˈkrɪptɪkəlɪ] adv (*mysteriously*) énigmatiquement; (*tersely*) laconiquement.

crypto- [krɪptəʊ] pref crypto-. **~communist** *etc* cryptocommuniste *etc*.

cryptogram [ˈkrɪptəʊgræm] n cryptogramme *m*.

cryptographer [krɪpˈtɒgrəfəʳ] n cryptographe *mf*.

cryptographic(al) [ˌkrɪptəʊˈgræfɪk(əl)] adj cryptographique.

cryptography [krɪpˈtɒgrəfɪ] n cryptographie *f*.

crystal [ˈkrɪstl] 1 n a (*NonC*) cristal *m*; *see* **rock²**. b (*Chem, Min*) cristal *m*. **salt ~s** cristaux de sel. c (*US: watch glass*) verre *m* de montre. d (*Rad*) galène *f*. 2 comp (*lit*) *vase* de cristal; (*fig*) *waters, lake* de cristal (*fig, liter*) ▶ **crystal ball** boule *f* de cristal ▶ **crystal-clear** clair comme le jour *or* comme de l'eau de roche ▶ **crystal-gazer** voyant(e) *m(f)* (*qui lit dans la boule de cristal*) ▶ **crystal-gazing** (l'art *m* de la) voyance *f*; (*fig*) les prédictions *fpl*, les prophéties *fpl* ▶ **crystal set** (*Rad*) poste *m* à galène.

crystalline [ˈkrɪstəlaɪn] adj cristallin, clair *or* pur comme le cristal. (*Opt*) **~ lens** cristallin *m*.

crystallize [ˈkrɪstəlaɪz] 1 vi (*lit, fig*) se cristalliser. 2 vt cristalliser; *sugar* (faire) cuire au cassé. **~d fruits** fruits confits *or* candis.

crystallography [ˌkrɪstəˈlɒgrəfɪ] n cristallographie *f*.

CSC [ˌsiːesˈsiː] n (abbr of **Civil Service Commission**) *see* **civil**.

CSE [ˌsiːesˈiː] n (*Brit*) (abbr of **Certificate of Secondary Education**) ≃ BEPC *m*.

CSEU [ˌsiːesiːˈjuː] n (*Brit*) (abbr of **Confederation of Shipbuilding and Engineering Unions**) *syndicat*.

CS gas [ˌsiːesˈgæs] n (*Brit*) gaz *m* C.S.

CST [ˌsiːesˈtiː] n (*US*) (abbr of **Central Standard Time**) *see* **central**.

CSU [ˌsiːesˈjuː] n (*Brit*) (abbr of **Civil Service Union**) *syndicat*.

ct a abbr of **carat**. b abbr of **cent**.

CT n (*US*) abbr of **Connecticut**.

CTT [ˌsiːtiːˈtiː] n (*Brit*) abbr of **capital transfer tax**.

cub [kʌb] 1 n a *[animal]* petit(e) *m(f)*; (*: *youth*) gosse *m*, petit morveux (*pej*); *see* **bear²**, **fox**, **wolf** *etc*. b (*also* **~ scout**) louveteau *m* (*scout*). 2 comp ▶ **cub master** (*Scouting*) chef *m* ▶ **cub mistress** cheftaine *f* ▶ **cub reporter** (*Press*) jeune reporter *m*.

Cuba [ˈkjuːbə] n Cuba *f* (*no art*). **in ~** à Cuba.

Cuban [ˈkjuːbən] 1 adj cubain. 2 n Cubain(e) *m(f)*.

cubbyhole [ˈkʌbɪhəʊl] n (*cupboard*) débarras *m*, cagibi *m*; (*poky room*) cagibi; (*Brit Aut*) vide-poches *m inv*.

cube [kjuːb] 1 n (*gen, Culin, Math*) cube *m*. (*Math*) **~ root** racine *f* cubique; *see* **soup**, **stock**. 2 vt (*Math*) cuber; (*Culin*) couper en cubes *or* en dés.

cubic [ˈkjuːbɪk] adj (*of shape, volume*) cubique; (*of measures*) cube. **~ capacity** volume *m*; **~ centimetre** centimètre *m* cube; **~ content** contenance *f* cubique; **~ measure** mesure *f* de volume; **~ metre** mètre *m* cube; (*Math*) **~ equation** équation *f* du troisième degré.

cubicle [ˈkjuːbɪkəl] n *[hospital, dormitory]* box *m*, alcôve *f*; *[swimming baths]* cabine *f*.

cubism [ˈkjuːbɪzəm] n cubisme *m*.

cubist [ˈkjuːbɪst] adj, n cubiste (*mf*).

cuckold† [ˈkʌkəld] 1 n (mari *m*) cocu‡ *m*. 2 vt cocufier‡, faire cocu‡.

cuckoo [ˈkʊkuː] 1 n (*Orn*) coucou *m*. 2 adj (*: *mad*) piqué*, toqué*. **to go ~*** perdre la boule*. 3 comp ▶ **cuckoo clock** coucou *m* (*pendule*) ▶ **cuckoopint** (*Bot*) pied-de-veau *m* ▶ **cuckoo spit** (*Bot*) crachat *m* de coucou.

cucumber [ˈkjuːkʌmbəʳ] n concombre *m*; *see* **cool**.

cud [kʌd] n *see* **chew 1**.

cuddle [ˈkʌdl] 1 n étreinte *f*, caresse(s) *f(pl)*. **to have a ~** (se) faire (un) câlin*; **to give sb a ~** faire un câlin* à qn. 2 vt embrasser, caresser; *child* bercer, câliner. 3 vi s'enlacer, se serrer, se blottir l'un contre l'autre.

▶**cuddle down** vi *[child in bed]* se pelotonner. **cuddle down now!** maintenant allonge-toi (et dors)!

▶**cuddle up** vi se pelotonner (*to, against* contre).

cuddly [ˈkʌdlɪ] adj *child* caressant, câlin; *animal* qui donne envie de le caresser; *teddy bear, doll* doux (*f* douce), qu'on a envie de câliner. **~ toy** (jouet *m* en) peluche *f*.

cudgel [ˈkʌdʒəl] 1 n gourdin *m*, trique *f*. (*fig*) **to take up the ~s for** *or* **on behalf of** prendre fait et cause pour. 2 vt frapper à coups de trique. (*fig*) **to ~ one's brains** se creuser la cervelle *or* la tête (*for* pour).

cue [kjuː] 1 n a (*Theat*) (*verbal*) réplique *f* (*indiquant à un acteur qu'il doit parler*); (*action*) signal *m*; (*Mus*) signal d'entrée; (*Rad, TV*) signal. (*TV*) **~ card** (télé)prompteur *m*; (*Theat*) **to give sb his ~** donner la réplique à qn; (*fig*) faire un signal à qn; (*Theat*) **to take one's ~** entamer sa réplique; (*Theat*) **X's exit was the ~ for Y's entrance** la sortie d'X donnait à Y le signal de son entrée; (*fig*) **to take one's ~ from sb** emboîter le pas à qn (*fig*); (*fig*) **that was my ~ to ...** c'était mon signal pour ... . b (*Billiards etc*) queue *f* de billard. c *[wig]* queue *f* (*de perruque*). 2 vt (*Theat*) donner la réplique à.

▶**cue in** vt sep (*Rad, TV*) donner le signal à; (*Theat*) donner la réplique à. **to cue sb in on sth** mettre qn au courant de qch.

cuesta [ˈkwestə] n (*Geog, Geol*) cuesta *f*.

cuff [kʌf] 1 n a (*gen*) poignet *m*; *[shirt]* manchette *f*; *[coat]* parement *m*; (*US*) *[trousers]* revers *m inv* de pantalon. **~link** bouton *m* de manchette; (*fig*) **off the ~** à l'improviste, au pied levé (*see also* **off**); **to speak off the ~** improviser; (*US*) **to buy on the ~‡** acheter à crédit. b (*blow*) gifle *f*, calotte* *f*. c (*: *handcuffs*) **~s** menottes *fpl*. 2 vt (*strike*) gifler, calotter*.

cul-de-sac [ˈkʌldəˌsæk] n, pl **culs-de-sac** *or* **cul-de-sacs** (*esp Brit*) cul-de-sac *m*, impasse *f*. (*road sign*) "**~**" "voie sans issue".

culinary [ˈkʌlɪnərɪ] adj culinaire.

cull [kʌl] 1 vt a (*take samples from*) sélectionner. b (*remove inferior items, animals etc*) éliminer, supprimer; *seals* abattre, massacrer. c (*pick*) *flowers, fruit* cueillir. 2 n a (*killing*) massacre *m*; *see* **seal¹**. b (*animal*) animal *m* à éliminer (dans une portée).

culminate [ˈkʌlmɪneɪt] vi: **to ~ in sth** (*end in*) finir *or* se terminer par qch; (*lead to*) mener à qch; **it ~d in his throwing her out** pour finir il l'a mise à la porte.

culminating [ˈkʌlmɪneɪtɪŋ] adj culminant. **~ point** point culminant, sommet *m*.

culmination [ˌkʌlmɪˈneɪʃən] n (*Astron*) culmination *f*; (*fig*) *[success, career]* apogée *m*; *[disturbance, quarrel]* point culminant.

culotte(s) [kjuːˈlɒt(s)] n(pl) jupe-culotte *f*.

culpability [ˌkʌlpəˈbɪlɪtɪ] n culpabilité *f*.

culpable [ˈkʌlpəbl] adj coupable (*of* de), blâmable. (*Jur*) **~ homicide** homicide *m* volontaire; (*Scot*) homicide sans préméditation; (*Jur*) **~ negligence** négligence *f* coupable.

culprit [ˈkʌlprɪt] n coupable *mf*.

cult [kʌlt] 1 n (*Rel, fig*) culte *m* (*of* de). **he made a ~ of cleanliness** il avait le culte de la propreté. 2 comp ▶ **cult figure** objet *m* d'un culte, idole *f*; (*fig*) **he has become a cult figure** il est devenu l'objet d'un véritable culte *or* une véritable idole ▶ **cult film** (*Brit*) *or* **movie** (*US*) film-culte *m* ▶ **cult following: it is a film/book/group with a cult following** c'est un film-/livre-/groupe-culte.

cultivable [ˈkʌltɪvəbl] adj cultivable.

cultivar [ˈkʌltɪˌvɑːʳ] n variété cultivée.

cultivate [ˈkʌltɪveɪt] vt (*lit, fig*) cultiver. **to ~ the mind** se cultiver (l'esprit).

cultivated [ˈkʌltɪveɪtɪd] adj *land, person* cultivé; *voice* distingué. **~ pearls** perles *fpl* de culture.

cultivation [ˌkʌltɪˈveɪʃən] n culture *f*. **fields under ~** cultures *fpl*; **out of ~** en friche, inculte.

cultivator [ˈkʌltɪveɪtəʳ] n (*person*) cultivateur *m*, -trice *f*; (*machine*) cultivateur; (*power-driven*) motoculteur *m*.

cultural [ˈkʌltʃərəl] adj a *background, activities* culturel. **~ attaché** attaché culturel; **~ environment** environnement *or* milieu culturel; **~ integration** acculturation *f*; **the C~ Revolution** la Révolution Culturelle. b (*Agr*) de culture, cultural.

culture [ˈkʌltʃəʳ] 1 n a culture *f*. **physical ~** culture physique; **a woman of no ~** une femme sans aucune culture *or* complètement inculte; **French ~** la culture française. b (*Agr*) culture *f*; *[bees]* apiculture *f*; *[fish]* pisciculture *f*; *[farm animals]* élevage *m*. c (*Med*) culture *f*. 2 comp *tube* à culture ▶ **culture-fair test** *examen conçu pour ne pas défavoriser les minorités ethniques* ▶ **culture fluid** bouillon *m* de culture ▶ **culture-free test** = **culture-fair test** ▶ **culture gap** fossé culturel ▶ **culture medium** milieu *m* de culture ▶ **culture**

shock choc culturel ► **culture vulture*** (*hum*) fana *mf* de culture. 3 vt (*Bio*) cultiver.
cultured ['kʌltʃəd] adj cultivé. ~ **pearl** perle *f* de culture.
culvert ['kʌlvət] n caniveau *m*.
-cum- [kʌm] prep: **a carpenter-~-painter** un charpentier-peintre; **a typewriter-~-word processor** une machine à écrire avec traitement de texte; **a dining room-~-living room** une salle à manger-salon.
cumbersome ['kʌmbəsəm] adj, **cumbrous** ['kʌmbrəs] adj (*bulky*) encombrant, embarrassant; (*heavy*) lourd, pesant.
cumin ['kʌmɪn] n cumin *m*.
cum laude [kʊm 'laʊdeɪ] adj (*Univ*) avec distinction (*obtention d'un diplôme, d'un titre*).
cummerbund ['kʌməbʌnd] n ceinture *f* (*de smoking; aussi portée par les Hindous*).
cumulative ['kju:mjʊlətɪv] adj cumulatif. (*Jur*) ~ **evidence** preuve *f* par accumulation de témoignages; (*Fin*) ~ **interest** intérêt cumulatif; ~ **voting** vote plural.
cumulonimbus [ˌkju:mjələʊ'nɪmbəs] n cumulo-nimbus *m inv*.
cumulus ['kju:mjələs] n, pl **cumuli** ['kju:mjəˌlaɪ] cumulus *m*.
cuneiform ['kju:nɪfɔ:m] 1 adj cunéiforme. 2 n écriture *f* cunéiforme.
cunnilingus [ˌkʌnɪ'lɪŋgəs] n cunnilingus *m*.
cunning ['kʌnɪŋ] 1 n finesse *f*, astuce *f*; (*pej*) ruse *f*, fourberie *f*, duplicité *f*; (††: *skill*) habileté *f*, adresse *f*. 2 adj a astucieux, malin (*f* -igne); (*pej*) rusé, fourbe. **a ~ little gadget*** un petit truc astucieux*. b (*US* ‡) charmant, mignon.
cunningly ['kʌnɪŋlɪ] adv avec astuce, finement; (*pej*) avec ruse, avec fourberie; (*: *cleverly*) astucieusement.
cunt** [kʌnt] n con** *m*, chatte** *f*; (*woman*) nana‡ *f*; (*despicable person*) salaud‡ *m*, salope‡ *f*.
cup [kʌp] 1 n a tasse *f*; (*goblet*) coupe *f*; (*cupful*) tasse, coupe. ~ **of tea** tasse de thé; **he drank four ~s** *or* **~fuls** il (en) a bu quatre tasses; (*Culin*) **one ~** *or* **~ful of sugar/flour** *etc* une tasse de sucre/farine *etc*; **cider/champagne** *etc* ~ cup *m* au cidre/au champagne *etc*; (*fig*) **he was in his ~s** il était dans les vignes du Seigneur, il avait un verre dans le nez*; (*fig*) **that's just his ~ of tea*** c'est tout à fait à son goût, c'est exactement ce qui lui convient; (*fig*) **that's not my ~ of tea*** ce n'est pas du tout à mon goût, ça n'est vraiment pas mon genre*; (*fig*) **it isn't everyone's ~ of tea*** ça ne plaît pas à tout le monde; (*liter*) **his ~ of happiness was full** son bonheur était complet *or* parfait; (*liter*) **to drain the ~ of sorrow** vider *or* boire le calice (jusqu'à la lie); *see* **coffee, slip** *etc*.
b (*Tech*) godet *m*; [*flower*] corolle *f*; (*Rel: also* **communion** ~) calice *m*; (*Brit Sport etc: prize, competition*) coupe *f*; (*Geog*) cuvette *f*; (*Anat*) [*bone*] cavité *f* articulaire, glène *f*; (*Med: cupping glass*) ventouse *f*; [*brassière*] bonnet *m* (*de soutien-gorge*); *see* **world**.
2 vt a **to ~ one's hands** mettre ses mains en coupe; **to ~ one's hands round sth** mettre ses mains autour de qch; **to ~ one's hands round one's ear/one's mouth** mettre ses mains en cornet/en porte-voix.
b (*Med* ††) appliquer des ventouses sur.
c (*Golf*) **to ~ the ball** faire un divot.
3 comp ► **cup bearer** échanson *m* ► **cupcake** (*Culin*) petit gâteau ► **cup final** (*Brit Ftbl*) finale *f* de la coupe ► **cup-tie** (*Brit Ftbl*) match *m* de coupe *or* comptant pour la coupe.
cupboard ['kʌbəd] n (*esp Brit*) placard *m*. (*Brit*) ~ **love** amour intéressé; *see* **skeleton**.
cupful ['kʌpfʊl] n (*contenu d'une*) tasse *f*; *see* **cup**.
Cupid ['kju:pɪd] n (*Myth*) Cupidon *m*; (*Art: cherub*) amour *m*. **~'s darts** les flèches *fpl* de Cupidon.
cupidity [kju:'pɪdɪtɪ] n cupidité *f*.
cupola ['kju:pələ] n a (*Archit*) (*dome*) coupole *f*, dôme *m*; (*US: lantern, belfry*) belvédère *m*. b (*Naut*) coupole *f*. c (*Metal*) cubilot *m*.
cuppa‡ ['kʌpə] n (*Brit*) tasse *f* de thé.
cupric ['kju:prɪk] adj cuprique. ~ **oxide** oxyde *m* de cuivre.
cur [kɜ:ʳ] n a (*pej: dog*) sale chien *m*, sale cabot* *m*. b (* *pej: man*) malotru *m*, mufle* *m*, rustre *m*.
curable ['kjʊərəbl] adj guérissable, curable.
curare [kjʊə'rɑ:rɪ] n curare *m*.
curate ['kjʊərɪt] n vicaire *m*. (*Brit*) **it's like the ~'s egg** il y a du bon et du mauvais.
curative ['kjʊərətɪv] adj curatif.
curator [kjʊə'reɪtəʳ] n a [*museum etc*] conservateur *m*. b (*Scot Jur*) curateur *m* (*d'un aliéné ou d'un mineur*).
curb [kɜ:b] 1 n a [*harness*] gourmette *f*; (*fig*) frein *m*; (*on trade etc*) restriction *f*. (*fig*) **to put a ~ on** mettre un frein à.
b (*US: at roadside*) bord *m* du trottoir.
2 vt (*US*) *horse* mettre un mors à; (*fig*) *impatience, passion* refréner, maîtriser, contenir; *expenditure* réduire, restreindre.
3 comp ► **curb bit** mors *m* ► **curb chain** gourmette *f* ► **curb crawler** (*US*) dragueur motorisé, conducteur *m* qui accoste les femmes sur le trottoir ► **curb crawling** drague motorisée ► **curb reins** rênes *fpl* de filet ► **curb roof** (*Archit*) comble brisé ► **curb service** (*US*) service *m* au volant (dans un restaurant drive-in) ► **curbstone** (*US*) pavé *m* (*pour bordure de trottoir*) ► **curb(stone) market** (*US*) marché *m* après bourse ► **curb weight** (*US Aut*) poids *m* à vide.
curd [kɜ:d] n (*gen pl*) **~(s)** lait caillé; ~ **cheese** ≃ fromage blanc; *see* **lemon**.
curdle ['kɜ:dl] 1 vt *milk* cailler; *mayonnaise* faire tomber. **it was enough to ~ the blood** c'était à vous (faire) figer *or* glacer le sang dans les veines. 2 vi [*milk*] se cailler; [*mayonnaise*] tomber. (*fig*) **his blood ~d** son sang s'est figé dans ses veines; **it made my blood ~** cela m'a glacé *or* figé le sang dans les veines.
cure [kjʊəʳ] 1 vt a (*Med*) *disease, patient* guérir (*of* de); (*fig*) *poverty* éliminer; *unfairness* éliminer, remédier à. **to ~ an injustice** réparer une injustice; **to ~ an evil** remédier à un mal; **to be ~d (of)** guérir (de); **to ~ a child of a bad habit** faire perdre une mauvaise habitude à un enfant; **to ~ o.s. of smoking** se déshabituer du tabac, se guérir de l'habitude de fumer; (*Prov*) **what can't be ~d must be endured** il faut savoir accepter l'inévitable.
b *meat, fish* (*salt*) saler; (*smoke*) fumer; (*dry*) sécher; *skins* traiter.
2 n a (*Med*) (*remedy*) remède *m*, cure *f*; (*recovery*) guérison *f*. **to take** *or* **follow a ~** faire une cure; **past** *or* **beyond ~** *person* inguérissable, incurable; *state, injustice, evil* irrémédiable, irréparable; *see* **rest**.
b (*Rel*) cure *f*. ~ **of souls** charge *f* d'âmes.
3 comp ► **cure-all** panacée *f*.
curfew ['kɜ:fju:] n couvre-feu *m*. **to impose a/lift the ~** décréter/lever le couvre-feu.
curie ['kjʊərɪ] n (*Phys*) curie *m*.
curing ['kjʊərɪŋ] n (*see* **cure 1b**) salaison *f*, fumaison *f*, séchage *m*.
curio ['kjʊərɪəʊ] n bibelot *m*, curiosité *f*.
curiosity [ˌkjʊərɪ'ɒsɪtɪ] n a (*NonC: inquisitiveness*) curiosité *f* (*about* de). **out of ~** par curiosité; (*Prov*) ~ **killed the cat** la curiosité est toujours punie. b (*rare object*) curiosité *f*, rareté *f*. ~ **shop** magasin *m* de brocante *or* de curiosités.
curious ['kjʊərɪəs] adj a (*inquisitive*) curieux (*about* de). **I'm ~ to know what he did** je suis curieux de savoir ce qu'il a fait. b (*odd*) curieux, bizarre, singulier.
curiously ['kjʊərɪəslɪ] adv (*inquisitively*) avec curiosité; (*oddly*) curieusement, singulièrement. ~ **enough, he didn't come** chose bizarre, il n'est pas venu.
curium ['kjʊərɪəm] n curium *m*.
curl [kɜ:l] 1 n a [*hair*] boucle *f* (de cheveux).
b (*gen*) courbe *f*; [*smoke*] spirale *f*, volute *f*; [*waves*] ondulation *f*. (*fig*) **with a ~ of the lip** avec une moue méprisante.
2 comp ► **curling irons, curling tongs** fer *m* à friser ► **curl paper** papillote *f*.
3 vt *hair* (*loosely*) (faire) boucler; (*tightly*) friser. **she ~s her hair** elle frise *or* boucle ses cheveux; **he ~ed his lip in disdain** il a fait une moue méprisante; **the dog ~ed its lip menacingly** le chien a retroussé ses babines d'un air menaçant.
4 vi a [*hair*] (*tightly*) friser; (*loosely*) boucler. (*fig*) **it's enough to make your hair ~*** c'est à vous faire dresser les cheveux sur la tête; **his lip ~ed disdainfully** il a eu une moue de dédain; **the dog's lip ~ed menacingly** le chien a retroussé ses babines d'un air menaçant.
b [*person, animal*] = **curl up**.
►**curl up** 1 vi s'enrouler; [*person*] se pelotonner; (*: *from shame etc*) rentrer sous terre; [*cat*] se mettre en boule, se pelotonner; [*dog*] se coucher en rond; [*leaves*] se recroqueviller; [*paper*] se recourber, se replier; (*corners only*) se corner; [*stale bread*] se racornir. **he lay curled up on the floor** il était couché en boule par terre; **to curl up with laughter** se tordre de rire; **the smoke curled up** la fumée montait en volutes *or* en spirales. 2 vt sep enrouler. **to curl o.s. up** [*person*] se pelotonner; [*cat*] se mettre en boule, se pelotonner; [*dog*] se coucher en rond.
curler ['kɜ:ləʳ] n a [*hair*] rouleau *m*, bigoudi *m*. b (*Scot Sport*) joueur *m*, -euse *f* de curling.
curlew ['kɜ:lju:] n courlis *m*.
curlicue ['kɜ:lɪkju:] n [*handwriting*] fioriture *f*; [*skating*] figure *f* (*de patinage*).
curling ['kɜ:lɪŋ] n (*Sport*) curling *m*.
curly ['kɜ:lɪ] adj *hair* (*loosely*) bouclé; (*tightly*) frisé. ~ **eyelashes** cils recourbés; **~-haired, ~-headed** aux cheveux bouclés *or* frisés; ~ **lettuce** laitue frisée.
currant ['kʌrənt] n a (*Bot*) (*fruit*) groseille *f*; (*also* ~ **bush**) groseillier *m*; *see* **black, red**. b (*dried fruit*) raisin *m* de Corinthe. ~ **bun** petit pain *m* aux raisins; ~ **loaf** pain *m* aux raisins.
currency ['kʌrənsɪ] 1 n (*NonC*) a (*Fin*) monnaie *f*, devise *f*; (*money*) argent *m*. **the ~ is threatened** la monnaie est en danger; **this coin is no longer legal ~** cette pièce n'a plus cours (légal); **foreign ~** devise *or* monnaie étrangère; **I have no French ~** je n'ai pas d'argent français; *see* **hard, paper** *etc*.
b **this coin is no longer in ~** cette pièce n'est plus en circulation.
c (*acceptance, prevalence*) cours *m*, circulation *f*. **to gain ~** se répandre, s'accréditer; **to give ~ to** accréditer; **such words have short ~** de tels mots n'ont pas cours longtemps.
2 comp ► **currency exemptions** (*Fin, Jur*) dispenses *fpl* en matière

de réglementation des changes ▸ **currency market** (*Fin*) place financière ▸ **currency note** billet *m* ▸ **currency rate** cours *m* des devises ▸ **currency restrictions** contrôle *m* des changes ▸ **currency snake** serpent *m* monétaire ▸ **currency unit** unité *f* monétaire.

current ['kʌrənt] 1 adj *opinion* courant, commun, admis; *word, phrase* commun, courant; *price* courant, en cours; *fashion, tendency, popularity* actuel. **to be** ~ *[report, rumour]* avoir cours; *[phrase, expression]* être accepté *or* courant; **to be in** ~ **use** être d'usage courant; **at the** ~ **rate of exchange** au cours actuel du change; (*Brit Banking*) ~ **account** compte courant; ~ **affairs** questions *fpl or* problèmes *mpl* d'actualité, actualité *f* (*NonC*); (*Fin*) ~ **assets** actif *m* de roulement; (*Fin*) ~ **cost accounting** comptabilité *f* en coûts actuels; ~ **liabilities** passif *m* exigible *or* dettes *fpl* exigibles à court terme; ~ **events** événements actuels, actualité *f* (*NonC*); ~ **expenditure** dépenses *fpl* de fonctionnement *or* d'exploitation; (*Press*) ~ **issue** dernier numéro; ~ **month/year** mois/année en cours; (*St Ex*) ~ **yield** taux *m* de rendement courant, taux actuariel; ~ **week** semaine *f* en cours; **his** ~ **job** le travail qu'il fait *or* le poste qu'il occupe en ce moment; **her** ~ **boyfriend*** le copain* *or* petit ami* du moment.

2 n *[air, water]* courant *m* (*also Elec*); (*fig: of events etc*) cours *m*, tendance *f*; (*of opinions*) tendance. (*lit, fig*) **to go with the** ~ suivre le courant; **to drift with the** ~ (*lit*) se laisser aller au fil de l'eau; (*fig*) aller selon le vent; **to go against the** ~ (*lit*) remonter le courant; (*fig*) aller à contre-courant; *see* **alternating, direct**.

currently ['kʌrəntlɪ] adv actuellement, en ce moment. **it is** ~ **thought that ...** on pense maintenant *or* à présent que ... .

curriculum [kə'rɪkjʊləm] 1 n, pl ~s *or* **curricula** [kə'rɪkjʊlə] programme *m* scolaire *or* d'études. 2 comp ▸ **curriculum coordinator** responsable *m* des programmes scolaires ▸ **curriculum council** (*US Scol*) ≃ service *m* des programmes scolaires ▸ **curriculum vitae** (*US Scol*) (pl **curricula vitae**) curriculum vitae *m*, C.V. *m*.

curried ['kʌrɪd] adj au curry.

curry[1] ['kʌrɪ] (*Culin*) 1 n curry *m or* cari *m*. **beef** ~ curry de bœuf. 2 comp ▸ **curry powder** (poudre *f* de) curry *m*. 3 vt accommoder au curry.

curry[2] ['kʌrɪ] 1 vt *horse* étriller; *leather* corroyer. (*fig*) **to** ~ **favour with sb** chercher à gagner la faveur de qn. 2 comp ▸ **curry-comb** n étrille *f* ◊ vt étriller.

curse [kɜːs] 1 n a malédiction *f*. **a** ~ **on him!**† maudit soit-il!†; **to call down** *or* **put** *or* **lay a** ~ **on sb** maudire qn. b (*swearword*) juron *m*, imprécation *f*. ~**s!*** zut!* c (*fig: bane*) fléau *m*, malheur *m*, calamité *f*. **the** ~ **of drunkenness** le fléau de l'ivrognerie; **it has been the** ~ **of my life** c'est un sort qui m'a poursuivi toute ma vie; (*menstruation*) **she has the** ~* elle a ses règles; **this essay is a dreadful** ~* quelle corvée cette dissertation!; **the** ~* **of it is that ...** l'embêtant* c'est que ... . 2 vt maudire. ~ **the child!*** maudit enfant!; (*fig*) **to be** ~**d with** être affligé de. 3 vi jurer, sacrer.

cursed* ['kɜːsɪd] adj sacré*, maudit, satané (*all before n*).

cursive ['kɜːsɪv] 1 adj cursif. 2 n (écriture *f*) cursive *f*.

cursor ['kɜːsəʳ] n (*Comput*) curseur *m*.

cursorily ['kɜːsərɪlɪ] adv (*see* **cursory**) superficiellement; hâtivement, à la hâte.

cursory ['kɜːsərɪ] adj (*superficial*) superficiel; (*hasty*) hâtif. **to give a** ~ **glance at** *person, object* jeter un coup d'œil à; *book, essay, letter* lire en diagonale*.

curt [kɜːt] adj *person, manner* brusque, sec (*f* sèche), cassant; *explanation, question* brusque, sec. **in a** ~ **voice** d'un ton cassant; **with a** ~ **nod** avec un bref signe de tête.

curtail [kɜː'teɪl] vt *account* écourter, raccourcir, tronquer; *proceedings, visit* écourter; *period of time* écourter, raccourcir; *wages* rogner, réduire; *expenses* restreindre, réduire.

curtailment [kɜː'teɪlmənt] n (*see* **curtail**) raccourcissement *m*; réduction *f*.

curtain ['kɜːtn] 1 n a (*gen*) rideau *m*; (*fig*) rideau, voile *m*. **to draw** *or* **pull the** ~**s** tirer les rideaux; (*Mil*) ~ **of fire** rideau de feu; (*fig*) **it was** ~**s for him**‡ il était fichu* *or* foutu‡; *see* **iron, safety**.

b (*Theat*) rideau *m*; (*time when curtain rises or falls*) lever *m or* baisser *m* de rideau; (*also* ~ **call**) rappel *m*. **she took 3** ~**s** elle a été rappelée 3 fois; **the last** *or* **final** ~ le dernier rappel.

2 comp ▸ **curtain hook** crochet *m* de rideau ▸ **curtain pole** tringle *f* à rideau(x) ▸ **curtain raiser** (*Theat*) lever *m* de rideau (*pièce*) ▸ **curtain ring** anneau *m* de rideau ▸ **curtain rod** tringle *f* à rideau(x) ▸ **curtain-up** (*Theat*) lever *m* du rideau ▸ **curtain wall** (*Constr*) mur *m* rideau.

3 vt *window* garnir de rideaux.

▸**curtain off** vt sep *room* diviser par un *or* des rideau(x); *bed, kitchen area* cacher derrière un *or* des rideau(x).

curtly ['kɜːtlɪ] adv avec brusquerie, sèchement, d'un ton cassant.

curtness ['kɜːtnɪs] n brusquerie *f*, sécheresse *f*.

curtsey, curtsy ['kɜːtsɪ] 1 n révérence *f*. **to make** *or* **drop a** ~ faire une révérence. 2 vi faire une révérence (*to* à).

curvaceous [kɜː'veɪʃəs] adj *woman* bien balancée*, bien roulée*.

curvature ['kɜːvətʃəʳ] n courbure *f*; (*Med*) déviation *f*. ~ **of the spine** déviation de la colonne vertébrale, scoliose *f*; **the** ~ **of space** la courbure de l'espace.

curve [kɜːv] 1 n (*gen*) courbe *f*; *[arch]* voussure *f*; *[beam]* cambrure *f*; *[graph]* courbe. ~ **in the road** courbe, tournant *m*, virage *m*; **a woman's** ~**s*** les rondeurs *fpl* d'une femme. 2 vt courber; (*Archit*) *arch, roof* cintrer. 3 vi *[line, surface, beam]* se courber, s'infléchir; *[road etc]* faire une courbe, être en courbe. **the road** ~**s down into the valley** la route descend en courbe dans la vallée; **the river** ~**s round the town** la rivière fait un méandre autour de la ville.

curved [kɜːvd] adj (*gen*) courbe; *edge of table etc* arrondi; *road* en courbe; (*convex*) convexe.

curvet [kɜː'vet] (*Equitation*) 1 n courbette *f*. 2 vi faire une courbette.

curvilinear [,kɜːvɪ'lɪnɪəʳ] adj curviligne.

curvy ['kɜːvɪ] adj *girl, body* bien roulé*; (*gen*) courbe.

cushion ['kʊʃən] 1 n a coussin *m*. **on a** ~ **of air** sur un coussin d'air; *see* **pin** *etc*. b (*Billiards*) bande *f*. **stroke off the** ~ doublé *m*. 2 vt *sofa* mettre des coussins à; *seat* rembourrer; (*Tech*) matelasser; (*fig*) *shock* amortir; (*Fin*) *losses* atténuer. **to** ~ **sb's fall** amortir la chute de qn; (*fig*) **to** ~ **sb against sth** protéger qn contre qch; **to** ~ **one's savings against inflation** mettre ses économies à l'abri de l'inflation.

cushy‡ ['kʊʃɪ] adj (*Brit*) pépère‡, tranquille. **a** ~ **job** une bonne planque‡, un boulot pépère‡; **to have a** ~ **time** se la couler douce*; *see* **billet**[1].

cusp [kʌsp] n (*Bot*), *[tooth]* cuspide *f*; *[moon]* corne *f*.

cuspidor ['kʌspɪdɔːʳ] n (*US*) crachoir *m*.

cuss* [kʌs] (*US* = **curse**) 1 n a (*oath*) juron *m*. **he's not worth a tinker's** ~ il ne vaut pas un pet de lapin*. b (*gen pej: person*) individu *m* (*pej*), type* *m*, bonne femme (*gen pej*). **he's a queer** ~ c'est un drôle de type*. 2 vi jurer.

cussed* ['kʌsɪd] adj entêté, têtu comme une mule*.

cussedness* ['kʌsɪdnɪs] n esprit contrariant *or* de contradiction. **out of sheer** ~ histoire d'embêter le monde*.

custard ['kʌstəd] 1 n (*pouring*) crème anglaise; (*set*) crème renversée. 2 comp ▸ **custard apple** (*Bot*) anone *f* ▸ **custard cream (biscuit)** biscuit fourré ▸ **custard pie** tarte *f* à la crème ▸ **custard powder** crème instantanée (en poudre) ▸ **custard tart** flan *m*.

custodial [kʌs'təʊdɪəl] adj a (*Jur*) ~ **sentence** peine privative de liberté. b *[museum etc]* ~ **staff** personnel *m* de surveillance.

custodian [kʌs'təʊdɪən] n *[building]* concierge *mf*, gardien(ne) *m(f)*; *[museum]* conservateur *m*, -trice *f*; *[tradition etc]* gardien(ne), protecteur *m*, -trice *f*.

custody ['kʌstədɪ] n a (*Jur etc*) garde *f*. **in safe** ~ sous bonne garde; **the child is in the** ~ **of his aunt** l'enfant est sous la garde de sa tante; (*Jur*) **after the divorce she was given** ~ **of the children** après le divorce elle a reçu la garde des enfants. b (*gen*) garde *f* à vue; (*imprisonment*) emprisonnement *m*, captivité *f*; (*also* **police** ~) (*for short period*) garde à vue; (*before trial*) détention préventive. **in** ~ en détention préventive; **to be kept in (police)** ~ être mis en garde à vue; **to take sb into** ~ mettre qn en état d'arrestation; **to give sb into** ~ remettre qn aux mains de la police; *see* **protective, remand**.

custom ['kʌstəm] 1 n a (*established behaviour*) coutume *f*, usage *m*, pratique courante; (*habit*) coutume, habitude *f*. **as** ~ **has it** selon la coutume, selon les us et coutumes; **it was his** ~ **to rest each morning** il avait l'habitude de se reposer chaque matin. b (*Brit Comm*) clientèle *f*, pratique†† *f*. **the grocer wanted to get her** ~ l'épicier voulait obtenir sa clientèle; **he has lost a lot of** ~ il a perdu beaucoup de clients; **he took his** ~ **elsewhere** il est allé se fournir ailleurs. c (*Jur*) coutume *f*, droit coutumier. 2 comp ▸ **custom-built** (*Comm*) (fait) sur commande ▸ **custom-made** (*US Comm*) *clothes* (fait) sur mesure; *other goods* (fait) sur commande.

customarily ['kʌstəmərɪlɪ] adv habituellement, ordinairement.

customary ['kʌstəmərɪ] adj habituel, coutumier, ordinaire; (*Jur*) coutumier. (*Jur*) ~ **tenant** tenancier *m* censitaire; **it is** ~ **to do it** c'est ce qui se fait d'habitude, c'est la coutume.

customer ['kʌstəməʳ] n a (*Comm*) client(e) *m(f)*. ~ **appeal** facteur *m* de séduction du client; ~ **base** clientèle *f*; ~ **profile** profil *m* du consommateur; ~ **services** service *m* clientèle. b (*) type* *m*, individu *m* (*pej*). **he's an awkward** ~ il n'est pas commode; **queer** ~ drôle de type* *or* d'individu; **ugly** ~ sale type* *or* individu.

customize ['kʌstəmaɪz] vt fabriquer (*or* construire *or* arranger *etc*) sur commande. ~**d** *software, service* sur mesure.

customs ['kʌstəmz] 1 n a (*sg or pl: authorities, place*) douane *f*. **to go through (the)** ~ passer la douane; **at** *or* **in the** ~ à la douane.

b (*pl: duty payable*) droits *mpl* de douane.

2 comp *regulations, receipt etc* de la douane ▸ **customs border patrol** brigade volante des services du douane ▸ **customs clearance** dédouanement *m* ▸ **customs declaration** déclaration *f* de douane ▸ **customs duty** droit(s) *m(pl)* de douane ▸ **customs house** (poste *m or* bureaux *mpl* de) douane *f* ▸ **customs inspection** visite douanière *or* de douane ▸ **customs officer** douanier *m*, -ière *f* ▸ **customs post** = **customs house** ▸ **customs service** service *m* des douanes ▸ **customs shed** local *m* de la douane ▸ **customs union** union douanière.

cut [kʌt] (vb: pret, ptp **cut**) 1 n a (*stroke*) coup *m*; *[cards]* coupe *f*; (*mark, slit*) coupure *f*; (*notch*) entaille *f*; (*slash*) estafilade *f*; (*gash*) balafre *f*; (*Med*) incision *f*. **sabre ~** coup de sabre; **saw ~** trait *m* de scie; **a deep ~ in the leg** une profonde coupure à la jambe; **he had a ~ on his chin from shaving** il s'était coupé au menton en se rasant; **there is a ~ in his jacket** il y a une entaille à sa veste; (*fig*) **the ~ and thrust of modern politics** les estocades *fpl* de la politique contemporaine; (*fig*) **that remark was a ~ at me** cette remarque était une pierre dans mon jardin; (*fig*) **the unkindest ~ of all** le coup le plus perfide; (*fig*) **he is a ~ above the others*** il vaut mieux que les autres, il est supérieur aux autres; (*fig*) **that's a ~ above him*** ça le dépasse; *see* **short.**

b (*reduction: gen, esp Econ*) réduction *f* (*in* de), diminution *f* (*in* de); (*in staff*) compression *f* (*in* de). (*Fin*) **the ~s** les compressions budgétaires; **the ~s in the armed forces** la réduction *or* la compression (du personnel) *or* la diminution de l'effectif des forces armées; **the ~s in the defence budget** la diminution *or* la réduction du budget de la défense; **the ~s in education** les réductions dans les budgets scolaires; (*Econ*) **drastic ~s** coupes claires; **power** *or* **electricity ~** coupure *f* de courant; **to take a ~ in salary** subir une diminution *or* réduction de salaire; **to make ~s in a book/play** *etc* faire des coupures dans un livre/une pièce *etc*.

c [*meat*] (*piece*) morceau *m*; (*slice*) tranche *f*; (**: share*) part *f*. **a nice ~ of beef** un beau morceau de bœuf; **a ~ off** *or* **from the joint** un morceau de rôti; **they all want a ~ in the profits*** ils veulent tous leur part du gâteau* (*fig*).

d [*clothes*] coupe *f*; [*jewel*] taille *f*. **I like the ~ of this coat** j'aime la coupe de ce manteau; *see* **jib.**

e (*haircut*) **~ (and blow-dry)** coupe *f* (et brushing).

f (*US Typ: block*) cliché *m*.

g (*Cine, TV*) coupe *f* (*from* de, *to* à).

h (*US *: from school etc*) absence injustifiée.

i (*Comput*) **~ and paste** coupe *f* et insertion *f*.

2 **adj: ~ glass (n)** (*NonC*) cristal taillé; **(adj)** de *or* en cristal taillé; **~ flowers** fleurs coupées; **~ tobacco** tabac découpé; **~ prices** prix réduits; **well-~ coat** manteau bien coupé *or* de bonne coupe; (*fig*) **it was all ~ and dried** (*fixed beforehand*) c'était déjà décidé, tout était déjà arrangé; (*impossible to adapt*) il n'y avait pas moyen de changer quoi que ce soit; **~ and dried opinions** opinions toutes faites.

3 **comp ► cutaway (drawing** *or* **sketch)** (dessin *m*) écorché *m* **► cutback** (*reduction*) [*expenditure, production*] réduction *f*, diminution *f* (*in* de); (*in staff*) compressions *fpl* (*in* de); (*Cine: flashback*) flashback *m* (*to* sur); (*Econ etc*) **drastic cutbacks** coupes claires **► cutoff** (*short cut*) raccourci *m*; (*Tech: stopping*) arrêt *m*; **cutoff date** date *f* limite; **(automatic) cutoff device** système *m* d'arrêt (automatique); **cutoff point** (*in age etc*) limite *f*; (*in time*) dernier délai *m*; **cutoff switch** interrupteur *m*; **cutoffs** jeans coupés **► cutout** (*Elec*) disjoncteur *m*, coupe-circuit *m inv*; (*Aut*) échappement *m* libre; (*figure of wood or paper*) découpage *m*; **cutout book** livre *m* de découpages; (*Space*) **cutout point** point *m* de largage **► cut-price** (*Brit*) **adj** *goods, ticket* à prix réduit, au rabais; *shop* à prix réduits; *manufacturer, shopkeeper* qui vend à prix réduits ◊ **adv** *buy, get* à prix réduit; **cut-price shop** *or* **store** magasin *m* à prix réduits **► cut-rate** = **cut price ► cut-throat** assassin *m*; **cut-throat competition** compétition acharnée; (*Cards*) **cut-throat game** partie *f* à trois; (*Brit*) **cut-throat razor** rasoir *m* à main *or* de coiffeur **► cut up*** (*Brit: upset*) affligé; (*US: funny*) rigolo (*f* -ote), farceur.

4 **vt** a couper; *joint of meat* découper; (*slice*) découper en tranches; (*Med*) *abscess* inciser; *tobacco* découper; (*notch*) encocher; (*castrate*) châtrer. **to ~ one's finger** se couper le doigt *or* au doigt; **to ~ sb's throat** couper la gorge à qn, égorger qn; (*fig*) **he is ~ting his own throat** il prépare sa propre ruine (*fig*); **to ~ in half/in three** *etc* couper en deux/en trois *etc*; **to ~ in pieces** (*lit*) couper en morceaux; (*fig*) *army* tailler en pièces; *reputation* démolir; **to ~ open** (*with knife*) ouvrir au *or* avec un couteau; (*with scissors etc*) ouvrir avec des ciseaux *etc*; **he ~ his arm open on a nail** il s'est ouvert le bras sur un clou; **he ~ his head open** il s'est fendu le crâne; **to ~ sb free** délivrer qn en coupant ses liens; (*fig*) **to ~ short** abréger, couper court à; **to ~ a visit short** écourter une visite; **to ~ sb short** couper la parole à qn; **to ~ a long story short, he came** bref *or* pour en finir, il est venu.

b (*shape*) couper, tailler; *steps* tailler; *channel* creuser, percer; *figure, statue* sculpter (*out of* dans); (*engrave*) graver; *jewel, key, glass, crystal* tailler; *screw* fileter; *dress* couper. **to ~ a (gramophone) record** graver un disque; **to ~ one's way through** se frayer *or* s'ouvrir un chemin à travers; (*fig*) **to ~ one's coat according to one's cloth** vivre selon ses moyens.

c (*mow, clip, trim*) *hedge, trees* tailler; *corn, hay* faucher; *lawn* tondre. **to ~ one's nails/hair** se couper les ongles/les cheveux; **to have** *or* **get one's hair ~** se faire couper les cheveux.

d (*not to go*) *class etc* manquer, sécher*; *appointment* manquer exprès. (*ignore, avoid*) **to ~ sb (dead)** faire semblant de ne pas voir *or* reconnaître qn; **she ~ me dead** elle a fait comme si elle ne me voyait pas.

e (*cross, intersect*) couper, croiser, traverser; (*Math*) couper. **the path ~s the road here** le sentier coupe la route à cet endroit.

f (*reduce*) *profits, wages* réduire, diminuer; *text, book, play* réduire, faire des coupures dans. **to ~ prices** réduire les prix, vendre à prix réduit *or* au rabais; **we ~ the journey time by half** nous avons réduit de moitié la durée du trajet; (*Sport*) **he ~ 30 seconds off the record, he ~ the record by 30 seconds** il a amélioré le record de 30 secondes.

g (*fig: wound, hurt*) *person* blesser (profondément), affecter. **it ~ me to the heart** cela m'a profondément blessé; **the wind ~ his face** le vent lui coupait le visage; *see* **quick.**

h [*child*] **to ~ a tooth** percer une dent; **he is ~ting teeth** il fait ses dents; (*fig*) **to ~ one's teeth on sth** se faire les dents sur qch.

i *cards* couper.

j (*Sport*) **to ~ the ball** couper la balle.

k (*Cine etc*) *film* monter.

l (*dilute*) *drink* couper.

m (*phrases*) **he ~ a sorry figure** il faisait piètre figure; **she ~s a fine figure in that dress** elle a grand air (*frm*) *or* elle a beaucoup d'allure dans cette robe; **to ~ a dash** faire de l'effet; **to ~ it fine** compter un peu juste, ne pas (se) laisser de marge; **you're ~ting it too fine** vous comptez trop juste; **that ~s no ice** *or* **that doesn't ~ much ice with me** ça ne me fait aucun effet, ça ne m'impressionne guère; **to ~ the ground from under sb's feet** couper l'herbe sous le pied de qn; **to ~ one's losses** faire la part du feu, sauver les meubles*; (*Aut*) **to ~ a corner** prendre un virage à la corde; (*fig*) **to ~ corners** prendre des raccourcis (*fig*); (*fig: financially*) **to ~ corners (on sth)** rogner sur les coûts (de qch); **to ~ the Gordian knot** trancher le nœud gordien; **~ the cackle!**‡ assez bavardé comme ça!*; *see* **mustard.**

n (*Comput*) **~ and paste** *document etc* couper-coller.

5 **vi** a [*person, knife etc*] couper, tailler, trancher. **he ~ into the cake** il a fait une entaille dans le gâteau, il a entamé le gâteau; **~ along the dotted line** découper suivant le pointillé; **his sword ~ through the air** son épée fendit l'air; **this knife ~s well** ce couteau coupe bien; (*fig*) **this ~s across all I have learnt** ceci va à l'encontre de tout ce que j'ai appris; (*fig*) **what you say ~s both ways** ce que vous dites est à double tranchant; (*fig*) **that argument ~s both ways** c'est un argument à double tranchant; (*fig*) **to ~ and run*** mettre les bouts‡, filer*; (*Naut*) **to ~ loose** couper les amarres; (*fig*) **he ~ loose (from his family)** il a coupé les amarres (avec sa famille).

b [*material*] se couper. **paper ~s easily** le papier se coupe facilement; **this piece will ~ into 4** ce morceau peut se couper en 4.

c (*Math*) se couper. **lines A and B ~ at point C** les lignes A et B se coupent au point C.

d (*run, hurry*) **~ across the fields and you'll soon be there** coupez à travers champs et vous serez bientôt arrivé; **to ~ across country** couper à travers champs; **if you ~ through the lane you'll save time** si vous coupez *or* passez par la ruelle vous gagnerez du temps.

e (*Cine, TV*) **they ~ from the street to the shop scene** ils passent de la rue à la scène du magasin; **~!** coupez!

f (*Cards*) couper. **to ~ for deal** tirer pour la donne.

►cut along vi s'en aller, filer*.

►cut away 1 **vt sep** *branch* élaguer; *unwanted part* dégager, enlever (en coupant). 2 **cutaway n, adj** *see* **cut 3.**

►cut back 1 **vt sep** *plants, shrubs* élaguer, tailler; (*fig: also* **cut back on**) *production, expenditure* réduire, diminuer. 2 **vi** revenir (sur ses pas). **he cut back to the village and gave his pursuers the slip** il est revenu au village par un raccourci et a semé ses poursuivants. 3 **cutback n** *see* **cut 3.**

►cut down vt sep a *tree* couper, abattre; *corn* faucher; *person* (*by sword etc*) abattre (*d'un coup d'épée etc*); (*fig: through illness etc*) terrasser. **cut down by pneumonia** terrassé par la *or* une pneumonie.

b (*reduce*) réduire; *expenses* réduire, rogner; *article, essay* couper, tronquer; *clothes* (*gen*) rapetisser, diminuer. **she cut down the trousers to fit her son** elle a coupé le pantalon pour en faire un pour son fils; (*fig*) **to cut sb down to size*** remettre qn à sa place.

►cut down on vt fus *food* manger moins de; *alcohol* boire moins de; *cigarettes* fumer moins de; *expenditure, costs* réduire. **you should cut down on drink** vous devriez boire moins.

►cut in 1 **vi** (*into conversation*) se mêler à la conversation; (*Aut*) se rabattre. (*Aut*) **to cut in on sb** faire une queue de poisson à qn; (*Comm, Fin*) **to cut in on the market** s'infiltrer sur le marché. 2 **vt sep: to cut sb in on** *or* **into a deal*** intéresser qn à une affaire.

►cut off 1 **vi** (**†: leave*) filer*, se trotter‡.

2 **vt sep** a *piece of cloth, cheese, meat, bread* couper (*from* dans); *limbs* amputer, couper. **to cut off sb's head** trancher la tête de *or* à qn, décapiter qn; (*loc*) **to cut off one's nose to spite one's face** scier la branche sur laquelle on est assis, par dépit.

b (*disconnect*) *telephone caller, telephone, car engine, gas, electricity* couper. **our water supply has been cut off** on nous a coupé l'eau; (*Telec*) **we were cut off** nous avons été coupés; **to cut off sb's supplies** (*of food, money etc*) couper les vivres à qn.

c (*isolate*) isoler (*sb from sth* qn de qch). **to cut o.s. off from** rompre ses liens avec; **he feels very cut off in that town** il se sent très isolé dans cette ville; **town cut off by floods** ville isolée par des inondations; (*Mil*) **to cut off the enemy's retreat** couper la retraite à l'ennemi; (*fig*) **to cut sb off with a shilling** déshériter qn.

3 **cutoff n, adj, pl cutoffs** *see* **cut 3.**

►cut out 1 **vi** a (*Aut, Aviat*) [*engine*] caler.

b (‡: *leave*) filer*, se tailler‡.

2 vt sep a *picture, article* découper (*of, from* de); *statue, figure* sculpter, tailler (*of* dans); *coat* couper, tailler (*of, from* dans); (*Phot*) détourer. **to cut out a path through the jungle** se frayer un chemin à travers la jungle; (*fig*) **to be cut out for sth** avoir des dispositions pour qch; (*fig*) **he's not cut out for** *or* **to be a doctor** il n'est pas fait pour être médecin, il n'a pas l'étoffe d'un médecin; (*fig*) **he had his work cut out for him** il avait du pain sur la planche; (*fig*) **you'll have your work cut out to get there on time** vous n'avez pas de temps à perdre si vous voulez y arriver à l'heure; **you'll have your work cut out to persuade him to come** vous aurez du mal à le persuader de venir.

b (*fig*) *rival* supplanter.

c (*remove*) enlever, ôter; *intermediary, middleman* supprimer; *unnecessary detail* élaguer. **to cut sb out of one's will** déshériter qn; (*fig*) **cut it out!*** ça suffit!*, ça va comme ça!*; (*fig*) **cut out the talking!** assez bavardé!, vous avez fini de bavarder?; (*fig*) **you can cut out the tears for a start!*** et pour commencer arrête de pleurnicher!

d (*give up*) *tobacco* supprimer. **to cut out smoking/drinking** arrêter de fumer/boire.

3 **cutout** n, adj *see* **cut 3**.

►**cut up** 1 vi a (*Brit*) **to cut up rough*** se mettre en rogne* *or* en boule*; *see* **ugly**. b (*US: clown around*) faire le pitre. 2 vt sep a *wood, food* couper; *meat* (*carve*) découper; (*chop up*) hacher; (*fig*) *enemy, army* tailler en pièces, anéantir. b (*Brit* *: *pass only*) **to be cut up about sth** (*hurt*) être affecté *or* démoralisé par qch; (*annoyed*) être très embêté par qch*; **he's very cut up** il n'a plus le moral*; **he was very cut up by the death of his son** la mort de son fils l'a beaucoup affecté. 3 **cut-up**‡ adj *see* **cut 3**.

cutaneous [kjuː'teɪnɪəs] adj cutané.

cute* [kjuːt] adj a (*attractive*) mignon; (*pej*) affecté. b (*clever*) malin (*f* -igne), futé. **don't try and be ~ (with me)** ne fais pas le malin!

cutely ['kjuːtlɪ] adv (*cleverly*) d'un air malin. **to smile ~** faire un sourire mignon.

cuticle ['kjuːtɪkl] n (*skin*) épiderme *m*; *[fingernails]* petites peaux, envie *f*; (*Bot*) cuticule *f*. **~ remover** repousse-peaux *m*.

cutie‡ ['kjuːtɪ] n (*US*) (*girl*) jolie fille; (*shrewd person*) malin *m*, -igne *f*; (*shrewd action*) beau coup.

cutlass ['kʌtləs] n (*Naut*) coutelas *m*, sabre *m* d'abordage.

cutler ['kʌtləʳ] n coutelier *m*.

cutlery ['kʌtlərɪ] n a (*knives, forks, spoons etc*) couverts *mpl*; *see* **canteen**. b (*knives, daggers etc; also trade*) coutellerie *f*.

cutlet ['kʌtlɪt] n a (*gen*) côtelette *f*; *[veal]* escalope *f*. b (*US: croquette of meat, chicken etc*) croquette *f*.

cutter ['kʌtəʳ] n a (*person*) *[clothes]* coupeur *m*, -euse *f*; *[stones, jewels]* tailleur *m*; *[films]* monteur *m*, -euse *f*.

b (*tool*) coupoir *m*, couteau *m*, cutter *m*. **(pair of) ~s** (*for metal etc*) pinces *fpl* coupantes.

c (*sailing boat*) cotre *m*, cutter *m*; (*motor boat*) vedette *f*; *[coastguards]* garde-côte *m*; *[warship]* canot *m*.

d (*US: sleigh*) traîneau *m*.

cutting ['kʌtɪŋ] 1 n a (*NonC*) coupe *f*; *[diamond]* taille *f*; *[film]* montage *m*; *[trees]* coupe, abattage *m*.

b (*for road, railway*) tranchée *f*.

c (*piece cut off*) *[newspaper]* coupure *f*; *[cloth]* coupon *m*; (*Agr*) bouture *f*; *[vine]* marcotte *f*.

d (*reduction*) *[prices, expenditure]* réduction *f*, diminution *f*.

2 adj a *knife* coupant, tranchant. **the ~ edge** le tranchant; **~ pliers** pinces coupantes.

b (*fig*) *wind* glacial, cinglant; *rain* cinglant; *cold* piquant, glacial; *words* blessant, cinglant, incisif; *remark* mordant, caustique, blessant. **~ tongue** langue acérée.

3 comp ► **cutting board** planche *f* à découper ► **cutting-out scissors** (*Sewing*) ciseaux *mpl* à couture *or* de couturière ► **cutting room** (*Cine*) salle *f* de montage.

cuttlebone ['kʌtlbəʊn] n os *m* de seiche.

cuttlefish ['kʌtlfɪʃ] n seiche *f*.

CV [siː'viː] n abbr of **curriculum vitae**.

C & W ['siːən'dʌbljuː] (abbr of **country-and-western**) *see* **country**.

C.W.O. [siː,dʌbljuː'əʊ] a (abbr of **cash with order**) *see* **cash**. b (abbr of **chief warrant officer**) *see* **chief**.

CWS ['siː,dʌbljuː'es] (abbr of **Cooperative Wholesale Society**) *Coop*.

cwt abbr of **hundredweight(s)**.

cyanide ['saɪənaɪd] n cyanure *m*. **~ of potassium** cyanure de potassium.

cyanose ['saɪənəʊz] n cyanose *f*.

cybernetics [,saɪbə'netɪks] n (*NonC*) cybernétique *f*.

cyclamate ['saɪklə,meɪt, 'sɪklə,meɪt] n cyclamate *m*.

cyclamen ['sɪkləmən] n cyclamen *m*.

cycle ['saɪkl] 1 n a = **bicycle 1**. b *[poems, seasons etc]* cycle *m*. 2 vi faire de la bicyclette, faire du vélo. **he ~s to school** il va à l'école à bicyclette *or* à vélo *or* en vélo. 3 comp *lamp, chain, wheel* de bicyclette; *race* cycliste ► **cycle bell** sonnette *f or* timbre *m* de bicyclette ► **cycle clip** pince *f* à vélo ► **cycle path** piste *f* cyclable ► **cycle pump** pompe *f* à bicyclette ► **cycle rack** râtelier *m* à bicyclettes; (*on car roof*) porte-vélos *m inv* ► **cycle shed** abri *m* à bicyclettes ► **cycle track** piste *f* cyclable.

cycler ['saɪkləʳ] n (*US*) = **cyclist**.

cyclic(al) ['saɪklɪk(əl)] adj cyclique.

cycling ['saɪklɪŋ] 1 n cyclisme *m*. **to do a lot of ~** (*gen*) faire beaucoup de bicyclette *or* de vélo; (*Sport*) faire beaucoup de cyclisme. 2 comp de bicyclette ► **cycling clothes** tenue *f* cycliste ► **cycling holiday** *or* **tour: to go on a cycling holiday** *or* **tour** faire du cyclotourisme ► **cycling shorts: (pair of) cycling shorts** (short *m* de) cycliste *m* ► **cycling tour** circuit *m* à bicyclette ► **cycling track** vélodrome *m*.

cyclist ['saɪklɪst] n cycliste *mf*; *see* **racing**.

cyclone ['saɪkləʊn] n cyclone *m*. (*US*) **~ cellar** abri *m* anticyclone.

Cyclops ['saɪklɒps] n, pl **~es** *or* **Cyclopes** [saɪ'kləʊpiːz] cyclope *m*.

cyclorama [,saɪklə'rɑːmə] n (*also Cine*) cyclorama *m*.

cyclostyle ['saɪkləstaɪl] 1 n machine *f* à polycopier (*à stencils*). 2 vt polycopier.

cyclothymia [,saɪkləʊ'θaɪmɪə] n cyclothymie *f*.

cyclothymic [,saɪkləʊ'θaɪmɪk] adj, n cyclothymique (*mf*).

cyclotron ['saɪklətrɒn] n cyclotron *m*.

cygnet ['sɪgnɪt] n jeune cygne *m*.

cylinder ['sɪlɪndəʳ] 1 n a (*Aut, Math, Tech*) cylindre *m*. **a 6-~ car** une 6-cylindres; **to fire on all 4 ~s** (*lit*) avoir les 4 cylindres qui donnent; (*fig*) marcher *or* fonctionner à pleins gaz* *or* tubes*. b *[typewriter]* rouleau *m*; *[clock, gun]* barillet *m*. 2 comp ► **cylinder block** (*Aut*) bloc-cylindres *m* ► **cylinder capacity** cylindrée *f* ► **cylinder head** culasse *f*; **to take off the cylinder head** déculasser; **cylinder head gasket** joint *m* de culasse.

cylindrical [sɪ'lɪndrɪkəl] adj cylindrique.

cymbal ['sɪmbəl] n cymbale *f*.

cynic ['sɪnɪk] 1 n (*gen, Philos*) cynique *mf*. 2 adj = **cynical**.

cynical ['sɪnɪkəl] adj (*gen, Philos*) cynique.

cynically ['sɪnɪklɪ] adv cyniquement, avec cynisme.

cynicism ['sɪnɪsɪzəm] n (*gen, Philos*) cynisme *m*. **~s** remarques *fpl* cyniques, sarcasmes *mpl*.

cynosure ['saɪnəʃʊəʳ] n (*also* **~ of every eye**) point *m* de mire, centre *m* d'attraction.

CYO [siːwaɪ'əʊ] n (*US*) (abbr of **Catholic Youth Organization**) *mouvement catholique*.

cypher ['saɪfəʳ] = **cipher**.

cypress ['saɪprɪs] n cyprès *m*.

Cypriot ['sɪprɪət] 1 adj cypriote *or* chypriote. 2 n Cypriote *mf or* Chypriote *mf*.

Cyprus ['saɪprəs] n Chypre *f* (*no art*). **in ~** à Chypre.

Cyrillic [sɪ'rɪlɪk] adj cyrillique.

cyst [sɪst] n (*Med*) kyste *m*; (*Bio*) sac *m* (membraneux).

cystic fibrosis ['sɪstɪk,faɪ'brəʊsɪs] n fibrose *f* kystique.

cystitis [sɪs'taɪtɪs] n cystite *f*.

cytological [,saɪtə'lɒdʒɪkəl] adj cytologique.

cytology [saɪ'tɒlədʒɪ] n cytologie *f*.

CZ [siː'zed] (*US Geog*) (abbr of **Canal Zone**) *see* **canal**.

czar [zɑːʳ] n *see* **tsar**.

czarina [zɑː'riːnə] n *see* **tsarina**.

czarism ['zɑːrɪzəm] n *see* **tsarism**.

czarist ['zɑːrɪst] n, adj *see* **tsarist**.

Czech [tʃek] 1 adj tchèque. 2 n a Tchèque *mf*. b (*Ling*) tchèque *m*.

Czechoslovak [tʃekəʊ'sləʊvæk] 1 adj tchécoslovaque. 2 n Tchécoslovaque *mf*.

Czechoslovakia [tʃekəʊslə'vækɪə] n Tchécoslovaquie *f*.

Czechoslovakian [tʃekəʊslə'vækɪən] = **Czechoslovak**.

D

D, d [diː] 1 n a (*letter*) D, d *m*. **D for dog,** (*US*) **D for David** D comme Désirée; (*Cine etc*) **(in) 3-D** en relief. b (*Mus*) ré *m*; *see* **key**. c (*Scol: mark*) passable (≃ *10 sur 20*). d († *Brit*) **abbr of penny**†. e **abbr of died.** f (*US*) **abbr of Democrat(ic).** 2 **comp** ▸**D and C*** (*Med*) dilatation *f* et curetage *m* ▸**D-day** (*Mil*) le jour J.

D.A. [diːˈeɪ] **n abbr of District Attorney.**

dab¹ [dæb] 1 **n** a **a ~ of** un petit peu de; **a ~ of glue** une goutte de colle; **to give sth a ~ of paint** donner un petit coup *or* une petite touche de peinture à qch. b (*esp Brit: fingerprints*) **~s**⁑ empreintes digitales. 2 **vt** tamponner. **to ~ one's eyes** se tamponner les yeux; **to ~ paint on sth** donner un petit coup de peinture à qch, mettre un peu de peinture sur qch; **to ~ iodine on a wound** appliquer de la teinture d'iode à petits coups sur une blessure.

▸**dab off vt sep** enlever (en tamponnant).

▸**dab on vt sep** appliquer *or* mettre *or* étaler à petits coups.

dab² [dæb] **n** (*fish*) limande *f*.

dab³ [dæb] **adj** (*Brit*) **to be a ~ hand* at sth/at doing sth** être doué en qch/pour faire qch.

dabble [ˈdæbl] 1 **vt: to ~ one's hands/feet in the water** barboter dans l'eau avec les mains/les pieds. 2 **vi** (*fig*) **to ~ in sth** (*gen*) faire qch en amateur; **to ~ in politics** donner dans la politique; **to ~ in stocks and shares** *or* **on the Stock Exchange** boursicoter.

dabbler [ˈdæbləʳ] **n** (*often pej*) amateur *m*.

dabchick [ˈdæbtʃɪk] **n** petit grèbe.

Dacca [ˈdækə] **n** Dhaka, Dacca.

dace [deɪs] **n, pl ~** *or* **~s** vandoise *f*.

dacha [ˈdætʃə] **n** dacha *f*.

dachshund [ˈdækshʊnd] **n** teckel *m*.

Dacron [ˈdækrɒn] **n** ® tergal *m* ®.

dactyl [ˈdæktɪl] **n** dactyle *m*.

dactylic [dækˈtɪlɪk] **adj** dactylique.

dad [dæd] **n** a (*) papa *m*. b (⁑: *to old man*) **come on, ~!** allez viens pépé!*; (*hum*) **D~'s army** l'armée *f* de (grand-)papa (*hum*).

Dada [ˈdɑːdɑː] 1 **n** Dada *m*. 2 **comp** *school, movement* dada *inv*, dadaïste.

dadaism [ˈdɑːdɑːɪzəm] **n** dadaïsme *m*.

dadaist [ˈdɑːdɑːɪst] **adj, n** dadaïste *(mf)*.

daddy [ˈdædɪ] 1 **n** (*) papa *m*. 2 **comp** ▸**daddy-long-legs pl inv** (*harvestman*) faucheur *m or* faucheux *m*; (*Brit: cranefly*) tipule *f*.

dado [ˈdeɪdəʊ] **n, pl ~es** *or* **~s** plinthe *f*; *[pedestal]* dé *m*; *[wall]* lambris *m* d'appui.

Daedalus [ˈdiːdələs] **n** Dédale *m*.

daemon [ˈdiːmən] **n** démon *m*.

daffodil [ˈdæfədɪl] **n** jonquille *f*. **~ yellow** jonquille *inv* (jaune).

daffy⁑ [ˈdæfɪ] **adj** toqué*, timbré*.

daft [dɑːft] (*Brit*) **adj** *person* idiot, dingue⁑; *idea* stupide, idiot. **to be ~ about*** être fou (*f* folle) de.

dagger [ˈdægəʳ] **n** a poignard *m*, (*shorter*) dague *f*. (*fig*) **to be at ~s drawn with sb** être à couteaux tirés avec qn; **to look ~s at sb** lancer des regards furieux *or* meurtriers à qn, foudroyer qn du regard. b (*Typ*) croix *f*.

dago [ˈdeɪgəʊ] **n, pl ~s** *or* **~es** (*pej*) métèque *m* (*pej*) (*gén d'origine italienne ou espagnole etc*).

daguerreotype [dəˈgerəʊtaɪp] **n** daguerréotype *m*.

dahlia [ˈdeɪlɪə] **n** dahlia *m*.

Dail Eireann [dɔɪlˈɛərən] **n** *Chambre f des Députés de la république d'Irlande*.

daily [ˈdeɪlɪ] 1 **adj** *task, routine, walk* quotidien; *consumption, output, wage* journalier; (*everyday*) de tous les jours. (*Rel*) **our ~ bread** notre pain quotidien *or* de chaque jour; **~ consumption** consommation journalière; **~ dozen*** gymnastique *f* (quotidienne); (*pej*) **the ~ grind*** le train-train (quotidien); **~ paper** quotidien *m* (*see also* **3a**). 2 **adv** quotidiennement, tous les jours, journellement. **twice ~** deux fois par jour. 3 **n** a (*newspaper*) quotidien *m*. b (*Brit* *: *also* **~ help, ~ woman**) femme *f* de ménage.

daimon [ˈdaɪmɒn] **n = daemon.**

daintily [ˈdeɪntɪlɪ] **adv** *eat, hold* délicatement; *dress* coquettement; *walk* à petits pas élégants.

daintiness [ˈdeɪntɪnɪs] **n** (*see* **dainty a, b**) délicatesse *f*.

dainty [ˈdeɪntɪ] 1 **adj** a *food* de choix, délicat. **a ~ morsel** un morceau de choix. b *figure* menu; *handkerchief, blouse* délicat. **she is a ~ little thing** elle est mignonne à croquer. c (*difficult to please*) difficile. **he is a ~ eater** il est difficile (pour *or* sur la nourriture). 2 **n** mets délicat.

daiquiri [ˈdaɪkərɪ] **n** daiquiri *m*.

dairy [ˈdɛərɪ] 1 **n** (*on farm*) laiterie *f*; (*shop*) crémerie *f*, laiterie. 2 **comp** *cow, farm* laitier ▸**dairy butter** beurre fermier ▸**dairy farming** industrie laitière ▸**dairy herd** troupeau *m* de vaches laitières ▸**dairy ice cream** glace *f* faite à la crème ▸**dairymaid** fille *f* de laiterie ▸**dairyman** (*on farm etc*) employé *m* de laiterie; (*in shop*) crémier *m* ▸**dairy produce** produits laitiers.

dais [ˈdeɪɪs] **n** estrade *f*.

daisied [ˈdeɪzɪd] **adj** (*liter*) émaillé (*liter*) de pâquerettes.

daisy [ˈdeɪzɪ] 1 **n** pâquerette *f*; (*cultivated*) marguerite *f*; *see* **fresh, push up.** 2 **comp** ▸**daisy chain** guirlande *f or* collier *m* de pâquerettes; (*US fig*) série *f*, chapelet *m* ▸**daisy (ham)** (*US Culin*) jambon fumé désossé ▸**daisywheel** marguerite *f* ▸**daisywheel printer** imprimante *f* à marguerite.

Dakar [ˈdækəʳ] **n** Dakar.

Dakota [dəˈkəʊtə] **n** Dakota *m*. **North/South ~** Dakota du Nord/du Sud.

Dalai Lama [ˈdælaɪˈlɑːmə] **n** dalaï-lama *m*.

dale [deɪl] **n** (*N Engl, also liter*) vallée *f*, vallon *m*. (*Brit*) **the (Yorkshire) D~s** le pays vallonné du Yorkshire.

dalliance [ˈdælɪəns] **n** (*liter*) badinage *m* (amoureux).

dally [ˈdælɪ] **vi** (*dawdle*) lambiner*, lanterner (*over sth* dans *or* sur qch). **to ~ with an idea** caresser une idée; **to ~ with sb**† badiner (amoureusement) avec qn.

Dalmatian [dælˈmeɪʃən] **n** (*also* **d~**: *dog*) dalmatien *m*.

dalmatic [dælˈmætɪk] **n** dalmatique *f*.

daltonism [ˈdɔːltənɪzəm] **n** daltonisme *m*.

dam¹ [dæm] 1 **n** a (*wall*) *[river]* barrage *m* (de retenue), digue *f*; *[lake]* barrage (de retenue). b (*water*) réservoir *m*, lac *m* de retenue. 2 **vt** a (*also* **~ up**) *river* endiguer; *lake* construire un barrage sur. **to ~ the waters of the Nile** faire *or* construire un barrage pour contenir les eaux du Nil. b *flow of words, oaths* endiguer. 3 **comp** ▸**dambuster** (*bomb*) bombe *f* à ricochets; (*person*) (aviateur *m*) briseur *m* de barrages (*se réfère à un épisode de la Seconde Guerre mondiale*).

dam² [dæm] **n** (*animal*) mère *f*.

dam³⁑ [dæm] **adj, adv** a **= damn 4, 5.** b (*US*) **~Yankee** sale* Yankee *or* Nordiste.

damage [ˈdæmɪdʒ] 1 **n** a (*NonC*) dommage(s) *m(pl)*; (*visible, eg to car*) dégâts *mpl*, dommages; (*to ship, cargo*) avarie(s) *f(pl)*; (*fig*) préjudice *m*, tort *m*. **~ to property** dégâts matériels; **to make good the ~** réparer les dégâts; **the bomb did a lot of ~** la bombe a causé des dommages importants, la bombe a fait de gros dégâts; **there was a lot of ~ (done) to the house** la maison a beaucoup souffert; **there's no ~ done** il n'y a pas de mal; **the ~ is done (now)** le mal est fait; **that has done ~ to our cause** cela a fait du tort *or* porté préjudice à notre cause; **~ control, ~ limitation** limitation *f* des dégâts; (*fig: how much is it ?*) **what's the ~?*** cela se monte à combien?; (*Insurance*) **~ survey** expertise *f* d'avarie; *see* **storm 2.**

b (*Jur*) **~s** dommages *mpl* et intérêts *mpl*, dommages-intérêts *mpl*; **liable for ~s** tenu des dommages et intérêts; **war ~** dommages *or* indemnités *fpl* de guerre; *see* **sue.**

2 **vt** *furniture, goods, crops, machine, vehicle* endommager, causer des dégâts à, abîmer; *food* abîmer, gâter; *eyesight, health* abîmer; *good relations, reputation* nuire à, porter atteinte à; *cause, objectives* faire du tort à.

damageable ['dæmɪdʒəbl] adj dommageable.
damaging ['dæmɪdʒɪŋ] adj préjudiciable, nuisible (*to* à); (*Jur*) préjudiciable.
Damascus [də'mɑːskəs] n Damas.
damask ['dæməsk] 1 n a (*cloth*) [*silk*] damas *m*, soie damassée; [*linen*] (linge *m*) damassé *m*. b ~ **(steel)** (acier *m*) damasquiné *m*. 2 adj *cloth* damassé. (*liter*) **her ~ cheeks** ses joues vermeilles (*liter*). 3 comp ►**damask rose** rose *f* de Damas.
dame [deɪm] n a (*esp Brit*) (†, *liter, also hum*) dame *f*. (*Brit Theat*) **the ~** la vieille dame (*rôle féminin de farce bouffonne joué par un homme*); (*Hist*) ~ **school** école enfantine, petit cours privé; (†, *liter*) **D~ Fortune** Dame Fortune. b (*Brit: in titles*) **D~** *titre porté par une femme décorée d'un ordre de chevalerie (e.g. Dame Margot Fonteyn, Dame Margot)*. c (*US* ‡) fille *f*, nana‡ *f*.
damfool‡, damnfool‡ ['dæm'fuːl] adj (*Brit*) idiot, crétin, fichu*. **that ~ waiter** ce crétin de garçon, ce fichu* garçon.
dammit‡ ['dæmɪt] excl (*Brit*) bon sang!*, merde!‡ **it weighs 2 kilos as near as ~** cela pèse 2 kilos à un cheveu près *or* à un poil* près.
damn [dæm] 1 excl (‡: *also* ~ **it!**) bon sang!*, merde!‡; *see* **2c**.
2 vt a (*Rel*) damner; *book* condamner, éreinter. **to ~ with faint praise** faire de tièdes éloges à; **his long hair ~ed him from the start** ses cheveux longs le condamnaient dès le départ *or* d'avance.
b (*swear at*) pester contre, maudire.
c (‡) ~ **him!** qu'il aille au diable!, qu'il aille se faire fiche!*; **the boy pinched my book, ~ him!** il a fauché mon livre, le petit salaud!‡; ~ **it!** bon sang!*, merde!‡; **well I'll be** *or* **I'm ~ed!** ça c'est trop fort!; **I'll be** *or* **I'm ~ed if ...** je veux bien être pendu si ..., que le diable m'emporte si ...; ~ **this machine!** au diable cette machine!, il y en a marre de cette machine!‡
3 n (‡) **I don't care a ~, I don't give a ~** je m'en fous‡ pas mal, je n'en ai rien à foutre‡; **he just doesn't give a ~ about anything** il se fout‡ de tout; **it's not worth a ~** cela ne vaut pas un clou*, ça ne vaut strictement rien, c'est de la foutaise‡; *see also* **give 1a**.
4 adj (‡: *also* **dam³, damned**) fichu* (*before n*), sacré* (*before n*). **it is one ~ thing after another** quand ce n'est pas une chose c'est l'autre; **it's a ~ nuisance!** quelle barbe!*, c'est la barbe!*
5 adv a (‡: *also* **dam³, damned**) (*extremely*) vachement‡, sacrément*, rudement*.
b (*Brit: also* **dam³**) **I know ~ all about it** je n'en sais foutrement‡ rien; **can you see anything? — ~ all!** tu vois quelque chose? — zéro!* *or* rien de rien!*; **there's ~ all to drink in the house** il n'y a pas une goutte à boire dans la maison; **that's ~ all good** *or* **use** tu parles d'un truc utile!*, comme utilité c'est zéro!*; **he's done ~ all today** il n'a rien fichu* *or* foutu‡ aujourd'hui; **you know ~ well what I mean** tu sais foutrement‡ bien de quoi je parle.
damnable* ['dæmnəbl] adj détestable, odieux.
damnably* ['dæmnəblɪ] adv vachement‡, rudement*.
damnation [dæm'neɪʃən] 1 n (*Rel*) damnation *f*. 2 excl (‡) enfer et damnation! (*hum*), malheur!, misère!, merde!‡
damned [dæmd] 1 adj a *soul* damné, maudit. b (‡) *see* **damn 4**. 2 adv (‡) *see* **damn 5**. 3 n (*Rel, liter*) **the ~** les damnés.
damnedest‡ ['dæmdɪst] 1 n: **to do one's ~ to help/to get away** faire l'impossible *or* tout (son possible) pour aider/pour s'évader. 2 adj (†*) **he's the ~ eccentric** il est d'une excentricité folle* *or* renversante*.
damnfool‡ ['dæm'fuːl] adj = **damfool**.
damning ['dæmɪŋ] adj *words, facts, evidence* accablant. **the criticism was ~** c'était un éreintement.
Damocles ['dæməkliːz] n: **the Sword of ~** l'épée de Damoclès.
damp [dæmp] 1 adj *air, room, clothes, heat* humide; *skin* moite. (*Brit*) **that was a ~ squib*** c'est tombé à plat, ça a fait long feu. 2 n a [*atmosphere, walls*] humidité *f*. b (*Min*) (*choke* ~) mofette *f*; (*fire* ~) grisou *m*. 3 vt a *a cloth, ironing* humecter. b *sounds* amortir, étouffer; (*Mus*) étouffer; *fire* couvrir. c *enthusiasm, courage, ardour* refroidir. **to ~ sb's spirits** décourager *or* déprimer qn; **to ~ sb's appetite** faire passer l'envie de manger à qn. 4 comp ►**damp course** (*Brit Constr*) couche isolante ►**damp-dry** prêt à repasser (*encore humide*) ►**damp-proof** imperméable, étanche, hydrofuge ►**damp-proof course** = **damp course**.
►**damp down** vt sep *fire* couvrir; (*fig*) *crisis etc* décrisper; *consumption, demand* freiner, réduire.
dampen ['dæmpən] vt = **damp 3a, 3c**.
damper ['dæmpər] n, (*US*) **dampener** ['dæmpənər] n a [*chimney*] registre *m*. b (*: *depressing event*) douche *f* (froide)*. **to act as** *or* **put a ~ on** jeter un froid sur. c (*Mus*) étouffoir *m*. d (*Aut, Elec, Tech*) amortisseur *m*. e (*for stamps, envelopes, clothes*) mouilleur *m*.
dampish ['dæmpɪʃ] adj un peu humide.
damply ['dæmplɪ] adv sans (grand) enthousiasme, mollement.
dampness ['dæmpnɪs] n (*see* **damp**) humidité *f*; moiteur *f*.
damsel ['dæmzəl] 1 n (††, *liter, also hum*) damoiselle *f*. ~ **in distress** damoiselle en détresse. 2 comp ►**damsel-fly** (*Zool*) demoiselle *f*, libellule *f*.
damson ['dæmzən] n (*fruit*) prune *f* de Damas; (*tree*) prunier *m* de Damas.
dan [dæn] n (*Sport*) dan *m*.
dance [dɑːns] 1 n a (*movement*) danse *f*. **the D~ of Death** la danse macabre; (*Brit fig*) **to lead sb a (pretty) ~** donner à qn du fil à retordre; **may I have the next ~?** voudriez-vous m'accorder la prochaine danse?; *see* **folk, sequence** *etc*.
b (*social gathering*) bal *m*, soirée dansante, sauterie *f* (*more informal*). **to give** *or* **hold a ~** donner un bal; **to go to a ~** aller à un bal *or* à une soirée dansante.
2 vt *waltz etc* danser. (*fig*) **to ~ attendance on sb** être aux petits soins pour qn.
3 vi [*person, leaves in wind, boat on waves, eyes*] danser. **he ~d with her** il l'a fait danser; **she ~d with him** elle a dansé avec lui; (*fig*) **to ~ in/out** *etc* entrer/sortir *etc* joyeusement; **to ~ about, to ~ up and down** gambader, sautiller; **the child ~d away** *or* **off** l'enfant s'est éloigné en gambadant *or* en sautillant; **to ~ for joy** sauter de joie; **to ~ with rage** trépigner de colère; (*fig*) **to ~ to sb's tune** faire les quatre volontés de qn.
4 comp ►**dance band** orchestre *m* de danse ►**dance floor** piste *f* (de danse) ►**dance hall** dancing *m* ►**dance hostess** entraîneuse *f* ►**dance music** musique *f* de danse ►**dance programme** carnet *m* de bal ►**dance studio** cours *m* de danse; (*place*) salle *f* de danse.
dancer ['dɑːnsər] n danseur *m*, -euse *f*.
dancing ['dɑːnsɪŋ] 1 n (*NonC*) danse *f*. 2 comp *master, school* de danse ►**dancing-girl** danseuse *f* ►**dancing-partner** cavalier *m*, -ière *f*, partenaire *mf* ►**dancing shoes** [*men*] escarpins *mpl*; [*women*] souliers *mpl* de bal; (*for ballet*) chaussons *mpl* de danse.
dandelion ['dændɪlaɪən] n pissenlit *m*, dent-de-lion *f*.
dander* ['dændər] n: **to get sb's ~ up** mettre qn hors de lui *or* en rogne*; **to have one's ~ up** être hors de soi *or* en rogne*.
dandified ['dændɪfaɪd] adj vêtu en dandy, qui a une allure de dandy.
dandle ['dændl] vt *child* (*on knees*) faire sauter sur ses genoux; (*in arms*) bercer dans ses bras, câliner.
dandruff ['dændrəf] n (*NonC*) pellicules *fpl* (*du cuir chevelu*). ~ **shampoo** shampooing *m* antipelliculaire.
dandy ['dændɪ] 1 n dandy *m*, élégant *m*. 2 adj (*: *esp US*) épatant*.
Dane [deɪn] n a Danois(e) *m(f)*. b *see* **great 3**.
dang* [dæŋ] (*euph*) = **damn 1, 4, 5**.
danger ['deɪndʒər] 1 n danger *m*, péril *m*. **to be a ~ to** être un danger pour; **to put in ~** mettre en danger *or* en péril; **in ~** en danger; **he was in little ~** il ne courait pas grand risque; (*gen, Med*) **out of ~** hors de danger; **in ~ of invasion** menacé d'invasion; **he was in ~ of losing his job** il risquait de *or* il était menacé de perdre sa place; **he was in ~ of falling** il risquait de tomber; **there was no ~ that she would be recognized** *or* **of her being recognized** elle ne courait aucun risque d'être reconnue; (*lit*) **there's no ~ of that** il n'y a pas le moindre danger *or* risque; (*iro*) il n'y a pas de danger, aucune chance; **there is a ~ of fire** il y a un risque d'incendie; (*Rail*) **signal at ~** signal à l'arrêt; **"~ road up"** "attention (aux) travaux"; **"~ keep out"** "danger: défense d'entrer".
2 comp ►**danger area** = **danger zone** ►**danger list**: (*Med*) **to be on the danger list** être dans un état critique *or* très grave; (*Med*) **to be off the danger list** être hors de danger ►**danger money** prime *f* de risque ►**danger point** point *m* critique, cote *f* d'alerte ►**danger signal** signal *m* d'alarme; (*Rail*) arrêt *m* ►**danger zone** zone dangereuse.
dangerous ['deɪndʒrəs] adj *person, animal, behaviour, example, maxim, topic, river, event, tool* dangereux; *expedition* dangereux, périlleux; *illness* grave. **it is ~ to do that** il est dangereux de faire cela; **in a ~ situation** dans une situation périlleuse, dans un mauvais pas; (*fig*) **to be on ~ ground** être sur un terrain glissant.
dangerously ['deɪndʒrəslɪ] adv a (*in a dangerous way*) *live, sway, shake etc* dangereusement. b (*to a dangerous degree*) gravement, dangereusement, sérieusement. ~ **ill** gravement malade; ~ **wounded** grièvement *or* gravement blessé; **food supplies were ~ low** les vivres commençaient sérieusement à manquer; **he stood ~ near the fire** il se tenait dangereusement près du feu; (*fig*) **he came ~ close to admitting it** il s'en est fallu d'un doigt qu'il l'admette, il a été à deux doigts de l'admettre; **the date is getting ~ close** la date s'approche de manière menaçante *or* inquiétante.
dangle ['dæŋgl] 1 vt *object on string* balancer, suspendre; *arm, leg* laisser pendre, balancer; (*fig*) *prospect, offer* faire miroiter (*before sb* à qn). 2 vi [*object on string*] pendre, pendiller; [*arms, legs*] pendre, (se) balancer. **with arms dangling** les bras ballants; **with legs dangling** les jambes pendantes.
Daniel ['dænjəl] n Daniel *m*.
Danish ['deɪnɪʃ] 1 adj danois. 2 comp ►**Danish blue (cheese)** bleu *m* (du Danemark) ►**Danish pastry** feuilleté *m* (fourré aux fruits *etc*). 3 n a (*Ling*) danois *m*. b **the D~** les Danois *mpl*. c = **Danish pastry**; *see* **2**.
dank [dæŋk] adj *air, weather* humide et froid; *dungeon* humide et froid, aux murs suintants.
Dante ['dæntɪ] n Dante *m*.
Dantean ['dæntɪən], **Dantesque** [dæn'tesk] adj dantesque.
Danube ['dænjuːb] n Danube *m*.
Danzig ['dænsɪg] n Dan(t)zig.

Daphne ['dæfnɪ] n a (*name*) Daphné *f*. b (*plant*) **d~** daphné *f* lauréola, lauréole *f*.
daphnia ['dæfnɪə] n daphnie *f*.
dapper ['dæpəʳ] adj (*neat*) pimpant, soigné de sa personne; (*nimble*) fringant, sémillant.
dapple ['dæpl] 1 vt tacheter. 2 comp ▸ **dapple grey** (cheval *m*) gris pommelé *inv*.
dappled ['dæpld] adj *surface* tacheté, moucheté; *sky* pommelé; *horse* miroité; (*grey*) pommelé.
DAR [ˌdiːeɪ'ɑːʳ] (*US*) (abbr of **Daughters of the American Revolution**) *club de descendantes des combattants de la Révolution américaine*.
Darby ['dɑːbɪ] n: ~ **and Joan** ≈ Philémon et Baucis; (*Brit*) ~ **and Joan club** cercle *m* pour couples du troisième âge.
Dardanelles [ˌdɑːdə'nelz] n: **the** ~ les Dardanelles *fpl*.
dare [dɛəʳ] pret **dared** or **durst**††, ptp **dared** 1 vt modal aux vb a oser (*do, to do* faire). **he dare not** or **daren't climb that tree** il n'ose pas grimper à cet arbre; **he dared not do it, he didn't dare (to) do it** il n'a pas osé le faire; **dare you do it?** oserez-vous le faire?; **how dare you say such things?** comment osez-vous dire des choses pareilles?; **how dare you!** vous osez!, comment osez-vous?, vous (en) avez du culot!*; **don't dare say that!** je vous défends d'oser dire cela!; **don't you dare!** ose donc!, avise-toi donc!; **I daren't!** je n'ose pas!; **the show was, dare I say it, dull** le spectacle était, si je puis me permettre, ennuyeux.
b **I dare say he'll come** il viendra sans doute, il est probable qu'il viendra; **I dare say you're tired after your journey** vous êtes sans doute fatigué or j'imagine que vous êtes fatigué après votre voyage; **I dare say she's 40** elle pourrait bien avoir 40 ans, je lui donne dans les 40 ans; **he is very sorry** — (*iro*) **I dare say!** il le regrette beaucoup — c'est bien possible! (*iro*).
c (*face the risk of*) *danger, death* affronter, braver.
d (*challenge*) **to dare sb to do** défier qn de faire, mettre qn au défi de faire; **(I) dare you!** chiche!*
2 n défi *m*. **to do sth for a dare** faire qch pour relever un défi.
3 comp ▸ **daredevil** n casse-cou *m inv*, cerveau brûlé, risque-tout *m inv* ◊ adj *behaviour* de casse-cou; *adventure* fou (*f* folle), audacieux.
Dar-es-Salaam [ˌdɑːressə'lɑːm] n Dar Es-Salaam.
daring ['dɛərɪŋ] 1 adj *person, attempt* audacieux, téméraire, hardi; *dress, opinion, proposal* osé, audacieux, hardi. 2 n audace *f*, hardiesse *f*.
daringly ['dɛərɪŋlɪ] adv audacieusement, témérairement. ~ **low-cut** au décolleté provoquant.
dark [dɑːk] 1 adj a (*lacking light*) obscur, noir; *room* sombre, obscur; *dungeon* noir, ténébreux. **it is** ~ il fait nuit or noir; **it is getting** ~ il commence à faire nuit; **it is as** ~ **as pitch** or **night** il fait nuit noire; **the sky is getting** ~ le ciel s'assombrit; **the** ~ **side of the moon** la face cachée de la Lune.
b *colour* foncé, sombre. ~ **blue/green** bleu/vert foncé *inv*; ~ **brown hair** cheveux châtain foncé *inv*; **a** ~ **blue** un bleu sombre; ~ **glasses** lunettes noires; ~ **chocolate** chocolat *m* à croquer; *see also* **blue**.
c *complexion, skin, hair* brun. **she is very** ~ elle est très brune; **she has a** ~ **complexion** elle a le teint foncé or brun or basané; **she has** ~ **hair** elle est brune, elle a les cheveux bruns.
d mystérieux, obscur, secret (*f* -ète); (*sinister*) noir. **to keep sth** ~ tenir qch secret; **keep it** ~! pas un mot!, pas un mot à la Reine Mère!*; ~ **designs** noirs desseins; ~ **hint** allusion sibylline or énigmatique; ~ **threats** sourdes menaces; (*fig*) ~ **horse** (*gen*) quantité inconnue; (*US Pol*) candidat inattendu.
e (*gloomy, sad*) *thoughts* sombre, triste. **to look on the** ~ **side of things** voir tout en noir.
f (*Phon*) sombre.
2 n a (*absence of light*) nuit *f*, obscurité *f*, noir *m*. **after** ~ la nuit venue, après la tombée de la nuit; **until** ~ jusqu'à (la tombée de) la nuit; **to be afraid of the** ~ avoir peur du noir.
b (*fig*) **I am quite in the** ~ **about it** je suis tout à fait dans le noir là-dessus, j'ignore tout de cette histoire; **he has kept** or **left me in the** ~ **as to** or **about what he wants to do** il m'a laissé dans l'ignorance or il ne m'a donné aucun renseignement sur ce qu'il veut faire; **to work in the** ~ travailler à l'aveuglette; *see* **shot**.
3 comp ▸ **dark age** (*fig*) période *f* sombre; **the Dark Ages** l'âge *m* des ténèbres or de l'ignorance ▸ **dark-complexioned** brun (de teint), basané ▸ **the Dark Continent** le continent noir ▸ **dark-eyed** aux yeux noirs ▸ **dark-haired** aux cheveux bruns ▸ **dark room** (*Phot*) chambre noire ▸ **dark-skinned** *person* brun (de peau), à peau brune; *race* de couleur.
darken ['dɑːkən] 1 vt *room, landscape* obscurcir, assombrir; *sky* assombrir; *sun* obscurcir, voiler; *complexion* brunir, basaner; *colour* foncer; *brilliance* ternir; (*fig*) *reason* obscurcir; *future* assombrir; (*sadden*) assombrir, attrister. (††, *hum*) **never** ~ **my door again!** ne mettez plus les pieds chez moi!; **a** ~**ed house/room/street** une maison/pièce/rue sombre. 2 vi *[sky, evening]* s'assombrir; *[room]* s'obscurcir, s'assombrir; *[colours]* foncer. **the night** ~**ed gradually** la nuit s'assombrit peu à peu or se fit peu à peu plus épaisse; (*fig*) **his brow** ~**ed** sa mine s'est rembrunie.
darkey⁎⁎, **darkie**⁎⁎ ['dɑːkɪ] n (*pej*) moricaud(e)⁎⁎ *m(f)* (*pej*), nègre⁎⁎ *m* (*pej*), négresse⁎⁎ *f* (*pej*).
darkish ['dɑːkɪʃ] adj *sky* (un peu) sombre; *hair, person* plutôt brun.
darkly ['dɑːklɪ] adv a *outlined* obscurément. **hills rose** ~ des collines dressaient leurs silhouettes sombres. b *hint* mystérieusement, énigmatiquement. c (*gloomily*) tristement; (*sinisterly*) sinistrement, lugubrement.
darkness ['dɑːknɪs] n (*NonC*) a *[night, room]* (*also fig*) obscurité *f*, ténèbres *fpl*. **in total** or **utter** ~ dans une complète or totale obscurité; **the house was in** ~ la maison était plongée dans l'obscurité; *see* **prince**. b *[colour]* teinte foncée; *[face, skin]* teint brun or bronzé or basané.
darky⁎⁎ ['dɑːkɪ] n = **darkey**⁎⁎.
darling ['dɑːlɪŋ] 1 n bien-aimé(e)† *m(f)*, favori(te) *m(f)*. (*fig*) **the** ~ **of** la coqueluche de; **a mother's** ~ un chouchou*, une chouchoute*, un(e) enfant gâté(e); **she's a little** ~ c'est un petit amour, elle est adorable; **come here, (my)** ~ viens (mon) chéri or mon amour; (*to child*) viens (mon) chéri or mon petit chou; **be a** ~* **and bring me my glasses** sois un chou or un ange et apporte-moi mes lunettes; **she was a perfect** ~ **about it*** elle a été un ange (dans cette histoire). 2 adj *child* chéri, bien-aimé†; (*liter*) *wish* le plus cher. **a** ~ **little place*** un petit coin ravissant or adorable.
darn[1] [dɑːn] 1 vt *socks* repriser; *clothes etc* raccommoder. 2 n reprise *f*.
darn[2]* [dɑːn], **darned*** [dɑːnd] euph of **damn, damned**; *see* **damn 1, 2c, 3, 4, 5**.
darnel ['dɑːnl] n ivraie *f*, ray-grass *m*.
darning ['dɑːnɪŋ] 1 n a (*NonC*) raccommodage *m*, reprise *f*. b (*things to be darned*) raccommodage *m*, linge *m* or vêtements *mpl* à raccommoder. 2 comp ▸ **darning needle** aiguille *f* à repriser ▸ **darning stitch** point *m* de reprise ▸ **darning wool** laine *f* à repriser.
dart [dɑːt] 1 n a **to make a sudden** ~ **at** foncer* sur, se précipiter sur. b (*Sport*) fléchette *f*. **a game of** ~**s** une partie de fléchettes; **I like (playing)** ~**s** j'aime jouer aux fléchettes. c (*weapon*) trait *m*, javelot *m*; (*liter*) *[serpent, bee]* dard *m*; (*fig*) trait, flèche *f*; *see* **Cupid, paper**. d (*Sewing*) pince *f*. 2 vi se précipiter, s'élancer, foncer* (*at* sur). **to** ~ **in/out** *etc* entrer/sortir *etc* comme une flèche. 3 vt *rays* darder; *look* darder, décocher. 4 comp ▸ **dartboard** cible *f* (*de jeu de fléchettes*).
Darwinian [dɑː'wɪnɪən] adj darwinien.
Darwinism ['dɑːwɪnɪzəm] n darwinisme *m*.
dash [dæʃ] 1 n a (*sudden rush*) mouvement *m* brusque (*en avant*), élan *m*; *[crowd]* ruée *f*. **there was a** ~ **for the door** tout le monde se précipita or se rua vers la porte; **to make a** ~ se précipiter, se ruer, foncer* (*at* sur, *towards* vers); **to make a** ~ **for freedom** saisir l'occasion de s'enfuir; **he made a** ~ **for it*** il a pris ses jambes à son cou; (*Sport*) **the 100 metre** ~ le sprint, le 100 mètres; *see* **cut**.
b (*small amount*) petite quantité; *[spirits, flavouring]* goutte *f*, larme *f*, doigt *m*; *[seasonings etc]* pointe *f*; *[vinegar, lemon]* filet *m*; *[colour]* touche *f*, tache *f*. **a** ~ **of soda** un peu d'eau de Seltz.
c (*punctuation mark*) tiret *m*; (*in handwriting*) trait *m* de plume.
d (*Morse*) trait *m*.
e *see* **dashboard**.
2 vt a (*throw violently*) jeter or lancer violemment. **to** ~ **sth to pieces** casser qch en mille morceaux; **to** ~ **sth down** or **to the ground** jeter or flanquer* qch par terre; **to** ~ **one's head against** se cogner la tête contre; **the ship was** ~**ed against a rock** le navire a été jeté contre un écueil.
b (*fig*) *spirits* abattre; *person* démoraliser. **to** ~ **sb's hopes** anéantir les espoirs de qn.
3 vi a (*rush*) se précipiter, filer*. **to** ~ **away/back/up** *etc* s'en aller/revenir/monter *etc* à toute allure or en coup de vent; **to** ~ **into a room** se précipiter dans une pièce; **I must** ~* il faut que je file* (*subj*).
b (*crash*) *[waves]* se briser (*against* contre); *[car, bird, object]* se heurter (*against* à), se jeter (*against* contre).
4 excl (* euph of **damn**) ~ **(it)!**, ~ **it all!** zut alors!*, flûte!*; **but** ~ **it all*, you can't do that!** mais quand même, tu ne peux faire ça!
▸**dash off** 1 vi partir précipitamment. 2 vt sep *letter etc* faire en vitesse; *drawing* dessiner en un tour de main.
dashboard ['dæʃbɔːd] n (*Aut*) tableau *m* de bord.
dashed* [dæʃt] adj, adv euph of **damned**; *see* **damn 4, 5**.
dashiki [dɑː'ʃiːkɪ] n tunique africaine.
dashing ['dæʃɪŋ] adj a (*spirited*) *person, behaviour* impétueux, plein d'allant. b (*stylish*) *person, appearance* fringant, qui a grande allure, plein de panache.
dashingly ['dæʃɪŋlɪ] adv *behave* avec brio, avec fougue, avec panache; *dress* avec une élégance fringante.
das(s)n't ['dæsənt] (*US*) = **dare not**; *see* **dare**.
dastardly ['dæstədlɪ] adj († or *liter*) *person, action* lâche, ignoble.
DAT [diːeɪ'tiː] n (abbr of **digital audio tape**) *see* **digital**.
data ['deɪtə] 1 npl of **datum** (*sometimes with sg vb*) données *fpl*, information *f* (brute), informations (brutes); (*Comput*) données.
2 comp (*Comput*) *input, sorting etc* de(s) données ▸ **data bank** banque *f* de or des données ▸ **database** (*Comput*) base *f* de données ▸ **database management** gestion *f* de (base de) données ▸ **database management system** système *m* de gestion de données ▸ **data**

capture saisie *f* des données ▸**data carrier** support *m* d'informations *or* de données ▸**data collection** collecte *f* de données ▸**data directory, data dictionary** dictionnaire *m* de données ▸**data file** fichier *m* informatisé *or* de données ▸**data link** liaison *f* de transmission ▸**data pen** lecteur *m* optique (*pour code à barres*) ▸**Datapost** ® (*Brit Post*) ≃ Postexpress ® (PTT) ▸**data preparation** préparation *f* de données ▸**data processing** informatique *f*, traitement *m* de données ▸**data processor** (*machine*) machine *f* de traitement de données; (*person*) informaticien(ne) *m(f)* ▸**data protection act** ≃ loi *f* informatique et libertés ▸**data security** sécurité *f* des informations ▸**data transmission** transmission *f* de données.

3 **vt** (* *US*) *person etc* ficher.

datcha ['dætʃə] **n** = **dacha**.

date¹ [deɪt] 1 **n** a (*time of some event*) date *f*; (*Jur*) quantième *m* (du mois). ~ **of birth** date de naissance; **what is today's ~?** quelle est la date aujourd'hui?, nous sommes le combien aujourd'hui?; **what ~ is he coming (on)?** à quelle date vient-il?, quel jour arrive-t-il?; **what is the ~ of this letter?** de quand est cette lettre?; **to fix a ~ for a meeting** prendre date *or* convenir d'une date pour un rendez-vous; **to set a ~ for sth** fixer une date pour qch.

b *[coins, medals etc]* millésime *m*.

c (*phrases*) **the announcement of recent ~ that ...** l'annonce récente *or* de fraîche date que ...; **to ~ we have accomplished nothing** jusqu'ici *or* à ce jour nous n'avons rien accompli; **to be out of ~** *[document]* ne plus être applicable; *[building]* être démodé, ne plus être au goût du jour, être de conception dépassée; *[person]* retarder, ne pas être de son temps *or* à la page; **he's very out of ~** il retarde vraiment; **to be out of ~ in one's opinions** avoir des opinions complètement dépassées; **to be up to ~** *[document]* être à jour; *[building]* être moderne, être au goût du jour; *[person]* être moderne *or* à la page *or* dans le vent; **to be up to ~ in one's work** *etc* être à jour dans son travail *etc;* **to bring up to ~** *accounts, correspondence etc* mettre à jour; *method etc* moderniser; **to bring sb up to ~** mettre qn au courant (*about sth* de qch); *see also* **out, up.**

d (*: *appointment*) rendez-vous *m*, rancard⁑ *m*; (⁑: *person*) petit(e) ami(e) *m(f)*. **to have a ~ with sb** avoir (pris) rendez-vous avec qn; **they made a ~ for 8 o'clock** ils ont pris rendez-vous *or* fixé un rendez-vous pour 8 heures; **have you got a ~ for tonight?** as-tu (un) rendez-vous ce soir?; **he's my ~ for this evening** je sors avec lui ce soir; *see* **blind.**

2 **comp** ▸**date book** (*US*) agenda *m* ▸**date line** (*Geog*) ligne *f* de changement de date *or* de changement de jour; (*Press*) date *f* (d'une dépêche) ▸**date stamp n** *[library etc]* tampon *m* (encreur) (*pour dater un livre etc*), dateur *m*; (*Post*) tampon *or* cachet *m* (de la poste); (*for cancelling*) oblitérateur *m*; (*postmark*) cachet de la poste ▸**date-stamp vt** *library book* tamponner; *letter, document* (*gen*) apposer le cachet de la date sur; (*Post*) apposer le cachet de la poste sur; (*cancel*) *stamp* oblitérer.

3 **vt** a *letter* dater; *ticket, voucher* dater; (*with machine*) composter. **letter ~d August 7th** lettre datée du 7 août; **a coin ~d 1390** une pièce au millésime de 1390.

b *manuscript, ruins etc* donner *or* assigner une date à, fixer la date de. **his taste in ties certainly ~s him** son goût en matière de cravates trahit son âge; *see* **carbon.**

c (*: *esp US*) (*go out regularly with*) sortir avec; (*arrange meeting with*) prendre rendez-vous avec.

4 **vi** a **to ~ from, to ~ back to** dater de, remonter à.

b (*become old-fashioned*) *[clothes, expressions etc]*dater.

c (*: *esp US*) (*go out with sb*) **they're dating** ils sortent ensemble; **she has started dating** elle commence à sortir avec des garçons.

date² [deɪt] **n** (*fruit*) datte *f*; (*tree: also* ~ **palm**) dattier *m*.

dated ['deɪtɪd] **adj** démodé, qui date (*or* datait *etc*), suranné.

Datel, datel ['deɪtel] **n** ® ≃ Transpac ®, transmission *f* de données informatiques par la poste.

dateless ['deɪtlɪs] **adj** qui ne date jamais.

dating ['deɪtɪŋ] **n** a (*Archeol*) datation *f*. b ~ **agency** agence *f* matrimoniale.

dative ['deɪtɪv] 1 **n** datif *m*. **in the ~** au datif. 2 **adj:** ~ **case** (cas *m*) datif *m*; ~ **ending** flexion *f* du datif.

datum ['deɪtəm] **n, pl data** donnée *f*; *see* **data.**

DATV [diːeɪtiːˈviː] **n** (**abbr of digitally assisted television**) télévision *f* numérique.

daub [dɔːb] 1 **vt** (*pej*) (*with paint, make-up*) barbouiller, peinturlurer* (*with* de); (*with clay, grease*) enduire, barbouiller (*with* de). 2 **n** a (*Constr*) enduit *m*. b (*pej: bad picture*) croûte* *f*, barbouillage *m*.

daughter ['dɔːtəʳ] 1 **n** (*lit, fig*) fille *f*. 2 **comp** ▸**daughter-in-law** (**pl ~s-~-~**) belle-fille *f*, bru *f* ▸**daughterboard** (*Comput*) carte *f* fille.

daunt [dɔːnt] **vt** intimider, décourager, démonter. **nothing ~ed, he continued** sans se (laisser) démonter, il a continué.

daunting ['dɔːntɪŋ] **adj** décourageant, intimidant.

dauntless ['dɔːntlɪs] **adj** *person* intrépide; *courage* indomptable.

dauntlessly ['dɔːntlɪslɪ] **adv** intrépidement, avec intrépidité.

davenport ['dævnpɔːt] **n** a (*esp US: sofa*) canapé *m*. b (*Brit: desk*) secrétaire *m*.

David ['deɪvɪd] **n** David *m*.

davit ['dævɪt] **n** (*Naut*) bossoir *m*.

Davy ['deɪvɪ] **n** (**dim of David**) (*Naut*) **to go to ~ Jones' locker*** boire à la grande tasse⁑; (*Min*) ~ **lamp** lampe *f* de sécurité (*de mineur*).

dawdle ['dɔːdl] **vi** (*also* ~ **about,** ~ **around**) flâner, traîner, lambiner*. **to ~ on the way** s'amuser en chemin; **to ~ over one's work** traînasser sur son travail.

▸**dawdle away vt sep: to dawdle away one's time** passer *or* perdre son temps à flâner.

dawdler ['dɔːdləʳ] **n** traînard(e) *m(f)*, lambin(e)* *m(f)*, flâneur *m*, -euse *f*.

dawdling ['dɔːdlɪŋ] 1 **adj** lambin*, traînard. 2 **n** flânerie *f*.

dawn [dɔːn] 1 **n** a aube *f*, point *m* du jour, aurore *f*. **at ~** à l'aube, au point du jour; **from ~ to dusk** du matin au soir; **it was the ~ of another day** c'était l'aube d'un nouveau jour.

b (*NonC*) *[civilization]* aube *f*; *[an idea, hope]* naissance *f*.

2 **vi** a *[day]* poindre, se lever. **the day ~ed bright and clear** l'aube parut, lumineuse et claire; **the day ~ed rainy** le jour a commencé dans la pluie, il pleuvait au lever du jour; **the day will ~ when ...** un jour viendra où ... .

b (*fig*) *[era, new society]* naître, se faire jour; *[hope]* luire. **an idea ~ed upon him** une idée lui vint à l'esprit; **the truth ~ed upon him** il a commencé à entrevoir la vérité; **it suddenly ~ed on him that no one would know** il lui vint tout d'un coup à l'esprit que personne ne saurait.

3 **comp** ▸**dawn chorus** concert *m* (matinal) des oiseaux ▸**dawn raid** (*St Ex*) tentative *f* d'O.P.A. surprise, raid *m* ▸**dawn raider** (*St Ex*) raider *m*.

dawning ['dɔːnɪŋ] 1 **adj** *day, hope* naissant, croissant. 2 **n** = **dawn 1b.**

day [deɪ] 1 **n** a (*unit of time: 24 hours*) jour *m*. **3 ~s ago** il y a 3 jours; **to do sth in 3 ~s** faire qch en 3 jours, mettre 3 jours à faire qch; **he's coming in 3 ~s** *or* **3 ~s' time** il vient dans 3 jours; **what ~ is it today?** quel jour sommes-nous aujourd'hui?; **what ~ of the month is it?** nous sommes le combien?; **she arrived (on) the ~ they left** elle est arrivée le jour de leur départ; **on that ~** ce jour-là; **on a ~ like this** un jour comme aujourd'hui; **on the following ~** le lendemain; **twice a ~** deux fois par jour; **the ~ before yesterday** avant-hier; **the ~ before/two ~s before her birthday** la veille/l'avant-veille de son anniversaire; **the ~ after, the following ~** le lendemain; **two ~s after her birthday** le surlendemain de son anniversaire, deux jours après son anniversaire; **the ~ after tomorrow** après-demain; **this ~ week** d'aujourd'hui en huit; **from that ~ onwards** *or* **on** dès lors, à partir de ce jour(-là); (*frm*) **from this ~ forth** désormais, dorénavant; **2 years ago to the ~** il y a 2 ans jour pour jour *or* exactement; **he will come any ~ now** il va venir d'un jour à l'autre; **every ~** tous les jours; **every other ~** tous les deux jours; **one ~ we saw the king** un (beau) jour nous vîmes le roi; **one ~ she will come** un jour (ou l'autre) elle viendra; **one of these ~s** un de ces jours, un jour ou l'autre; **~ by ~** jour après jour; **~ in ~ out** tous les jours que (le bon) Dieu fait; **~ after ~** jour après jour; **for ~s on end** pendant des jours et des jours; **for ~s at a time** pendant des jours entiers; **to live from ~ to ~** vivre au jour le jour; **the other ~** l'autre jour, il y a quelques jours; **it's been one of those ~s** ça a été une de ces journées où tout va de travers *or* où rien ne va; **this ~ of all ~s** ce jour entre tous; **some ~** un de ces jours; **I remember it to this (very) ~** je m'en souviens encore aujourd'hui; **he's fifty if he's a ~*** il a cinquante ans bien sonnés*; **as of D~ 1*, from D~ 1*, on ~ 1*** dès le premier jour; **that'll be the ~!** j'aimerais voir ça!; (*Rel*) **D~ of Atonement** jour *m* du Pardon, fête *f* du Grand Pardon; (*Rel*) **the ~ of judgment, the ~ of reckoning** le jour du jugement dernier; (*fig*) **the ~ of reckoning will come** un jour il faudra rendre des comptes; *see* **Christmas, Easter** *etc.*

b (*daylight hours*) jour *m*, journée *f*. **during the ~** pendant la journée; **to work all ~** travailler toute la journée; **to travel by ~** voyager de jour; **to work ~ and night** travailler jour et nuit; (*liter*) **the ~ is done** le jour baisse, le jour tire à sa fin; **it's a fine ~** il fait beau aujourd'hui; **one summer's ~** un jour d'été; **on a wet ~** par une journée pluvieuse; (*Mil, fig*) **to carry** *or* **win the ~** remporter la victoire; (*Mil, fig*) **to lose the ~** perdre la bataille; (*US fig*) **to give sb a ~ in court*** donner à qn l'occasion de s'expliquer *or* de se faire entendre; *see* **break, good, time.**

c (*working hours*) journée *f*. **paid by the ~** payé à la journée; **it's all in the ~'s work!** ça fait partie de la routine!; **to take/get a ~ off** prendre/obtenir un jour de congé; **it's my ~ off** c'est mon jour de congé *or* mon jour libre; **~ of rest** jour de repos; **to work an 8-hour ~** travailler huit heures par jour, faire une journée de huit heures; *see* **call, working.**

d (*period of time: often pl*) époque *f*, temps *m*. **these ~s, in the present ~** à l'heure actuelle, de nos jours, actuellement; **in this ~ and age** par les temps qui courent; **in ~s to come** dans l'avenir, dans les jours à venir; **in his working ~s** au temps *or* à l'époque où il travaillait; **in his younger ~s** quand il était plus jeune; **in the ~s of Queen Victoria, in Queen Victoria's ~** du temps de *or* sous le règne de la reine Victoria; **in Napoleon's ~** à l'époque *or* du temps de Napoléon; **in those ~s** à l'époque; famous in her ~ célèbre à son époque; in the good old ~s au bon vieux temps; those were the ~s! c'était le bon vieux temps; they were sad ~s then c'était une époque sombre; the happiest ~s of my life les jours les plus heureux *or* la période la plus heureuse de ma vie; during the early ~s of the war tout au début *or* pendant les premiers temps de la guerre; it's early ~s (yet) (*too early to say*) c'est un peu tôt pour le dire; (*there's still time*) on n'en est encore qu'au début; to end one's ~s in misery finir ses jours dans la misère; that has had its ~ (*old-fashioned*) cela est passé de mode; (*worn out*) cela a fait son temps; his ~ will come son jour viendra; *see* dog, olden *etc.*

2 comp ▸**day bed** (*US*) banquette-lit *f* ▸**day boarder** (*Scol*) demi-pensionnaire *mf* ▸**daybook** (*Comm*) main courante *f*, brouillard *m* ▸**day boy** (*Brit Scol*) externe *m* ▸**daybreak** point *m* du jour, lever *m* du jour, aube *f*; at daybreak au point du jour, à l'aube ▸**day care** (*for children*) garderie *f*; (*for the old*) soins *mpl* journaliers (en foyer); day care centre (*Brit*) *or* center (*US*) ≃ garderie *f* ▸**day-care services** (*Brit*) *système de garderies* ▸**day centre** (*Brit*) *centre spécialisé de jour pour le troisième âge, les handicapés etc* ▸**daydream** n rêverie *f*, rêvasserie *f* ◊ vi rêvasser, rêver (tout éveillé) ▸**day girl** (*Brit Scol*) externe *f* ▸**day labourer** journalier *m*, ouvrier *m* à la journée ▸**day letter** (*US*) ≃ télégramme-lettre *m* ▸**daylight** *see* daylight ▸**daylong** (*liter*) continuel, qui dure toute la journée ▸**day nurse** infirmière *f* (de jour) ▸**day nursery** (*public*) ≃ garderie *f*; (*room in private house*) pièce *f* des enfants ▸**day-old** *bread* de la veille; (*yesterday's*) d'hier; day-old chick poussin *m* d'un jour ▸**day-pass** (*Ski*) carte journalière ▸**day pupil** (*Brit Scol*) externe *mf* ▸**day release:** (*Brit: Comm, Ind*) day release course ≃ cours professionnel (de l'industrie *etc*) à temps partiel; to be on day release faire un (*or* deux) jour(s) par semaine de stage (de formation) ▸**day return (ticket)** (*Brit Rail*) (billet *m* d')aller et retour *m* (*valable pour la journée*) ▸**day room** (*in hospital etc*) salle *f* de séjour commune ▸**day school:** to go to day school être externe *mf* (*Scol*) ▸**day shift** (*workers*) équipe *f or* poste *m* de jour; to be on day shift, to work day shift travailler de jour, être de jour ▸**day-ticket** (*Ski*) = day-pass ▸**daytime** n jour *m*, journée *f* ◊ adj de jour; in the daytime le jour, de jour, dans *or* pendant la journée ▸**day-to-day** *occurrence* qui se produit tous les jours, journalier; *routine* journalier, ordinaire; on a day-to-day basis au jour le jour ▸**day trip** excursion *f* (d'une journée); to go on a day trip to Calais faire une excursion (d'une journée) à Calais ▸**day-tripper** excursionniste *mf*.

daylight ['deɪlaɪt] 1 n a = daybreak; *see* day 2. b (lumière *f* du) jour *m*. in (the) ~ à la lumière du jour, au grand jour; it is still ~ il fait encore jour; I'm beginning to see ~* (*understand*) je commence à voir clair; (*see the end appear*) j'en aperçois la fin; to beat *or* knock *or* thrash the (living) ~s out of sb‡ (*beat up*) rosser* qn, tabasser‡ qn; (*knock out*) mettre qn K.O.; to scare *or* frighten the (living) ~s out of sb‡ flanquer une peur bleue *or* la frousse* à qn; *see* broad. 2 comp *attack* de jour ▸**daylight robbery***: (*Brit*) it's daylight robbery c'est du vol caractérisé, c'est de l'arnaque‡ ▸**daylight-saving time** (*Brit*) heure *f* d'été.

daze [deɪz] 1 n (*after blow*) étourdissement *m*; (*at news*) stupéfaction *f*, ahurissement *m*, confusion *f*; (*from drug*) hébétement *m*. in a ~ étourdi, stupéfait, ahuri, hébété, médusé. 2 vt [*drug*] stupéfier, hébéter; [*blow*] étourdir; [*news etc*] abasourdir, méduser, sidérer.

dazed [deɪzd] adj (*see* daze) hébété; tout étourdi; abasourdi, sidéré.

dazzle ['dæzl] 1 vt (*lit*) éblouir, aveugler; (*fig*) éblouir. to ~ sb's eyes éblouir qn. 2 n lumière aveuglante, éclat *m*. blinded by the ~ of the car's headlights ébloui par les phares de la voiture.

dazzling ['dæzlɪŋ] adj (*lit*) éblouissant, aveuglant; (*fig*) éblouissant.

dazzlingly ['dæzlɪŋlɪ] adv *shine* de manière éblouissante. ~ beautiful d'une beauté éblouissante.

dB (abbr of decibel) dB.

DBMS [di:bi:em'es] n (abbr of database management system) *see* data 2.

DBS [di:bi:'es] n a (abbr of direct broadcasting by satellite) *see* direct 1. b (abbr of direct broadcasting satellite) *see* direct 1.

DC [di:'si:] a (abbr of direct current) *see* direct 1. b (*US*) (abbr of District of Columbia) *district fédéral*.

DD (*Comm*) (abbr of direct debit) *see* direct 1.

dd (*Comm*) a (abbr of delivered) livré. b (abbr of dated) en date du ... .

D.D. [di:'di:] a (*Univ*) (abbr of Doctor of Divinity) *doctorat en théologie*. b (*US Mil*) (abbr of dishonourable discharge) *see* dishonourable.

d.d. (*Comm*) (abbr of demand draft) *see* demand 3.

D-day ['di:deɪ] n (*Mil*) le jour J.

DDT [di:di:'ti:] n (abbr of dichlorodiphenyltrichloroethane) D.D.T. *m*.

DE[1] [di:'i:] n (abbr of Department of Employment) *see* employment 1.

DE[2], **De** (*US Post*) abbr of Delaware.

de... [di:] pref de..., dé..., des..., dés... .

DEA [di:i:'eɪ] n abbr (*US*) (abbr of Drug Enforcement Administration) ≃ Brigade *f* des stupéfiants.

deacon ['di:kən] n diacre *m*. (*US*) ~'s bench siège *m* à deux places (de style colonial).

deaconess ['di:kənes] n diaconesse *f*.

dead [ded] 1 adj a *person* mort, décédé; *animal, plant* mort. ~ or alive mort ou vif; more ~ than alive plus mort que vif; (*lit, fig*) ~ and buried *or* gone mort et enterré; to drop down ~, to fall (stone) ~ tomber (raide) mort; as ~ as a doornail *or* as mutton *or* as the dodo tout ce qu'il y a de plus mort; to wait for a ~ man's shoes* attendre que quelqu'un veuille bien mourir (pour prendre sa place); will he do it? — over my ~ body!* il le fera? — pas question!* *or* il faudra d'abord qu'il me passe (*subj*) sur le corps!; (*fig*) to flog (*Brit*) *or* beat (*US*) a ~ horse s'acharner inutilement, perdre sa peine et son temps; (*Prov*) ~ men tell no tales les morts ne parlent pas; he's/it's a ~ duck* il/c'est fichu* *or* foutu‡; to leave sb for ~ laisser qn pour mort; (*at hospital*) he was found to be ~ on arrival les médecins n'ont pu que constater le décès; I wouldn't be seen ~ wearing that hat *or* in that hat!* jamais je ne porterais ce chapeau!; *see* drop, strike *and* 4 *below*.

b *limbs* engourdi. my fingers are ~ j'ai les doigts gourds; he's ~ from the neck up‡ il n'a rien dans la tête, il a la cervelle vide; he was ~ to the world* (*asleep*) il dormait comme une souche; (*drunk*) il était ivre mort.

c (*fig*) *custom* tombé en désuétude; *fire* mort, éteint; *cigarette* éteint; *battery* à plat; *town* mort, triste; *colour* éteint, terne; *sound* sourd, feutré. (*Fin*) ~ account compte dormant *or* inactif; ~ language langue morte; (*Telec*) the line has gone ~ *or* is ~ on n'entend plus rien (sur la ligne); the engine's ~ le moteur est kaputt.

d (*absolute, exact*) ~ calm calme plat; to hit sth in the ~ centre frapper qch au beau milieu *or* en plein milieu; it's a ~ cert‡ that he'll come il viendra à coup sûr, sûr qu'il viendra*; this horse is a ~ cert‡ ce cheval est le gagnant sûr; in ~ earnest avec le plus grand sérieux, très sérieusement; he's in ~ earnest il ne plaisante pas; on a ~ level with exactement au même niveau que; a ~ loss (*Comm etc*) une perte sèche; (*: *person*) un bon à rien; that idea was a ~ loss* cette idée n'a absolument rien donné; this book/knife is a ~ loss* ce livre/couteau ne vaut rien; to be a ~ shot être un tireur d'élite; ~ silence silence *m* de mort; he's the ~ spit of his father* c'est son père tout craché; to come to a ~ stop s'arrêter net *or* pile; *see* catch.

2 adv (*Brit: exactly, completely*) absolument, complètement. ~ ahead tout droit; ~ broke‡ fauché (comme les blés)*; to be ~ certain about sth* être absolument certain *or* convaincu de qch, être sûr et certain de qch*; your guess was ~ on tu as deviné juste; ~ drunk* ivre mort; it's ~ easy *or* simple* c'est simple comme bonjour*, il n'y a rien de plus facile *or* simple; to be/arrive ~ on time être/arriver juste à l'heure *or* à l'heure pile; it was ~ lucky‡ c'était le coup de pot monstre‡; (*order*) ~ slow (*Aut*) roulez au pas; (*Naut*) en avant lentement; to go ~ slow aller aussi lentement que possible; to stop ~ s'arrêter net *or* pile; ~ tired claqué*, éreinté, crevé*; he went ~ white il est devenu pâle comme un mort; *see* stop 4a.

3 n a the ~ les morts *mpl*; (*Rel*) office *or* service for the ~ office *m* des morts *or* funèbre.

b at ~ of night, in the ~ of night au cœur de *or* au plus profond de la nuit; in the ~ of winter au plus fort de l'hiver, au cœur de l'hiver.

4 comp ▸**dead-and-alive** *town* triste, mort; a dead-and-alive little place un trou perdu ▸**dead ball** (*Ftbl*) ballon sorti ▸**dead-ball line** (*Rugby*) ligne *f* du ballon mort ▸**dead-beat*** n chiffe molle; (*US*) parasite *m*, pique-assiette *mf inv* ◊ adj éreinté, crevé*, claqué*; I'm dead-beat* je suis claqué* *or* mort* *or* sur les rotules* ▸**dead centre** (*Tech*) point mort ▸**dead end** (*lit, fig*) impasse *f*; (*fig*) to come to a dead end être dans une impasse; a dead-end job un travail sans débouchés ▸**dead-head** vt enlever les fleurs fanées de (*see also* deadhead*) ▸**dead heat:** the race was a dead heat ils sont arrivés ex-aequo; (*Racing*) la course s'est terminée par un dead-heat ▸**dead letter** (*Post*) lettre tombée au rebut; (*: *useless thing*) chose *f* du passé; (*Jur*) to become a dead letter tomber en désuétude, devenir lettre morte ▸**dead-letter office** (*Post*) bureau *m* des rebuts ▸**deadline** (*Press etc*) date *f or* heure *f* limite, dernière limite; (*US: boundary*) limite *f* (qu'il est interdit de franchir); to work to a deadline travailler en vue d'une date *or* d'une heure limite; he was working to a 6 o'clock deadline son travail devait être terminé à 6 heures dernière limite ▸**deadlock** impasse *f*; to reach (a) deadlock aboutir à une impasse; to be at (a) deadlock être dans une impasse, être au point mort ▸**dead march** marche *f* funèbre ▸**dead matter** matière inanimée; (*Typ*) composition *f* à distribuer ▸**dead men*** (*fig: empty bottles*) bouteilles *fpl* vides, cadavres‡ *mpl* ▸**deadnettle** ortie blanche ▸**deadpan** adj *face* sans expression, figé, de marbre; *humour* pince-sans-rire *inv* ◊ adv sans expression ▸**dead reckoning** (*Naut*) estime *f*; by dead reckoning à l'estime ▸**Dead Sea** mer Morte; Dead Sea Scrolls manuscrits *mpl* de la mer Morte ▸**dead season** (*Comm, Press*) morte-saison *f* ▸**dead set***: to make a dead set at sth s'acharner comme un beau diable pour avoir qch; to make a dead set at sb chercher à mettre le grappin sur qn*; to be dead set on doing sth vouloir faire qch à tout prix; to be dead set against sth s'opposer absolument à qch ▸**dead soldiers*** (*US fig*) bouteilles *fpl* vides, cadavres‡ *mpl* ▸**dead stock** invendu(s) *m(pl)*, rossignols* *mpl* ▸**dead weight** poids mort *or* inerte; (*Naut*) charge *f or* port *m* en lourd ▸**dead wire** (*Elec*) fil *m* sans courant ▸**deadwood** (*lit, fig*) bois mort; (*fig*) to get rid of the deadwood in the office* se débarrasser du personnel improductif *or* inutile.

deaden ['dedn] vt *shock, blow* amortir; *feeling* émousser; *sound* assourdir, feutrer; *passions* étouffer; *pain* calmer; *nerve* endormir.

deadening ['dednɪŋ] 1 n (*see* **deaden**) amortissement *m*; assourdissement *m*. 2 adj *boredom, task* abrutissant.

deadhead* ['dedhed] (*US*) 1 n a (*person using free ticket*) (*Rail*) personne *f* possédant un titre de transport gratuit; (*Theat*) personne possédant un billet de faveur. b (*stupid person*) nullité *f*. c (*empty truck/train etc*) camion *m*/train *m etc* roulant à vide. 2 adj *truck etc* roulant à vide.

deadliness ['dedlɪnɪs] n *[poison]* caractère mortel; *[aim]* précision *f* infaillible; (*boredom*) ennui mortel.

deadly ['dedlɪ] 1 adj a *blow, poison, sin, enemy* mortel; *hatred* mortel, implacable; *wit* caustique, implacable; *aim* qui ne rate jamais; *weapon* meurtrier; *pallor* de mort. (*Bot*) ~ **nightshade** belladone *f*; **the seven ~ sins** les sept péchés capitaux; **in ~ earnest** avec le plus grand sérieux, très sérieusement. b (*: *boring*) casse-pieds* *inv*, rasoir* *inv*. 2 adv *dull* mortellement, terriblement. ~ **pale** d'une pâleur mortelle, pâle comme un(e) mort(e) *or* la mort; **it's/I'm ~ serious** c'est/je suis tout ce qu'il y a de plus sérieux; ~ **cold** terriblement froid.

deadness ['dednɪs] n (*fig*) *[place]* absence *f* de vie *or* de vitalité; *[limbs]* engourdissement *m*; *[colour]* fadeur *f*.

deaf [def] 1 adj a sourd. ~ **in one ear** sourd d'une oreille; ~ **as a (door)post** *or* **a stone** sourd comme un pot; (*Prov*) **there are none so ~ as those who will not hear** il n'y a pire sourd que celui qui ne veut pas entendre (*Prov*). b (*unwilling to listen*) sourd, insensible (*to* à). **to be ~ to sth** rester sourd à qch; **to turn a ~ ear to sth** faire la sourde oreille à qch. 2 n: **the ~** les sourds *mpl*. 3 comp ►**deaf-aid** appareil *m* acoustique, audiophone *m* ►**deaf-and-dumb** sourd-muet; **deaf-and-dumb alphabet** alphabet *m* des sourds et muets ►**deaf-mute** sourd(e)-muet(te) *m(f)*.

deafen ['defn] vt (*lit*) rendre sourd; (*fig*) assourdir, rendre sourd, casser les oreilles à*.

deafening ['defnɪŋ] adj (*lit, fig*) assourdissant.

deafness ['defnɪs] n surdité *f*.

deal[1] [di:l] (vb: pret, ptp dealt) 1 n a (*NonC*) **a good ~ of, a great ~ of, a ~ of** une grande quantité de, beaucoup de, pas mal de*, énormément de; **to have a great ~ to do** avoir beaucoup à faire, avoir bien des choses à faire; **a good ~ of the work is done** une bonne partie du travail est terminée; **that's saying a good ~** ce n'est pas peu dire; **there's a good ~ of truth in what he says** il y a beaucoup de vrai dans ce qu'il dit; **to think a great ~ of sb** avoir beaucoup d'estime pour qn; **to mean a great ~ to sb** compter beaucoup pour qn; (*adv phrase*) **a good ~** nettement, beaucoup; **she's a good ~ cleverer than her brother** elle est nettement plus intelligente que son frère; **she's a good ~ better today** elle va beaucoup mieux aujourd'hui; **they've travelled a good ~** ils ont beaucoup voyagé.

b (*agreement*) marché *m*, affaire *f*; (*pej*) coup *m*; (*Comm, Fin: also* **business ~**) affaire, marché; (*St Ex*) opération *f*, transaction *f*. **to do a ~ with sb** (*gen*) conclure un marché avec qn; (*Comm etc*) faire *or* passer un marché avec qn, faire (une) affaire avec qn; **we might do a ~?** on pourrait (peut-être) s'arranger?; **it's a ~!*** d'accord!, marché conclu!; (*fig: treatment*) **he got a very bad ~ from them** ils se sont très mal conduits envers lui, ils ont agi très malhonnêtement avec lui; (*Pol etc*) **a new ~** un programme de réformes; (*iro*) **big ~!** la belle affaire!, tu parles!*; **don't make such a big ~ out of it!*** n'en fais pas toute une histoire! *or* tout un plat!*; *see* **fair**[1], **raw** *etc*.

c (*Cards*) donne *f*, distribution *f*. **it's your ~** à vous la donne, à vous de distribuer *or* donner.

2 vt a (*also* **~ out**) *cards* donner, distribuer.

b **to ~ sb a blow** porter *or* assener un coup à qn; (*fig*) **this dealt a nasty blow to individual freedom** cela a porté un coup très dur aux libertés individuelles.

3 vi a (*Brit*) **to ~ well/badly by sb** agir bien/mal avec qn.

b *[business firm]* **this company has been ~ing for 80 years** cette société est en activité depuis 80 ans; **to ~ in wood/property** *etc* être dans le commerce du bois/dans l'immobilier *etc*; **to ~ on the Stock Exchange** faire *or* conclure des opérations de bourse.

c (*Cards*) donner, distribuer.

►**deal out** vt sep *gifts, money* distribuer, répartir, partager (*between* entre). **to deal out justice** rendre (la) justice; *see* **deal**[1] **2a**.

►**deal with** vt fus a (*have to do with*) *person* avoir affaire à, traiter avec. **teachers who have to deal with very young children** les enseignants qui ont affaire à de très jeunes enfants; **workers dealing with the public** les employés qui sont en contact avec le public *or* qui ont affaire au public; **they refused to deal with him because of this** ils ont refusé de traiter avec lui *or* d'avoir affaire à lui à cause de cela; **he's not very easy to deal with** il n'est pas commode *or* facile.

b (*be responsible for*) *person* s'occuper de; *task, problem* se charger de, s'occuper de; (*take action as regards*) *person, problem* s'occuper de, prendre des mesures concernant. **I'll deal with it/him** je me charge de cela/lui; **I can deal with that alone** je peux m'en occuper tout seul; **in view of the situation he had to deal with** vu la situation qu'il avait sur les bras; **he dealt with the problem very well** il a très bien résolu le problème; **you naughty boy, I'll deal with you later!** vilain garçon, tu vas avoir affaire à moi *or* tu vas avoir de mes nouvelles tout à l'heure!; **the headmaster dealt with the culprits individually** le directeur s'est occupé des coupables un par un; **the committee deals with questions such as ...** le comité s'occupe de questions telles que ...; **the police officer dealing with crime prevention** l'agent chargé de la prévention des crimes; (*treat*) **to know how to deal with sb** savoir s'y prendre avec qn; **they dealt with him very fairly** ils ont été très corrects avec lui; **you must deal with them firmly** il faut vous montrer fermes à leur égard; **the firm deals with over 1,000 orders every week** l'entreprise traite plus de 1000 commandes par semaine.

c (*be concerned with, cover*) *[book, film etc]* traiter de; *[speaker]* parler de. **the next chapter deals with ...** le chapitre suivant traite de ...; **I shall now deal with ...** je vais maintenant vous parler de ... .

d (*buy from or sell to*) **a list of the suppliers our company deals with** une liste des fournisseurs de notre société; **I won't deal with that firm again** je ne m'adresserai plus à cette société; **I always deal with the same butcher** je me sers *or* me fournis toujours chez le même boucher.

deal[2] [di:l] n (*plank*) planche *f*; (*thicker*) madrier *m*; (*planks collectively*) plot *m*.

dealer ['di:lər] n a (*Comm: gen*) marchand *m* (*in* de), négociant *m* (*in* en); (*wholesaler*) stockiste *m*, fournisseur *m* (en gros) (*in* de); (*St Ex*) opérateur *m*. **Citroën ~** concessionnaire *mf* Citroën; *see* **double, secondhand**. b (*Cards*) donneur *m*.

dealership ['di:ləʃɪp] n (*Comm*) concession *f*. ~ **network** réseau *m* de concessionnaires.

dealing ['di:lɪŋ] n a (*NonC*) (*also* **~ out**) distribution *f*; *[cards]* donne *f*. b (*St Ex*) opérations *fpl*, transactions *fpl*; *see* **wheel**.

dealings ['di:lɪŋz] npl (*gen*) relations *fpl* (*with sb* avec qn); (*Comm, St Ex*) transactions *fpl* (*in sth* en qch); (*trafficking*) trafic *m* (*in sth* de qch).

dealmaker ['di:l,meɪkər] n (*St Ex*) opérateur *m*, -trice *f*.

dealt [delt] pret, ptp of **deal**[1].

dean [di:n] n (*Rel, fig*) doyen *m*; (*Brit Univ*) doyen; (*US Scol*) conseiller *m*, -ère *f* (principal(e)) d'éducation; (*US Univ*) ~ **of education** directeur *m* d'école normale d'instituteurs, directrice *f* d'école normale d'institutrices; (*US Univ*) **~'s list** liste *f* des meilleurs étudiants.

deanery ['di:nərɪ] n (*Univ*) demeure *f or* résidence *f* du doyen; (*Rel*) doyenné *m*, demeure du doyen.

deanship [di:nʃɪp] n (*Rel, fig etc*) décanat *m*.

dear [dɪər] 1 adj a (*loved*) *person, animal* cher; (*precious*) *object* cher, précieux; (*lovable*) adorable; *child* mignon, adorable. **she is very ~ to me** elle m'est très chère; **a ~ friend of mine** un de mes meilleurs amis, un de mes amis les plus chers; **to hold sb/sth ~** chérir qn/qch; **his ~est wish** son plus cher désir, son souhait le plus cher; **what a ~ child!** quel amour d'enfant!; **what a ~ little dress!*** quelle ravissante *or* mignonne petite robe!

b (*in letter-writing*) cher. **D~ Daddy** Cher Papa; **My ~ Anne** Ma chère Anne; **D~ Alice and Robert** Chère Alice, cher Robert, Chers Alice et Robert; **D~est Paul** Bien cher Paul; **D~ Mr Smith** Cher Monsieur; **D~ Mr & Mrs Smith** Cher Monsieur, chère Madame; **D~ Sir** Monsieur; **D~ Sirs** Messieurs; **D~ Sir or Madam** Madame, Monsieur; (*fig*) **D~ John letter*** lettre *f* de rupture.

c (*expensive*) *prices, goods* cher, coûteux; *price* élevé; *shop* cher. **to get ~er** *[goods]* augmenter, renchérir; *[prices]* augmenter.

2 excl (*surprise: also* **~ ~!, ~ me!**) mon Dieu!, vraiment!, pas possible!; (*regret: also* **oh ~!**) oh là là!, oh mon Dieu!

3 n cher *m*, chère *f*, chéri(e) *m(f)*. **my ~** mon ami(e), mon cher ami, ma chère amie; (*to child*) mon petit; **my ~est** mon chéri, mon amour; **poor ~** (*to child*) pauvre petit, pauvre chou*; (*to woman*) ma pauvre; **your mother is a ~*** votre mère est un amour; **give it to me, there's a ~!*** sois gentil, donne-le-moi!, donne-le-moi, tu seras (bien) gentil!

4 adv (*lit, fig*) *buy, pay, sell* cher.

dearest ['dɪərɪst] n chéri(e) *m(f)*.

dearie* ['dɪərɪ] 1 n mon petit chéri, ma petite chérie. 2 excl (*) **~ me!** Grand Dieu!, Dieu du ciel!

dearly ['dɪəlɪ] adv a (*tenderly*) tendrement, avec tendresse. **he loves this country ~** il est très attaché à ce pays; **I should ~ like to live here** j'aimerais infiniment habiter ici. b (*lit, fig*) **to pay ~ for sth** payer qch cher; (*fig*) **~ bought** chèrement payé.

dearness ['dɪənɪs] n a (*expensiveness*) cherté *f*. b (*lovableness*) **your ~ to me** la tendresse que j'ai pour vous.

dearth [dɜ:θ] n *[food]* disette *f*; *[money, resources, water]* pénurie *f*; *[ideas etc]* stérilité *f*, pauvreté *f*. **there is no ~ of young men** les jeunes gens ne manquent pas.

deary* ['dɪərɪ] = **dearie***.

death [deθ] 1 n mort *f*, décès *m* (*Jur, frm*); *[plans, hopes]* effondrement *m*, anéantissement *m*. **to be burnt to ~** mourir carbonisé; **he drank himself to ~** c'est la boisson qui l'a tué; **starved/frozen to ~** mort de faim/de froid; **he was stabbed to ~** il a été poignardé mortellement; **he jumped to his ~** il a sauté dans le vide et il s'est tué; **to be bored to ~*** s'ennuyer à mourir *or* à crever*; **you look tired to ~*** tu as l'air crevé*; **I'm sick to ~*** *or* **tired to ~* of all this** j'en ai par-dessus la tête *or* j'en ai marre* de tout ceci; **to be at ~'s door** être à (l'article de) la mort; (*Jur*) **to sentence sb to ~** condamner qn à mort; (*Jur*) **to put sb**

to ~ mettre qn à mort, exécuter qn; **a fight to the ~** une lutte à mort; (*fig*) **to be in at the ~** assister au dénouement (d'une affaire); (*lit*) **it will be the ~ of him** il le paiera de sa vie, cela va l'achever; (*fig*) **he will be the ~ of me** il me fera mourir, il sera ma mort; (*fig*) **he died the ~*** il aurait voulu rentrer sous terre; **to look/feel like ~** (**warmed up** *or US* **warmed over**)* avoir l'air/se sentir complètement nase*; *see* **catch, dance, do**[1].

2 **comp** ▸**deathbed n** lit *m* de mort ◊ **adj** *repentance* de la dernière heure; (*Theat*) **this is a deathbed scene** la scène se passe au chevet du mourant ▸**death benefit** (*Insurance*) capital *m* décès ▸**death-blow** (*lit, fig*) coup mortel *or* fatal ▸**death camp** camp *m* de la mort ▸**death cell** cellule *f* de condamné à mort ▸**death certificate** acte *m* de décès ▸**death duty** *or* **duties** (†: *Brit Fin*) droits *mpl* de succession ▸**death grant** allocation *f* de décès ▸**death house** (*US: in jail*) quartier *m* des condamnés à mort ▸**death knell** *see* **knell** ▸**deathlike** semblable à la mort, de mort ▸**death march** marche *f* de la mort ▸**death mask** masque *m* mortuaire ▸**death penalty** (*Jur*) peine *f* de mort ▸**death rate** (taux *m* de) mortalité *f* ▸**death rattle** râle *m* (d'agonie) ▸**death ray** rayon *m* de la mort, rayon qui tue ▸**death roll** liste *f* des morts ▸**death row** (*US*) = **death house** ▸**death sentence** (*lit*) condamnation *f* à mort, arrêt *m* de mort; (*fig*) arrêt de mort ▸**death's-head** tête *f* de mort ▸**death's-head moth** (sphinx *m*) tête *f* de mort ▸**death squad** escadron *m* de la mort ▸**death throes** affres *fpl* de la mort, agonie *f*; (*fig*) agonie ▸**death toll** chiffre *m* des morts ▸**deathtrap** endroit (*or* véhicule *etc*) dangereux; **that corner is a real deathtrap** ce tournant est mortel ▸**death warrant** (*Jur*) ordre *m* d'exécution; (*fig*) **to sign the death warrant of a project** condamner un projet, signer la condamnation d'un projet ▸**death-watch beetle** vrillette *f*, horloge *f* de la mort ▸**death wish** (*Psych, also fig*) désir *m* de mort.

deathless [ˈdeθlɪs] **adj** immortel, impérissable, éternel. (*iro, hum*) **~ prose** prose *f* impérissable.

deathly [ˈdeθlɪ] 1 **adj** *appearance* semblable à la mort, de mort, cadavérique. **~ hush, ~ silence** silence mortel *or* de mort. 2 **adv** comme la mort. **~ pale** au teint blafard *or* cadavérique, d'une pâleur mortelle.

deb* [deb] **n abbr of débutante.**

debacle, débâcle [deɪˈbɑːkl] **n** fiasco *m*; (*Mil*) débâcle *f*.

debag* [diːˈbæg] **vt** (*Brit*) déculotter.

debar [dɪˈbɑːʳ] **vt** (*from club, competition*) exclure (*from* de). **to ~ sb from doing** interdire *or* défendre à qn de faire.

debark [dɪˈbɑːk] **vti** (*US*) débarquer.

debarkation [ˌdiːbɑːˈkeɪʃən] **n** (*US*) débarquement *m*.

debarment [dɪˈbɑːmənt] **n** exclusion *f* (*from* de).

debase [dɪˈbeɪs] **vt** a *person* avilir, ravaler. **to ~ o.s.** s'avilir *or* se ravaler (*by doing* en faisant). b (*reduce in value or quality*) *word, object* dégrader; *metal* altérer; (*Fin*) *coinage* déprécier, dévaloriser.

debasement [dɪˈbeɪsmənt] **n** (*see* **debase**) avilissement *m*; dégradation *f*; altération *f*; dépréciation *f*.

debatable [dɪˈbeɪtəbl] **adj** discutable, contestable. **it's a ~ point** c'est discutable; **it is ~ whether** on est en droit de se demander si.

debate [dɪˈbeɪt] 1 **vt** *question* discuter, débattre. *subject, theme etc* **much ~d** très discuté. 2 **vi** discuter (*with* avec, *about* sur). **he was debating with himself whether to refuse or not** il se demandait bien s'il refuserait ou non, il s'interrogeait pour savoir s'il refuserait ou non. 3 **n** discussion *f*, débat *m*, délibération *f*; (*Parl*) débat(s); (*esp in debating society*) conférence *f or* débat *m* contradictoire. **to hold long ~s** discuter longuement; **after much ~** après de longues discussions; **the ~ was on** *or* **about** la discussion portait sur; **the death penalty was under ~** on délibérait sur la peine de mort; [*fact, statement*] **to be in ~** être controversé.

debater [dɪˈbeɪtəʳ] **n** maître *m* dans l'art de la discussion. **he is a good ~** c'est un bon argumentateur *or* dialecticien.

debating [dɪˈbeɪtɪŋ] **n** art *m* de la discussion. **~ society** société *f* de conférences *or* débats contradictoires.

debauch [dɪˈbɔːtʃ] 1 **vt** *person* débaucher, corrompre; *morals* corrompre; *woman* séduire; *taste* corrompre, vicier. 2 **n** débauche *f*.

debauched [dɪˈbɔːtʃd] **adj** débauché.

debauchee [ˌdebɔːˈtʃiː] **n** débauché(e) *m(f)*.

debaucher [dɪˈbɔːtʃəʳ] **n** [*person, taste, morals*] corrupteur *m*, -trice *f*; [*woman*] séducteur *m*.

debauchery [dɪˈbɔːtʃərɪ] **n** (*NonC*) débauche *f*, dérèglement *m* de(s) mœurs.

debenture [dɪˈbentʃəʳ] 1 **n** (*Customs*) certificat *m* de drawback; (*Fin*) obligation *f*, bon *m*. (*Fin*) **the conversion of ~s into equity** la conversion d'obligations en actions. 2 **comp** ▸**debenture bond** titre *m* d'obligation ▸**debenture holder** obligataire *mf* ▸**debenture stock** obligations *fpl* sans garantie.

debilitate [dɪˈbɪlɪteɪt] **vt** débiliter.

debilitating [dɪˈbɪlɪteɪtɪŋ] **adj** débilitant; (*fig*) *effect* fragilisant, affaiblissant.

debility [dɪˈbɪlɪtɪ] **n** (*Med*) débilité *f*, faiblesse *f*.

debit [ˈdebɪt] 1 **n** (*Comm*) débit *m*. 2 **comp** *account* débiteur ▸**debit balance** solde débiteur ▸**debit card** carte *f* de paiement (*à retrait non différé*) ▸**debit entry** inscription *f or* écriture *f* au débit ▸**debit side**: **on the debit side** au débit; (*fig*) **on the debit side there is the bad weather** à mettre au passif, il y a le mauvais temps. 3 **vt**: **to ~ sb's account with a sum, to ~ a sum against sb's account** porter une somme au débit du compte de qn; **to ~ sb with a sum, to ~ a sum to sb** porter une somme au débit de qn, débiter qn d'une somme.

debonair [ˌdebəˈnɛəʳ] **adj** raffiné, doucereux.

debouch [dɪˈbaʊtʃ] (*Geog, Mil*) 1 **vi** déboucher. 2 **n** débouché *m*.

debrief [ˌdiːˈbriːf] **vt** (*Mil etc*) *patrol, astronaut, spy* faire faire un compte rendu oral (de fin de mission) à; *freed hostages etc* recueillir le témoignage de. (*Mil*) **to be ~ed** faire un compte rendu oral.

debriefing [ˌdiːˈbriːfɪŋ] **n** (*see* **debrief**) compte rendu *m* (de fin de mission); témoignage *m*.

debris [ˈdebriː] **n** débris *mpl*; (*Geol*) roches *fpl* détritiques.

debt [det] 1 **n** (*payment owed*) dette *f*, créance *f*. **bad ~s** créances irrécouvrables; **~ of honour** dette d'honneur; **outstanding ~** créance à recouvrer; **to be in ~** avoir des dettes, être endetté; **he is in ~ to everyone** il doit à tout le monde; **I am £5 in ~** je dois 5 livres; **to be out of sb's ~** être quitte envers qn; **to get** *or* **run into ~** faire des dettes, s'endetter; **to get out of ~** s'acquitter de ses dettes; **to be out of ~** n'avoir plus de dettes; (*fig*) **to repay a ~** acquitter une dette; (*fig*) **I am greatly in your ~ for sth/for having done** je vous suis très redevable de qch/d'avoir fait; *see* **eye, head, national** *etc*.

2 **comp** ▸**debt collection agency** agence *f* de recouvrement de créances ▸**debt collector** agent *m* de recouvrement de créances ▸**debt consolidation** consolidation *f* de la dette ▸**debt-ridden** criblé de dettes.

debtor [ˈdetəʳ] **n** débiteur *m*, -trice *f*.

debug [diːˈbʌg] **vt** a (*Comput, fig*) mettre au point. b (*remove microphones from*) *room etc* enlever les micros cachés dans.

debugging [diːˈbʌgɪŋ] **n** (*Comput*) mise *f* au point.

debunk* [ˌdiːˈbʌŋk] **vt** *person* déboulonner*; *claim* démentir; *institution* discréditer; *theories, beliefs, religion* démystifier, démythifier.

début [ˈdeɪbjuː] **n** (*Theat*) début *m*; (*in society*) entrée *f* dans le monde. **he made his ~ as a pianist** il a débuté comme pianiste.

débutante [ˈdebjuːtɑ̃ːnt] **n** débutante *f* (*jeune fille qui fait son entrée dans le monde*).

Dec. **abbr of December.**

dec. **abbr of deceased.**

decade [ˈdekeɪd] **n** a décennie *f*, décade *f*. b [*rosary*] dizaine *f*.

decadence [ˈdekədəns] **n** décadence *f*.

decadent [ˈdekədənt] 1 **adj** *person, civilization* en décadence, décadent; *book, attitude* décadent. 2 **n** (*Literat*) décadent *m*.

decaffeinate [ˌdiːˈkæfɪneɪt] **vt** décaféiner.

decagramme, (*US*) **decagram** [ˈdekəgræm] **n** décagramme *m*.

decal [dɪˈkæl] **n** (*US*) décalcomanie *f*.

decalcification [ˈdiːˌkælsɪfɪˈkeɪʃən] **n** décalcification *f*.

decalcify [ˌdiːˈkælsɪfaɪ] **vt** décalcifier.

decalitre, (*US*) **decaliter** [ˈdekəˌliːtəʳ] **n** décalitre *m*.

Decalogue [ˈdekəlɒg] **n** décalogue *m*.

decametre, (*US*) **decameter** [ˈdekəˌmiːtəʳ] **n** décamètre *m*.

decamp [dɪˈkæmp] **vi** a (*) décamper, ficher le camp*. b (*Mil*) lever le camp.

decant [dɪˈkænt] **vt** a *wine* décanter. **he ~ed the solution into another container** il a transvasé la solution. b (*fig: rehouse*) reloger.

decanter [dɪˈkæntəʳ] **n** carafe *f* (à liqueur *or* à vin); (*small*) carafon *m*.

decapitate [dɪˈkæpɪteɪt] **vt** décapiter.

decapitation [dɪˌkæpɪˈteɪʃən] **n** décapitation *f*, décollation *f* (*liter etc*).

decapod [ˈdekəpɒd] **n** décapode *m*.

decarbonization [ˈdiːˌkɑːbənaɪˈzeɪʃən] **n** (*Aut*) décalaminage *m*; [*steel*] décarburation *f*.

decarbonize [ˌdiːˈkɑːbənaɪz] **vt** (*Aut*) décalaminer; *steel* décarburer.

decartelize [dɪˈkɑːtəlaɪz] **vt** décartelliser.

decasualization [ˌdɪkæʒjʊlaɪˈzeɪʃən] **n** (*US*) (*abolition*) suppression *f* du travail temporaire; (*redeployment*) transformation *f* de la main-d'oeuvre temporaire en main-d'oeuvre permanente.

decasualize [ˌdɪˈkæʒjʊˌlaɪz] **vt** *workers* rendre permanent.

decathlete [dɪˈkæθliːt] **n** décathlonien *m*.

decathlon [dɪˈkæθlən] **n** décathlon *m*.

decay [dɪˈkeɪ] 1 **vi** a (*go bad etc*) [*food*] pourrir, se gâter; [*flowers, vegetation, wood*] pourrir; [*tooth*] se carier, se gâter; [*stone, work of art*] s'altérer, se détériorer.

b (*crumble*) [*building*] se délabrer, tomber en ruines.

c (*Phys*) [*radioactive nucleus*] se désintégrer.

d (*fig*) [*hopes*] s'enfuir; [*beauty*] se faner; [*civilization*] décliner; [*race, one's faculties*] s'affaiblir.

2 **vt** *food, wood* faire pourrir; *tooth* carier.

3 **n** a (*Culin*) pourrissement *m*; (*Bot*) pourrissement, dépérissement *m*; (*Med*) carie *f*.

b (*Archit*) délabrement *m*, décrépitude *f*. **to fall into ~** tomber en ruines, se délabrer.

c (*Phys*) désintégration *f*.

d (*fig*) [*hopes, friendship, beauty*] ruine *f*; [*civilization*] décadence *f*, déclin *m*; [*race*] affaiblissement *m*, déchéance *f*; [*faculties*] affaiblissement, déclin.

decayed [dɪˈkeɪd] adj *tooth* carié, gâté; *wood* pourri; *food* gâté, pourri; *building* délabré; (*Phys*) partiellement désintégré; *faculty, health, civilization* en déclin; *hopes, friendship* en ruines.

decaying [dɪˈkeɪɪŋ] adj *food* en train de s'avarier; *vegetation etc* pourrissant; *flesh* en pourriture; *tooth* qui se carie; *building* en état de délabrement; *stone* qui s'altère; *civilization* en décadence.

decease [dɪˈsiːs] (*Admin, frm*) 1 n décès *m*. 2 vi décéder.

deceased [dɪˈsiːst] (*Admin, frm*) 1 adj décédé, défunt. **John Brown ~** feu John Brown. 2 n: **the ~** le défunt, la défunte.

deceit [dɪˈsiːt] n a supercherie *f*, tromperie *f*, duperie *f*. b (*NonC*) = **deceitfulness**.

deceitful [dɪˈsiːtfʊl] adj *person* trompeur, faux (*f* fausse), fourbe; *words, conduct* trompeur, mensonger.

deceitfully [dɪˈsiːtfəlɪ] adv avec duplicité, faussement, par supercherie.

deceitfulness [dɪˈsiːtfʊlnɪs] n fausseté *f*, duplicité *f*.

deceive [dɪˈsiːv] 1 vt tromper, abuser, duper; *spouse* tromper; *hopes* tromper, décevoir. **to ~ sb into doing** amener qn à faire (en le trompant); **he ~d me into thinking that he had bought it** il m'a (faussement) fait croire qu'il l'avait acheté; **I thought my eyes were deceiving me** je n'en croyais pas mes yeux; **to be ~d by appearances** être trompé par *or* se tromper sur les apparences; **to ~ o.s.** s'abuser, se faire illusion. 2 vi tromper, être trompeur. **appearances ~** les apparences sont trompeuses.

deceiver [dɪˈsiːvəʳ] n trompeur *m*, -euse *f*, imposteur *m*, fourbe *m*.

decelerate [diːˈseləreɪt] vti ralentir.

deceleration [ˈdiːˌseləˈreɪʃən] n *[engine, programme]* ralentissement *m*; *[car]* décélération *f*, freinage *m*.

December [dɪˈsembəʳ] n décembre *m*; *for phrases see* **September**.

decency [ˈdiːsənsɪ] n a (*NonC*) *[dress, conversation]* décence *f*, bienséance *f*; *[person]* pudeur *f*. **to have a sense of ~** avoir de la pudeur. b (*good manners*) convenances *fpl*. **to observe the decencies** observer *or* respecter les convenances; **common ~** la simple politesse, le simple savoir-vivre; **for the sake of ~** par convenance, pour garder les convenances; **to have the ~ to do sth** avoir la décence de faire qch; **you can't in all ~ do that** tu ne peux pas décemment faire ça; **sheer human ~ requires that ...** le respect de la personne humaine exige que ... . c (*: *niceness*) gentillesse *f*.

decent [ˈdiːsənt] adj a (*respectable*) *person* convenable, honnête, bien* *inv*; *house, shoes* convenable; (*seemly*) *language, behaviour, dress* décent, bienséant. **no ~ person would do it** jamais une personne convenable ne ferait cela, quelqu'un de bien* ne ferait jamais cela; **to do the ~ thing (by sb)** agir comme il se doit (à l'égard de qn); (*dressed*) **are you ~?*** es-tu présentable?
b (*: *good, pleasant*) *person* bon, brave. **a ~ sort of fellow** un bon *or* brave garçon, un type bien*; **it was ~ of him** c'était chic* de sa part; **I've got quite a ~ flat** j'ai un appartement qui n'est pas mal; **I could do with a ~ meal** un bon repas ne me ferait pas de mal.
c (* *US: great*) formidable, terrible*.

decently [ˈdiːsəntlɪ] adv *dress, behave* décemment, convenablement, avec bienséance. **you can't ~ ask him that** décemment vous ne pouvez pas lui demander cela.

decentralization [diːˌsentrəlaɪˈzeɪʃən] n décentralisation *f*.

decentralize [diːˈsentrəlaɪz] vt décentraliser.

deception [dɪˈsepʃən] n a (*NonC*) (*deceiving*) tromperie *f*, duperie *f*; (*being deceived*) illusion *f*, erreur *f*. **he is incapable of ~** il est incapable de tromperie; **to obtain money by ~** obtenir de l'argent par des moyens frauduleux. b (*deceitful act*) supercherie *f*.

deceptive [dɪˈseptɪv] adj *distance, speed, tone, attitude* trompeur; *cheerfulness, energy* trompeur, illusoire.

deceptively [dɪˈseptɪvlɪ] adv: **the village looks ~ near** le village donne l'illusion d'être proche; **he was ~ quiet/obedient** *etc* il était calme/obéissant *etc*, mais ce n'était qu'en apparence.

deceptiveness [dɪˈseptɪvnɪs] n caractère trompeur *or* illusoire.

decibel [ˈdesɪbel] n décibel *m*.

decide [dɪˈsaɪd] 1 vt a (*make up one's mind*) se décider (*to do* à faire), décider (*to do* de faire), se résoudre (*to do* à faire). **I ~d to go** *or* **that I would go** je me suis décidé à y aller, j'ai décidé d'y aller; **what made you ~ to go?** qu'est-ce qui vous a décidé à y aller?; **it has been ~d that** on a décidé *or* il a été décidé que.
b (*settle*) *question* décider, trancher; *quarrel* décider, arbitrer; *piece of business* régler; *difference of opinion* juger; *sb's fate, future* décider de. (*Jur*) **to ~ a case** statuer sur un cas.
c (*cause to make up one's mind*) décider, déterminer (*sb to do* qn à faire).
2 vi se décider. **you must ~** il vous faut prendre une décision, il faut vous décider; **to ~ for sth** se décider pour qch *or* en faveur de qch; **to ~ against sth** se décider contre qch; *[judge, arbitrator, committee]* **to ~ for/against sb** donner raison/tort à qn; **to ~ in favour of sb** décider en faveur de qn, donner gain de cause à qn.

►**decide (up)on** vt fus *thing, course of action* se décider pour, choisir (finalement). **to decide on doing** se décider à faire.

decided [dɪˈsaɪdɪd] adj *improvement, progress* incontestable; *difference* net, marqué; *refusal* catégorique; *character, person* résolu, décidé, déterminé; *manner, tone, look* résolu, décidé; *opinion* arrêté.

decidedly [dɪˈsaɪdɪdlɪ] adv *act, reply* résolument, avec décision, d'une façon marquée. **~ lazy** incontestablement paresseux.

decider [dɪˈsaɪdəʳ] n (*goal*) but décisif; (*point*) point décisif; (*factor*) facteur décisif. (*game*) **the ~** la belle.

deciding [dɪˈsaɪdɪŋ] adj *factor, game, point* décisif.

deciduous [dɪˈsɪdjʊəs] adj *tree* à feuilles caduques; *leaves, antlers* caduc (*f* -uque).

decilitre, (*US*) **deciliter** [ˈdesɪˌliːtəʳ] n décilitre *m*.

decimal [ˈdesɪməl] 1 adj *number, system, coinage* décimal. **~ fraction** fraction décimale; **to three ~ places** (jusqu')à la troisième décimale; **~ point** virgule *f* (*de fraction décimale*); *see* **fixed, floating**. 2 n décimale *f*. **~s** le calcul décimal, la notation décimale; *see* **recurring**.

decimalization [ˌdesɪməlaɪˈzeɪʃən] n décimalisation *f*.

decimalize [ˈdesɪməlaɪz] vt décimaliser.

decimate [ˈdesɪmeɪt] vt (*lit, fig*) décimer.

decimation [ˌdesɪˈmeɪʃən] n décimation *f*.

decimetre, (*US*) **decimeter** [ˈdesɪˌmiːtəʳ] n décimètre *m*.

decipher [dɪˈsaɪfəʳ] vt (*lit, fig*) déchiffrer.

decipherable [dɪˈsaɪfərəbl] adj déchiffrable.

decision [dɪˈsɪʒən] 1 n a (*act of deciding*) décision *f*; (*Jur*) jugement *m*, arrêt *m*. **to come to a ~** arriver à *or* prendre une décision, prendre (un) parti, se décider; **his ~ is final** sa décision est irrévocable *or* sans appel; (*Jur*) **to give a ~ on a case** statuer sur un cas. b (*NonC*) décision *f*, résolution *f*, fermeté *f*. **a look of ~** un air décidé *or* résolu. 2 comp ►**decision-maker** décideur *m* ►**decision-making: he's good at decision-making** il sait prendre des décisions ►**decision table** (*Comput*) table *f* de décision.

decisive [dɪˈsaɪsɪv] adj a *battle, experiment, victory* décisif, concluant; *factor* décisif. b *manner, answer* décidé, catégorique. **he is very ~** il a de la décision; **a ~ woman** une femme décidée.

decisively [dɪˈsaɪsɪvlɪ] adv *speak* d'un ton décidé *or* catégorique; *act* avec décision, sans hésiter.

decisiveness [dɪˈsaɪsɪvnɪs] n (*NonC*) *[experiment]* caractère décisif *or* concluant; *[person]* ton *or* air décidé *or* catégorique.

deck [dek] 1 n a (*Naut*) pont *m*. **to go up on ~** monter sur le pont; **below ~s** sous le pont, en bas; **between ~s** dans l'entrepont; (*US fig*) **on ~** prêt à l'action; *see* **after, clear, flight[1], hand**.
b *[vehicle]* plate-forme *f*. **top ~, upper ~** *[bus]* impériale *f*; *[jumbo jet]* étage *m*.
c (*US*) **~ of cards** jeu *m* de cartes.
d *[record player etc]* table *f* de lecture; (*for recording*) platine *f* magnétophone; *see also* **cassette**.
e (*US : Drugs sl*) sachet *m* d'héroïne.
2 vt a (*also* **~ out**) orner, parer, agrémenter (*with* de). **to ~ o.s. (out) in one's Sunday best** se mettre sur son trente et un, s'endimancher (*pej*).
b (‡ *US*) flanquer* par terre.
3 comp ►**deck cabin** cabine *f* (de pont) ►**deck cargo** pontée *f* ►**deckchair** chaise longue, transat* *m*, transatlantique *m* ►**deck hand** matelot *m* ►**deckhouse** rouf *m* ►**decklid** (*US Aut*) capot *m* du coffre à bagages.

-decker [ˈdekəʳ] n ending in comps: (*Naut*) **a three-decker** un vaisseau à trois ponts, un trois-ponts; (*bus*) **a single-decker** un autobus sans impériale; *see* **double** *etc*.

deckle [ˈdekl] n (*also* **~ edge**) barbes *fpl*.

deckle-edged [ˌdeklˈedʒd] adj *paper* non ébarbé.

declaim [dɪˈkleɪm] vti (*lit, fig*) déclamer (*against* contre), s'indigner (*that* que).

declamation [ˌdekləˈmeɪʃən] n déclamation *f*.

declamatory [dɪˈklæmətərɪ] adj déclamatoire.

declaration [ˌdekləˈreɪʃən] n *[love, war, intentions, taxes, goods at Customs]* déclaration *f*; (*Cards*) annonce *f*; (*public announcement*) proclamation *f*, déclaration (publique). (*US Hist*) **D~ of Independence** Déclaration d'indépendance.

declarative [dɪˈklærətɪv] adj (*Gram*) déclaratif, assertif.

declaratory [dɪˈklærətərɪ] adj (*Jur*) **~ judgment** jugement *m* déclaratoire.

declare [dɪˈklɛəʳ] 1 vt a *intentions,* (*Fin etc*) *income* déclarer; *results* proclamer. (*Customs*) **have you anything to ~?** avez-vous quelque chose à déclarer?; *[suitor]* **to ~ o.s.** faire sa déclaration, se déclarer; **to ~ war (on)** déclarer la guerre (à); **to ~ a state of emergency** déclarer l'état d'urgence. b (*assert*) déclarer (*that* que). **to ~ o.s. for/against** se déclarer *or* se prononcer *or* prendre parti en faveur de/contre; **to ~ sb president/bankrupt** déclarer qn président/en faillite. 2 vi a **well I (do) ~!*** (ça) par exemple! b (*US Pol*) *[presidential candidate]* annoncer sa candidature.

declared [dɪˈklɛəd] adj déclaré, avoué, ouvert.

declaredly [dɪˈklɛərɪdlɪ] adv ouvertement, formellement, de son propre aveu.

declarer [dɪˈklɛərəʳ] n (*Cards*) déclarant(e) *m(f)*.

declassify [diːˈklæsɪfaɪ] vt *information, document* rayer de la liste des documents secrets, ne plus classer comme confidentiel.

declension [dɪˈklenʃən] n (*Gram*) déclinaison *f*.

declinable [dɪ'klaɪnəbl] adj (*Gram*) déclinable.

declination [ˌdeklɪ'neɪʃən] n (*Astron*) déclinaison *f*.

decline [dɪ'klaɪn] 1 n *[day, life]* déclin *m*; *[empire]* déclin, décadence *f*. **~ in price** baisse *f* de prix; **to be on the ~** *[prices]* être en baisse, baisser; *[fame, health]* décliner; **cases of real poverty are on the ~** les cas d'indigence réelle sont de moins en moins fréquents *or* sont en diminution; (*Med*) **to go into a ~** dépérir.
2 vt a (*gen*) refuser (*to do* de faire); *invitation, honour* refuser, décliner; *responsibility* décliner, rejeter. **he ~d to do it** il a refusé (poliment) de le faire; **he offered me a lift but I ~d** il a proposé de m'emmener mais j'ai refusé; (*Jur*) **to ~ a jurisdiction** se déclarer incompétent.
b (*Gram*) décliner.
3 vi a *[health, influence]* décliner, baisser; *[empire]* tomber en décadence; *[prices]* baisser, être en baisse; *[business]* être en baisse, péricliter, décliner. **to ~ in importance** perdre de l'importance.
b (*slope*) s'incliner, descendre.
c *[sun]* décliner, se coucher; *[day]* tirer à sa fin, décliner.
d (*Gram*) se décliner.

declining [dɪ'klaɪnɪŋ] 1 adj sur son déclin. **in his ~ years** au déclin de sa vie; **in ~ health** d'une santé devenue chancelante *or* qui décline. 2 n *[invitation]* refus *m*; *[empire]* décadence *f*; (*Gram*) déclinaison *f*.

declivity [dɪ'klɪvɪtɪ] n déclivité *f*, pente *f*.

declutch ['diː'klʌtʃ] vi débrayer; *see* **double**.

decoction [dɪ'kɒkʃən] n décoction *f*.

decode ['diː'kəʊd] vt a déchiffrer, traduire (en clair), décoder. b (*Comput, Ling*) décoder. c (*fig*) (*understand*) comprendre; (*explain*) expliquer.

decoder [diː'kəʊdəʳ] n (*Comput, TV*) décodeur *m*.

decoding [diː'kəʊdɪŋ] n (*Comput*) décodage *m*.

decoke [diː'kəʊk] (*Brit Aut*) 1 vt décalaminer. 2 ['diːkəʊk] n décalaminage *m*.

decollate [dɪ'kɒleɪt] vt (*Comput*) déliasser.

décolletage [deɪ'kɒltɑːʒ] n, **décolleté** [deɪ'kɒlteɪ] n décolletage *m*, décolleté *m*.

décolleté(e) [deɪ'kɒlteɪ] adj décolleté.

decolonize [diː'kɒləˌnaɪz] vt décoloniser.

decommission [ˌdiːkə'mɪʃən] vt a *nuclear power station* fermer. b *warship, aircraft* retirer de la circulation.

decompartmentalization [ˌdiːkɒmpɑːtˌmentəlaɪ'zeɪʃən] n (*Soc*) décloisonnement *m*.

decompartmentalize [ˌdiːkɒmpɑːt'mentəlaiz] vt (*Soc*) décloisonner.

decompose [ˌdiːkəm'pəʊz] 1 vt décomposer. 2 vi se décomposer.

decomposition [ˌdiːkɒmpə'zɪʃən] n décomposition *f*.

decompress [ˌdiːkəm'pres] vt décompresser.

decompression [ˌdiːkəm'preʃən] 1 n (*Med, Phys, Tech*) décompression *f*. 2 comp ▸**decompression chamber** caisson *m* de décompression ▸**decompression illness** *or* **sickness** maladie *f* des caissons.

decongestant [ˌdiːkən'dʒestənt] adj, n décongestionnant (*m*).

decontaminate [ˌdiːkən'tæmɪneɪt] vt décontaminer, désinfecter.

decontamination ['diːkənˌtæmɪ'neɪʃən] n décontamination *f*, désinfection *f*.

decontrol [ˌdiːkən'trəʊl] 1 vt (*Admin, Comm*) libérer des contrôles gouvernementaux. **to ~ (the price of) butter** libérer le prix du beurre, lever *or* supprimer le contrôle du prix du beurre; **~led road** route non soumise à la limitation de vitesse. 2 n *[price]* libération *f*.

décor ['deɪkɔːʳ] n décor *m*.

decorate ['dekəreɪt] 1 vt a orner, décorer (*with* de); *cake* décorer; (*paint etc*) *room* décorer, peindre (et tapisser). **to ~ with flags** pavoiser. b *soldier* décorer, médailler. **he was ~d for gallantry** il a été décoré pour son acte de bravoure. 2 vi (*paint etc*) peindre (et tapisser).

decorating ['dekəreɪtɪŋ] n a **(painting and) ~** décoration intérieure; **they are doing some ~** ils sont en train de refaire les peintures. b *[cake etc]* décoration *f*.

decoration [ˌdekə'reɪʃən] n a (*NonC*) *[cake]* décoration *f*; *[hat]* ornementation *f*; *[room]* (*act*) décoration (intérieure); (*state*) décoration, décor *m*; *[town]* décoration; (*with flags*) pavoisement *m*. b (*ornament*) *[hat]* ornement *m*; (*in streets*) décoration *f*. **Christmas ~s** décorations de Noël. c (*Mil*) décoration *f*, médaille *f*.

decorative ['dekərətɪv] adj décoratif.

decorator ['dekəreɪtəʳ] n (*designer*) décorateur *m*, -trice *f*, ensemblier *m*; (*esp Brit: also* **painter-and-decorator**) peintre-décorateur *m*.

decorous ['dekərəs] adj *action* convenable, bienséant, comme il faut; *behaviour, person* digne.

decorously ['dekərəslɪ] adv (*see* **decorous**) convenablement, avec bienséance, comme il faut; avec dignité, d'un air digne.

decorum [dɪ'kɔːrəm] n décorum *m*, étiquette *f*, bienséance *f*. **with ~** avec bienséance, comme il faut; **a breach of ~** une inconvenance; **to have a sense of ~** avoir le sens des convenances.

decoy ['diːkɔɪ] 1 n (*bird*) (*live*) appeau *m*, chanterelle *f*; (*artificial*) leurre *m*; (*animal*) proie *f* (servant d'appât); (*person*) compère *m*. **police ~** policier *m* en civil (*servant à attirer un criminel dans une souricière*). 2 comp ▸**decoy duck** (*lit*) appeau *m*, chanterelle *f*; (*fig*) compère *m*. 3 *also* [dɪ'kɔɪ] vt [(*see* 1) attirer avec un appeau *or* une chanterelle *or* un leurre; (*fig*) attirer dans un piège. **to ~ sb into doing sth** faire faire qch à qn en le leurrant.

decrease [diː'kriːs] 1 vi *[amount, numbers, supplies]* diminuer, décroître, s'amoindrir; *[birth rate, population]* décroître, diminuer; *[power]* s'affaiblir; *[strength, intensity]* s'affaiblir, décroître, aller en diminuant; *[price, value]* baisser; *[enthusiasm]* se calmer, se refroidir; (*Knitting*) diminuer.
2 vt diminuer, réduire.
3 ['diːkriːs] n *[amount, supplies]* diminution *f*, amoindrissement *m* (*in* de); *[numbers]* diminution, décroissance *f* (*in* de); *[birth rate, population]* diminution (*in* de); *[power]* affaiblissement *m* (*in* de); *[strength, intensity]* diminution, décroissance (*in* de); *[price, value]* baisse *f* (*in* de); *[enthusiasm]* baisse, refroidissement *m* (*in* de). **~ in speed** ralentissement *m*; **~ in strength** affaiblissement.

decreasing [diː'kriːsɪŋ] adj *amount, numbers, population* décroissant; *power* qui s'affaiblit; *enthusiasm, strength, intensity* décroissant, diminué; *price, value* en baisse.

decreasingly [diː'kriːsɪŋlɪ] adv de moins en moins.

decree [dɪ'kriː] 1 n (*Pol, Rel*) décret *m*; *[tribunal]* arrêt *m*, jugement *m*; (*municipal*) arrêté *m*. **by royal/government ~** par décret du roi/du gouvernement; *[divorce]* **~ absolute** jugement définitif; **~ nisi** jugement provisoire de divorce. 2 vt (*gen; also Pol, Rel*) décréter (*that* que + *indic*); (*Jur*) ordonner (*that* que + *subj*); *[mayor, council etc]* arrêter (*that* que + *indic*). (*frm*) **to ~ an end to** décréter la fin de.

decrepit [dɪ'krepɪt] adj *objet* délabré; *building* délabré, décrépit; (*) *person* décrépit, décati*.

decrepitude [dɪ'krepɪtjuːd] n (*see* **decrepit**) délabrement *m*; décrépitude *f*.

decretal [dɪ'kriːtl] n décrétale *f*.

decriminalize [diː'krɪmɪnəlaɪz] vt décriminaliser.

decry [dɪ'kraɪ] vt décrier, dénigrer, déprécier.

decumulation [ˌdɪkjuːmjʊ'leɪʃən] n *[capital]* réduction *f*, diminution *f*; *[stocks]* contraction *f*, réduction *f*. **stock ~** déstockage *m*.

dedicate ['dedɪkeɪt] vt *church, shrine, book* dédier (*to* à); *one's life* consacrer (*to sth* à qch, *to doing* à faire); (*consecrate*) *church* consacrer; (*open officially*) *building* inaugurer officiellement. **to ~ o.s. to sth/to doing** se vouer *or* se consacrer à qch/à faire; **I'd like to ~ this song to Eva** (*singer*) je voudrais jouer (*or* chanter) cette chanson pour Eva; (*DJ*) voici une chanson *or* un disque pour Eva.

dedicated ['dedɪˌkeɪtɪd] adj *attitude* consciencieux; *thoroughness* scrupuleux; *word processor* dédié; *flash* automatique. **she's very ~** elle est très consciencieuse *or* dévouée.

dedication [ˌdedɪ'keɪʃən] n a *[church]* dédicace *f*, consécration *f*. b (*in book, on radio*) dédicace *f*. **to write a ~ in a book** dédicacer un livre; (*Rad*) **if you want a ~ just write in** si vous voulez faire une dédicace, écrivez-nous. c (*quality: devotion*) dévouement *m*.

deduce [dɪ'djuːs] vt déduire, inférer, conclure (*from* de, *that* que).

deducible [dɪ'djuːsɪbl] adj que l'on peut déduire *or* inférer (*from* de).

deduct [dɪ'dʌkt] vt *amount* déduire, retrancher, défalquer (*from* de); *numbers* retrancher, soustraire (*from* de); *tax* retenir, prélever (*from* sur). **to ~ something from the price** faire une réduction sur le prix; **to ~ sth for expenses** retenir qch pour les frais; **to ~ 5% from the wages** faire une retenue de *or* prélever 5 % sur les salaires; **after ~ing 5%** déduction faite de 5 %.

deductible [dɪ'dʌktəbl] 1 adj à déduire, à retrancher, à défalquer (*from* de); (*Tax*) *expenses* déductible. 2 n (*US Insurance*) franchise *f*. **a 50 dollar ~** une franchise de 50 dollars.

deduction [dɪ'dʌkʃən] n a (*sth deducted*) déduction *f*, défalcation *f* (*from* de); (*from wage*) retenue *f*, prélèvement *m* (*from* sur). b (*sth deduced*) déduction *f*, raisonnement déductif.

deductive [dɪ'dʌktɪv] adj déductif.

deed [diːd] 1 n a (*action*) action *f*, acte *m*. **brave ~** haut fait, exploit *m*. **good ~(s)** bonne(s) action(s); (*hum*) **to do one's good ~ for the day** *or* **today** faire sa B.A. quotidienne; *see* **word**. b **in ~** de fait, en fait; **master in ~ if not in name** maître de *or* en fait sinon de *or* en titre. c (*Jur*) acte notarié, contrat *m*. **~ of covenant** *or* **gift** (acte de) donation *f*; **~ of partnership** contrat de société. 2 comp ▸**deed box** coffre *m* *or* mallette *f* pour documents (officiels) ▸**deed poll**: **to change one's name by deed poll** ≃ changer de nom officiellement. 3 vt (*US Jur*) transférer par acte notarié.

deejay* ['diːˌdʒeɪ] n disc-jockey *m*, animateur *m*.

deem [diːm] vt juger, estimer, considérer. **to ~ it prudent to do** juger prudent de faire; **to be ~ed worthy of (doing) sth** être jugé digne de (faire) qch.

deep [diːp] 1 adj a (*extending far down*) *water, hole, wound* profond; *snow* épais (*f* -aisse). **the water/pond was 4 metres ~** l'eau/l'étang avait 4 mètres de profondeur; **he was ankle-~ in water** l'eau lui arrivait aux chevilles; (*fig*) **to be in ~ water(s)** avoir de gros ennuis, être en mauvaise posture, être dans de vilains draps; *[swimming pool]* **the ~ end** le grand bain; (*fig*) **to go off (at) the ~ end*** (*excited*) se mettre dans tous ses états; (*angry*) se flanquer* *or* se ficher* en colère; (*fig*) **he went in** *or* **plunged in** *or* **jumped in** *or* **was thrown in at the ~ end**

cela a été le baptême du feu (pour lui); **the snow lay ~** il y avait une épaisse couche de neige; **the streets were 2 feet ~ in snow** les rues étaient sous 60 cm *or* étaient recouvertes de 60 cm de neige.

b (*extending far back*) *shelf, cupboard* large, profond. **a plot of ground 15 metres ~** un terrain de 15 mètres de profondeur; **the spectators stood 10 ~** il y avait 10 rangs de spectateurs debout; **~ space** espace intersidéral or interstellaire; (*US Geog*) **the ~ South** le Sud profond (des États-Unis), les États *mpl* les plus au sud.

c (*broad*) *edge, border* large, haut.

d (*fig*) *sound* grave; *voice, tones* grave, profond; (*Mus*) *note, voice* bas (*f* basse), grave; *sorrow, relief* profond, intense; *concern, interest* vif; *colour* intense, profond; *mystery, darkness* profond, total; *sleep* profond; *writer, thinker, book* profond; (**: crafty*) *person* malin (*f* -igne), rusé. **~ in thought/in a book** plongé *or* absorbé dans ses pensées/dans un livre; **~ in debt** criblé de dettes, dans les dettes jusqu'au cou; **~ breathing** (*action, sound*) respiration profonde; (*exercises*) exercices *mpl* respiratoires; **he's a ~ one*** il est plus malin qu'il n'en a l'air, il cache bien son jeu; *see* **mourning**.

e (*Gram*) **~ structure** structure profonde; **~ grammar** grammaire profonde.

2 **adv** profondément. **don't go in too ~ if you can't swim** ne va pas trop loin si tu ne sais pas nager; **to go ~ into the forest** pénétrer profondément *or* très avant dans la forêt; **to read ~ into the night** lire tard dans la nuit; **to drink ~** boire à longs traits; **to breathe ~** respirer profondément *or* à pleins poumons; *[crisis, tendency]* **to go** *or* **run ~** être profond; **to thrust one's hands ~ in one's pockets** enfoncer ses mains dans ses poches; **he's in it pretty ~*, he's pretty ~ in*** il s'est engagé très loin *or* à fond là-dedans, (*pej*) il est dedans jusqu'au cou; (*fig*) **~ down she still mistrusted him** en son for intérieur elle se méfiait encore de lui; **she seems abrupt, but ~ down she's kind** sous son air *or* son extérieur brusque, c'est quelqu'un de gentil; *see* **knee, skin, still**[2] *etc*.

3 **n** a (*liter*) **the ~** (les grands fonds de) l'océan *m*, les grandes profondeurs.

b (*rare: also* **depth**) **in the ~ of winter** au plus fort *or* au cœur de l'hiver.

4 **comp** ▸**deep-chested** *person* large de poitrine; *animal* à large poitrail ▸**deep-discount bond** (*Fin*) obligation *f* à forte décote ▸**deep-freeze** **n** (*also* **Deepfreeze** ® *in US*) congélateur *m* ◊ **vt** surgeler ▸**deep freezer** (*US*) congélateur *m* ▸**deep-freezing** congélation *f*; (*industrially*) surgélation *f* ▸**deep-frozen foods** aliments surgelés ▸**deep-fry** faire frire (en friteuse) ▸**deep ray therapy** radiothérapie destructrice *or* à rayons X durs ▸**deep-rooted** *affection, prejudice* profond, profondément enraciné, vivace; *habit* invétéré, ancré; *tree* aux racines profondes ▸**deep-sea** *animal, plant* pélagique, abyssal; *current* pélagique; **deep-sea diver** plongeur sous-marin; **deep-sea diving** plongée sous-marine; **deep-sea fisherman** pêcheur hauturier *or* de haute mer; **deep-sea fishing** pêche hauturière, grande pêche ▸**deep-seated** *prejudice, dislike* profond, profondément enraciné; *conviction* fermement ancré; **deep-seated cough** toux bronchiale *or* caverneuse ▸**deep-set** *eyes* très enfoncé, creux, cave; *window* profond ▸**deep-six**‡ (*US*) (*throw out*) balancer‡; (*kill*) liquider‡ ▸**deep therapy** = **deep ray therapy**.

deepen ['di:pən] 1 **vt** *hole* approfondir; *sorrow, interest* rendre plus intense *or* vif, augmenter; *darkness* épaissir, approfondir; *sound* rendre plus grave; *colour* foncer. 2 **vi** (*see* **1**) devenir *or* se faire plus profond (*or* plus foncé *etc*), s'approfondir; *[night, mystery]* s'épaissir; *[voice]* se faire plus profond *or* plus grave.

deepening ['di:pənɪŋ] (*see* **deepen**) 1 **adj** qui s'approfondit; qui se fonce, qui se fait plus intense *etc*. 2 **n** *[meaning, mystery etc]* intensification *f*; *[colour, sound]* augmentation *f* d'intensité.

deeply ['di:plɪ] **adv** a *dig, cut* profondément, à une grande profondeur; (*fig*) *drink* abondamment, à longs traits; *think, consider* profondément. (*fig*) **to go ~ into sth** approfondir qch. b (*very much*) *grateful, moving, concerned* infiniment, extrêmement. **~ offended** profondément offensé; **to regret ~** regretter vivement.

deer [dɪəʳ] 1 **n, pl ~** *or* **~s** cerf *m*, biche *f*; (*red ~*) cerf; (*fallow ~*) daim *m*; (*roe ~*) chevreuil *m*. **certain types of ~** certains types de cervidés *mpl*; **look at those ~!** regardez ces cerfs! *or* ces biches! 2 **comp** ▸**deerhound** limier *m* ▸**deerskin** peau *f* de daim ▸**deerstalker** (*hat*) casquette *f* à la Sherlock Holmes; (*hunter*) chasseur *m* de cerf ▸**deer-stalking** chasse *f* au cerf à pied.

de-escalate [di:'eskə,leɪt] **vt** *tension* faire baisser, diminuer; *situation* détendre, décrisper.

de-escalation [di:,eskə'leɪʃən] **n** (*Mil, Pol*) désescalade *f*; (*in industrial relations*) décrispation *f*.

deface [dɪ'feɪs] **vt** *monument, door* dégrader; *work of art* mutiler; *poster* barbouiller; *inscription* barbouiller, rendre illisible.

de facto [deɪ'fæktəʊ] **adj, adv** de facto.

defamation [,defə'meɪʃən] **n: ~ (of character)** diffamation *f*.

defamatory [dɪ'fæmətərɪ] **adj** diffamatoire, diffamant.

defame [dɪ'feɪm] **vt** diffamer.

default [dɪ'fɔ:lt] 1 **n** a (*Jur*) (*failure to appear: in civil cases*) défaut *m*, non-comparution *f*; (*in criminal cases*) contumace *f*; (*failure to meet financial obligation*) défaillance *f*, manquement *m*. **judgment by ~** jugement *m or* arrêt *m* par contumace *or* par défaut.

b **we must not let it go by ~** ne laissons pas échapper l'occasion (faute d'avoir agi); (*Sport*) **match won by ~** match gagné par forfait *or* par walk-over*.

c (*lack, absence*) manque *m*, carence *f*. **in ~ of** à défaut de, faute de.

d (*Fin*) cessation *f* de paiements.

e (*Comput*) position *f* par défaut. **~ option/value** option *f*/valeur *f* par défaut.

2 **vt** (*Jur*) condamner par défaut *or* par contumace, rendre un jugement par défaut contre.

3 **vi** a (*Jur*) faire défaut, être en état de contumace.

b (*gen*) manquer à ses engagements, être en défaut.

c (*Fin*) manquer à ses engagements.

d (*Comput*) **to ~ to a value** prendre une valeur par défaut; **it ~s to drive C** ça se positionne par défaut sur le disque C.

defaulter [dɪ'fɔ:ltəʳ] **n** (*gen*) coupable *mf*; (*offender*) délinquant(e) *m(f)*; (*Mil, Naut*) soldat *m* (*or* marin *m*) en infraction; (*Mil, Naut: undergoing punishment*) consigné *m*; (*Jur*) contumace *mf*; (*Fin, St Ex*) défaillant(e) *m(f)*, débiteur *m*, -trice *f* (qui n'acquitte pas une dette); (*defaulting tenant*) locataire *mf* qui ne paie pas son loyer.

defaulting [dɪ'fɔ:ltɪŋ] **adj** a (*St Ex etc*) défaillant, en défaut. b (*Jur*) défaillant, qui n'a pas comparu.

defeat [dɪ'fi:t] 1 **n** (*act, state*) *[army, team]* défaite *f*; *[project, ambition]* échec *m*, insuccès *m*; *[legal case, appeal]* rejet *m*. 2 **vt** *opponent* vaincre, battre; *army* battre, défaire, mettre en déroute; *team* battre; *hopes* frustrer, ruiner; *ambitions, plans, efforts, attempts* faire échouer; (*Parl*) *government, opposition* mettre en minorité; *bill, amendment* rejeter. **~ed in his attempts to** ... n'ayant pas réussi à ...; **to ~ one's own ends** *or* **object** aller à l'encontre du but que l'on s'est (*or* s'était *etc*) proposé; **that plan will ~ its own ends** ce plan sera autodestructeur.

defeated [dɪ'fi:tɪd] **adj** *army* vaincu; *team, player* battu, vaincu.

defeatism [dɪ'fi:tɪzəm] **n** défaitisme *m*.

defeatist [dɪ'fi:tɪst] **adj, n** défaitiste (*mf*).

defecate ['defəkeɪt] **vti** déféquer.

defecation [,defə'keɪʃən] **n** défécation *f*.

defect ['di:fekt] 1 **n** (*gen*) défaut *m*, imperfection *f*, faute *f*; (*in workmanship*) défaut, malfaçon *f*. **physical ~** vice *m or* défaut de conformation; **hearing/sight ~** défaut de l'ouïe/de la vue; **speech ~** difficulté *f* du langage; **mental ~** anomalie *or* déficience mentale; **moral ~** défaut; *see* **latent**. 2 [dɪ'fekt] **vi** (*Pol*) faire défection. **to ~ from one country to another** s'enfuir d'un pays pour aller dans un autre (*pour raisons politiques*); **to ~ to the West/to another party/to the enemy** passer à l'Ouest/à un autre parti/à l'ennemi.

defection [dɪ'fekʃən] **n** (*Pol*) défection *f*; (*Rel*) apostasie *f*. **his ~ to the East was in all the papers** quand il est passé à l'Est, tous les journaux en ont parlé; **after his ~ from Russia, he lost contact with his family** quand il s'est enfui d'Union Soviétique, il a été coupé de sa famille.

defective [dɪ'fektɪv] 1 **adj** *machine* défectueux; *reasoning* mauvais; (*Med*) déficient; (*Gram*) défectif. **to be ~ in sth** manquer de qch; **~ workmanship** malfaçons *fpl*; *see* **mental, mentally**. 2 **n** (*Med*) déficient(e) *m(f)*; (*Gram*) mot défectif.

defector [dɪ'fektəʳ] **n** (*Pol*) transfuge *mf*; (*Rel*) apostat *m*.

defence, (US) defense [dɪ'fens] 1 **n** a (*NonC*) défense *f*, protection *f*; *[action, belief]* justification *f*; (*Jur, Physiol, Psych, Sport*) défense. **in ~ of** à la défense de, pour défendre; (*Brit*) **Secretary (of State) for** *or* **Minister of D~**, (*US*) **Secretary of Defense** ministre *m* de la Défense nationale; (*Brit*) **Department** *or* **Ministry of D~**, (*US*) **Department of Defense** ministère *m* de la Défense nationale; *see* **civil, self 2**.

b défense *f*. **~s** (*gen, also Mil: weapons etc*) moyens *mpl* de défense; (*Mil: constructions*) ouvrages défensifs; **the body's ~s against disease** la défense de l'organisme contre la maladie; **as a ~ against** pour se défendre *or* se protéger contre, en guise de défense contre; **to put up a stubborn ~** se défendre obstinément; **to come to sb's ~** venir au secours de qn; **his conduct needs no ~** sa conduite n'a pas à être justifiée; **in his ~** (*Jur*) à sa décharge; (*gen*) à sa décharge, pour sa défense; (*Jur*) **witness for the ~** témoin *m* à décharge; (*Jur*) **the case for the ~** la défense.

c *[argument, decision]* justification *f*; (*Univ*) *[thesis]* soutenance *f*.

2 **comp** (*gen*) de défense; *industry, manufacturer etc* travaillant pour la défense nationale; *product, contract* destiné à la défense nationale ▸**defence counsel** avocat *m* de la défense ▸**defence expenditure** dépenses *fpl* militaires ▸**defence forces** (*Mil*) forces *fpl* défensives, défense *f* ▸**defence mechanism** (*Physiol*) système *m* de défense; (*Psych*) défenses *fpl*.

defenceless [dɪ'fenslɪs] **adj** (*lit, fig*) sans défense (*against* contre). **he is quite ~** il est incapable de se défendre, il est sans défense.

defend [dɪ'fend] 1 **vt** *country, town, person* défendre (*against* contre); (*Chess, Jur, Sport*) défendre; (*fig*) *friend* défendre, prendre le parti de; *action, decision, opinion* défendre, justifier. **to ~ o.s.** se défendre (*against* contre); **he is well able to ~ himself** il est très capable de *or* il sait se défendre; **he can't ~ himself** il est incapable de se défendre;

(*Univ*) **to ~ a thesis** soutenir une thèse. 2 **vi** (*Sport*) être en défense, défendre. **the ~ing team** l'équipe en défense; **they ~ed very well** ils ont très bien défendu; *[champion]* **to ~ against sb** défendre son titre contre qn, remettre son titre en jeu contre qn.

defendant [dɪ'fendənt] **n** (*Jur*) défendeur *m*, -deresse *f*; (*on appeal*) intimé(e) *m(f)*; (*in criminal case*) prévenu(e) *m(f)*; (*in assizes court*) accusé(e) *m(f)*.

defender [dɪ'fendəʳ] **n** (*lit, fig*) défenseur *m*; (*Sport*) *[record, title]* détenteur *m*, -trice *f*. (*Brit Hist*) **~ of the faith** défenseur de la foi.

defending [dɪ'fendɪŋ] **adj** (*Sport*) **~ champion** champion(ne) *m(f)* en titre; (*Jur*) **~ counsel** avocat *m* de la défense.

defense [dɪ'fens] (*US*) = **defence**.

defensible [dɪ'fensɪbl] **adj** (*lit*) défendable; (*fig*) justifiable, soutenable, défendable.

defensive [dɪ'fensɪv] 1 **adj** (*Mil, fig*) défensif. 2 **n** (*Mil, fig*) défensive *f*. (*lit, fig*) **to be on the ~** être sur la défensive; **to put sb/go on the ~** mettre qn/se mettre sur la défensive.

defensively [dɪ'fensɪvlɪ] **adv** *act, talk, reply etc* de façon défensive, défensivement.

defensiveness [dɪ'fensɪvnɪs] **n**: **his ~ (when we talk about ...)** sa façon d'être sur la défensive (chaque fois que nous parlons de ...).

defer¹ [dɪ'fɜːʳ] **vt** a *journey* différer, reporter, remettre (à plus tard); *meeting* ajourner, reporter; *business* renvoyer; *payment* différer, reculer, retarder; *decision, judgment* suspendre, différer. **to ~ doing** différer de *or* à faire; (*Fin*) **~red annuity** rente *f* à paiement différé; (*Jur, Fin*) **~red liabilities** dettes *fpl* chirographaires; (*Comm etc*) **~red payment** paiement *m* par versements échelonnés. b (*Mil*) **to ~ sb's call-up** mettre qn en sursis (d'incorporation); **to ~ sb on medical grounds** réformer qn (pour raisons médicales).

defer² [dɪ'fɜːʳ] **vi** (*submit*) **to ~ to sb** déférer (*frm*) à qn, s'incliner devant *or* s'en remettre à la volonté de qn; **to ~ to sb's knowledge** s'en remettre aux connaissances de qn; (*Jur*) **to ~ to California jurisdiction** accepter la compétence des tribunaux californiens.

deference ['defərəns] **n** déférence *f*, égards *mpl* (*to* pour). **in ~ to, out of ~ for** par déférence *or* égards pour; **with all due ~ to you** avec tout le respect que je vous dois, sauf votre respect.

deferential [ˌdefə'renʃəl] **adj** *person, attitude* respectueux, plein de déférence *or* d'égards; *tone* de déférence. **to be ~ to sb** se montrer plein de déférence pour *or* envers qn.

deferentially [ˌdefə'renʃəlɪ] **adv** avec déférence.

deferment [dɪ'fɜːmənt] **n** (*see* **defer¹**) report *m*; ajournement *m*; renvoi *m*; retard *m* (*of* dans); suspension *f*. (*Mil*) **to apply for ~** faire une demande de sursis (d'incorporation).

deferral [dɪ'ferəl] **n** = **deferment**.

defiance [dɪ'faɪəns] **n** défi *m*. **a gesture/act of ~** un geste/acte de défi; **a ~ of our authority** un défi à notre autorité; **his ~ of my orders caused the accident** le fait qu'il a défié mes ordres a causé l'accident; **I won't tolerate this ~ of my orders** je ne peux pas tolérer cette façon de défier mes ordres; **to act in ~ of** défier, braver, narguer; **in ~ of** *the law, instructions* au mépris de; *person* en dépit de, au mépris de.

defiant [dɪ'faɪənt] **adj** *attitude, tone* de défi, provocant; *reply* provocant; *person* rebelle, intraitable. **to be ~ of sth** défier qch.

defiantly [dɪ'faɪəntlɪ] **adv** d'un air *or* d'un ton provocant *or* de défi.

deficiency [dɪ'fɪʃənsɪ] 1 **n** a *[goods]* manque *m*, insuffisance *f*, défaut *m* (*of* de); (*Med*) (*of iron etc*) carence *f* (*of* en); (*of liver etc*) déficience *f* (*of* de); *see* **mental, vitamin** *etc*. b (*in character, system*) imperfection *f*, faille *f*, faiblesse *f* (*in* dans). **his ~ as an administrator** son incompétence en tant qu'administrateur. c (*Fin*) déficit *m*, découvert *m*. 2 **comp ▸deficiency disease** (*Med*) maladie *f* de carence ▸**deficiency payment** (*Econ*) paiement *m* différentiel.

deficient [dɪ'fɪʃənt] **adj** (*defective*) défectueux; (*inadequate*) faible (*in* en), insuffisant. **to be ~ in sth** manquer de qch.

deficit ['defɪsɪt] **n** (*Fin etc*) déficit *m*. **in ~** en déficit.

defile¹ ['diːfaɪl] 1 **n** (*procession; place*) défilé *m*. 2 [dɪ'faɪl] **vi** (*march in file*) défiler.

defile² [dɪ'faɪl] **vt** (*pollute: lit, fig*) souiller (*liter*), salir; (*desecrate*) profaner.

defilement [dɪ'faɪlmənt] **n** (*pollution: lit, fig*) souillure *f* (*liter*); (*desecration*) profanation *f*.

definable [dɪ'faɪnəbl] **adj** définissable.

define [dɪ'faɪn] **vt** a *word, feeling* définir; *attitude* préciser, définir; *functions* définir; *responsibilities, conditions* définir, déterminer; *boundaries, powers, duties* délimiter, définir. b (*outline*) dessiner *or* dégager (les formes de). **the tower was clearly ~d against the sky** la tour se détachait nettement sur le ciel.

definite ['defɪnɪt] **adj** a (*exact, clear*) *decision, agreement* bien déterminé, précis, net; *stain, mark* très visible; *improvement* net, manifeste; *intention, order, sale* ferme; *plan* déterminé, précis. **to come to a ~ understanding** parvenir à un accord précis *or* à une entente précise (*on sth* sur qch).
b (*certain*) certain, sûr; *manner, tone* assuré, positif. **is that ~?** (*gen*) c'est certain?, c'est sûr?; (*of sth official*) c'est confirmé?; **it is ~ that** il est certain que + *indic*; **is it ~ that ...?** est-il certain que ...? + *subj*; **she was very ~ about it** elle a été catégorique *or* très nette sur la question.
c (*Gram*) **~ article** article défini; **past ~ (tense)** prétérit *m*.
d (*Math*) **~ integral** intégrale définie.

definitely ['defɪnɪtlɪ] **adv** a (*without doubt*) sans aucun doute, certainement. **he is ~ leaving** il part, c'est certain; **oh ~!** absolument!, bien sûr! b (*appreciably*) nettement, manifestement. **she is ~ more intelligent than ...** elle est nettement *or* manifestement plus intelligente que ... . c (*emphatically*) catégoriquement, d'une manière précise *or* bien déterminée. **she said very ~ that she was not going out** elle a déclaré catégoriquement qu'elle ne sortirait pas.

definition [ˌdefɪ'nɪʃən] **n** a *[word, concept]* définition *f*. **by ~** par définition. b *[powers, boundaries, duties]* délimitation *f*. c (*Phot*) netteté *f*; (*TV*) définition *f*; (*Rad etc*) *[sound]* netteté; (*Opt*) *[lens]* (pouvoir *m* de) résolution *f*.

definitive [dɪ'fɪnɪtɪv] **adj** *study, work* définitif, qui fait autorité; *result* décisif.

definitively [dɪ'fɪnɪtɪvlɪ] **adv** définitivement.

deflate [diː'fleɪt] 1 **vt** a *tyre* dégonfler. **~d tyre** pneu dégonflé *or* à plat. b (*Fin*) **to ~ the currency** provoquer la déflation monétaire; **to ~ prices** faire tomber *or* faire baisser les prix. c (*) *person* démonter, rabattre le caquet à. 2 **vi** se dégonfler.

deflation [diː'fleɪʃən] **n** a (*Econ*) déflation *f*. b *[tyre, ball]* dégonflement *m*.

deflationary [diː'fleɪʃənərɪ] **adj** *measures, policy* déflationniste.

deflationist [diː'fleɪʃənɪst] **adj** déflationniste.

deflator [diː'fleɪtəʳ] **n** déflateur *m*, mesure *f* déflationniste.

deflect [dɪ'flekt] 1 **vt** *ball, projectile* faire dévier; *stream* dériver, détourner; *person* détourner (*from* de). 2 **vi** dévier; *[magnetic needle]* décliner.

deflection [dɪ'flekʃən] **n** *[projectile]* déviation *f*; *[light]* déflexion *f*, déviation; *[magnetic needle]* déclinaison *f* (magnétique), déviation.

deflector [dɪ'flektəʳ] **n** déflecteur *m* (*sauf au sens Aut*).

defloration [ˌdiːflɔː'reɪʃən] **n** (*lit, fig*) défloration *f*.

deflower [diː'flaʊəʳ] **vt** a *girl* déflorer. b (*Bot*) défleurir.

defoliant [diː'fəʊlɪənt] **n** défoliant *m*.

defoliate [diː'fəʊlɪeɪt] **vt** défolier.

defoliation [ˌdiːfəʊlɪ'eɪʃən] **n** défoliation *f*.

deforest [diː'fɒrɪst] **vt** déboiser.

deforestation [diːˌfɒrɪst'eɪʃən] **n** déboisement *m*.

deform [dɪ'fɔːm] **vt** *outline, structure* déformer; (*Tech*) fausser; (*Anat, Phys*) déformer; *mind, tastes* déformer; *town* défigurer, enlaidir.

deformation [ˌdiːfɔː'meɪʃən] **n** déformation *f*.

deformed [dɪ'fɔːmd] **adj** *limb, body* difforme; *person* difforme, contrefait; *mind, structure* déformé, tordu.

deformity [dɪ'fɔːmɪtɪ] **n** *[body]* difformité *f*; *[mind]* déformation *f*.

defraud [dɪ'frɔːd] **vt** *Customs, state* frauder; *person* escroquer. **to ~ sb of sth** escroquer qch à qn, frustrer qn de qch (*Jur*); *see* **conspiracy**.

defrauder [dɪ'frɔːdəʳ] **n** fraudeur *m*, -euse *f*.

defray [dɪ'freɪ] **vt** (*reimburse*) *expenses* payer, rembourser; (*cover*) *cost* couvrir. **to ~ sb's expenses** défrayer qn, rembourser ses frais à qn.

defrayal [dɪ'freɪəl] **n**, **defrayment** [dɪ'freɪmənt] **n** paiement *m or* remboursement *m* des frais.

defrock [diː'frɒk] **vt** défroquer.

defrost [diː'frɒst] 1 **vt** *refrigerator, windscreen* dégivrer; *meat, vegetables* décongeler. 2 **vi** *[fridge]* se dégivrer; *[frozen food]* se décongeler.

defroster [diː'frɒstəʳ] **n** (*Aut*) dégivreur *m*; (*US*) dispositif *m* antibuée.

deft [deft] **adj** *hand, movement* habile, preste, adroit. **to be ~** avoir la main preste.

deftly ['deftlɪ] **adv** adroitement, prestement.

deftness ['deftnɪs] **n** adresse *f*, habileté *f*, dextérité *f*.

defunct [dɪ'fʌŋkt] 1 **adj** (*lit*) défunt, décédé; (*fig*) défunt. 2 **n**: **the ~** le défunt, la défunte.

defuse [diː'fjuːz] **vt** *bomb* désamorcer. (*fig*) **to ~ the situation** désamorcer la situation.

defy [dɪ'faɪ] **vt** a *person, law, danger, death* braver, défier. b *attack* défier. **it defies description** cela défie toute description; **the window defied all efforts to open it** la fenêtre a résisté à tous nos (*or* leurs) efforts pour l'ouvrir. c (*challenge*) **to ~ sb to do** défier qn de faire, mettre qn au défi de faire.

degeneracy [dɪ'dʒenərəsɪ] **n** dégénérescence *f*.

degenerate [dɪ'dʒenəreɪt] 1 **vi** *[race, people]* dégénérer (*into* en), s'abâtardir. (*fig*) **the expedition ~d into a farce** l'expédition a dégénéré en farce. 2 [dɪ'dʒenərɪt] **adj** dégénéré. 3 [dɪ'dʒenərɪt] **n** dégénéré(e) *m(f)*.

degeneration [dɪˌdʒenə'reɪʃən] **n** *[mind, body, morals, race, people]* dégénérescence *f*.

degenerative [dɪ'dʒenərɪtɪv] **adj** dégénératif.

degradable [dɪ'greɪdəbl] **adj** dégradable.

degradation [ˌdegrə'deɪʃən] **n** *[person]* déchéance *f*; *[character]* avilissement *m*; (*Chem, Geol, Mil, Phys*) dégradation *f*. **the ~ of having to accept charity** l'humiliation d'avoir à accepter la charité; (*poverty*) **a scene of utter ~** une scène de misère absolue.

degrade [dɪ'greɪd] **vt** a *official* dégrader; (*Mil*) dégrader, casser. b (*debase*) dégrader. **he felt ~d** il se sentait avili *or* dégradé; **he ~d himself by accepting it** il s'est dégradé en l'acceptant; **I wouldn't ~ myself to do that** je n'irais pas m'abaisser *or* m'avilir à faire cela. c (*Chem, Geol, Phys*) dégrader.

degrading [dɪˈgreɪdɪŋ] adj dégradant, avilissant, humiliant.

degree [dɪˈgriː] 1 n a (*Geog, Math*) degré *m*. **angle of 90 ~s** angle *m* de 90 degrés; **40 ~s east of Greenwich** à 40 degrés de longitude est de Greenwich; **20 ~s of latitude** 20 degrés de latitude; (*fig*) **a 180-~ turn** un virage à 180 degrés.
b [*temperature*] degré *m*. **it was 35 ~s in the shade** il faisait *or* il y avait 35 (degrés) à l'ombre.
c (*step in scale*) degré *m*, rang *m*, échelon *m*. **to do sth by ~s** faire qch par degrés *or* petit à petit; (*esp Brit*) **to a ~** énormément, extrêmement, au plus haut point *or* degré; **to some ~, to a certain ~** à un certain degré, jusqu'à un certain point, dans une certaine mesure; **to a high ~** au plus haut degré, au suprême degré; *stupid etc* **to the last ~** au dernier degré; **not in the least ~ angry** pas le moins du monde fâché; **to such a ~ that** à (un) tel point que; (*Med*) **first-/second-/third-~ burns** brûlures *fpl* au premier/deuxième/troisième degré; (*US Jur*) **first-~ murder** assassinat *m*; (*US Jur*) **second-~ murder** meurtre *m*; **~s of kinship** degrés de parenté; *see* **third**.
d (*amount*) **some ~ of freedom, a (certain) ~ of freedom** une certaine liberté; **a fairly high ~ of error** d'assez nombreuses erreurs, un taux d'erreurs assez élevé; **a considerable ~ of doubt** des doutes considérables; **his ~ of commitment was low** il ne se sentait pas vraiment engagé à fond.
e (*Univ*) diplôme *m* (universitaire). (*Arts, Science, Law*) **first ~** ≈ licence *f*; **higher ~** (*master's*) ≈ maîtrise *f*; (*doctorate*) ≈ doctorat *m*; **~ in** licence de; **I'm taking a science ~** *or* **a ~ in science** je fais une licence de sciences; **he got his ~** il a eu son diplôme; **he got his ~ in geography** il a eu sa licence de géographie; *see* **honorary**.
f (*Gram*) degré *m*. **three ~s of comparison** trois degrés de comparaison.
g (*liter: position in society*) rang *m*. **of high ~** de haut rang.
2 comp ▸**degree course:** (*Brit Univ*) **to do a degree course (in)** faire une licence (de); **the degree course consists of ...** le cursus (universitaire) consiste en ... ▸**degree mill** (*US pej*) usine *f* à diplômes.

degressive [dɪˈgresɪv] adj *taxation* dégressif.

dehumanization [diːˌhjuːmənaɪˈzeɪʃən] n déshumanisation *f*.

dehumanize [diːˈhjuːmənaɪz] vt déshumaniser.

dehumanizing [diːˈhjuːmənaɪzɪŋ] adj déshumanisant.

dehydrate [ˌdiːhaɪˈdreɪt] vt déshydrater.

dehydrated [ˌdiːhaɪˈdreɪtɪd] adj *person, skin, vegetables* déshydraté; *milk, eggs* en poudre.

dehydration [ˌdiːhaɪˈdreɪʃən] n déshydratation *f*.

de-ice [ˈdiːˈaɪs] vt (*Aut, Aviat*) dégivrer.

de-icer [ˈdiːˈaɪsəʳ] n (*Aut, Aviat*) dégivreur *m*.

de-icing [ˈdiːˈaɪsɪŋ] n (*Aut, Aviat*) dégivrage *m*. (*Aut*) **~ spray** bombe *f* antigel.

deictic [ˈdaɪktɪk] n (*Ling*) déictique *m*.

deification [ˌdiːɪfɪˈkeɪʃən] n déification *f*.

deify [ˈdiːɪfaɪ] vt déifier, diviniser.

deign [deɪn] vt daigner (*to do* faire), condescendre (*to do* à faire).

de-indexation [ˌdiːɪndekˈseɪʃən] n désindexation *f*.

deism [ˈdiːɪzəm] n déisme *m*.

deist [ˈdiːɪst] n déiste *mf*.

deity [ˈdiːɪtɪ] n a (*Myth, Rel*) dieu *m*, déesse *f*, divinité *f*, déité *f*. **the D~** Dieu *m*. b (*NonC*) divinité *f*.

deixis [ˈdaɪksɪs] n (*Ling*) déixis *f*.

déjà vu [ˌdeɪʒɑːˈvuː] n déjà(-)vu *m*.

dejected [dɪˈdʒektɪd] adj abattu, découragé. **to become** *or* **get ~** se décourager, se laisser abattre.

dejectedly [dɪˈdʒektɪdlɪ] adv *say, talk* d'un ton abattu; *look* d'un air abattu.

dejection [dɪˈdʒekʃən] n abattement *m*, découragement *m*.

de jure [ˌdeɪˈdʒʊərɪ] adj, adv de jure.

dekko‡ [ˈdekəʊ] n (*Brit*) petit coup d'œil. **let's have a ~** fais voir ça, on va (y) jeter un œil*.

Del. (*US*) abbr of **Delaware**.

Delaware [ˈdeləˌwɛəʳ] n Delaware *m*. **in ~** dans le Delaware.

delay [dɪˈleɪ] 1 vt a (*postpone*) *action, event* retarder, différer; *payment* différer. **~ed effect** effet *m* à retardement; **to ~ doing sth** tarder *or* différer (*frm*) à faire qch, ne pas faire qch à temps.
b (*keep waiting, hold up*) *person* retarder, retenir; *train, plane* retarder; *traffic* retarder, ralentir, entraver. **I don't want to ~ you** je ne veux pas vous retenir *or* retarder.
2 vi s'attarder (*in doing* en faisant). **don't ~!** dépêchez-vous!
3 n a (*waiting period*) délai *m*, retard *m*. **with as little ~ as possible** dans les plus brefs délais; **without ~** sans délai; **without further ~** sans plus tarder *or* attendre, sans autre délai; **they arrived with an hour's ~** ils sont arrivés avec une heure de retard.
b (*postponement*) retardement *m*, arrêt *m*. **after 2 or 3 ~s** après 2 ou 3 arrêts; **there will be ~s to trains on the London-Brighton line** on prévoit des retards pour les trains de la ligne Londres-Brighton; **there will be ~s to traffic** la circulation sera ralentie.
4 comp ▸**delayed-action** adj *bomb, fuse* à retardement ▸**delayed-action shutter** (*Phot*) obturateur *m* à retardement.

delayering [diːˈleɪərɪŋ] n écrasement *m* des niveaux hiérarchiques.

delaying [dɪˈleɪɪŋ] adj *action* dilatoire, qui retarde. **~ tactics** moyens *mpl* dilatoires.

delectable [dɪˈlektəbl] adj délectable, délicieux.

delectation [ˌdiːlekˈteɪʃən] n délectation *f*.

delegate [ˈdelɪgeɪt] 1 vt *authority, power* déléguer (*to* à). **to ~ responsibility** déléguer les responsabilités; **to ~ sb to do sth** déléguer qn *or* se faire représenter par qn pour faire qch. 2 vi déléguer ses responsabilités. 3 [ˈdelɪgɪt] n délégué(e) *m(f)* (*to* à). **~ to a congress** congressiste *mf*.

delegation [ˌdelɪˈgeɪʃən] n a (*NonC*) [*power*] délégation *f*; [*person*] nomination *f*, désignation *f* (*as* comme). b (*group of delegates*) délégation *f*.

delete [dɪˈliːt] vt (*gen*) effacer (*from* de); (*score out*) barrer, rayer (*from* de), biffer; (*Gram, Comput*) supprimer, effacer. (*on forms etc*) **"~ where inapplicable"** "rayer les mentions inutiles".

deleterious [ˌdelɪˈtɪərɪəs] adj *effect, influence* nuisible, délétère (*to* à); *gas* délétère.

deletion [dɪˈliːʃən] n a (*NonC*) effacement *m*. b (*thing deleted*) rature *f*.

delft [delft] n faïence *f* de Delft. **D~ blue** (*colour*) bleu *m* (de) faïence.

Delhi [ˈdelɪ] n Delhi. **~ belly*** turista* *f*, maladie *f* du touriste.

deli* [ˈdelɪ] n (abbr of **delicatessen**) épicerie fine-traiteur *f*.

deliberate [dɪˈlɪbərɪt] 1 adj a (*intentional*) *action, insult, lie* délibéré, voulu, intentionnel. **it wasn't ~** ce n'était pas fait exprès. b (*cautious, thoughtful*) *action, decision* bien pesé, mûrement réfléchi; *character, judgment* réfléchi, circonspect, avisé; (*slow, purposeful*) *air, voice* décidé; *manner, walk* mesuré, posé. 2 [dɪˈlɪbəreɪt] vi a (*think*) délibérer, réfléchir (*upon* sur). b (*discuss*) délibérer, tenir conseil. 3 [dɪˈlɪbəreɪt] vt a (*study*) réfléchir sur, considérer, examiner. b (*discuss*) délibérer sur, débattre.

deliberately [dɪˈlɪbərɪtlɪ] adv a (*intentionally*) *do, say* exprès, à dessein, délibérément, de propos délibéré. b (*slowly, purposefully*) *move, talk* avec mesure, posément.

deliberation [dɪˌlɪbəˈreɪʃən] n a (*consideration*) délibération *f*, réflexion *f*. **after due** *or* **careful ~** après mûre réflexion. b (*discussion: gen pl*) **~s** débats *mpl*, délibérations *fpl*. c (*slowness*) mesure *f*, manière posée.

deliberative [dɪˈlɪbərətɪv] adj a *speech* mûrement réfléchi. b **~ assembly** assemblée délibérante.

delicacy [ˈdelɪkəsɪ] n a (*NonC: see* **delicate**) délicatesse *f*, finesse *f*; fragilité *f*; sensibilité *f*; tact *m*. b (*tasty food*) mets délicat, friandise *f*. **it's a great ~** c'est un mets très délicat. c (*Gram*) syntaxe fine, finesse *f*.

delicate [ˈdelɪkɪt] adj a (*fine, exquisite*) *silk, work* délicat, fin; *china, flower* délicat, fragile; *colour* délicat. **of ~ workmanship** d'un travail délicat. b (*Med*) *health, person, liver* fragile. (*hum*) **in a ~ condition** dans une position intéressante (*hum*). c (*sensitive*) *instrument* délicat; *compass* sensible; *touch* léger, délicat; *person* délicat, sensible; (*tactful*) plein de tact, délicat, discret (*f* -ète). d (*requiring skilful handling*) *operation, subject, question, situation* délicat. e *food, flavour* fin, délicat.

delicately [ˈdelɪkɪtlɪ] adv (*see* **delicate**) *touch* délicatement; *act, say, express* avec délicatesse (*or* finesse *or* tact *etc*).

delicatessen [ˌdelɪkəˈtesn] n a (*shop*) épicerie fine-traiteur *f*. b (*food*) plats cuisinés, charcuterie *f*.

delicious [dɪˈlɪʃəs] adj *dish, smell, person* délicieux, exquis.

deliciously [dɪˈlɪʃəslɪ] adv *smell, look, creamy etc* délicieusement. **to smile ~** avoir un sourire exquis; **~ innocent** d'une innocence exquise.

delight [dɪˈlaɪt] 1 n a (*intense pleasure*) grand plaisir, joie *f*, délectation *f*. **to my ~** à *or* pour ma plus grande joie *or* mon plus grand plaisir; **to take ~ in sth/in doing** prendre grand plaisir à qch/à faire; **with ~** (*gen*) avec joie; (*more sensual: taste, smell*) avec délices; **to give ~** charmer.
b (*source of pleasure: often pl*) délice *m* (*f in pl*), joie *f*, charme *m*. **she is the ~ of her mother** elle fait les délices *or* la joie de sa mère; **this book is a great ~** ce livre est vraiment merveilleux; **a ~ to the eyes** un régal *or* un plaisir pour les yeux; **he's a ~ to watch** il fait plaisir à voir; **the ~s of life in the open** les charmes *or* les délices de la vie en plein air.
2 vt *person* réjouir, enchanter, faire les délices de; *see* **delighted**.
3 vi prendre plaisir (*in sth* à qch, *in doing* à faire), se délecter, se complaire (*in doing* à faire). **she ~s in him/it** il/cela lui donne beaucoup de joie.

delighted [dɪˈlaɪtɪd] adj ravi, enchanté (*with, at, by* de, par; *to do* de faire; *that* que + *subj*). **absolutely ~!** tout à fait ravi!; **~ to meet you!** enchanté (de faire votre connaissance)!; **will you go? — (I shall be) ~** voulez-vous y aller? — avec grand plaisir *or* je ne demande pas mieux *or* très volontiers.

delightedly [dɪˈlaɪtɪdlɪ] adv avec ravissement.

delightful [dɪ'laɪtfʊl] **adj** *person, character, smile* délicieux, charmant; *evening, landscape, city, appearance, dress* ravissant. **it's ~ to live like this** c'est merveilleux de vivre ainsi.

delightfully [dɪ'laɪtfəlɪ] **adv** *friendly, vague* délicieusement; *arranged, decorated* d'une façon ravissante; *smile, behave* de façon charmante.

Delilah [dɪ'laɪlə] **n** Dalila *f*.

delimit [diː'lɪmɪt] **vt** délimiter.

delimitation [ˌdiːlɪmɪ'teɪʃən] **n** délimitation *f*.

delineate [dɪ'lɪnɪeɪt] **vt** a (*lit*) *outline etc* délinéer, tracer. **mountains clearly ~d** montagnes qui se détachent clairement à l'horizon. b *plan etc* (*present*) présenter; (*in more detail*) énoncer en détail; (*with diagram etc*) représenter graphiquement. c (*fig*) *character* représenter, dépeindre, décrire.

delineation [dɪˌlɪnɪ'eɪʃən] **n** *[outline]* dessin *m*, tracé *m*; *[plan]* présentation *f* (détaillée); *[character]* description *f*, peinture *f*.

delinquency [dɪ'lɪŋkwənsɪ] **n** a (*NonC*) délinquance *f*; *see* **juvenile**. b (*act of ~*) faute *f*, délit *m*. c (*US Fin: failure to pay*) défaillance *f*, défaut *m* de paiement.

delinquent [dɪ'lɪŋkwənt] 1 **adj** a délinquant; *see* **juvenile**. b (*US Fin*) *debtor* défaillant; *payment* arriéré, impayé, échu. 2 **n** a délinquant(e) *m(f)*; (*fig*) coupable *mf*, fautif *m*, -ive *f*. b (*US Fin*) défaillant(e) *m(f)*.

deliquescence [ˌdelɪ'kwesəns] **n** déliquescence *f*.

delirious [dɪ'lɪrɪəs] **adj** (*Med*) qui a le délire, délirant; (*fig: very excited*) en proie au délire. **to be ~** (*Med*) délirer, avoir le délire; (*fig*) *[individual]* délirer de joie; *[crowd]* être en délire; (*Med, fig*) **to become** *or* **grow ~** être pris de délire; **~ with joy** délirant de joie.

deliriously [dɪ'lɪrɪəslɪ] **adv** (*Med*) en délire; (*fig*) frénétiquement. **~ happy** débordant *or* transporté de joie.

delirium [dɪ'lɪrɪəm] **n, pl ~** *or* **deliria** [dɪ'lɪrɪə] (*Med, fig*) délire *m*. **bout of ~** accès *m* de délire; **~ tremens** delirium *m* tremens.

delist [dɪ'lɪst] **vt** (*US St Ex*) *security* radier du registre (des valeurs cotées en Bourse).

deliver [dɪ'lɪvəʳ] 1 **vt** a (*take*) remettre (*to* à); *letters etc* distribuer (*à domicile*); *goods* livrer. **to ~ a message to sb** remettre un message à qn; **milk is ~ed each day** le lait est livré tous les jours; (*Comm*) **"we ~ daily"** "livraisons quotidiennes"; **"~ed free"** "livraison gratuite"; **I will ~ the children to school tomorrow** j'emmènerai les enfants à l'école demain; **to ~ a child (over) into sb's care** confier un enfant aux soins de qn; (*fig*) **to ~ the goods*** tenir parole, tenir ses promesses.

b (*rescue*) délivrer, sauver, retirer (*sb from sth* qn de qch). **~ us from evil** délivrez-nous du mal.

c (*utter*) *speech, sermon* prononcer. **to ~ an ultimatum** lancer un ultimatum; (*frm*) **to ~ o.s. of an opinion** émettre une opinion.

d (*Med*) *baby* mettre au monde; *woman* (faire) accoucher. (*frm*) **to be ~ed of a son** accoucher d'un fils.

e (*hand over: also* **~ over, ~ up**) céder, remettre, transmettre. **to ~ a town (up** *or* **over) into the hands of the enemy** livrer une ville à l'ennemi; *see* **stand**.

f *blow* porter, assener.

2 **vi** (**: keep promise*) *[person, nation]* tenir parole, tenir ses promesses (*on sth* quant à qch); *[machine etc]* faire le travail.

deliverance [dɪ'lɪvərəns] **n** a (*NonC*) délivrance *f*, libération *f* (*from* de). b (*statement of opinion*) déclaration *f* (formelle); (*Jur*) prononcé *m* (du jugement).

deliverer [dɪ'lɪvərəʳ] **n** a (*saviour*) sauveur *m*, libérateur *m*, -trice *f*. b (*Comm*) livreur *m*.

delivery [dɪ'lɪvərɪ] 1 **n** a *[goods]* livraison *f*; *[parcels]* remise *f*, livraison; *[letters]* distribution *f*. **to take ~ of** prendre livraison de; **to pay on ~** payer à la *or* sur livraison; **payable on ~** payable à la livraison; (*Comm*) **price on ~** (*gen*) prix *m* à la livraison; *[car]* prix clés en main; *see* **charge, free** *etc*.

b (*Med*) accouchement *m*.

c (*NonC*) *[speaker]* débit *m*, élocution *f*; *[speech]* débit. **his speech was interesting but his ~ dreary** son discours était intéressant mais son débit monotone.

2 **comp** ►**delivery man** livreur *m* ►**delivery note** bulletin *m* de livraison ►**delivery order** bon *m* de livraison ►**delivery room** (*Med*) salle *f* de travail *or* d'accouchement ►**delivery service** service *m* de livraison ►**delivery time** délai *m* de livraison ►**delivery truck** (*esp US*), **delivery van** (*Brit*) camionnette *f* de livraison.

dell [del] **n** vallon *m*.

delouse ['diː'laʊs] **vt** *person, animal* épouiller; *object* ôter les poux de.

Delphi ['delfaɪ] **n** Delphes.

Delphic ['delfɪk] **adj** *oracle* de Delphes; (*fig liter*) obscur.

delphinium [del'fɪnɪəm] **n, pl ~s** *or* **delphinia** [del'fɪnɪə] pied-d'alouette *m*, delphinium *m*.

delta ['deltə] 1 **n** delta *m*. 2 **comp** ►**delta-winged** (*Aviat*) à ailes (en) delta.

deltoid ['deltɔɪd] **adj, n** deltoïde (*m*).

delude [dɪ'luːd] **vt** tromper, duper (*with* par), induire en erreur (*with* par). **to ~ sb into thinking that** amener qn à penser (par des mensonges) que, faire croire à qn (par des mensonges) que; **to ~ o.s.** se faire des illusions, se leurrer, se bercer d'illusions.

deluded [dɪ'luːdɪd] **adj: to be ~** être victime d'illusions, avoir été induit en erreur; **the poor ~ boy said ...** le pauvre garçon, dans son erreur, dit ... .

deluding [dɪ'luːdɪŋ] **adj** trompeur, illusoire.

deluge ['deljuːdʒ] 1 **n** (*lit*) déluge *m*, inondation *f*; (*fig*) déluge. **the D~** le déluge; **a ~ of rain** une pluie diluvienne; **a ~ of protests** un déluge de protestations; **a ~ of letters** une avalanche de lettres. 2 **vt** (*lit, fig*) inonder, submerger (*with* de).

delusion [dɪ'luːʒən] **n** (*false belief*) illusion *f*; (*Psych*) fantasme *m*, hallucination *f*, psychose *f* paranoïaque. **to suffer from ~s** être en proie à des fantasmes; **to be under a ~** se faire illusion, s'abuser; **~s of grandeur** illusions de grandeur; **happiness is a ~** le bonheur est une illusion.

delusive [dɪ'luːsɪv] **adj** = **deluding**.

delusiveness [dɪ'luːsɪvnɪs] **n** caractère trompeur *or* illusoire.

de luxe [dɪ'lʌks] **adj** (*gen*) de luxe, somptueux. **a ~ flat** un appartement (de) grand standing; (*car, machine*) **~ model** modèle *m* (de) grand luxe.

delve [delv] **vi** a (*into book etc*) fouiller (*into* dans). **to ~ into a subject** creuser *or* approfondir un sujet, étudier un sujet à fond; **to ~ (down) into the past** fouiller le passé. b (*in drawer etc*) fouiller (*into* dans). **to ~ into one's pockets** (*lit*) fouiller dans ses poches; (*fig*) mettre la main au portefeuille. c (*dig*) creuser (*into* dans); (*with spade*) bêcher.

Dem. (*US Pol*) 1 **n abbr of Democrat.** 2 **adj abbr of Democratic.**

demagnetize [ˌdiː'mægnɪtaɪz] **vt** démagnétiser.

demagogic [ˌdemə'gɒgɪk] **adj** démagogique.

demagogue ['deməgɒg] **n** démagogue *m*.

demagoguery [ˌdemə'gɒgərɪ] **n** (*US*) agissements *mpl or* méthodes *fpl* de démagogue, démagogie *f*.

demagogy ['deməgɒgɪ] **n** démagogie *f*.

de-man [ˌdiː'mæn] **vt** a (*Brit Ind: reduce manpower*) réduire *or* dégraisser les effectifs de. b (*deprive of virility*) déviriliser.

demand [dɪ'mɑːnd] 1 **vt** *money, explanation, help* exiger, réclamer (*from, of* de); *higher pay etc* revendiquer, réclamer. **to ~ to do** exiger de faire, demander expressément à faire; **he ~s to be obeyed** il exige qu'on lui obéisse; **he ~s that you leave at once** il exige que vous partiez (*subj*) tout de suite; **a question/situation that ~s our attention** une question/une situation qui réclame *or* exige notre attention.

2 **n** a *[person]* exigence(s) *f(pl)*, demande *f*; *[duty, problem, situation etc]* exigence(s); (*claim*) (*for better pay etc*) revendication *f*, réclamation *f*; (*for help, money*) demande. **payable on ~** payable sur demande *or* sur présentation; **final ~ (for payment)** dernier avertissement (d'avoir à payer); **to make ~s on sb** exiger beaucoup de qn *or* de la part de qn; **you make too great ~s on my patience** vous abusez de ma patience; **the ~s of the case** les nécessités *fpl* du cas; **I have many ~s on my time** je suis très pris, mon temps est très pris.

b (*NonC: Comm, Econ*) demande *f*. **to be in great ~** être très demandé *or* recherché; **the ~ for this product increases** ce produit est de plus en plus demandé; **to create a ~ for a product** créer la demande pour un produit; **do you stock suede hats? — no, there's no ~ for them** avez-vous des chapeaux en daim? — non, ils ne sont pas demandés; *see* **supply**[1].

3 **comp** ►**demand bill, demand draft** (*Fin*) bon *m or* effet *m* à vue ►**demand feeding** alimentation *f* libre ►**demand liabilities** engagements *mpl* à vue ►**demand management** (*Econ*) contrôle *m* (gouvernemental) de la demande ►**demand note** = **demand bill**.

demanding [dɪ'mɑːndɪŋ] **adj** *person* exigeant, difficile; *work* exigeant, astreignant. **physically ~** qui demande beaucoup de résistance (physique).

de-manning [ˌdiː'mænɪŋ] **n** (*Brit Ind*) licenciements *mpl*, réduction *f* des effectifs.

demarcate ['diːmɑːkeɪt] **vt** tracer la *or* une ligne de démarcation entre *or* de, délimiter.

demarcation [ˌdiːmɑː'keɪʃən] **n** démarcation *f*, délimitation *f*. **~ line** ligne *f* de démarcation; **~ dispute** conflit *m* d'attributions.

démarche ['deɪmɑːʃ] **n** démarche *f*, mesure *f*.

demean [dɪ'miːn] **vt** *person* avilir, dégrader; *thing* rabaisser. **to ~ o.s.** s'abaisser (*to do* à faire), s'avilir, se ravaler.

demeaning [dɪ'miːnɪŋ] **adj** avilissant, abaissant.

demeanour, (*US*) **demeanor** [dɪ'miːnəʳ] **n** (*behaviour*) comportement *m*, attitude *f*, conduite *f*; (*bearing*) maintien *m*.

demented [dɪ'mentɪd] **adj** (*Med*) dément, en démence; (*) fou (*f* folle), insensé. (*Med*) **to become ~** tomber en démence; **to drive sb ~** rendre qn fou, faire perdre la tête à qn.

dementedly [dɪ'mentɪdlɪ] **adv** comme un fou (*f* une folle).

dementia [dɪ'menʃɪə] **n** démence *f*. **~ praecox** démence précoce; *see* **senile**.

demerara [ˌdemə'reərə] **n** (*Brit: also* **~ sugar**) sucre roux (cristallisé), cassonade *f*.

demerge [ˌdiː'mɜːdʒ] **vt** *company* défusionner.

demerger [ˌdiː'mɜːdʒəʳ] **n** scission *f*, déconcentration *f*, démantèlement *m*.

demerit [diː'merɪt] **n** démérite *m*, tort *m*, faute *f*. (*US Scol*) **~ (point)**

avertissement *m*, blâme *m*.

demesne [dɪˈmeɪn] n domaine *m*, terre *f*; (*Jur*) possession *f*. (*Jur*) **to hold sth in ~** posséder qch en toute propriété.

demi... [ˈdemɪ] pref demi-. **~god** demi-dieu *m*.

demijohn [ˈdemɪdʒɒn] n dame-jeanne *f*, bonbonne *f*.

demilitarization [ˈdiːˌmɪlɪtəraɪˈzeɪʃən] n démilitarisation *f*.

demilitarize [diːˈmɪlɪtəraɪz] vt démilitariser.

demise [dɪˈmaɪz] 1 n a (*death: frm, hum*) décès *m*, mort *f*; (*fig: of institution, custom etc*) mort, fin *f*. b (*Jur*) (*by legacy*) cession *f or* transfert *m* par legs, transfert par testament; (*by lease*) transfert par bail. **~ of the Crown** transmission *f* de la Couronne (*par décès ou abdication*). 2 vt (*Jur*) *estate* léguer; *the Crown, sovereignty* transmettre.

demisemiquaver [ˈdemɪsemɪˌkweɪvəʳ] n (*Brit*) triple croche *f*.

demist [diːˈmɪst] vt désembuer.

demister [diːˈmɪstəʳ] n (*Brit Aut*) dispositif *m* antibuée.

demisting [diːˈmɪstɪŋ] n désembuage *m*.

demitasse [ˈdemɪtæs] n (*US*) (*cup*) tasse *f* (à moka); (*contents*) (tasse de) café noir.

demo* [ˈdeməʊ] n a (*Brit*) (abbr of **demonstration**) manif* *f*. b (*US*) = **demonstration model**; *see* **demonstration 2**. c (*US*) = **demolition worker**; *see* **demolition 2**. d = **demonstration record/tape**; *see* **demonstration 2**.

demob* [ˈdiːˈmɒb] vt, n (*Brit*) abbr of **demobilize, demobilization**.

demobilization [ˈdiːˌməʊbɪlaɪˈzeɪʃən] n démobilisation *f*.

demobilize [diːˈməʊbɪlaɪz] vt démobiliser.

democracy [dɪˈmɒkrəsɪ] n démocratie *f*. **they are working towards ~** ils sont en train de se démocratiser; *see* **people**.

Democrat [ˈdeməkræt] n a (*Brit Pol*) (Libéral) Démocrate *mf*. b (*US Pol*) Démocrate *mf*.

democrat [ˈdeməkræt] n démocrate *mf*.

democratic [ˌdeməˈkrætɪk] adj *institution, spirit* démocratique; (*believing in democracy*) démocrate. (*US Pol*) **the D~ Party** le parti démocrate; **The D~ Republic of ...** la République démocratique de ... .

democratically [ˌdeməˈkrætɪkəlɪ] adv démocratiquement. **to be ~ minded** avoir l'esprit démocrate.

democratize [dɪˈmɒkrətaɪz] 1 vt démocratiser. 2 vi se démocratiser.

demographer [dɪˈmɒgrəfəʳ] n démographe *mf*.

demographic [ˌdeməˈgræfɪk] adj démographique.

demographics [ˌdeməˈgræfɪks] n pl données *fpl* démographiques; *[market]* profil *m* démographique. **the ~ of housing demand** les données démographiques concernant la demande de logement.

demography [dɪˈmɒgrəfɪ] n démographie *f*.

demolish [dɪˈmɒlɪʃ] vt *building* démolir, abattre; *fortifications* démanteler; (*fig*) *theory* démolir, détruire; (*) *cake* liquider*, dire deux mots à*.

demolisher [dɪˈmɒlɪʃəʳ] n (*lit, fig*) démolisseur *m*.

demolition [ˌdeməˈlɪʃən] 1 n démolition *f*. 2 comp ►**demolition area** = **demolition zone** ►**demolition squad** équipe *f* de démolition ►**demolition work** démolition *f* ►**demolition worker** démolisseur *m* ►**demolition zone** zone *f* de démolition.

demon [ˈdiːmən] n (*all senses*) démon *m*. **the D~** le Démon; **the D~ drink** le démon de la boisson; **that child's a ~!*** cet enfant est un petit démon!; **to be a ~ for work** être un bourreau de travail; **a ~ driver** un as* du volant; (*dangerous*) un conducteur pris de folie; **he's a ~ squash player** *etc* il joue au squash *etc* comme un dieu.

demonetization [diːˌmʌnɪtaɪˈzeɪʃən] n démonétisation *f*.

demonetize [diːˈmʌnɪtaɪz] vt démonétiser.

demoniac [dɪˈməʊnɪæk] adj, n démoniaque (*mf*).

demoniacal [ˌdiːməʊˈnaɪəkəl] adj démoniaque, diabolique. **~ possession** possession *f* diabolique.

demonic [diːˈmɒnɪk, dɪˈmɒnɪk] adj démoniaque, diabolique.

demonology [ˌdiːməˈnɒlədʒɪ] n démonologie *f*.

demonstrable [ˈdemənstrəbl] adj démontrable.

demonstrably [ˈdemənstrəblɪ] adv visiblement, manifestement, de façon évidente. **a ~ false statement** une affirmation dont la fausseté est facilement démontrable.

demonstrate [ˈdemənstreɪt] 1 vt a *truth, need* démontrer, prouver. **to ~ that ...** démontrer *or* prouver que ... . b *appliance* faire une démonstration de; *system* expliquer, décrire. **to ~ how sth works** montrer le fonctionnement de qch, faire une démonstration de qch; **to ~ how to do sth** montrer comment faire qch. 2 vi (*Pol etc*) manifester, faire *or* organiser une manifestation (*for* pour, *in favour of* en faveur de, *against* contre).

demonstration [ˌdemənˈstreɪʃən] 1 n a (*NonC*) *[truth etc]* démonstration *f*. b (*Comm*) démonstration *f*. **to give a ~ (of)** faire une démonstration (de). c (*Pol etc*) manifestation *f*. **to hold a ~** manifester, faire *or* organiser une manifestation. d *[love, affection]* manifestations *fpl*, témoignage(s) *m(pl)*. 2 comp *car, lecture, tape, diskette* de démonstration ►**demonstration model** modèle *m* de démonstration.

demonstrative [dɪˈmɒnstrətɪv] adj *behaviour, person* démonstratif, expansif; (*Gram, Math, Philos*) démonstratif.

demonstrator [ˈdemənstreɪtəʳ] n a (*person*) (*Comm*) démonstrateur *m*, -trice *f*; (*Educ*) préparateur *m*, -trice *f*; (*Pol*) manifestant(e) *m(f)*. b (*appliance*) appareil *m* (*or* article *m*) de démonstration; (*car*) voiture *f* de démonstration.

demoralization [dɪˌmɒrəlaɪˈzeɪʃən] n démoralisation *f*.

demoralize [dɪˈmɒrəlaɪz] vt démoraliser. **to become ~d** perdre courage *or* le moral*.

demoralizing [dɪˈmɒrəlaɪzɪŋ] adj démoralisant.

demote [dɪˈməʊt] vt (*also Mil*) rétrograder.

demotic [dɪˈmɒtɪk] 1 adj a (*of the people*) populaire. b (*Ling*) démotique. 2 n démotique *m*.

demotion [dɪˈməʊʃən] n rétrogradation *f*.

demulcent [dɪˈmʌlsənt] adj, n (*Med*) émollient (*m*), adoucissant (*m*).

demur [dɪˈmɜːʳ] 1 vi hésiter (*at sth* devant qch, *at doing* à faire), faire *or* soulever des difficultés (*at doing* pour faire), élever des objections (*at sth* contre qch); (*Jur*) opposer une exception. 2 n hésitation *f*, objection *f*. **without ~** sans hésiter, sans faire de difficultés.

demure [dɪˈmjʊəʳ] adj *smile, look* modeste, sage, réservé; *girl* modeste, sage; *child* très sage. **a ~ hat** un petit chapeau bien sage.

demurely [dɪˈmjʊəlɪ] adv modestement, sagement, avec réserve; (*coyly*) avec une modestie affectée.

demureness [dɪˈmjʊənɪs] n (*see* **demure**) air *m* modeste; sagesse *f*.

demurrage [dɪˈmʌrɪdʒ] n (*Jur*) surestarie *f*. **goods in ~** marchandises *fpl* en souffrance (sur le quai).

demurrer [dɪˈmʌrəʳ] n (*Jur*) ≃ exception *f* péremptoire.

demystification [diːˌmɪstɪfɪˈkeɪʃən] n démystification *f*.

demystify [diːˈmɪstɪˌfaɪ] vt démystifier.

demythification [diːˌmɪθɪfɪˈkeɪʃən] n démythification *f*.

demythify [diːˈmɪθɪˌfaɪ] vt démythifier.

den [den] n a *[lion, tiger]* tanière *f*, antre *m*; *[thieves]* repaire *m*, antre. (*lit, fig*) **the lion's ~** l'antre du lion; **~ of iniquity** *or* **vice** lieu *m* de perdition *or* de débauche; *see* **gambling, opium**. b (*: *room, study*) antre *m*, turne* *f*, piaule* *f*.

►**den up*** vi (*US*) se retirer dans sa piaule*.

denationalization [ˈdiːˌnæʃnəlaɪˈzeɪʃən] n dénationalisation *f*.

denationalize [diːˈnæʃnəlaɪz] vt dénationaliser.

denature [ˌdiːˈneɪtʃəʳ] vt dénaturer.

dengue [ˈdeŋgɪ] n dengue *f*.

denial [dɪˈnaɪəl] n a *[rights, truth]* dénégation *f*; *[report, accusation]* démenti *m*; *[guilt]* dénégation; *[authority]* répudiation *f*, rejet *m*, reniement *m*. **~ of justice** déni *m* (de justice); **~ of self** abnégation *f*; **he met the accusation with a flat ~** il a nié catégoriquement l'accusation; **to issue a ~** publier un démenti. b **Peter's ~ of Christ** le reniement du Christ par Pierre.

denier [ˈdenɪəʳ] n a (*weight*) denier *m*. **25 ~ stockings** bas *mpl* de 25 deniers. b (*coin*) denier *m*.

denigrate [ˈdenɪgreɪt] vt dénigrer, discréditer.

denigration [ˌdenɪˈgreɪʃən] n dénigrement *m*.

denim [ˈdenɪm] n (*for jeans, skirts etc*) (toile *f* de) jean *m*; (*heavier: for uniforms, overalls etc*) treillis *m*. (*Dress*) **~s** (*trousers*) blue-jean *m*, jean; (*workman's overalls*) bleus *mpl* de travail.

denizen [ˈdenɪzn] n a (*inhabitant*) habitant(e) *m(f)*. **~s of the forest** habitants *or* hôtes *mpl* (*liter*) des forêts. b (*Brit Jur*) étranger *m*, -ère *f* (ayant droit de cité). c (*naturalized plant/animal*) plante *f*/animal *m* acclimaté(e).

Denmark [ˈdenmɑːk] n Danemark *m*.

denominate [dɪˈnɒmɪneɪt] vt dénommer.

denomination [dɪˌnɒmɪˈneɪʃən] n a (*group*) groupe *m*, catégorie *f*; (*Rel*) confession *f*; *[money]* valeur *f*; *[weight, measure]* unité *f*. b (*NonC*) dénomination *f*, appellation *f*.

denominational [dɪˌnɒmɪˈneɪʃənl] adj (*Rel*) confessionnel, appartenant à une confession. (*US*) **~ college** université confessionnelle; (*US*) **~ school** école *f* libre *or* confessionnelle.

denominative [dɪˈnɒmɪnətɪv] adj, n dénominatif (*m*).

denominator [dɪˈnɒmɪneɪtəʳ] n dénominateur *m*; *see* **common**.

denotation [ˌdiːnəʊˈteɪʃən] n a (*NonC*) (*gen, also Ling, Philos*) dénotation *f*; (*meaning*) signification *f*. b (*symbol*) indices *mpl*, signes *mpl*.

denotative [dɪˈnəʊtətɪv] adj (*Ling*) dénotatif.

denote [dɪˈnəʊt] vt (*indicate*) dénoter, marquer, indiquer; (*mean*) signifier; (*Ling, Philos*) dénoter.

denounce [dɪˈnaʊns] vt a (*speak against*) *person* dénoncer (*to* à); *action* dénoncer. **to ~ sb as an impostor** accuser publiquement qn d'imposture. b (*repudiate*) *treaty* dénoncer.

denouncement [dɪˈnaʊnsmənt] n = **denunciation**.

denouncer [dɪˈnaʊnsəʳ] n dénonciateur *m*, -trice *f*.

dense [dens] adj a *fog, forest* dense, épais (*f* -aisse); *crowd* dense, compact; *population* nombreux, dense. b (*Opt, Phot*) opaque. c (*: *stupid*) *person* bête, obtus, bouché*. d (*US: meaningful*) profond.

densely [ˈdenslɪ] adv: **~ wooded** couvert de forêts épaisses; **~ populated** très peuplé, à forte densité de population.

denseness [ˈdensnɪs] n a = **density**. b (*) stupidité *f*.

densitometer [ˌdensɪˈtɒmɪtəʳ] n densitomètre *m*.

density ['densɪtɪ] n (*Phys*) densité *f*; *[fog]* densité, épaisseur *f*; *[population]* densité. **double/high/single ~ diskette** disquette *f* double/haute/simple densité.

dent [dent] 1 n (*in wood*) entaille *f*; (*in metal*) bosse *f*, bosselure *f*. (*Aut*) **to have a ~ in the bumper** avoir le pare-choc bosselé *or* cabossé; **his holiday in Rome made a ~ in his savings*** ses vacances à Rome ont fait un trou dans *or* ont écorné ses économies. 2 vt *hat* cabosser; *car* bosseler, cabosser; *wood* entailler.

dental ['dentl] 1 adj a *treatment, school* dentaire. **~ floss** fil *m* dentaire; **~ hygienist** hygiéniste *mf* dentaire; **~ nurse** assistant(e) *m(f)* dentaire *or* de dentiste; **~ receptionist** réceptionniste *f* dans un cabinet dentaire; **~ surgery** cabinet *m* dentaire *or* de dentiste; **~ surgeon** chirurgien *m* dentiste; **~ technician** mécanicien *m* dentiste. b (*Ling*) dental. 2 n (*Ling*) dentale *f*.

dentifrice ['dentɪfrɪs] n dentifrice *m*.

dentine ['denti:n] n dentine *f*.

dentist ['dentɪst] n dentiste *mf*. **~'s chair** fauteuil *m* de dentiste; **~'s surgery** cabinet *m* dentaire *or* de dentiste; **to go to the ~('s)** aller chez le dentiste.

dentistry ['dentɪstrɪ] n dentisterie *f*. **to study ~** faire des études dentaires, faire l'école dentaire.

dentition [den'tɪʃən] n dentition *f*.

denture ['denʧəʳ] n dentier *m*, râtelier *m* (†, *hum*).

denude [dɪ'nju:d] vt (*lit, fig*) dénuder, dépouiller. **~d landscape** paysage nu *or* dépouillé; **area ~d of trees** région dépouillée d'arbres.

denunciation [dɪ,nʌnsɪ'eɪʃən] n a *[person]* dénonciation *f*; (*in public*) accusation publique, condamnation *f*; *[action]* dénonciation. b *[treaty]* dénonciation *f*.

denunciator [dɪ'nʌnsɪeɪtəʳ] n dénonciateur *m*, -trice *f*.

deny [dɪ'naɪ] vt a (*repudiate*) nier (*having done* avoir fait, *that* que + *indic or subj*); *fact, accusation* nier, refuser d'admettre; *sb's authority* rejeter. **there is no ~ing it** c'est indéniable; **I'm not ~ing the truth of it** je ne nie pas que ce soit vrai. b (*refuse*) **to ~ sb sth** refuser qch à qn, priver qn de qch; **he was denied admittance** on lui a refusé l'entrée; **to ~ o.s. cigarettes** se priver de cigarettes; **to ~ sb the right to do** refuser *or* dénier à qn le droit de faire. c (*disown*) *leader, religion* renier.

deodorant [di:'əʊdərənt] adj, n déodorant *(m)*, désodorisant *(m)*.

deodorize [di:'əʊdəraɪz] vt désodoriser.

deontology [,di:ɒn'tɒlədʒɪ] n déontologie *f*.

deoxidize [di:'ɒksɪdaɪz] vt désoxyder.

deoxyribonucleic [di:,ɒksɪ,raɪbəʊnju:'kleɪɪk] adj: **~ acid** acide *m* désoxyribonucléique.

depart [dɪ'pɑ:t] 1 vi a (*go away*) *[person]* partir, s'en aller; *[bus, plane, train etc]* partir. **to ~ from a city** quitter une ville, partir *or* s'en aller d'une ville; **to be about to ~** être sur le *or* son départ; (*on timetable etc*) **"~ing London at 12.40"** "départ de Londres (à) 12.40". b (*fig*) **to ~ from** (*gen*) s'écarter de; (*from habit, principle, the truth*) faire une entorse à. 2 vt (*liter*) **to ~ this world** *or* **this life** quitter ce monde, trépasser (*liter*).

departed [dɪ'pɑ:tɪd] 1 adj a (*liter: dead*) défunt. **the ~ leader** le chef défunt, le défunt chef. b (*bygone*) *glory, happiness* passé; *friends* disparu. 2 n (*liter*) **the ~** le défunt, la défunte, les défunts *mpl*.

department [dɪ'pɑ:tmənt] 1 n (*government ~*) ministère *m*, département *m*; (*Ind*) service *m*; *[shop, store]* rayon *m*; *[smaller shop]* comptoir *m*; (*Scol*) section *f*; (*Univ*) ≃ U.E.R. *f* (*Unité d'études et de recherches*), département; (*French Admin, Geog*) département; (*fig: field of activity*) domaine *m*, rayon. (*Brit Admin*) **D~ of Health** ministère de la Santé; (*Ind*) **he works in the sales ~** il travaille au service des ventes; **which government ~ is involved?** de quel ministère *or* département cela relève-t-il?; **in all the ~s of public service** dans tous les services publics; (*Comm*) **the shoe ~** le rayon des chaussures; **the French D~** (*Scol*) la section de français; (*Univ*) l'U.E.R. *or* le département de français; **gardening is my wife's ~*** le jardinage c'est le rayon de ma femme; *see* **head, state, trade** *etc*.

2 comp ►**department chairman, department head** (*Univ*) ≃ directeur *m*, -trice *f* d'U.E.R ►**department store** grand magasin.

departmental [,di:pɑ:t'mentl] adj (*see* **department**) d'un *or* du ministère *or* département *or* service; d'une *or* de la section; *[France]* départemental. *[shop]* **~ manager** chef *m* de rayon.

departmentalization [,di:pɑ:t,mentəlaɪ'zeɪʃən] n organisation *f* en départements.

departmentalize [,di:pɑ:t'mentə,laɪz] vt organiser en départements.

departure [dɪ'pɑ:tʃəʳ] 1 n a (*from place*) *[person, vehicle]* départ *m*; (*from job*) départ, démission *f*. **on the point of ~** sur le point de partir, sur le départ; *see* **arrival** *etc*.

b (*from custom, principle*) dérogation *f*, entorse *f* (*from* à); (*from law*) manquement *m* (*from* à). **a ~ from the norm** une exception à la règle, un écart par rapport à la norme; **a ~ from the truth** une entorse à la vérité.

c (*change of course, action*) nouvelle voie *or* orientation *or* direction; (*Comm: new type of goods*) nouveauté *f*, innovation *f*. **it's a new ~ in biochemistry** c'est une nouvelle voie qui s'ouvre en *or* pour la biochimie.

d (*liter: death*) trépas *m* (*liter*).

2 comp *preparations etc* de départ ►**departure board** (*Aviat, Rail*) horaire *m* des départs ►**departure gate** (*Aviat*) porte *f* (de départ) ►**departure indicator** (*Aviat, Rail*) horaire *m* des départs ►**departure language** (*Ling*) langue-source *f* ►**departure lounge** (*Aviat*) salle *f* d'embarquement ►**departure platform** (*Rail*) quai *m* de départ ►**departure signal** (*Rail*) signal *m* de départ ►**departure time** heure *f* de départ.

depend [dɪ'pend] impers vi dépendre (*on sb/sth* de qn/qch). **it all ~s, that ~s** cela dépend, c'est selon*; **it ~s on you whether he comes or not** cela dépend de vous *or* il ne tient qu'à vous qu'il vienne ou non; **it ~s (on) whether he will do it or not** cela dépend s'il veut le faire ou non; **it ~s (on) what you mean** cela dépend de ce que vous voulez dire (*by* par); **~ing on the weather** selon le temps; **~ing on what happens tomorrow ...** selon ce qui se passera demain ... .

►**depend (up)on** vt fus a (*rely on*) compter sur, se fier à, se reposer sur. **you can always depend (up)on him** on peut toujours compter sur lui *or* se fier à lui; **you may depend (up)on his coming** vous pouvez compter qu'il viendra *or* compter sur sa venue; **I'm depending (up)on you to tell me what he wants** je me fie à vous *or* je compte sur vous pour savoir ce qu'il veut; **you can depend (up)on it** soyez-en sûr, je vous le promets *or* garantis; **you can depend (up)on it that he'll do it wrong again** tu peux être sûr (et certain*) qu'il le fera de nouveau de travers.

b (*need support or help from*) dépendre de. **he depends (up)on his father for pocket money** il dépend de son père pour son argent de poche; **I'm depending (up)on you for moral support** votre appui moral m'est indispensable; **your success depends (up)on your efforts** votre succès dépendra de vos efforts.

dependability [dɪ,pendə'bɪlɪtɪ] n *[machine]* sécurité *f* de fonctionnement; *[person]* sérieux *m*. **his ~ is well-known** tout le monde sait que l'on peut compter sur lui.

dependable [dɪ'pendəbl] adj *person* sérieux, sûr, sur qui on peut compter; *mechanism* fiable; *information* sûr. **this is a really ~ car** on peut vraiment avoir confiance en cette voiture, c'est vraiment une voiture solide; **he is not ~** on ne peut pas compter sur lui *or* se fier à lui *or* lui faire confiance.

dependance [dɪ'pendəns] n = **dependence**.

dependant [dɪ'pendənt] n personne *f* à charge, charge *f* de famille. **he had many ~s** il avait de nombreuses personnes à (sa) charge.

dependence [dɪ'pendəns] n a (*state of depending: also* **dependency**) dépendance *f* (*on* à, à l'égard de, envers), sujétion *f* (*on* à). **~ on one's parents** dépendance à l'égard de *or* envers ses parents; **~ on drugs** (situation *f or* état *m* de) dépendance à l'égard de la drogue; **to place ~ on sb** faire confiance à *or* se fier à qn. b **~ of success upon effort** rapport *m or* dépendance *f* entre le succès et l'effort.

dependency [dɪ'pendənsɪ] n a = **dependence a**. (*Jur*) **~ allowance** indemnité *f* pour charges de famille. b (*Ling*) dépendance *f*. **~ grammar** grammaire dépendancielle. c (*country*) dépendance *f*, colonie *f*.

dependent [dɪ'pendənt] 1 adj a *person* dépendant (*on* de); *child, relative* à charge; *condition, decision* dépendant (*on* de), subordonné (*on* à). **to be ~ on charity** dépendre de la charité, subsister de charité; **to be (financially) ~ on sb** vivre aux frais de qn, être à la charge de qn, dépendre de qn financièrement; **to be ~ on one another** dépendre l'un de l'autre; **to be ~ on drugs** avoir une dépendance psychologique à l'égard de la drogue.

b (*contingent*) **~ on** tributaire de; **tourism is ~ on the climate** le tourisme est tributaire du climat; **the time of his arrival will be ~ on the weather** son heure d'arrivée dépendra du temps.

c (*Gram*) *clause* subordonné.

d (*Math*) dépendant. **~ variable** variable dépendante, fonction *f*.

2 n = **dependant**.

depersonalize [di:'pɜ:sənəlaɪz] vt dépersonnaliser.

depict [dɪ'pɪkt] vt (*in words*) peindre, dépeindre, décrire; (*in picture*) représenter. **surprise was ~ed on his face** la surprise se lisait sur son visage, son visage exprimait la surprise.

depiction [dɪ'pɪkʃən] n (*see* **depict**) peinture *f*; représentation *f*.

depilate ['depɪleɪt] vt épiler.

depilatory [dɪ'pɪlətərɪ] adj, n dépilatoire *(m)*.

deplane [,di:'pleɪn] vi (*US*) descendre d'avion.

deplenish [dɪ'plenɪʃ] vt (*reduce*) dégarnir; (*empty*) vider.

deplete [dɪ'pli:t] vt a (*reduce*) *supplies* réduire; *strength* diminuer, réduire; (*exhaust*) *supplies, strength* épuiser. (*Comm*) **our stock is very ~d** nos stocks sont très bas; (*Mil*) **the regiment was greatly ~d** (*by cuts etc*) l'effectif du régiment était très réduit; (*by war, sickness*) le régiment a été décimé; **numbers were greatly ~d** les effectifs étaient très réduits. b (*Med*) décongestionner.

depletion [dɪ'pli:ʃən] n (*see* **deplete**) réduction *f*; diminution *f*; épuisement *m*. (*Jur*) **~ allowance** reconstitution *f* des gisements.

deplorable [dɪ'plɔ:rəbl] adj déplorable, lamentable.

deplorably [dɪ'plɔ:rəblɪ] adv déplorablement, lamentablement.

deplore [dɪ'plɔ:ʳ] vt déplorer, regretter vivement. **to ~ the fact that** déplorer le fait que + *indic*, regretter vivement que + *subj*.

deploy [dɪ'plɔɪ] 1 vt (*Mil*) *missiles, ships, tanks, troops etc* déployer; (*gen*) *resources, equipment* faire usage de, utiliser; *staff* utiliser (les services de); *skills, talents* déployer, faire preuve de. 2 **vi** (*Mil*) être déployé.

deployment [dɪ'plɔɪmənt] **n** (*Mil*) déploiement *m*; (*fig*) usage *m*, utilisation *f*; *see* **rapid**.

depolarization ['diːˌpəʊləraɪ'zeɪʃən] **n** dépolarisation *f*.

depolarize [diː'pəʊləraɪz] **vt** dépolariser.

deponent [dɪ'pəʊnənt] 1 **n** a (*Gram*) déponent *m*. b (*Jur*) déposant(e) *m(f)*. 2 **adj** (*Gram*) déponent.

depopulate [ˌdiː'pɒpjʊleɪt] **vt** dépeupler. **to become ~d** se dépeupler.

depopulation ['diːˌpɒpjʊ'leɪʃən] **n** dépopulation *f*, dépeuplement *m*. **rural ~** exode rural.

deport [dɪ'pɔːt] **vt** a (*expel*) expulser (*from* de); (*transport*) déporter (*from* de; *to* à); (*Hist*) *prisoner* déporter. b (*behave*) **to ~ o.s.** se comporter, se conduire.

deportation [ˌdiːpɔː'teɪʃən] **n** expulsion *f*; (*Hist*) déportation *f*. (*Jur*) **~ order** arrêt *m* d'expulsion.

deportment [dɪ'pɔːtmənt] **n** maintien *m*, tenue *f*. **~ lessons** leçons *fpl* de maintien.

depose [dɪ'pəʊz] 1 **vt** *king* déposer, détrôner; *official* destituer. 2 **vti** (*Jur*) déposer, attester par déposition.

deposit [dɪ'pɒzɪt] 1 **vt** a (*put down*) *parcel etc* déposer, poser.

b *money* (*in bank account*) verser, déposer; *money, valuables* déposer, laisser *or* mettre en dépôt (*in or with the bank* à la banque; *with sb* chez qn), confier (*sth with sb* qch à qn). **I ~ed £200 in my account** j'ai versé 200 livres à mon compte, j'ai déposé *or* mis 200 livres sur mon compte.

c (*Geol*) déposer, former un dépôt de.

2 **n** a (*in bank*) dépôt *m*. **to make a ~ of £50** déposer *or* verser 50 livres; **loan on ~** prêt *m* en nantissement.

b (*part payment*) arrhes *fpl*, acompte *m*, provision *f*; (*in hire purchase: down payment*) premier versement comptant; (*in hiring goods, renting accommodation: against damage etc*) caution *f*, cautionnement *m*; (*on bottle etc*) consigne *f*; (*Brit Pol*) cautionnement ((*à verser pour faire acte de candidature*)). (*Comm*) **to leave a ~ of £2** *or* **a £2 ~ on a dress** verser 2 livres d'arrhes *or* d'acompte sur une robe; (*Comm*) **"a small ~ will secure any goods"** "on peut faire mettre tout article de côté moyennant (le versement d')un petit acompte"; (*Brit Pol*) **to lose one's ~** perdre son cautionnement.

c (*Chem*) dépôt *m*, précipité *m*, sédiment *m*; (*in wine*) dépôt; (*Geol*) (*alluvial*) dépôt; *[mineral, oil]* gisement *m*. **to form a ~** se déposer.

3 **comp** ►**deposit account** (*Brit Banking*) compte *m* sur livret ►**deposit bank** banque *f* de dépôt ►**deposit loan** prêt *m* en nantissement ►**deposit slip** bulletin *m* de versement.

depositary [dɪ'pɒzɪtərɪ] **n** a (*person*) dépositaire *mf*. b = **depository**.

deposition [ˌdiːpə'zɪʃən] **n** a (*NonC*) *[king, official]* déposition *f*. b (*Jur*) déposition *f* sous serment, témoignage *m*.

depositor [dɪ'pɒzɪtə^r] **n** déposant(e) *m(f)*.

depository [dɪ'pɒzɪtərɪ] **n** dépôt *m*, entrepôt *m*.

depot ['depəʊ] 1 **n** a (*Mil*) dépôt *m*. b (*Brit: garage*) garage *m*, dépôt *m*. c (*Brit*) ['depəʊ], (*US*) ['diːpəʊ] (*warehouse*) dépôt *m*, entrepôt *m*. **coal ~** dépôt *or* entrepôt de charbon. d (*US*) ['diːpəʊ] (*railway station*) gare *f*; (*bus station*) dépôt *m*. 2 **comp** ►**depot ship** (navire *m*) ravitailleur *m*.

depravation [ˌdeprə'veɪʃən] **n** dépravation *f*, corruption *f*.

deprave [dɪ'preɪv] **vt** dépraver, corrompre.

depraved [dɪ'preɪvd] **adj** dépravé, perverti, vicié. **to become ~** se dépraver.

depravity [dɪ'prævɪtɪ] **n** dépravation *f*, perversion *f*.

deprecate ['deprɪkeɪt] **vt** *action, behaviour* désapprouver, s'élever contre. **I ~ his having spoken to you** j'estime qu'il n'aurait pas dû vous parler.

deprecating ['deprɪkeɪtɪŋ] **adj** a (*disapproving*) *air, voice* désapprobateur (*f* -trice), de reproche. b (*apologetic*) *smile* d'excuse, humble.

deprecatingly ['deprɪkeɪtɪŋlɪ] **adv** (*see* **deprecating**) d'un ton désapprobateur; avec l'air de s'excuser, humblement.

deprecatory ['deprɪkətərɪ] **adj** = **deprecating**.

depreciate [dɪ'priːʃɪeɪt] 1 **vt** (*Fin*) *property, currency* déprécier, dévaloriser; (*write off*) *asset, investment* amortir; (*fig*) *help, talent* déprécier, dénigrer. **to ~ sth by 25% a year** amortir qch de 25% *or* à un rythme de 25% par an. 2 **vi** (*Fin, fig*) se déprécier, se dévaloriser.

depreciation [dɪˌpriːʃɪ'eɪʃən] **n** *[property, car]* dépréciation *f*, perte *f* de valeur; *[currency]* dépréciation, dévalorisation *f*; (*Comm, Econ*) *[goods]* moins-value *f*; (*writing off*) *[asset, investment]* amortissement *m*; (*fig*) *[talent etc]* dépréciation, dénigrement *m*.

depredation [ˌdeprɪ'deɪʃən] **n** (*gen pl*) déprédation(s) *f(pl)*, ravage(s) *m(pl)*.

depress [dɪ'pres] **vt** a *person* déprimer, donner le cafard* à; (*Med*) déprimer. b (*press down*) *lever* appuyer sur, abaisser. c *status* réduire; *trade* réduire, (faire) diminuer; *the market, prices* faire baisser.

depressant [dɪ'presnt] **adj, n** (*Med*) dépresseur *(m)*.

depressed [dɪ'prest] **adj** a *person* déprimé, abattu, découragé (*about* à cause de); (*Med*) déprimé. **to feel ~** se sentir déprimé *or* démoralisé, avoir le cafard*; **to get ~** se décourager, se laisser abattre. b *industry, area* en déclin, touché par la crise; (*Fin*) *market, trade* en crise, languissant; *business* dans le marasme, languissant; (*Soc*) *class, group* économiquement faible.

depressing [dɪ'presɪŋ] **adj** déprimant, décourageant. **I find it very ~** je trouve cela très déprimant *or* décourageant, ça me donne le cafard*.

depressingly [dɪ'presɪŋlɪ] **adv** *sigh, say* d'un ton découragé; *point out, conclude* de façon déprimante *or* décourageante. **~ weak/monotonous** *etc* d'une faiblesse/monotonie *etc* déprimante.

depression [dɪ'preʃən] **n** a (*NonC*) *[person]* découragement *m*; (*Med*) dépression *f*, état dépressif. (*Med*) **to suffer from ~** faire de la dépression. b (*in ground*) creux *m*; (*Geog*) dépression *f*; (*Met*) dépression (atmosphérique); (*Econ*) crise *f*, dépression, récession *f*. (*Met*) **a deep/shallow ~** une forte/faible dépression; (*Hist*) **the D~** la Crise (de 1929); **the country's economy was in a state of ~** l'économie du pays était dans le marasme *or* en crise. c *[lever, key etc]* abaissement *m*.

depressive [dɪ'presɪv] **adj, n** (*Med*) dépressif *(m)*, -ive *(f)*.

depressurization [dɪˌpreʃəraɪ'zeɪʃən] **n** dépressurisation *f*.

depressurize [dɪ'preʃəˌraɪz] **vt** (*Phys etc*) dépressuriser; (*fig: take strain off*) *person* faciliter la vie à.

deprivation [ˌdeprɪ'veɪʃən] **n** (*act, state*) privation *f*; (*loss*) perte *f*; (*Psych*) carence affective. (*Jur*) **~ of office** destitution *f* de fonction; *see* **maternal**.

deprive [dɪ'praɪv] **vt** (*of sleep, food, company*) priver (*of* de); (*of right*) priver, déposséder (*of* de); (*of asset*) ôter, enlever (*sb of sth* qch à qn). **to ~ o.s. of** se priver de; (*Soc*) **~d child/family** enfant/famille déshérité(e).

dept. **abbr of department**.

depth [depθ] 1 **n** a *[water, hole]* profondeur *f*; *[shelf, cupboard]* profondeur, largeur *f*; *[snow]* épaisseur *f*; *[edge, border]* largeur, hauteur *f*, épaisseur; *[voice, tone]* registre *m* grave; *[knowledge, feeling]* profondeur; *[sorrow, relief]* profondeur, intensité *f*, acuité *f*; *[concern, interest]* acuité, intensité; *[colour]* intensité. **at a ~ of 3 metres** à 3 mètres de profondeur, par 3 mètres de fond; **the water is 3 metres in ~** l'eau a 3 mètres de profondeur, il y a 3 mètres de fond; (*lit, fig*) **to get out of one's ~** perdre pied; (*in swimming pool etc*) **don't go out of your ~** ne va pas là où tu n'as pas pied; (*fig*) **I am quite out of my ~** je nage complètement*, je suis complètement dépassé*; **the ~s of the ocean** les profondeurs océaniques; **from the ~s of the earth** des profondeurs *or* des entrailles *fpl* de la terre; **a great ~ of feeling** une grande profondeur de sentiment; **to study in ~** étudier en profondeur; **in-~ interview** interview *f* en profondeur; (*Phot*) **~ of field/of focus** profondeur de champ/de foyer.

b (*fig*) **~s** fond *m*; **to be in the ~s of despair** toucher le fond du désespoir; **I would never sink to such ~s as to do that** je ne tomberais jamais assez bas pour faire cela; **in the ~ of winter** au plus fort *or* au cœur de l'hiver; **in the ~ of night** au milieu *or* au plus profond de la nuit; **in the ~s of the forest** au plus profond *or* au cœur de la forêt.

2 **comp** ►**depth charge** grenade sous-marine ►**depth psychology** psychologie *f* des profondeurs.

deputation [ˌdepjʊ'teɪʃən] **n** délégation *f*, députation *f*.

depute [dɪ'pjuːt] **vt** *power, authority* déléguer; *person* députer, déléguer (*sb to do* qn pour faire).

deputize ['depjʊtaɪz] 1 **vi** assurer l'intérim (*for sb* de qn). 2 **vt** députer (*sb to do* qn pour faire).

deputy ['depjʊtɪ] 1 **n** a (*second in command*) adjoint(e) *m(f)*; (*replacement*) remplaçant(e) *m(f)*, suppléant(e) *m(f)*; (*in business*) fondé *m* de pouvoir; (*member of deputation*) délégué(e) *m(f)*. b (*French Pol*) député *m*. c (*US*) shérif adjoint, ≃ gendarme *m*. 2 **adj** adjoint. **~ chairman** vice-président *m*; **~ director** sous-directeur *m*, -trice *f*; (*Scol*) **~ head** (*gen*) directeur, -trice adjoint(e), (*of lycée*) censeur *m*; (*Scol*) **~ headmaster, ~ headmistress** = **deputy head; ~ judge** juge suppléant; **~ mayor** maire adjoint; (*US*) **D~ Secretary** ministre adjoint; (*US*) **~ sheriff** = **deputy 1c**.

derail [dɪ'reɪl] 1 **vt** faire dérailler. 2 **vi** dérailler.

derailleur [də'reɪljə^r] **n** (*also* **~ gears**) dérailleur *m*.

derailment [dɪ'reɪlmənt] **n** déraillement *m*.

derange [dɪ'reɪndʒ] **vt** a *plan* déranger, troubler; *machine* dérégler. b (*Med*) déranger (le cerveau de), aliéner. **~d person/mind** personne *f*/esprit *m* dérangé(e); **to be (mentally) ~d** avoir le cerveau dérangé.

derangement [dɪ'reɪndʒmənt] **n** a (*Med*) aliénation mentale. b *[machine]* dérèglement *m*.

derate [diː'reɪt] **vt** (*Tax*) *land, property* dégrever.

Derby ['dɑːbɪ,] (*US*) ['dɜːbɪ] **n** a (*Brit*) (*Horse-racing*) **the ~** le Derby (d'Epsom); (*Sport*) **local ~** match *m* entre équipes voisines. b (*US*) **d~ (hat)** (chapeau *m*) melon *m*.

Derbys. (*Brit*) **abbr of Derbyshire**.

deregulate [dɪ'regjʊˌleɪt] **vt** *prices* libérer; *transport system* déréglementer.

deregulation [dɪˌregjʊ'leɪʃən] **n** *[prices]* libération *f*; *[transport system]* déréglementation *f*.

derelict ['derɪlɪkt] 1 adj a (*abandoned*) abandonné, délaissé; (*ruined*) (tombé) en ruines. b (*frm: neglectful of duty*) négligent. 2 n a (*Naut*) navire abandonné (*en mer*). b (*person*) épave *f* (humaine).

dereliction [,derɪ'lɪkʃən] n *[property]* état *m* d'abandon; *[person]* délaissement *m*. ~ **of duty** négligence *f* (dans le service), manquement *m* au devoir.

derestricted [,di:rɪ'strɪktɪd] adj (*Brit*) *road, area* sans limitation de vitesse.

deride [dɪ'raɪd] vt rire de, railler, tourner en ridicule.

derision [dɪ'rɪʒən] n dérision *f*. **object of** ~ objet *m* de dérision *or* de risée.

derisive [dɪ'raɪsɪv] adj a *smile, person* moqueur, railleur. b *amount, offer* dérisoire.

derisively [dɪ'raɪsɪvlɪ] adv d'un ton railleur *or* moqueur, d'un air *or* d'un ton de dérision.

derisory [dɪ'raɪsərɪ] adj a *amount, offer* dérisoire. b *smile, person* moqueur, railleur.

derivation [,derɪ'veɪʃən] n dérivation *f*.

derivative [dɪ'rɪvətɪv] 1 adj (*Chem, Ling, Math*) dérivé; (*fig*) *literary work etc* peu original. 2 n (*Chem, Ling*) dérivé *m*; (*Math*) dérivée *f*.

derive [dɪ'raɪv] 1 vt *profit, satisfaction* tirer (*from* de), trouver (*from* dans); *comfort, ideas* puiser (*from* dans); *name, origins* tenir (*from* de); *word* (faire) dériver (*from* de). **to** ~ **one's happiness from** devoir son bonheur à, trouver son bonheur dans; **to be ~d from** *see* **2**. 2 vi: **to** ~ **from** (*also* **be ~d from**) dériver de, provenir de, venir de; *[power, fortune]* provenir de; *[idea]* avoir sa source *or* ses origines dans; *[word]* dériver de; **it all ~s from the fact that** tout cela tient au fait que *or* provient du fait que.

dermatitis [,dɜ:mə'taɪtɪs] n dermatite *f*, dermite *f*.

dermatologist [,dɜ:mə'tɒlədʒɪst] n dermatologue *mf*, dermatologiste *mf*.

dermatology [,dɜ:mə'tɒlədʒɪ] n dermatologie *f*.

dermis ['dɜ:mɪs] n derme *m*.

derogate ['derəgeɪt] vi: **to** ~ **from** porter atteinte à; **without derogating from his authority/his merits** sans rien enlever à *or* sans vouloir diminuer son autorité/ses mérites; (*liter*) **to** ~ **from one's position** déroger (à son rang) (*liter*).

derogation [,derə'geɪʃən] n (*see* **derogate**) atteinte *f* (*from* à), diminution *f* (*from* de); (*liter*) dérogation *f* (*liter*) (*from* à).

derogatory [dɪ'rɒgətərɪ] adj *remark* désobligeant (*of, to* à), peu flatteur, dénigrant; *attitude* de dénigrement.

derrick ['derɪk] n (*lifting device, crane*) mât *m* de charge; (*above oil well*) derrick *m*.

derring-do†† ['derɪŋ'du:] n bravoure *f*. **deeds of** ~ hauts faits, prouesses *fpl*.

derringer ['derɪndʒə^r] n (*US*) pistolet *m* (court et à gros calibre), derringer *m*.

derv [dɜ:v] n (*Brit Aut*) gas-oil *m*.

dervish ['dɜ:vɪʃ] n derviche *m*.

DES [,di:i:'es] (abbr of **Department of Education and Science**) *ministère de l'Éducation*.

desalinate [di:'sælɪneɪt] vt dessaler.

desalination [di:,sælɪ'neɪʃən] n dessalement *m*. ~ **plant** usine *f* de dessalement.

descale [di:'skeɪl] vt détartrer. **descaling agent** *or* **product** (produit *m*) détartrant *m*.

descant ['deskænt] n déchant *m*. **to sing** ~ chanter une partie du déchant.

descend [dɪ'send] 1 vi a (*go down*) *[person, vehicle, road, hill etc]* descendre (*from* de); *[rain, snow]* tomber. **to** ~ **into oblivion** tomber dans l'oubli; **sadness ~ed upon him** la tristesse l'a envahi; **in ~ing order of importance** par ordre d'importance décroissante.
b (*by ancestry*) descendre, être issu (*from* de); *[plan, event etc]* tirer son origine (*from* de).
c (*pass by inheritance*) *[property, customs, rights]* passer (par héritage) (*from* de, *to* à).
d (*attack suddenly*) s'abattre, se jeter, tomber (*on, upon* sur); (*Mil, fig*) faire une descente (*on* sur). (*fig*) **visitors ~ed upon us** des gens sont arrivés (chez nous) sans crier gare.
e (*lower o.s. to*) **to** ~ **to lies** *or* **to lying** s'abaisser à mentir, descendre jusqu'à mentir; **I'd never** ~ **to that** je refuserais de m'abaisser ainsi *or* de descendre si bas.
2 vt a *stairs* descendre.
b **to be ~ed from** *species* descendre de; *person* descendre de, être issu de.

descendant [dɪ'sendənt] n descendant(e) *m(f)*.

descendeur [desɑ:n'dɜ:^r] n (*Climbing*) descendeur *m*.

descendible [dɪ'sendəbl] adj (*Jur*) transmissible.

descent [dɪ'sent] n a (*going down*) *[person]* descente *f* (*into* dans); (*fig: into crime etc*) chute *f*; (*Aviat, Sport*) descente; *[hill]* descente, pente *f*. **the street made a sharp** ~ la rue était très en pente *or* descendait en pente très raide; ~ **by parachute** descente en parachute.
b (*ancestry*) origine *f*, famille *f*. **of noble** ~ de noble extraction; **to trace one's** ~ **back to** faire remonter sa famille à; **to trace back the** ~ **of** établir la généalogie de.
c *[property, customs etc]* transmission *f* (par héritage) (*to* à).
d (*Mil etc: attack*) descente *f*, irruption *f*. (*Mil*) **to make a** ~ **on the enemy camp** faire une descente sur *or* faire irruption dans le camp ennemi; (*Mil*) **to make a** ~ **on the enemy** faire une descente sur l'ennemi.

describe [dɪs'kraɪb] vt a *scene, person* décrire, faire la description de, dépeindre. ~ **what it is like** racontez *or* dites comment c'est; ~ **him for us** décrivez-le-nous; **which cannot be ~d** indescriptible, qu'on ne saurait décrire. b (*represent*) décrire, représenter (*as* comme), qualifier (*as* de). **he ~s himself as a doctor** il se dit *or* se prétend docteur; **she ~s herself as ordinary** elle se présente *or* se décrit comme quelqu'un d'ordinaire. c (*Math*) décrire.

description [dɪs'krɪpʃən] n a *[person]* description *f*, portrait *m*; (*Police*) signalement *m*; *[scene, object]* description; *[event, situation]* description, exposé *m*. **to give an accurate/lively** ~ faire *or* donner une description exacte/vivante; **beyond** ~ indescriptible, qu'on ne saurait décrire; **it beggars** *or* **defies** ~ cela défie toute description; *see* **answer**. b (*sort*) sorte *f*, espèce *f*, genre *m*. **vehicles of every** ~ véhicules de toutes sortes.

descriptive [dɪs'krɪptɪv] adj (*gen, also Ling*) descriptif. ~ **geometry/linguistics** géométrie/linguistique descriptive.

descriptivism [dɪ'skrɪptɪvɪzəm] n (*Ling*) descriptivisme *m*.

descriptivist [dɪ'skrɪptɪvɪst] n (*Ling*) descriptiviste *mf*.

descry [dɪs'kraɪ] vt discerner, distinguer.

desecrate ['desɪkreɪt] vt *shrine, memory* profaner, souiller (*liter*).

desecration [,desɪ'kreɪʃən] n profanation *f*.

deseed [di:'si:d] vt *fruit* épépiner.

desegregate [,di:'segrɪgeɪt] vt abolir *or* supprimer la ségrégation raciale dans. **~d schools** écoles *fpl* où la ségrégation raciale n'est plus pratiquée.

desegregation ['di:,segrɪ'geɪʃən] n déségrégation *f*.

deselect [,di:sɪ'lekt] vt (*Brit Pol*) *candidate* ne pas resélectionner.

desensitize [,di:'sensɪtaɪz] vt désensibiliser.

desert[1] ['dezət] 1 n (*lit, fig*) désert *m*. 2 comp *region, climate, animal, plant* désertique ► **desert boot** chaussure montante (en daim à lacets) ► **desert island** île déserte ► **desert rat** (*Zool*) gerboise *f* ► **Desert Rats*** (*Brit Mil*) *forces britanniques combattant en Libye (Seconde Guerre mondiale)*.

desert[2] [dɪ'zɜ:t] 1 vt *post, people, land* déserter, abandonner; *cause, party* déserter; *spouse, family* abandonner; *friend* délaisser. **his courage ~ed him** son courage l'a abandonné; **the place was ~ed** l'endroit était désert. 2 vi (*Mil*) déserter; (*from one's party*) faire défection. **to** ~ **to the rebels** passer du côté des rebelles.

deserted [dɪ'zɜ:tɪd] adj *road, place* désert; *wife etc* abandonné.

deserter [dɪ'zɜ:tə^r] n (*Mil*) déserteur *m*; (*to the enemy*) transfuge *m*.

desertion [dɪ'zɜ:ʃən] n (*see* **desert**[2]) désertion *f*; abandon *m*; défection *f*; délaissement *m*; (*Mil*) désertion; (*Jur*) *[spouse]* abandon du conjoint *or* du domicile conjugal. ~ **to the enemy** désertion *or* défection à l'ennemi; ~ **of one's family** abandon de sa famille.

deserts [dɪ'zɜ:ts] npl dû *m*, ce que l'on mérite; (*reward*) récompense méritée; (*punishment*) châtiment mérité. **according to his** ~ selon ses mérites; **to get one's (just)** ~ avoir *or* recevoir ce que l'on mérite.

deserve [dɪ'zɜ:v] 1 vt *[person]* mériter, être digne de; *[object, suggestion]* mériter. **he ~s to win** il mérite de gagner; **he ~s to be pitied** il mérite qu'on le plaigne, il est digne de pitié; **he ~s more money** il mérite d'être mieux payé; **he got what he ~d** il n'a eu que ce qu'il méritait, il ne l'a pas volé*; **the idea ~s consideration** l'idée mérite réflexion; *see* **well**[2] *etc*. 2 vi: **to** ~ **well of one's country** bien mériter de la patrie; **man deserving of more respect** homme digne d'un plus grand respect.

deservedly [dɪ'zɜ:vɪdlɪ] adv à bon droit, à juste titre (*also pej*).

deserving [dɪ'zɜ:vɪŋ] adj *person* méritant; *action, cause* méritoire, louable. **she's a** ~ **case** c'est une personne méritante; **the** ~ **poor** les pauvres méritants; *see* **deserve**.

deshabille [,dezə'bi:l] n = **dishabille**.

desiccant ['desɪkənt] n dessiccatif *m*.

desiccate ['desɪkeɪt] vt dessécher, sécher. **~d coconut** noix de coco séchée.

desiccation [,desɪ'keɪʃən] n dessiccation *f*.

desiderata [dɪ,zɪdə'rɑ:tə] npl desiderata *mpl*.

design [dɪ'zaɪn] 1 n a (*intention*) dessein *m*, intention *f*, projet *m*. **by** ~ à dessein, exprès, de propos délibéré; **his ~s became obvious when ...** ses intentions *or* ses projets sont devenu(e)s manifestes quand ...; **to form a** ~ **to do** former le projet *or* concevoir le dessein de faire; **to have ~s on sb/sth** avoir des desseins *or* des visées *fpl* sur qn/qch; **imperialist ~s against** *or* **on Ruritania** les visées impérialistes sur la Ruritanie.
b (*plan drawn in detail*) *[building, machine, car etc]* plan *m*, dessin *m* (*of, for* de); *[dress, hat]* croquis *m*, dessin (*of, for* de); (*preliminary sketch*) ébauche *f*, étude *f* (*for* de). **have you seen the** ~ **for the new cathedral?** avez-vous vu les plans *or* les dessins *or* les ébauches de la nouvelle cathédrale?

c (*way in which sth is planned and made*) *[building, book]* plan *m*, conception *f* (*of* de); *[dress etc]* style *m*, ligne *f* (*of* de); *[car, machine etc]* conception; (*look*) esthétique *f*, design *m*, look* *m*. **computer-aided ~** conception assistée par ordinateur; **the ~ of the apartment facilitates ...** le plan de l'appartement facilite ...; **the ~ of the car allows ...** la conception de la voiture *or* la façon dont la voiture est conçue permet ...; **the latest ~ in ...** le dernier modèle de ...; **the general ~ of "Paradise Lost"** le plan général *or* l'architecture *f* du "Paradis Perdu"; **the grand** *or* **overall ~** le plan d'ensemble; **this is a very practical ~** c'est conçu de façon très pratique; **the ~ was wrong** la conception était défectueuse, c'était mal conçu.

d (*subject of study*) (*for furniture, housing*) design *m*; (*for clothing etc*) stylisme *m*. **industrial ~** l'esthétique *or* la création industrielle; **his real interest is ~** ce qui l'intéresse vraiment, c'est le design.

e (*ornamental pattern*) motif *m*, dessin *m* (*on* sur); (*geometric*) dessin. **the ~ on the material/the cups** le dessin *or* le motif du tissu/des tasses.

2 comp ▸**design award** prix *m* de la meilleure conception *or* du meilleur dessin ▸**Design Office** (*Ind*) bureau *m* d'études.

3 vt (*think out*) concevoir; (*draw on paper*) *object* concevoir, dessiner; *building* concevoir, dessiner, faire le plan de; *dress, hat* créer, dessiner; *scheme* élaborer. **well-~d** bien conçu; **this machine was ~ed for a special purpose** cette machine a été conçue pour un usage spécifique; **room ~ed as a study** pièce conçue pour être un cabinet de travail; **~ed to hold wine** fait *or* conçu pour contenir du vin.

designate ['dezɪgneɪt] 1 vt a (*indicate, specify, appoint*) *person, thing* désigner (*as* comme; *to sth* à qch; *to do* pour faire). **he was ~d to take charge of the operations** on l'a désigné comme responsable des opérations; **these posts ~ the boundary between ...** ces poteaux montrent la frontière entre ... . b (*entitle*) *person, thing* désigner. **this area was ~d a priority development region** cette région a été classée *or* choisie comme zone à développer en priorité. 2 ['dezɪgnɪt] adj désigné. **the chairman ~** le président désigné.

designation [ˌdezɪg'neɪʃən] n (*gen*) désignation *f*. (*Jur, Comm*) **~ of origin** appellation *f* d'origine.

designedly [dɪ'zaɪnɪdlɪ] adv à dessein, exprès.

designer [dɪ'zaɪnəʳ] 1 n (*Archit, Art*) dessinateur *m*, -trice *f*, créateur *m*, -trice *f*; (*Comm, Ind*) concepteur-projeteur *m*; (*esp Advertising*) créatif *m*; (*for furniture etc*) designer *m*; (*for dress*) styliste *mf*, modéliste *mf*; (*very famous*) couturier *m*; (*Cine, Theat*) décorateur *m*, -trice *f*; *see* **industrial** *etc*. 2 comp *jeans, gloves, scarves etc* haute couture; (*: *fashionable*) *lager, mineral water* branché* ▸**designer drug** (*synthetic narcotic*) drogue *f* de synthèse ▸**designer stubble** barbe *f* de trois jours (*d'un négligé savamment entretenu*).

designing [dɪ'zaɪnɪŋ] adj (*scheming*) intrigant; (*crafty*) rusé.

desirability [dɪˌzaɪərə'bɪlɪtɪ] n *[plan]* avantages *mpl*; *[person]* charmes *mpl*, sex-appeal *m*.

desirable [dɪ'zaɪərəbl] adj *position, offer* désirable, enviable, tentant; *person* désirable, séduisant; *action, progress* désirable, à désirer, souhaitable. **it is ~ that** il est désirable *or* souhaitable que + *subj*; **~ residence for sale** belle propriété à vendre.

desirably [dɪ'zaɪərəblɪ] adv avantageusement. **~ located** très bien situé; **~ priced** à un prix intéressant *or* avantageux.

desire [dɪ'zaɪəʳ] 1 n désir *m*, envie *f* (*for* de, *to do* de faire); (*sexual*) désir. **a ~ for peace** un désir (ardent) de paix; **it is my ~ that** c'est mon désir que + *subj*; **I have no ~** *or* **I haven't the least ~ to do it** je n'ai nullement envie de le faire. 2 vt a (*want*) désirer, vouloir (*to do* faire, *that* que + *subj*), avoir envie (*to do* de faire); *object, person* avoir envie de, désirer; *peace* désirer. **his work leaves much to be ~d** son travail laisse beaucoup à désirer; **the ~d effect/result** l'effet/le résultat voulu *or* escompté. b (*request*) prier (*sb to do* qn de faire).

desirous [dɪ'zaɪərəs] adj désireux (*of* de). **to be ~ of sth/of doing** désirer qch/faire.

desist [dɪ'zɪst] vi cesser, s'arrêter (*from doing* de faire). **to ~ from sth** cesser qch; (*Jur*) se désister de qch; **to ~ from criticism** renoncer à *or* cesser de critiquer; **to ~ from one's efforts** abandonner ses efforts.

desk [desk] 1 n a (*for pupil*) pupitre *m*; (*for teacher*) bureau *m*, chaire *f*; (*in office, home*) bureau; (*bureau-type*) secrétaire *m*; (*Mus*) pupitre; *see* **roll** *etc*.

b (*Brit: in shop, restaurant*) caisse *f*; (*in hotel, at airport*) réception *f*. **ask at the ~** demandez à la caisse (*or* à la réception); (*Press*) **the ~** le secrétariat de rédaction; (*Press*) **the news/city ~** le service des informations/financier; *[Foreign Office, State Department]* **he's on the West African ~** il est à la direction des affaires ouest-africaines; *see* **cash** *etc*.

2 comp ▸**desk blotter** sous-main *m inv* ▸**desk-bound** sédentaire ▸**desk clerk** (*US*) réceptionniste *mf* ▸**desk diary** agenda *m* (de bureau) ▸**desk job**: **he's got a desk job** il fait un travail de bureau ▸**desk lamp** lampe *f* de bureau ▸**desk pad** bloc *m* (de bureau), bloc-notes *m* ▸**deskside computer** ordinateur *m* type "tower" ▸**desk study** (*Brit fig: Econ etc*) étude *f* sur documents ▸**desktop** *model, computer* de table, de bureau ▸**desktop publishing** publication *f* assistée par ordinateur, P.A.O. *f*, microédition *f*.

deskill [dɪ'skɪl] vt déqualifier.

deskilling [dɪ'skɪlɪŋ] n déqualification *f*.

desolate ['desəlɪt] 1 adj a *place* (*empty*) désolé, désert; (*in ruins*) ravagé, dévasté; (*fig*) *outlook, future* sombre, morne. b (*grief-stricken*) affligé, au désespoir; (*friendless*) délaissé, solitaire. **a ~ cry** un cri de désespoir. 2 ['desəleɪt] vt *country* désoler, ravager; *person* désoler, affliger.

desolately ['desəlɪtlɪ] adv *say etc* d'un air désolé *or* affligé.

desolation [ˌdesə'leɪʃən] n a (*grief*) désolation *f*, affliction *f*; (*friendlessness*) solitude *f*; *[landscape]* aspect désert, solitude. b (*of country, by war*) désolation *f* (*liter*), dévastation *f*.

despair [dɪs'pɛəʳ] 1 n a (*NonC*) désespoir *m* (*about, at, over* au sujet de, *at having done* d'avoir fait). **to be in ~** être au désespoir, être désespéré; **in ~ she killed him** de désespoir elle l'a tué; **to drive sb to ~** réduire qn au désespoir, désespérer qn. b (*cause of ~*) désespoir *m*. **this child is the ~ of his parents** cet enfant fait *or* est le désespoir de ses parents. 2 vi (se) désespérer, perdre l'espoir. **don't ~!** ne te désespère pas!; **to ~ of (doing) sth** désespérer de (faire) qch; **his life was ~ed of** on désespérait de le sauver.

despairing [dɪs'pɛərɪŋ] adj *person* désespéré; *look, gesture* de désespoir, désespéré; (*) *situation, sb's work* catastrophique*.

despairingly [dɪs'pɛərɪŋlɪ] adv *say* d'un ton désespéré; *look* d'un air désespéré; *agree, answer* avec désespoir; *look for* désespérément.

despatch [dɪs'pætʃ] n = **dispatch**.

desperado [ˌdespə'rɑːdəʊ] n, pl **~(e)s** hors-la-loi *m inv*, desperado *m*.

desperate ['despərɪt] adj a *person, animal, measure, attempt, situation* désespéré; *fight, effort* désespéré, acharné; *criminal* capable de tout, prêt à tout. **to feel ~** être désespéré; **to do something ~** commettre un acte de désespoir; **he's a ~ man** c'est un désespéré; **I am ~ for money/a rest** il me faut absolument de l'argent/du repos, j'ai désespérément besoin d'argent/de repos; **to be ~ to do sth** mourir d'envie de faire qch; **I'm ~ (for the toilet)*** j'ai une envie pressante*. b (*: *very bad*) atroce*, abominable.

desperately ['despərɪtlɪ] adv a *struggle* désespérément, avec acharnement, en désespéré; *regret* désespérément; *say, look* avec désespoir. b *cold, needy* terriblement, désespérément; *funny* extrêmement. **~ in love** éperdument amoureux; **~ ill** très gravement malade; **~ shy/thin** d'une timidité/maigreur maladive.

desperation [ˌdespə'reɪʃən] n (*NonC*) a (*state*) désespoir *m*. **to be in ~** être au désespoir; **to drive sb to ~** pousser qn à bout; **in ~ she killed him** poussée à bout elle l'a tué; **in sheer ~** en désespoir de cause. b (*recklessness*) désespoir *m*, rage *f or* fureur *f* du désespoir. **to fight with ~** combattre avec la rage du désespoir.

despicable [dɪs'pɪkəbl] adj *action, person* ignoble, abject, méprisable.

despicably [dɪs'pɪkəblɪ] adv d'une façon méprisable *or* ignoble, bassement.

despise [dɪs'paɪz] vt *danger, person* mépriser. **to ~ sb for sth/for doing sth** mépriser qn pour qch/pour avoir fait qch.

despisingly [dɪs'paɪzɪŋlɪ] adv avec mépris, dédaigneusement.

despite [dɪs'paɪt] 1 prep malgré, en dépit de. **~ our objecting to this, they decided ...** bien que nous ayons fait des objections *or* malgré nos objections, ils ont décidé ... . 2 n (*liter*) dépit *m*.

despoil [dɪs'pɔɪl] vt (*liter*) *person* dépouiller, spolier (*of* de); *country* piller.

despoiler [dɪs'pɔɪləʳ] n (*liter*) spoliateur *m*, -trice *f*.

despoiling [dɪs'pɔɪlɪŋ] n spoliation *f*.

despondence [dɪs'pɒndəns] n, **despondency** [dɪs'pɒndənsɪ] n découragement *m*, abattement *m*.

despondent [dɪs'pɒndənt] adj découragé, abattu, déprimé (*about* par).

despondently [dɪs'pɒndəntlɪ] adv d'un air *or* d'un ton découragé *or* abattu.

despot ['despɒt] n (*lit, fig*) despote *m*, tyran *m*.

despotic [des'pɒtɪk] adj (*lit*) despotique; (*fig*) despote.

despotically [des'pɒtɪkəlɪ] adv *behave* d'une manière despotique, despotiquement; *govern* despotiquement, en despote.

despotism ['despətɪzəm] n despotisme *m*.

des res [dez rez] n abbr of **desirable residence**.

dessert [dɪ'zɜːt] 1 n dessert *m*. 2 comp ▸**dessert apple** pomme *f* à couteau ▸**dessert chocolate** chocolat *m* à croquer ▸**dessert plate** assiette *f* à dessert ▸**dessertspoon** (*Brit*) cuiller *f* à dessert ▸**dessert wine** vin doux.

destabilization [diːˌsteɪbɪlaɪ'zeɪʃən] n déstabilisation *f*.

destabilize [diː'steɪbɪˌlaɪz] vt (*Pol*) *regime etc* déstabiliser.

de-Stalinization [diːˌstɑːlɪnaɪ'zeɪʃən] n déstalinisation *f*.

de-Stalinize [diː'stɑːlɪˌnaɪz] vt déstaliniser.

destination [ˌdestɪ'neɪʃən] n destination *f*.

destine ['destɪn] vt *person, object* destiner (*for* à).

destined ['destɪnd] adj a (*by fate*) destiné (*to* à). **they were ~ to meet again later** ils étaient destinés à se rencontrer plus tard; **I was ~ never to see them again** je devais ne plus jamais les revoir; (*liter*) **at the ~ hour** à l'heure fixée par le destin. b (*heading for*) **~ for London** à destination de Londres; **a letter ~ for her** une lettre qui lui est (*or* était *etc*) destinée.

destiny ['destɪnɪ] n destin *m*, destinée *f*, sort *m*. **D~** le destin, le sort, la destinée; the destinies of France during this period le destin de la France pendant cette période; it was his ~ to die in battle il était écrit qu'il devait mourir au combat; a man of ~ un homme promis à une grande destinée.

destitute ['destɪtju:t] 1 adj a (*poverty-stricken*) indigent, sans ressources. to be utterly ~ être dans le dénuement le plus complet. b (*lacking*) dépourvu, dénué (*of* de). 2 npl: the ~ les pauvres *mpl*, les indigents *mpl*.

destitution [ˌdestɪ'tju:ʃən] n dénuement *m*, indigence *f*, misère noire.

destroy [dɪs'trɔɪ] vt a (*spoil completely*) *town, forest* détruire, ravager; *building* démolir; *toy, gadget* démolir; *document* détruire. ~ed by bombing détruit par bombardement; the village was ~ed by a fire un incendie a ravagé le village. b (*kill*) *enemy* détruire, anéantir; *population* détruire, exterminer, décimer; *dangerous animal, injured horse* abattre; *cat, dog* supprimer, faire piquer. to ~ o.s. se suicider, se tuer. c (*put an end to*) *reputation, mood, beauty, influence, faith* détruire; *hope, love* anéantir, détruire.

destroyer [dɪs'trɔɪəʳ] n a (*Naut*) contre-torpilleur *m*, destroyer *m*. ~ escort escorteur *m*. b (*person*) destructeur *m*, -trice *f*; (*murderer*) meurtrier *m*, -ière *f*.

destruct [dɪs'trʌkt] 1 vt *missile* détruire volontairement. 2 vi être détruit volontairement. 3 n destruction *f* volontaire. 4 comp ▶**destruct button/mechanism** télécommande *f*/mécanisme *m* de destruction.

destructible [dɪs'trʌktəbl] adj destructible.

destruction [dɪs'trʌkʃən] n a (*NonC: act*) *[town, building]* destruction *f*; *[enemy]* destruction, anéantissement *m*; *[people, insects]* destruction, extermination *f*; *[documents]* destruction; *[reputation, hope]* destruction, ruine *f*; *[character, soul]* ruine, perte *f*. ~ by fire destruction par un incendie *or* par le feu. b (*NonC: damage: from war, fire*) destruction *f*, dégâts *mpl*, dommages *mpl*.

destructive [dɪs'trʌktɪv] adj a (*causing actual destruction*) *person, wind, fire etc* destructeur (*f* -trice); (*potentially destroying*) *power, instinct* destructif. *[child]* he's very ~ c'est un brise-fer, il casse tout; a ~ effect on ... un effet destructeur sur ...; (*fig*) it was a very ~ piece of writing c'était vraiment un écrit destructeur *or* accablant. b (*not constructive*) *criticism, comment, idea* destructif.

destructively [dɪs'trʌktɪvlɪ] adv de façon destructrice.

destructiveness [dɪ'strʌktɪvnɪs] n *[fire, war, criticism etc]* caractère *or* effet destructeur; *[child etc]* penchant destructeur.

destructor [dɪs'trʌktəʳ] n (*Brit: also* refuse ~) incinérateur *m* (à ordures).

desuetude [dɪ'sjʊɪtju:d] n (*liter*) désuétude *f*.

desultory ['desəltərɪ] adj *reading* décousu, sans suite, sans méthode; *attempt* peu suivi, peu soutenu; *firing, contact* irrégulier, interrompu, intermittent. to have a ~ conversation échanger des propos décousus.

det. abbr of detective.

detach [dɪ'tætʃ] vt *hook, rope, cart* détacher, séparer (*from* de). to ~ o.s. from a group se détacher d'un groupe; a section became ~ed from ... une section s'est détachée de ...; troops were ~ed to protect the town on a envoyé un détachement de troupes pour protéger la ville; *see also* detached.

detachable [dɪ'tætʃəbl] adj *part of machine, section of document* détachable (*from* de); *collar, lining* amovible. (*Phot*) ~ lens objectif *m* mobile.

detached [dɪ'tætʃt] adj a (*separate*) *part, section* détaché, séparé. (*Brit*) ~ house maison individuelle (entourée d'un jardin), ≃ pavillon *m*, petite villa; ~ retina décollement *m* de la rétine; ~ from the world of racing coupé du monde des courses; ~ from reality coupé de la réalité. b (*unbiased*) *opinion* désintéressé, objectif, sans préjugés; (*unemotional*) *manner* détaché, indifférent, dégagé. he seemed very ~ about it il semblait ne pas du tout se sentir concerné.

detachment [dɪ'tætʃmənt] n a (*NonC*) *[part, section etc]* séparation *f* (*from* de). (*Med*) ~ of the retina décollement *m* de la rétine. b (*NonC: fig: in manner*) détachement *m*, indifférence *f*; (*towards pleasure, friends*) indifférence (*towards* à, à l'égard de). c (*Mil*) détachement *m*.

detail ['di:teɪl] 1 n a (*also Archit, Art*) détail *m*; (*information on sth wanted*) renseignements *mpl*. in ~ en détail; in great ~ dans les moindres détails; his attention to ~ l'attention qu'il apporte au détail; to go into ~s entrer dans les détails; in every ~ it resembles ... de point en point *or* dans le moindre détail cela ressemble à ...; but that's a tiny ~! mais ce n'est qu'un (petit) détail!; let me take down the ~s je vais noter les renseignements nécessaires; (*Comm etc*) please send me ~s of ... veuillez m'envoyer des renseignements sur *or* concernant ...; *see* personal.

b (*Mil*) détachement *m*.

2 comp ▶**detail drawing** (*Archit, Tech*) épure *f*.

3 vt a *reason, fact* exposer en détail; *story, event* raconter en détail; *items, objects* énumérer, détailler.

b (*Mil*) *troops* affecter (*for* à, *to do* à *or* pour faire), détacher, désigner (*for* pour, *to do* pour faire).

detailed ['di:teɪld] adj *work* détaillé, minutieux; *account* détaillé, circonstancié. (*Surv*) a ~ survey un levé de détail.

detain [dɪ'teɪn] vt a (*keep back*) retenir, garder. Mr X has been ~ed at the office M. X a été retenu au bureau; I don't want to ~ you any longer je ne veux pas vous retarder *or* retenir plus longtemps. b (*in captivity*) détenir; (*Scol*) mettre en retenue, consigner.

detainee [ˌdi:teɪ'ni:] n détenu(e) *m(f)*; (*political*) prisonnier *m* politique.

detect [dɪ'tekt] vt (*perceive presence of*) *substance, gas* détecter, découvrir; *explosive* découvrir; *disease* dépister; *sadness* déceler; (*see or hear*) distinguer, discerner. they ~ed traces of poison in the body on a découvert des traces de poison dans le cadavre; I thought I could ~ a note of sarcasm in his voice j'avais cru déceler une note sarcastique dans sa voix; I could just ~ his pulse je sentais tout juste son pouls.

detectable [dɪ'tektəbl] adj (*see* detect) qu'on peut détecter *or* découvrir *etc*.

detection [dɪ'tekʃən] n *[criminal, secret]* découverte *f*; *[gas, mines]* détection *f*; (*Med*) dépistage *m*. the ~ of crime la chasse aux criminels; the bloodstains led to the ~ of the criminal les taches de sang ont mené à la découverte du criminel; to escape ~ *[criminal]* échapper aux recherches; *[mistake]* passer inaperçu.

detective [dɪ'tektɪv] 1 n policier *m* (en civil); (*also* private ~) détective *m* (privé). 2 comp ▶**detective chief inspector** (*Brit*) ≃ inspecteur *m* de police principal ▶**detective chief superintendent** (*Brit*) ≃ commissaire *m* divisionnaire (de police judiciaire) ▶**detective constable** (*Brit*) ≃ inspecteur *m* de police ▶**detective device** dispositif *m* de détection *or* de dépistage ▶**detective inspector** (*Brit*) ≃ inspecteur de police principal ▶**detective sergeant** (*Brit*) ≃ inspecteur(-chef) *m* de police ▶**detective story** roman *m* policier, polar* *m* ▶**detective superintendent** (*Brit*) ≃ commissaire *m* de police judiciaire ▶**detective work** (*fig*) enquêtes *fpl*.

detector [dɪ'tektəʳ] 1 n (*device, person*) détecteur *m*; *see* lie², mine² *etc*. 2 comp ▶**detector van** (*Brit TV*) voiture *f* gonio.

detente [deɪ'tɑ:nt] n détente *f* (*Pol*).

detention [dɪ'tenʃən] 1 n (*captivity*) *[criminal, spy]* détention *f*; (*Mil*) arrêts *mpl*; (*Scol*) retenue *f*, consigne *f*. to give a pupil 2 hours' ~ donner à un élève 2 heures de retenue *or* de consigne; *see* preventive. 2 comp ▶**detention centre** (*Brit*), **detention home** (*US*) (*Jur*) centre *m* de détention pour mineurs.

deter [dɪ'tɜ:ʳ] vt (*prevent*) détourner (*from sth* de qch); dissuader, empêcher (*from doing* de faire); (*discourage*) décourager (*from doing* de faire); (*Mil*) *attack* prévenir; *enemy* dissuader. I was ~red by the cost le coût m'a fait reculer; don't let the weather ~ you ne vous laissez pas arrêter par le temps; a weapon which ~s no one une arme qui ne dissuade personne.

detergent [dɪ'tɜ:dʒənt] adj, n détersif (*m*), détergent (*m*).

deteriorate [dɪ'tɪərɪəreɪt] 1 vt *material, machine* détériorer, abîmer. 2 vi *[material]* se détériorer, s'altérer, s'abîmer; *[species, morals]* dégénérer; *[one's health, relationships, weather]* se détériorer; *[situation]* se dégrader. his schoolwork is deteriorating il y a un fléchissement dans son travail scolaire.

deterioration [dɪˌtɪərɪə'reɪʃən] n *[goods, weather, friendship]* détérioration *f*; *[situation, relations]* dégradation *f*; *[species]* dégénération *f*; (*in morality*) dégénérescence *f*; (*in taste, art*) déchéance *f*, décadence *f*.

determinable [dɪ'tɜ:mɪnəbl] adj a *quantity* déterminable. b (*Jur*) résoluble.

determinant [dɪ'tɜ:mɪnənt] adj, n déterminant (*m*).

determination [dɪˌtɜ:mɪ'neɪʃən] n (*NonC*) a (*firmness of purpose*) détermination *f*, résolution *f* (*to do* de faire). an air of ~ un air résolu. b (*gen, Math etc*) détermination *f*; *[frontiers]* délimitation *f*.

determinative [dɪ'tɜ:mɪnətɪv] 1 adj déterminant; (*Gram*) déterminatif. 2 n facteur déterminant; (*Gram*) déterminant *m*.

determine [dɪ'tɜ:mɪn] vt a (*settle, fix*) *conditions, policy, date* fixer, déterminer; *price* fixer, régler; *frontier* délimiter; *cause, nature, meaning* déterminer, établir; *sb's character, future* décider de, déterminer; (*Jur*) *contract* résoudre. b (*resolve*) décider (*to do* de faire), se déterminer, se résoudre (*to do* à faire); (*cause to decide*) *person* décider, amener (*to do* à faire).

▶**determine (up)on** vt fus décider de, résoudre de (*doing* faire); *course of action* se résoudre à; *alternative* choisir.

determined [dɪ'tɜ:mɪnd] adj a *person, appearance* décidé, déterminé, résolu. to be ~ to do être déterminé *or* bien décidé à faire; to be ~ that être déterminé *or* décidé à ce que + *subj*; he's a very ~ person il est très décidé *or* volontaire *or* résolu, il a de la suite dans les idées. b *quantity* déterminé, établi.

determiner [dɪ'tɜ:mɪnəʳ] n (*Gram*) déterminant *m*.

determining [dɪ'tɜ:mɪnɪŋ] adj déterminant.

determinism [dɪ'tɜ:mɪnɪzəm] n déterminisme *m*.

determinist [dɪ'tɜ:mɪnɪst] adj, n déterministe (*mf*).

deterministic [dɪˌtɜ:mɪ'nɪstɪk] adj déterministe.

deterrence [dɪ'terəns] n (*Mil*) force *f* de dissuasion.

deterrent [dɪ'terənt] 1 n (*also Mil*) force *f* de dissuasion. to act as a ~ exercer un effet de dissuasion; *see* nuclear, ultimate. 2 adj de dissuasion, préventif.

detest [dɪ'test] vt détester, avoir horreur de, haïr. to ~ doing détester (de) *or* avoir horreur de faire; I ~ that sort of thing! j'ai horreur de ce genre de chose!

detestable [dɪ'testəbl] adj détestable, odieux.

detestably [dɪ'testəblɪ] adv détestablement, d'une manière détestable *or* odieuse.

detestation [ˌdiːtes'teɪʃən] n a (*NonC*) haine *f*. b (*object of hatred*) abomination *f*, chose *f* détestable.

dethrone [diː'θrəʊn] vt détrôner.

dethronement [diː'θrəʊnmənt] n déposition *f* (*d'un souverain*).

detonate ['detəneɪt] 1 vi détoner. 2 vt faire détoner *or* exploser.

detonation [ˌdetə'neɪʃən] n détonation *f*, explosion *f*.

detonator ['detəneɪtər] n détonateur *m*, amorce *f*, capsule fulminante; (*Rail*) pétard *m*.

detour ['diːˌtʊər] 1 n (*in river, road; also fig*) détour *m*; (*for traffic*) déviation *f*. 2 vi faire un détour. 3 vt (*US*) *traffic* dévier.

detox‡ [diː'tɒks] abbr of **detoxicate, detoxication, detoxification, detoxify.**

detoxicate [diː'tɒksɪkeɪt] vt, **detoxify** [diː'tɒksɪfaɪ] vt désintoxiquer.

detoxi(fi)cation [diːˌtɒksɪ(fɪ)'keɪʃən] n désintoxication *f*. ~ **centre** centre *m* de désintoxication.

detract [dɪ'trækt] vi: **to ~ from** *quality, merit* diminuer; *reputation* porter atteinte à; **it ~s from the pleasure of walking** cela diminue le plaisir de se promener.

detraction [dɪ'trækʃən] n détraction *f*.

detractor [dɪ'træktər] n détracteur *m*, -trice *f*, critique *m*.

detrain [diː'treɪn] 1 vt débarquer (*d'un train*). 2 vi *[troops]* débarquer (*d'un train*); (*US*) *[passengers]* descendre (*d'un train*).

detriment ['detrɪmənt] n détriment *m*, préjudice *m*, tort *m*. **to the ~ of** au détriment de, au préjudice de; **without ~ to** sans porter atteinte *or* préjudice à; **that is no ~ to ...** cela ne nuit en rien à ... .

detrimental [ˌdetrɪ'mentl] adj (*to health, reputation*) nuisible, préjudiciable, qui nuit (*to* à); (*to a case, a cause, one's interests*) qui nuit, qui fait tort, qui cause un préjudice (*to* à). **to have a ~ effect on, to be ~ to** nuire à.

detritus [dɪ'traɪtəs] n (*Geol*) roches *fpl* détritiques, pierraille *f*; (*fig*) détritus *m*.

deuce[1] [djuːs] n a (*Cards, Dice etc*) deux *m*. b (*Tennis*) égalité *f*. **to be at ~** être à égalité.

deuce[2]†* [djuːs] n euph of **devil**; *see* **devil 1c**.

deuced†* ['djʊsɪd] 1 adj satané (*before n*), sacré* (*before n*). 2 adv diablement†. **what ~ bad weather!** quel sale temps!

deuterium [djuː'tɪərɪəm] n deutérium *m*. ~ **oxide** eau lourde.

Deuteronomy [ˌdjuːtə'rɒnəmɪ] n le Deutéronome.

devaluate [diː'væljʊeɪt] vt = **devalue**.

devaluation [ˌdɪvæljʊ'eɪʃən] n dévaluation *f*.

devalue ['diː'væljuː] vt (*Fin, fig*) dévaluer.

devastate ['devəsteɪt] vt *town, land* dévaster, ravager; *opponent, opposition* anéantir; (*fig*) *person* terrasser, foudroyer. **he was absolutely ~d when he heard the news** cette nouvelle lui a porté un coup terrible.

devastating ['devəsteɪtɪŋ] adj *wind, storm, power, passion* dévastateur (*f* -trice), ravageur; *news, grief* accablant; *argument, reply, effect* accablant, écrasant; *wit, humour, charm, woman* irrésistible.

devastatingly ['devəsteɪtɪŋlɪ] adv *beautiful, funny* irrésistiblement.

devastation [ˌdevə'steɪʃən] n dévastation *f*.

develop [dɪ'veləp] 1 vt a *mind, body* développer, former; (*Math, Phot*) développer; *argument, thesis* développer, exposer (en détail), expliquer (en détail); *business, market* développer; *see also* **developed**.

b *region* exploiter, mettre en valeur; (*change and improve*) aménager (*as* en). **this ground is to be ~ed** on va construire *or* bâtir sur ce terrain; *see also* **developed**.

c (*acquire, get*) *tic, boil, cold* attraper; *symptoms, signs* présenter; *disease, swollen ankles etc* commencer à souffrir de; *habit* contracter. **to ~ a taste for** acquérir *or* contracter le goût de; **to ~ a talent for** faire preuve de talent pour; **to ~ a tendency to** manifester une tendance à.

2 vi *[person, region]* se développer; *[illness, tendency, talent]* se manifester, se déclarer; *[feeling]* se former; (*Phot*) se développer; *[plot, story]* se développer; *[event, situation]* se produire. **to ~ into** devenir; **it later ~ed that he had never seen her** plus tard il est devenu évident qu'il ne l'avait jamais vue.

developed [dɪ'veləpt] adj *girl, breasts, adolescent* bien développé; *market* développé; *country* industrialisé. **highly ~** *ideas, theories* mûrement pensé; *sense of humour, sense of the absurd* très développé.

developer [dɪ'veləpər] n a (*also* **property ~**) promoteur *m* (de construction). b (*Phot*) révélateur *m*, développateur *m*.

developing [dɪ'veləpɪŋ] 1 adj *crisis, storm* qui se prépare; *country* en voie de développement; *industry* en expansion. 2 n a = **development 1a.** b (*Phot*) développement *m*. **"~ and printing"** "développement et tirage", "travaux photographiques". 3 comp ▸**developing bath** (*Phot*) (bain *m*) révélateur *m* ▸**developing tank** cuve *f* à développement.

development [dɪ'veləpmənt] 1 n a (*NonC*) *[person, body]* développement *m*; *[mind]* développement, formation *f*; (*Math, Mus, Phot*) développement; *[subject, theme]* développement, exposé *m*; *[ideas]* développement, évolution *f*, progrès *m*; *[plot, story]* déroulement *m*, développement; *[region]* exploitation *f*, aménagement *m* (*as* en), mise *f* en valeur; *[site]* mise en exploitation; *[industry]* développement, expansion *f*. **at every stage in his ~** à chaque stade de son développement.

b (*change in situation*) fait nouveau. **to await ~s** attendre la suite des événements; **an unexpected** *or* **a surprise ~** un rebondissement; **there have been no ~s** il n'y a pas de changements, il n'y a rien de nouveau.

c (*US: also* **housing ~**) cité *f*; (*also* **industrial ~**) zone industrielle.

2 comp ▸**development area** (*Brit*) zone *f* à urbaniser en priorité, Z.U.P. *f* ▸**development bank** banque *f* de développement ▸**development company** société *f* d'exploitation ▸**development grant** subvention *f or* allocation *f* pour le développement, aide *f* au développement ▸**development period** *[project, company]* phase *f* de démarrage ▸**development planning** planification *f* du développement.

developmental [dɪˌveləp'mentl] adj de croissance.

deviance ['diːvɪəns], **deviancy** ['diːvɪənsɪ] n (*gen, also Psych*) déviance *f* (*from* de).

deviant ['diːvɪənt] 1 adj *behaviour* déviant, qui s'écarte de la norme; *development* anormal; (*sexually*) perverti; (*Ling*) *sentence, form* déviant. 2 n déviant(e) *m(f)*.

deviate ['diːvɪeɪt] vi a (*from truth, former statement etc*) dévier, s'écarter (*from* de). **to ~ from the norm** s'écarter de la norme. b *[ship, plane]* dévier, dériver; *[projectile]* dévier.

deviation [ˌdiːvɪ'eɪʃən] n a (*Math, Med, Philos: also from principle, custom*) déviation *f* (*from* de); (*from law, instructions*) dérogation *f* (*from* à); (*from social norm*) déviance *f* (*from* de). **there have been many ~s from the general rule** on s'est fréquemment écarté de la règle générale; **standard ~** écart type *m*. b *[ship, plane]* déviation *f*, dérive *f*; *[projectile]* déviation, dérivation *f*. c (*Aut*) déviation *f*.

deviationism [ˌdiːvɪ'eɪʃənɪzəm] n déviationnisme *m*.

deviationist [ˌdiːvɪ'eɪʃənɪst] adj, n déviationniste *(mf)*.

device [dɪ'vaɪs] n a (*mechanical*) appareil *m*, engin *m*, mécanisme *m* (*for* pour); (*Comput*) dispositif *m*, unité *f* physique. **a clever ~** une invention astucieuse; *see* **safety**. b (*scheme, plan*) formule *f*, truc* *m* (*to do* pour faire), moyen *m* (*to do* de faire). **to leave sb to his own ~s** laisser qn se débrouiller. c (*Her*) devise *f*, emblème *m*. d (*bomb*) engin *m* (explosif). **nuclear ~** engin *m* nucléaire.

devil ['devl] 1 n a (*evil spirit*) diable *m*, démon *m*. **the D~** le Diable, Satan *m*.

b (*) **poor ~!** pauvre diable!; **he's a nice little ~** c'est un bon petit diable; **you little ~!** petit monstre, va!; (*hum*) **go on, be a ~!** fais donc une folie!, laisse-toi tenter!

c (*: *as intensifier: also* **deuce**[2], **dickens**) **he had the ~ of a job to find it** il a eu toutes les peines du monde *or* un mal fou à le trouver; **the ~ of a wind** un vent du diable *or* de tous les diables; **he lives the ~ of a long way away** il habite au diable*; **it's the very ~** *or* **it's the ~ of a job to get him to come** c'est toute une affaire *or* c'est le diable pour le faire venir; **why the ~ didn't you say so?** pourquoi diable ne l'as-tu pas dit?; **how the ~ would I know?** comment voulez-vous que je (le) sache?; **where the ~ is he?** où diable peut-il bien être?; **what the ~ are you doing?** mais enfin que diable fais-tu? *or* qu'est-ce que tu fabriques?* *or* qu'est-ce que tu fiches?*; **who the ~ are you?** qui diable êtes-vous donc?; **to work/run/shout** *etc* **like the ~** travailler/courir/crier *etc* comme un fou; **to be in a ~ of a mess** être dans de beaux draps, être dans un sacré pétrin*; (*fig*) **there will be the ~ to pay** cela va faire du grabuge*, ça va barder‡; **they were making the ~ of a noise** ils faisaient un chahut de tous les diables.

d (*phrases*) **between the ~ and the deep blue sea** entre Charybde et Scylla; (*Prov*) **the ~ finds work for idle hands** l'oisiveté est la mère de tous les vices (*Prov*); **it will play the ~ with all your plans*** cela va bousiller* *or* foutre en l'air‡ tous vos projets; **go to the ~!‡** va te faire voir!*, va te faire foutre!‡; **he is going to the ~*** il court à sa perte; **his work has gone to the ~*** son travail ne vaut plus rien; **he has the ~ in him today** il a le diable au corps aujourd'hui; **speak** *or* **talk of the ~!** quand on parle du loup (on en voit la queue)!; **to play** *or* **be the ~'s advocate** se faire l'avocat du diable; **to give the ~ his due ...** pour être honnête il faut reconnaître que ...; **he has the luck of the ~*** *or* **the ~'s own luck*** il a une veine insolente *or* une veine de pendu* *or* une veine de cocu‡; (*Prov*) **better the ~ you know (than the ~ you don't)** mieux vaut un danger que l'on connaît qu'un danger que l'on ne connaît pas, ≃ un homme averti en vaut deux.

e (*printer's ~*) apprenti imprimeur; (*hack writer*) nègre* *m* (*d'un écrivain etc*); (*Jur*) ≃ avocat *m* stagiaire.

2 vi: **to ~ for sb** (*Literat etc*) servir de nègre* à qn; (*Jur*) ≃ faire office d'avocat stagiaire auprès de qn.

3 vt a (*Culin*) *kidneys* (faire) griller au poivre et à la moutarde. **devilled** (*Brit*) *or* **deviled** (*US*) **egg** œuf *m* à la diable.

b (*US* *: *nag*) harceler (*verbalement*).

4 comp ▸**devilfish** mante *f* ▸**Devil's Island** île *f* du Diable ▸**devil-may-care** insouciant, je-m'en-foutiste‡ ▸**devil's food cake** (*US*) (sorte *f* de) gâteau *m* au chocolat.

devilish ['devlɪʃ] 1 adj a *invention* diabolique, infernal. b satané* (*before n*), maudit* (*before n*), sacré* (*before n*), du diable. 2 adv *difficult, beautiful* rudement*, diablement. **it's ~ cold** il fait un froid du diable *or* de canard*.

devilishly ['devlɪʃlɪ] **adv** a *behave* diaboliquement. b = **devilish**.

devilishness ['devlɪʃnɪs] **n** *[invention]* caractère *m* diabolique; *[behaviour]* méchanceté *f* diabolique.

devilment ['devlmənt] **n** (*NonC*) (*mischief*) diablerie *f*, espièglerie *f*; (*spite*) méchanceté *f*, malice *f*. **a piece of ~** une espièglerie; **out of sheer ~** par pure malice *or* méchanceté.

devilry ['devlrɪ], (*US*) **deviltry** ['devltrɪ] **n** (*daring*) (folle) témérité *f*; (*mischief*) diablerie *f*, espièglerie *f*; (*black magic*) magie noire, maléfices *mpl*; (*wickedness*) malignité *f*, méchanceté *f* (diabolique).

devious ['di:vɪəs] **adj** *route* détourné; *path, mind* tortueux; *means, method* détourné, tortueux; *character* dissimulé, sournois (*pej*). **he's very ~** il a l'esprit tortueux, il n'est pas franc.

deviously ['di:vɪəslɪ] **adv** *act, behave* d'une façon détournée.

deviousness ['di:vɪəsnɪs] **n** *[person]* sournoiserie *f*; *[scheme, method]* complexité(s) *f(pl)*.

devise [dɪ'vaɪz] 1 **vt** *scheme, style* imaginer, inventer, concevoir; *plot* tramer, ourdir; *escape* combiner, machiner; (*Jur*) léguer. **of his own devising** de son invention. 2 **n** (*Jur*) legs *m* (de biens immobiliers).

devisee [dɪvaɪ'zi:] **n** (*Jur*) légataire *mf* (*qui reçoit des biens immobiliers*).

deviser [dɪ'vaɪzə^r] **n** *[scheme, plan]* inventeur *m*, -trice *f*, auteur *m*.

devisor [dɪ'vaɪzə^r] **n** (*Jur*) testateur *m*, -trice *f* (*qui lègue des biens immobiliers*).

devitalization [di:,vaɪtəlaɪ'zeɪʃən] **n** affaiblissement *m*.

devitalize [di:'vaɪtəlaɪz] **vt** affaiblir.

devoiced [di:'vɔɪst] **adj** (*Phon*) *consonant* dévoisé.

devoicing [di:'vɔɪsɪŋ] **n** (*Phon*) dévoisement *m*.

devoid [dɪ'vɔɪd] **adj**: **~ of ornament/imagination** *etc* dépourvu *or* dénué d'ornement/d'imagination *etc*, sans ornement/imagination *etc*; **~ of sense** dénué de (bon) sens; **~ of error/guilt** *etc* exempt d'erreur/de culpabilité *etc*.

devolution [,di:və'lu:ʃən] **n** *[power, authority]* délégation *f*; (*Jur*) *[property]* transmission *f*, dévolution *f*; (*Pol etc*) décentralisation *f*; (*Bio*) dégénérescence *f*.

devolve [dɪ'vɒlv] 1 **vi** a *[duty]* incomber (*on, upon* à); (*by chance*) retomber (*on, upon* sur), échoir (*on, upon* à). **it ~s on you to take this step** c'est à vous qu'il incombe de faire cette démarche; **all the work ~s on me** tout le travail retombe sur moi. b (*Jur*) *[property]* passer (*on, upon* à), être transmis (*on, upon* à). 2 **vt** déléguer, transmettre, remettre (*on, upon* à).

Devonian [də'vəʊnɪən] **adj** (*Geol*) *period* dévonien.

devote [dɪ'vəʊt] **vt** *time, life, book, magazine* consacrer (*to* à); *resources* affecter (*to* à), consacrer (*to* à), réserver (*to* pour). **to ~ o.s. to** *a cause* se vouer à, se consacrer à; *pleasure* se livrer à; *study, hobby* s'adonner à, se consacrer à, se livrer à; **the money ~d to education** l'argent consacré à *or* (*Admin*) les crédits affectés à l'éducation; **2 chapters ~d to his childhood** 2 chapitres consacrés à son enfance; (*Rad, TV*) **they ~d the whole programme to ...** ils ont consacré toute l'émission à ... .

devoted [dɪ'vəʊtɪd] **adj** *husband, friend* dévoué; *admirer* fervent; *service, friendship* loyal, fidèle, dévoué. **to be ~ to** être dévoué *or* très attaché à.

devotedly [dɪ'vəʊtɪdlɪ] **adv** avec dévouement.

devotee [,devəʊ'ti:] **n** *[doctrine, theory]* partisan(e) *m(f)*; *[religion]* adepte *mf*; *[sport, music, poetry]* passionné(e) *m(f)*, fervent(e) *m(f)*.

devotion [dɪ'vəʊʃən] **n** a (*NonC*) (*to duty*) dévouement *m* (*to* à); (*to friend*) dévouement (*to* à, envers), (profond) attachement *m* (*to* pour); (*to work*) dévouement (*to* à), ardeur *f* (*to* pour, à); (*Rel*) dévotion *f*, piété *f*. **with great ~** avec un grand dévouement. b (*Rel*) **~s** dévotions *fpl*, prières *fpl*.

devotional [dɪ'vəʊʃənl] **adj** *book* de dévotion, de piété; *attitude* de prière, pieux.

devour [dɪ'vaʊə^r] **vt** a *food* dévorer, engloutir; (*fig*) *money* engloutir, dévorer; *book* dévorer. **to ~ sb with one's eyes** dévorer qn des yeux. b *[fire]* dévorer, consumer. (*fig*) **~ed by jealousy** dévoré de jalousie.

devouring [dɪ'vaʊərɪŋ] **adj** *hunger, passion* dévorant; *zeal, enthusiasm* ardent.

devout [dɪ'vaʊt] **adj** *person* pieux, dévot; *prayer, attention, hope* fervent.

devoutly [dɪ'vaʊtlɪ] **adv** *pray* dévotement, avec dévotion; *hope* sincèrement, bien vivement.

DEW, dew[1] [dju:] (*US*) (**abbr of distant early warning**) **~ line** DEW *f*, (*système de radars*).

dew[2] [dju:] 1 **n** rosée *f*; *see* **mountain**. 2 **comp** ►**dew claw** ergot *m* ►**dewdrop** goutte *f* de rosée ►**dewlap** *[cow, person]* fanon *m* ►**dewpoint** point *m* de saturation ►**dewpond** mare *f* (*alimentée par les eaux de condensation*).

dewy ['dju:ɪ] 1 **adj** *grass* couvert de *or* humide de rosée. (*liter*) **~ lips** lèvres fraîches. 2 **comp** ►**dewy-eyed** (*innocent*) aux grands yeux ingénus; (*credulous*) (trop) naïf (*f* naïve); **to be dewy-eyed** faire l'ingénu(e); être (trop) naïf.

dex [deks] **n** (*Drugs sl*) Dexédrine *f* ®.

Dexedrine [deksɪ'dri:n] **n** ® Dexédrine *f* ®.

dexie ['deksɪ] **n** (*Drugs sl*) comprimé *m* de Dexédrine ®.

dexterity [deks'terɪtɪ] **n** dextérité *f*, adresse *f*, habileté *f*. **~ in doing** habileté à faire, adresse avec laquelle on fait; **a feat of ~** un tour d'adresse.

dexterous ['dekstrəs] **adj** *person* adroit, habile; *movement* adroit, agile. **by the ~ use of** par l'habile emploi de.

dexterously ['dekstrəslɪ] **adv** adroitement, habilement, avec dextérité.

dextrin ['dekstrɪn] **n** dextrine *f*.

dextrose ['dekstrəʊs] **n** dextrose *m*.

dextrous(ly) ['dekstrəs(lɪ)] = **dexterous(ly)**.

D.F. [di:'ef] (**abbr of direction finder**) *see* **direction**.

dg abbr of decigram(s).

D.G. [di:'dʒi:] a (**abbr of director general**) *see* **director**. b (**abbr of Deo gratias**) par la grâce de Dieu.

DH [di:eɪtʃ] **n** (*Brit*) **abbr of Department of Health**.

dhoti ['dəʊtɪ] **n** dhotî *m*.

DHSS† [,di:eɪtʃes'es] **n** (*Brit*) (**abbr of Department of Health and Social Security**) *see* **health**.

DI [di:'aɪ] **n** (**abbr of Donor Insemination**) *see* **donor**.

di... [daɪ] **pref** di... .

diabetes [,daɪə'bi:ti:z] **n** diabète *m*. **to have ~** être diabétique, avoir du diabète.

diabetic [,daɪə'betɪk] 1 **n** diabétique *mf*. 2 **adj** a (*person*) diabétique. b (*for diabetics*) *chocolate, dessert, jam etc* pour diabétiques.

diabolic(al) [,daɪə'bɒlɪk(əl)] **adj** a *action, invention, plan, power* diabolique, infernal, satanique; *laugh, smile* satanique, diabolique. b (**: dreadful*) *child* infernal*; *weather* atroce*, épouvantable.

diabolically [,daɪə'bɒlɪkəlɪ] **adv** *behave etc* diaboliquement, d'une manière diabolique; (*) *hot, late etc* rudement*.

diachronic [,daɪə'krɒnɪk] **adj** diachronique.

diacid [daɪ'æsɪd] **n** biacide *m*, diacide *m*.

diacritic [,daɪə'krɪtɪk] 1 **adj** diacritique. 2 **n** signe *m* diacritique.

diacritical [,daɪə'krɪtɪkəl] **adj** diacritique.

diadem ['daɪədem] **n** (*lit, fig*) diadème *m*.

diaeresis, (*US*) **dieresis** [daɪ'erɪsɪs] **n, pl diaereses,** (*US*) **diereses** [daɪ'erɪ,si:z] (*Ling*) diérèse *f*; (*sign for this*) tréma *m*.

diagnose ['daɪəgnəʊz] **vt** (*Med, fig*) diagnostiquer. **his illness was ~d as bronchitis** on a diagnostiqué une bronchite, on a diagnostiqué que c'était d'une bronchite qu'il souffrait.

diagnosis [,daɪəg'nəʊsɪs] **n, pl diagnoses** [,daɪəg'nəʊsi:z] (*Med, fig*) diagnostic *m*; (*Bio, Bot*) diagnose *f*.

diagnostic [,daɪəg'nɒstɪk] **adj** diagnostique. (*Comput*) **~ program** programme *m* de diagnostic.

diagnostician [,daɪəgnɒs'tɪʃən] diagnostiqueur *m*.

diagnostics [,daɪəg'nɒstɪks] **n** (*NonC: Comput etc*) diagnostic *m*.

diagonal [daɪ'ægənl] 1 **adj** diagonal. 2 **n** diagonale *f*.

diagonally [daɪ'ægənəlɪ] **adv** *cut, fold* en diagonale, obliquement, diagonalement. **the bank is ~ opposite the church** la banque est diagonalement opposée à l'église; **to cut ~ across a street** traverser une rue en diagonale; **the car was struck ~ by a lorry** la voiture a été prise en écharpe par un camion; **ribbon worn ~ across the chest** ruban porté en écharpe sur la poitrine.

diagram ['daɪəgræm] **n** (*gen*) diagramme *m*, schéma *m*; (*Math*) diagramme, figure *f*. **as shown in the ~** comme le montre le diagramme *or* le schéma.

diagrammatic [,daɪəgrə'mætɪk] **adj** schématique.

dial ['daɪəl] 1 **n** cadran *m*; (*‡: face*) tronche‡ *f*; *see* **sun**. 2 **vt** (*Telec*) *number* faire, composer. **you must ~ 336-1295** il faut faire le 336-12-95; **to ~ 999** ≃ appeler police-secours; **to ~ a wrong number** faire un faux *or* mauvais numéro; **to ~ direct** appeler par l'automatique; **can I ~ London from here?** est-ce que d'ici je peux avoir Londres par l'automatique? 3 **comp** ►**Dial-a-record** *etc* (*Telec*) le disque *etc* du jour par téléphone ►**dial code** (*US Telec*) indicatif *m* ►**dial tone** (*US Telec*) tonalité *f* ►**dial-up service** (*Comput*) service *m* de télétraitement.

dial. abbr of dialect.

dialect ['daɪəlekt] 1 **n** (*regional*) dialecte *m*, parler *m*; (*local, rural*) patois *m*. **the Norman ~** le dialecte normand, les parlers normands; **in ~** en dialecte, en patois. 2 **comp** *word* dialectal ►**dialect atlas** atlas *m* linguistique ►**dialect survey** étude *f* de géographie linguistique *or* de dialectologie.

dialectal [,daɪə'lektl] **adj** dialectal, de dialecte.

dialectical [,daɪə'lektɪkəl] **adj** dialectique. **~ materialism** matérialisme *m* dialectique.

dialectician [,daɪəlek'tɪʃən] **n** dialecticien(ne) *m(f)*.

dialectic(s) [,daɪə'lektɪk(s)] **n** (*NonC*) dialectique *f*.

dialectology [,daɪəlek'tɒlədʒɪ] **n** (*NonC*) dialectologie *f*.

dialling, (*US*) **dialing** ['daɪəlɪŋ] (*Telec*) 1 **n** composition *f* d'un numéro (de téléphone). 2 **comp** ►**dialling code** (*Brit*) indicatif *m* ►**dialling tone** (*Brit*) tonalité *f*.

dialogue, (*US*) **dialog** ['daɪəlɒg] **n** (*lit, fig*) dialogue *m*.

dialysis [daɪ'æləsɪs] **n, pl dialyses** [daɪ'ælɪ,si:z] dialyse *f*. **~ machine** rein artificiel.

diamagnetism [ˌdaɪəˈmægnɪtɪzəm] n diamagnétisme *m*.
diamanté [ˌdaɪəˈmæntɪ] n tissu diamanté.
diameter [daɪˈæmɪtəʳ] n diamètre *m*. **the circle is one metre in ~** le cercle a un mètre de diamètre.
diametrical [ˌdaɪəˈmetrɪkəl] adj (*Math, fig*) diamétral.
diametrically [ˌdaɪəˈmetrɪkəlɪ] adv (*Math, fig*) diamétralement.
diamond [ˈdaɪəmənd] 1 n a (*stone*) diamant *m*; *see* **rough.** b (*shape, figure*) losange *m*. c (*Cards*) carreau *m*. **the ace/six of ~s** l'as/le six de carreau; *see* **club 1b.** d (*Baseball*) diamant *m*, terrain *m* (de base-ball). 2 comp *clip, ring* de diamant(s) ▸**diamond-cutting** taille *f* du diamant ▸**diamond drill** foreuse *f* à pointe de diamant ▸**diamond jubilee** (célébration *f* du) soixantième anniversaire *m* (*d'un événement*) ▸**diamond merchant** diamantaire *m* ▸**diamond necklace** rivière *f* de diamants ▸**diamond-shaped** en losange(s), (taillé) en losange ▸**diamond wedding** noces *fpl* de diamant.
diamorphine [ˌdaɪəˈmɔːfiːn] n (*Med*) diamorphine *f*.
Diana [daɪˈænə] n Diane *f*.
diapason [ˌdaɪəˈpeɪzən] n diapason *m*. *[organ]* **open/stopped ~** diapason large/étroit.
diaper [ˈdaɪəpəʳ] n (*US*) couche *f* (*de bébé*). **~ service** service *m* de couches à domicile.
diaphanous [daɪˈæfənəs] adj (*lit, fig*) diaphane.
diaphoretic [ˌdaɪəfəˈretɪk] adj, n diaphorétique (*m*).
diaphragm [ˈdaɪəfræm] n (*all senses*) diaphragme *m*.
diarist [ˈdaɪərɪst] n *[personal events]* auteur *m* d'un journal intime; *[contemporary events]* mémorialiste *mf*, chroniqueur *m*.
diarrhoea, (*US*) **diarrhea** [ˌdaɪəˈriːə] n diarrhée *f*. **to have ~** avoir la diarrhée *or* la colique.
diarrhoeal, (*US*) **diarrheal** [ˌdaɪəˈrɪəl] adj diarrhéique.
diary [ˈdaɪərɪ] n (*record of events*) journal *m* (intime); (*for engagements*) agenda *m*. **to keep a ~** tenir un journal; **I've got it in my ~** je l'ai noté sur mon agenda.
Diaspora [daɪˈæspərə] n Diaspora *f*; (*fig*) diaspora.
diastole [daɪˈæstəlɪ] n diastole *f*.
diatonic [ˌdaɪəˈtɒnɪk] adj diatonique.
diatribe [ˈdaɪətraɪb] n diatribe *f* (*against* contre).
dibasic [ˌdaɪˈbeɪsɪk] adj dibasique.
dibber [ˈdɪbəʳ] n = **dibble 1.**
dibble [ˈdɪbl] 1 n plantoir *m*. 2 vt repiquer au plantoir.
dibs [dɪbz] npl a (*game, knucklebones*) osselets *mpl*; (*Cards: counters*) jetons *mpl*. b (*Brit* ‡†) (*money*) fric‡ *m*. c (*US*) **to have ~ on sth‡** avoir des droits sur qch; **~ on the cookies!‡** prem'‡ pour les petits gâteaux!
dice [daɪs] 1 n, pl inv dé *m* (à jouer). **to play ~** jouer aux dés; (*fig: esp US*) **no ~!*** pas question!; *see* **load.** 2 vi jouer aux dés. (*fig*) **he was dicing with death** il jouait avec la mort. 3 vt *vegetables* couper en dés *or* en cubes.
dicey* [ˈdaɪsɪ] adj (*Brit*) risqué. **it's ~, it's a ~ business** c'est bien risqué.
dichotomy [dɪˈkɒtəmɪ] n dichotomie *f*.
Dick [dɪk] n (**dim of Richard**) Richard *m*.
dick [dɪk] 1 n a (‡: *detective*) détective *m*; *see* **clever.** b (*‡*: *penis*) bitte*‡* *f*. 2 comp ▸**dickhead*‡*** tête *f* de nœud*‡*.
dickens* [ˈdɪkɪnz] n (**euph of devil**) *see* **devil 1c.**
Dickensian [dɪˈkenzɪən] adj à la Dickens.
dicker [ˈdɪkəʳ] vi (*US*) marchander.
dickey, dicky[1] [ˈdɪkɪ] n a (*also* **~ bird:** *baby talk*) petit zoziau. **I won't say a ~-bird*† about it** je n'en piperai pas mot. b (*Brit: also* **~ seat**) strapontin *m*; (*Aut*) spider *m*. c (*) *[shirt]* faux plastron (*de chemise*).
dicky[2] [ˈdɪkɪ] adj (*Brit*) *person* patraque*, pas solide*; *health, heart* qui flanche*, pas solide*; *situation* pas sûr*, pas solide*.
dicta [ˈdɪktə] npl of **dictum.**
Dictaphone [ˈdɪktəfəʊn] n ® Dictaphone *m* ®. **~ typist** dactylo *f* qui travaille au dictaphone.
dictate [dɪkˈteɪt] 1 vt *letter, passage* dicter (*to* à); *terms, conditions* dicter, prescrire, imposer. **his action was ~d by circumstances** il a agi comme le lui dictaient les circonstances. 2 vi a dicter. **he spent the morning dictating to his secretary** il a passé la matinée à dicter des lettres (*or* des rapports *etc*) à sa secrétaire. b (*order about*) **to ~ to sb** imposer sa volonté à qn, régenter qn; **I won't be ~d to** je n'ai pas d'ordres à recevoir; **I don't like to be ~d to** je n'aime pas qu'on me commande (*subj*). 3 [ˈdɪkteɪt] n (*gen pl*) **~s** ordre(s) *m(pl)*, précepte(s) *m(pl)* (*de la raison etc*); **the ~s of conscience** la voix de la conscience.
dictation [dɪkˈteɪʃən] n (*in school, office etc*) dictée *f*. **to write to sb's ~** écrire sous la dictée de qn; **at ~ speed** à une vitesse de dictée.
dictator [dɪkˈteɪtəʳ] n (*fig, Pol*) dictateur *m*.
dictatorial [ˌdɪktəˈtɔːrɪəl] adj (*fig, Pol*) dictatorial.
dictatorially [ˌdɪktəˈtɔːrɪəlɪ] adv (*fig, Pol*) autoritairement, dictatorialement, en dictateur.
dictatorship [dɪkˈteɪtəʃɪp] n (*fig, Pol*) dictature *f*.
diction [ˈdɪkʃən] n a (*Literat*) style *m*, langage *m*. **poetic ~** langage poétique. b diction *f*, élocution *f*. **his ~ is very good** il a une très bonne diction *or* une élocution très nette.
dictionary [ˈdɪkʃənrɪ] 1 n dictionnaire *m*. **to look up a word in a ~** chercher un mot dans un dictionnaire; **French ~** dictionnaire de français. 2 comp ▸**dictionary-maker** lexicographe *mf* ▸**dictionary-making** lexicographie *f*.
dictum [ˈdɪktəm] n, pl **~s** *or* **dicta** (*maxim*) dicton *m*, maxime *f*; (*pronouncement*) proposition *f*, affirmation *f*; (*Jur*) remarque *f* superfétatoire.
did [dɪd] pret of **do**[1].
didactic [dɪˈdæktɪk] adj didactique.
didactically [dɪˈdæktɪkəlɪ] adv didactiquement.
diddle* [ˈdɪdl] vt (*Brit*) rouler*, escroquer. **you've been ~d** tu t'es fait rouler* *or* avoir*; **to ~ sb out of sth** souffler qch à qn*; **to ~ sth out of sb** soutirer *or* carotter* qch à qn.
diddler‡ [ˈdɪdləʳ] n (*Brit*) carotteur* *m*, -euse* *f*, escroc *m*.
didn't [ˈdɪdənt] = **did not;** *see* **do**[1].
Dido [ˈdaɪdəʊ] n Didon *f*.
die[1] [daɪ] vi a *[person]* mourir (*of* de), décéder (*frm*), s'éteindre (*euph*); *[animal, plant]* mourir, crever; *[engine, motor]* caler, s'arrêter. **to be dying** être à l'agonie *or* à la mort, se mourir; **they were left to ~** ils furent abandonnés à la mort; **to ~ of hunger** mourir de faim; **to ~ a natural/violent death** mourir de sa belle mort/de mort violente; **to ~ by one's own hand** se suicider, mettre fin à ses jours; (*fig*) **to ~ with one's boots on*** mourir debout *or* en pleine activité; **he ~d a hero** il est mort en héros; **they were dying like flies** ils mouraient *or* tombaient comme des mouches; **never say ~!** il ne faut jamais désespérer; **you only ~ once** on ne meurt qu'une fois; (*fig*) **I nearly** *or* **could've ~d** (*from laughing*) j'ai failli mourir de rire; (*from fear*) j'ai failli mourir de peur; (*from embarrassment*) je voulais rentrer sous terre; **to ~ a thousand deaths** être au supplice, souffrir mille morts (*liter*); (*fig*) **to be dying to do*** mourir d'envie de faire; **I'm dying* for a cigarette** j'ai une envie folle d'une cigarette.
b *[fire, love, memory, daylight]* s'éteindre, mourir; *[custom]* mourir, disparaître. **the secret ~d with him** il a emporté le secret dans la tombe; **rumours/bad habits ~ hard** les bruits qui courent/les mauvaises habitudes ont la vie dure.
▸**die away** vi *[sound, voice]* s'éteindre, mourir, s'affaiblir.
▸**die down** vi *[plant]* se flétrir, perdre ses feuilles et sa tige; *[emotion, protest]* se calmer, s'apaiser; *[wind]* tomber, se calmer; *[fire]* (*in blazing building*) diminuer, s'apaiser; (*in grate etc*) baisser, tomber; *[noise]* diminuer.
▸**die off** vi mourir *or* être emportés les uns après les autres.
▸**die out** vi *[custom, race]* disparaître, s'éteindre; *[showers etc]* disparaître.
die[2] [daɪ] 1 n a (*pl* **dice** [daɪs]) dé *m* (à jouer). **the ~ is cast** le sort en est jeté, les dés sont jetés; *see* **dice.** b (*pl* **~s**) (*in minting*) coin *m*; (*Tech*) matrice *f*. **stamping ~** étampe *f*. 2 comp ▸**die-casting** moulage *m* en coquille ▸**die-sinker** graveur *m* de matrices ▸**die-stamp** graver ▸**die-stock** (*frame*) cage *f* (de filière à peignes); (*tool*) filière *f* à main.
diectic [daɪˈektɪk] n (*Ling*) diectique *m*.
dièdre [dɪˈedəʳ] n (*Climbing*) dièdre *m*.
diehard [ˈdaɪhɑːd] 1 n (*one who resists to the last*) jusqu'au-boutiste *mf*; (*opponent of change*) conservateur *m*, -trice *f* (à tout crin); (*obstinate politician etc*) dur(e) à cuire* *m(f)*, réactionnaire *mf*. 2 adj intransigeant, inébranlable; (*Pol*) réactionnaire.
dielectric [ˌdaɪəˈlektrɪk] adj, n diélectrique (*m*).
dieresis [daɪˈerɪsɪs] n (*US*) = **diaeresis.**
diesel [ˈdiːzəl] 1 n a diesel *m*. b = **diesel fuel, diesel oil.** 2 comp ▸**diesel-electric** diesel-électrique ▸**diesel engine** (*Aut*) moteur *m* diesel; (*Rail*) motrice *f* ▸**diesel fuel, diesel oil** gas-oil *m* ▸**diesel train** autorail *m*.
diet[1] [ˈdaɪət] 1 n a (*restricted food*) régime *m*; (*light*) diète *f*. **milk ~** régime lacté; **to be/go on a ~** être/se mettre au régime *or* à la diète; **~ bread/drink** *etc* pain *m*/boisson *f* basses calories. b (*customary food*) alimentation *f*, nourriture *f*. **to live on a (constant) ~ of** vivre *or* se nourrir de. 2 vi suivre un régime *or* une diète. 3 vt mettre au régime *or* à la diète.
diet[2] [ˈdaɪət] n (*esp Pol*) diète *f*.
dietary [ˈdaɪətərɪ] 1 adj (*gen*) de régime, diététique. **~ fibre** cellulose végétale. 2 n régime *m* alimentaire (*d'un hôpital, d'une prison etc*).
dietetic [ˌdaɪəˈtetɪk] adj diététique.
dietetics [ˌdaɪəˈtetɪks] n (*NonC*) diététique *f*.
dietician [ˌdaɪəˈtɪʃən] n spécialiste *mf* de diététique, diététicien(ne) *m(f)*.
differ [ˈdɪfəʳ] vi (*be different*) différer, être différent, se distinguer (*from* de); (*disagree*) ne pas être d'accord, ne pas s'entendre (*from sb* avec qn, *on or about sth* sur qch). **the two points of view do not ~ much** les deux points de vue ne se distinguent guère l'un de l'autre *or* ne sont pas très différents l'un de l'autre; **they ~ in their approach to the problem** ils diffèrent en *or* sur leur manière d'appréhender le problème; **I beg to ~** permettez-moi de ne pas partager cette opinion *or* de ne pas être de votre avis; **the texts ~** les textes ne s'accordent pas; (*Jur*) **to ~ from the rules** déroger aux règles; *see* **agree.**

difference ['dɪfrəns] n différence *f*; (*in ideas, character, nature*) différence, divergence *f* (*in* de, *between* entre); (*in age, height, value, weight etc*) écart *m*, différence (*in* de, *between* entre); (*between numbers, amounts*) différence. **that makes a big ~ to me** c'est très important pour moi, ça ne m'est pas du tout égal, cela compte beaucoup pour moi; **to make a ~ in sb/sth** changer qn/qch; **that makes all the ~** voilà qui change tout; **what ~ does it make if ...?** qu'est-ce que cela peut faire que ...? + *subj*, quelle importance cela a-t-il si ...? + *indic*; **it makes no ~** peu importe, cela ne change rien (à l'affaire); **it makes no ~ to me** cela m'est égal, ça ne (me) fait rien; **for all the ~ it makes** pour ce que cela change *or* peut changer; **with this ~ that** à la différence que, à ceci près que; **a car with a ~** une voiture pas comme les autres*; **~ of opinion** différence *or* divergence d'opinions; (*quarrel*) différend *m*; **to pay the ~** payer la différence; *see* **know, split.**

different ['dɪfrənt] adj a (*not the same*) différent (*from, to, US than** de), autre. **completely ~ (from)** totalement différent (de), tout autre (que); **he wore a ~ tie each day** il portait chaque jour une cravate différente; **go and put on a ~ tie** va mettre une autre cravate; **I feel a ~ person** je me sens tout autre; (*rested etc*) j'ai l'impression de faire peau neuve; **let's do something ~** faisons quelque chose de nouveau; **quite a ~ way of doing** une tout autre manière de faire; **that's quite a ~ matter** ça c'est une autre affaire, c'est tout autre chose; **she's quite ~ from what you think** elle n'est pas du tout ce que vous croyez; **he wants to be ~** il veut se singulariser.
b (*various*) différent, divers, plusieurs. **~ people had noticed this** plusieurs personnes l'avaient remarqué; **in the ~ countries I've visited** dans les différents *or* divers pays que j'ai visités.

differential [ˌdɪfə'renʃəl] 1 adj différentiel. (*Math*) **~ calculus/operator** calcul/opérateur différentiel; **~ equation** équation différentielle; **~ gear** (engrenage *m*) différentiel *m*; **~ housing** boîtier *m* de différentiel. 2 n (*Math*) différentielle *f*; (*in pay*) écart salarial; (*Aut*) différentiel *m*.

differentially [ˌdɪfə'renʃəlɪ] adv (*Tech*) par action différentielle.

differentiate [ˌdɪfə'renʃɪeɪt] 1 vi faire la différence *or* la distinction (*between* entre). **he cannot ~ between red and green** il ne fait pas la différence entre le rouge et le vert; **in his article he ~s between ...** dans son article, il fait la distinction entre ...; **we must ~ between the meanings of this term** il nous faut différencier les sens de ce mot.
2 vt *people, things* différencier, distinguer (*from* de); (*Math*) différentier, calculer la différentielle de. **this is what ~s the 2 brothers** c'est ce qui différencie les 2 frères; **this is what ~s one brother from the other** c'est ce qui distingue *or* différencie un frère de l'autre.

differentiation [ˌdɪfərenʃɪ'eɪʃən] n différenciation *f*; (*Math*) différentiation *f*.

differently ['dɪfrəntlɪ] adv différemment, d'une manière différente (*from* de), autrement (*from* que). **he thinks ~ from you** sa façon de penser n'est pas la même (que la vôtre); (*doesn't agree*) il n'est pas de votre avis.

difficult ['dɪfɪkəlt] adj *problem, undertaking* difficile, dur, ardu; *writer, music, book* difficile; *person, character* difficile, peu commode; *child* difficile. **~ to live with, ~ to get on with** difficile à vivre; **this work is ~ to do** ce travail est difficile à faire *or* est ardu; **it is ~ to know** il est difficile de savoir; **it's ~ to deny that ...** on ne peut guère *or* on ne saurait (*frm*) nier que ... + *indic or subj*; **it is ~ for me** *or* **I find it ~ to believe** il m'est difficile de croire, j'ai de la peine *or* du mal à croire; **there's nothing ~ about it** cela ne présente aucune difficulté; **the ~ thing is to begin** le (plus) difficile *or* dur c'est de commencer.

difficulty ['dɪfɪkəltɪ] n a (*NonC*) [*problem, undertaking, writing*] difficulté *f*. **with/without ~** avec/sans difficulté *or* peine; **it's feasible, but with ~** c'est faisable, mais ce sera difficile; **she has ~ in walking** elle marche difficilement *or* avec difficulté, elle a de la difficulté *or* elle éprouve de la difficulté *or* elle a du mal à marcher; **a slight ~ in breathing** un peu de gêne dans la respiration; **there was some ~ in finding him** on a eu du mal à le trouver; **the ~ is in choosing** *or* **to choose** le difficile *or* la difficulté c'est de choisir.
b difficulté *f*, obstacle *m*. **to make difficulties for sb** créer des difficultés à qn; **without meeting any difficulties** sans rencontrer d'obstacles *or* la moindre difficulté, sans accrocs; **to get into ~** *or* **difficulties** se trouver en difficulté; **to get into all sorts of difficulties** se trouver plongé dans toutes sortes d'ennuis; **to get o.s. into ~** se créer des ennuis; **to get out of a ~** se tirer d'affaire *or* d'embarras; **I am in ~** j'ai des difficultés, j'ai des problèmes; **to be in (financial) difficulties** être dans l'embarras, avoir des ennuis d'argent; **he was in ~** *or* **difficulties over the rent** il était en difficulté pour son loyer; **he was working under great difficulties** il travaillait dans des conditions très difficiles; **I can see no ~ in what you suggest** je ne vois aucun obstacle à ce que vous suggérez; **he's having ~** *or* **difficulties with his wife/his car** il a des ennuis *or* des problèmes avec sa femme/sa voiture.

diffidence ['dɪfɪdəns] n manque *m* de confiance en soi, manque d'assurance, défiance *f* de soi.

diffident ['dɪfɪdənt] adj *person* qui se défie de soi, qui manque de confiance *or* d'assurance; *smile* embarrassé. **to be ~ about doing** hésiter à faire (par modestie *or* timidité).

diffidently ['dɪfɪdəntlɪ] adv avec (une certaine) timidité, de façon embarrassée.

diffract [dɪ'frækt] vt diffracter.

diffraction [dɪ'frækʃən] n diffraction *f*. **~ grating** réseau *m* de diffraction.

diffuse [dɪ'fju:z] 1 vt *light, heat, perfume, news* diffuser, répandre. **~d lighting** éclairage diffus *or* indirect. 2 vi se diffuser, se répandre. 3 [dɪ'fju:s] adj *light, thought* diffus; *style, writer* prolixe, diffus.

diffuseness [dɪ'fju:snɪs] n prolixité *f*, verbiage *m* (*pej*).

diffuser [dɪ'fju:zə^r] n (*for light*) diffuseur *m*.

diffusion [dɪ'fju:ʒən] n diffusion *f*.

dig [dɪg] (vb: pret, ptp **dug**) 1 n a (*with hand/elbow*) coup *m* de poing/de coude. **to give sb a ~ in the ribs** donner un coup de coude dans les côtes de qn, pousser qn du coude.
b (**: sly remark*) coup *m* de patte. **to have** *or* **take a ~ at sb** donner un coup de patte *or* de griffe à qn; **that's a ~ at John** c'est une pierre dans le jardin de Jean.
c (*with spade*) coup *m* de bêche.
d (*Archeol*) fouilles *fpl*. **to go on a ~** aller faire des fouilles.
2 vt a *ground* (*gen*) creuser, (*with spade*) bêcher; *grave, trench, hole* creuser; *tunnel* creuser, percer, ouvrir; *potatoes etc* arracher. **they dug their way out of prison** ils se sont évadés de prison en creusant un tunnel; (*fig*) **to ~ one's own grave** se mettre la corde au cou.
b (*thrust*) *fork, pencil etc* enfoncer (*sth into sth* qch dans qch). (*fig*) **to ~ sb in the ribs** donner un coup de coude dans les côtes de qn, pousser qn du coude.
c (‡) (*understand*) piger‡; (*take notice of*) viser‡. **~ that guy!** vise un peu le mec!‡; **I ~ that!** ça me botte!‡; **he really ~s jazz** il est vraiment fou de jazz; **I don't ~ football** le football ne me dit rien *or* me laisse froid.
3 vi a [*dog, pig*] fouiller, fouir; [*person*] creuser (*into* dans); (*Tech*) fouiller; (*Archeol*) faire des fouilles. **to ~ for minerals** (creuser pour) extraire du minerai; (*fig*) **to ~ in one's pockets for sth** fouiller dans ses poches pour trouver qch; (*fig*) **to ~ into the past** fouiller dans le passé.
b (*Brit ‡: lodge*) loger (en garni) (*with* chez).

►**dig in** 1 vi a (*Mil*) se retrancher; (*fig*) tenir bon, se braquer, se buter (*pej*). b (**: eat*) attaquer* un repas (*or* un plat *etc*). **dig in!** allez-y, mangez! 2 vt sep *compost etc* enterrer; *blade, knife* enfoncer. **to dig in one's spurs** éperonner son cheval, enfoncer ses éperons; (*fig*) **to dig one's heels in** se braquer, se buter (*pej*).

►**dig into** vt fus *sb's past* fouiller dans; (*) *cake, pie* dire deux mots à*, entamer sérieusement*.

►**dig out** vt sep *tree, plant* déterrer; *animal* déterrer, déloger; (*fig*) *facts, information* déterrer, dénicher. **to dig sb out of the snow** sortir qn de la neige (à coups de pelles et de pioches); **where did he dig out* that old hat?** où a-t-il été pêcher *or* dénicher ce vieux chapeau?

►**dig over** vt sep *earth* retourner; *garden* bêcher, retourner.

►**dig up** vt sep *weeds, vegetables* arracher; *treasure, body* déterrer; *earth* retourner; *garden* bêcher, retourner; (*fig*) *fact, solution, idea* déterrer, dénicher.

digest [daɪ'dʒest] 1 vt *food, idea* digérer, assimiler; *insult* digérer*. **this kind of food is not easily ~ed** ce genre de nourriture se digère mal *or* est un peu lourd. 2 vi digérer. 3 ['daɪdʒest] n [*book, facts*] (*summary*) sommaire *m*, résumé *m*; (*magazine*) digest *m*; (*Jur*) digeste *m*. **in ~ form** en abrégé.

digestible [dɪ'dʒestəbl] adj (*lit, fig*) facile à digérer *or* à assimiler, digeste.

digestion [dɪ'dʒestʃən] n (*Anat, Chem, fig*) digestion *f*.

digestive [dɪ'dʒestɪv] adj digestif. **~ system** système digestif; **~ tract** appareil digestif; (*Brit*) **~ (biscuit)** (sorte *f* de) sablé *m*; *see* **juice.**

digger ['dɪgə^r] n (*machine*) excavatrice *f*, pelleteuse *f*; (*miner*) ouvrier mineur *m*; (*navvy*) terrassier *m*; (*‡: Australian/New Zealander*) Australien *m*/Néo-Zélandais *m*; *see* **gold.**

digging ['dɪgɪŋ] n a (*NonC*) (*with spade*) bêchage *m*; [*hole etc*] forage *m*; (*Min*) terrassement *m*, creusement *m*, excavation *f*. b **~s** (*Miner*) placer *m*; (*Archeol*) fouilles *fpl*.

digit ['dɪdʒɪt] n (*Math*) chiffre *m*; (*finger*) doigt *m*; (*toe*) orteil *m*; (*Astron*) doigt. **double-/triple-~** (adj) à deux/trois chiffres.

digital ['dɪdʒɪtəl] adj (*Comput etc*) *readout, recording etc* numérique; *tape, recorder* audio-numérique; (*Anat etc*) digital; *clock, watch* à affichage numérique. **~ computer** calculateur *m* numérique.

digitalin [ˌdɪdʒɪ'teɪlɪn] n digitaline *f*.

digitalis [ˌdɪdʒɪ'teɪlɪs] n (*Bot*) digitale *f*; (*Pharm*) digitaline *f*.

digitize ['dɪdʒɪtaɪz] vt (*Comput*) digitaliser.

digitizer [ˌdɪdʒɪtaɪzə^r] n (*Comput*) digitaliseur *m*, convertisseur *m* numérique.

diglossia [daɪ'glɒsɪə] n diglossie *f*.

dignified ['dɪgnɪfaɪd] adj *person, manner* plein de dignité, digne, grave; *pause, silence* digne. **a ~ old lady** une vieille dame très digne; **he is very ~** il a beaucoup de dignité; **it is not very ~ to do that** cela manque de dignité (de faire cela).

dignify ['dɪgnɪfaɪ] vt donner de la dignité à. **to ~ with the name of** honorer du nom de.

dignitary ['dɪgnɪtərɪ] n dignitaire *m*.

dignity [ˈdɪgnɪtɪ] n a (*NonC*) *[person, occasion, character, manner]* dignité *f*. **it's beneath his ~ (to do that)** il se croit au-dessus de ça; **it would be beneath his ~ to do such a thing** faire une chose pareille serait au-dessous de lui, il s'abaisserait en faisant une chose pareille; *see* **stand.** b (*high rank*) dignité *f*, haut rang, haute fonction; (*title*) titre *m*, dignité.

digress [daɪˈgres] vi s'écarter, s'éloigner (*from* de), faire une digression.

digression [daɪˈgreʃən] n digression *f*. **this by way of ~** ceci (soit) dit en passant.

digs* [dɪgz] npl (*Brit: lodgings*) chambre meublée, logement *m* (*avec ou sans pension*), piaule‡ *f*. **I'm looking for ~** je cherche une chambre *or* une piaule‡ à louer; **to be in ~** avoir une chambre (chez un particulier).

dihedral [daɪˈhiːdrəl] adj, n dièdre (*m*).

dike [daɪk] n = **dyke.**

dilapidated [dɪˈlæpɪdeɪtɪd] adj *house* délabré; *clothes* dépenaillé*; *book* déchiré. **in a ~ state** dans un état de délabrement.

dilapidation [dɪˌlæpɪˈdeɪʃən] n *[buildings]* délabrement *m*, dégradation *f*; *[clothes]* état dépenaillé*; (*Jur: gen pl*) détérioration *f* (*causée par un locataire*); (*Geol*) dégradation.

dilate [daɪˈleɪt] 1 vt dilater. 2 vi a se dilater. b (*talk at length*) **to ~ (up)on sth** s'étendre sur qch, raconter qch en détail.

dilation [daɪˈleɪʃən] n dilatation *f*. (*Med*) **~ and curettage** (dilatation et) curetage *m*.

dilatoriness [ˈdɪlətərɪnɪs] n lenteur *f* (*in doing* à faire), caractère *m* dilatoire.

dilatory [ˈdɪlətərɪ] adj *person* traînard, lent; *action, policy* dilatoire. **they were very ~ about it** ils ont fait traîner les choses (en longueur); (*Pol*) **~ motion** manœuvre *f* dilatoire.

dildo [ˈdɪldəʊ] n godemiché *m*.

dilemma [daɪˈlemə] n dilemme *m*. **to be in a ~** *or* **on the horns of a ~** être pris dans un dilemme.

dilettante [ˌdɪlɪˈtæntɪ] 1 n, pl **~s** *or* **dilettanti** [ˌdɪlɪˈtæntɪ] dilettante *mf*. 2 comp de dilettante.

dilettantism [ˌdɪlɪˈtæntɪzəm] n dilettantisme *m*.

diligence [ˈdɪlɪdʒəns] n soins assidus *or* attentifs, zèle *m*, assiduité *f*. **his ~ in trying to save the child** les efforts assidus qu'il a déployés *or* le zèle dont il a fait preuve en essayant de sauver l'enfant; **his ~ in his work** le zèle *or* l'assiduité qu'il apporte à son travail.

diligent [ˈdɪlɪdʒənt] adj *student, work* appliqué, assidu; *person, search* laborieux. **to be ~ in doing sth** mettre du zèle à faire qch, faire qch avec assiduité *or* zèle.

diligently [ˈdɪlɪdʒəntlɪ] adv avec soin *or* application *or* assiduité, assidûment.

dill [dɪl] n aneth *m*, fenouil bâtard.

dilly* [ˈdɪlɪ] n (*US*) **it's/he's a ~** c'est/il est sensationnel* *or* vachement* bien; **we had a ~ of a storm** nous avons eu une sacrée* tempête; *[problem]* **it's a ~** c'est un casse-tête.

dillydally [ˈdɪlɪdælɪ] vi (*dawdle*) lanterner, lambiner*; (*fritter time away*) musarder; (*vacillate*) tergiverser, atermoyer. **no ~ing!** ne traînez pas!

dillydallying [ˈdɪlɪdælɪɪŋ] n (*hesitating*) tergiversation(s) *f(pl)*.

dilute [daɪˈluːt] 1 vt *liquid* diluer, couper d'eau; *sauce* délayer, allonger; *colour* délayer; (*Pharm*) diluer; (*fig*) diluer, édulcorer. **"~ to taste"** "à diluer selon votre goût"; (*fig*) **to ~ the workforce** adjoindre de la main-d'œuvre non qualifiée. 2 adj *liquid* coupé *or* étendu d'eau, dilué; (*fig*) dilué, édulcoré.

diluter [daɪˈluːtəʳ] n diluant *m*.

dilution [daɪˈluːʃən] n dilution *f*; *[wine, milk]* coupage *m*, mouillage *m*; (*fig*) édulcoration *f*.

dim [dɪm] 1 adj *light* faible, pâle; *lamp* faible; *room, forest etc* sombre; *sight* faible, trouble; *colour, metal* terne, mat (*f* mate), sans éclat; *sound* vague, indistinct; *memory, outline* vague, incertain, imprécis; (*Brit *: stupid*) bouché*, borné. **~ shapes** formes indécises; **to have a ~ remembrance of** avoir un vague souvenir de; **to take a ~ view of sth*** voir qch d'un mauvais œil; **to take a ~ view of sb*** avoir une piètre opinion de qn; **she took a ~ view of his selling the car*** elle n'a pas du tout apprécié qu'il ait vendu la voiture; *see also* **4.**

2 comp ►**dim-out** (*US*) black-out partiel ►**dim-sighted** à la vue basse ►**dimwit‡** imbécile *mf*, crétin(e)* *m(f)* ►**dim-witted*** gourde*, idiot; **a dim-witted* mechanic** un crétin* de mécanicien.

3 vt *light* réduire, baisser; *lamp* mettre en veilleuse; *sight* brouiller, troubler; *colours, metals, beauty* ternir, obscurcir; *sound* affaiblir; *memory, outline* effacer, estomper; *mind, senses* affaiblir, troubler; *glory* ternir. (*Theat*) **to ~ the lights** baisser les lumières; (*US Aut*) **to ~ the headlights** se mettre en code.

4 vi (*also* **grow ~**) *[light]* baisser, décliner; *[sight]* baisser, se troubler; *[metal, beauty, glory]* se ternir; *[colours]* devenir terne; *[outlines, memory]* s'effacer, s'estomper.

►**dim out** (*US*) 1 vt sep *city* plonger dans un black-out partiel. 2 **dim-out** n *see* **dim 2.**

dime [daɪm] (*Can, US*) 1 n a (pièce *f* de) dix cents. **it's not worth a ~*** cela ne vaut pas un clou* *or* un radis*; (*fig*) **they're a ~ a dozen*** il y en a *or* on en trouve à la pelle. b = **dime bag;** *see* **2.** 2 comp ►**dime bag** (*Drugs sl*) sachet *m* de marijuana à dix dollars ►**dime novel** roman *m* de gare, roman de quatre sous ►**dime store** ≃ Prisunic *m* ®.

dimension [daɪˈmenʃən] n (*size, extension in space*) dimension *f*; (*Archit, Geom*) dimension, cote *f*; (*fig: scope, extent*) *[problem, epidemic]* étendue *f*.

-dimensional [daɪˈmenʃənl] adj ending in comps: **two-dimensional** à deux dimensions; *see* **three** *etc.*

diminish [dɪˈmɪnɪʃ] 1 vt *cost, speed* réduire, diminuer; *effect, enthusiasm, strength* diminuer, amoindrir; *staff* réduire; (*Mus*) diminuer. 2 vi diminuer, se réduire, s'amoindrir. **to ~ in numbers** diminuer en nombre, devenir moins nombreux.

diminished [dɪˈmɪnɪʃt] adj *numbers, speed, strength* diminué, amoindri, réduit; *character, reputation* diminué, rabaissé; *value* réduit; (*Mus*) diminué. **a ~ staff** un personnel réduit; (*Jur*) **~ responsibility** responsabilité atténuée.

diminishing [dɪˈmɪnɪʃɪŋ] 1 adj *amount, importance, speed* qui diminue, qui va en diminuant; *value, price* qui baisse, en baisse. (*Art*) **~ scale** échelle fuyante *or* de perspective; (*Econ*) **law of ~ returns** loi *f* des rendements décroissants. 2 n diminution *f*, affaiblissement *m*, atténuation *f*.

diminuendo [dɪˌmɪnjʊˈendəʊ] 1 n diminuendo *m inv*. 2 vi faire un diminuendo.

diminution [ˌdɪmɪˈnjuːʃən] n *[value]* baisse *f*, diminution *f*; *[speed]* réduction *f*; *[strength, enthusiasm]* diminution, affaiblissement *m* (*in* de); *[temperature]* baisse, abaissement *m* (*in* de); *[authority]* baisse (*in* de); (*Mus*) diminution.

diminutive [dɪˈmɪnjʊtɪv] 1 adj a *person, object* tout petit, minuscule; *house, garden* tout petit, exigu (*f* -guë), minuscule. b (*Ling*) diminutif. 2 n (*Ling*) diminutif *m*.

dimity [ˈdɪmɪtɪ] n basin *m*.

dimly [ˈdɪmlɪ] adv *shine* faiblement, sans éclat; *see* indistinctement, vaguement; *recollect* vaguement, imparfaitement. **~ lit room** pièce mal *or* faiblement éclairée.

dimmer [ˈdɪməʳ] n (*Elec: also* **~ switch**) variateur *m* (de lumière). (*US Aut*) **~s** phares *mpl* code *inv*; (*parking lights*) feux *mpl* de position.

dimming [ˈdɪmɪŋ] n *[light]* affaiblissement *m*, atténuation *f*; *[mirror, reputation]* ternissement *m*; *[headlights]* mise *f* en code.

dimness [ˈdɪmnɪs] n *[light, sight]* faiblesse *f*; *[room, forest]* obscurité *f*; *[outline, memory]* imprécision *f*, vague *m*; *[colour, metal]* aspect *m* terne; *[intelligence]* faiblesse *f*, manque *m* de clarté; (*: stupidity*) intelligence bornée.

dimorphism [ˌdaɪˈmɔːfɪzəm] n dimorphisme *m*.

dimple [ˈdɪmpl] 1 n *[chin, cheek]* fossette *f* (*on* à); *[water]* ride *f*. 2 vi *[cheeks]* former des fossettes; *[water]* se rider. **she ~d** un petit sourire creusa deux fossettes dans ses joues. 3 vt: **the wind ~d the water** le vent ridait la surface de l'eau.

dimpled [ˈdɪmpld] adj *cheek, chin* à fossettes; *hand, arm* potelé; *water* (doucement) ridé.

DIN [dɪn] n (abbr of **Deutsche Industrie Normen**) DIN.

din [dɪn] 1 n (*from people*) vacarme *m*, tapage *m*; (*from factory, traffic*) vacarme; (*esp in classroom*) chahut *m*. **the ~ of battle** le fracas de la bataille; **to make** *or* **kick up* a ~** faire un boucan monstre*; (*esp Scol*) chahuter, faire un chahut monstre*. 2 vt: **to ~ cleanliness into sb** dresser qn à être propre; **she ~ned into the child that he mustn't speak to strangers** elle ne cessait de dire et de répéter à l'enfant de ne pas parler à des inconnus; **try to ~ it into her that ...** essayez de lui faire entrer dans la tête le fait que ... .

dine [daɪn] 1 vi dîner (*off, on* de). **to ~ out** dîner en ville *or* dehors; (*fig*) **he ~d out on that story for a long time afterwards** il a resservi cette histoire x fois par la suite. 2 vt offrir à dîner à; *see* **wine.**

diner [ˈdaɪnəʳ] n a (*person*) dîneur *m*, -euse *f*. b (*Rail*) wagon-restaurant *m*. c (*US*) petit restaurant.

dinero* [dɪˈnɛərəʊ] n (*US*) pognon* *m*, fric* *m*.

dinette [daɪˈnet] n coin-repas *m*; *see* **kitchen.**

ding-a-ling [ˈdɪŋəˈlɪŋ] n a *[bell, telephone]* dring dring *m*. b (*US ‡: fool*) cloche* *f*.

dingbat‡ [ˈdɪŋˌbæt] n (*US*) imbécile *mf*, andouille‡ *f*.

ding-dong [ˈdɪŋˈdɒŋ] 1 n ding dong *m*. 2 adj (*) *fight* acharné, dans les règles (*fig*). 3 adv ding dong.

dinghy [ˈdɪŋgɪ] n youyou *m*, petit canot; (*collapsible*) canot pneumatique; (*also* **sailing ~**) dériveur *m*.

dinginess [ˈdɪndʒɪnɪs] n aspect minable* *or* miteux.

dingo [ˈdɪŋgəʊ] n, pl **~es** dingo *m*.

dingus‡ [ˈdɪŋgəs] n (*US*) truc* *m*, machin* *m*.

dingy [ˈdɪndʒɪ] adj (*dark*) lugubre; (*seedy*) minable*, miteux.

dining car [ˈdaɪnɪŋkɑːʳ] n (*Brit Rail*) wagon-restaurant *m*.

dining hall [ˈdaɪnɪŋhɔːl] n réfectoire *m*, salle *f* à manger.

dining room [ˈdaɪnɪŋrʊm] 1 n salle *f* à manger; (*in hotel*) salle *f* de restaurant. 2 comp *table, chairs* de salle à manger ►**dining room suite** salle *f* à manger (*meubles*).

dink* [dɪŋk] n (*US baby talk: penis*) zizi* *m*.

dinkie* [ˈdɪŋkɪ] (abbr of **double income no kids**) 1 n: **~s** jeune(s) couple(s) *m(pl)* salarié(s) sans enfant, ≃ couple(s) yuppie. 2 **adj** *attitude, lifestyle* ≃ de yuppie.

dinky* ['dɪŋkɪ] **adj** a (*Brit*) mignon, gentil. b (*US pej*) de rien du tout.

dinner ['dɪnəʳ] 1 **n** (*meal; occasion*) dîner *m*; (*regional use: lunch*) déjeuner *m*; (*for dog, cat*) pâtée *f*. **have you given the dog his ~?** tu as donné à manger au chien?; **he was at ~, he was having his ~** il était en train de dîner; **we're having people to ~** nous avons du monde à dîner; **~'s ready!** le dîner est prêt!, à table!; **we had a good ~** nous avons bien dîné *or* mangé; **to go out to ~** (*in restaurant*) dîner dehors *or* en ville; (*at friends*) dîner chez des amis; **to give a (public) ~ in sb's honour** donner un banquet en l'honneur de qn; **a formal ~** un dîner officiel, un grand dîner.

2 **comp** ▸**dinner bell**: **the dinner bell has gone** on a sonné (pour) le dîner ▸**dinner dance** dîner-dansant *m* ▸**dinner duty** (*Scol*) service *m* de réfectoire; (*Scol*) **to do dinner duty, to be on dinner duty** être de service *or* de surveillance au réfectoire ▸**dinner jacket** (*Brit*) smoking *m* ▸**dinner knife** grand couteau ▸**dinner lady** (*Brit Scol*) femme *f* de service (*à la cantine*) ▸**dinner party** dîner *m* (*sur invitation*); **to give a dinner party** avoir du monde à dîner, donner un dîner ▸**dinner plate** (grande) assiette *f* ▸**dinner roll** petit pain ▸**dinner service** service *m* de table ▸**dinner table**: **at the dinner table** pendant le dîner, au dîner, à table ▸**dinner time**: **at dinner time** à l'heure du dîner; **it's dinner time** c'est l'heure du *or* de dîner ▸**dinner trolley, dinner wagon** table roulante ▸**dinnerware** (*US*) vaisselle *f*.

dinosaur ['daɪnəsɔːʳ] **n** dinosaure *m*.

dint [dɪnt] 1 **n** a = **dent 1**. b **by ~ of (doing) sth** à force de (faire) qch. 2 **vt** = **dent 2**.

diocesan [daɪ'ɒsɪsən] 1 **adj** diocésain. 2 **n** (évêque *m*) diocésain *m*.

diocese ['daɪəsɪs] **n** diocèse *m*.

diode ['daɪəʊd] **n** diode *f*.

dioptre, (*US*) **diopter** [daɪ'ɒptəʳ] **n** dioptrie *f*.

diorama [daɪə'rɑːmə] **n** diorama *m*.

dioxide [daɪ'ɒksaɪd] **n** bioxyde *m*, déoxyde *m*.

dioxin [daɪ'ɒksɪn] **n** dioxine *f*.

DIP [dɪp] **n** (*Comput*) (**abbr of Dual-In-Line Package**)**~ switch** interrupteur *m* à positions multiples.

dip [dɪp] 1 **vt** a (*into liquid*) *pen, hand, clothes* tremper, plonger (*into* dans); (*Tech*) tremper, décaper; *sheep* laver. **she ~ped her hand into the bag** elle a plongé la main dans le sac; **to ~ a spoon into a bowl** plonger une cuiller dans un bol; **to ~ water from a lake** puiser de l'eau dans un lac.

b (*Brit Aut*) **to ~ one's headlights** se mettre en code; **~ped headlights** codes *mpl*, feux *mpl* de croisement; **to drive on ~ped headlights** rouler en code; (*Naut*) **to ~ one's flag** saluer avec le pavillon.

2 **vi** a *[ground]* descendre, s'incliner; *[road]* descendre; *[temperature, pointer on scale etc]* baisser; *[prices]* fléchir, baisser; *[sun]* baisser, descendre à l'horizon; *[boat, raft]* tanguer, piquer du nez*.

b puiser. **she ~ped into her handbag for money** elle a cherché de l'argent dans son sac à main; (*lit, fig*) **to ~ into one's pockets** puiser dans ses poches; **to ~ into one's savings** puiser dans ses économies; **to ~ into a book** feuilleter un livre.

3 **n** a (**: in sea etc*) baignade *f*, bain *m* (*de mer etc*). **to have a (quick) ~** prendre un bain rapide (*en mer etc*), faire trempette (*hum*).

b (*for cleaning animals*) bain *m* parasiticide.

c (*in ground*) déclivité *f*; (*Geol*) pendage *m*; (*Phys: also* **angle of ~**) inclinaison *f* magnétique.

d (*Culin*) (*cheese: hot*) fondue savoyarde *ou* au fromage; (*cheese: cold*) hors d'œuvre *m* au fromage (*que l'on mange sur des biscuits salés, des chips etc*); (*anchovy/shrimp etc*) mousse *f* aux anchois/aux crevettes *etc*.

e *see* **lucky**.

4 **comp** ▸**dip needle, dipping needle** aiguille aimantée (de boussole) ▸**dipstick**, (*US*) **diprod** (*Aut*) jauge *f* (*de niveau d'huile*) ▸**dip switch** (*Aut*) basculeur *m* de phares.

Dip. **abbr of diploma**.

diphtheria [dɪf'θɪərɪə] **n** diphtérie *f*. **~ vaccine** vaccin *m* antidiphtérique.

diphthong ['dɪfθɒŋ] **n** diphtongue *f*.

diphthongize ['dɪfθɒŋaɪz] 1 **vt** diphtonguer. 2 **vi** se diphtonguer.

diploid ['dɪplɔɪd] **adj** diploïde.

diploma [dɪ'pləʊmə] **n** diplôme *m*. **teacher's/nurse's ~** diplôme d'enseignement/d'infirmière; **to hold** *or* **have a ~ in** être diplômé de *or* en.

diplomacy [dɪ'pləʊməsɪ] **n** (*Pol, fig*) diplomatie *f*. (*fig*) **to use ~** user de diplomatie.

diplomat ['dɪpləmæt] **n** (*Pol*) diplomate *m*, femme *f* diplomate; (*fig*) diplomate *mf*.

diplomatic [ˌdɪplə'mætɪk] **adj** a *mission, relations* diplomatique. **~ bag**, (*US*) **~ pouch** valise *f* diplomatique; **~ corps** corps *m* diplomatique; **~ immunity** immunité *f* diplomatique; **~ service** diplomatie *f*, service *m* diplomatique; **~ shuttle** navette *f* diplomatique. b (*fig: tactful*) *person* diplomate; *action, behaviour* diplomatique, plein de tact; *answer* diplomatique, habile. **to be ~ in dealing with sth** s'occuper de qch avec tact *or* en usant de diplomatie.

diplomatically [ˌdɪplə'mætɪkəlɪ] **adv** (*Pol*) diplomatiquement; (*fig*) diplomatiquement, avec diplomatie.

diplomatist [dɪ'pləʊmətɪst] **n** = **diplomat**.

dipole ['daɪˌpəʊl] **n** dipôle *m*.

dipper ['dɪpəʳ] **n** (*ladle*) louche *f*; *[mechanical shovel]* godet *m* (de pelleteuse); (*for river, sea*) benne *f* (de drague), hotte *f* à draguer; (*at fairground*) montagnes *fpl* russes; (*Aut: for headlamps*) basculeur *m* (de phares); (*Orn*) cincle *m* (plongeur). (*US Astron*) **the Big** *or* **Great D~** la Grande Ourse; **the Little D~** la Petite Ourse.

dippy‡ ['dɪpɪ] **adj** toqué*.

dipso‡ ['dɪpsəʊ] **n** (**abbr of dipsomaniac**) soûlard(e)‡ *m(f)*.

dipsomania [ˌdɪpsəʊ'meɪnɪə] **n** (*Med*) dipsomanie *f*, alcoolisme *m*.

dipsomaniac [ˌdɪpsəʊ'meɪnɪæk] **n** (*Med*) dipsomane *mf*, alcoolique *mf*.

diptera ['dɪptərə] **npl** diptères *mpl*.

dipterous ['dɪptərəs] **adj** diptère.

dir. **abbr of director**.

dire ['daɪəʳ] **adj** *event* terrible, affreux; *poverty* extrême, noir; *prediction* sinistre. **~ necessity** dure nécessité; **they are in ~ need of food** ils ont un besoin urgent *or* extrême de nourriture; **in ~ straits** dans une situation désespérée.

direct [dɪ'rekt] 1 **adj** *link, road, responsibility, attack, reference, train* direct; *cause, result* direct, immédiat; *refusal, denial* direct, catégorique, absolu; *danger* immédiat, imminent; *person, character, question, answer* franc (*f* franche), direct. (*Comput*) **~ access/addressing** accès/adressage direct; (*Ind etc*) **~ action** action directe; **~ broadcasting by satellite** diffusion *f* en direct par satellite; **~ broadcasting satellite** satellite *m* de diffusion directe; **to be a ~ descendant of sb** descendre de qn en ligne directe; (*Elec*) **~ current** courant continu; (*Comm*) **~ debit** prélèvement *m*; **~ dialling** composition *f* directe (*d'un numéro de téléphone*); (*Brit*) **~ grant school**† *établissement scolaire sous contrat avec l'État;* **keep away from ~ heat** éviter l'exposition directe à la chaleur; **~ heating** chauffage direct; (*Mil*) **~ hit** coup *m* au but; **to make a ~ hit** porter un coup au but, frapper de plein fouet; *[bomb, projectile]* toucher *or* atteindre son objectif; **~-mail advertising** publicité *f* par courrier individuel; **~ method of teaching a language** méthode directe pour l'enseignement d'une langue; (*Astron*) **~ motion** mouvement direct; (*Gram*) **~ object** complément (d'objet) direct; (*Pol*) **~ rule** administration *f* directe (*par le pouvoir central*); **~ sales, ~ selling** vente *f* directe; (*Gram*) **~ speech**, (*US*) **~ discourse** discours *or* style direct; **~ tax** impôt direct.

2 **vt** a (*address, aim, turn*) *remark, letter* adresser (*to* à); *torch* diriger (*on* sur); *efforts* orienter (*towards* vers). **to ~ one's steps to(wards)** diriger ses pas *or* se diriger vers; **to ~ sb's attention to** attirer *or* appeler l'attention de qn sur; **can you ~ me to the town hall?** pourriez-vous m'indiquer le chemin de la mairie?

b (*control*) *sb's work* diriger; *conduct* diriger, gouverner; *business* diriger, gérer, administrer; *movements* guider; (*Theat*) *play* mettre en scène; (*Cine, Rad, TV*) *film, programme* réaliser; *group of actors* diriger.

c (*instruct*) charger (*sb to do* qn de faire), ordonner (*sb to do* à qn de faire). (*Jur*) **the judge ~ed the jury to find the accused not guilty** le juge imposa au jury un verdict de non-coupable; (*US Jur*) **~ed verdict** verdict rendu par le jury sur la recommandation du juge; **he did it as ~ed** il l'a fait comme on le lui avait dit *or* comme on l'en avait chargé; (*Med*) **"as ~ed"** "suivre les indications du médecin".

3 **vi**: **who is ~ing?** (*Theat*) qui est le metteur en scène?; (*Ciné, Rad, TV*) qui est le réalisateur?

4 **adv** *go, write* directement.

direction [dɪ'rekʃən] 1 **n** a (*way*) direction *f*, sens *m*; (*fig*) direction, voie *f*. **in every ~** dans toutes les directions, en tous sens; **in the wrong/right ~** (*lit*) dans le mauvais/bon sens, dans la mauvaise/bonne direction; (*fig*) sur la mauvaise/bonne voie; (*fig*) **it's a step in the right ~** voilà un pas dans la bonne direction; **in the opposite ~** en sens inverse; **in the ~ of** dans la direction de, en direction de; **what ~ did he go in?** quelle direction a-t-il prise?; **a sense of ~** le sens de l'orientation.

b (*management*) direction *f*, administration *f*. **under the ~ of** sous la direction de, sous la conduite de.

c (*Theat*) mise *f* en scène; (*Cine, Rad, TV*) réalisation *f*. **"under the ~ of"** (*Theat*) "mise en scène de"; (*Cine, Rad, TV*) "réalisation de".

d (*instruction*) ordre *m*, indication *f*, instruction *f*. (*Comm*) **~s for use** mode *m* d'emploi; (*Theat*) **stage ~s** indications scéniques.

2 **comp** ▸**direction finder** radiogoniomètre *m* ▸**direction finding** radiogoniométrie *f* ▸**direction indicator** (*Aut*) clignotant *m*.

directional [dɪ'rekʃənl] **adj** directionnel. **~ antenna** antenne directionnelle.

directive [dɪ'rektɪv] **n** directive *f*, instruction *f*.

directly [dɪ'rektlɪ] 1 **adv** a (*without deviating*) directement; *go, return etc* directement, tout droit. **to be ~ descended from** descendre en droite ligne *or* en ligne directe de; **he's not ~ involved** cela ne le concerne pas directement, il n'est pas directement en cause.

b (*frankly*) *speak* sans détours, sans ambages, franchement. **to come ~ to the point** aller droit au fait.

c (*completely*) *opposite* exactement; *opposed* diamétralement, directement. ~ **contrary to** diamétralement opposé à, exactement contraire à.

d (*Brit: immediately*) tout de suite, sur-le-champ, immédiatement.

2 **conj** (*esp Brit*) aussitôt que, dès que. **he'll come ~ he's ready** il viendra dès qu'il sera prêt.

directness [dɪ'rektnɪs] **n** *[character, reply]* franchise *f*; *[remarks]* absence *f* d'ambiguïté; *[person]* franchise, franc-parler *m*; *[attack]* caractère direct. **to speak with great ~** parler en toute franchise.

director [dɪ'rektəʳ] 1 **n** a (*person*) (*Brit: of company*) directeur *m*, -trice *f*, administrateur *m*, -trice *f*; *[institution]* directeur, -trice; (*Theat*) metteur *m* en scène; (*Cine, Rad, TV*) réalisateur *m*, -trice *f*; (*Rel*) directeur de conscience. ~ **general** directeur général; (*US: Univ etc*) ~ **of admissions** responsable *mf* du service des inscriptions; (*Brit*) **D~ of Education** ≃ recteur *m* d'académie; (*Mil*) ~ **of music** chef *m* de musique; (*Brit Jur*) **D~ of Public Prosecutions** ≃ procureur général; (*Univ*) ~ **of studies** (*for course*) directeur, -trice d'études *or* de travaux; (*for thesis*) directeur, -trice *or* patron(ne) *m(f)* de thèse; *see* **board, managing, stage** *etc.* b (*device*) guide *m*.

directorate [dɪ'rektərɪt] **n** (*board of directors*) conseil *m* d'administration.

directorial [ˌdɪrek'tɔːrɪəl] **adj** directorial, de directeur.

directorship [dɪ'rektəʃɪp] **n** poste *m or* fonctions *fpl* de directeur *or* d'administrateur, direction *f*.

directory [dɪ'rektərɪ] 1 **n** a *[addresses]* répertoire *m* (d'adresses); (*also* **street** ~) guide *m* des rues; (*Telec*) annuaire *m* (des téléphones); (*Comm*) annuaire du commerce; (*Comput*) répertoire *m* (de dossiers). b (*Hist*) **D~** Directoire *m*. 2 **comp** ▸**directory inquiries** (*Brit*), **directory assistance** (*US*) (*Telec*) (service *m* des) renseignements *mpl*.

directrix [dɪ'rektrɪks] **n** (*Math*) (ligne *f*) directrice *f*.

direful ['daɪəfʊl] **adj** sinistre, menaçant.

dirge [dɜːdʒ] **n** (*lit*) hymne *m or* chant *m* funèbre; (*fig*) chant lugubre.

dirigible ['dɪrɪdʒəbl] **adj, n** dirigeable *(m)*.

dirk [dɜːk] **n** (*Scot*) dague *f*, poignard *m*.

dirndl ['dɜːndəl] **adj, n:** ~ **(skirt)** large jupe froncée.

dirt [dɜːt] 1 **n** a (*on skin, clothes, objects*) saleté *f*, crasse *f*; (*earth*) terre *f*; (*mud*) boue *f*; (*excrement*) crotte *f*, ordure *f*. **covered with** ~ (*gen*) très sale, couvert de crasse; *clothes, shoes, mudguards* couvert de boue, tout crotté; *cog, stylus* encrassé; **a layer of** ~ une couche de saleté *or* de crasse; **dog** ~ crotte de chien; **horse** ~ crottin *m* de cheval; **cow** ~ bouse *f* de vache; (*fig*) **to eat** ~* faire ses excuses les plus plates, ramper; **to treat sb like** ~* traiter qn comme un chien; (*US fig*) **to do the ~ on sb*, to do sb ~*** faire une vacherie‡ *or* une saloperie‡ à qn, jouer un tour de cochon* à qn.

b (*fig*) (*obscenity*) obscénité *f*; (*: *scandal*) cancans *mpl*, ragots *mpl*, calomnies *fpl*. (*fig*) **to spread the ~* about sb** cancaner sur qn, calomnier qn; **what's the ~ on ...?*** qu'est-ce que l'on raconte sur ...?

c (*Ind*) impuretés *fpl*, corps étrangers; (*on machine, in engine*) encrassement *m*.

2 **comp** ▸**dirt-cheap*** **adv** pour rien, pour une bouchée de pain ◊ **adj** très bon marché *inv*; **it was dirt-cheap*** c'était donné, c'était pour (presque) rien ▸**dirt farmer** (*US*) petit fermier (*sans ouvriers*) ▸**dirt road** chemin non macadamisé ▸**dirt track** (*gen*) piste *f*; (*Sport*) cendrée *f* ▸**dirt track racing** courses *fpl* motocyclistes *or* de motos sur cendrée.

dirtily ['dɜːtɪlɪ] **adv** *eat, live* salement, malproprement; (*fig*) *act, behave* bassement; *play, fight* déloyalement.

dirtiness ['dɜːtɪnɪs] **n** saleté *f*.

dirty ['dɜːtɪ] 1 **adj** a *hands, clothes, house, person, animal* sale, malpropre, crasseux; *shoes* sale, (*mucky*) couvert de boue, crotté; *job, work* salissant; *machine, plug* encrassé; *cut, wound* infecté; *bomb* sale; *colour* sale, terne. **to get** ~ se salir; **to get sth** ~ salir qch; **that coat gets ~ very easily** ce manteau est très salissant.

b (*fig: lewd*) grossier, sale, cochon*. **to have a ~ mind** avoir l'esprit mal tourné; ~ **old man** vieux cochon*; ~ **remarks** propos orduriers; ~ **story** histoire sale *or* cochonne* *or* graveleuse; ~ **word** mot grossier, terme offensant; (*fig*) **"communist" is a ~ word* there** le mot "communiste" est une insulte là-bas; **"work" is a ~ word* for them** ils ne veulent pas entendre parler de travail.

c (*unpleasant, dishonest*) sale (*before n*). **that was a ~ business** c'était une sale affaire *or* histoire; **politics is a ~ business** la politique est un sale métier; ~ **crack** vacherie‡ *f*; **it was a very ~ election** c'était *or* ce fut une élection très déloyale; (*US*) ~ **dozen‡** duel *m* d'obscénités; **he's a ~ fighter** il se bat en traître; **to give sb a ~ look** regarder qn d'un sale œil; ~ **money** argent mal acquis; (*US*) ~ **pool‡** tour *m* de cochon*; **he's a ~ rat*** c'est un sale type* *or* un salaud‡; **to play a ~ trick on sb** jouer un sale tour *or* un tour de cochon* à qn; ~ **weather** sale *or* vilain temps; **he left the ~ work for me to do** il m'a laissé le plus embêtant du boulot* à faire.

2 **adv** a (*: *unfairly*) *play, fight* déloyalement.

b (‡: *intensifier*) ~ **great** vachement‡ grand (*or* gros *etc*).

3 **vt** *hands, clothes* salir; *reputation* salir, souiller (*liter*); *machine* encrasser.

4 **n** (*Brit*) **to do the ~ on sb‡** faire une vacherie‡ *or* une saloperie‡ à qn, jouer un tour de cochon* à qn.

5 **comp** ▸**dirty-faced** à *or* qui a la figure sale ▸**dirty-minded** à *or* qui a l'esprit mal tourné ▸**dirty weekend*** partie *f* de jambes en l'air*.

disability [ˌdɪsə'bɪlɪtɪ] 1 **n** a (*NonC*) (*physical*) invalidité *f*, incapacité *f*; (*mental*) incapacité. ~ **for work** incapacité de travail; **complete/partial** ~ incapacité totale/partielle. b (*infirmity*) infirmité *f*; (*handicap*) désavantage *m*, handicap *m*. **the disabilities of old age** les infirmités de la vieillesse; **this ~ made him eligible for a pension** cette infirmité lui donnait droit à une pension, étant infirme *or* invalide il avait droit à une pension; **to be under a** ~ être dans une position désavantageuse, avoir un handicap. 2 **comp** ▸**disability allowance** allocation *f* d'invalidité ▸**disability pension** pension *f* d'invalidité.

disable [dɪs'eɪbl] **vt** *[illness, accident, injury]* rendre infirme, (*stronger*) rendre impotent; (*maim*) estropier, mutiler; *tank, gun* mettre hors d'action; *ship* (*gen*) avarier, mettre hors d'état; (*by enemy action*) mettre hors de combat, désemparer; (*Jur: make/pronounce incapable*) rendre/prononcer inhabile (*from doing* à faire).

disabled [dɪs'eɪbld] 1 **adj** a (*permanently*) infirme, handicapé; (*esp Admin: unable to work*) invalide; (*maimed*) estropié, mutilé; (*Mil*) mis hors de combat. ~ **ex-servicemen** mutilés *mpl or* invalides *mpl* de guerre. b (*Naut*) *[ship]* **to be** ~ avoir des avaries, être avarié *or* désemparé; *[propeller]* être immobilisé. c (*Jur*) incapable (*from* de), inhabile (*from* à). 2 **npl: the** ~ les handicapés *mpl*, les infirmes *mpl*, les invalides *mpl*; **the war** ~ les mutilés *mpl or* les invalides de guerre.

disablement [dɪs'eɪblmənt] **n** invalidité *f*. ~ **insurance** assurance *f* invalidité; ~ **pension/benefit** pension *f*/allocation *f* d'invalidité.

disabuse [ˌdɪsə'bjuːz] **vt** détromper, désenchanter (*of* de).

disadvantage [ˌdɪsəd'vɑːntɪdʒ] 1 **n** a (*NonC*) désavantage *m*, inconvénient *m*. **to be at a** ~ être dans une position désavantageuse; **you've got me at a** ~ vous avez l'avantage sur moi; **to catch sb at a** ~ prendre qn en position de faiblesse; **to put sb at a** ~ désavantager qn, mettre qn en position de faiblesse. b (*prejudice, injury*) préjudice *m*, désavantage *m*; (*Comm: loss*) perte *f*. **it would be *or* work to your ~ to be seen with him** cela vous porterait préjudice *or* vous ferait du tort qu'on vous voie avec lui; **to sell at a** ~ vendre à perte. 2 **vt** désavantager, défavoriser.

disadvantaged [ˌdɪsəd'vɑːntɪdʒd] **adj** (*Econ, Soc*) (*financially etc*) déshérité. **educationally** *etc* ~ défavorisé sur le plan scolaire *etc*; **the** ~ les classes défavorisées, les économiquement faibles.

disadvantageous [ˌdɪsædvɑːn'teɪdʒəs] **adj** désavantageux, défavorable (*to* à).

disadvantageously [ˌdɪsædvɑːn'teɪdʒəslɪ] **adv** d'une manière désavantageuse, désavantageusement.

disaffected [ˌdɪsə'fektɪd] **adj** (*discontented*) mécontent, mal disposé; (*disloyal*) rebelle.

disaffection [ˌdɪsə'fekʃən] **n** désaffection *f*, mécontentement *m*.

disagree [ˌdɪsə'griː] **vi** a ne pas être d'accord (*with* avec, *on, about* sur), ne pas être du même avis (*with* que, *on, about* sur), se trouver *or* être en désaccord (*with* avec, *on, about* sur). **I ~** je ne suis pas de cet avis, je ne suis pas d'accord; **I ~ completely with you** je ne suis pas du tout d'accord avec vous *or* pas du tout de votre avis; **they always ~ (with each other)** ils ne sont jamais du même avis *or* d'accord; (*always quarrelling*) ils sont incapables de s'entendre; **to ~ with the suggestion that** être contre la suggestion que; **she ~s with everything he has done** elle se trouve en désaccord avec tout ce qu'il a fait.

b (*be different*) *[explanations, reports, sets of figures]* ne pas concorder.

c *[climate, food]* **to ~ with sb** ne pas convenir à qn, être nuisible à qn; **mutton ~s with him** il ne digère pas le mouton, le mouton ne lui réussit pas; **the mutton ~d with him** il a mal digéré le mouton, le mouton n'est pas bien passé*.

disagreeable [ˌdɪsə'grɪəbl] **adj** *smell, work* désagréable, déplaisant; *experience* désagréable, fâcheux; *person, answer* désagréable, désobligeant, maussade (*towards* envers).

disagreeableness [ˌdɪsə'grɪəblnɪs] **n** *[work, experience]* nature désagréable *or* fâcheuse; *[person]* mauvaise humeur, maussaderie *f*, attitude *f or* manière(s) *f(pl)* désagréable(s).

disagreeably [ˌdɪsə'grɪəblɪ] **adv** désagréablement, d'un air *or* d'une manière désagréable *or* désobligeant(e).

disagreement [ˌdɪsə'griːmənt] **n** a (*of opinion, also between accounts etc*) désaccord *m*, différence *f*. b (*quarrel*) désaccord *m*, différend *m*, différence *f* d'opinion. **to have a ~ with sb** avoir un différend avec qn (*about* à propos de); *[people]* **to be in ~ (over)** être en désaccord (sur).

disallow [ˌdɪsə'laʊ] **vt** (*gen*) rejeter; (*Sport*) *goal etc* refuser; (*Jur*) débouter, rejeter.

disambiguate [ˌdɪsæm'bɪgjʊˌeɪt] **vt** désambiguïser.

disambiguation [ˌdɪsæmˌbɪgjʊ'eɪʃən] **n** désambiguïsation *f*.

disappear [ˌdɪsə'pɪəʳ] **vi** *[person, vehicle]* disparaître; *[lost object]* disparaître, s'égarer; *[snow, objection]* disparaître; *[memory]* disparaître, s'effacer; *[difficulties]* disparaître, s'aplanir; *[custom]* disparaître, tomber en désuétude; (*Ling*) s'amuïr. **he ~ed from sight** on l'a perdu de vue; **the ship ~ed over the horizon** le navire a disparu à l'horizon; (*fig*) **to do a ~ing trick*** s'éclipser*, s'esquiver; **to make sth ~** faire

disparaître qch; *[conjurer]* escamoter qch.
disappearance [ˌdɪsəˈpɪərəns] **n** disparition *f*; (*Ling*) *[sound]* amuïssement *m*.
disappoint [ˌdɪsəˈpɔɪnt] **vt** *person* décevoir, désappointer, tromper dans ses espoirs *or* son attente; (*after promising*) manquer de parole à; *hope* décevoir; *expectations* tromper. **he promised to meet me but ~ed me several times** il m'a promis de me rencontrer mais il m'a fait faux bond plusieurs fois; **his schemes were ~ed** on a contrecarré ses plans.
disappointed [ˌdɪsəˈpɔɪntɪd] **adj** *person* déçu, désappointé; *hope, ambition* déçu; *plan* contrecarré. **I'm very ~ in you** vous m'avez beaucoup déçu *or* désappointé; **he was ~ with her reply** sa réponse l'a déçu; **I was ~ to learn that ...** *or* **when I learned that ...** j'ai été déçu *or* désappointé d'apprendre que ... **we were ~ at not seeing her** *or* **not to see her** cela a été une déception pour nous *or* nous avons été déçus de ne pas la voir; **to be ~ in one's hopes/in love** être déçu dans ses espoirs/en amour.
disappointing [ˌdɪsəˈpɔɪntɪŋ] **adj** décevant. **how ~!** quelle déception!, comme c'est décevant!
disappointingly [ˌdɪsəˈpɔɪntɪŋlɪ] **adv: it was ~ small** c'était bien petit (ma foi); **~ ordinary** très ordinaire; **~, he couldn't come** hélas, il n'a pas pu venir.
disappointment [ˌdɪsəˈpɔɪntmənt] **n** **a** (*NonC*) déception *f*,contrariété *f*, désappointement *m*. **to my great ~** à ma grande déception *or* contrariété *or* déconvenue. **b** déception *f*, déboires *mpl*, désillusion *f*. **after a series of ~s** après une succession de déboires; **~s in love** chagrins *mpl* d'amour; **he/that was a great ~ to me** il/cela a été une grosse déception pour moi, il/cela m'a beaucoup déçu.
disapprobation [ˌdɪsæprəˈbeɪʃən] **n** (*liter*), **disapproval** [ˌdɪsəˈpruːvəl] **n** désapprobation *f*; (*stronger*) réprobation *f*. **murmur** *etc* **of ~** murmure *etc* désapprobateur *or* de désapprobation; **to show one's ~ of sb/sth** marquer sa désapprobation *or* sa réprobation à l'égard de qn/qch.
disapprove [ˌdɪsəˈpruːv] **1** **vi: to ~ of sb/sth** désapprouver qn/qch, trouver à redire à qn/qch; **to ~ of sb's doing sth** désapprouver *or* trouver mauvais que qn fasse qch; **your mother would ~** ta mère serait contre*, ta mère ne trouverait pas ça bien; **he entirely ~s of drink** il est tout à fait contre la boisson. **2** **vt** *action, event* désapprouver.
disapproving [ˌdɪsəˈpruːvɪŋ] **adj** désapprobateur (*f* -trice), de désapprobation.
disapprovingly [ˌdɪsəˈpruːvɪŋlɪ] **adv** avec désapprobation, d'un air *or* d'un ton désapprobateur.
disarm [dɪsˈɑːm] **vti** (*also fig*) désarmer.
disarmament [dɪsˈɑːməmənt] **n** désarmement *m*. **~ talks** conférence *f* sur le désarmement.
disarmer [dɪsˈɑːməʳ] **n: (nuclear) ~** partisan(e) *m(f)* du désarmement nucléaire.
disarming [dɪsˈɑːmɪŋ] **1** **n** (*Mil*) désarmement *m*. **2** **adj** *smile* désarmant.
disarmingly [dɪsˈɑːmɪŋlɪ] **adv** d'une manière désarmante.
disarrange [ˈdɪsəˈreɪndʒ] **vt** déranger, mettre en désordre.
disarranged [ˈdɪsəˈreɪndʒd] **adj** *bed* défait; *hair, clothes* en désordre.
disarray [ˌdɪsəˈreɪ] **n** désordre *m*, confusion *f*. **the troops were in (complete) ~** le désordre *or* la confusion régnait parmi les troupes, les troupes étaient en déroute; **a political party in ~** un parti politique en plein désarroi *or* en proie au désarroi; **thoughts in complete ~** pensées très confuses; **she was** *or* **her clothes were in ~** ses vêtements étaient en désordre.
disassemble [ˈdɪsəˈsembl] **vt** désassembler, démonter.
disassociate [ˈdɪsəˈsəʊʃɪeɪt] **vt** = **dissociate**.
disassociation [ˌdɪsəsəʊsɪˈeɪʃən] **n** = **dissociation**.
disaster [dɪˈzɑːstəʳ] **1** **n** (*gen, also fig*) désastre *m*, catastrophe *f*; (*from natural causes*) catastrophe, sinistre *m*. **air ~** catastrophe aérienne; **the Madrid airport ~** la catastrophe de l'aéroport de Madrid; **financial ~** désastre financier; **a record of ~s** une série de désastres *or* de calamités *or* de malheurs; **attempt doomed to ~** tentative vouée à l'échec (total) *or* à la catastrophe; **on the scene of the ~** sur les lieux du désastre *or* de la catastrophe *or* du sinistre; **their marriage/her hair style was a ~*** leur mariage/sa coiffure était une catastrophe* *or* un (vrai) désastre.
2 **comp ▸disaster area** région sinistrée **▸disaster fund** collecte *f* au profit des sinistrés; **earthquake disaster fund** collecte *f* au profit des victimes du tremblement de terre **▸disaster-victim** sinistré(e) *m(f)*, victime *f* de la catastrophe.
disastrous [dɪˈzɑːstrəs] **adj** désastreux, funeste; (*) catastrophique*.
disastrously [dɪˈzɑːstrəslɪ] **adv** désastreusement.
disavow [ˈdɪsəˈvaʊ] **vt** *one's words, opinions* désavouer, renier; *faith, duties* renier.
disavowal [ˌdɪsəˈvaʊəl] **n** désaveu *m*, reniement *m*.
disband [dɪsˈbænd] **1** **vt** *army, corporation, club* disperser. **2** **vi** *[army]* se débander, se disperser; *[organization]* se disperser.
disbar [dɪsˈbɑːʳ] **vt** *barrister* rayer du tableau de l'ordre (des avocats). **to be ~red** se faire rayer du tableau de l'ordre (des avocats).
disbarment [dɪsˈbɑːmənt] **n** radiation *f* (du barreau *or* du tableau de l'ordre).
disbelief [ˈdɪsbəˈliːf] **n** incrédulité *f*. **in ~** avec incrédulité.
disbelieve [ˈdɪsbəˈliːv] **1** **vt** *person* ne pas croire; *news etc* ne pas croire à. **2** **vi** (*also Rel*) ne pas croire (*in* à).
disbeliever [ˈdɪsbəˈliːvəʳ] **n** (*also Rel*) incrédule *mf*.
disbelieving [ˈdɪsbəˈliːvɪŋ] **adj** incrédule.
disbud [dɪsˈbʌd] **vt** ébourgeonner.
disburden [dɪsˈbɜːdn] **vt** (*lit, fig*) décharger, débarrasser (*of* de); (*relieve*) soulager. **to ~ one's conscience** se décharger la conscience.
disburse [dɪsˈbɜːs] **vti** débourser, décaisser.
disbursement [dɪsˈbɜːsmənt] **n** (*paying out*) déboursement *m*, décaissement *m*; (*money paid*) débours *mpl*.
disc [dɪsk] **1** **n** **a** (*also of moon etc*) disque *m*. **b** (*Anat*) disque *m* (intervertébral); *see* **slip**. **c** (*Mil: also* **identity ~**) plaque *f* d'identité. **d** (*gramophone record*) disque *m*. **2** **comp ▸disc brakes** (*Brit*) freins *mpl* à disque(s) **▸disc camera** appareil-photo *m* disque **▸disc film** film *m* disque **▸disc harrow** pulvériseur *m* **▸disc jockey** disc-jockey *m*, animateur *m*, -trice *f* **▸disc shutter** (*Cine*) *[projector]* obturateur *m* à disque.
discard [dɪsˈkɑːd] **1** **vt** **a** (*get rid of*) se débarrasser de; (*throw out*) jeter; *jacket etc* se débarrasser de; *idea, plan* renoncer à, abandonner; *rocket, part of spacecraft* larguer. **b** (*Bridge etc*) se défausser de, défausser; (*Cribbage*) écarter. **he was ~ing clubs** il se défaussait à trèfle; **he ~ed the three of hearts** il s'est défaussé du trois de cœur. **2** **vi** (*Bridge etc*) se défausser; (*Cribbage*) écarter. **3** [ˈdɪskɑːd] **n** **a** (*Bridge*) défausse *f*; (*Cribbage*) écart *m*. **b** (*Comm, Ind*) pièce *f* de rebut, déchet *m*.
discern [dɪˈsɜːn] **vt** *person, object, difference* discerner, distinguer, percevoir; *feelings* discerner.
discernible [dɪˈsɜːnəbl] **adj** *object* visible; *likeness, fault* perceptible, sensible.
discernibly [dɪˈsɜːnəblɪ] **adv** visiblement, perceptiblement, sensiblement.
discerning [dɪˈsɜːnɪŋ] **adj** *person* judicieux, sagace, doué de discernement; *taste* délicat; *look* clairvoyant, perspicace.
discernment [dɪˈsɜːnmənt] **n** (*fig*) discernement *m*, pénétration *f*.
discharge [dɪsˈtʃɑːdʒ] **1** **vt** **a** *ship, cargo* décharger; *[bus etc] passengers* débarquer; *liquid* déverser; (*Elec*) décharger. (*Med*) **to ~ pus** suppurer.
b *employee* renvoyer, congédier; (*Mil*) *soldier* rendre à la vie civile; (*for health reasons*) réformer; (*Jur*) *prisoner* libérer, mettre en liberté, élargir; (*Jur*) *jury* congédier; (*Jur*) *accused* relaxer; *bankrupt* réhabiliter; (*Med*) *patient* renvoyer (guéri) de l'hôpital. **the patient ~d himself** le malade est sorti en signant une décharge.
c *gun* décharger, faire partir; *arrow* décocher.
d (*Fin*) *debt, bill* acquitter, régler; *obligation, duty* remplir, s'acquitter de; *function* remplir.
2 **vi** *[wound]* suinter.
3 [ˈdɪstʃɑːdʒ] **n** **a** (*NonC*) *[cargo]* déchargement *m*; (*Elec*) décharge *f*; *[weapon]* décharge; *[liquid]* écoulement *m*; *[duty]* accomplissement *m*, exécution *f*, exercice *m*; *[debt]* acquittement *m*; *[employee]* renvoi *m*; *[prisoner]* libération *f*, élargissement *m*, mise *f* en liberté; *[patient]* renvoi. **the soldier got his ~ yesterday** le soldat a été libéré hier.
b (*Med*) (*gen*) suintement *m*; (*vaginal*) pertes *fpl* (blanches); *[pus]* suppuration *f*.
disciple [dɪˈsaɪpl] **n** disciple *m*.
disciplinarian [ˌdɪsɪplɪˈnɛərɪən] **n** personne stricte en matière de discipline.
disciplinary [ˈdɪsɪplɪnərɪ] **adj** *action* disciplinaire; *committee* de discipline. (*Jur*) **~ complaint** recours *m* hiérarchique.
discipline [ˈdɪsɪplɪn] **1** **n** **a** (*NonC*) discipline *f*. **to keep ~** maintenir la discipline. **b** (*branch of knowledge*) discipline *f*, matière *f*. **2** **vt** (*control*) *person* discipliner; *mind* former, discipliner; (*punish*) punir.
disciplined [ˈdɪsɪplɪnd] **adj** discipliné; *vie* rangé; *attitude* rigoureux.
disclaim [dɪsˈkleɪm] **vt** **a** *news, statement* démentir; *responsibility* rejeter, nier; *authorship* nier; *paternity* désavouer. **to ~ all knowledge of** désavouer *or* nier toute connaissance de. **b** (*Jur*) se désister de, renoncer à.
disclaimer [dɪsˈkleɪməʳ] **n** désaveu *m*, dénégation *f*, démenti *m*; (*Jur*) désistement *m* (*of* de), renonciation *f* (*of* à). **to issue a ~** démentir officiellement, publier un démenti.
disclose [dɪsˈkləʊz] **vt** *secret* divulguer, dévoiler, mettre au jour; *news* divulguer; *intentions* révéler; *contents of envelope, box etc* exposer, montrer, laisser voir. (*Dentistry*) **disclosing agent** révélateur *m* de plaque dentaire.
disclosure [dɪsˈkləʊʒəʳ] **n** **a** (*NonC*) (*by newspaper etc*) divulgation *f*, révélation *f*; (*by individual to press etc*) communication *f* (de renseignements) (*to* à). **b** (*fact etc revealed*) révélation *f*.
disco* [ˈdɪskəʊ] **1** **n** (**abbr of discotheque**) disco *m*. **2** **comp ▸disco dancing** disco *m* **▸disco jockey** (*US*) animateur *m* de disco.
discography [dɪsˈkɒgrəfɪ] **n** discographie *f*.
discolour, (*US*) **discolor** [dɪsˈkʌləʳ] **1** **vt** (*change, spoil colour of, fade*) décolorer; *white material, teeth* jaunir. **2** **vi** se décolorer, passer, s'altérer; *[white material, teeth]* jaunir; *[mirror]* se ternir.
discolo(u)ration, (*US*) **discoloration** [dɪsˌkʌləˈreɪʃən] **n** (*see* **dis-**

colour) décoloration *f*; jaunissement *m*; ternissure *f*.

discombobulate [ˌdɪskəm'bɒbjʊˌleɪt] **vt** (*US*) *person, plans* chambouler*.

discomfit [dɪs'kʌmfɪt] **vt** (*disappoint*) décevoir, tromper les espoirs de; (*confuse*) déconcerter, décontenancer, confondre.

discomfiture [dɪs'kʌmfɪtʃəʳ] **n** (*disappointment*) déconvenue *f*; (*confusion*) embarras *m*, déconfiture* *f*.

discomfort [dɪs'kʌmfət] **n** **a** (*NonC: physical, mental*) malaise *m*, gêne *f*, manque *m* de bien-être *or* de confort. (*Med*) **he is in some ~** il a assez mal; **I feel some ~ from it but not real pain** ça me gêne mais ça ne me fait pas vraiment mal; **this ~ will pass** cette gêne va passer. **b** (*cause of ~*) inconvénient *m*, inconfort *m*, incommodité *f*.

discomposure [ˌdɪskəm'pəʊʒəʳ] **n** trouble *m*, confusion *f*.

disconcert [ˌdɪskən'sɜːt] **vt** déconcerter, décontenancer.

disconcerting [ˌdɪskən'sɜːtɪŋ] **adj** déconcertant, troublant, déroutant.

disconcertingly [ˌdɪskən'sɜːtɪŋlɪ] **adv** d'une manière déconcertante *or* déroutante.

disconnect ['dɪskə'nekt] **vt** (*gen*) détacher, séparer, disjoindre; *railway carriages* décrocher; *pipe, radio, television* débrancher; *gas, electricity, water supply, telephone* couper. (*Telec*) **to ~ a call** couper *or* interrompre une communication; (*Telec*) **we've been ~ed** (*for non-payment etc*) on nous a coupé le téléphone; (*in mid-conversation*) nous avons été coupés.

disconnected ['dɪskə'nektɪd] **adj** *speech, thought* décousu, sans suite; *facts* sans rapport.

disconsolate [dɪs'kɒnsəlɪt] **adj** inconsolable.

disconsolately [dɪs'kɒnsəlɪtlɪ] **adv** inconsolablement.

discontent ['dɪskən'tent] **n** mécontentement *m*; (*Pol*) malaise *m* (social). **cause of ~** grief *m*.

discontented ['dɪskən'tentɪd] **adj** mécontent (*with, about* de).

discontentedly ['dɪskən'tentɪdlɪ] **adv** d'un air mécontent.

discontentment ['dɪskən'tentmənt] **n** mécontentement *m*.

discontinuance [ˌdɪskən'tɪnjʊəns], **discontinuation** [ˌdɪskənˌtɪnjʊ'eɪʃən] **n** (*gen*) interruption *f*; *[production etc]* arrêt *m*.

discontinue ['dɪskən'tɪnjuː] **vt** (*gen*) cesser, interrompre; *production etc* abandonner; *series* interrompre; *magazine* interrompre la publication de; (*Jur*) *case* abandonner. **to ~ one's subscription to a newspaper** (*permanently*) cesser de s'abonner à un journal; (*temporarily*) suspendre *or* interrompre son abonnement à un journal; (*Comm*) **a ~d line** une série *or* un article qui ne se fait plus; (*on sale article*) **"~d"** "fin de série".

discontinuity [ˌdɪskɒntɪ'njuːɪtɪ] **n** (*gen, Math*) discontinuité *f*; (*Geol*) zone *f* de discontinuité.

discontinuous ['dɪskən'tɪnjʊəs] **adj** discontinu (*also Ling*).

discord ['dɪskɔːd] **n** discorde *f*, dissension *f*, désaccord *m*; (*Mus*) dissonance *f*. **civil ~** dissensions civiles.

discordant [dɪs'kɔːdənt] **adj** *opinions* incompatible; *sounds, colours* discordant; (*Mus*) dissonant.

discotheque ['dɪskəʊtek] **n** discothèque *f* (*dancing*).

discount ['dɪskaʊnt] **1** **n** escompte *m*; (*on article*) remise *f*, rabais *m*; (*rebate on transaction not shown on invoice*) ristourne *f*; (*St Ex: also* **share ~**) décote *f*; (*in forward markets*) déport *m*. **to give a ~** faire une remise (*on* sur); **to buy at a ~** acheter au rabais; **~ for cash** escompte au comptant; **at a ~** (*Fin*) en perte, au-dessous du pair; (*in forward markets*) avec un déport; (*fig*) mal coté; (*St Ex*) **a ~ of 25% below the nominal value of the shares** une décote de 25 % par rapport à la valeur nominale de l'action.

2 **comp** ▸**discount house** magasin *m* de vente au rabais ▸**discount rate** taux *m* d'escompte ▸**discount store** = **discount house**.

3 [dɪs'kaʊnt] **vt** *sum of money* faire une remise de, escompter; *bill, note* prendre à l'escompte, escompter; (*fig*) ne pas tenir compte de. **I ~ half of what he says** je divise par deux tout ce qu'il dit.

discounter [dɪs'kaʊntəʳ] **n** (*Fin, Banking*) escompteur *m*; (*Comm*) magasin *m* discount.

discourage [dɪs'kʌrɪdʒ] **vt** **a** (*dishearten*) décourager, abattre. **to become ~d** se laisser décourager *or* rebuter, se laisser aller au découragement; **he isn't easily ~d** il ne se décourage pas facilement. **b** (*advise against*) décourager, détourner, (essayer de) dissuader (*sb from sth/from doing* qn de qch/de faire). **c** *suggestion* déconseiller; *offer of friendship* repousser. **she ~d his advances** elle a repoussé *or* découragé ses avances.

discouragement [dɪs'kʌrɪdʒmənt] **n** (*act*) désapprobation *f* (*of* de); (*depression*) découragement *m*, abattement *m*.

discouraging [dɪs'kʌrɪdʒɪŋ] **adj** décourageant, démoralisant.

discourse ['dɪskɔːs] **1** **n** **a** discours *m*; (*written*) dissertation *f*, traité *m*. **b** (††) conversation *f*. **2** **comp** ▸**discourse analysis** (*Ling*) analyse *f* du discours. **3** [dɪs'kɔːs] **vi** **a** discourir (*on* sur), traiter (*on* de). **b** (††) s'entretenir (*with* avec).

discourteous [dɪs'kɜːtɪəs] **adj** impoli, peu courtois, discourtois (*towards* envers, avec).

discourteously [dɪs'kɜːtɪəslɪ] **adv** d'une manière peu courtoise, de façon discourtoise. **to behave ~ towards** manquer de politesse envers, se montrer impoli *or* discourtois avec.

discourtesy [dɪs'kɜːtɪsɪ] **n** incivilité *f*, manque *m* de courtoisie, impolitesse *f*.

discover [dɪs'kʌvəʳ] **vt** *country, planet* découvrir; *treasure* découvrir, trouver; *secret, person hiding* découvrir, surprendre; *reason, cause* découvrir, comprendre, pénétrer; *mistake, loss* s'apercevoir de, se rendre compte de; (*after search*) *house, book* dénicher. **to ~ that** (*find out*) apprendre que; (*notice*) s'apercevoir que; (*understand*) comprendre que.

discoverer [dɪs'kʌvərəʳ] **n**: **the ~ of America/penicillin** celui qui le premier a découvert l'Amérique/la pénicilline.

discovery [dɪs'kʌvərɪ] **n** **a** (*NonC*) *[fact, place, person]* découverte *f*. **it led to the ~ of penicillin** cela a conduit à la découverte de la pénicilline, cela a fait découvrir la pénicilline; *see* **voyage**. **b** (*happy find*) trouvaille *f*. **c** (*Jur*) **~ of documents** communication *f* des pièces du dossier avant l'audience. **d** (*Scol: subject*) activités *fpl* d'éveil. **to learn through ~** apprendre par des activités d'éveil.

discredit [dɪs'kredɪt] **1** **vt** (*cast slur on*) discréditer, déconsidérer; (*disbelieve*) ne pas croire, mettre en doute. **2** **n** discrédit *m*, déconsidération *f*. **to bring ~ upon sb** jeter le discrédit sur qn; **without any ~ to you** sans que cela nuise à votre réputation; **to be a ~ to** être une honte pour, faire honte à; **to be to sb's ~** discréditer qn.

discreditable [dɪs'kredɪtəbl] **adj** peu honorable, indigne, déshonorant.

discreet [dɪs'kriːt] **adj** *person, silence, inquiry etc* discret (*f* -ète); *decor, colour* discret, sobre.

discreetly [dɪs'kriːtlɪ] **adv** *speak, behave* discrètement; *dress* sobrement.

discrepancy [dɪs'krepənsɪ] **n** contradiction *f*, désaccord *m*, divergence *f* (*between* entre). **there is a slight ~ between the two explanations** les deux explications divergent légèrement *or* ne cadrent pas tout à fait.

discrete [dɪs'kriːt] **adj** (*gen, Math, Med*) discret (*f* -ète).

discretion [dɪs'kreʃən] **n** **a** (*tact*) discrétion *f*, réserve *f*, retenue *f*; (*prudence*) discrétion, sagesse *f*. (*Prov*) **~ is the better part of valour** prudence est mère de sûreté (*Prov*). **b** (*freedom of decision*) discrétion *f*, arbitraire *m*, liberté *f* d'agir. **to leave sth to sb's ~** laisser qch à la discrétion de qn; **use your own ~** faites comme bon vous semblera, c'est à vous de juger; **at the ~ of the judge/the chairman** *etc* **it is possible to ...** c'est au juge/au président *etc* de décider s'il est possible de ...; **the age of ~** l'âge de raison.

discretionary [dɪs'kreʃənərɪ] **adj** *powers* discrétionnaire.

discriminant [dɪs'krɪmɪnənt] **n** (*Math*) discriminant *m*.

discriminate [dɪs'krɪmɪneɪt] **1** **vi** **a** (*distinguish*) distinguer, établir une distinction, faire un choix (*between* entre). **the public should ~** le public ne devrait pas accepter n'importe quoi *or* devrait exercer son sens critique. **b** (*make unfair distinction*) établir une discrimination (*against* contre, *in favour of* en faveur de). **to be ~d against** être victime de la discrimination. **2** **vt** distinguer (*from* de), discriminer (*liter*).

discriminating [dɪs'krɪmɪneɪtɪŋ] **adj** *judgment, mind* judicieux, sagace; *taste* fin, délicat; *tariff, tax* différentiel. **he's not very ~, he watches every television programme** il ne fait guère preuve d'esprit critique, il regarde tous les programmes de la télévision.

discrimination [dɪsˌkrɪmɪ'neɪʃən] **n** **a** (*distinction*) distinction *f* (*between* entre), séparation *f* (*of one thing from another* d'une chose d'avec une autre); (*judgment*) discernement *m*, jugement *m*. **b** discrimination *f* (*against* contre, *in favour of* en faveur de). **racial ~** discrimination raciale, racisme *m*; **sexual ~** discrimination sexuelle, sexisme *m*.

discriminatory [dɪs'krɪmɪnətərɪ] **adj** discriminatoire.

discursive [dɪs'kɜːsɪv] **adj**, **discursory** [dɪs'kɜːsərɪ] **adj** discursif, décousu (*pej*).

discus ['dɪskəs] **n**, *pl* **~es** *or* **disci** ['dɪskaɪ] disque *m*. **~ thrower** lanceur *m* de disque, discobole *m* (*Hist*).

discuss [dɪs'kʌs] **vt** (*examine in detail*) discuter, examiner; (*talk about*) *problem, project, price* discuter; *topic* discuter de *or* sur, débattre de. **we were ~ing him** nous parlions *or* discutions de lui; **I ~ed it with him** j'en ai discuté avec lui; **I won't ~ it any further** je ne veux plus (avoir à) revenir là-dessus.

discussant [dɪs'kʌsənt] **n** (*US*) participant(e) *m(f)* (*à une discussion etc*).

discussion [dɪs'kʌʃən] **n** discussion *f*, échange *m* de points de vue, débat *m* (*of, about* sur, au sujet de). **under ~** en discussion; **a subject for ~** un sujet de discussion.

disdain [dɪs'deɪn] **1** **vt** dédaigner (*to do* de faire). **2** **n** dédain *m*, mépris *m*. **in ~** avec dédain.

disdainful [dɪs'deɪnfʊl] **adj** *person* dédaigneux; *tone, look* dédaigneux, de dédain.

disdainfully [dɪs'deɪnfəlɪ] **adv** dédaigneusement, avec dédain.

disease [dɪ'ziːz] **n** (*Med: mental, physical*) maladie *f*, affection *f*; (*Bot, Vet*) maladie; (*fig*) maladie, mal *m*; *see* **occupational, venereal, virus** *etc*.

diseased [dɪ'ziːzd] **adj** malade.

diseconomy [ˌdɪsɪ'kɒnəmɪ] **n** déséconomie *f*.

disembark [ˌdɪsɪm'bɑːk] **vti** débarquer.

disembarkation [ˌdɪsembɑː'keɪʃən] **n** débarquement *m*.

disembodied ['dɪsɪm'bɒdɪd] **adj** désincarné.

disembowel [ˌdɪsɪmˈbaʊəl] vt éventrer, éviscérer, étriper*.
disenchant [ˈdɪsɪnˈtʃɑːnt] vt désabuser, désenchanter, désillusionner.
disenchantment [ˌdɪsɪnˈtʃɑːntmənt] n désenchantement *m*, désillusion *f*.
disencumber [ˌdɪsɪnˈkʌmbəʳ] vt *mortgage* payer; *property* déshypothéquer.
disenfranchise [ˈdɪsɪnˈfrænʃaɪz] vt = **disfranchise**.
disengage [ˌdɪsɪnˈgeɪdʒ] 1 vt *object, hand* dégager, libérer (*from* de); (*Tech*) *machine* déclencher, débrayer. **to ~ o.s. from** se dégager de; (*Aut*) **to ~ the clutch** débrayer. 2 vi (*Fencing*) dégager (le fer); (*Tech*) se déclencher.
disengaged [ˌdɪsɪnˈgeɪdʒd] adj libre, inoccupé; (*Tech*) débrayé.
disengagement [ˌdɪsɪnˈgeɪdʒmənt] n (*Pol*) désengagement *m*.
disentangle [ˈdɪsɪnˈtæŋgl] 1 vt *wool, problem, mystery* débrouiller, démêler; *plot* dénouer. (*lit, fig*) **to ~ o.s. from** se dépêtrer de, se sortir de. 2 vi se démêler.
disequilibrium [ˌdɪsekwɪˈlɪbrɪəm] n instabilité *f*.
disestablish [ˈdɪsɪsˈtæblɪʃ] vt *the Church* séparer de l'État.
disestablishment [ˌdɪsɪsˈtæblɪʃmənt] n séparation *f* (de l'Église et de l'État).
disfavour, (*US*) **disfavor** [dɪsˈfeɪvəʳ] 1 n défaveur *f*, désapprobation *f*, mécontentement *m*. **to fall into ~** tomber en défaveur *or* en disgrâce; **to fall into ~ with sb** mécontenter qn; **to be in ~ with sb** être mal vu de qn; **to incur sb's ~** s'attirer la défaveur de qn, encourir la désapprobation de qn; **to look with ~ on sth** regarder qch avec mécontentement *or* désapprobation. 2 vt a (*dislike*) désapprouver, voir avec mécontentement. b (*US: disadvantage*) être défavorable à, défavoriser.
disfigure [dɪsˈfɪgəʳ] vt *face* défigurer; *scenery* défigurer, déparer.
disfigured [dɪsˈfɪgəd] adj défiguré (*by* par).
disfigurement [dɪsˈfɪgəmənt] n défigurement *m*, enlaidissement *m*.
disfranchise [ˈdɪsˈfrænʃaɪz] vt *person* priver du droit électoral; *town* priver de ses droits de représentation.
disgorge [dɪsˈgɔːdʒ] 1 vt *food* dégorger, rendre; *contents, passengers* déverser. 2 vi *[river]* se dégorger, se décharger.
disgrace [dɪsˈgreɪs] 1 n a (*NonC*) (*dishonour*) honte *f*, déshonneur *m*; (*disfavour*) disgrâce *f*, défaveur *f*. **there is no ~ in doing** il n'y a aucune honte à faire; **to be in ~** *[politician etc]* être en disgrâce *or* en défaveur; *[child, dog]* être en pénitence; **to bring ~ on sb** déshonorer qn.
b (*cause of shame*) honte *f*. **it is a ~ to the country** cela est une honte pour *or* cela déshonore le pays; **the price of butter is a ~** le prix du beurre est une honte *or* un scandale; **she's a ~ to her family** elle est la honte de sa famille.
2 vt *family etc* faire honte à; *name, country* déshonorer, couvrir de honte *or* d'opprobre (*liter*). **don't ~ us** ne nous fais pas honte; **he ~d himself by drinking too much** il s'est très mal tenu *or* conduit en buvant trop; *[officer, politician]* **to be ~d** être disgracié.
disgraceful [dɪsˈgreɪsfʊl] adj honteux, scandaleux, déshonorant; (*) honteux, scandaleux. **it was ~ of him** c'était scandaleux de sa part.
disgracefully [dɪsˈgreɪsfəlɪ] adv *act* honteusement, scandaleusement. **~ badly paid** scandaleusement mal payé.
disgruntled [dɪsˈgrʌntld] adj *person* (*discontented*) mécontent (*about, with* de); (*in bad temper*) de mauvaise humeur, mécontent (*about, with* à cause de); *expression* maussade, renfrogné.
disguise [dɪsˈgaɪz] 1 vt *person* déguiser (*as* en); *mistake, voice* déguiser, camoufler; *building, vehicle, ship* camoufler (*as* en); *facts, feelings* masquer, dissimuler, déguiser. **to ~ o.s. as a woman** se déguiser en femme; **there is no disguising the fact that ...** on ne peut pas se dissimuler que ..., il faut avouer que ... . 2 n déguisement *m*; (*fig*) masque *m*, voile *m*, fausse apparence. **in ~** déguisé; **in the ~ of** déguisé en.
disgust [dɪsˈgʌst] 1 n dégoût *m*, aversion *f*, répugnance *f* (*for, at* pour). (*lit, fig*) **he left in ~** il est parti dégoûté *or* écœuré; **to his ~ they left** écœuré, il les a vus partir; **to my ~ he refused to do it** j'ai trouvé dégoûtant qu'il refuse (*subj*) de le faire. 2 vt inspirer du dégoût à, dégoûter, écœurer; (*infuriate*) dégoûter, révolter.
disgusted [dɪsˈgʌstɪd] adj dégoûté, écœuré (*at* de, par).
disgustedly [dɪsˈgʌstɪdlɪ] adv avec écœurement, avec dégoût. **... he said ~** ... dit-il, écœuré.
disgusting [dɪsˈgʌstɪŋ] adj *food* dégoûtant, écœurant; *smell* nauséabond; *behaviour* révoltant, choquant; *work* abominable. **what a ~ mess!** (*of room etc*) quelle pagaïe!*, quel bazar!*; (*of situation*) c'est dégoûtant!, c'est du propre! (*iro*); **it is quite ~ to have to pay ...** c'est tout de même écœurant d'avoir à payer ... .
disgustingly [dɪsˈgʌstɪŋlɪ] adv d'une manière dégoûtante. **~ dirty** d'une saleté dégoûtante *or* répugnante.
dish [dɪʃ] 1 n a plat *m*; (*in laboratory etc*) récipient *m*; (*Phot*) cuvette *f*. **vegetable ~** plat à légumes, légumier *m*; **the ~es** la vaisselle; **to do the ~es** faire la vaisselle.
b (*food*) plat *m*, mets *m*. (*fig*) **she's quite a ~*** c'est vraiment une belle fille, elle est rudement bien roulée*; (*US fig*) **this is not my ~*** ce n'est pas dans mes goûts, ce n'est pas mon truc*.
2 comp ▸**dish aerial**, (*US*) **dish antenna** antenne *f* parabolique ▸**dishcloth** (*for washing*) lavette *f*; (*for drying*) torchon *m* (à vaisselle) ▸**dishmop** lavette *f* ▸**dishpan** (*US*) bassine *f* (à vaisselle) ▸**dishrack** égouttoir *m* (à vaisselle) ▸**dishrag** lavette *f* ▸**dishtowel** torchon *m* (à vaisselle) ▸**dishwasher** (*machine*) machine *f* à laver la vaisselle, lave-vaisselle *m inv*; (*person*) laveur *m*, -euse *f* de vaisselle; (*in restaurant*) plongeur *m*, -euse *f*; **to work as a dishwasher** travailler à la plonge ▸**dishwater** eau *f* de vaisselle; **this coffee's like dishwater*** ce café est de la lavasse* *or* de l'eau de vaisselle*; *see* **dull**.
3 vt a *food, meal* verser dans un plat.
b (‡) *opponent* enfoncer*; *sb's chances, hopes* foutre en l'air‡, flanquer par terre*.
▸**dish out** vt sep *food* servir; (*: *fig*) *money, sweets, books etc* distribuer; *punishment* administrer. **to dish out a hiding to sb*** flanquer* une correction à qn; (*fig*) **to dish it out to sb*** (*smack etc*) flanquer* une correction à qn; (*verbally*) passer un savon* à qn.
▸**dish up** vt sep a *food, meal* servir, verser dans un plat. **the meal was ready to dish up** le repas était prêt à servir; **I'm dishing it up!** je sers!
b (*) *facts, statistics* sortir tout un tas de*.
dishabille [ˌdɪsəˈbiːl] n peignoir *m*, négligé *m*. **in ~** en déshabillé, en négligé.
disharmony [ˈdɪsˈhɑːmənɪ] n désaccord *m*, manque *m* d'harmonie; *[sound]* dissonance *f*.
dishearten [dɪsˈhɑːtn] vt décourager, abattre, démoraliser. **don't be ~ed** ne vous laissez pas décourager *or* abattre.
disheartening [dɪsˈhɑːtnɪŋ] adj décourageant, démoralisant.
dished [dɪʃt] adj a (*dish-shaped*) concave. b (*Aut*) **~ wheel** roue désaxée *or* gauchie. c (*: *fig*) *person, hopes* fichu*, foutu‡.
dishevelled [dɪˈʃevəld] adj *person* échevelé, ébouriffé; *hair* ébouriffé; *clothes* en désordre; (*scruffy*) *person, clothes* débraillé.
dishoard [dɪsˈhɔːd] vt *money* déthésauriser, remettre en circulation.
dishonest [dɪsˈɒnɪst] adj malhonnête; (*insincere*) déloyal, de mauvaise foi. **to be ~ with sb** être de mauvaise foi avec qn, être déloyal envers qn.
dishonestly [dɪsˈɒnɪstlɪ] adv *act* malhonnêtement; *say* en mentant.
dishonesty [dɪsˈɒnɪstɪ] n (*see* **dishonest**) malhonnêteté *f*; déloyauté *f*, mauvaise foi. **an act of ~** une malhonnêteté.
dishonour [dɪsˈɒnəʳ] 1 n déshonneur *m*, infamie *f*, opprobre *m* (*liter*).
2 vt a *family* déshonorer, porter atteinte à l'honneur de; *woman* déshonorer, séduire. b *bill, cheque* refuser d'honorer. **a ~ed cheque** un chèque impayé *or* refusé *or* non honoré.
dishonourable [dɪsˈɒnərəbl] adj *person* peu honorable; *action, conduct etc* déshonorant. (*Mil*) **~ discharge** renvoi *m* à la vie civile pour manquement à l'honneur.
dishonourably [dɪsˈɒnərəblɪ] adv avec déshonneur, de façon déshonorante. (*Mil*) **to be ~ discharged** être renvoyé à la vie civile pour manquement à l'honneur.
dishy‡ [ˈdɪʃɪ] adj (*Brit*) *person* excitant, sexy*, appétissant.
disillusion [ˌdɪsɪˈluːʒən] 1 vt désillusionner, désabuser. **to be ~ed** être désillusionné *or* désabusé *or* désenchanté (*with* en ce qui concerne, quant à); **to grow ~ed** perdre ses illusions. 2 n désillusion *f*, désenchantement *m*, désabusement *m* (*liter*).
disillusionment [ˌdɪsɪˈluːʒənmənt] n = **disillusion 2**.
disincentive [ˌdɪsɪnˈsentɪv] 1 n: **it's a real ~** cela a un effet dissuasif *or* de dissuasion; **this is a ~ to work** cela n'incite pas à travailler *or* au travail. 2 adj dissuasif.
disinclination [ˌdɪsɪnklɪˈneɪʃən] n manque *m* d'enthousiasme (*to do* à faire, *for sth* pour qch).
disinclined [ˈdɪsɪnˈklaɪnd] adj peu disposé, peu porté, peu enclin (*for* à, *to do* à faire).
disinfect [ˌdɪsɪnˈfekt] vt désinfecter.
disinfectant [ˌdɪsɪnˈfektənt] adj, n désinfectant (*m*).
disinfection [ˌdɪsɪnˈfekʃən] n désinfection *f*.
disinflation [ˌdɪsɪnˈfleɪʃən] n déflation *f*.
disinflationary [ˌdɪsɪnˈfleɪʃənərɪ] adj de déflation, déflationniste.
disinformation [ˌdɪsɪnfəˈmeɪʃən] n désinformation *f*.
disingenuous [ˌdɪsɪnˈdʒenjʊəs] adj déloyal, insincère, (*stronger*) fourbe.
disingenuousness [ˌdɪsɪnˈdʒenjʊəsnɪs] n déloyauté *f*, manque *m* de sincérité, fourberie *f*.
disinherit [ˈdɪsɪnˈherɪt] vt déshériter.
disintegrate [dɪsˈɪntɪgreɪt] 1 vi se désintégrer, se désagréger; (*Phys*) se désintégrer. 2 vt désintégrer, désagréger; (*Phys*) désintégrer.
disintegration [dɪsˌɪntɪˈgreɪʃən] n désintégration *f*, désagrégation *f*; (*Phys*) désintégration.
disinter [ˈdɪsɪnˈtɜːʳ] vt déterrer, exhumer.
disinterest [dɪsˈɪntrɪst] n (*impartialité*) désintéressement *m*; (*: *lack of interest*) indifférence *f*.
disinterested [dɪsˈɪntrɪstɪd] adj (*impartial*) désintéressé; (*: *uninterested*) indifférent.
disinterestedness [dɪsˈɪntrɪstɪdnɪs] n (*impartiality*) désintéressement *m*, altruisme *m*; (*: *lack of interest*) indifférence *f*.
disinterment [ˌdɪsɪnˈtɜːmənt] n déterrement *m*, exhumation *f*.
disintoxicate [ˌdɪsɪnˈtɒksɪkeɪt] vt désintoxiquer.
disintoxication [dɪsɪnˌtɒksɪˈkeɪʃən] n désintoxication *f*.

disinvest [ˌdɪsɪn'vest] vi désinvestir (*from* de).
disinvestment [ˌdɪsɪn'vestmənt] n désinvestissement *m* (*from* de).
disjoint [dɪs'dʒɔɪnt] adj (*Math*) disjoint.
disjointed [dɪs'dʒɔɪntɪd] adj *lecture, account, conversation* sans suite, décousu, incohérent; *style* haché, décousu.
disjunction [dɪs'dʒʌŋkʃən] n disjonction *f*.
disjunctive [dɪs'dʒʌŋktɪv] adj disjonctif. ~ **pronoun** forme *f* tonique du pronom.
disk [dɪsk] 1 n a (*esp US*) = **disc.** b (*Comput*) disque *m*. **on ~** sur disque; *see* **double, floppy, hard** *etc.* 2 comp ▸**disk capacity** (*Comput*) capacité *f* du disque ▸**disk drive** lecteur *m* de disques ▸**disk pack** unité *f* de disques.
diskette [dɪs'ket] n (*Comput*) disquette *f*.
dislike [dɪs'laɪk] 1 vt *person, thing* ne pas aimer, avoir de l'aversion pour. **to ~ doing** ne pas aimer faire; **I don't ~ it** cela ne me déplaît pas, je ne le déteste pas; **I ~ her** je la trouve antipathique *or* désagréable, elle ne me plaît pas, je ne l'aime pas; **I ~ this intensely** j'ai cela en horreur. 2 n aversion *f*, antipathie *f*. **his ~ of sb/sth** l'aversion qu'il ressent *or* l'antipathie qu'il éprouve pour qn/qch; **one's likes and ~s** ce que l'on aime et ce que l'on n'aime pas; **to take a ~ to sb/sth** prendre qn/qch en grippe.
dislocate ['dɪsləʊkeɪt] vt a *limb etc [person]* se disloquer, se démettre, se luxer; *[fall, accident]* disloquer, démettre, luxer. b (*fig*) *traffic, business* désorganiser; *plans, timetable* bouleverser.
dislocation [ˌdɪsləʊ'keɪʃən] n (*see* **dislocate**) dislocation *f*, luxation *f*, déboîtement *m*; bouleversement *m*.
dislodge [dɪs'lɒdʒ] vt *stone* déplacer, faire bouger; *cap, screw, nut* débloquer; *enemy* déloger; *person* faire bouger (*from* de).
disloyal ['dɪs'lɔɪəl] adj *person, behaviour* déloyal, infidèle (*to* à, envers).
disloyalty ['dɪs'lɔɪəltɪ] n déloyauté *f*, infidélité *f*.
dismal ['dɪzməl] adj *prospects, person, mood* lugubre, sombre, morne; *weather* maussade, morne. **the ~ science** la science funeste.
dismally ['dɪzməlɪ] adv lugubrement, d'un air sombre *or* maussade. **to fail ~** échouer lamentablement.
dismantle [dɪs'mæntl] vt *machine, furniture* démonter; *company, department* démanteler (*also Mil*).
dismantling [dɪs'mæntəlɪŋ] n *[company, department]* démantèlement *m*.
dismast [dɪs'mɑːst] vt démâter.
dismay [dɪs'meɪ] 1 n consternation *f*, désarroi *m*. **to my great ~** à ma grande consternation; **in ~** d'un air consterné. 2 vt consterner.
dismember [dɪs'membəʳ] vt démembrer (*also fig*).
dismemberment [dɪs'membəmənt] n démembrement *m*.
dismiss [dɪs'mɪs] vt a *employee* renvoyer, congédier, licencier; *official, officer* destituer, casser; *class, visitors* laisser partir,congédier; *assembly* dissoudre; *troops* faire rompre les rangs à. (*Mil*) **to be ~ed (from) the service** être renvoyé de l'armée *or* rayé des cadres; (*Mil*) **~!** rompez (les rangs)!; (*Scol*) **class ~!** partez!
b *subject of conversation* écarter, abandonner; *thought, possibility* écarter; *request* rejeter; *suggestion* écarter, exclure.
c (*gen*) *sb's appeal, claim* rejeter; (*Jur*) *accused* relaxer; *jury* congédier. (*Jur*) **to ~ sb's appeal** débouter qn de son appel; **to ~ a case** rendre une fin de non-recevoir; **to ~ a charge** rendre un (arrêt de *or* une ordonnance de) non-lieu.
dismissal [dɪs'mɪsəl] n (*see* **dismiss**) a licenciement *m*, renvoi *m*, congédiement *m*; destitution *f*; départ *m*; dissolution *f*. **he made a gesture of ~** d'un geste il les (*or* nous *etc*) a congédiés. b rejet *m*, abandon *m*, exclusion *f*. c (*Jur*) relaxe *f*; rejet *m*; *[jury]* congédiement *m*. **~ of case** fin *f* de non-recevoir; **~ of charge** non-lieu *m*.
dismissive [dɪs'mɪsɪv] adj dédaigneux.
dismissively [dɪs'mɪsɪvlɪ] adv dédaigneusement.
dismount [dɪs'maʊnt] 1 vi descendre (*from* de), mettre pied à terre. 2 vt *rider* démonter, désarçonner; *troops, gun, machine* démonter (*from* de).
disobedience [ˌdɪsə'biːdɪəns] n (*NonC*) désobéissance *f*, insoumission *f* (*to* à). **an act of ~** une désobéissance.
disobedient [ˌdɪsə'biːdɪənt] adj *child* désobéissant (*to* à); *soldier* indiscipliné, insubordonné. **he has been ~** il a été désobéissant, il a désobéi.
disobey ['dɪsə'beɪ] vt *parents, officer* désobéir à, s'opposer à; *law* enfreindre, violer.
disobliging ['dɪsə'blaɪdʒɪŋ] adj désobligeant, peu agréable.
disorder [dɪs'ɔːdəʳ] 1 n a (*NonC*) *[room, plans etc]* désordre *m*, confusion *f*. **to throw sth into ~** semer *or* jeter le désordre dans qch; **in ~** en désordre; (*Mil*) **to retreat in ~** être en déroute *or* en débâcle. b (*Pol etc: rioting*) désordres *mpl*, émeute *f*. c (*Med*) troubles *mpl*. **kidney/stomach/mental ~** troubles rénaux/gastriques/psychiques; **speech ~** difficulté *f* de langage. 2 vt *room* mettre en désordre; (*Med*) troubler, déranger.
disordered [dɪs'ɔːdəd] adj *room* en désordre; *imagination, existence* désordonné; (*Med*) *stomach* dérangé, malade; *mind* malade, déséquilibré.
disorderly [dɪs'ɔːdəlɪ] adj *room etc* en désordre; *flight, mind* désordonné; *behaviour, life* désordonné, déréglé; *crowd, meeting* désordonné, tumultueux. **~ house** (*brothel*) maison *f* de débauche; (*gambling den*) maison de jeu, tripot *m*; (*Jur*) **~ conduct** conduite *f* contraire aux bonnes mœurs; *see* **drunk.**
disorganization [dɪsˌɔːgənaɪ'zeɪʃən] n désorganisation *f*.
disorganize [dɪs'ɔːgənaɪz] vt désorganiser, déranger. **~d** *person* désorganisé; *room* mal rangé.
disorient [dɪs'ɔːrɪent] vt désorienter.
disorientate [dɪs'ɔːrɪənteɪt] vt désorienter.
disorientation [dɪs'ɔːrɪən'teɪʃən] n désorientation *f*.
disown [dɪs'əʊn] vt *child, country, opinion, document* désavouer, renier; *debt, signature* nier, renier.
disparage [dɪs'pærɪdʒ] vt dénigrer, décrier, déprécier.
disparagement [dɪs'pærɪdʒmənt] n dénigrement *m*, dépréciation *f*.
disparaging [dɪs'pærɪdʒɪŋ] adj peu flatteur, désobligeant, (plutôt) méprisant (*to* pour). **to be ~ about** faire des remarques désobligeantes *or* peu flatteuses sur.
disparagingly [dɪs'pærɪdʒɪŋlɪ] adv *look, speak* de façon désobligeante *or* peu flatteuse.
disparate ['dɪspərɪt] adj disparate.
disparity [dɪs'pærɪtɪ] n disparité *f*, inégalité *f*, écart *m*.
dispassionate [dɪs'pæʃənɪt] adj (*unemotional*) calme, froid; (*unbiased*) impartial, objectif.
dispassionately [dɪs'pæʃənɪtlɪ] adv (*unemotionally*) sans émotion, avec calme; (*unbiasedly*) impartialement, sans parti pris.
dispatch [dɪs'pætʃ] 1 vt a (*send*) *letter, goods* expédier, envoyer; *messenger* dépêcher; (*Mil*) *troops* envoyer, faire partir; *convoy* mettre en route; (*fig*) *food, drink* expédier.
b (*finish off*) *job* expédier, en finir avec; (*kill*) *person, animal* tuer, abattre.
2 n a *[letter, messenger, telegram etc]* envoi *m*, expédition *f*. **date of ~** date *f* d'expédition; **office of ~** bureau *m* d'origine.
b (*official report: also Mil*) dépêche *f*; (*Press*) dépêche (de presse). (*Mil*) **mentioned** *or* **cited in ~es** cité à l'ordre du jour.
c (*promptness*) promptitude *f*.
3 comp ▸**dispatch box** (*Brit Parl*) ≃ tribune *f* (*d'où parlent les membres du gouvernement*); (*case*) valise officielle (*à documents*) ▸**dispatch case** serviette *f*, porte-documents *m inv* ▸**dispatch documents** (*Comm*) documents *mpl* d'expédition ▸**dispatch rider** estafette *f*.
dispatcher [dɪs'pætʃəʳ] n expéditeur *m*, -trice *f*.
dispel [dɪs'pel] vt dissiper, chasser.
dispensable [dɪs'pensəbl] adj dont on peut se passer; (*Rel*) dispensable.
dispensary [dɪs'pensərɪ] n (*Brit*) (*in hospital*) pharmacie *f*; (*in chemist's*) officine *f*; (*clinic*) dispensaire *m*.
dispensation [ˌdɪspen'seɪʃən] n a (*handing out*) *[food]* distribution *f*; *[justice, charity]* exercice *m*, pratique *f*. b (*exemption*) (*gen, Jur, Rel*) dispense *f* (*from* de); (*Univ, Scol : from exam etc*) dispense *f*, dérogation *f*.
dispense [dɪs'pens] vt a *food* distribuer; *charity* pratiquer; *justice, sacrament* administrer; *hospitality* accorder, offrir. **to ~ alms** faire l'aumône (*to sb* à qn). b (*Pharm*) *medicine, prescription* préparer. **dispensing chemist** (*person*) pharmacien(ne) *m(f)*; (*shop*) pharmacie *f*. c (*also Rel: exempt*) dispenser, exempter (*sb from sth/from doing* qn de qch/de faire).
▸**dispense with** vt fus (*do without*) se passer de; (*make unnecessary*) rendre superflu.
dispenser [dɪs'pensəʳ] n (*Brit*) (*person*) pharmacien(ne) *m(f)*; (*device*) distributeur *m*.
dispersal [dɪs'pɜːsəl] n dispersion *f*.
dispersant [dɪs'pɜːsənt] n (*Chem*) dispersant *m*.
disperse [dɪs'pɜːs] 1 vt *crowd, mist* disperser; *sorrow* dissiper, chasser; *paper, seeds* disperser, éparpiller; *knowledge* disséminer, répandre, propager; (*Chem, Opt*) décomposer. *family, friends* **~d** dispersé. 2 vi se disperser; se dissiper; se disséminer, se propager; se décomposer.
dispersion [dɪs'pɜːʃən] n (*also Phys*) dispersion *f*. (*Hist*) **the D~** la dispersion des Juifs.
dispirit [dɪs'pɪrɪt] vt décourager, déprimer, abattre.
dispirited [dɪs'pɪrɪtɪd] adj découragé, déprimé, abattu.
dispiritedly [dɪs'pɪrɪtɪdlɪ] adv d'un air *or* d'un ton découragé, avec découragement.
dispiriting [dɪs'pɪrɪtɪŋ] adj décourageant, désolant.
displace [dɪs'pleɪs] vt a (*move out of place*) *refugees* déplacer; *furniture* déplacer, changer de place. **~d person** personne déplacée. b (*deprive of office*) *officer* destituer; *official* déplacer; (*replace*) supplanter, remplacer. c (*Naut, Phys*) *water* déplacer.
displacement [dɪs'pleɪsmənt] 1 n (*see* **displace**) déplacement *m*; destitution *f*; remplacement *m* (*by* par); (*Geol*) faille *f*. 2 comp ▸**displacement activity** (*Zool*) activité *f* de substitution; (*Psych*) déplacement *m* ▸**displacement tonnage** (*Naut*) déplacement *m*.
display [dɪs'pleɪ] 1 vt a (*show*) *object* montrer; (*pej: ostentatiously*) exhiber (*pej*). **he ~ed his medals proudly** il arborait fièrement ses

médailles; **she ~ed the letter she had received from the President** elle a montré *or* brandi la lettre qu'elle avait reçue du président; **she bought a cabinet to ~ her china collection in** elle a acheté une vitrine pour y exposer sa collection de porcelaines.

b (*set out visibly*) exposer; *goods for sale* exposer, mettre à l'étalage; *items in exhibition* exposer; *notice, results, poster* afficher.

c (*give evidence of*) *courage, interest, ignorance* faire preuve de; (*pej*) faire parade de, exhiber.

d (*Comput*) visualiser; *[electronic device, watch etc]* afficher.

e *[peacock]* étaler.

2 vi (*Zool*) parader.

3 n a (*NonC*) *[one's possessions, medals etc]* exposition *f*, déploiement *m*; (*pej: ostentatious*) étalage *m*; *[goods for sale]* étalage, exposition; *[items in exhibition]* exposition; *[notices, results, posters]* affichage *m*; *[courage, interest etc]* manifestation *f*. **on ~** exposé; (*Mil*) **a ~ of force** démonstration *f or* déploiement de force; (*pej*) **to make a great ~ of learning** faire parade de son érudition; **a fine ~ of paintings/china** *etc* une belle exposition de tableaux/de porcelaines *etc;* (*in shop window*) **the ~ of fruit** *etc* l'étalage de fruits *etc,* les fruits *etc* exposés.

b (*group, arrangement*) arrangement *m*.

c (*event, ceremony*) **~ of gymnastics/dancing** *etc* exhibition *f* de gymnastique/de danse *etc;* **military ~** parade *f* militaire; *see* **air**.

d (*Comput*) (*device*) écran *m* de visualisation, visuel *m*; (*visual information*) affichage *m*.

e (*Zool*) parade *f*.

4 comp (*Comm*) *goods* d'étalage ►**display advertising** (*Press*) placards *mpl* (publicitaires) ►**display cabinet, display case** vitrine *f* (*meuble*) ►**display pack** (*dummy*) emballage *m* de démonstration; (*attractive*) emballage de luxe ►**display panel** écran *m* d'affichage ►**display unit** (*Comput*) écran *m* de visualisation ►**display window** étalage *m*, vitrine *f* (*de magasin*).

displease [dɪs'pliːz] vt déplaire à, mécontenter, contrarier. **~d at** *or* **with** mécontent de.

displeasing [dɪs'pliːzɪŋ] adj désagréable (*to* à), déplaisant (*to* pour). **to be ~ to sb** déplaire à qn.

displeasure [dɪs'pleʒəʳ] n mécontentement *m*, déplaisir *m*. **to incur sb's ~** provoquer le mécontentement de qn; **to my great ~** à mon grand mécontentement *or* déplaisir.

disport [dɪs'pɔːt] vt: **to ~ o.s.** s'amuser, s'ébattre, folâtrer.

disposable [dɪs'pəʊzəbl] 1 adj a (*not reusable*) à jeter, à usage unique. **~ nappy** couche *f* à jeter, couche-culotte *f*; (*Comm*) **~ wrapping** emballage perdu. b (*available*) *objects, money* disponible. (*Fin*) **~ income** revenu *m* net (d'impôts et de retenues). 2 npl: **~s** (*containers*) emballage perdu *or* à jeter; (*bottles*) verre perdu; (*nappies*) couches *fpl* à jeter, couches-culottes *fpl*.

disposal [dɪs'pəʊzəl] 1 n a *[rubbish]* (*collection*) enlèvement *m*; (*destruction*) destruction *f*; *[goods for sale]* vente *f*; *[bomb]* désamorçage *m*; (*Jur*) *[property]* disposition *f*, cession *f*; *[problem, question]* résolution *f*; *[matters under discussion, current business]* expédition *f*, exécution *f*; *see* **bomb, refuse**[2]. b (*arrangement*) *[ornaments, furniture]* disposition *f*, arrangement *m*; *[troops]* disposition; (*control*) *[resources, funds, personnel]* disposition *f*. **the means at one's ~** les moyens à sa disposition *or* dont on dispose; **to put o.s./be at sb's ~** se mettre/être à la disposition de qn. 2 comp ►**(waste) disposal unit** broyeur *m* (d'ordures).

dispose [dɪs'pəʊz] vt a (*arrange*) *papers, ornaments* disposer, arranger; *troops* disposer; *forces* déployer. (*Prov*) **man proposes, God ~s** l'homme propose, Dieu dispose (*Prov*). b disposer, porter (*sb to do* qn à faire). **this does not ~ me to like him** ceci ne me rend pas bien disposé à son égard.

►**dispose of** vt fus a (*get rid of*) *sth no longer wanted or used* se débarrasser de, se défaire de, (*by selling*) vendre; *workers, staff* congédier, renvoyer, larguer*; *rubbish [householder etc]* jeter, se débarrasser de; *[refuse collection services]* (*remove*) enlever, (*destroy*) se débarrasser de, détruire; *[shop] stock* écouler, vendre; (*give away*) *one's property, money* disposer de (*to sb* à qn); (*fig: kill*) liquider*; (*Jur*) *property* aliéner.

b (*deal with*) *bomb* désamorcer; *question, problem* résoudre, expédier; *business* expédier; *one's opponent, opposing team* régler son compte à; *meal* liquider*, expédier. (*Jur*) **to dispose of a case** trancher une affaire, statuer.

c (*control*) *time, money* disposer de, avoir à sa disposition; (*settle*) *sb's fate* décider de.

disposed [dɪs'pəʊzd] adj disposé, enclin (*to do* à faire). **well-/ill-~ towards sb** bien/mal disposé *or* intentionné envers qn *or* à l'égard de qn.

disposer [dɪs'pəʊzəʳ] n (*also* **waste ~**) broyeur *m* (d'ordures).

disposition [ˌdɪspə'zɪʃən] n a (*temperament*) naturel *m*, caractère *m*, tempérament *m*. b (*readiness*) inclination *f* (*to do* à faire). c (*arrangement*) *[ornaments etc]* disposition *f*, arrangement *m*; *[troops]* disposition.

dispossess ['dɪspə'zes] vt déposséder, priver (*of* de); (*Jur*) exproprier.

dispossession [ˌdɪspə'zeʃən] n dépossession *f*; (*Jur*) expropriation *f*.

disproportion [ˌdɪsprə'pɔːʃən] n disproportion *f*.

disproportionate [ˌdɪsprə'pɔːʃnɪt] adj disproportionné (*to* à, avec).

disproportionately [ˌdɪsprə'pɔːʃnɪtlɪ] adv *react etc* d'une façon disproportionnée. **~ large** *etc* d'une grandeur *etc* disproportionnée.

disprove [dɪs'pruːv] vt établir *or* démontrer la fausseté de, réfuter.

disputable [dɪs'pjuːtəbl] adj discutable, contestable, douteux.

disputably [dɪs'pjuːtəblɪ] adv de manière contestable.

disputant [dɪs'pjuːtənt] n (*US Jur*) **the ~s** les parties *fpl* en litige.

disputation [ˌdɪspjuː'teɪʃən] n (*argument*) débat *m*, controverse *f*, discussion *f*; (††: *formal debate*) dispute†† *f*.

disputatious [ˌdɪspjuː'teɪʃəs] adj raisonneur.

dispute [dɪs'pjuːt] 1 n a (*NonC*) discussion *f*. **beyond ~** (adj) incontestable; (adv) incontestablement; **without ~** sans contredit; **there is some ~ about why he did it/what he's earning** on n'est pas d'accord sur ses motifs/le montant de son salaire; **there is some ~ about which horse won** il y a contestation sur le gagnant; **in** *or* **under ~** *matter* en discussion; *territory, facts, figures* contesté; (*Jur*) en litige; **statement open to ~** affirmation sujette à contradiction, affirmation contestable; **it is open to ~ whether he knew** on peut se demander s'il savait.

b (*quarrel*) dispute *f*; (*argument*) discussion *f*, débat *m*; (*Jur*) litige *m*; (*Ind, Pol*) conflit *m*. **to have a ~ with sb about sth** se disputer avec qn à propos de qch; (*Ind*) **industrial ~** conflit social; **the miners'/postal workers' ~** le conflit des mineurs/des employés des postes; **the transport/Post Office ~** le conflit dans les transports/dans les services postaux; **the United Shipping Company ~** le conflit chez United Shipping; **wages ~** conflit salarial *or* sur les salaires.

2 vt a (*cast doubt on*) *statement, claim* contester, mettre en doute; (*Jur*) *will* attaquer, contester. **I do not ~ the fact that ...** je ne conteste pas (le fait) que ... + *subj*.

b (*debate*) *question, subject* discuter, débattre.

c (*try to win*) *victory, possession* disputer (*with sb* à qn).

disputed [dɪs'pjuːtɪd] adj *decision* contesté, en discussion; *territory, fact* contesté; (*Jur*) en litige.

disqualification [dɪsˌkwɒlɪfɪ'keɪʃən] n disqualification *f* (*also Sport*), exclusion *f* (*from* de); (*Jur*) incapacité *f*. **his ~ (from driving)** le retrait de son permis (de conduire).

disqualify [dɪs'kwɒlɪfaɪ] vt a (*debar*) rendre inapte (*from sth* à qch, *from doing* à faire); (*Jur*) rendre inhabile (*from sth* à qch, *from doing* à faire); (*Sport*) disqualifier. (*Jur*) **to ~ sb from driving** retirer à qn son *or* le permis de conduire; (*Jur*) **he was disqualified for speeding** on lui a retiré son permis pour excès de vitesse; (*Jur*) **he was accused of driving while disqualified** il a été accusé d'avoir conduit alors qu'on lui avait retiré son permis. b (*incapacitate*) rendre incapable, mettre hors d'état (*from doing* de faire).

disquiet [dɪs'kwaɪət] 1 vt inquiéter, troubler, tourmenter. **to be ~ed about** s'inquiéter de. 2 n (*NonC*) inquiétude *f*, trouble *m*; (*unrest*) agitation *f*.

disquieting [dɪs'kwaɪətɪŋ] adj inquiétant, alarmant, troublant.

disquietude [dɪs'kwaɪɪtjuːd] n (*NonC*) inquiétude *f*, trouble *m*.

disquisition [ˌdɪskwɪ'zɪʃən] n (*treatise*) traité *m*, dissertation *f*, étude *f* (*on* sur); (*discourse*) communication *f* (*on* sur); (*investigation*) étude approfondie (*on* de).

disregard ['dɪsrɪ'gɑːd] 1 vt *fact, difficulty, remark* ne tenir aucun compte de, ne pas s'occuper de; *danger* mépriser, ne pas faire attention à; *feelings* négliger, faire peu de cas de; *authority, rules, duty* méconnaître, passer outre à. 2 n *[difficulty, comments, feelings]* indifférence *f* (*for* à); *[danger]* mépris *m* (*for* de); *[money]* mépris, dédain *m* (*for* de); *[safety]* négligence *f* (*for* en ce qui concerne); *[rule, law]* désobéissance *f* (*for* à), non-observation *f* (*for* de).

disrepair ['dɪsrɪ'pɛəʳ] n (*NonC*) mauvais état, délabrement *m*, dégradation *f*. **in a state of ~** *building* délabré; *road* en mauvais état; **to fall into ~** *[building]* tomber en ruines, se délabrer; *[road]* se dégrader.

disreputable [dɪs'repjʊtəbl] adj *person* de mauvaise réputation, louche, peu recommandable; *behaviour* honteux, déshonorant; *clothes* minable*, miteux; *area* louche, malfamé. **a ~ crowd** une bande d'individus louches *or* peu reluisants.

disreputably [dɪs'repjʊtəblɪ] adv *behave* d'une manière honteuse *or* peu honorable; *dress* minablement*.

disrepute ['dɪsrɪ'pjuːt] n discrédit *m*, déconsidération *f*, déshonneur *m*. **to bring into ~** faire tomber dans le discrédit; **to fall into ~** tomber en discrédit.

disrespect ['dɪsrɪs'pekt] n manque *m* d'égards *or* de respect, irrespect *m*, irrévérence *f*. **to show ~ to** manquer de respect envers.

disrespectful [ˌdɪsrɪs'pektfʊl] adj irrespectueux, irrévérencieux (*towards, to* envers). **to be ~ to** manquer de respect envers, se montrer irrespectueux envers.

disrespectfully [ˌdɪsrɪs'pektfəlɪ] adv irrespectueusement. **..., he said ~** ..., dit-il de façon irrespectueuse.

disrobe ['dɪs'rəʊb] 1 vi se dévêtir, enlever ses vêtements; (*undress*) se déshabiller. 2 vt enlever les vêtements (de cérémonie) à, dévêtir; déshabiller.

disrupt [dɪs'rʌpt] vt *peace, relations, train service* perturber; *conversation* interrompre; *plans* déranger, (*stronger*) mettre *or* semer la confusion dans; *communications* couper, interrompre.

disruption [dɪs'rʌpʃən] n (*see* **disrupt**) perturbation *f*; interruption *f*;

dérangement *m*.
disruptive [dɪsˈrʌptɪv] adj *element, factor* perturbateur (*f* -trice); (*Elec*) disruptif.
dissatisfaction [ˈdɪsˌsætɪsˈfækʃən] n mécontentement *m*, insatisfaction *f*. **growing/widespread ~** mécontentement croissant/général (*at, with* devant, provoqué par).
dissatisfied [ˈdɪsˈsætɪsfaɪd] adj mécontent, peu satisfait (*with* de).
dissect [dɪˈsekt] vt *animal, plant, truth* disséquer; *book, article* éplucher.
dissected [dɪˈsektɪd] adj (*Bot*) découpé.
dissection [dɪˈsekʃən] n (*Anat, Bot, fig*) dissection *f*.
dissemble [dɪˈsembl] 1 vt (*conceal*) dissimuler; (*feign*) feindre, simuler. 2 vi (*in speech*) dissimuler *or* déguiser *or* masquer sa pensée; (*in behaviour*) agir avec dissimulation.
disseminate [dɪˈsemɪneɪt] vt disséminer, semer. (*Med*) **~d sclerosis** sclérose *f* en plaques.
dissemination [dɪˌsemɪˈneɪʃən] n *[seeds]* dissémination *f*; *[ideas]* dissémination, propagation *f*.
dissension [dɪˈsenʃən] n dissension *f*, discorde *f*.
dissent [dɪˈsent] 1 vi différer (d'opinion *or* de sentiment) (*from sb* de qn); (*Rel*) être en dissidence, être dissident. (*US Jur*) **~ing opinion** avis *m* minoritaire de l'un des juges (*divergeant sur des questions de fond*). 2 n dissentiment *m*, différence *f* d'opinion; (*Rel*) dissidence *f*.
dissenter [dɪˈsentəʳ] n (*esp Rel*) dissident(e) *m(f)*.
dissentient [dɪˈsenʃɪənt] 1 adj dissident, opposé. 2 n dissident(e) *m(f)*, opposant(e) *m(f)*.
dissenting [dɪˈsentɪŋ] adj *voice* dissident. **a long ~ tradition** une longue tradition de dissidence.
dissertation [ˌdɪsəˈteɪʃən] n a (*written*) mémoire *m* (*on* sur); (*spoken*) exposé *m* (*on* sur). b (*Univ*) (*Brit*) mémoire *m*; (*US*) thèse *f* (de doctorat).
disservice [ˈdɪsˈsɜːvɪs] n mauvais service. **to do sb a ~** *[person]* ne pas rendre service à qn, rendre un mauvais service à qn; *[appearance etc]* constituer un handicap pour qn.
dissidence [ˈdɪsɪdəns] n dissidence *f* (*also Pol*), désaccord *m*, divergence *f* d'opinion.
dissident [ˈdɪsɪdənt] adj, n dissident(e) *m(f)*.
dissimilar [ˈdɪˈsɪmɪləʳ] adj dissemblable (*to* à), différent (*to* de).
dissimilarity [ˌdɪsɪmɪˈlærɪtɪ] n différence *f*, dissemblance *f* (*between* entre).
dissimulate [dɪˈsɪmjʊleɪt] vti dissimuler.
dissimulation [dɪˌsɪmjʊˈleɪʃən] n dissimulation *f*.
dissipate [ˈdɪsɪpeɪt] 1 vt *fog, clouds, fears, suspicions* dissiper; *hopes* anéantir; *energy, efforts* disperser, gaspiller; *fortune* dissiper, dilapider. 2 vi se dissiper.
dissipated [ˈdɪsɪpeɪtɪd] adj *life, behaviour* déréglé, de dissipation; *person* débauché. **to lead** *or* **live a ~ life** mener une vie déréglée *or* une vie de bâton de chaise.
dissipation [ˌdɪsɪˈpeɪʃən] n *[clouds, fears]* dissipation *f*; *[energy, efforts]* gaspillage *m*; *[fortune]* dilapidation *f*; (*debauchery*) dissipation, débauche *f*.
dissociate [dɪˈsəʊʃɪeɪt] vt dissocier, séparer (*from* de); (*Chem, Psych*) dissocier. **to ~ o.s. from** se dissocier de, se désolidariser de.
dissociation [dɪˌsəʊsɪˈeɪʃən] n (*all senses*) dissociation *f*.
dissoluble [dɪˈsɒljʊbl] adj soluble.
dissolute [ˈdɪsəluːt] adj *person* débauché, dissolu (*liter*); *way of life* dissolu, déréglé, de débauche.
dissolution [ˌdɪsəˈluːʃən] n (*all senses*) dissolution *f*.
dissolvable [dɪˈzɒlvəbl] adj soluble (*in* dans).
dissolve [dɪˈzɒlv] 1 vt a *[water etc] substance* dissoudre (*in* dans); *[person] chemical etc* faire dissoudre (*in* dans); (*Culin*) *sugar etc* faire fondre (*in* dans). b *alliance, marriage, assembly* dissoudre. 2 vi a (*Chem*) se dissoudre; (*Culin*) fondre. b (*fig*) *[hopes, fears]* disparaître, s'évanouir; (*Jur, Pol*) se dissoudre. (*fig*) **to ~ into thin air** s'en aller *or* partir en fumée; (*fig*) **to ~ into tears** fondre en larmes. c (*Cine*) se fondre. 3 n (*Cine, TV*) fondu *m* (enchaîné). **~ in/out** ouverture *f*/fermeture *f* en fondu.
dissolvent [dɪˈzɒlvənt] 1 adj dissolvant, dissolutif. 2 n dissolvant *m*, solvant *m*.
dissonance [ˈdɪsənəns] n dissonance *f*, discordance *f*.
dissonant [ˈdɪsənənt] adj dissonant, discordant.
dissuade [dɪˈsweɪd] vt dissuader (*sb from doing* qn de faire), détourner (*sb from sth* qn de qch). **to try to ~ sb from doing** déconseiller à qn de faire.
dissuasion [dɪˈsweɪʒən] n dissuasion *f*.
dissuasive [dɪˈsweɪsɪv] adj (*gen*) dissuasif; *voice, person* qui cherche à dissuader; *powers* de dissuasion.
distaff [ˈdɪstɑːf] n quenouille *f*. (*fig*) **on the ~ side** du côté maternel *or* des femmes.
distance [ˈdɪstəns] 1 n a (*in space*) distance *f* (*between* entre). **the ~ between the boys/the houses/the towns** la distance qui sépare les garçons/les maisons/les villes; **the ~ between the eyes/rails/posts** *etc* l'écartement *m* des yeux/des rails/des poteaux *etc;* **at a ~** assez loin, à quelque distance; **at a ~ of 2 metres** à une distance de 2 mètres; **what ~ is it from London?** c'est à quelle distance de *or* c'est à combien de Londres?; **what ~ is it from here to London?** nous sommes *or* on est à combien de Londres?; **it's a good ~** c'est assez loin; **in the ~** au loin, dans le lointain; **from a ~** de loin; **seen from a ~** vu de loin; **it's within walking/cycling ~** on peut y aller à pied/en vélo; **a short ~ away** à une faible distance; **within hailing ~** à portée de voix; **it's no ~*** c'est à deux pas, c'est tout près; **to cover the ~ in 2 hours** franchir *or* parcourir la distance en deux heures; **to go part of the ~ alone** faire une partie du trajet seul; (*Sport, fig*) **to go the ~** tenir la distance; **at an equal ~ from each other** à égale distance l'un de l'autre; *see* **long[1]**, **middle** *etc*.
b (*in time*) distance *f*, intervalle *m*, écart *m*. **at a ~ of 400 years** à 400 ans d'écart; **at this ~ in time** après un tel intervalle de temps, après tant d'années.
c (*in rank etc*) distance *f*. **to keep sb at a ~** tenir qn à distance *or* à l'écart; **to keep one's ~** garder ses distances.
2 vt (*Sport etc*) distancer. (*fig*) **to ~ o.s. from sth** se distancier de qch.
3 comp ▸**distance learning** (*Educ*) enseignement *m* à distance ▸**(long-)distance race** (*Sport*) épreuve *f* de fond ▸**distance teaching** (*Educ*) enseignement *m* à distance.
distancing [ˈdɪstənsɪŋ] n distanciation *f*.
distant [ˈdɪstənt] adj a *country, town* lointain, éloigné. **we had a ~ view of the church** nous avons vu l'église de loin; **the school is 2 km ~ from the church** l'école est à (une distance de) 2 km de l'église; (*US Mil*) **~ early warning line** DEW *f* (*système de radars*). b (*in time, age*) éloigné, reculé; *recollection* lointain. **in the ~ future/past** dans un avenir/un passé lointain. c (*fig*) *cousin, relationship* éloigné; *likeness* vague, lointain. d (*reserved*) *person, manner* distant, froid.
distantly [ˈdɪstəntlɪ] adv a *resemble* vaguement, un peu. **~ related** d'une parenté éloignée. b (*haughtily*) *smile, say* froidement, avec hauteur, d'une manière distante.
distaste [ˈdɪsˈteɪst] n dégoût *m*, répugnance *f* (*for* pour).
distasteful [dɪsˈteɪstfʊl] adj déplaisant, désagréable. **to be ~ to** déplaire à, être désagréable à.
distemper[1] [dɪsˈtempəʳ] 1 n (*paint*) détrempe *f*, badigeon *m*. 2 vt peindre en détrempe *or* à la détrempe, badigeonner.
distemper[2] [dɪsˈtempəʳ] n (*Vet*) maladie *f* des jeunes chiens *or* de Carré.
distend [dɪsˈtend] 1 vt distendre. (*Med*) **~ed stomach** ventre dilaté. 2 vi se distendre, se ballonner.
distension [dɪsˈtenʃən] n distension *f*, dilatation *f*.
distich [ˈdɪstɪk] n distique *m*.
distil, (*US*) **distill** [dɪsˈtɪl] 1 vt a *alcohol, knowledge* distiller. (*Aut etc*) **~led water** eau déminéralisée. b (*drip slowly*) laisser couler goutte à goutte. 2 vi se distiller; couler goutte à goutte.
distillation [ˌdɪstɪˈleɪʃən] n (*Chem etc, fig*) distillation *f*.
distiller [dɪsˈtɪləʳ] n distillateur *m*.
distillery [dɪsˈtɪlərɪ] n distillerie *f*.
distinct [dɪsˈtɪŋkt] adj a (*clear*) *landmark, voice, memory* distinct, clair, net; *promise, offer* précis, formel; *preference, likeness* marqué, net; *increase, progress* sensible, net (*before n*). b (*different*) distinct, différent, séparé (*from* de). **as ~ from** par opposition à.
distinction [dɪsˈtɪŋkʃən] n a (*difference*) distinction *f*, différence *f*; (*act of keeping apart*) distinction (*of ... from* de ... et de, *between* entre). **to make a ~ between two things** faire la *or* une distinction entre deux choses. b (*NonC*) (*pre-eminence*) distinction *f*, mérite *m*; (*refinement*) distinction. **to win ~** se distinguer, acquérir une *or* de la réputation; **a pianist of ~** un pianiste réputé *or* de marque; **she has great ~** elle est d'une grande distinction. c (*Univ etc*) **he got a ~ in French** il a été reçu en français avec mention très bien.
distinctive [dɪsˈtɪŋktɪv] adj distinctif, caractéristique; (*Phon*) distinctif; (*Semantics*) pertinent. **to be ~ of sth** caractériser qch.
distinctively [dɪsˈtɪŋktɪvlɪ] adv: **~ English/masculine** *etc* distinctement anglais/masculin; **~ patterned** au motif caractéristique.
distinctly [dɪsˈtɪŋktlɪ] adv a (*clearly etc*) *speak, hear, see* distinctement, clairement; *promise* sans équivoque; *stipulate* expressément, formellement. **he was told ~ that** on lui a bien précisé que, on lui a formellement stipulé que. b (*very*) *cold, frightening etc* vraiment. **~ better** incontestablement *or* sensiblement mieux.
distinguish [dɪsˈtɪŋgwɪʃ] 1 vt a (*discern*) *landmark* distinguer, apercevoir; *change* discerner, percevoir. b *object, series, person* (*make different*) distinguer (*from* de); (*characterize*) caractériser. **to ~ o.s.** se distinguer (*as* en tant que); (*iro*) **you've really ~ed yourself!** tu t'es vraiment distingué! (*iro*); *see also* **distinguished, distinguishing.** 2 vi: **to ~ between A and B** distinguer *or* faire la distinction entre A et B, distinguer A de B.
distinguishable [dɪsˈtɪŋgwɪʃəbl] adj a (*which can be differentiated*) *problems, people* qui peut être distingué, que l'on peut distinguer (*from* de). **easily ~ from each other** faciles à distinguer l'un de l'autre. b (*discernible*) *landmark, change* visible, perceptible.
distinguished [dɪsˈtɪŋgwɪʃt] adj (*refined etc*) distingué, qui a de la distinction; (*eminent*) *pianist, scholar* distingué. **~ for his bravery** remarquable par *or* remarqué pour son courage; (*US Univ*) **~ service professor** professeur *m* à titre personnel.

distinguishing [dɪsˈtɪŋgwɪʃɪŋ] adj distinctif, caractéristique. ~ **mark** caractéristique *f*; (*on passport*) signe particulier.
distort [dɪsˈtɔːt] 1 vt (*physically*) déformer, altérer; (*fig*) *truth* défigurer, déformer; *text* déformer; *judgment* fausser; *words, facts* dénaturer, déformer. 2 vi *[face]* se crisper.
distorted [dɪˈstɔːtɪd] adj (*lit*) déformé, altéré; (*fig*) *report, impression* faux (*f* fausse). **he gave us a ~ed version of the events** il a dénaturé les événements en les racontant.
distortion [dɪsˈtɔːʃən] n (*gen, Electronics, Med, Opt*) distorsion *f*; *[tree etc]* déformation *f*; *[features]* distorsion, altération *f*, décomposition *f*; *[shape, facts, text]* déformation, altération. **by ~ of the facts** en dénaturant les faits.
distract [dɪsˈtrækt] vt *person* (*interrupt*) distraire; (*destroy sb's concentration*) empêcher de se concentrer. **the noise ~ed him from working** le bruit le distrayait de son travail; **the noise ~ed him** le bruit l'empêchait de se concentrer; **he's busy, you mustn't ~ him** il est occupé, il ne faut pas le déranger; **to ~ sb's attention** détourner *or* distraire l'attention de qn (*from sth* de qch).
distracted [dɪsˈtræktɪd] adj éperdu, fou (*f* folle), égaré; *look* égaré, affolé. **to drive sb ~** faire perdre la tête à qn, rendre qn fou; **~ with worry** *etc* fou d'anxiété *etc*; **she was quite ~** elle était dans tous ses états.
distractedly [dɪsˈtræktɪdlɪ] adv *behave, run* comme un fou (*or* une folle), d'un air affolé; *love, weep* éperdument.
distracting [dɪsˈtræktɪŋ] adj gênant, qui empêche de se concentrer.
distraction [dɪsˈtrækʃən] n a (*NonC: lack of attention*) distraction *f*, inattention *f*. b (*interruption: to work etc*) interruption *f*; (*entertainment*) divertissement *m*, distraction *f*. c (*NonC: perplexity*) confusion *f*, trouble *m* d'esprit; (*madness*) affolement *m*. **to love to ~** aimer à la folie; **to drive sb to ~** *[noise etc]* rendre qn fou (*f* folle); *[love etc]* faire perdre la tête à qn.
distrain [dɪsˈtreɪn] vi (*Jur*) **to ~ upon sb's goods** saisir les biens de qn, opérer la saisie des biens de qn.
distrainee [ˌdɪstreɪˈniː] n (*Jur*) saisi *m*.
distrainor [dɪsˈtreɪnəʳ] n (*Jur*) saisissant *m*.
distraint [dɪsˈtreɪnt] n (*Jur*) saisie *f*, saisie-exécution *f* (*sur les meubles d'un débiteur*).
distraught [dɪsˈtrɔːt] adj éperdu (*with, from* de), égaré, affolé.
distress [dɪsˈtres] 1 n a (*physical*) douleur *f*; (*mental*) douleur, chagrin *m*, affliction *f*. **to be in great ~** (*physical*) souffrir beaucoup; (*mental*) être bouleversé, être (plongé) dans l'affliction; **to be in great ~ over sth** être bouleversé *or* profondément affligé de qch; **to cause ~ to** causer une grande peine *or* douleur à.
b (*great poverty*) détresse *f*, misère *f*. **in ~** dans la détresse.
c (*danger*) péril *m*, détresse *f*. **a ship in ~** un navire en perdition; **a plane in ~** un avion en détresse; **comrades in ~** compagnons *mpl* d'infortune.
d (*Jur*) saisie *f*.
2 vt affliger, peiner.
3 comp ►**distress rocket** = **distress signal** ►**distress sale** vente *f* de biens saisis ►**distress signal** signal *m* de détresse.
distressed [dɪsˈtrest] adj affligé, peiné (*by* par, de). **she was very ~** elle était bouleversée; (*Brit*) **~ area** zone sinistrée; **in ~ circumstances** dans la détresse *or* la misère; **~ gentlewomen** dames *fpl* de bonne famille dans le besoin.
distressful [dɪsˈtresfʊl] adj = **distressing**.
distressing [dɪsˈtresɪŋ] adj *situation, experience* pénible; *poverty, inadequacy* lamentable.
distressingly [dɪsˈtresɪŋlɪ] adv *poor, inadequate* lamentablement.
distributary [dɪsˈtrɪbjʊtərɪ] 1 n (*Geog*) défluent *m*. 2 adj de distribution.
distribute [dɪsˈtrɪbjuːt] vt *leaflets, prizes, type* distribuer; *dividends, load, weight* répartir; *money* distribuer, partager, répartir; (*Comm*) *goods* être concessionnaire de; *films* être distributeur de. **to ~ into categories** répartir en catégories.
distribution [dɪstrɪˈbjuːʃən] n (*see* **distribute**) distribution *f* (*also Comm, Ling, Econ*); répartition *f*. (*Econ*) **the ~ of wealth** la répartition *or* distribution des richesses; **~ network** réseau *m* de distribution.
distributional [ˌdɪstrɪˈbjuːʃənəl] adj (*Comm*) de distribution; (*Ling*) distributionnel.
distributive [dɪsˈtrɪbjʊtɪv] 1 adj (*Comm, Gram, Philos etc*) distributif. (*Econ*) **the ~ trades** le secteur de la distribution. 2 n (*Gram*) pronom *or* adjectif distributif.
distributor [dɪsˈtrɪbjʊtəʳ] n a (*Comm*) *[goods over an area]* concessionnaire *mf*; *[films]* distributeur *m*. **~ network** réseau *m* de distributeurs. b (*Tech: device*) distributeur *m*; (*Aut*) Delco *m* ®, distributeur. (*Aut*) **~ cap** tête *f* de Delco ®.
district [ˈdɪstrɪkt] 1 n (*of a country*) région *f*; (*in town*) quartier *m*; (*administrative area*) district *m*, (*in Paris etc*) arrondissement *m*; (*US Pol*) circonscription électorale (*or* administrative); *see* **electoral, postal.** 2 comp ►**district attorney** (*US Jur*) représentant *m* du ministère public, ≃ procureur *m* de la République ►**district commissioner** (*Brit*) commissaire *m* ►**district council** (*Brit: Local Govt*) ≃ conseil général ►**district court** (*US Jur*) cour fédérale (de grande instance) ►**district heating** ≃ chauffage urbain ►**district manager** (*Comm*) directeur régional ►**district nurse** infirmière visiteuse.
distrust [dɪsˈtrʌst] 1 vt se méfier de, se défier de. **a ~ed method** une méthode dont tout le monde se méfie *or* qui n'inspire pas confiance. 2 n méfiance *f*. **to feel some ~ of sb/sth** éprouver de la méfiance à l'égard de qn/qch.
distrustful [dɪsˈtrʌstfʊl] adj méfiant, qui se méfie (*of* de).
disturb [dɪsˈtɜːb] vt a (*inconvenience*) *person* déranger. **don't ~ yourself!** ne vous dérangez pas!; **sorry to ~ you** excusez-moi de vous déranger; (*on notice*) **"please do not ~"** "prière de ne pas déranger". b (*alarm*) *person* troubler, inquiéter. **the news ~ed him greatly** la nouvelle l'a beaucoup troublé *or* ébranlé. c (*interrupt*) *silence, balance* troubler, rompre; *sleep, rest* troubler. d (*disarrange*) *waters, sediment* troubler, remuer; *air, atmosphere* perturber. **don't ~ those papers** ne dérangez pas ces papiers, laissez ces papiers comme ils sont.
disturbance [dɪsˈtɜːbəns] n a (*political, social*) troubles *mpl*, émeute *f*; (*in house, street*) bruit *m*, tapage *m*. **to cause a ~** faire du bruit *or* du tapage; (*Jur*) **~ of the peace** tapage injurieux *or* nocturne. b (*NonC*) *[routine, papers]* dérangement *m*; *[liquid]* agitation *f*; *[air, atmosphere]* perturbation *f*. c (*NonC: alarm, uneasiness*) trouble *m* (d'esprit), perturbation *f* (de l'esprit).
disturbed [dɪsˈtɜːbd] adj a *person* agité, troublé; (*Psych*) perturbé, troublé. **to be greatly ~** être très troublé (*at, by* par). b *waters* troublé; *night, sleep* agité, troublé.
disturbing [dɪsˈtɜːbɪŋ] adj (*alarming*) inquiétant, troublant; (*distracting*) gênant, ennuyeux.
disturbingly [dɪsˈtɜːbɪŋlɪ] adv de façon inquiétante. **a ~ high number/percentage** un nombre/pourcentage inquiétant.
disunite [ˈdɪsjuːˈnaɪt] vt désunir.
disunity [ˌdɪsˈjuːnɪtɪ] n désunion *f*.
disuse [ˈdɪsˈjuːs] n désuétude *f*. **to fall into ~** tomber en désuétude.
disused [ˈdɪsˈjuːzd] adj *building* désaffecté, abandonné.
disyllabic [ˌdɪsɪˈlæbɪk] adj dissyllabe, dissyllabique.
ditch [dɪtʃ] 1 n (*by roadside, between fields etc*) fossé *m*; (*for irrigation*) rigole *f*; (*around castle*) douve *f*. (*Aviat sl*) **the ~** la patouille‡, la baille (*sl*); *see* **last¹**. 2 vt a (**: get rid of*) *person* plaquer*, laisser tomber*; *car etc* abandonner. **to ~ a plane** faire un amerrissage forcé. b (*US*) *class* sécher*.
ditcher [ˈdɪtʃəʳ] n terrassier *m*.
ditching [ˈdɪtʃɪŋ] n a creusement *m* de fossés. **hedging and ~** entretien *m* des haies et fossés. b (*Aviat*) amerrissage forcé (*d'un avion*).
dither* [ˈdɪðəʳ] (*esp Brit*) 1 n panique *f*. **to be in a ~, to be all of a ~** être dans tous ses états, paniquer*. 2 vi hésiter, se tâter. **to ~ over a decision** se tâter pour prendre une décision; **stop ~ing and get on with it!** il n'y a pas à tortiller*, il faut que tu t'y mettes!
►**dither about*, dither around*** vi tourner en rond (*fig*).
ditherer [ˈdɪðərəʳ] n (*Brit*) indécis(e) *m(f)*. **don't be such a ~!** ne sois pas si indécis!
ditto [ˈdɪtəʊ] 1 adv idem. **you made a mistake and Robert ~*** tu t'es trompé et Robert idem* *or* aussi. 2 comp ►**ditto mark, ditto sign** guillemets *mpl* de répétition.
ditty [ˈdɪtɪ] n chansonnette *f*.
diuresis [ˌdaɪjʊˈriːsɪs] n diurèse *f*.
diuretic [ˌdaɪjʊəˈretɪk] adj, n diurétique (*m*).
diurnal [daɪˈɜːnl] 1 adj (*Astron, Bot*) diurne. 2 n (*Rel*) diurnal *m*.
diva [ˈdiːvə] n, pl **~s** *or* **dive** diva *f*, grande cantatrice.
divan [dɪˈvæn] 1 n divan *m*. 2 comp ►**divan bed** divan-lit *m*.
dive¹ [daɪv] 1 n a *[swimmer, goalkeeper]* plongeon *m*; *[submarine, deep-sea diver etc]* plongée *f*; *[aircraft]* piqué *m*. (*fig*) **to make a ~** foncer (tête baissée); *[profits, sales etc]* **to take a ~, go into a ~** dégringoler, plonger, chuter.
b (‡ *pej: club, café etc*) bouge *m*.
2 comp ►**dive-bomb** bombarder en piqué ►**dive bomber** bombardier *m* (*qui bombarde en piqué*) ►**dive bombing** bombardement *m* en piqué.
3 vi a *[swimmer etc]* plonger, faire un plongeon; *[submarine]* plonger, s'immerger; *[aircraft]* piquer du nez, plonger, descendre en piqué. **he ~d in head first** il a piqué une tête dans l'eau; **to ~ for pearls** pêcher des perles.
b **to ~ in/out** *etc* entrer/sortir *etc* tête baissée; **he ~d for the exit** il a foncé (tête baissée) vers la sortie; **he ~d into the crowd** il s'est engouffré dans la foule; **he ~d under the table** il s'est jeté sous la table; **to ~ for cover** se précipiter pour se mettre à l'abri; (*Ftbl*) **the goalie ~d for the ball** le gardien de but a plongé pour bloquer le ballon; (*fig*) **to ~ into one's pocket** plonger la main dans sa poche.
►**dive in** vi a *[swimmer]* plonger. b (‡: *start to eat*) **dive in!** attaquez!*
dive² [ˈdiːvɪ] npl of **diva**.
diver [ˈdaɪvəʳ] n a (*person*) plongeur *m*; (*in suit*) scaphandrier *m*; (*in diving bell*) plongeur (sous-marin); *see* **skin.** b (*Orn*) plongeon *m*, plongeur *m*.
diverge [daɪˈvɜːdʒ] vi *[lines, paths]* diverger, s'écarter; *[opinions, stories, explanations]* diverger.

divergence [daɪˈvɜːdʒəns] n divergence *f*.
divergent [daɪˈvɜːdʒənt] adj divergent. ~ **thinking** raisonnement divergent.
divers [ˈdaɪvɜːz] adj (*liter*) divers, plusieurs.
diverse [daɪˈvɜːs] adj divers, différent.
diversification [daɪˌvɜːsɪfɪˈkeɪʃən] n diversification *f*.
diversify [daɪˈvɜːsɪfaɪ] vt diversifier, varier.
diversion [daɪˈvɜːʃən] n a (*Brit: redirecting*) *[traffic]* déviation *f*; *[stream]* dérivation *f*, détournement *m*. b (*relaxation*) divertissement *m*, distraction *f*, diversion *f*. **it's a ~ from work** cela change *or* distrait du travail. c (*Mil etc*) diversion *f*. **to create a ~** (*Mil*) opérer une diversion; (*in class, during argument etc*) faire diversion.
diversionary [daɪˈvɜːʃnərɪ] adj *remark, behaviour* destiné à faire diversion; (*Mil*) *landing, manoeuvre* de diversion.
diversity [daɪˈvɜːsɪtɪ] n diversité *f*, variété *f*.
divert [daɪˈvɜːt] vt a (*turn away*) *stream* détourner, dériver; *train, plane, ship* dérouter, détourner; (*Brit*) *traffic* dévier; *attention, eyes* détourner; *conversation* détourner, faire dévier; *blow* écarter. b (*amuse*) divertir, distraire, amuser.
diverting [daɪˈvɜːtɪŋ] adj divertissant, amusant.
divest [daɪˈvest] vt (*of clothes, weapons*) dévêtir, dépouiller (*of* de); (*of rights, property*) dépouiller, priver (*of* de); *room* dégarnir.
divide [dɪˈvaɪd] 1 vt a (*separate*) séparer (*from* de). **the Pyrenees ~ France from Spain** les Pyrénées séparent la France de l'Espagne. b (*split: often ~* **up**: *gen*) diviser (*into* en; *among, between* entre); *money, work* diviser, partager, répartir; *property, kingdom* diviser, démembrer, morceler; *house* diviser, partager (*into* en); *apple, room* diviser, couper (*into* en); *one's time, attention* partager (*between* entre). **they ~d it (amongst themselves)** ils se le sont partagé. c (*Math*) diviser. **to ~ 6 into 36, to ~ 36 by 6** diviser 36 par 6. d (*cause disagreement among*) *friends, political parties etc* diviser. (*Pol etc*) **policy of ~ and rule** politique *f* consistant à diviser pour mieux régner. e (*Brit Parl*) **to ~ the House** faire voter la Chambre. 2 vi a *[river]* se diviser; *[road]* bifurquer. b (*also ~* **up**) *[people]* se diviser, se séparer (*into groups* en groupes); (*Bio*) *[cells etc]* se diviser. c (*Math*) être divisible (*by* par). d (*Brit Parl*) **the House ~d** la Chambre a procédé au vote *or* a voté. 3 n (*Geog*) ligne *f* de partage des eaux. **the Great D~** ligne de partage des montagnes Rocheuses.
▸**divide off** 1 vi se séparer (*from* de). 2 vt sep séparer (*from* de).
▸**divide out** vt sep répartir, distribuer (*among* entre).
▸**divide up** 1 vi = **divide 2b**. 2 vt sep = **divide 1b**.
divided [dɪˈvaɪdɪd] adj a (*lit*) divisé; (*Bot*) découpé. (*US*) ~ **highway** route *f* à chaussées séparées *or* à quatre voies; ~ **skirt** jupe-culotte *f*. b (*fig: in disagreement*) *people* divisé; *opinion* partagé; *couple, country* désuni. **they were ~ on (the question of) the death penalty** ils étaient divisés sur la question de la peine de mort; **opinions are ~ on that** les avis sont partagés là-dessus. c (*vacillating*) indécis. **I feel ~ (in my own mind) about this** je me sens partagé *or* indécis à cet égard.
dividend [ˈdɪvɪdend] n (*Fin, Math*) dividende *m*; *see* **pay**.
divider [dɪˈvaɪdəʳ] n a **~s** compas *m* à pointes sèches. b *see* **room 3**.
dividing [dɪˈvaɪdɪŋ] adj *wall, fence* mitoyen. ~ **line** ligne *f* de démarcation.
divination [ˌdɪvɪˈneɪʃən] n (*lit, fig*) divination *f*.
divine¹ [dɪˈvaɪn] 1 adj (*Rel, fig*) divin. **D~ Providence** la divine Providence; (*Hist*) ~ **right of kings** le droit divin des rois; **by ~ right** de droit divin; (*Rel*) ~ **service/office** service/office divin; **my wife/that music** *etc* **is ~*** ma femme/cette musique *etc* est divine. 2 n ecclésiastique *m*, théologien *m*.
divine² [dɪˈvaɪn] 1 vt a (*foretell*) *the future* présager, prédire. b (*make out*) *sb's intentions* deviner, pressentir. c (*find*) *water, metal* découvrir par la radiesthésie. 2 comp ▸**divining rod** baguette *f* divinatoire *or* de sourcier.
divinely [dɪˈvaɪnlɪ] adv (*Rel, fig*) divinement.
diviner [dɪˈvaɪnəʳ] n *[future etc]* devin *m*, devineresse *f*; *[water]* radiesthésiste *mf*.
diving [ˈdaɪvɪŋ] 1 n a (*underwater*) plongée sous-marine; (*skill*) art *m or* (*trade*) métier *m* du plongeur *or* du scaphandrier; *see* **skin**. b (*from diving board*) plongeon(s) *m(pl)*. (*Sport*) **platform high ~** plongée *f* de haut vol. 2 comp ▸**diving bell** cloche *f* à plongeur ▸**diving board** plongeoir *m*; (*springboard*) tremplin *m* ▸**diving suit** scaphandre *m*.
divinity [dɪˈvɪnɪtɪ] n a (*quality; god*) divinité *f*. **the D~** la Divinité. b (*theology*) théologie *f*.
divisible [dɪˈvɪzəbl] adj divisible (*by* par).
division [dɪˈvɪʒən] 1 n a (*act, state*) division *f*, séparation *f* (*into* en); (*sharing*) partage *m*, répartition *f*, distribution *f* (*between, among* entre); (*Bot, Math*) division. ~ **of labour** division du travail; *see* **long¹ 1a, short 1a, simple 1a**. b (*part: gen, Admin, Comm, Mil, Naut*) division *f*; (*Brit Police*) circonscription administrative; (*category*) classe *f*, catégorie *f*, section *f*; (*Ftbl etc*) division; (*in box, case*) division, compartiment *m*. c (*that which divides*) séparation *f*; (*in room*) cloison *f*; (*fig: between social classes etc*) barrière *f*; (*dividing line: lit, fig*) division *f*. d (*discord*) division *f*, désaccord *m*, brouille *f*. e (*Brit Parl*) **to call a ~** passer au vote; **to call for a ~** demander la mise aux voix; **the ~ took place at midnight** la Chambre a procédé au vote à minuit; **without a ~** sans procéder au vote; **to carry a ~** avoir la majorité des voix. 2 comp ▸**division bell** (*Brit Parl*) sonnerie *f* qui annonce la mise aux voix ▸**division sign** (*Math*) symbole *m* de division.
divisional [dɪˈvɪʒənl] adj divisionnaire. ~ **coin** monnaie *f* divisionnaire.
divisive [dɪˈvaɪsɪv] adj qui entraîne la division, qui sème la discorde.
divisiveness [dɪˈvaɪsɪvnɪs] n: **the ~ of this decision** les dissensions causées par cette décision.
divisor [dɪˈvaɪzəʳ] n (*Math*) diviseur *m*.
divorce [dɪˈvɔːs] 1 n (*Jur, fig*) divorce *m* (*from* d'avec). **to get a ~ from** obtenir le divorce d'avec. 2 vt (*Jur*) divorcer avec *or* d'avec; (*fig*) séparer (*from* de). **SHE ~d HIM** c'est elle qui a demandé le divorce *or* a voulu divorcer; (*fig*) **one cannot ~ this case from ...** on ne peut pas séparer ce cas de ... . 3 vi divorcer. 4 comp ▸**divorce court** ≃ tribunal *m* de grande instance ▸**divorce proceedings** procédure *f* de divorce; **to start divorce proceedings** former une requête de divorce, demander le divorce.
divorced [dɪˈvɔːst] adj (*Jur*) divorcé (*from* d'avec).
divorcee [dɪˌvɔːˈsiː] n divorcé(e) *m(f)*.
divot [ˈdɪvɪt] n (*esp Golf*) motte *f* de gazon.
divulge [daɪˈvʌldʒ] vt divulguer, révéler.
divvy [ˈdɪvɪ] 1 n (*Brit* *) abbr of **dividend**. 2 vt (*US* ⁑: *also* ~ **up**) partager.
Dixie [ˈdɪksɪ] 1 n (*US*) États *mpl* du Sud. 2 comp ▸**Dixie Democrat** (*US Pol*) démocrate *mf* du Sud.
dixie [ˈdɪksɪ] n (*Brit Mil sl: also ~* **can**) gamelle *f*.
Dixieland [ˈdɪksɪlænd] 1 n = **Dixie 1**. 2 comp ▸**Dixieland jazz** le jazz (genre) Dixieland.
DIY [diːaɪˈwaɪ] (*Brit*) abbr of **do-it-yourself**.
dizzily [ˈdɪzɪlɪ] adv a (*giddily*) *walk* avec un sentiment de vertige; *rise, fall, spin* d'une façon vertigineuse, vertigineusement. b (*fig: foolishly*) bêtement, de façon étourdie, étourdiment.
dizziness [ˈdɪzɪnɪs] n (*state*) vertige(s) *m(pl)*; (*also* **attack of ~**) vertige, étourdissement *m*, éblouissement *m*.
dizzy [ˈdɪzɪ] 1 adj a (*Med*) *person* pris de vertiges *or* d'étourdissements. **to feel ~** (*gen: unwell*) être pris de vertiges *or* d'étourdissements; (*from fear of heights*) avoir le vertige; **it makes me ~** cela me donne le vertige, j'en ai la tête qui tourne; **it makes one ~ to think of it** c'est à donner le vertige (rien que d'y penser); ~ **spell** étourdissement *m*, vertige *m*. b *height, speed, rise in price* vertigineux. c (*fig: heedless etc*) *person* tête de linotte *inv*, étourdi. 2 vt (*confuse*) *person* étourdir, donner des vertiges à.
DJ [diːˈdʒeɪ] n (abbr of **disc jockey**) disc-jockey *m*, animateur *m*, -trice *f*.
Djakarta [dʒəˈkɑːtə] n Jakarta.
Djibouti [dʒɪˈbuːtɪ] n Djibouti. **in ~** à Djibouti.
djinn [dʒɪn] n djinn *m*.
dl (abbr of **decilitre(s)**) dl.
D Lit(t) [diːˈlɪt] n (abbr of **Doctor of Literature** *and* **Doctor of Letters**) *doctorat ès Lettres*.
dm (abbr of **decimetre(s)**) dm.
DMus n (abbr of **Doctor of Music**) *doctorat de musique*.
DNA [diːenˈeɪ] n (*Med*) (abbr of **deoxyribonucleic acid**) A.D.N. *m*.
Dnieper [ˈdniːpəʳ] n Dniepr *m*.
do. (abbr of **ditto**) id., idem.
do¹ [duː] 3rd person sg present **does**, pret **did**, ptp **done** 1 aux vb a (*used to form interrog and neg in present and pret verbs*). **~ you understand?** comprenez-vous?, (est-ce que) vous comprenez?; **I ~ not** *or* **don't understand** je ne comprends pas; **didn't you** *or* **did you not speak?** n'avez-vous pas parlé?; **never did I see so many** jamais je n'en ai autant vu. b (*for emphasis: with stress on "do"*) **DO come!** venez donc, je vous en prie!; **DO tell him that ...** dites-lui bien que ...; **but I DO like it!** mais si je l'aime!, mais bien sûr que je l'aime!; **he DID say it** bien sûr qu'il l'a dit, il l'a bien dit; **so you DO know them!** alors c'est vrai que vous les connaissez!; **I DO wish I could come with you** je voudrais tant pouvoir vous accompagner; **do you like Paris? — do I like PARIS!**⁑ Paris te plaît-il? — ah si Paris me plaît!* c (*vb substitute: used to avoid repeating verb*) **you speak better than I ~** vous parlez mieux que moi *or* que je ne le fais; **she always says she will go but she never does** elle dit toujours qu'elle ira mais elle n'y va jamais; **so ~ I** moi aussi; **she used to like him and so did I** elle l'aimait bien et moi aussi (je l'aimais); **neither ~ I** ni moi, moi non plus; **he doesn't like butter and neither ~ I** il n'aime pas le beurre et moi non plus; **he said he would write to me and I believe he will ~ (so)** il a dit qu'il m'écrirait et je crois qu'il le fera; **they said he would go and so he did** on a dit qu'il s'en irait et c'est ce qui est arrivé *or* et c'est bien ce qu'il a fait; **you know him, don't you?** vous le connaissez, n'est-ce pas?; **(so) you know him, ~ you?** alors vous le connaissez?; **you DO agree, don't you?** vous êtes bien d'accord, n'est-ce pas?; **he didn't go,**

did he? il n'y est pas allé, tout de même?; **she said that, did she?** elle a vraiment dit ça?, elle a osé dire ça?; **she said that, didn't she?** elle a bien dit ça, n'est-ce pas?; **I like them, don't you?** je les aime, pas vous?; **~ you see them often? — yes, I ~** vous les voyez souvent? — oui bien sûr *or* oui (je les vois souvent); **they speak French — oh, ~ they?** ils parlent français — ah oui? *or* vraiment? *or* c'est vrai?; **they speak French — ~ they really?** ils parlent français — non, c'est vrai? *or* vraiment?; **may I come in? — ~!** puis-je entrer? — bien sûr! *or* je vous en prie! (*frm*); **shall I open the window? — no, don't!** si j'ouvrais la fenêtre? — ah non!; **I'll tell him — don't!** je vais le lui dire — surtout pas!; **who broke the mirror? — I did** qui est-ce qui a cassé le miroir? — (c'est) moi.

2 **vt** a (*be busy with, involved in, carry out*) faire. **what are you ~ing (now)?** qu'est-ce que tu fais? *or* qu'es-tu en train de faire?; **what are you ~ing (these days** *or* **with yourself)?** qu'est-ce que tu deviens?; **what do you ~ (for a living)?** que faites-vous dans la vie?; **what shall I ~ next?** qu'est-ce que je dois faire ensuite?; **I've got plenty to ~** j'ai beaucoup à faire, j'ai largement de quoi m'occuper; **there's nothing to ~ here** il n'y a rien à faire ici; **I don't know what to ~** je ne sais que faire, je ne sais pas quoi faire; **are you ~ing anything this evening?** êtes-vous pris ce soir?, vous faites quelque chose ce soir?; **I shall ~ nothing of the sort** je n'en ferai rien; **don't ~ too much!** n'en faites pas trop!; (*don't overwork*) ne vous surmenez pas!; **he does nothing but complain** il ne fait que se plaindre, il ne cesse (pas) de se plaindre; **what must I ~ to get better?** que dois-je faire pour guérir?; **what shall we ~ for money?** comment allons-nous faire pour trouver de l'argent?; **what have you done with my gloves?** qu'avez-vous fait de mes gants?

b (*perform, accomplish*) faire, accomplir, rendre. **I'll ~ all I can** je ferai tout mon possible; **to ~ one's best** faire (tout) son possible, faire de son mieux; **I'll ~ my best to come** je ferai (tout) mon possible *or* je ferai de mon mieux pour venir; **how do you ~ it?** comment faites-vous?, comment vous y prenez-vous?; **what's to be done?** que faire?; **what can I ~ for you?** en quoi puis-je vous aider? *or* vous être utile?; **what do you want me to ~ (about it)?** qu'est-ce que vous voulez que je fasse? *or* que j'y fasse?; **to ~ sth again** refaire qch; **it's all got to be done again** tout est à refaire *or* à recommencer; **~ something for me, will you?** rends-moi (un) service, veux-tu?; **what's done cannot be undone** ce qui est fait est fait; **that's just not done!** cela ne se fait pas!; **well done!** bravo!, très bien!; **that's done it!*** (*dismay*) il ne manquait plus que ça!; (*satisfaction*) (voilà) ça y est!; **it's as good as done** c'est comme si c'était fait; **no sooner said than done** aussitôt dit aussitôt fait; **it's easier said than done** c'est plus facile à dire qu'à faire; **I've done a stupid thing** j'ai fait une bêtise; (*Theat*) **to ~ a play** monter une pièce; (*Cine*) **to ~ a film** tourner un film; **to ~ one's military service** faire son service militaire; **to ~ 6 years (in jail)** faire 6 ans de prison; *see* **bit²**, **credit**, **good** *etc*.

c (*make, produce*) faire. **~ this letter and 6 copies** faites cette lettre et 6 copies; **I'll ~ a translation for you** je vais vous (en) faire *or* donner la traduction, je vais vous le traduire; *see* **wonder** *etc*.

d (*Scol etc: study*) faire, étudier. **we've done Milton** nous avons étudié *or* fait Milton; **I've never done any German** je n'ai jamais fait d'allemand.

e (*solve*) faire. **to ~ a crossword/a problem** faire des mots croisés/un problème; (*Math*) **to ~ a sum** faire un calcul *or* une opération.

f (*translate*) traduire, mettre (*into* en).

g (*arrange*) **to ~ the flowers** arranger les fleurs (dans les vases); **to ~ one's hair** se coiffer; **I can't ~ my tie** je n'arrive pas à faire mon nœud de cravate.

h (*clean, tidy*) faire, laver, nettoyer. **to ~ one's nails** se faire les ongles; **to ~ one's teeth** se laver *or* se brosser les dents; **to ~ the shoes** cirer les chaussures; **this room needs ~ing today** cette pièce est à faire aujourd'hui; **to ~ the dishes/housework** faire la vaisselle/le ménage; *see* **washing** *etc*.

i (*deal with*) faire, s'occuper de. **the barber said he'd ~ me next** le coiffeur a dit qu'il me prendrait après *or* qu'il s'occuperait de moi après; **he does the film criticism for the "Gazette"** il fait la critique du cinéma dans la "Gazette"; (*Comm*) **we only ~ one make of gloves** nous n'avons *or* ne faisons qu'une marque de gants; **I'll ~ you‡ if I get hold of you!** tu vas le payer cher *or* tu auras affaire à moi si je t'attrape!; **he's hard done by** on le traite durement; **he's been badly done by** on s'est très mal conduit à son égard.

j (*complete, accomplish*) faire; (*use up*) finir. **the work's done now** le travail est fait maintenant; **I've only done 3 pages** je n'ai fait que 3 pages; **a woman's work is never done** une femme n'est jamais au bout de sa tâche; **the soap is (all) done** il ne reste plus de savon; **I haven't done telling you what I think of you*** je n'ai pas fini de vous dire ce que je pense de vous; (*Comm*) **done!** marché conclu!, entendu!; (*frm*) **have done!** finissez donc!; **when all's said and done** tout compte fait, en fin de compte; **it's all over and done (with)** tout ça c'est fini *or* classé; **to ~ sb to death** tuer qn, frapper qn à mort; **this theme has been done to death** ce thème est rebattu; **to get done with sth** en finir avec qch.

k (*visit, see sights of*) *city, country, museum* visiter, faire*.

l (*Aut etc*) faire; rouler; parcourir. **the car was ~ing 100** la voiture roulait à 100 à l'heure *or* faisait du 100 (à l'heure); **this car does** *or* **can ~** *or* **will ~ 100** cette voiture fait *or* peut faire du 100; **we did London to Edinburgh in 8 hours** nous avons fait (le trajet) Londres-Édimbourg en huit heures; **we've done 200 km since 2 o'clock** nous avons fait *or* parcouru 200 km depuis 2 heures.

m (*suit*) aller à; (*be sufficient for*) suffire à. **that will ~ me nicely** (*that's what I want*) cela fera très bien mon affaire, ça m'ira bien; (*that's enough*) cela me suffit.

n (*Theat, fig*) (*play part of*) faire, jouer le rôle de; (*pretend to be*) faire; (*mimic*) faire. **she does the worried mother very convincingly** elle joue à la mère inquiète avec beaucoup de conviction; **he does his maths master to perfection** il fait *or* imite son professeur de math à la perfection.

o (*Brit *: cheat*) avoir*, refaire*. **you've been done!** on vous a eu!* *or* refait!*; **to ~ sb out of £10** carotter* 10 livres à qn, refaire* qn de 10 livres; **to ~ sb out of a job** prendre à qn son travail.

p (**: provide food, lodgings for*) **they ~ you very well at that restaurant** on mange rudement* bien à ce restaurant; **she does her lodgers proud** elle mitonne *or* dorlote ses pensionnaires; **to ~ o.s. well** *or* **proud** ne se priver de rien.

q (*Culin*) (*cook*) faire (cuire); (*prepare*) *vegetables* éplucher, préparer; *salad* faire, préparer. **to ~ the cooking** faire la cuisine; **to ~ an omelette** faire une omelette; **how do you like your steak done?** comment aimez-vous votre bifteck?; **steak well done** bifteck bien cuit; **steak done to a turn** bifteck à point.

r (*‡: tire out*) éreinter*. **I'm absolutely done!** je n'en peux plus!, je suis crevé!*

s (*phrases*) **what am I to ~ with you?** qu'est-ce que je vais bien pouvoir faire de toi?; **he didn't know what to ~ with himself all day** il ne savait pas quoi faire de lui-même *or* de sa peau* toute la journée; **tell me what you did with yourself last week** raconte-moi ce que tu as fait *or* fabriqué* la semaine dernière; **what have you been ~ing with yourself?** (*greeting*) qu'est-ce que vous devenez?; (*mother to child*) qu'est-ce que tu as bien pu fabriquer?*; **I shan't know what to ~ with my free time** je ne saurai pas quoi faire de *or* comment occuper mon temps libre.

3 **vi** a (*act: be occupied*) faire, agir. **~ as your friends ~** faites comme vos amis; (*Prov*) **~ as you would be done by** ne faites pas aux autres ce que vous ne voudriez pas qu'on vous fasse; **he did well by his mother** il a bien agi envers sa mère; **he did well to take advice** il a bien fait de demander des conseils; **you would ~ well to rest more** vous feriez bien de vous reposer davantage; **he did right** il a bien fait; **he did right to go** il a bien fait d'y aller; **she was up and ~ing at 6 o'clock** elle était (debout et) à l'ouvrage dès 6 heures du matin.

b (*get on, fare*) aller, marcher, se porter; être. **how do you ~?** (*greeting*) bonjour, comment allez-vous?; (*on being introduced*) très heureux *or* enchanté (de faire votre connaissance); **how are you ~ing?*** comment ça va?, comment ça marche?*; **the patient is ~ing very well** le malade est en très bonne voie; **the patient is ~ing better now** le malade va mieux; **he's ~ing well at school** il marche bien* en classe; **he** *or* **his business is ~ing well** ses affaires vont *or* marchent bien; **the roses are ~ing well this year** les roses viennent bien cette année.

c (*finish*) finir, terminer. **have you done?** (vous avez) terminé?, ça y est?; **I've done with all that nonsense** je ne veux plus rien avoir à faire avec toutes ces bêtises; **have you done with that book?** vous n'avez plus besoin de ce livre?; **I've done with smoking** je ne fume plus.

d (*suit, be convenient*) convenir, aller. **that will never ~!** (ah non!) ça ne peut pas aller!; **this room will ~** cette chambre ira bien *or* fera l'affaire; **will it ~ if I come back at 8?** ça (vous) va si je reviens à 8 heures?; **it doesn't ~ to tell him what you think of him** ce n'est pas (la chose) à faire (que) de lui dire ce que vous pensez de lui; **these shoes won't ~ for walking** ces chaussures ne conviennent pas *or* ne vont pas pour la marche; **this coat will ~ for** *or* **as a cover** ce manteau servira de couverture; **nothing would ~ but that he should come** il a fallu absolument qu'il vienne; (*fig*) **to make ~ and mend** faire des économies de bouts de chandelle; **you'll have to make ~ with £10** il faudra vous contenter de *or* vous débrouiller* avec 10 livres; **she hadn't much money but she made ~ with what she had** elle n'avait pas beaucoup d'argent mais elle s'en est tirée *or* elle s'est débrouillée* *or* elle a fait aller* avec ce qu'elle avait.

e (*be sufficient*) suffire. **half a kilo of flour will ~ (for the cake/for the weekend)** un demi-kilo de farine suffira (pour le gâteau/pour le week-end); **can you lend me some money? — will £1 ~?** pouvez-vous me prêter de l'argent? — une livre, ça suffit? *or* ça (vous) va?; **that will ~!** ça suffit!, assez!

f (*do housework*) faire le ménage (et la cuisine) (*for* chez). **the woman who does for me** ma femme de ménage.

g (*phrases*) **what's ~ing?*** qu'est-ce qu'on fait?, qu'est-ce qui se passe?; **there's nothing ~ing in this town*** il n'y a rien d'intéressant *or* il ne se passe rien dans cette ville; **could you lend me £5? — nothing ~ing!‡** tu pourrais me prêter 5 livres? — rien à faire!* *or* pas question! *or* tu peux toujours courir!*; **this debate has to ~ with the cost of living** ce débat a à voir avec *or* concerne le coût de la vie; **a doctor has to ~ with all kinds of people** un médecin a affaire à toutes sortes de gens; **his business activities have nothing to ~ with how much I earn** ses affaires n'ont aucune influence sur ce que je touche; **money has a lot to ~ with it** l'argent y est pour beaucoup, c'est surtout une question d'argent; **he has something to ~ with the government** il a quelque chose à voir dans *or* avec le gouvernement; **he has to ~ with the steel industry** il est dans la sidérurgie; **what has that got to ~ with it?** et alors, qu'est-ce que cela a à voir?; **that has nothing to ~ with it!** cela n'a rien à voir!, cela n'y est pour rien!, cela n'a aucun rapport!; **that's got a lot to ~ with it!** cela y est pour beaucoup!; **that has nothing to ~ with the problem** cela n'a rien à voir avec le problème; **that has nothing to ~ with you!** cela ne vous regarde pas!; **I won't have anything to ~ with it** je ne veux pas m'en mêler.

4 n (*) a (*Brit*) (*party*) soirée *f*; (*ceremony*) fête *f*, grand tralala*. **there's a big ~ at the Ritz tonight** il y a (un) grand tralala* ce soir au Ritz; **there's a big Air Force ~ tomorrow at noon** l'armée de l'air organise une grande fête demain à midi.

b (*Brit: swindle*) escroquerie *f*. **the whole business was a real ~ from start to finish** tout ça, c'était une escroquerie du début jusqu'à la fin.

c (*phrases*) **it's a poor ~!** c'est plutôt minable!*; **the ~s and don'ts** ce qu'il faut faire ou ne pas faire; **fair ~s all round** à chacun son dû; *see* **hair** *etc*.

▶**do away with** vt fus a (*get rid of*) *custom, law, document* supprimer; *building* démolir. b (*kill*) *person* liquider*, supprimer. **to do away with o.s.** se suicider, se supprimer, mettre fin à ses jours.

▶**do down*** vt sep (*Brit*) *person* rouler*, refaire*.

▶**do for‡** vt fus *person* (*finish off*) démolir*, (*ruin*) ruiner; *project* flanquer en l'air*, bousiller*; *ambition* mettre fin à. **he/it is done for** il/cela est fichu* *or* foutu‡; *see also* **do[1] 3f**.

▶**do in‡** vt sep a (*kill*) supprimer, liquider*. b (*gen pass: exhaust*) éreinter. **to be** *or* **feel (quite) done in** être claqué* *or* éreinté.

▶**do out** vt sep *room* faire *or* nettoyer (à fond).

▶**do over** vt sep a (*redecorate*) refaire. b (‡: *beat up*) passer à tabac, tabasser‡.

▶**do up** 1 vi [*dress etc*] s'attacher, se fermer. 2 vt sep a (*fasten*) *buttons* boutonner; *zip* fermer, remonter; *dress* attacher; *shoes* attacher (les lacets de). b (*parcel together*) *goods* emballer, empaqueter. **to do sth up in a parcel** emballer *or* empaqueter qch; **to do up a parcel** faire un paquet; **books done up in brown paper** des livres emballés *or* empaquetés dans du papier d'emballage. c (*renovate*) *house, room* remettre à neuf, refaire; *old dress etc* rafraîchir. **to do o.s. up** se faire beau (*f* belle).

▶**do with** vt fus a (*with "can" or "could": need*) avoir besoin de, avoir envie de. **I could do with a cup of tea** je prendrais bien une tasse de thé. b (*in neg, with "can" or "could": tolerate*) supporter, tolérer. **I can't do with whining children** je ne peux pas supporter les enfants qui pleurnichent. c = **make do**; *see* **do[1] 3d**.

▶**do without** vt fus se passer de, se priver de. **I can do without your advice!** je vous dispense de vos conseils!; **I could well have done without that!** je m'en serais très bien passé!; **you'll have to do without then!** alors il faudra bien que tu t'en passes (*subj*)! *or* que tu en fasses ton deuil!*

do[2] [dəʊ] n (*Mus*) do *m*, ut *m*.

DOA (abbr of **dead on arrival**) *see* **dead 1a**.

d.o.b. (abbr of **date of birth**) *see* **date[1]**.

Doberman ['dəʊbəmən] n (*also* **~ pinscher**) doberman *m*.

doc* [dɒk] n (*US*) (abbr of **doctor**) toubib* *m*. **yes ~*** oui docteur.

docile ['dəʊsaɪl] adj docile, maniable.

docilely ['dəʊsaɪlɪ] adv docilement.

docility [dəʊ'sɪlɪtɪ] n docilité *f*, soumission *f*.

dock[1] [dɒk] 1 n (*for berthing*) bassin *m*, dock *m*; (*for loading, unloading, repair: often pl*) dock(s). (*Brit fig*) **my car is in ~*** ma voiture est en réparation; *see* **dry, graving** *etc*. 2 comp ▶**dock house** bureaux *mpl* des docks ▶**dock labourer** docker *m*, débardeur *m* ▶**the dockland** le quartier des docks, les docks *mpl* ▶**dock strike** grève *f* des dockers ▶**dockwalloper*** (*US*), **dock-worker** = **dock labourer** ▶**dockyard** chantier naval *or* de constructions navales (*see* **naval**). 3 vt mettre à quai. 4 vi a (*Naut*) entrer au bassin *or* aux docks, arriver *or* se mettre à quai. **the ship has ~ed** le bateau est à quai. b (*Space*) [*two spacecraft*] s'arrimer, s'amarrer.

dock[2] [dɒk] n (*Brit Jur*) banc *m* des accusés *or* des prévenus. **"prisoner in the ~ ..."** "accusé ...".

dock[3] [dɒk] vt a *animal's tail* écourter, couper. b (*Brit*) *wages* rogner, faire une retenue sur. **to ~ £5 off sb's wages** retenir *or* rogner 5 = livres sur le salaire de qn; **he had his wages ~ed for being late** on lui a fait une retenue sur son salaire pour retard; **to ~ a soldier of 2 days' pay/leave** supprimer 2 jours de solde/de permission à un soldat.

dock[4] [dɒk] n (*Bot*) patience *f*.

docker ['dɒkəʳ] n docker *m*, débardeur *m*.

docket ['dɒkɪt] 1 n a (*paper: on document, parcel etc*) étiquette *f*, fiche *f* (*indiquant le contenu d'un paquet etc*). b (*Jur*) (*register*) registre *m* des jugements rendus; (*list of cases*) rôle *m* des causes; (*abstract of letters patent*) table *f* des matières, index *m*. c (*Brit: Customs certificate*) récépissé *m* de douane, certificat *m* de paiement des droits de douane. 2 vt a *contents* résumer; (*Jur*) *judgment* enregistrer *or* consigner sommairement; (*fig*) *information etc* consigner, prendre note de. b *packet, document* faire une fiche pour, étiqueter.

docking ['dɒkɪŋ] n (*Space*) arrimage *m*, amarrage *m*.

doctor ['dɒktəʳ] 1 n a (*Med*) docteur *m*, médecin *m*. **who is your ~?** qui est votre docteur?, qui est votre médecin traitant?; **D~ Smith** le docteur Smith; (*more formally*) Monsieur *or* Madame le docteur Smith; **yes ~** oui docteur; **to send for the ~** appeler *or* faire venir le médecin *or* le docteur; **he/she is a ~** il/elle est médecin *or* docteur; **a woman ~** une femme docteur, une femme médecin; **he's under the ~ *** il est suivi par le docteur, il est entre les mains du docteur; (*Scol etc*) (*Brit*) **~'s line** *or* **note**, (*US*) **~'s excuse** dispense *f*; (*US*) **~'s office** cabinet *m* médical; (*fig*) **it's just what the ~ ordered*** c'est exactement ce qu'il me (*or* te *etc*) fallait; *see* **Dr.**

b (*Univ etc*) docteur *m*. (*Univ*) **~'s degree** doctorat *m*; **D~ of Law/of Science** *etc* docteur en droit/ès sciences *etc;* **D~ of Philosophy** ≃ titulaire *m* d'un doctorat d'État; *see* **medicine**.

2 vt a *sick person* soigner.

b (* *Brit*) *cat etc* châtrer (*un animal*).

c (* *pej: mend*) rafistoler* (*pej*).

d (*tamper with*) *wine* frelater; *food* altérer; *text, document* arranger, tripatouiller*; *figures, accounts* falsifier, tripatouiller*.

doctoral ['dɒktərəl] adj de doctorat. (*Univ*) (*Brit*) **~ thesis**, (*US*) **~ dissertation** thèse *f* de doctorat.

doctorate ['dɒktərɪt] n doctorat *m*. **~ in science/in philosophy** doctorat ès sciences/en philosophie.

doctrinaire [ˌdɒktrɪ'nɛəʳ] adj, n doctrinaire (*mf*).

doctrinal [dɒk'traɪnl] adj doctrinal.

doctrine ['dɒktrɪn] n (*Philos, Rel*) doctrine *f*.

docudrama [ˌdɒkjʊ'drɑːmə] n (*TV etc*) docudrame *m*.

document ['dɒkjʊmənt] 1 n (*gen, also Comput*) document *m*. **~s relating to a case** dossier *m* d'une affaire; **official ~** document officiel; (*Jur*) acte authentique public; (*Jur*) **judicial ~** acte *m* judiciaire. 2 ['dɒkjʊment] vt a *case* documenter. (*Jur*) **complaints must be ~ed** les plaintes doivent être accompagnées de pièces justificatives. b *ship* munir des papiers nécessaires. 3 comp ▶**document case** porte-documents *m inv* ▶**document reader** (*Comput*) lecteur *m* de documents.

documentary [ˌdɒkjʊ'mentərɪ] 1 adj documentaire. (*Jur*) **~ evidence** documents *mpl*, preuve *f* documentaire *or* par écrit; **~ letter of credit** crédit *m* documentaire. 2 n (*Cine, TV*) (film *m*) documentaire *m*.

documentation [ˌdɒkjʊmen'teɪʃən] n documentation *f*; (*Comm*) documents *mpl* (à fournir *etc*).

DOD [ˌdiːəʊ'diː] (*US*) abbr of **Department of Defense**.

do-dad‡ ['duːdæd] n = **doodah**.

dodder ['dɒdəʳ] vi ne pas tenir sur ses jambes, marcher d'un pas branlant; (*fig*) tergiverser, atermoyer.

dodderer ['dɒdərəʳ] n vieux (*or* vieille) gaga*, croulant(e)* *m(f)*, gâteux *m*, -euse *f*.

doddering ['dɒdərɪŋ] adj, **doddery** ['dɒdərɪ] adj (*trembling*) branlant; (*senile*) gâteux.

doddle* ['dɒdəl] n (*Brit*) **it's a ~** c'est simple comme bonjour*, c'est du gâteau*.

Dodecanese [ˌdəʊdɪkə'niːz] n Dodécanèse *m*.

dodge [dɒdʒ] 1 n a (*movement*) mouvement *m* de côté, détour *m*; (*Boxing, Ftbl*) esquive *f*.

b (*Brit* *) (*trick*) tour *m*, truc* *m*; (*ingenious scheme*) combine* *f*, truc*. **he's up to all the ~s** il connaît (toutes) les ficelles; **that's an old ~** c'est le coup classique*; **I've got a good ~ for making money** j'ai une bonne combine* pour gagner de l'argent.

2 vt *blow, ball* esquiver; *pursuer* échapper à; (*fig: avoid ingeniously*) *question* esquiver, éluder; *difficulty* esquiver; *tax* éviter de payer; (*shirk*) *work, duty* esquiver, se dérober à. **he ~d the issue** il est volontairement passé à côté de la question; **I managed to ~ him before he saw me** j'ai réussi à l'éviter avant qu'il ne me voie.

3 vi faire un saut de côté *or* un brusque détour; (*Boxing, Ftbl*) faire une esquive. **to ~ out of sight** *or* **out of the way** s'esquiver; **to ~ behind a tree** disparaître derrière un arbre; **to ~ through the traffic/the trees** se faufiler entre les voitures/les arbres; **he saw the police and ~d round the back (of the house)** il a vu les agents et s'est esquivé (en faisant le tour de la maison) par derrière.

▶**dodge about** vi aller et venir, remuer.

dodgems ['dɒdʒəmz] npl (*Brit*) autos tamponneuses.

dodger ['dɒdʒəʳ] n a (*: *trickster*) roublard(e)* *m(f)*, finaud(e) *m(f)*; (*shirker*) tire-au-flanc *m inv*; *see* **artful**. b (*Naut*) toile *f* de passerelle de commandement. c (*US: handbill*) prospectus *m*.

dodgy* ['dɒdʒɪ] adj a (*Brit: tricky*) *situation* délicat, épineux, pas commode*. **the whole business seemed a bit ~** toute cette affaire était un peu risquée *or* douteuse; **he's very ~** *or* **in a very ~ situation financially** il est dans une mauvaise passe financièrement. b (*artful*) malin (*f* -igne), rusé.

dodo ['dəʊdəʊ] n, pl **~s** *or* **~es** dronte *m*, dodo *m*; *see* **dead**.

DOE [ˌdiːəʊ'iː] a (*Brit*) (abbr of **Department of the Environment**) *see* **en-**

vironment. b (*US*) (abbr of **Department of Energy**) *ministère de l'Énergie*.
doe [dəʊ] n, pl ~s or ~ a (*deer*) biche *f*. b (*rabbit*) lapine *f*; (*hare*) hase *f*. **~-eyed** (*person*) aux yeux de biche; *look* de biche.
doer ['du(:)ər] n a (*author of deed*) auteur *m* de l'action (*or* de cette action *etc*). **~s of good deeds often go unrewarded** ceux qui font le bien souvent ne sont pas récompensés; **he's a great ~ of crosswords*** c'est un cruciverbiste fervent; **he's a great ~ of jigsaw puzzles*** il adore faire *or* il se passionne pour les puzzles; *see* **evil**. b (*active person*) personne *f* efficace *or* dynamique.
does [dʌz] *see* **do**¹.
doeskin ['dəʊskɪn] n peau *f* de daim.
doesn't ['dʌznt] = **does not**; *see* **do**¹.
doff [dɒf] vt (†, *hum*) *garment, hat* ôter, enlever.
dog [dɒg] 1 n a chien(ne) *m(f)*. **the ~'s dinner, the ~'s food** la pâtée du chien (*see also* 2); (*fig*) **it's a real ~'s dinner*** *or* **~'s breakfast*** ça a l'air de Dieu sait quoi; **he's all done up like a ~'s dinner*** regarde comme il est attifé, il est attifé n'importe comment; **to lead a ~'s life** mener une vie de chien; **she led him a ~'s life** elle lui a fait une vie de chien; (*Brit Sport*) **the ~s*** les courses *fpl* de lévriers; (*fig*) **to go to the ~s*** *[person]* gâcher sa vie, mal tourner; *[institution, business]* aller à vau-l'eau, péricliter; **he is being a ~ in the manger** il fait l'empêcheur de tourner en rond; (*Prov*) **every ~ has his day** à chacun vient sa chance, à chacun son heure de gloire; **he hasn't a ~'s chance*** il n'a pas la moindre chance (de réussir); **it's (a case of) ~ eat ~** c'est un cas où les loups se mangent entre eux; (*Prov*) **give a ~ a bad name (and hang him)** qui veut noyer son chien l'accuse de la rage (*Prov*); (*US*) **to put on the ~‡** faire de l'épate*; *see* **cat, hair** *etc*.
b (*male*) *[fox etc]* mâle *m*.
c (**: person*) **lucky ~** veinard(e)* *m(f)*; **gay ~** joyeux luron; **dirty ~** sale type* *m*; **sly ~** (petit) malin *m*, (petite) maligne *f*.
d (*‡: unattractive woman*) fille *f* moche*.
e (*Tech*) (*clamp*) crampon *m*; (*pawl*) cliquet *m*.
f (*feet*) **~s‡** panards‡ *mpl*.
2 comp ▸**dog basket** panier *m* de chien ▸**dog biscuit** biscuit *m* pour chien ▸**dog breeder** éleveur *m*, -euse *f* de chiens ▸**dog-cart** charrette anglaise, dog-cart *m* ▸**dog collar** (*lit*) collier *m* de chien; (*hum: clergyman's*) col *m* de pasteur, (faux-)col *m* d'ecclésiastique ▸**dog days** canicule *f* ▸**dog-eared** écorné ▸**dog fancier** (*connoisseur*) connaisseur *m*, -euse *f* en chiens; (*breeder*) éleveur *m*, -euse *f* de chiens ▸**dogfight** (*lit*) bataille *f* de chiens; (*Aviat*) combat *m* entre avions de chasse; (*between people*) bagarre *f* ▸**dogfish** chien *m* de mer, roussette *f* ▸**dogfood** nourriture *f* pour chiens ▸**dog fox** renard *m* (mâle) ▸**dog guard** (*Aut*) barrière *f* pour chien (*à l'arrière d'une voiture*) ▸**dog handler** (*Police etc*) maître-chien *m* ▸**doghouse** chenil *m*, niche *f* à chien; (*fig*) **he is in the doghouse*** il n'est pas en odeur de sainteté ▸**dog Latin** latin *m* de cuisine ▸**dog leg** n (*in road etc*) coude *m*, angle abrupt ◊ adj qui fait un coude ▸**dog licence** permis *m* de posséder un chien ▸**dog-paddle** n nage *f* en chien ◊ vi nager en chien ▸**dog rose** (*flower*) églantine *f*; (*bush*) églantier *m* ▸**dogsbody***: **she's the general dogsbody** elle fait le factotum, elle est la bonne à tout faire ▸**dogshow** exposition canine ▸**Dog Star** Sirius *m* ▸**dog tag** (*US Mil sl*) plaque *f* d'identification (*portée au cou par les militaires*) ▸**dog-tired*** claqué*, crevé* ▸**dog track** piste *f* (pour les courses de lévriers) ▸**dogtrot** petit trot; (*US: passageway*) passage couvert ▸**dog-watch** (*Naut*) petit quart, quart de deux heures ▸**dog wolf** loup *m* ▸**dogwood** cornouiller *m*.
3 vt a (*follow closely*) *person* suivre (de près). **he ~s my footsteps** il marche sur mes talons, il ne me lâche pas d'une semelle.
b (*harass*) harceler. **~ged by ill fortune** poursuivi par la malchance.
doge [dəʊdʒ] n doge *m*.
dogged ['dɒgɪd] adj *person, character* déterminé, tenace, persévérant; *courage* opiniâtre, obstiné.
doggedly ['dɒgɪdlɪ] adv obstinément, avec ténacité *or* obstination.
doggedness ['dɒgɪdnɪs] n obstination *f*, entêtement *m*, ténacité *f*.
Dogger Bank ['dɒgəbæŋk] n Dogger Bank *m*.
doggerel ['dɒgərəl] n vers *mpl* de mirliton.
doggie ['dɒgɪ] n = **doggy 1**.
doggo* ['dɒgəʊ] adv (*Brit*) **to lie ~** se tenir coi; *[fugitive, criminal]* se terrer.
doggone(d)* [ˌdɒg'gɒn(d)] adj (*US*) euph of **damn, damned**; *see* **damn 1, 2c, 3, 4, 5**.
doggy ['dɒgɪ] 1 n (*baby talk*) chienchien* *m*, toutou* *m* (*langage enfantin*). 2 adj *smell* de chien. **she is a very ~ woman** elle a la folie des chiens. 3 comp ▸**doggy bag*** petit sac pour emporter les restes ▸**doggy paddle*** n nage *f* en chien ◊ vi nager en chien.
dogie ['dəʊgɪ] n (*US*) veau *m* sans mère.
doglike ['dɒglaɪk] adj de bon chien.
dogma ['dɒgmə] n, pl ~s *or* **dogmata** ['dɒgmətə] dogme *m*.
dogmatic [dɒg'mætɪk] adj (*Rel, fig*) dogmatique. **to be very ~ about sth** être très dogmatique sur qch.
dogmatically [dɒg'mætɪkəlɪ] adv (*gen*) dogmatiquement; *say, remark* d'un ton autoritaire.
dogmatism ['dɒgmətɪzəm] n (*Philos, Rel*) dogmatisme *m*; (*fig*) caractère *m* *or* esprit *m* dogmatique.
dogmatize ['dɒgmətaɪz] vi (*Rel, fig*) dogmatiser.
do-gooder ['du:'gʊdər] n (*slightly pej*) pilier *m* de bonnes œuvres, bonne âme (*iro*).
doh [dəʊ] n (*Mus*) = **do²**.
doily ['dɔɪlɪ] n (*under plate*) napperon *m*; (*on plate*) dessus *m* d'assiette.
doing ['du:ɪŋ] n a action *f* de faire. **this is your ~** c'est vous qui avez fait cela; **it was none of my ~** je n'y suis pour rien, ce n'est pas moi qui l'ai fait; **that takes some ~** ce n'est pas facile *or* commode, (il) faut le faire!* b **~s** faits *mpl* et gestes *mpl*. c (*Brit ‡: thingummy*) **~s** machin* *m*, truc* *m*; **that ~s over there** ce machin* là-bas.
do-it-yourself ['du:ɪtjə'self] 1 n bricolage *m*. 2 adj a *shop* de bricolage. **~ enthusiast** bricoleur *m*, -euse *f*; **the ~ craze** la passion du bricolage, l'engouement *m* pour le bricolage; **~ kit** kit *m* (prêt-à-monter). b (*fig*) *divorce, conveyancing* que l'on conduit soi-même (*sans employer les services d'un professionnel*).
do-it-yourselfer* [ˌdu:ɪtjɔ:'selfər] n bricoleur *m*, -euse *f*.
doldrums ['dɒldrəmz] npl (*area*) zone *f* des calmes; (*weather*) calme équatorial. (*fig*) **to be in the ~** *[person]* avoir le cafard*, broyer du noir; *[business]* être dans le marasme.
dole [dəʊl] n allocation *f* *or* indemnité *f* de chômage. (*Brit*) **to go/be on the ~** s'inscrire/être au chômage.
▸**dole out** vt sep distribuer *or* accorder au compte-gouttes.
doleful ['dəʊlfʊl] adj *face, tone* dolent, plaintif, morne; *prospect, song* lugubre, morne.
dolefully ['dəʊlfəlɪ] adv d'un ton *or* d'une manière lugubre *or* morne, plaintivement.
dolichocephalic ['dɒlɪkəʊse'fælɪk] adj dolichocéphale.
doll [dɒl] n a poupée *f*. **to play with a ~** *or* **~s** jouer à la poupée; **~'s house/pram** maison *f*/voiture *f* de poupée; (*US*) **~ carriage** *or* **buggy** voiture *f* de poupée. b (*‡: esp US: girl*) nana‡ *f*, pépée‡ *f*; (*pretty girl*) poupée* *f*. (*attractive person*) **he's/she's a ~** il/elle est chou*, il/elle est adorable; (*US*) **you're a ~* to help me** tu es un ange de m'aider.
▸**doll up‡** vt sep *person, thing* bichonner. **to doll o.s. up, to get dolled up** se faire (tout) beau* (*or* (toute) belle*), se bichonner; **all dolled up** sur son trente et un.
dollar ['dɒlər] 1 n dollar *m*. (*US*) **it's ~s to doughnuts that ...** c'est du tout cuit‡ que ...; *see* **half, sixty**. 2 comp ▸**dollar area** zone *f* dollar ▸**dollar bill** billet *m* d'un dollar ▸**dollar diplomacy** (*US Pol*) diplomatie *f* à coups de dollars ▸**dollar gap** déficit *m* de la balance dollar ▸**dollar rate** (*Fin*) cours *m* du dollar ▸**dollar sign** signe *m* du dollar.
dollop* ['dɒləp] n *[butter, cheese etc]* gros *or* bon morceau; *[cream, jam etc]* bonne cuillerée.
dolly ['dɒlɪ] 1 n a (**: doll*) poupée *f*. b (*for washing clothes*) agitateur *m*. **~ tub** (*for washing*) baquet *m* à lessive; (*Min*) cuve *f* à rincer. c (*wheeled frame*) chariot *m*; (*Cine, TV*) chariot, travelling *m* (*dispositif*); (*Rail: truck*) plate-forme *f*. 2 adj (*Sport *: easy*) facile. 3 vt (*Cine, TV*) **to ~ the camera in/out** avancer/reculer la caméra. 4 comp ▸**dolly bird‡** (*Brit*) jolie nana‡, poupée* *f*.
dolman ['dɒlmən] n dolman *m*. **~ sleeve** (sorte *f* de) manche *f* kimono *inv*.
dolmen ['dɒlmen] n dolmen *m*.
dolomite ['dɒləmaɪt] n dolomite *f*, dolomie *f*. (*Geog*) **the D~s** les Dolomites *fpl*.
dolphin ['dɒlfɪn] n (*Zool*) dauphin *m*.
dolphinarium [ˌdɒlfɪ'nɛərɪəm] n aquarium *m* pour dauphins savants.
dolt [dəʊlt] n balourd(e) *m(f)*.
doltish ['dəʊltɪʃ] adj gourde*, cruche*.
domain [dəʊ'meɪn] n (*liter*) domaine *m* (*also fig, Math etc*), propriété *f*, terres *fpl*. **in the ~ of science** dans le domaine des sciences.
dome [dəʊm] n (*Archit: on building*) dôme *m*, coupole *f*; (*liter: stately building*) (noble) édifice *m*; *[hill]* sommet arrondi, dôme; *[skull]* calotte *f*; *[heaven, branches]* dôme.
domed [dəʊmd] adj *forehead* bombé; *building* à dôme, à coupole.
Domesday Book ['du:mzdeɪˌbʊk] n Domesday Book *m*, *recueil cadastral établi par Guillaume le Conquérant*.
domestic [də'mestɪk] 1 adj a *duty, happiness* familial, de famille, domestique. **his public and his ~ life** sa vie publique et sa vie privée; **everything of a ~ nature** tout ce qui se rapporte au ménage; **~ chores** travaux *mpl* du ménage; **~ heating oil** fuel *m* domestique; **do you have ~ help?** avez-vous une aide ménagère?; (*esp Brit*) **~ science** arts *mpl* ménagers; **~ science college** école *f* ménagère *or* d'art ménager; **~ science teaching** enseignement *m* ménager; **~ servants** domestiques *mfpl*, employé(e)s *m(f)pl* de maison; **she was in ~ service** elle était employée de maison *or* domestique; **~ staff** *[hospital, institution]* personnel *m* auxiliaire; *[private house]* domestiques *mfpl*.
b (*Econ, Pol*) *policy, affairs, flights* intérieur; *currency, economy* national. **~ quarrels** querelles intestines; **~ rates** tarifs *mpl* en régime intérieur.
c *animal* domestique.
2 n domestique *mf*.
domestically [də'mestɪkəlɪ] adv *produced, consumed etc* au niveau

national, nationalement. ~ **inclined** axé sur les travaux domestiques.
domesticate [də'mestɪkeɪt] vt *person* habituer à la vie domestique; *animal* domestiquer.
domesticated [də'mestɪkeɪtɪd] adj *person* qui aime son intérieur, pantouflard* (*pej*), pot-au-feu *inv* (*slightly pej*); *animal* domestiqué. **she's very** ~ elle est très femme d'intérieur *or* femme au foyer.
domestication [dəmestɪ'keɪʃən] n *[animal]* domestication *f.*
domesticity [ˌdəumes'tɪsɪtɪ] n (*home life*) vie *f* de famille, vie casanière (*slightly pej*); (*love of household duties*) attachement *m* aux tâches domestiques.
domicile ['dɒmɪsaɪl] (*Brit Admin, Fin, Jur*) 1 n domicile *m.* 2 vt domicilier. *[person]* **~d at** domicilié à, demeurant à; **to ~ a bill with a bank** domicilier un effet à une banque.
domiciliary [ˌdɒmɪ'sɪlɪərɪ] adj domiciliaire.
domiciliation [ˌdɒmɪsɪlɪ'eɪʃən] n *[bill, cheque]* domiciliation *f.*
dominance ['dɒmɪnəns] n (*gen: Ecol, Genetics, Psych*) dominance *f* (*over* sur); *[person, country etc]* prédominance *f.*
dominant ['dɒmɪnənt] 1 adj a *nations, species* dominant; (*Genetics*) dominant; *feature* dominant, principal; *position* dominant, élevé; *personality, tone* dominateur (*f* -trice). b (*Mus*) de dominante. 2 n (*Mus*) dominante *f*; (*Ecol, Genetics*) dominance *f.*
dominate ['dɒmɪneɪt] vti dominer.
dominating ['dɒmɪneɪtɪŋ] adj *character, personality* dominateur (*f* -trice).
domination [ˌdɒmɪ'neɪʃən] n domination *f.*
domineer [ˌdɒmɪ'nɪə^r^] vi agir en maître (autoritaire), se montrer autoritaire (*over* avec).
domineering [ˌdɒmɪ'nɪərɪŋ] adj dominateur (*f* -trice), impérieux, autoritaire.
Dominica [ˌdɒmɪ'niːkə] n (*Geog*) Dominique *f.*
Dominican[1] [də'mɪnɪkən] 1 adj (*Geog*) dominicain. ~ **Republic** République dominicaine. 2 n Dominicain(e) *m(f).*
Dominican[2] [də'mɪnɪkən] adj, n (*Rel*) dominicain(e) *m(f).*
dominion [də'mɪnɪən] n a (*NonC*) domination *f*, empire *m* (*over* sur). **to hold ~ over sb** maintenir qn sous sa domination *or* sous sa dépendance. b (*territory*) territoire *m*, possessions *fpl*; (*Brit Pol*) dominion *m.* (*Can*) **D~ Day** fête *f* de la Confédération.
domino ['dɒmɪnəu] 1 n, pl **~es** a domino *m.* **to play ~es** jouer aux dominos. b (*costume, mask, person*) domino *m.* 2 comp ▸**domino effect** effet *m* d'entraînement ▸**domino theory** (*Pol*) théorie *f* des dominos, théorie du proche en proche.
Don [dɒn] n (*river*) Don *m.*
don[1] [dɒn] n a (*Brit Univ*) professeur *m* d'université (*surtout à Oxford et à Cambridge*). b (*Spanish title*) don *m.* **a D~ Juan** un don Juan. c (*US*) chef *m* de la Mafia.
don[2] [dɒn] vt *garment* revêtir, mettre.
donate [dəu'neɪt] vt faire don de. **to ~ blood** donner son sang.
donation [dəu'neɪʃən] n (*act of giving*) donation *f*; (*gift*) don *m.* **to make a ~ to a fund** faire un don *or* une contribution à une caisse.
done [dʌn] 1 ptp of **do**[1]. 2 adj (*see* **do**[1]) a **the ~ thing** ce qui se fait. b (*: *tired out*) claqué*, crevé*. c (*used up*) fini. **the butter is** ~ le beurre est terminé, il n'y a plus de beurre.
donee [ˌdəu'niː] n (*Jur*) donataire *mf.*
doner ['dɒnə^r^] n: ~ **kebab** brochette *f.*
dongle ['dɒŋgl] n (*Comput*) boîtier *m* de sécurité.
donjon ['dʌndʒən] n donjon *m.*
donkey ['dɒŋkɪ] 1 n a âne(sse) *m(f)*, baudet* *m.* (*Brit*) **she hasn't been here for ~'s years*** il y a une éternité qu'elle n'est pas venue ici; *see* **hind**[2]. b (*: *fool*) âne *m*, imbécile *mf.* 2 comp ▸**donkey engine** (*Tech*) auxiliaire *m*, petit cheval, cheval alimentaire ▸**donkey jacket** grosse veste ▸**donkey ride** promenade *f* à dos d'âne ▸**the donkey work** le gros du travail.
donnish ['dɒnɪʃ] adj *look, tone* d'érudit, de savant; *person* érudit; (*pej*) pédant.
donor ['dəunə^r^] n (*to charity etc*) donateur *m*, -trice *f*; (*Med*) *[blood, organ for transplant]* donneur *m*, -euse *f.* **D~ Insemination** insémination artificielle.
don't [dəunt] 1 vb = **do not**; *see* **do**[1]. 2 n: **~s** choses *fpl* à ne pas faire; *see* **do**[1] **4c.** 3 comp ▸**don't knows** (*gen*) sans-opinion *inv*; (*voters*) indécis *mpl.*
donut ['dəunʌt] n (*US*) = **doughnut**; *see* **dough 2.**
doodah‡ ['duːdɑː] n (*gadget*) petit bidule*.
doodle ['duːdl] 1 vi griffonner (distraitement). 2 n griffonnage *m.* 3 comp ▸**doodlebug*** (*Brit*) bombe volante; (*US*) petit véhicule.
doohickey* [ˌduː'hɪkɪ] n (*US*) machin* *m*, truc* *m*, bidule* *m.*
doolally‡ [ˌduː'lælɪ] adj dingo‡, barjo‡.
doom [duːm] 1 n (*ruin*) ruine *f*, perte *f*; (*fate*) destin *m*, sort *m.* 2 vt condamner (*to* à), destiner (*to* à). **~ed to failure** voué à l'échec; **the project was ~ed from the start** le projet était voué à l'échec dès le début. 3 comp ▸**doom-laden** lugubre, sinistre ▸**doomwatch** attitude *f* pessimiste, catastrophisme *m* ▸**doomwatcher** prophète *m* de malheur.
doomsday ['duːmzdeɪ] n jour *m* du Jugement dernier. (*fig*) **till** ~ jusqu'à la fin des siècles *or* des temps; **D~ Book** = **Domesday Book.**

door [dɔː^r^] 1 n a *[house, room, cupboard]* porte *f*; *[railway carriage, car]* portière *f.* **he shut** *or* **closed the ~ in my face** il m'a fermé la porte au nez; **he came through the ~** il est passé par la porte; **in the ~(way)** dans (l'embrasure de) la porte; (*outside door*) sous le porche; (*Theat etc*) **"pay at the ~"** "billets à l'entrée"; **to go from ~ to ~** (*gen*) aller de porte en porte; *[salesman]* faire du porte à porte (*see also* **2**); **he lives 2 ~s down the street** il habite 2 portes plus loin; **out of ~s** (au-)dehors; *see* **answer, front, next door** *etc.*

b (*phrases*) **to lay sth at sb's ~** imputer qch à qn, charger qn de qch; **to open the ~ to further negotiations** ouvrir la voie à des négociations ultérieures; **to leave** *or* **keep the ~ open for further negotiations** laisser la porte ouverte à des négociations ultérieures; **to close** *or* **shut the ~ on** *or* **to sth** barrer la route à qch, rendre qch irréalisable; (*Theat etc*) **to be on the ~** être à l'entrée; (*fig*) **to open ~s** ouvrir des portes; *see* **death, show** *etc.*

2 comp ▸**doorbell** sonnette *f*; **there's the doorbell!** on sonne (à la porte)! ▸**door chain** chaîne *f* de sûreté ▸**door curtain** portière *f* (*tenture*) ▸**doorframe** chambranle *m*, châssis *m* de porte ▸**door handle** poignée *f or* bouton *m* de porte; (*Aut*) poignée de portière ▸**doorjamb** montant *m* de porte, jambage *m* ▸**doorkeeper** = **doorman** ▸**doorknob** poignée *f or* bouton *m* de porte ▸**door-knocker** marteau *m* (de porte), heurtoir *m* ▸**door-locking mechanism** (*Aut*) dispositif *m* de verrouillage des portières ▸**doorman** *[hotel]* portier *m*; *[block of flats]* concierge *m* ▸**doormat** (*lit*) paillasson *m* (d'entrée), essuie-pieds *m inv*; (*: *downtrodden person*) chiffe molle ▸**doornail** clou *m* de porte (*see* **dead**) ▸**doorpost** montant *m* de porte, jambage *m* (*see* **deaf**) ▸**door scraper** grattoir *m* ▸**doorstep** (*lit*) pas *m* de porte, seuil *m* de porte; (* *hum: hunk of bread*) grosse tartine; **he left it on my doorstep** il l'a laissé devant ma porte; **the bus-stop is just at my doorstep** l'arrêt du bus est (juste) à ma porte; (*fig*) **we don't want trouble/a motorway on our doorstep** nous ne voulons pas d'embêtements dans notre voisinage/d'autoroute dans notre arrière-cour ▸**doorstep salesman** (*Brit*) démarcheur *m*, vendeur *m* à domicile ▸**doorstep selling** (*Brit*) démarchage *m*, vente *f* à domicile, porte à porte *m inv* ▸**door-to-door: door-to-door delivery** livraison *f* à domicile; **we deliver door-to-door** nous livrons à domicile; **door-to-door salesman** = **doorstep salesman; door-to-door selling** = **doorstep selling** ▸**doorstop(per)** butoir *m* de porte ▸**doorway** (*gen*) porte *f*; **in the doorway** dans l'embrasure de la porte; *see* **central.**
dopamine ['dəupəmiːn] n dopamine *f.*
dope [dəup] 1 n a (‡: *drugs*) drogue *f*, dope‡ *f*; (*for athlete, horse*) dopant *m*, doping *m*; (*US* ‡: *drug addict*) drogué(e) *m(f)*, toxico* *mf.* **to take ~, to be on ~,** (*US*) **to do ~** se droguer, se doper*.

b (‡ *NonC: information*) tuyaux* *mpl.* **to give sb the ~** tuyauter* qn, affranchir‡ qn; **what's the ~ on ...?** qu'est-ce qu'on a comme tuyaux* sur ... ?

c (‡: *stupid person*) andouille‡ *f*, nouille* *f.*

d (*varnish*) enduit *m*; (*Aut, Chem*) dopant *m.*

e (*for explosives*) absorbant *m.*

2 comp ▸**dope fiend**‡ toxicomane *mf*, drogué(e) *m(f)* ▸**dope peddler**‡, **dope pusher**‡ revendeur *m*, -euse *f* de stupéfiants *or* de drogue ▸**dope-test*** n test *m* anti-doping *inv* ◊ vt faire subir le test anti-doping à.

3 vt *horse, person* doper; *food, drink* mettre une drogue *or* un dopant dans. **he was ~d (up) to the eyeballs*** il était complètement pété‡.
▸**dope out*** vt sep (*US*) deviner, piger*.
dopey ['dəupɪ] adj (*drugged*) drogué, dopé; (*very sleepy*) (à moitié) endormi; (‡: *stupid*) abruti*.
doping ['dəupɪŋ] n dopage *m.*
Doppler effect ['dɒplərɪˌfekt] n effet *m* Doppler-Fizeau.
dopy ['dəupɪ] adj = **dopey.**
Dordogne [dɔr'dɒɲ] n (*region*) Dordogne *f.* (*river*) **the ~** la Dordogne.
Doric ['dɒrɪk] adj (*Archit*) dorique.
dorm [dɔːm] n (*Scol sl*) = **dormitory.**
dormant ['dɔːmənt] adj *energy, passion* en veilleuse, qui sommeille; (*Bio, Bot*) dormant; *volcano* en repos, en sommeil; *rule, law* inappliqué; *title* tombé en désuétude; (*Her*) dormant. **to let a matter lie ~** laisser une affaire en sommeil.
dormer (window) ['dɔːmə('wɪndəu)] n lucarne *f.*
dormice ['dɔːmaɪs] npl of **dormouse.**
dormie ['dɔːmɪ] adj (*Golf*) dormie.
dormitory ['dɔːmɪtrɪ] 1 n (*Brit*) dortoir *m*; (*US Univ*) résidence *f* universitaire. 2 comp ▸**dormitory suburb** (*esp Brit*) banlieue *f* dortoir ▸**dormitory town** ville *f* dortoir.
Dormobile ['dɔːməbiːl] n ® (*Brit*) camping-car *m*, auto-camping *f*, voiture-camping *f.*
dormouse ['dɔːmaus] n, pl **dormice** loir *m.*
dorsal ['dɔːsl] adj dorsal.
dory[1] ['dɔːrɪ] n (*fish*) dorée *f*, saint-pierre *m inv.*
dory[2] ['dɔːrɪ] n (*boat*) doris *m.*
DOS [dɒs] n (**abbr of disk operating system**) DOS, SED *m.*
dosage ['dəusɪdʒ] n (*dosing*) dosage *m*; (*amount*) dose *f*; (*on medicine bottle*) posologie *f.*

dose [dəʊs] 1 n a (*Pharm*) dose *f*. **give him a ~ of medicine** donne-lui son médicament; **in small/large ~s** à faible/haute dose; (*hum*) **it went through her like a ~ of salts*** ça lui a donné la courante‡; **she's all right in small ~s*** elle est supportable à petites doses; (*fig*) **to give sb a ~ of his own medicine** rendre à qn la monnaie de sa pièce. b (*bout of illness*) attaque *f* (*of* de). **to have a ~ of flu** avoir une bonne grippe*. c (*‡: venereal disease*) vérole‡ *f*. 2 vt *person* administrer un médicament à. **she's always dosing herself (up)** elle se bourre de médicaments.

dosh‡ [dɒʃ] n (*Brit: money*) fric ‡, pognon‡.

doss‡ [dɒs] (*Brit*) 1 n (*cheap bed for night*) pieu‡ *m*; (*sleep*) roupillon* *m*, somme *m*. 2 comp ▸**doss house** asile *m* (de nuit). 3 vi coucher à l'asile (de nuit).

▸**doss down‡** vi crécher‡ (quelque part). **to doss down for the night** (trouver à) crécher‡ quelque part pour la nuit.

dosser‡ ['dɒsə^r] n (*Brit*) clochard(e) *m(f)*.

dossier ['dɒsɪeɪ] n dossier *m*, documents *mpl*.

Dosto(y)evsky [ˌdɒstɔɪ'efskɪ] n Dostoïevski *m*.

DOT [ˌdiːəʊ'tiː] n (*US*) (abbr of **Department of Transportation**) see **transportation**.

dot [dɒt] 1 n (*over i, on horizon, Math, Mus*) point *m*; (*on material*) pois *m*. (*Morse*) **~s and dashes** points et traits *mpl*; (*in punctuation*) "~, ~, ~" "points de suspension"; (*fig*) **on the ~*** à l'heure pile* *or* tapante; (*Brit*) **in the year ~*** il y a des siècles, dans la nuit des temps.

2 comp ▸**dot-matrix printer** (*Comput*) imprimante matricielle.

3 vt a *paper, wall* marquer avec des points, pointiller. **to ~ an i** mettre un point sur un i; (*fig*) **to ~ one's i's (and cross one's t's)** mettre les points sur les i; **to ~ and carry one** (*Math*) reporter un chiffre; (*: limp*) boiter, clopiner; **field ~ted with flowers** champ parsemé de fleurs; **cars ~ted along the route** des voitures échelonnées sur le parcours; see also **dotted**.

b **to ~ sb one‡** flanquer un gnon à qn‡.

dotage ['dəʊtɪdʒ] n a (*senility*) gâtisme *m*, seconde enfance. **to be in one's ~** être gâteux. b (*blind love*) adoration folle (*on* pour).

dote [dəʊt] vi (*be senile*) être gâteux, être gaga*.

▸**dote on** vt fus *person, thing* aimer à la folie, être fou (*f* folle) de, raffoler de.

doting ['dəʊtɪŋ] adj a (*adoring*) qui aime follement, qui adore. **her ~ father** son père qui l'adore. b (*senile*) gâteux.

dotted ['dɒtɪd] adj a **~ line** ligne pointillée *or* en pointillé; (*Aut*) ligne discontinue; **to tear along the ~ line** détacher suivant le pointillé; **to sign on the ~ line** (*lit*) signer à l'endroit indiqué *or* sur la ligne pointillée *or* sur les pointillés; (*fig*) (*agree officially*) donner son consentement (en bonne et due forme); (*accept uncritically*) s'incliner (*fig*). b (*Mus*) **~ note** note pointée; **~ rhythm** notes pointées.

dotterel ['dɒtrəl] n pluvier *m* (guignard).

dotty‡ ['dɒtɪ] adj (*Brit*) toqué*, piqué*. **to be ~ about sb/sth** être toqué* de qn/qch.

double ['dʌbl] 1 adj a (*twice as much: also Bot*) double (*usu before n*). **a ~ amount of work** une double quantité de travail; (*Ind*) **to earn ~ time (on Sundays** *etc*) être payé (au tarif) double (le dimanche *etc*); see also **4**.

b (*twofold; having two similar parts; in pairs*) deux fois, double (*usu before n*). (*in numerals*) **~ seven five four** (*7754*) deux fois sept cinq quatre, (*as telephone number*) soixante-dix-sept cinquante-quatre; **spelt with a ~ "p"** écrit avec deux "p"; (*Dominoes*) **the ~ 6** le double 6; **box with a ~ bottom** boîte à double fond; (*Aut*) **~ yellow lines** double bande *f* jaune (*marquant l'interdiction de stationner*); **~ white lines** lignes blanches continues; see also **4**.

c (*made for two users*) pour *or* de deux personnes; see also **4**.

d (*for two purposes*) double (*usu before n*). **with a ~ meaning** à double sens; **~ advantage** double avantage *m*; **that table serves a ~ purpose** cette table a une double fonction; see also **4**.

e (*underhand, deceptive*) double (*usu before n*), à double face, faux (*f* fausse), trompeur. **to lead a ~ life** mener une double vie; **to play a ~ game** jouer un double jeu; see also **4**.

2 adv a (*twice*) deux fois. **that costs ~ what it did last year** cela coûte deux fois plus que l'année dernière, cela a doublé de prix depuis l'année dernière; **I've got ~ what you've got** j'en ai deux fois plus que toi, j'ai le double de ce que tu as; **her salary is ~ what it was 10 years ago** son salaire est le double de ce qu'il était il y a 10 ans; **he did it in ~ the time it took me** il a mis deux fois plus de temps que moi à le faire; **he's ~ your age** il est deux fois plus âgé que vous, il a le double de votre âge; **~ 6 is 12** deux fois 6 font 12, le double de 6 est 12; see also **4**.

b (*in twos; twofold*) *fold etc* en deux. **to see ~** voir double; **bent ~ with pain** plié en deux de douleur; see also **4**.

3 n a (*twice a quantity, number, size etc, whisky etc*) double *m*. **12 is the ~ of 6** 12 est le double de 6; **~ or quits** quitte ou double; **he earns the ~ of what I do** il gagne le double de ce que je gagne *or* deux fois plus que moi; (*fig: quickly*) **at** *or* **on the ~** au pas de course.

b (*exactly similar thing*) réplique *f*; (*exactly similar person*) double *m*, sosie *m*; (*Cine: stand-in*) doublure *f*; (*Theat: actor taking two parts*) acteur *m*, -trice *f* qui tient deux rôles (*dans la même pièce*); (*Cards*) contre *m*; (*other games*) double; (*Betting*) pari doublé (*sur deux chevaux de deux courses différentes*).

c (*Tennis*) **~s** double *m*; **mixed ~s** double mixte; **ladies'/men's ~s** double dames/messieurs; **a ~s player** un joueur (*f* une joueuse) de double.

d (*double bedroom*) chambre *f* pour deux personnes.

4 comp ▸**double-acting** à double effet ▸**double agent** agent *m* double ▸**double bar** (*Mus*) double barre *f* ▸**double-barrelled** *gun* à deux coups; (*Brit fig*) *surname* à rallonges*, à tiroir* ▸**double bass** (*instrument, player*) contrebasse *f* ▸**double bassoon** contrebasson *m* ▸**double bed** grand lit, lit de deux personnes ▸**double bend** (*Brit Aut*) virage *m* en S ▸**double bill** (*Cine etc*) double programme *m* ▸**double bind*** situation *f* insoluble *or* sans issue, impasse *f* ▸**double-blind** *test, experiment* en double aveugle; *method* à double insu, à double anonymat ▸**double bluff** *du bluff qui n'en est pas;* **it's actually a double bluff** il (*or* elle *etc*) dit la vérité en faisant croire que c'est du bluff ▸**double boiler** = **double saucepan** ▸**double-book** vi [*hotel/airline etc*] faire du surbooking, réserver deux fois la même chambre/place *etc* ◊ vt *room, seat* réserver pour deux personnes différentes ▸**double booking** double réservation *f*, surbooking *m* ▸**double bounce** (*Tennis*) double *m* ▸**double-breasted** (*Dress*) croisé ▸**doublecheck** vti revérifier ◊ n revérification *f* ▸**double chin** double menton *m* ▸**double-chinned** qui a un double menton ▸**double consonant** consonne *f* double *or* redoublée *or* géminée ▸**double cream** (*Brit*) crème fraîche épaisse *or* à fouetter ▸**double-cross*** vt trahir, doubler* ◊ n traîtrise *f*, duplicité *f* ▸**double-date** (*US*) vi sortir à deux couples ▸**double-dealer** fourbe *m* ▸**double-dealing** n double jeu *m*, duplicité *f* ◊ adj hypocrite, faux (*f* fausse) comme un jeton* ▸**double-decker** (*bus*) autobus *m* à impériale; (*aircraft*) deux-ponts *m inv*; (*sandwich*) sandwich *m* à deux garnitures (superposées) ▸**double-declutch** (*Aut*) faire un double débrayage ▸**double density** see **density** ▸**double-digit** adj à deux chiffres; *inflation* égal ou supérieur à 10 % ▸**double-dipper** (*US pej*) cumulard *m* ▸**double-dipping** (*US pej*) cumul *m* d'emplois *or* de salaires ▸**double door** porte *f* à deux battants ▸**double Dutch*** (*Brit*) baragouin* *m*, charabia* *m*; **to talk double Dutch** baragouiner; **it was double Dutch to me** pour moi c'était de l'hébreu* ▸**double eagle** (*Golf*) albatros *m* ▸**double-edged** (*lit, fig*) à double tranchant, à deux tranchants ▸**double entendre** ambiguïté *f*, double entente *f* ▸**double entry book-keeping** comptabilité *f* en partie double ▸**double exposure** (*Phot*) surimpression *f*, double exposition *f* ▸**double-faced** *material* réversible; (*pej*) *person* hypocrite ▸**double fault** (*Tennis*) n double faute *f* ◊ vi faire *or* servir une double faute ▸**double feature** (*Cine*) programme *m* de deux longs métrages ▸**double-figure** adj = **double-digit** ▸**double first** (*Univ*) n double mention *f* très bien (dans deux disciplines) ▸**double flat** (*Mus*) double bémol *m* ▸**double-glaze:** (*Brit*) **to double-glaze a window** poser une double fenêtre ▸**double glazing** (*Brit*) (*gen*) double vitrage *m*; **to put in double glazing** (faire) installer des doubles fenêtres *or* un double vitrage ▸**double helix** double hélice *f* ▸**double indemnity** (*US Insurance*) indemnité *f* double ▸**double jeopardy** (*US Jur*) *mise en cause de l'autorité de la chose jugée* ▸**double-jointed** désarticulé ▸**double-knit(ting)** n (*wool*) laine *f* sport ◊ adj en laine sport ▸**double knot** double nœud *m* ▸**double-lock** fermer à double tour ▸**double lock** serrure *f* de sécurité ▸**double major** (*US Univ*) double *f* dominante ▸**double marking** (*Educ*) double correction *f* ▸**double negative** double négation *f* ▸**double-park** (*Aut*) stationner en double file ▸**double-parking** (*Aut*) stationnement *m* en double file ▸**double pneumonia** (*Med*) pneumonie *f* double ▸**double-quick** (*also* **in double-quick time**) *run etc* au pas de course *or* de gymnastique; *do, finish* en vitesse, en deux temps trois mouvements* ▸**double room** chambre *f* pour deux personnes ▸**double saucepan** casserole *f* à double fond ▸**double sharp** (*Mus*) double dièse *m* ▸**double-sided disk** (*Comput*) disque *m* double ▸**double-space** (*Typ*) vt taper avec un double interligne; **double-spaced, in double spacing** à double interligne ▸**double standard: to have double standards** *or* **a double standard** avoir deux poids, deux mesures ▸**double star** étoile *f* double ▸**double stopping** (*Mus*) doubles cordes *fpl* ▸**double take*: to do a double take** devoir y regarder à deux fois ▸**double talk** paroles ambiguës *or* trompeuses ▸**double taxation agreement** (*Fin, Jur*) convention relative aux doubles impositions ▸**double think*: to do a double think** *tenir un raisonnement ou suivre une démarche où l'on s'accommode (sans vergogne) de contradictions flagrantes* ▸**double time: to get/pay double time** gagner/payer le double; (*US Mil*) **in double time** au pas redoublé (*see also* **time**) ▸**double track** (*Cine*) double bande *f*; (*tape*) double piste *f* ▸**double track line** (*Rail*) ligne *f* à deux voies ▸**double vision** vision *f* double; **to get/have double vision** voir double ▸**double whisky** double whisky *m* ▸**double windows** doubles fenêtres *fpl* ▸**double yolk: egg with a double yolk** œuf *m* à deux jaunes.

5 vt a (*multiply by two*) *number* doubler; *salary, price* doubler, augmenter du double.

b (*fold in two: also* **~ over**) plier en deux, replier, doubler.

c (*Theat*) **he ~s the parts of courtier and hangman** il joue les rôles *or* il a le double rôle du courtisan et du bourreau; **he's doubling the**

hero's part for X il est la doublure de X dans le rôle du héros.

d (*Cards*) *one's opponent, his call* contrer; *one's stake* doubler. (*Bridge*) ~! contre!

6 vi a *[prices, incomes, quantity etc]* doubler.

b (*run*) courir, aller au pas de course.

c (*Cine*) **to ~ for sb** doubler qn.

d (*Bridge*) contrer.

e (*US fig*) **to ~ in brass**‡ avoir une corde supplémentaire à son arc.

▸**double back** 1 vi *[animal, person]* revenir sur ses pas; *[road]* faire un brusque crochet. *[line]* **to double back on itself** former une boucle en épingle à cheveux. 2 vt sep *blanket* rabattre, replier; *page* replier.

▸**double over** 1 vi = **double up a.** 2 vt sep = **double 5b.**

▸**double up** vi a (*bend over sharply*) se plier, se courber. **to double up with laughter/pain** être plié en deux *or* se tordre de rire/de douleur. b (*share room*) partager une chambre (*with* avec). c (*Brit Betting*) parier sur deux chevaux.

doublet ['dʌblɪt] n a (*Dress*) pourpoint *m*, justaucorps *m*. b (*Ling*) doublet *m*.

doubleton ['dʌbltən] n (*Cards*) deux cartes *fpl* d'une (même) couleur, doubleton *m*.

doubling ['dʌblɪŋ] n *[number, letter]* redoublement *m*, doublement *m*.

doubly ['dʌblɪ] adv (*twice as much*) *difficult, grateful* doublement, deux fois plus; (*in two ways*) *mistaken, justified etc* doublement. **to be ~ careful** redoubler de prudence.

doubt [daʊt] 1 n (*NonC*) doute *m*, incertitude *f*. **his honesty is in ~** (*in this instance*) son honnêteté est en doute; (*in general*) son honnêteté est sujette à caution; **I am in (some) ~ about his honesty** j'ai des doutes sur son honnêteté; **the outcome is in ~** l'issue est indécise *or* dans la balance; (*outcome, result etc*) **it is not in ~** cela ne fait aucun doute; **I am in no ~ as to** *or* **about what he means** je n'ai aucun doute sur ce qu'il veut dire; **to be in great ~ about sth** être dans une grande incertitude *or* dans le doute au sujet de qch; **there is room for ~** il est permis de douter; **there is some ~ about whether he'll come or not** on ne sait pas très bien s'il viendra ou non; **to have one's ~s about sth** avoir des doutes sur *or* au sujet de qch; **I have my ~s (about) whether he will come** je doute qu'il vienne; **to cast** *or* **throw ~(s) on sth** mettre qch en doute, jeter le doute sur qch; **I have no ~(s) about it** je n'en doute pas; **no ~ about it!** cela va sans dire!; **no ~** sans doute; **this leaves no ~ that ...** cela ne laisse plus de doute que ... + *subj*; **there is no ~ that ...** il n'y a pas de doute que ... + *indic*; **he'll come without any ~, there's no ~ that he'll come** il viendra sûrement, il n'y a pas de doute qu'il viendra; **no ~ he will come tomorrow** sans doute qu'il viendra demain; **without (a) ~** sans aucun doute, sans le moindre doute; **beyond ~** (adv) indubitablement, à n'en pas douter; (adj) indubitable; **if** *or* **when in ~** s'il y a (un) doute, en cas de doute; *see* **benefit.**

2 vt a *person, sb's honesty, truth of statement* douter de. **I ~ it (very much)** j'en doute (fort); **I ~ed my own eyes** je n'en croyais pas mes yeux.

b douter. **I ~ whether he will come** je doute qu'il vienne; **I don't ~ that he will come** je ne doute pas qu'il vienne; **she didn't ~ that he would come** elle ne doutait pas qu'il viendrait; **I ~ he won't come now** je crains qu'il ne vienne pas maintenant; **I ~ if that is what she wanted** je doute que ce soit ce qu'elle voulait.

3 vi douter (*of* de), avoir des doutes (*of* sur), ne pas être sûr (*of* de). **~ing Thomas** Thomas l'incrédule; **don't be a ~ing Thomas** ne fais pas ton (petit) saint Thomas.

doubter ['daʊtəʳ] n incrédule *mf*, sceptique *mf*.

doubtful ['daʊtfʊl] adj a (*undecided*) *person* incertain, indécis, peu convaincu; *question* douteux, discutable; *result* indécis. **to be ~ about sb/sth** douter de qn/qch, avoir des doutes sur qn/qch; **I'm a bit ~ (about it)** je n'en suis pas (si) sûr; **to be ~ about doing** hésiter à faire; **to look ~** avoir l'air peu convaincu; **it is ~ whether ...** il est douteux que ... + *subj*, on ne sait pas si ... + *indic*, on se demande si ... + *indic*; **it is ~ that ...** il est douteux que ... + *subj*. b (*questionable*) *person* suspect, louche; *affair* douteux, louche. **in ~ taste** d'un goût douteux.

doubtfully ['daʊtfəlɪ] adv (*unconvincedly*) d'un air *or* d'un ton de doute, avec doute; (*hesitatingly*) en hésitant, d'une façon indécise.

doubtfulness ['daʊtfʊlnɪs] n (*hesitation*) indécision *f*, irrésolution *f*; (*uncertainty*) incertitude *f*; (*suspicious quality*) caractère *m* équivoque *or* suspect *or* louche.

doubtless ['daʊtlɪs] adv (*probably*) très probablement; (*indubitably*) sans aucun doute, sûrement, indubitablement.

douceur [duːˈsɜːʳ] n (*gift, tip etc*) petit cadeau.

douche [duːʃ] 1 n (*shower bath*) douche *f*; (*Med*) lavage *m* interne. (*fig*) **it was (like) a cold ~** cela a été une douche froide*; (*US*) **take a ~!**‡ va te faire foutre!‡ 2 vt doucher.

dough [dəʊ] 1 n a pâte *f*. **bread ~** pâte à pain; (*fig*) **to be ~ in sb's hands** être comme une cire molle entre les mains de qn. b (‡: *money*) fric‡ *m*, pognon‡ *m*. 2 comp ▸**doughboy** (*Culin*) boulette *f* (de pâte); (‡: *US Mil*) sammy *m*, (*soldat américain de la Première Guerre mondiale*) ▸**dough-hook** crochet *m* de pétrissage ▸**doughnut** (*Brit*) beignet *m*; **jam** (*Brit*) *or* **jelly** (*US*) **doughnut** beignet *m* à la confiture.

doughty ['daʊtɪ] adj (*liter*) preux (*liter*), vaillant. **~ deeds** hauts faits (*liter*).

doughy ['dəʊɪ] adj *consistency* pâteux; *bread* mal cuit; (*pej*) *complexion* terreux.

dour ['dʊəʳ] adj austère, dur; (*stubborn*) buté. **a ~ Scot** un austère Écossais.

dourly [dʊəlɪ] adv *say* d'un ton dur *or* maussade.

douse [daʊs] vt a (*drench*) plonger dans l'eau, tremper, inonder; *head* tremper. b *flames, light* éteindre.

dove [dʌv] 1 n colombe *f*; (*fig: Pol, esp US*) colombe; *see* **turtle** *etc.* 2 comp ▸**dove-grey** gris perle *inv* ▸**dovecot(e)** colombier *m*, pigeonnier *m*.

Dover ['dəʊvəʳ] n Douvres; *see* **strait.**

dovetail ['dʌvteɪl] 1 n (*Carpentry*) queue *f* d'aronde. **~ joint** assemblage *m* à queue d'aronde. 2 vt (*Carpentry*) assembler à queue d'aronde; (*fig*) *plans etc* faire concorder, raccorder. 3 vi (*Carpentry*) se raccorder (*into* à); (*fig*) bien cadrer, concorder (*with* avec).

dovish* ['dʌvɪʃ] adj (*fig: esp US Pol*) *person* partisan(e) *m(f)* de la négociation et du compromis; *speech, attitude* de compromis.

dowager ['daʊədʒəʳ] n douairière *f*. **~ duchess** duchesse *f* douairière.

dowdiness ['daʊdɪnɪs] n manque *m* de chic.

dowdy ['daʊdɪ] adj *person* mal fagoté*, sans chic; *clothes* démodé, sans chic.

dowel ['daʊəl] 1 n cheville *f* en bois, goujon *m*. 2 vt assembler avec des goujons, goujonner.

dower house ['daʊəhaʊs] n (*Brit*) petit manoir (de douairière).

Dow-Jones average ['daʊ'dʒəʊnz'æv(ə)rɪdʒ] n (*US*) indice *m* Dow-Jones (*moyenne quotidienne des principales valeurs boursières*).

down¹ [daʊn] (*phr vb elem*) 1 adv a (*indicating movement to lower level*) en bas, vers le bas; (*~ to the ground*) à terre, par terre. (*said to a dog*) ~! couché!; **~ with traitors!** à bas les traîtres!; **to come** *or* **go ~** descendre; **to fall ~** tomber; **to go/fall ~ and ~** descendre/tomber de plus en plus bas; **to run ~** descendre en courant; *see* **bend down, knock down, slide down** *etc.*

b (*indicating position at lower level*) en bas. **~ there** en bas (là-bas); **I shall stay ~ here** je vais rester ici *or* en bas; **don't hit a man when he is ~** ne frappez pas un homme à terre; **the sun is ~** le soleil est couché; **the blinds were ~** les stores étaient baissés; **John isn't ~ yet** Jean n'est pas encore descendu; (*Boxing*) **to be ~ for the count** être mis knock-out; *see* **face, head, stay down** *etc.*

c (*from larger town, the north, university etc*) **he came ~ from London yesterday** il est arrivé de Londres hier; **we're going ~ to the sea tomorrow** demain nous allons à la mer; **we're going ~ to Dover tomorrow** demain nous descendons à Douvres; (*Univ*) **he came ~ from Oxford in 1973** il a terminé ses études à Oxford *or* il est sorti d'Oxford en 1973; (*US*) **~ East** (adj/adv) *du/au nord-est de la Nouvelle Angleterre;* **~ under** (*in Australia/New Zealand*) en Australie/Nouvelle-Zélande, aux antipodes; **from ~ under** de l'Australie/la Nouvelle-Zélande; *see* **come down, go down, send down** *etc.*

d (*indicating diminution in volume, degree, activity*) **his shoes were quite worn ~** ses chaussures étaient tout éculées; **the tyres are ~/right ~** les pneus sont dégonflés/à plat; **his temperature has gone ~** sa température a baissé; **I'm £2 ~ on what I expected** j'ai 2 livres de moins que je ne pensais; **she's very run ~** elle est en mauvaise forme, elle est très à plat*; *see* **close down, put down** *etc.*

e (*in writing*) **I've got it ~ in my diary** je l'ai (mis) *or* c'est inscrit sur mon agenda; **let's get it ~ on paper** mettons-le par écrit; **did you get ~ what he said?** as-tu noté ce qu'il a dit?; **to be ~ for the next race** être inscrit dans *or* pour la course suivante; *see* **note, take down, write down** *etc.*

f (*indicating a series or succession*) **~ to** jusqu'à; **from 1700 ~ to the present** de *or* depuis 1700 jusqu'à nos jours; **from the biggest ~ to the smallest** du plus grand (jusqu')au plus petit; **from the king ~ to the poorest beggar** depuis le roi jusqu'au plus pauvre des mendiants; **we are ~ to our last £5** il ne nous reste plus que 5 livres.

g (*phrases*) *[computer]* **to go ~** tomber en panne; **I've been ~ with flu** j'ai été au lit avec une grippe; **to be ~ on sb*** avoir une dent contre qn; **I know the subject ~ to the ground** je connais le sujet à fond; **I am ~ on my luck** je n'ai pas de chance *or* de veine; **it's ~ to him to do it** c'est à lui de le faire; **it's ~ to him now** c'est à lui de jouer maintenant; *see also* **6** *and* **cash, come down, put down, up** *etc.*

2 prep a (*indicating movement to lower level*) du haut en bas de. (*lit*) **he went ~ the hill** il a descendu la colline (*see also* **downhill**); **to slide ~ a wall** se laisser tomber d'un mur; **her hair hung ~ her back** ses cheveux lui tombaient dans le dos; **he ran his finger ~ the list** il a parcouru la liste du doigt.

b (*at a lower part of*) **he's ~ the hill** il est au pied *or* en bas de la côte; **she lives ~ the street (from us)** elle habite plus bas *or* plus loin (que nous) dans la rue; (*fig*) **~ the ages** au cours des siècles.

c (*along*) le long de. **he was walking ~ the street** il descendait la rue; **he has gone ~ town** il est allé *or* descendu *or* parti en ville; **let's go ~ the pub*** allons *or* descendons au pub; **looking ~ this street, you can see ...** si vous regardez le long de cette rue, vous verrez ... .

3 n (*Brit*) **to have a ~ on sb*** avoir une dent contre qn, en vouloir à qn; *see* **up.**

4 adj a **to be** *or* **feel** ~ avoir le cafard*, être déprimé. b (*Brit*) *train* en provenance de la grande ville. **the ~ line** la ligne de la grande ville. c *computer* en panne.
5 vt (*: *replacing vb + down*) **to ~ an opponent** terrasser *or* abattre un adversaire; **he ~ed 3 enemy planes** il a descendu* 3 avions ennemis; **to ~ tools** (*stop work*) cesser le travail; (*strike*) se mettre en grève, débrayer; **he ~ed a glass of beer** il a vidé *or* s'est envoyé* un verre de bière.
6 comp ▸**down-and-out: to be down-and-out** (*Boxing*) aller au tapis pour le compte, être hors de combat; (*destitute*) être sur le pavé; **he's a down-and-out(er)** c'est un clochard ▸**down-at-heel** *see* **heel**[1] ▸**down-bow** (*Mus*) tiré *m* ▸**down-cycle** (*Econ*) cycle *m* de récession ▸**down-home**‡ (*US*) (*from south*) du Sud, sudiste; (*pej*) péquenaud‡ ▸**down-in-the-mouth** abattu, tout triste; **to be down-in-the-mouth** être abattu *or* tout triste, avoir le moral à zéro*; **to look down-in-the-mouth** avoir l'air abattu, faire une sale tête ▸**down-market** (*fig*) *goods, car* bas de gamme *inv*; *newspaper* grande diffusion *inv*; **it's rather down-market** *[programme etc]* c'est plutôt du genre public de masse; **to go** *or* **move down-market** *[company]* se tourner vers le bas de gamme; *[house-purchaser etc]* acheter moins bien ▸**down payment** (*Fin*) acompte *m*, premier versement; **to make a down payment of £10** payer un acompte de 10 livres, payer 10 livres d'acompte ▸**down-river** = **downstream** ▸**down time** *see* **downtime** ▸**down-to-earth** terre à terre *inv or* terre-à-terre *inv*, réaliste; **it was a very down-to-earth plan** c'était un projet très terre à terre; **he's a very down-to-earth person** il a les pieds sur terre.

down[2] [daʊn] n *[bird, person, plant]* duvet *m*; *[fruit]* peau *f* (veloutée); *see* **eider, thistle** *etc.*

down[3] [daʊn] n a (*hill*) colline dénudée. (*Brit*) **the D~s** les Downs *fpl* (*collines herbeuses dans le sud de l'Angleterre*). b (*Brit Geog: Straits of Dover*) **the D~s** les Dunes *fpl*.

downbeat ['daʊn,biːt] 1 n (*Mus*) temps *m* frappé. 2 adj (*gloomy*) *person* abattu; *ending* pessimiste; (*relaxed*) flegmatique, imperturbable.

downcast ['daʊn,kɑːst] 1 adj (*discouraged*) abattu, démoralisé, découragé; (*looking down*) *look, eyes* baissé. 2 n (*Min*) puits *m* d'aérage.

downcry‡ ['daʊn,kraɪ] vt (*US: denigrate*) décrier, dénigrer.

downer* ['daʊnəʳ] n (*tranquilliser*) tranquillisant *m*, sédatif *m*; (*depressing experience*) expérience déprimante *or* démoralisante. **to be on a ~** faire de la déprime*.

downfall ['daʊn,fɔːl] n *[person, empire]* chute *f*, ruine *f*, effondrement *m*; *[hopes]* ruine; *[rain]* chute de pluie.

downgrade ['daʊn,greɪd] 1 vt *person* rétrograder; *hotel* déclasser; *work, job* dévaloriser, déclasser. 2 n (*Rail etc*) rampe descendante, descente *f*. (*fig*) **on the ~** sur le déclin.

downhearted [,daʊn'hɑːtɪd] adj abattu, découragé, déprimé. **don't be ~** ne te laisse pas décourager!

downhill ['daʊn'hɪl] 1 adj a *road etc* en pente, incliné; *walk* dans le sens de la descente (sur un terrain en pente). b (*Ski*) **~ race** descente *f*; **~ racer, ~ specialist** descendeur *m*, -euse *f*; **~ ski(ing)** (ski *m* de) descente *f*. 2 adv: **to go ~** *[road]* aller en descendant, descendre; *[person, car]* descendre la côte *or* la pente; (*fig: get worse*) *[person]* être sur le déclin; *[company, business etc]* péricliter.

Downing Street ['daʊnɪŋ,striːt] n (*Brit*) Downing Street (*résidence du Premier ministre britannique*).

downlighter ['daʊn,laɪtəʳ] n lampe *f or* applique *f* à faisceau descendant.

download ['daʊn,ləʊd] vt (*Comput*) transférer (*pour garder, ou exploiter avec limitation des fonctions*).

downloading ['daʊn,ləʊdɪŋ] n (*Comput*) transfert *m or* chargement *m* des programmes (*avec limitation des fonctions*).

downpipe ['daʊn,paɪp] n (*Brit*) (tuyau *m* de) descente *f*.

downplay‡ ['daʊn,pleɪ] vt (*US fig*) minimiser l'importance de.

downpour ['daʊn,pɔːʳ] n averse *f*, (chute *f* de) pluie torrentielle, déluge *m*.

downright ['daʊnraɪt] 1 adj *person* franc (*f* franche), direct; *refusal* catégorique; *lie* effronté. **it's ~ cheek on his part*** il a un sacré culot* *or* un fier toupet*; **it's a ~ lie to say ...** c'est mentir effrontément *or* c'est purement et simplement mentir que de dire ...; **it's a ~ lie for him to say ...** il ment carrément quand il dit ...; **it is ~ rudeness** c'est d'une impolitesse flagrante. 2 adv *rude* carrément, franchement; *refuse* catégoriquement. **it's ~ impossible** c'est purement et simplement impossible.

downshift ['daʊn,ʃɪft] 1 vi (*US Aut*) rétrograder. 2 n rétrogradation *f*.

downside ['daʊn,saɪd] n a (*US*) **~ up** sens dessus dessous. b (*negative aspect*) inconvénient *m*, désavantage *m*, mauvais côté *m*. **on the ~** côté inconvénients; *[investment]* **~ risk** risque *m* de baisse *or* de chute du cours.

downspout ['daʊn,spaʊt] n (*US*) = **downpipe**.

Down's syndrome ['daʊnz,sɪndrəʊm] n mongolisme *m*, trisomie *f*. **a ~ baby** un bébé mongolien *or* trisomique.

downstage ['daʊn,steɪdʒ] adv sur *or* vers le devant de la scène (*from* par rapport à).

downstairs ['daʊn'stɛəz] 1 adv (*gen*) en bas; (*to or on floor below*) à l'étage inférieur *or* en-dessous; (*to or on ground floor*) au rez-de-chaussée. **to go** *or* **come ~** descendre (l'escalier); **to run/crawl** *etc* **~** descendre (l'escalier) en courant/en rampant *etc*; **the people ~** les gens *mpl* (de l'appartement) du dessous. 2 adj *room etc* (*gen*) en bas; (*on floor below*) de l'étage inférieur *or* au-dessous; (*on ground floor*) du rez-de-chaussée. **a ~ flat** un appartement au rez-de-chaussée.

downstate ['daʊn,steɪt] (*US*) 1 n campagne *f*, sud *m* de l'État. 2 adj de la campagne, du sud de l'État. 3 adv *be* à la campagne, dans le sud; *go* à la campagne, vers le sud.

downstream ['daʊn,striːm] adj, adv en aval. **to go ~** descendre le courant; (*fig*) **~ industries** industries *fpl* en aval.

downstroke ['daʊn,strəʊk] n a (*in writing*) plein *m*. b *[piston etc]* course descendante, mouvement *m* de descente.

downswept ['daʊn,swept] adj (*Aviat*) *wings* surbaissé.

downswing ['daʊn,swɪŋ] n (*fig*) baisse *f*, passage *m* à la phase descendante.

downtime ['daʊntaɪm] n *[machine]* temps *m or* durée *f* d'immobilisation; (*Comput*) temps *m* d'arrêt.

downtown ['daʊn'taʊn] 1 adv en ville. 2 adj: **~ Chicago** le centre *or* le quartier commerçant de Chicago.

downtrodden ['daʊn,trɒdən] adj (*fig*) *person, nation* opprimé, tyrannisé.

downturn ['daʊn,tɜːn] n = **downswing**.

downward ['daʊnwəd] 1 adj *movement, pull* vers le bas; *road* qui descend en pente; *glance* baissé. (*fig*) **the ~ path** la pente fatale, le chemin qui mène à la ruine; (*St Ex*) **~ trend** tendance *f* à la baisse. 2 adv = **downwards**.

downwards ['daʊnwədz] (*phr vb elem*) adv *go* vers le bas, de haut en bas, en bas. **to slope (gently) ~** descendre (en pente douce); **to look ~** regarder en bas *or* vers le bas; **looking ~** les yeux baissés, la tête baissée; **place the book face ~** posez le livre face en dessous; (*fig*) **from the 10th century ~** à partir du 10ᵉ siècle; (*fig*) **from the king ~** depuis le roi (jusqu'au plus humble), du haut en bas de l'échelle sociale.

downwind ['daʊn,wɪnd] adv sous le vent (*from* par rapport à). (*Hunting etc*) **to be ~ of sth** avoir le vent *or* être sous le vent de qch.

downy ['daʊnɪ] adj a *skin, leaf* couvert de duvet, duveté; *softness* duveteux; *peach* duveté, velouté; *cushion* duveteux. b (*Brit* ‡: *sly, sharp*) malin (*f* -igne), roublard*.

dowry ['daʊrɪ] n dot *f*.

dowse [daʊz] 1 vi (*search for water*) faire de l'hydroscopie *or* de la radiesthésie; (*search for ore*) faire de la radiesthésie. **dowsing rod** baguette *f* (de sourcier). 2 vt = **douse**.

dowser ['daʊzəʳ] n (*for water*) sourcier *m*, radiesthésiste *mf*; (*for ore*) radiesthésiste.

doxology [dɒk'sɒlədʒɪ] n doxologie *f*.

doxy ['dɒksɪ] n (‡, †) catin† *f*.

doyen ['dɔɪən] n doyen *m* (d'âge).

doyenne ['dɔɪen] n doyenne *f*.

doz. [dʌz] abbr of **dozen**.

doze [dəʊz] 1 n somme *m*. **to have a ~** faire un petit somme. 2 vi sommeiller. **to be dozing** être assoupi.
▸**doze off** vi s'assoupir, s'endormir.

dozen ['dʌzn] n douzaine *f*. **3 ~** 3 douzaines; **a ~ shirts** une douzaine de chemises; **a round ~** une bonne douzaine; **half-a-~, a half-~** une demi-douzaine; **20p a ~** 20 pence la douzaine; **~s of times** des dizaines *or* douzaines de fois; **there are ~s like that** des choses (*or* des gens) comme cela, on en trouve à la douzaine; *see* **baker, nineteen**.

dozy ['dəʊzɪ] adj a (*sleepy*) à moitié endormi, somnolent. b (*: *stupid*) gourde*, pas très dégourdi*.

DP [diː'piː] n (abbr of **data processing**) *see* **data**.

DPh [diːpiː'eɪtʃ] n, **D Phil** [diː'fɪl] n (abbr of **Doctor of Philosophy**) ≃ doctorat en philosophie.

DPM [diːpiː'em] n (abbr of **Diploma in Psychiatric Medicine**) *diplôme de psychiatrie*.

DPP [diːpiː'piː] n (*Brit*) (abbr of **Director of Public Prosecutions**) *see* **director**.

Dr ['dɒktəʳ] abbr of **Doctor**. (*on envelope*) **~ J. Smith** Dr J. Smith; (*in letters*) **Dear ~ Smith** Monsieur, (*less formally*) Cher Monsieur; (*if known to writer*) Cher Docteur.

dr (*Comm*) abbr of **debtor**.

drab [dræb] 1 adj *colour* terne, fade; *surroundings, existence* terne, morne, gris. 2 n a (*NonC: Tex*) grosse toile bise. b (††) (*slattern*) souillon *f*; (*prostitute*) grue‡ *f*.

drabness ['dræbnɪs] n (*see* **drab 1**) caractère *m or* aspect *m* terne *or* morne; fadeur *f*.

drachm [dræm] n a (*Measure, Pharm*) drachme *f*. b = **drachma**.

drachma ['drækmə] n, pl **~s** *or* **~e** ['drækmiː] (*coin*) drachme *f*.

draconian [drə'kəʊnɪən] adj draconien.

Dracula ['drækjʊlə] n Dracula *m*.

draft [drɑːft] 1 n a (*outline*) (*gen*) avant-projet *m*; *[letter]* brouillon

m; *[novel]* premier jet, ébauche *f*.
b (*Comm, Fin: for money*) traite *f*, effet *m*. **to make a ~ on** tirer sur.
c (*Mil: group of men*) détachement *m*.
d (*US Mil: conscript intake*) contingent *m*. **to be ~ age** être en âge de faire son service.
e (*US*) = **draught.**
2 comp ▸draft board (*US Mil*) conseil *m* de révision **▸draft card** (*US Mil*) ordre *m* d'incorporation **▸draft dodger** (*US Mil*) insoumis *m* **▸draft letter** brouillon *m* de lettre; (*more frm*) projet de lettre **▸draft version** version *f* préliminaire.
3 vt a (*also* **~ out**) *letter* faire le brouillon de; *speech* (*gen*) écrire, préparer; (*first ~*) faire le brouillon de; (*final version*) rédiger; (*Parl*) *bill*, (*Comm, Fin*) *contract* rédiger, dresser; *plan* esquisser, dresser; *diagram* esquisser.
b (*US Mil*) *conscript* appeler (sous les drapeaux), incorporer. (*esp Mil*) **to ~ sb to a post/to do sth** détacher *or* désigner qn à un poste/pour faire qch.

draftee [dræf'tiː] **n** (*US: Mil, fig*) recrue *f*.
draftiness ['dræftɪnɪs] **n** (*US*) = **draughtiness.**
draftsman ['dræftsmən] **n** (*US*) = **draughtsman a.**
draftsmanship ['dræftsmənʃɪp] **n** (*US*) = **draughtsmanship.**
drafty ['dræftɪ] **adj** (*US*) = **draughty.**
drag [dræg] **1 n a** (*for dredging etc*) drague *f*; (*Naut: cluster of hooks*) araignée *f*; (*heavy sledge*) traîneau *m*; (*Agr: harrow*) herse *f*.
b = **dragnet;** *see* **2** *below*.
c (*Aviat, Naut etc: resistance*) résistance *f*, traînée *f*.
d (*Aut, Rail etc: brake*) sabot *m or* patin *m* de frein.
e (*Hunting*) drag *m*.
f (*hindrance*) boulet *m*, entrave *f*, frein *m* (*on* à); (*: *person*) raseur* *m*, -euse* *f*, casse-pieds* *mf inv*; (*tedium*) corvée *f*. **he's an awful ~ on them** ils le traînent comme un boulet; **what a ~ to have to go there!*** quelle corvée *or* quelle barbe* d'avoir à y aller!; **this thing is a ~!*** quelle barbe* ce truc-la!*, ce que c'est embêtant ce truc-là!*
g (‡: *pull on cigarette, pipe*) bouffée *f*. **here, have a ~** tiens, tire une bouffée.
h (‡: *women's clothing worn by men*) travesti *m*. **in ~** en travesti.
i (*US* ‡: *influence*) piston *m*. **to use one's ~** travailler dans la coulisse, user de son influence.
j (*US*) **the main ~** la grand-rue.
2 comp ▸drag coefficient, drag factor (*Aut*) coefficient *m* de pénétration dans l'air **▸drag lift** (*Ski*) tire-fesses *m inv* **▸dragnet** (*for fish*) seine *f*, drège *f*; (*for birds*) tirasse *f*; (*fig: by police*) rafle *f* (policière) **▸drag queen‡** travelo‡ *m* **▸drag race** (*US Aut*) course *f* de hot-rods à départ arrêté **▸drag shoe** (*Aut, Rail etc*) sabot *m or* patin *m* (de frein) **▸drag show‡** (*Theat*) spectacle *m* de travestis **▸dragstrip, dragway** (*US Aut*) piste *f* de vitesse (*pour voitures au moteur gonflé*).
3 vi a (*trail along*) *[object]* traîner (à terre); *[anchor]* chasser.
b (*lag behind*) rester en arrière, traîner.
c (*Aut*) *[brakes]* frotter, (se) gripper.
d (*fig*) *[time, work, an entertainment]* traîner; *[conversation]* traîner, languir.
4 vt a *person, object* traîner, tirer; *person* entraîner. **to ~ one's feet** (*scuff feet*) traîner les pieds; (*go slow*) traîner (exprès); (*fig: show reluctance*) **to ~ one's feet** *or* **one's heels** faire preuve de mauvaise volonté; (*Naut*) **to ~ anchor** chasser sur ses ancres; (*fig*) **to ~ the truth from sb** arracher la vérité à qn; (*US*) **to ~ ass‡** glander‡, traînasser.
b *river* draguer (*for* à la recherche de).
c (*fig: involve*) *person* entraîner; *issue, question etc* mêler. **don't ~ me into your affairs!** ne m'entraîne pas dans vos histoires; **to ~ politics into sth** mêler la politique à qch.

▸drag about 1 vi traîner. **2 vt sep** traîner, trimbaler*. **to drag o.s. about (in pain** *etc***)** se traîner péniblement (sous l'effet de la douleur *etc*).
▸drag along vt sep *person* entraîner (à contrecœur); *toy etc* tirer. **to drag o.s. along** se traîner, avancer péniblement.
▸drag apart vt sep séparer de force.
▸drag away vt sep arracher (*from* à), emmener de force (*from* de). **she dragged him away from the television*** elle l'a arraché à la télévision.
▸drag down vt sep tirer du haut, entraîner (en bas). (*fig*) **to drag sb down to one's own level** rabaisser qn à son niveau; **his illness is dragging him down** sa maladie l'affaiblit.
▸drag in vt sep (*fig*) *subject, remark* tenir à placer, amener à tout prix.
▸drag on vi *[meeting, conversation]* se prolonger, s'éterniser.
▸drag out 1 vi = **drag on. 2 vt sep** *discussion* faire traîner.
▸drag up vt sep a (‡ *pej*) *child* élever à la diable *or* tant bien que mal. **b** *scandal, story* remettre sur le tapis, déterrer.

dragoman ['drægəʊmən] **n** drogman *m*.
dragon ['drægən] **1 n a** (*Myth, Zool, also fig: fierce person*) dragon *m*. **b** (*Mil: armoured tractor*) tracteur blindé. **2 comp ▸dragonfly** libellule *f*, demoiselle *f*.
dragoon [drə'guːn] **1 n** (*Mil*) dragon *m*. **2 vt: to ~ sb into doing** contraindre *or* forcer qn à faire.
dragster ['drægstəʳ] **n** (*US Aut*) voiture *f* au moteur gonflé, hot-rod *m*.
dragsville‡ ['drægzvɪl] **n** (*US*) **it's just ~‡** c'est casse-pieds* *or* barbant*, on s'emmerde‡.
drain [dreɪn] **1 n a** (*in town*) égout *m*; (*in house*) canalisation *f* sanitaire, tuyau *m* d'écoulement; (*on washing machine etc*) tuyau d'écoulement; (*Agr, Med*) drain *m*; (*~ cover*) (*in street*) bouche *f* d'égout; (*beside house*) puisard *m*. **~s** (*in town*) égouts; (*in house*) canalisations *fpl* sanitaires; (*Agr*) drains; **open ~** canal *m or* fossé *m or* égout à ciel ouvert; (*fig*) **to throw one's money down the ~** jeter son argent par les fenêtres; **all his hopes have gone down the ~*** voilà tous ses espoirs fichus* *or* à l'eau*.
b (*fig*) (*on resources, manpower*) saignée *f* (*on* de), perte *f* (*on* en); (*on strength*) épuisement *m* (*on* de). **looking after her father has been a great ~ on her** s'occuper de son père l'a complètement épuisée; *see* **brain.**
2 comp ▸drainboard (*US*), **draining board** égouttoir *m*, paillasse *f* **▸draining spoon** écumoire *f* **▸drainpipe** tuyau *m* d'écoulement *or* de drainage **▸drainpipe trousers** (*Brit*) pantalon-cigarette *m*.
3 vt *land, marshes* drainer, assécher; *vegetables, dishes* égoutter; *mine* vider, drainer; *reservoir* mettre à sec, vider; *boiler* vider, vidanger; (*Med*) *wound* drainer; *glass* vider complètement; *wine in glass* boire jusqu'à la dernière goutte. (*Comm*) **~ed weight** poids net égoutté; (*fig*) **to ~ sb of strength** épuiser qn; (*fig*) **to ~ a country of resources** saigner un pays.
4 vi *[liquid]* s'écouler; *[stream]* s'écouler (*into* dans); *[vegetables]* (s')égoutter.

▸drain away, drain off 1 vi *[liquid]* s'écouler; *[strength]* s'épuiser. **2 vt sep** *liquid* faire couler (*pour vider un récipient*).

drainage ['dreɪnɪdʒ] **1 n** (*act of draining*) drainage *m*, assèchement *m*; (*system of drains*) (*on land*) système *m* de fossés *or* de tuyaux de drainage; *[town]* système d'égouts; *[house]* système d'écoulement des eaux; (*sewage*) eaux usées; (*Geol*) système hydrographique fluvial. **2 comp ▸drainage area, drainage basin** (*Geol*) bassin *m* hydrographique **▸drainage channel** (*Constr*) barbacane *f* **▸drainage tube** (*Med*) drain *m*.
drainer ['dreɪnəʳ] **n** égouttoir *m*.
drake [dreɪk] **n** canard *m* (mâle); *see* **duck¹.**
Dralon ['dreɪlɒn] **n** ® dralon *m* ®.
DRAM, D-RAM ['diːræm] (*Comput*) **abbr of dynamic random access memory.**
dram [dræm] **n** (*Brit*) **a** (*Measure, Pharm*) drachme *f*. **b** (*: *small drink*) goutte *f*, petit verre.
drama ['drɑːmə] **1 n a** (*NonC: gen*) théâtre *m*. **to study ~** étudier l'art *m* dramatique. **English ~** le théâtre anglais. **b** (*play*) drame *m*, pièce *f* de théâtre; (*fig*) drame. **c** (*NonC: quality of being dramatic*) drame *m*. **2 comp ▸drama critic** critique *m* dramatique.
dramatic [drə'mætɪk] **adj a** (*Literat, Theat*) *art, criticism, artist* dramatique. (*Literat*) **~ irony** ironie *f* dramatique; *see* **amateur. b** (*fig: theatrical*) *effect, entry* théâtral; (*spectacular*) *effect, situation, event* dramatique; *change* spectaculaire.
dramatically [drə'mætɪkəlɪ] **adv a** (*Literat, Theat*) *effective etc* du point du vue théâtral. **b** (*see* **dramatic b**) de manière théâtrale; dramatiquement, de manière dramatique.
dramatics [drə'mætɪks] **npl** (*Theat*) art *m* dramatique; (*) comédie *f* (*fig*); *see* **amateur.**
dramatis personae ['dræmətɪspɜː'səʊnaɪ] **npl** personnages *mpl* (*d'une pièce etc*).
dramatist ['dræmətɪst] **n** auteur *m* dramatique, dramaturge *m*.
dramatization [ˌdræmətaɪ'zeɪʃən] **n** (*see* **dramatize**) adaptation *f* pour la scène *etc;* dramatisation *f*.
dramatize ['dræmətaɪz] **vt a** *novel* adapter pour la scène *or* (*Cine*) pour l'écran *or* (*TV*) pour la télévision. **they ~d several episodes from his life** ils ont présenté plusieurs épisodes de sa vie sous forme de sketch. **b** (*make vivid*) *event* dramatiser, rendre dramatique *or* émouvant; (*exaggerate*) dramatiser, faire un drame de.
Drambuie [dræm'bjuːɪ] **n** ® Drambuie *f* ®.
drank [dræŋk] **pret of drink.**
drape [dreɪp] **1 vt** *window, statue, person* draper (*with* de); *room, altar* tendre (*with* de); *curtain, length of cloth* draper. **she ~d herself over the settee*** elle s'est étalée sur le canapé. **2 n: ~s** (*Brit: hangings*) tentures *fpl*; (*US: curtains*) rideaux *mpl*.
draper ['dreɪpəʳ] **n** (*Brit*) marchand(e) *m(f)* de nouveautés.
drapery ['dreɪpərɪ] **n a** (*material*) draperie *f*, étoffes *fpl*; (*hangings*) tentures *fpl*, draperies. **b** (*Brit: also* **draper's shop**) magasin *m* de nouveautés.
drastic ['dræstɪk] **adj** *remedy* énergique; *effect, change* radical; *measures* énergique, sévère, draconien; *price reduction* massif.
drastically ['dræstɪkəlɪ] **adv** *change etc* radicalement; *cut, reduce* radicalement, sévèrement; *raise or reduce prices* considérablement.
drat* [dræt] **excl** (*euph for* **damn**) sapristi!*, diable! **~ the child!** au diable cet enfant!, quelle barbe* que cet enfant!
dratted* ['drætɪd] **adj** sacré* (*before n*), maudit (*before n*).

draught, (*US*) **draft** [drɑːft] 1 n a courant *m* d'air; (*for fire*) tirage *m*; (*Naut*) tirant *m* d'eau. **beer on ~** bière *f* à la pression; (*fig: financially*) **to feel the ~** devoir se serrer la ceinture*; (*fig, esp US: unfriendliness*) **I felt a ~*** j'ai senti qu'il (*etc*) me traitait avec froideur.
b (*drink*) coup *m*; *[medicine]* potion *f*, breuvage *m*. **a ~ of cider** un coup de cidre; **to drink in long ~s** boire à longs traits.
c (*Brit*) **(game of) ~s** (jeu *m* de) dames *fpl*.
d (*rough sketch*) = **draft 1a**.
2 comp *animal* de trait; *cider, beer* à la pression ▸**draughtboard** (*Brit*) damier *m* ▸**draught excluder** bourrelet *m* (*de porte, de fenêtre*) ▸**draughtproof** adj calfeutré ◊ vt calfeutrer ▸**draughtproofing** calfeutrage *m*, calfeutrement *m*.

draughtiness, (*US*) **draftiness** ['drɑːftɪnɪs] n (*NonC*) courants *mpl* d'air.

draughtsman ['drɑːftsmən] n a ((*US*) **draftsman**) (*Art*) dessinateur *m*, -trice *f*; (*in drawing office*) dessinateur, -trice industriel(le). b (*Brit: in game*) pion *m*.

draughtsmanship, (*US*) **draftsmanship** ['drɑːftsmənʃɪp] n *[artist]* talent *m* de dessinateur, coup *m* de crayon; (*in industry*) art *m* du dessin industriel.

draughty, (*US*) **drafty** ['drɑːftɪ] adj *room* plein de courants d'air; *street corner* exposé à tous les vents *or* aux quatre vents.

draw [drɔː] pret **drew**, ptp **drawn** 1 vt a (*pull: gen*) *object, cord, string, bolt* tirer. **to ~ a bow** tirer à l'arc; **to ~ the curtains** (*open*) tirer *or* ouvrir les rideaux; (*shut*) tirer *or* fermer les rideaux; **to ~ one's hand over one's eyes** se passer la main sur les yeux; **I drew her arm through mine** j'ai passé *or* glissé son bras sous le mien; **to ~ a book towards one** tirer un livre vers soi; **to ~ one's finger along a surface** passer le doigt sur une surface; **to ~ one's hat over one's eyes** baisser son chapeau sur ses yeux; **to ~ one's belt tighter** serrer sa ceinture; (*Med*) **to ~ an abscess** faire mûrir un abcès; (*aim*) **to ~ a bead on sth** viser qch.
b (*pull behind*) *coach, cart* tirer, traîner; *train* tirer; *caravan, trailer* remorquer.
c (*extract, remove*) *teeth* extraire, arracher; *cork* retirer, enlever. (*fig*) **to ~ sb's teeth** mettre qn hors d'état de nuire; (*Sewing*) **to ~ threads** tirer des fils; **to ~ a ticket out of a hat** tirer un billet d'un chapeau; **to ~ one's gun** tirer son pistolet; **he drew a gun on me** il a tiré un pistolet et l'a braqué sur moi; (*fig*) **to ~ the sword** passer à l'attaque; **with ~n sword** l'épée dégainée.
d (*obtain from source*) *wine* tirer (*from* de); *water* (*from tap, pump*) tirer (*from* de); (*from well*) puiser (*from* dans). **to ~ a bath** faire couler un bain, préparer un bain; **the stone hit him and drew blood** la pierre l'a frappé et l'a fait saigner; (*Med*) **to ~ blood from sb's arm** faire une prise de sang à qn; (*fig*) **that remark drew blood** cette remarque a porté; (*fig*) **to ~ sb's fire** attirer les foudres de qn; **to ~ (a) breath** aspirer, respirer; (*fig*) souffler; **to ~ lots (for sth)** tirer (qch) au sort; **to ~ straws** tirer à la courte paille; **to ~ the short straw** (*lit*) tirer la paille la plus courte; (*fig*) tirer le mauvais numéro; **they drew lots as to who should do it** ils ont tiré au sort (pour décider) qui le ferait; **to ~ the first prize** gagner *or* décrocher le gros lot; **to ~ a card from the pack** tirer une carte du jeu; (*Cards*) **to ~ trumps** tirer *or* faire tomber les atouts; **to ~ inspiration from** tirer son inspiration de, puiser son inspiration dans; **to ~ comfort from** puiser une *or* sa consolation dans; **her singing drew tears from the audience** sa façon de chanter a fait pleurer les auditeurs; **her singing drew applause from the audience** sa façon de chanter a provoqué les applaudissements des auditeurs; **to ~ a smile/a laugh from sb** faire sourire/rire qn; **I could ~ no reply from him** je n'ai pu tirer de lui aucune réponse; **to ~ money from the bank** retirer de l'argent à la banque *or* de la banque; **to ~ a cheque on a bank** tirer un chèque sur une banque; **to ~ one's salary/pay** toucher son traitement/son salaire; *see* **blank**.
e (*attract*) *attention, customer, crowd* attirer. **the play has ~n a lot of criticism** la pièce a donné lieu à *or* s'est attiré de nombreuses critiques; **to feel ~n towards sb** se sentir attiré par *or* porté vers qn.
f (*cause to move, do, speak etc*) **her shouts drew me to the scene** ses cris m'ont attiré sur les lieux; **to ~ sb into a plan** entraîner qn dans un projet; **he refuses to be ~n** (*will not speak*) il refuse de parler; (*will not react*) il refuse de se laisser provoquer *or* de réagir; **to ~ sth to a close** *or* **an end** mettre fin à qch.
g *picture* dessiner; *plan, line, circle* tracer; (*fig*) *situation* faire un tableau de; *character* peindre, dépeindre. **to ~ sb's portrait** faire le portrait de qn; **to ~ a map** (*Geog*) dresser une carte; (*Scol*) faire *or* dessiner une carte; (*fig*) **I ~ the line at scrubbing floors** je n'irai pas jusqu'à *or* je me refuse à frotter les parquets; **I ~ the line at murder** (*personally*) je n'irai pas jusqu'au *or* je me refuse au meurtre; (*as far as others are concerned*) je n'admets pas *or* je ne tolère pas le meurtre; **we must ~ the line somewhere** il faut se fixer une limite, il y a des limites *or* une limite à tout; **it's hard to know where to ~ the line** il n'est pas facile de savoir où fixer les limites.
h (*establish, formulate*) *conclusion* tirer (*from* de); *comparison, parallel* établir, faire (*between* entre); *distinction* faire, établir (*between* entre).
i (*Naut*) **the boat ~s 4 metres** le bateau a un tirant d'eau de 4 mètres, le bateau cale 4 mètres.
j **to ~ (a match)** (*Sport*) faire match nul; (*Chess*) faire partie nulle.
k (*infuse*) *tea* faire infuser.
l (*Culin*) *fowl* vider; *see* **hang**.
m (*Hunting*) **to ~ a fox** débusquer *or* lancer un renard.
n *metal* étirer; *wire* tréfiler.
2 vi a (*move, come*) *[person]* se diriger (*towards* vers). **to ~ to one side** s'écarter; **to ~ round the table** se rassembler *or* s'assembler autour de la table; **the train drew into the station** le train est entré en gare; **the car drew over towards the centre of the road** la voiture a dévié vers le milieu de la chaussée; **he drew ahead of the other runners** il s'est détaché des autres coureurs; **the 2 horses drew level** les 2 chevaux sont arrivés à la hauteur l'un de l'autre; **to ~ near** *[person]* s'approcher (*to* de); *[time, event]* approcher; **to ~ nearer (to)** s'approcher un peu plus (de); **to ~ to an end** *or* **a close** tirer à *or* toucher à sa fin.
b *[chimney, pipe]* tirer; *[pump, vacuum cleaner]* aspirer.
c (*be equal*) *[two teams]* faire match nul; (*in exams, competitions*) être ex æquo *inv*. **the competitors/the teams drew for second place** les concurrents *mpl*/les équipes *fpl* sont arrivé(e)s deuxièmes ex æquo *or* ont remporté la deuxième place ex æquo.
d (*Cards*) **to ~ for partners** tirer pour les partenaires.
e (*Art*) dessiner. **he ~s well** il dessine bien, il sait bien dessiner.
f *[tea]* infuser.
3 n a (*lottery*) loterie *f*, tombola *f*; (*act of ~ing a lottery*) tirage *m* au sort; *see* **luck**.
b (*Sport*) match nul, partie nulle. **the match ended in a ~** ils ont fini par faire match nul; **5 wins and 2 ~s** 5 matches gagnés et 2 matches nuls.
c (*attraction*) attraction *f*, succès *m*; (*Comm*) réclame *f*. **Laurence Olivier was the big ~** Laurence Olivier était la grande attraction.
d **to beat sb to the ~** (*lit*) dégainer plus vite que qn; (*fig*) devancer qn; **to be quick on the ~** (*lit*) avoir la détente rapide; (*fig:* *) avoir la repartie facile.
4 comp ▸**drawback** (*disadvantage*) inconvénient *m*, désavantage *m* (*to* à); (*Tax: refund*) drawback *m* ▸**drawbridge** pont-levis *m*, pont basculant *or* à bascule ▸**draw poker** (*US*) *sorte de jeu de poker* ▸**draw-sheet** alaise *f* ▸**drawstring** cordon *m* ▸**draw(-top) table** table *f* à rallonge.

▸**draw along** vt sep *cart* tirer, traîner; (*fig*) *person* entraîner.

▸**draw apart** vi s'éloigner *or* s'écarter l'un de l'autre, se séparer.

▸**draw aside** 1 vi *[people]* s'écarter. 2 vt sep *person* tirer *or* prendre à l'écart; *object* écarter.

▸**draw away** 1 vi a *[person]* s'éloigner, s'écarter (*from* de); *[car etc]* démarrer. **to draw away from the kerb** s'éloigner du trottoir. b (*move ahead*) *[runner, racehorse etc]* se détacher (*from* de), prendre de l'avance (*from* sur). 2 vt sep *person* éloigner, emmener; *object* retirer, ôter.

▸**draw back** 1 vi (*move backwards*) (se) reculer (*from* de), faire un mouvement en arrière; (*fig*) se retirer, reculer (*at, before, from* devant). 2 vt sep *person* faire reculer; *object, one's hand* retirer. 3 **drawback** n *see* **draw 4**.

▸**draw down** vt sep *blind* baisser, descendre; (*fig*) *blame, ridicule* attirer (*on* sur).

▸**draw in** 1 vi a (*Aut*) **to draw in by the kerb** (*pull over*) se rapprocher du trottoir; (*stop*) s'arrêter le long du trottoir. b (*get shorter*) **the days are drawing in** les jours diminuent *or* raccourcissent. 2 vt sep a *air* aspirer, respirer. b (*attract*) *crowds* attirer. **the play is drawing in huge returns** la pièce fait des recettes énormes; (*fig*) **to draw sb in on a project** recruter qn pour un projet. c (*pull in*) rentrer; *reins* tirer sur. **to draw in one's claws** (*gen, also fig*) rentrer ses griffes; *[cat]* faire patte de velours; *see* **horn**.

▸**draw off** 1 vi *[army, troops]* se retirer. 2 vt sep *gloves* retirer, ôter; *garment* ôter, enlever; *pint of beer* tirer; (*Med*) *blood* prendre.

▸**draw on** 1 vi *[time]* s'avancer. 2 vt sep a *stockings, gloves, garment* enfiler; *shoes* mettre. b (*fig: encourage*) *person* entraîner, encourager. 3 vt fus = **draw upon**.

▸**draw out** 1 vi (*become longer*) **the days are drawing out** les jours rallongent. 2 vt sep a (*bring out, remove*) *handkerchief, purse* sortir, tirer (*from* de); *money from bank* retirer (*from* de); *secret, plan* soutirer (*from* à); (*fig*) *person* faire parler. **he's shy, try and draw him out (of his shell)** il est timide, essayez de le faire parler *or* de le faire sortir de sa coquille. b (*stretch, extend*) *wire* étirer, tréfiler; (*fig*) *speech, meeting* faire traîner, (faire) tirer en longueur; *meal* prolonger.

▸**draw up** 1 vi (*stop*) *[car etc]* s'arrêter, stopper. 2 vt sep a *chair* approcher; *troops* aligner, ranger; *boat* tirer à sec. **to draw o.s. up (to one's full height)** se redresser (fièrement). b (*formulate, set out*) *inventory* dresser; *list, contract, agreement* dresser, rédiger; *plan, scheme* formuler, établir; (*Fin*) *bill* établir, dresser.

▸**draw (up)on** vt fus: **to draw (up)on one's savings** prendre *or* tirer sur ses économies; **to draw (up)on one's imagination** faire appel à son imagination.

drawee [drɔːˈiː] n (*Fin*) tiré *m*.

drawer [drɔːʳ] n a *[furniture]* tiroir *m*; *see* **bottom, chest**[1] *etc.* b [ˈdrɔːəʳ] (*person*) *[cheque etc]* tireur *m*; (*Art*) *[pictures]* dessinateur *m*, -trice *f*.

drawers† [drɔːz] npl *[men]* caleçon *m*; *[women]* culotte *f*, pantalon(s)† *m(pl)*.

drawing [ˈdrɔːɪŋ] 1 n a (*Art*) dessin *m*. **a pencil ~** un dessin au crayon; **a chalk ~** un pastel; **rough ~** ébauche *f*, esquisse *f*, croquis *m*. b (*NonC: extending, tapering*) *[metals]* étirage *m*. 2 comp ▸**drawing board** planche *f* à dessin; (*fig*) **the scheme is still on the drawing board** le projet est encore à l'étude; (*fig*) **back to the drawing board!** retour à la case départ! ▸**drawing office** (*Brit*) bureau *m* de dessin industriel ▸**drawing paper** (*Art*) papier *m* à dessin ▸**drawing pen** (*Art*) tire-ligne *m* ▸**drawing pin** (*Brit*) punaise *f* (*à papier*) ▸**drawing room** salon *m*; (*larger*) salle *f* or salon de réception.

drawl [drɔːl] 1 vi parler d'une voix traînante. 2 vt dire *or* prononcer d'une voix traînante. 3 n débit traînant, voix traînante. **a slight American ~** un léger accent américain; **... he said with a ~ ...** dit-il d'une voix traînante.

drawn [drɔːn] 1 ptp of **draw**; *see also* **long**. 2 adj a (*haggard*) *features* tiré, crispé. **to look ~** avoir les traits tirés; **face ~ with pain** visage crispé par la douleur. b (*equal*) *game, match* nul. **~ battle** bataille indécise. 3 comp ▸**drawn butter** (*Culin*) beurre fondu ▸**drawn(-thread) work** (*Sewing*) ouvrage *m* à fils tirés *or* à jour(s).

dray [dreɪ] n *[brewer]* haquet *m*; *[wood, stones]* fardier *m*; *[quarry work]* binard *m*.

dread [dred] 1 vt redouter, appréhender. **to ~ doing** redouter de faire; **to ~ that ...** redouter que ... ne + *subj*; **the ~ed Mrs B** la redoutable Mme B; (*hum*) **the ~ed exam/medicine** l'examen/le médicament tant redouté (*hum*). 2 n terreur *f*, effroi *m*, épouvante *f*. **in ~ of doing** dans la crainte de faire; **to be** *or* **stand in ~ of** redouter, vivre dans la crainte de. 3 adj (*liter*) redoutable, terrible.

dreadful [ˈdredfʊl] adj *crime, sight, suffering* épouvantable, affreux, atroce; *weapon, foe* redoutable; (*less strong: unpleasant*) *weather* affreux, atroce; (*) *child* insupportable, terrible. **what a ~ nuisance!*** quelle barbe!*, c'est rudement embêtant!*; **it's a ~ thing but ...** c'est terrible mais ...; **what a ~ thing to happen!** quelle horreur!; **I feel ~!** (*ill*) je ne me sens pas bien (du tout)!; (*ashamed*) j'ai vraiment honte!; *see* **penny**.

dreadfully [ˈdredfəlɪ] adv *frightened, late* terriblement, affreusement, horriblement. **I'm ~ sorry but ...** je regrette infiniment mais ...; **I'm ~ sorry** je suis absolument désolé.

dreadlocks [ˈdred,lɒks] npl dreadlocks *fpl*.

dreadnought [ˈdrednɔːt] n (*Naut*) cuirassé *m* (d'escadre).

dream [driːm] (vb: pret, ptp **dreamed** *or* **dreamt**) 1 n a (*during sleep*) rêve *m*. **to have a ~ about sth** faire un rêve sur qch, rêver de qch; **I've had a bad ~** j'ai fait un mauvais rêve *or* un cauchemar; **the whole business was (like) a bad ~** toute cette affaire a été comme un mauvais rêve; **everything went like a ~*** tout s'est passé comme dans un rêve *or* à merveille; **it was like a ~ come true** c'était comme dans un rêve; **sweet ~s!** fais de beaux rêves!; **to see sth in a ~** voir qch en rêve; **life is but a ~** la vie n'est qu'un songe.

b (*when awake*) rêverie *f*, rêve *m*, songerie *f*. **half the time she goes around in a ~*** la moitié du temps elle est dans un rêve *or* elle est dans les nuages *or* elle rêvasse.

c (*fantasy*) rêve *m*, vision *f*. **the house of his ~s** la maison de ses rêves; **his fondest ~ was to see her again** son vœu le plus cher était de la revoir; **to have ~s of doing** rêver de faire; **all his ~s came true** tous ses rêves se sont réalisés; **idle ~s** rêvasseries *fpl*; **rich beyond his wildest ~s** plus riche qu'il n'aurait jamais pu rêver de l'être.

d (*: *lovely thing, person*) merveille *f*, amour* *m*. **a ~ of a hat** un amour de chapeau*, une merveille de petit chapeau; **isn't he a ~?** n'est-ce pas qu'il est adorable?

2 adj: **a ~ house** une maison de rêve; **his ~ house** la maison de ses rêves.

3 comp ▸**dreamboat***: **he's a dreamboat** il est beau à faire rêver ▸**dreamland** pays *m* des rêves *or* des songes ▸**dream world** (*ideal*) monde *m* utopique; (*imagination*) monde imaginaire; **he lives in a dream world** il plane complètement.

4 vi a (*in sleep*) rêver. **to ~ about** *or* **of sb/sth** rêver de qn/qch; **to ~ about** *or* **of doing** rêver que l'on a fait.

b (*when awake*) rêvasser, se perdre en rêveries. **I'm sorry, I was ~ing** excusez-moi, j'étais dans la lune *or* je rêvais.

c (*imagine, envisage*) songer, penser (*of* à), avoir l'idée (*of* de). **I should never have dreamt of doing such a thing** l'idée ne me serait jamais passée par la tête de faire une chose pareille, je n'aurais jamais songé *or* pensé à faire une chose pareille; **I shouldn't ~ of telling her!** jamais il ne me viendrait à l'idée de lui dire cela!; **will you come? — I shouldn't ~ of it!** vous allez venir? — jamais de la vie! *or* pas question!

5 vt a (*in sleep*) rêver, voir en rêve. **to ~ a dream** faire un rêve; **I dreamt that she came** j'ai rêvé qu'elle venait; **you must have dreamt it!** vous avez dû le rêver!

b (*imagine*) imaginer. **if I had dreamt you would do that ...** si j'avais pu imaginer un instant que tu ferais cela ...; **I didn't ~ he would come!** je n'ai jamais songé *or* imaginé un instant qu'il viendrait!

▸**dream away** vt sep *time, one's life* perdre en rêveries.

▸**dream up*** vt sep *idea* imaginer, concevoir. **where did you dream that up?** où est-ce que vous êtes allés pêcher cela?*

dreamer [ˈdriːməʳ] n (*lit*) rêveur *m*, -euse *f*; (*fig*) rêveur, songe-creux *m inv*; (*politically*) utopiste *mf*.

dreamily [ˈdriːmɪlɪ] adv (*see* **dreamy**) d'un air *or* d'un ton rêveur *or* songeur, rêveusement, d'une manière distraite.

dreamless [ˈdriːmlɪs] adj sans rêves.

dreamlike [ˈdriːmlaɪk] adj onirique.

dreamt [dremt] pret, ptp of **dream**.

dreamy [ˈdriːmɪ] adj a *nature* rêveur, romanesque, songeur. b (*absent-minded*) rêveur, distrait, dans la lune *or* les nuages; *expression* rêveur. c *music* langoureux. d (*: *adorable*) ravissant.

dreariness [ˈdrɪərɪnɪs] n (*see* **dreary**) aspect *m* morne *etc*; monotonie *f*.

dreary [ˈdrɪərɪ] adj *weather* morne, lugubre; *landscape* morne, désolé, monotone; *life* morne, monotone; *work* monotone, ennuyeux; *speech, person* ennuyeux (comme la pluie).

dredge[1] [dredʒ] 1 n (*net, vessel*) drague *f*. 2 vt *river, mud* draguer. 3 vi draguer.

▸**dredge up** vt sep (*lit*) draguer; (*fig*) *unpleasant facts* déterrer, ressortir.

dredge[2] [dredʒ] vt (*Culin*) saupoudrer (*with* de, *on to, over* sur).

dredger[1] [ˈdredʒəʳ] n (*Naut*) (*ship*) dragueur *m*; (*machine*) drague *f*.

dredger[2] [ˈdredʒəʳ] n (*Culin*) saupoudreuse *f*, saupoudroir *m*.

dredging[1] [ˈdredʒɪŋ] n (*Naut*) dragage *m*.

dredging[2] [ˈdredʒɪŋ] n (*Culin*) saupoudrage *m*.

dregs [dregz] npl lie *f* (*also fig*). **to drink sth to the ~** boire qch jusqu'à la lie; **the ~ of society** la lie de la société; **he is the ~*** c'est la dernière des crapules.

drench [drentʃ] 1 vt a tremper, mouiller. **to get ~ed to the skin** se faire tremper jusqu'aux os, se faire saucer*; *see* **sun**. b (*Vet*) administrer *or* faire avaler un médicament à. 2 n (*Vet*) (dose *f* de) médicament *m* (*pour un animal*).

drenching [ˈdrentʃɪŋ] 1 n: **to get a ~** se faire tremper *or* saucer*. 2 adj: **~ rain** pluie battante *or* diluvienne.

Dresden [ˈdrezdən] n (*also* **~ china**) porcelaine *f* de Saxe, saxe *m*. **a piece of ~** un saxe.

dress [dres] 1 n a robe *f*. **a long/silk/summer ~** une robe longue/de soie/d'été; *see* **cocktail, wedding** *etc.*

b (*NonC: clothing*) habillement *m*, tenue *f*, vêtements *mpl*; (*way of dressing*) tenue, mise *f*. **articles of ~** vêtements; **in eastern ~** en tenue orientale; **careless in one's ~** d'une tenue *or* mise négligée; *see* **evening, full, national** *etc.*

2 comp ▸**dress circle** premier balcon, corbeille *f* ▸**dress coat** habit *m*, queue-de-pie *f* ▸**dress designer** dessinateur *m*, -trice *f* de mode, modéliste *mf*, (*famous*) (grand) couturier *m* ▸**dress length** (*of material*) hauteur *f* (de robe) ▸**dressmaker** couturière *f* ▸**dressmaking** couture *f*, confection *f* de robes ▸**dress parade** (*US Mil*) défilé *m* en grande tenue ▸**dress rehearsal** (*Theat*) (répétition *f*) générale *f*; (*fig*) répétition générale ▸**dress shield** dessous-de-bras *m* ▸**dress shirt** chemise *f* de soirée ▸**dress suit** habit *m* *or* tenue *f* de soirée *or* de cérémonie ▸**dress uniform** (*Mil*) tenue *f* de cérémonie.

3 vt a (*clothe*) *child, family, recruits, customer* habiller. **to get ~ed** s'habiller; *[child]* **he's old enough to ~ himself** il est assez grand pour s'habiller tout seul; *see also* **dressed**.

b (*Theat*) *play* costumer.

c (*arrange, decorate*) *gown* parer, orner; (*Naut*) *ship* pavoiser. **to ~ a shop window** faire l'étalage, faire la vitrine; **to ~ sb's hair** coiffer qn.

d (*Culin*) *salad* assaisonner, garnir (*d'une vinaigrette, d'une sauce*); *food for table* apprêter, accommoder; *chicken* préparer. **~ed crab** du crabe tout préparé (*pour la table*).

e *skins* préparer, apprêter; *material* apprêter; *leather* corroyer; *timber* dégrossir; *stone* tailler, dresser.

f (*Agr*) *field* façonner.

g *troops* aligner.

h *wound* panser. **to ~ sb's wound** faire le pansement de qn.

4 vi a s'habiller, se vêtir. **to ~ in black** s'habiller de noir; **to ~ as a man** s'habiller en homme; **she ~es very well** elle s'habille avec goût; **to ~ for dinner** se mettre en tenue de soirée; *[man]* se mettre en smoking; *[woman]* se mettre en robe du soir; **we don't ~ (for dinner)** nous ne nous habillons pas pour le dîner.

b *[soldiers]* s'aligner. **right ~!** à droite, alignement!

▸**dress down** 1 vt sep a (*Brit* *: *scold*) passer un savon à*. b *horse* panser. 2 vi (*Brit*) s'habiller décontracté. 3 **dressing-down*** n *see* **dressing 2**.

▸**dress up** 1 vi a (*put on smart clothes*) s'habiller, se mettre en grande toilette, s'endimancher (*pej*). (*Brit*) **to be dressed up to the nines*** être sur son trente et un; **there's no need to dress up*** il n'y a pas besoin de vous habiller; *see also* **dressed**. b (*put on fancy dress*) se déguiser, se costumer (*as* en). **the children love dressing up** les enfants adorent se déguiser. 2 vt sep a (*disguise*) déguiser (*as* en). b **it dresses up the skirt** cela rend la jupe plus habillée.

dressage ['dresɑːʒ] n dressage *m*.

dressed [drest] adj habillé. **well-~** bien habillé; **to be ~ for the country/for town/for tennis** être en tenue de sport/de ville/de tennis; **~ as a man** habillé en homme; **~ in black** habillé de noir; **to be ~ to kill***, (*US*) **to be ~ fit to kill*** être sapé à mort*; **all ~ up*** bien sapé*; (*loc hum*) **all ~ up and nowhere to go*** fringué comme un prince, et tout ça pour rien; *see also* **dress 3a**.

dresser[1] ['dresəʳ] n a (*Theat*) habilleur *m*, -euse *f*; (*Comm: window* ~) étalagiste *mf*. **she's a stylish ~** elle s'habille avec chic; *see* **hair**. b (*tool*) (*for wood*) raboteuse *f*; (*for stone*) rabotin *m*.

dresser[2] ['dresəʳ] n a (*furniture*) buffet *m*, vaisselier *m*. b (*US*) = **dressing table**; *see* **dressing 2**.

dressing ['dresɪŋ] 1 n a (*providing with clothes*) habillement *m*. **~ always takes me a long time** je mets beaucoup de temps à m'habiller; *see* **hair** *etc*.

b (*Med*) pansement *m*.

c (*Culin*) (*presentation*) présentation *f*; (*seasoning*) assaisonnement *m*, sauce *f*; (*stuffing*) farce *f*. **oil and vinegar ~** vinaigrette *f*; *see* **salad**.

d (*manure*) engrais *m*, fumages *mpl*.

e (*for material, leather*) apprêt *m*.

f (*Constr*) parement *m*.

2 comp ▸**dressing case** nécessaire *m* de toilette, trousse *f* de toilette *or* de voyage ▸**dressing-down***: **to give sb a dressing-down** passer un savon à qn*; **to get a dressing-down** recevoir *or* se faire passer un savon*, se faire enguirlander* ▸**dressing gown** (*Brit*) robe *f* de chambre; (*made of towelling*) peignoir *m*; (*negligée*) déshabillé *m* ▸**dressing room** (*in house*) dressing(-room) *m*, garde-robe *f*, vestiaire *m*; (*Theat*) loge *f* (*d'acteur*); (*US: in shop*) cabine *f* d'essayage ▸**dressing table** coiffeuse *f*, (table *f* de) toilette *f* ▸**dressing table set** accessoires *mpl* pour coiffeuse ▸**dressing-up** déguisement *m*.

dressy* ['dresɪ] adj *person* chic *inv*, élégant; *party* (très) habillé; *clothes, material* (qui fait) habillé.

drew [druː] pret of **draw**.

dribble ['drɪbl] 1 vi *[liquids]* tomber goutte à goutte, couler lentement; *[baby]* baver; (*Sport*) dribbler. *[people]* **to ~ back/in** *etc* revenir/entrer *etc* par petits groupes *or* un par un. 2 vt a (*Sport*) *ball* dribbler. b **he ~d his milk all down his chin** son lait lui dégoulinait le long du menton. 3 n a *[water]* petite goutte. b (*Sport*) dribble *m*.

dribbler ['drɪbləʳ] n (*Sport*) dribbleur *m*.

driblet ['drɪblɪt] n *[liquid]* gouttelette *f*. **in ~s** (*lit*) goutte à goutte; (*fig*) au compte-gouttes.

dribs and drabs ['drɪbzən'dræbz] npl petites quantités. **in ~** (*gen*) petit à petit, peu à peu; *arrive* en *or* par petits groupes; *pay, give* au compte-gouttes.

dried [draɪd] 1 pret, ptp of **dry**. 2 adj *fruit, beans* sec (*f* sèche); *vegetables* séché, déshydraté; *eggs, milk* en poudre; *flowers* séché. **~ fruit** fruits secs. 3 comp ▸**dried out** *alcoholic* désintoxiqué.

drier ['draɪəʳ] n = **dryer**.

drift [drɪft] 1 vi a (*on sea, river etc*) aller à la dérive, dériver; (*in wind/current*) être poussé *or* emporté (par le vent/le courant); (*Aviat*) dériver; *[snow, sand etc]* s'amonceler, s'entasser. **to ~ downstream** descendre le courant à la dérive; *[person]* **to ~ away/out/back** *etc* s'en aller/sortir/revenir *etc* d'une allure nonchalante; **he was ~ing aimlessly about** il flânait (sans but), il déambulait.

b (*fig*) *[person]* se laisser aller, aller à la dérive; *[events]* tendre (*towards* vers). **to let things ~** laisser les choses aller à la dérive *or* à vau-l'eau; **he ~ed into marriage** il s'est retrouvé marié; **the nation was ~ing towards a crisis** le pays glissait vers une crise.

c (*Rad*) se décaler.

2 n a (*NonC: driving movement or force*) mouvement *m*, force *f*; *[air, water current]* poussée *f*. **the ~ of the current** (*speed*) la vitesse du courant; (*direction*) le sens *or* la direction du courant; **carried north by the ~ of the current** emporté vers le nord par le courant; (*fig*) **the ~ of events** le cours *or* la tournure des événements.

b (*mass*) *[clouds]* traînée *f*; *[dust]* nuage *m*; *[falling snow]* rafale *f*; *[fallen snow]* congère *f*, amoncellement *m*; *[sand, leaves]* amoncellement, entassement *m*; (*Geol: deposits*) apports *mpl*.

c (*NonC*) (*act of drifting*) *[ships, aircraft]* dérivation *f*; *[projectile]* déviation *f*; (*deviation from course*) dérive *f*; (*Ling*) évolution *f* (de la langue). **continental ~** dérive des continents.

d (*general meaning*) *[question etc]* but *m*, portée *f*, sens *m* (général). **I caught the ~ of what he said, I caught his general ~** j'ai compris le sens général de ses paroles, j'ai compris où il voulait en venir.

e (*Min*) galerie chassante.

3 comp ▸**drift anchor** ancre flottante ▸**drift(ing) ice** glaces flottantes *or* en dérive ▸**drift-net** filet dérivant, traîne *f* ▸**driftwood** bois flotté.

▸**drift apart** vi (*fig*) s'éloigner l'un de l'autre.

▸**drift off** vi (*fig: fall asleep*) se laisser gagner par le sommeil.

drifter ['drɪftəʳ] n (*boat*) chalutier *m*, drifter *m*; (*person*) personne *f* qui se laisse aller *or* qui n'a pas de but dans la vie. **he's a bit of a ~** il manque un peu de stabilité.

drill[1] [drɪl] 1 n (*for metal, wood*) foret *m*, mèche *f*; (*for oil well*) trépan *m*; (*complete tool*) porte-foret *m*, perceuse *f*; (*Min*) perforatrice *f*, foreuse *f*; (*for roads*) marteau-piqueur *m*; *[dentist]* roulette *f*, fraise *f* (de dentiste). **electric (hand) ~** perceuse électrique; *see* **pneumatic**. 2 vt *wood, metal* forer, driller, percer; *tooth* fraiser. **to ~ an oil well** forer un puits de pétrole; **to ~ sb full of holes‡** trouer qn de balles. 3 vi forer, effectuer des forages (d'exploitation) (*for* pour trouver).

drill[2] [drɪl] 1 n (*NonC*) (*esp Mil: exercises etc*) exercice(s) *m(pl)*, manœuvre(s) *f(pl)*; (*in grammar etc*) exercices. (*fig*) **what's the ~?*** quelle est la marche à suivre?; **he doesn't know the ~*** il ne connaît pas la marche à suivre *or* la marche des opérations.

2 vt *soldiers* faire faire l'exercice à. **these troops are well-~ed** ces troupes sont bien entraînées; **to ~ pupils in grammar** faire faire des exercices de grammaire à des élèves; **to ~ good manners into a child** apprendre à un enfant à bien se tenir; **I ~ed it into him that he must not ...** je lui ai bien fait entrer dans la tête qu'il ne doit pas ... .

3 vi (*Mil*) faire l'exercice, être à l'exercice.

4 comp ▸**drill sergeant** (*Mil*) sergent *m* instructeur.

drill[3] [drɪl] (*Agr*) 1 n (*furrow*) sillon *m*; (*machine*) drill *m*, semoir *m*. 2 vt *seeds* semer en sillons; *field* tracer des sillons dans.

drill[4] [drɪl] n (*Tex*) coutil *m*, treillis *m*.

drilling[1] ['drɪlɪŋ] 1 n (*NonC*) *[metal, wood]* forage *m*, perçage *m*, perforation *f*; (*by dentist*) fraisage *m*. **~ for oil** forage (pétrolier). 2 comp ▸**drilling platform** plate-forme *f* de forage ▸**drilling rig** derrick *m*; (*at sea*) plate-forme *f* ▸**drilling ship** navire *m* de forage.

drilling[2] ['drɪlɪŋ] n (*Mil*) exercices *mpl*, manœuvres *fpl*.

drillion‡ ['drɪljən] n (*US*) **a ~ dollars** des tonnes de dollars, des milliards et des milliards de dollars.

drily ['draɪlɪ] adv (*coldly*) sèchement, d'un ton sec; (*with dry humour*) d'un ton *or* d'un air pince-sans-rire.

drink [drɪŋk] (vb: pret **drank**, ptp **drunk**) 1 n a (*liquid to ~*) boisson *f*. **have you got ~s for the children?** est-ce que tu as des boissons pour les enfants?; **there's food and ~ in the kitchen** il y a de quoi boire et manger à la cuisine; **there's plenty of food and ~ in the house** il y a tout ce qu'il faut à boire et à manger dans la maison; **may I have a ~?** est-ce que je pourrais boire quelque chose?; **to give sb a ~** donner à boire à qn; **he's a long ~ of water*** c'est un grand échalas, c'est une asperge.

b (*glass of alcoholic ~*) verre *m*, coup* *m*, pot* *m*; (*before meal*) apéritif *m*; (*after meal*) digestif *m*. **have a ~!** tu prendras bien un verre?; **let's have a ~** on va prendre *or* boire quelque chose, on va prendre un verre *or* un pot*; **let's have a ~ on it** on va boire un coup* pour fêter ça; **I need a ~!** il me faut quelque chose à boire!, vite à boire!; **he likes a ~** il aime bien boire un verre *or* un coup*; **to ask friends in for ~s** inviter des amis à venir prendre un verre *or* boire un pot*; **to stand sb a ~** offrir un verre *or* un pot* à qn, offrir à boire à qn; **to stand a round of ~s, to stand ~s all round** payer une tournée*; **he had a ~ in him‡** il avait un verre dans le nez*; *see* **short, soft, strong** *etc*.

c (*NonC: alcoholic liquor*) la boisson, l'alcool *m*. **to be under the influence of ~, to be the worse for ~** être en état d'ébriété, être plutôt éméché* *or* parti*; **to take to ~** s'adonner à la boisson; **to smell of ~** sentir l'alcool; **his worries drove him to ~** ses soucis l'ont poussé à boire *or* à la boisson; **it's enough to drive you to ~!** ça vous pousserait un honnête homme à la boisson!*; *see* **demon**.

d (‡: *sea*) flotte* *f*. **to be in the ~** être à la baille‡ *or* à la patouille‡.

2 comp ▸**drink driving** conduite *f* en état d'ivresse ▸**drink driving campaign** campagne *f* contre l'alcool au volant ▸**drink problem**: **the drink problem** le problème de l'alcoolisme; **to have a drink problem** boire (trop).

3 vt *wine, coffee* boire, prendre; *soup* manger. **would you like something to ~?** voulez-vous boire quelque chose?; **give me something to ~** donnez-moi (quelque chose) à boire; **is the water fit to ~?** est-ce que l'eau est potable?; **this coffee isn't fit to ~** ce café n'est pas buvable; **to ~ sb's health** boire à (la santé de) qn; **this wine should be drunk at room temperature** ce vin se boit chambré; (*fig*) **he ~s all his wages** il boit tout ce qu'il gagne; **to ~ o.s. to death** se tuer à force de boire; **to ~ sb under the table** faire rouler qn sous la table; *see* **toast** *etc*.

4 vi boire. **he doesn't ~** il ne boit pas; **his father drank** son père buvait; **to ~ from the bottle** boire à (même) la bouteille; **to ~ out of a glass** boire dans un verre; (*notice*) **"don't ~ and drive"** "attention, au volant l'alcool tue"; **to ~ like a fish*** boire comme un trou*; **to ~ to sb/to sb's success** boire à *or* porter un toast à qn/au succès de qn.

▸**drink away** vt sep *fortune* boire; *sorrows* noyer (dans l'alcool).

▸**drink down** vt sep avaler, boire d'un trait.

▸**drink in** vt sep *[plants, soil]* absorber, boire; (*fig*) *story* avaler*. **he drank in the fresh air** il a respiré *or* humé l'air frais; (*fig*) **the children were drinking it all in** les enfants n'en perdaient pas une miette* *or* goutte*.

▸**drink up** 1 vi boire, vider son verre. **drink up!** finis *or* bois ton vin! (*or* ton café! *etc*). 2 vt sep boire (jusqu'au bout), finir.

drinkable ['drɪŋkəbl] adj (*not poisonous*) *water* potable; (*palatable*) *wine etc* buvable.

drinker ['drɪŋkəʳ] n buveur *m*, -euse *f*. **whisky ~** buveur de whisky;

he's a hard *or* **heavy** ~ il boit beaucoup, il boit sec.

drinking ['drɪŋkɪŋ] 1 n (fait *m* de) boire *m*; (*drunkenness*) boisson *f*. **eating and** ~ manger et boire; **he wasn't used to** ~ il n'avait pas l'habitude de boire; **there was a lot of heavy** ~ on a beaucoup bu; **his problem was** ~ son problème c'était qu'il buvait; **his** ~ **caused his marriage to break up** le fait qu'il buvait a fait des ravages dans son ménage; **I don't object to** ~ **in moderation** je ne vois pas d'inconvénient à boire *or* à ce que l'on boive avec modération; ~ **by the under-18s must be stopped** il faut empêcher les jeunes de moins de 18 ans de s'adonner à la boisson.

2 comp ▸**drinking bout** (séance *f* de) beuverie *f* ▸**drinking chocolate** chocolat *m* (en poudre) ▸**drinking companion**: **one of his drinking companions** un de ses compagnons de beuverie ▸**drinking fountain** (*in street*) fontaine publique; (*in toilets etc*) jet *m* d'eau potable ▸**drinking session** = **drinking bout** ▸**drinking song** chanson *f* à boire ▸**drinking straw** paille *f* ▸**drinking trough** abreuvoir *m*, auge *f* à boire ▸**drinking water** eau *f* potable.

drip [drɪp] 1 vi *[water, sweat, rain]* tomber goutte à goutte, dégoutter, dégouliner; *[tap]* couler, goutter; *[cheese, washing]* s'égoutter; *[hair, trees etc]* dégoutter, ruisseler (*with* de). **the rain was ~ping down the wall** la pluie dégouttait *or* dégoulinait le long du mur; **sweat was ~ping from his brow** il avait le front ruisselant de sueur; **to be ~ping with sweat** ruisseler de sueur, être en nage; **his hands were ~ping with blood** il avait les mains dégoulinantes de sang; **the walls were ~ping (with water)** les murs suintaient; **he's ~ping wet*** il est trempé jusqu'aux os; **my coat is ~ping wet*** mon manteau est trempé *or* est à tordre.

2 vt *liquid* faire tomber *or* laisser tomber goutte à goutte; *washing, cheese* égoutter. **you're ~ping paint all over the place** tu mets de la peinture partout.

3 n a (*sound*) *[water, rain]* bruit *m* de l'eau qui tombe goutte à goutte; *[tap]* bruit d'un robinet qui goutte; (*drop*) goutte *f*; (* *fig: spineless person*) lavette* *f*.

b (*Med*) (*liquid*) perfusion *f*; (*device*) goutte-à-goutte *m inv*. **to put up a** ~ mettre un goutte-à-goutte; **to be on a** ~ être sous perfusion, avoir le goutte-à-goutte.

c (*Archit: also* ~**stone**) larmier *m*.

4 comp ▸**drip-dry** *shirt* qui ne nécessite aucun repassage; (*Comm: on label*) "ne pas repasser" ▸**drip-feed** (*Med*) alimenter par perfusion ▸**drip mat** dessous-de-verre *m inv* ▸**drip pan** (*Culin*) lèchefrite *f*.

dripping ['drɪpɪŋ] 1 n a (*Culin*) graisse *f* (de rôti). **bread and** ~ tartine *f* à la graisse. b (*action*) *[water etc]* égouttement *m*, égouttage *m*. 2 adj *tap* qui goutte *or* fuit; *rooftop, tree* ruisselant, qui dégoutte; *washing* qui dégoutte, trempé; (*) *coat, hat* trempé, dégoulinant*, saucé*. 3 comp ▸**dripping pan** (*Culin*) lèchefrite *f*.

drivability [ˌdraɪvə'bɪlɪtɪ] n maniabilité *f*, manœuvrabilité *f*.

drive [draɪv] (vb: pret **drove**, ptp **driven**) 1 n a (*Aut: journey*) promenade *f* or trajet *m* en voiture. **to go for a** ~ faire une promenade en voiture; **it's about one hour's** ~ **from London** c'est à environ une heure de voiture de Londres.

b (*private road*) (*into castle*) allée *f*, avenue *f*; (*into house*) allée.

c (*Golf*) drive *m*; (*Tennis*) coup droit, drive.

d (*energy*) dynamisme *m*, énergie *f*; (*Psych etc*) besoin *m*, instinct *m*. **the sex** ~ les pulsions sexuelles; **to have plenty of** ~ avoir de l'énergie *or* du dynamisme *or* de l'allant, être dynamique *or* entreprenant; **to lack** ~ manquer d'allant *or* de dynamisme.

e (*Pol etc*) campagne *f*; (*Mil*) poussée *f*. **a** ~ **to boost sales** une promotion systématique de vente; **output** ~ effort *m* de production; *see* **export, whist** *etc*.

f (*Tech: power transmission*) commande *f*, transmission *f*, actionnement *m*. (*Aut*) **front-wheel** ~ traction *f* avant; **rear-wheel** ~ propulsion *f* arrière; **left-hand** ~ conduite *f* à gauche.

g (*Comput*) (*for disk*) unité *f* de disques; (*for tape*) dérouleur *m*.

h (*herding*) rassemblement *m*. **cattle** ~ rassemblement de bétail.

2 comp ▸**drive-in** adj, n drive-in (*m*) ▸**driveline** (*Aut*) transmission *f* ▸**driveshaft** (*Aut etc*) arbre *m* de transmission ▸**drive-time** (*US Rad*) heure *f* de pointe, heure d'encombrement ▸**drivetrain** = **driveline** ▸**drive-up window** (*US*) guichet *m* pour automobilistes ▸**driveway** = **drive 1b**.

3 vt a *people, animals* chasser *or* pousser (devant soi); (*Hunting*) *game* rabattre; *clouds* charrier, chasser, pousser; *leaves* chasser. **to** ~ **sb out of the country** chasser qn du pays; (*fig*) **to** ~ **sb into a corner** mettre qn au pied du mur (*fig*); **the dog drove the sheep into the farm** le chien a fait rentrer les moutons à la ferme; **the gale drove the ship off course** la tempête a fait dériver le navire; **the wind drove the rain against the windows** le vent rabattait la pluie contre les vitres.

b *cart, car, train* conduire; *racing car* piloter; *passenger* conduire, emmener (en voiture). **he ~s a lorry/taxi** (*for a living*) il est camionneur/chauffeur de taxi; **he ~s a Peugeot** il a une Peugeot; **he ~s racing cars** il est pilote de course; (*Aut*) **to** ~ **sb back/off** *etc* ramener/emmener *etc* qn en voiture; **I'll** ~ **you home** je vais vous ramener en voiture, je vais vous reconduire chez vous; **he drove me down to the coast** il m'a conduit *or* emmené (en voiture) jusqu'à la côte; **he drove his car straight at me** il s'est dirigé *or* il a dirigé sa voiture droit sur moi.

c (*operate*) *machine [person]* actionner, commander; *[steam etc]* faire fonctionner. **steam-driven train** locomotive *f* à vapeur; **machine driven by electricity** machine fonctionnant à l'électricité.

d *nail* enfoncer; *stake* enfoncer, ficher; *rivet* poser; (*Golf, Tennis*) driver; *tunnel* percer, creuser; *well* forer, percer. **to** ~ **a nail home** enfoncer un clou à fond; **to** ~ **this point home, he ...** pour bien se faire comprendre *or* pour souligner son argumentation, il ...; (*fig*) **to** ~ **a point home** réussir à faire comprendre un argument; (*fig*) **to** ~ **sth into sb's head** enfoncer qch dans la tête de qn; **to** ~ **sth out of sb's head** faire complètement oublier qch à qn; **to** ~ **a bargain** conclure un marché; **to** ~ **a hard bargain with sb** soutirer le maximum à qn; **he ~s a hard bargain** il ne fait pas de cadeau.

e (*fig*) **to** ~ **sb hard** surcharger qn de travail, surmener qn; **to** ~ **sb mad** rendre qn fou (*f* folle); **to** ~ **sb to despair** réduire qn au désespoir; **to** ~ **sb to rebellion** pousser *or* inciter qn à la révolte; **to** ~ **sb to do** *or* **into doing sth** pousser qn à faire qch; **I was driven to it** j'y ai été poussé malgré moi, j'y ai été contraint; *see* **distraction c**.

4 vi a (*Aut*) (*drive a car etc*) conduire (une voiture); (*go by car*) aller en voiture. **to** ~ **away/back** *etc* partir/revenir *etc* en voiture; **she drove down to the shops** elle est allée faire des courses en voiture; **can you** ~? savez-vous conduire?; **to** ~ **at 50 km/h** rouler à 50 km/h; **to** ~ **on the right** rouler à droite, tenir la droite; **did you come by train? — no, we drove** êtes-vous venus par le train? — non, (nous sommes venus) en voiture; **we have been driving all day** nous avons fait de la route *or* nous avons roulé toute la journée; **she was about to** ~ **under the bridge** elle s'apprêtait à s'engager sous le pont.

b **the rain was driving in our faces** la pluie nous fouettait le visage.

▸**drive along** 1 vi *[vehicle]* rouler, circuler; *[person]* rouler. 2 vt sep *[wind, current]* chasser, pousser.

▸**drive at** vt fus (*fig: intend, mean*) en venir à, vouloir dire. **what are you driving at?** où voulez-vous en venir?, que voulez-vous dire?

▸**drive away** 1 vi *[car]* démarrer; *[person]* s'en aller *or* partir en voiture. 2 vt sep (*lit, fig*) *person, suspicions, cares* chasser.

▸**drive back** 1 vi *[car]* revenir; *[person]* rentrer en voiture. 2 vt sep a (*cause to retreat*) (*Mil etc*) repousser, refouler, faire reculer. **the storm drove him back** la tempête lui a fait rebrousser chemin. b (*convey back*) ramener *or* reconduire en voiture.

▸**drive in** 1 vi *[car]* entrer; *[person]* entrer (en voiture). 2 vt sep *nail* enfoncer; *screw* visser. (*fig*) **to drive an idea into sb's head** enfoncer *or* faire entrer une idée dans la tête de qn. 3 **drive-in** adj, n *see* **drive 2**.

▸**drive off** 1 vi a = **drive away 1**. b (*Golf*) driver. 2 vt sep = **drive away 2**. 3 vt fus *ferry* débarquer de.

▸**drive on** 1 vi *[person, car]* poursuivre sa route; (*after stopping*) reprendre sa route, repartir. 2 vt sep (*incite, encourage*) pousser, inciter, entraîner (*to* à, *to do, to doing* à faire).

▸**drive on to** vt fus *ferry* embarquer sur.

▸**drive out** 1 vi *[car]* sortir; *[person]* sortir (en voiture). 2 vt sep *person* faire sortir, chasser; *thoughts, desires* chasser.

▸**drive over** 1 vi venir *or* aller en voiture. **we drove over in 2 hours** nous avons fait le trajet en deux heures. 2 vt sep (*convey*) conduire en voiture. 3 vt fus (*crush*) écraser.

▸**drive up** vi *[car]* arriver; *[person]* arriver (en voiture).

driveability [ˌdraɪvə'bɪlɪtɪ] n = **drivability**.

drivel ['drɪvl] 1 n (*NonC*) radotage *m*, sornettes *fpl*, imbécillités *fpl*. **what utter** ~! quelles imbécillités! *or* sornettes! 2 vi radoter. **what's he ~ling (on) about?** qu'est-ce qu'il radote?*

driven ['drɪvn] ptp of **drive**.

-driven ['drɪvn] adj ending in comps fonctionnant à, *e.g.* **chauffeur-driven** conduit par un chauffeur; **electricity-driven** fonctionnant à l'électricité; **steam-driven** à vapeur.

driver ['draɪvə^r] 1 n a *[car]* conducteur *m*, -trice *f*; *[taxi, truck, bus]* chauffeur *m*, conducteur, -trice; *[racing car]* pilote *m*; (*Brit*) *[locomotive]* mécanicien *m*, conducteur; *[cart]* charretier *m*; (*Sport: in horse race etc*) driver *m*. **car ~s** automobilistes *mpl*; **to be a good** ~ conduire bien; **he's a very careful** ~ il conduit très prudemment; (*US*) **~'s license** permis *m* de conduire; (*Aut*) **the ~'s** *or* **driving seat** la place du conducteur; **to be in the ~'s** *or* **driving seat** (*lit*) être au volant; (*fig*) tenir les rênes, être aux commandes, diriger les opérations; *see* **back, lorry, racing** *etc*.

b *[animals]* conducteur *m*; *see* **slave**.

c (*golf club*) driver *m*.

2 comp ▸**driver education** (*US Scol*) cours *mpl* de conduite automobile (dans les lycées).

driving ['draɪvɪŋ] 1 n (*Aut*) conduite *f*. **his** ~ **is awful** il conduit très mal; **bad** ~ conduite imprudente *or* maladroite; **dangerous** ~ conduite dangereuse; ~ **is his hobby** conduire est sa distraction favorite.

2 adj a *necessity* impérieux, pressant. **he is the** ~ **force** c'est lui qui est la force agissante, il est la locomotive*.

b ~ **rain** pluie battante.

3 comp ▸**driving belt** courroie *f* de transmission ▸**driving instructor** moniteur *m*, -trice *f* de conduite *or* d'auto-école ▸**driving lesson** leçon *f* de conduite ▸**driving licence** (*Brit*) permis *m* de

conduire ▸**driving mirror** rétroviseur *m* ▸**driving school** auto-école *f* ▸**driving seat** *see* **driver a** ▸**driving test** examen *m* du permis de conduire; **to pass one's driving test** avoir son permis; **to fail one's driving test** être refusé *or* recalé* à son permis ▸**driving wheel** (*Tech*) roue motrice.

drizzle [ˈdrɪzl] 1 n bruine *f*, crachin *m*. 2 vi bruiner, crachiner.

drizzly [ˈdrɪzlɪ] adj de bruine, de crachin.

droll [drəʊl] adj (*comic*) comique, drôle; (*odd*) bizarre, drôle, curieux.

dromedary [ˈdrɒmɪdərɪ] n dromadaire *m*.

drone [drəʊn] 1 n a (*bee*) abeille *f* mâle, faux-bourdon *m*; (*pej: idler*) fainéant(e) *m(f)*. b (*sound*) *[bees]* bourdonnement *m*; *[engine, aircraft]* ronronnement *m*, (*louder*) vrombissement *m*; (*fig: monotonous speech*) débit *m* soporifique *or* monotone, ronronnement. c (*Mus*) bourdon *m*. d (*robot plane*) avion téléguidé, drone *m*. 2 vi *[bee]* bourdonner; *[engine, aircraft]* ronronner, (*louder*) vrombir; (*speak monotonously: also* ~ **away**, ~ **on**) parler d'une voix monotone *or* endormante. **he ~d on and on for hours** il n'a pas cessé pendant des heures de parler de sa voix monotone. 3 vt: **to ~ (out) a speech** débiter un discours d'un ton monotone.

drool [dru:l] vi (*lit*) baver; (* *fig*) radoter. (*fig*) **to ~ over sth*** baver d'admiration *or* s'extasier devant qch.

droop [dru:p] 1 vi *[body]* s'affaisser; *[shoulders]* tomber; *[head]* pencher; *[eyelids]* s'abaisser; *[flowers]* commencer à se faner *or* à baisser la tête; *[feathers, one's hand]* retomber. **his spirits ~ed** il a été pris de découragement; **the heat made him ~** il était accablé par la chaleur. 2 vt *head* baisser, pencher. 3 n *[body]* attitude penchée *or* affaissée; *[eyelids]* abaissement *m*; *[spirits]* langueur *f*, abattement *m*.

droopy [ˈdru:pɪ] adj *moustache, tail, breasts* qui pendouille; (*hum: tired*) mou (*f* molle).

drop [drɒp] 1 n a *[water, rain etc]* goutte *f*; *[alcohol]* goutte, larme *f*. ~ **by** ~ goutte à goutte; (*Med*) ~**s** gouttes; **just a ~!** (juste) une goutte! *or* une larme!, une (petite) goutte!; **there's only a ~ left** il n'en reste qu'une goutte; **to fall in ~s** tomber en gouttes; **we haven't had a ~ of rain** nous n'avons pas eu une goutte de pluie; (*fig*) **it's a ~ in the ocean** c'est une goutte d'eau dans la mer; **he's had a ~ too much*** il a un verre dans le nez*; *see* **nose, tear**[2] *etc*.

b (*pendant*) *[chandelier]* pendeloque *f*; *[earring]* pendant *m*, pendeloque; *[necklace]* pendentif *m*. (*sweet*) **acid ~** bonbon acidulé.

c (*fall*) *[temperature]* baisse *f* (*in* de); *[prices]* baisse, chute *f* (*in* de). (*Elec*) ~ **in voltage** chute de tension; (*fig*) **at the ~ of a hat** *act, make speech etc* au pied levé; *leave, shoot, get angry* pour un oui pour un non.

d (*difference in level*) dénivellation *f*, descente *f* brusque; (*abyss*) précipice *m*; (*fall*) chute *f*; (*distance of fall*) hauteur *f* de chute; (*Climbing*) vide *m*; *[gallows]* trappe *f*; (*parachute jump*) saut *m* (en parachute); (*act of dropping: of supplies, arms*) parachutage *m*, droppage *m*; (*hiding place: for secret letter etc*) cachette *f*, dépôt clandestin. **there's a ~ of 10 metres between the roof and the ground** il y a (une hauteur de) 10 mètres entre le toit et le sol; **sheer ~** descente à pic; (*US fig*) **to have/get the ~ on sb** avoir/prendre l'avantage sur qn; *[gangster]* **to make a ~** déposer un colis.

e (*Theat: also* ~ **curtain**) rideau *m* d'entracte; *see* **back**.

2 comp ▸**drop-add** (*US Univ etc*) remplacement *m* d'un cours par un autre ▸**drop-cloth** (*US*) bâche *f* de protection ▸**drop-forge** marteau-pilon *m* ▸**drop goal** (*Rugby*) drop(-goal) *m*; **to score a drop goal** passer un drop ▸**drop-hammer** = **drop-forge** ▸**drop handlebars** guidon *m* de course ▸**drop kick** (*Rugby*) coup *m* de pied tombé, drop *m* (*coup de pied*) ▸**drop-leaf table** table *f* à volets, table anglaise ▸**drop-off** (*in sales, interest etc*) diminution *f* (*in* de) ▸**dropout** (*from society*) drop-out* *mf*, marginal(e) *m(f)*; (*from college etc*) étudiant(e) *m(f)* qui abandonne ses études ▸**drop-out** (*Rugby*) renvoi *m* aux 22 mètres ▸**dropping out** (*Univ etc*) abandon *m*, désistement *m* ▸**drop shipment** (*Comm*) drop shipment *m* ▸**drop shot** (*Tennis*) amorti *m* ▸**drop tag** (*US*) démarquer.

3 vt a *rope, ball, cup* (*let fall*) laisser tomber; (*release, let go*) lâcher; *one's trousers etc* laisser tomber; *bomb* lancer, larguer; *liquid* laisser tomber goutte à goutte; *price* baisser; (*from car*) *person, thing* déposer; (*from boat*) *cargo, passengers* débarquer. (*Aut*) **I'll ~ you here** je vous dépose *or* laisse ici; **to ~ one's eyes/voice** baisser les yeux/la voix; **to ~ a letter in the postbox** mettre *or* jeter une lettre à la boîte; **to ~ soldiers/supplies by parachute** parachuter des soldats/du ravitaillement; *[parachutist]* **to be ~ped** sauter; (*Tennis*) **he ~ped the ball over the net** son amorti a juste passé le filet; (*Naut*) **to ~ anchor** mouiller *or* jeter l'ancre; (*fig*) **to ~ a brick*** faire une gaffe* *or* une bourde*; (*Theat*) **to ~ the curtain** baisser le rideau; **to ~ a curtsy** faire une révérence; (*Rugby*) **to ~ a goal** marquer un drop; (*Knitting*) **to ~ a stitch** sauter *or* laisser échapper *or* laisser tomber une maille; **to ~ a hem** ressortir un ourlet.

b (*kill*) *bird* abattre; (‡) *person* descendre‡.

c (*utter casually*) *remark, clue* laisser échapper. **to ~ a hint about sth** (laisser) suggérer qch; **are you ~ping hints?** c'est une allusion?, ce sont des allusions?; **to ~ a word in sb's ear** glisser un mot à l'oreille de qn; **he let ~ that he had seen her** (*accidentally*) il a laissé échapper qu'il l'avait vue; (*deliberately*) il a fait comprendre qu'il l'avait vue.

d *letter, card* envoyer, écrire (*to* à). **to ~ sb a line** faire *or* écrire un (petit) mot à qn; ~ **me a note** écrivez-moi *or* envoyez-moi un petit mot.

e (*omit*) *word, syllable* (*spoken*) avaler, (*written*) omettre; (*intentionally*) *programme, word, scene from play* supprimer; (*unintentionally*) *word, letter in type* laisser tomber, omettre. **to ~ one's h's** *or* **aitches** ne pas aspirer les h, avoir un accent vulgaire.

f (*abandon*) *habit, idea* renoncer à; *work* abandonner; (*Scol etc*) *subject* abandonner, laisser tomber; *plan* renoncer à, ne pas donner suite à; *discussion, conversation* abandonner; *friend* laisser tomber, lâcher, cesser de voir; *girlfriend, boyfriend* rompre avec, lâcher, laisser tomber. (*Sport*) **to ~ sb from a team** écarter qn d'une équipe; **they had to ~ 100 workers** ils ont dû se défaire de 100 salariés; **let's ~ the subject** parlons d'autre chose, laissons ce sujet, ne parlons plus de cela; ~ **it!*** laisse tomber!*, finis!, assez!

g (*lose*) *money* perdre, laisser; (*Cards, Tennis etc*) *game* perdre. **to ~ a set/one's serve** perdre un set/son service.

h *[animal]* (*give birth to*) mettre bas.

i (*Drugs sl*) **to ~ acid** prendre *or* avaler du LSD.

4 vi a *[object]* tomber, retomber; *[liquids]* tomber goutte à goutte; *[person]* descendre, se laisser tomber; (*sink to ground*) se laisser tomber, tomber; (*collapse*) s'écrouler, s'affaisser. (*Theat*) **the curtain ~s** le rideau tombe; **you could have heard a pin ~** on aurait entendu voler une mouche; **to ~ into sb's arms** tomber dans les bras de qn; **to ~ on one's knees** se jeter *or* tomber à genoux; **I'm ready to ~*** je tombe de fatigue, je ne tiens plus debout, je suis claqué*; **people were ~ping like flies*** les gens tombaient comme des mouches*; **she ~ped into an armchair** elle s'est écroulée dans un fauteuil; ~ **dead!**‡ va te faire voir!*, va te faire foutre!‡; (*select*) **to ~ on sth*** choisir qch; **to ~ on sb (like a ton of bricks)*** passer un fameux savon à qn*, secouer les puces à qn*; *see* **penny**.

b (*decrease*) *[wind]* se calmer, tomber; *[temperature, voice]* baisser; *[price]* baisser, diminuer.

c (*end*) *[conversation, correspondence]* en rester là, être interrompu, cesser. **there the matter ~ped** l'affaire en est restée là; **let it ~!*** laisse tomber!*, finis!, assez!

▸**drop across*** vi: **we dropped across to see him** nous sommes passés *or* allés le voir; **he dropped across to see us** il est passé *or* venu nous voir.

▸**drop away** vi *[numbers, attendance]* diminuer, tomber.

▸**drop back, drop behind** vi rester en arrière, se laisser devancer *or* distancer; (*in work etc*) prendre du retard.

▸**drop by** vi: **to drop by somewhere/on sb** faire un saut* *or* passer quelque part/chez qn; **we'll drop by if we're in town** nous passerons si nous sommes en ville.

▸**drop down** vi tomber.

▸**drop in** vi: **to drop in on sb** passer voir qn, débarquer* chez qn; **to drop in at the grocer's** passer chez l'épicier; **do drop in if you're in town** passez à la maison si vous êtes en ville.

▸**drop off** 1 vi a (*fall asleep*) s'endormir; (*for brief while*) faire un (petit) somme. b *[leaves]* tomber; *[sales, interest]* diminuer. c (*: *alight*) descendre. 2 vt sep (*set down from car etc*) *person, parcel* déposer, laisser. 3 **drop-off** n *see* **drop 2**.

▸**drop out** 1 vi *[contents etc]* tomber; (*fig*) se retirer, renoncer; (*from college etc*) abandonner ses études. **to drop out of a competition** se retirer d'une compétition, abandonner une compétition *or* un concours; **to drop out of circulation** se mettre hors circuit; **to drop out of sight** disparaître de la circulation; **to drop out (of society)** choisir de vivre marginalement *or* en marge de la société. 2 **dropout** n *see* **drop 2**.

▸**drop round*** 1 vi = **drop across**. 2 vt sep déposer chez moi (*or* toi *etc*).

droplet [ˈdrɒplɪt] n gouttelette *f*.

dropper [ˈdrɒpəʳ] n (*Med*) compte-gouttes *m inv*.

droppings [ˈdrɒpɪŋz] npl *[birds]* fiente *f*; *[animals]* crottes *fpl*; *[flies]* chiures *fpl*, crottes.

dropsical [ˈdrɒpsɪkəl] adj hydropique.

dropsy [ˈdrɒpsɪ] n hydropisie *f*.

drosophila [drɒˈsɒfɪlə] n, pl ~**s** *or* ~**e** [drɒˈsɒfɪˌli:] drosophile *f*.

dross [drɒs] n (*NonC*) (*Metal*) scories *fpl*, crasse *f*, laitier *m*; (*Brit: coal*) menu *m* (de houille *or* de coke), poussier *m*; (*refuse*) impuretés *fpl*, déchets *mpl*; (*fig: sth worthless*) rebut *m*.

drought [draʊt] n sécheresse *f*.

drove [drəʊv] 1 pret of **drive**. 2 n a *[animals]* troupeau *m* en marche. ~**s of people** des foules *fpl* de gens; **they came in ~s** ils arrivèrent en foule. b (*channel*) canal *m or* rigole *f* d'irrigation.

drover [ˈdrəʊvəʳ] n toucheur *m or* conducteur *m* de bestiaux.

drown [draʊn] 1 vt *person, animal* noyer; *land* inonder, submerger; (*fig*) *sorrows* noyer; *noise, voice* couvrir, noyer, étouffer. **because he couldn't swim he was ~ed** il s'est noyé parce qu'il ne savait pas nager; **he ~ed himself in despair** il s'est noyé de désespoir; **he's like** *or* **he looks like a ~ed rat*** il est trempé jusqu'aux os *or* comme une soupe*; (*fig*) **to ~ one's sorrows** noyer son chagrin; (*of whisky etc*) **don't ~ it!*** n'y mets pas trop d'eau!, ne le noie pas!; (*fig*) **they were ~ed with offers of help*** ils ont été inondés *or* submergés d'offres d'assistance. 2 vi se noyer, être noyé.

drowning [ˈdraʊnɪŋ] 1 adj qui se noie. (*Prov*) **a ~ man will clutch at a**

straw un homme qui se noie se raccroche à un fétu de paille. 2 n (*death*) (mort *f or* asphyxie *f* par) noyade *f*; *[noise, voice]* étouffement *m*. **there were 3 ~s here last year** 3 personnes se sont noyées ici *or* il y a eu 3 noyades ici l'année dernière.

drowse [draʊz] vi être à moitié endormi *or* assoupi, somnoler. **to ~ off** s'assoupir.

drowsily ['draʊzɪlɪ] adv d'un air endormi, d'un air *or* d'un ton somnolent, à demi endormi.

drowsiness ['draʊzɪnɪs] n somnolence *f*, assoupissement *m*, engourdissement *m*.

drowsy ['draʊzɪ] adj *person* somnolent, qui a envie de dormir; *smile, look* somnolent; *afternoon, atmosphere* assoupissant, soporifique. **to grow ~** s'assoupir; **to feel ~** avoir envie de dormir.

drub [drʌb] vt (*thrash*) rosser*, rouer de coups; (*abuse*) injurier, traiter de tous les noms; (*defeat*) battre à plate(s) couture(s). (*fig*) **to ~ an idea into sb** enfoncer une idée dans la tête de qn; (*fig*) **to ~ an idea out of sb** arracher une idée de la tête de qn.

drubbing ['drʌbɪŋ] n (*thrashing*) volée *f* de coups, raclée* *f*; (*defeat*) raclée*. (*lit, fig*) **to give sb a ~** donner *or* administrer une belle raclée* à qn; (*fig*) **to take a ~** en prendre un coup*, en prendre pour son grade.

drudge [drʌdʒ] 1 n bête *f* de somme (*fig*). **the household ~** la bonne à tout faire, la Cendrillon de la famille. 2 vi trimer‡, peiner.

drudgery ['drʌdʒərɪ] n (*NonC*) grosse besogne, corvée *f*, travail pénible et ingrat *or* fastidieux. **it's sheer ~** c'est (une corvée) d'un fastidieux!

drug [drʌg] 1 n drogue *f*, stupéfiant *m*, narcotique *m*; (*Med, Pharm*) drogue, médicament *m*. **he's on ~s, he's taking ~s** (*gen*) il se drogue; (*Med*) il est sous médication, on lui fait prendre des médicaments; (*Drugs sl*) **to do ~s** se droguer; (*fig*) **a ~ on the market** un article *or* une marchandise invendable; **television is a ~** la télévision est comme une drogue; *see* **hard, soft** *etc*.

2 comp ▸**drug abuse** abus *m* de la drogue ▸**drug abuser** drogué(e) *m(f)* ▸**drug addict** drogué(e) *m(f)*, intoxiqué(e) *m(f)*, toxicomane *mf* ▸**drug addiction** toxicomanie *f* ▸**drug check** contrôle *m* anti-dopage ▸**drug company** compagnie *f* pharmaceutique; **the drug companies** l'industrie *f* pharmaceutique ▸**drug habit** accoutumance *f* à la drogue ▸**drug peddler, drug pusher** revendeur *m*, -euse *f* de drogue *or* de stupéfiants ▸**drug runner** trafiquant(e) *m(f)* (de la drogue) ▸**drug-running** = **drug traffic** ▸**Drug(s) Squad** (*Police*) brigade *f* des stupéfiants ▸**drugstore** (*US*) drugstore *m* ▸**drugstore cowboy*** (*US fig*) glandeur‡ *m*, traîne-savates* *m* ▸**drug-taker** consommateur *m*, -trice *f* de drogue *or* de stupéfiants ▸**drug-taking** usage *m* de la drogue *or* de stupéfiants ▸**drug traffic(king)** trafic *m* de la drogue *or* des stupéfiants ▸**drug user** = **drug-taker**.

3 vt *person* droguer (*also Med*); *food, wine etc* mêler un narcotique à. **to be in a ~ged sleep** dormir sous l'effet d'un narcotique; (*fig*) **to be ~ged with sleep/from lack of sleep** être abruti de sommeil/par manque de sommeil.

druggist ['drʌgɪst] n a (*Brit*) pharmacien(ne) *m(f)*. **~'s** pharmacie *f*, droguerie médicinale. b (*US*) droguiste-épicier *m*, -ière *f*.

druggy ['drʌgɪ] n, **drugster** ['drʌgstər] n (*Drugs sl*) camé(e)‡ *m(f)*, drogué(e) *m(f)*.

druid ['druːɪd] n druide *m*.

druidic [druː'ɪdɪk] adj druidique.

druidism ['druːɪdɪzəm] n druidisme *m*.

drum [drʌm] 1 n a (*Mus: instrument, player*) tambour *m*. **the big ~** la grosse caisse; (*Mil Mus, jazz*) **the ~s** la batterie; **to beat the ~** battre le *or* du tambour; *see* **kettle, tight** *etc*.

b (*for oil*) tonnelet *m*, bidon *m*; (*for tar*) gonne *f*; (*cylinder for wire etc*) tambour *m*; (*machine part*) tambour; (*Aut: brake ~*) tambour (de frein); (*Comput*) tambour magnétique; (*box: of figs, sweets*) caisse *f*.

c (*sound*) = **drumming**.

2 comp ▸**drumbeat** battement *m* de tambour ▸**drum brake** (*Aut*) frein *m* à tambour ▸**drumfire** (*Mil*) tir *m* de barrage, feu roulant ▸**drumhead** (*Mus*) peau *f* de tambour ▸**drumhead court-martial** (*Mil*) conseil *m* de guerre prévôtal ▸**drumhead service** (*Mil*) office religieux en plein air ▸**drum kit** batterie *f* ▸**drum machine** boîte *f* à rythme ▸**drum major** (*Brit Mil*) tambour-major *m*; (*US*) chef *m* des tambours ▸**drum majorette** (*US*) majorette *f* ▸**drum roll** roulement *m* de tambour ▸**drum set** = **drum kit** ▸**drumstick** (*Mus*) baguette *f* de tambour; *[chicken]* pilon *m*.

3 vi (*Mus*) battre le *or* du tambour; *[person, fingers]* tambouriner, pianoter (*with* de, avec; *on* sur); *[insect etc]* bourdonner. **the noise was ~ming in my ears** le bruit me tambourinait aux oreilles.

4 vt *tune* tambouriner. **to ~ one's fingers on the table** tambouriner *or* pianoter des doigts *or* avec les doigts sur la table; **to ~ one's feet on the floor** tambouriner des pieds sur le plancher; (*fig*) **to ~ sth into sb** enfoncer *or* fourrer* qch dans le crâne *or* la tête de qn, seriner* qch à qn; **I don't want to ~ it in but** ... je ne veux pas trop insister mais ... .

▸**drum out** vt sep (*Mil, also fig*) expulser (à grand bruit) (*of* de).

▸**drum up** vt sep (*fig*) *enthusiasm, support* susciter; *supporters* rassembler, racoler, battre le rappel de; *customers* racoler, raccrocher.

drumlin ['drʌmlɪn] n drumlin *m*.

drummer ['drʌmər] n a (joueur *m* de) tambour *m*; (*Jazz*) batteur *m*. **~ boy** petit tambour; (*fig*) **to march to** *or* **hear a different ~** marcher en dehors des sentiers battus. b (*US Comm* *) commis voyageur.

drumming ['drʌmɪŋ] n *[drum]* bruit *m* du tambour; *[insect]* bourdonnement *m*; (*in the ears*) bourdonnement; *[fingers]* tambourinage *m*, tambourinement *m*.

drunk [drʌŋk] 1 ptp of **drink**. 2 adj ivre, soûl*; (*fig*) ivre, enivré, grisé (*with* de, par). **to get ~** s'enivrer, se griser, se soûler* (*on* de); (*Jur*) **~ and disorderly, ~ and incapable** ≃ en état d'ivresse publique *or* manifeste; **as ~ as a lord** soûl comme une grive* *or* un Polonais*; **~ with success** enivré *or* grisé par le succès; *see* **blind, dead.** 3 n (*) ivrogne(sse) *m(f)*, homme *or* femme soûl(e)*, soûlard(e)‡ *m(f)*.

drunkard ['drʌŋkəd] n ivrogne(sse) *m(f)*, alcoolique *mf*, buveur *m*, -euse *f*, soûlard(e)‡ *m(f)*.

drunken ['drʌŋkən] adj *person* (*habitually drunk*) ivrogne; (*intoxicated*) ivre, soûl*; *orgy, quarrel* d'ivrogne(s); *fury* causé par la boisson, d'ivrogne; *voice* aviné. **a ~ old man** un vieil ivrogne, un vieux soûlard‡; **accused of ~ driving** accusé d'avoir conduit en état d'ivresse.

drunkenly ['drʌŋkənlɪ] adv *quarrel* comme un ivrogne; *sing* d'une voix avinée; *walk* en titubant, en zigzag.

drunkenness ['drʌŋkənnɪs] n (*state*) ivresse *f*, ébriété *f*; (*problem, habit*) ivrognerie *f*.

drunkometer [drʌŋ'kɒmɪtər] n (*US*) alcootest *m*.

druthers‡ ['drʌðəz] n (*US*) **if I had my ~**‡ s'il ne tenait qu'à moi.

dry [draɪ] 1 adj a *ground, climate, weather, skin, clothes* sec (*f* sèche); *day* sans pluie; *country* sec, aride; *riverbed, well* tari, à sec; (*Geol*) *valley* sec; (*Elec*) *cell* sec; *battery* à piles sèches. **on ~ land** sur la terre ferme; **as ~ as a bone** tout sec, sec comme de l'amadou; **to keep sth ~** tenir qch au sec; (*on label*) **"to be kept ~"** "craint l'humidité"; **to wipe sth ~** essuyer *or* sécher qch; **the river ran ~** la rivière s'est asséchée *or* s'est tarie *or* a tari; **his mouth was ~ with fear** la peur lui desséchait la bouche; **~ bread** pain sec; **piece of ~ toast** tartine *f* de pain grillé sans beurre; (*Met*) **a ~ spell** une période sèche *or* de sécheresse; *see also* **2**.

b *wine, vermouth etc* sec (*f* sèche); *champagne* brut, dry *inv*.

c *country, state* (qui a le régime) sec. (*fig: thirsty*) **to feel** *or* **to be ~** avoir le gosier sec*; **it's ~ work*** c'est un boulot* qui donne soif.

d *humour* pince-sans-rire *inv*; *sarcasm, wit* caustique, mordant. **he has a ~ sense of humour** il est pince-sans-rire, c'est un pince-sans-rire, il a l'esprit caustique.

e (*dull*) *lecture, book, subject* aride. **as ~ as dust** mortel*, ennuyeux comme la pluie.

f (*Brit Pol hum*) réactionnaire.

2 comp ▸**dry-as-dust** aride, dépourvu d'intérêt, sec (*f* sèche) ▸**dry-bulk cargo ship** vraquier *m* ▸**dry-clean** vt nettoyer à sec, dégraisser; (*on label*) **"dry-clean only"** "nettoyage à sec"; **to have a dress dry-cleaned** donner une robe à nettoyer *or* à la teinturerie, porter une robe chez le teinturier ▸**dry cleaner** teinturier *m*; **to take a coat to the dry cleaner's** porter un manteau à la teinturerie *or* chez le teinturier *or* au pressing ▸**dry cleaning** nettoyage *m* à sec, pressing *m*, dégraissage *m* ▸**dry dock** (*Naut*) cale sèche, bassin *m or* cale de radoub ▸**dry-eyed** les yeux secs, l'œil sec ▸**dry farming** (*Agr*) culture sèche, dry-farming *m* ▸**dry fly** (*Fishing*) mouche sèche ▸**dry ginger** ≃ Canada dry ® *m* ▸**dry goods** (*Comm*) tissus *mpl*, mercerie *f* ▸**dry goods store** (*US Comm*) magasin *m* de nouveautés ▸**dry ice** neige *f* carbonique ▸**dry measure** mesure *f* de capacité pour matières sèches ▸**dry rot** pourriture sèche (*du bois*) ▸**dry run** (*fig*) n (*trial, test*) galop *m* d'essai; (*rehearsal*) répétition *f* ◊ adj d'essai ▸**drysalter** (*Brit*) marchand *m* de couleurs ▸**dry shampoo** shampooing sec ▸**dry-shod** à pied sec ▸**dry ski slope** piste (de ski) artificielle ▸**dry(stone) wall** (*Constr*) mur *m* de pierres sèches.

3 n (*Brit Pol hum*) réactionnaire *mf*.

4 vt *paper, fruit, skin* sécher; (*with cloth*) essuyer, sécher; *clothes* (faire) sécher. (*on label*) **"~ away from direct heat"** "ne pas sécher près d'une source de chaleur"; **to ~ one's eyes** *or* **one's tears** sécher ses larmes *or* ses pleurs; **to ~ the dishes** essuyer la vaisselle; **to ~ o.s.** s'essuyer, se sécher, s'éponger.

5 vi sécher; (*) *[actor, speaker]* sécher*, rester sec*.

▸**dry off** vi, vt sep sécher.

▸**dry out** 1 vi a = **dry off.** b *[alcoholic]* se faire désintoxiquer, subir une cure de désintoxication. 2 vt sep *alcoholic* désintoxiquer.

▸**dry up** vi a *[stream, well]* se dessécher, (se) tarir; *[moisture]* s'évaporer; *[clay]* sécher; *[cow]* tarir; *[source of supply, inspiration]* se tarir. b (*dry the dishes*) essuyer la vaisselle. c (*: *be silent*) se taire; *[actor, speaker]* sécher*, rester sec*; *[writer etc]* s'essoufler. **dry up!*** tais-toi!, laisse tomber!*, boucle-la!‡

dryer ['draɪər] n a (*apparatus*) *[clothes]* séchoir *m* (à linge); *[hair]* (*gen*) séchoir (à cheveux), (*helmet type*) casque *m* (sèche-cheveux); *see* **spin, tumble** *etc*. b (*for paint*) siccatif *m*.

drying ['draɪɪŋ] 1 n *[river, clothes]* séchage *m*; (*with a cloth*) essuyage *m*. 2 comp ▸**drying cupboard, drying room** séchoir *m* ▸**drying-up**: **to do the drying-up** essuyer la vaisselle ▸**drying-up cloth** torchon *m* (à vaisselle).

dryly ['draɪlɪ] adv = **drily**.
dryness ['draɪnɪs] n *[soil, weather]* sécheresse *f*, aridité *f*; *[clothes, skin]* sécheresse; *[wit, humour]* causticité *f*; *[humorist]* ton *m* or air *m* pince-sans-rire.
D.Sc. n (*Univ*) (abbr of **Doctor of Science**) *doctorat ès sciences*.
DSS [,di:es'es] n (*Brit*) (abbr of **Department of Social Security**) *see* **social**.
D.S.T. (*US*) (abbr of **Daylight Saving Time**) *see* **daylight**.
DT (*Comput*) (abbr of **data transmission**) *see* **data**.
DTI [di:ti:'aɪ] n (*Brit Admin*) (abbr of **Department of Trade and Industry**) *see* **trade**.
DTP [,di:ti:'pi:] n (abbr of **desktop publishing**) PAO *f*.
D.T.'s [di:'ti:z] npl (abbr of **delirium tremens**) delirium tremens *m*.
dual ['djʊəl] 1 adj double, à deux. (*US Univ etc*) ~ **admissions** double système *m* d'inscriptions (*avec sélection moins stricte pour étudiants défavorisés*); (*Brit*) ~ **carriageway** route *f* à chaussées séparées or à quatre voies; (*Aut, Aviat*) ~ **controls** double commande *f*; ~**-control** (adj) à double commande; ~ **national** personne *f* ayant la double nationalité, binational(e) *m(f)*; ~ **nationality** double nationalité *f*; ~ **ownership** copropriété *f* (*à deux*); (*Psych*) ~ **personality** dédoublement *m* de la personnalité; ~**-purpose** (adj) à double usage, à double emploi. 2 n (*Gram*) duel *m*.
dualism ['djʊəlɪzəm] n (*Philos, Pol, Rel*) dualisme *m*.
dualist ['djʊəlɪst] adj, n (*Philos*) dualiste *(mf)*.
duality [djʊ'ælɪtɪ] n dualité *f*, dualisme *m*.
dub [dʌb] vt a to ~ **sb a knight** donner l'accolade à qn; (*Hist*) adouber or armer qn chevalier; (*nickname*) **to ~ sb "Ginger"** qualifier qn de or surnommer qn "Poil de Carotte". b (*Cine*) postsonoriser; (*into another language*) doubler (*dialogue*).
Dubai [du:'baɪ] n Dubaï *m*.
dubbin ['dʌbɪn] n dégras *m*, graisse *f* pour les chaussures.
dubbing ['dʌbɪŋ] n (*Cine*) doublage *m*.
dubiety [dju:'baɪətɪ] n doute *m*, incertitude *f*.
dubious ['dju:bɪəs] adj *company, offer, privilege* douteux, suspect; *reputation* douteux, équivoque; *person* qui doute (*of* de), hésitant, incertain (*of* de). **he was ~ (about) whether he should come or not** il se demandait s'il devait venir ou non; ~ **of success** incertain du succès; **I'm very ~ about it** j'en doute fort, je n'en suis pas du tout sûr; **with a ~ air** d'un air de doute.
dubiously ['dju:bɪəslɪ] adv avec doute, d'un ton or d'un air incertain or de doute.
Dublin ['dʌblɪn] n Dublin. ~ **Bay prawn** langoustine *f*.
Dubliner ['dʌblɪnəʳ] n habitant(e) *m(f)* or natif *m*, -ive *f* de Dublin.
ducal ['dju:kəl] adj ducal, de duc.
ducat ['dʌkɪt] n ducat *m*.
duchess ['dʌtʃɪs] n duchesse *f*.
duchy ['dʌtʃɪ] n duché *m*.
duck¹ [dʌk] 1 n, pl ~s or ~ a canard *m*; (*female*) cane *f*; (*Mil: vehicle*) véhicule *m* amphibie. **wild ~** canard sauvage; (*Culin*) **roast ~** canard rôti; **to play at ~s and drakes** faire des ricochets (sur l'eau); **to play at ~s and drakes with one's money** jeter son argent par les fenêtres*, gaspiller son argent; **he took to it like a ~ to water** il était comme un poisson dans l'eau, c'était comme s'il l'avait fait toute sa vie; (*Brit*) **yes ~s‡, yes duckie‡** (*to child, friend*) oui mon chou*; (*to unknown adult*) oui mon petit monsieur or ma petite dame or ma petite demoiselle; **he is a ~** c'est un chou* or un amour; *see* **Bombay, dying, lame** *etc*.
b (*Brit Cricket*) **to make a ~, to be out for a ~** faire un score nul.
c (*St Ex*) spéculateur *m*, -trice *f* insolvable.
2 comp ▸**duckbill, duck-billed platypus** ornithorynque *m* ▸**duckboard** caillebotis *m* ▸**duck-egg blue** bleu-vert (pâle) *inv* ▸**duck pond** mare *f* aux canards, canardière *f* ▸**duck shooting** chasse *f* au canard (sauvage) ▸**duck soup‡** (*US fig*) du gâteau* ▸**duckweed** lentille *f* d'eau, lenticule *f*.
3 vi (*also* ~ **down**) se baisser vivement or subitement; (*in fight etc*) esquiver un coup. **to ~ (down) under the water** plonger subitement sous l'eau.
4 vt a **to ~ sb** (*push under water*) plonger qn dans l'eau; (*as a joke*) faire faire le plongeon à qn; (*head only*) faire boire la tasse à qn*.
b *one's head* baisser vivement or subitement; *blow, question etc* éviter, esquiver.
duck² [dʌk] n (*Tex*) coutil *m*, toile fine. (*Brit*) ~s pantalon *m* de coutil.
duckie‡ ['dʌkɪ] 1 n (*Brit*) *see* **duck¹ 1**. 2 adj = **ducky**.
ducking ['dʌkɪŋ] n plongeon *m*, bain forcé. **to give sb a ~** faire faire le plongeon à qn; (*head only*) faire boire la tasse à qn*.
duckling ['dʌklɪŋ] n (*also Culin*) caneton *m*; (*female*) canette *f*; (*older*) canardeau *m*.
ducky* ['dʌkɪ] adj (*iro*) mimi*, mignon tout plein.
duct [dʌkt] n *[liquid, gas, electricity]* conduite *f*, canalisation *f*; (*Bot*) trachée *f*; (*Anat*) canal *m*, conduit *m*. **respiratory ~** conduit respiratoire.
ductile ['dʌktaɪl] adj *metal* ductile; *person* maniable, malléable, docile.
ductless ['dʌktlɪs] adj: ~ **gland** glande *f* endocrine.
dud* [dʌd] 1 adj *shell, bomb* non éclaté, qui a raté; *object, tool* mal fichu*, à la noix*; *note, coin* faux (*f* fausse); *cheque* sans provision, en bois*; *person* à la manque*, (très) mauvais, nul. (*Press*) ~ **(story)** canard* *m*. 2 n a (*shell*) obus non éclaté; (*bomb*) bombe non éclatée; (*person*) type nul*, raté(e) *m(f)*. **this coin is a ~** cette pièce est fausse; **this watch is a ~** cette montre ne marche pas; **to be a ~ at geography** être nul en géographie; **to be a ~ at tennis** être un zéro or une nullité au tennis. b (‡†: *clothes*) ~s nippes* *fpl*.
dude* [d(j)u:d] (*US*) 1 n a (*Easterner*) touriste *mf* de la côte Est (*à l'Ouest*). b (*man*) type* *m*, mec‡ *m*. c (*dandy*) dandy *m*, (*young*) gommeux* *m*. 2 comp ▸**dude ranch** (hotel *m*) ranch *m*.
dudgeon ['dʌdʒən] n: **in (high)** ~ offensé dans sa dignité, furieux.
due [dju:] 1 adj a (*owing*) *sum, money* dû (*f* due). **the sum which is ~ to him** la somme qui lui est due or qui lui revient; **our thanks are ~ to X** nous aimerions remercier X, notre gratitude va à X (*frm*); **to fall ~** échoir, venir à (l')échéance; ~ **on the 8th** payable le 8; **when is the rent ~?** quand faut-il payer le loyer?; **I am ~ 6 days' leave** on me doit 6 jours de permission; **he is ~ for a rise** (*will get it*) il doit recevoir une augmentation; (*should get it*) il devrait recevoir une augmentation; **I am ~ for a holiday in September** en principe j'aurai des vacances en septembre.
b (*proper, suitable*) *respect, regard* qu'on doit, qui convient. **he acted with ~ regard to the conditions** il a agi comme il convenait vu les circonstances; (*Jur*) **driving without ~ care and attention** conduite imprudente; **after ~ consideration** après mûre réflexion; **in ~ course** (*when the time is ripe*) en temps utile or voulu; (*in the long run*) à la longue; **it will come about in ~ course** cela arrivera en temps utile or voulu; **in ~ course it transpired that ...** à la longue il s'est révélé que ...; **in ~ time** à la longue, finalement; **in ~ form** en bonne et due forme; **with all ~ respect, I believe ...** sauf votre respect or sans vouloir vous contredire, je crois ... .
c **when is the plane ~ (in)?** à quelle heure l'avion doit-il atterrir?; **the train is ~ (in or to arrive) at midday** le train doit arriver à midi; **they are ~ to start at 6** l'heure du départ est fixée pour 6 heures, ils doivent partir à 6 heures; **I am ~ there tomorrow** je dois être là-bas demain, on m'attend là-bas demain.
d ~ **to** dû (*f* due) à, attribuable à; **it is ~ to his ineptitude that ...** c'est à cause de son incompétence que ...; **the accident was ~ to a drunken driver** l'accident a été provoqué par un conducteur en état d'ivresse; **the accident was ~ to the icy road** l'accident était dû au verglas; **it is ~ to you that he is alive today** c'est grâce à vous qu'il est en vie aujourd'hui; **what's it ~ to?** comment cela se fait-il?, quelle en est la cause?
2 adv (tout) droit. **to go ~ west** aller droit vers l'ouest, faire route plein ouest; **to sail ~ north** avoir le cap au nord; **to face ~ north** *[house]* être (en) plein nord; *[person]* faire face au nord; ~ **east of the village** plein est par rapport au village.
3 n a **to give sb his ~** être juste envers qn, faire or rendre justice à qn; **(to) give him his ~, he did try hard** il faut (être juste et) reconnaître qu'il a quand même fait tout son possible; *see* **devil**.
b (*fees*) ~s *[club etc]* cotisation *f*; *[harbour]* droits *mpl* (de port).
duel ['djʊəl] 1 n duel *m*, rencontre *f*; (*fig*) duel, lutte *f*. ~ **to the death** duel à mort; *see* **challenge, fight**. 2 vi se battre en duel (*with* contre, avec). 3 comp ▸**duelling pistols** pistolets *mpl* de duel.
duellist ['djʊəlɪst] n duelliste *m*.
duet [dju:'et] n duo *m*. **to sing/play a ~** chanter/jouer en duo; **violin ~** duo de violon; **piano ~** morceau *m* à quatre mains.
duff¹ [dʌf] n (*Culin*) pudding *m*; *see* **plum**.
duff² [dʌf] (*Brit*) 1 adj (*) (*out of order*) *machine, watch* déglingué*; *light bulb* mort; (*failed*) *shot etc* raté, loupé*; (*useless*) *suggestion, idea* stupide, inepte. 2 vt (‡: *alter, fake*) *stolen goods* maquiller, truquer.
▸**duff up‡** vt sep tabasser, casser la gueule à‡.
duff³‡ [dʌf] n (*US: buttocks*) postérieur *m*. **he just sits on his ~ all day** il ne fiche* rien de la journée; **get off your ~!** magne-toi le train!‡
duffel ['dʌfəl] adj: ~ **bag** sac *m* de paquetage, sac marin; ~ **coat** duffel-coat *m*.
duffer* ['dʌfəʳ] n cruche* *f*, gourde* *f*; (*Scol*) cancre* *m*, âne *m*. **he is a ~ at French** il est nul or c'est un cancre* en français; **to be a ~ at games** n'être bon à rien en sport.
duffle ['dʌfəl] adj = **duffel**.
dug¹ [dʌg] n mamelle *f*, tétine *f*; *[cow]* pis *m*.
dug² [dʌg] 1 pret, ptp of **dig**. 2 comp ▸**dugout** (*Mil*) tranchée-abri *f*; (*canoe*) pirogue *f*.
duke [dju:k] n a (*nobleman*) duc *m*. b (*esp US* ‡: *fists*) ~s poings *mpl*.
dukedom ['dju:kdəm] n (*territory*) duché *m*; (*title*) titre *m* de duc.
dulcet ['dʌlsɪt] adj (*liter*) suave, doux (*f* douce), harmonieux.
dulcimer ['dʌlsɪməʳ] n tympanon *m*.
dull [dʌl] 1 adj a *sight, hearing* faible; (*slow-witted*) *person, mind* borné, obtus. (*Scol*) **the ~ ones** les moins doués; **his senses/his intellectual powers are growing ~** ses sens/ses capacités intellectuelles s'émoussent or s'amoindrissent; **to be ~ of hearing** être dur d'oreille.
b (*boring*) *book, evening, lecture* ennuyeux, dépourvu d'intérêt; *style* terne; *person* terne, insignifiant. **deadly ~*** assommant*, mortel*; **as ~ as ditchwater or dishwater** ennuyeux comme la pluie; **a ~ old stick*** un vieux raseur*.

c (*not bright etc*) *colour, light, eyes, mirror* sans éclat, terne; *metal* terne; *sound* sourd, étouffé; *weather, sky* couvert, gris, sombre, maussade; *blade* émoussé; *pain* sourd, vague; (*St Ex*) *market* calme, terne, lourd; (*Comm*) *trade, business* lent, languissant, stagnant; *person* déprimé, las (*f* lasse) (d'esprit), triste; *mood, humour* déprimé, triste, las; *look* terne, atone. **it's ~ today** il fait un temps maussade *or* il fait gris aujourd'hui; **a ~ day** un jour maussade; **a ~ thud** un bruit sourd *or* mat.

2 **vt** *senses* émousser, engourdir; *mind* alourdir, engourdir; *pain, grief, impression* amortir, atténuer; *thing remembered* atténuer; *pleasure* émousser; *sound* assourdir, amortir; *edge, blade* émousser; *colour, mirror, metal* ternir.

3 **vi** s'émousser; s'engourdir; s'alourdir; s'atténuer; s'amortir; s'assourdir; se ternir.

dullard ['dʌləd] **n** lourdaud(e) *m(f)*, balourd(e) *m(f)*; (*Scol*) cancre* *m*, âne *m*.

dullness ['dʌlnɪs] **n** a (*slow-wittedness*) lourdeur *f* d'esprit; *[senses]* affaiblissement *m*. **~ of hearing** dureté *f* d'oreille. b (*tedium*) *[book, evening, lecture, person]* caractère ennuyeux, manque *m* d'intérêt. c *[colour, metal, mirror etc]* manque *m or* peu *m* d'éclat, aspect *m* terne; *[sound]* caractère sourd *or* étouffé; *[person]* ennui *m*, lassitude *f*, tristesse *f*; *[landscape, room]* tristesse. **the ~ of the weather** le temps couvert.

dullsville* ['dʌlzvɪl] **n** (*US*) **it's ~ here** on s'emmerde ici*, c'est pas la joie ici*.

dully ['dʌllɪ] **adv** (*depressedly*) *behave, walk* lourdement; *answer, listen* avec lassitude, avec découragement; (*boringly*) *talk, write* d'une manière ennuyeuse *or* insipide, avec monotonie.

duly ['dju:lɪ] **adv** (*properly*) comme il faut, ainsi qu'il convient; (*Jur etc*) dûment; (*on time*) en temps voulu, en temps utile. **he ~ protested** il a protesté comme on s'y attendait; **he said he would come and he ~ came at 6 o'clock** il avait promis de venir et est en effet venu à 6 heures; **everybody was ~ shocked** tout le monde a bien entendu été choqué.

dumb [dʌm] 1 **adj** a muet; (*with surprise, shock*) muet (*with, from* de), sidéré*, abasourdi (*with, from* de, par). **a ~ person** un(e) muet(te); **~ animals** les animaux *mpl*; **~ creatures** les bêtes *fpl*; **our ~ friends** nos amis les bêtes; **to be struck ~** rester muet, être sidéré*; *see* **deaf**.

b (*: *stupid*) *person* bête, nigaud, bêta* (*f* -asse), gourde*; *action* bête. **a ~ blonde** une blonde évaporée; **to act ~** faire l'innocent; (*US*) **~ ox*** ballot* *m*, andouille* *f*.

2 **comp** ▸**dumb-ass*** (*US*) **n** con* *m*, conne* *f* ◊ **adj** à la con* ▸**dumbbell** (*Sport*) haltère *m*; (*: *fool: also* **dumb cluck***) imbécile *mf* ▸**dumb show**: **in dumb show** en pantomime, par (des) signes ▸**dumb terminal** (*Comput*) terminal *m* passif ▸**dumbwaiter** (*US: lift*) monte-plats *m inv*; (*Brit: trolley*) table roulante; (*revolving stand*) plateau tournant.

dumbfound [dʌm'faʊnd] **vt** confondre, abasourdir, ahurir, sidérer*.

dumbfounded [dʌm'faʊndɪd] **adj** ahuri, sidéré*. **I'm ~** j'en suis ahuri *or* sidéré*, je n'en reviens pas.

dumbly ['dʌmlɪ] **adv** (*stupidly*) stupidement; (*in shock, surprise*) d'un air abasourdi.

dumbo* ['dʌmbəʊ] **n** (*US*) ballot* *m*, andouille* *f*.

dumbness ['dʌmnɪs] **n** (*Med*) mutisme *m*; (*: *stupidity*) bêtise *f*, niaiserie *f*.

dumbstruck ['dʌmstrʌk] **adj** muet de surprise.

dum-dum ['dʌmdʌm] **n** a (*bullet*) balle *f* dumdum *inv*. b (*: *stupid person*) crétin(e) *m(f)*, andouille* *f*.

dummy ['dʌmɪ] 1 **n** a (*Comm: sham object*) factice *m*; *[book]* maquette *f*; (*Comm, Sewing: model*) mannequin *m*; *[ventriloquist]* pantin *m*; (*Theat*) personnage muet, figurant *m*; (*Fin etc: person replacing another*) prête-nom *m*, homme *m* de paille; (*Bridge*) mort *m*; (*Sport*) feinte *f*. (*Sport*) **to sell (sb) the ~** feinter (qn); (*Bridge*) **to be ~** faire *or* être le mort; (*Bridge*) **to play from ~** jouer du mort.

b (*Brit: baby's teat*) sucette *f*, tétine *f*.

2 **adj** faux (*f* fausse), factice. (*Cards*) **~ bridge** bridge *m* à trois; (*Sport*) **~ pass** feinte *f* de passe; **~ run** (*Aviat*) attaque *f or* bombardement *m* simulé(e); (*Comm, Ind*) (coup *m* d')essai *m*; (*Ling*) **~ element, ~ symbol** postiche *m*.

3 **vi** (*Sport*) feinter, faire une feinte.

dump [dʌmp] 1 **n** a (*pile of rubbish*) tas *m or* amas *m* d'ordures; (*place*) décharge *f* (publique), dépotoir *m*, terrain *m* de décharge. (*fig*) **to be (down) in the ~s*** avoir le cafard*, broyer du noir.

b (*Mil*) dépôt *m*; *see* **ammunition**.

c (* *pej*) (*place*) trou* *m*, bled* *m*; (*house, hotel*) baraque* *f*, boîte* *f*.

d (*Comput*) vidage *m*.

2 **vt** a (*get rid of*) *rubbish* déposer, jeter; (*Comm*) *goods* vendre *or* écouler à bas prix (*sur les marchés extérieurs*), pratiquer le dumping pour; (*) *person* larguer*, plaquer*; (*) *thing* larguer*, bazarder*.

b (*put down*) *package* déposer; *sand, bricks* décharger, déverser; (*) *passenger* déposer. **~ your bag on the table** plante *or* fiche* ton sac sur la table.

c (*Comput*) *data, file etc* vider. **to ~ to the printer** transférer sur l'imprimante.

3 **comp** ▸**dump bin, dump display** (*Comm*) présentoir *m* d'articles en vrac ▸**dump truck** = **dumper**.

dumper ['dʌmpə^r] **n** (*also* **~ truck**) tombereau *m* automoteur, dumper *m*.

dumping ['dʌmpɪŋ] 1 **n** *[load, rubbish]* décharge *f*; (*Ecol: in sea etc*) déversement *m* (de produits nocifs); (*Comm*) dumping *m*. 2 **comp** ▸**dumping ground** (*also fig*) dépotoir *m*.

dumpling ['dʌmplɪŋ] **n** (*Culin: savoury*) boulette *f* (de pâte); (*: *person*) boulot(te) *m(f)*; *see* **apple**.

dumpy ['dʌmpɪ] **adj** courtaud, boulot (*f* -otte).

dun¹ [dʌn] 1 **adj** (*colour*) brun foncé *inv*, brun grisâtre *inv*. 2 **n** cheval louvet, jument louvette.

dun² [dʌn] 1 **n** (*claim*) demande *f* de remboursement. 2 **vt** *debtor* harceler, relancer. **to ~ sb for money owed** harceler *or* relancer qn pour lui faire payer ses dettes.

dunce [dʌns] **n** (*Scol*) âne *m*, cancre* *m*. **to be a ~ at maths** être nul *or* un cancre* en math; **~'s cap** bonnet *m* d'âne.

dunderhead ['dʌndəhed] **n** imbécile *mf*, souche* *f*.

Dundonian [dʌn'dəʊnɪən] 1 **n** habitant(e) *m(f) or* natif (*f* native) de Dundee. 2 **adj** de Dundee.

dune [dju:n] **n** dune *f*. **~ buggy** buggy *m*.

dung [dʌŋ] 1 **n** (*NonC*) (*excrement*) excrément(s) *m(pl)*, crotte *f*; *[horse]* crottin *m*; *[cattle]* bouse *f*; *[bird]* fiente *f*; *[wild animal]* fumées *fpl*; (*manure*) fumier *m*, engrais *m*. 2 **comp** ▸**dung beetle** bousier *m* ▸**dunghill** (tas *m* de) fumier *m*.

dungarees [,dʌŋgə'ri:z] **npl** *[workman]* bleu(s) *m(pl)* (de travail); (*Brit*) *[child, woman]* salopette *f*.

dungeon ['dʌndʒən] **n** (*underground*) cachot *m* (souterrain); (*Hist: castle tower*) donjon *m*.

dunk [dʌŋk] **vt** tremper. **to ~ one's bread in one's coffee** *etc* faire trempette.

Dunkirk [dʌn'kɜ:k] **n** Dunkerque.

dunlin ['dʌnlɪn] **n** bécasseau *m* variable.

dunno* [də'nəʊ] = **don't know**.

dunnock ['dʌnək] **n** (*Brit*) accenteur *m* mouchet, fauvette *f* d'hiver *or* des haies.

dunny* ['dʌnɪ] **n** (*Austral*) chiottes* *fpl*, W.-C.* *mpl*.

Duns Scotus ['dʌnz'skɒtəs] **n** Duns Scot *m*.

duo ['dju:əʊ] **n, pl ~s** *or* **dui** ['dju:i:] (*Mus, Theat*) duo *m*.

duodecimal [,dju:əʊ'desɪməl] **adj** duodécimal.

duodenal [,dju:əʊ'di:nl] **adj** duodénal. **~ ulcer** ulcère *m* du duodénum.

duodenum [,dju:əʊ'di:nəm] **n, pl duodena** [,dju:əʊ'di:nə] *or* **~s** duodénum *m*.

duopoly [djʊ'ɒpəlɪ] **n** duopole *m*.

dupe [dju:p] 1 **vt** duper, tromper. **to ~ sb into doing sth** amener qn à faire qch en le dupant. 2 **n** dupe *f*.

duple ['dju:pl] **adj** (*gen*) double; (*Mus*) binaire. (*Mus*) **~ time** rythme *m or* mesure *f* binaire.

duplex ['dju:pleks] 1 **adj** (*gen*) duplex *inv*. (*Phot*) **~ paper** bande *f* protectrice. 2 **n** (*US*) (*also* **~ house**) maison jumelée; (*also* **~ apartment**) duplex *m*.

duplicate ['dju:plɪkeɪt] 1 **vt** *document, map, key* faire un double de; *film* faire un contretype de; (*on machine*) *document* polycopier; *action etc* répéter exactement. **duplicating machine** machine *f* à polycopier; **that is merely duplicating work already done** cela fait double emploi avec ce qu'on a déjà fait.

2 ['dju:plɪkɪt] **n** *[document, map]* double *m*, copie exacte; (*Jur etc*) duplicata *m inv*, ampliation *f*; *[key, ornament, chair]* double. **in ~** en deux exemplaires, (*Jur etc*) en *or* par duplicata.

3 ['dju:plɪkɪt] **adj** *copy* en double; *bus, coach* supplémentaire. **a ~ receipt** un reçu en duplicata; **a ~ cheque** un duplicata; **I've got a ~ key** j'ai un double de la clef; **~ bridge** bridge *m* de compétition *or* de tournoi.

duplication [,dju:plɪ'keɪʃən] **n** (*NonC*) *[document]* action *f* de copier, (*on machine*) polycopie *f*; *[efforts, work]* répétition *f*, reproduction *f*. **there is some ~ between television and magazine advertising** il y a un certain recoupement entre la publicité télévisée et la publicité dans les magazines.

duplicator ['dju:plɪkeɪtə^r] **n** duplicateur *m*.

duplicity [dju:'plɪsɪtɪ] **n** duplicité *f*, fausseté *f*, double jeu *m*.

Dur. (*Brit*) **abbr of Durham**.

durability [,djʊərə'bɪlɪtɪ] **n** (*see* **durable**) solidité *f*, résistance *f*; durabilité *f*.

durable ['djʊərəbl] 1 **adj** *material, metal* solide, résistant; *friendship* durable, de longue durée. (*Comm*) **~ goods** biens *mpl* de consommation durable, articles *mpl* d'équipement; **"~ press"** (**adj**: *gen*) "repassage superflu"; *trousers* "pli permanent". 2 **npl**: **~s** = **~ goods**; *see* **1**.

Duralumin [djʊə'ræljʊmɪn] **n** ® duralumin *m*.

duration [djʊə'reɪʃən] **n** durée *f*. **of long ~** de longue durée; **for the ~ of the war** jusqu'à la fin de la guerre; **for the ~*** (*for ages*) jusqu'à la saint-glinglin*.

Durban ['dɜ:bæn] **n** Durban.

duress [djʊəˈres] **n** contrainte *f*, coercition *f*. **under ~** sous la contrainte, contraint et forcé (*Jur*).
Durex [ˈdjʊəreks] **n, pl inv** ® préservatif *m*.
during [ˈdjʊərɪŋ] **prep** pendant, durant; (*in the course of*) au cours de.
durst†† [dɜːst] **pret of dare.**
dusk [dʌsk] **n** (*twilight*) crépuscule *m*; (*gloom*) (semi-)obscurité *f*. **at ~** au crépuscule, entre chien et loup, à la brune (*liter*); **in the ~** dans la semi-obscurité, dans l'obscurité.
duskiness [ˈdʌskɪnɪs] **n** *[complexion]* teint foncé *or* mat *or* bistré.
dusky [ˈdʌskɪ] **adj** *complexion* foncé, mat, bistré; *person* au teint foncé *or* mat *or* bistré; *colour* sombre, brunâtre; *room* sombre, obscur. **~ pink** vieux rose *inv*.
dust [dʌst] 1 **n** (*NonC*) (*on furniture, ground*) poussière *f*; *[coal, gold]* poussière, poudre *f*; *[dead body]* poudre. **there was thick ~, the ~ lay thick** il y avait une épaisse couche de poussière; **I've got a speck of ~ in my eye** j'ai une poussière dans l'œil; **to raise a lot of ~** (*lit*) faire de la poussière; (*fig*) faire tout un scandale, faire beaucoup de bruit; **to lay the ~** (*lit*) mouiller la poussière; (*fig*) ramener le calme, dissiper la fumée; (*fig*) **to throw ~ in sb's eyes** jeter de la poudre aux yeux de qn; **to kick up** *or* **raise a ~**‡ faire un *or* du foin*; *see* **ash², bite, shake off** *etc.*
2 **comp ▸dust bag** sac *m* à poussière (*d'aspirateur*) **▸dust bath:** *[bird]* **to take a dust bath** s'ébrouer dans la poussière, prendre un bain de poussière **▸dustbin** (*Brit*) poubelle *f*, boîte *f* à ordures **▸dustbin man** (*Brit*) = **dustman ▸dust bowl** (*Geog*) désert *m* de poussière, cratère(s) *m(pl)* de poussière **▸dustcart** (*Brit*) tombereau *m* aux ordures, camion *m* des boueux **▸dust cloth** (*US*) chiffon *m* (à poussière) **▸dustcloud** nuage *m* de poussière **▸dust cover** *[book]* jaquette *f*; *[furniture]* housse *f* (de protection) **▸dustheap** (*lit*) tas *m* d'ordures; (*fig*) poubelle *f* (*fig*), rebut *m* **▸dust jacket** jaquette *f* **▸dustman** (*Brit*) boueux *m*, éboueur *m* **▸dustmen's strike** (*Brit*) grève *f* des éboueurs **▸dustpan** pelle *f* à poussière **▸dustproof** anti-poussière **▸dust sheet** housse *f* (de protection) **▸dust storm** tourbillon *m* de poussière **▸dust-up*** (*Brit*) accrochage* *m*, bagarre* *f*; (*Brit*) **to have a dust-up with sb** avoir un accrochage* *or* se bagarrer* avec qn.
3 **vt** a *furniture* épousseter, essuyer; *room* essuyer la poussière dans.
b (*with talc, sugar etc*) saupoudrer (*with* de).
4 **vi** épousseter.
▸dust down vt sep (*with brush*) brosser, épousseter; (*with hand*) épousseter.
▸dust off vt sep *dust, crumbs* enlever (*en époussetant*); *object* épousseter.
▸dust out vt sep *box, cupboard* épousseter.
duster [ˈdʌstəʳ] **n** a (*Brit*) chiffon *m* (à poussière); (*blackboard ~*) chiffon (à effacer); *see* **feather.** b (*esp US*) (*overgarment*) blouse *f* de protection; (*housecoat*) robe-tablier *f*. c (*device: also* **crop ~**) pulvérisateur *m* d'insecticide (*NB souvent un avion*).
dusting [ˈdʌstɪŋ] 1 **n** a *[furniture]* époussetage *m*. **to do the ~** épousseter, essuyer (la poussière); **to give sth a ~** donner un coup de chiffon à qch. b (*Culin etc: sprinkling*) saupoudrage *m*. 2 **comp ▸dusting down: to give sb a dusting down** passer un savon à qn; **to get a dusting down** recevoir un savon **▸dusting powder** (poudre *f* de) talc *m*.
dusty [ˈdʌstɪ] **adj** a *table, path* poussiéreux, couvert de *or* plein de poussière. **to get ~** se couvrir de poussière; **not so ~*** pas mal; **to get a ~ answer*** en être pour ses frais; **to give sb a ~ answer*** envoyer promener qn. b **~ pink** vieux rose *inv*, rose fané *inv*; **~ blue** bleu cendré *inv*.
Dutch [dʌtʃ] 1 **adj** hollandais, de Hollande, néerlandais, des Pays-Bas. **the ~ government** le gouvernement néerlandais *or* hollandais; **the ~ embassy** l'ambassade néerlandaise *or* des Pays-Bas; **the ~ East Indies** les Indes néerlandaises; (*Art*) **the ~ School** l'école hollandaise; **~ cheese** fromage *m* de Hollande, hollande *m*.
2 **comp ▸Dutch auction** (*fig*) enchères *fpl* au rabais **▸Dutch barn** hangar *m* à récoltes **▸Dutch cap** diaphragme *m* **▸Dutch courage** (*fig*) courage puisé dans la bouteille; **the drink gave him Dutch courage** il a trouvé du courage dans la bouteille **▸Dutch door** (*US*) porte *f* à double vantail, porte d'étable **▸Dutch elm disease** champignon *m* parasite de l'orme **▸Dutch oven** (*casserole*) grosse cocotte (*en métal*) **▸Dutch treat: to go on a Dutch treat** partager les frais **▸Dutch uncle*: to talk to sb like a Dutch uncle** dire à qn ses quatre vérités.
3 **n** a **the ~** les Hollandais *mpl*, les Néerlandais *mpl*.
b (*Ling*) hollandais *m*, néerlandais *m*. (*fig*) **it's (all) ~ to me*** c'est du chinois *or* de l'hébreu pour moi; *see* **double.**
c (*US fig*) **to be in ~ with sb**‡ être en difficulté avec *or* en disgrâce auprès de qn; **to get one's ~ up**‡ se mettre en rogne*; **to get into ~**‡ avoir des ennuis, se mettre dans le pétrin*.
4 **adv** (*paying one's share*) **to go ~*** partager les frais.
Dutchman [ˈdʌtʃmən] **n** Hollandais *m*. **he did say that or I'm a ~*** il a bien dit ça, j'en mettrais ma tête à couper; *see* **flying.**
Dutchwoman [ˈdʌtʃˌwʊmən] **n** Hollandaise *f*.
dutiable [ˈdjuːtɪəbl] **adj** taxable; (*Customs*) soumis à des droits de douane.
dutiful [ˈdjuːtɪfʊl] **adj** *child* obéissant, respectueux, soumis; *husband* plein d'égards; *employee* consciencieux.
dutifully [ˈdjuːtɪfəlɪ] **adv** *obey, act* avec soumission, respectueusement; *work* consciencieusement.
duty [ˈdjuːtɪ] 1 **n** a (*NonC: moral, legal*) devoir *m*, obligation *f*. **to do one's ~** s'acquitter de *or* faire son devoir (*by sb* envers qn); **it is my ~ to say that ..., I feel (in) ~ bound to say that ...** il est de mon devoir de faire remarquer que ...; **~ calls** le devoir m'appelle; **one's ~ to one's parents** le respect dû à *or* son devoir envers ses parents; **what about your ~ to yourself?** et ton devoir envers toi-même?; **to make it one's ~ to do** se faire un devoir *or* prendre à tâche de faire.
b (*gen pl: responsibility*) fonction *f*, responsabilité *f*. **to take up one's duties** assumer ses fonctions, commencer *or* prendre son service; **to neglect one's duties** négliger ses fonctions; **my duties consist of ...** mes fonctions consistent en ...; **his duties have been taken over by his colleague** ses fonctions ont été reprises par son collègue.
c (*NonC*) **on ~** (*Mil, Admin etc*) de service; (*Med*) de garde; (*Admin, Scol*) de jour, de service; **to be on ~** être de service (*or* de garde *or* de jour *or* de permanence); **to be off ~** être libre, n'être pas de service (*or* de garde *or* de jour); (*Mil*) avoir quartier libre; **to go on/off ~** prendre/quitter le service (*or* la garde); **in the course of ~** (*Mil, Police etc*) en service commandé; (*civilian*) dans l'accomplissement de mes (*or* ses *etc*) fonctions; **to do ~ for sb, to do sb's ~** remplacer qn; (*fig*) **the box does ~ for a table** la boîte fait fonction *or* office de table, la boîte sert de table; *see* **spell², tour.**
d (*Fin: tax*) droit *m*, impôt *m* (indirect), taxe *f* (indirecte); (*at Customs*) frais *mpl* de douane. **to pay ~ on** payer un droit *or* une taxe sur; *see* **death, estate** *etc.*
2 **comp ▸duty call** visite *f* de politesse **▸duty-free** hors taxe **▸duty-free allowance** quantités autorisées de produits hors taxe **▸duty-free shop** magasin *m* hors-taxe **▸duty officer** (*Mil etc*) officier *m* de permanence; (*Police*) officier *m* de police de service; (*Admin*) officiel *m or* préposé *m* de service **▸duty paid** dédouané **▸duty roster, duty rota** liste *f* de service, (*esp Mil*) tableau *m* de service.
duvet [ˈduːveɪ] **n** (*Brit*) couette *f* (*édredon*). **~ cover** housse *f* de couette.
DV [diːˈviː] **adv** (**abbr of Deo volente**) Dieu voulant.
DVM [ˌdiːviːˈem] **n** (*US Univ*) (**abbr of Doctor of Veterinary Medicine**) *doctorat vétérinaire*.
dwarf [dwɔːf] 1 **n, pl ~s** *or* **dwarves** [dwɔːvz] (*person, animal*) nain(e) *m(f)*; (*tree*) arbre nain. 2 **adj** *person, tree, star* nain. 3 **vt** a *[skyscraper, person]* rapetisser, écraser (*fig*); *[achievement]* écraser, éclipser. b *plant* rabougrir, empêcher de croître.
dwarfish [ˈdwɔːfɪʃ] **adj** (*pej*) nabot.
dwell [dwel] **pret, ptp dwelt** *or* **dwelled vi** (*liter*) habiter (*in* dans), demeurer, résider (*frm*) (*in* à); (*fig*) *[interest, difficulty]* résider (*in* dans). **the thought dwelt in his mind** la pensée lui resta dans l'esprit, la pensée demeura dans son esprit.
▸dwell (up)on vt fus (*think about*) s'arrêter sur, arrêter sa pensée sur; (*talk at length on*) s'étendre sur; (*Mus*) *note* appuyer sur. **to dwell (up)on the past** s'appesantir sur le passé, revenir sans cesse sur le passé; **to dwell (up)on the fact that ...** insister *or* appuyer *or* s'appesantir sur le fait que ...; **don't let's dwell (up)on it** passons là-dessus, glissons.
dweller [ˈdweləʳ] **n** habitant(e) *m(f)*; *see* **country** *etc.*
dwelling [ˈdwelɪŋ] 1 **n** (*Admin or liter: also* **~ place**) habitation *f*, résidence *f*. **to take up one's ~** s'installer, élire domicile (*Admin*). 2 **comp ▸dwelling house** maison *f* d'habitation.
dwelt [dwelt] **pret, ptp of dwell.**
dwindle [ˈdwɪndl] **vi** *[strength]* diminuer, décroître, s'affaiblir; *[numbers, resources]* diminuer, tomber (peu à peu); *[supplies, interest]* diminuer, baisser.
▸dwindle away vi diminuer; *[person]* dépérir.
dwindling [ˈdwɪndlɪŋ] 1 **n** diminution *f* (graduelle). 2 **adj** *interest* décroissant, en baisse; *strength* décroissante; *resources* en diminution.
dye [daɪ] 1 **n** (*substance*) teinture *f*, colorant *m*; (*colour*) teinte *f*, couleur *f*, ton *m*. **hair ~** teinture pour les cheveux; **fast ~** grand teint; **the ~ will come out in the wash** la teinture ne résistera pas au lavage, cela déteindra au lavage; (*fig liter*) **a villain of the deepest ~** une canaille *or* crapule de la pire espèce. 2 **vt** teindre. **to ~ sth red** teindre qch en rouge; **to ~ one's hair** se teindre les cheveux; *see also* **4** *and* **dyed, tie.** 3 **vi** *[cloth etc]* prendre la teinture, se teindre. 4 **comp ▸dyed-in-the-wool** (*fig*) bon teint *inv*, invétéré **▸dyestuffs** matières colorantes, colorants *mpl* **▸dyeworks** teinturerie *f*.
dyed [daɪd] **adj** *hair, fabric* teint. **~ blond/blue** teint en blond/bleu.
dyeing [ˈdaɪɪŋ] **n** (*NonC*) teinture *f*.
dyer [ˈdaɪəʳ] **n** teinturier *m*. **~'s and cleaner's** teinturier (dégraisseur).
dying [ˈdaɪɪŋ] 1 **adj** *person* mourant, agonisant, moribond; *animal, plant* mourant; (*fig*) *custom* en train de disparaître. **to my ~ day** jusqu'à ma dernière heure *or* mon dernier jour; (*hum*) **he looked like a ~ duck (in a thunderstorm)*** il avait un air lamentable *or* pitoyable. 2

n **a** (*death*) mort *f*; (*just before death*) agonie *f*. **b** **the** ~ les mourants *mpl*, les agonisants *mpl*, les moribonds *mpl*; **prayer for the** ~ prière *f* des agonisants.

dyke [daɪk] n **a** (*channel*) fossé *m*; (*wall, barrier*) digue *f*; (*causeway*) levée *f*, chaussée *f*; (*Geol*) filon *m* stérile, dyke *m*; (*Scot dial: wall*) mur *m*. **b** (‡: *lesbian*) gouine‡ *f*.

dynamic [daɪ'næmɪk] adj (*Phys etc*) dynamique; *person etc* dynamique, énergique, plein d'entrain.

dynamically [daɪ'næmɪkəlɪ] adv dynamiquement.

dynamics [daɪ'næmɪks] n (*NonC*) dynamique *f* (*also Mus*).

dynamism ['daɪnəmɪzəm] n dynamisme *m*.

dynamite ['daɪnəmaɪt] **1** n **a** (*NonC*) dynamite *f*; *see* **stick**. **b** (*fig: dangerous*) **that business is** ~* ça pourrait t'exploser dans les mains (*fig*); **it's political** ~ politiquement c'est un sujet explosif (*or* une affaire explosive). **c** (*fig*) **he's** ~* (*terrific*) il est super* *or* du tonnerre*; (*full of energy etc*) il pète le feu*, il est d'un dynamisme! **2** vt faire sauter à la dynamite, dynamiter.

dynamo ['daɪnəməʊ] n (*esp Brit*) dynamo *f*. **he is a human** ~ il déborde d'énergie.

dynastic [daɪ'næstɪk] adj dynastique.

dynasty ['dɪnəstɪ], (*US*) ['daɪnəstɪ] n dynastie *f*.

dyne [daɪn] n dyne *f*.

d'you [djuː] (abbr of **do you**) *see* **do**[1].

dysenteric [ˌdɪsən'terɪk] adj dysentérique.

dysentery ['dɪsɪntrɪ] n dysenterie *f*.

dysfunction [dɪs'fʌŋkʃən] n dysfonction *f*.

dysfunctional [dɪs'fʌŋkʃənl] adj dysfonctionnel.

dyslexia [dɪs'leksɪə] n dyslexie *f*.

dyslexic [dɪs'leksɪk] adj, n dyslexique (*mf*).

dysmenorrhoea, (*US*) **dysmenorrhea** [ˌdɪsmenə'rɪə] n dysménorrhée *f*.

dyspepsia [dɪs'pepsɪə] n dyspepsie *f*.

dyspeptic [dɪs'peptɪk] adj, n dyspepsique (*mf*), dyspeptique (*mf*).

dysphasia [dɪs'feɪzɪə] n dysphasie *f*.

dysprosium [dɪs'prəʊsɪəm] n dysprosium *m*.

dystrophy ['dɪstrəfɪ] n dystrophie *f*; *see* **muscular**.

E

E, e [iː] 1 **n** a (*letter*) E, e *m*. **E for Easy** E comme Eugène (*or* É comme Émile). b (*Mus*) mi *m*; *see* **key**. c (**abbr of East**) E, est. d (*Scol*) ≈ faible. e (*Brit*) (**abbr of elbow**) **to give sb/get the big E*** *lover* plaquer‡ *or* laisser tomber qn*/se faire plaquer‡; *employee* virer qn*/se faire virer*. f (*Drugs sl*) **E** ecstasy *m*. 2 **comp** (*on food packets*) E ►**E 25/132** E 25/132 ►**E number** ≈ additif *m* (alimentaire).

E.A. [ˌiːˈeɪ] **n** (*US Scol*) (**abbr of educational age**) *see* **educational**.

each [iːtʃ] 1 **adj** chaque. ~ **passport** chaque passeport, tout passeport; ~ **day** chaque jour, tous les jours; ~ **one of us** chacun(e) de *or* d'entre nous; ~ **(and every) one of us,** ~ **and all of us** chacun(e) de nous sans exception.

2 **pron** a (*thing, person, group*) chacun(e) *m(f)*. ~ **of the boys** chacun des garçons; ~ **of us** chacun(e) de *or* d'entre nous; ~ **of them gave their*** *or* **his opinion** chacun a donné son avis, ils ont donné chacun leur avis; **we** ~ **had our own idea about it** nous avions chacun notre idée là-dessus; ~ **more beautiful than the next** *or* **the other** tous plus beaux les uns que les autres; ~ **of them was given a present** on leur a offert à chacun un cadeau, chacun d'entre eux a reçu un cadeau; **a little of** ~ **please** un peu de chaque s'il vous plaît.

b (*apiece*) chacun(e). **we gave them one apple** ~ nous leur avons donné une pomme chacun; **2 classes of 20 pupils** ~ 2 classes de chacune 20 élèves *or* de 20 élèves chacune; **the books are £2** ~ les livres coûtent 2 livres chacun *or* chaque; **carnations at one franc** ~ des œillets à un franc (la) pièce.

c ~ **other** l'un(e) l'autre *m(f)*, mpl les uns les autres, *fpl* les unes les autres; **they love** ~ **other** ils s'aiment (l'un l'autre); **they write to** ~ **other often** ils s'écrivent souvent; **they were sorry for** ~ **other** ils avaient pitié l'un de l'autre; **they respected** ~ **other** ils avaient du respect l'un pour l'autre, ils se respectaient mutuellement; **you must help** ~ **other** il faut vous entraider; **separated from** ~ **other** séparés l'un de l'autre; **they used to carry** ~ **other's books** ils s'aidaient à porter leurs livres.

eager [ˈiːgəʳ] **adj** (*keen*) désireux, avide (*for* de, *to do* de faire); (*impatient*) impatient, pressé (*to do* de faire); *scholar, supporter* passionné; *lover* ardent, passionné; *desire* ardent, passionné, violent; *search, glance* avide; *pursuit, discussion* âpre. **to be** ~ **for** *happiness* rechercher avidement; *affection* être avide de; *power, vengeance, pleasure* être assoiffé de; *praise, fame, knowledge* avoir soif de; *nomination, honour* désirer vivement, ambitionner; ~ **for profit** âpre au gain; **to be** ~ **to do** (*keen*) être extrêmement désireux *or* avoir très envie de faire, désirer vivement faire; (*impatient*) brûler *or* être impatient *or* être pressé de faire; **to be** ~ **to help** être empressé à *or* très désireux d'aider; **to be an** ~ **student of** se passionner pour l'étude de; ~ **beaver*** (*gen*) personne *f* enthousiaste et consciencieuse; (*at work*) **he's an** ~ **beaver*** il en veut*, il se donne du mal pour réussir.

eagerly [ˈiːgəlɪ] **adv** (*see* **eager**) avidement; avec impatience, avec empressement; passionnément; ardemment; âprement.

eagerness [ˈiːgənɪs] **n** (*see* **eager**) (vif) désir *m*, avidité *f* (*for* de) (*liter*), désir ardent (*to do* de faire, *for* de); impatience *f* (*to do* de faire), empressement *m* (*to do* à faire); ardeur *f* (*for* à); âpreté *f* (*for* à).

eagle [ˈiːgl] 1 **n** (*Orn*) aigle *mf* (*gen m*); (*Rel: lectern*) aigle *m*; (*Her, Hist, Mil*) aigle *f*; (*Golf*) eagle *m*; (*US* †*: coin*) *pièce de 10 dollars*; *see* **golden.** 2 **comp** ►**eagle eye** œil *m* de lynx ►**eagle-eyed** à l'œil d'aigle, aux yeux de lynx ►**eagle owl** grand-duc *m* ►**eagle ray** aigle *m* de mer.

eaglet [ˈiːglɪt] **n** aiglon(ne) *m(f)*.

E & OE [ˌiːəndˈəʊiː] (**abbr of errors and omissions excepted**) se & o.

ear¹ [ɪəʳ] 1 **n** oreille *f*. (*fig*) **to keep one's ~s open** ouvrir l'oreille; (*fig*) **to close** *or* **shut one's ~s to sth** faire la sourde oreille à qch; **to keep one's** ~ **to the ground** être aux écoutes; **to be all ~s*** être tout oreilles *or* tout ouïe; (*fig*) **that set them by the ~s!** ça a semé la zizanie (entre eux)!, cela les a mis aux prises!; (*US fig*) **to set** *or* **put sb on his** ~ (*irritate*) exaspérer qn; (*shock*) atterrer qn; **your ~s must have been burning** les oreilles ont dû vous tinter; **if that came to his ~s** si cela venait à ses oreilles; **it goes in one** ~ **and out of the other** cela lui (*or* vous *etc*) entre par une oreille et lui (*or* vous *etc*) sort par l'autre; **you'll be out on your ~*** **if you're not careful** tu vas te faire vider* si tu ne fais pas attention; **he has the** ~ **of the President** il a l'oreille du Président; **to be up to the** *or* **one's ~s in work** avoir du travail par-dessus la tête; **to be up to the** *or* **one's ~s in debt** être endetté jusqu'au cou; **to have an** ~ **for music** avoir l'oreille musicale; (*Mus*) **to have a good** ~ avoir une bonne oreille; **to have an ~/a good** ~ **for languages** avoir de l'oreille/une bonne oreille pour les langues; (*Mus*) **to play by** ~ jouer d'instinct *or* à l'oreille; (*fig*) **I'll play it by** ~ je déciderai quoi faire *or* j'improviserai le moment venu, j'aviserai selon les circonstances; *see* **bend, box², deaf, half** *etc*.

2 **comp** *operation* à l'oreille ►**earache** mal *m* d'oreille(s); **to have earache** avoir mal à l'oreille *or* aux oreilles ►**eardrops** (*Med*) gouttes *fpl* pour les oreilles ►**eardrum** tympan *m* (*de l'oreille*) ►**earful***: **to give sb an earful** (*talk a lot*) en raconter de belles* à qn; (*scold*) passer un savon* à qn ►**earlobe** lobe *m* d'oreille ►**earmark n** (*fig*) marque *f*, signe distinctif, caractéristique *f* ◊ **vt** *cattle* marquer (au fer rouge); (*fig*) *object, seat* réserver (*for* à); *funds, person* assigner, affecter, destiner (*for* à) ►**earmuff** serre-tête *m inv* ►**ear, nose and throat department** (*Med*) service *m* d'oto-rhino-laryngologie ►**ear, nose and throat specialist** oto-rhino-laryngologiste *mf*, oto-rhino* *mf* ►**earphone** (*Rad, Telec etc*) écouteur *m*; **to listen on earphones** écouter au casque ►**earpiece** (*Rad, Telec etc*) écouteur *m* ►**ear piercing n** perçage *m* d'oreilles ►**ear-piercing adj** = **ear-splitting** ►**earplugs** (*for sleeping*) boules *fpl* Quiès ®; (*for underwater*) protège-tympans *mpl* ►**earring** boucle *f* d'oreille ►**ear shell** (*Zool*) ormeau *m* ►**earshot: out of earshot** hors de portée de voix; **within earshot** à portée de voix ►**ear-splitting** *sound, scream* strident; *din* fracassant ►**ear stoppers** = **earplugs** ►**ear trumpet** cornet *m* acoustique ►**ear wax** cérumen *m*, cire *f* ►**earwig** perce-oreille *m*.

ear² [ɪəʳ] **n** *[grain, plant]* épi *m*.

earl [ɜːl] **n** comte *m*.

earldom [ˈɜːldəm] **n** (*title*) titre *m* de comte; (*land*) comté *m*.

early [ˈɜːlɪ] 1 **adj** a (*in day etc*) de bonne heure. **we've got an** ~ **start tomorrow** nous partons tôt *or* de bonne heure demain; **I caught an** ~ **train** j'ai pris un train tôt le matin; **I caught the** ~ **train** j'ai pris le premier train (du matin); **it was** ~ **in the morning/afternoon** c'était tôt le matin/l'après-midi; **in the** ~ **morning** de bon *or* grand matin; **very** ~ **in the morning** de très bonne heure le matin; **at an** ~ **hour** de bonne heure, très tôt; **at an** ~ **hour of the morning** à une heure matinale; **don't go, it's still** ~ ne t'en va pas, il est encore tôt *or* il n'est pas tard; **it is too** ~ **to say that,** (*Brit*) **it's** ~ **in the day** *or* **it's** ~ **days to say that** il est un peu tôt pour dire ça; (*Brit*) **it's** ~ **closing (day) today** aujourd'hui les magasins ferment l'après-midi; (*Prov*) **it's the** ~ **bird that catches the worm** l'avenir appartient à qui se lève matin (*Prov*); **to be an** ~ **riser** *or* **an** ~ **bird*** être matinal, se lever tôt *or* de bonne heure; **to keep** ~ **hours** être un(e) couche-tôt (*pl inv*), se coucher tôt.

b (*before expected time*) *departure etc* de bonne heure; *death* prématuré. **Easter is** ~ **this year** Pâques est tôt cette année; **raspberries are** ~ **this year** les framboises ont mûri tôt cette année (*see also* **e**); **you're** ~ **today** vous arrivez de bonne heure *or* tôt aujourd'hui; **he's always** ~ il est toujours en avance; **we're having an** ~ **holiday this year** nous partons tôt en vacances cette année; **to have an** ~ **night** (aller) se coucher tôt; **his** ~ **arrival** son arrivée de bonne heure, le fait qu'il arrive (*or* est arrivé *etc*) de bonne heure; (*Admin*) ~ **retirement** préretraite *f* (*Admin*), retraite anticipée; (*Admin*) **to take** ~ **retirement** partir en préretraite (*Admin*), prendre sa retraite anticipée; (*US Univ*) ~ **admission** inscription *f* anticipée; (*Mil*) ~ **warning system** système *m* de première alerte.

c (*towards the start of sth*) **in the** ~ **afternoon/spring** *etc* au début *or* au commencement de l'après-midi/du printemps *etc;* **in the** ~ **part of the century** au début *or* au commencement du siècle; **in the** ~ **days** au début, au commencement (*of sth* de qch); **the ~ days** *or* **stages of a project** les débuts d'un projet; **in the ~ Forties** (*years*) au début des années 40; **she's in her ~ forties** elle a juste dépassé la quarantaine; **from an ~ age** dès l'enfance, de bonne heure; **in his ~ youth** dans sa première *or* prime jeunesse; **his ~ life** sa jeunesse, ses premières années; **in (his** *etc***) ~ life** tôt dans la vie, de bonne heure.

d (*near the first etc*) *settlers, aeroplanes etc* premiers; *man, Church* primitif. **an ~ text** un texte très ancien, un des premiers textes; **in an ~ film** dans un premier film; **the ~ Tudors** les premiers Tudors; **~ Christian** (*adj, n*) paléochrétien(ne) *m(f)*; **the ~ Victorians** les Victoriens *mpl* du début du règne; **an ~ Victorian table** une table du début de l'époque victorienne; (*Archit*) **E~ English** premier gothique anglais.

e *apples etc* précoce, hâtif. (*Comm*) **~ fruit/vegetables** primeurs *mpl*; **Worcesters are an ~ apple** la Worcester est une pomme précoce *or* hâtive; **the ~ apples are in the shops now** les premières pommes sont en vente maintenant.

f (*in future time*) **at an ~ date** bientôt, prochainement; **at an earlier date** à une date plus rapprochée; **at the earliest** au plus tôt; **at the earliest possible moment** le plus tôt possible, au plus tôt, dès que possible; (*Comm*) **at your earliest convenience** dans les meilleurs délais; (*Comm*) **to promise ~ delivery** promettre une livraison rapide; (*Comm*) **the earliest delivery time** le délai de livraison le plus court, le meilleur délai de livraison; (*Comm*) **hoping for an ~ reply** dans l'espoir d'une prompte réponse.

g (*in past time*) **earlier** précédent; **at an earlier date** précédemment; **in earlier times** à une époque précédente.

2 **adv** a (*in day etc*) *get up, set off etc* de bonne heure, tôt. **too ~** trop tôt, de trop bonne heure; **as ~ as possible** le plus tôt possible, dès que possible; **~ next day** le lendemain de bonne heure; **I get up earlier in summer** je me lève plus tôt en été; (*Prov*) **~ to bed, ~ to rise** tôt couché, tôt levé; **as ~ as 1978** dès 1978.

b (*before expected time*) de bonne heure, tôt. **they always come ~** ils arrivent toujours de bonne heure *or* en avance; **five years ~** avec cinq ans d'avance; **he arrived 10 minutes/two days ~** il est arrivé avec 10 minutes/deux jours d'avance, il est arrivé 10 minutes/deux jours à l'avance; **he took his summer holiday ~ this year** il a pris ses vacances d'été tôt cette année; **the peaches are ripening ~ this year** les pêches seront mûres tôt cette année.

c (*towards the start of sth*) **~ in the year/book** *etc* au commencement *or* au début de l'année/du livre *etc*; **~ in the meeting** vers le commencement de la réunion, peu après le commencement de la réunion; **~ in the morning** de bon *or* grand matin; **~ in the day** (*lit*) de bonne heure (*see also* **1a**); **~ in (his** *etc***) life** dans *or* dès sa (*etc*) jeunesse.

d (*in good time*) (longtemps) à l'avance. **post ~** expédiez votre courrier à l'avance; **book ~** réservez longtemps à l'avance.

e **earlier** (*before, previously*) auparavant, plus tôt; **she had left 10 minutes earlier** elle était partie 10 minutes plus tôt *or* 10 minutes auparavant; **earlier on** plus tôt, précédemment; **I said earlier that ...** tout à l'heure j'ai dit que ...; **not earlier than Thursday** pas avant jeudi; **the earliest he can come is Monday** le plus tôt qu'il puisse venir c'est lundi.

earn [ɜːn] 1 **vt** *money* gagner; *salary* toucher; (*Fin*) *interest* rapporter; *praise, rest* mériter, gagner. **to ~ one's living** gagner sa vie; (*hum*) **to ~ an honest crust** gagner honnêtement sa vie *or* son pain; **his success ~ed him praise** sa réussite lui a valu des éloges; **~ed income** revenus salariaux, traitement(s) *m(pl)*, salaire(s) *m(pl)*; **~ing power** (*Econ*) productivité financière; **his ~ing power** son salaire (*etc*) potentiel. 2 **vi**: **to be ~ing** gagner sa vie.

earner [ˈɜːnəʳ] **n**: **high/low ~s** gens *mpl* qui gagnent bien leur vie/qui ont des revenus modestes; **it's a nice little ~*** ça rapporte (bien).

earnest [ˈɜːnɪst] 1 **adj** (*conscientious*) sérieux, consciencieux; (*eager*) ardent; (*sincere*) sincère; *prayer* fervent; *desire, request* pressant. 2 **n** a **in ~** (*with determination*) sérieusement; (*without joking*) sans rire. **this time I am in ~** cette fois je ne plaisante pas; **it is snowing in ~** il neige pour de bon. b (*also* **~ money**) arrhes *fpl*; (*fig: guarantee*) garantie *f*, gage *m*. **as an ~ of his good intentions** en gage de ses bonnes intentions.

earnestly [ˈɜːnɪstlɪ] **adv** *speak* avec conviction, avec (grand) sérieux; *work* consciencieusement, avec ardeur; *beseech* instamment; *pray* avec ferveur.

earnestness [ˈɜːnɪstnɪs] **n** *[person, tone]* gravité *f*, sérieux *m*; *[effort]* ardeur *f*; *[demand]* véhémence *f*.

earnings [ˈɜːnɪŋz] **npl** *[person]* salaire *m*, gain(s) *m(pl)*; *[business]* profits *mpl*, bénéfices *mpl*. **~-related** *pension, contributions* proportionnel au salaire.

earth [ɜːθ] 1 **n** a (*the world*) terre *f*, monde *m*. **(the) E~** la Terre; **on ~** sur terre; **here on ~** ici-bas, en ce bas monde; (*fig*) **it's heaven on ~** c'est le paradis sur terre; **to the ends of the ~** au bout du monde; **where/why/how on ~ ...?** où/pourquoi/comment diable ...?; **nowhere on ~ will you find ...** nulle part au monde vous ne trouverez ...; **nothing on ~** rien au monde; **she looks nothing on ~!** à quoi elle ressemble!; **it tasted like nothing on ~** ça avait un goût abominable; (*fig*) **to promise sb the ~** promettre la lune à qn; **it must have cost the ~ !*** ça a dû coûter les yeux de la tête!*

b (*NonC*) (*ground*) terre *f*, sol *m*; (*soil*) terre; (*Brit Elec*) masse *f*, terre; (*Art: also* **~ colour**) terre, couleur minérale. **to fall to ~** tomber à terre *or* par terre *or* au sol; (*lit, fig*) **to come back to ~** redescendre sur terre; **my boots are full of ~** j'ai les bottes pleines de terre; (*hum, euph*) **the ~ moved** ça a été le grand frisson; *see* **down¹**.

c *[fox, badger etc]* terrier *m*, tanière *f*. (*lit, fig*) **to run** *or* **go to ~** se terrer; (*fig*) **to run sth/sb to ~** découvrir *or* dépister *or* dénicher qch/qn.

2 **comp** ►**earthborn** (*liter*) humain ►**earthbound** (*moving towards ~*) qui se dirige vers la terre; (*stuck on ~*) attaché à la terre; (*fig: unimaginative*) terre à terre *inv or* terre-à-terre *inv* ►**earth closet** fosse *f* d'aisances ►**earthman** terrien *m* (*par opposition à extra-terrestre*) ►**earth mother** (*Myth*) déesse *f* de la fertilité; (*fig*) mère nourricière ►**earthmover** bulldozer *m* ►**earth-moving equipment** engins *mpl* de terrassement ►**earthquake** tremblement *m* de terre, séisme *m* ►**earth sciences** sciences *fpl* de la terre ►**earth-shaking, earth-shattering** (*fig*) stupéfiant ►**earth tremor** secousse *f* sismique ►**earthwork** (*Mil, Archeol*) ouvrage *m* de terre; (*Constr*) terrassement *m* ►**earthworm** ver *m* de terre.

3 **vt** (*Brit, Elec*) *apparatus* mettre à la masse *or* à la terre.

►**earth up** **vt sep** *plant* butter.

earthen [ˈɜːθən] 1 **adj** de terre, en terre. 2 **comp** ►**earthenware** poterie *f*; (*glazed*) faïence *f* ►**earthenware jug** *etc* cruche *f etc* en faïence *or* en terre (cuite).

earthiness [ˈɜːθɪnɪs] **n** (*fig*) *[person]* caractère *m* terre à terre *or* terre-à-terre; (*fig*) *[humour]* truculence *f*.

earthling [ˈɜːθlɪŋ] **n** terrien(ne) *m(f)* (*par opposition à extra-terrestre*).

earthly [ˈɜːθlɪ] 1 **adj** *being, paradise, possessions* terrestre. (*fig*) **there is no ~ reason to think** il n'y a pas la moindre raison de croire; **for no ~ reason** sans aucune raison; **he hasn't an ~ chance of succeeding** il n'a pas la moindre chance de réussir; **of no ~ use** d'aucune utilité, sans aucun intérêt; **it's no ~ use telling him that** ça ne sert absolument à rien de lui dire ça. 2 **n** (*Brit*) **not an ~‡** pas la moindre chance, pas l'ombre d'une chance.

earthscape [ˈɜːθskeɪp] **n** vue *f* de la terre prise d'un engin spatial *etc*.

earthward(s) [ˈɜːθwəd(z)] **adv** dans la direction de la terre, vers la terre.

earthy [ˈɜːθɪ] **adj** *taste, smell* terreux, de terre; (*fig*) *person* matériel, terre à terre *inv or* terre-à-terre *inv*; *humour* truculent.

ease [iːz] 1 **n** (*NonC*) a (*mental*) tranquillité *f*; (*physical*) bien-être *m*. **at (one's) ~** à l'aise; **to put sb at (his) ~** mettre qn à l'aise; **not at ~, ill-at-~** mal à son aise, mal à l'aise; **my mind is at ~** j'ai l'esprit tranquille; **to put sb's mind at ~** tranquilliser qn; **the feeling of ~ after a good meal** la sensation de bien-être qui suit un bon repas; **to take one's ~** prendre ses aises; **he lives a life of ~** il a une vie facile; (*Mil*) **(stand) at ~!** repos!

b (*lack of difficulty*) aisance *f*, facilité *f*. **with ~** facilement, aisément, sans difficulté.

2 **vt** a *pain* atténuer, soulager; *mind* calmer, rassurer, tranquilliser; (*liter*) *person* délivrer, soulager (*of a burden* d'un fardeau); *cord* détendre, desserrer; *strap* relâcher; *dress, coat* donner plus d'ampleur à; *pressure, tension* diminuer, modérer; *speed* ralentir. (*Naut*) **to ~ a rope** donner du mou à *or* mollir un cordage.

b **to ~ a key into a lock** introduire doucement *or* délicatement une clef dans une serrure; (*Aviat*) **to ~ back the stick** redresser doucement le manche (à balai); (*Aut*) **to ~ in the clutch** embrayer en douceur; (*Aut*) **he ~d the car into gear** il a passé la première en douceur; **he ~d out the screw** il a desserré délicatement la vis; **he ~d himself into the chair** il s'est laissé glisser dans le fauteuil; **he ~d himself through the gap in the fence** il s'est glissé par le trou de la barrière; **he ~d himself into his jacket** il a passé *or* enfilé doucement sa veste.

3 **vi** se détendre. **the situation has ~d** une détente s'est produite; **prices have ~d** les prix ont baissé, il y a eu une baisse des prix.

►**ease back** **vi** (*US*) **to ease back on sb/sth** se montrer moins strict envers qn/en ce qui concerne qch.

►**ease off** 1 **vi** (*slow down*) ralentir; (*work less hard*) se relâcher; *[situation]* se détendre; *[pressure]* diminuer; *[work, business]* devenir plus calme; *[traffic]* diminuer; *[pain]* se calmer; *[demand]* baisser. 2 **vt sep** *bandage, stamp etc* enlever délicatement; *lid* enlever doucement.

►**ease up** **vi** *[person]* se détendre, se reposer, dételer; *[situation]* se détendre. **ease up a bit!** vas-y plus doucement!; **to ease up on sb/sth** se montrer moins strict envers qn/en ce qui concerne qch.

easel [ˈiːzl] **n** chevalet *m*.

easement [ˈiːzmənt] **n** (*US Jur*) droit *m* de passage.

easily [ˈiːzɪlɪ] **adv** a (*without difficulty*) facilement, sans difficulté, aisément. **the engine was running ~** le moteur tournait régulièrement. b (*unquestionably*) sans aucun doute, de loin; (*with amounts, measurements etc*) facilement. **he is ~ the best** il est de loin *or* sans aucun doute le meilleur; **that's ~ 4 km** cela fait facilement 4 km. c (*possibly*) bien. **he may ~ change his mind** il pourrait bien changer d'avis; **he could ~ be right** il pourrait bien avoir raison. d (*calmly*) *smile etc* avec calme, tranquillement. **"yes" he said ~** "oui" dit-il tranquillement.

easiness [ˈiːzɪnɪs] **n** facilité *f*.

east [iːst] 1 n est *m*, orient *m* (*frm*), levant† *m*. **the E~** (*gen*) l'Orient; (*Pol*) les pays *mpl* de l'Est; (*US Geog*) (les états *mpl* de) l'Est; **the mysterious E~** l'Orient mystérieux; **to the ~ of** à l'est de; **in the ~ of Scotland** dans l'est de l'Écosse; **house facing the ~** maison exposée à l'est; *[wind]* **to veer to the ~, to go into the ~** tourner à l'est; **the wind is in the ~** le vent est à l'est; **the wind is (coming** *or* **blowing) from the ~** le vent vient *or* souffle de l'est; **to live in the ~** habiter dans l'Est; *see* **far, middle** *etc*.

2 adj est *inv*, de *or* à l'est, oriental. **~ wind** vent *m* d'est; **~ coast** côte est *or* orientale; **on the ~ side** du côté est; **in ~ Devon** dans l'est du Devon; **in ~ Leeds** dans les quartiers est de Leeds; **room with an ~ aspect** pièce exposée à l'est; (*Archit*) **~ transept/door** transept/portail est *or* oriental; *see also* **4**.

3 adv *go* à *or* vers l'est, en direction de l'est; *be* à *or* dans l'est. **further ~** plus à l'est; **the town lies ~ of the border** la ville est située à l'est de la frontière; **we drove ~ for 100 km** nous avons roulé pendant 100 km en direction de l'est; **go ~ till you get to Crewe** allez en direction de l'est jusqu'à Crewe; **to sail due ~** aller droit vers l'est; (*Naut*) avoir le cap à l'est; **~ by north** est quart nord; **~ by south** est quart sud; **~ by north-~** est quart nord-est.

4 comp ►**East Africa** l'Afrique orientale, l'Est *m* de l'Afrique ►**East African** adj d'Afrique orientale ◊ n Africain(e) *m(f)* de l'Est ►**East Berlin** Berlin-Est ►**East Berliner** n habitant(e) *m(f)* de Berlin-Est ►**eastbound** *traffic, vehicles* (se déplaçant) en direction de l'est; *carriageway* est *inv* ►**the East End** *[London]* les quartiers *mpl* est de Londres (*quartiers pauvres*) ►**east-facing** exposé à l'est ►**East Germany** Allemagne *f* de l'Est ►**East German** adj est-allemand ◊ n Allemand(e) *m(f)* de l'Est ►**East Indies** Indes orientales ►**east-north-east** est-nord-est (*m*) ►**the East Side** *[New York]* les quartiers *mpl* est de New York ►**east-south-east** est-sud-est (*m*).

Easter ['iːstəʳ] 1 n Pâques *fpl or msg*. **at ~** à Pâques; **Happy ~!** joyeuses Pâques!; **~ is celebrated between ...** Pâques est célébré entre ... . 2 comp *egg* de Pâques; *holidays* pascal, de Pâques ►**Easter bonnet** chapeau *m* de printemps ►**Easter communion: to make one's Easter communion** faire ses pâques *fpl* ►**Easter Day** le jour de Pâques ►**Easter Island** Ile *f* de Pâques ►**Easter Monday** le lundi de Pâques ►**Easter parade** défilé pascal ►**Easter Sunday** le dimanche de Pâques ►**Eastertide** le temps pascal, la saison de Pâques ►**Easter week** la semaine pascale.

easterly ['iːstəli] 1 adj *wind* d'est; *situation* à l'est, à l'orient (*frm*). **in an ~ direction** en direction de l'est, vers l'est; **~ aspect** exposition *f* à l'est. 2 adv vers l'est.

eastern ['iːstən] 1 adj est *inv*, de l'est. **the ~ coast** la côte est *or* orientale; **house with an ~ outlook** maison exposée à l'est; **~ wall** mur exposé à l'est; **~ Africa** Afrique orientale; **~ France** la France de l'est, l'Est *m* de la France; (*Pol*) **the E~ bloc** le bloc de l'Est; **the E~ Church** l'Église d'Orient; (*US*) **E~ Daylight Time** heure *f* d'été de l'Est; **E~ European Time** heure *f* de l'Europe orientale; (*US*) **E~ Standard Time** heure *f* de l'Est. 2 comp ►**easternmost** le plus à l'est.

easterner ['iːstənəʳ] n (*esp US*) homme *m or* femme *f* de l'Est. **he is an ~** il vient de l'Est; **the ~s** les gens *mpl* de l'Est.

eastward ['iːstwəd] 1 adj à l'est. 2 adv (*also* **~s**) vers l'est.

easy ['iːzɪ] 1 adj a (*not difficult*) *problem, sum, decision* facile; *person* facile, accommodant. **as ~ as anything*, as ~ as pie*, as ~ as falling off a log*** facile comme tout *or* comme bonjour; **it is ~ to see that ...** on voit bien que ..., cela se voit que ...; **it is ~ for him to do that** il lui est facile de faire cela; **it's ~ to see why** il est facile de comprendre pourquoi; **it was ~ to get them to be quiet** on a eu vite fait de les faire taire; **it's easier said than done!** c'est vite dit!, c'est plus facile à dire qu'à faire!; **it's no ~ task, it's none too ~** ce n'est pas simple *or* évident; **you've got an ~ life** tu as une vie sans problèmes, tu n'as pas de problèmes; **it's an ~ house to run** c'est une maison facile à tenir; **it's ~ money** c'est comme si on était payé à ne rien faire; **within ~ reach of** à distance commode de; **in ~ stages** *travel* par petites étapes; *learn* par degrés; **to have an ~ time (of it)** ne pas avoir beaucoup de mal *or* de problèmes; **to take the ~ way out** choisir la solution de facilité; **he is ~ to work with** il est agréable *or* accommodant dans le travail; **~ to get on with** facile à vivre; **to be ~ on the eye*** (*Brit*) *or* **on the eyes*** (*US*) *[person]* être bien balancé*; *[thing]* être drôlement* joli; (*Brit*) **I'm ~*** ça m'est égal; **woman of ~ virtue** femme *f* facile *or* de petite vertu; **she's an ~ lay** *or* (*US*) **make**‡ elle couche avec n'importe qui*; **he came in an ~ first** il est arrivé bon premier *or* dans un fauteuil*.

b (*relaxed, comfortable*) aisé, facile, tranquille; *manners* aisé, naturel; *life* tranquille, sans souci; *style* facile, aisé, coulant; *conditions* favorable. **to feel ~ in one's mind** être tout à fait tranquille, ne pas se faire de souci; **in ~ circumstances** dans l'aisance; **to be on ~ street*** être financièrement à l'aise; **at an ~ pace** à une allure modérée; **to be on ~ terms with** avoir des relations cordiales avec; (*Comm*) **on ~ terms, by ~ payments** avec facilités *fpl* de paiement; (*St Ex*) **~ market** marché tranquille *or* mou; **prices are ~ today** les prix sont un peu moins hauts aujourd'hui; *see* **mark[2]**.

2 adv doucement, tranquillement. **to take things** *or* **it ~** ne pas se fatiguer, en prendre à son aise (*pej*), se la couler douce*; **take it ~!** (*don't worry*) ne vous en faites pas!; (*calm down*) ne vous emballez pas!; (*relax*) ne vous fatiguez pas!; (*go slow*) ne vous pressez pas!; **go ~ on** *or* **with the sugar** ne mets pas trop de sucre, vas-y doucement avec le sucre; **go ~ on** *or* **with the whisky** ne verse pas trop de whisky, vas-y doucement *or* mollo‡ avec le whisky; **to go ~ on** *or* **with sb** ne pas être trop dur envers qn, ménager qn, traiter qn avec ménagement; (*Prov*) **~ come, ~ go** ce n'est que de l'argent!, c'est fait pour être dépensé! (*see also* **3**); **~ does it!** allez-y doucement! *or* mollo!‡; **~ there!** tout doucement!; (*Mil*) **stand ~!** repos!

3 comp ►**easy-care** d'entretien facile ►**easy chair** fauteuil *m* (rembourré) ►**easy come-easy go*: to be easy come-easy go** gagner et dépenser sans compter ►**easy-going** accommodant, facile à vivre, qui ne s'en fait pas; *attitude* complaisant.

eat [iːt] pret **ate**, ptp **eaten** 1 vt *food* manger. **to ~ (one's) breakfast** déjeuner, prendre son petit déjeuner; **to ~ (one's) lunch** déjeuner; **to ~ (one's) dinner** dîner; **to ~ a meal** prendre un repas; **to have nothing to ~** n'avoir rien à manger *or* à se mettre sous la dent; **to ~ one's fill** manger à sa faim; (*lit*) **fit to ~** mangeable, bon à manger; (*fig*) **she looks good enough to ~** elle est belle à croquer; (*fig*) **to ~ one's words** se rétracter, ravaler ses paroles; (*fig*) **to make sb ~ his words** faire rentrer ses mots dans la gorge à qn; **I'll ~ my hat if ...*** je veux bien être pendu si ...; **I could ~ a horse*** je pourrais avaler un bœuf*; **he won't ~ you*** il ne va pas te manger; **what's ~ing you?**‡ qu'est ce qui ne va pas?, qu'est-ce qui te tracasse?

2 vi manger. **we ~ at 8** nous dînons à 20 heures; **to ~ like a horse** manger comme quatre *or* comme un ogre; **he is ~ing us out of house and home*** son appétit va nous mettre à la rue; (*fig*) **to ~ out of sb's hand** faire les quatre volontés de qn; **I've got him ~ing out of my hand** il fait tout ce que je lui dis *or* tout ce que je veux.

3 n (*Brit*) **~s*** bouffe‡ *f*; (*on notice*) snacks *mpl*; **the ~s* were very good** tout ce qu'il y avait à manger était très bon; **let's get some ~s*** mangeons quelque chose *or* un morceau.

►**eat away** vt sep *[sea]* saper, éroder; *[acid, mice]* ronger.

►**eat in** 1 vi manger chez soi. 2 vt consommer sur place.

►**eat into** vt fus *[acid, insects]* ronger; *[moths]* manger; *[expenditure] savings* entamer, écorner.

►**eat out** 1 vi aller au restaurant, déjeuner *or* dîner en ville. 2 vt sep (*fig*) **to eat one's heart out** se ronger d'inquiétude.

►**eat up** 1 vi: **eat up!** mangez! 2 vt sep a finir. **eat up your meat** finis ta viande; **eat up your meal** finis ton repas, finis de manger; (*fig*) **to be eaten up with envy** être dévoré d'envie *or* rongé par l'envie. b (*fig: usually fus*) *fuel* consommer; *resources, profits* absorber; *savings* engloutir. **this car eats up the miles** cette voiture dévore la route; **this car eats up petrol** cette voiture bouffe‡ l'essence *or* consomme beaucoup; **it eats up the electricity/coal** cela consomme beaucoup d'électricité/de charbon.

eatable ['iːtəbl] 1 adj (*fit to eat*) mangeable, bon à manger; (*edible*) comestible. 2 n: **~s*** comestibles *mpl*, victuailles *fpl* (*hum*).

eaten ['iːtn] ptp of **eat**.

eater ['iːtəʳ] n a (*person*) mangeur *m*, -euse *f*. **to be a big ~** être un grand *or* gros mangeur; **to be a big meat ~** être un gros mangeur de viande. b (*eating apple/pear*) pomme *f*/poire *f* à couteau *or* de dessert.

eatery* ['iːtərɪ] n (*US*) (café-)restaurant *m*.

eating ['iːtɪŋ] 1 n: **these apples make good ~** ces pommes sont bonnes à manger. 2 comp *apple* à couteau, de dessert ►**eating chocolate** chocolat *m* à croquer ►**eating hall** (*US*) réfectoire *m* ►**eating house, eating place** restaurant *m*.

eau de Cologne ['əʊdəkə'ləʊn] n eau *f* de Cologne.

eaves [iːvz] 1 npl avant-toit(s) *m(pl)*. 2 comp ►**eavesdrop** écouter de façon indiscrète; **to eavesdrop on a conversation** écouter une conversation privée ►**eavesdropper** oreille indiscrète.

ebb [eb] 1 n *[tide]* reflux *m*, (*Naut*) jusant *m*. **~ and flow** le flux et le reflux; **the tide is on the ~** la marée descend; (*fig*) **to be at a low ~** *[person]* être bien bas; *[business]* aller mal; **his spirits were at a low ~** il avait le moral très bas *or* à zéro*; **his funds were at a low ~** ses fonds étaient bien bas *or* bien dégarnis. 2 comp ►**ebb tide** marée descendante, reflux *m*; (*Naut*) jusant *m*. 3 vi a *[tide]* refluer, descendre. **to ~ and flow** monter et baisser. b (*fig: also* **~ away**) *[enthusiasm, strength etc]* décliner, baisser, être sur le déclin.

ebonite ['ebənaɪt] n ébonite *f*.

ebony ['ebənɪ] 1 n ébène *f*. 2 comp (*~-coloured*) noir d'ébène; (*made of ~*) en ébène, d'ébène.

ebullience [ɪ'bʌlɪəns] n exubérance *f*.

ebullient [ɪ'bʌlɪənt] adj *person* plein de vie, exubérant; *spirits, mood* exubérant.

EC [ˌiː'siː] n (abbr of **European Community**) CE *f*.

eccentric [ɪk'sentrɪk] 1 adj (*fig*) *person, behaviour, clothes, ideas* excentrique, original, bizarre; (*Math, Tech*) *orbit, curve, circles* excentrique. 2 n (*person*) original(e) *m(f)*, excentrique *mf*; (*Tech*) excentrique *m*.

eccentrically [ɪk'sentrɪkəlɪ] adv (*see* **eccentric**) excentriquement, avec excentricité, d'une manière originale, bizarrement.

eccentricity [ˌeksən'trɪsɪtɪ] n a (*see* **eccentric**) excentricité *f*, originalité *f*, bizarrerie *f*. b *[action, whim]* excentricité *f*.

Ecclesiastes [ɪˌkliːzɪ'æstiːz] n (*Bible*) **(the Book of)** ~ (le livre de l')Ecclésiaste *m*.
ecclesiastic [ɪˌkliːzɪ'æstɪk] adj, n ecclésiastique *(m)*.
ecclesiastical [ɪˌkliːzɪ'æstɪkəl] adj ecclésiastique.
ecdysis ['ekdɪsɪs] n, pl **ecdyses** ['ekdɪˌsiːz] ecdysis *f*.
ECG [ˌiːsiː'dʒiː] n abbr of **electrocardiogram**.
echelon ['eʃəlɒn] n échelon *m*.
echinoderm [ɪ'kiːnədɜːm] n échinoderme *m*.
echo ['ekəʊ] 1 n, pl **~es** écho *m*; (*fig*) écho, rappel *m*. **to cheer to the ~** applaudir à tout rompre. 2 vt (*lit*) répercuter, renvoyer. (*fig*) **he ~ed my words incredulously** il a répété ce que j'avais dit d'un ton incrédule; **"go home?" he ~ed** "rentrer?" répéta-t-il; **to ~ sb's ideas** se faire l'écho de la pensée de qn. 3 vi *[sound]* (*resonate*) retentir, résonner; (*bounce back*) se répercuter, faire écho; *[place]* renvoyer l'écho. (*liter*) **to ~ with music** retentir de musique; (*liter*) **the valley ~ed with their laughter** la vallée résonnait *or* retentissait de leurs rires. 4 comp ►**echo chamber** (*Rad, TV*) chambre *f* sonore ►**echo-sounder** (*Naut*) sondeur *m* (à ultra-sons).
éclair [eɪ'klɛəʳ, ɪ'klɛəʳ] n (*Culin*) éclair *m* (à la crème).
eclampsia [ɪ'klæmpsɪə] n éclampsie *f*.
eclectic [ɪ'klektɪk] adj, n éclectique *(mf)*.
eclecticism [ɪ'klektɪsɪzəm] n éclectisme *m*.
eclipse [ɪ'klɪps] 1 n (*Astron, fig*) éclipse *f*. (*Astron, fig*) **to be in** *or* **go into ~** être éclipsé; **partial/total ~** éclipse partielle/totale. 2 vt (*Astron*) éclipser; (*fig*) éclipser, faire pâlir, surpasser. **eclipsing binary** étoile *f* double.
ecliptic [ɪ'klɪptɪk] adj écliptique.
eclogue ['eklɒg] n églogue *f*.
eclosion [ɪ'kləʊʒən] n éclosion *f*.
eco... ['iːkəʊ] pref éco... .
ecocide ['iːkəˌsaɪd] n écocide *m*.
eco-friendly ['iːkəʊˌfrendlɪ] adj *detergent, hairspray etc* non nuisible à *or* qui ne nuit pas à l'environnement.
ecological [ˌiːkə'lɒdʒɪkəl] adj écologique.
ecologically [ˌiːkə'lɒdʒɪkəlɪ] adv écologiquement.
ecologist [ɪ'kɒlədʒɪst] n écologiste *mf*.
ecology [ɪ'kɒlədʒɪ] n écologie *f*. (*Pol*) **the E~ Party** le parti écologique.
ecomovement ['iːkəʊˌmuːvmənt] n (*Pol*) mouvement *m* écologique.
econometer [ˌɪkə'nɒmətəʳ] n (*Aut*) économètre *m*.
econometric [ɪˌkɒnə'metrɪk] adj économétrique.
econometrician [ɪˌkɒnəmə'trɪʃən] n économétricien(ne) *m(f)*.
econometrics [ɪˌkɒnə'metrɪks] n (*NonC*) économétrie *f*.
econometrist [ɪˌkɒnə'metrɪst] = **econometrician**.
economic [ˌiːkə'nɒmɪk] adj a *development, geography, factor* économique. **the ~ system of a country** l'économie *f* d'un pays; **the ~ crisis** la crise (économique); **~ analyst** spécialiste *mf* de l'analyse économique; **~ indicator** indicateur *m* économique *or* de conjoncture; **~ management** gestion *f* de l'économie; **~ performance** performance *f* de l'économie.
b (*profitable*) rentable, qui rapporte. **~ rate of return** taux *m* de rentabilité économique; **an ~ rent** un loyer rentable; **this business is no longer ~** *or* **an ~ proposition** cette affaire n'est plus rentable; **it isn't ~** *or* **it isn't an ~ proposition** *or* **it doesn't make ~ sense to own a car in town** si l'on habite en ville il n'est pas intéressant d'avoir une voiture.
economical [ˌiːkə'nɒmɪkəl] adj *person* économe; *method, appliance, speed* économique. **to be ~ with** économiser, ménager; **to be ~ with the truth** ne pas dire toute la vérité.
economically [ˌiːkə'nɒmɪkəlɪ] adv économiquement. **to use sth ~** économiser qch, ménager qch.
economics [ˌiːkə'nɒmɪks] n (*NonC*) (*science*) économie *f* politique, (science *f*) économique *f*; (*financial aspect*) côté *m* économique. **the ~ of the situation/the project** le côté économique de la situation/du projet; *see* **home**.
economist [ɪ'kɒnəmɪst] n économiste *mf*, spécialiste *mf* d'économie politique.
economize [ɪ'kɒnəmaɪz] 1 vi économiser (*on* sur), faire des économies. 2 vt *time, money* économiser, épargner. **to ~ 20% on the costs** faire une économie de 20% sur la dépense.
economy [ɪ'kɒnəmɪ] 1 n a (*saving: in time, money etc*) économie *f* (*in* de). **to make economies in** faire des économies de; **economies of scale** économies d'échelle. b (*NonC: system*) économie *f*, système *m* économique. **the country's ~ depends on ...** l'économie du pays dépend de ...; *see* **black, political** *etc*. 2 comp ►**economy class** (*esp Aviat*) classe *f* touriste ►**economy drive** *[government, firm]* (campagne *f* de) restrictions *fpl* budgétaires; **I'm having an economy drive this month** ce mois-ci je m'efforce de faire des économies ►**economy pack/size** (*Comm*) paquet *m*/taille *f* économique.
ecosphere ['iːkəʊˌsfɪə] n écosphère *f*.
ecosystem ['iːkəʊˌsɪstəm] n écosystème *m*.
ecotone ['iːkəˌtəʊn] n écotone *m*.
eco-tourism [ˌiːkəʊ'tʊərɪzəm] n écotourisme *m*.
ecotype ['iːkəˌtaɪp] n écotype *m*.
ecru ['ekruː] adj, n écru *(m)*.
ECSC [ˌiːsiːes'siː] n (abbr of **European Coal and Steel Community**) C.E.C.A. *f*.
ecstasy ['ekstəsɪ] n extase *f* (*also Rel*), ravissement *m*, transport *m* (de joie) (*liter*); (*drug*) ecstasy *m*. **with ~** avec ravissement, avec extase; **to be in ecstasies over** *object* s'extasier sur; *person* être en extase devant.
ecstatic [eks'tætɪk] adj extasié. **to be ~ over** *or* **about** *object* s'extasier sur; *person* être en extase devant.
ecstatically [eks'tætɪkəlɪ] adv avec extase, avec ravissement, d'un air extasié.
ECT [ˌiːsiː'tiː] n (abbr of **electroconvulsive therapy**) *see* **electroconvulsive**.
ectomorph ['ektəʊˌmɔːf] n ectomorph *m*.
ectopic [ek'tɒpɪk] adj: **~ pregnancy** grossesse extra-utérine.
ectoplasm ['ektəʊplæzəm] n ectoplasme *m*.
ECU ['eɪkjuː, ˌiːsiː'juː] n (abbr of **European Currency Unit**) ECU *m*, écu *m*. **hard ~** écu fort; **weights of currencies in the ~** pieds *m* des devises au sein de l'écu.
Ecuador ['ekwədɔːʳ] n Équateur *m*.
Ecuador(i)an [ˌekwə'dɔːr(ɪ)ən] 1 adj équatorien. 2 n Équatorien(ne) *m(f)*.
ecumenical [ˌiːkjʊ'menɪkəl] adj œcuménique.
ecumenicism [ˌiːkjʊ'menɪsɪzəm] n, **ecumenism** [iː'kjuːmənɪzəm] n œcuménisme *m*.
eczema ['eksɪmə] n eczéma *m*. **~-sufferer** personne sujette à l'eczéma.
EDC [ˌiːdiː'siː] n (abbr of **European Defence Community**) C.E.D. *f*.
eddy ['edɪ] 1 n *[water, air]* remous *m*, tourbillon *m*; *[snow, dust, smoke]* tourbillon; *[leaves]* tournoiement *m*, tourbillon. 2 vi *[air, smoke, leaves]* tourbillonner; *[people]* tournoyer; *[water]* faire des remous *or* des tourbillons.
edelweiss ['eɪdlvaɪs] n edelweiss *m inv*.
edema [ɪ'diːmə] n, pl **edemata** [ɪ'diːmətə] (*esp US*) œdème *m*.
Eden ['iːdn] n Eden *m*, paradis *m* terrestre. **the garden of ~** le jardin d'Éden.
edentate [ɪ'denteɪt] adj, n édenté *(m)*.
edge [edʒ] 1 n a *[knife, razor]* tranchant *m*, fil *m*. **a blade with a sharp ~** une lame bien affilée; **to put an ~ on** aiguiser, affiler, affûter; **to take the ~ off** *knife, sensation* émousser; *appetite* calmer, émousser; **it sets my teeth on ~** cela m'agace les dents; **he is on ~** il est énervé *or* à cran*; **my nerves are all on ~*** j'ai les nerfs à vif *or* en pelote* *or* en boule*; (*fig*) **to have the** *or* **an ~ on** être légèrement supérieur à, l'emporter de justesse *or* d'un poil* sur.
b *[table, plate]* bord *m*; *[river, lake]* bord, rive *f*; *[sea]* rivage *m*, bord; *[cliff]* bord; *[forest]* lisière *f*, orée *f*; *[road]* bord, côté *m*; *[town]* abords *mpl*; *[cloth]* (*uncut*) lisière, bord, (*cut*) bord; *[coin]* tranche *f*; *[page]* bord, (*margin*) marge *f*; *[cube, brick]* arête *f*; (*distance round the ~ of an object*) pourtour *m*. **a book with gilt ~s** un livre doré sur tranches; **to stand sth on its ~** poser qch de chant; **the trees at the ~ of the road** les arbres en bordure de la route; (*fig*) **to be on the ~ of disaster** être au bord du désastre, courir au désastre; (*fig*) **that pushed him over the ~** ça a été plus qu'il ne pouvait supporter.
c *[ski]* arête *f*; (*metal strip*) carre *f*.
2 comp ►**edgeways, edgewise** de côté; **I couldn't get a word in edgeways*** je n'ai pas réussi à placer un mot.
3 vt a (*put a border on*) border (*with* de). **to ~ a collar with lace** border un col de dentelle.
b (*sharpen*) *tool, blade* aiguiser, affiler, affûter.
c **to ~ up/down** *salaries, inflation etc* augmenter/diminuer peu à peu; **to ~ one's chair nearer the door** rapprocher sa chaise tout doucement de la porte; **to ~ sb out of his/her job** déloger progressivement qn de son poste; **to ~ one's way through** *etc* = **to edge through** *etc; see* **4**.
4 vi se glisser, se faufiler. **to ~ through/into** *etc* se glisser *or* se faufiler à travers/dans *etc;* **to ~ forward** avancer petit à petit; **to ~ away** s'éloigner tout doucement *or* furtivement; **to ~ up to sb** s'approcher tout doucement *or* furtivement de qn; **share prices ~d up** il y a eu une tendance à la hausse de valeurs boursières; **to ~ out of a room** se glisser hors d'une pièce, sortir furtivement d'une pièce.
-edged [edʒd] adj ending in comps a *paper, fabric* bordé de, avec une bordure de. b *knife etc* **blunt/sharp-edged** émoussé/bien aiguisé.
edginess ['edʒɪnɪs] n (*NonC*) nervosité *f*, énervement *m*, irritation *f*.
edging ['edʒɪŋ] 1 n a (*gen*) bordure *f*; *[ribbon, silk]* liseré *m or* liséré *m*. b (*Ski*) prise *f* de carres. 2 comp ►**edging shears** cisaille *f* de jardinier *or* d'horticulteur.
edgy ['edʒɪ] adj énervé, à cran*, crispé.
edibility [ˌedɪ'bɪlɪtɪ] n comestibilité *f*.
edible ['edɪbl] adj *mushroom, berry* comestible, bon à manger; *meal* mangeable. **~ snail** escargot *m* comestible; **~ crab** dormeur *m*, tourteau *m*.
edict ['iːdɪkt] n (*gen, Jur, Pol*) décret *m*; (*Hist*) édit *m*.
edification [ˌedɪfɪ'keɪʃən] n édification *f*, instruction *f*.
edifice ['edɪfɪs] n édifice *m*.
edify ['edɪfaɪ] vt édifier (*moralement*).
Edinburgh ['edɪnbərə] n Édimbourg.
edit ['edɪt] 1 vt *magazine, review* diriger; *daily newspaper* être le rédacteur *or* la rédactrice en chef de; *article* mettre au point, préparer;

series of texts diriger la publication de; *text, author* éditer, donner une édition de; *film* monter; *tape* mettre au point, couper et recoller; *dictionary, encyclopedia* assurer la rédaction de; *Rad or TV programme* réaliser; (*Comput*) *file* éditer. 2 n révision *f*.

editing ['edɪtɪŋ] n *[magazine]* direction *f*; *[newspaper, dictionary]* rédaction *f*; *[article, series of texts, tape]* mise *f* au point; *[text, author]* édition *f*; *[film]* montage *m*; (*Comput*) édition.

edition [ɪ'dɪʃən] n *[newspaper, book]* édition *f*; *[print, etching]* tirage *m*. **limited ~** édition à tirage restreint *or* limité; **revised ~** édition revue et corrigée; **to bring out an ~ of a text** publier *or* faire paraître l'édition d'un texte; **a one volume ~ of Corneille** une édition de Corneille en un volume.

editor ['edɪtə^r] n *[daily newspaper]* rédacteur *m*, -trice *f* en chef; *[magazine, review]* directeur *m*, -trice *f*; *[text]* éditeur *m*, -trice *f*; *[series]* directeur, -trice de la publication; *[dictionary, encyclopaedia]* rédacteur, -trice; *[Rad or TV programme]* réalisateur *m*, -trice *f*. (*Press*) **political ~** rédacteur, -trice politique; **sports ~** rédacteur sportif, rédactrice sportive; *see* **news** *etc*.

editorial [,edɪ'tɔːrɪəl] 1 adj *office* de (la) rédaction; *comment, decision* de la rédaction, du rédacteur. **~ staff** rédaction *f*; **the ~ "we"** le "nous" de modestie *or* d'auteur. 2 n *[newspaper etc]* éditorial *m*, article *m* de tête.

editorialist [,edɪ'tɔːrɪəlɪst] n (*US*) éditorialiste *mf*.

editorialize [,edɪ'tɔːrɪəlaɪz] vi exprimer une opinion.

editorship ['edɪtəʃɪp] n (*see* **editor**) rédaction *f*; direction *f*. **under the ~ of** sous la direction de.

Edmund ['edmənd] n Edmond *m*.

EDP [,iːdiː'piː] n abbr of **Electronic Data Processing**.

EDT [,iːdiː'tiː] n (*US*) (abbr of **Eastern Daylight Time**) *see* **eastern**.

educable ['edjʊkəbl] adj éducable.

educate ['edjʊkeɪt] vt *pupil* instruire, donner de l'instruction à; *the mind, one's tastes* former; (*bring up*) *family, children* élever, éduquer. **he is being ~d in Paris** il fait ses études à Paris; **to ~ the public** éduquer le public; (*fig*) **to ~ sb to believe that ...** enseigner à qn que ... .

educated ['edjʊkeɪtɪd] 1 ptp of **educate**. 2 adj *person* instruit, cultivé; *handwriting* distingué; *voice* cultivé. **hardly ~ at all** qui n'a guère d'instruction; *see* **guess, well**.

education [,edjʊ'keɪʃən] 1 n (*gen*) éducation *f*; (*teaching*) instruction *f*, enseignement *m*; (*studies*) études *fpl*; (*training*) formation *f*; (*knowledge*) culture *f*; (*Univ etc subject*) pédagogie *f*. **Department** *or* **Ministry of E~** ministère *m* de l'Éducation nationale; (*Brit*) **Secretary of State for** *or* **Minister of E~**, (*US*) **Secretary for E~** ministre *m* de l'Éducation (nationale); (*Brit*) **Department of E~ and Science** ≃ ministère *m* de l'Éducation nationale (*et de la Recherche scientifique*); **primary/secondary ~** enseignement primaire/secondaire; **physical/political ~** éducation physique/politique; **literary/professional ~** formation littéraire/professionnelle; **~ is free** l'instruction est gratuite, l'enseignement est gratuit; **he has had very little ~** c'est un homme sans instruction; **man with a sound ~** homme qui a une solide instruction; **he had a good ~** il a reçu une bonne éducation; **the ~ he received at school** l'instruction qu'il a reçue à l'école (*or* au lycée *etc*); **his ~ was neglected** on a negligé son éducation; **his ~ was interrupted** ses études ont été interrompues; **the crisis in ~, the ~ crisis** la crise de l'enseignement; **the system of ~, the ~ system** (*gen*) le système éducatif *or* d'éducation; **the French system of ~, the ~ system in France** le système éducatif *or* l'enseignement en France; **people working in ~** les gens qui travaillent dans l'enseignement; (*Univ etc*) **diploma in ~** diplôme *m* de pédagogie; *see* **adult, further** *etc*.

2 comp *theory, method* d'enseignement, pédagogique; *standards* d'instruction, scolaire; *costs* de l'enseignement; (*Pol etc*) *budget, minister* de l'Éducation nationale ►**the Education Act** (*Brit Parl*) la loi sur l'enseignement ►**education authority** (*Brit*) ≃ délégation départementale de l'enseignement ►**Education Committee** (*Brit: Scol Admin*) commission *f* du conseil régional chargée des affaires scolaires *etc* ►**education correspondent** (*Press*) correspondant(e) *m(f)* chargé(e) des questions de l'enseignement ►**Education Department** (*ministry*) ministère *m* de l'Éducation nationale ►**education department** (*Brit: of local authority*) ≃ délégation départementale de l'enseignement ►**education page** (*Press*) rubrique *f* de l'enseignement ►**Education Welfare Officer** (*Brit: Scol Admin*) assistant(e) social(e) scolaire.

educational [,edjʊ'keɪʃənl] adj a *methods* pédagogique; *establishment, institution* d'enseignement, scolaire; *system* d'éducation; *supplies* scolaire; *film, games, visit* éducatif; *role, function* éducateur (*f* -trice). **~ standards are rising/falling** le niveau d'instruction monte/baisse; **his ~ standard** son niveau scolaire; (*Brit: Scol Admin*) **~ adviser** conseiller *m*, -ère *f* pédagogique; (*US Scol*) **~ age** niveau *m* scolaire (*d'un élève*); **~ psychologist** psychologue *mf* scolaire; **~ psychology** psychopédagogie *f*; (*US*) **~ park** complexe *m* d'écoles primaires et secondaires; **~ qualifications** titres *mpl* scolaires, diplômes *mpl*; (*US*) **~ television** *chaîne de télévision scolaire et culturelle*.

b *experience, event* instructif. **we found the visit very ~** cette visite a été très instructive.

education(al)ist [,edjʊ'keɪʃn(əl)ɪst] n éducateur *m*, -trice *f*, pédagogue *mf*.

educationally [,edjʊ'keɪʃnəlɪ] adv (*as regards teaching methods*) du point de vue pédagogique, pédagogiquement; (*as regards education, schooling*) sous l'angle scolaire *or* de l'éducation. **it is ~ wrong to do so** il est faux d'un point de vue pédagogique *or* il est pédagogiquement faux de procéder ainsi; **~ subnormal** arriéré; **~ deprived children** enfants déshérités sous l'angle scolaire *or* de l'éducation, enfants sous-scolarisés.

educative ['edjʊkətɪv] adj éducatif, éducateur (*f* -trice).

educator ['edjʊkeɪtə^r] n éducateur *m*, -trice *f*.

educe [ɪ'djuːs] vt dégager, faire sortir.

Edward ['edwəd] n Édouard *m*. (*Brit Hist*) **~ the Confessor** Édouard le Confesseur.

Edwardian [ed'wɔːdɪən] (*Brit*) 1 adj *lady, architect, society* de l'époque du roi Édouard VII; *clothes, manners, design* dans le style 1900. **in ~ days** à l'époque d'Édouard VII, juste après 1900; **the ~ era** ≃ la Belle Époque. 2 n *personne qui vivait sous le règne d'Édouard VII ou qui a les caractéristiques de cette époque*.

EEC [,iːiː'siː] n (abbr of **European Economic Community**) C.E.E. *f*.

EEG [,iːiː'dʒiː] n abbr of **electroencephalogram**.

eel [iːl] n anguille *f*. **~worm** anguillule *f*; *see* **electric, slippery**.

e'en [iːn] adv (*liter*) = **even² 2**.

EEOC [,iːiːəʊ'siː] n (*US*) (abbr of **Equal Employment Opportunity Commission**) *see* **equal 4**.

e'er [ɛə^r] adv (*liter*) = **ever 1**.

eerie, eery ['ɪərɪ] adj inquiétant, sinistre, qui donne le frisson.

eerily ['ɪərɪlɪ] adv sinistrement.

EET [,iːiː'tiː] n (abbr of **Eastern European Time**) *see* **eastern**.

eff* [ef] vi: **he was ~ing and blinding** il jurait comme un charretier*.

►**eff off*** vi aller se faire voir*; *see* **effing***.

efface [ɪ'feɪs] vt (*lit, fig*) effacer, oblitérer (*liter*).

effect [ɪ'fekt] 1 n a (*result*) effet *m*, conséquence *f* (*on* sur); (*Phys*) effet; *[wind, chemical, drug]* action *f* (*on* sur). **to have an ~ on** avoir *or* produire un effet sur; **to have no ~** ne produire aucun effet, rester sans effet *or* sans suite; **it won't have any ~ on him** ça ne lui fera aucun effet, ça n'aura aucun effet sur lui; **this rule will have the ~ of preventing ..., the ~ of this rule will be to prevent ...** cette règle aura pour conséquence *or* effet d'empêcher ...; **the ~ of all this is that ...** il résulte de tout ceci que ...; **to feel the ~s of an accident** ressentir les effets d'un accident, se ressentir d'un accident; **the ~s of the new law are already being felt** les effets de la nouvelle loi se font déjà sentir; (*Phys*) **the Doppler ~** l'effet Doppler-Fizeau; **to little ~** sans grand résultat; **to no ~** en vain; **to use to good** *or* **great ~** savoir tirer avantage de; **to such good ~ that** si bien que; **to put into ~** mettre à exécution *or* en application; *[drug]* **to take ~** produire *or* faire son effet, agir; *[law]* **to come into ~, take ~** prendre effet, entrer en vigueur; **to be of no ~** être inefficace *or* inopérant; **to come into ~** entrer en vigueur; (*frm*) **with ~ from April** à compter du mois d'avril; (*frm*) **with immediate ~** avec effet immédiat; **in ~** en fait, en réalité.

b (*impression*) effet *m*. (*Theat*) **stage ~s** effets scéniques; **sound ~s** bruitage *m*; **to make an ~** faire effet *or* de l'effet; **to give a good ~** faire (un) bon effet; **literary ~** effet littéraire; (*Art*) **~s of light** effets de lumière; **he said it just for ~** il ne l'a dit que pour faire de l'effet *or* pour impressionner; *see* **special**.

c (*meaning*) sens *m*. **his letter is to the ~ that ...** sa lettre nous apprend que ...; **an announcement to the ~ that ...** un communiqué déclarant que *or* dont la teneur est que ...; **orders to the ~ that ...** ordres suivant lesquels ...; **he used words to that ~** il s'est exprimé dans ce sens; **... or words to that ~** ... ou quelque chose d'analogue *or* de ce genre; **we got a letter to the same ~** nous avons reçu une lettre dans le même sens.

d (*property*) **~s** biens *mpl*; (*Banking*) **"no ~s"** "sans provision"; *see* **personal**.

2 vt (*gen*) *reform, reduction, payment* effectuer; *cure* obtenir; *improvement* apporter; *transformation* opérer, effectuer; *reconciliation, reunion* amener; *sale, purchase* réaliser, effectuer. **to ~ a saving (in** *or* **of)** faire une économie (de); **to ~ a settlement** arriver à un accord; **to ~ an entry** entrer de force.

effective [ɪ'fektɪv] 1 adj a (*efficient*) *cure* efficace; *word, remark* qui porte, qui a de l'effet. **the measures were ~** les mesures ont été efficaces *or* ont fait leur effet; **the system is ~** le système fonctionne bien; **an ~ argument** un argument décisif; **to become ~** *[law, regulation, insurance cover]* prendre effet, entrer en vigueur (*from* à partir de); *[ticket]* être valide (*from* à partir de); **it was an ~ way of stopping him** c'était une bonne façon *or* une façon efficace de l'arrêter.

b (*striking, impressive*) frappant, saisissant, qui fait *or* qui produit de l'effet.

c (*actual*) *aid, contribution* effectif. **the ~ head of the family** le chef réel *or* véritable de la famille; (*Mil*) **~ troops** hommes *mpl* valides.

d (*Econ, Fin*) *demand* solvable; *interest rate* réel. **~ date** date *f* d'entrée en vigueur.

2 npl (*Mil*) **~s** effectifs *mpl*.

effectively [ɪ'fektɪvlɪ] adv (*efficiently*) efficacement, d'une manière effective; (*usefully*) utilement; (*strikingly*) d'une manière frappante, avec beaucoup d'effet; (*in reality*) effectivement, réellement.

effectiveness [ɪ'fektɪvnɪs] **n** (*efficiency*) efficacité *f*; (*striking quality*) effet frappant *or* saisissant.

effector [ɪ'fektəʳ] 1 **adj** effecteur (*f* -trice). 2 **n** effecteur *m*.

effectual [ɪ'fektjʊəl] **adj** *remedy, punishment* efficace, qui produit l'effet voulu; *document, agreement* valide.

effectually [ɪ'fektjʊəlɪ] **adv** efficacement.

effectuate [ɪ'fektjʊeɪt] **vt** effectuer, opérer, réaliser.

effeminacy [ɪ'femɪnəsɪ] **n** caractère efféminé.

effeminate [ɪ'femɪnɪt] **adj** efféminé.

efferent ['efərənt] **adj** efférent.

effervesce [ˌefə'ves] **vi** *[liquids]* être *or* entrer en effervescence; *[drinks]* pétiller, mousser; *[gas]* se dégager (en effervescence); (*fig*) *[person]* déborder (*with* de), être tout excité.

effervescence [ˌefə'vesns] **n** effervescence *f*, pétillement *m*; (*fig*) excitation *f*.

effervescent [ˌefə'vesnt] **adj** *liquid, tablet* effervescent; *drink* gazeux; (*fig*) plein d'entrain.

effete [ɪ'fiːt] **adj** *person* mou (*f* molle), veule; *empire, civilization* décadent; *government* affaibli; *method* (devenu) inefficace, stérile.

effeteness [ɪ'fiːtnɪs] **n** (*see* **effete**) veulerie *f*; décadence *f*; inefficacité *f*.

efficacious [ˌefɪ'keɪʃəs] **adj** *cure, means* efficace; *measure, method* efficace, opérant.

efficacy ['efɪkəsɪ] **n**, **efficaciousness** [ˌefɪ'keɪʃəsnɪs] **n** efficacité *f*.

efficiency [ɪ'fɪʃənsɪ] 1 **n** *[person]* capacité *f*, compétence *f*; *[method]* efficacité *f*; *[organization, system]* efficacité, bon fonctionnement; *[machine]* bon rendement, bon fonctionnement. 2 **comp** ►**efficiency apartment** (*US*) studio *m*.

efficient [ɪ'fɪʃənt] **adj** *person* capable, compétent, efficace; *method, system* efficace, opérant; *plan, organization* efficace; *machine* d'un bon rendement, qui fonctionne bien. **the ~ working of a machine** le bon fonctionnement d'une machine.

efficiently [ɪ'fɪʃəntlɪ] **adv** (*see* **efficient**) avec compétence, efficacement. *[machine]* **to work ~** bien fonctionner, avoir un bon rendement.

effigy ['efɪdʒɪ] **n** effigie *f*. **in ~** en effigie.

effing⁑ ['efɪŋ] 1 **adj**: **what an ~ waste of time!** purée!⁑ quelle perte de temps!; **don't be ~ stupid** arrête de faire le connard⁑; **it's ~ ridiculous!** c'est complètement dingue!*; **this ~ phone!** ce purée⁑ de téléphone; *see* **eff**⁑. 2 **n**: **~ and blinding** grossièretés *fpl*.

effloresce [ˌeflɒ'res] **vi** (*Chem*) effleurir.

efflorescence [ˌeflɔː'resns] **n** (*Chem, Med: also liter*) efflorescence *f*; (*Bot*) floraison *f*.

efflorescent [ˌeflɔː'resnt] **adj** (*Chem*) efflorescent; (*Bot*) en fleur(s).

effluence ['eflʊəns] **n** émanation *f*, effluence *f* (*liter, rare*).

effluent ['eflʊənt] **adj**, **n** effluent (*m*).

effluvium [e'fluːvɪəm] **n**, *pl* **~s** *or* **effluvia** [e'fluːvɪə] effluve(s) *m(pl)*, émanation *f*, exhalaison *f*; (*pej*) exhalaison *or* émanation fétide.

efflux ['eflʌks] **n**: **~ of capital** fuite *f or* exode *m* de capitaux.

effort ['efət] **n** effort *m*. **to make an ~ to do** faire un effort pour faire, s'efforcer de faire; **to make every ~** *or* **a great ~ to do** (*try hard*) faire tous ses efforts *or* (tout) son possible pour faire, s'évertuer à faire; (*take great pains*) se donner beaucoup de mal *or* de peine pour faire; **to make an ~ to concentrate/to adapt** faire un effort de concentration/d'adaptation; **do make some ~ to help!** fais un petit effort pour aider!, essaie d'aider un peu!; **he made no ~ to be polite** il ne s'est pas donné la peine d'être poli; (*Scol*) **he makes no ~** il ne fait aucun effort, il ne s'applique pas; **it's not worth the ~** cela ne vaut pas la peine; **without ~** sans peine, sans effort; **to do sth by ~ of will** faire qch dans un effort de volonté; **in an ~ to solve the problem/be polite** *etc* pour essayer de résoudre le problème/d'être poli *etc*; **the government's ~ to avoid ...** les efforts *or* les tentatives *fpl* du gouvernement pour éviter ...; **it's an awful ~ to get up!** il en faut du courage pour se lever!; **what do you think of his latest ~?*** qu'est-ce que tu penses de ce qu'il vient de faire?; **it's not bad for a first ~** ça n'est pas (si) mal pour un coup d'essai; **that's a good ~*** ça n'est pas mal (réussi); **it's a pretty poor ~*** ça n'est pas une réussite *or* un chef-d'œuvre.

effortless ['efətlɪs] **adj** *success, victory* facile; *style, movement* aisé.

effortlessly ['efətlɪslɪ] **adv** sans effort, sans peine, aisément, facilement.

effrontery [ɪ'frʌntərɪ] **n** effronterie *f*.

effusion [ɪ'fjuːʒən] **n** *[liquid]* écoulement *m*; *[blood, gas]* effusion *f*; (*fig*) effusion, épanchement *m*.

effusive [ɪ'fjuːsɪv] **adj** *person, character* expansif, démonstratif; *welcome* chaleureux; *style* expansif; *thanks, apologies* sans fin.

effusively [ɪ'fjuːsɪvlɪ] **adv** *greet, praise* avec effusion. **to thank sb ~** se confondre *or* se répandre en remerciements auprès de qn.

EFL [ˌiːef'el] **n** (**abbr of English as a Foreign Language**) *see* **English**.

eft [eft] **n** (*Zool*) triton *m* (crêté), salamandre *f* d'eau.

EFTA ['eftə] **n** (**abbr of European Free Trade Association**) A.E.L.E. *f*, Association européenne de libre-échange.

EFTPOS ['eftpɒs] **n** (**abbr of electronic funds transfer at point of sale**) TEF/TPV *m*.

EFTS [ˌiːeftiː'es] **n** (**abbr of electronic funds transfer system**) *see* **electronic**.

eg, e.g. [ˌiː'dʒiː] **adv** (**abbr of exempli gratia = for example**) ex.

EGA [ˌiːdʒiː'eɪ] **n** (**abbr of enhanced graphics adaptor**) *see* **enhance**.

egad†† [ɪ'gæd] **excl** ciel!

egalitarian [ɪˌgælɪ'tɛərɪən] 1 **n** égalitariste *mf*. 2 **adj** *person* égalitariste; *principle* égalitaire.

egalitarianism [ɪˌgælɪ'tɛərɪənɪzəm] **n** égalitarisme *m*.

egest [ɪ'dʒest] **vt** évacuer.

egg [eg] 1 **n** (*Culin, Zool*) œuf *m*. **in the ~** dans l'œuf; **~s and bacon** œufs au bacon; **to lay an ~** *[hen etc]* pondre (un œuf); (⁑: *fig: fail*) faire un fiasco *or* un bide⁑; (*fig*) **to put all one's ~s in one basket** mettre tous ses œufs dans le même panier; **as sure as ~s is ~s**⁑ c'est sûr et certain*; (*fig*) **to have ~ on one's face** avoir l'air plutôt ridicule; **he's a good/bad ~***† c'est un brave/sale type*; *see* **boil**[1], **Scotch** *etc*.

2 **comp** ►**eggbeater** (*rotary*) batteur *m* (à œufs); (*whisk*) fouet *m* (à œufs); (⁑: *US: helicopter*) hélico* *m*, hélicoptère *m* ►**eggcup** coquetier *m* ►**egg custard** ≈ crème renversée ►**egg flip** (*with milk*) lait *m* de poule; (*with spirits*) eggflip *m* ►**egghead*** intellectuel(le) *m(f)*, cérébral(e) *m(f)* ►**eggnog** eggflip *m* ►**eggplant** (*esp US*) aubergine *f* ►**egg roll** (*bread*) petit pain *m* aux œufs (durs); (*Chinese*) pâté *or* rouleau impérial ►**egg sandwich** sandwich *m* aux œufs (durs) ►**egg-shaped** ovoïde ►**eggshell** coquille *f* (d'œuf); **eggshell china** coquille *f* d'œuf (*porcelaine*); **eggshell paint** peinture coquille d'œuf ►**egg timer** (*sand*) sablier *m*; (*automatic*) minuteur *m* ►**egg whisk** fouet *m* (à œufs) ►**egg white** blanc *m* d'œuf ►**egg yolk** jaune *m* d'œuf.

3 **vt** (*) pousser, inciter (*to do* à faire).

►**egg on vt sep** pousser, inciter (*to do* à faire).

eglantine ['egləntaɪn] **n** (*flower*) églantine *f*; (*bush*) églantier *m*.

EGM [ˌiːdʒiː'em] **n** (**abbr of extraordinary general meeting**) AGE *f*.

ego ['iːgəʊ] 1 **n** (*Psych*) **the ~** le moi, l'ego *m*. 2 **comp** ►**ego trip***: **to be on an ego trip** planer,* se sentir gonflé à bloc*; **having his name all over the papers is a great ego trip for him** le fait d'avoir son nom dans tous les journaux est pour lui une grande satisfaction d'amour-propre, depuis qu'il a son nom dans tous les journaux, il plane*.

egocentric(al) [ˌegəʊ'sentrɪk(əl)] **adj** égocentrique.

egocentricity [ˌegəʊsen'trɪsɪtɪ] **n** égocentrisme *m*.

egoism ['egəʊɪzəm] **n** égoïsme *m*.

egoist ['egəʊɪst] **n** égoïste *mf*.

egoistic(al) [ˌegəʊ'ɪstɪk(əl)] **adj** égoïste.

egomania [ˌegəʊ'meɪnɪə] **n** manie *f* égocentrique.

egomaniac [ˌegəʊ'meɪnɪæk] **n** égotiste *mf*.

egotism ['egəʊtɪzəm] **n** égotisme *m*.

egotist ['egəʊtɪst] **n** égotiste *mf*.

egotistic(al) [ˌegəʊ'tɪstɪk(əl)] **adj** égotiste.

egregious [ɪ'griːdʒəs] **adj** (*pej*) énorme (*iro*), fameux* (*iro: before n*); *folly, blunder* insigne. **he's an ~ ass** c'est un fameux* imbécile.

egress ['iːgres] **n** (*gen: frm*) sortie *f*, issue *f*; (*Astron*) émersion *f*.

egret ['iːgrɪt] **n** aigrette *f*.

Egypt ['iːdʒɪpt] **n** Égypte *f*.

Egyptian [ɪ'dʒɪpʃən] 1 **adj** égyptien, d'Égypte. 2 **n** Égyptien(ne) *m(f)*.

Egyptologist [ˌiːdʒɪp'tɒlədʒɪst] **n** égyptologue *mf*.

Egyptology [ˌiːdʒɪp'tɒlədʒɪ] **n** égyptologie *f*.

eh [eɪ] **excl** a (*what did you say?*) comment?, quoi?, hein?* b **you'll do it for me, ~?** tu le feras pour moi, n'est-ce pas? *or* hein?*

eider ['aɪdəʳ] **n** eider *m*. **~down** (*quilt*) édredon *m*; (*NonC: down*) duvet *m* (d'eider).

eidetic [aɪ'detɪk] **adj** eidétique.

Eiffel Tower [ˌaɪfəl'taʊəʳ] **n** tour *f* Eiffel.

Eiger ['aɪgəʳ] **n** Eiger *m*.

eight [eɪt] 1 **adj** huit *inv*. (*Ind etc*) **an ~-hour day** la journée de huit heures; (*Ind etc*) **to do** *or* **work ~-hour shifts** faire des postes *mpl or* des roulements *mpl* de huit heures; *for other phrases see* **six**. 2 **n** huit *m inv* (*also Rowing*). (*fig*) **he's had one over the ~*** il a du vent dans les voiles*, il a un verre dans le nez*; *see* **figure**. 3 **pron** huit *mfpl*. **there are ~** il y en a huit.

eighteen ['eɪ'tiːn] 1 **adj** dix-huit *inv*. 2 **n** dix-huit *m inv*; *for phrases see* **six**. 3 **pron** dix-huit *mfpl*. **there are ~** il y en a dix-huit.

eighteenth ['eɪ'tiːnθ] 1 **adj** dix-huitième. 2 **n** dix-huitième *mf*; (*fraction*) dix-huitième *m*; *for phrases see* **sixth**.

eighth [eɪtθ] 1 **adj** huitième. (*US Mus*) **~ note** croche *f*. 2 **n** huitième *mf*; (*fraction*) huitième *m*; *for phrases see* **sixth**.

eightieth ['eɪtɪəθ] 1 **adj** quatre-vingtième. 2 **n** quatre-vingtième *mf*; (*fraction*) quatre-vingtième *m*; *for phrases see* **sixth**.

eighty ['eɪtɪ] 1 **adj** quatre-vingts *inv*. **about ~ books** environ *or* à peu près quatre-vingts livres; *for other phrases see* **sixty**. 2 **n** quatre-vingts *m*. **about ~** environ *or* à peu près quatre-vingts; **~-one** quatre-vingt-un; **~-two** quatre-vingt-deux; **~-first** quatre-vingt-unième; **page ~** page quatre-vingt; (*US*) **to ~-six sb**⁑ (*refuse to serve*) refuser de servir qn; (*eject*) vider* qn; *for other phrases see* **sixty**. 3 **pron** quatre-vingts *mfpl*. **there are ~** il y en a quatre-vingts.

Einsteinian [aɪn'staɪnɪən] **adj** einsteinien.

einsteinium [aɪn'staɪnɪəm] **n** einsteinium *m*.

Eire [ˈɛərə] n République *f* d'Irlande.
eisteddfod [aɪˈstedfəd] n concours *m* de musique et de poésie (*en gallois*).
either [ˈaɪðəʳ, ˈiːðəʳ] 1 adj a (*one or other*) l'un(e) ou l'autre, n'importe lequel (*f* laquelle) (des deux). ~ **day would suit me** l'un ou l'autre jour *or* l'un de ces deux jours me conviendrait; **do it ~ way** faites-le de l'une ou l'autre façon; ~ **way* I can't do anything about it** de toute façon *or* quoi qu'il arrive je n'y peux rien; **I don't like ~ book** je n'aime ni l'un ni l'autre de ces livres.
b (*each*) chaque. **in ~ hand** dans chaque main; **on ~ side of the street** des deux côtés *or* de chaque côté de la rue; **on ~ side lay fields** de part et d'autre s'étendaient des champs.
2 pron l'un(e) *m(f)* ou l'autre, n'importe lequel *m* (*or* laquelle *f*) (des deux). **which bus will you take?** — ~ quel bus prendrez-vous? — l'un ou l'autre *or* n'importe lequel (des deux); **there are two boxes on the table, take ~** il y a deux boîtes sur la table, prenez celle que vous voulez *or* n'importe laquelle *or* l'une ou l'autre; **I don't admire ~** je n'admire ni l'un ni l'autre; **I don't believe ~ of them** je ne les crois ni l'un ni l'autre; **give it to ~ of them** donnez-le soit à l'un soit à l'autre; **if ~ is attacked the other helps him** si l'un des deux est attaqué l'autre l'aide.
3 adv (*after neg statement*) non plus. **he sings badly and he can't act ~** il chante mal et il ne sait pas jouer non plus *or* et il ne joue pas mieux; **I have never heard of him — no, I haven't ~** je n'ai jamais entendu parler de lui — moi non plus.
4 conj a ~ ... **or** ou (bien) ... ou (bien), soit ... soit; (*after neg*) ni ... ni; **he must be ~ lazy or stupid** il doit être ou paresseux ou stupide; **he must ~ change his policy or resign** il faut soit qu'il change (*subj*) de politique soit qu'il démissionne (*subj*); ~ **be quiet or go out!** tais-toi ou sors d'ici!, ou (bien) tu te tais ou (bien) tu sors d'ici!; **I have never been ~ to Paris or to Rome** je ne suis jamais allé ni à Paris ni à Rome; **it was ~ he or his sister** c'était soit lui soit sa sœur, c'était ou (bien) lui ou (bien) sa sœur.
b (*moreover*) **she got a sum of money, and not such a small one ~** elle a reçu une certaine somme, pas si petite que ça d'ailleurs.
ejaculate [ɪˈdʒækjʊleɪt] vti (*cry out*) s'exclamer, s'écrier; (*Physiol*) éjaculer.
ejaculation [ɪˌdʒækjʊˈleɪʃən] n (*cry*) exclamation *f*, cri *m*; (*Physiol*) éjaculation *f*.
ejaculatory [ɪˈdʒækjʊlətərɪ] adj (*Physiol*) éjaculatoire.
eject [ɪˈdʒekt] 1 vt (*Aviat, Tech etc*) éjecter; *tenant, troublemaker* expulser; *trespasser* chasser, reconduire; *customer* expulser, vider*. 2 vi [*pilot*] utiliser le mécanisme d'éjection.
ejection [ɪˈdʒekʃən] n (*NonC*) [*person*] expulsion *f*; (*Aviat, Tech*) éjection *f*.
ejector [ɪˈdʒektəʳ] n (*Tech*) éjecteur *m*. (*Aviat*) ~ **seat** siège *m* éjectable.
eke [iːk] vt: **to ~ out** (*by adding*) accroître, augmenter; (*by saving*) économiser, faire durer; **to ~ out one's pension by doing ...** étirer sa pension de retraite en faisant ...; **to ~ out a living** vivoter.
el [ɛl] n (*US*) (abbr of **elevated railroad**) métro *m* aérien.
elaborate [ɪˈlæbərɪt] 1 adj *scheme, programme* complexe; *ornamentation, design, sewing* détaillé, compliqué; *preparations* minutieux; *pattern, joke, excuse* compliqué, recherché; *meal* soigné, raffiné; *style* recherché, travaillé; *clothes* recherché, raffiné; *sculpture* ouvragé, travaillé; *drawing* minutieux, travaillé. **with ~ care** très soigneusement, minutieusement; **he made an ~ plan for avoiding ...** il a établi un projet détaillé *or* minutieux pour éviter ...; **his plan was so ~ that I couldn't follow it** son projet était si complexe *or* compliqué que je n'arrivais pas à le comprendre; **the work was so ~ that it took her years to finish it** le travail était si complexe *or* minutieux qu'elle a mis des années à le finir.
2 [ɪˈlæbəreɪt] vt élaborer. (*Ling*) **~d code** code *m* élaboré.
3 [ɪˈlæbəreɪt] vi donner des détails (*on* sur), entrer dans *or* expliquer les détails (*on* de).
elaborately [ɪˈlæbərɪtlɪ] adv (*see* **elaborate**) en détail; minutieusement; soigneusement, avec soin; avec recherche.
elaboration [ɪˌlæbəˈreɪʃən] n élaboration *f*.
élan [eɪˈlɑːn, eɪˈlæn] n (*liter*) allant *m*.
elapse [ɪˈlæps] vi s'écouler, (se) passer.
elastic [ɪˈlæstɪk] 1 adj élastique (*also fig*). (*Brit*) ~ **band** élastique *m*, caoutchouc *m*; ~ **stockings** bas *mpl* à varices. 2 n a (*NonC*) élastique *m*. b (*also* **baggage** *or* **luggage** ~) tendeur *m*, sandow *m* ®.
elasticated [ɪˈlæstɪkeɪtɪd] adj élastiqué, à élastique.
elasticity [ˌiːlæsˈtɪsɪtɪ] n élasticité *f*.
Elastoplast [ɪˈlæstəˌplɑːst] n ® sparadrap *m*.
elate [ɪˈleɪt] vt transporter, ravir, enthousiasmer.
elated [ɪˈleɪtɪd] adj transporté (de joie), rempli d'allégresse. **to be ~** exulter.
elation [ɪˈleɪʃən] n allégresse *f*, exultation *f*.
Elba [ˈelbə] n l'île *f* d'Elbe.
Elbe [elb] n Elbe *f* (*fleuve*).
elbow [ˈelbəʊ] 1 n [*person, road, river, pipe*] coude *m*. **to lean one's ~s on** s'accouder à *or* sur, être accoudé à; **to lean on one's ~** s'appuyer sur le coude; **at his ~** à ses côtés; **out at the ~s** *garment* percé *or* troué aux coudes; *person* déguenillé, loqueteux; (*Brit*) **to give sb/get the ~*** *lover* plaquer‡ *or* laisser tomber qn*/se faire plaquer‡; *employee* virer qn*/se faire virer*; (*euph*) **he lifts his ~* a bit** il lève le coude*, il picole‡.
2 comp ►**elbow grease: to use a bit of elbow grease** mettre de l'huile de coude* ►**elbow joint** articulation *f* du coude ►**elbow-rest** accoudoir *m*; [*armchair*] bras *m* ►**elbow room: to have enough elbow room** (*lit*) avoir de la place pour se retourner; (*fig*) avoir les coudées franches; **to have no elbow room** (*lit*) être à l'étroit; (*fig*) ne pas avoir de liberté d'action.
3 vi: **to ~ through** se frayer un passage à travers (en jouant des coudes); **to ~ forward** avancer en jouant des coudes.
4 vt: **to ~ sb aside** écarter qn du coude *or* d'un coup de coude; **to ~ one's way through** *etc* = **to elbow through** *etc; see* **3**.
elder¹ [ˈeldəʳ] 1 adj aîné (*de deux*). **my ~ sister** ma sœur aînée; **Pliny the ~** Pline l'Ancien; **Alexandre Dumas the ~** Alexandre Dumas père; ~ **statesman** vétéran *m* de la politique, homme politique chevronné. 2 n aîné(e) *m(f)*; [*Presbyterian Church*] membre *m* du conseil d'une église presbytérienne. [*tribe, Church*] **~s** anciens *mpl*; **one's ~s and betters** ses aînés.
elder² [ˈeldəʳ] 1 n (*Bot*) sureau *m*. 2 comp ►**elderberry** baie *f* de sureau; **elderberry wine** vin *m* de sureau.
elderly [ˈeldəlɪ] 1 adj assez âgé. **he's getting ~** il prend de l'âge, il se fait vieux. 2 npl: **the ~** les personnes âgées.
eldest [ˈeldɪst] adj, n aîné(e) *m(f)* (*de plusieurs*). **their ~ (child)** leur aîné(e), l'aîné(e) de leurs enfants; **my ~ brother** l'aîné de mes frères.
Eleanor [ˈelɪnəʳ] n Éléonore *f*.
elec abbr of **electric, electricity**.
elect [ɪˈlekt] 1 vt a (*by vote*) élire; (*more informally*) nommer. **he was ~ed chairman/M.P.** il a été élu président/député; **to ~ sb to the senate** élire qn au sénat; (*Brit: Local Govt*) **~ed member** conseiller *m*, -ère *f* municipal(e) *or* régional(e); **~ed official** élu(e) *m(f)*. b (*choose*) choisir, opter (*to do* de faire). **to ~ French nationality** opter pour *or* choisir la nationalité française. 2 adj futur (*before n*). **the president ~** le président désigné, le futur président. 3 npl (*esp Rel*) **the ~** les élus *mpl*.
election [ɪˈlekʃən] 1 n élection *f*. **to hold an ~** procéder à une élection; **to stand for ~ to Parliament** se porter candidat *or* se présenter aux élections législatives; *see* **general**. 2 comp *campaign, speech, agent* électoral; *day, results* du scrutin; *publication* de propagande électorale ►**elections judge** (*US*) scrutateur *m*.
electioneer [ɪˌlekʃəˈnɪəʳ] vi mener une campagne électorale, faire de la propagande électorale.
electioneering [ɪˌlekʃəˈnɪərɪŋ] 1 n (*campaign*) campagne électorale; (*propaganda*) propagande électorale. 2 comp *propaganda, publicity* électoral; *speech* de propagande électorale.
elective [ɪˈlektɪv] 1 adj (*with power to elect*) *body, assembly, power* électoral; (*elected*) *official, body* électif, élu; (*Chem, fig*) électif; (*optional*) *class, course* facultatif. (*US Pol*) ~ **office** charge *f* élective. 2 n (*Scol, Univ*) cours *m* facultatif.
elector [ɪˈlektəʳ] n (*gen, Parl*) électeur *m*, -trice *f*; (*US Parl*) membre *m* du collège électoral. (*Hist*) E~ Électeur *m*, prince électeur.
electoral [ɪˈlektərəl] adj électoral. ~ **college** (*gen*) collège électoral; (*US*) collège électoral (présidentiel); ~ **district** *or* **division** circonscription électorale; ~ **roll** liste électorale; ~ **umbrella** étiquette électorale; (*US*) ~ **vote** vote *m* des grands électeurs.
electorally [ɪˈlektərəlɪ] adv sur le plan électoral.
electorate [ɪˈlektərɪt] n électorat *m*, électeurs *mpl*.
Electra [ɪˈlektrə] n Électre *f*.
electric [ɪˈlektrɪk] 1 adj *appliance, current, wire* électrique; *meter, account, generator* d'électricité, électrique; *car etc* (à propulsion) électrique. (*fig*) **the atmosphere was ~** il y avait de l'électricité dans l'air*.
2 npl (*Brit* *) **the ~s** l'installation *f* électrique.
3 comp ►**electric (arc) welding** soudure *f* électrique (à l'arc) ►**electric blanket** couverture chauffante ►**electric blue** n, **electric-blue** adj bleu (*m*) électrique ►**electric chair** chaise *f* électrique ►**electric charge/current** charge *f*/courant *m* électrique ►**electric eel** (*Zool*) anguille *f* électrique, gymnote *m* ►**electric eye** cellule *f* photoélectrique ►**electric fence** clôture électrifiée ►**electric field** champ *m* électrique ►**electric fire** (*Brit*) radiateur *m* électrique ►**electric furnace** four *m* électrique ►**electric guitar** guitare *f* électrique ►**electric heater** = **electric fire** ►**electric light** lumière *f* électrique; (*NonC: lighting*) éclairage *m* électrique *or* à l'électricité ►**electric organ** (*Mus*) orgue *m* électronique; (*in fish*) organe *m* électrique ►**electric piano** piano *m* électronique ►**electric potential** potentiel *m* électrique ►**electric ray** (*Zool*) raie *f* électrique ►**electric shock** décharge *f* électrique; **to get an electric shock** recevoir une décharge électrique, recevoir le courant, prendre le jus*; **to give sb an electric shock** donner une décharge électrique à qn; (*Med*) **electric shock treatment*** électrochoc(s) *m(pl)* ►**electric storm** orage *m* magnétique.
electrical [ɪˈlektrɪkəl] adj électrique. ~ **engineer** ingénieur *m* électricien; ~ **engineering** électrotechnique *f*; ~ **failure** panne *f* d'élec-

tricité; ~ **fitter** monteur *m* électricien.

electrically [ɪ'lektrɪkəlɪ] **adv** à l'électricité; (*Phys*) électriquement.

electrician [ɪlek'trɪʃən] **n** électricien *m*. **electricians' dispute/strike** conflit *m*/grève *f* des employés de l'électricité.

electricity [ɪlek'trɪsətɪ] 1 **n** (*gen*) électricité *f*. (*also fig*) **to switch off/on the ~** couper/rétablir le courant; *see* **supply**[1]. 2 **comp** ►**electricity board** (*Brit*) office régional de l'électricité ►**electricity dispute/strike** conflit *m*/grève *f* des employés de l'électricité.

electrification [ɪ,lektrɪfɪ'keɪʃən] **n** électrification *f*.

electrify [ɪ'lektrɪfaɪ] **vt** a (*Rail*) électrifier; (*charge with electricity*) électriser. **electrified fence** barrière *f* électrifiée; *[village etc]* **to be electrified** avoir l'électricité. b (*fig*) *audience* électriser, galvaniser.

electrifying [ɪ'lektrɪfaɪɪŋ] **adj** (*fig*) électrisant, galvanisant.

electro... [ɪ,lektrəʊ] **pref** électro... .

electrocardiogram [ɪ,lektrəʊ'kɑːdɪəgræm] **n** électrocardiogramme *m*.

electrocardiograph [ɪ,lektrəʊ'kɑːdɪəgræf] **n** électrocardiographe *m*.

electrochemical [ɪ,lektrəʊ'kemɪkəl] **adj** électrochimique.

electrochemistry [ɪ,lektrəʊ'kemɪstrɪ] **n** électrochimie *f*.

electroconvulsive [ɪ,lektrəkən'vʌlsɪv] **adj**: ~ **therapy** électrochocs *mpl*; **to give sb/have ~ therapy** traiter qn/être traité par électrochocs.

electrocute [ɪ'lektrəkjuːt] **vt** électrocuter.

electrocution [ɪ,lektrə'kjuːʃən] **n** électrocution *f*.

electrode [ɪ'lektrəʊd] **n** électrode *f*.

electrodialysis [ɪ,lektrəʊdaɪ'ælɪsɪs] **n** électrodialyse *f*.

electrodynamic [ɪ,lektrəʊdaɪ'næmɪk] **adj** électrodynamique.

electrodynamics [ɪ,lektrəʊdaɪ'næmɪks] **n** (*NonC*) électrodynamique *f*.

electrodynamometer [ɪ,lektrəʊ,daɪnə'mɒmɪtə^r] **n** électrodynamomètre *m*.

electroencephalogram [ɪ,lektrəʊen'sefələ,græm] **n** électroencéphalogramme *m*.

electroencephalograph [ɪ,lektrəʊen'sefələ,græf] **n** électroencéphalographie *f*.

electroforming [ɪ'lektrəʊ,fɔːmɪŋ] **n** électroformage *m*.

electrolyse [ɪ'lektrəʊ,laɪz] **vt** électrolyser.

electrolyser [ɪ'lektrəʊ,laɪzə^r] **n** électrolyseur *m*.

electrolysis [ɪlek'trɒlɪsɪs] **n** électrolyse *f*.

electrolyte [ɪ'lektrəʊ,laɪt] **n** électrolyte *m*.

electrolytic [ɪ,lektrəʊ'lɪtɪk] **adj** électrolytique.

electrolyze [ɪ'lektrəʊ,laɪz] *etc* (*US*) = **electrolyse** *etc*.

electromagnet [ɪ,lektrəʊ'mægnɪt] **n** électro-aimant *m*.

electromagnetic [ɪ,lektrəʊmæg'netɪk] **adj** électromagnétique. ~ **wave** faisceau *m* hertzien.

electromagnetism [ɪ,lektrəʊ'mægnɪ,tɪzəm] **n** électromagnétisme *m*.

electromechanical [ɪ,lektrəʊmɪ'kænɪkəl] **adj** électromécanique.

electromechanics [ɪ,lektrəʊmɪ'kænɪks] **n** (*NonC*) électromécanique *f*.

electrometallurgical [ɪ,lektrəʊ,metə'lɜːdʒɪkəl] **adj** électrométallurgique.

electrometallurgist [ɪ,lektrəʊmɪ'tælədʒɪst] **n** électrométallurgiste *m*.

electrometallurgy [ɪ,lektrəʊmɪ'tælədʒɪ] **n** électrométallurgie *f*.

electrometer [ɪlek'trɒmɪtə^r] **n** électromètre *m*.

electromotive [ɪ,lektrəʊ'məʊtɪv] **adj** électromoteur (*f* -trice).

electron [ɪ'lektrɒn] 1 **n** électron *m*. 2 **comp** *telescope* électronique ►**electron beam** faisceau *m* électronique ►**electron camera** caméra *f* électronique ►**electron engineering** génie *m* électronique ►**electron gun** canon *m* à électrons ►**electron microscope** microscope *m* électronique.

electronegative [ɪ,lektrəʊ'negətɪv] **adj** électronégatif.

electronic [ɪlek'trɒnɪk] **adj** électronique. ~ **computer** ordinateur *m* électronique; ~ **data processing** traitement *m* électronique de données; ~ **flash** flash *m* électronique; ~ **funds transfer system** transfert *m* électronique de fonds, télévirement *m*; ~ **keyboard** clavier *m* électronique; (*Comput*) ~ **mail** courrier *m* électronique; (*Comput*) ~ **mailbox** boîte *f* aux lettres électronique; ~ **music/organ** musique *f*/orgue *m* électronique; ~ **news gathering** collecte *f* électronique d'informations; ~ **point of sale** point *m* de vente électronique; ~ **publishing** l'édition électronique; ~ **surveillance** surveillance *f* électronique; (*Penal System*) ~ **tag** signal *m* électronique; (*Penal System*) ~ **tagging** filature *f* électronique; ~ **transfer of funds** transfert *m* électronique de fonds, télévirement *m*.

electronics [ɪlek'trɒnɪks] **n** (*NonC*) électronique *f*. ~ **engineer** électronicien(ne) *m(f)*.

electrophysiological [ɪ,lektrəʊ,fɪzɪəʊ'lɒdʒɪkəl] **adj** électrophysiologique.

electrophysiologist [ɪ,lektrəʊ,fɪzɪ'ɒlədʒɪst] **n** électrophysiologiste *mf*.

electrophysiology [ɪ,lektrəʊ,fɪzɪ'ɒlədʒɪ] **n** électrophysiologie *f*.

electroplate [ɪ'lektrəʊpleɪt] 1 **vt** plaquer par galvanoplastie; (*with gold*) dorer *or* (*with silver*) argenter par galvanoplastie. **~d nickel silver** ruolz *m*. 2 **n** (*NonC*) articles plaqués *etc* par galvanoplastie; (*silver*) articles de ruolz.

electropositive [ɪ,lektrəʊ'pɒzɪtɪv] **adj** électropositif.

electropuncture [ɪ,lektrəʊ'pʌŋktʃə^r] **n** électroponcture *f*.

electroshock [ɪ'lektrəʊʃɒk] 1 **n** électrochoc *m*. 2 **comp** ►**electroshock therapy, electroshock treatment** (traitement *m* par) électrochocs *mpl*; **to give sb electroshock treatment** traiter qn par électrochocs.

electrostatic [ɪ,lektrəʊ'stætɪk] **adj** électrostatique.

electrostatics [ɪ,lektrəʊ'stætɪks] **n** (*NonC*) électrostatique *f*.

electrosurgery [ɪ,lektrəʊ'sɜːdʒərɪ] **n** électrochirurgie *f*.

electrosurgical [ɪ,lektrəʊ'sɜːdʒɪkəl] **adj** électrochirurgical.

electrotechnological [ɪ,lektrəʊ,teknə'lɒdʒɪkəl] **adj** électrotechnique.

electrotechnology [ɪ,lektrəʊtek'nɒlədʒɪ] **n** électrotechnique *f*.

electrotherapeutic [ɪ,lektrəʊ,θerə'pjuːtɪk] **adj** électrothérapeute.

electrotherapeutics [ɪ,lektrəʊ,θerə'pjuːtɪks] **n** (*NonC*) électrothérapie *f*.

electrotherapist [ɪ,lektrəʊ'θerəpɪst] **n** électrothérapeute *mf*.

electrotherapy [ɪ,lektrəʊ'θerəpɪ] **n** électrothérapie *f*.

electrotype [ɪ'lektrəʊ,taɪp] 1 **n** galvanotype *m*, galvano* *m*. 2 **vt** clicher par galvanotypie.

electrovalency [ɪ,lektrəʊ'veɪlənsɪ] **n** électrovalence *f*.

electrovalent [ɪ,lektrəʊ'veɪlənt] **adj**: ~ **bond** liaison *f* électrostatique.

electrum [ɪ'lektrəm] **n** électrum *m*.

eleemosynary [,eliː'mɒsɪnərɪ] **adj** (*frm*) de bienfaisance, charitable.

elegance ['elɪgəns] **n** (*see* **elegant**) élégance *f*; chic *m*; distinction *f*; grâce *f*.

elegant ['elɪgənt] **adj** *person, clothes* élégant, chic *inv*, distingué; *style, design* élégant, chic; *proportions, building* élégant, harmonieux; *manners, movement* élégant, gracieux.

elegantly ['elɪgəntlɪ] **adv** (*see* **elegant**) élégamment, avec élégance; avec chic *or* distinction; avec grâce.

elegiac [,elɪ'dʒaɪək] 1 **adj** élégiaque. ~ **couplet** distique *m* élégiaque. 2 **n**: **~s** poèmes *mpl* élégiaques.

elegy ['elɪdʒɪ] **n** élégie *f*.

element ['elɪmənt] **n** (*Chem, Gram, Med, Phys, fig*) élément *m*; *[heater, kettle]* résistance *f*. (*Met*) **the ~s** les éléments; **the ~s of mathematics** les éléments *or* les rudiments *mpl* des mathématiques; **an ~ of danger/truth** une part de danger/de vérité; **the ~ of chance** le facteur chance; **it's the personal ~ that matters** c'est le rapport personnel qui compte; **the comic/tragic ~ in X's poetry** le comique/le tragique dans la poésie de X; **the communist ~ in the trade unions** l'élément communiste dans les syndicats; **to be in/out of one's ~** être/ne pas être dans son élément; (*Rel*) **the E~s** les Espèces *fpl*.

elemental [,elɪ'mentl] 1 **adj** *forces* des éléments, élémentaire; (*Chem, Phys*) élémentaire; (*basic*) essentiel. ~ **truth** vérité première. 2 **n** (*Occult*) esprit *m* (élémental).

elementary [,elɪ'mentərɪ] **adj** (*gen*) élémentaire. (*Math*) ~ **particle** particule *f* élémentaire; ~ **geometry course** cours élémentaire *or* fondamental de géométrie; ~ **science** les rudiments *mpl* de la science; (*US; also Brit* †) ~ **school/education** école *f*/enseignement *m* primaire; ~ **politeness requires that ...** la plus élémentaire politesse exige que ... + *subj*; ~, **my dear Watson!** c'est tout ce qu'il y a de plus simple, mon cher Watson!

elephant ['elɪfənt] **n, pl ~s** *or* ~ (*bull* ~) éléphant *m* (mâle); (*cow* ~) éléphant *m* (femelle); (*young* ~) éléphanteau *m*. ~ **seal** éléphant de mer; **African/Indian ~** éléphant d'Afrique/d'Asie; *see* **white**.

elephantiasis [,elɪfən'taɪəsɪs] **n** éléphantiasis *f*.

elephantine [,elɪ'fæntaɪn] **adj** (*heavy, clumsy*) gauche, lourd; (*large*) éléphantesque; (*iro*) *wit* lourd. **with ~ grace** avec la grâce d'un éléphant.

elevate ['elɪveɪt] **vt** hausser, élever (*also fig, Rel*); *voice* hausser; *mind* élever; *soul* élever, exalter. **to ~ to the peerage** élever à la pairie, anoblir.

elevated ['elɪveɪtɪd] **adj** *position* élevé; *railway* aérien; *rank* éminent; *style* soutenu; *thoughts* noble, sublime. (*US*) ~ **railroad** métro *m* aérien.

elevating ['elɪveɪtɪŋ] **adj** *reading* qui élève l'esprit.

elevation [,elɪ'veɪʃən] **n** a (*NonC*: *see* **elevate**; *also Archit, Gunnery, Surv*) élévation *f*. **angle of ~** angle *m* d'élévation; (*Archit*) **front ~** façade *f*; **sectional ~** coupe verticale. b (*altitude*) altitude *f*, hauteur *f*; (*hill*) hauteur, éminence *f*. **at an ~ of 1000 metres** à 1000 mètres d'altitude.

elevator ['elɪveɪtə^r] **n** a élévateur *m*; (*esp US*: *lift*) ascenseur *m*; (*hoist*) monte-charge *m inv*; (*grain storehouse*) silo *m* (à élévateur pneumatique), élévator *m*; (*Aviat*) gouvernail *m* de profondeur. (*US*) ~ **car/shaft** cabine *f*/cage *f* d'ascenseur. b (*US*: *also* ~ **shoe**) soulier *m* à talonnette.

eleven [ɪ'levn] 1 **adj** onze *inv*; *for phrases see* **six**. 2 **n** a (*number*) onze *m inv*. **number ~** le numéro onze, le onze; (*Brit Scol*) **the ~ plus** ≃ l'examen *m* d'entrée en sixième. b (*Sport*) **the French ~** le onze de France; **the first ~** le onze, la première équipe; **the second ~** la deuxième équipe. 3 **pron** onze *mfpl*. **there are ~** il y en a onze.

elevenses* [ɪ'levnzɪz] **npl** (*Brit*) ≃ pause-café *f* (*dans la matinée*).

eleventh [ɪ'levnθ] 1 **adj** onzième. (*fig*) **at the ~ hour** à la onzième heure, à la dernière minute. 2 **n** onzième *mf*; (*fraction*) onzième *m*; *for phrases see* **sixth**.

elf [elf] **n, pl elves** (*lit*) elfe *m*, lutin *m*, farfadet *m*; (*fig*) lutin.

elfin ['elfɪn] **adj** d'elfe, de lutin; *light, music* féerique.

El Greco [el'grekəʊ] **n** Le Greco.

elicit [ɪ'lɪsɪt] **vt** *truth* arracher (*from sb* à qn), mettre à jour; *admission* arracher (*from* à), provoquer; *reply, explanation, information* tirer, obtenir (*from* de); *smile* faire naître; *secret* tirer (*from* de), arracher (*from* à). **to ~ the facts of a case** tirer au clair les faits dans une affaire, tirer une affaire au clair; **to ~ the truth about a case** faire le jour *or* la clarté sur une affaire.

elide [ɪ'laɪd] **vt** élider. **to be ~d** s'élider.

eligibility [ˌelɪdʒə'bɪlɪtɪ] **n** (*for election*) éligibilité *f*; (*for employment*) admissibilité *f*.

eligible ['elɪdʒəbl] **adj** (*for membership, office*) éligible (*for* à); (*for job*) admissible (*for* à). **to be ~ for a pension** avoir droit à la retraite, pouvoir faire valoir ses droits à la retraite (*frm*); **to be ~ for promotion** remplir les *or* satisfaire aux conditions requises pour obtenir de l'avancement; **an ~ young man** un beau *or* bon parti; **he's very ~*** c'est un parti très acceptable.

Elijah [ɪ'laɪdʒə] **n** Elie *m*.

Elisha [ɪ'laɪʃə] **n** Elisée *m*.

eliminate [ɪ'lɪmɪneɪt] **vt** *alternative, suspicion, competitor, candidate* éliminer, écarter; *possibility* écarter, exclure; *competition, opposition, suspect* éliminer; *mark, stain* enlever, faire disparaître; *bad language, expenditure, detail* éliminer, supprimer; (*Math, Physiol*) éliminer; (*kill*) supprimer.

elimination [ɪˌlɪmɪ'neɪʃən] **n** élimination *f*. **by (the process of) ~** par élimination.

elision [ɪ'lɪʒən] **n** élision *f*.

elite [ɪ'li:t] **1 n a** (*select group*) élite *f*. **b** (*Typ*) caractères *mpl* élite. **2 adj a** *regiment, troops* d'élite; *school etc* réservé à l'élite. **b** (*Typ*) élite *inv*.

elitism [ɪ'li:tɪzəm] **n** élitisme *m*.

elitist [ɪ'li:tɪst] **adj, n** élitiste *(mf)*.

elixir [ɪ'lɪksəʳ] **n** élixir *m*. **~ of life** élixir de longue vie.

Elizabeth [ɪ'lɪzəbəθ] **n** Élisabeth *f*.

Elizabethan [ɪˌlɪzə'bi:θən] **1 adj** élisabéthain. **2 n** Élisabéthain(e) *m(f)*.

elk [elk] **n, pl ~** *or* **~s** (*Zool*) élan *m*. **Canadian ~** orignac *m or* orignal *m*.

ellipse [ɪ'lɪps] **n** (*Math*) ellipse *f*.

ellipsis [ɪ'lɪpsɪs] **n, pl ellipses** [ɪ'lɪpsi:z] (*Gram*) ellipse *f*.

ellipsoid [ɪ'lɪpsɔɪd] **adj, n** ellipsoïde *(m)*.

elliptic(al) [ɪ'lɪptɪk(əl)] **adj** (*Gram, Math, fig*) elliptique.

elliptically [ɪ'lɪptɪk(ə)lɪ] **adv** elliptiquement.

elm [elm] **n** (*tree, wood*) orme *m*. **young ~** ormeau *m*; *see* **Dutch**.

elocution [ˌelə'kju:ʃən] **n** élocution *f*, diction *f*.

elocutionist [ˌelə'kju:ʃənɪst] **n** (*teacher*) professeur *m* d'élocution *or* de diction; (*entertainer*) diseur *m*, -euse *f*.

elongate ['i:lɒŋgeɪt] **1 vt** (*gen*) allonger, étirer; *line* prolonger. **2 vi** s'allonger, s'étirer.

elongation [ˌi:lɒŋ'geɪʃən] **n** (*gen*) allongement *m*; *[line etc]* prolongement *m*; (*Astron, Med*) élongation *f*.

elope [ɪ'ləʊp] **vi: to ~ with sb** *[woman]* se faire *or* se laisser enlever par qn; *[man]* enlever qn; **they ~d** ils se sont enfuis (ensemble).

elopement [ɪ'ləʊpmənt] **n** fugue *f* (amoureuse).

eloquence ['eləkwəns] **n** éloquence *f*.

eloquent ['eləkwənt] **adj** *person* éloquent, qui a le don de la parole; *speech* éloquent; *words* entraînant; (*fig*) *look, gesture* éloquent, expressif, parlant. **his silence was ~** son silence en disait long; *see* **wax²**.

eloquently ['eləkwəntlɪ] **adv** éloquemment, avec éloquence.

El Salvador [el'sælvəˌdɔ:ʳ] **n** Le Salvador.

else [els] **1 adv a** (*other, besides, instead*) autre, d'autre, de plus. **if all ~ fails** si rien d'autre ne marche; **anybody ~ would have done it** tout autre *or* n'importe qui d'autre l'aurait fait; **is there anybody ~ there?** y a-t-il quelqu'un d'autre?, y a-t-il encore quelqu'un?; **I'd prefer anything ~** je préférerais n'importe quoi d'autre; **have you anything ~ to say?** avez-vous encore quelque chose à dire?, avez-vous quelque chose à ajouter?; **will there be anything ~ sir?** *[shop assistant]* désirez-vous quelque chose d'autre monsieur?, et avec ça* monsieur?; *[servant]* monsieur ne désire rien d'autre?; **nothing ~, thank you** plus rien, merci; **I couldn't do anything ~ but leave** il ne me restait plus qu'à partir; **anywhere ~ nobody would have noticed, but ...** n'importe où ailleurs personne ne s'en serait aperçu mais ...; **can you do it anywhere ~?** pouvez-vous le faire ailleurs?; **you won't find this flower anywhere ~** vous ne trouverez cette fleur nulle part ailleurs; **how ~ can I do it?** de quelle autre façon est-ce que je peux le faire?, comment est-ce que je peux le faire autrement?; **nobody ~, no one ~** personne d'autre; **nothing ~** rien d'autre; **it was fun if nothing ~** c'était marrant au moins; **nowhere ~** nulle part ailleurs; **someone** *or* **somebody ~** quelqu'un d'autre; **may I speak to someone ~?** puis-je parler à quelqu'un d'autre?; **this is someone ~'s umbrella** c'est le parapluie de quelqu'un d'autre; **something ~** autre chose, quelque chose d'autre; (*fig*) **she is/it is something ~*** elle est/c'est vraiment fantastique *or* terrible*; **somewhere ~, (*US*) someplace ~** ailleurs, autre part; **where ~?** à quel autre endroit?, où encore?; **who ~?** qui encore?, qui d'autre?; **what ~?** quoi encore, quoi d'autre?; **what ~ could I do?** que pouvais-je faire d'autre *or* de plus?; **they sell books and toys and much ~** ils vendent des livres, des jouets et bien d'autres choses (encore) *or* et que sais-je encore; **there is little ~ to be done** il n'y a *or* il ne reste pas grand-chose d'autre à faire.

b or ~ ou bien, sinon, autrement; **do it or ~ go away** faites-le, ou bien allez-vous-en; **do it now or ~ you'll be punished** fais-le tout de suite, sans ça *or* sinon tu seras puni; **do it or ~!*** faites-le sinon ...!

2 comp ▸elsewhere ailleurs, autre part; **from elsewhere** (venu) d'ailleurs *or* d'un autre endroit (*or* pays *etc*).

ELT [ˌi:el'ti:] **n** (**abbr of English Language Teaching**) *see* **English**.

elucidate [ɪ'lu:sɪdeɪt] **vt** *text* élucider, expliquer, dégager le sens de; *mystery* élucider, tirer au clair, éclaircir.

elucidation [ɪˌlu:sɪ'deɪʃən] **n** explication *f*, éclaircissement *m*, élucidation *f*.

elude [ɪ'lu:d] **vt** *enemy, pursuit, arrest* échapper à; *question* éluder; *sb's gaze, police, justice* se dérober à; *obligation, responsibility* se soustraire à, se dérober à; *blow* esquiver, éviter. **to ~ sb's grasp** échapper aux mains de qn; **the name ~s me** le nom m'échappe; **success ~d him** le succès restait hors de sa portée.

elusive [ɪ'lu:sɪv] **adj** *enemy, prey, thoughts* insaisissable; *word, happiness, success* qui échappe; *glance, personality* fuyant; *answer* évasif.

elusively [ɪ'lu:sɪvlɪ] **adv** de façon insaisissable *or* évasive.

elusiveness [ɪ'lu:sɪvnɪs] **n** nature *f* insaisissable, caractère évasif.

elusory [ɪ'lu:sərɪ] **adj** = **elusive**.

elver ['elvəʳ] **n** civelle *f*.

elves [elvz] **npl of elf**.

Elysian [ɪ'lɪzɪən] **adj** élyséen.

elytron ['elɪtrɒn] **n, pl elytra** ['elɪtrə] élytre *m*.

EM [ˌi:'em] **n** (*US*) **a** (**abbr of Engineer of Mines**) *see* **engineer**. **b** (**abbr of enlisted man**) *see* **enlist**.

em [em] **n** (*Typ*) cicéro *m*.

emaciated [ɪ'meɪsɪeɪtɪd] **adj** *person, face* émacié, amaigri; *limb* décharné. **to become ~** s'émacier, s'amaigrir, se décharner.

emaciation [ɪˌmeɪsɪ'eɪʃən] **n** émaciation *f*, amaigrissement *m*.

e-mail ['i:meɪl] **n** (*Comput*) (**abbr of electronic mail**) courrier *m* électronique.

emanate ['eməneɪt] **vi** *[light, odour]* émaner (*from* de); *[rumour, document, instruction]* émaner, provenir (*from* de).

emanation [ˌemə'neɪʃən] **n** émanation *f*.

emancipate [ɪ'mænsɪpeɪt] **vt** *women* émanciper; *slaves* affranchir; (*fig*) émanciper, affranchir, libérer (*from* de). **to be ~d from** s'affranchir de, s'émanciper de.

emancipated [ɪ'mænsɪpeɪtɪd] **adj** (*fig*) émancipé, libéré.

emancipation [ɪˌmænsɪ'peɪʃən] **n** (*see* **emancipate**) émancipation *f*; affranchissement *m*; libération *f*.

emasculate [ɪ'mæskjʊleɪt] **1 vt** (*lit, fig*) émasculer. **2** [ɪ'mæskjʊlɪt] **adj** (*lit, fig*) émasculé.

emasculation [ɪˌmæskjʊ'leɪʃən] **n** (*lit, fig*) émasculation *f*.

embalm [ɪm'bɑ:m] **vt** (*all senses*) embaumer.

embalmer [ɪm'bɑ:məʳ] **n** embaumeur *m*.

embalming [ɪm'bɑ:mɪŋ] **1 n** embaumement *m*. **2 comp ▸embalming fluid** bain *m* de natron.

embankment [ɪm'bæŋkmənt] **n** *[path, railway line]* talus *m*, remblai *m*; *[road]* banquette *f* (de sûreté); *[canal, dam]* digue *f*, chaussée *f* (de retenue); *[river]* berge *f*, levée *f*, quai *m*. *[London]* **the E~** *l'un des quais le long de la Tamise;* (*fig*) **to sleep on the E~** ≃ coucher sous les ponts.

embargo [ɪm'bɑ:gəʊ] **1 n, pl ~es a** (*Pol, Comm, Naut etc*) embargo *m*. **to lay** *or* **put an ~ on** mettre l'embargo sur; **arms ~** embargo sur les armes; **to lift an ~** lever l'embargo. **b** (*fig*) interdiction *f*, restriction *f*. **to put an ~ on sth** interdire qch. **2 vt** (*Pol etc*) mettre l'embargo sur; (*fig*) interdire. (*Press: esp US*) **the story has been ~ed until noon Saturday** la nouvelle a été mise sous embargo jusqu'à samedi midi.

embark [ɪm'bɑ:k] **1 vt** *passengers* embarquer, prendre à bord; *goods* embarquer, charger. **2 vi** (*Aviat, Naut*) (s')embarquer (*on* à bord de, sur). (*fig*) **to ~ on** *journey* commencer; *business undertaking, deal* s'engager dans, se lancer dans; *doubtful or risky affair, explanation, story* se lancer dans, s'embarquer dans*; *discussion* entamer.

embarkation [ˌembɑ:'keɪʃən] **n** *[passengers]* embarquement *m*; *[cargo]* embarquement *m*, chargement *m*. (*Aviat, Naut*) **~ card** carte *f* d'embarquement.

embarrass [ɪm'bærəs] **vt** (*disconcert*) embarrasser, gêner, déconcerter; (*hamper*) *[clothes, parcels]* embarrasser, gêner, encombrer. **I feel ~ed about it** j'en suis gêné, cela m'embarrasse; **to be (financially) ~ed** avoir des embarras *or* des ennuis d'argent, être gêné *or* à court.

embarrassing [ɪm'bærəsɪŋ] **adj** embarrassant, gênant. **to get out of an ~ situation** se tirer d'embarras.

embarrassingly [ɪm'bærəsɪŋlɪ] **adv: ~ short/few** si court/peu que c'en était (*or* est) embarrassant; **~, he had forgotten his wallet** comble de l'embarras, il avait oublié son portefeuille.

embarrassment [ɪm'bærəsmənt] **n a** (*emotion*) embarras *m*, gêne *f*, confusion *f* (*at* devant). **to cause sb ~** embarrasser qn; **financial ~** des embarras d'argent *or* financiers. **b** (*person or thing causing it*) **her son is an ~ to her** son fils lui fait honte; **her scar is an ~ to her** sa cicatrice est gênante *or* embarrassante pour elle.

embassy ['embəsɪ] **n** ambassade *f*. **the French E~** l'ambassade de

France.

embattled [ɪm'bætld] adj *army* rangé *or* formé en bataille; *town, camp* fortifié; (*fig*) *person, campaigner* aguerri, rompu aux conflits.

embed [ɪm'bed] vt (*in wood*) enfoncer; (*in cement*) noyer; (*in stone*) sceller; *jewel* enchâsser; (*encrust*) incruster; (*Ling*) enchâsser. (*fig*) **~ded in the memory/mind** fixé *or* gravé dans la mémoire/l'esprit.

embedding [ɪm'bedɪŋ] n action *f* de sceller; fixation *f*; (*Ling*) enchâssement *m*.

embellish [ɪm'belɪʃ] vt (*adorn*) embellir, orner, décorer (*with* de); *manuscript* relever, rehausser, enjoliver (*with* de); (*fig*) *tale, account* enjoliver; *truth* broder sur, orner.

embellishment [ɪm'belɪʃmənt] n (*see* **embellish**) embellissement *m*, ornement *m*, décoration *f*; enjolivement *m*; *[style, handwriting]* fioritures *fpl* (*gen pej*).

Ember ['embəʳ] adj (*Rel*) **~ days** Quatre-Temps *mpl*.

ember ['embəʳ] n charbon ardent. **~s** braise *f*; **the dying ~s** les tisons *mpl*; *see* **fan¹**.

embezzle [ɪm'bezl] vt détourner, escroquer (*des fonds*). **he has been embezzling** il a détourné des fonds.

embezzlement [ɪm'bezlmənt] n détournement *m* de fonds.

embezzler [ɪm'bezləʳ] n escroc *m*.

embitter [ɪm'bɪtəʳ] vt *person* aigrir, remplir d'amertume; *relations, disputes* envenimer.

embittered [ɪm'bɪtəd] adj *person* aigri, plein d'amertume.

embittering [ɪm'bɪtərɪŋ] adj qui laisse amer.

embitterment [ɪm'bɪtəmənt] n amertume *f*, aigreur *f*.

emblazon [ɪm'bleɪzən] vt (*extol*) chanter les louanges de; (*Her*) blasonner.

emblem ['embləm] n (*all senses*) emblème *m*.

emblematic [ˌemblə'mætɪk] adj emblématique.

embodiment [ɪm'bɒdɪmənt] n **a** incarnation *f*, personnification *f*. **to be the ~ of progress** incarner le progrès; **he is the ~ of kindness** c'est la bonté incarnée *or* personnifiée. **b** (*inclusion*) incorporation *f*.

embody [ɪm'bɒdɪ] vt **a** *spirit, quality* incarner; *one's thoughts, theories [person]* exprimer, concrétiser, formuler (*in* dans, en); *[work]* exprimer, donner forme à, mettre en application (*in* dans). **b** (*include*) *[person] ideas* résumer (*in* dans); *[work] ideas* renfermer; *[machine] features* réunir.

embolden [ɪm'bəʊldən] vt **a** enhardir. **to ~ sb to do** donner à qn le courage de faire, enhardir qn à faire. **b** (*Typ*) imprimer en gras (*or* mi-gras).

embolism ['embəlɪzəm] n embolie *f*.

emboss [ɪm'bɒs] vt *metal* travailler en relief, repousser, estamper; *leather, cloth* frapper, gaufrer; *velvet, paper* frapper.

embossed [ɪm'bɒst] adj *metal* estampé; *velvet, leather* frappé. **~ wallpaper** papier gaufré; **~ writing paper** papier à lettres à en-tête en relief.

embouchure [ˌɒmbʊ'ʃʊəʳ] n (*Mus*) embouchure *f*.

embrace [ɪm'breɪs] **1** vt **a** *hug* embrasser, étreindre, enlacer. **b** (*fig*) *religion* embrasser; *opportunity* saisir; *cause* épouser, embrasser; *offer* profiter de. **c** (*include*) *[person] theme, experience* embrasser; *topics, hypotheses* inclure; *[work] theme, period* embrasser, englober; *ideas, topics* renfermer, comprendre. **his charity ~s all mankind** sa charité s'étend à l'humanité tout entière; **an all-embracing review** une revue d'ensemble. **2** vi s'étreindre, s'embrasser. **3** n (*hug*) étreinte *f*, enlacement *m*. **they were standing in a tender ~** ils étaient tendrement enlacés; **he held her in a tender ~** il l'a enlacée tendrement.

embrasure [ɪm'breɪʒəʳ] n embrasure *f*.

embrocation [ˌembrəʊ'keɪʃən] n embrocation *f*.

embroider [ɪm'brɔɪdəʳ] **1** vt broder; (*fig: also* **~ on**) *facts, truth* broder sur; *story* enjoliver. **2** vi faire de la broderie.

embroidery [ɪm'brɔɪdərɪ] **1** n broderie *f*. **2** comp ▸**embroidery frame** métier *m or* tambour *m* à broder ▸**embroidery silk/thread** soie *f*/coton *m* à broder.

embroil [ɪm'brɔɪl] vt entraîner (*in* dans), mêler (*in* à). **to get (o.s.) ~ed in** se laisser entraîner dans, se trouver mêlé à.

embroilment [ɪm'brɔɪlmənt] n implication *f* (*in* dans), participation *f* (*in* à).

embryo ['embrɪəʊ] n (*lit, fig*) embryon *m*. **in ~** (*lit*) à l'état *or* au stade embryonnaire; (*fig*) en germe.

embryological [ˌembrɪə'lɒdʒɪkəl] adj embryologique.

embryologist [ˌembrɪ'ɒlədʒɪst] n embryologiste *mf*, embryologue *mf*.

embryology [ˌembrɪ'ɒlədʒɪ] n embryologie *f*.

embryonic [ˌembrɪ'ɒnɪk] adj embryonnaire; (*fig*) en germe.

embus [ɪm'bʌs] **1** vt (faire) embarquer dans un car. **2** vi s'embarquer dans un car.

emcee ['em'siː] (abbr of **master of ceremonies**) **1** n (*gen*) maître *m* de cérémonies; (*in show etc*) animateur *m*, meneur *m* de jeu. **2** vt *show etc* animer.

emend [ɪ'mend] vt *text* corriger.

emendation [ˌiːmen'deɪʃən] n correction *f*.

emerald ['emərəld] **1** n (*stone*) émeraude *f*; (*colour*) (vert *m*) émeraude *m*. **2** comp (*set with ~s*) (serti) d'émeraudes; (*also* **emerald green**) émeraude *inv* ▸**the Emerald Isle** l'île *f* d'Émeraude (*Irlande*) ▸**emerald necklace** collier *m* d'émeraudes.

emerge [ɪ'mɜːdʒ] vi (*gen*) apparaître, surgir (*from* de, *from behind* de derrière); (*from water*) émerger, surgir, s'élever (*from* de); (*from hole, room*) sortir, surgir (*from* de); (*from confined space*) déboucher, sortir (*from* de); (*fig*) *[truth]* émerger (*from* de), apparaître, se faire jour; *[facts]* émerger (*from* de), apparaître; *[difficulties]* surgir, s'élever, apparaître; *[new nation]* naître; *[theory, school of thought]* apparaître, naître. **it ~s that** il ressort que, il apparaît que.

emergence [ɪ'mɜːdʒəns] n *[truth, facts]* apparition *f*; *[theory, school of thought]* naissance *f*.

emergency [ɪ'mɜːdʒənsɪ] **1** n cas urgent, imprévu *m* (*NonC*). **in case of ~, in an ~** en cas d'urgence *or* d'imprévu *or* de nécessité; **to be prepared for any ~** être prêt à *or* parer à toute éventualité; **in this ~** dans cette situation critique, dans ces circonstances critiques; **state of ~** état *m* d'urgence; **to declare a state of ~** déclarer l'état d'urgence. **2** comp *measures, treatment, operation, repair* d'urgence; *brake, airstrip* de secours; (*improvised*) *mast* de fortune ▸**emergency blinkers** (*Aut*) feux *mpl* de détresse ▸**an emergency case** (*Med*) une urgence ▸**emergency centre** poste *m* de secours ▸**emergency exit** issue *f or* sortie *f* de secours ▸**emergency force** (*Mil*) force *f* d'urgence *or* d'intervention ▸**emergency landing** (*Aviat*) atterrissage forcé ▸**emergency powers** pouvoirs *mpl* extraordinaires ▸**emergency rations** vivres *mpl* de réserve ▸**emergency room** (*US Med*) = **emergency ward** ▸**emergency service** (*Med*) service *m* des urgences; (*Aut*) service de dépannage ▸**emergency services** (*Police etc*) ≃ police-secours *f* ▸**emergency tax** impôt *m* extraordinaire ▸**emergency telephone** téléphone *m* d'urgence ▸**emergency ward** (*Med*) salle *f* des urgences.

emergent [ɪ'mɜːdʒənt] adj qui émerge; (*Opt, Philos*) émergent. **~ nations** pays *mpl* en voie de développement.

emeritus [ɪ'merɪtəs] adj (*Univ*) **~ professor, professor ~** professeur *m* émérite† *or* honoraire.

emery ['emərɪ] n émeri *m*. **~ board** lime *f* à ongles; **~ cloth** toile *f* (d')émeri; **~ paper** papier *m* (d')émeri, papier de verre.

emetic [ɪ'metɪk] adj, n émétique (*m*).

emigrant ['emɪgrənt] **1** n (*just leaving*) émigrant(e) *m(f)*; (*established*) émigré(e) *m(f)*. **2** comp ▸**emigrant ship** bateau *m* d'émigrants. **3** adj *worker* émigré.

emigrate ['emɪgreɪt] vi émigrer.

emigration [ˌemɪ'greɪʃən] n émigration *f*.

émigré ['emɪgreɪ] n émigré(e) *m(f)*.

Emilia-Romagna [ɪ'miːlɪərəʊ'mɑːnjə] n Émilie-Romagne *f*.

eminence ['emɪnəns] n **a** (*NonC: distinction*) distinction *f*. **to achieve ~ in one's profession** parvenir à un rang éminent dans sa profession; **to win ~ as a surgeon** acquérir un grand renom comme chirurgien; **the ~ of his position** sa position éminente; (*Rel*) **His/Your E~** Son/Votre Éminence. **b** (*high ground*) éminence *f*, élévation *f*, butte *f*.

eminent ['emɪnənt] adj *person* éminent, très distingué; *quality, services* éminent, insigne. (*Rel*) **Most E~** éminentissime.

eminently ['emɪnəntlɪ] adv éminemment, parfaitement, admirablement. **~ suitable** qui convient admirablement *or* parfaitement; **an ~ respectable gentleman** un monsieur des plus respectables *or* éminemment respectable.

emir [e'mɪəʳ] n émir *m*.

emirate [e'mɪərɪt] n émirat *m*.

emissary ['emɪsərɪ] n émissaire *m*.

emission [ɪ'mɪʃən] **1** n **a** (*NonC*) (*release*) dégagement *m*. **b** (*substance(s)*) **~s** émissions *fpl*. **2** comp ▸**emission spectrum** spectre *m* d'émission.

emit [ɪ'mɪt] vt *gas, heat, smoke* émettre, dégager; *sparks* lancer, jeter; *light, electromagnetic waves, banknotes* émettre; *vapour, smell* dégager, répandre, exhaler; *lava* émettre, cracher, vomir; *cry* laisser échapper; *sound* rendre, émettre.

emitter [ɪ'mɪtəʳ] n (*Electronics*) émetteur *m*.

Emmanuel [ɪ'mænjʊəl] n Emmanuel *m*.

Emmy ['emɪ] n, pl **~s** *or* **Emmies** Oscar *m* de la télévision américaine.

emollient [ɪ'mɒlɪənt] adj, n émollient (*m*).

emolument [ɪ'mɒljʊmənt] n émoluments *mpl*, rémunération *f*; (*fee*) honoraires *mpl*; (*salary*) traitement *m*.

emote* [ɪ'məʊt] vi donner dans le sentiment* *or* dans le genre exalté*.

emotion [ɪ'məʊʃən] n **a** (*NonC*) émotion *f*. **voice full of ~** voix émue. **b** (*jealousy, love etc*) sentiment *m*.

emotional [ɪ'məʊʃənl] adj *shock, disturbance* émotif; *reaction* émotionnel, affectif; *moment* d'émotion profonde *or* intense; *story, writing* qui fait appel aux sentiments *or* à l'émotion. **he's very ~, he's a very ~ person** il est facilement ému *or* très sensible; **he was being very ~ or he was in a very ~ state about it** il prenait cela très à cœur, il laissait paraître son émotion *or* ses sentiments à ce sujet; **his ~ state** son état émotionnel.

emotionalism [ɪ'məʊʃnəlɪzəm] n émotivité *f*, sensiblerie *f* (*pej*). **the article was sheer ~** l'article n'était qu'un étalage de sensiblerie.

emotionally [ɪ'məʊʃnəlɪ] adv *speak* avec émotion. **~ worded article** article qui fait appel aux sentiments; **~ deprived** privé d'affection; **to be ~ disturbed** avoir des troubles émotifs *or* de l'affectivité; **an ~ dis-**

turbed child un(e) enfant caractériel(le); **he is ~ involved** ses sentiments sont en cause.
emotionless [ɪ'məʊʃənlɪs] adj *face etc* impassible, qui ne montre aucune émotion; *person* indifférent.
emotive [ɪ'məʊtɪv] adj *word, expression* chargé de connotations; *issue, subject* délicat.
empanel [ɪm'pænl] vt (*Jur*) *jury* constituer. **to ~ a juror** inscrire quelqu'un sur la liste du jury.
empanelment [ɪm'pænlmənt] n *[jury]* constitution *f*.
empathetic [ˌempə'θetɪk] adj compréhensif, ouvert à autrui.
empathetically [ˌempə'θetɪkəlɪ] adv avec compréhension *or* sympathie *or* empathie.
empathic [em'pæθɪk] adj = **empathetic.**
empathize ['empəθaɪz] vi sympathiser.
empathy ['empəθɪ] n empathie *f*, communion *f* d'idées (*or* de sentiments *etc*). **our ~ with the pain she was suffering** notre compassion *f* pour la douleur qui était la sienne.
emperor ['empərəʳ] 1 n empereur *m*. 2 comp ▸**emperor (moth)** paon *m* de nuit ▸**emperor penguin** manchot *m* empereur.
emphasis ['emfəsɪs] n, pl **emphases** ['emfəsiːz] (*in word, phrase*) accentuation *f*, accent *m* d'intensité; (*fig*) accent. **to speak with ~** parler sur un ton d'insistance; **the ~ is on the first syllable** l'accent d'intensité *or* l'accentuation tombe sur la première syllabe; **to lay ~ on a word** souligner un mot, insister sur *or* appuyer sur un mot; (*fig*) **to lay ~ on one aspect of ...** mettre l'accent sur *or* insister sur *or* attacher de l'importance à un aspect de ...; **the ~ is on sport** on accorde une importance particulière au sport; **this year the ~ is on femininity** cette année l'accent est sur la féminité; *see* **shift.**
emphasize ['emfəsaɪz] vt (*stress*) *word, fact, point* appuyer sur, insister sur, souligner; *syllable* insister sur, appuyer sur; (*draw attention to*) (*gen*) accentuer, *sth pleasant or flattering* mettre en valeur, faire valoir. **this point cannot be too strongly ~d** on ne saurait trop insister sur ce point; **I must ~ that ...** je dois souligner le fait que ...; **the long coat ~d his height** le long manteau faisait ressortir sa haute taille; **to ~ the eyes with mascara** mettre les yeux en valeur *or* souligner les yeux avec du mascara.
emphatic [ɪm'fætɪk] adj *tone, manner* énergique; *denial, speech, condemnation* catégorique, énergique; *person* vigoureux, énergique. **I am ~ about this point** j'insiste sur ce point, sur ce point je suis formel.
emphatically [ɪm'fætɪkəlɪ] adv *speak* énergiquement; *deny, refuse* catégoriquement, énergiquement. **yes, ~!** oui, absolument!; **~ no!** non, en aucun cas!, non, absolument pas!; **I must say this ~** je ne saurais trop insister sur ceci, sur ce point je suis formel.
emphysema [emfɪ'siːmə] n emphysème *m*.
empire ['empaɪəʳ] 1 n (*all senses*) empire *m*. 2 comp ▸**Empire** *costume, furniture* Empire *inv* ▸**empire-builder** (*fig*) bâtisseur *m* d'empires ▸**empire-building:** (*fig*) **he is empire-building, it is empire-building on his part** il joue les bâtisseurs d'empire ▸**the Empire State** (*US*) l'État *m* de New York.
empiric [em'pɪrɪk] 1 adj empirique. 2 n empiriste *mf*; (*Med*) empirique *m*.
empirical [em'pɪrɪkəl] adj empirique.
empirically [em'pɪrɪkəlɪ] adv empiriquement.
empiricism [em'pɪrɪsɪzəm] n empirisme *m*.
empiricist [em'pɪrɪsɪst] adj, n empiriste *(mf)*.
emplacement [ɪm'pleɪsmənt] n (*Mil*) emplacement *m* (*d'un canon*).
employ [ɪm'plɔɪ] 1 vt *person* employer (*as* comme); *means, method, process* employer, utiliser; *time* employer (*in or by doing* à faire); *force, cunning* recourir à, employer; *skill* faire usage de, employer. **to be ~ed in doing** être occupé à faire. 2 n: **to be in the ~ of** être employé par, travailler chez *or* pour; *[domestic staff]* être au service de.
employable [ɪm'plɔɪəbəl] adj *person* susceptible d'être employé; *skill* utilisable.
employee [ˌɪmplɔɪ'iː] n salarié(e) *m(f)*. (*US*) **~ stock ownership plans** actionnariat *m* ouvrier *or* des salariés.
employer [ɪm'plɔɪəʳ] n (*Comm, Ind; also domestic*) patron(ne) *m(f)*; (*Jur*) employeur *m*, -euse *f*. (*Ind: collectively*) **~s** le patronat; **~s' federation** syndicat patronal, fédération patronale; (*Insurance*) **~'s contribution** cotisation patronale.
employment [ɪm'plɔɪmənt] 1 n (*NonC: jobs collectively*) emploi *m* (*NonC*); (*a job*) emploi, travail *m*; (*modest*) place *f*; (*important*) situation *f*. **full ~** le plein emploi; **to take up ~** prendre un emploi; **in ~** qui travaille, qui a un emploi; **the numbers in ~** les actifs *mpl*; **without ~** sans emploi, au *or* en chômage; **to seek/find ~** chercher/trouver un emploi *or* du travail; **in sb's ~** employé par qn; *domestic staff* au service de qn; **conditions/place of ~** conditions *fpl*/lieu *m* de travail; (*Brit*) **Secretary (of State) for** *or* **Minister of E~**, (*US*) **Secretary for E~** ministre *m* de l'Emploi; **Department** *or* **Ministry of E~** ministère *m* de l'Emploi.
2 comp ▸**employment agency** agence *f* de placement ▸**employment exchange** (*Brit:* †) bourse *f* du travail ▸**employment office** (*Brit*) ≃ Agence *f* Nationale pour l'Emploi ▸**Employment Service** (*US*) agence *f* nationale pour l'emploi ▸**Employment Trainee** (*Brit*) jeune stagiaire *mf* (*dans le cadre du Plan Avenir Jeunes*) ▸**Employment Training** (*Brit*) ≃ Plan *m* Avenir Jeunes.
emporium [em'pɔːrɪəm] n, pl **~s** *or* **emporia** [em'pɔːrɪə] (*shop*) grand magasin, bazar *m*; (*market*) centre commercial, marché *m*.
empower [ɪm'paʊəʳ] vt: **to ~ sb to do** autoriser qn à faire; (*Jur*) habiliter qn à faire; **to be ~ed to do** avoir pleins pouvoirs pour faire.
empress ['emprɪs] n impératrice *f*.
emptiness ['emptɪnɪs] n vide *m*; *[pleasures etc]* vanité *f*. **the ~ of life** le vide de l'existence.
empty ['emptɪ] 1 adj *jar, box, car* vide; *house, room* inoccupé, vide; *lorry, truck* vide, sans chargement; *ship* lège; *post, job* vacant; *town, theatre* vide, désert; (*Ling*) vide. **~ of** vide de, dénué de, sans; **on an ~ stomach** à jeun; **my stomach is ~** j'ai le ventre *or* l'estomac creux; (*Prov*) **~ vessels make most noise** les grands diseurs ne sont pas les grands faiseurs; **~ words** paroles creuses, discours *mpl* creux; **~ talk** verbiage *m*; **~ promises** promesses *fpl* en l'air; **~ threats** menaces en l'air; (*fig*) **it's an ~ gesture** c'est un geste qui ne veut rien dire; **to look into ~ space** regarder dans le vide.
2 n: **empties** (*bottles*) bouteilles *fpl* vides; (*boxes etc*) boîtes *fpl or* emballages *mpl* vides; (*in pub etc*) verres *mpl* vides.
3 comp ▸**empty-handed** les mains vides; **to return empty-handed** revenir bredouille *or* les mains vides ▸**empty-headed** sot (*f* sotte), sans cervelle; **an empty-headed girl** une écervelée, une évaporée.
4 vt a *box, glass* vider; *pond, tank* vider, vidanger; *vehicle* décharger. **the burglars emptied the shop** les voleurs ont dévalisé *or* nettoyé* le magasin; **television has emptied the cinemas** la télévision a vidé les cinémas.
b (*also* **~ out**) *box, tank, pocket* vider; *bricks, books* sortir (*of, from* de, *into* dans); *liquid* vider (*of, from* de), verser (*of, from* de, *into* dans), transvaser (*into* dans).
5 vi *[water]* se déverser, s'écouler; *[river]* se jeter (*into* dans); *[building, container]* se vider.
empyema [ˌempaɪ'iːmə] n, pl **~s** *or* **empyemata** [ˌempaɪ'iːmətə] empyème *m*.
EMS [ˌiːem'es] n (abbr of **European Monetary System**) S.M.E. *m*.
emu ['iːmjuː] n émeu *m or* émou *m*.
emulate ['emjʊleɪt] vt (*imitate*) imiter, essayer d'égaler; (*successfully*) être l'émule de.
emulation [ˌemjʊ'leɪʃən] n émulation *f*.
emulator ['emjʊleɪtəʳ] n (*Comput*) émulateur *m*.
emulsifier [e'mʌlsɪˌfaɪəʳ] n émulsifiant *m*.
emulsify [ɪ'mʌlsɪfaɪ] vti émulsionner.
emulsion [ɪ'mʌlʃən] n émulsion *f*. **~ (paint)** peinture *f* mate *or* à émulsion.
en [en] n (*Typ*) n *m*, lettre moyenne.
enable [ɪ'neɪbl] vt: **to ~ sb to do** (*give opportunity*) permettre à qn de faire, donner à qn la possibilité de faire; (*give means*) permettre à qn de faire, donner à qn le moyen de faire, mettre qn à même de faire; (*Jur etc: authorize*) habiliter qn à faire, donner pouvoir à qn de faire; **enabling legislation** loi habilitante.
enact [ɪ'nækt] vt a (*Jur*) (*make into law*) promulguer, donner force de loi à; (*decree*) décréter, ordonner, arrêter. **as by law ~ed** aux termes de la loi, selon la loi; **~ing terms** dispositif *m* d'un jugement. b (*perform*) *play* représenter, jouer; *part* jouer. (*fig*) **the drama which was ~ed yesterday** le drame qui s'est déroulé hier.
enactment [ɪ'næktmənt] n promulgation *f*.
enamel [ɪ'næməl] 1 n a (*NonC: most senses*) émail *m*. **nail ~** vernis *m* à ongles (laqué). b (*Art*) **an ~** un émail. 2 vt émailler. 3 comp *saucepan, ornament, brooch* en émail ▸**enamel paint** peinture laquée, Ripolin *m* ® ▸**enamel painting** (*Art*) peinture *f* sur émail ▸**enamelware** articles *mpl* en métal émaillé.
enamelled [ɪ'næməld] adj *brooch* en émail; *metal* émaillé; *saucepan* en émail, émaillé.
enamelling [ɪ'næməlɪŋ] n émaillage *m*.
enamoured, (*US*) **enamored** [ɪ'næməd] adj: **to be ~ of** *person* être amoureux *or* épris de, s'être amouraché de (*pej*); *thing* être enchanté de, être séduit par; **she was not ~ of the idea** l'idée ne l'enchantait pas.
encamp [ɪn'kæmp] 1 vi camper. 2 vt faire camper.
encampment [ɪn'kæmpmənt] n campement *m*.
encapsulate [ɪn'kæpsjʊleɪt] vt (*Pharm, Space*) mettre en capsule; (*fig*) renfermer, résumer.
encase [ɪn'keɪs] vt (*contain*) enfermer, enchâsser (*in* dans); (*cover*) entourer, recouvrir (*in* de).
encash [ɪn'kæʃ] vt (*Brit*) *cheque* encaisser, toucher.
encashable [ɪn'kæʃəbl] adj (*Brit*) encaissable.
encashment [ɪn'kæʃmənt] n (*Brit*) encaissement *m*.
encaustic [en'kɔːstɪk] 1 adj *painting* encaustique; *tile, brick* céramique. 2 n (*painting*) encaustique *f*.
encephalic [ensɪ'fælɪk] adj encéphalique.
encephalitis [ˌensefə'laɪtɪs] n encéphalite *f*.
encephalogram [en'sefələgræm] n encéphalogramme *m*.
encephalon [en'sefəlɒn] n, pl **encephala** [en'sefələ] encéphale *m*.
enchain [ɪn'tʃeɪn] vt enchaîner; (*fig*) enchaîner, retenir.
enchant [ɪn'tʃɑːnt] vt (*put under spell*) enchanter, ensorceler,

charmer; (*delight*) enchanter, ravir, charmer. **the ~ed wood** le bois enchanté.
enchanter [ɪn'tʃɑːntəʳ] n enchanteur *m*.
enchanting [ɪn'tʃɑːntɪŋ] adj enchanteur (*f* -eresse), charmant, ravissant.
enchantingly [ɪn'tʃɑːntɪŋlɪ] adv *smile, dance* d'une façon ravissante. **she is ~ beautiful** elle est belle à ravir.
enchantment [ɪn'tʃɑːntmənt] n (*see* **enchant**) enchantement *m*; ensorcellement *m*; ravissement *m*.
enchantress [ɪn'tʃɑːntrɪs] n enchanteresse *f*.
enchilada* [ˌentʃɪ'lædə] n (*US*) **big ~** huile* *f*, grosse légume*, gros bonnet*.
encircle [ɪn'sɜːkl] vt (*gen*) entourer; *[troops, men, police]* encercler, cerner, entourer; *[walls, belt, bracelet]* entourer, ceindre.
encirclement [ɪn'sɜːklmənt] n encerclement *m*.
encircling [ɪn'sɜːklɪŋ] 1 n encerclement *m*. 2 adj qui encercle. **~ movement** manœuvre *f* d'encerclement.
enc(l). (abbr of **enclosure(s)**) P.J., pièce(s) jointe(s).
enclave ['enkleɪv] n enclave *f*.
enclitic [ɪn'klɪtɪk] n enclitique *m*.
enclose [ɪn'kləʊz] vt a (*fence in*) enclore, clôturer; (*surround*) entourer, ceindre (*with* de); (*Rel*) cloîtrer. **to ~ within** enfermer dans; **an ~d space** un espace clos; **an ~d community** une communauté retirée; (*Rel*) **~d order** ordre cloîtré. b (*with letter etc*) joindre (*in, with* à). **to ~ sth in a letter** joindre qch à une lettre, inclure qch dans une lettre; **letter enclosing a receipt** lettre contenant un reçu; **please find ~d** veuillez trouver ci-joint *or* sous ce pli; **the ~d cheque** le chèque ci-joint *or* ci-inclus.
enclosure [ɪn'kləʊʒəʳ] 1 n a (*NonC*) *[land]* fait *m* de clôturer; (*Brit Hist*) enclosure *f*, clôture *f* des terres. b (*document etc enclosed*) pièce jointe, document ci-joint *or* ci-inclus; (*ground enclosed*) enclos *m*, enceinte *f*; *[monastery]* clôture *f*; (*fence etc*) enceinte, clôture. *[racecourse]* **the ~** le pesage; **the public ~** la pelouse; **royal ~** enceinte réservée à la famille royale. 2 comp ►**enclosure wall** mur *m* d'enceinte.
encode [ɪn'kəʊd] vti coder; (*Comput*) coder, encoder; (*Ling*) encoder.
encoder [ɪn'kəʊdəʳ] n (*Comput*) encodeur *m*.
encoding [ɪn'kəʊdɪŋ] n *[message]* codage *m*; (*Comput, Ling*) encodage *m*.
encomium [ɪn'kəʊmɪəm] n, pl **~s** *or* **encomia** [ɪn'kəʊmɪə] panégyrique *m*, éloge *m*.
encompass [ɪn'kʌmpəs] vt (*lit*) entourer, ceindre, environner (*with* de); (*fig*) (*include*) contenir, inclure; (*beset*) assaillir.
encore [ɒŋ'kɔːʳ] 1 excl bis! 2 ['ɒŋkɔːʳ] n bis *m*. **to call for an ~** bisser, crier "bis"; **the pianist gave an ~** le pianiste a joué un (morceau en) bis. 3 vt *song, act* bisser.
encounter [ɪn'kaʊntəʳ] 1 vt *person* rencontrer (à l'improviste), tomber sur; *enemy* affronter, rencontrer; *opposition* se heurter à; *difficulties* affronter, rencontrer, éprouver; *danger* affronter. **to ~ enemy fire** essuyer le feu de l'ennemi. 2 n rencontre *f* (inattendue); (*Mil*) rencontre, engagement *m*, combat *m*. 3 comp ►**encounter group** (*Psych*) atelier relationnel.
encourage [ɪn'kʌrɪdʒ] vt *person* encourager; *arts, industry, projects, development, growth* encourager, favoriser; *bad habits* encourager, flatter. **to ~ sb to do** encourager *or* inciter *or* pousser qn à faire; **to ~ sb in his belief that ...** confirmer qn dans sa croyance que ..., encourager qn à croire que ...; **to ~ sb in his desire to do** encourager le désir de qn de faire.
encouragement [ɪn'kʌrɪdʒmənt] n encouragement *m*; (*to a deed*) incitation *f* (*to* à); (*support*) encouragement, appui *m*, soutien *m*.
encouraging [ɪn'kʌrɪdʒɪŋ] adj encourageant.
encouragingly [ɪn'kʌrɪdʒɪŋlɪ] adv *speak etc* d'une manière encourageante. **we had ~ little difficulty** le peu de difficulté rencontré a été encourageant *or* nous a encouragés.
encroach [ɪn'krəʊtʃ] vi (*on sb's land, time, rights*) empiéter (*on* sur). **the sea is ~ing on the land** la mer gagne (du terrain); (*US fig*) **to ~ on sb's turf** marcher sur les plates-bandes de qn.
encroachment [ɪn'krəʊtʃmənt] n empiètement *m* (*on* sur).
encrust [ɪn'krʌst] vt (*with earth, cement*) encroûter, couvrir (d'une croûte) (*with* de); (*with jewels etc*) incruster (*with* de).
encrustation [ɪnkrʌ'steɪʃən] n *[earth, cement etc]* encroûtement *m*.
encumber [ɪn'kʌmbəʳ] vt *person, room* encombrer (*with* de). **estate ~ed with debts** succession grevée de dettes.
encumbrance [ɪn'kʌmbrəns] n (*burden*) fardeau *m*; (*inhibiting career etc*) handicap *m*, gêne *f*; (*furniture, skirts etc*) gêne; (*mortgage*) charge *f* hypothécaire. **to be an ~ to sb** être un fardeau pour qn; handicaper qn; gêner qn, être une gêne pour qn; *[heavy parcel]* embarrasser qn.
encyclical [ɪn'sɪklɪkəl] adj, n encyclique (*f*).
encyclop(a)edia [ɪnˌsaɪkləʊ'piːdɪə] n encyclopédie *f*; *see* **walking**.
encyclop(a)edic [ɪnˌsaɪkləʊ'piːdɪk] adj encyclopédique.
encyclop(a)edist [enˌsaɪkləʊ'piːdɪst] n encyclopédiste *m*.
end [end] 1 n a (*farthest part*) *[road, string, table, branch, finger]* bout *m*, extrémité *f*; *[procession, line of people]* bout, queue *f*; *[garden, estate]* bout, limite *f*. **the southern ~ of the town** l'extrémité sud de la ville; **the fourth from the ~** le quatrième avant la fin; **from ~ to ~** d'un bout à l'autre, de bout en bout; **on ~** debout (*see also* **1b**); **to stand a box *etc* on ~** mettre une caisse *etc* debout; **his hair stood on ~** ses cheveux se dressèrent sur sa tête; **the ships collided ~ on** les bateaux se sont heurtés de front *or* nez à nez; **~ to ~** bout à bout; **to the ~s of the earth** jusqu'au bout du monde; (*Sport*) **to change ~s** changer de côté *or* de camp; (*fig*) **to make (both) ~s meet** (faire) joindre les deux bouts; (*fig*) **the ~ of the road** la fin du voyage; (*fig*) **he can't see beyond the ~ of his nose** il ne voit pas plus loin que le bout de son nez; (*fig*) **to begin at the wrong ~** s'y prendre mal *or* par le mauvais bout; **to keep one's ~ up*** se défendre (assez bien); *see* **hair, loose, stick** *etc*.
b (*conclusion*) *[story, chapter, month]* fin *f*; *[work]* achèvement *m*; *[efforts]* fin, aboutissement *m*; *[meeting]* fin, issue *f*. **to read a book to the very ~** lire un livre de A à Z *or* jusqu'à la dernière page; **it succeeded in the ~** cela a réussi à la fin *or* finalement *or* en fin de compte; **he got used to it in the ~** il a fini par s'y habituer; **in the ~ they decided to use ...** ils ont décidé en définitive *or* ils ont fini par décider d'employer ...; **at the ~ of the day** à la fin de la journée; (*fig*) en fin de compte; **at the ~ of December** à la fin de décembre; (*Comm*) fin décembre; **at the ~ of the century** à *or* vers la fin du siècle; **at the ~ of the winter** à la fin *or* au sortir de l'hiver; **at the ~ of three weeks** au bout de trois semaines; **the ~ of a session** la clôture d'une séance; **the ~ of the world** la fin du monde; (*fig*) **it's not the ~ of the world*** ce n'est pas une catastrophe, ce n'est pas la fin du monde; **to *or* until the ~ of time** jusqu'à la fin des temps; **that was the ~ of my watch** ma montre était fichue*; **that was the ~ of that!** on n'en a plus reparlé; **that's the ~ of the matter, that's an ~ to the matter** un point c'est tout, on n'en parle plus; **that was the ~ of him** on n'a plus reparlé de lui, on ne l'a plus revu; (*fig*) **there is no ~ to it all** cela n'en finit plus; **to be at an ~** *[action]* être terminé *or* fini; *[time, period]* être écoulé; *[material, supplies]* être épuisé; **to be at the ~ of one's patience/strength** être à bout de patience/forces; **my patience is at an ~** ma patience est à bout; (*fig*) **to be at the ~ of one's tether** être à bout de nerfs; **to bring to an ~** *speech, writing* achever, conclure; *work* terminer; *relations* mettre fin à; **to come to an ~** prendre fin, se terminer, arriver à son terme (*liter, frm*); **to get to the ~ of** *supplies, food* finir; *work, essay* venir à bout de; *troubles* (se) sortir de; *holiday* arriver à la fin de; **to put an ~ to, to make an ~ of** mettre fin à, mettre un terme à; **to put an ~ to one's life** mettre fin à ses jours; (*euph, liter*) **to be nearing one's ~** être à (l'article de) la mort, se mourir (*liter*); **to come to a bad ~** mal finir; **we shall never hear the ~ of it** on n'a pas fini d'en entendre parler; **there was no ~* of ...** il y avait une masse* de *or* un tas de *or* énormément de ...; **it pleased her no ~*** cela lui a fait un plaisir fou *or* énorme; **that's the (bitter) ~!*** il ne manquait plus que cela!, c'est la fin de tout!, c'est le comble!; (*US: excellent*) **it's the ~!** c'est super* *or* terrible*; **he's (just) the ~!*** c'est une vraie plaie!*; **for two hours on ~** deux heures de suite *or* d'affilée; **for days on ~** jour après jour, pendant des jours et des jours; **for several days on ~** pendant plusieurs jours de suite; *see* **bitter, meet[1], sticky, untimely**.
c (*remnant*) *[rope, candle]* bout *m*; *[loaf, meat]* reste *m*, restant *m*; *see* **cigarette** *etc*.
d (*purpose*) but *m*, fin *f*, dessein *m*. **with this ~ in view** dans ce dessein *or* but, à cette fin, avec cet objectif en vue; **an ~ in itself** une fin en soi; **to no ~** en vain; (*Prov*) **the ~ justifies the means** la fin justifie les moyens (*Prov*).
e (*US Ftbl*) ailier *m*.
2 comp ►**end-all** *see* **be 5** ►**end game** (*Cards, Chess*) fin *f* de partie, phase finale du jeu ►**end house: the end house in the street** la dernière maison de la rue ►**end line** (*Basketball*) ligne *f* de fond ►**endpapers** (*Typ*) gardes *fpl*, pages *fpl* de garde ►**end product** (*Comm, Ind*) produit fini; (*fig*) résultat *m* ►**end result** résultat final *or* définitif ►**end run** (*US fig*) moyen détourné ►**end table** (*US*) table *f* basse ►**end user** (*Comput etc*) utilisateur final ►**endways** *see* **endways**.
3 vt *work* finir, achever, terminer; *period of service* accomplir; *speech, writing* conclure, achever (*with* avec, par); *broadcast, series* terminer (*with* par); *speculation, gossip, rumour* mettre fin à, mettre un terme à; *quarrel, war* mettre fin à, faire cesser. **to ~ one's days** finir *or* achever ses jours; **to ~ it all** en finir (avec la vie); **this is the dictionary to ~ all dictionaries*** c'est ce qu'il y a de mieux comme dictionnaire; **that was the lie to ~ all lies!*** comme mensonge on ne fait pas mieux!* (*iro*).
4 vi *[speech, programme, holiday, marriage, series]* finir, se terminer, s'achever; *[road]* se terminer; *[insurance cover etc]* expirer, arriver à échéance. **the winter is ~ing** l'hiver tire à sa fin; **where's it all going to ~?, how will it all ~?** comment tout cela finira-t-il?; **word ~ing in an s/ in -re** mot se terminant par un s/en -re; **stick which ~s in a point** bâton qui se termine en pointe; **it ~ed in a fight** cela s'est terminé par une bagarre*; **the plan ~ed in failure** le projet s'est soldé par un échec; **the film ~s with the heroine dying** le film se termine par la mort de l'héroïne.
►**end off** vt sep finir, achever, terminer.
►**end up** vi a finir, se terminer, s'achever (*in* en, par); *[road]* aboutir (*in* à). **it ended up in a fight** cela s'est terminé par une *or* en bagarre*.

b (*finally arrive at*) se retrouver, échouer (*in* à, en); (*finally become*) finir par devenir. **he ended up in Paris** il s'est retrouvé à Paris; **you'll end up in jail** tu vas finir *or* te retrouver *or* échouer en prison; **he ended up a rich man** il a fini (par devenir) riche; **the book she had planned ended up (being) an article** le livre qu'elle avait projeté a fini par n'être qu'un article.

endanger [ɪn'deɪndʒəʳ] vt *life, interests, reputation* mettre en danger, exposer; *future, chances, health* compromettre. **~ed species** espèce *f* en voie d'extinction.

endear [ɪn'dɪəʳ] vt faire aimer (*to* de). **this ~ed him to the whole country** cela l'a fait aimer de tout le pays; **what ~s him to me is ...** ce qui me plaît en lui c'est ...; **to ~ o.s. to everybody** se faire aimer de tout le monde; **that speech didn't ~ him to the public** ce discours ne l'a pas fait apprécier du public.

endearing [ɪn'dɪərɪŋ] adj *smile* engageant; *personality* attachant, qui inspire l'affection; *characteristic* (qui rend) sympathique. **she's a very ~ person** elle est très attachante *or* sympathique.

endearingly [ɪn'dɪərɪŋlɪ] adv de façon engageante *or* attachante *or* sympathique.

endearment [ɪn'dɪəmənt] n: **~s** (*words*) paroles affectueuses *or* tendres; (*acts*) marques *fpl* d'affection; **term of ~** terme *m* d'affection; **words of ~** paroles *fpl* tendres.

endeavour, (*US*) **endeavor** [ɪn'devəʳ] 1 n effort *m*, tentative *f* (*to do* pour faire). **to make an ~ to do** essayer *or* s'efforcer de faire, se donner la peine de faire; **he made every ~ to go** il a fait tout son possible pour y aller, il a tout fait pour y aller; **in an ~ to please** dans l'intention de plaire, dans un effort pour plaire. 2 vi essayer, s'efforcer, tenter (*to do* de faire), (*stronger*) s'évertuer, s'appliquer (*to do* à faire).

endemic [en'demɪk] 1 adj endémique. 2 n endémie *f*.

ending ['endɪŋ] n a *[story, book]* fin *f*, dénouement *m*; *[events]* fin, conclusion *f*; *[day]* fin; (*outcome*) issue *f*; *[speech etc]* conclusion. **story with a happy ~** histoire qui finit bien; *see* **nerve**. b (*Ling*) terminaison *f*, désinence *f*. **feminine ~** terminaison féminine; **accusative ~** flexion *f* de l'accusatif.

endive ['endaɪv] n (*curly*) chicorée *f*; (*smooth, flat*) endive *f*.

endless ['endlɪs] adj *road* interminable, sans fin; *plain* sans bornes, infini; *speech, vigil* interminable, qui n'en finit plus, sans fin; *times, attempts* innombrable, sans nombre; *discussion, argument* continuel, incessant; *chatter* intarissable; *patience* infini; *resources, supplies* inépuisable; *possibilities* illimité, sans limites. **this job is ~** c'est à n'en plus finir, on n'en voit pas la fin; (*Tech*) **~ belt** courroie *f* sans fin.

endlessly ['endlɪslɪ] adv *stretch out* interminablement, sans fin, à perte de vue; *chatter, argue* continuellement, interminablement; *speak* sans cesse, continuellement; *repeat* sans cesse, infatigablement. **~ kind/willing** d'une bonté/d'une bonne volonté à toute épreuve.

endocarditis [endəʊkɑː'daɪtɪs] n endocardite *f*.

endocardium [endəʊ'kɑːdɪəm] n, pl **endocardia** [endəʊ'kɑːdɪə] endocarde *m*.

endocarp ['endəkɑːp] n endocarpe *m*.

endocrine ['endəʊkraɪn] adj endocrine. **~ gland** glande *f* endocrine.

endocrinologist [ˌendəʊkraɪ'nɒlədʒɪst] n endocrinologue *mf*, endocrinologiste *mf*.

endogamy [en'dɒgəmɪ] n (*Sociol*) endogamie *f*.

endogenous [en'dɒdʒɪnəs] adj *factor* endogène.

endolymph ['endəʊˌlɪmf] n (*Anat*) endolymphe *f*.

endometrium [ˌendəʊ'miːtrɪəm] n, pl **endometria** [ˌendəʊ'miːtrɪə] (*Anat*) endomètre *m*.

endomorph ['endəʊˌmɔːf] n (*Anat*) endomorphe *mf*.

endorphin [ˌen'dɔːfɪn] n endorphine *f*.

endorse [ɪn'dɔːs] vt (*sign*) *document, cheque* endosser; (*guarantee*) *bill* avaliser; (*approve*) *claim, candidature* appuyer; *opinion* souscrire à, adhérer à; *action, decision* approuver, sanctionner. **to ~ an insurance policy** faire un avenant à une police d'assurance; (*Brit Jur*) **to ~ a driving licence** ≃ porter une contravention au permis de conduire; **he has had his licence ~d** une contravention a été portée à son permis de conduire.

endorsee [ˌɪndɔː'siː] n endossataire *mf*, bénéficiaire *mf* d'un endossement.

endorsement [ɪn'dɔːsmənt] n (*see* **endorse**) endossement *m*, endos *m*; aval *m*; appui *m* (*of* de); adhésion *f* (*of* à); approbation *f*, sanction *f* (*of* de); *[insurance policy]* avenant *m* (*to* à). **~ advertising** *technique publicitaire faisant intervenir des personnalités connues;* (*Brit Jur: on driving licence*) **she has had 2 ~s** ≃ elle a eu 2 contraventions portées à son permis.

endoscope ['endəʊˌskəʊp] n endoscope *m*.

endoscopy [ˌen'dɒskəpɪ] n endoscopie *f*.

endoskeleton [ˌendəʊ'skelɪtən] n squelette *m* interne, endosquelette *m*.

endothermic [ˌendəʊ'θɜːmɪk] adj endothermique.

endow [ɪn'daʊ] vt *institution, church* doter (*with* de); *hospital bed, prize, chair* fonder. (*fig*) **to be ~ed with brains/beauty** *etc* être doté d'intelligence/de beauté *etc*.

endowment [ɪn'daʊmənt] 1 n (*see* **endow**) dotation *f*, fondation *f*. 2 comp ►**endowment assurance, endowment insurance** assurance *f* à capital différé ►**endowment mortgage** hypothèque *f* liée à une assurance-vie ►**endowment policy** = **endowment assurance**.

endue [ɪn'djuː] vt revêtir, douer (*with* de).

endurable [ɪn'djʊərəbl] adj supportable, tolérable, endurable.

endurance [ɪn'djʊərəns] 1 n endurance *f*, résistance *f*. **to have great powers of ~ against pain** être dur au mal; **he has come to the end of his ~** il n'en peut plus, il est à bout; **beyond ~, past ~** intolérable, au-delà de ce que l'on peut supporter; **tried beyond ~** excédé. 2 comp ►**endurance race** (*Sport*) épreuve *f* de fond ►**endurance test** (*Sport, Tech, fig*) épreuve *f* de résistance; (*Aut*) épreuve d'endurance.

endure [ɪn'djʊəʳ] 1 vt *pain, insults* supporter, endurer, tolérer; *domination* subir; (*put up with*) supporter, souffrir (*doing* de faire). **she can't ~ being teased** elle ne peut pas supporter *or* souffrir qu'on la taquine (*subj*); **I cannot ~ him** je ne peux pas le supporter *or* le voir *or* le sentir*. 2 vi *[building, peace, friendship]* durer; *[book, memory]* rester.

enduring [ɪn'djʊərɪŋ] adj *friendship, fame, peace* durable; *government, regime* stable; *illness, hardship* persistant, qui persiste.

endways ['endweɪz] adv, **endwise** ['endwaɪz] adv (*~ on*) en long, par le petit bout; (*end to end*) bout à bout.

ENEA [ˌiːeniː'eɪ] n (**abbr of European Nuclear Energy Authority**) AENE *f*.

enema ['enɪmə] n, pl **~s** *or* **enemata** ['enɪmətə] (*act*) lavement *m*; (*apparatus*) poire *f or* bock *m* à lavement.

enemy ['enəmɪ] 1 n (*Mil*) ennemi *m*; (*gen*) ennemi(e) *m(f)*, adversaire *mf*. **to make enemies** se faire *or* s'attirer des ennemis; **to make an ~ of sb** (se) faire un ennemi de qn; **he is his own worst ~** il est son pire ennemi, il n'a de pire ennemi que lui-même; **they are deadly enemies** ils sont à couteaux tirés, ils sont ennemis jurés; (*fig*) **corruption is the ~ of the state** la corruption est l'ennemie de l'État; *see* **public**.

2 comp *tanks, forces, tribes* ennemi; *morale, strategy* de l'ennemi ►**enemy action** attaque ennemie; **killed by enemy action** tombé à l'ennemi ►**enemy alien** ressortissant(e) *m(f)* d'un pays ennemi ►**enemy-occupied territory** territoire occupé par l'ennemi.

energetic [ˌenə'dʒetɪk] 1 adj a *person* énergique, plein d'énergie, actif. **~ children** enfants pleins d'énergie *or* débordants d'activité; **I've had a very ~ day** je me suis beaucoup dépensé aujourd'hui; **do you feel ~ enough to come for a walk?** est-ce que tu te sens assez d'attaque* pour faire une promenade? b *measure* énergique, rigoureux; *denial, refusal* énergique, vigoureux; *government* énergique, à poigne. 2 n: **~s** (*NonC*) énergétique *f*.

energetically [ˌenə'dʒetɪkəlɪ] adv *move, behave* énergiquement, avec énergie, avec vigueur; *speak, reply* avec force, avec vigueur.

energize ['enədʒaɪz] vt *person* stimuler, donner de l'énergie à; (*Elec*) alimenter (en courant).

energizing ['enədʒaɪzɪŋ] adj *food* énergétique.

energy ['enədʒɪ] 1 n (*gen*) énergie *f*, vigueur *f*; (*Phys*) énergie. **potential/kinetic ~** énergie potentielle/cinétique; **he has a lot of ~** il a beaucoup d'énergie, il est très dynamique; (*Brit*) **Secretary (of State) for** *or* **Minister of E~** ministre *m* de l'Énergie; **Department** *or* **Ministry of E~** ministère *m or* direction *f* de l'Énergie; **in order to save ~** pour faire des économies d'énergie; **with all one's ~** de toutes ses forces; **to put all one's ~** *or* **energies into sth/into doing** se consacrer tout entier à qch/à faire, appliquer toute son énergie à qch/à faire; **I haven't the ~ to go back** je n'ai pas l'énergie *or* le courage de retourner; **he seems to have no ~ these days** il semble sans énergie *or* à plat* en ce moment; **don't waste your ~** ne te fatigue pas*, ne te donne pas du mal pour rien; **he used up all his ~** *or* **energies doing it** il a épuisé ses forces à le faire; *see* **atomic** *etc*.

2 comp ►**energy conservation** les économies *fpl* d'énergie ►**energy conversion** conversion *f* de l'énergie ►**energy crisis** crise *f* énergétique *or* de l'énergie ►**energy-giving** *food etc* énergétique ►**energy-intensive industry** industrie grande consommatrice d'énergie ►**energy level** niveau *m or* état *m* énergétique ►**energy-saving** n économies *fpl* d'énergie ◊ adj d'économie d'énergie.

enervate ['enɜːveɪt] vt affaiblir.

enervating ['enɜːveɪtɪŋ] adj débilitant, amollissant.

enfeeble [ɪn'fiːbl] vt affaiblir.

enfeeblement [ɪn'fiːblmənt] n affaiblissement *m*.

enfilade [ˌenfɪ'leɪd] (*Mil*) 1 vt soumettre à un tir d'enfilade. 2 n tir *m* d'enfilade.

enfold [ɪn'fəʊld] vt envelopper (*in* de). **to ~ sb in one's arms** entourer qn de ses bras, étreindre qn.

enforce [ɪn'fɔːs] vt *decision, policy* mettre en application *or* en vigueur, appliquer; *ruling, law* faire obéir *or* respecter; *discipline* imposer; *argument, rights* faire valoir. **to ~ obedience** se faire obéir.

enforceable [ɪn'fɔːsɪbl] adj *law, rules* exécutoire, applicable.

enforced [ɪn'fɔːst] adj forcé, obligé, obligatoire.

enforcement [ɪn'fɔːsmənt] n *[decision, policy, law]* mise *f* en application *or* en vigueur; *[discipline]* imposition *f*. (*Jur*) **~ action** mesure coercitive; (*Jur, Fin*) **~ of securities** réalisation *f* des sûretés; *see* **law**.

enfranchise [ɪn'frænʧaɪz] vt (*give vote to*) accorder le droit de vote à, admettre au suffrage; (*set free*) affranchir.

enfranchisement [ɪn'frænʧaɪzmənt] **n** (*see* **enfranchise**) admission *f* au suffrage; affranchissement *m*.

ENG [ˌiːen'dʒiː] **n** (**abbr of electronic news gathering**) *see* **electronic**.

engage [ɪn'geɪdʒ] **1 vt** *servant* engager; *workers* embaucher; *lawyer* prendre; (†) *room* retenir, réserver; (*fig*) *sb's attention, interest* éveiller, retenir; (*Mil*) *the enemy* engager le combat avec, attaquer; (*Tech*) engager; *gearwheels* mettre en prise. **to ~ sb in conversation** engager la *or* lier conversation avec qn; (*frm*) **to ~ o.s. to do** s'engager à faire; (*Aut*) **to ~ a gear** engager une vitesse; **to ~ gear** mettre en prise; **to ~ the clutch** embrayer.
2 vi *[person]* s'engager (*to do* à faire); (*Tech*) *[wheels]* s'engrener, s'engager, se mettre en prise; *[bolt]* s'enclencher. **the clutch didn't ~** l'embrayage n'a pas fonctionné; **to ~ in** *politics, transaction* se lancer dans; *controversy* s'engager dans, s'embarquer dans; **to ~ in a discussion/in a conversation/in competition** entrer en discussion/en conversation/en concurrence (*with* avec).

engaged [ɪn'geɪdʒd] **adj a** (*betrothed*) fiancé (*to* à, avec). **to get ~** se fiancer (*to* à, avec); **the ~ couple** les fiancés. **b** *seat* occupé, pris, retenu; *taxi* pris, pas libre; (*Brit*) *toilet* occupé; (*Brit Telec*) *number, line* occupé; *person* occupé, pris. **Mr Feri is ~ just now** M Feri est occupé *or* est pris *or* n'est pas libre en ce moment; **to be ~ in doing** être occupé à faire; **to be ~ on sth** s'occuper de qch; (*Brit Telec*) **the ~ signal** *or* **tone** la tonalité occupé *inv or* pas libre.

engagement [ɪn'geɪdʒmənt] **1 n a** (*appointment*) rendez-vous *m inv*; *[actor etc]* engagement *m*. **public ~** obligation officielle; **previous ~** engagement antérieur; **I have an ~** j'ai un rendez-vous, je ne suis pas libre, je suis pris. **b** (*betrothal*) fiançailles *fpl*. **to break off one's ~** rompre ses fiançailles. **c** (*frm: undertaking*) engagement *m*, obligation *f*, promesse *f*. **to give an ~ to do sth** s'engager à faire qch. **d** (*Mil*) action *f*, combat *m*, engagement *m*. **2 comp ▸engagement book** agenda *m* **▸engagement ring** bague *f* de fiançailles.

engaging [ɪn'geɪdʒɪŋ] **adj** *smile, look, tone* engageant; *personality* attirant, attachant.

engender [ɪn'dʒendəʳ] **vt** engendrer (*fig*), produire (*fig*).

engine ['endʒɪn] **1 n** (*Tech*) machine *f*, moteur *m*; *[ship]* machine; (*Rail*) locomotive *f*; (*Aut, Aviat*) moteur. (*Rail*) **to sit facing the ~/with one's back to the ~** être assis dans le sens de la marche/le sens contraire à la marche; *see* **jet**[1] *etc*. **2 comp ▸engine block** (*Aut*) bloc-moteur *m* **▸engine driver** (*Brit Rail*) mécanicien *m* **▸engine house** (*US Rail*) = **engine shed ▸engine room** (*Naut*) salle *f or* chambre *f* des machines **▸engine shed** (*Brit Rail*) rotonde *f* **▸engine unit** bloc-moteur *m*.

-engined ['endʒɪnd] **adj ending in comps: twin-engined** à deux moteurs, bimoteur; *see* **single** *etc*.

engineer [ˌendʒɪ'nɪəʳ] **1 n a** (*professional*) ingénieur *m*; (*tradesman*) technicien *m*; (*repairer: for domestic appliances etc*) dépanneur *m*, réparateur *m*. **woman ~** (femme *f*) ingénieur; (*Mil*) **the E~s** le génie; (*US*) **~ of mines** ingénieur des mines; **the TV ~ came** le dépanneur est venu pour la télé*; *see* **civil, highway** *etc*. **b** (*Merchant Navy, US Rail*) mécanicien *m*; (*Navy*) mécanicien de la marine; *see* **chief**. **2 vt** *sb's dismissal etc, scheme, plan* machiner, manigancer.

engineering [ˌendʒɪ'nɪərɪŋ] **1 n a** (*NonC*) ingénierie *f*, engineering *m*. **to study ~** faire des études d'ingénieur; *see* **civil, electrical, mechanical** *etc*. **b** (*fig, gen pej*) machination(s) *f(pl)*, manœuvre(s) *f(pl)*. **2 comp ▸engineering consultant** ingénieur-conseil *m* **▸engineering factory** atelier *m* de construction mécanique **▸engineering industries** industries *fpl* d'équipement **▸engineering works** = **engineering factory**.

England ['ɪŋglənd] **n** Angleterre *f*.

English ['ɪŋglɪʃ] **1 adj** anglais; *king, embassy* d'Angleterre.
2 n a npl: the ~ les Anglais *mpl*.
b (*Ling*) anglais *m*. **the King's** *or* **Queen's ~** l'anglais correct; **in plain** *or* **simple ~** en termes très simples, ≃ en bon français; **~ as a Foreign Language** l'anglais langue étrangère; **~ as a Second Language** l'anglais deuxième langue; **~ for Special Purposes** l'anglais appliqué; **~ Language Teaching** l'enseignement *m* de l'anglais.
c (*US Billiards, Bowling etc: often* **e~**) effet *m* (*donné à une boule*).
3 comp ▸English breakfast (*in hotel etc*) petit déjeuner anglais **▸the English Channel** la Manche **▸English horn** (*US*) cor *m* anglais **▸Englishman** Anglais *m*; (*Prov*) **an Englishman's home is his castle** charbonnier est maître chez soi (*Prov*) **▸English-speaker** anglophone *mf* **▸English-speaking** qui parle anglais; *nation etc* anglophone **▸Englishwoman** Anglaise *f*.

engraft [ɪn'grɑːft] **vt** (*Agr, Surg, fig*) greffer (*into, on* sur).

engram ['engræm] **n** engramme *m*.

engrave [ɪn'greɪv] **vt** *wood, metal, stone* graver; (*Typ*) graver au burin; (*fig*) graver, empreindre. **~d on the heart/the memory** gravé dans le cœur/la mémoire.

engraver [ɪn'greɪvəʳ] **n** graveur *m*.

engraving [ɪn'greɪvɪŋ] **n** gravure *f*. (*Typ*) **~ plate** cliché *m* typo; *see* **wood** *etc*.

engross [ɪn'grəʊs] **vt a** *attention, person* absorber, captiver. **to be ~ed in** *work* être absorbé par, s'absorber dans; *reading, thoughts* être plongé dans, s'abîmer dans (*liter*). **b** (*Jur*) grossoyer.

engrossing [ɪn'grəʊsɪŋ] **adj** *book, game* absorbant, captivant; *work* absorbant.

engrossment [ɪn'grəʊsmənt] **n** (*US Pol*) rédaction définitive d'un projet de loi.

engulf [ɪn'gʌlf] **vt** engouffrer, engloutir. **to be ~ed in** s'engouffrer dans, sombrer dans.

enhance [ɪn'hɑːns] **vt** *attraction, beauty* mettre en valeur, rehausser; *powers* accroître, étendre; *numbers, price, value* augmenter; *position, chances* améliorer; *prestige, reputation* accroître, rehausser; (*Admin: increase*) majorer (*by* de). **~d graphics adaptor** adaptateur *m* de graphique amélioré.

enhancement [ɪn'hɑːnsmənt] **n** (*Admin: of pension entitlement*) majoration *f*.

enharmonic [ˌenhɑː'mɒnɪk] **adj** enharmonique.

enigma [ɪ'nɪgmə] **n** énigme *f*. (*fig*) **he is an ~** cet homme est une énigme.

enigmatic [ˌenɪg'mætɪk] **adj** énigmatique.

enigmatically [ˌenɪg'mætɪkəlɪ] **adv** d'une manière énigmatique.

enjambement [ɪn'dʒæmmənt] **n** enjambement *m*.

enjoin [ɪn'dʒɔɪn] **vt a** (*urge*) *silence, obedience* imposer (*on* à); *discretion, caution* recommander (*on* à). **to ~ sb to do** ordonner *or* prescrire à qn de faire. **b** (*US: forbid*) **to ~ sb from doing** interdire à qn de faire, enjoindre à qn de ne pas faire.

enjoy [ɪn'dʒɔɪ] **vt a** (*take pleasure in*) *theatre, cinema, football, music* aimer; *game, pastime* aimer, trouver agréable; *evening, walk, holiday, company, conversation* aimer, prendre plaisir à; *book, meal* apprécier, trouver bon, goûter (*frm*). **to ~ doing** trouver du plaisir *or* prendre plaisir à faire, aimer faire, trouver agréable de faire; **I ~ed doing it** cela m'a fait (grand) plaisir de le faire; **to ~ greatly** se délecter (*sth* de qch, *doing* à faire); **to ~ life** jouir de *or* profiter de la vie; **to ~ a weekend/an evening/holidays** passer un bon weekend/une soirée très agréable/de bonnes vacances; **did you ~ the concert?** le concert vous a-t-il plu?; **to ~ one's dinner** bien manger *or* dîner; **the children ~ed their meal** les enfants ont bien mangé *or* ont mangé de bon appétit.
b to ~ o.s. s'amuser, prendre *or* se donner du bon temps; **did you ~ yourself in Paris?** est-ce que tu t'es bien amusé à Paris?; **~ yourself!** amusez-vous bien!; (*tonight/at weekend*) passez une bonne soirée/un bon week-end!; **she always ~s herself in the country** elle se plaît toujours à la campagne, elle est toujours contente d'être à la campagne.
c (*benefit from*) *income, rights, health, advantage* jouir de.

enjoyable [ɪn'dʒɔɪəbl] **adj** *visit, evening* agréable; *meal* excellent.

enjoyably [ɪn'dʒɔɪəblɪ] **adv** agréablement.

enjoyment [ɪn'dʒɔɪmənt] **n** (*NonC*) **a** plaisir *m*. **to get ~ from (doing) sth** trouver du plaisir à (faire) qch. **b** *[rights etc]* jouissance *f*, possession *f* (*of* de).

enlarge [ɪn'lɑːdʒ] **1 vt** *house, territory* agrandir; *empire, influence, field of knowledge, circle of friends* étendre; (*Med*) *organ* hypertrophier; *pore* dilater; (*Phot*) agrandir; *business* développer, agrandir; *hole* élargir, agrandir; *numbers* augmenter; *majority* accroître. **2 vi a** (*grow bigger*) s'agrandir; s'étendre; s'hypertrophier; se dilater; se développer; s'élargir; s'accroître. **b to ~ (up)on** *subject, difficulties etc* s'étendre sur; *idea* développer.

enlarged [ɪn'lɑːdʒd] **adj** *edition* augmenté; *majority* accru; *community etc* aggrandi; (*Med*) *organ* hypertrophié; *pore* dilaté.

enlargement [ɪn'lɑːdʒmənt] **n a** (*see* **enlarge**) agrandissement *m*; dilatation *f*; élargissement *m*; accroissement *m*; hypertrophie *f*. **b** (*Phot*) agrandissement *m*.

enlarger [ɪn'lɑːdʒəʳ] **n** (*Phot*) agrandisseur *m*.

enlighten [ɪn'laɪtn] **vt** éclairer (*sb on sth* qn sur qch).

enlightened [ɪn'laɪtnd] **adj** *person, views, mind* éclairé. (*gen iro*) **in this ~ age** dans notre siècle de lumières, à notre époque éclairée.

enlightening [ɪn'laɪtnɪŋ] **adj** révélateur (*f* -trice) (*about* au sujet de).

enlightenment [ɪn'laɪtnmənt] **n** (*explanations*) éclaircissements *mpl*; (*knowledge*) instruction *f*, édification *f*. **we need some ~ on this point** nous avons besoin de quelques éclaircissements *or* lumières *fpl* sur ce point; **the Age of E~** le Siècle des lumières.

enlist [ɪn'lɪst] **1 vi** (*Mil etc*) s'engager, s'enrôler (*in* dans). (*US Mil*) **~ed man** simple soldat *m*, militaire *m* du rang; (*woman*) ≃ caporal *m*. **2 vt** *recruits* enrôler, engager; *soldiers, supporters* recruter. **to ~ sb's support/sympathy** s'assurer le concours/la sympathie de qn.

enlistment [ɪn'lɪstmənt] **n** (*see* **enlist**) engagement *m*, enrôlement *m*; recrutement *m*.

enliven [ɪn'laɪvn] **vt** *conversation, visit, evening* animer; *décor, design* mettre une note vive dans, égayer.

enmesh [ɪn'meʃ] **vt** (*lit, fig*) prendre dans un filet. **to get ~ed in** s'empêtrer dans.

enmity ['enmɪtɪ] **n** inimitié *f*, hostilité *f* (*towards* envers, *for* pour).

enneathlon [ˌenɪ'æθlɒn] **n** (*Sport*) ennéathlon *m*.

ennoble [ɪ'nəʊbl] **vt** (*lit*) anoblir; (*fig*) *person, mind* ennoblir, élever.

enologist [iː'nɒlədʒɪst] (*US*) = **oenologist**.

enology [iː'nɒlədʒɪ] (*US*) = **oenology**.

enormity [ɪ'nɔːmɪtɪ] **n a** (*NonC*) *[action, offence]* énormité *f*. **b**

(*crime*) crime *m* très grave, outrage *m*; (*blunder*) énormité *f*.

enormous [ɪ'nɔːməs] **adj** *object, animal, influence, difference* énorme; *patience* immense; *strength* prodigieux; *stature* colossal. **an ~ quantity of** énormément de; **an ~ number of** une masse* *or* un tas de; **an ~ number of people** un monde fou, un tas de gens*; **an ~ great hole*** un super gros trou*.

enormously [ɪ'nɔːməslɪ] **adv** (+ *vb or ptp*) énormément; (+ *adj*) extrêmement. **the village has changed ~** le village a énormément changé; **he told an ~ funny story** il a raconté une histoire extrêmement drôle.

enosis ['enəʊsɪs] **n** Enosis *m*.

enough [ɪ'nʌf] **1 adj, n** assez (de). **~ books** assez de livres; **~ money** assez *or* suffisamment d'argent; **~ to eat** assez à manger; **he earns ~ to live on** il gagne de quoi vivre; **I've had ~** (*eating*) j'ai assez mangé; (*protesting*) j'en ai assez; **I've had ~ of this novel/of obeying him** j'en ai assez de ce roman/de lui obéir; **you can never have ~ of this music** on ne se lasse jamais de cette musique; **one song was ~ to show he couldn't sing** une chanson a suffi à prouver qu'il ne savait pas chanter; **it is ~ for us to know that ...** il nous suffit de savoir que ...; **that's ~, thanks** cela suffit *or* c'est assez, merci; **that's ~!** ça suffit!; **~ of this!** ça suffit comme ça!*; **~ said!** assez parlé! *or* causé!*; **this noise is ~ to drive you mad** ce bruit est à (vous) rendre fou; **I've had more than ~ wine** j'ai bu plus de vin que je n'aurais dû, j'ai bu un peu trop de vin; **there's more than ~ for all** il y en a largement (assez) *or* plus qu'assez pour tous; **~'s ~!** ça suffit comme ça!; (*Prov*) **~ is as good as a feast** il ne faut pas abuser des meilleures choses.

2 adv a (*sufficiently*) assez, suffisamment. **are you warm ~?** avez-vous assez chaud?; **he has slept long ~** il a suffisamment dormi; **he is old ~ to go alone** il est suffisamment *or* assez grand pour y aller tout seul; **your work is good ~** votre travail est assez bon *or* est honorable; **that's a good ~ excuse** c'est une excuse satisfaisante; **he knows well ~ what I've said** il sait très bien ce que j'ai dit; **I was fool ~** *or* **~ of a fool to believe him** j'ai été assez bête pour le croire.

b (*disparaging*) assez. **she is pretty ~** elle est assez jolie, elle n'est pas mal; **he writes well ~** il écrit assez bien, il n'écrit pas mal; **it's good ~ in its way** ce n'est pas (si) mal dans son genre*.

c (*intensifying*) **oddly** *or* **funnily ~, I saw him too** chose curieuse *or* c'est curieux, je l'ai vu aussi; *see* **sure**.

enprint ['enprɪnt] **n** (*Phot*) (photo *f*) format *m* normal.

enquire [ɪn'kwaɪəʳ] *etc* = **inquire** *etc*.

enrage [ɪn'reɪdʒ] **vt** mettre en rage *or* en fureur, rendre furieux. **~d** enragé; **it ~s me to think that ...** j'enrage *or* je rage* de penser que ... .

enrapture [ɪn'ræptʃəʳ] **vt** ravir, enchanter. **~d by** ravi de, enchanté par.

enrich [ɪn'rɪtʃ] **vt** *person, language, collection, mind* enrichir; *food* enrichir (*with* en); *soil* fertiliser, amender; (*Phys*) enrichir. **~ed uranium** uranium enrichi; **vitamin-/iron-~ed** enrichi en vitamines/en fer.

enrichment [ɪn'rɪtʃmənt] **n** enrichissement *m*; *[soil]* fertilisation *f*, amendement *m*.

enrol, (*gen US*) **enroll** [ɪn'rəʊl] **1 vt** *workers* embaucher; *students* immatriculer, inscrire; *members* inscrire; *soldiers* enrôler. (*US Pol*) **~ed bill** projet *m* de loi ratifié par les deux Chambres. **2 vi** *[labourer etc]* se faire embaucher (*as* comme); (*Univ etc*) se faire immatriculer *or* inscrire, s'inscrire (*in* à, *for* pour); (*Mil*) s'enrôler, s'engager (*in* dans). **to ~ as a member of a club/party** s'inscrire à un club/un parti.

enrolment, (*gen US*) **enrollment** [ɪn'rəʊlmənt] **n** (*NonC: see* **enrol**) embauchage *m*; immatriculation *f*; inscription *f*; enrôlement *m*. **school with an ~ of 600** une école avec un effectif de 600 élèves.

ensconce [ɪn'skɒns] **vt: to ~ o.s.** bien se caler, bien s'installer; **to be ~d** être bien installé *or* calé.

ensemble [ɑ̃ːnsɑ̃ːmbl] **n** (*Dress, Mus*) ensemble *m*.

enshrine [ɪn'ʃraɪn] **vt** (*Rel*) enchâsser; (*fig*) *memory* conserver pieusement *or* religieusement; *custom, principle* sauvegarder.

ensign ['ensaɪn] **n a** ['ensən] (*flag*) drapeau *m*; (*Naut*) pavillon *m*. (*Brit*) **Red/White E~** pavillon de la marine marchande/de la marine de guerre; **~-bearer** porte-étendard *m inv*. **b** (*emblem*) insigne *m*, emblème *m*. **c** (*Mil Hist*) (officier *m*) porte-étendard *m inv*. **d** (*US Naut*) enseigne *m* de vaisseau de deuxième classe.

enslave [ɪn'sleɪv] **vt** (*lit*) réduire en esclavage, asservir; (*fig*) asservir. **to be ~d by tradition** être l'esclave de la tradition.

enslavement [ɪn'sleɪvmənt] **n** asservissement *m*.

ensnare [ɪn'snɛəʳ] **vt** (*lit, fig*) prendre au piège; *[woman, charms]* séduire.

ensue [ɪn'sjuː] **vi** s'ensuivre, résulter (*from, on* de).

ensuing [ɪn'sjuːɪŋ] **adj** *event* qui s'ensuit; *year, day* suivant.

en suite [ɑ̃'swiːt] **adj: with bathroom ~, with an ~ bathroom** avec salle de bains attenante.

ensure [ɪn'ʃʊəʳ] **vt a** assurer, garantir. **he did everything to ~ that she came** il a tout fait pour qu'elle vienne *or* pour s'assurer qu'elle viendrait. **b** = **insure b**.

E.N.T. [ˌiːen'tiː] (*Med*) (**abbr of Ear, Nose and Throat**) O.R.L. *f*.

entail [ɪn'teɪl] **vt a** (*gen, also Philos*) entraîner; *expense, work, delay* occasionner; *inconvenience, risk, difficulty* comporter; *suffering, hardship* imposer, entraîner. **it ~ed buying a car** cela nécessitait l'achat d'une voiture. **b** (*Jur*) **to ~ an estate** substituer un héritage; **~ed estate** biens *mpl* inaliénables.

entangle [ɪn'tæŋgl] **vt** (*catch up*) empêtrer, enchevêtrer; (*twist together*) *hair* emmêler; *wool, thread* emmêler, embrouiller; (*fig*) *person* entraîner, impliquer (*in* dans), mêler (*in* à). **to become ~d in an affair** s'empêtrer *or* se laisser entraîner dans une affaire; **to become ~d in ropes/lies/explanations** s'empêtrer dans des cordages/des mensonges/des explications.

entanglement [ɪn'tæŋglmənt] **n** (*see* **entangle**) (*lit*) enchevêtrement *m*; emmêlement *m*; (*fig*) implication *f*. **his ~ with the police** son affaire *f* avec la police.

entente [ɒn'tɒnt] **n** entente *f*. **~ cordiale** entente *f* cordiale.

enter ['entəʳ] **1 vt a** (*come or go into*) *house etc* entrer dans, pénétrer dans; *vehicle* monter dans, entrer dans; *path, road etc* s'engager dans. **he ~ed the grocer's** il est entré chez l'épicier *or* dans l'épicerie; (*Naut*) **to ~ harbour** entrer au port *or* dans le port; **the thought never ~ed my head** cette pensée ne m'est jamais venue à l'esprit; **he is ~ing his sixtieth year** il entre dans sa soixantième année.

b (*become member of*) *a profession, the army etc* entrer dans; *university, college etc* s'inscrire à, se faire inscrire à *or* dans. **to ~ the Church** se faire prêtre, recevoir la prêtrise; **to ~ society** faire ses débuts dans le monde.

c (*submit, write down*) *amount, name, fact, order* (*on list etc*) inscrire; (*in notebook*) noter; (*Comput*) *data* introduire, entrer. **to ~ an item in the ledger** porter un article sur le livre de comptes; (*Comm*) **~ these purchases to me** mettez *or* portez ces achats à *or* sur mon compte; **to ~ a horse for a race** engager *or* inscrire un cheval dans une course; **to ~ a dog for a show** présenter un chien dans un concours; **to ~ a pupil for an exam/a competition** présenter un élève à un examen/à un concours; **he has ~ed his son for Eton** il a inscrit son fils (à l'avance) à Eton; **to ~ a protest** rédiger *or* élever *or* présenter une protestation; (*Jur*) **to ~ an appeal** interjeter appel; (*Jur*) **to ~ an appearance** comparaître (en justice).

2 vi a entrer. (*Theat*) **~ Macbeth** entre Macbeth.

b to ~ for a race s'inscrire pour une course; **to ~ for an examination** s'inscrire à un examen.

►enter into vt fus a *explanation, apology* se lancer dans; *correspondence, conversation* entrer en; *plot* prendre part à; *negotiations* entamer; *contract* passer; *alliance* conclure. **b** *sb's plans, calculations* entrer dans. (*lit, fig*) **to enter into the spirit of the game** entrer dans le jeu; **her money doesn't enter into it at all** son argent n'y est pour rien *or* n'a rien à voir là-dedans.

►enter up vt sep *sum of money, amount* inscrire; *diary, ledger* tenir à jour.

►enter (up)on vt fus *career* débuter dans, entrer dans; *negotiations* entamer; *alliance* conclure; *subject* aborder; *inheritance* prendre possession de.

enteric [en'terɪk] **adj** entérique. **~ fever** (fièvre *f*) typhoïde *f*.

enteritis [ˌentə'raɪtɪs] **n** entérite *f*.

enterostomy [ˌentə'rɒstəmɪ] **n** entérostomie *f*.

enterotomy [ˌentə'rɒtəmɪ] **n** entérotomie *f*.

enterovirus [ˌentərəʊ'vaɪrəs] **n** entérovirus *m*.

enterprise ['entəpraɪz] **n a** (*undertaking, company*) entreprise *f*. **b** (*NonC: initiative*) (esprit *m* d')initiative *f*, esprit entreprenant, hardiesse *f*. (*Brit*) **E~ Allowance Scheme** *aide à la création d'entreprise accordée aux chômeurs*; *see* **free** *etc*.

enterprising ['entəpraɪzɪŋ] **adj** *person* plein d'initiative, entreprenant; *venture* audacieux, hardi. **that was ~ of you!** vous avez fait preuve d'initiative!, vous avez eu de l'idée!*

enterprisingly ['entəpraɪzɪŋlɪ] **adv** (*showing initiative*) de sa (*etc*) propre initiative; (*daringly*) hardiment, audacieusement.

entertain [ˌentə'teɪn] **vt a** (*amuse*) *audience* amuser, divertir; *guests, children* distraire. **a novel should instruct and ~** un roman devrait instruire et divertir. **b** (*offer hospitality to*) *guests* recevoir. **to ~ sb to dinner** offrir un dîner à qn; (*at home*) recevoir qn à dîner; **they ~ a lot** ils reçoivent beaucoup. **c** (*bear in mind*) *thought* considérer, méditer; *intention, suspicion, doubt, hope* nourrir; *proposal* accueillir favorablement. **I wouldn't ~ it for a moment** je repousserais tout de suite une telle idée; **to ~ a claim** admettre une réclamation, faire droit à une réclamation.

entertainer [ˌentə'teɪnəʳ] **n** artiste *mf* (de music-hall *etc*), fantaisiste *mf*. **a well-known radio ~** un(e) artiste bien connu(e) à la radio; **he's a born ~** c'est un amuseur né.

entertaining [ˌentə'teɪnɪŋ] **1 adj** amusant, divertissant. **2 n: she does a lot of ~** elle reçoit beaucoup; **their ~ is always sumptuous** ils reçoivent toujours avec faste, leurs réceptions sont toujours fastueuses.

entertainingly [ˌentə'teɪnɪŋlɪ] **adv** d'une façon amusante *or* divertissante.

entertainment [ˌentə'teɪnmənt] **1 n a** (*NonC: see* **entertain**) amusement *m*, divertissement *m*; distraction *f*. **much to the ~ of** au grand amusement de; **for your ~ we have invited ...** pour vous distraire *or* amuser nous avons invité ...; **for my own ~** pour mon divertissement personnel; **the cinema is my favourite ~** le cinéma est ma distraction préférée. **b** (*performance*) spectacle *m*, attractions *fpl*. **musical ~** soirée musicale. **2 comp ►entertainment allowance** *or*

expenses frais *mpl* de représentation ▸**entertainment tax** taxe *f* sur les spectacles ▸**the entertainment world** le monde du spectacle.

enthral(l) [ɪn'θrɔːl] **vt** *[book, film, talk etc]* captiver, passionner; *[beauty, charm]* séduire, ensorceler; (*††: enslave*) asservir. **enthralled by what one is reading** captivé par une lecture.

enthralling [ɪn'θrɔːlɪŋ] **adj** *story, film* passionnant; *beauty* ensorcelant.

enthrone [ɪn'θrəʊn] **vt** *king* placer sur le trône, couronner, introniser; *bishop* introniser. (*liter*) **to sit ~d** trôner; (*fig*) **~d in the hearts of his countrymen** vénéré par ses compatriotes.

enthronement [ɪn'θrəʊnmənt] **n** (*lit*) couronnement *m*, intronisation *f*; (*fig*) consécration *f*.

enthuse [ɪn'θuːz] 1 **vi**: **to ~ over sb/sth** porter qn/qch aux nues, parler avec (beaucoup d')enthousiasme de qn/qch, être emballé* par qn/qch. 2 **vt** enthousiasmer.

enthusiasm [ɪn'θuːzɪæzəm] **n** (*NonC*) enthousiasme *m* (*for* pour). **to move** *or* **arouse to ~** enthousiasmer; **I haven't much ~ for going out** cela ne me dit pas grand-chose de sortir.

enthusiast [ɪn'θuːzɪæst] **n** enthousiaste *mf*. **he is a jazz/bridge/sport** *etc* **~** il se passionne pour le *or* il est passionné de jazz/bridge/sport *etc*; **all these football ~s** tous ces passionnés *or* enragés* de football; **a Vivaldi ~** un(e) fervent(e) de Vivaldi.

enthusiastic [ɪn,θuːzɪ'æstɪk] **adj** *person, attitude, response* enthousiaste; *welcome* enthousiaste, chaleureux; *shout* enthousiaste, d'enthousiasme. **an ~ swimmer** un nageur passionné *or* enragé*; **an ~ supporter** un partisan enthousiaste *or* fervent *or* passionné (*of* de); **to grow** *or* **wax ~ over** s'enthousiasmer *or* se passionner pour; **to be ~ about** *activity, hobby* être passionné de; *plan, suggestion* être enthousiasmé par; **he was very ~ about the plan** il a accueilli le projet avec enthousiasme; **I'm not very ~ about it** cela ne me dit pas grand-chose; **to make sb ~** enthousiasmer qn (*about* pour).

enthusiastically [ɪn,θuːzɪ'æstɪkəlɪ] **adv** *receive, speak, applaud* avec enthousiasme; *work* avec zèle, avec ferveur, avec élan; *support* avec enthousiasme, avec ferveur.

entice [ɪn'taɪs] **vt** attirer (*towards* vers; *into* dans), entraîner (*sb away from somewhere* qn à l'écart d'un endroit), éloigner (*sb away from sb* qn de qn); (*with food, prospects*) allécher; (*with false promises*) leurrer. **to ~ sb to do** entraîner qn (par la ruse) à faire.

enticement [ɪn'taɪsmənt] **n** (*act*) séduction *f*; (*attraction*) attrait *m*.

enticing [ɪn'taɪsɪŋ] **adj** *person* séduisant; *prospects, offer* attrayant; *food* alléchant, appétissant.

entire [ɪn'taɪə[r]] **adj** a (*whole*) entier, tout. **the ~ week** la semaine entière, toute la semaine; **the ~ world** le monde entier. b (*complete*) entier, complet (*f* -ète); (*unreserved*) entier (*before n*), total, absolu. **the ~ house** la maison (tout) entière; **the ~ text** le texte tout entier; (*unexpurgated*) le texte intégral; **my ~ confidence** mon entière confiance, ma confiance totale *or* absolue. c (*unbroken*) entier, intact.

entirely [ɪn'taɪəlɪ] **adv** entièrement, tout à fait, totalement, absolument, complètement; *change* du tout au tout.

entirety [ɪn'taɪərətɪ] **n** intégralité *f*, totalité *f*. **in its ~** en (son) entier, intégralement.

entitle [ɪn'taɪtl] **vt** a *book* intituler. **to be ~d** s'intituler.

b (*bestow right on*) autoriser, habiliter (*Jur*) (*to do* à faire). **to ~ sb to sth** donner droit à qch à qn; **to ~ sb to do** donner à qn le droit de faire; **this ticket ~s the bearer to do ...** ce billet donne au porteur le droit de faire ...; **to be ~d to sth** avoir droit à qch; **to be ~d to do** (*by position, qualifications*) avoir qualité pour faire, être habilité à faire (*Jur*); (*by conditions, rules*) avoir le droit *or* être en droit de faire; **you're ~d to a bit of fun!** tu as bien le droit de t'amuser un peu!; **he is quite ~d to believe that ...** il est tout à fait en droit de croire que ...; (*Jur etc*) **~d to vote** ayant voix délibérative; **these statements ~ us to believe that ...** ces déclarations nous autorisent à croire que ... .

entitlement [ɪn'taɪtəlmənt] **n** droit *m* (*to* à). (*US Pol*) **~ programs** grands programmes sociaux.

entity ['entɪtɪ] **n** entité *f*; *see* **legal**.

entomb [ɪn'tuːm] **vt** mettre au tombeau, ensevelir; (*fig*) ensevelir.

entombment [ɪn'tuːmmənt] **n** mise *f* au tombeau, ensevelissement *m*.

entomological [,entəmə'lɒdʒɪkəl] **adj** entomologique.

entomologist [,entə'mɒlədʒɪst] **n** entomologiste *mf*.

entomology [,entə'mɒlədʒɪ] **n** entomologie *f*.

entourage [,ɒntʊ'rɑːʒ] **n** entourage *m*.

entr'acte ['ɒntrækt] **n** entracte *m*.

entrails ['entreɪlz] **npl** (*lit, fig*) entrailles *fpl*.

entrain [ɪn'treɪn] 1 **vt** (faire) embarquer dans un train. 2 **vi** s'embarquer dans un train.

entrance[1] ['entrəns] 1 **n** a (*way in*) (*gen*) entrée *f* (*to* de); *[cathedral]* portail *m*; (*hall*) entrée, vestibule *m*; *see* **trade**.

b (*act*) entrée *f*. **on his ~** à son entrée; (*esp Theat*) **to make an ~** faire son entrée; **to force an ~ into** forcer l'entrée de; **door giving ~ to a room** porte qui donne accès à une pièce.

c (*right to enter*) admission *f*. **~ to a school** admission à *or* dans une école; **to gain ~ to a university** être admis à *or* dans une université.

2 **comp** ▸**entrance card** carte *f or* billet *m* d'entrée *or* d'admission ▸**entrance examination** examen *m* d'entrée; (*Admin*) concours *m* de recrutement ▸**entrance fee** (*at museum, cinema etc*) droit *m* d'entrée; (*Brit: for club, association etc*) droit *m* d'inscription ▸**entrance permit** visa *m* d'entrée ▸**entrance qualifications** *or* **requirements** (*Educ*) diplômes exigés à l'entrée ▸**entrance ramp** (*US Aut*) bretelle *f* d'accès ▸**entrance ticket** = **entrance card**.

entrance[2] [ɪn'trɑːns] **vt** transporter, ravir, enivrer. **she stood there ~d** elle restait là extasiée *or* en extase.

entrancing [ɪn'trɑːnsɪŋ] **adj** enchanteur (*f* -teresse), ravissant, séduisant.

entrancingly [ɪn'trɑːnsɪŋlɪ] **adv** *dance, sing* à ravir; *smile* d'une façon ravissante *or* séduisante. **she is ~ beautiful** elle est belle à ravir.

entrant ['entrənt] **n** (*to profession*) nouveau venu *m* (*to* dans, en); (*in race*) concurrent(e) *m(f)*, participant(e) *m(f)*; (*in competition*) candidat(e) *m(f)*, concurrent(e); (*in exam*) candidat(e).

entrap [ɪn'træp] **vt** prendre au piège. **to ~ sb into doing sth** amener qn à faire qch par la ruse *or* la feinte.

entrapment [ɪn'træpmənt] **n** (*US Jur*) *incitation policière à commettre un délit qui justifiera ensuite l'arrestation de son auteur*.

entreat [ɪn'triːt] **vt** supplier, implorer, prier instamment (*sb to do* qn de faire). **listen to him, I ~ you** écoutez-le, je vous en supplie *or* je vous en conjure; **to ~ sth of sb** demander instamment qch à qn; **to ~ sb for help** implorer le secours de qn.

entreating [ɪn'triːtɪŋ] 1 **adj** suppliant, implorant. 2 **n** supplications *fpl*.

entreatingly [ɪn'triːtɪŋlɪ] **adv** *look* d'un air suppliant; *ask* d'un ton suppliant, d'une voix suppliante.

entreaty [ɪn'triːtɪ] **n** prière *f*, supplication *f*. **at his (earnest) ~** sur ses (vives) instances *fpl*; **a look of ~** un regard suppliant.

entrée ['ɒntreɪ] **n** (*Culin*) entrée *f*.

entrench [ɪn'trentʃ] **vt** (*Mil*) retrancher.

entrenched [ɪn'trentʃd] **adj** (*Mil*) retranché; (*fig*) *person* indélogeable; *attitude* très arrêté. **he is ~ in the belief that ...** il ne veut pas démordre de l'idée que ...; **customs ~ by long tradition** coutumes implantées par une longue tradition.

entrenchment [ɪn'trentʃmənt] **n** (*Mil*) retranchement *m*.

entrepôt ['ɒntrəpəʊ] **n** entrepôt *m*.

entrepreneur [,ɒntrəprə'nɜː[r]] **n** entrepreneur *m* (*chef d'entreprise*).

entrepreneurial [,ɒntrəprə'nɜːrɪəl] **adj** animé de l'esprit d'entreprise.

entropy ['entrəpɪ] **n** entropie *f*.

entrust [ɪn'trʌst] **vt** *secrets, valuables, letters* confier (*to* à); *child* confier (*to sb* à qn, à la garde de qn); *prisoner* confier (*to* à la garde de). **to ~ sb/sth to sb's care** confier *or* remettre qn/qch aux soins de qn; **to ~ sb with a task** charger qn d'une tâche, confier à qn une tâche; **to ~ sb with the job of doing** charger qn de faire qch, confier à qn le soin de faire qch.

entry ['entrɪ] 1 **n** a (*action*) entrée *f*; (*in competition*) participation *f*. **to make an ~** faire son entrée; (*Theat*) **to make one's ~** entrer en scène; **"no ~"** (*on gate etc*) "défense d'entrer", "entrée interdite"; (*in one-way street*) "sens interdit".

b (*way in*) (*gen*) entrée *f*; *[cathedral]* portail *m*.

c (*item*) *[list]* inscription *f*; *[account book, ledger]* écriture *f*; *[dictionary]* (*term*) entrée *f*; (*headword*) adresse *f*, entrée; *[encyclopedia]* article *m*; (*piece of text*) article. (*Book-keeping*) **single/double ~** comptabilité *f* en partie simple/double; (*Naut*) **~ in the log** entrée du journal de bord.

d (*Sport etc*) **there is a large ~ for the 200 metres** il y a une longue liste de concurrents pour le 200 mètres; **there are only 3 entries** (*for race, competition*) il n'y a que 3 concurrents; (*for exam*) il n'y a que 3 candidats.

2 **comp** ▸**entry condition** (*Ling*) condition *f* d'admission (*à un système*) ▸**entry examination** examen *m* d'entrée; (*Admin*) concours *m* de recrutement ▸**entry fee** = **entrance fee** (*see* **entrance**[1] **2**) ▸**entry form** feuille *f* d'inscription ▸**entry-level** (*Comput*) de base ▸**entry permit** visa *m* d'entrée ▸**entry phone** interphone *m* ▸**entry qualifications** *or* **requirements** (*Educ*) diplômes exigés à l'entrée ▸**entry word** (*US Lexicography*) entrée *f*, adresse *f*.

entryism ['entrɪɪzəm] **n** entrisme *m*.

entryist ['entrɪɪst] **n, adj** entriste *(mf)*.

entwine [ɪn'twaɪn] 1 **vt** *stems, ribbons* entrelacer; *garland* tresser; (*twist around*) enlacer (*with* de). 2 **vi** s'entrelacer, s'enlacer, s'entortiller (*around* autour de).

enumerate [ɪ'njuːməreɪt] **vt** énumérer, dénombrer.

enumeration [ɪ,njuːmə'reɪʃən] **n** énumération *f*, dénombrement *m*.

enunciate [ɪ'nʌnsɪeɪt] **vt** *sound, word* prononcer, articuler; *principle, theory* énoncer, exposer. **to ~ clearly** bien articuler.

enunciation [ɪ,nʌnsɪ'eɪʃən] **n** *[sound, word]* articulation *f*; *[theory]* énonciation *f*, exposition *f*; *[problem]* énoncé *m*.

enuresis [,enjʊ'riːsɪs] **n** énurésie *f*.

enuretic [,enjʊ'retɪk] **adj** énurétique.

envelop [ɪn'veləp] **vt** envelopper (*also fig*). **~ed in a blanket** enveloppé dans une couverture; **~ed in clouds/snow** enveloppé de nuages/neige; **~ed in mystery** enveloppé *or* entouré de mystère.

envelope ['envələʊp] **n** *[letter, balloon, airship]* enveloppe *f*; (*Bio, Bot*) enveloppe, tunique *f*; (*Math*) enveloppe. **to put a letter in an ~** mettre une lettre sous enveloppe; **in a sealed ~** sous pli cacheté; **in the same**

~ sous le même pli.
envelopment [ɪn'veləpmənt] **n** enveloppement *m*.
envenom [ɪn'venəm] **vt** (*lit, fig*) envenimer.
enviable ['envɪəbl] **adj** *position, wealth, beauty* enviable; *fate* enviable, digne d'envie.
envious ['envɪəs] **adj** *person* envieux; *look, tone* envieux, d'envie. **to be ~ of sth** être envieux de qch; **to be ~ of sb** être jaloux de qn, envier qn; **to make sb ~** exciter *or* attirer l'envie de qn; **people were ~ of his success** son succès a fait des envieux *or* des jaloux.
enviously ['envɪəslɪ] **adv** avec envie.
environment [ɪn'vaɪərənmənt] **n** (*Bio, Bot, Geog*) milieu *m*; (*Admin, Pol, Ling*) environnement *m*; (*physical*) cadre *m*, milieu, environnement; (*social*) milieu, environnement; (*moral*) milieu, climat *m*, ambiance *f*. **cultural ~** climat *or* milieu culturel; **working ~** conditions *fpl* de travail; (*fig*) **hostile ~** climat d'hostilité, ambiance hostile; **natural ~** milieu naturel; **his normal ~** son cadre *or* son milieu normal; **working-class ~** milieu ouvrier; **heredity or ~** l'hérédité ou l'environnement; **pollution/protection of the ~** la pollution/la protection de l'environnement; **~-friendly** qui respecte l'environnement; (*Brit*) **Secretary (of State) for** *or* **Minister of the E~** ministre *m* de l'Environnement; **Department** *or* **Ministry of the E~** ministère *m* de l'Environnement.
environmental [ɪn,vaɪərən'mentl] **adj** *conditions, changes* écologique, du milieu; *influence* exercé par le milieu *or* l'environnement. **~ studies** études *fpl* de l'environnement; (*US Admin*) **E~ Protection Agency** ≃ Ministère de l'Environnement.
environmentalism [ɪn,vaɪrən'mentə,lɪzəm] **n** science *f* de l'environnement.
environmentalist [ɪn,vaɪərən'mentəlɪst] **n** écologiste *mf*.
environmentally [ɪn,vaɪərən'mentəlɪ] **adv** écologiquement. **~ friendly** qui respecte l'environnement.
environs [ɪn'vaɪərənz] **npl** environs *mpl*, alentours *mpl*, abords *mpl*.
envisage [ɪn'vɪzɪdʒ] **vt** (*foresee*) prévoir; (*imagine*) envisager. **it is ~d that ...** on prévoit que ...; **an increase is ~d next year** on prévoit une augmentation pour l'année prochaine; **it is hard to ~ such a situation** il est difficile d'envisager une telle situation.
envision [ɪn'vɪʒən] **vt** (*conceive of*) imaginer; (*foresee*) prévoir.
envoy[1] ['envɔɪ] **n** (*gen*) envoyé(e) *m(f)*, représentant(e) *m(f)*; (*diplomat, also* **~ extraordinary**) ministre *m* plénipotentiaire.
envoy[2] ['envɔɪ] **n** (*Poetry*) envoi *m*.
envy ['envɪ] **1 n** envie *f*, jalousie *f*. **out of ~** par envie, par jalousie; **filled with ~** dévoré de jalousie; **it was the ~ of everyone** cela faisait *or* excitait l'envie de tout le monde; *see* **green**. **2 vt** *person, thing* envier. **to ~ sb sth** envier qch à qn.
enzyme ['enzaɪm] **n** enzyme *f*.
EOC [,i:əʊ'si:] **n** (*Brit*) (**abbr of Equal Opportunities Commission**) *see* **equal 4**.
Eocene ['i:əʊ,si:n] **adj** (*Geol*) éocène.
eolithic [,i:əʊ'lɪθɪk] **adj** éolithique.
eon ['i:ɒn] = **aeon**.
eosin(e) ['i:əʊsɪn] **n** éosine *f*.
EPA [,i:pi:'eɪ] (**abbr of Environmental Protection Agency**) *see* **environmental**.
epaulet(te) ['epɔ:let] **n** épaulette *f*.
ephedrine ['efɪdrɪn] **n** éphédrine *f*.
ephemera [ɪ'femərə] **1 n, pl ~s** *or* **~e** [ɪ'femə,ri:] (*Zool*) éphémère *m*. **2 npl** (*transitory items*) choses *fpl* éphémères; (*collectables*) babioles *fpl* (*d'une époque donnée*).
ephemeral [ɪ'femərəl] **adj** (*Bot, Zool*) éphémère; (*fig*) éphémère, fugitif.
ephemerid [ɪ'femərɪd] **n** éphémère *m*.
ephemeris [ɪ'femərɪs] **n, pl ephemerides** [,efɪ'merɪ,di:z] éphéméride *f*.
Ephesians [ɪ'fi:ʒənz] **n** Ephésiens *mpl*.
Ephesus ['efɪsəs] **n** Ephèse.
epic ['epɪk] **1 adj** (*Literat*) épique; (*fig*) héroïque, épique; (*hum*) épique, homérique. **2 n** épopée *f*, poème *m or* récit *m* épique. (*Cine*) **an ~ of the screen** un film à grand spectacle.
epicarp ['epɪkɑ:p] **n** épicarpe *m*.
epicene ['epɪsi:n] **adj** *manners, literature* efféminé; (*Gram*) épicène.
epicentre, (*US*) **epicenter** ['epɪsentə^r] **n** épicentre *m*.
epicure ['epɪkjʊə^r] **n** (fin) gourmet *m*, gastronome *mf*.
epicurean [,epɪkjʊə'ri:ən] **adj, n** épicurien(ne) *m(f)*.
epicureanism [,epɪkjʊə'rɪənɪzəm] **n** épicurisme *m*.
Epicurus [,epɪ'kjʊərəs] **n** Épicure *m*.
epicyclic [epɪ'saɪklɪk] **adj: ~ gear** *or* **train** train épicycloïdal.
epidiascope [,epɪ'daɪə,skəʊp] **n** épidiascope *m*.
epidemic [,epɪ'demɪk] **1 n** épidémie *f*. **2 adj** épidémique. **to reach ~ proportions** atteindre des proportions épidémiques.
epidermis [,epɪ'dɜ:mɪs] **n** (*Anat, Bot, Zool*) épiderme *m*.
epididymis [,epɪ'dɪdɪmɪs] **n, pl epididymides** [,epɪdɪ'dɪmɪ,di:z] (*Anat*) épididyme *m*.
epidural [,epɪ'djʊərəl] **adj, n: ~ (anaesthetic)** péridurale *f*.
epigenesis [,epɪ'dʒenɪsɪs] **n** (*Biol*) épigénèse *f*; (*Geol*) épigénie *f*.
epiglottis [,epɪ'glɒtɪs] **n, pl ~es** *or* **epiglottides** [,epɪ'glɒtɪ,di:z] épiglotte *f*.
epigram ['epɪgræm] **n** épigramme *f*.
epigrammatic(al) [,epɪgrə'mætɪk(əl)] **adj** épigrammatique.
epigraph ['epɪgrɑ:f] **n** épigraphe *f*.
epilator ['epɪleɪtə^r] **n** épilateur *m*.
epilepsy ['epɪlepsɪ] **n** épilepsie *f*.
epileptic [,epɪ'leptɪk] **1 adj** épileptique. **~ fit** crise *f* d'épilepsie. **2 n** épileptique *mf*.
epilogue ['epɪlɒg] **n** (*Literat*) épilogue *m*.
epinephrine [,epə'nefrɪn] **n** (*US*) adrénaline *f*.
Epiphany [ɪ'pɪfənɪ] **n** Épiphanie *f*, fête *f* des Rois.
epiphytic [,epɪ'fɪtɪk] **adj** épiphyte.
episcopacy [ɪ'pɪskəpəsɪ] **n** épiscopat *m*.
episcopal [ɪ'pɪskəpəl] **adj** épiscopal. **~ ring** anneau pastoral *or* épiscopal; **the E~ Church** l'Église épiscopale.
episcopalian [ɪ,pɪskə'peɪlɪən] **1 adj** épiscopal (*de l'Église épiscopale*). **2 n** membre *m* de l'Église épiscopale. **the ~s** les épiscopaux *mpl*.
episcopate [ɪ'pɪskəpɪt] **n** épiscopat *m*.
episcope ['epi,skəʊp] **n** (*Brit*) épiscope *m*.
episiotomy [ə,pi:zɪ'ɒtəmɪ] **n** épisiotomie *f*.
episode ['epɪsəʊd] **n** épisode *m*.
episodic [,epɪ'sɒdɪk] **adj** épisodique.
epistemic [,epɪ'sti:mɪk] **adj** épistémique.
epistemological [ɪ,pɪstɪmə'lɒdʒɪkəl] **adj** épistémologique.
epistemology [ɪ,pɪstə'mɒlədʒɪ] **n** épistémologie *f*.
epistle [ɪ'pɪsl] **n** épître *f*; (*Admin: letter*) courrier *m*. (*Bible*) **E~ to the Romans/Hebrews** *etc* Épître aux Romains/Hébreux *etc*.
epistolary [ɪ'pɪstələrɪ] **adj** épistolaire.
epitaph ['epɪtɑ:f] **n** épitaphe *f*.
epithelium [,epɪ'θi:lɪəm] **n, pl ~s** *or* **epithelia** [,epɪ'θi:lɪə] épithélium *m*.
epithet ['epɪθet] **n** épithète *f*.
epitome [ɪ'pɪtəmɪ] **n** *[book]* abrégé *m*, résumé *m*; (*fig*) *[virtue, goodness]* modèle *m*, type *m or* exemple *m* même; *[idea, subject]* quintessence *f*.
epitomize [ɪ'pɪtəmaɪz] **vt** *book* abréger, résumer; *quality, virtue* incarner, personnifier.
EPNS [,i:pi:en'es] (**abbr of electroplated nickel silver**) *see* **electroplate**.
epoch ['i:pɒk] **1 n** époque *f*, période *f*. (*fig*) **to mark an ~** faire époque, faire date. **2 comp ▸epoch-making** qui fait époque, qui fait date.
eponym ['epənɪm] **n** éponyme *m*.
eponymous [ɪ'pɒnɪməs] **adj** éponyme.
EPOS ['i:pɒs] **n** (**abbr of electronic point of sale**) point *m* de vente électronique.
epoxide [ɪ'pɒksaɪd] **n** époxyde *m*. **~ resin** = **epoxy resin**.
epoxy [ɪ'pɒksɪ] **n: ~ resin** résine *f* époxyde.
Epsom salts ['epsəm'sɔ:ltz] **npl** sel *m* d'Epsom, sulfate *m* de magnésium.
equable ['ekwəbl] **adj** *temperament, climate* égal, constant. **he is very ~** il a un tempérament très égal.
equably ['ekwəblɪ] **adv** tranquillement.
equal ['i:kwəl] **1 adj a** (*Math, gen*) égal (*to* à). **~ in number** égal en nombre; **to be ~ to sth** égaler qch (*see also* **1b**); **~ pay for ~ work** à travail égal salaire égal; **~ pay for women** salaire égal pour les femmes; **other** *or* **all things (being) ~** toutes choses égales d'ailleurs; **an ~ sum of money** une même somme d'argent; **with ~ indifference** avec la même indifférence; (*in value etc*) **they are about ~** ils se valent à peu près; **to talk to sb on ~ terms** parler à qn d'égal à égal; **to be on an ~ footing (with sb)** être sur un pied d'égalité (avec qn); **to come ~ first/second** *etc* être classé premier/deuxième *etc* ex aequo; (*US Rad, TV*) **~ time** droit *m* de réponse (à l'antenne); **~ opportunities** chances égales, égalité *f* des chances; **~ rights** égalité *f* des droits; *see also* **4**.
b to be ~ to sth être à la hauteur de qch; **to be ~ to doing** être de force à *or* de taille à faire; **she did not feel ~ to going out** elle ne se sentait pas le courage *or* la force de sortir, elle ne se sentait pas capable de sortir.
c *temperament etc* égal.
2 n égal(e) *m(f)*, pair *m*, pareil(le) *m(f)*. **our ~s** nos égaux; **to treat sb as an ~** traiter qn d'égal à égal; **she has no ~** elle n'a pas sa pareille, elle est hors pair; (*in rank, standing*) **she is his ~** elle est son égale.
3 vt (*Math, gen*) égaler (*in* en). **not to be ~led** sans égal, qui n'a pas son égal; **there is nothing to ~ it** il n'y a rien de tel *or* de comparable; (*Math*) **let x ~ y** si x égale y.
4 comp ▸Equal Opportunities Commission (*Brit*), **Equal Employment Opportunity Commission** (*US*) commission *f* sur l'égalité des chances **▸equal opportunities** *or* **opportunity employer** employeur *m* qui ne fait pas de discrimination **▸Equal Rights Amendment** (*US*) *amendement constitutionnel en faveur de l'égalité des droits* **▸equal(s) sign** (*Math*) signe *m* d'égalité *or* d'équivalence.
equality [ɪ'kwɒlɪtɪ] **n** égalité *f*. **~ in the eyes of the law** égalité devant la loi; **~ of opportunity** l'égalité des chances; **the E~ State** le Wyoming.
equalization [i:kwəlaɪ'zeɪʃən] **n** (*see* **equalize**) égalisation *f*;

nivellement *m*; régularisation *f*.
equalize ['i:kwəlaɪz] 1 vt *chances, opportunities* égaliser; *wealth, possessions* niveler; *accounts* régulariser. 2 vi (*Sport*) égaliser.
equalizer ['i:kwəlaɪzəʳ] n a (*Sport*) but *or* point égalisateur. b (*US* *: *gun*) flingue* *m*, revolver *m*.
equally ['i:kwəlɪ] adv également. **to divide sth ~** diviser qch en parts *or* parties égales; **her mother was ~ disappointed** sa mère a été tout aussi déçue; **she did ~ well in history** elle a eu de tout aussi bons résultats en histoire; **it would be ~ wrong to suggest** il serait tout aussi faux de suggérer; **~ gifted brothers** frères également *or* pareillement doués; **they were ~ guilty** ils étaient également coupables *or* coupables au même degré.
equanimity [,ekwə'nɪmɪtɪ] n égalité *f* d'humeur, sérénité *f*, équanimité *f* (*frm*). **with ~** avec sérénité, d'une âme égale.
equate [ɪ'kweɪt] vt (*identify*) assimiler (*with* à); (*compare*) mettre sur le même pied (*with* que); (*Math*) mettre en équation (*to* avec); (*make equal*) égaler, égaliser. **to ~ Eliot with Shakespeare** mettre Eliot sur le même pied que Shakespeare; **to ~ black with mourning** assimiler le noir au deuil; **to ~ supply and demand** égaler *or* égaliser l'offre à la demande.
equation [ɪ'kweɪʒən] n (*see* **equate**) assimilation *f*; égalisation *f*; (*Chem, Math*) équation *f*. (*Astron*) **~ of time** équation du temps; *see* **quadratic, simple**.
equator [ɪ'kweɪtəʳ] n équateur *m* (terrestre), ligne équinoxiale. **at the ~** sous l'équateur.
equatorial [,ekwə'tɔ:rɪəl] adj équatorial. **E~ Guinea** Guinée équatoriale.
equerry [ɪ'kwerɪ] n écuyer *m* (*au service d'un membre de la famille royale*).
equestrian [ɪ'kwestrɪən] 1 adj équestre. 2 n (*gen*) cavalier *m*, -ière *f*; (*in circus*) écuyer *m*, -ère *f*.
equi... ['i:kwɪ] pref équi... .
equidistant ['i:kwɪ'dɪstənt] adj équidistant, à égale distance. **Orléans is ~ from Tours and Paris** Orléans est à égale distance de Tours et de Paris.
equilateral ['i:kwɪ'lætərəl] adj équilatéral.
equilibrium [,i:kwɪ'lɪbrɪəm] n, pl **~s** *or* **equilibria** [,i:kwɪ'lɪbrɪə] (*physical, mental*) équilibre *m*. **to lose one's ~** (*physically*) perdre l'équilibre; (*mentally*) devenir déséquilibré; **in ~** en équilibre.
equine ['ekwaɪn] adj *species, profile* chevalin.
equinoctial [,i:kwɪ'nɒkʃəl] adj équinoxial; *gales, tides* d'équinoxe.
equinox ['i:kwɪnɒks] n équinoxe *m*. **vernal** *or* **spring ~** équinoxe de printemps, point vernal; **autumnal ~** équinoxe d'automne.
equip [ɪ'kwɪp] vt a (*fit out*) *factory* équiper, outiller; *kitchen, laboratory* installer, équiper; *ship, soldier, worker, astronaut* équiper. **to ~ a room as a laboratory** aménager une pièce en laboratoire; **to ~ a household** monter un ménage; *[factory etc]* **to be ~ped to do** être équipé pour faire; (*fig*) **to be ~ped for a job** avoir les compétences nécessaires pour un emploi; (*fig*) **to be well ~ped to do** (*gen*) avoir tout ce qu'il faut pour faire; *[worker, employee]* avoir toutes les compétences *or* les qualités nécessaires pour faire; *see* **ill 5**.
b (*provide*) **to ~ with** *person* équiper de, pourvoir de, munir de; *ship, car, factory, army etc* équiper de, munir de, doter de; **to ~ o.s. with** s'équiper de, se munir de, se pourvoir de; **she is well ~ped with cookery books** elle est bien montée *or* pourvue en livres de cuisine; **to ~ a ship with radar** installer le radar sur un bateau.
equipage ['ekwɪpɪdʒ] n équipage *m* (*chevaux et personnel*).
equipment [ɪ'kwɪpmənt] n (*gen*) équipement *m*; (*for office, laboratory, camping etc*) matériel *m*. **factory ~** outillage *m*; **lifesaving ~** matériel *m* de sauvetage; **electrical ~** appareillage *m* électrique; **domestic ~** appareils ménagers; **~ grant** prime *f or* subvention *f* d'équipement.
equisetum [,ekwɪ'si:təm] n, pl **~s** *or* **equiseta** [,ekwɪ'si:tə] equisetum *m*, prèle *f*.
equitable ['ekwɪtəbl] adj équitable, juste.
equitably ['ekwɪtəblɪ] adv équitablement, avec justice.
equitation [,ekwɪ'teɪʃən] n (*frm*) équitation *f*.
equity ['ekwɪtɪ] n a (*NonC: fairness*) équité *f*. b (*Econ*) (*also* **owner's ~, shareholder's ~, ~ capital**) fonds *mpl or* capitaux *mpl* propres, capital *m* actions. **~ issue** émission *f* de capital; **~-linked policy** police *f* d'assurance-vie indexée sur le cours des valeurs boursières; (*Brit St Ex*) **equities** actions cotés en bourse. c (*Jur: system of law*) équité *f*. d (*Brit*) **E~** *syndicat des acteurs*.
equivalence [ɪ'kwɪvələns] n équivalence *f*.
equivalent [ɪ'kwɪvələnt] 1 adj équivalent. **to be ~ to** être équivalent à, équivaloir à. 2 n équivalent *m* (*in* en). **the French ~ of the English word** l'équivalent en français du mot anglais; (*Ind*) **man ~** unité-travailleur *f*.
equivocal [ɪ'kwɪvəkəl] adj (*ambiguous*) *attitude* équivoque, peu net; *words* équivoque, ambigu (*f* -guë); (*suspicious*) *behaviour* louche, douteux; (*unclear*) *outcome* incertain, douteux.
equivocally [ɪ'kwɪvəkəlɪ] adv d'une manière équivoque, avec ambiguïté.
equivocate [ɪ'kwɪvəkeɪt] vi user de faux-fuyants *or* d'équivoques, équivoquer (*liter*).
equivocation [ɪ,kwɪvə'keɪʃən] n (*often pl*) paroles *fpl* équivoques, emploi *m* d'équivoques.
ER (abbr of **Elizabeth Regina**) la reine Élisabeth.
er [ɜ:ʳ] interj euh.
ERA [,i:ɑ:'reɪ] a (*US*) (abbr of **Equal Rights Amendment**) *see* **equal 4**. b (*Brit*) (abbr of **Education Reform Act**) acte *m* de réforme de l'éducation.
era ['ɪərə] n (*Geol, Hist*) ère *f*; (*gen*) époque *f*, temps *m*. **the Christian ~** l'ère chrétienne; **the end of an ~** la fin d'une époque; **the ~ of crinolines** le temps des crinolines; **to mark an ~** marquer une époque, faire époque.
eradicate [ɪ'rædɪkeɪt] vt *vice, malpractices* extirper, supprimer; *disease* faire disparaître, supprimer; *superstition* bannir, mettre fin à; *weeds* détruire.
eradication [ɪ,rædɪ'keɪʃən] n (*see* **eradicate**) suppression *f*; fin *f*; destruction *f*.
erase [ɪ'reɪz] 1 vt a *writing, marks* effacer, gratter; (*with rubber*) gommer; (*Comput, Sound Recording; also from the mind*) effacer. b (*US* *: *kill*) liquider*, tuer. 2 comp ►**erase head** tête *f* d'effacement.
eraser [ɪ'reɪzəʳ] n (*rubber*) gomme *f*.
Erasmus [ɪ'ræzməs] n Érasme *m*.
erasure [ɪ'reɪʒəʳ] n rature *f*, grattage *m*, effacement *m*; (*act of erasing*) grattage, effacement.
erbium ['ɜ:bɪəm] n erbium *m*.
ere [ɛəʳ] (*liter*, ††) 1 prep avant. **~ now** déjà; **~ then** d'ici là; **~ long** sous peu. 2 conj avant que + *subj*.
erect [ɪ'rekt] 1 adj (*straight*) (bien) droit; (*standing*) debout; (*Physiol*) en érection. **to hold o.s. ~** se tenir droit; **with head ~** la tête haute; **with tail ~** la queue levée *or* dressée en l'air. 2 adv *walk* (*on hind legs*) debout; (*not stooping or drooping*) droit. 3 vt *temple, statue* ériger, élever; *wall, flats, factory* bâtir, construire; *machinery, traffic signs* installer; *scaffolding, furniture* monter; *altar, tent, mast, barricade* dresser; (*fig*) *theory* bâtir; *obstacles* élever.
erectile [ɪ'rektaɪl] adj érectile.
erection [ɪ'rekʃən] n a (*NonC: see* **erect**) érection *f*; construction *f*; installation *f*; montage *m*; dressage *m*; *[theory, obstacle]* édification *f*. b (*building, structure*) construction *f*, bâtiment *m*. c (*Physiol*) érection *f*.
erectly [ɪ'rektlɪ] adv droit.
erector [ɪ'rektəʳ] 1 n (*muscle*) érecteur *m*. 2 comp ►**erector set** (*US: toy*) jeu *m* de construction.
erg [ɜ:g] n erg *m*.
ergative ['ɜ:gətɪv] adj (*Ling*) ergatif.
ergo ['ɜ:gəʊ] conj (*frm, hum*) par conséquent.
ergonomic [,ɜ:gəʊ'nɒmɪk] adj ergonomique.
ergonomics [,ɜ:gəʊ'nɒmɪks] n (*NonC*) ergonomie *f*.
ergonomist [ɜ:'gɒnəmɪst] n ergonome *mf*.
ergot ['ɜ:gət] n (*Agr*) ergot *m*; (*Pharm*) ergot de seigle.
ergotism ['ɜ:gətɪzəm] n ergotisme *m*.
Erie ['ɪərɪ] n: **Lake ~** le lac Érié.
Erin ['ɪərɪn] n (*liter*, ††) Irlande *f*.
Eritrea [erɪ'treɪə] n Érythrée *f*.
Eritrean [erɪ'treɪən] 1 adj érythréen. 2 n (*person*) Érythréen(ne) *m(f)*.
erk* [ɜ:k] n (*Brit*) (*Aviat*) bidasse *m*; (*Naut*) mataf *m*.
ERM [,i:ɑ:'rem] n (abbr of **Exchange Rate Mechanism**) *see* **exchange 4**.
ermine ['ɜ:mɪn] n, pl **~s** *or* **~** (*animal, fur, robes*) hermine *f*.
ERNIE ['ɜ:nɪ] (*Brit*) (abbr of **Electronic Random Number Indicator Equipment**) *ordinateur qui sert au tirage des numéros gagnants des bons à lots*.
erode [ɪ'rəʊd] 1 vt *[water, wind, sea]* éroder, ronger; *[acid, rust]* ronger, corroder; (*fig*) ronger, miner, corroder. 2 vi s'éroder; se corroder.
►**erode away** 1 vt désagréger. 2 vi se désagréger.
erogenous [ɪ'rɒdʒənəs] adj érogène.
Eroica [ɪ'rəʊɪkə] n (*Mus*) **the ~ Symphony** la Symphonie Héroïque.
Eros ['i:rɒs] n Éros *m*.
erosion [ɪ'rəʊʒən] n (*see* **erode**) érosion *f*; corrosion *f*. **the ~ of the French franc through inflation** l'érosion *f or* l'effritement *m* du franc français du fait de l'inflation.
erosive [ɪ'rəʊzɪv] adj (*see* **erode**) érosif; corrosif.
erotic [ɪ'rɒtɪk] adj érotique.
erotica [ɪ'rɒtɪkə] npl (*Art*) art *m* érotique; (*Literat*) littérature *f* érotique.
erotically [ɪ'rɒtɪkəlɪ] adv érotiquement.
eroticism [ɪ'rɒtɪsɪzəm] n érotisme *m*.
err [ɜ:ʳ] vi (*be mistaken*) se tromper; (*sin*) pécher, commettre une faute. **to ~ in one's judgment** faire une erreur de jugement; **to ~ on the side of caution** pécher par excès de prudence; **to ~ is human** l'erreur est humaine.
errand ['erənd] n commission *f*, course *f*. **to go on** *or* **run ~s** faire des commissions *or* des courses; **to be on an ~** être en course; **~ of mercy** mission *f* de charité; **~ boy** garçon *m* de courses; *see* **fool**[1].
errant ['erənt] adj (*sinful*) dévoyé; (*wandering*) errant; *see* **knight**.
errata [e'rɑ:tə] npl of **erratum**.

erratic [ɪ'rætɪk] **adj** *person* fantasque, capricieux; *record, results* irrégulier; *performance* irrégulier, inégal; *mood* changeant; (*Geol, Med*) erratique. **his driving is ~** il conduit de façon déconcertante.
erratically [ɪ'rætɪkəlɪ] **adv** *act* capricieusement; *work* irrégulièrement, par à-coups. **to drive ~** conduire de façon déconcertante.
erratum [e'rɑːtəm] **n, pl errata** erratum *m*.
erroneous [ɪ'rəʊnɪəs] **adj** erroné, faux (*f* fausse).
erroneously [ɪ'rəʊnɪəslɪ] **adv** erronément, faussement, à tort.
error ['erəʳ] **n** **a** (*mistake*) erreur *f* (*also Math*), faute *f*. **to make** *or* **commit an ~** faire (une) erreur, commettre une erreur, se tromper; **it would be an ~ to underestimate him** on aurait tort de le sous-estimer; **~ of judgment** erreur de jugement; **~ in calculation** erreur de calcul; (*Naut*) **compass ~** variation *f* du compas; (*Comm*) **~s and omissions excepted** sauf erreur ou omission; (*Comput*) **~ message** message *m* d'erreur; *see* **margin, spelling** *etc*. **b** (*NonC*) erreur *f*. **in ~** par erreur, par méprise; (*Rel*) **to be in/fall into ~** être/tomber dans l'erreur; **to see the ~ of one's ways** revenir de ses erreurs.
ersatz ['ɛəzæts] **1** **n** ersatz *m*, succédané *m*. **2** **adj: this is ~ coffee** c'est de l'ersatz *or* du succédané de café; **this coffee is ~** ce café est un ersatz *or* de l'ersatz *or* un succédané.
erstwhile ['ɜːstwaɪl] (*liter*, †) **1** **adj** d'autrefois, d'antan (*liter*). **2** **adv** autrefois, jadis.
eructate [ɪ'rʌkteɪt] **vi** éructer.
erudite ['erʊdaɪt] **adj** *person, work* érudit, savant; *word* savant.
eruditely ['erʊdaɪtlɪ] **adv** d'une manière savante, avec érudition.
erudition [,erʊ'dɪʃən] **n** érudition *f*.
erupt [ɪ'rʌpt] **vi** *[volcano]* (*begin*) entrer en éruption; (*go on ~ing*) faire éruption; *[spots]* sortir, apparaître; *[teeth]* percer; *[anger]* exploser; *[war, fighting, quarrel]* éclater. **~ing volcano** volcan *m* en éruption; **he ~ed into the room** il a fait irruption dans la pièce.
eruption [ɪ'rʌpʃən] **n** *[volcano]* éruption *f*; *[spots, rash]* éruption, poussée *f*; *[teeth]* percée *f*; *[anger]* explosion *f*, accès *m*; *[violence]* accès. **a volcano in a state of ~** un volcan en éruption.
erysipelas [,erɪ'sɪpɪləs] **n** érysipèle *m or* érésipèle *m*.
erythrocyte [ɪ'rɪθrəʊ,saɪt] **n** (*Anat*) érythrocyte *m*.
ES [iː'es] **n** (**abbr of expert system**) SE *m*.
ESA [,iːes'eɪ] **n** (**abbr of European Space Agency**) ASE *f*.
Esau ['iːsɔː] **n** Ésaü *m*.
escalate ['eskəleɪt] **1** **vi** *[fighting, bombing, violence]* s'intensifier; *[costs]* monter en flèche. **the war is escalating** c'est l'escalade militaire; **prices are escalating** c'est l'escalade des prix. **2** **vt** *fighting etc* intensifier; *prices, wage claims* faire monter en flèche.
escalation [,eskə'leɪʃən] **n** (*see* **escalate**) escalade *f*, intensification *f*; montée *f* en flèche. **~ clause** clause *f* d'indexation *or* de révision.
escalator ['eskəleɪtəʳ] **1** **n** escalier roulant *or* mécanique, escalator *m*. **2** **comp ▸ escalator clause** (*Comm*) clause *f* d'indexation *or* de révision.
escalope [eskə'lɒp] **n** escalope *f*. **veal ~** escalope de veau.
escapade ['eskə,peɪd] **n** (*misdeed*) fredaine *f*; (*prank*) frasque *f*; (*adventure*) équipée *f*.
escape [ɪs'keɪp] **1** **vi** *[person, animal]* échapper (*from sb* à qn), s'échapper (*from somewhere* de quelque part); *[prisoner]* s'évader (*from* de); *[water, steam, gas]* s'échapper, fuir. **to ~ from sb/from sb's hands** échapper à qn/des mains de qn; **an ~d prisoner** un évadé; **to ~ to a neutral country** s'enfuir dans *or* gagner un pays neutre; **he ~d with a few scratches** il s'en est tiré avec quelques égratignures; **to ~ with a fright/a warning** en être quitte pour la peur/un avertissement; **to seek to ~ from the world/the crowd** fuir le monde/la foule; **to ~ from o.s.** se fuir; *see* **skin**.
2 **vt** **a** (*avoid*) *pursuit* échapper à; *consequences* éviter; *punishment* se soustraire à. **he narrowly ~d danger/death** il a échappé de justesse au danger/à la mort; **to ~ detection** ne pas se faire repérer; **to ~ observation** *or* **notice** passer inaperçu; **he narrowly ~d being run over** il a failli *or* manqué être écrasé.
b (*be unnoticed, forgotten by*) échapper à. **his name ~s me** son nom m'échappe; **nothing ~s him** rien ne lui échappe; **it had not ~d her notice that ...** elle n'avait pas été sans s'apercevoir que ..., il ne lui avait pas échappé que ...; **the thoughtless words which ~d me** les paroles irréfléchies qui m'ont échappé.
3 **n** *[person]* fuite *f*, évasion *f*; *[animal]* fuite; *[water, gas]* fuite; *[steam, gas in machine]* échappement *m*. **to plan an ~** combiner un plan d'évasion; **to make an** *or* **one's ~** s'échapper, s'évader; **to have a lucky** *or* **narrow ~** l'échapper belle, s'en tirer de justesse; (*fig*) **~ from reality** évasion hors de la réalité; (*Comput*) **~ (key)** touche *f* Esc *or* Échap.
4 **comp ▸ escape chute** (*Aviat*) toboggan *m* de secours **▸ escape clause** (*Jur*) clause *f* dérogatoire *or* de sauvegarde **▸ escape device** dispositif *m* de sortie *or* de secours **▸ escape hatch** (*Naut*) sas *m* de secours **▸ escape key** (*Comput*) *see* **3 ▸ escape mechanism** (*lit*) mécanisme *m* de défense *or* de protection; (*Psych*) fuite *f* (*devant la réalité*) **▸ escape pipe** tuyau *m* d'échappement *or* de refoulement, tuyère *f* **▸ escape plan** plan *m* d'évasion **▸ escape route** chemin *m* d'évasion **▸ escape valve** soupape *f* d'échappement **▸ escape velocity** (*Space*) vitesse *f* de libération.
escapee [ɪskeɪ'piː] **n** *[prison]* évadé(e) *m(f)*.
escapement [ɪs'keɪpmənt] **n** *[clock, piano]* échappement *m*.
escapism [ɪs'keɪpɪzəm] **n** (désir *m* d')évasion *f* de la réalité. **it's sheer ~!** c'est simplement s'évader du réel!
escapist [ɪs'keɪpɪst] **1** **n** personne *f* qui se complaît dans l'évasion. **2** **adj** *film, reading etc* d'évasion.
escapologist [,eskə'pɒlədʒɪst] **n** (*conjurer*) virtuose *m* de l'évasion; (*fig*) champion *m* de l'esquive.
escarpment [ɪs'kɑːpmənt] **n** escarpement *m*.
eschatology [,eskə'tɒlədʒɪ] **n** eschatologie *f*.
eschew [ɪs'tʃuː] **vt** (†, *frm*) éviter; *wine etc* s'abstenir de; *temptation* fuir.
escort ['eskɔːt] **1** **n** **a** (*Mil, Naut*) escorte *f*; (*guard of honour*) escorte, cortège *m*, suite *f*. **under the ~ of** sous l'escorte de; **under ~** sous escorte.
b (*male companion*) cavalier *m*; (*female*) hôtesse *f*.
2 **comp ▸ escort agency** bureau *m* d'hôtesses **▸ escort duty: to be on escort duty** *[soldiers]* être assigné au service d'escorte; *[ship]* être en service d'escorte **▸ escort vessel** (*Naut*) vaisseau *m or* bâtiment *m* d'escorte, (vaisseau) escorteur *m*.
3 [ɪs'kɔːt] **vt** (*Mil, Naut, gen*) escorter; (*accompany*) accompagner, escorter. **to ~ sb in** (*Mil, Police*) faire entrer qn sous escorte; (*gen: accompany*) faire entrer qn; **to ~ sb out** (*Mil, Police*) faire sortir qn sous escorte; (*gen*) raccompagner qn jusqu'à la sortie.
escrow ['eskrəʊ] **n** (*Jur*) dépôt fiduciaire *or* conditionnel. **in ~** en dépôt fiduciaire, en main tierce; (*Fin*) **~ account** compte bloqué.
escudo [es'kuːdəʊ] **n, pl ~s** escudo *m*.
escutcheon [ɪs'kʌtʃən] **n** (*Her*) écu *m*, écusson *m*; *see* **blot**.
esker ['eskəʳ] **n** (*Geol*) os *m*.
Eskimo ['eskɪməʊ] **1** **n** **a** Esquimau(de) *m(f)*. **b** (*Ling*) esquimau *m*. **2** **adj** esquimau (*f* -aude *or inv*), eskimo *inv*. **~ dogs** chiens esquimaux.
ESL [,iːes'el] **n** (*Educ*) (**abbr of English as a Second Language**) *see* **English**.
ESN [,iːes'en] **adj** (*Educ*) (**abbr of educationally subnormal**) *see* **educationally**.
esophagus [ɪ'sɒfəgəs] **n, pl ~es** *or* **esophagi** [ɪ'sɒfə,dʒaɪ] œsophage *m*.
esoteric [,esəʊ'terɪk] **adj** ésotérique, secret (*f* -ète).
esoterica [,esəʊ'terɪkə] **npl** objets *mpl* ésotériques.
ESP [,iːes'piː] **n** **a** (**abbr of extrasensory perception**) *see* **extrasensory**. **b** (**abbr of English for Special Purposes**) *see* **English**.
esp. **abbr of especially**.
espalier [ɪ'spæljəʳ] **1** **n** (*trellis*) treillage *m* d'un espalier; (*tree*) arbre *m* en espalier; (*method*) culture *f* en espalier. **2** **vt** cultiver en espalier.
esparto [e'spɑːtəʊ] **n** (*also* **~ grass**) alfa *m*.
especial [ɪs'peʃəl] **adj** particulier, exceptionnel, spécial.
especially [ɪs'peʃəlɪ] **adv** (*to a marked degree*) particulièrement, spécialement; (*principally*) particulièrement, spécialement, en particulier, surtout; (*expressly*) exprès. **more ~ as** d'autant plus que; **it is ~ awkward** c'est particulièrement fâcheux; **~ as it's so late** d'autant plus qu'il est si tard; **you ~ ought to know** tu devrais le savoir mieux que personne; **why me ~?** pourquoi moi en particulier *or* tout particulièrement?; **I came ~ to see you** je suis venu exprès pour vous voir.
Esperantist [,espə'ræntɪst] **n** espérantiste *mf*.
Esperanto [,espə'ræntəʊ] **1** **n** espéranto *m*. **2** **adj** en espéranto.
espionage [,espɪə'nɑːʒ] **n** espionnage *m*.
esplanade [,esplə'neɪd] **n** esplanade *f*.
espousal [ɪ'spaʊzəl] **n** *[cause]* adhésion *f* (*of* à).
espouse [ɪs'paʊz] **vt** *cause* épouser, embrasser; (††) *person* épouser.
espresso [es'presəʊ] **n** (café *m*) express *m*. **~ bar** café *m* (*où l'on sert du café express*).
espy [ɪs'paɪ] **vt** (†, *frm*) apercevoir, aviser (*frm*).
Esq. **n** (*Brit frm*) (**abbr of esquire**) **Brian Smith ~** M. Brian Smith (*sur une enveloppe etc*).
...esque [esk] **suf: Kafkaesque** kafkaïen.
esquire [ɪs'kwaɪəʳ] **n** **a** (*Brit: on envelope etc*) *see* **Esq.** **b** (*Brit Hist*) écuyer *m*.
essay ['eseɪ] **1** **n** **a** (*Literat*) essai *m* (*on* sur); (*Scol*) rédaction *f*, composition *f* (*on* sur); (*Brit Educ*) dissertation *f* (*on* sur); (*US Univ*) mémoire *m*. **b** (*attempt*) essai *m*. **2** **comp ▸ essay test** (*US Educ*) épreuve écrite. **3** [e'seɪ] **vt** (*try*) essayer, tenter (*to do* de faire); (*test*) mettre à l'épreuve.
essayist ['eseɪɪst] **n** essayiste *mf*.
essence ['esəns] **n** (*gen*) essence *f*, fond *m*, essentiel *m*; (*Chem*) essence; (*Culin*) extrait *m*; (*Philos*) essence, nature *f*. **in ~** par essence, essentiellement; **the ~ of what was said** l'essentiel de ce qui a été dit; **speed/precision is of the ~** la vitesse/la précision est essentielle *or* s'impose; **the ~ of stupidity*** le comble de la stupidité; **~ of violets** essence de violette; **meat ~** extrait de viande; **the divine ~** l'essence divine.
essential [ɪ'senʃəl] **1** **adj** *equipment, action* essentiel, indispensable (*to* à); *fact* essentiel; *role, point* capital, essentiel; *question* essentiel, fondamental; *commodities* essentiel, de première nécessité; (*Chem*)

essentiel. **it is ~ to act quickly** il est indispensable *or* essentiel d'agir vite; **it is ~ that ...** il est indispensable que ... + *subj*; **it's not ~** ce n'est pas indispensable; **the ~ thing is to act** l'essentiel est d'agir; **man's ~ goodness** la bonté essentielle de l'homme; (*Chem*) **~ oil** essence *f*, huile essentielle.

2 n qualité *f* (*or* objet *m etc*) indispensable. **the ~s** l'essentiel *m*; **in (all) ~s** pour l'essentiel, de manière générale; **to see to the ~s** s'occuper de l'essentiel; **accuracy is an ~ or one of the ~s** la précision est une des qualités indispensables; (*rudiments*) **the ~s of German grammar** les éléments *mpl or* les rudiments *mpl* de la grammaire allemande.

essentially [ɪ'senʃəlɪ] adv (*in essence*) essentiellement, fondamentalement, par essence; (*principally*) essentiellement, avant tout, principalement.

EST [ˌiːes'tiː] (*US*) (abbr of **Eastern Standard Time**) *see* **eastern.**

est. a (*Comm etc*) (abbr of **established**) **~ 1900** ≃ maison fondée en 1900. b abbr of **estimate(d).**

establish [ɪs'tæblɪʃ] vt a (*set up*) *government* constituer, établir; *state, business* fonder, créer; *factory* établir, monter; *society, tribunal* constituer; *laws, custom* instaurer; *relations* établir, nouer; *post* créer; *power, authority* affermir; *peace, order* faire régner; *list, sb's reputation* établir. **to ~ one's reputation as a scholar/as a writer** se faire une réputation de savant/comme écrivain; **to ~ o.s. as a grocer** s'établir épicier. b (*prove*) *fact, identity, one's rights* établir; *necessity, guilt* prouver, démontrer; *innocence* établir, démontrer.

established [ɪs'tæblɪʃt] adj *reputation* établi, bien assis; *fact* acquis, reconnu; *truth* établi, démontré; *custom, belief* établi, enraciné; *government* établi, au pouvoir; *laws* établi, en vigueur; *order* établi. (*Comm*) **E~ 1850** ≃ maison fondée en 1850; **well-~ business** maison solide; **the ~ Church** l'Église établie, la religion d'État *or* officielle.

establishment [ɪs'tæblɪʃmənt] 1 n a (*NonC*) (*see* **establish**) établissement *m*; fondation *f*, création *f*; constitution *f*; instauration *f*.

b (*institution etc*) établissement *m*. **commercial ~** établissement commercial, maison *f* de commerce, firme *f*; **teaching ~** établissement d'enseignement.

c (*Mil, Naut etc: personnel*) effectif *m*. **war/peace ~** effectifs de guerre/de paix; (*household*) **to keep up a large ~** avoir un grand train de maison.

d (*Brit*) **the E~** (*the authorities*) les pouvoirs établis, les milieux dirigeants, l'establishment *m*; (*their power*) le pouvoir effectif; (*the values they represent*) l'ordre établi, les valeurs reconnues; (*Rel*) l'Église établie; **these are the values of the E~** ce sont là les valeurs traditionnelles *or* conformistes *or* bien reconnues; **he has always been against the E~** il a toujours été anticonformiste; **he has joined the E~** il s'est rangé, il n'est plus rebelle; **the literary/political E~** ceux qui font la loi dans le monde littéraire/politique.

2 adj traditionnel, conformiste.

estate [ɪs'teɪt] 1 n a (*land*) propriété *f*, domaine *m*. **country ~** terre(s) *f(pl)*; (*esp Brit*) **housing ~** lotissement *m*, cité *f*; *see* **real** *etc*.

b (*Jur: possessions*) bien(s) *m(pl)*, fortune *f*; *[deceased]* succession *f*. **he left a large ~** il a laissé une grosse fortune (en héritage); **to liquidate the ~** liquider la succession.

c (*order, rank, condition*) état *m*, rang *m*, condition *f*. **the three ~s** les trois états; **the third ~** le Tiers État, la bourgeoisie; **the fourth ~** la presse, le quatrième pouvoir; (*liter*) **a man of high/low ~** un homme de haut rang/d'humble condition; (*liter*) **to reach man's ~** parvenir à l'âge d'homme.

2 comp ►**estate agency** (*esp Brit*) agence immobilière ►**estate agent** (*esp Brit*) agent immobilier ►**estate car** (*Brit*) break *m* ►**estate duty** (*Brit*), **estate tax** (*US*) droits *mpl* de succession.

esteem [ɪs'tiːm] 1 vt a (*think highly of*) *person* avoir de l'estime pour, estimer; *quality* estimer, apprécier. **our (highly) ~d colleague** notre (très) estimé collègue *or* confrère. b (*consider*) estimer, considérer. **I ~ it an honour (that)** je m'estime très honoré (que + *subj*); **I ~ it an honour to do** je considère comme un honneur de faire.

2 n estime *f*, considération *f*. **to hold in high ~** tenir en haute estime; **he went up/down in my ~** il a monté/baissé dans mon estime.

Esther ['estəʳ] n Esther *f*.

esthete ['iːsθiːt] *etc* = **aesthete** *etc*.

Esthonia [es'təʊnɪə] *etc* = **Estonia** *etc*.

estimable ['estɪməbl] adj estimable, digne d'estime.

estimate ['estɪmət] 1 n évaluation *f*, estimation *f*, calcul approximatif; (*Comm*) devis *m*. (*Comm*) **give me an ~ for (building) a greenhouse** donnez-moi *or* établissez-moi un devis pour la construction d'une serre; **give me an ~ of what your trip will cost** donnez-moi un état estimatif du coût de votre voyage; **this price is only a rough ~** ce prix n'est que très approximatif; **at a rough ~** approximativement, à vue de nez*; **at an optimistic ~** dans la meilleure des hypothèses; **at the lowest ~ it will cost 1,000 francs** cela coûtera 1.000 F au bas mot; (*Admin, Pol*) **the ~s** le budget, les crédits *mpl* budgétaires; **the Army ~s** le budget de l'armée; **to form an ~ of sb's capabilities** évaluer les capacités de qn; **his ~ of 400 people was very far out** il s'était trompé de beaucoup en évaluant le nombre de gens à 400; *see* **preliminary.**

2 ['estɪmeɪt] vt estimer, juger (*that* que); *cost, number, price, quantity* estimer, évaluer; *distance, speed* estimer, apprécier. **his fortune is ~d at ...** on évalue sa fortune à ...; **I ~ that there must be 40 of them** j'estime *or* je juge qu'il doit y en avoir 40, à mon avis il doit y en avoir 40; **an ~d 60,000 refugees have crossed the border** environ 60.000 réfugiés auraient traversé la frontière; **~d time of arrival/departure** horaire prévu d'arrivée/de départ; **~d cost** coût *m* estimatif.

estimator ['estɪmeɪtəʳ] n expert *m* (*de compagnie d'assurances*).

estimation [ˌestɪ'meɪʃən] n a jugement *m*, opinion *f*. **in my ~** à mon avis, selon moi. b (*esteem*) estime *f*, considération *f*. **he went up/down in my ~** il a monté/baissé dans mon estime.

Estonia [e'stəʊnɪə] n Estonie *f*.

Estonian [e'stəʊnɪən] 1 adj estonien. 2 n a Estonien(ne) *m(f)*. b (*Ling*) estonien *m*.

estrange [ɪs'treɪndʒ] vt brouiller (*from* avec), éloigner (*from* de). **to become ~d (from)** se brouiller (avec), se détacher (de); **the ~d couple** les époux désunis *or* séparés; **her ~d husband** son mari dont elle s'était (*or* s'est) séparée.

estrangement [ɪs'treɪndʒmənt] n (*see* **estrange**) brouille *f* (*from* avec), éloignement *m* (*from* de); désunion *f*, séparation *f*.

estrogen ['estrədʒən, 'iːstrədʒən] n (*US*) = **oestrogen.**

estrus ['iːstrəs] n (*US*) = **oestrus.**

estuary ['estjʊərɪ] n estuaire *m*.

ET [iː'tiː] a (*Brit*) (abbr of **Employment Training**) *see* **employment.** b (*US*) (abbr of **Eastern Time**) *heure sur la côte est.*

ETA [ˌiːtiː'eɪ] n abbr of **estimated time of arrival.**

et al [et'æl] (abbr of **and others**) et autres.

etc [ɪt'setərə] (abbr of **et cetera**) etc.

et cetera, etcetera [ɪt'setərə] 1 adv et caetera. 2 n: **the etceteras** les extras *mpl*, les et caetera *mpl*.

etch [etʃ] vti (*Art, Typ*) graver à l'eau forte. (*fig*) **~ed on his memory** gravé dans sa mémoire.

etching ['etʃɪŋ] n a (*NonC*) gravure *f* à l'eau forte. **~ needle** pointe *f* (sèche). b (*picture*) (gravure *f* à l')eau-forte *f*.

ETD [ˌiːtiː'diː] n abbr of **estimated time of departure.**

eternal [ɪ'tɜːnl] 1 adj (*Philos, Rel, gen*) éternel; (*pej*) *complaints, gossip etc* continuel, perpétuel, sempiternel (*pej*). **the ~ triangle** l'éternelle situation de trio, le ménage à trois. 2 n: **the E~** l'Éternel *m*.

eternally [ɪ'tɜːnəlɪ] adv (*see* **eternal**) éternellement; continuellement, perpétuellement, sempiternellement (*pej*).

eternity [ɪ'tɜːnɪtɪ] 1 n éternité *f*. **it seemed like an ~** on aurait dit une éternité; **we waited an ~*** nous avons attendu (toute) une éternité *or* des éternités*. 2 comp ►**eternity ring** bague *f* de fidélité (*offerte par un mari à sa femme*).

ETF [ˌiːtiː'ef] n (abbr of **electronic transfer of funds**) TEF *m*.

ethane ['iːθeɪn] n éthane *m*.

ethanol ['eθənɒl] n alcool *m* éthylique, éthanol *m*.

ether ['iːθəʳ] n (*Chem, Phys*) éther *m*. (*liter*) **the ~** l'éther, les espaces *mpl* célestes; (*Rad*) **over the ~** sur les ondes.

ethereal [ɪ'θɪərɪəl] adj (*delicate*) éthéré, aérien; (*spiritual*) éthéré, sublime.

ethic ['eθɪk] 1 n morale *f*, éthique *f*; *see* **work.** 2 adj = **ethical.**

ethical ['eθɪkəl] adj éthique (*frm*), moral. **not ~** contraire à la morale; (*Med*) **~ code** code *m* déontologique; **~ drug** médicament *m* sur ordonnance.

ethically ['eθɪklɪ] adv sur le plan éthique, d'un point de vue éthique.

ethics ['eθɪks] 1 n (*NonC*) (*study*) éthique *f*, morale *f*. 2 npl (*system, principles*) morale *f*; (*morality*) moralité *f*. **medical ~** code *m* déontologique *or* de déontologie; *see* **code.**

Ethiopia [ˌiːθɪ'əʊpɪə] n Éthiopie *f*.

Ethiopian [ˌiːθɪ'əʊpɪən] 1 adj éthiopien. 2 n Éthiopien(ne) *m(f)*.

ethnic ['eθnɪk] 1 adj ethnique. **~ minority** minorité *f* ethnique; **~ cleansing** purification *f* ethnique. 2 npl: **~s** (*esp US: people*) (*iro*) membres *mpl* de minorités ethniques blanches.

ethnically ['eθnɪklɪ] adv sur le plan ethnique.

ethnographer [eθ'nɒgrəfəʳ] n ethnographe *mf*.

ethnographic(al) [ˌeθnə'græfɪk(əl)] adv ethnographique.

ethnography [eθ'nɒgrəfɪ] n ethnographie *f*.

ethnolinguistics [ˌeθnəʊlɪŋ'gwɪstɪks] n (*NonC*) ethnolinguistique *f*.

ethnologic(al) [ˌeθnə'lɒdʒɪk(əl)] adj ethnologique.

ethnologist [eθ'nɒlədʒɪst] n ethnologue *mf*.

ethnology [eθ'nɒlədʒɪ] n ethnologie *f*.

ethologist [ɪ'θɒlədʒɪst] n éthologue *mf*.

ethology [ɪ'θɒlədʒɪ] n éthologie *f*, éthographie *f*.

ethos ['iːθɒs] n génie *m* (*d'un peuple, d'une culture*).

ethyl ['iːθaɪl] n éthyle *m*. **~ acetate** acétate *m* d'éthyle.

ethylene ['eθɪliːn] n éthylène *m*.

etiology [ˌiːtɪ'ɒlədʒɪ] n (*Med, gen*) étiologie *f*.

etiquette ['etɪket] n convenances *fpl*; (*protocol*) étiquette *f*. **~ demands that ...** les convenances exigent (*or* l'étiquette exige) que (+ *subj*); **diplomatic ~** protocole *m*; **court ~** cérémonial *m* de cour; **that isn't ~** c'est contraire aux convenances *or* au bon usage, cela ne se fait pas; **it's against medical ~** c'est contraire à la déontologie médicale; **it's not professional ~** c'est contraire aux usages de la profession.

Etna [ˈetnə] n (*also* **Mount ~**) l'Etna *m*.

étrier [eɪtrɪˈeɪ] n (*Climbing*) étrier *m*, escarpolette *f*.

Etruria [ɪˈtrʊərɪə] n Étrurie *f*.

Etruscan [ɪˈtrʌskən] 1 adj étrusque. 2 n a (*person*) Étrusque *mf*. b (*Ling*) étrusque *m*.

ETU [ˌiːtiːˈjuː] n (*Brit*) (abbr of **Electrical Trades Union**) *syndicat*.

ETV [ˌiːtiːˈviː] (*US TV*) (abbr of **Educational Television**) *see* **educational**.

etymological [ˌetɪməˈlɒdʒɪkəl] adj étymologique.

etymologically [ˌetɪməˈlɒdʒɪkəlɪ] adv étymologiquement.

etymology [ˌetɪˈmɒlədʒɪ] n étymologie *f*.

eucalyptus [ˌjuːkəˈlɪptəs] n, pl **~es** *or* **eucalypti** [ˌjuːkəˈlɪptaɪ] (*Bot, Pharm*) eucalyptus *m*. **~ oil** essence *f* d'eucalyptus.

Eucharist [ˈjuːkərɪst] n Eucharistie *f*.

euchre [ˈjuːkəʳ] (*US*) 1 n euchre *m* (*jeu de cartes*). 2 vt (*: *cheat*) **to ~ sb out of sth*** carotter* qch à qn.

Euclid [ˈjuːklɪd] n Euclide *m*.

Euclidean [juːˈklɪdɪən] adj euclidien.

eugenic [juːˈdʒenɪk] adj eugénique.

eugenics [juːˈdʒenɪks] n (*NonC*) eugénique *f*, eugénisme *m*.

eulogize [ˈjuːlədʒaɪz] 1 vt faire l'éloge *or* le panégyrique de. 2 vi faire l'éloge *or* le panégyrique (*about, over* de).

eulogy [ˈjuːlədʒɪ] n panégyrique *m*.

eunuch [ˈjuːnək] n eunuque *m*.

euphemism [ˈjuːfəmɪzəm] n euphémisme *m*.

euphemistic [ˌjuːfəˈmɪstɪk] adj euphémique.

euphemistically [ˌjuːfəˈmɪstɪkəlɪ] adv par euphémisme, euphémiquement.

euphonic [juːˈfɒnɪk] adj, **euphonious** [juːˈfəʊnɪəs] adj euphonique.

euphonium [juːˈfəʊnɪəm] n euphonium *m*.

euphony [ˈjuːfənɪ] n euphonie *f*.

euphorbia [juːˈfɔːbɪə] n euphorbe *f*.

euphoria [juːˈfɔːrɪə] n euphorie *f*.

euphoric [juːˈfɒrɪk] adj euphorique.

Euphrates [juːˈfreɪtiːz] n Euphrate *m*.

euphuism [ˈjuːfjuːɪzəm] n préciosité *f*, euphuisme *m*.

Eurasia [jʊəˈreɪʃə] n Eurasie *f*.

Eurasian [jʊəˈreɪʃn] 1 adj *population* eurasien; *continent* eurasiatique. 2 n Eurasien(ne) *m(f)*.

Euratom [jʊəˈrætəm] n (abbr of **European Atomic Energy Community**) Euratom *m*, CEEA *f*.

eureka [jʊəˈriːkə] excl eurêka!

eurhythmics [juːˈrɪðmɪks] n (*NonC*) gymnastique *f* rythmique.

Euripides [jʊˈrɪpɪdiːz] n Euripide *m*.

euro... [ˈjʊərəʊ] pref euro... .

euro-ad [ˈjʊərəʊˌæd] n pub *f* paneuropéenne.

Eurobonds [ˈjʊərəʊˌbɒndz] npl euro-obligations *fpl*.

Eurocheque [ˈjʊərəʊˌtʃek] n eurochèque *m*. **~ card** carte *f* Eurochèque.

Eurocommunism [ˈjʊərəʊˌkɒmjʊnɪzəm] n eurocommunisme *m*.

Eurocrat [ˈjʊərəʊˌkræt] n eurocrate *mf*.

eurocredit [ˈjʊərəʊˌkredɪt] n crédit *m* en eurodevises.

Eurocurrency [ˈjʊərəʊˌkʌrənsɪ] n eurodevise *f*, euromonnaie *f*.

Eurodollar [ˈjʊərəʊˌdɒləʳ] n eurodollar *m*.

Euromarket [ˈjʊərəʊˌmɑːkɪt], **Euromart** [ˈjʊərəʊˌmɑːt] n Communauté *f* Économique Européenne.

Euro MP [ˌjʊərəʊemˈpiː] n député(e) *m(f)* européen(ne).

Europe [ˈjʊərəp] n Europe *f*. (*Brit Pol*) **to go into ~, to join ~** entrer dans le Marché commun.

European [ˌjʊərəˈpiːən] 1 adj européen. **~ Atomic Energy Community** Communauté Européenne de l'Énergie Atomique; **~ Coal and Steel Community** Communauté *f* européenne du charbon et de l'acier; **~ Commission** Commission *f* des Communautés européennes, Commission *f* européenne; **~ Community** (abbr **EC**) Communauté Européenne (abbr CE *f*); **~ Court of Human Rights** Cour européenne des droits de l'homme; **~ Court of Justice** Cour *f* de justice européenne *or* des communautés européennes; **~ Currency Unit** unité *f* de compte européenne; **~ Defence Community** Communauté *f* européenne de défense; **~ Economic Community** (abbr **EEC**) Communauté Économique Européenne (abbr CEE *f*); **~ Free Trade Association** Association Européenne de Libre-Échange; **~ Monetary System** Système *m* monétaire européen; **~ Parliament** Parlement européen; (*US: in hotel*) **~ plan** chambre *f* sans les repas; **~ Regional Development Fund** Fonds *m* européen de développement régional; **~ Space Agency** Agence *f* spatiale européenne; **~ Union** Union *f* européenne.
2 n Européen(ne) *m(f)*.

Europeanize [ˌjʊərəˈpɪəˌnaɪz] vt européaniser.

europium [jʊˈrəʊpɪəm] n europium *m*.

eurosceptic [ˌjʊərəʊˈskeptɪk] n eurosceptique *mf*.

Euro-size [ˈjʊərəʊˌsaɪz] n (*Comm*) **~ 1** modèle *m* E 1.

Eurosterling [ˈjʊərəʊˌstɜːlɪŋ] n euro-sterling *m*.

Eurotunnel [ˈjʊərəʊˌtʌnl] n eurotunnel *m*.

Eurovision [ˈjʊərəʊˌvɪʒən] n Eurovision *f*. **~ song contest** concours *m* Eurovision de la chanson.

Eurydice [jʊˈrɪdɪsɪ] n Eurydice *f*.

Eustachian [juːˈsteɪʃən] adj: **~ tube** trompe *f* d'Eustache.

eustatic [juːˈstætɪk] adj eustatique.

euthanasia [ˌjuːθəˈneɪzɪə] n euthanasie *f*.

evacuate [ɪˈvækjʊeɪt] vt (*all senses*) évacuer.

evacuation [ɪˌvækjʊˈeɪʃən] n évacuation *f*.

evacuee [ɪˌvækjʊˈiː] n évacué(e) *m(f)*.

evade [ɪˈveɪd] vt *blow, difficulty* esquiver, éviter; *pursuers* échapper à, tromper; *obligation* éviter, esquiver, se dérober à; *punishment* échapper à, se soustraire à; *sb's gaze* éviter; *question* éluder; *law* tourner, contourner. **to ~ military service** se dérober à ses obligations militaires; **to ~ taxation/customs duty** frauder le fisc/la douane.

evaluate [ɪˈvæljʊeɪt] vt *damages, property, worth* évaluer (*at* à), déterminer le montant *or* la valeur *or* le prix de; *effectiveness, usefulness* mesurer; *evidence, reasons, argument* peser, évaluer; *achievement* porter un jugement sur la valeur de. **to ~ sth at £100** évaluer qch à 100 livres.

evaluation [ɪˌvæljʊˈeɪʃən] n évaluation *f*.

evanescent [evəˈnesnt] adj (*liter*) évanescent, fugitif, éphémère.

evangelical [ˌiːvænˈdʒelɪkəl] adj, n évangélique (*mf*).

evangelicalism [ˌiːvænˈdʒelɪkəlɪzəm] n évangélisme *m*.

evangelism [ɪˈvændʒəlɪzəm] n évangélisation *f*.

evangelist [ɪˈvændʒəlɪst] n (*Bible*) évangéliste *m*; (*preacher*) évangélisateur *m*, -trice *f*; (*itinerant*) évangéliste.

evangelize [ɪˈvændʒəlaɪz] 1 vt évangéliser, prêcher l'Évangile à. 2 vi prêcher l'Evangile.

evaporate [ɪˈvæpəreɪt] 1 vt *liquid* faire évaporer. **~d milk** lait condensé non sucré. 2 vi *[liquid]* s'évaporer; *[hopes, fear]* se volatiliser, s'évanouir, s'envoler.

evaporation [ɪˌvæpəˈreɪʃən] n évaporation *f*.

evasion [ɪˈveɪʒən] n a (*NonC*) fuite *f*, dérobade *f* (*of* devant); *see* **tax**. b (*excuse*) détour *m*, faux-fuyant *m*, échappatoire *f*.

evasive [ɪˈveɪzɪv] adj évasif. **to take ~ action** (*Mil*) effectuer une manœuvre dilatoire; (*gen*) prendre la tangente.

evasively [ɪˈveɪzɪvlɪ] adv évasivement; *reply* en termes évasifs, en Normand.

evasiveness [ɪˈveɪzɪvˌnɪs] n manière *f* évasive.

Eve [iːv] n Ève *f*.

eve[1] [iːv] n veille *f*; (*Rel*) vigile *f*. (*lit, fig*) **on the ~ of sth/of doing** à la veille de qch/de faire; *see* **Christmas**.

eve[2] [iːv] n (*liter: evening*) soir *m*.

even[1] [ˈiːvən] n = **eve**[2].

even[2] [ˈiːvən] 1 adj a (*smooth, flat*) *surface, ground* uni, plat, plan. **to make ~** égaliser, aplanir, niveler; *see* **keel**.
b (*regular*) *progress* régulier; *temperature, breathing, step, temper, distribution* égal. **his work is not ~** son travail est inégal *or* variable.
c (*equal*) *quantities, distances, values* égal. **our score is ~** nous sommes à égalité (de points); **they are an ~ match** (*Sport*) la partie est égale; (*fig*) ils sont (bien) assortis; **to get ~ with sb** se venger de qn; **I will get ~ with you for that** je vous revaudrai ça; (*fig*) **the odds** *or* **chances are about ~** les chances sont à peu près égales; **I'll give you ~ money** *or* **~s that ...** il y a cinquante pour cent de chances *or* une chance sur deux que ... + *subj*; **~s favourite** favori à un contre un; **the bookmakers are offering ~s** les bookmakers le donnent un contre un.
d **~ number/date** nombre/jour pair.
2 adv a même, jusqu'à. **~ in the holidays** même pendant les vacances; **~ the most optimistic** même les plus optimistes; **~ the guards were asleep** les gardes mêmes dormaient, même les gardes dormaient; **I have ~ forgotten his name** j'ai oublié jusqu'à son nom, j'ai même oublié son nom; **they ~ denied its existence** ils ont nié jusqu'à son existence, ils ont été jusqu'à nier *or* ils ont même nié son existence.
b (+ *compar adj or adv*) encore. **~ better** encore mieux; **~ more easily** encore plus facilement; **~ less money** encore moins d'argent.
c (+ *neg*) même, seulement. **without ~ saying goodbye** sans même *or* sans seulement dire au revoir; **he can't ~ swim** il ne sait même pas nager.
d (*phrases*) **~ if** même si + *indic*; **~ though** quand (bien) même + *cond*, alors même que + *cond*; **~ though** *or* **~ if he came himself I would not do it** il viendrait lui-même que je ne le ferais pas; **if he ~ made an effort** si encore *or* si au moins il faisait un effort; **~ then** même alors; **~ so** quand même, pourtant, cependant; **~ so he was disappointed** il a quand même *or* malgré tout été déçu, cependant *or* pourtant il a été déçu; **yes but ~ so ...** oui mais quand même ...; **~ as he spoke, the door opened** au moment même où il *or* alors même qu'il disait cela, la porte s'ouvrit; (*liter, frm*) **~ as he had wished it** précisément comme il l'avait souhaité; (*liter, frm*) **~ as ... so ...** de même que ... de même ... .
3 comp ►**even-handed** impartial, équitable ►**even-handedly** impartialement, équitablement ►**even-handedness** impartialité *f*, équité *f* ►**even-steven*** adv *divide* en deux (parts égales) ◊ adj (*quits*) quitte (*with* avec); **it's even-steven* whether we go or stay** qu'on parte ou qu'on reste, c'est kif-kif‡ *or* c'est du pareil au même ►**even-tempered** d'humeur égale, placide.
4 vt *surface* égaliser, aplanir, niveler.

►**even out** 1 vi *[prices]* s'égaliser; *[ground]* s'aplanir, s'égaliser, se niveler. 2 vt sep *prices* égaliser; *burden, taxation* répartir *or* distribuer plus également (*among* entre).

►**even up** vt sep égaliser. **that will even things up** cela rétablira l'équilibre; (*financially*) cela compensera.

evening ['i:vnɪŋ] 1 n soir *m*; (*length of time*) soirée *f*. **in the ~(s)** le soir; **to go out in the ~** sortir le soir; **let's have an ~ out** (*tonight*) si on sortait ce soir?; (*some time*) nous devrions sortir un soir; **6 o'clock in the ~** 6 heures du soir; **this ~** ce soir; **that ~** ce soir-là; **tomorrow ~** demain soir; **the previous ~** la veille au soir; **on the ~ of the next day** le lendemain soir; **on the ~ of the twenty-ninth** le vingt-neuf au soir; **on the ~ of his birthday** le soir de son anniversaire; **every ~** tous les soirs, chaque soir; **every Monday ~** tous les lundis soir(s); **one fine summer ~** (par) un beau soir d'été; **the warm summer ~s** les chaudes soirées d'été; **a long winter ~** une longue soirée *or* veillée d'hiver; **all ~** toute la soirée; **to spend one's ~ reading** passer sa soirée à lire; **where shall we finish off the ~?** où allons-nous terminer la soirée?; (*liter*) **in the ~ of life** au soir *or* au déclin de la vie; *see* **good** *etc*.

2 comp ►**evening class** cours *m* du soir ►**evening dress** *[man]* tenue *f* de soirée, habit *m*; *[woman]* robe *f* du soir; **in evening dress** *man* en tenue de soirée; *woman* en toilette de soirée, en robe du soir ►**evening fixture** *or* **match** (*Sport*) nocturne *f* ►**evening paper** journal *m* du soir ►**evening performance** (représentation *f* en) soirée *f* ►**evening prayer(s)** office *m* du soir ►**evening primrose oil** huile *f* d'onagre ►**evening service** (*Rel*) service *m* (religieux) du soir ►**evening star** étoile *f* du berger.

evenly ['i:vənlɪ] adv *spread, paint etc* de façon égale, uniment; *breathe, space* régulièrement; *distribute, divide* également.

evenness ['i:vənnɪs] n *[movements, performance]* régularité *f*; *[ground]* caractère uni, égalité *f*. **~ of temper** égalité d'humeur, sérénité *f*, calme *m*.

evensong ['i:vənsɒŋ] n (*Rel*) vêpres *fpl*, office *m* du soir (*de l'Église anglicane*).

event [ɪ'vent] 1 n a (*happening*) événement *m*. **course of ~s** suite *f* des événements, succession *f or* déroulement *m* des faits; **in the course of ~s** par la suite; **in the normal** *or* **ordinary course of ~s** normalement; **after the ~** après coup; **it's quite an ~** c'est un (véritable) événement; *see* **happy**.

b cas *m*. **in the ~ of death** en cas de décès; **in the ~ of his failing** au cas *or* dans le cas *or* pour le cas où il échouerait; **in the unlikely ~ that ...** s'il arrivait par hasard que ... + *subj*; **in the ~** en l'occurrence, en fait, en réalité; **in that ~** dans ce cas; **in any ~, at all ~s** en tout cas, de toute façon; **in either ~** dans l'un ou l'autre cas; (*Jur*) **~ of default** cas *m* de défaillance, manquement *m*.

c (*Sport*) épreuve *f*; (*Racing*) course *f*. **field ~s** épreuves d'athlétisme; **track ~s** épreuves de vitesse; *see* **three**.

2 comp ►**event horizon** (*Astron*) horizon *m* des événements.

eventer [ɪ'ventəʳ] n (*Horseriding*) participant(e) *m(f)* à un concours complet.

eventful [ɪ'ventfʊl] adj *life, day, period* mouvementé, fertile en événements; *journey* mouvementé, plein d'incidents; (*momentous*) mémorable, de grande importance.

eventide ['i:vəntaɪd] n (*liter*) tombée *f* du jour, soir *m*. **~ home** maison *f* de retraite.

eventing [ɪ'ventɪŋ] n (*Horseriding*) concours complet.

eventual [ɪ'ventʃʊəl] adj a (*resulting*) qui s'ensuit. **his many mistakes and his ~ failure** ses nombreuses erreurs et l'échec qui s'en est ensuivi *or* qui en a résulté *or* auquel elles ont mené; **it resulted in the ~ disappearance of ...** cela a abouti finalement à la disparition de ... . b (*possibly resulting*) éventuel, possible. **any ~ profits** les profits éventuels.

eventuality [ɪ,ventʃʊ'ælɪtɪ] n éventualité *f*.

eventually [ɪ'ventʃʊəlɪ] adv (*finally*) finalement, en fin de compte, en définitive; (*after interval*) à la longue, à la fin; (*sooner or later*) tôt ou tard. **to do sth ~** finir par faire qch, faire qch finalement *or* à la longue.

eventuate [ɪ'ventʃʊ,eɪt] vi (*US*) (finir par) se produire. **to ~ in** se terminer par.

ever ['evəʳ] 1 adv a (*with negation, doubt*) jamais; (*with interrogation*) jamais, déjà. **nothing ~ happens** il ne se passe jamais rien; **if you ~ see her** si jamais vous la voyez; **do you ~ see her?** est-ce qu'il vous arrive de la voir?; **have you ~ seen her?** l'avez-vous jamais *or* déjà vue?; **I haven't ~ seen her** je ne l'ai jamais vue; **we seldom if ~ go** nous n'y allons jamais ou rarement, nous n'y allons pour ainsi dire jamais; **now if ~ is the moment to ...** c'est le moment ou jamais de ...; **he's a liar if ~ there was one** c'est un menteur ou je ne m'y connais pas.

b (*after compar or superl*) jamais. **more beautiful than ~** plus beau que jamais; **faster than ~** plus vite que jamais; **the best meal I have ~ eaten** le meilleur repas que j'aie jamais fait; **the best grandmother ~** la meilleure grand-mère du monde; **the coldest night ~** la nuit la plus froide qu'on ait jamais connue.

c (*at all times*) toujours, sans cesse. **~ ready** toujours prêt; **~ after** à partir de ce jour; **they lived happily ~ after** ils vécurent (toujours) heureux; **~ since I was a boy** depuis mon enfance; **~ since I have lived here** depuis que j'habite ici; **~ since (then) they have been very careful** depuis (lors) *or* depuis ce moment-là ils sont très prudents; **all he ~ does is sleep** il passe tout son temps à dormir, tout ce qu'il sait faire c'est dormir; **as ~** comme toujours; (*in letters*) **yours ~** amical souvenir, cordialement (à vous); **~ increasing anxiety** inquiétude qui va (*or* allait) croissant; **~ present** constant; (†, *frm*) **he was ~ courteous** il était toujours poli.

d **for ~** (*for always*) *love etc* pour toujours; *leave* sans retour, pour toujours; (*a very long time*) *last, take, wait* une éternité; **for ~ and ~** à jamais, éternellement; **for ~ (and ~), amen** dans tous les siècles (des siècles), amen; **he has gone for ~** il est parti pour toujours *or* sans retour; (*liter*) **for ~ and a day** jusqu'à la fin des temps; (†, *liter*) **~ and anon** de temps à autre, parfois; *see also* **forever**.

e (*intensive*) **although he is** *or* (*frm*) **be he ~ so charming** quelque *or* si *or* pour charmant qu'il soit; **as quickly as ~ you can** aussi vite que vous le pourrez; **as soon as ~ he arrives** aussitôt *or* dès qu'il arrivera; **the first ~** le tout premier; **before ~ she came in** avant même qu'elle (ne) soit entrée; **he is ~ so slightly drunk** tant soit peu ivre; **~ so pretty** joli comme tout*; **he is ~ so nice** il est tout ce qu'il y a de plus gentil*; **I am ~ so sorry** je regrette infiniment, je suis (vraiment) désolé; **it's ~ such a pity** c'est vraiment dommage; **thank you ~ so much, thanks ~ so**‡ merci mille fois, merci bien; **she is ~ so much prettier than her sister** elle est autrement jolie que sa sœur; **as if I ~ would!** comme si je ferais ça moi!, moi faire ça!; **what ~ shall we do?** qu'est-ce que nous allons bien faire?; **where ~ can he have got to?** où a-t-il bien pu passer?; **when ~ will they come?** quand donc viendront-ils?; **why ~ not?** mais enfin, pourquoi pas?, pourquoi pas Grand Dieu?; **did you ~!*** a-t-on jamais vu cela!, (ça) par exemple!

2 comp ►**everglade** (*US*) terres marécageuses ►**Everglades** Everglades *mpl* ►**evergreen** *see* **evergreen** ►**everlasting** *see* **everlasting** ►**evermore** toujours; **for evermore** à tout jamais.

Everest ['evərɪst] n: **(Mount) ~** le mont Everest, l'Everest *m*.

evergreen ['evəgri:n] 1 adj *trees, shrubs* vert, à feuilles persistantes; *song* qui ne vieillit pas; *subject of conversation* éternel, qui revient toujours. **~ oak** yeuse *f*, chêne vert; (*US*) **the E~ State** le Washington. 2 n a (*tree*) arbre vert *or* à feuilles persistantes; (*plant*) plante *f* à feuilles persistantes; (*fig: song etc*) chanson *f etc* qui ne vieillit pas. b (*US*) crédit *m* permanent non confirmé.

everlasting [,evə'lɑ:stɪŋ] adj a *God* éternel; *gratitude, mercy* infini, éternel; *fame, glory* éternel, immortel; *materials* inusable, qui ne s'use pas. **~ flower** immortelle *f*. b (**: repeated*) perpétuel, éternel, sempiternel (*pej*).

everlastingly [,evə'lɑ:stɪŋlɪ] adv éternellement; sans cesse, sempiternellement (*pej*).

every ['evrɪ] adj a (*each*) tout, chaque; tous (*or* toutes) les. **~ shop in the town** tous les magasins de la ville; **not ~ child has the same advantages** les enfants n'ont pas tous les mêmes avantages; **not ~ child has the advantages you have** tous les enfants n'ont pas les avantages que tu as; **he spends ~ penny he earns** il dépense tout ce qu'il gagne (jusqu'au dernier sou); **I have ~ confidence in him** j'ai entièrement *or* pleine confiance en lui; **there is ~ chance that he will come** il y a toutes les chances *or* de fortes chances (pour) qu'il vienne; **you have ~ reason to complain** vous avez tout lieu de vous plaindre; **I have ~ reason to think that ...** j'ai de bonnes raisons *or* de fortes raisons *or* toutes les raisons de penser que ..., j'ai tout lieu de penser que ...; **we wish you ~ success** nous vous souhaitons très bonne chance, tous nos souhaits pour l'avenir; **there was ~ prospect of success** tout faisait croire au succès; **~ (single) one of them** chacun d'eux; **~ one of them had brought something** chacun d'entre eux avait apporté quelque chose, ils avaient tous apporté quelque chose; **~ child had brought something** chaque enfant avait apporté quelque chose; **~ movement is painful to him** chaque *or* tout mouvement lui fait mal; **from ~ country** de tous (les) pays; **at ~ moment** à tout moment, à chaque instant; **at ~ opportunity** à chaque occasion; **of ~ sort** de toute sorte; **from ~ side** de toutes parts; **of ~ age** de tout âge; **he became weaker ~ day** il devenait plus faible chaque jour *or* de jour en jour.

b (*showing recurrence*) tout. **~ fifth day, ~ five days** tous les cinq jours, un jour sur cinq; **~ second** *or* **~ other child** un enfant sur deux; **one man in ~ ten** un homme sur dix; **~ quarter of an hour** tous les quarts d'heure; **~ other day, ~ second day** tous les deux jours; **~ other Wednesday** un mercredi sur deux; **to write on ~ other line** écrire en sautant une ligne sur deux; **~ few days** tous les deux ou trois jours; **once ~ week** une fois par semaine; **~ 15 metres** tous les 15 mètres.

c (*after poss*) tout, chacun, moindre. **his ~ action** chacune de ses actions, tout ce qu'il faisait; **his ~ wish** son moindre désir, tous ses désirs.

d (*phrases*) **he is ~ bit as clever as his brother** il est tout aussi doué que son frère; **he is ~ bit as much of a liar as his brother** il est tout aussi menteur que son frère; **~ now and then, ~ now and again, ~ so often** de temps en temps, de temps à autre; **~ time (that) I see him** chaque fois *or* toutes les fois que je le vois; **~ single time** chaque fois sans exception; **you must examine ~ one** il faut les examiner tous; **~ single one of these peaches is bad** toutes ces pêches sans exception sont pourries; **~ last biscuit/chocolate** *etc* tous les biscuits/chocolats *etc* jusqu'au dernier; ~ **one of us is afraid of something** tous tant que nous sommes nous craignons quelque chose; ~ **one of them was there** ils étaient tous là (au grand complet); (*Prov*) ~ **little helps** les petits ruisseaux font les grandes rivières (*Prov*); ~ **man for himself** chacun pour soi; (excl) (*save yourself*) sauve qui peut!; ~ **man to his trade** à chacun son métier; ~ **man Jack of them** tous tant qu'ils sont (*or* étaient *etc*), tous sans exception; **in ~ way** (*from every point of view*) à tous (les) égards, en tous points, sous tous les rapports; (*by every means*) par tous les moyens; *see* **bit¹**.

everybody ['evrɪbɒdɪ] pron tout le monde, chacun. ~ **has finished** tout le monde a fini; ~ **has his** *or* **their* own ideas about it** chacun a ses (propres) idées là-dessus; ~ **else** tous les autres; ~ **knows ~ else here** tout le monde se connaît ici; ~ **knows that** tout le monde *or* n'importe qui sait cela; ~ **who is anybody** tous les gens qui comptent.

everyday ['evrɪdeɪ] adj (*daily*) quotidien; (*ordinary, usual*) *clothes* de tous les jours; *occurrence* banal; *experience* ordinaire, commun. **words in ~ use** mots d'usage courant; **it was an ~ event** c'était un événement banal, cela se produisait tous les jours; **it was not an ~ event** c'était un événement hors du commun.

everyone ['evrɪwʌn] pron = **everybody**.

everyplace ['evrɪpleɪs] adv (*US*) = **everywhere**.

everything ['evrɪθɪŋ] pron tout. ~ **is ready** tout est prêt; ~ **you have** tout ce que vous avez; **stamina is ~** c'est la résistance qui compte, l'essentiel c'est d'avoir de la résistance; **success isn't ~** réussir n'est pas l'essentiel *or* la chose la plus importante; **and ~ (like that)*** et tout et tout*.

everywhere ['evrɪwɛəʳ] adv partout, en tous lieux, de tous côtés. ~ **in the world** partout dans le monde, dans le monde entier; ~ **you go you meet the British** où qu'on aille *or* partout où on va on rencontre des Britanniques.

evict [ɪ'vɪkt] vt (*from house, lodgings*) expulser, chasser (*from* de); (*from meeting*) expulser (*from* de).

eviction [ɪ'vɪkʃən] n expulsion *f*. ~ **order** mandat *m* d'expulsion.

evidence ['evɪdəns] **1** n (*NonC*) **a** (*ground for belief*) évidence *f*; (*testimony*) témoignage *m*. **the clearest possible ~** la preuve manifeste; **the ~ of the senses** le témoignage des sens; **on the ~ of this document** à en croire ce document.

b (*Jur*) (*data*) preuve *f*; (*testimony*) témoignage *m*, déposition *f*. **to give ~** témoigner, déposer (en justice); **to give ~ for/against sb** témoigner *or* déposer en faveur de/contre qn; **to take sb's ~** recueillir la déposition de qn; (*Brit*) **to turn King's** *or* **Queen's ~**, (*US*) **to turn State's ~** témoigner contre ses complices; (*loc*) **whatever you say may be held in ~ against you** tout ce que vous direz pourrait être retenu contre vous.

c signe *m*, marque *f*. **to bear ~ of** porter la marque *or* les marques de; **to show ~ of** témoigner de, offrir des signes de, attester.

d to be in ~ *[object]* être en évidence; **his father was nowhere in ~** son père n'était nulle part dans les parages, il n'y avait pas trace de son père; **a man very much in ~ at the moment** un homme très en vue à l'heure actuelle.

2 vt manifester, témoigner de.

evident ['evɪdənt] adj évident, manifeste, patent. **that is very ~** c'est l'évidence même; **we must help her, that's ~** il faut l'aider, c'est évident *or* cela va de soi; **he's guilty, that's ~** il est coupable, c'est évident *or* cela saute aux yeux; **it was ~ from the way he walked** cela se voyait à sa démarche; **it is ~ from his speech that ...** il ressort de son discours que ... .

evidently ['evɪdəntlɪ] adv **a** (*obviously*) évidemment, manifestement, de toute évidence. **he was ~ frightened** il était évident qu'il avait peur. **b** (*apparently*) à ce qu'il paraît. **they are ~ going to change the rule** il paraît qu'ils vont changer le règlement; **are they going too? — ~** ils y vont aussi? — à ce qu'il paraît *or* on dirait.

evil ['iːvl] **1** adj *deed* mauvais; *person* mauvais, malveillant; *example, advice, reputation* mauvais; *influence* néfaste; *doctrine, spell, spirit* malfaisant; *course of action, consequence* funeste. **the E~ One** le Malin; **the ~ eye** le mauvais œil; **in an ~ hour** dans un moment funeste; (*hum*) **he had his ~ way with her** il est arrivé à ses fins avec elle.

2 n mal *m*. **to wish sb ~** vouloir du mal à qn; **to speak ~ of sb** dire du mal de qn; **of two ~s one must choose the lesser** de deux maux il faut choisir le moindre; **it's the lesser ~** c'est le moindre mal; **social ~s** maux sociaux, plaies sociales; **the ~s of drink** les conséquences *fpl* funestes de la boisson; **one of the great ~s of our time** un des grands fléaux de notre temps.

3 comp ▸**evildoer** scélérat *m*, méchant(e) *m(f)*, gredin(e) *m(f)* ▸**evil-minded** malveillant, mal intentionné ▸**evil-smelling** malodorant, nauséabond.

evilly ['iːvɪlɪ] adv avec malveillance.

evince [ɪ'vɪns] vt *surprise, desire* montrer, manifester; *qualities, talents* faire preuve de, manifester.

eviscerate [ɪ'vɪsəreɪt] vt éventrer, étriper.

evocation [ˌevə'keɪʃən] n évocation *f*.

evocative [ɪ'vɒkətɪv] adj *style, scent, picture, words* évocateur (*f* -trice); *incantation, magic* évocatoire.

evocatively [ɪ'vɒkətɪvlɪ] adv de façon évocatrice.

evoke [ɪ'vəʊk] vt *spirit, memories* évoquer; *admiration* susciter.

evolution [ˌiːvə'luːʃən] n **a** (*Bio, Zool etc*) évolution *f* (*from* à partir de); *[language, events]* évolution; *[culture, technology, machine]* évolution, développement *m*. **b** *[troops, skaters etc]* évolutions *fpl*.

evolutionary [ˌiːvə'luːʃnərɪ] adj évolutionniste.

evolve [ɪ'vɒlv] **1** vt *system, theory, plan* élaborer, développer. **2** vi (*gen, Bio*) évoluer. **to ~ from** se développer à partir de.

ewe [juː] n brebis *f*. ~ **lamb** (*lit*) agnelle *f*; (*fig*) trésor *m*.

ewer ['juːəʳ] n aiguière *f*.

ex [eks] **1** prep (*Comm*) ≃ départ, sortie. **price ~ factory,** (*Brit*) **price ~ works** prix *m* départ usine, prix sortie usine; **price ~ warehouse** prix départ *or* sortie entrepôt; *see* **ex dividend, ex officio** *etc*. **2** n (*) (*gen*) ex* *mf*; (*ex-husband*) ex*, ex-mari *m*; (*ex-wife*) ex*, ex-femme *f*.

ex- [eks] pref ex-, ancien, *e.g.* **~chairman** ancien président, ex-président *m*; **he's my ~boss** c'est mon ancien patron; *see* **ex-husband, ex-service** *etc*.

exacerbate [ɪg'zæsəˌbeɪt, ɪk'sæsəˌbeɪt] vt *pain, disease, hate* exacerber; *person* irriter, exaspérer.

exact [ɪg'zækt] **1** adj **a** (*accurate*) *description, time, measurements* exact, juste, précis; *forecast* juste, exact; *copy [picture]* exact, fidèle à l'original, *[document]* textuel; *transcript* littéral; *likeness* parfait. **that is ~** c'est exact *or* juste; **these were his ~ words** voilà textuellement ce qu'il a dit.

b (*precise*) *number, amount, value* exact, précis; *notions, meaning, time, moment, place, instructions* précis. **to give ~ details** donner des précisions; **he's 44 to be ~** il a très exactement 44 ans; **to be ~ it was 4 o'clock** il était 4 heures, plus précisément *or* plus exactement; **or, to be more ~ ...** ou pour mieux dire ...; **can you be more ~?** pouvez-vous préciser un peu?; **can you be more ~ about how many came?** pouvez-vous préciser le nombre des gens qui sont venus?

c (*rigorous*) *observation of rule etc* strict, exact; *analysis* exact; *study, work* rigoureux, précis; *instrument* de précision. **the ~ sciences** les sciences exactes.

2 vt *money, obedience etc* exiger (*from* de).

exacting [ɪg'zæktɪŋ] adj *person* exigeant; *profession* exigeant, astreignant; *task, activity, work* astreignant, qui exige beaucoup d'attention *or* d'efforts.

exaction [ɪg'zækʃən] n (*act*) exaction *f* (*pej*); (*money exacted*) impôt *m*, contribution *f*; (*excessive demand*) extorsion *f*.

exactitude [ɪg'zæktɪtjuːd] n exactitude *f*.

exactly [ɪg'zæktlɪ] adv **a** (*accurately*) avec précision, précisément, exactement. **b** (*precisely, quite*) exactement, précisément, justement, (tout) juste. ~ **the same thing** exactement *or* précisément la même chose; **we don't ~ know** nous ne savons pas au juste; **that's ~ what I thought** c'est exactement ce que je pensais; **I had ~ £3** j'avais 3 livres tout juste; **it is 3 o'clock ~** il est 3 heures juste(s); ~! précisément!, parfaitement!; ~ **so!** c'est précisément cela!, c'est cela même!

exactness [ɪg'zæktnɪs] n (*see* **exact**) exactitude *f*; justesse *f*; précision *f*; rigueur *f*.

exaggerate [ɪg'zædʒəreɪt] **1** vt (*overstate*) *dangers, fears, size, beauty* exagérer; *story* amplifier; (*give undue importance to*) s'exagérer; (*emphasize*) accentuer; *effect* outrer, forcer. **the dress ~d her paleness** la robe accentuait sa pâleur; **he ~s the importance of the task** il s'exagère l'importance de la tâche, il prête *or* attribue une importance excessive à la tâche. **2** vi exagérer, forcer la note. **he always ~s a little** il exagère *or* il en rajoute* toujours un peu.

exaggerated [ɪg'zædʒəreɪtɪd] adj exagéré; *praise, fashion* outré. **to have an ~ opinion of o.s.** avoir (une) trop bonne opinion de soi-même.

exaggeratedly [ɪg'zædʒəreɪtɪdlɪ] adv exagérément.

exaggeration [ɪgˌzædʒə'reɪʃən] n exagération *f*.

exalt [ɪg'zɔːlt] vt (*in rank, power*) élever (*à un rang plus important*); (*extol*) porter aux nues, exalter.

exaltation [ˌegzɔːl'teɪʃən] n (*NonC*) exaltation *f*.

exalted [ɪg'zɔːltɪd] adj (*high*) *rank, position, style* élevé; *person* haut placé, de haut rang; (*elated*) *mood, person* exalté, surexcité.

exam [ɪg'zæm] n (abbr of **examination 1a**) exam⁑ *m*.

examination [ɪgˌzæmɪ'neɪʃən] **1** n **a** (*Scol, Univ*) (*test*) examen *m*; (*each paper*) épreuve *f*. (*Scol*) **class ~** composition *f*; (*Univ etc*) **the June/September ~s** la session de juin/de septembre.

b (*study, inspection*) examen *m*; *[machine]* inspection *f*, examen; *[premises]* visite *f*, inspection; *[question]* étude *f*, considération *f*; *[accounts]* vérification *f*; *[passports]* contrôle *m*. **Custom's ~** fouille douanière; **close ~** examen rigoureux *or* minutieux; **expert's ~** expertise *f*; **on ~** après examen; *see* **medical** *etc*.

c (*Jur*) *[suspect, accused]* interrogatoire *m*; *[witness]* audition *f*; *[case, documents]* examen *m*. **legal ~** examen légal; *see* **cross**.

2 comp ▸**examination candidate** (*Scol etc*) candidat(e) *m(f)* à un (*or* l' *etc*) examen.

examine [ɪg'zæmɪn] vt **a** (*gen, Med*) examiner; *machine* inspecter; *proposition* examiner, étudier; *accounts* vérifier; *passport* contrôler; *dossier, documents* compulser, étudier, examiner; (*Customs*) *luggage* visiter, fouiller; *question, problem* examiner. **to ~ a question thoroughly** approfondir une question, examiner une question à fond.

b *pupil, candidate* examiner (*in* en); (*orally*) interroger (*on* sur).

examining board (*Brit Scol*) *comité responsable de l'organisation des examens nationaux;* (*Univ: for doctorates*) ≃ juré *m* de thèse.
c (*Jur*) *witness* interroger; *suspect, accused* interroger, faire subir un interrogatoire à; *case, document, evidence* examiner.

examinee [ɪɡ,zæmɪ'niː] **n** candidat(e) *m(f)*.

examiner [ɪɡ'zæmɪnəʳ] **n** examinateur *m*, -trice *f* (*in* de); *see* **board, oral, outside.**

example [ɪɡ'zɑːmpl] **n** (*model*) exemple *m*, modèle *m*; (*illustration*) exemple, cas *m*; (*sample*) spécimen *m*, exemple. **for ~** par exemple; **to set a good ~** donner l'exemple; **to be an ~** *[sb's conduct, deeds]* être un modèle; *[person]* être un exemple (*to* pour); **to take sb as an ~** prendre exemple sur qn; **to follow sb's ~** suivre l'exemple de qn; **following the ~ of** à l'exemple de; **to hold sb up as an ~** proposer qn en exemple; **to make an ~ of sb** faire un exemple en punissant qn; **to punish sb as an ~ to others** punir qn pour l'exemple; **to quote the ~ of ...** citer l'exemple de *or* le cas de ...; **to quote sth as an ~** citer qch en exemple; **here is an ~ of the work** voici un spécimen du travail.

exasperate [ɪɡ'zɑːspəreɪt] **vt** *person* exaspérer, mettre hors de soi, pousser à bout; *feeling* exaspérer, exacerber.

exasperated [ɪɡ'zɑːspəreɪtɪd] **adj** (*gen*) exaspéré. **to grow** *or* **become ~** s'exaspérer; **~ at** *or* **by** *or* **with sth** exaspéré par qch, poussé à bout par qch; **~ at** *or* **by** *or* **with sb** exaspéré par *or* contre qn.

exasperating [ɪɡ'zɑːspəreɪtɪŋ] **adj** exaspérant, énervant (au possible).

exasperatingly [ɪɡ'zɑːspəreɪtɪŋlɪ] **adv** d'une manière exaspérante. **~ slow/stupid** d'une lenteur/d'une stupidité exaspérante.

exasperation [ɪɡ,zɑːspə'reɪʃən] **n** exaspération *f*, irritation *f*. **"hurry!" he cried in ~** "dépêchez-vous!" cria-t-il, exaspéré.

ex cathedra [ekskə'θiːdrə] **adj, adv** ex cathedra.

excavate ['ekskəveɪt] 1 **vt** *ground* creuser, excaver; (*Archeol*) fouiller; *trench* creuser; *remains* dégager, déterrer. 2 **vi** (*Archeol*) faire des fouilles.

excavation [,ekskə'veɪʃən] **n** a (*NonC*) *[tunnel etc]* creusage *m*, creusement *m*, percement *m*. **~ work** travaux *mpl* de creusement. b (*Archeol: activity, site*) fouilles *fpl*.

excavator ['ekskəveɪtəʳ] **n** (*machine*) pelleteuse *f*; (*Archeol: person*) fouilleur *m*, -euse *f*.

exceed [ɪk'siːd] **vt** (*in value, amount, length of time etc*) dépasser, excéder (*in* en, *by* de); *powers* outrepasser, excéder; *instructions* outrepasser, dépasser; *expectations, limits, capabilities* dépasser; *desires* aller au-delà de, dépasser. (*Aut*) **to ~ the speed limit** dépasser la vitesse permise, commettre un excès de vitesse; (*Jur*) **a fine not ~ing £50** une amende ne dépassant pas 50 livres.

exceedingly [ɪk'siːdɪŋlɪ] **adv** extrêmement, infiniment.

excel [ɪk'sel] 1 **vi** briller (*at, in* en), exceller (*at or in doing* à faire). **he doesn't exactly ~ in Latin** on ne saurait dire qu'il brille en latin, on ne peut pas dire qu'il fasse des étincelles* en latin. 2 **vt** *person* surpasser, l'emporter sur (*in* en). (*often iro*) **to ~ o.s.** se surpasser, se distinguer.

excellence ['eksələns] **n** a (*NonC*) excellence *f*, supériorité *f*. b (*outstanding feature*) qualité *f* (supérieure).

Excellency ['eksələnsɪ] **n** Excellence *f*. **Your/His** *or* **Her ~** Votre/Son Excellence.

excellent ['eksələnt] **adj** excellent, admirable, parfait. **what an ~ idea!** (quelle) excellente idée!; **~!** parfait!; **that's ~!** c'est parfait!, c'est on ne peut mieux!

excellently ['eksələntlɪ] **adv** admirablement, parfaitement, excellemment (*liter*). **to do sth ~** faire qch à la perfection *or* on ne peut mieux.

excelsior [ek'selsjəʳ] **n** (*US: wood shavings*) copeaux *mpl* d'emballage.

except [ɪk'sept] 1 **prep** a sauf, excepté, à l'exception de, hormis. **all ~ the eldest daughter** tous excepté la fille aînée *or* la fille aînée exceptée; **~ (for)** à part, à l'exception de, si ce n'est; **~ (that)** sauf que, excepté que, sinon que, si ce n'est que, à cela près que; **~ if** sauf si; **~ when** sauf quand, excepté quand.
b (*after neg and certain interrogs*) sinon, si ce n'est. **what can they do ~ wait?** que peuvent-ils faire sinon *or* si ce n'est attendre?
2 **conj** (†, *liter*) à moins que + ne + *subj*. **~ he be a traitor** à moins qu'il ne soit un traître.
3 **vt** excepter, exclure (*from* de), faire exception de. **not** *or* **without ~ing** sans exclure, sans oublier; **always ~ing** à l'exception (bien entendu) de, exception faite (bien entendu) de; **present company ~ed** exception faite des personnes présentes.

excepting [ɪk'septɪŋ] **prep, conj** = **except 1, 2.**

exception [ɪk'sepʃən] **n** a (*NonC*) exception *f*. **without ~** sans (aucune) exception; **with the ~ of** à l'exception de, exception faite de; **to take ~ to** (*demur*) trouver à redire à, désapprouver; (*be offended*) s'offenser de, s'offusquer de; **I take ~ to that remark** je suis indigné par cette remarque.
b (*singularity*) exception *f*. **to make an ~** faire une exception (*to sth* à qch, *for sb/sth* pour qn/qch, en faveur de qn/qch); **these strokes of luck are the ~** ces coups de chance sont l'exception; **this case is an ~ to the rule** ce cas est *or* constitue une exception à la règle; **the ~ proves the rule** l'exception confirme la règle; **with this ~** à cette exception près, à ceci près; **apart from a few ~s** à part quelques exceptions, à de rares exceptions près.

exceptionable [ɪk'sepʃnəbl] **adj** (*open to objection*) *conduct* répréhensible, blâmable, condamnable; *proposal* inadmissible, inacceptable.

exceptional [ɪk'sepʃənl] **adj** (*unusual*) *weather, temperature* exceptionnel; (*outstanding*) *quality, talent* exceptionnel, peu commun, hors ligne; (*Jur*) *provisions etc* dérogatoire. (*Jur*) **to apply ~ arrangements** appliquer un régime dérogatoire (*to* à); (*US Scol etc*) **~ child** (*gifted*) enfant *mf* surdoué(e); (*handicapped*) enfant *mf* handicapé(e) mental(e).

exceptionally [ɪk'sepʃənəlɪ] **adv** (*unusually*) exceptionnellement, par exception; (*outstandingly*) exceptionnellement, extraordinairement.

excerpt ['eksɜːpt] **n** (*Literat, Mus etc*) extrait *m*, passage *m*, morceau *m*.

excess [ɪk'ses] 1 **n** a (*NonC*) *[precautions, enthusiasm]* excès *m*; *[details, adjectives]* luxe *m*, surabondance *f*. **to ~** (jusqu')à l'excès; **to carry to ~** pousser à l'excès, pousser trop loin; **carried to ~** outré; **in ~ of** qui dépasse, dépassant; **to drink to ~** boire à l'excès *or* avec excès, faire des excès de boisson; **the ~ of imports over exports** l'excédent *m* des importations sur les exportations.
b (*Brit Insurance*) franchise *f*.
c **~es** (*debauchery*) excès *mpl*, débauche *f*; (*cruelty, violence*) excès *mpl*, abus *m*, cruauté *f*; (*overindulgence*) excès *mpl*, écart *m*; **the ~es of the regime** les abus *or* excès du régime.
2 **comp** *weight, production* excédentaire ▸ **excess demand** (*Econ*) excès *m* de la demande ▸ **excess employment** suremploi *m* ▸ **excess fare** supplément *m* ▸ **excess luggage** excédent *m* de bagages ▸ **excess profits tax** impôt *m* sur les bénéfices exceptionnels ▸ **excess supply** (*Econ*) excès *m* de l'offre.

excessive [ɪk'sesɪv] **adj** *demands, price, use* excessif; *ambition* démesuré, sans mesure; *expenditure* immodéré; *praise* outré. **~ drinking** abus *m* de la boisson.

excessively [ɪk'sesɪvlɪ] **adv** a (*to excess*) *eat, drink, spend* avec excès, plus que de raison; *optimistic* par trop; *proud* démesurément. **I was not ~ worried** je ne m'inquiétais pas outre mesure. b (*extremely*) extrêmement, infiniment, excessivement; *pretty* extrêmement, infiniment; *boring, ugly* atrocement.

exchange [ɪks'tʃeɪndʒ] 1 **vt** *glances, gifts, letters, blows* échanger; *photographs, records, books* échanger, faire un *or* des échange(s) de; *houses, cars, jobs* faire un échange de. **to ~ one thing for another** échanger une chose contre une autre; **they ~d a few words** ils échangèrent quelques mots; (*euph: quarrel*) **they ~d words** ils se sont disputés, ils ont eu des mots ensemble*; (*Conveyancing*) **to ~ contracts** ≃ signer les contrats.
2 **vi** échanger. **to ~ with sb** échanger avec qn.
3 **n** a *[objects, prisoners, ideas, secrets, notes, greetings]* échange *m*. **in ~** en échange (*for* de), en retour (*for* de); **to gain/lose on the ~** gagner/perdre au change; (*Conveyancing*) **~ of contracts** ≃ signature *f* des contrats; *see* **fair¹, part** *etc.*
b (*Fin*) change *m*. **(foreign) ~ office** bureau *m* de change; **at the current rate of ~** au cours actuel du change; **the dollar ~** le change du dollar; **on the (stock) ~** à la Bourse; *see* **bill¹, foreign** *etc.*
c (*telephone ~*) central *m*; (*labour ~*) bourse *f* du travail.
4 **comp** *student, teacher* participant à un échange ▸ **exchange control** (*Fin*) contrôle *m* des changes; **exchange control regulations** réglementation *f* des changes ▸ **exchange law** droit *m* cambial ▸ **exchange rate** taux *m* de change; **exchange rate mechanism** mécanisme *m* du taux de change ▸ **exchange restrictions** restrictions *fpl* de change.

exchangeable [ɪks'tʃeɪndʒəbl] **adj** échangeable (*for* contre).

exchequer [ɪks'tʃekəʳ] **n** a (*Brit: state treasury*) **the E~** le ministère des finances, le Trésor public; (*in Britain*) l'Échiquier *m*; **~ bond** obligation *f* du Trésor; *see* **chancellor.** b (**: one's own funds*) fonds *mpl*, finances *fpl*.

excisable [ek'saɪzəbl] **adj** imposable, soumis aux droits de régie.

excise¹ ['eksaɪz] 1 **n** taxe *f* (*on* sur). (*Brit*) **the E~** la Régie. 2 **comp** ▸ **excise duties** (*Brit*) impôts prélevés par la régie, ≃ contributions indirectes ▸ **excise laws** (*US*) *lois sur le commerce des boissons* ▸ **exciseman** (*Brit*) employé *m* de la régie.

excise² [ek'saɪz] **vt** (*Med*) exciser; (*gen*) retrancher, supprimer.

excision [ek'sɪʒən] **n** (*see* **excise²**) excision *f*; retranchement *m*, suppression *f*.

excitability [ɪk,saɪtə'bɪlɪtɪ] **n** excitabilité *f*; nervosité *f*.

excitable [ɪk'saɪtəbl] **adj** *person* excitable, prompt à l'excitation, nerveux; *animal, temperament* nerveux; (*Med*) excitable.

excitableness [ɪk'saɪtəbəlnɪs] **n** = **excitability.**

excite [ɪk'saɪt] **vt** a (*gen*) exciter; (*rouse enthusiasm in*) passionner; (*move*) mettre en émoi, impressionner; *animal* exciter. **to ~ o.s.** s'exciter, s'énerver. b *sentiments, envy, attention, pity* exciter; *imagination, passion* exciter, enflammer; *desire, anger* exciter, aviver; *admiration* exciter, susciter; *curiosity* exciter, piquer. **to ~ enthusiasm/interest in sb** enthousiasmer/intéresser qn. c (*Med*) *nerve* exciter, stimuler.

excited [ɪk'saɪtɪd] **adj** *person, animal* excité, agité, énervé; *laughter* énervé; *crowd* excité, agité, en émoi; *voice* animé; *imagination* surexcité, enflammé; (*Phys*) *atom, molecule* excité. **to be ~ about sth** *promotion, holiday* être excité à l'idée de qch; *new product, project* être très enthousiaste sur; **to get ~** *[person]* s'exciter, s'énerver, se monter la tête (*about* au sujet de, à propos de); *[crowd]* s'agiter, devenir houleux; **don't get ~!** du calme!, ne t'énerve pas!; **to make ~ gestures** faire de grands gestes, gesticuler.

excitedly [ɪk'saɪtɪdlɪ] adv *behave* avec agitation, d'une manière agitée; *speak* sur un ton animé, avec agitation; *laugh* d'excitation. **to wave ~** faire de grands gestes, gesticuler.

excitement [ɪk'saɪtmənt] n (*agitation*) excitation *f*, agitation *f*, fièvre *f*; (*exhilaration*) vive émotion, exaltation *f*. **the ~ of the departure/elections** la fièvre du départ/des élections; **the ~ of victory** l'ivresse *f or* l'exaltation de la victoire; **to be in a state of great ~** être très agité, être en proie à une vive émotion; **the book caused great ~ in literary circles** le livre a fait sensation dans les milieux littéraires; **he likes ~** il aime les émotions fortes *or* l'aventure.

exciting [ɪk'saɪtɪŋ] adj *events, story, film* passionnant; *account* saisissant; *holiday, experience* excitant. **we had an ~ time** ça a été très excitant.

excitingly [ɪk'saɪtɪŋlɪ] adv passionnément.

excl. abbr of **excluding, exclusive (of).**

exclaim [ɪks'kleɪm] 1 vi (*gen*) s'exclamer. **he ~ed in surprise when he saw it** il s'est exclamé de surprise en le voyant; **to ~ at sth** (*indignantly*) se récrier (d'indignation) devant *or* contre qch; (*admiringly*) se récrier d'admiration devant qch. 2 vt s'écrier (*that* que). **"at last!" she ~ed** "enfin!" s'écria-t-elle.

exclamation [,ekskl ə'meɪʃən] 1 n exclamation *f*. 2 comp ▸**exclamation mark,** (*US*) **exclamation point** point *m* d'exclamation.

exclamatory [ɪks'klæmətərɪ] adj exclamatif.

exclude [ɪks'klu:d] vt (*from team, society*) exclure (*from* de), rejeter; (*Brit: from school*) exclure temporairement; (*from list*) écarter (*from* de), ne pas retenir; *doubt, possibility* exclure, écarter, éliminer. **he was ~d from the senior posts** il n'a jamais eu droit aux postes supérieurs; **he was ~d from taking part** il n'a pas eu le droit de participer; **to ~ from the jurisdiction of** soustraire à la compétence de.

exclusion [ɪks'klu:ʒən] n exclusion *f* (*from* de). **to the ~ of** à l'exclusion de; **~ clause** clause *f* d'exclusion.

exclusive [ɪks'klu:sɪv] 1 adj a (*excluding others*) *group, gathering* choisi; *club, society* fermé; *hotel, restaurant* huppé; *person, friendship, interest, occupation* exclusif; *see* **mutually.**

b (*owned by one person, one firm*) *rights, information, dress, design* exclusif. **to have/buy ~ rights for** avoir/acheter l'exclusivité de; (*Press*) **an interview ~ to X** une interview accordée exclusivement à X; (*Press*) **~ story** reportage exclusif.

c (*not including*) **from 15th to 20th June ~** du 15 (jusqu')au 20 juin exclusivement; **~ of** non compris, sans compter; **the price is ~ of transport charges** le prix ne comprend pas les frais de transport; (*Comm*) **~ of post and packing** frais d'emballage et d'envoi en sus *or* non compris.

2 n (*Press*) exclusivité *f*.

exclusively [ɪks'klu:sɪvlɪ] adv exclusivement.

exclusivity [ɪksklu:'sɪvətɪ] n exclusivité *f*.

excommunicate [,ekskə'mju:nɪkeɪt] vt excommunier.

excommunication ['ekskə,mju:nɪ'keɪʃən] n excommunication *f*.

ex-con [,eks'kɒn] n (*Prison etc sl*) ancien taulard‡.

excrement ['ekskrɪmənt] n excrément *m*.

excrescence [ɪks'kresns] n (*lit, fig*) excroissance *f*.

excreta [ɪks'kri:tə] npl excrétions *fpl*; (*excrement*) excréments *mpl*, déjections *fpl*.

excrete [ɪks'kri:t] vt excréter; *[plant]* sécréter.

excretion [ɪks'kri:ʃən] n excrétion *f*; sécrétion *f*.

excretory [ɪk'skri:tərɪ] adj (*Physiol*) excréteur, excrétoire.

excruciating [ɪks'kru:ʃɪeɪtɪŋ] adj *pain* atroce; *suffering* déchirant; *noise* infernal, insupportable; (**: unpleasant*) épouvantable, atroce.

excruciatingly [ɪks'kru:ʃɪeɪtɪŋlɪ] adv atrocement, affreusement. **it's ~ funny*** c'est désopilant, c'est à mourir de rire.

exculpate ['ekskʌlpeɪt] vt *person* disculper, innocenter (*from* de).

excursion [ɪks'kɜ:ʃən] 1 n excursion *f*, balade* *f*; (*in car, on cycle*) randonnée *f*; (*fig: digression*) digression *f*. 2 comp ▸**excursion ticket** billet *m* d'excursion ▸**excursion train** train spécial (*pour excursions*).

excusable [ɪks'kju:zəbl] adj excusable, pardonnable. **your hesitation is ~** votre hésitation s'excuse *or* est excusable.

excuse [ɪks'kju:z] 1 vt a (*justify*) *action, person* excuser, défendre. **such rudeness cannot be ~d** une telle impolitesse est sans excuse *or* inexcusable; **to ~ o.s.** s'excuser (*for* de, *for doing* de faire, d'avoir fait), présenter ses excuses.

b (*pardon*) excuser (*sb for having done* qn d'avoir fait). **to ~ sb's insolence** excuser l'insolence de qn, pardonner à qn son insolence; **one can be ~d for not understanding what he says** on est excusable de ne pas comprendre ce qu'il dit; **if you will ~ the expression** passez-moi l'expression; **and now if you will ~ me I have work to do** maintenant, si vous (le) permettez, j'ai à travailler; **~ me for wondering if ...** permettez-moi de me demander si ...; **~ me!** excusez-moi!, (je vous demande) pardon!; **~ me, but I don't think this is true** excusez-moi *or* permettez, mais je ne crois pas que ce soit vrai; **~ me for not seeing you out** excusez-moi si je ne vous raccompagne pas *or* de ne pas vous raccompagner; (*hum*) **~ my French** passez-moi l'expression.

c (*exempt*) exempter (*sb from sth* qn de qch), dispenser (*sb from sth* qn de qch, *sb from doing* qn de faire), excuser. (*to children*) **you are ~d** vous pouvez vous en aller; **he ~d himself after 10 minutes** au bout de 10 minutes, il s'est excusé et est parti; **to ask to be ~d** se faire excuser; **he was ~d from the afternoon session** on l'a dispensé d'assister à la séance de l'après-midi; **to ~ sb from an obligation** faire grâce à qn *or* exempter qn d'une obligation.

2 comp ▸**excuse-me (dance)** (*Brit*) danse *f* où l'on change de partenaire, ≃ danse du balai.

3 [ɪks'kju:s] n a (*reason, justification*) excuse *f*. **there is no ~ for it,** (*frm*) **it admits of no ~** cela est inexcusable *or* sans excuse; **his only ~ was that ...** il avait comme seule excuse le fait que ...; **that is no ~ for his leaving so abruptly** cela ne l'excuse pas d'être parti si brusquement; **in ~ for** pour excuser; **without ~** sans excuse, sans raison, sans motif valable; *see* **ignorance** *etc.*

b (*pretext*) excuse *f*, prétexte *m*. **lame ~** faible excuse, excuse boiteuse; **to find an ~ for sth** trouver une excuse à qch; **I have a good ~ for not going** j'ai une bonne excuse pour ne pas y aller; **to make an ~ for sth/for doing** (*gen*) trouver une *or* des excuse(s) à qch/pour faire; **he is only making ~s** il cherche tout simplement des prétextes *or* de bonnes raisons; **he is always making ~s to get away** il trouve *or* invente toujours des excuses pour s'absenter; **what's your ~ this time?** qu'avez-vous comme excuse cette fois-ci?; **he gave the bad weather as his ~ for not coming** il a prétexté *or* allégué le mauvais temps pour ne pas venir; **it's only an ~** ce n'est qu'un prétexte; **his success was a good ~ for a family party** sa réussite a servi de prétexte à une fête de famille.

ex-directory [,eksdɪ'rektərɪ] adj (*Brit Telec*) qui ne figure pas dans l'annuaire, qui est sur la liste rouge. **he's gone ~** il s'est fait mettre sur la liste rouge.

ex dividend ['eks'dɪvɪ,dend] adj (*St Ex*) ex-dividende.

execrable ['eksɪkrəbl] adj exécrable, affreux, détestable; *manners, temper* exécrable, épouvantable.

execrably ['eksɪkrəblɪ] adv exécrablement, détestablement.

execrate ['eksɪkreɪt] vt a (*hate*) exécrer, détester. b (*curse*) maudire.

execration [,eksɪ'kreɪʃən] n a (*NonC*) exécration *f*, horreur *f*. **to hold in ~** avoir en horreur *or* en exécration, exécrer. b (*curse*) malédiction *f*, imprécation *f*.

executant [ɪg'zekjʊtənt] n (*Mus*) interprète *mf*, exécutant(e) *m(f)*.

execute ['eksɪkju:t] vt a (*put to death*) exécuter. b (*carry out*) *order, piece of work, dance, movement* exécuter; *work of art* réaliser; *project, plan* exécuter, mettre à exécution, réaliser; *purpose, sb's wishes* accomplir; *duties* exercer, remplir, accomplir; *task* accomplir, s'acquitter de, mener à bien; (*Mus*) exécuter, interpréter; (*Jur*) *will* exécuter; *document* valider; *deed* signer; *contract* valider.

execution [,eksɪ'kju:ʃən] n a (*killing*) exécution *f*; *see* **stay 1b.** b (*see* **execute b**) exécution *f*; réalisation *f*; accomplissement *m*; validation *f*; (*Mus: of musical work*) exécution, interprétation *f*; (*Mus: performer's skill*) jeu *m*, technique *f*. **to put into ~** mettre à exécution; **in the ~ of his duties** dans l'exercice de ses fonctions; *see* **stay.**

executioner [,eksɪ'kju:ʃnəʳ] n (*also* **public ~**) bourreau *m*, exécuteur *m* des hautes œuvres.

executive [ɪg'zekjʊtɪv] 1 adj a *powers* exécutif; *talent, ability* d'exécution; *decision* de la direction. **the ~ arm of the organization** l'organe exécutif de cette organisation; (*US Pol*) **~ agreement** accord conclu par l'exécutif; (*Admin, Ind*) **~ board** conseil *m* de direction; **~ capability** capacité *f* d'exécution; **~ committee** comité exécutif; **~ council** (*gen*) conseil exécutif *or* de direction; (*US Pol*) conseil de l'exécutif; (*Can, US*) **~ director** directeur *m* (général), directrice *f*; (*US*) **the E~ Mansion** (*White House*) la Maison Blanche; (*Governor's house*) la résidence officielle du gouverneur (*d'un État*); (*US*) **E~ Office of the President** services administratifs de la présidence; **~ officer** *[organization]* cadre administratif; (*US: Mil, Naut*) commandant *m* en second; (*US*) **~ order** décret-loi *m*; (*US Pol*) **~ privilege** immunité *f* de l'exécutif; (*Comput*) **~ program** programme *m* superviseur; **~ secretary** secrétaire *m* général; (*Can, US: Parl*) **~ session** séance *f* parlementaire à huis clos.

b (*Ind etc*) *job, position* de cadre; *plane, car* de direction. **~ unemployment** chomâge *m* (des) cadres; **the ~ suite (of offices)** les bureaux *mpl* de la direction.

c (*up-market*) haut-de-gamme. **~ toy** gadget *m* de bureau.

2 n a (*Admin, Ind etc: person*) cadre *m*, supérieur *m*. **senior/junior ~** cadre supérieur/moyen; **a Shell/IBM ~** un cadre (de chez) Shell/IBM; **a sales/production ~** un cadre ventes/production; **a woman** *or* **female ~** un cadre femme; *see* **chief.**

b (*managing group: of organization*) bureau *m*. **to be on the ~** faire partie du bureau; **the trade union/party ~** le bureau du syndicat/du parti.

c (*part of government*) (pouvoir *m*) exécutif *m*.

executor [ɪgˈzekjʊtəʳ] n (*Jur*) exécuteur *m* testamentaire.

executrix [ɪgˈzekjʊtrɪks] n, pl ~es *or* executrices [ɪg͵zekjʊˈtraɪsiːz] (*Jur*) exécutrice *f* testamentaire.

exegesis [͵eksɪˈdʒiːsɪs] n, pl exegeses [͵eksɪˈdʒiːsiːz] exégèse *f*.

exemplary [ɪgˈzemplərɪ] adj *conduct, virtue* exemplaire; *pupil etc* modèle; *punishment* exemplaire. (*Jur*) ~ **damages** dommages-intérêts très élevés (à titre de réparation exemplaire).

exemplification [ɪg͵zemplɪfɪˈkeɪʃən] n exemplification *f*.

exemplify [ɪgˈzemplɪfaɪ] vt (*illustrate*) exemplifier, illustrer, démontrer; (*be example of*) servir d'exemple de, être un exemple de. (*Jur*) **exemplified copy** expédition *f*, copie certifiée.

exempt [ɪgˈzempt] 1 adj exempt (*from* de). 2 vt exempter (*from sth* de qch), dispenser (*from doing* de faire).

exemption [ɪgˈzempʃən] n exemption *f* (*from* de); (*Educ*) dispense *f* (*from* de); (*Jur*) dérogation *f*.

exercise [ˈeksəsaɪz] 1 n a (*NonC*) *[right, caution, power]* exercice *m*; *[religion]* pratique *f*, exercice. **in the ~ of his duties** dans l'exercice de ses fonctions; **physical ~** exercice physique; **to take ~** prendre de l'exercice.

b (*in gymnastics, school subjects*) exercice *m*. **a grammar ~** un exercice de grammaire; **to do (physical) ~s every morning** faire de la gymnastique tous les matins.

c (*Mil etc: gen pl*) exercice *m*, manœuvre *f*. **to go on (an) ~** (*Mil*) aller à la manœuvre, partir à l'exercice; (*Naut*) partir en exercice *or* en manœuvre; **NATO ~s** manœuvres de l'OTAN.

d (*sth carried out*) opération *f*. **an ~ in public relations/in management** *etc* une opération de relations publiques/de gestion des affaires *etc*; **a cost-cutting ~** une opération de réduction des coûts; **an ~ in futility** le type même de l'entreprise inutile.

e (*US: ceremony*) ~s cérémonies *fpl*.

2 comp ►**exercise bike** vélo *m* d'intérieur ►**exercise book** (*for writing in*) cahier *m* (de devoirs); (*book of exercises*) livre *m* d'exercices ►**exercise yard** cour *f* de prison.

3 vt a *body, mind* exercer; *troops* faire faire l'exercice à; *horse* exercer. **to ~ a dog** exercer *or* promener un chien.

b *one's authority, control, power* exercer; *a right* exercer, faire valoir, user de; *one's talents* employer, exercer; *patience, tact, restraint* faire preuve de. **to ~ care in doing** apporter du soin à faire, s'appliquer à bien faire.

c (*frm: preoccupy*) préoccuper. **the problem which is exercising my mind** le problème qui me préoccupe.

4 vi se donner de l'exercice. **you don't ~ enough** vous ne prenez pas assez d'exercice.

exert [ɪgˈzɜːt] vt a *pressure* exercer; *force* employer; *talent, influence* exercer, déployer; *authority* exercer, faire sentir. b **to ~ o.s.** (*physically*) se dépenser; (*take trouble*) se donner du mal, s'appliquer; **to ~ o.s. to do** s'appliquer à *or* s'efforcer de faire; **he didn't ~ himself unduly** il ne s'est pas donné trop de mal, il ne s'est pas trop fatigué; (*iro*) **don't ~ yourself!** ne vous fatiguez pas!

exertion [ɪgˈzɜːʃən] n a effort *m*. **by his own ~s** par ses propres moyens; **after the day's ~s** après les fatigues *fpl* de la journée; **it doesn't require much ~** cela n'exige pas un grand effort. b (*NonC*) *[force, strength]* emploi *m*; *[authority, influence]* exercice *m*. **by the ~ of a little pressure** en exerçant une légère pression.

exeunt [ˈeksɪʌnt] vi (*Theat*) ils sortent. ~ **Macbeth and Lady Macbeth** Macbeth et Lady Macbeth sortent.

exfoliate [eksˈfəʊlɪeɪt] 1 vt (*Bio, Geol*) exfolier. (*Cosmetics*) **exfoliating cream** crème *f* exfoliante. 2 vi (*Bio, Geol*) s'exfolier; (*Cosmetics*) se faire un gommage de peau.

exfoliation [eks͵fəʊlɪˈeɪʃən] n (*Bio, Geol*) exfoliation *f*. (*Cosmetics*) **frequent ~ is good for the skin** un gommage fréquent est bon pour la peau.

ex gratia [͵eksˈgreɪʃə] adj *payment* à titre gracieux.

exhalation [͵eks*h*ˈleɪʃən] n (*act*) exhalation *f*; (*odour, fumes etc*) exhalaison *f*.

exhale [eksˈheɪl] 1 vt a (*breathe out*) expirer (*Physiol*). b (*give off*) *smoke, gas, perfume* exhaler. 2 vi expirer. ~ **please** expirez s'il vous plaît; **he ~d slowly in relief** il a laissé échapper un long soupir de soulagement.

exhaust [ɪgˈzɔːst] 1 vt a (*use up*) *supplies, energy, mine, subject* épuiser. **to ~ sb's patience** épuiser la patience de qn, mettre qn à bout de patience. b (*tire*) épuiser, exténuer. **to ~ o.s. (doing)** s'épuiser (à faire). 2 n (*Aut etc*) (*also* ~ **system**) échappement *m*; (*also* ~ **pipe**) tuyau *m or* pot *m* d'échappement; (*also* ~ **fumes**) gaz *m* d'échappement.

exhausted [ɪgˈzɔːstɪd] adj *person* épuisé, exténué, brisé de fatigue; *supplies, oil well, mine* épuisé. **I'm ~** je n'en peux plus, je suis à bout, je tombe de fatigue; **my patience is ~** ma patience est à bout; **until funds are ~** jusqu'à épuisement des fonds.

exhaustible [ɪgˈzɔːstɪbl] adj *resources* non renouvelable; *patience* limité, qui a des limites.

exhausting [ɪgˈzɔːstɪŋ] adj *climate, activity* épuisant; *work* exténuant, épuisant.

exhaustion [ɪgˈzɔːstʃən] n (*NonC: tiredness*) épuisement *m*, fatigue *f* extrême.

exhaustive [ɪgˈzɔːstɪv] adj *account, report* complet (*f* -ète); *study, description, list* complet, exhaustif; *inquiry, inspection* minutieux; *research* approfondi; *search* poussé; *grammar, analysis* exhaustif. **to make an ~ study of** étudier à fond.

exhaustively [ɪgˈzɔːstɪvlɪ] adv *search* à fond; *study* à fond, exhaustivement; *list, describe* exhaustivement.

exhaustiveness [[ɪgˈzɔːstɪvnɪs] n exhaustivité *f*.

exhibit [ɪgˈzɪbɪt] 1 vt *painting, handicrafts* exposer; *merchandise* exposer, étaler; *document, identity card* montrer, présenter, produire; *courage, skill, ingenuity* faire preuve de, déployer. 2 n (*in exhibition*) objet exposé; (*Jur*) pièce *f* à conviction. ~ **A** première pièce à conviction.

exhibition [͵eksɪˈbɪʃən] n a (*show*) *[paintings, furniture etc]* exposition *f*; *[articles for sale]* étalage *m*. **the Van Gogh ~** l'exposition Van Gogh; (*fig*) **to make an ~ of o.s.** se donner en spectacle. b (*act of exhibiting*) *[technique etc]* démonstration *f*; *[film]* présentation *f*. **what an ~ of bad manners!** quelle belle démonstration d'impolitesse!, quel étalage de mauvaise éducation! c (*Brit Univ*) bourse *f* (d'études).

exhibitioner [͵eksɪˈbɪʃənəʳ] n (*Brit Univ*) boursier *m*, -ière *f*.

exhibitionism [͵eksɪˈbɪʃənɪzəm] n exhibitionnisme *m*.

exhibitionist [͵eksɪˈbɪʃənɪst] adj, n exhibitionniste (*mf*).

exhibitor [ɪgˈzɪbɪtəʳ] n exposant(e) *m(f)* (*dans une exposition*).

exhilarate [ɪgˈzɪləreɪt] vt *[sea air etc]* vivifier; *[music, wine, good company]* rendre euphorique. **to be** *or* **feel ~d** être en pleine euphorie.

exhilarating [ɪgˈzɪləreɪtɪŋ] adj *air, wind etc* vivifiant; *music* enivrant, grisant; *conversation, work* stimulant, passionnant. **she found his presence very ~** elle trouvait sa présence très stimulante.

exhilaration [ɪg͵zɪləˈreɪʃən] n ivresse *f*, euphorie *f*.

exhort [ɪgˈzɔːt] vt (*urge*) exhorter, inciter, appeler (*sb to sth* qn à qch, *sb to do* qn à faire); (*advise*) conseiller *or* recommander vivement (*sb to do* à qn de faire).

exhortation [͵egzɔːˈteɪʃən] n (*see* **exhort**) exhortation *f* (*to* à), incitation *f* (*to* à); conseil *m*, recommandation *f*.

exhumation [͵ekshjuːˈmeɪʃən] n exhumation *f*. (*Jur*) ~ **order** autorisation *f* d'exhumer.

exhume [eksˈhjuːm] vt exhumer.

ex-husband [͵eksˈhʌzbənd] n ex-mari *m*.

exigence [ˈeksɪdʒəns] n, **exigency** [ɪgˈzɪdʒənsɪ] n (*urgency*) urgence *f*; (*emergency*) circonstance *f or* situation *f* critique; (*gen pl: demand*) exigence *f*. **according to the exigencies of the situation** selon les exigences de la situation.

exigent [ˈeksɪdʒənt] adj (*urgent*) urgent, pressant; (*exacting*) exigeant.

exiguity [͵egzɪˈgjuːɪtɪ] n exiguïté *f*.

exiguous [ɪgˈzɪgjʊəs] adj *space* exigu (*f* -guë), minuscule, fort petit; *income, revenue* modique.

exile [ˈeksaɪl] 1 n a (*person*) (*voluntarily*) exilé(e) *m(f)*, expatrié(e) *m(f)*; (*expelled*) exilé(e), expulsé(e) *m(f)*, banni(e) *m(f)*. b (*NonC: condition: lit, fig*) exil *m*. **in ~** en exil; **to send into ~** envoyer en exil, exiler, bannir; **to go into ~** partir *or* s'en aller en exil, s'exiler, s'expatrier. 2 vt exiler, bannir (*from* de).

exiled [ˈeksaɪld] adj exilé, en exil.

exist [ɪgˈzɪst] vi a *[person, animal, plant, belief, custom]* exister; (*Philos etc*) exister, être. **everything that ~s** tout ce qui existe *or* est; **it only ~s in her imagination** cela n'existe que dans son imagination; **to continue to ~** exister encore, subsister; **doubt still ~s** le doute subsiste; **the understanding which ~s between the two countries** l'entente qui règne *or* existe entre les deux pays; **the tradition ~s that ...** il existe une tradition selon laquelle ...; **can life ~ on Mars?** la vie existe-t-elle sur Mars?, y a-t-il de la vie sur Mars?

b (*live*) vivre, subsister. **we cannot ~ without water** nous ne pouvons pas vivre *or* subsister sans eau; **she ~s on very little** elle vit de très peu; **we manage to ~** nous subsistons tant bien que mal, nous vivotons; **can one ~ on such a small salary?** est-il possible de subsister avec un salaire aussi modique?

existence [ɪgˈzɪstəns] n a (*NonC*) *[God, person, object, institution]* existence *f*. **to be in ~** exister; **to come into ~** naître, être créé; **to call into ~** faire naître, créer; **it came into ~ 30 years ago** cela a été créé il y a 30 ans, cela existe depuis 30 ans; **it went out of ~ 10 years ago** cela n'existe plus depuis 10 ans; **the only one in ~** le seul *or* la seule qui existe (*subj*) *or* qui soit. b (*life*) existence *f*, vie *f*.

existent [ɪgˈzɪstənt] adj existant.

existential [͵egzɪˈstenʃəl] adj existentiel.

existentialism [͵egzɪˈstenʃəlɪzəm] n existentialisme *m*.

existentialist [͵egzɪˈstenʃəlɪst] adj, n existentialiste (*mf*).

existing [ɪgˈzɪstɪŋ] adj *law* existant; *state of affairs, regime* actuel; *circumstances* présent, actuel.

exit [ˈeksɪt] 1 n a (*from stage*) sortie *f*. **to make one's ~** (*Theat*) quitter la scène; (*gen*) sortir, faire sa sortie. b (*way out, door*) sortie *f*, issue *f*; *see* **emergency**. c (*voluntary euthanasia society*) **E~** ≃ Mourir dans la Dignité. 2 vi a (*Theat*) ~ **the King** le roi sort. b (*: *leave*) sortir, faire sa sortie. c (*Comput*) sortir. 3 comp ►**exit permit/visa** permis *m*/visa *m* de sortie ►**exit poll** (*at election*) sondage fait à la sortie de l'isoloir ►**exit ramp** (*US Aut*) bretelle *f* d'accès.

ex nihilo [ˌeks'nɪhɪləʊ] **adv** ex nihilo.

exocrine ['eksəʊˌkraɪn] **adj** exocrine.

exodus ['eksədəs] **n** exode *m*. **there was a general ~** il a y eu un véritable exode; (*Bible*) **E~** l'Exode.

ex officio [ˌeksə'fɪʃɪəʊ] 1 **adv** *act* ex officio. 2 **adj** *member* ex officio, de plein droit, ès qualités.

exonerate [ɪg'zɒnəreɪt] **vt** (*prove innocent*) disculper, justifier (*from* de), innocenter; (*release from obligation*) exempter, dispenser, décharger (*from* de).

exoneration [ɪgˌzɒnə'reɪʃən] **n** (*see* **exonerate**) disculpation *f*, justification *f*; exemption *f*, dispense *f*, décharge *f* (*from* de).

exorbitance [ɪg'zɔːbɪtəns] **n** *[demands]* outrance *f*; *[price]* énormité *f*.

exorbitant [ɪg'zɔːbɪtənt] **adj** *price* exorbitant, excessif, exagéré; *demands, pretensions* exorbitant, démesuré, extravagant.

exorbitantly [ɪg'zɔːbɪtəntlɪ] **adv** démesurément.

exorcise ['eksɔːsaɪz] **vt** exorciser.

exorcism ['eksɔːsɪzəm] **n** exorcisme *m*.

exorcist ['eksɔːsɪst] **n** exorciste *mf*.

exoskeleton [ˌeksəʊ'skelɪtən] **n** exosquelette *m*.

exosphere ['eksəʊˌsfɪəʳ] **n** exosphère *f*.

exoteric [ˌeksəʊ'terɪk] **adj** *doctrine* exotérique; *opinions* populaire.

exothermic [ˌeksəʊ'θɜːmɪk] **adj** exothermique.

exotic [ɪg'zɒtɪk] 1 **adj** exotique. **an ~-sounding name** un nom aux consonances exotiques. 2 **n** (*Bot*) plante *f* exotique.

exotica [ɪg'zɒtɪkə] **npl** objets *mpl* exotiques.

exotically [ɪg'zɒtɪklɪ] **adv** exotiquement.

exoticism [ɪg'zɒtɪsɪzəm] **n** exotisme *m*.

expand [ɪk'spænd] 1 **vt** *gas, liquid, metal* dilater; *one's business, trade, ideas* développer; *production* accroître, augmenter; *horizons, study* élargir; *influence, empire, property, knowledge, experience* étendre; (*Math*) *formula* développer. **to ~ one's lungs** se dilater les poumons; **exercises to ~ one's chest** exercices physiques pour développer le torse; **to ~ a few notes into a complete article** développer quelques notes pour en faire un article complet. 2 **vi** a (*see* 1) se dilater; se développer; s'accroître, augmenter; s'élargir; s'étendre. **the market is ~ing** les débouchés se multiplient; *see also* **expanding**. b **to ~ (up)on** développer.

expanded [ɪk'spændɪd] **adj** (*Metal, Tech*) expansé. **~ polystyrene** polystyrène expansé.

expander [ɪk'spændəʳ] *see* **chest**.

expanding [ɪk'spændɪŋ] **adj** *metal etc* en expansion; *bracelet* extensible; *market* en expansion; *industry, profession* en développement rapide, en expansion. **the ~ universe** l'univers *m* en expansion; **the ~ universe theory** la théorie de l'expansion de l'univers; **~ file** classeur *m* extensible; **a job with ~ opportunities** un emploi qui offre un nombre croissant de débouchés; **a rapidly ~ industry** une industrie en pleine expansion *or* en plein essor.

expanse [ɪk'spæns] **n** étendue *f*.

expansion [ɪk'spænʃən] 1 **n** *[gas]* expansion *f*, dilatation *f*; *[business]* extension *f*, agrandissement *m*; *[trade]* développement *m*, essor *m*; *[production]* accroissement *m*, augmentation *f*; (*territorial, economic, colonial*) expansion; *[subject, idea]* développement; (*Math*) développement; (*Gram*) expansion. 2 **comp** ►**expansion bottle** *or* **tank** (*Aut*) vase *m* d'expansion.

expansionism [ɪk'spænʃənɪzəm] **n** expansionnisme *m*.

expansionist [ɪk'spænʃənɪst] **adj, n** expansionniste (*mf*).

expansive [ɪk'spænsɪv] **adj** a *person* expansif, démonstratif, communicatif; *smile, welcome* chaleureux. **to be in an ~ mood** être en veine d'épanchements *or* d'effusion(s). b (*Phys*) (*causing expansion*) expansif; (*capable of expanding*) expansible, dilatable.

expansively [ɪk'spænsɪvlɪ] **adv** (*in detail*) *relate* avec abondance; (*warmly*) *welcome, say* chaleureusement. **to gesture ~** faire de grands gestes; **he was smiling ~** il arborait un large sourire.

expansiveness [ɪk'spænsɪvnɪs] **n** *[person]* expansivité *f*; *[welcome]* chaleur *f*.

expat* [eks'pæt] **n** (**abbr of expatriate**) expatrié(e) *m(f)*. **the ~ community** la communauté des expatriés.

expatiate [ɪk'speɪʃɪeɪt] **vi** discourir, disserter, s'étendre (*upon* sur).

expatriate [eks'pætrɪət] 1 **n** expatrié(e) *m(f)*. **British ~s** ressortissants *mpl* britanniques établis à l'étranger. 2 **adj** expatrié. 3 **vt** [eks'pætrɪeɪt] expatrier.

expect [ɪk'spekt] **vt** a (*anticipate*) s'attendre à, attendre, prévoir; (*with confidence*) escompter; (*count on*) compter sur; (*hope for*) espérer. **to ~ to do** penser *or* compter *or* espérer faire, s'attendre à faire; **we were ~ing rain** nous nous attendions à de la pluie; **to ~ the worst** s'attendre au pire, prévoir le pire; **that was to be ~ed** c'était à prévoir, il fallait s'y attendre; **I ~ed as much** je m'y attendais; **I know what to ~** je sais à quoi m'attendre *or* m'en tenir; **well what do *or* did you ~?** il fallait t'y attendre!, ce n'est pas surprenant!; **I did not ~ that from him** je n'attendais pas cela de lui; **he did not have the success he ~ed** il n'a pas eu le succès qu'il escomptait; **we were ~ing war** on attendait la guerre; **to ~ that** s'attendre à ce que + *subj*, escompter que + *indic*; **it is ~ed that** il est vraisemblable que + *indic*, il y a des chances pour que + *subj*, il faut s'attendre à ce que + *subj*; **it is hardly to be ~ed that** il ne faut pas *or* guère s'attendre à ce que + *subj*, il y a peu de chances pour que + *subj*; **I ~ him to come, I ~ that he'll come** je m'attends à ce qu'il vienne; **this suitcase is not as heavy as I ~ed** cette valise n'est pas aussi lourde que je le croyais; **he failed, as we had ~ed** il a échoué, comme nous l'avions prévu; **as might have been ~ed, as was to be ~ed** comme il fallait *or* comme on pouvait s'y attendre; **as ~ed** comme on s'y attendait, comme prévu.

b (*suppose*) penser, croire, supposer, se douter de. **I ~ so** je (le) crois, je crois que oui; **this work is very tiring — yes, I ~ it is** ce travail est très fatigant — oui, je m'en doute *or* je veux bien le croire; **I ~ he'll soon have finished** je pense *or* suppose qu'il aura bientôt fini; **I ~ it was your father** je suppose que c'était ton père.

c (*demand*) exiger, attendre (*sth from sb* qch de qn), demander (*sth from sb* qch à qn). **to ~ sb to do sth** exiger *or* vouloir *or* demander que qn fasse qch; **you can't ~ too much from him** il ne faut pas trop lui en demander, on ne peut pas trop exiger de lui; **you can't ~ them to take it seriously** comment voulez-vous qu'ils le prennent au sérieux?; **I ~ you to tidy your own room** tu es censé ranger ta chambre toi-même, je compte que tu rangeras ta chambre toi-même; **what do you ~ me to do about it?** que voulez-vous que j'y fasse?; **what do you ~ of me?** qu'attendez-vous *or* qu'exigez-vous de moi?; **England ~s that every man will do his duty** l'Angleterre compte que chacun fera son devoir; **are we ~ed to leave now?** est-ce que nous sommes censés *or* est-ce qu'on doit partir tout de suite?

d (*await*) *person, baby, thing, action* attendre. **I am ~ing her tomorrow** je l'attends demain; (*Comm etc*) **we are ~ing it this week** nous espérons le recevoir cette semaine; **I am ~ing them for dinner** je les attends à dîner; **~ me when you see me!*** vous (me) verrez bien quand je serai là!*; **we'll ~ you when we see you*** on ne t'attend pas à une heure précise; **she is ~ing*** elle est enceinte, elle attend un bébé *or* un heureux événement.

expectancy [ɪk'spektənsɪ] **n** attente *f*; (*hopefulness*) espoir *m*. **air of ~** air *m* d'attente; **look of ~** regard plein d'espoir; **awaited with eager ~** attendu avec une vive impatience; *see* **life**.

expectant [ɪks'pektənt] **adj** *person, crowd* qui attend (quelque chose); *attitude* d'expectative. **with an ~ look** d'un air de quelqu'un qui attend quelque chose; **~ mother** femme enceinte, future maman.

expectantly [ɪk'spektəntlɪ] **adv** *look, listen* avec l'air d'attendre quelque chose. **to wait ~** être dans l'expectative, attendre avec espoir.

expectation [ˌekspek'teɪʃən] **n** a (*NonC*) prévision *f*, attente *f*, espoir *m*. **in ~ of** dans l'attente *or* l'espoir de, en prévision de; **to live in ~** vivre dans l'expectative; **happiness in ~** bonheur en perspective; **there is every ~ of/no ~ of a cold winter** il y a de grandes chances/peu de chances pour que l'hiver soit froid.

b (*sth expected*) attente *f*, espérance *f*. **contrary to all ~** contre toute attente *or* espérance; **to come up to sb's ~s** répondre à l'attente *or* aux espérances de qn, remplir les espérances de qn; **beyond ~** au-delà de mes (*or* de nos *etc*) espérances; **his (financial) ~s are good** ses espérances sont considérables; **~ of life** espérance de vie.

expectorant [ɪk'spektərənt] **n, adj** expectorant (*m*).

expectorate [ɪk'spektəreɪt] **vti** expectorer, cracher.

expedience [ɪk'spiːdɪəns] **n**, **expediency** [ɪk'spiːdɪənsɪ] **n** (*convenience*) convenance *f*; (*self-interest*) recherche *f* de l'intérêt personnel, opportunisme *m*; (*advisability*) *[project, course of action]* opportunité *f*.

expedient [ɪk'spiːdɪənt] 1 **adj** a (*suitable, convenient*) indiqué, opportun, expédient (*frm*). b (*politic*) politique, opportun. **this solution is more ~ than just** cette solution est plus politique que juste; **it would be ~ to change the rule** il serait opportun de changer le règlement. 2 **n** expédient *m*.

expedite ['ekspɪdaɪt] **vt** *preparations, process* accélérer; *work, operations, legal or official matters* activer, hâter; *business, deal* pousser; *task* expédier; († *or frm: dispatch*) expédier.

expedition [ˌekspɪ'dɪʃən] **n** a (*journey: gen, also Climbing*) expédition *f*; (*group of people*) (membres *mpl* d'une) expédition. b (*NonC:* † *or frm: speed*) promptitude *f*.

expeditionary [ˌekspɪ'dɪʃənrɪ] **adj** expéditionnaire. (*Mil*) **~ force** corps *m* expéditionnaire.

expeditious [ˌekspɪ'dɪʃəs] **adj** expéditif.

expeditiously [ˌekspɪ'dɪʃəslɪ] **adv** promptement, d'une façon expéditive.

expel [ɪk'spel] **vt** (*from country, meeting*) expulser (*from* de); (*from society, party*) exclure, expulser; (*from school*) renvoyer; *the enemy* chasser; *gas, liquid* évacuer, expulser; (*from the body*) éliminer, évacuer.

expend [ɪk'spend] **vt** a *time, energy, care* consacrer, employer (*on sth* à qch, *on doing* à faire); *money* dépenser (*on sth* pour qch, *on doing* à faire). b (*use up*) *ammunition, resources* épuiser.

expendability [ɪkˌspendə'bɪlɪtɪ] **n: its ~** le peu de valeur qu'on y attache, la possibilité de le sacrifier.

expendable [ɪk'spendəbl] 1 **adj** (*not reusable*) *equipment* non-réutilisable; (*Mil*) *troops* sacrifiable; (*of little value*) *person, object* remplaçable, dont on peut se passer. (*Mil*) ~ **stores** matériel *m* de consommation; **this watch is** ~ cette montre est facile à remplacer; **he is really** ~ il n'est vraiment pas irremplaçable, on peut se passer de lui. 2 **n** produit *m* jetable.

expenditure [ɪk'spendɪtʃəʳ] **n** (*NonC*) a (*money spent*) dépense(s) *f(pl)*; (*Bookkeeping: outgoings*) sortie *f*. **public** ~ dépenses publiques; **to limit one's** ~ limiter ses dépenses; **project which involves heavy** ~ projet qui entraîne une grosse dépense *or* de gros frais; **income and** ~ recettes *fpl* et dépenses. b *[money, time, energy]* dépense *f*; *[ammunition, resources]* consommation *f*. **the** ~ **of public funds on this project** l'utilisation *f* des fonds publics pour ce projet.

expense [ɪk'spens] 1 **n** a (*NonC*) dépense *f*, frais *mpl*; (*Accounting: on account statement*) charge *f*, frais *mpl*. **at my** ~ à mes frais; **at public** ~ aux frais de l'État; **at little** ~ à peu de frais; **at great** ~ à grands frais; **to go to the** ~ **of buying a car** faire la dépense d'une voiture; **to go to great** ~ **on sb's account** s'engager *or* se lancer dans de grosses dépenses pour qn; **to go to great** ~ **to repair the house** faire beaucoup de frais pour réparer la maison; **to go to some** ~ faire des frais; **don't go to any** ~ **over our visit** ne faites pas de frais pour notre visite; **regardless of** ~ sans regarder à la dépense; **to put sb to** ~ faire faire *or* causer des dépenses à qn; **that will involve him in some** ~ cela lui occasionnera des frais; **to meet the** ~ **of sth** faire face aux frais de qch *or* à la dépense occasionnée par qch, supporter les frais de qch; *see* **spare**.

b ~**s** frais *mpl*, débours *mpl*, dépenses *fpl*; **he gets all his** ~**s paid** il se fait rembourser tous ses frais; **your** ~**s will be entirely covered** vous serez défrayé entièrement *or* en totalité; **after all** ~**s have been paid** tous frais payés; (*Jur*) ~**s to be refunded** frais *mpl* remboursables.

c (*fig*) **to have a good laugh at sb's** ~ bien rire aux dépens de qn; **to get rich at other people's** ~ s'enrichir aux dépens d'autrui *or* au détriment des autres; **to live at other people's** ~ vivre aux dépens *or* à la charge *or* aux crochets des autres; **at the** ~ **of great sacrifices** au prix de grands sacrifices.

2 **comp** ►**expense account** (*Comm*) frais *mpl* de représentation; **this will go on his expense account** cela passera aux frais de représentation *or* sur sa note de frais; **expense account lunch** déjeuner *m* qui passe aux frais de représentation *or* sur la note de frais.

expensive [ɪk'spensɪv] **adj** *goods, seats, shop, restaurant* cher (*f* chère); *holidays, medicine, undertaking* coûteux; *tastes* dispendieux, de luxe; *journey* onéreux. **to be** ~ coûter cher *inv*, valoir cher *inv*; **that vase must be** ~ ce vase doit valoir cher, ce doit être un vase de prix; **this car comes** ~ cette voiture revient cher; **to be extremely** ~ être hors de prix, coûter les yeux de la tête*.

expensively [ɪk'spensɪvlɪ] **adv** (*sparing no expense*) *entertain* à grands frais; (*in costly way*) *dress* de façon coûteuse.

expensiveness [ɪk'spensɪvnɪs] **n** cherté *f*.

experience [ɪk'spɪərɪəns] 1 **n** a (*NonC: knowledge, wisdom*) expérience *f*. ~ **of life/of men** expérience du monde/des hommes; ~ **shows that ...** l'expérience démontre que ...; **I know by** ~ je (le) sais par expérience *or* pour en avoir fait l'expérience; **from my own** *or* **personal** ~ d'après mon expérience personnelle; **I know from bitter** ~ **that ...** j'ai appris à mes dépens que ...; **he has no** ~ **of real grief** il n'a jamais éprouvé *or* ressenti un vrai chagrin; **he has no** ~ **of living in the country** il ne sait pas ce que c'est que de vivre à la campagne; **the greatest disaster in the** ~ **of this nation** le plus grand désastre que cette nation ait connu.

b (*NonC: practice, skill*) pratique *f*, expérience *f*. **practical** ~ pratique; **business** ~ expérience des affaires; **he has a lot of teaching** ~ il a une longue pratique *or* expérience *or* habitude de l'enseignement; **he has considerable** ~ **in selecting ...** il possède une expérience considérable dans la sélection de ...; **he has considerable driving** ~ il a l'expérience de la route *or* du volant, c'est un conducteur expérimenté; **he lacks** ~ il manque d'expérience *or* de pratique; **have you any previous** ~ **(in this kind of work)?** avez-vous déjà fait ce genre de travail?; **I've (had) no** ~ **of driving this type of car** je n'ai jamais conduit une voiture de ce type.

c (*event experienced*) expérience *f*, aventure *f*, sensation *f*. **I had a pleasant/frightening** ~ il m'est arrivé une chose *or* une aventure agréable/effrayante; **she's had** *or* **gone through some terrible** ~**s** elle est passée par de rudes épreuves *fpl*, elle en a vu de dures*; **it was a new** ~ **for me** cela a été une nouveauté *or* une nouvelle expérience pour moi; **we had many unforgettable** ~**s there** nous y avons vécu *or* passé bien des moments inoubliables; **she swam in the nude and it was an agreeable** ~ elle a nagé toute nue et a trouvé cela agréable; **it wasn't an** ~ **I would care to repeat** ça n'est pas une aventure que je tiens à recommencer; **unfortunate** ~ mésaventure *f*.

2 **vt** a (*undergo*) *misfortune, hardship* connaître; *setbacks, losses* essuyer; *privations* souffrir de; *conditions* vivre sous *or* dans; *ill treatment* subir; *difficulties* rencontrer. **he doesn't know what it is like to be poor for he has never** ~**d it** il ne sait pas ce que c'est que d'être pauvre car il n'en a jamais fait l'expérience *or* cela ne lui est jamais arrivé; **he** ~**s some difficulty in speaking** il a *or* éprouve de la difficulté *or* du mal à parler.

b (*feel*) *sensation, terror, remorse* éprouver; *emotion, joy, elation* ressentir.

experienced [ɪk'spɪərɪənst] **adj** *teacher, secretary* expérimenté, qui a de l'expérience, qui a du métier; *technician etc* confirmé, expérimenté; *driver, politician* expérimenté, chevronné; *eye, ear* exercé. **wanted,** ~ **secretary/journalist** on cherche secrétaire/journaliste expérimenté(e); **she is not** ~ **enough** elle n'a pas assez d'expérience, elle est trop inexpérimentée; **someone** ~ **in the trade** quelqu'un qui a l'habitude du métier; **he is** ~ **in business/driving/teaching** il a de l'expérience en affaires/en matière de conduite/en matière d'enseignement, il est rompu aux affaires/à la conduite/à l'enseignement.

experiential [ɪk,spɪərɪ'enʃəl] **adj** (*frm, Philos*) qui résulte de l'expérience, dont on a fait l'expérience.

experiment [ɪk'sperɪmənt] 1 **n** (*Chem, Phys*) expérience *f*; (*fig*) expérience, essai *m*. **to carry out an** ~ faire une expérience; **by way of** ~, **as an** ~ à titre d'essai *or* d'expérience. 2 [ɪk'sperɪ,ment] **vi** (*Chem, Phys*) faire une expérience, expérimenter; (*fig*) faire une *or* des expérience(s). **to** ~ **with a new vaccine** expérimenter un nouveau vaccin; **to** ~ **on guinea pigs** faire des expériences sur des cobayes; **they are** ~**ing with communal living** ils font une expérience de vie communautaire.

experimental [ɪk,sperɪ'mentl] **adj** *laboratory, research, method, science* expérimental; *evidence* établi *or* confirmé par l'expérience; *engine, novel* expérimental; *cinema, period* d'essai. **at the** ~ **stage** au stade expérimental; **this system is merely** ~ ce système est encore à l'essai; ~ **chemist** chimiste *mf* de laboratoire.

experimentally [ɪk,sperɪ'mentəlɪ] **adv** (*by experimenting*) *test, establish, discover* expérimentalement; (*as an experiment*) *organize* à titre d'expérience.

experimentation [ɪk,sperɪmen'teɪʃən] **n** expérimentation *f*.

experimenter [ɪk'sperɪmentəʳ] **n** expérimentateur *m*, -trice *f*.

expert ['ekspɜːt] 1 **n** spécialiste *mf* (*in, on, at* de), connaisseur *m* (*in, on* de); (*officially qualified*) expert *m*. **he is an** ~ **on wines** *or* **a wine** ~ il est grand *or* fin connaisseur en vins; **he is an** ~ **on the subject** c'est un expert en la matière; ~ **at pigeon shooting** spécialiste du tir aux pigeons; **nineteenth century** ~ spécialiste du dix-neuvième siècle; **he's an** ~ **at repairing watches** il est expert à réparer les montres; **he's an** ~ **at that sort of negotiation** il est spécialiste de ce genre de négociations; **with the eye of an** ~ *examine* d'un œil *or* regard connaisseur; *judge* en connaisseur, en expert; ~**'s report** *or* **valuation** expertise *f*.

2 **adj** *person, worker* expert (*in sth* en qch; *at or in doing* à faire); *advice, knowledge,* (*Jur*) *evidence* d'expert. (*Jur*) ~ **witness** (témoin *m*) expert *m*; **to be** ~ **in an art/a science** être expert dans un art/une science; **he is** ~ **in this field** il est expert en la matière, il s'y connaît; **he is** ~ **in handling a boat** il est expert à manœuvrer un bateau; **to judge sth with an** ~ **eye** juger qch en connaisseur *or* en expert; **to cast an** ~ **eye on sth** jeter un coup d'œil connaisseur sur qch; **with an** ~ **touch** avec beaucoup d'habileté, avec une grande adresse; ~ **opinion believes that ...** d'après les avis autorisés ...; ~ **advice** l'avis *m* d'un expert; ~ **valuation** *or* **appraisal** expertise *f*; (*Comput*) ~ **system** système *m* expert.

expertise [,ekspə'tiːz] **n** compétence *f* (*in* en), adresse *f* (*in* à).

expertly ['ekspɜːtlɪ] **adv** de façon experte, habilement, adroitement.

expertness ['ekspɜːtnɪs] **n** = **expertise**.

expiate ['ekspɪeɪt] **vt** expier.

expiation [,ekspɪ'eɪʃən] **n** expiation *f*. **in** ~ **of** en expiation de.

expiatory ['ekspɪətərɪ] **adj** expiatoire.

expiration [,ekspaɪə'reɪʃən] **n** a = **expiry**. b (*breathing out*) expiration *f*. c (††: *death*) trépas *m* (*liter*), décès *m*.

expire [ɪk'spaɪəʳ] **vi** a *[lease, passport, licence]* expirer; *[period, time limit]* arriver à terme. b (*liter: die*) expirer, rendre l'âme *or* le dernier soupir. c (*breathe out*) expirer.

expiry [ɪk'spaɪərɪ] **n** *[time limit, period, term of office]* expiration *f*, fin *f*; *[passport, lease]* expiration. **date of** ~ **of the lease** expiration *or* terme *m* du bail; ~ **date** (*gen*) date *f* d'expiration; (*on label*) à utiliser avant ... .

explain [ɪk'spleɪn] **vt** a (*make clear*) *how sth works, rule, meaning of a word, situation* expliquer; *mystery* élucider, éclaircir; *motives, thoughts* expliquer, éclairer; *reasons, points of view* exposer. ~ **what you intend to do** expliquez ce que vous voulez faire; **"it's raining" she** ~**ed** "il pleut" expliqua-t-elle; **that is easy to** ~, **that is easily** ~**ed** cela s'explique facilement; **this may seem confused, I will** ~ **myself** ceci peut paraître confus, je m'explique donc (*see also* **b**); **I can** ~ je peux (m')expliquer; **let me** ~ je m'explique (*see also* **b**); **to** ~ **why/how** *etc* expliquer pourquoi/comment *etc*; **he** ~**ed to us why he had been absent** il nous a expliqué pourquoi il avait été absent; **to** ~ **to sb how to do sth** expliquer à qn comment (il faut) faire qch.

b (*account for*) *phenomenon* expliquer, donner l'explication de; *behaviour* expliquer, justifier. **the bad weather** ~**s why he is absent** le mauvais temps explique son absence *or* qu'il soit absent; **come now,** ~ **yourself!** allez, expliquez-vous!

►**explain away** **vt sep** justifier, trouver une explication convaincante de.

explainable [ɪk'spleɪnəbl] **adj** explicable. **that is easily** ~ cela s'explique facilement.

explanation [,eksplə'neɪʃən] **n** a (*act, statement*) explication *f*, éclaircissement *m*. **a long ~ of what he meant by democracy** une longue explication de ce qu'il entendait par la démocratie; **these instructions need some ~** ces instructions demandent quelques éclaircissements. b (*cause, motive*) explication *f*. **to find an ~ for sth** trouver l'explication de qch, s'expliquer qch. c (*NonC: justification*) explication *f*, justification *f*. **has he something to say in ~ of his conduct?** est-ce qu'il peut fournir une explication de sa conduite?; **what have you to say in ~?** qu'avez-vous à dire pour votre justification?

explanatory [ɪk'splænətərɪ] adj explicatif.

expletive [ɪk'spliːtɪv] 1 n (*exclamation*) exclamation *f*, interjection *f*; (*oath*) juron *m*; (*Gram*) explétif *m*. 2 adj (*Gram*) explétif.

explicable [ɪk'splɪkəbl] adj explicable.

explicably [ɪk'splɪkəblɪ] adv d'une manière explicable.

explicate ['eksplɪˌkeɪt] vt (*frm*) expliciter.

explicit [ɪk'splɪsɪt] adj (*plainly stated*) explicite (*also Math, sexually*); (*definite*) catégorique, formel. **the intention is ~ in the text** l'intention est explicite dans le texte; **in ~ terms** en termes explicites; **he was ~ on this point** il a été explicite sur ce point, il a été catégorique là-dessus; **~ denial/order** démenti/ordre formel.

explicitly [ɪk'splɪsɪtlɪ] adv (*see* **explicit**) explicitement; catégoriquement, formellement.

explode [ɪk'spləʊd] 1 vi [*bomb, boiler, plane*] exploser, éclater; [*gas*] exploser, détoner; [*building, ship, ammunition*] exploser, sauter; [*joy, anger*] éclater; [*person*] (**: from rage, impatience*) exploser. **to ~ with laughter** éclater de rire; (*Art etc*) **~d drawing** *or* **view** éclaté *m*. 2 vt (*see* 1) faire exploser *or* éclater *or* détoner *or* sauter; (*fig*) *theory, argument* discréditer, démontrer la fausseté de; *rumour* montrer la fausseté de. (*fig*) **to ~ the myth that ...** démolir *or* dégonfler le mythe selon lequel ... .

exploit ['eksplɔɪt] 1 n (*heroic*) exploit *m*, haut fait; (*feat*) prouesse *f*. (*adventures*) **~s** aventures *fpl*. 2 [ɪk'splɔɪt] vt a (*use unfairly*) *workers, sb's credulity* exploiter. b (*make use of*) *minerals, land, talent* exploiter; *situation* exploiter, profiter de, tirer parti *or* profit de.

exploitable [ɪk'splɔɪtəbl] adj exploitable.

exploitation [ˌeksplɔɪ'teɪʃən] n exploitation *f*.

exploitative [ɪk'splɔɪtətɪv] adj exploiteur *m* (*f* -trice).

exploration [ˌeksplə'reɪʃən] n (*lit, fig, Med*) exploration *f*. **voyage of ~** voyage *m* d'exploration *or* de découverte; [*ground, site*] **preliminary ~** reconnaissance *f*.

exploratory [ɪk'splɒrətərɪ] adj *expedition* d'exploration, de découverte; *step, discussion* préliminaire, exploratoire, préparatoire. (*Med*) **~ operation** sondage *m*; **~ surgery** chirurgie exploratrice; **~ drilling of a piece of land** sondage d'un terrain; (*Pol etc*) **~ talks** entretiens *mpl* préliminaires *or* préparatoires; (*Jur*) **~ study** étude prospective.

explore [ɪk'splɔːʳ] vt *territory, house, question, matter* explorer; (*Med*) sonder; (*fig*) *issue, proposal* étudier sous tous ses aspects. **to go exploring** partir en exploration *or* à la découverte; **to ~ every corner of** fouiller partout dans; (*lit, fig*) **to ~ the ground** tâter *or* sonder le terrain; (*fig*) **to ~ every avenue** examiner toutes les possibilités; **to ~ the possibilities** étudier les possibilités; **to ~ an agreement** examiner les modalités d'un éventuel accord.

explorer [ɪk'splɔːrəʳ] n a (*person*) explorateur *m*, -trice *f*. b (*US: dental probe*) sonde *f*.

explosion [ɪk'spləʊʒən] n (*see* **explode**) explosion *f*; éclatement *m*; [*joy, mirth*] explosion, débordement *m*. **noise of ~** détonation *f*; *see* **population**.

explosive [ɪk'spləʊsɪv] 1 adj *gas, matter* explosible; *weapons, force* explosif; *mixture* détonant; *situation, temper* explosif; (*Phon*) explosif. 2 n a (*gen, Chem*) explosif *m*; *see* **high**. b (*Phon*) consonne explosive.

explosively [ɪk'spləʊsɪvlɪ] adv de manière explosive.

expo ['ekspəʊ] n (abbr of **exposition b**) expo *f*.

exponent [ɪk'spəʊnənt] n [*theory etc*] interprète *m*; (*Math, Gram*) exposant *m*. **the principal ~ of this movement/this school of thought** le chef de file *or* le principal représentant de ce mouvement/de cette école de pensée.

exponential [ˌekspəʊ'nenʃəl] adj exponentiel. (*Statistics*) **~ distribution** distribution exponentielle.

exponentially [ˌekspəʊ'nenʃəlɪ] adv exponentiellement.

export [ɪk'spɔːt] 1 vti exporter (*to* vers). **countries which ~ coal** pays exportateurs de charbon.

2 ['ekspɔːt] n a (*NonC*) exportation *f*, sortie *f*. **for ~ only** réservé à l'exportation.

b (*object, commodity*) (article *m* d')exportation *f*. **invisible ~s** exportations invisibles; **ban on ~s** prohibition sur les sorties.

3 ['ekspɔːt] comp *goods, permit, agent* d'exportation; *manager, director* de l'export, des exportations ►**export credit** crédit *m* à l'exportation ►**export drive** campagne *f* pour (encourager) l'exportation ►**export duty** droit *m* de sortie ►**export earnings** recettes *fpl* d'exportation ►**export-orientated,** (*US*) **export-oriented** à vocation exportatrice ►**export reject** article *m* impropre à l'exportation ►**export trade** commerce *m* d'exportation.

exportable [ɪk'spɔːtəbl] adj exportable.

exportation [ˌekspɔː'teɪʃən] n (*NonC*) exportation *f*, sortie *f*.

exporter [ɪk'spɔːtəʳ] n (*person*) exportateur *m*, -trice *f*; (*country*) pays *m* exportateur.

expose [ɪk'spəʊz] vt a (*uncover; leave unprotected*) découvrir, exposer, mettre au jour; *wire, nerve* mettre à nu, dénuder; (*Phot*) exposer. **a dress which leaves the back ~d** une robe qui découvre *or* dénude le dos; **to ~ to radiation/rain/sunlight/danger** exposer à la radiation/à la pluie/au soleil/au danger; **not to be ~d to air** ne pas laisser *or* exposer à l'air; **to be ~d to view** s'offrir à la vue; **~d to the general view** exposé aux regards de tous; **digging has ~d the remains of a temple** les fouilles ont mis au jour les restes d'un temple; (*Tech*) **~d parts** parties apparentes; (*Hist*) **to ~ a child (to die)** exposer un enfant; **to ~ o.s. to criticism/censure** *etc* s'exposer à la critique/aux reproches *etc*; **he ~d himself to the risk of losing his job** il s'est exposé à perdre sa place; (*Jur: indecently*) **to ~ o.s.** commettre un outrage à la pudeur.

b (*display*) *goods* étaler, exposer; *pictures* exposer; *one's ignorance* afficher, étaler.

c (*unmask, reveal*) *vice* mettre à nu; *scandal, plot* révéler, dévoiler, exposer au grand jour; *secret* éventer; *person* démasquer, dénoncer.

exposé [eks'pəʊzeɪ] n révélation *f*.

exposed [ɪk'spəʊzd] adj *hillside, site* (*gen*) battu par les vents, mal abrité; (*Mil*) découvert; (*Climbing*) *passage, section* aérien; (*Tech*) *part* apparent; *wire* à nu; (*Phot*) exposé. (*Mil*) **~ position** lieu découvert; (*fig*) **he is in a very ~ position** il est très exposé; **~ ground** terrain découvert; **house ~ to the north** maison exposée au *or* orienté vers le nord.

exposition [ˌekspə'zɪʃən] n a (*NonC*) [*facts, theory, plan*] exposition *f*; [*text*] exposé *m*, commentaire *m*, interprétation *f*; (*Mus*) exposition. b (*exhibition*) exposition *f*.

expostulate [ɪk'spɒstjʊleɪt] 1 vt protester. 2 vi: **to ~ with sb about sth** faire des remontrances à qn au sujet de qch.

expostulation [ɪkˌspɒstjʊ'leɪʃən] n (*see* **expostulate**) protestation *f*; remontrances *fpl*.

exposure [ɪk'spəʊʒəʳ] 1 n a (*see* **expose**) découverte *f*; mise *f* à nu; exposition *f* (*to* à); étalage *m*; révélation *f*; dénonciation *f*. **this product has had good ~ in the press** ce produit a eu une bonne couverture publicitaire dans la presse; **to threaten sb with ~** menacer qn d'un scandale; **to die of ~** mourir de froid; *see* **indecent**.

b (*position of building*) exposition *f*. **southern/eastern ~** exposition au midi/à l'est; **house with a northern ~** maison exposée *or* orientée au nord.

c (*Phot*) (*length of ~: also* **~ time**) (temps *m* de) pose *f*; (*photo*) pose, vue *f*. **to make an ~** prendre un cliché; **film with 36 ~s** film de 36 poses *or* vues; *see* **double**.

2 comp ►**exposure index** (*Phot*) indice *m* de pose ►**exposure meter** posemètre *m*, photomètre *m* ►**exposure value** indice *m* de lumination.

expound [ɪk'spaʊnd] vt *theory* expliquer; *one's views* exposer; *the Bible* expliquer, interpréter.

ex-president [ˌeks'prezɪdənt] n ex-président *m*, ancien président.

express [ɪk'spres] 1 vt a (*make known*) *appreciation, feelings, sympathy* exprimer; *opinions* émettre, exprimer; *surprise, displeasure* exprimer, manifester; *thanks* présenter, exprimer; *a truth, proposition* énoncer; *wish* formuler. **to ~ o.s.** s'exprimer; **I haven't the words to ~ my thoughts** les mots me manquent pour traduire ma pensée; **they have ~ed interest in ...** ils se sont montrés intéressés par ..., ils ont manifesté de l'intérêt pour ... .

b (*in another language or medium*) rendre, exprimer; [*face, actions*] exprimer; (*Math*) exprimer. **this ~es exactly the meaning of the word** ceci rend exactement le sens du mot; **you cannot ~ that so succinctly in French** on ne peut pas exprimer cela aussi succinctement en français.

c *juice* exprimer, extraire; *breast milk* tirer.

d (*send*) *letter, parcel* expédier par exprès.

2 adj a (*clearly stated*) *instructions* exprès (*f* -esse), formel; *intention* explicite. **with the ~ purpose of** dans le seul but de, dans le but même de.

b (*fast*) extrêmement rapide; (*Brit*) *letter* exprès *inv*.

3 comp ►**express coach** (auto)car *m* express ►**express company** compagnie *f* de messageries exprès ►**express delivery** (*Brit Post*) distribution *f* exprès ►**expressman** (*US*) employé *m* de messageries exprès ►**express rifle** fusil *m* de chasse express ►**express train** rapide *m* ►**expressway** (*esp US*) voie *f* express (à plusieurs files).

4 adv très rapidement. **to send a parcel ~** envoyer un colis exprès; (*Rail*) **to travel ~** prendre le rapide.

5 n a (*train*) rapide *m*.

b **to send goods by ~** envoyer des marchandises par transport rapide *or* par messagerie exprès.

expressage [ɪk'spresɪdʒ] n (*US*) service *m* transport-express, colis-express *m*.

expression [ɪk'spreʃən] 1 n a (*NonC*) [*opinions*] expression *f*; [*friendship, affection*] témoignage *m*; [*joy*] manifestation *f*. **to give ~ to one's fears** formuler ses craintes; **to find ~ (in)** se manifester (dans *or* par).

b (*NonC: feeling*) expression *f*. **to play with ~** jouer avec expression.

c (*phrase etc*) expression *f*, tournure *f*, tour *m*, locution *f* (*frm*);

(*Math*) expression. **it's an ~ he's fond of** c'est une expression *or* une tournure qu'il affectionne; **a figurative ~** une expression figurée; **an original/common ~** une tournure originale/fréquente; (*Ling*) **set** *or* **fixed ~** expression consacrée, locution figée (*frm*).
d (*facial ~*) expression *f*.
2 **comp** ▶ **expression mark** (*Mus*) signe *m* d'expression.

expressionism [ɪk'spreʃə,nɪzəm] **n** expressionnisme *m*.

expressionist [ɪk'spreʃə,nɪst] **adj, n** expressionniste (*mf*).

expressionless [ɪk'spreʃənlɪs] **adj** *voice* sans expression, plat; *face* inexpressif, éteint; *style* dénué d'expression. **he remained ~** il est resté sans expression.

expressive [ɪk'spresɪv] **adj** *language, face, hands* expressif; *gestures, silence* éloquent; *look, smile* significatif. **poems ~ of despair** poèmes qui expriment le désespoir.

expressively [ɪk'spresɪvlɪ] **adv** avec expression, d'une manière expressive.

expressiveness [ɪk'spresɪvnɪs] **n** *[face]* caractère expressif, expressivité *f*; *[words]* force expressive. **picture remarkable for its ~** tableau remarquable par (la force de) l'expression.

expressly [ɪk'spreslɪ] **adv** expressément.

expresso [ɪk'spresəʊ] **n** = **espresso**.

expropriate [eks'prəʊprɪeɪt] **vt** *person, land* exproprier.

expropriation [eks,prəʊprɪ'eɪʃən] **n** expropriation *f*.

expulsion [ɪk'spʌlʃən] **n** expulsion *f*, bannissement *m*; (*Scol etc*) renvoi *m*, exclusion définitive. **~ order** arrêté *m* d'expulsion.

expunge [ɪk'spʌndʒ] **vt** (*from book*) supprimer. **to ~ sth from the record** supprimer *or* effacer qch.

expurgate ['ekspɜːgeɪt] **vt** expurger. **~d edition** édition expurgée.

exquisite [ɪk'skwɪzɪt] **adj** *sewing, painting, sweetness, politeness* exquis; *sensibility* raffiné, délicat; *sense of humour* exquis, subtil; *satisfaction, pleasure* vif (*f* vive); *pain* aigu (*f* -guë), vif. **woman of ~ beauty** femme d'une beauté exquise *or* exquise de beauté; **chair of ~ workmanship** chaise d'une facture exquise.

exquisitely [ɪk'skwɪzɪtlɪ] **adv** a *paint, embroider, decorate, dress* d'une façon exquise, exquisément; *describe* avec beaucoup de finesse. b (*extremely*) extrêmement, excessivement. **~ beautiful/polite** d'une beauté/d'une politesse exquise.

ex-service [,eks'sɜːvɪs] (*Brit*) 1 **adj** (*Mil*) ayant servi dans l'armée.
2 **comp** ▶ **ex-serviceman** ancien combattant.

ext (*Telec*) (**abbr of extension**) poste *m*.

extant [ek'stænt] **adj** qui existe encore, existant. **the only ~ manuscript** le seul manuscrit conservé; **a few examples are still ~** quelques exemples subsistent (encore).

extemporaneous [ɪk,stempə'reɪnɪəs] **adj, extemporary** [ɪk'stempərərɪ] **adj** improvisé, impromptu.

extempore [ɪk'stempərɪ] 1 **adv** impromptu, sans préparation. 2 **adj** improvisé, impromptu. **to give an ~ speech** improviser un discours, faire un discours au pied levé.

extemporize [ɪk'stempəraɪz] **vti** improviser.

extend [ɪk'stend] 1 **vt** a (*stretch out*) *arm* étendre. **to ~ one's hand (to sb)** tendre la main (à qn).
b (*prolong*) *street, line* prolonger (*by* de); *visit, leave* prolonger (*for 2 weeks* de 2 semaines).
c (*enlarge*) *house, property* agrandir; *research* porter *or* pousser plus loin; *powers* étendre, augmenter; *business* étendre, accroître; *knowledge* élargir, accroître; *limits* étendre; *period, time allowed* prolonger; *insurance cover etc* augmenter le montant de. **to ~ the frontiers of a country** reculer les frontières d'un pays; **to ~ the field of human knowledge/one's sphere of influence** agrandir le champ des connaissances humaines/sa sphère d'influence; **to ~ one's vocabulary** enrichir *or* élargir son vocabulaire; **to ~ a time limit (for payment)** proroger l'échéance (d'un paiement), accorder des délais (de paiement).
d (*offer, give*) *help* apporter; *hospitality, friendship* offrir; *thanks, condolences, congratulations* présenter; *credit, loan* consentir. **to ~ a welcome to sb** souhaiter la bienvenue à qn; **to ~ an invitation** faire *or* lancer une invitation.
e (*make demands on*) *person, pupil* pousser à la limite de ses capacités, faire donner son maximum à. **the staff are fully ~ed** le personnel travaille à la limite de ses possibilités *or* fournit un maximum d'effort; **the child is not being fully ~ed in this class** l'enfant ne donne pas son maximum dans cette classe.
2 **vi** *[wall, estate]* s'étendre (*to, as far as* jusqu'à); *[meeting, visit]* se prolonger, continuer (*over* pendant, *for* durant, *till* jusqu'à, *beyond* au-delà de). **holidays which ~ into September** des vacances qui durent *or* se prolongent jusqu'en septembre; **enthusiasm which ~s even to the children** enthousiasme qui gagne (*or* a gagné) les enfants eux-mêmes.

extendable [ɪk'stendəbl] **adj** *ladder* à rallonge; *contract, lease* renouvelable.

extended [ɪk'stendɪd] **adj** prolongé; *holiday, leave* longue durée. **for an ~ period** pendant une période supplémentaire; **an ~ play record** un disque double (durée); (*US Med*) **~ care facilities** soins *mpl* pour convalescents; (*Sociol*) **the ~ family** la famille étendue.

extendible [ɪk'stendəbl] **adj** = **extendable**.

extensible [ɪk'stensɪbl] **adj** extensible.

extension [ɪk'stenʃən] 1 **n** a (*NonC*) (*act of extending: see* **extend**) prolongation *f*; agrandissement *m*; extension *f*; augmentation *f*; prorogation *f*.
b (*addition*) (*to road, line*) prolongement *m*; (*for table, wire, electric flex*) rallonge *f*; (*to holidays, leave*) prolongation *f*. **to get an ~ (of time for payment)** obtenir un délai; (*Jur, Fin*) **~ of due date** report *m* d'échéance; **to have an ~ built on to the house** faire agrandir la maison; **there is an ~ at the back of the house** la maison a été agrandie par derrière; **come and see our ~** venez voir nos agrandissements *mpl*.
c (*telephone*) *[private house]* appareil *m* supplémentaire; *[office]* poste *m*. **I'm on ~ 21** je suis au poste 21.
2 **comp** ▶ **extension cable**, (*US*) **extension cord** (*Elec*) prolongateur *m* ▶ **(university) extension courses** cours publics du soir (*organisés par une université*) ▶ **extension ladder** échelle coulissante ▶ **extension lead** = **extension cable** ▶ **extension light** lampe baladeuse ▶ **extension tube** (*Phot*) bague *f* allonge.

extensive [ɪk'stensɪv] **adj** *estate, forest* étendu, vaste; *grounds, gardens* vaste, très grand; *knowledge* vaste, étendu; *study, research* approfondi; *investments, operations, alterations, damage* considérable, important; *plans, reforms, business* de grande envergure; *use* large, répandu, fréquent.

extensively [ɪk'stensɪvlɪ] **adv** *revise, alter* considérablement, largement; *review, discuss* abondamment; *advertise* largement. **~ used method** méthode très répandue; **he has travelled ~ in Asia** il a beaucoup voyagé en Asie.

extensor [ɪk'stensəʳ] **n** (muscle *m*) extenseur *m*.

extent [ɪk'stent] **n** a (*size*) étendue *f*, superficie *f*; (*length*) longueur *f*. **avenue bordered with trees along its entire ~** allée bordée d'arbres sur toute sa longueur; **to open to its fullest ~** ouvrir entièrement *or* tout grand; **over the whole ~ of the ground** sur toute la superficie du terrain; **she could see the full ~ of the park** elle voyait le parc dans toute son étendue.
b (*range, scope*) *[damage]* importance *f*, ampleur *f*; *[commitments, losses]* importance; *[knowledge, activities, power, influence]* étendue *f*.
c (*degree*) mesure *f*, degré *m*. **to what ~** dans quelle mesure; **to a certain ~** jusqu'à un certain point *or* degré, dans une certaine mesure; **to a large ~** en grande partie; **to a small** *or* **slight ~** dans une faible mesure, quelque peu; **to such an ~ that** à tel point que; **to the ~ of doing** au point de faire.

extenuate [ɪk'stenjʊ,eɪt] **vt** atténuer. **extenuating circumstances** circonstances atténuantes.

extenuation [ɪk,stenjʊ'eɪʃən] **n** atténuation *f*.

exterior [ɪk'stɪərɪəʳ] 1 **adj** *surface, paintwork* extérieur (*f* -eure); *decorating* du dehors. **~ to** extérieur à, en dehors de; **~ angle** angle *m* externe; **~ decoration** peintures *fpl* d'extérieur; **paint for ~ use** peinture *f* pour bâtiment. 2 **n** *[house, box]* extérieur *m*, dehors *m*; (*Art, Cine*) extérieur. **on the ~** à l'extérieur; **he has a rough ~** il a des dehors rudes, il a un extérieur rude.

exteriorize [ɪk'stɪərɪə,raɪz] **vt** extérioriser.

exterminate [ɪk'stɜːmɪ,neɪt] **vt** *pests, group of people* exterminer; *race* anéantir; *disease* abolir; *beliefs, ideas* supprimer, détruire, abolir.

extermination [ɪk,stɜːmɪ'neɪʃən] **n** (*see* **exterminate**) extermination *f*; anéantissement *m*; abolition *f*; suppression *f*; destruction *f*.

exterminator [ɪk'stɜːmɪ,neɪtəʳ] **n** (*US: rat-catcher etc*) employé(e) *m(f)* de la désinfection.

extern ['ekstɜːn] **n** (*US Med*) externe *mf*.

external [ɪk'stɜːnl] 1 **adj** externe, extérieur (*f* -eure); *wall* extérieur; *influences* du dehors; *factor* extérieur. (*Pharm*) **for ~ use only** pour (l')usage externe; (*Brit*) **~ degree from London University** diplôme de l'Université de Londres accordé à des étudiants extérieurs; (*Brit Univ etc*) **~ examiner** examinateur (venu) de l'extérieur (*d'une autre université*); (*US*) **~ trade** commerce extérieur. 2 **n** (*fig*) **the ~s** l'extérieur *m*, les apparences *fpl*.

externalize [ɪk'stɜːnə,laɪz] **vt** extérioriser.

externally [ɪk'stɜːnəlɪ] **adv** extérieurement. **he remained ~ calm** il gardait une apparence calme, il restait calme extérieurement; (*Pharm*) **to be used ~** pour (l')usage externe.

extinct [ɪk'stɪŋkt] **adj** *volcano* éteint; *feelings, passion* éteint, mort; *race, species* disparu.

extinction [ɪk'stɪŋkʃən] **n** (*NonC*) *[fire]* extinction *f*; *[race, family]* extinction, disparition *f*; *[hopes]* anéantissement *m*; *[debt]* amortissement *m*.

extinguish [ɪk'stɪŋgwɪʃ] **vt** *fire, light* éteindre; *candle* éteindre, souffler; *hopes* anéantir, mettre fin à; *debt* amortir.

extinguisher [ɪk'stɪŋgwɪʃəʳ] **n** extincteur *m*; *see* **fire**.

extirpate ['ekstə,peɪt] **vt** extirper.

extirpation [,ekstə'peɪʃən] **n** (*NonC*) extirpation *f*.

extirpator ['ekstə,peɪtəʳ] **n** (*Agr, Tech*) extirpateur *m*.

extn (*Telec*) (**abbr of extension**) poste *m*.

extol [ɪk'stəʊl] **vt** *person* louer, porter aux nues, chanter les louanges de; *act, quality* prôner, exalter.

extort [ɪk'stɔːt] **vt** *promise, money* extorquer, soutirer (*from* à); *consent, promise, confession, secret* arracher (*from* à); *signature* extorquer.

extortion [ɪk'stɔːʃən] n (*also Jur*) extorsion *f*. (*fig*) **this is sheer ~!** c'est du vol (manifeste)!
extortionate [ɪk'stɔːʃənɪt] adj *price* exorbitant, inabordable; *demand, tax* excessif, exorbitant.
extortioner [ɪk'stɔːʃənəʳ] n extorqueur *m*, -euse *f*.
extra ['ekstrə] 1 adj a (*additional*) supplémentaire, de plus, en supplément; *homework, credit, bus* supplémentaire. **an ~ chair** une chaise de plus *or* supplémentaire; **the ~ chair/money** la chaise/l'argent supplémentaire; **to work ~ hours** faire des heures supplémentaires; (*Ftbl*) **after ~ time** après prolongation *f*; **to make an ~ effort** faire un surcroît d'efforts; **I have had ~ work this week** j'ai eu plus de travail que d'habitude *or* un surcroît de travail cette semaine; **~ police/troops were called in** on a fait venir des renforts de police/de l'armée; **to order an ~ dish** commander un plat en supplément; **there is an ~ charge for wine, the wine is ~** le vin est en supplément, le vin n'est pas compris; **there will be no ~ charge** on ne vous comptera pas de supplément; **to go to ~ expense** faire des frais supplémentaires; **take ~ care!** faites particulièrement attention!; **~ pay** supplément *m* de salaire, sursalaire *m*; (*Mil*) supplément de solde; **for ~ safety** pour plus de sécurité, pour être plus sûr; **for ~ whiteness** pour plus de blancheur; **I have set an ~ place at (the) table** j'ai ajouté un couvert; **postage and packing ~** frais de port et d'emballage en plus *or* en sus.
b (*spare*) de trop, en trop, de réserve. **I bought a few ~ tins** j'ai acheté quelques boîtes de réserve *or* pour mettre en réserve; **these copies are ~** ces exemplaires sont en trop *or* en supplément.
2 adv plus que d'ordinaire *or* d'habitude, particulièrement. **she was ~ kind that day** elle fut plus gentille que d'habitude ce jour-là.
3 n a (*perk*) à-côté *m*; (*luxury*) agrément *m*. (*expenses*) **~s** frais *mpl or* dépenses *fpl* supplémentaires, faux frais *mpl*; **singing and piano are ~s** (*optional*) les leçons de chant et de piano sont en supplément; (*obligatory*) les leçons de chant et de piano ne sont pas comprises.
b (*in restaurant: ~ dish*) supplément *m*.
c (*Cine, Theat: actor*) figurant(e) *m(f)*.
d (*US: gasoline*) super(carburant) *m*.
extra... ['ekstrə] pref a (*outside*) extra-; *see* **extramarital** *etc*. b (*specially, ultra*) extra-. **~dry** *wine etc* très sec, extra-sec; *champagne, vermouth* extra-dry *inv*; **~fine** extra-fin; **~smart** ultra-chic *inv*; **~strong** *person* extrêmement fort; *material* extra-solide; *see* **extraspecial**.
extract [ɪk'strækt] 1 vt *juice, minerals, oil, bullet, splinter* extraire (*from* de); *tooth* arracher (*from* à); *cork* tirer; (*fig*) *secrets* extraire (*from* de), arracher (*from* à); *confession, permission, promise* arracher (*from* à); *information* tirer (*from* de); *money* tirer (*from* de), soutirer (*from* à); *meaning, moral* tirer, dégager (*from* de); *quotation, passage* extraire, relever (*from* de). **to ~ pleasure from sth** tirer du plaisir de qch; (*Math*) **to ~ the square root** extraire la racine carrée.
2 ['ekstrækt] n a [*book etc*] extrait *m*. **~s from Voltaire** morceaux choisis de Voltaire. b (*Pharm*) extrait *m*; (*Culin*) extrait, concentré *m*. **meat ~** extrait de viande.
extraction [ɪk'strækʃən] n a (*NonC*) (*see* **extract**) extraction *f*; arrachement *m*. b (*Dentistry*) extraction *f*, arrachement *m*. c (*NonC: descent*) origine *f*, extraction *f*. **of noble ~** d'origine noble; **of low/high ~** de basse/de haute extraction; **of Spanish ~** d'origine espagnole.
extractor [ɪk'stræktəʳ] n extracteur *m*. (*Brit*) **~ fan** ventilateur *m*.
extracurricular ['ekstrəkə'rɪkjʊləʳ] adj (*Scol etc: gen*) périscolaire, en dehors du programme, hors programme; *sports* en dehors des heures de classe.
extraditable ['ekstrə,daɪtəbl] adj *offence* qui peut donner lieu à l'extradition; *person* passible *or* susceptible d'extradition.
extradite ['ekstrə,daɪt] vt extrader.
extradition [,ekstrə'dɪʃən] n extradition *f*.
extragalactic [,ekstrəgə'læktɪk] adj extragalactique. **~ nebula** nébuleuse *f* extragalactique.
extralinguistic [,ekstrəlɪŋ'gwɪstɪk] adj extra-linguistique.
extramarital ['ekstrə'mærɪtl] adj en dehors du mariage.
extramural ['ekstrə'mjʊərəl] adj a (*esp Brit*) *course* hors faculté (*donné par des professeurs accrédités par la faculté et ouvert au public*). **~ lecture** conférence *f* publique; (*Brit Univ*) **Department of E~ Studies** ≃ Institut *m* d'éducation permanente; (*US Scol*) **~ sports** *sports pratiqués entre équipes de différents établissements*. b *district* extra-muros *inv*.
extraneous [ɪk'streɪnɪəs] adj (*non-essential*) *detail, idea* superflu; (*without much relevance*) *point* sans grande portée. **~ to** qui n'a aucun rapport avec, qui n'a rien à voir avec; **and other ~ points/suggestions** *etc* et autres points/suggestions *etc* divers(es).
extraordinarily [ɪk'strɔːdnrɪlɪ] adv extraordinairement, remarquablement.
extraordinary [ɪk'strɔːdnrɪ] adj a (*beyond the ordinary*) *measure* extraordinaire, d'exception; *success* remarquable, extraordinaire; *career, quality* remarquable, exceptionnel; *destiny* hors du commun; (*Admin etc*) extraordinaire. **envoy ~** délégué *or* ambassadeur extraordinaire; (*Brit*) **an ~ meeting of the shareholders** une assemblée extraordinaire des actionnaires; **~ general meeting** assemblée *f* générale extraordinaire.
b (*unusual, surprising*) *appearance, dress* extraordinaire, insolite, singulier; *tale, adventure* bizarre, curieux, invraisemblable; *action, speech, behaviour* étonnant, surprenant; *courage, skill* incroyable, extraordinaire; *insults, violence* inouï. **I find it ~ that he hasn't replied** je trouve extraordinaire *or* inouï qu'il n'ait pas répondu; **there's nothing ~ about that** cela n'a rien d'étonnant; **it's ~ to think that ...** il semble incroyable que ... + *subj*; **the ~ fact is that he succeeded** ce qu'il y a d'étonnant c'est qu'il a *or* ait réussi; **it's ~ how much he resembles his brother** c'est inouï ce qu'il peut ressembler à son frère.
extrapolate [ɪk'stræpəleɪt] vt extrapoler (*from* à partir de).
extrasensory ['ekstrə'sensərɪ] adj extra-sensoriel. **~ perception** perception extra-sensorielle.
extraspecial ['ekstrə'speʃəl] adj exceptionnel. **to take ~ care over sth** apporter un soin tout particulier à qch; **~ occasion** grande occasion; **to make something ~ to eat** préparer quelque chose de particulièrement bon.
extraterrestrial [,ekstrətɪ'restrɪəl] adj, n extraterrestre *(mf)*.
extraterritorial ['ekstrə,terɪ'tɔːrɪəl] adj d'exterritorialité, d'extraterritorialité.
extravagance [ɪk'strævəgəns] n (*excessive spending*) prodigalité *f*; (*wastefulness*) gaspillage *m*; (*thing bought*) dépense excessive, folie *f*; (*action, notion*) extravagance *f*, fantaisie *f*. **that hat was a great ~** ce chapeau était une vraie folie.
extravagant [ɪk'strævəgənt] adj a (*wasteful*) *person* dépensier, prodigue, gaspilleur; *taste, habit* dispendieux. **he is very ~ with his money** il gaspille son argent, il jette l'argent par les fenêtres*; **it was very ~ of him to buy this ring** il a fait une folie en achetant cette bague. b (*exaggerated*) *ideas, theories, behaviour* extravagant; *opinions, claims* exagéré; *praise* outré; *prices* exorbitant, inabordable; *dress* extravagant, excentrique. **~ talk** paroles excessives, propos extravagants *or* outranciers.
extravagantly [ɪk'strævəgəntlɪ] adv a (*lavishly*) *spend* largement, avec prodigalité; *furnish* avec luxe. **to use sth ~** gaspiller qch. b (*flamboyantly*) d'une façon extravagante. **to praise sth ~** louer qch à outrance; **to act *or* behave ~** faire des extravagances; **to talk ~** tenir des propos extravagants *or* outranciers.
extravaganza [ɪk,strævə'gænzə] n (*Literat, Mus*) fantaisie *f*; (*story*) histoire *f* extravagante *or* invraisemblable; (*show*) spectacle *m* somptueux; (*whim etc*) fantaisie, folie *f*, caprice *m*.
extravehicular [,ekstrəvɪ'hɪkjʊləʳ] adj (*Space*) extravéhiculaire.
extreme [ɪk'striːm] 1 adj a (*exceptional*) *courage, pleasure, concern, urgency* extrême; *joy* extrême, suprême, intense; (*exaggerated*) *praise, flattery* outré (*after n*), excessif; *measures* extrême, rigoureux, très sévère; *views, person* extrême (*after n*). **in ~ danger** en très grand danger; **of ~ importance** de (la) toute première importance; **the most ~ poverty** la plus grande misère, l'extrême misère; **an ~ case** un cas exceptionnel *or* extrême; **~ in one's opinions** d'opinions extrêmes, extrémiste; (*Pol*) **the ~ right** l'extrême droite *f*.
b (*furthest off*) extrême; *limit* dernier (*before n*), extrême. **to the ~ right** à l'extrême droite; **in the ~ distance** dans l'extrême lointain; **at the ~ end of the path** tout au bout du chemin, à l'extrémité du chemin; **at the ~ edge of the wood** tout à fait à la lisière du bois; **the ~ opposite** l'extrême opposé; **to carry sth to the ~ limits** pousser qch à son point extrême *or* à l'extrême.
c (*last, final*) dernier, extrême. **the ~ penalty** le dernier supplice; **~ old age** l'extrême vieillesse *f*; (*Rel*) **~ unction** extrême-onction *f*.
d (*ostentatious*) *hat, design* m'as-tu-vu* *inv*; *idea, suggestion* exagéré. **how ~!** c'est un peu fort!* *or* poussé!
2 n extrême *m*. **in the ~** *difficult, irritating, obstinate* à l'extrême, au possible; *wealthy, helpful, interesting* à l'extrême; **to go from one ~ to the other** passer d'un extrême à l'autre; **~s of temperature** températures *fpl* extrêmes; **~s meet** les extrêmes se touchent; **to go to ~s** pousser les choses à l'extrême; **I won't go to that ~** je ne veux pas aller jusqu'à ces extrémités.
extremely [ɪk'striːmlɪ] adv extrêmement, à l'extrême, au plus haut degré *or* point. **to be ~ talented** avoir un grand talent *or* énormément de talent; **he is ~ helpful** il est on ne peut plus serviable.
extremism [ɪk'striːmɪzəm] n extrémisme *m*.
extremist [ɪk'striːmɪst] 1 adj *opinion* extrême; *person* extrémiste. **an ~ party** un parti d'extrémistes. 2 n extrémiste *mf*.
extremity [ɪk'stremɪtɪ] n a (*furthest point*) extrémité *f*, bout *or* point le plus éloigné. (*hands and feet*) **extremities** extrémités. b [*despair, happiness*] extrême *or* dernier degré; (*extreme act*) extrémité *f*. **to drive sb to extremities** pousser qn à une extrémité. c (*danger, distress*) extrémité *f*. **to help sb in his ~** venir en aide à qn qui est aux abois.
extricate ['ekstrɪkeɪt] vt *object* dégager (*from* de). **to ~ o.s.** s'extirper (*from* de); (*fig*) se tirer (*from* de); **to ~ sb from a nasty situation** tirer qn d'un mauvais pas.
extrinsic [ek'strɪnsɪk] adj extrinsèque.
extroversion [,ekstrə'vɜːʃən] n extraversion *f*, extroversion *f*.
extrovert ['ekstrəʊ,vɜːt] 1 adj extraverti *or* extroverti. 2 n extraverti(e) *m(f)* *or* extroverti(e) *m(f)*. **he's an ~** il s'extériorise (beaucoup).
extrude [ɪk'struːd] vt rejeter (*from* hors de), expulser (*from* de);

metal, plastics extruder.
extrusion [ɪk'stru:ʒən] n (*Tech*) extrusion *f*.
extrusive [ɪk'stru:sɪv] adj extrusif.
exuberance [ɪg'zju:bərəns] n *[person]* exubérance *f*, trop-plein *m* de vie; *[vegetation]* exubérance, luxuriance *f*; *[words, images]* richesse *f*, exubérance.
exuberant [ɪg'zju:bərənt] adj *person* exubérant, débordant de vie; *mood* exubérant, expansif; *joy, imagination* exubérant, débordant; *style* abondant, exubérant; *vegetation* exubérant, luxuriant.
exuberantly [ɪg'zju:bərəntlɪ] adv avec exubérance.
exude [ɪg'zju:d] 1 vi suinter, exsuder (*from* de). 2 vt *resin, blood* exsuder. **to ~ water** *or* **moisture** suinter; **he ~d charm** le charme lui sortait par tous les pores; **he ~s confidence** il respire la confiance en soi.
exult [ɪg'zʌlt] vi (*rejoice*) se réjouir (*in* de, *over* à propos de), exulter; (*triumph*) jubiler, chanter victoire. **to ~ at finding** *or* **to find** se réjouir grandement *or* exulter de trouver.
exultant [ɪg'zʌltənt] adj *joy* triomphant; *expression, shout* de triomphe. **to be ~, to be in an ~ mood** jubiler, triompher, être transporté de joie.
exultantly [ɪg'zʌltəntlɪ] adv triomphalement.
exultation [,egzʌl'teɪʃən] n exultation *f*, jubilation *f*.
exurbia [eks'ɜ:bɪə] n (*US*) la banlieue résidentielle (*des nouveaux riches*).
ex-wife [,eks'waɪf] n ex-femme *f*.
ex-works [,eks'wɜ:ks] adj (*Brit Comm*) *price* départ *or* sortie usine; *see also* **ex 1**.
eye [aɪ] 1 n a *[person, animal]* œil *m* (*pl* yeux). **girl with blue ~s** fille aux yeux bleus; **to have brown ~s** avoir les yeux bruns; **with tears in her ~s** les larmes aux yeux; **with ~s half-closed** *or* **half-shut** les yeux à demi fermés, les paupières mi-closes (*liter*); **with one's ~s closed** *or* **shut** les yeux fermés; (*lit*) **to keep one's ~s wide open** garder les yeux grand(s) ouverts; **he couldn't keep his ~s open*** il dormait debout (*fig*), il sentait ses yeux se fermer (*see also* **1b**); **to have the sun in one's ~s** avoir le soleil dans les yeux; *see* **black**.

b (*phrases*) **before my very ~s** juste sous mes yeux; **it's there in front of your very ~s** tu l'as sous les yeux, c'est sous ton nez*; **for your ~s only** ultra-confidentiel; (*US: on documents*) **"~s only"** "ultra-confidentiel"; **as far as the ~ can see** à perte de vue; **in the ~s of** aux yeux de; **in his ~s** à ses yeux; **in the ~s of the law** aux yeux *or* au regard de la loi; **through someone else's ~s** par les yeux d'un autre; **to look at a question through the ~s of an economist** envisager une question du point de vue de l'économiste; **under the ~ of** sous la surveillance de, sous l'œil de; **with my own ~s** de mes propres yeux; **I saw him with my own ~s** je l'ai vu de mes yeux vu; **with a critical/jealous/uneasy ~** d'un œil critique/jaloux/inquiet; **with an ~ to the future** en prévision de l'avenir; **with an ~ to buying** en vue d'acheter; **that's one in the ~ for him*** c'est bien fait pour lui *or* pour sa poire‡; **to be all ~s** être tout yeux; **to be up to the** *or* **one's ~s in work/debts** être dans le travail/dans les dettes jusqu'au cou; **he's in it up to the ~s*** il est (compromis) dans l'affaire jusqu'au cou, il est dedans jusqu'au cou; **to close** *or* **shut one's ~s to sb's shortcomings** fermer les yeux sur les faiblesses de qn; **to close** *or* **shut one's ~s to the evidence** se refuser à l'évidence; **to close** *or* **shut one's ~s to the dangers of sth/the truth** se dissimuler les périls de qch/la vérité; **one can't close** *or* **shut one's ~s to the fact that ...** on ne peut pas se dissimuler que ..., on est bien obligé d'admettre que ...; (*fig*) **I could do it with my ~s shut** je pourrais le faire les yeux fermés; **his ~ fell on a small door** son regard est tombé sur *or* a rencontré une petite porte; **to get one's ~ in** ajuster son coup d'œil; (*US*) **to give sb the ~‡** faire de l'œil* à qn; **he's got his ~ on the championship** il guigne le championnat; **I've already got my ~ on a house** j'ai déjà une maison en vue; **to have an ~ on sb for a job** avoir qn en vue pour une place; **he had his ~ on a job in the Foreign Office** il visait un poste *or* il lorgnait* une place au ministère des Affaires étrangères; **to have an ~ to the main chance** ne jamais perdre de vue ses propres intérêts, ne négliger aucune occasion de soigner ses intérêts; **she has an ~ for a bargain** elle flaire *or* elle reconnaît tout de suite une bonne affaire; **she has got an ~ for antique furniture** elle a du coup d'œil pour les meubles anciens; **he had ~s for no one but her, he only had ~s for her** il n'avait d'yeux que pour elle; **to keep one's ~ on the ball** fixer la balle, regarder sa balle; **keeping his ~ on the beast, he seized his gun** sans quitter l'animal des yeux, il a empoigné son fusil; **keep your ~ on the main objective** ne perdez pas de vue le but principal; **to keep a watchful ~ on the situation** suivre de près la situation, avoir l'œil sur la situation; **to keep an ~ on things*** *or* **on everything** avoir l'œil (à tout); **to keep a strict ~ on sb** surveiller qn de près, avoir *or* tenir qn à l'œil*; **will you keep an ~ on the child/shop?** voudriez-vous surveiller l'enfant/le magasin?; **to keep an ~ on expenditure** surveiller la dépense; **to keep one's ~s open** *or* **peeled‡** *or* **skinned‡** être attentif (*for a danger* à un danger), être vigilant, ouvrir l'œil; **keep your ~s open for** *or* **keep an ~ out for* a hotel** essayez de repérer* un hôtel; **he went into it with his ~s wide open** *or* **with open ~s** il s'est lancé (là-dedans) en pleine connaissance de cause, (quand il a fait ça) il savait exactement ce qu'il faisait; **this will open his ~s to the truth** ça va lui ouvrir *or* dessiller (*liter*) les yeux (*about* au sujet de); **to let one's ~ rest on sth** poser *or* arrêter son regard sur qch; **to look sb straight in the ~** regarder qn dans les yeux *or* dans le blanc des yeux *or* bien en face; **to make ~s at*** faire de l'œil à*, lancer des œillades à; **to run** *or* **cast one's ~s over** jeter un coup d'œil sur; **he ran his ~ over the letter** il a parcouru la lettre (en diagonale); **to see ~ to ~ with sb** voir les choses exactement comme qn *or* du même œil que qn, partager les opinions *or* le point de vue de qn; **I've never set** *or* **clapped*** *or* **laid ~s on him** je ne l'ai jamais vu de ma vie; **he didn't take his ~s off her, he kept his ~s fixed on her** il ne l'a pas quittée des yeux; **she couldn't take her ~s off the cakes** elle ne pouvait pas s'empêcher de reluquer *or* lorgner les gâteaux, elle dévorait les gâteaux des yeux; **he never uses his ~s** il ne sait pas voir; **why don't you use your ~s?** tu es aveugle?, tu n'as donc pas les yeux en face des trous?‡; (*loc*) **an ~ for an ~ and a tooth for a tooth** œil pour œil, dent pour dent; (*Mil*) **~s right!** tête (à) droite!; (*Mil*) **~s front!** fixe!; **it's all my ~‡** tout ça, c'est des histoires*; **my ~!‡** mon œil!‡; *see* **catch, half, mind, open, private** *etc*.

c *[needle]* chas *m*, œil *m*, trou *m*; *[potato, peacock's tail]* œil; *[hurricane]* œil, centre *m*; (*photoelectric cell*) œil électrique.

2 vt *person* regarder, mesurer du regard; *thing* regarder, observer. **to ~ sb from head to toe** toiser qn de haut en bas; **he was eyeing (up)* the girls** il reluquait* les filles.

3 comp ► **eyeball** n globe *m* oculaire ◊ vt (*US* ‡) zieuter‡, regarder; (*fig*) **to stand eyeball to eyeball with sb*** se trouver nez à nez avec qn ► **eyebank** (*Med*) banque *f* des yeux ► **eyebath** (*esp Brit*) œillère *f* (*pour bains d'œil*) ► **eyebrow** sourcil *m*; **eyebrow pencil** crayon *m* (à sourcils); **eyebrow tweezers** pince *f* à épiler ► **eye-catcher** personne *f* *or* chose *f* qui tire l'œil *or* qui tape dans l'œil* ► **eye-catching** *dress, colour* qui tire l'œil, qui tape dans l'œil*, tape-à-l'œil* *inv* (*pej*); *publicity, poster* accrocheur ► **eye contact** le fait de regarder quelqu'un dans les yeux; **to establish/avoid eye contact with sb** regarder droit dans les yeux de qn/éviter de regarder qn dans les yeux ► **eyecup** (*US*) = **eyebath** ► **eye doctor** (*US*) oculiste *mf* ► **eyedrops** gouttes *fpl* pour les yeux ► **eyeglass** monocle *m* ► **eyeglasses** lorgnon *m*, binocle *m*, pince-nez *m inv*, lunettes *fpl* ► **eyelash** cil *m* ► **eye level: at eye level** au niveau de l'œil; **eye-level grill** gril surélevé ► **eyelid** paupière *f* ► **eyeliner** eye-liner *m* ► **eye-opener*** (*surprise*) révélation *f*, surprise *f*; (*US: drink*) petit verre pris au réveil; **that was an eye-opener for him** cela lui a ouvert les yeux; **his speech was an eye-opener** son discours a été très révélateur ► **eye-patch** cache *m*, bandeau *m* ► **eyepiece** oculaire *m* ► **eyeshade** visière *f* ► **eyeshadow** fard *m* à paupières ► **eyesight** vue *f*; **to have good eyesight** avoir une bonne vue *or* de bons yeux; **to lose one's eyesight** perdre la vue; **his eyesight is failing** sa vue baisse ► **eye socket** orbite *f* ► **eyesore** horreur *f*; **these ruins are an eyesore** ces ruines sont une horreur *or* sont hideuses, ces ruines choquent la vue; **her hat was an eyesore** son chapeau était une horreur ► **eyestrain: to have eyestrain** avoir la vue fatiguée ► **eye test** examen *m* de la vue ► **eyetooth** canine supérieure; (*fig*) **I'd give my eyeteeth* for a car like that/to go to China** qu'est-ce-que je ne donnerais pas pour avoir une voiture comme ça/pour aller en Chine ► **eyewash** (*Med*) collyre *m*; (*fig*) **that's a lot of eyewash‡** (*nonsense*) ce sont des fadaises, c'est du vent; (*to impress*) c'est de la frime*, c'est de la poudre aux yeux ► **eyewitness** témoin oculaire *or* direct; **eyewitness account** (*in media*) récit *m* de témoin; (*to police*) déposition *f* de témoin oculaire.
►**eye up*** vt sep reluquer*.
-eyed [aɪd] adj ending in comps: **big-eyed** aux grands yeux; **brown-eyed** aux yeux marron; **one-eyed** (*lit*) borgne, qui n'a qu'un œil; (* *fig*) miteux, minable; *see* **dry, hollow, wall** *etc*.
eyeful ['aɪfʊl] n: **he got an ~ of mud** il a reçu de la boue plein les yeux; **she's quite an ~*** cette fille, c'est un régal pour l'œil; **get an ~ of this!‡** vise ça un peu!‡
eyelet ['aɪlɪt] n œillet *m* (*dans du tissu etc*).
eyrie ['ɪərɪ] n aire *f* (*d'aigle*).
Ezekiel [ɪ'zi:kɪəl] n Ezéchiel *m*.

F, f [ef] n a (*letter*) F, f *m or f*. **F for Freddy,** (*US*) **F for fox** F comme François; *see also* **F-word.** b (*Mus*) fa *m*; *see* **key.** c (*Scol: mark*) faible. d abbr of **Fahrenheit.**
FA‡, f.a.‡ [ef'eɪ] (*Brit*) (abbr of **Fanny Adams**) *see* **Fanny.**
fa [fɑː] n (*Mus*) fa *m*.
F.A. [ef'eɪ] (*Brit*) (abbr of **Football Association**) fédération *f* anglaise et galloise de football.
FAA [ˌefeɪ'eɪ] (*US*) (abbr of **Federal Aviation Administration**) *see* **federal²**.
fab‡ [fæb] adj (*Brit*) (abbr of **fabulous**) sensass*, terrible‡.
Fabian ['feɪbɪən] 1 n (*Pol*) Fabien(ne) *m(f)*. 2 adj fabien. ~ **Society** Association fabienne.
fable ['feɪbl] n (*Literat*) fable *f*, légende *f*; (*fig*) fable; *see* **fact.**
fabled ['feɪbld] adj légendaire, fabuleux.
fabric ['fæbrɪk] n a (*cloth*) tissu *m*, étoffe *f*. **cotton/woollen ~s** cotonnades *fpl*/lainages *mpl*; ~ **conditioner** *or* **softener** produit *m* assouplissant. b *[building, system, society]* structure *f*.
fabricate ['fæbrɪkeɪt] vt *goods etc* fabriquer; (*fig*) *document* fabriquer, forger; *story, account* inventer, fabriquer. a **~d story** une histoire inventée *or* fabriquée *or* controuvée.
fabrication [ˌfæbrɪ'keɪʃən] n a (*NonC: see* **fabricate**) fabrication *f*; invention *f*. b (*false statement etc*) invention *f*. **it is (a) pure ~** c'est une pure invention, c'est de la fabrication pure (et simple).
fabulous ['fæbjʊləs] adj (*gen*) fabuleux; (**: wonderful*) fabuleux, formidable*, sensationnel*. a ~ **price*** un prix fou *or* fabuleux *or* astronomique; (*excl*) ~! chouette!*, sensass!*
fabulously ['fæbjʊləslɪ] adv fabuleusement, extraordinairement. ~ **rich** fabuleusement riche; ~ **successful** qui a (*or* a eu) un succès fabuleux.
façade [fə'sɑːd] n (*Archit, fig*) façade *f*.
face [feɪs] 1 n (*Anat*) visage *m*, figure *f*; (*expression*) mine *f*, physionomie *f*; *[building]* façade *f*, devant *m*, front *m*; *[clock]* cadran *m*; *[cliff]* paroi *f*; (*Climbing*) face *f*; *[coin]* côté *m*; *[the earth]* surface *f*; *[document]* recto *m*; *[type]* œil *m*; *[playing card]* face, dessous *m*; (*NonC: prestige*) face; (**: NonC: impertinence*) toupet* *m*. **a pleasant ~** un visage *or* une figure agréable; **to fall (flat) on one's ~** tomber à plat ventre, tomber face contre terre; **he was lying ~ down(wards)** (*on ground*) il était étendu (la) face contre terre *or* à plat ventre; (*on bed, sofa*) il était étendu à plat ventre, il était prosterné de tout son long; **he was lying ~ up(wards)** il était étendu sur le dos *or* le visage tourné vers le ciel (*or* le plafond *etc*); **it fell ~ up/down** (*gen*) c'est tombé du bon/du mauvais côté; *[playing card]* c'est tombé face en dessus/en dessous; **to turn sth ~ up** retourner *or* mettre qch à l'endroit; (*Med*) **injuries to the ~** blessures *fpl* à la face *or* au visage; **to have one's ~ lifted** se faire faire un lifting; **you can shout till you're black** *or* **blue in the ~, nobody will come** tu auras beau t'exténuer à crier, personne ne viendra; **to change the ~ of a town** changer le visage d'une ville; **he vanished off the ~ of the earth** il a complètement disparu; **I know that ~** je connais cette tête-là, cette tête-là me dit quelque chose; **I've got a good memory for ~s** j'ai la mémoire des visages, je suis physionomiste; **he's a good judge of ~s** il sait lire sur les visages; **the rain was blowing in our ~s** la pluie nous fouettait le visage *or* la figure; **it blew up in my ~** ça m'a explosé à la figure; **he laughed in my ~** il m'a ri au nez; **he won't show his ~ here again** il ne se montrera plus ici, il ne remettra plus le nez ici; **he told him the truth to his ~** il lui a dit la vérité sans ambages; **he told him so to his ~** il le lui a dit tout cru *or* sans ambages; **to come ~ to ~ with sb** se trouver face à face *or* nez à nez avec qn (*see also* **2**); **to bring two people ~ to ~** confronter deux personnes; **courage in the ~ of the enemy** courage *m* face à l'ennemi; **in the ~ of this threat** devant cette menace; **he succeeded in the ~ of great difficulties** il a réussi en dépit de grandes difficultés; **to set one's ~ against sth** s'élever contre qch; **to set one's ~ against doing** se refuser à faire; **to put a bold** *or* **brave ~ on things** faire bonne contenance *or* bon visage; **you'll just have to put a good ~ on it** tu n'auras qu'à faire contre mauvaise fortune bon cœur; **to put one's ~ on*** se faire le visage*; **to save (one's) ~** sauver la face; **to lose ~** perdre la face; **to make** *or* **pull ~s (at)** faire des grimaces (à); **to make** *or* **pull a (disapproving) ~** faire une moue de désapprobation; **on the ~ of it his evidence is false** à première vue son témoignage est faux; **to have the ~ to do*** avoir le toupet* de faire; *see* **coal, fly³, loss 1a, straight** *etc*.
2 comp ▸**face card** (*US*) figure *f* ▸**face cream** crème *f* pour le visage ▸**facecloth** (*Brit*), **face flannel** gant *m* de toilette ▸**faceguard** (*Baseball*) visière *f* de protection ▸**face lift** lifting *m*, déridage *m*; **to have a face lift** se faire faire un lifting; (*fig*) **to give a face lift* to** (*gen*) refaire une beauté* à; *house* ravaler, retaper; *car* refaire la carrosserie de; **the town/the park/the garden has been given a face lift*** la ville/le parc/le jardin a fait peau neuve ▸**face-off** (*US*) (*Hockey*) remise *f* en jeu; (*fig*) confrontation *f* ▸**face pack** masque *m* de beauté ▸**face powder** poudre *f* de riz ▸**face-saving** adj qui sauve la face; **it was clearly a piece of face-saving** *or* **a face-saver on their part** ils l'ont visiblement fait pour sauver la face ▸**face-to-face** face à face, nez à nez; (*TV etc*) **face-to-face discussion** face à face *m inv or* face-à-face *m inv* ▸**face value** valeur nominale; (*fig*) **to take a statement at its face value** prendre une déclaration pour argent comptant *or* au pied de la lettre; **to take sb at his face value** juger qn sur les apparences; **you can't take it at its face value** il ne faut pas vous laisser tromper par les apparences.
3 vt a (*turn one's face towards*) faire face à; (*have one's face towards: also* **to be facing**) faire face à, être en face de. **he turned and ~d the man** il se retourna et fit face à l'homme; ~ **this way!** tournez-vous de ce côté!; (*fig*) **to ~ both ways** ménager la chèvre et le chou; **he stood facing the wall** il se tenait face au mur; **he was facing the wall** il faisait face au mur, il était face au mur; **he was facing me** il me faisait face; **he was facing me at the dinner** il était assis en face de moi *or* il me faisait face *or* je l'avais comme vis-à-vis au dîner; **facing one another** en face l'un de l'autre, l'un vis-à-vis de l'autre, en vis-à-vis; **the two boys ~d each other** les deux garçons se faisaient face *or* étaient face à face; **when she entered, she was ~d by** *or* **with the headmaster** en entrant elle se trouva face à face *or* nez à nez avec le directeur.
b (*have its front towards: also* **to be facing**) (*gen*) faire face à; (*look out onto*) *[building, window]* faire face à, donner sur. **which way does the house ~?** comment la maison est-elle orientée?; **house facing north** maison exposée *or* orientée au nord; **the seats were all facing the platform** les sièges faisaient tous face à l'estrade; **the picture facing page 16** l'illustration en regard de *or* en face de la page 16.
c *[problem, task, situation]* se présenter à. **two problems/tasks** *etc* **~d them** deux problèmes/tâches *etc* se présentaient à eux, ils se trouvaient devant deux problèmes/tâches *etc*; **the problem facing us** le problème devant lequel nous nous trouvons *or* qui se pose à nous; **the economic difficulties facing the country** les difficultés économiques que rencontre le pays *or* auxquelles le pays doit faire face.
d (*have to deal with: also* **to be faced with** *or* **by**) être obligé de *or* contraint à faire face à, être confronté* à. **~d with the task of deciding, he ...** se trouvant dans l'obligation de prendre une décision, il ...; **he was ~d with having to pay £10** il se voyait contraint à payer 10 livres; **he was ~d with a bill for £10** il se voyait contraint à payer une note de 10 livres; **the government, ~d with renewed wage demands ...** le gouvernement, face aux nouvelles revendications salariales, ...; **he ~d** *or* **was ~d with a class who refused to cooperate** il se trouvait devant *or* face à *or* confronté* à une classe qui refusait de coopérer.
e *problem, difficulty, crisis* (*look at honestly*) faire face à; (*deal with, tackle*) s'attaquer à. **she ~d the problem at last** elle a enfin fait face au problème; **I could never ~ this alone** je ne pourrais jamais faire face à cela tout seul; **I can't ~ doing it** je n'ai pas *or* ne trouve pas le courage de le faire; **I can't ~ him/the washing up** je n'ai pas *or* je ne trouve pas le courage de le voir/de faire la vaisselle; (*fig*) **to ~ the music** braver l'orage *or* la tempête, ne pas reculer, ne pas se dérober; **we'll have to ~ the music** allons-y gaiement (*iro*), il ne faut pas reculer; **to ~ it out*** faire face, ne pas reculer, ne pas se dérober; **to ~ (the) facts** regarder

les choses en face, se rendre à l'évidence; **she won't ~ the fact that he will not come back** elle ne veut pas se rendre à l'évidence et comprendre *or* admettre qu'il ne reviendra pas; **let's ~ it*** regardons les choses en face, admettons-le.

f (*present sb with*) **you must ~ him with this choice/the decision** *etc* vous devez le contraindre à faire face à ce choix/cette décision *etc;* **you must ~ him with the truth** vous devez le contraindre à regarder la vérité en face.

g (*risk incurring etc*) *a fine, charges, prison, defeat, death* encourir; *unemployment, redundancy etc* être menacé de. **to ~** *or* **to be ~d with the possibility that sth might happen** encourir la possibilité que qch arrive; **he ~d** *or* **he was ~d with the prospect of doing it himself** il risquait d'avoir à le faire lui-même; **~d with the prospect of having to refuse, he ...** face à *or* devant la perspective d'avoir à refuser, il ...; **many people were facing redundancy** beaucoup de gens étaient menacés de chômage.

h (*line*) *wall* revêtir (*with* de). **coat ~d with silk** habit à revers de soie.

4 vi *[person]* (*turn one's face*) se tourner (*towards* vers); (*be turned: also* **to be facing**) être tourné (*towards* vers), faire face (*towards* à); *[house]* être exposé *or* orienté. **he was facing towards the audience** il faisait face au public; **room facing towards the sea** chambre donnant sur la mer, chambre face à la mer; (*US Mil*) **right ~!** à droite, droite!; (*US Mil*) **about ~!** demi-tour!

►**face about vi** (*Mil*) faire demi-tour.

►**face down vt sep** (*US*) défier du regard.

►**face up to vt fus** *danger, difficulty* faire face à, affronter. **to face up to the fact that** admettre *or* accepter (le fait) que.

faceless [ˈfeɪslɪs] **adj** anonyme.

facer* [ˈfeɪsəʳ] **n** (*Brit*) tuile* *f*, os* *m*. **well there's a ~ for us** nous sommes tombés sur un os*, voilà une belle tuile* qui nous tombe dessus.

facet [ˈfæsɪt] **n** (*lit, fig*) facette *f*.

faceted [ˈfæsɪtɪd] **adj** à facettes.

facetious [fəˈsiːʃəs] **adj** *person* facétieux, plaisant; *remark* plaisant, bouffon.

facetiously [fəˈsiːʃəslɪ] **adv** facétieusement.

facetiousness [fəˈsiːʃəsnɪs] **n** (*see* **facetious**) caractère facétieux *or* plaisant.

facia [ˈfeɪʃɪə] **n** = **fascia**.

facial [ˈfeɪʃəl] **1 adj** *nerve, massage* facial. **~ hair** poils *mpl* du visage. **2 n** (*) soin *m* (complet) du visage. **to have a ~** se faire faire un soin du visage; **to give o.s. a ~** se faire un nettoyage de peau.

facies [ˈfeɪʃɪiːz] **n, pl inv** faciès *m*.

facile [ˈfæsaɪl] **adj** (*gen pej*) *victory* facile; *talk, idea* superficiel, creux; *person* complaisant; *style, manner* aisé, coulant.

facilely [ˈfæsaɪllɪ] **adv** complaisamment.

facilitate [fəˈsɪlɪteɪt] **vt** faciliter.

facility [fəˈsɪlɪtɪ] **n a** (*NonC: ease, ability*) facilité *f*. **to write with ~/with great ~** écrire avec facilité/avec beaucoup de facilité; **~ in** *or* **for learning, learning ~** facilité pour apprendre; **~ in foreign languages** facilité *or* aptitude *f* pour les langues étrangères.

b (*often pl: equipment, means etc*) **facilities** (*equipment, material*) équipements *mpl* (*for* de); (*plant, installation*) installations *fpl*; (*means*) moyens *mpl* (*for* de); (*gen*) **facilities for** facilités *fpl* pour; **the main ~ is the library** le service principal est la bibliothèque, le service de la bibliothèque est particulièrement utile; **the museum has a ~ where students can work** le musée met à la disposition des étudiants un endroit où travailler; **recreational facilities** (*gen*) ce qu'il faut pour la détente *or* se détendre, les facilités pour la détente *or* le sport et les loisirs; **you will have all facilities** *or* **every ~ for study** vous aurez toutes facilités pour étudier; **books and other facilities** (les) livres et autres instruments de travail; **sports/educational facilities** équipements sportifs/scolaires; **transport/production facilities** moyens de transport/de production; **harbour facilities** installations portuaires; **the flat has no cooking facilities** l'appartement n'est pas équipé pour qu'on y fasse la cuisine; (*Mil*) **the use of this territory as an emergency ~ for the troops** l'utilisation de ce territoire par les troupes en cas d'urgence; (*Mil*) **the country's nuclear ~** la capacité nucléaire du pays.

c (*Admin etc: official method*) possibilité offerte (*for doing* de faire). **a ~ for converting part of one's pension into ...** la possibilité de convertir une partie de sa retraite en ...; **we offer this ~ to the general public** nous offrons cette possibilité au grand public; *see* **credit, loan, overdraft**.

d (*Tech etc: device*) mécanisme *m*; (*Comput*) fonction *f*. **the clock has a stopwatch ~** le réveil peut aussi servir de chronomètre; (*Comput*) **there's a ~ for storing data** il est possible de mettre en réserve les données; **the oven has an automatic timing ~** le four est doté d'un minuteur automatique.

facing [ˈfeɪsɪŋ] **n** (*Constr*) revêtement *m*; (*Sewing*) revers *m*.

-facing [ˈfeɪsɪŋ] **adj ending in comps: south-facing** exposé au sud.

facsimile [fækˈsɪmɪlɪ] **1 n** fac-similé *m*. **in ~** en fac-similé. **2 comp** ►**facsimile machine** télécopieur *m* ►**facsimile transmission** télécopie *f*.

fact [fækt] **1 n a** (*sth known, accepted as true*) fait *m*. **the ~ that he is here** le fait qu'il est là *or* qu'il soit là; **it is a ~ that** il est de fait que + *indic*; **is it a ~ that** est-il vrai que + *subj* (*often indic in conversation*); **(and) that's a ~** c'est certain *or* sûr; **I know it for a ~** c'est un fait certain, je le sais de source sûre; **to know (it) for a ~ that** savoir de science *or* source sûre que, savoir pertinemment que; **to stick to ~s** s'en tenir aux faits; **it's time he knew the ~s of life** il est temps de lui apprendre les choses de la vie *or* qu'on le mette devant les réalités de la vie; (*sex*) il est temps qu'il sache comment les enfants viennent au monde; (*iro*) **it's a ~ of life (that ...)** la vie est ainsi faite (que ...); *see* **face**.

b (*NonC: reality*) faits *mpl*, réalité *f*. **~ and fiction** le réel et l'imaginaire; (*fig*) **he can't tell ~ from fiction** *or* **from fable** il ne sait pas séparer le vrai du faux; **story founded on ~** histoire basée sur des faits *or* sur la réalité; **the ~ of the matter is that ...** le fait est que ..., la réalité c'est que ...; **I accept what he says as ~** je ne mets pas en doute la véracité de ses propos.

c in ~ (*gen*) en fait; (*reinforcing sth*) de fait, effectivement, en fait; (*giving more details*) en fait; (*contradicting or changing sth*) en fait, à vrai dire, en réalité; (*reinforcing*) **he had promised to send the books and in ~ they arrived the next day** il avait promis d'envoyer les livres et de fait *or* effectivement *or* en fait ils sont arrivés le lendemain; (*adding detail*) **he said that he'd gone to France, in ~ that he'd gone to Paris** il a dit qu'il était allé en France, en fait qu'il était allé à Paris; (*contradicting*) **he said he'd spoken to her, but in (actual) ~** *or* **in point of ~ he'd never even seen her** il a dit qu'il lui avait parlé mais en fait *or* à vrai dire *or* en réalité il ne l'avait jamais vue de sa vie.

d (*Jur*) fait *m*, action *f*; *see* **accessary**.

2 comp ►**fact-finding**: **fact-finding committee** commission *f* d'enquête; **they were on a fact-finding mission** *or* **tour to the war front** ils étaient partis enquêter au front; **fact-finding session** séance *f* d'information ►**fact sheet** fiche *f* d'informations.

faction¹ [ˈfækʃən] **n** (*group*) faction *f*; (*NonC: strife*) discorde *f*, dissension *f*.

faction² [ˈfækʃən] **n** (*Theat, Cine: mixture of fact and fiction*) docudrame *m*.

factious [ˈfækʃəs] **adj** factieux.

factitious [fækˈtɪʃəs] **adj** artificiel.

factitive [ˈfæktɪtɪv] **adj** (*Gram*) factitif.

factor [ˈfæktəʳ] **1 n a** facteur *m* (*also Bio, Math etc*), élément *m*. **determining ~** facteur décisif *or* déterminant; (*Tech*) **~ of safety, safety ~** facteur de sécurité; **human ~** élément humain; *[sun cream]* **(sun protection) ~ 9/17** *etc* indice *m* (de protection) 9/17 *etc; see* **common, prime**. **b** (*agent*) agent *m*; (*Scot: estate manager*) régisseur *m*, intendant *m*. **2 comp** ►**factor analysis** (*Statistics*) analyse factorielle ►**factor VIII** *or* **8** (*Med*) facteur *m* 8.

factorage [ˈfæktərɪdʒ] **n a** (*Comm*) commission *f*. **b** (*Fin*) commission *f* d'affacturage *or* de factoring.

factorial [fækˈtɔːrɪəl] **1 adj** factoriel. **2 n** factorielle *f*.

factoring [ˈfæktərɪŋ] **n** affacturage *m*, factoring *m*.

factorize [ˈfæktəˌraɪz] **vt** (*Math*) mettre en facteurs.

factory [ˈfæktərɪ] **1 n** usine *f*, (*gen smaller*) fabrique *f*; (*fig*) usine. **shoe/soap** *etc* **~** usine *or* fabrique de chaussures/de savon *etc;* **car/textile** *etc* **~** usine d'automobiles/de textile *etc;* **arms/china/tobacco ~** manufacture *f* d'armes/de porcelaine/de tabac.

2 comp ►**Factory Acts** législation industrielle ►**factory chimney** cheminée *f* d'usine ►**factory farm** ferme *f* industrielle ►**factory farming** élevage industriel ►**factory floor** ateliers *mpl*; **workers on the factory floor** ouvriers *mpl* ►**factory-fresh** tout droit sorti de l'usine ►**factory hand** = **factory worker** ►**factory inspector** inspecteur *m* du travail ►**factory outlet** magasin *m* d'usine ►**factory ship** navire-usine *m* ►**factory work** travail *m* en *or* d'usine ►**factory worker** ouvrier *m*, -ière *f* (d'usine).

factotum [fækˈtəʊtəm] **n** factotum *m*, intendant *m*; (*hum: man or woman*) bonne *f* à tout faire (*fig hum*).

factual [ˈfæktjʊəl] **adj** *report, description* factuel, basé sur les *or* des faits; *happening* réel; (*Philos*) factuel. **~ error** erreur *f* de fait *or* sur les faits.

factually [ˈfæktjʊəlɪ] **adv** en se tenant aux faits. **~ speaking** pour s'en tenir aux faits.

faculty [ˈfækəltɪ] **1 n a** faculté *f*. **the mental faculties** les facultés mentales; **to have all one's faculties** avoir toutes ses facultés; **critical ~** le sens critique. **b** (*NonC: aptitude*) aptitude *f*, facilité *f* (*for doing* à faire). **c** (*Univ*) faculté *f*. **the F~ of Arts** la faculté des Lettres; **the medical ~** la faculté de médecine; (*US*) **the F~** le corps enseignant; *see* **law, science** *etc.* **2 comp** ►**faculty advisor** (*US Univ*) (*for student*) directeur *m*, -trice *f* d'études; (*for club*) animateur *m*, -trice *f* ►**Faculty board** (*Univ*) Conseil *m* de faculté ►**Faculty (board) meeting** réunion *f* du Conseil de faculté ►**faculty lounge** (*US Scol*) salle *f* des professeurs.

fad [fæd] **n** (*personal*) marotte *f*, manie *f*; (*general*) engouement *m*, mode *f*. **she has her ~s** elle a ses (petites) marottes *or* manies; **a passing ~** un engouement (*for* pour), une lubie; **this ~ for long skirts** cette folie des *or* cet engouement pour les jupes longues.

faddish ['fædɪʃ], **faddy** ['fædɪ] adj (*Brit*) *person* maniaque, capricieux, à marottes; *distaste, desire* capricieux.

fade [feɪd] 1 vi a *[flower]* se faner, se flétrir; *[light]* baisser, diminuer, s'affaiblir; *[colour]* passer, perdre son éclat; *[material]* passer, se décolorer. (*Tex*) **guaranteed not to ~** garanti bon teint; **the daylight was fast fading** le jour baissait rapidement.

b (*also* ~ **away**) *[one's sight, memory, hearing etc]* baisser; *[thing remembered, vision]* s'effacer; *[hopes, smile]* s'éteindre, s'évanouir; *[interest, enthusiasm]* diminuer, décliner; *[sound]* s'affaiblir; *[person]* dépérir. **the castle ~d from sight** le château disparut aux regards; (*Rad*) **the sound is fading** il y a du fading, le son s'en va.

2 comp ▸**fade-in** (*Cine*) fondu *m* en ouverture; (*TV*) apparition graduelle; (*Rad*) fondu sonore ▸**fade in-fade out** fondu *m* enchaîné ▸**fade-out** (*Cine*) fondu *m* en fermeture; (*TV*) disparition graduelle; (*Rad*) fondu sonore; (*US fig: leave*) **to do a fade-out**‡ mettre les voiles*, se tirer‡.

3 vt a *curtains etc* décolorer; *colours, flowers* faner.

b (*Rad*) *conversation* couper par un fondu sonore. (*Cine, TV*) **to ~ one scene into another** faire un fondu enchaîné.

▸**fade away** vi = **fade 1b**.

▸**fade in** 1 vi (*Cine, TV*) apparaître en fondu. 2 vt sep (*Cine, TV*) faire apparaître en fondu; (*Rad*) monter. 3 **fade-in** n *see* **fade 2**.

▸**fade out** 1 vi *[sound]* s'affaiblir, disparaître; (*Cine, TV*) *[picture]* disparaître en fondu; (*Rad*) *[music, dialogue]* être coupé par fondu sonore; (*fig*) *[fashion]* passer; *[interest, enthusiasm]* tomber. 2 vt sep (*Cine, TV*) faire disparaître en fondu; (*Rad*) couper par un fondu sonore. 3 **fade-out** n *see* **fade 2**.

faded ['feɪdɪd] adj *material* décoloré, passé; *jeans etc* délavé; *flowers* fané, flétri; *beauty* défraîchi, fané.

faeces, (*US*) **feces** ['fiːsiːz] npl fèces *fpl*.

faerie, faery ['fɛərɪ] († *or liter*) 1 n féerie *f*. 2 adj imaginaire, féerique.

faff* [fæf] vi (*Brit*) **to ~ about** *or* **around** glandouiller‡.

fag [fæg] 1 n a (*NonC: Brit* ‡) corvée *f*. **what a ~!** quelle corvée! b (*Brit* ‡*: cigarette*) sèche‡ *f*. c (*Brit Scol*) petit *m* (*élève au service d'un grand*). d (‡*: esp US pej: homosexual*) pédé‡ *m*. 2 comp ▸**fag end** (*remainder*) restant *m*, reste *m*; *[material]* bout *m*; *[conversation]* dernières bribes; (‡) *[cigarette]* mégot* *m*, clope‡ *m*. 3 vt (*Brit: also* ~ **out**) *person, animal* éreinter, épuiser, fatiguer. **to ~ o.s. (out)** s'éreinter; **to be ~ged (out)*** être éreinté *or* claqué* *or* crevé*; **I can't be ~ged**‡ j'ai la flemme*. 4 vi a (*also* ~ **away**) s'échiner, s'éreinter (*at* à). b (*Brit Scol*) **to ~ for sb** faire les menues corvées de qn.

faggot[1], (*US*) **fagot** ['fægət] n (*wood*) fagot *m*; (*Brit Culin*) ≃ crépinette *f*.

faggot[2]‡ ['fægət] n (*esp US pej: homosexual*) pédé‡ *m*, tante‡ *f*.

fah [fɑː] n (*Mus*) fa *m*.

Fahrenheit ['færənhaɪt] adj Fahrenheit *inv*. **~ thermometer/scale** thermomètre *m*/échelle *f* Fahrenheit; **degrees ~** degrés *mpl* Fahrenheit.

fail [feɪl] 1 vi a (*be unsuccessful*) *[candidate]* échouer, être collé* *or* recalé* (*in an exam* à un examen, *in Latin* en latin); *[plans, attempts, treatment]* échouer, ne pas réussir; *[negotiations]* ne pas aboutir, échouer; *[play, show]* faire *or* être un four; *[bank, business]* faire faillite. **I ~ed (in my attempts) to see him** je n'ai pas réussi *or* je ne suis pas arrivé à le voir; **to ~ by 5 votes/by 10 minutes** échouer à 5 voix près/à 10 minutes près.

b (*grow feeble*) *[hearing, eyesight, health]* faiblir, baisser; *[person, invalid, voice]* s'affaiblir; *[light]* baisser; (*run short*) *[power, gas, electricity, water supply]* faire défaut, manquer; (*break down*) *[engine]* tomber en panne, flancher*; *[brakes]* lâcher. **his eyes are ~ing** sa vue faiblit *or* baisse; **crops ~ed because of the drought** la sécheresse a causé la perte des récoltes; **to ~ in one's duty** faillir à *or* manquer à son devoir.

2 vt a *examination* échouer à, être collé* *or* recalé* à; *candidate* refuser, coller*, recaler* (*in an exam* à un examen). **to ~ one's driving test** échouer à *or* être recalé* à son permis (de conduire); **he's a ~ed writer** c'est un écrivain raté, il n'a pas réussi comme écrivain; **he ~ed Latin** il a échoué en latin.

b (*let down*) (*gen*) décevoir; *friend, colleague* laisser tomber*; *partner* manquer à ses engagements envers. **don't ~ me!** ne me laissez pas tomber!*, je compte sur vous!; **his heart ~ed him** le cœur lui a manqué; **words ~ me!** les mots me manquent!; **his memory often ~s him** sa mémoire lui fait souvent défaut, sa mémoire le trahit souvent.

c (*omit*) manquer, négliger, omettre (*to do* de faire). **he never ~s to write** il ne manque jamais d'écrire; **he ~ed to visit her** il a négligé *or* omis de lui rendre visite; **he ~ed to keep his word** il a manqué à sa parole; (*Jur*) **to ~ to appear** faire défaut; **he ~ed to appear at the dinner** il ne s'est pas montré au dîner; **I ~ to see why** je ne vois pas pourquoi; **I ~ to understand** je n'arrive pas à comprendre.

3 n a **without ~** *come, do* à coup sûr, sans faute; *happen, befall* immanquablement, inévitablement.

b (*Scol, Univ*) échec *m*. **she got a ~ in history** elle a échoué *or* a été recalée* en histoire.

4 comp ▸**failsafe** (*Tech*) à sûreté intégrée.

failing ['feɪlɪŋ] 1 n défaut *m*. 2 prep à défaut de. **~ this** à défaut; **~ which we ...** faute de quoi nous ... . 3 adj *eyesight, health, memory* défaillant; *marriage* qui va à vau-l'eau. (*US Scol*) "~" "faible".

failure ['feɪljəʳ] n a (*lack of success*) échec *m* (*in an exam* à un examen); *[plan]* échec, insuccès *m*, avortement *m*; *[play, show etc]* échec; *[bank, business]* faillite *f*; *[discussions, negotiations]* échec, fiasco *m*. **academic ~** l'échec scolaire (*or* universitaire); **after two ~s he gave up** il a abandonné après deux échecs; **the play was a ~** la pièce a été un four *or* a fait un four *or* a été un fiasco *or* a fait fiasco; **this new machine/this plan is a total ~** cette nouvelle machine/ce projet est un fiasco complet; **his ~ to convince them** son incapacité *f* *or* son impuissance *f* à les convaincre; *see* **rate**[1].

b (*unsuccessful person*) raté(e) *m(f)*. **to be a ~ at maths** être nul en math; **to be a ~ at gardening** n'être pas doué pour le jardinage; **he's a ~ as a writer** il ne vaut rien comme écrivain.

c (*breakdown, insufficiency*) *[electricity, engine]* panne *f*. **~ of oil/water supply** manque *m* de pétrole/d'eau; **~ of the crops** perte *f* des récoltes; *see* **heart**.

d (*omission*) manquement *m*, défaut *m*. **his ~ to answer** le fait qu'il n'a pas répondu; **because of his ~ to help us** du fait qu'il ne nous a pas aidés; (*Jur*) **~ to appear** défaut *m* de comparution; **~ to observe a by-law** inobservation *f* d'un règlement (de police).

fain†† [feɪn] adv (used only with "would") volontiers.

faint [feɪnt] 1 adj a *breeze, smell, sound, hope, trace* (*slight*) faible; (*slight but hopeful*) léger; *colour* pâle, délavé; *voice* faible, éteint; *breathing* faible; *idea* vague, peu précis, flou. **I haven't the ~est idea (about it)** je n'en ai pas la moindre idée; **a ~ smile** (*indifferent*) un vague sourire; (*sad*) un pauvre sourire; **to make a ~ attempt at doing** essayer sans conviction de faire; **to grow ~(er)** s'affaiblir, diminuer; (*Prov*) **~ heart never won fair lady** la pusillanimité n'est point la clef des cœurs féminins.

b (*Med*) défaillant, prêt à s'évanouir. **to feel ~** se trouver mal, être pris d'un malaise; **~ with hunger/weariness** défaillant de faim/de fatigue.

2 n évanouissement *m*, défaillance *f*. **to fall in a ~** s'évanouir, avoir une défaillance.

3 comp ▸**fainthearted** *see* **fainthearted** ▸**fainting fit**, (*US*) **fainting spell** évanouissement *m* ▸**faint-ruled paper** papier réglé (en impression légère).

4 vi (*lose consciousness: also* ~ **away**) s'évanouir, tomber dans les pommes*. (*feel weak: from hunger etc*) **to be ~ing** défaillir (*from* de).

fainthearted [ˌfeɪnt'hɑːtɪd] adj pusillanime, timide, timoré.

faintheartedly [ˌfeɪnt'hɑːtɪdlɪ] adv timidement, avec pusillanimité.

faintheartedness [ˌfeɪnt'hɑːtɪdnɪs] n pusillanimité *f*, timidité *f*.

faintly ['feɪntlɪ] adv *call, say* d'une voix éteinte, faiblement; *breathe, shine* faiblement; *write, mark, scratch* légèrement; (*slightly*) légèrement, vaguement. **~ reminiscent of** qui rappelle vaguement; **in a ~ disappointed tone** d'un ton un peu déçu, avec une nuance de déception dans la voix.

faintness ['feɪntnɪs] n *[sound, voice etc]* faiblesse *f*; *[breeze etc]* légèreté *f*.

fair[1] [fɛəʳ] 1 adj a *person, decision* juste, équitable; *deal* équitable, honnête; *fight, game, match, player, competition* loyal, correct; *profit, comment* justifié, mérité. **he is strict but ~** il est sévère mais juste *or* équitable *or* impartial; **it's not ~** ce n'est pas juste; **to be ~ (to him)** *or* **let's be ~ (to him), he thought he had paid for it** rendons-lui cette justice, il croyait l'avoir payé; **it wouldn't be ~ to his brother** ce ne serait pas juste *or* honnête *or* équitable vis-à-vis de son frère; **as is (only) ~** et ce n'est que justice, comme de juste; **~'s ~!** ce n'est que justice!; **~ enough!** d'accord!, très bien!; (*loc*) **all's ~ in love and war** en amour comme à la guerre tous les coups sont permis; **it's (a) ~ comment** la remarque est juste; **to give sb ~ warning of sth** prévenir qn honnêtement de qch; **to get** *or* **have a ~ crack of the whip** avoir la chance de montrer de quoi on est capable; **to give sb a ~ deal** *or* (*US*) **a ~ shake** agir équitablement envers qn, être fair-play *inv* avec qn; **it's a ~ exchange** c'est équitable, c'est un échange honnête; (*loc*) **~ exchange is no robbery** échange n'est pas vol; **he was ~ game for the critics** c'était une proie rêvée *or* idéale pour les critiques; **by ~ means or foul** par tous les moyens, par n'importe quel moyen; **through ~ and foul** à travers toutes les épreuves; **~ play** fair-play *m*; **~ sample** échantillon représentatif; **he got his ~ share of the money** il a eu tout l'argent qui lui revenait (de droit); **he's had his ~ share of trouble*** il a eu sa part de soucis; **~ shares for all** (à) chacun son dû; **it was all ~ and square** tout était très correct *or* régulier; **he's ~ and square** il est honnête *or* franc *or* loyal.

b (*average*) *work, achievements* passable, assez bon. (*Scol: as mark*) "~" "passable"; **it's ~ to middling** c'est passable, ce n'est pas mal, c'est assez bien; **he has a ~ chance of success** il a des chances de réussir; **in ~ condition** en assez bon état.

c (*quite large*) *sum* considérable; *number* respectable. **to go at a ~ pace** aller bon train, aller à (une) bonne allure; **he is in a ~ way to doing** il y a de bonnes chances pour qu'il fasse; **he's travelled a ~ amount** il a pas mal voyagé; **there's a ~ amount of money left** il reste pas mal d'argent.

d (*light-coloured*) *hair etc* blond; *complexion, skin* clair, de blond(e). **she's ~** elle est blonde, c'est une blonde.

e (*fine*) *wind* propice, favorable; *weather* beau (*f* belle); (†: *beautiful*) beau. **it's set ~** le temps est au beau fixe; **the ~ sex** le beau sexe; **~ promises** belles promesses; **~ words** belles phrases *or* paroles.

f (*clean, neat*) propre, net. **to make a ~ copy of sth** recopier qch au propre *or* au net; **~ copy** (*rewritten*) copie *f* au propre *or* au net; (*model answer etc*) corrigé *m*.

2 **adv** a **to play ~** jouer franc jeu; **to act ~ and square** agir loyalement, faire preuve de loyauté, jouer cartes sur table; **the branch struck him ~ and square in the face** la branche l'a frappé au beau milieu du visage *or* en plein (milieu du) visage; **the car ran ~ and square into the tree** la voiture est entrée de plein fouet *or* en plein dans l'arbre.

b (‡ *or dial*) = **fairly c**.

c (††) *speak* courtoisement. **~ spoken** qui parle avec courtoisie.

3 **comp ▸fair-haired** blond, aux cheveux blonds; (*US: fig*) **the fair-haired boy*** le chouchou*, le chéri; **fair-haired girl** blonde *f* **▸fair-minded** impartial, équitable **▸fair-sized** assez grand, d'une bonne taille **▸fair-skinned** à la peau claire **▸fair-trade price** (*US*) prix imposé **▸fairway** (*Naut*) chenal *m*, passe *f*; (*Golf*) fairway *m* **▸fair-weather friends** (*fig*) les amis *mpl* des bons *or* beaux jours.

fair² [fɛəʳ] 1 **n** (*gen*) foire *f*; (*Comm*) foire; (*for charity*) fête *f*, kermesse *f*; (*Brit: funfair*) fête foraine. (*Comm*) **the Book F~** la Foire du livre; *see* **world** *etc*. 2 **comp ▸fairground** champ *m* de foire.

fairing ['fɛərɪŋ] **n** (*Aut, Aviat*) carénage *m*.

fairly ['fɛəlɪ] **adv** a (*justly*) *treat* équitablement, avec justice, impartialement; *obtain* honnêtement, loyalement; *compare, judge* impartialement, avec impartialité. b (*reasonably*) assez, moyennement. **it's ~ straightforward** c'est assez facile; **he plays ~ well** il joue passablement; **he's ~ good** il n'est pas mauvais; **they lead a ~ quiet life** ils mènent une vie plutôt tranquille; **I'm ~ sure that ...** je suis presque sûr que ..., j'ai bien l'impression que ... . c (*utterly*) absolument, vraiment. **he was ~ beside himself with rage** il était absolument hors de lui. d **~ and squarely** = **fair and square**; *see* **fair¹ 2a**.

fairness ['fɛənɪs] **n** a (*lightness*) *[hair]* couleur blonde, blond *m*, blondeur *f*; *[skin]* blancheur *f*. b (*honesty, justice*) justice *f*, honnêteté *f*; *[decision, judgment]* équité *f*, impartialité *f*. **in all ~** en toute justice; **in ~ to him** pour être juste envers lui.

fairy ['fɛərɪ] 1 **n** a fée *f*. **the wicked ~** la fée Carabosse; **she is his good/wicked ~** elle est son bon/mauvais ange; (*fig*) **he's away with the fairies** il rêve complètement, il n'a pas les pieds sur terre.

b (‡ *pej: homosexual*) pédé‡ *m*, tapette‡ *f*.

2 **adj** *helper, gift* magique; *child, dance, music* des fées.

3 **comp ▸fairy cycle** bicyclette *f* d'enfant **▸fairy footsteps** (*iro*) pas *mpl* (légers) de danseuse (*iro*) **▸fairy godmother** (*lit*) bonne fée; (*fig*) marraine *f* gâteau *inv* **▸fairyland** royaume *m* des fées; (*fig*) féerie *f* **▸fairy lights** guirlande *f* électrique **▸fairy-like** féerique, de fée **▸fairy queen** reine *f* des fées **▸fairy story, fairy tale** conte *m* de fées; (*untruth*) conte à dormir debout.

faith [feɪθ] 1 **n** a (*NonC: trust, belief*) foi *f*, confiance *f*. **F~, Hope and Charity** la foi, l'espérance et la charité; **~ in God** foi en Dieu; **to have ~ in sb** avoir confiance en qn; **I've lost ~ in him** je ne lui fais plus confiance; **to put one's ~ in, to pin one's ~ on*** mettre tous ses espoirs en.

b (*religion*) foi *f*, religion *f*.

c (*NonC*) **to keep ~ with sb** tenir ses promesses envers qn; **to break ~ with sb** manquer à sa parole envers qn.

d (*NonC*) **good ~** bonne foi; **to do sth in all good ~** faire qch en toute bonne foi; **bad ~** mauvaise foi; **to act in bad ~** agir de mauvaise foi.

2 **comp ▸faith healer** guérisseur *m*, -euse *f* (mystique) **▸faith healing** guérison *f* par la foi.

faithful ['feɪθfʊl] 1 **adj** a *person* fidèle (*to* à). b (*accurate*) *account, translation* fidèle, exact; *copy* conforme. 2 **n** a (**pl**) (*Rel*) **the ~** (*Christians*) les fidèles *mpl*; (*Muslims*) les croyants *mpl*. b (*Pol: gen pl*) **the (party) ~s** les fidèles du parti.

faithfully ['feɪθfəlɪ] **adv** *follow* fidèlement; *behave* loyalement; *translate* exactement, fidèlement. **to promise ~ that** donner sa parole que; (*Brit: in correspondence*) **yours ~** je vous prie (*or* nous vous prions), Monsieur (*or* Madame *etc*), d'agréer mes (*or* nos) salutations distinguées.

faithfulness ['feɪθfʊlnɪs] **n** fidélité *f* (*to* à), loyauté *f* (*to* envers); *[account, translation]* fidélité, exactitude *f*; *[copy]* conformité *f*.

faithless ['feɪθlɪs] **adj** déloyal, perfide.

faithlessness ['feɪθlɪsnɪs] **n** (*NonC*) déloyauté *f*, perfidie *f*.

fake [feɪk] 1 **n** a (*object*) article *or* objet truqué; (*picture*) faux *m*. **he's a ~** c'est un imposteur, il n'est pas ce qu'il prétend être.

b (*US Sport*) feinte *f*.

2 **adj** *document* maquillé, falsifié, faux (*f* fausse); *picture, beam, furniture* faux; *elections, trial, photograph* truqué; (*Rad, TV*) *interview* truqué, monté d'avance; *accounts* falsifié.

3 **vt** a *document* (*counterfeit*) faire un faux de; (*alter*) maquiller, falsifier; (*Art*) *picture* faire un faux de, contrefaire; *beam, furniture* imiter; *photograph, sound tape, elections, trial* truquer; *accounts* falsifier; (*Rad, TV*) *interview* truquer, monter d'avance. **to ~ illness/death** *etc* faire semblant d'être malade/mort *etc;* (*US Sport*) **to ~ a pass** feinter.

b (*US: ad-lib*) *tune* improviser.

4 **vi** faire semblant; (*US Sport*) feinter.

fakir ['fɑːkɪəʳ] **n** fakir *m*.

falcon ['fɔːlkən] **n** faucon *m*.

falconer ['fɔːlkənəʳ] **n** fauconnier *m*.

falconry ['fɔːlkənrɪ] **n** fauconnerie *f*.

Falkland ['fɔːlklənd] **comp ▸Falkland Islands** îles *fpl* Malouines *or* Falkland **▸Falkland Islander** habitant(e) *m(f)* des (îles) Malouines *or* Falkland **▸Falklands** = **Falkland Islands**.

fall [fɔːl] (**vb: pret fell, ptp fallen**) 1 **n** a (*lit, fig*) chute *f*; (*Mil*) chute, prise *f*. **to have a ~** tomber, faire une chute; **without a ~** sans tomber; (*fig*) **to be heading** *or* **riding for a ~** courir à l'échec, aller au-devant de la défaite; (*Rel*) **the F~ (of Man)** la chute (de l'homme); **the ~ of Saigon** la chute *or* la prise de Saigon; **the ~ of the Bastille** la prise de la Bastille; **~ of earth** éboulement *m* de terre, éboulis *m*; **~ of rock** chute de pierres; **there has been a heavy ~ of snow** il y a eu de fortes chutes de neige, il est tombé beaucoup de neige; *see* **free**.

b (*lowering: in price, demand, temperature*) baisse *f* (*in* de); (*more drastic*) chute *f*; (*Fin*) dépréciation *f*, baisse.

c (*slope: of ground, roof*) pente *f*, inclinaison *f*.

d (*waterfall*) **~s** chute *f* d'eau, cascade *f*; **the Niagara F~s** les chutes du Niagara.

e (*US: autumn*) automne *m*. **in the ~** en automne.

2 **vi** a *[person, object]* tomber; (*Rel etc: sin*) tomber, pécher; *[building]* s'écrouler, s'effondrer; *[rain, leaves, bombs, night, darkness, hair, garment, curtains]* tomber; *[temperature, price, level, voice, wind]* baisser, tomber; *[ground]* descendre, aller en pente; (*Mil*) *[soldier etc]* tomber (au champ d'honneur); *[country, city, fortress]* tomber; *[government]* tomber, être renversé. **he let ~ the cup, he let the cup ~** il a laissé tomber la tasse (*see also* **2b**); **he fell into the river** il est tombé dans la rivière; **to ~ out of a car/off a bike** tomber d'une voiture/d'un vélo; **to ~ over a chair** tomber en butant contre une chaise (*see also* **2b**); **to ~ flat** *[person]* tomber à plat ventre; *[event]* ne pas répondre à l'attente; *[scheme]* faire long feu, rater; *[joke]* tomber à plat; **to ~ (flat) on one's face** tomber face contre terre *or* à plat ventre; **he fell full length** il est tombé de tout son long; **to ~ to** *or* **on one's knees** tomber à genoux; (*lit, fig*) **to ~ on one's feet** retomber sur ses pieds; (*US: lit, fig*) **to ~ on one's ass**‡ se casser la gueule‡; **he fell into bed exhausted** il s'est jeté au lit épuisé; **they fell into each other's arms** ils sont tombés dans les bras l'un de l'autre; **her hair fell to her shoulders** les cheveux lui tombaient sur les épaules; *see* **neck, roll** *etc*.

b (*fig phrases*) **to ~ into a trap/an ambush** tomber *or* donner dans un piège/une embuscade; (*fig: in work etc*) **to ~ behind sb** prendre du retard sur qn; **he was ~ing over himself to be polite*** il se mettait en quatre pour être poli; **they were ~ing over each other to get it*** ils se battaient pour l'avoir; **to let ~ a hint that** laisser entendre que, donner à entendre que; **the accent ~s on the second syllable** l'accent tombe sur la deuxième syllabe; **strange sounds fell on our ears** des bruits étranges parvinrent à nos oreilles; **his face fell** son visage s'est assombri *or* s'est allongé; **her eyes fell on a strange object** son regard est tombé sur un objet étrange; **the students ~ into 3 categories** les étudiants se divisent en 3 catégories; **the responsibility ~s (up)on you** la responsabilité retombe sur vous; (*liter*) **the wrath of God fell (up)on them** la colère de Dieu s'abattit sur eux; **to ~ on bad times** tomber dans la misère, avoir des revers de fortune; **Christmas Day ~s on a Sunday** Noël tombe un dimanche; **he fell to wondering if ...** il s'est mis à se demander si ...; **it ~s to** *or* **(up)on me to say** il m'appartient de dire, c'est à moi de dire; **not a word fell from his lips** il n'a pas laissé échapper un mot; **to ~ by the way** abandonner en cours de route; **he fell among thieves** il est tombé aux mains de voleurs; **his work fell short of what we had expected** son travail n'a pas répondu à notre attente; **the copy fell far short of the original** la copie était loin de valoir l'original; **to ~ short of perfection** ne pas atteindre la perfection; *see* **foul, hard, stool** *etc*.

c (*become, find o.s. etc*) **to ~ asleep** s'endormir; **to ~ into a deep sleep** tomber dans un profond sommeil; **to ~ into bad habits** prendre *or* contracter de mauvaises habitudes; **to ~ into conversation with sb** entrer en conversation avec qn; **to ~ into despair** sombrer dans le désespoir; **to ~ into disgrace** tomber en disgrâce; **to ~ from grace** (*Rel*) perdre la grâce; (*fig*) tomber en disgrâce, ne plus avoir la cote; (*hum*) faire une gaffe*; *[rent, bill]* **to ~ due** venir à échéance; **to ~ into the hands of** tomber aux *or* entre les mains de; **to ~ heir to sth** hériter de qch; **to ~ ill** *or* **sick** tomber malade; **to ~ lame** se mettre à boiter; (*lit, fig*) **to ~ into line** s'aligner; (*fig*) **to ~ into line with sb** se ranger *or* se conformer à l'avis de qn; **to ~ in love** tomber amoureux (*with* de); **to ~ for sb*** tomber amoureux de qn; **to ~ for an idea*** *etc* s'enthousiasmer pour une idée *etc;* (*pej: be taken in by*) **to ~ for a suggestion** se laisser prendre à une suggestion; **he really fell for it!*** il s'est vraiment laissé prendre!, il s'est vraiment fait avoir!*; **to ~**

silent se taire; **to ~ under suspicion** devenir suspect; **to ~ vacant** *[job, position]* se trouver vacant; *[room, flat]* se trouver libre; **to ~ (a) victim to** devenir (la) victime de.

3 comp ▸**fallback** recul *m*, repli *m*; **as a fallback they will start building their own dealer network** ils vont mettre sur pied un réseau de distribution pour avoir une position de repli ▸**fall-back position** solution *f* de secours *or* de réserve ▸**fall guy**‡ (*US*) (*scapegoat*) bouc *m* émissaire; (*easy victim*) pigeon* *m*, dindon *m* (de la farce), dupe *f* ▸**falling-off** réduction *f*, diminution *f*, décroissance *f* (*in* de) ▸**falling star** étoile filante ▸**fall line** (*Geog*) ligne *f* de séparation entre un plateau et une plaine cotière; (*Ski*) ligne *f* de plus grande pente ▸**fall-off** = **falling-off** ▸**fallout** (*NonC*) retombées *fpl* (radioactives); (*fig*) retombées, répercussions *fpl* ▸**fallout shelter** abri *m* antiatomique.

▸**fall about*** vi (*fig: also* **fall about laughing**) se tordre (de rire).

▸**fall apart** vi *[object]* tomber en morceaux; *[scheme, plan, one's life, marriage]* se désagréger; *[deal]* tomber à l'eau, s'effondrer; *[person]* (*after tragedy*) s'effondrer; (*in an exam etc*) perdre tous ses moyens.

▸**fall away** vi *[ground]* descendre en pente; *[plaster]* s'écailler; *[supporters]* déserter; *[numbers, attendances]* diminuer; *[anxiety, fears]* se dissiper, s'évanouir.

▸**fall back** 1 vi (*retreat, also Mil*) reculer, se retirer. (*fig*) **to fall back on sth** avoir recours à qch; **a sum to fall back on** une somme en réserve, un matelas*; **gold shares fell back a point** les mines d'or ont reculé *or* se sont repliées d'un point. 2 **fallback** n *see* **fall 3**.

▸**fall behind** vi rester en arrière, être à la traîne; *[racehorse, runner]* se laisser distancer; (*in cycle race*) décrocher. **to fall behind with one's work** prendre du retard dans son travail; **she fell behind with the rent** elle était en retard pour son loyer; *see also* **fall 2b**.

▸**fall down** vi a *[person, book]* tomber (par terre); *[building]* s'effondrer, s'écrouler; *[tree]* tomber; *[plans]* s'effondrer, s'écrouler; *[hopes]* s'évanouir. b (*fig: fail*) échouer. **to fall down on the job** se montrer incapable de faire le travail, ne pas être à la hauteur; **he fell down badly that time** il a fait un vrai fiasco *or* il a vraiment raté son coup cette fois; **that was where we fell down** c'est là que nous avons achoppé *or* que nous nous sommes fichus dedans*; **she fell down on the last essay** elle a raté la dernière dissertation.

▸**fall in** 1 vi a *[building]* s'effondrer, s'écrouler, s'affaisser. **she leaned over the pool and fell in** elle s'est penchée au-dessus de la mare et est tombée dedans. b (*Mil*) *[troops]* former les rangs; *[one soldier]* rentrer dans les rangs. **fall in!** à vos rangs! 2 vt sep *troops* (faire) mettre en rangs.

▸**fall in with** vt fus a (*meet*) *person* rencontrer; *group* se mettre à frequenter. **he fell in with bad company** il a fait de mauvaises rencontres *or* connaissances. b (*agree to*) *proposal, suggestion* accepter, agréer. **to fall in with sb's views** entrer dans les vues de qn. c **this decision fell in very well with our plans** cette décision a cadré avec nos projets.

▸**fall off** 1 vi a (*lit*) tomber; (*Climbing*) dévisser. b *[supporters]* déserter; *[sales, numbers, attendances]* diminuer; *[curve on graph]* décroître; *[interest]* se relâcher, tomber; *[enthusiasm]* baisser, tomber. 2 **fall(ing)-off** n *see* **fall 3**.

▸**fall out** 1 vi a (*quarrel*) se brouiller, se fâcher (*with* avec). b (*Mil*) rompre les rangs. **fall out!** rompez! c (*come to pass*) advenir, arriver. **everything fell out as we had hoped** tout s'est passé comme nous l'avions espéré. 2 vt sep *troops* faire rompre les rangs à. 3 **fallout** n, adj *see* **fall 3**.

▸**fall over** vi tomber (par terre).

▸**fall through** vi *[plans]* échouer. **all their plans have fallen through** tous leurs projets ont échoué *or* sont (tombés) à l'eau.

▸**fall to** vi (*start eating*) se mettre à l'œuvre, attaquer (un repas).

▸**fall (up)on** vt fus a se jeter sur, se lancer sur. (*Mil*) **to fall (up)on the enemy** fondre *or* s'abattre sur l'ennemi. b (*find*) trouver, découvrir. **to fall (up)on a way of doing sth** trouver *or* découvrir un moyen de faire qch.

fallacious [fəˈleɪʃəs] adj fallacieux, faux (*f* fausse), trompeur.

fallaciousness [fəˈleɪʃəsnɪs] n caractère fallacieux, fausseté *f*.

fallacy [ˈfæləsɪ] n (*false belief*) erreur *f*, illusion *f*; (*false reasoning*) faux raisonnement, sophisme *m*.

fallen [ˈfɔːlən] 1 ptp of **fall**. 2 adj tombé; (*morally*) perdu; *angel, woman* déchu. **~ leaf** feuille morte; (*Med*) **~ arches** affaissement *m* de la voûte plantaire. 3 n (*Mil*) **the ~** ceux qui sont morts à la guerre, ceux qui sont tombés (au champ d'honneur).

fallibility [ˌfælɪˈbɪlɪtɪ] n faillibilité *f*.

fallible [ˈfæləbl] adj faillible. **everyone is ~** tout le monde peut se tromper.

falling [ˈfɔːlɪŋ] 1 prp of **fall**. 2 adj *prices, standards* en baisse. **"beware (of) ~ rocks"** "attention aux chutes de pierres"; (†: *epilepsy*) **~ sickness** *or* **evil** haut mal† *m*, mal caduc† *m*.

fallopian [fəˈləʊpɪən] adj: **~ tube** trompe utérine *or* de Fallope.

fallow[1] [ˈfæləʊ] 1 n (*Agr*) jachère *f*. 2 adj *land* en jachère. **the land lay ~** la terre était en jachère; **his mind lay ~ for years** il a laissé son esprit en friche pendant des années.

fallow[2] [ˈfæləʊ] adj: **~ deer** daim *m*.

false [fɔːls] 1 adj a (*mistaken, wrong*) *idea, information* faux (*f* fausse). (*lit, fig*) **~ alarm** fausse alerte; **~ dawn** lueurs annonciatrices de l'aube; (*fig*) lueur d'espoir trompeuse; **~ economy** fausse économie *f*; **to take a ~ step** faire un faux pas; **to put a ~ interpretation on sth** interpréter qch à faux; **in a ~ position** dans une position fausse; **~ ribs** fausses côtes; **~ report**, **~ rumour** canard *m*; (*Sport, also fig*) **~ start** faux départ; *see* **move 1c**.

b (*deceitful*) perfide, faux (*f* fausse), mensonger. **~ friend** faux ami *m*; **to be ~ to one's wife**† tromper sa femme; (*Jur*) **~ pretences** moyens *mpl* frauduleux; **on** *or* **under ~ pretences** (*Jur*) par des moyens frauduleux; (*by lying*) sous des prétextes fallacieux; **~ promises** promesses mensongères, fausses promesses; **~ witness** faux témoin; († *or frm*) **to bear ~ witness** porter un faux témoignage.

c (*counterfeit*) *coin* faux (*f* fausse); (*artificial*) artificiel; *ceiling* faux. **~ eyelashes** faux cils *mpl*; **a box with a ~ bottom** une boîte à double fond; **~ hem** faux ourlet; (*Brit*) **~ teeth** fausses dents, dentier *m*, râtelier *m*.

2 adv (*liter*) **to play sb ~** trahir qn.

3 comp ▸**false-hearted** fourbe.

falsehood [ˈfɔːlshʊd] n a (*lie*) mensonge *m*. **to tell a ~** mentir, dire un mensonge. b (*NonC*) faux *m*. **truth and ~** le vrai et le faux. c (*NonC*) = **falseness**.

falsely [ˈfɔːlslɪ] adv *claim, declare* faussement; *interpret* à faux; *accuse* à tort; *act* déloyalement.

falseness [ˈfɔːlsnɪs] n fausseté *f*; († *or liter: of lover etc*) infidélité *f*.

falsetto [fɔːlˈsetəʊ] 1 n (*Mus*) fausset *m*. 2 adj *voice, tone* de fausset, de tête.

falsies‡ [ˈfɔːlsɪz] npl soutien-gorge rembourré.

falsification [ˌfɔːlsɪfɪˈkeɪʃən] n falsification *f*.

falsify [ˈfɔːlsɪfaɪ] vt a (*forge*) *document* falsifier; *evidence* maquiller; (*misrepresent*) *story, facts* dénaturer; *accounts, figures, statistics* truquer. b (*disprove*) *theory* réfuter.

falsity [ˈfɔːlsɪtɪ] n = **falseness**.

falter [ˈfɔːltəʳ] 1 vi *[voice, speaker]* hésiter, s'entrecouper; (*waver*) vaciller, chanceler; *[sb's steps]* chanceler; *[courage, memory]* faiblir. 2 vt (*also* **~ out**) *words, phrases* bredouiller, prononcer d'une voix hésitante *or* entrecoupée.

faltering [ˈfɔːltərɪŋ] adj *voice* hésitant, entrecoupé; *steps* chancelant.

falteringly [ˈfɔːltərɪŋlɪ] adv *speak* d'une voix hésitante *or* entrecoupée; *walk* d'un pas chancelant *or* mal assuré.

fame [feɪm] n (*gen*) gloire *f*, célébrité *f*, (*slightly weaker*) renommée *f*, renom *m*. **this book brought him ~ (as a writer)** ce livre l'a rendu célèbre (en tant qu'écrivain), ce livre a fait sa renommée *or* son renom (d'écrivain); **he wanted ~** il était avide de gloire, il voulait se faire une renommée *or* un grand nom; **to win ~ for o.s.** bâtir sa renommée; **Margaret Mitchell of "Gone with the Wind" ~** Margaret Mitchell connue pour son livre "Autant en emporte le vent" *or* l'auteur célèbre de "Autant en emporte le vent"; **Bader of 1940 ~** Bader célèbre pour ses prouesses *or* exploits en 1940; († *or liter*) **of ill ~** mal famé.

famed [feɪmd] adj célèbre, renommé (*for* pour).

familiar [fəˈmɪljəʳ] 1 adj a (*usual, well-known*) *sight, scene, street* familier; *complaint, event, protest* habituel. **he's a ~ figure in the town** c'est un personnage bien connu *or* tout le monde le connaît de vue dans la ville; **it's a ~ feeling** c'est une sensation bien connue; **it's a ~ story: he wasted his time ...** c'est toujours la même histoire: il a perdu son temps ...; **his face is ~** je l'ai déjà vu (quelque part), sa tête me dit quelque chose*; **among ~ faces** parmi des visages familiers *or* connus; **his voice seems ~ (to me)** il me semble connaître sa voix; (*fig*) **now we're on ~ ground** nous sommes maintenant en terrain de connaissance.

b (*conversant*) **to be ~ with sth** bien connaître qch, être au fait de qch; **to make o.s. ~ with** se familiariser avec; **he is ~ with our customs** il connaît bien nos coutumes.

c (*intimate*) familier, intime. **~ language** langue familière; **to be on ~ terms with sb** être intime avec qn, avoir des rapports d'intimité avec qn; **~ spirit** démon familier; (*pej*) **he got much too ~, he was very ~** il s'est permis des familiarités (*with* avec).

2 n a (**~ spirit**) démon familier.

b (*friend*) familier *m*.

familiarity [fəˌmɪlɪˈærɪtɪ] n a (*NonC*) *[sight, event etc]* caractère familier *or* habituel. b (*NonC: with book, poem, customs etc*) familiarité *f* (*with* avec), (parfaite) connaissance *f* (*with* de). (*Prov*) **~ breeds contempt** la familiarité engendre le mépris. c (*pej: gen pl*) **familiarities** familiarités *fpl*, privautés *fpl*.

familiarize [fəˈmɪlɪəraɪz] vt a **to ~ sb with sth** familiariser qn avec qch, habituer qn à qch; **to ~ o.s. with** se familiariser avec. b *theory* répandre, vulgariser.

familiarly [fəˈmɪljəlɪ] adv familièrement.

family [ˈfæmɪlɪ] 1 n (*all senses incl Ling*) famille *f*. **has he any ~?** (*relatives*) a-t-il de la famille?; (*children*) a-t-il des enfants?; **it runs in the ~** cela tient de famille; **my ~ are all tall** dans ma famille tout le monde est grand; **to start a ~** avoir un enfant (*le premier*); **of good ~** de bonne famille; **he's one of the ~** il fait partie *or* il est de la famille.

2 comp *dinner, jewels, likeness, name* de famille; *Bible, life* familial, de famille ▸**family allowance** (†: *Brit Admin*) allocations familiales

▸**family business** affaire *f* de famille ▸**family butcher** boucher *m* de quartier ▸**family court** (*US Jur*) *tribunal pour tout ce qui touche aux enfants* ▸**family credit** (*Brit Admin*) ≃ complément familial ▸**Family Crisis Intervention Unit** (*US Police*) ≃ police-secours *m* (intervenant en cas de drames familiaux) ▸**family doctor** médecin *m* de famille, (médecin) généraliste *m* ▸**family friend** ami(e) *m(f)* de la famille ▸**family grouping** (*Scol*) *enseignement m dans des classes de primaire regroupant plusieurs années* ▸**family hotel** pension *f* de famille ▸**family income supplement** (†: *Brit Admin*) ≃ complément familial ▸**family man: he's a family man** c'est un bon père de famille, il aime la vie de famille ▸**family-minded: to be family-minded** avoir le sens de la famille ▸**family name** nom *m* de famille ▸**family planning** planning *or* planisme familial, orthogénie *f* ▸**family planning clinic** centre *m* de planning *or* planisme familial ▸**family practice** (*US Med*) médecine *f* générale ▸**family practitioner** (*esp US Med*) médecin *m* de famille, (médecin) généraliste *m* ▸**family-size(d) packet** (*Comm*) paquet familial ▸**family therapy** thérapie *f* familiale ▸**family tree** arbre *m* généalogique ▸**family unit** (*Sociol*) cellule *f* familiale ▸**family viewing:** (*TV*) **it's (suitable for) family viewing** c'est un spectacle familial, les enfants peuvent voir ça ▸**family way*†: she's in the family way** elle est enceinte, elle attend un bébé *or* un enfant.

famine ['fæmɪn] **n** famine *f*.

famished ['fæmɪʃt] **adj** affamé. **I'm absolutely ~*** je meurs de faim, j'ai une faim de loup; **~ looking** d'aspect famélique.

famishing ['fæmɪʃɪŋ] **adj: I'm ~*** je crève* de faim, j'ai une faim de loup.

famous ['feɪməs] **adj** célèbre, (bien) connu, renommé (*for* pour); (*†: *excellent*) fameux, formidable*. (*iro*) **~ last words!*** on verra bien!, c'est ce que tu crois!; (*iro*) **so much for his ~ motorbike!** maintenant on sait ce que vaut sa fameuse moto!

famously* ['feɪməslɪ] **adv** fameusement*, rudement bien*, à merveille. **they get on ~** ils s'entendent rudement bien* *or* comme larrons en foire.

fan¹ [fæn] **1 n** éventail *m*; (*mechanical*) ventilateur *m*; (*Agr*) tarare *m*. **electric ~** ventilateur électrique.

2 comp ▸**fan-(assisted) oven** four *m* à chaleur pulsée ▸**fan belt** (*Aut*) courroie *f* de ventilateur ▸**fanfold paper** (*Comput*) papier *m* en continu ▸**fan heater** (*Brit*) radiateur soufflant ▸**fan light** imposte *f* (*semi-circulaire*) ▸**fan-shaped** en éventail ▸**fantail (pigeon)** pigeon-paon *m* ▸**fan vaulting** (*Archit*) voûte(s) *f(pl)* en éventail.

3 vt a *person, object* éventer. **to ~ the fire** attiser le feu; **to ~ the embers** souffler sur la braise; **to ~ o.s.** s'éventer; (*fig*) **to ~ the flames** jeter de l'huile sur le feu (*fig*); **to ~ a quarrel** attiser une querelle.

b (*US* ‡: *smack*) corriger, flanquer* une fessée à.

▸**fan out 1 vi** *[troops, searchers]* se déployer (en éventail). **2 vt sep** *cards etc* étaler (en éventail).

fan² [fæn] **1 n** (*) enthousiaste *mf*; (*Sport*) supporter *m*; *[pop star etc]* fan *mf*, admirateur *m*, -trice *f*. **he is a jazz/bridge/sports/football** *etc* **~** il se passionne pour le *or* c'est un passionné du *or* c'est un mordu* du jazz/bridge/sport/football *etc*; **all these football ~s** tous ces enragés *or* mordus* *or* fanas* de football; **movie ~** cinéphile *mf*, passionné(e) *m(f)* du cinéma; **a Vivaldi ~** un(e) fervent(e) de Vivaldi; **I'm definitely not one of his ~s** je suis loin d'être un de ses admirateurs.

2 comp ▸**fan club** (*Cine etc*) cercle *m or* club *m* de fans; (*fig*) cercle d'adorateurs *or* de fervents (admirateurs); **the Colin Smith fan club** le club des fans de Colin Smith ▸**fan letters, fan mail: his fan mail** le courrier *or* les lettres *fpl* de ses admirateurs.

fanatic [fə'nætɪk] **n** fanatique *mf*.

fanatic(al) [fə'nætɪk(əl)] **adj** fanatique.

fanaticism [fə'nætɪsɪzəm] **n** fanatisme *m*.

fanciable* ['fænsɪəbl] **adj** (*Brit*) pas mal du tout*, plutôt chouette*.

fancied ['fænsɪd] **adj** imaginaire.

fancier ['fænsɪəʳ] **n: dog ~** (*connoisseur*) connaisseur *m*, -euse *f* en chiens; (*breeder*) éleveur *m*, -euse *f* de chiens.

fanciful ['fænsɪfʊl] **adj** (*whimsical*) *person* capricieux, fantasque; *ideas* fantasque; (*quaint*) *ideas etc* bizarre; *hat* extravagant; (*imaginative*) *design, drawing* plein d'imagination, imaginatif; (*imaginary*) *story, account* imaginaire.

fancy ['fænsɪ] **1 n a** (*whim*) caprice *m*, fantaisie *f*. **it was just a (passing) ~** ce n'était qu'un caprice (passager) *or* qu'une fantaisie (passagère) *or* qu'une lubie; **as the ~ takes her** comme l'idée la prend; **he only works when the ~ takes him** il ne travaille que quand cela lui plaît *or* lui chante*; **he took a ~ to go swimming** il a eu tout à coup envie *or* il lui a pris l'envie d'aller se baigner.

b (*taste, liking*) goût *m*, envie *f*. **to take a ~ to sb** se prendre d'affection pour qn; **to take a ~ to sth** se mettre à aimer qch, prendre goût à qch; **it took** *or* **caught** *or* **tickled his ~** d'un seul coup il en a eu envie; **the hat took** *or* **caught my ~** le chapeau m'a fait envie *or* m'a tapé dans l'œil‡; **it caught the public's ~** le public l'a tout de suite aimé; **he had a ~ for her** il a eu un petit béguin* *or* une toquade* pour elle; **he had a ~ for sports cars** il a eu une toquade* *or* un engouement pour les voitures de sport.

c (*NonC*) imagination *f*, fantaisie *f*. **that is in the realm of ~** cela appartient au domaine de l'imaginaire, c'est chimérique.

d (*delusion*) chimère *f*, fantasme *m*; (*whimsical notion*) idée *f* fantasque. **I have a ~ that ...** j'ai idée que ... .

e (*Culin*) gâteau à la crème (*fait de génoise fourrée*).

2 vt a (*imagine*) se figurer, s'imaginer; (*rather think*) croire, penser. **he fancies he can succeed** il se figure pouvoir réussir, il s'imagine qu'il peut réussir; **I rather ~ he's gone out** je crois (bien) qu'il est sorti; **he fancied he heard the car arrive** il a cru entendre arriver la voiture; **~ that!*** tiens!, voyez-vous cela!, vous m'en direz tant!*; **~ anyone doing that!** qu'est-ce que les gens vont imaginer de faire!; **~ seeing you here!*** tiens! c'est vous?, je ne m'imaginais pas vous voir ici!; **~ him winning!*** qui aurait cru qu'il allait gagner!

b (*want*) avoir envie de; (*like*) aimer. **do you ~ going for a walk?** as-tu envie *or* ça te dit* d'aller faire une promenade?; **I don't ~ the idea** cette idée ne me dit rien; **I don't ~ his books** ses livres ne me tentent pas *or* ne me disent rien; (*Brit*) **he fancies himself*** il ne se prend pas pour rien* (*iro*); **he fancies himself as an actor*** il ne se prend pas pour une moitié d'acteur* (*iro*); (*Brit*) **he fancies her*** il la trouve pas mal du tout*, elle lui plaît; (*Horseracing*) **Omar is strongly fancied for the next race** Omar est très coté *or* a la cote pour la prochaine course.

c (*imagine*) avoir l'impression (*that* que). **I ~ we've met before** j'ai l'impression que nous nous sommes déjà rencontrés.

3 adj a *hat, buttons, pattern* (de) fantaisie *inv*. **~ cakes** pâtisseries *fpl*; **~ dog** chien *m* de luxe.

b (*pej: overrated, too elaborate*) *idea, cure* fantaisiste. **a ~ price** un prix exorbitant; **it was all very ~** c'était très recherché, ça faisait très chic; **it is nothing ~** ce n'est rien de compliqué; **with his ~ house and his ~ car how can he know how the ordinary man lives?** avec sa belle maison et sa voiture grand luxe, comment peut-il se mettre à la place de l'homme de la rue?

c (*US: extra good*) *goods, foodstuffs* de qualité supérieure, de luxe.

4 comp ▸**fancy dress** travesti *m*, déguisement *m*; **in fancy dress** déguisé, travesti ▸**fancy-dress ball** bal masqué *or* costumé ▸**fancy-free: he is fancy-free** c'est un cœur à prendre (*see* **footloose**) ▸**fancy goods** (*Comm*) nouveautés *fpl*, articles *mpl* de fantaisie ▸**fancy man** (*pej*) amant *m*, jules* *m* ▸**fancy woman** (*pej*) maîtresse *f*, poule* *f* (*pej*) ▸**fancy work** ouvrages *mpl* d'agrément.

fandango [fæn'dæŋgəʊ] **n, pl ~s** fandango *m*.

fanfare ['fænfɛəʳ] **n** fanfare *f* (*morceau de musique*).

fang [fæŋ] **n** *[dog, vampire]* croc *m*, canine *f*; *[snake]* crochet *m*.

Fanny ['fænɪ] **n a abbr of Frances. b** (*Brit*) **sweet ~ Adams‡** que dal(le)‡, rien du tout.

fanny*‡ ['fænɪ] **n** (*buttocks*) cul*‡ *m*, fesses* *fpl*; (*vagina*) chatte*‡ *f*.

fantabulous‡ [fæn'tæbjʊləs] **adj** (*US*) superchouette*.

fantasia [fæn'teɪzjə] **n** (*Literat, Mus*) fantaisie *f*.

fantasize ['fæntəsaɪz] **vi** (*Psych etc*) se livrer à des fantasmes, fantasmer (*about* sur).

fantastic [fæn'tæstɪk] **adj** *story, adventure* fantastique, bizarre; *idea* impossible, invraisemblable; *success* inouï, fabuleux, fantastique; (*Comm*) *price cuts* phénoménal; (*fig: excellent*) *dress, plan, news, holiday* sensationnel, fantastique.

fantastically [fæn'tæstɪkəlɪ] **adv** fantastiquement, extraordinairement, terriblement. **he's ~ rich** il est extraordinairement *or* fabuleusement riche.

fantasy ['fæntəzɪ] **n a** (*NonC*) imagination *f*, fantaisie *f*. **b** idée *f* fantasque; (*Psych etc*) fantasme *m*. **c** (*Literat, Mus*) fantaisie *f*.

fanzine ['fænzi:n] **n** (**abbr of fan magazine**) fanzine *m*.

FAO [,efeɪ'əʊ] (**abbr of Food and Agriculture Organization**) F.A.O. *f*.

FAQ [,efeɪ'kju:] (*Comm*) (**abbr of free alongside quay**) FLQ.

far [fɑ:ʳ] **compar farther** *or* **further, superl farthest** *or* **furthest 1 adv a** (*lit*) loin. **how ~ is it to ...?** combien y a-t-il jusqu'à ...?; **is it ~?** est-ce loin?; **is it ~ to London?** c'est loin pour aller à Londres?; **we live not ~ from here** nous habitons pas loin d'ici; **we live quite ~** nous habitons assez loin; **have you come from ~?** vous venez de loin?; **how ~ are you going?** jusqu'où allez-vous?; *see also* **1c**.

b (*fig*) **how ~ have you got with your plans?** où en êtes-vous de vos projets?; **he is very gifted and will go ~** il est très doué et il ira loin *or* il fera son chemin; **to make one's money go ~** faire durer son argent; **£10 doesn't go ~ these days** 10 livres ne vont pas loin de nos jours; **that will go ~ towards placating him** cela contribuera beaucoup à le calmer; **this scheme does not go ~ enough** ce projet ne va pas assez loin; **I would even go so ~ as to say that ...** j'irais même jusqu'à dire que ..., je dirais même que ...; **that's going too ~** cela passe *or* dépasse les bornes *or* la mesure; **now you're going a bit too ~** alors là vous exagérez un peu; **he's gone too ~ this time!** il a vraiment exagéré cette fois!; **he has gone too ~ to back out now** il est trop engagé pour reculer maintenant; **he was ~ gone** (*ill*) il était bien bas; (*: *drunk*) il était bien parti*; **he carried** *or* **took the joke too ~** il a poussé trop loin la plaisanterie; **just so ~, so ~ and no further** jusque-là mais pas plus loin; **so ~ so good** jusqu'ici ça va; **so ~ this year** jusqu'ici cette année; **we have 10 volunteers so ~** nous avons 10 volontaires jusqu'ici *or* jusqu'à présent; **~ be it from me to try to dissuade you** loin de moi l'idée de vous dissuader.

c (*phrases*) **as ~ as** jusqu'à, autant que; **we went as ~ as the town** nous sommes allés jusqu'à la ville; **we didn't go as** *or* **so ~ as the others** nous ne sommes pas allés aussi loin que les autres; **as** *or* **so ~ as I know** (pour) autant que je (le) sache; **as ~ as I can** dans la mesure du possible; **as** *or* **so ~ as I can foresee** autant que je puisse (le) prévoir; **as ~ as the eye can see** à perte de vue; **as** *or* **so ~ as that goes** pour ce qui est de cela; **as** *or* **so ~ as I'm concerned** en ce qui me concerne, pour ma part; **as ~ back as I can remember** d'aussi loin que je m'en souvienne; **as ~ back as 1945** dès 1945, déjà en 1945; **~ and away** *see* **1d**; **~ and wide, ~ and near** de tous côtés, partout; **they came from ~ and wide** *or* **~ and near** ils sont venus de partout; **~ above** loin au-dessus; **~ above the hill** loin au-dessus de la colline; **he is ~ above the rest of the class** il est de loin supérieur au *or* il domine nettement le reste de la classe; **~ away in the distance** au loin, dans le lointain; **he wasn't ~ away when I saw him** il n'était pas loin quand je l'ai vu; **~ beyond** (*adv*) bien au-delà; **~ beyond the forest** très loin au-delà de la forêt; **it's ~ beyond what I can afford** c'est bien au-dessus de mes moyens; (*fig*) **I can't look ~ beyond May** je ne sais pas très bien ce qui se passera après le mois de mai; **~ from** loin de; **your work is ~ from satisfactory** votre travail est loin d'être satisfaisant, il s'en faut de beaucoup que votre travail soit satisfaisant (*frm*); **~ from it!** loin de là!, tant s'en faut!; **~ from liking him I find him rather objectionable** bien loin de l'aimer je le trouve (au contraire) tout à fait désagréable; **I am ~ from believing him** je suis très loin de le croire; **~ into** très avant dans; **~ into the night** tard dans la nuit, très avant dans la nuit; **I won't look so ~ into the future** je ne regarderai pas si avant dans l'avenir; **they went ~ into the jungle** ils ont pénétré très avant dans la jungle; **~ off** au loin, dans le lointain (*see also* **3**); **he wasn't ~ off when I caught sight of him** il n'était pas loin quand je l'ai aperçu; **his birthday is not ~ off** c'est bientôt son anniversaire, son anniversaire approche; **she's not ~ off fifty** elle n'est pas loin de la cinquantaine; **~ out at sea** au (grand) large; **~ out on the branch** tout au bout de la branche; (*fig: wrong*) **to be ~ out** *or* (*US*) **~ off** *[person]* se tromper lourdement, être loin du compte; *[estimates, guesses]* être loin du compte; *[opinion polls]* se tromper lourdement; *[calculations]* être complètement erroné; **to be not ~ wrong** *or* **out** *or* (*US*) **off** *[person]* ne pas s'être trompé de beaucoup, ne pas être très loin de la vérité; *[figures, change]* **it's not ~ wrong** *or* **out** il n'y a pas beaucoup de différence; **by ~** de loin, de beaucoup.

d (*very much*) beaucoup, bien. **~ too expensive/too slow/too dangerous** beaucoup *or* bien trop cher/trop lent/trop dangereux; **this is ~ better** ceci est beaucoup *or* bien mieux; **this is ~ (and away) the best, this is by ~ the best** *or* **the best by ~** ceci est de très loin ce qu'il y a de mieux; **it is ~ more serious** c'est (bien) autrement sérieux; **she is ~ prettier than her sister** elle est bien plus jolie que sa sœur.

2 adj a (*distant: liter*) *country, land* lointain, éloigné. (*not liter*) **it's a ~ cry from what he promised** on est loin de ce qu'il a promis.

b (*further away*) autre, plus éloigné. **on the ~ side of** de l'autre côté de; **at the ~ end of** à l'autre bout de, à l'extrémité de.

c (*Pol*) **the ~ right/left** l'extrême-droite/-gauche *f*.

3 comp ►**faraway** *country* lointain; *village, house* éloigné; *look* distrait, absent, perdu dans le vague; *voice* lointain; *memory* flou, vague ►**the Far East** l'Extrême-Orient *m* ►**the Far North** le Grand Nord ►**farsightedness** (*fig*) prévoyance *f*, clairvoyance *f*; (*lit*) hypermétropie *f*; (*in old age*) presbytie *f* ►**the Far West** (*US*) le far west, l'Ouest américain; *see also* **far-**.

far- [fɑːʳ] pref: **~-distant** lointain; **F~-Eastern** d'Extrême-Orient; **~-fetched** *explanation, argument* forcé, tiré par les cheveux; *idea, scheme, suggestion* bizarre; **~-flung** vaste, très étendu; **~-off** lointain, éloigné; **~-out*** (*modern*) d'avant-garde; (*superb*) super*, génial; (*fig*) **~-reaching** d'une portée considérable, d'une grande portée; **~-seeing, ~-sighted** *person* prévoyant, clairvoyant, qui voit loin; *decision, measure* pris avec clairvoyance; (*US*) (*lit*) **~-sighted** hypermétrope; (*in old age*) presbyte; *see also* **far 3**.

farad [ˈfærəd] n farad *m*.

farce [fɑːs] n (*Theat, fig*) farce *f*. **the whole thing's a~!, what a ~ it all is!** tout ça c'est une vaste rigolade* *or* ce n'est pas sérieux *or* c'est grotesque.

farcical [ˈfɑːsɪkəl] adj risible, grotesque, ridicule. **it's ~** cela tient de la farce, c'est vraiment grotesque.

fare [fɛəʳ] 1 n a (*charge*) (*on tube, subway, bus etc*) prix *m* du ticket *or* du billet; (*on train, boat, plane*) prix du billet; (*in taxi*) prix de la course. (*in bus*) **~s, please!** les places, s'il vous plaît!; **~s are going up** les (tarifs *mpl* des) transports *mpl* vont augmenter; **let me pay your ~** laissez-moi payer pour vous; **I haven't got the ~** je n'ai pas assez d'argent pour le billet; *see* **half, return** *etc*.

b (*passenger*) voyageur *m*, -euse *f*; *[taxi]* client(e) *m(f)*.

c (*food*) chère *f*, nourriture *f*. **hospital ~** régime *m* d'hôpital; *see* **bill**[1].

2 comp ►**fare stage** *[bus]* section *f* ►**fare war** guerre *f* des tarifs ►**farewell** *see* **farewell** ►**fare zone** (*US*) = **fare stage**.

3 vi: **he ~d well at his first attempt** il a réussi à sa première tentative; **we all ~d alike** nous avons tous partagé le même sort, nous étions tous au même régime*; **how did you ~?** comment cela s'est-il passé (pour vous)?, comment ça a marché?*; († *or hum*) **how ~s it with you?** les choses vont-elles comme vous voulez?; **it ~d well/badly with him** les choses se sont bien/mal passées pour lui.

fare-thee-well [fɛəðiːˈwel], **fare-you-well** [fɛəjuːˈwel] n (*US*) **to a ~** (*to perfection*) *imitate etc* à la perfection; (*very much, very hard etc*) au plus haut point.

farewell [fɛəˈwel] 1 n, excl adieu *m*. **to make one's ~s** faire ses adieux; **to take one's ~ of** faire ses adieux à; **to bid ~ to** dire adieu à; (*fig*) **you can say ~ to your wallet!** tu peux dire adieu à ton portefeuille!*, ton portefeuille tu peux en faire ton deuil!* 2 comp *dinner etc* d'adieu.

farinaceous [ˌfærɪˈneɪʃəs] adj farinacé, farineux.

farm [fɑːm] 1 n (*Agr*) ferme *f*, exploitation *f* agricole; (*fish ~ etc*) centre *m* d'élevage. **to work on a ~** travailler dans une ferme; *see* **sheep** *etc*. 2 comp ►**farm animal** animal *m* de la ferme ►**farm gate price** (*Econ*) prix *m* à la production *or* au producteur ►**farmhand** = **farm worker** ►**farmhouse** (maison *f* de) ferme *f* ►**farm labourer** = **farm worker** ►**farmland** terres cultivées *or* arables ►**farm produce** produits *mpl* agricoles *or* de ferme ►**farmstead** ferme *f* ►**farm worker** ouvrier *m*, -ière *f* agricole ►**farmyard** cour *f* de ferme. 3 vt cultiver. 4 vi être fermier, être cultivateur.

►**farm out** vt sep *shop* mettre en gérance. **to farm out work** céder un travail à un sous-traitant *or* en sous-traitance; **the firm farmed out the plumbing to a local tradesman** l'entreprise a confié la plomberie à un sous-traitant local; **to farm out children on sb*** donner des enfants à garder à qn, parquer* des enfants chez qn.

farmed [fɑːmd] adj *fish etc* d'élevage.

farmer [ˈfɑːməʳ] n fermier *m*, cultivateur *m*, agriculteur *m*. **~'s wife** fermière *f*, femme *f* du cultivateur.

farming [ˈfɑːmɪŋ] 1 n (*gen*) agriculture *f*. **he's always been interested in ~** il s'est toujours intéressé à l'agriculture; **vegetable/fruit ~** culture maraîchère/fruitière; **fish/mink ~** élevage *m* de poissons/de visons; **the ~ of this land** la culture *or* le faire-valoir *or* l'exploitation de cette terre; *see* **dairy, factory, mixed** *etc*. 2 comp *methods, techniques* de culture, cultural ►**farming communities** collectivités rurales.

Faroes [ˈfɛərəʊz] npl (*also* **Faroe Islands**) îles *fpl* Féroé *or* Faeroe.

farrago [fəˈrɑːgəʊ] n, pl **~s** *or* **~es** méli-mélo* *m*, mélange *m*.

farrier [ˈfærɪəʳ] n (*esp Brit*) maréchal-ferrant *m*.

farrow [ˈfærəʊ] 1 vti mettre bas. 2 n portée *f* (de cochons).

fart** [fɑːt] 1 n pet** *m*. (*pej: person*) **boring old ~** type *m* rasoir‡ *or* chiant‡. 2 vi péter**.

►**fart about****, **fart around**** vi glandouiller‡, glander** **to fart about** *or* **around with sth** faire le con** avec qch.

farther [ˈfɑːðəʳ] compar of **far** 1 adv plus loin. **how much ~ is it?** c'est encore à combien?; **it is ~ than I thought** c'est plus loin que je ne pensais; **have you got much ~ to go?** est-ce que vous avez encore loin à aller?; **we will go no ~** (*lit*) nous n'irons pas plus loin; (*fig*) nous en resterons là; **I got no ~ with him** je ne suis arrivé à rien de plus avec lui; **nothing could be ~ from the truth** rien n'est plus éloigné de la vérité; **nothing is ~ from my thoughts** rien n'est plus éloigné de ma pensée; **to get ~ and ~ away** s'éloigner de plus en plus; **~ back** plus (loin) en arrière; **push it ~ back** repousse-le plus loin; **move ~ back** reculez-vous; **~ back than 1940** avant 1940; **~ away, ~ off** plus éloigné, plus loin; **he went ~ off than I thought** il est allé plus loin que je ne pensais; **~ on, ~ forward** plus en avant, plus loin; (*fig*) **he is ~ on** *or* **~ forward than his brother** il est plus avancé que son frère, il est en avance sur son frère; (*fig*) **we're no ~ forward after all that** on n'est pas plus avancé, tout ça n'a rien donné.

2 adj plus éloigné, plus lointain. **at the ~ end of the room** à l'autre bout de la salle, au fond de la salle; **at the ~ end of the branch** à l'autre bout *or* à l'extrémité de la branche.

farthest [ˈfɑːðɪst] superl of **far** 1 adj le plus lointain, le plus éloigné. **in the ~ depths of the forest** au fin fond de la forêt; **the ~ way** la route la plus longue; **it's 5 km at the ~** il y a 5 km au plus *or* au maximum. 2 adv le plus loin.

farthing [ˈfɑːðɪŋ] n *quart d'un ancien penny*. **I haven't a ~** je n'ai pas le sou; *see* **brass** *etc*.

FAS [ˌefeɪˈes] (*Comm*) (abbr of **free alongside ship**) FLB.

fascia [ˈfeɪʃə] n, pl **fasciae** [ˈfeɪʃɪˌiː] a (*on building*) panneau *m*. b (*Brit Aut*) tableau *m* de bord.

fascicle [ˈfæsɪkl] n, **fascicule** [ˈfæsɪkjuːl] n (*Bot*) rameau fasciculé; *[book]* fascicule *m*.

fascinate [ˈfæsɪneɪt] vt *[speaker, tale]* fasciner, captiver; *[sight]* fasciner; *[snake etc]* fasciner.

fascinated [ˈfæsɪneɪtɪd] adj *person* fasciné, captivé; *look, smile* fasciné.

fascinating [ˈfæsɪneɪtɪŋ] adj *person* fascinant; *speaker, tale, book, film* fascinant, captivant, passionnant; *sight* fascinant.

fascination [ˌfæsɪˈneɪʃən] n fascination *f*, attrait *m* (irrésistible), charme *m*. **his ~ with the cinema** la fascination qu'exerce sur lui le cinéma.

fascism [ˈfæʃɪzəm] n fascisme *m*.

fascist [ˈfæʃɪst] adj, n fasciste *(mf)*.

fashion [ˈfæʃən] 1 n a (*NonC: manner*) façon *f*, manière *f*. **in a queer ~** d'une manière *or* façon bizarre; **after a ~** *finish, manage* tant bien que mal; *cook, paint* si l'on peut dire; **after the ~ of** à la manière de; **in the French ~** à la française; **in his own ~** à sa manière *or* façon; **it's not my ~ to lie** ce n'est pas mon genre de mentir.

b (*latest style*) mode *f*, vogue *f*. **in ~** à la mode, en vogue; **it's the latest ~** c'est la dernière mode *or* le dernier cri; **to dress in the latest ~** s'habiller à la dernière mode; **the Paris ~s** les collections (de mode) parisiennes; **~s have changed** la mode a changé; **out of ~** démodé, passé de mode; **to set the ~** donner le ton, lancer la mode; **to set the ~ for** lancer la mode de; **to bring sth into ~** mettre qch à la mode; **to come into ~** devenir à la mode; **to go out of ~** se démoder; **it is the ~ to say** il est bien porté *or* de bon ton de dire; **it's no longer the ~ to send children away to school** ça ne se fait plus de mettre les enfants en pension; **a man of ~** un homme élégant.

c (*habit*) coutume *f*, habitude *f*. **as was his ~** selon sa coutume *or* son habitude.

2 vt *carving* façonner; *model* fabriquer; *dress* confectionner.

3 comp ▸**fashion designer** (*gen*) modéliste *mf*; **the great fashion designers** les grands couturiers ▸**fashion editor** rédacteur *m*, -trice *f* de mode ▸**fashion house** maison *f* de couture ▸**fashion magazine** journal *m* de mode ▸**fashion model** mannequin *m* (*personne*) ▸**fashion parade** défilé *m* de mannequins ▸**fashion plate** gravure *f* de mode; **she's a real fashion plate*** à la voir on dirait une gravure de mode, on dirait qu'elle sort des pages d'un magazine ▸**fashion show** présentation *f* de modèles *or* de collections; **to go to the Paris fashion shows** faire les collections parisiennes.

fashionable ['fæʃnəbl] adj *dress* à la mode; *district, shop, hotel* chic *inv*; *dressmaker, subject* à la mode, en vogue. **the ~ world** les gens à la mode; **it is ~ to say** il est bien porté *or* de bon ton de dire; **it's no longer ~ to prefer ...** ça ne se fait plus de préférer ... .

fashionably ['fæʃnəblɪ] adv à la mode, élégamment.

fast[1] [fɑːst] 1 adj a (*speedy*) rapide. (*Aut*) **the ~ lane** ≃ la voie rapide; (*fig*) **to be in the ~ lane** avoir une vie trépidante, vivre à 100 à l'heure*; **life in the ~ lane** la vie trépidante; **~ train** rapide *m*; (*Phys*) **~ breeder (reactor)** réacteur *m* surgénérateur, surrégénérateur *m*; **he's a ~ thinker** il a l'esprit très rapide, il sait réfléchir vite; **he's a ~ talker** c'est un hâbleur; **he's a ~ worker** (*lit*) il va vite en besogne; (*: *with the girls*) c'est un tombeur* *or* un don Juan; **to pull a ~ one on sb*** rouler qn*, avoir qn*; (*Tennis*) **a grass court is ~er** le jeu est plus rapide sur gazon; (*Phot*) **~ film** pellicule *f* rapide; *see also* **2**.

b *[clock etc]* **to be ~** avancer; **my watch is 5 minutes ~** ma montre avance de 5 minutes.

c (*dissipated*) de mœurs légères, dissolu. **~ life** *or* **living** vie dissolue *or* de dissipation; **~ woman** femme légère *or* de mœurs légères; **a ~ set** une bande de viveurs *or* de noceurs*; **one of the ~ set** un viveur, un noceur (*or* une noceuse).

d (*firm*) *rope, knot* solide; *grip* tenace; *colour* bon teint *inv*, grand teint *inv*; *friend* sûr. **to make a boat ~** amarrer un bateau; **is the dye ~?** est-ce que ça déteindra?, est-ce que la teinture s'en ira?

2 comp ▸**fastback** (*Brit Aut*) voiture *f* à arrière profilé ▸**fast food** (*food*) prêt-à-manger *m*; (*place: also* **fast-food restaurant**) restaurant *m* rapide ▸**fast-food chain** chaîne *f* de restaurants rapides ▸**fast-food industry, fast-food trade** restauration *f* rapide ▸**fast forward** n avance *f* rapide ▸**fast-forward** vb (faire) avancer rapidement ▸**fast-moving** (*gen*) rapide; (*fig: active, rapidly-changing*) *industry, sector* en mouvement constant; **fast-moving consumer goods** biens *mpl* de consommation à rotation rapide ▸**fast-selling** à écoulement rapide ▸**fast-tracking** *[personnel]* avancement *m* rapide.

3 adv a (*quickly*) vite, rapidement. **he ran off as ~ as his legs could carry him** il s'est sauvé à toutes jambes; **don't speak so ~** ne parlez pas si vite; **how ~ can you type?** à quelle vitesse pouvez-vous taper (à la machine)?; (*interrupting*) **not so ~!** doucement!, minute!*; **he'd do it ~ enough if ...** il ne se ferait pas prier si ...; **as ~ as I advanced he drew back** à mesure que j'avançais il reculait; *see* **furious**.

b (*firmly, securely*) ferme, solidement. **to be ~ asleep** être profondément endormi, dormir à poings fermés; **a door shut ~** une porte bien close; **~ by**† **the church** qui jouxte l'église; *see* **hard, hold, play** *etc*.

fast[2] [fɑːst] 1 vi jeûner, rester à jeun; (*Rel*) jeûner, faire maigre. 2 n jeûne *m*. **to break one's ~** rompre le jeûne; (*Rel*) **~ day** jour *m* maigre *or* de jeûne.

fasten ['fɑːsn] 1 vt a (*lit*) attacher (*to* à); (*with rope, string etc*) lier (*to* à); (*with nail*) clouer (*to* à); (*with paste*) coller (*to* à); *box, door, window* fermer (solidement); *dress* fermer, attacher. **to ~ two things together** attacher deux choses ensemble *or* l'une à l'autre; **to ~ one's seat belt** attacher *or* mettre sa ceinture de sécurité; (*fig*) **to ~ one's eyes on sth** fixer son regard *or* les yeux sur qch. b (*fig*) *responsibility* attribuer (*on sb* à qn); *a crime* imputer (*on sb* à qn). **to ~ the blame on sb** rejeter la faute sur (le dos de) qn; **you can't ~ it on me!** tu ne peux pas me mettre ça sur le dos! 2 vi *[box, door, lock, window]* se fermer; *[dress]* s'attacher.

▸**fasten down** vt sep *blind, flap* fixer en place; *envelope* coller.

▸**fasten on** vt sep fixer (en place).

▸**fasten on to** vt fus a = **fasten (up)on**. b se cramponner à, s'accrocher à. **he fastened on to my arm** il s'est cramponné *or* accroché à mon bras.

▸**fasten up** vt sep *dress, coat* fermer, attacher.

▸**fasten (up)on** vt fus saisir. **to fasten (up)on an excuse** saisir un prétexte; **to fasten (up)on the idea of doing** se mettre en tête l'idée de faire.

fastener ['fɑːsnəʳ] n, **fastening** ['fɑːsnɪŋ] n attache *f*; *[box, door, window]* fermeture *f*; *[bag, necklace, book]* fermoir *m*; *[garment]* fermeture, (*button*) bouton *m*, (*hook*) agrafe *f*, (*press stud*) pression *f*, (*zip*) fermeture *f* éclair *inv*. **what kind of ~ has this dress got?** comment se ferme *or* s'attache cette robe?

fastidious [fæs'tɪdɪəs] adj a *work, research* minutieux. **you can see that he is very ~** (*from his work*) il est évident qu'il est très méticuleux *or* minutieux; (*from his appearance, house*) il est évident qu'il est très méticuleux *or* qu'il est d'une propreté méticuleuse.

b (*demanding about detail*) tatillon, pointilleux; (*particular about cleanliness*) délicat, tatillon; (*easily disgusted*) délicat. **their inspectors are very ~** leurs inspecteurs sont très pointilleux *or* tatillons *or* exigeants; **she's too ~ to eat there** elle est trop délicate pour manger là; **this film is not for the ~** ce film n'est pas pour les esprits délicats *or* pour les personnes trop délicates.

fastidiously [fæs'tɪdɪəslɪ] adv *examine, clean, check* méticuleusement, minutieusement.

fastidiousness [fæs'tɪdɪəsnɪs] n méticulosité *f* (*liter*), minutie *f*, caractère tatillon *or* délicat.

fastigiate [fæ'stɪdʒɪɪt] adj fastigié.

fastness ['fɑːstnɪs] n a (*stronghold*) place forte. **mountain ~** repaire *m* de montagne. b (*NonC: speed*) rapidité *f*, vitesse *f*. c *[colours]* solidité *f*.

fat [fæt] 1 n (*gen, also Anat*) graisse *f*; (*on raw meat*) graisse, gras *m*; (*on cooked meat*) gras *m*; (*for cooking*) matière grasse. **what kind of ~ did you use?** qu'avez-vous utilisé comme matière grasse *or* comme corps gras?; **the ~ will stain the tablecloth** la graisse tachera la nappe, il y aura une tache de graisse sur la nappe; **I must avoid all ~s** je dois éviter toutes les matières grasses *or* tous les corps gras; **to fry in deep ~** (faire) frire *or* cuire à la grande friture; **beef/mutton ~** graisse de bœuf/de mouton; **pork ~** saindoux *m*; **he's got rolls of ~ round his waist** il a des bourrelets de graisse autour de la taille; (*fig*) **the ~'s in the fire** le feu est aux poudres, ça va barder‡ *or* chauffer*; (*fig*) **to live off the ~ of the land** vivre grassement.

2 adj a *person* gras (*f* grasse); *limb* gros (*f* grosse), gras; *face* joufflu; *cheeks* gros; *meat, bacon* gras. **to get ~** grossir, engraisser, prendre de l'embonpoint; **she has got a lot ~ter** elle a beaucoup grossi; (*fig*) **he grew ~ on the profits** il s'est engraissé avec les bénéfices.

b (*thick, big*) *volume, cheque, salary* gros (*f* grosse). **he paid a ~ price for it*** il l'a payé un gros prix.

c *land* riche, fertile, gras (*f* grasse). **he's got a nice ~ job in an office*** il a un bon fromage* *or* une sinécure dans un bureau.

d (*: *phrases*) **a ~ lot you did to help!** tu as vraiment été d'un précieux secours! (*iro*), comme aide c'était réussi!*; **a ~ lot of good that did!** ça a bien avancé les choses! (*iro*); **and a ~ lot of good it did you!, that did you a ~ lot of good anyway!** ça t'a *or* te voilà bien avancé! (*iro*); **a ~ lot that's worth!** c'est fou ce que ça a comme valeur! (*iro*), ça ne vaut pas tripette!*; **that's a ~ lot of use** *or* **help to me!** c'est fou ce que ça m'aide!*; **a ~ lot he knows about it!** comme s'il en savait quelque chose!; **a ~ lot he cares!** comme si ça lui faisait quelque chose!; **a ~ chance he's got of getting rich!** tu parles qu'il a une chance de s'enrichir!*; **you've got a ~ chance of seeing her!** comme si tu avais une chance *or* la moindre chance de la voir!; **can't you get that into your ~ head?** tu peux pas te mettre ça dans la tête *or* la caboche*?

3 vt (††) = **fatten 1. to kill the ~ted calf** tuer le veau gras.

4 comp ▸**fatback** (sorte *f* de) lard *m* maigre ▸**fat cat** (*US*) gros richard*, huile* *f* ▸**fat city***: (*US*) **to be in fat city** être plein aux as ▸**fat farm‡** (*US*) clinique *f* d'amaigrissement ▸**fatfree** *diet* sans matières grasses, sans corps gras ▸**fathead*** idiot(e) *m(f)*, imbécile *mf*, cruche* *f* ▸**fat-headed*** idiot, imbécile ▸**fatless** = **fatfree** ▸**fatstock** (*Agr*) animaux *mpl* de boucherie.

fatal ['feɪtl] adj a (*lit: causing death*) *injury, disease, shot, accident* mortel; *blow* mortel, fatal; *consequences, result* fatal; (*fig*) *mistake* fatal; *decision* fatidique; *influence* néfaste, pernicieux. **his illness was ~ to their plans** sa maladie a porté un coup fatal *or* le coup de grâce à leurs projets; **it was absolutely ~ to mention that** c'était une grave erreur *or* c'était la mort que de parler de cela. b = **fateful**.

fatalism ['feɪtəlɪzəm] n fatalisme *m*.

fatalist ['feɪtəlɪst] n, adj fataliste (*mf*).

fatalistic [ˌfeɪtə'lɪstɪk] adj fataliste.

fatality [fə'tælɪtɪ] n (*fatal accident*) accident mortel; (*person killed*) mort *m*. **bathing fatalities** noyades *fpl*; **road fatalities** accidents mortels de la route; **luckily there were no fatalities** heureusement il n'y a pas eu de morts.

fatally ['feɪtəlɪ] adv *wounded* mortellement. **~ ill** condamné, perdu.

fate [feɪt] n a (*force*) destin *m*, sort *m*. (*Myth*) **the F~s** les Parques *fpl*; **what ~ has in store for us** ce que le destin *or* le sort nous réserve. b (*one's lot*) sort *m*. **to leave sb to his ~** abandonner qn à son sort;

to meet one's ~ trouver la mort; **it met with a strange ~** cela a eu une destinée curieuse; **that sealed his ~** ceci a décidé de son sort; **it was a ~ worse than death** c'était un sort pire que la mort, la mort eût été mille fois préférable.

fated ['feɪtɪd] **adj** *friendship, person* voué au malheur. **to be ~ to do** être destiné *or* condamné à faire.

fateful ['feɪtfʊl] **adj** *words* fatidique; *day, event, moment* fatal, décisif.

father ['fɑːðəʳ] 1 **n** a père *m*. (*Rel*) **Our F~** Notre Père; (*prayer*) **the Our F~** le Notre Père; **from ~ to son** de père en fils; (*Prov*) **like ~ like son** tel père tel fils (*Prov*); **to act like a ~** agir en père *or* comme un père; **he was like a ~ to me** il était comme un père pour moi; (*ancestors*) **~s** ancêtres *mpl*, pères; **there was the ~ and mother of a row!*** il y a eu une dispute à tout casser!* *or* une dispute maison!*; *see also* **3**.
b (*founder, leader*) père *m*, créateur *m*. **the F~s of the Church** les Pères de l'Église; *see* **city**.
c (*Rel*) père *m*. **F~ X** le (révérend) père X, l'abbé X; **yes, F~** oui, mon père; **the Capuchin F~s** les pères capucins; *see* **holy**.
2 **vt** a *child* engendrer; *idea, plan* concevoir, inventer.
b (*saddle with responsibility*) **to ~ sth on sb** attribuer la responsabilité de qch à qn; **to ~ the blame on sb** imputer la faute à qn, faire porter le blâme à qn.
3 **comp** ►**Father Christmas** (*Brit*) le père Noël ►**Father's Day** la Fête des Pères ►**father confessor** (*Rel*) directeur *m* de conscience, père spirituel ►**father-figure** personne *f* qui tient *or* joue le rôle du père; **he is the father-figure** il joue le rôle du père ►**father-in-law** (*pl* **~s-~-~**) beau-père *m* ►**fatherland** patrie *f*, mère *f* patrie ►**(Old) Father Time** le Temps.

fatherhood ['fɑːðəhʊd] **n** paternité *f*.

fatherless ['fɑːðəlɪs] **adj** orphelin de père, sans père.

fatherly ['fɑːðəlɪ] **adj** paternel.

fathom ['fæðəm] 1 **n** (*Naut*) brasse *f* (= *1,83m*). **a channel with 5 ~s of water** un chenal de 9m de fond; **to lie 25 ~s deep** *or* **down** reposer par 45m de fond. 2 **vt** (*Naut*) sonder; (*fig: also* **~ out**) *mystery, person* sonder, pénétrer. **I just can't ~ it (out)** je n'y comprends absolument rien.

fathomless ['fæðəmlɪs] **adj** (*lit*) insondable; (*fig*) insondable, impénétrable.

fatigue [fə'tiːg] 1 **n** a fatigue *f*, épuisement *m*. **metal ~** fatigue du métal. b (*Mil*) corvée *f*. **to be on ~** être de corvée. c (*Mil*) **~s** = **fatigue dress**. 2 **vt** fatiguer, lasser; (*Tech*) *metals etc* fatiguer. 3 **comp** ►**fatigue dress** (*Mil*) tenue *f* de corvée, treillis *m* ►**fatigue duty** (*Mil*) corvée *f* ►**fatigue limit** (*Tech*) limite *f* de fatigue ►**fatigue party** (*Mil*) corvée *f*.

fatigued [fə'tiːgd] **adj** las (*f* lasse), fatigué.

fatiguing [fə'tiːgɪŋ] **adj** fatigant, épuisant.

fatness ['fætnɪs] **n** *[person]* embonpoint *m*, corpulence *f*.

fatso‡ ['fætsəʊ] **n, pl ~s** *or* **~es** (*pej*) gros lard‡.

fatten ['fætn] 1 **vt** (*also* **~ up**) *cattle, chickens etc* engraisser; *geese* gaver. 2 **vi** (*also* **~ out**) engraisser, grossir.

fattening ['fætnɪŋ] 1 **adj** *food* qui fait grossir. 2 **n** (*also* **~-up**) *[cattle, chickens etc]* engraissement *m*; *[geese]* gavage *m*.

fatty ['fætɪ] 1 **adj** a (*greasy*) *chips etc* gras (*f* grasse), graisseux. **~ food** nourriture grasse, aliments gras; (*Chem*) **~ acid** acide gras. b *tissue* adipeux. (*Med*) **~ degeneration** dégénérescence graisseuse. 2 **n** (*) gros *m* (bonhomme), grosse *f* (bonne femme). **hey ~!** eh toi le gros! (*or* la grosse!).

fatuity [fə'tjuːɪtɪ] **n** imbécillité *f*, stupidité *f*, sottise *f*.

fatuous ['fætjʊəs] **adj** *person, remark* imbécile, sot (*f* sotte), stupide; *smile* stupide, niais.

fatuousness ['fætjʊəsnɪs] **n** = **fatuity**.

faucet ['fɔːsɪt] **n** (*US*) robinet *m*.

faugh [fɔː] **excl** pouah!

fault [fɔːlt] 1 **n** a (*in person, scheme*) défaut *m*; (*in machine*) défaut, anomalie *f*; (*mistake*) erreur *f*; (*Tennis*) faute *f*; (*Geol*) faille *f*. **in spite of all her ~s** malgré tous ses défauts; **her big ~ is ...** son gros défaut est ...; **there is a mechanical ~ in this hair-dryer** ce séchoir a un défaut mécanique; **a ~ has been found in the engine** une anomalie a été constatée dans le moteur; **there is a ~ in the gas supply** il y a un défaut dans l'arrivée du gaz; **to find ~ with sth** trouver à redire à qch, critiquer qch; **to find ~ with sb** critiquer qn; **I have no ~ to find with him** je n'ai rien à lui reprocher; **he is always finding ~** il trouve toujours à redire; **she is generous to a ~** elle est généreuse à l'excès; **to be at ~** être fautif, être coupable; **you were at ~ in not telling me** vous avez eu tort de ne pas me le dire; **he's at ~ in this matter** il est fautif *or* c'est lui le fautif en cette affaire; **my memory was at ~** ma mémoire m'a trompé *or* m'a fait défaut.
b (*NonC: blame, responsibility*) faute *f*. **whose ~ is it?** c'est la faute à qui?, qui est fautif?; (*iro*) **whose ~ is it if we're late?** et à qui la faute si nous sommes en retard?; **the ~ lies with him** c'est de sa faute, c'est lui le responsable; **it's not my ~** ce n'est pas (de) ma faute; **it's all your ~** c'est entièrement (de) ta faute; **it's your own ~** vous n'avez à vous en prendre qu'à vous-même; **it happened through no ~ of mine** ce n'est absolument pas de ma faute si c'est arrivé.
2 **vt**: **to ~ sth/sb** trouver des défauts à qch/chez qn; **you can't ~ him** on ne peut pas le prendre en défaut; **I can't ~ his reasoning** je ne trouve aucune faille dans son raisonnement.
3 **comp** ►**fault-finder** mécontent(e) *m(f)*, grincheux *m*, -euse *f* ►**fault-finding** **adj** chicanier, grincheux ◊ **n** critiques *fpl*; **she's always fault-finding** elle est toujours à critiquer ►**fault plane** (*Geol*) plan *m* de faille ►**fault-tolerant** (*Comput*) insensible aux défaillances.

faultless ['fɔːltlɪs] **adj** *person, behaviour* irréprochable; *work, manners, dress* impeccable, irréprochable. **he spoke ~ English** il parlait un anglais impeccable.

faulty ['fɔːltɪ] **adj** *work* défectueux, mal fait; *machine* défectueux; *style* incorrect, mauvais; *reasoning* défectueux, erroné.

faun [fɔːn] **n** faune *m*.

fauna ['fɔːnə] **n, pl ~s** *or* **faunae** ['fɔːniː] faune *f*.

Faust [faʊst] **n** Faust *m*.

Faustian ['faʊstɪən] **adj** faustien.

faux pas [fəʊ'pɑː] **n, pl inv** impair *m*, bévue *f*, gaffe *f*.

favor *etc* (*US*) = **favour** *etc*.

favour, (*US*) **favor** ['feɪvəʳ] 1 **n** a (*act of kindness*) service *m*, faveur *f*, grâce *f*. **to do sb a ~, to do a ~ for sb** rendre (un) service à qn, obliger qn; **to ask sb a ~, to ask a ~ of sb** demander un service à qn, solliciter une faveur *or* une grâce de qn (*frm*); **I ask you as a ~ to wait a moment** je vous demande d'avoir la gentillesse d'attendre un instant; **he did it as a ~ to his brother** il l'a fait pour rendre service à son frère; **I would consider it a ~ if ...** je vous serais très reconnaissant si ...; (*frm*) **do me the ~ of closing the door** soyez assez gentil pour fermer la porte; **do me a ~!*** je t'en prie!; **do me a ~ and ...** sois gentil et ...; **you're not doing yourself any ~s (by refusing to cooperate)** tu ne te facilites pas les choses (en refusant de coopérer); **a woman's ~s** les faveurs d'une femme; (*Comm*) **your ~ of the 7th inst** votre honorée du 7 courant; **I'll return this ~** je vous revaudrai ça.
b (*NonC: approval, regard*) faveur *f*, approbation *f*. **to be in ~** *[person]* être bien en cour *or* en faveur, avoir la cote*; *[style, fashion]* être à la mode *or* en vogue; **to be out of ~** *[person]* être mal en cour, ne pas avoir la cote*; *[style, fashion]* être démodé *or* passé de mode; **to be in ~ with sb** être bien vu de qn, être en faveur auprès de qn, jouir des bonnes grâces de qn; **to win sb's ~, to find ~ with sb** *[person]* s'attirer les bonnes grâces de qn; *[suggestion]* gagner l'approbation de qn; **to get back into sb's ~** rentrer dans les bonnes grâces de qn; **to look with ~ on sth** approuver qch; **to look with ~ on sb** bien considérer qn.
c (*NonC: support, advantage*) faveur *f*, avantage *m*. **the court decided in her ~** le tribunal lui a donné gain de cause; **will in ~ of sb** testament en faveur de qn; **cheque in ~ of sb** chèque payable à qn; (*Banking*) **"balance in your ~"** "à votre crédit"; **it's in our ~ to act now** c'est (à) notre avantage d'agir maintenant; **the exchange rate is in our ~** le taux de change joue en notre faveur *or* pour nous; **the traffic lights are in our ~** les feux sont pour nous; **that's a point in his ~** c'est quelque chose à mettre à son actif, c'est un bon point pour lui; **he's got** *or* **there is everything in his ~** il a tout pour lui.
d **to be in ~ of sth** être pour qch, être partisan(e) de qch; **to be in ~ of doing sth** être d'avis de faire qch.
e (*NonC: partiality*) faveur *f*, indulgence *f*. **to show ~ to sb** montrer un *or* des préjugé(s) en faveur de qn; *see* **curry²**, **fear**.
f (*ribbon, token*) faveur *f*.
2 **vt** *political party, scheme, suggestion* être partisan de; *undertaking* favoriser, appuyer; *person* préférer; *candidate, pupil* montrer une préférence pour; *team, horse* être pour; († *or dial: resemble*) ressembler à. **I don't ~ the idea** je ne suis pas partisan de cette idée; **he ~ed us with a visit** il a eu l'amabilité *or* la bonté de nous rendre visite; **to ~ sb with a smile** gratifier qn d'un sourire; (*iro*) **he did not ~ us with a reply** il n'a même pas eu l'amabilité *or* la bonté de nous répondre; **the weather ~ed the journey** le temps a favorisé *or* facilité le voyage; **circumstances that ~ this scheme** circonstances *fpl* favorables à ce projet.

favourable, (*US*) **favorable** ['feɪvərəbl] **adj** *reception, impression, report* favorable (*to* à); *weather, wind* propice (*for, to* à). **is he ~ to the proposal?** est-ce qu'il approuve la proposition?

favourably, (*US*) **favorably** ['feɪvərəblɪ] **adv** *receive, impress* favorablement; *consider* d'un œil favorable. **~ disposed** bien disposé (*towards sb* envers qn, à l'égard de qn, *towards sth* en ce qui concerne qch).

favoured, (*US*) **favored** ['feɪvəd] **adj** favorisé. **the ~ few** les élus; **ill-~** disgracieux; **most ~ nation clause** clause *f* de la nation la plus favorisée.

favourite, (*US*) **favorite** ['feɪvərɪt] 1 **n** (*gen*) favori(te) *m(f)*, préféré(e) *m(f)*; (*at court, Racing*) favori. **he's his mother's ~** c'est le préféré *or* le favori *or* le chouchou* de sa mère; **he is a universal ~** tout le monde l'adore; **that song is a great ~ of mine** cette chanson est une de mes préférées; **he sang a lot of old ~s** il a chanté beaucoup de vieux succès; *see* **hot**. 2 **adj** favori (*f* -ite), préféré. (*US*) **~ son** (*Pol*) *candidat à la présidence soutenu officiellement par son parti dans son État;* (*gen*) enfant chéri (*de sa ville natale etc*).

favouritism, (*US*) **favoritism** ['feɪvərɪtɪzəm] **n** favoritisme *m*.

fawn¹ [fɔːn] 1 **n** faon *m*. 2 **adj** (*colour*) fauve.

fawn² [fɔːn] vi: **to ~ (up)on sb** *[dog]* faire fête à qn; *[person]* flatter qn (servilement), lécher les bottes de qn*.
fawning [ˈfɔːnɪŋ] adj *person, manner* servile, flagorneur; *dog* trop démonstratif, trop affectueux.
fax [fæks] 1 n (*machine*) télécopieur *m*; (*transmission*) fax *m*, télécopie *f*. **~ number** numéro *m* de fax *or* de télécopie *or* de télécopieur; **by ~** par fax *or* télécopie. 2 vt *document* faxer, envoyer par fax *or* par télécopie *or* par télécopieur; *person* envoyer un fax à. **~ me your reply** répondez-moi par fax.
fay [feɪ] n (†† *or liter*) fée *f*.
faze [feɪz] vt (*US* *) déconcerter.
FBI [ˌefbiːˈaɪ] n (*US*) (abbr of **Federal Bureau of Investigation**) FBI *m*, ≃ police *f* judiciaire.
FCC [ˌefsiːˈsiː] (*US*) (abbr of **Federal Communications Commission**) *see* **federal**.
FCO [ˌefsiːˈəʊ] (*Brit*) (abbr of **Foreign and Commonwealth Office**) *see* **foreign**.
FD [efˈdiː] a (*US*) (abbr of **Fire Department**) *see* **fire**. b (*Brit*) (abbr of **Fidei Defensor**) Défenseur *m* de la foi. c (*Comm*) (abbr of **free delivered at dock**) livraison *f* franco à quai.
FDA [ˌefdiːˈeɪ] (*US*) (abbr of **Food and Drug Administration**) *see* **food**.
fealty [ˈfiːəltɪ] n (*Hist*) fidélité *f*, allégeance *f*.
fear [fɪəʳ] 1 n a (*fright*) crainte *f*, peur *f*. **he obeyed out of ~** il a obéi sous l'effet de la peur; **I couldn't move from** *or* **for ~** j'étais paralysé de peur; **a sudden ~ came over him** la peur s'est soudain emparée de lui; **grave ~s have arisen for the safety of the hostages** on est dans la plus vive inquiétude en ce qui concerne le sort des otages; **there are ~s that ...** on craint fort que ... + ne + *subj*; **he has ~s for his sister's life** il craint pour la vie de sa sœur; **to have a ~ of** avoir peur de; (*stronger*) avoir la phobie de; **have no ~(s)** ne craignez rien, soyez sans crainte; **without ~ or favour** impartialement, sans distinction de personnes; **to live** *or* **go in ~** vivre dans la peur; **to go in ~ of one's life** craindre pour sa vie; **he went in ~ of being discovered** il craignait toujours d'être découvert; **in ~ and trembling** en tremblant de peur, transi de peur; **for ~ of waking him** de peur de le réveiller; **for ~ (that)** de peur que + ne + *subj*; **~ of heights** vertige *m*.
b (*NonC: awe*) crainte *f*, respect *m*. **the ~ of God** le respect *or* la crainte de Dieu; **to put the ~ of God into sb*** (*frighten*) faire une peur bleue à qn; (*scold*) passer à qn une semonce *or* un savon* qu'il n'oubliera pas de si tôt.
c (*risk, likelihood*) risque *m*, danger *m*. **there's not much ~ of his coming** il est peu probable qu'il vienne, il ne risque guère de venir; **there's no ~ of that!** ça ne risque pas d'arriver!; **no ~!*** jamais de la vie!, pas de danger!*
2 vt a craindre, avoir peur de, redouter. **to ~ the worst** redouter *or* craindre le pire; **to ~ that** avoir peur que *or* craindre que + ne + *subj*; **I ~ he may come all the same** j'ai (bien) peur *or* je crains (bien) qu'il ne vienne quand même; **I ~ he won't come** j'ai (bien) peur *or* je crains (bien) qu'il ne vienne pas; **I ~ so** je crains que oui, hélas oui; **I ~ not** je crains que non, hélas non; (*apologizing*) **I ~ I'm late** je crois bien que je suis en retard, je suis désolé d'être en retard; **it's raining, I ~** il pleut, hélas; **he's a man to be ~ed** c'est un homme redoutable; **never ~!** ne craignez rien!, n'ayez crainte!, soyez tranquille!; **they did not ~ to die** ils ne craignaient pas la mort *or* de mourir, ils n'avaient pas peur de la mort *or* de mourir.
b (*feel awe for*) *God, gods* craindre, avoir le respect de.
3 vi: **to ~ for one's life** craindre pour sa vie; **I ~ for him** j'ai peur *or* je tremble pour lui; **he ~s for the future of the country** l'avenir du pays lui inspire des craintes *or* des inquiétudes; (†, *hum*) **~ not!** n'aies crainte!
fearful [ˈfɪəfʊl] adj a (*frightening*) *spectacle, noise* effrayant, affreux; *accident* épouvantable. b (*fig*) affreux. **it really is a ~ nuisance** c'est vraiment empoisonnant* *or* embêtant*; **she's a ~ bore** Dieu! qu'elle est *or* peut être ennuyeuse! c (*timid*) *person* peureux, craintif. **I was ~ of waking her** je craignais de la réveiller.
fearfully [ˈfɪəfəlɪ] adv a (*timidly*) peureusement, craintivement. b (*fig*) affreusement, terriblement. **she's ~ ugly** elle est laide à faire peur.
fearfulness [ˈfɪəfʊlnɪs] n (*fear*) crainte *f*, appréhension *f*; (*shyness*) extrême timidité *f*.
fearless [ˈfɪəlɪs] adj intrépide, courageux. (*liter*) **~ of** sans peur *or* appréhension de.
fearlessly [ˈfɪəlɪslɪ] adv intrépidement, avec intrépidité, courageusement.
fearlessness [ˈfɪəlɪsnɪs] n intrépidité *f*.
fearsome [ˈfɪəsəm] adj *opponent* redoutable; *apparition* terrible, effroyable.
fearsomely [ˈfɪəsəmlɪ] adv effroyablement, affreusement.
feasibility [ˌfiːzəˈbɪlɪtɪ] 1 n a (*practicability: of plan, suggestion*) faisabilité *f*, possibilité *f* (de réalisation). **~ of doing** possibilité de faire; **to doubt the ~ of a scheme** douter qu'un plan soit réalisable. b (*plausibility: of story, report*) vraisemblance *f*, plausibilité *f*. 2 comp ►**feasibility study** étude *f* de faisabilité.
feasible [ˈfiːzəbl] adj a (*practicable*) *plan, suggestion* faisable, possible, réalisable. **can we do it? — yes, it's quite ~** pouvons-nous le faire? — oui, c'est très faisable. b (*likely, probable*) *story, theory* plausible, vraisemblable.
feast [fiːst] 1 n a (*lit, fig*) festin *m*, banquet *m*. b (*Rel*) fête *f*. **~ day** (jour *m* de) fête; **the ~ of St John** la Saint-Jean; **the ~ of the Assumption** la fête de l'Assomption; *see* **movable**. 2 vi banqueter, festoyer. **to ~ on sth** se régaler de qch; (*fig*) se délecter de qch. 3 vt († *or liter*) *guest* fêter, régaler. **to ~ o.s.** se régaler; (*fig*) **to ~ one's eyes on** repaître ses yeux de, se délecter à regarder.
feat [fiːt] n exploit *m*, prouesse *f*. **~ of architecture** *etc* chef-d'œuvre *m or* réussite *f or* triomphe *m* de l'architecture *etc*; **~ of arms** fait *m* d'armes; **~ of skill** tour *m* d'adresse; **getting him to speak was quite a ~** cela a été un tour de force *or* un exploit de (réussir à) le faire parler.
feather [ˈfeðəʳ] 1 n plume *f*; *[wing, tail]* penne *f*. (*fig*) **to make the ~s fly** mettre le feu aux poudres (*fig*); **that smoothed her ruffled** *or* **rumpled ~s** cela lui a rendu le sourire; **in fine** *or* **high ~** en pleine forme; **that's a ~ in his cap** c'est une réussite dont il peut être fier *or* se féliciter, c'est un fleuron à sa couronne; **you could have knocked me over with a ~** les bras m'en sont tombés, j'en suis resté baba* *inv*; *see* **bird, light², white**.
2 vt a *arrow etc* empenner. (*fig*) **to ~ one's nest** faire sa pelote; **to ~ one's nest at sb's expense** s'engraisser sur le dos de qn.
b (*Aviat*) *propeller* mettre en drapeau. (*Rowing*) **to ~ an oar** plumer.
3 comp *mattress etc* de plumes; *headdress* à plumes ►**feather bed** n lit *m* de plume(s); (*: *sinecure*) sinécure *f*, bonne planque ►**featherbed** vt (*fig*) *person, project* protéger; *child* élever dans du coton; (*Ind*) protéger (*afin de lutter contre les licenciements pour raisons économiques*) ►**featherbedding** (*Ind*) protection *f* excessive de la main-d'œuvre ►**feather boa** boa *m* ►**featherbrain** hurluberlu *m*, écervelé(e) *m(f)* ►**featherbrained** étourdi, écervelé ►**feather duster** plumeau *m* ►**featheredge** (*Carpentry*) biseau *m* ►**feather-edged** en biseau ►**featherweight** (*Boxing*) n poids *m* plume *inv* ◊ adj *championship etc* poids plume *inv*.
feathered [ˈfeðəd] adj *bird* à plumes. **our ~ friends** nos amis à plumes.
feathering [ˈfeðərɪŋ] n plumage *m*, plumes *fpl*.
feathery [ˈfeðərɪ] adj *texture, feel* duveteux, doux (*f* douce) comme la plume; *mark, design* plumeté.
feature [ˈfiːtʃəʳ] 1 n a (*part of the face*) trait *m* (du visage). **the ~s** la physionomie; **delicate ~s** traits fins.
b *[person]* particularité *f*, caractéristique *f*, trait *m*; *[machine, countryside, building]* caractéristique, particularité. **her most striking ~ is her hair** son trait le plus frappant ce sont ses cheveux; **one of his most outstanding ~s is his patience** une de ses caractéristiques les plus remarquables est sa patience; **one of the main ~s in the kidnapping story was ...** un des traits les plus frappants dans l'affaire du kidnapping a été ...; **scepticism is a ~ of our age** le scepticisme est caractéristique *or* un trait de notre temps.
c (*Comm etc*) spécialité *f*. **this store makes a ~ of its ready-to-wear department** ce magasin se spécialise dans le prêt-à-porter.
d (*Cine*) grand film, long métrage; (*Press: column*) chronique *f*. **this cartoon is a regular ~ in "The Observer"** cette bande dessinée paraît régulièrement dans "The Observer".
e (*Ling*) (*also* **distinctive ~**) trait distinctif.
2 comp ►**feature article** (*Press*) article *m* de fond ►**feature(-length) film** (*Cine*) long métrage ►**feature story** = **feature article** ►**feature writer** (*Press*) journaliste *mf*.
3 vt a (*give prominence to*) *person, event, story* mettre en vedette; *name, news* faire figurer. **this film ~s an English actress** ce film a pour vedette une actrice anglaise; **the murder was ~d on the front page** le meurtre tenait la vedette (en première page) *or* était à la une.
b (*depict*) représenter.
c (*have as one of its features: of machine etc*) être doté *or* équipé de.
4 vi a (*Cine*) figurer, jouer (*in* dans).
b (*gen*) figurer. **fish often ~s on the menu** le poisson figure souvent au menu; **a lack of public concern ~d prominently in the car-bomb story** l'indifférence du public a été un trait frappant dans l'affaire des voitures piégées.
-featured [ˈfiːtʃəd] adj *ending in comps*: **delicate/heavy-featured** aux traits délicats/lourds.
featureless [ˈfiːtʃəlɪs] adj anonyme, sans traits distinctifs.
Feb. abbr of **February**.
febrifuge [ˈfebrɪfjuːdʒ] adj, n fébrifuge *(m)*.
febrile [ˈfiːbraɪl] adj fébrile, fiévreux.
February [ˈfebrʊərɪ] n février *m*; *for phrases see* **September**.
feces [ˈfiːsiːz] npl (*US*) = **faeces**.
feckless [ˈfeklɪs] adj *person* inepte, incapable; *attempt* maladroit. **a ~ girl** une tête sans cervelle, une évaporée.
fecund [ˈfiːkənd] adj fécond.
fecundity [fɪˈkʌndɪtɪ] n fécondité *f*.
Fed [fed] 1 (*esp US*) abbr of **Federal, Federated** *and* **Federation**. 2 n a (*US* *) (abbr of **federal officer**) agent *m or* fonctionnaire *m* fédéral. b (*US*) (abbr of **Federal Reserve Board**) banque *f* centrale américaine.

fed [fed] 1 pret, ptp of **feed**. **well** ~ bien nourri. 2 comp ▸**fed up***: **to be fed up** en avoir assez, en avoir marre*; **I'm fed up waiting for him** j'en ai assez *or* j'en ai marre* de l'attendre; **he got fed up with it** il en a eu assez, il en a eu marre*; **to be fed up to the back teeth**‡ en avoir ras le bol ‡ (*with doing* de faire).

fedayee [fə'dɑːjiː] n, pl ~n fedayin *m inv*.

federal ['fedərəl] 1 adj fédéral.

2 comp ▸**Federal Aviation Administration** (*US*) Direction générale de l'aviation civile ▸**Federal Bureau of Investigation** (*US*) FBI *m*, ≈ police *f* judiciaire ▸**Federal Communications Commission** (*US Admin*) haute autorité de l'audio-visuel ▸**Federal court** (*US Jur*) cour fédérale ▸**federal crop insurance** (*US*) *système fédéral d'indemnisation des agriculteurs en cas de catastrophe naturelle* ▸**Federal Housing Administration** (*US*) mission *f* de contrôle des prêts au logement ▸**federal land bank** (*US Fin*) banque fédérale agricole ▸**Federal Maritime Board** (*US*) Conseil supérieur de la Marine marchande ▸**Federal Republic of Germany** Allemagne fédérale, République fédérale d'Allemagne ▸**Federal Reserve Board** banque *f* centrale américaine.

3 n (*US Hist*) fédéral *m*, nordiste *m*.

federalism ['fedərəlɪzəm] n fédéralisme *m*.

federalist ['fedərəlɪst] adj, n fédéraliste *(mf)*.

federate ['fedəreɪt] 1 vt fédérer. 2 vi se fédérer. 3 ['fedərɪt] adj fédéré.

federation [ˌfedə'reɪʃən] n fédération *f*.

federative ['fedərətɪv] adj fédératif. **the F~ Republic of ...** la République fédérative de ... .

fedora [fə'dɔːrə] n (*US*) chapeau mou, feutre mou.

fee [fiː] 1 n *[doctor, lawyer etc]* honoraires *mpl*; *[artist, speaker, footballer etc]* cachet *m*; *[director, administrator etc]* honoraires, jeton *m*; *[private tutor]* appointements *mpl*; (*Scol, Univ etc*) (*for tuition*) frais *mpl* de scolarité; (*for examination*) droits *mpl*; (*for board*) prix *m* de la pension. **what's his ~?** combien prend-il?; **is there a ~?** est-ce qu'il faut payer?; **entrance** ~ prix *or* droit d'entrée; **membership** ~ montant *m* de la cotisation; **registration** ~ droits d'inscription; **retaining** ~ acompte *m*; (*to lawyer*) provision *f*; **one had to pay a ~ in order to speak at the meetings** il fallait payer une cotisation *or* participer aux frais pour prendre la parole aux réunions; **you can borrow more books for a small** ~ *or* **on payment of a small** ~ contre une somme modique vous pouvez emprunter d'autres livres; (*Jur*) ~ **or other charges** redevances *fpl* ou autres droits; (*Jur*) ~ **for appeal** taxe *f* de recours.

2 comp ▸**fee-paying school** établissement (d'enseignement) privé ▸**fee-splitting** (*US*) (*gen*) partage *m* des honoraires; *[doctors]* dichotomie *f*.

feeble ['fiːbl] 1 adj *person* faible, débile, frêle; *light, pulse, sound* faible; *attempt, excuse* pauvre, piètre; *joke* piteux, faiblard*. **a ~ old man** un frêle vieillard; **she's such a ~ sort of girl** c'est une fille si molle. 2 comp ▸**feeble-minded** imbécile ▸**feeble-mindedness** imbécillité *f*.

feebleness ['fiːblnɪs] n *[person, pulse etc]* faiblesse *f*.

feebly ['fiːblɪ] adv *stagger, smile* faiblement; *say, explain* sans grande conviction.

feed [fiːd] (vb: pret, ptp **fed**) 1 n a (*NonC: gen*) alimentation *f*, nourriture *f*; (*pasture*) pâture *f*; (*hay etc*) fourrage *m*. **he's off his ~**‡ (*not hungry*) il n'a pas d'appétit; (*dejected*) il a un peu le cafard*; (*unwell*) il est un peu patraque*.

b (*portion of food*) ration *f*. **the baby has 5 ~s a day** (*breastfeeds*) le bébé a 5 tétées par jour; (*bottles*) le bébé a 5 biberons par jour; (*solid feeds*) le bébé a 5 repas par jour; ~ **of oats** picotin *m* d'avoine; **we had a good ~*** on a bien mangé *or* bien boulotté* *or* bien bouffé‡.

c (*Theat* *) (*comedian's cue line*) réplique *f* (*donnée par un faire-valoir*); (*straight man*) faire-valoir *m inv*.

d (*part of machine*) mécanisme *m* d'alimentation. (*Comput*) **sheet paper** ~ chargeur *m* feuille à feuille.

2 comp ▸**feedback** (*Elec*) réaction *f*, (*unwanted*) réaction parasite; (*Cybernetics*) rétroaction *f*, feed-back *m*; (*gen*) feed-back, réactions *fpl* ▸**feedback information** information *f* en retour ▸**feedbag** musette *f* mangeoire ▸**feed grains** céréales *fpl* fourragères ▸**feedpipe** tuyau *m* d'amenée ▸**feedstuffs** nourriture *f or* aliments *mpl* (pour animaux).

3 vt a (*provide food for: gen*) nourrir; *army etc* ravitailler; (*give food to*) *child, invalid, animal* donner à manger à; (*Brit*) *baby* (*breastfed*) allaiter; (*bottle-fed*) donner le biberon à; *[mother bird]* *baby bird* donner la becquée à. **there are 6 people/mouths to ~ in this house** il y a 6 personnes/bouches à nourrir dans cette maison; **what do you ~ your cat on?** que donnez-vous à manger à votre chat?; **have you fed the horses?** avez-vous donné à manger aux chevaux?; *[child]* **he can ~ himself now** il sait manger tout seul maintenant; **to ~ sth to sb** donner qch à manger à qn, nourrir qn de qch; **you shouldn't ~ him that** vous ne devriez pas lui faire manger cela *or* lui donner cela à manger; **we've fed him all the facts*** nous lui avons fourni toutes les données.

b *fire* entretenir, alimenter; *furnace, machine* alimenter. **to ~ the flames** (*lit*) attiser le feu; (*fig*) jeter de l'huile sur le feu (*fig*); **2 rivers ~ this reservoir** 2 rivières alimentent ce réservoir; **to ~ the parking meter** rajouter une pièce dans le parcmètre; **to ~ sth into a machine** mettre *or* introduire qch dans une machine; **to ~ data into a computer** alimenter un ordinateur en données.

c (*Theat* *) *comedian* donner la réplique à (*pour obtenir de lui la réponse comique*); (*prompt*) souffler à.

4 vi *[animal]* manger, se nourrir; (*on pasture*) paître, brouter; *[baby]* manger, (*at breast*) téter. (*lit, fig*) **to ~ on** se nourrir de.

▸**feed back** 1 vt sep *information, results* donner (en retour). 2 **feedback** n *see* **feed 2**.

▸**feed in** vt sep *tape, wire* introduire (*to* dans); *facts, information* fournir (*to* à).

▸**feed up** 1 vt sep *animal* engraisser; *geese* gaver; *person* faire manger plus *or* davantage. 2 **fed up*** adj *see* **fed 2**.

feeder ['fiːdəʳ] 1 n a (*one who gives food*) nourrisseur *m*; (*eater: person, animal*) mangeur *m*, -euse *f*. **a heavy ~** un gros mangeur. b (*device*) (*for chickens*) mangeoire *f* automatique; (*for cattle*) nourrisseur *m* automatique; (*for machine*) chargeur *m*. c (*Elec*) conducteur *m* alimentaire. d (*Brit*) (*bib*) bavette *f*, bavoir *m*; (*bottle*) biberon *m*. 2 comp *canal* d'amenée; *railway* secondaire; *road* d'accès ▸**feeder primary (school)** (*Brit Scol*) *école primaire d'où sont issus les élèves d'un collège donné* ▸**feeder stream** affluent *m*.

feeding ['fiːdɪŋ] 1 n alimentation *f*. 2 comp ▸**feeding bottle** (*esp Brit*) biberon *m* ▸**feeding grounds** (*gen*) aire *f* d'alimentation; *[grazing animals]* aire *f* de pâture ▸**feeding stuffs** nourriture *f or* aliments *mpl* (pour animaux).

feel [fiːl] (vb: pret, ptp **felt**) 1 n a (*NonC*) (*sense of touch*) toucher *m*; (*sensation*) sensation *f*. **cold to the ~** froid au toucher; **at the ~ of** au contact de; **to know sth by the ~ (of it)** reconnaître qch au toucher; **I don't like the ~ of wool against my skin** je n'aime pas la sensation de la laine contre la peau; (*fig*) **I don't like the ~ of it** ça ne me dit rien de bon *or* rien qui vaille; **let me have a ~!*** laisse-moi toucher!

b (*familiarity*) **he wants to get the ~ of the factory** il veut se faire une impression générale de l'usine; **you have to get the ~ of a new car** il faut se faire à une nouvelle voiture; (*intuition*) **to have a ~ for doing** savoir s'y prendre pour faire; **to have a ~ for music/languages/English** sentir la musique/avoir le sens des langues/avoir le sens de l'anglais.

2 vt a (*touch, explore*) palper, tâter. **the blind man felt the object to find out what it was** l'aveugle a palpé *or* tâté l'objet pour découvrir ce que c'était; **to ~ sb's pulse** tâter le pouls à qn; **~ the envelope and see if there's anything in it** palpez l'enveloppe pour voir s'il y a quelque chose dedans; (*lit*) **to ~ one's way** avancer *or* marcher à tâtons; (*fig*) **you'll have to ~ your way** il faut y aller à tâtons; **we are ~ing our way towards an agreement** nous tâtons le terrain pour parvenir à un accord; (*fig*) **I'm still ~ing my way around** j'essaie de m'y retrouver.

b (*experience, be aware of*) *blow, caress* sentir; *pain* sentir, ressentir; *sympathy, grief* éprouver, ressentir. **I can ~ something pricking me** je sens quelque chose qui me pique; **I'm so cold I can't ~ anything** j'ai si froid que je ne sens plus rien; **I felt the water getting hot** j'ai senti que l'eau devenait chaude; **she could ~ the heat from the radiator** elle sentait la chaleur du radiateur; **to ~ the heat/cold** être sensible à la chaleur/au froid; **I don't ~ the heat much** la chaleur ne me gêne pas beaucoup; **she ~s the cold terribly** elle est terriblement frileuse; **I felt a few drops of rain** j'ai senti quelques gouttes de pluie; **he felt it move** il l'a senti bouger; **I ~ no interest in it** cela ne m'intéresse pas du tout; **to ~ o.s. doing sth** (*involuntarily*) se sentir faire qch, se rendre compte que l'on fait qch; **he felt a great sense of relief** il a éprouvé *or* ressenti un grand soulagement; **they couldn't help ~ing the justice of his remarks** ils ne pouvaient qu'apprécier la justesse de ses paroles, ils étaient pleinement conscients de la justesse de ses paroles; **I do ~ the importance of this** j'ai pleinement conscience de l'importance de ceci; **you must ~ the beauty of this music before you can play it** il faut que vous sentiez (*subj*) la beauté de la musique avant de pouvoir la jouer vous-même; (*US*) **to ~ one's oats*** (*feel high-spirited*) se sentir en pleine forme; (*feel important*) faire l'important; **the effects will be felt later** les effets se feront sentir plus tard; **he ~s his position very much** il est très conscient de la difficulté de sa situation; **she felt the loss of her father greatly** elle a été très affectée par la mort de son père, elle a vivement ressenti la perte de son père.

c (*think*) avoir l'impression, considérer, estimer. **I ~ he has spoilt everything** j'ai l'impression *or* il me semble qu'il a tout gâché; **I ~ that he ought to go** je considère *or* j'estime qu'il devrait y aller; **I ~ it in my bones that I am right** quelque chose (en moi) me dit que j'ai raison; **he felt it necessary to point out ...** il a jugé *or* estimé nécessaire de faire remarquer ...; **I ~ strongly that** je suis convaincu que; **if you ~ strongly about it** si cela vous tient à cœur, si cela vous semble important; **what do you ~ about this idea?** que pensez-vous de cette idée?, quel est votre sentiment sur cette idée?

3 vi a (*of physical state*) se sentir. **to ~ cold/hot/hungry/thirsty/sleepy** avoir froid/chaud/faim/soif/sommeil; **to ~ old/ill** se sentir vieux/malade; **he felt like a young man again** il se sentait redevenu jeune homme; **I ~ (like) a new man (*or* woman)** je me sens renaître *or* revivre; **how do you ~ today?** comment vous sentez-vous aujourd'hui?; **I ~ much better** je me sens beaucoup mieux; **you'll ~ all the better for a rest** vous vous sentirez mieux après vous être reposé; **he doesn't ~ quite himself today** il ne se sent pas tout à fait dans son assiette

aujourd'hui; **I felt as if I was going to faint** j'avais l'impression que j'allais m'évanouir; **to ~ up to doing** se sentir capable de faire; **I'm afraid I don't ~ up to it** je crois malheureusement que je ne m'en sens pas capable; *see* **equal.**

b (*of mental or moral state*) être. **I ~ sure that ...** je suis sûr que ...; **they don't ~ able to recommend him** ils estiment qu'ils ne peuvent pas le recommander; **he ~s confident of success** il s'estime capable de réussir; **we felt very touched by his remarks** nous avons été très touchés par ses remarques; **I don't ~ ready to see her again yet** je ne me sens pas encore prêt à la revoir; **I ~ very bad about leaving you here** cela m'ennuie beaucoup de vous laisser ici; **how do you ~ about him?** que pensez-vous de lui?; **how do you ~ about (going for) a walk?** est-ce que cela vous dit d'aller vous promener?; **I ~ as if there's nothing we can do** j'ai le sentiment que nous ne pouvons rien faire; **she felt as if she could do whatever she liked** elle avait l'impression qu'elle pouvait faire tout ce qu'elle voulait; **what does it ~ like** *or* **how does it ~ to know that you are a success?** quel effet cela vous fait-il de savoir que vous avez réussi?; **to ~ like doing** avoir envie de faire; **he felt like an ice cream*** il avait envie d'une glace; **if you ~ like it** si le cœur vous en dit; **I don't ~ like it** je n'en ai pas envie, cela ne me dit rien; **to ~ for sb** compatir aux malheurs de qn; **we ~ for you in your sorrow** nous partageons votre douleur; **I ~ for you!** comme je vous comprends!; *see* **sorry** *etc.*

c *[objects]* **to ~ hard/soft** être dur/doux (*f* douce) au toucher; **the house ~s damp** la maison donne l'impression d'être humide; **the box ~s as if** *or* **as though it has been mended** au toucher on dirait que la boîte a été réparée; **this material is so soft it ~s like silk** ce tissu est si doux qu'on dirait de la soie; **the car travelled so fast it felt like flying** la voiture filait si rapidement qu'on se serait cru en avion; **it ~s like rain** on dirait qu'il va pleuvoir; **it ~s like thunder** il y a de l'orage dans l'air.

d (*grope: also* **~ about, ~ around**) tâtonner, fouiller. **she felt (about** *or* **around) in her pocket for some change** elle a fouillé dans sa poche pour trouver de la monnaie; **he was ~ing (about** *or* **around) in the dark for the door** il tâtonnait dans le noir pour trouver la porte.

►**feel out*** vt sep (*US*) *person* sonder, tâter le terrain auprès de.

►**feel up‡** vt sep: **to feel sb up** peloter* qn.

feeler ['fiːləʳ] 1 n *[insect]* antenne *f*; *[octopus etc]* tentacule *m.* (*fig*) **to throw out** *or* **put out a ~** *or* **~s** tâter le terrain (*to discover* pour découvrir), tâter l'opinion, lancer un ballon d'essai. 2 comp ►**feeler gauge** (*Tech*) calibre *m* (d'épaisseur).

feeling ['fiːlɪŋ] n a (*NonC: physical*) sensation *f.* **I've lost all ~ in my right arm** j'ai perdu toute sensation dans le bras droit, mon bras droit ne sent plus rien; **a ~ of cold, a cold ~** une sensation de froid.

b (*awareness, impression*) sentiment *m.* **a ~ of isolation** un sentiment d'isolement; **he had the ~ (that) something dreadful would happen to him** il avait le sentiment *or* le pressentiment que quelque chose de terrible lui arriverait; **I've a funny ~ she will succeed** j'ai comme l'impression *or* comme le sentiment qu'elle va réussir; **I know the ~!** je sais ce que c'est *or* ce que ça fait!; **the ~ of the meeting was against the idea** le sentiment *or* l'opinion *f* de l'assemblée était contre l'idée; **there was a general ~ that ...** on avait l'impression que ..., le sentiment général a été que ...; *see* **strong.**

c (*emotions*) **~s** sentiments *mpl*, sensibilité *f*; **he appealed to their ~s rather than their reason** il faisait appel à leurs sentiments plutôt qu'à leur raison; **a ~ of joy came over her** la joie l'a envahie; **you can imagine my ~s** tu t'imagines ce que je ressens (*or* j'ai ressenti *etc*); **~s ran high about the new motorway** la nouvelle autoroute a déchaîné les passions; **his ~s were hurt** on l'avait blessé *or* froissé (dans ses sentiments); *see* **hard.**

d (*NonC*) (*sensitivity*) sentiment *m*, émotion *f*, sensibilité *f*; (*compassion*) sympathie *f.* **a woman of great ~** une femme très sensible; **she sang with ~** elle a chanté avec sentiment; **he spoke with great ~** il a parlé avec chaleur *or* avec émotion; **he doesn't show much ~ for his sister** il ne fait pas preuve de beaucoup de sympathie pour sa sœur; **he has no ~ for the suffering of others** les souffrances d'autrui le laissent insensible *or* froid; **he has no ~ for music** il n'apprécie pas du tout la musique; **he has a certain ~ for music** il est assez sensible à la musique; **ill** *or* **bad ~** animosité *f*, hostilité *f.*

feelingly ['fiːlɪŋlɪ] adv *speak, write* avec émotion, avec chaleur.

feet [fiːt] npl of **foot.**

feign [feɪn] vt *surprise* feindre; *madness* simuler. **to ~ illness/sleep** faire semblant d'être malade/de dormir; **~ed modesty** fausse modestie, modestie feinte.

feint [feɪnt] 1 n (*Boxing, Fencing, Mil*) feinte *f.* **to make a ~** faire une feinte (*at* à). 2 vi feinter. 3 comp ►**feint-ruled paper** papier réglé (en impression légère).

feist* [faɪst] n (*US*) roquet *m* (*chien*).

feisty* ['faɪstɪ] adj (*US*) (*lively*) fringant; (*quarrelsome*) bagarreur*.

feldspar ['feldspɑːʳ] n = **felspar.**

felicitate [fɪ'lɪsɪteɪt] vt féliciter, congratuler.

felicitous [fɪ'lɪsɪtəs] adj (*happy*) heureux; (*well-chosen*) bien trouvé, à propos, heureux.

felicity [fɪ'lɪsɪtɪ] n (*happiness*) félicité *f*, bonheur *m*; (*aptness*) bonheur, justesse *f*, à-propos *m.*

feline ['fiːlaɪn] adj, n félin(e) *m(f).*

fell[1] [fel] pret of **fall.**

fell[2] [fel] vt *tree, enemy* abattre; *ox* assommer, abattre.

fell[3] [fel] n (*Brit*) (*mountain*) montagne *f*, mont *m.* (*moorland*) **the ~s** la lande.

fell[4] [fel] adj (*liter*) *blow* féroce, cruel; *disease* cruel; *see* **swoop.**

fell[5] [fel] n (*hide, pelt*) fourrure *f*, peau *f* (d'animal).

fella‡ ['felə] n (*Brit*) (*chap*) type* *m*; (*boyfriend*) petit ami.

fellatio [fɪ'leɪʃɪəʊ], **fellation** [fɪ'leɪʃən] n fellation *f.*

fellow ['feləʊ] 1 n a homme *m*, type* *m*, individu *m* (*pej*). **a nice ~** un brave garçon, un brave type*; **an old ~** un vieux (bonhomme); **a poor old ~** un pauvre vieux; **some poor ~ will have to rewrite this** il y aura un pauvre malheureux qui devra récrire ceci; **poor little ~** pauvre petit (bonhomme *or* gars); **a young ~** un jeune homme, un garçon; **a ~ must have a bit of a rest!*** il faut bien qu'on se repose (*subj*) un peu!; **my dear ~** *or* **good ~**† mon cher; **look here, old ~**† écoute, mon vieux; **this journalist ~** ce journaliste.

b (*comrade*) camarade *m*, compagnon *m*; (*equal, peer*) pair *m*, semblable *m.* **~s in misfortune** frères *mpl* dans le malheur, compagnons d'infortune; **I can't find the ~ to this glove** je ne trouve pas le deuxième gant de cette paire *or* le frère de ce gant; **the ~ to this sock** la deuxième chaussette de cette paire, la sœur de cette chaussette; *see* **school**[1] *etc.*

c *[association, society etc]* membre *m*, associé *m* (*d'une société savante, d'une académie*).

d (*US Univ*) boursier *m*, -ière *f*; (*Brit Univ*) chargé *m* de cours (*qui est aussi membre du conseil d'administration d'un collège*); *see* **research.**

2 comp ►**fellow being** semblable *mf*, pareil(le) *m(f)* ►**fellow citizen** concitoyen(ne) *m(f)* ►**fellow countryman/-woman** compatriote *mf* ►**fellow creature** semblable *mf*, pareil(le) *m(f)* ►**fellow feeling** sympathie *f* ►**fellow member** confrère *m*, consœur *f*, collègue *mf* ►**fellow men** semblables *mpl* ►**fellow passenger** compagnon *m* de voyage, compagne *f* de voyage ►**fellow traveller** (*lit*) compagnon *m* de voyage, compagne *f* de voyage; (*Pol: with communists*) communisant(e) *m(f)*, cryptocommuniste *mf*; (*gen*) sympathisant(e) *m(f)* ►**fellow worker** (*in office*) collègue *mf*; (*in factory*) camarade *mf* (de travail).

fellowship ['feləʊʃɪp] n a (*NonC: comradeship*) amitié *f*, camaraderie *f*; (*Rel etc*) communion *f.* b (*society etc*) association *f*, corporation *f*; (*Rel*) confrérie *f.* c (*membership of learned society*) titre *m* de membre *or* d'associé (*d'une société savante*). d (*US Univ: scholarship*) bourse *f* universitaire; (*Brit Univ: post*) poste *m* de "fellow"; *see* **fellow 1d.**

felon ['felən] n (*Jur*) criminel(le) *m(f).*

felonious [fɪ'ləʊnɪəs] adj (*Jur*) criminel.

felony ['felənɪ] n (*Jur*) crime *m*, forfait *m.*

felspar ['felspɑːʳ] n feldspath *m.*

felt[1] [felt] pret, ptp of **feel.**

felt[2] [felt] 1 n feutre *m*; *see* **roofing.** 2 comp de feutre ►**felt hat** feutre *m* (*chapeau*) ►**felt-tip (pen)** feutre *m* (*crayon*).

fem‡ [fem] n = **femme‡.**

fem. [fem] a abbr of **female.** b abbr of **feminine.**

female ['fiːmeɪl] 1 adj *animal, plant* femelle (*also Tech*); *subject, slave* du sexe féminin; *company, vote* des femmes; *sex, character, quality, organs* féminin. **a ~ child** une enfant, une fille, un enfant du sexe féminin; **~ students** étudiantes *fpl*; **~ labour** main-d'œuvre féminine; (*Theat*) **~ impersonator** travesti *m.* 2 n (*person*) femme *f*, fille *f*; (*animal, plant*) femelle *f.* (*pej*) **there was a ~ there who ...*** il y avait là une espèce de bonne femme qui ...* (*pej*).

feminine ['femɪnɪn] 1 adj (*also Gram*) féminin. 2 n (*Gram*) féminin *m.* **in the ~** au féminin.

femininity [ˌfemɪ'nɪnɪtɪ] n féminité *f.*

feminism ['femɪnɪzəm] n féminisme *m.*

feminist ['femɪnɪst] n, adj féministe *(mf).*

femlib‡ ['fem'lɪb] n (abbr of **female liberation**) M.L.F. *m.*

femme [fæm, fem] n a **~ fatale** femme fatale. b (‡: *US*) homosexuel *m* passif.

femoral ['femərəl] adj fémoral.

femur ['fiːməʳ] n, pl **~s** *or* **femora** ['femərə] fémur *m.*

fen [fen] n (*Brit: also* **fenland**) marais *m*, marécage *m.* **the F~s** les plaines marécageuses du Norfolk.

fence [fens] 1 n a barrière *f*, palissade *f*, clôture *f*; (*Racing*) obstacle *m.* (*fig*) **to sit on the ~** ménager la chèvre et le chou, s'abstenir de prendre position; (*fig*) **to mend one's ~s*** (*gen*) rétablir sa réputation; (*with sb*) se réconcilier (avec qn); (*US Pol*) veiller à ses intérêts électoraux; *see* **barbed.** b (*machine guard*) barrière protectrice. c (*‡: of stolen goods*) receleur *m*, fourgue *m.* 2 vt a (*also* **~ in**) *land* clôturer, entourer d'une clôture. b (*fig*) *question* éluder. 3 vi (*Sport*) faire de l'escrime; (*fig*) éluder la question, se dérober. (*Sport*) **to ~ with sword/sabre** *etc* tirer à l'épée/au sabre *etc.*

►**fence in** vt sep a (*lit*) = **fence 2a.** b (*fig*) **to feel fenced in by restrictions** se sentir gêné *or* entravé par des restrictions.

►**fence off** vt sep *piece of land* séparer par une clôture.
fencer ['fensəʳ] n escrimeur *m*, -euse *f*.
fencing ['fensɪŋ] 1 n a (*Sport*) escrime *f*. b (*for making fences*) matériaux *mpl* pour clôture. 2 comp ►**fencing master** maître *m* d'armes ►**fencing match** assaut *m* d'escrime ►**fencing school** salle *f* d'armes.
fend [fend] vi: **to ~ for o.s.** se débrouiller (tout seul).
►**fend off** vt sep *blow* parer; *attack* détourner; *attacker* repousser; *awkward question* écarter, éluder.
fender ['fendəʳ] 1 n (*in front of fire*) garde-feu *m inv*; (*US Aut*) aile *f*; (*US Rail*) chasse-pierres *m inv*; (*Naut*) défense *f*, pare-battage *m inv*. 2 comp ►**fender-bender***: **it was just a fender-bender** c'était seulement un accrochage *or* de la tôle froissée*.
fenestration [ˌfenɪs'treɪʃən] n (*Archit*) fenêtrage *m*; (*Med*) fenestration *f*; (*Bot, Zool*) aspect fenêtré.
fennel ['fenl] n fenouil *m*.
fenugreek ['fenjʊˌgriːk] n fenugrec *m*.
feral ['fɪərəl] adj sauvage.
ferment [fə'ment] 1 vi (*lit, fig*) fermenter. 2 vt (*lit, fig*) faire fermenter. 3 ['fɜːment] n (*lit*) ferment *m*; (*fig*) agitation *f*, effervescence *f*. **city in a state of ~** ville en effervescence.
fermentation [ˌfɜːmen'teɪʃən] n (*lit, fig*) fermentation *f*.
fermium ['fɜːmɪəm] n fermium *m*.
fern [fɜːn] n fougère *f*.
ferocious [fə'rəʊʃəs] adj féroce.
ferociously [fə'rəʊʃəslɪ] adv férocement, avec férocité.
ferociousness [fə'rəʊʃəsnɪs] n, **ferocity** [fə'rɒsɪtɪ] n férocité *f*.
Ferrara [fə'rɑːrə] n Ferrare.
ferret ['ferɪt] 1 n (*Zool*) furet *m*. 2 vi a (*also* **~ about**, **~ around**) fouiller, fureter. **she was ~ing (about *or* around) among my books** elle furetait dans mes livres. b **to go ~ing** chasser au furet.
►**ferret out** vt sep *secret, person* dénicher, découvrir.
Ferris wheel ['ferɪswiːl] n grande roue (*dans une foire*).
ferrite ['feraɪt] n ferrite *f*.
ferro- ['ferəʊ] pref ferro-.
ferroconcrete ['ferəʊ'kɒŋkriːt] n béton armé.
ferrous ['ferəs] adj ferreux.
ferrule ['feruːl] n virole *f*.
ferry ['ferɪ] 1 n a (*also* **~boat**) (*small: for people, cars*) bac *m*; (*Can*) traversier *m*; (*larger: for people, cars, trains*) ferry(-boat) *m*; (*between ship and quayside*) va-et-vient *m inv*. **~man** passeur *m*; *see* **air, car**. b (*place*) passage *m*. 2 vt a (*also* **~ across**, **~ over**) *person, car, train* faire passer (en bac *or* par bateau *or* par avion *etc*). b (*fig: transport*) *people* transporter, emmener, conduire; *things* porter, apporter. **he ferried voters to and from the polls** il a fait la navette avec sa voiture pour emmener les électeurs au bureau de vote.
fertile ['fɜːtaɪl] adj *land* fertile; *person, animal, mind, egg* fécond; *imagination* fécond, fertile.
fertility [fə'tɪlɪtɪ] 1 n (*see* **fertile**) fertilité *f*; fécondité *f*. 2 comp *cult, symbol* de fertilité ►**fertility drug** (*Med*) médicament *m* contre la stérilité.
fertilization [ˌfɜːtɪlaɪ'zeɪʃən] n *[land, soil]* fertilisation *f*; *[animal, plant, egg]* fécondation *f*.
fertilize ['fɜːtɪlaɪz] vt *land, soil* fertiliser, amender; *animal, plant, egg* féconder.
fertilizer ['fɜːtɪlaɪzəʳ] n engrais *m*. **artificial ~** engrais chimique.
fervent ['fɜːvənt] adj fervent, ardent.
fervently ['fɜːvəntlɪ] adv avec ferveur, ardemment.
fervid ['fɜːvɪd] adj = **fervent**.
fervour, (*US*) **fervor** ['fɜːvəʳ] n ferveur *f*.
fester ['festəʳ] vi *[cut, wound]* suppurer; *[anger, resentment]* couver. **the insult ~ed** l'injure lui est restée sur le cœur.
festival ['festɪvəl] n (*Rel etc*) fête *f*; (*Mus etc*) festival *m*. **the Edinburgh F~** le festival d'Édimbourg.
festive ['festɪv] adj de fête. **the ~ season** la période des fêtes; **to be in a ~ mood** être en veine de réjouissances.
festivity [fes'tɪvɪtɪ] n a (*also* **festivities**) fête *f*, réjouissances *fpl*. b (*festival*) fête *f*.
festoon [fes'tuːn] 1 n feston *m*, guirlande *f*. 2 vt festonner, orner de festons; *building, town* pavoiser. **a room ~ed with posters** une pièce tapissée d'affiches.
fetch [fetʃ] 1 vt a (*go and get*) *person, thing* aller chercher; (*bring*) *person* amener; *thing* apporter. (*fig*) **to ~ and carry for sb** faire la bonne pour qn; (*to dog*) **~ (it)!** rapporte!, va chercher! b *sigh, groan* pousser. c (*sell for*) *money* rapporter. **they won't ~ much** ils ne rapporteront pas grand-chose; **it ~ed a good price** ça a atteint *or* fait* une jolie somme *or* un joli prix, c'est parti pour une jolie somme. d *blow* flanquer*. 2 vi (*Naut*) manœuvrer. 3 n (*Naut*) fetch *m*.
►**fetch in** vt sep *person* faire (r)entrer; *thing* rentrer.
►**fetch out** vt sep *person* faire sortir; *thing* sortir (*of* de).
►**fetch up** 1 vi finir par arriver, se retrouver (*at* à, *in* dans). 2 vt sep a *object* apporter, monter; *person* faire monter. b (*Brit fig: vomit*) rendre, vomir.
fetching ['fetʃɪŋ] adj *smile* attrayant; *person* charmant, séduisant; *dress, hat* ravissant, très seyant.
fête [feɪt] 1 n (*Brit*) fête *f*; (*for charity*) fête, kermesse *f*. **village ~** fête de village. 2 vt *person* faire fête à; *success, arrival* fêter.
fetid ['fetɪd] adj fétide, puant.
fetish ['fetɪʃ] n fétiche *m* (*objet de culte*); (*Psych*) objet *m* de la fétichisation. (*fig*) **she makes a real ~ of cleanliness** elle est obsédée par la propreté, c'est une maniaque de la propreté.
fetishism ['fetɪʃɪzəm] n fétichisme *m*.
fetishist ['fetɪʃɪst] n fétichiste *mf*. **to be a silk/foot ~** être un(e) obsédé(e) *m(f)* de la soie/avoir une obsession sexuelle pour le pied.
fetishistic [ˌfetɪ'ʃɪstɪk] adj fétichiste.
fetlock ['fetlɒk] n (*joint*) boulet *m*; (*hair*) fanon *m*.
fetoscope ['fiːtəʊˌskəʊp] n fœtoscope *m*.
fetoscopy [fiː'tɒskəpɪ] n fœtoscopie *f*.
fetter ['fetəʳ] 1 vt *person* enchaîner, lier; *horse, slave* entraver; (*fig*) entraver. 2 npl: **~s** *[prisoner]* fers *mpl*, chaînes *fpl*; *[horse, slave]* (*also fig*) entraves *fpl*; **to put a prisoner in ~s** mettre un prisonnier aux fers; **in ~s** dans les fers *or* les chaînes.
fettle ['fetl] n: **in fine *or* good ~** en pleine forme, en bonne condition.
fetus ['fiːtəs] n (*US*) = **foetus**.
feu [fjuː] n (*Scot Jur*) bail perpétuel (*à redevance fixe*). **~ duty** loyer *m* (de la terre).
feud[1] [fjuːd] 1 n querelle *f*, (*stronger*) vendetta *f*. **family ~s** querelles de famille, dissensions *fpl* domestiques. 2 vi se quereller, se disputer. **to ~ with sb** être l'ennemi juré de qn, être à couteaux tirés avec qn.
feud[2] [fjuːd] n (*Hist*) fief *m*.
feudal ['fjuːdl] adj féodal. **the ~ system** le système féodal.
feudalism ['fjuːdəlɪzəm] n (*Hist*) féodalité *f*; (*fig*) *[society, institution etc]* féodalisme *m*.
fever ['fiːvəʳ] n (*Med, fig*) fièvre *f*. **a bout of ~** un accès de fièvre; **high ~** forte fièvre; **raging ~** fièvre de cheval*; **he has no ~** il n'a pas de fièvre *or* de température; (*fig*) **the gambling ~** le démon du jeu; **a ~ of impatience** une impatience fébrile; **enthusiasm reached ~ pitch** l'enthousiasme était à son comble; *see* **glandular, scarlet** *etc*.
fevered ['fiːvəd] adj *brow* brûlant de fièvre; (*fig*) *imagination* exalté.
feverish ['fiːvərɪʃ] adj (*Med*) *person* fiévreux; *condition* fiévreux, fébrile; *swamp, climate* malsain; (*fig*) *state, activity, excitement* fiévreux, fébrile.
feverishly ['fiːvərɪʃlɪ] adv fiévreusement, fébrilement.
feverishness ['fiːvərɪʃnɪs] n (*Med*) état *m* fébrile; (*fig*) fébrilité *f*.
few [fjuː] adj, pron a (*not many*) peu (de). **~ books** peu de livres; **very ~ books** très peu de livres; **~ of them came** peu d'entre eux sont venus, quelques-uns d'entre eux seulement sont venus; **~ (people) come to see him** peu de gens viennent le voir; **he is one of the ~ people who ...** c'est l'une des rares personnes qui ... + *indic or subj*; **we have travelled a lot in the past ~ days** nous avons beaucoup voyagé ces jours-ci *or* ces derniers jours; **these past ~ weeks** ces dernières semaines; **the next ~ days** les (quelques) jours qui viennent; **with ~ exceptions** à de rares exceptions près; **the exceptions are ~** les exceptions sont rares *or* peu nombreuses; **she goes to town every ~ days** elle va à la ville tous les deux ou trois jours; **~ and far between** rares; **such occasions are ~** de telles occasions sont rares; **we are very ~ (in number)** nous sommes peu nombreux; (*liter*) **our days are ~** nos jours sont comptés; **I'll spend the remaining ~ minutes alone** je passerai seul le peu de *or* les quelques minutes qui me restent; **there are always the ~ who think that ...** il y a toujours la minorité qui croit que ...; **the ~ who know him** les rares personnes qui le connaissent; (*Brit Aviat Hist*) **the F~** *les héros de la Bataille d'Angleterre*; *see* **happy, word** *etc*.
b (*after adv*) **I have as ~ books as you** j'ai aussi peu de livres que vous; **I have as ~ as you** j'en ai aussi peu que vous; **there were as ~ as 6 objections** il n'y a eu en tout et pour tout que 6 objections; **how ~ there are!** qu'il y en a peu!; **how ~ they are!** qu'ils sont peu nombreux!; **however ~ books you (may) buy** si peu de livres que l'on achète (*subj*), même si l'on achète peu de livres; **however ~ there may be** si peu qu'il y en ait; **I've got so ~ already (that ...)** j'en ai déjà si peu (que ...); **so ~ have been sold** si peu se sont vendus; **so ~ books** tellement peu *or* si peu de livres; **there were too ~** il y en avait trop peu; **too ~ cakes** trop peu de gâteaux; **there were 3 too ~** il en manquait 3; **10 would not be too ~** 10 suffiraient, il (en) suffirait de 10; **I've got too ~ already** j'en ai déjà (bien) trop peu; **he has too ~ books** il a trop peu de livres; **there are too ~ of you** vous êtes trop peu nombreux, vous n'êtes pas assez nombreux; **too ~ of them realize that ...** trop peu d'entre eux sont conscients que ... .
c (*some, several*) **a ~** quelques(-uns), quelques(-unes); **a ~ books** quelques livres; **I know a ~ of these people** je connais quelques-uns de ces gens; **a ~ *or* (*liter*) some ~ thought otherwise** quelques-uns pensaient autrement; **I'll take just a ~** j'en prendrai quelques-uns (*or* quelques-unes) seulement; **I'd like a ~ more** j'en voudrais quelques-un(e)s de plus; **quite a ~ books** pas mal* de livres; **quite a ~ did not believe him** pas mal* de gens ne l'ont pas cru; **I saw a good ~ *or* quite a ~ people there** j'y ai vu pas mal* de gens; **he has had a good ~ (drinks)** il a pas mal* bu; **we'll go in a ~ minutes** nous partirons dans quelques minutes; **a ~ of us** quelques-un(e)s d'entre nous; **there were only a ~ of us** nous n'étions qu'une poignée; **a good ~ of the books are**

... bon nombre de ces livres sont ...; **we must wait a ~ more days** il nous faut attendre encore quelques jours *or* attendre quelques jours de plus.

fewer ['fju:ər] **adj, pron** (**compar of few**) moins (de). **we have sold ~ this year** nous en avons moins vendu cette année; **he has ~ books than you** il a moins de livres que vous; **we are ~ (in number) than last time** nous sommes moins nombreux que la dernière fois; **~ people than we expected** moins de gens que nous (ne) l'escomptions; **there are ~ opportunities for doing it** les occasions de le faire sont plus rares, il y a moins d'occasions de le faire; **no ~ than 37 pupils were ill** il y a eu pas moins de 37 élèves malades; **the ~ the better** moins il y en a mieux c'est *or* mieux ça vaut; **few came and ~ stayed** peu sont venus et encore moins sont restés.

fewest ['fju:ɪst] **adj, pron** (**superl of few**) le moins (de). **he met her on the ~ occasions possible** il l'a rencontrée le moins souvent possible; **we were ~ in number then** c'est à ce moment-là que nous étions le moins nombreux; **we sold ~ last year** c'est l'année dernière que nous en avons le moins vendu; **I've got (the) ~** c'est moi qui en ai le moins; **he has (the) ~ books** c'est lui qui a le moins de livres.

fey [feɪ] **adj** extra-lucide, visionnaire.

fez [fez] **n, pl fezzes** fez *m*.

F.F.A. [ˌefef'eɪ] (**abbr of Future Farmers of America**) *club agricole*.

F.F.V. [ˌefef'viː] (**abbr of First Families of Virginia**) *descendants des premiers colons de Virginie*.

FH (**abbr of fire hydrant**) *see* **fire**.

FHA (*US*) (**abbr of Federal Housing Administration**) **~ loan** *prêt à la construction*.

fiancé [fɪ'ɑ̃:ŋseɪ] **n** fiancé *m*.

fiancée [fɪ'ɑ̃:ŋseɪ] **n** fiancée *f*.

fiasco [fɪ'æskəʊ] **n, pl ~s** *or* **~es** fiasco *m*. **the play was a ~** la pièce a fait un four *or* a été un four *or* a été un fiasco; **the whole undertaking was a ~** *or* **ended in a ~** l'entreprise tout entière a tourné au désastre *or* a fait fiasco.

fiat ['faɪæt] **n** décret *m*, ordonnance *f*.

fib* [fɪb] **1 n** bobard* *m*, blague* *f*, mensonge *m*. **2 vi** raconter des bobards* *or* des blagues*. **you're ~bing!** ce que tu racontes c'est des blagues!*

fibber ['fɪbər] **n** blagueur* *m*, -euse *f*, menteur *m*, -euse *f*. **you ~!** espèce de menteur!

fibre, (*US*) **fiber** ['faɪbər] **1 n a** *[wood, cotton, muscle etc]* fibre *f*. **cotton ~** fibre de coton; **synthetic ~s** fibres synthétiques, synthétiques *mpl*; (*fig*) **a man of ~** un homme qui a de la trempe; **a man of great moral ~** un homme d'une grande force morale.

b (*dietary*) fibres *fpl*, cellulose *f* végétale.

2 comp ▸fibreboard panneau fibreux **▸(high) fibre diet** alimentation *f* riche en fibres **▸fibrefill,** (*US*) **fiberfill** rembourrage *m* synthétique **▸fibreglass,** (*US*) **fiberglass, Fiberglas** ® fibre *f* de verre **▸fibreoptic cable** câble *m* en fibres optiques **▸fibreoptic link** liaison *f* par fibre optique **▸fibre optics** la fibre optique **▸fibrescope,** (*US*) **fiberscope** fibroscope *m* **▸fibre-tip (pen)** (*Brit*) stylo *m* pointe fibre.

fibril ['faɪbrɪl], **fibrilla** [faɪ'brɪlə] **n** fibrille *f*.

fibrillation [ˌfaɪbrɪ'leɪʃən] **n** fibrillation *f*.

fibrin ['fɪbrɪn] **n** fibrine *f*.

fibrinogen [fɪ'brɪnədʒən] **n** fibrinogène *m*.

fibroid ['faɪbrɔɪd] **n = fibroma.**

fibroma [faɪ'brəʊmə] **n, pl ~s** *or* **fibromata** [ˌfaɪ'brəʊmətə] (*Med*) fibrome *m*.

fibrositis [ˌfaɪbrə'saɪtɪs] **n** aponévrite *f*.

fibrous ['faɪbrəs] **adj** fibreux.

fibula ['fɪbjʊlə] **n, pl ~s** *or* **fibulae** ['fɪbjʊˌliː] péroné *m*.

fickle ['fɪkl] **adj** inconstant, volage.

fickleness ['fɪklnɪs] **n** inconstance *f*.

fiction ['fɪkʃən] **n a** (*NonC: Literat*) **(works of) ~** romans *mpl*; **a writer of ~** un romancier; **light ~** romans faciles à lire; **romantic ~** romans à l'eau-de-rose (*pej*); **truth is stranger than ~** les faits dépassent la fiction; *see* **science. b** (*sth made up*) fiction *f*, création *f* de l'imagination. **a legal ~** une fiction légale; **his account was a complete ~** son récit était fictif; (*unjustified belief*) **there is still this ~ that you can find a job if you try hard enough** il y a encore des gens qui croient qu'en se donnant du mal, on arrive à trouver du travail. **c** (*NonC: the unreal*) le faux; *see* **fact.**

fictional ['fɪkʃənl] **adj** fictif. **a ~ character** un personnage imaginaire *or* fictif.

fictionalize ['fɪkʃənəlaɪz] **vt** romancer.

fictitious [fɪk'tɪʃəs] **adj** (*false, not genuine*) fictif; (*imaginary*) fictif, imaginaire.

Fid. Def. (**abbr of Fidei Defensor = Defender of the Faith**) Défenseur *m* de la foi.

fiddle ['fɪdl] **1 n a** (*violin*) violon *m*, crincrin* *m* (*pej*); *see* **fit[1], long[1], second[1].**

b (*esp Brit *: cheating*) truc* *m*, combine* *f*. **it was all a ~** tout ça c'était une combine*; **tax ~** fraude fiscale; **he's on the ~** il traficote*.

2 comp ▸fiddle-faddle!*, fiddlesticks!* quelle blague!*

3 vi a (*Mus*) jouer du violon, violoner*. **to ~ while Rome burns** se perdre en futilités en face de l'adversité.

b do stop fiddling (about *or* **around)!** tiens-toi donc tranquille!; **to ~ (about** *or* **around) with a pencil** tripoter un crayon; **he's fiddling (about** *or* **around) with the car** il tripote *or* bricole la voiture; **stop fiddling (about** *or* **around) over that job** arrête de perdre ton temps à faire ça.

c (*esp Brit *: cheat*) faire de la fraude, traficoter*.

4 vt a (*esp Brit **) *accounts, expenses claim* truquer. **to ~ one's tax return** truquer sa déclaration d'impôts; **he's ~d himself (into) a job** il s'est débrouillé* pour se faire nommer à un poste.

b (*Mus*) violoner*.

▸fiddle about, fiddle around vi: he's fiddling about in the garage il est en train de s'occuper vaguement *or* de bricoler dans le garage; **we just fiddled about yesterday** on n'a rien fait de spécial hier, on a seulement traînassé hier; *see also* **fiddle 3b.**

fiddler ['fɪdlər] **n a** joueur *m*, -euse *f* de violon, violoneux* *m* (*often pej*). **b** (*esp Brit *: cheat*) combinard* *m*.

fiddling ['fɪdlɪŋ] **1 adj** futile, insignifiant. **~ little jobs** menus travaux sans importance. **2 n** (**: dishonesty*) combine(s)* *f(pl)*.

fiddly ['fɪdlɪ] **adj** *task* minutieux, délicat (*et* agaçant); *object* délicat à utiliser, embêtant* à manier.

fidelity [fɪ'delɪtɪ] **n a** fidélité *f*, loyauté *f* (*to* à); (*in marriage*) fidélité. **b** *[translation etc]* exactitude *f*, fidélité *f*; *see* **high.**

fidget ['fɪdʒɪt] **1 vi** (*wriggle: also* **~ about, ~ around**) remuer, gigoter*; (*grow impatient*) donner des signes d'impatience. **stop ~ing!** reste donc tranquille!, arrête de bouger!; **to ~ (about** *or* **around) with sth** tripoter qch. **2 n: to be a ~** *[child]* être très remuant, ne jamais se tenir tranquille; *[adult]* être très nerveux, ne jamais tenir en place; **to have the ~s** avoir la bougeotte*.

fidgety ['fɪdʒɪtɪ] **adj** *child etc* remuant, agité. **to feel ~** ne plus tenir en place, s'impatienter.

fiduciary [fɪ'djuːʃɪərɪ] **adj, n** fiduciaire *(mf)*.

fief [fiːf] **n** fief *m*.

field [fiːld] **1 n a** (*Agr etc*) champ *m*; (*Miner*) gisement *m*. **in the ~s** dans les champs, aux champs; **this machine had a year's trial in the ~** cette machine a eu un an d'essais sur le terrain; (*Comm*) **to be first in the ~ with sth** être le premier à lancer qch; **work in the ~** enquête *f* sur place *or* sur le terrain; (*Mil*) **~ of battle** champ de bataille; **~ of honour** champ d'honneur; (*Mil*) **to take the ~** entrer en campagne (*see also* **1b**); **to hold the ~** (*Mil*) se maintenir sur ses positions; (*fig*) tenir tête à l'adversaire; (*Mil*) **to die in the ~** tomber *or* mourir au champ d'honneur; *see* **coal, gold, oil** *etc.*

b (*Sport*) terrain *m*. **the ~** (*Racing*) les concurrents *mpl* (*sauf le favori*); (*Hunting*) les chasseurs *mpl*; **football ~** terrain de football; **to take the ~** entrer en jeu; *see* **play.**

c (*sphere of activity etc*) domaine *m*, sphère *f*. **in the ~ of painting** dans le domaine de la peinture; **it's outside my ~** ce n'est pas de mon domaine *or* de ma compétence *or* dans mes cordes; **his particular ~ is Renaissance painting** la peinture de la Renaissance est sa spécialité.

d (*Phys: also* **~ of force**) champ *m*. **~ of vision** champ visuel *or* de vision; **gravitational ~** champ de gravitation; *see* **magnetic.**

e (*Comput*) champ *m*. (*Ling*) **(semantic) ~** champ (sémantique).

f (*expanse*) étendue *f*; (*Her*) champ *m*. (*Her*) **on a ~ of blue** en champ d'azur.

2 vt (*Sport*) *ball* attraper; *team* faire jouer. (*fig*) *[speaker etc]* **to ~ questions** répondre au pied levé (à des questions).

3 vi (*Sport*) être joueur de champ.

4 comp ▸field day (*Mil*) jour *m* de grandes manœuvres; (*gen*) grande occasion, grand jour; (*fig*) **the ice-cream sellers had a field day*** les marchands de glaces s'en sont donné à cœur joie **▸field engineering** (*Mil*) génie *f* d'opération **▸field event** (*Sport*) concours *m* **▸fieldfare** (*Orn*) litorne *f* **▸field glasses** jumelles *fpl* **▸field grown** de plein champ **▸field gun** canon *m* (de campagne) **▸field hand** (*US*) ouvrier *m*, -ière *f* agricole **▸field hockey** (*US*) hockey *m* sur gazon **▸field hospital** (*Mil*) antenne chirurgicale; (*Hist*) hôpital *m* de campagne **▸field house** (*US*) (*for changing*) vestiaire *m*; (*sports hall*) complexe sportif couvert **▸field kitchen** (*Mil*) cuisine roulante **▸field label** (*Ling*) domaine *m* **▸field marshal** (*Brit Mil*) ≃ maréchal *m* (de France) **▸fieldmouse** (*Zool*) mulot *m*, rat *m* des champs **▸field officer** (*Mil*) officier supérieur **▸field service** (*US Admin*) antenne *f* (*d'un service administratif*) **▸field sports** activités *fpl* de plein air (*surtout la chasse et la pêche*) **▸fieldsman** (*Cricket*) joueur *m* de champ **▸fieldstrip** (*US Mil*) *firearm* démonter (pour inspection) **▸field study** étude *f* *or* enquête *f* sur le terrain **▸field term** (*US Univ*) stage *m* pratique **▸field-test** (*Tech etc*) soumettre aux essais sur le terrain, tester (*Tech*) **▸field tests** (*Tech etc*) essais *mpl* sur le terrain **▸field trials** *[gundogs etc]* field trials *mpl*; *[machine etc]* essais *mpl* sur le terrain; (*Med*) essais cliniques **▸field trip** (*Educ*) sortie éducative, (*longer*) voyage *m* d'étude **▸field work** (*Archeol, Geol etc*) recherches *fpl* *or* enquête *f* sur le terrain; (*Soc*) travail *m* avec des cas sociaux **▸field worker** (*Archeol, Geol etc*) archéologue *mf* (*or* géologue *mf etc*) qui travaille sur le terrain; (*Soc*) ≃ assistant(e) *m(f)* de service social, assistant social.

fielder ['fiːldər] **n** (*Cricket*) joueur *m* de champ.

fiend [fi:nd] n a démon *m*; (*cruel person*) monstre *m*, démon. (*Rel: the Devil*) **the F~** le Malin; **that child's a real ~*** cet enfant est un petit monstre *or* est infernal*. b (*: *fanatic*) enragé(e) *m(f)*, mordu(e)* *m(f)*. **tennis ~** enragé *or* mordu* du tennis; **drug ~**† toxicomane *mf*; *see* **sex**.

fiendish ['fi:ndɪʃ] adj *cruelty, smile, plan* diabolique; (*: *unpleasant*) *evening, person, visit* sale* (*before n*), abominable. **to take a ~ delight in doing** prendre un plaisir diabolique à faire; **I had a ~ time* getting him to agree** j'ai eu un mal fou *or* un mal de chien* à obtenir son accord.

fiendishly ['fi:ndɪʃlɪ] adv diaboliquement; (*) *expensive, difficult* abominablement.

fierce [fɪəs] adj *animal, person, look, tone, gesture* féroce; *wind* furieux; *desire* ardent; (*lit*) *attack* violent; (*fig*) *speech* virulent, violent; *hatred* implacable; *heat* intense, torride; *competition, fighting* serré, acharné; *opponent, partisan, advocate* acharné.

fiercely ['fɪəslɪ] adv *behave* férocement; *attack* violemment; *fight, pursue, argue, advocate, oppose* avec acharnement; *speak* d'un ton féroce; *look* d'un air féroce *or* farouche.

fierceness ['fɪəsnɪs] n (*see* **fierce**) férocité *f*; fureur *f*; ardeur *f*; violence *f*; virulence *f*; implacabilité *f*; intensité *f*; acharnement *m*. **his ~ of manner** la violence de son comportement.

fiery ['faɪərɪ] adj *coals, sun* ardent; *heat, sands* brûlant; *sky* rougeoyant, embrasé; *person* fougueux, ardent; *speech* fougueux; *temper* violent. **~ eyes** des yeux qui étincellent *or* brillent de colère (*or* d'enthousiasme *etc*); **~-tempered** irascible, coléreux.

fiesta [fɪ'estə] n fiesta *f*.

FIFA ['fi:fə] n FIFA *f*, (*Fédération internationale de football-association*).

fife [faɪf] n fifre *m* (*instrument*).

FIFO ['faɪfəʊ] (abbr of **first in, first out**) PEPS.

fifteen [fɪf'ti:n] 1 adj quinze *inv*. **about ~ books** une quinzaine de livres. 2 n a quinze *m inv*. **about ~** une quinzaine. b (*Rugby*) quinze *m*. **the French ~** le quinze de France; *for other phrases see* **six**. 3 pron quinze *mfpl*. **there are ~** il y en a quinze.

fifteenth [fɪf'ti:nθ] 1 adj quinzième. 2 n quinzième *mf*; (*fraction*) quinzième *m*; *for phrases see* **sixth**.

fifth [fɪfθ] 1 adj cinquième. (*US Jur*) **to plead the F~ Amendment** invoquer le cinquième amendement pour refuser de répondre; (*fig: Pol etc*) **~ column** cinquième colonne *f*; (*fig*) **~-rate** de dernier ordre, de dernière catégorie; *for other phrases see* **sixth**. 2 n a (*gen*) cinquième *mf*; (*fraction*) cinquième *m*. (*US*) **to take the F~** (*Jur*) invoquer le cinquième amendement pour refuser de répondre; (* *fig*) refuser de parler; *for other phrases see* **sixth**. b (*Mus*) quinte *f*. c (*US*) (*measurement*) le cinquième d'un gallon (≃ 75 *cl*); (*bottle*) bouteille *f* (*d'alcool*).

fiftieth ['fɪftɪɪθ] 1 adj cinquantième. 2 n cinquantième *mf*; (*fraction*) cinquantième *m*.

fifty ['fɪftɪ] 1 adj cinquante *inv*. **about ~ books** une cinquantaine de livres. 2 n cinquante *m inv*. **about ~** une cinquantaine; (*fig*) **to go ~-~ with sb** se mettre de moitié avec qn, partager moitié-moitié avec qn; **we have a ~-~ chance of success** nous avons cinquante pour cent de chances *or* une chance sur deux de réussir; **it was a ~-~ deal** ils ont (*or* nous avons *etc*) fait moitié-moitié *or* cinquante-cinquante; *for other phrases see* **sixty**. 3 pron cinquante *mfpl*. **there are ~** il y en a cinquante.

fig [fɪg] 1 n (*fruit*) figue *f*; (*also* **~ tree**) figuier *m*. (*fig*) **I don't care a ~*** je m'en fiche*; **I don't give a ~ for that*** je m'en moque comme de ma première chemise*; **a ~ for all your principles!**† zut à tous vos principes!*. 2 comp ▸**fig leaf** (*Bot*) feuille *f* de figuier; (*on statue etc*) feuille de vigne.

fig. abbr of **figure 1b**.

fight [faɪt] (vb: pret, ptp **fought**) 1 n a (*between persons*) bagarre* *f*; (*brawl*) rixe *f*; (*Mil*) combat *m*, bataille *f*; (*Boxing*) combat; (*against disease, poverty etc*) lutte *f* (*against* contre); (*quarrel*) dispute *f*. (*lit, fig*) **he put up a good ~** il s'est bien défendu; **to have a ~ with sb** se battre avec qn, se bagarrer* avec qn; (*argue*) se disputer avec qn; **we're going to make a ~ of it** nous n'allons pas nous laisser battre comme ça, nous allons contre-attaquer; *see* **pick**.

b (*NonC: spirit*) **there was no ~ left in him** il n'avait plus envie de lutter, il n'avait plus de ressort; **he certainly shows ~** il faut reconnaître qu'il sait montrer les dents *or* qu'il ne se laisse pas faire.

2 comp ▸**fightback** (*Sport*) reprise *f*.

3 vi [*person, animal*] se battre (*with* avec, *against* contre); [*troops, countries*] se battre (*against* contre); (*fig*) lutter (*for* pour, *against* contre); (*quarrel*) se disputer (*with* avec). **the boys were ~ing in the street** les garçons se battaient dans la rue; **the dogs were ~ing over a bone** les chiens se disputaient un os; (*fig*) **to ~ shy of sth/sb** fuir devant qch/qn, tout faire pour éviter qch/qn; **to ~ shy of doing** éviter à tout prix de *or* répugner à faire; **to ~ against sleep** lutter contre le sommeil; **to ~ against disease** lutter contre *or* combattre la maladie; (*lit, fig*) **to ~ for sb** se battre pour qn; (*lit, fig*) **to ~ for one's life** lutter pour la *or* sa vie; **to be ~ing for breath** respirer à grand-peine; **he went down ~ing** il s'est battu jusqu'au bout.

4 vt *person, army* se battre avec *or* contre; *fire, disease* lutter contre, combattre. **to ~ a battle** livrer bataille; (*fig*) **to ~ a losing battle against sth** combattre qch en pure perte, se battre en pure perte contre qch; **we're ~ing a losing battle** nous livrons une bataille perdue d'avance; **to ~ a duel** se battre en duel; (*Pol etc*) **to ~ a campaign** mener une campagne, faire campagne; (*Jur*) **to ~ a case** défendre une cause; **we shall ~ this decision all the way** nous combattrons cette décision jusqu'au bout; **to ~ one's way out through the crowd** sortir en se frayant un passage à travers la foule.

▸**fight back** 1 vi (*in fight*) rendre les coups, répondre; (*Mil*) se défendre, résister; (*in argument*) répondre, se défendre; (*after illness*) se remettre, réagir; (*Sport*) se reprendre, effectuer une reprise. 2 vt sep *tears* refouler; *despair* lutter contre; *doubts* vaincre. 3 **fightback** n *see* **fight 2**.

▸**fight down** vt sep *anxiety, doubts* vaincre; *desire* refouler, réprimer.

▸**fight off** vt sep (*Mil*) *attack* repousser; (*fig*) *disease, sleep* lutter contre, résister à; *criticisms* répondre à.

▸**fight on** vi continuer le combat *or* la lutte.

▸**fight out** vt sep: **they fought it out** ils se sont bagarrés* pour régler la question; **leave them to fight it out** laissez-les se bagarrer* entre eux.

fighter ['faɪtə^r] 1 n a (*Boxing*) boxeur *m*, pugiliste *m*. (*fig*) **he's a ~** c'est un lutteur; *see* **prize**[1] *etc*. b (*also* **~ aircraft, ~ plane**) avion *m* de chasse, chasseur *m*. 2 comp ▸**fighter-bomber** (*Aviat*) chasseur bombardier *m*, avion *m* de combat polyvalent ▸**fighter pilot** pilote *m* de chasse.

fighting ['faɪtɪŋ] 1 n (*Mil*) combat *m*; (*in classroom, pub etc*) bagarres* *fpl*. **there was some ~ in the town** il y a eu des échauffourées dans la ville; *see* **bull**[1], **street** *etc*. 2 adj *person* combatif; (*Mil*) *troops* de combat. (*Mil*) **~ soldier, ~ man** combattant *m*; **he's got a lot of ~ spirit** c'est un lutteur, il a du cran*; **there's a ~ chance for her recovery** elle a une assez bonne chance de s'en tirer; **~ cock** coq *m* de combat; **to live like a ~ cock** vivre comme un coq en pâte; **~ fit** en pleine forme; (*Mil*) **~ forces** forces armées; **~ fund** fonds *m* de soutien; **~ line** front *m*; **~ strength** effectif *m* mobilisable; **~ words** paroles *fpl* de défi.

figment ['fɪgmənt] n: **a ~ of the imagination** une invention *or* création de l'imagination; **it's all a ~ of his imagination** il l'a purement et simplement inventé, il a inventé ça de toutes pièces.

figurative ['fɪgjʊrətɪv] adj a *language* figuré, métaphorique. **in the literal and in the ~ meaning** au (sens) propre et au (sens) figuré. b (*Art*) figuratif.

figuratively ['fɪgjʊrətɪvlɪ] adv *speak, write, mean* métaphoriquement, au sens figuré. **~ speaking, ...** métaphoriquement parlant, ...

figure ['fɪgə^r] 1 n a chiffre *m*. **in round ~s** en chiffres ronds; **I can't give you the exact ~s** je ne peux pas vous donner les chiffres exacts; **the crime/unemployment** *etc* **~s** le taux de la criminalité/du chômage *etc*; **to put a ~ to sth** chiffrer qch; **can you put a ~ to that?** est-ce que vous pouvez me donner un chiffre?; **he's good at ~s** il est doué pour le calcul; **there's a mistake in the ~s** il y a une erreur de calcul; **to get into double ~s** atteindre la dizaine; **to reach three ~s** atteindre la centaine; **to bring** *or* **get inflation/unemployment** *etc* **down to single ~s** faire passer l'inflation/le chômage *etc* en dessous (de la barre) des 10%; **a 3-~ number** un nombre *or* un numéro de 3 chiffres; **to sell sth for a high ~** vendre qch cher *or* à un prix élevé; **I got it for a low ~** je l'ai eu pour pas cher *or* pour peu de chose; **he earns well into five ~s** il gagne bien plus de dix mille livres.

b (*diagram, drawing*) (*Math*) figure *f*; [*animal, person etc*] figure, image *f*. **to draw a ~ on the blackboard** tracer une figure au tableau; **he drew the ~ of a bird** il a dessiné (l'image d')un oiseau; **draw a ~ of eight** dessinez un huit (*see also* **1h**).

c (*human form*) forme *f*, silhouette *f*. **I saw a ~ approach** j'ai vu une forme *or* une silhouette s'approcher de moi; **she's a fine ~ of a woman** c'est une belle femme; **he cut a poor ~** il faisait piètre figure.

d [*shape: of person*] ligne *f*, formes *fpl*. **to improve one's ~** soigner sa ligne; **to keep one's ~** garder la ligne; **she has a good ~** elle est bien faite *or* bien tournée; **remember your ~!** pense à ta ligne!

e (*important person*) figure *f*, personnage *m*. **the great ~s of history** les grandes figures *or* les grands personnages de l'histoire; **a ~ of fun** un guignol; *see* **public**.

f (*Literat*) figure *f*. **~ of speech** figure de rhétorique; (*fig*) **it's just a ~ of speech** ce n'est qu'une façon de parler.

g (*Mus*) figure *f* mélodique.

h (*Dancing, Skating*) figure *f*. **~ of eight,** (*US*) **~ eight** huit *m*.

2 comp ▸**figure-conscious***: **to be figure-conscious** penser à sa ligne ▸**figurehead** (*lit*) figure *f* de proue; (*pej: person*) prête-nom *m* (*pej*), homme *m* de paille (*pej*) ▸**figure-skate** (*in competition*) faire les figures imposées (*en patinage*); (*in display etc*) faire du patinage artistique ▸**figure skating** figures imposées; patinage *m* artistique.

3 vt a (*represent*) représenter; (*illustrate by diagrams*) illustrer par un *or* des schéma(s), mettre sous forme de schéma.

b (*decorate*) orner; *silk etc* brocher, gaufrer. **~d velvet** velours façonné.

c (*Mus*) **~d bass** basse chiffrée.

d (*imagine*) penser, s'imaginer.

e (*US: guess*) penser, supposer. **I ~ it like this** je vois la chose comme ceci; **I ~ he'll come** je pense *or* suppose qu'il va venir.

4 **vi** a (*appear*) figurer. **he ~d in a play of mine** il a joué *or* tenu un rôle dans une de mes pièces; **his name doesn't ~ on this list** son nom ne figure pas sur cette liste.

b (*US *: make sense*) **it doesn't ~** ça n'a pas de sens, ça ne s'explique pas; **that ~s** ça cadre, ça se tient, ça s'explique.

▸**figure in*** **vt sep** (*US*) inclure, compter. **it's figured in** c'est inclus, c'est compris.

▸**figure on** **vt fus** (*US*) (*take account of*) tenir compte de; (*count on*) compter sur; (*expect*) s'attendre (*doing* à faire). **you can figure on 30** tu peux compter sur 30; **I was figuring on doing that tomorrow** je pensais faire ça demain; **I hadn't figured on that** je n'avais pas tenu compte de ça; **I was not figuring on having to do that** je ne m'attendais pas à devoir faire ça.

▸**figure out** **vt sep** a (*understand*) arriver à comprendre, résoudre. **I can't figure that fellow out at all** je n'arrive pas du tout à comprendre ce type*; **I can't figure out how much money we need** je n'arrive pas à (bien) calculer la somme qu'il nous faut; **I can't figure it out** ça me dépasse*. b (*work out, plan*) calculer. **they had it all figured out** ils avaient calculé leur coup.

figurine [ˌfɪgəˈriːn] **n** figurine *f*.

Fiji [ˈfiːdʒiː] **n** (*also* **the ~ Islands**) (les îles *fpl*) Fidji *fpl*. **in ~** à Fidji.

Fijian [fɪˈdʒiːən] 1 **adj** fidjien. 2 **n** a Fidjien(ne) *m(f)*. b (*Ling*) fidjien *m*.

filament [ˈfɪləmənt] **n** filament *m*.

filariasis [ˌfɪləˈraɪəsɪs] **n** filariose *f*.

filbert [ˈfɪlbɜːt] **n** aveline *f*.

filch* [fɪltʃ] **vt** voler, chiper*.

file¹ [faɪl] 1 **n** (*for wood, fingernails etc*) lime *f*. **triangular ~** tiers-point *m*; *see* **nail**. 2 **vt** limer. **to ~ one's nails** se limer les ongles; **to ~ through the bars** limer les barreaux.

▸**file away** **vt sep** limer (*pour enlever*).

▸**file down** **vt sep** limer (*pour raccourcir*).

file² [faɪl] 1 **n** (*folder*) dossier *m*, chemise *f*; (*with hinges*) classeur *m*; (*for drawings: also in filing drawers*) carton *m*; (*for card index*) fichier *m*; (*cabinet*) classeur; (*papers*) dossier; (*Comput*) fichier *m*. **have we a ~ on her?** est-ce que nous avons un dossier sur elle?; **there's something in** *or* **on the file about him** le dossier contient des renseignements sur lui; **to put a document on the ~** joindre une pièce au dossier; (*fig*) **they closed the ~ on that question** ils ont classé le dossier *or* l'affaire; (*Comput*) **data on ~** données fichées; **to keep a ~ on sb/sth** tenir à jour un dossier sur qn/qch; **to be on police ~s** être fiché par la police; *see* **student**.

2 **comp** ▸**file cabinet** (*US*) classeur *m*, fichier *m* (*meuble*) ▸**file clerk** (*US*) documentaliste *mf* ▸**file management** (*Comput*) gestion *f* de fichiers ▸**filename** (*Comput*) nom *m* de fichier.

3 **vt** a (*also* **~ away**) *notes* classer; *letters* ranger, classer; (*into file*) joindre au dossier; (*on spike*) enfiler.

b (*Comput*) classer, stocker.

c (*Jur*) **to ~ a claim** déposer *or* faire enregistrer une requête *or* demande; **to ~ a claim for damages** intenter un procès en dommages-intérêts; (*Insurance*) **to ~ an accident claim** faire une déclaration d'accident; **to ~ a petition** déposer *or* faire enregistrer une requête *or* demande; **to ~ a petition (in bankruptcy)** déposer son bilan; **to ~ a suit against sb** intenter un procès à qn; *see* **submission**.

file³ [faɪl] 1 **n** file *f*. **in Indian ~** à la *or* en file indienne; **in single ~** à la *or* en file; *see* **rank¹**. 2 **vi** marcher en file. **to ~ in/out** *etc* entrer/sortir *etc* en file; **to ~ past** défiler; **the soldiers ~d past the general** les soldats ont défilé devant le général; **they ~d slowly past the ticket collector** ils sont passés lentement un à un devant le poinçonneur.

filial [ˈfɪlɪəl] **adj** filial.

filiation [ˌfɪlɪˈeɪʃən] **n** filiation *f*.

filibuster [ˈfɪlɪbʌstəʳ] 1 **n** a (*US Pol*) obstruction *f* parlementaire (*par quelqu'un qui conserve la parole interminablement*). b (*pirate*) flibustier *m*. 2 **vi** (*US Pol*) faire de l'obstruction parlementaire.

filibusterer [ˈfɪlɪˌbʌstərəʳ] **n** (*US Pol*) obstructionniste *mf* (*qui conserve la parole interminablement*).

filigree [ˈfɪlɪgriː] 1 **n** filigrane *m* (*en métal*). 2 **comp** en filigrane.

filing [ˈfaɪlɪŋ] 1 **n** [*documents*] classement *m*; [*claim etc*] enregistrement *m*. **to do the ~** s'occuper du classement. 2 **comp** ▸**filing box** fichier *m* (*boîte*) ▸**filing cabinet** classeur *m*, fichier *m* (*meuble*) ▸**filing clerk** (*Brit*) documentaliste *mf*.

filings [ˈfaɪlɪŋz] **npl** limaille *f*. **iron ~** limaille de fer.

Filipino [ˌfɪlɪˈpiːnəʊ] 1 **adj** philippin. 2 **n** a (*person*) Philippin(e) *m(f)*. b (*Ling*) tagalog *m*.

fill [fɪl] 1 **vt** a *bottle, bucket* remplir (*with* de); *hole* remplir (*with* de), boucher (*with* avec); *cake, pastry* fourrer (*with* de); *teeth* plomber. **smoke ~ed the room** la pièce s'est remplie de fumée; **the wind ~ed the sails** le vent a gonflé les voiles; **to ~ o.s. with** *chocolate etc* se gaver de; **they ~ed the air with their cries** l'air s'emplissait de leurs cris; **~ed with admiration** rempli *or* plein d'admiration; **~ed with anger** très en colère; **~ed with despair** en proie au désespoir, plongé dans le désespoir; **~d with emotion** très ému; **the thought ~s me with pleasure** cette pensée me réjouit.

b *post, job* remplir. **to ~ a vacancy** [*employer*] pourvoir à un emploi; [*employee*] prendre un poste vacant; **the position is already ~ed** le poste est déjà pris; **he ~s the job well** il remplit bien ses fonctions; **he ~s all our requirements** il répond à tous nos besoins; **to ~ a need** répondre à un besoin; **to ~ a void** *or* **a gap** remplir *or* combler un vide; **that ~s the bill** cela fait l'affaire; (*Comm*) **to ~ an order** livrer une commande.

2 **vi** (*also* **~ up**) [*bath etc*] se remplir, s'emplir; [*bus*] se remplir; [*hall*] se remplir, se garnir. [*hole*] **to ~ with water/mud** se remplir d'eau/de boue; **her eyes ~ed with tears** ses yeux se sont remplis de larmes.

3 **n: to eat one's ~** manger à sa faim, se rassasier; **he had eaten his ~** il était rassasié; **to drink/have one's ~** boire/avoir tout son content; **I've had my ~ of listening to her!** j'en ai assez de l'écouter, j'en ai jusque-là* de l'écouter; **a ~ of tobacco** une pipe, de quoi bourrer sa pipe.

4 **comp** ▸**fill-in** (*gen: temporary employee*) remplaçant(e) *m(f)*; (*fig*) **I'm only a fill-in** je fais office de bouche-trou.

▸**fill in** 1 **vi: to fill in for sb** remplacer qn (temporairement).

2 **vt sep** a *form, questionnaire* remplir; *account, report* mettre au point, compléter. (*fig*) **would you fill in the details for us?** voudriez-vous nous donner les détails?; **to fill sb in on sth*** mettre qn au courant de qch.

b *hole* boucher. **we had that door filled in** nous avons fait murer *or* condamner cette porte; **to fill in gaps in one's knowledge** combler des lacunes dans ses connaissances; **he was trying to fill in the day** il essayait de trouver à s'occuper jusqu'au soir; **draw the outline in black and fill it in in red** dessinez le contour en noir et remplissez-le en rouge.

c (*‡ fig: beat up*) casser la gueule à‡.

3 **fill-in** **n** *see* **fill 4**.

▸**fill out** 1 **vi** a [*sails etc*] gonfler, s'enfler. b (*become fatter*) [*person*] forcir, se fortifier. **her cheeks** *or* **her face had filled out** elle avait pris de bonnes joues. 2 **vt sep** a (*esp US*) *form, questionnaire* remplir. b *story, account, essay* étoffer.

▸**fill up** 1 **vi** a = **fill 2**. b (*Aut*) faire le plein (d'essence). 2 **vt sep** a *tank, cup* remplir. **to fill up to the brim** remplir jusqu'au bord *or* à ras bord; **to fill o.s. up with** *chocolates etc* se gaver de; (*Aut*) **fill it** *or* **her up!*** (faites) le plein! b *hole* boucher. c (*Brit*) *form, questionnaire* remplir.

-filled [fɪld] **adj ending in comps, e.g. cream-filled** fourré à la crème; **foam-filled** rempli de mousse; **tear-filled** plein de larmes.

filler [ˈfɪləʳ] **n** a (*utensil*) récipient *m* (de remplissage); [*bottle*] remplisseuse *f*; (*funnel*) entonnoir *m*. *Aut* **~ cap** bouchon *m* de réservoir. b (*NonC: for cracks in wood etc*) reboucheur *m*, mastic *m*; (*Press*) article *m* bouche-trou *inv*.

fillet [ˈfɪlɪt] 1 **n** a (*Culin*) [*beef, pork, fish*] filet *m*. **veal ~** (*NonC*) longe *f* de veau; (*one piece*) escalope *f* de veau; **~ steak** (*NonC*) filet de bœuf, tournedos *m*; (*one slice*) bifteck *m* dans le filet, (*thick*) chateaubriand *m*. b (*for the hair*) serre-tête *m inv*. 2 **vt** *meat* désosser; *fish* découper en filets. **~ed sole** filets *mpl* de sole.

filling [ˈfɪlɪŋ] 1 **n** a (*in tooth*) plombage *m*. **my ~'s come out** mon plombage est parti *or* a sauté. b (*in pie, tart, sandwich*) garniture *f*; (*in tomatoes etc*) farce *f*. **chocolates with a coffee ~** chocolats fourrés au café. 2 **adj** *food* substantiel. 3 **comp** ▸**filling station** poste *m* d'essence, station-service *f*.

fillip [ˈfɪlɪp] **n** (*with finger*) chiquenaude *f*, pichenette *f*; (*fig*) coup *m* de fouet (*fig*). **our advertisements gave a ~ to our business** notre publicité a donné un coup de fouet à nos affaires.

filly [ˈfɪlɪ] **n** pouliche *f*; (*†: *girl*) jeune fille *f*.

film [fɪlm] 1 **n** a (*Cine: motion picture*) film *m*. (*esp Brit*) **to go to the ~s** aller au cinéma; **the ~ is on at the Odeon just now** le film passe actuellement à l'Odéon; **he's in ~s** il travaille dans le cinéma; **he's been in many ~s** il a joué dans beaucoup de films; *see* **feature** *etc*.

b (*Phot*) (*material*) pellicule *f* (photographique); (*spool*) pellicule, film *m*; (*Cine*) (*material*) film *or* pellicule (cinématographique); (*spool*) film; (*Typ*) film.

c (*for wrapping food*) scellofrais *m* ®; (*in goods packaging etc*) pellicule *f* de plastique.

d (*thin layer*) (*of dust, mud*) couche *f*, pellicule *f*; (*of mist*) voile *m*.

2 **vt** (*gen*) *news, event, sb's arrival, play* filmer; *scene* [*director*] filmer, tourner; [*camera*] enregistrer.

3 **vi** a [*windscreen, glass*] (*also* **~ over**) se voiler, s'embuer.

b (*Cine*) (*make a film*) faire un film. **they were ~ing all day** ils ont tourné toute la journée; **they were ~ing in Spain** le tournage avait lieu en Espagne; **the story ~ed very well** l'histoire a bien rendu au cinéma *or* en film; **she ~s well** elle est photogénique.

4 **comp** *archives, history etc* du cinéma ▸**film camera** (*Cine*) caméra *f* ▸**film chain** (*US TV*) télécinéma *m* ▸**film fan** cinéphile *mf*, amateur *mf* de cinéma ▸**film festival** festival *m* du cinéma *or* du film ▸**film library** cinémathèque *f* ▸**film-maker** cinéaste *mf* ▸**film-making** tournage *m*, (*more gen*) le cinéma ▸**film première** première *f* ▸**film rights** droits *mpl* d'adaptation (cinématographique) ▸**film script** scénario *m* ▸**film sequence** séquence *f* ▸**film set** (*Cine*) plateau *m* de tournage ▸**filmset** **vt** (*Typ*) photocomposer ▸**filmsetter**

(*Typ*) photocomposeuse *f* ►**filmsetting** (*Typ*) photocomposition *f* ►**film speed** sensibilité *f* de la pellicule ►**film star** vedette *f* (de cinéma), star *f* ►**filmstrip** film *m* (pour projection) fixe ►**film studio** studio *m* (de cinéma) ►**film test** bout *m* d'essai; **to give sb a film test** faire tourner un bout d'essai à qn.

filming [ˈfɪlmɪŋ] n (*Cine*) tournage *m*.

filmography [fɪlˈmɒɡrəfɪ] n (*esp US*) filmographie *f*.

filmy [ˈfɪlmɪ] adj *clouds, material* léger, transparent, vaporeux; *glass* embué.

Filofax [ˈfaɪləʊ,fæks] n ® Filofax *m*.

filter [ˈfɪltəʳ] 1 n a (*gen, also Phot*) filtre *m*; *see* **colour, oil** *etc*.

b (*Brit: in traffic lights*) flèche *f* (*permettant à une file de voitures de passer*).

2 comp ►**filter bed** bassin *m* de filtration ►**filter cigarette** cigarette *f* (à bout) filtre ►**filter coffee** café *m* filtre ►**filter lane** (*Aut*) voie *f* d'accès (*sur l'autoroute*) ►**filter light** (*Aut*) flèche *f* ►**filter paper** papier *m* filtre ►**filter tip** (*cigarette, tip*) bout *m* filtre ►**filter-tipped** à bout filtre.

3 vt *liquids* filtrer; *air* purifier, épurer.

4 vi *[light, liquid, sound]* filtrer. **the light ~ed through the shutters** la lumière filtrait à travers les volets; (*Aut*) **to ~ to the left** tourner à gauche à la flèche; *[people]* **to ~ back/in/out** revenir/ entrer/sortir par petits groupes (espacés).

►**filter in** vi: **the news of the massacre began to filter in** on a commencé petit à petit à avoir des renseignements sur le massacre.

►**filter out** vt sep *impurities* éliminer par filtrage; (*fig*) éliminer.

►**filter through** vi *[light]* filtrer. **the news filtered through at last** les nouvelles ont fini par se savoir.

filth [fɪlθ] n (*lit*) saleté *f*, crasse *f*; (*excrement*) ordure *f*; (*fig*) saleté, ordure (*liter*). (*fig*) **this book is sheer ~** ce livre est une vraie saleté; **the ~ shown on television** les saletés *or* les grossièretés *fpl* que l'on montre à la télévision; **all the ~ he talks** toutes les grossièretés qu'il débite.

filthy [ˈfɪlθɪ] adj *room, clothes, face, object* sale, crasseux, dégoûtant; *language* ordurier, obscène; (*) *weather etc* affreux, abominable. **~ talk** grossièretés *fpl*, propos grossiers *or* orduriers; **it's a ~ habit** c'est une habitude dégoûtante *or* répugnante; **she's got a ~ mind** c'est une cochonne‡; **to give sb a ~ look** jeter un regard menaçant à qn; **he's ~ rich‡** il est pourri de fric‡.

filtrate [ˈfɪltreɪt] n filtrat *m*.

filtration [fɪlˈtreɪʃən] n filtration *f*.

fin [fɪn] n a *[fish, whale, seal]* nageoire *f*; *[shark]* aileron *m*; *[aircraft, spacecraft]* empennage *m*; *[ship]* dérive *f*; *[radiator etc]* ailette *f*. *[diver etc]* **~s** palmes *fpl*. b (*US* ‡: *5-dollar bill*) billet *m* de 5 dollars.

finagle [fɪˈneɪɡəl] (*US*) 1 vi resquiller. 2 vt: **to ~ sb out of sth** carotter* qch à qn.

finagler [fɪˈneɪɡləʳ] n (*US*) resquilleur *m*, -euse *f*.

final [ˈfaɪnl] 1 adj a (*last*) dernier. **to put the ~ touches to a book** *etc* mettre la dernière main à un livre *etc*; (*in speech, lecture*) **one ~ point** ... enfin ..., un dernier point ...; (*Univ etc*) **~ examinations** examens *mpl* de dernière année; (*Fin*) **~ instalment** versement *m* libératoire; (*Comm*) **~ demand** *or* **notice** dernière demande (de règlement), dernier avertissement; (*Pol*) **the F~ Solution** la solution finale.

b (*conclusive*) *decree, version* définitif; *answer* définitif, décisif; *judgment* sans appel, irrévocable. **the umpire's decision is ~** la décision de l'arbitre est sans appel; **and that's ~!** un point c'est tout!

c (*Philos*) *cause* final.

2 n a (*Univ*) **the ~s** les examens *mpl* de dernière année.

b (*Sport: US* **~s**) finale *f*.

c (*Press*) **late night ~** dernière édition (du soir).

finale [fɪˈnɑːlɪ] n (*Mus, fig*) finale *m*. (*fig*) **the grand ~** l'apothéose *f*.

finalist [ˈfaɪnəlɪst] n (*Sport*) finaliste *mf*.

finality [faɪˈnælɪtɪ] n *[decision etc]* caractère définitif, irrévocabilité *f*. **with an air of ~** avec fermeté, avec décision.

finalization [,faɪnəlaɪˈzeɪʃən] n (*see* **finalize**) rédaction définitive; dernière mise au point; confirmation définitive.

finalize [ˈfaɪnəlaɪz] vt *text, report* rédiger la version définitive de; *arrangements, plans* mettre au point les derniers détails de, parachever, mettre la dernière main à; *preparations* mettre la dernière main à; *details* mettre au point, arrêter définitivement; *decision* rendre définitif, confirmer de façon définitive; *date* fixer de façon définitive.

finally [ˈfaɪnəlɪ] adv a (*lastly*) enfin, en dernier lieu, pour terminer. **~ I would like to say** ... pour terminer je voudrais dire ... . b (*eventually*) enfin, finalement. **they ~ decided to leave** ils se sont finalement décidés à partir, ils ont fini par décider de partir. c (*once and for all*) définitivement. **~ and for ever** pour toujours.

finance [faɪˈnæns] 1 n a (*NonC*) finance *f*. **high ~** la haute finance; **Minister/Ministry of F~** ministre *m*/ministère *m* des Finances. b **~s** finances *fpl*; **his ~s aren't sound** ses finances ne sont pas solides; **the country's ~s** la situation financière du pays; **he hasn't the ~s to do that** il n'a pas les finances *or* les fonds *mpl* pour cela. 2 vt *scheme etc* (*supply money for*) financer, commanditer; (*obtain money for*) trouver des fonds pour. 3 comp (*Press*) *news, page* financier ►**finance bill** (*Parl*) projet *m* de loi de finances ►**finance company, finance house** compagnie financière, société *f* de financement.

financial [faɪˈnænʃəl] adj (*gen*) financier; (*Fin, Econ*) *plan* de financement. **~ aid** aide financière (*to* à); (*US Univ Admin*) **~ aid office** service *m* des bourses; **they are in ~ difficulties** ils ont des problèmes de trésorerie; (*Brit St Ex*) **F~ Times index** indice *m* F.T. (*moyenne quotidienne des principales valeurs boursières*); (*Brit*) **the ~ year** l'exercice *m*.

financially [faɪˈnænʃəlɪ] adv financièrement.

financier [faɪˈnænsɪəʳ] n financier *m*.

finch [fɪntʃ] n fringillidé *m* (*pinson, bouvreuil, gros-bec etc*).

find [faɪnd] pret, ptp **found** 1 vt a (*gen sense*) trouver; *lost person or object* retrouver. **he was trying to ~ his gloves** il cherchait ses gants, il essayait de retrouver ses gants; **I never found my book** je n'ai jamais retrouvé mon livre; **your book is not to be found** on ne parvient pas à retrouver votre livre, votre livre reste introuvable; **to ~ one's place in a book** retrouver sa page dans un livre; **they soon found him again** ils l'ont vite retrouvé; **he found himself in Paris** il s'est retrouvé à Paris; (*fig*) **he found himself at last** il a enfin trouvé sa voie; **to ~ one's voice** (*lit*) retrouver sa voix; (*fig*) trouver sa voix *or* son style; **they couldn't ~ the way back** ils n'ont pas pu trouver le chemin du retour; **I'll ~ my way about all right by myself** je trouverai très bien mon chemin tout seul; **can you ~ your own way out?** pouvez-vous trouver la sortie tout seul?; **to ~ one's way into a building** trouver l'entrée d'un bâtiment; **it found its way into my handbag** ça s'est retrouvé *or* ça a atterri* dans mon sac; **it found its way into his essay** ça s'est glissé dans sa dissertation; **we left everything as we found it** nous avons tout laissé tel quel; **he was found dead in bed** on l'a trouvé mort dans son lit; **the castle is to be found near Tours** le château se trouve près de Tours; **this flower is found all over England** on trouve cette fleur *or* cette fleur se trouve partout en Angleterre; **to ~ one's** *or* **its mark** atteindre son but.

b (*fig: gen*) trouver (*that* que); (*perceive, realize*) s'apercevoir, constater (*that* que); (*discover*) découvrir, constater (*that* que); *cure* découvrir; *solution* trouver, découvrir; *answer* trouver. **I can never ~ anything to say to him** je ne trouve jamais rien à lui dire; (*in health*) **how did you ~ him?** comment l'avez-vous trouvé?; **how did you ~ the steak?** comment avez-vous trouvé le bifteck?; **you will ~ that I am right** vous verrez *or* vous constaterez *or* vous vous apercevrez que j'ai raison; **I ~ that I have plenty of time** je m'aperçois *or* je constate que j'ai tout le temps qu'il faut; **it has been found that one person in ten does so** on a constaté qu'une personne sur dix le fait; **to ~ a house damp** trouver une maison humide; **I ~ her very pleasant** je la trouve très agréable; **I went there yesterday, only to ~ her out** j'y suis allé hier, pour constater qu'elle était sortie; **I found myself quite at sea among all those scientists** je me suis trouvé *or* senti complètement dépaysé *or* perdu au milieu de tous ces scientifiques; **he ~s it impossible to leave** il ne peut se résoudre à partir; **he ~s it impossible/difficult** *etc* **to walk** il lui est impossible/difficile *etc* de marcher; **he ~s it tiring/encouraging** *etc* il trouve que c'est fatigant/encourageant *etc*; **to ~ the courage to do** trouver le courage de faire; **you won't ~ it easy** vous ne le trouverez pas facile; **to ~ some difficulty in doing** éprouver une certaine difficulté à faire; (*fig*) **to ~ one's feet** s'adapter, s'acclimater; **I couldn't ~ it in my heart to refuse** je n'ai pas eu le cœur de refuser; **I can't ~ time to read** je n'arrive pas à trouver le temps de lire; **to ~ favour with sb** *[person]* s'attirer les bonnes grâces de qn; *[idea, suggestion, action]* recevoir l'approbation de qn; *see* **fault, expression 1a**.

c (*Jur*) **to ~ sb guilty** prononcer qn coupable; **how do you ~ the accused?** quel est votre verdict?; **to ~ a verdict of guilty** retourner un verdict de culpabilité; **the court found that** ... le tribunal a conclu que ... .

d (*supply*) fournir; (*obtain*) obtenir, trouver. **wages £50 all found** salaire de 50 livres logé (et) nourri; (*US*) **wages 100 dollars and found** salaire de 100 dollars logé (et) nourri; **you'll have to ~ yourself in clothes** vous aurez à fournir vos propres vêtements; **who will ~ the money for the journey?** qui va fournir l'argent pour le voyage?; **where will they ~ the money for the journey?** où est-ce qu'ils trouveront *or* obtiendront l'argent pour le voyage?; **I can't ~ the money to do it** je ne peux pas trouver l'argent nécessaire; **go and ~ me a needle** va me chercher une aiguille; **can you ~ me a pen?** peux-tu me trouver un stylo?; **there are no more to be found** il n'en reste plus.

2 vi (*Jur*) **to ~ for/against the accused** se prononcer en faveur de/contre l'accusé.

3 n trouvaille *f*. **that was a lucky ~** nous avons (*or* vous avez *etc*) eu de la chance de trouver *or* de découvrir cela.

►**find out** 1 vi a (*make enquiries*) se renseigner (*about* sur).

b (*discover*) **we didn't find out about it in time** nous ne l'avons pas su *or* appris à temps; **your mother will find out if you** ... ta mère le saura si tu ... .

2 vt sep a (*discover*) découvrir (*that* que); *answer* trouver; *sb's secret, character* découvrir. **I found out what he was really like** j'ai découvert son vrai caractère.

b (*discover the misdeeds etc of*) *person* démasquer. **he thought we wouldn't know, but we found him out** il pensait que nous ne saurions rien, mais nous l'avons démasqué *or* nous avons découvert le pot aux roses; **this affair has really found him out** il s'est bel et bien révélé tel qu'il est *or* sous son vrai jour dans cette affaire.

finder ['faɪndəʳ] n a (*of lost object*) celui *or* celle qui a trouvé (*or* qui trouvera *etc*); (*Jur*) inventeur *m*, -trice *f*. (*US*) **~'s fee** prime *f* d'intermédiaire; **~s keepers (losers weepers)!** (celui) qui le trouve le garde (et tant pis pour celui qui l'a perdu)! b *[telescope etc]* chercheur *m*; *see* **view**.

findings ['faɪndɪŋz] npl (*conclusions, deductions etc*) *[person, committee]* conclusions *fpl*, constatations *fpl*; *[scientist etc]* conclusions, résultats *mpl* (des recherches); (*Jur*) conclusions *fpl*, verdict *m*; (*sth found*) découvertes *fpl*.

fine¹ [faɪn] 1 n amende *f*, contravention *f* (*esp Aut*). **I got a ~ for going through a red light** j'ai attrapé une contravention pour avoir brûlé un feu rouge. 2 vt (*see* **1**) condamner à une amende, donner une contravention à. **he was ~d £10** il a eu une amende de 10 livres, il a eu 10 livres d'amende; **they ~d him heavily** ils l'ont condamné à une grosse amende.

fine² [faɪn] 1 adj a (*not coarse*) *cloth, dust, needle, rain, rope* fin; *metal* (*gen*) pur; *workmanship, feelings* délicat; *distinction* subtil (*f* subtile); *taste* raffiné, délicat. **~ gold** or fin; **~ handwriting** écriture fine *or* délicate; **he has no ~r feelings** il n'a aucune noblesse de sentiments; **not to put too ~ a point on it** ... disons *or* enfin ...; **the ~r points of** les subtilités *fpl* de; **~ art, the ~ arts** les beaux arts; **he's got it down to a ~ art** il le fait à la perfection, il est expert en la matière; *see* **print**.

b *weather* beau (*f* belle). **it's going to be ~ this afternoon** il va faire beau cet après-midi; **one ~ day** (*lit*) par une belle journée; (*fig*) un beau jour; (*fig*) **one of these ~ days** un de ces quatre matins, un de ces jours; **the weather is set ~** le temps est au beau (fixe); **I hope it keeps ~ for you!** je vous souhaite du beau temps!

c (*excellent*) beau (*f* belle); *musician, novelist* excellent, admirable. **~ clothes** de beaux vêtements; **meat of the finest quality** viande de première qualité; **you have a ~ future ahead of you** un bel avenir vous attend; **it's a ~ thing to help others** c'est beau d'aider autrui; **it's ~ for two** c'est très bien pour deux personnes; **it's ~ by me** d'accord, ça me convient; **(that's) ~!** très bien!; (*agreeing*) **~!** entendu!, d'accord!; (*iro*) **a ~ thing!*** c'est du beau! *or* du propre!*; (*iro*) **you're a ~ one!** tu en as de bonnes!*; (*iro*) **you're a ~ one to talk!** c'est bien à toi de le dire!; (*iro*) **that's a ~ excuse** en voilà une belle excuse; (*iro*) **a ~ friend you are!** c'est beau l'amitié!; **that's all very ~ but** ... tout cela (c')est bien beau *or* bien joli mais ...; **she likes to play at being the ~ lady** elle aime jouer les grandes dames; *see also* **figure, finest** *etc*.

2 adv a (très) bien. **you're doing ~!** ce que tu fais est très bien!, tu te débrouilles bien!*, ça va!; **I'm feeling ~ now** je me sens très bien maintenant; **that suits me ~** ça me convient très bien.

b finement, fin. **to cut/chop sth up ~** couper/hacher qch menu; (*fig*) **you've cut it a bit ~** vous avez calculé un peu juste; **he writes so ~ I can hardly read it** il écrit si fin *or* si petit que je peux à peine le lire.

3 comp ▸**fine-drawn** *wire, thread* finement étiré; *features* délicat, fin ▸**fine-grained** au grain fin *or* menu; (*Phot*) à grain fin ▸**fine-spun** *yarn etc* très fin, ténu; (*fig*) *hair* très fin ▸**fine-tooth comb** peigne fin; (*fig*) **he went through the document with a fine-tooth comb** il a passé les documents au peigne fin *or* au crible ▸**fine-tune** vt (*fig*) *production, the economy* régler avec précision ▸**fine-tuning** réglage *m* minutieux.

▸**fine down** 1 vi (*get thinner*) s'affiner. 2 vt sep (*reduce*) réduire; (*simplify*) simplifier; (*refine*) raffiner.

finely ['faɪnlɪ] adv a (*splendidly*) *written, painted* admirablement; *dressed* magnifiquement. b **to chop up ~** hacher menu *or* fin; **the meat was ~ cut up** la viande était coupée en menus morceaux; **~ ground** fin moulu. c (*delicately*) *adjusted* délicatement. (*fig*) **the distinction was ~ drawn** la distinction était très subtile.

fineness ['faɪnnɪs] n a (*see* **fine²**) finesse *f*; pureté *f*; délicatesse *f*; subtilité *f*; raffinement *m*. b (*Metal*) titre *m*.

finery ['faɪnərɪ] n parure *f*. **she wore all her ~** elle s'était parée de ses plus beaux atours.

finesse [fɪ'nes] 1 n finesse *f*; (*Cards*) impasse *f*. 2 vi (*Cards*) **to ~ against the King** faire l'impasse au roi. 3 vt (*Cards*) **to ~ the Queen** faire l'impasse en jouant la dame.

finest ['faɪnɪst] npl (*US iro: police*) **Chicago's/the city's ~** la police de Chicago/de la ville; **one of New York's ~** un agent de police new-yorkais.

finger ['fɪŋgəʳ] 1 n (*Anat*) doigt *m*; (*of cake etc*) petite part, petit rectangle. **first** *or* **index ~** index *m*; **little ~** auriculaire *m*, petit doigt; **middle ~** médius *m*, majeur *m*; **ring ~** annulaire *m*; **between ~ and thumb** entre le pouce et l'index; **to count on one's ~s** compter sur ses doigts; (*fig*) **I can count on the ~s of one hand the number of times he has** ... je peux compter sur les doigts de la main le nombre de fois où il a ...; (*fig*) **to work one's ~s to the bone** s'user au travail; **to point one's ~ at sb** (*lit*) montrer qn du doigt; (*fig*) (*identify*) identifier qn; (*accuse*) accuser qn; (*fig*) **to point the ~ of scorn at sb** pointer un doigt accusateur vers qn; **to put one's ~ on the difficulty** mettre le doigt sur la difficulté; **there's something wrong, but I can't put my ~ on it** il y a quelque chose qui cloche* mais je ne peux pas mettre le doigt dessus; (*fig*) **to have** *or* **keep one's ~ on the pulse** se tenir à la page; **to keep one's ~s crossed** dire une petite prière (*fig*) (*for sb* pour qn); **keep your ~s crossed!** dis une petite prière!, touchons du bois!; **his ~s are all thumbs** il est très maladroit de ses mains, il est adroit de ses mains comme un cochon de sa queue*; **she can twist** *or* **wind him round her little ~** elle fait de lui ce qu'elle veut, elle le mène par le bout du nez; **Robert has a ~ in the pie** (*gen*) il y a du Robert là-dessous, Robert y est pour quelque chose; (*financially*) Robert a des intérêts là-dedans *or* dans cette affaire; **he's got a ~ in every pie** il se mêle de tout, il est mêlé à tout; **he wouldn't lift a ~ to help me** il ne lèverait pas le petit doigt pour m'aider; **to pull one's ~ out‡** se décarcasser*, faire un effort; (*fig*) **to put the ~ on sb‡** (*betray*) moucharder* qn; (*indicate as victim*) désigner qn comme victime; (*Brit*) **to put two ~s up at sb‡**, (*US*) **to give sb the ~‡** ≃ faire un bras d'honneur* à qn; *see* **fish, green, lay¹, snap, thumb 1** *etc*.

2 vt a (*touch*) toucher *or* manier (des doigts), (*pej*) tripoter; *money* palper; *keyboard, keys* toucher.

b (*Mus: mark fingering on*) doigter, indiquer le doigté sur.

c (‡: *esp US: betray*) moucharder*, balancer ‡.

3 comp ▸**finger alphabet** alphabet *m* des sourds-muets ▸**finger board** (*Mus*) touche *f* (*de guitare ou de violon etc*) ▸**finger bowl** rince-doigts *m inv* ▸**finger exercises** (*for piano etc*) exercices *mpl* de doigté ▸**fingermark** trace *f* de doigt ▸**fingernail** ongle *m* (*de la main*) ▸**finger painting** peinture *f* avec les doigts ▸**finger plate** (*on door*) plaque *f* de propreté ▸**fingerprint** n empreinte digitale ◊ vt *car, weapon* relever les empreintes digitales sur; *person* prendre les empreintes digitales de ▸**fingerprint expert** spécialiste *mf* en empreintes digitales, expert *m* en dactyloscopie ▸**fingerstall** doigtier *m* ▸**fingertip** *see* **fingertip**.

fingering ['fɪŋgərɪŋ] n a (*Mus*) doigté *m*. b (*fine wool*) laine *f* (fine) à tricoter. c (*of goods in shop etc*) maniement *m*.

fingertip ['fɪŋgətɪp] 1 n bout *m* du doigt. **he has the whole matter at his ~s** il connaît l'affaire sur le bout du doigt; **he's a Scot right to his ~s** il est écossais jusqu'au bout des ongles; **a machine with ~ control** une machine d'un maniement (très) léger. 2 comp ▸**fingertip hold** (*Climbing*) gratton *m*.

finial ['faɪnɪəl] n fleuron *m*, épi *m* (de faîtage).

finicky ['fɪnɪkɪ] adj *person* pointilleux, tatillon; *work, job* minutieux, qui demande de la patience. **don't be so ~!** ne fais pas le (*or* la) difficile!; **she is ~ about her food** elle est difficile pour *or* sur la nourriture.

finish ['fɪnɪʃ] 1 n a (*end*) fin *f*; *[race]* arrivée *f*; (*Climbing*) sortie *f*; (*Hunting*) mise *f* à mort. (*fig*) **to be in at the ~** assister au dénouement (d'une affaire); **to fight to the ~** se battre jusqu'au bout; **from start to ~** du début jusqu'à la fin; *see* **photo**.

b *[woodwork, manufactured articles etc]* finition *f*. **it's a solid car but the ~ is not good** la voiture est solide mais les finitions sont mal faites; **a car with a two-tone ~** une voiture (peinte) en deux tons; **paint with a matt ~** peinture mate; **paint with a gloss ~** laque *f*; **table with an oak ~** (*stained*) table teintée chêne; (*veneered*) table plaquée *or* à placage chêne; **a table with rather a rough ~** une table à la surface plutôt rugueuse.

2 vt (*end*) *activity, work, letter, meal, game* finir, terminer, achever; (*use up*) *supplies, cake* finir, terminer. **~ your soup** finis *or* mange ta soupe; **to ~ doing sth** finir de faire qch; **I'm in a hurry to get this job ~ed** je suis pressé de finir *or* de terminer *or* d'achever ce travail; **to ~ a book** *[reader]* finir (de lire) un livre; *[author]* finir *or* terminer *or* achever un livre; **~ing school** institution *f* pour jeunes filles (de bonne famille); **to put the ~ing touch** *or* **touches to sth** mettre la dernière main *or* la touche finale à qch; (*fig*) **that last mile nearly ~ed me*** ces derniers quinze cents mètres ont failli m'achever *or* m'ont mis à plat*; *see also* **finished**.

3 vi a *[book, film, game, meeting]* finir, s'achever, se terminer; *[holiday, contract]* prendre fin; *[runner, horse]* arriver, terminer; (*St Ex*) clôturer, terminer; (*Climbing*) sortir. **the meeting was ~ing** la réunion tirait à sa fin; (*St Ex*) **our shares ~ed at $70** nos actions cotaient 70 dollars en clôture *or* en fin de séance; **he ~ed by saying that** ... il a terminé en disant que ...; (*in race*) **to ~ well** arriver en bonne position; **to ~ first** arriver *or* terminer premier; (*race*) **~ing line** ligne *f* d'arrivée.

b **I've ~ed with the paper** je n'ai plus besoin du journal; **I've ~ed with politics once and for all** j'en ai fini avec la politique, j'ai dit une fois pour toutes adieu à la politique; **she's ~ed with him** elle a rompu avec lui; **you wait till I've ~ed with you!*** attends un peu que je t'aie réglé ton compte!*.

▸**finish off** 1 vi terminer, finir. **let's finish off now** maintenant finissons-en; **to finish off with a glass of brandy** terminer (le repas) par *or* sur un verre de cognac; **the meeting finished off with a prayer** la réunion a pris fin sur une prière, à la fin de la réunion on a récité une prière. 2 vt sep a *work* terminer, mettre la dernière main à. b *food, meal* terminer, finir. **finish off your potatoes!** finis *or* mange tes pommes de terre! c (*fig: kill*) *person, wounded animal* achever. **his illness last year almost finished him off** sa maladie de l'année dernière a failli l'achever.

▸**finish up** 1 vi a = **finish off 1**. b se retrouver. **he finished up in Rome** il s'est retrouvé à Rome, il a fini par arriver à Rome. 2 vt sep = **finish off 2b**.

finished ['fɪnɪʃt] adj a *woodwork* poli; *performance* accompli; *appear-*

ance soigné. **the ~ product** le produit fini; **a well -~ dress** une robe bien finie *or* aux finitions bien faites. b (*done for*) fichu*, fini. **as a politician he's ~** sa carrière politique est finie. c (*: *tired*) à plat*, crevé*.

finite ['faɪnaɪt] adj a fini, limité. **a ~ number** un nombre fini. b (*Gram*) *mood, verb* fini. **~ state grammar** grammaire *f* à états finis.

fink‡ [fɪŋk] (*US pej*) 1 n (*strikebreaker*) jaune* *m*; (*informer*) mouchard* *m*, indic‡ *m*; (*unpleasant person*) sale type *m*. 2 vt moucharder, dénoncer.

▸fink out vi échouer, laisser tomber.

Finland ['fɪnlənd] n Finlande *f*.

Finn [fɪn] n (*gen*) Finlandais(e) *m(f)*; (*Finnish speaker*) Finnois(e) *m(f)*.

Finnish ['fɪnɪʃ] 1 adj (*gen*) finlandais; *ambassador, embassy* de Finlande; *teacher, dictionary* de finnois; *literature, culture, civilization* finnois. 2 n (*Ling*) finnois *m*.

Finno-Ugric ['fɪnəʊ'uːgrɪk], **Finno-Ugrian** ['fɪnəʊ'uːgrɪən] n, adj (*Ling*) finno-ougrien (*m*).

fiord [fjɔːd] n fjord *m or* fiord *m*.

fir [fɜːʳ] n (*also* **~ tree**) sapin *m*. **~ cone** pomme *f* de pin.

fire [faɪəʳ] 1 n a (*gen*) feu *m*; (*house-~ etc*) incendie *m*. (*excl*) ~! au feu!; **the house was on ~** la maison était en feu *or* en flammes; **the chimney was on ~** il y avait un feu de cheminée; (*fig*) **he's playing with ~** il joue avec le feu; **forest ~** incendie de forêt; **to insure o.s. against ~** s'assurer contre l'incendie; (*fig*) **~ and brimstone** les tourments *mpl* de l'enfer (*see also* **2**); **by ~ and sword** par le fer et par le feu; (*fig*) **he would go through ~ and water for her** il se jetterait au feu pour elle; **to set ~ to sth, set sth on ~** mettre le feu à qch; (*fig*) **to set the world on ~** révolutionner le monde; (*fig*) **he'll never set the Thames** (*Brit*) *or* **the world on ~** il n'a pas inventé la poudre *or* le fil à couper le beurre; **to lay/light/make up the ~** préparer/allumer/faire le feu; **come and sit by the ~** venez vous installer près du feu *or* au coin du feu; **I was sitting in front of a roaring ~** j'étais assis devant une belle flambée; *see* **catch** *etc*.

b (*Brit: heater*) radiateur *m*; *see* **electric** *etc*.

c (*Mil*) feu *m*. **to open ~** ouvrir le feu, faire feu; ~! feu!; (*also fig*) **between two ~s** entre deux feux; (*also fig*) **running ~** feu roulant; **under ~** sous le feu de l'ennemi; **to come under ~** (*Mil*) essuyer le feu (de l'ennemi); (*fig: be criticized*) être (vivement) critiqué; **to return ~** riposter par le feu; **to hold one's ~** (*stop firing*) suspendre le tir; (*hold back*) ne pas tirer; **to fight ~ with ~** combattre le feu par le feu; *see* **cease, hang, line¹**.

d (*NonC: passion*) ardeur *f*, fougue *f*, feu *m*. **to speak with ~** parler avec feu *or* avec ardeur *or* avec fougue.

2 comp **▸fire alarm** avertisseur *m* d'incendie **▸fire-and-brimstone** *sermon, preacher* apocalyptique **▸firearm** arme *f* à feu **▸fireback** contrecœur *m*, contre-feu *m* **▸fireball** (*meteor*) bolide *m*; (*lightning, nuclear*) boule *f* de feu; (*Mil*) bombe explosive; (*fig*) **he's a real fireball** il a un dynamisme à tout casser* **▸the Firebird** (*Mus*) l'Oiseau *m* de feu **▸firebomb** n bombe *f* incendiaire ◊ vt lancer une (*or* des) bombe(s) incendiaire(s) sur **▸firebrand** (*lit*) brandon *m*, tison *m*; **he's a real firebrand** (*energetic person*) il pète le feu; (*causing unrest*) c'est un brandon de discorde **▸firebreak** pare-feu *m inv*, coupe-feu *m inv* **▸firebrick** brique *f* réfractaire **▸fire brigade** (*Brit*) (sapeurs-)pompiers *mpl* **▸firebug*** incendiaire *mf*, pyromane *mf* **▸fire chief** (*US*) capitaine *m* de pompiers **▸fire clay** (*Brit*) argile *f* réfractaire **▸firecracker** (*US*) pétard *m* **▸fire curtain** (*Theat*) rideau *m* de fer **▸firedamp** (*Min*) grisou *m* **▸fire department** (*US*) = **fire brigade** **▸firedogs** chenets *mpl* **▸fire door** porte *f* anti-incendie *or* coupe-feu **▸fire drill** exercice *m* d'évacuation (*incendie*) **▸fire-eater** (*lit*) avaleur *m* de feu; (*fig*) belliqueux *m*, -euse *f* **▸fire engine** (*vehicle*) voiture *f* de pompiers; (*apparatus*) pompe *f* à incendie **▸fire escape** (*staircase*) escalier *m* de secours; (*ladder*) échelle *f* d'incendie **▸fire exit** sortie *f* de secours **▸fire extinguisher** extincteur *m* (d'incendie) **▸fire fighter** (*fireman*) pompier *m*; (*volunteer*) volontaire *mf* dans la lutte contre l'incendie **▸fire-fighting** n lutte *f* anti-incendie ◊ adj *equipment, team* de lutte anti-incendie **▸firefly** luciole *f* **▸fireguard** (*in hearth*) garde-feu *m inv*, pare-étincelles *m inv*; (*in forest*) pare-feu *m inv*, coupe-feu *m inv* **▸fire hazard: it's a fire hazard** ça constitue un danger d'incendie **▸firehouse** (*US*) = **fire station** **▸fire hydrant** bouche *f* d'incendie **▸fire insurance** assurance-incendie *f* **▸fire irons** garniture *f* de foyer **▸firelight** lueur *f* du feu; **by firelight** à la lueur du feu **▸firelighter** allume-feu *m inv*, ligot *m* **▸fireman** (*in fire brigade*) pompier *m*, sapeur-pompier *m*; (*Rail*) chauffeur *m* **▸fireplace** cheminée *f*, foyer *m* **▸fireplug** (*US*) = **fire hydrant** **▸fire power** (*Mil*) puissance *f* de feu **▸fire practice** = **fire drill** **▸fire prevention** mesures *fpl* de sécurité contre l'incendie **▸fireproof** vt ignifuger ◊ adj *material* ignifugé **▸fireproof dish** (*Culin*) plat *m* à feu *or* allant au feu **▸fireproof door** porte ignifugée *or* à revêtement ignifuge **▸fire-raiser** (*Brit*) incendiaire *mf*, pyromane *mf* **▸fire-raising** (*Brit*) pyromanie *f* **▸fire regulations** consignes *fpl* en cas d'incendie **▸fire risk** = **fire hazard** **▸fire sale** vente *f* de marchandises légèrement endommagées dans un incendie **▸fire screen** écran *m* de cheminée **▸fire service** = **fire brigade** **▸fireside** foyer *m*, coin *m* du feu; **fireside chair** fauteuil *m* club; (*without arms*) chauffeuse *f* **▸fire station** caserne *f* de pompiers **▸firestorm** incendie *m* dévastateur **▸fire trap: it's a fire trap** c'est une véritable souricière en cas d'incendie **▸fire warden** (*US*) responsable *mf* de la lutte anti-incendie **▸fire watcher** guetteur *m* des incendies **▸fire watching** guet *m or* surveillance *f* contre les incendies **▸firewater*** (*US*) alcool *m*, gnôle* *f* **▸firewood** bois *m* de chauffage, bois à brûler **▸firework** (fusée *f* de) feu *m* d'artifice **▸fireworks (display)** feu *m* d'artifice.

3 vt a (*set ~ to*) incendier, mettre le feu à; (*fig*) *imagination, passions, enthusiasm* enflammer, échauffer, exciter; *pottery* cuire; *furnace* chauffer. (*fig*) **~d with the desire to do** brûlant de faire; *see* **gas, oil** *etc*.

b *gun* décharger, tirer; *rocket* tirer; (‡: *throw*) balancer*. **to ~ a gun at sb** tirer (un coup de fusil) sur qn; **to ~ a shot** tirer un coup de feu (*at* sur); **without firing a shot** sans tirer un coup (de feu); **to ~ a salute** *or* **a salvo** lancer *or* tirer une salve; **to ~ a salute of 21 guns** saluer de 21 coups de canon; (*fig*) **to ~ (off) questions at sb** bombarder qn de questions; **"your name?" he suddenly ~d at me** "votre nom?" me demanda-t-il à brûle-pourpoint; **~ me over that book‡** balance-moi ce bouquin*.

c (*: *dismiss*) renvoyer, flanquer à la porte*, vider*, licencier (*Ind*). **you're ~d!** vous êtes renvoyé! *or* vidé!*

4 vi a [*person*] (*gen*) tirer; (*Mil, Police*) tirer, faire feu (*at* sur); [*gun*] partir. **the revolver failed to ~** le coup n'est pas parti; (*fig*) **~ away** vas-y!, tu peux y aller.

b (*engine*) tourner. **it's only firing on two cylinders** il n'y a que deux cylindres qui marchent; **the engine is firing badly** le moteur tourne mal.

▸fire away vi *see* **fire 4a**.

▸fire off vt sep *see* **fire 3b**.

firing ['faɪrɪŋ] 1 n a [*pottery*] cuite *f*, cuisson *f*. b (*Mil*) tir *m*; (*gun battle*) fusillade *f*. 2 comp **▸firing hammer** [*firearm*] percuteur *m* **▸firing line** ligne *f* de tir **▸firing pin** = **firing hammer** **▸firing squad** peloton *m* d'exécution.

firm¹ [fɜːm] n (*Comm*) compagnie *f*, firme *f*, maison *f* (de commerce). (*Brit Med*) **there are 4 doctors in the ~*** 4 médecins se partagent le cabinet.

firm² [fɜːm] 1 adj a *table, rock, tomato* ferme. **on ~ ground** (*lit*) sur le sol ferme, sur la terre ferme; (*fig*) sur une base solide; (*fig*) **I'm on ~ ground** je suis sûr de ce que j'avance; **he's as ~ as a rock** il est ferme comme le *or* un roc.

b (*unshakeable, stable*) *faith, friendship* constant, solide; *character* résolu, déterminé; *intention, purpose* ferme, résolu; *step, voice* ferme, assuré; *look* résolu; (*Comm, Fin*) *market* ferme. (*Comm*) **~ offer** offre *f* ferme; (*Comm*) **~ offer for a week** offre valable une semaine; **you must be ~ with your children** il vous faut être ferme avec vos enfants; **I am a ~ believer** *or* **I have a ~ belief in telling the truth** je crois fermement qu'il faut dire la vérité; (*fig*) **to stand ~** tenir bon, tenir ferme.

c (*definite*) *date* ferme, sûr; *sale, offer* ferme.

2 comp **▸firmware** (*Comput*) microprogramme *m*.

3 vt *gatepost etc* rendre ferme.

▸firm up 1 vi [*plans, programme*] s'affermir, se préciser. 2 vt sep *plans etc* établir, affermir.

firmament ['fɜːməmənt] n firmament *m*.

firmly ['fɜːmlɪ] adv *close, screw* fermement; *speak* d'une voix ferme, d'un ton ferme, avec fermeté; *maintain, insist* fermement, dur comme fer. **I ~ believe he's right** je crois fermement *or* je suis convaincu qu'il a raison.

firmness ['fɜːmnɪs] n (*see* **firm²**) fermeté *f*; solidité *f*; résolution *f*; détermination *f*; assurance *f*.

first [fɜːst] 1 adj premier. **the ~ of May** le premier mai; **the twenty-~ time** la vingt et unième fois; **Charles the F~** Charles Premier, Charles 1er; **in the ~ place** en premier lieu, d'abord; **~ principles** principes premiers; (*Climbing*) **~ ascent** première *f*; **he did it the very ~ time** il l'a fait du premier coup; **it's not the ~ time and it won't be the last** ce n'est pas la première fois et ce ne sera pas la dernière; **they won for the ~ and last time in 1932** ils ont gagné une seule et unique fois en 1932 *or* pour la première et dernière fois en 1932; **I haven't got the ~ idea*** je n'en ai pas la moindre idée; **she doesn't know the ~ thing about it** elle est complètement ignorante là-dessus; **he goes out ~ thing in the morning** il sort dès le matin; **I'll do it ~ thing in the morning** *or* **~ thing tomorrow** je le ferai dès demain matin, je le ferai demain à la première heure; **take the pills ~ thing in the morning** prenez les pilules dès le réveil; **~ things first!** les choses importantes d'abord! (*hum*); **she's past her ~ youth** elle n'est plus de la première *or* prime jeunesse; (*fig*) **of the ~ water** de tout premier ordre; *see also* **4** *and* **first-class, floor, love, sight** *etc*.

2 adv a (*at first*) d'abord; (*firstly*) d'abord, premièrement; (*in the beginning*) au début; (*as a preliminary*) d'abord, au préalable. **~ you take off the string, then you ...** d'abord on enlève la ficelle, ensuite on ..., premièrement on enlève la ficelle, deuxièmement on ...; **when we ~ lived here** quand nous habitions ici; **he accepted but ~ he wanted ...** il a accepté mais au préalable *or* d'abord il voulait ...; **~ of all** tout d'abord, pour commencer; **~ and foremost** tout d'abord, en tout premier lieu; **he's a patriot ~ and a socialist second** il est patriote avant

d'être socialiste, chez lui, le patriote l'emporte sur le socialiste; **she arrived** ~ elle est arrivée la première; **to come** ~ (*arrive*) arriver le premier; (*in exam, competition*) être reçu premier; (*fig*) **my family comes** ~ ma famille vient en premier *or* passe avant tout *or* compte le plus; **one's health comes** ~ il faut penser à sa santé d'abord, la santé est primordiale; **she/it comes** ~ **with him** c'est elle/c'est ce qui vient en premier *or* passe avant tout *or* compte le plus à ses yeux; ~ **come** ~ **served** les premiers arrivés seront les premiers servis; **you go** ~! (*gen*) allez-y d'abord; (*in doorway etc*) passez devant!, après vous!; **ladies** ~! les dames d'abord!, place aux dames!; **women and children** ~ les femmes et les enfants d'abord; **he says** ~ **one thing and then another** il se contredit sans cesse, il dit tantôt ceci, tantôt cela; **she looked at** ~ **one thing then another** elle regardait tantôt ceci tantôt cela, elle a regardé plusieurs choses l'une après l'autre; ~ **you agree, then you change your mind!** d'abord *or* pour commencer tu acceptes, et ensuite tu changes d'avis!; ~ **and last** avant tout; **I must finish this** ~ il faut que je termine (*subj*) ceci d'abord.

b (*for the first time*) pour la première fois. **when did you** ~ **meet him?** quand est-ce que vous l'avez rencontré pour la première fois?

c (*in preference*) plutôt. **I'd die** ~! plutôt mourir!; **I'd resign** ~! je préférerais démissionner!; **I'd give up my job** ~, **rather than do that** j'aimerais mieux renoncer à mon travail que de faire cela.

3 **n** **a** premier *m*, -ière *f*. **he was among the very** ~ **to arrive** il est arrivé parmi les tout premiers; **they were the** ~ **to come** ils sont arrivés les premiers; **he was among the** ~ **to meet her** il a été l'un des premiers à la rencontrer, il a été l'un des premiers qui l'ont *or* l'aient rencontrée; (*achievement*) **another** ~ **for Britain** une nouvelle première pour la Grande-Bretagne; (*Ind*) ~ **in**, ~ **out** premier entré, premier sorti.

b (*NonC*) commencement *m*, début *m*. **at** ~ d'abord, au commencement, au début; **from** ~ **to last** du début *or* depuis le début (jusqu')à la fin; **they liked him from the** ~ ils l'ont aimé dès le début *or* dès le premier jour *or* d'emblée; **the** ~ **we'd heard of it** la première fois que nous en avons entendu parler.

c (*Aut: also* ~ **gear**) première *f* (vitesse). **in** ~ en première.

d (*Brit Univ*) **he got a** ~ ≃ il a eu sa licence avec mention très bien; **to get a double** ~ obtenir sa licence avec mention très bien dans deux disciplines.

4 **comp** ▸**first aid, first aider** *see* **first aid** ▸**first base** (*Baseball*) première base; (*US fig*) **he didn't even get to first base*** il n'a même pas franchi le premier obstacle (*fig*); **these ideas didn't even get to first base** ces idées n'ont jamais rien donné ▸**first-born** **adj, n** premier-né (*m*), première-née (*f*) ▸**first-class** *see* **first-class** ▸**the first couple** (*US*) le couple présidentiel ▸**first cousin** cousin(e) *m(f)* germain(e) *or* au premier degré ▸**first-day cover** (*Post*) émission *f* du premier jour ▸**first-degree burns** brûlures *fpl* du premier degré ▸**first-degree murder** homicide *m* volontaire ▸**first edition** première édition, (*valuable*) édition originale *or* princeps ▸**first-ever** tout premier ▸**the first family** (*US*) la famille du président ▸**first floor: on the first floor** (*Brit*) au premier (étage); (*US*) au rez-de-chaussée ▸**first-foot** (*Scot*) **n** première personne à franchir le seuil d'une maison le premier janvier ◊ **vi** rendre visite à ses parents ou amis après minuit la Saint-Sylvestre ▸**first-footing** (*Scot*) *coutume écossaise de rendre visite à ses parents ou amis après minuit la Saint-Sylvestre* ▸**first form** (*Brit Scol*) ≃ sixième *f* ▸**first fruits** **npl** (*fig*) premiers résultats *mpl* ▸**first-generation: he's a first-generation American** il appartient à la première génération d'Américains de sa famille ▸**first grade** (*US Scol*) cours *m* préparatoire ▸**first-hand** *article, news, information* de première main; **I got it at first-hand** je l'ai appris de première main ▸**first lady** première dame; (*US Pol*) présidente *f* des États-Unis (*ou personne servant d'hôtesse à sa place*); (*fig*) **the first lady of jazz** la grande dame du jazz ▸**first language** première langue *f* ▸**first lieutenant** (*Brit Naut*) lieutenant *m* de vaisseau; (*US Aviat*) lieutenant ▸**first mate** (*Naut*) second *m* ▸**first name** prénom *m*, nom *m* de baptême; **my first name is Ellis** je m'appelle Ellis de mon prénom *or* de mon petit nom, mon prénom est Ellis; **to be on first-name terms with sb** appeler qn par son prénom ▸**the first-named** (*frm*) le premier, la première ▸**first night** (*Theat etc*) première *f* ▸**first-nighter** (*Theat etc*) habitué(e) *m(f)* des premières ▸**first offender** (*Jur*) délinquant *m* primaire ▸**first officer** (*Naut*) = **first mate** ▸**first-past-the-post system** (*Pol*) système *m* majoritaire ▸**first performance** (*Cine, Theat*) première *f*; (*Mus*) première audition ▸**first person** (*Gram*) première personne ▸**first-rate** *see* **first-rate** ▸**first school** école *f* primaire (*pour enfants de 5 à 8-9 ans*) ▸**first strike capability** (*Mil*) capacité *f* de première frappe ▸**first-time buyer** personne *f* achetant une maison (*or* un appartement *etc*) pour la première fois ▸**first violin** premier violon ▸**the First World** (*Pol*) les pays industrialisés ▸**the First World War** la première guerre mondiale ▸**first year infants** (*Brit Scol*) cours *m* préparatoire.

-first [fɜːst] **adv ending in comps: feet-first** les pieds devant; *see* **head 1a**.

first aid [ˈfɜːstˈeɪd] **1** **n** premiers secours *or* soins, secours d'urgence; (*subject of study*) secourisme *m*. **to give** ~ donner les soins *or* secours d'urgence. **2** **comp** ▸**first-aid box** = **first-aid kit** ▸**first-aid classes** cours *mpl* de secourisme ▸**first aider** secouriste *mf* ▸**first-aid kit** trousse *f* de premiers secours *or* à pharmacie ▸**first-aid post, first-aid station** poste *m* de secours ▸**first-aid worker** secouriste *mf*.

first-class [ˌfɜːstˈklɑːs] **1** **adj** **a** (*Aviat, Naut, Rail etc*) *seat, ticket* de première (classe); *hotel* de première catégorie. ~ **mail** *or* **post** courrier (tarif) normal (*rapide*); ~ **stamp** timbre *m* à tarif normal (*rapide*). **b** = **first-rate**. **c** (*Univ*) ~ **honours (degree)** ≃ (licence *f* avec) mention *f* très bien. **2** **adv** *travel* en première (classe). (*Post*) **to send/go** ~ envoyer/partir en courrier normal (*rapide*).

firstly [ˈfɜːstlɪ] **adv** premièrement, en premier lieu, primo.

first-rate [ˈfɜːstˈreɪt] **adj** (*gen*) de premier ordre, excellent; *food* excellent, de premier ordre, extra*; *produce* de première qualité; *student, work* excellent, remarquable, exceptionnel; *holiday, visit* excellent, merveilleux. ~ **wine** vin *m* de haute qualité; ~ **idea** excellente idée; **there is some** ~ **photography in that film** il y a des prises de vues excellentes *or* exceptionnelles dans ce film; **he is** ~ il est de premier ordre, il est formidable*; **he is a** ~ **engineer** c'est un ingénieur de premier ordre; **he's** ~ **at his job/at tennis** il est de premier ordre *or* de première force *or* de première* dans son travail/au tennis; (*iro*) **that's** ~! c'est absolument parfait! (*iro*); ~! de première!*

firth [fɜːθ] **n** (*gen Scot*) estuaire *m*, bras *m* de mer. **the F~ of Clyde** l'estuaire *m* de la Clyde.

FIS [ˌefaɪˈes] (*Brit*) (**abbr of Family Income Supplement**) *see* **family**.

fiscal [ˈfɪskəl] **1** **adj** fiscal. ~ **drag** fiscalisation excessive entraînant un ralentissement de l'économie; ~ **year** exercice *m*; *see* **procurator**. **2** **n** (*Scot Jur*) ≃ procureur *m* de la République.

fiscalist [ˈfɪskəlɪst] **n** fiscaliste *mf*.

fish [fɪʃ] **1** **n, pl** ~ *or* ~**es** **a** poisson *m*. **I caught 2** ~ j'ai pris 2 poissons; (*fig*) **I've got other** ~ **to fry** j'ai d'autres chats à fouetter; (*loc*) **there are plenty more** ~ **in the sea** (*gen*) les occasions ne manquent pas; (*relationship*) un(e) de perdu(e) dix de retrouvé(e)s; (*fig*) **it's neither** ~ **nor fowl** (*or* **nor flesh**) **nor good red herring** ce n'est ni chair ni poisson; **he's like a** ~ **out of water** il est comme un poisson hors de l'eau; **he's a big** ~* c'est un gros poisson* *or* un gros bonnet*; **he's a queer** ~!* c'est un drôle de numéro* *or* de lascar* (celui-là)!; **poor** ~!* pauvre type!*; (*Astron*) **the F~es** les Poissons; *see* **cold, drink, gold, kettle** *etc*.

b (*NonC: Culin*) poisson *m*.

2 **comp** ▸**fish and chips** poisson frit et frites ▸**fish-and-chip shop** débit *m* de fritures ▸**fishbone** arête *f* (de poisson) ▸**fishbowl** bocal *m* (à poissons) ▸**fish cake** (*Culin*) croquette *f* de poisson ▸**fish-eye** (*in door*) œil *m* panoramique ▸**fish-eye lens** (*Phot*) objectif *m* à (champ de) 180° ▸**fish factory** conserverie *f* de poisson ▸**fish farm** centre *m* de pisciculture, centre piscicole ▸**fish farmer** pisciculteur *m*, -trice *f* ▸**fish farming** pisciculture *f*, élevage *m* de poissons (*see* **sea**) ▸**fish fingers** (*Brit*) bâtonnets *mpl* de poisson ▸**fish fry** (*US*) pique-nique *m* (*où l'on fait frire du poisson*) ▸**fish glue** colle *f* de poisson ▸**fish hook** hameçon *m* ▸**fish kettle** (*Culin*) poissonnière *f* ▸**fish knife** couteau *m* à poisson; **fish knife and fork** couvert *m* à poisson ▸**fish ladder** échelle *f* à poissons ▸**fish manure** engrais *m* de poisson ▸**fish market** marché *m* au poisson ▸**fish meal** guano *m* de poisson ▸**fishmonger** marchand(e) *m(f)* de poisson, poissonnier *m*, -ière *f* ▸**fish net** (*on fishing boat*) filet *m* (de pêche); *[angler]* épuisette *f* ▸**fishnet tights** collant *m* en résille ▸**fish paste** (*Culin*) pâte *f* d'anchois (*or* de homard *or* d'écrevisse *etc*) ▸**fishplate** (*Rail*) éclisse *f* ▸**fish-pole** (*US*) canne *f* à pêche ▸**fishpond** étang *m* à poissons; (*in fish farming*) vivier *m* ▸**fish shop** poissonnerie *f* ▸**fish slice** (*Brit Culin*) pelle *f* à poisson ▸**fish sticks** (*US*) = **fish fingers** ▸**fish store** (*US*) = **fish shop** ▸**fish story*** (*US*) histoire *f* de pêcheur, histoire marseillaise ▸**fish-tail** **vi** (*US Aut*) *[car]* chasser ▸**fish tank** aquarium *m* ▸**fishwife** marchande *f* de poisson, poissonnière *f*; (*pej*) harengère *f*, poissarde *f*; (*pej*) **she gossips like a fishwife** elle est bavarde comme une concierge; (*pej*) **she talks like a fishwife** elle a un langage de poissarde *or* de charretier.

3 **vi** pêcher. **to go** ~**ing** aller à la pêche; **to go salmon** ~**ing** aller à la pêche au saumon; **to** ~ **for trout** pêcher la truite; (*fig*) **to** ~ **in troubled waters** pêcher en eau trouble (*fig*); **to** ~ **for compliments** chercher les compliments; **to** ~ **for information from sb** tâcher de tirer des renseignements de qn; (*US*) ~ **or cut bait**‡ allez, décide-toi!

4 **vt** *trout, salmon* pêcher; *river, pool* pêcher dans; (*fig: find*) pêcher*. **they** ~**ed the cat from the well** ils ont repêché le chat du puits; **he** ~**ed a handkerchief from his pocket** il a extirpé un mouchoir de sa poche; **where on earth did you** ~ **that (up) from?*** où diable as-tu été pêcher ça?*

▸**fish out** **vt sep** (*from water*) sortir, repêcher; (*from box, drawer etc*) sortir, extirper (*from* de). **he fished out a piece of string from his pocket** il a extirpé un bout de ficelle de sa poche; **to fish sb out of a river** repêcher qn d'une rivière; *see also* **fish 4**.

▸**fish up** **vt sep** (*from water*) pêcher, repêcher; (*from bag etc*) sortir; *see also* **fish 4**.

fisher [ˈfɪʃə[r]] **n** pêcheur *m*.

fisherman [ˈfɪʃəmən] **n** pêcheur *m*. **he's a keen** ~ il aime beaucoup la pêche; (*Brit fig*) ~**'s tale** histoire *f* de pêcheur, histoire marseillaise.

fishery [ˈfɪʃərɪ] **n** pêcherie *f*, pêche *f*.

fishing [ˈfɪʃɪŋ] **1** **n** pêche *f*. **"~ prohibited"** "pêche interdite", "défense de pêcher"; **"private ~"** "pêche réservée". 2 comp ▸**fishing boat** barque *f* de pêche, (*bigger*) bateau *m* de pêche ▸**fishing expedition**: **to go on a fishing expedition** (*lit*) aller à la pêche; (*fig*) chercher à en savoir plus long ▸**fishing fleet** flottille *f* de pêche ▸**fishing grounds** pêches *fpl*, lieux *mpl* de pêche ▸**fishing harbour** port *m* de pêche ▸**fishing line** ligne *f* de pêche ▸**fishing net** (*on fishing boat*) filet *m* (de pêche); *[angler]* épuisette *f* ▸**fishing port** port *m* de pêche ▸**fishing rod** canne *f* à pêche ▸**fishing tackle** attirail *m* de pêche.

fishy ['fɪʃɪ] adj a *smell* de poisson. **it smells ~ in here** ça sent le poisson ici. b (*: *suspicious*) suspect, douteux, louche. **the whole business seems very ~ to me** toute cette histoire m'a l'air bien louche; **it seems rather ~** ça ne me paraît pas très catholique*.

fissile ['fɪsaɪl] adj fissile.

fission ['fɪʃən] n fission *f*; *see* **nuclear**.

fissionable ['fɪʃnəbl] adj fissible.

fissure ['fɪʃəʳ] n (*gen*) fissure *f*, fente *f*, crevasse *f*; (*Anat: in brain*) scissure *f*.

fissured ['fɪʃəd] adj fissuré.

fist [fɪst] 1 n a poing *m*. **he hit me with his ~** il m'a donné un coup de poing; **he shook his ~ at me** il m'a menacé du poing. b (*: *handwriting*) écriture *f*. 2 comp ▸**fist fight** pugilat *m*, bagarre *f* à coups de poing; **to have a fist fight (with sb)** se battre à coups de poing (avec qn).

-fisted ['fɪstɪd] adj ending in comps: aux poings ...; *see* **ham, tight** *etc*.

fistful ['fɪstfʊl] n poignée *f*.

fisticuffs ['fɪstɪkʌfs] npl coups *mpl* de poing.

fistula ['fɪstjʊlə] n, pl **~s** *or* **fistulae** ['fɪstjʊliː] fistule *f*.

fit[1] [fɪt] 1 adj a (*suitable, suited*) *person* capable (*for* de); *time, occasion* propice; (*worthy*) digne (*for* de); (*right and proper*) convenable, correct. **~ to eat** (*palatable*) mangeable; (*not poisonous*) comestible, bon à manger; **a meal ~ for a king** un repas digne d'un roi, un festin de roi; (*qualified etc*) **to be ~ for a job** avoir la compétence nécessaire pour faire un travail; **he isn't ~ to rule the country** il n'est pas capable *or* digne de gouverner; **he's not ~ to drive** il n'est pas capable de *or* pas en état de conduire; **I'm not ~ to be seen** je ne suis pas présentable; **that shirt isn't ~ to wear** cette chemise n'est pas mettable; **the house is ~ for habitation** cette maison est habitable; (*frm*) **it is not ~ that you should be here** il est inconvenant que vous soyez ici (*frm*); **it is not a ~ moment to ask that question** ce n'est pas le moment de poser cette question; **to see** *or* **think ~ to do** trouver *or* juger bon de faire; **I'll do as I think ~** je ferai comme bon me semblera; **he's not ~ company for my son** ce n'est pas une compagnie pour mon fils.

b (*in health*) en bonne santé, en pleine forme. **he is not a ~ man** il n'est pas en bonne santé; **she is not yet ~ to travel** elle n'est pas encore en état de voyager; (*after illness*) **~ for duty** en état de reprendre le travail; (*Mil*) en état de reprendre le service; **to be as ~ as a fiddle** être en pleine forme, se porter comme un charme; *see* **keep**.

c (*: *ready*) **~ to laugh ~ to burst** rigoler* comme un fou (*f* une folle) *or* un(e) bossu(e)*, se tenir les côtes; **she was crying ~ to break one's heart** elle sanglotait à (vous) fendre le cœur; **she goes on until she's ~ to drop** elle continue jusqu'à tomber *or* jusqu'à ce qu'elle tombe (*subj*) de fatigue; (*US: angry*) **~ to be tied‡** furibard‡.

2 n: **your dress is a very good ~** votre robe est tout à fait à votre taille; **it's rather a tight ~** c'est un peu juste.

3 vt a *[clothes etc]* aller à. **this coat ~s you (well)** ce manteau vous va bien *or* est bien à votre taille; **the key doesn't ~ the lock** la clef ne va pas pour *or* ne correspond pas à la serrure; *see* **cap**.

b (*correspond to, match*) *description* répondre à. **his account doesn't ~ the facts** son explication ne concorde pas *or* ne colle* pas avec les faits; **the punishment should ~ the crime** la punition doit être proportionnée à l'offense; **the curtains won't ~ the colour scheme** les rideaux n'iront pas avec les couleurs de la pièce, la couleur des rideaux va jurer avec le reste; (*fig*) **that ~s the bill** ça fera l'affaire.

c *garment* adapter, ajuster. **her sister ~ted the dress on her** sa sœur a ajusté la robe sur elle.

d (*put*) mettre; (*fix*) fixer (*on* sur); (*install*) poser, mettre. **he ~ted it to the side of the instrument** il l'a mis *or* fixé sur le côté de l'instrument; **to ~ a key in the lock** engager une clef dans la serrure; **to ~ a handle on a broom** emmancher un balai; **to ~ 2 things together** assembler *or* ajuster 2 objets; **I'm having a new window ~ted** je suis en train de faire poser une nouvelle fenêtre; **car ~ted with a radio** voiture équipée d'une radio; **he has been ~ted with a new hearing aid** on lui a mis *or* posé un nouvel appareil auditif.

e **to ~ sb for sth/to do** préparer qn *or* rendre qn apte à qch/à faire; **to ~ o.s. for a job** se préparer à un travail.

4 vi a *[clothes etc]* aller. **the dress doesn't ~ very well** la robe n'est pas très bien ajustée; **these shoes ~ very badly** ces souliers chaussent très mal; **it ~s like a glove** *[clothes]* cela me (*or* vous *etc*) va comme un gant; *[suggestion]* cela me (*or* leur *etc*) convient parfaitement.

b *[key, spare part]* entrer, aller. **this key doesn't ~** cette clef n'entre pas, ce n'est pas la bonne clef; **the saucepan lid doesn't ~ any more** le couvercle ne va plus sur la casserole; **that lid won't ~ on this saucepan** ce couvercle ne va pas avec cette casserole.

c *[facts etc]* s'accorder, cadrer. **if the description ~s, he must be the thief** si la description est la bonne, ce doit être lui le voleur; **it all ~s now!** tout s'éclaire!; **it doesn't ~ with what he said to me** ceci ne correspond pas à *or* ne s'accorde pas avec *or* ne cadre pas avec ce qu'il m'a dit; (*fig*) **his face doesn't ~ there** il fait fausse note là, il détonne là.

▸**fit in** 1 vi a *[fact]* s'accorder (*with* avec). **this doesn't fit in with what I myself learnt** ceci ne correspond pas à *or* ne s'accorde pas avec *or* ne cadre pas avec ce que j'ai appris de mon côté.

b *[remark]* être en harmonie (*with* avec). **he left the firm because he didn't fit in** il a quitté la compagnie parce qu'il n'arrivait pas à s'intégrer; **he doesn't fit in with our group** il n'est pas au diapason de notre groupe.

c entrer. **this dictionary won't fit in on the shelf** ce dictionnaire n'entre pas sur le rayon.

2 vt sep a faire entrer. **can you fit another book in?** pouvez-vous faire entrer encore un livre?

b adapter, faire concorder. **I'll try to fit my plans in with yours** je tâcherai de faire concorder mes projets avec les tiens.

c prendre, caser*. **the doctor can fit you in tomorrow at 3** le docteur peut vous prendre *or* vous caser* demain à 15 heures.

▸**fit on** 1 vi: **this bottle top won't fit on any more** cette capsule ne ferme plus; **it should fit on this end somewhere** cela doit aller *or* se mettre là au bout (quelque part). 2 vt sep mettre, fixer, poser (*to* sur).

▸**fit out** vt sep *expedition, person* équiper; *ship* armer.

▸**fit up** vt sep pourvoir (*with* de). **they have fitted their house up with all modern conveniences** ils ont pourvu leur maison de tout le confort moderne.

fit[2] [fɪt] n a (*Med*) accès *m*, attaque *f*. **~ of coughing** quinte *f* de toux; **to have** *or* **throw* a ~** avoir *or* piquer* une crise; **to fall down in a ~** tomber en convulsions; (*fig*) **she'll have a ~ when we tell her*** elle aura une attaque *or* elle piquera une crise quand on lui dira ça*; *see* **blue, epileptic, faint**. b (*outburst*) mouvement *m*, accès *m*. **in a ~ of anger** dans un mouvement *or* accès de colère; **~ of crying** crise *f* de larmes; **to be in ~s (of laughter), to get a ~ of the giggles** avoir le fou rire; **he has ~s of enthusiasm** il a des accès d'enthousiasme; **in ~s and starts** par à-coups.

fitful ['fɪtfʊl] adj *showers* intermittent; *wind* capricieux, changeant; *sleep* troublé, agité. **~ enthusiasm/anger** des accès *mpl* d'enthousiasme/de colère.

fitfully ['fɪtfəlɪ] adv *move, work* par à-coups; *sleep* de façon intermittente.

fitment ['fɪtmənt] n a (*Brit: built-in furniture*) meuble encastré; (*cupboard*) placard encastré; (*in kitchen*) élément *m* (de cuisine). **you can't move the table, it's a ~** on ne peut pas déplacer la table, elle est encastrée. b (*for vacuum cleaner, mixer etc*) accessoire *m*. **it's part of the light ~** cela fait partie de l'appareil d'éclairage.

fitness ['fɪtnɪs] n a (*health*) santé *f* *or* forme *f* (physique). b (*suitability*) *[remark]* à-propos *m*, justesse *f*; *[person]* aptitudes *fpl* (*for* pour).

fitted ['fɪtɪd] adj a *garment* ajusté. (*Brit*) **~ carpet** moquette *f*; (*Brit*) **to lay a ~ carpet in a room** moquetter une pièce; **the room has a ~ carpet** la pièce est moquettée; (*Brit*) **~ kitchen** cuisine *f* aménagée; **~ sheet** drap-housse *m*; (*Brit*) **~ wardrobe** armoire *f* incorporée. b (*suitable*) **to be ~ for sth/to do** être apte à qch/à faire, être fait pour qch/ pour faire.

fitter ['fɪtəʳ] n a (*Dress*) essayeur *m*, -euse *f*. b (*of machine, device*) monteur *m*; (*of carpet*) poseur *m*.

fitting ['fɪtɪŋ] 1 adj *remark* approprié (*to* à), juste. 2 n a (*Dress*) essayage *m*. **~ room** salon *m* d'essayage. b (*Brit: gen pl: in house etc*) **~s** installations *fpl*; **bathroom ~s** installations sanitaires; **electrical ~s** installations électriques, appareillage *m* électrique; **furniture and ~s** mobilier *m* et installations; **office ~s** équipement *m* de bureau; *see* **light**[1].

-fitting ['fɪtɪŋ] adj ending in comps: **ill-fitting** qui ne va pas; **wide-fitting** large; *see* **close**[1] **3, loose 2, tight 3**.

fittingly ['fɪtɪŋlɪ] adv *dress* convenablement (pour l'occasion); *speak* à propos; *say* avec justesse, avec à-propos.

five [faɪv] 1 adj cinq *inv*. (*Rugby*) **Five Nations Tournament** tournoi *m* des cinq nations; *for other phrases see* **six**.

2 n a cinq *m*. (*esp US*) **to take ~*** faire une pause; *for other phrases see* **six**.

b (*Sport*) **~s** *sorte de jeu de pelote (à la main)*.

3 pron cinq *mfpl*. **there are ~** il y en a cinq.

4 comp ▸**five-and-dime, five-and-ten** (*US*) bazar *m*, Prisunic *m* ® ▸**five-a-side (football)** (*Brit*) football *m* à cinq ▸**five-by-five*** (*US fig*) aussi gros que grand ▸**fivefold** adj quintuple ◊ adv au quintuple ▸**five-o'clock shadow** barbe *f* d'un jour ▸**five spot*** (*US*) billet *m* de cinq dollars ▸**five-star restaurant** ≃ restaurant *m* (à) trois étoiles ▸**five-star hotel** palace *m* ▸**five-year** quinquennal ▸**five-year man*** (*US Univ: hum*) éternel redoublant *m* ▸**five-year plan** plan quinquennal.

fiver* ['faɪvəʳ] n (*Brit*) billet *m* de cinq livres; (*US*) billet de cinq dollars.

fix [fɪks] 1 vt a (*make firm*) (*with nails etc*) fixer; (*with ropes etc*) attacher. **to ~ a stake in the ground** enfoncer un pieu en terre; (*Mil*) **to ~ bayonets** mettre (la) baïonnette au canon; *see also* **fixed**.

b *attention* fixer (*on* sur). **to ~ one's eyes on sth** fixer qch du regard; **he ~ed his eye on me** son regard s'est fixé sur moi; **all eyes were ~ed on her** tous les regards *or* tous les yeux étaient fixés sur elle; **he ~ed him with an angry glare** il l'a fixé d'un regard furieux, il a dardé sur lui un regard furieux; **to ~ sth in one's mind** graver *or* imprimer qch dans son esprit; **to ~ one's hopes on sth** mettre tous ses espoirs en qch; **to ~ the blame on sb** attribuer la responsabilité à qn, mettre la responsabilité sur le dos de qn.

c (*arrange, decide*) décider, arrêter; *time, price* fixer, arrêter; *limit* fixer, établir. **on the date ~ed** à la date convenue; **nothing has been ~ed yet** rien n'a encore été décidé, il n'y a encore rien d'arrêté.

d (*Phot*) fixer. **~ing bath** (*liquid*) bain *m* de fixage; (*container*) cuvette *f* de fixage.

e (*US **) arranger, préparer. **to ~ one's hair** se passer un coup de peigne; **can I ~ you a drink?** puis-je vous offrir un verre?; **I'll go and ~ us something to eat** je vais vite nous faire quelque chose à manger.

f (*deal with*) arranger; (*mend*) réparer. **don't worry, I'll ~ it all** ne vous en faites pas, je vais tout arranger; **he ~ed it with the police before he called the meeting** il a attendu d'avoir le feu vert* de la police *or* il s'est arrangé avec la police avant d'organiser la réunion; **I'll soon ~ him***, (*US*) **I'll ~ his wagon*** je vais lui régler son compte; **to ~ a flat tyre** réparer un pneu.

g (**: bribe etc*) *person, witness, juror* acheter, soudoyer; *match, fight, election, trial* truquer.

2 n a (*) ennui *m*, embêtement* *m*. **to be in/get into a ~** être/se mettre dans le pétrin *or* dans de beaux draps; **what a ~!** nous voilà dans de beaux draps! *or* dans le pétrin!

b (*Drugs sl: injection*) piqûre *f*, piquouse *f* (*sl*). **to get *or* give o.s. a ~** se shooter (*sl*), se piquer.

c (*Aviat, Naut*) position *f*. **I've got a ~ on him now** j'ai sa position maintenant; (*Naut*) **to take a ~ on** déterminer la position de; (*fig*) **I can't get a ~* on it** je n'arrive pas à m'en faire une idée claire.

d (*US: trick*) **it's a ~*** c'est truqué, c'est une combine.

▸**fix on** 1 vt fus choisir. **they finally fixed on that house** leur choix s'est finalement arrêté sur cette maison-là. 2 vt sep *lid* fixer, attacher.

▸**fix up** 1 vi s'arranger (*to do* pour faire). 2 vt sep arranger, combiner. **I'll try to fix something up** je tâcherai d'arranger quelque chose; **let's fix it all up now** décidons tout de suite des détails; **to fix sb up with sth** faire avoir qch à qn, obtenir qch pour qn; **I fixed him up with a job** je lui ai trouvé un travail; **we fixed them up for one night** nous leur avons trouvé à coucher pour une nuit.

fixation [fɪk'seɪʃən] n (*Chem, Phot, Psych*) fixation *f*; (*fig*) obsession *f*. **to have a ~ about** (*Psych*) avoir une fixation à; (*fig*) être obsédé par.

fixative ['fɪksətɪv] n fixatif *m*.

fixed [fɪkst] adj a *star, stare* fixe; *idea* arrêté; *smile* figé; *determination* inébranlable; (*Ling*) *stress, word order* fixe. (*Jur*) **of no ~ abode** sans domicile fixe; (*Mil*) **with ~ bayonets** baïonnette au canon; **~ menu** (menu *m* à) prix *m* fixe; **~ price** prix *m* fixe *or* imposé; (*Fin*) **~ assets** immobilisations *fpl*; (*Fin*) **~ costs** frais *mpl* fixes; **~ cost contract** marché *m* à prix forfaitaire; **~ (decimal) point** virgule *f* fixe; (*Comput*) **~ disk** disque *m* fixe; (*Comput*) **~-point notation, ~-point representation** notation *f* en virgule fixe; **~-rate financing** financement *m* à taux fixe; **~ term contract** contrat *m* de durée déterminée.

b (*) **how are we ~ for time?** on a combien de temps?; **how are you ~ for cigarettes?** vous avez des cigarettes?; **how are you ~ for tonight?** qu'est-ce que vous faites ce soir?, vous êtes libre ce soir?

fixedly ['fɪksɪdlɪ] adv fixement.

fixer ['fɪksəʳ] n a (*Phot*) fixateur *m*. b (*‡: person*) combinard(e)‡ *m(f)*.

fixings ['fɪksɪŋz] npl (*US Culin*) garniture *f*, accompagnement *m*.

fixity ['fɪksɪtɪ] n *[stare]* fixité *f*. **his ~ of purpose** sa détermination inébranlable.

fixture ['fɪkstʃəʳ] n a (*gen pl: in building etc*) installation *f*; (*Jur*) immeuble *m* par destination. (*Brit*) **the house was sold with ~s and fittings** on a vendu la maison avec toutes les installations; (*Brit*) **£2000 for ~s and fittings** 2000 livres de reprise; (*fig*) **she's a ~*** elle fait partie du mobilier*; **lighting ~s** appareillage *m* électrique. b (*Brit Sport*) match *m* (prévu), rencontre *f*. **~ list** calendrier *m*.

fizz [fɪz] 1 vi *[champagne etc]* pétiller, mousser; *[steam etc]* siffler. 2 n a pétillement *m*; sifflement *m*. b (‡) champagne *m*, champ‡ *m*; (*US*) eau *or* boisson gazeuse.

▸**fizz up** vi monter (en pétillant), mousser.

fizzle ['fɪzl] vi pétiller.

▸**fizzle out** vi *[firework]* rater (*une fois en l'air*); *[party, event]* finir en eau de boudin; *[book, film, plot]* se terminer en queue de poisson; *[business started]* s'en aller en eau de boudin; *[plans]* aller à vau-l'eau, ne rien donner; *[enthusiasm, interest]* tomber.

fizzy ['fɪzɪ] adj *soft drink* pétillant, gazeux; *wine* mousseux, pétillant.

fjord [fjɔːd] n = **fiord**.

FL (*US Post*) abbr of **Florida**.

Fla. (*US*) abbr of **Florida**.

flab* [flæb] n (*fat*) graisse *f* superflue, lard* *m*.

flabbergast* ['flæbəgɑːst] vt sidérer*, époustoufler*, ahurir. **I was ~ed at this** j'ai été sidéré* *or* époustouflé* d'apprendre ça.

flabby ['flæbɪ] adj *handshake* mou (*f* molle); *muscle, flesh, person* flasque; (*fig*) *character* mou, mollasse, indolent.

flaccid ['flæksɪd] adj *muscle, flesh* flasque, mou (*f* molle).

flaccidity [flæk'sɪdɪtɪ] n flaccidité *f*.

flack [flæk] 1 n (*US Cine, Press*) agent *m* de presse. 2 vi servir d'agent de presse.

flag¹ [flæg] 1 n a drapeau *m*; (*Naut*) pavillon *m*. **~ of truce, white ~** drapeau blanc; *[pirates]* **black ~** pavillon noir; **red ~** drapeau rouge; **"The Red F~"** *hymne du parti travailliste*; **~ of convenience**, (*US*) **~ of necessity** pavillon de complaisance; (*fig*) **with (all) ~s flying** en pavoisant; **to go down with ~s flying** (*Naut*) couler pavillon haut; (*fig*) mener la lutte jusqu'au bout; (*fig*) **to keep the ~ flying** maintenir les traditions; *see* **show**.

b *[taxi]* **the ~ was down** ≃ le taxi était pris.

c (*for charity*) insigne *m* (*d'une œuvre charitable*).

d (*Comput*) drapeau *m*.

2 vt a orner *or* garnir de drapeaux; *street, building, ship* pavoiser.

b (*also* **~ down**) *taxi, bus, car* héler, faire signe à; *[police]* faire signe de s'arrêter à.

c (*mark*) *page* signaler (*avec une marque*); (*Comput*) signaler (*avec un drapeau*).

3 comp ▸**flag carrier** (*airline*) compagnie *f* nationale ▸**flag day** (*Brit*) journée *f* de vente d'insignes (*pour une œuvre charitable*); (*Brit*) **flag day in aid of the war-blinded** journée *f* des *or* pour les aveugles de guerre ▸**Flag Day** (*US*) le 14 juin (*anniversaire du drapeau américain*) ▸**flag officer** (*Naut*) officier supérieur ▸**flagpole** mât *m* (*pour drapeau*) ▸**flagship** (*Naut*) vaisseau *m* amiral; (*Comm*) produit *m* vedette ▸**flagstaff** mât *m* (*pour drapeau*); (*Naut*) mât de pavillon ▸**flag stop** (*US*) arrêt facultatif ▸**flag-waving** (*fig*) n déclarations *fpl* cocardières ◊ adj *politicians, patriots etc* cocardier.

flag² [flæg] vi *[plants etc]* languir, dépérir; *[athlete, walker, health]* s'affaiblir, s'alanguir; *[worker, zeal, courage etc]* fléchir, se relâcher; *[conversation]* traîner, languir; *[interest, spirits]* faiblir; *[enthusiasm]* tomber. **his steps were ~ging** il commençait à traîner la jambe; (*gen*) **it's ~ging** ça ne va pas fort.

flag³ [flæg] n (*Bot*) iris *m* (des marais).

flag⁴ [flæg] n (*also* **~stone**) dalle *f*. **kitchen with a ~ floor** cuisine dallée.

flagellate ['flædʒəleɪt] 1 adj, n (*Bio*) flagellé (*m*). 2 vt flageller, fouetter.

flagellation [ˌflædʒə'leɪʃən] n flagellation *f*.

flagellum [flə'dʒeləm] n, pl **~s** *or* **flagella** [flə'dʒelə] flagelle *m*.

flageolet [ˌflædʒəʊ'let] n (*Mus, Culin*) flageolet *m*.

flagon ['flægən] n (*of glass*) (grande) bouteille *f*, (*larger*) bonbonne *f*; (*jug*) (grosse) cruche *f*.

flagrant ['fleɪgrənt] adj flagrant.

flagrante delicto [flə'græntɪdɪ'lɪktəʊ] adv: **in ~** en flagrant délit *m*.

flagrantly ['fleɪgrəntlɪ] adv *provocative* clairement. **~ unjust** d'une injustice flagrante.

flail [fleɪl] 1 n (*Agr*) fléau *m*. 2 vt (*Agr*) *corn* battre au fléau. 3 vi *[arms etc]* (*also* **~ about**) battre l'air.

flair [flɛəʳ] n a (*talent*) flair *m*; (*perceptiveness*) perspicacité *f*. **to have a ~ for** avoir du flair pour. b (*style, elegance*) style *m*.

flak [flæk] 1 n a (*Mil*) (*firing*) tir antiaérien *or* de D.C.A.; (*guns*) canons antiaériens *or* de D.C.A.; (*flashes*) éclairs *mpl*. **~ ship** bâtiment *m* de D.C.A. b (**: criticism*) critiques *fpl* (désobligeantes). **he got a lot of ~ from ...** il s'est fait éreinter par ... . 2 comp ▸**flak-jacket** gilet *m* pare-balles *inv*.

flake [fleɪk] 1 n *[snow, cereal etc]* flocon *m*; *[metal etc]* paillette *f*, écaille *f*; *see* **corn¹**. 2 comp ▸**flake-white** blanc *m* de plomb. 3 vi (*also* **~ off**) *[stone, plaster etc]* s'effriter, s'écailler; *[paint]* s'écailler; *[skin]* peler, se desquamer (*Med*). 4 vt (*also* **~ off**) effriter, écailler. (*Culin*) **~d almonds** amandes effilées.

▸**flake off** vi a *see* **flake 4**. b (*US*) **flake off!‡** fous le camp!‡, de l'air!*

▸**flake out‡** vi (*Brit*) (*faint*) tomber dans les pommes*, tourner de l'œil*; (*fall asleep*) s'endormir *or* tomber (tout d'une masse). **to be flaked out‡** être crevé* *or* à plat*.

flakey‡ ['fleɪkɪ] adj (*US*) bizarre, excentrique.

flaky ['fleɪkɪ] adj floconneux; *pastry, biscuit* feuilleté.

flambé ['flɒːmbeɪ] 1 adj flambé. 2 vt flamber. **~ed steaks** steaks flambés.

flamboyance [flæm'bɔɪəns] n extravagance *f*.

flamboyant [flæm'bɔɪənt] adj *colour* flamboyant, éclatant; *person, character* haut en couleur; *rudeness* ostentatoire; *speech* retentissant; *style, dress, manners* extravagant; (*Archit*) flamboyant.

flame [fleɪm] 1 n a flamme *f*; (*fig*) *[passion, enthusiasm]* flamme, ardeur *f*, feu *m*. **in ~s** en flammes, en feu; **to burst into ~s, to go up in ~s** (*lit*) s'enflammer (brusquement), prendre feu (tout à coup), s'embraser; *see* **fan¹, fuel**. b **she's one of his old ~s*** c'est un de ses anciens béguins*. 2 comp ▸**flame-coloured** (rouge) feu *inv* ▸**flame gun** = **flamethrower** ▸**flame-proof dish** plat *m* à feu *or* allant au feu

▸**flame red** n, **flame-red** adj rouge *(m)* vif ▸**flamethrower** lance-flammes *m inv*. 3 vi *[fire]* flamber; *[passion]* brûler. **her cheeks ~d** ses joues se sont empourprées.

▸**flame up** vi *[fire]* flamber; (*fig*) *[anger]* exploser; *[quarrel, dispute]* éclater; *[person]* exploser*, se mettre en colère.

flamenco [flə'meŋkəʊ] adj, n flamenco *(m)*.

flaming ['fleɪmɪŋ] 1 adj a *sun, fire etc* ardent, flamboyant. b (*Brit *: furious*) furibard*, furax*. c (‡) fichu*, foutu‡. **you and your ~ radio!** toi et ta fichue* *or* foutue‡ radio!; **it's a ~ nuisance!** c'est empoisonnant!*, ce que c'est enquiquinant!* 2 adv‡: **he's ~ stupid!** il est complètement con!‡

flamingo [flə'mɪŋgəʊ] n, pl **~s** *or* **~es** flamant *m* (rose).

flammable ['flæməbl] adj inflammable (*lit*).

flan [flæn] n (*Brit Culin*) tarte *f*; (*savoury*) ≃ quiche *f*.

Flanders ['flɑːndəz] n Flandre(s) *f(pl)*. **~ poppy** coquelicot *m*.

flange [flændʒ] n (*on wheel*) boudin *m*; (*on pipe*) collerette *f*, bride *f*; (*on I-beam*) aile *f*; (*on railway rail*) patin *m*; (*on tool*) rebord *m*, collet *m*.

flanged [flændʒd] adj *wheel etc* à boudin, à rebord; *tube etc* à brides; *radiator* à ailettes.

flank [flæŋk] 1 n (*Anat, Geog, Mil*) flanc *m*; (*Culin*) flanchet *m*. 2 vt a flanquer. **~ed by 2 policemen** flanqué de *or* encadré par 2 gendarmes. b (*Mil*) flanquer; (*turn the ~ of*) contourner le flanc de.

flanker ['flæŋkə^r] n (*Rugby*) ailier *m*.

flannel ['flænl] 1 n a (*Tex: NonC*) flanelle *f*; (*Brit: face ~*) gant *m* de toilette; (*Brit * fig: waffle*) baratin *m*. b (*Brit: trousers*) **~s** pantalon *m* de flanelle. 2 comp de flanelle. 3 vi (*Brit *: waffle*) baratiner‡.

flannelette [ˌflænə'let] 1 n finette *f*, pilou *m*. 2 comp *sheet* de finette, de pilou.

flap [flæp] 1 n a *[wings]* battement *m*, coup *m*; *[sails]* claquement *m*; (*Phon*) battement *m*.

b *[pocket, envelope, hat, tent]* rabat *m*; *[counter, table]* abattant *m*; (*door in floor*) trappe *f*; (*for cats*) ouverture *f* à abattant; (*Aviat*) volet *m*.

c (*: *panic*) panique *f*. **to be in a ~** être affolé *or* dans tous ses états; **to get into a ~** s'affoler, se mettre dans tous ses états, paniquer*.

2 comp ▸**flapjack** (*Culin*) (*pancake*) crêpe épaisse; (*biscuit*) galette *f*.

3 vi a *[wings]* battre; *[shutters]* battre, claquer; *[sails]* claquer. **his cloak ~ped about his legs** sa cape lui battait les jambes; (*: *fig*) **his ears must be ~ping** ses oreilles doivent siffler*.

b (*: *be panicky*) paniquer*. **don't ~!** pas de panique!, pas d'affolement!

4 vt *[bird]* **to ~ its wings** battre des ailes.

flapdoodle* ['flæpˌduːdəl] n blague* *f*, balivernes *fpl*.

flapper*† ['flæpə^r] n jeune fille délurée (des années 1920).

flare [flɛə^r] 1 n a (*light*) *[torch, fire]* flamme *f*, éclat *m*, flamboiement *m*; *[sun]* éclat, flamboiement.

b (*signal*) feu *m*, signal *m* (lumineux); (*Mil*) fusée éclairante, fusée-parachute *f*; (*Aviat: for target*) bombe éclairante *or* de jalonnement; (*for runway*) balise *f*.

c (*Dress*) évasement *m*. **~s*** = **~d trousers**; *see* **4**.

2 comp ▸**flare path** (*Aviat*) piste *f* balisée ▸**flare-up** *[fire]* flambée *f* (soudaine); *[war]* intensification soudaine; *[quarrel, fighting]* recrudescence *f*; (*outburst of rage*) crise *f* de colère; (*sudden dispute*) altercation *f*, prise *f* de bec*.

3 vi a *[match]* s'enflammer; *[candle]* briller; *[sunspot]* brûler.

b *[sleeves, skirt]* s'évaser, s'élargir.

4 vt *skirt, trouser legs* évaser. **~d skirt** jupe évasée; **~d trousers** pantalon *m* à pattes d'éléphant.

▸**flare out** vi *see* **flare 3b**.

▸**flare up** 1 vi *[fire]* s'embraser, prendre (brusquement); *[person]* se mettre en colère, s'emporter; *[political situation]* exploser; *[anger, fighting, revolt]* éclater; *[disease]* se réveiller, reprendre; *[epidemic]* éclater, se déclarer (soudain). (*fig*) **he flares up at the slightest thing** il est très soupe au lait. 2 **flare-up** n *see* **flare 2**.

flash [flæʃ] 1 n a *[flame, jewels]* éclat *m*. **~ of lightning** éclair *m*; **~ of wit** saillie *f*, boutade *f*; **it happened in a ~** c'est arrivé en un clin d'œil; **it came to him in a ~ that ...** l'idée lui est venue tout d'un coup que ...; (*fig*) **a ~ in the pan** un feu de paille (*fig*); **~ of inspiration** éclair de génie; *see* **hot 1a**.

b (*also* **news~**) flash *m* (d'information). **we've just had a ~ that ...** nous venons de recevoir un flash *or* une dépêche indiquant que ... .

c (*Mil*) parement *m*.

d (*Phot*) flash *m*. **did you use a ~?** tu l'as faite *or* prise au flash?

e (*US: bright student*) petit(e) doué(e) *m(f)*.

2 vi a *[jewels]* étinceler, briller; *[light, traffic lights etc]* clignoter; *[eyes]* lancer des éclairs. **lightning was ~ing** il y avait des éclairs; (*Aut*) **~ing light** (*gen*) clignotant *m*; *[police car etc]* rotophare *m*.

b *[person, vehicle]* **to ~ in/out/past** *etc* entrer/sortir/passer *etc* comme un éclair; **the news ~ed round** la nouvelle s'est répandue comme un éclair *or* comme une traînée de poudre; **the day ~ed by** *or* **past** on n'a pas senti la journée passer; **the thought ~ed through his mind that ...** un instant, il a pensé que ...; **his whole life ~ed before him** il a revu le film de sa vie; **it ~ed upon me** *or* **into my mind that ...** l'idée m'est venue tout d'un coup que ... .

c (*Brit* ‡: *expose o.s. indecently*) s'exhiber.

3 vt a *light* projeter. **to ~ a torch on** diriger une lampe (de poche) sur; **she ~ed him a look of contempt** elle lui a jeté un regard de mépris; **to ~ a smile at sb** lancer un sourire éclatant à qn; (*Aut*) **to ~ one's headlights,** (*US*) **to ~ the high beams** faire un appel de phares (*at sb* à qn).

b (*flaunt*) *diamond ring* étaler (aux yeux de tous), mettre (bien) en vue. **don't ~ all that money around** n'étale pas tout cet argent comme ça.

4 comp ▸**flashback** (*Cine*) flashback *m inv*, retour *m* en arrière ▸**flash bulb** (*Phot*) ampoule *f* de flash ▸**flash burn** (*Med*) brûlure *f* de la peau (*causée par un flux thermique*) ▸**flash card** (*Scol*) carte *f* (*support visuel*) ▸**flash cube** (*Phot*) cube-flash *m* ▸**flash flood** crue subite ▸**flash gun** (*Phot*) flash *m* ▸**flashlight** (*Phot*) flash *m*; (*torch*) lampe *f* électrique *or* de poche; (*on lighthouse etc*) fanal *m* ▸**flash meter** (*Phot*) flashmètre *m* ▸**flash pack** emballage *m* promotionnel ▸**flash photography** (*Phot*) photographie *f* au flash ▸**flash point** (*Chem*) point *m* d'ignition; (*fig*) **the situation had nearly reached flash point** la situation était sur le point d'exploser ▸**flash powder** (*Phot*) photopoudre *m*.

5 adj (*) = **flashy**.

flasher ['flæʃə^r] n a (*light, device*) clignotant *m*. b (*Brit *: person committing indecent exposure*) exhibitionniste *m*.

flashing ['flæʃɪŋ] n a (*on roof*) revêtement *m* de zinc (*pour toiture*), noue *f*. b (*Brit *: indecent exposure*) exhibitionnisme *m*.

flashy ['flæʃɪ] adj (*pej*) *person* tapageur; *jewellery, car* tape-à-l'œil *inv*, clinquant; *dress* tapageur, tape-à-l'œil *inv*, voyant; *colour, taste* criard, tapageur.

flask [flɑːsk] n (*Pharm*) fiole *f*; (*Chem*) ballon *m*; (*bottle*) bouteille *f*; (*for pocket*) flasque *f*; (*also* **vacuum ~**) (bouteille) Thermos *f* ®.

flat¹ [flæt] 1 adj a *countryside, surface, the earth* plat; *tyre* dégonflé, à plat. **as ~ as a pancake*** *tyre* plat comme une galette; *surface, countryside* tout plat; (*after bombing*) complètement rasé; **a ~ dish** un plat creux; **~ roof** toit plat *or* en terrasse; **~ nose** nez épaté *or* camus; **a ~ stomach** un ventre plat; **to have ~ feet** avoir les pieds plats; **he was lying ~ on the floor** il était (étendu) à plat par terre; **the blow laid him ~** le coup l'a terrassé; **to fall ~ on one's face** tomber à plat ventre *or* sur le nez; **to fall ~** *[event, joke]* tomber à plat; *[scheme]* ne rien donner; **lay the book ~ on the table** pose le livre à plat sur la table; **the earthquake laid the whole city ~** le tremblement de terre a rasé la ville entière; (*Sport*) **a ~ race** une course de plat; (* *fig*) **to be in a ~ spin** être dans tous ses états; *see also* **4**.

b (*dull*) *taste, style* monotone, plat; (*unexciting*) *event, experience* terne, anodin; *battery* à plat; *beer etc* éventé. **I was feeling rather ~** je me sentais sans ressort, je me sentais plutôt vidé* *or* à plat*; **the beer tastes ~** la bière a un goût fade *or* d'éventé.

c (*Mus*) faux (*f* fausse), trop bas. **B ~** si *m* bémol.

d *refusal, denial* net (*f* nette), catégorique. **and that's ~!*** un point c'est tout!*; *see also* **4**.

e (*Comm*) **~ rate of pay** salaire *m* fixe; *[price, charge]* **~ rate** taux *m* fixe.

f (*not shiny*) *colour* mat.

g (*US: penniless*) **to be ~‡** être fauché (comme les blés)*, n'avoir plus un rond*.

2 adv a carrément, nettement, sans ambages. **he told me ~ that ...** il m'a dit carrément *or* sans ambages que ...; **he turned it down ~** il l'a carrément refusé, il l'a refusé tout net; (*Brit*) **to be ~ broke‡** être fauché (comme les blés)*, n'avoir plus un rond*; **in 10 seconds ~** en 10 secondes pile.

b **to go ~ out** *[runner in race]* donner son maximum; *[person running in street]* courir comme un dératé; *[car]* être à sa vitesse de pointe; **to go ~ out for sth** faire tout son possible pour avoir qch; **to be working ~ out** travailler d'arrache-pied; **to be lying ~ out** être étendu *or* couché de tout son long; **to be ~ out** (*exhausted*) être à plat* *or* vidé*; (*asleep*) dormir, ronfler* (*fig*); (*drunk*) être complètement rétamé, être K.-O.*; *see also* **4**.

c (*Mus*) *sing* faux, trop bas.

3 n a *[hand, blade]* plat *m*.

b (*Geog*) (*dry land*) plaine *f*; (*marsh*) marécage *m*; *see* **salt**.

c (*Mus*) bémol *m*. **A ~** la *m* bémol.

d (*US Aut*) crevaison *f*, pneu crevé.

e (*Racing*) **the ~** = **flat racing, the flat season** (*see* **4**); **on the ~** sur le plat.

4 comp ▸**flat bed** *[lorry]* plateau *m* ▸**flat-bed lorry** camion *m* à plateau ▸**flat-bottomed boat** bateau *m* à fond plat ▸**flat cap** (*Brit*) casquette *f* ▸**flat car** (*US Rail*) wagon-plateforme *m* ▸**flat-chested: she is flat-chested** elle est plate (comme une limande*), elle n'a pas de poitrine ▸**flat fish** poisson plat ▸**flatfoot‡** (*US: policeman*) flic* *m* ▸**flatfooted** adj (*lit*) aux pieds plats; (* *fig*) (*tactless*) *person, approach* maladroit; (*unequivocal*) *answer* clair et net ◊ adv (*wholeheartedly*) tout de go*; (*US fig*) **to catch sb flatfooted*** prendre qn par sur-

prise ▸**flatiron** fer *m* à repasser ▸**flat-out*** (*US*) **adj** complet, absolu ◊ **adv** complètement ▸**flat racing** (*Racing*) plat *m* ▸**flat rate amount** (*Fin, Jur*) montant *m* forfaitaire ▸**flat screen** (*TV*) écran *m* plat ▸**flat season** (*Racing*) (saison *f* du) plat *m* ▸**flat silver** (*US*) couverts *mpl* en argent ▸**flattop*** (*US*) porte-avions *m* ▸**flat top** (*haircut*) coupe *f* à la brosse ▸**flatware** (*plates*) plats *mpl* et assiettes *fpl*; (*cutlery*) couverts *mpl* ▸**flatworm** plathelminthe *m*.

flat² [flæt] **n** (*Brit*) appartement *m*. **to go ~-hunting** chercher un appartement; **my ~mate** la fille (*or* le garçon *or* la personne) avec qui je partage l'appartement.

flatlet ['flætlɪt] **n** (*Brit*) studio *m*.

flatly ['flætlɪ] **adv** *deny, oppose, refuse* catégoriquement, absolument. **"I'm not going" he said ~** "je n'y vais pas" dit-il tout net.

flatness ['flætnɪs] **n** *[countryside, surface]* égalité *f*, aspect *m* plat; *[curve]* aplatissement *m*; *[refusal]* netteté *f*; (*dullness*) monotonie *f*.

flatten ['flætn] **vt** a *path, road* aplanir; *metal* aplatir. b *[wind, storm etc] crops* coucher, écraser; *tree* abattre; *town, building* raser; (*: *knock over*) *person* étendre*. **to ~ o.s. against** s'aplatir *or* se plaquer contre. c (*: *defeat*) écraser*. d (*: *snub*) *person* clouer le bec à*, river son clou à. **that'll ~ him!** ça lui clouera le bec!*

▸**flatten out** 1 **vi** *[countryside, road]* s'aplanir; *[aircraft]* se redresser; *[curve]* s'aplatir. 2 **vt sep** *path* aplanir; *metal* aplatir; *map etc* ouvrir à plat.

flatter ['flætəʳ] **vt** (*all senses*) flatter. **he ~s himself he's a good musician** il se flatte d'être bon musicien; **you ~ yourself!** tu te flattes!

flatterer ['flætərəʳ] **n** flatteur *m*, -euse *f*, flagorneur *m*, -euse *f* (*pej*).

flattering ['flætərɪŋ] **adj** *person, remark* flatteur. **that's not very ~** ce n'est pas très flatteur; **she wears very ~ clothes** elle porte des vêtements très seyants *or* qui l'avantagent.

flatteringly ['flætərɪŋlɪ] **adv** flatteusement.

flattery ['flætərɪ] **n** flatterie *f*.

flatties* [flætɪz] **npl** chaussures *fpl* basses *or* à talon plat.

flatulence ['flætjʊləns] **n** flatulence *f*.

flatulent ['flætjʊlənt] **adj** flatulent.

flaunt [flɔːnt] **vt** *wealth* étaler, afficher; *jewels* faire étalage de; *knowledge* faire étalage *or* parade de; *boyfriend etc* afficher. **she ~ed her femininity at him** elle lui jetait sa féminité à la tête; **to ~ o.s.** poser (pour la galerie).

flautist ['flɔːtɪst] **n** (*Brit*) flûtiste *mf*.

flavour, (*US*) **flavor** ['fleɪvəʳ] 1 **n** goût *m*, saveur *f*; *[ice cream]* parfum *m*. **with a rum ~** (parfumé) au rhum; (*fig*) **a slight ~ of irony** une légère pointe d'ironie; **the film gives the ~ of Paris in the twenties** le film rend bien l'atmosphère *f* du Paris des années vingt; (*fig*) **to be (the) flavour of the month*** être la coqueluche du moment; **~ enhancer** agent *m* de sapidité. 2 **vt** (*give ~ to*) donner du goût à; (*with fruit, spirits*) parfumer (*with* à); (*with herbs, salt etc*) assaisonner. **to ~ a sauce with garlic** relever une sauce avec de l'ail; **pineapple-~ed** (parfumé) à l'ananas.

flavourful, (*US*) **flavorful** ['fleɪvəˌfəl] **adj** goûteux.

flavouring, (*US*) **flavoring** ['fleɪvərɪŋ] **n** (*Culin*) (*in sauce etc*) assaisonnement *m*; (*in cake etc*) parfum *m*. **vanilla ~** essence *f* de vanille.

flavourless, (*US*) **flavorless** ['fleɪvəlɪs] **adj** insipide, sans saveur, sans goût.

flaw [flɔː] 1 **n** (*in character, argument etc*) défaut *m*, imperfection *f*; (*in jewel, crystal, marble*) défaut *m*, imperfection *f*, crapaud *m*; (*Jur: in contract, procedure etc*) vice *m* de forme; (*obstacle*) inconvénient *m*. **everything seems to be working out, but there is just one ~** tout semble s'arranger, il n'y a qu'un seul inconvénient *or* qu'un hic*. 2 **vt: it is ~ed by ...** le (seul) défaut, c'est ... .

flawed [flɔːd] **adj** imparfait.

flawless ['flɔːlɪs] **adj** parfait, sans défaut. **he spoke ~ English** il parlait un anglais impeccable, il parlait parfaitement l'anglais.

flax [flæks] **n** lin *m*.

flaxen ['flæksən] **adj** *hair* blond, de lin; (*Tex*) de lin. **~-haired** aux cheveux de lin.

flay [fleɪ] **vt** *animal* (*skin*) écorcher; (*beat*) fouetter, rosser; *person* (*beat*) fouetter, rosser, battre (comme plâtre); (*criticize*) éreinter.

flea [fliː] 1 **n** puce *f*. **to send sb off with a ~ in his ear*** envoyer promener* qn; *see* **sand**. 2 **comp** ▸**fleabag*** (*Brit: person*) souillon *mf*; (*US: hotel*) hôtel *m* minable, écurie *f* ▸**fleabite** (*lit*) piqûre *f* de puce; (*fig*) vétille *f*, broutille *f* ▸**fleabitten** (*lit*) infesté de puces; (*fig*) miteux ▸**flea collar** *[dog, cat]* collier *m* anti-puces ▸**flea market** marché *m* aux puces ▸**flea-pit*** (*Brit: cinema*) ciné* miteux ▸**flea-ridden** (*lit*) *person, animal* couvert de puces; *place* infesté de puces; (*fig*) miteux.

fleck [flek] 1 **n** *[colour]* moucheture *f*; *[sunlight]* petite tache; *[dust]* particule *f*. 2 **vt** tacheter, moucheter. **dress ~ed with mud** robe éclaboussée de boue; **blue ~ed with white** bleu moucheté de blanc; **sky ~ed with little clouds** ciel pommelé; **hair ~ed with grey** cheveux qui commencent à grisonner.

fled [fled] **pret, ptp of flee**.

fledged [fledʒd] **adj: fully-~ bird** oiseau *m* qui a toutes ses plumes; **he's now a fully-~ doctor/architect** il est maintenant médecin/architecte diplômé; **a fully-~ British citizen** un citoyen britannique à part entière.

fledg(e)ling ['fledʒlɪŋ] **n** (*Orn*) oiselet *m*, oisillon *m*; (*fig: novice*) novice *mf*, débutant(e) *m(f)*. (*fig*) **a ~ industry** une industrie encore jeune.

flee [fliː] **pret, ptp fled** 1 **vi** fuir (*before, in face of* devant), s'enfuir (*from* de), se réfugier (*to* auprès de). **they fled** ils ont fui, ils se sont enfuis, ils se sont sauvés; **I fled when I heard she was expected** je me suis sauvé *or* j'ai pris la fuite lorsque j'ai appris qu'elle devait venir; **to ~ from temptation** fuir la tentation. 2 **vt** *town, country* s'enfuir de; *temptation, danger* fuir. **to ~ the country** quitter le pays, s'enfuir du pays.

fleece [fliːs] 1 **n** toison *f*; *see* **golden**. 2 **comp** ▸**fleece-lined** doublé de mouton. 3 **vt** a (*rob*) voler; (*swindle*) escroquer, filouter; (*overcharge*) estamper*, tondre*. b *sheep* tondre.

fleecy ['fliːsɪ] **adj** *clouds, snow* floconneux; *blanket* laineux.

fleet¹ [fliːt] 1 **n** (*Naut*) flotte *f*. (*fig*) **a ~ of vehicles** un parc automobile; **the company has a ~ of cars/coaches/taxis** la compagnie possède un certain nombre de voitures/d'autocars/de taxis; **their ~ of cars** (*or* **coaches** *or* **taxis**) leur parc automobile; *see* **admiral, fishing** *etc*. 2 **comp** ▸**fleet admiral** (*US*) amiral *m* (à cinq étoiles) ▸**Fleet Air Arm** (*Brit*) aéronavale *f* ▸**fleet chief petty officer** (*Brit*) major *m*.

fleet² [fliːt] **adj** (*also* **~-footed, ~ of foot**) rapide, au pied léger.

fleeting ['fliːtɪŋ] **adj** *time, memory* fugace, fugitif; *beauty, pleasure* éphémère, passager. **for a ~ moment** pendant un bref instant *or* moment; **a ~ visit** une visite éclair *or* en coup de vent*; (*liter*) **the ~ years** les années qui s'enfuient.

fleetingly ['fliːtɪŋlɪ] **adv** *think, smile, appear* un court instant, fugitivement.

Fleet Street ['fliːtˌstriːt] **n** (*Brit*) *les milieux de la presse*.

Fleming ['flemɪŋ] **n** Flamand(e) *m(f)*.

Flemish ['flemɪʃ] 1 **adj** flamand. 2 **n** a **the ~** les Flamands *mpl*. b (*Ling*) flamand *m*.

flesh [fleʃ] 1 **n** *[person, animal]* chair *f*; *[fruit, vegetable]* chair, pulpe *f*. **to put on ~** *[animal]* engraisser; *[person]* grossir, engraisser, prendre de l'embonpoint; (*fig*) **to make sb's ~ creep** donner la chair de poule à qn; **creatures of ~ and blood** êtres *mpl* de chair et de sang; **I'm only ~ and blood** je ne suis qu'un homme (*or* qu'une femme) comme les autres; **my own ~ and blood** les miens *mpl*, la chair de ma chair; **it is more than ~ and blood can stand** c'est plus que la nature humaine ne peut endurer; **in the ~** en chair et en os, en personne; **he's gone the way of all ~** il a payé le tribut de la nature; (*Rel*) **the sins of the ~** les péchés *mpl* de la chair; (*Rel*) **the ~ is weak** la chair est faible; *see* **fish, pound** *etc*.

2 **comp** ▸**flesh colour** couleur *f* (de) chair; (*Art*) carnation *f* ▸**flesh-coloured** (couleur *f*) chair *inv* ▸**fleshpots** lieux *mpl* de plaisir ▸**flesh tints** (*Art*) carnations *fpl* ▸**flesh wound** blessure *f* superficielle.

▸**flesh out** **vt sep** (*fig*) *essay etc* étoffer.

fleshings ['fleʃɪŋz] **npl** (*tights*) collant *m* (de danseuse).

fleshly ['fleʃlɪ] **adj** *creature, love* charnel; *pleasures* charnel, de la chair.

fleshy ['fleʃɪ] **adj** charnu.

flew [fluː] **pret of fly³**.

flex [fleks] 1 **vt** *body, knees* fléchir, ployer (*pour assouplir*); *muscle* faire jouer, bander (*liter*). 2 **n** (*Brit*) *[lamp, iron]* fil *m* (souple); *[telephone]* cordon *m*; (*heavy duty*) câble *m*.

flexibility [ˌfleksɪ'bɪlɪtɪ] **n** (*see* **flexible**) flexibilité *f*; souplesse *f*; élasticité *f*.

flexible ['fleksəbl] **adj** *wire, branch* flexible, souple; *shoes, sole etc* flexible, souple, élastique; (*fig*) *person* maniable, flexible, souple; *plans, attitude* flexible, souple; *room, building* polyvalent; *timetable* flexible, aménageable. (*in offices*) **~ time scheme, ~ working hours** horaire *m* mobile; **my working hours are very ~** j'ai des horaires souples *or* élastiques; (*gen*) **I'm ~** je peux toujours m'arranger (pour être libre *or* disponible); (*Mil*) **~ response** riposte graduée; *see* **link**.

flexion ['flekʃən] **n** flexion *f*, courbure *f*.

flexitime ['fleksɪˌtaɪm] **n** horaire *m* variable *or* à la carte. **to work ~** avoir un horaire variable *or* à la carte.

flexor ['fleksəʳ] **adj, n** fléchisseur *(m)*.

flibbertigibbet ['flɪbətɪ'dʒɪbɪt] **n** tête *f* de linotte, étourdi(e) *m(f)*.

flick [flɪk] 1 **n** a *[tail, duster]* petit coup; (*with finger*) chiquenaude *f*, pichenette *f*; (*with wrist*) petit mouvement (rapide). **at the ~ of a switch** ... rien qu'en appuyant sur un bouton ... .

b (*Brit *: film*) film *m*. **the ~s*** le ciné*, le cinoche*.

2 **comp** ▸**flick knife** (*Brit*) couteau *m* à cran d'arrêt.

3 **vt** donner un petit coup à. **he ~ed the horse lightly with the reins** il a donné au cheval un (tout) petit coup avec les rênes; **I'll just ~ a duster round the sitting room** je vais donner *or* passer un petit coup de chiffon au salon; **to ~ a ball of paper at sb** envoyer d'une chiquenaude une boulette de papier à qn; **he ~ed his cigarette ash into the fire** il a fait tomber la cendre de sa cigarette dans le feu.

▸**flick off** **vt sep** *dust, ash* enlever d'une chiquenaude.

▸**flick out** **vi, vt sep: the snake's tongue flicked out, the snake flicked its tongue out** le serpent a dardé sa langue.

▸**flick over** **vt sep** *pages of book* feuilleter, tourner rapidement.

►flick through vt fus *pages of book, document* feuilleter, lire en diagonale.

flicker ['flɪkəʳ] 1 vi *[flames, light]* danser, (*before going out*) trembloter, vaciller; *[needle on dial]* osciller; *[eyelids]* ciller. **the snake's tongue ~ed in and out** le serpent a dardé sa langue. 2 n *[flames, light]* danse *f*; (*before going out*) vacillement *m*. **in the ~ of an eyelid** en un clin d'œil; (*fig*) **without a ~** sans sourciller *or* broncher; **a ~ of hope/doubt** une lueur d'espoir/d'hésitation; **a ~ of annoyance** un geste d'humeur. 3 vt: **to ~ one's eyelids** battre des cils.

flickering ['flɪkərɪŋ] adj (*gen*) qui tremble (*or* tremblait *etc*); *flames* dansant, (*before going out*) vacillant; *needle* oscillant.

flickertail ['flɪkəˌteɪl] 1 n (*US*) spermophile *m* d'Amérique du Nord. 2 comp **►the F~ State** le Dakota du Nord.

flier ['flaɪəʳ] n a (*Aviat: person*) aviateur *m*, -trice *f*. *[passenger]* **to be a good ~** supporter (bien) l'avion; **to be a bad ~** ne pas supporter *or* mal supporter l'avion; *see* **high**. b (*esp US: fast train*) rapide *m*; (*fast coach*) car *m* express. c **to take a ~** (*leap*) sauter avec élan; (* *fig*) foncer tête baissée, risquer le tout pour le tout; (*US: take a risk*) (*gen*) se mouiller*; *[investor etc]* se lancer dans un investissement risqué. d (*St Ex*) (folle) aventure *f*. e (*handbill*) prospectus *m*.

flight¹ [flaɪt] 1 n a (*NonC: action, course*) *[bird, insect, plane etc]* vol *m*; *[ball, bullet]* trajectoire *f*. **the principles of ~** les rudiments *mpl* du vol *or* de la navigation aérienne; **in ~** en plein vol; (*Mus*) **the F~ of the Bumblebee** le Vol du bourdon.

b (*Aviat*) vol *m*. **~ number 776 from/to Madrid** le vol numéro 776 en provenance/à destination de Madrid; **did you have a good ~?** le vol s'est bien passé?, vous avez fait bon voyage?; *see* **reconnaissance, test** *etc*.

c (*group*) *[birds]* vol *m*, volée *f*; *[planes]* escadrille *f*. (*fig*) **in the first** *or* **top ~ of scientists/novelists** parmi les scientifiques/les romanciers les plus marquants; **a firm in the top ~** une compagnie de pointe.

d *[fancy, imagination]* élan *m*, envolée *f*.

e **~ of stairs** escalier *m*, volée *f* d'escalier; **we had to climb 3 ~s to get to his room** nous avons dû monter 3 étages pour arriver à sa chambre; **he lives three ~s up** il habite au troisième; **~ of hurdles** série *f* de haies; **~ of terraces** escalier *m* de terrasses.

2 comp **►flight attendant** (*US*) steward *m*/hôtesse *f* de l'air **►flight bag** sac *m* avion **►flight crew** équipage *m* **►flight deck** *[plane]* poste *m or* cabine *f* de pilotage; *[aircraft carrier]* pont *m* d'envol **►flight engineer** mécanicien *m* de bord **►flight lieutenant** (*Brit Aviat*) capitaine *m* (de l'armée de l'air) **►flight log** (*Aviat*) suivi *m* de vol **►flight path** trajectoire *f* (de vol) **►flight plan** plan *m* de vol **►flight recorder** (*Aviat*) enregistreur *m* de vol **►flight sergeant** (*Brit Aviat*) ≃ sergent-chef *m* (de l'armée de l'air) **►flight simulator** simulateur *m* de vol **►flight-test** vt essayer en vol.

flight² [flaɪt] n (*NonC: act of fleeing*) fuite *f*. **to put to ~** mettre en fuite; **to take (to) ~** prendre la fuite, s'enfuir; (*Fin*) **the ~ of capital abroad** la fuite *or* l'exode *m* des capitaux à l'étranger.

flightless ['flaɪtlɪs] adj (*bird*) coureur.

flighty ['flaɪtɪ] adj (*gen*) frivole; (*in love*) volage, inconstant.

flimflam‡ ['flɪmˌflæm] 1 n (*US: nonsense*) balivernes *fpl*, blague* *f*. 2 adj: **a ~ man** *or* **artist** un filou, un escroc. 3 vt (*swindle*) rouler*, blouser*.

flimsily ['flɪmzɪlɪ] adv: **~ built** *or* **constructed** (d'une construction) peu solide.

flimsiness ['flɪmzɪnɪs] n *[dress]* fragilité *f*; *[house]* construction *f* peu solide; *[paper]* minceur *f*; *[excuse, reasoning]* faiblesse *f*, futilité *f*.

flimsy ['flɪmzɪ] 1 adj *dress* trop léger; *cloth, paper* mince; *house* peu solide; *excuse, reasoning* piètre, pauvre. 2 n (*Brit: type of paper*) papier *m* pelure *inv*.

flinch [flɪntʃ] vi broncher, tressaillir. **to ~ from a task** reculer devant une tâche; **he didn't ~ from warning her** il ne s'est pas dérobé au devoir de la prévenir; **without ~ing** sans sourciller *or* broncher.

flinders ['flɪndəz] npl: **to break** *or* **fly into ~** voler en éclats.

fling [flɪŋ] (vb: pret, ptp **flung**) 1 n (*throw*) lancer *m*; (*brief love affair*) aventure *f*. (*fig*) **to have one's ~** s'en payer, se payer du bon temps; **youth must have its ~** il faut que jeunesse se passe (*Prov*); **to go on a ~** aller faire la noce *or* la foire*; (*in shops*) faire des folies; (*attempt*) **to have a ~** tenter sa chance; **to have a ~ at sth** s'essayer la main à qch; **to have a ~ at doing** essayer de faire; *see* **highland**.

2 vt *stone etc* jeter, lancer (*at sb* à qn, *at sth* sur qch); (*fig*) *remark, insult, accusation* lancer (*at sb* à qn). **he flung his opponent to the ground** il a jeté son adversaire à terre; **to ~ sb into jail** jeter *or* flanquer* qn en prison; **to ~ the window open** ouvrir toute grande la fenêtre; **the door was flung open** la porte s'est ouverte à la volée; **to ~ one's arms round sb's neck** sauter *or* se jeter au cou de qn; **to ~ a coat over one's shoulders** jeter un manteau sur ses épaules; **to ~ on/off one's coat** enfiler/enlever son manteau d'un geste brusque; **to ~ sb a look of contempt** lancer un regard de mépris à qn; **to ~ an accusation at sb** lancer une accusation à la tête de qn; **to ~ o.s. into a job/a hobby** se jeter *or* se lancer à corps perdu dans un travail/une activité; (*fig*) **she flung herself* at him** elle s'est jetée à sa tête.

3 vi: **to ~ off/out** *etc* partir/sortir *etc* brusquement; **he was ~ing about like a madman** il gesticulait *or* se démenait comme un possédé.

►fling away vt sep *unwanted object* jeter, ficher en l'air*; (*fig*) *money* gaspiller, jeter par les fenêtres.

►fling back vt sep *ball etc* renvoyer; *one's head* rejeter en arrière; *curtains* ouvrir brusquement.

►fling off vt sep (*fig liter*) se débarrasser de.

►fling out vt sep *person* flanquer* *or* mettre à la porte; *unwanted object* jeter, ficher en l'air*.

►fling up vt sep jeter en l'air. **to fling one's arms up in exasperation** lever les bras en l'air *or* au ciel d'exaspération; **he flung up his head** il a brusquement relevé la tête.

flint [flɪnt] 1 n (*gen: also tool, weapon*) silex *m*; (*for cigarette lighter*) pierre *f* (à briquet); *see* **clay**. 2 comp *axe* de silex **►flint glass** flint(-glass) *m*.

flintlock ['flɪntlɒk] n fusil *m* à silex.

flinty ['flɪntɪ] adj *soil* à silex; *rocks* siliceux; *heart* dur, insensible, de pierre.

flip [flɪp] 1 n a chiquenaude *f*, pichenette *f*, petit coup. **to decide/win sth on the ~ of a coin** décider/gagner qch en tirant à pile ou face.

b (*Aviat* *) petit tour en zinc‡.

2 comp **►flipboard** chevalet *m* (*tableau à feuilles mobiles*) **►flip-flop** *see* **flip-flop** **►flip side** *[record]* autre face *f*, face *f* B; (*fig*) envers *m*.

3 vt donner un petit coup à, donner une chiquenaude *or* une pichenette à; (*US*) *pancake etc* faire sauter. **to ~ a coin** tirer à pile ou face; **to ~ a book open** ouvrir un livre d'une chiquenaude *or* d'une pichenette; **he ~ped the letter over to me** il m'a passé la lettre d'une pichenette *or* d'une chiquenaude; (*Brit*) **to ~ one's lid‡**, (*US*) **to ~ one's wig‡** *or* **one's top‡** éclater, exploser (*fig*).

4 vi (‡: *also* **~ out**) (*angrily*) se mettre en rogne* (*over* à cause de); (*ecstatically*) devenir dingue* (*over* de).

5 adj *remark, repartee* désinvolte.

6 excl (*) zut!*.

►flip off vt sep *cigarette ash* secouer, faire tomber.

►flip out vi *see* **flip 4**.

►flip over vt sep *stone* retourner d'un coup léger; *pages* feuilleter.

►flip through vt fus *book* feuilleter.

flip-flop ['flɪpˌflɒp] 1 n a (*sandals*) **~s** tongs *fpl*. b (*Comput*) bascule *f* (bistable). c (*fig: esp US: change of opinion*) volte-face *f*. 2 vi (*US fig*) faire volte-face.

flippancy ['flɪpənsɪ] n *[attitude]* désinvolture *f*; *[speech, remark]* irrévérence *f*, légèreté *f*.

flippant ['flɪpənt] adj *remark* désinvolte, irrévérencieux; *person, tone, attitude* cavalier, (trop) désinvolte, irrévérencieux.

flippantly ['flɪpəntlɪ] adv avec désinvolture; irrévérencieusement; cavalièrement.

flipper ['flɪpəʳ] n *[seal etc]* nageoire *f*. *[swimmer]* **~s** palmes *fpl*.

flipping* ['flɪpɪŋ] 1 adj (*Brit*) fichu* (*before n*), maudit (*before n*). 2 adv (*Brit*) sacrément*, vachement*.

flirt [flɜːt] 1 vi flirter (*with* avec). **to ~ with an idea** caresser une idée. 2 n: **he's a ~** il adore flirter, il est très flirteur.

flirtation [flɜːˈteɪʃən] n flirt *m*, amourette *f*.

flirtatious [flɜːˈteɪʃəs] adj flirteur.

flit [flɪt] 1 vi a *[bats, butterflies etc]* voleter, voltiger. **the idea ~ted through his head** l'idée lui a traversé l'esprit. b *[person]* **to ~ in/out** *etc* (*Brit: lightly*) entrer/sortir *etc* avec légèreté; (*US: affectedly*) entrer/sortir *etc* à petits pas maniérés; **to ~ about** (*Brit*) se déplacer avec légèreté; (*US*) marcher à petits pas maniérés. c (*Brit: move house stealthily*) déménager à la cloche de bois; (*N Engl, Scot: move house*) déménager. 2 n a (*N Engl, Scot: house move*) déménagement *m*. (*Brit*) **to do a (moonlight) ~** déménager à la cloche de bois. b (*US* ‡: *homosexual*) pédale‡ *f*, tapette‡ *f*.

flitch [flɪtʃ] n flèche *f* (de lard).

flitting ['flɪtɪŋ] n (*N Engl, Scot*) déménagement *m*.

flivver‡ ['flɪvəʳ] n (*US*) tacot* *m*, guimbarde* *f*.

float [fləʊt] 1 n a (*Fishing, Plumbing*) flotteur *m*, flotte *f*; (*of cork*) bouchon *m*; *[seaplane etc]* flotteur *m*.

b (*vehicle in a parade*) char *m*; *see* **milk**.

c (*also* **cash ~**) fonds *m* de caisse.

d (*US: drink*) *milk shake ou soda contenant une boule de glace*.

2 vi (*on water, in air*) flotter; *[ship]* être à flot; *[bather]* faire la planche; *[vision etc]* planer; (*Fin*) *[currency]* flotter. **the raft ~ed down the river** le radeau a descendu la rivière; **to ~ back up to the surface** remonter à la surface (de l'eau).

3 vt a *boat* faire flotter, mettre à flot *or* sur l'eau; (*refloat*) remettre à flot *or* sur l'eau; *wood etc* faire flotter; (*fig*) *idea etc* lancer. **to ~ logs downstream** faire flotter des rondins au fil de l'eau.

b (*Fin*) *currency* laisser flotter; *company* fonder, créer, constituer. **to ~ a share issue** émettre des actions; **to ~ a loan** lancer *or* émettre un emprunt.

►float (a)round* vi *[rumour, news]* circuler, courir.

►float away vi dériver, partir à la dérive.

►float off 1 vi *[wreck etc]* se renflouer, se déséchouer. 2 vt sep renflouer, déséchouer, remettre à flot *or* sur l'eau.

floatation [fləʊ'teɪʃən] n = **flotation**.

floating ['fləʊtɪŋ] 1 adj *debris etc* flottant; *population* instable. (*Fin*) ~ **assets** capitaux circulants; ~ **currency** devise flottante; (*Fin*) ~ **currency rate** taux *m* de change flottant; ~ **debt** dette *f* à court terme *or* flottante; ~ **decimal (point)** virgule flottante; (*Naut*) ~ **dock** dock flottant; ~ **exchange** change flottant; (*Comput*) ~ **point representation** notation *f* en virgule flottante; (*Anat*) ~ **rib** côte flottante; (*Pol*) ~ **vote** vote flottant; ~ **voter** électeur *m*, -trice *f* indécis(e) *or* non-engagé(e).
2 n *[boat]* mise *f* en flottement; *[loan]* lancement *m*; *[currency]* flottement *m*, flottaison *f*.

flocculent ['flɒkjʊlənt] adj floconneux.

flock¹ [flɒk] 1 n *[animals, geese]* troupeau *m*; *[birds]* vol *m*, volée *f*; *[people]* foule *f*, troupeau (*pej*); (*Rel*) ouailles *fpl*. **they came in ~s** ils sont venus en masse. 2 vi aller *or* venir en masse *or* en foule, affluer. **to ~ in/out** *etc* entrer/sortir *etc* en foule; **to ~ together** s'assembler; **to ~ round sb** s'attrouper *or* s'assembler *or* se grouper autour de qn.

flock² [flɒk] n (*NonC*) (*wool*) bourre *f* de laine; (*cotton*) bourre de coton. ~ **paper** papier *m* velouté *or* tontisse.

floe [fləʊ] n banquise *f*, glaces flottantes.

flog [flɒg] vt a flageller, fustiger. (*fig*) **to ~ an idea to death*** *or* **into the ground*** rabâcher une idée; *see* **dead**. b (*Brit* ‡) vendre, refiler*, fourguer‡. **how much did you ~ it for?** tu en as tiré combien?*.

flogging ['flɒgɪŋ] n flagellation *f*, fustigation *f*; (*Jur*) fouet *m* (*sanction*).

flood [flʌd] 1 n a (*gen*) inondation *f*; (*flood tide*) marée *f* haute. (*notice on road*) "~" ≃ "attention route inondée"; (*Bible*) **the F~** le déluge; **river in ~** rivière en crue; **~s of tears** un torrent *or* déluge de larmes; **a ~ of light** un flot de lumière; **a ~ of letters/protests** un déluge de lettres/de protestations; **a ~ of immigrants** une marée d'immigrants.
b = **floodlight**.
2 comp ▸**flood control** prévention *f* des inondations ▸**flood damage** dégâts *mpl* des eaux ▸**floodgate** vanne *f*, porte *f* d'écluse; (*fig*) **to open the floodgates** ouvrir les vannes (*to* à) ▸**floodlight** *see* **floodlight** ▸**floodlighting** *see* **floodlighting** ▸**flood plain** lit *m* majeur, plaine *f* inondable ▸**flood tide** marée *f* haute ▸**floodwater(s)** eau *f* de la crue.
3 vt a *fields, town* inonder, submerger; (*Aut*) *carburettor* noyer; (*fig*) inonder. **he was ~ed with letters/with applications** il a été inondé de lettres/de demandes; **room ~ed with light** pièce inondée de lumière.
b *[storm, rain] river, stream* faire déborder. (*Comm*) *[suppliers, goods]* **to ~ the market** inonder le marché (*with* de).
4 vi *[river]* déborder, être en crue; *[people]* affluer, aller *or* venir en foule. **the crowd ~ed into the streets** la foule a envahi les rues *or* s'est répandue dans les rues.

▸**flood back** vi *[memories, worries]* (*also* **come flooding back**) resurgir. **it brought all the memories flooding back** cela a fait resurgir tous les souvenirs.

▸**flood in** vi *[sunshine]* entrer à flots; *[people]* entrer en foule, affluer.

▸**flood out** vt sep *house* inonder. **the villagers were flooded out** les inondations ont forcé les villageois à évacuer leurs maisons.

flooding ['flʌdɪŋ] n inondation *f*.

floodlight ['flʌdlaɪt] pret, ptp **floodlit** 1 vt *buildings* illuminer; (*Sport*) *match* éclairer (aux projecteurs); (*fig*) mettre en lumière, éclairer. 2 n (*device*) projecteur *m*; (*light*) lumière *f* (des projecteurs). **to play a match under ~s** jouer un match en nocturne.

floodlighting ['flʌdlaɪtɪŋ] n *[building]* illumination *f*; *[match]* éclairage *m* (aux projecteurs). **let's go and see the ~** allons voir les illuminations.

floodlit ['flʌdlɪt] pret, ptp of **floodlight**.

flooey‡ ['flu:ɪ] adj: **to go ~** se détraquer*.

floor [flɔ:ʳ] 1 n a (*gen*) sol *m*; (*~boards*) plancher *m*, parquet *m*; (*for dance*) piste *f* (de danse); (*fig*) *[prices etc]* plancher. **stone/tiled ~** sol dallé/carrelé; **put it on the ~** pose-le par terre *or* sur le sol; **she was sitting on the ~** elle était assise par terre *or* sur le sol; (*fig*) **a question from the ~ of the house** une question de l'auditoire *m or* de l'assemblée *f*; **to take the ~** (*speak*) prendre la parole; (*dance*) (aller) faire un tour de piste; **sea ~** fond *m* de la mer; *see* **cross, wipe** *etc*.
b (*storey*) étage *m*. **first ~** (*Brit*) premier étage, (*US*) rez-de-chaussée *m*; **on the first ~** (*Brit*) au premier (étage), (*in two-storey building*) à l'étage; (*US*) au rez-de-chaussée; **he lives on the second ~** il habite au deuxième étage *or* au second; **we live on the same ~** nous habitons au même étage *or* sur le même palier; *see* **ground¹** *etc*.
c (*St Ex*) enceinte *f* de la Bourse. **on/off the floor** en/hors Bourse.
2 vt a faire le sol de; (*with boards*) planchéier, parqueter.
b (*knock down*) *opponent* terrasser; (*Boxing*) envoyer au tapis.
c (**: defeat*) (*in argument etc*) réduire au silence; (*Sport*) battre à plates coutures. **this argument ~ed him** il n'a rien trouvé à répondre.
d (**: baffle, perplex*) désorienter, dérouter.
3 comp ▸**floor area** *[flat, offices etc]* surface *f* au sol ▸**floorboard** planche *f* (*de plancher*), latte *f* (de plancher) ▸**floorcloth** serpillière *f* ▸**floor covering** revêtement *m* de sol ▸**floor exercises** (*Gym*) exercices *mpl* au sol ▸**floor lamp** (*US*) lampadaire *m* ▸**floor leader** (*US Pol*) serre-file *m* ▸**floor manager** (*TV*) régisseur *m* de plateau; (*in shop*) chef *m* de groupe ▸**floor plan** (*Archit*) plan *m* (d'architecte) ▸**floor polish** encaustique *f*, cire *f* ▸**floor polisher** (*tool*) cireuse *f* ▸**floor show** attractions *fpl*, spectacle *m* de variétés (*dans un restaurant, cabaret etc*) ▸**floor space** place *f* (par terre) ▸**floorwalker** (*US Comm*) chef *m* de rayon.

flooring ['flɔ:rɪŋ] n (*floor*) sol *m*; (*made of wood*) plancher *m*, parquet *m*; (*tiled*) carrelage *m*; (*material*) revêtement *m* (de sol).

floozy‡ ['flu:zɪ] n poule* *f*, pouffiasse‡ *f*.

flop [flɒp] 1 vi a (*drop etc*) s'effondrer, s'affaler. **he ~ped down on the bed** il s'est affalé *or* s'est effondré sur le lit; **I'm ready to ~*** je suis claqué* *or* crevé* *or* sur les rotules*; **the fish ~ped feebly in the basket** le poisson s'agitait faiblement dans le panier.
b (*US* ‡*: sleep*) dormir, crécher*.
c (*fail*) *[play]* faire un four; *[scheme etc]* faire fiasco, être un fiasco *or* un bide‡. **he ~ped as Hamlet** il a complètement raté son interprétation d'Hamlet.
2 n (**: failure*) *[business venture, scheme]* fiasco *m*. **the play was a ~** la pièce a été un four *or* a fait fiasco *or* un bide‡; **he was a terrible ~** il s'est payé un échec monumental*, il a échoué dans les grandes largeurs*.
3 adv: **the whole business went ~** toute l'affaire s'est effondrée.
4 comp ▸**flophouse** (*US*) asile *m* de nuit ▸**flopover*** (*US TV*) cascade *f* d'images.

▸**flop over** 1 vi (*US*) **to flop over to a new idea*** adopter une nouvelle idée. 2 **flopover*** *see* **flop 4**.

floppy ['flɒpɪ] 1 adj *hat* à bords flottants; *clothes* lâche, flottant, flou; *[rabbit, dog] ears* tombant. (*Comput*) ~ **disk** disque *m* souple, disquette *f*. 2 n = ~ **disk**; *see* **1**.

flora ['flɔ:rə] n, pl ~s *or* **florae** ['flɔ:ri:] flore *f*.

floral [flɔ:rəl] adj floral. **material with a ~ pattern** étoffe *f* à ramages *or* à motifs floraux; (*bouquet: gen*) ~ **tribute** bouquet *m* de fleurs; (*at funerals*) ~ **tributes** fleurs *fpl* et couronnes *fpl*.

Florence ['flɒrəns] n Florence.

Florentine ['flɒrəntaɪn] adj florentin.

floribunda [flɔrə'bʌndə] n polyanta floribunda *m*.

florid ['flɒrɪd] adj *person, complexion* rubicond, rougeaud; *literary style* fleuri, plein de fioritures; *architecture* tarabiscoté, très chargé *or* orné.

Florida ['flɒrɪdə] n Floride *f*. **in ~** en Floride.

florin ['flɒrɪn] n florin *m* (*ancienne pièce de deux shillings*).

florist ['flɒrɪst] n fleuriste *mf*. **~'s shop** magasin *m or* boutique *f* de fleuriste.

floss [flɒs] n bourre *f* de soie; (*also* **dental ~**) fil *m* dentaire; *see* **candy**.

flossy* [flɒsɪ] adj (*US*) ultra-chic *inv*, d'un brillant superficiel.

flotation [fləʊ'teɪʃən] n a (*lit*) *[boat etc]* action *f* de flotter; *[log]* flottage *m*. (*Space*) ~ **collar** flotteur *m* (*de module lunaire*); ~ **compartment**, ~ **tank** caisse *f* de flottaison. b (*Fin etc*) *[shares, loan]* émission *f*; *[company]* constitution *f*, création *f*.

flotilla [flə'tɪlə] n flottille *f*.

flotsam ['flɒtsəm] n épave *f* (flottante). (*fig*) **the ~ and jetsam of our society** les épaves de notre société.

flounce [flaʊns] 1 vi: **to ~ in/out** *etc* entrer/sortir *etc* dans un mouvement d'humeur (*or* d'indignation *etc*). 2 n a (*gesture*) geste impatient, mouvement vif. b (*Dress*) volant *m*.

flounced [flaʊnst] adj *skirt, dress* à volants.

flounder¹ ['flaʊndəʳ] n, pl ~ *or* ~s (*fish*) flet *m*.

flounder² ['flaʊndəʳ] vi (*in mud etc*) patauger (péniblement), patouiller*, barboter; (*violently*) se débattre. **we ~ed along in the mud** nous avons poursuivi notre chemin en pataugeant dans la boue; **I watched him ~ing about in the water** je le regardais se débattre dans l'eau; (*fig*) **he was ~ing about upstairs** il allait et venait bruyamment en haut; **he ~ed through the rest of the speech** il a fini le discours en bredouillant; **he ~ed on in bad French** il continuait de patauger* *or* baragouiner en mauvais français.

flour ['flaʊəʳ] 1 n farine *f*. 2 vt fariner. 3 comp ▸**flour-bin** boîte *f* à farine ▸**flour mill** minoterie *f* ▸**flour shaker** saupoudreuse *f* (à farine) ▸**flour sifter** tamis *m* à farine.

flourish ['flʌrɪʃ] 1 vi *[plants etc]* bien venir, se plaire; *[business etc]* prospérer; *[writer, artist etc]* avoir du succès; *[literature, the arts, painting]* fleurir, être en plein essor. **the children were all ~ing** les enfants étaient tous en pleine forme *or* d'une santé florissante.
2 vt *stick, book etc* brandir.
3 n (*curve, decoration*) fioriture *f*, ornement *m*; (*in handwriting*) fioriture; (*under signature*) parafe *m or* paraphe *m*; (*Mus*) fioriture. **with a ~ of his stick** en faisant un moulinet avec sa canne; **he took the lid off with a ~** il a enlevé le couvercle avec un grand moulinet du bras *or* un geste du bras; **a ~ of trumpets** une fanfare, un air de trompettes.

flourishing ['flʌrɪʃɪŋ] adj *business* prospère, florissant; *plant* florissant, en très bon état; *person* resplendissant de santé, d'une santé florissante.

floury ['flaʊərɪ] adj *hands* enfariné; *potatoes* farineux; *loaf, dish* saupoudré de farine, fariné.

flout [flaʊt] vt *orders, advice* faire fi de, se moquer de, passer outre à; *conventions, society* mépriser, se moquer de.

flow [fləʊ] 1 vi *[river, blood from wound]* couler; *[electric current, blood* *in veins]* circuler; *[tide]* monter, remonter; *[dress, hair etc]* flotter, ondoyer; (*fig: result*) découler, résulter, provenir (*from* de). *[people]* **to ~ in** affluer, entrer à flots; *[liquid]* **to ~ out of** s'écouler de, sortir de; **the money keeps ~ing in** l'argent rentre bien; **to ~ past sth** passer devant qch; **to ~ back** refluer; **the water ~ed over the fields** l'eau s'est répandue dans les champs; **let the music ~ over you** laisse la musique t'envahir; **the river ~s into the sea** le fleuve se jette dans la mer; **tears were ~ing down her cheeks** les larmes coulaient *or* ruisselaient sur ses joues; **a land ~ing with milk and honey** une terre d'abondance.

2 **n** *[tide]* flux *m*; *[river]* courant *m*; *[electric current, blood in veins]* circulation *f*; *[traffic]* écoulement *m*; *[donations, orders, replies, words]* flot *m*; *[music]* déroulement *m*. **the interruption in the ~ of oil from Iran** l'arrêt de l'approvisionnement *m* en pétrole iranien; **he always has a ready ~ of conversation** il a toujours la conversation facile; *[speaker]* **to be in full ~** être sur sa lancée; **he stopped the ~ of blood** il a arrêté l'écoulement *m or* l'épanchement *m* du sang, il a étanché le sang; **(menstrual) ~** pertes *fpl*; *see* **ebb**.

3 **comp ▸flow chart, flow diagram, flow sheet** (*Comput*) organigramme *m*, ordinogramme *m*; (*Admin, Ind*) organigramme.

flower [ˈflaʊəʳ] 1 **n** fleur *f*. **in ~** en fleurs; **to say sth with ~s** dire qch avec des fleurs; **"no ~s by request"** "ni fleurs ni couronnes"; (*fig*) **the ~ of the army** la (fine) fleur *or* l'élite *f* de l'armée; **~s of rhetoric** fleurs de rhétorique; *see* **bunch**.

2 **vi** (*lit, fig*) fleurir.

3 **comp ▸flower arrangement** (*art*) art *m* de faire des bouquets; (*exhibit*) composition florale **▸flower bed** plate-bande *f*, parterre *m* **▸flower children** = **flower people** **▸flower garden** jardin *m* d'agrément **▸flower head** capitule *m* **▸flower people** (*fig*) hippies *mpl* **▸flowerpot** pot *m* (à fleurs) **▸flower power** *message d'amour et de paix des hippies* **▸flower-seller** bouquetière *f* **▸flower shop** (boutique *f* de) fleuriste *mf*; **at the flower shop** chez le marchand (*or* la marchande) de fleurs, chez le *or* la fleuriste **▸flower show** floralies *fpl*; (*smaller*) exposition *f* de fleurs.

flowered [ˈflaʊəd] **adj** *cloth, shirt etc* à fleurs.

flowering [ˈflaʊərɪŋ] 1 **n** (*lit*) floraison *f*; (*fig*) floraison, épanouissement *m*. 2 **adj** (*in flower*) en fleurs; (*which flowers*) à fleurs. **~ shrub** arbuste *m* à fleurs.

flowery [ˈflaʊərɪ] **adj** *meadow* fleuri, couvert *or* émaillé (*liter*) de fleurs; *material* à fleurs; *style, essay, speech* fleuri, orné.

flowing [ˈfləʊɪŋ] **adj** *movement* gracieux; *beard, dress, hair* flottant; *style* coulant; *tide* montant.

flown [fləʊn] **ptp of fly**[3]; *see* **high 4**.

fl. oz (**abbr of fluid ounce**) *see* **fluid 1**.

flu [fluː] **n** (**abbr of influenza**) grippe *f*; *see* **Asian**.

flub* [flʌb] (*US*) 1 **vt** louper*, rater*. 2 **vi** échouer. 3 **n** ratage* *m*, erreur *f*.

fluctuate [ˈflʌktjʊeɪt] **vi** *[prices, temperature etc]* varier, fluctuer; *[person, attitude]* varier (*between* entre).

fluctuation [ˌflʌktjʊˈeɪʃən] **n** fluctuation *f*, variation *f*.

flue [fluː] **n** *[chimney]* conduit *m* (de cheminée); *[stove]* tuyau *m* (de poêle). **~ brush** hérisson *m* (*de ramoneur*).

fluency [ˈfluːənsɪ] **n** (*in speech*) facilité *f or* aisance *f* (d'élocution); (*in writing*) facilité, aisance. **his ~ in English** son aisance à s'exprimer en anglais.

fluent [ˈfluːənt] **adj** *style* coulant, aisé. **to be a ~ speaker** avoir la parole facile; **he is ~ in Italian, he speaks ~ Italian, his Italian is ~** il parle couramment l'italien.

fluently [ˈfluːəntlɪ] **adv** *speak a language* couramment; *speak, write, express o.s.* avec facilité, avec aisance.

fluff [flʌf] 1 **n** (*NonC*) (*on birds, young animals*) duvet *m*; (*from material*) peluche *f*; (*dust on floors*) mouton(s) *m(pl)* (*de poussière*). (*fig: girl*) **a bit of ~**‡ une nénette‡. 2 **vt** a (*also* **~ out**) *feathers* ébouriffer; *pillows, hair* faire bouffer. b (*: *do badly*) *audition, lines in play, exam* rater, louper*.

fluffy [ˈflʌfɪ] **adj** *bird* duveteux; *animal* soyeux; *hair* bouffant; *toy* en peluche; *material* pelucheux; *cake* léger, aéré; *beaten eggs* mousseux.

fluid [ˈfluːɪd] 1 **adj** *substance* fluide, liquide; *situation* fluide, indécis; *drawing, outline, style* fluide, coulant. **~ ounce** *mesure de capacité* (*Brit:* ≃ *0,028 litres, US:* ≃ *0,030 litres*); **my plans are still fairly ~** je n'ai pas encore de plans très fixes; (*US Fin*) **~ assets** liquidités *fpl*, disponibilités *fpl*. 2 **n** fluide *m* (*also Chem*), liquide *m*. (*as diet*) **he's on ~s only** il ne peut prendre que des liquides.

fluidity [fluːˈɪdɪtɪ] **n** *[gas, liquid, situation etc]* fluidité *f*; *[style, speech]* aisance *f*, coulant *m*.

fluke[1] [fluːk] **n** coup *m* de chance *or* de veine* extraordinaire, hasard *m* extraordinaire. **by a (sheer) ~** par raccroc, par un hasard extraordinaire.

fluke[2] [fluːk] **n** *[anchor]* patte *f* (*d'ancre*); *[arrow harpoon etc]* barbillon *m*.

fluke[3] [fluːk] **n** (*Zool*) douve *f* (du foie *etc*).

fluky [ˈfluːkɪ] **adj** *wind* capricieux. **~ shot** raccroc *m*.

flummery [ˈflʌmərɪ] **n** (*Culin*) bouillie *f*; (*fig*) flagornerie *f*.

flummox* [ˈflʌməks] **vt** *person* démonter, couper le sifflet à*. **he was ~ed** ça lui avait coupé le sifflet*, il était complètement démonté.

flung [flʌŋ] **pret, ptp of fling**; *see* **far 3**.

flunk* [flʌŋk] 1 **vi** (*fail*) être recalé* *or* collé*; (*shirk*) se dégonfler*, caner‡. 2 **vt** a (*fail*) **to ~ French/an exam** être recalé* *or* être collé* *or* se faire étendre* en français/à un examen; **they ~ed 10 candidates** ils ont recalé* *or* collé* 10 candidats. b (*give up*) laisser tomber.

▸flunk out‡ 1 **vi** se faire virer* (*of* de). 2 **vt sep** virer*, renvoyer.

flunk(e)y [ˈflʌŋkɪ] **n** (*lit*) laquais *m*; (*fig*) larbin* *m*.

fluorescein [ˌflʊəˈresɪɪn] **n** fluorescéine *f*.

fluorescence [flʊəˈresns] **n** fluorescence *f*.

fluorescent [flʊəˈresnt] **adj** *lighting* fluorescent. **~ strip** tube fluorescent *or* au néon.

fluoridation [ˌflʊərɪˈdeɪʃən] **n** traitement *m* au fluor.

fluoride [ˈflʊəraɪd] **n** fluorure *m*. **~ toothpaste** dentifrice *m* fluoré *or* au fluor.

fluorine [ˈflʊəriːn] **n** fluor *m*.

fluorite [ˈflʊəraɪt] **n** (*US*) fluorine *f*, spath *m* fluor.

fluorspar [ˈflʊəspɑːʳ] **n** spath *m* fluor, fluorine *f*.

flurry [ˈflʌrɪ] 1 **n** *[snow]* rafale *f*; *[wind]* rafale, risée *f*; (*fig*) agitation *f*, émoi *m*. **a ~ of activity** une soudaine poussée *or* un soudain accès d'activité; **a ~ of protest** un concert de protestations; **in a ~ of excitement** dans un frisson d'agitation. 2 **vt** agiter, effarer. **to get flurried** perdre la tête, s'affoler (*at* pour).

flush[1] [flʌʃ] 1 **n** a (*in sky*) lueur *f* rouge, rougeoiement *m*; *[blood]* flux *m*; (*blush*) rougeur *f*. (*Med*) **(hot) ~es** bouffées *fpl* de chaleur.

b *[beauty, health, youth]* éclat *m*; *[joy]* élan *m*; *[excitement]* accès *m*. **in the (first) ~ of victory** dans l'ivresse de la victoire; **she's not in the first ~ of youth** elle n'est pas de la première jeunesse.

c *[lavatory]* chasse *f* (d'eau).

2 **vi** a *[face, person]* rougir. **to ~ crimson** s'empourprer, piquer un fard*; **to ~ with shame/anger** rougir de honte/de colère.

b *[lavatory]* **the toilet won't ~** la chasse d'eau ne marche pas.

3 **vt** nettoyer à grande eau; *drain, pipe* curer à grande eau. **to ~ the lavatory** *or* **toilet** tirer la chasse (d'eau); **to ~ sth down the lavatory** *or* **toilet** faire passer qch dans les toilettes; (*US: expressing disbelief*) **~ it**‡! et puis quoi encore?, tu te fous de moi?‡.

▸flush away vt sep (*down sink/drain*) faire partir par l'évier/par l'égout; (*down lavatory*) faire partir (en tirant la chasse d'eau).

▸flush out vt sep nettoyer à grande eau.

flush[2] [flʌʃ] 1 **adj** a au même niveau (*with* que), au *or* à ras (*with* de). **~ with the ground** à ras de terre, au ras de terre; **rocks ~ with the water** des rochers à *or* au ras de l'eau, des rochers à fleur d'eau *or* qui affleurent; **a door ~ with the wall** une porte dans l'alignement du mur; **a cupboard ~ with the wall** un placard encastré dans le mur; **~ against** tout contre. b **to be ~ (with money)**‡ être en fonds. 2 **vt: to ~ a door** rendre une porte plane.

flush[3] [flʌʃ] **vt** (*also* **~ out**) *game, birds* lever; *person* forcer à se montrer.

flush[4] [flʌʃ] **n** (*Cards*) flush *m*; *see* **royal** *etc*.

flushed [ˈflʌʃt] **adj** *person, face* (tout) rouge. **~ with fever** rouge de fièvre; **they were ~ with success** le succès leur tournait la tête.

fluster [ˈflʌstəʳ] 1 **vt** énerver, agiter, troubler. **don't ~ me!** ne me trouble pas!, ne m'énerve pas!; **to get ~ed** s'énerver, se troubler. 2 **n** agitation *f*, trouble *m*. **in a ~** énervé, troublé, agité.

flute [fluːt] **n** (*musical instrument, wine glass*) flûte *f*.

fluted [ˈfluːtɪd] **adj** a *pillar* cannelé, strié; *flan dish* à cannelures. b (*Mus*) *tone, note* flûté.

fluting [ˈfluːtɪŋ] **n** (*Archit etc*) cannelures *fpl*.

flutist [ˈfluːtɪst] **n** (*US*) flûtiste *mf*.

flutter [ˈflʌtəʳ] 1 **vi** a *[flag, ribbon]* flotter, voleter, s'agiter; *[bird, moth, butterfly]* voltiger, voleter; *[wings]* battre. **the bird ~ed about the room** l'oiseau voletait çà et là dans la pièce; **the butterfly ~ed away** le papillon a disparu en voltigeant; **a leaf came ~ing down** une feuille est tombée en tourbillonnant.

b *[person]* papillonner, virevolter, aller et venir dans une grande agitation. **she ~ed into the room** elle a fait une entrée très agitée dans la pièce.

c *[heart]* palpiter; *[pulse]* battre (faiblement).

2 **vt** *fan, paper* jouer de. **the bird ~ed its wings** l'oiseau a battu des ailes; **to ~ one's eyelashes** battre des cils (*at sb* dans la direction de qn).

3 **n** a *[eyelashes, wings]* battement *m*; *[heart]* palpitation *f*; *[pulse]* (faible) battement; (*nervousness*) agitation *f*, émoi *m*, trouble *m*. **(all) in a ~** tout troublé, dans un grand émoi.

b (*Brit: gamble*) **to have a ~*** parier *or* risquer (de petites sommes) (*on* sur); (*St Ex*) boursicoter.

fluvial [ˈfluːvɪəl] **adj** fluvial.

flux [flʌks] **n** (*NonC*) a changement continuel, fluctuation *f*. **to be in a state of ~** changer sans arrêt, fluctuer continuellement. b (*Med*) flux *m*, évacuation *f* (*de sang etc*); (*Phys*) flux; (*Metal*) fondant *m*.

fly[1] [flaɪ] 1 **n** (*insect: also Fishing*) mouche *f*. **the epidemic killed them off like flies** ils mouraient *or* tombaient comme des mouches, frappés par l'épidémie; **he wouldn't harm** *or* **hurt a ~** il ne ferait pas de mal à une mouche; (*fig*) **I wish I were a ~ on the wall** j'aimerais être une petite souris (pour pouvoir écouter *or* voir) (*see also* **2**); (*fig*) **there's a**

~ **in the ointment** il y a un ennui *or* un hic* *or* un os*; **he's the ~ in the ointment** le gros obstacle c'est lui, c'est lui l'empêcheur de tourner en rond; **there are no flies on him**‡ il n'est pas né d'hier, il n'est pas tombé de la dernière averse *or* pluie; *see* **die**[1], **house**.

2 comp ▸**fly-blown** (*lit*) couvert *or* plein de chiures de mouches; (*fig*) très défraîchi ▸**flycatcher** (*bird*) gobe-mouches *m inv*; (*plant*) plante *f* carnivore; (*trap*) attrape-mouches *m inv* ▸**fly fishing** pêche *f* à la mouche ▸**fly killer** insecticide *m* ▸**fly-on-the-wall documentary** (*TV*) document *m* pris sur le vif ▸**fly paper** papier *m* tue-mouches ▸**fly rod** (*Fishing*) canne *f* à mouche ▸**fly spray** bombe *f* insecticide ▸**fly swat(ter)** tapette *f* ▸**fly trap** *see* **Venus** ▸**flyweight** (*Boxing*) poids *m* mouche.

fly[2] [flaɪ] adj (*esp Brit: astute*) malin (*f* -igne), rusé, astucieux.

fly[3] [flaɪ] pret **flew**, ptp **flown** 1 vi a *[bird, insect, plane]* voler; *[air passenger]* aller *or* voyager en avion; *[pilot]* piloter un (*or* des) avions. **I don't like ~ing** je n'aime pas (prendre) l'avion; **I always ~** je voyage toujours en avion, je prends toujours l'avion; **how did you get here? — I flew** comment es-tu venu? — par *or* en avion; **to ~ over London** survoler Londres, voler au-dessus de Londres; **the planes flew past** *or* **over at 3 p.m.** les avions sont passés (au-dessus de nos têtes) à 15 heures; **to ~ over the Channel** survoler la Manche; **to ~ across the Channel** *[bird, plane]* traverser la Manche; *[passenger]* traverser la Manche en avion; *[bird]* **to ~ away** s'envoler; (*fig*) **all her worries flew away** tous ses soucis se sont envolés; **we flew in from Rome this morning** nous sommes venus de Rome en *or* par avion ce matin; **to ~ off** *[bird, plane]* s'envoler; *[passenger]* partir en avion, s'envoler (*to* pour); **a bee flew in through the window** une abeille est entrée par la fenêtre; (*fig*) **he is ~ing high** il voit grand, il vise haut; (*fig*) **to find that the bird has flown** trouver l'oiseau envolé; (*US fig*) **~ right, sonny*** conduis-toi bien, mon gars; *see* **fury**.

b (*fig*) *[time]* passer vite, filer*; *[sparks]* jaillir, voler; *[car, people]* filer*. *[person]* **to ~ in/out/back** *etc* entrer/sortir/ retourner *etc* à toute vitesse *or* à toute allure *or* comme un bolide; **it's late, I must ~!** il est tard, il faut que je me sauve! (*subj*) *or* que je file*! (*subj*); **to ~ to sb's assistance** voler au secours de qn; **to ~ in the face of danger** lancer un défi au danger; **to ~ in the face of authority** battre en brèche l'ordre établi; **to ~ into a rage** *or* **a passion** s'emporter, se mettre dans une violente colère; (*fig*) **to ~ off the handle** s'emporter, sortir de ses gonds; **to let ~ at sb** (*in angry words*) s'en prendre violemment à qn, prendre qn violemment à partie, traiter qn de tous les noms; (*by shooting*) tirer sur qn; **to let ~ a stone** jeter une pierre; **to ~ at sb** sauter *or* se ruer sur qn; **to ~ at sb's throat** sauter à la gorge de qn; **the door flew open** la porte s'est ouverte brusquement *or* soudain *or* en coup de vent; **the handle flew off** la poignée s'est détachée brusquement *or* soudain; **the lid and the box flew apart** le couvercle et la boîte se sont brusquement *or* soudain séparés; **the cup flew to bits** *or* **into pieces** la tasse a volé en éclats; *see* **feather, send, spark**.

c (*flee*) fuir (*before* devant), s'enfuir (*from* de), se réfugier (*to* auprès de). **to ~ from temptation** fuir la tentation; **~ for your life!** fuyez!

d *[flag]* se déployer. **her hair was ~ing in the wind** ses cheveux flottaient au vent; *see* **flag**[1].

2 vt a *aircraft* piloter; *person* emmener par avion; *goods* transporter par avion; *standard, admiral's flag etc* arborer. (*Naut*) **to ~ the French flag** battre pavillon français; **the building was ~ing the French flag** le drapeau français flottait sur l'immeuble; **to ~ a kite** (*lit*) faire voler un cerf-volant; (*fig*) lancer un ballon d'essai (*fig*); **to ~ great distances** faire de longs voyages en avion; **to ~ the Atlantic/the Channel** *etc* traverser l'Atlantique/ la Manche *etc* en avion; **to ~ Air France** voler sur Air France; **we will ~ you to Italy and back for £200** nous vous offrons un aller et retour en Italie par avion pour 200 livres.

b **to ~ the country** quitter le pays, s'enfuir du pays.

3 n a (*on trousers: also* **flies**) braguette *f*; (*on tent*) auvent *m*.

b (*vehicle*) fiacre *m*.

c *[flag]* battant *m*.

d (*Theat*) **flies** cintres *mpl*, dessus *mpl*.

4 comp ▸**flyaway** *hair* rebelle, intraitable*; (*frivolous*) frivole, futile ▸**flyboy**‡ (*US*) pilote *m* (*de l'armée de l'air*) ▸**fly-button** bouton *m* de braguette ▸**flyby** (*US*) (pl **~s**) = **flypast** ▸**fly-by-night** n (*irresponsible person*) tout-fou* *m*, écervelé(e) *m(f)*; (*decamping debtor*) débiteur *m*, -trice *f* qui déménage à la cloche de bois *or* qui décampe en douce* ◊ adj *person* tout-fou* (*m only*), écervelé; (*Comm, Fin*) *firm, operation* véreux ▸**fly-drive** (*Travel*) formule *f* avion plus voiture ▸**fly hack** (*Rugby*) = **fly kick** ▸**fly half** (*Rugby*) demi *m* d'ouverture ▸**fly kick** (*Rugby*) coup *m* de pied à suivre ▸**flyleaf** page *f* de garde ▸**flyover** (*Brit Aut*) autopont *m*; (*temporary*) toboggan *m*; (*US Aviat*) défilé aérien ▸**flypast** (*Brit*) défilé aérien ▸**fly-post** (*Brit*) coller des affiches illégalement ▸**flyposting** (*Brit*) affichage illégal ▸**fly sheet** (*Brit*) feuille volante ▸**fly-tipping** décharge *f* sauvage ▸**flywheel** volant *m* (*Tech*).

flyer ['flaɪəʳ] n = **flier**.

flying ['flaɪɪŋ] 1 n (*action*) vol *m*; (*activity*) aviation *f*. **he likes ~** il aime l'avion; **to go ~** (*lit*) faire du vol; (*fig: fall over*) aller valdinguer*; *see* **formation, stunt**.

2 adj volant. (*fig*) **to come through with ~ colours** réussir de façon éclatante; **~ insect** insecte volant; **~ jump** saut *m* avec élan; **to take a ~ jump** sauter avec élan; (*Sport*) **~ start** départ lancé; (*fig*) **to get off to a ~ start** *[racing car, runner]* prendre un départ très rapide *or* en flèche; *[scheme, plan]* prendre un bon *or* un excellent départ; **~ visit** visite *f* éclair *inv*.

3 comp ▸**flying ambulance** (*plane*) avion *m* sanitaire; (*helicopter*) hélicoptère *m* sanitaire ▸**flying boat** hydravion *m* ▸**flying bomb** bombe volante, V1 *m* ▸**flying buttress** arc-boutant *m* ▸**flying doctor** médecin volant ▸**the Flying Dutchman** (*legend*) le Hollandais volant; (*opera*) le Vaisseau fantôme ▸**flying fish** poisson volant, exocet *m* ▸**flying fortress** forteresse volante ▸**flying fox** roussette *f* ▸**flying machine** machine volante, appareil volant ▸**flying officer** (*Brit*) lieutenant *m* de l'armée de l'air ▸**flying picket** (*Ind*) piquet *m* de grève volant ▸**flying saucer** soucoupe volante ▸**Flying Squad** (*Police*) brigade volante (*de la police judiciaire*) ▸**flying suit** combinaison *f* ▸**flying time** heures *fpl* de vol ▸**flying trapeze** trapèze volant.

FM [ef'em] a (abbr of **Field Marshal**) *see* **field**. b (abbr of **frequency modulation**) F.M.

FMB [ˌefem'biː] (*US*) (abbr of **Federal Maritime Board**) *see* **federal**.

FMCG, f.m.c.g. [ˌefemsiː'dʒiː] (abbr of **fast-moving consumer goods**) *see* **fast**[1] **2**.

F.O. [ef'əʊ] (*Brit*) (abbr of **Foreign Office**) *see* **foreign**.

foal [fəʊl] 1 n (*horse*) poulain *m*; (*donkey*) ânon *m*. **the mare is in ~** la jument est pleine. 2 vi mettre bas (*un poulain etc*), pouliner.

foam [fəʊm] 1 n *[beer etc]* mousse *f*; *[sea]* écume *f*; (*in fire fighting*) mousse (*carbonique*); (*at mouth*) écume. (*liter*) **the ~** les flots *mpl* (*liter*). 2 comp ▸**foam-backed** *carpet* à sous-couche de mousse ▸**foam bath** bain *m* moussant, bain (de) mousse ▸**foam plastic** mousse *f* de plastique ▸**foam rubber** caoutchouc *m* mousse ▸**foam sprayer** extincteur *m* à mousse. 3 vi *[sea]* écumer, moutonner; *[soapy water]* mousser, faire de la mousse. **to ~ at the mouth** *[animal]* baver, écumer; *[person]* (*lit*) avoir de l'écume aux lèvres; (*fig*) écumer de rage; **he was absolutely ~ing**‡ il écumait (de rage).

▸**foam up** vi *[liquid in container]* mousser.

foamy ['fəʊmɪ] adj *sea* écumeux; *beer* mousseux.

FOB [efəʊ'biː] (*Comm*) (abbr of **free on board**) FOB.

fob [fɒb] 1 vt: **to ~ sth off on sb, to ~ sb off with sth** refiler* *or* fourguer‡ qch à qn; **to ~ sb off with promises** se débarrasser de qn par de belles promesses. 2 n (†) (*pocket*) gousset *m* (de pantalon); (*ornament*) breloque *f*. **~ watch** montre *f* de gousset.

FOC [efəʊ'siː] (*Comm*) (abbr of **free of charge**) *see* **free**.

focal ['fəʊkəl] adj focal. **~ length** *or* **distance** distance focale, focale *f*; (*Med*) **~ infection** infection focale; **~ plane** plan focal; (*Phot*) **~ plane shutter** obturateur focal *or* à rideau; **~ point** (*Opt*) foyer *m*; (*in buildings, gardens*) point *m* de convergence; (*fig: main point: of meeting, discussions etc*) point *m* central; **~ ratio** diaphragme *m*.

foci ['fəʊkaɪ] npl of **focus**.

fo'c'sle ['fəʊksl] n = **forecastle**.

focus ['fəʊkəs] 1 n, pl **~es** *or* **foci** (*Math, Phys*) foyer *m*; *[interest]* centre *m*; *[illness, unrest]* foyer, siège *m*. (*Phot*) **the picture is in/out of ~** l'image est nette/floue, l'image est/n'est pas au point; (*Phot*) **to bring a picture into ~** mettre une image au point; **he was the ~ of attention** il était le point de mire *or* le centre d'attention *or* le centre d'intérêt.

2 vt a *instrument, camera* mettre au point. **to ~ the camera** faire le point.

b (*direct etc*) *light, heat rays* faire converger; *beam, ray* diriger (*on* sur); (*fig*) *attention* concentrer (*on* sur). **to ~ one's eyes on sth** fixer ses yeux sur qch; **all eyes were ~ed on him** il était le point de mire de tous.

3 vi a (*Phot*) mettre au point (*on* sur).

b **to ~ on** *[eyes]* (*gen*) se fixer sur; (*fml*) accommoder sur; *[person]* fixer son regard sur; **my eyes won't ~, I can't ~ properly** (*gen*) je vois trouble, j'ai du mal à distinguer, (*more formally*) je ne peux pas accommoder.

c *[heat, light, rays]* converger (*on* sur).

d (*fig*) **we must ~ on raising funds** il faut nous concentrer sur la collecte des fonds; **the meeting ~ed on the problems of the unemployed** la réunion a surtout porté sur les problèmes des chômeurs.

fodder ['fɒdəʳ] n fourrage *m*; *see* **cannon**.

FOE, FoE (abbr of **Friends of the Earth**) *see* **friend**.

foe [fəʊ] n (*liter: lit, fig*) ennemi(e) *m(f)*, adversaire *mf*.

foetal ['fiːtl] adj fœtal. **in a ~ position** dans la position du fœtus, dans une position fœtale.

foetid ['fiːtɪd] adj = **fetid**.

foetus ['fiːtəs] n fœtus *m*.

fog [fɒg] 1 n a (*Met*) brouillard *m*; (*Naut*) brume *f*, brouillard (de mer); (*fig*) brouillard, confusion *f*. (*fig*) **to be in a ~** être dans le brouillard, ne plus savoir où l'on en est.

b (*Phot*) voile *m*.

2 vt *mirror, glasses* embuer; *person* embrouiller, brouiller les idées à; *photo* voiler. **to ~ the issue** (*accidentally*) embrouiller *or* obscurcir la question; (*purposely*) brouiller les cartes.

3 vi *[mirror, glasses]* (*also* ~ **over** *or* **up**) s'embuer; *[landscape]* s'embrumer; (*Phot*) *[negative]* se voiler.

4 comp ▸**fog bank** banc *m* de brume ▸**fogbound** pris dans la brume, bloqué par le brouillard ▸**foghorn** corne *f or* sirène *f* de brume; **she has a voice like a foghorn** elle a une voix tonitruante *or* de stentor ▸**foglamp** (*Brit*), **foglight** (*US*) (*Aut*) feu *m* de brouillard ▸**fog signal** (*Naut*) signal *m* de brume; (*Rail*) pétard *m*.

fogey* ['fəʊgɪ] n: **old** ~ vieille baderne*, vieux bonze*; **Young F~** *personne très classique dans ses goûts et ses opinions.*

foggy ['fɒgɪ] adj *landscape, weather* brumeux; *ideas, reasoning* confus. **it was ~ yesterday** hier il a fait du brouillard; **on a ~ day** par un jour de brouillard; **I haven't the foggiest (idea** *or* **notion)!*** aucune idée!, pas la moindre idée!

foible ['fɔɪbl] n marotte *f*, petite manie.

foil[1] [fɔɪl] n a (*NonC: metal sheet*) feuille *f or* lame *f* de métal; (*also* **cooking** *or* **kitchen** ~) papier *m* d'aluminium, (papier) alu* *m*. (*Culin*) **fish cooked in** ~ poisson cuit (au four) dans du papier d'aluminium; *see* **tin** *etc.* b (*fig*) repoussoir *m*. **to act as a ~ to sb/sth** servir de repoussoir à qn/qch, mettre qn/qch en valeur.

foil[2] [fɔɪl] n (*Fencing*) fleuret *m*.

foil[3] [fɔɪl] vt *attempts* déjouer; *plans* contrecarrer.

foist [fɔɪst] vt: **to ~ sth (off) on sb** refiler* *or* repasser* qch à qn; **this job was ~ed (off) on to me** c'est moi qui ai hérité de ce boulot*; **to ~ o.s. on (to) sb** s'imposer à qn; (*as uninvited guest*) s'imposer *or* s'installer chez qn.

fold[1] [fəʊld] 1 n (*in paper, cloth, skin, earth's surface*) pli *m*. (*Geol*) **~s** plissement *m*.

2 comp ▸**foldaway** *bed etc* pliant, escamotable ▸**foldout** dépliant *m* (encarté dans une revue), encart *m* ▸**fold-up** *chair etc* pliant, escamotable.

3 vt a *paper, blanket, bed, chair* plier; *wings* replier. **to ~ a sheet in two** plier un drap en deux; **to ~ one's arms** (se) croiser les bras; **to ~ one's hands** (*in prayer*) joindre les mains.

b (*wrap up*) envelopper (*in* dans), entourer (*in* de). **to ~ sb/sth in one's arms** serrer qn/qch dans ses bras, étreindre qn/qch; **to ~ sb to one's heart** serrer qn sur son cœur; (*liter*) **hills ~ed in mist** des collines enveloppées dans la brume *or* de brume.

c (*Culin*) *eggs, sugar* incorporer (*into* à).

4 vi a *[chair, table]* se (re)plier.

b (*: *fail*) *[newspaper]* disparaître, cesser de paraître; *[business]* fermer (ses portes); *[play]* quitter l'affiche, être retiré de l'affiche. *[business etc]* **they ~ed last year** ils ont mis la clé sous la porte l'année dernière.

▸**fold away** 1 vi *[table, bed]* (être capable de) se (re)plier. 2 vt sep *clothes, one's book, newspaper* plier et ranger. 3 **foldaway** adj *see* **fold**[1] **2.**

▸**fold back** vt sep *shutters* ouvrir, rabattre; *bedclothes, collar* replier, rabattre, retourner.

▸**fold down** vt sep *chair* plier. **to fold down the corner of a page** corner une page.

▸**fold in** vt sep (*Culin*) *eggs, sugar* incorporer.

▸**fold over** vt sep *paper* plier, replier; *blanket* replier, rabattre, retourner.

▸**fold up** 1 vi (* *fig*) *[plan, business venture]* faire fiasco, s'écrouler; *[play etc]* échouer, faire un four. **to fold up with laughter*** se tordre (de rire), être plié (en deux)*. 2 vt sep *paper etc* plier, replier.

fold[2] [fəʊld] n (*enclosure*) parc *m* à moutons; (*Rel*) sein *m* de l'Église. (*fig*) **to come back to the ~** rentrer au bercail.

...fold [fəʊld] suf: **twenty~** (adj) par vingt; (adv) vingt fois; *see* **two** *etc.*

folder ['fəʊldəʳ] n a (*file*) chemise *f*; (*with hinges*) classeur *m*; (*for drawings*) carton *m*; (*papers*) dossier *m*. b (*leaflet*) dépliant *m*, brochure *f*.

folding ['fəʊldɪŋ] adj *bed etc* pliant. **~ chair** (*with back*) chaise pliante; (*with back and arms*) fauteuil pliant; **~ door** porte *f* (en) accordéon; (*US*) **~ money*** billets *mpl* de banque; **~ seat** (*gen: also* **~ stool**) pliant *m*; (*Aut, Theat*) strapontin *m*; **~ table** table pliante.

foliage ['fəʊlɪɪdʒ] n feuillage *m*.

foliation [ˌfəʊlɪ'eɪʃən] n (*Bot*) foliation *f*, feuillaison *f*; *[book]* foliotage *m*; (*Geol*) foliation; (*Archit*) rinceaux *mpl*.

folic ['fəʊlɪk, 'fɒlɪk] adj: **~ acid** acide *m* folique.

folio ['fəʊlɪəʊ] n (*sheet*) folio *m*, feuillet *m*; (*volume*) (volume *m*) in-folio *m*.

folk [fəʊk] 1 n a (*pl: people: also* **~s**) gens *mpl* (*adj fem if before n*). **they are good ~(s)** ce sont de braves gens, ce sont de bonnes gens, ce sont des gens gentils; **a lot of ~(s) believe ...** beaucoup de gens croient ...; **there were a lot of ~ at the concert** il y avait beaucoup de gens *or* de monde au concert; **old ~(s)** les vieux, les vieilles gens; **young ~(s)** les jeunes *mpl*, les jeunes gens; **the old ~s stayed at home** les vieux* sont restés à la maison; **hullo ~s!*** bonjour tout le monde!*; *see* **country, old** *etc.*

b (*pl: people in general: also* **~s**) les gens, on. **what will ~(s) think?** qu'est-ce que les gens vont penser?, qu'est-ce qu'on va penser?; **~ get worried when they see that** les gens s'inquiètent quand ils voient ça.

c (*pl: relatives*) **~s*** famille *f*, parents *mpl*; **my ~s** ma famille, mes parents, les miens.

d (*NonC*) = **~ music;** *see* **2.**

2 comp ▸**folk art** art *m* populaire ▸**folk dance, folk dancing** danse *f* folklorique ▸**folk etymology** étymologie *f* populaire ▸**folklore** folklore *m* ▸**folk music** (*gen*) musique *f* folklorique; (*contemporary*) musique folk *inv*, folk *m* ▸**folk rock** folk-rock *m* ▸**folk singer** (*gen*) chanteur *m*, -euse *f* de chansons folkloriques; (*contemporary*) chanteur, -euse folk ▸**folksong** (*gen*) chanson *f or* chant *m* folklorique; (*contemporary*) chanson folk *inv* ▸**folk tale** conte *m* populaire *or* folklorique ▸**folk wisdom** la croyance populaire.

folksy* ['fəʊksɪ] adj *story, humour* populaire; *person* bon enfant *inv*, sans façon.

follicle ['fɒlɪkl] n follicule *m*.

follow ['fɒləʊ] 1 vt a *person, road, vehicle, roadsigns* suivre; (*in procession*) aller *or* venir à la suite de, suivre; *suspect* filer. **to ~ sb in/out** *etc* suivre qn (qui entre/sort *etc*); **he ~ed me into the room** il m'a suivi dans la pièce; **we're being ~ed** on nous suit; **~ that car!** suivez cette voiture!; **~ me** suivez-moi; **the child ~s him everywhere** l'enfant le suit partout, l'enfant est toujours sur ses talons; **they ~ed the guide** ils ont suivi le guide; (*fig*) **he'll be a difficult man to ~** il sera difficile de lui succéder *or* de le remplacer; **to have sb ~ed** faire filer qn; **the detectives ~ed the suspect for a week** les détectives ont filé le suspect pendant une semaine; **a bodyguard ~ed the president everywhere** un garde du corps accompagnait le président partout; **he was ~ed by one of our staff** il a été suivi par l'un de nos employés; **he arrived first, ~ed by the ambassador** il est arrivé le premier, suivi de l'ambassadeur *or* et après lui est venu l'ambassadeur; **this was ~ed by a request for ...** ceci a été suivi d'une demande de ...; **the boat ~ed the coast** le bateau suivait *or* longeait la côte; **~ your nose*** continuez tout droit; **he ~ed his father into the business** il est entré dans l'affaire sur les traces de son père; **the earthquake was ~ed by an epidemic** une épidémie a suivi le tremblement de terre; **the dinner will be ~ed by a concert** le dîner sera suivi d'un concert; **the years ~ed one another** les années se suivirent *or* se succédèrent; **night ~s day** la nuit succède au jour.

b *fashion* suivre, se conformer à; *instructions, course of study* suivre; *sb's orders* exécuter; *serial, strip cartoon* lire (régulièrement); *speech, lecture* suivre, écouter (attentivement). **to ~ sb's advice/example** suivre les conseils/l'exemple de qn; **to ~ suit** (*Cards*) fournir (*in clubs etc* à trèfle *etc*); (*fig*) en faire autant, faire de même; **do you ~ football?** vous suivez le football?; **which team do you ~?** tu es supporter de quelle équipe?

c *profession* exercer, suivre; *career* poursuivre. (*liter*) **to ~ the sea** être *or* devenir *or* se faire marin.

d (*understand*) suivre, comprendre. **do you ~ me?** vous me suivez?; **I don't quite ~ (you)** je ne vous suis pas bien *or* pas tout à fait.

2 vi a (*come after*) suivre. **as ~s** (*gen*) comme suit; **his argument was as ~s** son raisonnement était le suivant; **to ~ right behind sb, to ~ hard on sb's heels** être sur les talons de qn; (*fig*) **to ~ in sb's footsteps** *or* **tracks** suivre les traces *or* marcher sur les traces de qn; (*at meals*) **what is there to ~?** qu'est-ce qu'il y a après?, qu'est-ce qui suit?

b (*result*) s'ensuivre, résulter (*from* de). **it ~s that** il s'ensuit que + *indic*; **it doesn't ~ that** il ne s'ensuit pas nécessairement que + *subj or indic*, cela ne veut pas forcément dire que + *subj or indic*; **that doesn't ~** pas forcément, les deux choses n'ont rien à voir (l'une avec l'autre); **that ~s from what he said** cela découle de ce qu'il a dit.

c (*understand*) suivre, comprendre.

3 comp ▸**follow-my-leader** *jeu où les enfants doivent imiter tous les mouvements d'un joueur désigné* ▸**follow-on** (*Cricket*) *nouveau tour à la défense du guichet* ▸**follow-through** (*Billiards*) coulé *m*; (*Golf, Tennis*) accompagnement *m* (du coup); (*to a project, survey*) suite *f*, continuation *f* ▸**follow-up** (*Admin, Comm: on file, case*) suivi *m* (*on, of* de); (*event, programme etc coming after another*) suite *f* (*to* de); (*letter, circular*) rappel *m*; (*Med, Soc etc*) visite *f* de contrôle ▸**follow-up care** (*Med*) soins post-hospitaliers ▸**follow-up interview** entretien *m* complémentaire, second entretien ▸**follow-up letter** lettre *f* de rappel *or* relance ▸**follow-up study** *or* **survey** étude *f* complémentaire ▸**follow-up (telephone) call: to make a follow-up call** passer un coup de téléphone pour donner suite à une lettre *etc* ▸**follow-up visit** (*Med, Soc etc*) visite *f* de contrôle.

▸**follow about, follow around** vt sep suivre (partout), être toujours sur les talons de.

▸**follow on** vi a (*come after*) suivre. **you go ahead and I'll follow on when I can** allez-y, je vous suivrai quand je pourrai. b (*result*) résulter (*from* de). **it follows on from what I said** cela découle de ce que j'ai dit, c'est la conséquence logique de ce que j'ai dit.

▸**follow out** vt sep *idea, plan* poursuivre jusqu'au bout *or* jusqu'à sa conclusion; *an order* exécuter; *instructions* suivre.

▸**follow through** 1 vi (*Billiards*) faire *or* jouer un coulé; (*Golf, Tennis*) accompagner son coup *or* sa balle. 2 vt sep *idea, plan* poursuivre jusqu'au bout *or* jusqu'à sa conclusion. 3 **follow-through** n *see* **follow 3.**

▸**follow up** 1 vi a (*pursue an advantage*) exploiter un *or* tirer parti d'un avantage.

b (*Ftbl etc*) suivre l'action.

2 **vt sep** a (*benefit from*) *advantage, success, victory* exploiter, tirer parti de; *offer* donner suite à.

b (*not lose track of*) suivre; *[social worker]* maintenir une liaison avec, suivre, surveiller. **we must follow this business up** il faudra suivre cette affaire; **this is a case to follow up** c'est un cas à suivre; **"to be followed up"** "cas à suivre".

c (*reinforce*) *victory* asseoir; *remark* faire suivre (*with* de), compléter (*with* par). **they followed up the programme with another equally good** ils ont donné à cette émission une suite qui a été tout aussi excellente; **they followed up the insults with threats** ils ont fait suivre leurs insultes de menaces.

3 **follow-up n, adj** *see* **follow 3.**

follower ['fɒləʊə^r] **n** a partisan(e) *m(f)*, disciple *m*. **the ~s of fashion** ceux qui suivent la mode; **as all football ~s know** comme le savent tous ceux qui s'intéressent au football. b (†: *admirer*) amoureux *m*, -euse *f*, admirateur *m*, -trice *f*.

following ['fɒləʊɪŋ] 1 **adj** suivant. **the ~ day** le jour suivant, le lendemain; **he made the ~ remarks** il a fait les remarques suivantes *or* les remarques que voici; **~ wind** vent *m* arrière.

2 **n** a *[idea, doctrine]* partisans *mpl*, disciples *mpl*, adeptes *mpl*. **he has a large ~** il a de nombreux partisans *or* disciples *or* fidèles.

b **he said the ~** il a dit ceci; (*in documents etc*) **see the ~ for an explanation** voir ce qui suit pour toute explication; **his argument was the ~** son raisonnement était le suivant; *[people, books etc]* **the ~ have been chosen** les suivants *mpl* ont été choisis.

3 **prep** a (*after*) après. **~ the concert there will be ...** après le concert il y aura ... .

b (*as a result of*) (comme) suite à. (*Comm*) **~ your letter ...** (comme) suite à *or* en réponse à votre lettre ...; **~ our meeting** (comme) suite à notre entretien.

folly ['fɒlɪ] **n** a (*NonC: foolishness*) folie *f*, sottise *f*. **it's sheer ~ to do that** c'est de la pure folie *or* de la démence de faire cela. b (*foolish thing, action*) sottise *f*, folie *f*. c (*Archit*) (*gen*) extravagance *f* architecturale; (*specifically house; also in place names*) folie *f*.

foment [fəʊ'ment] **vt** (*lit, fig*) fomenter.

fomentation [ˌfəʊmen'teɪʃən] **n** (*lit, fig*) fomentation *f*.

fond [fɒnd] **adj** a **to be ~ of sb** aimer beaucoup qn, avoir de l'affection pour qn; **to be very ~ of music** aimer beaucoup la musique, être très amateur de musique; **to be ~ of sweet things** être friand de sucreries, aimer les sucreries. b (*loving*) *husband, friend* affectueux, tendre; *parent* (trop) bon, (trop) indulgent; *look* tendre; *hope* fervent; *ambition, wish* cher. **it is my ~est hope that ...** mon espoir le plus cher est que ... . c (*foolish*) *hope, ambition, wish* naïf (*f* naïve).

fondant ['fɒndənt] **n** (bonbon *m*) fondant *m*. **~ icing** glaçage *m* fondant.

fondle ['fɒndl] **vt** caresser.

fondly ['fɒndlɪ] **adv** a (*lovingly*) tendrement, affectueusement. b (*foolishly, credulously*) *believe, think, imagine* naïvement. **he ~ expected to learn it quickly** il avait la naïveté de croire qu'il l'apprendrait vite; **after that, he ~ imagined that** après cela, il était allé s'imaginer que *or* il s'imaginait naïvement que.

fondness ['fɒndnɪs] **n** (*for things*) prédilection *f*, penchant *m* (*for* pour); (*for people*) affection *f*, tendresse *f* (*for* pour).

fondue ['fɒnduː] **n** fondue *f*.

font [fɒnt] **n** a (*Rel*) fonts baptismaux. b (*US Typ*) = **fount b.**

fontanel(le) [ˌfɒntə'nel] **n** fontanelle *f*.

food [fuːd] 1 **n** a (*NonC: sth to eat*) nourriture *f*. **there was no ~ in the house** il n'y avait rien à manger *or* il n'y avait pas de nourriture dans la maison; **there's not enough ~** il n'y a pas assez à manger, il n'y a pas assez de nourriture; **most of the ~ had gone bad** la plus grande partie de la nourriture *or* des vivres *mpl* s'était avariée; **to give sb ~** donner à manger à qn; **to give the horses their ~** faire manger les chevaux, donner à manger aux chevaux; **what's that? — it's ~ for the horse** qu'est-ce que c'est? — c'est de la nourriture pour *or* c'est de quoi manger pour le cheval; **to buy ~** acheter à manger, faire des provisions; **the cost of ~** le prix des denrées *fpl* alimentaires *or* de la nourriture; **~ and clothing** la nourriture et les vêtements; **to be off one's ~*** avoir perdu l'appétit, n'avoir plus d'appétit; **the ~ is very good here** la cuisine est excellente ici, on mange très bien ici; **he likes plain ~** il aime la cuisine simple, il aime se nourrir simplement; (*fig*) **it gave me ~ for thought** cela m'a donné à penser *or* à réfléchir.

b (*specific substance*) (*gen*) aliment *m*; (*soft, moist: for poultry, dogs, cats, pigs etc*) pâtée *f*. **a new ~ for babies/for pigs** *etc* un nouvel aliment pour les bébés/pour les cochons *etc*; **pet ~** aliments pour animaux; **tins of dog/cat** *etc* **~** des boîtes de pâtée pour chiens/chats *etc*; **all these ~s must be kept in a cool place** tous ces aliments doivent être conservés au frais; *see* **frozen, health** *etc*.

c (*for plants*) engrais *m*.

2 **comp** ►**food additive** additif *m* alimentaire ►**Food and Agriculture Organization** Organisation *f* des Nations Unies pour l'alimentation et l'agriculture ►**Food and Drug Administration** (*US*) *office du contrôle pharmaceutique et alimentaire* ►**food chain** (*Ecol*) chaîne *f* alimentaire ►**food colouring** colorant *m* alimentaire ►**food counter** (*in shop*) rayon *m* (d')alimentation ►**food crop** culture *f* vivrière ►**food grains** céréales *fpl* vivrières ►**food mixer** mixe(u)r *m* ►**food parcel** colis *m* de vivres ►**food poisoning** intoxication *f* alimentaire ►**food prices** prix *mpl* des denrées alimentaires *or* de la nourriture ►**food processing** (*gen*) préparation *f* des aliments; (*Ind*) industrie *f* alimentaire ►**food processor** robot *m* de cuisine ►**food rationing** rationnement *m* alimentaire ►**food shares** (*St Ex*) valeurs *fpl* de l'agro-alimentaire ►**food stamps** (*US*) bons *mpl* de nourriture (*pour indigents*) ►**foodstuffs** denrées *fpl* alimentaires, aliments *mpl*, comestibles *mpl* ►**food subsidy** subvention *f* sur les denrées alimentaires ►**food supplies** vivres *mpl* ►**food value** valeur nutritive.

foodie* ['fuːdɪ] **n** fana* *mf* de la (grande) cuisine.

foofaraw ['fuːfəˌrɔː] **n** histoires* *fpl*, cirque* *m*, pétard* *m*.

fool[1] [fuːl] 1 **n** a imbécile *mf*, idiot(e) *m(f)*, sot(te) *m(f)*. **stupid ~!** espèce d'imbécile!* *or* d'idiot(e)! *or* d'abruti(e)!*; **don't be a ~!** ne sois pas stupide!, ne fais pas l'idiot(e)!; **I felt such a ~** je me suis vraiment senti bête; **some ~ of a doctor, some ~ doctor**‡ un imbécile *or* un abruti* de médecin; **he was a ~ not to accept** il a été idiot *or* stupide de ne pas accepter; **what a ~ I was to think ...** ce que j'ai pu être bête de penser ...; **he's more of a ~ than I thought** il est (encore) plus idiot que je ne pensais; **he was ~ enough to accept** il a été assez stupide pour accepter, il a eu la bêtise d'accepter; **to play** *or* **act the ~** faire l'imbécile *or* le pitre; **he's no ~** il est loin d'être bête; **he's nobody's ~** il n'est pas né d'hier *or* tombé de la dernière pluie; **more ~ you!*** tu n'avais qu'à ne pas faire l'idiot! *or* être idiot!; **he made himself look a ~** *or* **he made a ~ of himself in front of everybody** il s'est rendu ridicule devant tout le monde; **to make a ~ of sb** (*ridicule*) ridiculiser qn, se payer la tête de qn*; (*trick*) avoir* *or* duper qn; **I went on a ~'s errand** j'y suis allé pour rien, je me suis dépensé en pure perte; **any ~ can do that** n'importe quel imbécile peut le faire; (*Geol*) **~'s gold** chalcopyrite *f*; **to live in a ~'s paradise** se bercer d'illusions *or* d'un bonheur illusoire, poursuivre un rêve; (*Prov*) **a ~ and his money are soon parted** aux idiots l'argent file entre les doigts; (*Prov*) **there's no ~ like an old ~** il n'y a pire imbécile qu'un vieil imbécile.

b (*jester*) bouffon *m*, fou *m*.

2 **comp** ►**fooling about, fooling around** bêtises *fpl* ►**foolproof** *method* infaillible, à toute épreuve; *piece of machinery* indétraquable, indéréglable.

3 **vi** faire l'imbécile *or* l'idiot(e). **stop ~ing!** arrête de faire l'idiot(e)! *or* l'imbécile!; **no ~ing*, he really said it** sans blague*, il a vraiment dit ça; **I was only ~ing** je ne faisais que plaisanter, c'était pour rire.

4 **vt** avoir*, berner, duper. **you won't ~ me so easily!** vous ne m'aurez pas comme ça!* *or* si facilement!*; **it ~ed nobody** personne n'a été dupe.

►**fool about, fool around** 1 **vi** a (*waste time*) perdre son temps. **stop fooling about and get on with your work** cesse de perdre ton temps et fais ton travail. b (*play the fool*) faire l'idiot(e) *or* l'imbécile *or* le pitre. **stop fooling about!** arrête de faire l'idiot! *or* l'imbécile! *or* le pitre!, cesse tes idioties!; **to fool about with sth** faire l'imbécile avec qch. c (*have an affair*) avoir une liaison *or* une aventure; (*have affairs*) avoir des liaisons *or* des aventures. 2 **fooling about** *or* **around n** *see* **fool**[1] **2.**

►**fool away vt sep** *time, money* perdre *or* gaspiller (en futilités).

fool[2] [fuːl] **n** (*Brit Culin: also* **fruit ~**) (sorte de) mousse *f* de fruits. **gooseberry ~** ≃ mousse de groseilles à maquereaux.

foolery ['fuːlərɪ] **n** (*NonC*) (*foolish acts*) sottises *fpl*, bêtises *fpl*; (*behaviour*) bouffonnerie *f*, pitrerie(s) *f(pl)*.

foolhardiness ['fuːlˌhɑːdɪnɪs] **n** témérité *f*, imprudence *f*.

foolhardy ['fuːlˌhɑːdɪ] **adj** téméraire, imprudent.

foolish ['fuːlɪʃ] **adj** idiot, bête, insensé. **it would be ~ to believe her** ce ne serait pas (très) malin de la croire; **don't be so ~** ne fais pas l'idiot(e), ne sois pas bête; **that was very ~ of you** ça n'a pas été très malin de votre part, (*more formally*) vous avez vraiment été imprudent; **to look ~** avoir l'air idiot *or* tout bête*; **to make sb look ~** rendre qn ridicule; **I felt very ~** je me suis senti plutôt idiot *or* bête; **she did something very ~** elle a fait une grosse bêtise.

foolishly ['fuːlɪʃlɪ] **adv** sottement, bêtement. **and ~ I believed him** et je l'ai cru comme un(e) imbécile *or* un(e) idiot(e) (que j'étais).

foolishness ['fuːlɪʃnɪs] **n** (*NonC*) bêtise *f*, sottise *f*.

foolscap ['fuːlskæp] 1 **n** (*also* **~ paper**) ≃ papier *m* ministre. 2 **comp** ►**foolscap envelope** enveloppe longue ►**foolscap sheet** feuille *f* de papier ministre ►**foolscap size** format *m* ministre.

foot [fʊt] 1 **n, pl feet** a *[person, horse, cow etc]* pied *m*; *[dog, cat, bird]* patte *f*. **to be on one's feet** (*lit*) être *or* se tenir debout; (*fig: after illness*) être sur pied, être rétabli *or* remis; **I'm on my feet all day long** je suis debout toute la journée; (*fig*) **to think on one's feet** agir sur le moment; **to go on ~** aller à pied; **to get** *or* **to rise to one's feet** se lever, se mettre debout; **to bring sb to his feet** faire lever qn; (*fig*) **to put** *or* **set sb on his feet again** (*healthwise*) remettre qn d'aplomb *or* d'attaque*; (*financially*) remettre qn en selle; **to keep one's feet** garder l'équilibre; **feet first** les pieds devant; **it's very wet under ~** c'est très mouillé par terre; **he was trampled under ~ by the horses** les chevaux l'ont piétiné; **the children have been under my feet the whole day** les enfants ont été dans mes jambes toute la journée; (*fig*) **to get under sb's feet** venir dans les jambes de qn; (*fig*) **you've got to put your ~ down** il faut faire acte d'autorité, il faut être catégorique; **he let it go on for several weeks before finally putting his ~ down** il l'a supporté pendant plusieurs semaines avant d'y mettre le holà; (*Aut *: accelerate*) **to put one's ~ down** appuyer sur le champignon*; (*fig*) **to put one's ~ in it*** gaffer; (*fig*) **to put one's best ~ forward** (*hurry*) se dépêcher, allonger *or* presser le pas; (*do one's best*) faire de son mieux; (*fig*) **he didn't put a ~ wrong** il n'a pas commis la moindre erreur *or* maladresse; *[people, relationship]* **to start off** *or* **get off on the right/wrong ~** être bien/mal parti; **I got off on the wrong ~ with him** j'ai mal commencé avec lui; (*fig*) **to get one's** *or* **a ~ in the door** faire le premier pas, établir un premier contact; **to put one's feet up*** (s'étendre *or* s'asseoir pour) se reposer un peu; **to take the weight off one's feet** (s'asseoir pour) se reposer un peu; (*fig*) **to have one ~ in the grave*** avoir un pied dans la tombe; **he's dying on his feet*** (*exhausted*) il n'en peut plus; (*really ill*) il n'en a plus pour longtemps; (*fig*) **the business is dying on its feet*** c'est une affaire moribonde; **to set ~ on land** poser le pied sur la terre ferme; **I've never set ~ there** je n'y ai jamais mis le(s) pied(s); **never set ~ here again!** ne remettez pas les pieds ici!; (*excl*) **my ~!*** allons donc!, à d'autres!; (*Brit*) **the boot** *or* (*US*) **the shoe is on the other ~** les rôles sont inversés; *see* **cold, drag, fall, find** *etc.*

b *[hill, bed, stocking]* pied *m*; *[table]* (bas) bout *m*; *[page, stairs]* bas *m*. **at the ~ of the page** au *or* en bas de la page.

c (*measure*) pied *m* (anglais) (= *30,48 cm*); (*Poetry*) pied.

d (*NonC: Mil*) infanterie *f*. **ten thousand ~** dix mille fantassins *mpl* *or* soldats *mpl* d'infanterie; **the 91st of ~** le 91e (régiment) d'infanterie.

2 **vt: to ~ the bill*** payer (la note *or* la douloureuse*), casquer‡; **to ~ it*** (*walk*) (y) aller à pied *or* à pattes*; (*dance*) danser.

3 **comp ▸foot-and-mouth (disease)** fièvre aphteuse **▸football** *see* **football ▸footbath** bain *m* de pieds **▸footboard** marchepied *m* **▸footbrake** frein *m* à pied **▸footbridge** passerelle *f* **▸foot-dragging** lenteurs *fpl*, atermoiements *mpl* **▸footfall** (bruit *m* de) pas *m* **▸foot fault** (*Tennis*) faute *f* de pied; **foot fault judge** juge *m* de fond **▸footgear** chaussures *fpl* **▸foothills** contreforts *mpl* **▸foothold** prise *f* (de pied); **to get** *or* **gain a foothold** (*lit*) prendre pied; (*fig*) *[newcomer]* se faire accepter; *[idea, opinion]* s'imposer, prendre; *[fascism etc]* se répandre, prendre de l'importance; (*Comm*) **to gain a foothold in a market** prendre pied sur un marché **▸footlights** (*Theat*) rampe *f*; (*fig*) **the lure of the footlights** l'attrait du théâtre *or* des planches* **▸footlocker** (*US Mil*) cantine *f* **▸footloose** libre de toute attache; (*fig*) **footloose and fancy-free** libre comme l'air **▸footman** valet *m* de pied **▸footmark** empreinte *f* (de pied) **▸footnote** (*lit*) note *f* en bas de (la) page; (*fig*) post-scriptum *m* **▸foot passengers** *[ferry boat]* passagers *mpl* sans véhicule **▸footpath** (*path*) sentier *m* (*see also* **public**); (*Brit: pavement*) trottoir *m*; (*by highway*) chemin *m* **▸foot patrol** (*Police, Mil*) patrouille *f* à pied **▸foot patrolman** (*US Police*) agent *m* de police **▸footplate** (*esp Brit Rail*) plate-forme *f* (*d'une locomotive*) **▸footplatemen, footplate workers** agents *mpl* de conduite **▸footprint** (*lit*) empreinte *f* (*de pied*); (*fig*) *[computer]* surface *f* d'encombrement **▸footpump** pompe *f* à pied **▸footrest** (*part of chair*) repose-pieds *m inv*; (*footstool*) tabouret *m* (*pour les pieds*) **▸footrot** piétin *m* **▸footslog‡** s'envoyer* de la marche à pied **▸footslogger‡** (*walker*) marcheur *m*, -euse *f*; (*soldier*) pousse-cailloux‡† *m inv* **▸foot soldier** fantassin *m* **▸footsore** aux pieds endoloris; **to be footsore** avoir mal aux pieds **▸footstep** pas *m* (*see* **follow**) **▸footstool** tabouret *m* (*pour les pieds*) **▸footway** = **footpath** **▸footwear** (*NonC*) chaussure *f* (*NonC*), chaussures *fpl* **▸footwork** (*NonC: Sport, Dancing*) jeu *m* de jambes.

footage ['fʊtɪdʒ] **n** (*gen, also Cine: length*) ≃ métrage *m*; (*Cine: material on film*) séquences *fpl* (*about, on* sur).

football ['fʊtbɔːl] 1 **n** a (*sport*) (*Brit*) football *m*; (*US*) football américain; *see* **table**.

b (*ball*) ballon *m* (de football), balle *f*. (*fig*) **he/this charter is being used as a political ~** il/cette charte est le prétexte à des débats politiciens.

2 **comp** *ground, match, team* de football **▸football coupon** (*Brit*) fiche *f* de pari (sur les matchs de football) **▸football hooligan** (*Brit*) vandale *m* (*qui assiste à un match de football*) **▸football hooliganism** (*Brit*) vandalisme *m* (*lors d'un match de football*) **▸football league** (*Brit*) championnat *m* de football; (*Brit*) **the Football League** ≃ la Fédération française de football **▸football player** (*Brit*) joueur *m* de football, footballeur *m*; (*US*) joueur *m* de football américain **▸football pools** (*Brit*) ≃ loto *m* sportif, pronostics *mpl* (sur les matchs de football); (*Brit*) **to do the football pools** ≃ jouer au loto sportif; (*Brit*) **he won £200 on the football pools** ≃ il a gagné 200 livres au loto sportif **▸football season** saison *f* du football **▸football special** (*Brit Rail*) train *m* de supporters (*d'une équipe de football*).

footballer ['fʊtbɔːlə^r] **n** joueur *m* de football, footballeur *m*.

-footed ['fʊtɪd] **adj ending in comps: light-footed** au pied léger; *see* **four** *etc.*

footer ['fʊtə^r] **n** a (*Typ, Comput*) titre *m* en bas de page. b (*Brit* ‡) foot* *m*, football *m*.

-footer ['fʊtə^r] **n ending in comps:** (*boat*) **a 15-footer** ≃ un bateau de 5 mètres de long; *see* **six** *etc.*

footing ['fʊtɪŋ] **n** (*lit*) prise *f* (de pied); (*fig*) position *f*, relations *fpl*. **to lose** *or* **miss one's ~** perdre pied *or* son équilibre *or* l'équilibre; **to get a ~ in society** se faire une position dans le monde; **to be on a friendly ~ with sb** être traité en ami par qn, avoir des relations d'amitié avec qn; **on an equal ~** sur un pied d'égalité; **on a war ~** sur le pied de guerre; **we should put this on a regular ~** (*do it regularly*) nous devrions faire ceci régulièrement; (*make it official*) nous devrions régulariser ceci; **to put sth on an official ~** officialiser qch, rendre qch officiel; (*Jur*) **on the ~ that** en supposant que.

footle* ['fuːtl] **vi: to ~ about** faire l'âne, perdre son temps à des futilités.

footling ['fuːtlɪŋ] **adj** insignifiant, futile.

footsie‡ ['fʊtsɪ] **n: to play ~ with sb‡** faire du pied à qn.

fop [fɒp] **n** dandy *m*.

foppish ['fɒpɪʃ] **adj** *man* dandy; *manners, behaviour, clothes* de dandy.

FOR [ˌefəʊ'ɑː^r] (*Comm*) (**abbr of free on rail**) franco sur wagon.

for [fɔː^r] (*phr vb elem*) 1 **prep** a (*indicating intention*) pour, à l'intention de; (*destination*) pour, à destination de, dans la direction de. **a letter ~ you** une lettre pour toi; **is this ~ me?** c'est pour moi?; **I sent a present ~ the child** j'ai envoyé un cadeau pour l'enfant; **he put it aside ~ me** il l'a mis de côté pour moi *or* à mon intention; **votes ~ women!** le droit de vote pour les femmes!; **clothes ~ children** vêtements pour enfants; **~ sale** à vendre; **~ example** par exemple; **it's time ~ dinner** c'est l'heure du dîner, il est l'heure de dîner; **I've got news ~ you** j'ai du nouveau à t'apprendre; **a job ~ next week** un travail à faire la semaine prochaine; **to write ~ the papers** faire des articles pour les journaux; **6 children to provide ~** 6 enfants à élever; **she's the wife ~ me** voilà *or* c'est la femme qu'il me faut; **he's the man ~ the job** il est l'homme idéal *or* c'est l'homme qu'il (nous) faut pour ce travail; **a weakness ~ sweet things** un faible pour les sucreries; **a liking ~ work** le goût du travail; **a gift ~ languages** un don pour les langues; **he's got a genius ~ saying the wrong thing** il a le don de *or* un don pour dire ce qu'il ne faut pas; **he left ~ Italy** il est parti pour l'Italie; **trains ~ Paris** trains en direction de *or* à destination de Paris; **the train ~ Paris** le train pour *or* de Paris; **the ship left ~ Australia** le navire est parti pour l'Australie; **ship bound ~ Australia** (*before sailing*) navire en partance pour l'Australie; (*en route*) navire à destination de *or* en route pour l'Australie; **he swam ~ the shore** il a nagé dans la direction du rivage *or* vers le rivage; **to make ~ home** prendre la direction de la maison; **to make ~ the open sea** mettre le cap sur le (grand) large; **where are you ~?** où allez-vous?; **destined ~ greatness** promis à la célébrité; *see* **head** *etc.*

b (*indicating purpose*) pour. **what ~?** pourquoi?; **what did you do that ~?** pourquoi avez-vous fait cela?; **what's this knife ~?** à quoi sert ce couteau?; **it's not ~ cutting wood** ça n'est pas fait pour couper du bois; **it's been used ~ a hammer** on s'en est servi comme d'un marteau, ça a servi de marteau; **this will do ~ a hammer** ça ira comme marteau, ça servira de *or* comme marteau; **a room ~ studying in** une pièce réservée à l'étude *or* comme salle d'étude; **a bag ~ carrying books in** un sac pour porter des livres; **we went there ~ our holidays** nous y sommes allés pour les vacances; **he went there ~ a holiday/a rest** il y est allé pour des vacances/pour se reposer; **he does it ~ pleasure** il le fait par plaisir *or* pour son plaisir; **to work ~ exams** travailler pour des examens; **to work ~ one's living** travailler pour gagner sa vie; **to get ready ~ a journey** se préparer pour un voyage; **do you feel ready ~ bed now?** vous voulez aller vous coucher tout de suite?; **fit ~ nothing** bon à rien; **eager ~ praise** avide d'éloges; **a collection ~ the blind** une quête pour les *or* en faveur des aveugles; **a campaign ~ free education** une campagne pour la gratuité de l'enseignement; **to pray ~ peace** prier pour la paix; **to hope ~ news** espérer des nouvelles; **to look ~ sth** chercher qch; *see* **ask, good** *etc.*

c (*as representing*) **D ~ Daniel** D comme Daniel; (*Parl*) **member ~ Brighton** député *m* de Brighton; **agent ~ Ford cars** concessionnaire *mf* Ford; **I'll see her ~ you if you like** je la verrai à ta place si tu veux; **will you go ~ me?** voulez-vous y aller à ma place?; **the government will do it ~ them** le gouvernement le fera à leur place; **to act ~ sb** agir pour qn *or* au nom de qn *or* pour le compte de qn; **what is G.B. ~?** qu'est-ce que G.B. veut dire?; **I took you ~ a burglar** je vous ai pris pour un cambrioleur.

d (*in exchange for*) **I'll give you this book ~ that one** je vous échange ce livre-ci contre celui-là; **to exchange one thing ~ another** échanger une chose contre une autre; **to pay 5 francs ~ a ticket** payer 5 F le billet; **I sold it ~ £2** je l'ai vendu 2 livres; **he'll do it ~ £5** il le fera pour 5 livres; **word ~ word** mot à mot; **there is one French passenger ~ every 10 English** sur 11 passagers il y a un Français et 10 Anglais, il y a un passager français pour 10 Anglais; **~ one man like that there are 10 his opposite** pour un homme comme lui il y en a 10 qui sont (tout à fait) l'opposé; **what's (the) German ~ "dog"?** comment est-ce qu'on dit "chien" en allemand?

e (*in favour of*) pour. **~ or against** pour ou contre; **I'm ~ the government** je suis pour le *or* partisan du gouvernement; **I'm (all) ~ helping him if we can** je suis (tout à fait) partisan de l'aider si cela peut se faire; **I'm all ~ it*** je suis tout à fait pour*; **they voted ~ the**

bill ils ont voté en faveur de la loi.

f (*because of*) pour, en raison de. ~ **this reason** pour cette raison; ~ **fear of being left behind** de peur d'être oublié; **noted** ~ **his jokes** connu pour ses plaisanteries; **famous** ~ **its church** célèbre pour son église; **to shout** ~ **joy** hurler de joie; **to weep** ~ **rage** pleurer de rage; **to go to prison** ~ **theft/**~ **stealing** aller en prison pour vol/pour avoir volé; ~ **old times' sake** en souvenir du passé; ~ **my sake** pour moi; **to choose sb** ~ **his ability** choisir qn en raison de sa compétence; **if it weren't** ~ **him, but** ~ **him** sans lui.

g (*considering; with regard to*) pour. **anxious** ~ **sb** inquiet pour qn; ~ **my part** pour ma part, quant à moi; **as** ~ **him** quant à lui; **as** ~ **that** pour ce qui est de cela, quant à cela; ~ **sure** à coup sûr; **it is warm** ~ **January** il fait bon pour (un mois de) janvier; **he's tall** ~ **his age** il est grand pour son âge; **he's small** ~ **a policeman** il est petit pour un agent de police; **he's young** ~ **a prime minister** il est jeune pour un *or* pour être premier ministre.

h (*in spite of*) ~ **all his wealth** malgré toute sa richesse, tout riche qu'il soit; ~ **all that, you should have warned me** malgré tout vous auriez dû me prévenir, vous auriez néanmoins dû me prévenir; ~ **all he promised to come, he didn't** en dépit de *or* malgré ses (belles) promesses il n'est pas venu.

i (*in time*) (*future*) pour, pendant; (*past: completed action*) pendant; (*not yet completed action*) depuis. **I am going away** ~ **a few days** je pars pour quelques jours; **I shall be away** ~ **a month** je serai absent (pendant) un mois; **he won't be back** ~ **a week** il ne sera pas de retour avant huit jours; **that's enough** ~ **the moment** cela suffit pour le moment; **he's gone** ~ **good** il est parti pour de bon; **he went away** ~ **two weeks** il est parti (pendant) quinze jours; **I worked there** ~ **3 months** j'y a travaillé pendant 3 mois; **I have been working here** ~ **3 months** je travaille ici depuis 3 mois; **I had been working there** *or* **I had worked there** ~ **3 months when** ... je travaillais là depuis 3 mois quand ...; **I have not seen her** ~ **2 years** voilà 2 ans *or* il y a 2 ans *or* cela fait 2 ans que je ne l'ai vue; **he's been here** ~ **10 days** il est ici depuis 10 jours; **I had known her** ~ **years** je la connaissais depuis des années.

j (*distance*) pendant. **a road lined with trees** ~ **3 km** une route bordée d'arbres pendant *or* sur 3 km; **we walked** ~ **2 km** nous avons marché (pendant) 2 km; **we drove** ~ **50 km** nous avons roulé pendant 50 km; **there was nothing to be seen** ~ **miles** il n'y avait rien à voir pendant des kilomètres; **there were small drab houses** ~ **mile upon mile** de petites maisons monotones se succédaient kilomètre après kilomètre, c'était pendant des kilomètres un défilé de petites maisons monotones.

k (*with infin phrases*) pour que + *subj*. ~ **this to be possible** pour que cela se puisse, pour que cela puisse être; **it's easy** ~ **him to do it** il lui est facile de le faire; **I brought it** ~ **you to see** je l'ai apporté pour que vous le voyiez (*subj*); **it's not** ~ **you to blame him** ce n'est pas à vous de le critiquer, il ne vous appartient pas de le critiquer (*frm*); **it's not** ~ **me to say** ce n'est pas à moi de le dire; **the best would be** *or* **it would be best** ~ **you to go away** le mieux serait que vous vous en alliez (*subj*); **there is still time** ~ **him to come** il a encore le temps d'arriver; **their one hope is** ~ **him to return** leur seul espoir est qu'il revienne; *see* **arrange, wait** *etc*.

l (*phrases*) **now** ~ **it!** (bon alors) allons-y!; **you're** ~ **it!*** qu'est-ce que tu vas prendre!*, ça va être ta fête!⁑; **I'll be** ~ **it if he catches me here!*** qu'est-ce que je vais prendre* *or* dérouiller⁑ s'il me trouve ici!; **oh** ~ **a cup of tea!** je donnerais n'importe quoi pour une tasse de thé!; **oh** ~ **a horse!** si seulement j'avais un cheval!

2 **conj** car.

forage ['fɒrɪdʒ] 1 **n** fourrage *m*. (*Mil*) ~ **cap** calot *m*. 2 **vi** fourrager, fouiller (*for* pour trouver).

foray ['fɒreɪ] 1 **n** incursion *f*, raid *m*, razzia *f* (*into* en); (*fig*) incursion (*into* dans). **to go on** *or* **make a** ~ faire une incursion *or* un raid. 2 **vi** faire une incursion *or* un raid.

forbad(e) [fə'bæd] **pret of forbid.**

forbear [fɔː'bɛəʳ] **pret forbore, ptp forborne vi** s'abstenir. **to** ~ **from doing, to** ~ **to do** s'abstenir *or* se garder de faire; **he forbore to make any comment** il s'abstint de tout commentaire.

forbearance [fɔː'bɛərəns] **n** patience *f*, tolérance *f*.

forbearing [fɔː'bɛərɪŋ] **adj** patient, tolérant.

forbears ['fɔːbɛəz] **npl = forebears.**

forbid [fə'bɪd] **pret forbad(e), ptp forbidden vt** a (*not allow*) défendre, interdire (*sb to do* à qn de faire). **to** ~ **sb alcohol** interdire l'alcool à qn; **I** ~ **you to!** je vous l'interdis!; **employees are** ~**den to do this** il est interdit aux employés de faire cela, les employés n'ont pas le droit de faire cela; **it is** ~**den to talk** il est défendu de parler; (*on signs*) "défense de parler"; **smoking is strictly** ~**den** il est formellement interdit de fumer, défense absolue de fumer; **that's** ~**den** c'est défendu.

b (*prevent*) empêcher. **my health** ~**s my attending the meeting** ma santé m'empêche d'assister à la réunion; (*liter*) **God** ~ **that this might be true!** à Dieu ne plaise que ceci soit vrai! (*liter*); **God** ~**!*** pourvu que non!, j'espère bien que non!

forbidden [fə'bɪdn] 1 **pret of forbid.** 2 **adj** interdit. (*lit, fig*) ~ **fruit** fruit *m* défendu; (*fig*) **that's** ~ **territory** *or* **ground** c'est un sujet tabou.

forbidding [fə'bɪdɪŋ] **adj** *building, cliff, cloud* menaçant; *person* sévère. **a** ~ **look** un air *or* un aspect rébarbatif.

forbore [fɔː'bɔːʳ] **pret of forbear.**

forborne [fɔː'bɔːn] **ptp of forbear.**

force [fɔːs] 1 **n** a (*NonC: strength*) force *f*, violence *f*; (*Phys*) force; [*phrase, word etc*] importance *f*, force, poids *m*. (*Phys*) ~ **of gravity** pesanteur *f*; **centrifugal/centripetal** ~ force centrifuge/centripète; **to use** ~ employer la force (*to do* pour faire); **by sheer** ~ de vive force; **by** ~ **of** à force de; ~ **of circumstances** contrainte *f* *or* force des circonstances; **from** ~ **of habit** par la force de l'habitude; **through** *or* **by sheer** ~ **of will** purement à force de volonté; **by (sheer)** ~ **of personality** uniquement grâce à sa personnalité; ~ **of a blow** violence d'un coup; **to resort to** ~ avoir recours à la force *or* à la violence; **to settle a dispute by** ~ régler une querelle par la force *or* par la violence; **his argument lacked** ~ son argument manquait de conviction; **I don't quite see the** ~ **of his argument** je ne vois pas bien la force de son argument; **I can see the** ~ **of that** je comprends la force que cela peut avoir; [*law, prices etc*] **to come into** ~ entrer en vigueur *or* en application; **the rule is now in** ~ le règlement est actuellement en vigueur; **the police were there in** ~ la police était là en force *or* en grand nombre; **they came in** ~ **to support him** ils sont arrivés en force pour lui prêter leur appui; *see* **brute.**

b (*power*) force *f*. ~**s of Nature** forces de la nature; **he is a powerful** ~ **in the Trade Union movement** il exerce une influence puissante dans le mouvement syndical; **there are several** ~**s at work** plusieurs influences se font sentir; *see* **life.**

c (*body of men*) force *f*. (*Brit Mil*) **the** ~**s** les forces armées; (*Brit Mil*) **allied** ~**s** armées alliées; (*Police*) **the** ~***** la police (*see also* **police**); (*Comm*) **our sales** ~ (l'effectif *m* de) nos représentants *mpl* de commerce; *see* **join, land.**

2 **comp** ►**force-feed** nourrir de force; **he was force-fed** on l'a nourri de force ►**forcemeat** farce *f* ►**forcing bid** (*Bridge*) annonce forcée *or* de forcing ►**forcing house** (*Agric etc*) forcerie *f*; (*fig*) pépinière *f*.

3 **vt** a (*constrain*) contraindre, forcer, obliger (*sb to do* qn à faire). **to be** ~**d to do** être contraint *or* forcé *or* obligé de faire; **to** ~ **o.s. to do** se forcer *or* se contraindre à faire; **I find myself** ~**d to say that** force m'est de dire que, je me vois contraint de dire que; **he was** ~**d to conclude that** il a été forcé de conclure que, force lui a été de conclure que.

b (*impose*) *conditions, obedience* imposer (*on sb* à qn). **the decision was** ~**d on me by events** la décision m'a été imposée par les événements, les événements ont dicté ma décision; **they** ~**d action on the enemy** ils ont contraint l'ennemi à la bataille; **I don't want to** ~ **myself on you, but** ... je ne veux pas m'imposer (à vous), mais ... .

c (*push, thrust*) pousser. **to** ~ **books into a box** fourrer des livres dans une caisse; **he** ~**d himself through the gap in the hedge** il s'est frayé un passage par un trou dans la haie; **to** ~ **one's way into** entrer *or* pénétrer de force dans; **to** ~ **one's way through** se frayer un passage à travers; **to** ~ **a bill through Parliament** forcer la Chambre à voter une loi; **to** ~ **sb into a corner** (*lit*) pousser qn dans un coin; (*fig*) acculer qn; **the lorry** ~**d the car off the road** le camion a forcé la voiture à quitter la route.

d (*break open*) *lock etc* forcer. **to** ~ **open a drawer/a door** forcer un tiroir/une porte; (*fig*) **to** ~ **sb's hand** forcer la main à qn.

e (*extort*) arracher; (*stronger*) extorquer (*from* à). **he** ~**d a confession from me** il m'a arraché *or* extorqué une confession; **we** ~**d the secret out of him** nous lui avons arraché le secret.

f *plants etc* forcer, hâter. **to** ~ **the pace** forcer l'allure *or* le pas.

g *smile, answer* forcer. **he** ~**d a reply** il s'est forcé à répondre.

4 **vi** (*Bridge*) faire un forcing.

►**force back vt sep** a (*Mil*) *enemy* obliger à reculer, faire reculer; *crowd* repousser, refouler, faire reculer. b **to force back one's desire to laugh** réprimer son envie de rire; **to force back one's tears** refouler ses larmes.

►**force down vt sep** a *aircraft* forcer à atterrir. b **to force food down** se forcer à manger. c **if you force the clothes down you will get more into the suitcase** si tu tasses les vêtements tu en feras entrer plus dans la valise.

►**force out vt sep** a faire sortir (de force). **he forced the cork out** il a sorti le bouchon en forçant; **they forced the rebels out into the open** ils ont forcé *or* obligé les insurgés à se montrer; **small farmers will be forced out of the market** les petits exploitants seront éliminés du marché. b **he forced out a reply/an apology** il s'est forcé à répondre/à s'excuser.

forced [fɔːst] **adj** *laughter, smile* forcé, contraint, artificiel; *plant* forcé. (*Aviat*) ~ **landing** atterrissage forcé; (*Mil*) ~ **march** marche forcée; (*Econ etc*) ~ **savings** épargne forcée.

forceful ['fɔːsfʊl] **adj** *person, character* énergique; *argument, reasoning* vigoureux, puissant; *influence* puissant.

forcefully ['fɔːsfəlɪ] **adv** avec force, avec vigueur.

forcemeat ['fɔːsmiːt] **n** (*Culin*) farce *f*, hachis *m* (*de viande et de fines herbes*).

forceps ['fɔːseps] **npl** (*also* **pair of** ~) forceps *m*. ~ **delivery** accouchement *m* au forceps.

forcible ['fɔːsəbl] **adj** a (*done by force*) de *or* par force. ~ **entry** (*by* *police etc*) perquisition *f*; (*by thief etc*) effraction *f*; ~ **feeding** alimentation forcée. **b** (*powerful*) *language, style* vigoureux, énergique; *argument* vigoureux, puissant; *personality* puissant, fort; *speaker* percutant, puissant.

forcibly ['fɔːsəblɪ] **adv** **a** (*by force*) de force, par la force. **the prisoner was ~ fed** le prisonnier a été nourri de force. **b** (*vigorously*) *speak, object* énergiquement, avec véhémence, avec vigueur.

ford [fɔːd] **1** **n** gué *m*. **2** **vt** passer à gué.

fordable ['fɔːdəbl] **adj** guéable.

fore [fɔːʳ] **1** **adj** à l'avant, antérieur. (*Naut*) ~ **and aft rig** gréement *m* aurique; (*Naut*) ~ **and aft sail** voile *f* aurique; *see* **foreleg** *etc*. **2** **n** (*Naut*) avant *m*. (*fig*) **to come to the ~** *[person]* se mettre en évidence, se faire remarquer; *[sb's courage etc]* se manifester; **he was well to the ~ during the discussion** il a été très en évidence pendant la discussion; (*at hand*) **to the ~** à portée de main. **3** **adv** (*Naut*) à l'avant. ~ **and aft** de l'avant à l'arrière. **4** **excl** (*Golf*) gare!, attention!

forearm ['fɔːrɑːm] **n** avant-bras *m inv*.

forebears ['fɔːbɛəz] **npl** aïeux *mpl* (*liter*), ancêtres *mpl*.

forebode [fɔː'bəʊd] **vt** présager, annoncer.

foreboding [fɔː'bəʊdɪŋ] **n** pressentiment *m*, prémonition *f* (*néfaste*). **to have a ~ that** avoir le pressentiment que, pressentir que; **to have ~s** avoir des pressentiments *or* des prémonitions; **with many ~s he agreed to do it** il a consenti à le faire en dépit de *or* malgré toutes ses appréhensions.

forecast ['fɔːkɑːst] **pret, ptp forecast** **1** **vt** (*also Met*) prévoir. **2** **n** prévision *f*; (*Betting*) pronostic *m*. **according to all the ~s** selon toutes les prévisions; (*Comm*) **sales ~** prévisions de vente; **the racing ~** les pronostics hippiques *or* des courses; **weather ~** bulletin *m* météorologique, météo* *f*; (*Met*) **the ~ is good** les prévisions sont bonnes, la météo* est bonne.

forecaster ['fɔːˌkɑːstəʳ] **n** (*Met*) journaliste *mf* météorologique; (*Econ, Pol*) prévisionniste *mf*; (*Sport*) pronostiqueur *m*, -euse *f*.

forecastle ['fəʊksl] **n** (*Naut*) gaillard *m* d'avant; (*Merchant Navy*) poste *m* d'équipage.

foreclose [fɔː'kləʊz] **1** **vt** (*Jur*) saisir. **to ~ (on) a mortgage** saisir un bien hypothéqué. **2** **vi** *[bank etc]* saisir le bien hypothéqué. **to ~ on** = **to ~**; *see* **1**.

foreclosure [fɔː'kləʊʒəʳ] **n** forclusion *f*.

forecourt ['fɔːkɔːt] **n** avant-cour *f*, cour *f* de devant; *[filling station]* devant *m*.

foredoomed [fɔː'duːmd] **adj** condamné d'avance, voué à l'échec.

forefathers ['fɔːˌfɑːðəz] **npl** aïeux *mpl* (*liter*), ancêtres *mpl*.

forefinger ['fɔːˌfɪŋgəʳ] **n** index *m*.

forefoot ['fɔːfʊt] **n** *[horse, cow etc]* pied antérieur *or* de devant; *[cat, dog]* patte antérieure *or* de devant.

forefront ['fɔːfrʌnt] **n**: **in the ~ of** au premier rang *or* premier plan de.

foregather [fɔː'gæðəʳ] **vi** se réunir, s'assembler.

forego [fɔː'gəʊ] **pret forewent, ptp foregone** **vt** renoncer à, se priver de, s'abstenir de.

foregoing ['fɔːgəʊɪŋ] **adj** précédent, déjà cité, susdit. **according to the ~** d'après ce qui précède.

foregone ['fɔːgɒn] **adj**: **it was a ~ conclusion** c'était à prévoir, c'était réglé *or* couru d'avance.

foreground ['fɔːgraʊnd] **n** (*Art, Phot*) premier plan. **in the ~** au premier plan.

forehand ['fɔːhænd] (*Tennis*) **1** **adj**: ~ **drive** coup *m* droit; ~ **volley** volée *f* de face. **2** **n** coup *m* droit de face.

forehead ['fɒrɪd] **n** front *m*.

foreign ['fɒrən] **1** **adj** **a** *language, visitor* étranger; *goods* de l'étranger; *visit* à l'étranger; *politics, trade* extérieur. **he comes from a ~ country** il vient de l'étranger; **our relations with ~ countries** nos rapports avec l'étranger *or* l'extérieur; ~ **affairs** affaires étrangères; **Minister of F~ Affairs, F~ Minister,** (*Brit*) **Secretary (of State) for F~ Affairs, F~ Secretary** ministre *m* des Affaires étrangères; **Ministry of F~ Affairs, F~ Ministry,** (*Brit*) **F~ Office** ministère *m* des Affaires étrangères; (*Brit*) **F~ and Commonwealth Office** ministère *m* des Affaires étrangères et du Commonwealth; ~ **agent** (*spy*) agent étranger; (*Comm*) représentant *m* à l'étranger; (*Press, Rad, TV*) ~ **correspondent** correspondant(e) *m(f)* *or* envoyé(e) *m(f)* permanent(e) à l'étranger; ~ **currency** devises étrangères; **the ~ exchange market** le marché des changes; **F~ Legion** Légion *f* (étrangère); ~ **national** ressortissant étranger, ressortissante étrangère; ~ **policy** politique étrangère *or* extérieure; ~ **produce** produit(s) *m(pl)* de l'étranger; ~ **relations** relations *fpl* avec l'étranger *or* l'extérieur; **the ~ service** le service diplomatique; ~ **travel** voyages *mpl* à l'étranger.

b (*not natural*) étranger (*to* à). **lying is quite ~ to him** *or* **to his nature** le mensonge lui est (complètement) étranger; (*Med*) ~ **body** corps étranger.

2 **comp** ▸**foreign-born** né à l'étranger ▸**foreign-owned** (*Econ, Comm*) sous contrôle étranger.

foreigner ['fɒrənəʳ] **n** étranger *m*, -ère *f*.

foreknowledge ['fɔː'nɒlɪdʒ] **n** fait *m* de savoir à l'avance, connaissance anticipée. **I had no ~ of his intentions** je ne savais pas à l'avance ce qu'il voulait faire; **it presupposes a certain ~ of ...** ceci présuppose une certaine connaissance anticipée de ... .

foreland ['fɔːlənd] **n** cap *m*, promontoire *m*, pointe *f* (de terre).

foreleg ['fɔːleg] **n** *[horse, cow etc]* jambe antérieure; *[dog, cat etc]* patte *f* de devant.

forelock ['fɔːlɒk] **n** mèche *f*, toupet *m*. **to touch one's ~ to sb** saluer qn en portant la main à son front; (*fig*) **to take time by the ~** saisir l'occasion par les cheveux*, sauter sur l'occasion*.

foreman ['fɔːmən] **n, pl foremen** **a** (*Ind*) contremaître *m*, chef *m* d'équipe. **b** *[jury]* président *m*.

foremast ['fɔːmɑːst] **n** (*Naut*) mât *m* de misaine.

foremen ['fɔːmən] **npl of foreman**.

foremost ['fɔːməʊst] **1** **adj** (*fig*) *writer, politician* principal, le plus en vue; (*lit*) le plus en avant. **2** **adv**: **first and ~** tout d'abord, en tout premier lieu.

forename ['fɔːneɪm] **n** prénom *m*.

forenoon ['fɔːnuːn] **n** matinée *f*.

forensic [fə'rensɪk] **adj** **a** *eloquence* du barreau. **b** *chemistry etc* légal. ~ **evidence** expertise médico-légale; ~ **expert** expert *m* en médecine légale; ~ **laboratory** laboratoire médico-légal; ~ **medicine** *or* **science** médecine légale; ~ **scientist** médecin *m* légiste.

foreplay ['fɔːpleɪ] **n** prélude *m* (*stimulation érotique*).

forequarters ['fɔːˌkwɔːtəz] **npl** quartiers *mpl* de devant.

forerunner ['fɔːˌrʌnəʳ] **n** **a** (*thing: sign, indication*) signe *m* avant-coureur, présage *m*; (*person*) précurseur *m*. **b** (*Ski*) ouvreur *m*.

foresail ['fɔːseɪl] **n** (*Naut*) (voile *f* de) misaine *f*.

foresee [fɔː'siː] **pret foresaw, ptp foreseen** **vt** prévoir, présager.

foreseeable [fɔː'siːəbl] **adj** prévisible. **in the ~ future** dans un avenir prévisible.

foreshadow [fɔː'ʃædəʊ] **vt** *[event etc]* présager, annoncer, laisser prévoir.

foreshore ['fɔːʃɔːʳ] **n** (*beach*) plage *f*; (*Geog, Jur*) laisse *f* de mer.

foreshorten [fɔː'ʃɔːtn] **vt** *[telephoto lens]* (*horizontally*) réduire; (*vertically*) écraser; *[artist]* faire un raccourci de. **to be ~ed** (*horizontally*) être réduit; (*vertically*) être écrasé (par la perspective).

foreshortening [fɔː'ʃɔːtnɪŋ] **n** (*see* **foreshorten**) réduction *f*; écrasement *m*; raccourci *m*.

foresight ['fɔːsaɪt] **n** prévoyance *f*. **lack of ~** imprévoyance *f*.

foreskin ['fɔːskɪn] **n** prépuce *m*.

forest ['fɒrɪst] **n** forêt *f*. (*US: fig*) **he can't see the ~ for the trees** les arbres lui cachent la forêt; ~ **ranger** garde *m* forestier.

forestall [fɔː'stɔːl] **vt** *competitor* devancer; *desire, eventuality, objection* anticiper, prévenir, devancer.

forester ['fɒrɪstəʳ] **n** (garde *m or* agent *m*) forestier *m*.

forestry ['fɒrɪstrɪ] **n** sylviculture *f*. (*Brit*) **the F~ Commission** ≃ les Eaux et Forêts *fpl*.

foresummit ['fɔːˌsʌmɪt] **n** antécime *f*.

foretaste ['fɔːteɪst] **n** avant-goût *m*.

foretell [fɔː'tel] **pret, ptp foretold** **vt** prédire.

forethought ['fɔːθɔːt] **n** prévoyance *f*.

forever [fər'evəʳ] **adv** **a** (*incessantly*) toujours, sans cesse, continuellement, à tout bout de champ. **she's ~ complaining** elle se plaint toujours (*etc*), elle est toujours à se plaindre; **they are ~ quarrelling** ils ne font que se disputer, ils ne cessent de se disputer.

b (*for always*) (pour) toujours. **I'll love you ~** je t'aimerai (pour) toujours; **he loved her ~ (after)** il l'a aimée toute sa vie *or* toujours; **he left ~** il est parti pour toujours *or* sans retour; **he was trying ~ after to do the same** et après cela, il a toujours essayé de faire la même chose; **it won't last ~** cela ne durera pas toujours.

c (**: a very long time*) une éternité, très longtemps; **it'll take ~*** ça va durer *or* prendre des heures, ça va durer une éternité; **it lasted ~*** ça n'en finissait pas; **we had to wait ~*** nous avons dû attendre une éternité *or* jusqu'à la saint-glinglin*.

forewarn [fɔː'wɔːn] **vt** prévenir, avertir. (*Prov*) **~ed is forearmed** un homme averti en vaut deux (*Prov*).

foreword ['fɔːwɜːd] **n** avant-propos *m inv*, avis *m* au lecteur, avertissement *m* (au lecteur).

forfeit ['fɔːfɪt] **1** **vt** (*Jur*) *property* perdre (par confiscation); *one's rights* perdre; (*fig*) *one's life, health* payer de; *sb's respect* perdre. **2** **n** **a** (*gen*) prix *m*, peine *f*. **b** (*for non-performance of contract*) dédit *m*. (*game*) **~s** gages *mpl* (*jeu de société*); (*in game*) **to pay a ~** avoir un gage. **3** **adj** (*liter*) (*liable to be taken*) susceptible d'être confisqué; (*actually taken*) confisqué. **his life was ~** (*he died*) il le paya de sa vie; (*he might die*) il pourrait le payer de sa vie.

forfeiture ['fɔːfɪtʃəʳ] **n** *[property]* perte *f* (par confiscation) (*of* de); *[right etc]* renoncement *m* (*of* à).

forgather [fɔː'gæðəʳ] **vi** = **foregather**.

forgave [fə'geɪv] **pret of forgive**.

forge [fɔːdʒ] **1** **vt** **a** (*counterfeit*) *signature, banknote* contrefaire; *document* faire un faux de; (*alter*) maquiller, falsifier; (*Art*) *picture* faire un faux de, contrefaire; *evidence* fabriquer; (*invent*) *story* inventer, fabriquer. **a ~d passport/ticket** *etc* un faux passeport/billet *etc*; **it's ~d** c'est un faux. **b** *metal, friendship, plan* forger. **2** **vi**: **to ~ ahead** prendre de l'avance, pousser de l'avant; (*Racing*) foncer. **3** **n** forge *f*.

forger ['fɔːdʒəʳ] n faussaire *mf*; (*Jur*) contrefacteur *m*.

forgery ['fɔːdʒərɪ] n a (*NonC*) *[banknote, signature]* contrefaçon *f*; *[document, will]* falsification *f*; *[story]* invention *f*; (*Jur*) contrefaçon (frauduleuse). **to prosecute sb for ~** poursuivre qn pour faux (et usage de faux). b (*thing forged*) faux *m*.

forget [fə'get] pret **forgot**, ptp **forgotten** 1 vt a *name, fact, experience* oublier. **I shall never ~ what he said** je n'oublierai jamais ce qu'il a dit; **on that never-to-be-forgotten day** ce jour (à jamais) inoubliable; **I've forgotten all my Spanish** j'ai oublié tout l'espagnol que je savais *or* tout mon espagnol; **I ~ who said ...** je ne sais plus qui a dit ...; **she never ~s a face** elle a la mémoire des visages; **he quite forgot himself** *or* **his manners and behaved abominably** il s'est tout à fait oublié *or* il a oublié toutes ses bonnes manières et s'est comporté abominablement; **he works so hard for others that he ~s himself** il travaille tant pour autrui qu'il en oublie son propre intérêt; **don't ~ the guide!** n'oubliez pas le guide!; **not ~ting ...** sans oublier ...; **we quite forgot the time** nous avons complètement oublié l'heure; **and don't you ~ it!*** et tâche de ne pas l'oublier!, et tâche de te le rappeler!; **she'll never let him ~ it** elle n'est pas près de le lui laisser oublier; **let's ~ it!** passons *or* on passe l'éponge!; (*let's drop the subject*) ça n'a aucune importance; **~ it!** (*to sb thanking*) ce n'est rien!; (*to sb pestering*) laissez tomber!; (*to sb hopeful*) n'y comptez pas!; **to ~ to do** oublier *or* omettre de faire; **I've forgotten how to do it** je ne sais plus comment on fait; **it's easy to ~ how to do it** c'est facile d'oublier comment on fait; **I forgot I'd seen her** j'ai oublié que je l'avais vue.

b (*leave behind*) oublier, laisser. **she forgot her umbrella in the train** elle a oublié *or* laissé son parapluie dans le train.

2 vi oublier. **I quite forgot** j'ai complètement oublié, ça m'est complètement sorti de l'esprit*.

3 comp ►**forget-me-not** (*Bot*) myosotis *msg* ►**forget-me-not blue** (bleu *m*) myosotis *m inv*.

►**forget about** vt fus oublier. **I forgot all about it** je l'ai complètement oublié; **I've forgotten all about it (already)** je n'y pense (déjà) plus; **forget about it!*** n'y pensez plus!; **he seemed willing to forget about the whole business** il semblait prêt à passer l'éponge sur l'affaire.

forgetful [fə'getfʊl] adj (*absent-minded*) distrait; (*careless*) négligent, étourdi. **he is very ~** il a très mauvaise mémoire, il oublie tout; **how ~ of me!** que je suis étourdi!; **~ of the danger** oublieux du danger.

forgetfulness [fə'getfʊlnɪs] n (*absent-mindedness*) manque *m* de mémoire; (*carelessness*) négligence *f*, étourderie *f*. **in a moment of ~** dans un moment d'oubli *or* d'étourderie.

forgettable [fə'getəbəl] adj peu mémorable.

forgivable [fə'gɪvəbl] adj pardonnable.

forgive [fə'gɪv] pret **forgave**, ptp **forgiven** [fə'gɪvn] vt a *person, sin, mistake* pardonner. **to ~ sb (for) sth** pardonner qch à qn; **to ~ sb for doing** pardonner à qn de faire *or* d'avoir fait; **you must ~ him his rudeness** pardonnez-lui son impolitesse; **one can be ~n for thinking ...** on est excusable *or* pardonnable de penser ...; **~ me, but ...** pardonnez-moi *or* excusez-moi, mais ...; **we must ~ and forget** nous devons pardonner et oublier. b **to ~ (sb) a debt** faire grâce (à qn) d'une dette.

forgiveness [fə'gɪvnɪs] n (*NonC*) (*pardon*) pardon *m*; (*compassion*) indulgence *f*, clémence *f*, miséricorde *f*.

forgiving [fə'gɪvɪŋ] adj indulgent, clément.

forgo [fɔː'gəʊ] pret **forwent**, ptp **forgone** vt = **forego**.

forgot [fə'gɒt] pret of **forget**.

forgotten [fə'gɒtn] ptp of **forget**.

fork [fɔːk] 1 n a (*at table*) fourchette *f*; (*Agr*) fourche *f*. b *[branches]* fourche *f*; *[roads, railways]* embranchement *m*. (*in road*) **take the left ~** prenez à gauche à l'embranchement. 2 comp ►**forkful** ≃ bouchée *f* ►**fork-lift truck** chariot *m* de levage (à fourche), chariot élévateur ►**fork luncheon** (*Brit*) buffet *m* (*repas*). 3 vt a (*also* **~ over**) *hay, ground* fourcher. b **he ~ed the food into his mouth** il enfournait* la nourriture (à coups de fourchette). 4 vi *[roads]* bifurquer. **we ~ed right on leaving the village** nous avons pris *or* bifurqué à droite à la sortie du village; **~ left for Oxford** prenez *or* bifurquez à gauche pour Oxford.

►**fork out*** 1 vi casquer‡. 2 vt sep *money* allonger‡, abouler‡.

►**fork over** vt sep = **fork 3a**.

►**fork up** vt sep a *soil* fourcher. b (*) = **fork out 2**.

forked [fɔːkt] adj fourchu. **~ lightning** éclair *m* en zigzags; (*US fig: lie*) **to speak with a ~ tongue** mentir.

forlorn [fə'lɔːn] adj (*miserable*) *person, sb's appearance* mélancolique; (*deserted*) *person* abandonné, délaissé; (*despairing*) *attempt* désespéré. **he looked very ~** il avait un (petit) air triste; *[house etc]* **~ look, ~ appearance** air abandonné *or* négligé; **it is a ~ hope** c'est un mince espoir.

forlornly [fə'lɔːnlɪ] adv (*stand, sit*) tristement; (*say, look*) d'un (petit) air triste.

form [fɔːm] 1 n a (*type, particular kind*) forme *f*, genre *m*, espèce *f*. **a new ~ of government** une nouvelle forme *or* un nouveau système de gouvernement; **a different ~ of life** une autre forme *or* un autre genre de vie; **the various ~s of energy** les différentes formes *or* espèces d'énergie; **you could say it was a ~ of apology** on pourrait appeler cela une sorte d'excuse.

b (*style, condition*) forme *f*. **in the ~ of** sous forme de; **medicine in the ~ of tablets** *or* **in tablet ~** médicament sous forme de comprimés; **the first prize will take the ~ of a trip to Rome** le premier prix sera un voyage à Rome; **what ~ should my application take?** comment dois-je présenter *or* formuler ma demande?; **the same thing in a new ~** la même chose sous une forme nouvelle *or* un aspect nouveau; **their discontent took various ~s** leur mécontentement s'est manifesté de différentes façons; (*Gram*) **the plural ~** la forme du pluriel.

c (*NonC: Art, Literat, Mus etc*) forme *f*. **~ and content** la forme et le fond.

d (*NonC: shape*) forme *f*. **to take ~** prendre forme; **his thoughts lack ~** il n'y a aucun ordre dans ses pensées.

e (*figure*) forme *f*. **the human ~** la forme humaine; **I saw a ~ in the fog** j'ai vu une forme *or* une silhouette dans le brouillard.

f (*Philos*) (*structure, organization*) forme *f*; (*essence*) essence *f*; (*Ling*) forme.

g (*NonC: etiquette*) forme *f*, formalité *f*. **for ~'s sake, as a matter of ~** pour la forme; **it's good/bad ~ to do that** cela se fait/ne se fait pas.

h (*formula, established practice*) forme *f*, formule *f*. **he pays attention to the ~s** il respecte les formes; **choose another ~ of words** choisissez une autre expression *or* tournure; **the correct ~ of address for a bishop** le titre à utiliser en s'adressant *or* la manière correcte de s'adresser à un évêque; **~s of politeness** formules de politesse; **~ of worship** liturgie *f*, rites *mpl*; **what's the ~?*** quelle est la marche à suivre?

i (*document*) (*gen: for applications etc*) formulaire *m*; (*for telegram, giro transfer etc*) formule *f*; (*for tax returns etc*) feuille *f*; (*card*) fiche *f*. **telegraph ~** formule de télégramme; **printed ~** imprimé *m*; **to fill up** *or* **in** *or* (*US*) **out a ~** remplir un formulaire; *see* **application, tax** *etc*.

j (*NonC: fitness*) forme *f*, condition *f*. **on ~** en forme; **he is not on ~, he is off ~, he is out of ~** il n'est pas en forme; **in fine ~** en pleine forme, en excellente condition; **he was in great ~** *or* **on top ~** il était en pleine forme; **in good ~** en bonne forme.

k **to study (the) ~** (*Brit Racing*) ≃ préparer son tiercé; (*fig*) établir un pronostic.

l (*Brit: bench*) banc *m*.

m (*Brit Scol: class*) classe *f*. **he's in the sixth ~** ≃ il est en première.

n (*NonC: Brit Prison etc sl: criminal record*) **he's got ~** il a fait de la taule‡.

2 comp ►**form feeder** (*Comput*) dispositif *m* de changement de page ►**form leader** (*Brit Scol*) ≃ chef *m* de classe ►**form master** *or* **mistress** ≃ professeur *m* principal ►**form room** salle *f* de classe (*affectée à une classe particulière*) ►**form tutor** = **form master** *or* **mistress**.

3 vt a (*shape*) former, construire. (*Gram*) **~ the plural** formez le pluriel; **he ~s his sentences well** il construit bien ses phrases; **he ~s his style on that of Dickens** il forme *or* modèle son style sur celui de Dickens; **he ~ed it out of a piece of wood** il l'a façonné *or* fabriqué *or* sculpté dans un morceau de bois; **he ~ed the clay into a ball** il a roulé *or* pétri l'argile en boule.

b (*train, mould*) *child* former, éduquer; *sb's character* former, façonner.

c (*develop*) *habit* contracter; *plan* arrêter. **to ~ an opinion** se faire *or* se former une opinion; **to ~ an impression** avoir une impression; **you mustn't ~ the idea that ...** il ne faut pas que vous ayez l'idée que ... .

d (*organize*) *government* former; *classes, courses* organiser, instituer; (*Comm*) *company* former, fonder, créer. **to ~ a committee** former un comité.

e (*constitute*) composer, former. **to ~ part of** faire partie de; **the ministers who ~ the government** les ministres qui composent *or* constituent le gouvernement; **those who ~ the group** les gens qui font partie du groupe; **to ~ a** *or* **the basis for** former *or* constituer la base de, servir de base à.

f (*take the shape or order of*) former, faire, dessiner. (*Mil*) **to ~ fours** se mettre par quatre; **to ~ a line** se mettre en ligne, s'aligner; **~ a circle please** mettez-vous en cercle s'il vous plaît; **to ~ a queue** se mettre en file, former la queue; **the road ~s a series of curves** la route fait *or* dessine une série de courbes.

4 vi a (*take shape*) prendre forme, se former. **an idea ~ed in his mind** une idée a pris forme dans son esprit.

b (*also* **~ up**) se former. **to ~ (up) into a square** se former en carré.

►**form up** vi a se mettre *or* se ranger en ligne, s'aligner. **form up behind your teacher** mettez-vous *or* rangez-vous en ligne derrière votre professeur. b *see* **form 4b**.

formal ['fɔːməl] adj a (*austere; not familiar or relaxed*) *person* formaliste, compassé (*pej*), guindé (*pej*); *manner, style* soigné, ampoulé (*pej*). **he is very ~** il est très à cheval sur les convenances; **don't be so ~** ne faites pas tant de cérémonies; **in ~ language** dans la (*or* une) langue soignée.

b (*in design*) *gardens* à la française; *square* à l'agencement très régulier.

c (*ceremonious*) *bow, greeting, welcome* cérémonieux; *function* officiel, protocolaire. **a ~ dance** un grand bal; **a ~ dinner** un grand dîner, un dîner officiel; **~ dress** tenue *f* de cérémonie; (*evening dress*) tenue de soirée.

d (*in the accepted form*) *announcement* officiel; *acceptance* dans les règles, en bonne et due forme; (*specific*) formel, explicite, clair. **~ agreement** accord *m* en bonne et due forme (*see also* **e**); **~ denial** démenti formel; **~ surrender** reddition *f* dans les règles; **~ instructions** instructions formelles *or* explicites; **he had little ~ education** il a reçu une éducation scolaire très réduite; **she has no ~ training in teaching** elle n'a reçu aucune véritable formation pédagogique.

e (*superficial, in form only*) de forme. **a ~ agreement** un accord de forme; **a certain ~ resemblance** une certaine ressemblance dans la forme; **a lot of ~ handshaking** beaucoup de poignées de mains échangées pour la forme; **he is the ~ head of state** c'est lui qui est théoriquement chef d'État *or* qui est le chef d'État officiel.

f (*Philos etc*) formel. **~ grammar** grammaire formelle.

formaldehyde [fɔː'mældɪhaɪd] **n** formaldéhyde *m*.

formalin(e) ['fɔːməlɪn] **n** formol *m*.

formalism ['fɔːməlɪzəm] **n** formalisme *m*.

formalist ['fɔːməlɪst] **adj, n** formaliste *(mf)*.

formalistic [ˌfɔːmə'lɪstɪk] **adj** formaliste.

formality [fɔː'mælɪtɪ] **n** **a** (*NonC*) (*convention*) formalité *f*; (*stiffness*) raideur *f*, froideur *f*; (*ceremoniousness*) cérémonie *f* (*NonC*). **b** formalité *f*. **it's a mere ~** ce n'est qu'une simple formalité; **the formalities** les formalités; **let's do without the formalities!** trêve de formalités!, dispensons-nous des formalités!

formalize ['fɔːməlaɪz] **vt** formaliser.

formally ['fɔːməlɪ] **adv** **a** (*ceremoniously*) cérémonieusement. **to be ~ dressed** être en tenue de cérémonie (*or* de soirée). **b** (*officially*) officiellement, en bonne et due forme, dans les règles. **to be ~ invited** recevoir une invitation officielle.

format ['fɔːmæt] **1 n** (*size*) format *m*; (*layout*) présentation *f*. **2 vt** **a** (*Comput*) formater, mettre en forme. **b** (*gen*) concevoir le format (*or* la présentation) de.

formation [fɔː'meɪʃən] **1 n** **a** (*NonC*) *[child, character]* formation *f*; *[plan]* élaboration *f*, mise *f* en place; *[government]* formation; *[classes, courses]* création *f*, organisation *f*, mise en place; *[club]* création; *[committee]* formation, création, mise en place. **b** (*NonC: Mil etc*) formation *f*, disposition *f*. **battle ~** formation de combat; **in close ~** en ordre serré. **c** (*Geol*) formation *f*. **2 comp ▸formation dance, formation dancing** danse *f* de groupe **▸formation flying** (*Aviat*) vol *m* en formation.

formative ['fɔːmətɪv] **1 adj** formateur (*f* -trice). **~ years** années formatrices. **2 n** (*Gram*) formant *m*, élément formateur.

formatting ['fɔːmætɪŋ] **n** (*Comput*) formatage *m*.

-formed ['fɔːmd] **adj ending in comps: fully-formed** (*baby, animal*) complètement formé *or* développé; **half-formed** à moitié formé *or* développé; *see* **well 6**.

former¹ ['fɔːməʳ] **n** (*Tech*) gabarit *m*.

former² ['fɔːməʳ] **1 adj** **a** (*earlier, previous*) ancien (*before n*), précédent. **the ~ mayor** l'ancien maire, le maire précédent; **he is a ~ mayor of Brighton** c'est un ancien maire de Brighton; **my ~ husband** mon ex-mari; **in a ~ life** au cours d'une vie antérieure; **in ~ times, in ~ days** autrefois, dans le passé; **he was very unlike his ~ self** il ne se ressemblait plus du tout; (*Scol*) **~ pupil** ancien(ne) élève *m(f)*.

b (*as opposed to latter*) premier. **the ~ method seems better** la première méthode semble préférable; **your ~ suggestion** votre première suggestion.

2 pron celui-là, celle-là. **the ~ ... the latter** celui-là ... celui-ci; **of the two ideas I prefer the ~** des deux idées je préfère celle-là *or* la première; **the ~ seems more likely** la première hypothèse (*or* explication *etc*) est plus vraisemblable.

-former ['fɔːməʳ] **n ending in comps** (*Scol*) élève *mf* de ... . **fourth-former** ≃ élève de troisième.

formerly ['fɔːməlɪ] **adv** autrefois, anciennement, jadis.

formic ['fɔːmɪk] **adj** formique.

Formica [fɔː'maɪkə] **n** ® Formica *m* ®, plastique laminé.

formidable ['fɔːmɪdəbl] **adj** *person, enemy, opposition* redoutable, effrayant, terrible; *obstacles, debts* terrible, énorme.

formless ['fɔːmlɪs] **adj** informe.

Formosa [fɔː'məʊsə] **n** Formose *f*.

Formosan [fɔː'məʊsən] **adj** formosan.

formula ['fɔːmjʊlə] **n** **a** **pl ~s** *or* **formulae** ['fɔːmjʊliː] (*gen, also Chem, Math etc*) formule *f*. (*fig*) **a ~ for averting** *or* **aimed at averting the strike** une formule *or* une solution visant à éviter la grève; **they are seeking a ~ to allow ...** ils cherchent une nouvelle formule qui permette ...; (*Aut*) **F~ One** la formule un; **a ~-one car** une voiture de formule un. **b** (*US: baby's feed*) lait *m* en poudre.

formulaic [ˌfɔːmjʊ'leɪɪk] **adj: ~ phrase** *or* **expression** formule *f*.

formulate ['fɔːmjʊleɪt] **vt** formuler.

formulation [ˌfɔːmjʊ'leɪʃən] **n** formulation *f*, expression *f*.

fornicate ['fɔːnɪkeɪt] **vi** forniquer.

fornication [ˌfɔːnɪ'keɪʃən] **n** fornication *f*.

forsake [fə'seɪk] **pret forsook, ptp forsaken vt** *person* abandonner, délaisser; *place* quitter; *habit* renoncer à. **my willpower ~s me on these occasions** la volonté me fait défaut dans ces cas-là.

forsaken [fə'seɪkən] **1 pret of forsake**; *see* **god**. **2 adj: an old ~ farmhouse** une vieille ferme abandonnée.

forsook [fə'sʊk] **pret of forsake**.

forsooth [fə'suːθ] **adv** (†† *or hum*) en vérité, à vrai dire. (*excl*) **~!** par exemple!

forswear [fɔː'swɛəʳ] **pret forswore, ptp forsworn vt** (*frm*) (*renounce*) renoncer à, abjurer; (*deny*) désavouer. (*perjure*) **to ~ o.s.** se parjurer.

forsythia [fɔː'saɪθɪə] **n** forsythia *m*.

fort [fɔːt] **n** (*Mil*) fort *m*; (*small*) fortin *m*; *see* **hold**.

forte¹ ['fɔːtɪ], (*US*) [fɔːt] **n** fort *m*. **generosity is not his ~** la générosité n'est pas son fort.

forte² ['fɔːtɪ] **adj, adv** (*Mus*) forte.

forth [fɔːθ] (*phr vb elem*) **adv** **a** en avant. **to set ~** se mettre en route; (*frm*) **to stretch ~ one's hand** tendre la main; **to go back and ~ between** aller et venir entre, faire la navette entre; *see* **bring forth, sally forth** *etc*. **b and so ~** et ainsi de suite; (*frm*) **from this day ~** dorénavant, désormais.

forthcoming [fɔːθ'kʌmɪŋ] **adj** **a** *book* qui va paraître, à paraître; *film* qui va sortir; *play* qui va débuter; *event* à venir, prochain (*before n*). **his ~ film** son prochain film; **in a ~ film he studies ...** dans un film qui va bientôt sortir il examine ...; **in the ~ celebrations** dans les festivités qui vont bientôt avoir lieu, au cours des prochaines festivités; (*Theat etc*) **"~ attractions"** "prochains spectacles", "prochainement".

b (*available etc*) **if help is ~** si on nous (*or* les *etc*) aide; **if funds are ~** si on nous (*or* leur *etc*) donne de l'argent, si on met de l'argent à notre (*or* leur *etc*) disposition; **no answer was ~** il n'y a pas eu de réponse; **this was not ~** ceci ne nous (*or* leur *etc*) a pas été accordé.

c (*friendly, sociable*) *person* ouvert, communicatif; *manners* accueillant, cordial. **I asked him what his plans were but he wasn't ~ about them** je lui ai demandé quels étaient ses projets mais il s'est montré peu disposé à en parler.

forthright ['fɔːθraɪt] **adj** *answer, remark* franc (*f* franche), direct; *person* direct, carré; *look* franc. **he is very ~** il ne mâche pas ses mots.

forthwith ['fɔːθ'wɪθ] **adv** sur-le-champ, aussitôt, tout de suite.

fortieth ['fɔːtɪɪθ] **1 adj** quarantième. **2 n** quarantième *mf*; (*fraction*) quarantième *m*.

fortification [ˌfɔːtɪfɪ'keɪʃən] **n** fortification *f*.

fortify ['fɔːtɪfaɪ] **vt** **a** *place* fortifier, armer (*against* contre); *person* réconforter. **fortified place** place forte; **have a drink to ~ you*** prenez un verre pour vous remonter. **b** *wine* accroître la teneur en alcool de; *food* renforcer en vitamines. **fortified wine** ≃ vin *m* de liqueur.

fortitude ['fɔːtɪtjuːd] **n** courage *m*, fermeté *f* d'âme, force *f* d'âme.

fortnight ['fɔːtnaɪt] **n** (*esp Brit*) quinzaine *f*, quinze jours *mpl*. **a ~'s holiday** quinze jours de vacances; **a ~ tomorrow** demain en quinze; **adjourned for a ~** remis à quinzaine; **for a ~** pour une quinzaine, pour quinze jours; **in a ~, in a ~'s time** dans quinze jours; **a ~ ago** il y a quinze jours.

fortnightly ['fɔːtnaɪtlɪ] (*esp Brit*) **1 adj** bimensuel. **2 adv** tous les quinze jours.

FORTRAN, Fortran ['fɔːtræn] **n** fortran *m*.

fortress ['fɔːtrɪs] **n** (*prison*) forteresse *f*; (*mediaeval castle*) château fort; *see* **flying**.

fortuitous [fɔː'tjuːɪtəs] **adj** fortuit, imprévu, accidentel.

fortuitously [fɔː'tjuːɪtəslɪ] **adv** fortuitement, par hasard.

fortunate ['fɔːtʃənɪt] **adj** *person* heureux, chanceux; *circumstances, meeting, event* heureux, favorable, propice. **to be ~** avoir de la chance; **we were ~ enough to meet him** nous avons eu la chance *or* le bonheur de le rencontrer; **how ~!** quelle chance!

fortunately ['fɔːtʃənɪtlɪ] **adv** heureusement, par bonheur.

fortune ['fɔːtʃən] **1 n** **a** (*chance*) fortune *f*, chance *f*, hasard *m*. **the ~s of war** la fortune des armes; **by good ~** par chance, par bonheur; **I had the good ~ to meet him** j'ai eu la chance *or* le bonheur de le rencontrer; **to try one's ~** tenter sa chance; **~ favoured him** la chance *or* la fortune lui a souri; **to tell sb's ~** dire la bonne aventure à qn; **to tell ~s** dire la bonne aventure; **whatever my ~ may be** quel que soit le sort qui m'est réservé; *see* **seek**.

b (*riches*) fortune *f*. **to make a ~** faire fortune; **he made a ~ on it** il a gagné une fortune avec ça; **to come into a ~** hériter d'une fortune, faire un gros héritage; **a man of ~** un homme d'une fortune *or* d'une richesse considérable; **to marry a ~** épouser une grosse fortune *or* un sac‡; **to spend/cost/lose** *etc* **a (small) ~** dépenser/coûter/perdre *etc* une (petite) fortune *or* un argent fou*.

2 comp ▸fortune cookie (*US*) beignet *m* chinois (*renfermant un horoscope ou une devise*) **▸fortune hunter** (*man*) coureur *m* de dot, (*woman*) femme intéressée **▸fortuneteller** diseur *m*, -euse *f* de bonne aventure; (*with cards*) tireuse *f* de cartes **▸fortunetelling** pratique *f* de dire la bonne aventure; (*with cards*) cartomancie *f*.

forty ['fɔːtɪ] **1 adj** quarante *inv*. **about ~ books** une quarantaine de livres; **to have ~ winks*** faire un petit somme, piquer un roupillon*. **2 n** quarante *m inv*. **about ~** une quarantaine; (*US: states*) **the lower ~-eight** les quarante-huit États américains (à l'exclusion de l'Alaska et de Hawaï); *for other phrases see* **sixty**. 3 **pron** quarante *mfpl*. **there are** ~ il y en a quarante. 4 **comp** ▸**forty-niner** (*US*) prospecteur *m* d'or (*de la ruée vers l'or de 1849*).

forum ['fɔːrəm] **n, pl** ~**s** *or* **fora** ['fɔːrə] (*Hist*) forum *m*; (*fig*) tribune *f* (*sur un sujet d'actualité*).

forward ['fɔːwəd] (*phr vb elem*) 1 **adv** (*also* ~**s**) en avant. **to rush** ~ se précipiter *or* s'élancer (en avant); **to go** ~ avancer; **to go straight** ~ aller droit devant soi; ~!, (*Mil*) ~ **march!** en avant, marche!; **from this time** ~ à partir de maintenant, désormais, à l'avenir, dorénavant (*frm*); (*lit, fig*) **to push o.s.** ~ se mettre en avant; (*fig*) **to come** ~ s'offrir, se présenter, se proposer; **he went backward(s) and** ~**(s) between the station and the house** il allait et venait entre *or* il faisait la navette entre la gare et la maison; *see* **bring forward, look forward** *etc*.

2 **adj** a (*in front, ahead*) *movement* en avant, vers l'avant. **the** ~ **ranks of the army** les premiers rangs de l'armée; **I am** ~ **with my work** je suis en avance dans mon travail; **this seat is too far** ~ cette banquette est trop en avant; ~ **gears** vitesses *fpl* avant; ~ **line** (*Mil*) première ligne; (*Sport*) ligne des avants; (*Rugby*) ~ **pass** (passe *f*) en-avant *m inv*; (*Admin*) ~ **planning** planning *m* à long terme; (*Mil*) ~ **post** avant-poste *m*, poste avancé.

b (*well-advanced*) *season, plant* précoce; *child* précoce, en avance.

c (*pert*) effronté, insolent.

d (*Comm etc*) *prices* à terme. ~ **buying** vente *f* à terme; ~ **delivery** livraison *f* à terme.

3 **n** (*Sport*) avant *m*.

4 **vt** a (*advance*) *career etc* favoriser, avancer.

b (*dispatch*) *goods* expédier, envoyer; (*send on*) *letter, parcel* faire suivre. **please** ~ faire suivre S.V.P., prière de faire suivre.

5 **comp** ▸**forwarding address** (*gen*) adresse *f* (pour faire suivre le courrier); (*Comm*) adresse pour l'expédition; **he left no forwarding address** il est parti sans laisser d'adresse ▸**forwarding agent** (*Comm*) transitaire *m* ▸**forward-looking** *person* ouvert sur *or* tourné vers les possibilités de l'avenir; *plan* tourné vers l'avenir *or* le progrès.

forwardness ['fɔːwədnɪs] **n** *[seasons, children etc]* précocité *f*; (*pertness*) effronterie *f*, audace *f*.

forwards ['fɔːwədz] **adv** = **forward 1**.

Fosbury flop ['fɒzbərɪˌflɒp] **n** (*Sport*) rouleau dorsal.

fossil ['fɒsl] 1 **n** fossile *m*. (*fig*) **he's an old** ~**!*** c'est un vieux fossile!* *or* une vieille croûte!* 2 **adj** *insect* fossilisé. ~ **energy/fuel** énergie *f*/combustible *m* fossile.

fossilized ['fɒsɪlaɪzd] **adj** fossilisé; (*fig*) *person, customs* fossilisé, figé; (*Ling*) *form, expression* figé.

foster ['fɒstəʳ] 1 **vt** a (*Jur: care for*) *child* élever (*sans obligation d'adoption*). **the authorities** ~**ed the child with Mr and Mrs X** les autorités ont placé l'enfant chez M et Mme X. b (*encourage*) *friendship, development* favoriser, encourager, stimuler. c (*entertain*) *idea, thought* entretenir, nourrir. 2 **comp** *child* (*gen, Admin, Soc: officially arranged*) adoptif; (*where wet-nursed*) nourricier, de lait; *father, parents, family* adoptif; nourricier; *brother, sister* adoptif; de lait ▸**foster home** famille adoptive; famille nourricière ▸**foster mother** mère adoptive; (*wet-nurse*) nourrice *f*.

fought [fɔːt] **pret, ptp of fight**.

foul [faʊl] 1 **adj** *food, meal, taste* infect; *place* immonde, crasseux; *smell* infect, nauséabond, fétide; *breath* fétide; *water* croupi; *air* vicié, pollué; *calumny, behaviour* vil (*f* vile), infâme; *language* ordurier, grossier; *person* infect, ignoble; (*unfair*) déloyal. **to taste** ~ avoir un goût infect; **to smell** ~ puer; **a** ~ **blow** un coup en traître; (*liter*) ~ **deed** scélératesse *f* (*liter*), acte crapuleux; ~ **play** (*Sport*) jeu irrégulier *or* déloyal; (*Cards*) tricherie *f*; (*fig*) **he suspected** ~ **play** il soupçonnait qu'il y avait quelque chose de louche; (*fig*) **the explosion was put down to** ~ **play** l'explosion a été attribuée à la malveillance *or* à un acte criminel *or* à un geste criminel; **the police found a body but do not suspect** ~ **play** la police a découvert un cadavre mais écarte l'hypothèse d'un meurtre; ~ **weather** (*Naut etc*) gros temps, (*gen*) sale temps, temps de chien; **the weather was** ~ le temps était infect; **I've had a** ~ **day** j'ai eu une sale journée; **to fall** ~ **of sb** se mettre qn à dos, s'attirer le mécontentement de qn; **to fall** ~ **of the law/the authorities** *etc* avoir des démêlées avec la justice/les autorités *etc*; **to fall** ~ **of a ship** entrer en collision avec un bateau; *see* **fair**[1].

2 **n** (*Sport*) coup défendu *or* interdit *or* irrégulier; (*Boxing*) coup bas; (*Ftbl*) faute *f*; (*Basketball*) **technical/personal** ~ faute *f* technique/personnelle; *see* **fair**[1].

3 **comp** ▸**foulmouthed** au langage ordurier *or* grossier, qui parle comme un charretier ▸**foul-smelling** puant, nauséabond, fétide ▸**foul-tempered: to be foul-tempered** (*habitually*) avoir un caractère de chien; (*on one occasion*) être d'une humeur massacrante ▸**foul-up*** confusion *f*.

4 **vt** (*pollute*) *air* polluer, infecter; (*clog*) *pipe, chimney, gun barrel* encrasser, obstruer; (*collide with*) *ship* entrer en collision avec; (*entangle*) *fishing line* embrouiller, emmêler, entortiller; *propeller* s'emmêler dans; (*tarnish*) *reputation* salir. *[dog]* **to** ~ **the pavement** souiller le trottoir.

5 **vi** *[rope, line]* s'emmêler, s'entortiller, s'embrouiller.

▸**foul out** **vi** (*Basketball*) être exclu (*pour 5 fautes personnelles*).

▸**foul up** 1 **vt sep** *river* polluer; (‡) *relationship* ficher en l'air*. **that has fouled things up‡** ça a tout mis *or* flanqué par terre*, ça a tout fichu en l'air*. 2 **foul-up n** *see* **foul 3**.

found[1] [faʊnd] **pret, ptp of find**.

found[2] [faʊnd] **vt** *town, school etc* fonder, créer; *hospital* fonder; *business enterprise* fonder, constituer, établir; *colony* établir, fonder; (*fig*) *belief, opinion* fonder, baser, appuyer (*on* sur). **my suspicions were** ~**ed on the fact that ...** mes soupçons étaient basés sur le fait que ...; **our society is** ~**ed on this** notre société est fondée là-dessus; **the novel is** ~**ed on fact** le roman est basé sur des faits réels.

found[3] [faʊnd] **vt** (*Metal*) fondre.

foundation [faʊn'deɪʃən] 1 **n** a (*NonC: act of founding*) *[town, school]* fondation *f*, création *f*, établissement *m*; *[hospital, business enterprise]* fondation, création.

b (*establishment*) fondation *f*, institution dotée. **Carnegie F**~ fondation Carnegie.

c (*Constr*) ~**s** fondations *fpl*; **to lay the** ~**s** (*lit*) poser les fondations (*of* de); (*fig*) *see* **1d**.

d (*fig: basis*) *[career, social structure]* assises *fpl*, base *f*; *[idea, religious belief, theory]* base, fondement *m*. **his work laid the** ~**(s) of our legal system** son travail a posé les bases de notre système judiciaire; **the rumour is entirely without** ~ la rumeur est dénuée de tout fondement.

e (*also* ~ **cream**) fond *m* de teint.

2 **comp** ▸**foundation course** (*Brit Univ*) cours *m* d'initiation *or* d'introduction ▸**foundation garment** gaine *f*, combiné *m* ▸**foundation stone** (*Brit*) pierre commémorative; (*lit, fig*) **to lay the foundation stone** poser la première pierre.

founder[1] ['faʊndəʳ] **n** fondateur *m*, -trice *f*. (*Brit*) ~ **member** membre *m* fondateur.

founder[2] ['faʊndəʳ] **vi** *[ship]* sombrer, chavirer, couler; *[horse]* (*in mud etc*) s'embourber, s'empêtrer; (*from fatigue*) (se mettre à) boiter; *[plans etc]* s'effondrer, s'écrouler; *[hopes]* s'en aller en fumée.

founding ['faʊndɪŋ] 1 **n** = **foundation 1a**. 2 **adj** (*US*) ~ **fathers** pères fondateurs (*qui élaborèrent la Constitution Fédérale des États-Unis*).

foundling ['faʊndlɪŋ] **n** enfant trouvé(e) *m(f)*. ~ **hospital** hospice *m* pour enfants trouvés.

foundry ['faʊndrɪ] **n** fonderie *f*.

fount [faʊnt] **n** a (*liter: spring*) source *f*. **the** ~ **of knowledge/wisdom** la source du savoir/de la sagesse. b (*Brit Typ*) fonte *f*.

fountain ['faʊntɪn] 1 **n** (*natural*) fontaine *f*, source *f*; (*artificial*) fontaine, jet *m* d'eau; (*fig*) source; (*also* **drinking** ~) jet *m* d'eau potable; *see* **soda**. 2 **comp** ▸**fountainhead** source *f*, origine *f*; **to go to the fountainhead** aller (directement) à la source, retourner aux sources ▸**fountain pen** stylo *m* (*à encre*).

four [fɔːʳ] 1 **adj** quatre *inv*. **to the** ~ **corners of the earth** aux quatre coins du monde; **it's in** ~ **figures** c'est dans les milliers (*see also* **4**); **open to the** ~ **winds** ouvert à tous les vents *or* aux quatre vents; (*US*) **the F**~ **Hundred** *l'élite sociale*; *see* **stroke**.

2 **n** quatre *m inv*. **on all** ~**s** à quatre pattes; (*Rowing*) **a** ~ un quatre; **will you make up a** ~ **for bridge?** voulez-vous faire le quatrième au bridge?; (*Cricket*) **to hit a** ~ marquer quatre courses *or* points; **he hit 3** ~**s** il a marqué 3 fois quatre courses *or* points; *see* **form**; *for other phrases see* **six**.

3 **pron** quatre *mfpl*. **there are** ~ il y en a quatre.

4 **comp** ▸**four-ball** (*Golf*) **adj, n** fourball *(m)* ▸**four-colour (printing) process** (*Typ*) quadrichromie *f* ▸**four-door** (*Aut*) à quatre portes ▸**four-engined** (*Aviat*) à quatre moteurs ▸**four-engined plane** quadrimoteur *m* ▸**four-eyes‡** binoclard(e)* *m(f)* ▸**four-F** (*US Mil*) réformé *m* ▸**four-figure salary** traitement annuel de plus de mille ▸**four-flush‡** (*US*) bluffer* ▸**fourflusher‡** (*US*) bluffeur* *m*, -euse* *f* ▸**fourfold** **adj** quadruple ◊ **adv** au quadruple ▸**fourfooted** quadrupède, à quatre pattes ▸**four-four time:** (*Mus*) **in four-four time** à quatre/quatre ▸**Four-H club** (*US*) *club éducatif de jeunes ruraux* ▸**four-handed** (*Mus*) à quatre mains ▸**four-in-hand** (*coach*) attelage *m* à quatre ▸**four-leaf clover, four-leaved clover** trèfle *m* à quatre feuilles ▸**four-letter word** (*fig*) obscénité *f*, gros mot, mot grossier; **he let out a four-letter word** il a sorti le mot de cinq lettres (*euph*) ▸**four-minute mile** (*Sport*) course d'un mille courue en quatre minutes ▸**four-part** *song* à quatre voix; *serial* en quatre épisodes ▸**fourposter** lit *m* à baldaquin *or* à colonnes ▸**fourscore** (*liter*) **adj, n** quatre-vingts ▸**four-seater** (*Aut*) (voiture *f* à) quatre places *f inv* ▸**foursome** (*game*) partie *f* à quatre; (*two women, two men*) deux couples; **we went in a foursome** nous y sommes allés à quatre ▸**foursquare** (*square*) carré; (*firm*) *attitude, decision* ferme, inébranlable; (*forthright*) *account, assessment* franc (*f* franche) ▸**four-star** **adj** (*high-quality*) de première qualité ▸**four-star general** (*US*) général *m* à quatre étoiles ▸**four-star petrol** (*Brit*) super(carburant) *m* ▸**four-stroke** (*Aut*) **adj, n** (moteur *m*) à quatre temps ▸**four-wheel drive** (*Aut*) propulsion *f* à quatre roues motrices; **with four-wheel drive** à quatre roues motrices.

fourchette [fʊə'ʃet] **n** fourchette *f* vulvaire.

fourteen ['fɔː'tiːn] 1 **adj, n** quatorze (*m inv*); *for phrases see* **six**. 2 **pron** quatorze *mfpl*. **there are** ~ il y en a quatorze.

fourteenth [ˈfɔːˈtiːnθ] 1 adj quatorzième. **Louis the F~** Louis Quatorze. 2 n quatorzième *mf*; (*fraction*) quatorzième *m*. **the ~ of July** le quatorze juillet, la fête du quatorze juillet; *for other phrases see* **sixth**.

fourth [fɔːθ] 1 adj quatrième. **the ~ dimension** la quatrième dimension; **he lives on the ~ floor** il habite (*Brit*) au quatrième *or* (*US*) au cinquième (étage); (*Aut*) **to change into ~ gear** passer en quatrième; **the ~ estate** la presse (toute puissante); **~ finger** annulaire *m*; (*Pol*) **the F~ World** le quart-monde.
2 n quatrième *mf*; (*fraction*) quart *m*; (*Mus*) quarte *f*. **we need a ~ for our game of bridge** il nous faut un quatrième pour notre bridge; (*US*) **the F~ (of July)** le quatre juillet (*Fête de l'Indépendance américaine*); *for other phrases see* **sixth**.
3 comp ►**fourth-class matter** (*US Post*) paquet-poste *m* ordinaire ►**fourth-floor flat** (appartement *m* au) quatrième *m* (*or* (*US*) cinquième) ►**fourth-rate** (*fig*) de dernier ordre, de dernière catégorie.

fourthly [ˈfɔːθlɪ] adv quatrièmement, en quatrième lieu.

fowl [faʊl] 1 n a (*hens etc*) (*collective n*) volaille *f*, oiseaux *mpl* de basse-cour; (*one bird*) volatile *m*, volaille. (*Culin*) **roast ~** volaille rôtie, poulet rôti. b (††) oiseau *m*. (*liter*) **the ~s of the air** les oiseaux; *see* **fish, water, wild** *etc*. 2 vi: **to go ~ing** chasser le gibier à plumes. 3 comp ►**fowling piece** fusil *m* de chasse léger, carabine *f* ►**fowl pest** peste *f* aviaire.

fox [fɒks] 1 n a (*animal*) renard *m*. (*fig*) **a (sly) ~** un rusé, un malin, un fin renard. b (*US* ‡: *girl*) jolie fille, fille sexy*. 2 vt (*puzzle*) rendre perplexe, mystifier; (*deceive*) tromper, berner. 3 comp ►**fox cub** renardeau *m* ►**fox fur** renard *m* ►**foxglove** (*Bot*) digitale *f* (pourprée) ►**foxhole** terrier *m* de renard, renardière *f*; (*Mil*) gourbi *m* ►**foxhound** chien courant, fox-hound *m* ►**foxhunt(ing)** chasse *f* au renard; **to go foxhunting** aller à la chasse au renard ►**fox terrier** fox *m*, fox-terrier *m* ►**foxtrot** fox-trot *m*.

foxed [fɒkst] adj *book, paper* marqué de rousseurs.

foxy [ˈfɒksɪ] adj a (*crafty*) rusé, malin (*f* -igne), finaud. b **~ lady*** jolie fille, fille sexy*.

foyer [ˈfɔɪeɪ] n *[theatre]* foyer *m*; *[hotel]* vestibule *m*, foyer, hall *m*; (*US*) *[house]* vestibule, entrée *f*.

F.P. [efˈpiː] (*US*) (abbr of **fireplug**) *see* **fire**.

F.P.A. [efˌpiːˈeɪ] (abbr of **Family Planning Association**) Mouvement *m* pour le planning familial.

Fr. (*Rel*) (abbr of **Father** (*on envelope*)) **~ R. Frost** le Révérend Père R. Frost.

fr. (abbr of **franc**) F. **10 fr** 10 F.

fracas [ˈfrækɑː] n (*scuffle*) rixe *f*, échauffourée *f*, bagarre *f*; (*noise*) fracas *m*.

fraction [ˈfrækʃən] n (*Math*) fraction *f*; (*fig*) fraction, partie *f*. **for a ~ of a second** pendant une fraction de seconde; **she only spends a ~ of what she earns** elle ne dépense qu'une partie infime de ce qu'elle gagne; *see* **decimal, vulgar**.

fractional [ˈfrækʃənl] adj (*Math*) fractionnaire; (*fig*) infime, tout petit. (*US*) **~ note** petite coupure *f*; **~ part** fraction *f*; (*Chem*) **~ distillation** distillation fractionnée.

fractionally [ˈfrækʃnəlɪ] adv un tout petit peu.

fractious [ˈfrækʃəs] adj *child* grincheux, pleurnicheur; *old person* grincheux, hargneux.

fracture [ˈfræktʃəʳ] 1 n fracture *f*. 2 vt a fracturer. **she ~d her leg** elle s'est fracturé la jambe. b (*US* ‡: *make laugh*) faire rire aux éclats. 3 vi se fracturer.

frag‡ [fræg] (*US Mil*) 1 n grenade *f* offensive. 2 vt tuer *or* blesser d'une grenade (*un officier etc*). tuer *ou* blesser d'une grenade (*un officier etc*).

fragile [ˈfrædʒaɪl] adj *china* fragile; *complexion, health* fragile, délicat; *person* fragile, (*from age, ill-health*) frêle; *happiness* fragile, précaire. (*hum*) **I feel ~ this morning** je me sens déliquescent* ce matin.

fragility [frəˈdʒɪlɪtɪ] n fragilité *f*.

fragment [ˈfrægmənt] 1 n *[china, paper]* fragment *m*, morceau *m*; *[shell]* éclat *m*. **he smashed it to ~s** il l'a réduit en miettes *or* en mille morceaux; **~s of conversation** bribes *fpl* de conversation. 2 [frægˈment] vt fragmenter. 3 [frægˈment] vi se fragmenter.

fragmental [frægˈmentl] adj fragmentaire; (*Geol*) clastique.

fragmentary [ˈfrægməntərɪ] adj fragmentaire.

fragmentation [ˌfrægmenˈteɪʃən] n fragmentation *f*. (*Mil*) **~ grenade** grenade *f* offensive.

fragmented [frægˈmentɪd] adj *story, version* morcelé, fragmentaire.

fragrance [ˈfreɪgrəns] n parfum *m*, senteur *f*, fragrance *f* (*liter*). (*Comm*) **a new ~ by X** un nouveau parfum de X.

fragrant [ˈfreɪgrənt] adj parfumé, odorant. (*fig liter*) **~ memories** doux souvenirs.

fraidy* [ˈfreɪdɪ] adj (*US: children's language*) **~ cat** trouillard(e)‡ *m(f)*, poule mouillée.

frail [freɪl] adj *person* frêle, fragile; *health* délicat, fragile; *happiness* fragile, éphémère; *excuse* piètre. **it's a ~ hope** c'est un espoir fragile.

frailty [ˈfreɪltɪ] n *[person, health, happiness]* fragilité *f*; (*morally*) faiblesse *f*.

frame [freɪm] 1 n *[building]* charpente *f*; *[ship]* carcasse *f*; *[car]* châssis *m*; *[bicycle]* cadre *m*; *[window]* châssis, chambranle *m*; *[door]* encadrement *m*, chambranle; *[picture]* cadre, encadrement; *[embroidery, tapestry]* cadre; (*Tech*) métier *m*; *[spectacles]* (*also* **~s**) monture *f*; (*Cine*) image *f*, photogramme *m*; (*in garden*) châssis, cloche *f*; *[racket]* armature *f*, cadre; *[human, animal]* charpente, ossature *f*, corps *m*. **her ~ was shaken by sobs** toute sa personne était secouée par les sanglots; **his large ~** son grand corps; **~ of mind** humeur *f*, disposition *f* d'esprit; **I'm not in a ~ of mind for singing** je ne suis pas d'humeur à chanter; (*Math, fig*) **~ of reference** système *m* de référence.
2 comp ►**frame house** maison *f* à charpente de bois ►**frame rucksack** sac *m* à dos à armature ►**frame-up‡** coup monté, machination *f* ►**framework** (*lit: see* **frame 1**) charpente *f*; carcasse *f*; ossature *f*; encadrement *m*; châssis *m*; chambranle *m*; (*fig*) *[society, government etc]* structure *f*, cadre *m*, ossature; *[play, novel]* structure, ossature; **in the framework of a totalitarian society** dans le cadre d'une société totalitaire ►**framework agreement** (*Ind, Pol etc*) accord-cadre *m*.
3 vt a *picture* encadrer. **he appeared ~d in the door** il apparut dans l'encadrement de la porte; **a face ~d in a mass of curls** un visage encadré par une profusion de boucles.
b (*construct*) *house* bâtir *or* construire la charpente de; *idea, plan* concevoir, formuler; *plot* combiner, ourdir (*liter*); *sentence* construire.
c (‡: *also* **~ up**) **to ~ sb (up), to have sb ~d** monter un coup contre qn (*pour faire porter l'accusation contre lui*); **he claimed he had been ~d** il a prétendu être victime d'un coup monté.
4 vi (*develop*) **the child is framing well** l'enfant montre des dispositions *or* fait des progrès; **his plans are framing well/badly** ses projets se présentent bien/mal, ses projets prennent une bonne/une mauvaise tournure.

framer [ˈfreɪməʳ] n (*also* **picture ~**) encadreur *m*.

framing [ˈfreɪmɪŋ] n a (*also* **picture ~**) encadrement *m*. b (*Art, Phot*) cadrage *m*.

franc [fræŋk] n franc *m*. **~ area** zone *f* franc.

France [frɑːns] n France *f*. **in ~** en France.

Frances [ˈfrɑːnsɪs] n Françoise *f*.

franchise [ˈfræntʃaɪz] n a (*Pol*) droit *m* de suffrage *or* de vote. b (*Comm*) franchise *f*.

franchisee [ˌfræntʃaɪˈziː] n franchisé(e) *m(f)*.

franchiser [ˈfræntʃaɪzəʳ] n franchiseur *m*.

Francis [ˈfrɑːnsɪs] n François *m*, Francis *m*. **Saint ~ of Assisi** saint François d'Assise.

Franciscan [frænˈsɪskən] adj, n franciscain *(m)*.

francium [ˈfrænsɪəm] n francium *m*.

Franco* [ˈfræŋkəʊ] adj (*Can*) canadien français.

Franco... [ˈfræŋkəʊ] pref franco-. **~-British** franco-britannique.

franco [ˈfræŋkəʊ] adv (*Comm*) franco. **~ frontier/domicile** franco frontière/domicile.

francophile [ˈfræŋkəʊfaɪl] adj, n francophile *(mf)*.

francophobe [ˈfræŋkəʊfəʊb] adj, n francophobe *(mf)*.

frangipane [ˈfrændʒɪpeɪn] n, **frangipani** [ˌfrændʒɪˈpɑːnɪ] n, pl **~s** *or* **~** (*perfume, pastry*) frangipane *f*; (*shrub*) frangipanier *m*.

Franglais* [frɑ̃ˈglɛ] n franglais *m*.

Frank [fræŋk] n a (*Hist*) Franc *m*, Franque *f*. b (*name*) François *m*, Frank *m*.

frank¹ [fræŋk] adj *person* franc (*f* franche), direct, ouvert; *comment, admission* franc. **I'll be quite ~ with you** je vais être très franc *or* tout à fait sincère avec vous, je vais vous parler franchement *or* en toute franchise.

frank² [fræŋk] vt *letter* affranchir. **~ing machine** machine *f* à affranchir.

frank³* [fræŋk] n (*US*) (saucisse *f* de) Francfort *f*.

Frankenstein [ˈfræŋkənstaɪn] n Frankenstein *m*.

Frankfurt(-on-Main) [ˈfræŋkfɜːtˌɒnˈmeɪn] n Francfort(-sur-le-Main).

frankfurter [ˈfræŋkˌfɜːtəʳ] n (*Culin*) (saucisse *f* de) Francfort *f*.

frankincense [ˈfræŋkɪnsens] n encens *m*.

Frankish [ˈfræŋkɪʃ] 1 adj (*Hist*) franc (*f* franque). 2 n (*Ling*) francique *m*, langue franque.

frankly [ˈfræŋklɪ] adv franchement, sincèrement. **~, I don't think that ...** franchement, je ne pense pas que ... .

frankness [ˈfræŋknɪs] n franchise *f*.

frantic [ˈfræntɪk] adj *agitation, activity, cry, effort* frénétique; *need, desire, effort* effréné; *person* hors de soi, fou (*f* folle). **she's ~** elle est hors d'elle, elle est dans tous ses états; **~ with joy/rage** fou de joie/de rage; **she was ~ with pain** la douleur la rendait folle; **he was driven ~ by anxiety** il était fou d'inquiétude, il était dans tous ses états, il commençait à paniquer*; **the noise was driving him ~** le bruit l'exaspérait *or* le rendait fou; **he drives me ~*** il me rend dingue*.

frantically [ˈfræntɪkəlɪ] adv *wave* frénétiquement; *run* comme un fou (*or* une folle); *applaud* avec frénésie. **to try ~ to do** faire des efforts frénétiques pour faire.

frappé [ˈfræpeɪ] n (*US*) boisson glacée.

fraternal [frəˈtɜːnl] adj fraternel.

fraternity [frəˈtɜːnɪtɪ] n a (*NonC*) fraternité *f*. b (*community*) confrérie *f*, communauté *f*; (*US Univ*) confrérie (d'étudiants). (*US*

Univ) ~ **pin** insigne *m* de confrérie.

fraternization [ˌfrætənaɪˈzeɪʃən] **n** fraternisation *f*.

fraternize [ˈfrætənaɪz] **vi** fraterniser (*with* avec).

fratricidal [ˌfrætrɪˈsaɪdl] **adj** fratricide.

fratricide [ˈfrætrɪsaɪd] **n** (*act*) fratricide *m*; (*frm, liter: person*) fratricide *mf*.

fraud [frɔːd] **n** **a** (*criminal deception*) supercherie *f*, imposture *f*, tromperie *f*; (*financial*) escroquerie *f*; (*Jur*) fraude *f*. (*Police*) **F~ Squad** service *m* de la répression des fraudes. **b** (*person*) imposteur *m*, fraudeur *m*, -euse *f*; (*object*) attrape-nigaud *m*. **he isn't a doctor, he's a ~** ce n'est pas un médecin, c'est un imposteur; **he's not ill, he's a ~** il n'est pas malade, il joue la comédie* *or* c'est un simulateur; **this whole thing is a ~!** c'est de la frime!* *or* de la fumisterie!*

fraudulence [ˈfrɔːdjʊləns] **n**, **fraudulency** [ˈfrɔːdjʊlənsɪ] **n** caractère frauduleux.

fraudulent [ˈfrɔːdjʊlənt] **adj** frauduleux. (*Jur*) **~ conversion** malversation *f*, détournement *m* de fonds.

fraught [frɔːt] **adj** plein, chargé, lourd (*with* de); (*tense*) tendu. **situation ~ with danger** situation pleine de danger *or* dangereuse; **atmosphere ~ with hatred** atmosphère chargée de haine; **silence ~ with menace** silence chargé de *or* gros de *or* lourd de menaces; **the situation/discussion was very ~** la situation/discussion était très tendue; **the whole business is a bit ~*** tout ça c'est un peu risqué*.

fray¹ [freɪ] **n** rixe *f*, échauffourée *f*, bagarre *f*; (*Mil*) combat *m*. (*lit, fig*) **ready for the ~** prêt à se battre; (*fig*) **to enter the ~** descendre dans l'arène, entrer en lice.

fray² [freɪ] **1 vt** *cloth, garment* effilocher, effiler; *cuff* user le bord de, effranger; *trousers* user le bas de, effranger; *rope* user, raguer (*Naut*). **tempers were getting ~ed** tout le monde commençait à perdre patience *or* s'énerver; **my nerves are quite ~ed** je suis à bout de nerfs. **2 vi** *[cloth, garment]* s'effilocher, s'effiler; *[rope]* s'user, se raguer (*Naut*). **his sleeve was ~ing at the cuff** sa manche était usée *or* s'effrangeait *or* s'effilochait au poignet.

frazzle* [ˈfræzl] **1 n**: **worn to a ~** éreinté, claqué*, crevé*; **burnt to a ~** carbonisé, calciné; **to beat sb to a ~** battre qn à plate(s) couture(s). **2 vt a** (*US: exhaust*) éreinter*, crever*. **b** (*burn*) (faire) carboniser, (faire) cramer*.

freak [friːk] **1 n a** (*abnormal person or animal*) monstre *m*, phénomène *m*; (*eccentric*) phénomène; (*absurd idea*) lubie *f*, idée saugrenue *or* farfelue*; (*anomalous idea*) anomalie *f*. **~ of nature** accident *m* de la nature; **~ of fortune** caprice *m* de la fortune; **he won by a ~** il a gagné grâce à un hasard extraordinaire.
b (‡) hippie *mf*.
c (‡) **he's an acid ~** il se drogue au LSD, c'est un habitué du LSD; **a jazz ~** un(e) dingue* *or* un(e) fana* du jazz; **a health food ~** un(e) fana* des aliments naturels.
d (*US:* ‡) homosexuel(le) *m(f)*.
2 adj *storm, weather* anormal, insolite; *error* bizarre; *victory* inattendu; (‡) *culture, clothes* hippie.
3 comp ▸freak-out‡ partie *f* de came‡ **▸freak show** exposition *f* de monstres.

▸freak out‡ 1 vi (*abandon convention*) se défouler*; (*get high on drugs*) se défoncer‡, flipper*; (*drop out of society*) devenir marginal, se mettre en marge de la société; (*get angry*) piquer une de ces crises‡. **to freak out on LSD** se défoncer* au LSD. **2 vt sep** (*surprise*) asseoir*; (*anger*) foutre en boule‡ *or* en pétard‡; (*upset*) foutre les boules à‡; (*excite*) brancher*. **3 freak-out‡ n** *see* **freak 3**.

freakish [ˈfriːkɪʃ] **adj** (*gen*) bizarre; *weather* anormal; *idea* saugrenu, insolite.

freaky* [ˈfriːkɪ] **adj** bizarre, original.

freckle [ˈfrekl] **1 n** tache *f* de rousseur *or* de son. **2 vi** se couvrir de taches de rousseur.

freckled [ˈfrekld] **adj** plein de taches de rousseur, taché de son.

Fred [fred] **n** (**dim of Frederick** *or* **Alfred**) Freddy *m*.

Frederick [ˈfredrɪk] **n** Frédéric *m*.

free [friː] **1 adj a** (*at liberty, unrestricted*) *person, animal, object, activity, translation, choice* libre; *government* autonome, libre; *gas* libre, non combiné; (*Ling*) *morpheme* libre. **they tied him up but he managed to get ~** ils l'ont attaché mais il a réussi à se libérer; **to set a prisoner ~** libérer *or* mettre en liberté un prisonnier; **her aunt's death set her ~ to follow her own career** la mort de sa tante lui a donné toute liberté pour poursuivre sa carrière; **the ~ world** le monde libre; (*fig*) **it's a ~ country!** on est en république!*, on peut faire ce qu'on veut ici!; (*Hist*) **the F~ French** les Français libres; *[prisoner]* **to go ~** être relâché, être mis en liberté; **and all these dangerous people still go ~** et tous ces gens dangereux sont encore en liberté; **you're ~ to choose** vous êtes libre de choisir, libre à vous de choisir; **I'm not ~ to do it** je ne suis pas libre de le faire, j'ai les mains liées et je ne peux pas le faire; **the fishing is ~** la pêche est autorisée; **he left one end of the string ~** il a laissé un bout de la ficelle flotter libre; **a dress which leaves my arms ~** une robe qui me laisse les bras libres; **I am leaving you ~ to do as you please** je vous laisse libre de faire comme bon vous semble; **he was ~ to refuse** il était libre de refuser, il avait le droit de refuser; **he is ~ to refuse** il est libre de refuser, libre à lui de refuser, il a le droit de refuser; **to be ~ from care/responsibility** être dégagé de tout souci/de toute responsabilité; **to be ~ from pain** ne pas souffrir; **~ from the usual ruling** non soumis au règlement habituel; **a surface ~ from dust** une surface dépoussiérée; **to get ~ of sb** se débarrasser de qn; **to be ~ of sb** être débarrassé de qn; **area ~ of malaria** zone non touchée par la malaria; **we chose a spot ~ of tourists** nous avons choisi un endroit sans touristes; **~ of tax** *or* **duty** exonéré, hors taxe; **to be a ~ agent** avoir toute liberté d'action; **~ and easy** décontracté, désinvolte, à l'aise; **~ access to** libre accès *m* à; (*Psych*) **~ association** association *f* libre; (*Pol etc*) **~ elections** élections *fpl* libres; **to have a ~ hand to do sth** avoir carte blanche pour faire qch; **to give sb a ~ hand** donner carte blanche à qn (*see also* **1c, 5**); (*newspapers etc*) **~ press** presse *f* libre; **to give ~ rein to** donner libre cours à; **~ speech** liberté *f* de parole; **~ translation** traduction *f* libre; (*Parl: not party-political*) **~ vote** vote *m* de conscience; *see also* **break** *etc*.
b (*costing nothing*) *object, ticket* gratuit. **admission ~** entrée gratuite *or* libre; **we got in ~** *or* **for ~*** nous sommes entrés gratuitement *or* gratis *or* à l'œil*; **they'll send it ~ on request** ils l'enverront gratuitement *or* franco sur demande; **~ of charge (adj)** gratuit; **(adv)** gratuitement, gratis (*see also* **5**); (*Comm*) **~ delivery, delivery ~** livraison gratuite, franco de port; (*Comm*) **~ gift, ~ offer** prime *f*; **as a ~ gift** en prime; (*Comm*) **~ sample** échantillon gratuit; (*Comm: on packets etc*) **~ mug with each towel** une chope gratuite pour tout achat d'une serviette; **he got a ~ ticket** il a eu un billet gratuit *or* gratuitement *or* sans payer; *see* **post³**.
c (*not occupied*) *room, seat, hour, person* libre. **there are 2 ~ rooms left** il reste 2 chambres de libre; **is this table ~?** cette table est-elle libre?; **I wasn't able to get ~ earlier** je n'ai pas pu me libérer plus tôt; **I will be ~ at 2 o'clock** je serai libre à 2 heures; (*lit, fig*) **to have one's hands ~** avoir les mains libres.
d (*lavish, profuse*) généreux, prodigue, large. **to be ~ with one's money** dépenser son argent sans compter; (*iro*) **you're very ~ with your advice** vous êtes particulièrement prodigue de conseils (*iro*); **he makes ~ with all my things** il ne se gêne pas pour se servir de mes affaires; **to make ~ with a woman†** prendre des libertés *or* se permettre des familiarités avec une femme; **feel ~!** je t'en prie!; **feel ~ to interrupt me** n'hésitez pas à m'interrompre.
2 adv a (*without payment*) *give, obtain, travel* gratuitement, gratis.
b (*without restraint*) *run about* en liberté. *[sth caught]* **to work itself ~** se dégager.
3 vt *nation, slave* affranchir, libérer; *caged animal* libérer; *prisoner* libérer, élargir (*frm*), mettre en liberté; (*untie*) *person, animal* détacher, dégager; *knot* défaire, dénouer; *tangle* débrouiller; (*unblock*) *pipe* débloquer, déboucher; (*rescue*) sauver (*from* de); *sb trapped in wreckage* dégager (*from* de); (*from burden*) soulager, débarrasser (*from* de); (*from tax*) exempter, exonérer (*from* de). **to ~ sb from anxiety** libérer *or* délivrer qn de l'angoisse; (*lit, fig*) **to ~ o.s. from** se débarrasser de, se libérer de.
4 n: **the land of the ~** le pays de la liberté.
5 comp ▸free alongside quay (*Comm*) franco long du quai **▸free alongside ship** (*Comm*) franco long du bord **▸freeboard** (hauteur *f* de) franc-bord *m* **▸freebooter** (*buccaneer*) pirate *m*; (*Hist*) flibustier *m* **▸Free Church** (*Brit*) **n** église *f* non-conformiste ◊ **adj** non-conformiste **▸free climbing** escalade *f* libre, libre *m* **▸free clinic** (*US Med*) dispensaire *m* **▸free collective bargaining** (*Ind*) négociation salariale libre (*sans limite imposée par l'État*) **▸free delivered at dock** (*Comm*) livraison *f* franco à quai **▸free enterprise** libre entreprise *f* **▸free-enterprise economy** économie *f* de marché **▸free fall** (*Space, Parachuting*) chute *f* libre; **in free fall** en chute libre **▸free fight** mêlée générale **▸free-fire zone** (*Mil*) secteur *m or* zone *f* de tir libre **▸free flight** (*Aviat*) vol *m* libre **▸free-floating** (*in water*) qui flotte *or* flottant librement; (*in outer space*) qui flotte *or* flottant librement dans l'espace; (*fig*) *person* sans attaches **▸freefone** ® (*Brit Telec*) ≃ numéro vert **▸free-for-all** mêlée générale **▸freehand adj, adv** à main levée **▸free hit** (*Sport*) coup franc **▸freehold** (*Brit*) **n** propriété foncière libre (*de toute obligation*) ◊ **adv** en propriété libre **▸freeholder** (*Brit*) propriétaire foncier (sans obligation) **▸free house** (*Brit*) pub *m* en gérance libre **▸free kick** (*Sport*) coup franc **▸free labour** (*Ind*) main-d'œuvre non syndiquée **▸freelance** *see* **freelance** **▸freeload*** (*US*) grappiller, resquiller **▸freeloader*** (*US*) parasite *m*, resquilleur *m*, -euse *f* **▸free love** amour *m* libre, union *f* libre **▸freeman** (*Hist*) homme *m* libre **▸freeman of a city** citoyen(ne) *m(f)* d'honneur d'une ville **▸free market, free-market economy** économie *f* de marché **▸freemason** franc-maçon *m* **▸freemasonry** franc-maçonnerie *f* **▸free of charge adv** (*Comm*) gratuitement **▸free on board** (*Comm*) franco à bord **▸free on rail** (*Comm*) franco sur wagon **▸free period** (*Educ*) heure *f* de libre *or* sans cours **▸freephone** ® (*Brit Telec*) ≃ numéro vert **▸free port** port *m* franc **▸Freepost** ® (*Brit Post*) port payé **▸free-range eggs/poultry** œufs *mpl*/poulets *mpl* fermiers *or* de ferme **▸free school** (*Educ*) *école privée qui utilise des méthodes nouvelles* **▸free spirit** esprit *m* libre **▸free-standing** *furniture* sur pied, non-encastré **▸the Free State** (*US*) le Maryland **▸freestone** (*NonC*) pierre *f* de taille **▸freestyle (swimming)** (*Sport*) nage *f* libre **▸free-styling** (*Ski*) ski *m* acrobatique

▸**freethinker** libre-penseur *m*, -euse *f* ▸**freethinking** adj libre penseur ◊ n libre pensée *f* ▸**free throw** (*US Sport*) lancer *m* franc; **free throw shot** lancer *m* franc, coup *m* franc ▸**free trade** (*Econ*) libre-échange *m* ▸**free-trade zone** zone franche ▸**free-trader** (*Econ*) libre-échangiste *m* ▸**free verse** (*Literat*) vers *m* libre ▸**freeway** (*US*) autoroute *f* (*sans péage*) ▸**freewheel** (*Brit*) vi *[cyclist]* se mettre en roue libre, être en roue libre; *[motorist]* rouler au point mort ◊ n *[bicycle]* roue *f* libre ▸**freewheeler** (*fig*) personne indépendante qui ne se soucie pas des autres ▸**freewheeling** *person* indépendant; *scheme* hardi; *discussion* libre ▸**free will** (*Philos*) libre arbitre *m*; **he did it of his own free will** il l'a fait de son propre gré; **free-will gift/offering** don *m*/offrande *f* volontaire.

-free [friː] adj ending in comps, e.g. **salt-free** sans sel; **stress-free** dépourvu de stress; **trouble-free** sans problèmes.

freebee*, freebie* n ['friːbɪ] faveur *f*, extra *m*.

freedom ['friːdəm] 1 n liberté *f*. ~ **of action** liberté d'action *or* d'agir; ~ **of association** liberté d'association; ~ **of information** liberté d'information; ~ **of the press** liberté de la presse; ~ **of speech** liberté de parole; ~ **of worship** liberté religieuse *or* du culte; ~ **of the seas** franchise *f* des mers; **to give sb ~ to do as he wishes** laisser les mains libres à qn, donner carte blanche à qn; **to speak with ~** parler en toute liberté; ~ **from care/responsibility** le fait d'être dégagé de tout souci/de toute responsabilité; **to give sb the ~ of a city** nommer qn citoyen d'honneur d'une ville; **he gave me the ~ of his house** il m'a permis de me servir comme je voulais de sa maison, il m'a dit de faire comme chez moi.

2 comp ▸**freedom fighter** guérillero *m*, partisan *m*.

freelance ['friːlɑːns] 1 n collaborateur *m*, -trice *f* indépendant(e), free-lance *m*. 2 adj *journalist, designer, player etc* indépendant, free-lance *inv*. 3 vi travailler en indépendant *or* en free-lance. 4 adv (*work*) en indépendant, en free-lance.

freely ['friːlɪ] adv a (*lavishly*) *give* libéralement, à profusion. **he spends his money ~** il dépense son argent sans compter, il est dépensier. b (*unrestrictedly*) *speak* franchement, sans contrainte, à cœur ouvert; *act* sans contrainte, librement, en toute liberté; *grow* avec luxuriance. **to move ~** (*of person: without hindrance*) se déplacer en toute liberté; (*of person: walk without pain etc*) bouger sans gêne; *[machine part, object etc]* bouger sans accrocher; **traffic is moving ~** la circulation est fluide; **I ~ admit that ...** je reconnais volontiers que ... .

freesia ['friːzɪə] n freesia *m*.

freeze [friːz] pret froze, ptp frozen 1 vi (*Met*) geler; *[liquids, pipes, lakes, rivers etc]* geler; (*fig*) se figer. **it will ~ hard tonight** il gèlera dur cette nuit; **to ~ to death** mourir de froid; **the lake has frozen** le lac est pris *or* gelé; (*Aut*) **the windscreen was frozen** le pare-brise était givré; (*fig*) **his smile froze on his lips** son sourire s'est figé sur ses lèvres; **he froze (in his tracks)** il est resté figé sur place; **~!** pas un geste!; **to ~ on to sb*** se cramponner à qn; (*Culin*) **meat ~s well but lettuce won't ~** la viande se congèle bien mais la laitue se congèle mal; **his boots had frozen to the pavement** ses bottes étaient collées au trottoir par le gel; *see also* **freezing, frozen**.

2 vt *water etc* geler; *food* congeler; (*industrially*) surgeler; (*Econ*) *assets, credits* geler, bloquer; *prices, wages* bloquer, stabiliser. (*fig*) **she froze him with a look** elle lui a lancé un regard qui l'a glacé sur place; (*Cine: hold image*) **can you ~ it?** tu peux t'arrêter sur l'image?; *see also* **frozen**.

3 n a (*Met*) temps *m* de gelée, gel *m*. **the big ~ of 1948** le gel rigoureux *or* le grand gel de 1948; *see* **deep**.

b (*Econ*) *[prices, wages]* blocage *m*; *[credits]* gel *m*, blocage.

4 comp ▸**freeze-dry** vt lyophiliser ▸**freeze-frame** *[film, video]* arrêt *m* sur image ▸**freeze-up** (*Met*) gel *m*.

▸**freeze over** vi *[lakes, rivers]* geler, se prendre en glace; (*Aut*) *[windscreen etc]* givrer. **the river has frozen over** *or* **up** la rivière est gelée *or* est prise (en glace).

▸**freeze up** 1 vi a = **freeze over**. b *[pipes]* geler. 2 vt sep: **the pipes** *or* **we were frozen up last winter** les conduits ont gelé l'hiver dernier. 3 **freeze-up** n *see* **freeze 4**.

freezer ['friːzəʳ] n a (*domestic*) congélateur *m*; (*industrial*) surgélateur *m*. ~ **film/foil** plastique *m*/aluminium *m* spécial congélation. b (*in fridge: also* ~ **compartment**) (*one-star*) freezer *m*; (*two-star*) conservateur *m*; (*three-star*) congélateur *m*. c (*US: ice cream maker*) sorbetière *f*.

freezing ['friːzɪŋ] 1 adj (*very cold*) *person* gelé, glacé; *room, weather, conditions, look* glacial. **I'm ~** je suis gelé *or* glacé, je crève* de froid; **my hands are ~** j'ai les mains gelées *or* glacées; **it's ~ in here** c'est glacial ici, on crève* de froid ici; (*Met*) ~ **fog** brouillard givrant. 2 n congélation *f*, gel *m*. ~ **point** point *m* de congélation; **below ~ point** au-dessous de zéro (centigrade).

freight [freɪt] 1 n (*transporting*) transport *m* par petite vitesse *or* en régime ordinaire; (*price, cost*) fret *m*; (*goods moved*) fret, cargaison *f*; (*esp Brit: ship's cargo*) fret. (*Comm*) ~ **paid** port payé; (*US Comm*) ~ **and delivery paid** franco de port; **to send sth by ~** faire transporter qch par petite vitesse *or* en régime ordinaire; **air ~** transport *or* fret par avion.

2 vt *goods* transporter.

3 comp ▸**freight agent** (*US*) transitaire *m* ▸**freight car** (*US Rail*) wagon *m* de marchandises, fourgon *m* ▸**freight charges** frais *mpl* de transport, fret *m* ▸**freight forwarder** transporteur *m* ▸**freightliner** train *m* de marchandises en conteneurs ▸**freight note** bordereau *m* d'expédition ▸**freight plane** avion-cargo *m*, avion *m* de fret ▸**freight terminal** terminal *m* de fret ▸**freight train** (*esp US*) train *m* de marchandises ▸**freight yard** dépôt *m or* cour *f* des marchandises.

freightage ['freɪtɪdʒ] n (*charge*) fret *m*; (*goods*) fret, cargaison *f*.

freighter ['freɪtəʳ] n (*Naut*) cargo *m*, navire *m* de charge; (*Aviat*) avion-cargo *m*, avion *m* de fret.

French [frentʃ] 1 adj (*gen*) français; *king, embassy, ambassador* de France; *teacher, dictionary* de français. **the ~ Academy** l'Académie française; **the ~ way of life** la vie française; ~ **cooking** cuisine française; **the ~ people** les Français *mpl*; **the ~ Riviera** la Côte d'Azur; *see also* **3**.

2 n a **the ~** les Français *mpl*; *see* **free**.

b (*Ling*) français *m*. (*apologizing for swearing*) **excuse my ~*** passez-moi l'expression.

3 comp ▸**French bean** haricot vert ▸**French bread** pain *m* (*à la française*) ▸**French Canadian** adj canadien français ◊ n (*person*) Canadien(ne) français(e) *m(f)*; (*Ling*) français canadien ▸**French chalk** craie *f* de tailleur ▸**French door** (*US*) porte-fenêtre *f* ▸**French dressing** (*Culin*) (*oil and vinegar*) vinaigrette *f*; (*US: salad cream*) crème *f* à salade ▸**French Equatorial Africa** Afrique équatoriale française ▸**French fried (potatoes)**, (*esp US*) **French fries** (pommes *fpl* de terre) frites *fpl* ▸**french-fry** (*US*) frire à la friteuse ▸**French Guiana** Guyane française ▸**French horn** (*Mus*) cor *m* d'harmonie ▸**French kiss*** n patin* *m* ▸**French knickers** culotte-caleçon *f* ▸**French leave**: (*fig*) **to take French leave** filer à l'anglaise* ▸**French letter*** (*contraceptive*) capote anglaise* ▸**French loaf** baguette *f* (*de pain*) ▸**Frenchman** Français *m* ▸**French marigold** œillet *m* d'Inde ▸**French pastry** pâtisserie *f* ▸**French polish** (*Brit*) vernis *m* (à l'alcool) ▸**French-polish** (*Brit*) vernir (à l'alcool) ▸**French seam** (*Sewing*) couture anglaise ▸**French-speaking** qui parle français; *nation etc* francophone (*see* **Switzerland**) ▸**French stick** = **French loaf** ▸**French toast** (*Brit: toast*) pain grillé d'un seul côté; (*fried bread in egg*) pain perdu ▸**French West Africa** Afrique occidentale française ▸**French window** porte-fenêtre *f* ▸**Frenchwoman** Française *f*.

Frenchify ['frentʃɪfaɪ] vt franciser. (*pej*) **his Frenchified ways** ses maniérismes copiés sur les Français.

frenetic [frə'netɪk], **frenzied** ['frenzɪd] adj *person* très agité; *crowd* en délire; *applause, rhythm, shouts* frénétique; *efforts* désespéré; *joy, passion* frénétique.

frenzy ['frenzɪ] n frénésie *f*. ~ **of delight** transport *m* de joie.

frequency ['friːkwənsɪ] 1 n fréquence *f*; *see* **high, ultrahigh, very**. 2 comp ▸**frequency band** (*Elec*) bande *f* de fréquence ▸**frequency distribution** (*Statistics*) distribution *f* des fréquences ▸**frequency modulation** (*Elec*) modulation *f* de fréquence.

frequent ['friːkwənt] 1 adj (*numerous, happening often*) *visits, rests, changes* fréquent, nombreux; (*common*) *objection, criticism* fréquent, habituel, courant. **it's quite ~** c'est très courant, cela arrive souvent; **he is a ~ visitor (to our house)** c'est un habitué (de la maison). 2 [frɪ'kwent] vt fréquenter, hanter, courir.

frequentative [frɪ'kwentətɪv] adj, n (*Gram*) fréquentatif (*m*), itératif (*m*).

frequenter [frɪ'kwentəʳ] n *[house etc]* familier *m*, habitué(e) *m(f)*; *[pub etc]* habitué(e). **he was a great ~ of night clubs** il courait les boîtes de nuit, c'était un pilier de boîtes de nuit.

frequently ['friːkwəntlɪ] adv fréquemment, souvent.

fresco ['freskəʊ] n, pl ~**es** *or* ~**s** (*pigment, picture*) fresque *f*. **to paint in ~** peindre à fresque.

fresh [freʃ] 1 adj a (*recent, new*) *news, report, paint, make-up, flowers* frais (*f* fraîche); *wound* récent; (*not stale*) *air, milk, eggs, butter, food* frais; *food* (*not frozen*) frais, non congelé, non surgelé; (*not tinned*) frais; (*additional*) *supplies* nouveau (*f* nouvelle), supplémentaire; (*new, different*) *horse* nouveau; *clothes* nouveau, propre, de rechange. **milk ~ from the cow** lait fraîchement trait; ~ **butter** (*not stale*) beurre frais; (*unsalted*) beurre sans sel; **the bread is ~ from the oven** le pain est tout frais, le pain sort (à l'instant) du four; (*US*) ~ **paint** peinture fraîche; **is there any ~ news?** y a-t-il du nouveau? *or* des nouvelles fraîches?; **a ~ sheet of paper** une nouvelle feuille de papier; **he put ~ courage into me** il m'a redonné courage, il m'a insufflé un courage nouveau; (*fig*) **to break ~ ground** faire œuvre de pionnier, faire quelque chose d'entièrement nouveau; **he has had a ~ heart attack** il a eu une nouvelle crise cardiaque; **it's nice to see some ~ faces here** c'est agréable de voir des visages nouveaux ici; **to make a ~ start** prendre un nouveau départ; ~ **water** (*not salt*) eau douce (*see also* **3**); **it is still ~ in my memory** j'en ai encore le souvenir tout frais *or* tout récent; **I'm going out for some ~ air** *or* **for a breath of ~ air** je sors prendre l'air *or* le frais; **in the ~ air** au grand air, en plein air (*see also* **3**); **let's have some ~ air!** un peu d'air!

b (*Met: cool*) *wind* frais (*f* fraîche). **it is getting ~** il commence à faire frais; (*Naut*) ~ **breeze** vent frais.

c *colours* frais (*f* fraîche), gai; *complexion* frais. **she was as ~ as a daisy** elle était fraîche comme une rose.
d (*lively*) *person* plein d'entrain, fringant, sémillant; *horse* fougueux, fringant.
e (*: *cheeky*) familier, trop libre, culotté* (*with* envers). **don't get ~ with me!** pas d'impertinences!; **he's very ~!** il a du toupet!*, il est culotté!*
2 **adv: boy ~ from school** garçon frais émoulu du lycée; **~ from Scotland** nouvellement *or* fraîchement arrivé d'Écosse; **he's just come ~ from a holiday by the sea** il revient de vacances au bord de la mer; **we're ~ out of cream*** nous venons de vendre le dernier pot de crème.
3 **comp ►fresh-air fiend*** (*pej*) mordu(e)* *m(f)* du grand air **►freshman** (*US Univ*) bizut(h) *m*, nouveau *m*, nouvelle *f* (*étudiant(e) de première année*) **►freshwater fish** poisson *m* d'eau douce.

freshen ['freʃn] **vi** (*Met*) *[wind, air]* fraîchir.

►freshen up 1 **vi** (*wash o.s.*) faire un brin de toilette *or* une petite toilette; *[woman]* se refaire une beauté*, faire un raccord (à son maquillage)*. 2 **vt sep** *invalid etc* faire un brin de toilette à, faire une petite toilette à; *child* débarbouiller; *dress, room, paintwork* rafraîchir. **to freshen o.s. up** = **to freshen up** (*see* **1**); **that will freshen you up** cela vous ravigotera* *or* vous requinquera*.

freshener ['freʃnəʳ] **n** (*also* **skin ~**) lotion *f* tonique; (*also* **air ~**) désodorisant *m*.

fresher* ['freʃəʳ] **n** (*Brit Univ*) bizut(h) *m*, nouveau *m*, nouvelle *f* (*étudiant(e) de première année*). (*Brit Univ*) **~s' week** semaine *f* d'accueil des étudiants.

freshet ['freʃɪt] **n** (*flood*) crue *f* rapide, inondation brutale; (*into sea*) cours *m* d'eau qui se jette dans la mer.

freshly ['freʃlɪ] **adv** nouvellement, récemment. **~-cut flowers** des fleurs fraîches cueillies *or* nouvellement cueillies; **it's ~ made** c'est tout frais.

freshness ['freʃnɪs] **n** *[air, food, fruit, milk, wind etc]* fraîcheur *f*; *[manner]* franchise *f*, spontanéité *f*, naturel *m*; *[outlook, approach]* fraîcheur, jeunesse *f*; *[colour]* fraîcheur, gaieté *f or* gaîté *f*.

fret¹ [fret] 1 **vi** a (*become anxious*) s'agiter, se tourmenter, se tracasser; *[baby]* pleurer, geindre. **don't ~!** ne t'en fais pas!, ne te tracasse pas!; **she ~s over trifles** elle se fait du mauvais sang pour des vétilles; **the child is ~ting for its mother** le petit pleure parce qu'il veut sa mère. b *[horse]* **to ~ (at the bit)** ronger le mors. 2 **vt: to ~ o.s.*** se tracasser, se faire de la bile, se biler*. 3 **n: to be in a ~*** se faire du mauvais sang *or* de la bile, se biler*.

fret² [fret] 1 **vt** *wood etc* découper, chantourner. **the stream has ~ted its way through the rock** le ruisseau s'est creusé un chenal dans le rocher. 2 **comp ►fretsaw** scie *f* à découper **►fretwork** (*piece*) pièce chantournée; (*work*) découpage *m*.

fret³ [fret] **n** (*for guitar*) frette *f*, touche *f*.

fretful ['fretfʊl] **adj** *person* agité, énervé; *baby, child* grognon, pleurnicheur; *sleep* agité.

fretfully ['fretfəlɪ] **adv** *do* avec agitation *or* énervement, d'un air énervé; *say* d'un ton agité. *[baby]* **to cry ~** pleurnicher, être grognon.

fretfulness ['fretfʊlnɪs] **n** irritabilité *f*.

Freudian ['frɔɪdɪən] 1 **adj** (*Psych, fig*) freudien. **~ slip** lapsus *m*. 2 **n** disciple *mf* de Freud.

FRG [ˌefɑː'dʒiː] **n** (**abbr of Federal Republic of Germany**) R.F.A. *f*.

friable ['fraɪəbl] **adj** friable.

friar ['fraɪəʳ] **n** moine *m*, frère *m*, religieux *m*. **F~ John** Frère Jean.

friary ['fraɪərɪ] **n** confrérie *f*.

fricassee ['frɪkəsiː] **n** fricassée *f*.

fricative ['frɪkətɪv] (*Ling*) 1 **adj** spirant, fricatif. 2 **n** spirante *f*, fricative *f*.

friction ['frɪkʃən] 1 **n** a (*Phys etc*) friction *f*, frottement *m*; (*Ling*) friction; (*fig*) désaccord *m*, frottement, friction. (*fig*) **there is a certain amount of ~ between them** il y a des frottements *or* des désaccords *or* de la friction entre eux. b (*also* **~ climbing**) adhérence *f*. 2 **comp ►friction feed** (*on printer*) entraînement *m* par friction **►friction tape** (*US*) chatterton *m*.

Friday ['fraɪdɪ] **n** vendredi *m*. **~ the thirteenth** vendredi treize; *see* **good**; *for other phrases see* **Saturday**.

fridge [frɪdʒ] **n** (*Brit*) (**abbr of refrigerator**) frigo* *m*, frigidaire *m* ®. **~-freezer** réfrigérateur *m* avec partie congélateur.

fried [fraɪd] **pret, ptp of fry²**.

friend [frend] **n** ami(e) *m(f)*; (*schoolmate, workmate etc*) camarade *mf*, copain* *m*, copine* *f*; (*helper, supporter*) ami(e), bienfaiteur *m*, -trice *f*. **a ~ of mine** un de mes amis; **~s of ours** des amis (à nous); **he's one of my son's ~s** c'est un ami *or* un camarade *or* un copain* de mon fils; **her best ~** sa meilleure amie; (*fig*) **it's a girl's best ~** c'est le rêve de chaque femme; **he's no ~ of mine** je ne le compte pas au nombre de mes amis; **to make ~s with sb** devenir ami avec qn, se lier d'amitié avec qn; **he made a ~ of him** il en a fait son ami; **he makes ~s easily** il se fait facilement des amis, il se lie facilement; **to be ~s with sb** être ami *or* lié avec qn; **let's be ~s again** on fait la paix?; **close ~s** amis intimes; **we're just good ~s** nous sommes simplement bons amis; **we're all ~s here** nous sommes entre amis; **a ~ of the family** un ami de la famille *or* de la maison; (*Prov*) **a ~ in need is a ~ indeed** c'est dans le besoin que l'on connaît ses vrais amis; (*loc*) **the best of ~s must part** il n'est si bonne compagnie qui ne se sépare (*Prov*); **he's been a true ~ to us** il a fait preuve d'une véritable amitié envers nous; (*fig*) **a ~ at court** un ami influent; (*fig*) **to have ~s at court** avoir des amis influents *or* des protections; (*Parl*) **my honourable ~**, (*Jur*) **my learned ~** mon cher *or* distingué confrère, ma distinguée collègue; **~ of the poor** bienfaiteur *or* ami des pauvres; **F~s of the Earth** les Amis de la Terre; **F~s of the National Theatre** (Société *f* des) Amis du Théâtre National; (*Rel*) **Society of F~s** Société *f* des Amis, Quakers *mpl*.

friendless ['frendlɪs] **adj** seul, isolé, sans amis.

friendliness ['frendlɪnɪs] **n** attitude amicale, bienveillance *f*.

friendly ['frendlɪ] **adj** *person, attitude, feelings* amical; *child, dog* gentil, affectueux; *nation* ami; *hotel* accueillant; *advice* d'ami; *smile, welcome* amical; (*from superiors*) bienveillant, aimable. **people here are so ~** les gens sont si gentils ici; **I am quite ~ with her** je suis (assez) ami(e) avec elle; **to be on ~ terms with sb** être en termes amicaux *or* avoir des rapports d'amitié avec qn; **that wasn't a very ~ thing to do** ce n'était pas très gentil de faire cela; (*Sport*) **~ match** match amical; (*Brit*) **F~ Society** Société *f* de prévoyance, (société) mutuelle *f*; (*Geog*) **the F~ Islands** les îles *fpl* des Amis, Tonga *m*; (*Mil*) **~ fire** tir(s) *m(pl)* de son propre camp; *see* **neighbourhood**.

-friendly ['frendlɪ] **adj ending in comps, e.g. dolphin-friendly tuna** thon *m* produit sans danger pour les dauphins; **reader-friendly** qui tient compte du lecteur, qui prend le lecteur en considération; *see* **environment, ozone, user**.

friendship ['frendʃɪp] **n** amitié *f*. **out of ~** par amitié.

Friesian ['friːʒən] = **Frisian**.

frieze¹ [friːz] **n** (*Archit*) frise *f*.

frieze² [friːz] **n** (*Tex*) ratine *f*.

frig‡ [frɪg] **vi: to frig about** *or* **around** déconner‡.

frigate ['frɪgɪt] **n** frégate *f* (*Naut*).

frigging‡ ['frɪgɪŋ] 1 **adv** foutrement**‡**, vachement*. 2 **adj** foutu‡.

fright [fraɪt] **n** a effroi *m*, peur *f*. **to take ~** prendre peur, s'effrayer (*de* at); **to get** *or* **have a ~** avoir peur; **to get the ~ of one's life** avoir la peur de sa vie; **to give sb a ~** faire peur à qn; **it gave me such a ~** ça m'a fait une de ces peurs* *or* une belle peur; *see* **stage**. b (*: *person*) horreur* *f*, épouvantail *m*. **she's** *or* **she looks a ~** elle est à faire peur.

frighten ['fraɪtn] **vt** effrayer, faire peur à. **did he ~ you?** est-ce qu'il vous a fait peur?; **it nearly ~ed him out of his wits** *or* **his skin** cela lui a fait une peur bleue; **to ~ the life out of sb** faire une peur bleue à qn*; **to ~ sb into doing sth** effrayer qn pour lui faire faire qch, faire faire qch à qn par (l')intimidation; **he was ~ed into doing it** il l'a fait sous le coup de la peur; **to be ~ed of (doing) sth** avoir peur de (faire) qch; **I'm ~ed to death** je meurs de peur; **I'm ~ed to death of spiders** j'ai une peur bleue des araignées; **I was ~ed to death when I saw him** j'ai failli mourir de peur en le voyant; **she is easily ~ed** elle prend peur facilement, elle est peureuse; *see* **living**.

►frighten away, frighten off vt sep *birds* effaroucher; *children etc* chasser (en leur faisant peur).

frightened ['fraɪtnd] **adj** effrayé. **don't be ~** n'ayez pas peur, ne vous effrayez pas.

frightening ['fraɪtnɪŋ] **adj** effrayant.

frighteningly ['fraɪtnɪŋlɪ] **adv** *ugly, thin etc* à faire peur; *expensive, uncertain* terriblement.

frightful ['fraɪtfʊl] **adj** (*gen*) épouvantable, affreux; (*stronger*) effroyable. **she looks ~ in that hat*** elle est affreuse avec ce chapeau.

frightfully ['fraɪtfəlɪ] **adv** affreusement, effroyablement. **I am ~ late** je suis terriblement *or* affreusement en retard; **I am ~ sorry** je regrette énormément, je suis (absolument) désolé; **it's ~ good of you** c'est vraiment trop gentil à vous *or* de votre part, vous êtes vraiment trop bon; **~ ugly** affreusement *or* effroyablement laid; **he's ~ sweet** il est terriblement mignon.

frightfulness ['fraɪtfʊlnɪs] **n** *[crime etc]* atrocité *f*, horreur *f*.

frigid ['frɪdʒɪd] **adj** (*Geog, Met*) glacial; *manner, reaction, welcome* froid, glacé; (*Psych*) *woman* frigide.

frigidity [frɪ'dʒɪdɪtɪ] **n** (*sexual*) frigidité *f*; (*gen*) froideur *f*.

frill [frɪl] **n** *[dress]* ruche *f*, volant *m*; *[shirt front]* jabot *m*; *[cuff]* ruche; (*Culin*) papillote *f*; (*Orn*) collerette *f*. (*fig*) **~s** manières *fpl*, façons *fpl*, chichis* *mpl*; (*fig*) **without any ~s** simple, sans manières, sans façons; *see* **furbelow, no**.

frilly ['frɪlɪ] **adj** *dress* à fanfreluches; (*fig*) *speech* à fioritures, fleuri.

fringe [frɪndʒ] 1 **n** *[rug, shawl]* frange *f*; (*Brit*) *[hair]* frange *f*; *[forest]* bord *m*, bordure *f*, lisière *f*; *[crowd]* derniers rangs. **on the ~ of the forest** en bord *or* bordure de forêt, à la lisière *or* à l'orée de la forêt; **to live on the ~ of society** vivre en marge de la société; **the outer ~s** *[large town]* la grande banlieue; *[town]* la périphérie; *see* **lunatic**.
2 **vt** *shawl etc* franger (*with* de). (*fig*) **road ~d with trees** route bordée d'arbres; (*Geog*) **fringing reef** récif frangeant.
3 **comp ►fringe area** (*TV*) zone *f* limitrophe (de réception) **►fringe benefits** avantages *mpl* sociaux, avantages en nature, indemnités *fpl*, avantages divers **►fringe group** groupe marginal **►fringe theatre** (*Brit*) théâtre *m* d'avant-garde *or* expérimental *or* off.

frippery ['frɪpərɪ] **n** (*pej*) (*cheap ornament*) colifichets *mpl*; (*on dress*) fanfreluches *fpl*; (*ostentation*) préciosité *f*, maniérisme *m*.

Frisbee ['frɪzbɪ] n ® Frisbee *m* ®.

Frisian ['frɪʒən] 1 adj frison. ~ **Islands** îles Frisonnes. 2 n a Frison(ne) *m(f)*. b (*Ling*) frison *m*.

frisk [frɪsk] 1 vi gambader, batifoler*, folâtrer. 2 vt *criminal, suspect* fouiller.

friskiness ['frɪskɪnɪs] n vivacité *f*.

frisky ['frɪskɪ] adj vif (*f* vive), sémillant, fringant.

fritillary [frɪ'tɪlərɪ] n fritillaire *f*.

fritter[1] ['frɪtəʳ] vt (*also* ~ **away**) *money, time* gaspiller, perdre; *energy* gaspiller.

fritter[2] ['frɪtəʳ] n (*Culin*) beignet *m*. **apple** ~ beignet aux pommes.

fritz‡ [frɪts] (*US*) n: **on the** ~ en panne.

▸**fritz out‡** vi tomber en panne.

frivolity [frɪ'vɒlɪtɪ] n frivolité *f*.

frivolous ['frɪvələs] adj *person, behaviour* frivole, léger; *remark* frivole, superficiel.

frizz [frɪz] vt *hair* faire friser *or* frisotter.

frizzle ['frɪzl] 1 vi grésiller. 2 vt (*also* ~ **up**) *food* faire trop griller, laisser brûler *or* calciner. **the joint was all ~d (up)** le rôti était complètement calciné.

frizzly ['frɪzlɪ] adj, **frizzy** ['frɪzɪ] adj *hair* crépu, crêpelé.

fro [frəʊ] adv: **to and** ~ de long en large; **to go to and** ~ **between** aller et venir entre, faire la navette entre; **journeys to and** ~ **between London and Edinburgh** allers *mpl* et retours *mpl* entre Londres et Édimbourg; *see also* **to**.

frock [frɒk] n *[woman, baby]* robe *f*; *[monk]* froc *m*. ~ **coat** redingote *f*.

frog[1] [frɒg] 1 n a (*Zool*) grenouille *f*. (*fig*) **to have a** ~ **in one's throat** avoir un chat dans la gorge. b (*pej*) **F~‡** Français(e) *m(f)*. 2 comp ▸**frogman** homme-grenouille *m* ▸**frog-march: to frog-march sb in/out** *etc* (*hustle*) amener/sortir *etc* qn de force; (*carry*) amener/ sortir *etc* qn en le prenant par les quatre membres ▸**frogspawn** frai *m* de grenouille ▸**frogspit** crachat *m* de coucou.

frog[2] [frɒg] n (*Dress*) brandebourg *m*, soutache *f*.

frolic ['frɒlɪk] 1 vi (*also* ~ **about**, ~ **around**) folâtrer, batifoler*, gambader. 2 n ébats *mpl*, gambades *fpl*; (*prank*) espièglerie *f*, gaminerie *f*; (*merry-making*) ébats.

frolicsome ['frɒlɪksəm] adj folâtre, gai, espiègle.

from [frɒm] prep a (*place: starting point*) de. ~ **house to house** de maison en maison; **to jump** ~ **a wall** sauter d'un mur; **to travel** ~ **London to Paris** voyager de Londres à Paris; **train** ~ **Manchester** train (en provenance) de Manchester; **programme transmitted** ~ **Lyons** programme retransmis de *or* depuis Lyon; **he comes** ~ **London** il vient de Londres, il est (originaire) de Londres; **he comes** ~ **there** il en vient; **where are you** ~? d'où êtes-vous *or* venez-vous?

b (*time: starting point*) à partir de, de. **(as)** ~ **the 14th July** à partir du 14 juillet; ~ **that day onwards** à partir de ce jour-là; ~ **beginning to end** du début jusqu'à la fin; ~ **his childhood** dès son enfance; ~ **time to time** de temps en temps; ~ **year to year** d'année en année; **counting** ~ **last Monday** à dater de lundi dernier.

c (*distance: lit, fig*) de. **the house is 10 km** ~ **the coast** la maison est à 10 km de la côte; **it is 10 km** ~ **there** c'est à 10 km de là; **to go away** ~ **home** quitter la maison; **not far** ~ **here** pas loin d'ici; **far** ~ **blaming you** loin de vous le reprocher.

d (*origin*) de, de la part de, d'après. **a letter** ~ **my mother** une lettre de ma mère; **tell him** ~ **me** dites-lui de ma part; **an invitation** ~ **the Smiths** une invitation (de la part) des Smith; **painted** ~ **life** peint d'après nature; ~ **a picture by Picasso** d'après un tableau de Picasso.

e (*used with prices, numbers*) à partir de, depuis. **wine** ~ **6 francs a bottle** vins à partir de *or* depuis 6 F la bouteille; **there were** ~ **10 to 15 people there** il y avait là de 10 à 15 personnes.

f (*source*) **to drink** ~ **a brook** boire à un ruisseau; **to drink** ~ **a glass** boire dans un verre; **to drink straight** ~ **the bottle** boire à (même) la bouteille; **he took it** ~ **the cupboard** il l'a pris dans le placard, il l'a sorti du placard; **he put the box down and took a book** ~ **it** il a posé la caisse et en a tiré un livre; **to pick sb** ~ **the crowd** choisir qn dans la foule; **a quotation** ~ **Racine** une citation (tirée) de Racine; **here's an extract** ~ **it** en voici un extrait; **to speak** ~ **notes** parler avec des notes; **to judge** ~ **appearances** juger d'après les apparences; ~ **your point of view** à *or* de votre point de vue; **to draw a conclusion** ~ **the information** tirer une conclusion des renseignements.

g (*prevention, escape, deprivation etc*) à, de. **take the knife** ~ **this child!** ôtez *or* enlevez *or* prenez le couteau à cet enfant!; **he prevented me** ~ **coming** il m'a empêché de venir; **he took/stole it** ~ **them** il le leur a pris/volé; **the news was kept** ~ **her** on lui a caché la nouvelle; **to shelter** ~ **the rain** s'abriter de la pluie.

h (*change*) de. ~ **bad to worse** de mal en pis; **price increase** ~ **one franc to one franc fifty** augmentation de prix d'un franc à un franc cinquante; **he went** ~ **office boy to director in 5 years** de garçon de bureau il est passé directeur en 5 ans.

i (*cause, reason*) **to act** ~ **conviction** agir par conviction; **to die** ~ **fatigue** mourir de fatigue; **he died** ~ **his injuries** il est décédé des suites de ses blessures; ~ **what I heard** ... d'après ce que j'ai entendu ...; ~ **what I can see** ... à ce que je vois ...; ~ **the look of things** ... à en juger par les apparences ...; ~ **the way he talks you would think that** ... à l'entendre on penserait que ... .

j (*difference*) de. **he is quite different** ~ **the others** il est complètement différent des autres; **to distinguish the good** ~ **the bad** distinguer le bon du mauvais.

k (*with other preps and advs*) **seen** ~ **above** vu d'en haut; ~ **above the clouds** d'au-dessus des nuages; ~ **henceforth** à partir d'aujourd'hui, désormais, dorénavant (*frm*); **I saw him** ~ **afar** je l'ai vu de loin; **she was looking at him** ~ **over the wall** elle le regardait depuis l'autre côté du mur; ~ **under the table** de dessous la table.

frond [frɒnd] n *[fern]* fronde *f*; *[palm]* feuille *f*.

front [frʌnt] 1 n a (*leading section*) *[boat, car, train etc]* avant *m*; *[class, crowd, audience]* premier rang; (*part facing forward*) *[cupboard, shirt, dress]* devant *m*; *[building]* façade *f*, devant, front *m*; *[book]* (*beginning*) début *m*; (*cover*) couverture *f*; *[postcard, photo]* recto *m*. **in** ~ *be, stand, walk, put* devant; *send, move, look* en avant; **in** ~ **of the table** devant la table; **to send sb on in** ~ envoyer qn en avant; **he was walking in** ~ il marchait devant; (*Sport*) **to be in** ~ mener; (*fig*) **to come to the** ~ se faire connaître *or* remarquer, percer; **to sit in the** ~ **(of the car), to sit in** ~ être assis à l'avant (de la voiture); **to sit in the** ~ **of the train/bus** s'asseoir en tête de *or* du train/à l'avant de l'autobus; **in the** ~ **of the class** au premier rang de la classe; **in the** ~ **of the book** au début du livre; **she was lying on her** ~* elle était couchée sur le ventre; **it fastens at the** ~ cela se ferme devant; **she spilt it down the** ~ **of her dress** elle l'a renversé sur le devant de sa robe; **he pushed his way to the** ~ **of the crowd** il s'est frayé un chemin jusqu'au premier rang de la foule; (*fig*) **to put on a bold** ~ faire bonne contenance.

b (*Met, Mil, Pol*) front *m*. **to fall at the** ~ mourir au front; **there was fighting on several** ~**s** on se battait sur plusieurs fronts; (*gen, Mil, Pol etc*) **on all** ~**s** partout, de tous côtés; **cold/warm** ~ front froid/ chaud; **popular** ~ front populaire; (*Pol, fig*) **we must present a common** ~ nous devons offrir un front commun, il faut faire front commun; *see* **home** *etc*.

c (*Brit: also* **sea** ~) (*beach*) bord *m* de mer, plage *f*; (*prom*) front *m* de mer. **along the** ~ (*on the beach*) en bord de mer; (*on the prom*) sur le front de mer; **a house on the** ~ une maison sur le front de mer.

d (*liter: forehead*) front *m*.

e *[spy, criminal]* couverture *f* (*fig*). (*fig*) **it's all just a** ~ **with him** tout ça n'est que façade chez lui.

2 adj a de devant, (en) avant, premier. **on the** ~ **cover** en couverture; ~ **door** *[house]* porte d'entrée *or* principale; *[car]* portière *f* avant; **in the** ~ **end of the train** en tête de *or* du train, à l'avant du train; ~ **garden** jardin *m* de devant; (*Mil*) ~ **line(s)** front *m*; (*fig*) **to be in the** ~ **line** être en première ligne, être aux avant-postes; (*Press*) **the** ~ **page** la première page, la une*; (*Press*) **on the** ~ **page** en première page, à la une* (*see also* **6**); *[machine]* **the** ~ **panel** le panneau de devant, la face avant; (*fig*) **in the** ~ **rank** parmi les premiers; ~ **room** pièce *f* donnant sur la rue, pièce de devant; (*lounge*) salon *m*; **in the** ~ **row** au premier rang; **to have a** ~ **seat** (*lit*) avoir une place (assise) au premier rang; (*fig*) être aux premières loges (*fig*); ~ **tooth** dent *f* de devant; ~ **wheel** roue *f* avant (*see also* **6**); (*fig*) **it's on my** ~ **burner*** je vais m'en occuper tout de suite; *see* **row[1]** *etc*.

b de face. ~ **view** vue *f* de face; (*Archit*) ~ **elevation** élévation frontale.

3 adv par devant. **to attack** ~ **and rear** attaquer par devant et par derrière; (*Mil*) **eyes** ~! fixe!

4 vi a **to** ~ **on to** donner sur; **the house** ~**s north** la maison fait face *or* est exposée au nord; **the windows** ~ **on to the street** les fenêtres donnent sur la rue.

b **to** ~ **for sb** servir de façade à qn.

5 vt a *building* donner une façade à. **house** ~**ed with stone** maison avec façade en pierre.

b *TV show* présenter.

6 comp ▸**the front bench** (*Brit Parl: people*) (*government*) les ministres *mpl*; (*opposition*) les membres *mpl* du cabinet fantôme ▸**the front benches** (*Brit Parl: place*) le banc des ministres et celui des membres du cabinet fantôme ▸**frontbencher** (*Brit Parl*) (*government*) ministre *m*; (*opposition*) membre *m* du cabinet fantôme ▸**front-end financing** financement *m* initial ▸**front-end payment** versement *m* initial ▸**front-end processor** (*Comput*) (processeur *m*) frontal *m* ▸**front-line** *troops, news* du front; *countries, areas* limitrophe d'un pays hostile ▸**front-line player** (*US Sport*) avant *m* ▸**front-loader, front-loading washing machine** lave-linge *m* à chargement frontal ▸**frontman** (*TV etc*) présentateur *m* ▸**front money** acompte *m*, avance *f* ▸**front organization: it's merely a front organization** cette organisation n'est qu'une façade *or* une couverture ▸**front-page news** gros titres, manchettes *fpl*; **it was front-page news for a month** cela a été à la une* (des journaux) pendant un mois ▸**front-rank** de premier plan ▸**front runner** (*Athletics*) coureur *m* de tête; (*fig*) **he is a front runner for the party leadership** il est un des favoris pour être leader du parti ▸**front-to-back engine** (*Aut*) moteur longitudinal ▸**front vowel** (*Ling*) voyelle antérieure ▸**front-wheel drive** (*Aut*) traction *f* avant ▸**front-wheel drive car** traction *f* avant.

frontage ['frʌntɪdʒ] n *[shop]* devanture *f*, façade *f*; *[house]* façade.

(*US*) ~ **road** contre-allée *f*.

frontal [ˈfrʌntl] 1 adj (*Mil*) *attack* de front; (*Anat, Med etc*) frontal; see **full 4.** 2 n (*Rel*) parement *m*.

frontier [ˈfrʌntɪəʳ] 1 n frontière *f*. (*US Hist*) **the** ~ *la limite des terres colonisées*. 2 comp *town, zone* frontière *inv*; *tribe* frontalier ►**frontier dispute** incident *m* de frontière ►**frontier economy** (*Econ*) économie *f* d'avant-poste ►**frontier post** = **frontier station** ►**frontiersman** (*US Hist*) habitant *m* de la "frontier" (*see* **1**) ►**frontier station** poste *m* frontière ►**frontier technology** (*fig*) technologie *f* de pointe.

frontispiece [ˈfrʌntɪspiːs] n frontispice *m*.

frontwards [ˈfrʌntwədz] adv en avant, vers l'avant.

frost [frɒst] 1 n gel *m*, gelée *f*; (*also* **hoar**~) givre *m*, gelée blanche. **late** ~**s** gelées tardives *or* printanières *or* de printemps; (*Brit*) **10 degrees of** ~ 10 degrés au-dessous de zéro; *see* **ground¹, jack** *etc*. 2 vt (*freeze*) *plants, vegetables* geler; (*US: ice*) *cake* glacer; *see also* **frosted**. 3 comp ►**frostbite** gelure *f*; **to get frostbite in one's hands** avoir les mains qui gèlent ►**frostbitten** *hands, feet* gelé; *rosebushes, vegetables* gelé, grillé par la gelée *or* le gel ►**frostbound** *ground* gelé ►**frost-free** *fridge* qui ne forme pas de givre ►**frostproof** incongelable.

►**frost over, frost up** vi *[window, path]* se givrer, se couvrir de givre.

frosted [ˈfrɒstɪd] adj *plants, vegetables* gelé; *windscreen* givré; *nail varnish* nacré; (*US*) *cake* recouvert de glaçage. ~ **glass** (*for window*) verre dépoli; (*for drink*) verre givré.

frosting [ˈfrɒstɪŋ] n (*US Culin: icing*) glace *f*, glaçage *m*.

frosty [ˈfrɒstɪ] adj *morning, weather etc* de gelée, glacial; *window* couvert de givre; (*fig*) *welcome, look* glacial, froid. **it is going to be** ~ **tonight** il va geler cette nuit.

froth [frɒθ] 1 n *[liquids in general]* écume *f*, mousse *f*; *[beer]* mousse; (*fig: frivolities*) futilités *fpl*, vent *m* (*fig*), paroles creuses. 2 vi écumer, mousser. **this detergent does not** ~ **(up)** ce détergent ne mousse pas; **the beer** ~**ed over the edge of the glass** la mousse débordait du verre (de bière); **to** ~ **at the mouth** *[dog etc]* avoir de l'écume à la gueule; *[angry person]* écumer de rage.

frothy [ˈfrɒθɪ] adj *water* mousseux, écumeux; *sea* écumeux; *beer* mousseux; (*fig*) *lace, nightdress* léger, vaporeux; *play, entertainment* léger, vide (*pej*), creux (*pej*).

frown [fraʊn] 1 n froncement *m* (de sourcils). **to give a** ~ froncer les sourcils; **he looked at her with a disapproving** ~ il l'a fixée avec un froncement de sourcils désapprobateur. 2 vi froncer les sourcils, se renfrogner. **to** ~ **at sb** regarder qn en fronçant les sourcils, regarder qn de travers; **to** ~ **at a child** faire les gros yeux à un enfant; **he** ~**ed at the news/the interruption** l'information/l'interruption lui a fait froncer les sourcils.

►**frown (up)on** vt fus (*fig*) *person, suggestion, idea* désapprouver.

frowning [ˈfraʊnɪŋ] adj *face, look* renfrogné, sombre; *forehead* plissé, orageux.

frowsty* [ˈfraʊstɪ] adj (*Brit*) = **frowsy a**.

frowsy, frowzy [ˈfraʊzɪ] adj a *room* qui sent le renfermé. b *person, clothes* sale, négligé, peu soigné.

froze [frəʊz] pret of **freeze**.

frozen [ˈfrəʊzn] 1 ptp of **freeze**. 2 adj a *pipes, river* gelé; (*) *person* gelé, glacé. **I am** ~ je suis gelé *or* glacé; **my hands are** ~ j'ai les mains gelées *or* glacées; **to be** ~ **stiff** être gelé jusqu'aux os; **it's** ~ **solid** c'est complètement gelé; ~ **food** aliments congelés; (*industrially* ~) aliments surgelés; (*in fridge*) ~ **food compartment** = **freezer b**; *see* **marrow**. b (*Econ*) *prices, wages* bloqué; *credit, assets* gelé, bloqué.

F.R.S. [ˌefˌɑːrˈes] (abbr of **Fellow of the Royal Society**) ≃ membre de l'Académie des sciences.

fructification [ˌfrʌktɪfɪˈkeɪʃən] n fructification *f*.

fructify [ˈfrʌktɪfaɪ] vi fructifier.

frugal [ˈfruːgəl] adj *person* économe (*with* de); *meal* frugal, simple.

frugality [fruːˈgælɪtɪ] n *[meal]* frugalité *f*; *[person]* frugalité; (*fig*) parcimonie *f*.

frugally [ˈfruːgəlɪ] adv *give out* parcimonieusement; *live* simplement, avec simplicité.

fruit [fruːt] 1 n a (*collective pl inv*) fruit *m*. **may I have some** ~? puis-je avoir un fruit?; **a piece of** ~ un fruit; **more** ~ **is eaten nowadays** on mange actuellement plus de fruits; ~ **is good for you** les fruits sont bons pour la santé; **several** ~**s have large stones** plusieurs espèces de fruits ont de gros noyaux; **the** ~**s of the earth** les fruits de la terre; (*lit, fig*) **to bear** ~ porter fruit; *[tree, bush]* **to be in** ~ porter des fruits; **it is the** ~ **of much hard work** c'est le fruit d'un long travail; **hullo, old** ~!†‡ salut, mon pote!‡; *see* **dried, forbidden** *etc*.
b (*US* ‡) pédé‡ *m*, tapette‡ *f*.
2 vi *[tree]* donner.
3 comp ►**fruit basket** corbeille *f* à fruits ►**fruit bowl** coupe *f* à fruits ►**fruit cake** cake *m* ►**fruit cocktail** macédoine *f* de fruits (en boîte) ►**fruit cup** (*drink*) boisson *f* aux fruits (*parfois faiblement alcoolisée*); (*US*) (coupe *f* de) fruits rafraîchis ►**fruit dish** (*for dessert*) (*small*) petite coupe *or* coupelle *f* à fruits; (*large*) coupe à fruits, compotier *m*; (*basket etc*) corbeille *f* à fruits ►**fruit drop** bonbon *m* au fruit ►**fruit farm** exploitation *or* entreprise fruitière ►**fruit farmer** arboriculteur *m* (fruitier) ►**fruit farming** arboriculture *f* (fruitière) ►**fruit fly** mouche *f* du vinaigre, drosophile *f* ►**fruit gum** (*Brit*) boule *f* de gomme (*bonbon*) ►**fruit juice** jus *m* de fruit ►**fruit knife** couteau *m* à fruits ►**fruit machine** (*Brit*) machine *f* à sous ►**fruit salad** salade *f* de fruits ►**fruit salts** (*Med*) sels purgatifs ►**fruit tree** arbre fruitier.

fruiterer [ˈfruːtərəʳ] n (*Brit*) marchand(e) *m(f)* de fruits, fruitier *m*, -ière *f*. **at the** ~**'s (shop)** chez le fruitier, à la fruiterie.

fruitful [ˈfruːtfʊl] adj *plant* fécond; *soil* fertile, fécond; *career, attempt* fructueux; *discussion, investigation* fructueux, utile.

fruitfully [ˈfruːtfəlɪ] adv (*fig*) fructueusement, avec profit.

fruitfulness [ˈfruːtfʊlnɪs] n *[soil]* fertilité *f*, fécondité *f*; *[plant]* fécondité; *[discussion etc]* caractère fructueux *or* profitable, profit *m*.

fruition [fruːˈɪʃən] n *[aims, plans, ideas]* réalisation *f*. **to bring to** ~ réaliser, concrétiser; **to come to** ~ se réaliser.

fruitless [ˈfruːtlɪs] adj *plant* stérile, infécond; *attempt, discussion, investigation* stérile, vain, sans résultat.

fruity [ˈfruːtɪ] adj a *flavour* fruité, de fruit. **it has a** ~ **taste** cela a un goût de fruit; **it has a** ~ **smell** cela sent le fruit. b *voice* bien timbré, posé. c (‡) *joke* corsé, raide*.

frump [frʌmp] n bonne femme mal fagotée *or* mal ficelée*. **old** ~ vieux tableau, vieille sorcière *or* rombière*.

frumpish [ˈfrʌmpɪʃ] adj, **frumpy** [ˈfrʌmpɪ] adj mal fagoté, mal ficelé*.

frustrate [frʌsˈtreɪt] vt *attempts, plans* contrecarrer, faire échouer; *plot* déjouer, faire échouer, faire avorter; *person* décevoir, frustrer. **he was** ~**d in his efforts to win** il a été frustré dans les tentatives qu'il a faites pour gagner; **to** ~ **sb's hopes** frustrer qn dans ses espoirs, tromper les espoirs de qn.

frustrated [frʌsˈtreɪtɪd] adj *person* (*disappointed*) frustré, déçu; (*sexually*) frustré; (*irked*) agacé. **he feels very** ~ **in his present job** il se sent très insatisfait dans son poste actuel; **in a** ~ **effort to speak to him** dans un vain effort pour lui parler.

frustrating [frʌsˈtreɪtɪŋ] adj irritant, déprimant. **it's very** ~ **having** *or* **to have no money** c'est vraiment pénible de ne pas avoir d'argent.

frustration [frʌsˈtreɪʃən] n a (*NonC*) frustration *f* (*also Psych*), déception *f*. b déception *f*. **many** ~**s** de nombreux déboires, de nombreuses déceptions.

fry¹ [fraɪ] collective n *[fish]* fretin *m*; *[frogs]* têtards *mpl*. **small** ~ (*unimportant people*) le menu fretin; (*children*) les gosses* *mfpl*, les mioches* *mfpl*, la marmaille*.

fry² [fraɪ] pret, ptp **fried** 1 vt *meat, fish etc* faire frire, frire. **to** ~ **eggs** faire des œufs sur le plat; **fried eggs** œufs sur le plat; **fried fish** poisson frit; **fried food is fattening** les fritures *fpl* font grossir; **fried potatoes** (*chips*) pommes (de terre) frites, frites *fpl*; (*sauté*) pommes (de terre) sautées; **fried rice** ≃ pilaf *m*; *see* **fish, French**. 2 vi frire. 3 n friture *f*. (*US*) ~**-pan** poêle *f* (à frire); (*Brit: dish*) **fry-up*** *saucisses, œufs, bacon etc frits ensemble*.

frying [ˈfraɪɪŋ] n: **there was a smell of** ~ il y avait une odeur de friture; ~ **pan** poêle *f* (à frire); (*fig*) **to jump out of the** ~ **pan into the fire** tomber de Charybde en Scylla; ~ **steak** steak *m* (à frire).

ft. abbr of **foot** *or* **feet**.

F.T. [efˈtiː] (abbr of **Financial Times**) *see* **financial**.

fuchsia [ˈfjuːʃə] n fuchsia *m*.

fuck** [fʌk] 1 n a (*act*) baisage** *m*. **she's a good** ~ elle baise bien**. b **charge me? Like** ~ **(you will)!** moi payer? mon cul!**; ~ **knows!** je n'en sais foutrement rien!‡ 2 comp ►**fuck-all**** (*Brit*) rien de rien; **I know fuck-all about it** je n'en sais foutrement rien‡ ►**fuckwit**** peigne-cul** *m*. 3 vt baiser**. ~!, ~ **it!** putain de merde**; ~ **me!** putain!‡, merde alors!‡; ~ **you!** va te faire foutre!**. 4 vi baiser**.

►**fuck about****, **fuck around**** 1 vi déconner‡. **to fuck about** *or* **around with sth** tripatouiller* qch. 2 vt sep emmerder‡.

►**fuck off**** vi foutre le camp‡.

►**fuck up**** vt sep *plans* foutre la merde dans ‡; *people* foutre dans la merde‡.

fucker** [ˈfʌkəʳ] n connard‡ *m*, connasse‡ *f*.

fucking** [ˈfʌkɪŋ] 1 adj: ~ **hell!** putain de bordel!**, putain de merde!**; ~ **bastard/bitch** espèce de salaud**/salope**; **this** ~ **machine** cette putain de machine‡; **this** ~ **phone** ce putain *or* ce bordel de téléphone ‡; **where's the** ~ **phonebook?** où est le foutu‡ annuaire?; **I haven't a** ~ **clue** je n'en sais foutrement‡ rien. 2 adv vachement‡. **it's** ~ **cold** il fait un putain de froid‡; **it's** ~ **brilliant/incredible!** putain, c'est génial!**/chié!**; **don't be** ~ **stupid!** fais pas le con‡; **a** ~ **awful film** un film complètement con‡; **you** ~ **well know what I mean!** mais putain** tu sais très bien de quoi je parle!; **I don't** ~ **know!** mais j'en sais rien nom de Dieu!**

fuddled [ˈfʌdld] adj *ideas* embrouillé, confus; *person* (*muddled*) désorienté, déconcerté; (*tipsy*) éméché, gris.

fuddy-duddy* [ˈfʌdɪˌdʌdɪ] 1 adj (*old-fashioned*) vieux jeu *inv*; (*fussy*) tatillon, maniaque. 2 n vieux machin‡, vieux (*f* vieille) schnock‡ *mf or* schnoque‡ *mf*.

fudge [fʌdʒ] 1 n a (*Culin*) caramel(s) *m(pl)*. **a piece of** ~ un caramel. b (*Press*) (*space for stop press*) emplacement *m* de la dernière heure; (*stop press news*) (insertion *f* de) dernière heure, dernières nouvelles. c (*dodging*) faux-fuyants *mpl*, échappatoires *fpl*.

2 excl (*) balivernes! 3 vt a (*fake up*) *story, excuse* monter; (*tamper with*) *accounts, figures, results* truquer. b (*dodge*) *question, issue* esquiver, tourner. 4 vi (*dodge issue*) esquiver le problème.

fuel [fjʊəl] 1 n (*NonC: also Aviat, Space*) combustible *m*; (*for car engine*) carburant *m*; (*specifically coal*) charbon *m*; (*wood*) bois *m*. **what kind of ~ do you use in your central heating?** quel combustible utilisez-vous dans votre chauffage central?; **it's no longer a cheap ~** ce n'est plus une forme *or* une source d'énergie économique; (*fig*) **to add ~ to the flames** *or* **fire** jeter de l'huile sur le feu; **the statistics gave him ~ for further attacks on the government** les statistiques sont venues alimenter ses attaques *or* lui ont fourni des munitions pour continuer ses attaques contre le gouvernement; *see* **aviation, diesel, solid** *etc*.

2 vt *stove, furnace etc* alimenter (en combustible); *ships, aircraft etc* ravitailler en combustible *or* carburant.

3 vi *[ship, engine, aircraft]* s'approvisionner *or* se ravitailler en combustible *or* en carburant. (*Aviat etc*) a **~ling stop** une escale technique.

4 comp *bill, costs* de chauffage ►**fuel-efficient** économique (*qui ne consomme pas beaucoup*) ►**fuel injection** injection *f* (de carburant); **fuel injection engine** moteur *m* à injection ►**fuel injector** injecteur *m* (de carburant) ►**fuel oil** mazout *m*, fuel *m* ►**fuel pump** pompe *f* d'alimentation ►**fuel rod** crayon *m* combustible ►**fuel saving** n économies *fpl* de carburant (*or* de combustible *etc*) ►**fuel-saving** adj qui réduit la consommation de carburant (*or* de combustible *etc*) ►**fuel-saving device** (*Aut*) économiseur *m* de carburant ►**fuel tank** réservoir *m* à carburant; *[ship]* soute *f* à mazout.

fug* [fʌg] n (*esp Brit*) forte odeur de renfermé. **what a ~!** (ce que) ça pue le renfermé!

fuggy* ['fʌgɪ] adj (*esp Brit*) *room* qui sent le renfermé, mal aéré; *atmosphere* confiné.

fugitive ['fju:dʒɪtɪv] 1 n fugitif *m*, -ive *f*, fuyard(e) *m(f)*; (*refugee*) refugié(e) *m(f)*. **he was a ~ from justice** il fuyait la justice. 2 adj *thought, impression* fugitif; (*liter*) *happiness* fugace, éphémère; (*running away*) fugitif.

fugue [fju:g] n (*Mus, Psych*) fugue *f*.

fulcrum ['fʌlkrəm] n, pl **~s** *or* **fulcra** ['fʌlkrə] pivot *m*, point *m* d'appui (*de levier*).

fulfil, (*US*) **fulfill** [fʊl'fɪl] vt *task, prophecy* accomplir, réaliser; *order* exécuter; *condition, function* remplir; *plan, ambition* réaliser; *norm* obéir à, répondre à; *desire* satisfaire, répondre à; *promise* tenir; *one's duties* s'acquitter de, remplir; *contract* remplir, respecter. **all my prayers have been ~led** toutes mes prières ont été exaucées; **he ~s all my hopes** il répond à *or* satisfait toutes mes espérances, il comble tous mes espoirs; **to feel** *or* **be ~led** se sentir profondément satisfait, se réaliser (dans la vie).

fulfilling [fʊl'fɪlɪŋ] adj *work etc* profondément satisfaisant.

fulfilment, (*US*) **fulfillment** [fʊl'fɪlmənt] n *[duty, desire]* accomplissement *m*; *[prayer, wish]* exaucement *m*; *[conditions, plans]* réalisation *f*, exécution *f*; (*satisfied feeling*) (sentiment *m* de) contentement *m*. **sense of ~** sentiment de contentement *or* de complétude.

full [fʊl] 1 adj a (*filled*) *container, stomach* plein, rempli (*of* de); *room, hall, theatre* comble, plein; *hotel, bus, train* complet (*f* -ète). **pockets ~ of money** des poches pleines d'argent; **the house was ~ of people** la maison était pleine de monde; **~ to overflowing** plein à déborder; **he's had a ~ life** il a eu une vie (bien) remplie; **I have a ~ day ahead of me** j'ai une journée chargée devant moi; **look ~ of hate** regard plein *or* chargé de haine; **he's ~ of good ideas** il est plein de *or* il déborde de bonnes idées; **he's ~ of hope** il est rempli *or* plein d'espoir; (*liter*) **to die ~ of years** mourir chargé d'ans (*liter*); **his heart was ~** il avait le cœur gros; (*Theat*) **"house ~"** "complet"; (*Theat*) **to play to a ~ house** jouer à bureaux fermés; **we are ~ (up) for July** nous sommes complets pour juillet; **you'll work better on a ~ stomach** tu travailleras mieux après avoir mangé *or* le ventre plein; (*not hungry*) **I am ~ (up)!*** je n'en peux plus!, j'ai trop mangé!; **~ of life** qui déborde d'entrain; **~ of oneself** imbu de soi-même, plein de soi; **~ of one's own importance** imbu *or* pénétré de sa propre importance; **she was/the papers were ~ of the murder** elle ne parlait/les journaux ne parlaient que du meurtre; *see* **house** *etc*.

b (*maximum, complete*) **the ~ particulars** tous les détails; **ask for ~ information** demandez des renseignements complets; **we must have ~er information** il nous faut des informations plus complètes *or* un complément d'information, il nous faut un plus ample informé; **until ~er information is available** jusqu'à plus ample informé; **~ and frank discussions** un franc échange de vues; **I waited 2 ~ hours** j'ai attendu 2 bonnes heures *or* 2 grandes heures *or* pas moins de 2 heures; **a ~ 10 kilometres** 10 bons kilomètres, pas moins de 10 kilomètres; (*Mil*) **a ~ colonel** un colonel; **a ~ general** un général d'armée, ≃ un général à cinq étoiles; (*Univ, esp US*) **~ professor** professeur *m* (titulaire d'une chaire); (*Comput*) **~ adder** plein additionneur; **to go (at) ~ blast*** *[car etc]* aller à toute pompe* *or* à toute bitture*; *[radio, television]* marcher à pleins tubes*; **a radio on at ~ blast** une radio (marchant) à pleins tubes*; **roses in ~ bloom** roses épanouies; (*fig*) **the wheel has come ~ circle** la boucle est bouclée; (*Hunting*) **the pack was in ~ cry** toute la meute donnait de la voix; **the crowd was in ~ cry after the thief** la foule poursuivait le voleur en criant; **~ dress** (*Mil etc*) grande tenue; (*evening dress*) tenue *f* de soirée (*see also* **4**); **~ employment** plein emploi; **to pay ~ price for sth** acheter qch au prix fort; **to pay ~ fare** *[child]* payer place entière; (*gen*) payer plein tarif; **in ~ flight** en plein vol; **to fall ~ length** tomber de tout son long (*see also* **4**); (*Scol*) **he got ~ marks** il a eu dix sur dix (*or* vingt sur vingt *etc*); (*fig*) **he deserves ~ marks** il mérite vingt sur vingt; **~ marks to him for achieving so much** on ne peut que le féliciter de tout ce qu'il a accompli; **~ member** membre *m* à part entière; **~ moon** pleine lune; **~ name** nom et prénom(s); (*Mus*) **~ score** grande partition; **at ~ speed** à toute vitesse; **~ speed ahead**, (*Naut*) **~ steam ahead!** en avant toute!; (*Brit Gram*) **~ stop** point *m*; (*fig*) **I'm not going, ~ stop!*** je n'y vais pas, un point c'est tout!; **working at the factory came to a ~ stop** ça a été l'arrêt complet du travail à l'usine; **battalion at ~ strength** bataillon *m* au (grand) complet; **party in ~ swing** soirée qui bat son plein; **~ time** *see* **4**; **in ~ uniform** en grande tenue; (*Ling*) **~ word** mot plein; *see also* **4**, *and* **coverage, tilt** *etc*.

c (*rounded; ample*) *lips* charnu; *face* plein, rond, joufflu; *figure* replet (*f* -ète), rondelet; *skirt etc* large, ample; (*Naut*) *sails* plein, gonflé. **clothes for the ~er figure** des vêtements pour fortes tailles.

2 adv: **~ well** fort bien, parfaitement; **to hit sb ~ in the face** frapper qn en plein visage; **to look sb ~ in the face** regarder qn droit dans les yeux; **to go ~ out** aller à toute vitesse, filer à toute allure; **to turn the volume/sound up ~** mettre le volume/le son à fond.

3 n: **to write one's name in ~** écrire son nom en toutes lettres; **to publish a letter in ~** publier une lettre intégralement; **text in ~** texte intégral; **he paid in ~** il a tout payé; **to the ~** complètement, tout à fait; *see* **life**.

4 comp ►**fullback** (*Sport*) arrière *m* ►**full-blooded** (*vigorous*) *person* vigoureux, robuste; (*of unmixed race*) de race pure ►**full-blown** *flower* épanoui; (*fig*) **he's a full-blown doctor/architect** il est médecin/architecte diplômé ►**full-bodied** *wine* qui a du corps ►**full-cream milk** lait *m* entier ►**full-dress** adj (*for n see* **1b**) *clothes* de cérémonie; (*Parl*) **full-dress debate** débat *m* dans les règles; **they had a full-dress discussion on what to do** ils ont eu un débat en règle pour décider de ce qu'il fallait faire ►**full-face** *photograph* de face; *helmet* intégral ►**full-fledged** (*US*) = **fully-fledged** (*see* **fully 2**) ►**full frontal** n nu *m* intégral de face ►**full-frontal** adj *photograph* d'un nu intégral de face; *view* de face; **full-frontal assault** *or* **attack** attaque *f* de front ►**full-grown** *child* grand, qui est parvenu au terme de sa croissance; *animal, man, woman* adulte ►**full house** (*Cards*) full *m* ►**full-length** *portrait* en pied; *film* (de) long métrage ►**full-page** *advert, article* pleine page ►**full-scale** *see* **full-scale** ►**full-sized** *model, drawing* grandeur nature *inv* ►**full-strength** *cigarettes* très fort; *solution* non dilué ►**full-throated** *laugh, shout* retentissant ►**full time** adv *work* à temps plein, à plein temps ◊ n (*Sport*) fin *f* de match ►**full-time** adj *employment* à plein temps; **she's a full-time secretary** elle est secrétaire à plein temps; **it's a full-time job looking after those children*** il faut s'occuper de ces enfants 24 heures sur 24; (*Sport*) **full-time score** score final.

fuller ['fʊləʳ] n: **~'s earth** terre savonneuse.

ful(l)ness ['fʊlnɪs] n *[details etc]* abondance *f*; *[voice, sound, garment]* ampleur *f*. **out of the ~ of his heart** le cœur débordant de joie (*or* de chagrin *etc*); **out of the ~ of his sorrow** le cœur débordant de chagrin; **in the ~ of time** (*eventually*) avec le temps; (*at predestined time*) en temps et lieu.

full-scale ['fʊl'skeɪl] adj a *drawing, replica* grandeur nature *inv*. b (*fig*) *operation, retreat* de grande envergure. **to mount a ~ search for** mettre sur pied des recherches de grande envergure pour trouver; **~ fighting** une *or* la bataille rangée; **the factory starts ~ operations next month** l'usine va commencer à marcher à plein régime le mois prochain.

fully ['fʊlɪ] 1 adv a (*completely*) *use, load* au maximum, à plein; *justify* complètement; *understand* très bien; *convinced, satisfied* entièrement, complètement; *see* **laden**.

b (*at least*) au moins, bien, largement. **~ 600** 600 au moins; **~ half** une bonne moitié, la moitié au moins; **it is ~ 2 hours since he went out** il y a au moins *or* bien *or* largement 2 heures qu'il est sorti.

2 comp ►**fully-fashioned** (entièrement) diminué ►**fully-fitted kitchen** cuisine *f* tout équipée ►**fully-fledged**: **fully-fledged bird** oiseau *m* qui a toutes ses plumes; (*Brit*) **he's now a fully-fledged doctor/architect** il est maintenant médecin/architecte diplômé; (*Brit*) **a fully-fledged British citizen** un citoyen britannique à part entière.

fulmar ['fʊlməʳ] n fulmar *m*.

fulminate ['fʌlmɪneɪt] 1 vi fulminer, pester (*against* contre). 2 n: **~ of mercury** fulminate *m* de mercure.

fulsome ['fʊlsəm] adj (*pej*) *praise* excessif, exagéré; *manner, tone, welcome* plein d'effusions. **~ compliments** (*or* **thanks** *or* **praises** *etc*) effusions *fpl*.

fumarole ['fju:mə,rəʊl] n fumerolle *f*.

fumble ['fʌmbl] 1 vi (*also* **~ about, ~ around**) (*in the dark*) tâtonner; (*in one's pockets*) fouiller. **to ~ (about) for sth in the dark** chercher qch à tâtons dans l'obscurité; **to ~ (about) for sth in a pocket/a drawer**

fouiller dans une poche/un tiroir pour trouver qch; **to ~ with sth** manier *or* tripoter qch (maladroitement); **to ~ for words** chercher ses mots.

2 vt *object* manier gauchement *or* maladroitement. **to ~ an answer/a situation** répondre/agir avec maladresse; (*Sport*) **to ~ the ball** mal attraper la balle.

fume [fju:m] 1 vi a *[liquids, gases]* exhaler des vapeurs, fumer. b (*: *be furious*) rager. **he is fuming** il est furibard* *or* furax* *inv*.

2 n: **~s** (*gen*) exhalaisons *fpl*, émanations *fpl*; **factory ~s** fumées *fpl* d'usine; **petrol ~s** vapeurs *fpl* d'essence.

fumigate ['fju:mɪgeɪt] vt désinfecter par fumigation, fumiger (*frm*).

fun [fʌn] 1 n (*NonC*) (*amusement*) amusement *m*; (*joke*) plaisanterie *f*. **he had great** *or* **good ~** il s'est bien *or* beaucoup amusé; **have ~!*** amuse-toi bien!; **he's great** *or* **good ~** il est très drôle, on s'amuse bien avec lui; **the book is great** *or* **good ~** le livre est très amusant; **sailing is good ~** on s'amuse bien en faisant de la voile; **what ~!** ce que c'est drôle! *or* amusant!; **for ~, in ~** pour rire, par plaisanterie, en plaisantant; **I don't see the ~ of it** je ne trouve pas cela drôle; **I only did it for the ~ of it** je ne l'ai fait que pour m'amuser; **I'm not doing this for the ~ of it** je ne fais pas cela pour m'amuser *or* pour mon plaisir; **it's not much ~ for us** ce n'est pas très amusant, cela ne nous amuse pas beaucoup; **it's only his ~** il fait cela pour rire, c'est tout; **to spoil the ~, to spoil his** (*or* **our** *etc*) **~** *[person]* jouer les trouble-fête *or* les rabat-joie; *[event, weather]* gâter *or* gâcher son (*or* notre *etc*) amusement; **the children had ~ and games at the picnic** les enfants se sont follement amusés pendant le pique-nique; (*iro*) **there'll be ~ and games over this decision*** cette décision va faire du potin* *or* du boucan*; (*euph*) **he's having ~ and games with the au pair girl*** il ne s'ennuie pas avec la jeune fille au pair (*euph*); (*difficulty*) **she's been having ~ and games with the washing machine*** la machine à laver lui en a fait voir de toutes les couleurs*; (*difficulty*) **we had a bit of ~ getting the car started*** pour faire partir la voiture ça n'a pas été de la rigolade* *or* ça n'a pas été une partie de plaisir *or* on a rigolé* cinq minutes; **to make ~ of** *or* **poke ~ at sb/sth** rire *or* se moquer de qn/qch; **did he go? — like ~ he did!**‡ y est-il allé? — je t'en fiche!* *or* tu rigoles!* *or* tu parles!*

2 adj (‡) marrant*, rigolo*, amusant. **it's a ~ thing to do** c'est marrant à faire*; **she's a really ~ person** elle est vraiment marrante* *or* rigolote*.

3 comp ►**fun fair** fête *f* (foraine) ►**fun fur** n similifourrure *f* ◊ adj en similifourrure ►**fun-loving** aimant s'amuser, aimant les plaisirs ►**fun run** course *f* de fond pour amateurs.

function ['fʌŋkʃən] 1 n a *[heart, tool etc]* fonction *f*; *[person]* fonction, charge *f*. **in his ~ as judge** en sa qualité de juge; **it is not part of my ~ to do that** cela n'entre pas dans mes fonctions, il ne m'appartient pas de faire cela. b (*meeting*) réunion *f*; (*reception*) réception *f*; (*official ceremony*) cérémonie publique. c (*Math, Ling*) fonction *f*. (*fig: depend on*) **to be a ~ of sth** être en fonction de qch.

2 comp ►**function key** (*Comput*) touche *f* de fonction ►**function word** (*Ling*) mot fonctionnel. 3 vi fonctionner, marcher. *[person, thing]* **to ~ as** faire fonction de, servir de, jouer le rôle de.

functional ['fʌŋkʃnəl] adj fonctionnel.

functionary ['fʌŋkʃənərɪ] n employé(e) *m(f)* (*d'une administration*); (*in civil service, local government*) fonctionnaire *mf*.

fund [fʌnd] 1 n a (*Fin*) caisse *f*, fonds *m*. **to start a ~** lancer une souscription; **~s** fonds *mpl*; **to be in ~s** être en fonds; **the public ~s** les fonds publics; (*Banking*) **no ~s** défaut *m* de provision; **he hasn't the ~s to buy a house** il n'a pas assez de capitaux pour acheter une maison; *see* **raise, secret**.

b (*supply*) *[humour, good sense etc]* fond *m*. **a ~ of knowledge** un trésor de connaissances; **he has a ~ of stories** il connaît des quantités d'histoires.

2 vt *debt* consolider; *project* financer, assurer le financement de; *firm* doter en capital; *account* alimenter.

3 comp ►**fundholder** (*gen*) rentier *m*, -ière *f*; *[public funds]* détenteur *m*, -trice *f* de fonds publics ►**fund manager** gestionnaire *mf* de fonds *or* de portefeuille ►**fund-raiser** (*person*) collecteur *m*, -trice *f* de fonds; (*dinner/sale of work etc*) dîner *m*/vente *f* de charité *etc* organisé(e) pour collecter des fonds ►**fund-raising** n collecte *f* de fonds ◊ adj *dinner, event* organisé pour collecter des fonds.

fundamental [ˌfʌndə'mentl] 1 adj *rule, question* fondamental, de base; *quality* fondamental, essentiel; (*Mus*) fondamental. **it is ~ to our understanding of the problem** c'est fondamental *or* essentiel si nous voulons comprendre le problème. 2 n (*often pl*) les principes essentiels *or* de base; (*Mus*) fondamental *m*. **when you get down to (the) ~s** quand on en vient à l'essentiel.

fundamentalism [ˌfʌndə'mentəlɪzəm] n (*Rel*) fondamentalisme *m*; (*Moslem*) intégrisme *m*.

fundamentalist [ˌfʌndə'mentəlɪst] adj, n (*Rel*) fondamentaliste (*mf*); (*Moslem*) intégriste (*mf*).

fundamentally [ˌfʌndə'mentəlɪ] adv fondamentalement, essentiellement. **there is something ~ wrong in what he says** il y a quelque chose de radicalement *or* fondamentalement faux dans ce qu'il dit; **he is ~ good** il a un bon fond.

funding ['fʌndɪŋ] n financement *m*.

fundus ['fʌndəs] n, pl **fundi** ['fʌndaɪ] fond *m* (de l'utérus).

funeral ['fju:nərəl] 1 n enterrement *m*, obsèques *fpl* (*frm*); (*grander*) funérailles *fpl*; (*in announcements*) obsèques. **my uncle's ~** l'enterrement de mon oncle; **Churchill's ~** les funérailles de Churchill; **that's his ~ if he wants to do it*** s'il veut le faire c'est tant pis pour lui; **that's your ~!*** tant pis pour toi!, tu te débrouilles!*; *see* **state**.

2 comp ►**funeral director** entrepreneur *m* de pompes funèbres ►**funeral home** (*US*) = **funeral parlour** ►**funeral march** marche *f* funèbre ►**funeral oration** oraison *f* funèbre ►**funeral parlour** dépôt *m* mortuaire ►**funeral procession** (*on foot*) cortège *m* funèbre; (*in car*) convoi *m* mortuaire ►**funeral pyre** bûcher *m* (funéraire) ►**funeral service** service *m or* cérémonie *f* funèbre.

funereal [fju:'nɪərɪəl] adj *expression* funèbre, lugubre; *voice* sépulcral, lugubre.

fungal ['fʌŋgəl] adj *infection* fongique.

fungi ['fʌŋgaɪ] npl of **fungus**.

fungible ['fʌndʒɪbəl] adj fongible.

fungicide ['fʌndʒɪsaɪd] n fongicide. *m*.

fungoid ['fʌŋgɔɪd] adj, **fungous** ['fʌŋgəs] adj (*Med*) fongueux; (*Bot*) cryptogamique.

fungus ['fʌŋgəs] n, pl **fungi** *or* **~es** (*Bot*) (*generic term: mushrooms etc*) champignon *m*; (*mould*) moisissure *f*; (*Med*) fongus *m*; (‡ *hum: whiskers etc*) excroissance *f* (*hum*).

funicular [fju:'nɪkjʊlə^r] 1 adj funiculaire. 2 n (*also* **~ railway**) funiculaire *m*.

funk[1] [fʌŋk] n (*Mus*) **~ (music)** funk *m*.

funk[2]* [fʌŋk] 1 n (*Brit* †) **to be in a (blue) ~** (*frightened*) avoir la trouille‡.

2 vt: **he ~ed (doing) it** il s'est dégonflé*, il a cané*; **he ~ed his exams** il s'est dégonflé* *or* il a cané* et il n'a pas passé ses examens.

funky[1] ['fʌŋkɪ] adj (*Mus*) funky *inv*.

funky[2]* ['fʌŋkɪ] adj a (*US*) (*excellent*) super* *inv*, génial*; (*fashionable*) à la page, qui a le look*.

b (*Brit* †: *fearful*) trouillard‡.

c (*US: smelly*) qui cocotte‡, qui pue.

funnel ['fʌnl] 1 n a (*for pouring through*) entonnoir *m*. b (*Brit*) *[ship, engine etc]* cheminée *f*. **a two-~led liner** un paquebot à deux cheminées. 2 vt (faire) passer dans un entonnoir; (*fig*) canaliser.

funnily ['fʌnɪlɪ] adv a (*amusingly*) drôlement, comiquement. b (*strangely*) curieusement, bizarrement. **~ enough ...** chose curieuse ..., c'est drôle ... .

funny ['fʌnɪ] 1 adj a (*comic*) drôle, amusant, comique. **~ story** histoire *f* drôle; **he was always trying to be ~** il cherchait toujours à faire de l'esprit; **don't try anything ~!*** ne fais pas le malin!; **don't (try to) be ~!*** ce n'est pas le moment de plaisanter *or* de faire de l'esprit!; **don't get ~ with me!*** un peu de respect!, ne t'amuse pas à ça avec moi!; **it's not ~** ça n'a rien de drôle.

b (*strange*) curieux, bizarre, drôle. **a ~ idea** une drôle d'idée; **the ~ thing about it is ...** ce qu'il y a de drôle *or* de bizarre *or* de curieux c'est ...; **he is ~ that way*** il est comme ça*; **the meat tastes ~** la viande a un drôle de goût; **I find it ~ that he should want to see her** je trouve (cela) bizarre qu'il veuille la voir; **there's something ~ about this affair** il y a quelque chose de bizarre *or* qui cloche* dans cette affaire; **there's something ~** *or* **some ~ business* going on** il se passe quelque chose de louche; **I felt ~*** je me suis senti tout chose*; **it gave me a ~ feeling** cela m'a fait tout drôle; **~! I thought he'd left** c'est drôle *or* c'est curieux, je pensais qu'il était parti; **~-peculiar or ~-haha?*** qu'est ce que tu veux dire par drôle?, drôle bizarre ou drôle marrant?*; (*mental hospital*) **~ farm**‡ maison *f* de fous; **~ money*** des sommes astronomiques.

c **~ bone*** petit juif*.

2 n (*US Press: gen pl*) **the funnies**‡ les bandes dessinées.

fur [fɜ:^r] 1 n a *[animal]* poil *m*, pelage *m*, fourrure *f*. (*fig*) **it will make the ~ fly** *or* **set the ~ flying** cela va faire du grabuge*; **the ~ was flying** ça bardait‡, il y avait du grabuge*, les plumes volaient.

b (*animal skins: often pl*) fourrure(s) *f(pl)*. **she was dressed in ~s** elle portait des fourrures *or* de la fourrure.

c (*in kettle etc*) incrustation *f*, (dépôt *m* de) tartre *m*. (*Med*) **to have ~ on one's tongue** avoir la langue pâteuse *or* chargée.

2 comp *jacket etc* de fourrure ►**fur coat** manteau *m* de fourrure ►**fur trade** industrie *f* de la fourrure.

3 vi: **to ~ (up)** *[kettle, boiler]* s'entartrer, s'incruster; *[tongue]* se charger; **his tongue is ~red** sa langue est chargée *or* pâteuse.

furbelow† ['fɜ:bɪləʊ] n falbala *m*. **(frills and) ~s** fanfreluches *fpl*, falbalas.

furbish ['fɜ:bɪʃ] vt (*polish*) fourbir, astiquer, briquer; (*smarten*) remettre à neuf, retaper*; (*revise*) revoir, repasser*.

furious ['fjʊərɪəs] adj *person* furieux (*with sb* contre qn, *at having done* d'avoir fait); *storm, sea* déchaîné; *struggle* acharné; *speed* fou (*f* folle). **to get ~** se mettre en rage (*with sb* contre qn); **the fun was fast**

and ~ la fête battait son plein.

furiously ['fjʊərɪəslɪ] **adv** (*violently, angrily*) furieusement; *fight* avec acharnement; *drive* à une allure folle; *ride a horse* à bride abattue.

furl [fɜːl] **vt** (*Naut*) *sail* ferler, serrer; *umbrella, flag* rouler. **the flags are ~ed** les drapeaux sont en berne.

furlong ['fɜːlɒŋ] **n** furlong *m* (*201,17 mètres*).

furlough ['fɜːləʊ] **n** (*esp Admin, Mil*) permission *f*, congé *m*. **on ~** en permission.

furnace ['fɜːnɪs] **n** (*Ind etc*) fourneau *m*, four *m*; (*for central heating etc*) chaudière *f*. **this room is like a ~** cette pièce est une vraie fournaise; **~ room** chaufferie *f*.

furnish ['fɜːnɪʃ] **vt** **a** *house* meubler (*with* de). (*Brit*) **~ed flat**, (*US*) **~ed apartment** appartement meublé; **in ~ed rooms** en meublé. **b** (*supply*) *object, information, excuse, reason* fournir, donner. **to ~ sb with sth** pourvoir *or* munir qn de qch; **to ~ an army with provisions** ravitailler une armée.

furnishing ['fɜːnɪʃɪŋ] **n**: **~s** mobilier *m*, ameublement *m*; **house sold with ~s and fittings** maison vendue avec objets mobiliers divers; **~ fabrics** tissus *mpl* d'ameublement.

furniture ['fɜːnɪtʃəʳ] **1** **n** (*NonC*) meubles *mpl*, mobilier *m*, ameublement *m*. **a piece of ~** un meuble; **I must buy some ~** il faut que j'achète des meubles; **the ~ was very old** les meubles étaient très vieux, le mobilier était très vieux; **the ~ was scanty** l'ameublement était insuffisant, c'était à peine meublé; **one settee and three chairs were all the ~** un sofa et trois chaises constituaient tout l'ameublement *or* le mobilier; **he treats her as part of the ~** il la traite comme si elle faisait partie du décor; **dining-room ~** des meubles *or* du mobilier de salle à manger; **Empire ~** mobilier *or* meubles Empire.

2 **comp** ▸**furniture depot** garde-meubles *m inv* ▸**furniture mover** (*US*) déménageur *m* ▸**furniture polish** encaustique *f* ▸**furniture remover** déménageur *m* ▸**furniture shop** magasin *m* d'ameublement *or* de meubles ▸**furniture store** = **furniture depot** *or* **furniture shop** ▸**furniture van** camion *m* de déménagement.

furore [fjʊə'rɔːrɪ] **n**, (*US*) **furor** [fjʊ'rɔːʳ] **n** (*protests*) scandale *m*; (*enthusiasm*) débordement *m* d'enthousiasme.

furrier ['fʌrɪəʳ] **n** fourreur *m*.

furrow ['fʌrəʊ] **1** **n** (*Agr*) sillon *m*; (*in garden etc*) rayon *m*; (*on brow*) ride *f*, ligne *f*, sillon; (*liter: on sea*) sillage *m*; *see* **ridge**. **2** **vt** *earth* sillonner, labourer; *face, brow* rider.

furry ['fɜːrɪ] **adj** **a** *animal* à poil; *toy* en peluche; (*fig*) *kettle* entartré; *tongue* chargé, pâteux.

b (*US* ‡: *frightening*) effrayant.

further ['fɜːðəʳ] **compar of far** **1** **adv** **a** = **farther 1**.

b (*more*) davantage, plus. **he questioned us no ~** il ne nous a pas interrogés davantage, il ne nous a pas posé d'autres questions; **without troubling any ~** sans se tracasser davantage, sans plus se tracasser; **I got no ~ with him** je ne suis arrivé à rien de plus avec lui; **unless I hear any ~** à moins qu'on ne me prévienne du contraire, sauf avis contraire; **until you hear ~** jusqu'à nouvel avis; **we heard nothing ~ from him** nous n'avons plus rien reçu de lui, nous n'avons pas eu d'autres nouvelles de lui; (*fig*) **this mustn't go any ~** il ne faut pas que cela aille plus loin; **I think we should take this matter ~** je pense que nous devrions poursuivre cette affaire *or* que nous ne devrions pas nous en tenir là; **and ~ I believe** ... et de plus je crois ...; **he said that he would do it and ~ that he WANTED to** il a dit qu'il le ferait et en outre *or* et en plus *or* ajoutant qu'il avait envie de le faire; (*Comm*) **~ to your letter** par suite à votre lettre.

2 **adj** **a** = **farther 2**.

b (*additional*) nouveau (*f* nouvelle), additionnel, supplémentaire. **~ education** enseignement *m* postscolaire (*see also* **college**); **until ~ notice** jusqu'à nouvel ordre; (*Jur*) **to refer** *or* **remand a case for ~ inquiry** renvoyer une cause pour complément d'information *or* d'instruction; **without ~ delay** sans autre délai, sans plus attendre; **without ~ ado** sans plus de cérémonie; **upon ~ consideration** après plus ample réflexion, à la réflexion; **awaiting ~ details** en attendant de plus amples détails; **one or two ~ details** un ou deux autres points; (*Comm*) **please send me ~ details of** ... veuillez m'envoyer de plus amples renseignements sur *or* concernant ...; **there are one or two ~ things I must say** il y a encore une ou deux remarques à faire.

3 **vt** *one's interests, a cause* servir, avancer, favoriser.

4 **comp** ▸**furthermore** en outre, de plus, qui plus est, par ailleurs ▸**furthermost** le plus éloigné, le plus reculé, le plus lointain.

furtherance ['fɜːðərəns] **n** avancement *m*. **in ~ of sth** pour avancer *or* servir qch.

furthest ['fɜːðɪst] = **farthest**.

furtive ['fɜːtɪv] **adj** *action, behaviour, look* furtif; *person* sournois.

furtively ['fɜːtɪvlɪ] **adv** furtivement, à la dérobée.

fury ['fjʊərɪ] **n** [*person*] fureur *f*, furie *f*; [*storm, wind*] fureur, violence *f*; [*struggle*] acharnement *m*. **to be in a ~** être en furie, être dans une rage *or* colère folle; **to put sb into a ~** mettre qn dans une colère folle; **to fly into a ~** entrer en fureur *or* en furie, se mettre dans une rage folle, faire une colère terrible; **she's a little ~** c'est une petite furie *or* harpie; (*Myth*) **the Furies** les Furies *fpl*, les Euménides *fpl*; **to work like ~*** travailler d'arrache-pied *or* comme un nègre; **to run like ~*** courir comme un dératé.

furze [fɜːz] **n** (*NonC*) ajoncs *mpl*.

fuse, (*US*) **fuze** [fjuːz] **1** **vt** **a** (*unite*) *metal* fondre, mettre en fusion; (*fig*) fusionner, unifier, amalgamer.

b (*Brit Elec*) faire sauter. **to ~ the television** *or* **the iron** *or* **the lights** *etc* faire sauter les plombs.

c *bomb* amorcer.

2 **vi** **a** [*metals*] fondre; (*fig: also* **~ together**) s'unifier, fusionner.

b (*Brit Elec*) **the television** (*or* **the lights** *etc*) **~d** les plombs ont sauté.

3 **n** **a** (*Elec: wire*) plomb *m*, fusible *m*. **to blow a ~** faire sauter un plomb *or* un fusible; **there's been a ~ somewhere** il y a un plomb de sauté quelque part; (*fig*) **to have a short ~*** se mettre facilement en rogne*, être soupe au lait.

b [*bomb etc*] amorce *f*, détonateur *m*, fusée(-détonateur) *f*; (*Min*) cordeau *m*.

4 **comp** ▸**fuse box** (*gen*) boîte *f* à fusibles, coupe-circuit *m inv*; (*Aut*) porte-fusibles *m* ▸**fuse wire** fusible *m*.

fused [fjuːzd] **adj** (*Elec*) avec fusible incorporé. **~ plug** prise *f* avec fusible incorporé.

fusel ['fjuːzl] **n**: **~ oil** fusel *m*, huile *f* de fusel.

fuselage ['fjuːzəlɑːʒ] **n** fuselage *m*.

fusible ['fjuːzɪbl] **adj**: **~ metal** *or* **alloy** alliage *m* fusible.

fusilier [ˌfjuːzɪ'lɪəʳ] **n** (*Brit*) fusilier *m*.

fusillade [ˌfjuːzɪ'leɪd] **n** fusillade *f*.

fusion ['fjuːʒən] **n** (*Metal*) fonte *f*, fusion *f*; (*Phys*) fusion; (*Mus*) fusion; [*parties, races*] fusion, fusionnement *m*.

fuss [fʌs] **1** **n** (*NonC*) (*excitement*) tapage *m*, agitation *f*; (*activity*) façons *fpl*, embarras *m*, cérémonie *f*. **a lot of ~ about very little** beaucoup d'agitation *or* de bruit pour pas grand-chose; **to make a ~**, **to kick up a ~*** faire un tas d'histoires*; **to make a ~ about** *or* **over sth** faire des histoires pour qch, faire tout un plat de qch*; **you were quite right to make a ~** vous avez eu tout à fait raison de protester *or* de ne pas laisser passer ça; **what a ~ just to get a passport!** que d'histoires rien que pour obtenir un passeport!; **don't make such a ~ about accepting** ne faites pas tant d'embarras *or* de manières pour accepter; **to make a ~ of sb** être aux petits soins pour qn.

2 **comp** ▸**fusspot***, (*US*) **fussbudget*** (*nuisance*) enquiquineur* *m*, -euse* *f*; (*finicky person*) coupeur *m*, -euse *f* de cheveux en quatre; **don't be such a fusspot!*** ne fais pas tant d'histoires!, arrête d'enquiquiner le monde!*

3 **vi** (*become excited*) s'agiter; (*rush around busily*) s'affairer, faire la mouche du coche; (*worry*) se tracasser, s'en faire*. **to ~ over sb** être aux petits soins pour qn; (*pej*) embêter* qn (par des attentions excessives); **don't ~ over him** laisse-le tranquille.

4 **vt** *person* ennuyer, embêter*.

▸**fuss about, fuss around** **vi** faire l'affairé, s'affairer, faire la mouche du coche.

fussily ['fʌsɪlɪ] **adv** (*see* **fussy**) de façon tatillonne *or* méticuleuse *or* tarabiscotée.

fussy ['fʌsɪ] **adj** *person* tatillon, méticuleux, pointilleux; *dress* surchargé de fanfreluches, tarabiscoté; *style* trop orné, tarabiscoté. **she's very ~ about what she eats/what she wears** elle fait très attention à *or* elle est très tatillonne sur ce qu'elle mange/ce qu'elle porte; **what do you want to do? — I'm not ~*** que veux-tu faire? — ça m'est égal.

fustian ['fʌstɪən] **n** futaine *f*.

fusty ['fʌstɪ] **adj** *smell* de renfermé, de moisi; *room* qui sent le renfermé; (*fig*) *idea, outlook* suranné, vieillot (*f* -otte).

futile ['fjuːtaɪl] **adj** *remark* futile, vain; *attempt* vain.

futility [fjuː'tɪlɪtɪ] **n** futilité *f*; **the ~ of this attempt/measure** l'inutilité de cette tentative/mesure.

futon ['fuːtɒn] **n** futon *m* ®.

future ['fjuːtʃəʳ] **1** **n** **a** avenir *m*. **in (the) ~** à l'avenir; **in the near ~**, **in the not too distant ~** bientôt, (*more formally*) dans le *or* un proche avenir; **what the ~ holds for us** ce que l'avenir nous réserve; **his ~ is assured** son avenir est assuré; **there is a real ~ for bright boys in this firm** cette firme offre de réelles possibilités d'avenir pour des jeunes gens doués; **there's no ~ in this type of research** ce type de recherche n'a aucun avenir; **there's no ~ in it*** [*product, method*] ça n'a aucun avenir; [*measures, way of behaving*] ça n'aboutira à rien, ça ne servira à rien.

b (*Gram*) futur *m*. **in the ~** au futur; **~ perfect** futur antérieur.

c (*St Ex*) **~s** marchandises (achetées) à terme; **~s market** marché *m* à terme; **coffee ~s** café *m* (acheté) à terme.

2 **adj** futur (*gen before n*); (*Comm*) *delivery* à terme. **her ~ husband** son futur (époux); **~ generations** générations futures *or* à venir; **at some ~ date** à une date ultérieure (non encore précisée); **to file sth away/keep sth for ~ reference** classer/garder qch pour référence ultérieure; (*hum*) **I'll remember that for ~ reference** je garde ça à l'esprit; (*Gram*) **the ~ tense** le futur.

futurism ['fjuːtʃərɪzəm] **n** futurisme *m*.

futurist ['fjuːtʃərɪst] **n** **a** (*futurologist*) futurologue *mf*.

b (*Art*) futuriste *mf*.
futuristic [ˌfjuːtʃəˈrɪstɪk] adj futuriste.
futurologist [ˌfjuːtʃərˈɒlədʒɪst] n futurologue *mf*.
futurology [ˌfjuːtʃərˈɒlədʒɪ] n futurologie *f*, prospective *f*.
fuze [fjuːz] (*US*) = **fuse**.
fuzz [fʌz] n a (*NonC*) (*frizzy hair*) cheveux crépus *or* crêpelés (et bouffants); (*whiskers etc*) excroissance *f* (*hum*). b (*light growth*) (*on body*) duvet *m*, poils fins; (*on head*) duvet, cheveux fins. c (*‡: collective: police*) **the ~** la flicaille‡, les flics*.
fuzzy [ˈfʌzɪ] adj a *hair* crépu, crêpelé.
b (*Phot*) flou.
c (*muddled*) *ideas* confus; (*person: also* **~-headed**) désorienté, déconcerté; (**: tipsy*) pompette*, un peu parti*. **I feel ~** j'ai la tête qui tourne.
fwd. (*esp Comm*) abbr of **forward**.
f-word [ˈefˌwɜːd] n (*euph for* **fuck**) **the ~** le mot "fuck"*‡, une grossièreté.
FYI (abbr of **for your information**) *see* **information**.

G

G, g [dʒiː] 1 n a (*letter*) G, g *m*. **G for George** ≃ G comme Gaston. b (*Mus*) sol *m*; *see* **key**. c (*Phys: gravity, acceleration*) g *m*. d (*Cine*) (**abbr of general (audience)**) ≃ pour tous. e (‡) (**abbr of grand**) (*Brit*) mille livres *fpl*; (*US*) mille dollars *mpl*. f (*Scol*) (*mark*) (**abbr of good**) bon. 2 **comp** ►**G3/7** *etc* G3/7 *m etc* ►**G3/7** *etc* **summit** sommet *m* du G3/7 *etc* ►**G-force** force *f* gravitationnelle ►**G-man**‡ (*US*) agent *m* du FBI ►**G spot** *[woman]* point *m* G ►**G-string** (*Mus*) (corde *f* de) sol *m*; (*garment*) cache-sexe *m inv* ►**G-suit** (*Space*) combinaison spatiale *or* anti-g (*anti-gravité*).

g. a (**abbr of gram(s)**) g. b (**abbr of gravity**) g.

GA. (*US*) **abbr of Georgia**.

gab‡ [gæb] 1 n bagou(t)* *m*. **shut your ~!** la ferme!‡; *see* **gift**. 2 vi jacasser, bavasser‡.

gabardine [ˌgæbəˈdiːn] n gabardine *f*.

gabble [ˈgæbl] 1 vti (*talk indistinctly*) bafouiller; (*talk unintelligibly*) baragouiner*. (*talk quickly*) **he ~d on about the accident** il nous a fait une description volubile de l'accident; **he ~d (out) an excuse** il a bafouillé une excuse. 2 n baragouin* *m*, charabia* *m*, flot *m* de paroles (inintelligibles).

►**gabble away** vi jacasser sans arrêt. **they were gabbling away in French** ils jacassaient en français.

gabbro [ˈgæbrəʊ] n gabbro *m*.

gabby‡ [ˈgæbɪ] adj jacasseur, bavard comme une pie, bavasson‡.

gable [ˈgeɪbl] 1 n pignon *m*. 2 comp ►**gable end** pignon *m* ►**gable roof** comble *m* sur pignon(s).

gabled [ˈgeɪbld] adj à pignon(s).

Gabon [gəˈbɒn] n Gabon *m*.

Gabonese [ˌgæbəˈniːz] 1 adj gabonais. 2 n Gabonais(e) *m(f)*.

gad¹ [gæd] 1 n (*Agr*) aiguillon *m*. 2 comp ►**gadfly** taon *m*; (*fig: harassing person*) mouche *f* du coche.

gad² [gæd] 1 vi: **to ~ about** vadrouiller*, (se) baguenauder; **she's been ~ding about town all day** elle a couru la ville *or* elle a vadrouillé* en ville toute la journée. 2 comp ►**gadabout** vadrouilleur* *m*, -euse* *f*.

gad³* [gæd] excl (*also* **by ~**) sapristi!†, bon sang!

gadget [ˈgædʒɪt] n (*device*) gadget *m*, (petit) instrument *m or* dispositif *m*; (*: *thingummy*) (petit) truc* *m or* machin* *m or* bidule* *m*, gadget.

gadgetry [ˈgædʒɪtrɪ] n *[car etc]* tous les gadgets *mpl*.

gadolinium [ˌgædəˈlɪnɪəm] n gadolinium *m*.

Gael [geɪl] n Gaël *mf*.

Gaelic [ˈgeɪlɪk, ˈgælɪk] 1 adj gaélique. 2 n (*Ling*) gaélique *m*.

gaff¹ [gæf] 1 n (*Fishing*) gaffe *f*; (*Naut*) corne *f*. (*US fig*) **to stand the ~**‡ encaisser*, tenir. 2 vt gaffer, harponner.

gaff²‡ [gæf] n (*Brit: music hall etc*) (sorte *f* de) beuglant‡ *m*.

gaff³‡ [gæf] n (*nonsense*) foutaises‡ *fpl*; *see* **blow¹**.

gaffe [gæf] n gaffe *f*, bévue *f*.

gaffer‡ [ˈgæfəʳ] n a (*old man*) vieux *m*. **this old ~** ce vieux (bonhomme). b (*Brit*) (*foreman*) contremaître *m*; (*boss*) patron *m*, chef *m*. c (*US Cine*) chef-électricien *m*.

gag [gæg] 1 n a (*in mouth*) bâillon *m*; (*Med*) ouvre-bouche *m inv*. (*fig*) **it put an effective ~ on press reports of the incident** ceci a eu pour effet de bâillonner très efficacement la presse dans sa façon de rapporter l'incident.

b (*Theat*) (*joke*) plaisanterie *f*, blague* *f*; (*unscripted*) improvisation *f* comique; (*visual*) gag *m*.

c (**gen*) (*joke*) blague *f*, plaisanterie *f*; (*hoax*) canular *m*. **is this a ~?** c'est une plaisanterie?; **it's a ~ to raise funds** c'est un truc* comique pour ramasser de l'argent.

2 vt (*silence*) bâillonner; (*fig*) *press etc* bâillonner, museler.

3 vi a (*Theat*) faire une *or* des improvisation(s) comique(s).

b (*: *joke*) plaisanter, blaguer.

c (*: *retch*) avoir des haut-le-cœur.

4 comp ►**gag law*** (*US*) loi *f* sur le secret des délibérations.

gaga‡ [ˈgɑːgɑː] adj (*senile*) gaga* (*fem inv*), gâteux; (*crazy*) cinglé*.

gage [geɪdʒ] 1 n a (*challenge*) défi *m*; (*glove*) gant *m*. b (*pledge*) gage *m*, garantie *f*; (*article pledged*) gage. c (*US Tech*) = **gauge 1**. 2 vt (*US Tech*) = **gauge 2**.

gaggle [ˈgægl] 1 n *[geese etc]* troupeau *m*; (*hum*) *[girls etc]* (petite) troupe *f*, troupeau (*hum*). 2 vi *[geese]* cacarder.

gaiety [ˈgeɪɪtɪ] n a (*NonC*) gaieté *f or* gaîté *f*; (*in dress etc*) gaieté, couleur *f*. b (*gen pl*) **gaieties** réjouissances *fpl*.

gaily [ˈgeɪlɪ] adv *behave, speak* gaiement, avec bonne humeur; *decorate* de façon gaie. **to dress ~** porter des couleurs gaies; **~ coloured** aux couleurs vives.

gain [geɪn] 1 n (*Comm, Fin*) (*profit*) gain *m*, profit *m*, bénéfice *m*; (*increase in value of asset*) plus-value *m*; (*fig*) avantage *m*; (*increase*) augmentation *f*; (*in wealth*) accroissement *m* (*in* de); (*in knowledge etc*) acquisition *f* (*in* de). **to do sth for ~** faire qch pour le profit; **his loss is our ~** là où il perd nous gagnons; **~s** (*profits*) bénéfices *mpl*, gains *mpl*; (*winnings*) gains; **~ in weight** augmentation de poids; (*St Ex*) **there have been ~s of up to 3 points** des hausses allant jusqu'à 3 points ont été enregistrées; (*in election*) **Labour made ~s in the South** les travaillistes ont progressé *or* sont en progression dans le sud.

2 vt a (*obtain: gen*) *money, approval, respect* gagner, obtenir; *liberty* conquérir; *support, supporters* s'attirer; *friends* se faire. **to ~ experience** acquérir de l'expérience; **to ~ a hearing** (*make people listen*) se faire écouter; (*with king etc*) obtenir une audience; **to ~ sb's goodwill** se concilier qn, gagner les bonnes grâces de qn; (*fig*) **to ~ ground** gagner du terrain, progresser; **to ~ one's objective** atteindre son objectif; **the idea slowly ~ed popularity** l'idée gagna petit à petit en popularité; **to ~ time** gagner du temps (*by doing* en faisant); **what have you ~ed by doing it?** qu'est-ce que tu as gagné à faire ça?; **he'll ~ nothing by being rude** il ne gagnera rien à être impoli.

b (*increase*) (*St Ex*) **these shares have ~ed 3 points** ces valeurs ont enregistré une hausse de 3 points; **to ~ speed** prendre de la vitesse; **to ~ weight** prendre du poids; **she's ~ed 3 kg (in weight)** elle a pris 3 kg; **my watch has ~ed 5 minutes** ma montre a pris 5 minutes d'avance.

c (*win*) *battle* gagner. (*in election*) **Labour has ~ed three seats** les travaillistes ont gagné trois nouveaux sièges; **Labour has ~ed three seats from the Conservatives** les travaillistes ont pris trois sièges aux conservateurs; **to ~ the day** (*Mil*) remporter la victoire; (*fig*) l'emporter; **to ~ the upper hand** prendre le dessus.

d (*reach*) *place* atteindre, parvenir à.

3 vi *[watch]* avancer; *[runners]* prendre de l'avance. **to ~ in prestige** gagner en prestige; **to ~ in weight** prendre du poids; **he hasn't ~ed by the exchange** il n'a rien gagné au change.

►**gain (up)on** vt fus a (*Sport, fig*) (*catch up with*) rattraper; (*outstrip*) prendre de l'avance sur. b *[sea]* gagner sur.

gainer [ˈgeɪnəʳ] n gagnant(e) *m(f)*. **he is the ~ by it** c'est lui qui y gagne.

gainful [ˈgeɪnfʊl] adj *occupation etc* (*worthwhile*) utile, profitable; (*lucrative*) lucratif, rémunérateur (*f* -trice); *business* rentable. (*Admin etc*) **to be in ~ employment** avoir un emploi rémunéré.

gainfully [ˈgeɪnfʊlɪ] adv: **to be ~ employed** (*in paid work*) avoir un emploi rémunéré; (*doing sth useful*) être utilement employé.

gainsay [ˌgeɪnˈseɪ] pret, ptp **gainsaid** [ˌgeɪnˈsed] vt *person* contredire; *account, statement* contredire, démentir; *fact* nier. **facts that cannot be gainsaid** faits *mpl* indéniables; **evidence that cannot be gainsaid** preuve *f* irrécusable; **argument that cannot be gainsaid** argument *m* irréfutable; **it cannot be gainsaid, there's no ~ing it** c'est indéniable, on ne peut pas le nier; **I don't ~ it** je ne dis pas le contraire.

gait [geɪt] n démarche *f*. **with an awkward ~** d'une démarche *or* d'un pas gauche; **to know sb by his ~** reconnaître qn à sa démarche.

gaiter [ˈgeɪtəʳ] 1 n guêtre *f*. 2 vt guêtrer.

gal* [gæl] n († *or hum*) = **girl 1**.

gal., pl **~** *or* **gals. abbr of gallon**.

gala [ˈgɑːlə] 1 n fête *f*, gala *m*. **swimming/sports ~** grand concours de natation/d'athlétisme. 2 comp ►**gala day** jour *m* de gala *or* de fête ►**gala dress** tenue *f* de gala ►**gala night** (*Theat*) soirée *f* de gala

▸ **gala occasion** grande occasion.

galactic [gəˈlæktɪk] adj galactique.

galantine [ˈgælənti:n] n galantine *f*.

Galapagos [gəˈlæpəgəs] npl: the ~ (Islands) les (îles *fpl*) Galapagos *fpl*.

Galatians [gəˈleɪʃənz] npl (*Bible*) Galates *mpl*.

galaxy [ˈgæləksɪ] n (*Astron*) galaxie *f*; (*fig*) [*beauty, talent*] constellation *f*, brillante assemblée.

gale [geɪl] 1 n coup *m* de vent, grand vent. (*Met*) a force 8 ~ un vent de force 8; it was blowing a ~ le vent soufflait très fort; there's a ~ blowing in through that window c'est une véritable bourrasque qui entre par cette fenêtre; (*fig*) ~s of laughter grands éclats de rire. 2 comp ▸ **gale force winds** vent *m* soufflant en tempête, coups *mpl* de vent ▸ **gale warning** (*Met*) avis *m* de coup de vent.

galena [gəˈli:nə] n galène *f*.

Galicia [gəˈlɪʃɪə] n [*Central Europe*] Galicie *f*; [*Spain*] Galice *f*.

Galilean [ˌgæləˈli:ən] 1 adj (*Bible, Geog*) galiléen; (*Astron*) de Galilée. 2 n Galiléen(ne) *m(f)*. (*Bible*) the ~ le Galiléen.

Galilee [ˈgælɪli:] n Galilée *f*. the Sea of ~ le lac de Tibériade, la mer de Galilée.

Galileo [ˌgælɪˈleɪəʊ] n Galilée *m*.

gall[1] [gɔ:l] 1 n (*Med*) bile *f*; (*Zool*) bile, fiel *m*; (*fig: bitterness*) fiel, amertume *f*; (**: impertinence*) effronterie *f*, culot* *m*. she had the ~ to say that* ... elle a eu l'effronterie *or* le culot* de dire que ... . 2 comp ▸ **gall-bladder** vésicule *f* biliaire ▸ **gallstone** calcul *m* biliaire.

gall[2] [gɔ:l] 1 n (*on animal*) écorchure *f*, excoriation *f*; (*Bot*) galle *f*. 2 vt (*fig*) irriter, ulcérer, exaspérer. it ~s me to have to admit it je suis ulcéré d'avoir à le reconnaître.

gall., pl ~ *or* galls. abbr of **gallon**.

gallant [ˈgælənt] 1 adj a (*noble, brave*) *person* courageux, brave, vaillant (*liter*); *horse* noble, vaillant (*liter*); *appearance, dress* élégant, magnifique, superbe. ~ deed action *f* d'éclat. b [gəˈlænt] (*attentive to women*) galant, empressé auprès des dames. 2 [gəˈlænt] n galant *m*.

gallantly [ˈgæləntlɪ] adv (*see* **gallant**) a courageusement, bravement, vaillamment. b [gəˈlæntlɪ] galamment.

gallantry [ˈgæləntrɪ] n (*see* **gallant**) a courage *m*, bravoure *f*, vaillance *f* (*liter*). b galanterie *f*.

galleon [ˈgælɪən] n galion *m*.

gallery [ˈgælərɪ] n a (*Archit*) (*passageway, long room, also outside balcony*) galerie *f*; (*inside balcony*) tribune *f*; (*in cave, mine*) galerie; *see* **minstrel, press, shooting** *etc*. b (*art* ~) (*state-owned*) musée *m* (d'art); (*private*) galerie *f* (de tableaux *or* d'art); (*US: auction room*) salle *f* des ventes. c (*Theat*) dernier balcon *m*, poulailler* *m*. in the ~ au dernier balcon, au poulailler*; (*fig*) to play to the ~ poser *or* parler pour la galerie.

galley [ˈgælɪ] n a (*ship*) galère *f*; (*ship's kitchen*) coquerie *f*. ~ slave galérien *m*. b (*Typ*) galée *f*. ~ (proof) (épreuve *f* en) placard *m*.

galley west [ˈgælɪˌwest] adv (*US*) to knock sth ~ chambarder* qch, mettre la pagaille dans qch.

Gallic [ˈgælɪk] adj (*of Gaul*) gaulois; (*French*) français. ~ charm charme latin.

gallic [ˈgælɪk] adj (*Chem*) gallique.

gallicism [ˈgælɪsɪzəm] n gallicisme *m*.

gallimaufry [ˌgælɪˈmɔ:frɪ] n fatras *m*.

galling [ˈgɔ:lɪŋ] adj (*irritating*) irritant, exaspérant; (*humiliating*) blessant, humiliant.

gallinule [ˈgælɪnju:l] n: common ~ poule *f* d'eau.

gallium [ˈgælɪəm] n gallium *m*.

gallivant [ˌgælɪˈvænt] vi (*also* ~ about, ~ around) (*on pleasure*) courir le guilledou*; (**: busily*) courir. I've been ~ing about the shops all day* j'ai couru les magasins toute la journée.

gallon [ˈgælən] n gallon *m* (*Brit* = *4,546 litres, US* = *3,785 litres*).

gallop [ˈgæləp] 1 n galop *m*. to go for a ~ faire un temps de galop; to break into a ~ prendre le *or* se mettre au galop; at a *or* the ~ au galop; at full ~ [*horse*] au grand galop, ventre à terre; [*rider*] au grand galop, à bride abattue. 2 vi [*horse, rider*] galoper. to ~ away/back *etc* partir/revenir *etc* au galop; (*fig*) to go ~ing down the street descendre la rue au galop; to ~ through a book* lire un livre à toute allure *or* à la va-vite*, lire un livre en diagonale. 3 vt *horse* faire galoper.

galloping [ˈgæləpɪŋ] adj *horse* au galop; (*fig*) *inflation* galopant; *pneumonia, pleurisy* galopant. ~ consumption phtisie galopante.

gallows [ˈgæləʊz] 1 n, pl ~es *or* ~ (*NonC: also* ~ tree) gibet *m*, potence *f*. he'll end up on the ~ il finira à la potence *or* par la corde; to send sb to the ~ envoyer qn à la potence *or* au gibet. 2 comp ▸ **gallows bird*** gibier *m* de potence ▸ **gallows humour** (*fig*) humour *m* macabre.

Gallup poll [ˈgæləpˌpəʊl] n sondage *m* Gallup.

galoot‡ [gəˈlu:t] n (*US*) balourd* *m*.

galop [ˈgæləp] n galop *m* (*danse*).

galore [gəˈlɔ:ʳ] adv en abondance, à gogo*, à la pelle*.

galosh [gəˈlɒʃ] n (*gen pl*) ~es caoutchoucs *mpl* (*enfilés par-dessus les souliers*).

galumph* [gəˈlʌmf] vi cabrioler *or* caracoler lourdement *or* avec la légèreté d'un éléphant. to go ~ing in/out *etc* entrer/sortir *etc* en cabriolant *or* caracolant comme un (gros) balourd.

galvanic [gælˈvænɪk] adj (*Elec*) galvanique; *jerk* crispé; (*fig*) *effect* galvanisant, électrisant.

galvanism [ˈgælvənɪzəm] n galvanisme *m*.

galvanization [ˌgælvənaɪˈzeɪʃən] n galvanisation *f*.

galvanize [ˈgælvənaɪz] vt (*Elec, Med*) galvaniser; (*fig*) *discussions, debate* animer; *worker, speaker* galvaniser. ~d iron fer galvanisé; (*fig*) to ~ sb into action donner un coup de fouet à qn.

galvanometer [ˌgælvəˈnɒmɪtəʳ] n galvanomètre *m*.

galvanoscope [ˈgælvənəˌskəʊp] n galvanoscope *m*.

Gambia [ˈgæmbɪə] n: (The) ~ la Gambie.

Gambian [ˈgæmbɪən] 1 n Gambien(ne) *m(f)*. 2 adj gambien.

gambit [ˈgæmbɪt] n (*Chess*) gambit *m*. (*fig*) (opening) ~ manœuvre *f* *or* ruse *f* (stratégique).

gamble [ˈgæmbl] 1 n entreprise risquée. life's a ~ la vie est un jeu de hasard; it's a pure ~ c'est affaire de chance; the ~ came off *or* paid off le jeu en a valu la chandelle, ça a payé de prendre ce risque*; (*Racing, St Ex*) to have a ~ on jouer. 2 vi a (*lit*) jouer (*on* sur, *with* avec). to ~ on the stock exchange jouer à la Bourse. b (*fig*) to ~ on compter sur; (*less sure*) miser sur; we had been gambling on fine weather nous avions compté sur le beau temps; (*less sure*) nous avions misé sur le beau temps; he was gambling on her being late il comptait qu'elle allait être en retard, il escomptait son retard.

▸ **gamble away** vt sep *money etc* perdre *or* dilapider au jeu.

gambler [ˈgæmbləʳ] n joueur *m*, -euse *f*; *see* big 3.

gambling [ˈgæmblɪŋ] 1 n jeu *m*, jeux d'argent. his ~ ruined his family sa passion du jeu a *or* ses pertes de jeu ont entraîné la ruine de sa famille. 2 comp ▸ **gambling debts** dettes *fpl* de jeu ▸ **gambling den** (*pej*), **gambling hell*** (*pej*), **gambling house**, (*US*) **gambling joint**‡ maison *f* de jeu, tripot *m* (*pej*) ▸ **gambling losses** pertes *fpl* au jeu.

gamboge [gæmˈbu:ʒ] n gomme-gutte *f*.

gambol [ˈgæmbəl] 1 n gambade *f*, cabriole *f*. 2 vi gambader, cabrioler, faire des cabrioles. to ~ away/back *etc* partir/revenir *etc* en gambadant *or* cabriolant.

gambrel [ˈgæmbrəl] n (*also* ~ roof) toit *m* à deux pentes.

game[1] [geɪm] 1 n a (*gen*) jeu *m*; [*football, rugby, cricket etc*] match *m*; [*tennis*] partie *f*; [*billiards, chess*] partie. ~ of cards partie de cartes; card ~ jeu de cartes (*belote, bridge etc*); ~ of skill/of chance jeu d'adresse/de hasard; he plays a good ~ of football il est bon au football; to have *or* play a ~ of faire une partie de, jouer un match de; (*Scol*) ~s sport *m*, (activités *fpl* de) plein air; to be good at ~s être sportif; (*Scol*) we get ~s on Thursdays nous avons plein air le jeudi; that's ~ (*Tennis*) jeu; (*Bridge*) ça fait la manche; they were ~ all (*Tennis*) on était à un jeu partout; (*Bridge*) on était manche A, on était à une manche partout; (*Tennis*) ~, set and match jeu, set, et match; (*Tennis*) ~ to Johnston jeu Johnston; he's off his ~ il n'est pas en forme; to put sb off his ~ troubler qn; this isn't a ~! on n'est pas en train de jouer!, c'est sérieux!; it's all part of the ~ cela fait partie des règles du jeu; (*fig*) he's just playing (silly) ~s il n'est pas sérieux; (*lit, fig*) to have the ~ in one's hands être sur le point de gagner; *see* high-land, indoor, play 3 *etc*.

b (*fig*) (*scheme, plan*) plan *m*, projet *m*; (*dodge, trick*) (petit) jeu *m*, manège *m*, combinaison *f*; (**: occupation*) travail *m*, boulot* *m*. it's a profitable ~ c'est une entreprise rentable; the ~ is up tout est fichu* *or* à l'eau; they saw the ~ was up ils ont vu que la partie était perdue; I'll play his ~ for a while je ferai son jeu pendant un certain temps; don't play his ~ n'entre pas dans son jeu; we soon saw through his ~ nous avons vite vu clair dans son (petit) jeu; two can play at that ~ à bon chat bon rat (*Prov*); what's the ~?* (*what's happening?*) qu'est-ce qui se passe?; (*what are you doing?*) à quoi tu joues?*; what's your (little) ~?* à quoi tu joues?*; I wonder what his ~ is* je me demande ce qu'il mijote* *or* manigance; to beat sb at his own ~ battre qn sur son propre terrain; to spoil sb's ~ déjouer les combinaisons *or* manigances (*pej*) *or* machinations de qn; how long have you been in this ~?* cela fait combien de temps que vous faites ça?; [*prostitute*] to be on the ~‡ faire le trottoir*; the ~ isn't worth the candle le jeu n'en vaut pas la chandelle; to make a ~ of sb/sth se moquer de qn/qch, tourner qn/qch en dérision; *see* fun, play 3, waiting *etc*.

c (*Culin, Hunting*) gibier *m*. big/small ~ gros/petit *or* menu gibier; *see also* big, fair[1].

2 comp ▸ **gamebag** gibecière *f*, carnier *m*, carnassière *f* ▸ **game birds** gibier *m* (*NonC*) à plume ▸ **gamecock** coq *m* de combat ▸ **game fish** poissons *mpl* d'eau douce ▸ **gamekeeper** garde-chasse *m* ▸ **game laws** réglementation *f* de la chasse ▸ **game park** = game reserve ▸ **game pie** (*Culin*) pâté *m* de gibier en croûte ▸ **game plan** (*esp US lit, fig*) stratégie *f*; (*fig*) what's the game plan? comment va-t-on s'organiser? ▸ **game reserve** réserve *f* naturelle ▸ **game show** (*TV*) jeu *m* télévisé; (*Rad*) jeu *m* radiophonique ▸ **games master, games mistress** (*Scol*) professeur *m* d'éducation physique ▸ **games theory** théorie *f* des jeux ▸ **game warden** garde-chasse *m*; (*on reserve*) gardien *m* chargé de la protection des animaux.

3 vi (*gamble*) jouer.

4 adj a (*brave*) courageux. to be ~ avoir du cran*, avoir du cœur au ventre.

b (*ready, prepared*) prêt (*to do* à faire). **are you ~?** tu en as envie?; **I'm ~ if you are** je marche si tu marches; **he's ~ for anything** il est prêt à tout, il ne recule devant rien.

game[2] [geɪm] adj (*lame*) *arm, leg* estropié. **to have a ~ leg** être boiteux, boiter.

gamely ['geɪmlɪ] adv (*bravely*) courageusement; (*resolutely*) résolument; (*willingly*) avec bonne volonté.

gamesmanship ['geɪmzmənʃɪp] n art *m* de gagner par des astuces. **to be good at ~** savoir utiliser les règles (du jeu) à son avantage; **it's a piece of ~ on his part** c'est une de ses ruses pour gagner.

gamester ['geɪmstəʳ] n joueur *m*, -euse *f*.

gamete ['gæmi:t] n gamète *m*.

gamin ['gæmɛ̃] n gamin *m*.

gamine [gæ'mi:n] 1 n (*cheeky girl*) gamine *f* (espiègle); (*tomboy*) garçon manqué. 2 comp *appearance, hat* gamin ► **gamine haircut**: **she had a gamine haircut** elle avait les cheveux coupés très court ► **gamine look** style *m* gavroche.

gaming ['geɪmɪŋ] 1 n = **gambling**. 2 comp ► **gaming laws** réglementation *f* des jeux de hasard.

gamma ['gæmə] n gamma *m*. **~ radiation** *or* **rays** rayons *mpl* gamma.

gammon ['gæmən] n (*Brit*) (*bacon*) quartier *m* de lard fumé; (*ham*) jambon fumé. **~ steak** (épaisse) tranche *f* de jambon fumé *or* salé.

gammy* ['gæmɪ] adj (*Brit*) = **game[2]**.

gamp⁑ [gæmp] n (*Brit hum*) pépin* *m*, parapluie *m*.

gamut ['gæmət] n (*Mus, fig*) gamme *f*. (*fig*) **to run the ~ of** passer par toute la gamme de.

gamy ['geɪmɪ] adj *meat etc* faisandé.

gander ['gændəʳ] n a (*bird*) jars *m*; *see* **sauce**. b (*look*) **to take a ~**⁑ filer* un coup d'œil (*at* vers).

ganef⁑ ['gɑ:nəf] n (*US*) escroc *m*, filou *m*.

gang [gæŋ] 1 n *[workmen]* équipe *f*; *[criminals]* bande *f*, gang *m*; *[youths, friends etc]* bande, clique *f*; *[prisoners]* convoi *m*; (*Tech*) série *f* (d'outils multiples). **the little boy wanted to be like the rest of his ~** le petit garçon voulait être comme le reste de sa bande; **he's one of the ~ now*** il fait partie de la bande maintenant; (*Pol*) **the G~ of Four** la bande des Quatre; *see* **chain** *etc*.

2 comp ► **gangbang**⁑ copulation *f* en chaîne; (*rape*) viol *m* collectif ► **gangland***: **gangland boss** chef *m* de gang; **gangland killing** règlement *m* de comptes (entre gangs) ► **gangplank** passerelle *f* (de débarquement); (*Navy*) échelle *f* de coupée ► **gang rape** viol *m* collectif ► **gangway** (*gen*) passage *m* (planchéié); (*Naut*) = **gangplank**; (*in bus etc*) couloir *m*; (*in theatre*) allée *f*; (*excl*) **gangway!** dégagez!

► **gang together*** vi se mettre à plusieurs (*to do* pour faire).

► **gang up*** vi se mettre à plusieurs (*to do* pour faire). **to gang up on** *or* **against sb**⁑ se liguer contre qn, se mettre à plusieurs contre qn.

ganger ['gæŋəʳ] n (*Brit*) chef *m* d'équipe (*de travailleurs*).

Ganges ['gændʒi:z] n Gange *m*.

ganglia ['gæŋglɪə] npl of **ganglion**.

gangling ['gæŋglɪŋ] adj *person* dégingandé. **a ~ boy** un échalas, une perche (*hum*).

ganglion ['gæŋglɪən] n, pl **ganglia** *or* **~s** ganglion *m*; (*fig*) *[activity]* centre *m*; *[energy]* foyer *m*.

gangrene ['gæŋgri:n] n gangrène *f*.

gangrenous ['gæŋgrɪnəs] adj gangreneux. **to go ~** se gangrener.

gangster ['gæŋstəʳ] 1 n gangster *m*, bandit *m*. 2 comp *story, film* de gangsters.

gangsterism ['gæŋstərɪzəm] n gangstérisme *m*.

gannet ['gænɪt] n (*Orn*) fou *m* (de Bassan).

gantry ['gæntrɪ] n (*for crane*) portique *m*; (*Space*) tour *f* de lancement; (*Rail*) portique à signaux; (*for barrels*) chantier *m*.

gaol [dʒeɪl] (*Brit*) = **jail**.

gaoler ['dʒeɪləʳ] (*Brit*) = **jailer**.

gap [gæp] 1 n a trou *m*, vide *m*; (*in wall*) trou, brèche *f*, ouverture *f*; (*in hedge*) trou, ouverture; (*in print, text*) intervalle *m*, blanc *m*; (*between floorboards*) interstice *m*, jour *m*; (*in pavement*) brèche; (*between curtains*) intervalle, jour; (*in clouds, fog*) trouée *f*; (*between teeth*) écart, interstice; (*mountain pass*) trouée. **to stop up** *or* **fill in a ~** boucher un trou *or* une brèche, combler un vide; **leave a ~ for the name** laissez un blanc pour (mettre) le nom.

b (*fig*) vide *m*; (*in education*) lacune *f*, manque *m*; (*in time*) intervalle *m*; (*in timetable*) trou *m*; (*in conversation, narrative*) interruption *f*, vide. **a ~ in his memory** un trou de mémoire; **he left a ~ which will be hard to fill** il a laissé un vide qu'il sera difficile de combler; **to close the ~ between two points of view** supprimer l'écart entre *or* rapprocher deux points de vue; **the ~ between the rich and the poor** l'écart (qui existe) entre les riches et les pauvres; **this shows up the ~ between us** cela montre bien ce qui nous sépare; **to close the ~ in the balance of payments** supprimer le déficit dans la balance des paiements; (*Comm*) **a ~ in the market** un créneau; **the software ~ is the biggest problem** l'insuffisance *f* en matière de logiciel constitue le problème majeur; *see* **bridge[1]**, **credibility**, **generation**.

2 comp ► **gap financing** (*Fin*) crédit *m* (de) relais ► **gap-toothed** *person* (*teeth wide apart*) aux dents écartées; (*teeth missing*) brèche-dent *inv*, (*liter*) à qui il manque une (*or* des) dent(s); *smile, grin* montrant des dents écartées *or* manquantes.

gape [geɪp] 1 vi a (*open mouth*) *[person]* bâiller, ouvrir la bouche toute grande; *[bird]* ouvrir le bec tout grand; *[seam etc]* bâiller; *[chasm etc]* être ouvert *or* béant. b (*stare*) rester bouche bée (*at* devant), bayer aux corneilles. **to ~ at sb/sth** regarder qn/qch bouche bée. 2 n a *[chasm etc]* trou béant. b (*stare*) regard ébahi.

gaping ['geɪpɪŋ] adj *hole, chasm, wound* béant; *seam* qui bâille; *person* bouche bée *inv*.

gappy ['gæpɪ] adj *teeth* écartés.

garage ['gærɑ:ʒ] 1 n garage *m*. 2 vt garer, mettre au garage. 3 comp *door, wall* de garage ► **garageman, garage mechanic** mécanicien *m* ► **garageman, garage proprietor** garagiste *m* ► **garage sale** vente *f* d'objets usagés (*chez un particulier*) ► **garage space** de la place *f* pour se garer; **there is garage space for 3 cars** on peut y garer 3 voitures.

garaging ['gærədʒɪŋ] n (*NonC*) = **garage space**; *see* **garage 3**.

garb [gɑ:b] 1 n (*NonC: often hum*) costume *m*, mise *f*, atours *mpl* (*hum*). **in medieval ~** en costume médiéval. 2 vt (*gen pass*) vêtir (*in* de). **to ~ o.s. in** se revêtir de, s'affubler de (*hum*).

garbage ['gɑ:bɪdʒ] 1 n (*NonC*) ordures *fpl*, détritus *mpl*; (*food waste*) déchets *mpl*; (*fig*) (*worthless objects*) rebut *m*; (*nonsense*) foutaises⁑ *fpl*; (*Comput*) (informations *fpl*) parasites *mpl*. (*Comput*) **~ in, ~ out** qualité d'entrée égale qualité de sortie, garbage in garbage out. 2 comp ► **garbage can** (*US*) boîte *f* à ordures, poubelle *f* ► **garbage chute** *or* **shute** (*US*) vide-ordures *m inv* ► **garbage collector** (*US*) boueur *m or* boueux *m*, éboueur *m* ► **garbage disposal unit** broyeur *m* d'ordures ► **garbage man** (*US*) = **garbage collector** ► **garbage truck** (*US*) camion *m* des boueurs.

garble ['gɑ:bl] vt *story* raconter de travers; *quotation* déformer; *facts* dénaturer; *instructions* embrouiller; *foreign language* massacrer.

garbled ['gɑ:bld] adj *account* embrouillé; *text* altéré; *instructions* confus; *words, speech* incompréhensible.

Garda[1] ['gɑ:də] n: **Lake ~** le lac de Garde.

Garda[2] ['gɑ:də] n (*Irish Police*) *police irlandaise*.

garden ['gɑ:dn] 1 n jardin *m*. **the G~ of Eden** le jardin d'Éden, le Paradis terrestre; **~s** (*public*) parc *m*, jardin public; *[manor house etc]* jardin; **~ of remembrance** jardin du souvenir (*dans un cimetière*); (*fig*) **to lead sb up the ~ path*** mener qn en bateau*; (*fig*) **everything in the ~'s lovely** tout va pour le mieux; *see* **back, flower, kitchen** *etc*.

2 vi jardiner, faire du jardinage. **I like ~ing** j'aime le jardinage, j'aime jardiner.

3 comp ► **garden centre** garden-centre *m*, pépinière *f* ► **garden city** (*Brit*) cité-jardin *f* ► **garden flat** appartement *m* en rez-de-jardin ► **garden hose** tuyau *m* d'arrosage ► **garden(ing) tools** outils *mpl* de jardinage ► **garden party** garden-party *f*, réception *f* en plein air ► **garden path** *see* **1** ► **garden produce** produits maraîchers ► **garden seat** banc *m* de jardin ► **garden shears** cisaille *f* de jardinier ► **garden snail** escargot *m* ► **the Garden State** (*US*) le New Jersey ► **garden suburb** banlieue résidentielle (*dont l'environnement est aménagé par un paysagiste*) ► **garden wall**: **he lives just over the garden wall from us** il habite juste à côté de chez nous.

gardener ['gɑ:dnəʳ] n jardinier *m*, -ière *f*. **I'm no ~** je ne connais rien au jardinage; **he's a good ~** il est très bon jardinier; *see* **landscape**.

gardenia [gɑ:'di:nɪə] n gardénia *m*.

gardening ['gɑ:dnɪŋ] n jardinage *m*; *see also* **garden** *and* **landscape**.

garfish ['gɑ:,fɪʃ] n orphie *f*.

gargantuan [gɑ:'gæntjʊən] adj gargantuesque.

gargle ['gɑ:gl] 1 vi se gargariser, se faire un gargarisme. 2 vt: **to ~ one's throat** se gargariser, se faire un gargarisme. 3 n gargarisme *m*.

gargoyle ['gɑ:gɔɪl] n gargouille *f*.

garish ['gɛərɪʃ] adj *colour, decorations* voyant, criard, tapageur; *clothes* voyant, aux couleurs criardes; *light* cru, éblouissant.

garishly ['gɛərɪʃlɪ] adv: **~ coloured** aux couleurs criardes *or* voyantes; **~ decorated/painted/dressed** décoré aux/peint aux/habillé de couleurs criardes; **~ lit** brutalement éclairé.

garishness ['gɛərɪʃnɪs] n *[clothes, décor]* aspect criard *or* tapageur; *[colours, light]* crudité *f*, violence *f*.

garland ['gɑ:lənd] 1 n guirlande *f*, couronne *f* de fleurs. (*fig*) **a ~ of verse** un florilège (de poèmes). 2 vt orner de guirlandes, enguirlander.

garlic ['gɑ:lɪk] 1 n (*NonC*) ail *m*; *see* **clove[1]**. 2 comp ► **garlic bread** pain *m* frit à l'ail ► **garlic press** presse-ail *m* ► **garlic salt** sel *m* d'ail ► **garlic sausage** saucisson *m* à l'ail.

garlicky ['gɑ:lɪkɪ] adj *flavour, smell* d'ail; *sauce* à l'ail; *food* aillé; *breath* qui sent l'ail.

garment ['gɑ:mənt] n vêtement *m*.

garner ['gɑ:nəʳ] 1 vt (*also* **~ in, ~ up**) *grain etc* engranger, mettre en grenier; (*fig*) *memories etc* recueillir. 2 n (*liter*) (*granary*) grenier *m*; (*anthology*) recueil *m*.

garnet ['gɑ:nɪt] 1 n (*gem, colour*) grenat *m*. 2 comp *ring* de grenat(s) ► **garnet(-coloured)** grenat *inv*.

garnish ['gɑ:nɪʃ] 1 vt garnir, orner, parer (*with* de); (*Culin*) garnir (*with* de). 2 n garniture *f*.

garnishee [ˌgɑːnɪˈʃiː] n *(Jur)* saisi *m*.
garnishing [ˈgɑːnɪʃɪŋ] n garnissage *m*, embellissement *m*; *(Culin)* garniture *f*; *[style]* ornement *m*, floriture *f*.
garnishment [ˈgɑːnɪʃmənt] n *(Jur)* saisie-arrêt *f*.
garnishor [ˈgɑːnɪʃəʳ] n *(Jur)* saisissant *m*.
garotte [gəˈrɒt] = **garrotte**.
garret [ˈgærət] n *(room)* mansarde *f*; *(attic)* grenier *m*.
garrison [ˈgærɪsən] 1 n garnison *f*. 2 vt *fort etc* placer une garnison dans; *troops* mettre en garnison; *[regiment]* être en garnison dans. 3 comp ▸**garrison duty** service *m* de garnison *or* de place ▸**garrison life** vie *f* de garnison ▸**garrison town** ville *f* de garnison ▸**garrison troops** troupes *fpl* de garnison.
garrotte [gəˈrɒt] 1 vt *(strangle)* étrangler *(au cours d'un vol)*; *(Spanish Hist)* faire périr par le garrot. 2 n *(gen)* cordelette *f* *(pour étrangler)*; *(Spanish Hist)* garrot *m*.
garrulity [gəˈruːlɪtɪ] n *(NonC)* *[person]* loquacité *f*; *[style]* verbosité *f*.
garrulous [ˈgærʊləs] adj *person* loquace, volubile, bavard; *style* verbeux; *(liter)* *stream* babillard *(liter)*, jaseur *(liter)*.
garrulously [ˈgærʊləslɪ] adv avec volubilité.
garter [ˈgɑːtəʳ] 1 n *(gen)* jarretière *f*; *(for men's socks)* fixe-chaussette *m*; *(US: from belt)* jarretelle *f*. *(Brit)* **Order of the G~** Ordre *m* de la Jarretière; *(Brit)* **Knight of the G~** chevalier *m* de l'Ordre de la Jarretière. 2 comp ▸**garter belt** *(US)* porte-jarretelles *m inv* ▸**garter stitch** *(Knitting)* point *m* mousse.
gas [gæs] 1 n, pl ~(s)es a *(Chem, Culin, Phys etc)* gaz *m inv*; *(Min)* méthane *m*, grisou *m*; *(Mil)* gaz (asphyxiant *or* vésicant *etc*); *(anaesthetic)* (gaz) anesthésique *m*. **to cook by** *or* **with** ~ faire la cuisine au gaz; **to turn on/off the** ~ allumer/fermer *or* éteindre le gaz; *(Med etc)* **I had** ~ j'ai eu une anesthésie au masque; **(combined)** ~ **and electric cooker** cuisinière *f* mixte; *see* **laughing, natural, supply** *etc*.
b *(US: gasoline)* essence *f*. **to step on the** ~* *(Aut)* appuyer sur le champignon*; *(fig)* se magner‡, se presser; **to take one's foot off the** ~* ralentir.
c (‡: *idle words*) bla-bla-bla* *m*. *(chat)* **to have a** ~ avoir une bonne parlotte *(about* à propos de).
d (‡: *fun*) rigolade* *f*. **to do sth for a** ~ faire qch pour rigoler* *or* pour se marrer‡; **what a** ~ **it was!** quelle rigolade!*, ce qu'on s'est marrés!‡
2 comp *industry* du gaz, gazier; *engine* à gaz ▸**gasbag** (enveloppe *f* de) ballon *m* à gaz; (‡ *pej: talkative person*) moulin *m* à paroles* *(pej)*; *(boastful)* baratineur‡ *m*, -euse‡ *f* ▸**gas bracket** applique *f* à gaz ▸**gas burner** = **gas jet** ▸**gas carrier** *(ship)* méthanier *m* ▸**gas chamber** chambre *f* à gaz ▸**gas cooker** cuisinière *f* à gaz, gazinière *f*; *(portable)* réchaud *m* à gaz ▸**gas-cooled reactor** réacteur *m* à refroidissement au gaz carbonique ▸**gas explosion** *(gen)* explosion *f* (causée par une fuite) de gaz; *(in coal mine)* explosion *or* coup *m* de grisou ▸**gas fire** appareil *m* de chauffage à gaz; **to light the gas fire** allumer le gaz ▸**gas-fired** chauffé au gaz; **gas-fired central heating** chauffage central au gaz ▸**gas fitter** ajusteur-gazier *m* ▸**gas fittings** appareillage *m* du gaz ▸**gas fixture** *(US)* = **gas bracket** ▸**gas guzzler**‡ *(US: car)* voiture *f* qui consomme énormément d'essence, vorace *f* ▸**gas heater** appareil *m* de chauffage à gaz; *(for heating water)* chauffe-eau *m inv* (à gaz) ▸**gas hog*** *(US)* = **gas guzzler**‡ ▸**gasholder** gazomètre *m* ▸**gas jet** brûleur *m* à gaz ▸**gas lamp** lampe *f* à gaz ▸**gaslight** lumière *f* du gaz; **by gaslight** au gaz, à la lumière du gaz ▸**gas lighter** *(for cooker etc)* allume-gaz *m inv*; *(for cigarettes)* briquet *m* à gaz ▸**gas lighting** éclairage *m* au gaz ▸**gas line** *(US)* queue *f* (devant une pompe à essence) ▸**gaslit** éclairé au gaz ▸**gas main** canalisation *f* de gaz ▸**the gasman*** l'employé *m* du gaz ▸**gas mantle** manchon *m* à incandescence ▸**gasmask** masque *m* à gaz ▸**gas meter** compteur *m* à gaz ▸**gas mileage** *(US Aut)* consommation *f* *(d'essence)* ▸**gas oil** gas-oil *m* ▸**gas oven** four *m* à gaz; **he put his head in the gas oven** il s'est suicidé en se mettant la tête dans le four à gaz; **she felt like putting her head in the gas oven** elle avait envie de se jeter par la fenêtre ▸**gas pedal** *(US Aut)* accélérateur *m* ▸**gas-permeable** *lens* perméable à l'oxygène ▸**gas pipe** tuyau *m* à gaz ▸**gas pipeline** gazoduc *m* ▸**gas pump** *(US Aut)* pompe *f* à essence ▸**gas range** fourneau *m* à gaz ▸**gas ring** *(part of cooker)* brûleur *m*; *(small stove)* réchaud *m* à gaz ▸**gas station** *(US)* poste *m* d'essence, station-service *f* ▸**gas stove** *(portable)* réchaud *m* à gaz; *(larger)* cuisinière *f or* fourneau *m* à gaz ▸**gas tank** *(US)* réservoir *m* à essence ▸**gas tap** *(on pipe)* robinet *m* à gaz; *(on cooker)* bouton *m* (de cuisinière à gaz) ▸**gas turbine** turbine *f* à gaz ▸**gas worker** gazier *m* ▸**gasworks** sg inv usine *f* à gaz.
3 vt *(gen)* asphyxier; *(Mil)* gazer. **to** ~ **o.s.** *(gen)* s'asphyxier; *(commit suicide)* se suicider au gaz.
4 vi a *(Chem)* dégager des gaz.
b (‡: *talk*) parler; *(chat)* bavarder.
▸**gas up*** vi *(US Aut)* faire le plein (de carburant).
Gascon [ˈgæskən] 1 adj gascon. 2 n Gascon(ne) *m(f)*.
Gascony [ˈgæskənɪ] n Gascogne *f*.
gaseous [ˈgæsɪəs] adj gazeux.
gash [gæʃ] 1 n *(in flesh)* entaille *f*, estafilade *f*; *(on face)* balafre *f*; *(in cloth, leather)* (grande) déchirure *f*, (grand) accroc *m*. 2 vt *flesh* entailler, entamer; *face* balafrer; *cloth, leather* déchirer, faire un (grand) accroc à. 3 adj (‡ *Brit*) de trop, en surplus. **if that box is** ~ **I'll take it** si vous n'avez plus besoin de cette boîte, je la prends.
gasket [ˈgæskɪt] n a *[piston]* garniture *f* de piston; *[joint]* joint *m* d'étanchéité; *[cylinder head]* joint de culasse; *see* **blow¹**. b *(Naut)* raban *m* de ferlage.
gasohol [ˈgæsəʊhɒl] n *(US)* carburol *m*.
gasoline [ˈgæsəʊliːn] 1 n *(US)* essence *f*. 2 comp ▸**gasoline-powered** *(US)* à essence.
gasometer [gæˈsɒmɪtəʳ] n *(Brit)* gazomètre *m*.
gasp [gɑːsp] 1 n halètement *m*. **to give a** ~ **of surprise/fear** *etc* avoir le souffle coupé par la surprise/la peur *etc*; **to be at one's last** ~ *(lit)* être à l'agonie, agoniser, être à la dernière extrémité; (* *fig*) n'en pouvoir plus; *(lit, fig)* **to the last** ~ jusqu'au dernier souffle.
2 vi *(choke)* haleter, suffoquer; *(from astonishment)* avoir le souffle coupé. *(lit, fig)* **to make sb** ~ couper le souffle à qn; **to** ~ **for breath** *or* **air** haleter, suffoquer, chercher sa respiration; *(want desperately)* **to be** ~**ing for* a drink/cup of tea/cigarette** mourir de soif/d'envie de boire une tasse de thé/d'envie de fumer une cigarette; **I'm** ~**ing*** je meurs de soif.
3 vt: **"no!" she** ~**ed** "pas possible!" souffla-t-elle.
▸**gasp out** vt sep *plea* dire dans un souffle *or* d'une voix entrecoupée; *word* souffler.
gasper‡ [ˈgɑːspəʳ] n *(Brit)* sèche‡ *f*, clope‡ *f*.
gassed‡ [gæst] adj *(drunk)* bourré‡, ivre.
gassy [ˈgæsɪ] adj *(Chem etc)* gazeux; *drink* gazeux; (‡ *pej*) *person* bavard, jacasseur.
gastric [ˈgæstrɪk] adj gastrique. ~ **flu** grippe gastro-intestinale; ~ **juices** sucs *mpl* gastriques; ~ **ulcer** ulcère *m* de l'estomac.
gastritis [gæsˈtraɪtɪs] n gastrite *f*.
gastro... [ˈgæstrəʊ] pref gastro... .
gastroenteritis [ˌgæstrəʊˌentəˈraɪtɪs] n gastro-entérite *f*.
gastronome [ˈgæstrənəʊm] n gastronome *mf*.
gastronomic [ˌgæstrəˈnɒmɪk] adj gastronomique.
gastronomist [gæsˈtrɒnəmɪst] n gastronome *mf*.
gastronomy [gæsˈtrɒnəmɪ] n gastronomie *f*.
gastropod [ˈgæstrəpɒd] n gastéropode *m*.
gat¹†† [gæt] pret of **get**.
gat²‡† [gæt] n *(US: gun)* flingue‡ *m*, pétard‡ *m*.
gate [geɪt] 1 n a *[castle, town]* porte *f*; *[field, level crossing]* barrière *f*; *[garden]* porte, portail *m*; *(large, metallic)* grille *f* (d'entrée); *(low)* portillon *m*; *(tall, into courtyard etc)* porte cochère; *(Rail: in Underground)* portillon; *[lock, sluice]* vanne *f*, porte (d'écluse); *[sports ground]* entrée *f*. *(entrance)* **at the factory/castle** *etc* ~ à l'entrée de l'usine/du château *etc*; *(at airport)* ~ **5** porte 5; **five-bar** ~ = barrière; *(US)* **to give sb the** ~‡ *(employee)* virer* qn; *(boyfriend etc)* plaquer* qn; *(US: be dismissed)* **to get the** ~‡ être viré*.
b *(Sport)* *(attendance)* spectateurs *mpl*; *(money)* recette *f*, entrées *fpl*. **there was a** ~ **of 5,000** il y a eu 5 000 spectateurs; **the match got a good** ~ le match a fait de grosses entrées*.
c *(Ski)* porte *f*.
d *(Comput)* porte *f*.
2 vt *(Brit *: Scol, Univ)* consigner, coller*. **to be** ~**d** se faire consigner *or* coller*.
3 comp ▸**gatecrash** vi *(without invitation)* s'introduire sans invitation; *(without paying)* resquiller ◊ vt: **to gatecrash a party** s'introduire dans une réception sans invitation; **to gatecrash a match** assister à un match sans payer ▸**gatecrasher** *(without invitation)* intrus(e) *m(f)*; *(without paying)* resquilleur *m*, -euse *f* ▸**gatefold** *(US Publishing)* encart *m* à volets ▸**gatehouse** *[castle]* corps *m* de garde; *[park etc]* loge *f* ▸**gatekeeper** *[block of flats etc]* portier *m*, -ière *f*; *[factory etc]* gardien *m*, -ienne *f*; *(Rail)* garde-barrière *mf* ▸**gate-leg(ged) table** table anglaise ▸**gate money** *(Sport)* recette *f*, (montant *m* des) entrées *fpl* ▸**gatepost** montant *m* (de porte); *(fig)* **between you, me and the gatepost*** soit dit entre nous, entre quat'z'yeux‡ ▸**gateway** porte *f*, entrée *f*, portail *m*; **New York, the gateway to America** New York, porte de l'Amérique; *(fig)* **it proved the gateway to success/fame/fortune** cela s'avéra être la porte ouverte au succès/à la gloire/à la fortune.
gâteau [ˈgætəʊ] n, pl ~x [ˈgætəʊz] *(Brit)* grand gâteau fourré.
gather [ˈgæðəʳ] 1 vt a *(also* ~ **together)** *people* rassembler, grouper, réunir; *objects* rassembler, ramasser; *(Typ)* *pages* assembler; *troops* amasser. **the accident** ~**ed quite a crowd** l'accident a provoqué *or* causé un grand rassemblement.
b *(collect)* *flowers* cueillir; *wood, sticks, mushrooms* ramasser; *taxes etc* percevoir; *information* recueillir. **to** ~ **dirt** s'encrasser; **to** ~ **dust** ramasser la poussière; **to** ~ **one's energies** rassembler *or* ramasser ses forces; **to** ~ **one's senses** *or* **one's thoughts** méditer, s'absorber, se concentrer; **to** ~ **speed,** *(Naut)* **to** ~ **way** prendre de la vitesse; **to** ~ **strength** *[person]* reprendre des forces; *[feeling, movement]* se renforcer; **to** ~ **volume** croître en volume.
c **she** ~**ed him in her arms/to her** elle l'a serré dans ses bras/contre elle; **he** ~**ed his cloak around him** il a resserré sa cape contre lui; **she** ~**ed (up) her skirts** elle a ramassé ses jupes; **her hair was** ~**ed (up) into**

a bun ses cheveux étaient ramassés en chignon; (*liter: euph*) **he was ~ed to his fathers** il alla rejoindre ses ancêtres *or* aïeux.

d (*Sewing*) froncer. **~ed skirt** jupe froncée; **to ~ one's brows** froncer le(s) sourcil(s).

e (*infer*) déduire, conclure. **I ~ from this/this report** je conclus *or* je déduis de ceci/de ce rapport; **I ~ from the papers ...** d'après ce que disent les journaux, je déduis *or* je crois comprendre ...; **I ~ from him that ...** je comprends d'après ce qu'il me dit que ...; **what are we to ~ from that?** que devons-nous en déduire?; **as far as I can ~** à ce que je comprends; **I ~ she won't be coming** je crois comprendre qu'elle ne viendra pas; **as you will have ~ed** comme vous avez dû le deviner; **as will be ~ed from my report** comme il ressort de mon rapport.

2 **vi** a (*collect*) *[people]* s'assembler, se rassembler, se réunir, se grouper; *[crowd]* se former, se masser; *[troops etc]* s'amasser; *[objects]* s'accumuler, s'amonceler, s'amasser; *[clouds]* se former, s'amonceler; *[dust]* s'accumuler, s'amasser. **they ~ed round him** ils se sont groupés *or* se sont rassemblés autour de lui.

b (*increase*) (*in volume, intensity etc*) croître, grandir; (*in size, content etc*) grossir; *see also* **gathering**.

c *[abscess etc]* mûrir; *[pus]* se former. **tears ~ed in her eyes** ses yeux se remplirent de larmes.

3 **n** (*Sewing*) fronce *f*.

►**gather in** **vt sep** *crops* rentrer, récolter; *money, taxes* faire rentrer, percevoir; *contributions* recueillir; *papers, essays* ramasser.

►**gather round** **vi** faire cercle, s'approcher. **gather round!** approchez-vous!

►**gather together** 1 **vi** s'amasser, se rassembler. 2 **vt sep** = **gather 1a.** **to gather o.s. together** (*collect one's thoughts*) se recueillir, se concentrer; (*for jump etc*) se ramasser.

►**gather up** **vt sep** *papers, essays, toys* ramasser. **to gather up the threads of a discussion** rassembler les principaux points d'une discussion; **to gather up one's strength** rassembler ses forces; (*for jump etc*) **to gather o.s. up** se ramasser; **he gathered himself up to his full height** il s'est redressé de toute sa stature; *see also* **gather 1c**.

gathering ['gæðərɪŋ] 1 **n** a (*NonC: act*) *[people]* rassemblement *m*; *[objects]* accumulation *f*, amoncellement *m*; *[fruits etc]* cueillette *f*; *[crops]* récolte *f*; (*Typ*) assemblage *m*. **~ of speed** accélération *f*. b (*group*) *[people]* assemblée *f*, réunion *f*, rassemblement *m*; *[objects]* accumulation *f*, amoncellement *m*. **family ~** réunion de famille. c (*NonC: Sewing*) fronces *fpl*, froncis *m*. 2 **adj** *darkness, force, speed etc* croissant. **the ~ storm** l'orage qui se prépare (*or* se préparait).

GATT [gæt] **n** (**abbr of General Agreement on Tariffs and Trade**) GATT *m*, accord *m* général sur les tarifs douaniers et le commerce.

gauche [gəʊʃ] **adj** gauche, maladroit, inhabile.

gaucheness ['gəʊʃnɪs] **n** gaucherie *f*, maladresse *f*.

gaucho ['gaʊtʃəʊ] **n** gaucho *m*.

gaudily ['gɔːdɪlɪ] **adv**: **~ coloured** aux couleurs criardes *or* voyantes; **~ decorated/painted/dressed** décoré aux/peint aux/habillé de couleurs criardes; **~ patterned** aux motifs voyants.

gaudy ['gɔːdɪ] 1 **adj** *colour* voyant, criard; *display etc* tapageur, de mauvais goût. 2 **n** (*Brit Univ*) fête annuelle (*de collège*).

gauge [geɪdʒ] 1 **n** (*standard measure: also of gun*) calibre *m*; (*Rail*) écartement *m*; (*Tex*) jauge *f*; (*instrument*) jauge, indicateur *m*. (*Aut, Aviat*) **fuel ~** jauge de carburant; (*Aviat etc*) **height ~** altimètre *m*; **oil ~** indicateur *or* jauge du niveau d'huile; (*Aut*) **petrol ~**, (*US*) **gasoline ~** jauge d'essence; **pressure ~** manomètre *m*; **temperature ~** indicateur de température; **tyre ~** indicateur de pression des pneus; (*Aut*) **wheel ~** écartement des essieux; **rain ~** pluviomètre *m*; **wind ~** anémomètre *m*; (*fig*) **it is a ~ of his experience** c'est un test qui permettra de juger *or* de jauger *or* d'évaluer son expérience; **the incident was a ~ of public feeling on the subject** l'incident a permis de jauger *or* d'évaluer le sentiment du public sur le sujet.

2 **vt** a (*measure*) *nut, temperature* mesurer; *oil* jauger; *wind* mesurer la vitesse de; *screw, gun* calibrer; *sb's capacities* jauger, mesurer; *course of events* prévoir. **to ~ the distance with one's eye** jauger *or* mesurer la distance de l'œil; **he was trying to ~ how far he should move it** il essayait d'évaluer de combien il devait le déplacer; **to ~ the right moment** calculer le bon moment; **we must try to ~ how strong public opinion is** nous devons essayer de jauger *or* de mesurer la force de l'opinion publique.

b *tools* standardiser.

3 **comp** ► **narrow-/standard-/broad-gauge railway** voie étroite/à écartement normal/à grand écartement.

Gaul [gɔːl] **n** (*country*) Gaule *f*; (*person*) Gaulois(e) *m(f)*.

gaullist ['gəʊlɪst] **adj, n** gaulliste *(mf)*.

gaunt [gɔːnt] **adj** (*very thin*) *person* émacié, décharné; *face* creux; (*grim*) *building* sévère, lugubre; *landscape* désolé.

gauntlet ['gɔːntlɪt] **n** (*glove*) gant *m* (à crispin); (*part of glove*) crispin *m*; *[armour]* gantelet *m*. (*Hist, also fig*) **to throw down/take up the ~** jeter/relever le gant; **to run the ~** (*Mil Hist*) passer par les baguettes; (*Naut Hist*) courir la bouline; (*fig*) **he had to run the ~ through the crowd** il a dû foncer à travers une foule hostile; (*fig*) **he ran the ~ of public criticism** il essuya le feu des critiques du public.

gauss [gaʊs] **n, pl inv** gauss *m*.

gauze [gɔːz] **n** (*all senses*) gaze *f*.

gave [geɪv] **pret of give.**

gavel ['gævl] **n** marteau *m* (*de président de réunion, de commissaire-priseur*).

gavotte [gə'vɒt] **n** gavotte *f*.

Gawd‡ [gɔːd] **excl** (*Brit* = **God**) mon Dieu!, bon Dieu!‡

gawk [gɔːk] 1 **n** godiche* *mf*, grand dadais*. 2 **vi** rester bouche bée (*at* devant).

gawker* ['gɔːkə^r] **n** badaud *m*.

gawky ['gɔːkɪ] **adj** godiche*, gauche.

gawp* [gɔːp] **vi** = **gape 1.**

gay [geɪ] 1 **adj** a (*homosexual*) *person* homosexuel, gay *inv*; *club, bar etc* gay *inv*, pour homosexuels.

b (*liter or* †: *cheerful*) *person, music* gai, joyeux; *appearance* gai; *company, occasion* joyeux; *laughter* enjoué; *colour* éclatant, vif; (*pleasure-loving*) adonné aux plaisirs. **~ with lights** resplendissant de lumières; **~ with flowers** égayé de fleurs; **to become ~(er)** s'égayer; **with ~ abandon** avec une belle désinvolture; **they danced with ~ abandon** ils se sont abandonnés joyeusement au plaisir de la danse; **to lead a** *or* **the ~ life** mener une vie de plaisirs, mener joyeuse vie; **to have a ~ time** prendre du bon temps.

2 **n** homosexuel(le) *m(f)*. **G~ Liberation (Movement), Gay Lib*** (mouvement *m* pour) la libération des homosexuels *or* la libération gay.

gayness ['geɪnɪs] **n** *[homosexual]* homosexualité *f*.

Gaza strip ['gɑːzə'strɪp] **n** bande *f* *or* territoire *m* de Gaza.

gaze [geɪz] 1 **n** regard *m* (fixe). **his ~ met mine** son regard a croisé le mien. 2 **vi** regarder. **to ~ into space** regarder dans *or* fixer le vide; **to ~ at** *or* (*liter*) **upon sth** regarder *or* contempler qch.

►**gaze about, gaze around** **vi** regarder autour de soi.

gazebo [gə'ziːbəʊ] **n, pl ~s** *or* **~es** belvédère *m* (*pavillon*).

gazelle [gə'zel] **n, pl ~s** *or* **~** gazelle *f*.

gazette [gə'zet] 1 **n** (*official publication*) (journal *m*) officiel *m*; (*newspaper*) gazette *f*. 2 **vt** publier à l'Officiel. (*Mil etc*) **to be ~d** avoir sa nomination publiée à l'Officiel.

gazetteer [ˌgæzɪ'tɪə^r] **n** index *m* (géographique).

gazpacho [gəz'pætʃəʊ] **n** gaspacho *m*.

gazump [gə'zʌmp] 1 **vi** (*Brit*) *revenir sur une promesse de vente pour accepter un prix plus élevé*. 2 **vt** (*Brit*) **he was ~ed** il n'a pas pu acheter la maison parce que quelqu'un a fait une offre plus élevée au vendeur.

gazumping [gə'zʌmpɪŋ] **n** (*Brit*) *le fait de revenir sur une promesse de vente d'une maison pour accepter une offre plus élevée*.

GB [dʒiː'biː] (**abbr of Great Britain**) G.B.

G.B.H. [ˌdʒiːbiː'eɪtʃ] (*Brit: crime*) (**abbr of grievous bodily harm**) *see* **grievous**.

GBS [dʒiːbiː'es] (*Brit*) (**abbr of George Bernard Shaw**) *écrivain*.

G.C. [dʒiː'siː] **n** (*Brit*) (**abbr of George Cross**) *see* **George**.

GCE [dʒiːsiː'iː] **n** (*Brit Educ*) (**abbr of General Certificate of Education**) **~ "O" level**† ≃ brevet *m*; **~ "A" level** ≃ baccalauréat *m*.

GCHQ [ˌdʒiːsiːeɪtʃ'kjuː] **n** (*Brit*) (**abbr of Government Communications Headquarters**) *service gouvernemental d'écoutes et de transmissions*.

GCSE [ˌdʒiːsiːes'iː] **n** (*Brit Educ*) (**abbr of General Certificate of Secondary Education**) *certificat passé à l'âge de 16 ans sanctionnant les connaissances de l'élève dans une matière*.

Gdansk [gdænsk] **n** Gdansk.

GDI [dʒiːdiː'aɪ] (**abbr of gross domestic income**) *see* **gross**.

Gdns. **abbr of Gardens** (*dans les adresses*).

GDP [dʒiːdiː'piː] (**abbr of gross domestic product**) *see* **gross**.

GDR [dʒiːdiː'ɑː^r] (*Hist*) (**abbr of German Democratic Republic**) *see* **German**.

gear [gɪə^r] 1 **n** a (*NonC*) (*equipment*) équipement *m*, matériel *m*, attirail *m*; (*harness*) harnachement *m*; *[camping, skiing, climbing, photography]* matériel, équipement; *[sewing, painting]* matériel; *[gardening]* matériel, outils *mpl*. **fishing** *etc* **~** matériel *or* équipement de pêche *etc*; **the kitchen ~ is in this cupboard** les ustensiles *mpl* de cuisine sont dans ce placard.

b (*, *NonC: belongings*) effets *mpl* (personnels), affaires *fpl*. **he leaves his ~ all over the house** il laisse traîner ses affaires dans toute la maison.

c (*Brit: NonC: clothing*) vêtements *mpl*. **he had his tennis ~ on** il était en tenue de tennis; **put on your tennis ~** mets tes affaires de tennis.

d (*Brit* ‡: *NonC: modern clothes*) fringues‡ *fpl* à la mode.

e (*NonC: apparatus*) mécanisme *m*, dispositif *m*. **safety ~** mécanisme *m* *or* dispositif *m* de sécurité; *see* **landing, steering** *etc*.

f (*Tech*) engrenage *m*. **in ~** engrené, en prise; **it's out of ~** c'est désengrené, ce n'est pas *or* plus en prise.

g (*Aut*) (*mechanism*) embrayage *m*; (*speed*) vitesse *f*. **in ~** en prise; **not in ~** au point mort; **he put the car into ~** il a mis (la voiture) en prise; **the car slipped** *or* **jumped out of ~** la vitesse a sauté; **neutral ~** point mort; **to change** *or* (*US*) **to shift ~** changer de vitesse; **first** *or* **bottom** *or* **low ~** première vitesse; **second/third/fourth ~** deuxième/troisième/quatrième vitesse; (*Brit*) **top ~**, (*US*) **high ~**

(*fourth*) quatrième vitesse; (*fifth*) cinquième vitesse; **in second ~** en seconde; **to change** *or* (*US*) **to shift into third ~** passer en troisième (vitesse); (*fig*) (*Brit*) **to change ~,** (*US*) **to shift ~s** se réadapter; **you're in too high a ~** tu devrais rétrograder; (*fig*) **production has moved into high** *or* **top ~** la production a atteint sa vitesse maxima; *see* **engage, reverse** *etc.*

2 **comp** ▶**gearbox** (*Brit Aut*) boîte *f* de vitesses ▶**gear change** (*Brit*) changement *m* de vitesse ▶**gear lever** (*Brit*) levier *m* de (changement de) vitesse ▶**gear ratio** *[cycle]* braquet *m* ▶**gearshift** (*US*) = **gear lever, gear change** ▶**gearwheel** *[cycle]* pignon *m.*

3 **adj** (*US* ‡: *great*) formid*, super*.

4 **vt** a adapter. **they ~ed their output to seasonal demands** ils ont adapté leur production à la demande saisonnière; **he ~ed his timetable to collecting his children from school** il a adapté *or* combiné son emploi du temps de façon à pouvoir aller chercher les enfants à l'école; **they were not ~ed to cope with the influx of immigrants** ils n'étaient pas préparés pour cet afflux d'immigrants; **the factory was not ~ed to cope with an increase of production** la capacité de l'usine n'était pas calculée pour une production supérieure; (*Econ, Ind*) **~ed to the cost of living** indexé.

b *wheel* engrener.

5 **vi** s'engrener.

▶**gear down** **vi** (*Tech*) démultiplier.

▶**gear up** 1 **vi** a (*Tech*) produire une multiplication. b (*get ready*) **they are gearing up to a war** ils se préparent à la guerre. c (*Brit Fin*) *[company]* s'endetter, augmenter le taux d'endettement. 2 **vt sep** (*: *make ready*) **he geared himself up for the interview** il s'est préparé pour l'entrevue; **we're geared up (and ready) to do it** nous sommes tout prêts à le faire; **they were all geared up for the new sales campaign** ils étaient parés* *or* fin prêts pour la nouvelle promotion de vente.

gearing ['gɪərɪŋ] **n** (*Brit Fin*) rapport *m* des fonds propres sur fonds empruntés.

gecko ['gekəʊ] **n, pl ~s** *or* **~es** gecko *m.*

gee[1]* [dʒiː] **excl** (**esp US*) eh bien! **~ whiz!*** mince alors!*

gee[2] [dʒiː] 1 **n** (‡: *also* **~-~**: *baby talk*) dada *m.* 2 **excl** (*to horse*) **~ up!** hue!

geese [giːs] **npl of goose.**

geezer‡ ['giːzəʳ] **n** (*Brit*) type* *m.* **(silly) old ~** vieux schnock‡.

gefilte [gəˈfɪltə] **adj** (*US*) **~ fish** ≃ boulettes *fpl* de poisson.

Geiger counter ['gaɪgəˌkaʊntəʳ] **n** compteur *m* Geiger.

geisha ['geɪʃə] **n, pl ~** *or* **~s** geisha *f or* ghesha *f.*

gel[1] [dʒel] 1 **n** (*Chem*) colloïde *m*; (*for hair*) gel *m* (coiffant); (*gen*) gelée *f.* 2 **vi** *[jelly etc]* prendre, épaissir; *[plan etc]* prendre tournure.

gel[2] [gel] **n** († *or hum*) = **girl 1.**

gelatin(e) ['dʒelətiːn] **n** gélatine *f.*

gelatinous [dʒɪˈlætɪnəs] **adj** gélatineux.

geld [geld] **vt** *horse* hongrer; *pig etc* châtrer.

gelding ['geldɪŋ] **n** a (*horse*) (cheval *m*) hongre *m.* b (*NonC*) castration *f.*

gelignite ['dʒelɪgnaɪt] **n** plastic *m.*

gelt‡ [gelt] **n** (*US*) fric* *m.*

gem [dʒem] 1 **n** gemme *f*, pierre précieuse; (*fig: work of art*) (vrai) bijou *m*, chef-d'œuvre *m*, merveille *f.* **his painting was the ~ of the collection** son tableau était le joyau de la collection; **it's a little ~ of a house** la maison est un vrai petit bijou; **this miniature is a perfect ~** cette miniature est une vraie merveille; **your char's a ~*** votre femme de ménage est une perle; **her aunt's a real ~*** sa tante est un chou*; **I must read you this ~* from the newspaper** il faut que je te lise cette perle dans le journal. 2 **comp** ▶**the Gem State** (*US*) l'Idaho *m* ▶**gemstone** pierre *f* gemme *inv.*

Gemini ['dʒemɪnaɪ] **npl** (*Astron*) les Gémeaux *mpl.* (*Astrol*) **I'm (a) ~** je suis (des) Gémeaux.

Geminian [ˌdʒemɪˈnaɪən] **n: to be a ~** être (des) Gémeaux.

gemology [dʒeˈmɒlədʒɪ] **n** gemmologie *f.*

gen* [dʒen] (*Brit*) 1 **n** coordonnées* *fpl.* **to give sb the ~ on sth** donner à qn les coordonnées* *or* tous les tuyaux* de qch, rencarder‡ qn sur qch; **what's the ~ on this?** qu'est-ce qu'on doit savoir *or* qu'on sait là-dessus?; **I want all the ~ on him** je voudrais avoir toutes ses coordonnées*; **have you got the ~ on the new house?** avez-vous une documentation sur la nouvelle maison? 2 **adj** vrai, vrai de vrai‡, véritable.

▶**gen up**‡ 1 **vi: to gen up on sth** se rencarder sur qch‡. 2 **vt sep: to gen sb up on sth** mettre qn au parfum‡ de qch, rencarder‡ qn sur qch, donner à qn les coordonnées* de qch; **to be genned up on** être tout à fait au courant de, être bien renseigné sur.

Gen. (*Mil*) (**abbr of general**) (*on envelope*) **Gen. J. Smith** le général Smith.

gen. **abbr of general** *and* **generally.**

gendarme ['dʒɒndɑːm] **n** (*Climbing*) gendarme *m.*

gender ['dʒendəʳ] 1 **n** (*Gram*) genre *m*; (*: *sex*) sexe *m.* **common ~** genre commun; **of common ~** épicène; (*Gram*) **to agree in ~** s'accorder en genre. 2 **comp** ▶**gender bender**‡ *personne qui s'habille de façon asexuée* ▶**gender bias** parti pris *m* contre les femmes (*or* les hommes) ▶**the gender gap** les préjugés *mpl* contre les femmes.

gene [dʒiːn] **n** gène *m.* **~ therapy** thérapie *f* génétique; **~ pool** bagage *m or* patrimoine *m* héréditaire (de l'espèce).

genealogical [ˌdʒiːnɪəˈlɒdʒɪkəl] **adj** généalogique.

genealogist [ˌdʒiːnɪˈælədʒɪst] **n** généalogiste *mf.*

genealogy [ˌdʒiːnɪˈælədʒɪ] **n** généalogie *f.*

genera ['dʒenərə] **npl of genus.**

general ['dʒenərəl] 1 **adj** a (*common, not limited or specialized*) général; (*not in detail*) *view, plan, inquiry* d'ensemble. **in a ~ way** d'une manière générale; **as a ~ rule** en règle générale; **in ~ use** d'usage courant, généralement répandu; **for ~ use** à l'usage du public; **if you go in the ~ direction of the church** si vous allez grosso modo dans la direction de l'église; **he was a ~ favourite** il était universellement aimé *or* aimé par tout le monde; **the book was a ~ favourite** le livre a été très apprécié du (grand) public; **~ meeting** assemblée générale (*see* **annual**); **the ~ public** le grand public; **the ~ reader** le lecteur moyen; **~ servant** bonne *f* à tout faire; **there has been ~ opposition to the scheme** l'opposition à ce plan a été générale; **this type of behaviour is fairly ~ amongst young people** ce genre de comportement est assez répandu parmi les jeunes; **the rain has been fairly ~** il a plu un peu partout; **to give sb a ~ idea** *or* **outline of a subject** donner à qn un aperçu (d'ensemble) sur un sujet; **I've got the ~ idea** j'ai une idée d'ensemble sur la question; **I get the ~ idea** je vois.

b (*specific terms*) (*Med*) **~ anaesthetic** anesthésie générale; **~ assembly** assemblée générale; (*Brit Scol*) **G~ Certificate of Education** ≃ baccalauréat *m*; (*Rel*) **~ confession** (*Church of England*) confession collective (*lors de la prière en commun*); (*Roman Catholic Church*) confession générale; (*US*) **~ dealer = ~ shop;** (*Univ*) **~ degree** ≃ licence *f* libre; (*US, Can: Post*) **~ delivery** poste restante; **~ election** élections législatives *or* générales; (*Brit*) **~ factotum** (*lit*) factotum *m*; (*fig*) bonne *f* à tout faire; (*Mil*) **~ headquarters** quartier général; **~ holiday** fête publique, jour férié; **~ hospital** centre hospitalier; **~ insurance** assurances *fpl* IARD (*incendies, accidents, risques, divers*); **~ knowledge** connaissances générales, culture générale; **~ linguistics** linguistique générale; **~ manager** directeur général; (*Med*) **~ medicine** médecine générale; (*Mil*) **G~ Officer Commanding** général *m* commandant en chef; **there was ~ post within the department** (*changing desks*) tout le monde dans le service a changé de bureau; (*changing jobs*) il y a eu une réorganisation complète du personnel dans le service; **G~ Post Office** (*Admin*) Postes et Télécommunications; (*building*) poste centrale; (*Jur, Fin*) **general partnership** société *f* en nom collectif; (*Med*) **to be in ~ practice** faire de la médecine générale; **~ practitioner** (médecin *m*) généraliste *m*, omnipraticien *m*, -ienne *f*; (*Scol*) **general science** les sciences (*la physique, la chimie et les sciences naturelles*); **~ shop** magasin *m* qui vend de tout; (*Mil etc*) **~ staff** état-major *m*; **~ store** (*department store*) grand magasin; (*small shop*) épicerie *f* générale; **~ strike** grève générale; *see* **paralysis** *etc.*

c (*after official title*) général, en chef; *see* **secretary** *etc.*

d (*not belonging to anyone in particular*) *laundry, vehicle* communal; *typist* pour tout le service (*or* la section *etc*).

2 **comp** ▶**general-purpose** *tool, substance* universel, multi-usages; *dictionary* général.

3 **n** a général *m.* **in ~** en général; **the particular and the ~** le particulier et le général.

b (*Mil: Brit, US etc*) général *m.* (*US*) **~ (of the Air Force)** général *m* de l'armée de l'air; *see* **brigadier** *etc.*

c (*: *servant*) bonne *f* à tout faire.

generality [ˌdʒenəˈrælɪtɪ] **n** a (*gen pl*) généralité *f*, considération générale. **we talked only of generalities** nous n'avons parlé que de généralités *or* qu'en termes généraux *or* que de questions *fpl* d'ordre général. b (*most of*) **the ~ of** la plupart de. c (*NonC*) caractère général. **a rule of great ~** une règle très générale.

generalization [ˌdʒenərəlaɪˈzeɪʃən] **n** généralisation *f.*

generalize ['dʒenərəlaɪz] **vti** généraliser.

generally ['dʒenərəlɪ] **adv** (*usually*) généralement, en général; (*for the most part*) dans l'ensemble. **~ speaking** en général, d'une manière générale.

generalship ['dʒenərəlʃɪp] **n** (*Mil*) tactique *f.*

generate ['dʒenəreɪt] 1 **vt** *children* engendrer; *electricity, heat* produire; (*Ling*) générer; (*fig*) *hope, fear* engendrer, donner naissance à; *work etc* générer*, produire. 2 **comp** ▶**generating set** groupe *m* électrogène ▶**generating station** centrale *f* électrique ▶**generating unit** groupe *m* électrogène.

generation [ˌdʒenəˈreɪʃən] 1 **n** a génération *f.* **the younger ~** la jeune génération; **the postwar ~** la génération d'après-guerre; **a ~ ago** il y a une génération; (*fig*) **it's ~s since ...*** ça fait des siècles que ...; **first-/second-~** (**adj**) (*Comput etc*) de la première/de la seconde génération; **he is a first-/second-~ American** il appartient à la première/seconde génération d'Américains de sa famille; *see* **rising.** b (*NonC*) *[electricity, heat]* production *f*; (*Ling*) génération *f*; *[hatred etc]* engendrement *m.* 2 **comp** ▶**the generation gap** le conflit *or* l'opposition *f* des générations.

generative ['dʒenərətɪv] **adj** (*Ling*) génératif. **~ grammar** grammaire générative.

generator ['dʒenəreɪtəʳ] **n** a (*apparatus*) (*Elec*) groupe *m* électrogène, génératrice *f*; *[steam]* générateur *m*, chaudière *f*; *[gas]* gazogène *m*; *[lighting]* dynamo *f* (d'éclairage). **b** (*person*) générateur *m*, -trice *f*.

generatrix ['dʒɛnəˌreɪtrɪks] **n, pl generatrices** ['dʒɛnəˌreɪtrɪˌsiːz] (*Math*) génératrice *f*.

generic [dʒɪ'nerɪk] **adj** générique (*also Ling*).

generically [dʒɪ'nerɪkəlɪ] **adv** génériquement.

generosity [ˌdʒenə'rɒsɪtɪ] **n** (*NonC*) générosité *f*, libéralité *f*.

generous ['dʒenərəs] **adj** *person, character, action, wine* généreux; *gift, donation, quantity* généreux; *supply, harvest* abondant; *meal* copieux, abondant; *size* ample. **he is very ~ with his time** il est très généreux de son temps; **he took a ~ helping of carrots** il s'est servi abondamment de carottes; **a ~ spoonful of sugar** une bonne cuillerée de sucre; **the seams in this dress are very ~** les coutures de cette robe ont une bonne largeur.

generously ['dʒenərəslɪ] **adv** *give etc* généreusement; *say, offer* avec générosité; *pardon, reprieve* avec magnanimité. **a dress cut ~ around the waist** une robe ample à la taille; **you've salted this meat rather ~** tu as eu la main un peu lourde en salant cette viande.

genesis ['dʒenɪsɪs] **n, pl geneses** ['dʒenɪsiːz] genèse *f*, origine *f*. (*Bible*) **G~** la Genèse.

genetic [dʒɪ'netɪk] **adj** (*Bio: of the genes*) génétique, génique; (*hereditary*) génétique; (*Philos*) génétique. (*Bio*) **~ code** code *m* génétique; **~ counselling** conseil *m* génétique; **~ engineering** génie *m* génétique; **~ fingerprint** empreinte *f* génétique; **~ fingerprinting** système *m* d'empreinte génétique; **~ map** carte *f* génétique; **~ screening test** *m* de dépistage génétique.

genetically [dʒɪ'netɪkəlɪ] **adv** (*gen*) génétiquement. **~ engineered** obtenu par manipulation génétique.

geneticist [dʒɪ'netɪsɪst] **n** généticien(ne) *m(f)*.

genetics [dʒɪ'netɪks] **n** (*NonC*) génétique *f*.

Geneva [dʒɪ'niːvə] **n** Genève. **Lake ~** le lac Léman *or* de Genève; **~ Convention** convention *f* de Genève.

genial ['dʒiːnɪəl] **adj** **a** (*kindly, pleasant*) *person* cordial, affable, aimable; *climate* doux (*f* douce), clément, agréable; *smile, look, voice* chaleureux, cordial; *warmth* réconfortant, vivifiant. **b** (*having genius*) génial.

geniality [ˌdʒiːnɪ'ælɪtɪ] **n** *[person, smile]* cordialité *f*, chaleur *f*; *[climate]* douceur *f*, clémence *f*.

genially ['dʒiːnɪəlɪ] **adv** **a** (*pleasantly*) cordialement. **b** (*as a genius*) génialement.

genie ['dʒiːnɪ] **n, pl genii** génie *m*, djinn *m*.

genii ['dʒiːnɪaɪ] **npl of genie** *and* **genius d**.

genital ['dʒenɪtl] **1** **adj** génital. **~ herpes** herpès *m* génital; **~ warts** vésicules *fpl* génitales. **2** **npl: ~s** organes *mpl* génitaux.

genitalia [ˌdʒenɪ'teɪlɪə] **npl** organes *mpl* génitaux.

genitive ['dʒenɪtɪv] (*Gram*) **1** **adj** *case* génitif. **~ ending** flexion *f* du génitif. **2** **n** génitif *m*. **in the ~** au génitif.

genius ['dʒiːnɪəs] **n** **a** (*NonC*) (*cleverness*) génie *m*; (*ability, aptitude*) génie (*for* de), don *m* extraordinaire (*for* pour). **man of ~** (homme *m* de) génie; **his ~ lay in his ability to assess ...** il était supérieurement doué pour juger ...; **he has a ~ for publicity** il a le génie de la publicité; **he's got a ~ for saying the wrong thing** il a le génie de *or* un certain génie pour dire ce qu'il ne faut pas. **b** **pl ~es** génie *m*. **he's a ~** c'est un génie, il est génial. **c** (*NonC: distinctive character*) *[period, country etc]* génie *m* (particulier). **d** **pl genii** (*spirit*) génie *m*. **evil ~** mauvais génie.

genned up ['dʒend'ʌp] **adj** *see* **gen up‡ 2.**

Genoa ['dʒenəʊə] **n** Gênes.

genocidal [ˌdʒenəʊ'saɪdl] **adj** génocide.

genocide ['dʒenəʊsaɪd] **n** génocide *m*.

Genoese [ˌdʒenəʊ'iːz] **1** **adj** génois. **2** **n, pl inv** Génois(e) *m(f)*.

genotype ['dʒenəʊtaɪp] **n** génotype *m*.

genre ['ʒɑ̃ːŋrə] **n** genre *m*. **~ (painting)** tableau *m* de genre.

gent [dʒent] **n abbr of gentleman.** **a** (*Comm*) **~s' outfitters** magasin *m* d'habillement *or* de confection pour hommes; (*Comm*) **~s' shoes/suitings** *etc* chaussures/tissus *etc* (pour) hommes; **the ~s** les toilettes *fpl* (pour hommes); (*sign*) **"~s"** "messieurs". **b** (‡) monsieur *m*, type* *m*. **he's a (real) ~‡** c'est un monsieur (tout ce qu'il y a de) bien.

genteel [dʒen'tiːl] **adj** **a** (*frm, liter*) *person, behaviour, family* distingué, élégant; *life, upbringing* très convenable. **b** (*iro*) *person, behaviour, upbringing, school* très comme il faut. **~ poverty** une misère distinguée; **she has a very ~ way of holding her glass** elle a une façon qu'elle croit distinguée de tenir son verre; *see* **shabby.**

genteelly [dʒen'tiːlɪ] **adv** *sit, eat, drink etc* de façon très convenable (*also iro*). (*iro*) **to be ~ poor** vivre dans une misère distinguée; (*iro*) **she coughed ~ behind her hand** elle toussa de manière très délicate derrière sa main.

gentian ['dʒenʃɪən] **n** gentiane *f*. **~ blue** bleu *m* gentiane; **~ violet** bleu de méthylène.

Gentile ['dʒentaɪl] **1** **n** Gentil(e) *m(f)*. **2** **adj** des Gentils.

gentility [dʒen'tɪlɪtɪ] **n** (*iro*) prétention *f* à la distinction *or* au bon ton; (*†: good birth*) bonne famille, bonne naissance. (*†: gentry*) **the ~** la haute bourgeoisie, la petite noblesse.

gentle ['dʒentl] **1** **adj** **a** (*kind, not rough*) *person, disposition* doux (*f* douce), aimable; *voice, animal* doux. (*liter*) **the ~ sex** le beau sexe; **to be ~ with one's hands** avoir la main douce; **to use ~ methods** employer la douceur; **~ as a lamb** doux comme un agneau. **b** (*not violent or strong*) *rebuke* gentil, peu sévère; *exercise, heat* modéré; *slope* doux (*f* douce); *tap, breeze, push, sound, touch* léger; *progress* mesuré; *transition* sans heurts; *hint, reminder* discret (*f* -ète). **the car came to a ~ stop** la voiture s'est arrêtée doucement; **try a little ~ persuasion and he ...** essaie de le persuader en douceur et il ... . **c** (*†: wellborn*) noble, bien né, de bonne famille. **of ~ birth** bien né; (*† or hum*) **~ reader** aimable lecteur; (*Hist*) **~ knight** noble chevalier *m*. **2** **comp** ►**gentlefolk** gens *mpl* de bonne famille ►**gentleman** *see* **gentleman** ►**gentlewoman** (*by birth*) dame *f or* demoiselle *f* de bonne famille; (*in manner*) dame *or* demoiselle très bien *or* comme il faut*; (*at court*) dame d'honneur *or* de compagnie.

gentleman ['dʒentlmən], **pl gentlemen** **1** **n** **a** (*man*) monsieur *m*. **there's a ~ to see you** il y a un monsieur qui voudrait vous voir; (*US Pol*) **the gentleman from ...** Monsieur le député de ...; **the ~ I was speaking to** le monsieur à qui je parlais; (*sign*) **"gentlemen"** "messieurs". **b** (*man of breeding*) homme bien élevé, gentleman *m*. **he is a perfect ~** c'est un vrai gentleman; **a ~ never uses such language** un monsieur bien élevé ne se sert jamais de mots pareils; **one of nature's gentlemen** un gentleman né; **~'s agreement** accord *m* reposant sur l'honneur; (*Comm*) **gentlemen's shoes/suitings** *etc* chaussures/tissus *etc* (pour) hommes; (*hum*) **~'s ~** valet *m* de chambre; **be a ~ and give her your seat** montre-toi bien élevé et donne-lui ta place; **he's no ~!** ce n'est pas un monsieur! **c** (*man of substance*) rentier *m*. **to lead the life of a ~** vivre de ses rentes. **d** (*at court etc*) gentilhomme *m*. **2** **comp** ►**gentleman-at-arms** (**pl gentlemen-~-~**) gentilhomme *m* de la garde ►**gentleman-farmer** (**pl gentlemen-~s**) gentleman-farmer *m* ►**gentleman-in-waiting** (**pl gentlemen-~-~**) gentilhomme *m* (*attaché à la personne du roi etc*).

gentlemanly ['dʒentlmənlɪ] **adj** *person, manner* bien élevé, courtois; *voice, appearance* distingué; *behaviour* courtois.

gentlemen ['dʒentlmən] **npl of gentleman.**

gentleness ['dʒentlnɪs] **n** *[person, animal, character]* douceur *f*, bonté *f*; *[action, touch]* douceur.

gently ['dʒentlɪ] **adv** *push, touch, stroke* doucement, avec douceur; *say, smile, rebuke* avec douceur, gentiment; *remind, suggest* gentiment; *walk, move* (tout) doucement; *exercise* doucement, sans forcer. **the road slopes ~ down to the river** la route descend doucement *or* va en pente douce vers la rivière; **~ does it!** (allons-y) doucement!; **to go ~ with** *or* **on sth*** y aller doucement *or* mollo* avec qch; **to deal ~ with sb** ménager qn, ne pas bousculer qn; **~ born†** bien né, de bonne naissance†.

gentrification [ˌdʒentrɪfɪ'keɪʃən] **n** (*Brit*) *[area of a town or city]* embourgeoisement *m*.

gentrified [ˌdʒentrɪˌfaɪd] **adj** *area, houses etc* embourgeoisé.

gentry ['dʒentrɪ] **n** (*Brit*) (*of good birth*) petite noblesse; (*fig pej: people*) gens *mpl*.

genuflect ['dʒenjʊflekt] **vi** faire une génuflexion.

genuflexion, (*US*) genuflection [ˌdʒenjʊ'flekʃən] **n** génuflexion *f*.

genuine ['dʒenjʊɪn] **1** **adj** **a** (*authentic*) *wool, silver, jewel etc* véritable; *manuscript, antique* authentique; *coin* de bon aloi; (*Comm*) *goods* garanti d'origine. **a ~ Persian rug** un authentique tapis persan; **I'll only buy the ~ article** (*of furniture etc*) je n'achète que de l'authentique; (*of jewellery, cheeses etc*) je n'achète que du vrai; **that's the ~ article!*** ça c'est du vrai! **b** (*sincere*) *laughter* franc (*f* franche); *tears* vrai, sincère; *emotion, belief* sincère; *simplicity* vrai, franc; *person* franc, sincère. **he is a very ~ person** il est très (simple et) direct; (*Comm*) **~ buyer** acheteur sérieux. **2** **comp** ►**genuine assets** (*Accounting*) actif *m* réel.

genuinely ['dʒenjʊɪnlɪ] **adv** *prove, originate* authentiquement; *feel, think* sincèrement; *sorry, surprised, unable* vraiment.

genuineness ['dʒenjʊɪnˌnɪs] **n** **a** (*authenticity*) authenticité *f*. **b** (*sincerity*) sincérité *f*.

genus ['dʒenəs] **n, pl genera** *or* **~es** (*Bio*) genre *m*.

ge(o)... ['dʒiː(əʊ)] **pref** géo... .

geocentric [ˌdʒiːəʊ'sentrɪk] **adj** géocentrique.

geochemical [ˌdʒiːəʊ'kemɪkəl] **adj** géochimique.

geochemist [ˌdʒiːəʊ'kemɪst] **n** géochimiste *mf*.

geochemistry [ˌdʒiːəʊ'kemɪstrɪ] **n** géochimie *f*.

geode ['dʒiːəʊd] **n** géode *f*.

geodesic [ˌdʒiːəʊ'desɪk] **adj** géodésique. **~ dome** dôme *m* géodésique; **~ line** géodésique *f*.

geodesy [dʒiː'ɒdɪsɪ] **n** géodésie *f*.

geodetic [ˌdʒiːəʊ'detɪk] **adj** = **geodesic.**

geographer [dʒɪ'ɒgrəfə^r] **n** géographe *mf*.

geographic(al) [dʒɪə'græfɪk(əl)] **adj** géographique. **~ mile** mille marin *or* nautique.

geographically [dʒɪəˈgræfɪkəlɪ] **adv** géographiquement. ~ **speaking** du point de vue géographique.
geography [dʒɪˈɒgrəfɪ] **n** (*science*) géographie *f*. **I don't know the ~ of the district** je ne connais pas la topographie de la région.
geological [dʒɪəʊˈlɒdʒɪkəl] **adj** géologique. (*US*) ~ **survey** Bureau *m* de Recherches Géologiques et Minières.
geologically [dʒɪəˈlɒdʒɪkəlɪ] **adv** géologiquement. ~ **speaking** du point de vue géologique.
geologist [dʒɪˈɒlədʒɪst] **n** géologue *mf*.
geology [dʒɪˈɒlədʒɪ] **n** géologie *f*.
geomagnetic [ˌdʒiːəʊmægˈnetɪk] **adj** géomagnétique. ~ **storm** orage *m* géomagnétique.
geomagnetism [ˌdʒiːəʊˈmægnɪˌtɪzəm] **n** géomagnétisme *m*.
geometric(al) [dʒɪəʊˈmetrɪk(əl)] **adj** géométrique. (*Math*) ~ **mean** moyenne *f* géométrique; **by ~ progression** par progression géométrique; ~ **series** série *f* géométrique.
geometrically [ˌdʒɪəˈmetrɪkəlɪ] **adv** géométriquement.
geometrician [ˌdʒɪˌɒmɪˈtrɪʃən] **n** géomètre *mf*.
geometry [dʒɪˈɒmɪtrɪ] **n** géométrie *f*.
geomorphic [ˌdʒiːəʊˈmɔːfɪk] **adj** géomorphique.
geomorphologic(al) [ˌdʒiːəʊˈmɔːfəˈlɒdʒɪkəl] **adj** géomorphologique.
geomorphology [ˌdʒiːəʊmɔːˈfɒlədʒɪ] **n** géomorphologie *f*.
geonomics [ˌdʒiːəʊˈnɒmɪks] **n** (*NonC*) géographie *f* économique.
geophysical [ˌdʒiːəʊˈfɪzɪkəl] **adj** géophysique.
geophysicist [ˌdʒiːəʊˈfɪzɪsɪst] **n** géophysicien *m*, -ienne *f*.
geophysics [ˌdʒiːəʊˈfɪzɪks] **n** (*NonC*) géophysique *f*.
geopolitical [ˌdʒiːəʊpəˈlɪtɪkəl] **adj** géopolitique.
geopolitics [ˌdʒiːəʊˈpɒlɪtɪks] **n** (*NonC*) géopolitique *f*.
Geordie* [ˈdʒɔːdɪ] **n** (*Brit*) *natif m, -ive f de Tyneside*.
George [dʒɔːdʒ] **n** Georges *m*. **by ~!*** mon Dieu!; (*Brit*) ~ **Cross** *or* **Medal** ≃ médaille *f* du courage.
georgette [dʒɔːˈdʒet] **n** (*also* ~ **crêpe**) crêpe *m* georgette.
Georgia [ˈdʒɔːdʒɪə] **n** (*US and USSR*) Géorgie *f*. **in ~** en Géorgie.
Georgian [ˈdʒɔːdʒɪən] **adj** **a** (*Brit Hist*) du temps des rois George I-IV (*1714-1830*). (*Brit Archit*) ~ **style** *style anglais (environ 1720-1830) d'inspiration classique*. **b** (*Geog*) géorgien.
geoscience [ˌdʒiːəʊˈsaɪəns] **n** science(s) *f(pl)* de la terre.
geoscientist [ˌdʒiːəʊˈsaɪəntɪst] **n** spécialiste *mf* des sciences de la terre.
geostationary [ˌdʒiːəʊˈsteɪʃənərɪ] **adj** géostationnaire.
geosynchronous [ˌdʒiːəʊˈsɪŋkrənəs] **adj** géosynchrone.
geosyncline [ˌdʒiːəʊˈsɪnklaɪn] **n** géosynclinal *m*.
geothermal [ˌdʒiːəʊˈθɜːməl] **adj** géothermal, géothermique.
geothermally [ˌdʒiːəʊˈθɜːməlɪ] **adj** géothermiquement.
geotropic [ˌdʒiːəʊˈtrɒpɪk] **adj** géotropique.
geotropically [ˌdʒiːəʊˈtrɒpɪkəlɪ] **adv** géotropiquement.
geotropism [dʒɪˈɒtrəpɪzəm] **n** géotropisme *m*.
geranium [dʒɪˈreɪnɪəm] **1 n** géranium *m*. **2 adj** (*colour: also* ~ **red**) rouge vif *inv*, rouge géranium *inv*.
gerbil [ˈdʒɜːbɪl] **n** gerbille *f*.
geriatric [ˌdʒerɪˈætrɪk] **1 adj** gériatrique, des vieillards. ~ **hospital** hôpital *m* gériatrique; ~ **medicine** gériatrie *f*; ~ **nursing** soins *mpl* aux vieillards; ~ **social work** aide sociale aux vieillards; ~ **ward** salle *f* du service gériatrique. **2 n** (*Med*) malade *mf* gériatrique; (*pej: gen*) vieillard(e) *m(f)*.
geriatrics [ˌdʒerɪˈætrɪks] **n** (*NonC*) (*Med*) gériatrie *f*.
germ [dʒɜːm] **1 n a** (*Bio, also fig*) germe *m*. **the ~ of an idea** un embryon d'idée, le germe d'une idée. **b** (*Med*) microbe *m*, germe *m*. **2 comp ▸ germ carrier** (*Med*) porteur *m* de microbes **▸ germ cell** (*Bio*) cellule germinale *or* reproductrice, gamète *m* **▸ germ-free** (*Med*) stérile, stérilisé **▸ germ-killer** antiseptique *m*, germicide *m*, microbicide *m* **▸ germproof** résistant aux microbes **▸ germ warfare** guerre *f* bactériologique.
German [ˈdʒɜːmən] **1 adj** (*gen*) allemand; *king, ambassador, embassy* d'Allemagne; *dictionary, teacher* d'allemand. (*Hist*) ~ **Democratic Republic** République démocratique allemande; (*Hist*) **East/West ~** d'Allemagne de l'Est/de l'Ouest, Est-/Ouest-allemand; (*Med*) ~ **measles** rubéole *f*; (*US*) ~ **sheep dog**, ~ **shepherd** chien *m* loup, berger allemand; ~ **speaker** germanophone *mf*; **~-speaking** qui parle allemand; *nation etc* germanophone; *see* **Switzerland**. **2 n a** Allemand(e) *m(f)*. **b** (*Ling*) allemand *m*.
germane [dʒɜːˈmeɪn] **adj** allié, apparenté, se rapportant (*to* à).
Germanic [dʒɜːˈmænɪk] **adj** germanique.
germanium [dʒɜːˈmeɪnɪəm] **n** germanium *m*.
germanophile [dʒɜːˈmænəʊfaɪl] **n** germanophile *mf*.
germanophobe [dʒɜːˈmænəʊfəʊb] **n** germanophobe *mf*.
Germany [ˈdʒɜːmənɪ] **n** Allemagne *f*. (*Hist*) **East/West ~** Allemagne de l'Est/de l'Ouest; **Federal Republic of ~** République fédérale d'Allemagne.
germicidal [ˌdʒɜːmɪˈsaɪdl] **adj** antiseptique, germicide.
germicide [ˈdʒɜːmɪsaɪd] **n** antiseptique *m*, germicide *m*.
germinal [ˈdʒɜːmɪnəl] **adj** embryonnaire.
germinate [ˈdʒɜːmɪneɪt] **1 vi** germer. **2 vt** faire germer; (*fig*) donner naissance à, engendrer.
germination [ˌdʒɜːmɪˈneɪʃən] **n** germination *f*.
gerontocracy [ˌdʒerɒnˈtɒkrəsɪ] **n** gérontocratie *f*.
gerontologist [ˌdʒerɒnˈtɒlədʒɪst] **n** gérontologue *mf*.
gerontology [ˌdʒerɒnˈtɒlədʒɪ] **n** gérontologie *f*.
gerrymander [ˈdʒerɪmændəʳ] **1 vi** faire du charcutage électoral. **2 vt** *area* découper tendancieusement. **3 n = gerrymandering**.
gerrymandering [ˈdʒerɪmændərɪŋ] **n** charcutage *m* électoral.
gerund [ˈdʒerənd] **n** (*in English*) gérondif *m*, substantif verbal; (*in Latin*) gérondif.
gerundive [dʒɪˈrʌndɪv] **1 adj** du gérondif. **2 n** adjectif verbal.
gesso [ˈdʒesəʊ] **n** *[moulding etc]* plâtre *m* (de Paris); (*Art*) enduit *m* au plâtre.
Gestalt [gəˈʃtɑːlt] **n, pl ~s** *or* **~en** [gəˈʃtɑːltən] gestalt *f*. ~ **psychology** gestaltisme *m*.
Gestapo [gesˈtɑːpəʊ] **n** Gestapo *f*.
gestate [dʒesˈteɪt] **1 vi** être en gestation. **2 vt** (*Bio*) garder en gestation; (*fig*) mûrir.
gestation [dʒesˈteɪʃən] **n** gestation *f*.
gesticulate [dʒesˈtɪkjʊleɪt] **1 vi** gesticuler. **2 vt** mimer, exprimer par gestes.
gesticulation [dʒesˌtɪkjʊˈleɪʃən] **n** gesticulation *f*.
gestural [ˈdʒestʃərəl] **adj** gestuel.
gesture [ˈdʒestʃəʳ] **1 n** (*lit, fig*) geste *m*. **a ~ of refusal** un geste de refus; (*fig*) **friendly ~** geste *or* témoignage *m* d'amitié; **they did it as a ~ of support** ils l'ont fait pour manifester leur soutien; **an empty ~** un geste qui ne signifie rien; **what a nice ~!** c'est un très joli geste! **2 vi: to ~ to sb to do sth** faire signe à qn de faire qch; **he ~d towards the door** il désigna la porte d'un geste. **3 vt** mimer, exprimer par gestes.
get [get] **pret, ptp got**, (*US*) **ptp gotten** **1 vt a** (*obtain: gen*) avoir, trouver, (*through effort*) se procurer, obtenir; *permission, result* obtenir (*from* de); *commodity* (se) procurer, trouver, avoir; (*Rad*) *station* avoir, capter; (*Telec*) *person, number* avoir, obtenir; (*Scol*) *marks* obtenir, avoir. **to ~ sth cheap** avoir qch (à) bon marché; **I ~ my meat from the local butcher** je me fournis chez le boucher du quartier; **I must go and ~ some bread** il faut que j'aille acheter du pain; **I'll ~ some milk as well** je prendrai aussi du lait; **to ~ something to eat** (*find food*) chercher de quoi manger; (*prepare sth*) préparer de quoi manger; (*eat*) manger quelque chose; **I'm going to ~ a new hat** je vais acheter un nouveau chapeau; **where did you ~ that hat?** où as-tu trouvé ce chapeau?; **I don't ~ much from his lectures** je ne tire pas grand-chose de ses cours; **to ~ sth for sb** trouver qch pour qn, procurer qch à qn; **he got the book for me** il m'a trouvé le livre; **he got me a job** il m'a trouvé un emploi; (*fig*) **we'll never ~ anything out of him** nous ne tirerons jamais rien de lui; *see* **answer, right, sleep** *etc*.
b (*acquire, win*) *power, wealth* acquérir, accéder à; *ideas, reputation* se faire; *wages, salary* recevoir, gagner, toucher; *prize* gagner. **if I'm not working I ~ no pay** si je ne travaille pas ma paye ne tombe pas*; **to ~ sth for nothing** avoir *or* obtenir qch pour rien; *[collection, set]* **I've still 3 to ~** il m'en manque encore 3; **it got him fame/glory** *etc* cela lui a valu *or* rapporté la célébrité/la gloire *etc;* **he got fame/glory** *etc* il a connu la célébrité/la gloire *etc;* **he got help from the others** il s'est fait aider par les autres; **he got himself a wife** il a trouvé à se marier; *see* **best** *etc*.
c (*receive*) *letter, present* recevoir, avoir; *shock* recevoir, ressentir, avoir; *surprise* avoir; *wound, punishment* recevoir. (*selling sth*) **I didn't ~ much for it** on ne m'en a pas donné grand-chose, je ne l'ai pas vendu cher; **to ~ one in the eye⁑** recevoir *or* prendre un coup dans l'œil; **you'll ~ it!*** tu vas te faire passer un (bon) savon!*, tu vas écoper!*; **to ~ 2 years (in prison)** écoper* de *or* attraper* 2 ans (de prison); **he ~s it from his mother** il le tient de sa mère; **this room ~s all the sun** cette pièce reçoit tout le soleil; *see* **neck, sack[1], worst** *etc*.
d (*catch*) *ball, disease* attraper; *quarry* attraper, prendre; *person* prendre, attraper. *[pain]* **it ~s me here** cela me prend ici; **I've got him** *or* **it!** ça y est (je l'ai)!, je le tiens!; **got you at last!** enfin je te tiens!; **we'll ~ them yet!** on les aura!; **I'll ~ you!*** je t'aurai!, j'aurai ta peau!⁑; **he'll ~ you for that!*** qu'est-ce que tu vas prendre!*; (*phone, ring at door*) **I'll ~ it!** j'y vais!; **to ~ religion*** devenir bigot *or* calotin⁑; **he's got it bad (for her)*** il en pince sérieusement (pour elle)⁑.
e (*hit*) *target etc* atteindre, avoir. **the bullet got him in the arm** il a pris la balle dans le bras.
f (*seize*) prendre, saisir. **to ~ sb round the neck/by the throat** saisir *or* prendre qn au cou/à la gorge; **to ~ sb by the arm** saisir le bras de qn, attraper *or* saisir qn par le bras; *see* **grip, hold**.
g (*fetch*) *person* aller chercher; *doctor* aller chercher, faire venir; *object* chercher, apporter. **(go and) ~ my books** allez chercher mes livres; **can I ~ you a drink?** voulez-vous boire quelque chose?
h (*have, possess*) **to have got** avoir, posséder; **I've got toothache** j'ai mal aux dents; **I have got 3 sisters** j'ai 3 sœurs; **how many have you got?** combien en avez-vous?; **she's got too much to do** elle a trop (de choses) à faire; **you ~ different kinds of ...** on trouve plusieurs sortes de ...; *see also* **have**.
i (*causative etc*) **to ~ sb to do sth** persuader qn de faire qch, faire faire qch à qn, obtenir que qn fasse qch; **to ~ sth done** faire faire qch; **to ~ sth going** faire démarrer qch; **to ~ one's hair cut** se faire couper

les cheveux; **I got him to cut my hair** je me suis fait couper les cheveux par lui; **~ him to clean the car** fais-lui laver la voiture; **he knows how to ~ things done!** il sait faire activer les choses!; **you can't ~ anything done round here** (*do anything*) il est impossible de travailler par ici; (*get others to do sth*) il est impossible d'obtenir ce que l'on veut par ici; **she got her arm broken** elle a eu le bras cassé.

j (*cause to be: gen + adj*) **to ~ sth ready** préparer qch; **to ~ o.s. ready** se préparer; **to ~ sb drunk** enivrer *or* soûler qn; **to ~ one's hands dirty** se salir les mains; **to ~ o.s into a good/bad position** se placer dans une bonne/mauvaise situation; **try to ~ him into a good humour** essaie de le mettre de bonne humeur; **to ~ sb into trouble** attirer des ennuis à qn; (*euph*) **he got her into trouble*** il l'a mise dans une situation intéressante (*euph*); **to ~ sb alone** être seul à seul avec qn; **to ~ sb to o.s.** avoir qn tout à soi; **we got him on to the subject of the war** nous l'avons amené à parler de la guerre; *see* **straight** *etc*.

k (*put, take*) faire parvenir. **they got him home somehow** ils l'ont ramené (chez lui) tant bien que mal; **I'll come if you can ~ me home** je veux bien venir si vous pouvez me ramener; **how can we ~ it home?** comment faire pour le rapporter à la maison?; **this car may be old, but it ~s you there** la voiture a beau être vieille, elle vous amène à destination; **to ~ sth to sb** faire parvenir qch à qn; **to ~ a child to bed** (faire) coucher un enfant; **to ~ sb upstairs** faire monter l'escalier à qn, aider qn à monter l'escalier; **to ~ sth upstairs/downstairs** monter/descendre qch; **he managed to ~ the card into the envelope** il a réussi à faire entrer la carte dans l'enveloppe; **I'll never ~ the car through here** je n'arriverai jamais à faire passer la voiture par ici; **to ~ a horse/vehicle over a bridge** faire franchir un pont à un cheval/un véhicule; **to ~ sth past the customs** passer qch à la douane; (*fig*) **to ~ something off one's chest** dire ce que l'on a sur le cœur; **he got the blood off his hand** il a fait disparaître le sang de sa main; (*fig*) **to ~ sth off one's hands** se débarrasser de qch (*fig*); **shouting/rudeness** *etc* **will ~ you nowhere** ce n'est pas en criant/en étant grossier que vous obtiendrez qch; crier/la grossièreté ne vous mènera nulle part; (*hum*) **flattery will ~ you everywhere** on peut tout obtenir par des flatteries; **where does that ~ us?** où est-ce que ça nous mène?; *see* **nowhere a**.

l (*†† or liter: beget*) engendrer.

m (*understand*) *meaning* comprendre, saisir. **~ it?*, do you ~ me?*** tu saisis?*; **(I've) got it!** j'y suis!, ça y est!; **you've got it in one!*** tu as tout compris!; **I don't ~ it*** je ne comprends pas, je ne saisis pas*, je n'y suis pas (du tout); **I don't ~ you** *or* **your meaning*** je ne vous suis pas; **let me ~ this right** attendez, j'essaie de comprendre; **don't ~ me wrong** comprenez-moi bien.

n (*take note of*) observer, remarquer. **I didn't ~ your name** je n'ai pas saisi votre nom; (*to secretary etc*) **did you ~ that last sentence?** avez-vous pris la dernière phrase?; **~ (a load of) that!‡** regarde-moi ça!, vise-moi ça!‡; **~ her!‡** (*look*) regardez-la donc!; (*listen*) écoutez-la donc!

o (**: annoy: also* **get to**) ennuyer, chiffonner*, embêter*, (*stronger*) mettre en rogne* *or* en boule*. **it ~s (to) me*** ça m'énerve; **don't let it ~ (to) you** ne t'énerve pas pour ça; **that's what ~s (to) me in all this business** c'est ça qui me chiffonne* *or* me met en rogne* dans cette histoire; *see* **goat** *etc*.

p (**: impress, thrill*) **that tune ~s me!** cet air me fait quelque chose!; **that really ~s me!** ça m'emballe!*

2 vi a (*go*) aller, se rendre (*to, at* à, *from* de); (*arrive*) arriver. **how do you ~ there?** comment fait-on pour y aller?; **can you ~ there from London by bus?** est-ce qu'on peut y aller de Londres en autobus?; **he should ~ here soon** il devrait être là *or* arriver bientôt; **how did that box ~ here?** comment se fait-il que cette boîte se trouve ici?; **to ~ to the top** (*lit*) arriver au *or* atteindre le sommet; (*fig: also* **to ~ there**) arriver, réussir; (*fig*) **now we're ~ting somewhere!*** enfin on avance!; (*fig*) **we're ~ting nowhere, we're ~ting nowhere fast‡** on fait du sur place*; (*fig*) **you won't ~ anywhere if you behave like that** tu n'arriveras à rien en te conduisant comme ça; (*fig*) **we'll ~ nowhere** *or* **we won't ~ anywhere with him** nous n'arriverons à rien *or* nous perdons notre temps avec lui; **where did you ~ to?** où êtes-vous allé?; (*in book, work etc*) **where have you got to?** où en êtes-vous?; **where has he got to?, where can he have got to?** qu'est-ce qu'il est devenu?, où est-il passé?; **what's got into him?** qu'est-ce qui lui prend?; **I got as far as speaking to him** je suis allé jusqu'à lui parler; (*excl*) **~!‡** fous le camp!‡; (*fig*) **to ~ ahead** obtenir de l'avancement; *see* **above** *etc*.

b (*+ adj or ptp: become, be*) devenir, se faire. **to ~ old** devenir vieux, vieillir; **to ~ fat** devenir gros (*f* grosse), grossir; **he's ~ting* to be an old man** il se fait vieux; **it's ~ting* to be impossible** cela devient impossible; **to ~ paid** se faire payer; **to ~ killed** se faire tuer; **to ~ used to sth/to doing** s'habituer à qch/à faire; **to ~ married** se marier; **it's ~ting late** il se fait tard; **you're ~ting grey** vous commencez à grisonner; **how do people ~ like that?** comment peut-on en arriver là?; **how lucky/stupid can you ~?** il y en a qui ont vraiment de la chance!/qui sont vraiment stupides!; **to ~ with it‡** se mettre à la mode *or* dans le vent*; (*excl*) **~ with it!‡** mets-toi un peu à la mode!, sois un peu dans le vent!*; *see* **catch** *etc*.

c (*+ infin*) parvenir à. **to ~ to know sb** parvenir *or* apprendre à connaître qn; **we soon got to like them** nous nous sommes vite mis à les apprécier *or* aimer; **we got to like him in the end** nous avons fini par l'aimer, finalement nous nous sommes mis à l'aimer; **it got to be quite pleasant after a while** après un certain temps c'est devenu assez agréable.

d (*+ prp: begin*) se mettre à. **to ~ going** commencer, s'y mettre; **I got talking to him in the train** je me suis mis à parler avec lui *or* je suis entré en conversation avec lui dans le train; **to ~ working** se mettre au travail; **I got to thinking*** je me suis dit comme ça‡; *see* **crack, weave** *etc*.

e **to ~ to sb*** *see* **1 o**.

f (**: be allowed to*) **she never ~s to drive the car** on ne la laisse jamais conduire.

3 **modal auxiliary usage:** *la forme* **have got to** *est moins littéraire que la forme* **have to** *et la remplace généralement au présent en anglais parlé* **you've got to come** il faut absolument que vous veniez, il vous faut absolument venir; **I haven't got to leave yet** je ne suis pas obligé de partir tout de suite; **have you got to go and see her?** est-ce que vous êtes obligé d'aller la voir?; *see also* **have 2**.

4 **comp** ▸**get-at-able*** *place* accessible, d'accès facile; *person* accessible ▸**getaway** (*Aut*) démarrage *m*; (*Racing*) départ *m*; *[criminals]* fuite *f*; **to make a** *or* **one's getaway** filer, décamper; **they had a getaway car waiting** ils avaient une voiture pour filer; **the gangsters' getaway car was later found abandoned** on a retrouvé plus tard, abandonnée, la voiture qui avait permis aux gangsters de s'enfuir ▸**get-rich-quick scheme*** projet *m* pour faire fortune rapidement ▸**get-together** (petite) réunion *f* ▸**getup*** (*clothing*) mise *f*, tenue *f*, accoutrement *m* (*pej*); (*fancy dress*) déguisement *m*; (*presentation*) présentation *f*; **he's got lots of get-up-and-go*** il a un allant *or* un dynamisme fou*, il est très dynamique ▸**get-well card** carte *f* de vœux (de bon rétablissement).

▸**get about** vi a (*move about*) *[person]* se déplacer. **she gets about quite well despite her lameness** elle se déplace très bien malgré son infirmité; **he gets about with a stick/on crutches** il marche *or* se déplace avec une canne/avec des béquilles; (*after illness*) **he's getting about again now** il est de nouveau sur pied. b (*travel*) voyager. (*on business etc*) **she gets about a lot** elle voyage beaucoup, elle est souvent en déplacement. c *[news]* se répandre, circuler, s'ébruiter. **it has got about that ...** le bruit court que ... .

▸**get above** vt fus: **to get above o.s.** se prendre pour plus important qu'on n'est; **you're getting above yourself!** pour qui te prends-tu?

▸**get across** 1 vi (*lit*) traverser, passer d'un côté à l'autre; (*fig*) *[play]* passer la rampe; *[speaker]* se faire comprendre, se faire accepter; *[meaning, message]* passer*. **he didn't get across to the audience** il n'a pas réussi à établir la communication avec le public; **he managed to get across to her at last** il a enfin réussi à s'en faire entendre. 2 vt sep (*lit*) *load* traverser; *person* faire traverser, faire passer; (*fig*) *play, song* faire passer la rampe à; *ideas, intentions, desires* communiquer (*to sb* à qn). **to get sth across to sb** faire comprendre qch à qn. 3 vt fus (*annoy*) **to get across sb** se faire mal voir de qn.

▸**get after** vt fus (*run after*) courir après*.

▸**get ahead** vi (*lit, fig*) prendre de l'avance.

▸**get along** 1 vi a (*go*) aller, s'en aller, se rendre (*to* à). **I must be getting along** il faut que je m'en aille; **get along with you!*** (*go away*) va-t-en!, file!; (*Brit: stop joking*) ça va, hein!, allons (allons)!

b (*manage*) se débrouiller. **to get along without sth/sb** se passer de *or* se débrouiller sans qch/qn.

c (*progress*) *[work]* avancer; *[student]* faire des progrès. **he's getting along well in French** il fait de gros progrès en français; *[invalid etc]* **he's getting along nicely** il est en bonne voie, il fait des progrès.

d (*be on good terms*) s'entendre (bien). **they get along very well** ils s'entendent très bien; **I don't get along with him at all** je ne m'entends pas du tout avec lui.

2 vt sep faire avancer, faire venir, amener.

▸**get around** 1 vi = **get about**. 2 vt sep = **get round 2**. 3 vt fus = **get round 3**.

▸**get at** 1 vt fus a (*reach*) *high object, shelf* atteindre; *place* parvenir à, atteindre; *person* accéder jusqu'à. **house difficult to get at** maison difficile à atteindre *or* difficile d'accès, maison peu *or* difficilement accessible; **the dog got at the meat** le chien a touché à (*or* a pris) la viande; **put the meat where the dog can't get at it** mets la viande là où le chien ne pourra l'atteindre *or* hors de portée du chien; **he's not easy to get at** il est d'un abord peu facile; **let me get at him!*** que je l'attrape! (*subj*), que je mette la main sur lui!

b (*find, ascertain*) *facts, truth* parvenir à, découvrir.

c (*suggest*) **what are you getting at?** où voulez-vous en venir?

d (*attack, jibe at*) s'en prendre à, en avoir à‡. **she's always getting at her brother** elle est toujours sur le dos de son frère *or* après son frère*; **who are you getting at?** qui est-ce que vous visez?; **I feel got at** je me sens visé.

e (**: bribe*) acheter, suborner.

f (*start work on*) se mettre à. **I must get at this essay tonight** il faut que je me mette à cette dissertation ce soir; **I want to get at the redecorating this weekend** je veux commencer à refaire les peintures ce week-end.

2 **get-at-able*** adj *see* **get 4.**

▸**get away** 1 vi a (*leave*) s'en aller, partir; *[vehicle]* partir, démarrer. **to get away from a place** quitter un endroit; **to get away from work** quitter son travail; **I couldn't get away any sooner** je n'ai pas pu m'échapper *or* me libérer plus tôt; **can you get away for a holiday?** pouvez-vous vous libérer pour partir en vacances?; **get away!** allez-vous-en!; **get away (with you)!*** (*go away*) va-t-en!, file!*; (*stop joking*) ça va, hein!, allons (allons)!

b (*escape*) s'échapper, se sauver (*from* de). **to get away from one's environment** se soustraire à *or* échapper à son environnement; **to get away from sb** échapper à qn; **he went to the Bahamas to get away from it all** il est allé aux Bahamas pour laisser tous ses ennuis *or* problèmes derrière lui; **the doctor told her she must get away from it all** le médecin lui a ordonné de partir se reposer loin de tout; **the thief got away with the money** le voleur est parti avec l'argent; **he got away with a mere apology** il en a été quitte pour une simple excuse; (*fig*) **to get away with it** s'en tirer à bon compte; **you'll never get away with that!** on ne te laissera pas passer ça!*; (*fig*) **he'd get away with murder*** il tuerait père et mère qu'on lui pardonnerait; (*fig*) **you can't get away from it!, there's no getting away from it!** il faut bien le reconnaître!, le fait est là, on ne peut rien y changer!

2 vt sep a *person* faire partir, emmener, entraîner, éloigner. **you must get her away to the country for a while** il faut que vous l'emmeniez (*subj*) un peu à la campagne; **I must get this letter away today** il faut que je mette cette lettre à la poste *or* que je fasse partir cette lettre aujourd'hui.

b (*remove*) **to get sth away from sb** arracher qch à qn.

3 **getaway** n, adj *see* **get 4.**

▸**get back** 1 vi a (*return*) revenir, retourner. **to get back (home)** rentrer chez soi; **to get back to bed** se recoucher, retourner au lit; **to get back upstairs** remonter, retourner en haut; **to get back to work** (*after pause*) se remettre au travail; (*after illness, holiday*) retourner au travail; **to get back to the point** revenir au sujet; **let's get back to why you didn't come yesterday** revenons à la question de savoir pourquoi vous n'êtes pas venu hier; **to get back to sb*** recontacter qn, (*on phone also*) rappeler qn; **can I get back to you on that?*** puis-je vous recontacter *or* (*on phone*) rappeler à ce sujet?; *see also* **get on 3.**

b (*move backwards*) reculer. (*excl*) **get back!** reculez!

2 vt sep a (*recover*) *sth lent* se faire rendre, reprendre possession de, récupérer; *sth lost* retrouver, récupérer; *possessions* recouvrer; *good opinion* retrouver; *strength* reprendre, récupérer; *one's husband, girlfriend etc* faire revenir. **now that we've got you back** maintenant que tu nous es revenu; **to get one's money back** se faire rembourser, (*with difficulty*) récupérer son argent; *see* **own.**

b (*replace*) remettre, replacer.

c (*return*) *object* renvoyer; *person* raccompagner, reconduire, faire reconduire (chez lui).

▸**get back at*** vt fus (*retaliate against*) se venger de, rendre la monnaie de sa pièce à.

▸**get by** vi a (*pass*) passer. **let me get by** laissez-moi passer; **this work just gets by** ce travail est tout juste passable *or* acceptable. b (*manage*) se débrouiller, s'en sortir*, s'en tirer*. **she gets by on very little money** elle s'en tire* *or* elle s'en sort* *or* elle se débrouille* avec très peu d'argent; **he'll get by!** il s'en sortira!*, il se débrouillera toujours!*

▸**get down** 1 vi a descendre (*from, off* de). (*at table*) **may I get down?** est-ce que je peux sortir (de table)?; **to get down on one's knees** se mettre à genoux; **get down!** (*climb down*) descends!; (*lie down*) couche-toi!

b (*esp US* ‡: *dance*) se défoncer‡ (sur de la musique).

2 vt sep a *book, plate* descendre; *hat, picture* décrocher. **get that child down off the table!** descends cet enfant de (sur) la table!

b *bird, game* abattre, descendre*.

c (*swallow*) *food, pill* avaler, faire descendre.

d (*make note of*) noter, prendre (en note).

e (*: *depress*) déprimer, démoraliser. **he gets me down** il me fiche le cafard*; **all that worry has got him down** tous ces soucis l'ont déprimé *or* lui ont mis le moral à zéro*; **don't let it get you down!** ne vous laissez pas abattre!, du cran!*

▸**get down to** vt fus: **to get down to doing sth** se mettre à faire qch; **to get down to work** se mettre au travail; **to get down to a task** s'attaquer *or* s'atteler à une besogne; **you'll have to get down to it** il faut vous y mettre; **when you get down to it there's not much difference between the two** tout bien considéré il n'y a pas beaucoup de différence entre les deux; **to get down to business** se mettre au travail, passer aux choses sérieuses; **let's get down to the facts** venons-en aux faits.

▸**get in** 1 vi a *[person]* (*enter*) entrer, réussir à entrer; (*be admitted*) se faire admettre; (*reach home*) rentrer; *[sunshine, air, water]* pénétrer, entrer, s'introduire. **to get in between two people** se glisser *or* s'introduire entre deux personnes.

b (*arrive*) *[train, bus, plane]* arriver.

c (*Parl: be elected*) *[member]* être élu; *[party]* accéder au pouvoir.

2 vt sep a (*lit*) *object* rentrer; *person* faire entrer; *crops, harvest* rentrer, engranger; *taxes* percevoir; *debts* recouvrer. (*into case etc*) **I managed to get it in** j'ai réussi à le caser; **did you get your essay in in time?** as-tu rendu *or* remis ta dissertation à temps?

b (*plant*) *seeds* planter, semer; *bulbs* planter.

c (*buy, obtain*) *groceries, coal* acheter, faire rentrer. **to get in supplies** s'approvisionner, faire des provisions.

d (*summon*) *doctor, police, tradesman* faire venir.

e (*insert etc*) glisser. **to get a word in edgeways** glisser *or* placer un mot; **he got in a reference to his new book** il a glissé une allusion à son dernier livre; (*fig*) **to get one's hand in** se faire la main; **he managed to get in a couple of blows on his opponent's head** il a réussi à frapper deux fois son adversaire à la tête; *see* **eye.**

▸**get in on*** vt fus **he managed to get in on the deal/trip** il s'est débrouillé pour se joindre à *or* il a réussi à s'imposer dans l'affaire/le voyage; *see also* **act 1c.**

▸**get into** vt fus a (*enter*) *house, park* entrer dans, pénétrer dans; *car, train* monter dans. (*fig*) **to get into a club** se faire accepter comme membre d'un club; **he got into a good school** il a été accepté dans une bonne école; (*fig*) **how did I get into all this?** comment me suis-je fourré dans un pareil pétrin?, que suis-je allé faire dans cette galère?; **to get into the way of doing sth** (*become used to*) s'habituer à faire qch; (*make a habit of*) prendre l'habitude de faire qch; *see* **company, habit, mischief** *etc.* b *clothes* mettre, enfiler*; *coat, dressing gown* endosser, mettre.

▸**get in with** vt fus a (*gain favour of*) (réussir à) se faire bien voir de, s'insinuer dans les bonnes grâces de. **he tried to get in with the headmaster** il a essayé de se faire bien voir du directeur. b (*become friendly with*) **he got in with a bad crowd** il s'est mis à avoir de mauvaises fréquentations.

▸**get off** 1 vi a (*from vehicle*) descendre. (*fig*) **to tell sb where to get off*** envoyer qn sur les roses*, envoyer promener qn; **he was told where he got off*** on lui a fait comprendre que la plaisanterie avait assez duré.

b (*depart*) *[person]* partir, filer, se sauver; *[car]* démarrer; *[plane]* décoller. (*fig*) **to get off to a good start** prendre un bon départ; **to get off (to sleep)** s'endormir.

c (*escape*) s'en tirer. **to get off lightly** s'en tirer à bon compte; **to get off with a reprimand/a fine** en être quitte pour une semonce/une amende.

d (*leave work*) sortir, s'en aller; (*have free time*) se libérer. **I can't get off early today** je ne peux pas m'en aller de bonne heure aujourd'hui; **can you get off tomorrow?** est-ce que tu peux te libérer *or* être libre demain?; **we get off at 5 o'clock** nous sortons à 5 heures.

2 vt sep a (*remove*) *clothes, shoes* ôter, enlever; *jewellery* enlever; *stains* faire partir, faire disparaître, enlever.

b (*despatch*) *mail* expédier, envoyer, mettre à la poste. **to get the children off to school** expédier les enfants à l'école; **to get sb off to work** faire partir qn au travail; **to get a child off to sleep** endormir un enfant.

c (*save from punishment*) (*in court*) faire acquitter; (*gen*) tirer d'affaire *or* de là*. **a good lawyer will get him off** un bon avocat le tirera d'affaire *or* le fera acquitter.

d (*learn*) **to get sth off (by heart)** apprendre qch (par cœur).

e (*from shore*) *boat* renflouer; (*from boat*) *crew, passengers* débarquer.

3 vt fus a **to get off a bus/a cycle** descendre d'un autobus/d'une bicyclette; **to get off a ship** descendre à terre; **he got off his horse** il est descendu de cheval; **to get off a chair** se lever d'une chaise; **get (up) off the floor!** levez-vous!; (*fig*) **I wish you would get off my back!*** ne sois donc pas constamment sur mon dos!, vas-tu me laisser tranquille!; **let's get off this subject of conversation** parlons d'autre chose; **we've rather got off the subject** nous nous sommes plutôt éloignés du sujet.

b (*: *avoid etc*) **to get off doing the homework/washing up** se faire dispenser de (faire ses) devoirs/(faire la) vaisselle; **he got off visiting his aunt** il s'est fait dispenser d'aller rendre visite à sa tante; **to get off work** se libérer.

▸**get off on**‡ vt fus *pornography, violence, power, loud music etc* prendre son pied avec‡. **he gets off on watching people undress** il prend son pied en regardant les gens se déshabiller.

▸**get off with*** vt fus: **he got off with a blonde he met on a bus** il s'est tapé‡ une blonde qu'il a rencontrée dans un autobus.

▸**get on** 1 vi a (*on to bus etc*) monter; (*on to ship*) monter à bord.

b (*advance, make progress*) avancer, progresser, faire des progrès. **how are you getting on?** comment ça marche?*; **how did you get on?** ça a bien marché?*, comment ça c'est passé?; **to be getting on (in years)** se faire vieux; **he's getting on for forty** il frise la quarantaine; **time is getting on** il se fait tard; **it's getting on for 3 o'clock** il est bientôt 3 heures, il n'est pas loin de 3 heures; **there were getting on for 100 people** il y avait pas loin de 100 personnes; **we have getting on for 500 books** nous avons près de *or* pas loin de 500 livres.

c (*succeed*) réussir, arriver, faire son chemin. **if you want to get on, you must ...** si tu veux réussir, tu dois ...; **to get on in life** *or* **in the world** faire son chemin *or* réussir dans la vie; **the art of getting on** le moyen de parvenir dans la vie *or* de réussir dans la vie *or* d'arriver.

d (*continue, proceed*) continuer. **I must be getting on now** il faut que je parte maintenant; **get on (with you)!*** (*go away*) va-t-en!, file!*; (*stop joking*) ça va, hein!, allons (allons)!; **get on with it!, get on with the job!** allez, au travail!; **he got on with the job** *or* **his work** il s'est (re)mis au travail; **while he was getting on with the job** pendant qu'il travaillait; **this will do to be getting on with** ça ira pour le moment.

e (*agree*) s'accorder, s'entendre, faire bon ménage (*with* avec). **we don't get on** nous ne nous entendons pas; **I get on well with her** je m'entends bien avec elle.

2 **vt sep** *clothes, shoes* mettre, enfiler*; *lid, cover* mettre.

3 **vt fus: to get on a horse** monter (sur un cheval); **to get on a bicycle** monter sur *or* enfourcher une bicyclette; **to get on a ship** monter à bord (d'un navire); **to get on a bus/train** monter dans un autobus/un train; **to get on one's feet** se mettre debout, se lever; (*after illness, setback*) **to get back on one's feet** se remettre.

►**get on to vt fus** a = **get on 3.** b (*find, recognize*) *facts, truth* découvrir. **the police got on to him at once** la police l'a dépisté *or* a été sur sa trace immédiatement. c (*nag*) **she's always getting on to me** elle est toujours après moi*. d (*get in touch with*) se mettre en rapport avec; (*speak to*) parler à; (*Telec*) téléphoner à.

►**get out** 1 **vi** a sortir (*of* de); (*from vehicle*) descendre (*of* de). **get out!** sortez!, fichez le camp!*; **get out of here!** (*lit*) sors d'ici!; (* *US fig: I don't believe it*) tu me prends pour un imbécile?

b (*escape*) s'échapper (*of* de). (*fig*) **to get out of** *obligation* se dérober à, échapper à; *duty* se soustraire à; *difficulty* se tirer de; **there's no getting out of it, he's just not good enough** il n'y a pas à dire, il n'est pas à la hauteur; **you'll have to do it, there's no getting out of it** il faut que tu le fasses, il n'y a pas moyen d'y échapper; *see* **clutch, depth, trouble** *etc.*

c *[news etc]* se répandre, s'ébruiter; *[secret]* être éventé.

2 **vt sep** a (*bring etc out*) *chair* sortir; *person* faire sortir. **he got his diary out of his pocket** il sortit son agenda de sa poche.

b (*remove*) *plug* enlever; *tooth* enlever, arracher; *stain* enlever, faire partir, faire disparaître. **to get a cork out of a bottle** déboucher une bouteille; **I can't get it out of my mind** je ne peux m'empêcher d'y penser, cela me trotte par la tête*.

c (*bring out*) *object* sortir (*of* de); *words, speech* prononcer, sortir*; *book [publisher]* publier, sortir; *[author]* publier; *[library-user]* emprunter, sortir. **get the cards out and we'll have a game** sors les cartes et on va faire une partie.

d (*free*) *person* faire sortir (*of* de).

e (*prepare*) *plan, scheme* préparer, mettre sur pied; *list* établir, dresser.

f (*solve*) *problem, puzzle* venir à bout de.

►**get over** 1 **vi** (*lit*) traverser; *[message, meaning]* passer*.

2 **vt fus** a (*cross*) *river, road* franchir, traverser; *fence [horse]* franchir, passer par-dessus; *[person]* escalader, passer par-dessus.

b (*recover from*) **to get over an illness** guérir *or* se remettre d'une maladie; **to get over a loss** se consoler *or* se remettre d'une perte; **to get over a surprise** revenir d'une surprise; **I can't get over it** je n'en reviens pas; **I can't get over the fact that ...** je n'en reviens pas que ... + *subj*; **you'll get over it!** tu n'en mourras pas!, on n'en meurt pas!; **she never really got over him*** elle ne l'a jamais vraiment oublié.

c (*overcome*) *obstacle* surmonter; *objections, difficulties* triompher de, venir à bout de.

3 **vt sep** a (*lit*) *person, animal, vehicle* faire passer. **we couldn't get the car over** nous n'avons pas pu (faire) passer la voiture.

b (*swallow*) *food, pill* avaler.

c (*have done with*) en finir avec. **let's get it over (with)** finissons-en (avec*); **I was glad to get that over (with)** j'étais ravi d'en avoir fini (avec*).

d (*Theat*) *play* faire passer la rampe à; *song etc* faire accepter; (*gen: communicate*) faire comprendre. **he couldn't get his ideas over to his readers** il était incapable de faire comprendre *or* de communiquer ses idées à ses lecteurs; **I couldn't get it over to him that he must come** je n'ai pas pu lui faire comprendre qu'il devait venir.

►**get round** 1 **vi** = **get about.** 2 **vt sep** a *unconscious person* ranimer. b **to get sb round to one's way of thinking** amener qn à partager sa façon de voir. 3 **vt fus** a (*circumvent*) *obstacle* contourner; *difficulty, law, regulation* tourner. b (*coax, persuade*) entortiller*, embobiner*. **he knows how to get round her** il sait la prendre; **she got round him in the end** elle a fini par l'entortiller*.

►**get round to* vt fus: to get round to doing sth** arriver à faire qch; **if I get round to it** si j'y arrive; **I never got round to going to see her** jamais je n'ai réussi à aller la voir; **I shan't get round to that before next week** je n'arriverai pas à trouver l'occasion *or* le temps de m'en occuper avant la semaine prochaine.

►**get through** 1 **vi** a *[message, news]* parvenir (*to* à); *[signal]* être reçu.

b (*be accepted, pass*) *[candidate]* être reçu, réussir; *[motion, bill]* passer, être voté. *[football team etc]* **to get through to the third round** se classer pour le troisième tour.

c (*Telec*) obtenir la communication (*to* avec). **I phoned you several times but couldn't get through** je t'ai téléphoné plusieurs fois mais je n'ai pas pu t'avoir; **could you get through to him straight away?** pouvez-vous le contacter immédiatement?

d (*communicate with*) **to get through to sb** se faire comprendre de qn; **he can't get through to his son at all** il n'arrive pas à se faire comprendre de son fils, il n'est pas sur la même longueur d'onde que son fils; **she was so angry I couldn't get through to her** elle était tellement en colère que je ne pouvais rien lui faire entendre.

e (*finish*) terminer, finir. **I shan't get through before 6 o'clock** je n'aurai pas terminé *or* fini avant 6 heures; **to get through with sth*** en finir avec qch.

2 **vt fus** a *hole, window* passer par; *hedge* traverser, passer à travers; *crowd* se frayer un chemin dans *or* à travers; (*Mil*) *enemy lines* percer, franchir.

b (*finish*) *task* accomplir, achever, venir au bout de; *book* achever, finir; *supplies, sugar, fuel* venir au bout de. **he got through a lot of work** il a abattu de la besogne; **to get through all one's money** (*salary*) dépenser tout ce qu'on gagne; (*inheritance etc*) manger toute sa fortune; **I've got through the £20 you lent me** je suis venu à bout des 20 livres *or* j'ai dépensé les 20 livres *or* il ne reste plus rien des 20 livres que vous m'avez prêtées; **how can I get through the week without you?** comment vais-je pouvoir vivre une semaine sans toi?

c (*consume, use*) *food, drink, coal, supplies* consommer. **we get through 10 bottles a week** il nous faut 10 bouteilles par semaine; **we get through £50 per week** nous n'avons pas trop de 50 livres par semaine.

3 **vt sep** a (*lit*) *person, object* faire passer; (*fig*) *message* faire parvenir (*to* à). **can you get this message through to him?** pouvez-vous lui transmettre *or* faire passer ce message?; **I can't get it through to him that ...** je n'arrive pas à lui faire comprendre que ...; (*Telec*) **to get sb through to** passer qn à, donner à qn la communication avec; (*Telec*) **get me through to Paris at once** donnez-moi *or* passez-moi Paris tout de suite.

b (*fig*) **to get a bill through** faire adopter un projet de loi; **he got his pupils through** ses élèves ont été reçus grâce à lui; **it was his English that got him through** c'est à son anglais qu'il doit d'avoir été reçu.

►**get together** 1 **vi** se rassembler, se réunir. **let's get together on Thursday and decide what to do** on se retrouve jeudi pour décider ce qu'il faut faire; **you'd better get together with him before you decide** vous feriez bien de le consulter *or* de vous entendre avec lui avant de décider. 2 **vt sep** *people* rassembler, réunir; *things* ramasser, rassembler; *thoughts, ideas* rassembler. 3 **get-together n** *see* **get 4.**

►**get under** 1 **vi** (*pass underneath*) passer par-dessous. 2 **vt fus: to get under a fence/a rope** *etc* passer sous une barrière/une corde *etc.* 3 **vt sep** (*lit*) mettre dessous, faire passer par-dessous; (*fig: control*) *fire, revolt* maîtriser.

►**get up** 1 **vi** a (*rise*) *[person]* se lever (*from* de), se mettre debout; *[wind]* se lever. **the sea is getting up** la houle se lève; **get up out of bed!** sors du lit!

b (*on horse*) monter. (*on horse, cycle*) **to get up behind sb** monter en croupe derrière qn.

2 **vt fus** *tree, ladder* monter à; *hill* gravir.

3 **vt sep** a (*lit*) *person* (*on to ladder etc*) faire monter; (*from chair etc*) faire lever; *thing* monter; *sail* hisser. **to get sb's back up*** mettre qn en boule*, braquer qn; **to get sb's temper up** mettre qn en colère; **to get up speed** prendre de la vitesse; *see* **steam.**

b (*from bed*) *person* faire lever; (*wake*) réveiller.

c (*organize*) *play* monter; *entertainment* monter, organiser; *plot* ourdir, monter; *story* fabriquer, forger. **to get up a petition** mettre sur pied *or* organiser une pétition.

d (*prepare, arrange*) *article for sale* apprêter, préparer; (*Comm*) *book* présenter. **to get o.s. up as** se déguiser en, se travestir en; **to get o.s. up beautifully** se faire beau (*f* belle), se mettre sur son trente et un; **she was very nicely got up** elle était très bien habillée.

e (*study*) *history, literature etc* travailler, bûcher*; *speech, lecture* préparer.

4 **getup* n** *see* **get 4.**

►**get up to vt fus** a (*catch up with*) rattraper. b (*reach*) arriver à. **I've got up to page 17** j'en suis à la page 17; **where did we get up to last week?** où en sommes-nous arrivés la semaine dernière? c (*be involved in, do*) **to get up to mischief** faire des bêtises *or* des sottises; **you never know what he'll get up to next** on ne sait jamais ce qu'il va encore inventer *or* fabriquer*, on ne sait jamais ce qu'il va encore trouver moyen de faire.

Gethsemane [geθ'semənɪ] **n** Gethsémani *m.*

geum ['dʒiːəm] **n** benoîte *f.*

gewgaw ['gjuːgɔː] **n** bibelot *m*, babiole *f.*

geyser ['giːzəʳ] **n** (*Geol*) geyser *m*; (*Brit: in house*) chauffe-eau *m inv.*

Ghana ['gɑːnə] **n** Ghana *m.*

Ghanaian [gɑː'neɪən] 1 **adj** ghanéen. 2 **n** Ghanéen(ne) *m(f).*

ghastly ['gɑːstlɪ] **adj** (*pale*) *appearance* blême, livide, mortellement pâle; *pallor* mortel; *light* blafard, spectral; (*horrible, frightening*) horrible, effrayant, affreux; (*unpleasant*) horrible, affreux, épouvantable.

he looked ~ il avait une mine de déterré.
ghee [giː] n beurre *m* clarifié.
Ghent [gent] n Gand.
gherkin ['gɜːkɪn] n (*Culin*) cornichon *m*.
ghetto ['getəʊ] 1 n, pl ~s *or* ~es (*lit, fig*) ghetto *m*. 2 comp ▸**ghetto-blaster*** (gros) radio-cassette *m*.
ghettoization [ˌgetəʊaɪ'zeɪʃən] n (*US*) ségrégation *f* (dans des ghettos).
ghettoize ['getəʊˌaɪz] vt (*US*) enfermer *or* isoler dans de véritables ghettos.
Ghibelline ['gɪbɪˌlaɪn] n Gibelin *m*.
ghost [gəʊst] 1 n (*apparition*) fantôme *m*, revenant *m*, spectre *m*; (*fig*) ombre *f*; (*TV*) image *f* secondaire; (††: *soul*) âme *f*. **I don't believe in ~s** je ne crois pas aux fantômes; **the ~ of a smile** une ombre de sourire, un pâle *or* vague sourire; **I haven't the ~ of a chance** je n'ai pas la moindre chance *or* pas l'ombre d'une chance; (*liter, hum*) **to give up the** ~ rendre l'âme; **you look as if you've seen a ~!** on dirait que tu as vu un revenant *or* un fantôme!; *see* **holy** *etc*.
2 vt: **to ~ a book/an article** servir de nègre pour un livre/un article; **his book was ~ed by a journalist** c'est un journaliste qui lui a servi de nègre pour (écrire) son livre.
3 comp *film, story* de revenants, de fantômes; *ship, train* fantôme ▸**ghost image** (*Cine, TV*) filage *m* ▸**ghost town** ville morte ▸**ghost-write** = **ghost 2** ▸**ghost writer** nègre *m*.
ghostly ['gəʊstlɪ] adj a spectral, fantomatique. b (††: *Rel etc*) spirituel.
ghoul [guːl] n goule *f*, vampire *m*; (*grave robber*) déterreur *m* de cadavres. (*fig*) **he's a** ~ il est morbide, il a des goûts dépravés.
ghoulish ['guːlɪʃ] adj (*lit*) de goule, vampirique; (*fig*) *humour, tastes* morbide, macabre.
ghoulishly ['guːlɪʃlɪ] adv sinistrement, d'un air macabre.
GHQ [ˌdʒiːeɪtʃ'kjuː] n (*Mil etc*) (abbr of **General Headquarters**) GQG *m*.
G.I.* [ˌdʒiː'aɪ] (*US*) 1 n (*also* **GI Joe***) soldat *m or* bidasse* *m* (américain), G.I. *m*. 2 adj militaire. (*US Univ*) ~ **bill** *loi sur les bourses pour anciens combattants;* ~ **bride** *épouse étrangère d'un G.I.*
giant ['dʒaɪənt] 1 n géant *m*. (*Ir Geog*) **the G~'s Causeway** la chaussée des Géants; (*fig*) **electronics/chemicals** ~ géant de l'electronique/de l'industrie chimique. 2 adj *tree, star etc* géant; *strides* de géant; *helping, amount* gigantesque; (*Comm*) *packet, size* géant. (*Ski*) ~ **slalom** slalom *m* géant.
giantess ['dʒaɪəntɪs] n géante *f*.
gibber ['dʒɪbəʳ] vi *[person, ape etc]* baragouiner*. **to ~ with rage** bégayer *or* bafouiller de colère; **~ing idiot*** crétin patenté*.
gibberish ['dʒɪbərɪʃ] n (*NonC*) charabia* *m*, baragouin* *m*.
gibbet ['dʒɪbɪt] n potence *f*, gibet *m*.
gibbon ['gɪbən] n gibbon *m*.
gibbous ['gɪbəs] adj (*hump-backed*) gibbeux (*liter*), bossu. ~ **moon** lune *f* dans le deuxième *or* troisième quartier.
gibe [dʒaɪb] 1 vi a **to ~ at sb** railler qn, se moquer de qn. b (*Naut*) *[boat]* virer lof pour lof; *[sail]* passer d'un bord à l'autre du mât. 2 n raillerie *f*, moquerie *f*, sarcasme *m*.
giblets ['dʒɪblɪts] npl abattis *mpl or* abats *mpl* (*de volaille*).
Gibraltar [dʒɪ'brɔːltəʳ] n Gibraltar *m*. **in** ~ à Gibraltar; *see* **rock²**, **strait**.
giddily ['gɪdɪlɪ] adv (*lit*) vertigineusement; (*light-heartedly*) à la légère; (*heedlessly*) avec insouciance, à l'étourdie.
giddiness ['gɪdɪnɪs] n (*NonC*) (*Med*) vertiges *mpl*, étourdissements *mpl*; (*lightheartedness*) légèreté *f*; (*heedlessness*) étourderie *f*. **a bout of** ~ un vertige, un étourdissement.
giddy¹ ['gɪdɪ] adj *person* (*dizzy*) pris de vertige *or* d'un étourdissement; (*heedless*) étourdi, écervelé; (*not serious*) léger; *height* vertigineux, qui donne le vertige. **I feel** ~ la tête me tourne; **to turn** *or* **go** ~ être pris de vertige; **to make sb** ~ donner le vertige à qn; ~ **round of pleasure** tourbillon *m* de plaisirs; (*fig, iro*) **the ~ heights of senior management** les hautes sphères de la direction générale; **that's the ~ limit!**⁑ ça c'est le bouquet!*; *see* **goat, spell²**.
giddy² ['gɪdɪ] excl (*US: to horse*) ~ **up!** hue!
Gideon Bible ['gɪdɪən ˌbaɪbəl] n bible *f* (*placée dans les hôtels etc par la Gideon Society*).
GIFT [gɪft] n (abbr of **Gamete In** (*or* **Intra-**)**Fallopian Transfer**) GIFT *m*.
gift [gɪft] 1 n a (*present*) cadeau *m*, présent *m*; (*Comm*) prime *f*, cadeau. **New Year** ~ étrennes *fpl*; (*in shop*) **is it for a ~?** c'est pour offrir?; **it was a** ~ (*lit*) on me l'a offert; (*: *fig: it was easy*) c'était du gâteau*; **I wouldn't have it as a** ~ on m'en ferait cadeau que je n'en voudrais pas; **he thinks he's God's ~* to the human race** il se prend pour le nombril du monde*; **people like us are God's ~* to dentists** des gens comme nous c'est le rêve* pour les dentistes; (*Comm*) **"free ~ inside the packet"** "ce paquet contient un cadeau".
b (*Jur etc*) don *m*, donation *f*. **to make sb a ~ of sth** faire don *or* cadeau de qch à qn; **by free** ~ à titre gratuit; **in the ~ of** à la discrétion de; *see* **deed**.
c (*talent*) don *m* (*for* de, pour), talent *m* (*for* pour). **he has a ~ for maths** il a un don pour les maths *or* le don des maths; **he has great artistic ~s** il a de grands dons artistiques; **to have the ~ of the gab*** avoir la langue bien pendue, avoir du bagou*.
2 vt (*esp Jur*) donner. (*fig*) **to be ~ed with patience** *etc* être doué de patience *etc*.
3 comp ▸**gift coupon** (*Comm*) bon-prime *m* ▸**gift horse**: (*Prov*) **don't look a gift horse in the mouth** à cheval donné on ne regarde pas la bride (*Prov*), on ne critique pas le cadeau qu'on reçoit ▸**gift shop** boutique *f* de cadeaux ▸**gift token, gift voucher** chèque-cadeau *m* ▸**giftwrap: to giftwrap a package** faire un paquet-cadeau ▸**gift-wrapped** sous emballage-cadeau ▸**giftwrapping** emballage-cadeau *m*.
gifted ['gɪftɪd] adj (*fig*) doué (*for* pour). **the ~ child** l'enfant surdoué.
gig [gɪg] n a (*vehicle*) cabriolet *m*; (*boat*) petit canot, youyou *m*. b (*Mus sl: jazz, pop concert*) concert *m*. **they had a regular ~ at the Cavern** ils jouaient régulièrement au Cavern. c (*) (*US fig*) job *m* temporaire, engagement *m*.
gigabyte ['dʒɪgəˌbaɪt] n gigaoctet *m*.
gigaflop ['gaɪgəˌflɒp] n milliard *m* d'opérations en virgule flottante par seconde.
gigantic [dʒaɪ'gæntɪk] adj géant, gigantesque.
gigantically [dʒaɪ'gæntɪkəlɪ] adv: ~ **fat/swollen** démesurément *or* (*less frm*) énormément gros/enflé.
gigantism [dʒaɪ'gæntɪzəm] n gigantisme *m*.
gigawatt ['dʒɪgəˌwɒt] n gigawatt *m*.
giggle ['gɪgl] 1 vi pouffer de rire, rire sottement, glousser. **stop giggling!** ne riez pas sottement comme ça!; **she was giggling helplessly** elle ne pouvait pas se retenir de pouffer, elle avait le fou rire; **"stop that!" she ~d** "arrête!" dit-elle en pouffant de rire. 2 n petit rire sot *or* nerveux, gloussement sot *or* nerveux. **to have/get the ~s** avoir/attraper le fou rire; (*Brit*) **it was a bit of a ~*** ça nous a bien fait rigoler*; (*Brit*) **he did it for a ~*** il a fait ça pour rigoler*.
giggly ['gɪglɪ] adj qui glousse sans arrêt, qui glousse pour un rien.
GIGO ['giːgəʊ, ˌdʒiːˌaɪdʒiː'əʊ] (abbr of **garbage in, garbage out**) *see* **garbage 1**.
gigolo ['ʒɪgələʊ] n (*sexually*) gigolo *m*; (*dancing partner*) danseur mondain.
gigot ['ʒiːgəʊ, 'dʒɪgət] n (*Culin*) gigot *m*.
Gila ['hiːlə] n (*US*) ~ **monster** grand lézard venimeux.
Gilbertian [gɪl'bɜːtɪən] adj (*Brit*) ≃ vaudevillesque.
gild [gɪld] pret **gilded**, ptp **gilded** *or* **gilt** vt dorer. (*fig*) **to ~ the lily** renchérir sur la perfection; **to ~ the pill** dorer la pilule; **~ed youth** la jeunesse dorée.
gilding ['gɪldɪŋ] n dorure *f*.
Giles [dʒaɪlz] n Gilles *m*.
gill¹ [gɪl] n *[mushrooms]* lamelle *f*. *[fish]* **~s** ouïes *fpl*, branchies *fpl*; **he was looking rather green around the ~s*** il était vert (*de peur etc*).
gill² [dʒɪl] n (*Brit: measure*) quart *m* de pinte (= *0,142 litre*).
gillie ['gɪlɪ] n (*Scot*) gillie *m*, accompagnateur *m* (*d'un chasseur, d'un pêcheur etc*).
gillyflower ['dʒɪlɪˌflaʊəʳ] n giroflée *f*.
gilt [gɪlt] 1 ptp of **gild**. 2 n a (*gold*) dorure *f*. (*fig*) **to take the ~ off the gingerbread** enlever tout le charme, gâter le plaisir. b (*Brit Fin*) **~s** = **gilt-edged securities**; *see* **4**. 3 adj doré. 4 comp ▸**gilt-edged** *book* doré sur tranche; (*fig*) de tout premier ordre; (*Brit Fin*) **gilt-edged securities** *or* **stock** (*government-issued*) fonds *mpl or* titres *mpl* d'État; (*safe investment*) valeurs *fpl* de premier ordre *or* de tout repos *or* de père de famille ▸**gilt-head** (*fish*) daurade *f*, dorade *f*.
gimbal(s) ['dʒɪmbəl(z)] n (*Aut, Naut*) cardan *m*.
gimcrack ['dʒɪmkræk] adj *furniture* de camelote, de pacotille; *jewellery* en toc; *house* de carton.
gimlet ['gɪmlɪt] n vrille *f*. **to have eyes like ~s, to be ~-eyed** avoir des yeux perçants, avoir un regard perçant comme une vrille.
gimmick ['gɪmɪk] n (*gen*) truc* *m*, trouvaille *f*, gadget *m*; (*Theat: catchphrase*) réplique *f* à effet; (*gadget*) machin* *m*, truc*; (*US: trick*) truc*, combine *f*. **advertising** ~ trouvaille *or* truc* *or* gadget publicitaire; **it's just a sales** ~ c'est simplement un gadget promotionnel *or* une astuce promotionnelle; **the comedian put on a Scots accent as a** ~ le comique a pris un accent écossais pour l'effet; **her glasses are just a ~ to make her look intellectual** ses lunettes sont simplement un truc* pour lui donner l'air intellectuel.
gimmickry ['gɪmɪkrɪ] n (recherche *f* d')astuces *fpl*, trucs* *mpl*.
gimmicky ['gɪmɪkɪ] adj (*pej*) *photography* à trucs*; *presentation* à astuces.
gimp* [gɪmp] (*US*) 1 n (*person*) boiteux *m*, -euse *f*. **to walk with a** ~ boiter. 2 vi boiter.
gimpy ['gɪmpɪ] adj (*US*) boiteux.
gin¹ [dʒɪn] 1 n a gin *m*. ~ **and tonic** gin-tonic *m*; (*Brit*) ~ **and it** gin-vermouth *m*; *see* **pink**. b (*Cards also:* ~ **rummy**) *variante du rami*. 2 comp ▸**gin mill**⁑ (*US*) bar *m*, saloon *m*.
gin² [dʒɪn] n a (*Brit: also* ~ **trap**) piège *m*. b (*Tech: also* **cotton** ~) égreneuse *f* (de coton).
ginger ['dʒɪndʒəʳ] 1 n gingembre *m*; (*fig*) dynamisme *m*, énergie *f*, vitalité *f*. (*nickname*) **G~** Poil de Carotte. 2 adj a *hair* roux (*f* rousse), rouquin*. b (*Culin*) *biscuit etc* au gingembre. 3 comp ▸**ginger ale,** (*Brit*) **ginger beer** boisson gazeuse au gingembre

►**gingerbread** n pain *m* d'épice ◊ adj (*Culin*) en pain d'épice; (**: Archit*) *style* tarabiscoté; **gingerbread man** bonhomme *m* en pain d'épice ►**ginger group** (*Brit: esp Pol*) groupe *m* de pression ►**gingernut** gâteau sec au gingembre ►**ginger pop*** = **ginger ale** ►**gingersnap** = **gingernut**.

►**ginger up** vt sep (*Brit*) *person* secouer, secouer les puces à‡; *action, event* mettre de la vie *or* de l'entrain dans. **he gingered up his talk with a few jokes** il a relevé *or* égayé sa causerie de quelques plaisanteries.

gingerly [ˈdʒɪndʒəlɪ] 1 adj *prod* léger, doux (*f* douce); *touch* délicat. 2 adv *touch, move* précautionneusement, avec précaution. **to walk** *or* **tread** ~ (*lit*) marcher à pas précautionneux *or* avec précaution *or* comme sur des œufs; (*fig*) y aller avec des gants* *or* doucement.

gingery [ˈdʒɪndʒərɪ] adj a (*colour*) *hair* avec des reflets roux; *cloth etc* dans les tons roux. b *taste* de gingembre. **it tastes (very)** ~ ça a (fort) goût de gingembre.

gingham [ˈgɪŋəm] n (*Tex*) vichy *m*.

gingivitis [ˌdʒɪndʒɪˈvaɪtɪs] n gingivite *f*.

gink‡ [gɪŋk] n (*US pej*) (drôle de) type* *m*.

ginormous* [dʒaɪˈnɔːməs] adj énorme, maous* (*f* -se).

ginseng [dʒɪnˈseŋ] 1 n ginseng *m*. 2 comp *tea, tablets* au ginseng.

Gioconda [dʒoˈkonda] n: **La** ~ la Joconde; ~ **smile** sourire *m* énigmatique *or* sibyllin.

gipsy [ˈdʒɪpsɪ] 1 n (*gen*) bohémien(ne) *m(f)*; (*Spanish*) gitan(e) *m(f)*; (*Central European*) Tsigane *mf*; (*pej*) romanichel(le) *m(f)*. **she's so dark she looks like a** ~ elle est si foncée de peau qu'elle a l'air d'une bohémienne *or* d'une gitane. 2 comp *caravan, custom* de bohémien, de gitan, tsigane, de romanichel (*pej*); *music* des gitans, tsigane ►**gipsy cab** (*US*) taxi *m* clandestin ►**gipsy driver** (*US*) chauffeur *m* de taxi clandestin ►**gipsy moth** zigzag *m* (*Zool*).

giraffe [dʒɪˈrɑːf] n, pl ~**s** *or* ~ girafe *f*. **baby** ~ girafeau *m*.

gird [gɜːd] pret, ptp **girded** *or* **girt** vt (*liter*) (*encircle*) ceindre (*liter*); (*†: clothe*) revêtir (*with* de). (*fig: get ready*) **to** ~ **o.s. for a fight** se préparer au combat.

►**gird on** vt sep *sword etc* ceindre (*liter*).

►**gird up** vt sep *robe* ceindre. (*Bible*) **to gird up one's loins** se ceindre les reins.

girder [ˈgɜːdəʳ] n poutre *f*; (*smaller*) poutrelle *f*.

girdle[1] [ˈgɜːdl] 1 n (*belt: lit, fig*) ceinture *f*; (*corset*) gaine *f*. 2 vt (*fig liter*) ceindre (*with* de).

girdle[2] [ˈgɜːdl] n (*Culin*) = **griddle 1**.

girl [gɜːl] 1 n a (*jeune ou petite*) fille *f*. **it's not a** ~, **it's a boy** ce n'est pas une fille, c'est un garçon; **the** ~ **who looks after the children** la jeune fille qui s'occupe des enfants; **a little** ~ une petite fille, une fillette; **that** ~ **gets on my nerves** cette jeune fille *or* cette fille (*pej*) m'énerve; **a** ~ **of 17** une (jeune) fille de 17 ans; **an English** ~ une jeune Anglaise; **a little English** ~ une petite Anglaise; **poor little** ~ pauvre petite; **the Smith** ~**s** les filles des Smith; **the little Smith** ~**s** les petites Smith; ~**s' school** école *f* (*or* lycée *m etc*) de filles; **you were very rude, my** ~ tu as été très grossière, ma fille.
b (*daughter*) fille *f*; (*pupil*) élève *f*; (*servant*) bonne *f*; (*factory-worker*) ouvrière *f*; (*shop assistant*) vendeuse *f*, jeune fille; (**: sweetheart*) petite amie. (*Brit Scol*) **old** ~ ancienne élève; **yes, old** ~‡ oui, ma vieille*; **the old** ~‡ (*wife*) la patronne‡, la bourgeoise*; (*mother*) ma mère, ma vieille‡; **the old** ~* **next door** la vieille (dame) d'à côté.
2 comp ►**girl Friday** (*in office*) aide *f* de bureau ►**girlfriend** *[boy]* petite amie; *[girl]* amie *f*, camarade *f*, copine* *f* ►**girl guide** (*Brit*), (*US*) **girl scout** éclaireuse *f*; (*Roman Catholic*) guide *f* ►**girl-watching**: (*US*) **to go girl-watching** aller reluquer‡ les filles.

girlhood [ˈgɜːlhʊd] n enfance *f*, jeunesse *f*.

girlie* [ˈgɜːlɪ] n fillette *f*. ~ **magazine** magazine *m* de fesse*.

girlish [ˈgɜːlɪʃ] adj *boy* efféminé; *behaviour, appearance* (*woman's*) de petite fille, de jeune fille; (*man's, boy's*) de fille, efféminé.

giro [ˈdʒaɪrəʊ] n (*Brit*) (**: also* ~ **cheque**) ≃ chèque *m* postal (*pour versement d'indemnités chômage ou maladie*). **bank** ~ **system** système *m* de virement bancaire; **National G**~ ≃ Comptes Chèques Postaux; (*Fin*) **by** ~ **transfer** par virement postal (*or* bancaire).

girt [gɜːt] 1 pret, ptp of **gird**. 2 n = **girth b**.

girth [gɜːθ] n a (*circumference*) *[tree]* circonférence *f*; *[waist/hips etc]* tour *m* (de taille/de hanches *etc*). **in** ~ de circonférence, de tour; **his (great)** ~ sa corpulence. b *[saddle]* sangle *m*. **to loosen the** ~**s** dessangler.

gist [dʒɪst] n (*NonC*) *[report, conversation etc]* fond *m*, essentiel *m*; *[question]* point principal. **to get the** ~ **of sth** comprendre l'essentiel de qch; **give me the** ~ **of what he said** mettez-moi au courant de ce qu'il a dit, en deux mots.

git‡ [gɪt] n (*Brit: pej*) a (*idiot*) (*man*) con‡ *m*, connard‡ *m*; (*woman*) conne‡ *f*, connasse‡ *f*. **stupid** ~! espèce de con(ne)!‡. b (*unpleasant person*) (*man*) salaud‡ *m*, salopard‡ *m*; (*woman*) salope‡ *f*.

give [gɪv] pret **gave**, ptp **given** 1 vt a (*bestow, confer*) donner (*to* à); (*as gift*) donner, faire don *or* cadeau de, offrir (*to* à); *honour, title* conférer (*to* à), donner; *help, support* prêter (*to* à); *food, hospitality* donner, offrir; *meal* offrir; (*dedicate*) *one's time, fortune, energies* donner, consacrer (*to* à). **to** ~ **alms** faire l'aumône; **to** ~ **sb one's hand** donner *or* tendre la main à qn; (*†: in marriage*) accorder sa main à qn†; **to** ~ **one's daughter in marriage†** donner sa fille en mariage†; **to** ~ **sb one's trust** donner sa confiance à qn, reposer sa confiance en qn; **to** ~ **sb good day††** souhaiter le bonjour à qn; **one must** ~ **and take** il faut faire des concessions (*see also* **4**); (*fig*) ~ **or take a few minutes** à quelques minutes près; (*fig*) **he gave as good as he got** il a rendu coup pour coup (*fig*); **to** ~ **sb something to eat/drink** donner à manger/boire à qn; **can you** ~ **him something to do?** pouvez-vous lui donner *or* trouver quelque chose à faire?; (*fig*) ~ **it all you've got!*** mets-y le paquet!*; **what name will you** ~ **him?** quel nom lui donnerez-vous?; **can you** ~ **me a bed for the night?** pouvez-vous me loger pour la nuit?; **I wouldn't have it if you gave it to me*** tu m'en ferais cadeau que je n'en voudrais pas; **you've** ~**n me your cold** tu m'as donné *or* passé ton rhume; **he gave all his free time to golf** il consacrait tout son temps libre au golf; **he gave his life/himself to helping the needy** il a consacré sa vie/il s'est consacré aux nécessiteux; (*euph*) **she gave herself to him** elle s'est donnée à lui; (*Telec*) ~ **me Mr. Smith/Newtown 231** passez-moi M. Smith/le 231 à Newtown; **I'll** ~ **him something to cry about!*** je lui apprendrai à pleurer!; **to** ~ **sb what for‡**, **to** ~ **it to sb‡** passer un savon à qn*, faire sa fête à qn‡; **I don't** ~ **a damn*** *or* **a hoot* for culture** la culture j'en ai rien à faire* *or* à foutre‡ (*see also* **damn**); **don't** ~ **me that!*** ne me raconte pas d'histoires!* *or* de salades!*; (*US*) **O.K., now** ~!‡ allez, crache!‡ *or* accouche!‡; *see* **arm, thank, thought** *etc*.
b (*grant; cause to have*) donner; *pain, pleasure* occasionner (*to* à); *punishment*, (*Scol*) *order mark, demerit point* infliger (*to* à); *time* donner, laisser (*to* à); *damages* accorder (*to* à). **(God)** ~ **me strength to do it!** que Dieu me donne la force de le faire!; (*liter*) **it was not** ~**n to him to achieve happiness** il ne lui fut pas donné de trouver le bonheur; (*in age*) **I can** ~ **him 10 years** il est de 10 ans mon cadet; **the judge gave him 5 years** le juge l'a condamné à 5 ans de prison; **the doctors gave him 2 years (to live)** les médecins lui ont donné 2 ans (à vivre); **how long do you** ~ **that marriage?** combien de temps crois-tu que ce mariage tiendra?; **a hundred people** — ~ **or take a few** à peu près cent personnes; **I can't** ~ **you any longer, you must pay me now** je ne peux plus vous accorder de délai, il faut que vous payiez maintenant; **I can** ~ **you half an hour tomorrow** je peux vous consacrer une demi-heure demain; (*fig: agreeing*) **I'll** ~ **you that** je vous accorde cela; (*iro*) **he wants £10? I'll** ~ **him £10 (indeed)!*** il veut 10 livres? tu penses comme je vais lui donner 10 livres!*; ~ **him time to get home** laissez-lui le temps de rentrer; ~ **yourself time to think about it before you decide** accordez-vous le temps d'y réfléchir *or* de la réflexion avant de prendre une décision; **(just)** ~ **me time!** attends un peu!, ne me bouscule pas!; ~ **me time and I'll manage it** laissez-moi du temps et j'y arriverai; ~ **me Mozart every time!*** pour moi, rien ne vaut Mozart; *see* **due, ground**[1] *etc*.
c (*state, deliver*) donner; *message* remettre (*to* à); *description, particulars* donner, fournir (*to* à). **to** ~ **sb to understand that ...** donner à entendre à qn que ...; **to** ~ **sb to believe sth** faire croire *or* faire supposer qch à qn; (*Jur etc*) **to** ~ **the case for/against sb** décider en faveur de/contre qn; (*Jur*) ~**n under my hand and seal** signé et scellé par moi; **what name did he** ~? quel nom a-t-il donné?; (*lit, fig*) **he gave no sign of life** il n'a pas donné signe de vie; **to** ~ **a decision** donner *or* faire connaître sa décision; (*Jur*) prononcer *or* rendre un arrêt; ~ **him my love** faites-lui mes amitiés; *see* **account, evidence, hint** *etc*.
d (*pay, exchange*) donner, payer, offrir. **what will you** ~ **me for it?** combien m'en offrez-vous *or* m'en donnez-vous?; **what did you** ~ **for it?** combien l'avez-vous payé?; **to** ~ **one thing in exchange for another** échanger une chose pour *or* contre une autre; **I'd** ~ **a lot/anything to know** je donnerais gros/n'importe quoi pour savoir.
e (*perform etc*) *jump, gesture* faire; *answer, lecture* faire, donner; *sigh, cry, laugh* pousser; (*Theat*) *play* donner, présenter. **to** ~ **a party/ball** *etc* donner une soirée/un bal *etc*; **to** ~ **sb a look** jeter *or* lancer un regard à qn; **to** ~ **sb a blow** porter un coup à qn; **to** ~ **sb a slap** donner *or* allonger* *or* flanquer* une gifle à qn; **to** ~ **sb's hand a squeeze** presser la main à qn; **to** ~ **one's hair a brush** donner un coup de brosse à ses cheveux; **to** ~ **sb a smile** adresser *or* faire un sourire à qn; **she gave a little smile** elle a eu un petit sourire; **to** ~ **a recitation** dire des vers; ~ **us a song** chantez-nous quelque chose; ~ **us a laugh*** faites-nous rire; (*frm*) **I** ~ **you the Queen!** je lève mon verre à la santé de la Reine!
f (*produce, provide, supply*) donner, rendre; *sound* rendre; (*Math etc*) *result, answer* donner. **it** ~**s 16% per annum** cela rapporte 16% par an; **this lamp** ~**s a poor light** cette lampe éclaire mal; **5 times 4** ~**s 20** 5 fois 4 font *or* égalent 20; **it** ~**s a total of 100** cela fait 100 en tout; ~ **the answer to the 4th decimal place/in pence** donnez la réponse à la 4e décimale/en pence.
g **to** ~ **way** (*collapse*) *[building, bridge, beam, ceiling]* céder, s'effondrer, s'affaisser; (*beneath, under* sous); *[ground]* céder, s'affaisser, se dérober (*beneath, under* sous); *[plaster]* s'effriter; *[cable, rope, ladder etc]* céder, (se) casser, se rompre; *[legs]* fléchir, mollir; *[health]* s'altérer. **my legs are giving way*** mes jambes se dérobent sous moi; **his strength gave way** ses forces lui ont manqué; *see also* **1h**.
h **to** ~ **way** *[person]* (*stand back*) s'écarter, se pousser, reculer; (*yield*) céder, lâcher pied (*to sth* devant qch); (*agree*) donner son

accord, consentir; (*surrender*) céder, se rendre; *[troops]* (*withdraw*) reculer, se retirer; *[car, traffic]* céder *or* laisser la priorité (*to* à). (*Aut*) "~ **way**" "cédez la priorité"; (*Aut*) "~ **way to traffic from the right**" "priorité à droite"; **he gave way to their demands** il a cédé à leurs revendications; **she gave way to tears** elle s'est laissée aller à pleurer; **don't ~ way to despair** ne vous abandonnez pas au désespoir; **the storm gave way to sunshine** l'orage a fait place au soleil; **radio gave way to television** la radio a fait place à la télévision.

2 **vi** a (*collapse, yield*) *[road, ground, beam etc]* céder (*to* à, *beneath, under* sous), s'affaisser (*under* sous); (*lose firmness*) *[cloth, elastic etc]* prêter, se détendre, se relâcher. **the frost is giving** il commence à dégeler.

b (*esp US*) **what ~s?*** alors, qu'est-ce qui se passe?

3 **n** (*) élasticité *f*, souplesse *f*. **there is not much ~ in this cloth** ce tissu ne prête pas.

4 **comp** ►**give-and-take** concessions mutuelles; **there must be a certain amount of give-and-take** il faut que chacun fasse des concessions *or* y mette un peu du sien ►**giveaway** (*fig*) **n** révélation *f* involontaire; (*Comm: free gift*) prime *f*, cadeau *m* publicitaire; (*US: Rad, TV*) jeu radiophonique *or* télévisé (*doté de prix*) ◊ **adj** *price* dérisoire; **it was a real giveaway when he said that ...** il s'est vraiment trahi en disant que ...; **the fact that she knew his name was a giveaway** le simple fait qu'elle sache son nom était révélateur.

►**give away** 1 **vt sep** a (*bestow, distribute*) *prizes* distribuer; *bride* conduire à l'autel; *money, goods* donner, faire cadeau de. **I'm giving it away** j'en fais cadeau. b (*tell, betray*) *names, details* révéler. **to give sb away** *[person, accomplice]* dénoncer *or* donner* qn; *[mistake, reaction, expression]* trahir qn; **to give o.s. away** se trahir, se révéler; **don't give anything away** ne dis rien; **his face gave nothing away** son visage ne trahissait rien; (*fig*) **to give the game** *or* **show away*** vendre la mèche*. 2 **giveaway n, adj** *see* **give 4**.

►**give back vt sep** *object, health, freedom* rendre (*to* à); *property* restituer (*to* à); *echo* renvoyer; *image* refléter.

►**give forth vt sep** *sound* émettre, faire entendre.

►**give in** 1 **vi** (*yield*) renoncer, abandonner, s'avouer vaincu. **to give in to sb** céder à qn; **I give in!** (*in games etc*) je renonce; (*in guessing*) je donne ma langue au chat!* 2 **vt sep** *parcel, document* remettre; *essay, exam paper* rendre; *one's name* donner; *accounts* rendre.

►**give off vt sep** *heat* émettre, dégager; *smell* émettre, exhaler; (*Chem*) *gas* dégager; (*Bot*) *shoots* former.

►**give on to vt fus** *[door, window]* donner sur.

►**give out** 1 **vi** *[supplies]* s'épuiser, manquer; *[patience]* être à bout; (*) *[car, engine]* tomber en panne. **my strength is giving out** je suis à bout de forces, je n'en peux plus; **my patience gave out** j'ai perdu patience, la patience m'a manqué; **my watch is giving out*** ma montre est en train de rendre l'âme (*hum*). 2 **vt sep** a (*distribute*) *books, food etc* distribuer. b (*announce*) *news* annoncer, proclamer; *list etc* faire connaître. **it was given out that ...** on a annoncé que ... . c (*Rad*) *signal* émettre. d = **give off**.

►**give over** 1 **vt sep** (*dedicate, devote*) donner, consacrer (*to* à); (*transfer*) affecter (*to* à). **this building is now given over to offices** ce bâtiment est maintenant affecté à des bureaux; **to give o.s. over to** s'adonner à, s'abandonner à; **to give over all one's time to doing** consacrer tout son temps à faire. 2 **vt fus** (*: *stop*) cesser, finir. **to give over doing** cesser de faire, arrêter de faire*; **give over!** arrête!, assez!, finis donc!

►**give up** 1 **vi** abandonner, renoncer. **don't give up!** tenez bon!; **I give up** j'y renonce, je renonce; (*in guessing etc*) je donne ma langue au chat*.

2 **vt sep** a (*devote*) vouer, consacrer. **to give up one's life to music** vouer *or* consacrer sa vie à la musique; **to give o.s. up to sth** se livrer à qch, se plonger dans qch.

b (*renounce, part with*) *friends, interests* abandonner, délaisser; *seat, place* céder; *habit, idea* abandonner, renoncer à; *job* quitter; *appointment* démissionner de; *business* se retirer de; *subscription* cesser. **he'll never give her up** il ne renoncera jamais à elle; **to give up doing** renoncer à *or* cesser de faire; **to give up smoking** renoncer au tabac, cesser de fumer; (*fig*) **to give up the game** *or* **the struggle** abandonner la partie; **I gave it up as a bad job** (comme ça ne menait à rien) j'ai laissé tomber*; **she gave him up as a bad job*** comme elle n'arrivait à rien avec lui elle l'a laissé tomber*.

c (*deliver, hand over*) *prisoner* livrer (*to* à); *authority* se démettre de; *keys of city etc* rendre. **to give o.s. up** se livrer (*to the police* à la police), se rendre, se constituer prisonnier.

d (*abandon hope for*) *patient* condamner; *expected visitor* ne plus attendre, ne plus espérer voir; *problem, riddle* renoncer à (résoudre). **to give sb up for lost** considérer qn comme perdu; **to give o.s. up for lost** se croire perdu; **to give sb up for dead** croire qn mort.

►**give up on vt fus** a (*renounce*) *idea, attempt* abandonner, renoncer à. **the car/washing machine has given up on me*** la voiture/la machine à laver m'a lâché*. b (*abandon hope for*) *expected visitor* ne plus attendre, ne plus espérer voir; (*lose faith in*) perdre espoir en.

given ['gɪvn] 1 **ptp of give**. 2 **adj** a donné, déterminé. **at a ~ time** à une heure déterminée, à un moment donné; **of a ~ size** d'une taille donnée *or* bien déterminée; **under the ~ conditions** dans les conditions données *or* requises; (*Scot, US*) ~ **name** prénom *m*, nom *m* de baptême. b ~ **the triangle ABC** soit *or* étant donné le triangle ABC; ~ **that he is capable of learning** supposé qu'il soit capable d'apprendre. c (*having inclination*) adonné, enclin (*to* à). **I am not ~ to doing** je n'ai pas l'habitude de faire, je ne suis pas enclin à faire.

giver ['gɪvəʳ] **n** donateur *m*, -trice *f*; (*St Ex*) preneur *m*, -euse *f* d'option, optionnaire *mf*.

gizmo‡ ['gɪzməʊ] **n** (*US*) machin* *m*, truc* *m*.

gizzard ['gɪzəd] **n** gésier *m*; *see* **stick**.

glacé ['glæseɪ] **adj** (*Culin*) *fruit* glacé, confit. ~ **icing** glaçage *m*.

glacial ['gleɪsɪəl] **adj** (*Geol*) glaciaire; *wind, winter* glacial; (*Chem*) cristallisé, en cristaux.

glaciated ['gleɪsɪeɪtɪd] **adj** (*Geol*) ~ **landscape** relief *m* glaciaire.

glaciation [ˌgleɪsɪ'eɪʃən] **n** glaciation *f*.

glacier ['glæsɪəʳ] **n** glacier *m*.

glaciological [ˌglæsɪə'lɒdʒɪkəl] **adj** glaciologique.

glaciologist [ˌglæsɪ'ɒlədʒɪst] **n** glaciologue *mf*.

glaciology [ˌglæsɪ'ɒlədʒɪ] **n** glaciologie *f*.

glad [glæd] 1 **adj** *person* content, heureux (*of, about* de); *news* heureux; *occasion* joyeux. **I am ~ about it** cela me fait plaisir, j'en suis bien content; **I'm ~ (that) you came** je suis ravi que tu sois venu; **I'm ~ to hear it** je suis ravi de l'apprendre; **I shall be ~ to come** je serai heureux de venir; **he was only too ~ to help** il ne demandait pas mieux que d'aider; ~ **to know you!*** ravi!*, enchanté!, très heureux!; ~ **tidings**, ~ **news** heureuses *or* bonnes nouvelles; (*esp US*) **to give sb the ~ hand*** accueillir qn les bras ouverts (*see also* **2**); ~ **rags**‡ beaux atours, belles fringues‡, belles frusques‡; **she's in her ~ rags**‡ elle est en grand tralala‡, elle est sur son trente et un; **to give sb the ~ eye**‡ faire de l'œil* à qn.

2 **comp** ►**glad-hand*** (*US*) **vt** accueillir avec effusion.

gladden ['glædn] **vt** *person* rendre heureux; *heart, occasion* réjouir, égayer.

glade [gleɪd] **n** clairière *f*.

gladiator ['glædɪeɪtəʳ] **n** gladiateur *m*, belluaire *m*.

gladiatorial [ˌglædɪə'tɔːrɪəl] **adj** (*fig*) conflictuel. ~ **politics** politique *f* de la confrontation.

gladiolus [ˌglædɪ'əʊləs] **n, pl** ~ *or* ~**es** *or* **gladioli** [ˌglædɪ'əʊlaɪ] glaïeul *m*.

gladly ['glædlɪ] **adv** (*joyfully*) avec joie; (*willingly*) avec plaisir, volontiers, de bon cœur. **will you help me?** — ~ voulez-vous m'aider? — volontiers *or* avec plaisir.

gladness ['glædnɪs] **n** joie *f*, contentement *m*.

glam* [glæm] **adj abbr of glamorous**.

glamorize ['glæməraɪz] **vt** *place, event, act etc* montrer *or* présenter sous des couleurs séduisantes.

glamorous ['glæmərəs] **adj** *spectacle, life* brillant; *production* à grand spectacle; *dress, photo* splendide, glamoureux*; *person* séduisant, fascinant; *job* prestigieux.

glamour ['glæməʳ] 1 **n** *[person]* séductions *fpl*, fascination *f*; *[occasion]* éclat *m*; *[situation etc]* prestige *m*; *[distant countries, journeys]* fascination *f*. **the ~ of life in Hollywood** la vie brillante d'Hollywood; **the ~ of being an M.P.** la gloire d'être membre du parlement; **to lend ~ to sth** prêter de l'éclat à qch. 2 **comp** ►**glamour boy*** beau gars*, beau mec‡ ►**glamour girl*** pin-up‡ *f inv*, beauté *f*.

glance [glɑːns] 1 **n** a regard *m*, coup *m* d'œil. **at a ~** d'un coup d'œil; **at first ~** au premier coup d'œil, à première vue; **without a backward ~** (*lit*) sans se retourner; (*fig*) sans plus de cérémonies; **to have** *or* **take a ~ at** jeter un coup d'œil sur.

b (*gleam*) (*of light*) lueur *f*; (*of metal*) reflet *m*. **a ~ of sunlight** un rayon de soleil.

2 **vi** a (*look*) jeter un coup d'œil (*at* sur, à), lancer un regard (*at* à). **she ~d in my direction** elle a jeté un coup d'œil vers moi; **she ~d over her shoulder** elle a jeté un coup d'œil par-dessus son épaule; **he ~d over the paper** il a parcouru le journal du regard, il a lu le journal en diagonale; **he ~d through the book** il a jeté un coup d'œil sur *or* feuilleté le livre.

b (*glint*) étinceler.

c **to ~ off** *[bullet]* ricocher sur; *[arrow, sword]* dévier sur.

►**glance away vi** détourner le regard.

►**glance down vi** jeter un coup d'œil en bas, regarder en bas.

►**glance off vi** *[bullet etc]* ricocher, dévier; *[arrow, sword]* dévier.

►**glance round vi** (*behind*) regarder en arrière; (*round about*) jeter un coup d'œil autour de soi.

►**glance up vi** (*raise eyes*) lever les yeux; (*look upwards*) regarder en l'air.

glancing ['glɑːnsɪŋ] **adj** a *blow* oblique. b (*glinting*) *metal etc* étincelant.

gland [glænd] **n** glande *f*.

glanders ['glændəz] **n** (*Vet*) morve *f*.

glandes ['glændiːz] **npl of glans**.

glandular ['glændjʊləʳ] **adj** glandulaire. ~ **fever** mononucléose infectieuse.

glans [glænz] **n, pl glandes**: ~ **(penis)** gland *m*.

glare [glɛəʳ] 1 vi a *[person]* lancer un regard furieux *or* de colère (*at* à). b *[sun, lights]* éblouir, briller d'un éclat éblouissant *or* aveuglant. 2 vt: **to ~ defiance** *etc* **at sb** lancer un regard plein de défi *etc* à qn. 3 n a *[person]* regard furieux. **"no" he said with a ~** "non" jeta-t-il avec un regard furieux; **he gave me an angry ~** il m'a jeté un regard furieux. b *[light]* éclat aveuglant, lumière éblouissante; (*Aut*) éblouissement *m*; *[publicity]* feux *mpl*.

glaring ['glɛərɪŋ] adj *light* éblouissant, éclatant; *sun* aveuglant; *colour* hurlant, criard; *eyes* furieux, flamboyant (de colère); (*fig*) *fact, mistake* (plus qu')évident, qui saute aux yeux, qui crève les yeux; *injustice, lie* flagrant.

glaringly ['glɛərɪŋlɪ] adv (*fig*): **it is ~ obvious** cela saute aux yeux; **it is/it is becoming ~ obvious** *or* **apparent that ...** il est/devient manifeste que ... .

glasnost ['glæznɒst] n glasnost *f*.

glass [glɑːs] 1 n a (*NonC*) verre *m*. **pane of ~** carreau *m*, vitre *f*; **window ~** verre à vitre; **I cut myself on some broken ~** je me suis coupé avec un éclat de verre; **there was some broken ~ on the pavement** il y avait des éclats de verre sur le trottoir; *see* **cut, plate** *etc*. b (*tumbler*) verre *m*; (*glassful*) (plein) verre. **a ~ of wine** un verre de vin; **a wine ~** un verre à vin; *see* **balloon, beer, champagne**. c (*NonC: also* **~ware**) (*gen*) verrerie *f*; (*glasses*) gobeleterie *f*. d (*mirror*) miroir *m*, glace *f*; (*Opt*) lentille *f*; (*magnifying ~*) verre grossissant, loupe *f*; (*telescope*) longue-vue *f*; (*barometer*) baromètre *m*; (*for plants*) cloche *f*, châssis *m*; (*Comm etc*) vitrine *f*. (*Met*) **the ~ is falling** le baromètre baisse; **grown under ~** cultivé sous verre; **object displayed under ~** objet exposé en vitrine; **~es** (*spectacles*) lunettes *fpl*; (*binoculars*) jumelles *fpl*; *see* **sun** *etc*.
2 vt (*also* **~ in**) *door, shelves* vitrer; *picture* mettre sous verre.
3 comp *bottle, ornament* de verre, en verre ►**glassblower** verrier *m*, souffleur *m* (de verre) ►**glassblowing** soufflage *m* (du verre) ►**glass case** (*Comm*) vitrine *f*; *[clock etc]* globe *m*; **to keep sth in a glass case** garder qch sous verre *or* sous globe ►**glasscloth** essuie-verres *m inv*, torchon *m* à verres ►**glasscutter** (*tool*) diamant *m*, coupe-verre *m inv*; (*person*) vitrier *m* ►**glass door** porte vitrée ►**glass eye** œil *m* de verre ►**glass factory** = **glassworks** ►**glass fibre** n fibre *f* de verre ◊ comp en fibre de verre ►**glasshouse** (*Brit: for plants*) serre *f*; (*US: glassworks*) verrerie *f* (*fabrique*); (*Brit Mil sl*) **in the glasshouse** au trou‡; (*Prov*) **people in glass houses shouldn't throw stones** critiquer les autres, c'est s'exposer à la critique ►**glass industry** industrie *f* du verre, verrerie *f* ►**glasspaper** (*Brit*) papier *m* de verre ►**glass slipper** pantoufle *f* de verre ►**glass wool** laine *f* de verre ►**glassworks** sg inv verrerie *f* (*fabrique*).

glassful ['glɑːsfʊl] n (plein) verre *m*.

glassy ['glɑːsɪ] 1 adj semblable au verre, qui ressemble au verre; *substance* vitreux; *surface* uni, lisse; *water, sea* transparent, uni comme un miroir. **~ eyes** *or* **look** regard perdu *or* vague; (*from drink, drugs*) regard vitreux *or* terne; (*from displeasure*) regard froid. 2 comp ►**glassy-eyed** à l'air perdu *or* vague; (*from drugs, drink*) au regard terne *or* vitreux; (*from displeasure*) au regard froid.

Glaswegian [glæs'wiːdʒjən] 1 n: **he's a ~** (*living there*) c'est un habitant de Glasgow, il habite Glasgow; (*born there*) il est originaire de Glasgow. 2 adj de Glasgow.

glaucoma [glɔː'kəʊmə] n glaucome *m*.

glaucous ['glɔːkəs] adj glauque.

glaze [gleɪz] 1 vt a (*Brit*) *door, window* vitrer; *picture* mettre sous verre; *see* **double**. b *pottery* vernisser; *tiles* vitrifier, vernisser; *leather* vernir; *cotton etc* satiner, lustrer; *paper, photograph, cake, meat* glacer. 2 vi (*also* **~ over**) *[eyes]* devenir vitreux *or* terne. 3 n a (*NonC*) (*on pottery, leather, tiles etc*) vernis *m*; (*on cotton etc*) lustre *m*; (*on paper, photograph*) glacé *m*; (*Culin*) glaçage *m*. b (*substance*) (*for tiles etc*) enduit vitrifié; (*for pottery*) vernis *m*. c (*US: ice*) verglas *m*.

glazed [gleɪzd] adj a (*Brit*) *door, window etc* vitré; *picture* sous verre. b *pottery* émaillé, vernissé; *tiles* vernissé, vitrifié; *leather* glacé, verni; *material* lustré, satiné; *paper, photograph* brillant; *cake, meat* glacé; (*US* ‡: *drunk*) bourré‡, ivre. **his eyes** *or* **he had a ~ look** il avait les yeux ternes *or* vitreux.

glazier ['gleɪzɪəʳ] n (*Brit*) vitrier *m*.

glazing ['gleɪzɪŋ] n a (*act*) *[windows]* vitrage *m*, pose *f* de vitres; *[pottery]* vernissage *m*. b (*glass*) vitrage *m*, vitres *fpl*; *see also* **double 4, secondary, triple 2**.

G.L.C. [ˌdʒiːel'siː] n (*Brit* †) (abbr of **Greater London Council**) *administration f du grand Londres*.

gleam [gliːm] 1 n lueur *f*, rayon *m* (de lumière); *[metal]* reflet *m*; *[water]* miroitement *m*. **~ of hope** lueur d'espoir, rayon d'espérance; **~ of humour/of intelligence** lueur d'humour/d'intelligence; **she had a dangerous ~ in her eye** il y avait une lueur dangereuse dans ses yeux *or* dans son regard. 2 vi *[lamp, star, eyes etc]* luire; *[polished metal, shoes etc]* reluire; *[knife, blade etc]* luire, briller; *[water]* miroiter. **his eyes ~ed with delight/mischief** la joie/la malice luisait dans ses yeux.

gleaming ['gliːmɪŋ] adj *lamp, star* brillant; *polished metal, shoes etc* reluisant, brillant; *kitchen* étincelant; *water* miroitant.

glean [gliːn] vti (*lit, fig*) glaner.

gleaner ['gliːnəʳ] n glaneur *m*, -euse *f*.

gleanings ['gliːnɪŋz] npl glanure(s) *f(pl)*.

glebe [gliːb] n (*Rel*) terre attachée à un bénéfice ecclésiastique; (†† *or liter*) terre, glèbe *f* (*liter*).

glee [gliː] n a (*NonC*) joie *f*, jubilation *f*. **in great** *or* **high ~** jubilant, débordant *or* plein d'allégresse. b (*Mus*) chant choral à plusieurs voix. **~ club** chorale *f*.

gleeful ['gliːfʊl] adj joyeux, jubilant.

gleefully ['gliːfəlɪ] adv joyeusement, en jubilant.

glen [glen] n vallée encaissée, vallon *m*; (*steep-sided*) gorge *f*.

glib [glɪb] adj *person* qui a la parole facile, qui a du bagou*; *tongue* délié, affilé; *speech, style* facile, désinvolte; *excuse* désinvolte, spécieux; *lie* désinvolte. **he's very ~** il est beau parleur.

glibly ['glɪblɪ] adv *speak* avec aisance, facilement; *reply* sans hésiter; *make excuses, lie* avec désinvolture.

glibness ['glɪbnɪs] n *[person]* facilité *f* de parole, bagou* *m*; *[excuses, lies, style etc]* désinvolture *f*.

glide [glaɪd] 1 vi a **to ~ in/out** *etc [person]* (*silently*) entrer/sortir *etc* sans bruit; (*in stately way, gracefully*) entrer/sortir *etc* avec grâce; *[ghost]* entrer/sortir *etc* comme en flottant; *[car, ship]* entrer/sortir *etc* comme en glissant *or* en douceur; (*fig*) **time ~d past** le temps s'écoula. b (*Ski*) glisser. c *[birds]* planer; (*Aviat*) planer, faire du vol plané. (*Aviat*) **he ~d down to land** il a atterri en vol plané. 2 vt faire glisser, faire avancer sans heurts *or* en douceur. 3 n a glissement *m*; (*Dancing*) glissé *m*, glissade *f*; (*Ski*) glisse *f*. b (*Mus*) port *m* de voix; (*Phon*) glissement *m*. c (*Aviat*) vol plané.

glider ['glaɪdəʳ] n a (*Aviat*) planeur *m*. **~ pilot** pilote *m* de planeur. b (*US: swing*) balancelle *f*.

gliding ['glaɪdɪŋ] 1 n (*Sport*) vol *m* à voile; (*Aviat*) vol plané; (*gen: movement*) glissement *m*. 2 adj (*Anat*) **~ joint** arthrodie *f*.

glimmer ['glɪməʳ] 1 vi *[lamp, light, fire]* luire faiblement; *[water]* miroiter; *[sea]* miroiter, brasiller (*liter*). 2 n *[light, candle etc]* faible *or* petite lueur; *[water]* miroitement *m*; (*fig: of hope, intelligence etc*) (faible) lueur.

glimmering ['glɪmərɪŋ] 1 n = **glimmer 2**. 2 adj étincelant, scintillant.

glimpse [glɪmps] 1 n *[the truth, the future, sb's meaning]* aperçu *m*. **to catch a ~ of** *person, thing* entrevoir *or* entr'apercevoir (un bref instant); *the truth, the future etc* entrevoir, pressentir. 2 vt entrevoir *or* entr'apercevoir (un bref instant).

glint [glɪnt] 1 n *[light]* trait *m* de lumière, éclair *m*; *[metal]* reflet *m*. **he had a ~ in his eye** il avait une étincelle *or* une lueur dans le regard. 2 vi *[metal object, glass, wet road]* luire, briller; *[eyes, dewdrop]* briller.

glissade [glɪ'seɪd] (*Climbing*) 1 n (*also* **standing ~**) ramasse *f*. 2 vi descendre en ramasse.

glissando [glɪ'sændəʊ] adv glissando.

glisten ['glɪsn] 1 vi *[water]* miroiter, scintiller, chatoyer; *[wet surface]* luire; *[light]* scintiller; *[metal object]* briller, miroiter. **her eyes ~ed (with tears)** ses yeux brillaient (de larmes). 2 n miroitement *m*; chatoiement *m*; scintillement *m*.

glister†† ['glɪstəʳ] = **glitter**.

glitch [glɪtʃ] n (*esp US* ‡: *hiccup*) pépin *m*; (*Comput, Elec etc*) problème *m* technique.

glitter ['glɪtəʳ] 1 vi *[snow, ice, lights]* scintiller, briller; *[jewel]* chatoyer, rutiler, scintiller; *[water]* miroiter, scintiller. **her eyes ~ed** ses yeux brillaient *or* flambaient de haine (*or* de convoitise *etc*); (*Prov*) **all that ~s is not gold** tout ce qui brille n'est pas or (*Prov*). 2 n scintillement *m*; (*fig*) éclat *m*.

glitterati* [ˌglɪtə'rɑːtiː] npl: **the ~** le beau monde, les rupins* *mpl* (*pej*).

glittering ['glɪtərɪŋ] adj étincelant, scintillant; *eyes* brillant, étincelant; (*fig*) éclatant, resplendissant. **~ prizes** prix *mpl* fabuleux; (*fig*) prix miroitants.

glittery ['glɪtərɪ] adj étincelant, scintillant.

glitz* [glɪts] n faste *m*; (*pej*) faste *or* luxe *m* tapageur.

glitzy* ['glɪtsɪ] adj fastueux, au faste *or* au luxe tapageur (*pej*).

gloaming ['gləʊmɪŋ] n (*liter*) crépuscule *m*. **in the ~** au crépuscule, entre chien et loup.

gloat [gləʊt] vi (*pej*) exulter, jubiler*; (*maliciously*) se réjouir avec malveillance (*over, upon* de). **to ~ over** *money, possessions* jubiler* à la vue (*or* à l'idée) de; **he was ~ing over his success** son succès l'avait fait jubiler*; **it's nothing to ~ over** il n'y a pas de quoi jubiler* *or* de quoi se frotter les mains.

gloating ['gləʊtɪŋ] (*pej*) 1 n exultation *f or* jubilation *f* malveillante. 2 adj jubilatoire.

glob [glɒb] n *[liquid]* globule *m*; *[clay etc]* petite boule.

global ['gləʊbl] adj a (*worldwide*) *peace* universel, mondial. **the ~ village** le village planétaire; **~ warming** réchauffement *m* de la planète. b (*comprehensive*) *sum, view* global, entier. (*Comput*) **~ search and replace** recherche *f* et remplacement *m* automatiques. c (*globe-shaped*) globulaire, en forme de globe.

globally ['gləʊbəlɪ] adv a (*worldwide*) mondialement, dans le monde. b (*universally*) globalement.

globe [gləʊb] 1 n (*sphere*) globe *m*, sphère *f*; (*with map on it*) globe; (*lampshade etc*) globe; (*fishbowl*) bocal *m*; (*Anat*) globe. **terrestrial/celestial ~** globe terrestre/céleste; (*Geog*) **the ~** le globe, la terre; **all**

over the ~ sur toute la surface du globe. 2 comp ▸**globe artichoke** artichaut *m* ▸**globefish** poisson-globe *m* ▸**globe lightning** éclair *m* en boule ▸**globe-trotter** globe-trotter *m* ▸**globe-trotting** voyages *mpl* à travers le monde.

globular ['glɒbjʊləʳ] adj a (*composed of globules*) globuleux. b (*globe-shaped*) globulaire, en forme de globe, sphérique.

globule ['glɒbjuːl] n gouttelette *f*.

glockenspiel ['glɒkən,spiːl] n glockenspiel *m*.

gloom [gluːm] n (*darkness*) obscurité *f*, ténèbres *fpl*; (*melancholy*) mélancolie *f*, tristesse *f*. **to cast a ~ over sth** assombrir qch, jeter une ombre sur qch; **to cast a ~ over sb** rendre qn triste *or* sombre *or* mélancolique, attrister qn; **it was all ~ and doom*** tout était sombre, l'avenir se présentait sous les plus sombres couleurs.

gloomily ['gluːmɪlɪ] adv tristement, mélancoliquement, d'un air sombre *or* morne *or* lugubre.

gloomy ['gluːmɪ] adj a *person, character* sombre, triste, mélancolique, (*stronger*) lugubre; *tone, voice, look* morne, triste, mélancolique, (*stronger*) lugubre; *atmosphere, place* morne, (*stronger*) lugubre; *forecast, future, prospects* sombre; *thoughts* sombre, noir; *weather, day* sombre, morne. **he took a ~ view of everything** il voyait tout en noir; **to feel ~** avoir des idées noires. b (*dark*) obscur, sombre, ténébreux (*liter*).

glorification [,glɔːrɪfɪ'keɪʃən] n glorification *f*.

glorify ['glɔːrɪfaɪ] vt *God* glorifier, rendre gloire à; *person* glorifier, célébrer, chanter les louanges de; (*fig*) *event, place etc* glorifier, embellir. **the "luxury hotel" was nothing but a glorified boarding house** c'était en fait une pension de famille qui n'avait d'hôtel de luxe que le nom.

gloriole ['glɔːrɪəʊl] n nimbe *m*.

glorious ['glɔːrɪəs] adj *saint, martyr* glorieux; *person* illustre; *victory* éclatant; *weather, clothes, view, countryside* magnifique, splendide; *holiday etc* merveilleux, sensationnel*. **~ deed** action *f* d'éclat; (*Brit Hist*) **the G~ Revolution** la révolution en Angleterre (1688-89); **we had a ~ evening*** nous avons passé une soirée sensationnelle*; (*iro*) **a ~ mess** un joli *or* beau gâchis.

gloriously ['glɔːrɪəslɪ] adv *succeed, win* glorieusement. **~ sunny/warm** splendidement ensoleillé/bon.

glory ['glɔːrɪ] 1 n a (*NonC*) gloire *f* (*also Rel*); (*magnificence*) splendeur *f*, magnificence *f*, éclat *m*. **to give ~ to God** rendre gloire à Dieu; **to the greater ~ of God** pour la plus grande gloire de Dieu; **Christ in ~** le Christ en majesté *or* en gloire; **the saints in ~** les glorieux *mpl*; **Solomon in all his ~** Salomon dans toute sa gloire; **covered with ~** couvert de gloire; **Rome at the height of its ~** Rome à l'apogée *or* au sommet de sa gloire; **there she was in all her ~*, dressed in gold from head to foot** elle était là dans toute sa splendeur, vêtue d'or de la tête aux pieds; **she was in her ~* as president of the club** elle était tout à fait à son affaire en tant que présidente du club; (*die*) **to go to ~*†** aller ad patres*; **~ be!*** Seigneur!, grand Dieu!; (*US*) **Old G~*** le drapeau américain.

b (*object etc*) gloire *f*. **the church was the village's greatest ~** l'église était le principal titre de gloire du village; **her hair was her greatest *or* crowning ~** sa chevelure était sa gloire; **this sonnet is one of the glories of English poetry** ce sonnet est un des fleurons de la poésie anglaise; **the glories of Nature** les splendeurs *fpl* de la nature.

2 vi: **to ~ in sth** (*be proud of*) être très fier de qch; (*enjoy*) savourer; (*iro*) **the café glories in the name of "The Savoy"** le café porte le nom ronflant de "Savoy".

3 comp ▸**glory hole*** capharnaüm* *m*; (*Naut*) cambuse *f*.

Glos. (*Brit*) abbr of **Gloucestershire**.

gloss¹ [glɒs] 1 n (*shine*) lustre *m*, vernis *m*, brillant *m*, éclat *m*; (*on cloth*) cati *m*. **to take the ~ off** *metal etc* dépolir, délustrer; *cloth* décatir; (*fig*) *event, success* retirer *or* enlever tout son charme *or* attrait à; *victory, compliment* gâcher; **to lose its ~** *[metal etc]* se dépolir, se délustrer; *[cloth]* se décatir; (*fig*) *[event, success]* perdre tout son charme *or* son attrait; *[victory, compliment]* être gâché. 2 comp *paint* brillant, laqué; *paper* glacé, brillant ▸**gloss finish** brillant *m*; (*Phot*) glaçage *m*. 3 vt *metal etc* faire briller, polir; *material* catir, lustrer.

gloss² [glɒs] 1 n (*insertion*) glose *f*; (*note*) commentaire *m*; (*translation*) traduction *f* (interlinéaire); (*interpretation*) paraphrase *f*, interprétation *f*. 2 vt commenter, gloser.

▸**gloss over** vt fus (*play down*) atténuer, glisser sur, passer sur; (*cover up*) dissimuler.

glossary ['glɒsərɪ] n glossaire *m*, lexique *m*.

glossematics [,glɒsə'mætɪks] n (*NonC*) glossématique *f*.

glossily ['glɒsɪlɪ] adv: **~ packaged** luxueusement conditionné; **~ presented *or* produced brochure** brochure *f* luxueusement présentée.

glossolalia [,glɒsə'leɪlɪə] n glossolalie *f*.

glossy ['glɒsɪ] 1 adj *fur, material* luisant, lustré; *photograph* glacé; *paint* brillant, laqué; *hair* brillant; *leaves etc* vernissé; *metal* brillant, poli. **~ magazine/brochure** magazine *m*/brochure *f* de luxe (*sur papier couché*); **~ paper** (*Typ*) papier couché; (*esp Phot*) papier brillant *or* glacé; (*film*) **~ production** superproduction *f* (luxueuse). 2 n: **the glossies*** les magazines *mpl* de luxe.

glottal ['glɒtl] adj (*Anat*) glottique; (*Ling*) glottal. (*Ling*) **~ stop** coup *m* de glotte.

glottis ['glɒtɪs] n, pl **~es** *or* **glottides** ['glɒtɪ,diːz] glotte *f*.

glove [glʌv] 1 n a (*gen, also Baseball, Boxing*) gant *m*. **to put on one's ~s** mettre *or* enfiler ses gants; **to take off one's ~s** enlever *or* retirer ses gants; **he had ~s on** il portait des gants, il avait mis des gants; (*fig*) **the ~s are off!** j'y vais (*or* il y va *etc*) sans gants! *or* sans prendre de gants!; *see* **fit, hand, kid**. b (*US* ⁑: *condom*) capote *f* anglaise⁑. 2 vt ganter. **~d hand** main gantée; **white-~d hand** main gantée de blanc. 3 comp ▸**glove box, glove compartment** (*Aut*) boîte *f* à gants, vide-poches *m inv* ▸**glove factory** ganterie *f* (*fabrique*) ▸**glove maker** gantier *m*, -ière *f* ▸**glove puppet** marionnette *f* (à gaine) ▸**glove shop** ganterie *f* (*magasin*).

glover ['glʌvəʳ] n gantier *m*, -ière *f*.

glow [gləʊ] 1 vi *[coal, fire]* rougeoyer; *[sky]* rougeoyer, s'embraser; *[metal]* luire rouge, être incandescent; *[cigarette end, lamp]* luire; *[colour, jewel]* rutiler; *[complexion, face]* rayonner; *[eyes]* rayonner, flamboyer. **her cheeks ~ed** elle avait les joues en feu; **he was ~ing with health** il était florissant (de santé); (*fig*) **to ~ with enthusiasm/love** *etc* brûler d'enthousiasme/d'amour *etc*; **~ing with admiration** transporté d'admiration; **a walk in the cold makes your body ~** une marche par temps froid vous fouette le sang; **the compliment made her ~ (with pleasure)** le compliment la rendit radieuse.

2 n *[coal, fire]* rougeoiement *m*; *[metal]* rougeoiement, incandescence *f*; *[sun]* feux *mpl*, embrasement *m*; *[complexion, skin]* éclat *m*; *[colour, jewel]* éclat; *[lamp]* lueur *f*; *[passion]* feu *m*; *[youth]* ardeur *f*. **a ~ of enthusiasm** un élan d'enthousiasme.

3 comp ▸**glow-worm** (*Brit*) ver *m* luisant.

glower ['glaʊəʳ] 1 vi: **to ~ at sb/sth** lancer à qn/qch des regards mauvais *or* noirs, regarder qn/qch de travers; **he sat there ~ing silently** il était assis là en silence, jetant à la ronde des regards mauvais *or* noirs. 2 n regard noir.

glowering ['glaʊərɪŋ] adj *look* hostile, mauvais, noir; *person* à l'air mauvais *or* hostile.

glowing ['gləʊɪŋ] adj *coals, fire* rougeoyant; *sky* rougeoyant, embrasé; *colour, jewel* rutilant; *lamp, cigarette end* luisant; *eyes* brillant, flamboyant, de braise; *complexion, skin* rayonnant, éclatant; *person* florissant (de santé); *words etc* chaleureux. **to give a ~ account/description of sth** raconter/décrire qch en termes chaleureux *or* avec enthousiasme; (*fig*) **to paint sth in ~ colours** présenter qch en rose.

gloxinia [glɒk'sɪnɪə] n gloxinia *m*.

glucose ['gluːkəʊs] n glucose *m*.

glue [gluː] 1 n colle *f*, glu *f*.

2 comp ▸**glue-sniffer** sniffeur* *m* ▸**glue-sniffing** intoxication *f* à la colle *or* aux solvants.

3 vt coller (*to, on* à). **to ~ sth together** recoller qch; **you must ~ down the envelope** il faut que tu colles (*subj*) l'enveloppe; **it's broken off! – ~ it back on then!** c'est cassé! – eh bien! recolle-le!; (*fig*) **her face was ~ed to the window** son visage était collé au carreau (de la fenêtre); **to keep one's eyes ~d to sb/sth*** avoir les yeux fixés sur qn/qch, ne pas détacher les yeux de qn/qch; **he stood there ~d to the spot*** il était là comme s'il avait pris racine; (*fig*) **~d* to the television** cloué devant *or* rivé à la télévision.

gluey ['gluːɪ] adj gluant, collant, poisseux.

glum [glʌm] adj *person, face* mélancolique, triste, (*stronger*) lugubre; *appearance* triste, morne, sombre; *thoughts* noir. **to feel ~** avoir des idées noires, avoir le cafard.

glumly ['glʌmlɪ] adv *walk, shake one's head* d'un air triste; *answer* d'un ton *or* d'une voix triste; *look, inspect* d'un œil *or* d'un regard morne.

glut [glʌt] 1 vt rassasier, gaver, gorger; (*Comm*) *the market* saturer, encombrer (*with* de). **~ted with food** repu, gavé (de nourriture); **~ted with pleasure** rassasié *or* gavé de plaisirs. 2 n *[appetite etc]* rassasiement *m*; *[foodstuffs, goods]* surplus *m*, excès *m*, surabondance *f*. **a ~ on the market** un surplus *or* un excès *or* une surabondance sur le marché; **there is a ~ of ...** il y a surplus *or* excès *or* surabondance de ... .

glutamic [gluː'tæmɪk] adj: **~ acid** acide *m* glutamique.

gluteal [gluː'tiːəl] adj fessier.

gluten ['gluːtən] 1 n gluten *m*. 2 comp ▸**gluten-free** sans gluten.

glutenous ['gluːtənəs] adj glutineux.

gluteus [gluː'tiːəs] n, pl **glutei** [gluː'tiːaɪ] fessier *m*. **~ maximus/medius/minimus** grand/moyen/petit fessier.

glutinous ['gluːtɪnəs] adj visqueux, gluant.

glutton ['glʌtn] n glouton(ne) *m(f)*, gourmand(e) *m(f)*. (*fig*) **to be a ~ for work** être un bourreau de travail; **he's a ~ for punishment** c'est un masochiste (*fig*).

gluttonous ['glʌtənəs] adj glouton, gourmand, goulu.

gluttony ['glʌtənɪ] n gloutonnerie *f*, gourmandise *f*.

glycerin(e) [,glɪsə'riːn] n glycérine *f*.

glycerol ['glɪsərɒl] n glycérine *f*, glycérol *m*.

glycin(e) ['glaɪsiːn] n glycine *f*.

glycogen ['glaɪkəʊdʒen] n glycogène *m*.

glycol ['glaɪkɒl] n glycol *m*.

GM [,dʒiː'em] n a (abbr of **General Manager**) D.G. *m*. b (abbr of **George Medal**) *see* **George**.

gm (*abbr of* **gram(me)**) g *inv*.
GMT [ˌdʒiːemˈtiː] (*abbr of* **Greenwich Mean Time**) G.M.T.
GMWU [ˌdʒiːemdʌbljuːˈjuː] *n* (*Brit*) (*abbr of* **General and Municipal Workers Union**) *syndicat*.
gnarled [nɑːld] *adj wood, hand* noueux.
gnash [næʃ] 1 *vt*: **to ~ one's teeth** *[person]* grincer des dents; *[animal]* montrer ses dents en grognant. 2 *vi [person's teeth]* grincer. *[animal's teeth]* **its teeth were ~ing** il (*or* elle) montrait ses dents en grognant.
gnashing [ˈnæʃɪŋ] 1 *n*: **~ of teeth** grincement *m* de dents. 2 *adj* grinçant.
gnat [næt] *n* moucheron *m*.
gnaw [nɔː] 1 *vi* (*lit, fig*) ronger. **to ~ at** *or* **on a bone** ronger un os; **the rat had ~ed through the chair-leg** le rat avait coupé le pied de la chaise à force de ronger; **to ~ a hole in sth** faire un trou dans qch à force de ronger; **remorse/desire** *etc* **~ed at him constantly** le remords/le désir *etc* le rongeait sans cesse. 2 *vt bone etc* ronger. (*fig*) **~ed by hunger** tenaillé par la faim; **~ed by remorse** rongé par le remords.
►**gnaw away** 1 *vt sep* (*partially*) ronger; (*completely*) ronger complètement. 2 *vi* (*lit, fig*) **to gnaw away at** *or* **on a bone** ronger un os; **remorse was gnawing away at him** le remords le rongeait.
►**gnaw off** *vt sep* ronger complètement.
gnawing [ˈnɔːɪŋ] *adj sound* comme une bête qui ronge; (*fig*) *remorse, anxiety etc* torturant, tenaillant; *hunger* dévorant, tenaillant; *pain* harcelant. **I had a ~ feeling that something had been forgotten** j'étais tenaillé par le sentiment qu'on avait oublié quelque chose.
gneiss [naɪs] *n* gneiss *m*.
gnome [nəʊm] *n* gnome *m*, lutin *m*. (*Brit fig: bankers*) **the G~s of Zurich** les gnomes de Zurich.
gnomic [ˈnəʊmɪk] *adj* gnomique.
gnostic [ˈnɒstɪk] *adj, n* gnostique (*m*).
gnosticism [ˈnɒstɪˌsɪzəm] *n* gnosticisme *m*.
GNP [ˌdʒiːenˈpiː] *n* (*Econ*) (*abbr of* **gross national product**) P.N.B. *m*; *see* **gross**.
gnu [nuː] *n, pl* **~s** *or* **~** gnou *m*.
go [gəʊ] *3rd person sg* **goes**, *pret* **went**, *ptp* **gone** 1 *vi* a (*proceed, travel, move*) aller, se rendre (*to* à, en; *from* de); *[vehicle]* aller, rouler. **to ~ to France/to Canada/to London** aller en France/au Canada/à Londres; **he went to Paris/to his aunt's** il est allé *or* il s'est rendu à Paris/chez sa tante; **to ~ for a walk** (aller) se promener, (aller) faire une promenade; **to ~ on a journey** faire un voyage; **to ~ up/down the hill** monter/descendre la colline; **to ~ fishing/shooting** aller à la pêche/à la chasse; **to ~ riding** faire du cheval *or* de l'équitation, monter (à cheval); **to ~ swimming** faire de la natation, (aller) nager; **to ~ looking for sth** aller *or* partir à la recherche de qch; **we can talk as we ~** nous pouvons parler chemin faisant *or* en chemin; **what shall I ~ in?** qu'est-ce que je mets *or* vais mettre pour y aller?; **~ after him!** suivez-le!, poursuivez-le!; **there he ~es!** le voilà (qui passe)!; **there he ~es again!** (*there he is*) le voilà qui repasse!; (*fig: he's at it again*) le voilà qui recommence!; **there ~es my chance of winning a prize!** adieu ma chance de gagner un prix!, ma chance de gagner un prix vient de s'envoler!; **here ~es!*** allez, on y va!; (*US: in café*) **two hotdogs to ~** deux hotdogs à emporter; (*Mil*) **who ~es there?** qui va là?, qui vive?; (*esp US: fig*) **what ~es?*** quoi de neuf?; (*fig*) **where do we ~ from here?** que faisons-nous maintenant?; **you ~ first** passe devant, vas-y le premier; **you ~ next** à toi après; (*in games etc*) **whose turn is it to ~?** à qui le tour?; **~ and shut the door** va fermer la porte; **~ and get me it** va me le chercher; **don't ~ doing that!, don't ~ and do that!** ne va pas faire ça!, ne fais pas ça!; **don't ~ and say ...** ne va pas dire ...; **you've gone and torn my dress!** il a fallu que tu déchires (*subj*) ma robe!; **she went and broke a cup** elle a trouvé le moyen de casser une tasse; **to ~ to do sth** aller faire qch; **the child went to his mother** l'enfant est allé vers sa mère; **she went to the headmaster** elle est allée voir *or* trouver le directeur; **to ~ to the doctor** aller voir le médecin; **to ~ to sb for sth** aller demander qch à qn, aller trouver qn pour avoir qch; **the train ~es at 90 km/h** le train fait (du) *or* roule à 90 km/h; **the train ~es from London to Glasgow** le train va de Londres à Glasgow; **we had gone only 3 km** nous n'avions fait que 3 km; **I wouldn't ~ as far as to say that** je n'irais pas jusqu'à dire cela; **that's ~ing too far!** c'est un peu poussé!, il y a de l'exagération!, il y a de l'abus!; **you've gone too far!** tu exagères!, tu as été trop loin!; (*at auction*) **I went up to £100 but didn't get it** je suis monté jusqu'à 100 livres mais je ne l'ai pas eu; (*in buying*) **I'll ~ as high as £100** j'irai *or* je mettrai jusqu'à 100 livres; (*US: fail*) **to ~ down the tubes**‡ se casser la gueule‡ (*fig*); (*in gambling, also fig*) **to ~ for broke**‡ jouer le grand jeu *or* son va-tout; *see* **far, place, school**[1] *etc*.

b (*depart*) partir, s'en aller; (*disappear*) disparaître; (*euph: die*) s'éteindre (*euph*), disparaître (*euph*); *[time]* passer, s'écouler; (*be dismissed*) s'en aller; (*be abolished*) être aboli *or* supprimé, disparaître; (*be sold*) se vendre; (*be finished*) *[money]* disparaître, filer; *[strength]* manquer; *[hearing, sight etc]* baisser. **when does the train ~?** quand part le train?; **my voice has gone** j'ai une extinction de voix, je suis aphone; **my voice is going** je deviens aphone; **his health is ~ing** il n'a plus la santé*, sa santé se détériore; **his mind is ~ing** (*losing ability*) il commence à baisser, il n'a plus toute sa tête *or* toutes ses facultés; (*losing reason*) il perd l'esprit *or* la raison; **my hat has gone** mon chapeau n'est plus là; **the coffee has all gone** il n'y a plus de café; **the trees have been gone for years** cela fait des années qu'il n'y a plus d'arbres; **he is gone** (*lit*) il est parti; (*euph: dead*) il n'est plus; **after I ~** *or* **have gone** (*lit*) après mon départ; (*euph: death*) après ma mort, quand je ne serai plus là (*euph*); **gone are the days when** le temps n'est plus où; **we** (*or* **I** *etc*) **must ~** *or* **must be ~ing** il faut partir; (*Sport*) **~!** partez!; (*fig*) **from the word ~** dès le départ, dès le commencement; (*hum*) **how ~es the time?** quelle heure est-il?; (*US*) **it's ~ing on 3** il va être 3 heures; **to let sb ~** (*allow to leave*) laisser partir qn; (*stop gripping*) lâcher qn; **never let me ~!** ne me quitte pas!, ne m'abandonne pas!; **to let ~** *or* **leave ~** lâcher prise; **let ~!, leave ~!** lâchez!; **to let ~** *or* **leave ~ of sth/sb** lâcher qch/qn; **to let o.s. ~** (*lose control of o.s.*) se laisser aller; (*burst into tears*) se laisser aller à pleurer; (*lose interest in one's appearance etc*) se laisser aller, se négliger; **they have let their garden ~** ils ont laissé leur jardin à l'abandon; **I've let my music ~ as I've been so busy** j'ai eu trop à faire et je n'ai pas travaillé (à) ma musique; **to ~ to the bad** mal tourner; **to ~ to ruin** tomber en ruine(s); **we'll let it ~ at that** ça ira comme ça; **you're wrong, but let it ~** vous avez tort, mais passons; (†† *or hum*) **be gone!** partez!, allez-vous-en!; **he'll have to ~** il va falloir se débarrasser de lui; **"X must ~!"** "à bas X!"; **luxuries will have to ~** il va falloir se priver *or* se passer de tout ce qui est luxe; **it was ~ing cheap** cela se vendait à bas prix; **~ing, ~ing, gone!** une fois, deux fois, adjugé!; (*fig*) **7 down and 3 to ~** 7 de faits il n'en reste plus que 3; *see* **here, ready, song, west** *etc*.

c (*start up*) *[car]* partir; *[machine]* démarrer; (*function*) *[machine, watch, car etc]* marcher, fonctionner. **to ~ by steam** marcher à la vapeur; **it ~es on petrol** ça marche *or* fonctionne à l'essence; *[machine, engine]* **to be ~ing** marcher, être en marche; **to set** *or* **get ~ing** *machine* mettre en marche, faire démarrer; *work, business* mettre en train; **to keep ~ing** *[person]* se maintenir en activité, continuer ses activités; *[business]* se maintenir à flot; *[machine]* continuer à marcher, marcher toujours; **he's not well but he manages to keep ~ing** il n'est pas en bonne santé mais il se maintient *or* se défend*; **to keep a factory ~ing** maintenir une usine en activité; **to keep the fire ~ing** entretenir le feu; **she needs these pills/his friendship to keep her ~ing** elle a besoin de ces pilules/de son amitié pour tenir le coup; **this medicine/prospect** *etc* **kept her ~ing** elle a tenu le coup grâce à ce médicament/à cette perspective *etc*; **to keep sb ~ing in food/money** *etc* donner à qn ce qu'il lui faut de nourriture/d'argent *etc*; **to make the party ~** animer la soirée; **to get things ~ing** faire démarrer les choses; **to make things ~** faire marcher les choses, mener les choses rondement; **to get ~ing on** *or* **with sth** commencer à *or* se mettre à faire qch, s'attaquer à qch; **once he gets ~ing** ... une fois lancé ... .

d (*progress*) aller, marcher; (*turn out*) *[events]* se passer, se développer, se dérouler, se présenter. **how did your holiday ~?** comment se sont passées tes vacances?; **the evening went very well** la soirée s'est très bien passée; **the project was ~ing well** le projet marchait bien *or* était en bonne voie; **how's it ~ing?**, (*hum*) **how ~es it?** (comment) ça va?*; **the decision/judgment went in his favour** la décision/le jugement lui a été favorable; **how does the story ~?** comment c'est* cette histoire?; **the tune ~es like this** voici *or* écoutez l'air; **let's wait and see how things ~** attendons de voir ce qui va se passer *or* comment ça va tourner*; **as things ~** dans l'état actuel des choses; **the way things are ~ing*** si ça continue comme ça; **I don't know how things will ~** je ne sais pas comment les choses vont tourner*; **I hope that all will ~ well** j'espère que tout ira bien; **all went well for him until** ... tout a bien marché *or* s'est bien passé pour lui jusqu'à ce que ...; *see* **bomb, clockwork, strong** *etc*.

e (*be, become*) devenir, se faire. **the children went in rags** les enfants étaient en haillons; **to ~ hungry** n'avoir pas *or* jamais assez à manger; **he must not ~ unpunished** il ne faut pas qu'il s'en tire (*subj*) sans châtiment; **to ~ armed** porter une arme; **to ~ red** rougir; **the constituency went Labour at the last election** aux dernières élections la circonscription est passée aux travaillistes; **we never went short** nous n'avons jamais manqué du nécessaire; **to ~ short of** manquer de; *see* **free, piece, sick** *etc*.

f (*be about to, intend to*) **to be ~ing to do** aller faire, être sur le point de faire, avoir l'intention de faire; **I'm ~ing to do it tomorrow** je vais le faire demain; **it's ~ing to rain** il va pleuvoir; **I was just ~ing to do it** j'allais le faire, j'étais sur le point de le faire; **I was ~ing to do it yesterday but he stopped me** j'allais le faire *or* j'étais sur le point de le faire *or* j'avais l'intention de le faire hier mais il m'en a empêché; **I was ~ing to do it yesterday but I forgot** j'allais le faire hier *or* j'avais l'intention de le faire hier mais j'ai oublié; **I'm ~ing to do as I please** je ferai *or* je vais faire ce qu'il me plaira.

g (*be current, be accepted*) *[story, rumour]* circuler, passer; *[money]* avoir cours. **the story** *or* **rumour ~es that** ... le bruit court que ...; **anything ~es these days*** tout est permis de nos jours; **that ~es without saying** cela va sans dire; **what he says ~es** c'est lui qui fait la loi, tout le monde fait ce qu'il dit; **what I say ~es!** faites ce que je dis!; **that ~es for me too** (*that applies to me*) cela s'applique à moi aussi; (*I agree with that*) je suis (aussi) de cet avis.

h (*break, yield*) *[rope, cable]* céder; *[fuse]* sauter; *[lamp, bulb]* sauter, griller*; *[material]* s'user. **the skirt went at the seams** la jupe a craqué aux coutures; **this jacket has gone at the elbows** cette veste est percée aux coudes; **there ~es another button!** voilà encore un bouton de sauté!

i (*extend or cover a certain distance*) aller, s'étendre. **the garden ~es as far as the river** le jardin va *or* s'étend jusqu'à la rivière; (*fig*) **as far as that ~es** pour ce qui est de cela; **this book is good, as far as it ~es** c'est un bon livre, compte tenu de ses limites; **he's not bad, as boys ~** il n'est pas trop mal, pour un garçon; **it's a fairly good garage as garages ~** comme garage cela peut aller *or* ce n'est pas trop mal; **money does not ~ very far nowadays** l'argent ne va pas loin aujourd'hui; **a pound note does not ~ very far** on ne va pas loin avec un billet d'une livre; **the difference between them ~es deep** il y a une profonde différence entre eux; *see* **expense, length, trouble** *etc.*

j (*have recourse*) avoir recours (*to* à); *see* **country, law, war.**

k (*be placed, contained, arranged*) aller, se mettre, se ranger. **4 into 12 ~es 3 times** 12 divisé par 4 égale 3; **2 won't ~ exactly into 11** 11 n'est pas exactement divisible par 2; **4 into 3 won't ~** 3 divisé par 4 (il) n'y va pas; **the books ~ in that cupboard** les livres se rangent *or* se mettent *or* vont dans ce placard-là; **where does this box ~?** où est-ce que l'on met cette boîte?; **this screw ~es here** cette vis va là.

l *[prize, reward etc]* aller, être donné (*to* à); *[inheritance]* passer (*to* à).

m (*be available*) **are there any houses ~ing?** y-a-t-il des maisons à vendre (*or* à louer)?, trouve-t-on des maisons (à acheter *or* à louer)?; **are there any jobs ~ing?** y a-t-il des postes vacants?, peut-on trouver du travail?; **is there any coffee ~ing?** est-ce qu'il y a du café?; **I'll have what's ~ing** donnez-moi *or* je prendrai de ce qu'il y a.

n (*contribute*) contribuer, servir (*to* à). **that will ~ to make him happy** cela contribuera à son bonheur *or* à le rendre heureux; **the qualities that ~ to make a great man** les qualités qui font un grand homme; **the money will ~ towards a new car** l'argent sera consacré à l'achat d'une nouvelle auto; *see* **show.**

o (*make specific sound or movement*) faire; *[bell, clock]* sonner. **~ like that with your left foot** faites comme ça du pied gauche; **to ~ bang** faire "pan"; **he went "psst"** "psst" fit-il.

2 **vt: the car was fairly ~ing it*** la voiture roulait *or* filait à une bonne vitesse; **he was fairly ~ing it*** (*driving fast*) il allait bon train, il filait à toute allure; (*working hard*) il travaillait d'arrache-pied; (*having fun*) il faisait la noce*; **to ~ it alone** (*gen*) se débrouiller tout seul; (*Pol etc*) faire cavalier seul; **to ~ one better** faire (*or* dire) mieux (*than sb* que qn); **to ~ one better than sb** damer le pion à qn; (*Cards*) **he went 3 spades** il a annoncé *or* demandé *or* dit 3 piques; (*Gambling*) **he went £10 on the red** il a misé 10 livres sur le rouge; **I can only ~ £5** je ne peux mettre que 5 livres; **I could ~ a beer**‡ je m'enverrais‡ bien une bière; *see* **bail¹, half, share** *etc.*

3 **n, pl ~es** a (*NonC: energy*) dynamisme *m*, entrain *m*, allant *m*. **to be full of ~** être plein d'énergie, avoir beaucoup de dynamisme; **there's no ~ about him** il n'a aucun ressort, il est mou comme une chiffe*.

b (*NonC: activity, motion*) **to be always on the ~** être toujours sur la brèche *or* en mouvement; **to keep sb on the ~** ne pas laisser souffler qn; **he has 2 books on the ~ at the moment** il a 2 livres en train *or* en chantier en ce moment; **it's all ~!*** ça n'arrête pas!

c (*Brit: attempt*) coup *m*, essai *m*, tentative *f*. **to have a ~** essayer, tenter le coup; **to have a ~ at sth** essayer de faire qch; **to have a ~ at sb*** s'en prendre à qn*; **to have another ~** faire une nouvelle tentative, ressayer; **have another ~!** encore un coup!*; **at one *or* a ~** d'un seul coup, d'un seul trait; (*in games*) **it's your ~** c'est à toi (de jouer).

d (*Med *: attack*) accès *m*, attaque *f*.

e (*: event, situation*) **that was a near ~** on l'a échappé belle, il s'en est fallu de peu.

f (*success*) **to make a ~ of sth** réussir qch; **no ~!*** rien à faire!; **it's all the ~*** ça fait fureur, c'est le dernier cri.

4 **adj** (*: esp Space*) paré (à démarrer), en bon état de marche *or* de fonctionnement. **all systems (are) ~** tout est O.K.; **you are ~ for moon-landing** vous êtes "bon" *or* vous êtes "go" *or* vous avez le feu vert pour l'alunissage.

5 **comp ▶go-ahead adj** *person, government* dynamique, entreprenant, plein d'allant, qui va de l'avant; *business, attitude* dynamique ◊ **n to give sb the go-ahead (for sth/to do)*** donner à qn le feu vert (pour qch/pour faire) **▶go-between** intermédiaire *mf* **▶go-by*: to give sth/sb the go-by** laisser tomber qch/qn **▶go-cart** (*vehicle: also* **go-kart**) kart *m*; (*toy*) chariot *m* (*que se construisent les enfants*); (*handcart*) charrette *f*; (*pushchair*) poussette *f*; (*baby-walker*) trotteur *m*, trotte-bébé *m inv* **▶go-carting** (*Sport*) karting *m* **▶go-getter*** (*esp US*) battant(e)* *m(f)*, fonceur *m*, -euse *f* **▶go-go** *see* **go-go ▶go-karting** = **go-carting ▶go-slow (strike)** (*Brit*) ≃ grève perlée.

▶go about 1 **vi** a circuler, aller (çà et là). *[sick person]* **to be going about again** être de nouveau sur pied; **he goes about in a Rolls** il roule *or* circule en Rolls; **to go about barefoot/in torn jeans** se promener pieds nus/en jean déchiré; **they go about in gangs** ils vont *or* circulent en *or* par bandes; **he's going about with an unpleasant set of people** il fréquente des gens peu recommandables; **she's going about with Paul now** elle sort avec Paul en ce moment; **he always goes about telling people what to do** il est toujours là en train de dire aux gens ce qu'ils doivent faire.

b *[rumour]* courir, se répandre.

c (*Naut: change direction*) virer de bord.

2 **vt fus** a (*set to work at*) *task, duties* se mettre à. **he knows how to go about it** il sait s'y prendre; **we must go about it carefully** nous devons y aller *or* nous y prendre avec précaution; **how does one go about getting seats?** comment doit-on s'y prendre *or* comment fait-on pour avoir des places?

b (*be occupied with*) *affairs, business* s'occuper de. **to go about one's normal work** vaquer à ses occupations habituelles.

▶go across 1 **vi** (*cross*) traverser. **she went across to Mrs. Smith's** elle a fait un saut chez Mme Smith en face. 2 **vt fus** *river, road* traverser.

▶go after vt fus: to go after a girl faire la cour à *or* courir après* une fille; **to go after a job** essayer d'obtenir un emploi, viser un poste; **he went after first prize** il a essayé d'avoir *or* il a visé le premier prix.

▶go against vt fus a (*prove hostile to*) *[luck, events etc]* tourner contre, être hostile *or* contraire à; *[appearance, evidence]* militer contre, nuire à, être préjudiciable à. **the decision went against him** la décision lui a été défavorable, la décision a été prise contre lui; **if fate goes against us** si la fortune nous est contraire; **this behaviour will go against his chances of promotion** cette conduite nuira à ses chances de promotion.

b (*oppose*) (*fig*) **to go against the tide** aller contre le courant; **to go against public opinion** aller à l'encontre de *or* heurter l'opinion publique; **to go against sb's wishes** aller contre *or* contrarier les désirs de qn; **it goes against my conscience** ma conscience s'y oppose; *see* **grain.**

▶go ahead 1 **vi** (*also* **go on ahead**) passer devant *or* en tête. (*fig*) **go ahead!** allez-y!; **to go ahead with sth** aller de l'avant avec qch, mettre qch à exécution. 2 **go-ahead adj, n** *see* **go 5.**

▶go along vi aller, avancer. **I'll tell you as we go along** je vous le dirai chemin faisant *or* en cours de route *or* en chemin; (*lit*) **to go along with sb** aller avec qn, accompagner qn; (*fig*) **I'll go along with you on this** je vous soutiendrai *or* donnerai mon appui; **I don't go along with you on that** là, je ne vous suis pas; **I can't go along with that at all** je ne suis pas du tout d'accord là-dessus, je suis tout à fait contre*; **no one will mind if you go along too** personne n'y verra d'objection si vous y allez aussi; (*fig*) **I check as I go along** je vérifie au fur et à mesure; *see* **along 1a.**

▶go around vi = **go about 1a, 1b, go round;** *see also* **along 1a.**

▶go at vt fus (*attack*) *person* attaquer, se jeter sur; (*undertake*) *task* s'attaquer à; *meal* attaquer. **he went at it with a will** il s'y est mis *or* attaqué avec acharnement; **he was still going at it 3 hours later** il était toujours à la tâche 3 heures plus tard.

▶go away vi partir, s'en aller. **he's gone away with my keys** il est parti avec mes clefs; **don't go away with the idea that*** ... n'allez pas penser que ... .

▶go back vi a (*return*) revenir, retourner, s'en retourner. **to go back on one's steps** revenir sur ses pas, rebrousser chemin; **to go back to a subject** revenir sur un sujet; **to go back to the beginning** recommencer.

b (*retreat*) reculer.

c (*in time*) remonter. **my memory doesn't go so far back** ma mémoire ne remonte pas si loin; **the family goes back to the Norman Conquest** la famille remonte à la conquête normande; **we go back a long way** on se connaît depuis longtemps.

d (*revert*) revenir (*to* à). **I don't want to go back to coal fires** je ne veux pas en revenir aux feux de charbon; **to go back to one's former habits** retomber dans ses anciennes habitudes; **he's gone back to childhood** il est retombé en enfance.

e (*extend*) s'étendre. **the garden goes back to the river** le jardin s'étend jusqu'à la rivière; **the cave goes back 300 metres** la grotte a 300 mètres de profondeur.

▶go back on vt fus *decision* revenir sur; *promise* revenir sur, se dédire de, manquer à; *friend* trahir, faire faux bond à.

▶go before vi (*lit*) aller au devant. (*fig: happen earlier*) **all that has gone before** tout ce qui s'est passé avant; (*euph: dead*) **those who are *or* have gone before** les générations qui nous ont précédés; *see* **before 1d.**

▶go below vi (*Naut*) descendre dans l'entrepont.

▶go by 1 **vi** *[person]* passer; *[period of time]* (se) passer, s'écouler. **we've let the opportunity go by** nous avons manqué *or* raté *or* laissé échapper l'occasion; **as time goes by** à mesure que le temps passe, avec le temps; **in days (*or* years) gone by** autrefois.

2 **vt fus** (*base judgment or decision on*) juger d'après, (se) fonder sur; (*be guided by*) suivre, se régler sur. **that's nothing to go by** ce n'est pas une preuve*, on ne peut rien fonder là-dessus; **I'll go by what he does** j'agirai en fonction de ce qu'il fera; **I go by what I'm told** je me fonde sur ce qu'on me dit; **you can never go by what he says** on ne peut jamais se fonder sur *or* se fier à ce qu'il dit; **to go by appearances** juger d'après *or* selon les apparences; **to go by the instructions** suivre les instructions; **the only thing we've got to go by** la seule chose qui puisse nous guider *or* sur laquelle nous puissions nous baser, le seul indice sérieux que nous ayons.

3 **go-by** n *see* **go 5.**

►**go down** vi a (*descend*) descendre. **to go down to the country/the sea** aller à la campagne/au bord de la mer; (*Scol*) **to go down a class** descendre d'une classe.

b (*fall*) *[person]* tomber; *[building]* s'écrouler; *see* **knee, nine.**

c (*sink*) *[ship]* couler, sombrer; *[person]* couler, disparaître (*sous les flots*). (*Naut*) **to go down by the bows** sombrer par l'avant.

d (*Brit Univ*) *[student]* (*go on holiday*) terminer (le trimestre), partir en vacances; (*finish studies*) terminer (ses études), quitter l'université. **the university goes down on June 20th** les vacances universitaires commencent le 20 juin.

e (*set*) *[sun, moon]* se coucher.

f (*be swallowed*) **to go down the wrong way** passer de travers; **it went down the wrong way** j'ai (*or* il a *etc*) avalé de travers; **the cake just won't go down** le gâteau n'arrive pas à descendre.

g (*be accepted, approved*) être accepté, plaire. **that won't go down with me** ça ne prend pas avec moi, je n'avalerai pas ça*; **to go down well/badly** être bien/mal reçu; **his speech didn't go down at all in Exeter** son discours a été très mal reçu à Exeter; **he didn't go down at all well in Exeter** il n'a pas été du tout apprécié à Exeter; *see* **lead[2].**

h (*lessen etc*) *[wind, storm]* baisser, tomber; *[tide]* descendre; *[floods, temperature]* baisser, s'abaisser; *[amount, numbers, subscriptions]* diminuer; *[value, price, standards]* baisser. **the picture has gone down in value** le tableau a perdu de sa valeur; **this neighbourhood has gone down** ce quartier n'est plus ce qu'il était.

i (*be defeated, fail*) s'incliner (*to* devant), être battu (*to* par); (*Bridge*) chuter; (*fail examination*) échouer, être refusé, se faire coller* (*in* en). (*Ftbl*) **Spain went down to Scotland 2-1** l'Espagne s'est inclinée devant l'Écosse par 2 à 1.

j (*Theat*) *[curtain]* tomber. **when the curtain goes down** au tomber du rideau, quand le rideau tombe.

k (*go as far as*) aller, continuer. **go down to the bottom of the page** continuez jusqu'au bas de la page; **this history book goes down to the present day** ce livre d'histoire va jusqu'à nos jours.

l *[balloon, tyre]* se dégonfler; *[swelling]* désenfler, (se) dégonfler.

m (*be noted, remembered*) être noté, être pris par écrit. **to go down to posterity** passer à la postérité; *see* **history.**

n (*become ill*) **to go down with flu** attraper la grippe.

o (*Mus: lower pitch*) **can you go down a bit?** vous ne pouvez pas chanter (*or* jouer) un peu plus bas?

►**go for** vt fus a (*attack*) *person* tomber sur, fondre sur, s'élancer sur; (*verbally*) s'en prendre à; (*in newspaper*) attaquer. **they went for each other** (*physically*) ils en sont venus aux coups, ils se sont empoignés; (*verbally*) ils ont eu une prise de bec*; (*to dog*) **go for him!** mors-le! b (*: *admire*) *person, object* s'enticher de, se toquer de*. **he rather goes for that** il adore ça*; **I don't go much for television** la télévision ne me dit pas grand-chose. c (*strive for*) essayer d'avoir; (*choose*) choisir, préférer. **go far it!*** fonce!*. d (*fig*) **he's got a lot going for him*** il a beaucoup d'atouts.

►**go forth** vi (*liter, frm*) a *[person]* sortir. b *[order]* paraître, être promulgué. **the order went forth that ...** il fut décrété que ... .

►**go forward** vi *[person, vehicle]* avancer. (*fig*) **they let the suggestion go forward that ...** ils ont transmis la proposition que ... .

►**go in** vi a (*enter*) entrer, rentrer. **I must go in now** il faut que je rentre (*subj*) maintenant; **go in and win!** (allez,) bonne chance!; **what time does the theatre go in?** à quelle heure commence la pièce?; **the troops are going in tomorrow** les troupes attaquent demain. b *[sun, moon]* (*behind clouds*) se cacher (*behind* derrière).

►**go in for** vt fus (*fig*) a *examination* se présenter à; *appointment* poser sa candidature à, être candidat à; *competition, race* prendre part à.

b *sport, hobby* pratiquer, s'adonner à, faire; *style, idea, principle, cause* adopter; *lectures* s'inscrire à, suivre; *profession* entrer dans, se consacrer à; *politics* s'occuper de, se mêler de, faire. **she goes in for tennis/painting** *etc* elle fait du tennis/de la peinture *etc;* **I don't go in for bright colours** je ne suis pas (très) porté sur les couleurs vives, je n'aime pas beaucoup les couleurs vives; **we don't go in for that sort of thing here** nous n'aimons pas beaucoup ce genre de chose ici; **he doesn't go in much for reading** il ne s'intéresse pas beaucoup à la lecture; **he's going in for science** il va se spécialiser dans les sciences, il va faire des sciences; **he's going in for vegetables** *[grower]* il va cultiver *or* il va faire* des légumes; *[merchant]* il va vendre des légumes, il va faire* les légumes.

►**go into** vt fus a (*join, take up*) entrer à *or* dans; *see* **church, parliament** *etc.*

b (*embark on*) (se mettre à) donner, se lancer dans. **he went into a long explanation** il s'est lancé *or* embarqué dans une longue explication; **let's not go into that now** laissons cela pour le moment; **to go into fits of laughter** être pris de fou rire; *see* **action, decline, detail, hysterics** *etc.*

c (*investigate*) examiner, étudier. **to go into a question closely** approfondir une question; **this matter is being gone into** on s'occupe de *or* on étudie cette affaire, cette affaire est à l'étude.

d (*begin to wear*) (se mettre à) porter. **she goes into woollen stockings in September** elle se met à porter des bas en laine en septembre; *see* **mourning.**

►**go in with** vt fus se joindre à (*in* dans, *to do* pour faire). **she went in with her sister to buy the present** elle s'est mise* *or* cotisée avec sa sœur pour acheter le cadeau.

►**go off** 1 vi a (*leave*) partir, s'en aller; (*Theat*) quitter la scène. **to go off with sth** enlever *or* emporter qch; **to go off with sb** partir avec qn; **they went off together** ils sont partis ensemble; (*off duty*) **she went off at 3 o'clock** elle est partie à 3 heures, elle a quitté son travail à 3 heures; *see* **deep.**

b *[alarm clock]* sonner; *[gun]* partir. **the gun didn't go off** le coup n'est pas parti; **the pistol went off in his hand** le pistolet lui est parti dans la main.

c (*stop*) *[light, radio, TV]* s'éteindre; *[heating]* s'arrêter, s'éteindre.

d (*Brit: lose excellence*) *[meat]* s'avarier, se gâter; *[milk]* tourner; *[butter]* rancir; *[sportsman, athlete]* perdre de sa forme, baisser; *[woman]* perdre de sa beauté, se défraîchir.

e (*lose intensity*) *[feeling, effect]* passer.

f (*go to sleep*) s'endormir.

g *[event]* se passer. **the evening went off very well** la soirée s'est très bien passée; **how did it go off?** comment cela s'est-il passé?

2 vt fus (*Brit: lose liking for*) perdre le goût de. **I've gone off skiing** je n'ai plus envie de faire du ski, j'ai perdu le goût (de faire) du ski; **I've gone off my boyfriend/Dickens** *etc* je n'ai plus envie de sortir avec mon petit ami/de lire Dickens *etc.*

►**go on** 1 vi a (*be placed*) **the lid won't go on** le couvercle ne va pas (dessus); **these shoes won't go on** je n'entre pas dans ces chaussures.

b (*proceed on one's way*) (*without stopping*) poursuivre son chemin; (*after stopping*) repartir, se remettre en route, poursuivre sa course; *see* **go ahead.**

c (*continue*) continuer (*doing* de *or* à faire). **go on with your work** continuez votre travail; **to go on speaking** continuer de parler; (*after pause*) reprendre (la parole); **go on trying!** essaie encore!; **go on!** continuez!; **go on (with you)!*** allons donc!, à d'autres!*; **the war went on until 1945** la guerre a continué *or* s'est prolongée jusqu'en 1945; **if you go on doing that, you'll be punished** si tu continues *or* persistes à faire cela, tu seras puni; **you have enough to go on with** *or* **be going on with** tu as de quoi faire* pour le moment.

d (*talk*) **to go on about sth** (*boringly*) s'étendre à n'en plus finir sur qch; (*naggingly*) faire sans cesse des remarques sur qch; **don't go on about it!** arrête!, laisse tomber!; **she just goes on and on*** elle ne cesse pas de parler, c'est un moulin à paroles*; **he goes on and on about it*** il ne finit pas d'en parler, il est intarissable sur le sujet; (*nag*) **to go on at sb** s'en prendre à qn; **she went on (and on) at him** elle n'a pas cessé de s'en prendre à lui; **she's always going on at him (about ...)** elle est toujours sur son dos* *or* après lui* (au sujet de ...); **she's always going on at him to do his homework** elle est toujours après lui pour qu'il fasse ses devoirs.

e (*proceed*) passer. **to go on to another matter** passer à une autre question; **he went on to say that ...** puis il a dit que ..., il a dit ensuite que ... .

f (*happen*) se passer, se dérouler. **while this was going on** pendant que cela se passait, au même moment, pendant ce temps; **this has been going on for a long time** cela dure depuis longtemps; **how long will this go on for?** combien de temps cela va-t-il durer?; **several arguments were going on at the same time** plusieurs disputes étaient en train à la fois; **what's going on here?** qu'est-ce qui se passe ici?

g (*pass*) *[time]* passer; *[years]* s'écouler, passer. **as the years went on he ...** avec le passage des années, il ... .

h (*gen pej: behave*) se conduire. **what a way to go on!** en voilà des manières!; **she went on in a dreadful way** elle nous a fait une scène épouvantable*.

i (*Theat: enter*) entrer en scène; (*Sport*) *[substitute]* prendre sa place, entrer en jeu.

j (*progress*) *[person, esp patient]* se porter, aller; *[life, affairs]* marcher, continuer, aller son train.

k (*approach*) **she's going on fifty*** elle va sur la cinquantaine, elle frise* la cinquantaine.

2 vt fus a (*be guided by*) se fonder sur, se laisser guider par, s'appuyer sur. **what have you to go on?** sur quoi vous fondez-vous?; **the police had no clue to go on** la police n'avait aucun indice sur lequel s'appuyer; **we don't have much to go on yet** nous ne pouvons pas encore nous fonder sur grand-chose.

b (*: *appreciate, be impressed by*) s'intéresser à. **I don't go much on that** ça ne me dit pas grand-chose*.

3 **goings-on** npl *see* **going 3.**

►**go on for** vt fus: **to be going on for** approcher de, être près de; **he's going on for fifty** il frise la cinquantaine, il va sur la cinquantaine; **it's going on for 5 o'clock** il est presque 5 heures *or* près de 5 heures.

►**go out** vi a (*leave*) sortir. **to go out of a room** quitter une pièce, sortir d'une pièce; **to go out riding** faire une sortie *or* sortir à cheval; **to go out for a meal** manger en ville (*or* chez des amis); **he goes out a lot** il sort beaucoup; **she doesn't go out with him any more** elle ne sort plus avec lui; **to go out to work** travailler au dehors; **to go out charring** aller faire des ménages; **she doesn't want to go out to work** elle ne veut pas travailler hors de chez elle *or* au dehors; since she's gone out of his life depuis qu'elle est sortie de sa vie; *see* mind, way.

b *[fashion]* passer de mode, se démoder; *[custom]* disparaître; *[fire, light]* s'éteindre. he was so tired he went out like a light* il était si fatigué qu'il s'est endormi comme une masse*; the happiness went out of his face le bonheur a disparu de son visage.

c (*depart*) partir (*to* pour, à); (*emigrate, travel*) émigrer (*to* à, en). he's gone out to the Middle East with his regiment il est parti (servir) au Moyen-Orient avec son régiment.

d *[sea, tide]* descendre, se retirer. the tide is going out la marée descend, la mer se retire; the tide *or* the sea goes out 2 km la mer se retire à 2 km.

e my heart went out to him in his sorrow j'ai été de tout cœur avec lui dans son chagrin; all our sympathy goes out to you toute notre sympathie va vers vous.

f (*Cards etc*) terminer.

g (*be issued*) *[pamphlet, circular]* être distribué (*to* à).

h (*end*) *[year, month]* finir, se terminer.

►**go over** 1 vi a (*cross*) to go over to America aller aux États-Unis; how long does it take to go over? combien de temps faut-il pour faire la traversée?; she went over to Mrs. Smith's elle a fait un saut chez Mme Smith en face; (*fig*) his speech went over well son discours a été très bien reçu.

b (*change allegiance*) passer, se joindre (*to* à). to go over to the other side changer de parti (*or* de religion), passer de l'autre côté (de la barrière); to go over to the enemy passer à l'ennemi.

c (*be overturned*) *[vehicle etc]* verser, se retourner; *[boat]* chavirer, se retourner.

2 vt fus a (*examine*) *accounts, report* examiner, vérifier; *[doctor] patient* examiner. to go over a house *[visitor]* parcourir *or* visiter une maison; *[purchaser]* examiner une maison; (*lit, fig*) to go over the ground reconnaître le terrain; I went over his essay with him j'ai regardé sa dissertation avec lui.

b (*rehearse, review*) *lesson, rôle* repasser, revoir; *speech* revoir; *facts etc* revoir, récapituler. to go over sb's faults passer au crible *or* éplucher les défauts de qn; to go over sth in one's mind repasser qch dans son esprit; to go over the events of the day retracer les événements de la journée; let's go over the facts again reprenons les faits; let's go over what happened again récapitulons les faits *or* les événements.

c (*touch up*) retoucher, faire des retouches à. to go over a drawing in ink repasser un dessin à l'encre.

3 **going-over** n *see* going 3.

►**go round** vi a (*turn*) tourner. the wheels go round les roues tournent; my head is going round j'ai la tête qui tourne.

b (*make a detour*) faire un détour, faire le tour. to go a long way round faire un grand détour; to go the long way round prendre le chemin le plus long *or* le chemin des écoliers; there's no bridge, we'll have to go round il n'y a pas de pont, il faut faire le tour; we went round by Manchester nous avons fait le détour par Manchester.

c to go round to sb's house/to see sb passer chez qn/voir qn.

d (*be sufficient*) suffire (pour tout le monde). there's enough food to go round il y a assez de nourriture pour tout le monde; to make the money go round ménager son argent, s'arranger pour joindre les deux bouts*.

e (*circulate*) *[bottle, document, story]* circuler; *[rumour]* courir, circuler.

f = go about 1a.

►**go through** 1 vi (*gen*) être accepté; (*be agreed, voted etc*) *[law, bill]* passer, être voté; *[business deal]* être conclu, être fait, se faire. the deal did not go through l'affaire n'a pas été conclue *or* ne s'est pas faite.

2 vt fus a (*suffer, endure*) subir, souffrir, endurer. we've all gone through it nous avons tous passé par là; the experiences I have gone through les épreuves que j'ai subies; after all he's gone through après tout ce qu'il a subi *or* enduré.

b (*examine carefully*) *list, book* éplucher; *mail* dépouiller; *subject* discuter *or* examiner à fond; *clothes, wardrobe* trier; *one's pockets* fouiller dans, explorer; (*Customs*) *suitcases, trunks* fouiller. to go through sb's pockets faire les poches à qn*; I went through his essay with him j'ai regardé sa dissertation avec lui.

c (*use up*) *money* dépenser; (*wear out*) user. to go through a fortune engloutir une fortune; he goes through a pair of shoes a month il use une paire de chaussures par mois; (*hum*) he has gone through four cars/secretaries *etc* il a épuisé quatre voitures/secrétaires *etc;* he has gone through the seat of his trousers il a usé *or* troué le fond de son pantalon; this book has already gone through 13 editions il y a déjà eu 13 éditions de ce livre.

d (*perform, accomplish, take part in*) *lesson* réciter; *formalities* remplir, accomplir; *programme, entertainment* exécuter; *course of study* suivre; *apprenticeship* faire; *see* motion *etc.*

►**go through with** vt fus (*complete*) *plan, crime, undertaking* aller jusqu'au bout de, réaliser, exécuter. in the end she couldn't go through with it en fin de compte elle n'a pas pu aller jusqu'au bout; they nevertheless went through with their marriage ils se sont mariés malgré tout.

►**go to** 1 vi (*excl*) go to!†† allons donc!, laissez donc! 2 vt fus: go to it! allez-y!, au travail!

►**go together** vi *[people]* aller ensemble; *[colours, ideas]* s'accorder, s'harmoniser, aller bien ensemble; *[events, conditions]* marcher ensemble, aller de pair. they go well together ils vont bien ensemble; Ann and Peter are going together Ann et Peter sortent ensemble.

►**go under** vi a (*sink*) *[ship]* sombrer, couler; *[person]* couler, disparaître (*sous les flots*). b (*fail*) *[person]* succomber, être vaincu; *[business etc]* couler.

►**go up** 1 vi a (*rise*) *[price, value, temperature]* monter, être en hausse, s'élever; (*Theat*) *[curtain]* se lever. when the curtain goes up au lever du rideau; to go up in price augmenter, renchérir; (*Scol*) to go up a class monter d'une classe; *see* estimation *etc.* b (*ascend, climb*) monter, aller en haut; (*go upstairs to bed*) monter se coucher. c (*explode, be destroyed*) sauter, exploser; *see* flame, smoke. d (*Brit Univ*) entrer à l'université. he went up to Oxford il est entré à Oxford.

2 vt fus *hill* monter.

►**go with** vt fus a (*accompany*) *[circumstances, event, conditions]* marcher *or* aller (de pair) avec. poverty goes with laziness la pauvreté va de pair avec la paresse; the house goes with the job le logement va avec le poste; (*fig*) to go with the times marcher avec son temps; to go with the crowd suivre la foule.

b (*harmonize with, suit*) *[colours]* s'assortir avec, se marier avec; *[furnishings]* aller avec, être assorti à, s'accorder avec; *[behaviour, opinions]* cadrer avec, s'accorder avec. I want a hat to go with my new coat je cherche un chapeau assorti à mon *or* qui aille avec mon nouveau manteau; his accent doesn't go with his appearance son accent ne va pas *or* ne s'accorde pas avec son allure.

c (*agree with*) avoir les mêmes idées que, être du même avis que. I'll go with you there là, je suis de votre avis.

d (**: also* go steady with) sortir avec.

►**go without** 1 vi s'en passer. 2 vt fus se passer de, se priver de.

goad [gəʊd] 1 n aiguillon *m.* 2 vt *cattle* aiguillonner, piquer; (*fig*) aiguillonner, stimuler. to ~ sb into doing talonner *or* harceler qn jusqu'à ce qu'il fasse; he was ~ed into replying ... il a été piqué au point de répondre ...; fright ~ed him into action l'aiguillon de la peur le fit passer à l'action.

►**goad on** vt sep aiguillonner, stimuler. to goad sb on to doing inciter qn à faire.

goal [gəʊl] 1 n a but *m*, objectif *m.* his ~ was to become president son ambition *or* son but était de devenir président, il avait pour ambition *or* pour but de devenir président; his ~ was in sight il approchait du but.

b (*Sport*) but *m.* to keep ~, to play in ~ être gardien de but; to win by 3 ~s to 2 gagner par 3 buts à 2; the ball went into the ~ le ballon est entré dans le but *or* est allé au fond du filet.

2 comp ►goal-area (*Sport*) surface *f* de but ►goalkeeper gardien *m* de but, goal* *m* ►goal-kick (*Ftbl*) coup *m* (de pied) de but ►goal-line ligne *f* de but ►goalmouth: in the goalmouth juste devant les poteaux ►goal post montant *m or* poteau *m* de but; (*fig*) to move the goal posts modifier les objectifs (en chemin) ►goal scorer buteur *m*; the main goal scorer was Jones c'est Jones qui a marqué le plus de buts.

goalie* ['gəʊlɪ] n (abbr of goalkeeper) goal* *m.*

goat [gəʊt] 1 n a chèvre *f*, (*he-goat*) bouc *m.* young ~ chevreau *m*, chevrette *f*; *see* sheep. b (**: silly person*) imbécile *mf*, andouille* *f.* (*Brit*) to act *or* play the (giddy) ~* faire l'imbécile *or* l'andouille*. c (*fig: irritate*) to get sb's ~* énerver qn*, taper sur le système* *or* les nerfs* de qn; it gets my ~* ça me tape sur les nerfs*. 2 comp ►the goat God (*Myth*) le divin chèvre-pied, le dieu Pan ►goatherd chevrier *m*, -ière *f* ►goatskin (*clothing*) peau *f* de chèvre *or* de bouc; (*container*) outre *f* en peau de bouc.

goatee [gəʊ'tiː] n barbiche *f*, bouc *m.*

gob [gɒb] 1 n a (*‡: spit*) crachat *m*, mollard** *m.* b (*‡: esp Brit: mouth*) gueule‡ *f.* shut your ~! ferme-la!‡, ta gueule!‡ c (*‡: US Navy*) marin *m*, mataf‡ *m.* 2 vi (*‡: spit*) cracher (*at* sur). 3 comp ►gob-stopper* (*Brit*) (gros) bonbon *m.*

gobbet* ['gɒbɪt] n petit morceau.

gobble ['gɒbl] 1 n *[turkey]* glouglou *m.* 2 vi *[turkey]* glousser, glouglouter. 3 vt (*also* ~ down, ~ up) *food* engloutir, engouffrer, avaler gloutonnement. don't ~! ne mange pas si vite!

gobbledegook, gobbledygook* ['gɒbldɪguːk] n charabia* *m.*

gobbler* ['gɒblər] n (*turkey*) dindon *m.*

Gobi ['gəʊbɪ] n: ~ Desert désert *m* de Gobi.

goblet ['gɒblɪt] n verre *m* à pied; († *liter*) coupe *f.*

goblin ['gɒblɪn] n lutin *m*, farfadet *m.*

gobshite** ['gɒb,ʃaɪt] n (*Ir: idiot*) peigne-cul** *m.*

gobsmacked‡ [gɒb,smækd] adj (*Brit*) sidéré*, estomaqué*.

goby ['gəʊbɪ] n, pl ~ *or* gobies gobie *m.*

G.O.C. [dʒiːəʊ'siː] (*Mil*) (abbr of General Officer Commanding) *see* general.

god [gɒd] 1 n a G~ Dieu *m*; G~ the Father, the Son, the Holy Spirit

Dieu le Père, le Fils, le Saint-Esprit; **for G~'s sake!** (*imploringly*) pour l'amour du ciel!; (‡: *crossly*) nom d'un chien!*; **(my) G~!‡** mon Dieu!, bon Dieu!‡; **G~ (only) knows‡** Dieu seul le sait, allez donc savoir*; ... **and G~ (only) knows what else** ... et allez (donc) savoir quoi d'autre; **G~ knows‡ I've tried** Dieu sait si j'ai essayé; **G~ knows‡ where he's gone to** où est-il passé, ça Dieu seul le sait; **he went G~ knows where‡** il est parti Dieu sait où; **G~ forbid!*** à Dieu ne plaise!, Dieu m'en garde!; **G~ forbid that she should come!** prions le ciel *or* Dieu veuille qu'elle ne vienne pas!; **G~ help him!** (que) Dieu lui vienne en aide *or* l'assiste!; **G~ willing** s'il plaît à Dieu, Dieu voulant, si le ciel ne me (*or* nous) tombe pas sur la tête* (*hum*); (*pej*) **to play G~** se prendre pour Dieu, jouer au démiurge; **would to G~ that** plût à Dieu que + *subj*; (*fig*) **G~'s acre** cimetière *m*; (*US*) **G~'s own country‡** les États-Unis; *see* **gift, help, hope, love, man, name, thank.**

b dieu *m*, divinité *f*; (*fig*) dieu, idole *f*. **ye ~s!*** grands dieux!; (*fig*) **money is his ~** l'argent est son dieu *or* son idole; (*fig*) **to make a little tin ~ of sb** dresser des autels à qn, mettre qn sur un piédestal.

c (*Brit Theat*) **the ~s*** le poulailler*.

2 **comp ▸god-awful‡** (*gen*) vraiment affreux (*f* -euse); *weather, place* pourri; *book, film etc* complètement nul(le) **▸godchild** filleul(e) *m(f)* **▸goddam(n)‡, goddamned‡** sacré, fichu*, foutu‡ (*all before noun*); **it's no goddam(ned) use!‡** ça ne sert à rien de rien!* **▸goddammit!‡** (*US*) nom de Dieu!*, bon sang!* **▸goddaughter** filleule *f* **▸godfather** (*lit, fig*) parrain *m*; **to stand godfather to a child** être parrain d'un enfant; (*at ceremony*) tenir un enfant sur les fonts baptismaux **▸god-fearing** (très) religieux, (très) croyant; **any god-fearing man** tout croyant digne de ce nom **▸godforsaken** *town, place* perdu, paumé‡; *person* malheureux, misérable; **godforsaken existence** chienne *f* de vie*; **godforsaken spot** trou perdu *or* paumé*, bled* *m* **▸godhead** divinité *f* **▸godlike** divin; *stature etc* de dieu **▸godmother** marraine *f* (*see* **fairy 3**); **to stand godmother to a child** être marraine d'un enfant; (*at ceremony*) tenir un enfant sur les fonts baptismaux **▸godparents: his godparents** son parrain et sa marraine **▸godsend** aubaine *f*, bénédiction *f*, don *m* (du ciel); **to be a** *or* **come as a godsend** être une bénédiction *or* aubaine (*to* pour) **▸god-slot*** (*Brit TV*) créneau *m* horaire des émissions religieuses **▸godson** filleul *m* **▸godspeed!†** bonne chance!, bon voyage! **▸godsquad*** (*pej*) bande *f* d'illuminés (*pej*), ≃ les cathos* *mpl* (*pej*).

goddess [ˈgɒdɪs] **n** déesse *f*; (*fig*) idole *f*.

godless [ˈgɒdlɪs] **adj** *person, action, life* impie.

godly [ˈgɒdlɪ] **adj** *person* dévot, pieux, religieux; *actions, life* pieux.

goer [ˈgəʊəʳ] **n** a (*horse, runner*) fonceur *m*, -euse *f*; (*Austral* *: *feasible idea*) bon plan* *m*, bonne idée *f*. b (‡) [*woman*] **she's a real ~** elle démarre au quart de tour‡.

...goer [ˈgəʊəʳ] **n ending in comps: cinemagoer** cinéphile *mf*; *see* **opera, theatre** *etc*.

goes [gəʊz] *see* **go**.

Goethe [ˈgøːtə] **n** Goethe *m*.

gofer [ˈgəʊfəʳ] **n** (*US*) coursier *m*, -ière *f*.

goggle [ˈgɒgl] 1 **vi** [*person*] rouler de gros yeux ronds; [*eyes*] être saillants *or* exorbités, sortir de la tête. **to ~ at sb/sth** regarder qn/qch en roulant de gros yeux ronds, regarder qn/qch des yeux en boules de loto*. 2 **n: ~s** [*motorcyclist*] (grosses) lunettes protectrices *or* de motocycliste; [*skindiver*] lunettes de plongée; (*industrial*) lunettes protectrices *or* de protection; (*: *glasses*) lunettes, besicles *fpl* (*hum*).

3 **comp ▸goggle-box‡** (*Brit*) télé* *f* **▸goggle-eyed** aux yeux saillants *or* exorbités *or* en boules de loto*.

go-go [ˈgəʊgəʊ] **adj** a *dancer, dancing* de night-club. b (*US St Ex*) *market, stocks* spéculatif. c (*US: dynamic*) *team etc* plein d'allant. d (*Brit Fin*) *investment, fund* à haut rendement et à haut risque, hautement spéculatif.

going [ˈgəʊɪŋ] 1 **n** a (*departure*) départ *m*; *see* **coming**.

b (*pace*) allure *f*, marche *f*, train *m*. (*lit, fig*) **that was good ~** ça a été rapide; **it was slow ~** (*traffic*) on n'avançait pas; (*work etc*) les progrès étaient lents.

c (*conditions*) état *m* du sol *or* du terrain (*pour la marche etc*). **it's rough ~** (*walking*) on marche mal; (*Aut etc*) la route est mauvaise; **let's cross while the ~ is good** traversons pendant que nous le pouvons *or* que la circulation le permet; (*lit, fig*) **he got out while the ~ was good** il est parti au bon moment *or* au moment où les circonstances le permettaient; *see* **heavy**.

2 **adj** a *price* existant, actuel. **the ~ rate** le taux en vigueur.

b **a ~ concern** une affaire prospère *or* qui marche *or* florissante; **the shop was sold as a ~ concern** le magasin a été vendu comme une affaire qui marche.

3 **comp ▸going-over** (**pl ~s-~**) [*accounts*] vérification *f*, révision *f*; (*medical*) examen *m*; [*rooms, house etc*] nettoyage *m*; (*fig: beating*) brutalités *fpl*, passage *m* à tabac*; **to give sth a good** *or* **thorough going-over** (*check*) inspecter qch soigneusement, soumettre qch à une inspection en règle; (*clean*) nettoyer qch à fond **▸goings-on** (* *pej: behaviour*) activités *fpl*, conduite *f*, manigances *fpl*; (*happenings*) événements *mpl*; **fine goings-on!*** en voilà du joli!; **your letters keep me in touch with goings-on at home** tes lettres me tiennent au courant de ce qui se passe à la maison.

-going [ˈgəʊɪŋ] 1 **adj ending in comps: church-going Christian** chrétien *m* pratiquant; **the theatre-going public** les gens qui vont (régulièrement) au théâtre, le public du théâtre; *see* **easy 3, ocean 2.** 2 **n ending in comps: church-going/theatre-going has declined over the last 10 years** depuis 10 ans les gens vont de moins en moins à l'église/au théâtre.

goitre, (*US*) **goiter** [ˈgɔɪtə] **n** goitre *m*.

Golan [ˈgəʊlæn] **n: the ~ Heights** le plateau du Golan.

gold [gəʊld] 1 **n** a (*NonC*) or *m*. **£500 in ~** 500 livres en or; (*fig*) **heart of ~** cœur *m* d'or; *see also* **2**, *and* **good, heart, rolled.**

b = **gold medal**; *see* **3**.

2 **adj** *watch, tooth* en or; *coin, cloth, ingot* d'or; (*also* **gold-coloured**) d'or, doré, (couleur d')or *inv*; *paint* doré; *see also* **3**.

3 **comp ▸gold braid** galon *m* d'or **▸goldbrick n** (*lit*) barre *f* d'or; (*US* *: *fig: good deal*) affaire *f* en or; (*US* *: *fig: shirker*) tire-au-flanc* *m* ◊ **vi** (*US* *: *shirk*) tirer au flanc* **▸Gold Card** (*Comm, Fin*) ≃ Gold Card ®, ≃ Gold Master Card ® **▸gold-clause loan** (*Jur, Fin*) emprunt *m* avec garantie-or **▸Gold Coast** (*Hist: in Africa*) Côte-de-l'Or *f*, (*ancien nom du Ghana*); (*US* *: *fig*) quartiers *mpl* chic (*souvent en bordure d'un lac*) **▸goldcrest** roitelet *m* huppé **▸gold digger*:** (*fig pej*) **she's a gold digger** c'est une aventurière **▸gold disc** (*Mus*) disque *m* d'or **▸gold dust** (*lit*) poudre *f* d'or; (*fig*) **to be like gold dust** être une denrée rare; **▸gold-exchange standard** (*Econ*) étalon *m* de change-or **▸gold fever** la fièvre de l'or **▸goldfield** région *f or* terrain *m* aurifère **▸gold-filled** *watch etc* en doublé (or); *tooth* aurifié **▸gold filling** (*Dentistry*) obturation *f* en or **▸goldfinch** (*Orn*) chardonneret *m* **▸goldfish** poisson *m* rouge, cyprin *m* (doré); **goldfish bowl** bocal *m* (à poissons); (*fig*) **to live in a goldfish bowl** vivre comme dans un bocal en verre **▸gold foil** feuille *f* d'or **▸gold-headed cane** canne *f* à pommeau d'or **▸gold lace** (*on uniform*) = **gold braid ▸gold leaf** feuille *f* d'or, or *m* en feuille **▸gold medal** médaille *f* d'or **▸gold mine** (*lit, fig*) mine *f* d'or; (*fig*) **he's sitting on a gold mine** il est assis sur une véritable mine d'or **▸gold miner** mineur *m* (dans une mine d'or) **▸gold mining** extraction *f* de l'or **▸gold plate** (*coating*) mince couche *f* d'or; (*dishes*) vaisselle *f* d'or; (*fig*) **to eat off gold plates** rouler sur l'or, nager dans l'opulence **▸gold-plated** (*lit*) plaqué or *inv*; (*fig* *: *deal, contract*) qui doit rapporter gros **▸the gold pool** (*Fin*) le pool de l'or **▸gold reserves** (*Econ*) réserves *fpl* d'or **▸gold-rimmed spectacles** lunettes *fpl* à montures en or **▸gold rush** ruée *f* vers l'or **▸goldsmith** orfèvre *m*; **goldsmith's shop** magasin *m or* atelier *m* d'orfèvre; **goldsmith's trade** orfèvrerie *f* **▸gold standard** étalon-or *m*; **to come off** *or* **leave the gold standard** abandonner l'étalon-or **▸Gold Star Mother** (*US Hist*) mère *f* d'un soldat mort au combat **▸gold stone** aventurine *f*.

golden [ˈgəʊldən] **adj** (*of a ~ colour*) d'or, doré, (couleur d')or; *hair* doré, d'or; (*made of gold*) en or, d'or; (*fig*) *voice etc* d'or, en or; (*happy, prosperous etc*) *era* idéal. **~ age** âge *m* d'or; (*fig*) **~ boy/girl** enfant chéri(e); **the ~ calf** le veau d'or; **~ deed** action *f* d'éclat; **G~ Delicious (apple)** (pomme *f*) golden; [*pop star etc*] **~ disc** disque *m* d'or; **~ eagle** aigle royal; **The G~ Fleece** la Toison d'or; (*US Geog*) **G~ Gate** (détroit *m* du) Golden Gate *m*; (*fig*) **to kill the ~ goose** tuer la poule aux œufs d'or; (*Ind*) **~ handcuffs** contrat *m* très avantageux; (*Ind*) **~ handshake** (grosse) prime *f* de départ; (*Ind*) **~ hello** prime *f* d'embauche; **~ hours** heures précieuses *or* merveilleuses; **~ jubilee** fête *f* du cinquantième anniversaire; **~ legend** légende dorée; **the ~ mean** (*gen*) le juste milieu; **~ number** nombre *m* d'or; **~ oldie** classique *m*; **~ opportunity** occasion magnifique *or* rêvée; **it's your ~ opportunity to do it** c'est pour vous le moment ou jamais de le faire; **~ oriole** loriot *m* jaune; (*Ind*) **~ parachute** indemnité *f* de départ (*dans le cadre d'une OPA*); **~ pheasant** faisan doré; **~ remedy** remède souverain *or* infaillible; **~ retriever** golden retriever *m*; (*Bot*) **~ rod** solidage *f*, gerbe *f* d'or; **~ rule** règle *f* d'or; (*St Ex*) **~ share** action *f* privilégiée; (*US*) **the G~ State** la Californie; (*Brit*) **~ syrup** mélasse raffinée; **the ~ triangle** le triangle d'or; **~ wedding** noces *fpl* d'or; **~ yellow** jaune d'or.

Goldilocks [ˈgəʊldɪlɒks] **n** Boucles d'Or *f*.

golf [gɒlf] 1 **n** golf *m*; *see* **clock.** 2 **vi** faire du golf, jouer au golf. 3 **comp ▸golf ball** balle *f* de golf; (*on typewriter*) boule *f*, sphère *f*; **golf ball typewriter** machine *f* à écrire à boule *or* à sphère **▸golf club** (*stick*) club *m or* crosse *f or* canne *f* (de golf); (*place*) club de golf **▸golf course, golf links** (terrain *m* de) golf *m* **▸golf widow: she's a golf widow** son mari la délaisse pour aller jouer au golf *or* lui préfère le golf.

golfer [ˈgɒlfəʳ] **n** joueur *m*, -euse *f* de golf, golfeur *m*, -euse *f*.

golfing [ˈgɒlfɪŋ] 1 **adj** *equipment, trousers* de golf. **to go on a ~ holiday** partir en vacances faire du golf. 2 **n** golf *m*.

Golgotha [ˈgɒlgəθə] **n** Golgotha.

Goliath [gəʊˈlaɪəθ] **n** (*lit, fig*) Goliath *m*.

golliwog [ˈgɒlɪwɒg] (*Brit*) **n** poupée *f* nègre de chiffon (*aux cheveux hérissés*).

golly* [ˈgɒlɪ] 1 **excl (by) ~** mince (alors)!*, bon sang!*; **and by ~ he did it!** et il l'a fait nom de Dieu! 2 **n** (*Brit*) = **golliwog**.

golosh [gəˈlɒʃ] **n** = **galosh**.

Gomorrah [gəˈmɒrə] Gomorrhe.

gonad [ˈgəʊnæd] **n** (*Med*) gonade *f*.

gonadotropic [ˌgɒnədəʊˈtrəʊpɪk] **adj** gonadotrope.

gonadotropin [ˌgɒnədəʊ'trəʊpɪn] **n** gonadotrophine *f.*
gondola ['gɒndələ] **n** a gondole *f.* b *[balloon, airship]* nacelle *f.* c (*in supermarket*) gondole *f*; (*US Rail: also* ~ **car**) wagon-tombereau *m.*
gondolier [ˌgɒndə'lɪəʳ] **n** gondolier *m.*
Gondwana [gɒnd'wɑːnə] **n** (*also* **Gondwanaland**) continent *m* de Gondwana.
gone [gɒn] 1 **ptp of go.** 2 **adj** a **to be** ~ *[person]* être parti *or* absent; (*euph: dead*) être disparu *or* mort; *[object, enthusiasm etc]* avoir disparu; **to be far** ~ (*ill*) être très bas (*f* basse) *or* mal; (*: *drunk*) être parti* *or* beurré‡; (*Med*) **she was 6 months** ~* elle était enceinte de 6 mois; (*liter*) **she was far** ~ **with child** elle approchait de son terme; **to be** ~ **on sb**‡ en pincer pour qn‡; (†† *or hum*) **be** ~! allez-vous-en!; ~ **with the wind** autant en emporte le vent. b (*Brit*) **it's just** ~ **3** il vient de sonner 3 heures, 3 heures viennent de sonner; **it was** ~ **4 before he came** il était plus de 4 heures *or* passé 4 heures quand il est arrivé.
goner‡ ['gɒnəʳ] **n: to be a** ~ être fichu* *or* foutu‡.
gong [gɒŋ] **n** a (*also Boxing*) gong *m.* b (*Brit Mil sl: medal*) médaille *f.*
gonna* ['gənə] (*esp US*) = **going to.**
gonorrhoea [ˌgɒnə'rɪə] **n** blennorragie *f*, blennorrhée *f.*
gonzo ['gɒnzəʊ] **adj** (*US* ‡) bizarre, dingue*.
goo* [guː] **n** matière visqueuse *or* gluante; (*sentimentality*) sentimentalité *f* mièvre *or* à l'eau de rose.
good [gʊd] 1 **adj, compar better, superl best** a (*gen*) bon (*f* bonne); (*well-behaved*) *child, animal* sage; (*kind*) bon, gentil, bienveillant. **he's a** ~ **man** c'est un homme bien *or* quelqu'un de bien; **he's a** ~ **man but** ... c'est un brave homme mais ...; **he sounds too** ~ **to be true** mais il est parfait! — c'est trop beau pour être vrai (*see also* **1d**); **is he any** ~? *[worker/singer etc]* est-ce qu'il travaille/chante *etc* bien?; **all** ~ **people** toutes les braves gens; (*liter*) ~ **men and true** hommes vaillants; **a** ~ **and holy man** un saint homme; **to live** *or* **lead a** ~ **life** mener une vie vertueuse; **the child was as** ~ **as gold** l'enfant était sage comme une image; **be** ~! sois sage!; **be** ~ **to him** soyez gentil avec lui; **that's very** ~ **of you** c'est bien aimable *or* très gentil de votre part, vous êtes bien aimable *or* gentil; **would you be** ~ **enough to tell me** seriez-vous assez aimable pour *or* auriez-vous la bonté de me dire, voudriez-vous avoir l'obligeance (*frm*) de me dire; **he asked us to be** ~ **enough to sit** il nous a priés de bien vouloir nous asseoir; **she is a** ~ **mother** c'est une bonne mère; **she was a** ~ **wife to him** elle a été pour lui une épouse dévouée; **he's a** ~ **chap** *or* **sort*** c'est un brave *or* chic type*; **she's a** ~ **sort** c'est une brave *or* chic* fille; ~ **old Charles!*** ce (bon) vieux Charles!; **my** ~ **friend** (mon) cher ami; **your** ~ **lady**† votre épouse; **your** ~ **man**† votre époux; **yes, my** ~ **man** oui, mon brave; **the** ~ **ship Domino** le Domino; **very** ~, **sir!** (très) bien monsieur!; **to do** ~ **works** faire de bonnes œuvres; **the G**~ **Book** la Bible; **she was wearing a** ~ **dress** elle portait une robe de (belle) qualité; **she was wearing her** ~ **dress** elle portait sa belle robe; **nothing was too** ~ **for his wife** rien n'était trop beau pour sa femme; **he sat on the only** ~ **chair** il s'est assis sur la seule bonne chaise; (*in shop*) **I want something** ~ je veux quelque chose de bien; **that's not** ~ **enough** ça ne va pas; **it's just not** ~ **enough** ça laisse beaucoup à désirer; (*indignantly*) c'est lamentable, c'est déplorable; **that's** ~ **enough for me** cela me suffit; ~ **for YOU,** ~ **ON you!** bravo!; **(that's)** ~!, **very** ~! bon!, très bien!; (*joke, story*) **that's a** ~ **one!** elle est (bien) bonne celle-là!; (*iro*) à d'autres!*; (*well done, well said*) ~ **one!*** bravo! (*also iro*); ~ **gracious*,** ~ **heavens!*,** ~ **Lord!*** mon Dieu!, Seigneur!; **he's as** ~ **as you** il vous vaut, il vaut autant que vous; **he's as** ~ **a writer as his brother** il est aussi bon écrivain que son frère; **it's as** ~ **a way as any other** c'est une façon comme une autre *or* qui en vaut une autre; **he was as** ~ **as his word** il a tenu sa promesse; **his hearing/eyesight is** ~ il a l'ouïe fine/une bonne vue; **he came in a** ~ **third** il s'est honorablement classé troisième; *see* **form, part, Samaritan** *etc.*

b (*beneficial, wholesome*) bon (*for* pour), salutaire (*for* à). **milk is** ~ **for children** le lait est bon pour les enfants; **drink up your milk, it's** ~ **for you** bois ton lait, c'est bon pour toi *or* c'est bon pour la santé *or* ça te fait du bien; **oil of cloves is** ~ **for toothache** l'essence de girofle est bonne pour les maux de dents; **exercise is** ~ **for you** l'exercice vous fait du bien, il est sain de prendre de l'exercice; (*hum*) **it's** ~ **for the soul!** ça forme le caractère!; **you don't know what's** ~ **for you** (*of food etc*) tu ne sais pas apprécier les bonnes choses; (*fig*) tu ne sais pas profiter des bonnes occasions; **if you know what's** ~ **for you you'll say yes** si tu as le moindre bon sens tu accepteras; **the shock was** ~ **for him** le choc lui a été salutaire; **this climate is not** ~ **for one's health** ce climat est mauvais pour la santé *or* est insalubre; **all this running isn't** ~ **for me!** ce n'est pas bon pour moi de courir comme ça!; **to drink more than is** ~ **for one** boire plus qu'on ne le devrait *or* plus que de raison; **he's had more (to drink) than is** ~ **for him*** il a largement son compte*, il a trop bu; *[food]* **to keep** *or* **stay** ~ (bien) se conserver.

c (*efficient, competent*) bon, compétent, expert. **I've got a** ~ **teacher/doctor/lawyer** j'ai un bon professeur/médecin/avocat; **a** ~ **businessman** un excellent homme d'affaires; ~ **at French** bon *or* fort *or* calé* en français, doué pour le français; **he's** ~ **at everything** il est bon *or* il brille en tout; **she's** ~ **with children/dogs** elle sait s'y prendre avec les enfants/les chiens; **he's** ~ **at telling stories, he tells a** ~ **story** il sait bien raconter les histoires; **he's not** ~ **enough to do it alone** il n'est pas assez expert *or* il ne s'y connaît pas assez pour le faire tout seul; **he's too** ~ **for that** il mérite mieux que cela.

d (*pleasing, agreeable*) *visit, holiday* bon, agréable, plaisant; *weather, day* beau (*f* belle); *news* bon, heureux; *humour* bon, joyeux. **he has a** ~ **temper** il a bon caractère; **he's in a** ~ **temper** *or* **humour** il est de bonne humeur; **his** ~ **nature** son bon naturel *or* caractère; **we had a** ~ **time** nous nous sommes bien amusés; (*fig*) **there are** ~ **times ahead for** ... l'avenir est prometteur pour ... *or* sourit à ...; **I've had a** ~ **life** j'ai eu une belle vie; **it's too** ~ **to be true** c'est trop beau pour être vrai; **it's** ~ **to be alive** il fait bon vivre; **it's** ~ **to be here** cela fait plaisir d'être ici; **I feel** ~ je me sens bien; **I don't feel too** ~ **about that*** (*worried*) cela m'inquiète *or* m'ennuie un peu; (*ashamed*) j'en ai un peu honte; **Robert sends (his)** ~ **wishes** Robert envoie ses amitiés; (*in letter*) **with every** ~ **wish, with all** ~ **wishes** tous mes meilleurs vœux; *see* **cheer** *etc.*

e (*in greetings*) ~ **afternoon** (*early*) bonjour, (*later*) bonsoir, (*on leaving*) bonsoir; ~**bye** au revoir, adieu†; **to bid sb** ~**bye** faire ses adieux à qn, prendre congé de qn; ~**bye to all that!** fini tout cela!; **you can say** ~**bye to all your hopes** tu peux dire adieu à toutes tes espérances; ~ **day**† = ~**bye** *or* **morning**; ~ **evening** bonsoir; ~ **morning** bonjour; ~**night** bonsoir, bonne nuit; **to bid sb** ~**night** souhaiter le *or* dire bonsoir à qn; **to give sb a** ~**night kiss** embrasser qn (*en lui disant bonne nuit*).

f (*handsome, well-made*) *appearance etc* bon, beau (*f* belle), joli; *features* beau, joli. ~ **looks** beauté *f*; **you look** ~ **in that, that looks** ~ **on you** ça vous va bien; **you look** ~! tu es très bien!; **she's got a** ~ **figure** elle a la ligne, elle est bien faite; **she's got** ~ **legs** elle a les jambes bien faites *or* dessinées.

g (*advantageous, favourable*) *terms, contract, deal* avantageux, favorable; *offer* favorable, bon; *omen, chance* bon; *opportunity* bon, favorable. **to make a** ~ **marriage** faire un beau mariage; **to live at a** ~ **address** avoir une adresse chic; **people of** ~ **position** *or* **standing** des gens bien; (*Betting etc*) **I've had a** ~ **day** la chance était avec moi aujourd'hui; **you've never had it so** ~!* vous n'avez jamais eu la vie si belle!; **he thought it** ~ **to say** il crut bon *or* il jugea à propos de dire; **he's on to a** ~ **thing*** il a trouvé un filon*; **to make a** ~ **thing out of sth*** tirer bon parti de qch, faire de gros bénéfices sur qch; **it would be a** ~ **thing to ask him** il serait bon de lui demander; **it's a** ~ **thing I was there** heureusement que j'étais là, c'est une chance que j'aie été là; **that's a** ~ **thing!** tant mieux!, très bien!; **it's too much** *or* **you can have too much of a** ~ **thing** on se lasse des meilleures choses, il ne faut pas abuser des bonnes choses; **to put in a** ~ **word for sb** glisser un mot en faveur de qn; **this is as** ~ **a time as any to do it** autant le faire maintenant; *see* **fortune, job, time** *etc.*

h (*reliable, valid*) *car, tools, machinery* bon, sûr; *cheque* bon; *reason, excuse* bon, valable. (*Insurance*) **he is a** ~ **risk** il est un bon risque; (*Fin*) **is his credit** ~? peut-on lui faire crédit?; **he is** *or* **his credit is** ~ **for £3,000** on peut lui faire crédit jusqu'à 3 000 livres; **what** *or* **how much is he** ~ **for?** de combien (d'argent) dispose-t-il?; **how much will you be** ~ **for?** combien (d'argent) pouvez-vous mettre?; (*lending money*) **he's** ~ **for £500** il nous (*or* vous *etc*) prêtera bien 500 livres; **this ticket is** ~ **for 3 months** ce billet est bon *or* valable 3 mois; **this note is** ~ **for £5** ce bon vaut 5 livres; **he's** ~ **for another 20 years yet** il en a encore bien pour 20 ans; **my car is** ~ **for another few years** ma voiture fera *or* tiendra encore bien quelques années; **are you** ~ **for a long walk?** te sens-tu en état de *or* de taille à *or* de force à faire une longue promenade?; **I'm** ~ **for another mile or two** je me sens de force à faire encore un ou deux kilomètres; *see* **reason.**

i (*thorough*) bon, grand, complet (*f* -ète). **a** ~ **thrashing** une bonne correction; **to give sb a** ~ **scolding** passer un bon savon* à qn, tancer qn vertement; **to give sth a** ~ **clean*** nettoyer qch à fond, faire le nettoyage complet de qch; **to have a** ~ **cry** avoir une bonne crise de larmes, pleurer un bon coup *or* tout son soûl; **I've a** ~ **mind to tell him everything!** j'ai bien envie de tout lui dire!; *see* **care, grounding.**

j (*considerable, not less than*) bon, grand. **a** ~ **deal (of)** beaucoup (de); **a** ~ **many** beaucoup de, bon nombre de; **a** ~ **distance** une bonne distance; **a** ~ **way** un bon bout de chemin; **a** ~ **while** pas mal de temps, assez longtemps; **it will take you a** ~ **hour** vous n'aurez pas trop d'une heure, il vous faudra une bonne heure; **a** ~ **8 kilometres** 8 bons kilomètres, 8 kilomètres pour le moins; **that was a** ~ **10 years ago** il y a bien 10 ans de cela; **a** ~ **round sum** une somme rondelette; *see* **bit**[2].

k (*adv phrases*) **as** ~ **as** pour ainsi dire, à peu de choses près, pratiquement; **as** ~ **as new** comme neuf (*f* neuve); **to make sth as** ~ **as new** remettre qch à neuf; **the matter is as** ~ **as settled** c'est comme si l'affaire était réglée, l'affaire est pour ainsi dire *or* pratiquement réglée; **he's as** ~ **as lost it** c'est comme s'il l'avait perdu; **she as** ~ **as told me that** ... elle m'a dit à peu de chose près que ..., elle m'a pour ainsi dire déclaré que ...; **he as** ~ **as called me a liar** il n'a pas dit que je mentais mais c'était tout comme*; **it's as** ~ **as saying that** ... autant dire que ...; **it was as** ~ **as a play!** c'était une vraie comédie!; **it was as** ~ **as a holiday** c'était presque des vacances.

l **to make** ~ (*succeed*) faire son chemin, réussir; *[ex-criminal etc]* se refaire une vie, racheter son passé; **to make** ~ *deficit* combler; *deficiency, losses* compenser; *expenses* rembourser; *injustice, damage* réparer; **to make ~ a loss to sb** dédommager qn d'une perte; **to make ~ a promise** tenir *or* remplir une promesse; **to make ~ one's escape** réussir son évasion; **to make ~ an assertion** justifier une affirmation.

2 **adv** a bien. **a ~ strong stick** un bâton bien solide; **a ~ long walk** une bonne *or* une grande promenade; **we had a ~ long talk** nous avons discuté bien longuement; **in ~ plain English** en termes simples.

b **~ and*** bien, tout à fait; **the soup was served ~ and hot** la soupe a été servie bien chaude; **the house is ~ and clean** la maison est scrupuleusement propre; **I told him off ~ and proper‡** je lui ai passé un bon savon*, je l'ai bien engueulé‡.

c (*US*) **to be in ~ with sb‡** être dans les petits papiers de qn; (*US*) **you did ~*** tu as bien fait.

3 **n** a (*virtue, righteousness*) bien *m*. **to do ~** faire du bien *or* le bien; **to return ~ for evil** rendre le bien pour le mal; **he is a power for ~** il exerce une influence salutaire; **she's up to no ~*** elle prépare quelque mauvais coup; **there's some ~ in him** il a du bon; **for ~ or ill, for ~ or evil, for ~ or bad** que ce soit un bien ou un mal; **he'll come to no ~** il finira *or* tournera mal.

b (*collective n: people*) **the ~** les bons *mpl*, les gens *mpl* de bien, les gens vertueux; **the ~ and the bad** les bons et les méchants; (*loc*) **only the ~ die young** ce sont toujours les meilleurs qui partent les premiers.

c (*advantage, profit*) bien *m*, avantage *m*, profit *m*. **the common ~** l'intérêt commun; **I did it for your ~** je l'ai fait pour votre bien; **it's for his own ~** c'est pour son bien; **he went for the ~ of his health** il est parti pour des raisons de santé; **that will do you ~** cela vous fera du bien; **it does my heart ~ to see him** cela me réjouit *or* me réchauffe le cœur de le voir; **what ~ will that do you?** ça t'avancera à quoi?; **what's the ~?** à quoi bon?; **what's the ~ of hurrying?** à quoi bon se presser?; **a (fat) lot of ~ that will do (you)!*** tu seras bien avancé!, ça te fera une belle jambe!*; **much ~ may it do you!** grand bien vous fasse!; **a lot of ~ that's done!** nous voilà bien avancés!; **a lot of ~ that's done him!** le voilà bien avancé!; **it's not much ~ to me** *[advice, suggestion]* cela ne m'avance guère; *[object, money]* cela ne me sert pas à grand-chose; **so much to the ~** autant de gagné; **we were £5 to the ~** nous avions fait 5 livres de bénéfice, cela nous avait fait 5 livres de gagnées; **that's all to the ~!** tant mieux!, c'est autant de gagné!; **it's no ~** ça ne sert à rien, c'est en pure perte; **that's no ~** cela ne vaut rien, cela ne va pas, cela ne peut pas aller; **that won't be much ~** cela ne servira pas à grand-chose; **if that is any ~ to you** si ça peut vous être utile *or* vous rendre service; **it's no ~ saying that** ce n'est pas la peine de dire cela, inutile de dire cela.

d (*adv phrase*) **for ~** pour de bon, à jamais; **to settle down for ~** se fixer définitivement; **he's gone for ~** il est parti pour toujours *or* pour de bon *or* pour ne plus revenir; **for ~ and all** à tout jamais, une (bonne) fois pour toutes, pour tout de bon.

e *see* **goods**.

4 **comp** ►**goodbye** *see* **1e** ►**good-for-nothing adj** bon *or* propre à rien ◊ **n** propre *mf* à rien, vaurien(ne) *m(f)* ►**Good Friday** Vendredi saint ►**good-hearted** qui a bon cœur, bon, généreux ►**good-heartedness** bonté *f* ►**good-humoured** *person* de bonne humeur, jovial, bon enfant *inv*; *appearance, smile etc* plein de bonhomie, bonhomme *inv*, bon enfant *inv*; *joke* sans malice ►**good-humouredly** avec bonne humeur, avec bonhomie ►**good-looker*** (*man*) beau garçon, bel homme; (*woman*) belle *or* jolie femme; (*horse etc*) beau cheval *etc* ►**good-looking** beau (*f* belle), bien *inv*, joli ►**good-natured** *person* qui a un bon naturel, accommodant, facile à vivre; *smile, laughter* bon enfant *inv* ►**goodnight** *see* **1e** ►**good-tempered** *person* qui a bon caractère, de caractère égal; *smile, look* aimable, gentil ►**good-time girl*** (*pej*) fille *f* qui ne pense qu'à s'amuser *or* qu'à se donner du bon temps ►**goodwill** *see* **goodwill**.

goodie* ['gʊdɪ] = **goody**.

goodish ['gʊdɪʃ] **adj** assez bon *or* bien.

goodly ['gʊdlɪ] **adj** († *or liter*) a *appearance* beau (*f* belle), gracieux. b *size* grand, large, ample. **a ~ number** un nombre considérable; **a ~ heritage** un bel héritage.

goodness ['gʊdnɪs] **n** *[person]* bonté *f*; *[foodstuff]* valeur nutritive. **(my) ~!*, ~ gracious!*** Seigneur!, bonté divine!; **~ (only) knows*** Dieu (seul) sait; **for ~' sake*** pour l'amour de Dieu, par pitié; **I wish to ~ I had gone there!*** si seulement j'y étais allé!; (*frm*) **to have the ~ to do sth** avoir la bonté de faire qch; *see* **thank**.

goods [gʊdz] 1 **npl** a (*Comm*) marchandises *fpl*, articles *mpl*. **leather ~** articles de cuir, maroquinerie *f*; **knitted ~** articles en tricot; **that's/he's just the ~!‡** c'est/il est exactement ce qu'il (nous *or* vous *etc*) faut!; (*US*) **to have the ~ on sb‡** en savoir long sur qn; *see* **consumer, deliver** *etc*.

b (*Jur*) biens *mpl*, meubles *mpl*. **all his ~ and chattels** tous ses biens et effets.

2 **comp** ►**goods service:** (*Brit Rail*) **to send by fast/slow goods service** envoyer en grande/petite vitesse ►**goods siding** voie *f* de garage pour wagons de marchandises ►**goods station** gare *f* de marchandises ►**goods train** train *m* de marchandises ►**goods wagon** wagon *m* de marchandises ►**goods yard** dépôt *m or* cour *f* des marchandises.

goodwill [ˌgʊd'wɪl] **n** a bonne volonté, bon vouloir, bienveillance *f*. **to gain sb's ~** se faire bien voir de qn; (*Pol*) **~ mission** *or* **tour** visite *f* d'amitié. b (*willingness*) zèle *m*. **to work with ~** travailler de bon cœur *or* avec zèle. c (*Comm: customer connections*) (biens *mpl*) incorporels *mpl*, clientèle *f*; (*Accounting: intangible assets*) survaloir *m*, goodwill *m*. **the ~ goes with the business** les incorporels sont vendus *or* la clientèle est vendue avec le fonds de commerce.

goody* ['gʊdɪ] 1 **excl** (*also* ~ ~) chic!*, chouette!‡ 2 **n** a (*Cine*) **the goodies and the baddies*** les bons *mpl* et les méchants *mpl*. b (*Culin*) **goodies*** friandises *fpl*, bonnes choses.

goody-goody* ['gʊdɪˌgʊdɪ] 1 **adj** (*pej*) *[person]* **to be ~** *[child]* être l'image du petit garçon (*or* de la petite fille) modèle; *[adult]* être un vrai petit saint. 2 **n** modèle *m* de vertu (*iro*), petit saint, sainte nitouche *f*.

gooey* ['gu:ɪ] **adj** (*pej*) *substance* gluant; *cake* qui colle aux dents; (*fig*) *film, story* sentimental, à l'eau de rose.

goof‡ [gu:f] 1 **n** (*idiot*) toqué(e)‡ *m(f)*. 2 **comp** ►**goofball** (*drug*) barbiturique *m*; (*US: eccentric person*) fantaisiste *mf*, numéro* *m*. 3 **vi** faire une gaffe, mettre les pieds dans le plat.

►**goof around* vi** (*US*) faire l'imbécile.

►**goof off‡ vi** (*US*) tirer au flanc.

►**goof up‡** 1 **vi** (*US*) faire une gaffe, gaffer*. 2 **vt sep** foutre en l'air‡, bousiller‡.

goofy‡ ['gu:fɪ] **adj** maboul‡, toqué‡.

gook‡ [gu:k] **n** (*US*) a (*slime etc*) substance visqueuse; (*dirt*) crasse *f*. **what's this ~?** qu'est-ce que c'est que cette saloperie‡? b (*pej: Asian etc*) Asiate *mf* (*pej*).

goolies*‡ ['gu:lɪz] **npl** couilles*‡ *fpl*.

goon‡ [gu:n] **n** (*fool*) idiot(e) *m(f)*, imbécile *mf*; (*US: hired thug*) gangster *m*; (*prison camp guard*) surveillant *m*, garde-chiourme *m*.

gooney bird‡ ['gu:nɪˌbɜ:d] **n** (*US*) albatros *m*.

goosander [gu:'sændəʳ] **n** harle *m* bièvre.

goose [gu:s], **pl geese** 1 **n** oie *f*. (*fig*) **all his geese are swans** d'après lui tout ce qu'il fait tient du prodige; (*fig*) **to kill the ~ that lays the golden eggs** tuer la poule aux œufs d'or; **don't be such a ~!*** ne sois pas si bébête!* *or* si dinde!*; **silly little ~!*** petite dinde!*, petite niaise!*; *see* **boo, cook, mother** *etc*.

2 **comp** ►**gooseberry** *see* **gooseberry** ►**goose bumps** = **goose flesh** ►**goose chase** *see* **wild** ►**goose flesh, goose pimples: to come out in goose flesh** *etc* avoir la chair de poule; **that gives me goose flesh** *etc* cela me donne la chair de poule ►**goose-step** (*Mil*) **n** pas *m* de l'oie ◊ **vi** faire le pas de l'oie; **to goose-step along/in** *etc* avancer/entrer *etc* au pas de l'oie.

3 **vt** (*esp US* ‡: *prod*) donner un coup de doigt dans l'arrière-train à.

gooseberry ['gʊzbərɪ] **n** (*fruit*) groseille *f* à maquereau; (*also* **~ bush**) groseillier *m*. (*Brit*) **to play ~** tenir la chandelle.

goosegog‡ ['gʊzgɒg] (*Brit*) = **gooseberry**.

G.O.P. [ˌdʒi:əʊ'pi:] **n** (*US Pol*) (**abbr of Grand Old Party**) *parti républicain*.

gopher ['gəʊfəʳ] 1 **n** (*squirrel*) spermophile *m*; (*rodent*) geomys *m*. 2 **comp** ►**the Gopher State** (*US*) le Minnesota.

gorblimey‡ [ˌgɔ:'blaɪmɪ] **excl** (*Brit*) nom d'un chien!*

Gordian ['gɔ:dɪən] **n: to cut the ~ knot** trancher le nœud gordien.

gore¹ [gɔ:ʳ] **n** (*blood*) sang *m*.

gore² [gɔ:ʳ] **vt** (*injure*) encorner, blesser *or* éventrer d'un coup de corne. **~d to death** tué d'un coup de corne.

gore³ [gɔ:ʳ] 1 **n** (*Sewing*) godet *m*; *[sail]* pointe *f*. 2 **vt** *sail* mettre une pointe à. **~d skirt** jupe *f* à godets.

gorge [gɔ:dʒ] 1 **n** a (*Geog*) gorge *f*, défilé *m*. b (*Anat*) gorge *f*, gosier *m*. (*fig*) **it makes my ~ rise** cela me soulève le cœur. 2 **vt** *meal, food* engloutir, engouffrer*. **to ~ o.s.** se gaver, se rassasier (*with* de); **~d with cake** rassasié de gâteau. 3 **vi** se gaver, se rassasier (*on* de).

gorgeous ['gɔ:dʒəs] **adj** *sunset, colours* somptueux, splendide, magnifique, fastueux; *woman* magnifique, splendide; *weather* splendide, magnifique; (*) *holiday etc* sensationnel*, formidable*. **we had a ~ time*** on a passé un moment sensationnel*; **hullo there, ~!‡** bonjour, ma beauté! *or* ma belle! *or* ma mignonne!; **it was a ~ feeling** c'était une sensation merveilleuse.

gorgeously ['gɔ:dʒəslɪ] **adv** superbement. **~ coloured fabrics** des tissus aux couleurs superbes.

Gorgons ['gɔ:gənz] **npl** (*Myth*) Gorgones *fpl*.

gorilla [gə'rɪlə] **n** (*Zool*) gorille *m*; (‡ *pej: man*) brute *f*; (‡: *thug*) gangster *m*; (‡: *bodyguard*) gorille* *m*.

Gorki, Gorky ['gɔ:kɪ] (*writer*) Gorki *m*.

gormandize ['gɔ:məndaɪz] **vi** bâfrer‡, se goinfrer‡, s'empiffrer‡.

gormless* ['gɔ:mlɪs] **adj** (*Brit*) lourdaud, bêta (*f* -asse)*.

gorse [gɔ:s] **n** (*NonC*) ajoncs *mpl*. **~ bush** ajonc *m*.

gory ['gɔ:rɪ] **adj** *wound, battle etc* sanglant; *person* ensanglanté. (*fig*) **all the ~ details** tous les détails les plus horribles.

gosh* [gɒʃ] **excl** ça alors!*, mince (alors)!*, nom d'un chien!

goshawk ['gɒshɔ:k] **n** autour *m*.

gosling ['gɒzlɪŋ] **n** oison *m*.

gospel ['gɒspəl] 1 **n** a évangile *m*. **the G~ according to St John** l'Évangile selon St Jean; (*fig*) **that's ~*** c'est parole d'évangile, c'est la vérité pure; (*fig*) **to take sth for ~*** accepter qch comme *or* prendre qch pour parole d'évangile. **b** (*music*) gospel *m*. **2** **comp** ►**gospel music** gospel *m* ►**Gospel oath** serment prêté sur l'Évangile ►**gospel song** ≃ négro-spiritual *m* ►**gospel truth**: (*fig*) **it's the gospel truth*** c'est parole d'évangile, c'est la vérité pure.

gossamer ['gɒsəmə^r] **1** **n** (*NonC*) (*cobweb*) fils *mpl* de la Vierge; (*gauze*) gaze *f*; (*light fabric*) tulle *m*, gaze *f*; (*US: waterproof*) imperméable léger. **2** **adj** *curtains etc* de tulle; (*light*) arachnéen (*liter*), léger. **~ thin** très fin, fin comme de la gaze.

gossip ['gɒsɪp] **1** **n** **a** (*NonC*) (*chatter*) bavardage *m*, commérage *m* (*pej*), cancans *mpl* (*pej*), potins *mpl* (*pej*); (*in newspaper*) propos familiers, échos *mpl*. **I never listen to ~** je n'écoute jamais les cancans *or* les racontars *mpl*; **what's the latest ~?** quels sont les derniers potins?; **a piece of ~** un cancan, un ragot; **we had a good old ~** nous nous sommes raconté tous les potins, nous avons taillé une bonne bavette*.

b (*person*) bavard(e) *m(f)*, commère *f* (*pej*). **he's a real ~** c'est une vraie commère *or* un vrai pipelet*.

2 **vi** bavarder, papoter; (*maliciously*) potiner, cancaner, faire des commérages (*about* sur).

3 **comp** ►**gossip column** (*Press*) échos *mpl* ►**gossip columnist**, **gossip writer** échotier *m*, -ière *f*.

gossiping ['gɒsɪpɪŋ] **1** **adj** bavard, cancanier (*pej*). **2** **n** bavardage *m*, papotage *m*, commérage *m* (*pej*).

gossipy ['gɒsɪpɪ] **adj** *person* bavard, cancanier (*pej*); *style, book* anecdotique; *conversation* cancanier, de commère.

got [gɒt] **pret, ptp of get**; *for* **have ~** *see* **have**.

Goth [gɒθ] **n** Goth *m*.

Gothic ['gɒθɪk] **1** **adj** (*Archit etc*) gothique; (*Hist*) des Goths. **~ type** caractère *m* gothique. **2** **n** (*Archit, Ling etc*) gothique *m*.

gotta* ['gɒtə] (*esp US*) **modal aux vb** (*have* (*got*) *to*) **I/he's/they ~ go** je dois/il doit/ils doivent partir.

gotten ['gɒtn] (*US*) **ptp of get**.

gouache [gʊ'ɑːʃ] **n** gouache *f*.

gouge [gaʊdʒ] **1** **n** gouge *f*. **2** **vt** **a** *wood etc* gouger. **to ~ a hole in sth** creuser un trou dans qch. **b** (*US fig *: overcharge etc*) estamper‡, escroquer.

►**gouge out** **vt sep** (*with gouge*) gouger; (*with thumb, pencil etc*) évider. **to gouge sb's eyes out** arracher les yeux à qn.

goulash ['guːlæʃ] **n** goulache *f*.

gourd [gʊəd] **n** (*fruit*) gourde *f*; (*container*) gourde, calebasse *f*.

gourmand ['gʊəmənd] **n** gourmand(e) *m(f)*, glouton(ne) *m(f)*.

gourmet ['gʊəmeɪ] **n** gourmet *m*, gastronome *mf*.

gout [gaʊt] **n** (*Med*) goutte *f*.

gouty ['gaʊtɪ] **adj** *person, joint* goutteux.

gov‡ [gʌv] **n abbr of governor b**.

Gov. **n abbr of governor a**.

govern ['gʌvən] **1** **vt** **a** (*rule*) *country* gouverner; *province, city etc* administrer; *household* diriger, gérer; *affairs* administrer, gérer; *business, company* gérer, administrer, diriger. (*Jur*) **~ed by the laws of England** régi par le droit anglais. **b** (*Tech*) régler; (*fig: control*) *passions, emotions etc* maîtriser, contenir, gouverner, dominer. **to ~ one's tongue** tenir sa langue, contrôler ses paroles; **to ~ one's temper** se maîtriser. **c** (*influence*) *events* déterminer, régir; *opinions* guider; *speed* déterminer. **d** (*Gram*) régir. **2** **vi** (*Pol*) gouverner.

governess ['gʌvənɪs] **n** gouvernante *f*, institutrice *f* (*à domicile*).

governing ['gʌvənɪŋ] **adj** (*Pol etc*) gouvernant; (*fig*) *belief etc* dominant. (*Brit Scol*) **~ board** ≃ conseil *m* d'établissement; **~ body** conseil *m* d'administration, directeurs *mpl*; **~ principle** idée directrice *or* dominante.

government ['gʌvənmənt] **1** **n** **a** (*NonC: act: see* **govern 1**) gouvernement *m*; gestion *f*; direction *f*; administration *f*.

b (*Pol*) (*governing body*) gouvernement *m*, cabinet *m*, ministère *m*; (*system*) régime *m*, gouvernement; (*the State*) l'État *m*. **to form a ~** former un gouvernement *or* un cabinet *or* un ministère; **democratic ~** gouvernement *or* régime démocratique; **local ~** administration locale; **minority ~** gouvernement minoritaire; **~ by the people and for the people** gouvernement du peuple pour le peuple; **that country needs a strong ~** ce pays a besoin d'un gouvernement fort; **the ~ is taking measures to stop pollution** le gouvernement prend des mesures pour empêcher la pollution; **a dam built by the ~** un barrage construit par l'État; **the G~ and the Opposition** le gouvernement et l'opposition; **the ~ has fallen** le cabinet *or* le ministère *or* le gouvernement est tombé; **a socialist ~** un gouvernement *or* un ministère socialiste; **he was invited to join the ~** il a été invité à entrer dans le gouvernement.

2 **comp** *policy, decision, intervention, spending* gouvernemental, du gouvernement; *backing* du gouvernement; *grant* gouvernemental, d'État; *responsibility, loan* de l'État, public (*f* -ique) ►**Government Accounting Office** (*US*) ≃ Cour *f* des Comptes ►**government action** (*gen*) de l'action *f* gouvernementale; (*Insurance*) fait *m* du prince ►**government bond** (*Fin*) obligation *f* d'État ►**government corporation** (*US*) régie *f* d'État ►**government department** département *or* service gouvernemental ►**government expenditure** dépenses publiques ►**Government House** (*Brit*) palais *m* du gouverneur, résidence *f* ►**government issue** **adj** *equipment* fourni par le gouvernement; *bonds etc* émis par le gouvernement ►**government monopoly** monopole *m* d'État ►**government-owned corporation** établissement public autonome ►**Government Printing Office** (*US*) ≃ Imprimerie *f* nationale ►**government securities** (*Fin*) effets publics, titres *mpl* d'État ►**government stock** (*Fin*) fonds publics *or* d'État.

governmental [ˌgʌvən'mentl] **adj** gouvernemental, du gouvernement.

governor ['gʌvənə^r] **n** **a** *[state, bank]* gouverneur *m*; (*esp Brit*) *[prison]* directeur *m*, -trice *f*; *[institution]* administrateur *m*, -trice *f*; (*Brit Scol*) ≃ membre *m* d'un conseil d'établissement (*de lycée ou d'IUT*). (*Brit*) **~ general** (*pl* **~s ~** *or* **~ ~s**) gouverneur général. **b** (*Brit ‡*) (*employer*) patron *m*; (*father*) paternel‡ *m*. **thanks ~!** merci chef! *or* patron! **c** (*Tech*) régulateur *m*; (*Aut, Rail: speed control device*) limiteur *m* de vitesse.

governorship ['gʌvənəʃɪp] **n** fonctions *fpl* de gouverneur. **during my ~** pendant la durée de mes fonctions (de gouverneur).

govt. **abbr of government**.

gown [gaʊn] **1** **n** robe *f*; (*Jur, Univ*) toge *f*; *see* **town**. **2** **vt** (*liter*) revêtir (*in* de), habiller (*in* de).

goy [gɔɪ] **n, pl ~s** *or* **goyim** ['gɔɪɪm] goy *m or* goï *m* (*pl* goym *or* goyim).

GP [dʒiː'piː] **n** (**abbr of General Practitioner**) (médecin *m*) généraliste *m*, omnipraticien(ne) *m(f)*. **he's a ~** il est (médecin) généraliste; **go to your ~** allez voir votre médecin habituel *or* de famille; **who's your ~?** qui est votre médecin traitant?

GPO [dʒiːpiː'əʊ] **n** **a** (*Brit*) (**abbr of General Post Office**) *see* **general**. **b** (*US*) (**abbr of Government Printing Office**) *see* **government 2**.

gr. **abbr of gross 1d**.

grab [græb] **1** **n** **a** **to make a ~ for** *or* **at sth** faire un geste vif *or* un mouvement vif pour saisir qch; **to be up for ~s‡** (*gen*) être disponible; (*to the highest bidder*) être jeté en pâture au plus offrant.

b (*esp Brit: Tech*) benne preneuse.

2 **comp** ►**grab bag*** (*US*) sac *m* (pour jouer à la pêche miraculeuse) ►**grab strap** (*US Aut*) poignée *f* de maintien.

3 **vt** *object* saisir, agripper, empoigner; *seat* accaparer; (*fig*) *land* se saisir de, prendre, mettre la main sur; *power* se saisir de, prendre; *sb's attention* attirer, accaparer; *opportunity* saisir. **he ~bed the pen from me** il m'a arraché le stylo; **he ~bed (hold of) me** il m'a empoigné *or* saisi (par le bras, au cou *etc*); (*fig*) **I managed to ~ him before he left** j'ai réussi à lui mettre la main dessus avant qu'il s'en aille; (*fig*) **he ~bed* the audience at once** il a tout de suite captivé l'auditoire; **that really ~bed* me** ça m'a vraiment impressionné *or* emballé*; **how does that ~ you?‡** qu'est-ce que ça te dit?*

4 **vi**: **to ~ at a rope** essayer d'agripper une corde; (*to child*) **don't ~!** doucement!, ne te précipite pas dessus!, ne te jette pas dessus!

►**grab away** **vt sep**: **to grab sth away from sb** arracher qch à qn, enlever qch à qn d'un geste brusque.

grace [greɪs] **1** **n** **a** (*NonC*) *[person]* grâce *f*, charme *m*, distinction *f*, élégance *f*; *[animal, movement]* grâce.

b (*Rel*) grâce *f*. **by the ~ of God** par la grâce de Dieu; (*loc*) **there but for the ~ of God go I** cela aurait tout aussi bien pu être moi; **in a state of ~** en état de grâce; **to fall from ~** (*Rel*) perdre la grâce; (*fig hum*) tomber en disgrâce; **to say ~** (*before meals*) dire le bénédicité; (*after meals*) dire les grâces; *see* **year**.

c (*phrases*) **to be in sb's good/bad ~s** être bien/mal vu de qn, être en faveur/défaveur auprès de qn; **to get into sb's good/bad ~s** se faire bien/mal voir de qn; **to do sth with good/bad ~** faire qch de bonne/mauvaise grâce; **he had the ~ to apologize** il a eu la bonne grâce de s'excuser; **his saving ~** ce qui le rachète (*or* rachetait *etc*); *see* **air**.

d (*NonC: respite*) grâce *f*, répit *m*. **a day's ~** un jour de grâce *or* de répit; (*Comm*) **days of ~** jours de grâce; (*Jur*) **as an act of ~, he ...** en exerçant son droit de grâce, il ... .

e (*title*) **His G~ (the Archbishop)** Monseigneur l'Archevêque, Son Excellence l'Archevêque; **His G~ (the Duke)** Monsieur le duc; **Her G~ (the Duchess)** Madame la duchesse; **yes, your G~** oui, Monseigneur (*or* Monsieur le duc *or* Madame la duchesse).

f (*Myth*) **the (three) G~s** les trois Grâces *fpl*.

2 **comp** ►**grace and favour**: (*Brit*) **grace and favour residence** (*résidence attribuée à une personne pour la durée de sa vie par un roi ou un noble*); (*fig*) **he has the use of the room on a grace-and-favour basis** il a l'usage de cette pièce (à titre gratuit) ►**grace note** (*Mus*) (note *f* d')agrément *m*, (note *f* d')ornement *m* ►**grace period** (*Jur, Fin*) délai *m* de grâce *or* de carence.

3 **vt** **a** (*adorn*) orner, embellir (*with* de).

b honorer (*with* de). **the queen ~d the performance with her presence** la reine honora la représentation de sa présence.

graceful ['greɪsfʊl] **adv** *movement, animal, person* gracieux; *style, appearance etc* gracieux, élégant; *apology, retraction* élégant, plein d'élégance.

gracefully ['greɪsfəlɪ] **adv** *move, dance* gracieusement, élégamment, avec élégance, avec grâce; *apologize, withdraw* avec élégance, élégamment. **we cannot ~ refuse** nous ne pouvons pas trouver une excuse élégante pour refuser.

gracefulness ['greɪsfʊlnɪs] = **grace 1a**.

graceless ['greɪslɪs] **adj** *person, conduct* peu élégant, inélégant; *gesture* gauche.

gracious ['greɪʃəs] **adj** *person, smile, gesture* gracieux, bienveillant (*to* envers); *action* courtois, plein de bonne grâce; *God* miséricordieux (*to* envers); *house, room, gardens* d'une élégance raffinée. **our ~ Queen** notre gracieuse souveraine; (*frm*) **by the ~ consent of** par la grâce de; **he was very ~ to me** il s'est montré très affable *or* bienveillant envers moi; **Lord be ~ unto him** Seigneur soyez-lui miséricordieux; **~ living** vie élégante *or* raffinée; **(good) ~!*** juste ciel!, bonté divine!; **(good) ~ no!*** jamais de la vie!

graciously ['greɪʃəslɪ] **adv** *wave, smile* gracieusement, avec grâce; (*with good grace*) *agree etc* avec bonne grâce; *live* avec raffinement; (*frm*) *consent, allow* gracieusement; (*Rel*) miséricordieusement. **the king was ~ pleased to accept** le roi eut la bonté d'accepter, le roi accepta gracieusement.

graciousness ['greɪʃəsnɪs] **n** (*NonC*) *[person]* bienveillance *f* (*towards* envers); *[action, style]* grâce *f*, aménité *f*; *[house, room, gardens]* élégance raffinée; *[wave, smile]* grâce; *[God]* miséricorde *f*, clémence *f*.

grad* [græd] **n** (*US*) **abbr of graduate 3a.**

gradate [grə'deɪt] 1 **vt** graduer. 2 **vi** être gradué.

gradation [grə'deɪʃən] **n** gradation *f*, progression *f*, échelonnement *m*.

grade [greɪd] 1 **n** a (*in hierarchy*) catégorie *f*; (*on scale*) échelon *m*, grade *m*; (*Mil: rank*) rang *m*; (*Comm*) *[steel, butter, goods etc]* qualité *f*; (*Comm: size*) *[eggs, apples, anthracite, nuts etc]* calibre *m*; (*US: level*) niveau *m*; (*Climbing*) degré *m* (de difficulté). **the lowest ~ of skilled worker** la catégorie la plus basse des ouvriers qualifiés; **the highest ~ of clerical post** la catégorie supérieure *or* la plus élevée des employés de bureau; **~ C eggs** œufs *mpl* de calibre C; **~ B milk** lait *m* de qualité B; **high-~ meat/fruit** viande *f*/fruits *mpl* de premier choix *or* de première qualité; **high-~ steel/coal** acier *m*/charbon *m* de haute qualité; **he was classed as ~ 3 for physical fitness** on l'a mis en catégorie 3 en ce qui concerne la forme physique; (*US*) **at ~** au niveau du sol; (*fig*) **to make the ~** se montrer à la hauteur, y arriver*; **he'll never make the ~** il n'y arrivera jamais*, il ne sera jamais à la hauteur.

b (*US Scol: class*) classe *f*; (*mark*) note *f*. **~s for effort** *etc* note *f* d'application *etc*.

c (*US: slope*) rampe *f*, pente *f*.

2 **comp ▸grade book** (*US Scol*) registre *m* de notes **▸grade creep*** (*US Ind*) glissement *m* vers le haut d'un échelon salarial **▸grade crossing** (*US Rail*) passage *m* à niveau **▸grade inflation** (*US Educ*) surnotation *f* **▸grade point (average)** (*US Educ*) (note *f*) moyenne *f* **▸grade school** (*US*) école *f* primaire **▸grade separation** (*US Aut*) séparation *f* des niveaux de circulation **▸grade sheet** (*US Educ*) relevé *m* de notes.

3 **vt** a (*sort out*) *butter, milk, fruit, old clothes, accommodation, colours, questions* classer; (*by size*) *apples, eggs etc* calibrer. **the exercises are ~d according to difficulty** les exercices sont classés selon leur degré de difficulté; **~d reader** méthode *f* de lecture progressive.

b (*make progressively easier, more difficult, darker, lighter etc*) *work, exercises, colours etc* graduer. **~d** *charges, rates, tax* (*increasing*) progressif; (*decreasing*) dégressif; (*on graph*) **a nicely ~d curve** courbe *f* bien profilée; **a ~d series of transformations** une série progressive de transformations.

c (*Scol: mark*) *pupil, work* noter.

d (*Animal Husbandry: also* **~ up**) améliorer par sélection.

e (*US: level*) *ground* niveler.

f (*in hierarchy*) **to ~ according to performance/seniority** classer selon le rendement/l'ancienneté; **highly ~d** de haut niveau.

▸grade down **vt sep** classer *or* mettre *or* placer dans une catégorie inférieure.

▸grade up **vt sep** classer *or* mettre *or* placer dans une catégorie supérieure; *see also* **grade 3d.**

grader ['greɪdəʳ] **n** (*US Scol*) correcteur *m*; (*Constr*) niveleuse *f*.

gradient ['greɪdɪənt] **n** (*Brit*) rampe *f*, pente *f*, inclinaison *f*; (*Math, Phys*) gradient *m*. **a ~ of one in ten** une inclinaison de dix pour cent.

grading ['greɪdɪŋ] **n** (*gen*) classification *f*; (*by size*) calibration *f*; (*Scol etc*) notation *f*.

gradual ['grædjʊəl] 1 **adj** *change, improvement* graduel, progressif; *slope* doux (*f* douce). 2 **n** (*Rel*) graduel *m*.

gradually ['grædjʊəlɪ] **adv** graduellement, petit à petit, peu à peu.

graduate ['grædjʊeɪt] 1 **vt** a (*mark out*) *thermometer, container* graduer (*in* en).

b (*make progressively easier, more difficult, darker etc*) *work, exercises, colours etc* graduer. *[buyer]* **to ~ payments** payer par fractionnements progressifs (*or* dégressifs).

c (*US Scol, Univ*) conférer un diplôme à.

2 **vi** a (*Univ*) ≃ obtenir sa licence (*or* son diplôme *etc*); (*US Scol*) ≃ obtenir son baccalauréat. **he ~d as an architect/a teacher** *etc* il a eu son diplôme d'architecte/de professeur *etc*.

b *[colours etc]* se changer graduellement (*into* en), passer graduellement (*into* à).

3 ['grædjʊɪt] **n** a (*Univ*) ≃ licencié(e) *m(f)*, diplômé(e) *m(f)*.

b (*Pharm*) verre (*or* bocal *etc*) gradué.

4 ['grædjʊɪt] **adj** (*Univ*) *teacher, staff* ≃ diplômé, licencié. **~ assistant** étudiant(e) chargé(e) de travaux dirigés, moniteur *m*,-trice *f*; **~ course** études *fpl* de troisième cycle; (*US Univ*) **G~ Record Examination** *examen m d'entrée dans le second cycle;* (*US*) **~ school** troisième cycle *m* d'université; (*US*) **~ student** étudiant(e) *mf* de troisième cycle; **~ studies** études *fpl* de troisième cycle.

graduated ['grædjʊeɪtɪd] **adj** *tube, flask* gradué; *tax etc* progressif. **in ~ stages** par paliers, graduellement, progressivement; (*Brit*) **~ pension scheme** ≃ régime de retraite proportionnelle.

graduation [,grædjʊ'eɪʃən] **n** a (*see* **graduate 1a, 1b**) graduation *f*.

b (*Univ, also US Scol*) (*ceremony*) remise *f* des diplômes *etc;* (*by student*) réception *f* d'un diplôme *etc*. **~ day/ceremony** jour *m*/cérémonie *f* de la remise des diplômes.

graffiti [grə'fiːtɪ] **npl** graffiti *m*. **~ artist** graffiteur *m*, -euse *f* (*artiste*).

graft [grɑːft] 1 **n** a (*Agr*) greffe *f*, greffon *m*, ente *f*; (*Med*) greffe. **they did a skin ~** ils ont fait une greffe de la peau; **they did a kidney ~ on him** on lui a greffé un rein. b (*NonC: bribery etc*) corruption *f*. c (*Brit *: work*) dure besogne *f*. **hard ~*** boulot* acharné. 2 **vt** a (*Agr, Med*) greffer (*on* sur). b (*get by bribery etc*) obtenir par la corruption; (*get by swindling*) obtenir par (l')escroquerie. 3 **vi** (*engage in bribery*) donner (*or* recevoir) des pots-de-vin *mpl or* enveloppes* *fpl*; (*swindle*) faire de l'escroquerie.

grafter ['grɑːftəʳ] **n** a (*swindler etc*) escroc *m*, chevalier *m* d'industrie. b (**: Brit: hard worker*) bourreau *m* de travail.

graham ['greɪəm] **comp ▸graham cracker** (*US*) biscuit *m* de farine complète **▸graham flour** farine complète.

grail [greɪl] **n: the Holy G~** le Saint Graal.

grain [greɪn] 1 **n** a (*NonC*) grain(s) *m(pl)*, céréale(s) *f(pl)*; (*US*) blé *m*.

b (*single ~: of cereal, salt, sand etc*) grain *m*; *[sense, malice]* grain, brin *m*; *[truth]* ombre *f*, miette *f*. **a few ~s of rice** quelques grains de riz; **that's a ~ of comfort** c'est une petite consolation; *see* **salt.**

c (*in leather; also Phot*) grain *m*; (*in wood, meat*) fibre *f*; (*in cloth*) fil *m*; (*in stone, marble*) veine *f*. **with the ~** dans le sens de la fibre (*or* de la veine *etc*); **against the ~** en travers de la fibre (*or* de la veine *etc*); (*fig*) **it goes against the ~ for him to apologize** cela va à l'encontre de sa nature de s'excuser; **I'll do it, but it goes against the ~** je le ferai, mais pas de bon cœur *or* mais cela va à l'encontre de mes idées.

d (*weight*) *mesure de poids = 0,065 gramme*

2 **comp ▸grain alcohol** alcool *m* de grain **▸grain elevator** (*US*) silo *m* à céréales.

3 **vt** a *salt etc* grener, grainer, réduire en graine; *powder* granuler. **finely ~ed** à grain fin; **coarse ~ed** à gros grain.

b *leather, paper* greneler; (*paint in imitation of wood*) veiner.

graininess ['greɪnɪnɪs] **n** (*Phot*) grain *m*.

grainy ['greɪnɪ] **adj** (*Phot*) qui a du grain; *substance* granuleux.

gram [græm] **n** gramme *m*.

grammar ['græməʳ] 1 **n** a (*NonC*) grammaire *f*. **that is bad ~** cela n'est pas grammatical; *see* **generative** *etc*. b (*also* **~ book**) (livre *m* de) grammaire *f*. 2 **comp ▸grammar school** (*Brit*) ≃ lycée *m*; (*US*) ≃ école *f* primaire.

grammarian [grə'mɛərɪən] **n** grammairien(ne) *m(f)*.

grammatical [grə'mætɪkəl] **adj** grammatical.

grammaticality [grəmætɪ'kælɪtɪ] **n** grammaticalité *f*.

grammatically [grə'mætɪkəlɪ] **adv** grammaticalement.

grammaticalness [grə'mætɪkəlnɪs] **n** grammaticalité *f*.

grammatologist [,græmə'tɒlədʒɪst] **n** grammatologue *mf*.

grammatology [,græmə'tɒlədʒɪ] **n** grammatologie *f*.

gramme [græm] **n** (*Brit*) = **gram.**

Grammy ['græmɪ] **n, pl ~s** *or* **Grammies** (*US*) ≃ Victoire *f* de la musique.

gramophone† ['græməfəʊn] 1 **n** (*esp Brit*) phonographe *m*. 2 **comp ▸gramophone† needle** aiguille *f* de phonographe **▸gramophone† record** disque *m*.

Grampian ['græmpɪən] **n: the G~ Mountains, the G~s** les (monts *mpl*) Grampians *mpl*.

grampus ['græmpəs] **n, pl ~es** épaulard *m*, orque *m*; *see* **puff.**

gran* [græn] (*Brit*) **n** mémé* *f*, mamie* *f*, grand-maman *f*.

Granada [grə'nɑːdə] **n** Grenade (*en Espagne*).

granary ['grænərɪ] 1 **n** grenier *m* (*à blé etc*). 2 **comp** ® *bread, loaf, roll* complet (*f* -ète) (*avec grains concassés*).

grand [grænd] 1 **adj** a grand, magnifique, splendide; *person* magnifique, splendide; (*in official titles*) grand; *character* grand, noble; *style* grandiose, noble; *scenery, house* grandiose, magnifique, impressionnant; *job, post* important, considérable; *chorus, concert* grand. **in the ~ manner** dans un style de grand seigneur; **the ~ old man of music/French politics** *etc* le patriarche de la musique/de la politique française *etc;* (*US*) **G~ Old Party** parti républicain; *see also* **3.**

b (*excellent*) magnifique, sensationnel*, formidable*. **we had a ~ time** nous nous sommes formidablement* amusés; **it was a ~ game** le match a été magnifique.

2 **n** a (*US **) mille dollars *mpl*.

b piano *m* à queue *or* de concert; *see* **baby.**

3 **comp ▸the Grand Canyon** (*US*) le Grand Canyon; (*US*) **the**

Grand Canyon State l'Arizona *m* ▸**grandchild** petit(e)-enfant *m(f)*, petit-fils *m*, petite-fille *f* ▸**grandchildren** petits-enfants *mpl* ▸**grand(d)ad***, (*US*) **grand(d)addy*** grand-papa* *m*, pépé* *m*, bon-papa* *m* ▸**granddaughter** petite-fille *f* ▸**grand duke** grand duc ▸**grandfather** grand-père *m*; (*US fig: in law*) **grandfather clause** clause *f* d'antériorité; **grandfather clock** ≃ horloge *f* de parquet ▸**grand jury** (*US*) *(jury décidant de la mise en accusation)* ▸**grand larceny** (*US Jur*) vol qualifié ▸**grand mal** *see* **grand mal** ▸**grand(ma)ma*** grand-maman* *f*, mémé* *f*, mamie* *f*, bonne-maman* *f* ▸**grand master** (*Chess*) grand maître *m* ▸**grandmother** grand-mère *f* ▸**the Grand National** (*Racing*) le Grand National ▸**grand opera** grand opéra ▸**grand(pa)pa*** = **grand(d)ad** ▸**grandparents** grands-parents *mpl* ▸**grand piano** piano *m* à queue *or* de concert ▸**Grand Prix** *see* **Grand Prix** ▸**grand slam** (*Bridge, Sport*) grand chelem ▸**grandson** petit-fils *m* ▸**grand staircase** escalier *m* d'honneur ▸**grandstand** n (*Sport*) tribune *f* ◊ vi (*: *US fig*) jouer pour la galerie; (*US fig*) **grandstand play*** amusement *m* pour la galerie; (*fig*) **to have a grandstand view** être aux premières loges (*fig*) (*of sth* pour voir qch) ▸**grand total** (*gen*) somme globale; (*Math*) résultat final; (*fig*) **we get to the grand total of ...** nous arrivons au chiffre impressionnant de ... ▸**the Grand Tour** (*Hist*) le tour d'Europe; **we did a** *or* **the grand tour of the Louvre** nous avons fait le tour complet *or* une visite complète du Louvre ▸**grand vizier** grand vizir.

grandee [græn'di:] n (*in Spain*) grand *m* d'Espagne; (*fig*) grand manitou*.

grandeur ['grændjə^r] n *[person]* grandeur *f*; *[scenery, house etc]* splendeur *f*, magnificence *f*; *[character, style]* noblesse *f*; *[position]* éminence *f*. **an air of** ~ une allure grandiose.

grandiloquence [græn'dɪləkwəns] n grandiloquence *f*.

grandiloquent [græn'dɪləkwənt] adj grandiloquent.

grandiloquently [græn'dɪləkwəntlɪ] adv avec grandiloquence.

grandiose ['grændɪəʊz] adj grandiose; *style* grandiloquent, pompeux.

grandly ['grændlɪ] adv a (*splendidly*) **to live** ~ mener grand train; ~ **elegant/decorated** merveilleusement élégant/splendidement décoré. b (*rather pompously*) *speak, say* solennellement; *behave* avec majesté. ~ **called "The Palace"** grandiosement appelé "The Palace".

grand mal ['grɑ:*n*mæl] n épilepsie *f*, haut mal†.

Grand Prix [grɒ*n*'pri:] n (*Motor Racing*) Grand Prix *m*. **the French/Monaco** *etc* ~ le Grand Prix de France/de Monaco *etc*.

grange [greɪn*d*ʒ] n a (*esp Brit: country house*) château *m*, manoir *m*. b (*US: farm*) ferme *f*. **the G~** la fédération agricole. c (††) = **granary**.

granger ['greɪn*d*ʒə^r] n (*US*) fermier *m*.

granite ['grænɪt] 1 n granit *m*. 2 comp de granit ▸**the Granite City** (*Brit*) la cité de granit (*Aberdeen*) ▸**the Granite State** (*US*) le New Hampshire.

grannie, granny ['grænɪ] 1 n a (*) mémé *f*, mamie *f*, grand-maman *f*, bonne-maman *f*. 2 comp ▸**granny bond*** ≃ bon *m* du Trésor indexé ▸**granny flat*** petite annexe indépendante ▸**granny glasses*** petites lunettes cerclées de métal ▸**granny knot** nœud *m* de vache ▸**Granny Smith (apple)** granny smith *f inv* ▸**granny specs*** = **granny glasses**.

granola [græ'nəʊlə] n (*US*) muesli *m*.

grant [grɑ:nt] 1 vt a *favour, permission* accorder, octroyer; *prayer* exaucer; *wish* accorder; *request* accéder à, faire droit à; *pension etc* accorder, allouer. **to ~ sb permission to do** accorder à qn l'autorisation de faire; **to ~ sb his request** accorder à qn sa requête; **they were ~ed an extension of time** on leur a accordé un délai; **I beg your pardon! — ~ed!** je vous demande pardon! – je vous en prie!; **God ~ that** plaise à Dieu que + *subj*.

b (*admit*) admettre, accorder, concéder. **to ~ a proposition** admettre la vérité d'une proposition; **it must be ~ed that ...** il faut admettre *or* reconnaître que ...; **~ed that this is true** en admettant que ce soit vrai; **I ~ you that** je vous l'accorde; **I ~ that he is honest** je vous accorde qu'il est honnête; **~ed!** soit!, d'accord!; **he takes her for ~ed** il la considère comme faisant partie du décor; **stop taking me for ~ed!** j'existe moi aussi!, tu pourrais avoir quelques égards pour moi!; **to take details/sb's agreement** *etc* **for ~ed** considérer les détails/l'accord de qn *etc* comme allant de soi *or* admis; **we may take it for ~ed that he will come** nous pouvons tenir pour certain *or* compter qu'il viendra; **he takes it for ~ed that ...** il trouve tout naturel que ... (+ *subj*); **you take too much for ~ed** (*take too many liberties*) vous vous croyez tout permis, vous prenez trop de libertés; (*assume things are further forward than they are*) vous croyez que c'est si facile.

2 n a (*NonC*) *[favour, permission]* octroi *m*; *[land]* concession *f*; (*Jur*) *[property]* cession *f*; *[money, pension]* allocation *f*. (*Jur*) ~ **of a patent** délivrance *f* d'un brevet.

b (*sum given*) subvention *f*, allocation *f*; (*Brit: scholarship*) bourse *f*. **they have a government ~ to aid research** ils ont une subvention gouvernementale pour aider la recherche; **this student is on a ~ of £900** cet étudiant a une bourse de 900 livres; *see* **improvement**.

3 comp ▸**grant-aided** subventionné par l'État ▸**grant-in-aid** (pl **~s-~-~**) subvention *f* de l'État ▸**grant-maintained** subventionné (par l'État).

grantee [ˌgrɑ:n'ti:] n (*Jur*) (*gen*) bénéficiaire *mf*; *[patent]* impétrant *m*.

granular ['grænjʊlə^r] adj granuleux, granulaire.

granulate ['grænjʊleɪt] vt *metal, powder* granuler; *salt, sugar, soil* grener, grainer; *surface* rendre grenu. **~d paper** papier grenelé; **~d surface** surface grenue; **~d sugar** sucre *m* semoule.

granule ['grænju:l] n granule *m*.

grape [greɪp] 1 n (grain *m* de) raisin *m*, grume *f*. **~s** raisin (*NonC*), raisins; **to harvest the ~s** vendanger, faire la (*or* les) vendange(s); *see* **bunch, sour** *etc*. 2 comp ▸**grape harvest** vendange *f* ▸**grape hyacinth** muscari *m* ▸**grape juice** jus *m* de raisin ▸**grapeshot** mitraille *f* ▸**grapevine** (*lit*) vigne *f*; (*fig*) **I hear on** *or* **through the grapevine that ...** j'ai appris par le téléphone arabe *or* de mes sources personnelles que ..., mon petit doigt m'a dit que ... .

grapefruit ['greɪpfru:t] n, pl ~ *or* **~s** pamplemousse *m*.

graph [grɑ:f] 1 n (*gen*) graphique *m*; (*Ling*) graphe *m*. 2 comp ▸**graph paper** papier quadrillé; (*in millimetres*) papier millimétré ▸**graph plotter** table traçante. 3 vt tracer le graphique *or* la courbe de.

grapheme ['græfi:m] n graphème *m*.

graphic ['græfɪk] adj (*also Math*) graphique; (*fig*) *account, description of sth pleasant* pittoresque, vivant, animé; *of sth unpleasant* cru. ~ **artist** illustrateur *m*, -trice *f*; ~ **arts** arts *mpl* graphiques; ~ **design** graphisme *m*; ~ **designer** graphiste *mf*; ~ **equalizer** égaliseur *m* graphique; ~ **novel** roman *m* illustré, ≃ BD *f*; **in ~ detail** à grand renfort de détails.

graphical ['græfɪkəl] adj (*gen, also Math*) graphique. ~ **display unit** visuel *m* graphique.

graphically ['græfɪkəlɪ] adv (*in detail*) *describe, explain* à grand renfort de détails; (*clearly*) *convey, demonstrate, illustrate* très clairement.

graphics ['græfɪks] n a (*NonC*) (*art of drawing*) art *m* graphique; (*Math etc: use of graphs*) (utilisation *f* des) graphiques *mpl*; (*Comput*) traitement *m* graphique, graphiques *fpl*. b (*npl: sketches*) représentations *fpl* graphiques, graphisme *m*. (*TV etc*) ~ **by ...** art graphique (de) ...; *see* **computer**.

graphite ['græfaɪt] n graphite *m*, mine *f* de plomb, plombagine *f*.

graphologist [græ'fɒlədʒɪst] n graphologue *mf*.

graphology [græ'fɒlədʒɪ] n graphologie *f*.

grapnel ['græpnəl] n grappin *m*.

grapple ['græpl] 1 n (*Tech: also* **grappling iron**) grappin *m*. 2 vt (*Tech*) saisir avec un grappin *or* au grappin. 3 vi: **to ~ with** *person* lutter avec; *problem, task, book, subject* se colleter avec, se débattre avec.

grasp [grɑ:sp] 1 vt a (*seize*) *object* saisir, empoigner; (*fig*) *power, opportunity, territory* saisir, se saisir de, s'emparer de. **to ~ sb's hand** saisir *or* empoigner la main de qn; *see* **nettle**.

b (*understand*) saisir, comprendre.

2 n a poigne *f*. **a strong ~** une forte poigne.

b prise *f*, étreinte *f*. (*lit*) **to lose one's ~** lâcher prise; (*lit*) **to lose one's ~ on** *or* **of sth** lâcher qch; (*fig*) **to let sth/sb slip out of** *or* **from one's ~** laisser échapper qch/qn; (*lit, fig*) **to have sth within one's ~** avoir qch à portée de la main; **to have sb/sth in one's ~** avoir *or* tenir qn/qch en son pouvoir; **prosperity is within everyone's ~** la prospérité est à la portée de chacun.

c (*understanding*) compréhension *f*. **he has a good ~ of mathematics** il a une solide connaissance des mathématiques; **he has no ~ of our difficulties** il ne se rend pas compte de nos difficultés, il ne saisit pas la nature de nos difficultés; **it is beyond my ~** je n'y comprends rien, cela me dépasse; **this subject is within everyone's ~** ce sujet est à la portée de tout le monde.

grasping ['grɑ:spɪŋ] adj (*fig*) avare, cupide, avide.

grass [grɑ:s] 1 n a (*NonC*) herbe *f*; (*lawn*) gazon *m*, pelouse *f*; (*grazing*) herbage *m*, pâturage *m*. **"keep off the ~"** "défense de marcher sur le gazon"; (*fig*) **to let the ~ grow under one's feet** laisser traîner les choses, perdre son temps; **he can hear the ~ growing*** rien ne lui échappe; (*fig*) **the ~ is (always) greener on the other side of the fence** on jalouse (toujours) le sort du voisin; **at ~** au vert; **to put out to ~** *horse* mettre au vert; (*fig*) *person* mettre au repos; (*Agr*) **to put under ~** enherber, mettre en pré; *see* **blade, green, sparrow** *etc*.

b (*Bot*) **~es** graminées *fpl*.

c (*Drugs sl: marijuana*) herbe *f* (*sl*).

d (*Brit Prison sl: informer*) indic* *m* (*sl*), mouchard* *m*.

2 vt (*also* ~ **over**) *garden, square etc* gazonner; *field, land etc* couvrir d'herbe, enherber.

3 vi (*Brit Prison sl*) moucharder‡. **to ~ on sb** donner* *or* vendre* qn.

4 comp ▸**grass court** (*Tennis*) court *m* (en gazon); (*Tennis*) **to play on grass** *or* **on a grass court** jouer sur herbe *or* sur gazon ▸**grass cutter** (grosse) tondeuse *f* à gazon ▸**grass green** vert pré *inv* ▸**grasshopper** sauterelle *f* ▸**grassland** (*NonC*) prairie *f*, herbages *mpl* ▸**the grass roots** (*fig, esp Pol: of movement, party*) la base; (*Pol*) **grass-roots candidate/movement** *etc* candidat *m*/mouvement *m etc* populaire *or* du peuple *or* de la masse ▸**grass snake** couleuvre *f* ▸**grass widow** (*esp US*) divorcée *f*, femme séparée (de son mari); (*Brit fig*) **I'm a grass widow this week*** cette semaine je suis célibataire *f* (*hum*) *or* sans mari ▸**grass widower** (*esp US*) divorcé *m*, homme

séparé de sa femme.

grassy ['grɑːsɪ] adj herbeux, herbu.

grate[1] [greɪt] n (*metal framework*) grille *f* de foyer; (*fireplace*) cheminée *f*, âtre *m*, foyer *m*. **a fire in the ~** un feu dans la cheminée.

grate[2] [greɪt] 1 vt a (*Culin*) *cheese, carrot etc* râper. b *metallic object* faire grincer; *chalk* faire grincer *or* crisser. **to ~ one's teeth** grincer des dents. 2 vi *[metal]* grincer; *[chalk]* grincer, crisser (*on* sur). (*fig*) **to ~ on the ears** écorcher les oreilles; **it ~d on his nerves** cela lui tapait sur les nerfs* *or* le système*; **his constant chatter ~d on me** son bavardage incessant me tapait sur les nerfs* *or* m'agaçait.

grateful ['greɪtfʊl] adj reconnaissant (*to* à; *towards* envers; *for* de). **I am most ~ to you** je vous suis très reconnaissant; **I am ~ for your support** je vous suis reconnaissant de votre soutien; **he sent me a very ~ letter** il m'a envoyé une lettre exprimant sa vive reconnaissance; **I should be ~ if you would come** je vous serais reconnaissant de venir; **the ~ warmth of the fire** la chaleur réconfortante *or* l'agréable chaleur du feu; **with ~ thanks** avec mes (*or* nos *etc*) plus sincères remerciements.

gratefully ['greɪtfəlɪ] adv avec reconnaissance.

grater ['greɪtəʳ] n râpe *f*. **cheese ~** râpe à fromage.

gratification [ˌgrætɪfɪ'keɪʃən] n satisfaction *f*, plaisir *m*, contentement *m*; *[desires etc]* assouvissement *m*. **to his ~ he learnt that ...** à sa grande satisfaction il apprit que ... .

gratify ['grætɪfaɪ] vt *person* faire plaisir à, être agréable à; *desire etc* satisfaire, assouvir; *whim* satisfaire. **I was gratified to hear that** j'ai appris avec grand plaisir que, cela m'a fait plaisir d'apprendre que; **he was very gratified** il a été très content *or* très satisfait.

gratifying ['grætɪfaɪɪŋ] adj agréable, plaisant; *attentions etc* flatteur. **it is ~ to learn that** il est très agréable d'apprendre que, j'ai (*or* nous avons) appris avec plaisir que.

grating[1] ['greɪtɪŋ] n grille *f*, grillage *m*.

grating[2] ['greɪtɪŋ] 1 adj *sound* grinçant; *voice* discordant, de crécelle; (*annoying*) irritant, énervant, agaçant. 2 n (*NonC: sound*) grincement *m*.

gratis ['grætɪs] 1 adv gratis, gratuitement. 2 adj gratis *inv*, gratuit.

gratitude ['grætɪtjuːd] n reconnaissance *f*, gratitude *f* (*towards* envers, *for* de).

gratuitous [grə'tjuːɪtəs] adj a (*uncalled for*) gratuit, injustifié, sans motif. b (*freely given*) gratuit.

gratuitously [grə'tjuːɪtəslɪ] adv a (*for no reason*) gratuitement, sans motif. b (*without payment*) gratuitement, gratis.

gratuity [grə'tjuːɪtɪ] n a (*Brit Mil etc*) prime *f* de démobilisation. b (*tip*) pourboire *m*, gratification *f*. c (*to a retiring employee*) prime *f or* enveloppe *f* de départ.

gravamen [grə'veɪmen] n, pl **gravamina** [grə'væmɪnə] (*Jur*) ≃ principal chef *m* d'accusation.

grave[1] [greɪv] 1 n tombe *f*; (*more elaborate*) tombeau *m*. **from beyond the ~** d'outre-tombe; **he'll come to an early ~** il aura une fin prématurée; **he sent her to an early ~** il a sa mort sur la conscience; **someone is walking over my ~*** j'ai eu un frisson; **Mozart must be turning in his ~*** Mozart doit se retourner dans sa tombe*; *see* **dig, foot, silent** *etc*.

2 comp ▸**gravedigger** fossoyeur *m* ▸**graverobber** déterreur *m* de cadavres ▸**graveside: at the graveside** (*beside the grave*) près de la tombe; (*at the burial ceremony*) à l'enterrement ▸**gravestone** pierre tombale ▸**graveyard** cimetière *m*; (*fig*) **the graveyard of his hopes** l'enterrement *m* de ses espoirs; (*fig*) **a graveyard cough** une toux qui sent le sapin; (*US fig hum*) **graveyard shift*** le poste *or* l'équipe *f* de nuit.

grave[2] [greɪv] adj a *error, illness, misfortune, news* grave, sérieux; *matter* grave, important, de poids; *manner* grave, sérieux, solennel; *look* sérieux; *symptoms* grave, inquiétant. b [grɑːv] (*Ling*) *accent, sound* grave.

gravel ['grævəl] 1 n a (*NonC*) gravier *m*; (*finer*) gravillon *m*. b (*Med*) lithiase *f* urinaire. 2 vt couvrir de gravier. 3 comp ▸**gravel path** allée *f* de gravier ▸**gravel pit** carrière *f* de cailloux.

gravelly ['grævəlɪ] adj *road* caillouteux; *riverbed* pierreux, caillouteux; (*fig*) *voice* râpeux. **~ soil** gravier *m*.

gravely ['greɪvlɪ] adv *move, nod, beckon* gravement, sérieusement, solennellement; *speak* gravement, sérieusement, d'un ton grave *or* sérieux. **~ ill** gravement malade; **~ wounded** grièvement *or* gravement blessé; **~ displeased** extrêmement mécontent.

graven ['greɪvən] adj (††) taillé, sculpté. (*Rel etc*) **~ image** image *f*; (*fig*) **~ on his memory** gravé dans sa mémoire.

graveness ['greɪvnɪs] n (*NonC: all senses*) gravité *f*.

gravid ['grævɪd] adj gravide.

graving ['greɪvɪŋ] n (*Naut*) **~ dock** bassin *m* de radoub.

gravitate ['grævɪteɪt] vi (*Phys etc*) graviter (*round* autour de); (*fig*) graviter (*round* autour de), être attiré (*towards* par). **to ~ to the bottom** se déposer *or* descendre au fond (*par gravitation*).

gravitation [ˌgrævɪ'teɪʃən] n (*Phys, fig*) gravitation *f* (*round* autour de, *towards* vers).

gravitational [ˌgrævɪ'teɪʃənl] adj de gravitation, attractif. **~ constant/field/force** constante *f*/champ *m*/force *f* de gravitation; **~ pull** gravitation *f*.

gravity ['grævɪtɪ] n (*NonC*) a (*Phys*) pesanteur *f*. **the law of ~** la loi de la pesanteur; **~ feed** alimentation *f* par gravité; *see* **centre, specific.** b (*seriousness*) gravité *f*, sérieux *m*. **to lose one's ~** perdre son sérieux.

gravy ['greɪvɪ] 1 n a (*Culin*) sauce *f* au jus *m* de viande. b (*US* ‡) (*easy money*) profit *m* facile, bénef‡ *m*; (*dishonest money*) argent mal acquis. 2 comp ▸**gravy boat** saucière *f* ▸**gravy train‡**: (*fig*) **to be on** *or* **ride the gravy train** avoir une bonne planque‡, être planqué‡; (*fig*) **to get on the gravy train** trouver une bonne planque‡.

gray [greɪ] (*esp US*) = **grey**.

grayish ['greɪɪʃ] adj (*esp US*) = **greyish**.

grayling ['greɪlɪŋ] n, pl **~** *or* **~s** (*fish*) ombre *m* (de rivière).

graze[1] [greɪz] 1 vi brouter, paître. 2 vt a *[cattle] grass* brouter, paître; *field* pâturer (dans). b *[farmer] cattle* paître, faire paître.

graze[2] [greɪz] 1 vt a (*touch lightly*) frôler, raser, effleurer. (*Naut*) **to ~ bottom** labourer le fond; **it only ~d him** cela n'a fait que l'effleurer. b (*scrape*) *skin, hand etc* érafler, écorcher. **to ~ one's knees** s'écorcher les genoux; **the bullet ~d his arm** la balle lui a éraflé le bras. 2 n écorchure *f*, éraflure *f*.

grazing ['greɪzɪŋ] n (*NonC*) (*land: also* **~ land**) pâturage *m*; (*act*) pâture *f*.

grease [griːs] 1 n (*gen, also Culin*) graisse *f*; (*Aut, Tech*) lubrifiant *m*, graisse; (*dirt*) crasse *f*, saleté *f*. **to remove the ~ from sth** dégraisser qch; **his collar was thick with ~** son col était couvert d'une épaisse couche de crasse; *see* **axle, elbow** *etc*.

2 vt graisser; (*Aut etc*) lubrifier, graisser. **like ~d lightning*** à toute allure, en quatrième vitesse*, à toute pompe*, tel l'éclair (*hum*); *see* **palm**[1], **wheel** *etc*.

3 comp ▸**grease gun** (pistolet *m*) graisseur *m* ▸**grease monkey‡** mécano* *m* ▸**grease nipple** (*Aut*) graisseur *m* ▸**greasepaint** fard gras, maquillage *m* de théâtre; **stick of greasepaint** crayon gras ▸**greaseproof** (*Brit*) imperméable à la graisse; **greaseproof paper** papier sulfurisé ▸**grease remover** dégraisseur *m* ▸**grease-stained** graisseux.

greaser‡ ['griːsəʳ] n a (*mechanic*) mécano*. b (*motorcyclist*) motard* *m*. c (*pej: ingratiating person*) lèche-bottes* *m*. d (*US pej: Latin American*) Latino-Américain *m* (*surtout Mexicain*), ≃ métèque*.

greasiness ['griːsɪnɪs] n graisse *f*, nature graisseuse, état graisseux; *[ointment etc]* onctuosité *f*; (*slipperiness*) *[road etc]* surface grasse *or* glissante.

greasy ['griːsɪ] adj *substance, hair, food* graisseux, gras (*f* grasse), huileux; *tools* graisseux; *ointment* gras, huileux; (*slippery*) *surface, road etc* gras, glissant; *clothes, collar* (*oily*) taché de graisse; (*grubby*) sale, crasseux. **~ hands** mains pleines de graisse, mains graisseuses; (*fig*) **a ~ character** un personnage fuyant; **~ pole** mât *m* de cocagne; (*esp US*) **~ spoon*** gargote *f* (*pej*).

great [greɪt] 1 adj a *building, tree, fire, height, depth* grand; *cliff* grand, haut, élevé; *parcel* grand, gros (*f* grosse); *crowd, swarm* grand, gros, nombreux; *number, amount* grand, élevé; *heat* grand, gros, fort, intense; *pain* fort, intense; *pleasure, satisfaction, annoyance* grand, intense; *power* grand, énorme; *determination, will-power* fort; *person* (*in achievement*) grand, éminent, insigne; (*in character*) grand, supérieur, noble; (*in appearance*) magnifique, splendide; (*in importance*) grand, important, notable; (*chief*) grand, principal. **Alexander the G~** Alexandre le Grand; **a ~ man** un grand homme; **she's a ~ lady** c'est une grande dame; **the ~ masters** les grands maîtres; **a ~ painter** un grand peintre; **Dickens is a ~ storyteller** Dickens est un grand conteur; **the ~est names in football/poetry** *etc* les plus grands noms du football/de la poésie *etc*; **a ~ deal (of)** beaucoup (de); **a ~ many** beaucoup (de); **to a ~ extent** en grande partie; **to reach a ~ age** parvenir à un âge avancé; **~ big** énorme, immense; **with ~ care** avec grand soin, avec beaucoup de soin; **with ~ difficulty** à grand-peine, avec grande difficulté; **I envisage ~ difficulties** je prévois de grosses *or* grandes difficultés; **they are ~ friends** ce sont de grands amis; **Robert is my ~ friend** Robert est mon grand ami; **he has a ~ future** il a un bel *or* grand avenir (devant lui); **to take a ~ interest in** prendre grand intérêt à; **I have a ~ liking for/hatred of** j'éprouve une grande affection pour/une violente haine pour; **I have a ~ mind to do it** j'ai bien *or* très envie de le faire; **I have no ~ opinion of ...** je n'ai pas une haute opinion de ...; **at a ~ pace** à vive allure; **with ~ pleasure** avec grand plaisir, avec beaucoup de plaisir; **with the ~est pleasure** avec le plus grand plaisir; **a ~ while ago** il y a bien longtemps; (*Math etc*) **whichever is the ~er** on retiendra le montant le plus élevé; *see also* **3**.

b (*: *excellent*) *holiday, results etc* merveilleux, magnifique, sensationnel*, génial*, terrible‡. **it was a ~ joke** c'était une bonne blague* *or* une excellente plaisanterie; (*lit, iro*) **(that's) ~!** (c'est) super!* *or* génial!*; **you were ~!** tu as été magnifique! *or* merveilleux! *or* sensationnel!* *or* terrible!‡; **you look ~** (*healthy*) tu as vraiment bonne mine; (*attractive*) tu es très bien comme ça; **we had a ~ time** nous nous sommes follement amusés; **wouldn't it be ~ to do that** ce serait merveilleux de faire cela; **he's a ~ angler** (*keen*) il est passionné de pêche; (*expert*) c'est un pêcheur émérite; **he's ~ at football/maths** *etc* il est doué pour le football/les maths *etc*; **he's a ~ one* for cathedrals** il adore visiter les cathédrales; **he's a ~ one* for criticizing others** il ne rate pas une occasion de critiquer les autres; **he's a ~ arguer** il est toujours prêt à discuter; **he's ~ on jazz*** (*knowledgeable*) il connaît à fond le jazz; (*US: keen*) il est mordu* de jazz; **~ Scott!*†** grands dieux!†; **he's a ~ guy*** c'est un type sensass⁑ *or* génial* *or* terrible⁑; **he's the ~est!⁑** c'est lui le roi!⁑, il est champion!⁑; *see* **gun**.

2 **n** a **the ~** les grands *mpl*.

b (*Oxford Univ*) **G~s** ≃ licence *f* de lettres classiques.

3 **comp ▸great-aunt** grand-tante *f* **▸the Great Australian Bight** la Grande Baie Australienne **▸the Great Barrier Reef** la Grande Barrière de corail **▸Great Bear** (*Astron*) Grande Ourse **▸Great Britain** Grande-Bretagne *f* **▸greatcoat** pardessus *m*; (*Mil*) manteau *m*, capote *f* **▸Great Dane** (*dog*) danois *m* **▸the Great Dividing Range** la cordillère australienne **▸Greater London** (*Brit*) le grand Londres **▸Greater Manchester** *etc* l'agglomération *f* de Manchester *etc* **▸greatest common factor, greatest common divisor** (*Math*) plus grand commun diviseur **▸great-grandchild** arrière-petit(e)-enfant *m(f)* **▸great-granddaughter** arrière-petite-fille *f* **▸great-grandfather** arrière-grand-père *m*, bisaïeul *m* (*liter*) **▸great-grandmother** arrière-grand-mère *f*, bisaïeule *f* (*liter*) **▸great-grandson** arrière-petit-fils *m* **▸great-great-grandfather** arrière-arrière-grand-père *m*, trisaïeul *m* **▸great-great-grandson** arrière-arrière-petit-fils *m* **▸great-hearted** au grand cœur, magnanime **▸the Great Lakes** les Grands Lacs **▸great-nephew** petit-neveu *m* **▸great-niece** petite-nièce *f* **▸the Great Plains** les Grandes Plaines **▸the Great Powers** (*Pol*) les grandes puissances **▸great tit** (*Orn*) mésange *f* charbonnière **▸great-uncle** grand-oncle *m* **▸the Great Wall of China** la Grande Muraille de Chine **▸the Great War** la Grande Guerre, la guerre de 1914-18.

greater ['greɪtəʳ], **greatest** ['greɪtɪst] **adj compar, superl of great;** *see* **great**.

greatly ['greɪtlɪ] **adv** *love, regret, surprise etc* beaucoup; *loved, regretted, surprised* très, fort; *superior etc* de beaucoup, bien; *prefer* de beaucoup; *improve, increase etc* considérablement. **it is ~ to be feared/regretted** *etc* il est fort *or* bien à craindre/à regretter *etc*, il y a tout lieu de craindre/de regretter *etc*.

greatness ['greɪtnɪs] **n** a (*in size*) grandeur *f*; (*hugeness*) énormité *f*, immensité *f*; (*in degree*) intensité *f*. b (*of person: see* **great 1a**) grandeur *f*, éminence *f*; noblesse *f*; splendeur *f*, importance *f*.

grebe [gri:b] **n** grèbe *m*.

Grecian ['gri:ʃən] (*liter*) 1 **adj** grec (*f* grecque). **hair in a ~ knot** coiffure *f* à la grecque. 2 **n** (*Greek*) Grec(que) *m(f)*.

Greece [gri:s] **n** Grèce *f*.

greed [gri:d] **n** (*NonC*) (*for money, power etc*) avidité *f*, cupidité *f*; (*for food*) gourmandise *f*, gloutonnerie *f*.

greedily ['gri:dɪlɪ] **adv** avidement, cupidement; *eat* voracement, gloutonnement; *drink* avidement, avec avidité. **he eyed the food ~** il a regardé la nourriture d'un air vorace; **he licked his lips ~** il s'est léché les babines *or* les lèvres d'un air vorace.

greediness ['gri:dɪnɪs] = **greed**.

greedy ['gri:dɪ] **adj** (*for money, power etc*) avide (*for* de), rapace, cupide; (*for food*) vorace, glouton, goulu. **~ for gain** âpre au gain; **don't be ~!** (*at table*) ne sois pas si gourmand!; (*gen*) n'en demande pas tant!; (*pej*) **~ guts⁑** goinfre *m*, empiffreur⁑ *m*, -euse⁑ *f*; *see* **hog**.

Greek [gri:k] 1 **adj** grec (*f* grecque); *ambassador, king* de Grèce; *teacher, dictionary* de grec. **~ scholar** *or* **expert** helléniste *mf*; (*on china etc*) **~ key pattern, ~ fret** grecque *f*; (*US Univ*) **~ letter society** confrérie *f* (d'étudiants); **the ~ Orthodox Church** l'Église orthodoxe grecque. 2 **n** a Grec(que) *m(f)*. b (*Ling*) grec *m*. **ancient/modern ~** grec classique/moderne; (*fig*) **that's (all) ~ to me*** tout ça c'est de l'hébreu *or* du chinois pour moi*.

green [gri:n] 1 **adj** a (*colour*) vert; *complexion* vert, verdâtre. **light/dark ~** vert clair *inv*/vert foncé *inv*; **to turn ~** verdir; **he looked quite ~** il était vert; **she went ~** elle *or* son visage a verdi; (*fig*) **to be ~ with envy** être vert de jalousie; **to make sb ~ with envy** faire pâlir *or* loucher qn de jalousie; *see also* **4** *and* **baize** *etc*.

b (*Ecol*) (*ecological*) *issues, policies etc* écologique; (*: *ecologically aware*) *attitude, company, government etc* écologique; *person* écolo* *inv*; (*: *not harmful to the environment*) *product, washing powder etc* écologique; (*Pol*) *vote, voters* vert. **the G~s** les Verts *mpl*; (*Brit Pol*) **the G~ Party** le parti écologiste; **~ awareness** prise *f* de conscience des problèmes écologiques.

c (*unripe*) *fruit etc* vert, pas mûr; *bacon* non fumé; *wood* vert. **~ corn** blé *m* en herbe; **~ meat** viande trop fraîche.

d (*inexperienced*) jeune, inexpérimenté; (*naïve*) naïf (*f* naïve). **I'm not as ~ as I look!*** je ne suis pas si naïf que j'en ai l'air!; **he's as ~ as grass*** il ne connaît rien de la vie, c'est un innocent.

e (*flourishing*) vert, vigoureux. **~ old age** verte vieillesse; **to keep sb's memory ~** chérir la mémoire de qn; **memories still ~** souvenirs encore vivaces *or* vivants.

2 **n** a (*colour*) vert *m*. **dressed in ~** habillé de *or* en vert.

b pelouse *f*, gazon *m*; (*also* **village ~**) ≃ place *f* (du village) (*gazonnée*); (*Golf*) vert *m*; (*bowling ~*) *terrain gazonné pour le jeu de boules*.

c (*Brit: vegetables*) **~s** légumes verts.

3 **adv** (*Pol*) **to vote ~** voter vert; **to think ~** penser vert *or* environnement.

4 **comp ▸greenback** (*US*) (*: *dollar*) dollar *m* **▸green bean** haricot vert **▸green belt** (*Brit: Town Planning*) ceinture verte **▸the Green Berets** (*Mil*) les bérets verts **▸green card** (*Brit Aut*) carte verte; (*US: work permit*) permis *m* de travail **▸Green Cross Code** (*Brit*) code *m* de prévention routière destiné aux enfants **▸green currency** monnaie verte **▸green-eyed** aux yeux verts; (*fig*) jaloux, envieux; (*fig*) **the green-eyed monster** la jalousie **▸greenfield site** (*Ind*) emplacement *m* en dehors de la ville **▸greenfinch** verdier *m* **▸green fingers:** (*Brit*) **he's got green fingers** il a la main verte, il a un don pour faire pousser les plantes **▸greenfly (pl ~** *or* **-flies)** puceron *m* (des plantes) **▸greengage** *see* **greengage ▸greengrocer** (*Brit*) marchand(e) *m(f)* de fruits et légumes; **greengrocer's (shop)** magasin *m* de fruits et légumes **▸greenhorn** jeunot *m* **▸greenhouse** serre *f*; (*Phys*) **the greenhouse effect** l'effet *m* de serre; (*Phys*) **greenhouse gas** gaz *m* contribuant à l'effet de serre **▸green light** (*Aut*) feu vert; (*fig*) **to give sb the green light** donner le feu vert à qn; **to get the green light from sb** obtenir *or* recevoir le feu vert de qn **▸greenmail** (*US St Ex*) chantage *m* financier (*pour revendre au prix fort à une société les actions qui ont été achetées lors d'un raid*) **▸green man;** (*at pedestrian crossing*) **it's the green man** c'est vert (pour les piétons) **▸Green Mountain State** (*US*) le Vermont **▸Green Paper** (*Brit Pol*) ≃ livre blanc **▸green peas** petits pois **▸green pepper** poivron vert **▸the green pound** (*Econ*) la livre verte **▸green power** (*US fig*) *[money]* puissance *f* de l'argent **▸green revolution** (*Econ, Agric*) révolution verte **▸green room** (*Theat*) foyer *m* des acteurs *or* des artistes **▸greenshank** chevalier *m* aboyeur **▸green salad** salade *f* (verte) **▸greenstick fracture** (*Med*) fracture incomplète **▸greenstuff** verdure *f*; (*Culin*) légumes verts, verdure **▸greensward††** pelouse *f*, gazon *m*, tapis *m* de verdure **▸green thumb** (*US*) = **green fingers ▸green vegetables** légumes verts **▸greenway** (*US*) espace vert (pour piétons et cyclistes) **▸greenwood††** forêt verdoyante **▸green woodpecker** pic *m* vert.

greenery ['gri:nərɪ] **n** verdure *f*.

greengage ['gri:n,geɪdʒ] **n** (*Brit*) reine-claude *f*.

greening ['gri:nɪŋ] **n** (*NonC*) sensibilisation *f* à la cause verte *or* à l'environnement.

greenish ['gri:nɪʃ] **adj** tirant sur le vert, verdâtre (*pej*). **~-blue/-yellow/-brown** bleu/jaune/brun tirant sur le vert.

Greenland ['gri:nlənd] 1 **n** Groenland *m*. 2 **adj** groenlandais.

Greenlander ['gri:nləndəʳ] **n** Groenlandais(e) *m(f)*.

greenness ['gri:nnɪs] **n** couleur verte, vert *m*; *[countryside etc]* verdure *f*; *[wood, fruit etc]* verdeur *f*; *[person]* (*inexperience*) inexpérience *f*, manque *m* d'expérience; (*naïvety*) naïveté *f*.

Greenpeace ['gri:n,pi:s] **n** Greenpeace.

Greenwich ['grenɪtʃ, 'grenɪdʒ] **n: ~ (mean) time** heure *f* de Greenwich.

greeny* ['gri:nɪ] **adj** = **greenish**.

greet¹ [gri:t] **vt** *person* saluer, accueillir. **they ~ed him with cries of delight** ils l'ont salué *or* accueilli avec des cris de joie; **he ~ed me with the news that ...** il m'a accueilli en m'apprenant que ...; **the statement was ~ed with laughter** la déclaration fut accueillie *or* saluée par des rires; **this was ~ed with relief by everyone** ceci a été accueilli avec soulagement par tous; **to ~ the ear** parvenir à l'oreille; **an awful sight ~ed me** *or* **my eyes** un spectacle affreux s'offrit à mes regards.

greet² [gri:t] **vi** (*Scot: weep*) pleurer.

greeting ['gri:tɪŋ] **n** salut *m*, salutation *f*; (*welcome*) accueil *m*. **~s** compliments *mpl*, salutations; **Xmas ~s** souhaits *mpl or* vœux *mpl* de Noël; **~(s) card** carte *f* de vœux; **he sent ~s to my brother** il s'est rappelé au bon souvenir de mon frère; **my mother sends you her ~s** ma mère vous envoie son bon souvenir.

gregarious [grɪ'gɛərɪəs] **adj** *animal, instinct, tendency* grégaire; *person* sociable. **men are ~** l'homme est un animal grégaire.

Gregorian [grɪ'gɔ:rɪən] **adj** grégorien. **~ calendar/chant** calendrier/chant grégorien.

Gregory ['gregərɪ] **n** Grégoire *m*.

gremlin* ['gremlɪn] **n** (*hum*) diablotin *m* (malfaisant).

Grenada [gre'neɪdə] **n** la Grenade (*Antilles*). **in ~** à la Grenade.

grenade [grɪ'neɪd] **n** (*Mil*) grenade *f*; *see* **hand, stun**.

Grenadian [gre'neɪdɪən] 1 **adj** grenadin. 2 **n** Grenadin(e) *m(f)*.

grenadier [,grenə'dɪəʳ] **n** grenadier *m* (*soldat*).

grenadine ['grenədi:n] **n** grenadine *f*.

grew [gru:] **pret of grow**.

grey [greɪ] 1 **adj** gris; *hair* gris, grisonnant; *complexion* blême; (*fig*) *outlook, prospect* sombre, morne; *city* morne, triste. **he/his hair is going** *or* **turning ~** il grisonne/ses cheveux grisonnent; **he nearly went ~ over it** il s'en est fait des cheveux blancs; **he turned quite ~ when he heard the news** il a blêmi en apprenant la nouvelle; **~ skies** ciel gris *or* morne; **it was a ~ day** (*lit*) c'était un jour gris; (*fig*) c'était un jour triste; (*fig*) **~ matter*** matière grise, cervelle* *f*; (*fig*) **~ area** zone *f* d'incertitude, zone de flou; *see also* **4**.

2 **n** a gris *m*. **dressed in ~** habillé de *or* en gris; **hair touched with ~** cheveux grisonnants.

b (*horse*) cheval gris.

3 vi *[hair]* grisonner. **~ing hair** cheveux *mpl* grisonnants; **a ~ing man** un homme aux cheveux grisonnants; **he was ~ing at the temples** il avait les tempes grisonnantes.

4 comp ▸**greybeard** vieil homme ▸**grey-flannel:** (*US fig: pej*) **grey-flannel conformity** le conformisme des cadres ▸**Grey Friar** franciscain *m* ▸**grey-haired** aux cheveux gris, grisonnant ▸**greyhound** (*dog*) lévrier *m*; (*bitch*) levrette *f* ▸**grey lag goose** oie cendrée ▸**grey market** (*St Ex*) marché *m* gris ▸**grey mullet** mulet *m*, muge *m* ▸**grey squirrel** écureuil gris, petit-gris *m* ▸**grey wagtail** bergeronnette *f* des ruisseaux ▸**grey wolf** loup *m* (gris).

greyish [ˈgreɪɪʃ] adj tirant sur le gris, grisâtre (*pej*); *hair, beard* grisonnant.

greyness [ˈgreɪnɪs] n couleur *f* grise; *[hair]* couleur *f* grise, grisonnement *m* (*liter*); *[sky, weather]* grisaille *f*; (*fig: colourlessness*) grisaille *f*, morosité *f*.

grid [grɪd] 1 n a (*grating*) grille *f*, grillage *m*; (*network of lines on chart, map etc; also Rad*) grille; (*Culin: utensil*) gril *m*; (*Theat*) gril (*pour manœuvrer les décors*); (*Aut: on roof*) galerie *f*, porte-bagages *m inv*; (*electrode*) grille; (*Brit Elec: system*) réseau *m*; (*Surv*) treillis *m*. (*Brit Elec*) **the (national)** ~ le réseau électrique (national). b = **gridiron.** 2 comp ▸**gridiron** (*utensil*) gril *m*; (*US Ftbl*) terrain *m* de football américain ▸**gridlock** (*US*) *see* **gridlock** ▸**grid map** carte *f* (*or* plan *m*) quadrillé(e) *or* à grille ▸**grid reference** référence *f* de grille.

griddle [ˈgrɪdl] 1 n (*Culin*) plaque *f* en fonte (*pour cuire*); (*part of stove*) plaque chauffante. ~ **cake** (sorte *f* de) crêpe épaisse. 2 vt (*Culin*) cuire sur une plaque.

gridlock [ˈgrɪdlɒk] (*US*) n gros embouteillage *m* (*à un carrefour*).

grief [griːf] 1 n a (*NonC*) chagrin *m*, douleur *f*, peine *f*, (*stronger*) affliction *f*, désolation *f*. **to come to ~** *[person]* avoir un malheur *or* des ennuis; *[vehicle, rider, driver]* avoir un accident; *[plan, marriage etc]* tourner mal, échouer; **we came to ~** il nous est arrivé malheur; **good ~!*** ciel!, grands dieux! b (*cause of grief*) (cause *f* de) chagrin *m*. 2 comp ▸**grief-stricken** accablé de douleur, affligé.

grievance [ˈgriːvəns] n (*ground for complaint*) grief *m*, sujet *m* de plainte; (*complaint*) doléance *f*; (*injustice*) injustice *f*, tort *m*; (*Ind*) différend *m*, conflit *m*. **to have a ~ against sb** avoir un grief *or* un sujet de plainte contre qn, en vouloir à qn; **he was filled with a sense of ~** il avait le sentiment profond d'être victime d'une injustice; *see* **redress.**

grieve [griːv] 1 vt peiner, chagriner; (*stronger*) affliger, désoler. **it ~s us to see** nous sommes peinés de voir; **we are ~d to learn that ...** nous avons la douleur d'apprendre que ..., c'est avec beaucoup de peine que nous apprenons que ...; **in ~d astonishment** étonné et peiné, étonné et chagriné; **in a ~d tone** d'un ton peiné *or* chagriné. 2 vi avoir de la peine *or* du chagrin (*at, about, over* à cause de); (*stronger*) s'affliger, se désoler (*at, about, over* de). **to ~ for sb/sth** pleurer qn/qch.

grievous [ˈgriːvəs] adj *pain* affreux, cruel; *loss, blow* cruel; *wounds, injury* grave, sérieux; *fault* grave, lourd, sérieux; *wrongs* grave; *crime, offence* atroce, odieux; *news* pénible, cruel; *cry* douloureux. (*Jur*) ~ **bodily harm** coups *mpl* et blessures *fpl*.

grievously [ˈgriːvəslɪ] adv *hurt, offend* gravement, cruellement; *err, be mistaken* sérieusement, lourdement. ~ **wounded** grièvement blessé.

griffin [ˈgrɪfɪn] n (*Myth*) griffon *m*.

griffon [ˈgrɪfən] n (*Myth, Zool*) griffon *m*.

grift‡ [grɪft] (*US*) 1 n filouterie* *f*, escroquerie *f*. 2 vi filouter*, vivre d'escroquerie.

grifter‡ [ˈgrɪftəʳ] n (*US*) estampeur* *m*, filou *m*.

grill [grɪl] 1 n a (*Culin*) (*cooking utensil*) gril *m*; (*food*) grillade *f*; (*restaurant: also* **~room**) rôtisserie *f*, grill *m*. (*Culin*) **brown it under the ~** faites-le dorer au gril; *see* **mixed.** b = **grille.** 2 vt a (*Culin*) (faire) griller. **~ed fish** poisson grillé. b (*fig: interrogate*) faire subir un interrogatoire serré à, cuisiner*, mettre sur la sellette. 3 vi (*Culin*) griller.

grille [grɪl] n (*grating*) grille *f*, grillage *m*; *[convent etc]* grille; *[door]* judas *m* (grillé); (*Aut: also* **radiator ~**) calandre *f*.

grilling [ˈgrɪlɪŋ] 1 n (*fig: interrogation*) interrogatoire serré. **to give sb a ~** faire subir un interrogatoire serré à qn, mettre qn sur la sellette. 2 adj: **it's ~ (hot)* in here** on grille* ici.

grilse [grɪls] n, pl **~s** *or* ~ grilse *m*.

grim [grɪm] adj a *aspect* menaçant, sinistre; *outlook, prospects* sinistre; *landscape, building* lugubre; *joke* macabre; *smile* sardonique; *face* sévère, rébarbatif; *silence* sinistre. **to look ~** avoir une mine sinistre *or* sévère; ~ **reality** la dure réalité; ~ **necessity** la dure *or* cruelle nécessité; **the ~ truth** la vérité brutale; **with ~ determination** avec une volonté inflexible; **to hold on to sth like ~ death** rester cramponné à qch de toutes ses forces *or* comme quelqu'un qui se noie; *see* **reaper.**

b (*: *unpleasant*) désagréable. **life is rather ~ at present** les choses vont plutôt mal à présent, la vie n'est pas drôle actuellement*; **she's feeling pretty ~*** (*ill*) elle ne se sent pas bien du tout; (*depressed*) elle se sent très déprimée, elle n'a pas le moral*.

grimace [grɪˈmeɪs] 1 n grimace *f*. 2 vi (*from disgust, pain etc*) grimacer, faire la grimace; (*for fun*) faire des grimaces. **he ~d at the taste/the sight of ...** il a fait une grimace en goûtant/voyant ... .

grime [graɪm] n (*NonC*) crasse *f*, saleté *f*.

grimly [ˈgrɪmlɪ] adv *frown, look* d'un air mécontent; *continue, hold on* inexorablement, inflexiblement; *fight, struggle* avec acharnement. **"no surrender" they said ~** "nous ne nous rendrons pas" dirent-ils d'un air résolu; **"this is not good enough" he said ~** "ceci est insuffisant" dit-il d'un air mécontent.

grimness [ˈgrɪmnɪs] n *[situation]* réalité accablante; *[landscape]* aspect *m* lugubre *or* sinistre; *[sb's appearance, expression]* sévérité *f*, aspect lugubre *or* sinistre.

grimy [ˈgraɪmɪ] adj *place, building* sale, encrassé, noirci; (*with soot*) noir; *face, hands* crasseux, sale, noir.

grin [grɪn] 1 vi a (*smile*) sourire; (*broadly*) avoir un large *or* grand sourire. *face, person* **~ning** souriant; (*broader*) arborant un large *or* grand sourire; **to ~ broadly at sb** adresser un large sourire à qn; **to ~ like a Cheshire cat** avoir un sourire fendu jusqu'aux oreilles; **we must just ~ and bear it** il faut le prendre avec le sourire, il faut faire contre mauvaise fortune bon cœur. b (*in pain*) avoir un rictus, grimacer; *[snarling dog]* montrer les dents. 2 vt: **he ~ned his approval** il a manifesté son approbation d'un large sourire. 3 n (*smile*) (large) sourire *m*; (*in pain*) rictus *m*, grimace *f* de douleur.

grind [graɪnd] (vb: pret, ptp **ground**) 1 n a (*sound*) grincement *m*, crissement *m*.

b (*: *dull hard work*) boulot* *m* pénible; (*particular task*) (lourde) corvée *f*. **the daily ~** le boulot* quotidien, (*stronger*) le labeur quotidien; **I find maths/this essay a dreadful ~** pour moi les maths sont/cette dissertation est une vraie corvée; **it was an awful ~ for the exam** il a fallu bûcher ferme pour l'exam*.

c (*US *: swot*) bûcheur *m*, -euse *f*.

2 comp ▸**grindstone** meule *f* (à aiguiser); *see* **nose.**

3 vt a *corn, coffee, pepper etc* moudre; (*crush*) écraser, broyer; (*US*) *meat* hacher; (*in mortar*) piler, concasser; (*rub together*) écraser l'un contre l'autre; (*fig: oppress*) écraser, opprimer. **to ~ sth to pieces** réduire qch en pièces par broyage *or* en le broyant *or* en l'écrasant; **to ~ sth to a powder** pulvériser qch, réduire qch en poudre; **to ~ one's teeth** grincer des dents; **dirt ground into the carpet** saleté incrustée dans le tapis; **he ground his heel into the soil** il a enfoncé son talon dans la terre; (*fig*) **to ~ facts into sb's head** enfoncer des connaissances dans la tête de qn; (*loc*) **to ~ the faces of the poor** opprimer les pauvres; *see also* **ground²**.

b *gems* égriser, polir; *knife, blade* aiguiser *or* affûter (à la meule), meuler; *lens* polir; *see* **axe.**

c *handle* tourner; *barrel organ* faire jouer, jouer de. **to ~ a pepper mill** tourner un moulin à poivre.

4 vi a grincer. **the ship was ~ing against the rocks** le navire heurtait les rochers en grinçant; **to ~ to a halt** *or* **to a standstill** *[vehicle]* s'arrêter *or* s'immobiliser dans un grincement de freins; *[traffic]* se bloquer peu à peu; *[process, production, negotiations etc]* s'enrayer peu à peu.

b (*: *work hard*) bûcher‡ *or* boulonner‡ (dur *or* ferme).

▸**grind away*** vi bûcher‡ *or* boulonner‡ (dur *or* ferme). **to grind away at grammar** bûcher‡ *or* potasser‡ la grammaire.

▸**grind down** vt sep (*lit*) pulvériser; (*fig: oppress*) opprimer, écraser; (*wear down*) *one's opponents etc* avoir à l'usure. (*fig*) **they were ground down by taxation** ils étaient accablés *or* écrasés d'impôts; **ground down by poverty** accablé par la misère; **he gradually ground down all opposition to his plans** il a écrasé petit à petit toute tentative d'opposition à ses plans; *see also* **grind 3a.**

▸**grind on** vi *[person]* continuer péniblement *or* laborieusement; *[year, week, day etc]* s'écouler péniblement; *[war]* s'éterniser implacablement.

▸**grind out** vt sep: **to grind out a tune on a barrel organ** jouer un air sur un orgue de Barbarie; (*fig*) **he ground out an oath** il a proféré un juron entre ses dents; **he managed to grind out 2 pages of his essay** il est laborieusement arrivé à pondre‡ *or* à écrire 2 pages de sa dissertation.

▸**grind up** vt sep pulvériser.

grinder [ˈgraɪndəʳ] n a (*apparatus*) broyeur *m*, machine *f or* moulin *m* à broyer; (*in kitchen*) broyeur, moulin; (*tool*) meuleuse *f*; (*for sharpening*) affûteuse *f*, appareil *m* à aiguiser *or* à meuler. b (*person*) broyeur *m*, -euse *f*; (*for knives*) rémouleur *m*, -euse *f*; *see* **organ.** c (*tooth*) molaire *f*. d (*US* ‡: *Culin*) grand sandwich *m* mixte.

grinding [ˈgraɪndɪŋ] 1 n (*NonC: sound*) grincement *m*. 2 adj *hard work* écrasant, accablant. ~ **poverty** misère noire; **to bring to a ~ halt** *vehicle* arrêter dans un grincement de freins; *traffic* bloquer *or* paralyser peu à peu; *process, production, negotiations etc* enrayer peu à peu; **to come to a ~ halt** *[vehicle]* s'arrêter *or* s'immobiliser dans un grincement de freins; *[traffic]* se bloquer peu à peu; *[process, production, negotiations etc]* s'enrayer peu à peu.

grindingly [ˈgraɪndɪŋlɪ] adv: ~ **dull** d'une insipidité lancinante; **a ~ familiar routine** une routine d'une familiarité lancinante.

gringo [ˈgrɪŋgəʊ] n (*US pej*) gringo *m*, Ricain(e) *m(f)*.

grip [grɪp] 1 n a (*handclasp*) poigne *f*; (*hold*) prise *f*, étreinte *f*; (*Wrestling*) prise. **he has a strong ~** il a la poigne forte; **he held my arm in a vice-like ~** il me tenait le bras d'une poigne d'acier, il me serrait le bras comme un étau; (*Wrestling*) **arm** *etc* ~ prise de bras *etc*; **to get a ~ on** *or* **of sth** empoigner qch; (*fig*) **to get a ~ on** *or* **of o.s.*** se secouer*, se ressaisir; **get a ~ on yourself!*** secoue-toi un peu!*, ressaisis-toi!; **to keep a ~ on o.s.*** se maîtriser, se contrôler; (*lit*) **to lose one's ~** lâcher prise; **he lost his ~ on the rope** il a lâché la corde; **the tyres lost their ~ on the icy road** les pneus perdirent leur adhérence sur la chaussée gelée; (*fig*) **he's losing his ~*** il baisse*; (*hum*) **I must be losing my ~!*** je ne fais que des bêtises!; **to lose one's ~ on reality** perdre le sens de la réalité; (*fig*) **he had a good ~ on his audience** il tenait (parfaitement) son auditoire; **he had lost his ~ on his audience** il ne tenait plus son auditoire; **he has a good ~ on** *or* **of his subject** il possède bien son sujet, il connaît à fond son sujet; **he came to ~s with the intruder** il en est venu aux mains avec l'intrus; **to come** *or* **get to ~s with a problem** s'attaquer à un problème, s'efforcer de résoudre un problème; **we have never had to come to ~s with such a situation** nous n'avons jamais été confrontés à pareille situation; (*fig*) **to fall into the ~ of sb** tomber aux mains de qn; **in the ~ of winter** paralysé par l'hiver; **country in the ~ of a general strike** pays en proie à *or* pays paralysé par une grève générale.

b (*device*) serrage *m*.

c (*handle*) poignée *f*.

d (*suitcase*) valise *f*; (*bag: also US* **~sack**) sac *m* de voyage.

e (*Sport*) (*on racket*) prise *f* de raquette; (*on golf club, bat*) prise *f*.

f (*TV, Cine*) (*Brit*) ~, (*US*) **key ~** machiniste *mf* caméra.

2 **comp ▸grip strip** (*for carpet*) bande adhésive (*pour tapis*).

3 **vt** a (*grasp*) *rope, handrail, sb's arm* saisir; *pistol, sword etc* saisir, empoigner; (*hold*) serrer, tenir serré. **to ~ sb's hand** (*grasp*) saisir *or* prendre la main de qn; (*hold*) tenir la main de qn serrée; *[tyres]* **to ~ the road** adhérer à la chaussée; **the car ~s the road well** la voiture colle à la route.

b *[fear etc]* saisir, étreindre. **~ped by terror** saisi de terreur.

c (*interest strongly*) *[film, story etc]* empoigner. **a film that really ~s you** un film vraiment palpitant, un film qui vous empoigne vraiment.

4 **vi** *[wheels]* adhérer, mordre; *[screw, vice, brakes]* mordre; *[anchor]* crocher (sur le fond).

gripe [graɪp] 1 **vt** (*Med*) donner des coliques à. (*‡: anger*) **this ~d him** cela lui a mis l'estomac en boule*. 2 **vi** (*: *grumble*) ronchonner, rouspéter* (*at* contre). 3 **n** a (*Med: also* **~s**) coliques *fpl*. b (*: *complaint*) (*gen*) rogne* *f* (*NonC*), rouspétance* *f* (*NonC*). **his main ~ was that ...** son principal sujet de plainte *or* de rogne* était que ... . 4 **comp ▸gripe water** (*Brit*) calmant *m* (*pour coliques infantiles*).

griping ['graɪpɪŋ] 1 **adj** *pain* lancinant. 2 **n** (*: *NonC: grumbling*) rouspétance* *f*, ronchonnements* *mpl*.

grippe [grɪp] **n** (*US*) grippe *f*.

gripping ['grɪpɪŋ] **adj** *story, play* passionnant, palpitant.

grisly ['grɪzlɪ] **adj** (*gruesome*) macabre, sinistre; (*terrifying*) horrible, effroyable.

grist [grɪst] **n** blé *m* (à moudre). (*fig*) **that's all ~ to his mill** tout cela apporte de l'eau à son moulin.

gristle ['grɪsl] **n** (*NonC*) tendons *mpl*, nerfs *mpl* (*surtout dans la viande cuite*).

gristly ['grɪslɪ] **adj** *meat* nerveux, tendineux.

grit [grɪt] 1 **n** a (*NonC*) (*sand*) sable *m*; (*gravel*) gravillon *m*; (*rock: also* **~stone**) grès *m*; (*for fowl*) gravier *m*; (*: *courage*) cran* *m*. **I've got (a piece of) ~ in my eye** j'ai une poussière dans l'œil; **he's got ~*** il a du cran*. b (*US*) **~s** gruau *m* de maïs. 2 **vi** craquer, crisser. 3 **vt** a **to ~ one's teeth** serrer les dents. b **to ~ a road** gravillonner une route, répandre du gravillon sur une route.

gritter ['grɪtəʳ] **n** gravillonneuse *f*.

gritty ['grɪtɪ] **adj** *path etc* (couvert) de gravier *or* de cailloutis; *fruit* graveleux, grumeleux; (*: *plucky*) *person* qui a du cran*.

grizzle ['grɪzl] **vi** (*Brit*) (*whine*) pleurnicher, geindre; (*complain*) ronchonner*.

grizzled ['grɪzld] **adj** *hair, person* grisonnant.

grizzly ['grɪzlɪ] 1 **adj** a (*grey*) grisâtre; *hair, person* grisonnant. b (*whining*) pleurnicheur, geignard. 2 **n** (*also* **~ bear**) ours gris.

groan [grəʊn] 1 **n** (*of pain etc*) gémissement *m*, plainte *f*; (*of disapproval, dismay*) grognement *m*. **this was greeted with ~s** ceci fut accueilli par des murmures (désapprobateurs). 2 **vi** a (*in pain*) gémir, pousser un *or* des gémissement(s) (*with* de); (*in disapproval, dismay*) grogner. **he ~ed inwardly at the thought** il étouffa un grognement à cette idée. b (*creak*) *[planks etc]* gémir; *[door]* crier. **the table ~ed under the weight of the food** la table ployait sous le poids de la nourriture; (*hum*) **the ~ing board** la table ployant sous l'amoncellement de victuailles. 3 **vt** (*in pain*) dire en gémissant; (*in disapproval, dismay*) dire en grommelant.

groat [grəʊt] **n** (*Brit*) *ancienne petite pièce de monnaie*.

groats [grəʊts] **npl** gruau *m* d'avoine *or* de froment.

grocer ['grəʊsəʳ] **n** (*esp Brit*) épicier *m*. **at the ~'s (shop)** à l'épicerie, chez l'épicier; **the ~'s wife** l'épicière *f*.

grocery ['grəʊsərɪ] **n** a (*esp Brit: shop*) épicerie *f*. **he's in the ~ business** il est dans l'épicerie. b **I spent £7 on groceries** j'ai dépensé 7 livres en épicerie (*NonC*) *or* en provisions; **all the groceries are in this basket** toute l'épicerie est dans ce panier.

grog [grɒg] **n** (*Brit*) grog *m*.

groggy* ['grɒgɪ] **adj** *person* (*weak*) faible; (*unsteady*) vacillant, chancelant, groggy*; (*from blow etc*) groggy*, sonné*. **I still feel a bit ~** j'ai toujours un peu les jambes comme du coton, je me sens toujours un peu sonné* *or* groggy*; **that chair looks rather ~** cette chaise a l'air un peu bancale.

grogram ['grɒgrəm] **n** gros-grain *m*.

groin [grɔɪn] **n** a (*Anat*) aine *f*. b (*Archit*) arête *f*. c = **groyne**.

grommet ['grɒmɪt] **n** (*ring of rope, metal*) erse *f*, erseau *m*; (*metal eyelet*) œillet *m*.

groom [gruːm] 1 **n** (*for horses*) valet *m* d'écurie, palefrenier *m*; (*bridegroom*) (*just married*) (jeune) marié *m*; (*about to be married*) (futur) marié; (*in royal household*) chambellan *m*. 2 **vt** *horse* panser. **the animal was ~ing itself** l'animal faisait sa toilette; **to ~ o.s.** se pomponner, s'arranger; **well-~ed** *person* très soigné; *hair* bien coiffé; (*fig*) **to ~ sb for a post** *etc* préparer *or* former qn pour un poste *etc*; (*Cine*) **she is being ~ed for stardom** on la façonne pour en faire une star; **he is ~ing him as his successor** il en a fait son poulain.

grooming ['gruːmɪŋ] **n** a (*gen*) soins *mpl* de toilette *or* de beauté; (*well-groomedness*) apparence *f* (impeccable). b *[horse]* pansage *m*; *[dog]* toilettage *m*.

groove [gruːv] 1 **n** a (*for sliding door etc*) rainure *f*; (*for pulley etc*) cannelure *f*, gorge *f*; (*in column, screw*) cannelure; (*in record*) sillon *m*; (*in penknife blade*) onglet *m*. **it's in the ~‡** (*up-to-date*) c'est dans le vent‡; (*functioning perfectly*) ça baigne dans l'huile*, ça marche comme sur des roulettes*; **to get into a ~*** s'encroûter, devenir routinier; **he's in a ~*** il est pris dans la routine, il s'est encroûté. b (*US: great*) **it's a ~‡** c'est sensationnel*, c'est le pied‡. 2 **vt** a (*put ~in*) canneler, rainer, rainurer. b (*‡ US: like*) aimer, trouver à son goût. 3 **vi** (*‡ US*) prendre son pied‡.

groovy‡ ['gruːvɪ] **adj** (*marvellous*) sensass‡, vachement bien‡; (*up-to-date*) dans le vent*.

grope [grəʊp] 1 **vi** tâtonner, aller à l'aveuglette. **to ~ for sth** chercher qch à tâtons *or* à l'aveuglette; **to ~ for words** chercher ses mots; **to ~ (one's way) towards** avancer à tâtons *or* à l'aveuglette vers; **to ~ (one's way) in/out** *etc* entrer/sortir *etc* à tâtons *or* à l'aveuglette. 2 **vt** (*, *pej: touch sexually*) peloter*, tripoter*. 3 **n** (*, *pej, sexual*) *[couple]* **to have a ~** se peloter*; **all he wanted was a quick ~** il voulait juste la peloter un peu*.

▸grope about, grope around **vi** tâtonner, aller à l'aveuglette. **to grope about for sth** chercher qch à tâtons *or* à l'aveuglette.

groping ['grəʊpɪŋ] 1 **adj** a (*tentative*) tâtonnant. b (*pej*) **~ hands*** mains *fpl* baladeuses. 2 **n** a (*tentative attempt*) tâtonnement *m*. b (*: *pej*) pelotage* *m*, tripotage* *m*. **she was getting fed up of all this ~** elle commençait à en avoir marre de se faire peloter*.

gropingly ['grəʊpɪŋlɪ] **adv** à tâtons, en tâtonnant, à l'aveuglette.

grosgrain ['grəʊgreɪn] **n** gros-grain *m*.

gross [grəʊs] 1 **adj** a (*coarse*) *person* grossier, fruste, sans délicatesse; *food* grossier; *joke etc* cru, grossier. **~ eater** goulu(e) *m(f)*, glouton(ne) *m(f)*.

b (*esp US *: disgusting*) dégueulasse‡, dégueu‡.

c (*flagrant*) *injustice* flagrant; *abuse* choquant; *error* gros (*f* grosse), lourd. **~ ignorance** ignorance *f* crasse; **~ negligence** négligence *f* coupable.

d (*fat*) *person* obèse, bouffi, adipeux.

e (*Comm, Econ, Fin*) *weight, income, product, tonnage* brut. **~ domestic income** revenue *m* intérieur brut; **~ domestic product** produit *m* intérieur brut; **~ national product** produit national brut; (*Ind, Econ*) **~ output** production *f* brute.

2 **n** a **in (the) ~** (*wholesale*) en gros, en bloc; (*fig*) en général, à tout prendre.

b (**pl inv**) (*twelve dozen*) grosse *f*, douze douzaines *fpl*.

3 **vt** (*Comm*) faire *or* obtenir une recette brute de. **the company ~ed £100,000 last year** la compagnie a fait *or* obtenu une recette brute de 100.000 livres l'an dernier.

▸gross out* **vt** (*US*) dégoûter, écœurer.

▸gross up **vt sep** *interest, dividend, amount* calculer le montant brut *or* la valeur brute de.

grossly ['grəʊslɪ] **adv** a (*very much*) *exaggerate, overrate etc* énormément, extrêmement; *undervalued, underpriced* scandaleusement. **~ unfair** d'une injustice criante; **~ overweight** obèse. b (*coarsely*) *behave, talk* grossièrement.

grossness ['grəʊsnɪs] **n** *[person]* (*coarseness*) grossièreté *f*; (*fatness*) obésité *f*, adiposité *f*; *[joke, language]* grossièreté, crudité *f*; *[crime, abuse etc]* énormité *f*.

grot* ['grɒt] **n** (*NonC*) cochonnerie* *f*.

grotesque [grəʊ'tesk] 1 **adj** *appearance* grotesque, monstrueux; *idea, suggestion* grotesque, saugrenu. 2 **n** grotesque *m*.

grotesquely [grəʊ'tesklɪ] **adv** grotesquement.

grotto ['grɒtəʊ] **n, pl ~s** *or* **~es** grotte *f*.

grotty* ['grɒtɪ] **adj** (*Brit*) *room, surroundings, food, evening* minable*, affreux. **he was feeling ~** il ne se sentait pas bien, il se sentait tout chose*.

grouch* [graʊtʃ] 1 **vi** rouspéter*, ronchonner. 2 **n** (*person*) rouspéteur* *m*, -euse* *f*; (*complaint*) (*gen*) rogne* *f* (*NonC*), rouspétance* *f* (*NonC*). **his main ~ is that ...** son principal sujet de plainte *or* de rogne* est que ... .

grouchy* ['graʊtʃɪ] adj ronchon*, grognon, maussade.

ground[1] [graʊnd] 1 n a (*NonC*) **the ~** la terre, le sol; **to lie/sit (down) on the ~** se coucher/s'asseoir par terre *or* sur le sol; **above ~** en surface (*du sol*); **below (the) ~** sous terre; (*fig*) **to have one's feet firmly on the ~** avoir (bien) les pieds sur terre; **to fall to the ~** (*lit*) tomber à *or* par terre; (*fig*) *[plans etc]* tomber à l'eau, s'écrouler; **burnt to the ~** réduit en cendres; **to dash sb's hopes to the ~** anéantir *or* ruiner les espérances de qn; **to get off the ~** (*Aviat*) décoller; (*fig*) *[scheme etc]* démarrer; (*fig*) **to get sth off the ~** (faire) démarrer qch; (*fig*) **to run** *or* **drive a car into the ~** user une voiture jusqu'à ce qu'elle soit bonne pour la casse; (*fig*) **to run a business into the ~** laisser péricliter une entreprise; (*fig*) **that suits me down to the ~*** ça me va tout à fait; (*Naut*) **to touch ~** toucher le fond; *see* **thick, thin** *etc*.

b (*NonC: soil*) sol *m*, terre *f*, terrain *m*. **to till the ~** labourer la terre; **stony ~** terre(s) caillouteuse(s), sol *or* terrain caillouteux (*see also* **stony**); (*fig*) **to prepare the ~** préparer le terrain (*for* pour); *see* **break**.

c (*NonC*) (*piece of land*) terrain *m*, (*larger*) domaine *m*, terres *fpl*; (*territory*) territoire *m*, sol *m*. **hilly ~** contrée vallonnée, pays vallonné; **all this ~ is owned by X** c'est X qui possède toutes ces terres *or* tout ce domaine; **to hold** *or* **stand one's ~** tenir bon *or* ferme, ne pas lâcher pied; (*fig*) **to change** *or* **shift one's ~** changer son fusil d'épaule; **to gain ~** (*Mil*) gagner du terrain; *[idea etc]* faire son chemin; (*Mil, also fig*) **to give ~** céder du terrain; **to lose ~** (*Mil, also gen*) perdre du terrain; *[party, politician]* être en perte de vitesse; (*Econ*) **sterling lost ~ against the other European currencies** la livre a perdu du terrain face aux autres monnaies européennes; (*fig*) **to be on dangerous ~** être sur un terrain glissant; (*fig*) **forbidden ~** domaine interdit; (*fig*) **to be on sure** *or* **firm ~** être sûr de ce qu'on avance; **to be sure of one's ~** être sûr de son fait, parler en connaissance de cause; (*fig*) **to meet sb on his own ~** rencontrer qn sur son propre terrain; (*fig: in discussion etc*) **to go over the same ~ again** traiter les mêmes questions; *see* **common, cover, cut** *etc*.

d (*area for special purpose*) terrain *m*. **football ~** terrain de football; *see* **landing, parade, recreation** *etc*.

e (*gardens etc*) **~s** parc *m*.

f (*US Elec*) masse *f*, terre *f*.

g (*reason: gen* **~s**) motif *m*, raison *f*. **on personal/medical ~s** pour (des) raisons personnelles/médicales; **~s for divorce** motifs de divorce; **on what ~s?** à quel titre?; **on the ~(s) of** pour raison de; **on the ~s that** ... en raison du fait que ...; (*Jur*) **on the ~ that** au motif que; (*Jur*) **~s on which the application is based** moyens *mpl* invoqués à l'appui de la requête; **~ for complaint** grief *m*; **there are ~s for believing that** ... il y a des raisons de penser que ...; **the situation gives ~s for anxiety** la situation est (nettement) préoccupante.

h (*background*) fond *m*. **on a blue ~** sur fond bleu.

2 vt a *plane, pilot* empêcher de voler, interdire de voler à; (*keep on ground*) retenir au sol; (*US fig*) *student etc* consigner. **all aircraft have been ~ed** tous les avions ont reçu l'ordre de ne pas décoller.

b *ship* échouer.

c (*US Elec*) mettre une prise de terre à.

d (*fig*) *hopes etc* fonder (*on* sur). **well-~ed belief/rumour** croyance/rumeur bien fondée; **well ~ed in Latin** ayant de solides connaissances *or* bases en latin, possédant bien *or* à fond le latin.

3 vi *[ship]* s'échouer.

4 comp ►**ground angle shot** (*Phot, Cine*) contre-plongée *f* ►**ground attack** (*Mil*) offensive *f* au sol ►**ground bait** (*Fishing*) amorce *f* de fond ►**ground bass** (*Mus*) basse contrainte, basso *m* ostinato ►**ground cloth** (*US*) = **groundsheet** ►**ground colour** (*base coat*) première couche; (*background colour*) teinte *f* de fond ►**ground control** (*Aviat*) contrôle *m* au sol ►**ground crew** (*Aviat*) équipe *f* au sol ►**ground floor** (*Brit*) rez-de-chaussée *m* ►**ground-floor** (*Brit*) adj *flat* au rez-de-chaussée; (*fig*) **he got in on the ground floor** il est là depuis le début ►**ground forces** (*Mil*) armée *f* de terre ►**ground frost** gelée blanche ►**ground hog** (*US*) marmotte *f* d'Amérique; (*US*) **Ground Hog Day** le 2 (ou le 14) février (*date à laquelle on croit pouvoir prédire si les grands froids sont terminés*) ►**ground ice** glaces *fpl* de fond ►**ground ivy** lierre *m* terrestre ►**groundkeeper** gardien *m* de parc (*or* de cimetière, stade *etc*) ►**ground level**: **at ground level** au ras du sol, à fleur de terre ►**groundnut** (*Brit*) arachide *f*; (*Brit*) **groundnut oil** huile *f* d'arachide ►**ground plan** (*Archit*) plan *m*, projection horizontale; (*fig*) plan de base ►**ground pollution** pollution *f* des sols ►**ground rent** (*esp Brit*) redevance foncière ►**ground rules** (*gen*) procédure *f*; (*fig*) **we can't change the ground rules at this stage** on ne peut pas changer les règles du jeu maintenant ►**groundsheet** tapis *m* de sol ►**groundsman** (*Brit*) gardien *m* de stade ►**groundspeed** (*Aviat*) vitesse-sol *f* ►**ground staff** (*Aviat*) personnel *m* au sol ►**groundswell** *[sea]* lame *f* de fond; (*fig*) vague *f* de fond ►**ground-to-air missile** (*Mil*) engin *m* sol-air ►**ground-to-ground missile** (*Mil*) engin *m* sol-sol ►**ground water** (*Geol*) nappe *f* phréatique ►**ground wire** (*US Elec*) fil *m* de terre ►**groundwork** *[undertaking]* travail *m* préparatoire, préparation *f*; *[novel, play etc]* plan *m*, canevas *m* ►**ground zero** (*Mil: of nuclear explosion*) point *m* de radiation maximum au sol.

ground[2] [graʊnd] 1 pret, ptp of **grind**. 2 adj *coffee etc* moulu. (*US Culin*) **~ beef** viande hachée (de bœuf); **~ glass** (*rough surface*) verre dépoli; (*powdered*) verre pilé; **~ rice** semoule *f or* farine *f* de riz.

grounding ['graʊndɪŋ] n a *[ship]* échouage *m*. b *[plane]* interdiction *f* de vol. c (*in education*) connaissances fondamentales *or* de fond, base *f* (*in* en). **she had a good ~ in French** elle avait une base solide *or* de solides connaissances en français.

groundless ['graʊndlɪs] adj sans fond, mal fondé, sans motif.

grounds [graʊndz] n a (*coffee ~*) marc *m* (de café). b *see* **ground**[1] **1g**.

groundsel [graʊnsl] n séneçon *m*.

group [gru:p] 1 n (*gen, also Gram*) groupe *m*; *[mountains]* massif *m*. **to form a ~** (*lit*) se grouper; (*for discussion etc*) former un groupe; **to stand in ~s** se tenir par groupes; **literary ~** cercle *m* littéraire; **nominal/verbal ~** groupe nominal/verbal; *see* **blood, in, pressure** *etc*.

2 comp ►**group booking** (*Tourism*) réservation *f* de groupes ►**group captain** (*Brit Aviat*) colonel *m* de l'armée de l'air ►**group dynamics** la dynamique de(s) groupe(s) ►**Group of Three/Seven** *etc* (*Pol*) groupe *m* des trois/sept *etc* nations ►**group practice** (*Med*) cabinet *m* collectif; (*Med*) **group practice is expanding in this country** la médecine de groupe est en expansion dans notre pays ►**group sex**: **to take part in group sex** faire l'amour à plusieurs, se livrer à des rapports sexuels en groupe (*frm*) ►**group theory** (*Math*) théorie *f* des ensembles ►**group therapist** (*Psych*) (psycho)thérapeute *mf* de groupe ►**group therapy** (*Psych*) (psycho)thérapie *f* de groupe ►**group work** (*Soc*) travail *m* en groupe *or* en équipe.

3 vi (*also* **~ together**) *[people]* se grouper, former un groupe. **to ~ round sth/sb** se grouper *or* se rassembler autour de qch/de qn.

4 vt (*also* **~ together**) *objects, people* grouper, rassembler, réunir; *ideas, theories, numbers* grouper.

grouper ['gru:pəʳ] n mérou *m*.

groupie‡ ['gru:pɪ] n groupie‡ *f*.

grouping ['gru:pɪŋ] n groupement *m*. (*Fin, Jur*) **~s of companies** regroupements *mpl* de sociétés.

grouse[1] [graʊs] (*Orn*) 1 n, pl **~** *or* **~s** grouse *f*; *see* **black, red.** 2 comp ►**grouse-beating**: **to go grouse-beating** faire le rabatteur ►**grouse moor** chasse réservée (*où l'on chasse la grouse*) ►**grouse-shooting**: **to go grouse-shooting** chasser la grouse, aller à la chasse à la grouse.

grouse[2]* [graʊs] 1 vi (*grumble*) rouspéter*, râler*, récriminer (*at, about* contre). **stop grousing!** pas de rouspétance!* 2 n motif *m* de râler*, motif à rouspétance*, grief *m*.

grout [graʊt] 1 n enduit *m* de jointoiement. 2 vt mastiquer.

grouting ['graʊtɪŋ] n jointoiement *m*.

grove [grəʊv] n bocage *m*, bosquet *m*. **olive ~** oliveraie *f*; **chestnut ~** châtaigneraie *f*; **pine ~** pinède *f*.

grovel ['grɒvl] vi (*lit*) être à plat ventre, se vautrer (*in* dans); (*fig*) se mettre à plat ventre, ramper, s'aplatir (*to, before* devant, aux pieds de).

grovelling ['grɒvlɪŋ] adj (*lit*) rampant; (*fig*) rampant, servile.

grow [grəʊ] pret **grew**, ptp **grown** 1 vi a *[plant]* pousser, croître; *[hair]* pousser; *[person]* grandir, se développer; *[animal]* grandir, grossir. **she's letting her hair ~** elle se laisse pousser les cheveux; **that plant does not ~ in England** cette plante ne pousse pas en Angleterre; **how you've ~n** comme tu as grandi *or* poussé*; **he has ~n 5cm** il a grandi de 5cm; **to ~ into a man** devenir un homme; **he's ~n into quite a handsome boy** il est devenu très beau garçon en grandissant (*see also* **grow into**); (*liter*) **to ~ in wisdom/beauty** croître en sagesse/beauté; **she has ~n in my esteem** elle est montée dans mon estime; **we have ~n away from each other** nous nous sommes éloignés l'un de l'autre avec les années.

b *[numbers, amount]* augmenter, grandir; *[club, group]* s'agrandir; *[rage, fear, love, influence, knowledge]* augmenter, croître, s'accroître. **their friendship grew as time went on** leur amitié grandit avec le temps; **our friendship grew from a common love of gardening** notre amitié s'est développée à partir d'un amour partagé pour le jardinage.

c **to ~ to like/dislike/fear sth** finir par aimer/détester/redouter qch.

d (*+ adj = become: often translated by vi or vpr*) devenir. **to ~ big(ger)** grandir; **to ~ red(der)** rougir; **to ~ fat(ter)** grossir; **to ~ old(er)** vieillir; **to ~ angry** se fâcher, se mettre en colère; **to ~ rare(r)** se faire (plus) rare; **to ~ better** s'améliorer; **to ~ worse** empirer; **to ~ dark(er)** s'assombrir, s'obscurcir; **to ~ tired** se fatiguer, se lasser; **to ~ used to sth** s'habituer *or* s'accoutumer à qch.

2 vt *plants, crops* cultiver, faire pousser *or* venir; *one's hair, beard, nails etc* laisser pousser. **she has ~n her hair long** elle s'est laissé pousser les cheveux; **it's ~n a new leaf** une nouvelle feuille vient de pousser *or* d'apparaître; **to ~ horns** commencer à avoir des cornes; **compost-~n vegetables** légumes *mpl* cultivés dans le compost.

3 comp ►**grow bag** (*Gardening*) *sac contenant du terreau enrichi où l'on peut faire pousser directement des légumes, fleurs etc.*

►**grow apart** vi *[two people]* devenir peu à peu étranger l'un pour l'autre; *[group of people]* devenir peu à peu étrangers les uns pour les autres.

►**grow in** vi *[nail]* s'incarner; *[hair]* repousser.

►**grow into** vt fus *clothes* devenir assez grand pour mettre. **he grew into**

the job c'est en forgeant qu'il devint forgeron, il a petit à petit appris le métier *or* les ficelles du métier; **to grow into the habit of doing** acquérir (avec le temps) l'habitude de faire, prendre le pli de faire; *see also* **grow 1a**.

►**grow on** vt fus *[habit etc]* s'imposer petit à petit à; *[book, music etc]* plaire de plus en plus à. **his paintings grow on one** on finit par se faire à ses tableaux, plus on voit ses tableaux plus on les apprécie.

►**grow out of** vt fus *clothes* devenir trop grand pour. **he's grown out of this jacket** cette veste est trop petite pour lui; **he grew out of (his) asthma/acne** son asthme/acné lui a passé avec le temps; **to grow out of the habit of doing** perdre (en grandissant *or* avec l'âge) l'habitude de faire.

►**grow up** 1 vi a *[person, animal]* devenir adulte. **when I grow up I'm going to be a doctor** quand je serai grand je serai médecin; **grow up!*** ne sois pas si enfant! *or* si gamin! b *[friendship, hatred etc]* naître, se développer; *[custom]* naître, se répandre. 2 **grown-up** adj, n *see* **grown-up**.

grower ['grəʊəʳ] n a (*person*) producteur *m*, -trice *f*, cultivateur *m*, -trice *f*. **vegetable ~** maraîcher *m*, -ère *f*; *see* **rose**[2] *etc*. b **this plant is a slow ~** cette plante pousse lentement.

growing ['grəʊɪŋ] 1 adj a *plant* qui pousse. **~ crops** récoltes *fpl* sur pied; **fast-/slow- ~** à croissance rapide/lente.

b *child* en cours de croissance, qui grandit. **he's a ~ boy** c'est un enfant qui grandit.

c (*increasing*) *number, amount* grandissant, qui augmente; *club, group* qui s'agrandit; *friendship, hatred* grandissant, croissant. **a ~ opinion** opinion de plus en plus répandue; **a ~ feeling of frustration** un sentiment croissant *or* grandissant de frustration; **to have a ~ desire to do sth** avoir de plus en plus envie de faire qch.

2 n (*act*) croissance *f*; (*Agr*) culture *f*. (*Agr*) **~ season** période *f* de pousse; **~ pains*** (*Med*) douleurs *fpl* de croissance; (*fig*) *[business, project]* difficultés *fpl* de croissance.

growl [graʊl] 1 vi *[animal]* grogner, gronder (*at* contre); *[person]* grogner, ronchonner*; *[thunder]* tonner, gronder. 2 vt *reply etc* grogner, grommeler. 3 n grognement *m*, grondement *m*. **to give a ~** grogner.

grown [grəʊn] 1 ptp of **grow**; *see also* **home 3**. 2 adj a (*also* **fully ~**) *person, animal* adulte, qui a fini sa croissance. **he's a ~ man** il est adulte. b **wall ~ over with ivy** mur (tout) couvert de lierre; **weed-~** envahi par les mauvaises herbes; *see also* **grow 2**.

grown-up [,grəʊn'ʌp] 1 adj *behaviour* de grande personne, adulte. **when he is ~** quand il sera grand; **she is very ~** elle est très sérieuse *or* elle a beaucoup de maturité pour son âge; **she looks very ~** elle fait très grande personne; **a ~ daughter** une fille adulte; **try to be more ~ about it** ne sois pas aussi puéril, essaie de faire preuve d'un peu plus de maturité. 2 n grande personne *f*, adulte *mf*. **the ~s** les grandes personnes.

growth [grəʊθ] 1 n a (*NonC: development*) *[plant]* croissance *f*, développement *m*; *[person]* croissance. **to reach full ~** *[plant]* arriver à maturité; *[person]* avoir fini sa croissance.

b (*NonC: increase*) *[numbers, amount]* augmentation *f*; *[business, trade]* expansion *f*, croissance *f* (*in* de); *[club, group]* croissance; *[fear, love]* croissance, poussée *f*; *[influence, economy, knowledge, friendship]* croissance, développement *m*. (*Econ*) **these measures encourage ~** ces mesures favorisent la croissance; **the ~ of public interest in ...** l'intérêt croissant du public pour ... .

c (*what has grown*) pousse *f*, poussée *f*. **a thick ~ of weeds** des mauvaises herbes qui ont poussé dru; **a 5 days' ~ of beard** une barbe de 5 jours; **a new ~ of hair** une nouvelle pousse *or* poussée de cheveux.

d (*Med*) grosseur *f*, excroissance *f*, tumeur *f*. **benign/malignant ~** tumeur bénigne/maligne.

2 comp *market, point* n voie de développement *or* de croissance, en (pleine) expansion ►**growth hormone** hormone *f* de croissance ►**growth industry** industrie *f* en pleine expansion ►**growth rate** taux *m* de croissance ►**growth shares** (*Brit*), **growth stock** (*US*) actions *fpl* susceptibles d'une hausse rapide.

groyne [grɔɪn] n (*esp Brit*) brise-lames *m inv*.

grub [grʌb] 1 n a (*larva*) larve *f*; (*in apple etc*) ver *m*, asticot *m*. b (‡: *NonC: food*) boustifaille‡ *f*, bouffe‡ *f*. **~ up!** à la soupe!* 2 comp ►**grubstake*** (*US*) (*Hist*) n avance *f* faite à un prospecteur ◊ vt accorder une avance à; (*Fin*) financer (*pendant la phase de lancement*); (*Fin*) **to put up a grubstake for sb** fournir les fonds nécessaires à qn (pour le lancement d'une entreprise ou d'un projet). 3 vt *[animal] ground, soil* fouir. 4 vi (*also* **~ about, ~ around**) fouiller, fouiner (*in, among* dans). **he was ~bing (about *or* around) in the earth for a pebble** il fouinait dans la terre *or* fouillait le sol pour trouver un caillou.

►**grub up** vt sep *soil* fouir; *object* déterrer.

grubbiness ['grʌbɪnɪs] n saleté *f*.

grubby ['grʌbɪ] adj sale, pas très propre *or* net.

grudge [grʌdʒ] 1 vt donner *or* accorder à contrecœur *or* en rechignant *or* à regret. **to ~ doing** faire à contrecœur, rechigner à faire; **he ~s her even the food she eats** il lui mesure jusqu'à sa nourriture, il lésine même sur sa nourriture; **do you ~ me these pleasures?** me reprochez-vous ces (petits) plaisirs?; **they ~d him his success** ils lui en voulaient de sa réussite; **she ~s paying £2 a ticket** cela lui fait mal au cœur de *or* elle la trouve mauvaise de payer 2 livres un billet; **I shan't ~ you £5** je ne vais pas te refuser 5 livres; **it's not the money I ~ but the time** ce n'est pas la dépense mais le temps que je plains.

2 n rancune *f*. **to bear *or* have a ~ against sb** en vouloir à qn, garder rancune à qn, avoir une dent contre qn; **to pay off a ~** satisfaire une rancune.

grudging ['grʌdʒɪŋ] adj *person, attitude* radin*, mesquin, peu généreux; *contribution* parcimonieux; *gift, praise etc* accordé *or* donné à regret *or* à contrecœur. **with ~ admiration** avec une admiration réticente.

grudgingly ['grʌdʒɪŋlɪ] adv *give, help* à contrecœur, de mauvaise grâce; *say, agree* de mauvaise grâce.

gruel [grʊəl] n gruau *m*.

gruelling, (*US*) **grueling** ['grʊəlɪŋ] adj *march, match, race etc* exténuant, épuisant, éreintant*.

gruesome ['gru:səm] adj horrible, épouvantable, infâme, révoltant. **in ~ detail** jusque dans les plus horribles détails.

gruff [grʌf] adj *person* brusque, bourru; *voice* gros (*f* grosse), bourru.

gruffly ['grʌflɪ] adv d'un ton bourru *or* rude, avec brusquerie.

gruffness ['grʌfnɪs] n *[person, manner]* brusquerie *f*; *[voice]* ton *m* bourru.

grumble ['grʌmbl] 1 vi *[person]* grogner, grommeler, maugréer, ronchonner, rouspéter* (*at, about* contre), se plaindre (*about, at* de); *[thunder]* gronder. **he's always grumbling** il est toujours à grommeler. 2 n grognement *m*, ronchonnement* *m*. **to do sth without a ~** faire qch sans murmurer; **after a long ~ about ...** après une longue lamentation à propos de ...; **~s** récriminations *fpl*.

grumbling ['grʌmblɪŋ] 1 n (*NonC*) récriminations *fpl*. 2 adj *person* grognon, grincheux, bougon. **a ~ sound** un grondement; (*Med*) **~ appendix** appendicite *f* chronique.

grummet ['grʌmɪt] n = **grommet**.

grumpily ['grʌmpɪlɪ] adv d'un ton *or* d'une façon maussade, en bougonnant *or* ronchonnant.

grumpiness ['grʌmpɪnɪs] n (*permanent*) mauvais caractère *m*. (*temporary*) **sorry for my ~ yesterday** désolé d'avoir été grognon *or* grincheux hier.

grumpy ['grʌmpɪ] adj grognon, grincheux, renfrogné.

grungy* ['grʌndʒɪ] adj (*US*) minable*.

grunt [grʌnt] 1 vi *[pig, person]* grogner. 2 vt grogner. **to ~ a reply** grommeler *or* grogner une réponse; **"no" he ~ed** "non" grommela-t-il. 3 n a grognement *m*. **to give a ~** pousser *or* faire entendre un grognement; (*in reply*) répondre par un grognement; **with a ~ of distaste** avec un grognement dégoûté *or* de dégoût. b (*US* ‡: *soldier*) fantassin *m*, troufion* *m*, bidasse* *m*.

gruppetto [gru:'petəʊ] n, pl **gruppetti** [gru:'peti:] (*Mus*) gruppetto *m*.

gryphon ['grɪfən] n = **griffin**.

GT ['dʒi:'ti:] n (abbr of **gran turismo**) GT *f*.

GTi [,dʒi:ti:'aɪ] n (abbr of **gran turismo injection**) GTi *f*.

GU (*US Post*) abbr of **Guam**.

guacamole [,gwɑ:kə'məʊlɪ] n (*US Culin*) purée *f* d'avocats (fortement assaisonnée).

Guadeloupe [,gwɑ:də'lu:p] n la Guadeloupe.

Guam [gwɑ:m] n Guam *f*.

guano ['gwɑ:nəʊ] n (*NonC*) guano *m*.

guarantee [,gærən'ti:] 1 n a (*Comm etc: promise, assurance*) garantie *f*. **there is a year's ~ on this watch** cette montre est garantie un an, cette montre a une garantie d'un an; **a ~ against defective workmanship** une garantie contre les malfaçons; **"money-back ~ with all items"** "remboursement garanti sur tous articles"; **you must read the ~ carefully** il faut lire attentivement la garantie; **you have/I give you my ~ that ...** vous avez/je vous donne ma garantie que ...; **there's no ~ that it will happen** il n'est pas garanti *or* dit que cela arrivera; **there's no ~ that it actually happened** il n'est pas certain que cela soit arrivé; **health is not a ~ of happiness** la santé n'est pas une garantie de bonheur.

b (*Jur etc: pledge, security*) garantie *f*, caution *f*. (*Fin*) **~ for a bill** aval *m* d'une traite; **to give sth as (a) ~** donner qch en caution; **he left his watch as a ~ of payment** il a laissé sa montre en garantie de paiement *or* en gage; **what ~ can you offer?** quelle caution pouvez-vous donner?

c = **guarantor**.

2 comp ►**guarantee form** garantie *f* (*fiche*).

3 vt *goods etc* garantir, assurer (*against* contre, *for 2 years* pendant 2 ans). **~d waterproof** garanti imperméable; **~d not to rust** garanti inoxydable; **~d price** prix garanti; **~d loan** prêt privilégié; (*US Univ*) **~d student loan** prêt *m* d'honneur (*à un étudiant*); **I will ~ his good behaviour** je me porte garant de sa bonne conduite; **to ~ a loan** se porter garant *or* caution d'un emprunt; **I will ~ him for a £500 loan** je lui servirai de garant *or* de caution pour un emprunt de 500 livres; **I ~ that it won't happen again** je garantis *or* certifie que cela ne se reproduira pas; **I can't ~ that he will come** je ne peux pas garantir sa venue *or* qu'il viendra, je ne peux pas certifier qu'il viendra; **I can't ~ that he did it** je ne peux pas certifier qu'il l'ait fait; **we can't ~ good weather** nous ne pouvons pas garantir le beau temps *or* certifier qu'il

fera beau.

guarantor [ˌgærən'tɔːʳ] n garant(e) *m(f)*, caution *f*. **to stand ~ for sb** se porter garant *or* caution de qn; **will you be my ~ for the loan?** me servirez-vous de garant *or* de caution pour l'emprunt?

guaranty ['gærəntɪ] n (*Fin*) garantie *f*, caution *f*; (*agreement*) garantie; (*sth held as security*) garantie, caution.

guard [gɑːd] 1 n a (*NonC*) garde *f*, surveillance *f*; (*Boxing, Fencing, Mil etc*) garde. **to go on/come off ~** prendre/finir son tour de garde; **to be on ~** être de garde *or* de faction; **to keep** *or* **stand ~** être de garde, monter la garde; **to keep** *or* **stand ~ on** (*against attack*) garder; (*against theft, escape*) surveiller; **to stand ~ over sb/sth** monter la garde auprès de qn/qch; **to be under ~** être sous surveillance *or* sous bonne garde; **he was taken under ~ to ...** il a été emmené sous escorte à ...; **to keep sb under ~** garder qn sous surveillance; **to put a ~ on sb/sth** faire surveiller qn/qch; (*Sport*) **on ~!** en garde!; **to be on one's ~** se méfier (*against* de), être *or* se tenir sur ses gardes (*against* contre); **to put sb on his ~** mettre qn en garde (*against* contre); **to be off (one's) guard** ne pas être *or* ne pas se tenir sur ses gardes; **to put sb off (his) ~** tromper la vigilance de qn; **to catch sb off his ~** prendre qn au dépourvu; **he wears goggles as a ~ against accidents** il porte des lunettes protectrices par précaution contre les accidents; *see* **mount** *etc*.

b (*Mil etc*) (*squad of men*) garde *f*; (*one man*) garde *m*. (*lit, fig*) **~ of honour** garde *f* d'honneur; (*on either side*) haie *f* d'honneur; **one of the old ~** un vieux de la vieille*; (*Brit Mil*) **the G~s** les régiments *mpl* de la garde royale; *see* **change, life, security** *etc*.

c (*Brit Rail*) chef *m* de train.

d (*on machine*) dispositif *m* de sûreté; (*on sword*) garde *f*; *see* **fire** *etc*.

e (*Basketball*) **left/right ~** arrière *m* gauche/droit.

2 comp ▸**guard dog** chien *m* de garde ▸**guard duty**: (*Mil*) **to be on guard duty** être de garde *or* de faction ▸**guardhouse** (*Mil*) (*for guards*) corps *m* de garde; (*for prisoners*) salle *f* de police ▸**guardrail** barrière *f* de sécurité ▸**guardroom** (*Mil*) corps *m* de garde ▸**guardsman** (*Brit Mil*) garde *m* (*soldat m de la garde royale*); (*US*) soldat de la garde nationale ▸**guard's van** (*Brit Rail*) fourgon *m* du chef de train.

3 vt (*against attack*) garder (*from, against* contre); (*against theft, escape*) surveiller; (*Cards, Chess*) garder; (*fig*) *one's tongue, passions etc* surveiller. **the frontier is heavily ~ed** la frontière est solidement gardée; **the dog ~ed the house** le chien gardait la maison; **~ it with your life!** veillez bien dessus!; (*fig*) **to ~ o.s. against sth** se prémunir contre qch, se garder contre qch.

▸**guard against** vt fus se protéger contre, se défendre contre, se prémunir contre. **to guard against doing** (bien) se garder de faire; **in order to guard against this** pour éviter cela; **we must try to guard against this happening** nous devons essayer d'empêcher que cela ne se produise.

guarded ['gɑːdɪd] adj *machinery* protégé; *prisoner* sous surveillance, gardé à vue; *remark, smile* prudent, circonspect, réservé.

guardedly ['gɑːdɪdlɪ] adv avec réserve, avec circonspection, prudemment.

guardedness ['gaːdɪdnɪs] n circonspection *f*, prudence *f*.

guardian ['gɑːdɪən] 1 n a gardien(ne) *m(f)*, protecteur *m*, -trice *f*. b [*minor*] tuteur *m*, -trice *f*. 2 adj gardien. **~ angel** ange gardien.

Guatemala [ˌgwɑːtɪ'mɑːlə] n Guatemala *m*.

Guatemalan [ˌgwɑːtɪ'mɑːlən] 1 adj guatémaltèque. 2 n Guatémaltèque *mf*.

guava ['gwɑːvə] n (*fruit*) goyave *f*; (*tree*) goyavier *m*.

gubbins* ['gʌbɪnz] n (*Brit*) a (*thing*) machin* *m*, truc* *m*. b (*silly person*) crétin *m*, imbécile *m*.

gubernatorial [ˌguːbənə'tɔːrɪəl] adj (*esp US*) de *or* du gouverneur.

guddle ['gʌdl] vi (*Scot*): **to ~ for fish** pêcher à mains nues.

gudgeon¹ ['gʌdʒən] n (*fish*) goujon *m*.

gudgeon² ['gʌdʒən] n (*Tech*) tourillon *m*; (*Naut*) goujon *m*. (*Brit Aut*) **~ pin** goupille *f*.

guelder rose [ˌgeldə'rəʊz] n (*Bot*) boule-de-neige *f*.

Guelf, Guelph [gwelf] n guelfe *m*.

Guernsey ['gɜːnzɪ] n a (*Geog*) Guernesey *f*. **in ~** à Guernesey. b (*cow*) vache *f* de Guernesey. c (*garment*) **g~** jersey *m*.

guerrilla [gə'rɪlə] 1 n guérillero *m*. 2 comp *tactics etc* de guérilla ▸**guerrilla band** guérilla *f* (*troupe*) ▸**guerrilla financing** (*US*) financement *m* indépendant ▸**guerrilla group** = **guerrilla band** ▸**guerrilla strike** (*Ind*) grève *f* sauvage ▸**guerrilla war(fare)** guérilla *f* (*guerre*).

guess [ges] 1 n supposition *f*, conjecture *f*. **to have** *or* **make a ~** tâcher de *or* essayer de deviner; **to have** *or* **make a ~ at sth** essayer de deviner qch; **I give you three ~es!, have a ~!** essaie de deviner!, devine un peu!; **that was a good ~** tu as deviné juste, ton intuition ne t'a pas trompé; **that was a good ~ but ...** c'était une bonne intuition *or* idée mais ...; **it was just a lucky ~** j'ai (*or* il a *etc*) deviné juste, c'est tout; **an educated ~** une supposition éclairée; **he made a wild ~** il a lancé une réponse à tout hasard; **at a ~ I would say there were 200** au jugé je dirais qu'il y en avait 200; **at a rough ~** à vue de nez, approximativement, grosso modo; **my ~ is that he refused** d'après moi il aura refusé; **your ~ is as good as mine!*** tu en sais autant que moi!, je n'en sais pas plus que toi!; **it's anyone's ~ who will win*** impossible de prévoir *or* allez donc savoir qui va gagner; **will he come tomorrow? – it's anyone's ~*** viendra-t-il demain? – qui sait? *or* Dieu seul le sait; **by ~ and by God*** Dieu sait comment.

2 comp ▸**guesswork** conjecture *f*, hypothèse *f*; **it was sheer guesswork** ce n'étaient que des conjectures, on n'a fait que deviner; **by guesswork** en devinant, par flair.

3 vt a *answer, sb's name etc* deviner; (*estimate: also* **guess at**) *height, numbers etc* estimer, évaluer; (*surmise*) supposer, conjecturer (*that* que). **to ~ sb's age** deviner l'âge de qn; (*make a rough guess*) évaluer l'âge de qn; **I ~ed him to be about 20** j'estimais *or* je jugeais qu'il avait à peu près 20 ans; **~ how heavy he is** devine combien il pèse; **I'd already ~ed who had done it** j'avais déjà deviné qui l'avait fait; **you've ~ed (it)!** tu as deviné!, c'est ça!; **to ~ the answer** deviner la réponse; **I haven't a recipe, I just ~ the quantities** je n'ai pas de recette, je mesure à vue de nez; **can you ~ what it means?** peux-tu arriver à deviner ce que cela veut dire?; **~ what*** devine quoi*; **I ~ed as much** je m'en doutais; **~ who!*** devine qui c'est!; **you'll never ~ who's coming to see us!** tu ne devineras jamais qui va venir nous voir!

b (*esp US: believe, think*) croire, penser. **he'll be about 40 I ~** il doit avoir dans les 40 ans je pense *or* j'imagine, moi je lui donne *or* donnerais la quarantaine; **I ~ it's going to rain** j'ai l'impression *or* je crois qu'il va pleuvoir; **I ~ so** je crois que oui, probablement; **I ~ not** j'ai l'impression que non, je ne crois pas.

4 vi deviner. **try to ~!** essaie de deviner!, devine un peu!; **you'll never ~!** tu ne devineras jamais!; **to ~ right** deviner juste; **to ~ wrong** tomber à côté*; **to keep sb ~ing** laisser qn dans le doute; **to ~ at the height of a building/the number of people present** *etc* évaluer *or* estimer (au jugé) la hauteur d'un bâtiment/le nombre de personnes présentes *etc*.

guesstimate* ['gestɪmɪt] 1 n calcul *m* au pifomètre*. 2 vt calculer au pifomètre*.

guest [gest] 1 n (*at home*) invité(e) *m(f)*, hôte *mf*; (*at table*) convive *mf*; (*in hotel*) client(e) *m(f)*; (*in boarding house*) pensionnaire *mf*; (*TV, Rad*) invité(e) *m(f)*. **~ of honour** invité(e) d'honneur; **we were their ~s last summer** nous avons été leurs invités l'été dernier; **be my ~!*** fais comme chez toi!*; *see* **house, paying**.

2 comp ▸**guest artist** (*Theat*) artiste *mf* (*or* chanteur *m etc*) en vedette américaine; (*in credits*) avec la participation de ▸**guest appearance: to make a guest appearance on sb's show** être invité sur le plateau de qn ▸**guest book** livre *m* d'or ▸**guest-house** (*gen*) pension *f* de famille; (*in monastery etc*) maison *f* des hôtes ▸**guest list** liste *f* des invités ▸**guest night** *soirée f où les membres d'un club peuvent inviter des non-membres* ▸**guest room** chambre *f* d'amis ▸**guest speaker** conférencier *m*, -ière *f* (*invité(e) par un club, une organisation*) ▸**guestworker** travailleur *m*, -euse *f* immigré(e).

3 vi (*TV, Rad*) être un(e) invité(e) (*on* à). **to ~ on sb's show** être invité sur le plateau de qn; **and ~ing on tonight's show we have John Brown** et notre invité à l'émission de ce soir est John Brown.

guff‡ [gʌf] n (*NonC*) bêtises *fpl*, idioties *fpl*.

guffaw [gʌ'fɔː] 1 vi rire bruyamment, pouffer (de rire), partir d'un gros rire. 2 vt pouffer. 3 n gros (éclat de) rire.

Guiana [gaɪ'ænə] n les Guyanes *fpl*.

guidance ['gaɪdəns] 1 n a conseils *mpl*. **for your ~** pour votre gouverne, à titre d'indication *or* d'information; **he needs some ~ about** *or* **as to how to go about it** il a besoin de conseils quant à la façon de procéder; **your ~ was very helpful** vos conseils ont été très utiles; *see* **child, vocational**. b [*rocket etc*] guidage *m*. 2 comp ▸**guidance counselor** (*US Scol*) conseiller *m*, -ère *f* d'orientation ▸**guidance system** (*Tech*) système *m* de guidage.

guide [gaɪd] 1 n a (*gen, also for climbers, tourists etc*) guide *m*; (*spiritualism*) esprit *m*; (*fig*) guide, indication *f*. **you must let reason be your ~** il faut vous laisser guider par la raison; **this figure is only a ~** ce chiffre n'est qu'une indication; **last year's figures will be a good ~** les statistiques de l'année dernière serviront de guide; **these results are not a very good ~ as to his ability** ces résultats ne donnent pas d'indication sûre touchant ses compétences; **as a rough ~, count 4 apples to the pound** comptez en gros *or* à peu près 4 pommes par livre.

b (*also* **~book**) guide *m*. **~ to Italy** guide d'Italie.

c (*book of instructions*) guide *m*, manuel *m*. **beginner's ~ to sailing** manuel d'initiation à la voile.

d (*for curtains etc*) glissière *f*; (*on sewing machine*) pied-de-biche *m*.

e (*also* **girl ~**) éclaireuse *f*; (*Roman Catholic*) guide *f*.

2 vt a *blind man* conduire, guider; *stranger, visitor* guider, piloter. **he ~d us through the town** il nous a pilotés *or* guidés à travers la ville; **he ~d us to the main door** il nous a montré le chemin jusqu'à la porte d'entrée; (*lit, fig*) **to be ~d by sb/sth** se laisser guider par qn/qch.

b *rocket, missile* guider.

3 comp ▸**guidebook** *see* **1b** ▸**guide dog** chien *m* d'aveugle ▸**guide line** (*for writing*) ligne *f* (*permettant une écriture horizontale régulière*); (*fig: hints, suggestions*) ligne *f* directrice; (*rope*) main

courante ▸**guidepost** poteau *m* indicateur ▸**guide price** prix *m* indicatif.

guided [ˈgaɪdɪd] **adj** a *rocket etc* téléguidé. ~ **missile** engin téléguidé. b (*US*) ~ **tour** visite guidée.

guiding [ˈgaɪdɪŋ] **adj**: ~ **principle** principe *m* directeur; (*fig*) ~ **star** guide *m*; **he needs a ~ hand from time to time** il a besoin qu'on l'aide (*subj*) de temps en temps.

guild [gɪld] 1 **n** a (*Hist*) guilde *f*, corporation *f*. **goldsmiths' ~** guilde des orfèvres. b association *f*, confrérie *f*. **the church ~** le cercle paroissial; **women's ~** association féminine. 2 **comp** ▸**guildhall** (*Hist*) palais *m* des corporations; (*town hall*) hôtel *m* de ville.

guilder [ˈgɪldəʳ] **n, pl ~s** *or* ~ florin *m*.

guile [gaɪl] **n** (*NonC*) (*deceit*) fourberie *f*, tromperie *f*; (*cunning*) ruse *f*, astuce *f*.

guileful [ˈgaɪlfʊl] **adj** (*deceitful*) fourbe, trompeur; (*cunning*) rusé, astucieux.

guileless [ˈgaɪllɪs] **adj** (*straightforward*) sans astuce, candide; (*open*) franc (*f* franche), loyal, sincère.

guillemot [ˈgɪlɪmɒt] **n** guillemot *m*.

guillotine [ˌgɪləˈtiːn] 1 **n** (*for beheading*) guillotine *f*; (*for paper-cutting*) massicot *m*. (*Parl*) **a ~ was imposed on the bill** une limite de temps a été imposée au débat sur le projet de loi. 2 **vt** *person* guillotiner; *paper* massicoter. (*Parl*) **to ~ a bill** imposer une limite de temps au débat sur un projet de loi.

guilt [gɪlt] **n** (*NonC*) culpabilité *f*. **he was tormented by ~** il était torturé par un sentiment de culpabilité; (*Psych*) **to have ~ feelings about sb/sth** se sentir coupable *or* avoir des sentiments de culpabilité vis-à-vis de qn/qch; (*Psych*) ~ **complex** complexe *m* de culpabilité.

guiltily [ˈgɪltɪlɪ] **adv** *say, do* d'un air coupable; *hope, think* se sentant coupable.

guiltless [ˈgɪltlɪs] **adj** innocent (*of* de).

guilty [ˈgɪltɪ] **adj** a (*Jur etc*) *person* coupable (*of* de). ~ **person** *or* **party** coupable *mf*; **to plead ~/not ~** plaider coupable/non coupable; **to find sb ~/not ~** déclarer qn coupable/non coupable; **verdict of ~/not ~** verdict *m* de culpabilité/d'acquittement; **"not ~" he replied** "non coupable" répondit-il; **he was ~ of taking the book without permission** il s'est rendu coupable de prendre le livre sans permission; **I have been ~ of that myself** j'ai moi-même commis la même erreur; **I feel ~ about the letter** j'ai des remords en ce qui concerne la lettre; **I feel very ~ about not writing to her** je suis plein de remords de ne pas lui avoir écrit; **to make sb feel ~** culpabiliser qn, donner mauvaise conscience à qn.
b *look* coupable, confus; *thought, act* coupable. ~ **conscience** conscience lourde *or* chargée *or* coupable; **I have a ~ conscience about not writing** j'ai mauvaise conscience de ne pas avoir écrit.

Guinea [ˈgɪnɪ] 1 **n** (*Geog*) **(Republic of) ~** (République *f* de) Guinée *f*; *see* **equatorial.** 2 **comp** ▸**Guinea-Bissau** Guinée-Bissau *f* ▸**guinea-fowl pl inv** pintade *f* ▸**guinea-pig** (*Zool*) cochon *m* d'Inde, cobaye *m*; (*fig*) cobaye; (*fig*) **to be a guinea-pig** servir de cobaye.

guinea [ˈgɪnɪ] **n** (*Brit: money*) guinée *f* (= *21 shillings*).

Guinean [ˈgɪnɪən] 1 **adj** guinéen. 2 **n** Guinéen(ne) *m(f)*.

guise [gaɪz] **n**: **in the ~ of a soldier** sous l'aspect d'un soldat; **in** *or* **under the ~ of friendship** sous l'apparence *or* les traits de l'amitié.

guitar [gɪˈtɑːʳ] **n** guitare *f*.

guitarist [gɪˈtɑːrɪst] **n** guitariste *mf*.

Gujarat, Gujerat [ˌgʊdʒəˈrɑːt] **n** Gujarat *m*, Gujrat *m*.

Gujarati, Gujerati [ˌgʊdʒəˈrɑːtɪ] 1 **adj** du Guj(a)rat. 2 **n** a (*person*) Gujarati *mf*. b (*Ling*) gujarati *m*.

gulch [gʌlʃ] **n** (*US*) ravin *m*.

gulf [gʌlf] **n** a (*in ocean*) golfe *m*. **the (Persian) G~** le golfe Persique; **the G~ War** la guerre du Golfe; **G~ of Aden** golfe d'Aden; **G~ of Alaska** golfe d'Alaska; **G~ of Mexico** golfe du Mexique; *[Middle East]* **the G~ States** les États *mpl* du Golfe; (*US*) **the G~ states** les États du golfe du Mexique; **G~ Stream** Gulf Stream *m*. b (*abyss: lit, fig*) gouffre *m*, abîme *m*.

gull¹ [gʌl] **n** (*bird*) mouette *f*, goéland *m*. **common ~** goéland cendré; (*Aut*) **~-wing door** porte *f* papillon.

gull² [gʌl] (*dupe*) 1 **vt** duper, rouler‡. 2 **n** jobard‡ *m*, dindon‡ *m*.

gullet [ˈgʌlɪt] **n** (*Anat*) œsophage *m*; (*throat*) gosier *m*. (*fig*) **it really stuck in my ~** je ne l'ai vraiment pas digéré*.

gulley [ˈgʌlɪ] **n** = **gully.**

gullibility [ˌgʌlɪˈbɪlɪtɪ] **n** crédulité *f*.

gullible [ˈgʌlɪbl] **adj** crédule, facile à duper.

gully [ˈgʌlɪ] **n** a (*ravine*) ravine *f*, couloir *m*; (*Climbing*) couloir. b (*drain*) caniveau *m*, rigole *f*.

gulp [gʌlp] 1 **n** a (*action*) coup *m* de gosier; (*from emotion*) serrement *m* de gorge. **to swallow sth at one ~** avaler qch d'un seul coup; **he emptied the glass at one ~** il a vidé le verre d'un (seul) trait; **"yes" he replied with a ~** "oui" répondit-il la gorge serrée *or* avec une boule dans la gorge.
b (*mouthful*) *[food]* bouchée *f*, goulée* *f*; *[drink]* gorgée *f*, lampée *f*. **he took a ~ of milk** il a avalé une gorgée de lait.
2 **vt** a (*also ~ down*) *food* avaler à grosses bouchées, engloutir, enfourner*; *drink* avaler à pleine gorge, lamper. **don't ~ your food** mâche ce que tu manges.
b **"I'm sorry," he ~ed** "désolé", répondit-il la gorge serrée *or* avec une boule dans la gorge.
3 **vi** essayer d'avaler; (*from emotion etc*) avoir un serrement *or* une contraction de la gorge. **he ~ed** sa gorge s'est serrée *or* s'est contractée.

▸**gulp back vt sep**: **to gulp back one's tears/sobs** ravaler *or* refouler ses larmes/sanglots.

gum¹ [gʌm] 1 **n** (*Anat*) gencive *f*. 2 **comp** ▸**gumboil** fluxion *f* dentaire, abcès *m* à la gencive.

gum² [gʌm] 1 **n** a (*NonC*) (*Bot*) gomme *f*; (*Brit: glue*) gomme, colle *f*; (*rubber*) caoutchouc *m*.
b (*NonC*) chewing-gum *m*.
c (*sweet: also* **~drop**) boule *f* de gomme.
2 **comp** ▸**gum arabic** gomme *f* arabique ▸**gumboots** (*Brit*) bottes *fpl* de caoutchouc ▸**gum disease** gingivite *f* ▸**gum shield** protège-dents *m* ▸**gumshoe** (*US* ‡: *detective*) privé* *m* ▸**gumshoes** (*US*) (*overshoes*) caoutchoucs *mpl*; (*sneakers*) (chaussures *fpl* de) tennis *mpl* ▸**gum tree** gommier *m*; (*Brit fig*) **to be up a gum tree‡** être dans le lac (*fig*), être dans la merde‡.
3 **vt** (*put ~ on*) gommer; (*stick*) coller (*to* à). **~med envelope/label** enveloppe/étiquette collante *or* gommée; **to ~ sth back on** recoller qch; **to ~ down an envelope** coller *or* cacheter une enveloppe.

▸**gum up‡ vt sep** *machinery, plans* abîmer, bousiller*. (*fig*) **it's gummed up the works** ça a tout bousillé*.

gum³* [gʌm] **n** (*euph of* **God**) **by ~!** nom d'un chien!*, mince alors!*

gumbo [ˈgʌmbəʊ] **n** (*Bot*) gombo *m*; (*Culin*) soupe *f* au gombo.

gummy [ˈgʌmɪ] **adj** gommeux; (*sticky*) collant, gluant.

gumption* [ˈgʌmpʃən] **n** (*NonC: Brit*) jugeote* *f*, bon sens. **use your ~!** aie un peu de jugeote!*; **he's got a lot of ~** il sait se débrouiller; **he's got no ~** il n'a pas deux sous de jugeote* *or* de bon sens.

gun [gʌn] 1 **n** a (*handgun*) revolver *m*, pistolet *m*; (*rifle*) fusil *m*; (*cannon*) canon *m*. **he's got a ~!** il est armé!, il a un revolver!; **the thief was carrying a ~** le voleur avait une arme (à feu); **to draw a ~ on sb** braquer une arme sur qn; **a 21-~ salute** une salve de 21 coups de canon; (*Mil*) **the ~s** les canons, l'artillerie *f*; **the big ~s** (*Mil*) les gros canons, l'artillerie lourde; (*: *fig: people*) les grosses légumes*, les huiles* *fpl*; (*fig: in argument etc*) **to bring up one's big ~s** sortir son (*or* ses) argument(s) massue; **to be going great ~s‡** *[business]* marcher à pleins gaz*; *[person]* être en pleine forme (*see also* **blow¹**); (*fig*) **he's the fastest ~ in the West** de tous les cowboys il est le plus rapide sur la détente; *see* **jump, son, stick** *etc.*
b (*Brit: member of shooting party*) fusil *m*.
c (*US* ‡: *gunman*) bandit armé.
d (*Tech*) pistolet *m*. **paint ~** pistolet à peinture; *see* **grease.**
2 **comp** ▸**gunboat** (*Naut*) canonnière *f*; **gunboat diplomacy** diplomatie appuyée par la force armée ▸**gun carriage** affût *m* de canon; (*at funeral*) prolonge *f* d'artillerie ▸**gun cotton** fulmicoton *m*, coton-poudre *m* ▸**gun crew** (*Mil*) peloton *m* *or* servants *mpl* de pièce ▸**gun dog** chien *m* de chasse ▸**gunfight** échange *m* de coups de feu ▸**gunfire** *[rifles etc]* coups *mpl* de feu, fusillade *f*; *[cannons]* feu *m* *or* tir *m* d'artillerie ▸**the gun laws** (*US*) les lois sur le port d'armes ▸**gun licence** permis *m* de port d'armes ▸**gunman** bandit armé; (*Pol etc*) terroriste *m* ▸**gunmetal n** bronze *m* à canon ◊ **adj** (*colour*) vert-de-gris *inv* ▸**gunplay** (*US*) échange *m* de coups de feu ▸**gunpoint**: **to have** *or* **hold sb at gunpoint** tenir qn sous son revolver *or* au bout de son fusil; **he did it at gunpoint** il l'a fait sous la menace du revolver ▸**gunpowder** poudre *f* à canon; (*Brit Hist*) **the Gunpowder Plot** la conspiration des Poudres ▸**gun room** (*in house*) armurerie *f*; (*Brit Naut*) poste *m* des aspirants ▸**gunrunner** trafiquant *m* d'armes ▸**gunrunning** contrebande *f* *or* trafic *m* d'armes ▸**gunship** hélicoptère *m* de combat ▸**gunshot** *see* **gunshot** ▸**gun-shy** qui a peur des coups de feu *or* des détonations ▸**gunslinger‡** (*US*) bandit armé ▸**gunsmith** armurier *m* ▸**gun turret** (*Mil etc*) tourelle *f*.
3 **vt** a (*also ~ down*) abattre, tuer (à coups de pistolet *etc*).
b (*Aut*) **to ~ the engine** faire ronfler le moteur; **to ~ it‡** appuyer sur le champignon*.
4 **vi**: (*fig*) **to be ~ning for sb*** chercher qn, essayer d'avoir qn; **watch out, he's ~ning for you!** fais gaffe, il te cherche!

gunge* [gʌndʒ] **n** (*Brit*) magma *m* infame*.

gung ho* [ˈgʌŋ ˈhəʊ] **adj** enthousiaste et naïf.

gunk* [gʌŋk] **n** (*NonC*) = **gunge***.

gunner [ˈgʌnəʳ] **n** (*Mil, Naut*) artilleur *m*; (*Brit Mil*) canonnier *m*.

gunnery [ˈgʌnərɪ] 1 **n** a (*science, art, skill*) tir *m* au canon, canonnage *m*. b (*Mil: collective n: guns*) artillerie *f*. 2 **comp** ▸**gunnery officer** (*Mil*) officier *m* de tir.

gunny [ˈgʌnɪ] **n** (*NonC*) toile *f* de jute grossière; (*also* **~ bag, ~ sack**) sac *m* de jute.

gunshot [ˈgʌnʃɒt] 1 **n** (*sound*) coup *m* de feu. **within ~** à portée de fusil; **out of ~** hors de portée de fusil. 2 **comp** ▸**gunshot wound** blessure *f* de *or* par balle; **to get a gunshot wound** être blessé par une balle, recevoir un coup de feu.

gunwale [ˈgʌnl] **n** (*Naut*) plat-bord *m*.

guppy [ˈgʌpɪ] **n** guppy *m*.

gurgle [ˈgɜːgl] 1 **n** *[water]* glouglou *m*, gargouillis *m*, gargouillement *m*; *[rain]* gargouillis, gargouillement; *[stream]* murmure *m*; (*of laughter*) gloussement *m*; *[baby]* gazouillis *m*. **to give a ~ of delight** gazouiller de joie. 2 **vi** *[water]* glouglouter, gargouiller; *[rain]* gargouiller; *[stream]* murmurer; *[person]* (*with delight*) gazouiller; (*with laughter*) glousser.

gurnard ['gɜːnəd] **n** grondin *m*.

guru ['gʊruː] **n** (*lit, fig*) gourou *m*, maître *m* à penser.

gush [gʌʃ] 1 **n** *[oil, water, blood]* jaillissement *m*, bouillonnement *m*; *[tears, words]* flot *m*; (* *pej*) effusion(s) *f(pl)*, épanchement(s) *m(pl)*. 2 **vi** a (*lit, fig*) jaillir. *[water etc]* **to ~ in/out/through** *etc* entrer/sortir/traverser *etc* en bouillonnant. b (* *pej*) *[person]* se répandre en compliments (*over* sur; *about* à propos de, au sujet de), en remettre*.

gusher* ['gʌʃəʳ] **n** a (*oil well*) puits *m* jaillissant (de pétrole). b (*effusive person*) **to be a ~** en remettre*.

gushing ['gʌʃɪŋ] **adj** *water etc* jaillissant, bouillonnant; (*pej*) *person* trop exubérant, trop démonstratif, trop expansif.

gusset ['gʌsɪt] **n** (*Sewing*) soufflet *m*.

gussy ['gʌsɪ] **vt** (*US*) **to ~ sth up*** retaper qch, refaire une beauté à qch.

gust [gʌst] 1 **n** *[wind]* coup *m* de vent, rafale *f*, bourrasque *f*; *[smoke]* bouffée *f*; *[flame]* jet *m*; (*fig*) *[rage etc]* accès *m*, crise *f*, bouffée. **~ of rain** averse *f*; **there was a ~ of laughter from the audience** un grand éclat de rire s'est élevé du public. 2 **vi** *[wind]* souffler en bourrasque. (*Met*) **wind ~ing to force 7** vent (soufflant en bourrasque) atteignant force 7.

gusto ['gʌstəʊ] **n** (*NonC*) enthousiasme *m*, plaisir *m*. **... he said with ~** ... dit-il vivement; **he ate his meal with great ~** il a dévoré son repas.

gusty ['gʌstɪ] **adj** *weather* venteux. **a ~ day** un jour de grand vent *or* à bourrasques; **~ wind** des rafales *fpl* de vent.

gut [gʌt] 1 **n** a (*Anat*) boyau *m*, intestin *m*; (*Med: for stitching*) catgut *m*; (*Mus etc*) (corde *f* de) boyau. **~s** (*Anat*) boyaux; (*fig*) (*central point*) point *m* fondamental, cœur *m*; **he stuck his bayonet into my ~s** il m'a enfoncé sa baïonnette dans le ventre; (*fig*) **to work** *or* **sweat one's ~s out**⁑ se tuer de travail; **I hate his ~s**⁑ je ne peux pas le blairer⁑, je ne peux pas le voir en peinture*; **the ~s of his speech/of the problem** le point fondamental de son discours/du problème.
b (*: *courage*) **~s** cran* *m*; **he's got ~s*** il a du cran*, il a du cœur au ventre*; **he's got no ~s*** il n'a rien dans le ventre*, il manque de cran*; **it takes a lot of ~s* to do that** il faut beaucoup de cran* *or* d'estomac pour faire ça.
2 **adj** (*fig*) *reaction* instinctif; (*negative*) viscéral; *issues, problem* fondamental. **I've got a ~ feeling about it** je le sais au fond de moi-même; **she had a ~ feeling that it was wrong** elle sentait instinctivement que c'était mal, quelque chose en elle lui disait que c'était mal; (*US Univ*) **~ course*** cours fondamental.
3 **vt** (*Culin*) *animal* vider, étriper; *fish* vider; (*) *book etc* piller*. **fire ~ted the house** le feu n'a laissé que les quatre murs de la maison; **the vandals ~ted the hall** les vandales n'ont laissé de la salle que les murs; *see also* **gutted**.

gutless* ['gʌtlɪs] **adj** (*cowardly*) qui a les foies blancs⁑.

gutsy⁑ ['gʌtsɪ] **adj** *person, advertising, style* qui a du punch.

gutta-percha [ˌgʌtə'pɜːtʃə] **n** (*NonC*) gutta-percha *f*.

gutted⁑ ['gʌtɪd] **adj** (*Brit*) (*very disappointed*) complètement dégoûté*.

gutter ['gʌtəʳ] 1 **n** *[roof]* gouttière *f*; *[road]* caniveau *m*; (*ditch*) rigole *f*. (*fig*) **language of the ~** langage *m* de corps de garde; **to rise from the ~** sortir de la boue *or* du ruisseau. 2 **vi** *[candle]* couler; *[flame]* vaciller, crachoter. 3 **comp ▶ gutter-press** presse *f* de bas étage *or* à scandales, bas-fonds *mpl* du journalisme **▶ guttersnipe** gamin(e) *m(f)* des rues.

guttering ['gʌtərɪŋ] **n** (*NonC*) gouttières *fpl*.

guttural ['gʌtərəl] 1 **adj** guttural. 2 **n** (*Ling*) gutturale *f*.

guv⁑ [gʌv] **n = gov.**

guvnor⁑ ['gʌvnəʳ] **n = governor b.**

Guy [gaɪ] **n** Guy *m*. (*Brit*) **~ Fawkes Day** le cinq novembre (*anniversaire de la conspiration des Poudres*).

guy¹ [gaɪ] 1 **n** a (*: *esp US*) type* *m*, mec* *m*. **the good/bad ~s** les bons *mpl*/les méchants *mpl*; **nice ~** chic type*, type bien*; **smart** *or* **wise ~** malin *m*, type qui fait le malin*; **tough ~** dur* *m*; **hi, ~s!** salut les mecs!*; **what are you ~s doing tonight?** qu'est-ce que vous faîtes ce soir, les mecs?*; (*US: friends*) **the ~s** les copains *mpl*. *see* **fall, great.** b (*Brit*) effigie *f* (*de Guy Fawkes, brûlée en plein air le 5 novembre*); (*oddly dressed person*) épouvantail *m* (*fig*). 2 **vt** (*gen*) tourner en ridicule. (*Theat*) **to ~ a part** travestir un rôle.

guy² [gaɪ] **n** (*also* **~-rope**) corde *f* de tente.

Guyana [gaɪ'ænə] **n** Guyane *f*.

Guyanese [ˌgaɪə'niːz] 1 **adj** guyanais. 2 **n** Guyanais(e) *m(f)*.

guzzle ['gʌzl] 1 **vi** (*eat*) s'empiffrer*; (*drink*) siffler* du vin *etc*. 2 **vt** *food* bâfrer*, bouffer*; *drink* siffler*. 3 **n** glouton(ne) *m(f)*, goinfre *m*.

guzzler ['gʌzləʳ] **n** glouton(ne) *m(f)*; *see* **gas.**

gybe [dʒaɪb] **= gibe 1b.**

gym [dʒɪm] 1 **n** a (**abbr of gymnastics**) gymnastique *f*, gym* *f*. b (**abbr of gymnasium**) gymnase *m*; (*Scol*) gymnase, salle *f* de gym*. 2 **comp ▶ gym shoes** (chaussures *fpl* de) tennis *fpl*, chaussures de gym* **▶ gym slip** (*Brit*), (*US*) **gym suit** tunique *f* (*d'écolière*).

gymkhana [dʒɪm'kɑːnə] **n** (*esp Brit*) gymkhana *m*.

gymnasium [dʒɪm'neɪzɪəm] **n, pl ~s** *or* **gymnasia** [dʒɪm'neɪzɪə] gymnase *m*; (*Scol*) gymnase, salle *f* de gymnastique.

gymnast ['dʒɪmnæst] **n** gymnaste *mf*.

gymnastic [dʒɪm'næstɪk] **adj** gymnastique.

gymnastics [dʒɪm'næstɪks] **n** a (*pl: exercises*) gymnastique *f*. **to do ~** faire de la gymnastique; **mental ~** gymnastique intellectuelle. b (*NonC: art, skill*) gymnastique *f*.

gynae* ['gaɪnɪ] **abbr of gynaecological, gynaecology.**

gynaecological, (*US*) **gynecological** [ˌgaɪnɪkə'lɒdʒɪkəl] **adj** gynécologique.

gynaecologist, (*US*) **gynecologist** [ˌgaɪnɪ'kɒlədʒɪst] **n** gynécologue *mf*.

gynaecology, (*US*) **gynecology** [ˌgaɪnɪ'kɒlədʒɪ] **n** gynécologie *f*.

gyp [dʒɪp] 1 **n** a (*US* ⁑) (*swindler*) carotteur *m*, escroc *m*; (*swindle*) escroquerie *f*. b (*Brit* ⁑) **he gave me ~** il m'a passé une engueulade⁑; **my leg is giving me ~** j'ai atrocement *or* sacrément* mal à la jambe. c (*Brit Univ* *) domestique *m* (de collège). 2 **vt** (*US*) **to ~ sb out of sth**⁑ escroquer qch à qn.

gypsophila [dʒɪp'sɒfɪlə] **n** gypsophile *f*.

gypsum ['dʒɪpsəm] **n** (*NonC*) gypse *m*.

gypsy ['dʒɪpsɪ] **= gipsy.**

gyrate [ˌdʒaɪə'reɪt] **vi** tournoyer, décrire des girations.

gyration [ˌdʒaɪə'reɪʃən] **n** giration *f*.

gyratory [ˌdʒaɪə'reɪtərɪ] **adj** giratoire.

gyro ['dʒaɪərəʊ] **n abbr of gyrocompass, gyroscope.**

gyro... ['dʒaɪə'rəʊ] **pref** gyro ... .

gyrocompass ['dʒaɪərəʊ'kʌmpəs] **n** gyrocompas *m*.

gyrofrequency [ˌdʒaɪərəʊ'friːkwənsɪ] **n** gyrofréquence *f*.

gyromagnetic [ˌdʒaɪrəʊmæg'netɪk] **adj** gyromagnétique.

gyroscope ['dʒaɪərəskəʊp] **n** gyroscope *m*.

gyrostabilizer [ˌdʒaɪərəʊ'steɪbɪlaɪzəʳ] **n** gyrostabilisateur *m*.

gyrostat ['dʒaɪrəʊˌstæt] **n** gyrostat *m*.

H

H, h [eɪtʃ] 1 n a (*letter*) H, h *m or f*. **aspirate/silent h** h aspiré/muet; **H for Harry,** (*US*) **H for How** H comme Henri; *see* **drop.** b (*Drugs sl*) H poudre *f*, héroïne *f*. 2 comp ▸**H-bomb** bombe *f* H ▸**H grade** (*Scot Scol*) = **Higher Grade**; *see* **higher.**
ha [hɑː] excl ha!, ah! ~, ~! (*surprise, irony*) ha! ha!; (*laughter*) hi! hi! hi!
habeas corpus ['heɪbɪəs'kɔːpəs] n (*Jur*) habeas corpus *m*; *see* **writ**[1].
haberdasher ['hæbədæʃər] n (*Brit*) mercier *m*, -ière *f*; (*US*) chemisier *m*, -ière *f*.
haberdashery [ˌhæbə'dæʃərɪ] n (*Brit*) mercerie *f*; (*US*) chemiserie *f*.
habit ['hæbɪt] 1 n a (*custom*) habitude *f*, coutume *f*. **to be in the ~** *or* **to make a ~ of doing** avoir l'habitude *or* avoir pour habitude de faire; **I don't make a ~ of it** je le fais rarement, je ne le fais pas souvent; **don't make a ~ of it!** et ne recommence pas!; **let's hope he doesn't make a ~ of it** espérons qu'il n'en prendra pas l'habitude; **to get** *or* **fall into bad ~s** prendre *or* contracter de mauvaises habitudes; **to get into/out of the ~ of doing** prendre/perdre l'habitude de faire; **to get sb into the ~ of doing** habituer qn à faire, faire prendre à qn l'habitude de faire; **to get out of a ~** perdre une habitude, se débarrasser *or* se défaire d'une habitude; **to have a ~ of doing** avoir l'habitude *or* la manie (*slightly pej*) de faire; **to grow out of the ~ of doing** perdre en grandissant *or* avec l'âge l'habitude de faire; **by** *or* **out of** *or* **from (sheer) ~** par (pure) habitude; **their ~ of shaking hands surprised him** cette habitude qu'ils avaient de donner des poignées de main l'a surpris; (*drug-taking*) **they couldn't cure him of the ~*** ils n'ont pas réussi à le désaccoutumer *or* faire décrocher*; (*Drugs sl*) **to have a ~** être accroché *or* accro *inv* (*sl*); **~ of mind**† tournure *f* d'esprit; **to be a creature of ~** avoir ses (petites) habitudes; *see* **force.**
b (*costume*) habit *m*, tenue *f*. **(nun's) ~** habit (de religieuse); **(riding) ~** tenue de cheval *or* d'équitation.
2 comp ▸**habit-forming** qui crée une accoutumance.
habitable ['hæbɪtəbl] adj habitable.
habitat ['hæbɪtæt] n habitat *m*.
habitation [ˌhæbɪ'teɪʃən] n a (*NonC*) habitation *f*. **the house showed signs of ~** la maison avait l'air habitée; **fit for ~** habitable. b (*house etc*) habitation *f*, demeure *f*, domicile *m*; (*settlement*) établissement *m*, colonie *f*.
habitual [hə'bɪtjʊəl] adj *smile, action, courtesy* habituel, accoutumé; *smoker, liar, drinker* invétéré. (*criminal*) **~ offender** multirécidiviste *mf*; **this had become ~** ceci était devenu une habitude.
habitually [hə'bɪtjʊəlɪ] adv habituellement, d'habitude, ordinairement.
habituate [hə'bɪtjʊeɪt] vt habituer, accoutumer (*sb to sth* qn à qch).
hacienda [ˌhæsɪ'endə] n (*US*) hacienda *f*, grande propriété agricole.
hack[1] [hæk] 1 n a (*cut*) entaille *f*, taillade *f*, coupure *f*; (*blow*) (grand) coup *m*; (*kick*) coup *m* de pied.
b (*cough*) toux sèche.
c (*Comput* ‡) piratage *m* informatique.
2 comp ▸**hacksaw** scie *f* à métaux.
3 vt a (*cut*) hacher, tailler, taillader. **to ~ sth to pieces** tailler qch en pièces; **the regiment was ~ed to pieces** le régiment fut mis *or* taillé en pièces; (*fig*) **the editor ~ed his story to pieces** le rédacteur a fait des coupes sombres dans son reportage; **to ~ one's way in/out** entrer/sortir en se taillant un chemin à coups de couteau (*or* de hache *or* d'épée *etc*).
b (*Brit*) (*strike*) frapper; (*kick*) donner des coups de pied à.
c (*US*) **I can't ~ it**‡ (*can't manage it*) je n'y arrive pas; (*can't stand it*) je déteste ça, je supporte pas ça*.
d (*Brit*) **I'm ~ed off**‡ (*fed up*) j'en ai marre‡ *or* ras le bol‡ (*with* de); (*annoyed*) je l'ai mauvaise*.
e (*Comput*) *system, file* faire effraction dans, pirater.
4 vi a (*cut*) **to ~ at sth** (essayer de) couper qch (à la hache *etc*).
b (*cough: also* **~ away**) tousser sans arrêt.
c (*Comput*) (*gen*) passer tout son temps devant un ordinateur, être un mordu des ordinateurs; (*break into systems*) pirater, faire du piratage. **to ~ into a system** faire effraction dans *or* pirater un système.
▸**hack around** vi (*US*) fainéanter*, glander‡.
▸**hack down** vt sep abattre à coups de couteau (*or* de hache *or* d'épée *etc*).
▸**hack out** vt sep enlever grossièrement à coups de couteau (*or* de hache *or* d'épée *etc*).
▸**hack up** vt sep hacher, tailler en pièces.
hack[2] [hæk] 1 n a (*Brit: horse*) cheval *m* de selle; (*hired*) cheval de louage; (*worn-out*) haridelle *f*, rosse *f*; (*ride*) promenade *f* à cheval. **to go for a ~** (aller) se promener à cheval.
b (*pej*) (*journalist*) journaleux *m*, -euse *f*. **~ writer, (literary) ~** écrivaillon *m*, plumitif *m*; **as a writer/painter he was just a ~** il ne faisait que de la littérature/qu'une peinture alimentaire.
c (*US* ‡) taxi *m*; (*driver*) chauffeur *m* de taxi.
2 vi a (*Brit*) monter (à cheval). **to go ~ing** (aller) se promener à cheval.
b (*US: operate cab*) conduire un taxi.
3 comp ▸**hackman** (*US: cabdriver*) chauffeur *m* de taxi ▸**hack reporter: to be a hack reporter** faire la chronique des chiens écrasés ▸**hackwork** = **hack writing** ▸**hack writer** (*pej*) *see* **1** ▸**hack writing** écrits *mpl* alimentaires; (*pej*) travail *m* d'écrivaillon.
hacker ['hækər] n (*Comput*) (*enthusiast*) passionné(e) *m(f)* *or* mordu(e)* *m(f)* d'ordinateurs; (*pirate*) pirate *m* informatique.
hacking[1] ['hækɪŋ] 1 adj: **~ cough** toux *f* sèche et opiniâtre. 2 n (*Comput*) (*enthusiasm*) engouement *m* pour les ordinateurs; (*piracy*) effraction *f* informatique, piratage *m*.
hacking[2] ['hækɪŋ] adj (*Brit*) **~ jacket** veste *f* de cheval *or* d'équitation.
hackle ['hækl] n plume *f* du cou (*des gallinacés*). **~s** camail *m* (*NonC*); (*fig*) **his ~s rose at the very idea** il se hérissait rien que d'y penser; **with his ~s up** en colère, en fureur; **to get sb's ~s up** mettre qn en colère *or* en fureur.
hackney ['hæknɪ] adj: **~ cab** fiacre *m*; **~ carriage** voiture *f* de place *or* de louage.
hackneyed ['hæknɪd] adj *subject* rebattu; *phrase, metaphor* usé, galvaudé. **~ expression** cliché *m*.
had [hæd] pret, ptp of **have.**
haddock ['hædək] n, pl **~** *or* **~s** églefin *m* *or* aiglefin *m*. **smoked ~** haddock *m*.
Hades ['heɪdiːz] n (*Myth*) les Enfers *mpl*.
hadj [hædʒ] = **hajj.**
hadn't ['hædnt] = **had not;** *see* **have.**
Hadrian ['heɪdrɪən] n Hadrien *m*. (*Brit*) **~'s Wall** le mur d'Hadrien.
haematemesis [ˌhiːmə'temɪsɪs] n hématémèse *f*.
haematic [hiː'mætɪk] adj hématique.
haematite ['hiːməˌtaɪt] n hématite *f*.
haematological [ˌhiːmətə'lɒdʒɪkəl] adj hématologique.
haematologist [ˌhiːmə'tɒlədʒɪst] n hématologue *mf*, hématologiste *mf*.
haematology [ˌhiːmə'tɒlədʒɪ] n hématologie *f*.
haematolysis [ˌhiːmə'tɒlɪsɪs] = **haemolysis.**
haematoma [ˌhiːmə'təʊmə] n, pl **~s** *or* **haematomata** [ˌhimə'təʊmətə] (*SPEC*) hématome *m*.
haemodialyser [ˌhiːməʊ'daɪəˌlaɪzər] n rein artificiel.
haemodialysis [ˌhiːməʊdaɪ'ælɪsɪs] n hémodialyse *f*.
haemoglobin [ˌhiːməʊ'gləʊbɪn] n hémoglobine *f*.
haemolysis [hɪ'mɒlɪsɪs] n, pl **haemolyses** [hɪ'mɒlɪˌsiːz] hémolyse *f*.
haemophilia [ˌhiːməʊ'fɪlɪə] n hémophilie *f*.
haemophiliac [ˌhiːməʊ'fɪlɪæk] adj, n hémophile *(mf)*.
haemoptysis [hɪ'mɒptɪsɪs] n, pl **haemoptyses** [hɪ'mɒptɪˌsiːz] hémoptysie *f*.
haemorrhage ['hemərɪdʒ] 1 n hémorragie *f*. 2 vi faire une hémorragie.
haemorrhoids ['hemərɔɪdz] npl hémorroïdes *fpl*.
haemostasis [ˌhiːməʊ'steɪsɪs] n hémostase *f*, hémostasie *f*.

hafnium ['hæfnɪəm] n hafnium *m*.

haft [hɑːft] 1 n *[knife]* manche *m*; *[sword]* poignée *f*. 2 vt emmancher, mettre un manche à.

hag [hæg] 1 n (*ugly old woman*) vieille sorcière, vieille harpie; (*witch*) sorcière; (**: unpleasant woman*) chameau* *m*. **she's a real ~*** c'est un vrai chameau*. 2 comp ▸ **hag-ridden** tourmenté, obsédé.

haggard ['hægəd] adj (*careworn*) défait, abattu, blême; (*wild in appearance*) égaré. **to be ~** avoir l'air défait *or* égaré.

haggis ['hægɪs] n (*Culin*) haggis *m* (*plat national écossais*).

haggish ['hægɪʃ] adj (*see* **hag**) de (vieille) sorcière; (**: nasty*) vache*.

haggle ['hægl] vi marchander. **to ~ about** *or* **over the price** chicaner sur le prix, débattre le prix; **I'm not going to ~ over a penny here or there** je ne vais pas chicaner sur un centime par-ci par-là.

haggling ['hæglɪŋ] n marchandage *m*.

hagiographer [ˌhægɪ'ɒgrəfəʳ] n hagiographe *mf*.

hagiography [ˌhægɪ'ɒgrəfɪ] n hagiographie *f*.

Hague [heɪg] n: **The ~** La Haye.

ha-ha ['hɑː'hɑː] n (*Brit*) (*fence*) clôture *f* en contrebas; (*ditch*) saut-de-loup *m*.

hail[1] [heɪl] 1 n (*Met*) grêle *f*; (*fig*) grêle, pluie *f*. (*fig*) **a ~ of bullets** une pluie *or* grêle de balles. 2 comp ▸ **hailstone** grêlon *m* ▸ **hailstorm** averse *f* de grêle. 3 vi grêler. **it is ~ing** il grêle.

▸**hail down** 1 vi: **stones hailed down on him** il reçut une pluie de cailloux. 2 vt sep (*liter*) **to hail down curses on sb** faire pleuvoir des malédictions sur qn.

hail[2] [heɪl] 1 vt a (*greet*) saluer; (*acknowledge*) acclamer (*as* comme). **he was ~ed (as) emperor** (*saluted*) ils le saluèrent aux cris de "vive l'empereur"; (*fig: acknowledged*) on l'acclama *or* il fut acclamé comme empereur; (*excl*) **~!** salut à vous!, je vous salue!

b (*call loudly*) *ship, taxi, person* héler. **within ~ing distance** à portée de (la) voix.

2 vi (*Naut*) être en provenance (*from* de); *[person]* être originaire (*from* de). **a ship ~ing from London** un navire en provenance de Londres; **they ~ from Leeds** ils viennent de Leeds; **where do you ~ from?** d'où êtes-vous?

3 n appel *m*. **within ~** à portée de (la) voix.

4 comp ▸ **hail-fellow-well-met: to be hail-fellow-well-met** être liant *or* exubérant, tutoyer tout le monde (*fig*) ▸ **Hail Mary** (*Rel*) "Je vous salue Marie" *m*, Avé Maria *m*.

hair [hɛəʳ] 1 n a (*NonC*) *[head]* cheveux *mpl*. **he has black ~** il a les cheveux noirs; **a man with long ~** un homme aux cheveux longs; **a fine head of ~** une belle chevelure; **to wash one's ~** se laver les cheveux *or* la tête; **to do one's ~** se coiffer; **she always does my ~ very well** elle me coiffe toujours très bien; **her ~ is always very well done** *or* **very neat** *or* **very nice** elle est toujours très bien coiffée; **to have one's ~ done** se faire coiffer; **to have one's ~ set** se faire faire une mise en plis; **to get one's ~ cut** se faire couper les cheveux; **to make sb's ~ stand on end** faire dresser les cheveux sur la tête à qn; **it was enough to make your ~ stand on end** il y avait de quoi vous faire dresser les cheveux sur la tête; **his ~ stood on end at the sight** le spectacle lui a fait dresser les cheveux sur la tête; **to remove sb's unwanted ~** épiler qn; **to get rid of unwanted ~** s'épiler; **to put up one's ~** mettre ses cheveux en chignon, se faire un chignon; (*fig*) **to let one's ~ down*** se laisser aller, se défouler*; **his ~ is getting thin, he's losing his ~** il perd ses cheveux; (*Brit*) **keep your ~ on!*** du calme!, ne t'excite pas!; **he gets in my ~*** il me tape sur les nerfs* *or* sur le système*; *see* **part, tear**[1] *etc.*

b (*single hair*) *[head]* cheveu *m*; *[body]* poil *m*. **not a ~ of his head was harmed** on ne lui a pas touché un cheveu; **not a ~ out of place** tiré à quatre épingles; (*hum*) **this will put ~s on your chest*** ça va te mettre les veines en feu; **it was hanging by a ~** cela ne tenait qu'à un cheveu; (*fig*) **he won the race by a ~** il a gagné la course à un millimètre près *or* à un quart de poil*; *see* **hairbreadth, split, turn** *etc.*

c *[animal]* (*single ~*) poil *m*; (*NonC*) *[any animal]* pelage *m*; *[horse]* pelage, robe *f*; (*bristles*) soies *fpl*. **to stroke an animal against the ~** caresser un animal à rebrousse-poil *or* à rebours; (*fig*) **try a ~ of the dog that bit you*** reprends un petit verre (pour faire passer ta gueule de bois*).

2 comp *sofa, mattress etc* de crin ▸ **hair appointment** rendez-vous *m* chez le coiffeur ▸ **hairball** *[cat etc]* boule *f* de poils ▸ **hairband** bandeau *m* ▸ **hairbrained** = **harebrained;** *see* **hare 2** ▸ **hairbreadth** *see* **hairbreadth** ▸ **hairbrush** brosse *f* à cheveux ▸ **hair bulb** bulbe *m* pileux ▸ **hair clippers** npl tondeuse *f* ▸ **haircloth** étoffe *f* de crin ▸ **hair conditioner** baume *m* démêlant ▸ **hair cream** brillantine *f*, crème *f* capillaire ▸ **hair-curler** bigoudi *m* ▸ **haircut: to have** *or* **get a haircut** se faire couper les cheveux; **I'd like a haircut** je voudrais une coupe; **I like your haircut** j'aime ta coupe de cheveux; **he's got a dreadful haircut** on lui a très mal coupé les cheveux ▸ **hairdo*** coiffure *f*; **I'm going to have a hairdo** je vais me faire coiffer; **do you like my hairdo?** tu aimes ma coiffure?, tu aimes mes cheveux comme ça?* ▸ **hairdresser** coiffeur *m*, -euse *f* ▸ **hairdresser's (salon** *or* **shop)** salon *m* de coiffure; **I'm going to the hairdresser's** je vais chez le coiffeur ▸ **hairdressing** (*skill, job*) coiffure *f* (*métier*) ▸ **hairdressing appointment** rendez-vous *m* chez le coiffeur ▸ **hairdressing salon** salon *m* de coiffure ▸ **hair-dryer** (*hand-held*) séchoir *m* à cheveux, sèche-cheveux *m inv*; (*freestanding*) casque *m* ▸ **hair follicle** follicule pileux ▸ **hair gel** gel *m* pour cheveux ▸ **hair grip** (*Brit*) pince *f* à cheveux ▸ **hair implant** greffe *f* de cheveux ▸ **hair lacquer** laque *f* (*capillaire*) ▸ **hairline** (*on head*) naissance *f* des cheveux; (*in handwriting*) délié *m*; **he has a receding hairline** son front se dégarnit ▸ **hairline crack** mince *or* légère fêlure ▸ **hairline fracture** (*Med*) fêlure *f* ▸ **hairnet** résille *f*, filet *m* à cheveux ▸ **hair oil** huile *f* capillaire ▸ **hairpiece** postiche *m* ▸ **hairpin** épingle *f* à cheveux ▸ **hairpin bend** (*Brit*) *or* **curve** (*US*) virage *m* en épingle à cheveux ▸ **hair-raising** horrifique, à (vous) faire dresser les cheveux sur la tête; **prices are hair-raising* these days** le coût de la vie est affolant* en ce moment; **driving in Paris is a hair-raising business** conduire dans Paris c'est à vous faire dresser les cheveux sur la tête ▸ **hair remover** crème *f* épilatoire *or* à épiler ▸ **hair restorer** régénérateur *m* des cheveux ▸ **hair roller** rouleau *m* ▸ **hair's breadth** *see* **hairbreadth** ▸ **hair set** mise *f* en plis ▸ **hair shirt** (*Rel*) haire *f*, cilice *m* ▸ **hair slide** (*Brit*) barrette *f* ▸ **hair specialist** capilliculteur *m*, -trice *f* ▸ **hair-splitter** coupeur *m*, -euse *f* de cheveux en quatre ▸ **hair-splitting** n ergotage *m*, pinaillage* *m*, chicanerie *f* ◊ adj ergoteur, pinailleur*, chicanier ▸ **hair spray** laque *f* (en aérosol *or* en bombe); **a can of hair spray** un aérosol *or* une bombe de laque ▸ **hairspring** (ressort *m*) spiral *m* (*de montre*) ▸ **hair style** coiffure *f* (*arrangement des cheveux*) ▸ **hair stylist** coiffeur *m*, -euse *f* ▸ **hair transplant** greffe *f* de cheveux ▸ **hair-trigger** adj *temper* instable, changeant; *balance* instable, précaire.

hairbreadth ['hɛəbretθ] n (*also* **hair's breadth, hairsbreadth**) **by a ~** d'un cheveu, tout juste, de justesse; **the bullet missed him by a ~** la balle l'a manqué d'un cheveu; **we missed death by a ~** nous avons frisé la mort, nous étions à deux doigts de la mort, il s'en est fallu d'un cheveu qu'on y reste (*subj*); **the car missed the taxi by a ~** la voiture a évité le taxi de justesse; **to have a ~ escape** l'échapper belle; **he was within a ~ of giving in** il a tenu à un cheveu qu'il ne cède (*subj*); **he was within a ~ of bankruptcy** il était à deux doigts de la faillite.

-haired [hɛəd] adj ending in comps: **long-haired** *person* aux cheveux longs; *animal* à longs poils; **short-haired** *person* aux cheveux courts; *animal* à poils ras; *see* **curly, fair**[1] *etc.*

hairless ['hɛəlɪs] adj *head* chauve; *face, chin* glabre; *body, animal* sans poils.

hairy ['hɛərɪ] adj a *body, animal* velu, poilu; *scalp* chevelu; *person* hirsute; (*Bot*) velu; *wool* à longs poils. b (** fig*) (*frightening*) horrifique, à (vous) faire dresser les cheveux sur la tête; (*difficult*) hérissé de difficultés, épouvantable. **they had a few ~ moments*** ils ont eu des sueurs froides.

Haiti ['heɪtɪ] n Haïti *m*. **in ~** à Haïti.

Haitian ['heɪʃɪən] 1 adj haïtien. 2 n Haïtien(ne) *m(f)*.

hajj [hædʒ] n, pl **~es** hadj(i) *m*.

hake [heɪk] n, pl **~** *or* **~s** (*Brit*) colin *m*, merlu *m*, merluche *f*.

halal [hæ'læl] adj *meat, butcher* halal *inv*.

halberd ['hælbəd] n hallebarde *f*.

halcyon ['hælsɪən] 1 n (*Myth, Orn*) alcyon *m*. 2 adj paisible, serein. **~ weather** temps paradisiaque *or* enchanteur; **~ days** jours de bonheur, jours heureux.

hale [heɪl] adj vigoureux, robuste. **to be ~ and hearty** être vigoureux, être en pleine santé, se porter comme un charme.

half [hɑːf], pl **halves** 1 n a (*in quantity*) moitié *f*; demi(e) *m(f)*. **to cut in ~** couper en deux; *costs etc* **to cut in** *or* **by ~** réduire de moitié; **it broke in ~** cela s'est cassé en deux; **will you have one ~ of my apple?** veux-tu une *or* la moitié de ma pomme?; **to take ~ of** prendre la moitié de; **two halves make a whole** deux demis font un tout; **he doesn't do things by halves** il ne fait pas les choses à moitié *or* à demi; **two and a ~** deux et demi; **two and a ~ hours, two hours and a ~** deux heures et demie; **two and a ~ kilos, two kilos and a ~** deux kilos et demi; **will you go halves with me in buying the book?** est-ce que tu te mettras de moitié avec moi pour acheter le livre?; **they had always gone halves in everything** ils avaient toujours tout partagé (également); **bigger by ~** moitié plus grand; **he is too clever by ~*** il est un peu trop malin; **and that's not the ~ of it!*, I haven't told you the ~ of it yet!*** et ce n'est pas le mieux!, que je te raconte (*subj*) le meilleur!*; **that was a day/an exam and a ~!*** ça a été une sacrée journée/un sacré examen!*; **it was a laugh and a ~!*** qu'est-ce qu'on a pu rire!*; (*hum*) **my better** *or* **other ~*** ma (douce) moitié* (*hum*); (*fig*) **to see how the other ~ lives*** aller voir comment vivent les autres; *[rail ticket]* **outward/return ~** billet *m or* coupon *m* aller/retour.

b (*in number*) **~ of the books are in French** la moitié des livres sont en français; **they don't know how to drive, ~ of them** la plupart d'entre eux ne savent pas conduire.

c (*Sport*) (*player*) demi *m*; (*part of match*) mi-temps *f*. (*Ftbl*) **left/right ~** demi-gauche *m*/-droit *m*; **the first/second ~** la première/seconde mi-temps.

d (*Scol: term*) semestre *m*.

e (*Brit: half-pint*) **a ~ of Guinness please** un bock de Guinness, s'il vous plaît.

2 adj demi. **a ~ cup, ~ a cup** une demi-tasse; **two and a ~ cups** deux tasses et demie; (*fig*) **in ~ a second*** en moins de rien; **~ one thing ~ another** ni chair ni poisson; **~ man ~ beast** mi-homme mi-bête; **to**

listen with ~ an ear n'écouter que d'une oreille; **you can see that with ~ an eye** cela saute aux yeux, cela crève les yeux; **to go at ~ speed** aller à une vitesse modérée; **she was working with ~ her usual energy** elle travaillait avec moitié moins d'énergie que de coutume; **I don't like ~ measures** je n'aime pas faire les choses à moitié; **the dress had ~-sleeves** la robe avait des manches mi-longues; *see also* **5**, *and* **tick**[1].

3 **adv** a (à) moitié; à demi. **~ asleep** à moitié endormi; **the work is only ~ done** le travail n'est qu'à moitié fait; **~ French ~ English** mi-français mi-anglais, moitié français moitié anglais; **~ laughing ~ crying** moitié riant moitié pleurant; **I've only ~ read it** je ne l'ai qu'à moitié lu; **he ~ rose to his feet** il s'est levé à demi; **I ~ think** je serais tenté de penser; **I'm ~ inclined to do it** je suis tenté de le faire; **he only ~ understands** il ne comprend qu'à moitié; **I ~ suspect that ...** je soupçonne presque que ...; (*rather, somewhat*) **I'm ~ afraid that** j'ai un peu peur *or* quelque crainte que + ne + *subj*; **he was ~ ashamed to admit it** il avait quelque peu honte de l'admettre; **she has only ~ recovered from her illness** elle n'est qu'à moitié remise de sa maladie, elle est loin d'avoir entièrement récupéré depuis sa maladie; *see also* **5**.

b (*Brit* ‡: *intensive*) **he's not ~ rich!** il est rudement* *or* drôlement* riche!, il n'est pas à plaindre!; **she didn't ~ swear!** elle a juré comme un charretier!; **she didn't ~ cry!** elle a pleuré comme une madeleine; **not ~!** tu parles!*, et comment!*

c **it is ~ past three** il est trois heures et demie.

d **he is ~ as big as his sister** il est moitié moins grand que sa sœur; **~ as big again** moitié plus grand; **he earns ~ as much as you** il gagne moitié moins que vous; **~ as much again** moitié plus.

4 **pref: half-** à moitié, à demi; *eg* **half-buried** à moitié *or* à demi enterré; *see also* **5**.

5 **comp** ▸**half-adder** (*Comput*) demi-additionneur *m* ▸**half-and-half** **adv** moitié-moitié ◊ **n** (*US: milk and cream*) *mélange mi-crème mi-lait* ▸**half-assed**‡ (*US*) foireux‡, nul ▸**halfback** (*Sport*) demi *m* ▸**half-baked** (*Culin*) à moitié cuit; (*fig pej*) *person* mal dégrossi*; *plan, idea* qui ne tient pas debout, à la noix*; **a half-baked philosopher/politician** un philosophe/politicien à la manque* ▸**half-binding** *[book]* demi-reliure *f* ▸**half-blind** à moitié aveugle ▸**half-blood** (*US*) = **half-breed** ▸**half-board** (*in hotel*) demi-pension *f* ▸**half-breed** **n** *person* métis(se) *m(f)* ◊ **adj** (*also* **half-bred**) *person* métis; *animal* hybride ▸**half-brother** demi-frère *m* ▸**half-caste** **adj, n** métis(se) *m(f)* ▸**half-century** demi-siècle *m* ▸**half-circle** demi-cercle *m* ▸**half-clad** à demi vêtu ▸**half-closed** à demi fermé, à moitié fermé ▸**half-cock:** (*fig*) **to go off at half-cock** rater ▸**half-cocked** *gun* à moitié armé, au cran de sûreté; *plan, scheme* mal préparé, bâclé ▸**half-conscious** à demi conscient ▸**half-convinced** à demi convaincu, à moitié convaincu ▸**half-cooked** à moitié cuit ▸**half-crazy** à moitié fou ▸**half-crown:** (*Brit* †) **a half-crown** (*coin*), **half-a-crown** (*value*) une demi-couronne ▸**half-cup bra** soutien-gorge *m* à balconnet ▸**half-day** demi-journée *f*; **(to have a) half-day (holiday)** (prendre une) demi-journée (de congé) ▸**half-dazed** à demi hébété ▸**half-dead** (*lit, fig*) à moitié mort, à demi mort (*with* de), plus mort que vif ▸**half-deaf** à moitié sourd ▸**half-deck** (*Naut*) demi-pont *m* ▸**half-digested** (*lit, fig*) mal digéré ▸**half-dollar:** (*US*) **a half-dollar** (*coin*), **half-a-dollar** (*value*) un demi-dollar; (*Brit* ‡†) une demi-couronne ▸**half-dozen:** **a half-dozen, half-a-dozen** une demi-douzaine ▸**half-dressed** à demi vêtu ▸**half-drowned** quasi noyé ▸**half-educated:** **he is half-educated** il a reçu une éducation limitée, il n'est pas très instruit ▸**half-empty** **adj** à moitié vide ◊ **vt** vider à moitié ▸**half-fare** **n** demi-place *f*, demi-tarif *m* ◊ **adv** à demi-tarif ▸**half-fill** remplir à moitié ▸**half-forgotten** à moitié oublié ▸**half-frozen** à moitié gelé ▸**half-full** à moitié plein ▸**half-grown** à mi-croissance ▸**half-hearted** *manner, person* tiède, sans enthousiasme; *attempt* timide, sans conviction; *welcome* peu enthousiaste ▸**half-heartedly** avec tiédeur, sans enthousiasme, sans conviction ▸**half-heartedness** tiédeur *f*, manque *m* d'enthousiasme *or* de conviction ▸**half-hitch** demi-clef *f* ▸**half holiday** (*Brit*) demi-journée *f* de congé ▸**half-hour:** **a half-hour, half-an-hour** une demi-heure; **on the half-hour** à la demie ▸**half-hourly** **adv** toutes les demi-heures, de demi-heure en demi-heure ◊ **adj** (de) toutes les demi-heures ▸**half-jokingly** en plaisantant à moitié, sur un ton mi-moqueur ▸**half-length** **n** (*Swimming etc*) demi-longueur *f* ◊ **adj** *portrait* en buste ▸**half-lie** demi-mensonge *m* ▸**half-life** (*Phys*) demi-vie *f* ▸**half-light** demi-jour *m* ▸**half-mad** à moitié fou ▸**half-mast:** **at half-mast** en berne, à mi-mât ▸**half-monthly** bi-mensuel ▸**half-moon** demi-lune *f*; (*on fingernail*) lunule *f* ▸**half-naked** à demi nu, à moitié nu ▸**half-nelson** (*Wrestling*) clef *f* du cou ▸**half-note** (*US Mus*) blanche *f* ▸**half-open** *eye, mouth* entrouvert; *window* entrebâillé; *door* entrouvert, entrebâillé ▸**half open** entrouvrir, entrebâiller ▸**half-pay:** **on half-pay** (*gen*) à demi-salaire, à *or* en demi-traitement; (*Mil*) en demi-solde ▸**half-penny** [ˈheɪpnɪ] **n** (*coin: pl* **halfpennies;** *value: pl* **halfpence**) demi-penny *m* ◊ **adj** d'un demi-penny; **he hasn't got a halfpenny** il n'a pas le sou, il n'a pas un sou ▸**half-pint** ≃ quart *m* de litre; (*US* *: *fig: small person*) demi-portion* *f* (*personne*); **a half-pint (of beer)** ≃ un bock ▸**half-pleased** pas trop mécontent ▸**half-price:** **at half-price** à moitié prix; **the goods were reduced to half-price** le prix des articles était réduit de moitié; **children admitted (at) half-price** les enfants paient demi-tarif *or* demi-place; **a half-price hat** un chapeau à moitié prix ▸**half-raw** à moitié cru ▸**half-rest** (*Mus*) demi-pause *f* ▸**half seas over**‡ parti*, dans les vignes du Seigneur ▸**half-serious** pas entièrement sérieux ▸**half-shut** à moitié fermé ▸**half-sister** demi-sœur *f* ▸**half-size** *[shoes]* demi-pointure *f*; **half-size(d) model** modèle réduit de moitié ▸**half-staff:** (*US*) **at half-staff** en berne, à mi-mât ▸**half-starved** à demi mort de faim, affamé ▸**half term** (*Brit Scol etc*) congé *m* de demi-trimestre, petites vacances ▸**half-timbered** à colombage ▸**half-time** (*Sport*) mi-temps *f*; **at half-time** à la mi-temps; (*Ind*) **on half-time** à mi-temps; **they are working half-time** ils travaillent à mi-temps *or* à la demi-journée; **a half-time job** un poste à mi-temps; **half-time score** score *m* à mi-temps; **they are on half-time (work)** = **they are working half-time** ▸**half-tone** (*US Mus*) demi-ton *m*; (*Art*) demi-teinte *f*; (*Phot*) similigravure *f* ▸**half-track** (*tread*) chenille *f*; (*vehicle*) half-track *m* ▸**half-truth** demi-vérité *f* ▸**half-understood** compris à moitié, mal compris ▸**half-used** dont il ne reste que la moitié ▸**half volley** (*Tennis etc*) demi-volée *f* ▸**halfway** *see* **halfway** ▸**halfwit** idiot(e) *m(f)*, imbécile *mf* ▸**halfwitted** idiot, imbécile, faible d'esprit ▸**half-yearly** (*esp Brit*) **adj** semestriel ◊ **adv** tous les six mois, par semestre.

halfway [ˈhɑːfˈweɪ] 1 **adv** à mi-chemin. **~ to Paris** à mi-chemin de Paris; (*lit, fig*) **to be ~ between** être à mi-chemin entre; (*lit*) **to go ~** faire la moitié du chemin; (*fig*) **the decision goes ~ to giving the strikers what they want** avec cette décision on est à mi-chemin de donner satisfaction aux grévistes; **~ up (the hill)** à mi-côte; **~ down (the hill)** à mi-pente; **~ up** *or* **down (the pipe/tree/stairs** *etc*) à mi-hauteur (du tuyau/de l'arbre/de l'escalier *etc*); **~ up** *or* **along (the road)** à mi-chemin; **~ along (the line of cars** *etc*) vers le milieu (de la file de voitures *etc*); (*lit, fig*) **we're ~ there** nous n'avons plus que la moitié du chemin à faire; **I'll meet you ~** (*lit*) j'irai à votre rencontre, je ferai la moitié du chemin; (*fig*) coupons la poire en deux, faisons un compromis; (*fig*) **he agreed to meet them** (*or* **us** *etc*) **~** il a accepté de couper la poire en deux, il a accepté un compromis; (*fig*) **to meet trouble ~** (aller) chercher les ennuis, aller au-devant des ennuis; **~ through the book/film** à la moitié du livre/du film.

2 **comp** ▸**halfway house** maison *f or* bâtiment *m etc* à mi-chemin; (*Hist: inn*) hôtellerie *f* à mi-chemin entre deux relais; (*fig*) milieu *m*; (*also* **halfway hostel:** *for prisoners, mental patients etc*) centre *m* (ouvert) de réadaptation (*pour prisonniers, malades mentaux etc*) ▸**halfway line** (*Ftbl*) ligne *f* médiane.

halibut [ˈhælɪbət] **n, pl ~** *or* **~s** flétan *m* (holibut).

halitosis [ˌhælɪˈtəʊsɪs] **n** mauvaise haleine.

hall [hɔːl] 1 **n** a (*large public room*) salle *f*; *[castle, public building]* (grande) salle; (*village ~, church ~*) salle paroissiale; (*Brit Univ: refectory*) réfectoire *m*.

b (*mansion*) château *m*, manoir *m*. (*Theat*) **to play the ~s** faire du music-hall; *see* **concert, music, town** *etc*.

c (*entrance way*) *[house]* vestibule *m*, entrée *f*, hall *m*; *[hotel]* hall; (*corridor*) couloir *m*, corridor *m*.

d (*Univ: also* (*Brit*) **~ of residence,** (*US*) **residence ~**) résidence *f* universitaire.

2 **comp** ▸**hallmark** **n** *[gold, silver]* poinçon *m*; (*fig*) sceau *m*, marque *f* ◊ **vt** poinçonner; **the hallmark of genius** le sceau *or* la marque *or* l'empreinte *f* du génie ▸**hall porter** (*Brit*) (*in blocks of flats*) concierge *mf*; (*in hotel*) portier *m* ▸**hallstand,** (*US*) **hall tree** portemanteau *m* ▸**hallway** vestibule *m*; (*corridor*) couloir *m*.

hallelujah [ˌhælɪˈluːjə] **excl, n** alléluia (*m*).

hallo [həˈləʊ] **excl** (*in greeting*) bonjour!, salut!*; (*Telec*) allô!; (*to attract attention*) hé!, ohé!; (*in surprise*) tiens!

halloo [həˈluː] 1 **excl** (*Hunting*) taïaut!; (*gen*) ohé! 2 **vi** (*Hunting*) crier taïaut; (*gen*) appeler (à grands cris).

hallow [ˈhæləʊ] **vt** sanctifier, consacrer. **~ed be Thy name** que ton nom soit sanctifié; **~ed ground** terre sainte *or* bénie; (*fig*) **a ~ed right** un droit sacré.

Hallowe(')en [ˌhæləʊˈiːn] **n** veille *f* de la Toussaint.

hallucinant [həˈluːsɪnənt] **n** hallucinogène *m*.

hallucinate [həˈluːsɪˌneɪt] **vi** avoir des hallucinations.

hallucination [həˌluːsɪˈneɪʃən] **n** hallucination *f*.

hallucinatory [həˈluːsɪnətərɪ] **adj** hallucinatoire.

hallucinogenic [həˌluːsɪnəʊˈdʒenɪk] **adj** hallucinogène.

halo [ˈheɪləʊ] **n, pl ~(e)s** *[saint etc]* auréole *f*, nimbe *m*; (*Astron*) halo *m*.

halogen [ˈhæləˌdʒɛn] **n** halogène *m*. (*Aut*) **~ lamp** lampe *f* à iode.

halt[1] [hɔːlt] 1 **n** a halte *f*, arrêt *m*. **5 minutes' ~** 5 minutes d'arrêt; **to come to a ~** *[person]* faire halte, s'arrêter; *[vehicle]* s'arrêter; *[process]* être interrompu; **to call a ~** (*order a stop*) commander halte; (*stop*) faire halte; (*fig*) **to call a ~ to sth** mettre fin à qch. b (*Brit Rail*) halte *f*. 2 **vi** faire halte, s'arrêter. **~!** halte! 3 **vt** *vehicle* faire arrêter; *process* interrompre. 4 **comp** ▸**halt sign** (*Aut*) (panneau *m* de) stop *m*.

halt[2] [hɔːlt] 1 **adj** (††: *lame*) boiteux. 2 **npl: the ~** les estropiés *mpl*.

halter [ˈhɔːltəʳ] **n** *[horse]* licou *m*, collier *m*; (*hangman's noose*) corde *f* (*de pendaison*). **a dress with a ~ top** *or* **neckline** une robe dos nu *inv*.

halting [ˈhɔːltɪŋ] **adj** *speech, voice* hésitant, haché, entrecoupé; *progress* hésitant; *verse* boiteux; *style* heurté.

haltingly [ˈhɔːltɪŋlɪ] **adv** de façon hésitante, de façon heurtée.

halve [hɑːv] 1 **vt** *apple etc* partager *or* diviser en deux (moitiés égales); *expense, time* réduire *or* diminuer de moitié. 2 **vi** *[sales, figures]* être réduit de moitié.
halves [hɑːvz] **npl of half.**
halyard [ˈhæljəd] **n** (*Naut*) drisse *f*.
ham [hæm] 1 **n** a (*Culin*) jambon *m*. ~ **and eggs** œufs *mpl* au jambon. b (*Anat*) (*thigh*) cuisse *f*; (*buttock*) fesse *f*. c (*: *Theat: pej*) cabotin(e) *m(f)* (*pej*). d (*: *Rad*) radio-amateur *m*. 2 **comp** *sandwich* au jambon ▸**ham acting** cabotinage *m* ▸**ham-fisted, ham-handed** maladroit, gauche ▸**hamstring n** tendon *m* du jarret ◊ **vt** couper les jarrets à; (*fig*) couper ses moyens à, paralyser ▸**hamstring injury** claquage *m* tendineux (au jarret). 3 **vti** (*: *Theat: also* ~ **it up***) forcer son rôle.
Hamburg [ˈhæmbɜːg] **n** Hambourg.
hamburger [ˈhæm,bɜːgəʳ] **n** (*gen*) hamburger *m*; (*US: also* ~ **meat**) viande *f* hachée.
Hamitic [hæˈmɪtɪk] **adj** chamitique.
hamlet [ˈhæmlɪt] **n** hameau *m*. **H**~ Hamlet *m*.
hammer [ˈhæməʳ] 1 **n** (*gen, auctioneer's; Climbing, Mus, Sport, Tech etc*) marteau *m*; *[gun]* chien *m*. **the** ~ **and sickle** la faucille et le marteau; **they were going at it** ~ **and tongs** (*working*) ils y allaient de tout leur cœur *or* à bras raccourcis; (*arguing*) ils discutaient passionnément *or* avec feu; (*quarrelling*) ils se disputaient avec violence; (*at auction*) **to come under the** ~ être mis aux enchères; (*US: accelerate*) **to drop the** ~* appuyer sur le champignon*.
2 **comp** ▸**hammer drill** perceuse *f* à percussion ▸**hammerhead** (*shark*) requin *m* marteau ▸**hammertoe** orteil *m* en marteau ▸**hammertoed** aux orteils en marteau.
3 **vt** a battre au marteau, marteler. **to** ~ **a nail into a plank** enfoncer un clou dans une planche (à coups de marteau); **to** ~ **a nail home** enfoncer un clou (à fond); (*fig*) **to** ~ **sb/sth into the ground** venir à bout de qn/qch; (*fig*) **to** ~ **a point home** bien insister sur un point (pour le faire comprendre); **to** ~ **into shape** *metal* façonner au marteau; (*fig*) *plan, agreement* mettre au point; **I tried to** ~ **some sense into him** je me suis efforcé de lui faire entendre raison; **to** ~ **an idea into sb's head** enfoncer de force *or* faire entrer de force une idée dans la tête de qn.
b (* *fig*) (*defeat*) battre à plate(s) couture(s); (*criticize severely*) éreinter, démolir*. **the critics ~ed the film** les critiques ont éreinté *or* ont démoli* le film.
c (*St Ex*) *stockbroker* déclarer en faillite *or* failli.
4 **vi** (*also* ~ **away**) frapper au marteau. (*fig*) **he was ~ing (away) at the door** il frappait à la porte à coups redoublés; **he was ~ing (away) on the piano** il tapait sur le piano (à bras raccourcis); **to** ~ **(away) at a problem** s'acharner sur *or* travailler d'arrache-pied à un problème.
▸**hammer down vt sep** *nail* enfoncer; *metal* aplatir au marteau; *loose plank* fixer.
▸**hammer in vt sep** enfoncer (au marteau). **he hammered the nail in with his shoe** il a enfoncé le clou avec son soulier.
▸**hammer out vt sep** *metal* étendre au marteau; (*fig*) *plan, agreement* élaborer (avec difficulté); *difficulties* démêler, aplanir; *verse, music* marteler.
▸**hammer together** *pieces of wood etc* assembler au marteau.
hammering [ˈhæmərɪŋ] **n** (*action*) martelage *m*; (*sound*) martèlement *m*; (*: *fig*) (*defeat*) punition* *f*, dérouillée‡ *f*; (*criticism*) éreintement *m*. **to take a** ~* *[team, boxer, player]* prendre une punition* *or* une dérouillée‡; *[book, play, film]* se faire esquinter* *or* éreinter.
hammock [ˈhæmək] **n** hamac *m*.
hamper¹ [ˈhæmpəʳ] **n** panier *m* d'osier, manne *f*; (*for oysters, fish, game*) bourriche *f*. **a** ~ **of food** un panier garni (*de nourriture*); *see* **picnic.**
hamper² [ˈhæmpəʳ] **vt** *person* gêner; *movement* gêner, entraver.
hamster [ˈhæmstəʳ] **n** hamster *m*.
hand [hænd] 1 **n** a (*Anat*) main *f*. **on (one's) ~s and knees** à quatre pattes; **to have** *or* **hold in one's** ~ *book* tenir à la main; *money* avoir dans la main; (*fig*) *victory* tenir entre ses mains; **give me your** ~ donne-moi la main; **to take sb's** ~ prendre la main de qn; **he took her by the** ~ il l'a prise par la main; **to lead sb by the** ~ conduire *or* mener qn par la main; (*fig: in cash, not taxed*) **he got £100 in his** ~ il a eu 100 livres en cash; **to take sth with** *or* **in both ~s** prendre qch à deux mains; (*fig*) **he clutched at my offer with both ~s** il s'est jeté sur ma proposition; (*Mus*) **for four ~s** pour *or* à quatre mains; **~s up!** (*at gunpoint*) haut les mains!; (*in school etc*) levez la main!; **~s off!*** pas touche!*, bas les pattes!‡; **~s off the sweets!*** touche pas aux bonbons!*; (*fig*) **~s off our village*** laissez notre village tranquille; (*lit*) ~ **over** ~, ~ **over fist** main sur main; (*fig*) **he's making money** ~ **over fist** il fait des affaires d'or; **he's very good** *or* **clever with his ~s** il est très adroit de ses mains; **I'm no good with my ~s at all** je ne sais (strictement) rien faire de mes mains *or* de mes dix doigts; (*fig*) **I'm always putting my** ~ **in my pocket** je n'arrête pas de débourser *or* de mettre la main à la poche; (*fig*) **to sit on one's ~s** *[audience]* applaudir faiblement; *[committee etc]* se contenter d'attendre, ne rien faire; (*fig*) **you could see his** ~ **in everything the committee did** on reconnaissait son empreinte *or* influence dans tout ce que faisait le comité.
b (*phrases*) **at** ~ à portée de la main, sous la main; **to keep sth at** ~ garder qch à portée de la main; **he has enough money at** ~ il a assez d'argent disponible; **summer is (close) at** ~ l'été est (tout) proche; **at first** ~ de première main; **the information at** *or* **to** ~ les renseignements *mpl* disponibles; **by** ~ à la main; **made by** ~ fait à la main; **the letter was written by** ~ c'était une lettre manuscrite, la lettre était manuscrite *or* écrite à la main; **to send a letter by** ~ faire porter une lettre (*à la main*); **from** ~ **to** ~ de main en main (*see also* **2**); **to live from** ~ **to mouth** vivre au jour le jour (*see also* **2**); **pistol in** ~ pistolet *m* au poing; **in one's own ~s** entre ses mains; (*lit, fig*) **to put sth into sb's ~s** remettre qch entre les mains de qn; **to put o.s. in sb's ~s** s'en remettre à qn, se mettre entre les mains de qn; **my life is in your ~s** ma vie est entre vos mains; **to fall into the ~s of** tomber aux mains *or* entre les mains de; **to be in good ~s** être en bonnes mains; **I have this matter in** ~ **at the moment** je suis en train de m'occuper de cette affaire; **he had £6,000 in** ~ il avait 6 000 livres de disponibles; (*Comm*) **stock in** ~ existence *f or* marchandises *fpl* en magasin; **cash in** ~ encaisse *f*; **the matter in** *or* **on** ~ l'affaire en question; **it has got nothing to do with the matter in** ~ cela n'a rien à voir avec l'affaire en question *or* avec la question qui nous préoccupe; **he had the situation well in** ~ il avait la situation bien en main; **she took the child in** ~ elle a pris l'enfant en main; **to keep o.s. well in** ~ se contrôler; **work in** ~ travail *m* en cours *or* en chantier; **to have sth on one's ~s** avoir qch sur les bras (*see also* **time**); (*Comm*) **goods left on our ~s** marchandises invendues; **on the right/left** ~ du côté droit/gauche; **on my right** ~ à ma droite; **on every** ~, **on all ~s** partout, de tous (les) côtés; **on the one** ~ ... **on the other** ~ d'une part ... d'autre part; **yes, but on the other** ~ **he is very rich** oui, mais par contre il est très riche; **to get sth off one's ~s** se débarrasser *or* se décharger de qch; **I'll take it off your ~s** je m'en chargerai, je vous en déchargerai *or* débarrasserai; **his daughter was off his ~s** sa fille n'était plus à sa charge; **it is out of his ~s** ce n'est plus lui qui s'en occupe, il n'en a plus la responsabilité; (*gen: instantly*) **out of** ~ d'emblée; **to condemn sb out of** ~ condamner qn sans jugement; **to execute sb out of** ~ exécuter qn sommairement; **to get out of** ~ *[child, dog, situation]* devenir impossible; *[prices, spending etc]* déraper, échapper à tout contrôle; **this child/dog is quite out of** ~ il n'y a plus moyen de tenir cet enfant/ce chien; **to** ~ sous la main, à portée de la main; **I have not got the letter to** ~ je n'ai pas la lettre sous la main; (*Comm*) **your letter has come to** ~ votre lettre m'est parvenue; (*Comm*) **your letter of 6th inst. to** ~ en mains votre lettre du 6 courant (*Comm*); **he seized the first weapon to** ~ il s'est emparé de la première arme venue; **to rule with a firm** ~ gouverner d'une main ferme; **with a heavy** ~ avec poigne, à la cravache; **they are** ~ **in glove** ils s'entendent comme larrons en foire; **he's** ~ **in glove with them** il est de mèche avec eux; **he never does a** ~**'s turn** il ne remue pas le petit doigt, il n'en fiche pas une rame‡; **the hedgehog ate out of his** ~ le hérisson lui mangeait dans la main; (*fig*) **he's got the boss eating out of his** ~* il fait marcher le patron au doigt et à l'œil; **to force sb's** ~ forcer la main à qn; **to get one's** ~ **in** se faire la main; **to keep one's** ~ **in** garder *or* s'entretenir la main; **he can't keep his ~s off the money** il ne peut pas s'empêcher de toucher à l'argent; **I have my ~s full at the moment** je suis très occupé en ce moment; **to have one's ~s full with** avoir fort à faire avec, avoir du pain sur la planche avec; (*lit, fig*) **to have one's ~s tied** avoir les mains liées; **I can do it with one** ~ **tied behind my back** je peux le faire les doigts dans le nez‡, c'est un jeu d'enfant pour moi; **to have a** ~ **in** *piece of work, decision* être pour quelque chose dans, jouer un rôle dans; *crime* être mêlé à; *plot* tremper dans; **she had a** ~ **in it** elle y était pour quelque chose; **I have no** ~ **in it** je n'y suis pour rien; **I will have no** ~ **in it** je ne veux rien avoir à faire là-dedans; **to take a** ~ **in sth** se mêler de qch; **to take a** ~ **in doing sth** participer à qch, contribuer à qch; **to give sb a (helping)** ~ **(to do), to lend sb a** ~ **(to do)** donner un coup de main à qn (pour faire); **he got his brother to give him a** ~ il s'est fait aider par son frère, il a obtenu de son frère qu'il lui donne (*subj*) un coup de main; **give me a** ~, **will you?** tu peux me donner un coup de main?; (*Theat: applause*) **they gave him a big** ~* ils l'ont applaudi bien fort; (*Theat*) **give him a (big)** ~ **now!*** (et maintenant) on l'applaudit bien fort!; **to try one's** ~ **at sth** s'essayer à qch; **to get the upper** ~ **of sb** prendre l'avantage *or* le dessus sur qn; **to have the upper** ~ avoir le dessus; **to put** *or* **set one's** ~ **to sth** entreprendre qch; **he can set his** ~ **to most things** il y a peu de choses qu'il ne sache (pas) faire; (*fig liter*) **to put** *or* **set one's** ~ **to the plough** se mettre à l'ouvrage *or* à l'œuvre; **to hold** *or* (*liter*) **stay one's** ~ se retenir; (*fig*) **to show one's** ~ montrer *or* dévoiler son jeu; **to win sth ~s down** gagner qch haut la main; **to be waited on** ~ **and foot** se faire servir comme un prince; (*fig*) **he asked for her** ~ **(in marriage)** il a demandé sa main (en mariage); (*liter*) **she gave him her** ~ elle lui a accordé sa main; *see also* **1g** *and* **bite, free, high, lay¹** *etc.*
c (*worker*) travailleur *m*, -euse *f* manuel(le), ouvrier *m*, -ière *f*. **~s** (*Ind etc*) main-d'œuvre *f*; (*Naut*) équipage *m*, hommes *mpl*; **to take on ~s** embaucher (de la main-d'œuvre); (*Naut*) **all ~s on deck** tout le monde sur le pont; (*Naut*) **lost with all ~s** perdu corps et biens; (*fig*) **he's a great** ~ **at (doing) that** il a le coup de main pour (faire) cela, il est vraiment doué pour (faire) cela; (*fig*) **old** ~ vétéran *m*, vieux

routier; **he's an old ~ (at it)** il n'en est pas à son coup d'essai, il connaît la musique*; *see* **dab³**, **factory**, **farm** *etc*.

d *[clock etc]* aiguille *f*; (*Typ*) index *m*.

e (*Measure*) paume *f*. **a horse 13 ~s high** un cheval de 13 paumes.

f (*handwriting*) écriture *f*. **the letter was in his ~** la lettre était (écrite) de sa main; **he writes a good ~** il a une belle écriture *or* une belle main.

g (*Cards*) main *f*, jeu *m*; (*game etc*) partie *f*. **I've got a good ~** j'ai une belle main *or* un beau jeu; **we played a ~ of bridge** nous avons fait une partie de bridge; (*lit, fig*) **to show one's ~** montrer son jeu.

h (*Culin*) **~ of pork** jambonneau *m*; **~ of bananas** régime *m* de bananes.

2 **comp** ▶**handbag** sac *m* à main ▶**handball** (*Sport*) handball *m* ▶**handbasin** lavabo *m* ▶**handbell** sonnette *f*, clochette *f* ▶**handbill** prospectus *m* ▶**handblower** sèche-mains *m inv* ▶**handbook** (*instructions*) manuel *m* (*see also* **teacher**); *[tourist]* guide *m*; *[museum]* livret *m*, catalogue *m* ▶**handbrake** (*Brit Aut*) frein *m* à main ▶**handcar** (*Rail*) draisine *f* ▶**handcart** charrette *f* à bras ▶**handclasp** poignée *f* de main ▶**hand controls** (*Aut*) commandes *fpl* à main ▶**handcraft** = **handicraft** ▶**hand cream** crème *f* pour les mains ▶**handcuff** **n** menotte *f* ◊ **vt** mettre *or* passer les menottes à; **to be handcuffed** avoir les menottes aux poignets ▶**hand-drier, hand-dryer** sèche-mains *m inv* ▶**handful** *see* **handful** ▶**hand grenade** (*Mil*) grenade *f* (à main) ▶**handgrip** (*on cycle, machine etc*) poignée *f*; (*handshake*) poignée de main ▶**handgun** pistolet *m* ▶**hand-held** à main ▶**handhold** prise *f* de main ▶**hand-in-hand** (*lit*) la main dans la main; (*fig*) ensemble, de concert; (*fig*) **to go hand-in-hand (with)** aller de pair (avec) ▶**handiwork** *see* **handiwork** ▶**handjob****: **to have a handjob** se branler** ▶**hand-knitted** tricoté à la main ▶**hand lotion** lotion *f* pour les mains ▶**hand-luggage** bagages *mpl* à main ▶**handmade** fait (à la) main ▶**handmaid(en)** (*lit, fig*) servante *f* ▶**hand-me-down**: (*pej*) **it's a hand-me-down from my sister** c'est un vêtement qui me vient de ma sœur; **hand-me-downs*** **npl** vêtements *mpl* d'occasion; (*scruffier*) friperie *f* ▶**hand-out** (*leaflet*) prospectus *m*; (*at lecture, meeting*) polycopié *m*, documentation *f*; (*press release*) communiqué *m*; (*money*) (*from government, official body*) aide *f*, subvention *f*; (*alms*) charité *f*, aumône *f* ▶**hand-pick** trier sur le volet ▶**hand-picked** *fruit, vegetables etc* cueilli à la main; (*fig*) soigneusement sélectionné ▶**hand print** **n** empreinte *f* de main ▶**hand-printed** imprimé à la main ▶**hand puppet** marionnette *f* à gaine ▶**handrail** *[stairs etc]* rampe *f*, main courante, balustrade *f*; *[bridge, quay]* garde-fou *m* ▶**handsaw** scie *f* à main ▶**handset** (*Telec*) combiné *m* ▶**handshake** poignée *f* de main (*see* **golden**); (*Comput*) prise *f* de contact ▶**hands-off** (*fig*) *policy etc* de non-intervention ▶**hands-on** (*gen*) sur le tas; *experience* sur le tas; (*Comput etc*) appareil en main ▶**handsome** *see* **handsome** ▶**hand-spray** douchette *f* (amovible) ▶**handspring** saut *m* de mains ▶**handstand: to do a handstand** faire l'arbre droit ▶**hand-stitched** cousu main ▶**hand-to-hand: to fight hand-to-hand** combattre corps à corps; **a hand-to-hand fight** un corps à corps; **hand-to-hand fighting** du corps à corps ▶**hand-to-mouth: to lead a hand-to-mouth existence** vivre au jour le jour ▶**hand towel** essuie-mains *m inv* ▶**handwork** = **handiwork** ▶**hand-woven** tissé à la main ▶**handwrite** écrire à la main ▶**handwriting** écriture *f* ▶**handwritten** manuscrit, écrit à la main.

3 **vt** a (*give*) passer, donner (*to* à); (*hold out*) tendre (*to* à). (*fig*) **you've got to ~ it to him*, he did it very well** il faut bien reconnaître *or* il faut lui rendre cette justice qu'il l'a très bien fait; (*fig*) **it was ~ed to him (on a plate)*** ça lui a été apporté sur un plateau; (*fig*) **to ~ sb a line about sth**** raconter des bobards* à qn à propos de qch.

b **he ~ed the lady into/out of the car** il tendit sa main à la dame pour l'aider à monter dans/à descendre de la voiture.

▶**hand around vt sep** = **hand round**.

▶**hand back vt sep** rendre (*to* à).

▶**hand down vt sep** a (*lit*) **hand me down the vase** descends-moi le vase; **he handed me down the book from the shelf** il a descendu le livre du rayon et me l'a tendu. b (*fig*) transmettre. **the story/the sword was handed down from father to son** l'histoire/l'épée était transmise *or* se transmettait de père en fils. c (*US Jur*) *decision* rendre.

▶**hand in vt sep** remettre (*to* à). **hand this in at the office** remettez cela à quelqu'un au bureau.

▶**hand on vt sep** transmettre (*to* à). (*fig*) **to hand on the torch** passer *or* transmettre le flambeau.

▶**hand out** 1 **vt sep** distribuer. **to hand out advice*** prodiguer des conseils. 2 **handout** **n** *see* **hand 2**.

▶**hand over** 1 **vi** (*fig*) **to hand over to sb** passer le relais à qn. 2 **vt sep** *book, object* remettre (*to* à); *criminal, prisoner* livrer (*to* à); *authority, powers* (*transfer*) transmettre (*to* à); (*surrender*) céder (*to* à); *property, business* céder.

▶**hand round vt sep** *bottles, papers* faire circuler; *cakes* (faire) passer (à la ronde), *[hostess]* offrir.

▶**hand up vt sep** passer (*de bas en haut*).

-handed ['hændɪd] **adj ending in comps** qui a la main ... . **empty-handed** les mains vides; **heavy-handed** qui a la main lourde; *see* **left²**, **short** *etc*.

Handel ['hændəl] **n** Händel *m or* Haendel *m*.

handful ['hændfʊl] **n** *[coins, objects etc]* poignée *f*. **by the ~, in ~s** à *or* par poignées; **there was only a ~ of people at the concert** il n'y avait qu'une poignée de gens au concert, il y avait quatre pelés et un tondu au concert*; (*fig*) **the children are a ~*** les enfants ne me (*or* lui *etc*) laissent pas une minute de répit.

handicap ['hændɪkæp] 1 **n** a (*Sport*) handicap *m*. *[racehorse]* **weight ~** surcharge *f*; **time ~** handicap (de temps). b (*disadvantage*) handicap *m*, désavantage *m*. **his appearance is a great ~** son aspect physique le handicape beaucoup; **to be under a great ~** avoir un désavantage *or* un handicap énorme; *see* **physical**. 2 **vt** (*Sport, gen*) handicaper. **he was greatly ~ped by his accent** il était très handicapé par son accent.

handicapped ['hændɪkæpt] 1 **adj** handicapé. **~ children** enfants handicapés; **mentally/physically ~** handicapé mentalement/physiquement. 2 **npl: the ~** les handicapés *mpl*; **the mentally/physically ~** les handicapés mentaux/physiques.

handicraft ['hændɪkrɑːft] **n** (*work*) (travail *m* d')artisanat *m*; (*skill*) habileté manuelle. **exhibition of ~s** exposition *f* d'objets artisanaux.

handily ['hændɪlɪ] **adv** a (*conveniently*) *positioned etc* bien, d'une façon commode. b (*US: easily*) *win etc* facilement.

handiness ['hændɪnɪs] **n** (*see* **handy**) *[object, method]* commodité *f*, aspect *m* pratique; *[person]* adresse *f*, dextérité manuelle. **because of the ~ of the library** parce qu'il est si facile de se rendre à la bibliothèque.

handiwork ['hændɪwɜːk] **n** (*lit*) travail manuel, ouvrage *m*; (*fig*) œuvre *f*, ouvrage. (*fig*) **that is his ~** c'est son œuvre.

handkerchief ['hæŋkətʃɪf] **n** mouchoir *m*; (*fancy*) pochette *f*; (*for neck*) foulard *m*.

handle ['hændl] 1 **n** *[basket, bucket]* anse *f*; *[broom, spade, knife]* manche *m*; *[door, drawer, suitcase]* poignée *f*; *[handcart]* brancard *m*; *[saucepan]* queue *f*; *[pump, stretcher, wheelbarrow]* bras *m*; *[tap]* clef *f*, poignée *f*. *[car]* **(starting) ~** manivelle *f*; (*fig*) **to have a ~ to one's name*** avoir un titre; *see* **fly³**.

2 **vt** a (*touch*) *fruit, food etc* toucher à; (*move etc by hand: esp Ind*) manipuler, manier. **her hands are black from handling newsprint** elle a les mains noires d'avoir manié *or* manipulé des feuilles de journaux; **please do not ~ the goods** prière de ne pas toucher aux marchandises; (*label*) **"~ with care"** "fragile"; **the crowd ~d him roughly** (*lit*) la foule l'a malmené; (*fig*) la foule l'a hué; (*Ftbl*) **to ~ the ball** toucher le ballon de la main, faire une faute de mains.

b (*control, deal with*) *ship* manœuvrer, gouverner; *car* conduire, manœuvrer; *weapon* manier; *person, animal* manier, s'y prendre avec. **he knows how to ~ a gun** il sait se servir d'un revolver; **he ~d the situation very well** il a très bien conduit l'affaire; **I'll ~ this** je m'en charge, je vais m'en occuper; **he knows how to ~ his son** il sait très bien s'y prendre avec son fils; **this child is very hard to ~** cet enfant est très difficile *or* dur*; **can you ~ dogs?** savez-vous (comment) vous y prendre avec les chiens?; **she can certainly ~ children** il n'y a pas de doute qu'elle sait s'y prendre avec les enfants.

c (*Comm*) *commodity, product* avoir, faire. **we don't ~ that type of product** nous ne faisons pas ce genre de produit; **we don't ~ that type of business** nous ne traitons pas ce type d'affaires; **do you ~ tax matters?** est-ce que vous vous occupez de fiscalité?; **the treasurer ~s large sums of money** le trésorier a la responsabilité de grosses sommes d'argent; **to ~ stolen goods** receler des objets volés; **Orly ~s 5 million passengers a year** 5 millions de passagers passent par Orly chaque année; **we ~ 200 passengers a day** 200 voyageurs par jour passent par nos services; **can the port ~ big ships?** le port peut-il recevoir les gros bateaux?

3 **vi: to ~ well/badly** *[ship]* être facile/difficile à manœuvrer; *[car, gun]* être facile/difficile à manier; *[horse]* répondre bien/mal aux aides.

4 **comp** ▶**handlebar moustache** (*hum*) moustache *f* en crocs *or* en guidon de vélo* (*hum*) ▶**handlebars** **npl** guidon *m*.

-handled ['hændld] **adj ending in comps** au manche de, à la poignée de. **a wooden-handled spade** une pelle au manche de bois *or* avec un manche de bois.

handler ['hændləʳ] **n** a (*also* **dog ~**) maître-chien *m*. b *[stock]* manutentionnaire *mf*.

handling ['hændlɪŋ] **n** *[ship]* manœuvre *f*; *[car]* maniement *m*; *[goods, objects]* (*Ind*) manutention *f*; (*fingering*) maniement, manipulation *f*; *[stolen goods]* recel *m*. **his ~ of the matter** la façon dont il a traité l'affaire; *[person, object]* **to get some rough ~** se faire malmener; (*Comm*) **~ charges** frais *mpl* de manutention.

handsome ['hænsəm] **adj** a (*good-looking*) *person* beau (*f* belle); *furniture, building* beau, élégant; (*fig*) *conduct, compliment* généreux; *gift* riche, généreux. **~ apology** excuse *f* honorable. b (*considerable*) **a ~ amount** une jolie somme; **a ~ fortune** une belle fortune; **to make a ~ profit out of sth** réaliser de jolis bénéfices sur qch; **to sell sth for a ~ price** vendre qch un bon prix *or* pour une jolie somme.

handsomely ['hænsəmlɪ] **adv** (*elegantly*) élégamment, avec élégance; (*generously*) *contribute, donate* généreusement, avec générosité; *apologise, agree* avec bonne grâce, élégamment. **he behaved very ~** il s'est conduit très généreusement *or* élégamment.

handy ['hændɪ] 1 **adj** a *person* adroit. **he's a very ~ person** il est très

adroit de ses mains, il sait se servir de ses mains; **he's ~ with his fists*** il sait se servir de ses poings; **he's ~ with a gun*** il sait se servir d'un revolver; **she's ~ with a sewing machine*** elle sait très bien se servir d'une machine à coudre; **he's ~ in the kitchen*** il sait très bien se débrouiller dans la cuisine.
b (*close at hand*) *tool* accessible, sous la main, prêt. **in a ~ place** dans un endroit commode, à portée de la main; **I always have an aspirin ~** j'ai toujours une aspirine sous la main; **the shops are very ~** les magasins sont très accessibles; **the house is ~ for the shops** la maison est très bien placée *or* située pour les magasins.
c (*convenient*) *tool, method* commode, pratique. **a ~ little car** une petite voiture pratique; **that's ~!** ça tombe bien!; **that would come in very ~** cela tomberait bien.
d (*ship*) maniable.
2 comp ▸**handyman** (*servant*) factotum *m*, homme *m* à tout faire; (*do-it-yourself*) bricoleur *m* ▸**handy-pack** emballage *m* à poignée.

hang [hæŋ] pret, ptp **hung** 1 vt a (*suspend*) *lamp* suspendre, accrocher (*on* à); *curtains, hat, decorations* accrocher; *painting* accrocher, (*in gallery: exhibit*) exposer; *door* monter; *clothes* pendre (*on, from* à); *wallpaper* poser, tendre; (*Culin*) *game* faire faisander; *dangling object* laisser pendre. **he hung the rope over the side of the boat** il a laissé pendre le cordage par-dessus bord; **to ~ one's head** baisser la tête.
b (*decorate*) garnir, orner (*with* de). **trees hung with lights** arbres chargés de lumières; **balconies hung with flags** balcons pavoisés; **room hung with paintings** pièce ornée de tableaux *or* aux murs couverts de tableaux; **study/wall hung with hessian** bureau/mur tapissé *or* tendu de jute.
c **to ~ fire** *[guns]* faire long feu; *[plans etc]* traîner (en longueur).
d (*pret, ptp* **hanged**) *criminal* pendre. **he was ~ed for murder** il fut pendu pour meurtre; (*loc*) **(may) as well be ~ed for a sheep as a lamb** autant être pendu pour un mouton que pour un agneau; (*Hist*) **he was ~ed, drawn and quartered** il a été pendu, éviscéré et écartelé; **he ~ed himself from** *or* **out of despair** il s'est pendu de désespoir; **~ him!*** qu'il aille se faire voir!⁑; **(I'll be) ~ed if I know!*** je veux bien être pendu si je le sais!*; **~ it!***, **~ it all!*** zut!*
2 vi a *[rope, dangling object]* pendre, être accroché *or* suspendu (*on, from* à); *[drapery]* pendre, tomber, retomber. **her hair hung down her back** ses cheveux tombaient sur ses épaules *or* lui tombaient dans le dos; **a picture ~ing on the wall** un tableau accroché au mur; **to ~ out of the window** *[person]* se pencher par la fenêtre; *[thing]* pendre à la fenêtre; (*fig*) **to ~ by a hair** ne tenir qu'à un cheveu; (*fig: esp US*) **just ~ loose**⁑ essaie d'être relax⁑.
b planer, peser. **a fog ~s over the town** un brouillard plane *or* pèse sur la ville; **the hawk hung motionless in the sky** le faucon était comme suspendu immobile dans le ciel; (*fig*) **the threat which ~s over us** la menace qui plane *or* pèse sur nous, la menace qui est suspendue au-dessus de nos têtes; *see* **time**.
c *[criminal etc]* être pendu. **he ought to ~** il devrait être pendu; **he'll ~ for it** cela lui vaudra d'être pendu, cela lui vaudra la corde.
d (*US* ⁑) = **hang about**.
3 n a **to get the ~* of** (*learn to use*) *machine, tool, device* prendre le coup de main avec; (*learn to do*) *process, activity, work* attraper le coup pour faire; (*grasp meaning of*) *letter, book* (arriver à) comprendre; **to get the ~* of doing sth** attraper le coup pour faire qch; (*of device, process etc*) **you'll soon get the ~* of it** tu auras vite fait de t'y mettre; **I am getting the ~* of it!** ça y est je saisis!
b **I don't give** *or* **care a ~*** je m'en fiche*, je n'en ai rien à fiche⁑.
4 comp ▸**hangdog**: **to have a hangdog look** *or* **expression** avoir un air de chien battu ▸**hang-glider** (*person*) libériste *mf*; (*device*) deltaplane *m*, aile *f* delta *or* volante ▸**hang-gliding** deltaplane *m*, vol *m* libre; **to go hang-gliding** faire du deltaplane, pratiquer le vol libre ▸**hangman** bourreau *m* ▸**hangnail** petite peau, envie *f* ▸**hang-out**⁑ (*house, flat etc*) antre *m* favori ▸**hangover**: (*after drinking*) **to have a hangover** avoir une *or* la gueule de bois*; **this problem is a hangover from the previous administration** ce problème est un reliquat de l'administration précédente ▸**hang-up*** (*complex*) complexe *m*, fantasme *m* (*about* en ce qui concerne); (*obsession*) obsession *f* (*on* de); (*gen: hitch, difficulty*) os* *m*, contretemps *m*; **that was really the final hang-up** ça c'était vraiment le comble, il ne manquait plus que ça!

▸**hang about, hang around** 1 vi (*loiter, pass time*) rôder, errer, traîner; (*wait*) attendre. **he's always hanging about here** il est toujours à rôder *or* à errer par ici; **they always hang around together** ils sont toujours ensemble; **to keep sb hanging about** faire attendre qn, faire poireauter* qn; **this is where they usually hang about** c'est là qu'ils se trouvent habituellement; **hang about!**⁑ attends! 2 vt fus: **to hang about sb** coller à qn, être toujours sur le dos de qn; **he's always hanging about that café** il hante toujours ce café.

▸**hang back** vi (*in walking etc*) rester en arrière, hésiter à aller de l'avant. (*fig*) **she hung back from offering ...** elle ne voulait pas offrir ..., elle était réticente pour offrir ... .

▸**hang down** vi, vt sep pendre.

▸**hang in*** vi (*also* **hang in there**) s'accrocher, ne pas céder.

▸**hang on** 1 vi a (*: *wait*) attendre. **hang on!** attendez!; (*on phone*) ne quittez pas!; (*on phone*) **I had to hang on for ages** j'ai dû attendre des siècles.
b (*hold out*) tenir bon, résister. **he managed to hang on till help came** il réussit à tenir bon *or* à résister jusqu'à ce que des secours arrivent (*subj*); **hang on in there*** = **hang in there**;*see* **hang in***.
c **to hang on to sth*** (*keep hold of*) ne pas lâcher qch, rester cramponné à qch; (*keep*) garder qch; **hang on to the branch** tiens bien la branche, ne lâche pas la branche.
2 vt fus a (*lit, fig*) se cramponner à, s'accrocher à. **to hang on sb's arm** se cramponner au *or* s'accrocher au bras de qn; **to hang on sb's words** *or* **sb's every word** boire les paroles de qn, être suspendu aux lèvres de qn.
b (*depend on*) dépendre de, être suspendu à. **everything hangs on his decision** tout dépend de *or* est suspendu à sa décision; **everything hangs on whether he saw her or not** le tout est de savoir s'il l'a vue ou non.
3 vt sep (*fig, esp US*) **to hang one on*** se saouler, se biturer⁑.

▸**hang out** 1 vi a *[tongue]* pendre; *[shirt tails etc]* pendre (dehors), pendouiller*. (*fig*) **to let it all hang out*** se défouler. b (⁑) (*live*) percher*, crécher⁑; (*loiter aimlessly*) traîner. c (*: *resist, endure*) tenir bon, résister. **they managed to hang out till help came*** ils réussirent à tenir bon *or* à résister jusqu'à l'arrivée des secours; **they are hanging out for more pay*** ils tiennent bon pour avoir une augmentation. 2 vt sep *streamer* suspendre (dehors); *washing* étendre (dehors); *flag* arborer. 3 **hang-out**⁑ n *see* **hang 4**.

▸**hang together** vi a *[people]* se serrer les coudes. b *[argument]* se tenir; *[story]* tenir debout; *[statements]* s'accorder, concorder. **it all hangs together** tout ça se tient, c'est logique.

▸**hang up** 1 vi (*Telec*) raccrocher. **to hang up on sb** raccrocher. 2 vt sep *hat, picture* accrocher, pendre (*on* à, sur); (*Telec*) *receiver* raccrocher; (*fig: retire etc*) **to hang up one's hat** raccrocher*; *see* **hung 2**. 3 **hang-up*** n *see* **hang 4**.

hangar ['hæŋəʳ] n (*Aviat*) hangar *m*.

hanger ['hæŋəʳ] 1 n (*clothes ~*) cintre *m*, portemanteau *m*; (*hook*) crochet *m*. 2 comp ▸**hanger-on** (pl **~s-~**): (*fig*) **he's just one of the hangers-on** il fait juste partie de la suite; **there was a crowd of hangers-on** il y avait toute une suite.

hanging ['hæŋɪŋ] 1 n a (*execution*) pendaison *f*. b (*NonC*) accrochage *m*, suspension *f*; *[bells, wallpaper]* pose *f*; *[door]* montage *m*; *[picture]* accrochage. c (*curtains etc*) **~s** tentures *fpl*, draperies *fpl*; **bed ~s** rideaux *mpl* de lit. 2 adj a *bridge, staircase* suspendu; *door* battant; *lamp, light* pendant; *sleeve* tombant. **the ~ gardens of Babylon** les jardins suspendus de Babylone; **~ wardrobe** penderie *f*; (*Art*) **~ committee** jury *m* d'exposition. b (*Hist*) **~ judge** *juge m qui envoyait régulièrement à la potence*; (*lit*) **it's a ~ offence** c'est un crime pendable; (*fig*) **it's not a ~ matter** ce n'est pas grave, ce n'est pas un cas pendable.

hank [hæŋk] n *[wool etc]* écheveau *m*.

hanker ['hæŋkəʳ] vi: **to ~ for** *or* **after** aspirer à, avoir envie de, rêver de.

hankering ['hæŋkərɪŋ] n: **to have a ~ for sth/to do** avoir envie de qch/de faire, rêver de qch/de faire.

hankie*, **hanky*** ['hæŋkɪ] n abbr of **handkerchief**.

hanky-panky* ['hæŋkɪ'pæŋkɪ] n (*suspicious*) entourloupes* *fpl*; (*fooling around*) bêtises *fpl*; (*sexual*) batifolage *m*. (*suspicious*) **there's some ~ going on** il se passe quelque chose de louche, il y a là quelque chose de pas très catholique.

Hannibal ['hænɪbəl] n Annibal *m or* Hannibal *m*.

Hanoi [hæ'nɔɪ] n Hanoi.

Hanover ['hænəʊvəʳ] n Hanovre. (*Brit Hist*) **the house of ~** la maison *or* la dynastie de Hanovre.

Hanoverian [ˌhænəʊ'vɪərɪən] adj hanovrien.

Hansard ['hænsɑːd] n (le) Hansard (*sténographie des débats du parlement britannique*).

Hanseatic [ˌhænzɪ'ætɪk] adj: **the ~ League** la Hanse, la ligue hanséatique.

hansom ['hænsəm] n (*also ~ cab*) cab *m*.

Hants [hænts] (*Brit*) abbr of **Hampshire**.

ha'pence ['heɪpəns] npl of **ha'penny**.

ha'penny ['heɪpnɪ] n = **halfpenny**; *see* **half 4**.

haphazard [ˌhæp'hæzəd] adj (fait) au hasard, (fait) au petit bonheur. **a ~ arrangement** une disposition fortuite; **the whole thing was very ~** tout était fait au petit bonheur.

haphazardly [ˌhæp'hæzədlɪ] adv *arrange* au petit bonheur, au hasard; *select* à l'aveuglette, au petit bonheur, au hasard.

hapless ['hæplɪs] adj infortuné (*before n*), malchanceux (*after n*).

happen ['hæpən] vi a arriver, se passer, se produire. **something ~ed** il est arrivé *or* il s'est passé quelque chose; **what's ~ed?** qu'est-ce qui s'est passé *or* est arrivé?, qu'est-ce qu'il y a eu?; **just as if nothing had ~ed** tout comme si il n'était rien arrivé, comme si de rien n'était; **whatever ~s** quoi qu'il arrive (*subj*) *or* advienne; **don't let it ~ again!** et que ça ne se reproduise pas!; **these things ~** ce sont des choses qui arrivent, ça peut arriver; **what has ~ed to him?** (*befallen*) qu'est-ce qui lui est arrivé?; (*become of*) qu'est-ce qu'il est devenu?; **if anything**

~ed to me my wife would have enough money s'il m'arrivait quelque chose *or* si je venais à disparaître ma femme aurait assez d'argent; **something has ~ed to him** il lui est arrivé quelque chose; **a funny thing ~ed to me this morning** il m'est arrivé quelque chose de bizarre ce matin; **let's pretend it never ~ed** c'est *or* faisons comme si ça n'était pas arrivé; **it's all ~ing*** on est vraiment au cœur de l'action, tout arrive en même temps.

b (*come about, chance*) **how does it ~ that?** d'où vient que? + *indic*, comment se fait-il que? + *subj*; **it might ~ that** il pourrait se faire que + *subj*; **it so ~ed that** il s'est trouvé que + *indic*; **it so ~s that I'm going there today, as it ~s I'm going there today** il se trouve que *or* en l'occurrence j'y vais aujourd'hui; **he ~ed to call on me** il s'est trouvé qu'il est venu me voir; **do you ~ to have a pen?** aurais-tu par hasard un stylo?; **how did you ~ to go?** comment se fait-il que tu y sois allé?; **I ~ to know he is not rich** il se trouve que je sais qu'il n'est pas riche; **if he does ~ to see her** s'il lui arrive de la voir.

►**happen (up)on**† vt fus *object* trouver par hasard; *person* rencontrer par hasard.

happening ['hæpnɪŋ] 1 n événement *m*; (*Theat*) happening *m*. 2 adj (*) branché*.

happenstance* ['hæpənstæns] n (*US*) événement fortuit, circonstance fortuite.

happily ['hæpɪlɪ] adv a (*contentedly*) *play, walk, talk* tranquillement; *say, smile* joyeusement. **to live ~** vivre heureux (*see also* **live**); **she smiled ~** elle eut un sourire épanoui *or* de contentement. b (*fortunately*) heureusement, par bonheur. c (*felicitously*) *word, choose* heureusement, avec bonheur.

happiness ['hæpɪnɪs] n bonheur *m*, félicité *f*.

happy ['hæpɪ] 1 adj a (*contented*) heureux. **as ~ as a king** heureux comme un roi; **as ~ as a lark** *or* **a sandboy** gai comme un pinson; **a ~ marriage** un mariage heureux *or* réussi; **I'm not ~ about the plan** je ne suis pas très heureux de ce projet; **I'm not ~ about leaving him alone** je ne suis pas tranquille de le laisser seul; **I'll be quite ~ to do it** je le ferai volontiers, ça ne me dérange pas de le faire; **she was ~ to be able to help** elle a été heureuse *or* contente de pouvoir aider; **she was quite ~ to stay there alone** cela ne l'ennuyait pas (du tout) de rester là toute seule; **I'm ~ here reading** je suis très bien ici à lire; **the child is ~ playing in the sand** l'enfant est heureux *or* content de jouer dans le sable; **~ ending** fin heureuse; **the film has a ~ ending** le film se termine bien; **the ~ few** les rares privilégiés; **~ hour** (*US*) l'heure du cocktail *or* de l'apéritif, le 5 à 7; (*Brit*) *heure pendant laquelle les consommations sont à prix réduit*; **~ birthday!** bon *or* joyeux anniversaire!; **~ Christmas!** joyeux Noël!; **~ New Year!** bonne année!

b (*felicitous*) *phrase, gesture, words* heureux, à propos. (*euph*) **a ~ event** un heureux événement (*euph*); **a ~ thought** une heureuse inspiration; **a ~ medium** un moyen terme.

c (*: *tipsy*) (un peu) gai, (un peu) pompette*.

2 comp ►**happy families** (*card game*) jeu *m* des sept familles ►**happy-go-lucky** *person* insouciant, sans souci; *attitude* insouciant; **the arrangements were very happy-go-lucky** c'était organisé au petit bonheur (la chance), l'organisation était à la va comme je te pousse*; **to do sth in a happy-go-lucky way** faire qch au petit bonheur (la chance) *or* à la va comme je te pousse* ►**happy hunting ground** *[Amerindians]* paradis *m* des Indiens d'Amérique; (*fig*) **a happy hunting ground for collectors** une terre promise pour les collectionneurs, le paradis des collectionneurs.

Hapsburg ['hæpsbɜːg] n Habsbourg. **the ~s** les Habsbourgs *mpl*.

hara-kiri ['hærə'kɪrɪ] n hara-kiri *m*. **to commit ~** faire hara-kiri.

harangue [hə'ræŋ] 1 vt haranguer (*about* à propos de); *individuals* haranguer, sermonner (*about* à propos de). **he ~d her into getting her hair cut** il n'a eu de cesse qu'elle ne se fasse couper les cheveux. 2 n harangue *f*, sermon *m*.

harass ['hærəs] vt a (*harry*) *troops, the enemy, crowd etc* harceler. b (*worry*) tracasser, (*stronger*) harceler, tourmenter. **~ed by doubts** harcelé de doutes.

harassed ['hærəst] adj tracassé, surmené, (*stronger*) harcelé.

harassment ['hærəsmənt] n (*see* **harass**) harcèlement *m*; tracasseries *fpl*; *see* **sexual**.

harbinger ['hɑːbɪndʒəʳ] n (*liter*) avant-coureur *m* (*liter*), présage *m*. (*fig*) **a ~ of doom** un funeste présage.

harbour, (US) harbor ['hɑːbəʳ] 1 n (*for boats*) port *m*; (*fig*) port, havre *m* (*liter*), refuge *m*. (*in names*) **Dover-Harbour** Douvres-maritime; *see* **outer**.

2 comp ►**harbour dues, harbour fees** (*Jur, Comm*) droits *mpl* de port ►**harbour master** capitaine *m* de *or* du port ►**harbour station** gare *f* maritime.

3 vt a (*give shelter to*) héberger, abriter. **to ~ a criminal** receler un criminel.

b *suspicions* entretenir, nourrir; *fear, hope* entretenir. **to ~ a grudge against sb** garder rancune à qn.

c *dirt, dust* retenir, garder. **the river still ~s crocodiles** des crocodiles habitent encore le fleuve; **the cat's fur ~s various parasites** divers parasites trouvent refuge dans la fourrure du chat.

hard [hɑːd] 1 adj a *substance* dur; *mud, snow* durci; *muscle* ferme; (*Med*) *tissue* scléreux, sclérosé. **to get** *or* **become** *or* **grow ~** durcir; (*Tennis*) **~ court** court *m* en dur; **~ frost** forte gelée; *see also* **3**.

b (*fig*) *light, line, colour, outline* dur; (*Ling: consonant*) fort; (*St Ex*) *market* soutenu, ferme. **he's as ~ as nails** (*physically*) c'est un paquet de muscles; (*mentally*) il est dur; **children are ~ on their shoes** avec les enfants les chaussures ne durent pas longtemps; **it was a ~ blow** cela a été un coup dur *or* un rude coup; (*St Ex*) **~ cash** espèces *fpl*; (*Brit*) **~ cheese!**‡ pas de veine!*, pas de pot!*; (*Comput*) **~ copy** copie *f* papier; **~ core** (*material*) matériaux *mpl* pour assise, blocage *m*; (*fig*) *[argument]* fondement *m*; *[supporters, advocates, objectors etc]* noyau *m* (irréductible); (*part of organization etc*) éléments *mpl* durs, inconditionnels *mpl*; **the ~ core of the party** les éléments durs *or* les inconditionnels parmi les membres du parti (*see also* **3**); (*Pol*) **the ~ left/right** les (purs et) durs de la gauche/de la droite; (*Fin*) **~ currency** devise *f* forte; **~ drink** boisson *f* fortement alcoolisée; **he's a ~ drinker** c'est un gros buveur, il boit sec; **~ drug** drogue dure; **~ evidence** preuve(s) *f(pl)* concrète(s); **the ~ facts** la réalité brutale *or* non déguisée; **he had a ~ fall** il a fait une mauvaise chute; **there's still a lot of ~ feelings about it** il en reste encore beaucoup d'amertume; **no ~ feelings!** sans rancune!; (*lit, fig*) **it was ~ going** on a eu du mal, ça a été dur*; **he is ~ of hearing** il est dur d'oreille; **the ~-of-hearing** *npl* les mal-entendants *mpl*; (*Jur*) **~ labour** travaux *mpl* forcés; (*fig*) **to take a ~ line** adopter une ligne de conduite intransigeante, se montrer intransigeant (*on sth* en ce qui concerne qch; *with sb* envers qn); (*Brit*) **~ lines!*, ~ luck!*** pas de veine!*, pas de pot!*; (*Brit*) **it was ~ lines** *or* **~ luck that he didn't win*** c'est manque de pot* qu'il ait perdu; **it's ~ lines** *or* **~ luck on him*** il n'a pas de veine* *or* de pot*; **a ~ luck story** une histoire de malchance *or* de guigne*; **he told me another ~ luck story** il a encore essayé de m'apitoyer avec une de ses histoires; **~ liquor** = **~ drink**; (*Fin*) **~ loan** prêt *m* aux conditions commerciales *or* du marché; **he's a ~ (task)master** il mène ses subordonnés à la baguette; **duty is a ~ (task)master** le devoir est un maître exigeant; (*US*) **~ mint candy** bonbon *m* à la menthe; (*Press*) **what we want is ~ news** ce qu'il nous faut c'est de l'information sérieuse; **that's a ~ nut to crack*** ce n'est pas un petit problème; **he's a ~ nut to crack*** c'est un dur à cuire; (*Mus*) **~ rock** rock *m* hard, hard *m*; **~ sauce** crème *f* au beurre dure; (*Comm*) **~ sell** promotion (de vente) agressive; (*Brit Aut*) **hard shoulder** accotement stabilisé; **~ study** étude assidue; **the ~ stuff** (*whisky*) le whisky; (*drugs*) la *or* les drogue(s) dure(s); **to give sb a ~ time** en faire voir de toutes les couleurs à qn*, en faire baver à qn*; **she had a ~ time of it after her husband's death** elle a traversé des moments difficiles après la mort de son mari; **you'll have a ~ time of it trying to get him to help you** vous allez avoir du mal à lui persuader de vous aider; **these are ~ times** les temps sont durs; **she has fallen on ~ times** elle traverse des temps difficiles; **they fell upon ~ times** ils connurent des temps difficiles; **~ water** eau *f* calcaire *or* dure; **these are ~ words** c'est s'exprimer en termes très durs; *see also* **3** *and* **drive**.

c (*difficult*) *problem, examination* difficile, dur; *question* ardu, difficile; *task* pénible, dur. **to do sth the ~ way** faire qch à la dure; **to learn the ~ way** payer pour le savoir, l'apprendre à ses dépens; **it was ~ to understand** c'était difficile *or* dur à comprendre; **I find it ~ to explain** j'ai du mal à l'expliquer; **I find it ~ to believe that ...** j'ai du mal à croire que ... + *subj*, j'ai peine à croire que ... + *subj*; **he is ~ to please** il est exigeant *or* difficile; **he is ~ to get on with** il est difficile à vivre; **that is ~ to beat** on peut difficilement faire mieux; *see also* **3**.

d (*severe*) *person* dur, sévère, strict (*on, to* avec; *towards* envers); *master* sévère, exigeant; *voice, tone* dur, sec (*f* sèche); *face, expression* dur, sévère; *heart* dur, impitoyable; *treatment* sévère. **he's a ~ man** il est dur, c'est un homme impitoyable; **to be ~ on sb** être dur *or* sévère avec qn, traiter qn avec sévérité; **to grow ~** s'endurcir; *see also* **3**.

e (*harsh*) *life* dur, pénible, difficile; *fate* dur; *climate, winter* rude, rigoureux; *rule, decision* sévère; (*tough*) *battle, fight* acharné, âpre, rude; *match* âprement disputé; *work* dur; *worker* dur (à la tâche), endurant. **it's ~ work!** c'est dur!

2 adv a (*strongly, energetically*) **as ~ as one can** de toutes ses forces; **it's raining ~** il pleut à verse, il tombe des cordes*; **it's snowing ~** il neige dru; **it's freezing ~** il gèle fort *or* ferme *or* dur *or* à pierre fendre; **the lake was frozen ~** le lac était profondément gelé; **the ground was frozen ~** le sol était durci par le gel; **to beg ~** prier instamment, supplier; **he's drinking fairly ~ these days** il boit beaucoup *or* sec en ce moment; **to fall down ~** tomber durement; **to hit ~** frapper dur *or* fort, cogner dur; **to be ~ hit** être sérieusement touché; **to hold on ~** tenir bon *or* ferme; **to look ~ at** *person* regarder fixement, dévisager; *thing* regarder *or* examiner de près; **pull ~!** tirez fort!; **to run ~** courir à toutes jambes *or* comme un dératé*; **to think ~** réfléchir sérieusement *or* profondément; **to try ~** faire *or* fournir un gros effort; **to study ~** étudier assidûment *or* d'arrache-pied; **to work ~** travailler dur *or* d'arrache-pied; **to be ~ at work** *or* **at it*** être attelé à la tâche, travailler d'arrache-pied; (*Naut*) **~ a-port** (à) bâbord toute; (*Navy*) à gauche toute; *see* **drive, hold**.

b (*closely*) **~ by** tout près, tout contre, tout à côté; **to follow ~ upon sb's heels** suivre qn de très près, être sur les talons de qn; **the revolution followed ~ on (the heels of) the strike** la révolution suivit de très près la grève *or* suivit immédiatement la grève; **it was ~ on 10**

o'clock il était bientôt 10 heures.

c (*phrases*) **to be ~ put (to it)** *or* **pressed to do** avoir beaucoup de mal *or* de peine à faire, être bien en peine de faire, éprouver les plus grandes difficultés à faire; **to be ~ pressed for time/money** *etc* être vraiment à court de temps/d'argent *etc;* **I'm rather ~ pressed** (*for time*) je suis débordé; (*for money*) je suis à court; **she took it pretty ~** elle a été très affectée; **he took the news very ~** il a très mal pris la nouvelle; (*Brit*) **to be ~ done by** être traité injustement, être mal traité; **he feels very ~ done by** il a l'impression d'avoir été brimé *or* très mal traité; **it will go ~ for him if** ... cela tournera *or* ira mal pour lui si ... .

3 **comp** ▶ **hard-and-fast** strict, inflexible; *rule* absolu ▶ **hard-ass**** (*US*) dur(e) *m(f)* à cuire ▶ **hardback adj** *book* relié, cartonné ◊ **n** livre relié *or* cartonné ▶ **hardball** (*US*) base-ball *m*; (*US fig*) **to play hardball*** employer une tactique brutale ▶ **hard-bitten** (*fig*) dur à cuire* ▶ **hardboard** Isorel *m* ® ▶ **hard-boiled** *egg* dur; (*fig*) *person* dur à cuire* ▶ **hard core** (*supporters etc*) **n** noyau *m* dur ▶ **hard-core adj** *reactionary, Marxist etc* endurci, (pur et) dur, inconditionnel; *support, opposition* inconditionnel; **hard-core pornography** pornographie (dite) dure ▶ **hard disk** (*Comput*) disque *m* dur ▶ **hard disk drive** (*Comput*) unité *f* de disque dur ▶ **hard-earned** *money, salary* (si) durement gagné; *holiday* bien mérité ▶ **hard-faced, hard-featured** au visage sévère, aux traits durs ▶ **hard-fought** *battle* âprement mené; *election, competition* âprement disputé ▶ **hard hat** *[motorcyclist, construction worker etc]* casque *m*; (*riding hat*) bombe *f*; (*fig: construction worker*) ouvrier *m* du bâtiment ▶ **hard-hat adj** (*fig*) réactionnaire ▶ **hardhead** réaliste *mf*; **hard-headed** réaliste, à la tête froide; **hard-headed businessman** homme *m* d'affaires réaliste ▶ **hard-hearted** insensible, impitoyable, au cœur dur; **he was very hard-hearted towards them** il était très dur avec eux ▶ **hard-hitting** (*lit*) *person* cogneur; (*fig*) *report* sans complaisances ▶ **hard-line** (pur et) dur ▶ **hard-liner** (pur(e) *m(f)*) et dur(e) *m(f)* ▶ **hard-nosed** impitoyable, dur ▶ **hard-on****: **to have a hard-on** bander** ▶ **hard-packed snow** neige tassée; (*by wind*) congère *f* ▶ **hard palate** voûte *f* du palais, voûte palatine ▶ **hard porn*** le hard* ▶ **hardscrabble** *see* **hardscrabble** ▶ **hardsell tactics** (*Comm*) politique *f* de promotion (de vente) agressive ▶ **hard-shell* Baptist** (*US*) baptiste *mf* fondamentaliste ▶ **hardtack** (*Mil*) biscuit *m*; (*Naut*) galette *f* ▶ **hardtop** (*Aut*) voiture *f* à toit de tôle amovible ▶ **hard-up*** fauché*; **I'm hard-up** je suis fauché*, je suis à sec*; (*fig*) **they must be hard-up if** ... les choses doivent aller mal (pour eux) si ...; **to be hard-up for sth** (*gen*) être à court de qch, manquer de qch; **I'm hard-up for books about it** j'ai bien du mal à trouver des livres sur ce sujet ▶ **hardware** (*NonC*) (*Comm*) quincaillerie *f* (*marchandises*); (*Mil etc*) matériel *m*; (*Comput, Space*) matériel, hardware *m* ▶ **hardware dealer** quincaillier *m*, -ière *f* ▶ **hardware shop** quincaillerie *f* (*magasin*) ▶ **hardware specialist** (*Comput*) technicien(ne) *m(f)* du hardware ▶ **hardware store** = **hardware shop** ▶ **hard-wearing** solide, résistant ▶ **hard-wired** (*Comput*) câblé ▶ **hard-won** (si) durement gagné, remporté de haute lutte ▶ **hardwood** bois *m* de feuillu ▶ **hard-working** (*gen*) travailleur; *student, pupil* travailleur, bûcheur*.

harden ['hɑːdn] 1 **vt** durcir; *steel* tremper; *muscle* affermir, durcir; (*Med*) indurer, scléroser. **his years in the Arctic ~ed him considerably** les années qu'il a passées dans l'Arctique l'ont considérablement endurci; **to ~ o.s. to sth** s'endurcir *or* s'aguerrir à qch; **to ~ one's heart** s'endurcir; **this ~ed his heart** cela lui a endurci le cœur; (*Fin*) **to ~ credit** restreindre le crédit; *see also* **hardened**. 2 **vi** a *[substances]* durcir, s'affermir; (*Med*) s'indurer, se scléroser; *[steel]* se tremper. **his voice ~ed** sa voix se fit dure. b (*St Ex*) *[shares]* se raffermir; *[prices]* être en hausse. **the market ~ed** le marché s'affermit.

hardened ['hɑːdnd] **adj** durci; *steel* trempé; *criminal* endurci; *sinner* invétéré. **I'm ~ to it** j'y suis accoutumé *or* fait, j'ai l'habitude.

hardening ['hɑːdnɪŋ] **n** durcissement *m*, affermissement *m*; *[steel]* trempe *f*; (*Med*) induration *f*, sclérose *f*; (*fig*) durcissement *m*, endurcissement *m*; (*St Ex*) *[currency, prices]* raffermissement *m*. **I noticed a ~ of his attitude** je remarquais un durcissement de son attitude *or* que son attitude se durcissait; (*Med*) **~ of the arteries** durcissement des artères.

hardihood ['hɑːdɪhʊd] **n** hardiesse *f*.

hardiness ['hɑːdɪnɪs] **n** force *f*, vigueur *f*.

hardly ['hɑːdlɪ] **adv** a (*gen*) à peine, ne...; guère; (*only just*) à peine, tout juste. **he can ~ write** il sait à peine écrire, c'est à peine s'il sait écrire; **I can ~ hear you** je vous entends à peine, c'est à peine si je vous entends; **he had ~ spoken when** ... à peine eut-il parlé que ..., il n'eut pas plus tôt parlé que ...; **you'll ~ believe it** vous aurez de la peine *or* du mal à le croire; **it's ~ his business if** ... ce n'est guère son affaire si ...; **I need ~ point out that** je n'ai pas besoin de faire remarquer que; **I ~ know** je n'en sais trop rien; **~ anyone** presque personne; **~ anywhere** presque nulle part; **you have ~ eaten anything** tu n'as presque rien mangé; **~ ever** presque jamais; **~!** (*not at all*) certainement pas!; (*not exactly*) pas précisément!; **he would ~ have said that** il n'aurait tout de même pas dit cela.

b (*harshly*) durement, rudement, sévèrement. **to treat sb ~** être *or* se montrer sévère avec qn, traiter qn sévèrement.

hardness ['hɑːdnɪs] **n** (*see* **hard**) a dureté *f*; fermeté *f*; (*Med*) induration *f*. b difficulté *f*. c dureté *f*, sévérité *f*. d dureté *f*, difficulté *f*; rigueur *f*; sévérité *f*. (*St Ex*) **the ~ of the market** le raffermissement du marché; (*Med*) **~ of hearing** surdité *f* (partielle); (*fig*) **his ~ of heart** sa dureté de cœur, son insensibilité *f*.

hardscrabble ['hɑːdˌskræbəl] **adj** (*US*) *farmer, farm* misérable, très pauvre.

hardship ['hɑːdʃɪp] 1 **n** a (*NonC*) (*circumstances*) épreuves *fpl*; (*suffering*) souffrance *f*; (*poverty*) pauvreté *f*; (*deprivation*) privation *f*. **he has suffered great ~** il a connu de dures épreuves; **there's a certain amount of ~ involved but it's worth it** ça sera dur mais ça en vaut la peine; **a life of ~** une vie pleine d'épreuves; **it is no ~ to him to stop smoking** pour lui cesser de fumer n'est pas une privation; **it's no great ~ to go and see her once a month** ce n'est tout de même pas une épreuve *or* ce n'est pas la mer à boire* d'aller la voir une fois par mois.

b **~s** épreuves *fpl*, privations *fpl*; **the ~s of war** les privations *or* les rigueurs *fpl* de la guerre.

2 **comp** ▶ **hardship clause** (*Jur*) clause *f* de sauvegarde.

hardy ['hɑːdɪ] **adj** a (*strong*) *person* vigoureux, robuste; *plant* résistant (au gel); *tree* de plein vent. **~ perennial** plante *f* vivace; **~ annual** (*Bot*) plante annuelle résistante au gel; (* *fig*) (vieille) histoire *f* qui a la vie dure. b (*bold*) hardi, audacieux, intrépide.

hare [hɛəʳ] 1 **n, pl ~s** *or* **~** lièvre *m*. (*game*) **~ and hounds** (*sorte de*) jeu *m* de piste; *see* **jug, mad** *etc*. 2 **comp** ▶ **harebell** campanule *f* ▶ **harebrained** *person* écervelé; *plan* insensé; **to be harebrained** avoir *or* être une tête de linotte, être écervelé ▶ **hare coursing** chasse *f* au lièvre ▶ **harelip** (*Med*) bec-de-lièvre *m*. 3 **vi** (*Brit*) **to ~ in/out/through*** *etc* entrer/sortir/traverser *etc* en trombe *or* à fond de train.

harem [hɑːˈriːm] **n** harem *m*.

haricot ['hærɪkəʊ] **n** (*Brit*) **~ (bean)** haricot blanc; (*Culin*) **~ mutton** haricot de mouton.

hark [hɑːk] **vi** (*liter*) **to ~ to** écouter, prêter une oreille attentive à; (*liter*, †) **~!** écoutez!; **~ at him!*** mais écoutez-le (donc)!*

▶ **hark back vi** revenir (*to* à). **he's always harking back to that** il y revient toujours, il en est toujours à cette histoire.

harken ['hɑːkən] **vi** = **hearken**.

Harlequin ['hɑːlɪkwɪn] **n** (*Theat*) Arlequin *m*. **~ costume** costume bigarré *or* d'Arlequin.

Harley Street ['hɑːlɪˌstriːt] **n** (*Brit*) Harley Street (*haut lieu de la médecine privée à Londres*).

harlot†† ['hɑːlət] **n** courtisane *f*.

harm [hɑːm] 1 **n** mal *m*, tort *m*, dommage *m*. **to do sb ~** faire du mal *or* du tort à qn, nuire à qn; **what ~ has he done you?** quel mal vous a-t-il fait?, qu'est-ce qu'il vous a fait?*; **the ~'s done now** le mal est fait maintenant; **no ~ done!** il n'y a pas de mal!; **it can't do you any ~** ça ne peut pas te faire de mal; **it will do more ~ than good** cela fera plus de mal que de bien; **he means no ~** il n'a pas de mauvaises intentions, il a de bonnes intentions; **he meant no ~ by what he said** il ne l'a pas dit méchamment; **he doesn't mean us any ~** il ne nous veut pas de mal; **you will come to no ~** il ne t'arrivera rien; **I don't see any ~ in it, I see no ~ in it** je n'y vois aucun mal; **there's no ~ in an occasional drink** un petit verre de temps en temps ne peut pas faire de mal; **there's no ~ in doing that** il n'y a pas de mal à faire cela; **keep** *or* **stay out of ~'s way** (*out of danger*) mettez-vous en sûreté; (*out of the way*) ne restez pas dans les parages; **to keep a child out of ~'s way** mettre un enfant à l'abri du danger; **to put a vase out of ~'s way** mettre un vase en lieu sûr.

2 **vt** *person* faire du mal *or* du tort à, nuire à; *crops, harvest, building* endommager; *object* abîmer; *reputation* salir, souiller (*liter*); *sb's interests, a cause* causer du tort à *or* un dommage à. **this will ~ his case considerably** ceci sera très préjudiciable à sa cause; *see* **fly**.

harmful ['hɑːmfʊl] **adj** *person* malfaisant, nuisible; *influence, thing* nocif, nuisible (*to* à).

harmless ['hɑːmlɪs] **adj** *animal, joke* inoffensif, pas méchant; *person* sans méchanceté, sans malice, pas méchant; *action, game* innocent; *suggestion, conversation* anodin. **a ~ child** un enfant innocent; **it was all fairly ~** tout ça était assez innocent; (*Jur*) **to hold ~** tenir à couvert.

harmonic [hɑːˈmɒnɪk] 1 **adj** (*Math, Mus, Phys*) harmonique. 2 **n** a (*Mus*) **~s** (*NonC: science*) harmonie *f*; (*pl: overtones*) harmoniques *mpl*. b (*Phys*) **~s** harmoniques *mpl or fpl*.

harmonica [hɑːˈmɒnɪkə] **n** harmonica *m*.

harmonious [hɑːˈməʊnɪəs] **adj** (*Mus*) harmonieux, mélodieux; (*fig*) harmonieux.

harmoniously [hɑːˈməʊnɪəslɪ] **adv** (*Mus*) harmonieusement; (*fig*) *work* en harmonie; *combine* harmonieusement.

harmonium [hɑːˈməʊnɪəm] **n** harmonium *m*.

harmonize ['hɑːmənaɪz] 1 **vt** (*Mus*) harmoniser; (*fig*) *ideas, views* harmoniser, mettre en harmonie (*with* avec); *colours* assortir, harmoniser, marier; *texts, statements* faire accorder, concilier. 2 **vi** (*Mus*) chanter en harmonie; *[colours etc]* s'harmoniser (*with* avec), s'allier (*with* à), s'assortir (*with* à); *[person, facts]* s'accorder (*with* avec).

harmony ['hɑːmənɪ] **n** (*Mus*) harmonie *f*; (*fig*) harmonie, accord *m*. **in perfect ~** en parfaite harmonie, en parfait accord; **in ~ with** en harmonie *or* en accord avec; **his ideas are in ~ with mine** ses idées s'accordent avec les miennes, nos idées s'accordent; *see* **close**[1].

harness ['hɑːnɪs] 1 n *[horse]* harnais *m*, harnachement *m*; *[loom, parachute]* harnais; (*Climbing*) baudrier *m*. (*fig*) **to get back in(to) ~** reprendre le collier; (*fig*) **to die in ~** mourir debout *or* à la tâche; (*fig*) **to work in ~ (with sb)** travailler en tandem (avec qn). 2 vt a *horse* harnacher. **to ~ a horse to a carriage** atteler un cheval à une voiture. b (*fig*) *river, resources, energy etc* exploiter; *talents, energy* employer à bien.

Harold ['hærəld] n Harold *m*.

harp [hɑːp] 1 n harpe *f*. 2 vi a (*)**to ~ on (about) sth** rabâcher qch; **stop ~ing on (about) it!** cesse de répéter toujours la même chose!; **I don't want to ~ on about it** je ne veux pas revenir toujours là-dessus; **she's always ~ing on about her troubles** elle nous rebat les oreilles de ses malheurs. b (*Mus*) jouer de la harpe.

harpist ['hɑːpɪst] n harpiste *mf*.

harpoon [hɑː'puːn] 1 n harpon *m*. 2 vt harponner.

harpsichord ['hɑːpsɪkɔːd] n clavecin *m*.

harpsichordist ['hɑːpsɪkɔːdɪst] n claveciniste *mf*.

harpy ['hɑːpɪ] n (*Myth*) harpie *f*. **old ~** vieille harpie *or* sorcière.

harridan ['hærɪdən] n vieille harpie *or* sorcière.

harried ['hærɪd] adj *look, expression* tourmenté.

harrier ['hærɪəʳ] n a (*dog*) harrier *m*. **~s** meute *f*. b (*cross-country runners*) **~s** coureurs *mpl* de cross. c (*Orn*) busard *m*.

Harris ['hærɪs] adj: **~ tweed** ® (gros) tweed *m* (*des Hébrides*).

harrow ['hærəʊ] 1 n herse *f*. 2 vt (*Agr*) herser. (*fig*) **to ~ sb** *or* **sb's feelings** déchirer le cœur de qn, torturer qn.

harrowing ['hærəʊɪŋ] 1 adj *story* poignant, navrant; *cry* déchirant; *experience* extrêmement pénible, atroce. 2 n (*Agr*) hersage *m*.

Harry ['hærɪ] n a (**dim of Henry**) b **to play old ~ with*** *person* en faire voir des vertes et des pas mûres* à; *machine, sb's digestion* détraquer; *timetable, plans etc* chambouler*; *sb's chances* gâcher, bousiller*.

harry ['hærɪ] vt *country* dévaster, ravager; *person* harceler, tourmenter; (*Mil*) harceler.

harsh [hɑːʃ] adj a (*cruel, severe*) *person, punishment* dur, sévère; *words* dur, âpre; *tone, voice, reply* cassant, dur; *fate* cruel, dur; *climate* dur, rude, rigoureux. **to be ~ with sb** être dur avec *or* envers qn; **that's a ~ thing to say** c'est méchant de dire cela, (*more formally*) c'est une déclaration très dure. b (*to the touch*) *material* rêche; *surface* rugueux, râpeux, rude. c (*to the ear*) *woman's voice* criard, aigre; *man's voice* discordant; *bird cry* criard; *sound* discordant. **a ~ squeal of brakes** un grincement de freins strident. d (*to the eye*) *colours* criard; *contrast* dur, heurté. e (*to the taste*) âpre, râpeux; *wine* âpre.

harshly ['hɑːʃlɪ] adv *reply* rudement, durement; *treat* sévèrement.

harshness ['hɑːʃnɪs] n a (*severity, cruelty*) *[manner]* rudesse *f*; *[words]* dureté *f*; *[fate, climate]* rigueur *f*; *[punishment]* sévérité *f*. b (*to the eye*) aspect déplaisant *or* heurté; (*to the touch*) rudesse *f*, dureté *f*, rugosité *f*; (*to the taste*) âpreté *f*; (*to the ear*) discordance *f*.

hart [hɑːt] n, pl **~s** *or* **~** cerf *m*.

harum-scarum ['hɛərəm'skɛərəm] 1 adj écervelé, étourdi, tête de linotte *inv*. 2 n tête *f* en l'air, tête de linotte, écervelé(e) *m(f)*.

harvest ['hɑːvɪst] 1 n *[corn]* moisson *f*; *[fruit]* récolte *f*, cueillette *f*; *[grapes]* vendange *f*; (*fig*) moisson. **to get in the ~** faire la moisson, moissonner. 2 vt *corn* moissonner; *fruit* récolter, cueillir; *grapes* vendanger, récolter; (*fig*) *reward* moissonner; *insults* récolter. **to ~ the fields** faire les moissons, moissonner (les champs). 3 vi faire la moisson, moissonner. 4 comp ▸**harvest festival** fête *f* de la moisson ▸**harvest home** (*festival*) fête *f* de la moisson; (*season*) fin *f* de la moisson ▸**harvestman** (*insect*) faucheur *m* ▸**harvest moon** pleine lune (de l'équinoxe d'automne) ▸**harvest time: at harvest time** pendant *or* à la moisson.

harvester ['hɑːvɪstəʳ] n (*person*) moissonneur *m*, -euse *f*; (*machine*) moissonneuse *f*; *see* **combine**.

has [hæz] 1 *see* **have**. 2 comp ▸**has-been*** (*person*) type *m or* bonne femme *f* fini(e); (*hat, carpet etc*) vieillerie *f*, vieux truc*; **he's/she's/it's a has-been*** il/elle/ça a fait son temps.

hash [hæʃ] 1 n a (*Culin*) hachis *m*; (* *fig*) gâchis *m*; (*US Culin*) *mélange de pommes de terre et de viande hachée*. **he made a ~ of it*** il a saboté ça, il en a fait un beau gâchis; **a ~(-up)* of old ideas** un réchauffé *or* une resucée* de vieilles idées; *see* **settle**[2]. b (*Drugs sl: hashish*) hasch *m* (*sl*). 2 comp ▸**hash browns** (*US Culin*) pommes de terre sautées (*servies au petit déjeuner*) ▸**hash house*** (*US*) gargote *f* ▸**hash house slinger*** (*US*) serveur *m*, -euse *f* dans une gargote. 3 vt (*Culin*) hacher.

▸**hash out*** vt sep (*discuss*) discuter (en détail); (*solve*) finir par résoudre.

▸**hash over**‡ vt sep *problem, plan, difficulty* discuter ferme de. **they were hashing it over when I came** ils discutaient le coup* quand je suis arrivé.

▸**hash up** 1 vt sep a (*Culin*) hacher menu. b (‡: *spoil*) bousiller*, faire un beau gâchis de. 2 **hash-up*** n *see* **hash 1a**.

hashish ['hæʃɪʃ] n haschisch *m or* hachisch *m*.

hasn't ['hæznt] = **has not**; *see* **have**.

hasp [hɑːsp] n *[book cover, necklace]* fermoir *m*; *[door, lid, window]* moraillon *m*.

hassle* ['hæsl] 1 n (*squabble*) chamaillerie* *f*, bagarre* *f*; (*bustle, confusion*) pagaïe *f or* pagaille *f*; (*fuss, trouble*) histoire *f*, tracas *mpl*. **what a ~!** quelle histoire!, que de tracas!; **I had a ~ to be ready on time** ça a été toute une histoire pour être prêt à l'heure; **it's a ~!** c'est toute une histoire!, c'est beaucoup de tracas! 2 vt a (*harass*) tracasser, enquiquiner*. **don't ~ him** ne le tracasse pas, ne l'enquiquine* pas, fiche lui la paix*. b (*quarrel*) se battre (*with sb* avec qn; *over sth* au sujet de qch).

hassock ['hæsək] n coussin *m* (d'agenouilloir).

haste [heɪst] n hâte *f*, diligence *f*, célérité *f*; (*excessive*) précipitation *f*. **to do sth in ~** faire qch à la hâte *or* en hâte; **in great ~** en toute hâte; **to be in ~ to do** avoir hâte de faire; **to make ~** se hâter *or* se dépêcher (*to do* de faire); (*Prov*) **more ~ less speed** hâtez-vous lentement (*loc*); **why all this ~?** pourquoi tant de précipitation?

hasten ['heɪsn] 1 vi se hâter, se dépêcher, se presser, s'empresser (*to do* de faire). **I ~ to add ...** je m'empresse d'ajouter ..., j'ajoute tout de suite ...; **to ~ down/away** *etc* se hâter de descendre/partir *etc*, descendre/partir *etc* à la hâte. 2 vt (*gen*) hâter, accélérer; *reaction* activer. **to ~ one's steps** presser le pas, accélérer l'allure *or* le pas; **to ~ sb's departure** hâter le départ de qn.

hastily ['heɪstɪlɪ] adv a *leave, write, work* (*speedily*) en hâte, à la hâte; (*too speedily*) hâtivement, précipitamment. **he ~ suggested that ...** il s'est empressé de suggérer que ... . b (*without reflexion*) *speak, act* sans réfléchir, trop hâtivement.

Hastings ['heɪstɪŋz] n: **Battle of ~** bataille *f* d'Hastings.

hasty ['heɪstɪ] adj *departure, marriage* précipité, hâtif; *visit, glance, meal* rapide, hâtif; *sketch* fait à la hâte; *action, decision, move* hâtif, inconsidéré, irréfléchi. **don't be so ~!** ne va pas si vite (en besogne)!; **to have a ~ temper, to be ~-tempered** être (très) emporté, s'emporter facilement, être soupe au lait; **~ words** paroles irréfléchies, paroles lancées à la légère.

hat [hæt] 1 n chapeau *m*. **to put on one's ~** mettre son chapeau; *[man]* se couvrir; **to keep one's ~ on** garder son chapeau; *[man]* rester couvert; **to take off one's ~** enlever son chapeau; *[man]* se découvrir; **~ in hand** (*lit*) chapeau bas; (*fig*) obséquieusement; **~s off!** chapeau bas!; (*fig*) **to take off one's ~ to** tirer son chapeau à; **I take my ~ off to him!** chapeau!; **to keep sth under one's ~*** garder qch pour soi; **keep it under your ~!*** motus!; (*fig*) **to pass round the ~** *or* (*US*) **to pass the ~ for sb** faire la quête pour qn; (*fig*) **that's old ~!*** c'est vieux, c'est dépassé, c'est du déjà vu; **she's old ~** elle est vieux jeu; (*fig*) **she wears two ~s** elle a deux rôles *or* casquettes; (*fig*) **speaking with my accountant's/priest's ~ on ...** (si je te parlais) en tant que comptable/prêtre ...; *see* **bowler**[2], **eat, pull out, talk, top** *etc*.

2 comp ▸**hatband** ruban *m* de chapeau ▸**hatbox** carton *m* à chapeau ▸**hatcheck (man/girl)** (*US*) le préposé/la préposée au vestiaire ▸**hatpin** épingle *f* à chapeau ▸**hatrack** porte-chapeaux *m inv* ▸**hat shop** (*for women*) boutique *f* de modiste; (*for men*) chapellerie *f* ▸**hatstand,** (*US*) **hat tree** portemanteau *m* ▸**hat trick** (*Conjuring*) tour *m or* coup *m* du chapeau; **to score a hat trick** (*gen Sport*) réussir trois coups (*or* gagner trois matchs *etc*) consécutifs; (*Ftbl*) marquer trois buts dans un match; (*Cricket*) éliminer trois batteurs en trois balles.

hatch[1] [hætʃ] 1 vt a (*also* **~ out**) *chick, egg* faire éclore. (*loc*) **don't count your chickens before they are ~ed** il ne faut pas vendre la peau de l'ours avant de l'avoir tué. b *plot* ourdir, tramer; *plan* couver. **I wonder what he's ~ing (up)** je me demande ce qu'il manigance. 2 vi (*also* **~ out**) *[chick, egg]* éclore. 3 n (*act*) éclosion *f*; (*brood*) couvée *f*.

hatch[2] [hætʃ] 1 n a (*Naut: also* **~way**) écoutille *f*; (*floodgates*) vanne *f* d'écluse. **under ~es** dans la cale; (*fig*) **down the ~!**‡ cul sec!* b (*Brit*) **(service** *or* **serving) ~** passe-plats *m inv*, guichet *m*. c (*Aut*) = **hatchback**; *see* **2.** 2 comp ▸**hatchback** (*Aut*) (*two-door*) coupé *m* avec hayon (à l')arrière; (*four-door*) berline *f* avec hayon (à l')arrière ▸**hatchway** passe-plats *m inv*, guichet *m*.

hatch[3] [hætʃ] vt (*Art*) hachurer.

hatchery ['hætʃərɪ] n *[chicks]* couvoir *m*, incubateur *m*; *[fish]* appareil *m* à éclosion.

hatchet ['hætʃɪt] 1 n hachette *f*; *see* **bury**. 2 comp ▸**hatchet-faced** au visage en lame de couteau ▸**hatchet job** (*fig*) (entreprise *f* de) démolissage *m*; (*fig*) **to do a hatchet job on sb** démolir qn ▸**hatchet man*** (*US: hired killer*) tueur *m* (à gages); (*fig: in industry etc*) homme *m* de main; (*fig*) **he was the firm's hatchet man when they sacked 200 workers** c'est lui que la compagnie a chargé de faire tomber les têtes quand elle a licencié 200 travailleurs.

hatching[1] ['hætʃɪŋ] n *[chicks etc]* (*act*) éclosion *f*; (*brood*) couvée *f*.

hatching[2] ['hætʃɪŋ] n (*Art*) hachures *fpl*.

hate [heɪt] 1 vt haïr, avoir en horreur, exécrer; (*weaker*) détester, avoir horreur de. **she ~s him like poison** elle le hait à mort, (*weaker*) elle ne peut pas le voir en peinture*; **she ~s me for not helping her** elle m'en veut à mort de ne pas l'avoir aidée; **to hate o.s. for (not) doing sth)** s'en vouloir (de (ne pas) faire qch); **to ~ to do** *or* **doing** détester faire, avoir horreur de faire; **he ~s to be** *or* **being ordered about** il a horreur *or* il ne peut pas souffrir qu'on lui donne (*subj*) des ordres; **what he ~s most of all is ...** ce qu'il déteste le plus au monde c'est ...; **I**

~ **being late** je déteste être en retard, j'ai horreur d'être en retard; **I ~ to say so, I ~ having to say it** cela m'ennuie beaucoup de *or* je suis désolé de devoir le dire; **I ~ seeing her in pain** je ne peux pas supporter de la voir souffrir; **I should ~ to keep you waiting** je ne voudrais surtout pas vous faire attendre; **I should ~ it if he thought ..., I should ~ him to think ...** je détesterais qu'il vienne à penser ... .

2 **n** a (*NonC*) haine *f*. ~ **mail** lettres *fpl* d'injures.

b **one of my pet ~s*** une de mes bêtes noires.

hated ['heɪtɪd] **adj** haï, détesté.

hateful ['heɪtfʊl] **adj** haïssable, odieux, détestable.

hatless ['hætlɪs] **adj** sans chapeau, tête nue, nu-tête.

hatred ['heɪtrɪd] **n** (*NonC*) haine *f*. **out of ~ of** *or* **for sth/sb** en *or* par haine de qch/qn; **to feel ~ for sb/sth** haïr qn/qch.

hatter ['hætəʳ] **n** chapelier *m*; *see* **mad**.

haughtily ['hɔːtɪlɪ] **adv** avec hauteur, avec arrogance, hautainement.

haughtiness ['hɔːtɪnɪs] **n** hauteur *f*, morgue *f*, arrogance *f*.

haughty ['hɔːtɪ] **adj** hautain, plein de morgue, arrogant.

haul [hɔːl] 1 **n** a (*Aut etc*) **the long ~ between Paris and Grenoble** le long voyage entre Paris et Grenoble; (*lit, fig*) **it's a long ~** la route est longue.

b *[fishermen]* prise *f*; *[thieves]* butin *m*. (*Fishing*) **a good ~** une belle prise, un beau coup de filet; **the thieves made a good ~** les voleurs ont eu un beau butin; **a good ~ of jewels** un beau butin en bijoux; (*fig*) **a good ~ of presents*** une bonne récolte de cadeaux; (*fig*) **what a ~!*** quelle récolte!

2 **vt** a (*pull*) traîner, tirer. (*fig*) **to ~ sb over the coals** passer un savon* à qn, réprimander sévèrement qn; (*US*) **to ~ ass**⁑ se barrer⁑, mettre les bouts⁑.

b (*transport by truck*) camionner.

c (*Naut*) haler. **to ~ into the wind** faire lofer.

3 **vi** (*Naut*) *[boat]* lofer; *[wind]* refuser.

►**haul down** **vt sep** *flag, sail* affaler, amener; (*gen*) *object* descendre (*en tirant*).

►**haul in** **vt sep** *line, catch* amener; *drowning man* tirer (de l'eau).

►**haul up** **vt sep** *flag, sail* hisser; (*gen*) *object* monter (*en tirant*). **to haul o.s. up** se hisser; (*Naut*) **to haul up a boat** (*aboard ship*) rentrer une embarcation (à bord); (*on to beach*) tirer un bateau au sec; **to be hauled up in court** *etc* être traîné devant les tribunaux *etc*.

haulage ['hɔːlɪdʒ] **n** (*gen*) transport *m* routier, camionnage *m*, roulage *m*; (*charge*) camionnage, frais *mpl* de roulage *or* de transport. (*Brit*) ~ **company** entreprise *f* de transports (routiers); ~ **contractor** = **haulier**.

hauler ['hɔːləʳ] **n** (*US*) a = **haulier**. b (*vehicle*) camion *m*, poids *m* lourd.

haulier ['hɔːlɪəʳ] **n** (*Brit*) (*company*) entreprise *f* de transports (routiers); (*person in charge*) entrepreneur *m* de transports (routiers), transporteur *m*; (*driver*) camionneur *m*, routier *m*.

haunch [hɔːnʃ] **n** hanche *f*. *[animal]* **~es** derrière *m*, arrière-train *m*; **(squatting) on his ~es** *person* accroupi; *dog etc* assis (sur son derrière); (*Culin*) ~ **of venison** cuissot *m* de chevreuil.

haunt [hɔːnt] 1 **vt** (*lit, fig*) hanter. (*fig*) **he ~ed the café in the hope of seeing her** il hantait le café dans l'espoir de la voir; **to be ~ed by memories** être hanté *or* obsédé par des souvenirs; **he is ~ed by the fear of losing all his money** il est hanté par la peur de *or* il a la hantise de perdre tout son argent; *see also* **haunted**. 2 **n** *[criminals]* repaire *m*. **one of the favourite ~s of this animal is ...** un des lieux où l'on trouve souvent cet animal est ...; **it is a favourite ~ of artists** c'est un lieu fréquenté des artistes; **that café is one of his favourite ~s** ce café est un de ses coins favoris.

haunted ['hɔːntɪd] **adj** *house* hanté; *look, expression* égaré; *face* hagard, à l'air égaré.

haunting ['hɔːntɪŋ] 1 **adj** *tune* obsédant, qui vous trotte par la tête *or* qui vous hante; *doubt* obsédant. 2 **n**: **there have been several ~s here** il y a eu plusieurs apparitions *fpl* ici.

hauntingly ['hɔːntɪŋlɪ] **adv**: ~ **beautiful** d'une beauté envoûtante.

haute couture [ˌəʊt kuːˈtʊəʳ] **n** haute couture *f*.

haute cuisine [ˌəʊtˌkwɪˈziːn] **n** haute cuisine *f*.

Havana [həˈvænə] **n** a Havane *f*. b **a ~ (cigar)** un havane.

have [hæv] *3rd person sg pres* **has**, **pret, ptp had** 1 **aux vb** a avoir; être. **to have been** avoir été; **to have eaten** avoir mangé; **to have gone** être allé; **to have got up** s'être levé; **I have been** j'ai été; **I have eaten** j'ai mangé; **I have gone** je suis allé; **I have got up** je me suis levé; **I have not** *or* **I've not** *or* **I haven't seen him** je ne l'ai pas vu; **I had been** j'avais été; **I had eaten** j'avais mangé; **I had gone** j'étais allé; **I had got up** je m'étais levé; **I had not** *or* **I hadn't** *or* **I'd not seen him** je ne l'avais pas vu; **had I seen him** *or* **if I had seen him I should have spoken to him** si je l'avais vu je lui aurais parlé; **having seen him** l'ayant vu; **after** *or* **when I had seen him I went out** après l'avoir vu je suis sorti; **when he had seen me I went out** une fois qu'il m'eut vu je sortis; **I have lived** *or* **have been living here for 10 years/since January** j'habite ici depuis 10 ans/ depuis janvier; **I had lived** *or* **had been living there for 10 years** j'habitais là depuis 10 ans; **you HAVE grown!** ce que tu as grandi!; **have got** *see* **2, 3a, 3b, 3f, 3m**.

b (*in tag questions etc*) **you've seen her, haven't you?** vous l'avez vue, n'est-ce pas?; **you haven't seen her, have you?** vous ne l'avez pas vue, je suppose?; **you haven't seen her – yes I have!** vous ne l'avez pas vue – si!; **you've made a mistake – no I haven't!** vous vous êtes trompé – mais non!; **you've dropped your book – so I have!** vous avez laissé tomber votre livre – en effet! *or* c'est vrai!; **have you been there? if you have ...** y êtes-vous allé? si oui ...; **have you been there? if you haven't ...** y avez-vous été? si non ... .

c **to have just done sth** venir de faire qch; **I have just seen him** je viens de le voir; **I had just seen him** je venais de le voir; **I've just come from London** j'arrive à l'instant de Londres.

2 **modal aux usage** (+ *infin: be obliged*) (*au présent la forme* **have got** *to est plus usuelle en anglais parlé que la forme* **have to**) **to have (got) to** do devoir faire, être obligé *or* forcé de faire; **I have (got) to speak to you at once** je dois vous parler *or* il faut que je vous parle (*subj*) immédiatement; **I haven't got to do it, I don't have to do it** je ne suis pas obligé *or* forcé de le faire; **I've got** *or* **I have to hurry or I'll be late** il faut que je me dépêche (*subj*) sinon je serai en retard, si je ne me dépêche pas je serai en retard; **it has still** *or* **still has to be done** cela reste à faire; **do you have to go now?, have you got to go now?** est-ce que vous êtes obligé de *or* est-ce que vous devez partir tout de suite?; **do you have to make such a noise?** tu ne pourrais pas faire un peu moins de bruit?; **you didn't have to tell her!** tu n'avais pas besoin de le lui dire! *or* d'aller le lui dire!; **haven't you got to** *or* **don't you have to write to your mother?** est-ce que tu ne dois pas écrire à ta mère?; **if you go through Dijon you haven't got to** *or* **you don't have to go to Lyons** si vous passez par Dijon vous n'avez pas besoin d'aller à Lyon; **you haven't (got) to say a word about it!*** tu ne dois pas en dire un mot!; **he doesn't have to work, he hasn't got to work** il n'est pas obligé de travailler, il n'a pas besoin de travailler; **she was having to get up at 6 each morning** elle devait se lever *or* il fallait qu'elle se lève (*subj*) à 6 heures tous les matins; **we've had to go and see her twice this week** nous avons dû aller *or* il nous a fallu aller la voir deux fois cette semaine; **we shall have to leave tomorrow** nous devrons *or* nous serons obligés de *or* il nous faudra partir demain; **the letter will have to be written tomorrow** il va falloir que la lettre soit écrite demain; **I had to send for the doctor** j'ai été obligé d'appeler *or* j'ai dû appeler le médecin; (*US*) **it's got to be** *or* **it has to be the biggest scandal this year** ça doit être le plus grand scandale de l'année.

3 **vt** a (*also* **have got**: *possess*) avoir, posséder. **she has (got) blue eyes** elle a les yeux bleus; **he has (got) big feet** il a de grands pieds; **I have** *or* **I've got 3 books** j'ai 3 livres; **have you (got)** *or* (*esp US*) **do you have a suitcase?** avez-vous une valise?; **all I have (got)** tout ce que je possède; **I haven't (got) any more** je n'en ai plus; **she has (got) a shop** elle a *or* tient une boutique; **have you (got) any money? if you have ...** avez-vous de l'argent? si vous en avez ...; **have you got a cigarette?** (est-ce que) tu as une cigarette?; **have you got the time (on you)?** avez-vous *or* est-ce que vous avez l'heure?; **I have (got) no German** je ne parle pas un mot d'allemand; (*Cards*) **I had (got) no hearts** je n'avais pas de cœur; (*in shop*) **have you (got) any bananas?** avez-vous des bananes?; *see also* **3m**.

b *meals etc* avoir, prendre. **he has dinner at 8** il dîne à 8 heures; **he has had lunch** il a déjeuné; **to have tea with sb** prendre le thé avec qn; **will you have tea or coffee?** voulez-vous du thé ou du café?; **what will you have? – I'll have an egg** qu'est-ce que vous prendrez? – je prendrai *or* donnez-moi un œuf; **how will you have your eggs? – boiled** comment voulez-vous vos œufs? – à la coque; **he had eggs for breakfast** il a eu *or* mangé des œufs au petit déjeuner; **will you ~ some more?** en reprendrez-vous?; **I have had some more** j'en ai repris; **will you have a drink?** voulez-vous prendre *or* boire un verre?; **he had a cigarette** il a fumé une cigarette; **will you have a cigarette?** voulez-vous une cigarette?; **do you have coffee at breakfast?** est-ce que vous prenez du café au petit déjeuner?; **have you (got) coffee now or is that tea?** est-ce que c'est du café ou du thé que vous buvez là?

c (*receive, obtain, get*) avoir, recevoir, tenir. **to have news from sb** recevoir des nouvelles de qn; **I had a telegram from him** j'ai reçu un télégramme de lui; **I have it from my sister that ...** je tiens de ma sœur que ...; **I have it on good authority that ...** je tiens de bonne source que ...; **I shall let you have the books tomorrow** je vous donnerai les livres demain; **I must have them by this afternoon** il me les faut pour cet après-midi; **let me have your address** donnez-moi votre adresse; **let me have a reply soon** répondez-moi rapidement; **I shall let you have it for 10 francs** je vous le cède *or* laisse pour 10 F; **we had a lot of visitors** nous avons reçu beaucoup de visites; **I must have £5 at once** il me faut 5 livres immédiatement; **I must have more time** il me faut davantage de temps; **there are no newspapers to be had** on ne trouve pas de journaux; **it is to be had at the chemist's** cela se trouve en pharmacie.

d (*maintain, insist*) **he will have it that Paul is guilty** il soutient que Paul est coupable; **he won't have it that Paul is guilty** il n'admet pas que Paul soit coupable; **rumour has it that ...** le bruit court que ...; **as gossip has it** selon les racontars; **as the Bible has it** comme il est dit dans la Bible.

e (*neg: refuse to allow*) **I won't have this nonsense!** je ne tolérerai pas cette absurdité!; **I won't have this sort of behaviour!** je ne supporterai *or* tolérerai pas une pareille conduite!; **I won't have it!** je ne tolérerai pas ça!, cela ne va pas se passer comme ça!; **I won't have**

him hurt je ne veux pas qu'on lui fasse du mal.

f (*hold*) tenir. **he had (got) me by the throat/the hair** il me tenait à la gorge/par les cheveux; **the dog had (got) him by the ankle** le chien le tenait par la cheville; (*fig*) **I have (got) him where I want him!*** je le tiens (à ma merci)!

g (*to give birth to*) **to have a child** avoir un enfant; **she is having a baby in April** elle va avoir un bébé en avril; **our cat has had kittens** notre chatte a eu des petits.

h (+ *will or would: wish*) **which one will you have?** lequel voulez-vous?; **will you have this one?** voulez-vous (prendre) celui-ci?; **what more would you have?** que vous faut-il de plus?; **as fate would have it he did not get the letter** la fatalité a voulu qu'il ne reçoive pas la lettre; **what would you have me say?** que voulez-vous que je dise?; **I would have you know that ...** sachez que ... .

i (*causative*) **to have sth done** faire faire qch; **to have one's hair cut** se faire couper les cheveux; **I had my luggage brought up** j'ai fait monter mes bagages; **have it mended!** faites-le réparer!; **to have sb do sth** faire faire qch à qn; **I had him clean the car** je lui ai fait nettoyer la voiture.

j (*experience, suffer*) **he had his car stolen** il s'est fait voler sa voiture, on lui a volé sa voiture; **I've had 3 windows broken this week** on m'a cassé 3 fenêtres cette semaine.

k (+ *n* = *vb identical with n*) **to have a walk** faire une promenade, aller se promener; *see* **dream, sleep, talk** *etc*.

l (**: *have sex with*) avoir**, coucher* avec.

m (*phrases*) **I had better go now** je devrais partir (maintenant); **you'd better not tell him that!** tu ferais mieux de *or* tu as intérêt à ne pas lui dire ça!; **I had as soon not see him** j'aimerais autant ne pas le voir; **I had rather do it myself** j'aimerais mieux le faire moi-même; **I'd rather not speak to him** j'aimerais mieux *or* je préférerais ne pas lui parler; **to have a good time** bien s'amuser; **to have a pleasant evening** passer une bonne soirée; **to have good holidays** passer de bonnes vacances; **he has (got) flu** il a la grippe; **I've (got) a headache** j'ai mal à la tête; **I've (got) an idea** j'ai une idée; **I've (got) £6 left** il me reste 6 livres; **I've (got) a half left** il m'en reste la moitié; **I had my camera ready** j'avais mon appareil tout prêt; **I shall have everything ready** je veillerai à ce que tout soit prêt; **I have (got) letters to write** j'ai des lettres à écrire; (*fig*) **she has got it in her** elle en est capable; **to have (got) sth to do/to read** *etc* avoir qch à faire/à lire *etc;* **I have (got) nothing to do** je n'ai rien à faire; **I have (got) nothing to do with it** je n'y suis pour rien; **there you have me!** ça je n'en sais rien; **I have it!** j'y suis!, ça y est, j'ai trouvé!; **you've been had*** tu t'es fait avoir*, on t'a eu*; **I'm not having any‡** ça ne prend pas*; **I've had it*** (*lost, doomed etc*) je suis fichu* *or* foutu‡; (*US: fed up: also* **I've had it up to here*, I've had that***) j'en ai marre*, j'en ai ras-le-bol*!; *see* **cheek, cold, lesson** *etc*.

4 **n: the haves and the have-nots** les riches *mpl* et les pauvres *mpl*, les nantis *mpl* et les démunis *mpl*; **the have-nots** les démunis, les déshérités *mpl*.

►**have at** vt fus (*Fencing*) *person* attaquer. **have at thee!**† défends-toi!

►**have down** vt sep: **we are having the Smiths down for a few days** nous avons invité les Smith à venir passer quelques jours chez nous, les Smith viennent passer quelques jours chez nous.

►**have in** vt sep a *employee, caller* faire entrer; *doctor* faire venir. **I had the children in to speak to them** j'ai fait entrer les enfants pour leur parler; **we had him in for the evening** nous l'avons invité à venir passer la soirée chez nous. b **to have it in for sb*** garder *or* avoir une dent contre qn.

►**have off** vt sep (*Brit*) **to have it off with sb**** s'envoyer** qn, se taper** qn.

►**have on** vt sep a *clothes* porter. **he had (got) nothing on** il était tout nu. b (*Brit: be occupied or busy*) **I've got so much on this week that ...** j'ai tant à faire cette semaine que ...; **I have (got) nothing on (for) this evening** je ne suis pas pris ce soir, je n'ai rien ce soir. c (*Brit* ‡: *deceive, tease*) *person* faire marcher*.

►**have out** vt sep a **to have a tooth out** se faire arracher une dent. b **to have it out with sb** s'expliquer avec qn.

►**have up** vt sep *person* faire venir; (*from below*) faire monter. **I had him up to see me** je l'ai fait venir (*or* monter) me voir, je l'ai convoqué; **he was had up by the headmaster** il a été appelé chez le proviseur; **to be had up by the police** être arrêté (*for sth* pour qch; *for doing* pour avoir fait).

haven ['heɪvn] n (*harbour*) port *m*; (*safe place*) havre *m*, abri *m*, refuge *m*; *see* **tax**.

haven't ['hævnt] = **have not;** *see* **have**.

haver ['heɪvəʳ] vi (*N Engl, Scot*) dire des âneries.

haversack ['hævəsæk] n (*over shoulder*) musette *f*; (*on back*) sac *m* à dos; (*Mil*) havresac *m*, musette.

havoc ['hævək] n (*NonC*) ravages *mpl*, dégâts *mpl*. **to wreak ~ in, to make ~ of** ravager, causer des ravages dans; (*fig*) **to play ~ with** désorganiser complètement; *stomach etc* abîmer, bousiller*.

haw[1] [hɔː] n (*Bot*) cenelle *f*.

haw[2] [hɔː] vi: **to hem and ~, to hum and ~** bafouiller.

Hawaii [hə'waɪ] n Hawaii *m*. **in ~** à Hawaii.

Hawaiian [hə'waɪjən] 1 adj hawaïen. **~ Islands** îles *fpl* Hawaii *or* Hawaï; **~ guitar** guitare hawaïenne. 2 n a Hawaïen(ne) *m(f)*. b (*Ling*) hawaïen *m*.

hawfinch ['hɔːˌfɪntʃ] n gros-bec *m*.

hawk[1] [hɔːk] 1 n a (*Orn*) faucon *m*. **to have eyes like a ~** avoir un regard d'aigle *or* des yeux de lynx. b (*Pol fig*) faucon *m*. **~s and doves** faucons et colombes *fpl*. 2 vi chasser au faucon. 3 comp ►**Hawkeye** (*US*) habitant(e) *m(f)* de l'Iowa; (*US*) **the Hawkeye State** l'Iowa *m* ►**hawk-eyed** au regard d'aigle, aux yeux de lynx.

hawk[2] [hɔːk] vi (*clear one's throat*) se racler la gorge.

►**hawk up** vt sep expectorer.

hawk[3] [hɔːk] vt (*peddle*) colporter; (*in street*) crier (*des marchandises*).

hawker ['hɔːkəʳ] n (*street*) colporteur *m*; (*door-to-door*) démarcheur *m*, -euse *f*.

hawser ['hɔːzəʳ] n haussière *f or* aussière *f*.

hawthorn ['hɔːθɔːn] n aubépine *f*.

hay [heɪ] 1 n foin *m*. (*Agr*) **to make ~** faner, faire les foins; (*Prov*) **to make ~ while the sun shines** battre le fer pendant qu'il est chaud, profiter de l'occasion; **to make ~ of*** *argument* démolir*; *enemy, team* battre à plate(s) couture(s); (*US fig*) **that ain't ~‡** c'est pas rien*; *see* **hit, roll 1c**.

2 comp ►**haycock** meulon *m* (de foin) ►**hay fever** (*Med*) rhume *m* des foins ►**hay fork** fourche *f* à foin ►**hayloft** grenier *m* à foin, fenil *m* ►**haymaker** (*worker*) faneur *m*, -euse *f*; (*fig* ‡: *blow*) uppercut *m* magistral ►**haymaking** fenaison *f* ►**hayrick** = **haystack** ►**hayride** (*esp US*) promenade *f* dans une charrette de foin ►**hayseed‡** (*US pej*) péquenaud‡ *m* ►**haystack** meule *f* de foin ►**haywire***: **to go haywire** *[person]* perdre la tête *or* la boule*; *[plans etc]* mal tourner; *[equipment etc]* se détraquer; **to be haywire, to have gone haywire** *[person]* avoir perdu la tête *or* la boule*; *[plans etc]* être à l'eau; *[equipment etc]* être détraqué.

hazard ['hæzəd] 1 n a (*chance*) hasard *m*, chance *f*. **it was pure ~ that he ...** ce fut pur hasard qu'il ... + *subj*.

b (*risk*) risque *m*, (*stronger*) danger *m*, péril *m*; (*Golf*) hazard *m*. **natural ~s** risques naturels; **professional ~** risque du métier; **this constitutes a ~ for pedestrians** ceci constitue un danger pour les piétons; *see* **health**.

2 comp ►**hazard (warning) lights** (*Aut*) feux *mpl* de détresse.

3 vt a (*risk*) *life, reputation* hasarder, risquer; *one's fortune* risquer.

b (*venture to make*) *remark, forecast* hasarder. **to ~ a suggestion** hasarder une proposition; **to ~ an attempt** risquer une tentative; **to ~ a guess** faire une conjecture, hasarder *or* risquer une hypothèse; **if I might ~ a guess** si je peux me permettre de risquer une hypothèse; **"I could do it" she ~ed** "moi je pourrais bien le faire" se risqua-t-elle à dire *or* risqua-t-elle.

hazardous ['hæzədəs] adj a (*risky*) *enterprise, situation* hasardeux, risqué, périlleux. b (*problematical*) *outcome* aléatoire, incertain, hasardeux.

haze[1] [heɪz] n brume *f* (légère), vapeur *f*. **a ~ of tobacco filled the room** des vapeurs de tabac emplissaient la pièce; (*fig*) **to be in a ~** être dans le brouillard; *see* **heat**.

haze[2] [heɪz] vt (*US Univ etc*) bizuter.

hazel ['heɪzl] 1 n (*Bot*) noisetier *m*, coudrier *m*. 2 adj (*colour*) (couleur) noisette *inv*. **~ eyes** yeux (couleur) noisette. 3 comp ►**hazel grouse** gélinotte *f* (des bois) ►**hazel grove** coudraie *f* ►**hazelnut** noisette *f* ►**hazelwood** (bois *m* de) noisetier *m*.

haziness ['heɪzɪnɪs] n *[day, weather]* état brumeux; *[ideas etc]* vague *m*, flou *m*.

hazing ['heɪzɪŋ] n (*US Univ etc*) bizutage *m*.

hazy ['heɪzɪ] adj *day, weather* brumeux; *sun, moon* voilé; *outline, photograph* flou; *idea* vague, nébuleux; *thinking* fumeux. **he's ~ about dates** il ne se rappelle pas bien les dates; **I'm ~ about maths** j'ai des notions mathématiques (très) vagues; **I'm ~ about what really happened** j'ai une idée assez vague de *or* je ne sais pas (très) bien ce qui s'est vraiment passé.

HC, h. & c. (abbr of **hot and cold (water)**) *see* **hot**.

HDTV [ˌeɪtʃdiːˌtiː'viː] n (abbr of **high definition television**) TVHD *f*.

HE [eɪtʃ'iː] a (abbr of **His** *or* **Her Excellency**) SE. b (abbr of **high explosive**) *see* **high**.

he, (*Rel*) **He** [hiː] 1 pers pron a (*unstressed*) il. **~ has come** il est venu; **here ~ is** le voici; **~ is a doctor** il est médecin, c'est un médecin; **~ is a small man** c'est un homme petit. b (*stressed*) lui. (*frm*) **it is ~** c'est lui; (*frm*) **if I were ~** si j'étais lui, si j'étais à sa place; (*frm*) **younger than ~** plus jeune que lui; **HE didn't do it** ce n'est pas lui qui l'a fait. c (+ *rel pron*) celui. **~ who** *or* **that can** celui qui peut. 2 comp mâle ►**he-bear** ours *m* mâle ►**he-goat** bouc *m* ►**he-man*** (vrai) mâle *m*, macho* *m*. 3 n a (*) mâle *m*. **it's a ~** (*animal*) c'est un mâle; (*baby*) c'est un garçon. b (*Scol sl*) **you're ~!** (c'est toi le) chat!

head [hed] 1 n a (*Anat*) tête *f*. (*fig*) **to have a big** *or* **swollen ~** avoir la grosse tête*; **~ of hair** chevelure *f*; **covered** *etc* **from ~ to foot** couvert *etc* de la tête aux pieds; **armed from ~ to foot** armé de pied en cap; **~ down** (*upside down*) la tête en bas; (*looking down*) la tête baissée; ~ **hanging** la tête baissée; ~ **downwards** la tête en bas; ~ **first,** ~ **foremost** la tête la première (*see also* **2**); **my** ~ **aches, I've got a bad** ~ j'ai mal à la tête; **I've a bit of a** ~* j'ai un peu mal au crâne*; *[person, stone etc]* **to hit sb on the** ~ frapper qn à la tête; **to stand on one's** ~ faire le poirier; **I could do it standing on my** ~ c'est simple comme bonjour; **he stands** ~ **and shoulders above everybody else** (*lit*) il dépasse tout le monde d'une tête; (*fig*) il surpasse tout le monde; **she is** ~ **and shoulders above her sister in maths** elle est cent fois supérieure à sa sœur en maths; **she is a** ~ **taller than her sister, she is taller than her sister by a** ~ elle dépasse sa sœur d'une tête; *[horse]* **to win by a (short)** ~ gagner d'une (courte) tête; **to be** ~ **over ears in debt** être criblé *or* accablé de dettes, être dans les dettes jusqu'au cou; **to turn** *or* **go** ~ **over heels** (*accidentally*) faire la culbute; (*on purpose*) faire une galipette; **to be** ~ **over heels in love with sb** être follement *or* éperdument amoureux de qn; **to keep one's** ~ **above water** (*lit*) garder la tête au-dessus de l'eau; (*fig*) se maintenir à flot; (*fig*) **to put** *or* **lay one's** ~ **on the block** risquer gros; (*fig*) **he's got his** ~ **in the sand** il pratique la politique de l'autruche; (*fig*) **to have one's** ~ **in the clouds** être dans les nuages; **he was talking his** ~ **off*** il n'arrêtait pas de parler; **to sing/shout one's** ~ **off*** chanter/crier à tue-tête; **he's talking off the top of his** ~* il dit n'importe quoi; **I'm saying that off the top of my** ~* je dis ça sans savoir exactement; **to give a horse its** ~ lâcher la bride à un cheval; **to give sb his** ~ lâcher la bride à qn; **on your** ~ **be it!** à vos risques et périls!; *see* **bang[1], crown, hold, lion** *etc.*

b (*mind, intellect*) tête *f*. **to get sth into one's** ~ s'enfoncer *or* se mettre qch dans la tête; **I wish he would get it into his** ~ **that ...** j'aimerais qu'il se mette (bien) dans la tête que ...; **I can't get that into his** ~ je ne peux pas lui enfoncer *or* mettre ça dans la tête; **he has taken it into his** ~ **that ...** il s'est mis dans la tête que ...; **to take it into one's** ~ **to do** se mettre en tête de *or* s'aviser de faire; **it didn't enter his** ~ **that .../to do** il ne lui vint pas à l'idée *or* à l'esprit que .../de faire; **you never know what's going on in his** ~ on ne sait jamais ce qui lui passe par la tête; **what put that (idea) into his** ~? qu'est-ce qui lui a mis cette idée-là dans la tête?; **don't put ideas into his** ~* ne lui donnez pas des idées, ne lui mettez pas d'idées dans la tête; **I can't get it out of my** ~ je ne peux pas me sortir ça de la tête, ça me trotte par la tête; **his name has gone out of my** ~ son nom m'est sorti de la tête *or* de la mémoire; **it's gone right out of my** ~ ça m'est tout à fait sorti de la tête; **that tune has been running through my** ~ **all day** cet air m'a trotté* par la tête toute la journée; **she has a good** ~ **for figures** elle a des dispositions pour *or* elle est douée pour le calcul; **he has a good** ~ **for heights** il n'a jamais le vertige; **he has no** ~ **for heights** il a le vertige; **he has a good business** ~ il a le sens des affaires; **he has a good** ~ **(on his shoulders)** il a de la tête; **he's got his** ~ **screwed on (right)*** il a la tête sur les épaules, il a la tête bien plantée entre les deux épaules; (*Prov*) **two** ~**s are better than one** deux avis valent mieux qu'un; **we put our** ~**s together** (*gen*) nous nous sommes consultés, nous nous y sommes tous mis; *[two people]* nous nous y sommes mis à deux; **don't bother** *or* **worry your** ~ **about it** ne vous en faites pas pour cela; **to count in one's** ~ calculer mentalement *or* de tête; **I can't do it in my** ~ je ne peux pas faire *or* calculer ça de tête; (*fig*) **he spoke above** *or* **over their** ~**s** ce qu'il a dit les a complètement dépassés; (*fig*) **he gave orders over my** ~ il a donné des ordres sans me consulter; **he went over my** ~ **to the director** il m'a court-circuité pour parler au directeur; **it's quite above my** ~ cela me dépasse complètement; **to keep one's** ~ garder son sang-froid; **to lose one's** ~ perdre la tête; **the wine/his success went to his** ~ le vin/son succès lui est monté à la tête; **he has gone** *or* **he is off his** ~* il a perdu la boule*; **weak** *or* **soft*** **in the** ~ un peu demeuré, faible *or* simple d'esprit.

c (pl inv) **20** ~ **of cattle** 20 têtes *or* pièces de bétail; **20** ~ **of oxen** 20 bœufs; **they paid 10 francs a** ~ *or* **per** ~ ils ont payé 10 F par tête.

d (*specific part*) *[tree, flower, nail, pin, hammer, mast]* tête *f*; *[asparagus, arrow]* pointe *f*; *[spear]* fer *m*; *[cane]* pommeau *m*; *[bed]* chevet *m*, tête; *[violin]* crosse *f*; (*on beer*) mousse *f*, faux col* *m*; (*on tape recorder*) tête (*de lecture/d'enregistrement*). (*Naut*) ~ **to wind** vent debout; ~ **on** adv = **head-on**.

e (*highest etc end*) *[mountain]* faîte *m*, sommet *m*, haut *m*; *[page, staircase]* haut; *[pillar]* chapiteau *m*; *[jetty, pier]* extrémité *f*. **at the** ~ **of** *[lake]* à l'extrémité de, à l'amont de; *[valley]* à la tête *or* en tête de; *[table]* au haut bout de; (*fig: in charge of*) *[army, organization, company]* à la tête de; **at the** ~ **of the list/the queue** en tête de liste/de file.

f *[lettuce, cabbage]* pomme *f*; *[celery]* pied *m*; *[corn]* épi *m*. ~ **of steam** pression *f*; ~ **of water** colonne *f* d'eau, hauteur *f* de chute.

g *[abscess etc]* tête *f*. **it's coming to a** ~ (*fig, gen*) ça devient critique; *[abscess]* ça mûrit; **it all came to a** ~ **when he met her yesterday** les choses sont arrivées au point critique quand il l'a rencontrée hier; **to bring things to a** ~ précipiter une crise.

h (*leader*) *[family, business etc]* chef *m*. (*Scol*) **the** ~ = **the headmaster** *or* **headmistress** (*see* **2**); (*Scol*) ~ **of French/Maths** *etc* ≃ professeur *m* coordinateur de français/de maths *etc;* ~ **of department** *[business firm]* chef de service; *[shop]* chef de rayon; *[school, college etc]* chef de section; (*Pol*) ~ **of state** chef d'État; **the** ~ **of the government** le chef du gouvernement.

i (*title*) titre *m*; (*subject heading*) rubrique *f*. **under this** ~ sous ce titre *or* cette rubrique; **this comes under the** ~ **of** ceci se classe sous la rubrique de, ceci vient au chapitre de; **the speech/essay was divided into several** ~**s** le discours/la dissertation était divisé(e) en plusieurs têtes de chapitre *or* en plusieurs parties; *see* **letter**.

j *[coin]* face *f*. **to toss** ~**s or tails** jouer à pile ou face; ~**s or tails?** pile ou face?; ~**s I win!** face je gagne!; **he called** ~**s** il a annoncé "face"; **I can't make** ~ **(n)or tail of what he's saying** je ne comprends rien à ce qu'il dit; **I can't make** ~ **(n)or tail of it** je n'y comprends rien, pour moi ça n'a ni queue ni tête.

k (*Drugs sl: in comp*) drogué, camé(e), toxicomane; *see* **acid** *etc.*

l (*Comput*) tête *f*. **reading/writing** ~ tête de lecture/d'écriture.

2 comp *typist, assistant etc* principal ▸**headache** *see* **headache** ▸**headband** bandeau *m* ▸**head-banger*** (*heavy metal fan*) enragé(e)* *m(f)* de heavy metal; (*nutcase*) cinglé(e)* *m(f)* ▸**headboard** *[bed]* dosseret *m* ▸**head boy/girl** (*Brit Scol*) *élève de terminale chargé(e) d'un certain nombre de responsabilités* ▸**headbutt** n coup *m* de tête ◊ vt donner un coup de tête à ▸**headcase*** cinglé(e)* *m(f)* ▸**headcheese** (*US Culin*) fromage *m* de tête ▸**head clerk** (*Comm*) premier commis, chef *m* de bureau; (*Jur*) principal *m* ▸**head cold** rhume *m* de cerveau ▸**headcount** comptage *m*, vérification *f* du nombre de personnes présentes; **let's do a headcount** on va les compter *or* compter combien ils sont ▸**headdress** (*of feathers etc*) coiffure *f*; (*of lace*) coiffe *f* ▸**headfirst** (*lit*) la tête la première; (*fig*) **she rushed headfirst into marriage** elle s'est précipitée dans le mariage ▸**head gardener** jardinier *m* en chef ▸**headgear** (*NonC*) couvre-chef *m*; **I haven't any headgear for this weather** je n'ai rien à me mettre sur la tête par ce temps ▸**head-guard** (*Sport*) casque *m* de protection ▸**headhunt** (*fig*) vi recruter des cadres pour une entreprise ◊ vt recruter; **she was headhunted** elle a été recrutée par un chasseur de têtes ▸**headhunter** (*lit*) chasseur *m* de têtes; (*fig: in recruiting personnel*) chasseur de têtes, recruteur *m* de cadres ▸**headhunting** chasse *f* aux têtes ▸**headlamp** (*Brit Aut*) phare *m*; *[train]* fanal *m*, feu *m* avant ▸**headland** promontoire *m*, cap *m* ▸**headlight** = **headlamp** ▸**headline** *see* **headline** ▸**headlong** *see* **headlong** ▸**headman** chef *m* (*d'une tribu etc*) ▸**headmaster** (*Brit*) *[school]* directeur *m*; *[college]* principal *m*; (*US Scol*) directeur d'école privée ▸**headmistress** (*Brit*) (*gen*) directrice *f*; *[French lycée]* proviseur *m*; *[college]* principale *f*; (*US Scol*) directrice d'école privée ▸**head nurse** (*US*) infirmier *m*, -ière *f* en chef ▸**head office** siège social, agence centrale ▸**head-on** *see* **head-on** ▸**headphones** (*Rad, Telec*) casque *m* (à écouteurs) ▸**head post office** bureau central des postes, poste principale ▸**headquarters** *[bank, business company, political party]* siège *m*; (*Mil*) quartier *m* général ▸**headquarters staff** (*Mil*) état-major *m* ▸**headrest** appui-tête *m*, repose-tête *m* ▸**head restraint** (*Aut*) = **headrest** ▸**headroom:** (*on roadsign*) **5 metres headroom** hauteur *f* limite de 5 mètres; **there is not enough headroom** le plafond est trop bas *or* n'est pas assez haut; **have you got enough headroom?** est-ce que vous avez assez de place (pour ne pas vous cogner la tête)? ▸**headscarf** foulard *m*, (*triangular*) pointe *f* ▸**headset** = **headphones** ▸**headship** (*post*) poste *m* de directeur *or* de directrice (*school*) *or* de proviseur (*lycée*); **under the headship of X** sous la direction de X ▸**head shop** (*US*) boutique *f* hippie ▸**headshrinker**‡ psy‡ *m*, psychiatre *mf* ▸**headsman** bourreau *m* ▸**headsquare** foulard *m* ▸**headstand: to do a headstand** faire le poirier ▸**head start:** (*fig*) **to have a head start** être avantagé dès le départ (*over or on sb* par rapport à qn) ▸**headstone** *[grave]* pierre tombale (de tête); (*Archit*) clef *f* de voûte, pierre angulaire ▸**headstrong** (*obstinate*) têtu, entêté, volontaire, obstiné; (*rash*) impétueux ▸**head teacher** = **headmaster** *or* **headmistress** ▸**head waiter** maître *m* d'hôtel ▸**headwaters** sources *fpl* ▸**headway** progrès *m*; **to make headway** (*in journey, studies etc*) avancer, faire des progrès; *[ship]* faire route; **I didn't make much headway with him** je n'ai pas fait beaucoup de progrès avec lui ▸**headwind** vent *m* contraire; (*Naut*) vent debout ▸**headword** entrée *f*, adresse *f*.

3 vt **a** *procession, list, poll* venir *or* être en tête de; *group of people* être à la tête de.

b (*direct*) **he** ~**ed the car towards town** il a pris la direction de *or* il s'est dirigé vers la ville; (*Naut*) **to** ~ **a ship for port** mettre le cap sur le port; (*gen*) **to be** ~**ed** = **to head;** *see* **4**.

c (*put at* ~ *of*) *chapter* intituler. **to** ~ **a chapter/a letter** *etc* **with sth** mettre qch en tête d'un chapitre/d'une lettre *etc;* (*Brit*) ~**ed writing paper** *or* **note paper** papier *m* à lettres à en-tête.

d (*Ftbl*) **to** ~ **the ball** faire une tête.

4 vi (*also* **be headed**) **to** ~ **for** *[person, car etc]* se diriger vers; *[ship]* mettre le cap sur; **he** ~**ed up the hill** il s'est mis à monter la colline; **he was** ~**ing home(wards)** il était sur le chemin du retour; **they were** ~**ing back to town** ils rentraient *or* retournaient à la ville; (*fig*) **he's** ~**ing for a disappointment** il va vers une déception; **he's** ~**ing for a fall** il court à un échec.

▸**head off** **1** vi partir (*for* pour, *towards* vers). (*fig*) **he headed off on to the subject of ...** il est passé à la question de ... . **2** vt sep *enemy* forcer à se rabattre; *person* (*lit*) détourner de son chemin; (*fig*) détourner (*from* de); *questions* parer, faire dévier.

headache ['hedeɪk] n mal *m* de tête, (*worse*) migraine *f*; (*fig*) problème *m*. **to have a ~** avoir mal à la tête, avoir la migraine; **terrible ~s** de terribles maux de tête, des migraines affreuses; (*fig*) **that's his ~** c'est son problème (à lui); **the whole business was a ~ from beginning to end** nous n'avons (*or* ils n'ont *etc*) connu que des ennuis avec cette affaire, cette affaire a été un casse-tête du début à la fin; **geography is a ~ to me** la géographie est une de mes bêtes noires.

-headed ['hedɪd] **adj ending in comps: bare-headed** nu-tête *inv*; **curly-headed** frisé, aux cheveux frisés; *see* **hard** *etc*.

header ['hedəʳ] **n** a (*dive*) plongeon *m*; (*fall*) chute *f or* plongeon *or* dégringolade *f* (la tête la première). **to take a ~** (*fall*) piquer une tête, se flanquer* par terre la tête la première; **to take a ~ into the water** piquer une tête dans l'eau, se flanquer* à l'eau la tête la première. b (*Ftbl*) (coup *m* de) tête *f*. c (*Constr*) boutisse *f*. d (*Comput*) en-tête *f*.

headiness ['hedɪnɪs] **n** (*see* **heady**) a bouquet capiteux; qualité entêtante; griserie *f*, ivresse *f*. b impétuosité *f*.

heading ['hedɪŋ] **n** (*title: at top of page, chapter, article, column of figures etc*) titre *m*; (*subject title*) rubrique *f*; (*printed: on letter, document etc*) en-tête *m*. **chapter ~** (*gen*) tête *f* de chapitre; (*title*) titre; **under this ~** sous ce titre *or* cette rubrique; **this comes under the ~ of** ceci se classe sous la rubrique de, ceci vient au chapitre de; **under the ~ of "Science" may be found ...** sous la rubrique des "Sciences" on peut trouver ...; **the essay was divided into several ~s** la dissertation était divisée en plusieurs têtes de chapitre *or* en plusieurs parties; *see* **tariff**.

headless ['hedlɪs] **adj** *body, nail* sans tête; (*Zool*) acéphale.

headline ['hedlaɪn] 1 **n** [*newspaper*] manchette *f*, (gros) titre *m*; (*Rad, TV*) grand titre. **it's in the ~s in the papers** c'est en gros titre *or* en manchette dans les journaux; **to hit the ~s*** (*gen*) faire les gros titres, être en manchette; [*scandal, crime etc*] défrayer la chronique; **have you seen the ~s?** as-tu vu les (gros) titres?; **I've only glanced at the ~s** je n'ai fait que jeter un coup d'œil aux gros titres *or* sur les titres; (*Rad, TV*) **here are the news ~s** voici les grands titres de l'actualité; **here are the ~s again** et maintenant le rappel des (grands) titres; **I only heard the ~s** je n'ai entendu que les (grands) titres.
2 **vt** mettre en manchette.

headlong ['hedlɒŋ] 1 **adv** *fall* la tête la première; *run, rush* (*head down*) tête baissée; (*at uncontrollable speed*) à toute allure *or* vitesse. **the car drove ~ into the wall** la voiture s'est littéralement jetée contre le mur. 2 **adj** *fall etc* la tête la première. **~ flight** débandade *f*, sauve-qui-peut *m inv*; **there was a ~ dash for the gates** ce fut une ruée générale vers la sortie.

head-on ['hed'ɒn] 1 **adj** *collision* [*cars, planes*] frontal, de plein fouet, de front; [*ships*] par l'avant; (*fig*) *confrontation* direct, en front. 2 **adv: to collide with sth ~** [*car, plane*] heurter qch de plein fouet *or* de front; [*ship*] heurter qch par l'avant; [*person running*] rentrer dans qch en courant, heurter qch de front; (*fig*) **to meet sb/sth ~** s'attaquer de front à qn/qch.

heady ['hedɪ] **adj** a (*intoxicating*) *wine* capiteux, qui monte à la tête; *perfume* capiteux, entêtant; *success* grisant, enivrant. **the ~ delights of ...** les plaisirs grisants de ... . b (*impetuous*) emporté, impétueux.

heal [hiːl] 1 **vi** (*also* **~ over, ~ up**) [*wound*] se cicatriser. 2 **vt** (*Med*) *person* guérir (*of* de); *wound* cicatriser; (*fig*) *differences* régler; *troubles* apaiser. **time will ~ the pain** le temps guérit les chagrins; (*fig*) **to ~ the breach** combler le fossé, effectuer une réconciliation.

healer ['hiːləʳ] **n** guérisseur *m*, -euse *f*; *see* **faith**.

healing ['hiːlɪŋ] 1 **n** [*person*] guérison *f*; [*wound*] cicatrisation *f*. 2 **adj** (*Med*) *ointment* cicatrisant; *remedy* curatif; (*fig*) apaisant; *hands* de guérisseur.

health [helθ] 1 **n** a (*Med, fig*) santé *f*. **in good/bad ~** en bonne/mauvaise santé; **mental ~** [*person*] santé mentale; (*Admin etc*) prévention *f* en (matière de) médecine mentale; **to regain one's ~** recouvrer la santé, guérir, se remettre; **he enjoys good ~** il jouit d'une bonne santé; **from a ~ point of view** du point de vue de la santé; (*Brit* †) **Department of/Secretary of State for Health and Social Security**, (*US*) **Department/Secretary of Health and Human Services** ministère *m*/ministre *m* de la Santé et des Affaires Sociales; (*Brit*) **Minister/Ministry of Health** ≃ ministre/ministère de la Santé; (*fig*) **the ~ of the economy** la santé de l'économie; *see* **national, restore**.
b **to drink (to) sb's ~** boire à la santé de qn; **your ~!, good ~!** à votre santé!
2 **comp ▸Health Authority** (*Brit*) administration régionale de la santé publique **▸health benefits** prestations *fpl* maladie **▸health care** services *mpl* médicaux **▸health centre** ≃ centre médico-social **▸health education** (*Scol*) hygiène *f* **▸health farm** centre *m* de remise en forme, établissement *m* de cure (de rajeunissement *etc*) **▸health foods** aliments naturels *or* diététiques **▸health food shop,** (*US*) **health food store** centre *m* diététique, boutique *f* de produits diététiques **▸health-giving** *see* **healthful ▸health hazard** risque *m* pour la santé **▸health insurance** assurance *f* maladie **▸health officer** inspecteur *m*, -trice *f* de la santé (publique) **▸health resort** (*watering place*) station thermale, ville *f* d'eau; (*in mountains*) station climatique **▸health risk** = **health hazard ▸health service** (*US Univ*) infirmerie *f* **▸Health Service** (*Brit*) ≃ Sécurité *f* Sociale; **I got my glasses on the Health Service** ≃ la Sécurité Sociale m'a remboursé mes lunettes **▸Health Service doctor** ≃ médecin conventionné **▸Health Service nursing home** ≃ clinique conventionnée **▸health spa** (*US*) établissement *m* de cure de rajeunissement **▸health visitor** ≃ infirmière visiteuse.

healthful ['helθfʊl] **adj, health-giving** ['helθ,gɪvɪŋ] **adj** *air* salubre; *exercise etc* salutaire, bon pour la santé.

healthily ['helθɪlɪ] **adv** *live etc* sainement. (*fig*) **~ sceptical about ...** manifestant un *or* des doute(s) salutaire(s) à propos de ... .

healthy ['helθɪ] **adj** *person* sain, bien portant, en bonne santé; *animal, plant* en bonne santé; *climate, air* salubre; *food, skin, surroundings* sain; *appetite* robuste, bon; *exercise* bon pour la santé, salutaire; (*fig*) *economy, finances, attitude* sain; *doubts* de bon aloi, légitime. **he is very ~** il se porte très bien, il est très bien portant; **~ eating/living** une alimentation/une vie saine; **to make sth ~** *or* **healthier** assainir qch; (*fig*) **his interest in this is not very ~** l'intérêt qu'il porte à cela n'est pas très sain; (*fig*) **to have a ~ respect for sb/sth** éprouver un respect salutaire pour qn/qch.

heap [hiːp] 1 **n** a tas *m*, monceau *m*, amas *m*. **in a ~** en tas; [*person*] **to collapse/fall in a ~** s'effondrer/tomber comme une masse.
b (* *fig*) tas* *m*, masse* *f*. **~s of** *or* **a whole ~ of things to do** un tas* *or* des masses* de choses à faire; **~s of** des tas* de, des masses* de, des monceaux de; **she has ~s of money** elle a des tas* *or* des monceaux d'argent, elle a de l'argent à ne savoir qu'en faire; **we've got ~s of time** nous avons grandement *or* largement le temps, nous avons tout notre temps; **~s of times** des tas* de fois, mille fois; **~s better** drôlement* mieux; **a whole ~ of people** tout un tas* de gens; **a whole ~ of trouble** tout un tas* d'ennuis; **to be at the top/the bottom of the ~** être en haut/en bas de l'échelle sociale; (*fig*) [*person*] **to end up on the scrap** *or* **rubbish ~** être mis au rebut.
c (*‡: car etc*) tas *m* de ferraille*.
2 **vt** (*also* **~ up**) entasser, amonceler, empiler. **to ~ sth (up) on top of sth** empiler *or* entasser qch sur qch; **to ~ gifts on sb** couvrir qn de cadeaux; **to ~ praises/favours on sb** combler qn d'éloges/de faveurs; **to ~ insults on sb** accabler *or* couvrir qn d'injures; **to ~ work on sb** accabler qn de travail; (*fig*) **to ~ coals of fire (on sb)** rendre le bien pour le mal (à qn); **she ~ed (up) her plate with cakes** elle a empilé des gâteaux sur son assiette, elle a chargé son assiette de gâteaux; **shelves ~ed with piles of old books** des étagères croûlant sous des piles de vieux livres; **~ed baskets** paniers très chargés; (*Culin*) **~ed spoonful,** (*US*) **~ing spoonful** grosse cuillerée.

hear [hɪəʳ] **pret, ptp heard** 1 **vt** a entendre. **did you ~ what he said?** avez-vous entendu ce qu'il a dit?; **can you ~ him?** l'entendez-vous?, vous l'entendez bien?; **I can't ~ you!** je ne vous entends pas!, je n'entends pas ce que vous dites!; **I ~ you speaking** je vous entends parler; **I heard him say that ...** je l'ai entendu dire que ...; **I heard someone come in** j'ai entendu entrer quelqu'un *or* quelqu'un entrer; **a noise was heard** un bruit se fit entendre; **he was heard to say that ...** on l'a entendu dire que ...; **to make o.s. heard** se faire entendre; **I couldn't ~ myself think*** je ne m'entendais plus penser; **he likes to ~ himself talk** il aime s'écouter parler; **to ~ him (talk) you'd think he was an expert** à l'entendre vous le prendriez pour un expert; **I have heard it said that ..., I've heard tell that ...** j'ai entendu dire que ...; **I've heard tell of ...** j'ai entendu *or* ouï parler de ... .
b (*learn*) *piece of news, facts* apprendre. **have you heard the news?** connaissez-vous la nouvelle?; **have you heard the rumour that they're going to leave?** avez-vous entendu dire qu'ils partent?; **have you heard the story about her going to Paris?** tu as su l'histoire de son voyage à Paris?; **have you heard the one about the Scotsman who ...** tu connais l'histoire de l'Écossais qui ...; **we've heard it all before** ce n'est pas la première fois qu'on entend cette histoire; **I've heard bad reports of him** j'ai eu sur lui des échos défavorables; **I've never heard such rubbish!** c'est d'une imbécillité inouïe!, jamais je n'ai entendu pareilles âneries!; **he had heard that they had left** il avait appris qu'ils étaient partis; **I ~ you've been ill** il paraît que vous avez été malade.
c (*listen to*) *lecture etc* assister à, écouter. **to ~ a child's lessons** faire répéter *or* réciter ses leçons à un enfant; (*Jur*) **to ~ a case** entendre une cause; (*Rel*) **to ~ mass** assister à *or* entendre la messe; **Lord, ~ our prayers** Seigneur, écoutez *or* exaucez nos prières; (*excl*) **~, ~!** bravo!; (*call for applause*) **let's ~ it for ...*** un grand bravo pour ..., on applaudit bien fort ... .
2 **vi** a entendre. **he does not** *or* **cannot ~ very well** il n'entend pas très bien.
b (*get news*) recevoir *or* avoir des nouvelles (*from* de). **I ~ from my daughter every week** je reçois *or* j'ai des nouvelles de ma fille chaque semaine; **you will ~ from me soon** vous aurez bientôt de mes nouvelles; (*in letters*) **hoping to ~ from you** dans l'attente de vous lire; (*threatening*) **you'll be ~ing from me!** tu vas avoir de mes nouvelles!, tu vas entendre parler de moi!; **to ~ about** *or* **of sb/sth** (*gen*) entendre parler de qn/qch; (*have news of*) avoir des nouvelles de qn/qch; **I ~ about** *or* **of him from his mother** j'ai de ses nouvelles par sa mère, sa mère me donne de ses nouvelles; **he wasn't heard of for a long time** on n'entendit plus parler de lui pendant longtemps; **I've never heard of him!** je ne le connais pas!, connais pas!*; **everyone has heard of him** tout le monde a entendu parler de lui; **he was never heard of again** on

n'a jamais plus entendu parler de lui; **the ship was never heard of again** on n'a jamais retrouvé trace du navire; **I've never heard of such a thing!** je n'ai jamais entendu parler d'une chose pareille!; **the first I heard of it was when ...** la première fois que j'en ai entendu parler c'était lorsque ...; **that's the first I've heard of it!** c'est la première fois que j'entends parler de ça!; **I ~ of nothing but that!** j'en ai les oreilles rebattues!, je n'entends plus que cela!; **I won't ~ of you going there** je ne veux absolument pas que tu y ailles; **Mother won't ~ of it!** Maman ne veut pas en entendre parler!; **can I wash the dishes? — I wouldn't ~ of it!** puis-je faire la vaisselle? — (il n'en est) pas question!

►**hear out** vt sep *person, story* écouter *or* entendre jusqu'au bout.

heard [hɜːd] pret, ptp of **hear**.

hearer ['hɪərəʳ] n auditeur *m*, -trice *f*. **~s** auditoire *m*, auditeurs *mpl*.

hearing ['hɪərɪŋ] 1 n a (*NonC: sense*) ouïe *f*. **to have good ~** avoir l'oreille fine; **within ~ (distance)** à portée de voix; **in my ~** en ma présence, devant moi; *see* **hard**. b (*act*) audition *f*. (*Jur*) **~ of witnesses** audition des témoins; (*Jur*) **~ of the case** audience *f*; **to give sb a (fair) ~** écouter ce que qn a à dire; **he was refused a (fair) ~** on refusa de l'entendre; **to condemn sb without a (fair) ~** condamner qn sans entendre sa défense *or* sans l'entendre. c (*meeting: of commission, committee etc*) séance *f*. 2 comp ►**hearing aid** appareil *m* acoustique, audiophone *m*. 3 adj *person* qui entend (bien), (bien) entendant.

hearken ['hɑːkən] vi (*liter*, †) prêter l'oreille (*to* à).

hearsay ['hɪəseɪ] 1 n: **from** *or* **by ~** par ouï-dire; **it's only ~** ce ne sont que des rumeurs *or* des on-dit. 2 comp *report, account* fondé sur des ouï-dire ►**hearsay evidence** (*Jur*) déposition *f* sur la foi d'un tiers *or* d'autrui.

hearse [hɜːs] n corbillard *m*, fourgon *m* mortuaire.

heart [hɑːt] 1 n a (*Anat*) cœur *m*. (*Med*) **to have a weak ~** avoir le cœur malade, être cardiaque; **to clasp sb to one's ~** serrer qn sur son cœur; *see* **beat, cross, hole** *etc*.

b (*fig phrases*) **at ~** au fond; **a man after my own ~** un homme comme je les aime *or* selon mon cœur; **he knew in his ~** il savait instinctivement; **in his ~ (of ~s) he thought ...** en son for intérieur il pensait ...; **with all my ~** de tout mon cœur; **from the ~, from (the bottom of) one's ~** (du fond) du cœur; **to take sth to ~** prendre qch à cœur; **don't take it to ~** ne prenez pas cela trop à cœur; **I hadn't the ~ to tell him, I couldn't find it in my ~ to tell him** je n'ai pas eu le courage *or* le cœur de lui dire; **I have his future at ~** c'est son avenir qui me tient à cœur; **have a ~!*** pitié!*; **to sing to one's ~'s content** chanter tout son content *or* à cœur joie; **to eat/drink/sleep to one's ~'s content** manger/boire/dormir tout son soûl *or* tout son content; **it did my ~ good to see them** cela m'a réchauffé le cœur de les voir; **~ and soul** corps et âme; **he put his ~ and soul into his work** il s'est donné à son travail corps et âme, il a mis tout son cœur dans son travail; **his ~ isn't in his work** il n'a pas le cœur à l'ouvrage; **his ~ is not in it** le cœur n'y est pas; **to lose/take ~** perdre/prendre courage; **we may take ~ from the fact that ...** nous pouvons nous sentir encouragés du fait que ...; **to put new ~ into sb** donner du courage *or* du cœur à qn; **to be in good ~** avoir (un) bon moral; **to put** *or* **set sb's ~ at rest** calmer les inquiétudes de qn, tranquilliser qn; **to have a ~ of gold** avoir un cœur d'or; **his ~ is in the right place** il a bon cœur; **to have a ~ of stone** avoir un cœur de pierre; **to lose one's ~ to sb** tomber amoureux de qn; **the cause is close to** *or* **dear to** *or* **near his ~** c'est une cause chère à son cœur *or* qui lui est chère *or* qui lui tient à cœur; **it was his ~'s desire** c'était son plus cher désir *or* ce qu'il désirait le plus au monde; **he has set his ~ on** *or* **his ~ is set on a new car** il veut à tout prix une nouvelle voiture, il a jeté son dévolu sur une nouvelle voiture; **he has set his ~ on going to Paris** il veut à tout prix *or* désire absolument aller à Paris; **to have** *or* **wear one's ~ on one's sleeve** laisser voir ses sentiments; **his ~ was in his boots** il avait la mort dans l'âme; **my ~ sank** j'ai eu un coup au cœur; **my ~ sinks at the thought** rien que d'y penser cela me déprime; **she had her ~ in her mouth** son cœur battait la chamade; **to learn sth by ~** apprendre qch par cœur; **to know** *or* **have sth by ~** savoir qch par cœur; *see* **bless, break** *etc*.

c (*centre*) *[town etc]* cœur *m*, centre *m*; *[cabbage, lettuce]* cœur; *[artichoke]* fond *m*, cœur; *[celery]* cœur. **in the ~ of winter** au cœur de l'hiver, en plein hiver; **the ~ of the matter** le fond du problème, le vif du sujet; **in the ~ of the country** en pleine campagne; **in the ~ of the forest** au cœur *or* au (beau) milieu de la forêt, en pleine forêt; **in the ~ of the desert** au cœur *or* au (fin) fond du désert; **the H~ of Dixie** l'Alabama.

d (*Cards*) **~s** cœur *m*; **queen/six of ~s** dame *f*/six *m* de cœur; *for phrases see* **club**.

2 comp ►**heartache** chagrin *m*, douleur *f* ►**heart attack** crise *f* cardiaque ►**heartbeat** pulsation *f*, battement *m* de cœur ►**heartbreak** immense chagrin *m* *or* douleur *f* ►**heartbreaker** (*man*) bourreau *m* des cœurs; (*woman*) femme fatale ►**heartbreaking** *story, sight* navrant; *appeal, cry, sound* déchirant, qui fend le cœur; **it was heartbreaking to see him like that** c'était à fendre le cœur de le voir comme ça ►**heartbroken** navré, au cœur brisé; **to be heartbroken** avoir un immense chagrin, (*stronger*) avoir le cœur brisé; *[child]* avoir un gros chagrin; **she was heartbroken about it** elle en a eu un immense chagrin, (*stronger*) elle en a eu le cœur brisé ►**heartburn** (*Med*) brûlures *fpl* d'estomac ►**heartburning** (*ill-feeling*) animosité *f*, rancœur *f*; (*regret*) regret(s) *m(pl)* ►**heart case** (*Med*) cardiaque *mf* ►**heart complaint, heart condition** (*Med*) maladie *f* de cœur; **to have a heart complaint** *or* **condition** avoir une maladie de cœur, être cardiaque ►**heart disease** maladie *f* de cœur ►**heart failure** (*Med*) arrêt *m* du cœur ►**heartfelt** sincère, senti, qui vient du fond du cœur; **to make a heartfelt appeal** faire un appel bien senti; **heartfelt sympathy** condoléances *fpl* sincères ►**heartland** *[country, continent]* cœur *m*, centre *m*; (*fig*) **the Tory heartland** le pays des Conservateurs par excellence ►**heart-lung machine** cœur-poumon *m* (artificiel) ►**heart-rate** rythme *m* cardiaque; **heart-rate monitor** moniteur *m* cardiaque ►**heartrending** *cry, appeal* déchirant, qui fend le cœur; *sight* navrant; **it was heartrending to see him** c'était à fendre le cœur de le voir ►**heart-searching: after much heart-searching he ...** après s'être longuement interrogé, il ... ►**heart-shaped** en (forme de) cœur ►**heartsick: to be heartsick** avoir la mort dans l'âme ►**heartstrings: to pull at** *or* **touch** *or* **tug sb's heartstrings** toucher *or* faire vibrer les cordes sensibles de qn, prendre qn par les sentiments ►**heart surgeon** (*Med*) chirurgien *m* cardiologue ►**heart surgery** (*Med*) chirurgie *f* du cœur ►**heart-throb** (*: *person*) idole *f*, coqueluche *f* (*du cinéma, de la jeunesse etc*); (*US: heartbeat*) battement *m* de cœur ►**heart-to-heart** adj intime, à cœur ouvert ◊ adv à cœur ouvert; **to have a heart-to-heart*** parler à cœur ouvert ►**heart transplant** (*Med*) greffe *f* du cœur ►**heart trouble:** (*Med*) **to have heart trouble** souffrir du cœur, être cardiaque; **heart trouble in the over-50's** les troubles *mpl* cardiaques dont on souffre après la cinquantaine ►**heartwarming** réconfortant, qui réchauffe le cœur ►**heart-whole** (qui a le cœur) libre.

-hearted ['hɑːtɪd] adj ending in comps: **open-hearted** sincère; **warm-hearted** chaleureux, généreux; *see* **broken, hard** *etc*.

hearten ['hɑːtn] vt encourager, donner du courage à.

heartening ['hɑːtnɪŋ] adj encourageant, réconfortant. **I found it very ~** cela m'a donné du courage, j'ai trouvé cela très encourageant *or* réconfortant.

hearth [hɑːθ] n foyer *m*, cheminée *f*, âtre† *m*. **~ rug** devant *m* de foyer.

heartily ['hɑːtɪlɪ] adv *say, welcome* chaleureusement, de tout cœur; *laugh, work* de tout son cœur; *eat* avec appétit, de bon appétit. **I ~ agree** je suis on ne peut plus d'accord; **I'm ~ tired** *or* **sick* of ...** j'en ai par-dessus la tête* de ...; **to be ~ glad** être ravi.

heartless ['hɑːtlɪs] adj *person* sans cœur, sans pitié, insensible; *treatment* cruel.

heartlessly ['hɑːtlɪslɪ] adv sans pitié.

heartlessness ['hɑːtlɪsnɪs] n (*see* **heartless**) manque *m* de cœur, insensibilité *f*; cruauté *f*.

hearty ['hɑːtɪ] 1 adj *greeting, welcome* (très) cordial, chaleureux; *approval, support* chaleureux; *laugh* franc, gros; *meal* copieux; *appetite* gros, solide; *kick, slap* bien senti, vigoureux; *person* (*healthy*) vigoureux, robuste, solide; (*cheerful*) jovial. **he is a ~ eater** c'est un gros mangeur, il a un bon coup de fourchette; **to have a ~ dislike of sth** détester qch de tout son cœur; *see* **hale**. 2 npl (*: *esp Naut*) **... my hearties!** ... les gars!*

heat [hiːt] 1 n a (*NonC*) (*gen, Phys*) chaleur *f*; *[fire, flames, sun]* ardeur *f*; *[oven, kiln]* température *f*, chaleur. **extremes of ~ and cold** extrêmes *mpl* de chaleur et de froid; **I can't stand ~** je ne supporte pas la chaleur; (*fig*) **if you can't stand the ~ get out of the kitchen** que ceux qui trouvent la situation intenable s'en aillent; **in the ~ of the day** au (moment le) plus chaud de la journée; (*Culin*) **at low ~** à feu doux; (*Culin*) **lower the ~ and allow to simmer** réduire la chaleur et laisser frémir; **in the ~ of the moment** dans le feu de l'action; **in the ~ of the battle** dans le feu du combat; **in the ~ of his departure they forgot ...** dans l'agitation qui entoura son départ ils oublièrent ...; **in the ~ of the argument** dans le feu de la discussion; **to speak with (some) ~** parler avec feu *or* avec passion; **we had no ~ all day at the office** nous avons été sans chauffage toute la journée au bureau; **to turn on the ~** (*in house, office etc*) mettre le chauffage; (*fig*) **to put** *or* **turn the ~ on sb*** faire pression sur qn; (*fig*) **it'll take the ~ off us*** ça nous permettra de souffler *or* de respirer* un peu; *see* **red, specific, white** *etc*.

b (*Sport*) (épreuve *f*) éliminatoire *f*; *see* **dead**.

c (*NonC: Zool*) chaleur *f*, rut *m*. **in** *or* (*Brit*) **on ~** en chaleur, en rut.

d (*US*) **the ~**⁑ les flics⁑ *mpl*.

2 comp ►**heat constant** (*Phys*) constante *f* calorifique ►**heat efficiency** rendement *m* calorifique ►**heat exchanger** échangeur *m* de chaleur ►**heat exhaustion** (*Med*) épuisement *m* dû à la chaleur ►**heat haze** brume *f* de chaleur ►**heat lightning** éclair(s) *m(pl)* de chaleur ►**heat loss** perte *f* calorifique ►**heatproof** *material* résistant à la chaleur; *dish* allant au four ►**heatpump** pompe *f* à chaleur, thermopompe *f* ►**heat rash** (*Med*) irritation *f* *or* inflammation *f* (due à la chaleur) ►**heat-resistant, heat-resisting** = **heatproof** ►**heat seeking** *missile etc* thermoguidé, guidé par infrarouge ►**heat-sensitive** sensible à la chaleur ►**heat shield** (*Space*) bouclier *m* thermique ►**heatstroke** (*Med: NonC*) coup *m* de chaleur ►**heat treatment** (*Med*) traitement *m* par la chaleur, thermothérapie *f* ►**heatwave** vague *f* de chaleur.

3 **vt** (*Culin, Phys, Tech etc*) chauffer; (*Med*) *blood etc* échauffer; (*fig*) enflammer.

4 **vi** *[liquids etc]* chauffer; *[room]* se réchauffer.

►**heat up** **1** **vi** *[liquids etc]* chauffer; *[room]* se réchauffer. **2** **vt sep** réchauffer.

heated ['hi:tɪd] **adj** (*lit*) chauffé; (*fig*) *argument, discussion* passionné; *words* vif (*f* vive); *person* échauffé. **to get** *or* **grow ~** *[conversation etc]* s'échauffer; *[person]* s'échauffer, s'enflammer, s'exciter.

heatedly ['hi:tɪdlɪ] **adv** *speak, debate* avec passion; *deny, argue* farouchement, avec passion.

heater ['hi:təʳ] **n** (*gen: for room etc*) appareil *m* de chauffage; (*for water*) chauffe-eau *m inv*; *[car]* chauffage *m*; *see* **electric, immersion** *etc.*

heath [hi:θ] **n** (*moorland*) lande *f*; (*plant*) bruyère *f*.

heathen ['hi:ðən] **1** **adj** (*unbelieving*) païen; (*barbarous*) barbare, sauvage. **2** **n, pl ~s** *or* **~** païen(ne) *m(f)*. **the ~** les païens *mpl*; (*savages*) les barbares *mpl*, les sauvages *mpl*.

heathenish ['hi:ðənɪʃ] **adj** (*pej*) de païen, barbare.

heathenism ['hi:ðənɪzəm] **n** paganisme *m*.

heather ['heðəʳ] **n** bruyère *f*.

Heath Robinson* [hi:θ'rɒbɪnsən] **adj** (*Brit*) fait avec les moyens de bord.

heating ['hi:tɪŋ] **1** **n** chauffage *m*; *see* **central. 2** **comp** ►**heating apparatus** (*heater*) appareil *m* de chauffage; (*equipment*) appareillage *m* de chauffage ►**heating engineer** chauffagiste *m* ►**heating plant** système *m or* installation *f* de chauffage ►**heating power** pouvoir *m* calorifique ►**heating system** système *m* de chauffage.

heave [hi:v] (**vb: pret, ptp heaved,** (*Naut*) **hove**) **1** **n** *[sea]* houle *f*; *[bosom]* soulèvement *m*; (*retching*) haut-le-cœur *m inv*, nausée *f*; (*vomiting*) vomissement *m*. (*lift/throw/tug*) **to give a ~** faire un effort pour soulever/lancer/tirer; **to give sb the ~(-ho)**** *[employer]* sacquer* *or* virer* qn; *[girlfriend etc]* plaquer** qn.

2 **comp** ►**heave-ho!** (*Naut excl*) oh-hisse!

3 **vt** (*lift*) lever *or* soulever (avec effort); (*pull*) tirer (avec effort); (*drag*) traîner (avec effort); (*throw*) lancer. **to ~ a sigh** pousser un (gros) soupir; (*Naut*) **to ~ a boat astern/ahead** déhaler un bateau sur l'arrière/sur l'avant.

4 **vi** **a** *[sea, chest]* se soulever; *[person, horse]* (*pant*) haleter; (*retch*) avoir des haut-le-cœur *or* des nausées; (*vomit*) vomir. **his stomach was heaving** son estomac se soulevait.

b (*Naut*) *[ship]* **to ~ in(to) sight** poindre (à l'horizon), paraître.

►**heave to** (*Naut*) **1** **vi** se mettre en panne. **2** **vt sep** mettre en panne.

►**heave up** **vt sep** (*vomit*) vomir.

heaven ['hevn] **1** **n** **a** (*paradise*) ciel *m*, paradis *m*. **to go to ~** aller au ciel, aller au *or* en paradis; **in ~** au ciel, au *or* en paradis; **he was in ~** *or* **in the seventh ~ (of delight)** il était au septième ciel *or* aux anges, il nageait dans la félicité; **an injustice that cries out to ~** une injustice criante *or* flagrante; **~ help us/you** *etc*!* on n'est pas sorti de l'auberge!*; **~ forbid that I should accept** Dieu me garde d'accepter; **~ forbid that he should come here** Dieu fasse *or* veuille qu'il ne vienne pas ici; **~ forbid!*** mon Dieu non!, surtout pas!; **what in ~'s name does that mean?*** qu'est-ce que ça veut bien dire?; **~ (only) knows what/when** *etc* Dieu sait quoi/quand *etc*; **when will you come back? — ~ (only) knows!** quand reviendras-tu? – Dieu seul le sait!; **~ knows I've tried** Dieu sait *or* m'est témoin que j'ai essayé; **(good) ~s!*** mon Dieu!, Seigneur!, ciel! (*hum*); **for ~'s sake*** (*pleading*) pour l'amour de Dieu* *or* du ciel*; (*protesting*) zut alors!*; **I wish to ~* that he hadn't left!** comme je voudrais qu'il ne soit pas parti!; **it was ~*** c'était divin *or* merveilleux; **he found a ~ on earth** ce fut pour lui le paradis sur terre; **he's ~!**** il est divin! *or* merveilleux!; *see* **help, move, stink, thank** *etc.*

b (*gen liter: sky*) **the ~s** le ciel, le firmament (*liter*); **the ~s opened** le ciel se mit à déverser des trombes d'eau.

2 **comp** ►**heaven-sent** providentiel.

heavenly ['hevnlɪ] **adj** (*lit*) céleste, du ciel; (*fig: delightful*) divin, merveilleux. **~ body** corps *m* céleste; (*Rel*) **H~ Father** Père *m* céleste.

heavenward(s) ['hevnwəd(z)] **adv** *go* vers le ciel; *look* au ciel.

heavily ['hevɪlɪ] **1** **adv** *load, tax* lourdement; *underline* fortement; *sleep, sigh* profondément; *breathe* péniblement, bruyamment; *move* péniblement, avec difficulté; *walk* lourdement, d'un pas pesant; *lean* pesamment; *drink, smoke* beaucoup. **to be ~ in debt** être très endetté, avoir de lourdes dettes; **to lose ~** *[team]* se faire écraser; *[gambler]* perdre gros; **it was raining ~** il pleuvait à verse; **it was snowing ~** il neigeait dru *or* très fort; **... he said ~** ... dit-il d'une voix accablée; (*fig*) **he's ~ into* health foods** il donne à fond* dans les aliments naturels.

2 **comp** ►**heavily-built** solidement bâti, fortement charpenté ►**heavily-laden** lourdement chargé.

heaviness ['hevɪnɪs] **n** pesanteur *f*, lourdeur *f*, poids *m*. **~ of heart** tristesse *f*.

heavy ['hevɪ] **1** **adj** **a** (*gen*) lourd; *weight, parcel* lourd, pesant. **~ luggage** gros bagages *mpl*; (*Zool*) **~ with young** gravide, grosse; **to make heavier** alourdir; **how ~ are you?** combien pesez-vous?; (*Phys*) **~ bodies** corps *mpl* graves; **~ crude (oil)** brut lourd; **~ (goods) vehicle** poids lourd; **~ water** eau lourde; **heavier than air** plus lourd que l'air.

b (*fig*) *expenses, movement* lourd; *payments, charges* important, considérable; *step* pesant, lourd; *crop* abondant, gros (*f* grosse) (*before n*); *loss, fine* gros (*before n*), lourd; *rain, shower* fort (*before n*), gros (*before n*); *fog* épais (*f* -aisse), à couper au couteau; *meal, food* lourd, indigeste; *defeat* grave; *odour* fort, lourd; *book, film, lecture* (*not superficial*) profond; (*difficult, tedious*) indigeste; *evening* ennuyeux; *humour, irony* lourd, peu subtil (*f* subtile); (*Theat*) *part* (*demanding*) lourd, difficile, (*tragic*) tragique; *population* dense; *sigh* gros (*before n*), profond; *silence, sleep* lourd, pesant, profond; *sky* chargé, couvert, lourd; *soil* lourd, gras (*f* grasse); *task* lourd, pénible; *work* gros (*before n*). **to be a ~ drinker/smoker** *etc* boire/fumer *etc* beaucoup, être un grand buveur/fumeur *etc;* **to be a ~ sleeper** avoir le sommeil profond *or* lourd; **air ~ with scents** air chargé *or* lourd de parfums; **atmosphere ~ with suspicion** atmosphère pleine de soupçon; **eyes ~ with sleep** yeux lourds de sommeil; **~ eyes** yeux battus; **the car is ~ on petrol** la voiture consomme beaucoup (d'essence); **I've had a ~ day** j'ai eu une journée chargée; (*Mil*) **~ artillery, ~ guns** artillerie lourde, grosse artillerie; **~ (gun)fire** feu nourri; **~ blow** (*lit*) coup violent; (*fig: from fate etc*) rude coup; **man of ~ build** homme fortement charpenté *or* solidement bâti; **there were ~ casualties** il y a eu de nombreuses victimes; (*Med*) **~ cold** gros rhume; **a ~ concentration of** une forte concentration de; (*US*) **~ cream** crème fraîche épaisse *or* à fouetter; (*Naut*) **~ cruiser** croiseur lourd; **~ dew** rosée abondante; (*fig*) **to play the ~ father** jouer les pères nobles, faire l'autoritaire; **~ features** gros traits, traits épais *or* lourds; **~ fighting** combats *mpl* acharnés; **the going was ~ because of the rain** le terrain était lourd à cause de la pluie; **the conversation was ~ going** la conversation traînait; **this book is very ~ going** ce livre est très indigeste; **with a ~ heart** le cœur gros; **~ industry** industrie lourde; **~ line** gros trait, trait épais; **~ sea** grosse mer; **a ~ sea was running** la mer était grosse; (*fig*) **it is ~ stuff*** (*not superficial*) c'est du solide*; (*difficult, tedious*) c'est indigeste; **traffic was ~** la circulation était dense, il y avait une grosse circulation; (*Typ*) **~ type** caractères gras; (*Marketing*) **~ viewer** téléspectateur *m*, -trice *f* assidu(e); (*Naut etc*) **~ weather** gros temps; **the weather's ~ today** il fait lourd aujourd'hui; (*fig*) **he made ~ weather of it** il s'est compliqué la tâche *or* l'existence*; **he made ~ weather of cleaning the car** il a fait toute une histoire pour laver la voiture; **~ wine** vin corsé *or* lourd; **he did all the ~ work** c'est lui qui a fait le gros travail; (*Ind etc*) **~ workers** travailleurs *mpl* de force.

2 **adv** (*rare*) lourd, lourdement. **to weigh** *or* **lie ~ on** peser lourd sur; (*US fig*) **he's ~ into* health foods** il donne à fond* dans les aliments naturels; *see also* **lie¹**.

3 **n** **a** (*) = **heavyweight.**

b (*: *gangster*) gros dur* *m*, casseur* *m*.

4 **comp** ►**heavy-duty** (*carpet etc*) résistant; (*equipment*) à usage industriel ►**heavy-handed: to be heavy-handed** (*clumsy*) être maladroit; (*fig*) être maladroit, manquer de tact ►**heavy-hearted: to be heavy-hearted** avoir le cœur gros ►**heavy-laden** lourdement chargé ►**heavy metal** (*Mus*) heavy metal *m* ►**heavy-set** (*esp US*) costaud ►**heavyweight** *see* **heavyweight.**

heavyweight ['hevɪweɪt] **1** **n** (*Boxing*) poids lourd; (* *fig: influential person*) homme *m* de poids. **2** **adj** **a** (*Boxing*) *bout, champion* poids lourd. **in the ~ class** dans la catégorie (des) poids lourds. **b** *cloth* lourd.

Hebe** ['hi:bɪ] **n** (*US pej*) youpin(e)** *m(f)*.

Hebraic [hɪ'breɪk] **adj** hébraïque.

Hebrew ['hi:bru:] **1** **adj** hébreu (*m only*), hébraïque. **2** **n** **a** (*Hist*) Hébreu *m*, Israélite *mf*. (*Bible*) **~s** Hébreux *mpl*. **b** (*Ling*) hébreu *m*.

Hebrides ['hebrɪdi:z] **n: the ~** les Hébrides *fpl*.

heck* [hek] **1** **excl** zut!*, flûte!* **2** **n: a ~ of a lot** une sacrée quantité*; **what the ~ is he doing?** que diable* peut-il bien faire?; **what the ~!** et puis flûte!* *or* zut!*

heckle ['hekl] **1** **vi** (*Pol etc*) (*shout*) chahuter; (*interrupt*) interrompre bruyamment. **2** **vt** *speaker* interrompre, interpeller.

heckler ['hekləʳ] **n** (*Pol etc*) (élément *m*) perturbateur *m*.

heckling ['heklɪŋ] **n** (*Pol etc*) interpellations *fpl*, chahut *m* (*pour troubler l'orateur*).

hectare ['hektɑ:ʳ] **n** hectare *m*.

hectic ['hektɪk] **adj** **a** *period* très bousculé, très agité, trépidant; *traffic* intense, fou (*f* folle), terrible. **~ life** (*busy*) vie trépidante; (*eventful*) vie très mouvementée; **we had 3 ~ days** nous avons été très bousculés pendant 3 jours, nous avons passé 3 jours mouvementés; **the journey was fairly ~** le voyage a été assez mouvementé; **I've had a ~ rush** ça a vraiment été une course folle. **b** (*Med*) *person* fiévreux; *fever* hectique.

hectogramme, (*US*) **hectogram** ['hektəʊgræm] **n** hectogramme *m*.

hectolitre, (*US*) **hectoliter** ['hektəʊ,li:təʳ] **n** hectolitre *m*.

Hector ['hektəʳ] **n** Hector *m*.

hector ['hektəʳ] **1** **vt** malmener, rudoyer. **2** **vi** faire l'autoritaire, être tyrannique.

hectoring ['hektərɪŋ] **adj** tyrannique. **in a ~ voice** d'un ton autoritaire *or* impérieux.

Hecuba ['hekjʊbə] **n** Hécube.

he'd [hi:d] = **he had, he would;** *see* **have, would.**

hedge [hedʒ] 1 n haie *f*. **beech ~** haie *f* de hêtres; (*fig*) **a ~ against inflation** une sauvegarde *or* une sauvegarde contre l'inflation.

2 comp ►**hedge clippers** sécateur *m* à haie ►**hedgehog** *see* **hedgehog** ►**hedgehop** (*Aviat*) voler en rase-mottes, faire du rase-mottes ►**hedgerow(s)** haies *fpl* ►**hedgesparrow** fauvette *f* des haies *or* d'hiver, accenteur *m* mouchet.

3 vi (*in answering*) répondre à côté, éviter de répondre; (*in explaining/recounting etc*) expliquer/raconter avec des détours. **don't ~** dis-le franchement *or* directement.

4 vt a (*also* **~ about, ~ in**) entourer d'une haie, enclore. **~d (about or in) with difficulties** entouré de difficultés.

b *bet, risk* couvrir. (*fig*) **to ~ one's bets** se couvrir (*fig*).

c (*US*) **to ~ the issue** esquiver la question.

►**hedge off** vt sep *garden* entourer d'une haie; *part of garden* séparer par une haie (*from* de).

hedgehog ['hedʒ,hɒg] n hérisson *m*.

hedger ['hedʒəʳ] n (*St Ex, Fin*) arbitragiste *m* (*en couverture de risques*).

hedonism ['hi:dənɪzəm] n hédonisme *m*.

hedonist ['hi:dənɪst] adj, n hédoniste *(mf)*.

hedonistic [,hi:do'nɪstɪk] adj hédoniste.

heebie-jeebies‡ ['hi:bɪ'dʒi:bɪz] npl: **to have the ~** (*shaking*) avoir la tremblote*; (*fright, nerves*) avoir la frousse; **it gives me the ~** (*revulsion*) ça me donne la chair de poule; (*fright, apprehension*) ça me donne la frousse* *or* la trouille‡ *or* les chocottes‡.

heed [hi:d] 1 vt faire attention à, prendre garde à, tenir compte de. 2 n: **to take ~ of sth, to pay** *or* **give ~ to sth** faire attention *or* prendre garde à qch, tenir compte de qch; **take no ~ of what they say** ne faites pas attention à ce qu'ils disent; **he paid no ~ to the warning** il n'a tenu aucun compte de l'avertissement; **to take ~ to do** prendre garde *or* soin de faire.

heedless ['hi:dlɪs] adj (*not thinking*) étourdi; (*not caring*) insouciant. **~ of what was going on** inattentif à ce qui se passait; **~ of danger** sans se soucier du danger; **~ of complaints** sans tenir compte des réclamations.

heedlessly ['hi:dlɪslɪ] adv (*without reflection*) étourdiment, à la légère, sans (faire) attention; (*without caring*) avec insouciance.

heehaw ['hi:hɔ:] 1 n hi-han *m*. 2 vi faire hi-han, braire.

heel[1] [hi:l] 1 n a *[foot, sock, shoe, tool, golf club, bow etc]* talon *m*. **to be (hot) on** *or* **tread hard on sb's ~s** marcher sur les talons de qn; **they followed close** *or* **hard on his ~s** ils étaient sur ses talons; **to take to one's ~s, to show a clean pair of ~s** prendre ses jambes à son cou; **he turned on his ~ and departed** il a tourné les talons et est parti; **down-at-~,** (*US*) **down at the ~s** *person* miteux; *shoe* éculé; (*fig*) **under the ~ of** sous le joug *or* la botte de; (*to dog*) **~!** au pied!; **he brought the dog to ~** il a fait venir le chien à ses pieds; (*fig*) **to bring sb to ~** rappeler qn à l'ordre, faire rentrer qn dans le rang; *see* **cool, kick** *etc*.

b (**: unpleasant person*) (*man*) salaud‡ *m*; (*man or woman*) chameau* *m*.

2 vt *shoes, socks* remettre *or* refaire un talon à; (*Sport*) *ball* talonner.

3 comp ►**heel-bar** talon-minute *m* ►**heel-piece** (*Ski*) talonnière *f*.

heel[2] [hi:l] vi (*also* **~ over**) *[ship]* gîter, donner de la bande; *[truck, structure]* s'incliner *or* pencher (dangereusement).

heeled [hi:ld] adj a *see* **well.** b (*US ‡: armed*) armé, enfouraillé‡.

heeling ['hi:lɪŋ] n (*Rugby*) talonnage *m*.

heft* [heft] vt (*lift*) soulever; (*feel weight of*) soupeser.

hefty* ['heftɪ] adj *person* costaud*; *parcel* lourd; *part, piece, debt, price* gros (*f* grosse). **it's a ~ sum** c'est une grosse *or* une jolie somme.

Hegelian [hɪ'geɪlɪən] adj hégélien.

hegemony [hɪ'gemənɪ] n hégémonie *f*.

hegira ['hedʒɪrə] n hégire *f*.

heifer ['hefəʳ] n génisse *f*.

heigh [heɪ] excl hé!, eh!, oh!, hé là-bas! **~-ho!** eh bien!

height [haɪt] n a *[building]* hauteur *f*; *[person]* taille *f*, grandeur *f*; *[mountain, plane]* altitude *f*; *[star, sun]* élévation *f*. **what ~ are you?** combien mesurez-vous?; **he is 1 metre 80 in ~, his ~ is 1 metre 80** il fait 1 mètre 80; **of average ~** de taille moyenne; **he drew himself up to his full ~** il s'est dressé de toute sa hauteur; **a building 40 metres in ~** un bâtiment qui a *or* un bâtiment de 40 mètres de haut; **~ above sea level** altitude au-dessus du niveau de la mer; *[plane]* **to gain/lose ~** gagner *or* prendre/perdre de l'altitude.

b (*high ground*) éminence *f*, hauteur *f*. **the ~s** les sommets *mpl*; (*gen*) **fear of ~s** vertige *m*; **to have a fear of ~s** craindre le vertige; (*fig*) **his performance never reached the ~s** il n'a jamais brillé; *see* **giddy, head.**

c (*fig: highest point etc*) *[fortune]* apogée *m*; *[success]* point culminant; *[glory]* sommet *m*; *[grandeur]* sommet, faîte *m*, point culminant; *[absurdity, folly, ill manners]* comble *m*. **at the ~ of his power** au summum de sa puissance; (*abilities etc*) **he is at the ~ of his powers** il est en pleine possession de *or* à l'apogée de ses moyens; **at the ~ of summer/of the storm/of the battle** au cœur de l'été/de l'orage/de la bataille; **at the ~ of the season** en pleine saison; **the ~ of fashion** la toute dernière mode, le dernier cri; **the fair was at its ~** la fête battait son plein; **excitement was at its ~** l'animation était à son apogée *or* à son maximum.

heighten ['haɪtn] 1 vt (*lit: raise*) relever, rehausser; (*Med*) *fever* faire monter, aggraver; (*fig*) *effect, absurdity, interest, tension, fear* augmenter, intensifier; *flavour* relever. *emotions, sensations* **~ed** plus vif; **with ~ed interest** en manifestant un regain d'intérêt; *[person]* **with ~ed colour** le teint animé. 2 vi *[tension]* augmenter, monter; *[fear]* s'intensifier, devenir plus vif.

heinous ['heɪnəs] adj odieux, atroce, abominable.

heir [ɛəʳ] 1 n héritier *m*, légataire *mf* (*to* de). **he is ~ to a fortune** il héritera d'une fortune; **~ to the throne** héritier du trône *or* de la couronne; **rightful ~** héritier légitime *or* naturel; *see* **fall.** 2 comp ►**heir apparent** (pl **~s ~**) héritier *m* présomptif ►**heir-at-law** (*Jur*) (pl **~s-~-~**) héritier *m* légitime *or* naturel ►**heir presumptive** héritier *m* présomptif (*sauf naissance d'un héritier en ligne directe*).

heiress ['ɛəres] n héritière *f*.

heirloom ['ɛəlu:m] n héritage *m*. **this picture is a family ~** c'est un tableau de famille.

heist‡ [haɪst] (*US*) 1 n hold-up *m inv*; (*burglary*) casse‡ *m*. 2 vt voler.

held [held] pret, ptp of **hold.**

Helen ['helɪn] n Hélène *f*. **~ of Troy** Hélène de Troie.

helical ['helɪkəl] adj hélicoïdal. **~ spring** ressort *m* hélicoïdal.

helices ['helɪ,si:z] npl of **helix.**

helicopter ['helɪkɒptəʳ] 1 n hélicoptère *m*. **transfer** *or* **transport by ~** héliportage *m*; **transferred** *or* **transported by ~** héliporté. 2 comp *patrol, rescue* en hélicoptère; *pilot* d'hélicoptère ►**helicopter gunship** hélicoptère *m* de combat ►**helicopter station** héligare *f*. 3 vt (*esp US*) *person, goods* transporter en hélicoptère. **to ~ in/out** *etc* amener/évacuer *etc* par hélicoptère.

heliograph ['hi:lɪəʊgrɑ:f] n héliographe *m*.

heliostat ['hi:lɪəʊstæt] n héliostat *m*.

heliotrope ['hi:lɪətrəʊp] 1 n (*Bot*) héliotrope *m*. 2 adj (couleur d')héliotrope *inv*.

helipad ['helɪ,pæd] n plate-forme *f* pour hélicoptères.

heliport ['helɪpɔ:t] n héliport *m*.

helium ['hi:lɪəm] n hélium *m*.

helix ['hi:lɪks] n, pl **helixes** *or* **helices** ['helɪ,si:z] (*Anat*) hélix *m*.

hell [hel] 1 n a (*Rel etc*) enfer *m*; (*Myth*) les enfers. **in ~** (*Rel, gen*) en enfer; (*Myth*) aux enfers; **when ~ freezes over** quand les poules auront des dents, à la saint-glinglin*; **all ~ broke** *or* **was let loose*** ça a été une pagaïe* monstre; **when he heard about it all ~ broke** *or* **was let loose*** quand il l'a appris il y a eu une scène infernale; **life became ~** la vie est devenue infernale *or* un enfer; **it's ~ on earth*** c'est l'enfer; **come ~ or high water** en dépit de tout, contre vents et marées; **to ride ~ for leather** aller au triple galop *or* à bride abattue, aller à un train d'enfer; **he went off home ~ for leather** il est rentré chez lui au triple galop; **there'll be ~ to pay*, there'll be a ~ of a row*** ça va barder‡; *see* **raise.**

b (*‡: emphatic phrases*) **to make a ~ of a noise** faire un boucan *or* un raffut du diable*; **a ~ of a lot of cars** tout un tas de bagnoles*; **a ~ of a lot of people** des masses* de gens; **he's a ~ of a nice guy** c'est un type vachement bien*; **we had a ~ of a time** (*bad*) ça n'a pas été marrant‡, on en a bavé‡; (*good*) on s'est vachement marrés‡, ça a été terrible‡ *or* du tonnerre‡; **he did it for the ~ of it** (*gen*) il l'a fait parce que ça lui chantait; (*to annoy people*) il l'a fait pour embêter le monde; **to play (merry) ~ with sth***détraquer complètement qch; *rheumatism, bad tooth etc* ne pas arranger qch; **to work like ~** travailler comme un nègre *or* comme une brute; **to run like ~** courir comme un dératé* *or* comme un fou; **to give sb ~** (*make his life a misery*) faire mener une vie infernale à qn; (*scold*) faire sa fête à qn (*iro*), passer une engueulade‡ à qn; **oh ~!** flûte!*, merde!‡; **~'s bells!**‡, **~'s teeth!**‡ merde!‡; **to ~ with him!** qu'il aille se faire voir!*; **to ~ with it!** la barbe!*; **get the ~ out of here!** fous-moi le camp d'ici!‡; **let's get the ~ out of here** foutons le camp d'ici‡; **he got the ~ out** il a foutu le camp‡; **to scare the ~ out of sb** faire une peur bleue à qn*, ficher la frousse à qn*; **what the ~ does he want now?** qu'est-ce qu'il peut bien vouloir maintenant?; **what the ~ is he doing?** qu'est-ce qu'il peut bien fabriquer?* *or* foutre?‡; **where the ~ have I put it?** où est-ce que j'ai bien pu le fourrer?* *or* foutre?‡; **how the ~ did you get in?** mais enfin! *or* bon sang!* comment as-tu fait pour entrer?; **why the ~ did you do it?** qu'est-ce qui t'a pris de faire ça?; **go to ~!** va te faire voir!* *or* foutre!‡; **will you do it? — like ~ (I will)!** tu le feras? — tu parles!* *or* tu rigoles!‡ *or* pas si con! ‡*

2 comp ►**hellbent***: **hellbent on doing** *or* (*US*) **to do** acharné à faire ►**hellcat** harpie *f*, mégère *f* ►**hellfire** feu *m* de l'enfer ►**hellhole*** bouge *m* ►**hell-raiser**‡ (*US*) vrai démon* *m* ►**hell-raising**‡ (*US*) vie *f* démoniaque *or* de patachon* ►**hell's angel** blouson *m* noir.

he'll [hi:l] = **he will;** *see* **will.**

hellebore ['helɪ,bɔ:ʳ] n ellébore *m*.

Hellene ['heli:n] n Hellène *mf*.

Hellenic [he'li:nɪk] adj hellénique.

heller‡ ['heləʳ] n (*US*) vrai démon* *m*.

hellion* [ˈheljən] **n** (*US*) chahuteur *m*, trublion *m*.

hellish [ˈhelɪʃ] 1 **adj** *intentions, actions* diabolique; (**: unpleasant*) infernal. 2 **adv** (‡) vachement‡, atrocement*.

hellishly* [ˈhelɪʃlɪ] **adv** atrocement*, vachement‡.

hello [həˈləʊ] **excl** = **hallo.**

helluva‡ [ˈheləvə] = **hell of a;** *see* **hell 1b.**

helm [helm] 1 **n** (*Naut*) barre *f*. **to be at the ~** (*Naut*) être à *or* tenir la barre; (*fig*) être à *or* tenir la barre *or* les rênes; (*fig*) **to take over the ~** prendre la barre. 2 **comp** ►**helmsman** (*Naut*) timonier *m*, homme *m* de barre. 3 **vt** tenir la barre de. 4 **vi** être à *or* tenir la barre, barrer.

helmet [ˈhelmɪt] **n** casque *m*; *see* **crash1** *etc*.

helminth [ˈhelmɪnθ] **n** helminthe *m*.

help [help] 1 **n** a aide *f*, secours *m*, assistance *f*. (*excl*) **~!** (*in danger etc*) au secours!, à l'aide!; (*in dismay*) mince!; **thank you for your ~** merci de votre aide; **with his brother's ~** avec l'aide de son frère; **with the ~ of a knife** à l'aide d'un couteau; **he did it without ~** il l'a fait tout seul; **to shout for ~** appeler *or* crier au secours, appeler à l'aide; **to go to sb's ~** aller au secours de qn, prêter secours *or* assistance à qn; **to come to sb's ~** venir à l'aide de qn *or* en aide à qn; *[person, machine, training]* **to be of ~ to sb** rendre service à qn; **can I be of ~?** puis-je faire quelque chose pour vous?; **I was glad to be of ~** j'ai été content d'avoir pu rendre service; **it was of no ~ (at all)** cela n'a servi à rien (du tout); **he's a (great) ~ to me** il m'est d'un grand secours, il m'aide beaucoup; (*iro*) **you're a great ~!** tu es d'un précieux secours! (*iro*); **you can't get (domestic) ~ nowadays** on ne trouve plus à se faire aider de nos jours; **she has no ~ in the house** elle n'a personne pour l'aider à la maison; **we need more ~ in the shop** il nous faut davantage de personnel au magasin; (*fig*) **he's beyond ~** on ne peut plus rien pour lui; **there's no ~ for it** il n'y a rien à faire, on n'y peut rien; *see* **voluntary.**

b (*charwoman*) femme *f* de ménage; *see* **daily, home, mother** *etc*.

2 **comp** ►**helpline** ligne *f* d'assistance; (*Comm*) ≃ numéro *m* vert (*esp pour renseignements sur un produit*) ►**helpmate, helpmeet**† (*spouse*) époux *m*, épouse *f*; (*companion*) compagnon *m*, compagne *f*, aide *mf* ►**help menu** (*Comput*) menu *m* d'assistance.

3 **vt** a aider (*sb to do* qn à faire), secourir, venir à l'aide de. **let me ~ you with that suitcase** laissez-moi vous aider à porter votre valise; **she ~s her son with his homework** elle aide son fils à faire ses devoirs; **he got his brother to ~ him** il s'est fait aider par son frère; **that doesn't ~ much** cela ne sert pas à *or* n'arrange pas grand-chose; **that won't ~ you** cela ne vous servira à rien; (*Prov*) **God ~s those who ~ themselves** aide-toi et le ciel t'aidera (*Prov*); **so ~ me God!** je le jure devant Dieu!; **so ~ me* I'll kill him!** je le tuerai, je le jure!; **this money will ~ to save the church** cet argent contribuera à sauver l'église; (*loc*) **every little ~s** les petits ruisseaux font les grandes rivières (*Prov*); (*in shops etc*) **can I ~ you?** vous désirez?; **to ~ each other** *or* **one another** s'entraider; **he is ~ing the police with their inquiries** il est en train de répondre aux questions de la police; **it ~s industry/exports** *etc* cela favorise l'industrie/les exportations *etc*; **to ~ sb across/down/in** *etc* aider qn à traverser/à descendre/à entrer *etc*; **to ~ sb up/down/out with a suitcase** aider qn à monter/à descendre/à sortir une valise; **to help sb (up) to his** (*or* **her**) **feet** aider qn à se lever; **to ~ sb on/off with his coat** aider qn à mettre/à enlever son manteau.

b servir. **she ~ed him to potatoes** elle l'a servi de pommes de terre; **he ~ed himself to vegetables** il s'est servi de légumes; **~ yourself!** servez-vous!; **~ yourself to wine/bread** prenez du vin/du pain, servez-vous de vin/de pain; (*euph*) **he's ~ed himself to my pencil*** il m'a piqué mon crayon*.

c (*with "can" or "cannot"*) **I couldn't ~ laughing** je ne pouvais pas m'empêcher de rire; **one cannot ~ wondering whether ...** on ne peut s'empêcher de se demander si ...; **one can't ~ but wonder/be impressed** on ne peut pas ne pas se demander/être impressionné; **it can't be ~ed** tant pis!, on n'y peut rien!; **I can't ~ it if he always comes late, I can't ~ him** *or* **his always coming late** je n'y peux rien *or* ce n'est pas de ma faute s'il arrive toujours en retard; **he can't ~ it** ce n'est pas de sa faute, il n'y peut rien; **why are you laughing? — I can't ~ it** pourquoi riez-vous? — c'est plus fort que moi; **not if I can ~ it!** sûrement pas!, il faudra d'abord me passer sur le corps! (*hum*); **he won't come if I can ~ it** je vais faire tout mon possible pour l'empêcher de venir; **can I ~ it if it rains?** est-ce que c'est de ma faute s'il pleut?; **it's rather late now — I can't ~ that, you should have come earlier** il est un peu tard maintenant — je n'y peux rien, tu aurais dû venir plus tôt; **he can't ~ his nature** il ne peut rien (changer) à sa nature; **he can't ~ his deafness** ce n'est pas de sa faute s'il est sourd; **he can't ~ being stupid** ce n'est pas de sa faute s'il est idiot; **don't say more than you can ~** n'en dites pas plus qu'il ne faut.

►**help along vt sep** *person* aider à marcher; *scheme* (faire) avancer, faire progresser.

►**help out** 1 **vi** aider, donner un coup de main. 2 **vt sep** (*gen*) aider, donner un coup de main à; (*sb in trouble*) dépanner, tirer d'embarras. **to help each other out** s'entraider.

►**help up vt sep: to help sb up** aider qn à se lever.

helper [ˈhelpəʳ] **n** aide *mf*, assistant(e) *m(f)*, auxiliaire *mf*.

helpful [ˈhelpfʊl] **adj** *person* serviable, obligeant; *book, tool, gadget etc* utile; *medicine etc* efficace, salutaire; *advice* efficace, utile. *[person, thing]* **to be extremely ~** être d'un grand secours; **you have been most ~** votre aide m'a été très utile.

helpfully [ˈhelpfəlɪ] **adv** gentiment, avec obligeance.

helpfulness [ˈhelpfʊlnɪs] **n** obligeance *f*.

helping [ˈhelpɪŋ] 1 **n** (*at table*) portion *f*. **to take a second ~ of sth** reprendre de qch; **I've had three ~s** j'en ai repris deux fois. 2 **adj** secourable. **to give** *or* **lend a ~ hand (to)** aider, donner un coup de main (à).

helpless [ˈhelplɪs] **adj** (*powerless*) sans ressource, sans recours, sans appui; *baby, animal* sans défense; (*mentally, morally*) impuissant, incapable de s'en sortir; (*physically*) faible, impotent. **she looked at him with a ~ expression** elle lui jeta un regard où se lisait son impuissance; **~ as a child** aussi désarmé qu'un enfant; **he is quite ~ (in this matter)** il n'y peut rien, il est absolument impuissant; **we were ~ to do anything about it** nous avons été impuissants à y faire quoi que ce soit; **her illness has left her ~** sa maladie l'a laissée impotente; **she is a ~ invalid** elle est complètement impotente; (*fig*) **to feel ~** se sentir impuissant; **she was quite ~ (with laughter)** elle n'en pouvait plus de rire*, elle était malade de rire.

helplessly [ˈhelplɪslɪ] **adv** *struggle* en vain; *try, agree* désespérément. **he was lying there ~** il était allongé là sans pouvoir bouger; **... he said ~** ... dit-il d'un ton où se sentait son impuissance; **to laugh ~** être pris d'un fou rire, ne pas pouvoir s'empêcher de rire.

helplessness [ˈhelplɪsnɪs] **n** (*see* **helpless**) impuissance *f*, incapacité *f* à s'en sortir; impotence *f*.

Helsinki [helˈsɪŋkɪ] **n** Helsinki.

helter-skelter [ˈheltəˈskeltəʳ] 1 **adv** à la débandade, à la six-quatre-deux*. 2 **adj** désordonné, à la débandade. 3 **n** (*rush*) débandade *f*, bousculade *f*; (*Brit: in fairground*) toboggan *m*.

hem1 [hem] 1 **n** ourlet *m*; (*edge*) bord *m*. **I've let the ~ down on my skirt** j'ai défait l'ourlet de ma jupe pour la rallonger, j'ai rallongé ma jupe. 2 **comp** ►**hemline** (bas *m* de l')ourlet *m*; **hemlines are lower this year** les robes rallongent cette année ►**hemstitch vt** ourler à jour ◊ **n** ourlet *m* à jour. 3 **vt** (*sew*) ourler.

►**hem in vt sep** *[houses, objects, people]* cerner; *[rules etc]* entraver. **I feel hemmed in** ça me donne la claustrophobie, ça m'écrase *or* m'oppresse.

hem2 [hem] **vi** *see* **haw2**.

hema(t)... [ˈhiːmə(t)] **pref** (*US*) = **haema(t)...** .

hemato... [ˈhiːmətəʊ] **pref** (*US*) = **haemato...** .

hemicycle [ˈhemɪsaɪkl] **n** hémicycle *m*.

hemiplegia [hemɪˈpliːdʒɪə] **n** hémiplégie *f*.

hemiplegic [ˌhemɪˈpliːdʒɪk] **adj, n** hémiplégique (*mf*).

hemisphere [ˈhemɪsfɪəʳ] **n** hémisphère *m*. **the northern ~** l'hémisphère nord *or* boréal; **the southern ~** l'hémisphère sud *or* austral.

hemistich [ˈhemɪstɪk] **n** hémistiche *m*.

hemlock [ˈhemlɒk] **n** a ciguë *f*. b (*tree*) (*also* **~ spruce**) sapin *m* du Canada, sapin-ciguë *m*.

hem(o)... [ˈhiːm(əʊ)] **pref** (*US*) = **haem(o)...** .

hemp [hemp] **n** (*plant, fibre*) chanvre *m*; (*drug*) haschisch *m or* hachisch *m*, chanvre indien.

hen [hen] 1 **n** a poule *f*; (*female bird*) femelle *f*. **~ bird** oiseau *m* femelle. b (*Scot* ‡) **here you are, ~**‡ voici, ma cocotte*. 2 **comp** ►**henbane** (*Bot*) jusquiame *f* (noire), herbe *f* aux poules ►**hencoop** cage *f* à poules, mue *f* ►**hen harrier** busard *m* Saint-Martin ►**henhouse** poulailler *m* ►**hen night*, hen party*** soirée *f* entre femmes *or* filles ►**henpecked: he's henpecked** sa femme le mène par le bout du nez, c'est sa femme qui porte la culotte ►**henpecked husband** mari dominé par sa femme.

hence [hens] 1 **adv** a (*therefore*) d'où, de là. b (*from now on*) d'ici. **2 years ~** d'ici 2 ans, dans 2 ans (d'ici). c (†† *or liter: from here*) d'ici. **(get thee) ~!** hors d'ici! 2 **comp** ►**henceforth, henceforward** dorénavant, désormais, à l'avenir.

henchman [ˈhentʃmən] **n** (*pej*) acolyte *m* (*pej*), suppôt *m* (*pej*); (*supporter*) partisan *m*, adepte *m*; (*Hist*) écuyer *m*.

henna [ˈhenə] 1 **n** henné *m*. 2 **vt** *hair* teindre au henné. **to ~ one's hair** se faire un henné.

Henry [ˈhenrɪ] **n** Henri *m*; *see* **hooray.**

hep‡ [hep] **adj** dans le vent*. (*US*) **to be ~**‡ **to sth** être au parfum‡ de qch.

heparin [ˈhepərɪn] **n** héparine *f*.

hepatitis [ˌhepəˈtaɪtɪs] **n** hépatite *f*. **serum ~, ~ B** hépatite *f* (virale) B *or* sérique.

heptathlon [hepˈtæθlən] **n** heptathlon *m*.

her [hɜːʳ] 1 **pers pron** a (*direct*) (*unstressed*) la; (*before vowel*) l'; (*stressed*) elle. **I see ~** je la vois; **I have seen ~** je l'ai vue; **I know HIM but I have never seen HER** lui je le connais, mais elle je ne l'ai jamais vue.

b (*indirect*) lui. **I give ~ the book** je lui donne le livre; **I'm speaking to ~** je lui parle.

c (*after prep etc*) elle. **I am thinking of ~** je pense à elle; **without ~** sans elle; **she took her books with ~** elle a emporté ses livres; **if I were ~** si j'étais elle; **it's ~** c'est elle; **younger than ~** plus jeune qu'elle.

d celle. **to ~ who objects I would explain it thus** à celle qui n'est pas d'accord je l'expliquerais ainsi.

2 **poss adj** son, sa, ses. **~ book** son livre; **~ table** sa table; **~ friend** son ami(e); **~ clothes** ses vêtements.

Hera ['hɪərə] **n** Héra *f*.

Heracles ['herə,kli:z] **n** Héracles *m*.

Heraclitus [,herə'klaɪtəs] **n** Héraclite *m*.

herald ['herəld] 1 **n** héraut *m*. (*fig liter*) **the ~ of spring** le messager du printemps (*liter*). 2 **vt** annoncer. **to ~ (in)** annoncer l'arrivée de.

heraldic [he'rældɪk] **adj** héraldique. **~ bearing** armoiries *fpl*, blason *m*.

heraldry ['herəldrɪ] **n** (*NonC*) (*science*) héraldique *f*; (*coat of arms*) blason *m*; (*ceremonial*) pompe *f* héraldique. **book of ~** armorial *m*.

herb [hɜ:b] 1 **n** herbe *f*. (*Culin*) **~s** fines herbes; **pot ~s** herbes potagères; **medicinal ~s** herbes médicinales, simples *mpl*. 2 **comp** ►**herb garden** jardin *m* d'herbes aromatiques ►**herb tea** tisane *f*.

herbaceous [hɜ:'beɪʃəs] **adj** herbacé. **~ border** bordure *f* de plantes herbacées.

herbage ['hɜ:bɪdʒ] **n** (*Agr*) herbages *mpl*; (*Jur*) droit *m* de pâturage *or* de pacage.

herbal ['hɜ:bəl] 1 **adj** (*gen*) d'herbes. **~ medicine** phytothérapie *f*; **~ tea** tisane *f*. 2 **n** herbier *m* (*livre*).

herbalist ['hɜ:bəlɪst] **n** herboriste *mf*.

herbarium [hɜ:'bɛərɪəm] **n, pl ~s** *or* **herbaria** [hɜ:'bɛərɪə] herbier *m* (*collection*).

herbicide ['hɜ:bɪsaɪd] **n** herbicide *m*.

herbivore ['hɜ:bɪvɔ:ʳ] **n** herbivore *m*.

herbivorous [hɜ:'bɪvərəs] **adj** herbivore.

Herculean [,hɜ:kjʊ'li:ən] **adj** herculéen.

Hercules ['hɜ:kjuli:z] **n** Hercule *m*; (*fig: strong man*) hercule *m*.

herd [hɜ:d] 1 **n** a *[cattle etc]* troupeau *m*; *[stags]* harde *f*; *[horses]* troupe *f*, bande *f*; *[people]* troupeau, foule *f*; *see* **common**. b (*person*) pâtre *m* (*liter*); *see* **cow¹**, **goat** *etc*. 2 **comp** ►**herd instinct** instinct *m* grégaire ►**herdsman** gardien *m* de troupeau; (*shepherd*) berger *m*; (*cowman*) vacher *m*, bouvier *m*. 3 **vt** (*also:* **~ up**) *animals, people* mener, conduire (*along* le long de).

►**herd together** 1 **vi** *[animals, people]* s'attrouper, s'assembler en troupeau. 2 **vt sep** *animals, people* rassembler en troupeau.

here [hɪəʳ] 1 **adv** a (*place*) ici. **I live ~** j'habite ici; **come ~** venez ici; (*at roll call*) ~! présent!; **~ I am** me voici; **~ is my brother** voici mon frère; **~ are the others** voici les autres; **~ we are at last** nous voici enfin arrivés; (*bringing sth*) **~ we are!** voici!; (*giving sth*) **~ you are!** tenez!; **~ come my friends** voici mes amis qui arrivent; **he's ~ at last** le voici enfin, il est enfin là *or* arrivé; **spring is ~** c'est le printemps, le printemps est là; **my sister ~ says ...** ma sœur que voici dit ...; **this man ~ saw it** cet homme-ci l'a vu; **~'s to you!** à la tienne! *or* à la vôtre!; **~'s to your success!** à votre succès!; (*US*) **~ is you'll never do it!*** je te parie que tu n'y arriveras jamais; **about** *or* **around ~** par ici; **far from ~** loin d'ici; **put it in ~** mettez-le ici; **come in ~** venez (par) ici; **in ~ please** par ici s'il vous plaît; **near ~** près d'ici; **over ~** ici; **it's cold up ~** il fait froid ici (en haut); **up to** *or* **down to ~** jusqu'ici; **from ~ to there** d'ici (jusqu')à là-bas; **it's 10 km from ~ to Paris** il y a 10 km d'ici à Paris; **Mr X is not ~ just now** M. X n'est pas là *or* ici en ce moment; **are you there? — yes I'm ~** vous êtes là? — oui je suis là; **I shan't be ~ this afternoon** je ne serai pas là cet après-midi; **~ and there** çà et là, par-ci par-là; **~, there and everywhere** un peu partout; **I can't be ~, there and everywhere** je ne peux pas être partout (à la fois), je ne peux pas être à la fois au four et au moulin*; (*fig*) **it's neither ~ nor there** tout cela n'a aucun rapport; **~ goes!*** allons-y!, c'est parti!*; **~ we** *or* **I go again!** c'est reparti!*, (et) voilà que ça recommence!; **~ and now** sur-le-champ; **I must warn you ~ and now that ...** il faut que je vous prévienne sans plus tarder que ...; **~ below** ici-bas; **~ lies** ci-gît; *see* **look** *etc*.

b (*time*) alors, à ce moment-là. **and ~ I stopped work to answer the telephone** et alors j'ai laissé mon travail pour répondre au téléphone.

2 **excl** tenez!, écoutez! **~, I didn't promise that at all!** mais écoutez *or* dites donc, je n'ai jamais promis cela!; **~, you try to open it** tiens, essaie de l'ouvrir; **~, hold this a minute** tiens, prends ça une minute.

3 **comp** ►**hereabouts** par ici, près d'ici, dans les environs, dans les parages ►**hereafter** (*in the future*) après, plus tard; (*in books etc: following this*) ci-après; (*after death*) dans l'autre vie *or* monde ►**the hereafter** l'au-delà *m*, la vie future ►**the here and now** le présent, l'instant présent ►**hereby** (*Comm, Jur etc*) (*in letter*) par la présente; (*in document*) par le présent document; (*in act*) par le présent acte; (*in will*) par le présent testament; (*in declaration*) par la présente (déclaration) ►**herein** (*frm*) (*in this matter*) en ceci, en cela; (*in this writing*) ci-inclus ►**hereinafter** (*Jur*) ci-après, dans la suite des présentes ►**hereof** (*frm*) de ceci, de cela; (*Jur*) **the provisions hereof** les dispositions *fpl* des présentes ►**hereto** (*Jur*) à ceci, à cela; (*Jur*) **the parties hereto** les parties aux présentes ►**heretofore** (*frm*) jusque-là, jusqu'ici, ci-devant ►**hereupon** là-dessus, sur ce ►**herewith** avec ceci; **I am sending you herewith** je vous envoie ci-joint *or* sous ce pli; **I enclose herewith a copy of ...** veuillez trouver ci-joint une copie de ... .

hereditaments [,herɪ'dɪtəmənts] **npl** (*Jur*) *biens mpl meubles ou immeubles transmissibles par héritage*.

hereditary [hɪ'redɪtərɪ] **adj** héréditaire.

heredity [hɪ'redɪtɪ] **n** hérédité *f*.

heresy ['herəsɪ] **n** hérésie *f*. **an act of ~** une hérésie.

heretic ['herətɪk] **n** hérétique *mf*.

heretical [hɪ'retɪkəl] **adj** hérétique.

heritable ['herɪtəbl] **adj** *objects, property etc* dont on peut hériter; *person* qui peut hériter.

heritage ['herɪtɪdʒ] **n** (*lit, fig*) héritage *m*, patrimoine *m*. **our national ~** notre patrimoine national.

hermaphrodite [hɜ:'mæfrədaɪt] **adj, n** hermaphrodite (*m*).

Hermes ['hɜ:mi:z] **n** Hermès *m*.

hermetic [hɜ:'metɪk] **adj** (*gen, also Literat*) hermétique.

hermetically [hɜ:'metɪkəlɪ] **adv** hermétiquement. **~ sealed** bouché *or* fermé hermétiquement.

hermit ['hɜ:mɪt] **n** ermite *m*, solitaire *m*. **~ crab** bernard-l'ermite *m inv*.

hermitage ['hɜ:mɪtɪdʒ] **n** ermitage *m*.

hernia ['hɜ:nɪə] **n, pl ~s** *or* **herniae** ['hɜ:nɪ,i:]hernie *f*.

hero ['hɪərəʊ] **pl ~es** 1 **n** (*all senses*) héros *m*; *see* **land**. 2 **comp** ►**hero (sandwich)** (*US*) grand sandwich mixte ►**hero-worship** **n** culte *m* (du héros) ◊ **vt** aduler, idolâtrer.

Herod ['herəd] **n** Hérode *m*; *see* **out**.

heroic [hɪ'rəʊɪk] **adj** *act, behaviour, person* héroïque. (*Poetry*) **in ~ verse** en décasyllabes; **~ couplet** distique *m* héroïque.

heroically [hɪ'rəʊɪkəlɪ] **adv** héroïquement.

heroics [hɪ'rəʊɪks] **npl** (*slightly pej*) mélodrame *m*.

heroin ['herəʊɪn] 1 **n** héroïne *f*. 2 **comp** ►**heroin addict** héroïnomane *mf* ►**heroin addiction** héroïnomanie *f* ►**heroin user** personne *f* qui prend de l'héroïne.

heroine ['herəʊɪn] **n** héroïne *f* (*femme*).

heroism ['herəʊɪzəm] **n** héroïsme *m*.

heron ['herən] **n** héron *m*.

herpes ['hɜ:pi:z] **n** herpès *m*; *see* **genital**.

herring ['herɪŋ] 1 **n, pl ~s** *or* **~** hareng *m*; *see* **fish, red** *etc*. 2 **comp** ►**herring boat** harenguier *m* ►**herringbone** (*lit*) arête *f* de hareng; (*Archit*) appareil *m* en épi; (*Ski: also* **herringbone climb**) montée *f* en ciseaux; **herringbone pattern** (dessin *m* à) chevrons *mpl*; **herringbone stitch** point *m* d'épine (en chevron) ►**herring gull** goéland *m* argenté ►**the herring-pond**⁑ (*Atlantic*) la mare aux harengs (*hum*), l'Atlantique nord.

hers [hɜ:z] **poss pron** le sien, la sienne, les siens, les siennes. **my hands are clean, ~ are dirty** mes mains sont propres, les siennes sont sales; **~ is a specialized department** sa section est une section spécialisée; **this book is ~** ce livre est à elle, ce livre est le sien; **the house became ~** la maison est devenue la sienne; **it is not ~ to decide** ce n'est pas à elle de décider, il ne lui appartient pas de décider; **a friend of ~** un de ses amis (à elle); **it's no fault of ~** ce n'est pas de sa faute (à elle); **no advice of ~ could prevent him** aucun conseil de sa part ne pouvait l'empêcher; **is this poem ~?** ce poème est-il d'elle?; (*pej*) **that car of ~** sa fichue* voiture; (*pej*) **that stupid son of ~** son idiot de fils; (*pej*) **that temper of ~** son sale caractère.

herself [hɜ:'self] **pers pron** (*reflexive: direct and indirect*) se; (*emphatic*) elle-même; (*after prep*) elle. **she has hurt ~** elle s'est blessée; **she said to ~** elle s'est dit; **she told me ~** elle me l'a dit elle-même; **I saw the girl ~** j'ai vu la jeune fille elle-même *or* en personne; **she kept 3 for ~** elle s'en est réservé 3; **he asked her for a photo of ~** il lui a demandé une de ses photos *or* une photo d'elle; **(all) by ~** toute seule; **she is not ~ today** elle n'est pas dans son état normal *or* dans son assiette* aujourd'hui.

Herts [hɑ:ts] (*Brit*) **abbr of Hertfordshire.**

hertz [hɜ:ts] **n, pl inv** hertz *m*.

he's [hi:z] = **he is, he has**; *see* **be, have**.

hesitancy ['hezɪtənsɪ] **n** hésitation *f*.

hesitant ['hezɪtənt] **adj** hésitant, irrésolu, indécis. **I am ~ about offering him money** j'hésite à lui offrir de l'argent.

hesitantly ['hezɪtəntlɪ] **adv** avec hésitation; *speak, suggest* d'une voix hésitante.

hesitate ['hezɪteɪt] **vi** hésiter (*over, about, at* sur, devant; *to do* à faire). (*Prov*) **he who ~s is lost** une minute d'hésitation peut coûter cher, ≃ aux audacieux les mains pleines (*Prov*); **he ~s at nothing** il ne recule devant rien, rien ne l'arrête; **I ~ to condemn him** j'hésite à le condamner; **I am hesitating about what I should do** j'hésite sur ce que je dois faire; **don't ~ to ask me** n'ayez pas peur de *or* n'hésitez pas à me demander.

hesitation [,hezɪ'teɪʃən] **n** hésitation *f*. **without the slightest ~** sans la moindre hésitation; **I have no ~ in saying that ...** je n'hésite pas à dire que ... .

Hesperides [he'sperɪ,di:z] **npl** Hespérides *fpl*.

hessian ['hesɪən] 1 **n** (toile *f* de) jute *m*. 2 **comp** (*made of ~*) en (toile de) jute.

hetero... ['hetərəʊ] **pref** hétér(o)... .

hetero⁑ ['hetərəʊ] **n, adj** hétéro* (*mf*).

heterodox ['hetərədɒks] **adj** hétérodoxe.

heterodoxy ['hetərədɒksɪ] **n** hétérodoxie *f*.

heterogeneous [ˈhetərəʊˈdʒiːnɪəs] adj hétérogène.
heterosexual [ˈhetərəʊˈseksjʊəl] adj, n hétérosexuel(le) *(m(f))*.
heterosexuality [ˌhetərəʊˌseksjʊˈælɪtɪ] n hétérosexualité *f*.
het up* [ˈhetˈʌp] adj agité, excité, énervé. **he gets very ~ about it** cela le met dans tous ses états.
heuristic [hjʊəˈrɪstɪk] adj heuristique.
heuristics [hjʊəˈrɪstɪks] npl heuristique *f*.
hew [hjuː] 1 pret **hewed**, ptp **hewn** [hjuːn] or **hewed** vt *stone* tailler, équarrir; *wood* couper; *coal* abattre. **to ~ sth out of wood** *etc* tailler qch dans du bois *etc*; **to ~ one's way through the jungle** se tailler un chemin à travers la jungle (à coups de hache *etc*); (*fig*) **he ~ed out a position for himself in the company** il s'est taillé une bonne place dans la compagnie. 2 pret, ptp **hewed** vi (*US*) **to ~ to sth** se conformer à qch, suivre qch.
hewer [ˈhjuːəʳ] n *[stone]* tailleur *m*, équarrisseur *m*; *[wood]* équarrisseur; *[coal]* haveur *m*, piqueur *m*.
hex[1] [heks] (*US*) 1 n (*spell*) sort *m*; (*witch*) sorcière *f*. 2 vt jeter un sort sur.
hex[2] [heks] n (*Comput*) **~ code** code hexadécimal.
hexadecimal [ˌheksəˈdesɪməl] adj, n (*Comput*) (*also* **~ notation**) hexadécimal *(m)*.
hexagon [ˈheksəgən] n hexagone *m*.
hexagonal [hekˈsægənəl] adj hexagonal.
hexagram [ˈheksəˌgræm] n hexagramme *m*.
hexameter [hekˈsæmɪtəʳ] n hexamètre *m*.
hexathlon [hekˈsæθlən] n hexathlon *m*.
hey [heɪ] excl hé!, holà! **~ presto!** *[magician]* passez muscade!; (*fig*) ô miracle!
heyday [ˈheɪdeɪ] n *[the music hall, the railways etc]* âge *m* d'or, beaux jours. **in his ~** (*in his prime*) quand il était dans la force de l'âge; (*at his most famous*) à l'apogée de sa gloire; **in the ~ of the crinoline/the theatre** à l'âge d'or de la crinoline/du théâtre.
HGV [ˌeɪtʃdʒiːˈviː] (*Aut*) (abbr of **heavy goods vehicle**) *see* **heavy**.
HI (*US Post*) abbr of **Hawaii**.
hi* [haɪ] excl hé!, ohé!; (*: *greeting*) salut!*
hiatus [haɪˈeɪtəs] n, pl **~es** or **~** (*in series, manuscript etc*) lacune *f*; (*Ling, Phon, Poetry*) hiatus *m*; (*fig*) (*interruption*) interruption *f*, pause *f*; (*difference*) hiatus *m*, décalage *m*. (*Med*) **~ hernia** hernie hiatale.
hibernate [ˈhaɪbəneɪt] vi hiberner.
hibernation [ˌhaɪbəˈneɪʃən] n hibernation *f*.
hibiscus [hɪˈbɪskəs] n, pl **~es** hibiscus *m*.
hiccough†, hiccup [ˈhɪkʌp] 1 n a hoquet *m*. **to have ~s** avoir le hoquet; **to give a ~** hoqueter, avoir un hoquet. b (*minor setback*) contretemps *m*, ratés *mpl*. 2 vi hoqueter. 3 vt dire en hoquetant.
hick‡ [hɪk] (*US*) 1 n péquenaud(e)‡ *m(f)* (*pej*). 2 adj *ideas* de péquenaud‡ (*pej*). **~ town** bled‡ *m* (*pej*).
hickey* [ˈhɪkɪ] n (*US*) (*pimple*) petit bouton *m*; (*love bite*) suçon *m*.
hickory [ˈhɪkərɪ] n hickory *m*, noyer *m* blanc d'Amérique.
hid [hɪd] pret, (††) ptp of **hide**[1].
hidden [ˈhɪdn] ptp of **hide**[1].
hide[1] [haɪd] pret **hid**, ptp **hidden** or **hid††** 1 vt cacher (*from sb* à qn); *feelings* dissimuler (*from sb* à qn). **to ~ o.s.** se cacher; **I've got nothing to ~** je n'ai rien à cacher *or* à dissimuler; **he's hiding something** il nous cache quelque chose; **to ~ one's face** se cacher le visage; **to ~ sth from sight** dérober qch aux regards, cacher qch; **hidden from sight** dérobé aux regards, caché; (*fig*) **to ~ one's light under a bushel** cacher ses talents; (*fig*) **he doesn't ~ his light under a bushel** ce n'est pas la modestie qui l'étouffe; **clouds hid the sun** des nuages cachaient *or* voilaient le soleil; **a small village hidden in a valley** un petit village caché *or* niché dans une vallée; **a hidden meaning** un sens caché; **"no hidden extras"** "garanti sans suppléments"; **hidden tax** impôt déguisé; **hidden agenda** intentions *fpl* non déclarées.
2 vi se cacher (*from sb* de qn). (*fig*) **he's hiding behind his boss** il se réfugie derrière son patron (*fig*).
3 n (*Brit*) cachette *f*.
4 comp ►**hide-and-(go-)seek** cache-cache *m* ►**hideaway, hideout** cachette *f*, planque‡ *f*.
►**hide away** 1 vi se cacher (*from* de). 2 vt sep cacher. 3 **hideaway** n *see* **hide**[1] 4.
►**hide out, hide up** 1 vi se cacher (*from* de), rester caché (*from* de). 2 **hideout** n *see* **hide**[1] 4.
hide[2] [haɪd] 1 n (*skin*) peau *f*; (*leather*) cuir *m*. **to save one's ~*** sauver sa peau*; **they found neither ~ nor hair of him** ils n'ont pas trouvé la moindre trace de son passage; *see* **tan**. 2 comp *chair etc* de *or* en cuir ►**hidebound** *person* borné, obtus, à l'esprit étroit *or* limité; *view* étroit, borné, rigide.
hideous [ˈhɪdɪəs] adj *appearance, sight, person* hideux, affreux; *crime* atroce, abominable, horrible; (*fig*) terrible*. **it was a ~ disappointment** ce fut une terrible déception.
hideously [ˈhɪdɪəslɪ] adv hideusement, atrocement, affreusement; (*fig: very*) terriblement*, horriblement*.
hiding[1] [ˈhaɪdɪŋ] 1 n acte *m* de cacher; *[feelings etc]* dissimulation *f*; *[criminals]* recel *m*. **to be in ~** se tenir caché; **to go into ~** se cacher. 2 comp ►**hiding place** cachette *f*.
hiding[2] [ˈhaɪdɪŋ] n (*beating*) correction *f*, volée *f* de coups. **to give sb a good ~** donner une bonne correction à qn; (*fig*) **the team got a ~*** l'équipe a pris une raclée* *or* une déculottée‡.
hie [haɪ] vi (†† *or hum*) se hâter. **~ thee hence!** hors d'ici!
hierarchic(al) [ˌhaɪəˈrɑːkɪk(əl)] adj hiérarchique.
hierarchy [ˈhaɪərɑːkɪ] n hiérarchie *f*.
hieroglyph [ˈhaɪərəglɪf] n hiéroglyphe *m*.
hieroglyphic [ˌhaɪərəˈglɪfɪk] 1 adj hiéroglyphique. 2 n hiéroglyphe *m*.
hifalutin* [ˌhaɪfəˈluːtɪn] adj = **high falutin(g)**; *see* **high**.
hi-fi [ˈhaɪˈfaɪ] (abbr of **high fidelity**) 1 n a (*NonC*) hi-fi *f inv*, haute fidélité *inv*. b (*gramophone*) chaîne *f* (hi-fi) *inv*; (*radio*) radio *f* hi-fi *inv*. 2 comp *reproduction, record* hi-fi *inv*, haute fidélité *inv* ►**hi-fi equipment** matériel *m* hi-fi ►**hi-fi set** *or* **system** chaîne *f* (hi-fi).
higgledy-piggledy* [ˈhɪgldɪˈpɪgldɪ] adj, adv pêle-mêle *inv*, n'importe comment.
high [haɪ] 1 adj a *building, mountain, tide* haut; *altitude* haut, élevé. **building 40 metres ~** bâtiment haut de 40 mètres, bâtiment de 40 mètres de haut, bâtiment qui a *or* fait 40 mètres de haut; **how ~ is that tower?** quelle est la hauteur de cette tour?; **when he was so ~*** quand il était grand comme ça; **~ cheekbones** pommettes saillantes; *see also* **4**.
b (*fig*) *frequency, latitude, opinion* haut (*before noun*); *speed, value* grand (*before noun*); *fever* gros (*f* grosse) (*before noun*), fort (*before noun*), intense; *respect* grand (*before noun*), profond; *complexion* rougeaud; *colour* vif; *polish* brillant; *pressure* élevé, haut (*before noun*), fort (*before noun*); *salary* haut (*before noun*), élevé, gros (*before noun*); *rent, price* élevé; *tension* haut (*before noun*); *number* grand (*before noun*), élevé; *sound* aigu (*f* -guë); *note* haut; (*shrill*) aigu; *voice* aigu; (*Phon*) *vowel* fermé; *calling, character* noble; *ideal* noble, grand (*before noun*), élevé. **to have ~ blood pressure** avoir de la tension; **~ caste** caste supérieure; (*Math*) **the ~est common factor** le plus grand commun diviseur; **in the ~est degree** au plus haut degré, à l'extrême; (*Aut*) **in ~ gear** en quatrième (*or* cinquième) vitesse; **~ official** haut fonctionnaire; **to have a ~ opinion of sb/sth** avoir une haute opinion de qn/qch; **to buy sth at a ~ price** acheter qch cher; (*lit, fig*) **to pay a ~ price for sth** payer qch cher; **he has a ~ temperature** il a une forte température; **it boils at a ~ temperature** cela bout à une température élevée; **it's ~ time you went home** il est grand temps que tu rentres (*subj*); **to set a ~ value on sth** attacher une grande valeur à qch; **in a ~ voice** d'une voix aiguë; **a ~ wind was blowing** il soufflait un vent violent, il faisait grand vent; *see also* **4** *and* **lord, octane, profile, very** *etc*.
c (*Culin*) *game, meat* avancé, faisandé; *butter* fort, rance.
d (*: *intoxicated etc*) (*drunk*) paf* *inv*, parti*. **to be ~ (on drugs)** être défoncé* (par la drogue); **to be (as) ~ as a kite*** planer complètement*; **to get ~ on music/sports**prendre son pied‡ avec la musique/le sport.
e (*fig*) **to have a ~ old time*** s'amuser follement, faire la fête*; **there was a ~ old row about it*** cela a provoqué une sacrée bagarre* *or* un sacré chambard‡.
2 adv a (*lit*) haut, en haut; *fly etc* à haute altitude, à une altitude élevée. **~ up** (en) haut; **~er up** plus haut; **~er and ~er** de plus en plus haut; **the balloon rose ~ in the air** le ballon s'est élevé *or* est monté haut dans le ciel *or* dans les airs; **the kite sailed ~ over the house** le cerf-volant est passé très haut au-dessus de la maison; **~ above our heads** bien au-dessus de nos têtes; (*lit, fig*) **to aim ~** viser haut; (*US fig*) **to live ~ on the hog*** vivre comme un nabab.
b (*fig*) **the numbers go as ~ as 200** les nombres montent jusqu'à 200; **I had to go as ~ as 200 francs for it** j'ai dû aller *or* monter jusqu'à 200 F pour l'avoir; **the bidding went as ~ as 4.000 francs** les enchères sont montées jusqu'à 4 000 F; **to hunt** *or* **look ~ and low for sb** chercher qn un peu partout; **to hunt** *or* **look ~ and low for sth** chercher qch un peu partout *or* dans tous les coins; **to hold one's head (up) ~** avoir la tête haute; *[gambler etc]* **to play ~** jouer gros (jeu); (*fig*) **to fly ~** voir grand, viser haut; **to live ~** mener grand train, mener la grande vie; **the sea is running ~** la mer est grosse *or* houleuse; **the river is running ~** la rivière est en crue; **feelings ran ~** les esprits étaient échauffés.
3 n a **on ~** en haut, au ciel; **from on ~** (*lit*) d'en haut; (*fig*) en haut lieu.
b (*Rel*) **the Most H~** le Très-Haut.
c **the cost of living reached a new ~** le coût de la vie a atteint une nouvelle pointe *or* un nouveau plafond; (*Met*) **a ~ over the North Sea** une zone de haute pression sur la mer du Nord.
4 comp ►**high-ability** adj très doué ►**high altar** maître-autel *m* ►**high-angle shot** (*Cine*) plongée *f* ►**high and dry** *boat* échoué; (*fig*) **to leave sb high and dry** laisser qn en plan* ►**high and mighty***: **to be high and mighty** se donner de grands airs, faire le grand seigneur (*or* la grande dame) ►**highball** (*US*) n whisky *m* à l'eau (avec de la glace) ◊ vi (*US Aut* ‡) foncer ►**high beam** optique *f* feux de route ►**highborn** de haute naissance, bien né ►**highboy** (*US*) commode *f* (haute) ►**highbrow** (*slightly pej*) n intellectuel(le) *m(f)* ◊ adj *tastes, interests* intellectuel; *music* pour intellectuels ►**high**

camp *see* camp² ▸ **highchair** chaise haute (*pour enfants*) ▸ **High Church** (*Brit*) Haute Église ▸ **high-class** *hotel, food, service* de premier ordre; *house* très bourgeois; *neighbourhood, flat* (de) grand standing; *person* du grand monde; *prostitute* de luxe ▸ **high comedy** (*Theat*) comédie élevée; (*fig*) it was high comedy c'était du plus haut comique ▸ **high command** (*Mil*) haut commandement ▸ **High Commission** (*Admin*) haut commissariat *m* ▸ **High Commissioner** (*Admin*) haut commissaire ▸ **High Court** (*Jur*) cour *f* suprême ▸ **high definition** adj, n haute définition *(f)* ▸ **high density** *printing, disk* haute densité *f* ▸ **high density housing** grands ensembles *mpl* ▸ **high diving** (*Sport*) plongeon(s) *m(pl)* de haut vol (*see also* diving) ▸ **high-energy** *particle* de haute énergie; *music* énergétique ▸ **high explosive** explosif *m* (puissant) ▸ **high-explosive shell** obus *m* explosif ▸ **high-falutin(g)*** affecté, prétentieux, ampoulé ▸ **high fibre diet** alimentation *f* riche en fibres ▸ **high-fidelity** haute fidélité *inv* (*see* hi-fi) ▸ **high flier** (*fig*) ambitieux *m*, -euse *f*; (*gifted*) doué(e) *m(f)* ▸ **high-flown** *style* ampoulé; *discourse* ampoulé, boursouflé ▸ **high-flying** *aircraft* volant à haute altitude; (*fig*) *aim, ambition* extravagant; *person* ambitieux ▸ **high-frequency** de *or* à haute fréquence (*see also* ultrahigh, very) ▸ **High German** haut allemand ▸ **high-grade** *goods* de haute qualité, de premier choix ▸ **high-grade mineral** minerai *m* à haute teneur ▸ **high hand**: to rule sb with a high hand imposer sa loi à qn ▸ **high-handed** très autoritaire, tyrannique ▸ **high-handedly** très autoritairement ▸ **high hat** haut-de-forme *m* ▸ **high-hat*** adj snob, poseur ◊ vt snober, traiter de haut ◊ vi faire le snob (*f* la snobinette) ▸ **high-heeled shoes** chaussures *fpl* à hauts talons ▸ **high heels*** (*shoes*) hauts talons* ▸ **high horse**: (*fig*) to get up/be on one's high horse monter/être sur ses grands chevaux ▸ **high-income** adj *groups, country* à revenu(s) élevé(s) ▸ **high intensity lights** (*Aut*) phares *mpl* longue portée ▸ **highjack** = hijack ▸ **highjacker** = hijacker ▸ **highjacking** = hijacking ▸ **high jinks***: to have high jinks se payer du bon temps; there were high jinks last night on s'est amusé comme des fous hier soir ▸ **high jump** (*Sport*) saut *m* en hauteur; (*Brit fig*) he's for the high jump!* il est bon *or* mûr pour une engueulade*, qu'est-ce qu'il va prendre!*; (*going to be sacked*) il va se faire virer!* ▸ **highland** *see* highland ▸ **high-level** (*Admin, Ind, Pol etc*) adj *meeting, discussions* à un très haut niveau; (*Comput*) *language, programming* de haut niveau; high-level committee comité *m* de haute instance *or* formé de hauts responsables; high-level nuclear waste déchets *mpl* nucléaires à forte radioactivité ▸ **high life** vie mondaine, grande vie ▸ **highlight** *see* highlight ▸ **highlighter** *see* highlighter ▸ **high living** la grande vie ▸ **High Mass** grand-messe *f* ▸ **high-minded** *person* à l'âme noble, de caractère élevé; *ambition, wish* noble, élevé ▸ **high-necked** à col haut ▸ **high noon** plein midi ▸ **high-octane** adj *petrol* à indice d'octane élevé ▸ **high-performance** adj très performant, haute performance ▸ **high-pitched** (*Mus*) *song* (chanté) dans les aigus; *voice, sound, note* aigu (*f* -guë); (*Archit*) *roof* à forte pente; *ambitions etc* noble, haut (*before n*) ▸ **high point** *[show, evening]* point *m* culminant, zénith *m*, clou *m*; *[visit, holiday]* grand moment *m* ▸ **high-powered** *car* de haute puissance, très puissant; (*fig*) *person* très important; high-powered businessman important homme d'affaires, gros industriel ▸ **high-pressure** (*Tech*) à haute pression; (*Met*) high-pressure area anticyclone *m*, zone *f* de hautes pressions (atmosphériques); (*fig*) a high-pressure salesman vendeur *m* de choc*; high-pressure salesmanship technique *f* de la vente à l'arraché ▸ **high-priced** coûteux, cher (*f* chère) ▸ **high priest** grand prêtre ▸ **high priestess** grande prêtresse ▸ **high-principled** qui a des principes élevés ▸ **high-profile** *company, politician* très en vue; *role* très influant; *issue* très discuté ▸ **high-protein** adj riche en protéines ▸ **high-ranking** haut placé, de haut rang; high-ranking official haut fonctionnaire, fonctionnaire de haut rang ▸ **high resolution** n, **high-resolution** adj haute résolution *(f)* ▸ **high-rise block, high-rise flats** tour *f* (d'habitation) ▸ **high-risk** à haut risque ▸ **highroad** (*esp Brit*) (*lit*) grand-route *f*; the highroad to success (*fig*) la voie de la réussite ▸ **high roller*** (*US*) (*gen*) casse-cou* *m inv*; (*gambling*) flambeur⁑ *m* ▸ **high school** (*Brit*) lycée *m*; (*US*) collège *m or* établissement *m* d'enseignement secondaire; (*US*) high school diploma diplôme *m* de fin d'études secondaires, ≃ baccalauréat *m* ▸ **high seas**: on the high seas en haute mer ▸ **high season** (*Brit*) haute saison *f* ▸ **high society** haute société ▸ **high-sounding** sonore, grandiloquent (*pej*), ronflant (*pej*) ▸ **high-speed** ultra-rapide; high-speed lens objectif *m* à obturation (ultra-)rapide; high-speed train train *m* à grande vitesse, TGV *m* ▸ **high-spirited** *person* plein d'entrain *or* de vivacité; *horse* fougueux, fringant, vif ▸ **high spirits** entrain *m*, vivacité *f*, pétulance *f*; in high spirits plein d'entrain *or* de vivacité, tout joyeux ▸ **high spot**: (*fig: climax*) the high spot *[evening, show]* le clou, le point culminant; *[visit, holiday]* le grand moment; to hit the high spots* faire la foire⁑ *or* la noce* (*dans un night-club, restaurant etc*) ▸ **high stakes**: (*lit, fig*) to play for high stakes jouer gros (jeu) ▸ **high street** (*Brit*) *[village]* grand-rue *f*; *[town]* rue principale; the (little) high-street shops le petit commerce; the high-street banks les grandes banques (*qui ont des succursales un peu partout*) ▸ **high-strung** = highly strung (*see highly*) ▸ **high summer** le cœur *or* le plus chaud de l'été; in high summer en plein été, au cœur de l'été, au plus chaud de l'été ▸ **high table** (*gen*) table *f* d'honneur; (*Scol, Univ*) table des professeurs (*au réfectoire*) ▸ **hightail***: (*US*) they hightailed it back to town ils sont revenus à toute vitesse *or* blinde⁑ en ville ▸ **high tea** (*Brit*) goûter *m* dînatoire ▸ **high-tech** n (*furniture, decor*) high-tech *m* ◊ adj *industry, facilities, technique* de pointe; the high-tech age l'ère des techniques de pointe ▸ **high-technology** n technologie *f* avancée *or* de pointe ◊ comp *device* d'une haute technicité; *sector* de pointe ▸ **high-tension** (*Elec*) n haute tension *f* ◊ adj à haute tension ▸ **high tide** marée *f* haute; at high tide à marée haute ▸ **high treason** haute trahison ▸ **high-up** adj *person, post* de haut rang, très haut placé ◊ n grosse légume*, huile* *f* ▸ **high voltage** adj, n haut voltage *(m)* ▸ **high water** = high tide (*see also* hell); high-water mark niveau *m* des hautes eaux ▸ **highway** *see* highway ▸ **high wire** corde *f* raide ▸ **high yellow**⁑ (*US pej*) mulâtre *m* clair, mulâtresse *f* claire.

-high [haɪ] adj ending in comps: knee-/shoulder-high jusqu'au genou/à l'épaule.

higher ['haɪəʳ] compar of high 1 adj *mathematics, animals, post* supérieur (*f* -eure). any number ~ than 6 tout nombre supérieur à 6; ~ education enseignement supérieur; (*Scol*) the ~ forms *or* classes les grandes classes; the ~ income brackets les tranches de revenu(s) supérieur(s). 2 adv plus haut; *see* high. 3 n (*Scot Scol*) = Higher Grade; *see* 4. 4 comp ▸ **Higher Grade** (*Scot Scol*) diplôme *m* de fin d'études secondaires, ≃ baccalauréat *m* ▸ **Higher National Certificate** (*Brit*) ≃ BTS *m*, ≃ DUT *m* ▸ **Higher National Diploma** (*Brit*) ≃ DUT *m* ▸ **higher-up*** (*senior person*) supérieur(e) *m(f)*.

highland ['haɪlənd] 1 npl: ~s région montagneuse, montagnes *fpl*; (*Brit Geog*) the H~s les Highlands *mpl*. 2 adj (*Brit*) H~ *scenery, air* des Highlands; *holiday* dans les Highlands; H~ fling *danse écossaise*; H~ games jeux *mpl* écossais.

highlander ['haɪləndəʳ] n montagnard *m*. (*Brit*) H~ natif *m*, -ive *f* des Highlands.

highlight ['haɪlaɪt] 1 n (*Art*) rehaut *m*. to have ~s put in one's hair se faire faire des mèches *or* des reflets; (*fig*) the ~ of the evening le clou de la soirée; the ~s of the match les instants les plus marquants du match. 2 vt a (*lit, fig*) souligner, mettre en lumière. his report ~ed the lack of new houses son rapport a mis en lumière *or* a souligné le manque de maisons nouvelles. b (*with highlighter pen*) surligner; (*on Computer*) mettre en évidence.

highlighter ['haɪˌlaɪtəʳ] n (*pen*) surligneur *m*; (*for hair*) produit *m* éclaircissant.

highly ['haɪlɪ] adv très, fort, hautement, extrêmement; *recommend* chaudement. ~ interesting fort *or* très intéressant; ~ coloured (*lit*) haut en couleur; (*fig*) *description etc* exagéré, enjolivé; ~ paid *person, job* très bien payé *or* rémunéré; *[person]* to be ~ paid être très bien payé *or* rémunéré, toucher un gros salaire *or* traitement; he pays me very ~ il me paye très bien; ~ placed official officiel *m* de haut rang, officiel haut placé, (*in administration, government circles*) haut fonctionnaire; ~-regarded très bien considéré, très estimé; ~ seasoned fortement assaisonné; (*Brit*) ~ strung nerveux, toujours tendu; to praise sb ~ chanter (haut) les louanges de qn; to speak/think ~ of sb/sth dire/penser beaucoup de bien de qn/qch.

highness ['haɪnɪs] n a His *or* Her/Your H~ Son/Votre Altesse *f*; *see* royal. b *[building etc]* hauteur *f*; *[wind]* violence *f*, force *f*; *[fever]* intensité *f*.

highway ['haɪweɪ] 1 n grande route, route nationale; (*also* public ~) voie publique. the king's *or* queen's ~ la voie publique; through the ~s and byways of Sussex par tous les chemins du Sussex. 2 comp ▸ **highway code** (*Brit*) code *m* de la route ▸ **highwayman** voleur *m or* bandit *m* de grand chemin ▸ **(state) highway patrol** (*US*) police *f* de la route *or* des autoroutes ▸ **highway robbery** banditisme *m* de grand chemin; (*fig*) it's highway robbery c'est du vol manifeste ▸ **Highways Department** (*Admin*) administration *f* des Ponts et Chaussées ▸ **highways engineer** ingénieur *m* des Ponts et Chaussées.

hijack ['haɪdʒæk] 1 vt détourner (*par la force*). 2 n détournement *m*.

hijacker ['haɪdʒækəʳ] n *[plane]* pirate *m* (de l'air); *[coach, train]* terroriste *mf*, gangster *m*; *[truck]* gangster *m*.

hijacking ['haɪdʒækɪŋ] n détournement *m*.

hike [haɪk] 1 n a (*walk etc*) excursion *f* à pied; (*shorter*) promenade *f* (à pied); (*Mil, Sport*) marche *f* à pied. to go on *or* for a ~ faire une excursion *or* une promenade *or* une randonnée à pied. b (*US: increase: of prices etc*) hausse *f*, augmentation *f*. 2 vi a aller *or* marcher à pied. we spent our holidays hiking in France nous avons passé nos vacances à excursionner à pied à travers la France; they go hiking a lot ils font beaucoup d'excursions à pied. b (*US: increase*) *[price etc]* augmenter. 3 vt (*increase*) augmenter.

▸**hike up** vt sep *skirt* remonter; *prices, amounts* augmenter.

hiker ['haɪkəʳ] n excursionniste *mf* (à pied), marcheur *m*.

hiking ['haɪkɪŋ] n excursions *fpl or* randonnées *fpl* (à pied). ~ boots chaussures *fpl* de randonnée *or* de marche.

hilarious [hɪ'lɛərɪəs] adj (*merry*) hilare; (*funny*) hilarant, désopilant, tordant*.

hilariously [hɪ'lɛərɪəslɪ] adv *act etc* de façon hilarante. ~ funny vraiment hilarant.

hilarity [hɪ'lærɪtɪ] n hilarité *f*. it caused a lot of ~ cela a déchaîné l'hilarité.

hill [hɪl] 1 n colline *f*; (*gen lower*) coteau *m*; (*rounded*) mamelon *m*; (*slope*) côte *f*, pente *f*; (*up*) montée *f*; (*down*) descente *f*. **he was going up the ~** il montait la colline; **up ~ and down dale, over ~ and dale** par monts et par vaux; **as old as the ~s** vieux (*f* vieille) comme les chemins *or* comme Hérode; (*fig: old*) **he's over the ~*** il se fait vieux; **this car is not good on ~s** cette voiture ne grimpe pas bien; *see* **ant, mole[1], up** *etc*.

2 comp ▶**hillbilly*** (*US: often pej*) péquenaud* *m* (*pej*), rustaud *m* (*pej*) (*montagnard du sud des U.S.A.*) ▶**hillbilly music** musique *f* folk *inv* (*originaire des montagnes du sud des U.S.A.*) ▶**hill climb** (*Sport*) course *f* de côtes ▶**hill climber** = **hill walker** ▶**hill climbing** = **hill walking** ▶**hillside** (flanc *m* de) coteau *m*; **on the hillside** à flanc de coteau ▶**hill start** (*Aut*) démarrage *m* en côte ▶**hill station** (*esp in India*) station *f* dans les collines ▶**hilltop: on the hilltop** en haut de *or* au sommet de la colline ▶**hill walker** (grand(e)) randonneur *m*, -euse *f* (de basse montagne) ▶**hill walking** (grandes) randonnées *fpl* de basse montagne.

hilliness ['hɪlɪnɪs] n caractère accidenté, vallonnement *m*.

hillock ['hɪlək] n petite colline, tertre *m*, butte *f*; (*rounded*) mamelon *m*.

hilly ['hɪlɪ] adj *country* vallonné, accidenté; *road* accidenté, à fortes côtes, montueux (*liter*).

hilt [hɪlt] n *[sword]* poignée *f*, garde *f*; *[dagger etc]* manche *m*; *[pistol]* crosse *f*. (*fig*) **(up) to the ~** *in trouble, in debt, involved* jusqu'au cou; *mortgaged* au maximum; **to back sb up to the ~** être derrière qn quoiqu'il arrive, soutenir qn à fond.

him, (*Rel*) **Him** [hɪm] pers pron a (*direct*) (*unstressed*) le; (*before vowel*) l'; (*stressed*) lui. **I see ~** je le vois; **I have seen ~** je l'ai vu; **I know HER but I've never seen HIM** je la connais, elle, mais lui je ne l'ai jamais vu. b (*indirect*) lui. **I give ~ the book** je lui donne le livre; **I'm speaking to ~** je lui parle, c'est à lui que je parle. c (*after prep etc*) lui. **I am thinking of ~** je pense à lui; **without ~** sans lui; **if I were ~** si j'étais lui, si j'étais à sa place; **it's ~** c'est lui; **younger than ~** plus jeune que lui. d celui. **to ~ who objects I would explain it thus** à celui qui n'est pas d'accord je l'expliquerais ainsi.

Himalayan [ˌhɪmə'leɪən] adj *mountains, foothills, region* de l'Himalaya; *valley* himalayen; *expedition* sur l'Himalaya.

Himalayas [ˌhɪmə'leɪəz] npl (montagnes *fpl* de l')Himalaya *m*.

himself [hɪm'self] pers pron (*reflexive: direct and indirect*) se; (*emphatic*) lui-même; (*after prep*) lui. **he has hurt ~** il s'est blessé; **he said to ~** il s'est dit; **he told me ~** il me l'a dit lui-même; **I saw the teacher ~** j'ai vu le professeur lui-même *or* en personne; **he kept 3 for ~** il s'en est réservé 3; **she asked him for a photo of ~** elle lui a demandé une de ses photos *or* une photo de lui; **(all) by ~** tout seul; **he is not ~ today** il n'est pas dans son état normal *or* dans son assiette* aujourd'hui.

hind[1] [haɪnd] n, pl **~s** *or* **~** (*Zool*) biche *f*.

hind[2] [haɪnd] adj postérieur (*f* -eure), de derrière. **~ legs, ~ feet** pattes *fpl* de derrière; **to get up on one's ~ legs*** se lever (*pour parler*); **she could** *or* **would talk the ~ leg(s) off a donkey*** c'est un vrai moulin à paroles.

hinder[1] ['haɪndə^r] adj compar of **hind[2]**.

hinder[2] ['hɪndə^r] vt (*obstruct, impede*) gêner, entraver (*sb* qn); (*oppose*) faire obstacle à (*sth* qch); (*delay*) retarder; (*prevent*) empêcher, arrêter, retenir (*sb from doing* qn de faire). **you are ~ing my work** tu m'empêches de travailler, tu me gênes dans mon travail.

Hindi ['hɪndɪ] n (*Ling*) hindi *m*.

hindmost ['haɪndməʊst] adv dernier, ultime, le plus en arrière. (*Prov*) **every man for himself and the devil take the ~** sauve qui peut.

hindquarters ['haɪndˌkwɔːtəz] npl arrière-train *m*, train *m* de derrière.

hindrance ['hɪndrəns] n gêne *f*, entrave *f*, obstacle *m*. **to be a ~ (to sb/sth)** gêner (qn/qch); **he is more of a ~ than a help** il gêne plus qu'il n'aide.

hindsight ['haɪndsaɪt] n sagesse rétrospective. **with the benefit of ~** avec du recul, rétrospectivement.

Hindu ['hɪnduː] 1 adj (*gen*) hindou; *religion* hindou, hindouiste. 2 n (*all senses*) Hindou(e) *m(f)*; (*Rel*) hindou(e) *m(f)*, hindouiste *mf*.

Hinduism ['hɪndʊˌɪzəm] n hindouisme *m*.

Hindustan [ˌhɪndʊ'stɑːn] n Hindoustan *m*.

Hindustani [ˌhɪndʊ'stɑːnɪ] 1 adj hindou. 2 n a Hindoustani(e) *m(f)*. b (*Ling*) hindoustani *m*.

hinge [hɪndʒ] 1 n *[door]* gond *m*, charnière *f*; *[box]* charnière; (*fig*) pivot *m*, charnière; (*stamp ~*) charnière. **the door came off its ~s** la porte est sortie de ses gonds. 2 comp ▶**hinge joint** (*Anat*) diarthrose *f*. 3 vt *door* mettre dans ses gonds; *box* mettre des charnières à. **~d lid** couvercle *m* à charnière(s); *[counter]* **~d flap** battant *m* relevable; (*Tech*) **~d girder** poutre articulée. 4 vi (*Tech*) pivoter (*on* sur); (*fig*) dépendre (*on* de). **everything ~s on his decision** tout dépend de sa décision.

hint [hɪnt] 1 n a allusion *f*, insinuation *f* (*pej*). **to drop** *or* **throw out** *or* **let fall a ~** faire une allusion; **to drop a ~ that ...** faire une allusion au fait que ...; **he dropped me a ~ that he would like an invitation** il m'a fait comprendre (par une allusion) qu'il aimerait être invité; **he dropped a gentle ~ about it** il y a fait une allusion discrète; **broad ~** allusion transparente *or* à peine voilée; **no need to drop ~s!** pas la peine* de faire des allusions! *or* des insinuations! (*pej*); **he knows how to take a ~** il comprend à demi-mot, il comprend les allusions; **he took the ~ and left at once** il a compris sans qu'on ait besoin de lui expliquer et est parti sur-le-champ; **I can take a ~** (ça va) j'ai compris; **he can't take a ~** il ne comprend pas vite; (*in guessing etc*) **give me a ~** donne-moi une indication; **he gave no ~ of his feelings** il n'a donné aucune indication sur ce qu'il ressentait, il n'a rien laissé transparaître de ses sentiments; **~s for travellers** conseils *mpl* aux voyageurs; **~s on maintenance** conseils d'entretien.

b (*trace*) nuance *f*, trace *f*, soupçon *m*. **a ~ of garlic** un soupçon d'ail; **there was not the slightest ~ of a dispute** il n'y a pas eu l'ombre d'une dispute; **there was a ~ of sadness about him** il avait un je ne sais quoi de mélancolique; **there's a ~ of spring in the air** il y a un petit air printanier.

2 vt insinuer, suggérer (*that* que). **he ~ed to me that he was unhappy** il m'a laissé entendre *or* comprendre qu'il était malheureux.

3 vi: **to ~ at sth** faire (une) allusion à qch; **what are you ~ing at?** qu'est-ce que vous voulez dire par là?; **are you ~ing at something?** c'est une allusion?

hinterland ['hɪntəlænd] n arrière-pays *m inv*.

hip[1] [hɪp] 1 n a (*Anat*) hanche *f*. **with one's hands on one's ~s** les mains sur les hanches; **to break one's ~** se casser le col du fémur.

b (*Archit*) arête *f* (*d'un toit*).

2 comp ▶**hip bath** bain *m* de siège ▶**hipbone** os *m* iliaque *or* de la hanche ▶**hip flask** flacon *m* plat (pour la poche), flasque *f* ▶**hip joint** articulation *f* coxo-fémorale *or* de la hanche ▶**hip measurement** = **hip size** ▶**hip pocket** poche *f* revolver ▶**hip replacement (operation)** pose *f* d'une prothèse de la hanche; **she's waiting for/she's had a hip replacement** elle attend/on lui a posé une prothèse de la hanche ▶**hip size** tour *m* de hanches; **what is her hip size?** quel est son tour de hanches?, combien fait-elle de tour de hanches?

hip[2] [hɪp] n (*Bot*) fruit *m* d'églantier *or* de rosier, gratte-cul *m*, cynorrhodon *m*.

hip[3] [hɪp] excl: **~ ~ hurrah!** hip hip hip hourra!

hip[4]⁑ [hɪp] 1 adj (*up-to-date*) dans le vent*, à la page. 2 vt (*US*) mettre au courant *or* au parfum⁑.

hipped⁑ [hɪpt] adj (*interested*) mordu*, dingue* (*on* de); (*annoyed*) vexé. (*depressed*) **to be ~** avoir le cafard*.

-hipped [hɪpt] adj ending in comps: **broad-hipped** large de hanches.

hippie* ['hɪpɪ] adj, n hippie *(mf)*. **ageing ~** baba *m* cool*.

hippo* ['hɪpəʊ] n abbr of **hippopotamus**.

Hippocrates [hɪ'pɒkrəˌtiːz] n Hippocrate *m*.

Hippocratic [ˌhɪpəʊ'krætɪk] adj: **the ~ oath** le serment d'Hippocrate.

hippodrome ['hɪpədrəʊm] n hippodrome *m*.

Hippolytus [hɪ'pɒlɪtəs] n Hippolyte *m*.

hippopotamus [ˌhɪpə'pɒtəməs] n, pl **~es** *or* **hippopotami** [ˌhɪpə'pɒtəmaɪ] hippopotame *m*.

hippy[1]* ['hɪpɪ] = **hippie***.

hippy[2]* ['hɪpɪ] adj aux hanches larges, large de hanches.

hipster ['hɪpstə^r] n a (*Brit*) **~s** pantalon *m* taille basse; **~ skirt** jupe *f* taille basse. b (*US **) jeune homme branché⁑ *or* dans le vent (*1940-50*).

hire ['haɪə^r] 1 n a (*NonC: act of hiring*) *[car, clothes, hall, boat]* location *f*. **for ~** à louer; (*on taxi*) "libre"; **on ~** en location; **to let (out) sth on ~** louer qch; **car ~** location de voiture.

b (*money*) *[person]* paye *f*; *[car, hall etc]* prix *m* de (la) location.

2 comp ▶**hire car** (*Brit*) voiture *f* de location ▶**hire charges** frais *mpl or* droits *mpl* de location, prix *m* de (la) location ▶**hire purchase** (*Brit*) achat *m or* vente *f* à crédit, achat *or* vente à tempérament; **on hire purchase** à crédit ▶**hire purchase agreement** contrat *m* de crédit.

3 vt *thing,* (*Brit*) *car* louer; *person* engager, embaucher (*esp Ind*). **~d man** ouvrier *m* à la saison *or* à la journée; **~d car** voiture louée *or* de location; **~d killer** tueur *m* à gages.

▶**hire away** vt sep *workers* débaucher (de chez un autre employeur).

▶**hire out** vt sep *car, tools* louer, donner en location. (*US*) **he hires himself out as a gardener** il fait des journées (*or* des heures) de jardinier.

hireling ['haɪəlɪŋ] n (*pej*) larbin *m* (*pej*), laquais *m* (*pej*).

Hiroshima [ˌhɪrɒ'ʃiːmə] n Hiroshima.

hirsute ['hɜːsjuːt] adj hirsute, velu, poilu.

his [hɪz] 1 poss adj son, sa, ses. **~ book** son livre; **~ table** sa table; **~ friend** son ami(e); **~ clothes** ses vêtements; **HIS book** son livre à lui; **he has broken ~ leg** il s'est cassé la jambe.

2 poss pron le sien, la sienne, les siens, les siennes. **my hands are clean, ~ are dirty** mes mains sont propres, les siennes sont sales; **~ is a specialized department** sa section est une section spécialisée; **this book is ~** ce livre est à lui, ce livre est le sien; **this poem is ~** ce poème est de lui; **the house became ~** la maison est devenue la sienne; **it is not ~ to decide** ce n'est pas à lui de décider, il ne lui appartient pas de décider; **a friend of ~** un de ses amis (à lui); **it's no fault of ~** ce n'est pas de sa faute (à lui); **no advice of ~ could prevent her** aucun conseil de sa part ne pouvait l'empêcher; (*pej*) **that car of ~** sa fichue*

voiture; (*pej*) **that stupid son of ~** son idiot de fils; (*pej*) **that temper of ~** son sale caractère.

Hispanic [hɪˈspænɪk] 1 adj (*gen*) *culture etc* hispanique; (*South American*) latino-américain. 2 n (*US*) Latino-américain(e) *m(f)*, Hispano-américain(e) *m(f)*.

Hispano... [hɪˈspænəʊ] pref hispano-.

hiss [hɪs] 1 vi *[person, snake]* siffler; *[gas, steam]* chuinter, siffler. 2 vt *actor, speaker* siffler. **"come here," he ~ed** "viens ici", siffla-t-il. 3 n sifflement *m*. (*Theat etc*) **~es** sifflet(s) *m(pl)*.

histogram [ˈhɪstəgræm] n histogramme *m*.

histologist [hɪˈstɒlədʒɪst] n histologiste *mf*.

histology [hɪˈstɒlədʒɪ] n histologie *f*.

historian [hɪˈstɔːrɪən] n historien(ne) *m(f)*.

historic [hɪˈstɒrɪk] adj (*gen*) historique; (*important*) historique, qui fait date.

historical [hɪˈstɒrɪkəl] adj (*gen*) historique. (*Jur etc*) **the ~ background to the case** le rappel historique *or* l'historique *m* de l'affaire; **place of ~ interest** monument *m or* site *m* historique; **~ landmark** événement *m* historique marquant, jalon *m* dans l'histoire; **~ linguistics** linguistique *f* diachronique.

historically [hɪˈstɒrɪkəlɪ] adv (*gen*) du point de vue historique, historiquement; (*in the past*) dans *or* par le passé.

historiography [ˌhɪstɒrɪˈɒgrəfɪ] n historiographie *f*.

history [ˈhɪstərɪ] n a (*NonC*) histoire *f*. **to make ~** être historique; **he will go down in ~ for what he did** il entrera dans l'histoire pour ce qu'il a fait; (*fig*) *[event, day, decision]* **it will go down in ~** ce sera historique; (*fig*) **that's all (ancient) ~** c'est de l'histoire ancienne (tout cela); *see* **natural**. b **I don't know the ~ of this necklace** je ne connais pas l'histoire de ce collier; **the patient has a ~ of psychiatric disorders** le patient a dans son passé (médical) des désordres psychiatriques; **what is his medical ~?** quel est son passé médical?; *see* **case**[1].

histrionic [ˌhɪstrɪˈɒnɪk] adj théâtral; (*pej*) histrionique, de cabotin (*pej*). **~ ability** talent *m* dramatique.

histrionics [ˌhɪstrɪˈɒnɪks] npl art *m* dramatique. (*pej*) **to indulge in ~** prendre des airs dramatiques, cabotiner (*pej*); (*pej*) **I'm tired of his ~** j'en ai assez de ses airs dramatiques *or* de son cinéma* (*fig*).

hit [hɪt] (vb: pret, ptp **hit**) 1 n a (*stroke, blow*) coup *m*; (*Baseball, Cricket etc*) coup de batte *etc*; (*Tennis*) coup de raquette. (*fig*) **that's a ~ at me** ça c'est pour moi, c'est une pierre dans mon jardin; **he made a ~ at the government** il a attaqué le gouvernement; *see* **free**.

b (*successful stroke etc*) coup réussi, beau coup; (*Archery*) coup dans le mille; (*with bullet, shell etc*) tir réussi; (*Fencing*) touche *f*; (*good guess*) coup dans le mille (*fig*). (*gen*) **3 ~s and 3 misses** 3 succès et 3 échecs; (*Sport*) **direct ~** coup (en plein) dans le mille; *see* **score**.

c (*success*) coup réussi, beau coup; (*Theat*) (gros) succès *m*; (*song*) chanson *f* à succès, tube‡ *m*. **to make a ~ of sth*** réussir (pleinement) qch; **to make a ~ with sb*** faire une grosse impression sur qn, avoir un gros succès avec qn; **the play/song was a big ~** la pièce/chanson a eu un énorme succès.

2 comp ▸**hit-and-miss** = **hit-or-miss** ▸**hit-and-run accident** délit *m* de fuite ▸**hit-and-run driver** chauffard* *m* (coupable du délit de fuite) ▸**hit-and-run raid** (*Mil*) raid *m* éclair *inv* ▸**hit-and-run strike** grève *f* éclair ▸**hit list** liste *f* noire; (*fig*) **he's on her hit list** elle l'a dans le collimateur, il est sur sa liste noire ▸**hitman‡** tueur *m* ▸**hit-or-miss** adv au petit bonheur (la chance), un peu n'importe comment ◊ adj *work* fait au petit bonheur (la chance); *attitude* désinvolte; *technique* empirique; **it's a hit-or-miss affair** c'est une question de chance; **the way she painted the room was rather hit-or-miss** elle a peint la pièce un peu n'importe comment; **it was all rather hit-or-miss** tout se passait plutôt au petit bonheur (la chance), tout était à la va-comme-je-te-pousse ▸**hit parade** hit parade *m* ▸**hit show** (*Theat*) revue *f* à succès ▸**hit song** chanson *f* à succès, tube‡ *m* ▸**hit squad*** commando *m* (de tueurs).

3 vt a (*strike*) frapper, taper sur; (*knock against*) heurter, cogner; (*reach*) atteindre; (*Billiards, Fencing*) toucher; (*Typ, Comput etc*) *key* appuyer sur; (*fig: hurt, annoy*) affecter, blesser, piquer. **he ~ his brother** il a frappé son frère; **he ~ me!** il m'a frappé!, il m'a tapé dessus!; **his father used to ~ him** son père le battait; **to ~ sb where it hurts** (*lit: in fight*) frapper qn là où ça fait mal; (*fig: in argument, business rivalry etc*) toucher qn à son point faible *or* névralgique; **to ~ sb a blow** porter *or* donner *or* envoyer *or* flanquer* un coup à qn; (*fig*) **to ~ sb when he's (*or* she's) down** frapper qn à terre; **to ~ one's head/arm against sth** se cogner *or* se heurter la tête/le bras contre qch; **his head ~ the pavement, he ~ his head on the pavement** sa tête a donné contre *or* porté contre *or* heurté le trottoir; **the stone ~ the window** la pierre atteignit la fenêtre; **he was ~ by a stone** il fut atteint par une pierre, il reçut une pierre; (*fig*) **it ~s you in the eye** cela (vous) saute aux yeux; **he ~ the nail with a hammer** il a tapé sur le clou avec un marteau; (*fig*) **to ~ the nail on the head** mettre le doigt dessus, faire mouche; (*fig*) **to ~ the mark** atteindre le *or* son but; (*fig*) **that ~ home!** le coup a porté!; (*Shooting etc*) **you couldn't ~ an elephant!** tu raterais (même) un éléphant!; **the president was ~ by 3 bullets** le président reçut 3 balles; **the house was ~ by a bomb** la maison fut atteinte par *or* reçut une bombe; **my plane had been ~** mon avion avait été touché; (*fig*) **he was hard ~ by his losses** ses pertes l'ont durement touché *or* atteint; (*fig*) **the crops were ~ by the rain** la pluie a causé des dégâts aux récoltes; (*fig*) **production was ~ by the strike** la production a été atteinte *or* touchée par la grève; (*fig*) **the public was hardest ~ by the strike** c'est le public qui a été le plus atteint par la grève; (*fig*) **the rise in prices will ~ the poorest families first** la hausse des prix affectera *or* touchera d'abord les familles les plus pauvres.

b (*fig*) *[news, story]* **to ~ the papers** être à la une* des journaux, faire les gros titres des journaux; **what will happen when the story ~s the front page?** que se passera-t-il quand on lira cette histoire en première page des journaux?; (*realization*) **then it ~ me*** alors j'ai réalisé* d'un seul coup! *or* brusquement!; **you've ~ it!*** ça y est* tu as trouvé!; **~ it!‡** fiche le camp!*; **to ~ the bottle*** (se mettre à) picoler*; (*fig*) **to ~ the ceiling*** *or* **the roof*** sortir de ses gonds; **to ~ the deck‡** (*start work*) se mettre au boulot*; (*fall*) s'aplatir au sol; **to ~ the dirt‡** s'aplatir au sol; (*fig*) **to ~ the hay‡** *or* **the sack‡** se pieuter‡; **to ~ the road*** *or* **the trail*** se mettre en route, mettre les voiles*; **this car can ~* 160 km/h** cette voiture fait du 160 (km) à l'heure; **the troops ~ the beach at dawn*** les troupes ont débarqué sur la plage à l'aube; **when will Jim ~ town?*** quand est-ce que Jim va débarquer en ville?; (*fig*) **to ~ the shops*** sortir en magasin; (*fig*) *[new publication]* **to ~ the bookshops** *or* (*US*) **bookstores** sortir en librairie; (*US fig*) **it ~s the spot** c'est justement ce qu'il me faut!, ça me redonne le moral!; (*US Cards*) **he ~ me with a six of spades*** il m'a donné un six de pique; (*US fig*) **to ~ sb for 10 dollars‡** taper‡ qn de 10 dollars; (*fig*) **to ~ sb for six*** enfoncer* qn; *see* **headline, high, skid** *etc*.

c (*collide with*) entrer en collision avec, heurter, rentrer dans*.

d (*find*) trouver, tomber sur; *problems, difficulties* rencontrer. **at last we ~ the right road** nous sommes tombés enfin sur la bonne route.

4 vi (*collide*) se heurter, se cogner (*against* à, contre).

▸**hit back** 1 vi (*lit*) frapper en retour; (*fig*) riposter. (*fig*) **to hit back at sb** se venger de qn. 2 vt sep: **to hit sb back** frapper qn en retour.

▸**hit off** vt sep a **to hit off a likeness** saisir une ressemblance; **he hit him off beautifully** il l'a imité à la perfection. b **to hit it off with sb** bien s'entendre avec qn; **they hit it off well together** ils s'entendent très bien *or* comme larrons en foire; **they just don't hit it off** ils n'arrivent pas à s'entendre, entre eux ça n'accroche pas*.

▸**hit out at** vt fus (*lit*) envoyer un coup à; (*fig*) attaquer, lancer une attaque contre.

▸**hit (up)on** vt fus tomber sur, trouver.

hitch [hɪtʃ] 1 n a **to give sth a ~ (up)** remonter qch (d'une saccade).

b (*any knot*) nœud *m*; (*specific knot*) deux demi-clefs *fpl*.

c (*fig: obstacle*) anicroche *f*, contretemps *m*, os* *m*. **without a ~** sans accroc *or* anicroche; **there's been a ~** il y a eu une anicroche *or* un os*; **there was some ~ in their plans** il y a eu une anicroche *or* un contretemps quelconque dans leurs projets; **the ~ is that ...** l'ennui c'est que ...; *see* **technical**.

d (*US pej *: in army or in jail etc*) période passée dans l'armée (*or* en prison *etc*).

2 comp ▸**hitch-hike** faire du stop* *or* de l'auto-stop; **they hitch-hiked to Paris** ils sont allés à Paris en stop, ils ont fait du stop* *or* de l'auto-stop jusqu'à Paris ▸**hitch-hiker** auto-stoppeur *m*, -euse *f*, stoppeur* *m*, -euse* *f* ▸**hitch-hiking** auto-stop *m*, stop* *m*.

3 vt a (*also* **~ up**) remonter (d'une saccade).

b (*fasten*) accrocher, attacher, fixer; (*Naut*) amarrer. **to get ~ed‡** se marier.

c (*) **to ~ a lift** *or* **a ride to Paris** faire du stop* jusqu'à Paris; **I ~ed a lift to Paris with my father** je me suis fait emmener en voiture jusqu'à Paris par mon père.

4 vi (*) = **hitch-hike**; *see* **2**.

▸**hitch up** vt sep a *horses, oxen* atteler (*to* à). b *trousers* remonter (d'une saccade).

hi-tech [ˈhaɪˈtek] = **high-tech**; *see* **high**.

hither [ˈhɪðəʳ] 1 adv (††) ici. (*not* ††) **~ and thither** çà et là; (†† *or hum*) **come ~** venez çà (†† *or hum*); *see also* **come**. 2 adj (††) de ce côté-ci. 3 comp ▸**hitherto** jusqu'ici.

Hitler [ˈhɪtləʳ] n Hitler *m*.

Hitlerian [hɪtˈlɪərɪən] adj hitlérien.

Hitlerism [ˈhɪtlərɪzəm] n hitlérisme *m*.

Hittites [ˈhɪtaɪts] npl Hittites *mpl*.

HIV [ˌeɪtʃaɪˈviː] n (*Med*) (abbr of **human immunodeficiency virus**) HIV *m*, (*less common*) VIH *m*. **~-positive/-negative** séropositif/séronégatif; **~ virus** virus *m* HIV.

hive [haɪv] 1 n (*place, also fig*) ruche *f*; (*bees in it*) essaim *m*. (*fig*) **a ~ of industry** une vraie ruche. 2 vt mettre dans une ruche. 3 vi entrer à la ruche.

▸**hive off** (*Brit*) 1 vi a (*separate*) se séparer (*from* de), essaimer. b (‡: *rush off*) filer*, se tirer‡. 2 vt sep séparer (*from* de). **they hived off the infant school to a different building** ils ont décentralisé la maternelle pour l'installer dans un autre bâtiment; **this subsidiary will be hived off** cette filiale sera essaimée *or* deviendra indépendante; **to hive off state-owned companies to the private sector** rendre indépendantes des sociétés nationales pour qu'elles aillent dans le secteur privé.

hives [haɪvz] npl (*Med*) urticaire *f*.

hiya‡ ['haɪjə] excl salut!*

hl (abbr of **hectolitre(s)**) hl.

HM [eɪtʃ'em] n (abbr of **His** *or* **Her Majesty**) S.M., Sa Majesté.

HMG [ˌeɪtʃem'dʒiː] n (*Brit*) (abbr of **His** *or* **Her Majesty's Government**) *see* **majesty**.

HMI [ˌeɪtʃem'aɪ] n (*Brit Educ*) (abbr of **His** *or* **Her Majesty's Inspector**) ≃ inspecteur *m*, -trice *f* général(e) des lycées et collèges.

HMS [ˌeɪtʃem'es] n (*Brit*) (abbr of **His** *or* **Her Majesty's Ship**) *see* **ship**.

HMSO [ˌeɪtʃemes'əʊ] n (*Brit*) (abbr of **His** *or* **Her Majesty's Stationery Office**) *see* **stationery**.

HNC [ˌeɪtʃen'siː] n (*Brit Educ*) (abbr of **Higher National Certificate**) *see* **higher**.

HND [ˌeɪtʃen'diː] n (*Brit Educ*) (abbr of **Higher National Diploma**) *see* **higher**.

ho [həʊ] excl: ~ ~ ah ah (ah)!

hoard [hɔːd] 1 n réserves *fpl*, provisions *fpl*, stock *m* (*pej*); (*treasure*) trésor *m*. **a ~ (of money)** un trésor, un magot; **a ~ of food** des provisions, des réserves; **a squirrel's ~ of nuts** les réserves *or* provisions de noisettes d'un écureuil. 2 vt (*also* **~ up**) *food etc* amasser, mettre en réserve, stocker (*pej*); *money* accumuler, amasser.

hoarder ['hɔːdəʳ] n: **to be a ~** ne rien jeter.

hoarding¹ ['hɔːdɪŋ] n (*act of saving*) entassement *m*, accumulation *f*; *[capital]* thésaurisation *f*.

hoarding² ['hɔːdɪŋ] n (*Brit*) (*fence*) palissade *f*; (*for advertisements*) panneau *m* d'affichage *or* publicitaire.

hoarfrost ['hɔːˌfrɒst] n gelée blanche, givre *m*.

hoarse [hɔːs] adj *person* enroué; *voice* rauque, enroué. **to be ~** avoir la voix prise *or* enrouée *or* rauque, être enroué; **he shouted himself ~** il a tant crié qu'il a fini par s'enrouer.

hoarsely ['hɔːslɪ] adv d'une voix rauque *or* enrouée.

hoarseness ['hɔːsnɪs] n enrouement *m*.

hoary ['hɔːrɪ] adj *hair* blanchi, blanc neigeux *inv*; *person* (*lit: also* **~-headed**) chenu; (*fig*) vénérable; (*Bot*) couvert de duvet blanc. **a ~ old joke** une blague éculée.

hoax [həʊks] 1 n canular *m*. **to play a ~ on sb** monter *or* faire un canular à qn. 2 vt faire *or* monter un canular à. **we were completely ~ed** on nous a eus*.

hob [hɒb] n (*by fireplace*) plaque *f* (de foyer) (*où la bouilloire etc est tenue au chaud*); (*on old-fashioned cooker*) rond *m*; (*on modern cooker*) plaque (chauffante).

hobble ['hɒbl] 1 vi clopiner, boitiller. **to ~ along** aller clopin-clopant; **to ~ in/out** *etc* entrer/sortir *etc* en clopinant. 2 vt *horse* entraver. 3 n (*for horses*) entrave *f*. 4 comp ►**hobble skirt** jupe entravée.

hobbledehoy [ˌhɒbldɪ'hɔɪ] n grand dadais *or* niais.

hobby ['hɒbɪ] 1 n passe-temps *inv* favori, hobby *m*. **his ~ is sailing** son passe-temps favori *or* son hobby (c')est la voile; **he began to paint as a ~** il a commencé la peinture à titre de passe-temps; **he's got several hobbies** il a plusieurs passe-temps. 2 comp ►**hobby-horse** (*toy*) tête *f* de cheval (*sur un manche*); (*rocking horse*) cheval *m* à bascule; (*fig*) dada *m*; (*fig*) **he's off on his hobby-horse** le voilà reparti (sur son dada).

hobbyist ['hɒbɪɪst] n (*US*) amateur *m*. **a photo ~** un photographe amateur.

hobgoblin ['hɒbˌgɒblɪn] n (*elf*) lutin *m*; (*fig: bugbear*) croque-mitaine *m*.

hobnail ['hɒbneɪl] n caboche *f*, clou *m*. **~(ed) boots** souliers à clous *or* cloutés *or* ferrés.

hobnob ['hɒbnɒb] vi: **to ~ with** frayer avec.

hobo ['həʊbəʊ] n, pl **~(e)s** (*US*) a (*tramp*) (*in town*) clochard *m*, vagabond *m*; (*in country*) chemineau *m*, vagabond. b (*migratory worker*) saisonnier *m*.

Hobson's choice ['hɒbsənz'tʃɔɪs] n (*Brit*) **it's ~** c'est un choix qui n'en est pas un, ce n'est un choix qu'en apparence.

Ho Chi Minh City ['həʊ'tʃiː'mɪn'sɪtɪ] n Hô Chi Minh-Ville.

hock¹ [hɒk] n *[animal]* jarret *m*; *[human]* partie postérieure du genou; (*Culin*) jarret (de bœuf).

hock² [hɒk] n (*Brit: wine*) vin *m* du Rhin.

hock³‡ [hɒk] 1 vt (*pawn*) mettre au clou*. 2 n: **in ~** *object* au clou*, au mont-de-piété; *person* endetté.

hockey ['hɒkɪ] 1 n a (*Brit: also US* **field ~**) hockey *m*. b (*US: also Brit* **ice ~**) hockey *m* sur glace. 2 comp *match, pitch* de hockey ►**hockey player** hockeyeur *m*, -euse *f*; (*Can*) joueur *m*, -euse *f* de hockey ►**hockey stick** crosse *f* de hockey; (*Can*) hockey *m*.

hocus-pocus ['həʊkəs'pəʊkəs] n (*trickery*) supercherie *f*, attrape *f*; (*conjuring trick*) tour *m* de passe-passe; (*talk*) charabia* *m*, galimatias *m*.

hod [hɒd] n (*for coal*) seau *m* à charbon; (*for bricks, mortar*) oiseau *m*, hotte *f*.

hodgepodge ['hɒdʒpɒdʒ] n = **hotchpotch**.

hoe [həʊ] 1 n houe *f*, binette *f*. 2 vt *ground* biner; *vegetables, weeds* sarcler. 3 comp ►**hoedown** (*US*) danse *f* (de village).

hog [hɒg] 1 n a (*Zool*) cochon *m*, porc *m*; (*castrated*) verrat châtré. **he's a greedy ~** c'est un vrai goinfre, il se goinfre* comme un pourceau; *see* **high, road, whole**.

b (*US *: motorbike*) moto* *f*.

2 vt a (*) *food* se goinfrer* de; (*take selfishly*) *best chair etc* accaparer, monopoliser. **don't ~ all the sweets** ne garde pas tous les bonbons pour toi; **he was ~ging the only armchair** il accaparait *or* monopolisait le seul fauteuil; **to ~ the credit** s'attribuer tout le mérite.

b **they were ~ging it‡ in a dirty little room** ils vivaient comme des porcs dans un petit galetas.

3 comp ►**hogshead** barrique *f* ►**hogtie** (*US*) lier par les pieds et les poings; (*fig*) entraver ►**hogwash** (*pigswill*) eaux grasses (*pour nourrir les porcs*); (‡: *nonsense*) foutaises‡ *fpl*.

Hogarthian [həʊ'gɑːθɪən] adj (à la manière) de Hogarth.

Hogmanay [ˌhɒgmə'neɪ] n (*Scot*) la Saint-Sylvestre, le réveillon du jour de l'an.

hoi polloi [ˌhɔɪpə'lɔɪ] n (*pej*) **the ~** les gens *mpl* du commun, le commun (*pej*), la plèbe (*pej*).

hoist [hɔɪst] 1 vt hisser, remonter; *sails, flag* hisser. (*fig*) **~ with his own petard** pris à son propre piège. 2 n a (*equipment*) appareil *m* de levage, palan *m*; (*winch*) treuil *m*; (*crane*) grue *f*; (*for goods*) monte-charge *m inv*; (*made of rope*) corde *f*, palan. b **to give sth a ~ (up)** hisser *or* remonter qch.

hoity-toity ['hɔɪtɪ'tɔɪtɪ] 1 adj (*arrogant*) prétentieux, qui se donne de grands airs, bêcheur* (*f* -euse); (*touchy*) susceptible. 2 excl (†) taratata!†.

hoke‡ [həʊk] vt (*US*) **to ~ up a movie** forcer les effets (sentimentaux ou comiques) d'un film.

hokey-cokey ['həʊkɪ'kəʊkɪ] n hokey-cokey *m* (*chant et danse de groupe*).

hokum‡ ['həʊkəm] n (*US*) (*nonsense*) foutaises‡ *fpl*; (*sentimentality*) blablabla* sentimental, niaiseries *fpl*; (*US: Cine, Theat*) gros effets (sentimentaux *or* comiques).

hold [həʊld] (vb: pret, ptp **held**) 1 n a (*NonC*) prise *f*, étreinte *f*; (*fig*) prise, empire *m*, influence *f* (*over sb* sur qn). **to catch** *or* **lay** *or* **seize ~ of, to get** *or* **take (a) ~ of** saisir, se saisir de, s'emparer de; **catch ~!, take ~!** tiens!, attrape!; **he got** *or* **caught ~ of her arm** il lui a saisi le bras; (*fig*) **we're trying to get ~ of him** nous essayons de le contacter *or* joindre; **can you get** *or* **lay ~ of a piece of wire?** est-ce que tu peux dénicher* *or* te procurer un morceau de fil de fer?; **where did you get ~ of that hat?** où as-tu été trouver *or* dénicher* ce chapeau?; **where did you get ~ of that idea?** où as-tu été pêcher* cette idée?; (*fig*) **to get (a) ~ of o.s.** se maîtriser, se contrôler; **get (a) ~ of yourself!** ressaisis-toi!, ne te laisse pas aller!; **to have ~ of** tenir; **I've got a good** *or* **firm ~ on the rope** je tiens bien *or* bon la corde; **to keep ~ of** tenir fermement, ne pas lâcher; **keep ~ of the idea that ...** dites-vous bien que ...; (*fig*) **to have a ~ over sb** avoir barre *or* avoir prise sur qn; **I don't know what kind of a ~ he has over them but they all obey him** je ne sais pas quel pouvoir *or* quelle prise il a sur eux mais ils lui obéissent; (*fig: of custom, practice*) **to take ~** prendre, se répondre; *phone call, order etc* **on ~** en attente; (*US*) **to put sb/sth on ~** mettre qn/qch en attente.

b (*gen, also Climbing*) prise *f*. **the rock offered him few ~s** le rocher lui offrait peu de prises; *see* **foot, hand, press** *etc*.

c (*Wrestling*) prise *f*. (*fig*) **no ~s barred*** tous les coups sont permis.

d (*Naut*) cale *f*; (*Aviat*) soute *f*.

2 comp ►**holdall** (*Brit*) fourre-tout *m inv* ►**holdup** (*robbery*) hold-up *m inv*, attaque *f* à main armée; (*Brit*) (*delay*) retard *m*; (*in traffic*) embouteillage *m*, bouchon *m*; **there's been a holdup in ...** il y a eu un retard dans ...; **a big holdup owing to roadworks** un gros bouchon dû aux travaux.

3 vt a (*grasp, carry*) tenir. **she was ~ing a book in her hand** elle tenait un livre à la main; **she was ~ing a coin in her hand** elle tenait une pièce de monnaie dans la main; **~ this for a moment** tiens *or* prends ça un moment; (*lit, fig*) **she was ~ing her sister's hand** elle tenait la main de sa sœur; **they were ~ing hands** ils se tenaient par la main, ils s'étaient donné la main; **he held my arm** il me tenait le bras; **to ~ one's sides with laughter** se tenir les côtes de rire; **the dog held the stick in his mouth** le chien tenait le bâton dans sa gueule; **she held him tight for a moment** elle l'a serré très fort pendant un instant; **~ him tight or he'll fall** tenez-le bien (pour) qu'il ne tombe (*subj*) pas; **to ~ fast** tenir bien *or* bon *or* solidement; **the ladder won't ~ you** *or* **your weight** l'échelle ne supportera pas ton poids; **the nails ~ the carpet in place** les clous maintiennent la moquette en place; **he ~s the key to the mystery** il détient la clef du mystère; **to ~ o.s. upright** se tenir droit; (*lit, fig*) **to ~ one's head high** porter la tête haute.

b (*fig*) **to ~ o.s. ready** se tenir prêt; **he held us all spellbound** il nous tenait tous sous son charme; **can he ~ an audience?** est-ce qu'il sait tenir un auditoire?; **to ~ sb's attention/interest** retenir l'attention/ l'intérêt de qn; **to ~ sth against sb** en vouloir à qn de qch; **I don't ~ it against him** je ne lui en veux pas; **he was left ~ing the baby** *or* (*US*) **the bag** l'affaire lui est restée sur les bras, tout est retombé sur sa tête; **to ~ one's breath** retenir son souffle; **he can't ~ a candle to his brother** il n'arrive pas à la cheville de son frère; (*Naut*) **to ~ course** tenir le cap, continuer à faire route (*for* vers); **to ~ one's ground** tenir bon, tenir ferme; (*Telec*) **~ the line!** ne quittez pas!; (*Telec*) **I've been ~ing the line for several minutes** cela fait plusieurs minutes que je suis en ligne *or* que j'attends; **he can ~ his liquor!** il sait boire!; **to ~ in mind** garder en mémoire; (*Mus*) **to ~ a note** tenir une note; **to ~ an opinion** avoir une opinion; **to ~ one's own** (*gen*) tenir bon, tenir ferme; *[invalid]* se maintenir; **he can ~ his own with anybody** il ne s'en laisse pas remontrer; **he can ~ his own in German** il se débrouille très bien en allemand; **this car ~s the road well** cette voiture tient bien la route; (*Tennis*) **to ~ one's serve** défendre son service; **he held his tongue about it** il a tenu sa langue; **~ your tongue!** taisez-vous!

c *meeting, election, session, debate, conversation etc* tenir; (*Scol*) *examination* organiser. **the exhibition is always held here** l'exposition se tient toujours *or* a toujours lieu ici; **to ~ a check** faire un contrôle; (*Rel*) *[priest etc]* **to ~ a service** célébrer un office; **they are ~ing a service to mark the day when ...** il est prévu une cérémonie religieuse pour commémorer le jour où ...; *[employer etc]* **to ~ an interview** recevoir des candidats; **they are ~ing the interviews in London** ils organisent les entretiens à Londres; **when will the interviews be held?** quand auront lieu les entretiens?

d (*contain*) contenir. **this box will ~ all my books** cette boîte contiendra tous mes livres; **this bottle ~s one litre** cette bouteille contient un litre; **this room ~s 20 people** 20 personnes peuvent tenir dans cette salle; **what the future ~s (for him)** ce que l'avenir (lui) réserve; **to ~ no terrors for sb** ne pas faire peur du tout à qn; *see* **water** *etc.*

e (*believe, maintain*) tenir, maintenir, considérer, estimer, juger. **he ~s that matter does not exist** il maintient *or* considère que la matière n'existe pas; **to ~ sth to be true** considérer qch comme vrai; **this is held to be true** ceci passe pour vrai; **to ~ in high esteem** tenir en haute estime; (*Jur*) **it was held by the judge that** le juge a statué que; **the law ~s that ...** la loi prévoit *or* stipule que ...; **to ~ sb responsible for sth** tenir qn pour *or* considérer qn responsable de qch; **to ~ sb guilty** considérer qn coupable; **to ~ sb dear** aimer beaucoup qn; **all that he ~s dear** tout ce qui lui est cher.

f (*keep back, restrain*) *person* tenir, retenir. **I will ~ the money until ...** je garderai l'argent jusqu'à ce que ... + *subj*; **to ~ a train** empêcher un train de partir; **~ the letter until ...** n'envoyez pas la lettre avant que ... + *subj*; (*US: on letters*) **"~ for arrival"** "ne pas faire suivre"; **the police held him for 2 days** la police l'a gardé (à vue) pendant 2 jours; **there's no ~ing him** il n'y a pas moyen de le (re)tenir; (*fig*) **~ your horses!*** arrêtez!, minute!*; **~ it!*** (*stay still*) restez là!, ne bougez plus!; (*stop: also* **~ everything!***) arrêtez!, ne faites plus rien!; *see* **fire**.

g (*possess*) *ticket, card, permit* avoir, posséder; (*Mil*) tenir; *post, position* avoir, occuper; (*Fin*) *shares* détenir; (*Sport*) *record* détenir; (*Rel*) *living* jouir de. (*Parl*) **to ~ office** avoir *or* tenir un portefeuille; **he ~s the post of headmaster** il occupe le poste de directeur; **he ~s the record for the long jump** il détient le record du saut en longueur; **Spain held vast territories in South America** l'Espagne possédait de vastes territoires en Amérique du Sud; **the army held the castle against the enemy** l'armée a tenu le château fort malgré les attaques de l'ennemi; (*fig*) **to ~ the floor** garder la parole; (*fig*) **to ~ the fort** garder la maison, monter la garde (*hum*), assurer la permanence; (*fig*) **to ~ the stage** tenir le devant de la scène.

h (*keep, have charge of*) conserver, détenir. **the bank ~s these bills** la banque conserve ces effets; **my lawyer ~s these documents** mon avocat détient ces documents.

4 vi *[rope, nail etc]* tenir (bon), être solide; *[weather]* continuer, se maintenir; *[statement, argument]* (*also* **~ good**) valoir. **that objection does not ~ (good)** cette objection n'est pas valable; **his promise still ~s (good)** sa promesse tient *or* vaut toujours; **to ~ firm** *or* **tight** *or* **fast** tenir bon *or* ferme; **to ~ still** ne pas bouger; **~ hard!** arrêtez!, minute!*

►**hold back** 1 vi (*lit*) rester en arrière; (*fig*) se retenir (*from sth* de qch; *from doing* de faire). 2 vt sep a *fears, emotions* retenir, maîtriser. **the police held back the crowd** la police a contenu la foule; **to hold sb back from doing** retenir qn de faire; **they held back the names of the victims** on n'a pas donné le nom des victimes; **he was holding something back from me** il me cachait quelque chose. b (*US Scol*) *pupil* faire redoubler une classe à. **to be held back** redoubler.

►**hold down** vt sep a (*keep on ground*) *rug etc* maintenir à terre; *person* maintenir au sol, forcer à rester par terre; (*keep in place*) maintenir en place. **to hold one's head down** avoir *or* tenir la tête baissée; **we couldn't hold him down** nous ne pouvions arriver à le maintenir au sol. b *job* (*have*) avoir, occuper; (*keep*) garder. **he's holding down a good job** il occupe *or* a une belle situation; **he can't hold down a job** il ne garde jamais longtemps une situation.

►**hold forth** 1 vi pérorer, faire des discours (*on* sur), disserter. 2 vt sep (*frm: hold out*) tendre.

►**hold in** vt sep retenir. **hold your stomach in!** rentre ton ventre!; **to hold in one's temper, to hold o.s. in** se contenir, se retenir; **he managed to hold in his horse** il réussit à maîtriser *or* retenir son cheval.

►**hold off** 1 vi (*fig*) **the rain has held off so far** jusqu'ici il n'a pas plu. 2 vt sep tenir éloigné *or* à distance. **they held off the enemy** ils tenaient l'ennemi à distance; (*fig*) **I can't hold him off any longer, you'll have to see him** je ne peux pas le faire attendre plus longtemps, il faut que vous le voyiez (*subj*); **try to hold him off a little longer** essayez de le faire patienter encore un peu.

►**hold on** 1 vi (*endure*) tenir bon, tenir le coup; (*wait*) attendre. **hold on!** attendez!; (*Telec*) ne quittez pas!; (*Telec*) **I've been holding on for several minutes** j'attends depuis plusieurs minutes. 2 vt sep maintenir (à sa place), tenir en place. **this screw holds the lid on** cette vis maintient le couvercle (en place); **to hold one's hat on** tenir son chapeau sur sa tête.

►**hold on to** vt fus a (*cling to*) *rope, raft, branch* tenir bien, tenir bon à, se cramponner à, s'accrocher à; (*fig*) *hope, idea* se raccrocher à. b (*keep*) garder. **hold on to this for me** (*hold it*) tiens-moi ça; (*keep it*) garde-moi ça.

►**hold out** 1 vi a *[supplies etc]* durer. **how long will the food hold out?** combien de temps est-ce que les provisions vont durer?

b (*endure, resist*) tenir bon, tenir le coup. **to hold out against** *enemy, attacks* tenir bon devant; *change, improvements, progress, threats, fatigue* résister à; **they are holding out for more pay** ils tiennent bon pour avoir une augmentation.

2 vt sep a tendre, présenter, offrir (*sth to sb* qch à qn). **to hold out one's arms** ouvrir *or* étendre les bras.

b (*fig*) offrir. **his case holds out little hope of recovery** son cas offre peu d'espoir de guérison; **the doctor holds out little hope for him** le médecin laisse peu d'espoir à son sujet; **she's still holding out hope that ...** elle conserve toujours l'espoir que ... .

►**hold out on*** vt fus *price etc* s'en tenir à. **you've been holding out on me!** tu m'as caché quelque chose!

►**hold over** vt sep remettre. **the meeting was held over until Friday** la séance fut reportée *or* remise à vendredi.

►**hold to** vt fus s'en tenir à, rester attaché à. **I hold to what I said** je m'en tiens à ce que j'ai dit; **he held to his religious beliefs** il restait attaché à ses croyances religieuses.

►**hold together** 1 vi *[objects]* tenir (ensemble); *[groups, people]* rester unis. **this door hardly holds together any more** cette porte ne tient plus beaucoup; **we must hold together** il faut se serrer les coudes *or* rester unis. 2 vt sep *objects* maintenir (ensemble); (*fig*) *dissenting factions* assurer l'union de. (*Pol*) **this held the party together** ceci a maintenu l'union du parti.

►**hold up** 1 vi tenir bon, tenir le coup. **that building won't hold up much longer** ce bâtiment ne tiendra plus longtemps debout.

2 vt sep a (*raise*) lever, élever. **hold up your hand** levez la main; (*fig*) **I shall never hold up my head again** je ne pourrai plus jamais regarder personne en face; **to hold sth up to the light** élever qch à la lumière; (*fig*) **to hold sb up to ridicule** tourner qn en ridicule.

b (*support*) soutenir. **this pillar holds the roof up** cette colonne soutient le toit.

c (*stop*) arrêter; (*suspend*) différer, suspendre; (*cause delay to*) retarder. **the traffic was held up by the accident** la circulation fut retardée par l'accident; **I'm sorry, I was held up** excusez-moi, j'ai été mis en retard *or* retenu.

d *[robber] bank, shop* faire un hold-up dans, braquer*; *coach, person* attaquer (à main armée), braquer*.

3 **holdup** n *see* **hold 2**.

►**hold with*** vt fus: **I don't hold with that** je ne suis pas d'accord avec cela; **she doesn't hold with people smoking** elle est contre les gens qui fument, elle désapprouve que l'on fume (*subj*).

holder ['həʊldəʳ] n a *[ticket, card]* détenteur *m*, -trice *f*; *[passport, office, post, title of nobility, diploma]* titulaire *mf*; *[stocks]* porteur *m*, -euse *f*, détenteur, -trice; *[farm]* exploitant *m*; (*Sport*) *[record]* détenteur, -trice; *[title]* détenteur, -trice, tenant(e) *m(f)*. b (*object*) support *m*. **pen~** porte-plume *m inv*; *see* **cigarette** *etc.*

holding ['həʊldɪŋ] 1 n a (*act*) tenue *f*; (*Tech*) fixation *f*. b (*possession*) *[lands]* possession *f*, jouissance *f*; *[stocks]* possession. (*Fin*) **~s** (*lands*) avoirs *mpl* fonciers; (*stocks*) intérêts *mpl*, participations *fpl*; (*St Ex*) **cross ~s** participations *fpl* croisées. c (*farm*) propriété *f*, ferme *f*. 2 adj (*Fin*) **~ company** holding *m*, société *f* de portefeuille.

hole [həʊl] 1 n a (*in ground, road, wall, belt, strap etc; for mouse; also Golf*) trou *m*; (*in defences, dam*) brèche *f*; *[rabbit, fox]* terrier *m*. **these socks are in ~s** *or* **full of ~s** ces chaussettes sont toutes trouées *or* pleines de trous; **these socks got ~s in them** *or* **went into ~s** *or* **wore into ~s very quickly** ces chaussettes se sont trouées très vite; **to wear a ~ in sth** trouer qch; (*Golf*) **to get a ~ in one** faire le *or* un trou en un; **through a ~ in the clouds** par une trouée dans les nuages; (*fig*) **it made a ~ in his savings** cela a fait un trou dans ses économies; **there are ~s in his argument** il y a des failles *fpl* *or* des faiblesses *fpl* dans son argumentation; **he's talking through a ~ in his head**‡ il dit des idioties, il débloque‡; **I need it like a ~ in the head!**‡ je n'ai vraiment pas besoin de ça!; *see* **knock, pick** *etc.*

b (**: trouble*) **to be in a (nasty) ~** avoir des ennuis, être dans l'embarras; **he got me out of a ~** il m'a tiré d'embarras *or* d'un mauvais pas.

c (* *pej*) (*town*) trou *m* (paumé)‡; (*room, house*) bouge *m*.

2 comp ▸**hole-and-corner** (*pej*) (*secret*) clandestin, secret (*f* -ète); (*furtive*) furtif; (*underhand*) fait en douce* ▸**hole in one** (*Golf*) trou *m* en un ▸**hole-in-the-heart** (*Med*) communication *f* interventriculaire, maladie *f* bleue; **hole-in-the-heart baby** enfant *m(f)* bleu(e); **hole-in-the-heart operation** opération *f* pour communication interventriculaire.

3 vt a *socks etc* faire un trou dans, trouer.

b (*Golf*) *putt* enquiller. **to ~ one's ball in 3** faire un *or* le trou en 3; **he holed the 5th in 3** il a fait 3 sur le 5.

4 vi a *[socks etc]* se trouer.

b (*Golf: also* **~ out**) terminer le trou; (*Billiards*) bloquer. (*Golf*) **to ~ in one** faire le *or* un trou en un.

▸**hole up** vi *[animal]* se terrer; *[wanted man etc]* se terrer, se cacher.

holey ['həʊlɪ] adj plein de trous, (tout) troué.

holiday ['hɒlɪdeɪ] 1 n (*vacation*) vacances *fpl*; (*day off*) (jour *m* de) congé *m*. **tomorrow is a ~** demain c'est fête; **to take a ~** prendre des vacances *or* un congé; **on ~** en vacances, en congé; **to take a month's ~** prendre un mois de vacances; **~s with pay** congés payés; **school ~(s)** vacances scolaires; **Christmas ~(s)** vacances de Noël; *see* **bank**[2].

2 vi (*esp Brit*) passer les vacances. **they were ~ing at home** ils prenaient leurs vacances à la maison.

3 comp *mood etc* gai, joyeux ▸**holiday camp** (*Brit*) *[families]* camp *m* de vacances; *[children only]* colonie *f or* camp de vacances ▸**holiday clothes** tenue *f* de vacances ▸**holiday feeling** atmosphère *f or* ambiance *f* de vacances ▸**holiday home** maison *f or* résidence *f* secondaire ▸**holiday-maker** (*Brit*) vacancier *m*, -ière *f*; (*in summer*) estivant(e) *m(f)* ▸**holiday pay** salaire dû pendant les vacances ▸**holiday resort** villégiature *f*, lieu *m* de vacances ▸**holiday season** saison *f* des vacances ▸**holiday spirit** esprit *m* de vacances ▸**holiday traffic** circulation *f* des départs (*or* des rentrées) de vacances, rush *m* des vacances.

holier-than-thou* ['həʊlɪəðən'ðaʊ] adj supérieur (*f* -eure), satisfait de soi; (*in religious matters*) pharisien.

holiness ['həʊlɪnɪs] n sainteté *f*. **His H~** Sa Sainteté.

holism ['həʊlɪzəm] n holisme *m*.

holistic [həʊ'lɪstɪk] adj holistique.

Holland ['hɒlənd] n a Hollande *f*, Pays-Bas *mpl*. b (*Tex*) **h~** toile *f* de Hollande.

holler* ['hɒlə^r] 1 n braillement *m*. 2 vti (*also* **~ out**) brailler, beugler*.

hollow ['hɒləʊ] 1 adj *tooth, tree, cheeks* creux; *eyes* cave; *sound* (*from box*) creux, (*from hall, cave*) caverneux; *voice* caverneux; (*fig*) *sympathy, friendship, victory* faux (*f* fausse); *promise* vain, trompeur. *[object]* **to sound ~** sonner creux; (*hungry*) **to feel ~*** avoir le ventre *or* l'estomac creux; **to give a ~ laugh** rire jaune; *see* **beat**.

2 comp ▸**hollow-cheeked** aux joues creuses *or* creusées ▸**hollow-eyed** aux yeux caves *or* creux.

3 n *[back, hand, tree]* creux *m*; *[tooth]* cavité *f*; (*in ground*) dépression *f*, dénivellation *f*; (*valley*) cuvette *f*. (*fig*) **to hold sb in the ~ of one's hand** mener qn par le bout du nez; **they held the victory in the ~ of their hand** la victoire était à portée de leur main.

4 vt (*also* **~ out**) creuser, évider.

hollowly ['hɒləʊlɪ] adv: **to laugh ~** rire jaune.

holly ['hɒlɪ] 1 n houx *m*. 2 comp ▸**holly berry** baie *f* de houx.

hollyhock ['hɒlɪˌhɒk] n rose *f* trémière.

Hollywood ['hɒlɪˌwʊd] n Hollywood.

holmium ['hɒlmɪəm] n holmium *m*.

holm oak ['həʊm'əʊk] n chêne vert, yeuse *f*.

holocaust ['hɒləkɔːst] n holocauste *m*.

hologram ['hɒləˌgræm] n hologramme *m*.

holograph ['hɒləgrɑːf] 1 n document *m* (h)olographe. 2 adj (h)olographe.

holography [hɒ'lɒgrəfɪ] n holographie *f*.

holophrastic [ˌhɒlə'fræstɪk] adj holophrastique.

hols*† [hɒlz] n (*Brit*) (abbr of **holidays**) vacances *fpl*.

holster ['həʊlstə^r] n étui *m* de revolver; (*on saddle*) fonte *f*.

holy ['həʊlɪ] 1 adj *Bible, communion, Trinity, oil, person* saint (*before n*); *place, life, poverty* saint (*after n*); *bread, water* bénit; *ground* sacré. **H~ Bible** Sainte Bible; **H~ City** Ville sainte; **H~ Communion** Sainte communion; **the H~ Father** le Saint-Père; **the H~ Ghost** *or* **Spirit** le Saint-Esprit, l'Esprit Saint; **H~ Land** Terre Sainte; **~ matrimony** les liens sacrés du mariage; **~ orders** ordres *mpl* (majeurs) (*see also* **order**); **the H~ Roman Empire** l'Empire romain chrétien; **H~ Rood** Sainte Croix; **H~ Saturday** Samedi saint; **the H~ See** le Saint-Siège; **H~ Sepulchre** Saint Sépulcre; **H~ Trinity** Sainte Trinité; **H~ Week** la Semaine Sainte; **H~ Writ** Saintes Écritures, Écriture sainte; **that child is a ~ terror*** cet enfant est un vrai démon; **~ cow!‡**, **~ mackerel!***, **~ smoke!*** zut alors!*, mince alors!*, Seigneur!*; *see also* **innocent** *etc*.

2 n: **the ~ of holies** le Saint des Saints.

3 comp ▸**holystone** (*Naut*) n brique *f* à pont ◊ vt briquer.

homage ['hɒmɪdʒ] n (*NonC*) hommage *m*. **to pay** *or* **do ~ to** rendre hommage à.

homburg ['hɒmbɜːg] n chapeau mou, feutre *m* (souple).

home [həʊm] 1 n a maison *f*, foyer *m*, chez-soi *m inv*. **he left ~ in 1978** il est parti de chez lui *or* il a quitté la maison en 1978; **he was glad to see his ~ again** il était content de revoir sa maison; **it is quite near my ~** c'est tout près de chez moi; **his ~ is in Paris** il habite Paris; **we live in Paris but my ~ is in London** nous habitons Paris mais je suis de Londres; **~ for me is Edinburgh** c'est à Édimbourg que j'ai mes racines; **for some years he made his ~ in France** pendant quelques années il a habité en France *or* la France; **refugees who made their ~ in Britain** les réfugiés qui se sont installés en Grande-Bretagne; **~ for them is England now, they now call England ~** maintenant l'Angleterre c'est leur pays; **he is far from ~** il est loin de chez lui; **he has been away from ~ for some months** il est loin de chez lui depuis quelques mois; (*Prov*) **there's no place like ~** on n'est vraiment bien que chez soi; (*Prov*) **~ is where the heart lies** où le cœur aime, là est le foyer; **to have a ~ of one's own** avoir un foyer *or* un chez-soi; **he has no ~** il n'a pas de foyer *or* de chez-soi; **to give sb a ~** recueillir qn chez soi; **he needed a wife to make a ~ for him** il fallait qu'il se marie (*subj*) pour avoir un foyer; **she made a ~ for her brothers** elle a fait un (vrai) foyer pour ses frères; (*Brit*) **it's a ~ from ~** c'est un second chez-soi; **she has a lovely ~** elle a un joli intérieur; **he comes from a good ~** il vient d'une bonne famille; **"good ~ wanted for kitten"** "cherche foyer accueillant pour chaton"; **he comes from a broken ~** il vient d'un foyer désuni; **safety in the ~** prudence à la maison; **accidents in the ~** accidents domestiques; **at ~** chez soi, à la maison; (*Ftbl*) **Celtic are at ~ to Rangers, Celtic are playing Rangers at ~** le Celtic joue à domicile contre les Rangers, le Celtic reçoit les Rangers; (*fig*) **Mrs X is not at ~ to anyone** Mme X ne reçoit personne; (*fig*) **Mrs X is not at ~** Mme X ne reçoit pas; (*fig*) **Mrs X is at ~ on Fridays** Mme X reçoit le vendredi; **to be** *or* **feel at ~ with sb** se sentir à l'aise avec qn; **he doesn't feel at ~ in English** il n'est pas à l'aise en anglais; **to make o.s. at ~** se mettre à l'aise, faire comme chez soi; (*fig*) **to bring sth closer** *or* **nearer (to) ~ (for sb)** rendre qch plus réel (pour qn); *see* **spiritual 1**.

b (*country of origin*) pays natal, patrie *f*. **at ~ and abroad** chez nous *or* dans notre pays et à l'étranger; (*fig*) **let us consider something nearer ~** considérons quelque chose qui nous intéresse plus directement; (*fig*) **Scotland is the ~ of the haggis** l'Écosse est le pays du haggis.

c (*institution*) maison *f*, institution *f*; (*shorter-term*) foyer *m*. **children's ~** maison pour enfants; *see* **maternity, mental, nursing**.

d (*Bot, Zool*) habitat *m*.

e (*Racing*) arrivée *f*.

f (*Baseball*) base *f* de départ.

2 adv a chez soi, à la maison. **to go** *or* **get ~** rentrer (chez soi *or* à la maison); **I'll be ~ at 5 o'clock** je serai à la maison à 5 heures, je rentrerai (à la maison) à 5 heures; **I met him on the journey ~** je l'ai rencontré sur le chemin du retour; **to see sb ~** accompagner qn jusque chez lui, raccompagner qn; **I must write ~** il faut que j'écrive à la maison; **it's nothing to write ~ about*** ça ne casse rien*, c'est pas merveilleux*; (*fig*) **to be ~ and dry** *or* (*US*) **~ and free** être arrivé au bout de ses peines, être sauvé des eaux (*fig*).

b (*from abroad*) au pays natal. **he came ~ from abroad** il est rentré de l'étranger; **to send sb ~** rapatrier qn; **to go** *or* **return ~** rentrer dans son pays.

c (*right in etc*) à fond. **to drive a nail ~** enfoncer un clou à fond; **to bring sth ~ to sb** faire comprendre *or* faire voir qch à qn; **the horror of the situation was brought ~ to him when ...** l'horreur de la situation lui est apparue pleinement quand ...; (*fig*) **to drive** *or* **hammer sth ~** bien faire comprendre qch (avec insistance); **his words went ~ to her** ses paroles la touchèrent au vif; *see* **hit** *etc*.

3 comp *atmosphere* de famille, familial; *troubles* de famille, domestique; (*Econ, Pol etc*) du pays, national; *policy, market, sales etc* intérieur (*f* -eure) ▸**home address** (*on forms etc*) domicile *m* (permanent); (*as opposed to business address*) adresse personnelle ▸**home-baked** (fait à la) maison *inv*; **home-baked bread** pain *m* fait à la maison ▸**home baking** (*cakes etc*) pâtisseries *fpl* maison ▸**home banking** opérations *fpl* bancaires par télématique ▸**home base** (*Baseball*) base *f* de départ ▸**home birth** accouchement *m* à domicile ▸**homebody*** (*US*) = **home-lover** ▸**homebound** *see* **homebound** ▸**home brew (beer/wine** *etc*) bière *f*/vin *m etc* fait(e) à la maison ▸**home-buying** accession *f* à la propriété ▸**home comforts** confort *m* du foyer ▸**homecoming** (*gen*) retour *m* au foyer *or* à la maison *or* au pays; (*US Scol, Univ*) fête annuelle (*avec bal et match de football*) ▸**home computer** ordinateur familial ▸**home cooking** cuisine familiale ▸**the Home Counties** (*Brit Geog*) *les comtés qui entourent Londres* ▸**the home country** le vieux pays ▸**home economics** économie *f* domestique ▸**home front: on the home front** (*Pol, Mil etc*) à l'intérieur; (*hum *: at home*) à la maison ▸**home ground:** (*Sport*) **to play at one's home ground** jouer sur son terrain; (*fig*) **to be on home ground** *or* **territory** être sur son terrain ▸**home-grown** (*not foreign*) du pays; (*from own garden*) du jardin ▸**Home Guard** (*Brit*) *volontaires pour la défense du territoire (en 1940-45)* ▸**home heating oil** fuel *m* domestique ▸**home help** (*Brit: person*) aide ménagère; (*assistance*) **do you have any home help?** est-ce que vous avez

quelqu'un pour vous aider à la maison? ▸**home improvement loan/grant** prêt *m* pour/prime *f* à l'amélioration de l'habitat ▸**home improvements** réfection *f* de logements; (*DIY*) travaux *mpl* autour de la maison; (*DIY supplies*) articles *mpl* de bricolage ▸**homeland** (*gen*) patrie *f*; (*South Africa*) homeland *m*, région réservée aux noirs ▸**home leave** congé *m* de longue durée ▸**homeless** *see* **homeless** ▸**homelessness** *see* **homelessness** ▸**home life** vie *f* de famille ▸**homelike** accueillant, confortable; **it's very homelike here** on se sent vraiment chez soi *or* comme en famille ici ▸**home loan** prêt *m* immobilier ▸**home-lover** casanier *m*, -ière *f*; (*woman*) femme *f* d'intérieur ▸**home-loving** casanier ▸**home-made** (fait à la) maison *inv* ▸**home-maker** femme *f* d'intérieur ▸**home match** (*Sport*) match *m* (joué) à domicile *or* sur son (*or* notre *etc*) terrain ▸**home news** (*gen*) nouvelles *fpl* de chez soi; (*Pol*) nouvelles de l'intérieur ▸**Home Office** (*Brit*) ≃ ministère *m* de l'Intérieur ▸**home owners** ceux qui possèdent leur propre habitation ▸**home ownership** l'accession *f* à la propriété ▸**home port** (*Naut*) port *m* d'attache ▸**home posting** (*Brit: of diplomat etc*) affectation *f* au pays ▸**homeroom** (*US Scol*) salle *f* de classe (*affectée à une classe particulière*); (*US*) **homeroom teacher** ≃ professeur *m* principal ▸**home rule** autonomie *f* ▸**home run** *[ship, truck]* voyage *m* de retour; (*Baseball*) coup *m* de circuit ▸**home sales** ventes *fpl* sur le marché intérieur ▸**Home Secretary** (*Brit*) ≃ ministre *m* de l'Intérieur ▸**homesick** nostalgique; **to be homesick** (*gen*) s'ennuyer de sa famille *or* de son chez-soi; (*abroad*) avoir le mal du pays; **to be homesick for sth** avoir la nostalgie de qch ▸**homesickness** nostalgie *f* (*for* de), mal *m* du pays ▸**home side** (*Ftbl etc*) = **home team** ▸**homespun** adj *cloth* filé à la maison; (*fig*) simple, sans recherche ◊ n homespun *m* ▸**home State** (*US*) État *m* d'origine ▸**homestead** *etc see* **homestead** *etc* ▸**home straight: to be in the home straight** (*Sport*) être dans la (dernière) ligne droite; (*fig*) voir la lumière au bout du tunnel ▸**home stretch** = **home straight** ▸**home team** (*Ftbl etc*) équipe *f* qui reçoit ▸**home town: my home town** (*place of birth*) ma ville natale; (*where I grew up*) la ville où j'ai grandi ▸**home truth: I'll tell him a few home truths** je vais lui dire ses quatre vérités, je vais lui dire quelques vérités bien senties ▸**home visit** (*by doctor etc*) visite *f* à domicile ▸**home waters** (*Naut*) (*territorial waters*) eaux territoriales; (*near home port*) eaux voisines du port d'attache ▸**homework** (*Scol*) devoirs *mpl* (à la maison); **homework diary, homework notebook** cahier *m* de textes; **homework exercise** devoir *m* (à la maison) ▸**homeworker** travailleur *m*, -euse *f* à domicile ▸**homeworking** travail *m* à domicile.

4 vi revenir *or* rentrer chez soi; *[pigeons]* revenir au colombier.

▸**home in on, home on to** vt fus *[missile]* (*move towards*) se diriger (automatiquement) vers *or* sur; (*reach*) atteindre.

homebound ['həʊm'baʊnd] adj a (*on the way home*) *traveller* qui rentre chez soi. b (*kept at home*) **to be ~** devoir garder la maison; (*US*) **~ teacher** maître *m* à domicile.

homeless ['həʊmlɪs] 1 adj sans foyer, sans abri. 2 npl: **the ~** les sans-abri *mpl*; *see* **single**.

homelessness ['həʊmlɪsnɪs] n: **~ is on the increase** il y a de plus en plus de sans-abri; **what's the government doing about ~?** que fait le gouvernement pour les sans-abri?

homely ['həʊmlɪ] adj a *food* simple, ordinaire; *person* tout à fait simple, sans prétentions; *atmosphere* accueillant, confortable; *style* simple, sans recherche. b (*US: plain*) *person* laid, sans charme; *appearance* peu attrayant.

homeopath ['həʊmɪəʊpæθ] n homéopathe *mf*.

homeopathic [ˌhəʊmɪəʊ'pæθɪk] adj *medicine, methods* homéopathique; *doctor* homéopathe.

homeopathy [ˌhəʊmɪ'ɒpəθɪ] n homéopathie *f*.

Homer ['həʊmər] n Homère *m*.

homer ['həʊmər] n a (*US *: Baseball*) coup *m* de circuit. b (*Brit: homing pigeon*) pigeon *m* voyageur.

Homeric [həʊ'merɪk] adj homérique.

homestead ['həʊmˌsted] (*US*) 1 n (*house etc*) propriété *f*; (*farm*) ferme *f*. 2 comp ▸**the Homestead Act** *la loi agraire de 1862*.

homesteader ['həʊmˌstedər] n (*US*) colon *m* (*pionnier*).

homeward ['həʊmwəd] 1 adj du retour. **~ journey** (voyage *m* de) retour *m*. 2 adv (*also* **~s**) vers la maison *or* la patrie. **to be ~ bound** être sur le chemin de retour; *see* **head**.

homey ['həʊmɪ] adj (*US*) = **homelike**; *see* **home 3**.

homicidal [ˌhɒmɪ'saɪdl] adj homicide.

homicide ['hɒmɪsaɪd] n (*act*) homicide *m*; (*person*) homicide *mf*.

homily ['hɒmɪlɪ] n (*Rel*) homélie *f*; (*fig*) sermon *m*, homélie.

homing ['həʊmɪŋ] adj *missile* à tête chercheuse. **~ device** tête chercheuse; *[animal]* **~ instinct** instinct *m* de retour (à l'habitat d'origine); **~ pigeon** pigeon *m* voyageur.

hominy grits ['hɒmɪnɪ'grɪts] n (*US*) maïs *m* concassé et bouilli.

homo‡ ['həʊməʊ] adj, n (abbr of **homosexual**) pédé‡ *(m)*, homo* *(mf)*.

homoeopath *etc* = **homeopath** *etc*.

homogeneity [ˌhəʊməʊdʒɪ'niːɪtɪ] n homogénéité *f*.

homogeneous [ˌhəʊmə'dʒiːnɪəs] adj homogène.

homogenize [hə'mɒdʒənaɪz] vt homogénéiser.

homogenous [hə'mɒdʒɪnəs] adj = **homogeneous**.

homograph ['hɒməʊgrɑːf] n homographe *m*.

homographic [ˌhɒmə'græfɪk] adj homographique.

homography [hɒ'mɒgrəfɪ] n homographie *f*.

homonym ['hɒmənɪm] n homonyme *m*.

homonymic [ˌhɒmə'nɪmɪk] adj homonymique.

homonymy [hɒ'mɒnɪmɪ] n homonymie *f*.

homophobia [ˌhɒməʊ'fəʊbɪə] n homophobie *f*.

homophobic [ˌhɒməʊ'fəʊbɪk] adj homophobe.

homophone ['hɒməfəʊn] n homophone *m*.

homophonic [ˌhɒmə'fɒnɪk] adj homophone.

homophony [hɒ'mɒfənɪ] n homophonie *f*.

homo sapiens ['hɒməʊ'sæpɪˌenz] n homo sapiens *m*.

homosexual [ˌhɒməʊ'seksjʊəl] adj, n homosexuel(le) *m(f)*.

homosexuality [ˌhɒməʊseksjʊ'ælɪtɪ] n homosexualité *f*.

Hon. (*in titles*) abbr of **Honorary** *or* **Honourable**.

honcho* ['hɒntʃəʊ] n (*US*) patron *m*, grand chef *m*.

Honduran [hɒn'djʊərən] 1 adj hondurien. 2 n Hondurien(ne) *m(f)*.

Honduras [hɒn'djʊərəs] n Honduras *m*. **in ~** au Honduras.

hone [həʊn] 1 n pierre *f* à aiguiser. 2 vt (*lit*) affûter, affiler, aiguiser; (*fig*) *style, paragraph* polir.

honest ['ɒnɪst] 1 adj *person* honnête, probe, intègre; *action* honnête, loyal; *opinion* sincère, franc (*f* franche); *face* franc, ouvert; *money, profit* honnêtement acquis *or* gagné; (*Jur*) *goods* loyal et marchand. **they are ~ people** ce sont de braves *or* d'honnêtes gens; **the ~ truth** la pure vérité; **tell me your ~ opinion of it** dites-moi sincèrement ce que vous en pensez; **to be (quite *or* perfectly) ~ with you, I don't like it** à (vous) dire la vérité, je n'aime pas ça; **now, be ~!** (*say what you think*) allons, dis ce que tu penses!; (*tell the truth*) allons, sois franc!; (*be objective*) allons, sois objectif!; **you've not been ~ with me** tu n'as pas été franc avec moi; **to earn an ~ penny** *or* **crust** gagner honnêtement sa vie *or* son pain; **an ~ day's work** une bonne journée de travail; **by ~ means** par des moyens légitimes *or* honnêtes; **~ to goodness!*, ~ to God!**‡ ça alors! (*see also* **2**); **he made an ~ woman of her*** il a régularisé sa situation (*en l'épousant*).

2 comp ▸**honest-to-God*, honest-to-goodness*** adj très simple, sans chichi*.

honestly ['ɒnɪstlɪ] adv *act, behave* honnêtement. **I can ~ say that ...** en toute sincérité je peux dire que ...; **~, I don't care** franchement, ça m'est égal; **I didn't do it, ~** je ne l'ai pas fait, je vous le jure; **~?** c'est vrai?; (*exasperated*) **~!** ça alors!

honesty ['ɒnɪstɪ] n a (*see* **honest**) honnêteté *f*, probité *f*, intégrité *f*; loyauté *f*; *[words, report]* exactitude *f*, véracité *f*. **in all ~** en toute sincérité; (*Prov*) **~ is the best policy** l'honnêteté paie. b (*Bot*) monnaie-du-pape *f*, lunaire *f*.

honey ['hʌnɪ] 1 n a miel *m*. **clear/thick ~** miel liquide/solide; (*fig*) **he was all ~** il était (tout sucre) tout miel. b **yes, ~*** oui, chéri(e); **she's a ~*** elle est adorable, c'est un chou*. 2 comp ▸**honeybee** abeille *f* ▸**honeycomb** *see* **honeycomb** ▸**honeydew** miellée *f*; **honeydew melon** melon *m* d'hiver *or* d'Antibes ▸**honeymoon** *see* **honeymoon** ▸**honeypot** pot *m* à miel (*see* **bee**) ▸**honeysuckle** chèvrefeuille *m*.

honeycomb ['hʌnɪkəʊm] 1 n (*lit*) rayon *m* de miel; (*Tex*) nid *m* d'abeille; (*Metal*) soufflure *f*. 2 comp *textile, pattern* en nid d'abeille. 3 vt (*fig*) cribler (*with* de). **the palace was ~ed with corridors** le palais était un dédale de couloirs.

honeyed ['hʌnɪd] adj (*fig*) *words* mielleux, doucereux.

honeymoon ['hʌnɪˌmuːn] 1 n lune *f* de miel. **their ~ was spent in Paris** ils ont passé leur lune de miel à Paris, ils sont allés à Paris en voyage de noces; **we were on our ~** nous étions en voyage de noces; **while on ~ in Majorca they ...** pendant leur lune de miel *or* leur voyage de noces à Majorque, ils ... . 2 comp ▸**honeymoon couple, honeymooners** nouveaux mariés *mpl*; ▸**honeymoon period** (*fig*) (*gen*) lune *f* de miel; (*Pol: after election*) état *m* de grâce. 3 vi passer sa (*etc*) lune de miel. **while ~ing in Majorca we ...** pendant notre lune de miel *or* notre voyage de noces à Majorque, nous ... .

Hong Kong ['hɒŋ'kɒŋ] n Hong-Kong *f*. **in ~** à Hong-Kong.

honk [hɒŋk] 1 vi *[car]* klaxonner, corner; *[geese]* cacarder. 2 vt: **to ~ the horn** klaxonner, corner. 3 n *[car]* coup *m* de klaxon; *[geese]* cri *m*. **~, ~!** *[car]* tut-tut!; *[goose]* couin-couin!

honkie‡, **honky**‡ ['hɒŋkɪ] n (*US pej*) sale Blanc *m*, sale Blanche *f*.

honky-tonk* ['hɒŋkɪˌtɒŋk] n a (*US: club*) bastringue* *m*, beuglant‡ *m*. b (*Mus*) musique *f* de bastringue.

Honolulu [ˌhɒnə'luːluː] n Honolulu.

honor ['ɒnər] n (*US*) = **honour**.

honorable ['ɒnərəbl] adj (*US*) = **honourable**.

honorably ['ɒnərəblɪ] adv (*US*) = **honourably**.

honorarium [ˌɒnə'rɛərɪəm] n, pl **~s** *or* **honoraria** [ˌɒnə'rɛərɪə] honoraires *mpl* (*no sg*).

honorary ['ɒnərərɪ] adj *official, member* honoraire; *duties, titles* honorifique; *degree* accordé à titre honorifique. (*Univ*) **to be awarded an ~ doctorate** être nommé docteur honoris causa.

honorific [ɒnə'rɪfɪk] 1 adj honorifique. 2 n titre *m* honorifique.

honour, (*US*) **honor** ['ɒnər] 1 n a honneur *m*. **in ~ of** en l'honneur de; (*Prov*) **(there is) ~ among thieves** les loups ne se mangent pas entre eux; to lose one's ~ être déshonoré; for ~'s sake pour l'honneur; he is the soul of ~ c'est la probité même; on my ~!, ~ bright!*† parole d'honneur!; to be on one's ~ to do être engagé sur son honneur *or* sur l'honneur à faire; to put sb on his ~ to do engager qn sur son honneur *or* sur l'honneur à faire; it is a great ~ for me c'est un grand honneur pour moi; it does him ~ c'est tout à son honneur; (*frm*) I have the ~ to tell you j'ai l'honneur de vous dire; I had the ~ to do *or* of doing j'ai eu l'honneur de faire; (*frm*) may I have the ~? me ferez-vous l'honneur?; (*title*) Your/His H~ Votre/Son Honneur; he is an ~ to his father/his regiment il fait honneur à son père/son régiment; to do the ~s of one's house faire les honneurs de sa maison; (*introductions*) to do the ~s faire les présentations (*entre invités*); (*Mil etc*) the last ~s les derniers honneurs, le dernier hommage; with full military ~s avec les honneurs militaires; *see* debt, guard, word *etc*.

b (*Univ*) to take ~s in English ≃ faire une licence d'anglais; he got first-/second-class ~s in English ≃ il a eu sa licence d'anglais avec mention très bien/mention bien.

c (*Bridge*) honneur *m*.

d (*Brit: eg CBE etc*) distinction *f* honorifique.

2 comp ▸**honour-bound**: to be honour-bound to do être tenu par l'honneur de faire ▸**honours course** (*Brit Univ*) ≃ licence *f* ▸**honors course** (*US*) cours réservé aux meilleurs étudiants ▸**honours degree** (*Brit Univ*) ≃ licence *f* ▸**honors degree** (*US*) licence *f* avec mention ▸**honor guard** (*US*) membre *m* d'une garde d'honneur ▸**honor roll** (*US*) (*gen*) liste *f* honorifique; (*Mil*) liste d'anciens combattants; (*Scol*) liste des meilleurs élèves ▸**Honours List**: (*Brit*) Birthday Honours List *liste de distinctions honorifiques conférées par le monarque à l'occasion de son anniversaire officiel;* New Year Honours List *liste de distinctions honorifiques conférées par le monarque le 1er janvier* ▸**honor society** (*US Scol*) club *m* des meilleurs élèves ▸**honor system** (*US*) système *m* de l'autosurveillance.

3 vt a *person* honorer, faire honneur à. the Queen ~ed them with her presence la reine les honora de sa présence; since you have ~ed me with your confidence puisque vous m'avez fait l'honneur de m'accorder votre confiance; (*in dancing*) to ~ one's partner saluer son cavalier (*or* sa cavalière); ~ed guest invité(e) *m(f)* d'honneur.

b *cheque* honorer.

honourable, (*US*) **honorable** ['ɒnərəbl] adj *person, action* honorable. an ~ mention une mention honorable; (*title*) the H~ ... l'honorable ...; (*Brit Parl*) my (right) H~ friend ≃ mon cher (*or* ma chère) collègue; (*Brit Parl*) the (right) H~ member for Weston ≃ Monsieur (*or* Madame) le député de Weston; *see* right.

honourably, (*US*) **honorably** ['ɒnərəblɪ] adv honorablement.

hooch‡ [hu:tʃ] n gnôle* *f*.

hood [hʊd] 1 n a (*gen*) capuchon *m*; (*Ku Klux Klan type*) cagoule *f*; (*Univ*) épitoge *f*. rain-~ capuche *f*. b (*Brit Aut*) capote *f*; (*US Aut*) capot *m*; [*pram*] capote; (*over fire, cooker etc*) hotte *f*; [*falcon*] chaperon *m*; [*cobra*] capuchon *m*. c (*US* ‡) (abbr of hoodlum) truand *m*. 2 vt *falcon* chaperonner, enchaperonner.

hooded ['hʊdɪd] adj (*gen*) *monk, figure, gunman* encapuchonné; *prisoner* au visage couvert; *cloak etc* à capuchon. ~ crow corneille mantelée; ~ falcon faucon chaperonné *or* enchaperonné; with ~ eyes aux paupières tombantes.

hoodlum ['hu:dləm] n (*US*) truand *m*.

hoodoo* ['hu:du:] 1 n (*bad luck*) guigne* *f*, poisse* *f*; (*object, person*) porte-guigne* *m*. 2 vt porter la guigne* *or* la poisse* à.

hoodwink ['hʊd,wɪŋk] vt tromper, avoir*. to ~ sb into doing amener qn à faire en le trompant.

hooey‡ ['hu:ɪ] n (*US*) chiqué* *m*, blague* *f*, fumisterie* *f*. to talk a lot of ~ dire des bêtises.

hoof [hu:f] 1 n, pl ~s *or* hooves sabot *m* (*d'animal*). on the ~ sur pied; *see* cloven. 2 comp ▸**hoof and mouth disease** (*US*) fièvre aphteuse. 3 vt: to ~ it‡ (*walk*) aller à pinces‡; (*US: dance*) danser, se trémousser.

hoofed [hu:ft] adj à sabots.

hoofer‡ ['hu:fəʳ] n (*esp US: dancer*) danseur *m*, -euse *f* (de claquettes) professionnel(le).

hoo-ha* ['hu:,hɑ:] n (*noise*) brouhaha *m*, boucan* *m*; (*confusion*) pagaïe* *f or* pagaille* *f*; (*bustle*) tohu-bohu *m*; (*excitement*) animation *f*; (*pej: publicity*) battage *m* publicitaire, baratin* *m*. there was a great ~ about it on en a fait tout un foin‡ *or* tout un plat*.

hook [hʊk] 1 n a crochet *m*; (*for coats*) patère *f*; (*on dress*) agrafe *f*; (*Fishing*) hameçon *m*. (*Sewing*) ~s and eyes agrafes; (*fig*) to take the ~ avaler le morceau, mordre à *or* gober l'hameçon; he swallowed the story ~, line and sinker* il a gobé tout ce qu'on lui a raconté, il a tout avalé; by ~ or by crook coûte que coûte, par tous les moyens; to take the phone off the ~ décrocher le téléphone; the phone's off the ~ on a décroché le téléphone; (*fig*) to get sb off the ~* tirer qn d'affaire *or* d'un mauvais pas; to let sb off the ~* *wrongdoer* ficher la paix à qn*; *sb with problem* tirer une épine du pied à qn; he's off the ~* il est tiré d'affaire.

b (*Boxing*) crochet *m*; (*Golf*) coup hooké. (*Boxing*) right ~ crochet (du) droit.

c (*Agr*) faucille *f*.

2 comp ▸**hook-nosed** au nez recourbé *or* crochu ▸**the Hook of Holland** Hoek van Holland ▸**hookup*** (*Rad, TV etc*) relais *m* temporaire ▸**hookworm** ankylostome *m*.

3 vt a accrocher (*to* à); (*Naut*) gaffer; (*Boxing*) donner un crochet à; (*Fishing*) prendre; (*Golf*) hooker; *dress* agrafer. she finally ~ed him* elle a fini par lui passer la corde au cou; *see also* hooked.

b (*Rugby*) to ~ the ball talonner le ballon.

4 vi a (*Golf*) hooker.

b (*US* ‡) [*prostitute*] faire le tapin‡ *or* le trottoir*.

▸**hook on** 1 vi s'accrocher (*to* à). 2 vt sep accrocher (*to* à).

▸**hook up** 1 vi [*dress*] s'agrafer. 2 vt sep a *dress etc* agrafer.

b (*: *Rad, TV etc*) faire un duplex entre. 3 **hookup*** n *see* hook 2.

hookah ['hʊkɑ:] n narguilé *m*.

hooked [hʊkt] adj a (*hook-shaped*) *nose* recourbé, crochu. the end of the wire was ~ le bout du fil (de fer) était recourbé. b (*having hooks*) muni de crochets *or* d'agrafes *or* d'hameçons (*see* hook 1(a)).

c (* *fig*) (*fascinated*) fasciné (*on* par), accroché*, accro‡; (*dependent*) dépendant (*on* de). he's ~ on it il ne peut plus s'en passer; to get ~ on *drugs* se camer à*; *jazz, television* devenir enragé* de; he's really ~ on that girl il est complètement dingue‡ de cette fille; once I'd seen the first episode I was ~ après avoir vu le premier épisode j'étais accroché*. d (‡: *married*) casé*, marié.

hooker ['hʊkəʳ] n a (*Rugby*) talonneur *m*. b (‡: *prostitute*) putain‡ *f*.

hookey*, **hooky*** ['hʊkɪ] n (*esp US*) to play ~ sécher les cours, faire l'école buissonnière.

hooligan ['hu:lɪgən] n voyou *m*, vandale *m*, hooligan *m*.

hooliganism ['hu:lɪgənɪzəm] n vandalisme *m*.

hoop [hu:p] n [*barrel*] cercle *m*; (*toy; in circus; for skirt*) cerceau *m*; (*Croquet*) arceau *m*. (*fig*) they put him through the ~(s) ils l'ont mis sur la sellette.

hoopla ['hu:plɑ:] n a (*Brit*) jeu *m* d'anneaux (*dans les foires*). b (*US* *) = hoo-ha.

hoopoe ['hu:pu:] n huppe *f*.

hooray [hu:'reɪ] 1 excl hourra. 2 comp ▸**Hooray Henry** (*Brit pej*) *jeune homme des classes supérieures jovial et bruyant*.

hoosegow‡ ['hu:sgaʊ] n (*US*) taule‡ *f or* tôle‡ *f*, trou* *m*.

Hoosier ['hu:ʒəʳ] n (*US*) habitant(e) *m(f)* de l'Indiana. the ~ State l'Indiana *m*.

hoot [hu:t] 1 n [*owl*] hululement *m*; (*Aut*) coup *m* de klaxon; [*siren*] mugissement *m*; [*train*] sifflement *m*; (*jeer*) huée *f*. she gave a ~ of laughter elle s'est esclaffée; I don't care a ~* *or* two ~s* je m'en fiche* comme de ma première chemise, je n'en ai rien à fiche*; (*Brit*) it was a ~‡ c'était tordant* *or* marrant*. 2 vi [*owl*] hululer; (*Aut*) klaxonner, corner; [*siren*] mugir; [*train*] siffler; (*jeer*) huer, pousser des huées. to ~ with laughter s'esclaffer, rire aux éclats. 3 vt (*also:* ~ down) *actor, speaker* huer, conspuer.

hooter ['hu:təʳ] n a [*factory*] sirène *f*; (*Brit Aut*) klaxon *m*; [*train*] sifflet *m*. b (*Brit* ‡: *nose*) pif* *m*, blair‡ *m*. c (*US* ‡: *breasts*) ~s roberts‡ *mpl*.

Hoover ['hu:vəʳ] (*Brit*) ® 1 n aspirateur *m*. 2 vt: to h~ a carpet/a room passer l'aspirateur sur un tapis/dans une pièce.

hooves [hu:vz] npl of hoof.

hop¹ [hɒp] 1 n a [*person, animal*] saut *m*; [*person, bird*] sautillement *m*. ~ skip and jump, ~ step and jump (*Sport*) triple saut *m*; (*fig*) it's a ~ skip *or* step and jump from here c'est à un jet de pierre d'ici; with a ~ skip *or* step and jump he was gone une pirouette et il avait disparu; (*fig*) to catch sb on the ~ prendre qn au dépourvu; to be/keep sb on the ~*ne pas avoir/ne pas laisser à qn le temps de respirer*.

b (*: *dance*) sauterie *f*.

c (*Aviat*) étape *f*. from London to Athens in 2 ~s de Londres à Athènes en 2 étapes; it's a short ~ from Paris to Brussels ce n'est qu'un saut de Paris à Bruxelles.

2 comp ▸**hop-o'-my-thumb** le Petit Poucet ▸**hopscotch** marelle *f*.

3 vi [*person*] sauter à cloche-pied; (*jump*) sauter; [*animal*] sauter; [*bird*] sautiller. he ~ped over to the window il est allé à cloche-pied jusqu'à la fenêtre; (*in car etc*) ~ in! montez!; he ~ped out of bed il a sauté du lit; (*fig*) he ~ped onto a plane for London il a attrapé un avion pour Londres; *see* mad.

4 vt sauter. to ~ it* décamper, mettre les bouts* *or* les voiles*; ~ it!* fiche le camp!*; (*US*) he ~ped a flight to New York il a attrapé un vol pour New York.

▸**hop off*** vi (*leave*) décamper, ficher le camp*. he hopped off with all the silver il a fichu le camp* avec toute l'argenterie.

hop² [hɒp] 1 n (*Bot: also* ~s) houblon *m*. 2 comp ▸**hopfield** houblonnière *f* ▸**hop picker** cueilleur *m*, -euse *f* de houblon ▸**hop-picking** cueillette *f* du houblon ▸**hop pole** perche *f* à houblon.

hope [həʊp] 1 n espoir *m* (*of doing* de faire), espérance *f* (*liter, also Rel*). past *or* beyond (all) ~ sans espoir, désespéré; we must live in ~ nous devons vivre d'espoir; she lives in (the) ~ of seeing her son again c'est l'espoir de revoir son fils qui la fait vivre; in the ~ that/of sth/of doing dans l'espoir que/de qch/de faire; to have ~s of doing avoir l'espoir de faire; I haven't much ~ of succeeding je n'ai pas beaucoup d'espoir de réussir; **she hasn't (got) a ~ in hell of doing ...**‡ elle n'a pas la moindre chance de faire ...; **there is no ~ of that** c'est hors de question, n'y comptez pas; **not a ~* (in hell‡)!** penses-tu!, pas question!; **he set out with high ~s** il s'est lancé avec l'espoir de faire de grandes choses; **don't raise your ~s** ne te fais pas trop d'espoir *or* d'idées*; **to raise sb's ~s** faire naître l'espoir chez qn; **don't raise her ~s too much** ne lui laisse *or* donne pas trop d'espoir; **to lose (all) ~ of sth/of doing** perdre l'espoir *or* tout espoir de qch/de faire; **my ~ is that ...** ce que j'espère *or* mon espoir c'est que ...; **he's the ~ of his family** c'est l'espoir de sa famille; **you're my last ~** tu es mon dernier espoir; **what a ~!*, some ~(s)!*** tu parles!*, tu crois au père Noël!*; *see* **dash, faith, hold out 2.**

2 **vi** espérer. **to ~ in God** espérer en Dieu, mettre son espoir en Dieu; **to ~ for money/for success** espérer gagner de l'argent/avoir du succès; **if I were you I shouldn't ~ for too much from the meeting** à votre place je n'attendrais pas trop de la réunion; **don't ~ for too much** n'en attendez pas trop; **to ~ for better days** espérer (connaître) des jours meilleurs; **we must ~ for better things** il faut espérer que de meilleurs jours viendront *or* que ça ira mieux; **to ~ for the best** être optimiste; **to ~ against hope** espérer en dépit de tout *or* contre tout espoir.

3 **vt** espérer. **I ~ he comes** j'espère qu'il viendra; **I ~ to see you, I ~ I'll see you** j'espère te voir; **I ~ to God** *or* **hell* she remembers/he doesn't turn up** j'espère vraiment qu'elle s'en souvient/qu'il ne vienne pas; **hoping to hear from you** dans l'espoir d'avoir de vos nouvelles; **what do you ~ to gain by that?** qu'espères-tu obtenir par là?; **I ~ so** (*answer to question*) j'espère que oui; (*agreeing with sb's statement*) je l'espère, j'espère bien; **I ~ not** (*answer to question*) j'espère que non; (*agreeing: also* **I should ~ not**) j'espère bien que non!

4 **comp** ▸**hope chest** (*US*) (armoire *f* à) trousseau *m*.

hopeful ['həʊpfʊl] 1 **adj** *person* plein d'espoir; *situation* qui promet; *future* qui se présente bien; *response* encourageant, qui promet. **we are ~ about the results** nous attendons avec confiance les résultats; **I am ~ that ...** j'ai bon espoir que ...; **I'll ask her but I'm not too ~** je lui demanderai mais je n'ai pas tellement d'espoir; **it's a ~ sign** c'est bon signe. 2 **n**: **the young ~s** (*showing promise*) les jeunes espoirs *mpl*; (*ambitious*) les jeunes ambitieux *mpl*; (*hoping for sth*) les jeunes optimistes *mpl*.

hopefully ['həʊpfəlɪ] **adv** a *speak, assess, smile* avec (bon) espoir, avec optimisme; *develop, progress* d'une façon encourageante. **... he said ~ ...,** dit-il avec optimisme. b (*one hopes*) **~ it won't rain** on espère qu'il ne va pas pleuvoir; **three or ~ four ...** trois ou avec un peu de chance quatre ...; (*as answer*) ~ je l'espère.

hopeless ['həʊplɪs] **adj** a *person* sans espoir, désespéré; *task* impossible; *situation* désespéré, qui ne permet *or* ne laisse aucun espoir, irrémédiable; *outlook* désespéré. b (*bad, worthless*) *work* lamentable, nul; *person* bon à rien. **he's a ~ teacher** il est nul comme professeur; **I'm ~ at maths** je suis nul en maths; **it's ~!** c'est impossible! *or* désespérant! c *liar, drunkard etc* invétéré, incorrigible. **he's ~*, he's a ~ case*** c'est un cas désespéré.

hopelessly ['həʊplɪslɪ] **adv** *act* sans espoir; *speak* avec désespoir; *long for, regret* désespérément; *besotted etc* éperdument. **~ naïve** *etc* d'une naïveté *etc* désespérante; **~ in love** amoureux fou, éperdument amoureux; **they were ~ lost** ils étaient complètement perdus.

hopelessness ['həʊplɪsnɪs] **n** *[situation]* caractère *m* désespéré; *[person]* sensation *f* d'impuissance.

hopper ['hɒpəʳ] **n** (*person, animal, insect*) sauteur *m*, -euse *f*; (*: *Australia*) kangourou *m*; (*bin*) trémie *f*. (*Rail*) **~ car** wagon-trémie *m*.

Horace ['hɒrɪs] **n** Horace *m*.

Horae ['hɔːriː] **npl** (*Myth*) Heures *fpl*.

horde [hɔːd] **n** horde *f* (*also pej*), foule *f*. **~s of** des foules de; (*fig*) **~s* of books/cars** *etc* des tas de livres/de voitures *etc*.

horizon [hə'raɪzn] **n** (*lit*) horizon *m*; (*fig*) vue *f*, horizon. (*lit, fig*) **on the ~** à l'horizon; (*fig*) **a man of narrow ~s** un homme de vues étroites; (*fig*) **to enlarge** *or* **widen one's ~s** élargir ses horizons; **to open new ~s for sb** ouvrir des horizons à qn.

horizontal [,hɒrɪ'zɒntl] 1 **adj** horizontal. **~ bar** barre *f* fixe. 2 **n** horizontale *f*.

horizontally [,hɒrɪ'zɒntəlɪ] **adv** horizontalement.

hormonal [hɔː'məʊnəl] **adj** hormonal.

hormone ['hɔːməʊn] 1 **n** hormone *f*. 2 **comp** ▸**hormone replacement therapy** traitement hormonal substitutif ▸**hormone tablet** comprimé *m* d'hormones ▸**hormone treatment** traitement hormonal.

horn [hɔːn] 1 **n** a corne *f*. **~ of plenty** corne d'abondance; (*fig*) **to draw in** *or* **pull in one's ~s** (*back down*) diminuer d'ardeur; (*spend less*) restreindre son train de vie; *see* **dilemma.** b (*Mus*) cor *m*; *see* **French** *etc.* c (*Aut*) klaxon *m*, avertisseur *m*; (*Naut*) sirène *f*. **to blow** *or* **sound the ~** klaxonner, corner; *see* **fog.** d (*US* ‡: *telephone*) bigophone* *m*. **to get on the ~ to sb** bigophoner* à qn. e *[saddle]* corne *f*, pommeau *m*. 2 **comp** *handle, ornament* en corne ▸**hornbeam** (*Bot*) charme *m* ▸**hornbill** calao *m* ▸**hornpipe** (*Naut*) matelote *f* (*danse*) ▸**horn-rimmed spectacles** lunettes *fpl* à monture d'écaille *or* à grosse monture.

▸**horn in**‡ **vi** (*esp US*) mettre son grain de sel.

horned [hɔːnd] **adj** (*gen*) cornu. **~ owl** (*variété de*) duc *m* (*Orn*); **~ toad** crapaud cornu.

hornet ['hɔːnɪt] **n** frelon *m*. (*fig*) **his inquiries stirred up a ~'s nest** ses investigations ont mis le feu aux poudres.

hornless ['hɔːnlɪs] **adj** sans cornes.

horny ['hɔːnɪ] **adj** a (*like horn*) corné; *hands etc* calleux. b (‡: *sexually aroused*) en rut*, excité* (*sexuellement*).

horology [hɒ'rɒlədʒɪ] **n** horlogerie *f*.

horoscope ['hɒrəskəʊp] **n** horoscope *m*.

horrendous [hɒ'rendəs] **adj** horrible, affreux.

horrible ['hɒrɪbl] **adj** *sight, murder* horrible, affreux; (*less strong*) *holiday, weather, person* affreux, atroce. **it's ~** c'est affreux.

horribly ['hɒrɪblɪ] **adv** horriblement, affreusement. **I'm going to be ~ late** je vais être affreusement en retard.

horrid ['hɒrɪd] **adj** méchant, vilain; (†: *stronger*) horrible, affreux, hideux; *weather* épouvantable. **a ~ child** un méchant enfant, une horreur d'enfant*.

horrific [hɒ'rɪfɪk] **adj** horrible, terrifiant.

horrifically [hɒ'rɪfɪkəlɪ] **adv** horriblement.

horrified ['hɒrɪfaɪd] **adj** horrifié.

horrify ['hɒrɪfaɪ] **vt** horrifier.

horrifying ['hɒrɪfaɪɪŋ] **adj** horrifiant.

horrifyingly ['hɒrɪfaɪɪŋlɪ] **adv** = **horrifically**.

horror ['hɒrəʳ] 1 **n** (*feeling, object, person*) horreur *f*. **to have a ~ of sth/of doing** avoir horreur de qch/de faire; (*excl*) **~s!*** quelle horreur!, quelle chose affreuse!; **to my ~ I realized that ...** je me suis rendu compte avec horreur que ...; **to my ~ he returned with a knife** à ma grande horreur il est revenu un couteau à la main; **and then, ~ of ~s*, he said ...** et alors, pour comble de l'horreur, il a dit ...; **that child is a ~!*** cet enfant est un petit monstre!; **you ~!*** monstre!*; **that gives me the ~s*** cela me donne le frisson, cela me donne la chair de poule; **9 die in motorway ~** scènes d'horreur sur l'autoroute: 9 morts; *see* **chamber.**

2 **comp** *book, film, comic* d'épouvante ▸**horror story** (*lit*) histoire *f* d'épouvante; (*fig*) horreur *f* ▸**horror-stricken, horror-struck** glacé *or* frappé d'horreur.

horse [hɔːs] 1 **n** a cheval *m*. **to work like a ~** travailler comme un forcené; (*fig*) **(straight) from the ~'s mouth** de source sûre; (*lit, fig*) **to back the wrong ~** miser sur le mauvais cheval; (*fig*) **that's a ~ of a different colour** cela n'a rien à voir, nous ne parlons plus de la même chose; (*Prov*) **you can take** *or* **lead a ~ to water but you cannot make it drink** on ne peut pas forcer les gens; *see* **dark, eat, gift, white, willing** *etc.*

b (*Gymnastics*) cheval *m* d'arçons; *see* **clothes.**

c (*Mil: NonC*) cavalerie *f*. **light ~** cavalerie légère.

d (*Drugs sl: heroin*) cheval *m* (*sl*), héroïne *f*.

2 **comp** ▸**horse-artillery** artillerie montée ▸**horseback: on horseback** à cheval; (*esp US*) **horseback riding** équitation *f* ▸**horsebox** fourgon *m* à chevaux, van *m*; (*in stable*) box *m* ▸**horse brass** médaillon *m* de cuivre (fixé à une martingale) ▸**horse-breaker** dresseur *m*, -euse *f* de chevaux ▸**horse breeder** éleveur *m*, -euse *f* de chevaux ▸**horsecar** (*US*) van *m* ▸**horse chestnut** marron *m* (d'Inde) ▸**horse chestnut tree** marronnier *m* (d'Inde) ▸**horse-collar** collier *m* (*de harnais*) ▸**horse-dealer** maquignon *m* ▸**horse-doctor*** vétérinaire *mf* ▸**horse-drawn** tiré par des chevaux, à chevaux ▸**horseflesh** (*horses generally*) chevaux *mpl*; (*Culin: horsemeat*) viande *f* de cheval ▸**horsefly** taon *m* ▸**the Horse Guards** (*Brit Mil*) (le régiment de) la Garde à cheval ▸**horsehair** **n** crin *m* (de cheval) ◊ **comp** de *or* en crin (de cheval) ▸**horsehide** cuir *m* de cheval ▸**horse latitudes** ceintures subtropicales ▸**horse-laugh** gros rire ▸**horseman** cavalier *m*; **he's a good horseman** il est bon cavalier, il monte bien (à cheval) ▸**horsemanship** (*skill*) talent *m* de cavalier, monte *f* ▸**horse manure** crottin *m* de cheval ▸**horsemeat** (*Culin*) viande *f* de cheval ▸**horse opera*** (*US: Cine, TV*) western *m* ▸**horseplay** jeu *m* de mains, chahut *m* ▸**horsepower** puissance *f* (en chevaux); (*unit*) cheval-vapeur *m*; **a ten-horsepower car** une dix-chevaux ▸**horse-race** course *f* de chevaux ▸**horse-racing** courses *fpl* de chevaux, hippisme *m* ▸**horseradish** (*Bot*) raifort *m*; **horseradish sauce** sauce *f* au raifort ▸**horse-riding** (*Brit*) équitation *f* ▸**horse-sense*** (gros) bon sens ▸**horseshit*‡** (*lit*) crottin *m* (de cheval); (*fig: nonsense*) foutaises‡ *fpl* ▸**horseshoe** **n** fer *m* à cheval ◊ **comp** en fer à cheval ▸**horse show** concours *m* hippique ▸**horsetail** (*Bot*) prêle *f* ▸**horse-trade** (*lit, fig*) maquignonner ▸**horse-trader** (*lit, fig*) maquignon *m* ▸**horse-trading** (*lit, fig*) maquignonnage *m* ▸**horse trailer** (*US*) = **horsebox** ▸**horse trials** concours *m* hippique ▸**horse vaulting** (*Sport*) saut *m* de cheval ▸**horsewhip** **n** cravache *f* ◊ **vt** cravacher ▸**horsewoman** cavalière *f*, amazone *f*, écuyère *f*; **she's a good horsewoman** elle est bonne cavalière, elle monte bien (à cheval).

▸**horse about**‡, **horse around**‡ **vi** chahuter, jouer vivement.

horseless ['hɔːslɪs] **adj** sans cheval. **~ carriage**†† voiture *f* sans chevaux.

hors(e)y* ['hɔːsɪ] **adj** *person* féru de cheval; *appearance, face* chevalin. **~ people** les passionnés *mpl* de chevaux.

horticultural [,hɔːtɪ'kʌltʃərəl] **adj** horticole. **~ show** exposition *f* horticole *or* d'horticulture.

horticulture ['hɔːtɪkʌltʃəʳ] n horticulture *f*.

horticulturist [ˌhɔːtɪ'kʌltʃərɪst] n horticulteur *m*, -trice *f*.

hose¹ [həʊz] 1 n (*also Brit* **~pipe**) tuyau *m*; (*garden* ~) tuyau d'arrosage; (*fire* ~) tuyau d'incendie; (*Tech*) manche *f* (à eau *or* à air *etc*); (*Aut*) durite *f* ®. 2 vt (*in garden*) arroser au jet; [*firemen*] arroser à la lance.

▸**hose down, hose out** vt sep laver au jet.

hose² [həʊz] n, pl inv (*Comm: stockings etc*) bas *mpl*; (*Hist*) (*tights*) chausses *fpl*; (*knee breeches*) culotte courte (*jusqu'aux genoux*).

Hosea [həʊ'zɪə] n Osée *m*.

hosier ['həʊzɪəʳ] n bonnetier *m*, -ière *f*.

hosiery ['həʊzɪərɪ] n (*business*) bonneterie *f*; (*Comm: stocking department*) (rayon *m* des) bas *mpl*; (*stockings*) bas *mpl*.

hospice ['hɒspɪs] n (*gen*) hospice *m*; (*for terminally ill*) hospice pour incurables.

hospitable [hɒs'pɪtəbl] adj hospitalier, accueillant.

hospitably [hɒs'pɪtəblɪ] adv avec hospitalité, d'une façon accueillante.

hospital ['hɒspɪtl] 1 n hôpital *m*. **in** ~ à l'hôpital; **people** *or* **patients in** ~ (malades *mpl*) hospitalisés *mpl*; **to go into** ~ aller à l'hôpital, être hospitalisé; *see* **maternity, mental** *etc*.

2 comp *treatment, staff* hospitalier; *bed etc* d'hôpital; *dispute, strike* des hôpitaux ▸**hospital administration** gestion hospitalière ▸**hospital administrator** (*Brit*) administrateur *m*, -trice *f* d'hôpital; (*US*) directeur *m*, -trice *f* d'hôpital ▸**hospital board** conseil *m* d'administration de l'hôpital ▸**hospital case: 90 % of hospital cases are released within 3 weeks** 90 % des patients hospitalisés sortent dans les 3 semaines; **this is a hospital case** le patient doit être hospitalisé ▸**hospital doctor** médecin *m* d'hôpital; **junior hospital doctors** internes *mpl* des hôpitaux ▸**hospital facilities** service *m* hospitalier ▸**hospital nurse** infirmier *m*, -ière *f* (*d'hôpital*) ▸**hospital service** service *m* hospitalier ▸**hospital ship** navire-hôpital *m* ▸**hospital train** train *m* sanitaire.

hospitality [ˌhɒspɪ'tælɪtɪ] n hospitalité *f*. ~ **suite** salon *m* (*où sont offerts les rafraîchissements*).

hospitalize ['hɒspɪtəlaɪz] vt hospitaliser.

host¹ [həʊst] 1 n hôte *m*; (*in hotel etc*) patron *m*; (*Bot, Zool*) hôte. (*hum*) **mine** ~ notre hôte (*hum*). 2 comp *plant, animal* hôte; *town etc* qui reçoit ▸**host country** [*conference, games etc*] pays *m* d'accueil. 3 vt *TV show etc* animer.

host² [həʊst] n (*crowd*) foule *f*; (††) armée *f*. **a** ~ **of friends** une foule d'amis; **a whole** ~ **of reasons** toute une série *or* tout un tas* de raisons.

host³ [həʊst] n (*Rel*) hostie *f*.

hostage ['hɒstɪdʒ] n otage *m*. **to take/hold sb** ~ prendre/retenir qn en otage; (*fig*) **to be a** ~ **to fate** *or* **fortune** être le jouet du hasard.

hostel ['hɒstəl] 1 n a [*students, workers etc*] foyer *m*. **(youth)** ~ auberge *f* de jeunesse. b (††) auberge *f*. 2 vi: **to go (youth) ~ling** aller passer ses vacances en auberges de jeunesse.

hosteller ['hɒstələʳ] n ≃ ajiste *mf*.

hostelling ['hɒstəlɪŋ] n mouvement *m* des auberges de jeunesse.

hostelry ['hɒstəlrɪ] n hostellerie *f*.

hostess ['həʊstɪs] n hôtesse *f*; (*in night club*) entraîneuse *f*; *see* **air**.

hostile ['hɒstaɪl], (*US*) ['hɒstəl] adj hostile (*to* à).

hostility [hɒ'stɪlɪtɪ] n hostilité *f*.

hostler ['ɒsləʳ] n = **ostler**.

hot [hɒt] 1 adj a (*lit*) chaud. **to be** ~ [*person*] avoir (très *or* trop) chaud; [*thing*] être (très) chaud; (*Met*) faire (très) chaud; **this room is** ~ il fait (très *or* trop) chaud dans cette pièce; **it's too** ~ **in here** il fait trop chaud ici, on étouffe ici; **to get** ~ [*person*] s'échauffer; [*thing*] devenir chaud, chauffer; (*Met*) commencer à faire chaud; **it was a very** ~ **day** c'était un jour très chaud, c'était un jour de grande *or* de forte chaleur; **the** ~ **sun** le soleil brûlant; **in the** ~ **weather** pendant les chaleurs; **it was a** ~ **and tiring walk** ce fut une marche épuisante dans la grande chaleur; **bread** ~ **from the oven** pain tout chaud sorti du four; (*on menu*) ~ **dishes** plats chauds; **I can't drink** ~ **things** je ne peux pas boire chaud; **the food must be served** ~ la nourriture doit être servie bien chaude; (*fig*) **he's had more trips to Paris than I've had** ~ **dinners*** il va plus souvent à Paris que je ne change (*subj*) de chemise; ~ **and cold (running water)** (eau courante) chaude et froide; (*Med*) ~ **flush,** (*US*) ~ **flash** bouffée *f* de chaleur; (*fig*) **to be in/get into** ~ **water** être/se mettre dans une mauvaise passe *or* dans le pétrin; **to be (all)** ~ **and bothered** (*perspiring*) être en nage; (*flustered*) être dans tous ses états, être tourneboulé* (*about sth* au sujet de qch); **to be/get** ~ **under the collar* (about sth)** être/se mettre dans tous ses états *or* en colère (au sujet de qch); (*fig*) **to go** ~ **and cold** avoir des sueurs froides (*about* à la pensée de); *see also* 3, *and* **cake, coal, iron** *etc*.

b (*fig*) *food, curry* fort, épicé; *spices* fort; *news, report* tout frais (*f* fraîche); *struggle, contest, dispute* acharné; *temperament* passionné, violent; *supporter* enthousiaste, passionné. ~ **jazz** hot *m*; **he's got a** ~ **temper** il a un caractère violent, il est très colérique; (*Pol*) **a** ~ **war*** une guerre ouverte; (*Sport*) ~ **favourite** grand favori; ~ **tip** tuyau sûr *or* increvable*; **to be** ~ **on the trail** être sur la bonne piste; **to be** ~ **on sb's trail** être sur les talons de qn; (*in guessing games etc*) **you're getting** ~! tu brûles!; **news** ~ **from the press** informations de dernière minute; **he was** ~ **from Paris** il était tout frais arrivé de Paris; **he made the town too** ~ **for his enemies** il a rendu l'atmosphère de la ville irrespirable pour *or* à ses ennemis; **to make it** *or* **things** ~ **for sb*** mener la vie dure à qn, en faire baver à qn*; *see also* 3, *and* **pursuit** *etc*.

c (*: *very good*) (*gen*) terrible*, sensationnel*. (*esp US*) **that's** ~ c'est fantastique; **not so** ~ pas formidable*, pas merveilleux, pas fameux*; **how are things? — not so** ~ comment ça va? — pas fameux* *or* pas terrible; **he's pretty** ~ **at maths** c'est un crack* en maths; **he's pretty** ~ **at football** il est très calé en football; (*sexually*) **she's a** ~ **piece*** elle est (très) sexy*.

d (*successful*) *article for sale* très recherché, qui a beaucoup de succès.

e (*: *stolen*) volé. **it's** ~ ça a été volé.

2 adv: **he went at it** ~ **and strong** il n'y est pas allé de main morte*; **to give it to sb** ~ **and strong*** passer un savon à qn*, sonner les cloches à qn*; *see* **blow¹**.

3 comp ▸**hot air*** (*fig*) (*nonsense*) blablabla* *m*, foutaises* *fpl*; (*empty talk*) du vent; (*fig*) **to blow hot air*** brasser du vent ▸**hot-air balloon** ballon *m*, montgolfière *f* ▸**hotbed: a hotbed of vice/social unrest** *etc* un foyer de vice/de troubles sociaux *etc* ▸**hot-blooded** (*fig*) ardent, passionné ▸**hot cross bun** brioche *f* du Vendredi saint ▸**hot dog** (*Culin*) hot-dog *m* ▸**hot-dogging** (*Ski*) ski *m* acrobatique ▸**hot-foot** à toute vitesse, à toute allure; **to hotfoot it*** galoper ▸**hot gospeller** prêcheur enragé (du protestantisme) ▸**hothead** n (*fig*) tête brûlée ◊ adj (*also* **hotheaded**) *person* exalté, impétueux; *attitude* impétueux ▸**hothouse** n serre *f* (chaude) ◊ adj (*lit, fig*) de serre (chaude) ▸**hot issue** (*Fin*) émission *f* des valeurs vedettes ▸**hot key** (*Comput*) touche *f* directe ▸**hot line** (*Telec*) (*gen*) ligne ouverte vingt-quatre heures sur vingt-quatre (*to sb* avec qn); (*Pol*) téléphone *m* rouge (*to* avec) ▸**hot money** (*Fin*) capitaux *mpl* spéculatifs *or* fébriles; (*stolen*) argent volé ▸**hot pants*** mini-short *m* ▸**hotplate** plaque chauffante ▸**hotpot** (*esp Brit Culin*) ragoût *m* (*cuit au four avec des pommes de terre*) ▸**hot potato*** (*fig*) sujet brûlant; **he dropped the idea like a hot potato*** il a brusquement tout laissé tomber ▸**hotrod (car)** (*US*) hotrod *m*, voiture gonflée* ▸**hot seat** (*US: electric chair*) chaise *f* électrique; (*fig: in decision-making etc*) **to be in the hot seat** être en première ligne ▸**hot-selling** qui se vend comme des petits pains ▸**hot shit****: (*US fig*) **he really thinks he's hot shit** il ne se prend pas pour de la merde* ▸**hot-shoe** n sabot(-contact) *m*, porte-flash *m* ▸**hotshot*** (*esp US*) adj (*gen*) terrible*; *performance* de virtuose ◊ n (*expert*) as *m*, crack* *m*; (*important person*) gros bonnet *m* ▸**hot spot*** (*Brit*) (*trouble area*) point *m* névralgique *or* chaud; (*night club*) boîte *f* (de nuit) ▸**hot spring** source *f* chaude ▸**hot stuff***: **to be hot stuff** (*terrific*) être terrible*; (*daring: of film etc*) être audacieux ▸**hot-tempered** emporté, colérique ▸**hot tub** (*US*) jacuzzi *m* ▸**hot-water bag** *or* **bottle** bouillotte *f* ▸**hot-wire*** *car* démarrer en faisant se toucher les fils de contact.

4 n: **to have the ~s**** **for sb** [*man*] bander** pour qn; [*woman*] mouiller** pour qn.

▸**hot up*** 1 vi (*lit*) réchauffer; (*fig*) chauffer. **things are hotting up in the Middle East** cela commence à chauffer* au Moyen-Orient; (*at a party*) **things are hotting up** l'atmosphère commence à chauffer* *or* à balancer*. 2 vt sep a *food* faire chauffer, (faire) réchauffer. b (*fig*) *music* faire balancer*; *party* mettre de l'animation dans; *car engine* gonfler*. **he was driving a hotted-up Mini** ® il conduisait une Mini ® au moteur gonflé*; (*fig*) **to hot up the pace** forcer l'allure.

hotchpotch ['hɒtʃpɒtʃ] n salmigondis *m*, fatras *m*.

hotel [həʊ'tel] 1 n hôtel *m*. 2 comp *furniture, prices, porter* d'hôtel ▸**hotel industry** industrie *f* hôtelière ▸**hotelkeeper** hôtelier *m*, -ière *f*, patron(ne) *m(f)* (d'hôtel) ▸**hotel manager** gérant *m* *or* directeur *m* d'hôtel ▸**hotel receptionist** réceptionniste *mf* d'hôtel ▸**hotel room** chambre *f* d'hôtel ▸**hotel ship** navire-hôtel *m* ▸**hotel staff** personnel *m* hôtelier *or* de l'hôtel ▸**hotel work: he's looking for hotel work** il cherche un travail dans l'hôtellerie ▸**hotel workers** (le) personnel hôtelier.

hotelier [həʊ'telɪəʳ] n hôtelier *m*, -ière *f*.

hotly ['hɒtlɪ] adv avec feu, passionnément, violemment. **it was** ~ **disputed** ce fut contredit violemment.

Hottentot ['hɒtəntɒt] 1 adj hottentot. 2 n a Hottentot *mf*. b (*Ling*) hottentot *m*.

houm(o)us ['huːməs] n houmous *m*.

hound [haʊnd] 1 n a chien courant, chien de meute; (*often hum: any dog*) chien. (*Brit*) **the ~s** la meute; **to ride to ~s** chasser à courre; *see* **fox, master** *etc*. b (*pej: person*) canaille *f*, crapule *f*. 2 comp ▸**hounddog** (*US*) bâtard *m* (*chien*). 3 vt *debtor etc* poursuivre avec acharnement, s'acharner sur *or* contre, traquer. **they ~ed the lepers out of town** ils chassèrent les lépreux hors de la ville; **they ~ed him for the money** ils se sont acharnés contre lui pour lui soutirer l'argent.

▸**hound down** vt sep (traquer et) capturer.

▸**hound out** vt sep chasser.

hour ['aʊəʳ] 1 n a (*period*) heure *f*. **a quarter of an** ~ un quart d'heure; **half an** ~, **a half-**~ une demi-heure; **an** ~ **and a half** une heure et demie; ~ **by** ~ heure par heure; **80 km an** ~ 80 km à l'heure; **4 ~s' walk from here** (à) 4 heures de marche d'ici; **to do sth (for)** ~ **after**

faire qch heure après heure *or* des heures d'affilée; **to pay sb by the ~** payer qn à l'heure; **she is paid £8 an ~** elle est payée 8 livres (de) l'heure; **he took ~s to do it** il a mis des heures *or* un temps fou* à le faire; **she's been waiting for ~s** elle attend depuis des heures; **to be ~s late** (*lit*) être en retard de plusieurs heures; (*fig*) être terriblement en retard.

b (*time of day, point in time*) heure *f*; (*fig*) heure, moment *m*. **this clock strikes the ~s** cette horloge sonne les heures; **on the ~** toutes les heures (*à partir de 9 heures etc*); **at the ~ stated** à l'heure dite; **the ~ has come** l'heure est venue, c'est l'heure; **his ~ has come** son heure est venue; **he realized his last ~ had come** il comprit que sa dernière heure était venue *or* arrivée; **in the early *or* small ~s (of the morning)** au petit matin *or* jour, aux premières heures (du jour); **at all ~s (of the day and night)** à toute heure (du jour et de la nuit); **till all ~s** jusqu'à une heure avancée de la nuit; **not at this ~ surely!** tout de même pas à cette heure-ci! *or* à l'heure qu'il est!; (*fig*) **at this late ~** à ce stade avancé; **in the ~ of danger** à l'heure du danger; **the problems of the ~** les problèmes du jour *or* de l'heure; **Book of H~s** livre *m* d'Heures; *see* **eleventh**.

c **to keep regular ~s** avoir une vie réglée; **to work long ~s** avoir une journée très longue; (*Brit*) **after ~s** *[shops, pubs]* après l'heure de fermeture; *[offices]* après les heures de bureau; **out of ~s** en dehors des heures d'ouverture; **out of visiting ~s** en dehors des heures de visite; *see* **early, late, office, school**[1] *etc.*

2 **comp** ▸**hourglass** sablier *m* ▸**hourglass figure** (*fig*) taille *f* guêpe ▸**hour hand** *[watch etc]* petite aiguille.

hourly [ˈaʊəlɪ] 1 **adj** a (*every hour*) *bus service etc* toutes les heures. (*Ind*) **~ rate** taux *m* horaire. b (*fig: incessant*) *dread, fear* constant. 2 **adv** (*lit*) une fois par heure, toutes les heures; (*fig*) continuellement. **they expected him ~** ils l'attendaient d'une heure à l'autre *or* incessamment *or* à tout moment; (*Ind*) **~ paid workers** ouvriers payés à l'heure.

house [haʊs] 1 **n, pl houses** [ˈhaʊzɪz] a maison *f*. **at *or* to my ~** chez moi; **the H~ of God** la maison de Dieu; (*fig*) **they got on like a ~ on fire** ils s'entendaient à merveille *or* comme larrons en foire; **the children were playing at ~(s)** les enfants jouaient à papa et maman; **doll's ~** maison de poupée; **~ of cards** château *m* de cartes; (*US*) **~ of correction** maison d'arrêt; **she looks after the ~ herself** elle tient son ménage, c'est elle qui s'occupe de son ménage; **she needs more help in the ~** il faudrait qu'elle soit plus aidée à la maison; **to keep ~ (for sb)** tenir la maison *or* le ménage (de qn); **to set up ~** s'installer, monter son ménage; **they set up ~ together** ils se sont mis en ménage; (*fig*) **to put *or* set one's ~ in order** mettre de l'ordre dans ses affaires; *see* **eat 2, move, open, public, safe** *etc.*

b (*Parl etc*) **the H~** la Chambre; (*Brit*) **H~ of Commons/of Lords** Chambre des communes/des lords; (*US*) **H~ of Representatives** Chambre des députés; **the H~s of Parliament** (*building*) le Palais de Westminster; (*members*) le Parlement, les Chambres; *see* **floor**.

c (*Theat etc*) salle *f*, auditoire *m*, spectateurs *mpl*. **is there a doctor in the ~?** y a-t-il un médecin dans la salle?; **a full *or* good ~** une salle pleine; **to play to full *or* packed ~s** faire salle pleine, jouer à guichets fermés; **"~ full"** "complet"; **the second ~** la deuxième séance; (*fig*) **to bring the ~ down** faire crouler la salle sous les applaudissements; *see* **pack**.

d (*Comm*) maison *f* (de commerce), compagnie *f*; (*noble family*) maison; (*Rel*) maison religieuse; (*Brit Scol*) maison *f*. (*fig*) **on the ~*** aux frais de la maison; **the H~ of Windsor** la maison des Windsors; **banking ~** établissement *m* bancaire; **business ~** compagnie, maison (de commerce); **publishing ~** maison d'édition; **in-house** *see* **in**.

e (*Mus*) **H~ (music)** House *f*.

2 **comp** ▸**house agent** (*Brit*) agent *m* immobilier ▸**house arrest** assignation *f* à domicile *or* à résidence; **to put sb under house arrest** assigner qn à domicile *or* à résidence; **to be under house arrest** être assigné à domicile, être en résidence surveillée ▸**houseboat** houseboat *m*, péniche *f* (aménagée) ▸**housebound** confiné chez soi; **the housebound** les personnes isolées ▸**housebreaker** (*burglar*) cambrioleur *m*; (*Brit: demolition worker*) démolisseur *m* ▸**housebreaking** (*burglary*) cambriolage *m*; (*Brit: demolition*) démolition *f* ▸**house-broken** (*US*) = **house-trained** ▸**house-clean** (*US*) faire le ménage ▸**housecleaning** (*US*) ménage *m*, nettoyage *m* (*d'une maison*) ▸**housecoat** peignoir *m* ▸**housedress** robe *f* d'intérieur ▸**house-father** responsable *m* (de groupe) (*dans une institution*) ▸**housefly** mouche *f* (commune *or* domestique) ▸**houseguest** invité(e) *m(f)*; **I've got houseguests** j'ai des amis de passage ▸**household** *see* **household** ▸**househunt** (*Brit*) chercher un appartement *or* une maison, être à la recherche d'un appartement *or* d'une maison ▸**house-hunting** recherche *f* d'une maison (*or* d'un appartement) ▸**house-husband** homme *m* au foyer ▸**house journal** = **house magazine** ▸**housekeeper** (*in sb else's house*) gouvernante *f*; (*in institution*) économe *f*, intendante *f*; **his wife is a good housekeeper** sa femme est bonne ménagère *or* maîtresse de maison ▸**housekeeping** (*skill*) économie *f* domestique *or* ménagère; (*work*) ménage *m*; (*Comput*) gestion *f* des disques; **house-keeping (money)** argent *m* du ménage ▸**houselights** (*Theat*) lumières *fpl or* éclairage *m* de la salle ▸**house magazine** *[company, organization]* journal *m* d'entreprise ▸**housemaid** bonne *f*, femme *f* de chambre; (*Med*) **housemaid's knee** inflammation *f* du genou ▸**houseman** (*Brit: in hospital*) ≃ interne *m* ▸**house manager** (*Theat*) directeur *m* de théâtre ▸**housemartin** hirondelle *f* de fenêtre ▸**housemaster, housemistress** (*Brit Scol*) professeur *m* responsable d'une maison ▸**housemother** responsable *f* (de groupe) (*dans une institution*) ▸**house organ** = **house magazine** ▸**house-owner** propriétaire *mf* d'une (*or* de la) maison ▸**house painter** peintre *m* en bâtiments ▸**house party** partie *f* de campagne ▸**house physician** (*Brit: in hospital*) ≃ interne *mf* en médecine; (*in hotel etc*) médecin *m* (*attaché à un hôtel etc*) ▸**house plant** plante *f* d'intérieur ▸**house prices** prix immobiliers ▸**house-proud**: **to be house-proud** être fier de son intérieur; (*pej*) avoir la manie de l'astiquage ▸**house red** vin *m* rouge cuvée du patron ▸**houseroom** place *f* (*pour loger qch ou qn*); (*fig*) **I wouldn't give it houseroom** je n'en voudrais pas chez moi ▸**house rosé** vin *m* rosé cuvée du patron ▸**house sale** vente immobilière ▸**house-sit***: **to house-sit for sb** garder la maison de qn ▸**house sparrow** moineau *m* domestique ▸**house surgeon** (*Brit*) ≃ interne *mf* en chirurgie ▸**house-to-house** porte à porte *inv*; **house-to-house search** perquisition *f* systématique dans le quartier; **to make a house-to-house search for sb** aller de porte en porte à la recherche de qn ▸**housetop** toit *m*; **to proclaim sth from the housetops** crier qch sur les toits ▸**housetrain** (*Brit*) apprendre à être propre à ▸**house-trained** (*Brit*) *animal* propre; (*fig*) *person* docile, obéissant ▸**house-wares** articles *mpl* de ménage ▸**house-warming (party)** pendaison *f* de crémaillère; **to give a house-warming (party)** pendre la crémaillère ▸**housewife** *see* **housewife** ▸**housewifely** *see* **housewifely** ▸**house-wifery** *see* **housewifery** ▸**house wine** cuvée *f* du patron ▸**house white** vin *m* blanc cuvée du patron ▸**housework** (travaux *mpl* de) ménage *m*; **to do the housework** faire le ménage.

3 [haʊz] **vt** *person* loger, héberger, recevoir. **she was housing refugees** elle logeait *or* hébergeait des réfugiés; **the town offered to ~ six refugee families** la ville a proposé de loger six familles de réfugiés; **this building ~s 5 families/3 offices** ce bâtiment abrite 5 familles/3 bureaux; **the school can't ~ more than 100** l'école ne peut recevoir plus de 100 élèves; **the papers were ~d in a box** les papiers étaient rangés dans une boîte; **the freezer is ~d in the basement** on garde le congélateur au sous-sol.

houseful [ˈhaʊsfʊl] **n**: **a ~ of people** une pleine maisonnée de gens; **a ~ of dogs** une maison pleine de chiens.

household [ˈhaʊsˌhəʊld] 1 **n** (*persons*) (gens *mpl* de la) maison *f*, maisonnée *f*, ménage *m* (*also Admin, Econ etc*). **there were 7 people in his ~** sa maison était composée de 7 personnes; **the whole ~ was there to greet him** tous les gens de la maison étaient *or* toute la maisonnée était là pour l'accueillir; **give below details of your ~** indiquez ci-dessous le nom des personnes qui résident chez vous; **~s with more than 3 wage-earners** des ménages *or* des familles *fpl* à plus de 3 salariés; (*Brit*) **H~** maison royale.

2 **comp** *accounts, expenses, equipment* de *or* du ménage ▸**household ammonia** ammoniaque *f* (d'usage domestique) ▸**household arts** économie *f* domestique ▸**Household Cavalry** (*Brit*) la Cavalerie de la Garde Royale ▸**household chores** (travaux *mpl* du) ménage *m* ▸**household gods** pénates *mpl* ▸**household goods** (*gen, Comm*) appareils *mpl* ménagers; (*Econ*) biens *mpl* d'équipement ménager; (*more generally*) **all her household goods** toutes ses affaires ▸**house-hold linen** linge *m* de maison ▸**household name**: **she is a household name** elle est connue partout; **Kleeno is a household name** Kleeno est une marque très connue ▸**household soap** savon *m* de Marseille ▸**Household troops** (*Brit*) Garde Royale ▸**household word**: (*fig*) **it's a household word** c'est un mot que tout le monde connaît.

householder [ˈhaʊsˌhəʊldəʳ] **n** occupant(e) *m(f)*; (*owner*) propriétaire *mf*; (*lessee*) locataire *mf*; (*head of house*) chef *m* de famille.

housewife [ˈhaʊsˌwaɪf] **n, pl housewives** a ménagère *f*; (*as opposed to career woman*) femme *f* au foyer; **a born ~** une ménagère née, une femme au foyer type; **housewives refused to pay these prices** les ménagères ont refusé de payer ces prix; **we wish to see housewives paid for their work** nous voulons qu'on rémunère (*subj*) les femmes au foyer; **I'd rather be a ~** j'aimerais mieux être femme au foyer. b [ˈhʌzɪf] (*sewing box*) trousse *f* de couture.

housewifely [ˈhaʊsˌwaɪflɪ] **adj** de ménagère.

housewifery [ˈhaʊsˌwɪfərɪ] **n** économie *f* domestique, tenue *f* du ménage.

housewives [ˈhaʊsˌwaɪvz] **npl of housewife.**

housey-housey [ˈhaʊsɪˈhaʊsɪ] **n** (*Brit*) (*sorte de*) loto *m*.

housing [ˈhaʊzɪŋ] 1 **n** a logement *m*. (*Brit*) **Minister/Ministry of H~**, (*US*) **Secretary/Department of H~ and Urban Development** ministre *m*/ministère *m* de l'Urbanisme et du Logement; **there's a lot of new ~** il y a beaucoup de résidences *or* de constructions nouvelles; **the ~ of workers proved difficult** le logement des ouvriers a posé un problème; *see* **low**[1].

b (*Tech: for mechanism etc*) boîtier *m*; (*Archit, Constr*) encastrement *m*.

2 **comp** *matters, problem, crisis* de *or* du logement ▸**housing association** (*Brit*) (*for providing housing*) *société charitable*

fournissant des logements; (*for co-ownership*) association *f* de copropriétaires (*pour faciliter l'accession à la propriété privée*) ▸**housing benefit** (*Admin*) allocation *f* logement ▸**housing conditions** conditions *fpl* de logement ▸**housing development** (*US*) ensemble immobilier privé ▸**housing estate** (*Brit*) ≃ cité *f* (*usu council-owned flats*), lotissement *m* (*usu privately-owned houses*) ▸**housing project** (*US*) (*place*) ≃ cité *f*; (*planning*) programme *m* de construction de logements sociaux ▸**housing scheme** (*Scot*) = **housing estate** ▸**housing shortage** crise *f* du logement, manque *m* de logements.

hove [həʊv] **pret, ptp of heave.**

hovel ['hɒvəl] **n** taudis *m*, masure *f*.

hover ['hɒvəʳ] 1 **vi** a *[bird, butterfly]* voltiger (*about* autour de; *over* au-dessus de); *[bird of prey, helicopter, danger, threat]* planer (*above, over* au-dessus de); *[person]* (*also* ~ **about,** ~ **around**) rôder; *[smile]* errer. **a waiter ~ed over** *or* **round us** un garçon (de café) rôdait *or* tournait autour de nous; **he was ~ing between life and death** il restait suspendu entre la vie et la mort; (*fig*) **prices ~ing around ...** les prix tournant *or* oscillant autour de ... . b (*waver*) hésiter, vaciller (*between* entre). 2 **comp** ▸**hovercraft** aéroglisseur *m* ▸**hoverport** hoverport *m*.

how [haʊ] 1 **adv** a (*in what way*) comment. ~ **did you come?** comment êtes-vous venu?; **tell me ~ you came** dites-moi comment vous êtes venu; **to learn ~ to do sth** apprendre à faire qch; **I know ~ to do it** je sais le faire; ~ **do you like your steak?** comment aimez-vous votre bifteck?; ~ **did you like the steak?** comment avez-vous trouvé le bifteck?; ~ **was the play?** comment avez-vous trouvé la pièce?; ~ **is it that ...?** comment se fait-il que ...? + *subj*; ~ **so?,** ~ **can that be?** comment cela (se fait-il)?; ~ **come?*** comment ça se fait?*, comment cela?, pourquoi?; ~ **come you aren't going out?*** comment ça se fait que tu ne sors pas?*; ~**('s‡) about going for a walk?** si on allait se promener?; ~ **about you?** et toi?; **and ~!*** et comment!*

b ~**'s that?** (*how possible?, in what way?*) comment ça?; (*what is your opinion?*) qu'est-ce que tu en penses?; (*agreed?*) d'accord?, ça va?; ~**'s that for size/height** *etc?* ça va (du) point de vue taille/hauteur *etc?*; (*admiringly*) ~**'s that for clean** *etc!* c'est ce que j'appelle du propre *etc!*; (*unacceptable*) ~**'s that for cheek!** si ce n'est pas du culot!; (*please repeat*) ~ **was** *or* ~**'s that (again)?** vous pouvez répéter?

c (*health etc*) ~ **are you?** comment allez-vous?; **tell me ~ she is** dites-moi comment elle va; ~ **do you do?** (*greeting*) bonjour; (*on being introduced*) enchanté; ~ **are things?** comment ça va?; ~**'s business?** comment vont les affaires?

d (*with adj, adv: degree, quantity etc*) que, comme. ~ **big he is!** comme *or* qu'il est grand!; ~ **splendid!** c'est merveilleux!; ~ **kind of you!** c'est très aimable à vous; ~ **very astute of you (***or* **him** *etc***)!** quelle finesse! (*also iro*); ~ **very clever of you/her!** quelle intelligence!, ce que vous pouvez/ce qu'elle peut être intelligent(e)!; ~ **glad I am to see you!** que *or* comme je suis content de vous voir!; ~ **he has grown!** comme il a grandi!, ce qu'il a grandi!*, comme il est grand!; ~ **long is the boat?** quelle est la longueur du bateau?, quelle longueur fait le bateau?; ~ **long shall I make it?** je le fais de quelle longueur?, je le fais long comment?*; ~ **tall is he?** quelle est sa taille?, combien mesure-t-il?; ~ **old is he?** quel âge a-t-il?; ~ **soon can you come?** quand pouvez-vous venir?, quel est le plus tôt que vous puissiez venir?; ~ **much does this book cost?** combien coûte ce livre?; ~ **many days in a week?** combien de jours dans une semaine?

e (*that*) que. **she told me ~ she had seen the child lying on the ground** elle m'a raconté qu'elle avait vu l'enfant couché par terre.

2 **n: the ~ and the why of it** le comment et le pourquoi de cela.

3 **comp** ▸**how-d'ye-do*: here's a (fine) how-d'ye-do!** en voilà une affaire!, en voilà une histoire!*; **it was a real how-d'ye-do** c'était un joli gâchis!* ▸**however** *see* **however.**

howdy* ['haʊdɪ] **excl** (*US*) salut!

however [haʊ'evəʳ] 1 **adv** a de quelque manière *or* façon que + *subj*. ~ **you may do it, it will never be right** de quelque manière que vous le fassiez, ce ne sera jamais bien fait; ~ **that may be** quoi qu'il en soit. b (+ *adj*) quelque *or* si ... que + *subj*. ~ **tall he may be** *or* **is** quelque *or* si grand qu'il soit; ~ **much money he has** quelque argent qu'il ait, pour riche qu'il soit; ~ **little** si peu que ce soit; ~ **few people come, we'll do the play** pour peu nombreux que soit le public, nous jouerons la pièce. c (*: *in questions*) ~ **did you do it?*** comment avez-vous bien pu faire ça?* 2 **conj** pourtant, cependant, toutefois, néanmoins.

howitzer ['haʊɪtsəʳ] **n** obusier *m*.

howl [haʊl] 1 **n** *[person, animal]* hurlement *m*; *[baby]* braillement *m*, hurlement; *[wind]* mugissement *m*. **there were ~s of laughter** on entendit d'énormes éclats de rire. 2 **vi** *[person, animal]* hurler; (*: *cry*) pleurer; *[baby]* brailler; *[wind]* mugir. **to ~ with laughter** rire aux éclats *or* à gorge déployée; **to ~ with pain/fury** hurler de douleur/de rage; **to ~ with derision** lancer des huées. 3 **vt** (*also* ~ **out**) hurler, crier. **they ~ed their disapproval** ils hurlaient leur désapprobation.

▸**howl down vt sep: they howled the speaker down** ils ont réduit l'orateur au silence par leurs huées.

howler* ['haʊləʳ] **n** gaffe* *f*, bourde *f*. **schoolboy** ~ perle *f* (d'écolier).

howling ['haʊlɪŋ] 1 **n** *[person, animal]* hurlement(s) *m(pl)*; *[baby]* braillement(s) *m(pl)*; *[wind]* mugissement(s) *m(pl)*. 2 **adj** a *person, animal* hurlant. a ~ **gale** une violente tempête. b (* *fig*) *mistake* énorme. ~ **success** succès fou.

hoy [hɔɪ] **excl** ohé!

hoyden ['hɔɪdn] **n** garçon manqué.

hoydenish ['hɔɪdənɪʃ] **adj** garçonnier, de garçon manqué.

H.P.* [eɪtʃ'piː] **n** (*Brit*) (**abbr of hire purchase**) *see* **hire.**

hp [eɪtʃ'piː] **n** (**abbr of horsepower**) CV.

H.Q. [eɪtʃ'kjuː] **n** (**abbr of headquarters**) Q.G. *m*.

hr (**abbr of hour**) h. **28 hrs** 28 h.

H.R.H. (**abbr of His** *or* **Her Royal Highness**) S.A.R.

HRT [ˌeɪtʃɑː'tiː] **n abbr of hormone replacement therapy.**

H.S. (*US Scol*) (**abbr of high school**) *see* **high.**

HT (**abbr of high tension**) *see* **high.**

hub [hʌb] **n** *[wheel]* moyeu *m*; (*fig*) pivot *m*, centre *m*. (*Aut*) ~ **cap** enjoliveur *m*.

hubba-hubba* ['hʌbə'hʌbə] **excl** (*US*) (*gen*) bravo!; (*quick*) presto*!, vite!

hubbub ['hʌbʌb] **n** brouhaha *m*, vacarme *m*.

hubby‡ ['hʌbɪ] **n** (**abbr of husband**) petit mari*, bonhomme* *m*. **my** ~ le patron*.

hubris ['hjuːbrɪs] **n** orgueil *m* (démesuré).

huckleberry ['hʌklbərɪ] **n** (*US*) myrtille *f*, airelle *f*.

huckster ['hʌkstəʳ] **n** (*US*) (*hawker*) colporteur *m*; (*fig pej*) mercanti *m*; (*: *salesman*) vendeur *m* de choc*; (*in fairground*) bonimenteur *m*.

HUD [hʌd] **n** (*US*) (**abbr of Department of Housing and Urban Development**) *see* **housing.**

huddle ['hʌdl] 1 **n** *[people]* petit groupe (compact); *[books etc]* tas *m*, amas *m*. **a ~ of houses in the valley** quelques maisons blotties dans la vallée; **to go into a ~*** se réunir en petit comité (*fig*). 2 **vi** a (*lit*) se blottir (les uns contre les autres). **we ~d round the fire** nous nous sommes blottis près du feu; **the baby birds ~d in the nest** les oisillons se blottissaient les uns contre les autres dans le nid; *see also* **huddled.** b (*fig: US: meet and discuss*) se réunir en petit comité (*fig*).

▸**huddle down vi** (*crouch*) se recroqueviller, se faire tout petit; (*snuggle*) se blottir, se pelotonner.

▸**huddle together vi** se serrer *or* se blottir les uns contre les autres, se réunir en (un) petit groupe. **they were huddling together for warmth** ils se serraient *or* se blottissaient les uns contre les autres pour se tenir chaud; **they huddled together to discuss the proposal** ils ont formé un petit groupe pour discuter de la proposition; *see also* **huddled.**

▸**huddle up vi** se blottir, se pelotonner.

huddled ['hʌdld] **adj: the chairs were ~ in a corner** les chaises étaient rassemblées *or* groupées dans un coin; **houses ~ (together) round the church** des maisons blotties autour de l'église; **he lay ~ under the blankets** il était blotti *or* pelotonné sous les couvertures; **the children lay ~ under the blankets** les enfants étaient blottis *or* pelotonnés les uns contre les autres sous les couvertures; **he was ~ over his books** il était penché sur ses livres.

Hudson Bay ['hʌdsən'beɪ] **n** baie *f* d'Hudson.

hue¹ [hjuː] **n:** ~ **and cry** clameur *f*; **with ~ and cry** à cor et à cri; **to raise a ~ and cry** crier haro (*against* sur).

hue² [hjuː] **n** (*colour*) teinte *f*, nuance *f*.

-hued [hjuːd] **adj ending in comps: many-hued** multicolore.

huff¹* [hʌf] **n: to be in a ~** être froissé *or* fâché; **to get into a ~** prendre la mouche, s'offusquer; **he went off** *or* **left in a ~** il est parti froissé *or* fâché.

huff² [hʌf] **vi: to ~ and puff** (*lit*) souffler comme un bœuf*; (*: *show annoyance*) râler*.

huffed* [hʌft] **adj** froissé, fâché.

huffily* ['hʌfɪlɪ] **adv** *leave* avec humeur; *say* d'un ton froissé *or* fâché.

huffiness* ['hʌfɪnɪs] **n** mauvaise humeur.

huffy* ['hʌfɪ] **adj** (*annoyed*) froissé, fâché; (*sulky*) boudeur; (*touchy*) susceptible.

hug [hʌg] 1 **vt** a (*hold close*) serrer dans ses bras, étreindre; *[bear, gorilla]* écraser entre ses bras; (*fig*) *opinion etc* tenir à, ne pas démordre de. **to ~ one another** s'étreindre; (*fig*) **to ~ o.s. over** *or* **about sth** jubiler de qch. b serrer. (*Naut*) **to ~ the shore/wind** serrer la côte/le vent; *[car]* **to ~ the kerb** serrer le trottoir. 2 **vi** s'étreindre. 3 **n** étreinte *f*. **to give sb a ~** serrer qn dans ses bras, étreindre qn; **he gave the child a big (bear) ~** il a serré l'enfant bien fort dans ses bras.

huge [hjuːdʒ] **adj** *object, sum of money, helping* énorme; *house* immense, vaste; *man* énorme, gigantesque; *success* fou (*f* folle).

hugely ['hjuːdʒlɪ] **adv** énormément; (*very*) extrêmement.

hugeness ['hjuːdʒnɪs] **n** immensité *f*.

hugger-mugger* ['hʌgəˌmʌgəʳ] 1 **n** (*muddle*) fouillis *m*, pagaïe* *f* *or* pagaille* *f*, désordre *m*; (*secrecy*) secret *m*. 2 **adj** désordonné; secret (*f* -ète). 3 **adv** en désordre; en secret.

Hugh [hjuː] **n** Hugues *m*.

Huguenot ['hjuːgənəʊ] 1 **adj** huguenot. 2 **n** Huguenot(e) *m(f)*.

huh [hʌ] **excl** (*dismay*) oh!; (*surprise, disbelief*) hein?; (*disgust*) berk!*, beuh!

Hula Hoop ['huːləˌhuːp] ® **n** cerceau *m*.

hulk [hʌlk] **n** (*prison etc ship*) ponton *m*; (*wrecked ship*) épave *f*; (*ramshackle ship*) vieux rafiot‡; (*wrecked vehicle, building etc*) carcasse *f*.

(big) ~ **of a man** mastodonte* *m*, malabar* *m*.
hulking ['hʌlkɪŋ] **adj** balourd, lourdaud, gros (*f* grosse). **he was a ~ great brute*** c'était un gros malabar*.
hull [hʌl] 1 **n** a *[ship, plane]* coque *f*; *[tank]* caisse *f*. **a ship ~ down on the horizon** un navire coque noyée *or* dont la coque disparaissait sous l'horizon. b *[nuts]* coque *f*; *[peas, beans]* cosse *f*, gousse *f*. 2 **vt** a *peas* écosser; *barley* émonder; *oats, rice* décortiquer; *nuts* écaler; *berries* équeuter. b *ship, plane* percer la coque de.
hullabaloo* [ˌhʌləbə'lu:] **n** (*noise*) chambard* *m*, boucan* *m*, raffut* *m*. (*fuss*) **there was quite a ~ about the missing money** on a fait toute une histoire* *or* tout un foin‡ à propos de l'argent disparu.
hullo [hʌ'ləʊ] **excl** = **hallo**.
hum [hʌm] 1 **vi** a *[insect]* bourdonner; *[person]* fredonner, chantonner; *[aeroplane, engine, machine]* vrombir; *[top, wireless etc]* ronfler; *[wire]* bourdonner. (*fig*) **to make things ~*** mener *or* faire marcher les choses rondement; **then things began to ~*** alors les choses ont commencé à chauffer* *or* à s'animer; *see* **haw²**. b (‡: *stink*) puer, sentir mauvais, taper‡. 2 **vt** *tune* fredonner, chantonner. 3 **n** a *[insect, voices]* bourdonnement *m*; *[aeroplane, machine, engine]* vrombissement *m*; *[top etc]* ronflement *m*. b (‡: *stink*) puanteur *f*. 4 **excl** hem!, hum!
human ['hju:mən] 1 **adj** (*gen*) humain. ~ **nature** nature humaine; **it's only ~ nature to want revenge** c'est normal *or* humain de chercher à se venger; **he's only ~ after all** il n'est pas un saint, personne n'est parfait; **to lack the ~ touch** manquer de chaleur humaine; **it needs the ~ touch to bring the situation home to the public** le public ne comprend la situation que lorsqu'il la voit sous l'angle humain; *see* **decency**.
2 **n** humain *m*, être humain.
3 **comp** ►**human being** être *m* humain ►**human ecology** écologie *f* humaine ►**human engineering** ergonomie *f* ►**humankind** humanité *f*, genre *m* humain, race *f* humaine ►**human race** race *f* humaine, genre *m* humain ►**human resource management** gestion *f* des ressources humaines ►**human resources** ressources *fpl* humaines ►**human rights** droits *mpl* de l'homme ►**human rights campaigner** défenseur *m* des droits de l'homme.
humane [hju:'meɪn] **adj** a (*compassionate*) *person, attitude* humain, plein d'humanité; *method* humain. b ~ **studies** humanités *fpl*, sciences humaines.
humanely [hju:'meɪnlɪ] **adv** avec humanité, humainement.
humanism ['hju:mənɪzəm] **n** humanisme *m*.
humanist ['hju:mənɪst] **n** humaniste *mf*.
humanistic [ˌhju:mə'nɪstɪk] **adj** humaniste.
humanitarian [hju:ˌmænɪ'teərɪən] **adj, n** humanitaire (*mf*).
humanity [hju:'mænɪtɪ] **n** humanité *f*. **the humanities** les humanités, les sciences *fpl* humaines.
humanization [ˌhju:mənaɪ'zeɪʃən] **n** humanisation *f*.
humanize ['hju:mənaɪz] **vt** humaniser.
humanly ['hju:mənlɪ] **adv** humainement. **if it is ~ possible** si c'est humainement possible.
humanoid ['hju:mənɔɪd] **adj, n** humanoïde (*mf*).
humble ['hʌmbl] 1 **adj** humble, modeste. **of ~ birth** *or* **extraction** d'humble extraction; **of ~ origin** d'origine modeste; **in my ~ opinion** à mon humble avis; (*fig*) **to eat ~ pie** faire des excuses humiliantes; (*in letters: frm*) **I am, Sir, your ~ servant** veuillez agréer, Monsieur, l'assurance de ma considération très distinguée; (*hum: oneself*) **your ~ servant** votre serviteur (*hum*). 2 **vt** humilier, mortifier. **to ~ o.s.** s'humilier, s'abaisser. 3 **comp** ►**humble-bee** bourdon *m*.
humbleness ['hʌmblnɪs] **n** humilité *f*.
humbly ['hʌmblɪ] **adv** humblement, modestement.
humbug ['hʌmbʌg] **n** a (*person*) charlatan *m*, fumiste* *mf*; (*behaviour, talk*) blague* *f*, fumisterie* *f*. b (*Brit: sweet*) bonbon *m* à la menthe.
humdinger‡ ['hʌmdɪŋəʳ] **n** quelqu'un *or* quelque chose de terrible* *or* de sensationnel*. **it's a ~!** c'est terrible* *or* sensass!‡; **she's a ~** elle est extra* *or* terrible* *or* sensass‡; **a ~ of a speech** un discours sensationnel*; (*Sport*) **that shot was a real ~** c'est un coup sans bavure*.
humdrum ['hʌmˌdrʌm] 1 **adj** monotone, banal, routinier. 2 **n** monotonie *f*, banalité *f*.
humerus ['hju:mərəs] **n, pl humeri** ['hju:məˌraɪ] humérus *m*.
humid ['hju:mɪd] **adj** humide.
humidifier [hju:'mɪdɪfaɪəʳ] **n** humidificateur *m*.
humidity [hju:'mɪdɪtɪ] **n** humidité *f*.
humidor ['hju:mɪdɔ:ʳ] **n** boîte *f* à cigares.
humiliate [hju:'mɪlɪeɪt] **vt** humilier.
humiliating [hju:'mɪlɪeɪtɪŋ] **adj** humiliant.
humiliation [hju:ˌmɪlɪ'eɪʃən] **n** humiliation *f*.
humility [hju:'mɪlɪtɪ] **n** humilité *f*.
humming ['hʌmɪŋ] 1 **n** *[insect, voices]* bourdonnement *m*; *[aeroplane, engine, machine]* vrombissement *m*; *[person]* fredonnement *m*. 2 **comp** ►**hummingbird** oiseau-mouche *m*, colibri *m* ►**humming-top** toupie ronflante.
hummock ['hʌmək] **n** (*hillock*) mamelon *m*, tertre *m*, monticule *m*; (*in ice field*) hummock *m*.
humor **n** (*US*) = **humour**.
-humored ['hju:məd] **adj ending in comps** (*US*) = **-humoured**.
humorist ['hju:mərɪst] **n** humoriste *mf*.
humorless(ly) **adj, adv** (*US*) = **humourless(ly)**.
humorous ['hju:mərəs] **adj** *genre, book, story, writer* humoristique; *person, remark* plein d'humour, amusant.
humorously ['hju:mərəslɪ] **adv** avec humour.
humour ['hju:məʳ] 1 **n** a (*sense of fun*) humour *m*. **he has no sense of ~** il n'a pas le sens de l'humour; **I see no ~ in that** je ne vois pas où est l'humour; **this is no time for ~** ce n'est pas le moment de faire de l'humour; **the ~ of the situation** le comique de la situation. b (*temper*) humeur *f*, disposition *f*. **to be in a good/bad ~** être de bonne/mauvaise humeur; **he is in no ~ for working** il n'est pas d'humeur à travailler; **to be out of ~** être de mauvaise humeur. c (*Med* ††) humeur *f*. 2 **vt** *person* faire plaisir à, ménager; *sb's wishes, whims* se prêter à, se plier à.
-humoured ['hju:məd] **adj ending in comps: good-humoured** de bonne humeur; **bad-humoured** de mauvaise humeur.
humourless ['hju:məlɪs] **adj** *person* qui manque d'humour *or* du sens de l'humour; *attitude, book, voice* sans humour.
humourlessly ['hju:məlɪslɪ] **adv** sans humour.
hump [hʌmp] 1 **n** a (*Anat*) bosse *f*; *[camel]* bosse.
b (*hillock*) bosse *f*, mamelon *m*. (*fig*) **we're over the ~ now*** le plus difficile est passé *or* fait maintenant, on a doublé le cap maintenant.
c (*Brit* †‡) cafard* *m*. **he's got the ~** il a le cafard*, il a le moral à zéro*; **that gives me the ~** ça me donne le cafard*, ça me met le moral à zéro*.
2 **vt** a arrondir, voûter. **to ~ one's back** *[person]* arrondir *or* voûter le dos; *[cat]* faire le gros dos; **to ~ one's shoulders** voûter les épaules, rentrer la tête dans les épaules.
b (*: *carry*) porter, trimballer*.
c (*‡: *have sex with*) baiser*‡, sauter‡.
3 **vi** (*‡: *have sex*) baiser*‡.
4 **comp** ►**humpback** (*person*) bossu(e) *m(f)*; (*whale: also* **humpback whale**) baleine *f* à bosse; **to have a humpback** être bossu ►**humpbacked** *person* bossu; (*Brit*) *bridge* en dos d'âne.
humph [hʌmʃ] **excl** hum!
humpy ['hʌmpɪ] **adj** *ground* inégal, accidenté.
humus ['hju:məs] **n** humus *m*.
Hun [hʌn] **n** (*Hist*) Hun *m*; (* *pej*) Boche‡ *m* (*pej*).
hunch [hʌntʃ] 1 **vt** (*also* ~ **up**) *back* arrondir; *shoulders* voûter. **to ~ one's back** arrondir *or* voûter le dos, se voûter; **~ed shoulders** épaules voûtées *or* remontées; **with ~ed shoulders** la tête rentrée dans les épaules; **he sat ~ed (up) over his books** il était assis courbé *or* penché sur ses livres.
2 **n** a (*hump*) bosse *f*.
b (*hunk*) morceau *m*. ~ **of bread** (gros) morceau *or* quignon *m* de pain; ~ **of cheese** gros morceau de fromage.
c (*: *premonition*) pressentiment *m*, intuition *f*. **to have a ~ that ...** avoir (comme une petite) idée *or* comme un pressentiment que* ...; **you should follow your ~** il faut suivre son intuition; **it's only a ~** ce n'est qu'une idée (comme ça*); **~es sometimes pay off** on fait quelquefois bien de suivre son intuition; (*esp US*) **to play a ~** suivre son intuition.
3 **comp** ►**hunchback** bossu(e) *m(f)* ►**hunchbacked** bossu.
hundred ['hʌndrəd] 1 **adj** cent. **a ~ books/chairs** cent livres/chaises; **two ~ chairs** deux cents chaises; **about a ~ books** une centaine de livres.
2 **n** a cent *m*. **about a ~, a ~-odd*** une centaine; **I've got a ~** j'en ai cent; **a** *or* **one ~ and one** cent un; **two ~** deux cents; **two ~ and one** deux cent un; **the ~ and first** le *or* la cent unième; **a ~ per cent** cent pour cent; (*fig*) **it was a ~ per cent successful** cela a réussi à cent pour cent; **in seventeen ~** en dix-sept cents; **in seventeen ~ and ninety-six** en dix-sept cent quatre-vingt-seize; (*Comm*) **sold by the ~** vendus au cent; **to live to be a ~** devenir centenaire; **they came in (their) ~s** ils sont venus par centaines; (*Hist*) **the H~ Days** les Cent Jours; (*Hist*) **the H~ Years' War** la guerre de Cent Ans; *for other phrases see* **sixty**.
b (* *fig*) **~s of** des centaines de, des tas* de; **I've told you ~s of times!** je te l'ai dit cent fois!
3 **comp** ►**hundredfold** **adj** centuple ◊ **adv** au centuple ►**hundredweight** (*Brit, Can*) (poids *m* de) cent douze livres (*50,7 kg*); (*US*) (poids de) cent livres (*45,3 kg*) ►**hundred-year-old** centenaire, séculaire (*liter*).
hundredth ['hʌndrɪdθ] 1 **adj** centième. 2 **n** centième *mf*; (*fraction*) centième *m*.
hung [hʌŋ] 1 **pret ptp of hang.** 2 **adj:** ~ **jury** jury *m* sans majorité, jury qui ne parvient pas à une décision; ~ **parliament** parlement *m* sans majorité, parlement où aucun parti n'a la majorité. 3 **comp** ►**hung over***: **to be hung over** avoir la gueule de bois* ►**hung up*** (*tense*) complexé, inhibé; **he's hung up about it** il en fait tout un complexe*; (*obsessed*) **to be hung up on sb/sth** être fou (*f* folle) de qn/qch.
Hungarian [hʌŋ'geərɪən] 1 **adj** hongrois. 2 **n** a Hongrois(e) *m(f)*. b (*Ling*) hongrois *m*.

Hungary ['hʌŋɡərɪ] n Hongrie *f.*

hunger ['hʌŋɡəʳ] 1 n faim *f*; (*fig*) faim, soif *f*, désir ardent (*for* de). 2 comp ▸**the hunger marches** (*Brit Hist*) les marches *fpl* de la faim ▸**hunger strike** grève *f* de la faim; **to go on (a) hunger strike** faire la grève de la faim ▸**hunger striker** gréviste *mf* de la faim. 3 vi (*liter*) avoir faim. (*fig*) **to ~ for** *or* **after** avoir faim (*fig*) *or* soif (*fig*) de, désirer ardemment.

hungrily ['hʌŋɡrɪlɪ] adv (*lit*) voracement, avidement; (*fig*) avidement. **to look ~ at sth, to eye sth ~** convoiter qch du regard, jeter un regard de convoitise sur qch.

hungry ['hʌŋɡrɪ] adj: **to be ~** avoir faim, avoir l'estomac creux; **to be very ~** avoir très faim, être affamé; **to feel ~** avoir faim, se sentir (le ventre) creux; **to make sb ~** donner faim à qn; **to go ~** (*starve*) souffrir de la faim; (*miss a meal*) se passer de manger; **if you don't eat your spinach you'll have to go ~** si tu ne manges pas tes épinards tu n'auras rien d'autre; **you look ~** tu as l'air d'avoir faim; **it's ~ work** c'est un travail qui donne faim *or* qui creuse*; (*fig: eager*) **~ for** avide de.

hunk [hʌŋk] n a *see* **hunch 2(b)**. b (*: *attractive man*) beau mec‡.

hunkers ['hʌŋkəz] npl (*dial*) fesses *fpl*. **on one's ~** accroupi.

hunky* ['hʌŋkɪ] adj *man* (*attractive*) bien fait, bien foutu‡.

hunky-dory* ['hʌŋkɪ'dɔːrɪ] adj (*esp US*) chouette*, au poil*. **it's all ~** tout marche comme sur des roulettes*.

hunt [hʌnt] 1 n a (*Sport*) chasse *f*. **elephant/tiger ~** chasse à l'éléphant/au tigre; **the ~ rode by** les chasseurs sont passés à cheval; **the Beaufort ~** l'équipage *m* Beaufort.

b (*gen*) chasse *f*, recherche *f*. **the ~ for the murderer** la chasse au meurtrier; **we all went on a ~ for the missing key/child** nous nous sommes tous mis à la recherche de la clef perdue/de l'enfant disparu; **I've had a ~ for my gloves** j'ai cherché mes gants partout, j'ai tout retourné pour trouver mes gants; **to be on the ~ for a cheap house** chercher une *or* être à la recherche d'une maison pas chère; (*fig*) **the ~ is on for ...** on cherche ... .

2 vt (*Sport*) chasser, faire la chasse à; (*pursue*) poursuivre, pourchasser; (*seek*) chercher. (*Sport*) **to ~ a horse** monter un cheval à la chasse; **we ~ed the town for a green vase** nous avons fait* toute la ville à la recherche d'un vase vert; **I've ~ed my desk for it** j'ai retourné tout mon bureau pour le trouver.

3 vi (*Sport*) chasser. **to go ~ing** aller à la chasse; **to ~ for** (*Sport*) faire la chasse à, chasser; (*gen*) *object, details, facts* rechercher (partout), être à la recherche de; **he ~ed in his pocket for his pen** il a fouillé dans sa poche pour trouver son stylo; **I've been ~ing (about** *or* **around) for that book everywhere** j'ai cherché ce livre partout, j'ai tout retourné pour trouver ce livre.

▸**hunt down** vt sep *animal* forcer, pourchasser; *person* traquer, pourchasser; *object, facts, details, quotation* dénicher.

▸**hunt out** vt sep dénicher, découvrir.

▸**hunt up** vt sep rechercher.

hunter ['hʌntəʳ] 1 n (*person: Sport*) chasseur *m*; (*gen*) poursuivant *m*; (*horse*) cheval *m* de chasse; (*watch*) (montre *f* à) savonnette *f*; *see* **lion** *etc.* 2 comp ▸**hunter-killer submarine** sous-marin *m* nucléaire d'attaque.

hunting ['hʌntɪŋ] 1 n a (*Sport*) (*on foot*) chasse *f* à courre; (*on horseback*) chasse; (*fox ~*) chasse au renard. b (*gen: search*) chasse *f* (*for* à), recherche *f* (*for* de); *see* **bargain, house.** 2 comp ▸**hunting ground** (terrain *m* de) chasse *f* (*see* **happy**) ▸**hunting horn** cor *m or* trompe *f* de chasse ▸**hunting lodge** pavillon *m* de chasse ▸**hunting pink** rouge chasseur *inv* ▸**hunting season** saison *f* de la chasse.

huntress ['hʌntrɪs] n (*liter*) chasseresse *f*.

huntsman ['hʌntsmən] n, pl **huntsmen** ['hʌntsmən] chasseur *m*.

hurdle ['hɜːdl] 1 n (*for fences*) claie *f*; (*Sport*) haie *f*; (*fig*) obstacle *m*. (*Sport*) **the 100-metre ~s** le 100 mètres haies; **to take a ~** (*Sport*) franchir une haie; (*fig*) franchir un obstacle; **the ~s champion** le champion de course de haies; **~ race** course *f* de haies. 2 vi (*Sport*) faire de la course de haies.

hurdler ['hɜːdləʳ] n (*Sport*) coureur *m*, -euse *f* (qui fait des courses de haies).

hurdling ['hɜːdəlɪŋ] n course *f* de haies.

hurdy-gurdy ['hɜːdɪ'ɡɜːdɪ] n orgue *m* de Barbarie.

hurl [hɜːl] vt *stone* jeter *or* lancer (avec violence) (*at* contre). **they were ~ed to the ground by the blast** ils ont été précipités à terre par le souffle de l'explosion; **to ~ o.s. at sb/sth** se ruer sur qn/qch; **they ~ed themselves into the fray** ils se sont jetés dans la mêlée; **he ~ed himself over a cliff** il s'est jeté *or* précipité (du haut) d'une falaise; (*fig*) **to be ~ed into** être précipité dans; **to ~ abuse at sb** lancer des injures à qn, accabler *or* agonir qn d'injures.

hurly-burly ['hɜːlɪ'bɜːlɪ] n (*commotion*) tohu-bohu *m*; (*uproar*) tintamarre *m*, tumulte *m*, brouhaha *m*. **the ~ of politics** le tourbillon de la politique.

Huron ['hjʊərən] n: **Lake ~** le lac Huron.

hurrah [hʊ'rɑː] n, **hurray** [hʊ'reɪ] n hourra *m*. **~ for Robert!** vive Robert!; (*US*) **last ~** (*gen*) dernière tentative†; (*Pol*) dernière campagne *f*; *see* **hip³**.

hurricane ['hʌrɪkən] n ouragan *m*. **~ lamp** lampe-tempête *f*.

hurried ['hʌrɪd] adj *steps* précipité, pressé; *remark* dit à la hâte; *departure* précipité; *decision* pris à la hâte; *reading* très rapide; *work* fait à la hâte, fait à la va-vite* (*pej*), bâclé (*pej*). **a ~ line to tell you ...** un mot bref *or* à la hâte pour te dire ...; **to have a ~ meal** manger à la hâte; **we had a ~ discussion about it** nous en avons discuté rapidement.

hurriedly ['hʌrɪdlɪ] adv (*as fast as one can*) en toute hâte, vite; (*faster than one would wish*) précipitamment, à la hâte. **he changed his mind ~** il a changé d'avis précipitamment; **you've done it too ~** tu l'as fait à la hâte *or* à la va-vite*.

hurry ['hʌrɪ] 1 n (*haste*) hâte *f*, précipitation *f*; (*eagerness*) empressement *m*. **to be in a ~** être pressé; **to be in a ~ to do** avoir hâte de faire; **it was done in a ~** cela a été fait à la hâte; **I won't do that again in a ~!*, I'm in no ~ to do that again!*** je ne recommencerai pas de sitôt!, je ne suis pas près de recommencer!; **he won't come back here in a ~!*** il ne reviendra pas de sitôt!, il n'est pas près de revenir!; **are you in a ~ for this?** vous le voulez très vite?; **what's the** *or* **your ~?** qu'est-ce qui (vous) presse?; **there's no (great) ~** rien ne presse, il n'y a pas le feu*; **there's no ~ for it** ça ne presse pas.

2 vi a se dépêcher, se presser, se hâter (*to do* de faire). **do ~** dépêchez-vous; **don't ~** ne vous pressez *or* dépêchez pas; **I must ~** il faut que je me dépêche (*subj*) *or* presse (*subj*); **don't ~ over that essay** ne faites pas cette dissertation à la va-vite, prenez votre temps pour faire cette dissertation; **if we ~ over the meal** si nous mangeons rapidement, si nous nous dépêchons de manger.

b **to ~ in/out/through** *etc* entrer/sortir/traverser *etc* à la hâte *or* en toute hâte *or* précipitamment; **she hurried (over) to her sister's** elle s'est précipitée chez sa sœur, elle s'est rendue chez sa sœur en toute hâte; **he hurried (over) towards me** il s'est précipité vers moi; **he hurried after her** il a couru pour la rattraper; **they hurried up the stairs** ils ont monté l'escalier précipitamment *or* en toute hâte *or* quatre à quatre; **she hurried home** elle s'est dépêchée de rentrer, elle est rentrée en hâte.

3 vt a *person* faire presser, bousculer, faire se dépêcher; *piece of work* presser. **don't ~ your meal** ne mangez pas trop vite; **I don't want to ~ you** je ne veux pas vous bousculer; **you can't ~ him, he won't be hurried** vous ne le ferez pas se dépêcher; **this plan can't be hurried** ce projet prend du temps *or* exige d'être exécuté sans hâte; *see also* **hurried.**

b **to ~ sb in/out/through** *etc* faire entrer/sortir/traverser *etc* qn à la hâte *or* en (toute) hâte; **they hurried him to a doctor** ils l'ont emmené d'urgence chez un médecin; **troops were hurried to the spot** des troupes ont été envoyées d'urgence sur place.

▸**hurry along** 1 vi marcher d'un pas pressé. **hurry along please!** pressons un peu *or* activons*, s'il vous plaît! 2 vt sep = **hurry on 2.**

▸**hurry back** vi se presser de revenir (*or* de retourner). (*to guest*) **hurry back!** revenez-nous bientôt!; **don't hurry back, I shall be here till 6 o'clock** ne te presse pas de revenir, je serai ici jusqu'à 6 heures.

▸**hurry on** 1 vi se dépêcher, continuer à la hâte *or* en hâte. **she hurried on to the next stop** elle s'est pressée de gagner l'arrêt suivant; **they hurried on to the next question** ils sont vite passés à la question suivante. 2 vt sep *person* faire presser le pas à, faire se dépêcher, activer; *work etc* activer, accélérer. **we're trying to hurry things on a little** nous essayons d'accélérer *or* d'activer un peu les choses.

▸**hurry up** 1 vi se dépêcher, se presser. **hurry up!** dépêchez-vous!, activez!* 2 vt sep *person* faire se dépêcher, (faire) activer; *work* activer, pousser.

hurry-scurry ['hʌrɪ'skʌrɪ] 1 vi courir dans tous les sens. 2 n bousculade *f*, débandade *f*. 3 adv à la débandade.

hurt [hɜːt] pret, ptp **hurt** 1 vt a (*do physical damage to*) *person* faire du mal à, blesser. **to ~ o.s.** se blesser, se faire (du) mal; **to ~ one's arm** se blesser au bras; **I hope I haven't ~ you?** j'espère que je ne vous ai pas fait de mal *or* pas blessé?; **to get ~** se blesser, se faire (du) mal; **someone is bound to get ~** il va y avoir quelqu'un de blessé, quelqu'un va se faire du mal (*see also* **1(b), 1(c)**); **a little rest won't ~ him** un peu de repos ne lui fera pas de mal; **wine never ~ anyone** un peu de vin n'a jamais fait de mal à personne; *see* **fly¹**.

b (*cause physical pain to*) *person* faire mal à. **to ~ o.s.** se faire mal; **my arm ~s me** mon bras me fait mal; **where does it ~ you?** où est-ce que vous avez mal?, où cela vous fait-il mal?; **to get ~** se faire mal.

c (*mentally etc*) faire de la peine à. **in such cases someone is bound to get ~** en pareils cas il y a toujours quelqu'un qui pâtit *or* qui écope*; **what ~ most was ...** ce qui faisait le plus mal c'était ...; **to ~ sb's feelings** offenser *or* froisser *or* blesser qn; **his feelings were ~ by what you said** ce que vous avez dit l'a froissé.

d (*damage*) *thing* abîmer, endommager; *sb's reputation* nuire à. **moths can't ~ this material** les mites ne peuvent pas attaquer ce tissu; **it wouldn't ~ the grass to water it** ça ne ferait pas de mal au gazon d'être arrosé; **that rumour will ~ his business** cette rumeur fera du tort à *or* nuira à son commerce.

2 vi a faire mal. **that ~s** ça fait mal; **my arm ~s** mon bras me fait mal; **it doesn't ~ much** ça ne fait pas très mal; **where does it ~?** où avez-vous mal?; (*loc*) **nothing ~s like the truth** il n'y a que la vérité qui blesse (*loc*); **it won't ~ for being left for a while** il n'y aura pas de

mal à laisser cela de côté un instant.
b (*: *suffer emotionally*) souffrir.
3 n (*physical*) mal *m*, blessure *f*. (*fig*) **the real ~ lay in his attitude to her** ce qui la blessait réellement *or* lui faisait vraiment mal c'était l'attitude qu'il avait envers elle.
4 adj (*physically injured*) blessé; (*offended*) offensé, froissé, blessé. **with a ~ expression** avec un regard meurtri *or* blessé; **she's feeling ~ about it** elle en est *or* a été blessée.

hurtful ['hɜːtfʊl] adj nocif, nuisible (*to* à); *remark* blessant, offensant. **~ to his health** nuisible *or* préjudiciable à sa santé; **what a ~ thing to say!** comme c'est méchant *or* (*stronger*) cruel de dire cela!

hurtfully ['hɜːtfʊlɪ] adv de façon blessante.

hurtle ['hɜːtl] 1 vi *[car, person]* **to ~ along** avancer à toute vitesse *or* allure; **to ~ past sb** passer en trombe à côté de qn; **the stone ~d through the air** la pierre a fendu l'air; **great masses of snow ~d down the mountain** d'énormes masses de neige dévalèrent de la montagne; **she went hurtling down the hill** elle a dégringolé *or* dévalé la pente. 2 vt lancer (de toutes ses forces *or* violemment).

husband ['hʌzbənd] 1 n mari *m*; (*often Admin, Jur etc*) époux *m*. **now they're ~ and wife** ils sont maintenant mari et femme; **the ~ and wife** les conjoints *mpl*, les époux *mpl*; **they were living together as ~ and wife** ils vivaient maritalement *or* en ménage. 2 vt *strength* ménager, économiser; *supplies, resources* bien gérer.

husbandry ['hʌzbəndrɪ] n (*Agr*) agriculture *f*; (*fig*) économie *f*, gestion *f*. **good ~** bonne gestion; *see* **animal**.

hush [hʌʃ] 1 n calme *m*, silence *m*. **the ~ before the storm** le calme avant la tempête; **there was a sudden ~, a ~ fell** il y a eu un silence, tout à coup tout le monde s'est tu; **in the ~ of the night** dans le silence de la nuit; *see also* **hushed**. 2 excl chut! 3 comp ►**hush-hush*** (ultra-) secret (*f* -ète) ►**hush money*** pot-de-vin *m* (*pour acheter le silence*), prix *m* du silence; **to pay sb hush money** acheter le silence de qn ►**hush puppy** (*US Culin*) *espèce de beignet*. 4 vt (*silence*) faire taire; (*soothe*) apaiser, calmer. **she ~ed the baby to sleep** elle endormit le bébé en le berçant.

►**hush up** vt sep *scandal, news* étouffer; *fact* cacher; *person* faire taire, empêcher de parler.

hushed [hʌʃt] adj *voice, conversation* étouffé. **there was a ~ silence** il y eut un grand *or* profond silence; **in ~ amazement they ...** frappés de stupeur, ils ... .

husk [hʌsk] 1 n *[wheat]* balle *f*; *[maize, rice]* enveloppe *f*; *[chestnut]* bogue *f*; *[nut]* écale *f*; *[peas]* cosse *f*, gousse *f*. **rice in the ~** riz non décortiqué. 2 vt *maize, rice* décortiquer; *nut* écaler; *grain* vanner; *peas* écosser; *barley, oats* monder.

huskily ['hʌskɪlɪ] adv *speak, whisper* d'une voix rauque; *sing* d'une voix voilée.

huskiness ['hʌskɪnɪs] n enrouement *m*.

husky[1] ['hʌskɪ] adj a (*hoarse*) *person* enroué; *voice* rauque; *singer's voice* voilé. b (*burly*) costaud*.

husky[2] ['hʌskɪ] n (*dog*) chien *m* esquimau *or* de traîneau.

hussar [hʊ'zɑːʳ] n hussard *m*.

hussy ['hʌsɪ] n a (*minx*) coquine *f*, mâtine *f*. **you little ~!** petite coquine! b (*pej*) garce‡ *f*, traînée‡ *f*.

hustings ['hʌstɪŋz] npl (*esp Brit*) plate-forme électorale. **he said it on the ~** il l'a dit pendant *or* au cours de sa campagne électorale.

hustle ['hʌsl] 1 vt a *person* pousser, bousculer, presser. **to ~ sb in/out** *etc* (*push*) pousser *or* (*hurry*) bousculer qn pour le faire entrer/sortir *etc*; **they ~d him into a car** ils l'ont poussé *or* enfourné* dans une voiture; **I won't be ~d into anything** je ne ferai rien si on me bouscule; **I don't want to ~ you but ...** je ne veux pas vous bousculer mais ... .
b (*cause to proceed*) **to ~ legislation through** faire voter des lois à la hâte; **to ~ things (on** *or* **along)** faire activer les choses.
c (*US* ‡: *sell, pass off*) fourguer*, refiler*.
2 vi a **to ~ in/out/away** entrer/sortir/partir à la hâte.
b (*US* ‡) (*make efforts*) se manier‡, se dépenser sans compter; (*work hard*) trimer*, turbiner*.
c (*esp US* ‡) *[prostitute]* faire le trottoir*.
3 n a (*jostling*) bousculade *f*, presse *f*; (*activity*) grande activité. **~ and bustle** tourbillon *m* d'activité; **the ~ and bustle of city life** le tourbillon de la vie dans les grandes villes.
b (*US* ‡) racket *m*, activité *f* illégale.

hustler* ['hʌsləʳ] n (*go-getter*) type* *m* dynamique, débrouillard(e)* *m(f)*; (*swindler*) arnaqueur *m*, -euse *f*; (*prostitute*) prostitué(e) *m(f)*.

hut [hʌt] n (*primitive dwelling*) hutte *f*, case *f*; (*hovel*) masure *f*, baraque* *f*; (*shed*) cabane *f*; (*Mil*) baraquement *m*; *[climbers]* refuge *m*; *[shepherd]* cabane *f*, abri *m*; *see* **mud**.

hutch [hʌtʃ] n *[rabbit etc]* clapier *m*; (*US: dresser*) vaisselier *m*.

HV, h.v. abbr of **high voltage**.

hyacinth ['haɪəsɪnθ] n (*Bot*) jacinthe *f*; (*stone*) hyacinthe *f*. (*Bot*) **wild ~** jacinthe des bois *or* sauvage, endymion *m*.

hyaena [haɪ'iːnə] n hyène *f*.

hybrid ['haɪbrɪd] adj, n hybride (*m*). (*Comput*) **~ system** système *m* hybride.

hybridism ['haɪbrɪdɪzəm] n hybridisme *m*.

hybridization [ˌhaɪbrɪdaɪ'zeɪʃən] n hybridation *f*.

hybridize ['haɪbrɪdaɪz] vt hybrider, croiser.

hydra ['haɪdrə] n, pl **~s** *or* **hydrae** ['haɪdriː] hydre *f*.

hydrangea [haɪ'dreɪndʒə] n hortensia *m*.

hydrant ['haɪdrənt] n prise *f* d'eau; (*also* **fire ~**) bouche *f* d'incendie.

hydrate ['haɪdreɪt] 1 n hydrate *m*. 2 vt hydrater.

hydraulic [haɪ'drɒlɪk] adj (*gen*) hydraulique. (*Aut*) **~ brake/circuit/suspension** frein *m*/circuit *m*/suspension *f* hydraulique; (*Aut*) **~ ramp** pont *m* élévateur.

hydraulics [haɪ'drɒlɪks] n (*NonC*) hydraulique *f*.

hydro ['haɪdrəʊ] 1 n a (*Brit: hotel etc*) établissement thermal (*hôtel*). b (*Can*) (*power*) énergie *f* hydro-électrique; (*plant*) centrale *f* d'énergie hydro-électrique. 2 adj (*Can*) hydro-électrique.

hydr(o)... ['haɪdr(əʊ)] pref hydr(o)... .

hydrocarbon [ˌhaɪdrəʊ'kɑːbən] n hydrocarbure *m*.

hydrochloric [ˌhaɪdrəʊ'klɒrɪk] adj chlorhydrique.

hydrocyanic [ˌhaɪdrəʊsaɪ'ænɪk] adj cyanhydrique.

hydrodynamics [ˌhaɪdrəʊdaɪ'næmɪks] n (*NonC*) hydrodynamique *f*.

hydroelectric [ˌhaɪdrəʊɪ'lektrɪk] adj hydro-électrique. **~ power** énergie *f* hydro-électrique.

hydroelectricity [ˌhaɪdrəʊɪlek'trɪsɪtɪ] n hydro-électricité *f*.

hydrofoil ['haɪdrəʊˌfɔɪl] n hydrofoil *m*.

hydrogen ['haɪdrɪdʒən] n hydrogène *m*. **~ bomb** bombe *f* à hydrogène; **~ peroxide** eau *f* oxygénée.

hydrography [haɪ'drɒgrəfɪ] n hydrographie *f*.

hydrolysis [haɪ'drɒlɪsɪs] n hydrolyse *f*.

hydrometer [haɪ'drɒmɪtəʳ] n hydromètre *m*.

hydropathic [ˌhaɪdrəʊ'pæθɪk] adj hydrothérapique.

hydrophilic [ˌhaɪdrəʊ'fɪlɪk] adj hydrophile.

hydrophobia [ˌhaɪdrəʊ'fəʊbɪə] n hydrophobie *f*.

hydrophobic [ˌhaɪdrəʊ'fəʊbɪk] adj hydrophobe.

hydroplane ['haɪdrəʊˌpleɪn] n hydroglisseur *m*.

hydroponics [ˌhaɪdrəʊ'pɒnɪks] n (*NonC*) culture *f* hydroponique.

hydrotherapy [ˌhaɪdrəʊ'θerəpɪ] n hydrothérapie *f*.

hydroxide [haɪ'drɒksaɪd] n hydroxyde *m*, hydrate *m*.

hyena [haɪ'iːnə] n hyène *f*.

hygiene ['haɪdʒiːn] n hygiène *f*.

hygienic [haɪ'dʒiːnɪk] adj hygiénique.

hygienist ['haɪdʒiːnɪst] n hygiéniste *mf*.

hymen ['haɪmen] n (*Anat*) hymen *m*.

hymn [hɪm] 1 n hymne *m*, cantique *m*. **~ book** livre *m* de cantiques. 2 vt (*liter*) chanter un hymne à la gloire de.

hymnal ['hɪmnəl] n livre *m* de cantiques.

hype [haɪp] 1 n a (*) (*publicity drive*) battage *m* publicitaire; (*book, product*) livre *m* *or* produit *m* lancé à grand renfort de publicité. b (*Drugs sl*) (*syringe*) shooteuse‡ *f*, seringue *f*; (*injection*) shoot‡ *m*, piqûre *f*; (*addict*) toxico* *mf*, camé(e)* *m(f)*. 2 vt a (*: *publicize*) *book, product, film* lancer à grand renfort de publicité. b (‡: *also* **~ up**) (*excite*) *person* exciter; (*increase*) *numbers, attendance* augmenter. **to ~ the economy** stimuler l'économie. c (*US* ‡: *cheat*) *person* tromper, rouler*. 3 vi (*Drugs sl: also* **~ up**) se shooter‡, se piquer.

►**hype up** vi, vt sep *see* **hype 2(b), 3**.

hyper* ['haɪpəʳ] adj (*nervy, overexcited*) (tout) excité; (*hyperactive: child*) hyperactif.

hyper... ['haɪpəʳ] pref hyper... .

hyperacidity ['haɪpərə'sɪdɪtɪ] n hyperacidité *f*.

hyperactive [ˌhaɪpər'æktɪv] adj suractif; *child* hyperactif.

hyperactivity [ˌhaɪpəræk'tɪvɪtɪ] n suractivité *f*; *[child]* hyperactivité *f*.

hyperbola [haɪ'pɜːbələ] n, pl **~s** *or* **hyperbole** [haɪ'pɜːbəˌliː] (*Math*) hyperbole *f*.

hyperbole [haɪ'pɜːbəlɪ] n (*Literat*) hyperbole *f*.

hyperbolic(al) [ˌhaɪpə'bɒlɪk(əl)] adj hyperbolique.

hypercorrection [ˌhaɪpəkə'rekʃən] n hypercorrection *f*.

hypercritical [ˌhaɪpə'krɪtɪkəl] adj hypercritique.

hyperinflation [ˌhaɪpərɪn'fleɪʃən] n hyperinflation *f*.

hyperkinetic [ˌhaɪpəkɪ'netɪk] adj (*hyperactive*) suractif.

hypermarket ['haɪpəmɑːkɪt] n (*Brit*) hypermarché *m*.

hypermeter [haɪ'pɜːmɪtəʳ] n vers *m* hypermètre.

hypermetropia [ˌhaɪpəmɪ'trəʊpɪə], **hypermetropy** [ˌhaɪpə'metrəpɪ] n hypermétropie *f*.

hypernym ['haɪpənɪm] n hyperonyme *m*.

hyperrealism [ˌhaɪpə'rɪəlɪzəm] n hyperréalisme *m*.

hypersensitive [ˌhaɪpə'sensɪtɪv] adj hypersensible.

hypersonic [ˌhaɪpə'sɒnɪk] adj hypersonique.

hypertension [ˌhaɪpə'tenʃən] n hypertension *f*.

hypertrophy [haɪ'pɜːtrəfɪ] 1 n hypertrophie *f*. 2 vt hypertrophier. 3 vi s'hypertrophier.

hyperventilate [ˌhaɪpɜː'ventɪleɪt] vi hyperventiler.

hyperventilation [ˌhaɪpɜːventɪ'leɪʃən] n hyperventilation *f*.

hyphen ['haɪfən] n trait *m* d'union.

hyphenate ['haɪfəneɪt] vt mettre un trait d'union à. **~d word** mot *m* à trait d'union.

hypnagogic, hypnogogic [ˌhɪpnə'gɒdʒɪk] adj hypnagogique.

hypnosis [hɪp'nəʊsɪs] n, pl **hypnoses** [hɪp'nəʊsiːz] hypnose *f*. **under ~** en état d'hypnose, en état hypnotique.

hypnotherapy [ˌhɪpnəʊˈθerəpɪ] **n** hypnothérapie *f*.
hypnotic [hɪpˈnɒtɪk] 1 **adj** hypnotique. 2 **n** (*drug*) hypnotique; (*person*) sujet *m* hypnotique.
hypnotism [ˈhɪpnətɪzəm] **n** hypnotisme *m*.
hypnotist [ˈhɪpnətɪst] **n** hypnotiseur *m*, -euse *f*.
hypnotize [ˈhɪpnətaɪz] **vt** (*lit, fig*) hypnotiser. **to ~ sb into doing sth** faire faire qch à qn sous hypnose.
hypo... [ˈhaɪpəʊ] **pref** hypo... .
hypoallergenic [ˌhaɪpəʊæləˈgenɪk] **adj** hypoallergénique.
hypocentre [ˈhaɪpəʊˌsentəʳ] **n** *[earthquake]* hypocentre *m*; *[nuclear blast]* point *m* zéro.
hypochondria [ˌhaɪpəʊˈkɒndrɪə] **n** hypocondrie *f*.
hypochondriac [ˌhaɪpəʊˈkɒndrɪæk] 1 **adj** hypocondriaque. 2 **n** malade *mf* imaginaire, hypocondriaque *mf*. **he's a ~** il se croit toujours malade.
hypocrisy [hɪˈpɒkrɪsɪ] **n** hypocrisie *f*.
hypocrite [ˈhɪpəkrɪt] **n** hypocrite *mf*.
hypocritical [ˌhɪpəˈkrɪtɪkəl] **adj** hypocrite.
hypocritically [ˌhɪpəˈkrɪtɪkəlɪ] **adv** hypocritement.
hypodermic [ˌhaɪpəˈdɜːmɪk] 1 **adj** hypodermique. 2 **n** (*syringe*) seringue *f* hypodermique; (*needle*) aiguille *f* hypodermique; (*injection*) injection *f* hypodermique.
hypoglossal [ˌhaɪpəˈglɒsəl] **adj** hypoglosse.
hyponym [ˈhaɪpənɪm] **n** hyponyme *m*.
hyponymy [haɪˈpɒnɪmɪ] **n** hyponymie *f*.
hypostasis [haɪˈpɒstəsɪs] **n, pl hypostases** [haɪˈpɒstəsiːz] (*Rel*) hypostase *f*.
hypostatic [ˌhaɪpəʊˈstætɪk] **adj** (*Rel*) hypostatique.
hypotenuse [haɪˈpɒtɪnjuːz] **n** hypoténuse *f*.
hypothalamus [ˌhaɪpəˈθæləməs] **n, pl hypothalami** [ˌhaɪpəˈθæləmaɪ] hypothalamus *m*.
hypothermia [ˌhaɪpəʊˈθɜːmɪə] **n** hypothermie *f*.
hypothesis [ˌhaɪˈpɒθɪsɪs] **n, pl hypotheses** [haɪˈpɒθɪsiːz] hypothèse *f*; *see* **working**.
hypothesize [ˌhaɪˈpɒθɪˌsaɪz] **vi** formuler une (*or* des) hypothèse(s).
hypothetic(al) [ˌhaɪpəʊˈθetɪk(əl)] **adj** hypothétique.
hypothetically [ˌhaɪpəʊˈθetɪkəlɪ] **adv** hypothétiquement.
hyssop [ˈhɪsəp] **n** (*Bot*) hysope *f*.
hysterectomy [ˌhɪstəˈrektəmɪ] **n** hystérectomie *f*.
hysteria [hɪsˈtɪərɪə] **n** (*Psych*) hystérie *f*. **she felt a wave of mounting ~** (*panic*) elle sentait monter la crise de nerfs; (*laughter*) elle sentait qu'elle allait avoir le fou rire; **there were signs of ~ among the crowd** la foule semblait être sur le point de perdre tout contrôle; *see* **mass**[1].
hysterical [hɪsˈterɪkəl] **adj** (*Psych*) hystérique; (*gen*) *person* très nerveux, surexcité; (*with laughter*) en proie au fou rire; *laugh, sobs, weeping* convulsif. **to become ~** (*gen*) avoir une (violente) crise de nerfs; **~ laughter** fou rire *m*.
hysterically [hɪsˈterɪkəlɪ] **adv** (*Med, Psych*) hystériquement. **to weep ~** avoir une violente crise de larmes; **to laugh ~** rire convulsivement, être saisi d'un rire convulsif; **"come here," she shouted ~** "viens ici", hurla-t-elle comme une hystérique.
hysterics [hɪsˈterɪks] **npl** a (*tears, shouts etc*) (violente) crise *f* de nerfs. **to have ~, to go into ~** avoir une (violente) crise de nerfs; **she was nearly in ~** elle était au bord de la crise de nerfs. b (**: laughter*) crise *f* de rire. **to have ~, to go into ~** attraper un fou rire; **we were in ~ about it** on en était malade (de rire)*, on en a ri jusqu'aux larmes.
Hz (*Rad etc*) (**abbr of hertz**) hz.

I

I¹, i [aɪ] n a (*letter*) I, i *m*; **I for Isaac** (*Brit*) *or* **Item** (*US*) ≃ I comme Irma; *see* **dot**. b (*Geog*) (abbr of **Island** *and* **Isle**) île *f* (*cartographie*).

I² [aɪ] pers pron (*unstressed*) je, (*before vowel*) j'; (*stressed*) moi. **he and ~ are going to sing** lui et moi (nous) allons chanter; **no, I'll do it** non, c'est moi qui vais le faire; (*frm*) **it's ~** c'est moi.

IA (*US Post*) abbr of **Iowa**.

Ia. (*US*) abbr of **Iowa**.

IAEA [ˌaɪeɪiːˈeɪ] (abbr of **International Atomic Energy Agency**) A.I.E.A. *f*.

iambic [aɪˈæmbɪk] 1 adj iambique. **~ pentameter** pentamètre *m* iambique. 2 n iambe *m*, vers *m* iambique.

I.B.A. [ˌaɪbiːˈeɪ] n (*Brit*) (abbr of **Independent Broadcasting Authority**) *haute autorité contrôlant les sociétés indépendantes de radiodiffusion et de télévision*.

Iberia [aɪˈbɪərɪə] n Ibérie *f*.

Iberian [aɪˈbɪərɪən] 1 adj ibérique, ibérien. **~ Peninsula** péninsule *f* Ibérique. 2 n a Ibère *mf*. b (*Ling*) ibère *m*.

ibex [ˈaɪbeks] n, pl **~es** *or* **~** *or* **ibices** [ˈɪbɪˌsiːz] bouquetin *m*, ibex *m*.

ib(id). [ˈɪb(ɪd)] (abbr of **ibidem** = *from the same source*) ib(id).

ibis [ˈaɪbɪs] n, pl **~es** *or* **~** ibis *m*.

Ibiza [ɪˈbiːθə] n Ibiza *f*. **in ~** à Ibiza.

IBRD [ˌaɪbiːɑːrˈdiː] n (abbr of **International Bank for Reconstruction and Development**) BIRD *f*.

i/c (abbr of **in charge**) *see* **charge 1e**.

ICA [ˌaɪsiːˈeɪ] n a (*Brit*) abbr of **Institute of Contemporary Arts**. b (*Brit*) abbr of **Institute of Chartered Accountants**. c abbr of **International Co-operation Administration**.

ICAO [ˌaɪsiːeɪˈəʊ] n (abbr of **International Civil Aviation Organization**) OACI *f*.

Icarus [ˈɪkərəs] n Icare *m*.

ICBM [ˌaɪsiːbiːˈem] n (abbr of **intercontinental ballistic missile**) *see* **intercontinental**.

ice [aɪs] 1 n a (*NonC*) glace *f*; (*on road*) verglas *m*. **my hands are like ~** j'ai les mains glacées; (*fig*) **to be (skating** *or* **treading) on thin ~** s'aventurer en terrain glissant (*fig*); **to put on ~** (*lit*) *melon, wine* mettre à rafraîchir avec de la glace; *champagne* mettre à frapper; (*fig*) mettre en attente *or* au frigidaire*; **to keep sth on ~** garder qch sur *or* dans de la glace; (*Theat*) **"Cinderella on ~"** "Cendrillon, spectacle sur glace"; *see* **black, break, cold, cut** *etc*.
b (*Brit*: **~ cream**) glace *f*. **raspberry ~** glace à la framboise; *see* **water** *etc*.
c (*‡*: *diamonds*) diamant(s) *m(pl)*, diam(s)‡ *m(pl)*.
2 compar ▸**ice age** période *f* glaciaire ▸**ice-age** adj (qui date) de la période glaciaire ▸**ice axe** piolet *m* ▸**iceberg** iceberg *m*; (* *fig*: *person*) glaçon* *m* (*see also* **tip¹**) ▸**iceberg lettuce** laitue croquante ▸**ice blue** bleu glacier *inv* ▸**iceboat** (*Sport*) = **ice yacht**; (*Naut*) = **icebreaker** ▸**icebound** *harbour* fermé par les glaces; *ship* pris dans les glaces ▸**icebox** (*US*: *refrigerator*) Frigidaire *m* ®, réfrigérateur *m*; (*Brit*: *part of refrigerator*) compartiment *m* à glace, freezer *m*; (*insulated box*) glacière *f*; **this room is like an icebox** cette pièce est une vraie glacière, on gèle dans cette pièce ▸**icebreaker** (*Naut*) brise-glace(s) *m*; (*fig*: *at party, meeting etc*) façon *f* de briser la glace; **as an icebreaker** (*fig*) pour briser la glace ▸**ice bucket** seau *m* à glace *or* à champagne ▸**icecap** calotte *f* glaciaire ▸**ice climber** glaciériste *mf* ▸**ice-cold** *drink, hands* glacé; *room* glacial; *manners, person* glacé, glacial ▸**ice cream** glace *f*; **strawberry ice cream** glace *f* à la fraise ▸**ice-cream soda** (*US*) ice-cream soda *m* ▸**ice cube** glaçon *m*, cube *m* de glace ▸**ice dance** = **ice dancing** ▸**ice dancer** danseur (-euse) *m(f)* sur glace ▸**ice dancing** danse *f* sur glace ▸**ice field** champ *m* de glace ▸**ice floe** banquise *f* ▸**ice-hammer** marteau-piolet *m* ▸**ice hockey** hockey *m* sur glace ▸**icehouse** glacière *f* ▸**ice lolly** (*Brit*) ≃ esquimau *m* (*glace*) ▸**iceman** (*US*) marchand *m or* livreur *m* de glace ▸**ice pack** sachet *m* de glace ▸**ice pick** pic *m* à glace ▸**ice piton** broche *f* (à glace) ▸**ice rink** patinoire *f* ▸**ice show** (*Theat*) spectacle *m* sur glace ▸**iceskate** n patin *m* (à glace) ▸**ice-skate** vi patiner (sur glace), faire du patin (à glace) *or* du patinage (sur glace) ▸**ice-skating** patinage *m* (sur glace) ▸**ice-tray** (*in refrigerator*) bac *m* à glaçons ▸**ice yacht** yacht *m* à glace.
3 vt a *drink* (*chill*) (faire) rafraîchir, mettre à rafraîchir; (*put ~ cubes in*) mettre des glaçons dans, ajouter des glaçons à. **~d tea/coffee** thé/café glacé; **~d water/martini** de l'eau/un martini avec des glaçons; **~d champagne** champagne frappé; **~d melon** melon rafraîchi.
b *cake* glacer.
4 vi (*also* **~ over, ~ up**) *[aircraft wings, windscreen]* givrer.

▸**ice over** 1 vi *[windscreen, aircraft]* givrer; *[river]* geler. **the lake has iced over** le lac a gelé *or* est pris (de glace). 2 vt sep: **to be iced over** *[windscreen, aircraft]* être givré; *[river, lake]* être gelé, être pris (de glace).

▸**ice up** 1 vi *[windscreen, aircraft]* givrer. 2 vt sep: **to be iced up** être gelé.

Iceland [ˈaɪslənd] n Islande *f*.

Icelander [ˈaɪsləndəʳ] n Islandais(e) *m(f)*.

Icelandic [aɪsˈlændɪk] 1 adj islandais. 2 n (*Ling*) islandais *m*.

I Ching [ˈiː ˈtʃɪŋ] n Yi King *m*.

ichthyologist [ˌɪkθɪˈɒlədʒɪst] n ichtyologiste *mf*.

ichthyology [ˌɪkθɪˈɒlədʒɪ] n ichtyologie *f*.

ichthyosaurus [ˌɪkθɪəˈsɔːrəs] n, pl **~es** *or* **ichthyosauri** [ˌɪkθɪəˈsɔːraɪ] ichtyosaure *m*.

icicle [ˈaɪsɪkl] n glaçon *m* (*naturel*).

icily [ˈaɪsɪlɪ] adv *look, bow* d'un air glacial; *speak* d'une voix *or* d'un ton glacial(e).

iciness [ˈaɪsɪnɪs] n a (*lit*) *[road, surface]* état *m* verglacé. b (*fig*) *[manner, tone, stare etc]* froideur *f* extrême.

icing [ˈaɪsɪŋ] n a (*NonC*) (*Culin*) glace *f*, glaçage *m*. (*Brit*) **~ sugar** sucre *m* glace; **chocolate/coffee** *etc* **~** glaçage au chocolat/au café *etc*; *see* **butter**. b (*on aircraft etc*) givre *m*. c (*fig*) **the ~ on the cake** la cerise sur le gâteau.

icky‡ [ˈɪkɪ] adj (*US*) (*messy*) poisseux; (*fig*: *horrible*) dégueulasse‡.

icon [ˈaɪkɒn] n icône *f*.

iconoclast [aɪˈkɒnəklæst] n iconoclaste *mf*.

iconoclastic [aɪˌkɒnəˈklæstɪk] adj iconoclaste.

iconographer [ˌaɪkɒˈnɒgrəfəʳ] n iconographe *mf*.

iconography [ˌaɪkɒˈnɒgrəfɪ] n iconographie *f*.

ICU [ˌaɪsiːˈjuː] n (abbr of **intensive care unit**) USI *f*.

icy [ˈaɪsɪ] adj *wind, weather, stare, reception* glacial, glacé; *ground, hands* glacé; *road* couvert de verglas, verglacé. **it will be ~ cold today** aujourd'hui le temps sera glacial; **it's ~ cold in here** on gèle ici, il fait glacial ici; **her hands were ~ cold** elle avait les mains glacées.

ID [aɪˈdiː] n a (abbr of **identification, identity**) **ID disk/card** plaque *f*/carte *f* d'identité. b (*US Post*) abbr of **Idaho**.

id [ɪd] n (*Psych*) ça *m*.

I'd [aɪd] = **I had, I should, I would**; *see* **have, should, would**.

Ida. (*US*) abbr of **Idaho**.

Idaho [ˈaɪdəˌhəʊ] n Idaho *m*. **in ~** dans l'Idaho.

IDD [ˌaɪdiːˈdiː] n (*Brit Telec*) (abbr of **international direct dialling**) *automatique international*.

idea [aɪˈdɪə] n a (*thought, purpose*) idée *f*. **man/woman of ~s** homme *m*/femme *f* à idées; (*in firm*) **he's the ~s man*** (*his job*) c'est lui le concepteur; (*he's the one with the ideas*) c'est lui qui trouve les idées nouvelles; **he hasn't an ~ in his head** il n'a rien dans la tête; **brilliant** *or* **bright ~** idée géniale *or* de génie; **good ~!** bonne idée!; **what an ~!, the very ~ (of it)!** quelle idée!, en voilà une idée!; **I can't bear the ~ (of it)** je n'ose pas y penser; **I've got an ~ for a play** j'ai l'idée d'une pièce; **I hit (up)on** *or* **I suddenly had the ~ of going to see her** d'un seul coup l'idée m'est venue d'aller la voir; **I had an ~ of buying a car but didn't do so** j'avais l'idée d'acheter une voiture mais je ne l'ai pas fait; **it's an ~** *or* **a good ~ to book well in advance** c'est une (bonne) idée de réserver bien à l'avance; **it might not be a bad ~ to wait a few days** ce ne serait peut-être pas une mauvaise idée d'attendre quelques jours;

the ~ is to sell the car to him il s'agit de lui vendre la voiture; **whose ~ was it to take this route?** qui a eu l'idée de prendre ce chemin?; **it wasn't my ~!** ce n'est pas moi qui en ai eu l'idée!; **the ~ never entered my head** l'idée ne m'en est jamais venue *or* ne m'a jamais effleuré; **he got the ~ (into his head) that she wouldn't help him** il s'est mis en tête l'idée qu'elle ne l'aiderait pas; **where did you get that ~?** où est-ce que tu as pris cette idée-là?; **what gave you the ~ that I couldn't come?** qu'est-ce qui t'a fait penser que je ne pourrais pas venir?; **don't get any ~s!*** ne te fais pas d'illusions!, ce n'est pas la peine de t'imaginer des choses!*; **once he gets an ~ into his head** une fois qu'il s'est mis une idée en tête; **to put ~s into sb's head, to give sb ~s** mettre *or* fourrer des idées dans la tête de qn; **that gave me the ~ of inviting her** cela m'a donné l'idée de l'inviter.

b (*opinion*) idée *f*, opinion *f*; (*way of thinking*) conception *f*, façon *f* de penser. **she has some odd ~s about how to bring up children** elle a de drôles d'idées sur la façon d'élever les enfants; **according to his ~** selon sa façon de penser; **if that's your ~ of fun** si c'est ça que tu appelles t'amuser; **it wasn't my ~ of a holiday** ce n'était pas ce que j'appelle des vacances.

c (*vague knowledge*) idée *f*, notion *f*. **I've got some ~ of physics** j'ai quelques notions de physique; **have you any ~ of what he meant to do?** avez-vous la moindre idée de ce qu'il voulait faire?; **I haven't the least** *or* **slightest** *or* **foggiest* ~** je n'en ai pas la moindre idée; **I have an ~ that he was going to Paris** j'ai idée *or* j'ai dans l'idée qu'il allait à Paris; **I had no ~ they knew each other** je n'avais aucune idée *or* j'ignorais absolument *or* j'étais loin de soupçonner qu'ils se connaissaient; **he has no ~ what he's doing!** il fait n'importe quoi!*; **it was awful, you've no ~!** c'était terrible, tu ne peux pas t'imaginer!; **can you give me a rough ~ of how many you want?** pouvez-vous m'indiquer en gros *or* approximativement combien vous en voulez?; **he gave me a general ~ of what they would do** il m'a donné une indication générale sur ce qu'ils allaient faire; **it gives you an ~ of how much it will cost** cela permet de se faire une idée de *or* sur ce que ça va coûter; **you're getting the ~!*** tu y es!, tu as compris! *or* pigé!*; **I've got the general ~*** je vois à peu près (ce dont il s'agit); **that's the ~!*** c'est ça!; **what's the big ~?*** ça ne va pas, non?‡.

ideal [aɪˈdɪəl] 1 adj idéal. **her ~ man** son homme idéal; **it would be ~ if she could come with us** ce serait idéal *or* parfait si elle pouvait venir avec nous; **it's ~!** c'est (l')idéal! 2 n idéal *m*.

idealism [aɪˈdɪəlɪzəm] n idéalisme *m*.

idealist [aɪˈdɪəlɪst] adj, n idéaliste *(mf)*.

idealistic [aɪˌdɪəˈlɪstɪk] adj idéaliste.

idealize [aɪˈdɪəlaɪz] vt idéaliser.

ideally [aɪˈdɪəlɪ] adv *suited* idéalement; *placed, equipped, shaped* d'une manière idéale. **the village is ~ situated** le village jouit d'une situation idéale; **he is ~ suited to the job** il est parfait pour ce poste; **~ the house should have 4 rooms** l'idéal serait que la maison ait 4 pièces.

identical [aɪˈdentɪkəl] adj identique (*to* à). **~ twins** vrais jumeaux, vraies jumelles.

identically [aɪˈdentɪkəlɪ] adv identiquement.

identifiable [aɪˈdentɪˌfaɪəbl] adj *trait* distinctif; *goal, group* distinct; *person* repérable, reconnaissable; *criminal, dead body, virus etc* identifiable. **how is he ~?** comment est-ce qu'on peut l'identifier?; **~ as a Muscovite/an artist** reconnaissable en tant que *or* comme un Moscovite/artiste; **~ as being** repérable *or* reconnaissable comme étant; **he's easily ~** il est facilement repérable *or* reconnaissable (*as* comme).

identification [aɪˌdentɪfɪˈkeɪʃən] 1 n a (*NonC*) identification *f*. b (*papers etc*) pièce *f* d'identité. **have you got any (means of) ~ to back up this cheque?** avez-vous une pièce d'identité pour garantir la validité de ce chèque? 2 comp ▸**identification mark** signe *m* d'identification ▸**identification papers** pièces *fpl or* papiers *mpl* d'identité ▸**identification parade** (*Brit Police*) séance *f* d'identification (d'un suspect) ▸**identification tag** (*US*) plaque *f* d'identité.

identifier [aɪˈdentɪfaɪəʳ] n (*Comput*) identificateur *m*.

identify [aɪˈdentɪfaɪ] 1 vt a (*establish identity of*) identifier, établir l'identité de. **she identified him as the man who attacked her** elle l'a identifié comme étant l'homme qui l'a attaquée; **the police have identified the man they want to question** la police a identifié *or* établi l'identité de l'homme qu'elle veut interroger; **to ~ a body** identifier un cadavre.

b (*consider as the same*) identifier (*A with B* A avec *or* à *or* et B). **to ~ o.s. with** s'identifier à *or* avec, s'assimiler à; **he refused to ~ himself with the rebels** il a refusé de s'identifier avec les rebelles; **he refused to be identified with the rebels** il a refusé d'être identifié *or* assimilé aux rebelles.

2 vi s'identifier (*with* avec, à), s'assimiler (*with* à).

Identikit [aɪˈdentɪkɪt] n ®: **~ (picture)** portrait-robot *m*, photo-robot *f*.

identity [aɪˈdentɪtɪ] 1 n identité *f*. **show me some proof of ~** montrez-moi une pièce d'identité; **this is not a proof of ~** ceci ne constitue pas une preuve d'identité; **a case of mistaken ~** une erreur d'identité. 2 comp ▸**identity card** carte *f* d'identité ▸**identity crisis** (*Psych*) crise *f* d'identité ▸**identity disc** (*Mil etc*) plaque *f* d'identité ▸**identity papers** pièces *fpl or* papiers *mpl* d'identité ▸**identity parade** séance *f* d'identification (d'un suspect).

ideogram [ˈɪdɪəgræm] n, **ideograph** [ˈɪdɪəgrɑːf] n idéogramme *m*.

ideographic [ˌɪdɪəˈgræfɪk] adj idéographique.

ideological [ˌaɪdɪəˈlɒdʒɪkəl] adj idéologique.

ideologically [ˌaɪdɪəˈlɒdʒɪkəlɪ] adv du point de vue *or* sur le plan idéologique. **~ sound/unsound** correct/incorrect du point de vue idéologique.

ideologist [ˌaɪdɪˈɒlədʒɪst] n idéologue *mf*.

ideology [ˌaɪdɪˈɒlədʒɪ] n idéologie *f*.

ides [aɪdz] npl ides *fpl*.

idiocy [ˈɪdɪəsɪ] n (*NonC*) stupidité *f*, idiotie *f*, imbécillité *f*; (*Med* ††) idiotie. **a piece of ~** une stupidité, une idiotie.

idiolect [ˈɪdɪəʊlekt] n idiolecte *m*.

idiom [ˈɪdɪəm] n a (*phrase, expression*) expression *f or* tournure *f* idiomatique, locution *f*, idiotisme *m*. b (*language*) *[country]* idiome *m*, langue *f*; *[region]* idiome; *[person]* idiome, langue, parler *m*.

idiomatic [ˌɪdɪəˈmætɪk] adj idiomatique. **he speaks ~ French** il parle un français idiomatique; **~ expression** expression *f or* tournure *f* idiomatique, locution *f*, idiotisme *m*.

idiomatically [ˌɪdɪəˈmætɪkəlɪ] adv de façon idiomatique.

idiosyncrasy [ˌɪdɪəˈsɪŋkrəsɪ] n particularité *f*, caractéristique *f*. **one of his little idiosyncrasies** une de ses particularités *or* petites manies.

idiosyncratic [ˌɪdɪəsɪŋˈkrætɪk] adj particulier, caractéristique.

idiot [ˈɪdɪət] 1 n idiot(e) *m(f)*, imbécile *mf*, crétin(e)* *m(f)*; (*Med* ††) idiot(e) (de naissance). **to act/speak like an ~** faire/dire des idioties *or* des imbécillités; **to behave like an ~** se conduire en idiot *or* en imbécile *or* en crétin*, faire l'idiot *or* l'imbécile; **you ~!** espèce d'idiot! *or* d'imbécile!; **what an ~ I am!** que je suis idiot! *or* bête!, quel imbécile je fais!; *see* **village**. 2 comp ▸**idiot board** (*TV*) téléprompteur *m* ▸**idiot box‡** (*US TV*) télé* *f*.

idiotic [ˌɪdɪˈɒtɪk] adj idiot, bête, stupide. **that was ~ of you!** ce que tu as été idiot!

idiotically [ˌɪdɪˈɒtɪkəlɪ] adv bêtement, stupidement, idiotement. **to behave ~** se conduire en idiot *or* en imbécile, faire l'imbécile *or* l'idiot.

idle [ˈaɪdl] 1 adj a *person* (*doing nothing*) sans occupation, inoccupé, désœuvré; (*unemployed*) en chômage; (*lazy*) paresseux, fainéant, oisif. **the ~ rich** les riches désœuvrés, l'élite oisive; **in my ~ moments** à mes moments de loisir, à mes moments perdus; **~ life** vie oisive *or* d'oisiveté; (*Ind*) **to make sb ~** réduire qn au chômage.

b (*not in use*) *machine* au repos. **this machine is never ~** cette machine n'est jamais au repos *or* ne s'arrête jamais; **the whole factory stood ~** l'usine entière était arrêtée *or* chômait *or* était en chômage; **~ time** *[workers]* temps *m* chômé; *[machine]* temps *m* mort, arrêt *m* machine; *see* **lie¹**.

c *speculation, question, wish, threat* oiseux, futile, vain; *hope* vain, futile; *remark* fait en passant. **out of ~ curiosity** par curiosité pure et simple; **~ money** argent *m* qui dort; **~ promise** vaine promesse, promesse en l'air; **~ gossip** racontars *mpl*, ragots *mpl*; **~ words** *or* **talk** paroles oiseuses *or* en l'air; **~ fancy** rêve *m* chimérique, chimère *f*; **~ fear** crainte non justifiée *or* sans fondement; **~ pleasures** plaisirs *mpl* futiles; **it is ~ to hope that ...** il est inutile d'espérer que ... .

2 vi a (*also* **~ about, ~ around**) *[person]* paresser, fainéanter, se laisser aller à la paresse. **to ~ about the streets** traîner dans les rues.

b *[engine, machine]* tourner au ralenti.

▸**idle away** vt sep: **to idle away one's time** gaspiller *or* perdre son temps (à ne rien faire).

idleness [ˈaɪdlnɪs] n a (*state of not working*) oisiveté *f*, inaction *f*, inactivité *f*, désœuvrement *m*; (*unemployment*) chômage *m*; (*laziness*) paresse *f*, fainéantise *f*. **to live in ~** vivre oisif *or* dans l'oisiveté. b *[threat, wish, question, speculation]* futilité *f*, inutilité *f*; *[promises, pleasures]* futilité; *[fears]* manque *m* de justification; *[words]* manque de sérieux; *[effort]* inutilité.

idler [ˈaɪdləʳ] n a (*person*) (*doing nothing*) oisif *m*, -ive *f*, désœuvré(e) *m(f)*; (*lazy*) paresseux *m*, -euse *f*, fainéant(e) *m(f)*. b (*Tech*) (*wheel*) roue folle; (*pinion*) pignon *m* libre; (*pulley*) poulie-guide *f*, poulie folle.

idling [ˈaɪdlɪŋ] adj: **at ~ speed** au ralenti.

idly [ˈaɪdlɪ] adv (*without working*) sans travailler; (*lazily*) paresseusement; (*without thought*) *reply, say, suggest* négligemment.

idol [ˈaɪdl] n (*lit, fig*) idole *f*. (*Cine, TV etc*) **the current ~** l'idole du jour *or* du moment.

idolater [aɪˈdɒlətəʳ] n idolâtre *mf*.

idolatrous [aɪˈdɒlətrəs] adj idolâtre.

idolatry [aɪˈdɒlətrɪ] n idolâtrie *f*.

idolize [ˈaɪdəlaɪz] vt idolâtrer, adorer. **to ~ sb** idolâtrer *or* adorer qn, faire de qn son idole.

idyll [ˈɪdɪl] n (*Literat, also fig*) idylle *f*.

idyllic [ɪˈdɪlɪk] adj idyllique.

i.e. [ˌaɪˈiː] (abbr of *id est* = *that is*) c.-à-d., c'est-à-dire.

if [ɪf] 1 conj a (*condition: supposing that*) si. **I'll go ~ you come with me** j'irai si tu m'accompagnes; **~ it is fine I shall be pleased** s'il fait beau je serai content; **~ it were fine I should be pleased** s'il faisait beau je serais content; **~ it is fine and (~ it is) not too cold I shall go with you** s'il fait beau et (s'il ne fait *or* qu'il ne fasse) pas trop froid je vous accompagnerai; **~ I had known, I would have visited them** si j'avais su, je leur aurais rendu visite; ~ **you wait a minute, I'll come with you** si vous attendez *or* voulez attendre une minute, je vais vous accompagner; ~ **you were a bird you could fly** si tu étais (un) oiseau tu pourrais voler; ~ **I were you** si j'étais vous, (si j'étais) à votre place; **(even) ~ I knew I wouldn't tell you** quand même je le saurais *or* même si je le savais je ne te le dirais pas; ~ **they are to be believed** à les en croire; ~ **it is true that ...** s'il est vrai que ... + *indic*, si tant est que ... + *subj*; *see also* **1i**.

b (*whenever*) si. ~ **I asked him he helped me** si je le lui demandais il m'aidait; ~ **she wants any help she asks me** si elle a besoin d'aide elle s'adresse à moi.

c (*although*) si. **(even) ~ it takes me all day I'll do it** (même) si cela doit *or* quand bien même cela devrait me prendre toute la journée je le ferai; **(even) ~ they are poor at least they are happy** s'ils sont pauvres du moins ils sont *or* sont-ils heureux; **even ~ it is a good film it's rather long** c'est un bon film bien qu'(il soit) un peu long; **nice weather, even ~ rather cold** temps agréable, bien qu'un peu froid; **even ~ he tells me himself I won't believe it** même s'il me le dit lui-même je ne le croirai pas.

d (*granted that, admitting that*) si. ~ **I am wrong, you are wrong too** si je me trompe *or* en admettant que je me trompe (*subj*), vous vous trompez aussi; **(even) ~ he DID say that, he didn't mean to hurt you** quand (bien) même il l'aurait dit, il n'avait aucune intention de vous faire de la peine.

e (*whether*) si. **do you know ~ they have gone?** savez-vous s'ils sont partis?; **I wonder ~ it's true** je me demande si c'est vrai.

f (*unless*) ~ ... **not** si ... ne; **that's the house, ~ I'm not mistaken** voilà la maison, si je ne me trompe; **they're coming at Christmas ~ they don't change their minds** ils viennent à Noël à moins qu'ils ne changent (*subj*) d'avis.

g (*excl*) ~ **only I had known!** si seulement j'avais su!

h **as ~** comme, comme si; **he acts as ~ he were rich** il se conduit comme s'il était riche; **as ~ by chance** comme par hasard; **he stood there as ~ he were dumb** il restait là comme (s'il était) muet; **it isn't as ~ we were rich** ce n'est pas comme si nous étions riches, nous ne sommes pourtant pas riches.

i (*phrases*) ~ **anything, it's even smaller** c'est peut-être encore plus petit; ~ **anything, this one is bigger** c'est plutôt celui-ci qui est le plus grand; **underpaid, ~ they are paid at all** mal payés, si tant est qu'on les paie; ~ **necessary** s'il le faut, au besoin, s'il est nécessaire; ~ **so**, (*liter*) ~ **it be so** s'il en est ainsi, si c'est le cas; ~ **not** sinon; ~ **only for a moment** ne serait-ce *or* ne fût-ce que pour un instant; **well ~ he didn't try to steal my bag!*** (ne) voilà-t-il pas qu'il essaie de me voler mon sac!*; ~ **it isn't our old friend Smith!** tiens! *or* par exemple! ce vieux Smith!; ~ **I know HER, she'll refuse** telle que je la connais, elle refusera.

2 n: **~s and buts** les si *mpl* et les mais *mpl*; **it's a big ~** c'est un grand point d'interrogation.

iffy‡ ['ɪfɪ] adj *outcome, future* aléatoire, problématique; *method* douteux; *problem* plein d'inconnues. (*uncertain*) **it's arranged for 5 o'clock, but it's a bit ~** c'est prévu pour 5 heures, mais il n'est pas absolument certain que ça aura lieu.

igloo ['ɪglu:] n igloo *m or* iglou *m*.

Ignatius [ɪg'neɪʃɪəs] n Ignace *m*. **(St) ~ Loyola** saint Ignace de Loyola.

igneous ['ɪgnɪəs] adj igné.

ignite [ɪg'naɪt] 1 vt mettre le feu à, enflammer. 2 vi prendre feu, s'enflammer.

ignition [ɪg'nɪʃən] 1 n a ignition *f*. b (*Aut*) allumage *m*. **to switch on the ~** mettre le contact. 2 comp ▸**ignition coil** (*Aut*) bobine *f* d'allumage ▸**ignition key** clef *f* de contact ▸**ignition switch** contact *m*.

ignoble [ɪg'nəʊbl] adj ignoble, infâme, indigne, vil.

ignominious [ˌɪgnə'mɪnɪəs] adj ignominieux, honteux.

ignominiously [ˌɪgnə'mɪnɪəslɪ] adv ignominieusement, honteusement.

ignominy ['ɪgnəmɪnɪ] n ignominie *f*.

ignoramus [ˌɪgnə'reɪməs] n ignare *mf*, ignorant(e) *m(f)*.

ignorance ['ɪgnərəns] n a ignorance *f* (*of* de). **to be in ~ of sth** ignorer qch; **to keep sb in ~ of sth** tenir qn dans l'ignorance de qch, laisser ignorer qch à qn; ~ **of the law is no excuse** nul n'est censé ignorer la loi; **his ~ of chemistry astonished me** son ignorance en matière de chimie m'a ahuri; (*loc*) ~ **is bliss** il vaut mieux ne pas savoir. b (*lack of education*) ignorance *f*. **he was ashamed of his ~** il avait honte de son ignorance *or* de ne rien savoir; **don't show your ~!** ce n'est pas la peine d'étaler ton ignorance!

ignorant ['ɪgnərənt] adj a (*unaware*) ~ **of** ignorant de; **to be ~ of the facts** ignorer les faits, être ignorant des faits. b (*lacking education*) *person* ignorant; *words, behaviour* d'(un) ignorant, qui trahit l'ignorance; *see* **pig**.

ignorantly ['ɪgnərəntlɪ] adv par ignorance.

ignore [ɪg'nɔ:ʳ] vt a (*take no notice of*) *interruption, remark, objection* ne tenir aucun compte de, ne pas relever, passer sous silence; *sb's behaviour* ne pas prêter attention à, faire semblant de ne pas s'apercevoir de; *person* faire semblant de ne pas voir *or* entendre; *invitation, letter* ne pas répondre à; *facts* méconnaître; *rule, prohibition* ne pas respecter; *awkward fact* faire semblant de ne pas connaître, ne tenir aucun compte de. **I shall ~ your impertinence** je ne relèverai pas votre impertinence; **we cannot ~ this behaviour any longer** nous ne pouvons plus fermer les yeux sur ces agissements.

b (*Jur*) **to ~ a bill** prononcer un verdict d'acquittement.

iguana [ɪ'gwɑ:nə] n iguane *m*.

ikon ['aɪkɒn] n = **icon**.

IL (*US Post*) abbr of **Illinois**.

ILEA [aɪˌeli:'eɪ] n (*Brit Educ*) (abbr of **Inner London Education Authority**) *anciennement office londonien de l'enseignement*.

ileum ['ɪlɪəm] n (*Anat*) iléon *m*.

ilex ['aɪleks] n a (*holm oak*) yeuse *f*, chêne vert. b (*genus: holly*) houx *m*.

Iliad ['ɪlɪəd] n: **the ~** l'Iliade *f*.

Ilion ['ɪlɪən], **Ilium** ['ɪlɪəm] n Ilion.

ilium ['ɪlɪəm] n, pl **ilia** ['ɪlɪə] (*Anat*) ilion *m*.

ilk [ɪlk] n: **of that ~** (*fig*) de cet acabit; (*Scot: in names*) de ce nom.

ill [ɪl] 1 adj, compar **worse**, superl **worst** a (*sick*) malade, (*less serious*) souffrant. **to be ~** être malade; **to fall** *or* **be taken ~** tomber malade; **to feel ~** se sentir malade *or* souffrant; **to look ~** avoir l'air malade; ~ **with a fever** malade d'une fièvre; ~ **with anxiety/jealousy** *etc* malade d'inquiétude/de jalousie *etc*; **he's seriously ~ in hospital** il est à l'hôpital dans un état grave.

b (*bad*) mauvais, méchant. ~ **deed** mauvaise action, méfait *m*; ~ **effects** conséquences désastreuses; ~ **fame** mauvaise réputation; **house of ~ fame** *or* **repute** maison mal famée; ~ **feeling** ressentiment *m*, rancune *f*; **no ~ feeling!** sans rancune!; ~ **health** mauvaise santé; ~ **humour**, ~ **temper** mauvaise humeur; ~ **luck** malchance *f*; **by ~ luck** par malheur, par malchance; **as ~ luck would have it, he ...** le malheur a voulu qu'il ... + *subj*; ~ **nature** méchanceté *f*; ~ **omen** mauvais augure; ~ **repute** = ~ **fame**; ~ **will** (*gen*) malveillance *f*; (*grudge, resentment*) rancune; **I bear him no ~ will** je ne lui en veux pas; **just to show there's no ~ will, I'll do it** (*gen: to show I bear no grudge*) je vais le faire, pour bien montrer que je ne t'en (*or* lui en *etc*) veux pas; (*often hum: to show willing*) je vais le faire, pour faire preuve de bonne volonté; (*Prov*) **it's an ~ wind that blows nobody any good** à quelque chose malheur est bon (*Prov*); *see also* **4**.

2 n a (*NonC: evil, injury*) mal *m*. **to think/speak ~ of** penser/dire du mal de; *see* **good**.

b (*misfortunes*) ~**s** maux *mpl*, malheurs *mpl*.

3 adv mal. **he can ~ afford the expense** il peut difficilement se permettre la dépense; **he can ~ afford to refuse** il ne peut guère se permettre de refuser; (*liter*) **to take sth ~** prendre mal qch, prendre qch en mauvaise part; (*liter*) **to go ~ with** tourner mal pour, aller mal pour; (*frm, liter*) **it ~ becomes you to do that** il vous sied mal (*frm*) de faire cela.

4 comp ▸**ill-advised** *decision, remark, action* peu judicieux; **you would be ill-advised to do that** vous auriez tort de faire cela, vous seriez malavisé (*liter*) de faire cela ▸**ill-assorted** mal assorti ▸**ill-at-ease** mal à l'aise, gêné ▸**ill-bred** mal élevé ▸**ill-breeding** manque *m* de savoir-vivre *or* d'éducation, impolitesse *f* ▸**ill-concealed** *amusement, disdain, disgust* mal dissimulé ▸**ill-considered** *action, words* irréfléchi; *measures* hâtif ▸**ill-disposed** malintentionné, mal disposé; **ill-disposed towards** mal disposé *or* malintentionné envers ▸**ill-equipped** mal équipé (*with* en); (*fig*) **he's ill-equipped for the role of Macbeth** il n'a pas les qualités requises pour le rôle de Macbeth; **to be ill-equipped to do sth** (*lit*) être mal-équipé pour faire qch; (*fig: person*) ne pas avoir les qualités requises pour faire qch ▸**ill-fated** *person* infortuné, malheureux; *day* fatal, néfaste; *action, effort* malheureux ▸**ill-favoured** (*ugly*) laid; (*objectionable*) déplaisant, désagréable, (*stronger*) répugnant ▸**ill-fitting** *shoes* qui vont mal; *garment* qui ne va pas, qui va mal; *lid, stopper* qui ferme mal ▸**ill-formed** (*Ling*) mal formé, agrammatical ▸**ill-founded** *belief, argument* mal fondé; *rumour* sans fondement ▸**ill-gotten gains** biens *mpl* mal acquis ▸**ill-humoured** de mauvaise humeur, maussade, grincheux ▸**ill-informed** *person* mal renseigné, mal informé; *essay, speech* plein d'inexactitudes ▸**ill-judged** peu judicieux, peu sage ▸**ill-mannered** *person* mal élevé; *behaviour* grossier, impoli ▸**ill-natured** *person, reply* désagréable; *child* méchant, désagréable ▸**ill-nourished** mal nourri ▸**ill-omened** de mauvais augure ▸**ill-prepared** mal préparé ▸**ill-starred** (*liter*) *person* né sous une mauvaise étoile, infortuné; *day, undertaking* malheureux, néfaste ▸**ill-suited** mal assorti; **ill-suited to** qui ne convient guère à, qui convient mal à ▸**ill-tempered** (*habitually*) grincheux, désagréable, qui a mauvais caractère; (*on one occasion*) de mauvaise humeur, maussade, grincheux ▸**ill-timed** inopportun, malencontreux, intempestif, mal à propos ▸**ill-treat** maltraiter, brutaliser, rudoyer ▸**ill-treatment** mauvais traitements ▸**ill-use** = **ill-treat**.

I'll [aɪl] = **I shall, I will**; *see* **shall, will**.

Ill. (*US*) abbr of **Illinois**.

illegal [ɪ'li:gəl] adj illégal. (*Sport*) ~ **tackle** charge irrégulière.

illegality [ˌɪli:'gælɪtɪ] n illégalité *f*.

illegally [ɪ'li:gəlɪ] adv illégalement, d'une manière illégale *or* contraire à la loi.

illegible [ɪ'ledʒəbl] adj illisible.

illegibly [ɪ'ledʒəblɪ] adv illisiblement.

illegitimacy [ˌɪlɪ'dʒɪtɪməsɪ] n illégitimité *f*.

illegitimate [ˌɪlɪ'dʒɪtɪmɪt] adj *action* illégitime; *child* illégitime, naturel; (*fig*) *argument* illogique; *conclusion* injustifié.

illegitimately [ˌɪlɪ'dʒɪtɪmɪtlɪ] adv illégitimement.

illiberal [ɪ'lɪbərəl] adj **a** (*narrow-minded*) intolérant, à l'esprit étroit. **b** (†: *niggardly*) ladre (*liter*).

illicit [ɪ'lɪsɪt] adj illicite.

illicitly [ɪ'lɪsɪtlɪ] adv illicitement.

illimitable [ɪ'lɪmɪtəbl] adj illimité, sans bornes, sans limites.

Illinois [ˌɪlɪ'nɔɪ] n Illinois *m*. **in ~** dans l'Illinois.

illiteracy [ɪ'lɪtərəsɪ] n analphabétisme *m*.

illiterate [ɪ'lɪtərɪt] **1** adj *person* illettré, analphabète; *letter, sentence* plein de fautes. **in an ~ hand** dans une écriture de primaire. **2** n illettré(e) *m(f)*, analphabète *mf*.

illness ['ɪlnɪs] n maladie *f*. **to have a long ~** faire une longue maladie.

illocutionary [ˌɪlə'kjuːʃənərɪ] adj illocutionnaire.

illogical [ɪ'lɒdʒɪkəl] adj illogique.

illogicality [ɪˌlɒdʒɪ'kælɪtɪ] n illogisme *m*.

illogically [ɪ'lɒdʒɪkəlɪ] adv illogiquement.

illuminate [ɪ'luːmɪneɪt] vt **a** (*gen*) éclairer; (*for special occasion or effect*) *building etc* illuminer; (*fig*) *question, subject* éclairer, faire la lumière sur. **~d sign** enseigne lumineuse. **b** (*Art*) *manuscript* enluminer.

illuminating [ɪ'luːmɪneɪtɪŋ] adj (*lit, fig*) éclairant. (*fig*) **his comments proved very ~** ses commentaires se sont avérés très éclairants *or* ont beaucoup éclairci la question.

illumination [ɪˌluːmɪ'neɪʃən] n **a** (*NonC*) (*gen*) éclairage *m*; (*for special effect*) [*building etc*] illumination *f*; [*sky etc*] illumination, embrasement *m*; (*fig*) lumière *f*, inspiration *f*. **b** (*decorative lights*) **~s** illuminations *fpl*. **c** [*manuscript*] enluminure *f*.

illuminator [ɪ'luːmɪneɪtə^r] n **a** (*lighting device*) dispositif *m* d'éclairage. **b** [*manuscript*] enlumineur *m*.

illumine [ɪ'luːmɪn] vt éclairer, éclaircir, faire la lumière sur.

illusion [ɪ'luːʒən] n illusion *f*. **it gives an ~ of space** cela donne une illusion d'espace; **to be under an ~** avoir *or* se faire une illusion; **to be under the ~ that** avoir *or* se faire l'illusion que + *indic*; **to have or to be under no ~(s)** ne se faire aucune illusion; **I have no ~s about what will happen to him** je ne me fais aucune illusion sur le sort qui l'attend; **he cherishes the ~ that ...** il caresse l'illusion que ...; *see* **optical**.

illusive [ɪ'luːsɪv] adj, **illusory** [ɪ'luːsərɪ] adj (*unreal*) illusoire, irréel; (*deceptive*) illusoire, trompeur, chimérique.

illustrate ['ɪləstreɪt] vt **a** *book, story* illustrer. **~d paper** (journal *m or* magazine *m etc*) illustré *m*. **b** (*fig: exemplify*) *idea, problem* illustrer, éclairer, mettre en lumière; *rule* donner un exemple de. **I can best ~ this as follows** la meilleure façon d'illustrer ceci est la suivante.

illustration [ˌɪləs'treɪʃən] n (*lit, fig*) illustration *f*. (*fig*) **by way of ~** à titre d'exemple.

illustrative ['ɪləstrətɪv] adj *example* explicatif, servant d'explication, qui illustre *or* explique. **~ of this problem** qui sert à illustrer ce problème.

illustrator ['ɪləstreɪtə^r] n illustrateur *m*, -trice *f*.

illustrious [ɪ'lʌstrɪəs] adj illustre, célèbre.

illustriously [ɪ'lʌstrɪəslɪ] adv glorieusement.

ILO [aɪel'əʊ] n (abbr of **International Labour Organisation**) OIT *f*.

IM, i.m. ['aɪ'em] (abbr of **intramuscular(ly)**) IM, im.

I'm [aɪm] = **I am**; *see* **be**.

image ['ɪmɪdʒ] **1** n **a** (*gen*) image *f*. **God created man in his own ~** Dieu créa l'homme à son image; **real/virtual ~** image réelle/virtuelle; **~ in the glass/lake** *etc* réflexion *f* dans la vitre/à la surface du lac *etc*; (*fig*) **he is the (living or very or spitting*) ~ of his father** c'est le portrait (vivant) de son père, c'est son père tout craché*; **I had a sudden (mental) ~ of her, alone and afraid** soudain je l'ai vue en imagination, qui était seule et qui avait peur; **they had quite the wrong ~ of him** ils se faisaient une idée tout à fait fausse de lui; *see* **graven, mirror** *etc*.
b (*also* **public ~**) image *f* de marque (*fig*). **he has to think of his ~** il faut qu'il prenne en considération son image de marque; (*Cine, Theat etc*) **he's got the wrong ~ for that part** le public ne le voit pas dans ce genre de rôle, son image de marque ne convient guère à ce rôle; *see* **brand**.
2 comp ▸**image-building**: (*fig*) **it's just image-building** ça ne vise qu'à promouvoir son (*or* leur *etc*) image *f* de marque ▸**image-conscious**: **he is very image-conscious** il se soucie beaucoup de son image de marque ▸**image enhancement** (*Tech*) enrichissement *m* d'images.

imagery ['ɪmɪdʒərɪ] n (*Literat*) images *fpl*. **style/language full of ~** style/langage imagé.

imaginable [ɪ'mædʒɪnəbl] adj imaginable. **she's the quietest person ~** c'est la personne la plus silencieuse qu'on puisse imaginer; **the best thing ~ would be for him to leave at once** le mieux qu'on puisse imaginer serait qu'il parte tout de suite.

imaginary [ɪ'mædʒɪnərɪ] adj *danger* imaginaire; *character, place* imaginaire, fictif.

imagination [ɪˌmædʒɪ'neɪʃən] n (*NonC*) imagination *f*. **to have a lively or vivid ~** avoir l'imagination fertile; **he's got ~** il a de l'imagination; **she lets her ~ run away with her** elle se laisse emporter *or* entraîner par son imagination; **it existed only in his ~** cela n'existait que dans son imagination; **in (his) ~ he saw ...** en imagination il a vu ...; **it is only or all (your) ~!** vous vous faites des idées!, vous rêvez!; **haven't you got any ~?** tu n'as donc aucune imagination?; **use your ~!** aie donc un peu d'imagination!; *see* **appeal**.

imaginative [ɪ'mædʒɪnətɪv] adj *person* imaginatif, plein d'imagination; *book, film, approach* plein d'imagination.

imaginatively [ɪ'mædʒɪnətɪvlɪ] adv avec imagination.

imaginativeness [ɪ'mædʒɪnətɪvnɪs] n imagination *f*, esprit imaginatif *or* inventif.

imagine [ɪ'mædʒɪn] vt **a** (*picture to o.s.*) (s')imaginer, se figurer, se représenter. **~ life 100 years ago** imaginez(-vous) *or* représentez-vous *or* figurez-vous la vie il y a 100 ans; **try to ~ a huge house far from anywhere** essayez d'imaginer *or* de vous imaginer *or* de vous figurer *or* de vous représenter une immense maison loin de tout; **~ that you were or ~ yourself at school now** imagine que tu sois à l'école en ce moment; **I can't ~ myself at 60** je ne m'imagine *or* ne me vois pas du tout à 60 ans; **~ a situation in which ...** imaginez(-vous) une situation où ...; **(just) ~!** tu (t')imagines!; **(you can) ~ how I felt!** imaginez(-vous) *or* vous imaginez ce que j'ai pu ressentir!; **I can ~!** je m'en doute!; **you can ~ my fury when ...** vous imaginez *or* vous vous représentez ma rage quand ...; **(you can) ~ how pleased I was!** vous pensez si j'étais content!; **you can't ~ how difficult it is** vous ne pouvez pas (vous) imaginer *or* vous figurer combien c'est difficile; **did you ever ~ you'd meet her one day?** est-ce que tu t'étais jamais douté que tu la rencontrerais un jour?; **I can just ~ his reaction when he sees her** je me doute de sa réaction quand il la verra; **I can well ~ he's pleased** qu'il soit content, je m'en doute; **he's (always) imagining things** il se fait des idées.
b (*suppose, believe*) supposer, imaginer, penser (*that* que). **he's rich, I ~** il est riche, j'imagine *or* je suppose; **I didn't ~ he would come** je ne pensais pas qu'il viendrait.
c (*believe wrongly*) croire, s'imaginer, se figurer. **don't ~ that I can help you** n'allez pas croire que *or* ne vous imaginez pas que *or* ne vous figurez pas que je puisse vous aider; **he fondly ~d she was still willing to obey him** il s'imaginait naïvement qu'elle était encore prête à lui obéir; **I ~d I heard someone speak** j'ai cru entendre parler.

imam [ɪ'mɑːm] n imam *m*, iman *m*.

imbalance [ɪm'bæləns] n (*lit, fig*) déséquilibre *m*.

imbecile ['ɪmbəsiːl] **1** n imbécile *mf*, idiot(e) *m(f)*; (*Med* ††) imbécile. **to behave like an ~** se conduire comme un imbécile *or* en imbécile, se conduire comme un idiot *or* en idiot, faire l'imbécile *or* l'idiot; **to act/speak like an ~** faire/dire des imbécillités *or* des bêtises; **you ~!** espèce d'imbécile! *or* d'idiot!; **this ~ said ...** cette espèce d'imbécile! *or* d'idiot a dit ... . **2** adj *action, laugh, words* imbécile; *person* imbécile, idiot; (*Med* ††) imbécile.

imbecility [ˌɪmbɪ'sɪlɪtɪ] n **a** (*NonC*) imbécillité *f*, stupidité *f*; (*Med* ††) imbécillité. **b** (*act etc*) imbécillité *f*, stupidité *f*.

imbibe [ɪm'baɪb] **1** vt **a** (*drink*) boire, avaler, absorber; (*fig*) *ideas, information* absorber, assimiler. **b** (*absorb*) *water, light, heat* absorber. **2** vi (* *hum: drink to excess*) picoler‡.

imbroglio [ɪm'brəʊlɪəʊ] n imbroglio *m*.

imbue [ɪm'bjuː] vt (*fig*) imprégner (*with* de). **~d with** imbu de, imprégné de.

IMF [ˌaɪem'ef] (*Econ*) (abbr of **International Monetary Fund**) F.M.I. *m*.

imitable ['ɪmɪtəbl] adj imitable.

imitate ['ɪmɪteɪt] vt (*all senses*) imiter.

imitation [ˌɪmɪ'teɪʃən] **1** n (*all senses*) imitation *f*. **in ~ of** à l'imitation de, en imitant, sur le modèle de; (*Comm*) **"beware of ~s"** "se méfier des contrefaçons"; **it's only ~** c'est de l'imitation; (*loc*) **~ is the sincerest form of flattery** l'imitation est une des formes les plus sincères de l'admiration, l'hommage le plus sincère que l'on puisse rendre à quelqu'un c'est de l'imiter.
2 comp ▸**imitation fur coat** manteau *m* en fourrure synthétique *or* artificielle ▸**imitation gold** similor *m* ▸**imitation jewellery** faux bijoux ▸**imitation leather** imitation *f* cuir *inv*, similicuir *m* ▸**imitation marble** imitation *f* marbre, faux marbre, similimarbre *m* ▸**imitation mink coat** manteau *m* (en) imitation vison ▸**imitation pearl/stone** perle/pierre artificielle *or* d'imitation, fausse perle/pierre.

imitative ['ɪmɪtətɪv] adj *word, art* imitatif; *person* imitateur (*f* -trice).

imitator ['ɪmɪteɪtə^r] n imitateur *m*, -trice *f*.

immaculate [ɪ'mækjʊlɪt] adj *snow* immaculé; *dress, appearance* irréprochable, impeccable; *person* impeccable, tiré à quatre épingles; *room* impeccable, d'une propreté irréprochable; *behaviour, manners, courtesy* irréprochable, impeccable, parfait; (*Rel*) immaculé, sans tache. **the I~ Conception** l'Immaculée Conception.

immaculately [ɪ'mækjʊlɪtlɪ] adv *dress* avec un soin impeccable; *behave* de façon irréprochable, parfaitement.

immanent ['ɪmənənt] adj immanent.

Immanuel [ɪ'mænjʊəl] n Emmanuel *m*.

immaterial [ˌɪmə'tɪərɪəl] adj **a** (*unimportant*) négligeable, insignifiant, peu important, sans importance. **it is ~ whether he did or not** il importe peu *or* il est indifférent qu'il l'ait fait ou non; **that's (quite) ~** la question n'est pas là; **that is quite ~ to me** cela m'est tout à fait indifférent. b (*Philos etc*) immatériel.

immature [ˌɪməˈtjʊəʳ] **adj** *fruit* (qui n'est) pas mûr, vert; *animal, tree* jeune. **he's very ~** il manque vraiment de maturité, il est très immature.

immaturity [ˌɪməˈtjʊərɪtɪ] **n** manque *m* de maturité, immaturité *f*.

immeasurable [ɪˈmeʒərəbl] **adj** *amount, height, space* incommensurable; *joy* incommensurable, infini; *precautions, care* infini.

immeasurably [ɪˈmeʒərəblɪ] **adv** (*lit*) incommensurablement; (*fig*) infiniment.

immediacy [ɪˈmiːdɪəsɪ] **n** caractère immédiat *or* d'urgence.

immediate [ɪˈmiːdɪət] **adj** *successor, reaction, result, neighbour, risk* immédiat; *information, knowledge* immédiat, direct; *reply* immédiat, instantané; *measures, need* immédiat, urgent, pressant; (*Philos*) *cause, effect* immédiat. **I shall take ~ steps** *or* **action to ensure that ...** je vais agir immédiatement *or* tout de suite *or* sans retard pour m'assurer que ..., je vais prendre des mesures immédiates pour m'assurer que ...; **the ~ future** le futur proche, l'avenir immédiat; **in the ~ future** dans l'immédiat, dans un avenir immédiat; **my ~ object** mon premier but; **for ~ delivery** à livrer d'urgence; **in the ~ neighbourhood** dans le voisinage immédiat, dans le proche voisinage; **the ~ area** les environs immédiats *or* les plus proches; (*Gram*) **~ constituent** constituant immédiat.

immediately [ɪˈmiːdɪətlɪ] 1 **adv** a (*at once*) *reply, react, depart* immédiatement, tout de suite, aussitôt, instantanément. **~ after** aussitôt après. b (*directly*) directement. **it does not ~ concern you** cela ne vous regarde pas directement. 2 **conj** (*Brit*) dès que. **~ he had finished he went home** dès qu'il eut fini il rentra chez lui; **~ I returned** dès mon retour.

immemorial [ˌɪmɪˈmɔːrɪəl] **adj** immémorial. **from time ~** de toute éternité, de temps immémorial.

immense [ɪˈmens] **adj** *space* immense, vaste; *size* immense; *possibilities, achievements, fortune, difficulty* immense, énorme.

immensely [ɪˈmenslɪ] **adv** extrêmement, immensément. **~ rich** immensément *or* extrêmement riche; **to enjoy o.s. ~** s'amuser énormément.

immensity [ɪˈmensɪtɪ] **n** immensité *f*.

immerse [ɪˈmɜːs] **vt** immerger, plonger; (*Rel*) baptiser par immersion. **to ~ one's head in water** plonger la tête dans l'eau; (*fig*) **to ~ o.s. in** se plonger dans; **to be ~d in one's work/one's reading** être absorbé *or* plongé dans son travail/sa lecture.

immersion [ɪˈmɜːʃən] 1 **n** immersion *f*; (*fig*) absorption *f*; (*Rel*) baptême *m* par immersion. 2 **comp ▸immersion course** (*Educ*) stage *m or* cours *m* intensif (*in* de) **▸immersion heater** (*Brit*) chauffe-eau *m inv* électrique.

immigrancy [ˈɪmɪgrənsɪ] **n** (*US*) condition *f* d'immigrant.

immigrant [ˈɪmɪgrənt] **adj, n** (*newly arrived*) immigrant(e) *m(f)*; (*well-established*) immigré(e) *m(f)*. (*Ind*) **~ labour, ~ workers** main-d'œuvre immigrée.

immigrate [ˈɪmɪgreɪt] **vi** immigrer.

immigration [ˌɪmɪˈgreɪʃən] 1 **n** immigration *f*. **to go through customs and ~** passer la douane et l'immigration. 2 **comp ▸immigration authorities** (*Admin*) services *mpl* de l'immigration **▸immigration border patrol** (*US Police*) (services *mpl* de) l'immigration *f* **▸immigration control** = **Immigration (Department) ▸Immigration (Department)** (services *mpl* de) l'immigration *f*.

imminence [ˈɪmɪnəns] **n** imminence *f*.

imminent [ˈɪmɪnənt] **adj** imminent.

immobile [ɪˈməʊbaɪl] **adj** immobile.

immobility [ˌɪməʊˈbɪlɪtɪ] **n** immobilité *f*.

immobilize [ɪˈməʊbɪlaɪz] **vt** (*also Fin*) immobiliser.

immoderate [ɪˈmɒdərɪt] **adj** *desire, appetite* immodéré, démesuré; *conduct* déréglé.

immoderately [ɪˈmɒdərɪtlɪ] **adv** immodérément.

immodest [ɪˈmɒdɪst] **adj** a (*indecent*) immodeste, impudique, indécent. b (*presumptuous*) impudent, présomptueux.

immodestly [ɪˈmɒdɪstlɪ] **adv** a (*indecently*) immodestement, impudiquement, indécemment. **to behave ~** avoir une conduite indécente. b (*presumptuously*) impudemment, présomptueusement.

immodesty [ɪˈmɒdɪstɪ] **n** a (*indecency*) immodestie *f*, impudeur *f*, indécence *f*. b (*presumption*) impudence *f*, présomption *f*.

immolate [ˈɪməʊleɪt] **vt** immoler.

immoral [ɪˈmɒrəl] **adj** *action, suggestion, person* immoral. (*scandalous*) **it's ~!** c'est scandaleux!

immorality [ˌɪməˈrælɪtɪ] **n** immoralité *f*.

immortal [ɪˈmɔːtl] 1 **adj** *person, God* immortel; *fame* immortel, impérissable. 2 **n** immortel(le) *m(f)*.

immortality [ˌɪmɔːˈtælɪtɪ] **n** immortalité *f*.

immortalize [ɪˈmɔːtəlaɪz] **vt** immortaliser.

immovable [ɪˈmuːvəbl] 1 **adj** *object* fixe; (*Jur*) *belongings* immobilier; (*fig*) *courage, decision, person* inflexible, inébranlable. 2 **n** (*Jur*) **~s** immeubles *mpl*, biens immobiliers.

immune [ɪˈmjuːn] **adj** a (*Med*) *person* immunisé (*from* contre). **~ body** immunisine *f*, sensibilisatrice *f*; **~ response** réaction *f* immunitaire; **~ serum** sérum immunisant, immun-sérum *m*; **~ system** système *m* immunitaire; *see* **acquired.** b (*fig: secure from*) **~ from** *or* **to** *temptation, wish etc* immunisé contre, à l'abri de; **~ to inflation/criticism** à l'abri de l'inflation/de la critique. c (*fig: exempt from*) **~ from taxation** exempt d'impôts, qui bénéficie d'immunité fiscale; **~ from arrest** qui ne risque pas d'être arrêté.

immunity [ɪˈmjuːnɪtɪ] **n** (*Med, gen*) immunité *f* (*from* contre). **diplomatic/parliamentary ~** immunité diplomatique/parlementaire.

immunization [ˌɪmjʊnaɪˈzeɪʃən] **n** immunisation *f* (*against* contre).

immunize [ˈɪmjʊnaɪz] **vt** immuniser (*against* contre).

immunodeficiency [ɪˌmjʊnəʊdɪˈfɪʃənsɪ] **n** déficience *f* immunologique.

immunodepressant [ɪˌmjʊnəʊdɪˈpresnt] **n, adj** immunodépresseur *(m)*.

immunogenic [ˌɪmjʊnəʊˈdʒenɪk] **adj** immunogène.

immunoglobulin [ˌɪmjʊnəʊˈglɒbjʊlɪn] **n** immunoglobine *m*.

immunological [ɪˌmjʊnəʊˈlɒdʒɪkəl] **adj** immunologique.

immunologist [ˌɪmjʊˈnɒlədʒɪst] **n** immunologiste *mf*.

immunology [ˌɪmjʊˈnɒlədʒɪ] **n** immunologie *f*.

immunosuppressant [ˌɪmjʊnəʊsʌˈpresnt] 1 **n** immunosuppresseur *m*. 2 **adj** immunosuppressif.

immunosuppression [ˌɪmjʊnəʊsʌˈpreʃən] **n** immunosuppression *f*.

immunotherapy [ˌɪmjʊnəʊˈθerəpɪ] **n** immunothérapie *f*.

immure [ɪˈmjʊəʳ] **vt** (*lit*) emmurer; (*fig*) enfermer.

immutability [ɪˌmjuːtəˈbɪlɪtɪ] **n** immutabilité *f*, immuabilité *f* (*frm*).

immutable [ɪˈmjuːtəbl] **adj** immuable, inaltérable.

immutably [ɪˈmuːtəblɪ] **adv** immuablement.

imp [ɪmp] **n** diablotin *m*, lutin *m*; (*child*) petit(e) espiègle *m(f)*, petit diable.

impact [ˈɪmpækt] 1 **n** impact *m* (*on* sur), choc *m* (*on, against* contre); (*fig*) impact, effet *m* (*on* sur). (*Comput*) **~ printer** imprimante *f* à impact; (*fig*) **to make an ~ on sb** faire une forte impression sur qn. 2 [ɪmˈpækt] **vt** enfoncer, presser (*into* dans). 3 [ɪmˈpækt] **vi** (*fig*) influer.

impacted [ɪmˈpæktɪd] **adj** *tooth* inclus, enclavé; *fracture* engrené. (*US*) **~ area** quartier *m* surpeuplé.

impair [ɪmˈpɛəʳ] **vt** *abilities, faculties* détériorer, diminuer; *negotiations, relations* porter atteinte à; *health* abîmer, détériorer; *sight, hearing* abîmer, affaiblir; *mind, strength* diminuer.

impaired [ɪmˈpɛəd] **adj** *sight, hearing* abîmé, affaibli; *faculties, health* détérioré; *strength* diminué.

impala [ɪmˈpɑːlə] **n, pl ~s** *or* **~** impala *m*.

impale [ɪmˈpeɪl] **vt** empaler (*on* sur).

impalpable [ɪmˈpælpəbl] **adj** impalpable.

impanel [ɪmˈpænl] **vt** = **empanel.**

imparity [ɪmˈpærɪtɪ] **n** inégalité *f*.

impart [ɪmˈpɑːt] **vt** a (*make known*) *news* communiquer, faire connaître, faire part de; *knowledge* communiquer, transmettre. b (*bestow*) donner, transmettre.

impartial [ɪmˈpɑːʃəl] **adj** *person, attitude* impartial, objectif, équitable; *verdict, decision, speech* impartial, objectif.

impartiality [ɪmˌpɑːʃɪˈælɪtɪ] **n** impartialité *f*.

impartially [ɪmˈpɑːʃəlɪ] **adv** impartialement, objectivement, sans parti pris.

impassable [ɪmˈpɑːsəbl] **adj** *barrier, river* infranchissable; *road* impraticable.

impasse [æmˈpɑːs] **n** (*lit, fig*) impasse *f*.

impassioned [ɪmˈpæʃnd] **adj** *feeling* exalté; *plea, speech* passionné.

impassive [ɪmˈpæsɪv] **adj** *person, attitude, face* impassible, imperturbable.

impassively [ɪmˈpæsɪvlɪ] **adv** impassiblement, imperturbablement, sans s'émouvoir.

impatience [ɪmˈpeɪʃəns] **n** a impatience *f* (*to do* de faire). b (*intolerance*) intolérance *f* (*of sth* à l'égard de qch, *with sb* vis-à-vis de qn, à l'égard de qn).

impatiens [ɪmˈpeɪʃɪˌenz] **n, pl inv** (*Bot*) impatiente *f*.

impatient [ɪmˈpeɪʃənt] **n** a *person, answer* impatient. **~ to leave** impatient de partir; **to become** *or* **get** *or* **grow ~** s'impatienter. b intolérant (*of sth* à l'égard de qch, *with sb* vis-à-vis de qn, à l'égard de qn).

impatiently [ɪmˈpeɪʃəntlɪ] **adv** avec impatience, impatiemment.

impeach [ɪmˈpiːtʃ] **vt** a (*Jur: accuse*) *public official* mettre en accusation (*en vue de destituer*), (*US*) entamer la procédure d'impeachment contre; *person* accuser (*for sth, of sth* de qch, *for doing* de faire). b (*question, challenge*) *sb's character* attaquer; *sb's motives, honesty* mettre en doute. (*Jur*) **to ~ a witness** récuser un témoin.

impeachable [ɪmˈpiːtʃəbl] **adj** passible des tribunaux.

impeachment [ɪmˈpiːtʃmənt] **n** a (*Jur*) *[public official]* mise *f* en accusation (*en vue d'une destitution*); (*US*) procédure *f* d'impeachment; *[person]* accusation *f* (*for sth* de qch, *for doing* de faire). b *[sb's character etc]* dénigrement *m*; *[sb's honesty]* contestation *f*.

impeccable [ɪm'pekəbl] adj impeccable, irréprochable, parfait.

impeccably [ɪm'pekəblɪ] adv impeccablement, irréprochablement.

impecunious [ˌɪmpɪ'kjuːnɪəs] adj impécunieux, nécessiteux.

impedance [ɪm'piːdəns] n (*Elec*) impédance *f*.

impede [ɪm'piːd] vt empêcher (*sb from doing* qn de faire); *action, success, movement* gêner, faire obstacle à, entraver; *traffic* gêner, entraver.

impediment [ɪm'pedɪmənt] n **a** obstacle *m*. **b** (*also* **speech ~**) défaut *m* d'élocution. **c** **~s** = **impedimenta**.

impedimenta [ɪmˌpedɪ'mentə] npl (*also Mil*) impedimenta *mpl*.

impel [ɪm'pel] vt **a** (*drive forward*) pousser, faire avancer. **b** (*compel*) obliger, forcer (*to do* à faire); (*urge*) inciter, pousser (*to do* à faire). **to ~ sb to crime** pousser qn au crime.

impend [ɪm'pend] vi (*be about to happen*) être imminent; (*menace, hang over*) *[danger, storm]* menacer; *[threat]* planer.

impending [ɪm'pendɪŋ] adj (*about to happen*) *birth, arrival* imminent, prochain (*after noun*); (*threateningly close*) *danger, storm* imminent, menaçant, qui menace. **his ~ fate** le sort qui le menace (*or* menaçait *etc*); **his ~ retirement** la retraite qu'il va (*or* allait *etc*) prendre sous peu, sa retraite prochaine; **we discussed our ~ removal** nous avons parlé de notre déménagement imminent.

impenetrability [ɪmˌpenɪtrə'bɪlɪtɪ] n impénétrabilité *f*.

impenetrable [ɪm'penɪtrəbl] adj *substance* impénétrable (*to, by* à); *mystery, secret* insondable, impénétrable.

impenitence [ɪm'penɪtəns] n impénitence *f*.

impenitent [ɪm'penɪtənt] adj impénitent. **he was quite ~ about it** il ne s'en repentait nullement.

impenitently [ɪm'penɪtəntlɪ] adv sans repentir.

imperative [ɪm'perətɪv] **1** adj **a** *need, desire* urgent, pressant, impérieux; *order* impératif; *voice, manner* impérieux, autoritaire. **silence is ~** le silence s'impose; **it is ~ that you leave, it is ~ for you to leave** il faut absolument que vous partiez (*subj*), votre départ s'impose. **b** (*Gram*) impératif. **2** n (*Gram*) impératif *m*. **in the ~ (mood)** à l'impératif, au mode impératif.

imperatively [ɪm'perətɪvlɪ] adv *need* impérieusement; *order* impérativement; (*Gram*) *use verb* à l'impératif.

imperceptible [ˌɪmpə'septəbl] adj *sight, movement* imperceptible (*to* à); *sound* imperceptible, inaudible; *difference* imperceptible, insensible.

imperceptibly [ˌɪmpə'septəblɪ] adv imperceptiblement.

imperceptive [ˌɪmpə'septɪv] adj peu perspicace.

imperfect [ɪm'pɜːfɪkt] **1** adj **a** (*faulty*) *reasoning* imparfait; *car, machine* défectueux; (*incomplete*) incomplet (*f* -ète), inachevé. **b** (*Gram*) imparfait. **2** n (*Gram*) imparfait *m*. **in the ~ (tense)** à l'imparfait.

imperfection [ˌɪmpə'fekʃən] n (*see* **imperfect**) imperfection *f*; défauts *mpl*, défectuosité *f*; état imparfait *or* incomplet.

imperfectly [ɪm'pɜːfɪktlɪ] adv imparfaitement.

imperial [ɪm'pɪərɪəl] **1** adj **a** (*gen*) *territory, troops* impérial; (*of British Empire*) de l'Empire britannique. (*Brit Hist*) **~ preference** tarif préférentiel (*à l'intérieur de l'Empire britannique*). **b** (*lordly*) *splendour, dignity* majestueux, grandiose; *look, gesture* impérieux, autoritaire, hautain. **c** (*Brit*) *weight, measure* légal (*adopté dans tout le Royaume-Uni*). **2** n (*beard*) (barbe *f* à l')impériale *f*.

imperialism [ɪm'pɪərɪəlɪzəm] n impérialisme *m*.

imperialist [ɪm'pɪərɪəlɪst] adj, n impérialiste (*mf*).

imperialistic [ɪmˌpɪərɪə'lɪstɪk] adj impérialiste.

imperially [ɪm'pɪərɪəlɪ] adv majestueusement; *say, gesture* impérieusement.

imperil [ɪm'perɪl] vt mettre en péril *or* danger; *fortune, life* exposer, risquer; *health, reputation* compromettre.

imperious [ɪm'pɪərɪəs] adj *gesture, look, command* impérieux, autoritaire; *need, desire* urgent, pressant, impérieux.

imperiously [ɪm'pɪərɪəslɪ] adv *gesture, look* impérieusement, d'un air *or* d'un ton impérieux; *need* impérativement, de façon urgente.

imperishable [ɪm'perɪʃəbl] adj impérissable.

impermanent [ɪm'pɜːmənənt] adj éphémère, fugitif, transitoire, passager.

impermeable [ɪm'pɜːmɪəbl] adj *rock* imperméable; *wall, roof* étanche.

impersonal [ɪm'pɜːsnl] adj **a** *manner, style* impersonnel, froid; *decision, discussion, remark* impersonnel, objectif. **b** (*Gram*) impersonnel.

impersonality [ɪmˌpɜːsə'nælɪtɪ] n impersonnalité *f*, froideur *f*; objectivité *f*.

impersonalize [ˌɪm'pɜːsənəˌlaɪz] vt déshumaniser.

impersonally [ɪm'pɜːsnəlɪ] adv impersonnellement.

impersonate [ɪm'pɜːsəneɪt] vt (*gen*) se faire passer pour; (*Jur*) usurper l'identité de; (*Theat*) imiter.

impersonation [ɪmˌpɜːsə'neɪʃən] n (*Theat*) imitation *f*; (*Jur*) usurpation *f* d'identité, supposition *f* de personne. (*Theat*) **he does ~s** il fait des imitations (de personnages); **his ~ of his uncle caused him a lot of trouble** s'être fait passer pour son oncle lui a attiré beaucoup d'ennuis.

impersonator [ɪm'pɜːsəneɪtəʳ] n (*Theat*) imitateur *m*, -trice *f*; (*Jur*) usurpateur *m*, -trice *f* d'identité; *see* **female**.

impertinence [ɪm'pɜːtɪnəns] n impertinence *f*, insolence *f*, impudence *f*. **it's the height of ~** c'est le comble de l'impertinence; **a piece of ~** une impertinence; **it would be an ~ to say** il serait impertinent de dire.

impertinent [ɪm'pɜːtɪnənt] adj (*impudent*) impertinent, insolent, impudent. **to be ~ to sb** être *or* se montrer insolent envers qn; **don't be ~!** ne soyez pas impertinent!

impertinently [ɪm'pɜːtɪnəntlɪ] adv **a** (*impudently*) avec impertinence, d'un air insolent, avec impudence. **b** (*irrelevantly*) sans pertinence, hors de propos; *reply* en dehors de la question.

imperturbable [ˌɪmpə'tɜːbəbl] adj imperturbable.

imperturbably [ˌɪmpə'tɜːbəblɪ] adv imperturbablement.

impervious [ɪm'pɜːvɪəs] adj *substance, rock* imperméable (*to* à); *wall, roof* étanche (*to* à). (*fig*) **~ to the sufferings of others** imperméable *or* fermé aux souffrances d'autrui; **~ to reason/suggestions** inaccessible *or* sourd à la raison/aux suggestions; **~ to threats** indifférent aux menaces; **he is ~ to criticism** la critique le laisse indifférent *or* ne le touche pas; (*pej*) il est fermé *or* sourd à la critique.

impetigo [ˌɪmpɪ'taɪgəʊ] n (*Med*) impétigo *m*; (*in children*) gourme *f*.

impetuosity [ɪmˌpetjʊ'ɒsɪtɪ] n impétuosité *f*, fougue *f*.

impetuous [ɪm'petjʊəs] adj impétueux, fougueux.

impetuously [ɪm'petjʊəslɪ] adv impétueusement, fougueusement.

impetuousness [ɪm'petjʊəsnɪs] n = **impetuosity**.

impetus ['ɪmpɪtəs] n *[object]* force *f* d'impulsion; *[runner]* élan *m*; (*fig*) impulsion *f*, élan. (*fig*) **to give (an) ~ to** donner l'impulsion à, donner son élan à, mettre en branle.

impiety [ɪm'paɪətɪ] n impiété *f*.

impinge [ɪm'pɪndʒ] vi **a** (*make impression*) **to ~ on** affecter, toucher; **her death did not ~ on him** sa mort ne l'a pas affecté *or* touché; **it didn't ~ on his daily life** cela n'affectait pas sa vie quotidienne, cela n'avait pas de répercussion sur sa vie quotidienne; **what was happening around him suddenly ~d on him** il a pris brusquement conscience de ce qui se passait autour de lui. **b** **to ~ on sb's rights** empiéter sur les droits de qn. **c** **rays of light impinging on the eye** des rais de lumière qui frappent l'œil.

impingement [ɪm'pɪndʒmənt] n empiètement *m* (*of, on* sur).

impious ['ɪmpɪəs] adj impie.

impiously ['ɪmpɪəslɪ] adv avec impiété.

impish ['ɪmpɪʃ] adj espiègle, malicieux.

implacable [ɪm'plækəbl] adj implacable (*towards* envers).

implacably [ɪm'plækəblɪ] adv implacablement.

implant [ɪm'plɑːnt] **1** vt **a** *idea* implanter (*in sb* dans la tête de qn); *principle* inculquer (*in sb* à qn); *desire, wish* inspirer (*in sb* à qn). **b** (*Med*) implanter (*in* dans). **2** ['implɑːnt] n (*under skin*) implant *m*; (*graft*) greffe *f*.

implausible [ɪm'plɔːzəbl] adj peu plausible, peu vraisemblable.

implausibly [ɪm'plɔːzəblɪ] adv de façon peu plausible *or* peu vraisemblable.

implement ['ɪmplɪmənt] **1** n outil *m*, instrument *m*; (*fig*) instrument. **~s** équipement *m* (*NonC*), matériel *m* (*NonC*); (*for gardening, painting, carpentry*) matériel, outils; (*for cooking*) ustensiles *mpl*; **~s of war** matériel de guerre; **farm ~s** matériel *or* outillage *m* agricole. **2** ['ɪmplɪment] vt *contract* exécuter; *decision* donner suite à, exécuter; *promise* accomplir; *engagement* remplir, exécuter; *plan* réaliser; *law* appliquer; *ideas* mettre en pratique.

implementation [ˌɪmplɪmen'teɪʃən] n (*see* **implement 2**) exécution *f*; accomplissement *m*; réalisation *f*; (*Comput*) implémentation *f*.

implicate ['ɪmplɪkeɪt] vt impliquer, compromettre (*in* dans).

implication [ˌɪmplɪ'keɪʃən] n **a** insinuation *f*, implication *f*. **by ~** implicitement; **I know only from ~** je ne sais que d'après ce qui a été insinué; **there were ~s of dishonesty** on a insinué qu'il y avait eu de la malhonnêteté; **I don't like the ~s of that question** je n'aime pas ce que cette question insinue *or* sous-entend, je n'aime pas les implications contenues dans cette question; **he didn't realize the full ~s of his words** il n'avait pas pleinement mesuré la portée de ses paroles; **we shall have to study all the ~s** il nous faudra étudier toutes les conséquences (possibles); **this has serious ~s for the youth of the country** ceci pourrait avoir des répercussions sérieuses *or* un retentissement sérieux sur la jeunesse du pays. **b** (*NonC*) implication *f* (*in* dans).

implicit [ɪm'plɪsɪt] adj **a** (*implied*) implicite (*in* dans); *threat* implicite; *recognition* tacite. **b** (*unquestioning*) *belief, faith* absolu; *confidence* absolu, sans réserve, aveugle, parfait; *obedience* aveugle, parfait.

implicitly [ɪm'plɪsɪtlɪ] adv **a** *make known* implicitement, tacitement. **b** *believe* absolument, sans réserves. **to obey sb ~** obéir à qn aveuglément *or* au doigt et à l'œil.

implied [ɪm'plaɪd] adj implicite, tacite, sous-entendu.

implode [ɪm'pləʊd] **1** vi (*gen*) imploser. **2** vt (*gen*) causer l'implosion de. (*Phon*) **~d consonant** consonne *f* implosive.

implore [ɪm'plɔːʳ] vt implorer, conjurer, supplier (*sb to do* qn de faire). **to ~ sb's help** implorer le secours de qn; **I ~ you!** je vous en supplie! *or* conjure!

imploring [ɪm'plɔːrɪŋ] adj *look, voice* implorant, suppliant; *person* suppliant.

imploringly [ɪm'plɔːrɪŋlɪ] **adv** *ask* d'un ton implorant *or* suppliant. **to look ~ at sb** implorer *or* supplier qn du regard.

implosion [ɪm'pləʊʒən] **n** implosion *f*.

implosive [ɪm'pləʊzɪv] **1** **adj** implosif. **2** **n** (*Phon*) implosive *f*.

imply [ɪm'plaɪ] **vt** **a** *[person]* suggérer, laisser entendre, laisser supposer; (*insinuate*) insinuer (*pej*). **he implied that he would come** il a laissé entendre *or* laissé supposer qu'il viendrait; **he implied that I was lying** il a laissé entendre *or* insinué que je mentais; **are you ~ing that ...?** voulez-vous suggérer *or* insinuer que ...?; **it is implied that ...** il faut sous-entendre que ..., cela sous-entend que ...; *see also* **implied**.
b (*indicate*) suggérer, impliquer, (laisser) supposer. **that implies some intelligence** cela suppose *or* implique une certaine intelligence; **this fact implies that he was already aware of the incident** ce fait suggère *or* laisse supposer qu'il était déjà au courant de l'incident; *see also* **implied**.

impolite [ˌɪmpə'laɪt] **adj** impoli (*to, towards* envers).

impolitely [ˌɪmpə'laɪtlɪ] **adv** impoliment, d'une manière impolie, avec impolitesse.

impoliteness [ˌɪmpə'laɪtnɪs] **n** impolitesse *f* (*to, towards* envers).

impolitic [ɪm'pɒlɪtɪk] **adj** peu politique, impolitique.

imponderable [ɪm'pɒndərəbl] **adj, n** impondérable (*m*).

import ['ɪmpɔːt] **1** **n** **a** (*Comm*) importation *f* (*into* en). **~ of goods** importation de marchandises; **~s** articles *mpl or* marchandises *fpl* d'importation, importations; **~s from England** importations en provenance d'Angleterre.
b (*meaning*) *[action, decision, speech, words]* sens *m*, signification *f*; *[document]* teneur *f*.
c importance *f*. **questions of great ~** questions de grande importance.
2 **comp** ▸**import duty** (*Comm*) droits *mpl* d'importation, taxe *f* à l'importation ▸**import-export (trade)** import-export *m* ▸**import licence** licence *f* d'importation ▸**import quota** quota *m* à l'importation *or* d'importation ▸**import surcharge** surcharge *f* d'importation ▸**import trade** (commerce *m* d')importation *f*.
3 [ɪm'pɔːt] **vt** **a** (*Comm*) importer. **~ed goods** marchandises d'importation *or* importées.
b (*mean, imply*) signifier, vouloir dire.

importance [ɪm'pɔːtəns] **n** importance *f*. **to be of ~** avoir de l'importance; **of some ~** assez important, d'une certaine importance; **of great ~** très important, de grande importance; **it is of the highest ~ that ...** il est de la plus haute importance que ... + *subj*, il importe au premier chef que ... + *subj*; **it is of ~ to do** il est important de faire, il importe de faire (*frm*); **it is of no (great) ~** c'est sans (grande) importance; **to give ~ to sth** *[person]* accorder *or* attacher de l'importance à qch; *[event, development]* donner de l'importance à qch; **we give** *or* **attach the greatest ~ to establishing the facts** nous accordons *or* attachons la plus haute importance à l'établissement des faits; **man of ~** homme important, personnage (important); **person of no ~** personne *f* sans importance *or* de peu de conséquence; **his position gives him considerable ~** sa position lui donne une influence considérable; **he is full of his own ~** il est plein de lui-même, il est imbu *or* pénétré de sa propre importance; **the ~ of being/doing** l'importance d'être/de faire.

important [ɪm'pɔːtənt] **adj** important. **it is ~ that you (should) know** il importe (*frm*) *or* il est important que vous sachiez; **that's not ~** ça n'a pas d'importance, cela n'est pas important; **his presence is ~ to** *or* **for the success of our plan** sa présence est importante pour la réussite de notre projet; **he played an ~ part in abolishing slavery** il a joué un rôle important dans l'abolition de l'esclavage; **he was trying to look ~** il se donnait *or* il prenait des airs importants.

importantly [ɪm'pɔːtəntlɪ] **adv** (*pej*) d'un air important, d'un air d'importance.

importation [ˌɪmpɔː'teɪʃən] **n** (*Comm*) importation *f*.

importer [ɪm'pɔːtə^r] **n** (*person*) importateur *m*, -trice *f*; (*country*) (pays *m*) importateur *m*.

importunate [ɪm'pɔːtjʊnɪt] **adj** *visitor, demand* importun, gênant; *creditor* harcelant.

importune [ˌɪmpɔː'tjuːn] **1** **vt** *[questioner etc]* importuner, ennuyer; *[creditor]* harceler, presser; (*Jur*) *[prostitute etc]* racoler. **2** **vi** (*Jur*) racoler. **she was arrested for importuning** elle a été arrêtée pour racolage.

importunity [ˌɪmpɔː'tjuːnɪtɪ] **n** importunité *f*.

impose [ɪm'pəʊz] **1** **vt** **a** *task, conditions* imposer (*on* à); *sanctions* infliger (*on* à). **to ~ a penalty/a fine on sb** infliger une peine/une amende à qn, frapper qn d'une peine/d'une amende; **to ~ a tax on sth** imposer qch, taxer qch, mettre un impôt *or* une taxe sur qch; **to ~ itself** s'imposer; **to ~ o.s. (on sb)** s'imposer (à qn); **to ~ one's presence on sb** imposer sa présence à qn. **b** (*Typ*) imposer. **2** **vi**: **to ~ on sb** abuser de la gentillesse *or* de la bonté *or* de l'amabilité de qn; **to ~ on sb's generosity** abuser de la générosité de qn.

imposing [ɪm'pəʊzɪŋ] **adj** imposant, impressionnant. **~ height** *[person]* taille imposante; *[building etc]* hauteur impressionnante.

imposition [ˌɪmpə'zɪʃən] **n** **a** (*NonC*) *[tax, condition, sanction]* imposition *f*. **b** (*tax imposed*) impôt *m*, taxe *f*. **c** (*fig*) **it's rather an ~ on her** c'est abuser de sa gentillesse *or* de sa bonté *or* de son amabilité; **I'm afraid it's an ~ for you** je crains que cela ne vous dérange (*subj*). **d** (*Typ*) imposition *f*. **e** (*Scol*) punition *f*.

impossibility [ɪmˌpɒsə'bɪlɪtɪ] **n** impossibilité *f* (*of sth* de qch, *of doing* de faire). **the moral/physical ~ of** l'impossibilité morale/matérielle de; **it's a physical ~ for her to get there before 3 o'clock** elle est dans l'impossibilité matérielle *or* il lui est matériellement impossible d'y être avant 3 heures; **it's an ~** c'est une impossibilité, c'est une chose impossible, c'est quelque chose d'impossible.

impossible [ɪm'pɒsəbl] **1** **adj** **a** impossible. **it is ~ for him to leave** il lui est impossible *or* il est dans l'impossibilité de partir; **he made it ~ for me to accept** il m'a mis dans l'impossibilité d'accepter; **it is/is not ~ that ...** il est/n'est pas impossible que ... + *subj*; **I'm afraid it's quite ~!** c'est malheureusement absolument impossible! **b** *person, child, condition, situation* impossible, insupportable; *excuse, account, adventure, story, reason* impossible, invraisemblable, extravagant. **he made her life ~** il lui a rendu la vie *or* l'existence impossible. **2** **n** impossible *m*. **to do/ask for the ~** faire/demander l'impossible.

impossibly [ɪm'pɒsəblɪ] **adv** **a** (*lit*) **it was ~ small** c'était beaucoup trop petit *or* ridiculement petit; **if, ~, he were to succeed** si, par impossible, il réussissait; **an ~ difficult problem** un problème d'une difficulté insurmontable. **b** (*fig*) *dress* d'une façon invraisemblable; *behave* d'une façon impossible *or* insupportable. **we're ~ late** nous sommes incroyablement *or* épouvantablement en retard; **she is ~ eccentric** elle est incroyablement *or* follement excentrique.

impost ['ɪmpəʊst] **n** (*Admin, Fin, Jur*) impôt *m*; (*Customs*) taxe *f* douanière, droit *m* de douane.

imposter, impostor [ɪm'pɒstə^r] **n** (*impersonator*) imposteur *m*; (*fraud*) charlatan *m*.

imposture [ɪm'pɒstʃə^r] **n** imposture *f*.

impotence ['ɪmpətəns] **n** (*lit, fig*) impuissance *f*, faiblesse *f*; (*sexual*) impuissance; (*Med gen*) impotence *f*.

impotent ['ɪmpətənt] **adj** (*see* **impotence**) impuissant; faible; impotent.

impound [ɪm'paʊnd] **vt** (*Jur*) confisquer, saisir.

impoundment [ɪm'paʊndmənt] **n** (*US Fin*) *mise f en réserve de fonds votés (par le Congrès)*.

impoverish [ɪm'pɒvərɪʃ] **vt** appauvrir. **~ed** appauvri, pauvre.

impoverishment [ɪm'pɒvərɪʃmənt] **n** appauvrissement *m*.

impracticability [ɪmˌpræktɪkə'bɪlɪtɪ] **n** impraticabilité *f*.

impracticable [ɪm'præktɪkəbl] **adj** *idea, plan, scheme, suggestion* impraticable, irréalisable; *road etc* impraticable.

impractical [ɪm'præktɪkəl] **adj** *person* qui manque d'esprit pratique; *plan, idea* peu réaliste, pas pratique.

impracticality [ɪmˌpræktɪ'kælɪtɪ] **n** manque *m* de réalisme.

imprecation [ˌɪmprɪ'keɪʃən] **n** imprécation *f*, malédiction *f*.

imprecise [ˌɪmprɪ'saɪs] **adj** imprécis.

imprecision [ˌɪmprɪ'sɪʒən] **n** imprécision *f*, manque *m* de précision.

impregnable [ɪm'pregnəbl] **adj** (*Mil*) *fortress, defences* imprenable, inexpugnable; (*fig*) *position* inattaquable; *argument* irréfutable.

impregnate ['ɪmpregneɪt] **vt** **a** (*fertilize*) féconder. **b** (*saturate*) imprégner, imbiber (*with* de); (*fig*) imprégner, pénétrer (*with* de).

impregnation [ˌɪmpreg'neɪʃən] **n** (*see* **impregnate**) fécondation *f*; imprégnation *f*.

impresario [ˌɪmpre'sɑːrɪəʊ] **n** impresario *m*.

impress [ɪm'pres] **1** **vt** **a** *person* impressionner, faire impression sur. **how did he ~ you?** quelle impression vous a-t-il faite?; **he ~ed me favourably/unfavourably** il m'a fait une bonne/mauvaise impression; **his novel greatly ~ed me** son roman m'a beaucoup impressionné, son roman m'a fait une forte *or* grosse impression; **to be ~ed by sth** être impressionné par qch; **they were most ~ed by his having everything ready on time** ils ont été très impressionnés par le fait qu'il ait tout préparé à temps; **he is not easily ~ed** il ne se laisse pas facilement impressionner; (*negative opinion*) **I am not ~ed** ça ne m'impressionne pas, ça me laisse froid; (*annoyance*) **I am NOT ~ed!** (continue,) tu m'intéresses!* (*iro*); ça ne m'impressionne pas!; **he does it just to ~ people** il ne le fait que pour (impressionner) la galerie.
b imprimer, marquer (*on* sur). **to ~ a seal on wax** imprimer un sceau sur la cire; (*fig*) **to ~ sth on sb** faire (bien) comprendre qch à qn; **you must ~ on him that he should be on time** il faut que tu lui fasses (bien) comprendre qu'il doit arriver à l'heure; **his words are (forever) ~ed on my memory** ses paroles sont (à jamais) gravées dans ma mémoire.
2 ['ɪmpres] **n** marque *f*, empreinte *f*.

impression [ɪm'preʃən] **n** **a** (*effect*) impression *f*. **to make an ~** faire impression *or* de l'effet (*on sb* à qn); **to make a good/bad ~ on sb** faire une bonne/mauvaise impression à qn; **what ~ does he make on you?, what's your ~ of him?** quelle impression vous fait-il?; **the water made no ~ on the stains** l'eau n'a fait aucun effet sur *or* n'a pas agi sur les taches; **first ~s are most important** ce sont les premières impressions qui comptent (le plus); **he gave the ~ of power** il donnait une impression de puissance.
b (*vague idea*) impression *f*. **I am under the ~ that ..., my ~ is that ...** j'ai l'impression que ...; **that wasn't my ~!** ce n'est pas l'im-

pression que j'ai eue!; **his ~s of Paris** les impressions qu'il a gardées de Paris; **he had the ~ of falling** il avait l'impression de tomber.

c *[seal, stamp, footprint]* empreinte *f*, impression *f*, trace *f*, marque *f*; (*on wax*) impression.

d *[engraving etc]* impression *f*; (*esp Brit*) *[book etc]* tirage *m*, édition *f*.

impressionable [ɪm'preʃnəbl] adj impressionnable, sensible. **at an ~ age** à un âge où l'on est impressionnable.

impressionism [ɪm'preʃənɪzəm] n (*Art*) impressionnisme *m*.

impressionist [ɪm'preʃənɪst] adj, n (*Art*) impressionniste (*mf*).

impressionistic [ɪm,preʃə'nɪstɪk] adj *story, account* impressionniste, subjectif; (*Art*) impressionniste.

impressive [ɪm'presɪv] adj *appearance, building, ceremony, person, sight, sum* impressionnant, imposant; *amount, account, achievement, result* impressionnant; *speech* impressionnant, frappant. **~ height** *[person]* taille imposante; *[building]* hauteur impressionnante.

impressively [ɪm'presɪvlɪ] adv de façon impressionnante, d'une manière impressionnante.

impressment [ɪm'presmənt] n *[person]* enrôlement forcé; *[property, goods]* réquisition *f*.

imprint [ɪm'prɪnt] 1 vt imprimer, marquer (*on* sur); (*fig*) imprimer, graver, implanter (*on* dans). 2 ['ɪmprɪnt] n (*lit, fig*) marque *f*, empreinte *f*; (*Psych*) empreinte perceptive. **published under the Collins ~** édité chez Collins.

imprinting [ɪm'prɪntɪŋ] n (*Psych: NonC*) empreinte *f*.

imprison [ɪm'prɪzn] vt emprisonner, mettre en prison; (*fig*) emprisonner. **he had been ~ed for 3 months when ...** il avait été en prison 3 mois quand ..., il avait fait 3 mois de prison quand ...; **the judge ~ed him for 10 years** le juge l'a envoyé en prison pour 10 ans, le juge l'a condamné à 10 ans de prison.

imprisonment [ɪm'prɪznmənt] n (*action, state*) emprisonnement *m*. **to sentence sb to one month's ~/to life ~** condamner qn à un mois de prison/à la prison à vie; **sentence of life ~** condamnation *f* à la prison à perpétuité; **to serve a sentence of ~** faire de la prison.

improbability [ɪm,prɒbə'bɪlɪtɪ] n (*see* **improbable**) a improbabilité *f*. b invraisemblance *f*.

improbable [ɪm'prɒbəbl] adj a (*unlikely to happen*) improbable. **it is ~ that ...** il est improbable *or* il est peu probable que ... + *subj*. b (*of doubtful truth*) *story, excuse* invraisemblable.

improbably [ɪm'prɒbəblɪ] adv invraisemblablement. **this area is, ~, one of the most desirable in town** aussi invraisemblable que cela puisse paraître, ce quartier est l'un des plus recherchés de la ville.

impromptu [ɪm'prɒmptju:] 1 adv impromptu. 2 adj impromptu. **to make an ~ speech** faire un discours impromptu *or* au pied levé *or* à l'improviste. 3 n (*Mus*) impromptu *m*.

improper [ɪm'prɒpə^r] adj (*unsuitable*) déplacé, malséant, de mauvais goût; (*indecent*) indécent, inconvenant; *conduct, suggestion* indécent; *story* indécent, scabreux; (*dishonest*) malhonnête; (*wrong*) *diagnosis* incorrect, erroné; *term* inexact, impropre, incorrect; *use, interpretation* abusif, incorrect; (*Sport*) *play etc* incorrect.

improperly [ɪm'prɒpəlɪ] adv (*indecently*) d'une manière malséante *or* inconvenante, indécemment; (*wrongly*) incorrectement, à tort. **word ~ used** mot employé incorrectement *or* improprement *or* abusivement.

impropriety [,ɪmprə'praɪətɪ] n a *[behaviour etc]* inconvenance *f*. **to commit an ~** commettre une inconvenance; **to behave with ~** se conduire avec inconvenance. b (*Ling*) *[expression, phrase]* impropriété *f*.

improve [ɪm'pru:v] 1 vt a (*make better*) améliorer; *situation, position, one's work, health, wording, property, building* améliorer; *knowledge* améliorer, augmenter, accroître; *physique* développer; *machine, invention* améliorer, perfectionner; *site* aménager, embellir; *soil, land* amender, fertiliser, bonifier. **to ~ sb's looks** *or* **appearance** embellir *or* avantager qn; **to ~ one's looks** s'embellir; **that should ~ his chances of success** ceci devrait lui donner de meilleures chances de réussir; **she's trying to ~ her mind** elle essaie de se cultiver (l'esprit); **a book** *etc* **which ~s the mind** un livre *etc* édifiant; **he wants to ~ his French** il veut se perfectionner en français.

b (*make good use of*) tirer parti de, profiter de. **to ~ the occasion**, (*hum*) **to ~ the shining hour** tirer parti de l'occasion, mettre l'occasion à profit.

2 vi a (*see* **1a**) s'améliorer; s'augmenter, s'accroître; se développer; être amélioré, être perfectionné; s'embellir; s'amender, se bonifier. **this wine ~s with age** ce vin se bonifie *or* s'améliore en vieillissant; **to ~ with use** s'améliorer à l'usage; *[person, town etc]* **to ~ on acquaintance** gagner à être connu; **this book ~s on rereading** ce livre gagne à être relu; **his chances of success are improving** ses chances de réussir augmentent *or* s'améliorent; **she's improving in appearance, her appearance is improving** elle embellit; **the invalid is improving** l'état du malade s'améliore; **his work is improving** (la qualité de) son travail s'améliore; **he has ~d in maths, his maths have ~d** il a fait des progrès en maths; **his French is improving** son français s'améliore; **business is improving** les affaires reprennent; **things are improving** les choses vont mieux, la situation s'améliore; **this child is difficult but he's improving** c'est un enfant difficile mais il s'améliore *or* il fait des progrès; **the weather is improving** le temps s'améliore *or* s'arrange.

b **to ~ on sth** faire mieux que qch, apporter des améliorations à qch; **it can't be ~d on** on ne peut pas faire mieux; (*Comm, Fin*) **to ~ on sb's offer** enchérir sur qn.

improved [ɪm'pru:vd] adj meilleur. **much/slightly ~** très/peu amélioré; **this room looks much ~ after painting** la pièce est beaucoup mieux après avoir été repeinte; **his behaviour is much ~ on last year** sa conduite s'est nettement améliorée par rapport à l'an dernier; (*Comm*) **"new ~ formula"** "nouvelle formule".

improvement [ɪm'pru:vmənt] 1 n a (*NonC*) amélioration *f*; *[gifts, mind, physique]* développement *m*; *[studies]* progrès *m*; *[health, situation, land, soil]* amélioration; *[site]* aménagement *m*, embellissement *m*; *[machine]* perfectionnement *m*. (*gen*) **there's been quite an ~** il y a un *or* du mieux; **the ~ in the appearance of the house** l'embellissement de la maison; **there has been a great ~ in her looks since ...** elle a beaucoup embelli depuis ..., elle s'est beaucoup arrangée depuis ...; **there has been some ~ in the patient's condition** l'état du malade s'est un peu amélioré; **to be open to ~** être susceptible d'amélioration; **he has shown some ~ in French** il a fait quelques progrès en français; **this model is an ~ on the previous one** ce modèle marque un progrès sur le précédent; **there is room for ~** cela pourrait être mieux, on pourrait faire mieux.

b (*gen pl*) **~s** améliorations *fpl*; **to carry out ~s to a town/a house** apporter des améliorations à *or* faire des travaux *mpl* d'aménagement dans une ville/une maison.

2 comp ►**improvement grant** subvention *f* pour l'amélioration d'un logement, ≃ prime *f* à l'amélioration de l'habitat; **he got an improvement grant from the council for his kitchen** il a obtenu une aide financière de la ville pour la modernisation de sa cuisine.

improvidence [ɪm'prɒvɪdəns] n imprévoyance *f*, manque *m* de prévoyance.

improvident [ɪm'prɒvɪdənt] adj (*not providing for future*) imprévoyant; (*spendthrift*) prodigue, dépensier.

improvidently [ɪm'prɒvɪdəntlɪ] adv avec imprévoyance.

improving [ɪm'pru:vɪŋ] adj édifiant.

improvisation [,ɪmprəvaɪ'zeɪʃən] n improvisation *f*.

improvise ['ɪmprəvaɪz] vti improviser.

imprudence [ɪm'pru:dəns] n imprudence *f*.

imprudent [ɪm'pru:dənt] adj imprudent.

imprudently [ɪm'pru:dəntlɪ] adv imprudemment.

impudence ['ɪmpjʊdəns] n impudence *f*, effronterie *f*, insolence *f*.

impudent ['ɪmpjʊdənt] adj impudent, effronté, insolent.

impudently ['ɪmpjʊdəntlɪ] adv impudemment, effrontément, insolemment.

impugn [ɪm'pju:n] vt contester, attaquer.

impulse ['ɪmpʌls] 1 n a (*spontaneous act etc*) impulsion *f*, élan *m*. **rash ~** coup *m* de tête; **on a sudden ~ he ...** pris d'une impulsion soudaine il ...; **man of ~** impulsif *m*; **to act on (an) ~** agir par impulsion; **my first ~ was to refuse** ma première impulsion *or* réaction a été de refuser. b impulsion *f*, poussée *f*. **to give an ~ to business** donner une impulsion aux affaires. 2 comp ►**impulse buy** *or* **purchase** achat *m* d'impulsion, achat sur un coup de tête ►**impulse buying** (tendance *f* à faire des) achats *mpl* sur un coup de tête, achats d'impulsion.

impulsion [ɪm'pʌlʃən] n impulsion *f*.

impulsive [ɪm'pʌlsɪv] adj a (*spontaneous, acting on impulse*) *movement* impulsif; *temperament* primesautier; *temper, passion* fougueux; *action* impulsif, spontané, irréfléchi; *remark* irréfléchi. b (*impelling*) *force* irrésistible.

impulsively [ɪm'pʌlsɪvlɪ] adv *act, speak* par *or* sur impulsion.

impulsiveness [ɪm'pʌlsɪvnɪs] n (*NonC*) caractère impulsif, impulsivité *f*.

impunity [ɪm'pju:nɪtɪ] n impunité *f*. **with ~** impunément, avec impunité.

impure [ɪm'pjʊə^r] adj *air, water, milk, motive* impur; *thought, action* impur, impudique; (*Archit etc*) *style* bâtard.

impurity [ɪm'pjʊərɪtɪ] n a (*NonC: see* **impure**) impureté *f*; impudicité *f*. b (*in water etc*) **impurities** impuretés *fpl*.

imputation [,ɪmpjʊ'teɪʃən] n a (*accusation*) imputation *f*, accusation *f*. b (*NonC*) attribution *f*, imputation *f* (*of sth to sb/sth* de qch à qn/qch).

impute [ɪm'pju:t] vt imputer, attribuer (*sth to sb/sth* qch à qn/qch). (*Comm*) **~d rent/value** loyer *m*/valeur *f* imputé(e) *or* implicite; (*Comm*) **~d cost** coût *m* supplétif, charge *f* supplétive.

IN (*US Post*) abbr of **Indiana**.

in [ɪn] (*phr vb elem*) 1 prep a (*place: gen*) dans. **~ the box** dans la boîte; **put that ~ it** mets ça dedans; **there's something ~ it** il y a quelque chose dedans; **~ the garden** dans le *or* au jardin; **~ the country** à la campagne; **~ town** en ville; **~ here** ici; **~ there** là; (*inside sth*) là-dedans; **~ the street** dans la rue; **~ the shop window** à la vitrine, en vitrine; **sitting ~ the doorway** assis dans l'embrasure de la porte; **sitting ~ the window** assis devant la fenêtre; **~ school** à l'école; **~ the school** dans l'école; **~ a friend's house** chez un ami; *see* **bed, hand, place** *etc*.

b (*in geog names*) (*countries: gen; also fem French provinces, islands and fem US states*) en; (*countries: all plurals, and masc sing with initial consonant*) au *or* aux; (*towns: gen; also masc islands*) à; (*most departments; also masc French regions, Brit counties, masc US states, and islands with "île" in name*) dans le (*or* la *or* l' *or* les). **in England/France** *etc* en Angleterre/France *etc;* **in Iran/Israel** *etc* en Iran/Israël *etc;* **in Brittany/Provence** *etc* en Bretagne/Provence *etc;* **in Sicily/Crete** *etc* en Sicile/Crète *etc;* **in Louisiana/Virginia** *etc* en Louisiane/Virginie *etc;* **in Japan/the United States** *etc* au Japon/aux États-Unis *etc;* **in London/Paris** *etc* à Londres/Paris *etc;* **in Cuba/Malta** *etc* à Cuba/Malte *etc;* **in the Drôme/the Var** *etc* dans la Drôme/le Var *etc;* **in Seine-et-Marne** en Seine-et-Marne; **in Poitou/Berry** dans le Poitou/le Berry; **in Sussex/Yorkshire** *etc* dans le Sussex/le Yorkshire *etc;* **in the Isle of Man/the Ile de Ré** dans l'île de Man/l'île de Ré.

c (*people, works*) chez, en, dans. **we find it ~ Dickens** nous le trouvons chez *or* dans Dickens; **rare ~ a child of that age** rare chez un enfant de cet âge; **he has/hasn't got it ~ him to succeed** il est capable/incapable de réussir; **you find this instinct ~ animals** on trouve cet instinct chez les animaux; **they will have a great leader ~ him** ils trouveront en lui un excellent dirigeant.

d (*time: during*) **~ 1989** en 1989; **~ the sixties** dans les années soixante; **~ the reign of** sous le règne de; **~ June** en juin, au mois de juin; **~ spring** au printemps; **~ summer/autumn/winter** en été/automne/hiver; **~ the morning** le matin, dans la matinée; **~ the afternoon** l'après-midi, dans l'après-midi; **~ the mornings** le(s) matin(s); **~ the daytime** pendant la journée; **~ the evening** le soir, pendant la soirée; **~ the night** la nuit, pendant la nuit, de nuit; **3 o'clock ~ the afternoon** 3 heures de l'après-midi; **at any time ~ the day** à n'importe quelle heure du jour *or* de la journée; **~ those days** à cette époque-là; **~ these days** de nos jours, à notre époque, actuellement; **I haven't seen him ~ years** cela fait des années que je ne l'ai (pas) vu; *see* **end, future, life** *etc.*

e (*time: in the space of*) en. **I did it/will do it ~ 2 hours** je l'ai fait/je le ferai en deux heures, j'ai mis/je mettrai deux heures à le faire.

f (*time: at the end of*) dans, au bout de. **~ a moment** *or* **a minute** dans un moment *or* une minute; **~ a short time** sous peu, dans peu de temps; **~ a week's time** dans (l'espace d')une semaine; **he will arrive ~ a fortnight** il arrivera dans quinze jours; **he returned ~ a week** il est rentré au bout d'une semaine; *see* **time** *etc.*

g (*manner*) **~ a loud voice** d'une voix forte; **~ a soft voice** à voix basse; **to speak ~ a whisper** parler en chuchotant, chuchoter; **to dress ~ fashion** s'habiller à la mode; **~ self-defence** pour se défendre; (*Jur*) en légitime défense; **~ ink** à l'encre; **~ pencil** au crayon; **~ French** en français; **to reply ~ writing** répondre par écrit; **to paint ~ oils** peindre à l'huile; **to pay ~ cash/~ kind** payer (en argent) comptant/en nature; **it is written ~ black and white** c'est écrit noir sur blanc; **to stand ~ a row** être en ligne; **~ alphabetical order** par ordre alphabétique; **to walk ~ groups** se promener en *or* par groupes; **packed ~ hundreds** en *or* par paquets de cent; **~ rags** en haillons, en lambeaux; **dressed ~ white/black** habillé en *or* vêtu de blanc/noir; **~ his shirt** en chemise; **~ his slippers** en pantoufles; **you look nice ~ that dress** tu es jolie avec cette robe.

h (*substance, material*) en. **~ velvet** en velours; **~ marble** en marbre.

i (*physical surroundings, circumstances*) **~ the rain** sous la pluie; **~ the sun** au soleil; **~ the shade** à l'ombre; **~ darkness** dans l'obscurité; **~ the moonlight** au clair de (la) lune; **to go out ~ all weathers/~ a high wind** sortir par tous les temps/par grand vent; **~ itself** en soi.

j (*state, condition*) **~ good/bad health** en bonne/mauvaise santé; **~ tears** en larmes; **~ despair** au désespoir; **to be ~ a rage** être en rage, être furieux; **~ good repair** en bon état; **~ ruins** en ruines; **to live ~ luxury/poverty** vivre dans le luxe/la misère; **~ private** en privé; **~ public** en public; **~ secret** en secret; **~ fun** pour rire, par plaisanterie; **~ earnest** sérieusement, pour de bon.

k (*ratio*) **one man ~ ten** un homme sur dix; **once ~ a hundred years** une fois tous les cent ans; **a day ~ a thousand** un jour entre mille; **15 pence ~ the pound** 15 pence par livre sterling.

l (*degree, extent*) **~ large/small quantities** en grande/petite quantité; **~ some measure** dans une certaine mesure; **~ part** en partie; **~ hundreds** par centaines.

m (*in respect of*) **blind ~ the left eye** aveugle de l'œil gauche; **poor ~ maths** faible en maths; **10 metres ~ height by 30 ~ length** 10 mètres de haut sur 30 de long; **5 ~ number** au nombre de 5; **~ that, he resembles his father** en cela, il ressemble à son père; *see* **respect** *etc.*

n (*occupation, activity*) **he is ~ the army** il est dans l'armée; **he is ~ the motor trade** il travaille dans l'(industrie) automobile; **he spends his time ~ reading** il passe son temps à lire.

o (*after superlative*) de. **the best pupil ~ the class** le meilleur élève de la classe; **the highest mountain ~ Europe** la montagne la plus haute d'Europe, la plus haute montagne d'Europe.

p (*+ gerund*) **~ saying this, ~ so saying** en disant cela; **~ trying to save her he fell into the water himself** en essayant de la sauver il est tombé lui-même à l'eau.

q **~ that there are 5 of them** étant donné qu'il y en a 5; **~ so** *or* **as far as** dans la mesure où; **~ all** en tout.

r (*Jur*) **~ re: ...** objet: ... .

2 **adv** **a** dedans, à l'intérieur. **to be ~** (*at home*) être là, être à la maison, être chez soi; (*in room, office etc*) être là; **there is nobody ~** il n'y a personne (à la maison); **is Paul ~?** est-ce que Paul est là?; **they will be ~ at 6 o'clock** ils seront rentrés *or* là à 6 heures; **we were asked ~** on nous a invités à entrer; **the train is ~** le train est en gare *or* est arrivé; **the harvest is ~** la moisson est rentrée; **oranges are now ~** c'est maintenant la saison des oranges, les oranges sont maintenant en saison; **straw hats are ~** les chapeaux de paille sont en vogue *or* à la mode; **the socialists are ~** les socialistes sont au pouvoir; (*Pol*) **to put sb ~** porter qn au pouvoir; **the Communist candidate is ~** le candidat communiste a été élu; **the fire is still ~** le feu brûle encore, il y a encore du feu; *see* **call in, move in** *etc.*

b (*phrases*) **~ between** (*space*) entre, au milieu; (*time*) dans l'intervalle, entre-temps (*see also* **5**;) **we are ~ for trouble** nous allons avoir des ennuis; **we are ~ for rain** nous allons avoir de la pluie; **he's ~ for it!*** il va écoper!*, il va en prendre pour son grade!*; **you don't know what you're ~ for!*** tu ne sais pas ce qui t'attend!; **are you ~ for the race?** est-ce que tu es inscrit pour la course?; **he's ~ for the job of ...** il est candidat au poste de ...; **to have it ~ for sb*** avoir une dent contre qn*, garder une dent à qn*; **to be ~ on a plan/secret** être au courant d'un plan/d'un secret; **are you ~ on it?** tu es au courant?, tu es dans le coup?*; **to be (well) ~ with sb** être en bons termes avec qn, être bien avec qn; **day ~ day out** jour après jour; *see* **all, eye, luck** *etc.*

3 **adj** **a** **"~" door** porte *f* d'entrée; *see also* **5**.

b (*) **it's the ~ thing to ...** c'est très dans le vent* de ... + *infin*; **it's the ~ place to eat** c'est le restaurant dans le vent* *or* à la mode; **an ~ joke** une plaisanterie qui n'est comprise que des initiés.

4 **n** **a** **to know the ~s and outs of a matter** connaître une affaire dans ses moindres détails, connaître les tenants et les aboutissants d'une affaire; **all the ~s and outs of the question** les tenants et les aboutissants de la question.

b (*US Pol* *) **the ~s** le parti au pouvoir.

5 **comp** ►**in-between: the in-betweens** ceux qui sont entre les deux; **it's in-between** c'est entre les deux; **in-between times** dans les intervalles; **it was in-between* weather** il faisait un temps moyen; **a coat for in-between weather** un manteau de demi-saison ►**in-built** *feeling, tendency* inné; *flaw, limitation* qui en fait partie intégrante ►**in-car entertainment** détente *f* en voiture, détente-voiture *f* ►**in-depth** **adj** en profondeur ►**in-fighting** = **infighting** ►**in-flight** (*Aviat*) *see* **in-flight** ►**in-goal area** (*Rugby*) en-but *m* ►**in-group** noyau *m* (fermé) ►**in-house** **adj** (*designed for staff*) *publication* interne; *training* effectué sur place *or* dans le cadre de la compagnie; (*made within company*) *video etc* réalisé dans le cadre de la compagnie ◊ **adv** *train, produce etc* en interne ►**in-laws*** (*parents-in-law*) beaux-parents *mpl*; (*others*) belle-famille ►**in-patient** = **inpatient** ►**in-service education** (*US*) stage *m* de perfectionnement ►**in-service training** (*Ind etc*) formation *f* continue *or* en cours d'emploi; (*Ind, Scol etc*) **to have in-service training** *[new employee]* faire un stage d'initiation; *[present employee]* faire un stage de perfectionnement; (*new subject*) faire un stage de recyclage; **to have in-service training in the use of computers** faire un stage d'informatique ►**in-store** *detective* employé par le magasin; *theft* commis par un membre du personnel ►**in-tray** courrier *m* "arrivée".

-in [ɪn] **n ending in comps** *particule qui désigne une réunion ou un rassemblement, e.g.* **a talk-in** une réunion où l'on discute; *see* **sit-in, teach.**

in. **abbr of inch.**

inability [ˌɪnəˈbɪlɪtɪ] **n** incapacité *f* (*to do* de faire), impuissance *f* (*to do* à faire).

in abstentia [ˌɪnæbˈsentɪə] **adv** (*frm*) en votre (*or* leur *etc*) absence.

inaccessibility [ˈɪnækˌsesəˈbɪlɪtɪ] **n** inaccessibilité *f.*

inaccessible [ˌɪnækˈsesəbl] **adj** *country, town* inaccessible (*to* à); *forest* impénétrable (*to* par); *person* inabordable, inaccessible.

inaccuracy [ɪnˈækjʊrəsɪ] **n** **a** (*NonC*) *[calculation, information, translation, quotation, statement]* inexactitude *f*; *[person]* imprécision *f*, manque *m* de précision; *[expression, term, word]* inexactitude, impropriété *f*. **b** **there are several inaccuracies in his account/calculations** il y a plusieurs inexactitudes dans son rapport/ses calculs.

inaccurate [ɪnˈækjʊrɪt] **adj** *calculation, information* inexact, erroné; *word, expression* incorrect, impropre; *mind* manquant de précision; *account, statement, report, quotation, translation* inexact. **he is ~** il fait des erreurs; **the clock is ~** l'horloge n'est pas à l'heure.

inaccurately [ɪnˈækjʊrɪtlɪ] **adv** *answer, quote, report* avec inexactitude, inexactement; *multiply* incorrectement.

inaction [ɪnˈækʃən] **n** inaction *f*, inactivité *f*. **policy of ~** politique *f* de l'inaction *or* de non-intervention.

inactive [ɪnˈæktɪv] **adj** *person* inactif, peu actif; *life* peu actif; *mind* inerte; *volcano* qui n'est pas en activité, en léthargie.

inactivity [ˌɪnækˈtɪvɪtɪ] **n** (*see* **inactive**) inactivité *f*; manque *m* d'activité; inertie *f*.

inadequacy [ɪnˈædɪkwəsɪ] **n** *[heating, punishment, resources]* insuffisance *f*; *[piece of work]* insuffisance, médiocrité *f*; (*Psych*) inadaptation *or* insuffisance socio-affective.

inadequate [ɪn'ædɪkwɪt] adj *amount, measures, precautions, punishment, resources, supply, strength* insuffisant, inadéquat; *piece of work* insuffisant, médiocre; *tool* inadéquat; (*Psych*) mal adapté *or* inadapté (sur le plan socio-affectif). **the proposed legislation is quite ~ for this purpose** la législation en projet est tout à fait insuffisante *or* inadéquate pour atteindre ce but; **the amount offered is ~ to cover the expenses** la somme proposée ne suffit pas à couvrir les frais; **he felt/was totally ~** il ne se sentait/il n'était absolument pas à la hauteur.

inadequately [ɪn'ædɪkwɪtlɪ] adv insuffisamment.

inadmissible [ˌɪnəd'mɪsəbl] adj *attitude, opinion, behaviour* inadmissible; *suggestion, offer* inacceptable. (*Jur*) **~ evidence** témoignage *m* irrecevable.

inadvertence [ˌɪnəd'vɜːtəns] n inattention *f*, manque *m* d'attention, étourderie *f*. **by ~** par mégarde, par inadvertance, par étourderie.

inadvertent [ˌɪnəd'vɜːtənt] adj *person* (*inattentive*) inattentif, étourdi; (*heedless*) insouciant (*to* de); *action* commis par inadvertance *or* par mégarde. **an ~ insult** une insulte lâchée par étourderie.

inadvertently [ˌɪnəd'vɜːtəntlɪ] adv par inadvertance, par mégarde, par étourderie.

inadvisability ['ɪnədˌvaɪzə'bɪlɪtɪ] n inopportunité *f* (*of doing* de faire).

inadvisable [ˌɪnəd'vaɪzəbl] adj *action, scheme* inopportun, à déconseiller. **it is ~ to ...** il est déconseillé de ... + *infin.*

inalienable [ɪn'eɪlɪənəbl] adj (*Jur, fig*) *rights, affection* inaliénable.

inamorata [ɪnˌæmə'rɑːtə] n amoureuse *f*.

inane [ɪ'neɪn] adj *person, action* inepte, bête; *hope* vain, insensé. **~ remark** observation *f* inepte, ineptie *f*; **what an ~ thing to do!** faut-il être inepte *or* stupide pour faire une chose pareille!

inanely [ɪ'neɪnlɪ] adv bêtement, ineptement.

inanimate [ɪn'ænɪmɪt] adj inanimé.

inanition [ˌɪnə'nɪʃən] n inanition *f*.

inanity [ɪ'nænɪtɪ] n ineptie *f*.

inapplicable [ɪn'æplɪkəbl] adj inapplicable (*to* à).

inappropriate [ˌɪnə'prəʊprɪɪt] adj *action, behaviour, remark* inopportun, mal à propos; *word, expression* impropre; *name* mal choisi, impropre; *moment* inopportun, mauvais.

inappropriately [ˌɪnə'prəʊprɪɪtlɪ] adv *behave, remark, reply* mal à propos, inopportunément; *use word* improprement.

inappropriateness [ɪnə'prəʊprɪɪtnəs] n (*gen*) inopportunité *f*, manque *m* d'à-propos; *[word]* impropriété *f*.

inapt [ɪn'æpt] adj **a** *remark, behaviour* peu approprié. **b** *person* inapte, incapable.

inaptitude [ɪn'æptɪtjuːd] n **a** *[remark, behaviour]* manque *m* d'à-propos. **b** *[person]* inaptitude *f*, incapacité *f*.

inarticulate [ˌɪnɑː'tɪkjʊlɪt] adj **a** *person* incapable de s'exprimer, qui parle *or* s'exprime avec difficulté; *speech* mal prononcé, indistinct; *sound* inarticulé. **~ with anger** bafouillant *or* bégayant de colère; **his ~ fury** la rage qui le faisait bégayer; **she is a very ~ person** c'est une personne qui a beaucoup de difficulté *or* de mal à s'exprimer. **b** (*Anat, Bot*) *body, structure* inarticulé.

inarticulately [ˌɪnɑː'tɪkjʊlɪtlɪ] adv *mumble etc* de façon indistincte.

inartistic [ˌɪnɑː'tɪstɪk] adj *work* peu artistique, sans valeur artistique; *person* dépourvu de sens artistique, peu artiste.

inartistically [ˌɪnɑː'tɪstɪkəlɪ] adv sans talent (artistique), de façon peu artistique.

inasmuch [ɪnəz'mʌtʃ] adv: **~ as** (*seeing that*) attendu que, vu que; (*insofar as*) en ce sens que.

inattention [ˌɪnə'tenʃən] n manque *m* d'attention, inattention *f*. **~ to details** manque d'attention accordée aux détails.

inattentive [ˌɪnə'tentɪv] adj (*not paying attention*) inattentif, distrait; (*neglectful*) peu attentionné, négligent (*towards sb* envers qn). **~ to details** qui accorde peu d'attention aux détails.

inattentively [ˌɪnə'tentɪvlɪ] adv distraitement, sans prêter attention.

inaudible [ɪn'ɔːdəbl] adj *sound* inaudible, imperceptible; *voice* inaudible, faible. **an ~ whisper** un murmure inaudible *or* imperceptible; **he was almost ~** on l'entendait à peine.

inaudibly [ɪn'ɔːdəblɪ] adv de manière inaudible.

inaugural [ɪ'nɔːgjʊrəl] adj *meeting* inaugural; *address, speech* d'inauguration, inaugural. (*Univ*) **~ lecture** leçon inaugurale *or* d'ouverture.

inaugurate [ɪ'nɔːgjʊreɪt] vt **a** *policy* inaugurer, instaurer, mettre en vigueur *or* en application; *new rail service etc* inaugurer; *era* inaugurer, commencer. **b** *president, official* investir de ses fonctions; *bishop, king* introniser.

inauguration [ɪˌnɔːgjʊ'reɪʃən] n (*see* **inaugurate**) **a** inauguration *f*. **b** investiture *f*; intronisation *f*. (*US Pol*) **I~ Day** jour *m* de l'investiture présidentielle.

inauspicious [ˌɪnɔːs'pɪʃəs] adj *beginning, event* peu propice, de mauvais augure; *circumstances* malencontreux, fâcheux.

inauspiciously [ˌɪnɔːs'pɪʃəslɪ] adv d'une façon peu propice; malencontreusement.

inboard ['ɪnˌbɔːd] (*Naut*) **1** adv à l'intérieur, à bord. **2** prep à bord de. **3** adj intérieur (*f* -eure). **~ motor** (moteur *m*) inboard *m*.

inborn ['ɪnˌbɔːn] adj *feeling, desire* inné; *weakness* congénital.

inbred ['ɪnˌbred] adj *quality* inné, naturel. **an ~ family/tribe** une famille/tribu qui a un fort degré de consanguinité; **an ~ animal** une bête issue de parents consanguins.

inbreeding ['ɪnˌbriːdɪŋ] n *[animals]* croisement *m* d'animaux de même souche. **there is a lot of ~ in the tribe** il y a beaucoup d'unions consanguines au sein de la tribu.

Inc. (abbr of **Incorporated**) **Smith and Jones ~** Smith and Jones S.A.R.L.

inc. abbr of **including, inclusive.**

Inca ['ɪŋkə] **1** n, pl **~** *or* **~s** **a** Inca *mf*. **b** (*Ling*) quichua *m*. **2** adj inca *inv*.

incalculable [ɪn'kælkjʊləbl] adj (*amount, also Math*) incalculable; *consequences* incalculable, imprévisible; *person, character, mood* inégal, changeant.

incandescence [ˌɪnkæn'desns] n incandescence *f*.

incandescent [ˌɪnkæn'desnt] adj (*lit, fig*) incandescent.

incantation [ˌɪnkæn'teɪʃən] n incantation *f*.

incapability [ɪnˌkeɪpə'bɪlɪtɪ] n (*Jur, fig*) incapacité *f* (*of doing* de faire).

incapable [ɪn'keɪpəbl] adj *person* incapable (*of doing* de faire); (*Jur*) incapable, incompétent. **he was ~ of movement** il était incapable de bouger; **~ of tenderness** incapable de montrer de la tendresse *or* de faire preuve de tendresse; **~ of proof** impossible à prouver; *see* **drunk**.

incapacitate [ˌɪnkə'pæsɪteɪt] vt **a** rendre incapable. **to ~ sb for work** *or* **from working** mettre qn dans l'incapacité de travailler, rendre qn incapable de travailler; **he was ~d by his fall** sa chute l'a mis dans l'incapacité de poursuivre ses activités. **b** (*Jur*) frapper d'incapacité.

incapacity [ˌɪnkə'pæsɪtɪ] n **a** incapacité *f* (*to do* de faire), incompétence *f* (*to do* pour faire), impuissance *f* (*to do* à faire, *for sth* en matière de qch). **b** (*Jur*) incapacité *f* (légale).

incarcerate [ɪn'kɑːsəreɪt] vt incarcérer.

incarceration [ɪnˌkɑːsə'reɪʃən] n incarcération *f*.

incarnate [ɪn'kɑːnɪt] (*Rel, fig*) **1** adj incarné. (*Rel*) **the I~ Word** le Verbe incarné; **he's the devil ~** c'est le diable incarné; **liberty ~** la liberté incarnée. **2** ['ɪnkɑːneɪt] vt incarner.

incarnation [ˌɪnkɑː'neɪʃən] n (*Rel, fig*) incarnation *f*. **she is the ~ of virtue** c'est la vertu incarnée.

incautious [ɪn'kɔːʃəs] adj *person* imprudent; *remark, promise, action* irréfléchi, imprudent, inconsidéré.

incautiously [ɪn'kɔːʃəslɪ] adv imprudemment, sans réfléchir.

incendiary [ɪn'sendɪərɪ] **1** adj (*lit, fig*) incendiaire. **~ device** dispositif *m* incendiaire. **2** n (*bomb*) engin *m* or bombe *f* incendiaire; (*arsonist*) incendiaire *mf*; (*fig: agitator*) brandon *m* de discorde.

incense¹ [ɪn'sens] vt (*anger*) mettre en fureur, courroucer; (*stronger*) exaspérer. **he was quite ~d** il était dans une violente colère.

incense² ['ɪnsens] **1** n encens *m*. **2** vt encenser. **3** comp ► **incense bearer** thuriféraire *m* ► **incense burner** encensoir *m*.

incensed [ɪn'senst] adj outré (*at/by* de/par), révolté (*at, by* par).

incentive [ɪn'sentɪv] **1** n **a** (*NonC: reason for doing sth*) motivation *f*. **he has got no ~** il n'a aucune motivation, il n'est absolument pas motivé; **this gave me an ~** cela m'a motivé *or* m'a donné une motivation; **there is no ~ to hard work** *or* **to work hard** rien ne vous incite *or* ne vous pousse à travailler dur; **what ~ is there to work faster?** pour quelle (bonne) raison se mettrait-on à travailler plus vite? **b** (*promised reward for doing sth*) récompense *f*, prime *f*, carotte* *f*. **they offered him an ~** ils lui ont promis qu'il serait récompensé, ils lui ont offert une carotte*.

2 adj: (*Ind*) **~ bonus** *or* **payment** (*for office workers*) prime *f* d'encouragement; (*for manual workers*) prime de rendement; (*Comm*) **~ discount** remise *f* promotionnelle.

inception [ɪn'sepʃən] n commencement *m*, début *m*.

incertitude [ɪn'sɜːtɪtjuːd] n incertitude *f*.

incessant [ɪn'sesnt] adj *complaints* incessant, perpétuel; *rain, efforts* incessant.

incessantly [ɪn'sesntlɪ] adv sans cesse, incessamment, constamment.

incest ['ɪnsest] n inceste *m*.

incestuous [ɪn'sestjʊəs] adj incestueux.

inch [ɪntʃ] **1** n pouce *m* (= *2,54 cm*). **he has grown a few ~es since last year** il a grandi de quelques centimètres depuis l'année dernière; **not an ~ from my face** *or* **nose** en plein *or* juste devant mon nez; **he couldn't see an ~ in front of him** il n'y voyait pas à deux pas; **not an ~ of the cloth is wasted** on ne perd pas un centimètre de tissu; **not an ~ of French territory will be conceded** on ne cédera pas un pouce de territoire français; **he knows every ~ of the district** il connaît la région comme sa poche *or* (jusque) dans ses moindres recoins; **we searched every ~ of the room** nous avons cherché partout dans la pièce, nous avons passé la pièce au peigne fin; **he wouldn't budge an ~** (*lit*) il n'a pas voulu bouger d'un pouce; (*fig*) il n'a pas voulu faire la plus petite concession *or* céder d'un pouce; **he looked every ~ a king** son allure était en tous points celle d'un roi; **he's every ~ a soldier** il est soldat jusqu'à la moelle; **she's every ~ a lady** elle est raffinée jusqu'au bout des ongles; **within an ~ of succeeding/of death** *etc* à deux doigts *or* à un doigt *or* à un cheveu de réussir/de la mort *etc*; **he missed being run over by ~es** il a été à deux doigts de se faire écraser; **~ by ~** petit à petit; (*loc*) **give him an ~ and he'll take a yard** *or* **an ell** donnez-lui-en long comme le doigt et il en prendra long comme le bras.

2 comp ▸**inchtape** centimètre *m* (de couturière).

3 vi: **to ~ (one's way) forward/out/in** *etc* avancer/sortir/entrer *etc* peu à peu *or* petit à petit; **prices are ~ing up** les prix augmentent petit à petit.

4 vt: **to ~ sth forward/in/out** *etc* faire avancer/entrer/sortir *etc* qch peu à peu *or* petit à petit.

inchoate ['ɪnkəʊeɪt] adj (*just begun*) naissant, débutant; (*half-formed*) rudimentaire, fruste; (*unfinished*) incomplet (*f* -ète), inachevé.

inchoative [ɪn'kəʊətɪv] adj *aspect, verb* inchoatif.

incidence ['ɪnsɪdəns] n a *[crime, disease]* fréquence *f*, taux *m*. **the high ~ of heart trouble in men over 40** le taux élevé des troubles cardiaques chez les hommes de plus de 40 ans; **the low ~ of TB** la faible fréquence des cas de tuberculose. b (*Opt, Phys etc*) incidence *f*. **angle of ~** angle *m* d'incidence.

incident ['ɪnsɪdənt] 1 n incident *m*, événement *m*; (*in book, play etc*) épisode *m*, péripétie *f*. **a life full of ~** une vie mouvementée; **we arrived without ~** nous sommes arrivés sans incident *or* sans encombre *or* sans anicroche; **there were several ~s on the border last month** il y a eu plusieurs incidents *or* accrochages frontaliers le mois dernier; **this caused a diplomatic ~** cela provoqua un incident diplomatique; **the Birmingham ~** l'incident de Birmingham *or* qui a eu lieu à Birmingham. 2 adj a (*frm*) **~ to** qui s'attache à, attaché à. b (*Opt*) incident. 3 comp ▸**incident room** (*Police etc*) salle *f* d'opérations.

incidental [ˌɪnsɪ'dentl] 1 adj (*accompanying*) accessoire; (*secondary*) d'importance secondaire; (*unplanned*) accidentel, fortuit. (*Jur*) **~ damages** dommages-intérêts *mpl* accessoires; **~ expenses** faux frais *mpl*; **~ music** musique *f* de fond *or* d'accompagnement; (*Theat*) musique de scène; (*Cine*) musique de film; **the ~ music to the play** la musique qui accompagne la pièce; **~ to sth** qui accompagne qch; **the dangers ~ to such exploration** les dangers que suppose *or* que comporte une telle exploration; **but that is ~ to my purpose** mais ceci est en marge de mon propos *or* n'a qu'un rapport secondaire avec mon propos.

2 n (*event etc*) chose fortuite. **that's just an ~** ça n'a pas de rapport avec la question; **~s** (*expenses*) faux frais *mpl*; (*objects*) accessoires *mpl*.

incidentally [ˌɪnsɪ'dentəlɪ] adv a *happen etc* incidemment, accidentellement. **it was interesting only ~** cela n'avait qu'un intérêt secondaire. b (*by the way*) à propos, entre parenthèses.

incinerate [ɪn'sɪnəreɪt] vt incinérer.

incineration [ɪnsɪnə'reɪʃən] n incinération *f*.

incinerator [ɪn'sɪnəreɪtə^r] n (*also in garden*) incinérateur *m*; *[crematorium]* four *m* crématoire.

incipient [ɪn'sɪpɪənt] adj *quarrel, disease, revolt* naissant, qui commence. **the ~ uprising was suppressed** la révolte naissante a été étouffée, la révolte a été réprimée à ses débuts *or* écrasée dans l'œuf.

incise [ɪn'saɪz] vt a inciser, faire une incision dans. b (*Art*) graver.

incision [ɪn'sɪʒən] n incision *f*, coupure *f*, entaille *f*; (*Surg*) incision.

incisive [ɪn'saɪsɪv] adj (*trenchant*) *style, report, tone, person* incisif, acerbe, acéré, tranchant; (*biting*) *person, voice, tone, criticism* mordant, incisif; (*acute*) *criticism, mind, person* pénétrant, perspicace.

incisively [ɪn'saɪsɪvlɪ] adv (*see* **incisive**) d'une façon tranchante; d'un ton mordant *or* incisif; d'une façon pénétrante.

incisiveness [ɪn'saɪsɪvnɪs] n (*see* **incisive**) tranchant *m*; ton mordant *or* incisif; pénétration *f*, perspicacité *f*. **the ~ of his style** son style incisif *or* tranchant; **the ~ of his criticism** la pénétration *or* la perspicacité de sa critique.

incisor [ɪn'saɪzə^r] n (*tooth*) incisive *f*.

incite [ɪn'saɪt] vt pousser, inciter, entraîner (*to* à). **to ~ sb to violence/revolt** *etc* pousser *or* inciter qn à la violence/la révolte *etc*; **to ~ sb to do** pousser *or* entraîner *or* inciter qn à faire.

incitement [ɪn'saɪtmənt] n (*NonC*) incitation *f*, provocation *f* (*to* à).

incivility [ˌɪnsɪ'vɪlɪtɪ] n (*NonC*) impolitesse *f*, incivilité *f*. **a piece of ~** une impolitesse, une incivilité.

incl. abbr of **including, inclusive**.

inclemency [ɪn'klemənsɪ] n inclémence *f*, dureté *f*, rigueur *f*.

inclement [ɪn'klemənt] adj inclément, dur, rigoureux.

inclination [ˌɪnklɪ'neɪʃən] n a (*slope, leaning*) *[head, body]* inclination *f*; *[hill etc]* inclinaison *f*, pente *f*. b (*liking, wish etc*) inclination *f*, penchant *m*; (*tendency*) propension *f*. **my ~ is to leave** j'incline à partir; **I have no ~ to help him** je n'ai aucune envie *or* aucun désir de l'aider; **he has an ~ to(wards) meanness** il a tendance à être mesquin *or* à la mesquinerie; **to follow one's (own) ~** suivre son inclination *or* ses penchants (naturels); **to do sth from ~** faire qch par inclination *or* par goût.

incline [ɪn'klaɪn] 1 vt a (*bend, bow*) incliner, baisser, pencher. **~d plane** plan incliné; **~d at an angle of ...** incliné à un angle de ... .

b (*fig: gen pass*) **to ~ sb to do** incliner qn *or* porter qn *or* rendre qn enclin à faire; *[person]* **to be ~d to do** (*feel desire to*) incliner à *or* être enclin à *or* être porté à faire; (*have tendency to*) incliner à *or* avoir tendance à faire; **he is ~d to be lazy** il a tendance à être paresseux, il est enclin à la paresse; **it's ~d to break** cela se casse facilement, c'est fragile; **he's that way ~d** il a tendance à être comme ça; **if you feel (so) ~d** si le cœur vous en dit, si l'envie vous en prend; **to be well ~d towards sb** être bien disposé *or* être dans de bonnes dispositions à l'égard de qn.

2 vi a (*slope*) s'incliner; (*bend, bow*) s'incliner, pencher, se courber.

b (*tend towards*) **to ~ to an opinion/a point of view** *etc* pencher pour une opinion/un point de vue *etc*; **he ~s to laziness** il incline à la paresse, il a tendance à être paresseux; **the colour ~s towards blue** la couleur tend vers le bleu; **his politics ~ towards socialism** ses idées politiques tendent vers le socialisme.

3 ['ɪnklaɪn] n pente *f*, inclinaison *f*, déclivité *f*; (*Rail etc*) plan incliné.

inclose [ɪn'kləʊz] vt = **enclose**.

inclosure [ɪn'kləʊʒə^r] n = **enclosure**.

include [ɪn'klu:d] vt comprendre, compter, englober, embrasser, inclure. **your name is not ~d on the list** votre nom n'est pas inclus dans la liste, votre nom ne paraît pas *or* ne figure pas sur la liste, la liste ne comporte pas votre nom; **the tip is not ~d in the bill** le service n'est pas compris *or* compté *or* inclus dans la note; **the wine was ~d in the overall price** le vin était compris *or* compté *or* inclus dans le prix total; **all** *or* **everything ~d** tout compris; **does that remark ~ me?** est-ce que cette remarque s'applique aussi à moi?; **he ~d my mother in the invitation** ma mère était comprise dans son invitation; **the invitation ~s everybody** tout le monde est compris dans l'invitation, l'invitation s'adresse à *or* englobe tout le monde; **they were all ~d in the accusation** ils étaient tous visés par l'accusation; **the children/tables** *etc* **~d** y compris les enfants/les tables *etc*; (*Admin*) **not ~d elsewhere** non inclus ailleurs; **the district ~s ...** la région comprend *or* englobe ... .

▸**include out*** vt sep: **include me out!*** ne comptez pas sur moi!

including [ɪn'klu:dɪŋ] prep y compris, compris, inclus. **that comes to 200 francs ~ packing** cela fait 200 F y compris l'emballage *or* l'emballage compris *or* l'emballage inclus; **there were 6 rooms ~ the kitchen** il y avait 6 pièces en comprenant la cuisine *or* si on comprend la cuisine *or* la cuisine (y) comprise *or* y compris la cuisine; **~ the service charge** service compris; **not ~ tax** taxe non comprise; **up to and ~ chapter 5** jusqu'au chapitre 5 inclus, jusques et y compris le chapitre 5; **up to and ~ 4th May** jusqu'au 4 mai inclus; **several projects, ~ ...** plusieurs projets, dont ... *or* parmi lesquels ... .

inclusion [ɪn'klu:ʒən] n inclusion *f*.

inclusive [ɪn'klu:sɪv] adj a (*included*) inclus, compris. **from 1st to 6th May ~** du 1er au 6 mai inclus(ivement); **up to page 5 ~** jusqu'à la page 5 incluse *or* comprise; **cost ~ of travel** prix *m* voyage compris; **to be ~ of sth** inclure *or* comprendre qch. b (*comprehensive*) *amount, sum* forfaitaire, global; *rent, hire charge* tout compris *inv*. **for an ~ charge of £100** contre paiement de 100 livres tout compris; (*Comm etc*) **~ terms** (prix *m*) tout compris *m*.

inclusively [ɪn'klu:sɪvlɪ] adv inclusivement.

incognito [ɪnkɒg'ni:təʊ] 1 adv incognito. 2 adj *traveller* dans l'incognito. **to remain ~** garder l'incognito. 3 n incognito *m*.

incoherence [ˌɪnkəʊ'hɪərəns] n incohérence *f*.

incoherent [ˌɪnkəʊ'hɪərənt] adj *conversation, speech, person* incohérent; *style* décousu.

incoherently [ˌɪnkəʊ'hɪərəntlɪ] adv sans cohérence, d'une façon incohérente; d'une façon décousue.

incohesive [ˌɪnkəʊ'hi:sɪv] adj sans cohésion.

incombustible [ˌɪnkəm'bʌstəbl] adj incombustible.

income ['ɪnkʌm] 1 n revenu(s) *m(pl)*; *[company]* (*profit, earnings*) bénéfice *m*, résultat *m* bénéficiaire. **(private) ~** rente(s) *f(pl)*; **annual/taxable ~** revenu annuel/imposable; **to live beyond/within one's ~** dépasser/ne pas dépasser son revenu; *see* **price, upper** *etc*.

2 comp ▸**income group**: (*Econ*) **the lowest income group** les économiquement faibles *mpl*; **the middle income group** la classe à revenus moyens; **the upper** *or* **highest income group** la classe à revenus élevés ▸**incomes policy** politique *f* des revenus ▸**Income Support** (*Brit Admin*) ≃ revenu *m* minimum d'insertion, RMI *m* ▸**income tax** (*gen*) impôt *m* sur le revenu; *[corporations]* impôt sur les bénéfices ▸**income tax inspector** inspecteur *m* des contributions directes ▸**income tax return** déclaration *f* des revenus, feuille *f* d'impôts.

incomer ['ɪnˌkʌmə^r] n (*new arrival*) nouveau venu *m*, nouvelle venue *f*, nouvel(le) arrivant(e) *m(f)*; (*immigrant*) immigrant(e) *m(f)*.

incoming ['ɪnˌkʌmɪŋ] 1 adj *people, crowd* qui arrive, qui entre; *tenant, resident* nouveau (*f* nouvelle); *mayor, president* nouveau, entrant. **~ call** appel *m* de l'extérieur; **~ mail** courrier *m* du jour; **~ tide** marée montante. 2 n (*Book-keeping*) **~s** rentrées *fpl*, recettes *fpl*.

incommensurable [ˌɪnkə'menʃərəbl] adj (*lit, fig*) incommensurable (*with* avec).

incommensurate [ˌɪnkə'menʃərɪt] adj a (*out of proportion*) sans rapport (*to* avec), disproportionné (*to* à); (*inadequate*) insuffisant (*to* pour). b = **incommensurable**.

incommode [ˌɪnkə'məʊd] vt (†, *frm*) incommoder, gêner.

incommodious [ˌɪnkə'məʊdɪəs] adj (*inconvenient*) incommode; (*not spacious*) *house, room* où l'on est à l'étroit.

incommunicable [ɪnkə'mju:nɪkəbl] adj incommunicable.

incommunicado [ˌɪnkəmjʊnɪ'kɑ:dəʊ] 1 adj: **to be ~** (*against one's will*) être isolé; (*voluntarily*) ne pas être joignable. 2 adv: **to be kept** *or* **held ~** être tenu au secret.

incomparable [ɪn'kɒmpərəbl] adj incomparable (*to, with* à); *talent, beauty etc* incomparable, inégalable, sans pareil.
incomparably [ɪn'kɒmpərəblɪ] adv incomparablement, infiniment.
incompatibility ['ɪnkəm,pætə'bɪlɪtɪ] n *[people, aims, wishes]*, (*Med*) *[blood groups etc]*, (*Comput*) incompatibilité *f*. **divorce on the grounds of ~** divorce *m* pour incompatibilité d'humeur.
incompatible [,ɪnkəm'pætəbl] adj incompatible, inconciliable (*with* avec); (*Med, Comput*) incompatible.
incompetence [ɪn'kɒmpɪtəns] n, **incompetency** [ɪn'kɒmpɪtənsɪ] n a incompétence *f*, incapacité *f*, insuffisance *f*. b (*Jur*) incompétence *f*.
incompetent [ɪn'kɒmpɪtənt] 1 adj a incompétent, incapable. **to be ~ in business** être incompétent en *or* n'avoir aucune compétence en affaires; **he is ~ to teach** *or* **for teaching music** il n'a pas les compétences nécessaires pour enseigner la musique. b (*Jur*) incompétent. 2 n incompétent(e) *m(f)*, incapable *mf*.
incomplete [,ɪnkəm'pli:t] adj (*unfinished*) incomplet (*f* -ète), inachevé; (*with some parts missing*) *collection, series, kit, machine* incomplet.
incompletely [,ɪnkəm'pli:tlɪ] adv incomplètement.
incompleteness [,ɪnkəm'pli:tnɪs] n inachèvement *m*.
incomprehensible [ɪn,kɒmprɪ'hensəbl] adj *person, speech, reasoning* incompréhensible, inintelligible; *writing* indéchiffrable.
incomprehensibly [ɪn,kɒmprɪ'hensəblɪ] adv *behave etc* de manière incompréhensible, incompréhensiblement. **~ worded** formulé de façon inintelligible *or* incompréhensible; **~, he refused** inexplicablement, il a refusé.
incomprehension [ɪn,kɒmprɪ'henʃən] n incompréhension *f*.
inconceivable [,ɪnkən'si:vəbl] adj inconcevable.
inconceivably [,ɪnkən'si:vəblɪ] adv à un degré inconcevable. **~ stupid** d'une stupidité inconcevable; **~, he refused** inexplicablement, il a refusé.
inconclusive [,ɪnkən'klu:sɪv] adj *result, discussion* peu concluant; *evidence, argument* peu convaincant; *action* sans résultat concluant, qui n'aboutit pas; *fighting, skirmish* dont l'issue reste indécise.
inconclusively [,ɪnkən'klu:sɪvlɪ] adv *discuss* d'une manière peu concluante *or* peu convaincante; *close etc* sans résultat. **to end ~** ne pas produire de résultats tangibles, ne déboucher sur rien.
incongruity [,ɪnkɒŋ'gru:ɪtɪ] n *[situation]* absurdité *f*; *[behaviour, dress, remark]* incongruité *f*, inconvenance *f*; *[age, condition]* disproportion *f*, incompatibilité *f*.
incongruous [ɪn'kɒŋgrʊəs] adj (*out of place*) *remark, act, name* incongru, déplacé; (*absurd*) absurde, grotesque; (*incompatible*) disparate, incompatible. **it seems ~ that** il semble absurde que + *subj*; **~ with** *or* **to** peu approprié à, sans rapport avec.
incongruously [ɪn'kɒŋgrʊəslɪ] adv (*with verbs*) de façon incongrue. **he wore old jeans, with ~ smart shoes** il portait un vieux jean avec des chaussures d'une élégance incongrue.
inconsequent [ɪn'kɒnsɪkwənt] adj *person, remark, behaviour, reasoning* illogique, inconséquent.
inconsequential [ɪn,kɒnsɪ'kwenʃəl] adj a = **inconsequent**. b (*unimportant*) sans importance, sans conséquence.
inconsequentially [ɪn,kɒnsɪ'kwenʃəlɪ] adv *talk* de façon inconséquente.
inconsiderable [,ɪnkən'sɪdərəbl] adj insignifiant.
inconsiderate [,ɪnkən'sɪdərɪt] adj a (*thoughtless*) *person* qui manque d'égards *or* de considération; *action, reply* inconsidéré, irréfléchi. **to be ~ towards sb** manquer d'égards *or* de considération envers qn; **you were very ~, that was most ~ of you** tu as agi sans aucun égard *or* sans aucune considération; **it was a very ~ thing to do** c'était vraiment agir sans aucun égard *or* sans aucune considération. b (*hasty*) *action, words* inconsidéré, irréfléchi.
inconsistency [,ɪnkən'sɪstənsɪ] n *[person]* inconsistance *f*, inconséquence *f*; *[facts, accusation]* inconsistance; *[behaviour, reasoning]* inconsistance, inconséquence, illogisme *m*.
inconsistent [,ɪnkən'sɪstənt] adj *action, speech, attitude, person* inconséquent, inconsistant. **his report was ~** son rapport était inconsistant *or* présentait des contradictions; **~ with** en contradiction avec, incompatible avec; **this is ~ with what you told me** ceci ne concorde pas avec *or* ceci est incompatible avec ce que vous m'avez dit.
inconsolable [,ɪnkən'səʊləbl] adj inconsolable.
inconsolably [,ɪnkən'səʊləblɪ] adv inconsolablement.
inconspicuous [,ɪnkən'spɪkjʊəs] adj *person, action, dress* qui passe inaperçu, qui ne se fait pas remarquer. **he tried to make himself ~** il a essayé de passer inaperçu, il s'est efforcé de ne pas se faire remarquer.
inconspicuously [,ɪnkən'spɪkjʊəslɪ] adv *behave, move* sans se faire remarquer, discrètement; *dress* de façon discrète.
inconstancy [ɪn'kɒnstənsɪ] n (*see* **inconstant**) inconstance *f*; instabilité *f*.
inconstant [ɪn'kɒnstənt] adj *person* (*in friendship*) changeant, instable; (*in love*) inconstant, volage; (*unstable*) *weather* instable, changeant; (*variable*) *quality etc* variable.
incontestable [,ɪnkən'testəbl] adj incontestable, indiscutable.
incontinence [ɪn'kɒntɪnəns] n (*Med, fig*) incontinence *f*.
incontinent [ɪn'kɒntɪnənt] adj (*Med*) incontinent; (*fig*) intempérant.
incontrovertible [ɪn,kɒntrə'vɜ:təbl] adj *fact* indéniable; *argument, explanation* irréfutable; *sign, proof* irrécusable.
incontrovertibly [ɪn,kɒntrə'vɜ:təblɪ] adv indéniablement, irréfutablement.
inconvenience [,ɪnkən'vi:nɪəns] 1 n a inconvénient *m*, désagrément *m*, ennui *m*. **there are ~s in living in the country** il y a des inconvénients à habiter la campagne, habiter la campagne présente des inconvénients *or* des désagréments. b (*NonC*) dérangement *m*, gêne *f*. **to put sb to great ~** causer beaucoup de dérangement à qn; **I don't want to put you to any ~** je ne veux surtout pas vous déranger; **he went to a great deal of ~ to help me** il s'est donné beaucoup de mal pour m'aider. 2 vt déranger, incommoder; (*stronger*) gêner.
inconvenient [,ɪnkən'vi:nɪənt] adj *time, place* inopportun, mal choisi; *house, equipment* peu pratique, malcommode; *visitor* gênant, importun. **if it is not ~ (to you)** si cela ne vous dérange pas; **it is most ~** c'est très gênant; **it is very ~ for him to have to wait** cela le dérange *or* gêne beaucoup d'avoir à attendre.
inconveniently [,ɪnkən'vi:nɪəntlɪ] adv *design* incommodément; *happen* d'une manière gênante; *arrive* inopportunément, à contretemps.
inconvertibility ['ɪnkən,vɜ:tɪ'bɪlɪtɪ] n non-convertibilité *f*.
inconvertible [,ɪnkən'vɜ:təbl] adj (*Fin etc*) inconvertible.
incorporate[1] [ɪn'kɔ:pəreɪt] 1 vt a (*introduce as part*) *territory, suggestions, revisions* incorporer (*into* dans). **they ~d him into their group** ils l'ont incorporé dans *or* associé à leur groupe, ils l'ont pris dans leur groupe.
b (*include, contain*) contenir. **his book ~s his previous articles** son livre contient *or* englobe ses précédents articles; **this essay ~s all his thoughts on the subject** cette étude contient *or* rassemble toutes ses pensées sur la question.
c (*Comm, Jur*) se constituer en société (unique) avec. (*esp US*) **~d company** société *f* à responsabilité limitée; (*in names of firm*) **Smith Robinson I~d** Smith Robinson S.A.R.L.
d (*mix, add*) incorporer (*into* à). **to ~ eggs into a sauce** incorporer des œufs à une sauce.
2 vi *[business firm]* fusionner (*with* avec); *[two firms]* se constituer en (une seule) société.
incorporate[2] [ɪn'kɔ:pərɪt] adj (*Philos*) incorporel.
incorporation [ɪn,kɔ:pə'reɪʃən] n (*see* **incorporate**[1]) incorporation *f* (*into* dans, à); (*Comm, Jur*) constitution *f* en société (unique).
incorporator [ɪn'kɔ:pə,reɪtə[r]] n (*Jur, Fin*) fondateur *m* (d'une société).
incorrect [,ɪnkə'rekt] adj a (*wrong*) *wording, calculation, statement, opinion, assessment* incorrect, inexact, erroné; *text* fautif, inexact, erroné. (*Ling*) **~ expression** expression incorrecte, incorrection *f*, impropriété *f* (de langage); **you are ~** vous faites erreur, vous vous trompez; **he is ~ in stating that ...** il se trompe *or* il fait erreur quand il affirme que ...; **it would be ~ to say that ...** il serait inexact de dire que ...; **that's quite ~** c'est tout à fait inexact.
b (*out of place*) *behaviour* incorrect, déplacé; *dress* incorrect, indécent. **it would be ~ to mention it** il serait incorrect *or* déplacé d'en faire mention.
incorrectly [,ɪnkə'rektlɪ] adv a (*wrongly*) inexactement; *spell, address, translate* incorrectement, mal. **he was ~ reported as having said ...** on a faussement *or* inexactement raconté qu'il avait dit ... . b *behave, act* incorrectement, de façon déplacée.
incorrigible [ɪn'kɒrɪdʒəbl] adj incorrigible.
incorrigibly [ɪn'kɒrɪdʒəblɪ] adv incorrigiblement. **he's ~ romantic/sentimental** *etc* c'est un incorrigible romantique/sentimental *etc*, il est d'un romantisme/d'une sentimentalité *etc* incorrigible.
incorruptible [,ɪnkə'rʌptəbl] adj incorruptible.
increase [ɪn'kri:s] 1 vi *[taxes]* augmenter; *[pain]* augmenter, s'intensifier; *[amount, numbers]* augmenter, croître; *[price, sales]* augmenter, monter; *[demand, strength, supply]* augmenter, croître, s'accroître; *[speed]* augmenter, s'accroître; *[joy, rage]* augmenter, croître, s'intensifier; *[sorrow, surprise]* augmenter, croître; *[possessions, riches, trade]* s'accroître, augmenter; *[darkness, noise]* s'intensifier, grandir; *[pride]* croître, grandir; *[business firm, institution, town]* s'agrandir, se développer, croître; *[crime]* s'intensifier, augmenter; *[rain, wind]* augmenter, redoubler; *[population]* augmenter, croître, s'accroître; *[friendship]* se renforcer, se consolider; *[effort]* s'intensifier. **to ~ in volume** augmenter de volume, prendre du volume; **to ~ in weight** prendre du poids, s'alourdir; **to ~ in width** s'élargir; **to ~ in height** *[person]* grandir; *[tree]* pousser; *[building]* gagner de la hauteur.
2 vt *numbers, strength, taxes* augmenter (*by* de); *pain* augmenter, intensifier; *price, sales* augmenter, faire monter (*by* de); *demand, supply, population* augmenter, accroître (*by* de); *delight, joy, pride, rage* augmenter, ajouter à; *sorrow, surprise* augmenter, ajouter à, accroître; *possessions, riches, trade* accroître, augmenter (*by* de); *darkness, noise* intensifier; *business firm, institution, town* agrandir, développer; *rain, wind* faire redoubler; *friendship* renforcer, consolider; *effort* redoubler de, intensifier. **to ~ an amount to** porter un montant à; **he ~d his efforts** il redoubla ses efforts *or* d'effort; **to ~ speed** accélérer, augmenter *or* accroître la vitesse; (*Aut*) **he ~d his speed to 90 km/h** il

a accéléré jusqu'à 90 km/h, il a atteint le 90*.
3 ['ɪnkriːs] **n** (*gen*) augmentation *f* (*in, of* de); *[pain]* augmentation, intensification *f*; *[numbers]* augmentation, accroissement *m*, multiplication *f*; *[price, sales]* augmentation, montée *f*; *[demand, strength, supply]* augmentation, croissance *f*, accroissement; *[speed]* augmentation, accroissement; *[joy, rage]* intensification; *[possessions, riches, trade]* accroissement; *[darkness, noise]* intensification; *[pride]* accroissement; *[business firm, institution, town]* agrandissement *m*, développement *m*, croissance; *[crime]* intensification, augmentation; *[rain, wind]* redoublement *m*; *[population]* augmentation, croissance, accroissement; *[friendship]* renforcement *m*, consolidation *f*; *[effort]* redoublement, intensification. (*Fin*) ~ **in value** plus-value *f*; **he had a big ~ in his workload** il a vu une grosse augmentation *or* un gros accroissement de ses charges professionnelles; **there has been an ~ in police activity** la police a intensifié ses activités *or* redoublé d'activité; **an ~ in pay** une hausse de salaire, une augmentation (de salaire); **on the ~** en augmentation; **to be on the ~** augmenter, aller en augmentant, être en hausse; **the problem of crime is on the ~** le problème de la criminalité s'accentue.

increasing [ɪn'kriːsɪŋ] **adj** croissant. **an ~ number/amount of ...** un nombre/une quantité croissant(e) de ...; **law of ~ costs/returns** loi *f* des rendements décroissants/croissants.

increasingly [ɪn'kriːsɪŋlɪ] **adv** de plus en plus. **~ violent** de plus en plus violent, d'une violence croissante.

incredible [ɪn'kredəbl] **adj** *number, amount, error, behaviour* incroyable; *story* incroyable, invraisemblable, inimaginable.

incredibly [ɪn'kredəblɪ] **adv** incroyablement. **and, ~, he refused** et, chose incroyable, il a refusé.

incredulity [ˌɪnkrɪ'djuːlɪtɪ] **n** incrédulité *f*.

incredulous [ɪn'kredjʊləs] **adj** *person* incrédule; *look* incrédule, d'incrédulité.

incredulously [ɪn'kredjʊləslɪ] **adv** d'un air *or* d'un ton incrédule *or* d'incrédulité.

increment ['ɪnkrɪmənt] 1 **n** (*in salary*) augmentation *f*; (*Math*) différentielle *f*; (*Comput*) incrément *m*; *[employee]* augmentation *f*; *see* **unearned**. 2 **vt** (*gen*) augmenter; (*Comput*) incrémenter.

incremental [ˌɪnkrɪ'mentl] **adj** *benefits* supplémentaire; *cost* marginal, différentiel; *rise, increase* progressif; (*Comput*) incrémentiel. (*Comput*) **~ plotter** traceur incrémentiel; (*Comm: on index, scale*) **~ value** valeur *f* indiciaire *or* de l'augmentation.

incriminate [ɪn'krɪmɪneɪt] **vt** incriminer, compromettre, impliquer. **his evidence ~s his friends** son témoignage incrimine *or* implique *or* compromet ses amis; **don't say anything that could ~ you** ne dites rien qui puisse vous incriminer *or* vous compromettre.

incriminating [ɪn'krɪmɪneɪtɪŋ] **adj** compromettant. **~ document** *or* **evidence** pièce *f* à conviction.

incrimination [ɪnˌkrɪmɪ'neɪʃən] **n** accusation *f*, incrimination *f*.

incriminatory [ɪn'krɪmɪnətərɪ] **adj** = **incriminating**.

incrust [ɪn'krʌst] **vt** = **encrust**.

incrustation [ˌɪnkrʌs'teɪʃən] **n** incrustation *f*.

incubate ['ɪnkjʊbeɪt] 1 **vt** *eggs* couver, incuber; *bacteria cultures, disease* incuber; (*fig*) *plan, scheme* couver. 2 **vi** (*also fig*) couver; (*Med*) être en incubation.

incubation [ˌɪnkjʊ'beɪʃən] **n** *[eggs, disease, scheme etc]* incubation *f*. **~ period** période *f* d'incubation.

incubator ['ɪnkjʊbeɪtə^r] **n** *[chicks, eggs, infants]* couveuse *f*, incubateur *m*; *[bacteria cultures]* incubateur. **(to put) an infant in an ~** (mettre) un nouveau-né en couveuse.

incubus ['ɪŋkjʊbəs] **n, pl ~es** *or* **incubi** ['ɪŋkjʊˌbaɪ] (*demon*) incube *m*; (*fig*) cauchemar *m*.

incudes [ɪn'kjuːdiːz] **npl of incus**.

inculcate ['ɪnkʌlkeɪt] **vt** inculquer (*sth in sb, sb with sth* qch à qn).

inculcation [ˌɪnkʌl'keɪʃən] **n** inculcation *f*.

incumbency [ɪn'kʌmbənsɪ] **n** *[President, official]* période *f* de fonction, exercice *m*; (*Rel*) charge *f*. **during his ~** (*gen*) pendant la durée de ses fonctions; (*Rel*) pendant la durée de sa charge.

incumbent [ɪn'kʌmbənt] 1 **adj** a **to be ~ upon sb to do sth** incomber *or* appartenir à qn de faire qch. b (*in office*) *minister etc* en exercice. (*US Pol*) **the ~ President** le président en exercice; (*before elections*) le président sortant. 2 **n** (*Rel etc*) titulaire *m*. (*US Pol*) **the present ~ of the White House** l'occupant actuel de la Maison Blanche.

incunabula [ˌɪnkjʊ'næbjʊlə] **npl** incunables *mpl*.

incunabular [ˌɪnkjʊ'næbjʊlə^r] **adj** incunable.

incur [ɪn'kɜː^r] **vt** *anger, blame* s'attirer, encourir; *risk* courir; *obligation, debts* contracter; *loss* subir; *expenses* encourir.

incurable [ɪn'kjʊərəbl] 1 **adj** (*Med, fig*) incurable, inguérissable. 2 **n** incurable *mf*.

incurably [ɪn'kjʊərəblɪ] **adv** incurablement. **~ inquisitive** d'une curiosité incurable; **the ~ ill** les incurables.

incurious [ɪn'kjʊərɪəs] **adj** sans curiosité (*about* en ce qui concerne), incurieux (*liter*) (*about* de).

incuriously [ɪn'kjʊərɪəslɪ] **adv** sans curiosité.

incursion [ɪn'kɜːʃən] **n** incursion *f*.

incus ['ɪŋkəs] **n, pl incudes** (*Anat*) enclume *f*.

Ind. (*US*) **abbr of Indiana**.

indebted [ɪn'detɪd] **adj** (*Fin*) redevable (*to sb for sth* à qn de qch), endetté; (*fig*) redevable (*to sb for sth* à qn pour *or* de qch). **he was ~ to his brother for a large sum** il était redevable d'une grosse somme à son frère; **I am greatly ~ to him for his generosity** je lui dois beaucoup pour sa générosité; **I am ~ to him for pointing out that ...** je lui suis redevable d'avoir fait remarquer que ... .

indebtedness [ɪn'detɪdnɪs] **n** (*Fin, fig*) dette(s) *f(pl)*; (*Fin, Comm also*) endettement *m*. **my ~ to my friend** ma dette envers mon ami, ce dont je suis redevable à mon ami; (*Fin, Comm*) **the amount of our ~ to the bank is $ 15,000** le montant de notre endettement *or* dette envers la banque s'élève à 15 000 dollars.

indecency [ɪn'diːsnsɪ] **n** (*see* **indecent**) indécence *f*, inconvenance *f*; (*Jur*) outrage public à la pudeur, outrage aux bonnes mœurs.

indecent [ɪn'diːsnt] **adj** a (*offensive*) indécent, peu décent. (*Jur*) **~ assault (on sb)** attentat *m* à la pudeur (sur *or* contre qn); (*Jur*) **~ exposure** outrage public à la pudeur. b (*unseemly*) malséant, inconvenant. **with ~ haste** avec une précipitation malséante *or* inconvenante.

indecently [ɪn'diːsntlɪ] **adv** (*see* **indecent**) indécemment; de façon inconvenante. **he arrived ~ early** il est arrivé si tôt que c'en était inconvenant.

indecipherable [ˌɪndɪ'saɪfərəbl] **adj** indéchiffrable.

indecision [ˌɪndɪ'sɪʒən] **n** indécision *f*, irrésolution *f*.

indecisive [ˌɪndɪ'saɪsɪv] **adj** a (*hesitating*) *person, manner* indécis, irrésolu. b (*inconclusive*) *discussion, argument* peu concluant; *battle* indécis. c (*vague*) *outline* indécis, flou.

indecisively [ˌɪndɪ'saɪsɪvlɪ] **adv** de façon indécise.

indecisiveness [ˌɪndɪ'saɪsɪvnɪs] **n** = **indecision**.

indeclinable [ˌɪndɪ'klaɪnəbl] **adj** indéclinable.

indecorous [ɪn'dekərəs] **adj** peu convenable, inconvenant, incorrect, peu digne (*hum*).

indecorously [ɪn'dekərəslɪ] **adv** d'une manière incorrecte *or* inconvenante *or* peu convenable.

indecorum [ˌɪndɪ'kɔːrəm] **n** faute *f* contre le bon ton, manquement *m* aux usages.

indeed [ɪn'diːd] **adv** a (*really, in reality, in fact*) en effet, vraiment. **he promised to help and ~ he helped us a lot** il a promis de nous aider et en effet il nous a beaucoup aidés; **I feel, ~ I know he is right** je sens, et même je sais qu'il a raison; **I am ~ quite tired** je suis en effet assez fatigué; **he was ~ as tall as she had said** il était vraiment *or* en effet aussi grand qu'elle l'avait dit; **are you coming? — ~ I am!** *or* **yes ~!** vous venez? — mais certainement! *or* (mais) bien sûr!; **I may ~ come** il se peut effectivement *or* en effet que je vienne; **if ~ he were wrong** s'il est vrai qu'il a tort, si tant est qu'il ait tort.
b (*as intensifier*) **I am very pleased ~** je suis extrêmement content *or* vraiment très content; **he was very grateful ~** il était infiniment reconnaissant; **thank you very much ~** merci mille fois.
c (*showing interest, irony, surprise etc*) **(oh) ~?** vraiment?, c'est vrai?; **is it ~!, did you** (*or* **he** *etc*) **~!** vraiment?; **who is that man? — who is he ~?** qui est cet homme? — ah, là est la question!

indefatigable [ˌɪndɪ'fætɪgəbl] **adj** infatigable, inlassable.

indefatigably [ˌɪndɪ'fætɪgəblɪ] **adv** infatigablement, inlassablement.

indefensible [ˌɪndɪ'fensəbl] **adj** *action, behaviour* indéfendable, injustifiable, inexcusable; *crime* injustifiable; *cause, theory, argument* indéfendable, insoutenable; (*Mil etc*) indéfendable.

indefensibly [ɪndɪ'fensəblɪ] **adv** de manière inexcusable.

indefinable [ˌɪndɪ'faɪnəbl] **adj** indéfinissable, vague.

indefinably [ˌɪndɪ'faɪnəblɪ] **adv** vaguement.

indefinite [ɪn'defɪnɪt] **adj** a *intentions, doubts, feelings* incertain, indéfini, vague; *answer* vague; *outline* indistinct, mal défini; *size* indéterminé; *number, duration, period* indéterminé, illimité. **our plans are still somewhat ~** nos plans ne sont encore que mal définis *or* que peu précis, nos plans sont encore assez nébuleux; **~ leave of absence** congé illimité *or* indéfini. b (*Gram*) indéfini.

indefinitely [ɪn'defɪnɪtlɪ] **adv** a *wait etc* indéfiniment. **the meeting has been postponed ~** la réunion a été remise à une date indéterminée. b *speak etc* vaguement, avec imprécision.

indelible [ɪn'deləbl] **adj** a *stain, ink* indélébile. **~ pencil** crayon *m* à copier. b *impression* ineffaçable, indélébile; *memory* ineffaçable, inoubliable; *shame* ineffaçable.

indelibly [ɪn'delɪblɪ] **adv** de façon indélébile, ineffaçablement.

indelicacy [ɪn'delɪkəsɪ] **n** (*see* **indelicate**) a (*NonC*) *[person, behaviour, comment]* indélicatesse *f*, manque *m* de délicatesse; manque de discrétion. b *[action, remark etc]* inconvenance *f*; grossièreté *f*; indiscrétion *f*.

indelicate [ɪn'delɪkɪt] **adj** *person* indélicat, peu délicat; (*tactless*) manquant de tact, indiscret (*f* -ète); *act, remark* (*out of place*) indélicat, inconvenant, déplacé; (*tactless*) indiscret, manquant de tact; (*coarse*) grossier.

indemnification [ɪnˌdemnɪfɪ'keɪʃən] **n** a (*NonC*) indemnisation *f* (*for, against* de). b (*sum paid*) indemnité *f*, dédommagement *m*.

indemnify [ɪn'demnɪfaɪ] **vt** a (*compensate*) indemniser, dédommager (*sb for sth* qn de qch). b (*safeguard*) garantir, assurer (*sb against or* *for sth* qn contre qch).

indemnity [ɪn'demnɪtɪ] **n** a (*compensation*) indemnité *f*, dédommagement *m*, compensation *f*. b (*insurance*) assurance *f*, garantie *f*.

indent [ɪn'dent] 1 **vt** a *border* denteler, découper (*en dentelant*). **~ed edge** bord dentelé; **~ed coastline** littoral échancré *or* découpé. b (*Typ*) *word, line* renfoncer, mettre en alinéa *or* en retrait. **~ed line** ligne *f* en alinéa *or* en retrait; **~ 2 spaces** renfoncez de 2 espaces, mettez en alinéa *or* en retrait de 2 espaces. c (*make dent in*) faire *or* laisser une marque *or* une empreinte sur; *sheet of metal, car door etc* bosseler, cabosser. 2 **vi** (*Brit Comm*) **to ~ on sb for sth** passer une commande de qch à qn, commander qch à qn. 3 ['ɪndent] **n** a (*Brit Comm: see* **2**) commande *f*. b = **indentation**.

indentation [ˌɪnden'teɪʃən] **n** a (*act*) découpage *m*; (*notched edge*) dentelure *f*, découpure *f*; *[coastline]* échancrures *fpl*. b (*Typ*) renfoncement *m*, retrait *m*, alinéa *m*. c (*hollow mark*) empreinte *f*, impression *f* (en creux); (*in metal, car*) bosse *f*. **the ~ of tyres on the soft ground** l'empreinte des pneus sur le sol mou.

indenture [ɪn'dentʃəʳ] 1 **n** (*Jur*) contrat *m* synallagmatique; *[apprentice]* contrat d'apprentissage. 2 **vt** (*Jur*) lier par contrat (synallagmatique); *apprentice* mettre en apprentissage (*to* chez).

independence [ˌɪndɪ'pendəns] 1 **n** indépendance *f* (*from* par rapport à); (*Pol*) indépendance, autonomie *f*. **to show ~** faire preuve d'indépendance, manifester son indépendance; **the country got its ~ in 1970** le pays est devenu indépendant *or* autonome en 1970, le pays a obtenu son indépendance *or* son autonomie en 1970. 2 **comp** ▸**independence day** (*gen*) fête *f* de l'indépendance ▸**Independence Day** (*US*) fête *f or* anniversaire *m* de l'Indépendance américaine (*le 4 juillet*).

independent [ˌɪndɪ'pendənt] 1 **adj** a (*free*) *person, attitude, thinker, artist* indépendant; *country, nation* indépendant, autonome; *radio* libre. **to become ~** *[person]* devenir indépendant, s'affranchir; *[country, nation]* devenir indépendant *or* autonome, s'affranchir; **to be ~ of sb/sth** être indépendant de qn/qch, ne pas dépendre de qn/qch; **she is quite ~** elle est tout à fait indépendante; **he is an ~ thinker** c'est un penseur original; (*Pol*) **an I~ member** un député non inscrit *or* non affilié; **~ means** rentes *fpl*, revenus indépendants; **he has ~ means** il a une fortune personnelle, il vit de ses rentes; (*Brit*) **~ school** établissement *m* d'enseignement privé; (*Brit*) **I~ Television Commission** ≃ Conseil *m* supérieur de l'audiovisuel.
b (*unrelated*) *proof, research* indépendant; *opinions, reports* émanant de sources différentes. **to ask for an ~ opinion** demander l'avis d'un tiers; (*Aut*) **~ suspension** suspension indépendante.
c (*Gram*) indépendant.
2 **n** (*Pol*) **I~** non-inscrit(e) *m(f)*, non-affilié(e) *m(f)*.

independently [ˌɪndɪ'pendəntlɪ] **adv** de façon indépendante. **~ of** indépendamment de; **he acted ~** il a agi de son côté *or* de façon indépendante; **quite ~ he had offered to help** de façon tout à fait indépendante il avait proposé son aide.

indescribable [ˌɪndɪs'kraɪbəbl] **adj** *disorder, event* indescriptible; *emotion* indescriptible, inexprimable, indicible (*liter*).

indescribably [ˌɪndɪs'kraɪbəblɪ] **adv** (*see* **indescribable**) indescriptiblement; inexprimablement, indiciblement (*liter*). **it was ~ awful** c'était affreux au-delà de toute expression.

indestructibility [ˌɪndɪstrʌktə'bɪlɪtɪ] **n** indestructibilité *f*.

indestructible [ˌɪndɪs'trʌktəbl] **adj** indestructible.

indeterminable [ˌɪndɪ'tɜːmɪnəbl] **adj** indéterminable.

indeterminacy [ˌɪndɪ'tɜːmɪnəsɪ] **n** indétermination *f*.

indeterminate [ˌɪndɪ'tɜːmɪnɪt] **adj** *amount, sound* indéterminé; *shape* indéterminé, imprécis, vague; (*Ling, Math*) indéterminé. (*US Jur*) **~ sentence** peine *f* de prison de durée indéterminée.

indeterminately [ˌɪndɪ'tɜːmɪnɪtlɪ] **adv** de façon indéterminée, vaguement.

index ['ɪndeks] 1 **n** a (*pl* **~es**: *list*) (*in book etc*) index *m*, table *f* alphabétique; (*on cards, in files: in library etc*) catalogue *m or* répertoire *m* (alphabétique). (*Rel*) **to put a book on the I~** mettre un livre à l'Index.
b (*pl* **~es**: *pointer*) *[instrument]* aiguille *f*, index *m*.
c (*pl* **indices**: *number expressing ratio*) indice *m*. **cost-of-living ~** indice du coût de la vie; **~ of growth** indice de croissance; **~ of intelligence** *etc* taux *m* d'intelligence *etc;* (*Opt*) **~ of refraction** indice de réfraction.
d (*pl* **indices**: *fig*) indice *m*, signe *m* (révélateur *or* indicateur), indication *f*, symptôme *m*. **it was a true ~ of his character** c'était un signe bien révélateur de son caractère; **it is an ~ of how much poorer people were then** c'est un signe *or* une indication qui permet de se rendre compte combien les gens étaient plus pauvres en ce temps-là, c'est un signe révélateur de la plus grande pauvreté qui régnait alors.
e (*pl* **~es**) **~ (finger)** index *m*.
f (*pl* **~es**: *Typ*) index *m*.
g (*pl* **indices**: *Math*) exposant *m*.
2 **vt** a (*put an index in*) *book* mettre un index *or* une table alphabétique à. **the book is badly ~ed** l'index *or* la table alphabétique du livre est mal fait(e).
b (*put into an index*) *word* mettre dans l'index *or* la table alphabétique; (*on cards, in files etc*) *information* répertorier *or* cataloguer (alphabétiquement); *books, diskettes, articles* classer (*under* sous, à). **it is ~ed under "Europe"** c'est classé *or* ça se trouve sous *or* à "Europe", l'entrée est à "Europe".
c (*Fin, Econ*) *wages, prices* indexer.
3 **comp** ▸**index card** fiche *f* ▸**index figure** (*Statistics*) indice *m* ▸**index finger** index *m* ▸**index-linked** (*Brit Econ*) indexé ▸**index number** = **index figure** ▸**index-tied** = **index-linked**.

indexation [ˌɪndek'seɪʃən] **n** indexation *f*.

India ['ɪndɪə] 1 **n** Inde *f*; (*Hist*) Indes *fpl*. 2 **comp** ▸**India ink** encre *f* de Chine ▸**Indiaman** (*Naut Hist*) navire *m* faisant le voyage des Indes ▸**India paper** papier *m* bible ▸**India rubber** **n** (*NonC: substance*) caoutchouc *m*; (*eraser*) gomme *f* (*à effacer*) ◊ **comp** de *or* en caoutchouc.

Indian ['ɪndɪən] 1 **n** a (*in India*) Indien(ne) *m(f)*.
b (*in America*) Indien(ne) *m(f)* (d'Amérique).
c (*Ling*) amérindien *m*.
2 **adj** a (*in India*) indien, de l'Inde; (*Hist*) des Indes.
b **(American *or* Red) ~** indien, des Indiens (d'Amérique).
3 **comp** ▸**Indian clubs** massues *fpl* de gymnastique ▸**Indian elephant** éléphant *m* d'Asie ▸**Indian Empire** Empire *m* des Indes ▸**Indian file: in Indian file** en file indienne ▸**Indian giver*** (*US pej*) personne *f* qui reprend ses cadeaux ▸**Indian ink** encre *f* de Chine ▸**Indian Mutiny** (*Hist*) révolte *f* des Cipayes ▸**Indian National Congress** Congrès National Indien ▸**Indian Ocean** océan Indien ▸**Indian summer** (*fig*) été indien *or* de la Saint-Martin ▸**Indian tea** thé indien *or* de l'Inde ▸**Indian tonic (water)** Schweppes® *m* ▸**Indian wrestling** (*US Sport*) bras *m* de fer; *see also* **rope**.

Indiana [ˌɪndɪ'ænə] **n** Indiana *m*. **in ~** dans l'Indiana.

indicate ['ɪndɪkeɪt] **vt** a (*point to*) indiquer, montrer (*with one's hand* de la main). **he ~d the spot on the map** il indiqua *or* montra l'endroit sur la carte.
b (*be a sign of*) indiquer, dénoter, révéler, être l'indice de. **it ~s the presence of acid** ceci révèle la présence d'acide; **that ~s a clear conscience** cela dénote *or* révèle une conscience nette, c'est l'indice d'une conscience nette; **it ~s that he is dissatisfied** ceci indique *or* révèle qu'il est mécontent, ceci témoigne de son mécontentement.
c (*make known*) signaler, indiquer, faire connaître; *feelings, intentions* manifester, montrer. **he ~d that I was to leave** il m'a fait comprendre que je devais partir; (*Aut*) **he was indicating left** il avait mis son clignotant gauche.
d (*Med etc*) indiquer. **the use of penicillin is clearly ~d** le recours à la pénicilline est nettement indiqué; **a new approach to the wages problem is ~d** une approche nouvelle du problème salarial est indiquée *or* semble nécessaire.

indication [ˌɪndɪ'keɪʃən] **n** a (*sign, suggestion etc*) indice *m*, signe *m*, indication *f*. **there is every ~ that he is right** tout porte à croire *or* laisse à penser qu'il a raison; **there is no ~ that he will come** rien ne porte à croire qu'il vienne; **we had no ~ that it was going to take place** aucun signe ne nous permettait de prévoir *or* nous n'avions aucun indice nous permettant de prévoir que cela allait arriver; **it is some ~ of how much remains to be done** cela permet de se rendre compte de ce qu'il reste à faire; **if this result is any ~, he ...** à en juger par ce résultat, il ...; **he gave us some ~ of what he meant** il nous a donné quelque idée de ce qu'il voulait dire; **to give sb an ~ of one's feelings/intentions** manifester ses sentiments/ses intentions à qn; **it was an ~ of his guilt** c'était une indication *or* un signe *or* un indice de sa culpabilité; **all the ~s lead one to believe that ...** tout porte à croire que ..., il y a toute raison de croire que ... .
b (*NonC*) indication *f*.

indicative [ɪn'dɪkətɪv] 1 **adj** a indicatif (*of* de). **to be ~ of sth/of the fact that ...** montrer qch/que ... . b (*Gram*) indicatif. 2 **n** (*Gram*) **~ (mood)** (mode *m*) indicatif *m*; **in the ~** à l'indicatif.

indicator ['ɪndɪkeɪtəʳ] **n** (*device*) indicateur *m*; (*needle on scale etc*) aiguille *f*, index *m*; (*Brit Aut: also* **~ light**) (*flashing*) clignotant *m*; (*projecting*) flèche *f*; (*Ling*) indicateur. **altitude/pressure ~** indicateur d'altitude/de pression; **speed ~** indicateur *or* compteur *m* de vitesse; (*plan*) **town ~** table *f* d'orientation; (*Rail*) **arrival/departure ~** tableau *m or* indicateur des arrivées/des départs.

indices ['ɪndɪsiːz] **npl of index 1c, 1d, 1g**.

indict [ɪn'daɪt] **vt** a (*Jur*) accuser (*for, on a charge of* de), mettre en accusation. b (*fig*) accuser, porter une accusation contre.

indictable [ɪn'daɪtəbl] **adj** (*Jur*) *person, action* tombant sous le coup de la loi. **~ offence** délit pénal, délit punissable (par la loi).

indictment [ɪn'daɪtmənt] **n** (*Jur*) (*bill*) acte *m* d'accusation (*for* de); (*process*) mise *f* en accusation (*for* de); (*US*) mise en accusation (*par le grand jury*). (*Brit Hist*) **bill of ~** résumé *m* d'instruction (*présenté au grand jury*); **to bring an ~ against sb for sth** mettre qn en accusation pour qch; (*fig*) **such poverty is an ~ of the political system** une telle pauvreté constitue une mise en accusation *or* une condamnation du système politique.

Indies ['ɪndɪz] **npl** Indes *fpl*; *see* **east, west**.

indifference [ɪn'dɪfrəns] **n** a (*lack of interest, of feeling*) indifférence *f* (*to* à, *towards* envers), manque *m* d'intérêt (*to, towards* pour, à l'égard de). **he greeted the suggestion with ~** il a accueilli la suggestion avec indifférence *or* sans manifester d'intérêt; **it is a matter of supreme ~ to me** cela m'est parfaitement indifférent *or* égal. b (*poor quality*) médiocrité *f*.

indifferent [ɪn'dɪfrənt] adj a (*lacking feeling, interest*) indifférent (*to* à); (*impartial*) impartial, neutre. **it is quite ~ to me** cela m'est tout à fait indifférent *or* égal. b (*pej*) *talent, performance, player* médiocre, quelconque. **good, bad or ~** bon, mauvais ou quelconque.

indifferently [ɪn'dɪfrəntlɪ] adv a indifféremment. **she went ~ to one shop or the other** elle fréquentait indifféremment une boutique ou l'autre. b (*pej*) *paint, perform* médiocrement, de façon quelconque.

indigence ['ɪndɪdʒəns] n indigence *f*.

indigenous [ɪn'dɪdʒɪnəs] adj (*lit, fig*) indigène (*to* de); *population, language, customs* indigène, autochtone.

indigent ['ɪndɪdʒənt] adj (*frm*) indigent, nécessiteux.

indigestible [ˌɪndɪ'dʒestəbl] adj (*Med, fig*) indigeste.

indigestion [ˌɪndɪ'dʒestʃən] n (*NonC: Med*) dyspepsie *f*. **to have an attack of ~** avoir une indigestion; **she gets a lot of ~** elle a la digestion difficile, elle a une mauvaise digestion.

indignant [ɪn'dɪgnənt] adj indigné, plein *or* rempli d'indignation (*at sth* de *or* devant qch, *with sb* contre qn); *look* indigné, d'indignation. **to get** *or* **grow ~** s'indigner (*at sth* de *or* devant qch, *with sb about sth* contre qn à propos de qch); **to make sb ~** indigner qn.

indignantly [ɪn'dɪgnəntlɪ] adv avec indignation, d'un air *or* d'un ton indigné.

indignation [ˌɪndɪg'neɪʃən] n indignation *f* (*at* devant, *with* contre). **~ meeting*** réunion *f* de protestation.

indignity [ɪn'dɪgnɪtɪ] n a (*act etc*) indignité *f*, affront *m*, offense *f*, outrage *m*. **it was a gross ~** c'était un grave outrage; **he suffered the ~ of having to ...** il subit l'indignité d'avoir à ... . b (*NonC*) indignité *f*.

indigo ['ɪndɪgəʊ] 1 n, pl ~s *or* ~es indigo *m*. 2 adj: **~ (blue)** (bleu) indigo *inv*.

indirect [ˌɪndɪ'rekt] adj a (*gen*) indirect; *route, means etc* indirect, oblique, détourné; *consequence, reference* indirect. **~ lighting** éclairage indirect; **~ taxes** contributions indirectes; **~ taxation** imposition indirecte, impôts indirects. b (*Gram*) *object* indirect. **~ speech** discours indirect.

indirectly [ˌɪndɪ'rektlɪ] adv indirectement.

indirectness [ˌɪndɪ'rektnɪs] n caractère indirect; *[route etc]* détours *mpl*.

indiscernible [ˌɪndɪ'sɜːnəbl] adj indiscernable, imperceptible.

indiscipline [ɪn'dɪsɪplɪn] n indiscipline *f*.

indiscreet [ˌɪndɪs'kriːt] adj (*tactless*) indiscret (*f* -ète); (*rash*) imprudent, peu judicieux.

indiscreetly [ˌɪndɪs'kriːtlɪ] adv (*tactlessly*) indiscrètement; (*rashly*) imprudemment, avec imprudence.

indiscretion [ˌɪndɪs'kreʃən] n a (*NonC: see* **indiscreet**) manque *m* de discrétion, indiscrétion *f*; imprudence *f*. b (*action, remark*) indiscrétion *f*. **youthful ~** bêtise *f or* péché *m* de jeunesse.

indiscriminate [ˌɪndɪs'krɪmɪnɪt] adj *punishment, blows* distribué au hasard *or* à tort et à travers; *killings* commis au hasard; *person* manquant de discernement; *faith, admiration, confidence* aveugle.

indiscriminately [ˌɪndɪs'krɪmɪnɪtlɪ] adv *choose, kill* au hasard; *make friends* sans discrimination; *read, watch TV* sans aucun sens critique; *accept, admire* aveuglément.

indispensable [ˌɪndɪs'pensəbl] adj indispensable (*to* à). **you're not ~!** on peut se passer de toi!

indisposed [ˌɪndɪs'pəʊzd] adj a (*unwell*) indisposé, souffrant. b (*disinclined*) peu disposé, peu enclin (*to do* à faire).

indisposition [ˌɪndɪspə'zɪʃən] n a (*illness*) indisposition *f*, malaise *m*. b (*disinclination*) manque *m* d'inclination (*to do* à faire).

indisputable [ˌɪndɪs'pjuːtəbl] adj incontestable, indiscutable.

indisputably [ˌɪndɪs'pjuːtəblɪ] adv sans conteste, incontestablement, indiscutablement.

indissoluble [ˌɪndɪ'sɒljʊbl] adj *friendship etc* indissoluble; (*Chem*) insoluble.

indissolubly [ˌɪndɪ'sɒljʊblɪ] adv (*also Jur*) indissolublement.

indistinct [ˌɪndɪs'tɪŋkt] adj *object, voice, words* indistinct; *memory* vague, confus; *noise* confus, sourd. (*on telephone*) **you're very ~** je ne vous entends pas bien, je vous entends mal.

indistinctly [ˌɪndɪs'tɪŋktlɪ] adv *see, hear, speak* indistinctement; *feel* vaguement.

indistinguishable [ˌɪndɪs'tɪŋgwɪʃəbl] adj a indifférenciable (*from* de). b (*very slight*) *noise, difference, change* insaisissable, imperceptible, indiscernable.

indistinguishably [ˌɪndɪs'tɪŋgwɪʃəblɪ] adv au point de ne pouvoir être différencié.

indium ['ɪndɪəm] n indium *m*.

individual [ˌɪndɪ'vɪdjʊəl] 1 adj a (*separate*) *opinion, attention, portion* individuel. (*Sport*) **~ pursuit** poursuite individuelle; **~ sports** sports individuels. b (*distinctive, characteristic*) original, particulier. **he has an ~ style** il a un style particulier *or* personnel *or* bien à lui. 2 n individu *m*.

individualism [ˌɪndɪ'vɪdjʊəlɪzəm] n individualisme *m*.

individualist [ˌɪndɪ'vɪdjʊəlɪst] n individualiste *mf*.

individualistic [ˌɪndɪˌvɪdjʊə'lɪstɪk] adj individualiste.

individuality [ˌɪndɪˌvɪdjʊ'ælɪtɪ] n individualité *f*.

individualize [ˌɪndɪ'vɪdjʊəlaɪz] vt individualiser. (*US Scol*) **~d instruction** enseignement individualisé.

individually [ˌɪndɪ'vɪdjʊəlɪ] adv a (*separately*) individuellement. **he spoke to them ~** il leur a parlé à chacun individuellement *or* séparément; **they're all right ~** (pris chacun) individuellement ils sont très bien. b (*for o.s. alone*) pour soi-même. **he is speaking ~** il parle pour lui-même, il parle en son nom personnel.

indivisibility [ˌɪndɪˌvɪzə'bɪlɪtɪ] n indivisibilité *f*.

indivisible [ˌɪndɪ'vɪzəbl] adj indivisible; (*Math, Philos*) insécable.

indivisibly [ˌɪndɪ'vɪzəblɪ] adv indivisiblement, indissolublement.

Indo- ['ɪndəʊ] pref indo-; *see* **Indo-China** *etc*.

Indo-China ['ɪndəʊ'tʃaɪnə] n Indochine.

Indo-Chinese ['ɪndəʊtʃaɪ'niːz] 1 adj indochinois. 2 n Indochinois(e) *m(f)*.

indoctrinate [ɪn'dɒktrɪneɪt] vt endoctriner. **he's been well ~d** on l'a bien endoctriné; **to ~ sb with political ideas/with hatred of the enemy** inculquer des doctrines politiques/la haine de l'ennemi à qn.

indoctrination [ɪnˌdɒktrɪ'neɪʃən] n endoctrinement *m*.

Indo-European ['ɪndəʊˌjʊərə'pɪən] 1 adj indo-européen. 2 n (*Ling*) indo-européen *m*.

indolence ['ɪndələns] n indolence *f*, nonchalance *f*.

indolent ['ɪndələnt] adj indolent, nonchalant.

indolently ['ɪndələntlɪ] adv indolemment, nonchalamment.

indomitable [ɪn'dɒmɪtəbl] adj indomptable, invincible.

indomitably [ɪn'dɒmɪtəblɪ] adv *struggle, continue* sans jamais se laisser abattre.

Indonesia [ˌɪndəʊ'niːzɪə] n Indonésie *f*.

Indonesian [ˌɪndəʊ'niːzɪən] 1 adj indonésien. 2 n a Indonésien(ne) *m(f)*. b (*Ling*) indonésien *m*.

indoor ['ɪndɔːʳ] adj *shoes etc* d'intérieur; *plant* d'appartement; *swimming pool, tennis court* couvert; (*Cine, Theat*) *scene* d'intérieur. **it's an ~ hobby/occupation/job** c'est un passe-temps/une activité/un travail qui se pratique en intérieur; (*TV*) **~ aerial** antenne intérieure; **~ athletics** athlétisme *m* en salle; **~ games** (*squash etc*) sports pratiqués en intérieur; (*table games*) jeux *mpl* de société; **~ photography** photographie *f* d'intérieur *or* en studio.

indoors [ɪn'dɔːz] adv (*in building*) à l'intérieur; (*at home*) à la maison; (*under cover*) à l'abri. **to stay ~** rester à l'intérieur *or* à la maison; **to go ~** entrer, rentrer; **~ and outdoors** à l'intérieur et au-dehors, dedans et dehors.

indorse [ɪn'dɔːs] vt = **endorse**.

indrawn ['ɪndrɔːn] adj *cheeks* creux; *stomach* rentré. **he received the news with ~ breath** l'annonce de la nouvelle lui a coupé le souffle; **the nasty rumours were received with ~ breath** les méchantes rumeurs étaient reçues avec un léger choc; **the crowd gave a gasp of ~ breath** la foule a retenu sa respiration subitement; **oh, he said, after a long ~ breath** ah, dit-il, après une longue inspiration.

indubitable [ɪn'djuːbɪtəbl] adj indubitable, incontestable.

indubitably [ɪn'djuːbɪtəblɪ] adv indubitablement, sans aucun doute, sans conteste, incontestablement.

induce [ɪn'ˌdjuːs] vt a (*persuade*) persuader (*sb to do* qn de faire), décider, inciter (*sb to do* qn à faire). b (*bring about*) *reaction* produire, provoquer, amener; *sleep, illness, hypnosis* provoquer. (*Med*) **to ~ labour** déclencher l'accouchement (*artificiellement*); **~d labour** accouchement *m* déclenché; **she was ~d** elle a été déclenchée. c (*Philos: infer*) déduire, induire, conclure. d (*Elec*) produire par induction.

-induced [ɪn'djuːst] adj ending in comps causé *or* provoqué par, *e.g.* **drug~** *sleep, fit* causé *or* provoqué par la drogue; **self~** intentionnel, volontaire; *hypnosis* autosuggéré.

inducement [ɪn'djuːsmənt] n a (*NonC*) (*reason for doing sth*) motivation *f* (*to do* pour faire), encouragement *m*, incitation *f* (*to do* à faire). b (*reward*) récompense *f*; (*pej: bribe*) pot-de-vin *m*. **he can't work without ~s** il est incapable de travailler sans la promesse d'une récompense; **and as an added ~ we are offering ...** et comme avantage supplémentaire nous offrons ...; **he received £100 as an ~** il a reçu 100 livres à titre de gratification, il a reçu un pot-de-vin de 100 livres (*pej*).

induct [ɪn'dʌkt] vt a *clergyman* instituer, installer; *president etc* établir dans ses fonctions, installer. b **to ~ sb into the mysteries of ...** initier qn aux mystères de ... . c (*US Mil*) incorporer.

induction [ɪn'dʌkʃən] 1 n a (*NonC*) (*Elec, Philos*) induction *f*; *[sleep, hypnosis etc]* provocation *f*. b *[clergyman, president etc]* installation *f*. c *[new staff members]* insertion *f*, intégration *f*. d (*US Mil*) incorporation *f*. 2 comp ▸**induction coil** (*Elec*) bobine *f* d'induction ▸**induction course, induction training** (*Ind*) stage *m* préparatoire (d'intégration), stage *m* d'accueil et d'orientation ▸**induction year** (*Scol*) *[teacher]* ≃ année *f* (de stage) de CPR.

inductive [ɪn'dʌktɪv] adj a *reasoning, process* inductif. b (*Elec*) *current, charge* inducteur (*f* -trice).

indue [ɪn'djuː] vt = **endue**.

indulge [ɪn'dʌldʒ] 1 vt a *person (spoil)* gâter; (*give way to*) céder à; (*gratify*) *sb's desires, wishes* se prêter à; *one's own desires* satisfaire; *one's own laziness* s'abandonner à, se laisser aller à, donner libre cours à. **to ~ sb's whim** passer une fantaisie à qn, céder à un caprice de qn; **I'll ~ myself and have a chocolate** je vais me faire plaisir et manger un chocolat.
b (*Comm: extend time for payment*) *person, firm* accorder des délais de paiement à.
2 vi: **to ~ in doing sth** se livrer à qch, s'adonner à qch; **to ~ in a cigarette** se permettre une cigarette; **to ~ in sth to excess** abuser de qch; (*: *refusing cigarette etc*) **I'm afraid I don't ~** non merci, ce n'est pas un de mes vices; (*: *drink*) **he tends to ~** il est assez porté sur *or* il a un faible pour la bouteille*.

indulgence [ɪn'dʌldʒəns] n a (*NonC*) (*tolerance etc*) indulgence *f*, complaisance *f*; *[desires etc]* satisfaction *f*. b satisfaction *f*, gâterie *f*. **his little ~s** les petites douceurs qu'il se permet, les petites faiblesses qu'il s'autorise. c (*Rel*) indulgence *f*.

indulgent [ɪn'dʌldʒənt] adj (*not severe*) indulgent (*to* envers, pour), clément (*to* envers); (*permissive*) indulgent (*to* envers, pour), complaisant (*to* à l'égard de, pour), accommodant (*to* avec).

indulgently [ɪn'dʌldʒəntlɪ] adv (*see* **indulgent**) avec indulgence; complaisamment.

Indus ['ɪndəs] n Indus *m*.

industrial [ɪn'dʌstrɪəl] adj *application, experience, psychology, research, training* industriel; *expansion* industriel, de l'industrie; *worker* de l'industrie; *accident, injury, medicine* du travail; *fabric, equipment* pour l'industrie, industriel. **~ action** action revendicative; (*strike*) (mouvement *m* de) grève *f*; **to take ~ action** se mettre en grève; (*US*) **~ arts** enseignement *m* technique; (*Brit: Press, Rad, TV*) **~ correspondent** correspondant industriel; **~ design** design *m* industriel, esthétique *f* industrielle; **~ designer** concepteur-dessinateur industriel, designer *m*; **~ diamond** diamant naturel *or* industriel; **~ disease** maladie *f* professionnelle; (*Brit*) **~ dispute** conflit *m* social; **~ engineering** génie industriel; **~ espionage** espionnage *m* industriel; (*Brit*) **~ estate** zone industrielle; **~ hygiene** hygiène *f* du travail; **~ injury benefit** indemnité *f* d'accident du travail; **~ insurance** assurance *f* contre les accidents du travail, assurance des salariés de l'industrie; (*US*) **~ park** zone industrielle; **~ psychologist** psychologue *mf* d'entreprise; **~ rehabilitation** réadaptation fonctionnelle; **~ relations** relations *fpl* patronat-syndicats; (*field of study*) relations *fpl* sociales; (*Hist*) **the ~ revolution** la révolution industrielle; (*US*) **~ school** école *f* technique; **~ tribunal** ≃ conseil *m* de prud'hommes; **~ unrest** troubles sociaux, agitation ouvrière; (*Aut*) **~ vehicle** véhicule industriel; **~ waste** (*Brit*) *or* **wastes** (*US*) déchets industriels.

industrialism [ɪn'dʌstrɪəlɪzəm] n industrialisme *m*.

industrialist [ɪn'dʌstrɪəlɪst] n industriel *m*.

industrialization [ɪn,dʌstrɪəlaɪ'zeɪʃən] n industrialisation *f*.

industrialize [ɪn'dʌstrɪəlaɪz] vt industrialiser.

industrious [ɪn'dʌstrɪəs] adj industrieux, travailleur.

industriously [ɪn'dʌstrɪəslɪ] adv industrieusement.

industriousness [ɪn'dʌstrɪəsnɪs] n = **industry b**.

industry ['ɪndəstrɪ] n a industrie *f*. **basic** *or* **heavy ~** industrie lourde; **the hotel ~** l'hôtellerie *f*, l'industrie hôtelière; **tourist ~** tourisme *m*, industrie touristique; (*Brit*) **Secretary of State for/Department of I~** ministre *m*/ministère *m* de l'Industrie; *see* **coal, textile** *etc*. b (*NonC: industriousness*) zèle *m*, assiduité *f*, application *f*.

inebriate [ɪ'ni:brɪɪt] 1 n alcoolique *mf*. 2 adj ivre. 3 [ɪ'ni:brɪeɪt] vt (*lit, fig*) enivrer, griser.

inebriated [ɪ'ni:brɪ,eɪtɪd] adj (*drunk*) (*lit*) ivre; (*fig*) ivre, enivré, grisé (*by* de).

inebriation [ɪ,ni:brɪ'eɪʃən] n, **inebriety** [,ɪni:'braɪətɪ] n état *m* d'ébriété.

inedible [ɪn'edɪbl] adj (*not meant to be eaten*) non comestible; (*not fit to be eaten*) immangeable.

ineducable [ɪn'edjʊkəbl] adj inéducable.

ineffable [ɪn'efəbl] adj (*liter*) indicible (*liter*), ineffable, inexprimable.

ineffaceable [,ɪnɪ'feɪsəbl] adj ineffaçable, indélébile.

ineffective [,ɪnɪ'fektɪv] adj *remedy, measures, reasoning* inefficace, sans effet, sans résultat; *style* plat, fade, terne; *person* incapable, incompétent. **he made an ~ attempt to apologize** il a vainement *or* en vain essayé de s'excuser.

ineffectively [,ɪnɪ'fektɪvlɪ] adv *use* inefficacement; *try* vainement, en vain.

ineffectual [,ɪnɪ'fektjʊəl] adj = **ineffective**.

ineffectually [,ɪnɪ'fektjʊəlɪ] adv = **ineffectively**.

inefficacious [,ɪnefɪ'keɪʃəs] adj inefficace, sans effet, sans résultat.

inefficacy [ɪn'efɪkəsɪ] n inefficacité *f*.

inefficiency [,ɪnɪ'fɪʃənsɪ] n *[action, machine, measures]* inefficacité *f*, insuffisance *f*; *[person]* incompétence *f*, incapacité *f*, insuffisance.

inefficient [,ɪnɪ'fɪʃənt] adj *action, machine, measures* inefficace; *person* incapable, incompétent. **an ~ use of** une mauvaise utilisation de.

inefficiently [,ɪnɪ'fɪʃəntlɪ] adv (*see* **inefficient**) inefficacement; sans compétence. **work ~ done** travail mal exécuté.

inelastic [,ɪnɪ'læstɪk] adj inélastique; (*fig*) rigide, sans souplesse, sans élasticité. (*Econ*) **~ demand** demande *f* inélastique.

inelegant [ɪn'elɪgənt] adj inélégant, peu élégant, sans élégance.

inelegantly [ɪn'elɪgəntlɪ] adv inélégamment, sans élégance, peu élégamment.

ineligibility [ɪn,elɪdʒə'bɪlɪtɪ] n (*gen*) inéligibilité *f*; (*Fin*) irrecevabilité *f*.

ineligible [ɪn'elɪdʒəbl] adj *candidate* inéligible. **~ for military service** inapte au service militaire; **~ for social security benefits** n'ayant pas droit aux prestations de la Sécurité sociale; **he is ~ to vote** il n'a pas le (droit de) vote.

ineluctable [,ɪnɪ'lʌktəbl] adj (*frm*) inéluctable, inévitable.

inept [ɪ'nept] adj *behaviour* inapproprié, mal *or* peu à propos; *remark, refusal* inepte, stupide, absurde; *person* inepte, stupide.

ineptitude [ɪ'neptɪtju:d] n, **ineptness** [ɪ'neptnɪs] n *[behaviour]* manque *m* d'à-propos; *[remark, person]* ineptie *f*, sottise *f*, stupidité *f*.

ineptly [ɪ'neptlɪ] adv ineptement, stupidement.

inequality [,ɪnɪ'kwɒlɪtɪ] n inégalité *f*.

inequitable [ɪn'ekwɪtəbl] adj inéquitable, injuste.

inequity [ɪn'ekwɪtɪ] n injustice *f*, iniquité *f*.

ineradicable [,ɪnɪ'rædɪkəbl] adj indéracinable, tenace.

inert [ɪ'nɜ:t] adj (*gen, also Chem, Phys*) inerte.

inertia [ɪ'nɜ:ʃə] 1 n a *[person]* inertie *f*, apathie *f*. b (*Chem, Phys*) inertie *f*. 2 comp ►**inertia-reel seat belts** (*Aut*) ceintures *fpl* (de sécurité) à enrouleurs ►**inertia selling** (*Brit Comm*) vente(s) *f(pl)* par envoi forcé.

inescapable [,ɪnɪs'keɪpəbl] adj inéluctable, inévitable.

inessential [,ɪnɪ'senʃəl] adj superflu, non-essentiel.

inestimable [ɪn'estɪməbl] adj *gift, friendship* inestimable, inappréciable; *fortune, work* incalculable.

inevitability [ɪn,evɪtə'bɪlɪtɪ] n caractère *m* inévitable, inévitabilité *f*.

inevitable [ɪn'evɪtəbl] 1 adj *consequence* inévitable, inéluctable, fatal; *day, event* fatal. **the ~ result of this war** le résultat inéluctable *or* inévitable de cette guerre; **it was ~ that she should discover ...** elle devait inévitablement *or* fatalement *or* forcément découvrir ...; **I'm afraid it's ~** j'ai bien peur que ce ne soit inévitable *or* inéluctable; **the tourist had the ~ camera** le touriste avait l'inévitable appareil-photo. 2 n: **the ~** l'inévitable *m*.

inevitably [ɪn'evɪtəblɪ] adv inévitablement, immanquablement, fatalement.

inexact [,ɪnɪg'zækt] adj *information* inexact, erroné, incorrect; *description, measurement* inexact.

inexactitude [,ɪnɪg'zæktɪtju:d] n inexactitude *f*.

inexactly [,ɪnɪg'zæktlɪ] adv inexactement, incorrectement.

inexcusable [,ɪnɪks'kju:zəbl] adj inexcusable, impardonnable, injustifiable.

inexcusably [,ɪnɪks'kju:zəblɪ] adv inexcusablement. **~ lazy** d'une paresse inexcusable.

inexhaustible [,ɪnɪg'zɔ:stəbl] adj inépuisable.

inexorable [ɪn'eksərəbl] adj inexorable.

inexorably [ɪn'eksərəblɪ] adv inexorablement.

inexpedient [,ɪnɪks'pi:dɪənt] adj *action, decision, policy* inopportun, malavisé.

inexpensive [,ɪnɪks'pensɪv] adj bon marché *inv*, pas cher (*f* chère), peu coûteux.

inexpensively [,ɪnɪks'pensɪvlɪ] adv *buy* à bon marché, à bon compte; *live* à peu de frais.

inexperience [,ɪnɪks'pɪərɪəns] n inexpérience *f*, manque *m* d'expérience.

inexperienced [,ɪnɪks'pɪərɪənst] adj inexpérimenté, manquant d'expérience, novice. **I am very ~ in matters of this kind** j'ai très peu d'expérience en ces matières.

inexpert [ɪn'ekspɜ:t] adj inexpert, maladroit (*in* en).

inexpertly [ɪn'ekspɜ:tlɪ] adv maladroitement.

inexplicable [,ɪnɪks'plɪkəbl] adj inexplicable.

inexplicably [,ɪnɪks'plɪkəblɪ] adv inexplicablement.

inexpressible [,ɪnɪks'presəbl] adj inexprimable, indicible (*liter*).

inexpressive [,ɪnɪks'presɪv] adj inexpressif, sans expression.

inextinguishable [,ɪnɪks'tɪŋgwɪʃəbl] adj *passion etc* inextinguible; *fire* impossible à éteindre *or* à maîtriser.

in extremis [ɪnɪk'stri:mɪs] adv (*frm*) in extremis.

inextricable [,ɪnɪks'trɪkəbl] adj inextricable.

inextricably [,ɪnɪks'trɪkəblɪ] adv inextricablement.

infallibility [ɪn,fælə'bɪlɪtɪ] n (*also Rel*) infaillibilité *f*.

infallible [ɪn'fæləbl] adj infaillible.

infallibly [ɪn'fæləblɪ] adv a (*without error*) *pronounce, correct* infailliblement. b (*always*) infailliblement, immanquablement.

infamous ['ɪnfəməs] adj *conduct, person, thing* infâme.

infamy ['ɪnfəmɪ] n infamie *f*.

infancy ['ɪnfənsɪ] n (toute) petite enfance, bas âge; (*Jur*) minorité *f*; (*fig*) enfance, débuts *mpl*. **from his ~** depuis sa petite enfance; **child still in ~** enfant encore en bas âge; **this process is still in its ~** ce procédé en est encore à ses débuts, ce procédé est encore dans l'enfance.

infant ['ɪnfənt] 1 n (*newborn*) nouveau-né(e) *m(f)*; (*baby*) bébé *m*, nourrisson *m*; (*young child*) petit(e) enfant *m(f)*, enfant en bas âge; (*Jur*) mineur(e) *m(f)*; (*Brit Scol*) enfant, petit(e) *m(f)* (*de 5 à 7 ans*). 2 **comp** *disease etc* infantile; (*fig*) *industry etc* naissant ▸**infant class** (*Brit*) ≃ cours *m* préparatoire; **the infant classes** les classes enfantines, les petites classes ▸**infant education** enseignement *m* des petits (*entre 5 et 7 ans*) ▸**infant mortality** mortalité *f* infantile ▸**infant school** (*Brit*) ≃ classes *fpl* de onzième et de dixième (*entre 5 et 7 ans*) ▸**infant welfare clinic** centre *m* médico-social pédiatrique.

infanta [ɪn'fæntə] **n** infante *f*.

infante [ɪn'fæntɪ] **n** infant *m*.

infanticide [ɪn'fæntɪsaɪd] **n** (*act*) infanticide *m*; (*person*) infanticide *mf*.

infantile ['ɪnfəntaɪl] **adj** a (*childish*) enfantin, infantile, puéril. b (*Med*) infantile. ~ **paralysis**† paralysie *f* infantile†, poliomyélite *f*.

infantry ['ɪnfəntrɪ] **n** (*NonC: Mil*) infanterie *f* (*NonC*), fantassins *mpl*. **~man** fantassin *m*; *see* **light**[2].

infatuate [ɪn'fætjʊeɪt] **vt** (*gen pass*) tourner la tête à. **to be ~d with** *person* être entiché de, avoir le béguin* pour; *idea etc* avoir la tête pleine de, être engoué de; **to become ~d with** *person* s'enticher de, se toquer de*; *idea etc* s'engouer pour; **after he met her he was clearly ~d** après sa rencontre avec elle il était évident qu'il avait la tête tournée.

infatuation [ɪn,fætjʊ'eɪʃən] **n** a (*NonC: see* **infatuate**) engouement *m*; toquade* *f*; béguin* *m* (*with* pour). b (*object of* ~) folie *f*.

infect [ɪn'fekt] **vt** a (*Med*) *air, well, wound etc* infecter, contaminer. **his wound became ~ed** sa blessure s'infecta; **to ~ sb with a disease** transmettre *or* communiquer une maladie à qn; **~ed with leprosy** atteint de la lèpre, ayant contracté la lèpre; (*fig*) **to ~ sb with one's enthusiasm** communiquer son enthousiasme à qn. b (*fig pej*) *person* corrompre; *morals* corrompre, infecter (*liter*), souiller (*liter*).

infection [ɪn'fekʃən] **n** (*Med*) infection *f*, contagion *f*, contamination *f*; (*fig*) contagion. **she has a slight ~** elle est légèrement souffrante; **a throat ~** une angine; **an ear ~** une infection de l'oreille, une otite.

infectious [ɪn'fekʃəs] **adj** (*Med*) *disease* infectieux; *person* contagieux; (*fig*) *idea* contagieux; *enthusiasm, laughter* contagieux, communicatif.

infectiousness [ɪn'fekʃəsnɪs] **n** (*Med*) nature infectieuse; (*fig*) contagion *f*.

infelicitous [,ɪnfɪ'lɪsɪtəs] **adj** malheureux, fâcheux.

infelicity [,ɪnfɪ'lɪsɪtɪ] **n** a (*NonC: misfortune*) malheur *m*. b (*tactless act, remark*) maladresse *f*.

infer [ɪn'fɜː[r]] **vt** a (*conclude*) déduire, conclure, inférer (*sth from sth* qch de qch, *that* que). b (*: *imply*) laisser entendre, insinuer. **what are you ~ing?** qu'est-ce que vous insinuez?

inference ['ɪnfərəns] **n** déduction *f*, inférence *f*, conclusion *f*. **by ~** par déduction; **the ~ is that he is unwilling to help us** on doit en conclure qu'il n'est pas disposé à nous aider; **to draw an ~ from sth** tirer une conclusion de qch.

inferential [,ɪnfə'renʃəl] **adj** *method* déductif; *proof* obtenu par déduction.

inferentially [,ɪnfə'renʃəlɪ] **adv** par déduction.

inferior [ɪn'fɪərɪə[r]] 1 **adj** inférieur (*f* -eure) (*to* à); *products, goods* de qualité inférieure, de second choix; (*Bot*) infère. (*Typ*) ~ **letter** lettre inférieure; **he makes me feel ~** il me donne un sentiment d'infériorité. 2 **n** (*in quality, social standing*) inférieur(e) *m(f)*; (*in authority, rank: also Mil*) subalterne *mf*, subordonné(e) *m(f)*.

inferiority [ɪn,fɪərɪ'ɒrɪtɪ] **n** infériorité *f* (*to* par rapport à). ~ **complex** complexe *m* d'infériorité.

infernal [ɪn'fɜːnl] **adj** a (*liter*) *regions etc* infernal, de l'enfer; (*fig*) *cruelty* diabolique, abominable. b (*: *infuriating*) *noise, impudence* infernal*. **that ~ car** *etc* cette satanée *or* maudite voiture *etc*; **it's an ~ nuisance!** que c'est enquiquinant!*

infernally* [ɪn'fɜːnəlɪ] **adv** *difficult* abominablement, épouvantablement, atrocement. **it is ~ hot** il fait une chaleur infernale *or* à crever*.

inferno [ɪn'fɜːnəʊ] **n** a **a (blazing) ~** un brasier. b (*liter: hell*) enfer *m*.

infertile [ɪn'fɜːtaɪl] **adj** *land* stérile, infertile, infécond (*liter*); *person* stérile, infécond (*liter*).

infertility [,ɪnfɜː'tɪlɪtɪ] **n** (*see* **infertile**) infertilité *f*; stérilité *f*.

infest [ɪn'fest] **vt** infester (*with* de).

infestation [,ɪnfes'teɪʃən] **n** infestation *f*.

infidel ['ɪnfɪdəl] 1 **n** (*liter*) (*Hist Rel*) infidèle† *mf*; (*Rel*) incroyant(e) *m(f)*. 2 **adj** infidèle†; incroyant.

infidelity [,ɪnfɪ'delɪtɪ] **n** infidélité *f*. (*Jur*) **divorce on the grounds of ~** divorce *m* pour cause d'adultère.

infighting ['ɪn,faɪtɪŋ] **n** (*Mil*) (*hand-to-hand*) corps à corps *m*; (*close-range*) combat *m* rapproché; (*Boxing*) corps à corps; (*fig*) (*within group etc*) conflits *mpl or* querelles *fpl* internes, luttes *fpl* intestines (*within* au sein de).

infill ['ɪnfɪl] **n** (*Constr, Geol*) remplissage *m*.

infiltrate ['ɪnfɪl,treɪt] 1 **vi** *[troops, person, light, liquid, ideas]* s'infiltrer (*into* dans). 2 **vt** *liquid* infiltrer (*into* dans, *through* à travers). (*Mil*) **to ~ troops into a territory** faire s'infiltrer des troupes dans un territoire; (*Mil*) **to ~ the enemy lines** s'infiltrer dans les lignes ennemies; (*Pol*) **disruptive elements have ~d the group** des éléments perturbateurs se sont infiltrés dans le groupe *or* ont noyauté le groupe.

infiltration [,ɪnfɪl'treɪʃən] **n** (*see* **infiltrate**) infiltration *f*; (*Pol*) noyautage *m*. (*Mil*) ~ **course** parcours *m* du combattant.

infiltrator ['ɪnfɪl,treɪtə[r]] **n** (*inside organization, country*) agent *m* infiltré. **Western ~s** agents *mpl* de l'Occident.

infinite ['ɪnfɪnɪt] 1 **adj** (*Math, Philos, Rel etc*) infini; (*fig*) infini, illimité, sans bornes. **it gave her ~ pleasure** cela lui a fait infiniment plaisir; **he took ~ pains to do it** il mit un soin infini à le faire. 2 **n** infini *m*.

infinitely ['ɪnfɪnɪtlɪ] **adv** infiniment.

infiniteness ['ɪnfɪnɪtnɪs] **n** = **infinity c**.

infinitesimal [,ɪnfɪnɪ'tesɪməl] **adj** (*Math etc*) infinitésimal; (*gen*) *amount, majority etc* infinitésimal, infime.

infinitive [ɪn'fɪnɪtɪv] (*Gram*) 1 **n** infinitif *m*. **in the ~** à l'infinitif. 2 **adj** infinitif.

infinitude [ɪn'fɪnɪtjuːd] **n**: **an ~ of** une infinité de.

infinity [ɪn'fɪnɪtɪ] **n** a (*that which is infinite*) infinité *f*, infini *m*. **in time and space or in ~** dans le temps et dans l'espace ou dans l'infinité *or* l'infini. b (*infinite quantity, number etc*) infinité *f*. (*fig*) **an ~ of reasons** *etc* une infinité de raisons *etc*. c (*infiniteness*) infinitude *f*. **the ~ of God** l'infinitude de Dieu. d (*Math*) infini *m*. **to ~** à l'infini.

infirm [ɪn'fɜːm] **adj** a (*sick*) infirme. **the old and ~** ceux qui sont âgés et infirmes *or* âgés et invalides. b (*liter*) ~ **of purpose** irrésolu, indécis.

infirmary [ɪn'fɜːmərɪ] **n** (*hospital*) hôpital *m*; (*in school etc*) infirmerie *f*.

infirmity [ɪn'fɜːmɪtɪ] **n** a (*NonC*) infirmité *f*, débilité *f*, faiblesse *f*. (*liter*) ~ **of purpose** irrésolution *f*, indécision *f*. b infirmité *f*. **the infirmities of old age** les infirmités de l'âge.

infix [ɪn'fɪks] 1 **vt** *habit, idea* inculquer (*in* à), implanter (*in* dans); (*Ling*) insérer (*in* dans). 2 ['ɪn,fɪks] **n** (*Gram*) infixe *m*.

inflame [ɪn'fleɪm] 1 **vt** (*set alight*) enflammer, mettre le feu à; (*Med*) enflammer; (*fig*) *courage* enflammer; *anger, desire, hatred, discord* attiser, allumer. 2 **vi** s'enflammer, prendre feu; (*Med*) s'enflammer; (*fig*) s'allumer, s'échauffer.

inflammable [ɪn'flæməbl] **adj** (*lit, fig*) inflammable.

inflammation [,ɪnflə'meɪʃən] **n** (*also Med, fig*) inflammation *f*.

inflammatory [ɪn'flæmətərɪ] **adj** *speech etc* incendiaire; (*Med*) inflammatoire.

inflatable [ɪn'fleɪtɪbl] 1 **adj** *dinghy, mattress* pneumatique, gonflable; *toy, rubber ring* gonflable. 2 **n** objet *m* (*or* jouet *etc*) gonflable.

inflate [ɪn'fleɪt] **vt** *tyre, balloon* gonfler (*with* de); (*Med*) *lung* dilater; (*fig*) *prices* faire monter, hausser; *bill, account* grossir, charger. (*Econ*) **to ~ the currency** recourir *or* avoir recours à l'inflation.

inflated [ɪn'fleɪtɪd] **adj** *tyre etc* gonflé; (*Med*) *lung* dilaté; (*fig*) *style* enflé, boursouflé; *value* exagéré; *prices* exagéré, gonflé. ~ **with pride** bouffi *or* gonflé d'orgueil; **he has an ~ sense of his own importance** il a une idée exagérée de sa propre importance.

inflation [ɪn'fleɪʃən] **n** (*NonC*) (*Econ*) inflation *f*; *[tyre etc]* gonflement *m*; *[prices]* hausse *f*.

inflationary [ɪn'fleɪʃnərɪ] **adj** inflationniste.

inflationist [ɪn'fleɪʃənɪst] **n** partisan(e) *m(f)* de l'inflation.

inflect [ɪn'flekt] 1 **vt** a (*Ling*) *word* mettre une désinence à, modifier la désinence de, fléchir; (*conjugate*) conjuguer; (*decline*) décliner. **~ed form** forme fléchie; **~ed vowel** voyelle infléchie. b *voice* moduler; (*Mus*) *note* altérer. c (*bend*) courber, fléchir, infléchir. 2 **vi** (*Ling*) prendre une *or* des désinence(s), prendre une *or* des marque(s) flexionnelle(s). **a verb which ~s** un verbe flexionnel *or* qui prend des désinences *or* des marques flexionnelles; **a noun ~s in the plural** un nom prend le signe du pluriel; **an ~ing language** une langue désinentielle *or* flexionnelle.

inflection [ɪn'flekʃən] **n** = **inflexion**.

inflectional [ɪn'flekʃənəl] **adj** flexionnel. (*Ling*) **an ~ ending** une désinence; **an ~ language** une langue désinentielle *or* flexionnelle.

inflexibility [ɪn,fleksɪ'bɪlɪtɪ] **n** (*lit*) rigidité *f*; (*fig*) inflexibilité *f*, rigidité.

inflexible [ɪn'fleksəbl] **adj** *object* rigide; *person, attitude, opinion* inflexible, rigide.

inflexion [ɪn'flekʃən] **n** a (*NonC: Ling: see* **inflect 1a**) *[word]* flexion *f*, adjonction *f* de désinence, modification *f* de désinence; conjugaison *f*; déclinaison *f*; *[vowel]* inflexion *f*. **the ~ of nouns/verbs** la flexion nominale/verbale. b (*Ling: affix*) désinence *f*. c (*NonC*) *[voice]* inflexion *f*, modulation *f*; *[note]* altération *f*; *[body]* inflexion, inclination *f*; (*Geom, Opt etc*) inflexion, déviation *f*. d **the ~s of her voice** les inflexions *fpl* de sa voix.

inflict [ɪn'flɪkt] **vt** *punishment, fine, torture* infliger (*on* à); *pain, suffering* faire subir, infliger, occasionner (*on* à). **to ~ a wound on sb** blesser qn; **to ~ o.s.** *or* **one's company on sb** infliger *or* imposer sa compagnie à qn.

infliction [ɪn'flɪkʃən] **n** a (*NonC*) infliction *f*. **to avoid the unnecessary ~ of pain/punishment** éviter d'infliger inutilement la douleur/un châtiment. b (*misfortune*) affliction *f*.

in-flight ['ɪn,flaɪt] **adj** *refuelling* en vol. ~ **film/meal/entertainment** film *m* diffusé/repas *m* servi/distractions *fpl* pendant le vol *or* à bord.

inflow ['ɪnfləʊ] 1 **n** a *[water]* afflux *m*, arrivée *f*, flot *m*. b =

influx a. c *[capital]* entrée *f*. 2 **comp ▸inflow pipe** tuyau *m* d'arrivée; **water-inflow pipe** arrivée *f or* adduction *f* d'eau.

influence [ˈɪnflʊəns] 1 **n** (*gen*) influence *f* (*on* sur); (*power*) influence, autorité *f* (*on* sur). **under his ~** sous son influence; **under the ~ of drugs/anger** sous l'effet *m or* l'empire *m* des drogues/de la colère; **under the ~ of drink** sous l'effet *or* l'empire de la boisson, en état d'ébriété (*Jur*); (*Jur*) **convicted of driving under the ~ of drink** condamné pour avoir conduit en état d'ébriété *or* d'ivresse; **he was a bit under the ~*** il avait bu un coup de trop*, il était paf*; **his book had** *or* **was a great ~ on her** son livre a eu beaucoup d'influence sur elle *or* l'a beaucoup influencée; **I've got a lot of ~ with her** j'ai beaucoup d'influence *or* d'ascendant auprès d'elle; **to use one's ~ with sb to get sth** user de son influence auprès de qn pour obtenir qch; **I shall bring all my ~** *or* **every ~ to bear on him** j'essaierai d'exercer toute mon influence *or* toute l'influence dont je dispose sur lui; **he has got ~** il a de l'influence *or* de l'autorité *or* de l'importance *or* du crédit, il a le bras long; **a man of ~** un homme influent; **she is a good ~ in the school/on the pupils** elle a *or* exerce une bonne influence dans l'établissement/sur les élèves.

2 **comp ▸influence peddling** trafic *m* d'influence.

3 **vt** *attitude, behaviour, decision, person* influencer, influer sur, agir sur. **don't let him ~ you** ne le laissez pas vous influencer; **don't be ~d by him** ne vous laissez pas influencer par lui; **she's easily ~d** elle est très influençable, elle se laisse facilement influencer; **the artist has been ~d by Leonardo da Vinci** l'artiste a été influencé par *or* a subi l'influence de *or* a été sous l'influence de Léonard de Vinci.

influential [ˌɪnflʊˈenʃəl] **adj** influent. **to be ~** avoir de l'influence *or* du crédit *or* de l'autorité *or* de l'importance, avoir le bras long; **~ friends** amis influents *or* haut placés.

influenza [ˌɪnflʊˈenzə] **n** (*NonC*) grippe *f*. **he's got ~** il a la grippe.

influx [ˈɪnflʌks] **n** a *[people]* afflux *m*, flot *m*; *[new ideas, attitudes]* flot, flux *m*. **a great ~ of people into the neighbourhood** un gros afflux d'arrivants dans le voisinage; **the ~ of tourists/foreign workers** *etc* l'afflux *or* le flot de touristes/de travailleurs étrangers *etc*. b = **inflow 1a.** c (*meeting place of rivers etc*) confluent *m*.

info* [ˈɪnfəʊ] **n** (*NonC*) (**abbr of information 1a**) (*gen*) renseignements *mpl*; (*tips*) tuyaux* *mpl* (*about* sur).

inform [ɪnˈfɔːm] 1 **vt** informer, avertir, aviser (*of* de); renseigner (*about* sur). **to ~ sb of sth** informer *or* avertir *or* aviser qn de qch, faire savoir qch à qn, faire part de qch à qn; **I should like to be ~ed as soon as he arrives** j'aimerais être informé *or* averti *or* avisé dès qu'il sera là, prévenez-moi s'il vous plaît dès qu'il arrivera; **keep me ~ed (of what is happening)** tenez-moi au courant (de ce qui se passe); **why was I not ~ed?** pourquoi ne m'a-t-on rien dit?, pourquoi n'ai-je pas été averti? *or* informé? *or* tenu au courant?; **we must ~ the police** il (nous) faut avertir la police; **can you ~ me about the recent developments?** pouvez-vous me mettre au courant des *or* me faire connaître les derniers faits?; **he was well ~ed about what had been happening** il était bien informé sur *or* bien au courant de ce qui s'était passé; **he was ill ~ed** *or* **not well ~ed about what had been happening** il était mal informé *or* il n'était pas bien au courant de ce qui s'était passé; *see also* **informed.**

2 **vi: to ~ against sb** dénoncer qn, informer contre qn.

informal [ɪnˈfɔːməl] **adj** a (*simple, relaxed*) *tone, manner, style* simple, familier, sans façon. **~ language** le langage de la conversation; **he is very ~** il est très simple, il ne fait pas de façons; **we had an ~ talk about it** nous en avons discuté entre nous.

b (*without ceremony*) *welcome, greeting, visit* dénué de cérémonie *or* de formalité; *discussion* dénué de formalité, informel. **~ dance** sauterie *f* entre amis; **~ dinner** repas *m* simple (entre amis); **"dress ~"** "tenue de ville"; **~ meeting** réunion *f* sans caractère officiel; **it was a very ~ occasion** c'était une occasion dénuée de toute formalité *or* de toute cérémonie *or* de tout protocole; **it's just an ~ get-together*** ce ne sera qu'une réunion toute simple; **it will be quite ~** ce sera sans cérémonie *or* en toute simplicité *or* à la bonne franquette, on ne fera pas de cérémonies*.

c (*not official*) *announcement, acceptance, communication* officieux, non-officiel; *instructions, invitation* non-officiel, dénué de caractère officiel. **there was an ~ arrangement that ...** il y avait une entente officieuse selon laquelle ...; **we had an ~ agreement to do it this way** nous nous étions mis d'accord officieusement *or* entre nous pour le faire ainsi; **there is an ~ suggestion that ...** il est suggéré de façon officieuse que ... .

informality [ˌɪnfɔːˈmælɪtɪ] **n** *[person, manner, style]* simplicité *f*; *[visit, welcome etc]* simplicité, absence *f* de formalité *or* de cérémonie; *[arrangement, agreement etc]* caractère officieux. **we liked the ~ of the meeting** nous avons aimé l'absence de cérémonie qui a marqué la réunion.

informally [ɪnˈfɔːməlɪ] **adv** *invite* sans cérémonie; *arrange, agree, meet* officieusement, en privé; *behave, speak* de façon toute simple, sans cérémonie. **to dress ~** s'habiller simplement.

informant [ɪnˈfɔːmənt] **n** a informateur *m*, -trice *f*. **my ~ tells me ...** mon informateur me dit que ...; **who is your ~?** de qui tenez-vous cette information?, quelles sont vos sources?; **a reliable ~** un informateur bien renseigné. b (*Ling: also* **native ~**) informateur *m*, -trice *f*.

informatics [ˌɪnfəˈmætɪks] **n**(*NonC*) informatique *f*.

information [ˌɪnfəˈmeɪʃən] 1 **n** a (*NonC*) (*facts*) renseignements *mpl*, information(s) *f(pl)*. **a piece of ~** un renseignement, une information; **to give sb ~ about** *or* **on sth/sb** renseigner qn sur qch/qn; **to get ~ about** *or* **on sth/sb** se renseigner sur qch/qn; **to ask for ~ about** *or* **on sth/sb** demander des renseignements *or* des informations sur qch/qn; **I need more ~ about it** il me faut des renseignements plus complets *or* des informations plus complètes *or* une information plus complète là-dessus; **we are collecting as much ~ as we can on that organization** nous sommes en train de réunir le plus possible d'informations *or* de renseignements sur cette organisation; **we have no ~ on that point** nous n'avons aucune information *or* aucun renseignement là-dessus; **until more ~ is available** jusqu'à plus ample informé; **have you any ~ about the accident?** avez-vous des renseignements *or* des détails sur l'accident?; **the police are seeking ~ about ...** la police recherche des renseignements sur ..., la police enquête sur ... .

b (*knowledge*) connaissances *fpl*, savoir *m*, science *f*. **his ~ on the subject is astonishing** ses connaissances en la matière sont stupéfiantes, son savoir en la matière est stupéfiant; (*on document*) **"for ~"** "à titre d'information *or* de renseignement", "à titre indicatif"; **for your ~, he ...** (*gen*) nous vous signalons *or* informons qu'il ...; (*iro*) permettez-moi de vous dire qu'il ..., au cas où vous ne le sauriez pas (encore), il ...; **I enclose for your ~ a copy of ...** à titre d'information *or* de renseignement je joins une copie de ... .

c (*US Telec*) (service *m* des) renseignements *mpl*.

d (*Jur: pl* **~s**) (*denunciation*) dénonciation *f*; (*charge*) acte *m* d'accusation. **to lay an ~ against sb** (*bring charge against*) former *or* porter une accusation contre qn; (*denounce*) dénoncer qn à la police.

2 **comp ▸information bureau** bureau *m* de renseignements **▸information content** contenu *m* informationnel **▸information desk** accueil *m* **▸information office** = **information bureau ▸information processing** informatique *f* **▸information retrieval** recherche *f* documentaire, retrouve *f* de l'information **▸information retrieval system** système *m* de recherche documentaire **▸information room** (*Police*) (salle *f*) radio *f* **▸information science** informatique *f* **▸information scientist** informaticien(ne) *m(f)* **▸information service** bureau *m* de renseignements **▸information technology** informatique *f*, technologie *f* de l'information **▸information theory** théorie *f* de l'information; *see* **tourist.**

informative [ɪnˈfɔːmətɪv] **adj** *book, meeting* instructif. **he's not very ~ about his plans** il ne s'ouvre pas beaucoup de *or* il ne dit pas grand-chose de ses projets.

informatory [ɪnˈfɔːmətərɪ] **adj** (*Bridge*) d'information. **~ double** contre *m* d'appel.

informed [ɪnˈfɔːmd] **adj** informé, renseigné. **there is a body of ~ opinion which claims that ...** il y a une opinion (bien) informée selon laquelle ...; **~ observers believe that ...** des observateurs informés *or* bien renseignés croient que ...; **an ~ guess** une hypothèse fondée sur la connaissance des faits; *see also* **inform.**

informer [ɪnˈfɔːməʳ] **n** dénonciateur *m*, -trice *f*, délateur *m*, -trice *f*. **police ~** indicateur *m*, -trice *f* (de police); **to turn ~** dénoncer *or* vendre ses complices.

infraction [ɪnˈfrækʃən] **n** *[law, rule etc]* infraction *f* (*of* à).

infra dig* [ˈɪnfrəˈdɪg] **adj** au-dessous de sa (*or* ma *etc*) dignité, indigne *or* au-dessous de soi (*or* moi *etc*), déshonorant.

infrared [ˈɪnfrəˈred] **adj** infrarouge.

infrasonic [ˌɪnfrəˈsɒnɪk] **adj** infrasonore.

infrastructure [ˈɪnfrəˌstrʌktʃəʳ] **n** infrastructure *f*.

infrequency [ɪnˈfriːkwənsɪ] **n** rareté *f*.

infrequent [ɪnˈfriːkwənt] **adj** peu fréquent, rare.

infrequently [ɪnˈfriːkwəntlɪ] **adv** peu fréquemment, rarement.

infringe [ɪnˈfrɪndʒ] 1 **vt** *obligation* contrevenir à; *law, rule* enfreindre, transgresser, contrevenir à. **to ~ copyright** ne pas respecter les droits d'auteur; **to ~ a patent** commettre une contrefaçon (en matière) de brevet. 2 **vi: to ~ (up)on sb's rights** empiéter sur les droits de qn.

infringement [ɪnˈfrɪndʒmənt] **n** (*see* **infringe**) infraction *f* (*of* à); contravention *f* (*of* à); transgression *f* (*of* de). **~ of copyright** non-respect *m* des droits d'auteur; **~ of patent** contrefaçon *f* d'une invention brevetée *or* d'une fabrication brevetée.

infuriate [ɪnˈfjʊərɪeɪt] **vt** rendre furieux, mettre en fureur. **it ~s me** cela me rend fou, cela m'exaspère (*that* que + *subj*); **~d** furieux; **to be ~d to hear that** être furieux d'apprendre que; **to be ~d by sth/sb** être exaspéré par qch/qn.

infuriating [ɪnˈfjʊərɪeɪtɪŋ] **adj** exaspérant, rageant.

infuriatingly [ɪnˈfjʊərɪeɪtɪŋlɪ] **adv** de façon exaspérante. **~ slow** d'une lenteur exaspérante.

infuse [ɪnˈfjuːz] 1 **vt** infuser (*into* dans); (*Culin*) *tea, herbs* (faire) infuser; (*fig*) *ideas etc* infuser, insuffler (*into* à); *enthusiasm* inspirer, insuffler. 2 **vi** (*Culin*) *[tea, herbs]* infuser.

infusion [ɪnˈfjuːʒən] **n** infusion *f*.

ingenious [ɪnˈdʒiːnɪəs] **adj** ingénieux, astucieux.

ingeniously [ɪnˈdʒiːnɪəslɪ] **adv** ingénieusement, astucieusement.

ingenuity [ˌɪndʒɪ'nju:ɪtɪ] n ingéniosité *f*.

ingenuous [ɪn'dʒenjʊəs] adj (*naïve*) ingénu, naïf (*f* naïve), simple; (*candid*) sincère, franc (*f* franche), ouvert.

ingenuously [ɪn'dʒenjʊəslɪ] adv (*naïvely*) ingénument, naïvement; (*candidly*) sincèrement, franchement.

ingenuousness [ɪn'dʒenjʊəsnɪs] n (*see* **ingenuous**) ingénuité *f*, naïveté *f*, simplicité *f*; sincérité *f*, franchise *f*.

ingest [ɪn'dʒest] vt (*Med*) ingérer.

ingestion [ɪn'dʒestʃən] n (*Med*) ingestion *f*.

inglenook ['ɪŋglnʊk] n coin *m* du feu. ~ **fireplace** grande cheminée à l'ancienne.

inglorious [ɪn'glɔ:rɪəs] adj peu glorieux, (*stronger*) déshonorant, honteux.

ingoing ['ɪn,gəʊɪŋ] adj *people, crowd* qui entre; *tenant* nouveau (*f* nouvelle).

ingot ['ɪŋgət] n lingot *m*.

ingrained ['ɪn'greɪnd] adj *habit* invétéré; *prejudice* enraciné. **an ~ hatred of** une haine tenace pour; ~ **dirt** crasse *f*; ~ **with dirt** encrassé.

ingratiate [ɪn'greɪʃɪeɪt] vt: **to ~ o.s. with sb** se faire bien voir de qn, s'insinuer dans les bonnes grâces *or* dans la confiance de qn.

ingratiating [ɪn'greɪʃɪeɪtɪŋ] adj insinuant, patelin, doucereux.

ingratitude [ɪn'grætɪtju:d] n ingratitude *f*.

ingredient [ɪn'gri:dɪənt] n (*Culin etc*) ingrédient *m*; *[character etc]* élément *m*.

ingress ['ɪngres] n (*Jur*) entrée *f*. **to have free ~** avoir le droit d'entrée.

ingrowing ['ɪn,grəʊɪŋ] adj (*Med*) ~ **nail** ongle incarné.

ingrown ['ɪn,grəʊn] adj (*US*) = **ingrowing**.

inguinal ['ɪŋgwɪnl] adj inguinal.

inhabit [ɪn'hæbɪt] vt *town, country* habiter; *house* habiter (dans). **~ed** habité.

inhabitable [ɪn'hæbɪtəbl] adj habitable.

inhabitant [ɪn'hæbɪtənt] n habitant(e) *m(f)*.

inhalant [ɪn'heɪlənt] n inhalant *m*.

inhalation [ˌɪnhə'leɪʃən] n inhalation *f*, aspiration *f*.

inhalator ['ɪnhəleɪtə^r] n (appareil *m*) inhalateur *m*.

inhale [ɪn'heɪl] **1** vt *vapour, gas etc* inhaler; *[smoker]* avaler; *perfume* aspirer, respirer, humer. **2** vi (*in smoking*) avaler la fumée.

inhaler [ɪn'heɪlə^r] n = **inhalator**.

inharmonious [ˌɪnhɑ:'məʊnɪəs] adj inharmonieux, peu harmonieux.

inhere [ɪn'hɪə^r] vi être inhérent (*in* à); être intrinsèque (*to, in* à).

inherent [ɪn'hɪərənt] adj inhérent, naturel (*in, to* à); (*Jur*) propre (*in, to* à). **with all the ~ difficulties** avec toutes les difficultés qui s'y rattachent.

inherently [ɪn'hɪərəntlɪ] adv en soi, fondamentalement; (*Philos*) par inhérence; (*Jur*) en propre. **it's not ~ difficult** ce n'est pas difficile en soi; **he is ~ curious** il est fondamentalement curieux, il est né curieux.

inherit [ɪn'herɪt] vt hériter de, hériter. **to ~ a house/fortune** hériter (d')une maison/(d')une fortune; **to ~ a house/fortune from sb** hériter une maison/une fortune de qn; **he ~ed the estate from his father** il a succédé à son père à la tête du domaine, il a hérité le domaine de son père; **to ~ a title** succéder à un titre; **he is due to ~ on the death of his uncle** il doit hériter à la mort de son oncle; **she ~ed her mother's beauty** elle a hérité (de) la beauté de sa mère; **he ~s his patience/his red hair from his father** il tient sa patience/ses cheveux roux de son père; (*hum*) **I've ~ed my brother's coat** j'ai hérité du manteau de mon frère.

inheritance [ɪn'herɪtəns] n **a** (*NonC*) succession *f*. (*Jur*) **law of ~** droit *m* de succession; ~ **tax** droits *mpl* de succession. **b** héritage *m*, patrimoine *m*. **to come into an ~** faire un héritage; **he wasted all his ~** il a dilapidé tout son héritage; **our national ~** notre patrimoine national.

inheritor [ɪn'herɪtə^r] n (*lit, fig*) héritier *m*, -ière *f*.

inhibit [ɪn'hɪbɪt] vt **a** *[person] impulse, desire* dominer, maîtriser; *[situation, sb's presence]* gêner, entraver; (*Psych*) inhiber. **to ~ sb from doing** (*restrain*) retenir qn de faire; (*prevent*) empêcher qn de faire; **his presence ~ed the discussion** sa présence gênait *or* entravait la discussion; **he was greatly ~ed by his lack of education** son manque d'instruction le gênait beaucoup. **b** (*Jur: prohibit*) interdire, défendre (*sb from doing* à qn de faire).

inhibited [ɪn'hɪbɪtɪd] adj refoulé, inhibé. **he is very ~** il a beaucoup d'inhibitions.

inhibiting [ɪn'hɪbɪtɪŋ] adj inhibiteur (*f* -trice).

inhibition [ˌɪnhɪ'bɪʃən] n **a** (*Physiol, Psych*) inhibition *f*. **b** (*Jur: prohibition*) interdiction *f*.

inhibitory [ɪn'hɪbɪtərɪ] adj **a** (*Physiol, Psych*) inhibiteur (*f* -trice). **b** (*Jur*) prohibitif.

inhospitable [ˌɪnhɒs'pɪtəbl] adj *person, country, climate* inhospitalier; *attitude, remark* inamical, désobligeant.

inhospitably [ˌɪnhɒs'pɪtəblɪ] adv (*see* **inhospitable**) d'une manière inhospitalière *or* peu hospitalière; de façon inamicale *or* désobligeante.

inhospitality ['ɪn,hɒspɪ'tælɪtɪ] n (*see* **inhospitable**) inhospitalité *f*; inimitié *f*.

inhuman [ɪn'hju:mən] adj (*lit, fig*) inhumain.

inhumane [ˌɪnhju(:)'meɪn] adj inhumain, brutal, cruel.

inhumanity [ˌɪnhju:'mænɪtɪ] n inhumanité *f*, brutalité *f*, cruauté *f*.

inhumation [ˌɪnhju:'meɪʃən] n inhumation *f*, enterrement *m*.

inimical [ɪ'nɪmɪkəl] adj (*hostile*) hostile, inamical, ennemi. ~ **to** défavorable à, (l')ennemi de.

inimitable [ɪ'nɪmɪtəbl] adj inimitable.

inimitably [ɪ'nɪmɪtəblɪ] adv d'une façon inimitable.

iniquitous [ɪ'nɪkwɪtəs] adj inique, d'une injustice monstrueuse.

iniquitously [ɪ'nɪkwɪtəslɪ] adv iniquement, monstrueusement.

iniquity [ɪ'nɪkwɪtɪ] n iniquité *f*.

initial [ɪ'nɪʃəl] **1** adj initial, premier, du début; (*Phon*) initial. *[shop, firm etc]* ~ **expenses** frais *mpl* de premier établissement; **in the ~ stages** dans les débuts, au début, dans un premier temps; **my ~ reaction was to refuse** ma première réaction *or* ma réaction initiale a été de refuser; (*Typ*) ~ **letter** initiale *f*; (*Brit Scol*) **I~ Teaching Alphabet** *alphabet phonétique d'apprentissage de la lecture*. **2** n (lettre *f*) initiale *f*. **~s** initiales *fpl*; (*as signature*) parafe *m or* paraphe *m*. **3** vt *letter, document* parafer *or* parapher; (*approve*) viser.

initialize [ɪ'nɪʃə,laɪz] vt (*Comput*) initialiser.

initially [ɪ'nɪʃəlɪ] adv initialement, au commencement, au début, à l'origine.

initiate [ɪ'nɪʃɪeɪt] **1** vt **a** *reform* prendre l'initiative de, promouvoir; *negotiations* entreprendre, amorcer, engager; *enterprise* être à l'origine de, lancer; *scheme, programme* inaugurer, instaurer, mettre en action; *fashion* lancer. (*Jur*) **to ~ proceedings against sb** intenter un procès à qn. **b** (*Rel etc*) *person* initier. **to ~ sb into a society** admettre qn au sein d'une société (secrète); **to ~ sb into a science/a secret** initier qn à une science/un secret. **2** [ɪ'nɪʃɪɪt] adj, n initié(e) *m(f)*.

initiation [ɪ,nɪʃɪ'eɪʃən] **1** n **a** *[negotiations, enterprise]* commencement *m*, début *m*, amorce *f*; *[scheme]* inauguration *f*. **b** (*into society*) admission *f* (*into* dans), initiation *f*; (*into knowledge, secret*) initiation (*into* à). **2** comp ▸**initiation rite** rite *m* d'initiation.

initiative [ɪ'nɪʃətɪv] n initiative *f*. **to take the ~** prendre l'initiative (*in doing sth* de faire qch); **to use one's (own) ~** faire preuve d'initiative; **on one's own ~** de sa propre initiative, par soi-même; **he's got ~** il a de l'initiative.

initiator [ɪ'nɪʃɪ,eɪtə^r] n auteur *m*, instigateur *m*, -trice *f*.

inject [ɪn'dʒekt] vt *liquid, gas* injecter (*into* dans). (*Med*) **to ~ sb with sth** injecter qch à qn, faire une piqûre *or* une injection de qch à qn; **to ~ sb's arm with penicillin, to ~ penicillin into sb's arm** faire une piqûre *or* injection de pénicilline dans le bras de qn; **he ~s himself** il se fait ses piqûres lui-même, il se fait ses propres piqûres; (*fig*) **to ~ sb with enthusiasm** *etc* communiquer *or* insuffler de l'enthousiasme *etc* à qn; **to ~ new life into a club** insuffler une vie nouvelle à un club; **to ~ new capital into a company** injecter *or* apporter de l'argent frais dans une entreprise.

injection [ɪn'dʒekʃən] n (*lit, fig, also Fin: process*) injection *f*; (*Med, Brit Dentistry: shot*) injection, piqûre *f*. **an ~ of new capital** une injection *or* un apport de capital frais.

injector [ɪn'dʒektə^r] n (*Aut*) injecteur *m*; *see* **fuel**.

injudicious [ˌɪndʒʊ'dɪʃəs] adj peu judicieux, malavisé.

injudiciously [ˌɪndʒʊ'dɪʃəslɪ] adv peu judicieusement.

injunction [ɪn'dʒʌŋkʃən] n (*gen*) ordre *m*, recommandation formelle; (*Jur*) injonction *f*; (*court order*) ordonnance *f* (*to do* de faire, *against doing* de ne pas faire). **to give sb strict ~s to do** enjoindre formellement *or* strictement à qn de faire.

injure ['ɪndʒə^r] vt **a** (*Med*) *person, limb* blesser. **to ~ o.s.** se blesser, se faire du mal; **to ~ one's leg** se blesser à la jambe; **fatally ~d** blessé mortellement *or* à mort; **no one was ~d** il n'y a pas eu de blessés, personne n'a été blessé; *see also* **injured**. **b** (*wrong*) *person* faire du tort à, nuire à; (*Jur*) porter préjudice à, léser; (*offend*) blesser, offenser; (*damage*) *reputation, sb's interests, chances, trade* compromettre; (*Comm*) *cargo, goods* avarier. **to ~ sb's feelings** offenser *or* outrager *or* offusquer qn; **to ~ one's health** compromettre sa santé, se détériorer la santé; *see also* **injured**.

injured ['ɪndʒəd] **1** adj (*Med*) blessé; (*maimed*) estropié; (*in accident etc*) accidenté; *limb* blessé; (*fig*) *person* offensé; *look, voice* blessé, offensé; *wife, husband* outragé, trompé. (*Jur*) **the ~ party** la partie lésée. **2** n: **the ~** (*gen*) les blessés *mpl*; (*in road accident etc*) les accidentés *mpl*, les blessés.

injurious [ɪn'dʒʊərɪəs] adj nuisible, préjudiciable (*to* à). ~ **to the health** nuisible *or* préjudiciable à la santé, mauvais pour la santé.

injury ['ɪndʒərɪ] **1** n **a** (*Med*) blessure *f*, lésion *f* (*Med*). **to do sb an ~** blesser qn; **to do o.s. an ~** se blesser, se faire mal; (*Sport*) **3 players have injuries** il y a 3 joueurs (de) blessés; *see* **internal**. **b** (*wrong*) (*to person*) tort *m*, préjudice *m*; (*to reputation etc*) atteinte *f*; (*Jur*) lésion *f*, préjudice. **to the ~ of sb** au détriment *or* au préjudice de qn. **c** (*Comm, Naut*) avarie *f*. **2** comp ▸**injury time** (*Ftbl*) arrêts *mpl* de jeu; **to play injury time** jouer les arrêts de jeu.

injustice [ɪn'dʒʌstɪs] n injustice *f*. **to do sb an ~** être *or* se montrer injuste envers qn.

ink [ɪŋk] **1** n **a** encre *f*. **written in ~** écrit à l'encre; *see* **Indian, invisible** *etc*. **b** *[cuttlefish etc]* encre *f*, sépia *f*. **2** comp ▸**ink bag** (*Zool*) sac *m or* poche *f* d'encre ▸**ink blot** tache *f* d'encre, pâté *m* ▸**ink blot**

test (*Psych*) test *m* de la tache d'encre, test de Rorschach (*SPEC*) ►**ink bottle** bouteille *f* d'encre ►**ink eraser** gomme *f* à encre ►**ink-jet printer** (*Comput*) imprimante *f* à jet d'encre ►**inkpad** tampon *m* (encreur) ►**inkpot** encrier *m* ►**ink rubber** = **ink eraser** ►**inkstain** tache *f* d'encre ►**inkstand** (grand) encrier *m* (de bureau) ►**inkwell** encrier *m* (de pupitre *etc*). 3 **vt** a (*Typ*) *roller* encrer. b (*US* * *fig: sign*) signer.

►**ink in vt sep** repasser à l'encre.

►**ink out vt sep** raturer *or* barrer à l'encre.

►**ink over vt sep** = **ink in.**

inkling ['ɪŋklɪŋ] **n** soupçon *m*, vague *or* petite idée. **I had no ~ that ...** je n'avais pas la moindre idée que ..., je ne me doutais pas du tout que ..., j'étais à cent lieues de me douter que ...; **he had no ~ of it** il n'en avait pas la moindre idée, il ne s'en doutait pas le moins du monde; **we had some ~ of their plan** nous soupçonnions leur plan, nous avions une petite idée de leur plan; **there was no ~ of the disaster to come** rien ne laissait présager le désastre qui allait se produire.

inky ['ɪŋkɪ] **adj** taché *or* couvert d'encre; *book, hand* barbouillé d'encre; *pad, rubber stamp* encré; (*fig*) *darkness etc* noir comme de l'encre, noir d'encre.

inlaid ['ɪn'leɪd] **adj** *brooch, sword etc* incrusté (*with* de); *box, table* marqueté; *metal* damasquiné. **ivory ~ with gold** ivoire incrusté d'or; **~ floor** parquet *m*; **~ work** (*jewels*) incrustation *f*; (*wood*) marqueterie *f*.

inland ['ɪnlænd] 1 **adj** a (*not coastal*) *sea, town* intérieur (*f* -eure). **~ navigation** navigation fluviale; **~ waterways** canaux *mpl* et rivières *fpl*. b (*Brit: domestic*) *mail, trade* intérieur (*f* -eure). (*organization, system*) **I~ Revenue** fisc *m*; (*payments*) **~ revenue** contributions directes; **I~ Revenue stamp** timbre fiscal. 2 [ɪn'lænd] **adv** à l'intérieur. **to go ~** pénétrer à l'intérieur *or* dans les terres.

inlay ['ɪnleɪ] (**vb: pret, ptp inlaid**) 1 **n** incrustation *f*; *[table, box]* marqueterie *f*; *[floor]* parquet *m*; *[metal]* damasquinage *m*. 2 [,ɪn'leɪ] **vt** incruster (*with* de); *table, box* marqueter; *floor* parqueter; *metal* damasquiner; *see also* **inlaid.**

inlet ['ɪnlet] 1 **n** a *[sea]* crique *f*, anse *f*, bras *m* de mer; *[river]* bras de rivière. b (*Tech*) arrivée *f*, admission *f*; *[ventilator]* prise *f* (d'air). 2 **comp** ►**inlet pipe** tuyau *m* d'arrivée; *see* **valve.**

inmate ['ɪnmeɪt] **n** *[house]* occupant(e) *m(f)*, résident(e) *m(f)*; *[prison]* détenu(e) *m(f)*; *[asylum]* interné(e) *m(f)*; *[hospital]* malade *mf*, hospitalisé(e) *m(f)*, pensionnaire* *mf*.

inmost ['ɪnməʊst] **adj** *part* le plus profond; *corner, thoughts, feelings* le plus secret (*f* la plus secrète). **one's ~ being** le tréfonds de son être (*liter*); **in one's ~ heart** dans le fond de son cœur.

inn [ɪn] 1 **n** a (*small, wayside*) auberge *f*; (*larger, wayside*) hostellerie *f*; (*in town*) hôtel *m*; (†: *tavern*) cabaret† *m*. b (*Brit Jur*) **the I~s of Court** les (quatre) écoles de droit (*londoniennes*). 2 **comp** ►**innkeeper** aubergiste *mf*; hôtelier *m*, -ière *f* ►**inn sign** enseigne *f* d'auberge.

innards* ['ɪnədz] **npl** entrailles *fpl*, intérieurs* *mpl*.

innate [ɪ'neɪt] **adj** *knowledge, gift* inné, infus; *sense, wisdom, qualities* inné, naturel, foncier.

innately [ɪ'neɪtlɪ] **adv: ~ aggressive/generous** *etc* d'une agressivité/générosité *etc* innée, naturellement agressif/généreux *etc*.

inner ['ɪnəʳ] 1 **adj** a *room, court* intérieur (*f* -eure), interne, de dedans. **on the ~ side** à l'intérieur, en dedans; **they formed an ~ circle within the society** ils formaient un petit noyau *or* un petit cercle (fermé) *or* une chapelle à l'intérieur de la société; **~ city, ~-city areas** quartiers *mpl* déshérités (*à l'intérieur de la ville*); **~-city** *school, children, renewal* des quartiers déshérités (*à l'intérieur de la ville*); (*Naut*) **~ dock** arrière-bassin *m*; (*Anat*) **~ ear** oreille *f* interne; **~ harbour** arrière-port *m*; **the ~ man** (*spiritual self*) l'homme intérieur; (*hum: stomach*) l'estomac *m*; *[shoe]* **~ sole** semelle *f* (intérieure); *[tyre]* **~ tube** chambre *f* à air.

b (*fig*) *emotions, thoughts* intime, secret (*f* -ète), profond; *life* intérieur (*f* -eure). **~ meaning** sens *m* intime *or* profond.

2 **n** (*Archery etc*) zone *f* entourant le visuel.

3 **comp** ►**inner-city** *see* **1a** ►**inner-directed** (*esp US*) individualiste ►**innermost** = **inmost** ►**inner spring mattress** (*US*) matelas *m* à ressorts.

inning ['ɪnɪŋ] **n** (*Baseball*) tour *m* de batte.

innings ['ɪnɪŋz] **n (pl inv)** (*Cricket*) tour *m* de batte; (*fig*) tour. (*fig*) **I've had a good ~** j'ai bien profité de l'existence (*etc*).

innocence ['ɪnəsns] **n** (*gen, Jur*) innocence *f*; (*simplicity*) innocence, naïveté *f*, candeur *f*. **to put on an air of ~** faire l'innocent; **in all ~** en toute innocence; **in his ~ he believed it all** naïf comme il (l')est (*or* (l')était) *or* dans son innocence il a tout cru.

Innocent ['ɪnəsnt] **n** (*Papal name*) Innocent *m*.

innocent ['ɪnəsnt] 1 **adj** (*Jur etc*) innocent, non coupable (*of* de); (*Rel*) innocent, sans péché, pur; (*simple*) naïf (*f* naïve), candide, innocent; *question, remark* innocent, sans malice; *mistake* innocent; *amusement, pastime* innocent, inoffensif. **as ~ as a newborn babe** innocent comme l'enfant qui vient de naître; **to put on an ~ air** faire l'innocent; (*Jur: of patent*) **~ infringement** contrefaçon *f* involontaire; **he was ~ of any desire to harm her** il était dénué de tout désir de *or* il n'avait nulle intention de lui faire du mal; **she was dressed in black, ~ of all jewellery** elle était vêtue de noir et sans aucun bijou; **room ~ of all ornament** pièce dépourvue de tout ornement.

2 **n: he's one of Nature's ~s*, he's a bit of an ~*** c'est un grand innocent; (*Rel*) **Massacre of the Holy I~s** massacre *m* des saints Innocents; **Holy I~s' Day** jour *m* des saints Innocents.

innocently ['ɪnəsntlɪ] **adv** innocemment.

innocuous [ɪ'nɒkjʊəs] **adj** inoffensif.

innovate ['ɪnəʊveɪt] **vti** innover.

innovation [,ɪnəʊ'veɪʃən] **n** innovation *f* (*in* en, en matière de); changement *m* (*in* dans, en matière de). **to make ~s in sth** apporter des innovations *or* des changements à qch; **scientific/technical ~s** innovations scientifiques/techniques.

innovative ['ɪnəʊ,veɪtɪv] **adj** innovateur (*f* -trice), novateur (*f* -trice).

innovator ['ɪnəʊveɪtəʳ] **n** innovateur *m*, -trice *f*, novateur *m*, -trice *f*.

innovatory ['ɪnəʊ,veɪtərɪ] **adj** = **innovative.**

innuendo [,ɪnjʊ'endəʊ] **n, pl ~(e)s** insinuation *f*, allusion *f* (malveillante). **to make ~(e)s against sb** faire des insinuations (malveillantes) à l'égard de qn.

Innuit ['ɪnjuːɪt] = **Inuit.**

innumerable [ɪ'njuːmərəbl] **adj** innombrable, sans nombre. **there are ~ reasons** il y a une infinité de raisons; **I've told you ~ times** je te l'ai dit cent fois *or* trente-six fois.

inoculate [ɪ'nɒkjʊleɪt] **vt** a (*Med*) *person* vacciner (*against* contre). b (*in lab*) **to ~ a rat** *etc* **with sth** inoculer qch à un rat *etc*.

inoculation [ɪ,nɒkjʊ'leɪʃən] **n** (*Med*) inoculation *f*.

inoffensive [,ɪnə'fensɪv] **adj** inoffensif.

inoperable [ɪn'ɒpərəbl] **adj** inopérable.

inoperative [ɪn'ɒpərətɪv] **adj** inopérant.

inopportune [ɪn'ɒpətjuːn] **adj** *arrival, demand, request* inopportun, intempestif; *moment* inopportun, mal choisi, peu propice; *remark* déplacé.

inopportunely [ɪn'ɒpətjuːnlɪ] **adv** *speak* inopportunément, mal à propos; *arrive, demand* inopportunément, intempestivement.

inordinate [ɪ'nɔːdɪnɪt] **adj** *size* démesuré; *quantity, demands* excessif; *passion* immodéré. **an ~ amount of time** un temps fou*; **an ~ amount of butter** énormément de beurre; **an ~ sum (of money)** une somme exorbitante *or* astronomique.

inordinately [ɪ'nɔːdɪnɪtlɪ] **adv** (*too*) *hot, heavy etc* démesurément, immodérément, excessivement; (*very*) *pleased, rich etc* excessivement.

inorganic [,ɪnɔː'gænɪk] **adj** inorganique.

inpatient ['ɪn,peɪʃənt] **n** malade *mf* hospitalisé(e).

input ['ɪnpʊt] 1 **n** a (*contribution*) contribution *f*, participation *f*; (*of funds, labour*) apport *m*; (*ideas*) idées *fpl*. **~s** (*Econ*) facteurs *mpl* de production, (facteurs *mpl*) intrants *mpl*; (*Ind*) (*materials, parts*) consommations *fpl* intermédiaires; **we need a regular ~ of new ideas** nous avons besoin d'un flux constant de nouvelles idées.

b (*Elec*) énergie *f*, puissance *f*; (*Tech*) *[machine]* consommation *f*.

c (*Comput*) (*data*) données *fpl* à traiter; (*act of inputting*) entrée *f* (de données).

2 **comp** ►**input data** (*Comput*) données *fpl* en entrée ►**input/output** (*Comput*) entrée-sortie *f* ►**input/output device** (*Comput*) périphérique *m* entrée-sortie ►**input/output table** (*Econ*) tableau *m* des échanges interindustriels.

3 **vt** (*Comput*) entrer, introduire (*into* dans).

inquest ['ɪnkwest] **n** (*Jur*) enquête *f* (criminelle); *see* **coroner.**

inquietude [ɪn'kwaɪətjuːd] **n** inquiétude *f*.

inquire [ɪn'kwaɪəʳ] 1 **vi** se renseigner (*about* sur), s'informer (*about, after* de); (*ask*) demander. **to ~ after sb/sth** demander des nouvelles de qn/qch, s'informer *or* s'enquérir de qn/qch; **to ~ for sb** demander qn; **to ~ into** *subject* faire des recherches *or* des investigations sur; *possibilities* se renseigner sur, se documenter sur, examiner; (*Admin, Jur*) *event, situation* enquêter sur, faire une enquête sur; **to ~ into the truth of sth** vérifier la véracité de qch; **I'll go and ~** je vais demander; **~ at the office** demandez au bureau, renseignez-vous au bureau.

2 **vt** (*gen*) demander, s'informer de, s'enquérir de; *the time, a name* demander. **to ~ the way of** *or* **from sb** demander le (*or* son) chemin à qn; **to ~ the price of sth from sb** demander à qn le prix de qch, s'enquérir *or* s'informer du prix de qch auprès de qn; **"~ within"** "renseignements ici", "s'adresser ici"; **"~ at the information desk"** "s'adresser aux renseignements *or* au bureau de renseignements"; **he ~d how to get to the theatre** il a demandé le chemin du théâtre; **he ~d what she wanted** il a demandé ce qu'elle voulait.

inquiring [ɪn'kwaɪərɪŋ] **adj** *attitude, frame of mind* curieux, investigateur (*f* -trice); *look* interrogateur (*f* -trice).

inquiringly [ɪn'kwaɪərɪŋlɪ] **adv** *look* d'un air interrogateur; *say* d'un ton interrogateur. **to look ~ at sb** regarder qn d'un air interrogateur, interroger qn du regard.

inquiry [ɪn'kwaɪərɪ] 1 **n** a (*from individual*) demande *f* de renseignements. **to make inquiries about sb/sth (of sb)** se renseigner sur qn/qch (auprès de qn), demander des renseignements sur qn/qch (à qn) (*see also* **1b**); **on ~ he found that ...** renseignements pris il a découvert que ...; **a look of ~** un regard interrogateur; **he gave me a look of ~** il m'a interrogé du regard; **"all inquiries to ..."** "pour tous renseignements s'adresser à ...".

b (*Admin, Jur*) enquête *f*, investigation *f*. **to set up** *or* **open an ~ into** ouvrir une enquête sur; **committee of ~** commission *f* d'enquête; **to hold an ~ into** enquêter *or* faire une enquête sur; **judicial ~** enquête judiciaire; (*Jur*) **remanded for further ~** renvoyé pour complément d'instruction *or* d'information; **this is a fruitful line of ~** c'est une bonne direction dans laquelle pousser cette enquête; **there will have to be an ~ into this** il va falloir enquêter *or* faire une enquête sur cette affaire; **the police are making inquiries** la police enquête; *see* **help, officer.**
c (*Telec, Rail etc*) **the Inquiries** les renseignements *mpl*.
2 **comp ▸inquiry agent** détective privé **▸inquiry desk, inquiry office** (bureau *m* de) renseignements *mpl*.

inquisition [ˌɪnkwɪˈzɪʃən] **n** investigation *f*, recherches *fpl*; (*Jur*) enquête *f* (judiciaire). (*Rel*) **the I~** l'Inquisition *f*.

inquisitive [ɪnˈkwɪzɪtɪv] **adj** *person, mind* curieux; (*pej*) inquisiteur (*f* -trice), indiscret (*f* -ète), (trop) curieux.

inquisitively [ɪnˈkwɪzɪtɪvlɪ] **adv** avec curiosité; (*pej*) indiscrètement, trop curieusement.

inquisitiveness [ɪnˈkwɪzɪtɪvnɪs] **n** curiosité *f*; (*pej*) curiosité indiscrète, indiscrétion *f*.

inquisitor [ɪnˈkwɪzɪtəʳ] **n** (*Jur*) enquêteur *m*, -euse *f*; (*Rel*) inquisiteur *m*.

inquisitorial [ɪnˌkwɪzɪˈtɔːrɪəl] **adj** inquisitorial.

inquorate [ɪnˈkwɔːreɪt] **adj** (*Admin*) qui n'a pas le quorum, où le quorum n'est pas atteint.

inroad [ˈɪnrəʊd] **n** (*Mil*) incursion *f* (*into* en, dans). (*fig*) **to make ~s upon** *or* **into** *sb's rights* empiéter sur; *savings, majority, numbers* entamer, ébrécher; *supplies* entamer.

inrush [ˈɪnˌrʌʃ] **n** *[water, people etc]* irruption *f*.

ins. (**abbr of inches**) po.

insalubrious [ˌɪnsəˈluːbrɪəs] **adj** (*gen*) insalubre, malsain; (*fig*) *district* peu recommandable.

insane [ɪnˈseɪn] 1 **adj** (*Med*) aliéné, dément; (*gen*) *person, desire* fou (*f* folle), insensé; *project* démentiel. **to become ~** perdre la raison; **to drive sb ~** rendre qn fou; **he must be ~ to think of going** il faut qu'il soit fou pour envisager d'y aller; **you must be ~!** tu es fou!; (*US*) **~ asylum** asile *m* d'aliénés; *see* **certify.** 2 **npl** (*Med*) **the ~** les aliénés *mpl*, les malades *mpl* psychiatriques.

insanely [ɪnˈseɪnlɪ] **adv** *laugh* comme un fou (*f* une folle); *behave* de façon insensée. **to act/talk ~** faire/dire des insanités; **~ jealous** d'une jalousie maladive.

insanitary [ɪnˈsænɪtərɪ] **adj** insalubre, malsain.

insanity [ɪnˈsænɪtɪ] **n** (*Med*) aliénation mentale, démence *f*; (*gen*) folie *f*, démence, insanité *f*.

insatiable [ɪnˈseɪʃəbl] **adj** insatiable (*of* de).

insatiably [ɪnˈseɪʃəblɪ] **adv** *eat* avec une faim insatiable; *kiss* avec une passion insatiable. **to be ~ hungry/curious/greedy** avoir une faim/être d'une curiosité/être d'une avarice insatiable.

inscribe [ɪnˈskraɪb] **vt** a (*in book etc*) inscrire (*in* dans); (*on monument etc*) inscrire, graver (*on* sur); *surface etc* marquer, graver; (*fig*) *ideas* graver, inscrire, fixer (*on* sur). **to ~ a tomb with a name** *or* **a name on a tomb** graver un nom sur une tombe; **a watch ~d with his name** une montre gravée à son nom; (*Fin*) **~d stock** titres nominatifs *or* inscrits. b (*dedicate*) *book* dédier, dédicacer (*to* à).

inscription [ɪnˈskrɪpʃən] **n** (*on coin, monument etc*) inscription *f*; (*on cartoon*) légende *f*; (*dedication*) dédicace *f*.

inscrutability [ɪnˌskruːtəˈbɪlɪtɪ] **n** impénétrabilité *f* (*fig*).

inscrutable [ɪnˈskruːtəbl] **adj** impénétrable, insondable. **~ face** visage impénétrable *or* fermé.

insect [ˈɪnsekt] 1 **n** insecte *m*. 2 **comp ▸insect bite** piqûre *f*, morsure *f* d'insecte **▸insect eater** insectivore *m* **▸insect powder** poudre *f* insecticide **▸insect repellent adj** anti-insecte *inv* ◊ **n** (*cream, ointment etc*) crème *f* anti-insecte *inv* **▸insect spray** aérosol *m* *or* bombe *f* insecticide.

insecticide [ɪnˈsektɪsaɪd] **adj, n** insecticide (*m*).

insectivorous [ˌɪnsekˈtɪvərəs] **adj** insectivore.

insecure [ˌɪnsɪˈkjʊəʳ] **adj** a (*not firm, badly fixed*) *bolt, nail, padlock* peu solide, qui tient mal; *rope* mal attaché, peu solide; *foothold* mal assuré; *structure, ladder* branlant, mal affermi, qui tient mal; *lock* peu sûr; *door, window* qui ferme mal. b (*uncertain*) *career, future* incertain. c (*dangerous*) *place* peu sûr, exposé au danger. d (*worried*) *person* anxieux, inquiet (*f* -ète); (*Psych etc*) insécurisé. **he is very ~** c'est un anxieux.

insecurity [ˌɪnsɪˈkjʊərɪtɪ] **n** (*also Psych*) insécurité *f*.

inseminate [ɪnˈsemɪneɪt] **vt** inséminer.

insemination [ɪnˌsemɪˈneɪʃən] **n** insémination *f*; *see* **artificial.**

insensate [ɪnˈsenseɪt] **adj** (*senseless*) insensé; (*inanimate*) inanimé, insensible; (*unfeeling*) insensible.

insensibility [ɪnˌsensəˈbɪlɪtɪ] **n** a (*Med: unconsciousness*) insensibilité *f*, inconscience *f*. b (*fig: unfeelingness*) insensibilité *f* (*to* à), indifférence *f* (*to* à, pour).

insensible [ɪnˈsensəbl] **adj** a (*Med: unconscious*) inconscient, sans connaissance. **the blow knocked him ~** le coup lui fit perdre connaissance; **he drank himself ~** il a bu à en tomber ivre mort. b (*without sensation*) *limb etc* insensible. **~ to cold/heat** insensible au froid/à la chaleur. c (*emotionless*) insensible, indifférent (*to* à). d (*unaware*) **~ of danger** *etc* insensible *or* indifférent au danger *etc*. e (*imperceptible*) *change, shift* insensible, imperceptible. **by ~ degrees** petit à petit, insensiblement, imperceptiblement.

insensibly [ɪnˈsensɪblɪ] **adv** *change etc* insensiblement, imperceptiblement.

insensitive [ɪnˈsensɪtɪv] **adj** (*all senses*) insensible (*to* à).

insensitivity [ɪnˌsensɪˈtɪvɪtɪ] **n** insensibilité *f*.

inseparable [ɪnˈsepərəbl] **adj** inséparable (*from* de).

inseparably [ɪnˈsepərəblɪ] **adv** *join* indissolublement, inséparablement.

insert [ɪnˈsɜːt] 1 **vt** insérer (*in, into* dans, *between* entre); *paragraph, word etc* insérer, introduire (*in* dans), ajouter (*in* à); *key, knife, finger* insérer, introduire, enfoncer (*in* dans); (*Typ*) *page, leaflet* encarter, insérer; *advertisement* insérer (*in* dans). 2 [ˈɪnsɜːt] **n** (*extra pages*) encart *m*; (*in print: advertisement, note, word*) insertion *f*; (*Tech*) pièce insérée, ajout *m*; (*Sewing*) entre-deux *m inv*, incrustation *f*.

insertion [ɪnˈsɜːʃən] 1 **n** a (*NonC*) insertion *f*, introduction *f*. b = **insert 2.** 2 **comp ▸insertion mark** (*Typ etc*) signe *m* d'insertion.

inset [ˈɪnset] **pret, ptp inset** 1 **vt** *map, illustration* insérer en cartouche (*into* dans); *jewel, ornamentation* insérer (*into* dans), incruster (*into* sur); *lace* incruster (*into* sur); *leaflet* encarter, insérer (*into* dans); (*in typing, printing*) *word, line* rentrer. (*Sewing*) **to ~ a panel into a skirt** rapporter un panneau sur une jupe; **to ~ a map into the corner of a larger one** insérer une carte en cartouche sur une plus grande. 2 **n** (*diagram/map/portrait etc*) schéma *m*/carte *f*/portrait *m etc* en cartouche; (*Typ: leaflet, pages*) encart *m*; (*Sewing*) entre-deux *m inv*, incrustation *f*. 3 **adj** *gem, pearl etc* enchâssé, serti. **~ with** incrusté de.

inshore [ˈɪnˈʃɔːʳ] 1 **adj** *area, fisherman, navigation* côtier; *fishing boat* côtier, caboteur. **~ fishing, ~ fisheries** pêche côtière; **~ lifeboat** canot *m* de sauvetage côtier; **~ wind** vent *m* de mer. 2 **adv** *be, fish* près de la côte; *blow, flow, go* vers la côte.

inside [ˈɪnˈsaɪd] (*phr vb elem*) 1 **adv** a dedans, au-dedans, à l'intérieur. **~ and outside** au-dedans et au-dehors; **come** *or* **step ~!** entrez (donc)!; **it is warmer ~** il fait plus chaud à l'intérieur *or* dedans; **wait for me ~** attendez-moi à l'intérieur.
b (*⁑: in jail*) en taule⁑, à l'ombre*, au frais⁑.
2 **prep** a (*of place*) à l'intérieur de, dans. **he was waiting ~ the house** il attendait à l'intérieur (de la maison); **she was standing just ~ the gate** (*seen from inside*) elle était juste de ce côté-ci de la barrière; (*seen from outside*) elle était juste de l'autre côté de la barrière.
b (*of time*) en moins de. **he came back ~ 3 minutes** *or* (*US*) **~ of 3 minutes** il est revenu en moins de trois minutes; (*Sport*) **he was well ~ the record time** il avait largement battu le record.
3 **n** a dedans *m*, intérieur *m*; *[house, box]* intérieur. **on the ~** en dedans, au-dedans, à l'intérieur; **walk on the ~ of the pavement** *or* (*US*) **sidewalk** marchez sur le trottoir du côté maisons; **on the ~ of the road** (*Brit*) ≃ sur la gauche; (*US, Europe etc*) ≃ sur la droite; **the door is bolted on** *or* **from the ~** la porte est fermée au verrou du dedans; (*fig*) **to know the ~ of an affair** connaître les dessous *mpl* d'une affaire; **I see the firm from the ~** je vois la compagnie de l'intérieur.
b **your coat is ~ out** ton manteau est à l'envers; **the wind blew the umbrella ~ out** le vent a retourné le parapluie; **I turned the bag ~ out but there was no money in it** j'ai retourné le sac (entièrement) mais il n'y avait pas d'argent dedans; (*fig*) **the children turned everything ~ out** les enfants ont tout mis sens dessus dessous; **he knows his subject ~ out** il connaît son sujet à fond; **he knows the district ~ out** il connaît le quartier comme sa poche.
c (**: stomach: also ~s*) ventre *m*. **he's got a pain in his ~(s)** il a mal au ventre *or* aux entrailles (*hum*); **my ~ is playing me up** j'ai les intestins détraqués, je suis tout détraqué.
4 **adj** a intérieur (*f* -eure), d'intérieur. **~ pocket** poche intérieure; **~ leg measurement** mesure *f* *or* hauteur *f* de l'entrejambe; *[plane]* **~ seat** place *f* de fenêtre; (*fig*) **to get ~ information** obtenir des renseignements *mpl* à la source; (*Press*) **"the ~ story of the plot"** "le complot raconté par un des participants"; (*of theft etc*) **it must have been an ~ job*** c'est un coup qui a dû être monté de l'intérieur *or* par quelqu'un de la maison.
b (*Aut*) *wheel, headlight etc* (*Brit*) gauche; (*US, Europe etc*) droit. **the ~ lane** (*Brit*) ≃ la voie de gauche; (*US, Europe etc*) ≃ la voie de droite; **to be on** *or* **hold the ~ track** (*Sport*) être à la corde, tenir la corde; (*fig*) être le mieux placé pour l'emporter.
5 **comp ▸inside-forward** (*Sport*) intérieur *m*, inter* *m* **▸inside-left/-right** intérieur *m* gauche/droit.

insider [ɪnˈsaɪdəʳ] 1 **n** (*gen*) quelqu'un qui connaît les choses de l'intérieur; (*in firm, organization*) quelqu'un qui est dans la place; (*esp sb with influence, knowledge, also St Ex*) initié(e) *m(f)*. 2 **comp ▸insider dealing** *or* **trading** (*Jur, Fin*) délit *m* d'initiés.

insidious [ɪnˈsɪdɪəs] **adj** *promises, flattery* insidieux, traître (*f* traîtresse), trompeur; *enemy, disease* insidieux; *argument* insidieux, captieux, spécieux.

insidiously [ɪnˈsɪdɪəslɪ] **adv** insidieusement.

insight [ˈɪnsaɪt] **n** a (*discernment*) pénétration *f*, perspicacité *f*. b (*glimpse*) aperçu *m*, idée *f* (*into* de). **I got** *or* **gained an ~ into his way of thinking** cela m'a permis de comprendre *or* de pénétrer sa façon de penser; **that will give you an ~ into his reasons for doing it** cela vous éclairera sur les raisons qui l'ont poussé à le faire.

insignia [ɪn'sɪgnɪə] n, pl ~s *or* ~ insigne *m*.

insignificance [ˌɪnsɪg'nɪfɪkəns] n insignifiance *f*; *see* **pale**[1].

insignificant [ˌɪnsɪg'nɪfɪkənt] adj *detail, fact, person* insignifiant, sans importance; *amount, quantity* insignifiant, négligeable.

insincere [ˌɪnsɪn'sɪəʳ] adj *person* pas sincère, hypocrite, de mauvaise foi; *book, smile, remark* faux (*f* fausse), hypocrite.

insincerity [ˌɪnsɪn'serɪtɪ] n manque *m* de sincérité, fausseté *f*, hypocrisie *f*.

insinuate [ɪn'sɪnjʊeɪt] vt a insinuer (*into* dans). **to ~ o.s. into sb's favour** s'insinuer dans les bonnes grâces de qn. b (*hint, suggest*) laisser entendre, insinuer (*sth to sb* qch à qn, *that* que); sous-entendre (*sth* qch, *that* que). **what are you insinuating?** que voulez-vous dire *or* insinuer par là?

insinuating [ɪn'sɪnjʊeɪtɪŋ] adj insinuant.

insinuation [ɪnˌsɪnjʊ'eɪʃən] n a (*NonC*) insinuation *f*. b (*suggestion*) insinuation *f*, allusion *f*, sous-entendu *m*.

insipid [ɪn'sɪpɪd] adj insipide, fade.

insipidity [ˌɪnsɪ'pɪdɪtɪ] n insipidité *f*, fadeur *f*.

insist [ɪn'sɪst] 1 vi (*demand, urge*) insister; (*stress*) insister, appuyer. **to ~ on doing** insister pour faire, vouloir absolument faire, tenir à faire; **I ~ on your coming** je veux absolument que tu viennes; **he ~ed on my waiting for him** il a tenu à ce que *or* insisté pour que je l'attende; **they ~ed on silence/our help** ils ont exigé le silence/notre aide; **if you ~** si vous insistez, si vous y tenez; **I shan't ~ if you object** si vous avez des objections je n'insisterai pas; **please don't ~, I should like to pay for it!** inutile d'insister, je tiens à le payer!; **if he refuses, I will ~** s'il refuse, j'insisterai; **he ~s on the justice of his claim** il affirme *or* soutient *or* maintient que sa revendication est juste; **to ~ on a point in a discussion** appuyer *or* insister sur un point dans une discussion.

2 vt a insister. **I must ~ that you let me help** j'insiste pour que tu me permettes d'aider; **she ~ed that I should come** elle a insisté pour que je vienne; **I ~ that you should come** je veux absolument que tu viennes.

b affirmer, soutenir, maintenir. **he ~s that he has seen her before** il affirme *or* soutient *or* maintient qu'il l'a déjà vue.

insistence [ɪn'sɪstəns] n insistance *f*. **his ~ on coming with me** l'insistance qu'il met (*or* a mis *etc*) à vouloir venir avec moi; **his ~ on his innocence** ses protestations *fpl* d'innocence; **with ~** avec insistance, avec instance; **I did it on** *or* **at his ~** je l'ai fait parce qu'il a insisté.

insistent [ɪn'sɪstənt] adj *person* insistant, pressant; *demands etc* instant, insistant, pressant. **he was most ~ about it** il a beaucoup insisté là-dessus, il a été très pressant; **... he said in ~ tones** ... dit-il d'une voix pressante.

insistently [ɪn'sɪstəntlɪ] adv avec insistance, avec instance, instamment; (*repeatedly*) avec insistance, à maintes reprises.

insole ['ɪnˌsəʊl] n (*removable sole*) semelle intérieure; (*part of shoe*) première *f*.

insolence ['ɪnsələns] n (*NonC*) insolence *f* (*to* envers).

insolent ['ɪnsələnt] adj insolent (*to* envers).

insolently ['ɪnsələntlɪ] adv insolemment.

insolubility [ɪnˌsɒljʊ'bɪlɪtɪ] n insolubilité *f*.

insoluble [ɪn'sɒljʊbl] adj insoluble.

insolvable [ɪn'sɒlvəbl] adj insoluble.

insolvency [ɪn'sɒlvənsɪ] n (*gen*) insolvabilité *f*; (*bankruptcy*) faillite *f*.

insolvent [ɪn'sɒlvənt] adj (*gen*) insolvable; (*bankrupt*) en faillite, en état de cessation de paiement (*Jur*). **to become ~** *[trader etc]* tomber en *or* faire faillite; *[individual]* tomber en déconfiture; **to declare oneself ~** *[trader etc]* déposer son bilan; *[individual]* se déclarer insolvable.

insomnia [ɪn'sɒmnɪə] n insomnie *f*.

insomniac [ɪn'sɒmnɪæk] adj, n insomniaque (*mf*).

insomuch [ˌɪnsəʊ'mʌtʃ] adv: **~ that** à tel point *or* au point *or* tellement que; **~ as** d'autant que.

insouciance [ɪn'suːsɪəns] n insouciance *f*.

insp. abbr of **inspector**.

inspect [ɪn'spekt] vt a (*examine*) *document, object* examiner (avec attention *or* de près), inspecter; (*Brit*) *ticket* contrôler; (*Customs*) *luggage* visiter; *machinery* inspecter, vérifier; (*Mil, Pol*) *weapon sites* inspecter; *school, teacher* inspecter. (*Jur*) **right to ~** droit *m* de regard (*sth* sur qch). b (*formally*) *troops etc* (*check*) inspecter; (*review*) passer en revue.

inspection [ɪn'spekʃən] 1 n a *[document, object]* examen *m* (attentif); *[ticket]* contrôle *m*; *[machinery]* vérification *f*, inspection *f*; *[school]* (visite *f* d')inspection. **close ~** (*gen*) examen minutieux; (*for checking purposes*) inspection; **customs ~** visite douanière *or* de douane; **factory ~** inspection d'usine; **on ~ everything proved normal** une vérification a permis de s'assurer que tout était normal. b *[troops etc]* (*check*) inspection *f*; (*review*) revue *f*. 2 comp ▸**inspection pit** (*Aut*) fosse *f* (à réparations).

inspector [ɪn'spektəʳ] 1 n a (*gen*) inspecteur *m*, -trice *f*; (*Brit: on bus, train*) contrôleur *m*, -euse *f*. **tax ~**, (*Brit, frm*) **~ of taxes** contrôleur *m or* inspecteur *m* des impôts. b (*Brit*) **police ~** ≃ inspecteur *m* (de police); *see* **chief**. c (*Brit Scol*) **(schools) ~, ~ of schools** (*secondary*) ≃ inspecteur *m*, -trice *f* d'académie; (*primary*) ≃ inspecteur, -trice primaire. 2 comp ▸**inspector general** (pl **~s ~**) inspecteur *m* général; *see also* **1**.

inspectorate [ɪn'spektərɪt] n (*body of inspectors*) corps *m* des inspecteurs, inspection *f*; (*office*) inspection.

inspiration [ˌɪnspə'reɪʃən] n a (*NonC*) inspiration *f*. **to draw one's ~ from** s'inspirer de. b *[person, thing]* **to be an ~ to sb** être une source d'inspiration pour qn; **you've been an ~ to us all** vous avez été notre source d'inspiration à tous. c (*good idea*) inspiration *f*. **to have a sudden ~** avoir une inspiration subite.

inspirational [ˌɪnspə'reɪʃənl] adj *book, tale etc* qui suscite l'inspiration, inspirant; *leader* qui inspire ses adeptes; (*Rel*) édifiant. **to have ~ value** susciter l'inspiration, être inspirant.

inspire [ɪn'spaɪəʳ] vt *person* inspirer (*to do* à faire), stimuler, enthousiasmer; *work of art, action, decision* inspirer. **to ~ confidence in sb, to ~ sb with confidence** inspirer confiance à qn; **to ~ courage in sb** insuffler du courage à qn; **to ~ sb with an idea** inspirer une idée à qn; **her beauty ~d him** *or* **he was ~d by her beauty to write the song** inspiré par sa beauté il a écrit la chanson; **what ~d you to offer to help?** qu'est-ce qui vous a donné l'idée de *or* où avez-vous pris l'idée de proposer votre aide?

inspired [ɪn'spaɪəd] adj *poet, artist, book* inspiré; *moment* d'inspiration; (*fig*) *guess, idea, gesture* brillant. **an ~ idea** (*or* **guess** *or* **gesture** *etc*) une inspiration.

inspiring [ɪn'spaɪərɪŋ] adj *book, poem etc* qui suscite l'inspiration, inspirant; *leader* qui inspire ses adeptes. **this subject isn't particularly ~** ce sujet n'a rien de particulièrement inspirant *or* ne m'inspire pas particulièrement.

inst. adv (*Comm*) (abbr of **instant**) courant. **the 16th ~** le 16 courant *or* de ce mois.

instability [ˌɪnstə'bɪlɪtɪ] n instabilité *f*.

instal(l) [ɪn'stɔːl] vt (*also Rel*) installer. **to ~ o.s. in** s'installer dans.

installation [ˌɪnstə'leɪʃən] n (*all senses*) installation *f*.

instalment, (*US*) **installment** [ɪn'stɔːlmənt] 1 n a (*payment*) acompte *m*, versement partiel *or* échelonné; *[loan, investment, credit etc]* tranche *f*, versement. **to pay an ~** faire un versement partiel, verser un acompte *or* des arrhes *fpl*; **to pay in ~s** *or* **by ~s** payer en plusieurs versements *or* par acomptes *or* par traites échelonnées; **~ on account** acompte provisionnel; **annual ~** versement annuel, annuité *f*; **monthly ~** versement mensuel, mensualité *f*.

b *[story, serial]* épisode *m*; *[book]* fascicule *m*, livraison *f*. (*TV etc*) **this is the first ~ of a 6-part serial** voici le premier épisode d'un feuilleton qui en comportera 6; **this story will appear in ~s over the next 8 weeks** ce récit paraîtra par épisodes pendant les 8 semaines à venir; **to publish a work in ~s** publier un ouvrage par fascicules.

2 comp ▸**installment plan** (*US*) contrat *m* de crédit; **to buy on the installment plan** acheter à crédit.

instance ['ɪnstəns] 1 n a (*example*) exemple *m*, cas *m*; (*occasion*) circonstance *f*, occasion *f*. **for ~** par exemple; **in the present ~** dans le cas actuel *or* présent, dans cette circonstance; **in many ~s** dans bien des cas; **in the first ~** en premier lieu; **as an ~ of** comme exemple de; **let's take an actual ~** prenons un exemple *or* un cas concret; **this is an ~ of what I was talking about** c'est un exemple de ce dont je parlais. b (*Jur*) **at the ~ of** sur *or* à la demande de, sur l'instance de. 2 vt donner en exemple, citer en exemple, (*more formally*) faire état de.

instant ['ɪnstənt] 1 adj a *obedience, relief* immédiat, instantané; *need* urgent, pressant. **this calls for ~ action** ceci nécessite des mesures immédiates; **~ camera/photography** appareil *m* (photo)/photographie *f* à développement instantané; (*TV*) **~ replay** *répétition immédiate d'une séquence;* (*slow-motion*) ralenti *m*.

b (*Culin*) *coffee* soluble; *potatoes* déshydraté; *food* à préparation rapide. **~ soup** potage *m* (instantané) en poudre.

c (*Comm*) courant. **your letter of the 10th instant** votre lettre du 10 courant.

2 n instant *m*, moment *m*. **come here this ~** viens ici tout de suite *or* immédiatement *or* à l'instant; **for an ~** pendant un instant, l'espace d'un instant; **on the ~** tout de suite, à l'instant, immédiatement, sur-le-champ; **the next ~** l'instant d'après; **I did it in an ~** je l'ai fait en un instant; **I'll be ready in an ~** je serai prêt dans un instant; **he left the ~ he heard the news** il est parti dès qu'il *or* aussitôt qu'il a appris la nouvelle.

instantaneous [ˌɪnstən'teɪnɪəs] adj instantané.

instantaneously [ˌɪnstən'teɪnɪəslɪ] adv instantanément.

instantly ['ɪnstəntlɪ] adv à l'instant, sur-le-champ, immédiatement, tout de suite.

instead [ɪn'sted] adv au lieu de cela, plutôt. **the water is not good, drink wine ~** l'eau n'est pas bonne, buvez plutôt du vin; **if he isn't going, I shall go ~** s'il n'y va pas, j'irai à sa place; **I didn't go home, I went to the pictures ~** je ne suis pas rentré, au lieu de cela je suis allé au cinéma; **~ of** au lieu de; **~ of going to school** au lieu d'aller à l'école; **~ of sb** à la place de qn; **his brother came ~ of him** son frère est venu à sa place; **~ of it** à la place; **this is ~ of a birthday present** ceci tient lieu de cadeau d'anniversaire.

instep ['ɪnstep] n a (*Anat*) cou-de-pied *m*. **to have a high ~** avoir le

pied cambré. b *[shoe]* cambrure *f*.
instigate [ˈɪnstɪgeɪt] **vt** inciter, pousser (*sb to do* qn à faire); *rebellion etc* fomenter, provoquer, susciter; *plan* promouvoir, être à l'origine de.
instigation [ˌɪnstɪˈgeɪʃən] **n** instigation *f*, incitation *f*. **at sb's ~** à l'instigation de qn.
instigator [ˈɪnstɪgeɪtəʳ] **n** instigateur *m*, -trice *f*; *[riot, plot]* auteur *m*.
instil, (*US*) **instill** [ɪnˈstɪl] **vt** *courage etc* insuffler (*into sb* à qn); *knowledge, principles* inculquer (*into sb* à qn); *idea, fact* faire comprendre (*into sb* à qn). **to ~ into sb that ...** faire pénétrer dans l'esprit de qn que ... .
instinct [ˈɪnstɪŋkt] 1 **n** instinct *m*. **by** *or* **from ~** d'instinct; **to have an ~ for business** *or* **a good business ~** avoir l'instinct des affaires. 2 [ɪnˈstɪŋkt] **adj** (*liter*) **~ with** qui exhale *or* respire (*liter*), plein de.
instinctive [ɪnˈstɪŋktɪv] **adj** instinctif.
instinctively [ɪnˈstɪŋktɪvlɪ] **adv** instinctivement, d'instinct.
instinctual [ɪnˈstɪŋktʃʊəl] **adj** = **instinctive**.
institute [ˈɪnstɪtjuːt] 1 **vt** a (*establish*) *system, rules* instituer, établir; (*found*) *society* fonder, créer, constituer. **newly ~d** *post* récemment créé, de création récente; *organization* de fondation récente. b (*Jur etc*) *inquiry* ouvrir; *action* entreprendre (*against sb* à qn); *proceedings* entamer *or* engager (*against sb* contre qn). c (*Rel*) investir. 2 **n** a (*gen*) institut *m*. **I~ of Education** Institut de formation des maîtres; **I ~ of Linguistics** *etc* Institut de Linguistique *etc*. b (*US: course*) stage *m* (d'études).
institution [ˌɪnstɪˈtjuːʃən] **n** a (*NonC: see* **institute 1**) institution *f*, établissement *m*; fondation *f*, constitution *f*; (*Jur*) *[action, proceedings]* mise *f* en train; (*Rel*) investiture *f*.
b (*organization*) établissement *m*, organisme *m*, institution *f*; (*school, college*) établissement, (*private*) institution; (*mental hospital*) hôpital *m* psychiatrique; (*hospital*) hôpital; (*workhouse etc*) asile *m*, hospice *m*. **he has been in ~s all his adult life** il a passé toute sa vie d'adulte dans des établissements médico-sociaux ou autres.
c (*long-established structure, custom etc*) institution *f*. **the family is an important ~** la famille est une institution importante; **the morning coffee break is too much of an ~ to abolish** la pause café matinale est une telle institution qu'il serait impossible de la supprimer; **tea is a British ~** le thé est une institution britannique; **he's been with the firm so long that he's now an ~*** il fait partie de la compagnie depuis si longtemps qu'il en est devenu une véritable institution.
institutional [ˌɪnstɪˈtjuːʃənl] **adj** a *reform etc* institutionnel; (*pej*) *food* d'internat; *furniture* d'hospice. **she needs ~ care** (*in hospital*) elle a besoin de soins hospitaliers; (*in old people's home*) elle a besoin d'être placée dans une maison de retraite; **~ life** la vie (organisée) d'un établissement (*d'ordre social, médical ou pédagogique*); **~ life in hospital/in prison** la vie réglementée de l'hôpital/de la prison. b (*Comm, Fin: of large organizations*) *buying etc* institutionnel. **~ advertising** promotion *f* de l'image de marque.
institutionalize [ˌɪnstɪˈtjuːʃnəlaɪz] **vt** a *person* placer dans un établissement (*médical ou médico-social*). (*pej*) **to become ~d** être marqué par la vie en collectivité. b *procedure, custom, event etc* institutionnaliser, donner un caractère officiel à.
instruct [ɪnˈstrʌkt] **vt** a (*teach*) *person* instruire. **to ~ sb in sth** instruire qn en qch, enseigner *or* apprendre qch à qn; **to ~ sb in how to do sth** enseigner *or* apprendre à qn comment (il faut) faire qch. b (*order, direct*) *person* donner des instructions *or* des ordres à. **to ~ sb to do** charger qn de faire, donner pour instructions à qn de faire; (*frm*) **I am ~ed to inform you that ...** je suis chargé de *or* j'ai mission de vous informer que ... . c (*Jur*) (*Brit*) **to ~ a solicitor** donner ses instructions à un notaire; **to ~ counsel** constituer avocat; *[judge]* **to ~ the jury** donner des instructions au jury (*to do* pour qu'il fasse).
instruction [ɪnˈstrʌkʃən] 1 **n** a (*NonC: teaching*) instruction *f*, enseignement *m*. **to give ~ to sb (in sth)** instruire qn (en qch); **driving ~** leçons *fpl* de conduite.
b (*gen pl*) **~s** directives *fpl*, instructions *fpl*; (*Mil*) consigne *f*; (*Comm, Pharm, Tech*) indications *fpl*; (*Comm, Tech: on packet etc*) **"~s for use"** "mode d'emploi"; (*Comm, Tech*) **the ~s are on the back of the box** le mode d'emploi est (indiqué) au dos de la boîte; **he gave me careful ~s on what to do if ...** il m'a donné des directives *or* des instructions précises sur ce qu'il faut faire au cas où ...; **I gave ~s for him to be brought to me** j'ai donné des instructions *or* des directives pour qu'on me l'amène (*subj*); **he gave me ~s not to leave until ...** il m'a donné des instructions selon lesquelles je ne devais pas partir avant ...; **to act according to ~s** se conformer à la consigne.
2 **comp ▸instruction book** (*Comm, Tech*) manuel *m* (d'entretien).
instructive [ɪnˈstrʌktɪv] **adj** *speech, report* instructif; *book* éducatif.
instructor [ɪnˈstrʌktəʳ] **n** a maître *m*, professeur *m*; (*in prison*) éducateur *m*; (*Mil*) instructeur *m*; (*Ski, Gymnastics etc*) moniteur *m*. **the geography/tennis ~** le professeur de géographie/de tennis; *see* **driving** *etc*. b (*US Univ*) ≃ assistant *m*.
instructress [ɪnˈstrʌktrɪs] **n** maîtresse *f*, professeur *m*; (*in prison*) instructrice *f*; (*Ski, Gymnastics etc*) monitrice *f*.
instrument [ˈɪnstrʊmənt] 1 **n** (*Med, Mus, Tech etc*) instrument *m*; (*domestic*) ustensile *m*; (*fig*) instrument; (*Jur*) instrument, acte *m* juridique; (*Fin*) moyen *m* de paiement, titre *m*, effet *m*. **to fly by** *or* **on ~s** naviguer aux instruments; **~ of government** instrument du gouvernement; *see* **blunt, wind**[1] *etc*. 2 **comp** (*Aviat*) *flying, landing* aux instruments (de bord) **▸instrument board** (*Aut, Aviat*) tableau *m* de bord **▸instrument panel** (*Aviat, US Aut*) = **instrument board**. 3 [ˌɪnstrʊˈment] **vt** (*Mus*) orchestrer; (*Jur*) instrumenter.
instrumental [ˌɪnstrʊˈmentl] **adj** a **to be ~ in** contribuer à, être pour quelque chose dans; **he was ~ in founding the organization** il a contribué à la fondation de *or* à fonder l'organisation. b (*Mus*) instrumental. **~ music** musique instrumentale; **~ performer** instrumentiste *mf*.
instrumentalist [ˌɪnstrʊˈmentəlɪst] **n** (*Mus*) instrumentiste *mf*.
instrumentation [ˌɪnstrʊmenˈteɪʃən] **n** (*Mus*) orchestration *f*; (*Jur*) instrumentation *f*.
insubordinate [ˌɪnsəˈbɔːdənɪt] **adj** insubordonné, indiscipliné.
insubordination [ˈɪnsəˌbɔːdɪˈneɪʃən] **n** insubordination *f*, indiscipline *f*, désobéissance *f*.
insubstantial [ˌɪnsəbˈstænʃəl] **adj** *meal, work* peu substantiel; *structure* peu solide, léger; *argument* peu solide, sans substance; *evidence* insuffisant; *difference* négligeable; (*unreal*) *vision etc* imaginaire, chimérique, irréel.
insufferable [ɪnˈsʌfərəbl] **adj** insupportable, intolérable.
insufferably [ɪnˈsʌfərəblɪ] **adv** insupportablement, intolérablement. **~ rude** d'une grossièreté intolérable.
insufficiency [ˌɪnsəˈfɪʃənsɪ] **n** insuffisance *f*.
insufficient [ˌɪnsəˈfɪʃənt] **adj** insuffisant.
insufficiently [ˌɪnsəˈfɪʃəntlɪ] **adv** insuffisamment.
insular [ˈɪnsjələʳ] **adj** (*lit*) *administration, climate* insulaire; *attitude* d'insulaire; (*fig pej*) *mind, outlook* borné, étriqué; *person* aux vues étroites.
insularity [ˌɪnsjʊˈlærɪtɪ] **n** insularité *f*; (*fig pej*) *[person]* étroitesse *f* d'esprit; *[outlook, views]* étroitesse.
insulate [ˈɪnsjʊleɪt] **vt** (*Elec*) isoler; (*against cold, heat*) *room, roof* isoler; *water tank* calorifuger; (*against sound*) *room, wall* insonoriser; (*fig*) *person* (*separate*) séparer (*from* de); (*protect*) protéger (*against* de). **~d handle** manche isolant; **~d pliers** pince isolante; **insulating material** isolant *m*; (*Brit*) **insulating tape** (ruban *m*) isolant *m*; (*adhesive*) chatterton *m*.
insulation [ˌɪnsjʊˈleɪʃən] **n** a (*NonC*) (*Elec*) isolation *f*; *[house, room]* (*against cold*) calorifugeage *m*, isolation (calorifuge); (*against sound*) insonorisation *f*. **the ~ in this house is bad** l'isolation de cette maison est défectueuse. b (*NonC: material*) isolant *m*.
insulator [ˈɪnsjʊleɪtəʳ] **n** (*Elec*) (*device*) isolateur *m*; (*material*) isolant *m*.
insulin [ˈɪnsjʊlɪn] 1 **n** insuline *f*. 2 **comp** *treatment* à l'insuline; *injection* d'insuline **▸insulin shock** (*Med*) choc *m* insulinique **▸insulin treatment** insulinothérapie *f*.
insult [ɪnˈsʌlt] 1 **vt** (*with words, gestures*) insulter, injurier; (*offend*) faire (un) affront à. **she felt ~ed by his indifference** elle s'est sentie insultée par son indifférence. 2 [ˈɪnsʌlt] **n** insulte *f*, injure *f*, affront *m*. **to hurl ~s at sb** injurier qn, lancer des insultes à qn; **the book is an ~ to the reader's intelligence** le livre est une insulte à *or* fait affront à l'intelligence du lecteur; **these demands are an ~ to the profession** ces revendications sont un affront à la profession; *see* **add**.
insulting [ɪnˈsʌltɪŋ] **adj** insultant, injurieux, offensant. **to use ~ language to sb** adresser à qn des paroles offensantes *or* injurieuses *or* insultantes.
insultingly [ɪnˈsʌltɪŋlɪ] **adv** d'un ton *or* d'une voix insultant(e); d'une manière insultante.
insuperable [ɪnˈsuːpərəbl] **adj** insurmontable.
insuperably [ɪnˈsuːpərəblɪ] **adv** d'une façon insurmontable.
insupportable [ˌɪnsəˈpɔːtəbl] **adj** insupportable, intolérable.
insurable [ɪnˈʃʊərəbl] **adj** assurable.
insurance [ɪnˈʃʊərəns] 1 **n** (*gen*) assurance *f* (*on, for sth* pour qch, *against* contre); (*cover*) garantie *f* (d'assurances), couverture *f*; (*policy*) police *f* or contrat *m* d'assurances (*on, for sth* pour qch, *against* contre). **he pays £300 a year in ~** il paie 300 livres (de primes) d'assurance par an; **the ~ on a building against fire** *etc* la couverture *or* la garantie d'un immeuble contre l'incendie *etc*; **to take out ~** souscrire à une police d'assurances *or* un contrat d'assurances, contracter une assurance; **to take out (an) ~ against** s'assurer contre, se faire assurer contre; **what does your ~ cover?** qu'est-ce que votre contrat d'assurances couvre?; **we must extend our ~** nous devons augmenter le montant de notre garantie (d'assurances); **the ~ ends on 5th July** le contrat d'assurances *or* la police d'assurances expire le 5 juillet; (*fig*) **he buys property as an ~ against inflation** il achète de l'immobilier pour se protéger de l'inflation; *see* **fire, life** *etc*.
2 **comp ▸insurance agent** agent *m* d'assurances **▸insurance broker** courtier *m* d'assurances **▸insurance certificate** (*Aut*) carte *f* d'assurance (automobile) **▸insurance claim** (déclaration *f* de) sinistre *m* **▸insurance company** compagnie *f* *or* société *f* d'assurances **▸insurance office**: **to work in an insurance office** travailler pour une compagnie d'assurances **▸insurance policy** police *f* d'assurance, assurances* *fpl* **▸insurance premium** prime *f* (d'assurance) **▸insurance scheme** régime *m* d'assurances **▸insurance stamp** (*Brit*

Admin) vignette *f or* timbre *m* de contribution à la Sécurité sociale ▸**insurance underwriter** (*gen*) assureur *m*; (*underwriting company*) réassureur *m*.

insurant [ɪn'ʃʊərənt] **n** (*SPEC*) assuré(e) *m(f)*, souscripteur *m*, -trice *f*, preneur *m*, -euse *f* d'assurance.

insure [ɪn'ʃʊəʳ] **vt** a *car, house* (faire) assurer. **to ~ o.s.** *or* **one's life** s'assurer *or* se faire assurer sur la vie, prendre une assurance-vie; **I am ~d against fire** je suis assuré contre l'incendie; (*fig*) **we ~d (ourselves) against possible disappointment** nous avons paré aux déceptions possibles; **in order to ~ against any delay ...** pour nous (*or* les *etc*) garantir contre les délais ... . b *power, success* assurer, garantir. **this will ~ that you will be notified when ...** grâce à ceci vous êtes assuré d'être averti quand ... .

insured [ɪn'ʃʊəd] **adj, n** assuré(e) *m(f)*.

insurer [ɪn'ʃʊərəʳ] **n** assureur *m*.

insurgent [ɪn'sɜːdʒənt] **adj, n** insurgé(e) *m(f)*, révolté(e) *m(f)*.

insurmountable [ˌɪnsə'maʊntəbl] **adj** insurmontable.

insurrection [ˌɪnsə'rekʃən] **n** a (*NonC*) insurrection *f*. **to rise in ~** se soulever, s'insurger. b (*uprising*) insurrection *f*, émeute *f*, soulèvement *m*.

insurrectionary [ˌɪnsə'rekʃnərɪ] **adj** insurrectionnel.

insurrectionist [ˌɪnsə'rekʃənɪst] **n** insurgé(e) *m(f)*.

intact [ɪn'tækt] **adj** intact.

intake ['ɪnteɪk] 1 **n** a (*NonC: Tech*) *[water]* prise *f*, adduction *f*; *[gas, steam]* adduction, admission *f*. **air ~** admission d'air.
b (*Scol, Univ*) admission(s) *f(pl)*, (nombre *m* des) inscriptions *fpl*; (*Mil*) contingent *m*, recrues *fpl*. **there has been a big ~ of young graduates into our company** il y a eu un fort recrutement de jeunes diplômés dans notre société.
c *[protein, liquid etc]* consommation *f*. **food ~** *[animals]* ration *f* alimentaire; *[person]* consommation de nourriture.
d **she heard his ~ of breath as he noticed the damage** elle l'a entendu retenir sa respiration en constatant les dégâts.
2 **comp** ▸**intake class** (*Scol*) cours *m* préparatoire ▸**intake valve** (*Tech*) soupape *f* d'admission.

intangible [ɪn'tændʒəbl] 1 **adj** *quality, presence* intangible, impalpable. (*Jur*) **~ property** biens incorporels; (*Jur*) **~ assets** immobilisations incorporelles. 2 **n** impondérable *m*.

integer ['ɪntɪdʒəʳ] **n** (nombre *m*) entier *m*.

integral ['ɪntɪgrəl] 1 **adj** a *part* intégrant, constituant. **to be an ~ part of sth** faire partie intégrante de qch. b (*whole*) intégral, complet (*f* -ète), entier. **~ payment** paiement intégral. c (*Math*) intégral. **~ calculus** calcul intégral. 2 **n** (*Math, fig*) intégrale *f*.

integrate ['ɪntɪgreɪt] 1 **vt** a (*combine into a whole*) *people, objects, ideas* intégrer, incorporer (*in, into* dans).
b (*complete by adding parts*) compléter. (*Psych*) **an ~d personality** une personnalité bien intégrée.
c (*combine, desegregate*) *races, religions, ethnic groups etc* intégrer, unifier. **to ~ Catholic and non-Catholic schools** intégrer *or* unifier les établissements catholiques et non catholiques; (*US*) **to ~ a school** *etc* imposer la déségrégation raciale dans un établissement scolaire *etc*; (*US*) **~d school** établissement scolaire où se pratique la déségrégation raciale.
d (*Math*) intégrer.
2 **vi** a (*US: racially*) *[school, neighbourhood etc]* pratiquer la déségrégation raciale.
b *[person, religious or ethnic group etc]* s'intégrer (*into* dans).

integrated ['ɪntɪgreɪtɪd] **adj** (*gen*) intégré. **~ accounting package** logiciel *m* intégré de comptabilité; (*Elec*) **~ circuit** circuit intégré; (*Brit Educ*) **~ course** cours *m* de formation professionnelle (*pour apprentis*); (*Brit Scol*) **~ day** journée *f* sans emploi du temps structuré; **I~ Services Digital Network** Réseau *m* Numérique à l'Intégration de Services; (*Brit Scol*) **~ studies** études générales (*où les matières ne sont pas différenciées*).

integration [ˌɪntɪ'greɪʃən] **n** (*see* **integrate**) intégration *f* (*also Math, Psych*); incorporation *f*; unification *f*. **racial ~**, (*US*) **~** déségrégation raciale; **the ~ of the country's various ethnic groups** l'intégration des divers groupes ethniques du pays.

integrity [ɪn'tegrɪtɪ] **n** a (*honesty*) intégrité *f*, honnêteté *f*, probité *f*. **man of ~** homme *m* intègre. b (*totality*) intégrité *f*, totalité *f*. **in its ~** dans son intégrité, dans sa totalité, en entier; **territorial ~** l'intégrité du territoire.

integument [ɪn'tegjʊmənt] **n** tégument *m*.

intellect ['ɪntɪlekt] **n** a (*NonC*) (*reasoning power*) intellect *m*, intelligence *f*; (*cleverness*) intelligence, esprit *m*. **a man of (great) ~** un homme d'une grande intelligence. b (*person*) intelligence *f*, esprit *m*.

intellectual [ˌɪntɪ'lektjʊəl] 1 **adj** (*gen*) intellectuel; *family etc* d'intellectuels. **~ property** propriété *f* intellectuelle. 2 **n** intellectuel(le) *m(f)*.

intellectually [ˌɪntɪ'lektjʊəlɪ] **adv** intellectuellement.

intelligence [ɪn'telɪdʒəns] 1 **n** a (*NonC*) intelligence *f*. **man of little ~** homme peu intelligent; **he shows ~** il fait preuve d'intelligence; **his book shows ~** son livre est intelligent.
b (*information*) renseignement(s) *m(pl)*, information(s) *f(pl)*. (*Press*) **latest ~** informations de dernière minute.
c **Military/Naval I~** service *m* de renseignements de l'armée de Terre/de la Marine; **he was in I~ during the war** il était dans les services de renseignements pendant la guerre.
2 **comp** ▸**intelligence agent** agent *m* de renseignements, agent secret ▸**Intelligence Corps** (*Brit Mil*) *arme f du service de renseignements et de sécurité militaires* ▸**Intelligence officer** officier *m* du deuxième bureau *or* de renseignements ▸**intelligence quotient** quotient intellectuel ▸**Intelligence Service** (*Pol*) service secret *or* de renseignements ▸**intelligence test** test *m* d'aptitude intellectuelle ▸**intelligence work: to do Intelligence work** être dans *or* travailler dans les services de renseignements, être agent secret.

intelligent [ɪn'telɪdʒənt] **adj** (*gen*) intelligent. **~ credit card** carte *f* à mémoire; (*Comput*) **~ terminal** terminal intelligent.

intelligently [ɪn'telɪdʒəntlɪ] **adv** intelligemment, avec intelligence.

intelligentsia [ɪnˌtelɪ'dʒentsɪə] **n** (*collective sg*) **the ~** l'intelligentsia *f*, l'élite *f* intellectuelle.

intelligibility [ɪnˌtelɪdʒə'bɪlɪtɪ] **n** intelligibilité *f*.

intelligible [ɪn'telɪdʒəbl] **adj** intelligible.

intelligibly [ɪn'telɪdʒəblɪ] **adv** intelligiblement.

intemperance [ɪn'tempərəns] **n** (*lack of self-restraint*) intempérance *f*; (*lack of moderation*) manque *m* de modération.

intemperate [ɪn'tempərɪt] **adj** *climate* sévère, peu clément, rigoureux; *wind* violent; *haste, zeal* excessif; *rage* incontrôlé; *person* (*lacking self-restraint*) intempérant; (*lacking moderation*) immodéré.

intend [ɪn'tend] **vt** avoir l'intention, se proposer, projeter (*to do, doing* de faire), penser (*to do* faire); *gift etc* destiner (*for* à). **I ~ going to see him** *or* **to go and see him** j'ai l'intention d'aller le voir, je pense aller le voir; **I didn't ~ to let him know** je n'avais pas l'intention de lui en parler; **I ~ him to go with me, I ~ that he should go with me** j'ai (bien) l'intention qu'il m'accompagne (*subj*); **I fully ~ to punish him** j'ai la ferme intention de le punir; **he ~s to be a doctor** il a l'intention de *or* il projette de faire médecine, il se destine à la médecine; **we ~ him to be a doctor** nous le destinons à la médecine; **this scheme is ~ed to help the poor** ce projet est destiné à venir en aide aux indigents; **~d for** (*gen*) destiné à, conçu pour; **he ~ed that remark for you** sa remarque était à votre intention, c'est à vous qu'il destinait *or* adressait cette observation; **I ~ it as a present for Robert** c'est un cadeau que je destine à Robert; **I ~ed it as a compliment** (dans mon esprit) cela voulait être un compliment; **he ~ed no harm** il l'a fait sans mauvaise intention; **to ~ marriage** avoir des intentions de mariage; **what do you ~ by that?** que voulez-vous dire par là?; **did you ~ that?** est-ce que vous avez fait cela exprès? *or* à dessein? *or* avec intention?; *see also* **intended**.

intended [ɪn'tendɪd] 1 **adj** a (*deliberate*) *insult etc* intentionnel, fait intentionnellement. b (*planned*) *journey, enterprise* projeté; *effect* voulu. 2 **n** (†) **his ~** sa promise†, sa future (*hum*); **her ~** son promis†, son futur (*hum*).

intense [ɪn'tens] **adj** *cold, heat, sunlight* intense; *hatred, love, rage* intense, violent, profond; *enthusiasm, interest* vif, énorme; *person, tone* véhément. **~ expression** (*interested*) expression concentrée *or* d'intérêt profond; (*fervent*) expression exaltée *or* d'intense ferveur; **I find her too ~** je la trouve trop véhémente.

intensely [ɪn'tenslɪ] **adv** a *live, look, hate* intensément, avec intensité. b (*very*) *hot, cold, unpleasant* extrêmement; *moving, moved, affected* profondément.

intensification [ɪnˌtensɪfɪ'keɪʃən] **n** *[heat]* intensification *f*; *[production]* accélération *f*, intensification; (*Mil*) *[fighting]* intensification; (*Phot*) renforcement *m*.

intensifier [ɪn'tensɪfaɪəʳ] **n** (*Gram*) intensif *m*.

intensify [ɪn'tensɪfaɪ] 1 **vt** intensifier, augmenter; (*Mil*) *fighting* intensifier; *colour* intensifier, renforcer; *sound* intensifier. 2 **vi** (*see* **1**) s'intensifier; augmenter.

intensity [ɪn'tensɪtɪ] **n** *[anger, hatred, love]* intensité *f*, force *f*, violence *f*; *[cold, heat]* intensité; *[current, light, sound]* intensité, puissance *f*; *[tone]* véhémence *f*. **her ~ disturbs me** sa véhémence me met mal à l'aise; **capital/labour ~** intensité *f* capitalistique/travaillistique.

intensive [ɪn'tensɪv] **adj** (*also Ling*) intensif. **~ course in French** cours accéléré *or* intensif de français; (*Med*) **~ care unit** service *m* de réanimation, unité *f* de soins intensifs; **to be in ~ care** être en réanimation; **to need ~ care** demander des soins intensifs.

-intensive [ɪn'tensɪv] **adj ending in comps** à forte intensité de, *e.g.* **capital-intensive** à forte intensité de capital; *see* **energy, labour** *etc*.

intensively [ɪn'tensɪvlɪ] **adv** intensivement.

intent [ɪn'tent] 1 **n** intention *f*, dessein *m*, projet *m*. **to all ~s and purposes** en fait, pratiquement, virtuellement; **with ~ to do** dans l'intention *or* dans le dessein *or* dans le but de faire; **with good ~** dans une bonne intention; **to do sth with ~** faire qch de propos délibéré; (*Jur*) **with criminal ~** dans un but délictueux; *see* **loiter**.
2 **adj** (*concentrating*) attentif, absorbé. **~ stare** regard *m* fixe; **he was ~ on his work** il était absorbé par son travail; **~ on revenge** résolu *or* (bien) décidé à se venger; **I am ~ on leaving** je suis résolu *or* (bien) décidé à partir, j'ai la ferme intention de partir; **he was so ~ on catching the bus that he didn't see the car** dans sa préoccupation d'attraper

l'autobus il n'a pas vu la voiture.

intention [ɪn'tenʃən] n intention *f*, but *m*, dessein *m*. **to have the ~ of doing** avoir l'intention de faire; **to have no ~ of doing** n'avoir aucune intention de faire; **I haven't the least** *or* **slightest ~ of staying** je n'ai pas la moindre intention de rester ici, il n'est nullement dans mes intentions de rester ici; **with the ~ of doing** dans l'intention de *or* dans le but de *or* dans le dessein de faire; **with this ~** à cette intention, à cette fin; **with good ~s** avec de bonnes intentions; **with the best of ~s** avec les meilleures intentions (du monde); **what are your ~s?** quelles sont vos intentions?, que comptez-vous faire?; **I don't know what his ~s were when he did it** je ne sais pas quelles étaient ses intentions *or* quel était son dessein *or* quel était son but quand il l'a fait; **she thinks his ~s are honourable** elle pense qu'il a des intentions honorables.

intentional [ɪn'tenʃənl] adj intentionnel, voulu, délibéré. **it wasn't ~** ce n'était pas fait exprès, je ne l'ai (*or* il ne l'a *etc*) pas fait exprès.

intentionally [ɪn'tenʃnəlɪ] adv intentionnellement. **the wording was ~ vague** l'imprécision de l'énoncé était voulue *or* intentionnelle; **he did it ~** il l'a fait exprès *or* intentionnellement *or* de propos délibéré *or* à dessein.

intently [ɪn'tentlɪ] adv *listen, look* avec une vive attention.

intentness [ɪn'tentnɪs] n (*concentration*) préoccupation *f*; *[gaze]* intensité *f*. **~ of purpose** résolution *f*.

inter [ɪn'tɜːʳ] vt enterrer, ensevelir.

inter- [ˌɪntər] pref (+ n sing) entre + *npl*, *e.g.* **~-company** entre compagnies; inter ... + *adj*, *e.g.* **~-region** interrégional; *see* **inter-city, inter-school** *etc*.

interact [ˌɪntər'ækt] vi a *[substances]* (ré)agir réciproquement, avoir une action réciproque. b (*Comput*) dialoguer (*with* avec). (*fig*) **we don't ~ very well** le courant passe mal (entre nous).

interaction [ˌɪntər'ækʃən] n interaction *f*.

interactive [ˌɪntər'æktɪv] adj (*Comput, also gen*) interactif. **~ computing** traitement interactif, informatique conversationnelle; **~ mode** mode conversationnel *or* interactif; **~ video** vidéo *f* interactive.

interactively [ˌɪntər'æktɪvlɪ] adv (*Comput*) *work* en mode conversationnel *or* interactif.

inter alia [ˌɪntər'ælɪə] adv entre autres.

interbreed ['ɪntə'briːd] pret, ptp **interbred** 1 vt *animals* croiser. 2 vi se croiser (*with* avec).

intercalate [ɪn'tɜːkəleɪt] vt intercaler.

intercalation [ɪnˌtɜːkə'leɪʃən] n intercalation *f*.

inter-campus [ˌɪntə'kæmpəs] adj (*US Univ*) interuniversitaire.

intercede [ˌɪntə'siːd] vi intercéder (*with* auprès de, *for* pour, en faveur de).

intercensal [ˌɪntə'sensl] adj intercensitaire.

intercept [ˌɪntə'sept] 1 vt *message, light* intercepter, capter; *plane, suspect* intercepter; *person* arrêter au passage. 2 n interception *f*.

interception [ˌɪntə'sepʃən] n interception *f*.

interceptor [ˌɪntə'septəʳ] n (*Aviat*) intercepteur *m*. **~ (plane)** intercepteur.

intercession [ˌɪntə'seʃən] n intercession *f*.

interchange ['ɪntəˌtʃeɪndʒ] 1 n a (*NonC*) (*exchange*) échange *m*; (*alternation*) alternance *f*. b (*on motorway*) échangeur *m*. 2 [ˌɪntə'tʃeɪndʒ] vt (*exchange*) *gifts, letters, ideas* échanger (*with sb* avec qn); (*alternate*) faire alterner (*with* avec); (*change positions of*) changer de place, mettre à la place l'un de l'autre. 3 vi (*change position*) changer de place (*with* avec); (*alternate*) alterner (*with* avec).

interchangeable [ˌɪntə'tʃeɪndʒəbl] adj interchangeable.

interchangeably [ˌɪntə'tʃeɪndʒəblɪ] adv de façon interchangeable.

inter-city [ˌɪntə'sɪtɪ] 1 adj *travel* d'une grande ville à une autre; *communications* interurbain; *see also* **2**. 2 n (*Brit Rail: also* **~ train**) rapide *m*.

intercollegiate ['ɪntəkə'liːdʒɪɪt] adj entre collèges.

intercom ['ɪntəkɒm] n interphone *m*. **over** *or* **on the ~** à l'interphone.

intercommunicate [ˌɪntəkə'mjuːnɪkeɪt] vi communiquer (réciproquement).

intercommunication ['ɪntəkəˌmjuːnɪ'keɪʃən] n intercommunication *f*, communication *f* réciproque.

intercommunion [ˌɪntəkə'mjuːnɪən] n (*Rel*) intercommunion *f*; (*gen*) intercommunication *f*.

interconnect [ˌɪntəkə'nekt] 1 vt connecter (entre eux *or* elles). **~ed facts** faits intimement *or* étroitement liés; **~ed rooms** pièces communicantes. 2 vi *[rooms, tunnels]* communiquer (entre eux *or* elles); *[parts of a structure]* être relié(e)s (les un(e)s aux autres). **~ing wall** mur *m* mitoyen.

intercontinental ['ɪntəˌkɒntɪ'nentl] adj intercontinental. **~ ballistic missile** missile *m* balistique intercontinental.

intercostal [ˌɪntə'kɒstl] adj intercostal.

intercourse ['ɪntəkɔːs] n a (*NonC*) relations *fpl*, rapports *mpl*, commerce *m*. **business ~** relations commerciales; **human ~** relations humaines. b **(sexual) ~** rapports *mpl* (sexuels); **to have ~** avoir des rapports (*with* avec).

interdenominational ['ɪntədɪˌnɒmɪ'neɪʃənl] adj entre confessions, interconfessionnel.

interdepartmental ['ɪntəˌdiːpɑːt'mentl] adj (*within firm*) entre services; (*within ministry*) entre départements.

interdependence [ˌɪntədɪ'pendəns] n interdépendance *f*.

interdependent [ˌɪntədɪ'pendənt] adj interdépendant.

interdict ['ɪntədɪkt] 1 vt a (*Jur, frm*) interdire, prohiber. b (*Rel*) *priest, person* jeter l'interdit sur. 2 n a (*Jur*) prohibition *f*, interdiction *f*. b (*Rel*) interdit *m*.

interdiction [ˌɪntə'dɪkʃən] n (*Jur, Rel*) interdiction *f*.

interdisciplinarity [ˌɪntəˌdɪsɪplɪ'nærɪtɪ] n interdisciplinarité *f*.

interdisciplinary [ˌɪntə'dɪsɪplɪnərɪ] adj interdisciplinaire.

interest ['ɪntrɪst] 1 n a (*NonC: understanding etc*) intérêt *m*. **to take** *or* **have** *or* **feel an ~ in sb** s'intéresser à qn; **to take** *or* **have** *or* **feel an ~ in sth** s'intéresser à qch, prendre de l'intérêt à qch; **he took no further ~ in it** il ne s'y est plus intéressé; **to show an ~ in sb/sth** manifester *or* montrer de l'intérêt pour qn/qch; **to take a great ~ in sb/sth** s'intéresser vivement à qn/qch; **to arouse sb's ~** éveiller l'intérêt de qn; **that's of great ~ to me** ceci m'intéresse beaucoup, ceci a beaucoup d'intérêt pour moi; **that's of no ~ to me** ceci ne m'intéresse pas, ceci a peu d'intérêt pour moi; **a subject of little ~** un sujet présentant peu d'intérêt; **questions of public ~** questions d'intérêt public *or* qui intéressent le public (*see also* **1c**); **I'm doing it just for ~** *or* **just for ~'s sake** je le fais seulement parce que cela m'intéresse; **it adds ~ to the story** ça ajoute un certain intérêt à l'histoire; **matters of vital ~** questions d'un intérêt *or* d'une importance capital(e).

b (*hobby etc*) **my main ~ is reading** ce qui m'intéresse le plus c'est la lecture; **what are your ~s?** quelles sont les choses qui vous intéressent?, à quoi vous intéressez-vous?; **special ~ holidays** vacances *fpl* à thème.

c (*advantage, well-being*) intérêt *m*, avantage *m*, profit *m*. **in one's (own) ~(s)** dans son (propre) intérêt; **it is in your own ~ to do so** il est de votre (propre) intérêt d'agir ainsi, vous avez intérêt à agir ainsi; **to act in sb's ~(s)** agir dans l'intérêt de qn *or* au profit de qn *or* pour le compte de qn; **in the ~ of hygiene** par souci d'hygiène; **in the ~ of peace** dans l'intérêt de la paix; **in the public ~** dans l'intérêt public, pour le bien public.

d (*Comm, Jur etc: share, stake*) intérêts *mpl*, participation *f*. **I have an ~ in a hairdressing business** j'ai des intérêts dans un salon de coiffure; **he has business ~s abroad** il a des intérêts commerciaux à l'étranger; **Switzerland is looking after British ~s** la Suisse défend les intérêts britanniques; **he has sold his ~ in the company** il a vendu la participation *or* les intérêts qu'il avait dans la compagnie; (*fig*) **we have an ~ in knowing what is to happen** il est de notre intérêt de *or* nous avons intérêt à savoir ce qui va se produire; *see* **vest²**.

e (*people*) **the coal/oil ~(s)** les (gros) intérêts houillers/pétroliers; **shipping ~s** les intérêts maritimes; **the landed ~s** les propriétaires terriens.

f (*NonC: Fin*) intérêt(s) *m(pl)*. **simple/compound ~** intérêts simples/composés; **~ on an investment** intérêts d'un placement; **loan with ~** prêt à intérêt; **to lend at ~** prêter à intérêt; **at an ~ of 10%** à un taux d'intérêt de 10 %; **to bear ~** rapporter un intérêt; **to bear ~ at 8%** donner un intérêt de 8 %, porter intérêt à 8 %.

2 comp ▸**interest-bearing** (*Fin*) *loan* productif d'intérêt ▸**interest-free** (*Fin*) sans intérêt ▸**interest group** association *f* ▸**interest rate** (*Fin*) taux *m* d'intérêt.

3 vt a intéresser. **to be ~ed in sth/sb, to become** *or* **grow** *or* **get ~ed in sth/sb** s'intéresser à qch/qn; **I am not ~ed in football** le football ne m'intéresse pas, je ne m'intéresse pas au football; **the company is ~ed in buying land** cela intéresse la firme d'acheter des terrains; **I am ~ed in going** ça m'intéresse d'y aller; **she was ~ed to see what he would do** cela l'intéressait *or* elle était curieuse de voir ce qu'il ferait; **I am trying to ~ her in our sale of work** j'essaie de lui faire prendre un intérêt actif à notre vente de charité; **his teacher succeeded in ~ing him in geography** son professeur a réussi à l'intéresser *or* à le faire s'intéresser à la géographie; **can I ~ you in this problem?** puis-je attirer votre attention sur ce problème?; **can I ~ you in contributing to ...?** est-ce que cela vous intéresserait de contribuer à ...?

b (*concern*) intéresser, concerner, toucher. **the struggle against inflation ~s us all** la lutte contre l'inflation touche chacun d'entre nous *or* nous concerne tous, nous sommes tous intéressés par la lutte contre l'inflation.

interested ['ɪntrɪstɪd] adj (*see also* **interest 3a**) a (*attentive*) *look, attitude* d'intérêt. **~ spectators** spectateurs intéressés. b (*biased, involved*) *person, motive* intéressé. **~ party** partie intéressée; (*Jur*) ayant droit *m*; **the ~ parties** les intéressés *mpl*; (*Jur*) les ayants droit.

interesting ['ɪntrɪstɪŋ] adj *story, offer, proposition* intéressant. († *euph*) **she's in an ~ condition*** elle est dans une position intéressante (*euph*).

interestingly ['ɪntrɪstɪŋlɪ] adv de façon intéressante. **~ enough I saw him only yesterday** ce qui est très intéressant, c'est que je l'ai vu pas plus tard qu'hier.

interface ['ɪntəfeɪs] 1 n (*Comput, Tech*) interface *f*; (*fig*) intermédiaire *mf*. 2 vt connecter (*with* avec).

interfacing ['ɪntəfeɪsɪŋ] n entoilage *m*.

interfere [ˌɪntə'fɪəʳ] vi *[person]* s'immiscer, s'ingérer (*in* dans); (*Phys*) interférer. **to ~ in a quarrel** s'interposer dans une dispute; **stop interfering!** ne vous mêlez pas de mes (*or* leurs *etc*) affaires!; **he's always**

interfering il se mêle toujours de tout, il met *or* fourre* son nez partout; *[weather, accident, circumstances etc]* **to ~ with sb's plans** contrecarrer les *or* entraver les *or* se mettre en travers des projets de qn; **he never allows his hobbies to ~ with his work** il ne laisse jamais ses distractions empiéter sur son travail; (*sexually*) **to ~ with sb** abuser de qn; (*sexually*) **the child had been ~d with** l'enfant avait été abusé; **don't ~ with my camera*** ne touche pas à *or* ne tripote pas mon appareil, laisse mon appareil tranquille*.

interference [ˌɪntəˈfɪərəns] **n** (*NonC*) ingérence *f*, intrusion *f* (*in* dans); (*Phys*) interférence *f*; (*Rad*) parasites *mpl*, interférence. (*Econ*) **state ~** ingérence *f* de l'État; (*Jur*) **unwarrantable ~** immixtion *f*.

interfering [ˌɪntəˈfɪərɪŋ] **adj** *person* importun. **she's an ~ busybody** elle se mêle toujours de ce qui ne la regarde pas, elle fourre son nez partout*, il faut qu'elle mette partout son grain de sel*.

interferon [ˌɪntəˈfɪərɒn] **n** interféron *m*.

intergalactic [ˌɪntəgəˈlæktɪk] **adj** intergalactique.

intergovernmental [ˌɪntəgʌvnˈmentl] **adj** intergouvernemental.

interim [ˈɪntərɪm] **1 n** intérim *m*. **in the ~** dans l'intérim, entretemps. **2 adj** *administration, government* provisoire; *report, arrangements* provisoire, temporaire; *post, holder of post* par intérim, intérimaire. (*Fin*) **~ dividend** dividende *m* intérimaire; **~ financing** préfinancement *m*; **the ~ period** l'intérim *m*.

interior [ɪnˈtɪərɪəʳ] **1 adj** intérieur (*f* -eure). (*Math*) **~ angle** angle *m* interne. **2 n a** *[building, country]* intérieur *m*. **Minister/Ministry of the I~** ministre *m*/ministère *m* de l'Intérieur; (*US*) **Secretary/Department of the I~** *ministre/ministère de l'Environnement chargé des Parcs nationaux*. **b** (*Art*) (tableau *m* d')intérieur *m*. **3 comp ▸interior decoration** décoration *f* (d'intérieurs *or* d'appartements) **▸interior decorator** décorateur *m*, -trice *f* (d'intérieurs *or* d'appartements) **▸interior sprung mattress** matelas *m* à ressorts.

interject [ˌɪntəˈdʒekt] **vt** *remark, question* lancer, placer. **"yes" he ~ed** "oui" réussit-il à placer.

interjection [ˌɪntəˈdʒekʃən] **n** interjection *f*.

interlace [ˌɪntəˈleɪs] **1 vt** entrelacer, entrecroiser. **2 vi** s'entrelacer, s'entrecroiser.

interlard [ˌɪntəˈlɑːd] **vt** entrelarder, entremêler (*with* de).

interleave [ˌɪntəˈliːv] **vt** interfolier.

interline [ˌɪntəˈlaɪn] **vt a** (*Typ*) interligner. **b** (*Sewing*) mettre une doublure intermédiaire à.

interlinear [ˌɪntəˈlɪnɪəʳ] **adj** interlinéaire.

interlining [ˌɪntəˈlaɪnɪŋ] **n** (*Sewing*) doublure *f* intermédiaire.

interlink [ˌɪntəˈlink] **1 vi** *[parts of a structure]* se rejoindre; *[factors etc]* se lier. **2 vt** *[factors etc]* **to be ~ed** être lié (*with* à).

interlock [ˌɪntəˈlɒk] **1 vt** (*Tech*) enclencher. **2 vi** (*Tech*) s'enclencher; (*fig*) *[groups, companies, projects]* s'imbriquer.

interlocutor [ˌɪntəˈlɒkjʊtəʳ] **n** interlocuteur *m*, -trice *f*.

interloper [ˈɪntələʊpəʳ] **n** intrus(e) *m(f)*; (*Comm*) commerçant *m* marron.

interlude [ˈɪntəluːd] **n** intervalle *m*; (*Theat*) intermède *m*. **in the ~** (*gen*) dans l'intervalle, entre-temps; (*Theat*) pendant l'intermède; **musical ~** interlude *m*, intermède musical.

intermarriage [ˌɪntəˈmærɪdʒ] **n** (*NonC*) (*within family/tribe etc*) intermariage *m*; (*between families/tribes etc*) mariage *m* entre membres de familles/tribus *etc* différentes.

intermarry [ˈɪntəˈmærɪ] **vi** (*see* **intermarriage**) se marier. **these tribes do not ~** les membres de ces tribus ne se marient pas entre eux; **this tribe doesn't ~ with its neighbours** les membres de cette tribu ne se marient pas avec leurs voisins.

intermediary [ˌɪntəˈmiːdɪərɪ] **adj, n** intermédiaire (*mf*).

intermediate [ˌɪntəˈmiːdɪət] **1 adj a** intermédiaire. (*Econ*) **~ goods** biens *mpl* intermédiaires; *[ship, plane]* **~ stop** escale *f*; **the ~ stages of the project** les phases *fpl or* étapes *fpl* intermédiaires du projet. **b** (*Scol etc*) moyen. **~ course/exam** cours *m*/examen *m* (de niveau) moyen. **2 comp ▸intermediate-acting** *drug* à effet *m* tardif **▸intermediate range ballistic missile, intermediate range weapon** (*Mil*) missile *m* de moyenne portée. **3 n a** (*US: person*) intermédiaire *mf*. **b** (*US: car*) automobile *f* de taille moyenne. **c** (*substance*) substance *f or* produit *m* intermédiaire.

interment [ɪnˈtɜːmənt] **n** enterrement *m*, inhumation *f*.

intermezzo [ˌɪntəˈmetsəʊ] **n, pl ~s** *or* **intermezzi** [ˌɪntəˈmetsiː] intermède *m*; (*Mus*) intermezzo *m*.

interminable [ɪnˈtɜːmɪnəbl] **adj** interminable, sans fin.

interminably [ɪnˈtɜːmɪnəblɪ] **adv** (*gen*) interminablement. **it was ~ long** c'était interminable, ça n'en finissait pas.

intermingle [ˌɪntəˈmɪŋgl] **1 vt** entremêler (*with* de), mélanger. **2 vi** s'entremêler (*with* de), se confondre, se mélanger (*with* avec).

intermission [ˌɪntəˈmɪʃən] **n** interruption *f*, pause *f*; (*in hostilities, quarrel, work, session*) trêve *f*; (*US Cine, Theat*) entracte *m*; (*Med*) intermission *f*. **without ~** sans arrêt, sans relâche.

intermittent [ˌɪntəˈmɪtənt] **adj** intermittent. (*Aut*) **~ wipe** essuie-glace *m* à balayage intermittent.

intermittently [ˌɪntəˈmɪtəntlɪ] **adv** par intermittence, par intervalles.

intermodal [ɪntəˈməʊdəl] **adj** *transport* intermodal.

intern [ɪnˈtɜːn] **1 vt** (*Pol etc*) interner (*pour raisons de sécurité*). **2** [ˈɪntɜːn] **n** (*US Med*) interne *mf*.

internal [ɪnˈtɜːnl] **adj a** (*Math, Med, Tech*) interne. **~ combustion engine** moteur *m* à explosion, moteur à combustion interne; (*Med*) **~ examination** toucher *m* vaginal; **~ injuries** lésions *fpl* internes; (*US*) **~ medicine** médecine *f* interne. **b** (*Ind, Pol*) *dispute, trouble, reorganization* intérieur (*f* -eure), interne. (*Pol*) **~ wars** guerres intestines *or* intérieures *or* civiles; (*Pol*) **~ quarrels** querelles intestines; (*Fin*) **~ auditor** contrôleur financier; (*US*) **~ revenue** contributions *fpl* directes; (*US*) **I~ Revenue Service** ≃ fisc *m*. **c** (*intrinsic*) *proof, evidence* intrinsèque. **d** *hope* secret (*f* -ète). **~ conviction** conviction *f* intime.

internalize [ɪnˈtɜːnəˌlaɪz] **vt** *skill, fact* assimiler à fond; *problem* intérioriser; (*Ling*) intérioriser.

internally [ɪnˈtɜːnəlɪ] **adv** intérieurement. (*Pharm*) **"not to be taken ~"** "pour usage externe".

international [ˌɪntəˈnæʃnəl] **1 adj** international. **I~ Atomic Energy Agency** Agence internationale de l'énergie atomique; **I~ Bank for Reconstruction and Development** Banque *f* internationale pour la reconstruction et le développement; **I~ Court of Justice** Cour *f* internationale de Justice; **I~ Date Line** ligne *f* de changement de date *or* de changement de jour; **I~ Labour Organisation** Organisation *f* internationale du travail; **~ law** droit international; **I~ Modernism** = **I~ Style**; **I~ Monetary Fund** Fonds *m* monétaire international; **I~ Olympic Committee** Comité *m* international olympique; **I~ Phonetic Alphabet** Alphabet *m* phonétique international; **~ relations** relations *fpl* internationales; **~ reply coupon** coupon-réponse international; **I~ Standards Organization** Organisation *f* des normes internationales; (*Archit*) **I~ Style** style *m* international; *see* **road**. **2 n a** (*Sport: match, player*) international(e) *m(f)*. **b** (*Pol*) **I~** Internationale *f* (*association*).

Internationale [ˌɪntəˌnæʃəˈnɑːl] **n** Internationale *f* (*hymne*).

internationalism [ˌɪntəˈnæʃnəlɪzəm] **n** internationalisme *m*.

internationalize [ˌɪntəˈnæʃnəlaɪz] **vt** internationaliser.

internationally [ˌɪntəˈnæʃnəlɪ] **adv** *accepted, discussed* internationalement. **~ known** connu dans le monde entier, de réputation mondiale; **~ respected** respecté dans le monde entier.

internecine [ˌɪntəˈniːsaɪn] **adj** *feud, war, struggle* de destruction réciproque.

internee [ˌɪntɜːˈniː] **n** interné(e) *m(f)* (politique).

internist [ɪnˈtɜːnɪst] **n** (*US Med*) ≃ spécialiste *mf* des maladies organiques.

internment [ɪnˈtɜːnmənt] **n** internement *m* (politique). **~ camp** camp *m* d'internement.

internship [ˈɪntɜːnˌʃɪp] **n** (*US*) (*Med*) internat *m*; (*Univ etc*) stage *m* en entreprise.

interpersonal [ˌɪntəˈpɜːsnl] **adj**: **~ skills/relationships** compétences/relations interpersonnelles.

interplanetary [ˌɪntəˈplænɪtərɪ] **adj** *journey* interplanétaire. **~ vessel** vaisseau spatial.

interplay [ˈɪntəpleɪ] **n** (*NonC*) effet *m* réciproque, interaction *f*.

Interpol [ˈɪntəˌpɒl] **n** Interpol *m*.

interpolate [ɪnˈtɜːpəleɪt] **vt** (*gen*) interpoler (*into* dans); *text, manuscript* altérer par interpolation.

interpolation [ɪnˌtɜːpəˈleɪʃən] **n** interpolation *f*.

interpose [ˌɪntəˈpəʊz] **1 vt** *remark* intercaler; *objection, veto* opposer; *obstacle* interposer. **to ~ o.s. between** s'interposer entre. **2 vi** intervenir, s'interposer.

interpret [ɪnˈtɜːprɪt] **1 vt** (*all senses*) interpréter. **2 vi** interpréter, traduire, servir d'interprète, faire l'interprète.

interpretation [ɪnˌtɜːprɪˈteɪʃən] **n** (*all senses*) interprétation *f*. **what ~ am I to put *or* place on your conduct?** comment dois-je interpréter votre conduite?

interpretative [ɪnˈtɜːprɪtətɪv] **adj** interprétatif.

interpreter [ɪnˈtɜːprɪtəʳ] **n** (*person: lit, fig*) interprète *mf*; (*Comput*) interpréteur *m*.

interracial [ˌɪntəˈreɪʃəl] **adj** *marriage* mixte; *problems, violence* interracial.

interregnum [ˌɪntəˈregnəm] **n, pl ~s** *or* **interregna** [ˌɪntəˈregnə] interrègne *m*.

interrelate [ˌɪntərɪˈleɪt] **1 vt** mettre en corrélation. **~d** en corrélation, en relation mutuelle *or* réciproque; **~d facts** faits *mpl* en corrélation *or* étroitement liés. **2 vi** *[concepts]* être en corrélation.

interrelation [ˌɪntərɪˈleɪʃən], **interrelationship** [ˌɪntərɪˈleɪʃənʃɪp] **n** corrélation *f*, relation mutuelle *or* réciproque.

interrogate [ɪnˈterəgeɪt] **vt** interroger, soumettre à une interrogation *or* (*Police*) un interrogatoire; (*Comput*) interroger.

interrogation [ɪnˌterəˈgeɪʃən] **n** interrogation *f*; (*Police*) interrogatoire *m*. **~ mark, ~ point** point *m* d'interrogation.

interrogative [ˌɪntəˈrɒgətɪv] **1 adj** *look, tone* interrogateur (*f* -trice); (*Ling*) interrogatif. **2 n** (*Ling*) interrogatif *m*. **in the ~** à l'interrogatif.

interrogatively [ˌɪntəˈrɒgətɪvlɪ] **adv** d'un air *or* d'un ton interrogateur; (*Ling*) interrogativement.

interrogator [ɪnˈterəgeɪtəʳ] **n** interrogateur *m*, -trice *f*.

interrogatory [ˌɪntəˈrɒɡətərɪ] adj interrogateur (*f* -trice).
interrupt [ˌɪntəˈrʌpt] vt *speech, traffic, circuit* interrompre; *communication* interrompre, couper; *person* interrompre, couper la parole à; *view* gêner, boucher, cacher. **to ~ a private conversation** rompre un tête à tête; **don't ~!** n'interrompez pas!, pas d'interruptions!; **I don't want to ~, but** ... je ne voudrais pas vous interrompre, mais ... .
interruption [ˌɪntəˈrʌpʃən] n interruption *f*. **without ~** sans interruption, sans arrêt, d'affilée.
intersect [ˌɪntəˈsekt] 1 vt couper, croiser; (*Math*) intersecter. 2 vi *[lines, wires, roads etc]* s'entrecouper, s'entrecroiser, se couper, se croiser; (*Math*) s'intersecter. (*Math*) **~ing arcs/lines** arcs *mpl*/lignes *fpl* intersecté(e)s.
intersection [ˌɪntəˈsekʃən] n (*US: crossroads*) croisement *m*, carrefour *m*; (*Math*) intersection *f*.
interservice [ˌɪntəˈsɜːvɪs] adj (*Mil*) interarmes *inv*.
intersperse [ˌɪntəˈspɜːs] vt répandre, semer, parsemer (*among, between* dans, parmi). **book ~d with quotations** livre parsemé *or* émaillé de citations; **speech ~d with jokes** discours émaillé de plaisanteries; **lawns ~d with flowerbeds** pelouses agrémentées de parterres de fleurs.
interstate [ˌɪntəˈsteɪt] adj (*US*) *commerce etc* entre états.
interstellar [ˌɪntəˈstelər] adj interstellaire, intersidéral.
interstice [ɪnˈtɜːstɪs] n interstice *m*.
intertwine [ˌɪntəˈtwaɪn] 1 vt entrelacer. 2 vi s'entrelacer. **intertwining branches** branches entrelacées.
interurban [ˌɪntəˈɜːbən] adj interurbain.
interval [ˈɪntəvəl] n a (*in time*) intervalle *m*. **at ~s** par intervalles; **at frequent ~s** à intervalles rapprochés; **at rare ~s** à intervalles espacés, de loin en loin; **at regular ~s** à intervalles réguliers (*see also* **c**); **there was an ~ for discussion** il y eut une pause pour la discussion; (*Med*) **he has lucid ~s** il a des moments de lucidité; (*Met*) **bright ~s** (belles) éclaircies *fpl*; (*Met*) **showery ~s** averses *fpl*.
b (*Scol*) récréation *f*; (*Sport*) mi-temps *f*, pause *f*; (*Theat*) entracte *m*; (*Mus*) intervalle *m*. (*Mus*) **second/third ~** intervalle de seconde/de tierce.
c (*space between objects*) intervalle *m*, écartement *m*, distance *f*. **the ~s between the trees grew longer** les arbres s'espaçaient, la distance *or* l'intervalle entre les arbres grandissait; **lampposts (placed) at regular ~s along the road** des réverbères placés à intervalles réguliers *or* échelonnés régulièrement le long de la route.
intervene [ˌɪntəˈviːn] vi a *[person]* intervenir, s'interposer (*in* dans). b *[event, circumstances etc]* survenir, intervenir, arriver. **war ~d** survint la guerre; **if nothing ~s** s'il n'arrive *or* ne se passe rien entre-temps. c *[time]* s'écouler, s'étendre (*between* entre). **12 years ~ between the two events** 12 ans séparent les deux événements.
intervening [ˌɪntəˈviːnɪŋ] adj *event* survenu; *period of time* intermédiaire. **the ~ years were happy** les années qui s'écoulèrent entre-temps furent heureuses.
intervention [ˌɪntəˈvenʃən] n intervention *f*. (*Econ*) **~ price** prix *m* d'intervention.
interventionist [ˌɪntəˈvenʃənɪst] n, adj interventionniste *mf*.
interview [ˈɪntəvjuː] 1 n a (*gen*) entretien *m*, entrevue *f*; (*for job*) entretien *m* (d'embauche); (*sales*) entretien *m* (de vente). **to call** *or* **invite sb to an ~** convoquer qn (pour un entretien); **to come to (an) ~** venir pour *or* se présenter à un entretien; **I had an ~ with the manager** j'ai eu un entretien avec le directeur; **the ~s will be held next week** les entretiens auront lieu la semaine prochaine.
b (*Press, Rad, TV*) interview *f*.
2 vt a (*for job etc*) avoir un entretien avec. **he is being ~ed on Monday** on le convoque (pour) lundi; **we shall be ~ing throughout next week** nous faisons passer des entretiens toute la semaine prochaine.
b (*Press, Rad, TV*) interviewer. **he was ~ed by the police** il a été interrogé par les policiers; **the police want to ~ him** la police le recherche.
interviewee [ˌɪntəvjʊˈiː] n (*for job*) candidat(e) *m(f)* (*qui passe un entretien*); (*Press, Rad, TV*) interviewé(e) *m(f)*.
interviewer [ˈɪntəvjʊər] n (*Press, Rad, TV*) interviewer *m*; (*in market research, opinion poll*) enquêteur *m*, -euse *f*. (*for job etc*) **the ~ asked me** ... la personne qui me faisait passer un entretien m'a demandé ... .
inter vivos [ˈɪntəˈviːvɒs] adj (*Jur*) **~ gift** donation *f* entre vifs.
intervocalic [ˌɪntəvəʊˈkælɪk] adj intervocalique.
interwar [ˈɪntəˈwɔːr] adj: **the ~ period** *or* **years** l'entre-deux-guerres *m*.
interweave [ˌɪntəˈwiːv] 1 vt *threads* tisser ensemble; *lines etc* entrelacer; (*fig*) entremêler. 2 vi s'entrelacer, s'emmêler.
intestate [ɪnˈtestɪt] adj (*Jur*) intestat (*f inv*). **to die ~** mourir intestat; **~ estate** succession *f* ab intestat.
intestinal [ɪnˈtestɪnl] adj intestinal. **~ blockage** occlusion intestinale; (*US fig*) **to have ~ fortitude**‡ avoir quelque chose dans le ventre*.
intestine [ɪnˈtestɪn] n (*Anat*) intestin *m*. **small ~** intestin grêle; **large ~** gros intestin.
inti [ˈɪntɪ] n inti *m*.
intifada [ˌɪntɪˈfɑːdə] n intifada *f*.
intimacy [ˈɪntɪməsɪ] n a (*NonC*) intimité *f*. b (*NonC: euph: sexual*) rapports *mpl* (intimes *or* sexuels). c **intimacies** familiarités *fpl*, gestes familiers.
intimate [ˈɪntɪmɪt] 1 adj a (*close*) *friend* intime, proche; *friendship* profond. **to be on ~ terms with** être ami intime de, avoir des relations intimes avec; **to become ~ with sb** se lier (d'amitié) avec qn, devenir (ami) intime avec qn, devenir l'intime de qn; **they became ~** ils se sont liés d'amitié, ils sont devenus amis intimes.
b (*euph: sexually*) **he had been ~ with her** il avait eu des rapports (intimes) avec elle; **they were ~ several times** ils ont eu des rapports (intimes) plusieurs fois.
c (*private*) *feelings* intime, personnel, secret (*f* -ète); *beliefs, life* intime. **one's ~ affairs** ses affaires privées.
d (*cosy*) *restaurant etc* intime. **an ~ atmosphere** une atmosphère intime *or* d'intimité.
e (*detailed*) **to have an ~ knowledge of a subject** avoir une connaissance approfondie d'un sujet, connaître à fond un sujet; **a more ~ analysis** une analyse plus approfondie *or* plus détaillée.
2 n intime *mf*, familier *m*, -ière *f*.
3 [ˈɪntɪmeɪt] vt a (*make known officially*) annoncer, faire savoir, faire connaître (*that* que). **he ~d his approval** il annonça *or* fit connaître son approbation.
b (*make known indirectly*) suggérer, donner à entendre, laisser entendre.
intimately [ˈɪntɪmɪtlɪ] adv *know, talk* intimement. **to be ~ acquainted with a subject** connaître à fond *or* intimement un sujet; **to be ~ connected with sth** avoir un rapport très étroit avec qch; **to be ~ involved in sth** être mêlé de près à qch.
intimation [ˌɪntɪˈmeɪʃən] n (*announcement*) (*gen*) annonce *f*; *[death]* avis *m*; *[birth, wedding]* annonce; (*notice*) signification *f*, notification *f*; (*hint*) suggestion *f*; (*sign*) indice *m*, indication *f*. **this was the first ~ we had of their refusal/that they had refused** cela a été la première indication que nous avons eue de leur refus/du fait qu'ils avaient refusé; **we had had no previous ~ that** rien ne nous faisait pressentir que.
intimidate [ɪnˈtɪmɪdeɪt] vt intimider.
intimidating [ɪnˈtɪmɪdeɪtɪŋ] adj intimidant.
intimidation [ɪnˌtɪmɪˈdeɪʃən] n (*NonC*) intimidation *f*; (*Jur*) menaces *fpl*.
into [ˈɪntʊ] (*phr vb elem*) prep (*gen*) dans. **to come** *or* **go ~ a room** entrer dans une pièce; **to go ~ town** aller en ville; **to get ~ a car** monter dans une voiture *or* en voiture; **he helped his mother ~ the car** il a aidé sa mère à monter en voiture; **she fell ~ the lake** elle est tombée dans le lac; **he went off ~ the desert** il est parti dans le désert; **to put sth ~ a box** mettre qch dans une boîte; **put the book ~ it** mets le livre dedans; **it broke ~ a thousand pieces** ça s'est cassé en mille morceaux; **to change traveller's cheques ~ francs** changer des chèques de voyage contre des francs; **to translate** *or* **put sth ~ French** traduire qch en français; **he went further ~ the forest** il a pénétré *or* s'est enfoncé plus avant dans la forêt; **far ~ the night** très avant dans la nuit; **it was ~ 1986** c'était déjà 1986, on était déjà en 1986; **it continued well ~** *or* **far ~ 1986** cela a continué pendant une bonne partie de 1986; **let's not go ~ that again!** ne recommençons pas à discuter là-dessus!, ne revenons pas là-dessus!; **we must go ~ this very carefully** nous devons étudier la question de très près; **4 ~ 12 goes 3** 12 divisé par 4 donne 3; **the children are ~ everything*** les enfants touchent à tout; (*fig*) **she's ~**‡ **health foods/jazz/buying antiques** les aliments naturels/le jazz/acheter des antiquités, c'est son truc*; (*fig*) **to be ~ drugs**‡ toucher à la drogue*; *see* **burst, get into, grow** *etc*.
intolerable [ɪnˈtɒlərəbl] adj intolérable, insupportable. **it is ~ that** ... il est intolérable *or* il n'est pas tolérable que ... + *subj*.
intolerably [ɪnˈtɒlərəblɪ] adv intolérablement, insupportablement.
intolerance [ɪnˈtɒlərəns] n (*NonC: also Med*) intolérance *f*.
intolerant [ɪnˈtɒlərənt] adj intolérant (*of* de; (*Med*) *of* à).
intolerantly [ɪnˈtɒlərəntlɪ] adv avec intolérance.
intonation [ˌɪntəʊˈneɪʃən] n (*Ling, Mus*) intonation *f*.
intone [ɪnˈtəʊn] vt entonner; (*Rel*) psalmodier.
intoxicant [ɪnˈtɒksɪkənt] 1 adj enivrant, grisant. 2 n alcool *m*, boisson *f* alcoolique.
intoxicate [ɪnˈtɒksɪkeɪt] vt (*lit, fig*) enivrer, griser.
intoxicated [ɪnˈtɒksɪkeɪtɪd] adj (*lit*) ivre; (*Jur*) en état d'ivresse *or* d'ébriété; (*fig*) ivre, grisé. **~ with success** grisé par le succès, ivre de succès.
intoxicating [ɪnˈtɒksɪkeɪtɪŋ] adj *drink* alcoolisé; *effect* enivrant; *perfume* enivrant.
intoxication [ɪnˌtɒksɪˈkeɪʃən] n ivresse *f*; (*Med*) intoxication *f* (par l'alcool); (*fig*) ivresse, griserie *f*. (*Jur*) **in a state of ~** en état d'ivresse *or* d'ébriété.
intra... [ˈɪntrə] pref intra... .
intractability [ɪnˌtræktəˈbɪlɪtɪ] n (*see* **intractable**) caractère *m* intraitable, manque *m* de docilité; insolubilité *f*; opiniâtreté *f*.
intractable [ɪnˈtræktəbl] adj *child, temper* intraitable, indocile; *problem* insoluble; *illness* opiniâtre; *machine* difficile à régler *or* à manipuler.
intramural [ˌɪntrəˈmjʊərəl] 1 adj *studies, sports, competitions* à l'intérieur d'un même établissement. 2 npl: **~s** (*US Scol etc*) matchs *mpl* entre élèves (*or* étudiants) d'un même établissement.

intramuscular [ˌɪntrəˈmʌskjʊləʳ] adj intramusculaire.
intramuscularly [ˌɪntrəˈmʌskjʊləlɪ] adv par voie intramusculaire.
intransigence [ɪnˈtrænsɪdʒəns] n intransigeance *f*.
intransigent [ɪnˈtrænsɪdʒənt] adj, n intransigeant(e) *m(f)*.
intransitive [ɪnˈtrænsɪtɪv] adj, n (*Gram*) intransitif (*m*).
intrauterine [ˌɪntrəˈjuːtəraɪn] adj: ~ **device** stérilet *m*, dispositif anticonceptionnel intra-utérin.
intravenous [ˌɪntrəˈviːnəs] adj intraveineux.
intravenously [ˌɪntrəˈviːnəslɪ] adv par voie intraveineuse.
intrepid [ɪnˈtrepɪd] adj intrépide.
intrepidity [ˌɪntrɪˈpɪdɪtɪ] n intrépidité *f*.
intrepidly [ɪnˈtrepɪdlɪ] adv avec intrépidité, intrépidement.
intricacy [ˈɪntrɪkəsɪ] n *[problem, plot, pattern, mechanism]* complexité *f*, complication *f*. **the intricacies of the law** les complexités *or* les détours *mpl* de la loi.
intricate [ˈɪntrɪkɪt] adj *mechanism, pattern, style* compliqué; *plot, problem, situation* complexe. **all the ~ details** tous les détails dans leur complexité.
intricately [ˈɪntrɪkɪtlɪ] adv de façon complexe *or* compliquée.
intrigue [ɪnˈtriːg] 1 vi intriguer, comploter (*with sb* avec qn, *to do* pour faire). 2 vt intriguer, éveiller la curiosité de, intéresser. **she ~s me** elle m'intrigue; **go on, I'm ~d** continue, ça m'intrigue *or* m'intéresse; **I'm ~d to know whether he did arrive** je suis curieux de savoir s'il est vraiment arrivé; **your news ~s me** ce que vous m'annoncez m'intrigue; **we were ~d by a road sign** un panneau a éveillé notre curiosité *or* nous a intrigués. 3 n (*plot*) intrigue *f*; (*love affair*) intrigue, liaison *f*.
intriguer [ɪnˈtriːgəʳ] n intrigant(e) *m(f)*.
intriguing [ɪnˈtriːgɪŋ] 1 adj fascinant. 2 n (*NonC*) intrigues *fpl*.
intriguingly [ɪnˈtriːgɪŋlɪ] adv: ~ **different** étrangement différent; ~ **original** d'une originalité fascinante; **~-titled** au titre fascinant; ~, **this was never confirmed** très curieusement, ça n'a jamais été confirmé.
intrinsic [ɪnˈtrɪnsɪk] adj intrinsèque.
intrinsically [ɪnˈtrɪnsɪklɪ] adv intrinsèquement.
intro... [ˈɪntrəʊ] pref intro... .
introduce [ˌɪntrəˈdjuːs] vt a (*make acquainted*) présenter. **he ~d me to his friend** il m'a présenté à son ami; **I ~d myself to my new neighbour** je me suis présenté à mon nouveau voisin; **who ~d them?** qui les a présentés l'un à l'autre?; **we haven't been ~d** on ne nous a pas présentés (l'un à l'autre); (*frm*) **may I ~ Mr Smith?** puis-je (me permettre de) vous présenter M. Smith?; **he ~d me to the delights of skiing** il m'a initié aux plaisirs du ski; **I was ~d to Shakespeare too young** on m'a fait connaître Shakespeare quand j'étais trop jeune; **who ~d him to drugs?** qui est-ce qui lui a fait connaître la drogue?, qui est-ce qui lui a appris à se droguer?
b (*announce etc*) *speaker* présenter; *subject* présenter, aborder; (*Rad, TV*) *programme etc* présenter.
c *reform, new method, innovation* introduire, présenter; *subject, question* aborder, amener, présenter; *practice* faire adopter, introduire. (*Parl*) **to ~ a bill** présenter un projet de loi; **this ~d a new note into the conversation** ceci a donné un ton nouveau à la conversation.
d (*bring in or take in: gen*) introduire; *key etc* introduire, insérer (*into* dans). **he ~d the tape recorder surreptitiously into the meeting** il a introduit sans se faire remarquer le magnétophone dans la réunion; (*frm*) **we were ~d into a dark room** on nous introduisit dans une pièce sombre; **it was I who ~d him into the firm** c'est moi qui l'ai introduit *or* fait entrer dans la compagnie; **potatoes were ~d into Europe from America** la pomme de terre a été introduite d'Amérique en Europe.
introduction [ˌɪntrəˈdʌkʃən] n a (*NonC*) introduction *f* (*into* dans). **my ~ to chemistry/to life in London** mon premier contact avec la chimie/la vie londonienne. b présentation *f* (*of sb to sb* de qn à qn). **to give sb an ~** *or* **a letter of ~ to sb** donner à qn une lettre de recommandation auprès de qn; **will you make** *or* **do* the ~s?** voulez-vous faire les présentations? c (*to book etc*) avant-propos *m*, introduction *f*. d (*elementary course*) introduction *f* (*to* à), manuel *m* élémentaire. **"An ~ to German"** "Initiation à l'allemand".
introductory [ˌɪntrəˈdʌktərɪ] adj préliminaire, préalable, d'introduction. **a few ~ words** quelques mots d'introduction; **~ remarks** remarques *fpl* préliminaires *or* préalables, préambule *m*; (*Comm*) **~ offer** offre *f* de lancement.
introit [ˈɪntrɔɪt] n introït *m*.
introspection [ˌɪntrəʊˈspekʃən] n (*NonC*) introspection *f*.
introspective [ˌɪntrəʊˈspektɪv] adj introspectif, replié sur soi-même.
introspectiveness [ˌɪntrəʊˈspektɪvnɪs] n tendance *f* à l'introspection.
introversion [ˌɪntrəʊˈvɜːʃən] n introversion *f*.
introvert [ˈɪntrəʊvɜːt] 1 n (*Psych*) introverti(e) *m(f)*. **he's something of an ~** c'est un caractère plutôt fermé. 2 adj introverti. 3 vt *one's thoughts etc* tourner sur soi-même. (*Psych*) **to become ~ed** se replier sur soi-même.
introverted [ˈɪntrəʊvɜːtɪd] adj = **introvert 2**.
intrude [ɪnˈtruːd] 1 vt introduire de force (*into* dans), imposer (*into* à). **the thought that ~d itself into my mind** la pensée qui s'est imposée à mon esprit; **to ~ one's views (on sb)** imposer ses idées (à qn).
2 vi *[person]* être importun, s'imposer; *[feeling, emotion]* se manifester. **to ~ on sb's conversation** s'immiscer dans la conversation de qn; **to ~ on sb's privacy** s'ingérer dans la vie privée de qn; **to ~ on sb's time** empiéter sur le temps de qn; **to ~ into sb's affairs** s'immiscer *or* s'ingérer dans les affaires de qn; **sometimes a note of sentimentality ~s** quelquefois s'insinue une note sentimentale; **he lets no feelings of pity ~** il ne laisse intervenir aucun sentiment de pitié; **am I intruding?** est-ce que je (vous) dérange?, (*stronger*) est-ce que je (vous) gêne?
intruder [ɪnˈtruːdəʳ] n (*person*) intrus(e) *m(f)*; (*Aviat/Naut*) avion/navire isolé (*qui pénètre chez l'ennemi*); (*animal*) intrus(e). **the ~ fled when he heard the car** l'intrus s'enfuit quand il entendit la voiture; **she treated us like ~s** elle nous a traités comme des intrus *or* des étrangers; **I felt like an ~** je me sentais étranger *or* de trop.
intrusion [ɪnˈtruːʒən] n (*see* **intrude**) intrusion *f* (*into* dans); imposition *f* (*on* à). **~s on sb's privacy** ingérences *fpl* dans la vie privée de qn; **~s on sb's time** empiètement *m* sur le temps de qn; **his ~ into our conversation/meeting** son intrusion dans notre conversation/réunion; **excuse my ~** excusez-moi de vous déranger.
intrusive [ɪnˈtruːsɪv] adj *person, presence* importun, indiscret (*f* -ète), gênant. (*Ling*) **~ consonant** consonne *f* d'appui; (*Ling*) **the ~ "r"** *le "r" ajouté en anglais en liaison abusive*.
intuit [ɪnˈtjʊɪt] vt (*esp US*) **to ~ that ...** savoir intuitivement *or* par intuition que ..., avoir l'intuition que ... .
intuition [ˌɪntjuːˈɪʃən] n intuition *f*.
intuitive [ɪnˈtjuːɪtɪv] adj intuitif.
intuitively [ɪnˈtjuːɪtɪvlɪ] adv par intuition, intuitivement.
Inuit [ˈɪnjuːɪt] 1 n Inuit *mf*. **the ~(s)** les Inuit *mfpl*. 2 adj inuit *inv*.
inundate [ˈɪnʌndeɪt] vt (*lit, fig*) inonder (*with* de). **to be ~d with work** être débordé (de travail), être submergé de travail; **to be ~d with visits** être inondé de visiteurs, être débordé de visites.
inundation [ˌɪnʌnˈdeɪʃən] n inondation *f*.
inure [ɪnˈjʊəʳ] vt: **to be ~d to** être aguerri à; *sb's charms* être insensible à.
invade [ɪnˈveɪd] vt a (*gen, Mil, fig*) envahir. **city ~d by tourists** ville envahie par les touristes; **he was suddenly ~d by doubts** il fut soudain envahi de doutes. b *privacy* violer, s'ingérer dans. **to ~ sb's rights** empiéter sur les droits de qn.
invader [ɪnˈveɪdəʳ] n envahisseur *m*, -euse *f*. **the ~s were generally detested** les envahisseurs étaient haïs de tous, l'envahisseur était haï de tous.
invading [ɪnˈveɪdɪŋ] adj *army, troops* d'invasion. **the ~ Romans** l'envahisseur romain.
invalid[1] [ˈɪnvəlɪd] 1 n (*sick person*) malade *mf*; (*with disability*) invalide *mf*, infirme *mf*. **chronic ~** malade chronique. 2 adj (*ill*) malade; (*with disability*) invalide, infirme. 3 comp ▸**invalid car, invalid carriage** (*Brit*) voiture *f* d'infirme ▸**invalid chair** fauteuil *m* d'infirme *or* de malade ▸**invalid tricycle** (*Brit*) tricycle *m* pour infirme *or* invalide. 4 [ˌɪnvəˈliːd] vt (*esp Brit Mil*) **he was ~ed home from the front** il fut rapatrié du front pour blessures *or* pour raisons de santé.
▸**invalid out** vt sep (*Mil*) **to invalid sb out (of the army)** réformer qn (pour blessures *or* pour raisons de santé).
invalid[2] [ɪnˈvælɪd] adj (*esp Jur*) non valide, non valable; *argument* nul (*f* nulle). *[ticket]* **to become ~** ne plus être valable, se périmer.
invalidate [ɪnˈvælɪdeɪt] vt invalider, annuler; (*Jur*) *judgment* casser, infirmer; *will* rendre nul et sans effet; *contract etc* vicier; *statute* abroger.
invalidity [ɪnvəˈlɪdɪtɪ] n a (*disability*) invalidité *f*. (*Brit Admin*) **~ benefit** allocation *f* d'invalidité. b *[argument]* nullité *f*; *[law, election]* invalidité *f*.
invaluable [ɪnˈvæljʊəbl] adj (*lit, fig*) inestimable, inappréciable. **her help** *or* **she has been ~ to me** elle m'a été d'une aide inestimable *or* inappréciable.
invariable [ɪnˈvɛərɪəbl] adj invariable.
invariably [ɪnˈvɛərɪəblɪ] adv invariablement, immanquablement.
invasion [ɪnˈveɪʒən] n a (*Mil, fig*) invasion *f*, envahissement *m*. b *[rights]* empiètement *m* (*of* sur). **it is an ~ of his privacy to ask him such questions** c'est une incursion dans sa vie privée que de lui poser de telles questions.
invasive [ɪnˈveɪsɪv] adj *disease* (*gen*) qui gagne du terrain; *cancer* qui se généralise.
invective [ɪnˈvektɪv] n (*NonC*) invective *f*. **torrent** *or* **stream of ~** flot *m* d'invectives *or* d'injures.
inveigh [ɪnˈveɪ] vi: **to ~ against sb/sth** invectiver qn/qch; (*more violently*) fulminer *or* tonner contre qn/qch.
inveigle [ɪnˈviːgl] vt: **to ~ sb into sth** entraîner *or* attirer qn dans qch (sous de faux prétextes *or* par la flatterie *or* par la ruse); **to ~ sb into doing** entraîner *or* amener qn à faire (sous de faux prétextes *or* par la flatterie *or* par la ruse).
invent [ɪnˈvent] vt (*lit, fig*) inventer.
invention [ɪnˈvenʃən] n a invention *f*. **the ~ of the telephone** l'invention du téléphone; **one of his most practical ~s** une de ses inventions les plus pratiques. b (*falsehood*) invention *f*, mensonge *m*. **it was sheer ~ on her part** c'était pure invention de sa part; **it was (an) ~ from start to finish** c'était (une) pure invention du début à la fin.
inventive [ɪnˈventɪv] adj inventif.

inventiveness [ɪn'ventɪvnɪs] n (*NonC*) esprit inventif *or* d'invention.
inventor [ɪn'ventəʳ] n inventeur *m*, -trice *f*.
inventory ['ɪnvəntrɪ] 1 n inventaire *m*; (*US Comm*) stock *m*. **to draw up an ~ of sth** inventorier qch, faire *or* dresser un inventaire de qch; **~ of fixtures** état *m* des *or* de lieux. 2 comp ▸**inventory control** (*US Comm*) gestion *f* des stocks. 3 vt inventorier.
inverse ['ɪnvɜːs] 1 adj inverse. **in ~ order** en sens inverse; **in ~ proportion to** inversement proportionnel à; **in ~ ratio (to)** en raison inverse (de). 2 n inverse *m*, contraire *m*.
inversely [ɪn'vɜːslɪ] adv inversement.
inversion [ɪn'vɜːʃən] n (*gen*) inversion *f*; (*Mus*) renversement *m*; *[values, roles etc]* renversement.
invert [ɪn'vɜːt] 1 vt a *elements, order, words* inverser, intervertir; *roles* renverser, intervertir. **to ~ a process** renverser une opération; (*Mus*) **~ed chord** accord renversé; (*Brit*) **~ed commas** guillemets *mpl*; **in ~ed commas** entre guillemets; **~ed snobbery** snobisme *m* à l'envers. b *cup, object* retourner. 2 ['ɪnvɜːt] n (*Psych*) inverti(e) *m(f)*. 3 ['ɪnvɜːt] comp ▸**invert sugar** sucre inverti.
invertebrate [ɪn'vɜːtɪbrɪt] adj, n invertébré *(m)*.
invest [ɪn'vest] 1 vt a (*Fin*) *money* placer (*in* dans, en); *capital, funds* investir (*in* dans, en). **to ~ money** faire un *or* des placement(s), placer de l'argent; **they ~ed large sums in books** ils ont investi des sommes énormes dans l'achat de livres; **I have ~ed a lot of time in this project** j'ai consacré beaucoup de temps à ce projet.
b (*Mil: surround*) investir, cerner.
c (*endow*) revêtir, investir (*sb with sth* qn de qch). *[monarch, president etc]* **to ~ sb as ...** élever qn à la dignité de ...; **the event was ~ed with an air of mystery** l'événement revêtait un caractère de mystère; **she seems to ~ it with some importance** elle semble lui attribuer une certaine importance.
2 vi: **to ~ in shares/property** placer son argent en valeurs/dans l'immobilier; (*hum*) **I've ~ed in a new car** je me suis payé* *or* offert une nouvelle voiture.
investigate [ɪn'vestɪgeɪt] vt *question, possibilities* examiner, étudier; *motive, reason* scruter, sonder; *crime* se livrer à des investigations sur, enquêter sur, faire une enquête sur.
investigation [ɪn,vestɪ'geɪʃən] n a (*NonC*) *[facts, question]* examen *m*; *[crime]* enquête *f* (*of* sur). **the matter under ~** la question à l'étude.
b *[researcher]* investigation *f*, enquête *f*; *[policeman]* enquête. **his ~s led him to believe that ...** ses investigations l'ont amené à penser que ...; **criminal/scientific ~** enquête criminelle/scientifique; **to institute an ~** ouvrir une enquête; **preliminary ~** enquête *or* investigations préalable(s) *or* préparatoire(s); **it calls for (an) immediate ~** cela demande une étude immédiate *or* à être étudié immédiatement; **he called for (an) immediate ~ into** il a demandé qu'on fasse *or* ouvre (*subj*) immédiatement une enquête sur; **we have made ~s** nous avons fait une enquête *or* des recherches.
investigative [ɪn'vestɪ,geɪtɪv] adj *technique etc* d'investigation. **~ journalism** *or* **reporting** enquête-reportage *f*, journalisme *m* d'investigation *or* d'enquête; **~ journalist/reporter** journaliste *mf* reporter *m* d'investigation.
investigator [ɪn'vestɪgeɪtəʳ] n investigateur *m*, -trice *f*; *see* **private**.
investigatory [ɪn'vestɪ,geɪtərɪ] adj: **~ group/panel** groupe *m*/ commission *f* d'enquête.
investiture [ɪn'vestɪtʃəʳ] n investiture *f*.
investment [ɪn'vestmənt] 1 n a (*Fin*) investissement *m*, placement *m*; (*fig, esp Psych*) investissement. **by careful ~ of his capital/the money he inherited** en investissant *or* plaçant soigneusement son capital/ l'argent dont il a hérité; **he regretted his ~ in the company** il regrettait d'avoir investi dans la firme; **~ in shares** placement en valeurs; **~ in property** placement *or* investissement immobilier; **I have a large ~ in the business** j'ai une grosse somme investie dans cette affaire *or* de gros intérêts dans cette affaire; (*money invested*) **~s** placements, investissements; **he has large ~s in Africa** il a de grosses sommes investies en Afrique.
b (*Mil*) investissement *m*.
c = **investiture**.
2 comp ▸**investment analyst** analyste *mf* en placements ▸**investment bank** (*US Fin*) banque *f* d'acceptation ▸**investment company** société *f* de placement ▸**investment income** revenu *m* des placements *or* des investissements ▸**investment management** gestion *f* de portefeuille ▸**investment opportunities** investissements *mpl or* placements *mpl* intéressants ▸**investment trust** société *f* d'investissement.
investor [ɪn'vestəʳ] n (*gen*) investisseur *m*; (*shareholder*) actionnaire *mf*. **(the) big ~s** les gros actionnaires; **(the) small ~s** les petits actionnaires, la petite épargne (*NonC*).
inveterate [ɪn'vetərɪt] adj *habit* invétéré, (bien) enraciné; *hatred* opiniâtre, irréductible; *thief, smoker* invétéré; *gambler* invétéré, acharné. **an ~ liar** un fieffé menteur.
invidious [ɪn'vɪdɪəs] adj *decision, distinction, choice* injuste, propre à susciter la jalousie; *comparison* blessant, désobligeant; *task* ingrat, déplaisant.
invigilate [ɪn'vɪdʒɪleɪt] 1 vi (*Brit*) être de surveillance (à un examen). 2 vt *examination* surveiller.
invigilator [ɪn'vɪdʒɪleɪtəʳ] n (*Brit*) surveillant(e) *m(f)* (*à un examen*).
invigorate [ɪn'vɪgəreɪt] vt *person [drink, food, thought]* fortifier; *[fresh air, snack]* revigorer; *[climate, air]* vivifier, tonifier, donner du tonus à; *[exercise]* tonifier; *campaign* animer. **to feel ~d** se sentir revigoré *or* vivifié.
invigorating [ɪn'vɪgəreɪtɪŋ] adj *climate, air, walk* vivifiant, tonifiant; *speech* stimulant.
invincibility [ɪn,vɪnsɪ'bɪlɪtɪ] n invincibilité *f*.
invincible [ɪn'vɪnsəbl] adj invincible.
invincibly [ɪn'vɪnsəblɪ] adv: **~ established** inébranlablement établi; **~ stubborn** d'un entêtement inébranlable.
inviolability [ɪn,vaɪələ'bɪlɪtɪ] n inviolabilité *f*.
inviolable [ɪn'vaɪələbl] adj inviolable.
inviolably [ɪn'vaɪələblɪ] adv inviolablement.
inviolate [ɪn'vaɪəlɪt] adj inviolé.
invisibility [ɪn,vɪzə'bɪlɪtɪ] n invisibilité *f*.
invisible [ɪn'vɪzəbl] adj invisible. **~ ink** encre *f* sympathique; **~ mending** stoppage *m*; (*Econ*) **~ exports** exportations *fpl* invisibles.
invisibly [ɪn'vɪzəblɪ] adv invisiblement. **I've had my coat ~ mended** j'ai fait stopper mon manteau.
invitation [,ɪnvɪ'teɪʃən] 1 n invitation *f*. **~ to dinner** invitation à dîner; **at sb's ~** à *or* sur l'invitation de qn; **by ~ (only)** sur invitation (seulement); (*Fin*) **~ to bid** avis *m* d'appel d'offres; (*iro*) **this lock is an ~ to burglars!** cette serrure est une invite aux cambrioleurs! 2 comp ▸**invitation card** (carte *f* d')invitation *f*, carton *m*.
invite [ɪn'vaɪt] 1 vt a (*ask*) *person* inviter (*to do* à faire). **to ~ sb to dinner** inviter qn à dîner; **he ~d him for a drink** il l'a invité à prendre un verre; **I've never been ~d to their house** je n'ai jamais été invité chez eux; **they ~d him to give his opinion** ils l'ont invité à donner son avis; **he was ~d to the ceremony** il a été invité (à assister) à la cérémonie; **to ~ sb in/up/down** *etc* inviter qn à entrer/ monter/ descendre *etc*; (*fig*) **a shop like that just ~s people to steal** ce magasin est une véritable incitation au vol.
b (*ask for*) *sb's attention, subscriptions etc* demander, solliciter. **he ~d our opinion on ...** il nous a demandé notre avis sur ...; **he ~d questions at the end of his talk** il a invité le public à poser des questions à la fin de sa causerie.
c (*lead to*) *confidences, questions, doubts, ridicule* appeler; *discussion, step* inviter à; *trouble, failure, defeat* chercher. **you're inviting a break-in if you leave that door open** en laissant cette porte ouverte vous invitez les cambrioleurs à entrer, laisser cette porte ouverte est une invite aux cambrioleurs.
2 ['ɪnvaɪt] n (*) invitation *f*.
▸**invite out** vt sep inviter (à sortir). **he has invited her out several times** il l'a invitée à sortir (avec lui) *or* il lui a demandé de sortir (avec lui) plusieurs fois; **I've been invited out to dinner this evening** j'ai été invité à dîner ce soir.
▸**invite over** vt sep a inviter (à venir). **they often invite us over for a drink** ils nous invitent souvent à venir prendre un verre chez eux; **let's invite them over some time** invitons-les un de ces jours (à venir nous voir). b **he invited me over to his table** il (m'appela et) m'invita à venir m'asseoir à sa table.
inviting [ɪn'vaɪtɪŋ] adj *look, appearance* invitant, engageant, attrayant; *goods* attrayant; *gesture* encourageant; *meal, odour* appétissant, alléchant. **the sea looked very ~** la mer avait un aspect très tentant *or* engageant.
invitingly [ɪn'vaɪtɪŋlɪ] adv *describe* d'une manière attrayante; *speak* d'un ton encourageant.
in vitro [ɪn'viːtrəʊ] adj, adv in vitro. **~ fertilization** fécondation *f* in vitro.
invocation [,ɪnvəʊ'keɪʃən] n invocation *f*.
invoice ['ɪnvɔɪs] 1 n facture *f*. 2 vt *customer, goods* facturer. **they will ~ us for the maintenance** ils vont nous facturer l'entretien. 3 comp ▸**invoice clerk** facturier *m*, -ière *f* ▸**invoice typist** dactylo-facturière *f*.
invoicing ['ɪnvɔɪsɪŋ] n (*NonC*) facturation *f*.
invoke [ɪn'vəʊk] vt a (*call on*) *God, Muse, mercy, precedent, law* invoquer. **to ~ sb's help** invoquer *or* demander l'aide de qn; **to ~ vengeance on sb** appeler vengeance sur la tête de qn. b (*evoke*) *spirits, the devil* évoquer.
involuntarily [ɪn'vɒləntərɪlɪ] adv involontairement.
involuntary [ɪn'vɒləntərɪ] adj involontaire.
involve [ɪn'vɒlv] vt a (*implicate, associate*) impliquer (*in* dans), mêler (*in* à), entraîner (*in* dans). **to ~ sb in a quarrel** mêler qn à une querelle; **to get ~d in a quarrel** se laisser entraîner dans une querelle; **to be ~d in a quarrel** être mêlé à une querelle; **they are trying to ~ him in the theft** ils essaient de l'impliquer dans le vol; **he wasn't ~d in the plot** il n'était pour rien dans le complot, il n'était pas impliqué dans le complot *or* mêlé au complot; **don't try to ~ me in this scheme** n'essaie pas de me mêler à ce projet; **we would prefer not to ~ Robert** nous préférerions ne pas mêler Robert à l'affaire *or* ne pas impliquer Robert; **to ~ sb in expense** entraîner qn à faire des frais; **to ~ o.s.** *or* **to get ~d in expense** se laisser entraîner à des dépenses *or* à la

dépense; **how did you come to be ~d?** comment vous êtes-vous trouvé impliqué?; **we are all ~d** nous sommes tous concernés; **he was so ~d in politics that he had no time to ...** il était tellement engagé dans la politique qu'il n'avait pas le temps de ...; **the police became ~d** la police est intervenue; **a question of principle is ~d** c'est une question de principe qui est en jeu; **the factors/forces/principles ~d** les facteurs/forces/principes en jeu; **the vehicles ~d** les véhicules en cause; **the person ~d** l'intéressé(e) *m(f)*; **to feel personally ~d** se sentir concerné; **to get ~d with sb** (*gen*) se trouver mêlé aux affaires de qn; (*socially*) se trouver lié intimement à qn; (*fall in love with*) tomber amoureux de qn; **she likes him but she doesn't want to get (too) ~d*** elle a de l'affection pour lui mais elle ne veut pas (trop) s'engager.

b (*entail, imply*) entraîner, nécessiter. **does it ~ much trouble?** est-ce que cela nécessite *or* entraîne *or* occasionne beaucoup de dérangement?; **we apologize for the trouble ~d** nous vous prions de bien vouloir excuser le dérangement que ceci vous occasionne (*or* a occasionné); **it ~s a lot of expense** ceci entraîne beaucoup de frais; **the job ~s living in the country** le poste nécessite *or* exige que l'on réside (*subj*) à la campagne; **there's a good deal of work ~d** cela nécessite un gros travail.

involved [ɪn'vɒlvd] **adj** *situation, relationship, question* compliqué, complexe; *style* contourné, compliqué; *see also* **involve**.

involvement [ɪn'vɒlvmənt] **n** a (*NonC*) rôle *m* (*in* dans), participation *f* (*in* à). **we don't know the extent of his ~** nous ne savons pas dans quelle mesure il est impliqué; **his ~ in the affair/plot** *etc* son rôle dans l'affaire/le complot *etc*; **his ~ in politics** son engagement *m* dans la politique; **his ~ in social work** son action *f* en matière sociale; **one must avoid any ~ in their difficulties** il faut éviter de se trouver mêlé à leurs difficultés. b (*difficulty*) problème *m*, difficulté *f*. **financial ~s** difficultés financières, problèmes *or* embarras financiers. c (*NonC*) [*style etc*] complication(s) *f(pl)*.

invulnerability [ɪn,vʌlnərə'bɪlɪtɪ] **n** invulnérabilité *f*.

invulnerable [ɪn'vʌlnərəbl] **adj** invulnérable.

inward ['ɪnwəd] 1 **adj** *movement* vers l'intérieur; *happiness, peace* intérieur (*f* -eure); *thoughts, desire, conviction* intime, profond. 2 **adv** = **inwards**. 3 **comp** ►**inward-looking** replié sur soi(-même).

inwardly ['ɪnwədlɪ] **adv** a (*in the inside*) à l'intérieur, intérieurement, au-dedans. **the house was outwardly clean but ~ filthy** la maison était propre à l'extérieur mais dégoûtante à l'intérieur. b (*secretly, privately*) *feel, think, know* secrètement, en son (*or* mon *etc*) for intérieur.

inwards ['ɪnwədz] (*phr vb elem*) **adv** *move etc* vers l'intérieur. (*liter*) **his thoughts turned ~** il rentra en (dedans de) lui-même, il descendit en lui-même.

I/O [aɪ'əʊ] **n** (**abbr of input/output**) E/S *f*.

IOC [aɪəʊ'siː] **n** (**abbr of International Olympic Committee**) C.I.O. *m*.

iodine ['aɪədiːn] **n** iode *m*.

iodize ['aɪədaɪz] **vt** ioder.

iodoform [aɪ'ɒdəfɔːm] **n** iodoforme *m*.

I.O.M. (*Brit*) (**abbr of Isle of Man**) *see* **isle b**.

ion ['aɪən] **n** ion *m*.

Iona [aɪ'əʊnə] **n** (île *f* d')Iona.

Ionian [aɪ'əʊnɪən] **adj** ionien. **the ~ Islands** les îles Ioniennes; **the ~ (Sea)** la mer Ionienne.

Ionic [aɪ'ɒnɪk] **adj** (*Archit*) ionique.

ionic [aɪ'ɒnɪk] **adj** (*Chem, Phys*) ionique.

ionize ['aɪənaɪz] **vt** ioniser.

ionosphere [aɪ'ɒnəsfɪəʳ] **n** ionosphère *f*.

iota [aɪ'əʊtə] **n** (*letter*) iota *m*; (*fig: tiny amount*) brin *m*, grain *m*; (*in written matter*) iota. **he won't change an ~ (of what he has written)** il refuse de changer un iota (à ce qu'il a écrit); **if he had an ~ of sense** s'il avait un grain de bon sens; **not an ~ of truth** pas un brin de vérité, pas un mot de vrai.

IOU [,aɪəʊ'juː] **n** (**abbr of I owe you**) reconnaissance *f* de dette. **he gave me an ~ for £20** il m'a signé un reçu *or* un billet pour 20 livres.

I.O.W. (*Brit*) (**abbr of Isle of Wight**) *see* **isle b**.

Iowa ['aɪəʊə] **n** Iowa *m*. **in ~** dans l'Iowa.

IPA [,aɪpiː'eɪ] **n** (**abbr of International Phonetic Alphabet**) A.P.I. *m*.

ipecac(uanha) [,ɪpɪkæk(jʊ'ænə)] **n** ipéca(cuana) *m*.

ipso facto ['ɪpsəʊ' fæktəʊ] **adj, adv** ipso facto.

I.Q. [,aɪ'kjuː] **n** (**abbr of intelligence quotient**) Q.I. *m*.

IR [,aɪ'ɑːʳ] (*Brit*) (**abbr of Inland Revenue**) ≃ fisc *m*.

I.R.A. [,aɪɑːr'eɪ] **n** (**abbr of Irish Republican Army**) I.R.A. *f* (*organisation paramilitaire*).

Irak [ɪ'rɑːk] **n** = **Iraq**.

Iraki [ɪ'rɑːkɪ] = **Iraqi**.

Iran [ɪ'rɑːn] **n** Iran *m*. **in ~** en Iran.

Iranian [ɪ'reɪnɪən] 1 **adj** iranien. 2 **n** a Iranien(ne) *m(f)*. b (*Ling*) iranien *m*.

Iraq [ɪ'rɑːk] **n** Irak *m*, Iraq *m*. **in ~** en Irak.

Iraqi [ɪ'rɑːkɪ] 1 **adj** irakien, iraqien. 2 **n** Irakien(ne) *m(f)*, Iraqien(ne) *m(f)*.

irascibility [ɪ,ræsɪ'bɪlɪtɪ] **n** irascibilité *f*.

irascible [ɪ'ræsɪbl] **adj** irascible, coléreux, colérique.

irascibly [ɪ'ræsɪblɪ] **adv** irasciblement.

irate [aɪ'reɪt] **adj** furieux, courroucé (*liter*).

IRBM [,aɪɑː,biː'em] (**abbr of intermediate range ballistic missile**) *see* **intermediate**.

ire [aɪəʳ] **n** (*liter*) colère *f*, courroux *m* (*liter*). **to rouse sb's ~** mettre qn dans une grande colère *or* en courroux (*liter*), provoquer le courroux de qn (*liter*).

Ireland ['aɪələnd] **n** Irlande *f*. **Republic of ~** République *f* d'Irlande; *see* **northern**.

irides ['ɪrɪdiːz] **npl of iris a**.

iridescence [,ɪrɪ'desns] **n** irisation *f*; [*plumage etc*] chatoiement *m*.

iridescent [,ɪrɪ'desnt] **adj** irisé, iridescent; *plumage* chatoyant.

iridium [aɪ'rɪdɪəm] **n** iridium *m*.

iridology [,ɪrɪ'dɒlədʒɪ] **n** iridiologie *f*.

iris ['aɪərɪs] **n** a (*pl* **irides**) [*eye*] iris *m*. b (*pl* **~es**) (*Bot*) iris *m*.

Irish ['aɪərɪʃ] 1 **adj** irlandais. (*Hist*) **~ Free State** État *m* libre d'Irlande; **~man** Irlandais *m*; **~ Sea** mer *f* d'Irlande; (*Culin*) **~ stew** ragoût *m* de mouton (à l'irlandaise); **~ terrier** irish-terrier *m*; **~ wolfhound** lévrier irlandais; **~woman** Irlandaise *f*; **~ coffee** café irlandais, Irish coffee *m*. 2 **n** a **the ~** (*pl*) les Irlandais *mpl*. b (*Ling*) irlandais *m*.

irk [ɜːk] **vt** contrarier, ennuyer.

irksome ['ɜːksəm] **adj** *restriction, person* ennuyeux; *task* ingrat.

iron ['aɪən] 1 **n** a (*NonC: metal*) fer *m*. **old ~, scrap ~** ferraille *f* (*NonC*); (*fig*) **a man of ~** (*unyielding*) un homme de fer; (*cruel*) un homme au cœur de pierre; (*loc*) **to strike while the ~ is hot** battre le fer pendant qu'il est chaud; *see* **cast, pump, rod, wrought** *etc*.

b (*tool*) fer *m*; (*for laundry: also* **flat ~**) fer (à repasser). **electric ~** fer électrique; (*fig*) **to have too many ~s in the fire** mener trop de choses *or* d'affaires de front; (*fig*) **I've got a lot of ~s in the fire** j'ai des quantités d'affaires en train; (*fig liter*) **the ~ had entered his soul** il avait la mort dans l'âme; **to give a dress an ~*, to run the ~ over a dress** donner un coup de fer à une robe; *see* **fire, grapple, solder** *etc*.

c (*fetters*) **~s** fers *mpl*, chaînes *fpl*; **to put** *or* **clap sb in ~s** mettre qn aux fers; (*Naut*) **to be in ~s** faire chapelle.

d (*Golf*) fer *m*. **a number 3 ~** un fer 3.

e (*NonC: Med*) (sels *mpl* de) fer *m*.

f (*surgical appliance*) attelle-étrier *f*; *see* **leg**.

2 **comp** (*lit*) *tool, bridge* de *or* en fer; (*fig*) *determination* de fer, d'acier ►**the Iron Age** l'âge *m* de fer ►**iron and steel industry** l'industrie *f* sidérurgique ►**the Iron Chancellor** (*Hist*) le Chancelier de fer (*Bismarck*) ►**ironclad** **n** (*Naut*) cuirassé *m* ◊ **adj** (*lit*) *warship* cuirassé; (*fig*) *argument etc* à toute épreuve, en béton (armé); *rule* impératif ►**iron constitution**: **to have an iron constitution** avoir une santé de fer, être bâti à chaux et à sable *or* à chaux et à ciment ►**Iron Curtain**† (*Pol*) rideau *m* de fer; **the Iron Curtain countries** les pays *mpl* de l'Est, le bloc de l'Est ►**the Iron Duke** (*Brit Hist*) le Duc de fer (*Wellington*) ►**iron fist**: (*loc*) **an iron fist** *or* **hand in a velvet glove** une main de fer dans un gant de velours ►**iron foundry** fonderie *f* de fonte ►**iron grey** gris *inv* de fer, gris fer *inv*; *hair* gris acier *inv* ►**iron hand**: **to rule with an iron hand** gouverner d'une main *or* poigne de fer (*see also* **iron fist**) ►**the Iron Lady** (*Brit Pol*) la Dame de fer ►**iron lung** (*Med*) poumon *m* d'acier ►**iron mask**: **the man in the iron mask** l'homme *m* au masque de fer ►**ironmonger** *see* **ironmonger** ►**iron ore** minerai *m* de fer ►**iron oxide** oxyde *m* de fer ►**iron pyrite** pyrite *f* ►**iron rations** vivres *mpl* *or* rations *fpl* de réserve ►**ironstone (china)** terre *f* de fer ►**iron will** volonté *f* de fer ►**ironwork** (*NonC*) (*gates, railings etc*) ferronnerie *f*, serrurerie *f*; (*parts of construction*) ferronnerie, ferrures *fpl*; **heavy ironwork** grosse ferronnerie *or* serrurerie ►**ironworks** **pl inv** usine *f* sidérurgique; *see* **minimum, non-**.

3 **vt** *clothes etc* repasser; (*more sketchily*) donner un coup de fer à. **to ~ under a damp cloth** repasser à la pattemouille; (*on label*) **"no-~"** "repassage superflu".

4 **vi** [*clothes etc*] se repasser.

►**iron out** **vt sep** *creases* faire disparaître au fer; (*fig*) *difficulties* aplanir; *problems* faire disparaître.

ironic(al) [aɪ'rɒnɪk(əl)] **adj** ironique.

ironically [aɪ'rɒnɪkəlɪ] **adv** ironiquement.

ironing ['aɪənɪŋ] 1 **n** repassage *m*. **to do the ~** repasser, faire le repassage; **it needs no ~** cela n'a pas besoin d'être repassé, cela ne nécessite aucun repassage. 2 **comp** ►**ironing board** planche *f* à repasser.

ironmonger ['aɪən,mʌŋgəʳ] **n** (*Brit*) quincaillier *m*. **~'s (shop)** quincaillerie *f*.

ironmongery ['aɪən,mʌŋgərɪ] **n** (*Brit*) quincaillerie *f*.

irony ['aɪərənɪ] **n** ironie *f*. **the ~ of fate** l'ironie du sort; **the ~ of it is that ...** ce qu'il y a d'ironique (là-dedans) c'est que ...; *see* **dramatic**.

Iroquois ['ɪrəkwɔɪ] 1 **adj** iroquois. 2 **n, pl inv** a (*also* **~ Indian**) Iroquois(e) *m(f)*. b (*Ling*) iroquois *m*.

irradiate [ɪ'reɪdɪeɪt] 1 **vt** a (*illuminate: lit, fig*) illuminer. b **to ~ light** émettre de la lumière; **to ~ heat** dégager de la chaleur. c (*expose to radiation*) *food, population* irradier. 2 **vi** irradier.

irradiation [ɪ,reɪdɪ'eɪʃən] **n** (*see* **irradiate**) illumination *f*; irradiation *f*.

irrational [ɪ'ræʃənl] **adj** *person* qui n'est pas rationnel; *animal* dépourvu de raison; *belief* déraisonnable, absurde; *conduct* irrationnel; (*Math*) irrationnel. **she had become quite ~ about it** elle n'était plus du tout capable d'y penser rationnellement.

irrationality [ɪˌræʃəˈnælɪtɪ] n irrationalité *f*.

irrationally [ɪˈræʃnəlɪ] adv *believe* déraisonnablement; *behave* irrationnellement.

irreconcilable [ɪˌrekənˈsaɪləbl] adj *enemy, enemies* irréconciliable; *hatred* implacable; *belief, opinion* inconciliable, incompatible (*with* avec).

irrecoverable [ˌɪrɪˈkʌvərəbl] adj *object* irrécupérable; (*Fin*) irrécouvrable; (*fig*) *loss* irréparable, irrémédiable.

irredeemable [ˌɪrɪˈdiːməbl] adj a *person* incorrigible, incurable; *error* irréparable; *disaster* irrémédiable. b (*Fin*) *loan* non amortissable, non remboursable; *bond* irremboursable.

irredeemably [ˌɪrɪˈdiːməblɪ] adv: ~ **lost/ruined** irrémédiablement perdu/ruiné; ~ **evil** d'une méchanceté irrémédiable.

irreducible [ˌɪrɪˈdjuːsəbl] adj irréductible.

irrefutable [ˌɪrɪˈfjuːtəbl] adj *argument, evidence* irréfutable; *testimony* irrécusable.

irregular [ɪˈregjʊləʳ] 1 adj a *marriage, troops, situation, hours, behaviour* irrégulier. **to be ~ in one's attendance** assister *or* être présent de façon peu régulière *or* intermittente; **he leads a very ~ life** il mène une vie très déréglée; **all this is very ~** tout cela n'est pas du tout régulier. b *shape, pulse, handwriting* irrégulier; *surface* inégal; *object, outline* irrégulier, asymétrique. c (*Ling*) irrégulier. 2 npl (*Mil*) **the ~s** les irréguliers *mpl*.

irregularity [ɪˌregjʊˈlærɪtɪ] n (*see* **irregular**) irrégularité *f*; asymétrie *f*; (*Jur, Admin*) (*in procedure*) vice *m* de forme. **the ~ of the ground** les accidents *mpl* du terrain.

irregularly [ɪˈregjʊləlɪ] adv *do sth* irrégulièrement, de façon irrégulière. **I see her only ~** je ne la vois que très irrégulièrement *or* que de temps en temps; **~-shaped** à la forme irrégulière.

irrelevance [ɪˈreləvəns] n, **irrelevancy** [ɪˈreləvənsɪ] n a (*NonC*) manque *m* de rapport, manque d'à-propos (*to* avec). b **a report full of ~s** *or* **irrelevancies** un compte rendu qui s'écarte sans cesse du sujet.

irrelevant [ɪˈreləvənt] adj *facts, details* sans rapport; *question, remark* hors de propos. **that's ~** cela n'a rien à voir avec *or* cela est sans rapport avec la question; **~ to the subject** hors du sujet.

irrelevantly [ɪˈreləvəntlɪ] adv *say, add* hors de propos.

irreligion [ˌɪrɪˈlɪdʒən] n irréligion *f*.

irreligious [ˌɪrɪˈlɪdʒəs] adj irréligieux.

irremediable [ˌɪrɪˈmiːdɪəbl] adj irrémédiable, sans remède.

irremediably [ˌɪrɪˈmiːdɪəblɪ] adv irrémédiablement.

irremovable [ˌɪrɪˈmuːvəbl] adj *thing* immuable; *difficulty* invincible; *judge etc* inamovible.

irreparable [ɪˈrepərəbl] adj *harm, wrong* irréparable; *loss* irréparable, irrémédiable.

irreparably [ɪˈrepərəblɪ] adv irréparablement, irrémédiablement.

irreplaceable [ˌɪrɪˈpleɪsəbl] adj irremplaçable.

irrepressible [ˌɪrɪˈpresəbl] adj *envy, laughter* irrépressible. **she's quite ~** elle pétille d'entrain, elle fait preuve d'un entrain débridé *or* irrépressible; (*of child*) c'est un vrai petit diable.

irrepressibly [ˌɪrɪˈpresəblɪ] adv *laugh etc* de façon irrépressible. ~ **cheerful/enthusiastic** d'une gaîté/d'un enthousiasme irrépressible.

irreproachable [ˌɪrɪˈprəʊtʃəbl] adj irréprochable.

irresistible [ˌɪrɪˈzɪstəbl] adj irrésistible.

irresistibly [ˌɪrɪˈzɪstəblɪ] adv irrésistiblement.

irresolute [ɪˈrezəluːt] adj irrésolu, indécis, hésitant.

irresolutely [ɪˈrezəˌluːtlɪ] adv *hesitate, pause etc* d'un air irrésolu *or* indécis.

irresoluteness [ɪˈrezəluːtnɪs] n irrésolution *f*, indécision *f*.

irrespective [ˌɪrɪˈspektɪv] adj: ~ **of** sans tenir compte de; ~ **of whether they are needed** que l'on en ait besoin ou non.

irresponsibility [ˈɪrɪsˌpɒnsəˈbɪlɪtɪ] n *[person]* irresponsabilité *f* (*also Jur*), légèreté *f*; *[act]* légèreté.

irresponsible [ˌɪrɪsˈpɒnsəbl] adj *person* qui n'a pas le sens des responsabilités, irréfléchi; *act, remark* irréfléchi, léger; (*Jur*) irresponsable. **it was ~ of her to do that** elle a fait preuve de légèreté en faisant cela.

irresponsibly [ˌɪrɪsˈpɒnsɪblɪ] adv (*gen*) sans penser à ses (*or* leurs *etc*) responsabilités; (*without thinking enough*) à la légère.

irretrievable [ˌɪrɪˈtriːvəbl] adj *loss, damage* irréparable, irrémédiable; *object* introuvable.

irretrievably [ˌɪrɪˈtriːvəblɪ] adv irréparablement, irrémédiablement.

irreverence [ɪˈrevərəns] n irrévérence *f*.

irreverent [ɪˈrevərənt] adj irrévérencieux.

irreverently [ɪˈrevərəntlɪ] adv irrévérencieusement, avec irrévérence.

irreversible [ˌɪrɪˈvɜːsəbl] adj *movement, operation* irréversible; *decision, judgment* irrévocable.

irreversibly [ˌɪrɪˈvɜːsəblɪ] adv irréversiblement.

irrevocable [ɪˈrevəkəbl] adj irrévocable.

irrevocably [ɪˈrevəkəblɪ] adv irrévocablement.

irrigable [ˈɪrɪgəbl] adj irrigable.

irrigate [ˈɪrɪgeɪt] vt (*Agr, Med*) irriguer.

irrigation [ˌɪrɪˈgeɪʃən] n (*Agr, Med*) irrigation *f*.

irritability [ˌɪrɪtəˈbɪlɪtɪ] n (*see* **irritable**) irritabilité *f*; (*irascibility*) mauvais caractère, irascibilité *f* (*liter*).

irritable [ˈɪrɪtəbl] adj *person* (*cross*) irritable; (*irascible*) irascible, coléreux; *look, mood* irritable; *temperament, nature* irascible. **to get** *or* **grow ~** devenir irritable; **~ bowel syndrome** syndrome *m* du côlon irritable.

irritably [ˈɪrɪtəblɪ] adv *behave, nod* avec humeur; *speak* d'un ton irrité.

irritant [ˈɪrɪtənt] adj, n (*esp Med*) irritant (*m*).

irritate [ˈɪrɪteɪt] vt a (*annoy*) irriter, agacer. **to get** *or* **become ~d** s'irriter. b (*Med*) irriter.

irritating [ˈɪrɪteɪtɪŋ] adj a (*annoying*) irritant, agaçant. b (*Med*) irritant.

irritatingly [ˈɪrɪteɪtɪŋlɪ] adv: ~ **slow/smug** d'une lenteur/d'une autosuffisance irritante *or* agaçante.

irritation [ˌɪrɪˈteɪʃən] n (*also Med*) irritation *f*.

irruption [ɪˈrʌpʃən] n irruption *f*.

IRS [ˌaɪɑːˈres] (*US*) (abbr of **Internal Revenue Service**) ≃ fisc *m*.

is [ɪz] *see* **be**.

Isaac [ˈaɪzək] n Isaac *m*.

Isaiah [aɪˈzaɪə] n Isaïe *m*.

I.S.B.N. [ˌaɪesˌbiːˈen] n (abbr of **International Standard Book Number**) ISBN *m*.

ischium [ˈɪskɪəm] n, pl **ischia** [ˈɪskɪə] ischion *m*.

ISDN [ˌaɪesˌdiːˈen] n (abbr of **Integrated Services Digital Network**) RNIS *m*.

...ish [ɪʃ] suf a ...âtre. **blackish** plutôt noir, noirâtre (*pej*). b **she came at threeish** elle est venue vers trois heures *or* sur les trois heures; **it's coldish** il fait un peu froid *or* frisquet*; **she's fortyish** elle a dans les quarante ans*.

isinglass [ˈaɪzɪŋglɑːs] n ichtyocolle *f*; (*Culin*) gélatine *f*.

Isis [ˈaɪsɪs] n (*Myth*) Isis *f*.

Islam [ˈɪzlɑːm] n Islam *m*.

Islamic [ɪzˈlæmɪk] adj islamique. (*Geog: in names*) **the ~ Republic of ...** la République islamique de ... .

Islamism [ˈɪzləmɪzəm] n Islamisme *m*.

island [ˈaɪlənd] n a (*lit, fig*) île *f*. **small ~** îlot *m*; **an ~ people/community** un peuple/une communauté insulaire; **the ~ people/community** le peuple/la communauté de l'île. b (*also* **traffic** *or* **street ~**) refuge *m* (*pour piétons*); (*in centre of roundabout*) terre-plein *m* central.

islander [ˈaɪləndəʳ] n insulaire *mf*, habitant(e) *m(f)* d'une île *or* de l'île.

isle [aɪl] n a (*liter*) île *f*. b (*Geog*) **I~ of Man** île *f* de Man; **I~ of Wight** île de Wight; *see* **British**.

islet [ˈaɪlɪt] n îlot *m*.

ism [ˈɪzəm] n doctrine *f*, théorie *f*. **all the ~s of today** tous les mots en "isme" actuels.

...ism [ˈɪzəm] suf ...isme.

isn't [ˈɪznt] = **is not**; *see* **be**.

ISO [ˌaɪesˈəʊ] n (abbr of **International Standards Organization**) ISO *f*, Organisation *f* des normes internationales.

iso... [ˈaɪsəʊ] pref iso... .

isobar [ˈaɪsəʊbɑːʳ] n isobare *f*.

Isobel [ˈɪzəʊbel] n Isabelle *f*.

isogloss [ˈaɪsəʊˌglɒs] n isoglosse *f*.

isolate [ˈaɪsəʊleɪt] vt (*all senses*) isoler (*from* de).

isolated [ˈaɪsəʊleɪtɪd] adj (*Chem, Med etc*) isolé; *village* isolé, écarté. ~ **case** cas isolé; **to feel ~** se sentir isolé.

isolation [ˌaɪsəʊˈleɪʃən] 1 n a (*gen, Med*) isolement *m*; *[village etc]* isolement, solitude *f*. **splendid ~** splendide isolement. b (*in fig phrases*) **to act in ~** agir seul; **to deal with sth in ~** traiter de qch à part; **no social class can exist in ~** aucune classe sociale ne peut exister isolément. c (*Chem etc*) (*action*) isolation *f*; (*state*) isolement *m*. 2 comp ▸**isolation hospital** hôpital *m* d'isolement *or* de contagieux ▸**isolation ward** salle *f* des contagieux.

isolationism [ˌaɪsəʊˈleɪʃənɪzəm] n isolationnisme *m*.

isolationist [ˌaɪsəʊˈleɪʃənɪst] adj, n isolationniste (*mf*).

Isolde [iˈzɒldə] n Iseult *f or* Iseut *f*.

isometric [ˌaɪsəʊˈmetrɪk] 1 adj isométrique. 2 npl: **~s** exercices *mpl* musculaires isométriques.

isomorphic [ˌaɪsəʊˈmɔːfɪk] adj isomorphe.

isopluvial [ˌaɪsəʊˈpluːvɪəl] adj: ~ **map** carte *f* pluviométrique.

isosceles [aɪˈsɒsɪliːz] adj isocèle.

isotherm [ˈaɪsəʊθɜːm] n isotherme *f*.

isotope [ˈaɪsəʊtəʊp] adj, n isotope (*m*).

Israel [ˈɪzreəl] n Israël *m* (*never with article*). **in ~** en Israël.

Israeli [ɪzˈreɪlɪ] 1 adj israélien; *embassy* d'Israël. 2 npl **~s** *or* **~** Israélien(ne) *m(f)*.

Israelite [ˈɪzrɪəlaɪt] n Israélite *mf*.

issue [ˈɪʃuː] 1 n a (*matter, question*) question *f*, sujet *m*, problème *m*. **it is a very difficult ~** c'est une question *or* un sujet *or* un problème très complexe, c'est un point très délicat; **he raised several new ~s** il a soulevé plusieurs points nouveaux; **the ~ is whether ...** la question consiste à savoir si ...; **the main ~ is to discover if ...** la question centrale est de découvrir si ...; **that's the main ~** voilà la question *or* le problème principal(e); **it's not a political ~** ce n'est pas un problème politique; **to cloud** *or* **confuse** *or* **obscure the ~** brouiller les cartes; **to face the ~** regarder le problème en face; **to force the ~** forcer une décision; **to evade** *or* **avoid the ~** prendre la tangente, s'échapper par la tangente; **to make an ~ of sth** faire de qch un sujet de controverse, faire un problème de qch, monter qch en épingle; **he makes an ~ of every tiny detail** il fait une montagne du moindre détail; **I don't want to make an ~ of it but** ... je ne veux pas trop insister là-dessus mais ...; **the matter/factors at ~** l'affaire/les facteurs en jeu; **the point at ~** le point controversé, la question en litige *or* qui pose un problème; **his integrity is not at ~** son intégrité n'est pas (mise) en doute *or* en cause; **his political future is at ~** son avenir politique est (mis) en question *or* en cause; **they were at ~ over** ... ils étaient en désaccord sur ...; **to take** *or* **join ~ with sb** engager une controverse avec qn; **I feel I must take ~ with you on this** je me permets de ne pas partager votre avis là-dessus; *see also* **side**.

b (*outcome*) résultat *m*, aboutissement *m*, issue *f*. **in the ~** en fin de compte, à la fin; **until the ~ is known** jusqu'à ce qu'on sache le résultat; **favourable ~** résultat heureux, heureuse issue; **we brought the matter to a successful ~** nous avons mené l'affaire à une heureuse conclusion.

c *[book]* publication *f*, parution *f*, sortie *f*; *[magazine, newspaper]* livraison *f*; *[goods, tickets]* distribution *f*; *[passport, document]* délivrance *f*; *[banknote, cheque, shares, stamp]* émission *f*, mise *f* en circulation; *[proclamation]* parution; (*Jur*) *[warrant, writ, summons]* lancement *m*. **there has been a new ~ of banknotes/stamps/shares** il y a eu une nouvelle émission de billets/de timbres/d'actions; **there were several ~s of clothing to refugees** il y a eu plusieurs distributions de vêtements aux réfugiés; **these coins are a new ~** ces pièces viennent d'être émises; *see also* **2**.

d (*copy*) *[newspaper, magazine]* numéro *m*. **in this ~** dans ce numéro; **back ~** vieux numéro.

e (*Med*) écoulement *m*.

f (*NonC: Jur: offspring*) descendance *f*, progéniture *f* (*liter*). **without ~** sans enfants, sans progéniture (*liter*), sans descendance; **X and his ~** X et sa descendance *or* ses descendants.

2 **comp** (*esp Mil*) *clothing etc* réglementaire, d'ordonnance ►**issue price** (*St Ex*) prix *m or* cours *m* d'émission.

3 **vt** *book* publier, faire paraître; *order* donner; *goods, tickets* distribuer; *passport, document* délivrer; *banknote, cheque, shares, stamps* émettre, mettre en circulation; *proclamation* faire; (*Jur*) *warrant, warning, writ* lancer; (*Jur*) *verdict* rendre. **to ~ a statement** publier une mise au point, faire une déclaration; (*Jur*) **to ~ a summons** lancer une assignation; (*Fin*) **~d to bearer** émis au porteur; **to ~ sth to sb, to ~ sb with sth** fournir *or* donner qch à qn; **the children were ~d with pencils** on distribua *or* fournit *or* donna des crayons aux enfants.

issuer [ˈɪʃʊəʳ] **n** (*Fin, St Ex*) émetteur *m*, société *f* émettrice.

Istanbul [ˌɪstænˈbuːl] **n** Istamboul *or* Istanbul.

isthmus [ˈɪsməs] **n, pl ~es** *or* **isthmi** [ˈɪsmaɪ] isthme *m*.

Istria [ˈɪstrɪə] **n** Istrie *f*.

IT [ˈaɪˈtiː] (**abbr of information technology**) *see* **information**.

it¹ [ɪt] **pron** a (*specific*) (*nominative*) il, elle; (*accusative*) le, la, (*before vowel*) l'; (*dative*) lui. **where is the book? — ~'s on the table** où est le livre? — il est sur la table; **my machine is old but ~ works** ma machine est vieille mais elle marche; **here's the pencil — give ~ to me** voici le crayon — donne-le-moi; **if you can find the watch give ~ to him** si tu peux trouver la montre donne-la-lui; **he found the book and brought ~ to me** il a trouvé le livre et me l'a apporté; **let the dog in and give ~ a drink** fais entrer le chien et donne-lui à boire.

b **of ~, from ~, about ~, for ~** *etc* en; **he's afraid of ~** il en a peur; **I took the letter out of ~** j'en ai sorti la lettre; **I feel the better for ~** je m'en trouve mieux; **I don't care about ~** je ne m'en soucie pas, je m'en fiche*; **speak to him about ~** parlez-lui-en; **he didn't speak to me about ~** il ne m'en a pas parlé; (*following French verbs with "de"*) **I doubt ~** j'en doute.

c **in ~, to ~, at ~** *etc* y; **I'll see to ~** j'y veillerai; **he fell in ~** il y est tombé; (*meeting etc*) **he'll be at ~** il y sera; **he agreed to ~** il y a consenti; (*following French verbs with "à"*) **taste ~!** goutez-y!; **don't touch ~** n'y touche pas.

d **above ~, over ~** (au-)dessus; **below ~, beneath ~, under ~** (au-)dessous, (en-)dessous; **there's the table and your book is on ~** voilà la table et votre livre est dessus; **a table with a cloth over ~** une table avec une nappe dessus; **he drew a house with a cloud above ~** il a dessiné une maison avec un nuage au-dessus; **there is a fence but you can get under ~** il y a une barrière mais vous pouvez passer (en-)dessous.

e (*impers: non-specific*) il, ce, cela, ça. **~ is raining** il pleut; **~'s hot today** il fait chaud aujourd'hui; **~ was a warm evening** il faisait doux ce soir-là; **~ all frightens me** tout cela m'effraie; **~'s very pleasant here** c'est agréable *or* bien ici; **~'s Wednesday 16th October** nous sommes (le) mercredi 16 octobre; **~'s 3 o'clock** il est 3 heures; **who is ~?** qui est-ce?; **~'s me** c'est moi; **what is ~?** qu'est-ce que c'est?; **what's ~ all about?** qu'est-ce qui se passe?, de quoi s'agit-il?, de quoi est-il question?; **where is ~?** où est-ce?, où est-ce que c'est?; **that's ~!** (*approval*) c'est ça!; (*agreement*) c'est bien ça!, exactement!, tout à fait!; (*achievement*) ça y est!, c'est fait!; (*anger*) ça suffit!; (*dismay*) ça y est!; **how was ~?** comment ça s'est(-il) passé?, comment c'était?*; **what was that noise? — ~ was the cat** qu'est-ce que c'était que ce bruit? — c'était le chat; **~ isn't worth while** ce n'est pas la peine; **~'s no use trying to see him** ce n'est pas la peine de *or* ça ne sert à rien d'essayer de le voir; **~'s difficult to understand** c'est difficile à comprendre; **~'s difficult to understand why** il est difficile de comprendre pourquoi; **~'s a pity** c'est dommage; **I considered ~ pointless to protest** j'ai jugé (qu'il était) inutile de protester; **~'s fun to go for a swim** c'est amusant d'aller nager; **~ was your father who phoned** c'est ton père qui a téléphoné; **~ was Anne I gave it to** c'est à Anne que je l'ai donné; **~ can't be helped** on n'y peut rien, on ne peut rien y faire; **the best of ~ is that** ... ce qu'il y a de mieux (là-dedans) c'est que ...; **he's not got ~ in him to do this job properly** il est incapable de faire ce travail comme il faut, il n'a pas l'étoffe de mener la chose à bien; **he's got what ~ takes*** il est à la hauteur*; **keep at ~!** continuez!; (*after quarrel*) **they made ~ up** ils se sont réconciliés; **let's face ~** regardons les choses en face; **now you've done ~!** ça y est, regarde ce que tu as fait!; **you'll catch ~!** tu vas écoper!*; **he's had ~*** il est fichu*; **to be with ~*** être dans le vent* *or* à la page; **to get with ~*** se mettre à la page; **he's got ~ bad*** il est pincé*; **he's got ~ bad for her*** il en pince pour elle*, il l'a dans la peau*; **she's got ~ in for me** elle m'en veut, elle a une dent contre moi*.

f (*in games*) **you're ~!** c'est toi le chat!

g (*something special*) **she really thinks she's ~*** elle se prend vraiment pour le nombril du monde*; **she's got ~*** elle est sexy*.

it² [ɪt] **n** (**abbr of Italian**) **gin and ~** vermouth-gin *m*.

I.T.A. [ˌaɪtiːˈeɪ] (**abbr of initial teaching alphabet**) *see* **initial**.

Italian [ɪˈtæljən] 1 **adj** italien; *embassy* d'Italie. 2 **n** a Italien(ne) *m(f)*. b (*Ling*) italien *m*; *see* **Switzerland**.

italic [ɪˈtælɪk] 1 **adj** (*Typ*) italique. **~ script** écriture *f* italique. 2 **npl: ~s** italique *m*; **to put a word in ~s** mettre un mot en italique; **"my ~s"** "les italiques sont de moi".

italicize [ɪˈtælɪsaɪz] **vt** (*Typ*) mettre *or* imprimer en italique.

Italy [ˈɪtəlɪ] **n** Italie *f*.

ITC [ˌaɪtiːˈsiː] **n** (*Brit*) (**abbr of Independent Television Commission**) ≃ CSA *m*.

itch [ɪtʃ] 1 **n** (*lit*) démangeaison *f*. **I've got an ~ in my leg** ma jambe me démange; (*Med, Vet*) **the ~** la gale; (*fig*) **I've got an ~* to travel** l'envie de voyager me démange, je meurs d'envie de voyager.

2 **vi** a *[person]* éprouver des démangeaisons. **his legs ~** ses jambes le *or* lui démangent; **my back ~es** j'ai des démangeaisons dans le dos, le dos me démange.

b (* *fig*) **to be ~ing to do sth** avoir une envie qui vous démange de faire qch; **I am ~ing to tell him the news** la langue me démange de lui annoncer la nouvelle; **he's ~ing for a fight** ça le démange de se battre; **my hand is ~ing (to slap him)** la main me démange *or* j'ai la main qui me démange (de le gifler).

3 **vt** démanger.

itching [ˈɪtʃɪŋ] **n** démangeaison *f*. **~ powder** poil *m* à gratter.

itchy [ˈɪtʃɪ] **adj** qui démange. **I've got an ~ back** j'ai le dos qui me démange, j'ai des démangeaisons dans le dos; (*fig*) **he's got ~ feet*** il a la bougeotte*; (*fig*) **he's got ~ fingers*** il est chapardeur, il a les doigts collants*.

it'd [ˈɪtd] = **it had, it would**; *see* **have, would**.

item [ˈaɪtəm] 1 **n** (*Comm, Comput*) article *m*; (*in discussion, at meeting*) question *f*, point *m*; (*in variety show*) numéro *m*; (*in catalogue, newspaper*) article; (*Jur: in contract*) article; (*Book-keeping*) poste *m*. **an ~ of furniture** un meuble; **~s on the agenda** questions à l'ordre du jour; **the first ~ on the programme** le premier numéro du programme; **the first ~ on the list** (*gen*) la première chose sur la liste; (*on shopping list*) le premier article sur la liste; (*in discussion*) la première question *or* le premier point sur la liste; (*Rad, TV*) **the main ~ in the news** le titre principal des informations, la grosse nouvelle, le fait du jour; **it's an important ~ in our policy** c'est un point important de notre politique; **they're an ~*** ils sont ensemble.

2 **comp** ►**item veto** (*US Pol*) veto partiel (*sur un projet de loi*).

3 **adv** de plus, en outre; (*Comm etc: when enumerating*) item.

itemize [ˈaɪtəmaɪz] **vt** *bill etc* détailler, spécifier.

itinerant [ɪˈtɪnərənt] **adj** *preacher* itinérant; *actors, musician* ambulant. **~ lace-seller** colporteur *m*, -euse *f* de dentelle; (*US Scol*) **~ teacher** professeur *m* qui exerce sur plusieurs établissements.

itinerary [aɪˈtɪnərərɪ] **n** itinéraire *m*.

it'll [ˈɪtl] = **it will**; *see* **will**.

ITN [ˌaɪtiːˈen] **n** (*Brit*) (**abbr of Independent Television News**) *chaîne indépendante d'actualités télévisées*.

its [ɪts] 1 **poss adj** son *m* (*also f before vowel*), sa *f*, ses *pl*. 2 **poss pron** le sien, la sienne, les siens, les siennes.

it's [ɪts] = **it is, it has**; *see* **be, have**.

itself [ɪtˈself] **pron** a (*emphatic*) lui-même *m*, elle-même *f*. **the book ~ is not valuable** le livre (en) lui-même n'est pas de grande valeur; **the chair ~ was covered with ink** la chaise elle-même était couverte d'encre; **she is goodness ~** elle est la bonté même; **she fainted in the**

theatre ~ elle s'est évanouie en plein théâtre *or* dans le théâtre même; **the door closes by** ~ la porte se ferme automatiquement *or* toute seule; **by** ~ isolément, en soi; **this by** *or* **in** ~ **is not bad** ceci n'est pas un mal en soi. b (*reflexive*) se. **the dog hurt** ~ le chien s'est fait mal; **the computer can reprogram** ~ l'ordinateur peut se reprogrammer tout seul.

ITV [ˌaɪtiːˈviː] **n** (*Brit*) (**abbr of Independent Television**) *chaîne indépendante de télévision.*

IU(C)D [ˌaɪjuːsiːˈdiː] **n** (**abbr of intrauterine (contraceptive) device**) D.I.U. *m.*

IV, i.v. [ˈaɪˈviː] (**abbr of intravenous(ly)**) IV, iv.

Ivan [ˈaɪvən] **n** Ivan *m.* ~ **the Terrible** Ivan le Terrible.

I've [aɪv] = **I have;** *see* **have.**

IVF [ˌaɪviːˈef] (**abbr of in vitro fertilization**) FIV *f.*

ivory [ˈaɪvərɪ] 1 **n** a (*NonC*) ivoire *m.* b (objet *m* d')ivoire *m.* **an** ~ **of great worth** un ivoire de grande valeur; **ivories** (*: *piano keys*) touches *fpl*; (*Billiards* ⁑) boules *fpl* de billard; (*dice*) dés *mpl*; (⁑: *teeth*) dents *fpl.* 2 **comp** *statue, figure* en ivoire, d'ivoire; (*also* **ivory-coloured**) ivoire *inv* ▸**Ivory Coast** Côte *f* d'Ivoire ▸**ivory tower** (*fig*) tour *f* d'ivoire ▸**ivory trade** (*selling*) commerce *m* de l'ivoire; (*the industry*) industrie *f* de l'ivoire.

ivy [ˈaɪvɪ] **n** lierre *m.* ~**leaf geranium** géranium-lierre *m*; (*US*) **I~ League** (**n**) *les huit grandes universités privées du nord-est;* (**adj**) bon chic bon genre* (*style étudiant chic*).

J

J, j [dʒeɪ] n (*letter*) J, j *m*. **J for Jack, J for John,** (*US*) **J for Jig** ≃ J comme Joseph.

jab [dʒæb] 1 vt *knife, stick* enfoncer, planter (*into* dans). **he ~bed his elbow into my side** il m'a donné un coup de coude dans les côtes; **he ~bed the cushion with his stick** il a enfoncé son bâton dans le coussin; **he ~bed a finger at the map** il a planté son doigt sur la carte. 2 vi (*Boxing*) lancer un coup droit, envoyer un direct (*at* à). 3 n a coup *m* (*donné avec un objet pointu*), coup de pointe. b (*: *injection*) piqûre *f*. **I've had my ~** on m'a fait ma piqûre. c (*Boxing*) coup *m* droit, direct *m*.

jabber ['dʒæbəʳ] 1 vt *excuse, explanation* bafouiller; *foreign language* baragouiner. **to ~ (out) one's prayers** bredouiller *or* marmotter ses prières. 2 vi (*also* **~ away**) (*chatter*) bavarder, jacasser; (*speak unintelligibly*) baragouiner. **they were ~ing (away) in Chinese** ils baragouinaient en chinois.

jabbering ['dʒæbərɪŋ] n bavardage *m*, jacasserie *f*; baragouinage *m*.

jacaranda [ˌdʒækə'rændə] n jacaranda *m*.

jack [dʒæk] 1 n a (*Aut*) cric *m*.
b (*Bowling*) cochonnet *m*, bouchon* *m*.
c (*Cards*) valet *m*.
d (*flag*) *see* **union**.
e (**dim of John**) **J~ Frost** (le) Bonhomme Hiver; **J~ and the Beanstalk** Jack au pays des géants; **before you could say J~ Robinson*** en moins de temps qu'il n'en faut pour le dire.
f **every man ~** chacun; **every man ~ of them** tous tant qu'ils sont (*or* étaient *etc*).
g (*game*) **~s** osselets *mpl*.
2 comp ►**jackass** âne *m*, baudet* *m*; (* *fig*) crétin* *m* (*see* **laughing**) ►**jackboot** adj *discipline, method* autoritaire, dictatorial ►**jackboots** npl (*Mil etc*) bottes *fpl* à l'écuyère ►**jackdaw** choucas *m* ►**jackfruit** (*tree*) ja(c)quier *m*; (*fruit*) ja(c)que *m* ►**jackhammer** (*US*) marteau-piqueur *m* ►**jack-in-office*** (*pej*) gratte-papier *m inv or* rond-de-cuir *m* (qui joue à l'important) ►**jack-in-the-box** diable *m* (à ressort) ►**jack-knife** n couteau *m* de poche ◊ vi: **the lorry jack-knifed** la remorque (du camion) s'est mise en travers; **jack-knife dive** saut carpé *or* de carpe ►**jackleg** (*US*) (*not qualified*) *carpenter etc* amateur; (*dishonest*) *work* louche; (*makeshift*) *structure* de fortune ►**jack of all trades (and master of none)** touche-à-tout *m* ►**jack-o'-lantern** feu follet *m* ►**jack plug** prise *f* à fiche ►**jackpot** (*Betting*) gros lot; (*Cards*) pot *m*; (*lit, fig*) **to hit the jackpot** gagner le gros lot; **their last disc hit the jackpot** leur dernier disque a fait un malheur* *or* un tabac* ►**jack rabbit** gros lièvre (*de l'Ouest américain*) ►**jackstraw** (*fig*) nullité *f* ►**jackstraws** (*game*) (jeu *m* de) jonchets *mpl* ►**jack tar, Jack Tar** (*Naut* *) marin *m*, matelot *m*.

►**jack in**‡ vt sep plaquer‡.

►**jack up** vt sep *car* soulever avec un cric; (*: *raise*) *prices, wages* faire grimper. **the car was jacked up** la voiture était sur le cric.

jackal ['dʒækɔːl] n chacal *m*.

jackanapes ['dʒækəneɪps] n polisson(ne) *m(f)*.

jacket ['dʒækɪt] n a [*man*] veste *f*, veston *m*; [*woman*] veste, jaquette *f*; [*child*] paletot *m*; *see* **life**. b [*boiler etc*] enveloppe *f*, chemise *f*; [*book*] couverture *f*; [*record*] pochette *f*. (*Brit*) **~ potatoes, potatoes baked in their ~s** pommes de terre en robe des champs *or* en robe de chambre *or* au four.

Jacob ['dʒeɪkəb] n Jacob *m*. **Jacob's ladder** l'échelle *f* de Jacob.

Jacobean [ˌdʒækə'biːən] adj de l'époque de Jacques Iᵉʳ (*1603-1625*).

Jacobite ['dʒækəbaɪt] 1 n Jacobite *mf*. 2 adj jacobite.

Jacuzzi [dʒə'kuːzɪ] n ® Jacuzzi *m* ®, bain *m* à jet propulsé.

jade¹ [dʒeɪd] 1 n jade *m*. 2 adj (*colour*) (couleur de) jade *inv*. 3 comp ►**jade-green** vert (de) jade *inv*.

jade² [dʒeɪd] n (*horse*) haridelle *f*, rossinante *f*; († *pej: prostitute*) traînée‡ *f*; (†: *pert girl*) coquine *f*.

jaded ['dʒeɪdɪd] adj *person* las (*f* lasse) (*with or about* de), blasé; *palate* blasé. **his appetite was ~** il avait l'estomac fatigué.

jag [dʒæg] 1 n a pointe *f*, saillie *f*, aspérité *f*. b (*fig*) **drinking ~*** cuite* *f*; **they were on a drinking ~* last night** ils se sont bien cuités* *or* ils ont pris une fameuse cuite* hier soir; **she got a crying ~*** elle a eu une crise de larmes. c (*Scot*) injection *f*, piqûre *f*. 2 vt déchirer, déchiqueter, denteler.

jagged ['dʒægɪd] adj *tear, edge, hole* irrégulier, déchiqueté, dentelé.

jaguar ['dʒægjʊəʳ] n jaguar *m*.

jai alai ['haɪ əˌlaɪ] n (*US Sport*) ≃ pelote *f* basque.

jail [dʒeɪl] 1 n prison *f*. **he is in ~** il est en prison; **he was in ~ for 5 years** il a fait 5 ans de prison; **to put sb in ~** mettre qn en prison, emprisonner qn, incarcérer qn; **to send sb to ~** condamner qn à la prison; **to send sb to ~ for 5 years** condamner qn à 5 ans de prison. 2 vt emprisonner, mettre en prison, incarcérer. **to ~ sb for life** condamner qn (à la réclusion) à perpétuité; **to ~ sb for murder** condamner qn à la prison pour meurtre. 3 comp ►**jailbait**‡ (*US*) mineure *f* (*qui n'a pas atteint l'âge nubile légal*) ►**jailbird** récidiviste *mf* ►**jailbreak** évasion *f* (de prison) ►**jailbreaker** évadé(e) *m(f)*.

jailer ['dʒeɪləʳ] n geôlier *m*, -ière *f*.

jakes‡ [dʒeɪks] n: **the ~** les cabinets *mpl*.

jalop(p)y* [dʒə'lɒpɪ] n vieux tacot*, guimbarde *f*.

jalousie ['ʒæluːziː] n jalousie *f* (*store*).

jam¹ [dʒæm] 1 n a [*logs, vehicles etc*] embouteillage *m*, encombrement *m*. **there was a great ~ of people waiting to get in** il y avait toute une masse de gens *or* une foule de gens qui attendaient d'entrer; *see* **traffic**.
b (*) pétrin *m*. **to get into a ~** se mettre dans le pétrin; **to get sb out of a ~** tirer qn du pétrin.
c (*Climbing*) coincement *m*, verrou *m*.
2 comp ►**jam-full, jam-packed** *vehicle, room* comble, plein à craquer*, bondé; *street, pavements* noir de monde; *container, suitcase* plein à ras bord.
3 vt a (*crush, squeeze*) serrer, comprimer, écraser; (*wedge*) coincer. **to be ~med between the wall and the door** être coincé entre le mur et la porte; **ship ~med in the ice** navire bloqué par les glaces; **he got his finger ~med** *or* **he ~med his finger in the door** il s'est coincé le doigt dans la porte.
b (*make unworkable*) *brake, door* bloquer, coincer; *gun, machine* enrayer; (*Rad*) *station, broadcast* brouiller; (*Telec*) *line* encombrer.
c (*cram*) enfoncer, fourrer en forçant, tasser, entasser (*into* dans). **to ~ clothes into a suitcase** tasser des vêtements dans une valise; **the prisoners were ~med into a small cell** les prisonniers ont été entassés dans une petite cellule; **to ~ one's hat on one's head** enfoncer son chapeau sur sa tête; **to ~ one's foot on the brake** écraser le frein, freiner à bloc *or* à mort*.
d (*block*) [*crowd, cars etc*] *street, corridor* encombrer, embouteiller, obstruer; *door* encombrer. **a street ~med with cars** une rue embouteillée; **the street was ~med with people** la rue était noire de monde.
4 vi a (*press tightly*) [*crowd*] s'entasser (*into* dans).
b (*become stuck*) [*brake*] se bloquer; [*gun*] s'enrayer; [*door, switch, lever*] se coincer.

►**jam in** vt sep serrer, écraser, coincer. **the crowd jammed him in so that he couldn't move** la foule le bloquait *or* le coinçait tellement qu'il lui était impossible de bouger; **to be jammed in by the crowd** être écrasé *or* compressé par *or* dans la foule; **my car is jammed in** ma voiture est coincée *or* bloquée (entre deux autres).

►**jam on** vt sep a (*Aut*) **to jam on the brakes** freiner brutalement, freiner à bloc *or* à mort*. b **to jam on one's hat** enfoncer son chapeau sur sa tête.

jam² [dʒæm] 1 n confiture *f*. **cherry ~** confiture de cerises; (*Brit*) **it's real ~**‡ c'est du gâteau*; (*Brit*) **you want ~ on it!*** tu te contentes de peu! (*iro*), t'es pas difficile!* (*iro*), et avec ça?* (*iro*); *see* **money**. 2 comp *tart* à la confiture ►**jamjar, jampot** pot *m* à confitures ►**jam puff** feuilleté *m* à la confiture ►**jam roll** roulé *m* à la confiture.

jam³ [dʒæm] (*Mus*) 1 **n**: ~ **(session)** bœuf *m*. 2 **vi** faire un bœuf.
Jamaica [dʒə'meɪkə] **n** Jamaïque *f*. **in** ~ à la Jamaïque.
Jamaican [dʒə'meɪkən] 1 **adj** jamaïquain; *president, embassy* de la Jamaïque. 2 **n** Jamaïquain(e) *m(f)*.
jamb [dʒæm] **n** *[door etc]* jambage *m*, montant *m*.
jamboree [ˌdʒæmbə'riː] **n** grand rassemblement; (*merrymaking*) festivités *fpl*; (*fig*) réjouissances *fpl*; (*Scouts*) jamboree *m*.
James [dʒeɪmz] **n** Jacques *m*.
jamming ['dʒæmɪŋ] **n** a (*Rad*) brouillage *m*. b (*Climbing*) coincement *m*, verrou *m*.
jammy ['dʒæmɪ] **adj** a (*lit*) *fingers, hands* poisseux (*de confiture*). b (*Brit* ‡: *lucky*) verni*. **it was** ~ c'était un coup de veine* *or* de pot*; ~ **devil** *or* **so-and-so** veinard(e) *m(f)*.
JAN [ˌdʒeɪeɪ'en] **n** (*US*) (**abbr of Joint Army-Navy**) *organisation commune armée-marine*.
Jan. **abbr of January**.
Jane [dʒeɪn] **n** a Jeanne *f*; *see* **plain**. b (‡: *girl*) j~‡ pépée‡ *f*, nana‡ *f*. c (†: *Drugs sl*) marie-jeanne*† *f*, marijuana *f*.
jangle ['dʒæŋgl] 1 **vi** *[bells, saucepans]* retentir avec un bruit de ferraille *or* de casserole; *[bracelets, chains]* cliqueter. 2 **vt** faire retentir d'une façon discordante; faire cliqueter. ~**d nerves** nerfs en boule *or* en pelote. 3 **n** bruit discordant; cliquetis *m*.
jangling ['dʒæŋglɪŋ] 1 **adj** (qui fait un bruit) discordant, cacophonique. 2 **n** bruit(s) discordant(s); cliquetis *m*.
janitor ['dʒænɪtəʳ] **n** (*doorkeeper*) portier *m*; (*US, Scot: caretaker*) concierge *m*, gardien *m*.
Jansenism ['dʒænsəˌnɪzəm] **n** jansénisme *m*.
Jansenist ['dʒænsənɪst] **adj, n** janséniste *(mf)*.
January ['dʒænjʊərɪ] **n** janvier *m*; *for phrases see* **September**.
Janus ['dʒeɪnəs] **n** Janus *m*.
Jap [dʒæp] **n** (**abbr of Japanese**: *often pej*) Japonais(e) *m(f)*.
Japan [dʒə'pæn] **n** Japon *m*.
japan [dʒə'pæn] 1 **n** laque *f*. 2 **vt** laquer, vernir.
Japanese [ˌdʒæpə'niːz] 1 **adj** japonais, nippon; *embassy* du Japon. 2 **n** a (**pl inv**) Japonais(e) *m(f)*. b (*Ling*) japonais *m*.
jape [dʒeɪp] **n** (*trick*) farce *f*, tour *m*; (*joke*) blague* *f*.
japonica [dʒə'pɒnɪkə] **n** cognassier *m* du Japon.
jar¹ [dʒɑːʳ] 1 **n** (*harsh sound*) son discordant; (*jolt: lit, fig*) secousse *f*, choc *m*. **that gave him a nasty** ~ cela l'a sérieusement ébranlé *or* secoué.
2 **vi** a (*sound discordant*) rendre un son discordant, grincer, crisser; (*rattle, vibrate*) vibrer, trembler. **to** ~ **against sth** cogner sur qch *or* heurter qch (avec un bruit discordant).
b (*be out of harmony*) *[note]* détonner; *[colours]* jurer (*with* avec); (*fig*) *[ideas, opinions]* ne pas s'accorder (*with* avec), se heurter. **what he says** ~**s a little** ce qu'il dit sonne faux.
3 **vt** *structure* ébranler; *person* ébranler, secouer; (*fig*) commotionner, choquer. **the explosion** ~**red the whole building** l'explosion a ébranlé tout le bâtiment; **he was badly** ~**red by the blow** il a été sérieusement commotionné par le choc; **you** ~**red my elbow** tu m'as cogné le coude.
►**jar (up)on** **vt fus** irriter, agacer. **this noise jars (up)on my nerves** ce bruit me met les nerfs en boule* *or* me porte sur les nerfs*; **her screams jar (up)on my ears** ses cris m'écorchent *or* me percent les oreilles.
jar² [dʒɑːʳ] **n** a (*of stone, earthenware*) pot *m*, jarre *f*; (*of glass*) bocal *m*; *see* **jam²**. b (*Brit* ‡: *drink*) pot* *m*, verre *m*. **we had a few** ~**s** on a pris quelques verres*.
jargon ['dʒɑːgən] **n** (*technical language*) jargon *m*; (*pompous nonsense*) jargon, charabia* *m*, baragouin *m*.
jarring ['dʒɑːrɪŋ] **adj** *sound* discordant; *colour* qui jure. (*fig*) **it struck a** ~ **note** cela a sonné faux.
Jas. **abbr of James**.
jasmine ['dʒæzmɪn] **n** jasmin *m*. ~ **tea** thé *m* au jasmin.
Jason ['dʒeɪsən] **n** Jason *m*.
jasper ['dʒæspəʳ] **n** jaspe *m*.
jaundice ['dʒɔːndɪs] **n** (*Med*) jaunisse *f*; (*fig*) jalousie *f*, amertume *f*.
jaundiced ['dʒɔːndɪst] **adj** (*fig*) (*bitter*) amer, aigri; (*critical*) désapprobateur (*f* -trice). **to look on sth with a** ~ **eye, to take a** ~ **view of sth** voir qch d'un mauvais œil; **he has a fairly** ~ **view of things** il voit les choses en noir; **to give sb a** ~ **look** regarder qn d'un œil torve.
jaunt [dʒɔːnt] 1 **n** balade* *f*. **to go for a** ~ aller faire un tour, aller se balader*. 2 **comp** ►**jaunting car** carriole irlandaise (à deux roues).
jauntily ['dʒɔːntɪlɪ] **adv** (*see* **jaunty**) d'un pas vif; de façon désinvolte; d'un air crâneur*.
jauntiness ['dʒɔːntɪnɪs] **n** (*sprightliness*) insouciance *f*, légèreté *f*; (*offhand manner*) sans-gêne *m inv*, désinvolture *f*, allure *f* désinvolte *or* cavalière; (*swaggering*) crânerie* *f*, bravade *f*.
jaunty ['dʒɔːntɪ] **adj** (*sprightly*) *step* enjoué, vif; (*carefree*) *smile, air* désinvolte; (*swaggering*) crâneur*. ~ **car** carriole irlandaise (à deux roues).
Java ['dʒɑːvə] **n** Java *f*. **in** ~ à Java.
java* ['dʒɑːvə] **n** (*US: coffee*) café *m*.
Javanese [ˌdʒɑːvə'niːz] 1 **adj** javanais. 2 **n** a (**pl inv**) Javanais(e) *m(f)*. b (*Ling*) javanais *m*.
javelin ['dʒævlɪn] 1 **n** (*Mil*) javelot *m*, javeline *f*; (*Sport*) javelot. 2 **comp** ►**javelin thrower** (*Sport*) lanceur *m*, -euse *f* de javelot ►**javelin throwing** le lancement *or* le lancer du javelot.
jaw [dʒɔː] 1 **n** (*Anat*) mâchoire *f*; *[pincer, vice]* mâchoire; (‡: *moralizing*) sermon* *m*; (‡: *long-winded talk*) laïus* *m*. (*fig*) **his** ~ **dropped** il en est resté bouche bée; **the** ~**s of the valley** l'entrée *f* de la vallée; **the** ~**s of death** les griffes *fpl or* l'étreinte *f* de la mort; **the** ~**s of hell** les portes *fpl* de l'enfer; **I'll break your** ~ **for you!*** je vais te casser la figure!*; **we had a good old** ~ on a bien papoté*; **hold your** ~!‡ ferme-là!‡; *see* **lock¹**, **lower¹**.
2 **vi** (‡) (*chat*) bavarder, papoter; (*moralize*) faire un sermon*; (*talk at length*) laïusser*.
3 **vt** (‡) (*moralize at*) sermonner; (*scold*) enguirlander*.
4 **comp** ►**jawbone** **n** (os *m*) maxillaire *m* ◊ **vt** (*US fig*) chercher à convaincre, exercer des pressions sur ►**jawboning**‡ (*US Pol*) pressions gouvernementales ►**jawbreaker** (*US*) (*word*) mot très difficile à prononcer; (*sweet*) bonbon *m* à sucer ►**jawline** menton *m*.
-jawed [dʒɔːd] **adj ending in comps** au menton ... . **square-jawed** au menton carré.
jay [dʒeɪ] **n** (*Orn*) geai *m*.
Jayhawker ['dʒeɪˌhɔːkəʳ] **n** (*US*) habitant(e) *m(f)* du Kansas. **the** ~ **State** le Kansas.
jaywalk ['dʒeɪˌwɔːk] **vi** marcher *ou* se promener *etc* sur la chaussée (*au risque de provoquer un accident*).
jaywalker ['dʒeɪˌwɔːkəʳ] **n** piéton(ne) *m(f)* indiscipliné(e).
jaywalking ['dʒeɪˌwɔːkɪŋ] **n** (*gen*) indiscipline *f* des piétons. **to be accused of** ~ être accusé d'avoir marché sur la chaussée au risque de provoquer un accident.
jazz [dʒæz] 1 **n** (*Mus*) jazz *m*; (‡: *liveliness*) entrain *m*, allant *m*; (‡: *pretentious talk*) baratin* *m*. **he gave them a lot of** ~ **about his marvellous job**‡ il leur a fait tout un baratin* sur sa magnifique situation; ... **and all that** ~‡ ... et cetera, et tout le baratin* habituel; *see* **hot**. 2 **comp** *band, club, record etc* de jazz. 3 **vi** a (*dance*) danser (sur un rythme de jazz). b (*US* ‡: *exaggerate*) exagérer.
►**jazz up** **vt sep** a (*Mus*) **to jazz up the classics** (*play*) jouer les classiques en jazz; (*arrange*) adapter les classiques pour le jazz, jazzifier* les classiques. b (‡) animer. **to jazz up a party** mettre de l'entrain *or* de l'animation dans une soirée; **to jazz up an old dress** égayer *or* rajeunir une vieille robe.
jazzed‡ [dʒæzd] **adj**: (*US*) **to be** ~ **for sth** être plein d'entrain à la pensée de qch.
jazzy ['dʒæzɪ] **adj** a (*too vivid*) *colour* tapageur; *pattern* bariolé; *dress* voyant. b (*: *elegant*) qui a du chic *or* de la gueule‡.
J.C. **abbr of Jesus Christ**.
JCB [ˌdʒeɪsiː'biː] **n abbr** ® pelle *f* hydraulique automotrice.
JCS [ˌdʒeɪsiː'es] **n** (*US Mil*) (**abbr of Joint Chiefs of Staff**) *see* **joint**.
jct., jctn **abbr of junction**.
JD [ˌdʒeɪ'diː] **n** (*US*) (**abbr of Doctor of Laws**) ≃ doctorat *m* en droit.
jealous ['dʒeləs] **adj** a (*envious*) *person, look* jaloux (*of* de). b (*watchful, careful*) vigilant. **to keep a** ~ **watch over** *or* **a** ~ **eye on sb** surveiller qn avec un soin *or* d'un œil jaloux.
jealously ['dʒeləslɪ] **adv** (*enviously*) jalousement; (*attentively*) *guard etc* avec vigilance, avec un soin jaloux.
jealousy ['dʒeləsɪ] **n** jalousie *f*.
Jean [dʒiːn] **n** Jeanne *f*.
jeans [dʒiːnz] **npl**: **(pair of)** ~ jean *m*; *see* **blue 4**.
Jeep [dʒiːp] **n** ® Jeep *f* ®.
jeer [dʒɪəʳ] 1 **n** raillerie *f*, sarcasme *m*; (*from a crowd*) quolibet *m*, huée *f*. 2 **vi** *[individual]* railler; *[crowd]* huer, conspuer. **to** ~ **at sb** se moquer de qn, railler qn. 3 **vt** huer, conspuer.
jeering ['dʒɪərɪŋ] 1 **adj** railleur, moqueur, goguenard. 2 **n** sarcasmes *mpl*; *[crowd]* huées *fpl*.
Jeez‡ [dʒiːz] **excl** Bon Dieu!‡, merde (alors)!‡
jehad [dʒɪ'hæd] **n** = **jihad**.
Jehovah [dʒɪ'həʊvə] **n** Jéhovah *m*. ~**'s Witness** Témoin *m* de Jéhovah.
jejune [dʒɪ'dʒuːn] **adj** ennuyeux, plat.
jejunum [dʒɪ'dʒuːnəm] **n** jéjunum *m*.
jell [dʒel] **vi** *[jelly etc]* épaissir, prendre; (*) *[plan etc]* prendre tournure.
jellied ['dʒelɪd] **adj** *eels, meat etc* en gelée.
Jell-O, jello ['dʒeləʊ] **n** ® (*US Culin*) gelée *f*.
jelly ['dʒelɪ] 1 **n** a (*gen*) gelée *f*; (*US: jam*) confiture *f*. **blackcurrant** ~ gelée de cassis; *see* **petroleum**. b (‡) = **gelignite**. 2 **comp** ►**jelly baby** bonbon *m* à la gélatine (*en forme de bébé*) ►**jelly bean** dragée *f* à la gelée de sucre ►**jellyfish** méduse *f* ►**jelly roll** (*US Culin*) gâteau roulé.
jemmy ['dʒemɪ] **n** (*Brit*) pince-monseigneur *f*.
jeopardize ['dʒepədaɪz] **vt** mettre en danger, compromettre.
jeopardy ['dʒepədɪ] **n** (*NonC*) danger *m*, péril *m*. **his life is in** ~ sa vie est *or* ses jours sont en danger; **his happiness is in** ~ son bonheur est menacé *or* en péril; **my business is in** ~ mes affaires sont en mauvaise posture.
jerbil ['dʒɜːbɪl] **n** = **gerbil**.
jerboa [dʒɜː'bəʊə] **n** gerboise *f*.

jeremiad [ˌdʒerɪ'maɪəd] n jérémiade *f.*
Jeremiah [ˌdʒerɪ'maɪə] n Jérémie *m.*
Jericho ['dʒerɪˌkəʊ] n Jéricho.
jerk [dʒɜːk] 1 n (*push, pull, twist etc*) secousse *f*, saccade *f*, à-coup *m*; (*Med*) réflexe tendineux, crispation nerveuse; (*esp US* ‡ *pej: person*) pauvre type* *m.* **the car moved along in a series of ~s** la voiture a avancé par saccades *or* par à-coups *or* par soubresauts; **the train started with a series of ~s** le train s'est ébranlé avec une série de secousses *or* de saccades; *see* **physical, soda.**
2 vt (*pull*) tirer brusquement; (*shake*) secouer (par saccades), donner une secousse à. **she ~ed her head up** elle a brusquement redressé la tête; **he ~ed the book out of my hand** d'une secousse il m'a fait lâcher le livre; **he ~ed himself free** il s'est libéré d'une secousse; **to ~ out an apology** bafouiller une excuse.
3 vi a se mouvoir par saccades, cahoter. **the car ~ed along** la voiture roulait en cahotant; **he ~ed away (from me)** il a reculé brusquement.
b *[person, muscle]* se contracter, se crisper.
4 comp ▸**jerkwater**‡: (*US pej*) **a jerkwater town** un trou perdu.
▸**jerk off**** vi se branler**.
jerkily ['dʒɜːkɪlɪ] adv *move* par saccades, par à-coups; *speak* d'une voix saccadée.
jerkin ['dʒɜːkɪn] n blouson *m*; (*Hist*) justaucorps *m*, pourpoint *m.*
jerky ['dʒɜːkɪ] adj *motion* saccadé; (*fig*) *style* haché, heurté.
jeroboam [ˌdʒerə'bəʊəm] n jéroboam *m.*
Jerry*† ['dʒerɪ] n (*Brit: German*) Fritz‡ *m inv*, fridolin* *m.*
jerry¹‡ ['dʒerɪ] n (*Brit: chamberpot*) pot *m* (de chambre), Jules‡ *m.*
jerry² ['dʒerɪ] comp ▸**jerry-building** (*NonC*) construction *f* bon marché ▸**jerry-built** *house etc* (construit) en carton-pâte; (*fig*) *agreement, plan* cousu de fil blanc ▸**jerry-can** jerrycan *m.*
Jersey ['dʒɜːzɪ] n a (*Geog*) (île *f* de) Jersey *f.* **in ~** à Jersey. b (*Zool*) race *f* Jersey. **a ~ (cow)** une vache jersiaise *or* de Jersey.
jersey ['dʒɜːzɪ] n (*garment*) tricot *m*; (*material*) jersey *m.*
Jerusalem [dʒə'ruːsələm] 1 n Jérusalem. **the New/Heavenly ~** la Jérusalem nouvelle/céleste. 2 comp ▸**Jerusalem artichoke** topinambour *m.*
jessamine ['dʒesəmɪn] n = **jasmine.**
jest [dʒest] 1 n plaisanterie *f.* **in ~** pour rire, en plaisantant. 2 vi plaisanter, se moquer.
jester ['dʒestəʳ] n (*Hist*) bouffon *m*; (*joker*) plaisantin *m*, farceur *m*, -euse *f.* **the King's ~** le fou du Roi.
jesting ['dʒestɪŋ] 1 adj *person* porté à la plaisanterie; *remark* (fait) en plaisantant *or* pour plaisanter. 2 n plaisanterie(s) *f(pl).*
Jesuit ['dʒezjʊɪt] n, adj (*Rel, fig*) jésuite *(m).*
jesuitic(al) [ˌdʒezjʊ'ɪtɪk(əl)] adj (*Rel, fig*) jésuitique.
Jesus ['dʒiːzəs] 1 n Jésus *m.* **~ Christ** Jésus-Christ; (*excl*) **~!*‡** nom de Dieu!‡; *see* **society.** 2 comp ▸**Jesus freak**‡ membre *m* du Jesus Movement ▸**Jesus Movement** Jesus Movement *m* ▸**Jesus People** membres *mpl* du Jesus Movement ▸**Jesus sandals** (*Brit*), **Jesus shoes** (*US*) nu-pieds *mpl.*
jet¹ [dʒet] 1 n a *[liquids]* jet *m*, giclée *f*; *[gas]* jet.
b (*Aviat: also* **~ plane**) avion *m* à réaction, jet *m.*
c (*nozzle*) brûleur *m*; (*Aut*) gicleur *m.*
2 comp (*Aviat*) *travel* en jet ▸**jet engine** (*Aviat*) moteur *m* à réaction, réacteur *m*, jet *m* ▸**jet fighter** (*Aviat*) chasseur *m* à réaction ▸**jet-foil** hydroglisseur *m* ▸**jet fuel** kérosène *m* ▸**jet lag** (les troubles dûs *or* la fatigue due au) décalage *m* horaire ▸**jet-powered, jet-propelled** à réaction ▸**jet propulsion** propulsion *f* par réaction ▸**jet-set** adj *travellers etc* du *or* de la jet set ▸**jet set** n jet set *m or f* ▸**jet setter** membre *m* du *or* de la jet set ▸**jet ski** n scooter *m* des mers, jet-ski *m* ▸**jet-ski** vi faire du scooter des mers *or* du jet-ski ▸**jet skiing** jet-ski *m* ▸**jetway** (*Aviat*) passerelle *f* télescopique.
3 vi a *[liquids]* gicler, jaillir.
b (*Aviat* *) voyager en avion *or* en jet. **she ~s (around) all over the world** elle parcourt le monde en avion.
4 vt faire gicler, faire jaillir.
jet² [dʒet] n jais *m.* **~-black** de jais, noir comme jais.
jetsam ['dʒetsəm] n a (*NonC*) *objets jetés à la mer etc rejetés sur la côte*; *see* **flotsam.** b (*fig: down-and-outs*) épaves *fpl* (*fig*).
jettison ['dʒetɪsn] vt a (*Naut*) jeter par-dessus bord, jeter à la mer (*pour alléger le navire*), se délester de. b (*Aviat*) *bombs, fuel, cargo* larguer. c (*fig*) *hopes, chances* abandonner, renoncer à; *burden* se délester de.
jetty ['dʒetɪ] n (*breakwater*) jetée *f*, digue *f*; (*landing pier*) embarcadère *m*, débarcadère *m*; (*of wood*) appontement *m.*
Jew [dʒuː] n Juif *m.* **~-baiting** persécution *f* des Juifs; **~'s harp** guimbarde *f.*
jewel ['dʒuːəl] n bijou *m*, joyau *m*; (*gem*) pierre précieuse; (*Tech: in watch*) rubis *m*; (*fig*) bijou, trésor *m*, perle *f.* **~ box, ~ case** coffret *m* à bijoux.
jewelled, (*US*) **jeweled** ['dʒuːəld] adj orné *or* paré de bijoux *or* de pierreries; *watch* monté sur rubis.
jeweller, (*US*) **jeweler** ['dʒuːələʳ] n bijoutier *m*, joaillier *m.* **~'s (shop)** bijouterie *f*, joaillerie *f.*
jewellery, (*US*) **jewelry** ['dʒuːəlrɪ] n (*NonC*) bijoux *mpl*, joyaux *mpl*, bijouterie *f.* **a piece of ~** un bijou; (*US*) **jewelry store** bijouterie *f.*
Jewess ['dʒuːɪs] n Juive *f.*
Jewish ['dʒuːɪʃ] adj juif.
Jewry ['dʒʊərɪ] n la communauté juive, les Juifs *mpl.*
Jezebel ['dʒezəˌbel] n Jézabel *f.*
jib [dʒɪb] 1 n a (*Naut*) foc *m.* (*fig*) **the cut of his ~*** son allure, sa tournure. b *[crane]* flèche *f*, bras *m.* 2 vi *[person]* regimber, renâcler (*at sth* devant qch), répugner (*at sth* à qch), se refuser (*at doing* à faire); *[horse]* refuser d'avancer, regimber, se dérober. **the horse ~bed at the fence** le cheval a refusé la barrière.
jibe¹ [dʒaɪb] = **gibe.**
jibe²* [dʒaɪb] vi (*US: agree*) coller (*fig*).
jiffy* ['dʒɪfɪ] n: **wait a ~** attends une minute *or* une seconde; **half a ~!** une seconde!; **in a ~** en moins de deux*; **J~ bag** ® enveloppe *f* rembourrée.
jig [dʒɪg] 1 n a (*dance*) gigue *f.* (*US fig*) **the ~'s up**‡ c'est cuit* *or* foutu‡. b (*Tech*) calibre *m*, gabarit *m.* 2 vi (*dance*) danser la gigue; (*fig: also* **~ about, ~ around**) sautiller, gigoter*, se trémousser. **to ~ up and down** sautiller, se trémousser. 3 comp ▸**jigsaw** *see* **jigsaw.**
jigger¹ ['dʒɪgəʳ] n a (*whisky measure*) mesure *f* d'une once et demie (= 42 *ml*). b (*: *thingummy: esp US*) truc* *m*, machin* *m.*
jigger² ['dʒɪgəʳ] n (*sand flea*) pou *m* des sables.
jiggered‡ ['dʒɪgəd] adj (*Brit*) a (*astonished*) étonné. **well, I'm ~!** nom d'un chien!* b (*exhausted*) éreinté, crevé*.
jiggery-pokery‡ ['dʒɪgərɪ'pəʊkərɪ] n (*Brit: NonC*) entourloupettes* *fpl*, manigances *fpl*, micmac(s)* *m(pl).*
jiggle ['dʒɪgl] vt secouer légèrement.
jigsaw ['dʒɪgˌsɔː] n a **~ (puzzle)** puzzle *m.* b (*saw*) scie *f* à chantourner.
jihad [dʒɪ'hæd] n (*Rel*) jihad *m.*
jilt [dʒɪlt] vt *lover, girlfriend, boyfriend* rompre avec, laisser tomber*. **~ed** délaissé.
Jim [dʒɪm] n (**dim of James**) Jim *m.* (*US*) **~ Crow** (*policy*) politique *f* raciste (*envers les noirs*); (*pej: Negro*) nègre *m* (*pej*); (*US*) **jim-dandy*** excellent, formidable.
jimjams‡ ['dʒɪmdʒæmz] n: **to have the ~** (*from revulsion*) avoir des frissons *or* la chair de poule; (*from fear*) avoir les chocottes‡; (*from drink*) avoir une (*or* des) crise(s) de délirium tremens.
Jimmy ['dʒɪmɪ] n a (**dim of James**) Jimmy *m.* b (*US*) **j~** pince-monseigneur *f.*
jimson weed ['dʒɪmsənˌwiːd] n (*US Bot*) stramoine *f*, pomme épineuse.
jingle ['dʒɪŋgl] 1 n *[keys etc]* tintement *m*, cliquetis *m*; (*fig: catchy verse*) petit couplet. **advertising ~** couplet publicitaire. 2 vi tinter, cliqueter. 3 vt *keys, coins* faire tinter, faire sonner.
jingo ['dʒɪŋgəʊ] n, pl **~es** chauvin *m.* **by ~!*** ça alors!, nom d'une pipe!*
jingoism ['dʒɪŋgəʊɪzəm] n chauvinisme *m.*
jingoistic [ˌdʒɪŋgəʊ'ɪstɪk] adj chauvin.
jink* [dʒɪŋk] vi (*zigzag*) zigzaguer. **he ~ed out of the way** il a fait un bond sur le côté.
jinks [dʒɪŋks] npl *see* **high 4.**
jinx* [dʒɪŋks] 1 n porte-guigne* *m*, porte-poisse* *m.* **there's a ~ on this watch** on a jeté un sort à cette montre, cette montre est ensorcelée. 2 vt *project, game* porter la guigne* *or* la poisse* à; **to ~ sb's chances*** compromettre les chances de qn; **to be ~ed** avoir la guigne* *or* la poisse*.
jitney‡ ['dʒɪtnɪ] n (*US*) a pièce *f* de cinq "cents". b *véhicule à itinéraire fixe et à prix modique.*
jitterbug ['dʒɪtəbʌg] 1 n (*dance*) *danse acrobatique sur rythme de swing ou de boogie-woogie*; (*dancer*) fana* *mf* du jitterbug; (*: *panicky person*) froussard(e)* *m(f)*, trouillard(e)‡ *m(f)*, paniquard‡ *m.* 2 vi (*dance*) danser le jitterbug.
jitters* ['dʒɪtəz] npl frousse* *f.* **to have the ~** (*gen*) être nerveux *or* agité; (*before performance*) avoir le trac, avoir la frousse*; **to give sb the ~** rendre qn nerveux *or* agité, ficher la frousse à qn*.
jittery* ['dʒɪtərɪ] adj nerveux, agité. **to be ~** avoir la frousse*.
jiujitsu [dʒuː'dʒɪtsuː] n jiu-jitsu *m.*
jive [dʒaɪv] 1 n a (*music, dancing*) swing *m.* b (‡: *esp US*) (*big talk*) baratin* *m*; (*nonsense*) foutaises‡ *fpl*, conneries‡ *fpl.* **don't give me all that ~**‡ arrête ton baratin*, arrête de dire des conneries‡. c (*US*) (*type of speech*) argot *m* (*des Noirs surtout*). 2 vi a (*dance*) danser le swing. b (‡: *be kidding*) blaguer*. 3 vt (*tease etc*) blaguer*.
Jly abbr of **July.**
Jnr abbr of **junior.**
Joan [dʒəʊn] n Jeanne *f.* **~ of Arc** Jeanne d'Arc.
Job [dʒəʊb] n (*Bible*) Job *m.* **~'s comforter** piètre consolateur *m*, -trice *f.*
job [dʒɒb] 1 n a (*piece of work*) travail *m*, besogne *f*, tâche *f*, boulot* *m.* **I have a little ~ for you** j'ai un petit travail pour vous; **he has made a good ~ of it** il a fait du bon travail *or* de la bonne besogne *or* du bon boulot*; **he has made a bad ~ of it** il a saboté son travail*, il a fait du

sale boulot*; **he's done a good ~ (of work)** il a fait du bon travail; **it's not ideal but it'll do the ~*** ce n'est pas l'idéal mais ça fera l'affaire*; **this new airliner is a lovely ~*** ce nouvel avion c'est vraiment du beau travail*; **that red ~‡ over there** (*car/cycle/dress etc*) cette belle voiture/bicyclette/robe rouge *etc* là-bas; **who's the blonde ~‡ in the red dress?** c'est qui la nana blonde fringuée en rouge?‡; **to have a nose/chin** *etc* **~* (done)** se faire refaire le nez/menton *etc; see* **odd.**

b (*post, situation*) emploi *m*, travail *m*, poste *m*, boulot* *m*, job* *m*. **he found a ~ as a librarian** il a trouvé un poste *or* un emploi de bibliothécaire; **he has a ~ for the vacation** il a un emploi *or* un travail *or* un boulot* *or* un job* pour les vacances; **to look for a ~** chercher du travail *or* un emploi; **to be out of a ~** être au *or* en chômage; (*Ind, Press*) **7000 ~s lost** 7000 suppressions *fpl* d'emploi; **he has a very good ~** il a une belle situation; **on the ~** (*while working*) pendant le travail; (‡: *during sex*) en pleine action* (*hum*), en train de baiser*‡; **to stay** *or* **remain on the ~** rester à son poste; **off-the-~ training** formation *f* à l'extérieur; **on-the-~ training** formation *f* sur le tas; **~s for the boys*** des planques pour les (petits) copains*; *see* **cushy.**

c (*duty, responsibility*) travail *m*, boulot* *m*. **it's not my ~ to supervise him** ce n'est pas à moi *or* ce n'est pas mon travail de le surveiller; **he's got a ~ to do, he's only doing his ~** il ne fait que son boulot*; **he knows his ~** il connaît son affaire; **that's not his ~** ce n'est pas de son ressort, ce n'est pas son boulot*; **I had the ~ of telling them** c'est moi qui ai été obligé de le leur dire.

d (*state of affairs*) **it's a good ~ (that) he managed to meet you** c'est heureux *or* c'est une chance qu'il ait pu vous rencontrer; **and a good ~ too!** à la bonne heure!; **it's a bad ~** c'est une sale affaire, c'est une affaire enquiquinante*; **to give sth/sb up as a bad ~** renoncer à qch/qn en désespoir de cause; **this is just the ~*** c'est juste *or* exactement ce qu'il faut.

e (*difficulty*) **to have a ~ to do sth** *or* **doing sth** avoir du mal à faire qch; **I had a ~ to finish this letter** j'ai eu du mal à venir à bout de cette lettre; **it was a ~** *or* **an awful ~ to organize this party** ça a été un sacré* travail *or* tout un travail pour organiser cette soirée; **it's been quite a ~ getting him back home** ça a été toute une affaire pour le ramener chez lui; **you've got a real ~ there!** tu n'es pas au bout de tes peines!

f (*: *dishonest business*) combine* *f*, tripotage* *m*. **a put-up ~** un coup monté; **remember that bank ~?** tu te rappelles le coup de la banque?

2 comp ▸**job action** (*US Ind*) action *f* revendicative, (mouvement *m* de) grève *f* ▸**job analysis** (*Ind*) analyse *f* des tâches, analyse statique *or* par poste de travail ▸**job centre** (*Brit*) ≈ ANPE *f*, agence nationale pour l'emploi ▸**job club** (*Brit*) club *m* d'entraide pour chômeurs ▸**job control language** (*Comput*) langage *m* de contrôle de travaux ▸**job creation** création *f* d'emplois nouveaux ▸**job creation scheme** plan *m* de création d'emplois ▸**job description** description *f* de poste, profil *m* de l'emploi ▸**job evaluation** qualification *f* du travail ▸**jobholder** personne *f* qui occupe un emploi *or* qui travaille ▸**job hop*** changer d'emploi fréquemment ▸**job hopper*** personne qui change d'emploi fréquemment ▸**job hunting** chasse *f* à l'emploi ▸**job lot** lot *m* d'articles divers; **to sell/buy as a job lot** vendre/acheter par *or* en lot ▸**job offer** offre *f* d'emploi ▸**job queue** (*Comput*) file *f* d'attente des travaux ▸**job rotation** rotation *f* des tâches ▸**job satisfaction** satisfaction *f* au travail ▸**job security** garantie *f* de l'unité de l'emploi ▸**job-share** n partage *m* de poste ◊ vi partager un poste ▸**job sharing** partage *m* de poste ▸**job title** intitulé *m* de poste; **his job title is ...** l'intitulé de son poste est ... .

3 vi (*do casual work*) faire des petits travaux; (*St Ex*) négocier, faire des transactions; (*profit from public position*) tripoter*.

4 vt (*also* **~ out**) *work* sous-traiter.

jobber ['dʒɒbəʳ] n (*Brit St Ex*) *intermédiaire qui traite directement avec l'agent de change;* (*pieceworker*) ouvrier *m*, -ière *f* à la tâche; (*dishonest person*) tripoteur* *m*, -euse* *f*.

jobbery ['dʒɒbərɪ] n (*Brit: NonC*) tripotage* *m*, maquignonnage *m*.

jobbing ['dʒɒbɪŋ] 1 adj *gardener* à la journée; *workman* à la tâche. 2 n (*NonC*) (*St Ex*) transactions boursières; (*odd jobs*) tripotage* *m*, maquignonnage *m*.

jobless ['dʒɒblɪs] 1 adj sans travail, sans emploi, au *or* en chômage. 2 npl: **the ~** les chômeurs *mpl*, les sans-emploi *mpl*; **the ~ figures** le nombre des sans-emploi.

joblessness ['dʒɒblɪsnɪs] n chômage *m*.

jobsworth* ['dʒɒbz,wɜːθ] n (employé(e) *m(f)*) tatillon(ne) *m(f)* (*qui refuse de coopérer en invoquant le règlement*).

Jock [dʒɒk] n (*Mil sl*) soldat écossais; (*gen*) Écossais *m*.

jock [dʒɒk] 1 n a = **jockstrap.** b (*US*) sportif *m*. 2 comp ▸**jockstrap** (*Sport*) slip *m* de sport; (*Med*) suspensoir *m*.

jockey ['dʒɒkɪ] 1 n jockey *m*, femme *f* jockey. **J~ club** Jockey-Club *m*; **J~ Shorts** ® caleçon *m*. 2 vi: **to ~ about** se bousculer; (*lit, fig*) **to ~ for position** manœuvrer pour se placer avantageusement; **they were ~ing for office in the new government** ils intriguaient pour se faire donner des postes dans le nouveau gouvernement. 3 vt: **to ~ sb into doing** manœuvrer qn (habilement) pour qu'il fasse, amener adroitement qn à faire; **to ~ sb out of a job** réussir à (faire) évincer qn.

jocose [dʒə'kəʊs] adj (*merry*) joyeux, enjoué, jovial; (*jesting*) facétieux.

jocular ['dʒɒkjʊləʳ] adj (*merry*) joyeux, enjoué, jovial; (*humorous*) facétieux, badin, divertissant.

jocularity [,dʒɒkjʊ'lærɪtɪ] n jovialité *f*.

jocularly ['dʒɒkjʊləlɪ] adv jovialement.

jocund ['dʒɒkənd] adj gai, joyeux, jovial.

jodhpurs ['dʒɒdpəz] npl jodhpurs *mpl*, culotte *f* de cheval.

Joe [dʒəʊ] n (**dim of Joseph**) Jo *m*. (*Brit*) **~ Bloggs*,** (*US*) **~ Blow*** M Tout-le-monde, l'homme de la rue; (*US Univ*) **~ College*** l'étudiant-type *m* américain; (*Brit*) **~ Public*** le public, le quidam (*hum*); (*Brit*) **~ Soap*** Tout-le-monde, l'homme de la rue.

Joel ['dʒəʊəl] n Joël *m*.

jog [dʒɒg] 1 n a (*jerk*) secousse *f*, cahot *m*; (*nudge*) légère poussée; (*with elbow*) coup *m* de coude. b (*also* **~-trot**) petit trot. **to go along at a ~(-trot)** aller au petit trot. 2 vt (*shake*) secouer, bringuebaler*; (*jerk*) faire cahoter; (*nudge*) pousser. **to ~ sb's elbow** pousser le coude de qn; (*fig*) **to ~ sb's memory** rafraîchir la mémoire de qn; (*fig*) **to ~ sb into action** secouer qn, inciter qn à agir. 3 vi a cahoter. **the cart ~s along the path** la charrette cahote sur le chemin. b (*Sport*) faire du jogging.

▸**jog about** 1 vi sautiller. 2 vt sep remuer.

▸**jog along** vi (*lit*) *[person, vehicle]* aller son petit bonhomme de chemin, cheminer; (*fig*) *[person]* aller cahin-caha*; *[piece of work, course of action]* aller tant bien que mal.

▸**jog around** vti = **jog about.**

▸**jog on** vi = **jog along.**

jogger ['dʒɒgəʳ] n jogger *mf*. **~'s nipple*** inflammation *f* du bout des seins (*due au frottement du vêtement en courant*).

jogging ['dʒɒgɪŋ] 1 n (*Sport*) jogging *m*. 2 comp ▸**jogging shoes** chaussures *fpl* de jogging ▸**jogging suit** jogging *m*.

joggle ['dʒɒgl] 1 vt secouer. 2 vi bringuebaler, se mouvoir par saccades. 3 n légère secousse.

Johannesburg [dʒəʊ'hænɪs,bɜːg] n Johannesburg.

John [dʒɒn] 1 n a Jean *m*. b (*esp US* ‡: *lavatory*) **the ~** les cabinets *mpl*. c (*US* ‡: *prostitute's customer*) **j~** micheton‡ *m*. 2 comp ▸**(Saint) John the Baptist** Saint Jean-Baptiste ▸**John Bull** John Bull *m* (*l'Anglais type; la nation anglaise*) ▸**(Saint) John of the Cross** Saint Jean de la Croix ▸**John Dory** saint-pierre *m inv*, dorée *f* ▸**John Hancock*, John Henry*** (*US fig: signature*) signature *f*, paraphe *m* ▸**John Q. Public*** (*US*) le public, le quidam (*hum*).

Johnny ['dʒɒnɪ] n a (**dim of John.**) b **j~*‡** type* *m*; (*US*) **Johnny-come-lately** nouveau venu; (*upstart*) parvenu *m*. c (*Brit* ‡: *condom*) (*also* **rubber ~**) capote *f* (anglaise)‡.

join [dʒɔɪn] 1 vt a (*lit, fig: also* **~ together**) (*unite*) joindre, unir; (*link*) relier (*to* à); (*Carpentry*) *2 bits of wood* joindre; *broken halves of stick etc* raccorder; (*Elec*) *batteries* accoupler, connecter. **to ~ 2 things (together)** joindre *or* réunir 2 choses; **to ~ sth to sth** unir qch à qch; **the island was ~ed to the mainland by a bridge** l'île était reliée à la terre par un pont; (*Mil, fig*) **to ~ battle (with)** entrer en lutte *or* engager le combat (avec); **to ~ hands** se donner la main; (*Mil, fig*) **to ~ forces** unir leurs forces; (*fig*) **to ~ forces (with sb) to do** s'unir (à qn) pour faire; **~ed in marriage** *or* **matrimony** unis par les liens du mariage; (*Jur*) **~ed case** affaire jointe; *see* **issue.**

b (*become member of*) *club* devenir membre de; *political party* entrer à, s'inscrire à, adhérer à; *university* entrer à, s'inscrire à; *circus, religious order* entrer dans; *procession* se joindre à. **to ~ the army** *etc* s'engager *or* s'enrôler dans l'armée *etc;* (*fig*) **~ the club*!** tu es en bonne compagnie!; **to ~ the queue** prendre la queue.

c *person* rejoindre, retrouver. **to ~ one's regiment** rejoindre son régiment; **to ~ one's ship** rallier *or* rejoindre son bâtiment; **I'll ~ you in 5 minutes** je vous rejoins *or* retrouve dans 5 minutes; **Paul ~s me in wishing you ...** Paul se joint à moi pour vous souhaiter ...; **will you ~ us?** (*come with us*) voulez-vous venir avec nous?; (*be one of our number*) voulez-vous être des nôtres?; (*in restaurant etc*) voulez-vous vous asseoir à notre table?; (*in restaurant etc*) **may I ~ you?** je peux *or* puis-je m'asseoir avec vous?; **will you ~ me in a drink?** vous prendrez un verre avec moi?

d *[river] another river, the sea* rejoindre, se jeter dans; *[road] another road* rejoindre.

2 vi a (*also* **~ together;** *see* **1a**) se joindre, s'unir; s'associer, se joindre, s'unir (*with* à); *[lines]* se rejoindre, se rencontrer; *[roads]* se rejoindre; *[rivers]* se joindre, avoir leur confluent.

b (*Mil: also* **~ up**) entrer dans l'armée.

c *[club member]* se faire membre, devenir membre.

3 n (*in mended crockery etc*) ligne *f* de raccord; (*Sewing*) couture *f*.

▸**join in** 1 vi participer, se mettre de la partie*. (*in singing etc*) **join in!** chantez *etc* avec nous! 2 vt fus *game, activity* se mêler à, participer à; *conversation* se mêler à, prendre part à; *protest(s), shouts* joindre sa voix à; *thanks, wishes* s'associer à; *see* **chorus.**

▸**join on** 1 vi (*in queue*) prendre son rang dans la queue *or* dans la file; *[links, parts of structure]* se joindre (*to* à). 2 vt sep fixer; (*by tying*) attacher.

►**join together** 1 vi = **join 2a.** 2 vt sep = **join 1a.**
►**join up** 1 vi (*Mil*) s'engager, s'enrôler. 2 vt sep joindre, assembler; *pieces of wood or metal* abouter, rabouter; (*Elec*) *wires etc* connecter, accoupler.
joinder ['dʒɔɪndəʳ] n (*Jur*) jonction *f* d'instance.
joiner ['dʒɔɪnəʳ] n a (*Brit: carpenter*) menuisier *m.* b (*person who joins clubs etc*) **she's not really a ~*** elle n'a pas l'instinct grégaire, elle préfère rester en dehors des clubs *etc.*
joinery ['dʒɔɪnərɪ] n (*Brit*) menuiserie *f.*
joint [dʒɔɪnt] 1 n a (*Anat*) articulation *f.* **out of ~** *shoulder* démis, déboîté; *wrist* luxé; (*fig*) disloqué, de travers; **to put one's shoulder out of ~** se démettre *or* se déboîter l'épaule; **to put one's wrist out of ~** se luxer le poignet; *see* **ball, nose.**
b (*Carpentry*) articulation *f*, jointure *f*; (*in armour*) joint *m*, jointure, articulation; (*Geol: in rock*) diaclase *f*; *see* **mitre, universal.**
c (*Brit: of meat*) rôti *m.* **a cut off the ~** une tranche de rôti.
d (‡) (*place*) boîte* *f*; (*night club*) boîte de nuit; (*disreputable pub*) bistro(t)* mal famé; (*gambling den*) tripot *m.*
e (*Drugs sl: reefer*) joint *m* (*sl*).
2 adj commun, conjugué, réuni. (*in race, competition etc*) **to come ~ first/second** être classé premier/deuxième ex aequo; (*Fin*) **~ account** compte conjoint; (*Ind etc*) **~ agreement** convention *f* collective; **~ author** coauteur *m*; (*US*) **J~ Chiefs of Staff** chefs *mpl* d'état-major (des armées); **~ committee** (*gen*) commission *f* mixte, comité *m* paritaire; (*US Pol*) commission *f* interparlementaire; **~ communiqué** communiqué commun; **~ consultations** consultations bilatérales; **~ effort(s)** effort(s) conjugué(s); (*Jur*) **~ estate** biens communs; **~ financing** financement conjoint; (*Jur*) **~ heir** cohéritier *m*, -ière *f*; (*Brit Univ*) **~ honours** (*degree*) ≃ licence *f* préparée dans deux matières (*ayant égalité de coefficient*); (*Comm*) **~ manager** codirecteur *m*, -trice *f*, cogérant(e) *m(f)*; **~ mortgage** emprunt-logement *m* souscrit conjointement; *sign* **in ~ names** conjointement; **~ obligation** coobligation *f*; **~ ownership** copropriété *f*; **~ partner** coassocié(e) *m(f)*; **~ passport** passeport *m* conjoint (*pour mari et femme*); **~ responsibility** coresponsabilité *f*; **~ and several guarantee** caution *f* solidaire; **~ and several liability** responsabilité conjointe et solidaire; (*Fin*) **~-stock company** société *f* par actions; (*Jur, Fin*) **~ venture** (*operation*) joint-venture *m*, co-entreprise *f*; (*company*) joint-venture *m*, entreprise *f* en participation.
3 vt a (*Brit Culin*) découper (aux jointures).
b *pipes* joindre, articuler, emboîter.
jointed ['dʒɔɪntɪd] adj *doll etc* articulé; *fishing rod, tent pole* démontable.
jointly ['dʒɔɪntlɪ] adv en commun, conjointement. (*Jur*) **to be ~ liable (for)** être solidaire (de); (*Jur*) **~ and severally** conjointement et solidairement.
jointure ['dʒɔɪntʃəʳ] n douaire *m.*
joist [dʒɔɪst] n solive *f.*
jojoba [həʊ'həʊbə] n jojoba *m.*
joke [dʒəʊk] 1 n a (*sth causing amusement*) plaisanterie *f*, blague* *f.* **for a ~** par plaisanterie, pour rire, pour blaguer*; **to make a ~ about** plaisanter sur; **to make a ~ of sth** tourner qch à la plaisanterie; **he can't take a ~** il ne comprend pas la plaisanterie; **it's no ~!** (*it's not easy*) ce n'est pas une petite affaire!* (*doing* que de faire); (*it's not enjoyable*) ce n'est pas drôle *or* rigolo* *or* marrant‡ (*doing* (que) de faire); **what a ~!** ce que c'est drôle!; (*pej: useless*) **it's a ~!*** c'est de la blague!; **it's (getting) beyond a ~*** ça cesse d'être drôle; **the ~ is that** ... le plus drôle c'est que ..., ce qu'il y a de drôle *or* de rigolo* *or* de marrant‡ c'est que ...; *see* **standing.**
b (*trick*) tour *m*, farce *f.* **to play a ~ on sb** faire une farce à qn, jouer un tour à qn; *see* **practical.**
c (*object of amusement*) risée *f.* **he is the ~ of the village** il est la risée du village.
2 vi plaisanter, blaguer*. **you're joking!** vous voulez rire!, sans blague!*; **£100 for that? — you must be joking!** 100 livres pour ça? — vous n'êtes pas sérieux!, vous voulez rire!; **I am not joking** je ne plaisante pas, je suis parfaitement sérieux; **I was only joking** ce n'était qu'une plaisanterie; **you mustn't ~ about his accent** il ne faut pas se moquer de son accent.
joker ['dʒəʊkəʳ] n a (*one who jokes*) blagueur* *m*, -euse* *f.* b (‡: *person*) type* *m.* c (*Cards*) joker *m.* d (*in legal document*) clause *f* modifiant *or* annulant un document.
jokester ['dʒəʊkstəʳ] n humoriste *mf*, plaisantin *m.*
jokey* ['dʒəʊkɪ] adj (*amusing*) rigolo* (*f* -ote); (*jocular*) blagueur (*f* -euse), jovial. **in a ~ way** en plaisantant.
joking ['dʒəʊkɪŋ] 1 adj *tone* de plaisanterie. 2 n (*NonC*) plaisanterie *f*, blague* *f.* **~ apart** plaisanterie *or* blague* à part.
jokingly ['dʒəʊkɪŋlɪ] adv en plaisantant, à la blague*. **it was ~ called a luxury hotel** on l'avait baptisé, avec le plus grand sérieux, hôtel de luxe.
jollification* [,dʒɒlɪfɪ'keɪʃən] n partie *f* de plaisir *or* de rigolade*, réjouissances *fpl.*
jollity ['dʒɒlɪtɪ] n gaieté *f or* gaîté *f*, joyeuse humeur.
jolly ['dʒɒlɪ] 1 adj a (*merry*) enjoué, jovial. b (*pleasant*) agréable, amusant, plaisant. 2 comp ►**jolly boat** (*Naut*) canot *m* ►**Jolly Roger** pavillon noir. 3 adv (*Brit* *) drôlement*, rudement*, vachement‡. **he was ~ glad to come** il était drôlement* content de venir; **you are ~ lucky** tu as une drôle de veine*, tu as une sacrée veine*; **you ~ well will go!** pas question que tu n'y ailles pas! 4 vt enjôler, flatter. **they jollied him into joining them, they jollied him along until he agreed to join them** ils l'ont si bien enjôlé qu'il a fini par se joindre à eux. 5 n: (*US*) **to get one's jollies‡** prendre son pied‡ (*from doing* en faisant).
jolt [dʒəʊlt] 1 vi [*vehicle*] cahoter, tressauter. **to ~ along** avancer en cahotant; **to ~ to a stop** faire un arrêt brutal. 2 vt (*lit, fig*) secouer, cahoter. (*fig*) **to ~ sb into action** secouer qn, inciter qn à agir. 3 n a (*jerk*) secousse *f*, cahot *m*, à-coup *m.* **the train started with a series of ~s** le train s'est ébranlé avec une série de secousses *or* de saccades; **the car moved along in a series of ~s** la voiture a avancé par saccades *or* par à-coups *or* par soubresauts. b (*fig*) choc *m.* **it gave me a ~** ça m'a fait *or* donné un coup*.
jolting ['dʒəʊltɪŋ] 1 adj cahotant. 2 n (*NonC*) cahots *mpl.*
jolty ['dʒəʊltɪ] adj *car* cahotant, bringuebalant*; *road* cahoteux.
Jonah ['dʒəʊnə] n Jonas *m*; (*fig*) porte-malheur *m inv*, oiseau *m* de malheur.
Jonas ['dʒəʊnəs] n Jonas *m.*
Jonathan ['dʒɒnəθən] n Jonathan *m.*
jonquil ['dʒɒŋkwɪl] 1 n jonquille *f*, narcisse *m.* 2 adj jonquille *inv.*
Jordan ['dʒɔːdn] n (*country*) Jordanie *f*; (*river*) Jourdain *m.*
Jordanian [dʒɔː'deɪnɪən] 1 n Jordanien(ne) *m(f).* 2 adj jordanien; (*king, ambassador*) de Jordanie.
Joseph ['dʒəʊzɪf] n Joseph *m.*
Josephine ['dʒəʊzɪfiːn] n Joséphine *f.*
josh‡ [dʒɒʃ] (*US*) 1 vt taquiner, mettre en boîte*. 2 vi blaguer*. 3 n mise *f* en boîte*.
Joshua ['dʒɒʃʊə] n Josué *m.*
joss stick ['dʒɒsstɪk] n bâton *m* d'encens.
jostle ['dʒɒsl] 1 vi se cogner (*against* à), se bousculer. **he ~d against me** il m'a bousculé, il s'est cogné à moi; **to ~ through the crowd** se frayer un chemin (à coups de coudes) à travers la foule; **to ~ for sth** jouer des coudes pour obtenir qch. 2 vt bousculer. 3 n bousculade *f.*
jot [dʒɒt] 1 n brin *m*, iota *m.* **there is not a ~ of truth in this** il n'y a pas un grain de vérité là-dedans; **not one ~ or tittle** pas un iota, pas un brin. 2 vt noter, prendre note de.
►**jot down** vt sep noter, prendre note de. **to jot down notes** prendre *or* griffonner des notes; **to jot down a few points** prendre note de *or* noter quelques points.
jotter ['dʒɒtəʳ] n (*Brit*) (*exercise book*) cahier *m* (de brouillon); (*pad*) bloc-notes *m.*
jottings ['dʒɒtɪŋz] npl notes *fpl.*
joual [ʒwɑːl] n (*Can*) joual *m.*
joule [dʒuːl] n joule *m.*
journal ['dʒɜːnl] 1 n a (*periodical*) revue *f*; (*newspaper*) journal *m.* b (*Naut*) livre *m* de bord; (*Comm*) livre de comptes; (*Jur*) compte rendu. c (*diary*) journal *m.* 2 comp ►**journal bearing** (*Tech*) palier *m.*
journalese [,dʒɜːnə'liːz] n (*NonC: pej*) jargon *m* journalistique.
journalism ['dʒɜːnəlɪzəm] n journalisme *m.*
journalist ['dʒɜːnəlɪst] n journaliste *mf.*
journalistic [,dʒɜːnə'lɪstɪk] adj journalistique.
journey ['dʒɜːnɪ] 1 n (*gen*) voyage *m*; (*short, regular*) trajet *m*; (*distance covered*) trajet *m*, parcours *m.* **to go on a ~** partir en voyage; **to set out on one's ~** se mettre en route; **a 2 days' ~** un voyage de 2 jours; **to reach one's ~'s end** arriver à destination; **the ~ from home to office** le trajet de la maison au bureau; **the return ~, the ~ home** le (voyage de) retour; **a car ~** un voyage en voiture; **a long bus ~** un long trajet en autobus; *see* **outward.**
2 vi voyager. **to ~ on** continuer son voyage.
3 comp ►**journeyman** ouvrier *m*, compagnon *m* (*qui a fini son apprentissage*) ►**journeyman baker** ouvrier boulanger ►**journeyman joiner** compagnon charpentier ►**journey time** durée *f* du trajet.
joust [dʒaʊst] 1 n joute *f.* 2 vi jouter.
Jove [dʒəʊv] n Jupiter *m.* **by ~!*** sapristi!*, 'cré nom!‡
jovial ['dʒəʊvɪəl] adj jovial.
joviality [,dʒəʊvɪ'ælɪtɪ] n jovialité *f.*
jovially ['dʒəʊvɪəlɪ] adv jovialement.
jowl [dʒaʊl] n (*jaw*) mâchoire *f*; (*cheek*) bajoue *f*; *see* **cheek.**
-jowled [dʒaʊld] adj ending in comps: **square-jowled** à la mâchoire carrée.
joy [dʒɔɪ] 1 n a (*NonC*) joie *f.* **to my great ~** à ma grande joie; (*iro*) **I wish you ~ of it!** je vous souhaite du plaisir!; (*iro*) **I wish you ~ (of that job)** je vous souhaite bien du plaisir (avec ce travail); (*Brit*) **any ~?*** alors, c'est bon?*; (*Brit*) **I got no ~* out of it** ça n'a rien donné. b (*gen pl*) **~s** plaisirs *mpl*; **the ~s of the seaside** les plaisirs *or* les charmes *mpl* du bord de la mer; **it's a ~ to hear him** c'est un (vrai) plaisir *or* délice de l'entendre; **to be full of the ~s of spring** *or* **life** avoir le cœur joyeux. 2 comp ►**joyride** *etc see* **joyride** *etc* ►**joystick** (*Aviat*) manche *m* à balai; (*Comput*) manche à balai, manette *f* (de jeu).
joyful ['dʒɔɪfʊl] adj joyeux.
joyfully ['dʒɔɪfəlɪ] adv joyeusement.

joyfulness [ˈdʒɔɪfʊlnɪs] n grande joie, allégresse *f*, humeur joyeuse.
joyless [ˈdʒɔɪlɪs] adj sans joie.
joyous [ˈdʒɔɪəs] adj (*liter*) joyeux.
joyously [ˈdʒɔɪəslɪ] adv (*liter*) joyeusement.
joyride [ˈdʒɔɪˌraɪd] 1 n: **to go for a ~** (*gen*) faire une virée* *or* une balade* en voiture (pour le plaisir); (*in stolen car*) faire une virée* (dans une voiture volée). 2 vi (*also* **go joyriding**) faire une virée* (dans une voiture volée).
joyrider [ˈdʒɔɪˌraɪdəʳ] n voleur *m*, -euse *f* de voiture (*qui fait une virée dans le véhicule volé*).
joyriding [ˈdʒɔɪˌraɪdɪŋ] n vol *m* de voiture (*pour aller faire une virée*).
J.P. [dʒeɪˈpiː] n (*Brit Jur*) (abbr of **Justice of the Peace**) *see* **justice**.
Jr. (abbr of **Junior**) Jr.
jubilant [ˈdʒuːbɪlənt] adj *person, voice* débordant de joie; *face* épanoui, radieux. **he was ~** il jubilait.
jubilation [ˌdʒuːbɪˈleɪʃən] n a (*emotion*) allégresse *f*, exultation *f*, jubilation *f*. b (*celebration*) fête *f*, réjouissance(s) *f(pl)*.
jubilee [ˈdʒuːbɪliː] n jubilé *m*; *see* **diamond** *etc*.
Judaea [dʒuːˈdiːə] n Judée *f*.
Judah [ˈdʒuːdə] n Juda *m*.
Judaic [dʒuːˈdeɪɪk] adj judaïque.
Judaism [ˈdʒuːdeɪɪzəm] n judaïsme *m*.
Judas [ˈdʒuːdəs] n a (*name*) Judas *m*. **~ Iscariot** Judas Iscariote. b (*traitor*) judas *m*, traître *m*. c (*peephole*) **j~** judas *m*.
judder [ˈdʒʌdəʳ] (*Brit*) 1 vi vibrer, (*stronger*) trépider. 2 n vibration *f*, trépidation *f*.
Jude [dʒuːd] n Jude *m*.
judge [dʒʌdʒ] 1 n a (*Jur, Sport*) juge *m*; (*at show etc*) membre *m* du jury. (*Bible*) **(the book of) J~s** (le livre des) Juges *mpl*; (*Brit Police*) **the ~s' rules** le code de la police ayant trait aux suspects; *see also* **4**.
b (*fig*) connaisseur *m*, juge *m*. **to be a good ~ of character** être bon psychologue, savoir juger les gens; **to be a good ~ of wine** être bon juge en vins, s'y connaître en vins; **you are no ~ in this case** tu n'es pas à même de juger cette affaire; **I'll be the ~** *or* **let me be the ~ of that** c'est à moi de juger.
2 vt a (*assess*) *person, conduct, competition* juger; *qualities* apprécier.
b (*consider*) juger, estimer. **to ~ it necessary to do** juger *or* estimer nécessaire de faire; **he ~d the moment well (to do)** il a bien su choisir son moment (pour faire).
3 vi juger, rendre un jugement. **to ~ for oneself** juger par soi-même; **as far as one can ~, as far as can be ~d** autant qu'on puisse en juger; **judging by** *or* **from** à en juger par *or* d'après.
4 comp ▸**judge advocate** (*Mil Jur*) (pl **~ ~s**) assesseur *m* (*auprès d'un tribunal militaire*) ▸**judge of appeal** (*Jur*) conseiller *m* à la cour d'appel.
judg(e)ment [ˈdʒʌdʒmənt] 1 n a (*Jur, Rel*) jugement *m*. **to sit in ~ on** *or* **over** juger; **to give** *or* **pass ~ (on)** prononcer *or* rendre un jugement (sur); *see* **last¹**. b (*fig: opinion*) jugement *m*, opinion *f*, avis *m*. **to give one's ~ (on)** donner son avis (sur). c (*NonC: good sense*) jugement *m*, discernement *m*. **to have (sound) ~** avoir du jugement; **his ~ has gone** il n'a plus tout son discernement. 2 comp ▸**Judg(e)ment Day** (*Rel*) le jour du Jugement.
judg(e)mental [dʒʌdʒˈmentəl] adj: **he is very ~** il porte toujours des jugements catégoriques, il s'érige toujours en juge.
judicature [ˈdʒuːdɪkətʃəʳ] n a (*process of justice*) justice *f*. b (*body of judges*) magistrature *f*. c (*judicial system*) organisation *f* judiciaire.
judicial [dʒuːˈdɪʃəl] adj a (*Jur*) *power, function* judiciaire. **~ and extra-judicial documents** actes *mpl* judiciaires et extra-judiciaires; **~ proceedings** poursuites *fpl* judiciaires; **~ murder** assassinat *m* juridique *or* légal; (*US Jur*) **~ review** examen *m* de la constitutionnalité d'une loi; **~ sale** vente *f* forcée *or* judiciaire. b (*critical*) *mind* critique, impartial. **~ faculty** sens *m* critique.
judicially [dʒuːˈdɪʃəlɪ] adv judiciairement.
judiciary [dʒuːˈdɪʃɪərɪ] 1 adj judiciaire. 2 n a (*system*) organisation *f* judiciaire. b (*body of judges*) magistrature *f*. c (*branch of government*) pouvoir *m* judiciaire.
judicious [dʒuːˈdɪʃəs] adj judicieux.
judiciously [dʒuːˈdɪʃəslɪ] adv judicieusement.
Judith [ˈdʒuːdɪθ] n Judith *f*.
judo [ˈdʒuːdəʊ] n judo *m*.
judoka [ˈdʒuːdəʊˌkɑː] n judoka *m*.
Judy [ˈdʒuːdɪ] n a (dim of **Judith**) *see* **Punch**. b (*girl*) **j~**‡ nana‡ *f*.
jug [dʒʌg] 1 n a (*gen*) pot *m*; (*for wine*) pichet *m*; (*for washing water*) broc *m*; (*round, heavy, jar-shaped*) cruche *f*. b (*Prison sl: prison*) taule‡ *f* or tôle‡ *f*, bloc‡ *m*. **in ~** en taule‡, au bloc‡. 2 comp ▸**jug band** (*US*) orchestre *m* hillbilly improvisé (*utilisant des ustensiles ménagers*). 3 vt a (*Culin*) cuire à l'étuvée *or* à l'étouffée *or* en civet. **~ged hare** civet *m* de lièvre. b (*Prison sl: imprison*) coffrer*.
juggernaut [ˈdʒʌgənɔːt] n a (*fig: destructive force*) force *f or* poussée *f* irrésistible, forces aveugles. **the ~ of war** la force meurtrière de la guerre. b (*fig: cause, belief*) cause *f or* conviction *f* pour laquelle on est sacrifié *or* on se sacrifie soi-même. c (*truck*) énorme poids lourd *m or* semi-remorque *m*, mastodonte *m*. d (*Rel*) **J~** Jagannâth *m*.
juggins‡ [ˈdʒʌgɪnz] n niais(e) *m(f)*, jobard(e) *m(f)*, cruche* *f*.
juggle [ˈdʒʌgl] 1 vi (*lit, fig*) jongler (*with* avec). 2 vt *balls, plates, facts, figures* jongler avec.
juggler [ˈdʒʌgləʳ] n jongleur *m*, -euse *f*; (*conjurer*) prestidigitateur *m*, -trice *f*.
jugglery [ˈdʒʌglərɪ] n, **juggling** [ˈdʒʌglɪŋ] n (*NonC*) (*lit*) jonglerie *f*, tours *mpl* de prestidigitation *or* de passe-passe; (*fig: trickery*) tours de passe-passe.
Jugoslav [ˈjuːgəʊˌslɑːv] 1 adj yougoslave. 2 n Yougoslave *mf*.
Jugoslavia [ˌjuːgəʊˈslɑːvɪə] n Yougoslavie *f*.
jugular [ˈdʒʌgjʊləʳ] 1 adj jugulaire. 2 n (veine *f*) jugulaire *f*.
juice [dʒuːs] 1 n a [*fruit, meat*] jus *m*. **orange ~** jus d'orange. b (*Physiol*) suc *m*. **digestive ~s** sucs digestifs. c (*US* ‡: *alcohol*) alcool *m*. d (*: *electricity, gas etc*) jus‡ *m*; (*Brit: petrol*) essence *f*. 2 comp ▸**juice extractor** (*Brit*) centrifugeuse *f* électrique ▸**juicehead**‡ (*US*) poivrot* *m*, alcoolique *mf*.
juicer [ˈdʒuːsəʳ] n (*US*) centrifugeuse *f* électrique.
juiciness [ˈdʒuːsɪnɪs] n juteux *m*.
juicy [ˈdʒuːsɪ] adj *fruit* juteux; *meat* moelleux; (*fig* *) *story* savoureux.
juju [ˈdʒuːdʒuː] n *culte africain proche du vaudou*.
jujube [ˈdʒuːdʒuːb] n jujube *m*.
jujutsu [dʒuːˈdʒɪtsuː] n = **jiujitsu**.
jukebox [ˈdʒuːkbɒks] n juke-box *m*.
Jul. abbr of **July**.
julep [ˈdʒuːlep] n boisson sucrée, sirop *m*, julep *m*; *see* **mint²**.
Julian [ˈdʒuːlɪən] 1 n Julien *m*. 2 adj julien.
Juliet [ˈdʒuːlɪet] n Juliette *f*.
Julius [ˈdʒuːlɪəs] n Jules *m*. **~ Caesar** Jules César.
July [dʒuːˈlaɪ] n juillet *m*; *for phrases see* **September**.
jumble [ˈdʒʌmbl] 1 vt (*also* **~ up**) a (*lit*) brouiller, emmêler, mélanger. **to ~ everything (up)** tout mélanger; **~d (up)** en vrac; **his clothes are ~d (up) together on his bed** ses habits sont pêle-mêle sur son lit. b (*fig*) *facts, details* brouiller, embrouiller. 2 n a [*objects*] mélange *m*, fouillis *m*, salade* *f*, méli-mélo* *m*; [*ideas etc*] confusion *f*, enchevêtrement *m*, fouillis *m*. **in a ~** en vrac. b (*NonC: junk; goods at ~ sale*) bric-à-brac *m*. 3 comp ▸**jumble display** (*Comm*) présentation *f* en vrac ▸**jumble sale** (*Brit*) vente *f* de charité (*d'objets d'occasion*).
jumbo [ˈdʒʌmbəʊ] 1 n (*) éléphant *m*. 2 comp ▸**jumbo jet** (*Aviat*) jumbo-jet *m*, avion géant, avion gros porteur ▸**jumbo loan** prêt *m* géant *or* jumbo ▸**jumbo pack** (*gen*) paquet *m* géant; [*bottles, cans*] emballage *m* géant.
jump [dʒʌmp] 1 n a (*gen*) saut *m*; (*of fear, nervousness*) sursaut *m*. **to give a ~** faire un saut, sauter; (*nervously*) sursauter; **to be one ~ ahead** avoir une longueur d'avance (*of* sur); **at one ~** d'un (seul) bond; (*fig*) **the ~ in prices** la montée en flèche des prix, la hausse brutale des prix; **it gave him a ~** ça l'a fait sursauter; **to have the ~s**‡ avoir les nerfs à vif; *see* **high, running** *etc*.
b (*Comput*) saut *m*, rupture *f* de séquence.
c (*Showjumping*) obstacle *m*.
2 comp ▸**jumped-up*** (*pej: pushy*) parvenu; (*cheeky*) effronté; (*conceited*) prétentieux; **he is a jumped-up clerk** au fond, ce n'est qu'un petit employé ▸**jump-jet** avion *m* à décollage vertical ▸**jump leads** (*Brit Aut*) câbles *mpl* de démarrage (*pour batterie*) ▸**jump-off** (*Equitation*) (épreuve *f*) finale *f* (*d'un concours hippique*) ▸**jump rope** (*US*) corde *f* à sauter ▸**jump seat** (*Aut etc*) strapontin *m* ▸**jump-start** vt (*Aut*) démarrer en poussant ◊ n *démarrage d'une voiture en la poussant* ▸**jump suit** (*gen*) combinaison(-pantalon) *f*, combinaison de saut.
3 vi a (*leap*) sauter, bondir. **to ~ up and down** sautiller; **to ~ up and down with excitement/anger** bondir d'excitation/trépigner de colère; **to ~ in/out/across** *etc* entrer/sortir/traverser *etc* d'un bond; **to ~ into the bus/the river** sauter dans l'autobus/la rivière; **to ~ across the stream** franchir le ruisseau d'un bond; **to ~ off a bus/train** sauter d'un autobus/d'un train; **to ~ off a wall** sauter (du haut) d'un mur; **he ~ed over the wall** il a sauté par-dessus le mur; **he ~ed over the fence** d'un bond il a franchi la barrière; **~ to it!*** et plus vite que ça!*, et que ça saute!*
b (*fig*) sauter. **to ~ from one subject to another** sauter sans transition d'un sujet à un autre, passer du coq à l'âne; **to ~ at** *chance, suggestion, offer* sauter sur; **to ~ to a conclusion** conclure sans réflexion; **he ~ed to the conclusion that ...** il en a conclu tout de suite que ...; **you mustn't ~ to conclusions** il ne faut pas tirer des conclusions trop hâtives; **to ~ down sb's throat*** rabrouer qn.
c (*from nervousness*) sursauter, tressauter. **the shout made him ~** le cri l'a fait sursauter *or* tressauter; **it (almost) made him ~ out of his skin*** cela l'a fait sauter au plafond*; **his heart ~ed when ...** son cœur a fait *or* n'a fait qu'un bond quand ... .
d [*prices, shares*] monter en flèche, faire un bond.
4 vt a *ditch etc* sauter, franchir (d'un bond).
b *horse* faire sauter. **he ~ed his horse over the fence** il a fait sauter la barrière à son cheval; **he ~ed his son (up and down) on his knee** il

faisait sauter son fils sur ses genoux.

c (*phrases*) *[train]* **to ~ the rails** dérailler; **to ~ the points** dérailler à l'aiguillage; *[pickup]* **to ~ (a groove)** sauter; (*Draughts*) **to ~ a man** prendre *or* souffler un pion; (*Jur*) **to ~ bail** se soustraire à la justice (*après paiement de caution*); **to ~ a claim** s'emparer illégalement d'une concession minière; **to ~ the gun** (*Sport*) partir avant le départ; (** fig*) agir prématurément; **to ~ the gun on sb** couper l'herbe sous le pied de qn; (*Aut*) **to ~ the lights** passer au rouge; **to ~ the queue*** passer avant son tour, resquiller; **to ~ ship** déserter le navire; **to ~ sb‡** (*attack*) sauter sur qn; (*US*) **to ~ town‡** quitter la ville; **to ~ a train** (*get on*) sauter dans un train en marche (*pour voyager sans payer*); (*get off*) sauter d'un train en marche; (*US*) **to ~ ‡ a hotel bill** ne pas payer une note d'hôtel, commettre une grivèlerie.

►**jump about, jump around** vi sautiller.

►**jump down** vi (*gen*) descendre d'un bond (*from* de). (*from wall, bicycle etc*) **jump down!** sautez!

►**jump in** vi sauter dedans. **he came to the river and jumped in** arrivé à la rivière il a sauté dedans; **jump in!** (*into vehicle*) montez vite!; (*into swimming pool*) sautez!

►**jump off** 1 vi sauter. **he jumped off** il a sauté; (*from bicycle, wall etc*) **jump off!** sautez! 2 **jumping-off** adj *see* **jumping 2**. 3 **jump-off** n *see* **jump 2**.

►**jump on** 1 vi (*onto truck, bus*) **jump on!** montez vite!; **to jump on(to) one's bicycle** sauter sur son vélo. 2 vt fus a **to jump on(to) a bus** sauter dans un autobus. b (**: reprimand*) s'attaquer à, prendre à partie.

►**jump out** vi sauter (*of* de). **to jump out of bed** sauter (à bas) du lit; **to jump out of the window** sauter par la fenêtre; **to jump out of a car/train** sauter d'une voiture/d'un train; (*from car etc*) **jump out!** sortez *or* descendez (vite)!; (*fig*) **the mistake jumped out of the page at him** l'erreur dans la page lui a sauté aux yeux.

►**jump up** 1 vi sauter sur ses pieds, se (re)lever d'un bond. (*to fallen child*) **jump up now!** lève-toi! 2 **jumped-up*** adj *see* **jump 2**.

jumper ['dʒʌmpəʳ] n a (*garment*) (*Brit*) pull(over) *m*; (*US: dress*) robe-chasuble *f*. b (*one who jumps: person, animal*) sauteur *m*, -euse *f*. (*US Aut*) ~ **cables** câbles *mpl* de démarrage (*pour batterie*). c (*Comput*) cavalier *m*.

jumping ['dʒʌmpɪŋ] 1 n (*gen*) saut *m*; (*equitation*) jumping *m*, concours *m* hippique. 2 comp ►**jumping bean** fève *f* sauteuse ►**jumping-off place** *or* **point** (*fig*): **they used the agreement as a jumping-off place** *or* **point for further negotiations** ils se sont servis de l'accord comme d'un tremplin pour de plus amples négociations ►**jumping rope** (*US*) corde *f* à sauter. 3 adj (*US *: lively*) plein d'animation.

jumpy* ['dʒʌmpɪ] adj *person* nerveux; (*St Ex*) *market* instable.

Jun. a abbr of **June**. b (abbr of **Junior**) Jr.

junction ['dʒʌŋkʃən] 1 n a (*NonC*) jonction *f*. b (*Brit*) (*meeting place*) *[roads]* bifurcation *f*, (*crossroads*) carrefour *m*; *[rivers]* confluent *m*; *[railway lines]* embranchement *m*; *[pipes]* raccordement *m*; (*station*) gare *f* de jonction. 2 comp ►**junction box** (*Elec*) boîte *f* de dérivation.

juncture ['dʒʌŋktʃəʳ] n (*joining place*) jointure *f*, point *m* de jonction; (*Ling*) joncture *f*; (*fig: state of affairs*) conjoncture *f*. (*fig: point*) **at this ~** à ce moment.

June [dʒu:n] n juin *m*. ~ **bug** hanneton *m*; *for other phrases see* **September**.

Jungian [jʊŋɪən] 1 n (*follower of Jung*) Jungien(ne) *m(f)*. 2 adj jungien.

jungle ['dʒʌŋgl] 1 n (*lit, fig*) jungle *f*. 2 comp *animal, bird* de la jungle ►**jungle bunny*‡** (*pej: esp US*) Nègre *m*, Négresse *f*, Noir(e) *m(f)* ►**jungle gym** (*in playground*) cage *f* à poule *or* aux écureuils ►**jungle juice*** gnôle* *f* ►**jungle warfare** combat *m* de jungle.

junior ['dʒu:nɪəʳ] 1 adj a (*younger*) (plus) jeune, cadet. **he is ~ to me by 2 years** il est mon cadet de 2 ans, il est plus jeune que moi de 2 ans; **John Smith, J~** John Smith fils *or* junior; *see also* **2**.

b (*subordinate*) *employee, officer, job* subalterne. ~ **clerk** petit commis; ~ **executive** jeune cadre *m*; ~ **partner** associé(-adjoint) *m*; **he is ~ to me in the business** il est au-dessous de moi dans l'affaire; *see also* **2**.

c (*Sport*) ≃ minime. ~ **championship** championnat *m* des minimes.

2 comp ►**junior class: the junior classes** les petites classes (*de 7 à 11 ans*) ►**junior college** (*US*) institut *m* universitaire (du premier cycle) ►**junior high school** (*US*) ≃ collège *m* ►**junior minister** (*Parl*) sous-secrétaire *m* d'État ►**junior miss** (*Comm* †) fillette *f* (*de 11 à 14 ans*) ►**junior rating** (*Brit Navy*) matelot *m* ►**junior school** (*Brit*) école *f* primaire (*de 7 à 11 ans*) ►**junior secondary school** (*Brit* †) collège *m* d'enseignement secondaire ►**junior technician** (*Brit Aviat*) soldat *m* de première classe ►**junior training centre** (*Brit*) centre *m* médico-éducatif ►**junior varsity sports** (*US Univ*) *sports pratiqués entre équipes de différents établissements (deuxième catégorie)*.

3 n a cadet(te) *m(f)*. **he is my ~ by 2 years** il est plus jeune que moi de 2 ans, il est mon cadet de 2 ans.

b (*Brit Scol*) petit(e) élève *m(f)* (*de 7 à 11 ans*); (*US Scol*) élève *mf* de classe de première; (*US Univ*) étudiant(e) *m(f)* de troisième année.

c (*Sport*) ≃ cadet(te) *m(f)*, minime *mf*.

juniper ['dʒu:nɪpəʳ] n genévrier *m*. ~ **berry** baie *f* de genièvre; ~ **berries** genièvre *m* (*NonC*).

junk¹ [dʒʌŋk] 1 n (*NonC*) (*discarded objects*) bric-à-brac *m inv*, vieilleries *fpl*; (*metal*) ferraille *f*; (**: bad quality goods*) camelote* *f*; (**: worthless objects*) pacotille *f*; (*‡: nonsense*) âneries *fpl*; (*Drugs sl*) came *f* (*sl*).

2 comp ►**junk art** junk art *m*, sculptures *fpl* réalisées à l'aide de rebuts ►**junk bond** obligation *f* hautement spéculative (*à taux d'intérêt très élevé et à haut risque utilisée dans les OPA agressives*) ►**junk dealer** brocanteur *m*, -euse *f* ►**junk food*** aliments *mpl* sans valeur nutritive, snacks *mpl* vite prêts ►**junk heap** dépotoir *m* ►**junk mail** imprimés *mpl* publicitaires (*non sollicités, adressés par la poste*) ►**junk market** marché *m* aux puces ►**junkshop** (boutique *f* de) brocanteur *m* ►**junkyard** entrepôt *m* de chiffonnier-ferrailleur.

3 vt (*US **) balancer*.

junk² [dʒʌŋk] n (*boat*) jonque *f*.

junket ['dʒʌŋkɪt] 1 n a (*Culin*) (lait *m*) caillé *m*. b (*trip at public expense*) voyage *m* aux frais de la princesse*. 2 vi faire bombance.

junketing ['dʒʌŋkɪtɪŋ] n (*NonC*) (*merrymaking*) bombance *f*, bringue‡ *f*; (**: trip, banquet etc at public expense*) voyage *m or* banquet *m etc* aux frais de la princesse*.

junkie ['dʒʌŋkɪ] n (*Drugs sl*) drogué(e) *m(f)*, camé(e) *m(f)* (*sl*). **a television** *etc* ~ un mordu* de la télévision *etc*.

Juno ['dʒu:nəʊ] Junon *f*.

Junr. (abbr of **Junior**) Jr.

junta ['dʒʌntə] n junte *f*.

Jupiter ['dʒu:pɪtəʳ] n (*Myth*) Jupiter *m*; (*Astron*) Jupiter *f*.

Jura ['dʒʊərə] n: ~ **(Mountains)** Jura *m*.

Jurassic [dʒʊ'ræsɪk] adj (*Geol*) *period* jurassique.

juridical [dʒʊə'rɪdɪkəl] adj juridique.

jurisdiction [ˌdʒʊərɪs'dɪkʃən] n juridiction *f*. **to come** *or* **fall within** *or* **under sb's ~** tomber sous le coup de *or* relever de la juridiction de qn; **it comes within our ~** (*fig*) cela relève de notre compétence *or* de nos attributions, c'est de notre ressort; *see* **court**.

jurisdictional [ˌdʒʊərɪs'dɪkʃənl] adj (*US*) ~ **dispute** conflit *m* d'attributions.

jurisprudence [ˌdʒʊərɪs'pru:dəns] n jurisprudence *f*; *see* **medical**.

jurist ['dʒʊərɪst] n juriste *m*, légiste *m*.

juror ['dʒʊərəʳ] n juré *m*. **woman ~** femme *f* juré.

jury¹ ['dʒʊərɪ] 1 n (*Jur*) jury *m*, jurés *mpl*; *[examination, exhibition etc]* jury. **to be on the ~** faire partie du jury; **Gentlemen of the ~** Messieurs les jurés; *see* **coroner, grand**. 2 comp ►**jury box** banc *m* des jurés ►**jury duty: to have to report for jury duty** être convoqué comme juré ►**juryman** juré *m* ►**jury-rigging** *constitution d'un jury partisan* ►**jury shopping** (*US Jur*) *recherche f du jury idéal (par récusation de jurés)*.

jury² ['dʒʊərɪ] adj (*Naut*) de fortune, improvisé.

just¹ [dʒʌst] adv a (*exactly*) juste, exactement, justement, précisément. **it's ~ 9 o'clock** il est juste 9 heures, il est 9 heures juste(s) *or* sonnant(es) *or* tapant(es) (*see also* **j**); **it's ~ on 9** il est tout juste 9 heures; **it took me ~ 2 hours** il m'a fallu juste *or* exactement 2 heures; **it cost ~ on 50 francs** cela a coûté tout juste 50 F; **this is ~ what I want** c'est exactement *or* juste ce qu'il me faut; **that's ~ what I was going to say** c'est juste *or* justement *or* exactement ce que j'allais dire; ~ **what did he say?** qu'est-ce qu'il a dit exactement? *or* précisément?; **a doctor? — that's ~ what I am!** un docteur? — mais je suis justement *or* précisément docteur!; **that's ~ what I thought** c'est exactement ce que je pensais; **leave everything ~ as you find it** laissez tout exactement comme vous l'avez trouvé; (*fig*) **come ~ as you are*** venez comme vous êtes; ~ **as I thought, you aren't ready** c'est bien ce que je pensais, *or* je m'en doutais bien, tu n'es pas prêt; ~ **as you wish** (c'est) comme vous voulez *or* voudrez; ~ **then** *or* **at that moment** à ce moment même; ~ **when everything is going so well!** juste quand tout va si bien!; **that's ~ it!, that's ~ the point!** justement!; **that's ~ Robert, always late** c'est bien Robert, toujours en retard; ~ **how many came we don't know** nous ne savons pas exactement *or* au juste combien de gens sont venus; **it's ~ the same to me** cela m'est tout à fait égal; **yes, but ~ the same ...** oui, mais tout de même ...; ~ **so!** exactement!; **everything was ~ so*** tout était bien en ordre.

b (*indicating immediate past*) **to have ~ done** venir de faire; **he had ~ left** il venait de partir; **I have only ~ heard about it** je viens seulement de l'apprendre; **I've ~ this minute** *or* **this instant done it** je viens de le faire à l'instant; **this book is ~ out** ce livre vient de paraître; ~ **painted** fraîchement peint.

c (*at this or that moment*) juste. **we're ~ off** nous partons (à l'instant); **(I'm) ~ coming!** j'arrive!; **we're ~ about to start** nous sommes sur le point de commencer; **you're not interrupting us, I was ~ leaving** vous ne nous interrompez pas, je partais; ~ **as we arrived it began to rain** juste comme nous arrivions, il s'est mis à pleuvoir.

d (*almost not*) juste, de justesse. **we (only) ~ caught the train** nous avons eu le train de justesse, c'est tout juste si nous avons eu le train; **I'll ~ catch the train if I hurry** j'aurai tout juste le train si je me presse; **we only ~ missed the train** nous avons manqué le train de très peu; **you're ~ in time** vous arrivez juste à temps; **I will only ~ get there on**

time j'arriverai tout juste à l'heure; **I have only ~ enough money** j'ai tout juste assez d'argent; **he passed the exam but only ~** il a été reçu à l'examen mais de justesse *or* mais cela a été juste *or* mais il s'en est fallu de peu.

e (*with expressions of place*) juste. **~ here** juste ici, à cet endroit même; **~ over there/here** juste là/ici; **~ by the church** juste à côté de l'église; **~ past the station** juste après la gare.

f **~ about** à peu près; **~ about here** à peu près ici; **I've had ~ about enough!*** *or* **about as much as I can stand!*** j'en ai par-dessus la tête!*; **it's ~ about 3 o'clock** il est à peu près 3 heures; **it's ~ about 5 kilos** cela pèse 5 kilos à peu de chose près; **have you finished? — ~ about*** avez-vous fini? — à peu près *or* presque; **the incident ~ about ruined him** l'incident l'a ruiné ou presque *or* l'a quasiment* ruiné.

g (*in comparison*) **~ as** tout aussi; **this one is ~ as big as that** celui-ci est tout aussi grand que celui-là; **you sing ~ as well as I do** vous chantez tout aussi bien que moi.

h (+ *imper*) donc, un peu. **~ taste this!** goûte un peu à ça!*, goûte-moi ça!*; **~ come here a moment** viens ici un instant; **~ imagine!, ~ fancy!*** tu te rends compte!*, tu t'imagines un peu!*; **~ look at that!** regarde-moi ça!*; **~ you do!*, ~ you try it!*, ~ you dare!*** ose voir un peu!*; **~ shut up!*** veux-tu te taire!; **~ let me get my hands on him!*** que je l'attrape (*subj*) un peu!*

i (*slightly, immediately*) peu, juste. **~ over £10** un peu plus de 10 livres, 10 livres et des poussières*; **~ under £10** un peu moins de 10 livres; **~ after 9 o'clock he came in** peu *or* juste après 9 heures il est entré; **it's ~ after 9 o'clock** il est un peu plus de 9 heures, il est 9 heures et quelques; **~ after he came** juste après son arrivée; **~ before Christmas** juste avant Noël; **~ last week** pas plus tard que la semaine dernière; **~ afterwards** juste après, tout de suite après; **~ before it rained** peu *or* juste avant la pluie, peu *or* juste avant qu'il (ne) pleuve; **that's ~ over the kilo** cela fait tout juste un peu plus du kilo; **it's ~ to the left of the bookcase** c'est juste à gauche de la bibliothèque; **it's ~ on the left as you go in** c'est juste *or* tout de suite à gauche en entrant.

j (*only*) juste. **~ a moment please** un instant s'il vous plaît; **he's ~ a lad** c'est un gamin, ce n'est qu'un gamin; **don't go yet, it's ~ 9 o'clock** ne partez pas encore, il n'est que 9 heures; **I've come ~ to see you** je suis venu exprès pour te voir; **he did it ~ for a laugh*** il l'a fait histoire de rire*; **there will be ~ the two of us** il n'y aura que nous deux, il y aura juste nous deux; **~ a few** juste quelques-uns; **do you want any? — ~ a little bit** tu en veux? — juste un petit peu *or* rien qu'un petit peu; **~ a line to let you know that ...** juste un petit mot pour vous dire que ... .

k (*simply*) (tout) simplement, seulement. **I ~ told him to go away** je lui ai tout simplement dit de s'en aller; **you should ~ send it back** vous n'avez qu'à le renvoyer; **I would ~ like to say this** je voudrais seulement *or* simplement dire ceci; **I ~ can't imagine what's happened to him** je ne peux vraiment pas m'imaginer *or* je n'arrive pas à imaginer ce qui lui est arrivé; **we shall ~ drop in on him** nous ne ferons que passer chez lui; **I was ~ wondering if you knew ...** je me demandais simplement *or* seulement si vous saviez ...; **~ because YOU think so doesn't mean ...** ce n'est pas parce que toi tu penses cela que cela veut dire ...; **it's ~ one of those things*** c'est comme ça*, c'est la vie.

l (*positively*) absolument, tout simplement. **it was ~ marvellous!** c'était absolument merveilleux!; **it's ~ fine!** c'est parfait!

m (*emphatic*) **did you enjoy it? — did we ~!*** *or* **I should ~ say we did!*** cela vous a plu? — et comment!*

n (*other uses*) **it's ~ as well it's insured** heureusement que c'est assuré; **it would be ~ as well if he took it** il ferait aussi bien de le prendre; **we brought the umbrellas, and ~ as well** on a bien fait d'apporter les parapluies; **I'm busy ~ now** je suis occupé pour l'instant; **I saw him ~ now** je l'ai vu tout à l'heure; **not ~ yet** pas tout de suite, pas pour l'instant (*see also* **yet**); **~ in case it rains** juste au cas où il pleuvrait, si jamais il pleuvait; **I'm taking my umbrella, ~ in case** je prends mon parapluie, on ne sait jamais; **~ the same*, you shouldn't have done it** tout de même, tu n'aurais pas dû le faire; **I'd ~ as soon you kept quiet about it** j'aimerais autant que vous n'en disiez rien à personne.

just[2] [dʒʌst] **adj** *person, decision* juste, équitable (*to, towards* envers, avec); *punishment, reward* juste, mérité; *cause* juste; *anger* juste, légitime; *suspicion* justifié, bien fondé; *calculation* juste, exact. **it is only ~ to point out that ...** ce n'est que justice de faire remarquer que ... .

justice ['dʒʌstɪs] **n** **a** (*NonC: Jur*) justice *f*. **to bring sb to ~** traduire qn en justice, amener qn devant les tribunaux; (*US*) **Department of J~** ministère *m* de la Justice; *see* **poetic**.

b (*NonC: fairness*) équité *f*. **I must, in (all) ~, say ...** pour être juste, je dois dire ...; **in ~ to him he ..., to do him ~ he ...** pour être juste envers lui il ..., il faut lui rendre cette justice qu'il ...; **this photograph doesn't do him ~** cette photo ne le flatte pas *or* ne l'avantage pas; **she never does herself ~** elle ne se montre jamais à sa juste valeur; **to do ~ to a meal** faire honneur à un repas.

c (*judge*) (*Brit*) juge *m*; (*US*) juge de la Cour Suprême. **J~ of the Peace** juge de paix; *see* **lord**.

d (*justness: of cause etc*) justice *f*. **to dispute the ~ of a claim** contester le bien-fondé d'une réclamation.

justifiable [ˌdʒʌstɪ'faɪəbl] **adj** justifiable, légitime. (*Jur*) **~ homicide** homicide *m* justifiable.

justifiably [ˌdʒʌstɪ'faɪəblɪ] **adv** légitimement, avec raison.

justification [ˌdʒʌstɪfɪ'keɪʃən] **n** **a** (*gen, also Rel*) justification *f* (*of, for* de, à, pour). **as a ~ for his action** comme justification de *or* à son acte; **in ~ of** pour justifier; **he had no ~ for lying** son mensonge n'avait aucune justification, il n'avait aucune raison valable de mentir. **b** (*Typ, Comput : of text, page*) justification *f*, cadrage *m*.

justify ['dʒʌstɪfaɪ] **vt** **a** *behaviour, action* justifier, légitimer; *decision* prouver le bien fondé de. **to ~ o.s.** se justifier; **this does not ~ his being late** cela ne justifie pas son retard; **to be justified in doing** être en droit de faire, avoir de bonnes raisons pour faire; **you're not justified in talking to her like that** rien ne vous autorise à lui parler de cette façon; **am I justified in thinking ...?** est-ce que j'ai raison de penser ...? **b** (*Typ, Comput*) *paragraph, text etc* justifier. **justified left/right, left/right justified** justifié à gauche/à droite.

justly ['dʒʌstlɪ] **adv** avec raison, tout à fait justement.

justness ['dʒʌstnɪs] **n** *[cause]* justice *f*.

jut [dʒʌt] **vi** (*also* **~ out**) faire saillie, saillir, dépasser. **he saw a gun ~ting (out) from behind a wall** il a vu le canon d'un fusil dépasser de derrière un mur; **the cliff ~s (out) into the sea** la falaise avance dans la mer; **to ~ (out) over the street/the sea** surplomber la rue/la mer.

Jute [dʒuːt] **n** Jute *m*.

jute [dʒuːt] **n** jute *m*.

Juvenal ['dʒuːvɪnəl] **n** Juvénal *m*.

juvenile ['dʒuːvənaɪl] **1** **n** adolescent(e) *m(f)*, jeune *mf*. **2** **adj** juvénile; (*pej*) *behaviour, attitude* puéril (*f* puérile), juvénile. **~ books** livres *mpl* pour enfants; (*Jur*) **~ court** tribunal *m* pour enfants; **~ delinquency** délinquance *f* juvénile; **~ delinquent** mineur(e) *m(f)* délinquant(e), jeune délinquant(e) *m(f)*; **~ delinquents** l'enfance *or* la jeunesse délinquante; *see* **lead[1]**.

juxtapose ['dʒʌkstəpəʊz] **vt** juxtaposer.

juxtaposition [ˌdʒʌkstəpə'zɪʃən] **n** juxtaposition *f*. **to be in ~** se juxtaposer.

K

K, k [keɪ] **n** a (*letter*) K, k *m*. ~ **for King** ≃ K comme Kléber. b (**abbr of kilo**) mille. **he earns 30K*** il gagne 30K*. c (*Comput*) **K** K *m or* Ka *m*.
Kabala [kə'bɑːlə] **n** cabale *f*.
kabob [kə'bɒb] **n** = **kebab**.
Kabul [kə'bʊl] **n** Kaboul *or* Kabul.
Kaffeeklatsch ['kæfɪˌklætʃ] **n** (*US*) conversation *f* autour d'une tasse de café.
Kaffir ['kæfəʳ] (*usu pej*) 1 **n, pl ~s** *or* ~ Cafre *mf*. 2 **adj** cafre.
Kafkaesque [ˌkæfkə'esk] **adj** kafkaïen.
kaftan ['kæftæn] **n** kaftan *m*.
kail [keɪl] **n** = **kale**.
Kaiser ['kaɪzəʳ] **n** Kaiser *m*.
Kalahari [ˌkælə'hɑːrɪ] **n**: ~ **(Desert)** (désert *m* du) Kalahari.
kale [keɪl] **n** chou frisé.
kaleidoscope [kə'laɪdəskəʊp] **n** kaléidoscope *m*.
kaleidoscopic [kəˌlaɪdə'skɒpɪk] **adj** kaléidoscopique.
Kamasutra [ˌkɑːmə'suːtrə] **n** Kamasutra *m*.
kamikaze [ˌkæmɪ'kɑːzɪ] **n** kamikaze *m*. ~ **pilot/act/mission** pilote *m*/action *f*/mission *f* kamikaze.
Kampala [ˌkæm'pɑːlə] **n** Kampala.
Kampuchea [ˌkæmpʊ'tʃɪə] **n**: **(Democratic)** ~ Kampuchéa *m* (démocratique).
Kampuchean [ˌkæmpʊ'tʃɪən] **n, adj** Kampuchéen(ne) *m(f)*.
Kan. (*US*) **abbr of Kansas**.
Kanak [kə'næk] **n** canaque *mf*, kanak(e) *m(f)*.
kangaroo [ˌkæŋgə'ruː] **n** kangourou *m*. ~ **court** tribunal irrégulier.
Kans. (*US*) **abbr of Kansas**.
Kansas ['kænzəs] **n** Kansas *m*. **in** ~ dans le Kansas.
Kantian ['kæntɪən] **n, adj** Kantien.
kaolin ['keəlɪn] **n** kaolin *m*.
kapok ['keɪpɒk] 1 **n** kapok *m*. 2 **comp** *cushion* rembourré de kapok.
kaput* [kə'pʊt] **adj** *watch, car* fichu*, foutu‡, kaput‡ *inv*; *plan etc* fichu*, foutu‡, dans le lac*.
karabiner [ˌkæə'biːnəʳ] **n** (*Climbing*) mousqueton *m*.
karat ['kærət] **n** = **carat**.
karate [kə'rɑːtɪ] **n** (*NonC*) karaté *m*. ~ **chop** coup *m* de karaté (donné avec le tranchant de la main).
Kariba [kə'riːbə] **n**: **Lake** ~ le lac Kariba.
karma ['kɑːmə] **n** (*Rel*) karma *m*; (*fig*) aura *f*.
kart [kɑːt] 1 **n** kart *m*. 2 **vi**: **to go ~ing** faire du karting.
karting ['kɑːtɪŋ] **n** karting *m*.
Kashmir [kæʃ'mɪəʳ] **n** Cachemire *m*.
Kashmiri [kæʃ'mɪərɪ] 1 **n** a *person* Cachemirien(ne) *m(f)*. b (*Ling*) kashmiri *m*, cachemirien *m*. 2 **adj** cachemirien.
Kate [keɪt] **n** (**dim of Katharine**)
Katharine, Katherine ['kæθərɪn] **n, Kathleen** ['kæθliːn] **n** Catherine *f*.
katydid ['keɪtɪdɪd] **n** sauterelle *f* d'Amérique.
katzenjammer* ['kætsənˌdʒæməʳ] **n** (*US*) (*noise*) tapage *m*; (*hangover*) gueule *f* de bois*.
kayak ['kaɪæk] **n** kayak *m*.
Kazak(h) [kə'zɑːk] **n**: **the** ~ **SSR** la RSS du Kazakhastan.
Kazakhstan [ˌkɑːzɑːk'stæn] **n** Kazakhastan *m*.
kazoo [kə'zuː] **n** mirliton *m*.
KB (**abbr of kilobyte**) Ko *m*.
K.C. [keɪ'siː] **n** a (*Brit Jur*) (**abbr of King's Counsel**) *see* **counsel**. b (*US Geog*) **abbr of Kansas City**.
K.D. [keɪ'diː] **adj** (*US Comm*) (**abbr of knocked down**) livré démonté.
kebab [kə'bæb] **n** kébab *m*, brochette *f* (de viande).
kedge [kedʒ] (*Naut*) 1 **n** ancre *f* à jet. 2 **vt** haler (sur une ancre à jet).
kedgeree [ˌkedʒə'riː] **n** (*Brit*) pilaf *m* de poisson.
keel [kiːl] 1 **n** (*Naut*) quille *f*. **on an even** ~ (*Naut*) dans ses lignes, à égal tirant d'eau; (*fig*) stable; (*fig*) **to keep sth on an even** ~ maintenir qch en équilibre. 2 **comp** ▶**keelhaul** (*Naut*) faire passer sous la quille (*en guise de châtiment*); (* *fig*) passer un savon à*.
▶**keel over** 1 **vi** (*Naut*) chavirer; (*fig*) *[person]* tomber dans les pommes*, tourner de l'œil*. 2 **vt** (*Naut*) (faire) chavirer.
keen¹ [kiːn] **adj** a (*sharp*) *blade* aiguisé, affilé, tranchant; *point* aigu (*f* -guë); (*fig*) *wind, cold* piquant, cinglant; *air* vif; *sarcasm* mordant, caustique, âpre; *interest* vif; *pleasure, desire, feeling* vif, intense; *appetite* aiguisé; *grief, pain* cuisant, poignant; *sight, eye* pénétrant, perçant; *hearing, ear* fin; (*Brit*) *price* étudié (de près), serré; *competition* serré, acharné; *intelligence* vif, aigu, fin, pénétrant; *judgment* pénétrant. **he's a** ~ **judge of character** il a la pénétration *or* la finesse qui permet de juger les gens.
b (*Brit: enthusiastic*) *person* enthousiaste, ardent, zélé. **to be as** ~ **as mustard†** déborder d'enthousiasme, être plein de zèle; **he tried not to seem too** ~ il a essayé de ne pas se montrer trop enthousiaste *or* de ne pas montrer trop d'enthousiasme; **he's a** ~ **footballer** c'est un passionné du football; **she's a very** ~ **socialist** c'est une socialiste passionnée; **to be** ~ **to do** tenir (absolument) à faire; **to be** ~ **on music** avoir la passion de la musique; **to be** ~ **on an idea** être enthousiasmé par une idée; **to become** *or* **grow** ~ **on sth/sb** s'enthousiasmer *or* se passionner pour qch/qn; **I'm not too** ~ **on him** il ne me plaît pas beaucoup; **he's** ~ **on her*** il a un béguin* pour elle; **he's very** ~ **on Mozart** c'est un passionné de Mozart; **to be** ~ **on doing sth** aimer beaucoup faire qch; **he's not** ~ **on her coming** il ne tient pas tellement à ce qu'elle vienne; **he's very** ~ **that she should come** il tient beaucoup à ce qu'elle vienne; *see* **mad, madly**.
c (*US* ‡: *good*) chouette*.
keen² [kiːn] 1 **n** (*Ir Mus*) mélopée *f* funèbre (*irlandaise*). 2 **vi** chanter une mélopée funèbre.
keenly ['kiːnlɪ] **adv** a (*enthusiastically*) avec zèle, avec enthousiasme, ardemment. b (*acutely*) *interest, feel* vivement, profondément; *wish, desire* ardemment, profondément; *notice, remark, observe* astucieusement. **he looked at me** ~ il m'a jeté un regard pénétrant.
keenness ['kiːnnɪs] **n** a *[blade]* finesse *f*; *[cold, wind]* âpreté *f*; *[interest, pleasure, grief]* intensité *f*; *[pain]* violence *f*, acuité *f*; *[hearing]* finesse; *[intelligence, mind]* finesse, pénétration *f*, vivacité *f*. ~ **of sight** acuité visuelle. b (*eagerness*) ardeur *f*, enthousiasme *m*. **his** ~ **to leave** son empressement à partir.
keep [kiːp] **pret, ptp kept** 1 **vt** a (*retain: gen*) garder, (*more formally*) conserver. **you can** ~ **this book** tu peux garder ce livre; **you must** ~ **the receipt** il faut garder *or* conserver le reçu; ~ **the change!** gardez la monnaie!; **to** ~ **one's job** garder son travail; **to** ~ **control of** rester maître de; **this material will** ~ **its colour/texture** *etc* ce tissu gardera ses couleurs/sa texture *etc*; **I can't** ~ **that tune in my head** je n'arrive pas à retenir cet air; **to** ~ **sth for o.s.** garder qch; **she ~s herself to herself** elle fuit la compagnie, elle se tient à l'écart; **they** ~ **themselves to themselves** *[group]* ils font bande à part, ils restent entre eux; *[couple]* ils se tiennent à l'écart; *see* **cool, foot, goal** *etc*.
b (+ *adj, vb etc: maintain*) tenir, garder. **to** ~ **sth clean** tenir *or* garder qch propre; **to** ~ **o.s. clean** être toujours propre; **exercise will** ~ **you fit** l'exercice physique vous maintiendra en forme; **to** ~ **sth tidy** tenir qch en état; **well kept** *house, garden* bien entretenu, bien tenu; *hands, nails* soigné; *hair* bien entretenu; **"~ Britain tidy"** "pour une Grande-Bretagne propre"; **he kept them working** *or* **at work all night** il les a forcés à continuer de travailler toute la nuit; **they kept him at it** ils l'ont tenu attelé à la tâche *or* au travail; **to** ~ **a machine running** maintenir une machine en activité; **he kept the (car) engine running** il a laissé le moteur (de la voiture) en marche; **to** ~ **sb waiting** faire attendre qn; ~ **him talking while I ...** fais-lui la conversation pendant que je ...; **she managed to** ~ **the conversation going** elle a réussi à entretenir la conversation; **she kept him to his promise** elle l'a forcé à tenir sa promesse; ~ **me informed (of)** tenez-moi au courant (de); **to** ~ **a piece of news from sb** cacher une nouvelle à qn; ~ **it to yourself,** ~ **it under**

your hat* garde-le pour toi, ne le dis à personne; *see* **alive, quiet, secret, warm** *etc.*

c (*preserve, put aside*) garder, mettre de côté, mettre en réserve; (*store, hold in readiness*) avoir (en réserve); (*Comm: stock, sell*) vendre, avoir, stocker. **I've kept some for him** je lui en ai gardé; **I kept it for just this purpose** je l'ai gardé *or* mis de côté pour cela; **I'm ~ing some sugar in case there's a shortage** j'ai du sucre en réserve *or* une provision de sucre au cas où il viendrait à manquer; **~ it somewhere safe** mettez-le en lieu sûr; **you must ~ it in a cold place** il faut le garder *or* le conserver au froid; **where does he ~ his money?** où est-ce qu'il met son argent?; **where do you ~ your shoe polish?** où est-ce que tu ranges ton cirage?; (*in supermarket etc*) **where do you ~ the sugar?** où est-ce que vous mettez le sucre?

d (*detain*) garder, retenir. **to ~ sb in prison** détenir qn, garder qn en prison; **they kept him prisoner for some time** ils l'ont gardé prisonnier quelque temps; **they kept the prisoners in a dark room** les prisonniers étaient détenus dans une salle obscure; **what kept you?** qu'est-ce qui vous a retenu?; **I mustn't ~ you** je ne veux pas vous retarder *or* vous retenir; **they wanted to ~ me to dinner** ils ont voulu me garder à dîner; **illness kept her in bed** la maladie l'a forcée à rester au lit *or* à garder le lit.

e (*own; look after*) *shop, hotel, restaurant* tenir, avoir; *house, servant, dog, car* avoir; (*Agr*) *cattle, pigs, bees, chickens* élever, faire l'élevage de. **he ~s a good cellar** il a une bonne cave; *see* **house** *etc.*

f *accounts, diary* tenir. **I've kept a note of his name** j'ai pris note de *or* j'ai noté son nom; *see* **count[1], track** *etc.*

g (*support*) faire vivre, entretenir, subvenir aux besoins de. **I earn enough to ~ myself** je gagne assez pour vivre *or* pour subvenir à mes (propres) besoins; **I have 6 children to ~** j'ai 6 enfants à ma charge *or* à entretenir *or* à nourrir; **he ~s a mistress in Paris** il entretient une maîtresse à Paris; **to ~ sb in food/clothing** nourrir/habiller qn; **I can't afford to ~ you in cigarettes** je ne peux pas (me payer le luxe de) te fournir en cigarettes.

h (*restrain, prevent*) **to ~ sb from doing** empêcher qn de faire; **to ~ o.s. from doing** se retenir *or* s'empêcher de faire; **~ him from school for just now** ne l'envoyez pas à l'école pour le moment; **it kept him from despair** cela l'a sauvé *or* gardé (*frm*) du désespoir.

i (*observe, fulfil*) *promise* tenir; *law, rule* observer, respecter; *treaty* respecter; *vow* rester fidèle à; *obligations* remplir; *feast day* célébrer. **to ~ an appointment** se rendre à un rendez-vous; **she did not ~ her appointment with them** elle n'est pas venue à *or* elle n'a pas tenu son rendez-vous avec eux, elle leur a fait faux bond; **to ~ Lent/the Sabbath** observer le carême/le jour du sabbat; **to ~ sb's birthday** fêter l'anniversaire de qn; *see* **peace, word** *etc.*

j (†: *guard, protect*) garder, protéger; *sheep etc* garder. **God ~ you!** Dieu vous garde!

2 vi a (*continue*) garder, suivre, continuer. **~ on this road until you come to ...** suivez cette route jusqu'à ce que vous arriviez (*subj*) à ...; **to ~ (to the) left/right** garder sa gauche/droite; (*Aut*) tenir sa gauche/droite; **to ~ to** *or* **in the middle of the road** rester au *or* garder le milieu de la route; **to ~ straight on** continuer *or* suivre tout droit; **~ north till you get to ...** continuez vers le nord jusqu'à ce que vous arriviez (*subj*) à ...; **to ~ doing** continuer à *or* de faire, ne pas cesser de faire; **if you ~ complaining** si vous continuez à vous plaindre; **she ~s talking** elle n'arrête pas de parler; **he would ~ objecting** il ne cessait pas de faire des objections; **I ~ hoping she'll come back** j'espère toujours qu'elle reviendra; **to ~ standing** rester debout; **~ going!** allez-y!, continuez toujours!; **~ smiling!** gardez le sourire!

b (*remain*) rester, se tenir. **to ~ fit** se maintenir en forme (*see also* **4**); **he ~s in good health** il est toujours en bonne santé; **to ~ still** rester *or* se tenir tranquille; **to ~ silent** se taire, garder le silence, rester silencieux; **~ calm!** reste calme!, du calme!; **~ there for a minute** restez là une minute; **~ off the flowerbeds** ne marchez pas sur les plates-bandes; **"~ off the grass"** "défense de marcher sur les pelouses"; **she kept inside for 3 days** elle est restée chez elle *or* elle n'est pas sortie pendant 3 jours; **to ~ to one's bed/one's room** *etc* garder le lit/la chambre *etc*; **she ~s to herself** elle fuit la compagnie, elle ne fréquente presque personne; **they ~ to themselves** [*group*] ils font bande à part, ils restent entre eux; [*couple*] ils se tiennent à l'écart; *see* **alive, cool, quiet** *etc.*

c (*in health*) aller, se porter (*frm*). **how are you ~ing?** comment allez-vous?, comment vous portez-vous? (*frm*); **to ~ well** aller bien; **she's not ~ing very well** elle ne va pas très bien; **he's ~ing better** il va mieux.

d [*food etc*] se garder, se conserver, garder sa fraîcheur. **apples that ~ all winter** des pommes qui se gardent *or* se conservent tout l'hiver; **this ham will ~ up to 3 days in the fridge** ce jambon conservera sa fraîcheur 3 jours au réfrigérateur; (*fig*) **this business can ~** cette affaire peut attendre; **that will ~ till tomorrow** cela attendra demain, cela tiendra jusqu'à demain.

3 n a (*NonC: livelihood, food*) **to earn one's ~** gagner de quoi vivre; **I got £15 a week and my ~** je gagnais 15 livres par semaine logé et nourri; **he's not worth his ~** il ne vaut pas ce qu'on dépense pour lui *or* ce qu'on dépense pour l'entretenir, il ne vaut pas la dépense.

b (*Archit, Hist*) donjon *m.*

c **for ~s*** pour de bon, pour toujours.

4 comp ▸**keep-fit: she does keep-fit once a week** elle fait de la culture physique *or* de la gymnastique une fois par semaine; **keep-fit (classes)** cours *mpl* de gymnastique; **keep-fit exercises** culture *f* physique ▸**keepsake** souvenir *m* (*objet*).

▸**keep at** vt fus a (*continue*) continuer; (*work with persistence at*) travailler d'arrache-pied à, s'acharner à. **keep at it!** continuez! b (*nag at*) harceler, s'acharner sur. **she keeps at him all the time** elle le harcèle, elle est toujours après lui*; **you'll have to keep at him till he pays you** il va falloir le harceler jusqu'à ce qu'il vous paie (*subj*).

▸**keep away** 1 vi (*lit*) ne pas s'approcher (*from* de). **keep away from the fire** ne t'approche pas du feu; (*fig*) **to keep away from drink** s'abstenir de boire, ne pas boire. 2 vt sep (*gen*) empêcher de s'approcher (*from* de). **keep him away!** ne le laissez pas s'approcher, empêchez-le de s'approcher; **keep them away from each other!** empêchez-les de se rencontrer!

▸**keep back** 1 vi rester en arrière, ne pas avancer, ne pas approcher. **keep back!** restez en arrière! *or* où vous êtes!, n'approchez pas!

2 vt sep a (*withhold*) retenir. **they keep back 5% of my wages for national insurance** on me retient 5% de mon salaire pour la Sécurité sociale.

b (*conceal*) cacher, ne pas dire, ne pas révéler; *secrets* taire. **they are keeping back the names of the victims** ils ne communiquent pas les noms des victimes; **don't keep anything back** ne nous (*or* me *etc*) cachez rien, racontez tout.

c (*hinder, make late*) retarder. **I don't want to keep you back** je ne veux pas vous retarder; **have I kept you back in your work?** vous ai-je retardé dans votre travail?

d *crowd* empêcher de s'approcher (*from* de).

▸**keep down** 1 vi rester assis (*or* allongé *etc*). **keep down!** ne bougez pas!, restez assis (*or* allongé *etc*)!

2 vt sep a (*control*) retenir, maîtriser; *revolt, one's anger* réprimer, contenir; *dog* retenir, maîtriser. **you can't keep her down** elle ne se laisse jamais abattre; (*loc*) **you can't keep a good man down** un homme de valeur reprendra toujours le dessus.

b *spending* restreindre, limiter. **to keep prices down** maintenir les prix bas, empêcher les prix de monter, empêcher la hausse des prix.

c (*Scol*) **to keep a pupil down** faire redoubler une classe à un élève; **to be kept down** redoubler.

d (*Med*) **the sick man can't keep anything down** le malade ne garde rien, le malade vomit *or* rend tout ce qu'il prend.

▸**keep from** vt fus: **to keep from doing** s'abstenir *or* s'empêcher *or* se retenir de faire; **to keep from drink** s'abstenir de boire, ne pas boire.

▸**keep in** 1 vi: **to keep in with sb** rester en bons termes avec qn; (*for one's own purposes*) cultiver qn. 2 vt sep a *anger, feelings* contenir, réprimer. b *person* empêcher de sortir. (*Scol*) **to keep a child in** garder un enfant en retenue, consigner un enfant. c **keep your tummy in!** rentre ton *or* le ventre!; *see* **hand.**

▸**keep off** 1 vi [*person*] se tenir éloigné, rester à l'écart *or* à distance. **keep off!** n'approchez pas!; **if the rain keeps off** s'il ne pleut pas. 2 vt sep *dog* éloigner; *person* empêcher de s'approcher (*from* de), tenir à distance. **this weather will keep the crowds off** ce temps fera rester les gens chez eux; **keep your hands off!** ne touchez pas!; **keep your hat off** ne (re)mettez pas votre chapeau.

▸**keep on** 1 vi a continuer, ne pas cesser. **he kept on reading** il a continué à *or* de lire, il n'a pas cessé de lire; **don't keep on so!** arrête! (*see also* **1c**); **she does keep on about her rich friends** elle n'arrête pas de parler de ses riches amis; **the child kept on crying the whole night** l'enfant n'a fait que pleurer toute la nuit.

b (*keep going*) continuer (à avancer). **keep on past the church till you get to the school** continuez après l'église jusqu'à (ce que vous arriviez (*subj*) à) l'école; (*fig*) **if you keep on as you're doing now you'll pass the exam** si tu continues dans cette voie tu seras reçu à l'examen.

c (*Brit*) **to keep on at sb** harceler qn; **don't keep on so!** cesse de me (*or* le *etc*) harceler!

2 vt sep a *servant, employee* garder.

b **to keep one's hat on** garder son chapeau; [*man*] rester couvert; *see* **hair.**

▸**keep out** 1 vi rester en dehors. **"keep out"** "défense d'entrer", "accès interdit"; **to keep out of danger** rester *or* se tenir à l'abri du danger; **to keep out of a quarrel** ne pas se mêler à une dispute; **keep out of this!, you keep out of it!** mêlez-vous de ce qui vous regarde! *or* de vos (propres) affaires! *or* de vos oignons!* 2 vt sep *person, dog* empêcher d'entrer, ne pas laisser entrer. **that coat will keep out the cold** ce manteau protégera bien du froid.

▸**keep to** vt fus: **to keep to one's promise** tenir sa promesse, être fidèle à sa promesse; **to keep to the subject** ne pas s'écarter du sujet, rester dans le sujet; **to keep to the text** serrer le texte; **to keep to one's bed** garder le lit; **to keep to a/one's diet** suivre sérieusement un/son régime, ne pas faire d'écart à un/son régime; **to keep to one's ideal weight** rester *or* se maintenir à son poids idéal; **to keep to the rules** s'en tenir aux règles; **to keep to a/the schedule** respecter un/le programme; *see also* **keep 2b.**

►**keep together** 1 vi *[people]* rester ensemble, ne pas se séparer. 2 vt sep *objects* garder ensemble, (*keep fixed together*) maintenir ensemble; *people* garder ensemble *or* unis.

►**keep under** vt sep *anger, feelings* contenir, maîtriser; *passions* dominer; *people, race* soumettre, assujettir, asservir; *subordinates* dominer; *unruly pupils etc* tenir, mater.

►**keep up** 1 vi a continuer, se maintenir; *[prices]* se maintenir. **their spirits are keeping up** ils ne se découragent pas; **I hope the good weather will keep up** j'espère que le beau temps va continuer *or* se maintenir.

b **to keep up with sb** (*in race, walk etc*) aller aussi vite que qn, se maintenir à la hauteur de qn; (*in work, achievement*) se maintenir au niveau de qn; (*in comprehension*) suivre qn; **I couldn't keep up with what he was saying** je n'ai pas pu suivre ce qu'il disait; (*Scol*) **to keep up with the class** bien suivre (en classe); (*fig*) **to keep up with the Joneses** ne pas se trouver en reste avec les voisins; **to keep up with the times** être de son temps *or* époque; (*Ind*) **to keep up with demand** arriver à satisfaire la demande.

c (*stay friends with*) **to keep up with sb** rester en relations avec qn; **we haven't kept up at all since she went abroad** nous avons complètement perdu le contact depuis qu'elle est partie à l'étranger.

2 vt sep a continuer; *correspondence* entretenir; *study etc* continuer, ne pas interrompre *or* abandonner. **to keep up a subscription** maintenir un abonnement, continuer à payer une cotisation; **I try to keep up my Latin** j'essaie d'entretenir mon latin; **to keep up a custom** maintenir *or* respecter une tradition; **keep it up!** continuez!

b (*maintain*) *house, paintwork* maintenir en bon état; *engine, road* entretenir, maintenir en bon état.

keeper ['ki:pəʳ] n (*person*) gardien(ne) *m(f)*, surveillant(e) *m(f)*; (*in museum etc*) conservateur *m*, -trice *f*; (*in park, zoo etc*) gardien; (*gamekeeper*) garde-chasse *m*. **am I my brother's ~?** suis-je le gardien de mon frère?; *see* **bee, goal, shop** *etc.*

keeping ['ki:pɪŋ] n (*NonC*) a (*care*) garde *f*. **to put sb in sb's ~** confier qn à (la garde de) qn; **to put sth in sb's ~** confier qch à qn; *see* **safe** *etc.* b (*observing*) *[rule]* observation *f*; *[festival etc]* célébration *f*. c **to be in ~ with** s'accorder avec, être en rapport avec; **out of ~ with** en désaccord avec.

keester‡ ['ki:stəʳ] = **keister.**

keg [keg] n a (*barrel*) *[beer, brandy etc]* tonnelet *m*, baril *m*, petit fût; *[fish]* caque *f*. b (*also* **~ beer**) bière *f* en tonnelet.

keister‡ ['ki:stəʳ] n (*US*) (*buttocks*) derrière *m*, postérieur* *m*; (*case*) mallette *f*.

kelp [kelp] n (*NonC*) varech *m*.

ken [ken] 1 n: **that is beyond** *or* **outside my ~** je ne m'y connais pas, ce n'est pas dans mes cordes. 2 vt (*Scot*) = **know.**

Ken. (*US*) abbr of **Kentucky.**

kennel ['kenl] 1 n a *[dog]* niche *f*; *[hound]* chenil *m*; (*fig pej*) chenil (*fig*), tanière *f* (*fig*). **~s** (*for breeding*) élevage *m* (de chiens), chenil; (*for boarding*) chenil; **to put a dog in ~s** mettre un chien dans un chenil. b *[fox]* repaire *m*, tanière *f*. 2 comp ►**kennel maid** aide *f* de chenil.

Kentucky [ken'tʌkɪ] n Kentucky *m*. **in ~** dans le Kentucky.

Kenya ['kenjə] n Kenya *m*. **Mount ~** le mont Kenya.

Kenyan ['kenjən] 1 n Kényen(ne) *m(f)*. 2 adj kényen.

kepi ['keɪpɪ] n képi *m*.

kept [kept] pret ptp of **keep. a ~ man/woman** un homme/une femme entretenu(e).

keratin ['kerətɪn] n kératine *f*.

kerb [kɜ:b] (*Brit*) 1 n (bordure *f or* bord *m* du) trottoir *m*. **along the ~** le long du trottoir; (*Aut*) **to hit the ~** heurter le trottoir; (*St Ex*) **on the ~** en coulisse, après la clôture (*de la Bourse*). 2 comp ►**kerb broker** (*St Ex*) courtier *m* en valeurs mobilières, coulissier *m* ►**kerb crawler** dragueur* motorisé, conducteur *m* qui accoste les femmes sur le trottoir ►**kerb crawling** drague* motorisée ►**kerb drill** précautions *fpl* pour traverser la rue; **to learn one's kerb drill** apprendre à traverser la rue (en toute sécurité) ►**kerbstone** pierre *f or* pavé *m* de bordure (*de trottoir*).

kerchief ['kɜ:tʃɪf] n fanchon *f*, fichu *m*.

kerfuffle* [kə'fʌfl] n (*Brit*) histoire* *f*, affaire* *f*. **what a ~!** quelle histoire *or* que d'histoires pour si peu!*

kernel ['kɜ:nl] n a *[nut, fruitstone]* amande *f*; (*seed*) grain *m*. (*fig*) **there's a ~ of truth in what he says** il y a un grain de vérité dans ce qu'il dit; **the ~ of the question** le point fondamental de la question. b (*Ling, Comput*) noyau *m*. (*Ling*) **~ sentence, ~ string** phrase-noyau *f*, phrase *f* nucléaire.

kerosene ['kerəsi:n] 1 n (*aircraft fuel*) kérosène *m*; (*US: for stoves, lamps*) pétrole *m* (lampant). 2 comp *lamp* à pétrole.

kestrel ['kestrəl] n crécerelle *f*.

ketch [ketʃ] n ketch *m*.

ketchup ['ketʃəp] n ketchup *m*.

kettle ['ketl] 1 n a (*for water: also* (*US*) **tea~**) bouilloire *f*. **the ~'s boiling** l'eau bout (dans la bouilloire); **I'll just put the ~ on (for some tea)** je vais mettre l'eau à chauffer (pour le thé). b (*also* **fish ~**) poissonnière *f*. (*fig*) **that's a fine** *or* **a pretty ~ of fish** nous voilà dans de beaux draps *or* dans un joli pétrin; (*fig*) **that's another** *or* **a different ~ of fish** c'est une autre paire de manches*. 2 comp ►**kettledrum** (*Mus*) timbale *f*.

key [ki:] 1 n a *[door etc]* clef *f or* clé *f*. **to turn the ~ (in the door)** donner un tour de clef (dans la serrure); **leave the ~ in the door** laisse la clef sur la porte; *see* **latch, lock¹, master** *etc.*

b *[clock]* clef *f or* clé *f* de pendule, remontoir *m*; *[clockwork toy etc]* remontoir; (*Tech*) clef de serrage *or* à écrous.

c (*fig: to problem etc*) clef *f or* clé *f*. **the ~ to the mystery** la clef du mystère.

d (*answers*) solutions *fpl*; (*Scol*) (*crib*) corrigé *m*; (*translation*) traduction *f* (*toute faite*); (*for map, diagram etc*) légende *f*.

e *[piano, computer, typewriter etc]* touche *f*; *[wind instrument]* clef *f or* clé *f*; *see* **function.**

f (*Mus*) ton *m*. **to be in/off ~** être/n'être pas dans le ton; **to go off ~** sortir du ton; **to sing in/off ~** chanter juste/faux; **to play in/off ~** jouer dans le ton/dans le mauvais ton; **in the ~ of C/D** *etc* en do/ré *etc*; **in the major ~** dans le ton majeur; **change of ~** changement *m* de ton; *see* **low¹, minor.**

2 adj (*vital*) (*gen*) *industry, position* clef (*f inv*) *or* clé (*f inv*); *difference* fondamental; *problem, question* clef *or* clé, fondamental. **~ jobs** postes *mpl* clefs; **~ man** pivot *m*, cheville *f* (ouvrière); *[argument etc]* **~ point** point capital *or* essentiel; **~ speech** discours *m* clef; (*Ind*) **~ strike** grève-bouchon *f*; (*Ind*) **~ workers** travailleurs *mpl* clefs.

3 comp ►**keyboard** n *[piano, computer, typewriter etc]* clavier *m* ◊ vt (*Comput, Typ*) faire la saisie de ►**keyboarder** (*Comput*) opérateur-pupitre *m*, claviste *mf* ►**keyboard instruments** (*Mus*) instruments *mpl* à clavier ►**keyboard literate** (*Comput*) bien adapté à l'usage du clavier informatique ►**keyboard operator** (*Comput*) = **keyboarder** ►**keyboard player:** (*Mus*) **he's a keyboard player** il joue du piano (*or* clavecin *etc*) ►**keyboards** npl (*Mus*) orgue *m* (*or* piano *etc*) électronique; **he's on keyboards** il est à l'orgue (*or* piano *etc*) électronique ►**keyhole** trou *m* de serrure; **through the keyhole** par le trou de la serrure ►**keyhole saw** scie *f* à guichet ►**key money** pas *m* de porte (*fig*) ►**keynote** (*Mus*) tonique *f*; (*fig*) *[speech etc]* note dominante ►**keynote speaker,** (*US*) **keynoter*** (*Pol etc*) orateur chargé du discours-programme ►**keynote speech** discours-programme *m* ►**keypad** (*Comput*) clavier *m* ►**keyphone** (*Brit*) téléphone *m* à touches ►**key punch** (*Comput*) perforatrice *f* à clavier ►**key ring** porte-clefs *m inv* ►**key signature** (*Mus*) armature *f* ►**keystone** (*Archit, fig*) clef *f* de voûte ►**the Keystone State** (*US*) la Pennsylvanie ►**keystroke** (*Typ, Comput*) frappe *f*, manipulation *f* ►**keyword** mot-clé *m*.

4 vt a (*Comput, Typ*) (*also* **~ in** *or* **up**) *text, data* faire la saisie de.

b *speech etc* adapter (*to or for one's audience* à son auditoire). **the colour scheme was ~ed to brown** les coloris s'harmonisaient autour du brun *or* étaient dans les bruns.

►**key in** vt sep (*Comput, Typ*) *text, data* faire la saisie de.

►**key up** vt sep (*fig*) surexciter, tendre. **she was (all) keyed up about the interview** elle était surexcitée *or* tendue à la pensée de *or* dans l'attente de l'entrevue.

keying ['ki:ɪŋ] n saisie *f*.

Kg (abbr of **kilogram(s)**) kg.

KGB [keɪdʒi:'bi:] n (*in former USSR*) K.G.B. *m*.

khaki ['kɑ:kɪ] 1 adj kaki *inv*. 2 n kaki *m*.

Khartoum [kɑ:'tu:m] n Khartoum.

Khmer [kmeəʳ] 1 adj khmer (*f* khmère). **~ Republic** République *f* khmère. 2 n a Khmer *m*, Khmère *f*. **~ Rouge** Khmer *m* Rouge. b (*Ling*) khmer *m*, cambodgien *m*.

Khyber Pass [ˌkaɪbə'pɑ:s] n passe *f* de Khyber *or* Khaibar.

kHz abbr of **kilohertz.**

kibbutz [kɪ'bʊts] n, pl **kibbutzim** [kɪ'bʊtsɪm] kibboutz *m*.

kibitz* ['kɪbɪts] vi (*Cards*) regarder le jeu de quelqu'un par-dessus son épaule; (*US fig*) se mêler de ce qui ne vous regarde pas.

kibitzer* ['kɪbɪtsəʳ] n (*Cards*) spectateur *m*, -trice *f* (*qui regarde le jeu de quelqu'un par-dessus son épaule*); (*busybody*) mouche *f* du coche; (*pej: disruptive wisecracker*) petit malin, petite maligne.

kibosh‡ ['kaɪbɒʃ] n: **to put the ~ on sth**‡ mettre le holà à qch, mettre fin à qch.

kick [kɪk] 1 n a (*action*) coup *m* de pied. **to give the door a ~** donner un coup de pied dans la porte; **to aim** *or* **take a ~ at sb/sth** lancer un coup de pied à qn/qch *or* dans la direction de qn/qch; **to get a ~ on the leg** recevoir un coup de pied à la jambe; **to give sb a ~ in the pants*** donner un coup de pied au derrière à *or* de qn, botter* le derrière à *or* de qn; (*fig*) **he needs a ~ up the backside**‡ il a besoin de bons coups de pied au cul**‡; (*fig*) **this refusal was a ~ in the teeth**‡ *or* (*US*) **a ~ in the ass**‡ **for her** ce refus a été pour elle (comme) une gifle en pleine figure; *see* **free.**

b (** fig: thrill etc*) **she got quite a ~ out of seeing Paris** elle a été tout émoustillée *or* excitée de voir Paris; **he gets a ~ out of making his sister cry** il prend un malin plaisir à faire pleurer sa sœur; **I get a ~ out of it** je trouve ça stimulant *or* excitant; **he did it for ~s** il l'a fait pour le plaisir, (*stronger*) il l'a fait parce que ça l'excitait *or* ça le bottait*; **he has no ~ left, there's no ~ left in him** il ne lui reste plus aucune énergie *or* aucun allant; **this drink hasn't much ~ in it** cette boisson n'est pas très corsée, ça n'est pas cette boisson qui te (*or* me *etc*) montera à la tête; **a drink with plenty of ~ in it** une boisson qui vous donne un coup de fouet.

c *[gun]* recul *m*. (*Aut*) **a ~ of the starting handle** un retour de manivelle.

d (**: fig*) **he's on a fishing ~ now** il donne à plein* dans la pêche en ce moment.

e (*Ftbl etc*) **he's a good ~*** il a un bon dégagement.

2 **comp** ▸**kickback*** (*reaction*) réaction *f*, contrecoup *m*; (*percentage of money made, money paid as bribe or for information etc*) pourcentage *m* (*reçu*); (*rebate on sale*) ristourne *f*, rabais *m* ▸**kick boxing** boxe *f* française ▸**kick-off** (*Ftbl etc*) coup *m* d'envoi; (** fig: start*) *[meeting, ceremony etc]* démarrage* *m*; (*Ftbl*) **the kick-off is at 3 p.m.** le coup d'envoi est à 15h; (*fig*) **when's the kick-off?*** à quelle heure ça démarre?*; (*fig*) **for a kick-off*** d'abord, pour commencer ▸**kick pleat** pli *m* creux (à l'arrière) ▸**kick-stand** (*US*) *[motorcycle etc]* béquille *f* ▸**kick-start vt** *motorcycle* démarrer au pied; (*fig*) *economy* donner un coup de fouet à ▸**kick starter** *[motorcycle]* démarreur *m* au pied, kick *m* ▸**kick turn** (*Ski*) conversion *f*.

3 **vi** a *[person]* donner *or* lancer un coup de pied; *[footballer etc]* botter; *[baby]* gigoter*; *[horse etc]* ruer. **to ~ at sb/sth** *[person]* lancer un coup de pied à qn/qch *or* en direction de qn/qch; *[horse]* lancer une ruade à qn/qch *or* en direction de qn/qch (*see also* **3b**); (*Rugby*) **to ~ for touch** taper en touche; (*fig*) **to ~ against the pricks** regimber en pure perte; (*fig*) **to ~ over the traces** ruer dans les brancards (*fig*), regimber (*fig*), se cabrer (*fig*).

b (**: object to sth*) ruer dans les brancards, se rebiffer*. **to ~ at sth** se rebiffer contre qch*, regimber devant qch.

c *[gun]* reculer.

4 **vt** a *table, person [person]* donner un coup de pied à; *ball* donner un coup de pied à, botter; *[horse etc]* lancer une ruade à. **she ~ed him in the face/head/shin/stomach** elle lui a donné un coup de pied au visage/à la tête/dans le tibia/dans le ventre; **to ~ sb's bottom** botter* le derrière *or* les fesses à *or* de qn; **to ~ sb downstairs** faire descendre qn à coups de pied dans le derrière; **to ~ sb upstairs** (*lit*) faire monter qn à coups de pied dans le derrière; (** fig*) catapulter *or* bombarder* qn à un poste supérieur (pour s'en débarrasser); (*Brit Pol **) catapulter qn à la Chambre des lords (*un député dont on ne veut plus aux Communes*); (*Ftbl etc*) **to ~ a goal** marquer un but; (*fig*) **to ~ the bucket⁑** casser sa pipe*; **I could have ~ed myself*** je me serais flanqué* des coups *or* des gifles; (*fig*) **to ~ one's heels** faire le poireau* *or* le pied de grue, se morfondre, poireauter*; (*esp US, fig*) **I'm going to ~ (some) ass*⁑** il y a des coups de pied au cul qui se perdent*⁑.

b (*stop*) **to ~ the habit** (*gen*) arrêter; *[smoker]* arrêter de fumer; *[drug addict]* ne plus se droguer, renoncer à la drogue.

▸**kick about** (*Brit*), **kick around** 1 **vi** (⁑) *[books, clothes etc]* traîner; *[person]* traîner, traînasser (*pej*). 2 **vt sep: to kick a ball about** *or* **around** jouer au ballon, s'amuser avec un ballon; **he can't find anything better to do than kicking a ball about** tout ce qu'il sait faire c'est donner des coups de pied dans un ballon; (*fig*) **don't kick that book about** *or* **around** ne maltraite pas ce livre; (*fig*) **to kick an idea around*** (*reflecting*) tourner et retourner une idée; (*discussing*) débattre une idée; (*fig*) **to kick sb around** traiter qn sans ménagement, marcher sur les pieds de qn.

▸**kick away vt sep** a *object on ground* repousser du pied. b **he kicked away the last part of the fence** il a démoli à coups de pied ce qui restait de la clôture.

▸**kick back** 1 **vi** *[engine]* avoir un retour de manivelle. 2 **vt sep** a *ball etc* renvoyer (du pied). b (*US* ⁑) *money* ristourner. 3 **kickback* n** *see* **kick 2**.

▸**kick down vt sep** *door, hedge, barrier* démolir à coups de pied.

▸**kick in vt sep** a *door* enfoncer à coups de pied. **to kick sb's teeth in*** casser la figure* *or* la gueule⁑ à qn. b (*US* ⁑*: contribute*) cracher*, abouler⁑.

▸**kick off** 1 **vi** (*Ftbl*) donner le coup d'envoi; (** fig*) démarrer*. **the party kicked off in great style** la soirée a démarré* en beauté. 2 **vt sep** enlever (du pied *or* d'un coup de pied). 3 **kick-off n** *see* **kick 2**.

▸**kick out** 1 **vi** *[horse]* ruer. **the man kicked out at his assailants** l'homme envoyait de grands coups de pied à ses assaillants; (*fig*) **to kick out against one's lot/society** *etc* se révolter contre son sort/la société *etc*. 2 **vt sep** (*lit*) chasser à coups de pied, flanquer dehors* *or* vider* à coups de pied; (** fig*) mettre à la porte (*fig*), flanquer dehors* (*fig*), vider* (*fig*).

▸**kick up vt sep** *dust* faire voler. (*fig*) **to kick up a row*** *or* **a din*** *or* **a racket*** faire du chahut *or* du tapage *or* du boucan⁑; **to kick up a fuss*** faire des histoires *or* toute une histoire; **he kicked up a stink⁑ about it** il en a fait tout un plat* *or* tout un foin⁑.

kicker [ˈkɪkəʳ] **n** (*Rugby*) botteur *m*.

kicky⁑ [ˈkɪkɪ] **adj** excitant, palpitant.

kid [kɪd] 1 **n** a (*goat*) chevreau *m*, chevrette *f*.

b (*NonC: leather*) chevreau *m* (*NonC*).

c (**: child*) gosse* *mf*, gamin(e)* *m(f)*; (*teenager*) (petit(e)) jeune *m(f)*. **when I was a ~** quand j'étais gosse*; **that's ~'s stuff** (*easy to do*) un gamin* *or* un gosse* saurait faire ça; (*suitable for children*) c'est (tout juste) bon pour des gosses*; **hi, ~!** salut mon vieux (*or* ma vieille)!

2 **comp** ▸**kid brother*** petit frère *m* ▸**kid gloves/shoes** *etc* gants *mpl*/chaussures *fpl etc* de chevreau; (*fig*) **to handle with kid gloves** *person* ménager, traiter avec ménagements, prendre des gants avec*; *subject* traiter avec précaution.

3 **vt** (*) **to ~ sb** faire marcher qn*; **no ~ding!** sans blague!*; **you can't ~ me** tu ne me la feras pas⁑, je ne marche pas*; **to ~ o.s.** se faire des illusions; **to ~ o.s. that** s'imaginer que.

4 **vi** (*) (*also* **~ on**) raconter des blagues*. **he's just ~ding (on)** il te (*or* nous *etc*) fait marcher*, il te (*or* nous *etc*) raconte des blagues*; **I was only ~ding (on)** j'ai dit ça pour plaisanter *or* pour rigoler*.

▸**kid on** 1 **vi = kid 4**. 2 **vt sep** a **to kid sb on*** faire marcher qn*, raconter des blagues à qn*. b (*pretend*) **he was kidding on* that he was hurt** il essayait de faire croire qu'il était blessé.

kiddy* [ˈkɪdɪ] **n** gosse* *mf*, gamin(e)* *m(f)*, mioche* *mf*, mouflet(te)* *m(f)*.

kidnap [ˈkɪdnæp] **vt** kidnapper, enlever.

kidnapper, (*US*) **kidnaper** [ˈkɪdnæpəʳ] **n** kidnappeur *m*, -euse *f*, ravisseur *m*, -euse *f*.

kidnapping, (*US*) **kidnaping** [ˈkɪdnæpɪŋ] **n** enlèvement *m*, kidnapping *m*, rapt *m*.

kidney [ˈkɪdnɪ] 1 **n** (*Anat*) rein *m*; (*Culin*) rognon *m*. (*fig*) **of the same ~** du même acabit. 2 **comp** *disease etc* rénal, de(s) reins ▸**kidney bean** haricot *m* rouge *or* de Soissons ▸**kidney dish** petit plat *m* en forme de haricot ▸**kidney donor** donneur *m*, -euse *f* de rein(s) ▸**kidney machine** (*Med*) rein artificiel; **to be on a kidney machine** être sous rein artificiel *or* en hémodialyse, être en épuration extrarénale ▸**kidney-shaped** en forme de haricot ▸**kidney specialist** néphrologue *mf* ▸**kidney stone** calcul rénal *or* du rein ▸**kidney transplant** greffe *f* du rein.

kidology* [kɪˈdɒlədʒɪ] **n** (*Brit*) bluff *m*.

Kiel [kiːl] **n: ~ Canal** canal *m* de Kiel.

kike*⁑ [kaɪk] **n** (*US pej*) youpin(e)*⁑ *m(f)* (*pej*).

Kilimanjaro [ˌkɪlɪmənˈdʒɑːrəʊ] **n: Mount ~** le Kilimandjaro.

kill [kɪl] 1 **n** a (*at bullfight, hunt*) mise *f* à mort. **the wolves gathered round for the ~** les loups se sont rassemblés pour tuer leur proie; **the tiger had made a ~** le tigre avait tué; (*fig*) **to be in at the ~** assister au dénouement; (*for unpleasant event*) assister au coup de grâce (*fig*).

b (*NonC: animal(s) killed: Hunting*) pièces tuées, tableau *m* de chasse. **the lion crouched over his ~** le lion s'est accroupi sur la proie qu'il venait de tuer *or* sur sa proie.

2 **comp** ▸**killjoy** rabat-joie *m inv*.

3 **vt** a tuer; (*murder*) assassiner; (*gun down*) abattre; *animal* tuer; (*Hunting, Shooting; also in slaughterhouse*) abattre. **to be ~ed in action/battle** tomber au champ d'honneur/au combat; **thou shalt not ~** tu ne tueras point; (*Prov*) **to ~ two birds with one stone** faire d'une pierre deux coups (*Prov*); **her son's death/the shock ~ed her** c'est la mort de son fils/le choc qui l'a tuée; (*hum*) **it was ~ or cure** c'était un remède de cheval* (*fig*).

b (*fig*) *parliamentary bill, proposal, attempt* faire échouer; (*Press etc*) *paragraph, line* (faire) supprimer; *story* interdire la publication de; *rumour* étouffer, mettre fin à; *feeling, hope* détruire; *flavour, smell* tuer; *sound* étouffer, amortir; *engine, motor* arrêter. **to ~ time** tuer le temps; **the frost has ~ed my trees** le gel a tué *or* a fait mourir mes arbres; **this red ~s the other colours** ce rouge tue les autres couleurs; **to ~* a bottle of whisky** liquider* une bouteille de whisky.

c **to ~ o.s. with work** se tuer au *or* de travail; **he certainly wasn't ~ing himself*** le moins qu'on puisse dire c'est qu'il ne se tuait pas au *or* de travail; (*iro*) **don't ~ yourself!*** surtout ne te surmène pas! (*iro*); **I'll do it (even) if it ~s me** je le ferai même si je dois y laisser ma peau; **this heat is ~ing me*** cette chaleur me tue *or* me crève*; **my feet are ~ing me*** j'ai affreusement mal aux pieds; **she was laughing fit to ~ (herself)*, she was ~ing herself (laughing)*** elle riait comme une folle, elle était pliée en deux de rire; **this will ~ you!*** tu vas (mourir de) rire!; *see* **dress**.

▸**kill off vt sep** (*lit*) exterminer; (*fig*) éliminer.

killer [ˈkɪləʳ] 1 **n** tueur *m*, -euse *f*; (*murderer*) assassin *m*, meurtrier *m*, -ière *f*. **diphtheria was once a ~** autrefois la diphtérie tuait; (*fig*) **it's a ~*** (*hard work*) c'est tuant; (*very funny*) c'est tordant*; (*very impressive*) c'est terrible* *or* formidable; *see* **lady**. 2 **comp** ▸**killer disease** maladie *f* qui tue ▸**killer instinct** (*lit*) instinct *m* qui pousse à tuer; (*fig*) **he's got the killer instinct** il en veut*, c'est un gagneur; **he lacks the killer instinct** il manque de combativité ▸**killer satellite** (*Mil*) satellite-chasseur *m* ▸**killer whale** épaulard *m*, orgue *m*.

killing [ˈkɪlɪŋ] 1 **n** *[person]* meurtre *m*; *[people, group]* tuerie *f*, massacre *m*; *[animal]* (*Hunting*) mise *f* à mort; (*at abattoir*) abattage *m*. **all these ~s** tous ces meurtres; toutes ces tueries; **the ~ of stags is forbidden** il est interdit de tuer les cerfs; **all the ~ sickened him of war** le massacre *or* la tuerie lui fit prendre la guerre en horreur; (*during disturbances etc*) **there were 3 separate ~s during the night** 3 personnes ont été tuées pendant la nuit, il y a eu 3 morts pendant la nuit; (*fig: in buying and selling*) **to make a ~** réussir un beau coup (de filet).

2 **adj** a *blow, disease, shot* meurtrier. **~ fields** champs *mpl* de la

mort.

b (*: *exhausting*) *work* tuant, crevant*.

c (*: *funny*) tordant*, crevant*. **it was ~** c'était tordant* *or* crevant*, c'était à mourir de rire.

killingly ['kɪlɪŋlɪ] **adv: ~ funny** crevant*, tordant*; **it was ~ funny** c'était crevant* *or* tordant*, c'était à mourir de rire.

kiln [kɪln] **n** four *m*. **pottery ~** four céramique; **see lime**[1].

Kilner® jar ['kɪlnə,dʒɑːʳ] **n** (*Brit*) bocal *m* à conserves.

kilo ['kiːləʊ] **n** (**abbr of kilogram**) kilo *m*.

kiloampère ['kɪləʊ,æmpɛəʳ] **n** kiloampère *m*.

kilobar ['kɪləʊ,bɑːʳ] **n** kilobar *m*.

kilobyte ['kɪləʊ,baɪt] **n** (*Comput*) kilo-octet *m*.

kilocycle ['kɪləʊ,saɪkl] **n** kilocycle *m*.

kilogram(me) ['kɪləʊgræm] **n** kilogramme *m*.

kilohertz ['kɪləʊ,hɜːts] **n** kilohertz *m*.

kilolitre, (*US*) **kiloliter** ['kɪləʊ,liːtəʳ] **n** kilolitre *m*.

kilometre, (*US*) **kilometer** ['kɪləʊ,miːtəʳ, kɪ'lɒmɪtəʳ] **n** kilomètre *m*.

kilometric [,kɪləʊ'metrɪk] **adj** kilométrique.

kiloton ['kɪləʊ,tʌn] **n** kilotonne *f*.

kilovolt ['kɪləʊ,vəʊlt] **n** kilovolt *m*.

kilowatt ['kɪləʊwɒt] **n** kilowatt *m*. **~-hour** kilowatt-heure *m*.

kilt [kɪlt] **n** kilt *m*.

kilted ['kɪltɪd] **adj** *man* en kilt. **~ skirt** jupe-kilt *f*, kilt *m*.

kilter ['kɪltəʳ] **n** (*esp US*) **out of ~** détraqué, déglingué*.

kiltie* ['kɪltɪ] **n** homme *m* en kilt, Écossais *m* (en kilt); (*soldier*) soldat *m* en kilt.

kimono [kɪ'məʊnəʊ] **n** kimono *m*.

kin [kɪn] 1 **n** (*NonC*) parents *mpl*, famille *f*; **see kith, next.** 2 **comp** ▸**kin(s)folk** (*NonC*) parents *mpl*, famille *f* ▸**kinship see kinship** ▸**kinsman** parent *m* ▸**kinswoman** parente *f*.

kind [kaɪnd] 1 **n** a (*class, variety, sort, type*) genre *m*, espèce *f*, sorte *f*; (*make: of car, coffee etc*) marque *f*. **this ~ of book** ce genre *or* cette espèce *or* cette sorte de livre; **books of all ~s** des livres de tous genres *or* de toutes espèces *or* de toutes sortes; **this ~ of thing(s)** ce genre de chose(s); **what ~ of flour do you want? — the ~ you gave me last time** quelle sorte *or* quelle espèce *or* quel genre de farine voulez-vous? — la même que vous m'avez donnée (*or* le même que vous m'avez donné) la dernière fois; **what ~ do you want?** vous en (*or* le *or* la *etc*) voulez de quelle sorte?; **what ~ of car is it?** quelle marque de voiture est-ce?; **what ~ of dog is he?** qu'est-ce que c'est comme (race de) chien?; **what ~ of man is he?** quel genre *or* quel type d'homme est-ce?; **he is not the ~ of man to refuse** ce n'est pas le genre d'homme à refuser, il n'est pas homme à refuser; **he's not that ~ of person** ce n'est pas son genre; **I'm not that ~ of girl!*** ce n'est pas mon genre!, mais pour qui me prenez-vous?, je ne suis pas celle que vous croyez!; **that's the ~ of person I am** c'est comme ça que je suis (fait); **what ~ of people does he think we are?** (mais enfin,) pour qui nous prend-il?; **what ~ of a fool does he take me for?** (non mais*,) il me prend pour un imbécile!; **what ~ of behaviour is this?** qu'est-ce que c'est que cette façon de se conduire?; **what ~ of an answer do you call that?** vous appelez ça une réponse?; **classical music is the ~ she likes most** c'est la musique classique qu'elle préfère; **and all that ~ of thing** et autres choses du même genre, et tout ça*; **you know the ~ of thing I mean** vous voyez (à peu près) ce que je veux dire; **I don't like that ~ of talk** je n'aime pas ce genre de conversation; **he's the ~ that will cheat** il est du genre à tricher; **I know his ~!** je connais les gens de son genre *or* espèce; **your ~* never do any good** les gens de votre genre *or* espèce ne font rien de bien; **he's not my ~*** je n'aime pas les gens de son genre *or* de son espèce; **it's my ~* of film** c'est le genre de film que j'aime *or* qui me plaît.

b (*in phrases*) **something of the ~** quelque chose de ce genre(-là) *or* d'approchant; **this is wrong — nothing of the ~!** c'est faux — pas le moins du monde! *or* absolument pas!; **I shall do nothing of the ~!** je n'en ferai rien!, certainement pas!; **I will have nothing of the ~!** je ne tolérerai pas cela!; (*pej*) **it was beef of a ~** c'était quelque chose qui pouvait passer pour du bœuf.

c **a ~ of** une sorte *or* espèce de, un genre de; **there was a ~ of box in the middle of the room** il y avait une sorte *or* une espèce *or* un genre de boîte au milieu de la pièce, il y avait quelque chose qui ressemblait à une boîte au milieu de la pièce; **there was a ~ of tinkling sound** il y avait une sorte *or* une espèce de bruit de grelot, on entendait quelque chose qui ressemblait à un bruit de grelot; **in a ~ of way* I'm sorry** d'une certaine façon je le regrette; **I had a ~ of fear that, I was ~ of* frightened that** j'avais comme peur que + ne + *subj*; **I ~ of* like that** j'aime assez ça; **I ~ of* thought that he would come** j'avais un peu l'idée qu'il viendrait; **he was ~ of* worried-looking** il avait l'air un peu inquiet, il avait l'air comme qui dirait* inquiet; **it's ~ of* blue** c'est plutôt bleu; **aren't you pleased? — ~ of!*** tu n'es pas content? — assez! *or* ben si!‡

d (*race, species*) genre *m*, espèce *f*. **human ~** le genre humain; **they differ in ~** ils sont de genres différents *or* de natures différentes; **they're two of a ~** ils sont du même genre, (*pej*) ils sont du même acabit; **this painting is perfect of/the only one of its ~** ce tableau est parfait dans/unique en son genre; **see man** *etc*.

e (*NonC: goods as opposed to money*) nature *f*. **to pay/payment in ~** payer/paiement *m* en nature; (*fig*) **I shall repay you in ~** (*after good deed*) je vous le rendrai; (*after bad deed*) je vous rendrai la monnaie de votre pièce.

2 **adj** *person* gentil, bon, aimable. **they were ~ people** c'étaient de braves gens; **to be ~ to sb** être gentil avec qn, être bon pour *or* envers qn; **we must be ~ to animals** il faut être bon pour *or* envers les animaux; **they were ~ to the play in New York** ils ont fait bon accueil à la pièce à New York; **would you be ~ enough to** *or* **would you be so ~ as to open the door?** voulez-vous avoir l'amabilité d'ouvrir la porte?, voulez-vous être assez aimable *or* gentil pour ouvrir la porte?; **he was ~ enough to say** il a eu la gentillesse *or* l'amabilité *or* la bonté de dire; **it was very ~ of you to help me** vous avez été bien aimable *or* bien bon de m'aider, ça a été bien gentil à vous de m'aider; **that's very ~ of you** c'est très aimable *or* gentil à vous *or* de votre part; **you're too ~** vous êtes trop aimable *or* gentil; **how ~ of you!** comme c'est gentil *or* aimable à vous!; **that wasn't a very ~ thing to say** ce n'était pas très gentil de dire cela.

3 **comp** ▸**kind-hearted** bon, qui a bon cœur ▸**kind-heartedness** bonté *f*, bon cœur, grand cœur.

kinda‡ ['kaɪndə] = **kind of; see kind.**

kindergarten ['kɪndə,gɑːtn] **n** jardin *m* d'enfants.

kindle ['kɪndl] 1 **vt** *fire* allumer; *wood* enflammer; (*fig*) *passion, desire* allumer, enflammer; *heart* enflammer. 2 **vi** s'allumer; s'enflammer.

kindliness ['kaɪndlɪnɪs] **n** bienveillance *f*, bonté *f*.

kindling ['kɪndlɪŋ] **n** (*NonC: wood*) petit bois, bois d'allumage.

kindly ['kaɪndlɪ] 1 **adv** a *speak, act* avec bonté, avec gentillesse.

b **will you ~ do ...** voulez-vous avoir la bonté *or* l'obligeance de faire ..., je vous prie de (bien vouloir) faire ...; **~ shut the door** voulez-vous (bien) *or* veuillez (*frm*) fermer la porte, fermez la porte je vous prie; **~ be quiet!** voulez-vous *or* allez-vous vous taire!

c **to think ~ of sb** penser du bien de qn; **I don't take ~ to his doing that** je n'aime pas du tout qu'il fasse cela; **she didn't take it ~ when I said that** elle ne l'a pas bien pris *or* elle l'a mal pris quand j'ai dit cela; **I would take it ~ if you would do so** j'aimerais beaucoup que vous fassiez ainsi, vous m'obligeriez en agissant de la sorte (*frm*).

2 **adj** *person, advice* bienveillant; *voice* plein de bonté; *letter* gentil; *treatment* plein de gentillesse.

kindness ['kaɪndnɪs] **n** a (*NonC*) bonté *f* (*towards* pour), gentillesse *f* (*towards* pour, envers), bienveillance *f* (*towards* à l'égard de), amabilité *f* (*towards* envers). **to treat sb with ~, to show ~ to sb** être gentil avec *or* envers qn, avoir de la gentillesse pour qn; **out of the ~ of his heart** par (pure) bonté d'âme; **will you have the ~ to give me it?** voulez-vous avoir la bonté de *or* être assez gentil pour me le donner?

b (*act of ~*) bonté *f*, gentillesse *f*, service *m*. **to do sb a ~** rendre service à qn; **thank you for all your ~es** merci de toutes vos gentillesses; **it would be a ~ to tell him so** ce serait lui rendre service que de le lui dire.

kindred ['kɪndrɪd] 1 **n** (*NonC*) (*relatives*) parents *mpl*, famille *f*; (*relationship*) parenté *f*. 2 **adj** a (*related*) *languages, tribes* apparenté, de la même famille. b (*similar*) similaire, semblable, analogue. **~ spirits** âmes sœurs *fpl*; **to have a ~ feeling for sb** sympathiser avec qn.

kinetic [kɪ'netɪk] **adj** (*Phys, Art*) cinétique; (*dynamic*) dynamique.

kinetics [kɪ'netɪks] **n** (*NonC*) cinétique *f*.

king [kɪŋ] 1 **n** a (*lit, fig*) roi *m*. **K~ David** le roi David; (*Bible*) **(the Book of) K~s** le livre des Rois; **the ~ of beasts** le roi des animaux; (*fig*) **it cost a ~'s ransom** ça a coûté des sommes fabuleuses; **an oil ~** un roi *or* un magnat du pétrole.

b (*Brit*) (*Jur*) **K~'s Bench** cour supérieure de justice; (*Jur*) **K~'s Counsel** avocat *m* de la Couronne; (*Jur*) **to turn K~'s evidence** témoigner contre ses complices; **the K~'s highway** la voie publique; **K~'s Messenger** courrier *m* diplomatique.

c (*Cards, Chess*) roi *m*; (*Draughts*) dame *f*.

2 **comp** ▸**kingbolt** pivot central, cheville ouvrière ▸**king cobra** cobra royal ▸**kingcup** (*buttercup*) bouton *m* d'or; (*marsh marigold*) souci *m* d'eau ▸**kingdom see kingdom** ▸**kingfish*** (*US: leader*) caïd* *m* ▸**kingfisher** martin-pêcheur *m* ▸**kingmaker** homme *m* qui fait et défait les rois; (*fig: US Pol*) **the kingmakers** ceux dont dépend le succès d'un candidat ▸**king penguin** manchot royal ▸**kingpin** (*Tech*) pivot central, cheville ouvrière; (*fig*) pilier *m* ▸**kingship see kingship** ▸**king-size bed** grand lit *m* (*de 1,95m de large*) ▸**king-size(d)** (*Comm*) *cigarette* long (*f* longue); *packet* géant; **I've got a king-size(d) headache*** j'ai un mal de crâne à tout casser*.

kingdom ['kɪŋdəm] **n** royaume *m*; (*Bot, Zool*) règne *m*. **the plant ~** le règne végétal; **the K~ of God** le royaume de Dieu; **the K~ of Heaven** le royaume des cieux, le royaume céleste; **he's gone to ~ come*** il est parti dans l'autre monde *or* dans un monde meilleur; **to send sb to ~ come*** envoyer qn dans l'autre monde *or* dans un monde meilleur *or* "ad patres"*; **till ~ come*** jusqu'à la fin des siècles; **see animal, united** *etc*.

kingly ['kɪŋlɪ] **adj** (*lit, fig*) royal, de roi.

kingship ['kɪŋʃɪp] **n** royauté *f*.

kink [kɪŋk] 1 **n** (*in rope etc*) entortillement *m*; (*in paper etc*) défaut *m*;

(*fig*) anomalie *f*, aberration *f*, déséquilibre *m*; (*sexual*) aberration. **her hair has a ~ in it** ses cheveux frisent légèrement. 2 **vi** *[rope etc]* s'entortiller.

kinky [ˈkɪŋkɪ] **adj** a *hair* ondulé, (*tighter*) frisé. b (‡) *person* bizarre; (*unpleasantly so*) malade (*fig pej*); (*sexually*) qui a des goûts spéciaux; *underwear* coquin; *idea* biscornu*; *dress, fashion* bizarre, excentrique.

kinship [ˈkɪnʃɪp] **n** (*NonC*) parenté *f*.

kiosk [ˈkiːɒsk] **n** (*Brit: for selling; also bandstand*) kiosque *m*; (*Brit Telec*) cabine *f* téléphonique.

kip‡ [kɪp] (*Brit*) 1 **n** (*bed*) plumard‡ *m*, pieu‡ *m*; (*sleep*) roupillon* *m*. **to get some ~** piquer un somme *or* un roupillon*. 2 **vi** (*also* **~ down**) se pieuter‡.

kipper [ˈkɪpəʳ] (*Brit*) 1 **n** hareng fumé et salé, kipper *m*. 2 **vt** *herring* fumer et saler. (*fig*) **the room was so smoky we were nearly ~ed‡** la pièce était si enfumée qu'on a failli être transformés en harengs saurs.

kir [kɜːʳ, kɪəʳ] **n** kir *m*.

Kirbigrip ®, **kirbygrip** [ˈkɜːbɪˌgrɪp] **n** pince *m* à cheveux.

Kirghiz [ˈkɜːgɪz] **n**: **~ SSR** (RSS *f* de) Kirghizistan *m or* Kirghizie *f*.

kirk [kɜːk] **n** (*Scot*) église *f*. **the K~** l'Église presbytérienne (d'Écosse).

Kirsch, Kirschwasser [ˈkɪəʃ, ˈkɪəʃˌvɑːsə] **n** kirsch *m*.

kiss [kɪs] 1 **n** baiser *m*. **to give sb a ~** donner un baiser à qn, embrasser qn; **give me a ~** embrasse-moi; (*to child*) fais-moi une bise*; (*Brit Med*) **~ of life** bouche à bouche *m*; (*liter*) **the wind's ~ on her hair** le baiser du vent sur ses cheveux; (*in letter*) **love and ~es** bons baisers, grosses bises*; (*fig*) **to give the ~ of death to** porter le coup fatal à; *see* **blow**[1].

2 **comp** ▸**kiss curl** (*Brit*) accroche-cœur *m inv* ▸**kiss-off‡**: (*US*) **to give sb the kiss-off** (*employee*) virer qn; (*girlfriend etc*) plaquer‡ qn.

3 **vt** embrasser, donner un baiser à. **to ~ sb's cheek** embrasser qn sur la joue; **to ~ sb's hand** baiser la main de qn; (*Diplomacy etc*) **to ~ hands** être admis au baisemain (du roi *or* de la reine); **they ~ed each other** ils se sont embrassés; (*to hurt child*) **I'll ~ it better** un petit bisou* et ça ira mieux; **to ~ sb good night/goodbye** embrasser qn en lui souhaitant bonne nuit/en lui disant au revoir, souhaiter bonne nuit/dire au revoir à qn en l'embrassant; (*fig*) **you can ~ it goodbye!*** tu peux en faire ton deuil!; (*fig*) **to ~ the dust** *or* **ground** mordre la poussière.

4 **vi** s'embrasser. **to ~ and make up** faire la paix.

▸**kiss away** **vt sep**: **she kissed away the child's tears** elle a essuyé de ses baisers les larmes de l'enfant.

▸**kiss back** **vt sep** *person* rendre un baiser à.

kissagram [ˈkɪsəˌgræm] **n** *baiser envoyé à l'occasion d'une célébration par l'intermédiaire d'une personne employée à cet effet.*

kisser‡ [ˈkɪsəʳ] **n** gueule‡ *f*.

kit [kɪt] 1 **n** a (*NonC*) (*equipment, gear*) *[camping, skiing, climbing, photography etc]* matériel *m*, équipement *m*; (*Mil*) fourniment *m*, barda‡ *m*, fourbi* *m*; (*tools*) outils *mpl*; (*luggage*) bagages *mpl*. **fishing** *etc* **~** matériel *or* attirail *m or* équipement de pêche *etc*; (*US*) **the whole ~ and caboodle*** tout le bataclan*, tout le fourbi*.

b (*NonC: belongings, gear*) effets *mpl* (personnels), affaires *fpl*.

c (*NonC: gen Sport: Brit: clothes*) équipement *m*, affaires *fpl*. **have you got your gym/football ~?** tu as tes affaires de gym/de football?

d (*set of items*) trousse *f*. **tool~** trousse *f* à outils; **puncture-repair ~** trousse de réparations; **first-aid ~** trousse d'urgence *or* de premiers secours; *see* **survival** *etc*.

e (*parts for assembly*) kit *m*. **sold in ~ form** vendu en kit; **he built it from a ~** il l'a assemblé à partir d'un kit; **model aeroplane ~** maquette *f* d'avion (à assembler).

2 **comp** ▸**kitbag** sac *m* (*de voyage, de sportif, de soldat, de marin etc*) ▸**kit inspection** (*Mil*) revue *f* de détail.

▸**kit out, kit up** **vt sep** a (*Mil*) équiper (*with* de). b **to kit sb out with sth** équiper qn de qch; **he arrived kitted out in oilskins** il est arrivé équipé d'un ciré; **he had kitted himself out in a bright blue suit** il avait mis *or* il s'était acheté un costume bleu vif.

kitchen [ˈkɪtʃɪn] 1 **n** cuisine *f* (*pièce*); *see* **thief**.

2 **comp** *table, cutlery, scissors etc* de cuisine ▸**kitchen cabinet** buffet *m* de cuisine; (*fig Pol*) conseillers personnels *or* privés du Premier Ministre *or* (*US*) du Président ▸**kitchen-dinette** cuisine *f* avec coin-repas ▸**kitchen foil** papier *m* d'aluminium *or* d'alu* ▸**kitchen garden** (jardin *m*) potager *m* ▸**kitchenmaid** fille *f* de cuisine ▸**kitchen paper, kitchen roll** essuie-tout *m inv* ▸**kitchen police** (*US Mil*) corvée *f* de cuisine ▸**kitchen range** fourneau *m* (de cuisine), cuisinière *f* ▸**kitchen salt** sel *m* de cuisine, gros sel ▸**kitchen scales** balance *f* (de cuisine) ▸**kitchen sink** évier *m*; **I've packed everything but the kitchen sink*** j'ai tout empaqueté sauf les murs ▸**kitchen-sink* drama** (*Theat*) théâtre *m* naturaliste ▸**kitchen soap** savon *m* de Marseille ▸**kitchen unit** élément *m* de cuisine ▸**kitchen utensil** ustensile *m* de cuisine ▸**kitchenware** (*NonC*) (*dishes*) vaisselle *f or* faïence *f* (de cuisine); (*equipment*) ustensiles *mpl* de cuisine ▸**kitchen waste** *or* (*US*) **wastes** déchets *mpl* domestiques.

kitchenette [ˌkɪtʃɪˈnet] **n** kitchenette *f*.

kite [kaɪt] 1 **n** a (*Orn*) milan *m*; (*toy*) cerf-volant *m*; *see* **fly**[3]. b (*: *Fin*) (*cheque*) chèque *m* en bois*; (*bill*) effet *m* bidon*, traite *f* en l'air*. 2 **comp** ▸**kite balloon** (*Mil*) ballon *m* d'observation, saucisse *f* ▸**Kite mark** (*Brit Comm*) label *m* de qualité (*du British Standards Institution*).

kith [kɪθ] **n**: **~ and kin** amis *mpl* et parents *mpl*.

kitsch [kɪtʃ] 1 **n** (*NonC*) kitsch *m*, art kitsch *or* pompier. 2 **adj** kitsch *inv*, pompier.

kitten [ˈkɪtn] **n** chaton *m*, petit chat. (*Brit fig*) **to have ~s‡** piquer une crise*, être dans tous ses états.

kittenish [ˈkɪtənɪʃ] **adj** (*lit*) de chaton; (*fig*) de chaton, mutin.

kittiwake [ˈkɪtɪweɪk] **n** mouette *f* tridactyle.

kitty [ˈkɪtɪ] 1 **n** a (*Cards etc*) cagnotte *f*; (* *fig*) caisse *f*, cagnotte. **there's nothing left in the ~** il n'y a plus un sou dans la caisse *or* dans la cagnotte. b (*: *cat*) minet* *m*, minou* *m*. 2 **comp** ▸**Kitty Litter** ® (*US*) litière *f* pour chats.

kiwi [ˈkiːwiː] **n** a (*bird*) kiwi *m*, aptéryx *m*. b (*also* **~ fruit**) kiwi *m*. c (*: *New Zealander*) néo-zélandais(e) *m(f)*.

KKK [keɪkeɪˈkeɪ] (*US*) **abbr of Ku Klux Klan**.

klaxon [ˈklæksn] **n** klaxon *m*.

Kleenex [ˈkliːneks] **n, pl ~** *or* **~es** ® (*US*) Kleenex *m* ®.

kleptomania [ˌkleptəʊˈmeɪnɪə] **n** kleptomanie *f*.

kleptomaniac [ˌkleptəʊˈmeɪnɪæk] **adj, n** kleptomane *(mf)*.

klutz‡ [klʌts] **n** (*US*) empoté(e) *m(f)*, manche* *m*.

klystron [ˈklɪstrɒn] **n** klystron *m*.

km **n** (**abbr of kilometre(s)**) km.

kmh **n** (**abbr of kilometres per hour**) km/h.

knack [næk] **n** tour *m* de main, truc* *m*. **to learn** *or* **get the ~ of doing** attraper *or* saisir le tour de main *or* le truc* pour faire; **to have the ~ of doing** avoir le talent *or* le chic pour faire; **I've lost the ~** j'ai perdu le tour de main, j'ai perdu la main; **she's got a ~ of saying the wrong thing** elle a le chic pour dire *or* le don de dire ce qu'il ne faut pas; **there's a ~ in it** il y a un truc* *or* un tour de main à prendre; **you'll soon get the ~ of it** vous aurez vite fait d'attraper le truc* *or* le tour de main.

knacker [ˈnækəʳ] (*Brit*) 1 **n** a *[horses]* équarrisseur *m*. **to send a horse to the ~'s yard** envoyer un cheval à l'équarrissage. b *[boats, houses]* entrepreneur *m* de démolition, démolisseur *m*. 2 **vt** (‡) crever*.

knackered‡ [ˈnækəd] **adj** (*Brit*) crevé*, éreinté*.

knapsack [ˈnæpsæk] **n** sac *m* à dos, havresac *m*.

knave [neɪv] **n** († *pej*) filou *m*, fripon† *m*, coquin† *m*; (*Cards*) valet *m*.

knavery [ˈneɪvərɪ] **n** (*NonC: pej*) filouterie *f*, friponnerie† *f*, coquinerie† *f*.

knavish [ˈneɪvɪʃ] **adj** (*pej*) de filou, de coquin†.

knead [niːd] **vt** *bread dough* pétrir; *pastry dough* travailler; *muscles* masser.

knee [niː] 1 **n** genou *m*. **on one's ~s**, (*liter or hum*) **on bended ~(s)** à genoux; **to go (down) on one's ~s** s'agenouiller, tomber *or* se mettre à genoux; **to go down on one's ~s to sb** (*lit*) tomber *or* se mettre à genoux devant qn; (*fig*) se mettre à genoux devant qn (*fig*), supplier qn à genoux; (*fig*) **to bring sb to his ~s** forcer qn à capituler *or* à se rendre *or* à se soumettre; (*fig*) **it will bring the country/the steel industry** *etc* **to its ~s** ce sera la ruine du pays/de l'industrie sidérurgique; **he sank in up to the ~s** il s'est enfoncé jusqu'aux genoux; **these trousers are out at** *or* **have gone at the ~(s)** ce pantalon est usé aux genoux; **to put a child over one's ~** donner une fessée à un enfant; **to learn sth at one's mother's ~** apprendre qch à un âge tendre.

2 **comp** ▸**knee-bend** (*gen, Ski*) flexion *f* (du genou) ▸**knee breeches** culotte courte ▸**kneecap** **n** (*Anat*) rotule *f* ◊ **vt** tirer dans la rotule ▸**kneecapping** mutilation *f* par destruction de la rotule ▸**the water was knee-deep** l'eau arrivait aux genoux ▸**knee-deep**: **he was knee-deep in mud** la boue lui arrivait *or* venait (jusqu')aux genoux, il était dans la boue jusqu'aux genoux ▸**knee-high** à hauteur de genou; (*esp US*) **knee-high to a grasshopper*** haut comme trois pommes ▸**knee jerk** réflexe rotulien; (*: *fig pej*) (*also* **~ reaction**) réaction *f* instinctive; **he's a knee-jerk* conservative** il a le cœur à droite ▸**knee joint** (*Anat*) articulation *f* du genou ▸**knee level: at knee level** à (la) hauteur du genou ▸**kneepad** genouillère *f* ▸**knee pants** (*US*) bermuda(s) *m(pl)* ▸**knee reflex** réflexe rotulien ▸**knee-room** espace *m* pour les jambes ▸**knees-up‡** (**pl ~-~s**) (*Brit*) **n** pince-fesses *m*, fête *f*.

kneel [niːl] **pret, ptp knelt** *or* **kneeled** **vi** (*also* **~ down**) s'agenouiller, se mettre à genoux; (*position*) être agenouillé. **he had to ~ on his case to shut it** il a dû se mettre à genoux sur sa valise pour la fermer; (*lit, fig*) **to ~ (down) to** *or* **before sb** se mettre à genoux devant qn.

knell [nel] **n** glas *m*. **to sound** *or* **toll the (death) ~** sonner le glas.

knelt [nelt] **pret, ptp of kneel**.

knew [njuː] **pret of know**.

knickerbockers† [ˈnɪkəbɒkəz] **npl** knickerbockers *mpl*, culotte *f* de golf.

knickers [ˈnɪkəz] **npl** a (*Brit: woman's*) culotte *f*, slip *m* (*de femme*). (*excl*) **~!‡** merde!‡; (*fig*) **to get one's ~ in a twist‡** s'embrouiller *or* s'empêtrer* de belle façon. b (†) = **knickerbockers**.

knick-knack [ˈnɪknæk] **n** bibelot *m*, babiole *f*; (*on dress*) colifichet *m*.

knife [naɪf] 1 **n, pl knives** (*at table, in kitchen etc; also weapon*) couteau *m*; (*pocket* ~) canif *m*. **~, fork and spoon** couvert *m*; (*fig*) **to turn** *or* **twist the ~ in the wound** retourner le couteau dans la plaie (*fig*); (*fig*) **he's got his ~ into me*** il en a après moi*, il a une dent contre moi, il m'en veut; (*fig*) **it's war to the ~ between them** ils sont à couteaux tirés (*fig*), c'est la guerre ouverte entre eux (*fig*); (*Med*) **under the ~*** sur le billard*; **before you could say ~*** en moins de temps qu'il n'en faut pour le dire.

2 **vt** *person* donner un coup de couteau à. **she had been ~d** elle avait reçu un coup de couteau; (*to death*) elle avait été tuée à coups de couteau.

3 **comp** ▸**knife box** boîte *f* à couteaux ▸**knife edge** fil *m* d'un couteau; (*Tech*) couteau; (*fig: tense, anxious*) *person* **on a knife edge** sur des charbons ardents (*fig*); **the success of the scheme/the result was balanced on a knife edge** la réussite du projet/le résultat ne tenait qu'à un fil ▸**knife-edge(d)** *blade* tranchant, aiguisé; *crease* bien repassé, en lame de rasoir ▸**knife-grinder** rémouleur *m*, repasseur *m* de couteaux ▸**knife pleat** pli *m* en lame de rasoir ▸**knife point**: **at knife point** sous la menace du couteau ▸**knife rest** porte-couteau *m* ▸**knife-sharpener** (*on wall, on wheel etc*) affiloir *m*, aiguisoir *m*; (*long, gen with handle*) fusil *m* à repasser les couteaux.

knifing ['naɪfɪŋ] **n** attaque *f* au couteau.

knight [naɪt] 1 **n** chevalier *m*; (*Chess*) cavalier *m*. (*Brit*) **K~ of the Garter** Chevalier de (l'ordre de) la Jarretière; (*fig*) **a ~ in shining armour** (*romantic figure*) un prince charmant; (*saviour*) un sauveur, un redresseur de torts. 2 **comp** ▸**knight errant** (**pl ~s ~**) (*Hist*) chevalier errant ▸**knight-errantry** (*NonC*) chevalerie errante ▸**Knight Templar** (**pl ~s ~s** *or* **~s ~**) chevalier *m* de l'ordre du Temple, Templier *m*. 3 **vt** a (*Hist*) *squire etc* adouber, armer chevalier. b (*Brit*) *[sovereign]* donner l'accolade (de chevalier) à, faire chevalier. **he was ~ed for services to industry** il a été fait chevalier pour services rendus dans l'industrie.

knighthood ['naɪthʊd] **n** a (*knights collectively*) chevalerie *f*. b (*Brit: rank*) titre *m* de chevalier. **to get** *or* **receive a ~** être fait chevalier, recevoir le titre de chevalier.

knightly ['naɪtlɪ] **adj** *courtesy* chevaleresque; *armour* de chevalier.

knit [nɪt] **pret, ptp knitted** *or* **knit** 1 **vt** a tricoter. **"~ three, purl one"** "trois mailles à l'endroit, une maille à l'envers"; **~ted jacket** veste tricotée *or* en tricot; (*Comm*) **~ted goods** tricots *mpl*, articles *mpl* en tricot; *see* **thick** *etc*. b (*fig: also* **~ together**) lier, unir. **to ~ one's brows** froncer les sourcils; *see* **close**[1] *etc*. 2 **vi** tricoter; *[bone etc]* (*also* **~ together, ~ up**) se souder. **to ~ tightly** tricoter serré; **to ~ loosely** tricoter lâche, tricoter sans serrer les mailles. 3 **comp** ▸**knit stitch** maille *f* à l'endroit ▸**knitwear** (*Comm*) tricots *mpl*.

▸**knit together** 1 **vi** = **knit 2**. 2 **vt sep** a **"knit two together"** "tricoter deux mailles ensemble". b (*fig*) = **knit 1b**.

▸**knit up** 1 **vi** a = **knit 2**. b **this wool knits up very quickly** cette laine monte très vite, le tricot monte très vite avec cette laine. 2 **vt sep** *jersey* tricoter.

knitter ['nɪtəʳ] **n** tricoteur *m*, -euse *f*.

knitting ['nɪtɪŋ] 1 **n** (*NonC*) a (*gen*) tricot *m*; (*Ind*) tricotage *m*; **I like ~** j'aime tricoter; **where's my ~?** où est mon tricot?; *see* **double**. b *[bone etc]* soudure *f*. 2 **comp** ▸**knitting bag** sac *m* à ouvrage ▸**knitting machine** machine *f* à tricoter, tricoteuse *f* ▸**knitting needle, knitting pin** aiguille *f* à tricoter ▸**knitting wool** laine *f* à tricoter.

knives [naɪvz] **npl of knife**.

knob [nɒb] **n** a *[door, instrument etc]* bouton *m*; *[cane, walking stick]* pommeau *m*; (*small swelling*) bosse *f*, protubérance *f*; (*on tree*) nœud *m*. (*fig*) **with ~s on*** et encore plus. b (*small piece*) *[cheese etc]* petit morceau. **~ of butter** noix *f* de beurre. c (***: penis*) zob** *m*, bitte ** *f*.

knobbly ['nɒblɪ] **adj**, **knobby** ['nɒbɪ] **adj** noueux.

knobkerrie ['nɒb,kerɪ] **n** massue *f*.

knock [nɒk] 1 **n** a (*blow*) coup *m*; (*collision*) heurt *m*, choc *m*; (*in engine etc*) cognement *m*. **there was a ~ at the door** on a frappé (à la porte); **after several ~s at the door he went away** après avoir frappé plusieurs fois à la porte il s'est éloigné; **I heard a ~ (at the door)** j'ai entendu (quelqu'un) frapper (à la porte); **~, ~!** toc, toc, toc!; **I'll give you a ~ at 7 o'clock** je viendrai taper à la porte à 7 heures; **he got a ~ (on the head** *etc***)** il a reçu *or* attrapé *or* pris* un coup (sur la tête *etc*); **he gave himself a nasty ~ (on the head** *etc***)** il s'est cogné très fort (à la tête *etc*); **he gave the car a ~** il a cabossé la voiture.

b (*fig: setback etc*) revers *m*. (*criticism*) **~s*** critiques *fpl*; **to take a ~** recevoir un coup (*fig*); **that was a hard ~ for him** ça a été un coup pour lui; **his pride has taken a ~** son orgueil a été atteint, son orgueil en a pris un coup*.

2 **comp** ▸**knockabout** **n** (*Naut: esp US*) dériveur *m*, petit voilier ◊ **adj** (*boisterous*) turbulent, violent ▸**knockabout clothes** vieux vêtements (qui ne craignent rien) ▸**knockabout comedy** (*Theat*) (grosse) farce *f* ▸**knockdown** *see* **knockdown** ▸**knocked down** (*US Comm*) *table, shed etc* (livré) démonté ▸**knock-for-knock agreement** (*Insurance*) *accord entre compagnies d'assurance dans lequel chacune rembourse ses propres clients* ▸**knocking-off time*** (*Ind etc*) heure *f* de la sortie ▸**knock-kneed, knock-knees**: **to be knock-kneed, to have knock-knees** avoir les genoux cagneux ▸**knock-on** (*Rugby*) **n** en-avant *m inv* ▸**knock-on effect** (*fig: Econ etc*) réaction *f* en chaîne ▸**knock-out** *see* **knockout** ▸**knock-up**: (*Tennis*) **to have a knock-up** faire des balles.

3 **vt** a (*hit, strike*) frapper. **to ~ a nail into a plank** planter *or* enfoncer un clou dans une planche; **to ~ a nail in (with a hammer/shoe** *etc***)** enfoncer un clou (d'un coup *or* à coups de marteau/de chaussure *etc*); **he ~ed the ball into the hedge** il a envoyé la balle dans la haie; **to ~ the bottom out of a box** défoncer (le fond d')une boîte; **to ~ holes in sth** faire des trous dans qch, trouer qch, percer qch; (*fig*) **to ~ holes in an argument** souligner des failles dans un argument; (*fig*) **to ~ the bottom out of an argument** démolir un argument; (*St Ex*) **this ~ed the bottom out of the market** cela a provoqué l'effondrement des cours; **to ~ sb on the head** frapper qn sur la tête; (*stun*) assommer qn; **that ~ed his plans on the head*** cela a flanqué* par terre *or* démoli ses projets; **to ~ sb to the ground** jeter qn à terre, faire tomber qn; (*stun*) assommer qn; **to ~ sb unconscious** *or* **cold** *or* **senseless** *or* **silly** assommer qn; **she ~ed the knife out of his hand** elle lui a fait tomber le couteau des mains; **he ~ed the child out of the way** il a écarté brutalement l'enfant de son chemin; **to ~ a glass off a table** faire tomber un verre d'une table; **she ~ed the cup to the floor** elle a fait tomber la tasse (par terre); **I'll ~ the smile off your face!*** je vais te flanquer une raclée* qui t'enlèvera l'envie de sourire!; (*Brit*) **to ~ sb for six*** démolir* qn; **to ~ sb into the middle of next week*** faire voir trente-six chandelles à qn; (*US fig*) **to ~ sb for a loop*** époustoufler qn; **to ~ spots off sb*, to ~ sb into a cocked hat*** battre qn à plate(s) couture(s); (*astonish*) **to ~ sb sideways*** ébahir *or* ahurir qn; **to ~ some sense into sb, to ~ the nonsense out of sb** ramener qn à la raison (par la manière forte); *see* **stuffing**.

b (*collide with, strike*) *[vehicle]* heurter; *[person]* se cogner dans, heurter. **to ~ one's head on** *or* **against** se cogner la tête contre; **he ~ed his foot against a stone** il a donné du pied *or* a buté contre une pierre; **the car ~ed the gatepost** la voiture a heurté le poteau *or* est rentrée* dans le poteau; **I ~ed the car against the gatepost, I ~ed the gatepost with the car** je suis rentré* dans le poteau avec la voiture, j'ai heurté le poteau avec la voiture.

c (*‡: denigrate*) dire du mal de, critiquer, déblatérer* contre; (*in advertising*) faire de la contre-publicité à.

4 **vi** a (*strike, hit*) frapper, cogner. **to ~ at the door/window** *etc* frapper *or* cogner à la porte/la fenêtre *etc*; **he ~ed on the table** il a frappé la table, il a cogné sur la table; **he's ~ing on‡ fifty** il frise la cinquantaine; **his knees were ~ing** il tremblait de peur, il avait les chocottes‡.

b (*bump, collide*) **to ~ against** *or* **into sb/sth** se cogner *or* se heurter contre qn/qch, heurter qn/qch; **my hand ~ed against the shelf** ma main a heurté l'étagère, je me suis cogné la main contre l'étagère; **the car ~ed against** *or* **into the lamppost** la voiture a heurté le réverbère; **he ~ed into the table** il s'est cogné dans *or* contre la table, il s'est heurté contre la table, il a heurté la table; *see also* **knock into**.

c *[car engine etc]* cogner.

▸**knock about** (*Brit*), **knock around** 1 **vi** a (*travel, wander*) vagabonder, vadrouiller*, bourlinguer*; *[sailor]* bourlinguer. **he has knocked about a bit** il a beaucoup bourlingué* (*fig*), il a roulé sa bosse*.

b (*) traîner. **your socks are knocking about in the bedroom** tes chaussettes traînent dans la chambre.

2 **vt fus**: **to knock about the world** vadrouiller* *or* vagabonder de par le monde; **he's knocking about France somewhere*** il vadrouille* *or* il se balade* quelque part en France.

3 **vt sep** a (*ill-treat*) maltraiter, malmener. **he knocks her about** il lui flanque des coups*, il lui tape dessus*.

b ravager. **the harvest was badly knocked about by the storm** la récolte a été ravagée par l'orage.

4 **knockabout n, adj** *see* **knock 2**.

▸**knock back** 1 **vi** (*lit*) **he knocked on the wall and she knocked back** il a frappé *or* cogné au mur et elle a répondu de la même façon. 2 **vt sep** a (** fig*) (*drink*) s'enfiler*, s'envoyer*; (*eat*) avaler, engloutir*. b (*‡: cost*) coûter. **how much did it knock you back?** ça vous a coûté combien?; **this watch knocked me back £120** cette montre a fait un trou de 120 livres dans mes finances. c (* *fig: shock*) sonner*, ahurir, ébahir. **the news knocked her back a bit** la nouvelle l'a un peu sonnée*.

▸**knock down** 1 **vt sep** a *object* renverser; *building, wall etc* abattre, démolir; *tree* abattre; *door* (*remove*) démolir; (*kick in etc*) défoncer, enfoncer. **he knocked me down with one blow** il m'a jeté à terre *or* étendu* d'un seul coup; **you could have knocked me down with a feather!** les bras m'en sont tombés!, j'en étais comme deux ronds de flan!‡

b (*Aut etc*) renverser. **he got knocked down by a bus** il a été renversé par un autobus.

c *price* baisser, abaisser. **he knocked the price down by 10%** il a baissé le prix de 10%, il a fait une remise de 10% sur le prix.

d (*at auction*) **to knock down sth to sb** adjuger qch à qn; **it was knocked down for £10** ça a été adjugé et vendu 10 livres.

2 **knockdown adj, n** *see* **knockdown**.

3 **knocked down** adj *see* **knock 2.**

►**knock in** vt sep *nail* enfoncer.

►**knock into*** vt fus (*meet*) tomber sur.

►**knock off** 1 vi (*: *stop work*) s'arrêter (de travailler), cesser le travail; *[striker]* débrayer.
2 vt sep a (*lit*) *vase on shelf etc* faire tomber. **to knock sb's block off⁑** casser la figure* *or* la gueule⁑ à qn.
b (*reduce price by*) *percentage, amount* déduire, faire un rabais de. **I'll knock off £10** je vais baisser (le prix) de 10 livres, je vous fais un rabais de 10 livres.
c (*) *homework, correspondence, piece of work* (*do quickly*) expédier; (*do quickly and well*) trousser; (*do quickly and badly*) bâcler.
d (*Brit* ⁑: *steal*) piquer*.
e (⁑: *stop*) **to knock off smoking** arrêter de *or* cesser de fumer; **knock it off!** arrête!, suffit!*
f (⁑: *kill*) tuer, liquider*.
3 **knocking-off** adj *see* **knock 2.**

►**knock on** 1 vt sep: **to knock the ball on** faire un en-avant. 2 **knock-on** n, adj *see* **knock 2.**

►**knock out** 1 vt sep a *nail etc* faire sortir (*of* de); (* *fig*) *word, phrase, paragraph* barrer, biffer. **to knock out one's pipe** débourrer *or* éteindre sa pipe. b (*stun*) *[person]* assommer; (*Boxing*) mettre knock-out; *[drug]* sonner*, assommer. c (*) (*shock, overwhelm*) sonner*, ahurir, abasourdir; (*exhaust*) mettre à plat*. d (*from competition etc*) éliminer (*of* de). 2 **knockout** n, adj *see* **knockout.**

►**knock over** vt sep *table, stool etc* renverser, faire tomber; *object on shelf or table etc* faire tomber; (*Aut*) *pedestrian* renverser; *gatepost* faire tomber. **he was knocked over by a taxi** il a été renversé par un taxi.

►**knock together** 1 vi *[glasses, knees]* s'entrechoquer. 2 vt sep a (*lit*) *two objects* cogner l'un contre l'autre. **I'd like to knock their heads together!*** j'aimerais prendre l'un pour taper sur l'autre! b (*make hurriedly*) *table, shed etc* faire *or* bricoler à la hâte.

►**knock up** 1 vi (*Tennis*) faire des balles. 2 vt sep a (*lit*) *handle, lever etc* faire lever d'un coup. **to knock sb's arm up** faire voler le bras de qn en l'air. b (*Brit: waken*) réveiller (en frappant à la porte). c (*make hurriedly*) *meal* préparer en vitesse; *shed* construire à la hâte *or* à la va-vite; *furniture, toy* faire *or* fabriquer en un rien de temps. d (*Brit* *: *exhaust*) *person* éreinter, crever*. e (*Brit* *: *make ill*) rendre malade. **you'll knock yourself up if you go on like this** tu vas te rendre malade *or* t'esquinter* si tu continues comme ça. f (⁑: *make pregnant*) engrosser⁑. 3 **knock-up** n *see* **knock 2.** 4 **knocker-up** n *see* **knocker 2.**

►**knock up against** vt fus a (*bump into*) *table, chair* se cogner dans, se heurter contre, heurter. b (*: *meet*) tomber sur.

knockdown [ˈnɒkdaʊn] 1 adj a a ~ **blow** un coup qui assommerait un bœuf, un coup de boutoir. b (*Brit*) ~ **price** (*Comm*) prix très avantageux *or* intéressant; (*in posters, announcements*) (*Comm*) "~ **prices**" "prix imbattables"; **to sell at ~ prices** vendre pour une bouchée de pain. c (*easily dismantled*) *table, shed* démontable. 2 n (*price reduction*) réduction *f*, rabais *m*, remise *f*.

knocker [ˈnɒkəʳ] 1 n (*also* **door-~**) marteau *m* (de porte), heurtoir *m*. ~**s⁑** nichons⁑ *mpl*, roberts⁑ *mpl*. 2 comp ►**knocker-up** (*Brit*) *personne f qui réveille les gens en frappant à leur porte*.

knocking [ˈnɒkɪŋ] 1 n (*NonC*) a coups *mpl*. **I can hear ~ at the door** j'entends frapper à la porte. b (*in engine*) cognement *m*. 2 adj (*Advertising*) ~ **copy** contre-publicité *f* (*dénigrant le concurrent*); (*Brit*) ~**-shop⁑** bordel⁑ *m*.

knockout [ˈnɒkaʊt] 1 n a (*Boxing etc*) knock-out *m*. b (*: *overwhelming success*) *[person, record, achievement]* **to be a ~** être sensationnel* *or* formidable* *or* sensass⁑. c (*competition*) compétition *f* (avec épreuves éliminatoires). (*TV*) **"It's a ~"** "Jeux *mpl* sans frontières". 2 adj a ~ **blow** (*Boxing etc*) coup *m* qui (vous) met K.-O.; (*fig*) coup de grâce; (*Boxing*) **the ~ blow came in round 6** il a été mis knock-out au 6e round; (*Jur, Fin*) **knock-out agreement** entente *f* entre enchérisseurs. b (*) *pill, drug* qui (vous) assomme*. ~ **drops** soporifique *m*, narcotique *m*. c (*Sport*) ~ **competition** compétition *f* (avec épreuves éliminatoires).

knoll [nəʊl] n a (*hillock*) tertre *m*, monticule *m*. b (††: *bell stroke*) son *m* de cloche.

Knossos [ˈnɒsəs] n Cnossos.

knot [nɒt] 1 n a nœud *m*. **to tie/untie a ~** faire/défaire un nœud; **tight/slack ~** nœud serré/lâche; (*fig*) **the marriage ~** le lien du mariage; **Gordian ~** nœud gordien; *see* **granny, reef²**, **slip, tie** *etc*. b (*Naut*) nœud *m*. **to make 20 ~s** filer 20 nœuds; *see* **rate¹**. c (*in wood*) nœud *m*; (*fig*) *[problem etc]* nœud. a ~ **of people** un petit groupe de gens. 2 comp ►**knothole** (*in wood*) trou *m* (laissé par un nœud). 3 vt *rope* faire un nœud à, nouer. **he ~ted the piece of string to the rope** il a noué la ficelle à la corde; **get ~ted!⁑** va te faire voir!* *or* foutre!⁑ 4 vi faire un *or* des nœud(s).

►**knot together** vt sep attacher, nouer.

knotty [ˈnɒtɪ] adj *wood, hand* noueux; *rope* plein de nœuds; *problem* épineux, difficile.

knout [naʊt] n knout *m*.

know [nəʊ] pret **knew**, ptp **known** 1 vt a *facts, details, dates, results* savoir. **to ~ French** savoir le français; **I ~ (that) you're wrong** je sais que vous avez tort; **I ~ why he is angry** je sais pourquoi il est en colère; **do you ~ whether she's coming?** est-ce que tu sais si elle doit venir?; **I would have you ~ that ...** sachez que ...; **to ~ a lot about sth/sb** en savoir long sur qch/qn; **I don't ~ much about it/him** je ne sais pas grand-chose là-dessus/sur lui; **I'd like to ~ more (about it)** je voudrais en savoir davantage *or* plus long (là-dessus); **to ~ by heart** *text, song, poem* savoir par cœur; *subject, plan, route* connaître par cœur; **to get to ~ sth** apprendre qch (*see also* **1b**); **to ~ how to do sth** savoir faire qch; **I don't ~ where to begin** je ne sais pas par où commencer; **you don't** *or* **can't ~ how glad/sad/relieved** *etc* **I am to see you** vous ne pouvez pas savoir comme je suis content/triste/soulagé *etc* de vous voir; **he ~s all the answers** il s'y connaît, il sait tout; (*pej*) c'est un (monsieur) je-sais-tout*; **to ~ one's business, to ~ what's what*** connaître son affaire, s'y connaître, en connaître un bon bout*; **to ~ the difference between** connaître la différence entre; **she ~s what it means to suffer** *or* **what suffering means** elle sait ce que souffrir veut dire *or* ce qu'est la souffrance; **to ~ one's mind** savoir ce qu'on veut; **he ~s a thing or two*** il sait pas mal de choses; **he ~s what he's talking about** il sait de quoi il parle, il connaît son sujet; **(do) you ~ what, she's back/John's run off again** tu sais quoi, elle est rentrée/John s'est de nouveau sauvé; **I ~ (what), let's go for a walk/to the cinema** *etc* j'ai une idée, allons nous promener/au cinéma *etc*; **you ~ what I mean ...** tu vois ce que je veux dire ...; **that's worth ~ing** ça vaut la peine de le savoir, c'est bon à savoir; **there's no ~ing what he'll do** impossible de savoir ce qu'il va faire, on ne peut pas savoir ce qu'il va faire (*see also* **2a**); **I don't ~ if I can do it** je ne sais pas si je peux le faire; **I don't ~ that that is a very good idea** je ne sais pas si c'est une très bonne idée; **what do you ~!*** dites donc!, eh bien!, ça alors!; **I've been a fool and don't I ~ it!*** j'ai agi comme un idiot et je suis bien placé pour le savoir!; **she's angry! — don't I ~ it!*** *or* **I ~ all about that!*** elle est en colère! — à qui le dis-tu! *or* je suis bien placé pour le savoir!; **not if I ~ it!*** c'est ce qu'on va voir!, ça m'étonnerait!; **the Channel was rough, as I well ~!** *or* **as well I ~!** la Manche était houleuse, j'en sais quelque chose!; **it's no good lying, I ~ all about it** ce n'est pas la peine de mentir, je sais tout; **she ~s all about sewing** elle s'y connaît *or* elle est très forte *or* elle est très calée* en couture; **that's all you ~ (about it)!*** c'est ce que tu crois!; **you ~ what you can do with it!⁑** tu sais où tu peux te le mettre!⁑; **I ~ nothing about it** je n'en sais rien, je ne suis pas au courant; **it soon became ~n that ...** on a bientôt appris que ...; **it is well ~n that ...** il est (bien) connu que ..., tout le monde sait (bien) que ...; **to make sth ~n to sb** faire savoir qch à qn; **to let it be ~n that** faire savoir que; **to make one's presence ~n to sb** manifester sa présence à qn; **he is ~n to have been there/to be dishonest** on sait qu'il y a été/qu'il est malhonnête; **I ~ him to be a liar, I ~ him for a liar** je sais que c'est un menteur; **he knew himself (to be) guilty** il se savait coupable; **he soon let me ~ what he thought of it** il m'a fait bientôt savoir ce qu'il en pensait; **I'll let you ~** je vous le ferai savoir, je vous préviendrai; **when can you let me ~?** quand pourrez-vous me le dire? *or* me prévenir?; **let me ~ if I can help** si je peux me rendre utile dites-le-moi; *see* **rope.**
b (*be acquainted with*) *person, place, book, author, hunger, suffering, joy* connaître. **I ~ him well** je le connais bien; **I don't ~ him from Adam** je ne le connais ni d'Ève ni d'Adam; **do you ~ Paris?** connaissez-vous Paris?; **to ~ sb by sight/by name/by reputation** connaître qn de vue/de nom/de réputation; **I don't ~ her to speak to** je ne la connais pas (assez) pour lui parler; (*liter*) ~ **thyself** connais-toi toi-même; **I was glad to see someone I knew** j'étais content de voir une personne de connaissance; **to get to ~ sb** arriver à (mieux) connaître qn; **to make o.s. ~n to sb** se présenter à qn; **he is ~n as X** on le connaît sous le nom de X; **she wishes to be ~n as Mrs X** elle veut se faire appeler Mme X.
c (*be aware of*) **I have never ~n him to smile** je ne l'ai jamais vu sourire; **you have never ~n them to tell a lie** vous ne leur avez jamais entendu dire un mensonge; **I've ~n such things to happen before** j'ai déjà vu cela se produire; **I've never ~n it to rain like this** je n'ai jamais vu pleuvoir comme ça; **well, it has been ~n** enfin, ça c'est déjà vu *or* il y a un précédent.
d (*recognize*) reconnaître. **to ~ sb by his voice/his walk** reconnaître qn à sa voix/à sa démarche; **I knew him at once** je l'ai reconnu tout de suite; **you won't ~ him** tu ne le reconnaîtras pas; **he ~s a good horse when he sees one** il sait reconnaître un bon cheval; (*fig*) **she ~s a good thing when she sees it*** elle sait profiter des bonnes occasions, elle ne laisse pas échapper les bonnes occasions.
e (*distinguish*) reconnaître, distinguer. **I wouldn't ~ a spanner from a screwdriver** je ne sais pas reconnaître une clef à molette d'un tournevis; **he doesn't ~ one end of a horse/hammer** *etc* **from the other** c'est à peine s'il sait ce que c'est qu'un cheval/marteau *etc*; **you wouldn't ~ him from his brother** on le prendrait pour son frère.
2 vi a savoir. **as far as I ~** autant que je sache, à ma connaissance; **not as far as I ~** pas que je sache, pas à ma connaissance; **for all I ~** pour ce que j'en sais; **is he dead? — not that I ~ (of)** il est mort? — pas que je sache *or* pas à ma connaissance; **one never ~s, you never ~** on ne sait jamais; **who ~s?** qui sait?; **is she**

nice? — I don't ~ *or* **I wouldn't ~*** est-ce qu'elle est gentille? – je ne sais pas *or* je n'en sais rien; **how should I ~?** est-ce que je sais (moi)!, comment voulez-vous que je le sache?; **it's raining, you ~** il pleut, tu sais; **you ~, that's not a bad idea** tu sais, ce n'est pas une mauvaise idée; **will he help us? — there's no ~ing** va-t-il nous aider? – on ne peut pas savoir; **and afterwards they just don't want to ~*** et après ça ils font ceux qui n'en ont jamais entendu parler; **mummy ~s best!** maman a toujours raison!; **you ~ best, I suppose!** bien sûr, tu sais ce que tu dis!; **to ~ about** *or* **of sth** savoir qch, connaître qch, avoir entendu parler de qch; **I didn't ~ about that** je ne savais pas ça; **I'm going swimming — I don't ~ about that!*** je vais nager – c'est à voir!; **she ~s about cats** elle s'y connaît en (matière de) chats; **I knew of his death through a friend** j'ai appris sa mort par un ami; **I'd ~n of his death for some time** je savais depuis quelque temps qu'il était mort; **do you ~ about Paul?** tu es au courant pour Paul?*; **there were 10 in favour, 6 against, and 5 "don't ~s"** il y avait 10 pour, 6 contre et 5 "sans opinion".

b **I ~ better than to offer advice** je me garde bien de donner des conseils; **he ~s better than to touch his capital** il est trop prudent *or* avisé pour entamer son capital; **you ought to ~ better than to go out without a coat** tu ne devrais pas avoir la stupidité de sortir sans manteau; **you ought to have ~n better** tu aurais dû réfléchir; **he should ~ better at his age** à son âge il ne devrait pas être aussi bête *or* il devrait avoir un peu plus de bon sens; **they don't ~ any better** ils ne savent pas ce qu'ils font (*or* ce qu'il faut faire); **he says he didn't do it but I ~ better** il dit que ce n'est pas lui mais je ne suis pas dupe.

c **do you ~ of a good hairdresser?** connaissez-vous un bon coiffeur?; **I ~ of a nice little café** je connais un petit café sympathique; **I ~ of you through your sister** j'ai entendu parler de vous par votre sœur; **I don't know him but I ~ OF him** je ne le connais pas mais j'ai entendu parler de lui.

3 **comp ▸ know-all*** (Monsieur) je-sais-tout* *m*, (Madame *or* Mademoiselle) je-sais-tout* *f* **▸ know-how*: they have the materials to make the missile but they haven't got the know-how** ils ont le matériel nécessaire à la fabrication du missile mais ils n'ont pas la technique; **after years in the job he has acquired a lot of know-how** après des années dans cet emploi il a acquis beaucoup de technique *or* de savoir-faire *or* de métier; **you need quite a bit of know-how to operate this machine** il faut pas mal de* compétence pour faire marcher cette machine **▸ know-it-all*** (*US*) = **know-all***.

4 **n: to be in the ~*** être au courant *or* au parfum‡.

knowable ['nəʊəbl] **adj** connaissable.

knowing ['nəʊɪŋ] **adj** (*shrewd*) fin, malin (*f* -igne); (*wise*) sage; *look, smile* entendu.

knowingly ['nəʊɪŋlɪ] **adv** a (*consciously*) sciemment. b (*in knowing way*) *look, smile* d'un air entendu.

knowledge ['nɒlɪdʒ] 1 **n** (*NonC*) a (*understanding, awareness*) connaissance *f*. **to have ~ of** avoir connaissance de; **to have no ~ of** ne pas savoir, ignorer; **to (the best of) my ~** à ma connaissance, autant que je sache; **not to my ~** pas à ma connaissance, pas que je sache; **they had never to her ~ complained before** à sa connaissance ils ne s'étaient jamais plaints auparavant; **without his ~** à son insu; **without the ~ of her mother** à l'insu de sa mère; **to bring sth to sb's ~** porter qch à la connaissance de qn; **to bring to sb's ~ that ...** porter à la connaissance de qn le fait que ...; **it has come to my ~ that ...** j'ai appris que ...; **~ of the facts** la connaissance des faits; **it's common** *or* **public ~ that ...** il est de notoriété publique que ..., chacun sait que ... .

b (*learning, facts learnt*) connaissances *fpl*, science *f*, savoir *m*. **the advance of ~** le progrès du savoir *or* de la science *or* des connaissances; **his ~ will die with him** son savoir mourra avec lui; **my ~ of English is elementary** mes connaissances d'anglais sont élémentaires; **he has a working ~ of Japanese** il possède les éléments *mpl* de base du japonais, il se débrouille en japonais; **he has a thorough ~ of geography** il possède la géographie à fond.

2 **comp ▸ knowledge-based system** (*Comput*) système expert.

knowledgeable ['nɒlɪdʒəbl] **adj** *person* bien informé.

knowledgeably ['nɒlɪdʒəblɪ] **adv** en toute connaissance.

known [nəʊn] 1 **ptp of know**. 2 **adj** connu, reconnu. **he is a ~ thief/troublemaker** *etc* c'est un voleur/agitateur *etc* connu; **the ~ experts on this subject** les experts reconnus en la matière; **the ~ facts lead us to believe ...** les faits constatés *or* établis nous amènent à croire ...; **a ~ cure for ...** un remède qui existe déjà pour ...; **no ~ cure** aucun remède connu.

knuckle ['nʌkl] 1 **n** articulation *f or* jointure *f* du doigt. **to graze one's ~s** s'écorcher les articulations des doigts; *see* **rap**. 2 **comp ▸ knucklebone** (*Anat*) articulation *f* du doigt; (*Culin*) os *m* de jarret **▸ knuckleduster** coup-de-poing américain **▸ knucklehead‡** crétin(e)* *m(f)*, nouille* *f*.

▸knuckle down* **vi** s'y mettre. **to knuckle down to work** s'atteler au travail.

▸knuckle under* **vi** céder.

knurl [nɜːl] 1 **n** (*in wood*) nœud *m*; (*Tech*) moletage *m*. 2 **vt** (*Tech*) moleter.

KO* ['keɪ'əʊ] (**vb: pret, ptp KO'd** ['keɪ'əʊd]) (**abbr of knockout**) 1 **n, pl ~'s** (*blow*) K.-O. *m*, knock-out *m*. 2 **vt** (*Boxing*) mettre knock-out, battre par knock-out; (*gen*) mettre K.-O.* *or* knock-out*.

koala [kəʊ'ɑːlə] **n** (*also* **~ bear**) koala *m*.

kohl [keʊl] **n** khôl *m*. **~ pencil** crayon *m* khôl.

kohlrabi [keʊl'rɑːbɪ] **n, pl kohlrabies** chou-navet *m*.

kook‡ [kuːk] **n** (*US*) dingue* *mf*.

kookaburra ['kʊkə,bʌrə] **m** kookaburra *m*.

kookie‡, kooky‡ ['kuːkɪ] **adj** (*US*) dingue, cinglé.

Koran [kɒ'rɑːn] **n** Coran *m*.

Koranic [kɒ'rænɪk] **adj** coranique.

Korea [kə'rɪə] **n** Corée *f*. **North/South ~** Corée du Nord/du Sud.

Korean [kə'rɪən] 1 **adj** coréen. **North/South ~** nord-/sud-coréen. 2 **n** a Coréen(ne) *m(f)*. **North/South ~** Nord-/Sud-Coréen(ne). b (*Ling*) coréen *m*.

korma ['kɔːʳmə] **n** *type de curry souvent à la crème et à la noix de coco*.

kosher ['kəʊʃəʳ] **adj** kascher *inv*. (*fig*) **it's ~‡** c'est O.K.*

Kosovo ['kɒsɒ,vəʊ] **n** Kosovo *m*.

Kowloon ['kaʊ'luːn] **n: ~ Peninsula** péninsule *f* de Kowloon.

kowtow ['kaʊ'taʊ] **vi** se prosterner. **to ~ to sb** courber l'échine devant qn, faire des courbettes devant qn.

kph [,keɪpiː'aɪtʃ] **n** (**abbr of kilometres per hour**) km/h.

kraal [krɑːl] **n** kraal *m*.

Kraut‡ [kraʊt] **n** (*pej*) Boche‡ *mf*.

Kremlin ['kremlɪn] **n** Kremlin *m*.

kremlinologist ['kremlɪ'nɒlədʒɪst] **n** kremlinologue *mf*, kremlinologiste *mf*.

kremlinology ['kremlɪ'nɒlədʒɪ] **n** kremlinologie *f*.

krill [krɪl] **n, pl inv** krill *m*.

Krishna ['krɪʃnə] **n** (*deity*) Krisna *or* Krishna; (*river*) Kistna *f*.

Krishnaism ['krɪʃnə,ɪzəm] **n** Kris(h)naïsme.

Krugerrand ['kruːgə,rænd] **n** Krugerrand *m*.

Krum(m)horn ['krʌm,hɔːn] **n** (*Mus*) cromorne *m*.

krypton ['krɪptɒn] **n** krypton *m*.

KS (*US Post*) **abbr of Kansas**.

Kt (*Brit*) **abbr of knight** (*après le nom*).

kudos* ['kjuːdɒs] **n** (*NonC*) gloire *f*, lauriers *mpl*. **he got all the ~** c'est lui qui a récolté toute la gloire *or* tous les lauriers.

Ku Klux Klan ['kuː'klʌks'klæn] **n** (*US*) Ku Klux Klan *m*.

kummel ['kɪməl] **n** kummel *m*.

kumquat ['kʌmkwɒt] **n** kumquat *m*.

kung fu ['kʌŋ'fuː] **n** kung fu *m*.

Kuomintang ['kwəʊ'mɪn'tæŋ] **n** Kuo-min-tang *m*.

Kurd [kɜːd] **n** Kurde *mf*.

Kurdish ['kɜːdɪʃ] **adj** kurde.

Kurdistan [,kɜːdɪ'stɑːn] **n** Kurdistan *m*.

Kuwait [kʊ'weɪt] **n** Koweït *f or* Kuweit *f*.

Kuwaiti [kʊ'weɪtɪ] 1 **n** Koweïtien(ne) *m(f)*. 2 **adj** koweïtien.

kvas(s) [kvɑːs] **n** kwas *or* kvas *m*.

kvetch [kvetʃ] (*US* *) **vi** se plaindre (*about* de), râler*.

kW (**abbr of kilowatt**) kW.

kwashiorkor [,kwɑːʃɪ'ɔːkɔːʳ] **n** kwashiorkor *m*.

kWh (**abbr of kilowatt-hour(s)**) kWh.

KY (*US Post*) **abbr of Kentucky**.

L

L, l [el] n a (*letter*) L, l *m or f*. **L for London,** (*US*) **L for Love** ≈ L comme Louis; **L-shaped room** pièce *f* en (forme de) L. b (*Brit Aut*) (abbr of **learner**) **L-plate** plaque *f* d'apprenti conducteur *or* de conducteur débutant. c (abbr of **litre(s)**) l. d (*US*) **the L*** le métro aérien. e (*Geog*) (abbr of **Lake**) L. f (abbr of **left**) gauche. g (abbr of **large**: *pour indiquer la taille sur l'étiquette*) grand. h (*Ling*) abbr of **Latin**.

LA[1] [el'eɪ] (*US*) abbr of **Los Angeles**.

LA[2] (*US Post*) abbr of **Louisiana**.

La abbr of **Lane**.

La. (*US*) abbr of **Louisiana**.

lab* [læb] n (abbr of **laboratory**) labo* *m*, laboratoire *m*. (*Scol etc*) ~ **book** cahier *m* de travaux pratiques.

label ['leɪbl] 1 n (*lit, fig, Ling*) étiquette *f*; (*brand guarantee*) label *m*. **record on the Deltaphone** ~ disque *m* sorti chez Deltaphone, disque sous le label Deltaphone; *see* **luggage**.

2 vt a *parcel, bottle* coller une *or* des étiquette(s) sur; (*Comm*) *goods for sale* étiqueter. **every packet must be clearly ~led** tout paquet doit porter une *or* des étiquette(s) lisible(s) et précise(s); **the bottle was not ~led** il n'y avait pas d'étiquette sur la bouteille; **the bottle was ~led poison** sur la bouteille il y avait marqué poison.

b (*fig*) *person, group* étiqueter, cataloguer (*pej*) (*as* comme). **he was ~led (as) a revolutionary** on l'a étiqueté (comme) révolutionnaire.

c (*Ling*) marquer.

labia ['leɪbɪə] n (pl of **labium**) lèvres *fpl*. ~ **minora/majora** petites/grandes lèvres.

labial ['leɪbɪəl] (*Ling*) 1 adj (*Anat, Phon*) labial. 2 n (*Phon*) labiale *f*.

labiodental [ˌleɪbɪəʊ'dentəl] 1 adj labiodental. 2 n labiodentale *f*.

labiovelar [ˌleɪbɪəʊ'viːləʳ] adj, n labiovélaire (*f*).

labor ['leɪbəʳ] *etc* (*US*) = **labour** *etc*.

laboratory [lə'bɒrətərɪ], (*US*) ['læbrətərɪ] 1 n laboratoire *m*; *see* **language**. 2 comp *experiment, instrument, product* de laboratoire ▸**laboratory assistant** assistant(e) *m(f)* de laboratoire, laborantin(e) *m(f)* ▸**laboratory equipment** équipement *m* de laboratoire ▸**laboratory school** (*US*) école *f* d'application.

laborious [lə'bɔːrɪəs] adj laborieux.

laboriously [lə'bɔːrɪəslɪ] adv laborieusement.

labour, (*US*) **labor** ['leɪbəʳ] 1 n a (*hard work, task*) travail *m*. ~ **of love** travail fait par plaisir; **~s of Hercules** travaux *mpl* d'Hercule; *see* **hard, manual**.

b (*NonC: Ind: workers*) main-d'œuvre *f*, ouvriers *mpl*, travailleurs *mpl*. **Minister/Ministry of L~,** (*US*) **Secretary/Department of L~** ministre *m*/ministère *m* du Travail; *see* **management, skilled** *etc*.

c (*Pol*) **L~** les travaillistes *mpl*; **he votes L~** il vote travailliste.

d (*Med*) travail *m*. **in** ~ en travail, en train d'accoucher; **to go into** ~ commencer à avoir des contractions.

2 comp (*Ind*) *dispute, trouble* ouvrier; *relations* ouvriers-patronat *inv* ▸**Labour** (*Pol*) *leader, party* travailliste ▸**labo(u)r agreement** accord *m* sur les salaires, convention *f* collective ▸**labo(u)r camp** camp *m* de travaux forcés ▸**Labo(u)r Day** fête *f* du travail (*Brit*: 1er mai; *US, Can*: 1er lundi de septembre) ▸**Labour Exchange** (*Brit*) ≈ bourse *f* de l'emploi, Agence *f* pour l'emploi ▸**labo(u)r force** (*Ind*) (*number employed*) effectif(s) *m(pl)* en ouvriers; (*personnel*) main-d'œuvre *f* ▸**labo(u)r-intensive** qui nécessite l'emploi de beaucoup d'ouvriers *or* de main-d'œuvre ▸**labor laws** (*US*) législation industrielle *or* du travail ▸**labo(u)r-management relations** relations *fpl* patrons-ouvriers ▸**labo(u)r market** marché *m* du travail ▸**labo(u)r movement** (*Pol*) mouvement *m* ouvrier; **the Labo(u)r movement** le mouvement travailliste ▸**labo(u)r pains** (*Med*) douleurs *fpl* de l'accouchement ▸**labo(u)r-saving** qui allège le travail ▸**labo(u)r-saving device** (*in household*) appareil ménager ▸**labo(u)r shortage** (*Ind*) pénurie *f* de main-d'œuvre ▸**labo(u)r supply** (*Ind*) main-d'œuvre *f* disponible ▸**labor union** (*US*) syndicat *m* ▸**labo(u)r ward** (*Med*) salle *f* d'accouchement *or* de travail.

3 vi a (*work with effort*) travailler dur (*at* à); (*work with difficulty*) peiner (*at* sur). **to ~ to do** travailler dur *or* peiner pour faire.

b *[engine, motor]* peiner; *[ship, boat]* fatiguer. **to ~ under a delusion** être victime d'une illusion; **to ~ up a hill** *[person]* gravir *or* monter péniblement une côte; *[car]* peiner dans une montée; *see* **misapprehension**.

4 vt insister sur, s'étendre sur. **I won't ~ the point** je n'insisterai pas (lourdement) sur ce point, je ne m'étendrai pas là-dessus.

laboured, (*US*) **labored** ['leɪbəd] adj *style* (*clumsy*) lourd; (*showing effort*) laborieux; (*overelaborate*) ampoulé. ~ **breathing** respiration *f* pénible *or* difficile.

labourer, (*US*) **laborer** ['leɪbərəʳ] n ouvrier *m*, travailleur *m*; (*on farm*) ouvrier agricole; (*on roads, building sites etc*) manœuvre *m*; *see* **dock**[1].

labouring, (*US*) **laboring** ['leɪbərɪŋ] adj *class* ouvrier.

labourite, (*US*) **laborite** ['leɪbəraɪt] n (*Pol*) travailliste *mf*.

Labrador ['læbrəˌdɔːʳ] n a (*Geog*) Labrador *m*. b (*dog: also* **l~**) labrador *m*.

laburnum [lə'bɜːnəm] n cytise *m*, faux ébénier.

labyrinth ['læbɪrɪnθ] n labyrinthe *m*, dédale *m*.

labyrinthine [ˌlæbɪ'rɪnθaɪn] adj labyrinthique, labyrinthien.

lace [leɪs] 1 n a (*NonC: Tex*) dentelle *f*; (*pillow* ~) guipure *f*. **dress trimmed with** ~ robe bordée de dentelle(s); **a piece of** ~ de la dentelle; (*Mil*) **gold** ~ galon *m*. b *[shoe, corset]* lacet *m*. 2 comp *collar, curtains* de *or* en dentelle ▸**lacemaker** dentellière *f* ▸**lacemaking** fabrication *f* de la dentelle, dentellerie *f* (*rare*) ▸**lace-up shoes, lace-ups*** chaussures *fpl* à lacets. 3 vt a (*also* ~ **up**) *shoe, corset* lacer. b *drink* arroser (*with* de), corser. 4 vi (*also* ~ **up**) se lacer.

▸**lace into**‡ vt fus (*thrash*) rosser*; (*criticize*) éreinter, démolir.

lacerate ['læsəreɪt] vt (*lit*) *face, skin, clothes* lacérer; (*fig*) *person* déchirer, fendre le cœur de. **body ~d by pain** corps lacéré par la douleur.

laceration [ˌlæsə'reɪʃən] n (*act*) lacération *f*; (*tear: also Med*) déchirure *f*.

lachrymal ['lækrɪməl] adj lacrymal.

lachrymose ['lækrɪməʊs] adj (*liter*) larmoyant.

lack [læk] 1 n manque *m*. **through** *or* **for** ~ **of** faute de, par manque de; **there is a** ~ **of money** l'argent manque. 2 vt *confidence, friends, strength, interest* manquer de. **we ~ (the) time to do it** nous n'avons pas le temps de le faire, nous manquons de temps pour le faire; **he doesn't ~ talent** ce n'est pas le talent qui lui manque *or* qui lui fait défaut. 3 vi a *[food, money etc]* **to be ~ing** manquer, faire défaut. b *[person]* **to be ~ing in, to ~ for** manquer de.

lackadaisical [ˌlækə'deɪzɪkəl] adj (*listless*) nonchalant, apathique; (*lazy*) indolent; *work* fait à la va-comme-je-te-pousse*.

lackey ['lækɪ] n laquais *m* (*also pej*), larbin* *m* (*pej*).

lacking* ['lækɪŋ] adj (*stupid*) simplet, demeuré*, débile*.

lacklustre, (*US*) **lackluster** ['lækˌlʌstəʳ] adj terne, peu brillant.

laconic [lə'kɒnɪk] adj laconique.

laconically [lə'kɒnɪkəlɪ] adv laconiquement.

lacquer ['lækəʳ] 1 n (*substance: for wood, hair etc*) laque *f*; (*object*) laque *m*. ~ **ware** laques *mpl*. 2 vt *wood* laquer; (*Brit*) *hair* mettre de la laque sur.

lacrosse [lə'krɒs] n lacrosse *m*. ~ **stick** crosse *f*.

lactase ['lækteɪs] n lactase *f*.

lactate ['lækteɪt] 1 n (*Chem*) lactate *m*. 2 vi produire du lait.

lactation [læk'teɪʃən] n lactation *f*.

lacteal ['læktɪəl] 1 adj lacté. 2 npl: **~s** veines lactées.

lactic ['læktɪk] adj lacté. (*Chem*) ~ **acid** acide *m* lactique.

lactiferous [læk'tɪfərəs] adj lactifère.

lactogenic [ˌlæktə'dʒenɪk] adj lactogène.

lactose ['læktəʊs] n lactose *m*.

lacuna [lə'kjuːnə] n, pl **~s** *or* **lacunae** [lə'kjuːniː] lacune *f*.

lacustrine [lə'kʌstraɪn] adj lacustre.

lacy ['leɪsɪ] adj qui ressemble à la dentelle. **the frost made a ~ pattern** il y avait une dentelle de givre.

lad [læd] n (*boy*) garçon *m*, gars* *m*; (*: *son*) fiston* *m*. **when I was a ~** quand j'étais jeune, dans mon jeune temps; **he's only a ~** ce n'est qu'un gosse* *or* un gamin*; **I'm going for a drink with the ~s*** je vais boire un pot avec les copains*; **come on ~s!** allez les gars!*; **he's a bit of a ~*** il est un peu noceur*; *see* **stable[2]**.

ladder ['lædəʳ] 1 n a (*lit, fig*) échelle *f*. (*fig*) **to be at the top of the ~** être arrivé au sommet de l'échelle; *see* **rope, step.** b (*Brit: in stocking*) échelle *f*, maille filée. **to have a ~ in one's stocking** avoir une échelle à son bas, avoir un bas filé. 2 comp ►**ladderproof** (*Brit*) indémaillable. 3 vt (*Brit*) *stocking* filer, faire une échelle à. 4 vi (*Brit*) *[stocking]* filer.

laddie* ['lædɪ] n (*esp Scot and dial*) garçon *m*, (petit) gars* *m*. **look here, ~!** dis donc, mon petit!*, dis donc, fiston!‡

lade [leɪd] pret **laded**, ptp **laden** vt charger.

laden ['leɪdn] 1 ptp of **lade**. 2 adj chargé (*with* de). **fully ~ truck/ship** camion *m*/navire *m* en pleine charge.

la-di-da* ['lɑːdɪ'dɑː] adj *person* bêcheur*; *voice* maniéré, apprêté. **she's very ~** elle fait la prétentieuse; **in a ~ way** de façon maniérée.

lading ['leɪdɪŋ] n cargaison *f*, chargement *m*.

ladle ['leɪdl] 1 n louche *f*. 2 vt *soup* servir (à la louche).

►**ladle out** vt sep *soup* servir (à la louche); (* *fig*) *money* répandre à gogo*, allonger*; *advice* prodiguer à foison *or* en masse*.

lady ['leɪdɪ] 1 n dame *f*. **the ~ of the house** la maîtresse de maison; **Ladies and Gentlemen!** Mesdames, (Mesdemoiselles,) Messieurs!; **good morning, ladies and gentlemen** bonjour mesdames, bonjour mesdemoiselles, bonjour messieurs; **she's a real ~** c'est une vraie dame; **she's no ~** elle est très commune *or* fort peu distinguée; **your good ~*** votre dame‡ (*also hum*); **the headmaster and his ~†** le directeur et sa dame†; **young ~** (*married*) jeune femme *f*; (*unmarried*) jeune fille *f*; **look here, young ~!** dites donc, jeune fille!*; **this is the ~/the young ~ who served me** voilà la dame/la demoiselle qui m'a servi; **his young ~*†** (*girlfriend*) sa bonne amie†, sa petite amie; (*fiancée*) sa fiancée; **ladies' hairdresser** coiffeur *m*, -euse *f* pour dames; **~'s umbrella** parapluie *m* de dame *or* de femme; **he's a ladies' man** *or* **a ~'s man** c'est un homme à femmes; (*fig*) **a L~ Bountiful** une généreuse bienfaitrice; (*Rel*) **Our L~** Notre-Dame *f*; **listen here, ~‡** écoutez un peu, ma petite dame‡; (*public lavatory*) **ladies' room, ladies** toilettes *fpl* (pour dames); **where is the ladies' room, where is the ladies?** où sont les toilettes (pour dames)?; (*sign*) **"Ladies"** "Dames"; (*US Med*) **ladies' auxiliary** *association de bénévoles s'occupant d'œuvres de bienfaisance dans un hôpital;* (*Brit: in titles*) **L~ Davenport** lady Davenport; **Sir John and L~ Smith** sir John Smith et lady Smith; *see* **first, leading.**

2 comp *engineer etc* femme (*before noun*) (*but see below*) ►**ladybird** (*Brit*), **ladybug** (*US*) coccinelle *f*, bête *f* à bon Dieu ►**Lady Chapel** (*Rel*) chapelle *f* de la (Sainte) Vierge ►**Lady Day** (*Brit*) la fête de l'Annonciation ►**lady doctor** (*gen*) femme *f* médecin, doctoresse *f*; **I prefer to see a lady doctor** je préfère voir un médecin-femme ►**ladyfinger** (*US Culin*) boudoir *m* (*biscuit*) ►**lady friend*** petite amie ►**lady-in-waiting** (pl **ladies-~-~**) dame *f* d'honneur ►**ladykiller** (*fig*) don Juan *m*, tombeur* *m*, bourreau *m* des cœurs (*hum*) ►**ladylike** *person* bien élevée, distinguée; *manners* distingué; **it's not ladylike to yawn** une jeune fille bien élevée ne bâille pas, ce n'est pas poli *or* bien élevé de bâiller ►**lady-love**: († *or hum*) **his lady-love** sa bien-aimée†, la dame de ses pensées (*hum*) ►**Lady Mayoress** (*Brit*) femme *f* (*or* fille *f etc*) du Lord Mayor ►**lady's finger** okra *m* ►**lady's maid** femme *f* de chambre (*attachée au service particulier d'une dame*) ►**lady teacher** professeur-femme *m*.

ladyship ['leɪdɪʃɪp] n: **Her/Your L~** Madame *f* (la comtesse *or* la baronne *etc*).

lag[1] [læg] 1 n (*delay*) retard *m*; (*between two events*) décalage *m*; *see* **jet[1], time.** 2 vi rester en arrière, traîner. **he was ~ging behind the others** il traînait derrière les autres, il était à la traîne; (*fig*) **their country ~s behind ours in car exports** leur pays a du retard *or* est en retard sur le nôtre dans l'exportation automobile.

►**lag behind** vi rester en arrière, traîner. (*fig*) **we lag behind in space exploration** nous sommes en retard *or* à la traîne* dans l'exploration spatiale.

lag[2] [læg] vt *pipes* calorifuger.

lag[3] [læg] n (*esp Brit*) **old ~*** récidiviste *mf*, (vieux) cheval *m* de retour.

lager ['lɑːgəʳ] n lager *f*, ≃ bière blonde. **~ lout** jeune voyou *m* (*porté sur la boisson*).

laggard ['lægəd] n traînard(e) *m(f)*.

lagging ['lægɪŋ] n (*NonC*) (*material*) calorifuge *m*; (*act*) calorifugeage *m*.

lagniappe [læn'jæp] n (*US*) prime *f*, cadeau-réclame *m*.

lagoon [lə'guːn] n (*gen*) lagune *f*; (*coral*) lagon *m*.

Lagos ['leɪgɒs] n Lagos *m*.

lah [lɑː] n (*Mus*) la *m*.

laicize ['leɪɪsaɪz] vt laïciser.

laid [leɪd] 1 pret, ptp of **lay[1]**; *see* **new.** 2 comp ►**laid-back*** relax(e)*, décontracté.

lain [leɪn] ptp of **lie[1]**.

lair [lɛəʳ] n (*lit, fig*) tanière *f*, repaire *m*.

laird [lɛəd] n (*Scot*) laird *m*, propriétaire foncier.

laity ['leɪɪtɪ] npl: **the ~** les laïcs *mpl*.

lake[1] [leɪk] 1 n lac *m*. (*in Geog names*) **L~ Michigan** lac Michigan; **L~ Constance** lac de Constance; **L~ Geneva** lac Léman *or* de Genève. 2 comp ►**the Lake District** (*Brit Geog*) la région des lacs ►**lake dwellers** (*Hist*) habitants *mpl* d'un village *or* d'une cité lacustre ►**lake dwelling** (*Hist*) habitation *f* lacustre ►**Lakeland** (*Brit Geog*) = **the Lake District** ►**the Lake poets** (*Literat*) les lakistes *mpl* ►**the Lakes** (*Brit Geog*) = **the Lake District** ►**lakeside** n bord *m* de lac ◊ adj au bord du (*or* d'un) lac; **along the lakeside** le long du lac; **by** *or* **at the lakeside** au bord du lac.

lake[2] [leɪk] n (*Art*) laque *f*.

Lallans ['lælənz] 1 n Lallans *m* (*forme littéraire du dialecte parlé dans les Basses Terres d'Écosse*). 2 adj en Lallans.

lam[1]‡ [læm] 1 vt tabasser‡. 2 vi: **to ~ into sb** (*thrash*) rentrer dans qn*; (*scold*) engueuler qn‡.

lam[2]* [læm] n (*US*) **on the ~** en fuite, en cavale‡; **to take it on the ~** filer, partir en cavale‡.

lama ['lɑːmə] n lama *m* (*Rel*).

lamaism ['lɑːmə,ɪzəm] n (*Rel*) lamaïsme *m*.

lamaist ['lɑːmə,ɪst] adj, n (*Rel*) lamaïste *(mf)*.

lamb [læm] 1 n (*Culin, Zool*) agneau *m*. (*Rel*) **L~ of God** Agneau de Dieu; **my little ~!*** mon trésor!, mon agneau!, mon ange!; **poor ~!*** le (*or* la) pauvre!; (*fig*) **he took it like a ~** il l'a pris sans broncher, il s'est laissé faire, il n'a pas protesté; **like a ~ to the slaughter** comme un agneau que l'on mène à l'abattoir. 2 vi agneler, mettre bas. 3 comp ►**lamb chop, lamb cutlet** côtelette *f* d'agneau ►**lambskin** n (*skin itself*) peau *f* d'agneau; (*material*) agneau *m* (*NonC*) ◊ adj en agneau, d'agneau ►**lamb's lettuce** mâche *f*, doucette *f* ►**lamb's wool, lambswool** laine *f* d'agneau.

lambada [,læm'bɑːdə] n lambada *f*.

lambast* [læm'bæst] vt, **lambaste*** [læm'beɪst] vt (*beat*) rosser*; (*scold*) sonner les cloches à‡; (*criticize severely*) éreinter, démolir.

lambent ['læmbənt] adj chatoyant.

lambing ['læmɪŋ] n agnelage *m*. **~ time** (période *f* d')agnelage.

lambkin ['læmkɪn] n jeune agneau *m*, agnelet *m*.

lambrequin ['læmbrɪkɪn] n lambrequin *m*.

lame [leɪm] 1 adj a *animal, person* boiteux, estropié, éclopé. **to be ~** boiter; **to be slightly ~** boitiller; *[horse]* **to go ~** se mettre à boiter; **this horse is ~ in one leg** ce cheval boite d'une jambe; **~ duck** (*fig*) canard boiteux; (*US Pol*) *élu non réélu qui siège à titre provisoire jusqu'à l'instauration de son successeur.* b (*fig*) *excuse* faible, piètre (*before n*); *argument* faible, boiteux; (*Poetry*) *metre* boiteux, faux (*f* fausse). 2 vt *person, animal* estropier. 3 comp ►**lamebrain** idiot(e) *m(f)*, crétin(e) *m(f)* ►**lamebrained** idiot, crétin. 4 n (*US* ‡) personne *f* qui n'est pas dans le coup.

lamé ['lɑːmeɪ] 1 n lamé *m*. 2 comp en lamé. **gold lamé jacket** veste *f* lamée (d')or.

lamely ['leɪmlɪ] adv *say, argue* maladroitement, sans conviction.

lameness ['leɪmnɪs] n (*lit*) claudication *f* (*frm*), boiterie *f*; (*fig*) faiblesse *f*, pauvreté *f*, maladresse *f*.

lament [lə'ment] 1 n a lamentation *f*. b (*poem*) élégie *f*; (*song*) complainte *f*; (*at funerals*) chant *m* funèbre; (*for bagpipes etc*) plainte *f*. 2 vt pleurer, regretter, se lamenter sur. **our (late) ~ed sister** notre regrettée sœur (*frm*), notre pauvre sœur, la sœur que nous avons perdue. 3 vi se lamenter (*for, over* sur), s'affliger (*for, over* de).

lamentable ['læməntəbl] adj *state, condition, situation* déplorable, lamentable; *incident* fâcheux, regrettable; *results, performance* lamentable, déplorable.

lamentably ['læməntəblɪ] adv lamentablement.

lamentation [,læmən'teɪʃən] n lamentation *f*. (*Bible*) **(the Book of) L~s** le livre des Lamentations.

laminate ['læmɪneɪt] 1 vt laminer. 2 n stratifié *m*.

laminated ['læmɪneɪtɪd] adj *metal* laminé; *windscreen* (en verre) feuilleté; *book jacket* plastifié. **~ glass** verre *m* feuilleté; **~ wood** contre-plaqué *m*.

lamp [læmp] 1 n a (*light*) lampe *f*; (*Aut*) feu *m*; *see* **blow[1], safety, street** *etc.* b (*bulb*) ampoule *f*. **100-watt ~** ampoule de 100 watts. 2 comp ►**lampblack** noir *m* de fumée *or* de carbone ►**lamp bracket** applique *f* ►**lamplight**: **by lamplight** à la lumière de la lampe ►**lamplighter** allumeur *m* de réverbères ►**lamplit** éclairé (par une lampe) ►**lamppost** (*Brit*) réverbère *m*; (*fig*) **between you, me and the lamppost*** tout à fait entre nous, soit dit entre nous ►**lampshade** abat-jour *m inv* ►**lampstand** pied *m* de lampe ►**lamp standard** lampadaire *m* (*dans la rue*); (*very high*) pylône *m*.

lampern ['læmpən] n lamproie *f* de rivière.

lampoon [læm'puːn] 1 n (*gen*) virulente satire; (*written*) pamphlet *m*, libelle *m*; (*spoken*) diatribe *f*. 2 vt *person, action, quality* railler, tourner en dérision, faire la satire de; (*in song*) chansonner.

lampoonist [læm'puːnɪst] n (*gen*) satiriste *m*; (*writer*) pamphlétaire *m*; (*singer*) chansonnier *m*.

lamprey ['læmprɪ] n lamproie *f*.

LAN [læn] n (*Comput*) (abbr of **local area network**) réseau *m* local.

lanai [lə'naɪ] n (*US*) véranda *f*.

Lancaster [ˈlæŋkəstəʳ] **n** Lancastre.

Lancastrian [læŋˈkæstrɪən] **1 adj** lancastrien, de Lancastre. **2 n** Lancastrien(ne) *m(f)*, natif *m* (*f* -ive) *or* habitant(e) *m(f)* de Lancastre.

lance [lɑːns] **1 n a** (*weapon*) lance *f*; (*soldier*) lancier *m*. **b** (*Med*) lancette *f*, bistouri *m*. **2 vt** *abscess* percer, ouvrir; *finger* ouvrir. **3 comp ▸ lance corporal** (*Brit Mil*) caporal *m*.

lancer [ˈlɑːnsəʳ] **n** (*soldier*) lancier *m*.

lancet [ˈlɑːnsɪt] **1 n** (*Med*) lancette *f*, bistouri *m*. **2 comp ▸ lancet window** (*Archit*) fenêtre *f* en ogive.

Lancs. [læŋks] **n** (*Brit*) **abbr of Lancashire.**

land [lænd] **1 n a** (*NonC: opp of sea*) terre *f*. **dry ~** terre ferme; **on ~** à terre; **to go by ~** voyager par (voie de) terre; **over ~ and sea** sur terre et sur mer; (*Naut*) **to make ~** accoster; **we sighted ~ for the first time in 3 months** pour la première fois en 3 mois nous sommes arrivés en vue d'une terre; (*fig*) **to see how the ~ lies, to find out the lie of the ~** (*Brit*) *or* **the lay of the ~** (*US*) tâter le terrain, voir de quoi il retourne; (*US*) **(for) ~'s sake*** juste ciel!

b (*NonC: Agr*) terre *f*. **fertile ~** terre fertile; **to live off the ~** vivre de la terre; **to work on the ~** travailler la terre; **many people left the ~** beaucoup de gens ont quitté *or* déserté la campagne; **he bought ~ in Devon** il a acheté une terre dans le Devon.

c (*property*) (*gen large*) terre(s) *f(pl)*; (*not so large*) terrain *m*. **get off my ~!** sortez de mes terres! *or* de mon terrain!; **the ~ on which this house is built** le terrain sur lequel cette maison est construite.

d (*country, nation*) pays *m*. **people of many ~s** des gens de nationalités diverses; **throughout the ~** dans tout le pays; **~ fit for heroes** pays *m* digne de ses héros; **~ of milk and honey** pays de cocagne; (*fig*) **the L~ of Nod** le pays des rêves; **to be in the ~ of the living** être encore de ce monde; *see* **law, native, promised** *etc.*

2 comp *breeze* de terre; *prices* des terrains; *defences* terrestre; *law, policy, reform* agraire; *tax* foncier **▸ land agent** (*steward*) régisseur *m* d'un domaine; (*estate agent*) expert foncier **▸ land army** (*Brit*) corps *m* de travailleuses agricoles **▸ landfall** terre *f* (*aperçue d'un navire*); **to make landfall** accoster **▸ landfill** enfouissement *m* des déchets; **landfill site** centre *m* d'enfouissement des déchets **▸ land forces** armée *f* de terre, forces *fpl* terrestres **▸ land girl** (*Brit*) membre *m* du corps des travailleuses agricoles **▸ land grant college** (*US*) établissement *m* d'enseignement supérieur (*créé par donation foncière du gouvernement fédéral*) **▸ landlady** *see* **landlady ▸ landless** sans terre **▸ landlocked** (*totally enclosed*) enfermé dans les terres, sans littoral, sans accès à la mer; (*almost totally enclosed*) entouré par les terres **▸ landlord** *see* **landlord ▸ landmark** point *m* de repère; (*fig*) **to be a landmark in** faire date *or* faire époque dans **▸ land mass** bloc *m* continental **▸ landmine** (*Mil*) mine *f* terrestre **▸ land-office:** (*US fig*) **to do a land-office business*** faire d'excellentes affaires **▸ landowner** propriétaire *m* terrien **▸ land ownership n** propriété *f* foncière ◊ **comp** *policy, problem* foncier **▸ land patent** (*US*) titre *m* (constitutif) de propriété foncière **▸ land-poor farmer** (*US*) fermier *m* riche en terre mais pauvre en disponibilités **▸ land reform** réforme *f* agraire **▸ land registry** ≃ bureau *m* du cadastre **▸ Land's End** (*Geog*) le cap Land's End **▸ landslide** *see* **landslide ▸ landslip** glissement *m* de terrain; [*loose rocks etc*] éboulement *m* **▸ land worker** ouvrier *m*, -ière *f* agricole **▸ land yacht** char *m* à voile.

3 vt a *cargo* décharger, débarquer; *passengers* débarquer; *aircraft* poser; *fish* (*gen*) prendre; (*on deck*) amener à bord, hisser sur le pont; (*on shore, bank*) amener sur le rivage. **to ~ a blow** infliger un coup (*on* à).

b (**: obtain*) *job, contract, prize* décrocher*.

c (*Brit * fig*) **that will ~ you in trouble** ça va vous attirer des ennuis *or* vous mettre dans le pétrin; **to ~ sb in a mess/in debt** mettre qn dans de beaux draps/dans les dettes; **that's what ~ed him in jail** c'est comme ça qu'il s'est retrouvé en prison.

d (*Brit* *) **to be ~ed with sth** (*left with*) avoir qch *or* rester avec qch sur les bras; (*forced to take on*) récolter qch*, devoir se coltiner qch*; **now we're ~ed with all this extra work** maintenant il faut qu'on s'envoie (*subj*) tout ce boulot* en plus; **I've got ~ed with this job** on m'a collé* ce travail; **I got ~ed with him for 2 hours** je me le suis farci‡ pendant deux heures.

4 vi a [*aircraft etc*] atterrir, se poser; (*on sea*) amerrir; (*on ship's deck*) apponter. **to ~ on the moon** [*rocket, spacecraft*] alunir, se poser sur la lune; [*person*] atterrir sur la lune; **we ~ed at Orly** nous sommes arrivés *or* nous avons atterri à Orly; **as the plane was coming in to ~** comme l'avion s'apprêtait à atterrir.

b [*person, object*] (re)tomber, arriver, atterrir*; [*ski jumper, gymnast*] retomber, se recevoir. **to ~ on sth** [*falling object*] tomber sur qch; [*person or animal jumping*] retomber *or* atterrir* sur qch; [*bird, insect*] se poser sur qch; **the bomb ~ed square on target** la bombe est tombée en plein sur l'objectif; (*lit, fig*) **to ~ on one's feet** retomber sur ses pieds.

c (*from boat*) débarquer.

▸land up* **vi** atterrir*, échouer, (finir par) se retrouver. **to land up in Paris/in jail** atterrir* *or* finir par se retrouver à Paris/en prison; **the report landed up on my desk** le rapport a atterri* *or* a fini par arriver sur mon bureau; **he landed up with only £2** il s'est retrouvé avec 2 livres seulement; **we finally landed up in a small café** nous avons finalement échoué dans un petit café.

landau [ˈlændɔː] **n** landau *m* (*véhicule*).

landed [ˈlændɪd] **adj a** *proprietor* foncier, terrien; *property* foncier. **~ gentry** aristocratie terrienne. **b** (*Comm*) **~ price** prix *m* débarqué *or* au débarquement.

landing¹ [ˈlændɪŋ] **1 n a** [*aircraft, spacecraft etc*] atterrissage *m*; (*on sea*) amerrissage *m*; (*on moon*) alunissage *m*; (*on deck*) appontage *m*; *see* **crash, pancake, soft** *etc.*

b (*from ship*) débarquement *m*. (*Mil Hist*) **the Normandy ~s** le débarquement (du 6 juin 1944).

c [*high jumper, ski jumper, gymnast*] réception *f*.

2 comp ▸ landing card carte *f* de débarquement **▸ landing craft** (*Mil*) chaland *m* *or* navire *m* de débarquement **▸ landing field** terrain *m* d'aviation **▸ landing force** (*Mil*) troupes *fpl* de débarquement **▸ landing gear** (*Aviat*) train *m* d'atterrissage, atterrisseur *m* **▸ landing ground** terrain *m* d'atterrissage **▸ landing lights** (*on aircraft*) phares *mpl* d'atterrissage; (*on ground*) balises *fpl* (d'atterrissage) **▸ landing net** (*Fishing*) épuisette *f* **▸ landing party** (*Naut*) détachement *m* de débarquement **▸ landing stage** (*Brit*) débarcadère *m*, appontement *m* **▸ landing strip** (*Aviat*) piste *f* d'atterrissage **▸ landing wheels** roues *fpl* du train d'atterrissage.

landing² [ˈlændɪŋ] **n** (*between stairs*) palier *m*; (*floor*) étage *m*.

landlady [ˈlændˌleɪdɪ] **n** [*flat etc*] propriétaire *f*; (*Brit*) [*pub, guest house etc*] patronne *f*.

landlord [ˈlændˌlɔːd] **n** [*flat etc*] propriétaire *m*; (*Brit*) [*pub, guest house etc*] patron *m*.

landlubber* [ˈlændˌlʌbəʳ] **n** terrien(ne) *m(f)*. **he's a real ~** pour lui, il n'y a que le plancher des vaches* (qui compte).

Landrover [ˈlændˌrəʊvəʳ] **n** ® Land Rover *or* landrover *m or f*.

landscape [ˈlændˌskeɪp] **1 n** (*land, view, picture*) paysage *m*. **2 vt** *garden* dessiner; *bomb site, dirty place etc* aménager. **3 comp ▸ landscape architect** architecte *mf* paysagiste **▸ landscape gardener** jardinier *m*, -ière *f* paysagiste **▸ landscape gardening** jardinage *m* paysagiste, paysagisme *m* **▸ landscape mode:** (*Comput*) **to print sth in landscape mode** imprimer qch à l'italienne **▸ landscape painter** paysagiste *m*.

landscaping [ˈlændˌskeɪpɪŋ] **n** (*NonC*) aménagements paysagers.

landslide [ˈlændˌslaɪd] **1 n** glissement *m* de terrain; (*loose rocks etc*) éboulement *m*; (*fig Pol: also* **~ victory**) victoire *f* écrasante. **to win by a ~, to have a ~ victory** remporter une victoire écrasante; **~ majority** majorité écrasante. **2 vi** (*US Pol*) remporter une victoire électorale écrasante.

landward [ˈlændwəd] **1 adj** (situé *or* dirigé) du côté de la terre. **~ breeze** brise *f* de mer; **~ side** côté terre. **2 adv** (*also* **~s**) vers *or* en direction de la terre, vers l'intérieur.

lane [leɪn] **1 n a** (*in country*) chemin *m*, petite route; (*in town*) ruelle *f*.

b (*Aut*) (*part of road*) voie *f*; (*line of traffic*) file *f*. **"keep in ~"** "ne changez pas de file"; **"get into ~"** "mettez-vous dans *or* sur la bonne file"; **to take the left-hand ~** emprunter la voie de gauche, rouler sur la file de gauche; **3-~ road** route *f* à 3 voies; **I'm in the wrong ~** je suis dans *or* sur la mauvaise file; **traffic was reduced to a single ~** on ne circulait plus que sur une seule file; *see* **near** *etc.*

c (*for aircraft, ships, runners, swimmers*) couloir *m*. **air/shipping ~** couloir aérien/de navigation.

2 comp ▸ lane closure (*Aut*) fermeture *f* de voie(s) de circulation; **there'll be lane closures on the M1** certaines voies seront fermées à la circulation sur la M1 **▸ lane markings** signalisation horizontale.

langlauf [ˈlɑːŋˌlaʊf] **n** (*Ski*) ski *m* de fond. **~ specialist** fondeur *m*, -euse *f*; **~ skier** skieur *m*, -euse *f* de fond.

language [ˈlæŋgwɪdʒ] **1 n a** (*national etc tongue*) langue *f*. **the French ~** la langue française; **modern ~s** langues vivantes; **he studies ~s** il fait des (études de) langues; *see* **dead, source** *etc.*

b (*NonC*) (*means of communication; specialized terminology; way of expressing things; also Comput*) langage *m*; (*abstract linguistic system*) langue *f*. **the origin of ~** l'origine *f* du langage; **a child's use of ~** le langage de l'enfant, la façon dont l'enfant se sert du langage; **the ~ of birds/mathematics/flowers** le langage des oiseaux/des mathématiques/des fleurs; (*Ling*) **~, speaking and speech** la langue, la parole et le langage; (*Ling*) **speaking is one aspect of ~** la parole est l'un des aspects du langage; **he is studying ~** il fait de la linguistique; **scientific/legal ~** langage scientifique/juridique; (*fig*) **they do not speak the same ~** ils ne parlent pas le même langage; **try to express it in your own ~** essayez d'exprimer cela en votre propre langage *or* en vous servant de vos propres mots; **the formal ~ of official documents** le langage conventionnel des documents officiels; **bad** *or* **strong ~** gros mots, grossièretés *fpl*; **that's no ~ to use to your mother!** on ne parle pas comme ça à sa mère!; **(watch your) ~!** surveille ton langage!; *see* **machine, sign.**

2 comp *studies, textbooks, department* de langues; *students, degree* en langues; *development* linguistique; *ability* à s'exprimer, de communication **▸ language laboratory, language lab*** laboratoire *m* de langues; (*Scol, Univ etc*) **language lab training** *or* **practice** entraînement *m* en cabines.

languid ['læŋgwɪd] adj languissant.

languidly ['læŋgwɪdlɪ] adv languissamment.

languidness ['læŋgwɪdnɪs] n langueur *f*.

languish ['læŋgwɪʃ] vi (*gen*) (se) languir (*for, over* après); (*in prison*) se morfondre, dépérir.

languishing ['læŋgwɪʃɪŋ] adj languissant, langoureux.

languor ['læŋgəʳ] n langueur *f*.

languorous ['læŋgərəs] adj langoureux, alangui.

lank [læŋk] adj *hair* raide et terne; *grass, plant* long (*f* longue) et grêle.

lanky ['læŋkɪ] adj grand et maigre, dégingandé.

lanolin ['lænəʊlɪn] n lanoline *f*.

lantern ['læntən] 1 n (*all senses*) lanterne *f*; (*in paper*) lanterne vénitienne, lampion *m*; *see* **Chinese, magic.** 2 comp ▸**lantern-jawed** aux joues creuses ▸**lantern slide** plaque *f* de lanterne magique.

lanthanum ['lænθənəm] n lanthane *m*.

lanyard ['lænjəd] n (*gen, Mil*) cordon *m*; (*Naut*) ride *f* (de hauban).

Lao [laʊ] npl inv Lao *mpl*.

Laos [laʊs] n Laos *m*.

Laotian ['laʊʃɪən] 1 adj laotien. 2 n a (*person*) Laotien(ne) *m(f)*. b (*Ling*) laotien *m*.

Laotze ['laʊ'tzeɪ], **Lao-tzu** ['laʊ'tsu:] n Lao-tseu *m*.

lap[1] [læp] 1 n genoux *mpl*, giron *m* (*gen hum*). **sitting on his mother's ~** assis sur les genoux de sa mère; (*fig*) **it fell right into his ~*** ça lui est tombé tout cuit dans le bec*; (*fig*) **they dropped the problem in his ~** ils lui ont laissé *or* collé* le problème (à résoudre); (*fig*) **it's in the ~ of the gods** c'est entre les mains des dieux; (*fig*) **in the ~ of luxury** dans le plus grand luxe, dans un luxe inouï. 2 comp ▸**lap and shoulder belt** (*Aut*) ceinture *f* trois points ▸**lapdog** petit chien d'appartement, chien de manchon† ▸**lap robe** (*US*) plaid *m* (pour les genoux) ▸**laptop (computer)** (ordinateur *m*) portatif *m*.

lap[2] [læp] 1 n (*Sport*) tour *m* de piste. **to run a ~** faire un tour de piste; **10-~ race** course *f* en *or* sur 10 tours; **on the 10th ~** au 10e tour; **~ of honour** tour d'honneur; (*fig*) **we're on the last ~** on a fait le plus gros *or* le plus difficile, on tient le bon bout*. 2 vt (*Sport*) *runner, car* prendre un tour d'avance sur. 3 vi (*Racing*) **the car was ~ping at 200 km/h** la voiture faisait le circuit à 200 km/h de moyenne.

lap[3] [læp] 1 vt *milk* laper. 2 vi *[waves]* clapoter (*against* contre).

▸**lap up** vt sep *milk etc* laper; (* *fig*) *compliments* accueillir *or* accepter béatement, boire comme du petit-lait*. (*fig*) **he laps up everything you say** il gobe* tout ce qu'on lui dit; (*fig*) **he fairly lapped it up** il buvait du petit-lait*.

lap[4] [læp] vt (*wrap*) enrouler (*round* autour de); envelopper (*in* de).

▸**lap over** vi *[tiles etc]* se chevaucher.

laparoscopy [,læpə'rɒskəpɪ] n laparoscopie *f*, cœlioscopie *f*.

laparotomy [,læpə'rɒtəmɪ] n laparotomie *f*.

La Paz [læ'pæz] n La Paz.

lapel [lə'pel] n revers *m* (*de veston etc*). **~ microphone, ~ mike*** micro *m* cravate.

lapidary ['læpɪdərɪ] n (*craftsman*) lapidaire *m*; (*craft*) art *m or* métier *m* du lapidaire.

lapin ['læpɪn] n (*US*) (fourrure *f or* peau *f* de) lapin *m*.

lapis lazuli ['læpɪs'læzjʊlaɪ] n (*stone*) lapis(-lazuli) *m*; (*colour*) bleu *m* lapis(-lazuli).

Lapland ['læp,lænd] n Laponie *f*.

Laplander ['læp,lændəʳ] n Lapon(ne) *m(f)*.

Lapp [læp] 1 adj lapon. 2 n a Lapon(ne) *m(f)*. b (*Ling*) lapon *m*.

lapping ['læpɪŋ] n *[waves]* clapotis *m*.

Lappish ['læpɪʃ] = **Lapp 1, 2b.**

lapse [læps] 1 n a (*fault*) faute légère, défaillance *f*; (*in behaviour*) écart *m* (de conduite). **~ of memory** trou *m* de mémoire; **~ from truth/a diet** entorse *f* à la vérité/à un régime; **a ~ into bad habits** un retour à de mauvaises habitudes; **she behaved very well, with only a few ~s** elle s'est très bien conduite, à part quelques défaillances.

b (*passage of time*) intervalle *m*. **a ~ of time** un laps de temps; **after a ~ of 10 weeks** au bout de 10 semaines, après un intervalle de 10 semaines.

c (*falling into disuse*) *[custom etc]* disparition *f*, oubli *m*; *[right, privilege]* déchéance *f*.

2 vi a (*err*) (*gen*) faire une *or* des erreur(s) passagère(s); (*morally*) faire un *or* des écart(s) (de conduite).

b (*fall gradually*) tomber (*into* dans); (*Rel*) cesser de pratiquer. **to ~ from grace** (*Rel*) perdre l'état de grâce; (*fig*) déchoir, démériter; **to ~ into bad habits** prendre de mauvaises habitudes *or* un mauvais pli; **to ~ into silence** se taire, s'enfermer dans le mutisme; **to ~ into unconsciousness** (re)perdre connaissance; **he ~d into French** il est repassé au français, il s'est remis à parler français.

c *[act, law]* devenir caduc (*f* -uque), tomber en désuétude; *[contract]* expirer, venir à expiration; *[ticket, passport]* se périmer; *[subscription]* prendre fin. **her insurance policy has ~d** sa police d'assurance est périmée *or* n'est plus valable; **his membership ~d last month** son abonnement est venu à expiration *or* a pris fin le mois dernier, il n'est plus membre depuis le mois dernier.

lapsed [læpst] adj *contract, law* caduc (*f* -uque); *ticket, passport* périmé. **a ~ Catholic** un(e) catholique qui n'est plus pratiquant(e).

lapwing ['læpwɪŋ] n vanneau *m*.

larboard ['lɑ:bəd] (*Naut* ††) 1 n bâbord *m*. 2 adj de bâbord.

larceny ['lɑ:sənɪ] n (*Jur*) vol *m* simple. (*US Jur*) **to commit ~ by servant** commanditer un vol; *see* **grand, petty.**

larch [lɑ:tʃ] n mélèze *m*.

lard [lɑ:d] 1 n saindoux *m*. 2 vt (*Culin*) larder (*with* de). (*fig*) **to ~ one's speech with quotations** truffer son discours de citations.

larder ['lɑ:dəʳ] n (*cupboard*) garde-manger *m inv*; (*small room*) cellier *m*.

large [lɑ:dʒ] 1 adj a (*in size*) *town, house, parcel* grand; *garden, room* grand, vaste; *person, animal, slice, hand* gros (*f* grosse); *sum, loss* fort, gros, important; *amount* grand, important; *family* nombreux; *population* nombreuse, important; *meal* copieux. (*Anat*) **~ intestine** gros intestin; **a ~ number of them refused** beaucoup d'entre eux ont refusé, un grand nombre parmi eux a *or* ont refusé; **~ numbers of people came** les gens sont venus nombreux *or* en grand nombre; **a ~ slice of his savings** une bonne partie de ses économies; **a ~ proportion of the business** une part importante des affaires; (*Comm: of packet, tube*) **the ~ size** le grand modèle; (*Comm*) **a ~ size/the largest size of this dress** une grande taille/la plus grande taille dans ce modèle; (*on garment labels*) "~" "grande taille"; (*fig*) **there he was (as) ~ as life** c'était lui se conduisant comme si de rien n'était; (*fig*) **~r than life** plus grand que nature; **to grow** *or* **get ~(r)** grossir, grandir, s'agrandir; **to make ~r** agrandir.

b (*extensive*) **to do sth on a ~ scale** faire qch en grand *or* sur une grande échelle (*see also* **4**); **to a ~ extent** en grande mesure; **in (a) ~ measure** en grande mesure *or* partie, dans une large mesure; (*fig*) **to have ~ views** avoir des vues larges.

2 n: **at ~** (*at liberty*) en liberté; (*as a whole*) en général, dans son ensemble; (*at length*) tout au long; (*at random*) au hasard, sans (trop) préciser; (*US Pol*) *candidate, congressman* non rattaché à une circonscription électorale; **the prisoner is still at ~** le prisonnier est toujours en liberté *or* court toujours *or* n'a pas encore été repris; **the country at ~** le pays dans son ensemble; **he treated the subject at ~** il a traité le sujet dans son ensemble; **to scatter accusations at ~** lancer des accusations au hasard; *see* **ambassador.**

3 adv: **by and ~** généralement parlant; **taking it by and ~** à tout prendre.

4 comp ▸**large-handed** (*fig*) généreux ▸**large-hearted** (*fig*) au grand cœur ▸**large-minded** (*fig*) qui a l'esprit large ▸**large-mouth bass** achigan *m* à grande bouche ▸**large-print book** livre *m* en gros caractères ▸**large-scale** *drawing, map* à grande échelle; *business activities, reforms, relations* (fait) sur une grande échelle; *powers* étendu; (*Comput*) **very large-scale integration** intégration *f* à (très) grande échelle ▸**large-size(d)** grand.

largely ['lɑ:dʒlɪ] adv (*to a great extent*) en grande mesure *or* partie, dans une large mesure; (*principally*) pour la plupart, surtout; (*in general*) en général.

largeness ['lɑ:dʒnɪs] n (*see* **large**) grande taille; grandeur *f*; grosseur *f*; importance *f*.

largesse [lɑ:'ʒes] n (*NonC*) (*generosity*) largesse *f*; (*gifts*) largesses.

largish ['lɑ:dʒɪʃ] adj (*see* **large**) assez grand; assez gros (*f* grosse); de bonne taille; assez important; assez nombreux; assez copieux.

largo ['lɑ:gəʊ] adv, n largo (*m inv*).

lariat ['lærɪət] n (*lasso*) lasso *m*; (*tether*) longe *f*.

lark[1] [lɑ:k] 1 n (*Orn*) alouette *f*. **to rise with the ~** se lever au chant du coq; *see* **happy, sing.** 2 comp ▸**larkspur** (*Bot*) pied-d'alouette *m*, delphinium *m*.

lark[2]* [lɑ:k] n blague* *f*, niche* *f*. **we only did it for a ~** on l'a seulement fait pour rigoler*, on l'a seulement fait histoire de rigoler*; **what a ~!** quelle rigolade!*, la bonne blague!*; **what do you think of this dinner jacket ~?** qu'est-ce que tu penses de cette histoire de smoking?

▸**lark about*, lark around*** vi faire le petit fou (*f* la petite folle)*. **to lark about with sth** jouer avec qch.

larky ['lɑ:kɪ] adj espiègle.

larva ['lɑ:və] n, pl **larvae** ['lɑ:vi:] larve *f* (*Zool*).

larval ['lɑ:vəl] adj larvaire (*Zool*).

laryngitis [,lærɪn'dʒaɪtɪs] n laryngite *f*.

larynx ['lærɪŋks] n, pl **~es** *or* **larynges** [lə'rɪndʒi:z] larynx *m*.

lasagna, lasagne [lə'zænjə] n lasagne *f inv*.

lascivious [lə'sɪvɪəs] adj lascif, luxurieux.

lasciviously [lə'sɪvɪəslɪ] adv lascivement.

lasciviousness [lə'sɪvɪəsnɪs] n luxure *f*, lasciveté *f or* lascivité *f*.

laser ['leɪzəʳ] 1 n laser *m*. 2 comp ▸**laser beam** rayon *m* laser *inv* ▸**laser disk** disque *m* laser *inv* ▸**laser-guided** guidé par laser ▸**laser printer** (*Comput*) imprimante *f* à laser ▸**laser surgery** chirurgie *f* au laser ▸**laser weapon** arme *f* laser *inv*.

lash [læʃ] 1 n a (*thong*) mèche *f*, lanière *f*; (*blow from whip*) coup *m* de fouet. **sentenced to 10 ~es** condamné à 10 coups de fouet; (*fig*) **to feel the ~ of sb's tongue** essuyer les propos cinglants de qn; *see* **whip.**

b (*also* **eye~**) cil *m*.

2 vt a (*beat*) frapper (d'un grand coup de fouet), fouetter

violemment, cingler; (*flog*) flageller. (*fig*) **to ~ sb with one's tongue** faire des remarques cinglantes à qn; (*fig*) **to ~ o.s. into a fury** s'emporter violemment; (*fig*) **the wind ~ed the sea into a fury** le vent a déchaîné *or* démonté la mer; **the sea ~es (against) the cliffs** la mer bat *or* fouette les falaises; **the hailstones ~ed (against) my face** la grêle me cinglait le visage; **the rain was ~ing (at *or* against) the windows** la pluie fouettait *or* cinglait les carreaux; **the crocodile ~ed its tail** le crocodile a donné de grands coups de queue; **the lion ~ed its tail** le lion a fouetté l'air de sa queue.

b (*fasten*) attacher *or* fixer fermement; *cargo* arrimer; *load* attacher, amarrer. **to ~ sth to a post** attacher solidement qch à un piquet.

3 **vi**: **to ~ against** *or* **at** *see* **2a**.

▸**lash about vi** (*in bonds, in pain etc*) se débattre violemment.

▸**lash down** 1 **vi** [*rain*] tomber avec violence. 2 **vt sep** *cargo* amarrer, arrimer.

▸**lash out** 1 **vi** a **to lash out at sb** (*with fists*) envoyer un *or* de violent(s) coup(s) de poing à qn; (*with feet*) envoyer un *or* de violent(s) coup(s) de pied à qn; (*with both*) jouer violemment des pieds et des poings contre qn; (*fig: verbally*) se répandre en invectives contre qn, fustiger qn (*liter*). b (*: *spend a lot of money*) les lâcher*, les allonger*. **he lashed out and bought a car** il a lâché le paquet* et s'est payé une voiture; **now we can really lash out** maintenant on peut les faire valser*. 2 **vt sep** (*) *money* lâcher*, allonger*.

▸**lash up vt sep** attacher, amarrer, arrimer.

lashing ['læʃɪŋ] **n** a (*flogging*) flagellation *f*. **to give sb a ~** (*lit*) donner le fouet à qn; (*fig: verbally*) faire de vertes réprimandes à qn, tancer vertement qn. b (*rope*) corde *f*; (*Naut*) amarre *f*. c (*: *esp Brit: a lot*) **~s of** des tas de*, des masses de*; **with ~s of cream** avec des masses* *or* une montagne de crème.

lass [læs] **n** (*esp Scot and dial: girl*) jeune fille *f*; (††: *sweetheart*) bonne amie†.

Lassa fever ['læsə'fiːvəʳ] **n** fièvre *f* de Lassa.

lassie ['læsɪ] **n** (*esp Scot and dial*) gamine* *f*, gosse* *f*.

lassitude ['læsɪtjuːd] **n** lassitude *f*.

lasso [læ'suː] 1 **n, pl ~s** *or* **~es** a (*rope*) lasso *m*. b (*Climbing*) = **lassoing.** 2 **vt** prendre au lasso.

lassoing [læ'suːɪŋ] **n** (*Climbing*) lancer *m* de corde.

last¹ [lɑːst] 1 **adj** a (*in series*) dernier (*before n*). **the ~ Saturday of the month** le dernier samedi du mois; **the ~ 10 pages** les 10 dernières pages; **~ but one, second ~** avant-dernier, pénultième; **the ~ time but one** l'avant-dernière fois; **it's the ~ round but 3** il y a encore *or* il n'y a plus que 3 rounds après celui-ci; **his office is the second ~** son bureau est l'avant-dernier; **the third and ~ point is that ...** le troisième et dernier point est que ...; **to fight to the ~ man** se battre jusqu'au dernier; *see* **every**.

b (*past, most recent*) dernier (*usu after n*). **~ night** (*evening*) hier soir; (*night*) cette nuit, la nuit dernière; **~ week/year** la semaine/l'année dernière *or* passée; **~ month/summer** le mois/l'été dernier *or* passé; **~ Monday, on Monday ~** lundi dernier; **for the ~ few days** ces derniers jours, ces jours-ci, dernièrement; **for the ~ few weeks** ces dernières semaines, dernièrement; **he hasn't been seen these ~ 2 years** on ne l'a pas vu ces 2 dernières années; **for the ~ 2 years** depuis 2 ans; **the day before ~** avant-hier *m*; **the night/morning before ~** avant-hier soir/matin; **the week before ~** l'avant-dernière semaine; **what did you do ~ time?** qu'avez-vous fait la dernière fois?; **he was rather ill (the) ~ time I saw him** il était plutôt malade la dernière fois que je l'ai vu; **this time ~ year** (*last year about this time*) l'an dernier à pareille époque *or* à cette époque-ci; (*a year ago today*) il y a un an aujourd'hui.

c (*final*) *chance, hope* dernier. (*lit, fig*) **to fight to the ~ ditch** se battre dans ses derniers retranchements (*see also* **4**); **at one's ~ gasp** (*dying*) sur le point de mourir, à l'agonie; (*: *exhausted*) à bout; **he was on his ~ legs*** il était à bout; **the company is on its ~ legs*** la compagnie est au bord de la faillite; **the washing machine is on its ~ legs*** la machine à laver va bientôt nous lâcher* *or* rendre l'âme*; **at the ~ minute** à la dernière minute (*see also* **4**); (*Brit: bugle call*) **~ post** (sonnerie *f* de) l'extinction *f* des feux; (*at funerals*) sonnerie *f* aux morts; **in the ~ resort** *or* **resource** en dernier ressort, en désespoir de cause; (*Rel*) **~ rites** les derniers sacrements; (*Rel*) **L~ Supper** Cène *f*; **~ thing at night** juste avant de se coucher; **I'll get it, if it's the ~ thing I do** je l'aurai coûte que coûte *or* même si ça doit me coûter la vie; **for the ~ time, shut up!** pour la dernière fois, tais-toi!; **that was the ~ time I saw him** c'est la dernière fois que je l'ai vu; **that's the ~ time I lend you anything!** c'est la dernière fois que je te prête quelque chose; (*Rel*) **~ trump** *or* **trumpet** trompettes *fpl* du Jugement dernier; (*Rel*) **at the L~ Judgment** au Jugement dernier; **she always wants to have the ~ word** elle veut toujours avoir le dernier mot; **it's the ~ word in comfort** c'est ce que l'on fait de mieux *or* c'est le dernier cri en matière de confort; **I'm down to my ~ pound note** je n'ai plus *or* il ne me reste plus qu'une seule livre; *see* **degree, first, laugh, stand, straw** *etc*.

d (*least likely or desirable*) dernier. **he's the ~ person to ask** c'est la dernière personne à qui demander; **that's the ~ thing to worry about** c'est le dernier *or* le moindre *or* le cadet de mes (*or* tes *etc*) soucis.

2 **adv** a (*at the end*) en dernier. **she arrived ~** elle est arrivée en dernier *or* la dernière; **he arrived ~ of all** il est arrivé le tout dernier; **his horse came in ~** son cheval est arrivé (bon) dernier; **and ~ but not least** et en dernier mais non par ordre d'importance; **~ in, first out** dernier entré, premier sorti; **to leave sth/sb till ~** placer qch/qn en dernier *or* à la fin.

b (*most recently*) la dernière fois. **when I ~ saw him** quand je l'ai vu la dernière fois, la dernière fois que je l'ai vu; (*Cards*) **who dealt ~?** qui a donné en dernier?

c (*finally*) finalement, pour terminer. **~, I would like to say ...** pour terminer *or* enfin je voudrais dire ... .

3 **n** a dernier *m*, -ière *f*. **he was the ~ of the Tudors** ce fut lui le dernier des Tudors; **this is the ~ of the pears** (*one*) voici la dernière poire; (*several*) voici les dernières poires, voici le reste des poires; **this is the ~ of the cider** voici le reste du cidre, voici tout ce qui reste de *or* comme cidre; **the ~ but one** l'avant-dernier *m*, -ière *f*, le *or* la pénultième; **I'd be the ~ to criticize, but ...** bien que je sois le dernier à faire des critiques ..., j'ai horreur de critiquer, mais ...; **each one better than the ~** tous meilleurs les uns que les autres; **~ in, first out** dernier entré, premier sorti.

b (*phrases*) **at ~** enfin, à la fin; **at (long) ~** enfin; **at long ~ he came** il a enfin fini par arriver; **here he is! — at ~!** le voici! — enfin! *or* ce n'est pas trop tôt!; **to the ~** jusqu'au bout, jusqu'à la fin; **that was the ~ I saw of him** c'est la dernière fois que je l'ai vu, je ne l'ai pas revu depuis; **we shall never hear the ~ of this** on n'a pas fini d'en entendre parler; **you haven't heard the ~ of this!** vous n'avez pas fini d'en entendre parler!; (*threatening*) vous aurez de mes nouvelles! (*fig*); **the ~ I heard (of her), she was abroad** aux dernières nouvelles (que j'ai eues d'elle), elle était à l'étranger; **I shall be glad to see the ~ of this** je serai content de voir tout ceci terminé *or* de voir la fin de tout ceci *or* d'en avoir fini avec tout ceci; **we were glad to see the ~ of him** nous avons été contents de le voir partir *or* d'être débarrassés de lui; *see* **breathe.**

4 **comp** ▸**last-ditch adj** désespéré, ultime ▸**last-minute adj** de dernière minute.

last² [lɑːst] 1 **vi** a (*continue*) [*pain, film, supplies etc*] durer. **it's too good to ~** c'est trop beau pour durer *or* pour que ça dure (*subj*); **will this good weather ~ till Saturday?** est-ce que le beau temps va durer *or* tenir jusqu'à samedi?; **it ~ed 2 hours** cela a duré deux heures.

b (*hold out*) tenir. **no one ~s long in this job** personne ne reste longtemps dans ce poste; **after he got pneumonia he didn't ~ long** après sa pneumonie il n'en a pas eu pour longtemps*; **that whisky didn't ~ long** ce whisky n'a pas fait long feu *or* n'a pas duré longtemps.

c (*esp Comm: remain usable*) durer. **this table will ~ a lifetime** cette table vous fera toute une vie; **will this material ~?** ce tissu fera-t-il de l'usage?; **made to ~** fait pour durer.

2 **vt** durer. **this amount should ~ you (for) a week** cela devrait vous durer *or* vous faire huit jours; **the car ~ed me 8 years** la voiture m'a fait *or* duré 8 ans; **I have enough money to ~ me a lifetime** l'argent que j'ai me fera bien *or* me conduira bien jusqu'à la fin de mes jours; **she must have got enough chocolates to ~ her a lifetime** elle a dû recevoir des chocolats pour jusqu'à la fin de ses jours.

▸**last out** 1 **vi** [*person*] tenir (le coup); [*money*] suffire. 2 **vt sep** faire. **he won't last the winter out** il ne passera pas *or* ne fera pas l'hiver, il ne verra pas la fin de l'hiver; **my money doesn't last out the month** mon argent ne me fait pas le mois.

last³ [lɑːst] **n** [*cobbler*] forme *f*.

Lastex ['lasteks] **n** ® (*US*) Lastex *m* ®.

lasting ['lɑːstɪŋ] **adj** *benefit, friendship, good, peace* durable. **to his ~ shame** à sa plus grande honte.

lastly ['lɑːstlɪ] **adv** (enfin) pour terminer, en dernier lieu.

latch [lætʃ] 1 **n** clenche *f*, loquet *m*. **the door is on the ~** la porte n'est pas fermée à clef; **to leave the door on the ~** fermer la porte sans la verrouiller; **~key** clef *f* (de la porte d'entrée); **~key child** enfant *mf* à la clé (*qui rentre à la maison avant ses parents qui travaillent*). 2 **vt** fermer au loquet.

▸**latch on* vi** a (*grab*) s'accrocher (*to* à). b (*understand*) saisir, piger‡.

▸**latch on to* vt fus** a (*get possession of*) prendre possession de; (*catch hold of*) saisir; (*US: obtain*) se procurer. **he latched on to me as soon as I arrived** il s'est accroché *or* collé* à moi dès que je suis arrivé; **he latches on to the slightest mistake** il ne laisse pas passer la moindre erreur. b (*understand*) saisir, piger‡; (*realize*) se rendre compte de, réaliser*.

late [leɪt] 1 **adj** a (*not on time*) en retard. **to be ~** (*gen*) être en retard; (*arriving*) arriver en retard; **I'm ~** (*gen*) je suis en retard; (*menstrual period*) mes règles sont en retard; **I was ~ again yesterday** je suis de nouveau arrivé en retard hier; **I'm ~ for work/school** je ne serai pas au travail/à l'école (*or* au lycée *etc*) à l'heure; **I was ~ for work/an appointment** je suis arrivé au travail/à un rendez-vous en retard; **I'm a week ~** (*gen*) j'ai une semaine de retard; (*menstrual period*) mes règles ont une semaine de retard; **I'm/I was 2 hours ~ for work** je vais arriver/je suis arrivé au travail avec deux heures de retard; **he was ~ 4 times** il est arrivé 4 fois en retard; **to make sb ~** retarder qn, mettre qn en retard; **it made me an hour ~** j'ai eu une heure de retard à cause de ça; **the train is ~** le train est en retard *or* a du retard; **the train is 30 minutes ~** le train a trente minutes de retard; **your essay is ~** vous rendez votre dissertation en retard; **to be ~ in arriving** arriver avec du retard *or* en retard; **to be ~ with payments** avoir des paiements en retard *or* des arriérés; (*Scol*) **to get a ~ mark** avoir un retard; **spring was ~** le printemps était en retard *or* était tardif; **his ~ arrival** le fait qu'il est arrivé en retard; **we apologize for the ~ arrival of flight XY 709** nous vous prions d'excuser le retard du vol XY 709; **~ arrivals must sit at the back** les gens (qui arrivent) en retard doivent s'asseoir au fond; (*Scol*) **he's a ~ developer** (*gen*) il s'est développé sur le tard; (*academically*) il a été lent à s'épanouir.

b (*far on in day, season etc*) *delivery, edition, performance* dernier. **to have a ~ meal** manger tard; **~ hours** heures avancées *or* tardives; **to keep ~ hours** veiller tard, être un(e) couche-tard *inv*; **at this ~ hour** à cette heure tardive; **at this ~ stage** à ce stade avancé; **at a ~r stage in the discussions** à une étape plus avancée des discussions; **Easter is ~ this year** Pâques est tard cette année; **in ~ October** vers la fin (du mois) d'octobre, fin octobre; **in the ~ afternoon** en fin d'après-midi, vers la fin de l'après-midi; **~ opening Wednesdays until 10 p.m.** nocturne tous les mercredis soirs jusqu'à 22 heures; **the shop stays open ~ twice a week** le magasin reste ouvert tard le soir *or* est ouvert en nocturne 2 fois par semaine; **he is in his ~ sixties** il est plus près de soixante-dix ans que de soixante, il approche des soixante-dix ans; **in the ~ 1920s** vers la fin des années 1920; **in ~r life** plus tard dans la vie; **in his ~r years** vers la fin de sa vie, dans ses dernières années; **one of his ~(r) symphonies** une de ses dernières symphonies; **at a ~r date** à une date ultérieure; **we'll discuss it at a ~r meeting** nous en discuterons au cours d'une réunion ultérieure; **at a ~r meeting they decided** au cours d'une réunion qui eut lieu plus tard ils décidèrent; (*Press*) **a ~r edition** une édition postérieure *or* plus tardive (*see also* **1d**); **a ~r train** un train plus tard; **the ~r train** le deuxième train; **the latest time you may come is 4 o'clock** l'heure limite à laquelle vous pouvez arriver est 4 heures; **when *or* what is the latest you can come?** quand pouvez-vous venir, au plus tard?; **I'll be there by noon at the latest** j'y serai à midi au plus tard; **give me your essay by noon at the latest** rendez-moi votre dissertation à midi dernier délai *or* dernière limite *or* au plus tard; **the latest time for doing it is April** c'est en avril dernière limite qu'il faut le faire; **the latest date he could do it was 31st July** la dernière date à laquelle il pouvait le faire était le 31 juillet; **the latest date for applications** la date limite de dépôt de candidatures.

c (*former*) ancien (*before n*). **the ~ Prime Minister** l'ancien Premier ministre, l'ex-Premier ministre.

d (*recent*) **a ~r edition** une édition plus récente; **the latest edition** la dernière (édition); **the latest fashion** la dernière mode; **the latest news** les dernières nouvelles; (*Rad, TV*) **the latest news (bulletin)** les dernières informations; **of ~** récemment, dernièrement, ces derniers temps; **this version is ~r than that one** cette version est postérieure à celle-là *or* plus récente que celle-là; **this is the latest in a series of murders** c'est le dernier en date d'une série de meurtres; **his latest statement** sa dernière déclaration (en date).

e (*dead*) **the ~ Mr Black** feu M. Black; **our ~ colleague** notre regretté (*frm*) *or* défunt (*frm*) *or* pauvre collègue.

2 adv a (*not on time*) *arrive etc* en retard. **even ~r** encore plus en retard; **he arrived 10 minutes ~** il est arrivé dix minutes en retard *or* avec dix minutes de retard; (*Prov*) **better ~ than never** mieux vaut tard que jamais (*Prov*).

b (*far into day etc*) *get up etc* tard. **to work ~ at the office** rester tard au bureau pour travailler; **it's getting ~** il se fait tard; **~ at night** tard le soir; **~ into the night** tard dans la nuit; **~ in the afternoon** tard dans l'après-midi, vers la fin de l'après-midi; **~ in 1960** vers la fin de 1960, fin 1960; **~ in the year** tard dans l'année, vers la fin de l'année; **he decided ~ in life to become ...** sur le tard il a décidé de devenir ...; **2 weeks ~r** 2 semaines après *or* plus tard; **~r on** plus tard; (*fig*) **it is rather ~ in the day to change your mind** c'est un peu tard pour changer d'avis; (*fig*) **it was her intervention, ~ in the day, that saved the scheme** ce fut son intervention, assez tardive, qui sauva le projet; **not *or* no ~r than** (*gen*) pas plus tard que; **essays must be handed in not ~r than Monday morning** les dissertations devront être remises lundi matin dernier délai *or* dernière limite *or* au plus tard; **see you ~r!*** à tout à l'heure!, à plus tard!; (*when interrupted etc*) **~r!** tout à l'heure!

c (*recently*) **as ~ as last week** pas plus tard que la semaine dernière, la semaine dernière encore; **as ~ as 1950** en 1950 encore.

d (*formerly*) **Mr Colin, ~ of Paris** M. Colin, autrefois domicilié à Paris; **Acacia Avenue, ~ North Street** Acacia Avenue, anciennement North Street; **Smith, ~ of the Diplomatic Service** Smith, ancien membre du corps diplomatique.

3 comp ▸ **latecomer** (*lit*) retardataire *mf*; (*fig*) **he is a latecomer to politics** c'est un tard venu *or* il est venu tard à la politique ▸ **late-night opening** (*or* **show** *or* **session**) (*Comm etc*) nocturne *f*; **there's late-night opening *or* shopping on Thursdays** le magasin ouvre en nocturne le jeudi; **there's a late-night show/film on Saturdays** le théâtre/le cinéma est ouvert en nocturne le samedi.

lateen [lə'tiːn] n (*also* **~ sail**) voile *f* latine.

lately ['leɪtlɪ] adv (*recently*) dernièrement, récemment; (*these last few days*) ces jours-ci, ces derniers jours. **it's only ~ that** c'est seulement récemment que *or* depuis peu que; **till ~** jusqu'à ces de

latency ['leɪtənsɪ] n (*Med*) latence *f*.

lateness ['leɪtnɪs] n a (*not being on time*) *[person, ve* **punished for persistent ~** puni pour retards trop fréquent **the hour prevented us from going** vu l'heure tardive *or* a n'avons pas pu y aller; **the ~ of the concert lets us dine** tardive du concert nous permet de dîner avant.

latent ['leɪtənt] adj latent. (*Jur*) **~ defect** vice *m* caché; (*Med* période *f* de latence; (*Phys*) **~ heat** chaleur latente.

later ['leɪtər] adj, adv, compar of **late**.

lateral ['lætərəl] adj latéral (*also Ling*). **~ thinking** la pensée lat

laterally ['lætərəlɪ] adv latéralement.

latest ['leɪtɪst] 1 adj, adv, superl of **late**. 2 n (**: news*) **have you the ~?** tu connais la dernière?*; **what's the ~ on this affair?** qu'y de nouveau sur cette affaire?; (*Rad, TV*) **for the ~ on the riots, ove Ian** pour les dernières informations sur les émeutes, à vous, Ian; (*g friend*) **have you seen his ~?** tu as vu sa nouvelle?*; (*joke*) **have y heard his ~?** tu connais sa dernière?*; (*exploit*) **did you hear about h ~?** on t'a raconté son dernier exploit? *or* sa dernière prouesse? (*iro*).

latex ['leɪteks] n, pl **~es** *or* **latices** ['lætɪˌsiːz] latex *m*.

lath [lɑːθ] n, pl **~s** [lɑːðz] (*Constr*) latte *f*; *[Venetian blind]* lame *f*.

lathe [leɪð] n (*Tech*) tour *m*; *see* **capstan, power** *etc*.

lather ['lɑːðər] 1 n a *[soap]* mousse *f* (de savon). b (*sweat*) *[horse]* écume *f*. **in a ~** *horse* couvert d'écume; *person* (**: perspiring*) en nage; (*fig* ‡*: nervous, anxious*) agité, dans tous ses états. 2 vt a *one's face etc* savonner. b (**: thrash*) rosser*, tanner (le cuir à)‡. 3 vi *[soap]* mousser.

latifundia [ˌlætɪ'fʊndɪə] npl latifundia *mpl*.

Latin ['lætɪn] 1 adj (*Ling*) *text, poet* latin; *people, temperament* (*European*) latin, (*in US*) latino-américain. **~ quarter** quartier latin; (*US*) **~ school** ≃ lycée *m* classique. 2 comp ▸ **Latin-America** Amérique latine ▸ **Latin-American** adj latino-américain, d'Amérique latine ◊ n Latino-Américain(e) *m(f)*. 3 n a Latin(e) *m(f)*; (*in US*) Latino-Américain(e) *m(f)*. b (*Ling*) latin *m*. **late ~** latin décadent; **low ~** bas latin; **vulgar ~** latin vulgaire.

Latinist ['lætɪnɪst] n latiniste *mf*.

Latinization [ˌlætɪnaɪ'zeɪʃən] n latinisation *f*.

Latinize ['lætɪnaɪz] vt latiniser.

Latino-American [læ'tiːnəʊə'merɪkən] 1 adj latino-américain. 2 n (*US*) Latino-Américain(e) *m(f)*.

latish ['leɪtɪʃ] 1 adj *hour* assez avancé, assez tardif. **it's getting ~** il commence à se faire assez tard. 2 adv assez tard, plutôt tard.

latitude ['lætɪtjuːd] n a (*Geog*) latitude *f*. **at a ~ of 48° north** à *or* par 48° de latitude Nord; **in these ~s** à *or* sous ces latitudes. b (*NonC: freedom*) latitude *f*.

latitudinal [ˌlætɪ'tjuːdɪnl] adj latitudinal.

latrine [lə'triːn] n latrine(s) *f(pl)* (*gen pl*).

latter ['lætər] 1 adj a (*second*) deuxième, dernier (*both before n*). **the ~ proposition was accepted** cette dernière *or* la deuxième proposition fut acceptée.

b (*later*) dernier, deuxième (*both before n*). **the ~ half** la deuxième moitié; **the ~ half of the month** la deuxième quinzaine du mois; **the ~ part of the evening was quite pleasant** la fin de la soirée a été assez agréable; **in the ~ part of the century** vers la fin du siècle; **in the ~ years of his life, in his ~ years** dans les dernières années de sa vie, tard dans sa vie.

2 n: **the ~ is the more expensive of the two systems** ce dernier système est le plus coûteux des deux; **of these two books the former is expensive but the ~ is not** le premier de ces deux livres est cher mais le second *or* le deuxième ne l'est pas, de ces deux livres celui-là est cher mais celui-ci ne l'est pas.

3 comp ▸ **latter-day** moderne, d'aujourd'hui ▸ **Latter-Day Saints** (*Rel*) Saints *mpl* des Derniers Jours (*Mormons*).

latterly ['lætəlɪ] adv a (*recently*) dernièrement, récemment, depuis quelque temps. b (*towards the end of a period*) vers la fin, sur le tard. **he was a farmer but ~ became a writer** il était cultivateur mais devint écrivain sur le tard.

lattice ['lætɪs] 1 n treillis *m*; (*fence*) treillage *m*, claire-voie *f*; (*climbing-plant frame*) treillage. 2 comp ▸ **lattice girder** poutre *f* à treillis ▸ **lattice window** fenêtre treillissée ▸ **lattice work** treillis *m*.

latticed ['lætɪst] adj *window* treillissé; *fence, wall* treillagé.

Latvia ['lætvɪə] n Lettonie *f*.

Latvian ['lætvɪən] 1 adj lette, letton (*f* -one *or* -onne). **~ SSR** RSS *f* de Lettonie. 2 n a Lette *mf*, Letton *m*, Letton(n)e *f*, Latvien(ne) *m(f)*. b (*Ling*) lette *m*, letton *m*.

laud [lɔːd] vt (*liter*) louanger (*liter*); (*Rel*) louer, glorifier, chanter les louanges de.

laudable ['lɔːdəbl] adj louable, digne de louanges.

laudably ['lɔːdəblɪ] adv de manière louable *or* méritoire. **he was ~ calm** son calme était digne de louanges.

laudanum ['lɔːdnəm] n laudanum *m*.

laudatory ['lɔːdətərɪ] adj élogieux.

laugh [lɑːf] 1 n (*brief*) éclat *m* de rire; (*longer*) rire *m*. **with a ~** (*brief*) dans un éclat de rire; (*longer*) en riant; **with a scornful ~** avec

or **laugh a scornful ~** rire
~ il a un rire très
…nt c'est lui qui a bien
… qui rira le dernier; **to**
… qn; **to have a good ~ at**
… **got a ~** cela a fait rire; **if**
… tu veux t'amuser *or* rigoler*
…**ne ~ is on you*** c'est toi qui fais
… **~!*** ça, c'est marrant!*; (*iro*)
… rigoler!*; **just for a ~, for ~s*** rien
…**t was** *or* **we had a good ~** on a bien ri,
a (good) ~ il aime bien rire *or* s'amuser;
… nous fera toujours bien rire; **he's a good**
… amusant, on s'amuse bien avec lui; *see* **play,**

…e (*punchline of joke*) phrase-clef *f* qui fait rire;
d'expression ▶**laugh track** (*US Rad, TV*) (bande *f*
…nregistrés.

~ at a joke rire d'une plaisanterie; **he was so amusing** … **them all ~ing at him** il était si drôle que bientôt tous …ses plaisanteries (*see also* **laugh at**); **to ~ about** *or* **over sth** …ch; **there's nothing to ~ about** *or* **at** il n'y a pas de quoi rire; …**ut loud** rire tout haut, rire ouvertement; **to ~ inwardly** rire …ieurement; **he ~ed to himself** il a ri dans sa barbe *or* en lui-même; **~ed until he cried** il riait aux larmes, il pleurait de rire; **she was ~ing fit to burst*** elle riait comme une baleine*, elle riait à se faire mal aux côtes* *or* à en crever*; **he (nearly) split his sides ~ing** il se tordait de rire; (*Prov*) **he who ~s last ~s longest** rira bien qui rira le dernier (*Prov*); **to ~ in sb's face** rire au nez de qn; **he'll soon be ~ing on the other side of his face** il n'aura bientôt plus envie de rire, il va bientôt rire jaune; **I'll make you ~ on the other side of your face!** je vais t'apprendre à rire!; **he's ~ing all the way to the bank*** il n'a pas de problèmes de compte en banque!; (*fig*) **to ~ up one's sleeve** rire sous cape; *[man]* rire dans sa barbe; **it's all very well for you to ~!** tu peux toujours rire!; **he makes me ~*** il me fait rire; (*iro*) **don't make me ~*** laisse-moi rire, ne me fais pas rire; (*philosophical*) **you've got to** *or* **you have to ~*** il vaut mieux en rire; **it's all right for him, he's ~ing*** lui il s'en fiche*, il est tranquille *or* il est peinard*; **once we get this contract signed we're ~ing*** une fois ce contrat signé, on est tranquille *or* on tient le bon bout; *see* **burst out.**

4 **vt: he ~ed a jolly laugh** il eut un rire jovial; **they ~ed him to scorn** ils l'ont tourné en dérision; **his brothers ~ed him out of that idea** ses frères se sont tant moqués de lui qu'il a abandonné cette idée; (*fig*) **to ~ sb/sth out of court** tourner qn/qch en ridicule; **he ~ed himself silly*** il a ri comme un bossu* *or* comme une baleine*.

▶**laugh at vt fus** (*lit*) *person, sb's behaviour* rire de, se moquer de; (*fig*) *difficulty, danger* se rire de.

▶**laugh down vt sep: they laughed the speaker down** leurs moqueries ont réduit l'orateur au silence.

▶**laugh off vt sep** a **to ~ one's head off*** rire comme un fou *or* comme une baleine*. b *accusation* écarter d'une plaisanterie *or* d'une boutade. **to laugh off an embarrassing situation** se tirer d'une situation embarrassante par une boutade *or* par une plaisanterie; **she managed to laugh it off** elle a réussi à tourner la chose en plaisanterie; **you can't laugh this one off** cette fois tu ne t'en tireras pas par la plaisanterie.

laughable [ˈlɑːfəbl] **adj** *suggestion* ridicule, dérisoire; *amount* dérisoire. **it is ~ to hope that …** il est ridicule d'espérer que … .

laughing [ˈlɑːfɪŋ] **adj** riant, rieur. **this is no ~ matter** il n'y a pas de quoi rire; **I'm in no ~ mood** (*angry*) je ne suis pas d'humeur à rire; (*sad*) je n'ai pas le cœur à rire; **~ gas** gaz hilarant; (*Zool*) **~ hyena** hyène *f* (*africaine*); (*Orn*) **~ jackass** dacélo *m*; **he was the ~ stock of the class** il était la risée de la classe; **he made himself a ~ stock** il s'est couvert de ridicule.

laughingly [ˈlɑːfɪŋlɪ] **adv** *say etc* en riant. **it is ~ called …** l'ironie de la chose, c'est qu'on l'appelle … .

laughter [ˈlɑːftəʳ] 1 **n** (*NonC*) rire(s) *m(pl)*. **~ is good for you** cela fait du bien de rire; **at this there was ~** à ces mots il y a eu des rires *or* des rires ont fusé; **he said amid ~ that …** il dit au milieu des *or* parmi les rires que …; **their ~ could be heard in the next room** on les entendait rire dans la pièce à côté; **to roar with ~** rire aux éclats; **to burst into ~** éclater de rire; *see* **can²**. 2 **comp** ▶**laughter line** (*Brit: on face*) ride *f* d'expression.

launch [lɔːntʃ] 1 **n** a (*also* **motor ~**) (*for patrol duties etc*) vedette *f*, canot *m* automobile; (*pleasure boat*) bateau *m* de plaisance. **police ~** vedette de la police.

b (*boat carried by warship*) chaloupe *f*.

c *[ship, spacecraft, product]* lancement *m*; *see* **window.**

2 **comp** ▶**launch pad** (*Space*) = **launching pad** ▶**launch vehicle** (*Space*) fusée *f* de lancement.

3 **vt** *ship, satellite, missile, company* lancer; *shore lifeboat etc* faire sortir; *ship's boat* mettre à la mer; *product* lancer; *scheme, plan* mettre en action *or* en vigueur; *attack, offensive* lancer, déclencher. (*Fin*) **to ~ a share issue** émettre des actions, faire une émission d'actions; **to ~ sb on a career** lancer qn dans une carrière; **it would take £10,000 to ~ him as an architect** il faudrait 10 000 livres pour le lancer comme architecte; **once he is ~ed on this subject you can't stop him** une fois qu'il est lancé sur ce sujet on ne peut plus l'arrêter.

4 **vi** (*fig: also* **~ forth**) se lancer (*into, on* dans).

▶**launch forth vi** = **launch 4.**

▶**launch out vi** *[business, company]* se développer, prendre de l'extension. *[speaker, business]* **to ~ out into sth** se lancer dans qch.

launcher [ˈlɔːntʃəʳ] **n** (*Mil, Space*) lanceur *m*; *see* **missile, rocket.**

launching [ˈlɔːntʃɪŋ] 1 **n** *[new ship, missile, satellite, company, product]* lancement *m*; *[shore lifeboat]* sortie *f*; *[ship's boat]* mise *f* à la mer. 2 **comp** ▶**launching ceremony** cérémonie *f* de lancement ▶**launching pad** (*Space*) rampe *f* de lancement ▶**launching site** (*Mil, Space*) aire *f* de lancement.

launder [ˈlɔːndəʳ] 1 **vt** a *clothes etc* blanchir. **to send sth to be ~ed** envoyer qch à la blanchisserie *or* au blanchissage. b *stolen money* blanchir, rendre honorable. 2 **vi** *[shirt etc]* se laver.

launderette [ˌlɔːndəˈret] **n** (*Brit*) laverie *f* automatique (*à libre-service*).

laundering [ˈlɔːndərɪŋ] **n** blanchissage *m*.

laundress [ˈlɔːndrɪs] **n** blanchisseuse *f*.

Laundromat [ˈlɔːndrəmæt] **n** ® (*US*) = **launderette.**

laundry [ˈlɔːndrɪ] 1 **n** a (*clean clothes*) linge *m*; (*dirty clothes*) linge (sale). **to do the ~** faire la lessive, laver le linge (sale). b (*place*) blanchisserie *f*. 2 **comp** ▶**laundry basket** panier *m* à linge ▶**laundry list** (*lit*) liste *f* de blanchissage; (*fig pej*) liste *f* qui n'en finit pas ▶**laundry mark** marque *f* de la blanchisserie *or* du blanchissage ▶**laundry van** camionnette *f* du blanchisseur ▶**laundry worker** blanchisseur *m*, -euse *f*.

laureate [ˈlɔːrɪɪt] **adj, n** lauréat(e) *m(f)*. (*Brit*) **(poet) ~** poète lauréat.

laurel [ˈlɒrəl] 1 **n** (*Bot, fig*) laurier *m*. **to win one's ~s** se couvrir de lauriers; **to rest on one's ~s** se reposer sur ses lauriers; **you must look to your ~s** ne t'endors pas sur tes lauriers. 2 **comp** ▶**laurel wreath** couronne *f* de lauriers.

Laurence [ˈlɒrəns] **n** Laurent *m*.

lav* [læv] **n** (**abbr of lavatory**) cabs* *mpl*, cabinets *mpl*.

lava [ˈlɑːvə] 1 **n** lave *f*. 2 **comp** ▶**lava bed/flow** champ *m*/coulée *f* de lave.

lavalier(e) [ˌlævəˈlɪəʳ] **n** (*US*) pendentif *m*.

lavatorial [ˌlævəˈtɔːrɪəl] **adj** scatologique.

lavatory [ˈlævətrɪ] 1 **n** (*room*) toilettes *fpl*, W.-C. *mpl*, cabinets *mpl*; (*Brit: utensil*) (cuvette *f* et siège *m* de) W.-C. **to put sth down the ~** jeter qch dans les W.-C. *or* cabinets; *see* **public.** 2 **comp** ▶**lavatory bowl** cuvette *f* des W.-C. *or* cabinets ▶**lavatory humour*** (*fig pej*) humour *m* scatologique ▶**lavatory pan** = **lavatory bowl** ▶**lavatory paper** papier *m* hygiénique ▶**lavatory seat** siège *m* des W.-C. *or* cabinets.

lavender [ˈlævɪndəʳ] 1 **n** lavande *f*. 2 **comp** (*colour*) lavande *inv* ▶**lavender bag** sachet *m* de lavande ▶**lavender-blue** bleu lavande *inv* ▶**lavender water** eau *f* de lavande.

laverbread [ˈlɑːvəˌbred] **n** gâteau *m* d'algues.

lavish [ˈlævɪʃ] 1 **adj** a *person* prodigue (*of, with* de). **to be ~ with one's money** dépenser sans compter, se montrer prodigue. b (*abundant*) *expenditure* très considérable; *amount* gigantesque; *meal* plantureux, copieux; *helping, hospitality* généreux; *flat, surroundings* somptueux, luxueux. **to bestow ~ praise on sb** se répandre en éloges sur qn. 2 **vt** prodiguer (*sth on sb* qch à qn).

lavishly [ˈlævɪʃlɪ] **adv** *spend* sans compter; *give* généreusement, à profusion; *furnish* somptueusement, luxueusement.

lavishness [ˈlævɪʃnɪs] **n** *[spending]* extravagance *f*; *[furniture, surroundings etc]* luxe *m*, somptuosité *f*; (*prodigality*) prodigalité *f*.

law [lɔː] 1 **n** a (*NonC*) loi *f*. **the ~** la loi; **it's the ~** c'est la loi; **it's against the ~** c'est contraire à la loi, c'est illégal; **the ~ of the land** la législation *or* les lois du pays; **the ~ of the jungle** la loi de la jungle; **the L~ (of Moses)** la loi de Moïse; **the ~ as it stands** la législation en vigueur; **they are trying to change the ~ on this** ils essaient de changer la loi *or* la législation sur ce point; **~ and order** l'ordre public (*see also* **2**); **forces of ~ and order** forces *fpl* de l'ordre; (*Parl*) **a bill becomes ~** un projet de loi devient loi; **by ~** conformément à la loi; **by** *or* **under French ~** selon la loi *or* la législation française; **to be above the ~** être au-dessus des lois; **to have the ~ on one's side** avoir la loi pour soi; **to keep within the ~** rester dans (les limites de) la légalité; **to take the ~ into one's own hands** (se) faire justice soi-même; **he's a ~ unto himself** il ne connaît d'autre loi que la sienne, il fait ce qu'il veut; **his word is ~** sa parole fait loi; *see* **break, lay down, rule** *etc.*

b (*NonC: operation of the ~*) justice *f*. **court of ~** cour *f* de justice, tribunal *m*; **to go to ~** recourir à la justice; **to take a case to ~** porter une affaire devant les tribunaux; **to take sb to ~, to have the ~ on sb*** faire un procès à qn; **I'll have the ~ on you!*** je vous emmènerai devant la justice!, je vous traînerai devant les tribunaux!*; **here's the ~ arriving!*** voilà les flics!*; *see* **arm¹, brush, marshal, officer.**

c (*NonC: system, science, profession*) droit *m*. **to study** *or* **read ~** faire son *or* du droit; **he practises ~** il est homme de loi; (*Univ*) **Faculty of L~** faculté *f* de droit; **civil/criminal** *etc* **~** le droit civil/criminel *etc; see* **common, martial, point** *etc.*

d (*legal ruling*) loi *f*. **several ~s have been passed against pollution** plusieurs lois ont été votées pour combattre la pollution; **is there a ~ against it?** y a-t-il une loi qui s'y oppose *or* l'interdise?; **there's no ~ against it!*** il n'y a pas de loi contre!*; **framework** *or* **skeleton ~** loi-cadre *f*.

e (*principle, rule*) (*gen, Phys*) loi *f*; (*Sport*) règle *f*. **moral ~** principe *m*; **the ~s of nature** les lois de la nature; **~ of gravity** loi de la chute des corps *or* de la pesanteur; **~ of supply and demand** loi de l'offre et de la demande; **~ of diminishing returns** loi des rendements décroissants; **~ of averages** loi *f* des probabilités; *see* **Murphy, Parkinson, sod.**

2 **comp** ►**law-abiding** respectueux des lois ►**law-and-order issues** questions relatives à l'ordre public ►**lawbreaker** personne *f* qui viole *or* transgresse la loi ►**lawbreakers** ceux *mpl* qui violent la loi *or* qui ne respectent pas la loi ►**law clerk** (*US Jur*) jeune juriste *m* qui prépare le travail du juge ►**law court** cour *f* de justice, tribunal *m* ►**Law Courts** ≃ Palais *m* de Justice ►**law enforcement agency** service chargé de faire respecter la loi ►**law enforcement officer** représentant *m* d'un service chargé de faire respecter la loi ►**Law Faculty** (*Univ*) faculté *f* de droit ►**lawgiver** (*Brit*) législateur *m*, -trice *f* ►**Law Lords** (*Brit*) *juges siégeant à la Chambre des Lords* ►**lawmaker** législateur *m*, -trice *f* ►**lawman** (*US*) policier *m* ►**law school** (*Univ*) faculté *f* de droit; **he's at law school** il fait son droit ►**law student** étudiant(e) *m(f)* en droit ►**lawsuit** procès *m*; **to bring a lawsuit against sb** intenter un procès à qn, poursuivre qn en justice.

law-breaking ['lɔːˌbreɪkɪŋ] 1 **n** violation *f* de la loi. 2 **adj** violant *or* enfreignant la loi.

lawful ['lɔːfʊl] **adj** *action* légal, licite, permis; *marriage, child* légitime; *contract* valide. **it is not ~ to do that** il n'est pas légal de *or* il est illégal de faire cela; **to go about one's ~ business** vaquer à ses occupations; **~ currency** monnaie *f* ayant cours légal.

lawfully ['lɔːfəlɪ] **adv** légalement.

lawless ['lɔːlɪs] **adj** *country* sans loi, anarchique; *person* sans foi ni loi; *activity* illégal, contraire à la loi.

lawlessness ['lɔːlɪsnɪs] **n** *[person]* manque *m* de respect envers la loi; *[country]* anarchie *f*; *[activity]* illégalité *f*.

lawn[1] [lɔːn] 1 **n** pelouse *f*. 2 **comp** ►**lawnmower** tondeuse *f* (à gazon) ►**lawn tennis** (*on grass*) tennis *m* sur gazon; (*on hard surface*) tennis.

lawn[2] [lɔːn] **n** (*Tex*) batiste *f*, linon *m*.

Lawrence ['lɒrəns] **n** Laurent *m*.

Lawrencium [lɒ'rensɪəm] **n** lawrencium *m*.

lawyer ['lɔːjə[r]] **n** (*gen*) homme *m* de loi, juriste *m*; (*solicitor*) (*for sales, wills etc*) notaire *m*; (*in court for litigation*) avocat *m*; (*barrister*) avocat; (*in business firm etc*) conseiller *m* juridique. **he is a ~** il est homme de loi *or* juriste; **... or I shall put the matter in the hands of my ~** ... sinon je mets l'affaire entre les mains de mon avocat.

lax [læks] **adj** *behaviour, discipline, morals* relâché; *person* négligent; *government* laxiste, mou (*f* molle); (*Med*) *bowels* relâché; (*Ling*) *vowel* non tendu, relâché; *pronunciation* relâché. **to be ~ in doing sth** faire qch avec négligence *or* sans soin; **to be ~ about one's work/duties** négliger son travail/ses devoirs; **he's become very ~ recently** il s'est beaucoup relâché récemment.

laxative ['læksətɪv] **adj, n** laxatif *(m)*.

laxity ['læksɪtɪ] **n, laxness** ['læksnɪs] **n** (*see* **lax**) relâchement *m*; négligence *f*.

lay[1] [leɪ] **(vb: pret, ptp laid)** 1 **n** a *[countryside, district etc]* disposition *f*, configuration *f*. (*fig*) **to find out the ~ of the land** tâter le terrain.

b (**‡**) (*act*) baise**‡** *f* (*NonC*). **she's an easy ~** elle couche* avec n'importe qui, c'est une fille facile; **he's a good ~** il baise bien**‡**, c'est un bon coup**‡**.

2 **comp** ►**layabout*** (*Brit*) fainéant(e) *m(f)*, feignant(e)* *m(f)* ►**layaway plan** (*US Comm*) vente *f* à livraison différée ►**layback** (*Climbing*) dülfer *f* ►**lay-by** (*Brit Aut*) (petite) aire *f* de stationnement (*sur bas-côté*) ►**lay days** (*Jur*) jours *mpl* de planche, estarie *f* ►**lay-off** (*Ind*) licenciement *m*, mise *f* en chômage technique ►**layout** *[house, school]* disposition *f*, agencement *m*; *[garden]* plan *m*, dessin *m*, disposition; *[district]* disposition; *[essay]* plan; *[advertisement, newspaper article etc]* agencement, mise *f* en page; (*Press etc*) **the layout of page 4** la mise en page de la (page) 4; (*Cards*) **I don't like the layout of my hand** je n'aime pas la texture *or* la composition de mon jeu ►**layover** (*US*) halte *f*.

3 **vt** a (*put, place, set*) *cards, objects* mettre, poser; (*stretch out*) *cloth etc* étendre. **he laid his briefcase on the table** il a posé *or* mis sa serviette à plat sur la table; (*euph: buried*) **to be laid to rest** être enterré; **he laid his head on the table** il a appuyé son front sur la table; **she laid her head on the pillow** elle a posé sa tête sur l'oreiller; **she laid her hand on my shoulder** elle a posé *or* mis la main sur mon épaule; **I wish I could ~ my hands on a good dictionary** si seulement je pouvais mettre la main sur *or* dénicher un bon dictionnaire; (*Rel*) **to ~ hands on sb** faire l'imposition des mains à qn; (*seize*) **to ~ hands on a territory** *etc* s'emparer d'un territoire *etc;* (*strike*) **to ~ a hand** *or* **hands on sb** porter *or* lever la main sur qn; **I didn't ~ a finger on him** je ne l'ai pas touché; **if you so much as ~ a finger on me ...** si tu oses (seulement) lever la main sur moi ...; (*fig*) **to ~ sb by the heels** attraper qn; **the scene/story is laid in Paris** l'action/l'histoire se passe *or* se situe *or* se déroule à Paris; (*fig*) **to ~ sth at sb's door** tenir qn pour responsable de qch, faire porter la responsabilité de qch à qn; (*fig*) **to ~ it on the line** y aller carrément, ne pas y aller par quatre chemins; (*US fig: explain*) **he laid it on me*** il m'a tout expliqué; (*Brit*) **to ~ one on sb‡** (*hit*) filer un pain * *or* une châtaigne* à qn; (*trick*) jouer un sale tour à qn; *see* **curse, eye, hold, siege** *etc.*

b (*put down into position*) poser, mettre; *bricks, carpet, cable, pipe* poser; *mine* poser, mouiller. **to ~ the foundations of** (*lit*) faire *or* jeter les fondations de; (*fig*) poser les bases de; **to ~ the foundation stone** poser la première pierre; **to ~ a road** faire une route; **to ~ a floor with carpet** poser une moquette sur un sol.

c *eggs* pondre. **this bird ~s its eggs in the sand** cet oiseau pond (ses œufs) dans le sable; *see also* **egg, new** *etc.*

d (*prepare*) *fire* préparer; *snare, trap* tendre, dresser (*for* à); *plans* former, élaborer. (*Brit*) **to ~ the table for lunch** mettre la table *or* le couvert pour le déjeuner; **she laid the table for 5** elle a mis *or* dressé la table pour 5, elle a mis 5 couverts; **to ~ the tablecloth** mettre la nappe; **all our carefully-laid plans went wrong** tous nos plans si bien élaborés ont échoué.

e (*impose, place*) *tax* mettre, faire payer (*on sth* sur qch); *burden* imposer (*on sb* à qn); *see* **blame, emphasis, responsibility** *etc.*

f **(+ adj)** (*fig*) **to ~ bare one's innermost thoughts/feelings** mettre à nu *or* dévoiler ses pensées les plus profondes/ses sentiments les plus secrets; (*liter*) **to ~ bare one's soul** mettre son âme à nu; **the blow laid him flat** *or* **low** le coup l'étendit par terre *or* l'abattit *or* l'envoya au tapis; **the storm laid the town flat** la tempête a rasé la ville; **to be laid low** être immobilisé; **he was laid low with flu** il était immobilisé par la grippe, la grippe l'obligeait à garder le lit; **to ~ sb/to ~ o.s. open to criticism** *etc* exposer qn/s'exposer à la critique *etc;* **to ~ waste a town** ravager *or* dévaster une ville.

g (*wager*) *money* parier, miser (*on* sur). **to ~ a bet (on sth)** parier (sur qch); **I'll ~ you a fiver that ...** je vous parie cinq livres que ... .

h (*register, bring to sb's attention*) *accusation, charge* porter. (*Jur*) **to ~ a complaint** porter plainte (*against* contre; *with* auprès de); (*Police*) **to ~ information** donner des informations, servir d'indicateur (*f* -trice); (*Jur*) **to ~ a matter before the court** saisir le tribunal d'une affaire; **he laid his case before the commission** il a porté son cas devant *or* soumis son cas à la commission; **we shall ~ the facts before him** nous lui exposerons les faits; **they laid their plan before him** ils lui ont soumis leur projet; *see* **claim** *etc.*

i (*suppress*) *ghost* exorciser, conjurer; *doubt, fear* dissiper. **to ~ the dust** empêcher la poussière de voler, faire tomber la poussière.

j (**‡**) *have sex with* baiser**‡**.

4 **vi** a *[bird, fish, insect]* pondre.

b **he laid about him with a stick** il a distribué des coups de bâton tout autour de lui.

►**lay alongside** (*Naut*) **vi, vt sep** accoster.

►**lay aside** **vt sep** a (*save*) *money, supplies* mettre de côté. b (*put away temporarily*) *object* mettre de côté. **he laid aside his book to greet me** il a mis son livre de côté pour me recevoir. c (*abandon*) *prejudice, scruples* abandonner, oublier; *principles* se départir de. **we must lay aside our own feelings** nous devons faire abstraction de nos propres sentiments.

►**lay away** 1 **vt sep** (*US*) = **lay aside a.** 2 **layaway** **adj** *see* **lay**[1] **2.**

►**lay back** 1 **vt sep** remettre (*on* sur). 2 **layback** **n** *see* **lay**[1] **2.**

►**lay by** 1 **vt sep** = **lay aside a.** 2 **lay-by** **n** *see* **lay**[1] **2.**

►**lay down** 1 **vi** (*Cards*) étaler son jeu *or* ses cartes, montrer son jeu.

2 **vt sep** a (*deposit*) *object, parcel, burden* poser, déposer. **to lay down one's cards** étaler son jeu *or* ses cartes, montrer son jeu (*also fig*).

b *wine* mettre en cave.

c (*give up*) **to lay down one's arms** déposer ses *or* les armes; **to lay down one's life for sb** sacrifier sa vie pour qn; **to lay down (one's) office** se démettre de ses fonctions.

d (*establish, decide*) *rule* établir, poser; *condition, price* imposer, fixer. **he laid it down that ...** il décréta *or* stipula que ...; **it is laid down in the rules that ...** il est stipulé dans le règlement que ...; **to lay down a policy** dicter une politique; (*fig*) **to lay down the law to sb about sth** (essayer de) faire la loi à qn sur qch; **in our house it's my mother who lays down the law** c'est ma mère qui fait la loi à la maison.

►**lay in** **vt sep** *goods, reserves* faire provision de, emmagasiner. **to lay in provisions** faire des provisions; **I must lay in some fruit** il faut que je m'approvisionne (*subj*) en fruits *or* que je fasse provision de fruits.

►**lay into*** **vt fus** (*attack physically*) foncer sur, rentrer dans*; (*attack verbally*) prendre à partie; (*scold*) passer un savon à*. **we really laid into the beer last night** on a descendu pas mal de bière hier soir*.

►**lay off** 1 **vt sep** (*Ind*) *workers* licencier, débaucher. 2 **vt fus** (*) **lay off (it)!** (*stop*) tu veux t'arrêter?*; (*don't touch*) touche pas!*, pas touche!‡, bas les pattes!‡; **lay off him!** fiche-lui la paix!*; **I told him to lay off (it)** je lui ai dit d'arrêter. 3 **lay-off** **n** *see* **lay**[1] **2.**

►**lay on** **vt sep** a *tax* mettre. **they lay on an extra charge for tea** ils ajoutent à la note le prix du thé.

b (*Brit*) (*install*) *water, gas* installer, mettre; (*provide*) *facilities, entertainment* fournir. **a house with water/gas/electricity laid on** une maison qui a l'eau courante/le gaz/l'électricité; **I'll have a car laid on for you** je tiendrai une voiture à votre disposition; **everything will be laid on** il y aura tout ce qu'il faut; **it was all laid on (for us) so that we didn't have to buy anything** tout (nous) était fourni si bien qu'on n'a rien eu à acheter.

c *varnish, paint* étaler. (* *fig*) **he laid it on thick** *or* **with a shovel** *or* **with a trowel** (*flattered*) il a passé de la pommade*, il a manié l'encensoir*; (*exaggerated*) il en a rajouté*; *see* **lay 3a.**

▸**lay out** 1 vt sep a (*plan, design*) *garden* dessiner; *house* concevoir (le plan de); *essay* faire le plan de. **well-laid-out flat** appartement bien conçu; (*Typ*) **to lay out page 4** faire la mise en page de la (page) 4, monter la (page) 4.

b (*get ready, display*) *clothes* sortir, préparer; *goods for sale* disposer, étaler. **the meal that was laid out for them** le repas qui leur avait été préparé; **to lay out a body** faire la toilette d'un mort.

c (*fig*) (*recount systematically*) *reasons, events etc* exposer systématiquement.

d (*spend*) *money* débourser, dépenser (*on* pour).

e (*knock out*) mettre knock-out *or* K.-O.*

f (*do one's utmost*) **to lay o.s. out to do** faire tout son possible pour faire, se mettre en peine *or* en quatre pour faire.

2 **layout** n *see* **lay¹ 2.**

▸**lay over** (*US*) 1 vi s'arrêter, faire une halte. 2 **layover** n *see* **lay¹ 2.**

▸**lay to** (*Naut*) 1 vi être en panne. 2 vt sep mettre en panne.

▸**lay up** vt sep a *store, provisions* amasser, entasser, emmagasiner. **to lay up trouble for o.s.** se préparer des ennuis. b *car* remiser; *ship* désarmer. **he is laid up with flu** il est au lit avec la grippe, la grippe l'a forcé à s'aliter; **you'll lay yourself up if you carry on like this** tu vas te retrouver au lit si tu continues comme ça.

lay² [leɪ] pret of **lie¹**.

lay³ [leɪ] n (*Mus, Poetry*) lai *m*.

lay⁴ [leɪ] 1 adj *missionary, school, education* laïque. ~ **brother** frère convers; ~ **reader** prédicateur *m* laïque; ~ **sister** sœur converse; (*fig*) **to the ~ mind** aux yeux du profane, pour le profane; ~ **opinion on this** l'opinion des profanes sur la question. 2 comp ▸**layman** (*Rel*) laïc *m*; (*fig*) profane *m*; (*fig*) **to the layman it would appear that ...** aux yeux du profane il semblerait que ... ▸**lay person** profane *mf*, non initié(e) *m(f)*.

lay⁵ [leɪ] adj (*Art*) ~ **figure** mannequin *m*.

layer ['leɪəʳ] 1 n a *[atmosphere, paint, dust, sand]* couche *f*; (*Geol*) couche, strate *f*. b (*hen*) **a good ~** une bonne pondeuse. c (*Horticulture*) marcotte *f*. 2 vt a (*Horticulture*) marcotter. b *hair* couper en dégradé. 3 comp ▸**layer cake** gâteau fourré.

layette [leɪ'et] n layette *f*.

laying ['leɪɪŋ] 1 n *[carpet]* pose *f*. (*ceremony*) **the ~ of wreaths** le dépôt de gerbes; (*Rel*) **the ~ on of hands** l'imposition *f* des mains. 2 adj: ~ **hen** poule pondeuse.

Lazarus ['læzərəs] n Lazare *m*.

laze [leɪz] vi (*also* ~ **about,** ~ **around**) (*relax*) se reposer; (*be idle*) paresser, ne rien faire, traînasser (*pej*). **we ~d (about** *or* **around) in the sun for a week** nous avons passé une semaine au soleil à ne rien faire, nous avons eu une semaine de farniente au soleil; **stop lazing about** *or* **around and do some work!** cesse de perdre ton temps (à ne rien faire) et mets-toi au travail!

▸**laze away** vt sep: **to laze the time away** passer son temps à ne rien faire.

lazily ['leɪzɪlɪ] adv (*see* **lazy**) paresseusement; nonchalamment; avec indolence.

laziness ['leɪzɪnɪs] n paresse *f*, indolence *f*, fainéantise *f*.

lazy ['leɪzɪ] 1 adj *person* paresseux, indolent, fainéant; *attitude, gesture, smile* nonchalant, paresseux; *writing, work* peu soigné; *style* relâché; *hour, afternoon* de paresse; (*fig*) *river etc* paresseux, lent. **we had a ~ holiday** nous avons passé les vacances à ne rien faire. 2 comp ▸**lazybones** feignant(e)* *m(f)* ▸**lazy eye** (*Med*) amblyopie *f* ▸**lazy Susan** (*dish*) plateau tournant.

lb (abbr of *libra*) = **pound**; *see* **pound.**

l.b.w. [ˌelbiː'dʌbəljuː] n (*Cricket*) (abbr of **leg before wicket**) *faute du joueur qui met la jambe devant le guichet.*

L.C. [ˌel'siː] n (*US*) (abbr of **Library of Congress**) bibliothèque *f* du Congrès.

l.c. (*Typ*) (abbr of **lower case**) *see* **lower.**

L/C (abbr of **letter of credit**) *see* **letter 1b.**

L.C.C. [ˌelsiː'siː] n (*Brit*) (abbr of **London County Council**) *autorités régionales de Londres avant le G.L.C.*

LCD [ˌelsiː'diː] n a (abbr of **liquid crystal display**) *see* **liquid.** b (abbr of **lowest common denominator**) PPDC *m*.

lcd [ˌelsiː'diː] n = **LCD b.**

LCM, lcm [ˌelsiː'em] n (abbr of **lowest common multiple**) PPCM *m*.

Ld (*Brit*) abbr of **Lord.**

L-dopa [el'dəʊpə] n L-dopa *f*.

LDS [ˌeldiː'es] n (abbr of **Licentiate in Dental Surgery**) diplôme *m* de chirurgien dentiste.

LEA [ˌeliː'eɪ] n (*Brit Educ*) (abbr of **local education authority**) *see* **local.**

lea [liː] n (*liter*) pré *m*.

leach [liːtʃ] 1 vt *liquid* filtrer; *particles* lessiver. 2 vi *[ashes, soil]* être éliminé par filtration *or* filtrage; *[liquid]* filtrer.

lead¹ [liːd] (vb: pret, ptp **led**) 1 n a (*esp Sport*) (*front position*) tête *f*; (*distance or time ahead*) avance *f*. **to be in the ~** (*in match*) mener; (*in race, league*) être en tête; **to go into** *or* **take the ~** (*in race*) prendre la tête; (*in match*) mener; **to have a 3-point ~** avoir 3 points d'avance; **to have a 2-minute/10-metre ~ over sb** avoir deux minutes/10 mètres d'avance sur qn; *see* **widen.**

b initiative *f*, exemple *m*. **to take the ~ in doing sth** être le premier à faire qch; **thanks to his ~ the rest were able to ...** grâce à son initiative les autres ont pu ...; **to follow sb's ~** suivre l'exemple de qn; **to give the ~** donner le ton, montrer l'exemple; **to give sb a ~** montrer le chemin à qn (*fig*); *see also* **1c.**

c (*clue*) piste *f*. **the police have a ~** la police tient une piste; **the footprint gave them a ~** l'empreinte de pas les a mis sur la voie *or* sur la piste.

d (*Cards*) **whose ~ is it?** à qui est-ce de jouer?

e (*Theat*) rôle principal. **to play the ~** tenir *or* jouer *or* avoir le rôle principal; **to sing the ~** chanter le rôle principal; **male/female ~** premier rôle masculin/féminin; **juvenile ~** jeune premier *m*.

f (*leash*) laisse *f*. **dogs must be kept on a ~** les chiens doivent être tenus en laisse.

g (*Elec*) fil *m*.

h (*Press: also* ~ **story**) article *m* de tête. **what is the ~?** quel est l'article de tête?; **the financial crisis is the ~ (story) in this morning's papers** la crise financière est le gros titre des *or* est à la une des journaux de ce matin.

i (*Comm*) **~s and lags** termaillage *m*, jeu *m* de termes de paiement.

2 comp ▸**lead-in** introduction *f*, entrée *f* en matière ▸**lead story** (*Press*) *see* **1h** ▸**lead time** *[project, process]* délais *mpl* (d'exécution *or* de réalisation); *[stock]* délais (de réapprovisionnement); *[new product]* délais (de démarrage *or* de mise en production).

3 vt a (*conduct, show the way*) conduire, mener (*to* à). **to ~ sb in/out/across** *etc* faire entrer/sortir/traverser *etc* qn; **they led him into the king's presence** on le conduisit devant le roi; **to ~ sb into a room** faire entrer qn dans une pièce; **the guide led them through the courtyard** le guide leur a fait traverser la cour *or* les a fait passer par la cour; **the first street on the left will ~ you to the church** la première rue à gauche vous mènera à l'église; **what led you to Venice?** qu'est-ce qui vous a amené à Venise?; **each clue led him to another** chaque indice le menait à un autre; **one thing led to another** une chose en a amené *or* entraîné une autre; **this ~s me to an important point** cela m'amène à un point important; (*fig*) **he is easily led** il est très influençable; (*Jur*) **to ~ a witness** poser des questions tendancieuses à un témoin; (*lit, fig*) **to ~ the way** montrer le chemin; **he led the way to the garage** il nous (*or* les *etc*) a menés jusqu'au garage; **will you ~ the way?** vous passez devant et on vous suit; (*fig*) **to ~ sb astray** détourner qn du droit chemin, dévoyer qn (*liter*); (*fig*) **to ~ sb by the nose** mener qn par le bout du nez; **to ~ an army into battle** mener une armée au combat; **to ~ a team on to the field** conduire une équipe sur le terrain; **he led the party to victory** il a mené le parti à la victoire; **he will ~ us in prayer** il va diriger nos prières; *see* **garden.**

b (*be leader of*) *procession* (*be in charge of*) être à la tête de; (*be at head of*) être en tête de; *government, movement, party, team* être à la tête de, diriger; *expedition* être à la tête de, mener; *regiment* être à la tête de, commander; (*Ftbl etc*) *league* être en tête de; *orchestra* (*Brit*) être le premier violon de; (*US*) diriger. (*Comm*) **we are looking for someone to ~ our new department** nous recherchons quelqu'un pour assurer la direction de notre nouveau service.

c (*Sport, fig: be ahead of*) être en tête de. **they were ~ing us by 10 metres** ils avaient un avantage *or* une avance de 10 mètres sur nous; (*Sport, fig*) **to ~ the field** venir *or* être en tête; **this country ~s the world in textiles** ce pays est au *or* tient le premier rang mondial pour les textiles.

d (*Cards*) jouer; (*Bridge etc: at first trick*) attaquer de, entamer. **what is led?** qu'est-ce qui est joué? *or* demandé?

e *life, existence* mener. (*fig*) **to ~ sb a dance** faire la vie à qn*; *see* **dog** *etc.*

f (*induce, bring*) porter, amener. **I am led to the conclusion that ...** je suis amené à conclure que ...; **he led me to believe that he would help me** il m'a amené à croire qu'il m'aiderait; **what led you to think that?** qu'est-ce qui vous a porté à penser ça?; **his financial problems led him to steal** ses problèmes financiers l'ont poussé au vol.

4 vi a (*be ahead: esp Sport*) (*in match*) mener; (*in race*) être en tête. **which horse is ~ing?** quel est le cheval de tête?; **to ~ by half a length/3 points** avoir une demi-longueur/3 points d'avance; **to ~ (by) 4 goals to 3** mener (par) 4 buts à 3.

b (*go ahead*) aller devant. **you ~, I'll follow** passez *or* allez devant, je vous suis.

c (*Jur*) **to ~ for the defence** être l'avocat principal de la défense.

d (*Cards*) **who is it to ~?** c'est à qui de commencer?; (*Bridge*) **South to ~** sud joue.

e (*Dancing*) mener, conduire.

f *[street, corridor]* mener, conduire; *[door]* mener (*to* à), donner, s'ouvrir (*to* sur). **the streets that ~ into/off the square** les rues qui débouchent sur/partent de la place; **the rooms which ~ off the corridor** les pièces qui donnent sur le couloir.

g (*fig*) conduire, aboutir (*to* à). **it led to war** cela a conduit à la guerre; **it led to his arrest** cela aboutit à son arrestation; **that will ~ to his undoing** cela causera *or* sera sa perte; **it led to nothing** cela n'a mené à rien; **this led to their asking to see the president** ceci les a amenés à demander à voir le président; **it could ~ to some confusion** cela pourrait créer *or* occasionner une certaine confusion; **it led to a change in his attitude** cela a amené *or* causé un changement dans son attitude; **one story led to another** une histoire en a amené une autre; **one thing led to another and we ...** une chose en amenant une autre, nous ... .

►**lead away** vt sep emmener. **he was led away by the soldiers** il a été emmené par les soldats; **they led him away to the cells** ils l'ont conduit en cellule.

►**lead back** vt sep ramener, reconduire. **they led us back to the house** ils nous ont ramenés *or* reconduits à la maison; **this road leads (you) back to the town hall** cette route vous ramène à l'hôtel de ville.

►**lead off** 1 vi a (*begin*) commencer, débuter. b *[corridor, path]* partir. **a passage leading off the hall** un couloir qui part du foyer. 2 vt sep = **lead away**.

►**lead on** 1 vi marcher devant. **lead on!**, (*hum*) **lead on, Macduff!*** allez-y, je vous suis! 2 vt sep a (*tease*) taquiner, faire marcher*; (*fool*) duper, avoir*. b (*raise hopes of*) donner de faux espoirs à. c (*induce*) amener. **they led him on to talk about his experiences** ils l'ont amené à parler de ses expériences; **this led him on to say that ...** ceci l'amena à dire que ... .

►**lead up** vi a conduire. **this road leads up to the castle** cette route conduit *or* mène au château; **this staircase leads up to the roof** cet escalier conduit au *or* donne accès au toit; (*fig*) **his speech led up to a discussion of war** son discours nous (*or* les *etc*) a amenés *or* entraînés à parler de la guerre; **he led up carefully to his proposal** il a soigneusement amené sa proposition; **what are you leading up to?** où voulez-vous en venir?; **what's all this leading up to?** où est-ce qu'on veut en venir avec tout ça?

b (*precede*) précéder. **the years that led up to the war** les années qui ont précédé la guerre; **the events that led up to the revolution** les événements qui ont conduit à la révolution.

lead² [led] 1 n a (*NonC: metal*) plomb *m*. **they filled him full of ~‡** ils l'ont truffé de pruneaux‡, ils l'ont transformé en écumoire*; *see* **red** *etc*.

b (*NonC: graphite: also* **black ~**) mine *f* de plomb.

c *[pencil]* mine *f*; *[fishing line]* plomb *m*; (*for sounding*) plomb (de sonde); (*Aut*) (*for wheel balancing*) masselotte *f*; *see* **swing**.

d (*Typ*) interligne *f*, blanc *m*.

e (*Brit*) *[roof]* **~s** couverture *f* de plomb; **(window) ~s** plomburesfpl.

2 comp *object, weight etc* de *or* en plomb ►**lead acetate** acétate *m* de plomb ►**lead balloon: it went down like a lead balloon** c'est tombé à plat, ça a foiré‡ ►**lead-free** sans plomb ►**lead oxyde** oxyde *m* de plomb ►**lead paint** peinture *f* à base de carbonate de plomb ►**lead pencil** crayon *m* à mine de plomb *or* à papier ►**lead pipe** tuyau *m* de plomb ►**lead piping** tuyauterie *f* de plomb ►**lead poisoning** saturnisme *m*, coliques *fpl* de plomb ►**lead shot** grenaille *f* de plomb ►**lead works** (*NonC*) fonderie *f* de plomb.

leaded ['ledɪd] adj a **~ window** fenêtre *f* à tout petits carreaux; **~ lights** petits carreaux. b (*Typ*) interligné. c (*petrol*) au plomb, qui contient du plomb.

leaden ['ledn] 1 adj (*made of lead*) de *or* en plomb; (*in colour*) *sky* de plomb, plombé; (*fig: heavy*) lourd, pesant; *silence* de mort; *atmosphere* chargé. 2 comp ►**leaden-eyed** aux yeux ternes ►**leaden-limbed: to feel leaden-limbed** se sentir les membres en plomb.

leader ['liːdəʳ] n a *[expedition, gang, tribe]* chef *m*; *[club]* dirigeant(e) *m(f)*; (*guide*) guide *m*; (*Climbing*) premier *m* (de cordée); *[riot, strike]* meneur *m*, -euse *f*; (*Mil*) commandant *m*; (*Pol*) dirigeant(e), leader *m*, chef (de file). (*Brit Parl*) **L~ of the House** chef de la majorité ministérielle à la Chambre; (*Pol*) **the ~ of the Socialist Party** le leader *or* le chef (du parti) socialiste, le dirigeant socialiste; **the national ~s** les dirigeants *or* leaders nationaux; **political ~s** chefs politiques; **one of the ~s of the trade union movement** un des dirigeants *or* chefs de file *or* leaders du mouvement syndical; **he's a born ~** il est né pour commander; **the ~ of the orchestra** (*Brit*) le premier violon; (*US*) le chef d'orchestre; **she was a ~ of fashion** elle était de celles qui créent *or* font la mode; **one of the ~s in the scientific field** une des sommités du monde scientifique; (*Jur*) **the ~ for the defence** l'avocat principal de la défense; *see* **follow, youth** *etc*.

b (*Sport*) (*in race*) coureur *m* de tête; (*Horse-racing*) cheval *m* de tête; (*in league*) leader *m*. **he managed to stay up with the ~s** il a réussi à rester dans les premiers *or* dans le peloton de tête.

c (*Press*) (*Brit*) éditorial *m*; (*US*) article *m* de tête. (*Brit*) **~ writer** éditorialiste *mf*.

d *[film, tape etc]* amorce *f*; (*Fishing*) bas *m* de ligne.

e (*Comm: also* **loss leader**) article *m* pilote (*vendu à perte pour attirer les clients*).

f (*St Ex*) **~s** valeurs *fpl* vedettes.

leadership ['liːdəʃɪp] n a (*NonC*) (*position*) direction *f*, leadership *m*; (*action*) direction; (*quality*) qualités *fpl* de chef. **during** *or* **under his ~** sous sa direction; **to take over the ~ of the country** prendre la succession à la tête du pays; **they were rivals for the party ~** ils étaient candidats rivaux à la direction du parti; **to resign the party ~** démissionner de la tête du parti; **he has ~ potential** *or* **qualities of ~** il a des qualités de chef *or* l'étoffe d'un chef. b (*collective n: leaders*) dirigeants *mpl*. **the union ~ has** *or* **have agreed to arbitration** les dirigeants du syndicat ont accepté l'arbitrage.

leading¹ ['liːdɪŋ] adj a (*chief*) *person* de (tout) premier plan, principal; *position* dominant, de premier plan; *part* prépondérant, majeur (*f* -eure), de premier plan; (*Theat*) *role* premier, principal; *topic, theme* principal; *idea* majeur, dominant, principal. **he is one of the ~ writers in the country** c'est un des écrivains les plus importants *or* les plus en vue du pays; **he was one of the ~ figures of the twenties** c'était un personnage marquant *or* une figure marquante des années vingt; **he played a ~ part in getting the gang arrested** il a joué un rôle majeur dans l'arrestation du gang; **one of the ~ industries** une des industries de pointe; (*Press*) **~ article** (*Brit*) éditorial *m*; (*US*) article *m* de tête; (*Jur*) **~ case** précédent *m*; (*Cine*) **the ~ lady/man in the film** la vedette féminine/masculine du film; (*Cine*) **his ~ lady in that film was X** il avait X pour co-vedette dans ce film; (*Theat*) **the ~ lady/man was X** c'est X qui tenait le rôle principal féminin/masculin; **he is one of the ~ lights* in the town** c'est un des gros bonnets* *or* une des huiles* de la ville; **she was one of the ~ lights* in the local drama society** c'était une des étoiles du groupe d'art dramatique local; (*Comm*) **~ line** articles *mpl* en réclame; (*Mus*) **~ note** note *f* sensible; (*Brit Aviat*) **~ aircraftman/woman** ≃ soldat *m* (de l'armée de l'air); (*Brit Navy*) **~ rating** quartier-maître *m* de 1ère classe.

b (*in forward position*) (*gen*) de tête; (*winning: in race*) en tête. (*Aviat*) **the ~ edge** le bord d'attaque.

c **~ question** (*Jur*) question tendancieuse; (*gen*) question insidieuse; *[horse]* **~ rein** longe *f*.

leading² ['ledɪŋ] = **lead² d**.

leaf [liːf] pl **leaves** 1 n a *[tree, plant]* feuille *f*. **the leaves** les feuilles, le feuillage; **in ~** en feuilles; **to come into ~** se couvrir de feuilles; (*fig*) **to shake like a ~** trembler comme une feuille; *see* **fig**. b *[book]* feuillet *m*, page *f*. (*fig*) **you should take a ~ out of his book** vous devriez prendre exemple sur lui; (*fig*) **to turn over a new ~** changer de conduite; *see* **fly³**. c *[table]* (*on hinges*) rabat *m*, abattant *m*; (*in groove, removable*) rallonge *f*. d *[metal]* feuille *f*; *see* **gold**. 2 comp ►**leaf bud** bourgeon *m* (à feuilles) ►**leaf mould** (*Brit*), **leaf mold** (*US*) (*NonC*) terreau *m* (de feuilles) ►**leaf tobacco** tabac *m* en feuilles.

►**leaf through** vt fus *book* feuilleter, parcourir.

leafless ['liːflɪs] adj sans feuilles, dénudé.

leaflet ['liːflɪt] 1 n a (*publication*) prospectus *m*; (*Pol, Rel*) tract *m*; (*for publicity*) brochure *f*, dépliant *m*, prospectus; (*Comm etc: instruction sheet*) notice explicative, mode *m* d'emploi. b (*Bot*) foliole *f*. 2 vi distribuer des prospectus (*or* des tracts *etc*). 3 vt *area, street* distribuer des prospectus (*or* des tracts *etc*) dans.

leafy ['liːfɪ] adj *glade* entouré d'arbres feuillus; *tree* feuillu.

league¹ [liːg] 1 n a (*association*) ligue *f*. **to form a ~ against** se liguer contre; **to be in ~ with** être en coalition avec; **L~ of Nations** Société *f* des Nations.

b (*Ftbl*) championnat *m*; (*Baseball*) division *f*; (*fig*) classe *f*, catégorie *f*. (*Baseball*) **major/minor ~** première/deuxième division; (*fig*) **they're not in the same ~** ils ne sont pas de la même classe; (*fig*) **in the big ~** dans le peloton de tête, parmi les premiers; (*fig*) **it's out of his ~** il n'est pas à la hauteur; *see* **rugby** *etc*.

2 comp ►**league champions:** (*Brit Ftbl*) **they were the league champions last year** ils ont été champions l'année dernière ►**league championship** championnat *m* ►**league division one** (*Brit Ftbl*) première division du championnat ►**league leaders: they are the league leaders now** pour le moment ils sont en tête du championnat ►**league table** (*Ftbl*) classement *m* du championnat.

league² [liːg] n lieue *f*. **seven-~ boots** bottes *fpl* de sept lieues.

leak [liːk] 1 n (*in bucket, pipe, roof, balloon*) fuite *f*; (*in boat*) voie *f* d'eau; (*fig: of information etc*) fuite. **to spring a ~** *[boat]* commencer à faire eau; *[bucket, pipe]* se mettre à fuir; **the ship sprang a ~ in the bow** une voie d'eau s'est déclarée à l'avant du navire; **a gas ~** une fuite de gaz; (*fig*) **a Cabinet ~** une fuite ministérielle; **budget/security ~** fuite concernant le budget/la sécurité; (*fig*) **to go for** *or* **have a ~‡** aller pisser (un coup)‡; (*fig*) **to take a ~‡** pisser‡.

2 comp ►**leakproof** (*fig*) à l'abri des fuites.

3 vi a *[bucket, pen, pipe, bottle]* fuir; *[ship]* faire eau; *[shoes]* prendre l'eau. **the roof ~s** le toit fuit, il y a des fuites dans le toit.

b *[gas, liquid]* fuir, s'échapper. **the acid ~ed (through) on to the carpet** l'acide a filtré jusque dans le tapis.

4 vt *liquid* répandre, faire couler; (*fig*) *information* communiquer

clandestinement à la presse, divulguer. **it's ~ing acid all over the place** l'acide est en train de se répandre partout.

►**leak in** vi *[spilt liquid]* filtrer; *[water]* suinter, s'infiltrer. **the water is leaking in through the roof** l'eau entre *or* s'infiltre par le toit.

►**leak out** vi *[gas, liquid]* fuir, s'échapper; *[secret, news]* filtrer, transpirer, être divulgué. **it finally leaked out that** on a fini par savoir *or* apprendre que, il a fini par transpirer que.

leakage ['li:kɪdʒ] n (*leak*) *[gas, liquid, information]* fuite *f*; (*amount lost*) perte *f*. **some of the acid was lost through ~** un peu d'acide a été perdu par (suite d'une) fuite.

leaky ['li:kɪ] adj *bucket, kettle* percé, qui fuit; *roof* qui a une fuite; *shoe* qui prend l'eau; *boat* qui fait eau.

lean[1] [li:n] pret, ptp **leaned** *or* **leant** 1 vi a (*slope*) *[wall, construction etc]* pencher. (*fig*) **I ~ towards the belief that ...** je tends à *or* j'incline à croire que ...; **to ~ towards sb's opinion** tendre à partager l'opinion de qn; (*Pol*) **to ~ towards the left** pencher vers la gauche, avoir des sympathies pour la gauche *or* à gauche.

b (*support o.s., rest*) *[person]* s'appuyer (*against, up against* contre, à; *on* sur), prendre appui (*against, up against* contre; *on* sur); (*with one's back*) s'adosser (*against, up against* à), s'appuyer (*against, up against* contre, à); (*with elbows*) s'accouder (*on* à). **to be ~ing** être appuyé *or* adossé *or* accoudé; *[ladder, cycle etc]* **to be ~ing (up) against the wall** être appuyé contre le mur, être adossé au mur; **to ~ on one's elbows** s'appuyer *or* prendre appui sur les coudes; (*fig*) **to ~ on sb for help** *or* **support** s'appuyer sur qn (*fig*); (*fig*) **to ~ (heavily) on sb for advice** compter (beaucoup) sur qn pour ses conseils.

c (*: *put pressure on*) faire pression (*on* sur), forcer la main (*on* à). **they ~ed on him for payment** ils ont fait pression sur lui *or* ils lui ont forcé la main pour qu'il paie (*subj*); **the editor was ~ing on him for the article** l'éditeur faisait pression sur lui pour qu'il écrive l'article.

2 vt *ladder, cycle etc* appuyer (*against, up against* contre), adosser (*against, up against* à). **to ~ one's head on sb's shoulder** reposer sa tête sur l'épaule de qn.

3 n inclinaison *f*.

4 comp ►**lean-to** (pl **~-~s**) appentis *m*; **lean-to garage/shed** *etc* garage *m*/cabane *f etc* en appentis.

►**lean back** 1 vi se pencher en arrière. **to lean back in an armchair** se laisser aller en arrière dans un fauteuil; **to lean back against sth** s'adosser contre *or* à qch. 2 vt sep *chair* pencher en arrière. **to lean one's head back** pencher la tête en arrière, renverser la tête (en arrière).

►**lean forward** 1 vi se pencher en avant. 2 vt sep pencher en avant.

►**lean out** 1 vi se pencher au dehors. **to lean out of the window** se pencher par la fenêtre; **"do not lean out"** "ne pas se pencher au dehors". 2 vt sep pencher au dehors. **he leant his head out of the window** il a passé *or* penché la tête par la fenêtre.

►**lean over** vi *[person]* (*forward*) se pencher *or* se courber en avant; (*sideways*) se pencher sur le côté; *[object, tree]* pencher, être penché. **to lean over backwards** se pencher en arrière; (*fig*) **to lean over backwards to help sb*** se mettre en quatre *or* se décarcasser* *or* faire des pieds et des mains* pour aider qn.

►**lean up** vi, vt sep *see* **lean**[1] **1b, 2.**

lean[2] [li:n] 1 adj a *person, animal, meat* maigre. b (*unproductive*) *harvest* maigre, pauvre. **this is a ~ year for corn** c'est une mauvaise année pour le blé; **those were ~ years** c'étaient des années de vaches maigres; **~ diet** régime *m* maigre; **we had a ~ time** on a mangé de la vache enragée. 2 n *[meat]* maigre *m*.

leaning ['li:nɪŋ] 1 n tendance *f* (*towards* à), penchant *m* (*towards* pour). **he has artistic ~s** il a un penchant pour les arts, il a des tendances artistiques; **what are his political ~s?** quelles sont ses tendances politiques? 2 adj *wall, building* penché. **the L~ Tower of Pisa** la tour penchée de Pise.

leanness ['li:nnɪs] n maigreur *f*.

leant [lent] pret, ptp of **lean**[1].

leap [li:p] (vb: pret, ptp **leaped** *or* **leapt**) 1 n a (*lit*) saut *m*, bond *m*; (*fig*) bond, pas *m*. **to take a ~** bondir, sauter; **at one ~** d'un bond; (*fig*) **by ~s and bounds** à pas de géant; (*fig*) **a ~ in the dark** un saut dans l'inconnu; (*fig*) **a great ~ forward** un bond en avant; (*fig*) **a giant ~ for mankind** un pas de géant pour l'humanité; (*fig*) **there has been a ~ in profits this year** les profits ont fait un bond cette année.

b (*in place-names*) saut *m*; (*also* **salmon ~**) saut à saumons.

2 comp ►**leapfrog** *see* **leapfrog**.

3 vi *[person, animal, fish]* sauter, bondir; *[flames]* jaillir. **to ~ in/out** *etc* entrer/sortir *etc* d'un bond; **he leapt into/out of the car** il sauta dans/de la voiture; **to ~ over a ditch** franchir un fossé d'un bond, sauter (par-dessus) un fossé; **to ~ to one's feet** se lever d'un bond; (*Mil etc*) **to ~ to attention** se mettre vivement au garde-à-vous; **he leapt into the air** il fit un bond (en l'air); **the flames leapt into the air** les flammes ont jailli *or* se sont élevées dans l'air; **he leapt for joy** il sauta *or* bondit de joie; (*fig*) **the word leapt out at him** *or* **leapt off the page (at him)** le mot lui a sauté aux yeux; (*fig*) **her heart leapt** son cœur a bondi dans sa poitrine; (*fig*) **to ~ to the conclusion that ...** conclure immédiatement que ...; **you mustn't ~ to conclusions** il ne faut pas conclure trop hâtivement; **to ~ at the chance** sauter sur *or* saisir l'occasion, saisir la balle au bond; **to ~ at an offer** sauter sur *or* saisir une offre, saisir la balle au bond; *see* **look, mind.**

4 vt a *stream, hedge etc* sauter (par-dessus), franchir d'un bond. b *horse* faire sauter.

►**leap about** vi gambader. **to leap about with excitement** sauter de joie.

►**leap up** vi (*off ground*) sauter en l'air; (*to one's feet*) se lever d'un bond; *[flame]* jaillir; *[prices etc]* faire un bond. **the dog leapt up at him affectionately** le chien a sauté affectueusement après lui; **the dog leapt up at him and bit him** le chien lui a sauté dessus et l'a mordu; **he leapt up indignantly** il a bondi d'indignation.

leapfrog ['li:pˌfrɒg] 1 n saute-mouton *m*. 2 vi: **to ~ over** (*lit*) *person* sauter à saute-mouton par-dessus; *stool, object* franchir à saute-mouton; (*fig*) dépasser. 3 vt (*fig*) dépasser.

leapt [lept] pret, ptp of **leap**.

learn [lɜ:n] pret, ptp **learned** *or* **learnt** 1 vt a (*by study*) *language, lesson, musical instrument* apprendre. **to ~ (how) to do sth** apprendre à faire qch; **to ~ sth by heart** apprendre qch par cœur; (*fig*) **he's ~t his lesson** cela lui a servi de leçon; (*fig*) **I've ~t a lot since then** je sais à quoi m'en tenir maintenant, maintenant j'ai compris.

b (*find out*) *facts, news, results etc* apprendre. **I was sorry to ~ (that) you had been ill** j'ai appris avec regret que vous aviez été malade; **we haven't yet ~ed whether he recovered** nous ne savons toujours pas s'il est guéri.

c (‡: *teach*) apprendre. **I'll ~ you!** je vais t'apprendre, moi!*; **that'll ~ you!** ça t'apprendra!*

2 vi a apprendre. **we are ~ing about the Revolution at school** en classe on étudie *or* fait* la Révolution; **it's never too late to ~** il n'est jamais trop tard pour apprendre, on apprend à tout âge; **to ~ from experience** apprendre par l'expérience; **to ~ from one's mistakes** tirer la leçon de ses erreurs; (*fig iro*) **he'll ~!** un jour il comprendra!; *see* **live**[1].

b (*hear*) apprendre. **I was sorry to ~ of** *or* **about your illness** j'ai appris avec regret votre maladie.

►**learn off** vt sep apprendre par cœur.

►**learn up** vt sep *maths etc* travailler, bûcher*, bosser*. **she learnt up all she could about the district** elle a appris tout ce qu'elle a pu sur la région.

learned ['lɜ:nɪd] adj *person* (*in humanities*) érudit, savant; (*in sciences*) savant; *journal, society, remark, speech* savant; *profession* intellectuel. (*Brit Jur*) **my ~ friend** mon éminent confrère.

learnedly ['lɜ:nɪdlɪ] adv avec érudition, savamment.

learner ['lɜ:nəʳ] n apprenant(e) *m(f)*. (*Brit Aut*) **~ (driver)** (conducteur *m*, -trice *f*) débutant(e); **you are a quick ~** vous apprenez vite; **a ~s' dictionary** un dictionnaire pour apprenants; **language ~** étudiant(e) *m(f)* en langues; **a ~ of English** un apprenant *or* étudiant d'anglais.

learning ['lɜ:nɪŋ] 1 n (*NonC*) a (*fund of knowledge*) érudition *f*, savoir *m*, science *f*. **man of (great) ~** (*in humanities*) érudit *m*; (*in sciences*) savant *m*; *see* **little**[2], **seat.** b (*act*) apprentissage *m*, étude *f* (*of* de). **history** *etc* **~** apprentissage *or* étude de l'histoire *etc*; **~ develops the memory** apprendre développe la mémoire. 2 comp ►**learning difficulties, learning disabilities** troubles *mpl* *or* difficultés *fpl* scolaires, difficultés d'apprentissage ►**learning resources centre** (*Educ*) centre *m* de documentation et d'information.

learnt [lɜ:nt] 1 pret, ptp of **learn.** 2 adj (*Psych*) **~ behaviour** traits acquis.

lease [li:s] 1 n a (*Jur: contract, duration*) bail *m*. **long ~** bail à long terme; **99-year ~** bail de 99 ans; **to take a house on ~** prendre une maison à bail.

b (*fig*) **the antibiotics have given him a new ~ of life** (*Brit*) *or* **a new ~ on life** (*US*) les antibiotiques lui ont rendu sa vitalité; **the news gave him a new ~ of** *or* **on life** la nouvelle lui a donné un regain de vie, cela lui a donné une nouvelle vigueur; **to take on a new ~ of** *or* **on life** retrouver une nouvelle jeunesse.

2 vt a *[tenant etc] house, car* louer à bail.

b (*also* **~ out**) *[owner]* louer à bail.

3 comp ►**leaseback** cession-bail *f*; **leaseback scheme** *or* **contract** contrat *m* de cession-bail ►**leasehold** n (*contract*) bail *m*; (*property*) propriété louée à bail ◊ adj *property* loué à bail ◊ adv à bail; **leasehold reform** révision *f* du bail ►**leaseholder** preneur *m*, -euse *f*, locataire *mf* ►**lease-lend,** (*US*) **lend-lease** (*Econ*) prêt-bail *m*.

leash [li:ʃ] n (*for dog*) laisse *f*; (*for hawk*) filière *f*, créance *f*. **to keep a dog on a ~** tenir un chien en laisse; (*fig*) **to keep sb on a short ~** ne laisser à qn qu'une marge de manœuvre très étroite.

leasing ['li:sɪŋ] n crédit-bail *m*.

least [li:st] superl of **little**[2] 1 adj (*smallest amount of*) le moins de; (*smallest*) le moindre, la moindre, le plus petit, la plus petite. **he has (the) ~ money** c'est lui qui a le moins d'argent; **the ~ thing upsets her** la moindre chose *or* la plus petite chose la contrarie; **principle of ~ effort** principe *m* du moindre effort; (*Math*) **the ~ common denominator** le plus petit commun dénominateur; **with the ~ possible expenditure** avec le moins de dépenses possible; **that's the ~ of our worries** c'est le cadet de nos soucis; *see* **line**[1].

2 pron a le moins. **you've given me the ~** c'est à moi que tu en as donné le moins; **it's the ~ I can do** c'est le moins que je puisse faire,

c'est la moindre des choses; **it's the ~ one can expect** c'est la moindre des choses; **what's the ~ you are willing to accept?** quel prix minimum êtes-vous prêt à accepter?; *see* **say.**

b (*in phrases*) **at ~** (*with quantity, comparison*) au moins; (*parenthetically*) du moins, tout au moins; **it costs £5 at ~** cela coûte au moins *or* au bas mot 5 livres; **there were at ~ 8 books** il y avait au moins 8 livres; **he's at ~ as old as you** il a au moins votre âge; **he eats at ~ as much as I do** il mange au moins autant que moi; **at ~ it's not raining** du moins *or* au moins il ne pleut pas; **you could at ~ have told me!** tu aurais pu au moins me le dire!; **I can at ~ try** je peux toujours *or* du moins essayer; **he's ill, at ~ that's what he says** il est malade, du moins c'est ce qu'il dit; **at the very ~** au moins, au minimum; **not in the ~!** pas du tout!; **he was not in the ~ tired** *or* **not the ~ bit tired** *or* **not tired in the ~** il n'était pas le moins du monde fatigué; **it didn't surprise me in the ~** *or* **I wasn't the ~ bit surprised** cela ne m'a pas surpris le moins du monde; **it doesn't matter in the ~** cela n'a aucune importance *or* pas la moindre importance; (*Prov*) **~ said soonest mended** moins on en dit mieux on se porte, moins on en dit et mieux ça vaut; **that's the ~ of it!** s'il n'y avait que ça!, ça, ce n'est rien!; **I was annoyed, to say the ~ (of it)** j'étais mécontent, c'était le moins qu'on puisse dire.

3 **adv** le moins. **the ~ expensive** le moins cher, la moins chère; **the ~ expensive car** la voiture la moins chère; **he did it ~ easily of all** (*least easily of all he did*) c'est ce qu'il a eu le plus de mal à faire; (*least easily of all people involved*) il l'a fait le moins facilement de tous; **she is ~ able to afford it** c'est elle qui peut le moins se l'offrir; **when you are ~ expecting it** quand vous vous y attendez le moins; **he deserves it ~ of all** c'est lui qui le mérite le moins de tous; **nobody seemed amused, ~ of all John** cela ne semblait amuser personne et surtout pas John; **~ of all would I wish to offend him** je ne voudrais surtout pas le froisser; **all countries, not ~ the U.S.A.** tous les pays, et en particulier les USA; **not ~ because** entre autres parce que.

leastways* ['li:stweɪz] **adv**, **leastwise*** ['li:stwaɪz] **adv** du moins, ou plutôt.

leather ['leðəʳ] 1 **n** a (*NonC*) cuir *m*; *see* **hell, patent** *etc.* b (*also* **wash ~**) peau *f* de chamois; *see* **chamois.** c (*US* ‡: *wallet*) larfeuil‡ *m*, portefeuille *m*. 2 **comp** *boots, seat* de *or* en cuir ► **leather bar*** bar *m* cuir* *or* de cuirs* (*à clientèle sado-masochiste*) ► **leatherbound** *book* relié (en) cuir ► **leather goods** (*gen*) articles *mpl* en cuir; (*fancy goods*) maroquinerie *f* ► **leatherjacket** larve *f* de la tipule ► **leatherneck**‡ (*US*) marine *m*, fusilier marin américain. 3 **vt** (*) tanner le cuir à‡.

leatherette [ˌleðə'ret] **n** similicuir *m*, Skaï *m* ®.

leathering* ['leðərɪŋ] **n: to give sb a ~** tanner le cuir à qn‡.

leathern ['leðən] **adj** (*of leather*) de *or* en cuir; (*like leather*) tanné.

leathery ['leðərɪ] **adj** *meat, substance* coriace; *skin* parcheminé, tanné.

leave [li:v] (**vb: pret, ptp left**) 1 **n** a (*NonC: consent*) permission *f*. **by *or* with your ~** avec votre permission; **without so much as a by-your-~*** sans même demander la permission; **to ask ~ (from sb) to do sth** demander (à qn) la permission de faire qch.

b (*gen: holiday*) congé *m*; (*Mil*) permission *f*. **how much ~ do you get?** vous avez droit à combien de jours de congé (*or* de jours de permission)?; **to be on ~** être en permission *or* en congé; **6 weeks' ~** permission *or* congé de 6 semaines; **on ~ of absence** en congé exceptionnel; (*Mil*) en permission spéciale; *see* **absent, French, sick** *etc.*

c (*departure*) congé *m*. **to take (one's) ~ of sb** prendre congé de qn; **I must take my ~** il faut que je prenne congé; (*fig*) **have you taken ~ of your senses?** êtes-vous fou (*f* folle)?, avez-vous perdu la tête?

2 **comp** ► **leavetaking** adieux *mpl*.

3 **vt** a (*go away from*) *town* quitter, partir de, (*permanently*) quitter; *room, building* sortir de, quitter; *job* quitter; *person* (*gen*) quitter; (*abandon*) abandonner. **he left Paris in 1974** il a quitté Paris en 1974; **we left Paris at 6 o'clock** nous sommes partis de Paris *or* nous avons quitté Paris à 6 heures; **he left school in 1974** il a terminé ses études *or* fini sa scolarité en 1974; **he left school at 4 p.m.** il est sorti de l'école *or* il a quitté l'école à 16 heures; **he left home in 1969** il est parti de la maison en 1969; **I left home at 6 o'clock** je suis sorti de chez moi *or* j'ai quitté la maison à 6 heures; **he has left this address** il n'habite plus à cette adresse; **to ~ prison** sortir de prison; **to ~ hospital** sortir de *or* quitter l'hôpital; **to ~ the room** (*go out*) sortir de la pièce; (*Scol euph: go to toilet*) sortir (*euph*); **to ~ the table** se lever de table, quitter la table; **the ship left port** le navire a quitté le port; **the train left the station** le train est sorti de *or* a quitté la gare; (*Rail*) **to ~ the track** dérailler; **the car left the road** la voiture a quitté la route; **I must ~ you** il faut que je vous quitte (*subj*); (*frm*) **you may ~ us** vous pouvez vous retirer (*frm*); **to ~ one's wife** quitter sa femme; **they were left to die/to starve** *etc* ils ont été abandonnés à la mort/à la famine *etc*; *see* **love, lurch**[2].

b (*forget*) laisser, oublier. **he left his umbrella on the train** il a laissé *or* oublié son parapluie dans le train.

c (*deposit, put*) laisser. **I'll ~ the book for you with my neighbour** je laisserai le livre pour vous chez mon voisin; **to ~ the waiter a tip** laisser un pourboire au garçon; **has the postman left anything?** est-ce que le facteur a apporté *or* laissé quelque chose?; [*parcel*] **"to be left till called for"** "en consigne", "on passera prendre"; **can I ~ my camera with you?** puis-je vous confier mon appareil-photo?; **he left the children with a neighbour** il a laissé *or* confié les enfants à un voisin; **he ~s a widow and one son** il laisse une veuve et un fils; **to ~ a message for sb** laisser un message à qn; **to ~ word** laisser un mot *or* un message (*with sb for sb* à qn pour qn; *that* que); **he left word with me for Paul to go and see him** il m'a chargé de dire à Paul d'aller le voir; **he left word for Paul to go and see him** il a fait dire à Paul d'aller le voir.

d (*allow to remain*) laisser. **to ~ the door open** laisser la porte ouverte; **to ~ 2 pages blank** laisser 2 pages en blanc; **~ it where it is** laisse-le là où il est; **he left it lying on the floor** il l'a laissé par terre; **don't ~ that letter lying around** ne laissez pas traîner cette lettre; **to ~ the phone off the hook** laisser le téléphone décroché; **some things are better left unsaid** il vaut mieux passer certaines choses sous silence; **it left a good impression on me** cela m'a fait bonne impression; **let's ~ it at that** tenons-nous-en là; **I'll ~ it to you to decide** je te laisse le soin de décider; **I('ll) ~ you to judge** je vous laisse juger; **I wanted to ~ myself (with) at least £50 a week** je voulais garder *or* qu'il me reste (*subj*) au moins 50 livres par semaine; **I'll ~ the matter in your hands** je vous laisse vous occuper de l'affaire, je vous laisse le soin d'arranger cela; **shall we go via Paris? — I'll ~ it to you** passerons-nous par Paris? — je m'en remets à vous; **~ it to me!** laissez-moi faire!, je m'en charge!; **I'll ~ you to it*** je vous laisse (à vos occupations); **we left nothing to chance** nous n'avons rien laissé au hasard; **it ~s a lot to be desired** cela laisse beaucoup à désirer; **it left me free for the afternoon** cela m'a laissé l'après-midi de libre, cela m'a libéré pour l'après-midi; **this deal has left me in debt** cette affaire m'a laissé des dettes; **it ~s me cold*** cela me laisse froid *or* de marbre; **~ it alone** n'y touchez pas, laissez ça tranquille*; **~ me alone** laissez-moi tranquille; (*Prov*) **~ well alone** le mieux est l'ennemi du bien (*Prov*); **he was left a widower** il est devenu veuf; **to ~ sb on his own *or* to himself** laisser qn tout seul; **to ~ sb in peace *or* to himself** laisser qn tranquille; **left to himself *or* left to his own devices, he'd never have finished** (tout) seul *or* laissé à lui-même, il n'aurait jamais fini; **to ~ sb in charge of a house/shop** *etc* laisser à qn la garde d'une maison/d'une boutique *etc*; **the boss is out and he's left me in charge** le patron est sorti et m'a laissé la charge de tout; (*Typ etc*) **to ~ a space** laisser un blanc *or* un espace; **he left half his meal** il a laissé la moitié de son repas; **take it or ~ it** c'est à prendre ou à laisser; (*fig*) **I can take it or ~ it** cela me fait ni chaud ni froid; *see* **baby, go, shelf, stand, stone.**

e (*Math*) **3 from 6 ~s 3** 3 ôté de 6 égale *or* reste 3; **if you take 4 from 7, what are you left with?** si tu enlèves 4 de 7, qu'est-ce qu'il te reste?; *see also* **f.**

f **to be left** rester; **what's left?** qu'est-ce qui reste?; **who's left?** qui est-ce qui reste?; **there'll be none left** il n'en restera pas; **how many are (there) left?** combien est-ce qu'il en reste?; **I've no money left** il ne me reste plus d'argent, je n'ai plus d'argent; **I shall have nothing left** il ne me restera plus rien; **there are 3 cakes left** il reste 3 gâteaux; **are there any left?** est-ce qu'il en reste?; **have you (got) any left?** est-ce qu'il vous en reste?; **nothing was left for me but to sell the house** il ne me restait plus qu'à vendre la maison; **I was left with a lot of stock I couldn't sell** je me suis retrouvé avec un gros stock que je ne pouvais pas écouler.

g (*in will*) *money* laisser (*to* à); *object, property* laisser, léguer (*to* à).

4 **vi** (*go away*) [*person, train, ship etc*] partir, s'en aller; (*resign*) partir, démissionner, s'en aller. **it's time we left, it's time for us to ~** il est l'heure de partir *or* que nous partions (*subj*); **he left for Paris** il est parti pour Paris; **the ship left for Australia** le bateau est parti *or* a appareillé pour l'Australie; **the train ~s at 4 o'clock** le train part à 4 heures; **he's just left** il sort d'ici, il vient de partir.

► **leave about, leave around** **vt sep** *clothes, possessions etc* laisser traîner.

► **leave aside** **vt sep** laisser de côté.

► **leave behind** **vt sep** a (*not take*) *person* laisser, ne pas emmener; *object* laisser, ne pas prendre, ne pas emporter. **he left the children behind in Paris** il a laissé les enfants à Paris; **you'll get left behind if you don't hurry up** on va te laisser si tu ne te dépêches pas. b (*outdistance*) *opponent in race* distancer; *fellow students etc* dépasser. c (*forget*) *gloves, umbrella etc* laisser, oublier.

► **leave in** **vt sep** *paragraph, words etc* garder, laisser; *plug* laisser, ne pas enlever. (*Culin*) **leave the cake in for 50 minutes** laisser cuire le gâteau pendant 50 minutes.

► **leave off** 1 **vi** (*: *stop*) s'arrêter. (*in work, reading*) **where did we leave off?** où en étions-nous?, où nous sommes-nous arrêtés?; **leave off!** arrête!, ça suffit!* 2 **vt sep** a (*: *stop*) cesser, arrêter (*doing* de faire). b *lid* ne pas remettre; *clothes* (*not put back on*) ne pas remettre; (*stop wearing*) cesser de porter, abandonner; (*not put on*) ne pas mettre. c *gas, heating, tap* laisser fermé; *light* laisser éteint. c (*not add to list*) (*deliberately*) exclure; (*accidentally*) oublier, omettre.

► **leave on** **vt sep** a *one's hat, coat etc* garder, ne pas enlever; *lid* ne pas enlever, laisser. b *gas, heating, tap* laisser ouvert; *light* laisser allumé.

► **leave out** **vt sep** a (*omit*) (*accidentally*) oublier, omettre; (*deliberately*) exclure; *line in text,* (*Mus*) *note* sauter. **they left him out** ils ne l'ont pas inclus; **I'm feeling left out** j'ai l'impression d'être délaissé *or* exclu *or* tenu à l'écart. b (*not put back*) laisser sorti, ne pas ranger; (*leave visible*) *food, note, etc* laisser. **I left the box out on the table** j'ai laissé la boîte sortie sur la table; **to leave sth out in the rain** laisser qch dehors sous la pluie; **to leave sb out in the cold** (*lit*) laisser qn dans le froid; (*fig*) laisser qn à l'écart.

►**leave over** 1 **vt sep** a **this is all the meat that was left over** c'est toute la viande qui reste; **there's nothing left over** il ne reste plus rien; **there's never anything left over** il n'y a jamais de restes; **after each child has 3 there are 2 left over** quand chaque enfant en a pris 3 il en reste 2; **if there's any money left over** s'il reste de l'argent. b (*postpone*) remettre (à plus tard). **let's leave this over till tomorrow** remettons cela à demain. 2 **leftovers npl** *see* **leftover**.

-leaved [li:vd] **adj ending in comps: small-leaved** à petites feuilles; **round-leaved** à feuilles rondes; **five-leaved stem** tige *f* à cinq feuilles.

leaven ['levn] 1 **n** levain *m*. 2 **vt** (*lit*) faire lever. **~ed bread** pain *m* au levain; (*fig*) **his speech was ~ed by a few witty stories** son discours était relevé par quelques histoires spirituelles.

leavening ['levnıŋ] **n** (*lit, fig*) levain *m*.

leaves [li:vz] **npl of leaf**.

leaving ['li:vıŋ] **n** départ *m*. **a ~ present** un cadeau pour son (*or* mon *etc*) départ.

leavings ['li:vıŋz] **npl** restes *mpl*.

Lebanese [ˌlebə'ni:z] 1 **adj** libanais. 2 **n, pl inv** Libanais(e) *m(f)*.

Lebanon ['lebənən] **n** Liban *m*; *see* **cedar**.

lech* [letʃ] **vi: to ~ after sb** (*desire*) désirer qn; (*behave lecherously*) courir après qn (*fig*).

lecher ['letʃəʳ] **n** débauché *m*.

lecherous ['letʃərəs] **adj** lubrique, luxurieux, libidineux (*hum*); *look* lascif.

lecherously ['letʃərəslı] **adv** lubriquement, lascivement.

lechery ['letʃərı] **n** (*NonC*) luxure *f*, lubricité *f*.

lectern ['lektən] **n** lutrin *m*.

lector ['lektɔ:ʳ] **n** (*Univ*) lecteur *m*, -trice *f*.

lecture ['lektʃəʳ] 1 **n** a (*gen single occurrence*) conférence *f*; (*Univ etc: gen one of a series*) cours *m* (magistral). **to give a ~** faire *or* donner une conférence, faire un cours (*on* sur); **I went to the ~s on French poetry** j'ai suivi le cours de poésie française; *see* **inaugural**.

b (*fig: reproof*) réprimande *f*, sermon *m* (*pej*). **to give** *or* **read sb a ~** sermonner qn (*about* au sujet de).

2 **vi** faire *or* donner une conférence (*to* à, *on* sur), faire un cours (*to* à, *on* sur). (*Univ etc*) **he ~s at 10 o'clock** il fait son cours à 10 heures; **he ~s at Bristol** il est professeur à Bristol; (*Univ*) **he ~s in law** il est professeur de droit; **she ~s on Keats** elle fait cours sur Keats; (*Univ etc*) **he's lecturing at the moment** il fait (son) cours en ce moment.

3 **vt** (*reprove*) réprimander, sermonner (*pej*) (*sb for having done* qn pour avoir fait). **he ~d me for my clumsiness** il m'a réprimandé pour ma maladresse.

4 **comp** ►**lecture course** (*Univ*) cours magistral ►**lecture hall** amphithéâtre *m* ►**lecture notes** notes *fpl* de cours ►**lecture room, lecture theatre** (*gen*) salle *f* de conférences; (*Univ*) amphithéâtre *m*.

lecturer ['lektʃərəʳ] **n** a (*speaker*) conférencier *m*, -ière *f*. b (*Brit Univ*) ≃ assistant(e) *m(f)*; (*Brit Univ*) **senior ~** maître assistant *m*.

lectureship ['lektʃəʃıp] **n** (*see* **lecturer b**) poste *m* d'assistant(e). **he got a ~ at the university** il a été nommé assistant à l'université.

LED [ˌeli:'di:] **n** (**abbr of light-emitting diode**) (diode *f*) LED *f*, diode électroluminescente. **~ display** affichage *m* LED.

led [led] **pret, ptp of lead¹**.

ledge [ledʒ] **n** (*on wall*) rebord *m*, saillie *f*; (*also* **window ~**) rebord (de la fenêtre); (*on mountain*) saillie; (*Climbing*) vire *f*; (*under sea*) (*ridge*) haut-fond *m*; (*reef*) récif *m*.

ledger ['ledʒəʳ] 1 **n** (*Book-keeping*) grand livre (*Comptabilité*). 2 **comp** ►**ledger line** (*Mus*) ligne *f* supplémentaire.

lee [li:] 1 **n** côté *m* sous le vent. **in** *or* **under the ~ of** à l'abri de. 2 **adj** *side of ship, shore* sous le vent.

leech [li:tʃ] **n** (*lit, also fig pej*) sangsue *f*. **he clung like a ~ to me all evening** il m'a collé* comme une sangsue toute la soirée.

leek [li:k] **n** poireau *m*.

leer [lıəʳ] 1 **vi** lorgner. **to ~ at sb** lorgner qn. 2 **n** (*evil*) regard mauvais; (*lustful*) regard concupiscent.

leery* ['lıərı] **adj** (*esp US, Can*) **to be ~ about sth** se méfier de qch.

lees [li:z] **npl** *[wine]* lie *f* (*NonC*).

leeward ['li:wəd] (*esp Naut*) 1 **adj, adv** sous le vent. (*Geog*) **L~ Islands** îles *fpl* Sous-le-Vent. 2 **n** côté *m* sous le vent. **to ~** sous le vent.

leeway ['li:weı] **n** (*Naut*) dérive *f*. (*fig*) **that gives him a certain (amount of) ~** cela lui donne une certaine liberté d'action; (*fig*) **we had 10 minutes' ~ to catch the train** nous avions une marge (de sécurité) de dix minutes pour attraper le train; (*fig*) **there's a lot of ~ to make up** il y a beaucoup de retard à rattraper.

left¹ [left] 1 **pret, ptp of leave.** 2 **comp** ►**left luggage** (*Brit*) bagages *mpl* en consigne ►**left-luggage (office)** consigne *f* ►**left-luggage locker** (casier *m* à) consigne *f* automatique ►**left-over** *see* **leftover**; *see also* **leave**.

left² [left] 1 **adj** *bank, side, hand, ear etc* gauche. (*Aut*) **~ hand down!** braquez à gauche!; (*US fig*) **to be (way) out in ~ field*** être complètement à côté de la plaque✱; *see also* **4**.

2 **adv** *turn, look* à gauche. (*Mil*) **eyes ~!** tête gauche!; **go** *or* **bear** *or* **take** *or* **turn ~ at the church** tournez *or* prenez à gauche à l'église; *see* **right**.

3 **n** a gauche *f*. **on your ~** à *or* sur votre gauche; **on the ~** sur la gauche, à gauche; **the door on the ~** la porte de gauche; **to drive on the ~** conduire à gauche; (*Aut*) **to keep to the ~** tenir sa gauche; **turn it to the ~** tournez-le vers la gauche *or* à gauche.

b (*Pol*) **the L~** la gauche; **he's further to the L~ than I am** il est plus à gauche que moi; **the parties of the L~** (les partis *mpl* de) la gauche.

c (*Boxing*) gauche *m*. **he threw a ~ to the jaw** il a porté un direct du gauche à la mâchoire; **he hit him with his ~** il l'a frappé du gauche.

4 **comp** ►**left back** (*Sport*) arrière *m* gauche ►**left half** (*Sport*) demi *m* gauche ►**left-hand adj** à *or* de gauche; **the left-hand door/page** *etc* la porte/page *etc* de gauche; **left-hand drive car** conduite *f* à gauche (*véhicule*); **this car is left-hand drive** cette voiture a la conduite à gauche; **on the left-hand side** à gauche; **a left-hand turn** un virage à gauche ►**left-handed** *person* gaucher; *screw* fileté à gauche; *scissors etc* pour gaucher; (*fig*) **left-handed compliment** (*insincere*) compliment *m* hypocrite; (*ambiguous*) compliment ambigu ►**left-hander** (*person*) gaucher *m*, -ère *f*; (*: *blow*) gifle *f or* claque* *f* (assenée de la main gauche) ►**left-of-centre** (*Pol*) de centre gauche ►**left wing** (*Mil, Sport*) aile *f* gauche; (*Pol*) gauche *f* ►**left-wing** *newspaper, view* de gauche; **he's very left-wing** il est très à gauche ►**left-winger** (*Pol*) homme *m or* femme *f* de gauche; (*Sport*) ailier *m* gauche.

leftie* ['leftı] **n** a (*pej, Pol*) gaucho* *mf* (*pej*), gauchiste *mf*. b (*US: left-handed person*) gaucher *m*, -ère *f*.

leftism ['leftızəm] **n** (*NonC*) gauchisme *m*.

leftist ['leftıst] (*Pol*) 1 **n** gauchiste *mf*. 2 **adj** de gauche.

leftover ['leftˌəʊvəʳ] 1 **n** a (*throwback*) vestige *m*. b (*after meal*) **~s** *npl* restes *mpl*. 2 **adj** restant, qui reste. **a bottle of ~ wine** une bouteille avec un restant de vin.

leftward(s) ['leftwəd(z)] (*lit, Pol*) 1 **adj** orienté vers la gauche. 2 **adv** vers la gauche.

lefty* ['leftı] **n** = **leftie**.

leg [leg] 1 **n** a *[person, horse]* jambe *f*; *[other animal, bird, insect]* patte *f*. **my ~s won't carry me any further!** je ne tiens plus sur mes jambes!; **to stand on one ~** se tenir sur un pied *or* une jambe; **she's got nice** *or* **good ~s** elle a les jambes bien faites; **to give sb a ~ up** (*lit*) faire la courte échelle à qn; (* *fig*) donner un coup de pouce à qn; (*fig*) **he hasn't got a ~ to stand on** il ne peut s'appuyer sur rien, il n'a aucun argument valable; (*fig*) **to pull sb's ~** (*hoax*) faire marcher qn; (*tease*) taquiner qn; *see* **fast¹**, **hind²**, **last¹** *etc*.

b (*Culin*) *[lamb]* gigot *m*; *[beef]* gîte *m*, crosse *f*; *[veal]* sous-noix *f*; *[pork, chicken, frog]* cuisse *f*; *[venison]* cuissot *m*.

c *[table etc]* pied *m*; *[trousers, stocking etc]* jambe *f*; *see* **inside**.

d (*stage*) *[journey]* étape *f*. (*Ftbl etc*) **first ~** match *m* aller; **second** *or* **return ~** match retour; (*Sport: in relay*) **to run/swim the first ~** courir/nager la première distance *or* le premier relais.

2 **comp** ►**leg bone** tibia *m* ►**leg iron** (*Med*) appareil *m* (orthopédique) ►**legman*** (*Press*) reporter *m* débutant (qui va sur les lieux); (*gen*) garçon *m* de courses ►**leg muscle** muscle *m* de la jambe, muscle jambier (*frm*) ►**leg-pull*** canular *m* ►**leg-pulling*** mise *f* en boîte*, canulars *mpl* ►**legroom** place *f* pour les (*or* mes *etc*) jambes ►**leg shield** protège-jambe *m* ►**leg-warmers** jambières *fpl* ►**legwork*** *[reporter, investigator etc]* travail *m* de recherche sur place, déplacements *mpl*.

3 **vt: to ~ it*** (*run*) cavaler✱; (*flee*) se barrer✱; (*walk*) aller à pied, faire le chemin à pied.

legacy ['legəsı] **n** (*Jur*) legs *m* (*de biens mobiliers*); (*fig*) legs, héritage *m*. (*Jur*) **to leave a ~ to sb** laisser un héritage à qn, faire un legs à qn; **~ duty** *or* (*US*) **tax** impôt *m* sur les successions, droits *mpl* de succession; (*fig*) **this law is a ~ from medieval times** cette loi est un legs de l'époque médiévale; (*hum*) **this vase is a ~ from the previous tenants** on a hérité ce vase des précédents locataires.

legal ['li:gəl] **adj** a (*lawful*) *act, decision* légal; *requirements* légitime; *right* légal, légitime. **to acquire ~ status** acquérir un statut légal *or* judiciaire; (*Fin*) **~ currency, ~ tender** monnaie légale; **this note is no longer ~ currency** *or* **tender** ce billet n'a plus cours; **~ document** titre *m* authentique; (*US*) **~ holiday** jour férié.

b (*concerning the law*) *error* judiciaire; *affair, question* juridique. **to take ~ action against** intenter un procès à *or* contre; **I am considering taking ~ action** j'envisage d'intenter une action; **to take ~ advice** consulter un juriste *or* un avocat; **~ adviser** conseiller *m*, -ère *f* juridique; **~ aid** assistance *f* judiciaire; **~ costs** frais *mpl* de justice; *[bank, firm etc]* **~ department** service *m* du contentieux; **~ entity** personne *f* morale; **~ fiction** fiction *f* juridique; **it's a ~ matter** c'est une question juridique *or* de droit; **in ~ matters** en ce qui concerne le droit; **the ~ mind** l'esprit *m* juridique; **a ~ offence** une infraction à la loi; **~ opinion** avis *m* juridique; **~ proceedings** procès *m*, poursuites *fpl*; **the ~ process** la procédure; **the ~ profession** les hommes *mpl* de loi; **to go into the ~ profession** faire une carrière juridique *or* de juriste; **~ re-**

dress réparation *f* en justice; ~ **successor** ayant cause *m*.
legalese* [ˌliːgəˈliːz] n (*pej*) jargon *m* des juristes.
legalism [ˈliːgəˌlɪzəm] n (*pej*) a (*word, point, rule etc*) argutie *f* juridique. b (*turn of mind*) juridisme *m*, légalisme *m*.
legalistic [ˌliːgəˈlɪstɪk] adj (*pej*) légaliste, formaliste.
legalistically [ˌliːgəˈlɪstɪkəlɪ] adv au sens légal le plus strict.
legality [lɪˈgælɪtɪ] n légalité *f*.
legalization [ˌliːgəlaɪˈzeɪʃən] n légalisation *f*.
legalize [ˈliːgəlaɪz] vt légaliser.
legally [ˈliːgəlɪ] adv a (*lawfully*) *act etc* légalement. b (*in law, from point of view of law*) juridiquement, légalement. **this contract is ~ binding** c'est un contrat qui lie; ~ **valid** légalement valide; ~ **responsible** légalement *or* juridiquement responsable, responsable aux yeux de la loi.
legate [ˈlegɪt] n légat *m*.
legatee [ˌlegəˈtiː] n légataire *mf*.
legation [lɪˈgeɪʃən] n légation *f*.
legator [ˌlegəˈtɔːʳ] n testateur *m*, -trice *f*.
legend [ˈledʒənd] n (*all senses*) légende *f*. **a ~ in his own lifetime** une légende de son vivant.
legendary [ˈledʒəndərɪ] adj légendaire.
legerdemain [ˌledʒədəˈmeɪn] n prestidigitation *f*.
-legged [ˈlegɪd] adj ending in comps: **four-legged** à quatre pattes, quadrupède (*frm*); **bare-legged** aux jambes nues; *see* **three** *etc*.
leggings [ˈlegɪŋz] npl jambières *fpl*, leggin(g)s *mpl or fpl*; (*for baby*) culotte *f* (longue); (*thigh boots*) cuissardes *fpl*. **waterproof ~** jambières imperméables.
leggo‡ [leˈgəʊ] excl = **let go**; *see* **go 1b**.
leggy* [ˈlegɪ] adj *person* aux longues jambes; (*slightly pej*) *youth etc* tout en jambes; *animal* aux longues pattes, haut sur pattes. **a gorgeous ~ blonde** une magnifique blonde aux longues jambes.
Leghorn [ˈlegˌhɔːn] n (*Geog*) Livourne.
legibility [ˌledʒɪˈbɪlɪtɪ] n lisibilité *f*.
legible [ˈledʒəbl] adj lisible.
legibly [ˈledʒəblɪ] adv lisiblement.
legion [ˈliːdʒən] n légion *f* (*also fig*); *see* **foreign**.
legionary [ˈliːdʒənərɪ] 1 n légionnaire *m*. 2 adj de la légion.
legionella [ˌliːdʒəˈnelə] n légionellose *f*.
legionnaire [ˌliːdʒəˈnɛəʳ] n légionnaire *m*. (*Med*) **~'s disease** maladie *f* du légionnaire.
legislate [ˈledʒɪsleɪt] vi légiférer, faire des lois. **to ~ against** faire des lois contre.
legislation [ˌledʒɪsˈleɪʃən] n a (*body of laws*) législation *f*; (*single law*) loi *f*. **a piece of ~** une loi; **to bring in** *or* **introduce ~** faire des lois; **the government is considering ~ against ...** le gouvernement envisage de créer une législation contre ...; **we are in favour of ~ to abolish ...** nous sommes partisans d'une législation qui abolirait ...; **under the present ~** sous la législation actuelle. b (*NonC*) (*making laws*) élaboration *f* des lois; (*enacting*) promulgation *f* des lois.
legislative [ˈledʒɪslətɪv] adj législatif. **the ~ body** le (corps) législatif; (*US Pol*) ~ **drafting** rédaction *f* des projets de loi.
legislator [ˈledʒɪsleɪtəʳ] n législateur *m*, -trice *f*.
legislature [ˈledʒɪslətʃəʳ] n (corps *m*) législatif *m*.
legist [ˈliːdʒɪst] n légiste *mf*.
legit‡ [ləˈdʒɪt] adj abbr of **legitimate 1**.
legitimacy [lɪˈdʒɪtɪməsɪ] n légitimité *f*.
legitimate [lɪˈdʒɪtɪmɪt] 1 adj a (*Jur etc: lawful*) *action, right, ruler, child, authority* légitime. **for ~ purposes** dans un but légitime, pour des motifs valables. b (*fig*) *argument, cause, excuse* bon, valable; *complaint* légitime, fondé; *reasoning, conclusion* logique. **it would be ~ to think that ...** on serait en droit de penser que ...; **the ~ stage** *or* **theatre** (*gen*) le théâtre sérieux; (*as opp to cinema*) le théâtre (*par opposition au cinéma*). 2 [lɪˈdʒɪtɪmeɪt] vt légitimer.
legitimately [lɪˈdʒɪtɪmɪtlɪ] adv a (*lit*) *act* légitimement, dans son (*etc*) bon droit. b (*fig: justifiably*) *argue etc* de façon valable, légitimement, logiquement. **one might ~ believe/ask** *etc* on est en droit de croire/de demander *etc*.
legitimize [lɪˈdʒɪtɪmaɪz] vt légitimer.
legless [ˈleglɪs] adj a (*lit*) sans jambes, cul-de-jatte. **~ cripple** cul-de-jatte *mf*. b (*fig *: drunk*) bourré‡, rond*.
legume [ˈlegjuːm] n (*gen: plant*) légumineuse *f*; (*pod*) gousse *f*.
leguminous [leˈgjuːmɪnəs] adj légumineux.
Leibnitzian [laɪbˈnɪtsɪən] adj leibnitzien.
Leics. (*Brit*) abbr of **Leicestershire**.
Leipzig [ˈlaɪpsɪg] n Leipzig.
leisure [ˈleʒəʳ], (*US*) [ˈliːʒəʳ] 1 n (*NonC*) loisir *m*, temps *m* libre. **he had the ~ in which to go fishing** il avait le loisir d'aller à la pêche; (*hum*) **she's a lady of ~** elle est rentière (*fig hum*); **a life of ~** une vie pleine de loisirs, une vie d'oisiveté (*pej*); **do it at your ~** faites-le quand vous en aurez le temps *or* le loisir, faites-le quand vous aurez du temps libre; **he is not often at ~** il n'a pas souvent de temps libre; **think about it at ~** réfléchissez-y à tête reposée.
2 comp ►**leisure centre, leisure complex** centre *m* de loisirs ►**leisure moments: in my leisure moments** à mes moments de loisir, pendant mes loisirs ►**leisure occupations** loisirs *mpl* ►**leisure suit** costume *m* sport, costume décontracté ►**leisure time** loisir *m*, temps *m* libre ►**leisure wear** (*Comm*) vêtements *mpl* sport, vêtements décontractés.
leisured [ˈleʒəd] adj *person* qui a beaucoup de loisirs, qui n'a rien à faire; *life, existence* doux (*f* douce), peu fatigant. **the ~ classes** la classe oisive, le beau monde (*pej*).
leisurely [ˈleʒəlɪ] 1 adj *pace, movement* lent, mesuré, tranquille; *person* placide, calme, pondéré; *journey, stroll* peu fatigant, fait sans se presser; *occupation* qui ne demande pas beaucoup d'efforts, peu fatigant. **he moved in a ~ way towards the door** il se dirigea vers la porte sans se presser; **to work in a ~ way** travailler sans se dépenser *or* sans faire de gros efforts *or* sans se fouler*. 2 adv sans se presser.
leitmotiv [ˈlaɪtməʊˌtiːf] n (*Mus, fig*) leitmotiv *m*.
lem [lem] n (*Space*) lem *m*, module *m* lunaire.
lemma [ˈlemə] n, pl **~s** *or* **lemmata** [ˈlemətə] (*Ling: gen*) vocable *m*; (*Comput Ling*) lemme *m*.
lemmatization [leməˌtaɪˈzeɪʃən] n lemmatisation *f*.
lemmatize [ˈlemətaɪz] vt lemmatiser.
lemming [ˈlemɪŋ] n lemming *m*.
lemon [ˈlemən] 1 n a (*fruit, drink*) citron *m*; (*tree*) citronnier *m*; (*colour*) citron; *see* **bitter**.
b (*) cruche* *f*; (*idiot*) imbécile *mf*; (*defective object*) cochonnerie* *f*.
2 adj (*in colour*) citron *inv*.
3 comp ►**lemon balm** mélisse *f* ►**lemon cheese** (*Brit*), **lemon curd** (*Brit*) (sorte *f* de) crème *f* de citron ►**lemon drink** citronnade *f*, (*fresh lemon*) citron pressé ►**lemon drop** bonbon *m* (acidulé) au citron ►**lemon grass** lemon-grass *m* ►**lemon grove** plantation *f* de citronniers ►**lemon juice** jus *m* de citron; (*drink*) citron pressé ►**lemon soda** (*esp US*) limonade *f* ►**lemon sole** (*Brit*) limande-sole *f* ►**lemon squash** ≃ citronnade *f* ►**lemon squeezer** presse-citron *m inv* ►**lemon tea** thé *m* au citron ►**lemon tree** citronnier *m* ►**lemon yellow** adj, n jaune citron (*m*) *inv*.
lemonade [ˌleməˈneɪd] n (*still*) citronnade *f*; (*fizzy*) limonade *f*.
lemur [ˈliːməʳ] n maki *m*.
lend [lend] pret, ptp **lent** 1 vt a *money, possessions* prêter (*to sb* à qn). **to ~ money at 10%** prêter de l'argent à 10 %; *see* **lease**.
b (*fig*) *importance* prêter, accorder (*to* à); *dignity, authority, mystery* donner, conférer (*to* à). **to ~ an ear** écouter, prêter l'oreille; **to ~ one's name to** accorder son patronage à; **he refused to ~ his name to** il a refusé de prêter son nom *or* d'accorder son patronage à; **it would ~ itself to a different treatment** cela se prêterait à un autre traitement; **it doesn't ~ itself to being filmed** cela ne donnerait pas matière à un film; **I shall not ~ myself to your scheme** je ne me prêterai pas à votre projet; *see* **hand, support** *etc*.
2 comp ►**lend-lease** (*US*) = **lease-lend**; *see* **lease 3**.
►**lend out** vt sep *object, book* prêter.
lender [ˈlendəʳ] n prêteur *m*, -euse *f*; *see* **money**.
lending [ˈlendɪŋ] 1 n prêt *m*. **bank ~** prêt bancaire. 2 comp ►**lending library** bibliothèque *f* de prêt ►**lending limit** (*Fin*) plafond *m* de crédit ►**lending policy** (*Fin*) politique *f* de prêt ►**lending rate** (*Fin*) taux *m* de prêt, taux d'intérêt débiteur.
length [leŋ(k)θ] 1 n a (*NonC: in space*) longueur *f*. **its ~ was 6 metres, it was 6 metres in ~** cela avait 6 mètres de long; **what is the ~ of the field?, what ~ is the field?** quelle est la longueur du champ?; **overall ~** longueur totale, longueur hors tout; **along the whole ~ of the river** tout au long de la rivière; **what ~ do you want?** quelle longueur vous faut-il?, il vous en faut combien de long?; **what ~ (of cloth) did you buy?** quel métrage (de tissu) as-tu acheté?; **the ship turns in its own ~** le navire vire sur place; (*fig*) **over the ~ and breadth of England** partout dans l'Angleterre, dans toute l'Angleterre; **to go** *or* **measure one's ~ (on the ground), to fall full ~** tomber *or* s'étaler* de tout son long; *see* **arm¹, full** *etc*.
b (*NonC*) (*in time etc*) durée *f*; [*book, essay, letter, film, speech*] longueur *f*. **what ~ is the film?** quelle est la durée du film?; **~ of life** durée de vie; **for the whole ~ of his life** pendant toute la durée de sa vie; **for what ~ of time?** pour combien de temps?, pour quelle durée?; **for some ~ of time** pendant un certain temps, pendant quelque temps; **the ~ of time he took to do it** le temps qu'il a mis à le faire; (*Admin*) **~ of service** ancienneté *f*; [*essay, book*] **4,000 words in ~** de 4 000 mots; (*at last*) **at ~** enfin, à la fin; **at (great) ~** (*for a long time*) fort longuement; (*in detail*) dans le détail, à fond, en long et en large; (*fig*) **he went to the ~ of asking my advice** il est allé jusqu'à me demander conseil; **I've gone to great ~s to get it finished** je me suis donné beaucoup de mal pour le terminer; **he would go to any ~(s) to succeed** il ne reculerait devant rien pour réussir; **I didn't think he would go to such ~s to get the job** je n'aurais pas cru qu'il serait allé jusque-là pour avoir le poste.
c (*Sport*) longueur *f*. **to win by a ~** gagner d'une longueur; **he was 2 ~s behind** il avait un retard de 2 longueurs; **the race will be swum over 6 ~s** la course se nagera sur 6 longueurs; **4 ~s of the pool** 4 longueurs de piscine, 4 fois la longueur de la piscine; **he was about 3 car ~s behind me** il était à 3 longueurs de voiture derrière moi.

d (*Ling*) *[vowel]* quantité *f*; *[syllable]* longueur *f*.
e (*section*) *[rope, wire]* morceau *m*, bout *m*; *[wallpaper]* lé *m*, laize *f*; *[cloth]* pièce *f*, morceau; *[tubing]* morceau, bout, tronçon *m*; *[track]* tronçon. **cut into metre ~s** coupé en morceaux d'un mètre; **I bought several ~s of dress material** j'ai acheté plusieurs métrages *mpl or* hauteurs *fpl* de tissu pour faire une robe; (*Sewing*) **dress/skirt ~** hauteur de robe/de jupe.
2 **comp** ▸**length mark** (*Ling*) signe *m* diacritique de longueur.

-length [leŋ(k)θ] **adj ending in comps: ankle-length skirt** jupe *f* qui descend jusqu'aux chevilles; **elbow-length sleeve** manche *f* mi-longue; *see* **shoulder.**

lengthen ['leŋ(k)θən] 1 **vt** *object* allonger, rallonger; *visit, life* prolonger; (*Ling*) *vowel* allonger. 2 **vi** allonger, rallonger, s'allonger; *[skirts]* rallonger; *[visit etc]* se prolonger. **the days/nights are ~ing** les jours/nuits rallongent; **the intervals between his visits were ~ing** ses visites s'espaçaient.

lengthily ['leŋ(k)θılı] **adv** longuement.

lengthways ['leŋ(k)θ,weız], **lengthwise** ['leŋ(k)θ,waız] 1 **adv** dans le sens de la longueur, en long, longitudinalement. 2 **adj** longitudinal, en longueur.

lengthy ['leŋ(k)θı] **adj** (très) long (*f* longue); (*tedious*) interminable. **the book is ~ in places** ce livre a des longueurs.

lenience ['li:nıəns] **n**, **leniency** ['li:nıənsı] **n** (*see* **lenient**) indulgence *f*; clémence *f*.

lenient ['li:nıənt] **adj** *judge, parent* indulgent (*to* envers, pour); *government* clément (*to* envers).

leniently ['li:nıəntlı] **adv** (*see* **lenient**) avec indulgence; avec clémence (*liter*).

Lenin ['lenın] **n** Lénine *m*.

Leningrad ['lenıngræd] **n** Leningrad.

Leninism ['lenı,nızəm] **n** léninisme *m*.

Leninist ['lenınıst] **adj, n** léniniste (*mf*).

lens [lenz] 1 **n** (*for magnifying*) lentille *f*; *[camera]* objectif *m*; *[spectacles]* verre *m*; *[eye]* cristallin *m*; *see* **contact, telephoto, wide.** 2 **comp** ▸**lens cap** (*Phot*) bouchon *m* d'objectif ▸**lens field** angle *m* de couverture ▸**lens holder** porte-objectif *m inv* ▸**lens hood** parasoleil *m*.

lent [lent] **pret, ptp of lend.**

Lent [lent] **n** (*Rel*) le Carême. **in** *or* **during ~** pendant le Carême, en Carême; **to keep ~** observer le carême, faire carême; **I gave it up for ~** j'y ai renoncé pour le Carême.

Lenten ['lentən] **adj** de carême.

lentil ['lentl] **n** (*Bot, Culin*) lentille *f*. **~ soup** soupe *f* aux lentilles.

Leo ['li:əʊ] **n** (*Astron*) le Lion. **I'm (a) ~** je suis (du) Lion.

Leonard ['lenəd] **n** Léonard *m*.

Leonardo [,li:ə'nɑ:dəʊ] **n: ~ (da Vinci)** Léonard de Vinci *m*.

Leonian [li:'əʊnıən] **n: to be a ~** être (du) Lion.

leonine ['li:ənaın] **adj** léonin.

leopard ['lepəd] 1 **n** léopard *m*. (*Prov*) **the ~ cannot change its spots** on ne peut pas changer sa nature, chassez le naturel, il revient au galop. 2 **comp** ▸**leopardskin** peau *f* de léopard ▸**leopardskin coat** manteau *m* de léopard.

leopardess [,lepədes] **n** léopard *m* femelle.

leotard ['li:ətɑ:d] **n** collant *m* (*de danseur, d'acrobate*).

leper ['lepəʳ] **n** (*Med, fig*) lépreux *m*, -euse *f*. **~ colony** léproserie *f*.

lepidoptera [,lepı'dɒptərə] **npl** lépidoptères *mpl*.

lepidopterist [,lepı'dɒptərıst] **n** lépidoptériste *mf*.

leprechaun ['leprəkɔ:n] **n** (*Ir*) lutin *m*, farfadet *m*.

leprosy ['leprəsı] **n** lèpre *f*.

leprous ['leprəs] **adj** lépreux.

lesbian ['lezbıən] 1 **adj** lesbien. 2 **n** lesbienne *f*.

lesbianism ['lezbıənızəm] **n** lesbianisme *m*, homosexualité féminine.

lesion ['li:ʒən] **n** (*Med*) lésion *f*.

Lesotho [lı'su:tʊ] **n** Lesotho *m*.

less [les] **compar of little²** 1 **adj, pron** a (*in amount, size, degree*) moins (de). **~ butter** moins de beurre; **I have ~ than you** j'en ai moins que vous; **I need ~ than that** il m'en faut moins que cela; **even ~** encore moins; **even** *or* **still ~ butter** encore moins de beurre; **I have ~ money than you** j'ai moins d'argent que vous; **much ~ milk** beaucoup moins de lait; **a little ~ cream** un peu moins de crème; **~ and ~** de moins en moins; **~ and ~ money** de moins en moins d'argent; **it costs ~ than the export model** il coûte moins cher que le modèle d'exportation; **it was ~ money than I expected** c'était moins (d'argent) que je n'escomptais; **~ than half the audience** moins de la moitié de l'assistance *or* des auditeurs; **he has little but I have ~** il n'a pas grand-chose mais j'en ai encore moins; **he did ~ to help them than his brother did** il a moins fait *or* fait moins pour les aider que son frère; (*fig*) **he couldn't have done ~ if he'd tried** même en essayant il n'aurait pas pu faire moins *or* moins faire; **I got ~ out of it than you did** j'en ai tiré moins de profit que toi; **of ~ importance** de moindre importance, de moins d'importance; **it took ~ time than I expected** cela a pris moins de temps que je ne pensais; **I have ~ time for reading** j'ai moins le temps de lire, j'ai moins de temps pour lire; **we eat ~ bread than we used to** nous mangeons moins de pain qu'avant; **~ noise please!** moins de bruit s'il vous plaît!; **~ of that!** *or* **it!** assez!, ça suffit!; **with ~ trouble** avec moins de mal; **he knows little German and ~ Russian** il ne sait pas bien l'allemand et encore moins le russe; **we must see ~ of her** il faut que nous la voyions (*subj*) moins souvent; **it is ~ than perfect** on ne peut pas dire que ce soit parfait; **in ~ than a month** en moins d'un mois; **in ~ than no time*** en un rien de temps, en moins de deux*; **not ~ than one kilo** pas moins d'un kilo; **a sum ~ than 10 francs** une somme de moins de 10 F; **it's ~ than you think** c'est moins que vous ne croyez; **I won't sell it for ~ than £10** je ne le vendrai pas à *or* pour moins de 10 livres; **can't you let me have it for ~?** vous ne pouvez pas me le laisser à moins?; **~ of your cheek!*** un peu moins de toupet!*
b (*in phrases*) **with no ~ skill than enthusiasm** avec non moins d'habileté que d'enthousiasme; **no ~ a person than the Prime Minister** rien moins que le Premier ministre; **he's bought a car, no ~*** il s'est payé une voiture, rien que ça*; **I was told the news by the bishop, no ~*** c'est l'évêque, s'il vous plaît*, qui m'a appris la nouvelle; **he has no ~ than 4 months' holiday a year** il a au moins *or* au bas mot 4 mois de vacances par an; **it costs no ~ than £100** ça ne coûte pas moins de 100 livres; **I think no ~ of him** *or* **I think none the ~ of him** *or* **I don't think any (the) ~ of him for that** il n'est pas descendu dans mon estime pour autant; **I have so much ~ money nowadays** j'ai tellement moins d'argent maintenant; **there will be so much the ~ to pay** il y aura autant de moins à payer; **the ~ said about it the better** mieux vaut ne pas en parler; **the ~ you buy the ~ you spend** moins vous achetez moins vous dépensez; **nothing ~ than** rien moins que, tout simplement; **he's nothing ~ than a thief** c'est tout simplement un voleur, ce n'est qu'un voleur; **nothing ~ than a bomb would move them** il faudrait au moins une bombe pour les faire bouger; **nothing ~ than a public apology will satisfy him** il ne lui faudra rien moins que des excuses publiques pour le satisfaire; **it's nothing ~ than disgraceful** le moins qu'on puisse dire c'est que c'est une honte.
2 **adv** a moins. **you must eat ~** vous devez moins manger, il faut que vous mangiez (*subj*) moins; **I must see you ~** il faut que je vous voie moins souvent; **to grow ~** diminuer; **that's ~ important** c'est moins important, ça n'est pas si important; **~ and ~** de moins en moins; (*frm*) **still ~, much ~, even ~** encore moins; **~ regularly/often** moins régulièrement/souvent; **it's ~ expensive than you think** c'est moins cher que vous ne croyez; **whichever is (the) ~ expensive** le moins cher des deux; **he is ~ well known** il est moins (bien) connu; **he was ~ hurt than frightened** il a eu plus de peur que de mal; **the problem is ~ one of capital than of personnel** ce n'est pas tant *or* c'est moins un problème de capital qu'un problème de personnel.
b (*in phrases*) **the ~ he works the ~ he earns** moins il travaille moins il gagne; **the ~ you worry about it the better** le moins vous vous ferez du souci à ce sujet et le mieux ça vaudra; **he was (all) the ~ pleased as he'd refused to give his permission** il était d'autant moins content qu'il avait refusé son autorisation; **he wasn't expecting me but he was none the ~ pleased to see me** il ne m'attendait pas mais il n'en était pas moins content de me voir; **she is no ~ intelligent than you** elle n'est pas moins intelligente que vous; **he criticized the director no ~ than the caretaker** il a critiqué le directeur tout autant que le concierge; **he was ~ annoyed than amused** il était moins fâché qu'amusé; **it is ~ a short story than a novel** c'est moins une nouvelle qu'un roman; *see* **more.**
3 **prep** moins. **~ 10% discount** moins 10 % de remise; **in a year ~ 4 days** dans un an moins 4 jours.

...less [lıs] **adj ending in comps hatless** sans chapeau; **childless** sans enfants.

lessee [le'si:] **n** preneur *m*, -euse *f* (à bail).

lessen ['lesn] 1 **vt** (*gen*) diminuer; *cost* réduire; *anxiety, pain* atténuer; *effect, shock* amortir; (*Pol*) *tension* relâcher. 2 **vi** diminuer, s'amoindrir; *[pain]* s'atténuer; *[tension]* se relâcher.

lessening ['lesnıŋ] **n** (*NonC*) diminution *f*, amoindrissement *m*. (*Pol*) **~ of tension** détente *f*.

lesser ['lesəʳ] **adj** a moindre. **to a ~ degree** *or* **extent** à un moindre degré, à un degré moindre; **the ~ of two evils** le moindre de deux maux; (*hum*) **we ~ mortals*** *or* **beings*** nous (autres) simples mortels (*hum*).
b (*Bot, Zool, Geog*) petit. **~ celandine** ficaire *f*; **~ panda** petit panda *m*; **the ~ Antilles** les Petites Antilles.

lesson ['lesn] 1 **n** a (*gen*) leçon *f*; (*in school, college etc*) leçon, cours *m*. **a French/geography** *etc* **~** une leçon *or* un cours de français/de géographie *etc*; **swimming/driving ~** leçon de natation/de conduite; **to have** *or* **take ~s in** prendre des leçons de; **to give ~s in** donner des leçons de; **we have ~s from 9 to midday** nous avons classe *or* cours de 9 heures à midi; **~s start at 9 o'clock** la classe commence à 9 heures; (*fig*) **let that be a ~ to you!** que cela vous serve de leçon!; *see* **private, teach** *etc.* b (*Rel*) leçon *f*; *see* **read¹.** 2 **comp** ▸**lesson plans** (*US Scol*) dossier *m* pédagogique.

lessor [le'sɔ:ʳ] **n** bailleur *m*, -eresse *f*.

lest [lest] **conj** a (*for fear that*) de peur *or* de crainte de + *infin*, de peur *or* de crainte que (+ ne) + *subj*. **he took the map ~ he should get lost** il a pris la carte de peur *or* crainte de se perdre; **I gave him the map ~ he should get lost** je lui ai donné la carte de peur *or* de crainte qu'il (ne) se perde; (*on war memorial etc*) **"~ we forget"** "In memoriam".

b (*liter*) **I was afraid ~ he should** *or* **might fall** je craignais qu'il ne tombe (*subj*) *or* ne tombât (*subj: frm*).

let[1] [let] **pret, ptp let** 1 **vt** a (*allow*) laisser, permettre; (*cause to*) laisser, faire. **to ~ sb do sth** laisser qn faire qch; **he wouldn't ~ us** il n'a pas voulu (nous le permettre); **she wanted to help but her mother wouldn't ~ her** elle voulait aider mais sa mère ne l'a pas laissée faire; **I won't ~ you be treated like that** je ne permettrai pas qu'on vous traite (*subj*) de cette façon; **I won't ~ it be said that ...** je ne permettrai pas que l'on dise que ...; **who ~ you into the house?** qui vous a fait entrer dans la maison?; **to ~ sb into a secret** faire entrer qn dans un secret, mettre qn au courant d'un secret; (*fig*) **to ~ sb off (doing) sth** dispenser qn de (faire) qch; **don't ~ it get you down*** n'aie pas le cafard *or* ne te laisse pas démoraliser pour autant*; **don't ~ me forget** rappelle-moi, fais-moi penser; **don't ~ the fire go out** ne laisse pas s'éteindre le feu; **~ me have a look** laissez-moi regarder *or* voir, faites voir; **~ me help you** laissez-moi vous aider, attendez que je vous aide* (*subj*); **~ me tell you ...** que je vous dise ... *or* raconte (*subj*) ...; **when can you ~ me have it?** quand est-ce que je pourrai l'avoir? *or* le prendre?; **~ him have it!** (*give*) donnez-le-lui!; (*‡: shoot*) règle-lui son compte!*; **~ him be!** laisse-le (tranquille)!; **(just you) ~ me catch you stealing again*** que je t'attrape (*subj*) *or* t'y prenne encore à voler; **the hunted man ~ himself be seen** l'homme traqué s'est laissé repérer; **I ~ myself be persuaded** je me suis laissé convaincre; *see* **alone, drop, fall, fly**[3]**, go, know, lie** *etc*.

b (*used to form imper of 1st person*) **~ us** *or* **~'s go for a walk** allons nous promener; **~'s go!** allons-y!; **~'s get out of here!** filons!, fichons le camp (d'ici)!*; **don't ~'s** *or* **~'s not start yet** ne commençons pas encore; **don't ~ me keep you** que je ne vous retienne pas; **don't ~ me see you doing that again** que je ne t'y reprenne pas, que je ne te revois pas faire ça; **~ us pray** prions; **~ me see (now) ..., ~'s see (now) ...** voyons ...; **~ me think** laissez-moi réfléchir, que je réfléchisse*; *see* **say 1c, 1f**.

c (*used to form imper of 3rd person*) **if he wants the book, ~ him come and get it himself** s'il veut le livre, qu'il vienne le chercher lui-même *or* il n'a qu'à venir le chercher lui-même; **~ him say what he likes, I don't care** qu'il dise ce qu'il veut, ça m'est égal; **~ no one believe that I will change my mind** que personne ne s'imagine (*subj*) que je vais changer d'avis; **~ that be a warning to you** que cela vous serve d'avertissement; **~ there be light** que la lumière soit; **just ~ them try!** qu'ils essaient (*subj*) un peu!; (*Math*) **~ x equal 2** soit x égal à 2.

d (*Med*) **to ~ blood** tirer du sang, faire une saignée.

e **to ~ a window/door into a wall** percer *or* ouvrir une fenêtre/porte dans un mur.

f (*hire out*) *house etc* louer, mettre en location. **"flat to ~"** "appartement à louer"; **"to ~", "to be ~"** "à louer".

2 **n** *[house etc]* location *f*. **I'm looking for a long/short ~ for my villa** je cherche à louer ma villa pour une longue/brève période.

3 **comp ►let alone** (*used as conj*) *see* **alone d ►let-down** déception *f*; **what a let-down!*** quelle déception!, cela promettait pourtant bien!; **the film was a let-down* after the book** voir le film après avoir lu le livre, quelle déception! **►let-out** (*Brit*) échappatoire *m*, issue *f* **►let-up*** (*decrease*) diminution *f*; (*stop*) arrêt *m*; (*respite*) relâchement *m*, répit *m*; **if there is a let-up in the rain** si la pluie s'arrête un peu; **he worked 5 hours without (a) let-up** il a travaillé cinq heures d'affilée *or* sans s'arrêter; **he needs a let-up** il a besoin d'une détente *or* de se détendre un peu; **there will be no let-up in my efforts** je ne relâcherai pas mes efforts.

►let away vt sep (*allow to leave*) laisser partir. **the headmaster let the children away early today** le directeur a laissé partir *or* a renvoyé les enfants tôt aujourd'hui; (*fig*) **you can't let him away with that!** tu ne peux pas le laisser s'en tirer comme ça!

►let down 1 **vt sep** a *window* baisser; *one's hair* dénouer, défaire; *dress* rallonger; *hem* lâcher; *tyre* dégonfler; (*on rope etc*) *person, object* descendre. (*fig*) **he let me down gently** (*in giving bad news*) il me l'a dit *or* il m'a traité avec ménagement; (*in punishing etc*) il n'a pas été trop sévère avec moi; *see also* **hair**.

b (*disappoint, fail*) faire faux bond à, décevoir. **we're expecting you on Sunday, don't let us down** nous vous attendons dimanche, ne nous faites pas faux bond *or* nous comptons sur vous; **he's let me down several times** il m'a déçu plusieurs fois *or* à plusieurs reprises; **that shop has let me down before** j'ai déjà été déçu par cette boutique; **the car let me down** la voiture m'a joué un *or* des tour(s); **my watch never lets me down** ma montre ne se détraque jamais; **you've let the team down** ta façon de jouer a beaucoup déçu *or* desservi l'équipe; (*fig*) **you've let the side down** tu ne nous (*or* leur) as pas fait honneur; **the weather let us down** le beau temps n'a pas été de la partie.

2 **let-down* n** *see* **let**[1] **3**.

►let in vt sep a *person, cat* faire entrer, laisser entrer, ouvrir (la porte) à. **can you let him in?** pouvez-vous lui ouvrir (la porte)?; **the maid let him in** la bonne lui a ouvert la porte *or* l'a fait entrer; **he pleaded with us to let him in** il nous a suppliés de le laisser entrer *or* de lui ouvrir (la porte); **they wouldn't let me in** ils ne voulaient pas me laisser entrer; **he let himself in with a key** il a ouvert (la porte) *or* il est entré avec une clef; **to let in water** *[shoes, tent]* prendre l'eau; *[roof]* laisser entrer *or* passer la pluie; **the curtains let the light in** les rideaux laissent entrer la lumière; **this camera lets the light in** cet appareil-photo laisse passer la lumière; (*Aut*) **to let the clutch in** embrayer.

b (*fig*) **see what you've let me in for now!** tu vois dans quelle situation tu me mets maintenant!; **if I'd known what you were letting me in for I'd never have come** si j'avais su dans quoi tu allais m'entraîner je ne serais jamais venu; **you're letting yourself in for trouble** tu te prépares des ennuis; **you don't know what you're letting yourself in for** tu ne sais pas à quoi tu t'engages; **he let me in for helping at the camp** je me suis retrouvé à cause de lui contraint d'aider au camp; **I let myself in for doing the washing-up** je me suis laissé coincer pour la corvée de vaisselle; **I got let in for a £5 donation** j'ai dû donner 5 livres.

c **to let sb in on a secret/a plan** faire entrer qn dans un secret/un plan, mettre qn au courant d'un secret/d'un plan; **can't we let him in on it?** ne peut-on pas le mettre au courant?

►let off vt sep a (*cause to explode, fire etc*) *bomb* faire éclater; *firework* tirer, faire partir; *firearm* faire partir.

b (*release*) dégager, lâcher. **to let off steam** *[boiler, engine]* lâcher *or* dégager de la vapeur; (** fig*) *[person]* (*anger*) décharger sa bile; (*excitement*) se défouler*.

c (*allow to leave*) laisser partir. **they let the children off early today** aujourd'hui ils ont laissé partir *or* renvoyé les enfants de bonne heure; **will you please let me off at 3 o'clock?** pourriez-vous s'il vous plaît me laisser partir à 3 heures?; (*fig*) **if you don't want to do it, I'll let you off** si tu ne veux pas le faire, je t'en dispense.

d (*not punish*) ne pas punir, faire grâce à. **he let me off** il ne m'a pas puni; **I'll let you off this time** je vous fais grâce *or* je ferme les yeux pour cette fois; **the headmaster let him off with a warning** le directeur lui a seulement donné un avertissement; **he was let off with a fine** il s'en est tiré avec une amende, il en a été quitte pour une amende; **to let sb off lightly** laisser qn s'en tirer à bon compte.

e *rooms etc* louer. **the house has been let off in flats** la maison a été louée en plusieurs appartements.

►let on* 1 **vi** (*tell*) raconter, révéler, dire (*that* que). **don't let on about what they did** ne va pas raconter *or* dire ce qu'ils ont fait; **I won't let on** je ne dirai rien, je garderai ça pour moi; **they knew the answer but they didn't let on** ils connaissaient la réponse mais ils n'ont pas pipé; **don't let on!** motus!; **he passed me in the street but he didn't let on** il m'a croisé dans la rue mais il a fait comme s'il ne m'avait pas vu. 2 **vt sep** a (*admit, acknowledge*) dire, aller raconter (*that* que). b (*pretend*) prétendre, raconter (*that* que).

►let out 1 **vi: to let out at sb** (*with fists, stick etc*) envoyer des coups à qn; (*abuse*) injurier qn; (*speak angrily to*) attaquer qn; (*scold*) réprimander qn sévèrement.

2 **vt sep** a (*allow to leave*) *person, cat* faire *or* laisser sortir; (*release*) *prisoner* relâcher; *sheep, cattle* faire sortir (*of* de); *caged bird* lâcher. **let me out!** laissez-moi sortir!; **I'll let you out** je vais vous ouvrir la porte *or* vous reconduire; **the watchman let me out** le veilleur m'a fait sortir; **he let himself out quietly** il est sorti sans faire de bruit; **can you let yourself out?** vous m'excuserez de ne pas vous reconduire?; **they are let out of school at 4** on les fait sortir de l'école *or* on les libère à 16 heures; **to let the air out of a tyre** dégonfler un pneu; **to let the water out of the bath** vider l'eau de la baignoire; *see* **cat**.

b *fire, candle* laisser s'éteindre.

c (*reveal*) *secret, news* laisser échapper, révéler. **don't let it out that ...** ne va pas raconter que ... .

d *shout, cry* laisser échapper. **to let out a laugh** faire entendre un rire.

e *dress* élargir; *seam* lâcher. **to let one's belt out by 2 holes** desserrer sa ceinture de 2 crans.

f (*remove suspicion from*) disculper, mettre hors de cause; (*exclude*) exclure, éliminer. **his alibi lets him out** son alibi le met hors de cause; **if it's a bachelor you need that lets me out** si c'est un célibataire qu'il vous faut je ne peux pas faire votre affaire.

g *house etc* louer.

3 **let-out n** *see* **let**[1] **3**.

►let past vt sep *person, vehicle, animal, mistake* laisser passer.

►let through vt sep *vehicle, person, light* laisser passer.

►let up 1 **vi** *[rain]* diminuer; *[cold weather]* s'adoucir. **he didn't let up until he'd finished** il ne s'est accordé aucun répit avant d'avoir fini; **she worked all night without letting up** elle a travaillé toute la nuit sans relâche; **what a talker she is, she never lets up!** quelle bavarde, elle n'arrête pas!; **to let up on sb*** lâcher la bride à qn. 2 **vt sep** (*allow to rise*) **to let sb up** permettre à qn de se lever. 3 **let-up* n** *see* **let**[1] **3**.

let[2] [let] **n** a (*Tennis*) let *m*, balle *f* à remettre. **to play a ~** jouer un let, remettre le service; **~ ball** balle *f* de let; **~!** net!, let! b (*Jur*) **without ~ or hindrance** librement, sans empêchement aucun.

letch* [letʃ] **vi** = **lech***.

lethal [ˈliːθəl] **adj** *poison, dose, blow, wound* mortel, fatal; *effect* fatal; *weapon* meurtrier. (*fig*) **don't touch this coffee, it's ~!*** ne bois pas ce café, il est atroce!*

lethargic [lɪˈθɑːdʒɪk] **adj** *person, movement* léthargique; *atmosphere, heat* qui endort.

lethargy ['leθədʒɪ] n léthargie *f*.

Lett [let] = **Latvian.**

letter ['letəʳ] 1 n a (*of alphabet*) lettre *f*. **the ~ L** la lettre L; **it was printed in ~s 15 cm high** c'était écrit en lettres de 15 cm de haut; **he's got a lot of ~s after his name*** il a des tas* de diplômes (*or* de décorations *etc*); (*fig*) **the ~ of the law** la lettre de la loi; **he followed the instructions to the ~** il a suivi les instructions à la lettre *or* au pied de la lettre; *see* **block, capital, red** *etc*.

b (*written communication*) lettre *f*. **I wrote her a ~ yesterday** je lui ai écrit une lettre hier; **have you any ~s to post?** avez-vous des lettres à poster?; **were there any ~s for me?** y avait-il du courrier *or* des lettres pour moi?; **he was invited by ~** il a reçu une invitation écrite; **the news came in a ~ from her brother** une lettre de son frère annonçait la nouvelle; (*Comm*) **~ of acknowledgement** lettre accusant réception; (*Jur*) **~ of attorney** procuration *f*; (*Diplomacy*) **~(s) of credence** lettres de créance; (*Fin*) **~ of credit** lettre de crédit; **~ of intent** lettre d'intention; **~ of introduction** lettre de recommandation; **~s patent** lettres patentes; (*Jur*) **~ of request, ~ rogatory** commission *f* rogatoire; (*as publication*) **"The L~s of Virginia Woolf"** "La correspondance *or* Les lettres de Virginia Woolf"; *see* **covering, love, open** *etc*.

c (*learning*) **~s** (belles-)lettres *fpl*; **man of ~s** homme *m* de lettres.

d (*US Scol*) distinctions *fpl* (*pour succès sportifs*).

2 vt a (*put ~ on*) **I've ~ed the packets according to the order they arrived in** j'ai inscrit des lettres sur les paquets selon leur ordre d'arrivée; **she ~ed the envelopes from A to M** elle a marqué les enveloppes de A à M.

b (*engrave*) graver (des lettres sur). **the book cover was ~ed in gold** la couverture du livre portait une inscription en lettres d'or; **the case is ~ed with my initials** l'étui est gravé à mes initiales, mes initiales sont gravées sur l'étui.

3 comp ▸**letter bomb** lettre piégée ▸**letterbox** (*esp Brit*) boîte *f* aux *or* à lettres ▸**letter-card** (*Brit*) carte-lettre *f* ▸**letterhead** en-tête *m* ▸**letter opener** coupe-papier *m inv* ▸**letter paper** papier *m* à lettres ▸**letter-perfect:** (*US*) **to be letter-perfect in sth** savoir qch sur le bout du doigt ▸**letterpress** (*Typ*) (*method*) typographie *f*; (*text*) texte imprimé ▸**letter quality** (*Comput*) qualité *f* "courrier" ▸**letter-writer: he's a good/bad letter-writer** c'est un bon/mauvais correspondant *or* épistolier (*hum*).

lettered ['letəd] adj *person* lettré; *see also* **letter.**

lettering ['letərɪŋ] n (*NonC*) (*engraving*) gravure *f*; (*letters*) caractères *mpl*.

letting ['letɪŋ] n a [*flat etc*] location *f*. b *see* **blood 3.**

lettuce ['letɪs] n (*Bot*) laitue *f*; (*Culin*) laitue, salade *f*. **would you like some more ~?** veux-tu reprendre de la laitue? *or* de la salade?

leucocyte ['lu:kəˌsaɪt] n leucocyte *m*.

leucotomy [lu:'kɒtəmɪ] n leucotomie *f*, lobotomie *f* cérébrale.

leukaemia, (*esp US*) **leukemia** [lu:'ki:mɪə] n leucémie *f*.

leukocyte ['lu:kəˌsaɪt] n (*esp US*) = **leucocyte.**

leukotomy [lu:'kɒtəmɪ] n (*esp US*) = **leucotomy.**

Levant [lɪ'vænt] n Levant *m*.

levee[1] ['levɪ] n (*raised riverside of silt*) levée naturelle; (*man-made embankment*) levée, digue *f*; (*ridge surrounding field*) digue; (*landing place*) quai *m*.

levee[2] [le'veɪ] n (*Hist*) réception royale (*pour hommes*); (*at royal bedside*) lever *m* (du roi). (*US*) **a presidential ~** une réception présidentielle.

level ['levl] 1 n a (*height: lit, fig*) niveau *m*, hauteur *f*; (*scale*) niveau, échelon *m*. **the water reached a ~ of 10 metres** l'eau a atteint une hauteur de 10 mètres; **water finds its own ~** l'eau trouve son niveau; **the child will find his own ~** l'enfant trouvera son niveau; **at roof ~** au niveau du toit; (*fig*) **the teacher came down to their ~** le professeur s'est mis à leur niveau; (*fig*) **he's far above my ~** il est d'un niveau bien supérieur au mien; **I'm not on his ~ at all** je ne suis pas du tout à son niveau; **his ability is on a ~ with** *or* **on the same ~ as that of his schoolmates** ses capacités sont du même niveau que celles de ses camarades de classe; **that dirty trick is on a ~ with the other one he played** ce mauvais coup est (bien) à la hauteur du *or* vaut le précédent; **social/intellectual ~** niveau social/intellectuel; (*Admin, Pol etc*) **at a higher/lower ~** à un niveau *or* échelon supérieur/inférieur; (*Nuclear Ind*) **high-/intermediate-/low-~ waste** déchets *mpl* de haute/moyenne/faible activité; **top-~ talks** conférence *f* au niveau le plus élevé; **at departmental ~** à l'échelon départemental; *see* **eye, knee, sea** *etc*.

b (*Aut, Rail*) palier *m*. **speed on the ~** vitesse *f* en palier; (*fig*) **I'm telling you on the ~*** je te le dis franchement; (*fig*) **is this on the ~?*** est-ce que c'est régulier? *or* réglo?‡; (*fig*) **is he on the ~?*** est-ce qu'il joue franc-jeu?, est-ce qu'il est fair-play?

c (*also* **spirit ~**) niveau *m* à bulle (d'air).

d (*flat place*) terrain *m* plat.

2 adj a (*flat; not bumpy; not sloping*) *surface* plat, plan, uni. **~ ground** terrain plat *or* plan *or* uni; **it's dead ~** c'est parfaitement plat; **the tray must be absolutely ~** il faut que le plateau soit absolument horizontal; **hold the stick ~** tiens le bâton horizontal *or* à l'horizontale; **a ~ spoonful** une cuillerée rase; (*fig*) **to compete on a ~ playing field** jouer sur un terrain d'égalité, être sur un pied d'égalité; **to do one's ~ best (to do sth)*** faire tout son possible *or* faire de son mieux (pour faire qch).

b (*at same standard, equal*) à égalité. **the 2 contestants are dead ~** les 2 participants sont exactement à égalité; **to be ~ with** (*in race*) être à la hauteur de *or* à la même hauteur que; (*in league*) être à égalité avec, avoir le même nombre de points que; (*in one's studies, achievements etc*) être au niveau de *or* au même niveau que; (*in salary, rank*) être à l'échelon de *or* au même échelon que; **to draw ~ with** (*in race*) arriver à la hauteur de *or* à la même hauteur que, rejoindre, rattraper; (*in league*) arriver dans la même position que, arriver au même score que; (*in one's studies, achievements etc*) arriver au niveau de *or* au même niveau que; (*in salary, rank*) arriver au niveau de *or* au même niveau que, arriver au même échelon que; **to be ~ in seniority with** avoir la même ancienneté que, être au même niveau d'ancienneté que; **the dining room is ~ with the garden** la salle à manger est de plain-pied avec le jardin; **~ with the ground** au niveau du sol, à ras du sol; **hold the 2 sticks absolutely ~** tiens les 2 bâtons exactement à la même hauteur.

c (*steady*) *voice, tones* calme, égal, assuré; *judgment* sain, raisonné; *look* calme, assuré. (*fig*) **to keep a ~ head** garder tout son sang-froid; *see also* **3.**

d (*US *: honest*) *person, deal* honnête, régulier.

3 comp ▸**level crossing** (*Brit Rail*) passage *m* à niveau ▸**level-headed** équilibré ▸**level-pegging:** (*Brit*) **they were level-pegging** ils étaient à égalité.

4 vt a (*make level*) *site, ground* niveler, aplanir; *quantities* répartir également; (*demolish*) *building, town* raser. **to ~ sth to the ground** raser qch.

b **to ~ a blow at sb** allonger un coup de poing à qn; **to ~ a gun at sb** braquer *or* pointer un pistolet sur qn; **to ~ an accusation at sb** lancer *or* porter une accusation contre qn.

5 vi (*US* *) **I'll ~ with you** je vais être franc (*f* franche) avec vous, je ne vais rien vous cacher; **you're not ~ling with me about what you bought** tu ne me dis pas tout ce que tu as acheté.

▸**level down** 1 vt sep (*lit*) *surface* aplanir, raboter; (*fig*) *standards* niveler par le bas. 2 **levelling down** n *see* **levelling 3.**

▸**level off** 1 vi [*curve on graph, statistics, results, prices etc*] se stabiliser, se tasser; [*aircraft*] amorcer le vol en palier. 2 vt sep (*make flat*) *heap of sand etc* égaliser, niveler. 3 **levelling off** n *see* **levelling 3.**

▸**level out** 1 vi [*curve on graph, statistics, results, prices etc*] se stabiliser; [*road etc*] s'aplanir. 2 vt sep niveler, égaliser.

▸**level up** 1 vt sep (*lit*) *ground* niveler; (*fig*) *standards* niveler par le haut. 2 **levelling up** n *see* **levelling 3.**

leveller, (*US*) **leveler** ['levləʳ] n: **poverty is a great ~** tous les hommes sont égaux dans la misère.

levelling, (*US*) **leveling** ['levlɪŋ] 1 n (*NonC: lit, fig*) nivellement *m*. 2 adj (*fig*) *process, effect* de nivellement. 3 comp ▸**levelling down** nivellement *m* par le bas ▸**levelling off** (*gen*) égalisation *f*, nivellement *m*; (*Econ, Fin*) stabilisation *f*, tassement *m* ▸**levelling rod, levelling staff** mire *f*, jalon-mire *m* ▸**levelling up** nivellement *m* par le haut.

levelly ['levlɪ] adv *look* calmement; *speak* d'un ton calme *or* égal.

lever ['li:vəʳ] 1 n (*gen, also fig*) levier *m*; (*small, on machine etc*) manette *f*; *see* **gear.** 2 vt: **to ~ sth into position** mettre qch en place (à l'aide d'un levier).

▸**lever out** vt sep: **to lever sth out** extraire qch au moyen d'un levier; (*fig*) **he levered himself out of the chair** il s'est extirpé* du fauteuil; **they're trying to lever him out of his position as manager*** ils essaient de le déloger de son poste de directeur.

▸**lever up** vt sep soulever au moyen d'un levier. (*fig*) **he levered himself up on one elbow** il s'est soulevé sur un coude; (*fig*) **to lever up the bank rate** relever le taux d'escompte officiel.

leverage ['li:vərɪdʒ] 1 n (*lit*) force *f* (de levier); (*fig: influence*) influence *f*, prise *f* (*on or with sb* sur qn); (*US Fin*) effet *m* de levier. 2 vt (*Fin*) *company* augmenter le ratio d'endettement de. **~d buyout** rachat *m* d'entreprise financé par l'endettement.

leveret ['levərɪt] n levraut *m*.

leviathan [lɪ'vaɪəθən] n (*Bible*) Léviathan *m*; (*fig: ship/organization etc*) navire/organisme *etc* géant.

Levi's ['li:vaɪz] npl ® Levi's *mpl* ®.

levitate ['levɪteɪt] 1 vi se soulever *or* être soulevé par lévitation. 2 vt soulever *or* élever par lévitation.

levitation [ˌlevɪ'teɪʃən] n lévitation *f*.

Leviticus [lɪ'vɪtɪkəs] n Lévitique *m*.

levity ['levɪtɪ] n a (*frivolity*) manque *m* de sérieux, légèreté *f*. b (*fickleness*) inconstance *f*.

levy ['levɪ] 1 n a (*gen*) prélèvement *m* (*on* sur); (*tax*) impôt *m*, taxe *f* (*on* sur); (*amount, act of taxing*) taxation *f*. **import ~** prélèvement à l'importation; *see* **capital.** b (*Mil*) (*act*) levée *f*, enrôlement *m*; (*troops*) troupes enrôlées, levée. 2 vt a (*impose*) *tax* prélever, mettre (*on sth* sur qch); *fine* infliger, imposer (*on sb* à qn). b (*collect*) *taxes, contributions* lever, percevoir, recueillir. c (*Mil*) **to ~ troops/an army** lever des troupes/une armée; **to ~ war (on** *or* **against)** faire la

guerre (à).
►**levy on** vt fus (*Jur*) **to levy on sb's property** saisir (les biens de) qn.
lewd [lu:d] adj obscène, lubrique.
lewdly ['lu:dlɪ] adv de façon obscène.
lewdness ['lu:dnɪs] n *[person]* lubricité *f*; *[thing]* obscénité *f*.
lexeme ['leksi:m] n lexème *m*.
lexical ['leksɪkəl] adj lexical. ~ **item** unité lexicale, item lexical.
lexicalize ['leksɪkə,laɪz] vt lexicaliser.
lexicographer [,leksɪ'kɒgrəfə^r] n lexicographe *mf*.
lexicographical [,leksɪkəʊ'græfɪkəl] adj lexicographique.
lexicography [,leksɪ'kɒgrəfɪ] n lexicographie *f*.
lexicologist [,leksɪ'kɒlədʒɪst] n lexicologue *mf*.
lexicology [,leksɪ'kɒlədʒɪ] n lexicologie *f*.
lexicon ['leksɪkən] n lexique *m*.
lexis ['leksɪs] n (*Ling*) lexique *m*; (*study*) lexicologie *f*.
L.I. (*US*) abbr of **Long Island**.
liability [,laɪə'bɪlɪtɪ] n a (*NonC*) responsabilité *f*. **don't admit ~ for the accident** n'acceptez pas la responsabilité de l'accident; **his ~ for the company's debts was limited to £50,000** sa responsabilité quant aux dettes de la compagnie était limitée à 50 000 livres; ~ **insurance** assurance *f* responsabilité civile; *see* **joint, limited, strict** *etc*.
b (*NonC*) ~ **for tax/for paying tax** assujettissement *m* à l'impôt/au paiement de l'impôt; ~ **for military service** obligations *fpl* militaires.
c (*Fin: debts*) **liabilities** dettes *fpl*, engagements *mpl*, passif *m*; **assets and liabilities** actif *m* et passif; **to meet one's liabilities** faire face à ses engagements; (*Fin*) **current** ~ dettes à court terme; **non-current** ~ dettes à moyen et long terme.
d (*handicap*) handicap *m*, poids mort. **this car is a ~ for us** cette voiture est un poids mort pour nous; **he's a real ~** il nous handicape plutôt qu'autre chose*, c'est un vrai boulet.
liable ['laɪəbl] adj a (*likely*) *[person]* **to be ~ to do** (*gen*) risquer de faire; (*succeed, win etc*) risquer de faire, avoir des chances de faire; (*fall ill, hurt o.s. etc*) risquer de faire, (*more formally*) être susceptible de faire; *[thing]* **to be ~ to do** risquer de faire, (*more formally*) être susceptible de faire; **he's ~ to refuse to do it** il est possible qu'il refuse (*subj*) de le faire; **he is ~ not to come** il est possible qu'il ne vienne pas; **we are ~ to get shot at** on risque de se faire tirer dessus; **we are ~ to be in London next week** nous pourrions bien nous trouver à Londres la semaine prochaine; **it's ~ to be hot** il se peut qu'il fasse *or* il pourrait faire *or* il risque de faire très chaud.
b (*subject to*) *person* passible (*to* de), sujet (*to* à); *thing* assujetti (*to* à). ~ **to duty** *goods* assujetti à des droits; *person* passible de droits; ~ **to seasickness** sujet au mal de mer; **to be ~ to** *or* **for tax** *[person]* être imposable; *[thing]* être assujetti à la taxation; ~ **to a fine/imprisonment** passible d'une amende/d'emprisonnement; **to be ~ to prosecution** s'exposer à des poursuites; **every man of 20 is ~ for military service** tout homme de 20 ans est astreint au service militaire; **not ~ for military service** exempt d'obligations militaires; **the plan is ~ to changes** le projet est susceptible de changer; **the programme is ~ to alteration without notice** le programme peut être modifié sans préavis; *see* **damage**.
c (*Jur: responsible*) (civilement) responsable. **jointly and severally ~** responsable conjointement et solidairement; **to be ~ for sb** être (civilement) responsable de qn; **to be ~ for sb's debts** répondre des dettes de qn.
liaise [li:'eɪz] vi (*Brit*) se contacter. **to ~ with** (*co-operate with*) se concerter avec; (*act as go-between*) assurer la liaison avec; **to ~ between** assurer la liaison entre.
liaison [li:'eɪzɒn] 1 n (*Ling, Mil, gen*) liaison *f*. 2 comp ►**liaison committee** comité *m* de liaison ►**liaison officer** (*Mil, gen*) officier *m* de liaison.
liana [li:'ɑ:nə] n liane *f*.
liar ['laɪə^r] n menteur *m*, -euse *f*.
lib* [lɪb] n abbr of **liberation**.
libation [laɪ'beɪʃən] n libation *f*.
libber* ['lɪbə^r] n = **liberationist**.
libel ['laɪbəl] 1 n (*Jur*) (*act*) diffamation *f* (par écrit); (*document*) libelle *m*, pamphlet *m*, écrit *m* diffamatoire. **to sue sb for ~, to bring an action for ~ against sb** intenter un procès en diffamation à qn; (*fig*) **that's (a) ~!** c'est une calomnie! 2 comp ►**libel laws** (*Jur*) lois *fpl* contre la diffamation ►**libel proceedings, libel suit** procès *m* en diffamation. 3 vt (*Jur*) diffamer (par écrit); (*gen*) calomnier, médire de.
libellous, (*US*) **libelous** ['laɪbələs] adj diffamatoire.
liberal ['lɪbərəl] 1 adj a (*broad-minded*) *education* libéral; *ideas, mind, interpretation* libéral, large. ~ **arts** arts libéraux; (*Scol etc*) ~ **studies** ≃ programme *m* de culture générale. b (*generous*) *amount, contribution, offer* généreux; *person* prodigue (*with* de), généreux, libéral; (*copious*) *supply* ample, abondant. c (*Pol*) **L~** libéral. 2 n (*Pol*) **L~** libéral(e) *m(f)*. 3 comp ►**liberal-minded** libéral, large d'esprit.
liberalism ['lɪbərəlɪzəm] n (*Pol, gen*) libéralisme *m*.
liberality [,lɪbə'rælɪtɪ] n (*broad-mindedness*) libéralisme *m*; (*generosity*) libéralité *f*, générosité *f*.
liberalization [,lɪbərəlaɪ'zeɪʃən] n libéralisation *f*.
liberalize ['lɪbərəlaɪz] vt libéraliser.
liberally ['lɪbərəlɪ] adv (*gen*) libéralement; *help o.s., supply* amplement, abondamment.
liberate ['lɪbəreɪt] vt *prisoner, slave* libérer; *women etc* libérer, émanciper; (*Chem*) *gas* libérer, dégager; (*Fin*) *capital* dégager.
liberated ['lɪbəreɪtɪd] adj libéré.
liberation [,lɪbə'reɪʃən] 1 n libération *f*; (*Fin*) dégagement *m*. 2 comp ►**liberation theology** (*Rel*) théologie *f* de libération.
liberationist [,lɪbə'reɪʃənɪst] n (*active*) membre *m* d'un (*or* du) mouvement de libération; (*sympathiser*) partisan *m* de la libération (*des femmes etc*).
liberator ['lɪbəreɪtə^r] n libérateur *m*, -trice *f*.
Liberia [laɪ'bɪərɪə] n Libéria *m*, Liberia *m*.
Liberian [laɪ'bɪərɪən] 1 adj libérien; *embassy etc* du Libéria. 2 n Libérien(ne) *m(f)*.
libertarian [,lɪbə'tɛərɪən] adj, n libertaire *(mf)*.
libertarianism [,lɪbə'tɛərɪənɪzəm] n (*philosophy*) doctrine *f* libertaire; (*sb's characteristic*) idées *fpl* libertaires.
libertinage ['lɪbətɪnɪdʒ] n libertinage *m*.
libertine ['lɪbəti:n] adj, n libertin(e) *m(f)*.
liberty ['lɪbətɪ] 1 n a (*freedom*) liberté *f*. **at ~** (*not detained*) en liberté; (*not busy*) libre; **you are at ~ to choose** vous êtes libre de choisir, libre à vous de choisir; **you are not at ~ to change the wording** vous n'avez pas le droit de changer le texte; ~ **of the press** liberté de la presse; ~ **of conscience** liberté de conscience; *see* **civil**.
b (*presumption*) liberté *f*. **to take liberties (with sb)** prendre *or* se permettre des libertés (avec qn); **to take the ~ of doing** prendre la liberté *or* se permettre de faire; **that was rather a ~ on his part** il ne s'est pas gêné; **what a ~!*** quel toupet!*
2 comp ►**liberty bodice** chemise *f* américaine ►**liberty cap** (*Hist*) bonnet *m* phrygien ►**liberty hall:** (*fig*) **it's liberty hall here** ici tout est permis.
libidinous [lɪ'bɪdɪnəs] adj libidineux.
libido [lɪ'bi:dəʊ] n libido *f*.
Lib-Lab* ['lɪb,læb] adj (*Brit Pol*) (abbr of **Liberal-Labour**) ~ **pact** pacte *m* libéral-travailliste.
Libra ['li:brə] n (*Astron*) Balance *f*. **I'm (a) ~** je suis (de la) Balance.
Libran ['li:brən] n: **to be a ~** être (de la) Balance.
librarian [laɪ'brɛərɪən] n bibliothécaire *mf*.
librarianship [laɪ'brɛərɪənʃɪp] n (*job*) poste *m* de bibliothécaire; (*esp Brit: science*) bibliothéconomie *f*; (*knowledge*) connaissances *fpl* de bibliothécaire. **to do** *or* **study ~** faire des études de bibliothécaire *or* de bibliothéconomie.
library ['laɪbrərɪ] 1 n a (*building, room*) bibliothèque *f*. (*US*) **L~ of Congress** Bibliothèque du Congrès; *see* **mobile, public, reference** *etc*. b (*collection, also Comput*) bibliothèque *f*; (*published series*) collection *f*, série *f*, bibliothèque. 2 comp ►**library book** livre *m* de bibliothèque ►**library card** = **library ticket** ►**library edition** édition reliée pour bibliothèque ►**library science** bibliothéconomie *f* ►**library software** (*Comput*) logiciel-bibliothèque *m* ►**library ticket** carte *f* de lecteur *or* de bibliothèque.
librettist [lɪ'bretɪst] n librettiste *mf*.
libretto [lɪ'bretəʊ] n, pl ~**s** *or* **libretti** [lɪ'breti:] libretto *m*, livret *m*.
Librium ['lɪbrɪəm] n ® Librium *m* ®.
Libya ['lɪbɪə] n Libye *f*.
Libyan ['lɪbɪən] 1 n Libyen(ne) *m(f)*. 2 adj libyen, de Libye. ~ **Arab Jamahiriya** Jamahiriya *f* arabe libyenne; ~ **Desert** désert *m* de Libye.
lice [laɪs] npl of **louse**.
licence ['laɪsəns] 1 n a (*permit*) (*gen*) autorisation *f*, permis *m*; (*for manufacturing, trading etc*) licence *f*; (*Aut*) (*for driver*) permis; (*for car*) vignette *f*; (*for radio, TV*) redevance *f*; (*document itself*) fiche *f* de redevance. **driving ~** permis de conduire; **export/import ~** permis d'exporter/d'importer; **pilot's ~** brevet *m* de pilote; **have you got a ~ for this radio?** est-ce que vous avez payé la redevance pour cette radio?; **they were married by special ~** ils se sont mariés avec dispense (de bans); **to manufacture sth under ~** fabriquer qch sous licence; *see* **marriage, off** *etc*.
b (*NonC*) (*freedom*) licence *f*, liberté *f*; (*excess*) licence. **you can allow some ~ in translation** on peut tolérer une certaine licence *or* liberté dans la traduction; *see* **poetic**.
2 comp ►**licence number** (*Aut*) *[licence]* numéro *m* de permis de conduire; *[car]* numéro minéralogique *or* d'immatriculation *or* de police ►**licence plate** (*esp US*) plaque *f* minéralogique *or* d'immatriculation *or* de police.
license ['laɪsəns] 1 n (*US*) = **licence**.
2 vt a (*give licence to*) donner une licence à; *car [licensing authority]* délivrer la vignette pour; *[owner]* acheter la vignette de *or* pour. **is that gun ~d?** avez-vous un permis pour ce revolver?; **the shop is ~d to sell tobacco** le magasin détient une licence de bureau de tabac; **the shop is ~d for the sale of alcoholic liquor** le magasin détient une licence de débit de boissons; (*Brit*) ~**d victualler** patron *m or* gérant *m* d'un pub; (*Brit*) **(on) ~d premises** (dans un) établissement ayant une licence de débit de boissons; (*Jur*) ~**d product** produit *m* sous licence;

(*US*) ~d practical nurse infirmier *m*, -ière *f* auxiliaire; *see also* licensing.
b (*permit*) autoriser (*sb to do* qn à faire), permettre (*sb to do* à qn de faire).
3 comp ▸ license plate (*US*) = licence plate.

licensee [ˌlaɪsənˈsiː] n concessionnaire *mf* d'une licence, licencié *m*; (*Brit: of pub*) patron(ne) *m(f)*.

licenser [ˈlaɪsənsəʳ] n = licensor.

licensing [ˈlaɪsənsɪŋ] 1 adj: the ~ authority l'organisme *m or* le service délivrant les permis (*or* les licences *etc*). 2 comp ▸ licensing agreement (*Comm*) accord *m* de licence ▸ licensing hours (*Brit*) heures *fpl* d'ouverture légales (*des débits de boisson*) ▸ licensing laws (*Brit*) lois *fpl* réglementant la vente d'alcool.

licensor [ˈlaɪsənsəʳ] n (*Jur*) bailleur *m*, bailleresse *f* de licence.

licentiate [laɪˈsenʃɪɪt] n diplômé(e) *m(f)* (*pour pratiquer une profession libérale*).

licentious [laɪˈsenʃəs] adj licencieux.

licentiousness [laɪˈsenʃəsnɪs] n licence *f*.

lichee [ˌlaɪˈtʃiː] n = lychee.

lichen [ˈlaɪkən] n lichen *m*.

lichgate [ˈlɪtʃgeɪt] n porche *m* de cimetière.

licit [ˈlɪsɪt] adj licite.

lick [lɪk] 1 n a coup *m* de langue. give me *or* let me have a ~ laisse-moi lécher un coup*; give me a ~ of your lollipop laisse-moi sucer ta sucette un coup*; to give o.s. a ~ and a promise* faire un (petit) brin de toilette; a ~ of paint un (petit) coup de peinture.
b (*: *speed*) vitesse *f*. at full ~ en quatrième vitesse*, à toute vapeur*; (*Aut*) pleins gaz*; at a fair *or* good ~ à toute vapeur*, à toute blinde⁑.
c (*also* salt ~) salant *m* (*que les animaux viennent lécher*); (*block of rock salt*) pierre *f* à lécher.
d (*: *punch*) ramponneau⁑ *m*, pain* *m*.
2 comp ▸ lickspittle (*pej*) lèche-bottes* *mf inv*.
3 vt a [*person, animal, flames*] lécher. to ~ one's lips (*lit*) se lécher les lèvres; (*fig*) se frotter les mains (*fig*); to ~ one's chops* se lécher *or* se pourlécher les babines*; she ~ed the cream off her fingers elle a léché la crème qu'elle avait sur les doigts; to ~ sth clean nettoyer qch à coups de langue; (*fig*) to ~ sb's boots lécher les bottes à qn*, jouer les lèche-bottes* avec qn; to ~ sb's arse*⁑ lécher le cul à qn*⁑; (*fig*) to ~ one's wounds panser ses blessures (*fig*); *see* shape.
b (*) (*defeat*) écraser*, battre à plate(s) couture(s); (*outdo, surpass*) battre; (*thrash*) flanquer une correction à, tabasser⁑. I've got it ~ed *problem, puzzle etc* j'ai trouvé la solution; *bad habit* j'ai réussi à m'arrêter; [*problem etc*] it's got me ~ed cela me dépasse.

▸**lick off** vt sep enlever à coups de langue, lécher. lick it off! lèche-le!

▸**lick up** vt sep lécher; [*cat*] laper.

lickety-split* [ˈlɪkɪtɪˈsplɪt] adv (*US*) à fond de train.

licking* [ˈlɪkɪŋ] n (*whipping*) rossée* *f*, raclée* *f*; (*defeat*) déculottée⁑ *f*.

licorice [ˈlɪkərɪs] n (*US*) = liquorice.

lid [lɪd] n a [*pan, box, jar, piano*] couvercle *m*. (*fig*) the newspaper articles took *or* blew the ~ off his illegal activities les articles de presse ont étalé au grand jour ses activités illégales; that puts the ~ on it!* (*that's the end*) ça c'est un comble! *or* le pompon!*; (*US: act against sth*) to put the ~ on sth* prendre des mesures contre qch. b (*also* eye~) paupière *f*. c (⁑) (*helmet*) casque *m* (*de motocycliste etc*); (*esp US: hat*) galure⁑ *m*, chapeau *m*; *see* skid. d (*Drugs sl*) 25 *g de marijuana*.

lidded [ˈlɪdɪd] adj *container, jar* à couvercle. heavily ~ eyes yeux *mpl* aux paupières lourdes.

lido [ˈliːdəʊ] n (*resort*) complexe *m* balnéaire; (*Brit: swimming pool*) piscine *f* (*en plein air*).

lie[1] [laɪ] pret lay, ptp lain 1 vi a [*person etc*] (*also* ~ down) s'allonger, s'étendre, se coucher; (*state: gen* to be lying) être allongé *or* étendu *or* couché; (*in grave etc*) être enterré. go and ~ on the bed allez vous allonger *or* vous étendre sur le lit; don't ~ on the grass ne t'allonge pas *or* ne te couche pas sur l'herbe; he was lying on the floor (*resting etc*) il était allongé *or* étendu *or* couché par terre; (*unable to move*) il était étendu *or* il gisait par terre; she lay in bed until 10 o'clock elle est restée *or* a traîné (*pej*) au lit jusqu'à 10 heures; she was lying in bed reading elle lisait au lit; ~ on your side couche-toi *or* mets-toi *or* allonge-toi sur le côté; she was lying face downwards elle était (couchée *or* allongée *or* étendue) à plat ventre; he was lying asleep il était allongé et il dormait, il était allongé endormi; he lay asleep on the bed il dormait étendu *or* allongé sur le lit; he lay dead il était étendu mort; he lay dead at her feet il était étendu mort à ses pieds, il gisait à ses pieds; he lay helpless on the floor il était étendu par terre sans pouvoir faire quoi que ce soit; he was lying still il était étendu immobile; ~ still! ne bouge pas!, reste tranquille!; his body was lying on the ground son corps gisait sur le sol; he ~s in the churchyard il repose dans le *or* est enterré au cimetière; the body lay in the coffin/the tomb le corps reposait dans le cercueil/la tombe; to ~ in state être exposé solennellement; (*on tombstone*) here ~s ... ci-gît ...; (*fig*) he lay in prison for many years il est resté en prison pendant de nombreuses années; (*fig*) to ~ low (*hide*) se cacher, rester caché; (*stay out of limelight*) ne pas se faire remarquer, se tenir à carreau*; *see* ambush, sleeping, wait.
b [*object*] être; [*place, road*] se trouver, être; [*land, sea etc*] s'étendre; (*remain*) rester, être. the book lay on the table le livre était sur la table; the book lay unopened all day le livre est resté fermé toute la journée; the book lay open on the table le livre était ouvert sur la table; his food lay untouched while he told us the story il ne touchait pas à son assiette pendant qu'il nous racontait l'histoire; his clothes were lying on the floor ses vêtements étaient par terre; the whole contents of the box lay scattered on the carpet tout le contenu de la boîte était éparpillé *or* gisait éparpillé sur le tapis; our road lay along the river notre itinéraire longeait la rivière; the road ~s over the hills la route traverse les collines; the British team is lying third l'équipe britannique est troisième *or* en troisième position; the ship was lying in the harbour le navire était au port *or* avait mouillé dans le port; [*ship*] to ~ at anchor être à l'ancre, avoir mouillé; (*fig*) obstacles ~ in the way la route est semée d'embûches; the money is lying in the bank l'argent est en dépôt à la banque; the money is lying idle in the bank l'argent dort à la banque; the factory lay idle personne ne travaillait dans l'usine; the machines lay idle les machines étaient arrêtées; the snow lay 2 metres deep il y avait 2 mètres (d'épaisseur) de neige; the snow lay thick *or* deep on the ground il y avait une épaisse couche de neige sur le sol; the snow will not ~ la neige ne tiendra pas; the town lay in ruins la ville était en ruines; the meal lay heavy on his stomach le repas lui pesait sur l'estomac; the crime lay heavy on his conscience le crime lui pesait sur la conscience; the valley/lake/sea lay before us la vallée/le lac/la mer s'étendait devant nous; during the years that ~ before us pendant les années qui sont devant nous; a brilliant future ~s before you vous avez devant vous un brillant avenir; (*fig*) what ~s before him ce que lui réserve l'avenir; (*fig*) what ~s ahead ce qui reste à venir, ce que réserve l'avenir; (*fig*) the (whole) world lay at her feet toutes les portes lui étaient ouvertes; (*fig*) to let it *or* things ~ laisser les choses comme elles sont; *see* land.
c (*with abstract subject*) être, résider. he knows where his interests ~ il sait où sont *or* résident ses intérêts; what ~s behind his refusal? quelle est la véritable raison de son refus?; the real cause that lay behind the rise in divorce la vraie cause de la hausse du nombre des divorces; the trouble ~s in the engine le problème vient du moteur; the trouble ~s in his inability to be strict le problème provient de *or* réside dans son incapacité d'être sévère; the difference ~s in the fact that ... la différence vient de ce que ...; the real remedy ~s in education le vrai remède se trouve dans *or* réside dans l'enseignement; the blame ~s with you c'est vous qui êtes à blâmer, c'est à vous que la faute est imputable; a curse lay on the family une malédiction pesait sur la famille; it does not ~ within my power to decide il n'est pas en mon pouvoir de décider; it ~s with you to decide il vous appartient de décider, c'est à vous (qu'il incombe) de décider; (*liter, frm*) as far as in me ~s au mieux de mes possibilités, du mieux que je peux.
d (*Jur*) [*evidence, appeal*] être recevable.
2 n a (*Golf*) [*ball*] position *f*.
b [*land*] configuration *f*; *see* land.
3 comp ▸ lie-abed* flemmard(e)* *m(f)* (qui traîne au lit) ▸ lie-down*: (*Brit*) to have a lie-down s'allonger, se reposer ▸ lie-in*: (*Brit*) to have a lie-in faire la grasse matinée.

▸**lie about, lie around** vi a [*objects, clothes, books*] traîner. don't leave that money lying about ne laissez pas traîner cet argent. b [*person*] traîner, traînasser*. don't just lie about all day! tâche de ne pas traîner *or* traînasser toute la journée!

▸**lie back** vi (*in chair, on bed*) se renverser (en arrière). (*fig*) just lie back and enjoy yourself! laisse-toi (donc) vivre!

▸**lie down** 1 vi [*person, animal*] se coucher, s'allonger, s'étendre. she lay down for a while elle s'est allongée quelques instants; when I arrived she was lying down quand je suis arrivé elle était allongée; (*to dog*) lie down! couché!; to lie down on the job* tirer au flanc*, flemmarder*; (*fig*) to lie down under an insult courber la tête sous l'insulte; (*fig*) to take sth lying down encaisser qch* sans broncher, accepter qch sans protester, avaler des couleuvres; he won't take that lying down* il va se rebiffer*; I won't take it lying down* ça ne va pas se passer comme ça, je vais protester; he's not one to take things lying down* il n'est pas du genre à tout avaler* *or* à encaisser sans rien dire.
2 lie-down* n *see* lie[1] 3.

▸**lie in** 1 vi a (*stay in bed*) rester au lit, faire la grasse matinée. b (†: *in childbirth*) être en couches. 2 lie-in* n *see* lie[1] 3.

▸**lie off** vi (*Naut*) rester au large.

▸**lie over** vi (*be postponed*) être ajourné, être remis (à plus tard).

▸**lie to** vi (*Naut*) être *or* se tenir à la cape.

▸**lie up** vi a (*stay in bed*) garder le lit *or* la chambre. b (*hide*) se cacher, rester caché.

lie[2] [laɪ] (vb: pret, ptp lied) 1 n mensonge *m*. to tell ~s mentir, dire des mensonges; I tell a ~* je mens, je dis une bêtise; that's a ~! vous mentez!, c'est un mensonge!; to give the ~ to *person* accuser de mentir; *claim, account* démentir, contredire; *see* pack, white.
2 vi mentir. he's lying through *or* in his teeth* il ment effrontément

or comme un arracheur de dents.

3 **vt: he tried to ~ his way out of it** il a essayé de s'en sortir par des mensonges; **he managed to ~ his way into the director's office** il a réussi à s'introduire dans le bureau du directeur sous un prétexte mensonger; **he ~d his way into the job** il a obtenu le poste grâce à des mensonges.

4 **comp ▸lie detector** détecteur *m* de mensonges.

Liechtenstein ['lɪktən,staɪn] 1 **n** Liechtenstein *m*. **native** *or* **inhabitant of ~** Liechtensteinois(e) *m(f)*. 2 **adj** liechtensteinois.

lied [li:d] **n, pl lieder** ['li:dəʳ] lied *m* (*pl* lieder).

lief [li:f] **adv** (†† *or liter*) **I would as ~ die as tell a lie** j'aimerais autant mourir que mentir.

liege [li:dʒ] **n** (*Hist*) a (*also* **~ lord**) seigneur *m*, suzerain *m*. **yes, my ~!** oui, Sire! b (*also* **~ man**) vassal *m* (lige).

lien [lɪən] **n** (*Jur*) privilège *m*, droit *m* de gage. **to have a ~ on the estate of a debtor** avoir un privilège sur les biens d'un débiteur.

lienee [lɪə'ni:] **n** débiteur-gagiste *m*.

lienor ['lɪənəʳ] **n** créancier-gagiste *m*.

lieu [lu:] **n: in ~ of** au lieu de, à la place de; **one month's notice or £2,400 in ~** un mois de préavis ou bien 2 400 livres.

Lieut. (**abbr of Lieutenant**) (*on envelope*) **~ J Smith** Monsieur le lieutenant J. Smith.

lieutenant [lef'tenənt], (*US*) [lu:'tenənt] 1 **n** a (*Brit Army*) lieutenant *m*; (*Brit, US: Navy*) [lə'tenənt,] (*US*) [lu:'tenənt] lieutenant de vaisseau; (*fig: chief assistant*) second *m*. (*US Army*) **first ~** lieutenant *m*; *see* **lord.** b (*US Police*) (*uniformed*) officier *m* de paix; (*plain clothes*) inspecteur *m* de police. 2 **comp ▸lieutenant colonel** (*Brit, US: Army; also US Air Force*) lieutenant-colonel *m* **▸lieutenant commander** (*Navy*) capitaine *m* de corvette **▸lieutenant general** (*Brit, US: Army*) général *m* de corps d'armée; (*US Air Force*) général *m* de corps aérien **▸lieutenant-governor** (*Can*) lieutenant-gouverneur *m*.

life [laɪf] **pl lives** 1 **n** a (*NonC: in general*) vie *f*. **is there ~ on Mars?** la vie existe-t-elle sur Mars?; **animal and plant ~** vie animale et végétale; **bird ~** les oiseaux *mpl*; **insect ~** les insectes *mpl*; **there was no sign of ~** il n'y avait pas signe de vie; **a matter of ~ and death** une question de vie ou de mort (*see also* **2**); **he came to ~ again** il a repris conscience; **the town came to ~ when the sailors arrived** la ville s'éveillait à l'arrivée des marins; **to bring sb back to ~** ranimer qn; (*fig*) **she brought the party to ~** elle a animé la soirée (*see also* **d**); (*fig*) **his interpretation brings the character to ~** son interprétation fait vivre le personnage; **tired of ~** las de vivre; *see* **large, still²** *etc.*

b (*existence*) vie *f*. **he lived in France all his ~** il a vécu toute sa vie en France; **for the rest of his ~** pour le restant de ses jours; (*Jur*) **to be sent to prison for ~** être condamné à perpétuité *or* à la prison à vie; **friends for ~** amis pour toujours; **to be on trial for one's ~** risquer la peine capitale; **it will last you for ~** *or* **(for) all your ~** cela vous durera toute votre vie; **to have the time of one's ~** s'amuser follement; **at my time of ~** à mon âge; **she began ~ as a teacher** elle a débuté comme professeur; **never in (all) my ~ have I seen such stupidity** jamais de ma vie je n'ai vu une telle stupidité; **in early ~, early in ~** de bonne heure, tôt dans la vie; **in her early ~** dans sa jeunesse; **in later ~** plus tard (dans la vie); **in his later ~** plus tard dans sa vie; **late in ~** sur le tard, à un âge avancé; **loss of ~** perte *f* de vies humaines; **how many lives were lost?** combien de vies cela a-t-il coûté?; **many lives were lost** beaucoup ont trouvé la mort *or* péri; **no lives were lost** il n'y a eu aucun mort *or* aucune victime; **to lose one's ~** perdre la vie, périr; **he ran for dear ~*** *or* **for his ~*** il a pris ses jambes à son cou, il a foncé à bride abattue; **run for your lives!** sauve qui peut!; (*Rel*) **in this ~** en cette vie; (*on tombstone etc*) **departed this ~, May 10th 1842** qui a été enlevé(e) aux siens le 10 mai 1842; **is there (a) ~ after death?** y a-t-il une vie après la mort?; **I don't believe in ~ after death** je ne crois pas à la vie après la mort; **~ isn't worth living** la vie ne vaut pas la peine d'être vécue; **the cat has nine lives** le chat a neuf vies; **to take sb's ~** donner la mort à qn; **to take one's (own) ~** se donner la mort; **to take one's ~ in one's hands** jouer sa vie; (*liter*) **to lay down one's ~** se sacrifier, donner sa vie; (*Art*) **a portrait taken from ~** un portrait d'après nature; **it was Paul to the ~** c'était Paul tout craché*; **~ begins at forty** la vie commence à quarante ans; **I couldn't for the ~ of me tell you his name*** je ne pourrais absolument pas vous dire son nom; **I couldn't for the ~ of me understand ...*** je n'arrivais absolument pas à comprendre ..., j'avais beau m'évertuer, je ne pouvais comprendre ...; **upon** *or* **'pon my ~!†** seigneur!, diantre!†; **what a ~!** quelle vie!, quel métier!*; **how's ~?*** comment (ça) va?*; **such is ~!, that's ~!** c'est la vie!; **this is the ~!*** voilà comment je comprends la vie!; **not on your ~!*** jamais de la vie!; **I couldn't do it to save my ~*** je ne pourrais le faire pour rien au monde; *see* **after, risk, rose², true, worth 2b** *etc.*

c (*NonC: way of living*) vie *f*. **which do you prefer, town or country ~?** que préférez-vous, la vie à la ville ou la vie à la campagne?; **his ~ was very unexciting** sa vie n'avait rien de passionnant; **high ~** la vie mondaine; **the good ~** (*pleasant*) la belle vie; (*Rel*) la vie d'un saint, une vie sainte; **it's a good ~** c'est la belle vie; **home ~** vie de famille; **the private ~ of Henry VIII** la vie privée d'Henri VIII; **he is known in private ~ as ...** dans le privé *or* dans l'intimité on l'appelle ...; **to lead a charmed ~** avoir la chance avec soi; **to lead a quiet ~** mener une vie tranquille; **to live one's own ~** vivre sa vie; **to live the ~ of Riley*** mener la vie de château; **to make a new ~ for o.s., to start a new ~** commencer une nouvelle vie; (*US: of prostitute*) **she's in the ~‡** elle fait le trottoir; *see* **live 2, married, night, see¹** *etc.*

d (*NonC: liveliness*) vie *f*. **to be full of ~** être plein de vie; **you need to put a bit of ~ into it** il faut y mettre plus d'ardeur, il faut y aller avec plus d'entrain; **he's the ~ and soul of the party** c'est un boute-en-train, c'est lui qui met l'ambiance*; **it put new ~ into me** ça m'a fait revivre, ça m'a ragaillardi *or* revigoré; **there isn't much ~ in our village** notre village n'est pas très vivant *or* est plutôt mort; **there's ~ in the old dog yet*** le bonhomme a encore du ressort.

e (*biography*) vie *f*. **the lives of the Saints** la vie des saints.

f (*fig: validity, usefulness*) [*car, ship, government, licence, battery etc*] durée *f*.

g (*: *imprisonment*) **he got ~** il a été condamné à perpétuité *or* à perpète‡; **he's doing ~** il tire* une condamnation à perpétuité.

2 **comp** *subscription etc* à vie **▸life-and-death struggle** combat *m* à mort, lutte *f* désespérée **▸life annuity** rente viagère **▸life assurance** (*esp Brit*) assurance-vie *f* **▸lifebelt** bouée *f* de sauvetage **▸lifeblood** (*fig*) élément vital *or* moteur, âme *f* **▸lifeboat** (*from shore*) bateau *m* *or* canot *m* de sauvetage; (*from ship*) chaloupe *f* de sauvetage; **lifeboat station** centre *m* *or* poste *m* de secours en mer **▸lifeboatman** sauveteur *m* (en mer) **▸lifebuoy** bouée *f* de sauvetage **▸life cycle** cycle *m* de (la) vie **▸life expectancy** espérance *f* de vie; **life expectancy table** table *f* de survie **▸the life force** la force vitale **▸life form** forme *f* de vie **▸life-giving** vivifiant **▸lifeguard** (*on beach*) surveillant *m* de plage *or* de baignade; (*Mil: bodyguard*) garde *m* du corps **▸Life Guards** (*Brit Mil*) cavalerie *f* de la Garde (royale) **▸life imprisonment** (*gen*) prison *f* à vie; (*Jur*) réclusion *f* à perpétuité **▸life insurance** = **life assurance ▸life interest** (*Jur*) usufruit *m* **▸life jacket** gilet *m* de sauvetage, ceinture *f* de sauvetage; (*Navy*) brassière *f* (de sauvetage) **▸lifelike** qui semble vivant *or* vrai **▸lifeline** (*on ship*) main courante; (*in palmistry*) ligne *f* de vie; (*for diver*) corde *f* de sécurité; (*fig*) **it was his lifeline** c'était vital pour lui **▸lifelong** *ambition* de toute ma (*or* sa *etc*) vie; *friend, friendship* de toujours; **it is a lifelong task** c'est le travail de toute une vie **▸life member** membre *m* à vie **▸life membership** carte *f* de membre à vie; **to be given life membership** être nommé *or* fait membre à vie **▸life peer** (*Brit*) pair *m* à vie **▸life peerage** (*Brit*) pairie *f* à vie **▸life preserver** (*US: life jacket*) gilet *m* de sauvetage, ceinture *f* de sauvetage; (*Navy*) brassière *f* de sauvetage; (*Brit* ‡: *bludgeon*) matraque *f* **▸life president** président(e) *m(f)* à vie **▸life raft** radeau *m* de sauvetage **▸life-saver** (*person*) surveillant(e) *m(f)* de baignade; (*fig*) **that money was a life-saver** cet argent m'a (*or* lui a *etc*) sauvé la vie **▸life-saving n** (*rescuing*) sauvetage *m*; (*first aid*) secourisme *m* ◊ **adj** de sauvetage **▸the life sciences** les sciences *fpl* de la vie **▸life sentence** (*Jur*) condamnation *f* à perpétuité **▸life-sized** grandeur nature *inv* **▸life span** durée *f* *or* espérance *f* de vie **▸life story** biographie *f*; **his life story** sa biographie, l'histoire *f* de sa vie **▸life style** style *m* *or* mode *m* de vie **▸life support equipment, life support system** équipements *mpl* de vie; (*Med*) **he's on a life support system** il est sous assistance respiratoire; (*Med*) **to switch off the life support system** débrancher le respirateur artificiel **▸life's work** œuvre *f* de toute une (*or* ma *or* sa *etc*) vie **▸life tenancy: to hold a life tenancy of a house** être locataire d'une maison à vie **▸life-threatening** *disease, emergency* mortellement grave **▸lifetime** *see* **lifetime ▸life-vest** (*US*) = **life jacket.**

lifeless ['laɪflɪs] **adj** *body* sans vie, inanimé; *matter* inanimé; (*fig*) *style* sans vie, sans vigueur, mou (*f* molle).

lifelessness ['laɪflɪsnɪs] **n** (*lit*) absence *f* de vie; (*fig*) manque *m* de vigueur *or* d'entrain.

lifer‡ ['laɪfəʳ] **n** condamné(e) *m(f)* à perpète‡.

lifetime ['laɪftaɪm] **n** a vie *f*. **it won't happen in** *or* **during my ~** je ne verrai pas cela de mon vivant; **the chance of a ~** la chance de sa (*or* ma *etc*) vie; **once in a ~** une fois dans la *or* une vie; **the work of a ~** l'œuvre de toute une vie; **a ~'s experience** l'expérience de toute une vie; *see* **last².** b (*fig: eternity*) éternité *f*. **it seemed a ~** cela a semblé une éternité.

LIFO ['laɪfəʊ] (**abbr of last in, first out**) DEPS.

lift [lɪft] 1 **n** a (*Brit*) (*elevator*) ascenseur *m*; (*for goods*) monte-charge *m inv*; *see* **service.**

b (*Ski*) téléski *m*, tire-fesses* *m*.

c **give the box a ~** soulève la boîte; **give me a ~ with this trunk** aide-moi à soulever cette malle; **can you give me a ~ up, I can't reach the shelf** soulève-moi s'il te plaît, je n'arrive pas à atteindre l'étagère; *see* **air, face.**

d (*Brit: transport*) **can I give you a ~?** est-ce que je peux vous déposer quelque part?; **I gave him a ~ to Paris** je l'ai pris en voiture *or* je l'ai emmené jusqu'à Paris; **we didn't get any ~s** personne ne s'est arrêté pour nous prendre; **he stood there hoping for a ~** il était là (debout) dans l'espoir d'être pris en stop; *see* **hitch.**

e (*Aviat*) portance *f*.

f (*fig: boost*) **it gave us a ~** cela nous a remonté le moral *or* nous a encouragés.

2 comp ▸**lift attendant** (*Brit*) liftier *m*, -ière *f* ▸**liftboy** (*Brit*) liftier *m*, garçon *m* d'ascenseur ▸**lift cage** (*Brit*) cabine *f* d'ascenseur ▸**liftgate** (*Aut: esp US*) hayon *m* ▸**liftman** (*Brit*) = **liftboy** ▸**lift-off** (*Space*) décollage *m*; **we have lift-off!** décollage! ▸**lift shaft** (*Brit*) cage *f* d'ascenseur.

3 **vt** a (*raise*) lever, soulever; (*Agr*) *potatoes etc* arracher. **to ~ sth into the air** lever qch en l'air; **to ~ sb/sth onto a table** soulever qn/qch et le poser *or* pour le poser sur une table; **to ~ sb/sth off a table** descendre qn/qch d'une table; **to ~ sb over a wall** faire passer qn par-dessus un mur; **this suitcase is too heavy for me to ~** cette valise est trop lourde pour que je la soulève (*subj*); (*Sport*) **to ~ weights** faire de l'haltérophilie *or* des haltères; (*fig*) **he didn't ~ a finger to help** il n'a pas levé le petit doigt pour aider; **he ~ed his fork to his mouth** il a porté la fourchette à sa bouche; (*notice*) **"~ here"** "soulever ici"; *see* **face**.

b (*fig*) *restrictions* supprimer, abolir; *ban, blockade, siege* lever.

c (*: *steal*) piquer*, chiper*, barboter‡; *see* **shop**.

d *quotation, passage* prendre, voler. **he ~ed that idea from Sartre** il a volé *or* pris cette idée à Sartre, il a plagié Sartre.

4 **vi** *[lid etc]* se soulever; *[fog]* se lever.

▸**lift down** **vt sep** *box, person* descendre. **to lift sth down from a shelf** descendre qch d'une étagère.

▸**lift off** 1 **vi** (*Space*) décoller. 2 **vt sep** *lid* enlever; *person* descendre. 3 **lift-off** **n** *see* **lift 2**.

▸**lift out** **vt sep** *object* sortir; (*Mil*) *troops* (*by plane*) évacuer par avion, aéroporter; (*by helicopter*) héliporter, évacuer par hélicoptère. **he lifted the child out of his playpen** il a sorti l'enfant de son parc.

▸**lift up** 1 **vi** *[drawbridge etc]* se soulever, basculer. 2 **vt sep** *object, carpet, skirt, person* soulever. **to lift up one's eyes** lever les yeux; **to lift up one's head** lever *or* redresser la tête; (*liter*) **he lifted up his voice** il a élevé la voix.

ligament ['lɪgəmənt] **n** ligament *m*.

ligature ['lɪgətʃəʳ] **n** (*Surg, Typ: act, object*) ligature *f*; (*Mus*) coulé *m*, liaison *f*.

light¹ [laɪt] (**vb: pret, ptp lit** *or* **lighted**) 1 **n** a (*gen*) lumière *f*; (*from lamp*) lumière, éclairage *m*; (*from sun*) lumière; (*daylight*) lumière, jour *m*. **electric ~** éclairage *or* lumière électrique; **to put on** *or* **turn on** *or* **switch on the ~** allumer (la lumière); **to put off** *or* **put out** *or* **turn off** *or* **turn out** *or* **switch off** *or* **switch out the ~** éteindre (la lumière); **there were ~s on in several of the rooms** il y avait de la lumière dans plusieurs pièces; **he put out the ~s one by one** il a éteint les lumières une à une; **~s out at 9 o'clock** extinction *f* des feux à 21 heures; **~s out!** extinction des feux!, on éteint!; **we saw several ~s on the horizon** nous avons vu plusieurs lumières à l'horizon; **by the ~ of a candle/the fire/a torch** à la lumière *or* lueur d'une bougie/du feu/d'une lampe de poche; **with the ~ of battle in his eyes** (avec) une lueur belliqueuse dans le regard; **at first ~** au point du jour; **the ~ was beginning to fail** le jour commençait à baisser; **she was sitting with her back to the ~** *or* **with the ~ behind her** elle tournait le dos à la lumière; **to stand sth in the ~** mettre qch à la lumière; **you're holding it against the ~** vous le tenez à contre-jour; **to be** *or* **stand in one's own ~** se faire de l'ombre; **you're in my** *or* **the ~** (*daylight*) vous me cachez *or* bouchez le jour; (*electric*) vous me cachez la lumière; **get out of my** *or* **the ~!** pousse-toi, tu me fais de l'ombre!; **the ~ isn't good enough to take photographs** il ne fait pas assez clair *or* il n'y a pas assez de lumière pour prendre des photos; (*Art, Phot*) **~ and shade** les clairs *mpl* et les ombres *fpl*; (*fig*) **to see the ~** (*understand*) comprendre; (*see error of one's ways; also Rel*) trouver son chemin de Damas; (*fig*) **to see the ~ (of day)** (*be born*) venir au monde; (*be published etc*) paraître; (*fig*) **there is (a)** *or* **one can see the ~ at the end of the tunnel** on entrevoit la lumière au bout du tunnel; *see* **fire, go out, hide¹, moon** *etc*.

b (*fig*) lumière *f*, jour *m*. **to bring to ~** mettre en lumière, révéler; **to come to ~** être dévoilé *or* découvert; **new facts have come to ~** on a découvert des faits nouveaux; **can you throw any ~ on this question?** pouvez-vous éclaircir cette question?; **to shed** *or* **cast a new ~ on a subject** jeter un jour nouveau sur un sujet; **the incident revealed him in a new ~** l'incident l'a montré sous un jour nouveau; **in a good/bad ~** sous un jour favorable/défavorable; **in the ~ of what you say** à la lumière de *or* tenant compte de ce que vous dites; **I don't see things in that ~** je ne vois pas les choses sous cet angle-là *or* sous ce jour-là; **according to his ~s, by his own ~s** d'après sa façon de voir les choses; **in the cold ~ of day** à tête reposée.

c (*object: lamp etc*) lampe *f*. **desk/reading** *etc* **~** lampe de bureau/de lecture *etc*; **have you brought the ~ for the tent?** est-ce que tu as apporté la lampe *or* la lanterne pour la tente?

d *[motor vehicle]* (*gen*) feu *m*; (*headlamp*) phare *m*; *[cycle]* feu. **have you got your ~s on?** as-tu mis tes phares (*or* tes feux)?; **he saw the ~s of the cars** (*rear*) il a vu les feux des voitures; (*front*) il a vu les phares des voitures; *see* **parking, side** *etc*.

e (*traffic ~s*) **the ~s** (*gen*) les feux *mpl* (de circulation); **the ~s aren't working** les feux sont en panne; **the ~s were at red** le feu était (au) rouge; **to go through a red ~** griller* *or* brûler un feu rouge; **he stopped at the ~s** il s'est arrêté au feu (rouge).

f (*for cigarette etc*) feu *m*. **have you got a ~?** avez-vous du feu?; **to put a ~ to sth, to set ~ to sth** mettre le feu à qch; *see* **pilot, strike**.

g (*Archit: window*) fenêtre *f*, ouverture *f*, jour *m*; *see* **fan¹, leaded, sky**.

2 **adj** a *evening, room* clair. **it was growing ~** il commençait à faire jour *or* clair; **while it's still ~** pendant qu'il fait encore jour.

b *hair* clair, blond; *colour, complexion, skin* clair. **~ green** vert clair *inv*; **~ blue** bleu clair *inv*.

3 **comp** ▸**light bulb** ampoule *f*, lampe *f* ▸**light-coloured** clair, de couleur claire ▸**light effects** effets *mpl or* jeux *mpl* de lumière ▸**light-emitting diode** diode *f* électro-luminescente ▸**light fitting** appareil *m* d'éclairage ▸**light-haired** blond ▸**lighthouse** phare *m* ▸**lighthouse keeper** gardien *m* de phare ▸**light meter** (*Phot*) posemètre *m*, cellule *f* (photo-électrique) ▸**light pen, light pencil** (*Comput*) photostyle *m*, crayon *m* optique ▸**light-sensitive** photosensible ▸**lightship** bateau-phare *m*, bateau-feu *m* ▸**light wave** onde lumineuse ▸**light-year** année-lumière *f*; **3,000 light-years away** distant de 3 000 années-lumière; (*fig*) **that's light-years away** c'est à des années-lumière.

4 **vt** a *candle, cigarette, gas* allumer. **to ~ a match** frotter *or* craquer une allumette; **a ~ed match** une allumette enflammée; **he lit the fire** il a allumé le feu; **he lit a fire** il a fait du feu.

b *room, window* éclairer. **lit by electricity** éclairé à l'électricité; **this torch will ~ your way** *or* **the way for you** cette lampe de poche vous éclairera le chemin.

5 **vi** a *[match]* s'allumer; *[coal, wood]* prendre (feu).

b **to ~ into sb‡** tomber sur qn (à bras raccourcis).

▸**light out‡** **vi** partir à toute vitesse (*for* pour), se barrer‡.

▸**light up** 1 **vi** a *[lamp]* s'allumer; (*fig*) s'animer, s'éclairer. **her eyes/face lit up** son regard/visage s'est éclairé. b (*: *smoke*) allumer une cigarette *or* une pipe *etc*. 2 **vt sep** *[lighting, sun]* *room* éclairer. (*fig*) **a smile lit up her face** un sourire a éclairé *or* illuminé son visage; *see also* **lighting, lit**. 3 **lit up** **adj** *see* **lit 2**. 4 **lighting-up** **n** *see* **lighting 2**.

light² [laɪt] 1 **adj** a (*not heavy*) *parcel, weapon, clothes, sleep, meal, wine, soil* léger. **~er than air** plus léger que l'air; **as ~ as a feather** léger comme une plume; **to be ~ on one's feet** (*gen*) avoir le pas léger *or* la démarche légère; *[boxer]* avoir un très bon jeu de jambes; *[dancer]* être aérien; **to be a ~ sleeper** avoir le sommeil léger; (*Brit*) **~ ale** *sorte de bière blonde légère*; (*US*) **~ beer** bière *f* basses calories; **~ industry** industrie *f* légère; (*Mil*) **~ infantry** infanterie légère; (*Boxing*) **~ heavyweight** (**adj**) (poids *m*) mi-lourd; (**n**) (poids *m*) mi-lourd *m*; (*Boxing*) **~ middleweight** (**adj, n**) (poids *m*) super-welter *or* super-mi-moyen (*m*); (*Boxing*) **~ welterweight** (**adj, n**) (poids *m*) super-léger (*m*); **you've given me ~ weight** vous ne m'avez pas mis le poids (*see also* **4**); **~ aircraft** petit avion *m*; **~ vehicles** véhicules légers.

b (*fig*) *play, music, breeze, punishment, shower* léger; *rain* petit, fin; *work, task* (*easy*) facile; (*not strenuous*) peu fatigant. **~ comedy** comédie légère; **~ entertainment** spectacles *mpl* distrayants; **~ opera** opérette *f*; **~ reading** lecture distrayante; **~ verse** poésie légère; **it is no ~ matter** c'est sérieux, ça n'est pas une plaisanterie; **a ~ fall of snow** une légère chute de neige; **with a ~ heart** le cœur léger; **"woman wanted for ~ work"** "on demande employée de maison pour travaux légers"; **to make ~ work of sth** faire qch aisément *or* sans difficulté; **to make ~ of sth** prendre *or* traiter qch à la légère.

2 **adv**: **to sleep ~** avoir le sommeil léger; **to travel ~** voyager avec peu de bagages; **he got off ~*** il s'en est tiré à bon compte.

3 **npl**: (*meat*) **~s** mou *m* (*abats*).

4 **comp** ▸**light-fingered**: **to be light-fingered** être chapardeur, avoir les doigts crochus* ▸**light-footed** (*gen*) au pas léger, à la démarche légère; *dancer* aérien ▸**light-headed** (*dizzy*) étourdi, pris de vertige; (*unable to think clearly*) étourdi, hébété; (*excited*) exalté, grisé; (*thoughtless*) étourdi, écervelé ▸**light-hearted** *person* gai, aimable, enjoué; *laugh* joyeux, gai; *atmosphere* joyeux, gai, plaisant; *discussion* enjoué; *question, remark* plaisant, peu sérieux ▸**light-heartedly** (*happily*) joyeusement, allègrement; (*jokingly*) en plaisantant; (*cheerfully*) de bon cœur, avec bonne humeur ▸**lightweight** **adj** *jacket, shoes* léger; (*Boxing*) poids léger *inv* ◊ **n** (*Boxing*) poids léger; (*Boxing*) **European lightweight champion/championship** champion *m*/championnat *m* d'Europe des poids légers.

light³ [laɪt] **pret, ptp lighted** *or* **lit** **vi**: **to ~ (up)on sth** trouver qch par hasard, tomber par chance sur qch; **his eyes lit upon the jewels** son regard est tombé sur les bijoux.

lighten¹ ['laɪtn] 1 **vt** a (*light up*) *darkness, face* éclairer, illuminer. b (*make lighter*) *colour, hair* éclaircir. 2 **vi** a *[sky]* s'éclaircir; (*fig*) *[face]* s'éclairer. b (*Met: of lightning*) **it is ~ing** il fait *or* il y a des éclairs.

lighten² ['laɪtn] 1 **vt** (*make less heavy*) *cargo, burden* alléger; *tax* alléger, réduire. 2 **vi** *[load]* se réduire. **her heart ~ed at the news** la nouvelle lui a enlevé le poids qu'elle avait sur le cœur *or* lui a ôté un grand poids.

▸**lighten up*** **vt** se relaxer, se détendre.

lighter¹ ['laɪtəʳ] 1 **n** (*for gas cooker*) allume-gaz *m inv*; (*also* **cigarette ~**) briquet *m*; (*Aut: on dashboard*) allume-cigare *m inv*, allume-cigarette *m inv*; *see* **cigar, fire, lamp** *etc*. 2 **comp** ▸**lighter flint** pierre *f* à briquet ▸**lighter fuel** gaz *m* (*or* essence *f*) à briquet.

lighter[2] ['laɪtəʳ] n (*Naut*) péniche *f*, chaland *m*, allège *f*.

lighterage ['laɪtərɪdʒ] n (transport *m* par) ac(c)onage *m*; (*fee*) droit *m* d'ac(c)onage.

lighting ['laɪtɪŋ] 1 n (*NonC*) a (*Elec*) éclairage *m*; (*Theat*) éclairages. b (*act*) *[lamp, candle etc]* allumage *m*. 2 comp ▸**lighting effects** effets *mpl or* jeux *mpl* d'éclairage, éclairages *mpl* ▸**lighting engineer** éclairagiste *m* ▸**lighting fixture** appareil *m* d'éclairage ▸**lighting-up time** (*Brit Aut*) heure *f* de l'éclairage obligatoire des véhicules, tombée *f* du jour; (*duration*) heures d'obscurité.

lightly ['laɪtlɪ] adv a *walk, clothe* légèrement. **she touched his brow ~ with her hand** elle lui a effleuré le front de la main. b *behave, speak* légèrement, à la légère; *laugh* légèrement; *remark, say* d'un ton dégagé. c **to get off ~** s'en tirer à bon compte. d **~ boiled egg** ≃ œuf *m* mollet; **~ cooked** pas trop cuit.

lightness[1] ['laɪtnɪs] n (*brightness*) clarté *f*.

lightness[2] ['laɪtnɪs] n (*in weight, Culin*) légèreté *f*.

lightning ['laɪtnɪŋ] 1 n éclair *m*, foudre *f*. **we saw ~** nous avons vu un éclair *or* des éclairs; **there was a lot of ~** il y avait beaucoup d'éclairs; **a flash of ~** un éclair; **struck by ~** frappé par la foudre, foudroyé; **~ never strikes twice in the same place** la foudre ne frappe *or* ne tombe jamais deux fois à la même place; **like ~*** avec la vitesse de l'éclair; *see* **forked, grease, sheet.** 2 comp *attack* foudroyant; (*Ind*) *strike* surprise *inv*; *visit* éclair *inv* ▸**lightning bug** (*US*) luciole *f* ▸**lightning conductor**, (*US*) **lightning rod** paratonnerre *m*.

ligneous ['lɪgnɪəs] adj ligneux.

lignite ['lɪgnaɪt] n lignite *m*.

lignum vitae ['lɪgnəm'viːtaɪ] n (*tree*) gaïac *m*; (*wood*) bois *m* de gaïac.

Liguria [lɪ'gjʊərɪə] n Ligurie *f*.

Ligurian [lɪ'gjʊərɪən] adj ligurien.

likable ['laɪkəbl] adj = **likeable**.

like[1] [laɪk] 1 adj semblable, pareil, du même ordre, du même genre; (*stronger*) similaire, analogue. **they are as ~ as two peas (in a pod)** ils se ressemblent comme deux gouttes d'eau.

2 prep a comme, en. **he spoke ~ an aristocrat** il parlait comme un aristocrate; **he spoke ~ the aristocrat he was** il parlait comme l'aristocrate qu'il était, il parlait en aristocrate; **~ the fool he is, he ...** imbécile comme il l'est *or* (en) imbécile qu'il est, il ...; **he behaved ~ a fool** il s'est conduit comme un imbécile *or* en imbécile; **~ an animal in a trap he ...** telle une bête prise au piège, il ...; **the news spread ~ wildfire** la nouvelle s'est répandue comme une traînée de poudre; **it wasn't ~ that at all** ce n'était pas du tout comme ça; **you do it ~ so** *or* **~ this** tu fais comme ça; **it happened ~ this ...** voici comment ça s'est passé ..., ça s'est passé comme ceci ...; **it was ~ this, I'd just got home ...** voilà, je venais juste de rentrer ...; **I'm sorry I didn't come but it was ~ this ...** je m'excuse de ne pas être venu mais c'est que ...; **to tell it ~ it is*** dire les choses carrément; *see* **anything, crazy, hell, mad** *etc.*

b (*resembling*) comme, du même genre que, semblable à, pareil à. **to be ~ sb/sth** ressembler à qn/qch; **who is he ~?** à qui ressemble-t-il?; **they are very (much) ~ one another** ils se ressemblent beaucoup; **he is ~ his father** (*in appearance*) il ressemble à son père; (*in character*) il est comme son père, il ressemble à son père; **the portrait is not ~ him** le portrait ne lui ressemble pas *or* n'est pas ressemblant; **his work is rather ~ Van Gogh's** son œuvre est un peu dans le genre *or* le style de celle de Van Gogh, son œuvre ressemble un peu à celle de Van Gogh; **your writing is rather ~ mine** vous avez un peu la même écriture que moi, votre écriture ressemble assez à la mienne; **a house ~ mine** une maison pareille à *or* comme la mienne; **an idiot ~ you** un imbécile comme vous; **a hat rather** *or* **something ~ yours** un chapeau un peu comme le vôtre *or* dans le genre du vôtre; **I found one ~ it** j'en ai trouvé un pareil, j'ai trouvé le même; **I never saw anything ~ it!** je n'ai jamais rien vu de pareil!; **we heard a noise ~ a car backfiring** on a entendu comme une pétarade de voiture; **she was ~ a sister to me** elle était comme une sœur pour moi; **that's just ~ him!** c'est bien de lui!; **it's not ~ him to be late** ça ne lui ressemble pas *or* ça n'est pas son genre d'être en retard; **that's just ~ a woman!** voilà bien les femmes!; **he's just ~ anybody else** il est comme tout le monde *or* comme n'importe qui; **can't you just accept it ~ everyone else?** tu ne peux pas simplement l'accepter comme tout le monde?; **it cost something ~ £100** cela a coûté dans les 100 livres, cela a coûté quelque chose comme 100 livres; **he's called Middlewick or something ~ that** il s'appelle Middlewick ou quelque chose comme ça *or* quelque chose d'approchant; **I was thinking of giving her something ~ a necklace** je pensais lui offrir un collier ou quelque chose dans ce genre-là *or* quelque chose comme ça*; **that's something ~ a steak!*** voilà ce que j'appelle *or* ce qui s'appelle un bifteck!; **that's something ~ it!*** c'est ça!, voilà!; **that's more ~ it!** voilà qui est mieux!, il y a du progrès!; **that's nothing ~ it!** ça n'est pas du tout ça!; **there's nothing ~ real silk** rien de tel que la soie véritable, rien ne vaut la soie véritable; **some people are ~ that** il y a des gens comme ça; **people ~ that can't be trusted** on ne peut pas se fier à des gens pareils *or* à des gens comme ça; **his father is ~ that** son père est ainsi fait *or* est comme ça*; **you know what she's ~** vous savez comment elle est; **what's he ~?** comment est-il?; **what's he ~ as a teacher?** comment est-il *or* que vaut-il comme professeur?; **what's the film ~?** comment as-tu trouvé le film?; **what's the weather ~ in Paris?** quel temps fait-il à Paris?; *see* **feel, look, sound**[1] *etc.*

c comme, de même que. (*Prov*) **~ father, ~ son** tel père, tel fils (*Prov*); **~ me, he is fond of Brahms** comme moi *or* de même que moi, il aime Brahms; **he, ~ me, thinks that ...** comme moi *or* de même que moi, il pense que ...; **he thinks ~ us*** il pense comme nous; **do it ~ me*** fais-le comme moi.

d comme, tel que, par exemple. **there are many hobbies you might take up, ~ painting, gardening and so on** il y a beaucoup d'activités que tu pourrais entreprendre, par exemple *or* comme la peinture, le jardinage et cætera; **the basic necessities of life, ~ food and drink** les éléments indispensables à la vie, tels que *or* comme la nourriture et la boisson.

3 adv a (*) **~ enough, as ~ as not, very ~** probablement.

b (*near*) **that record's nothing ~ as good as this one** ce disque-là est loin d'être aussi bon que celui-ci; **she's more ~ 30 than 25** elle a plutôt 30 ans que 25, elle est plus près de 30 ans que de 25.

c (*Brit*) **he felt tired ~***, (*US*) **he felt ~* tired** il se sentait comme qui dirait* fatigué; **I had a fortnight's holiday, ~*, so I did a bit of gardening** j'avais quinze jours de vacances, alors comme ça* j'ai fait un peu de jardinage.

4 conj a (*: *as*) comme. **he did it ~ I did** il l'a fait comme moi; **he can't play poker ~ his brother can** il ne sait pas jouer au poker comme *or* aussi bien que son frère; **~ we used to** ainsi qu'on *or* comme on le faisait autrefois; **it's just ~ I say‡** c'est comme je vous le dis.

b (‡: *as if*) comme si. **he behaved ~ he was afraid** il s'est conduit comme s'il avait eu peur.

5 n (*similar thing*) chose pareille *or* semblable; (*person*) pareil *m*. **did you ever see the ~ (of it)?** a-t-on jamais vu chose pareille?; **oranges, lemons and the ~** *or* **and such~** des oranges, des citrons et autres fruits de ce genre; **the ~ of which we'll never see again** comme on n'en reverra plus jamais; **we shall not see his ~ again** jamais nous ne reverrons son pareil; **the ~s of him*** des gens comme lui *or* de son acabit (*pej*).

6 comp ▸**like-minded** de même opinion, animés des mêmes sentiments; **you and other like-minded individuals** vous et d'autres (gens) qui pensent comme vous.

like[2] [laɪk] 1 vt a *person* aimer (bien). **I ~ him** (*of relative, friend etc*) je l'aime bien; (*of casual acquaintance, colleague etc*) il me plaît; **I don't ~ him** je ne l'aime pas beaucoup, il me déplaît; **I've come to ~ him** il m'est devenu sympathique, maintenant je l'aime bien; **he is well ~d here** on l'aime bien ici, on le trouve sympathique ici; **how do you ~ him?** comment le trouvez-vous?; **I don't ~ the look of him** son allure ne me dit rien (qui vaille).

b *object, food, activity* aimer (bien). **I ~ that hat** j'aime bien ce chapeau, ce chapeau me plaît; **which do you ~ best?** lequel aimes-tu le mieux?, lequel préfères-tu?; **this plant doesn't ~ sunlight** cette plante ne se plaît pas à la lumière du soleil; **I ~ oysters but they don't ~ me*** j'aime bien les huîtres mais c'est elles qui ne m'aiment pas*; **I ~ music/Beethoven/football** j'aime bien la musique/Beethoven/le football; **I ~ having** *or* **to have a rest after lunch** j'aime (bien) me reposer après déjeuner; **he ~s to be** *or* **being obeyed** il aime être obéi *or* qu'on lui obéisse; **I ~ people to be punctual** j'aime (bien) que les gens soient à l'heure, j'aime les gens ponctuels; **I don't ~ it when he's unhappy** je n'aime pas qu'il soit malheureux; (*iro*) **well, I ~ that!*** ah ça, par exemple!; (*iro*) **I ~ your cheek!*** tu as quand même du toupet!*; **how do you ~ Paris?** comment trouvez-vous Paris?, que pensez-vous de Paris?, est-ce que Paris vous plaît?; **how do you ~ it here?** (est-ce que) vous vous plaisez ici?; **your father won't ~ it** cela ne plaira pas à ton père, ton père ne sera pas content; **whether he ~s it or not** que cela lui plaise ou non; **~ it or lump it*, you'll have to go** que tu le veuilles ou non *or* que ça te plaise ou non il faudra que tu y ailles; **if you don't ~ it, you can lump it*** si cela ne vous plaît pas, tant pis pour vous *or* c'est le même prix*.

c (*want, wish*) aimer (bien), vouloir, souhaiter. **I should ~ to go home** j'aimerais (bien) *or* je voudrais (bien) rentrer chez moi; **I should have ~d to be there** j'aurais (bien) aimé être là; **I didn't ~ to disturb you** je ne voulais pas vous déranger; **I thought of asking him but I didn't ~ to** j'ai bien pensé (à) le lui demander mais je n'ai pas osé; **would you ~ a drink?** voulez-vous boire quelque chose?; **I should ~ more time** je voudrais un peu plus de temps; **which one would you ~?** lequel voulez-vous *or* voudriez-vous?; **I would ~ you to speak to him** je voudrais que tu lui parles (*subj*); **would you ~ me to go and get it?** veux-tu que j'aille le chercher?; **would you ~ to go to Paris?** aimerais-tu aller à Paris?; **how would you ~ to go to Paris?** est-ce que cela te plairait *or* te dirait* d'aller à Paris?; **how would you ~ me to phrase it?** comment voudriez-vous que je le dise?; **how do you ~ your steak?** comment aimez-vous votre bifteck?; **how would you ~ a steak?** est-ce que ça te dirait* de manger un bifteck?; **I can do it when/where/as much as/how I ~** je peux le faire quand/où/autant que/comme je veux; **when would you ~ breakfast?** à quelle heure voulez-vous le petit-déjeuner?; **whenever you ~** quand vous voudrez; **"As You L~ It"** "Comme il vous plaira"; **don't think you can do as you ~** ne croyez pas que vous pouvez *or* puissiez faire comme vous voulez *or* comme bon vous semble; **I shall go out as much as I ~** je sortirai autant qu'il me plaira *or* autant que je voudrai; **come on Sunday if you ~** venez dimanche si vous voulez; **... if you ~** ... ... si tu veux ..., ... si vous voulez ...; **she can do what she ~s with him** elle fait tout ce qu'elle veut de lui; **(you can) shout as much as you ~, I won't open the door** crie tant que tu veux *or* voudras, je n'ouvrirai pas la porte; **he can say** *or* **let him say what he ~s, I won't change my mind** il peut dire ce qu'il veut, je ne changerai pas d'avis.

2 **n**: **~s** goûts *mpl*, préférences *fpl*; **he knows all my ~s and dislikes** il sait tout ce que j'aime et (tout) ce que je n'aime pas.

...like [laɪk] **adj ending in comps: childlike** enfantin; **statesmanlike** d'homme d'État; *see* **cat** *etc*.

likeable ['laɪkəbl] **adj** sympathique, agréable.

likeableness ['laɪkəblnɪs] **n** caractère *m* sympathique *or* agréable.

likelihood ['laɪklɪhʊd] **n** probabilité *f*, chance *f*. **there is little ~ of his coming** *or* **that he will come** il y a peu de chances *or* il est peu probable qu'il vienne; **there is a strong ~ of his coming** *or* **that he will come** il y a de fortes chances pour qu'il vienne, il est très probable qu'il viendra; **there is no ~ of that** cela ne risque pas d'arriver; **in all ~ she ...** selon toute probabilité elle ..., il est fort probable qu'elle ... .

likely ['laɪklɪ] 1 **adj** a *happening, outcome* probable; *explanation, excuse* plausible, vraisemblable. **which is the likeliest time to find him at home?** à quelle heure a-t-on le plus de chances de le trouver chez lui?; **this looks a ~ place for mushrooms** ça me paraît être un endroit à champignons *or* être un bon endroit pour les champignons; **the likeliest place to set up camp** l'endroit le plus propice où dresser la tente, le meilleur endroit pour dresser la tente; (*iro*) **a ~ story!** comme si j'allais croire ça!, elle est bien bonne! (*iro*); (*iro*) **a ~ excuse!** belle excuse!; **the most ~ candidates** les candidats qui ont le plus de chances de réussir; **I asked 6 ~ people** j'ai demandé à 6 personnes susceptibles de convenir *or* qui me semblaient pouvoir convenir; **he's a ~ young man** c'est un jeune homme qui promet; **it is ~ that** il est probable que + *fut indic*, il y a des chances pour que + *subj*; **it is not ~ that** il est peu probable que + *subj*, il y a peu de chances que + *subj*; **it is very ~ that** il est très possible que + *subj*, il y a de grandes chances que + *subj*; **it's hardly ~ that** il n'est guère probable que + *subj*; **is it ~ that he would forget?** risque-t-il d'oublier?; (*iro*) **is it ~ that I did?** aurais-je pu faire cela, moi? (*iro*).

b (*probable: gen*) **he/it is ~ to ...** il est bien possible qu'il/que cela ... + *subj*; (*of person: with pleasant outcome*) **to be ~ to win/succeed** *etc* avoir de fortes chances de gagner/réussir *etc*; (*with unpleasant outcome*) **to be ~ to fail/refuse** *etc* risquer d'échouer/de refuser *etc*; (*of thing: pleasant*) **it is ~ to sell well/to improve** *etc* il y a de fortes chances que cela se vende bien/que cela s'améliore (*subj*) *etc*; (*unpleasant*) **it is ~ to break/make a loss** *etc* cela risque de se casser/de se vendre à perte *etc*; **she is ~ to arrive at any time** elle va probablement arriver *or* elle risque d'arriver d'une minute à l'autre; **she is not ~ to come** il est peu probable *or* il y a peu de chances qu'elle vienne; **he is not ~ to succeed** il a peu de chances de réussir; **the man most ~ to succeed** l'homme qui a le plus de chances de réussir; **this incident is ~ to cause trouble** cet incident pourrait (bien) amener *or* risque d'amener *or* est de nature à amener des ennuis; **that is not ~ to happen** cela ne risque guère d'arriver.

2 **adv** probablement. **very** *or* **most ~** très probablement; **as ~ as not** sûrement, probablement; **are you going? — not ~!** tu y vas? — pas de danger!*; **I expect he'll let me off with a warning —** (*iro*) **not ~!** je pense qu'il me laissera m'en tirer avec un avertissement — tu crois ça!

liken ['laɪkən] **vt** comparer (*to* à), assimiler (*to* à). **to ~ sb to a fox** comparer qn à un renard; **X can be ~ed to Y** on peut comparer *or* assimiler X et Y.

likeness ['laɪknɪs] **n** a (*resemblance*) ressemblance *f* (*to* avec). **I can't see much ~ between them** je ne vois guère de ressemblance entre eux, je ne trouve pas qu'ils se ressemblent (*subj*) beaucoup; **a strong family ~** un air de famille très marqué; **to bear a ~ to** ressembler à. b (*appearance*) forme *f*, aspect *m*, apparence *f*. **in the ~ of** sous la forme *or* l'aspect de; **to assume the ~ of** prendre la forme *or* l'aspect *or* l'apparence de. c (*Art, Phot etc*) **to draw sb's ~** faire le portrait de qn; **to have one's ~ taken** se faire faire son portrait; **it is a good ~** c'est très ressemblant.

likewise ['laɪkwaɪz] **adv** (*similarly*) de même, également, pareillement; (*also*) aussi; (*moreover*) de plus, en outre. **to do ~** en faire autant, faire pareil *or* de même; **he suggested it, but I wish it ~** c'est lui qui l'a suggéré mais je le souhaite pareillement *or* également *or* aussi; **my wife is well, the children ~** ma femme va bien, les enfants aussi *or* également; **and ~, it cannot be denied that ...** et en outre *or* de plus, on ne peut nier que ... .

liking ['laɪkɪŋ] **n** (*for person*) sympathie *f*, affection *f* (*for* pour); (*for thing*) goût *m* (*for* pour), penchant *m* (*for* pour). **to take a ~ to sb** se prendre d'amitié pour qn; **to take a ~ to (doing) sth** se mettre à aimer (faire) qch; **to have a ~ for sb** tenir qn en affection, avoir de la sympathie pour qn; **to have a ~ for sth** avoir un penchant *or* du goût pour qch, aimer qch; **to your ~, for your ~** à votre goût.

lilac ['laɪlək] 1 **n** (*bush, colour, flower*) lilas *m*. **an avenue of mauve ~s** une avenue bordée de lilas mauves; **a bunch of white ~** un bouquet de lilas blanc. 2 **adj** (*in colour*) lilas *inv*.

Lilliputian [ˌlɪlɪ'pjuːʃɪən] 1 **adj** lilliputien. 2 **n** Lilliputien(ne) *m(f)*.

Lilo ['laɪˌləʊ] **n** ® matelas *m* pneumatique.

lilt [lɪlt] **n** *[speech, song]* rythme *m*, cadence *f*. **a song with a ~ to it** une chanson bien rythmée; **her voice had a pleasant ~ (to it)** sa voix avait des cadences mélodieuses.

lilting ['lɪltɪŋ] **adj** *song* cadencé; *voice* aux intonations mélodieuses; *movement* cadencé.

lily ['lɪlɪ] 1 **n** lis *m*. **~ of the valley** muguet *m*; *see* **water.** 2 **comp** ▸**lily-livered** (*liter*) poltron (*liter*) ▸**lily pad** feuille *f* de nénuphar ▸**lily-white** (*lit*) d'une blancheur de lis; (*fig: innocent*) blanc (*f* blanche) comme neige; (*US: for Whites only*) excluant totalement les Noirs.

Lima ['liːmə] **n** Lima. **~ bean** haricot *m* de Lima.

limb [lɪm] **n** (*Anat, Zool, also fig*) membre *m*; *[tree]* grosse branche; *[cross]* bras *m*. **to tear ~ from ~** *person* mettre en pièces; *animal* démembrer; (*fig*) **to be out on a ~** (*isolated*) être isolé; (*vulnerable*) être dans une situation délicate; (*fig*) **to go out on a ~** prendre des risques; **~ of Satan** suppôt *m* de Satan; *see* **risk.**

-limbed [lɪmd] **adj ending in comps: long-limbed** aux membres longs; **strong-limbed** aux membres forts.

limber[1] ['lɪmbər] **adj** *person* souple, agile, leste; *thing* souple, flexible.

▸**limber up** **vi** (*Sport etc*) se dégourdir, faire des exercices d'assouplissement; (*fig*) se préparer, se mettre en train. **limbering-up exercises** exercices *mpl* d'assouplissement.

limber[2] ['lɪmbər] **n** *[gun carriage]* avant-train *m*.

limbless ['lɪmlɪs] **adj** *tree* sans branches. **~ man** (*no limbs*) homme *m* sans membres, homme tronc; (*limb missing*) homme estropié, homme à qui il manque un bras *or* une jambe; (*after amputation*) amputé *m* (d'un membre); **~ ex-servicemen** ≃ (grands) mutilés *mpl* de guerre.

limbo[1] ['lɪmbəʊ] **n**: **in ~** (*forgotten*) tombé dans l'oubli; (*still undecided*) encore dans les limbes *mpl*; (*Rel*) dans les limbes; **in legal/social ~** dans un vide juridique/social.

limbo[2] ['lɪmbəʊ] **n** (*dance*) limbo *m*. **~ dancer** danseur *m*, -euse *f* de limbo.

lime[1] [laɪm] 1 **n** a (*Chem*) chaux *f*; *see* **quick** *etc*. b (*bird~*) glu *f*. 2 **vt** a *ground* chauler. b *twig* engluer; *bird* prendre à la glu, engluer. 3 **comp** ▸**lime kiln** four *m* à chaux ▸**limelight** *see* **limelight** ▸**limestone** pierre *f* à chaux, calcaire *m*.

lime[2] [laɪm] 1 **n** (*fruit*) citron *m* vert, lime *f*; (*tree: also* **~ tree**) lime *f*; (*drink*) jus *m* de citron vert. **vodka/lager and ~** vodka/bière citron vert. 2 **comp** ▸**lime cordial** jus *m* de citron vert ▸**lime green** vert jaune *inv* ▸**lime juice** jus *m* de citron vert.

lime[3] [laɪm] **n** (*linden: also* **~ tree**) tilleul *m*.

limelight ['laɪmlaɪt] **n** (*Theat*) feux *mpl* de la rampe. (*fig*) **to be in the ~** être en vedette *or* au premier plan; **to keep out of the ~** ne pas se faire remarquer.

limerick ['lɪmərɪk] **n** poème *m* humoristique (*de 5 vers*).

limey* ['laɪmɪ] **n** (*US, Austral*) Anglais(e) *m(f)*, Angliche‡ *mf*.

limit ['lɪmɪt] 1 **n** (*furthest point*) *[territory, experience, vision etc]* limite *f*; (*fig*) limite, borne *f*; (*restriction on amount, number etc*) limitation *f*, restriction *f*; (*permitted maximum*) limite. **outside/within the ~s of** en dehors des/dans les limites de; **within a 5-mile ~** dans un rayon de 8 kilomètres; **it is true within ~s** c'est vrai dans une certaine limite *or* mesure; **without ~** sans limitation, sans limite; **weight ~** limitation de poids; (*US*) **off ~s** *area, district* d'accès interdit; (*on sign*) "accès interdit"; **we must set a ~ to the expense** il faut limiter *or* restreindre les dépenses; (*Aut*) **the 60-km ~** la limitation (de vitesse) de 60 km à l'heure; (*Aut*) **there is a 60 km/h ~ on this road** la vitesse est limitée à 60 km/h sur cette route; (*Aut*) **to keep within/go over the speed ~** respecter/dépasser la limitation de vitesse; **over the ~** (*of lorry in weight*) en surcharge, surchargé; (*of driver on Breathalyser*) qui excède le taux légal (*de l'alcootest*); **to go to the ~ to help sb** faire tout son possible pour aider qn; **he is at the ~ of his patience/endurance** il est à bout de patience/de forces; **there is a ~ to my patience** ma patience a des limites *or* des bornes; **his anger knows no ~s** sa colère ne connaît pas de limites, sa colère est sans borne(s); **there are ~s!*** quand même il y a des limites!, il y a une limite à tout!; **there is no ~ on the amount you can import** la quantité que l'on peut importer n'est pas limitée; **there is a ~ to what one can do** il y a une limite à ce que l'on peut faire, on ne peut (quand même) pas faire l'impossible; **that's the ~!*** c'est le comble!, ça dépasse les bornes!; **he's the ~!*** (*goes too far*) il dépasse les bornes!; (*amusing*) il est impayable!*

2 **vt** a (*restrict*) *speed, time* limiter (*to* à); *expense, power* limiter, restreindre (*to* à); *person* limiter. **he ~ed questions to those dealing with education** il a accepté seulement les questions portant sur l'éducation; **he ~ed questions to 25 minutes** il a limité les questions à vingt-cinq minutes; **to ~ o.s. to a few remarks** se borner à (faire) quelques remarques; **to ~ o.s. to 10 cigarettes a day** se limiter à 10 cigarettes par jour; **we are ~ed in what we can do** nous sommes

limités dans ce que nous pouvons faire.

b (*confine*) limiter. **that plant is ~ed to Spain** cette plante ne se trouve qu'en Espagne; **our reorganization plans are ~ed to Africa** nos projets de réorganisation se limitent à *or* ne concernent que l'Afrique.

limitation [ˌlɪmɪ'teɪʃən] **n** a (*restriction*) limitation *f*, restriction *f*. **the ~ on imports** la limitation *or* la restriction des importations; **there is no ~ on the amount of currency you may take** il n'y a aucune restriction sur les devises que vous pouvez emporter; **he has/knows his ~s** il a/connaît ses limites. b (*Jur*) prescription *f*.

limited ['lɪmɪtɪd] **adj** a (*small*) *choice, means, resources* restreint, limité. **this book is written for a ~ readership** ce livre est destiné à un public restreint. b (*restricted*) *number* limité, restreint. **~ edition** édition *f* à tirage limité; **to a ~ extent** jusqu'à un certain point; **~-stop** *or* (*US*) **~ bus** autobus semi-direct. c (*narrow*) *intelligence, person* borné, limité. d (*esp Brit*) (*Comm, Jur*) **Smith and Sons L~** ≃ Smith et fils, Société anonyme; (*Fin*) **~ (liability) company** société *f* anonyme; **private ~ partnership** société *f* à responsabilité limitée.

limiting ['lɪmɪtɪŋ] **adj** restrictif, contraignant.

limitless ['lɪmɪtlɪs] **adj** *power* sans borne(s), illimité; *opportunities* illimité.

limo* ['lɪməʊ] **n** (*US*) (**abbr of limousine**) limousine *f*.

limousine ['lɪməziːn] 1 **n** (*gen*) limousine *f*; (*US: from airport etc*) (voiture-)navette *f*. 2 **comp** ▸**limousine liberal*** (*US*) libéral *m* de salon.

limp¹ [lɪmp] **adj** (*gen*) mou (*f* molle); (*pej*) *flesh, skin, body* flasque; (*pej*) *dress, hat* avachi, informe; *movement* mou, sans énergie; *person* (*from heat, exhaustion*) faible; *handshake* mou; *voice* faible; *style* mou, sans fermeté. *[book]* **~ cover(s)** reliure *f* souple; **to let one's body go ~** se décontracter; **let your arm go ~** décontractez votre bras; **I feel very ~ in this hot weather** je me sens tout ramolli *or* avachi par cette chaleur; (*fig: effeminate*) **to have a ~ wrist**‡ avoir des manières efféminées; (*fig*) **limp-wristed**‡ efféminé.

limp² [lɪmp] 1 **vi** *[person]* boiter, claudiquer (*frm*); (*fig*) *[vehicle etc]* marcher tant bien que mal. **to ~ in/out** *etc* entrer/sortir *etc* en boitant; **to ~ along** avancer en boitant, aller clopinant *or* clopin-clopant*; **he ~ed to the door** il est allé à la porte en boitant, il a clopiné jusqu'à la porte; **the plane managed to ~ home** l'avion a réussi à regagner sa base tant bien que mal. 2 **n** claudication *f*, boiterie *f*. **to have a ~, to walk with a ~** boiter, clopiner.

limpet ['lɪmpɪt] **n** a (*Zool*) chapeau *m* chinois, bernique *f*, patelle *f*; (*fig: person*) crampon *m*. **to cling** *or* **stick to sth like a ~** s'accrocher à qch comme une moule au rocher. b (*Mil: also* **~ mine**) mine-ventouse *f*.

limpid ['lɪmpɪd] **adj** (*lit, fig*) limpide.

limply ['lɪmplɪ] **adv** mollement, sans énergie.

limpness ['lɪmpnɪs] **n** (*see* **limp¹**) mollesse *f*; flaccidité *f* (*frm*); avachissement *m*, manque *m* d'énergie *or* de fermeté.

limy ['laɪmɪ] **adj** (*see* **lime¹**) calcaire; englué.

linchpin ['lɪntʃˌpɪn] **n** (*Aut*) esse *f*; (*fig*) pivot *m*, charnière *f*.

Lincs. [lɪŋks] (*Brit*) **abbr of Lincolnshire**.

linctus ['lɪŋktəs] **n, pl ~es** sirop *m* (contre la toux).

linden ['lɪndən] **n** (*also* **~ tree**) tilleul *m*.

line¹ [laɪn] 1 **n** a (*mark*) ligne *f*, trait *m*; (*Math, TV*) ligne; (*pen stroke*) trait; (*on face, palm*) ligne; (*wrinkle*) ride *f*; (*boundary*) frontière *f*; (*Ftbl, Tennis*) ligne. (*Geog*) **the L~** l'équateur *m*, la ligne; **to draw a ~ under sth** tirer *or* tracer un trait sous qch; **to put a ~ through sth** barrer *or* rayer qch; **the teacher put a red ~ through my translation** le professeur a barré *or* rayé ma traduction d'un trait rouge; (*Bridge*) **above/below the ~** (marqué) en points d'honneur/en points de marche; (*Book-keeping*) **below the ~** hors bilan; (*Book-keeping*) **~ by ~** ligne par ligne; (*Math*) **a straight ~** une (ligne) droite; (*Math*) **a curved ~** une (ligne) courbe; (*Mus*) **on the ~** sur la ligne; (*Aut*) **yellow/white ~** ligne jaune/blanche; (*Aut*) **double yellow ~s** *bandes fpl jaunes indiquant l'interdiction de stationner;* **broken white ~** ligne blanche discontinue; *see* **bottom, dot, draw, hard, state** *etc*.

b (*rope*) corde *f*; (*wire*) fil *m*; (*Fishing*) ligne *f*, fil; *[diver]* corde *f* (de sûreté); (*also* **clothes ~, washing ~**) corde (à linge). **the view was hidden by a ~ of washing** la vue était cachée par du linge étendu sur une corde; **to get a ~ to sb fallen overboard** lancer une corde *or* un bout à qn qui est tombé par-dessus bord; *see* **air, pipe** *etc*.

c (*pipe*) tuyau *m*; (*larger, esp for oil, gas etc*) pipeline *m*; (*Elec: cable*) ligne *f*. **to come on ~** *[refinery, oil rig]* entrer en service; *[crude oil]* jaillir.

d (*Telec*) ligne *f*. **the ~s are out of order** les lignes sont en dérangement; **the ~s are down** les lignes ont été abattues; **the ~'s gone dead** (*cut off*) on nous a coupés; (*no dialling tone*) il n'y a plus de tonalité; **give me a ~** donnez-moi une ligne; **can you get me a ~ to Chicago?** pouvez-vous m'avoir Chicago (au téléphone)?; **the ~s are open from 6 o'clock onwards** on peut téléphoner *or* appeler à partir de 6 heures; **the ~ is engaged** *or* (*US*) **busy** la ligne est occupée, c'est occupé; **Mr Smith is on the ~** (c'est) M. Smith au téléphone; **Mr Smith's ~ is engaged** la ligne de M. Smith est occupée; **he's on the ~ to the manager** il téléphone au directeur; **663-1111 5 ~s** 663-1111 5 lignes groupées; *see* **hold, hot** *etc*.

e (*Comput*) (*on screen*) ligne *f*. **on ~** en ligne; **to come on ~** se mettre en ligne.

f *[print, writing]* ligne *f*; *[poem]* vers *m*; (*: *letter*) mot *m*. (*esp Brit*) **(marriage) ~s** acte *m* de mariage; **a 6-~ stanza** une strophe de 6 vers; **30 ~s to a page** 30 lignes par page; **page 20, ~ 18** page 20, ligne 18; (*fig*) **to read between the ~s** lire entre les lignes; (*in dictation*) **new ~** à la ligne; **it's one of the best ~s in "Hamlet"** c'est l'un des meilleurs vers de "Hamlet"; (*Theat*) **to learn/forget one's ~s** apprendre/oublier son texte *or* son rôle; (*Scol: punishment*) **~s** lignes à copier, pensum *m*; (*Scol*) **take 100 ~s** vous (me) ferez 100 lignes; **drop me a ~** envoyez-moi un (petit) mot.

g (*row*) *[trees, parked cars]* rangée *f*; *[cars in traffic etc]* file *f*; *[hills]* chaîne *f*; *[people]* (*side by side*) rang *m*, rangée; (*behind one another*) file, colonne *f*; (*esp US: queue*) file, queue *f*; (*in factory*) chaîne. (*US*) **to stand in ~, to make a ~** faire la queue; **they were waiting in ~** ils attendaient en file *or* en colonne; **they were standing in a ~** ils étaient alignés *or* en ligne; **they were waiting in ~s** ils attendaient en rangs; **they moved along quietly in ~** ils avançaient tranquillement à la queue leu leu *or* les uns derrière les autres; **he got into ~** (*beside others*) il s'est mis dans le rang; (*behind others*) il s'est mis dans la file *or* la colonne; (*fig*) **to be in ~ for a job** *etc* être sur les rangs pour un emploi *etc;* (*fig*) **to bring sb into ~** mettre qn au pas; (*fig*) **to bring sth into ~ with sth** faire concorder qch avec qch, aligner qch sur qch; (*fig*) **to come** *or* **fall** *or* **step into ~** *[person, group]* se conformer (*with sth* à qch), tomber d'accord (*with sb* avec qn); *[plans, proposals]* concorder (*with* avec); (*fig*) **in ~ with** *person, group* en accord avec; *plans, policy* conforme à, qui va dans le sens de; (*fig*) **to keep the party in ~** maintenir la discipline dans le parti; **to be out of ~** (*in drill etc*) ne pas être à l'alignement; (*fig*) *[person]* être seul à penser (*or* agir) ainsi; *[action]* ne pas être conforme (*with* à); (*fig*) **he stepped out of ~** il a fait l'indépendant, il a refusé de se conformer, il a fait cavalier seul; (*fig*) **all along the ~** sur toute la ligne, complètement; (*fig*) **to reach the end of the ~** être au bout du rouleau, en avoir assez comme ça; *see* **assembly, bread, production** *etc*.

h (*direction*) ligne *f*, direction *f*. (*Mil*) **~ of fire** ligne de tir; **right in the ~ of fire** en plein champ de tir; (*Mil*) **~ of sight** ligne de visée; **~ of sight, ~ of vision** ligne de vision; (*fig*) **that's the ~ of least resistance** c'est la solution de facilité; (*fig*) **to take the ~ of least resistance** choisir la solution de facilité; *[policeman, ambassador etc]* **in the ~ of duty** dans l'exercice de ses (*or* mes *etc*) fonctions; **the soldier met his death in the ~ of duty** le soldat est tombé au champ d'honneur; **it's all in the ~ of duty** ça fait partie du travail *or* du boulot*; **~ of attack** (*Mil*) plan *m* d'attaque; (*fig*) plan d'action, ligne de conduite; **that is not my ~ of argument** ce n'est pas ce que je cherche à démontrer; **his ~ of argument was that ...** son raisonnement était que ...; **~ of research** ligne de recherche(s); **what is your ~ of thought?** qu'est-ce que vous envisagez de faire?, quels sont vos plans?; **to take a strong ~ on** adopter une attitude ferme sur; **somewhere along the ~** à un moment donné; (*all the time*) **all along the ~** tout le temps; **we are all thinking along the same ~s** nous pensons tous de la même façon, nous sommes tous d'accord; **the president and those who think along the same ~s** le président et ceux qui partagent son opinion; **your essay is more or less along the same ~s** votre dissertation suit plus ou moins le même plan; *[story, plan]* **the main** *or* **broad ~s** les grandes lignes; **I was thinking of something along** *or* **on those ~s** je pensais à quelque chose dans cet ordre d'idées *or* dans ce sens *or* dans ce style; **along political/racial ~s** (*gen*) pour des raisons politiques/raciales; *decide, divide* selon des critères politiques/raciaux; *organize, plan etc* dans une optique politique/raciale; **you're on the right ~s** vous êtes sur la bonne voie; *see* **bee, inquiry, party** *etc*.

i (*descent*) ligne *f*, lignée *f*. **in a direct ~ from** en droite ligne de, en ligne directe de; **in the male ~** par les hommes; **he comes from a long ~ of artists** il vient d'une longue lignée d'artistes; **the royal ~** la lignée royale.

j (*) (*information*) renseignement *m*, tuyau* *m*; (*clue*) indice *m*, tuyau*. **we've got a ~ on where he's gone to** nous croyons savoir où il est allé; **the police have got a ~ on the criminal** la police a une idée de *or* des indices sur l'identité du coupable; **I've got a ~ on a good used car** j'ai un tuyau* pour une voiture d'occasion en bon état; **to give sb a ~*** faire tout un baratin* à qn; **that's just a ~*** ça c'est du baratin*; *see* **hand, shoot**.

k (*also* **shipping ~**) (*company*) compagnie *f*; (*route*) ligne *f* (maritime). **the Cunard L~** la compagnie Cunard; **the New York-Southampton ~** la ligne New York-Southampton; *see* **air** *etc*.

l (*Rail*) (*route*) ligne *f* (de chemin de fer); *[underground]* ligne (de métro);*[bus]* ligne; (*track*) voie *f*. **the Brighton ~** la ligne de Brighton; **the ~ was blocked for several hours** la voie a été bloquée *or* la ligne a été interrompue pendant plusieurs heures; **cross the ~ by the footbridge** utilisez la passerelle pour traverser la voie; **the train left the ~** le train a déraillé; *see* **down¹, main, tram** *etc*.

m (*Art etc*) ligne *f* (*gen sg*). **I like the ~(s) of this car** j'aime la ligne de cette voiture; **the graceful ~s of Gothic churches** la ligne gracieuse des églises gothiques.

n (*Mil*) ligne *f*. (*Mil, fig*) **in the front ~** en première ligne; **behind the enemy ~s** derrière les lignes ennemies; **the Maginot ~** la ligne Maginot; **~ of battle** ligne de combat; (*Brit Mil*) **regiment of the ~** ≃ régiment *m* d'infanterie; (*Navy*) **~ abreast** ligne de front; (*Navy*) **~ astern** ligne de file; **ship of the ~** vaisseau *m* de ligne, navire *m* de haut bord.

o (*business*) affaires *fpl*; (*occupation*) métier *m*, partie *f*. **~ of business, ~ of work** branche *f*, type *m* d'activité; **what ~ are you in?, what's your ~ (of business *or* of work)?** que faites-vous (dans la vie)?, quelle est votre partie?; (*of companies*) **in the same ~ (of business)** ayant la même activité, de la même branche; **he's in the grocery ~** il est dans l'épicerie; **cocktail parties are not (in) my ~** les cocktails ne sont pas mon genre; **fishing's more (in) my ~ (of country)** la pêche est davantage mon rayon* *or* dans mes cordes.

p (*Comm: series of goods*) ligne *f* de produits. **they've brought out a new ~ in face cream** ils ont sorti une nouvelle ligne de crème pour le visage.

q (*Drugs sl*) *[cocaine]* rail *m* (*sl*).

2 comp ▶**line drawing** (*Art*) dessin *m* (au trait) ▶**line feed** (*Comput*) saut *m or* changement *m* de ligne ▶**line fishing** (*Sport*) pêche *f* à la ligne ▶**line judge** (*Tennis*) juge *m* de ligne ▶**lineman** (*Rail*) poseur *m* de rails; (*Telec*) ouvrier *m* de ligne ▶**line manager** chef *m* hiérarchique *or* direct ▶**line-out** (*Rugby*) touche *f* ▶**line printer** (*Comput*) imprimante *f* ligne par ligne ▶**linesman** (*Sport*) (*Tennis*) juge *m* de ligne; (*Ftbl, Rugby*) juge de touche ▶**line spacing** (*Typ, Comput*) interligne *m* ▶**line storm** (*US*) ouragan *m* ▶**line-up** (*row: of people etc*) file *f*; (*Police: identity parade*) séance *f* d'identification (d'un suspect); (*Ftbl etc*) (composition *f* de l')équipe *f*; (*fig: Pol etc*) **the new line-up** la nouvelle composition du Parlement (*or* du Congrès *etc*); **the President chose his line-up** le Président a choisi son équipe *f or* ses collaborateurs *mpl*; (*fig, Pol*) **the line-up of African powers** le front des puissances africaines.

3 vt *paper* régler, ligner; (*wrinkle*) *face* rider, marquer. **~d paper** papier réglé; **face ~d with sorrow** visage marqué par le chagrin; **the streets were ~d with cheering crowds** les rues étaient bordées d'une (double) haie de spectateurs enthousiastes; **cheering crowds ~d the route** une foule enthousiaste faisait la haie tout le long du parcours; **the road was ~d with trees** la route était bordée d'arbres.

▶**line up** 1 vi (*stand in row*) se mettre en rang(s), s'aligner; (*stand in queue*) faire la queue. **the teams lined up and waited for the whistle** les équipes se sont alignées et ont attendu le coup de sifflet; (*Sport fig*) **the teams lined up as follows ...** les équipes étaient constituées comme suit ... .

2 vt sep a *people, objects* aligner, mettre en ligne. **line them up against the wall** alignez-les le long du mur; (*fig: oppose*) **to line up against sb/sth** se liguer contre qn/qch; (*fig: support*) **to line up with *or* behind *or* alongside sb** se ranger au côté de qn, se rallier à qn; (*fig: ready*) **to be all lined up*** être fin prêt (*for* pour; *to do* pour faire).

b (*: *find*) trouver, dénicher*; (*have in mind*) prévoir, avoir en vue; (*organize*) *party etc* organiser. **we must line up a chairman for the meeting** il faut que nous trouvions (*subj*) *or* dénichions* (*subj*) un président pour la réunion; **have you got someone lined up?** avez-vous quelqu'un en vue?; **I wonder what he's got lined up for us** je me demande ce qu'il nous prépare.

3 **line-up** n *see* **line[1] 2.**

line[2] [laɪn] vt *clothes* doubler (*with* de); *[bird] nest* garnir, tapisser; (*Tech*) revêtir, chemiser; *brakes* garnir. (*fig*) **to ~ one's pockets** se garnir *or* se remplir les poches; **to ~ one's stomach*** se mettre quelque chose dans le ventre‡; **the walls were ~d with books and pictures** les murs étaient couverts *or* tapissés de livres et de tableaux; *see* **wool** *etc.*

lineage ['lɪnɪɪdʒ] n (*ancestry*) lignage†† *m*, famille *f*; (*descendants*) lignée *f*. **she can trace her ~ back to the 17th century** sa famille remonte au 17e siècle.

lineal ['lɪnɪəl] adj en ligne directe.

lineament ['lɪnɪəmənt] n (*feature*) trait *m*, linéament *m*. (*characteristics*) **~s** caractéristiques *fpl*, particularités *fpl*.

linear ['lɪnɪə[r]] adj linéaire. (*Econ*) **~ programming** programmation *f* linéaire.

linen ['lɪnɪn] 1 n a (*NonC: Tex*) (toile *f* de) lin *m*. b (*collective n*) (*sheets, tablecloths etc: often US* **~s**) linge *m* (de maison); (*underwear*) linge (de corps). **dirty *or* soiled ~** linge sale; *see* **household, wash.** 2 comp *sheet* de fil, pur fil; *suit, thread* de lin ▶**linen basket** panier *m* à linge ▶**linen closet, linen cupboard** armoire *f or* placard *m* à linge ▶**linen paper** papier *m* de lin.

liner ['laɪnə[r]] n a (*Naut*) paquebot *m* de grande ligne, liner *m*; *see* **air, Atlantic.** b **dustbin ~** sac *m* à poubelle. c *see* **eye 3.**

ling[1] [lɪŋ] n (*heather*) bruyère *f*.

ling[2] [lɪŋ] n, pl **~** *or* **~s** (*sea fish*) lingue *f*, julienne *f*; (*freshwater fish*) lotte *f* de rivière.

linger ['lɪŋgə[r]] vi (*also* **~ on**) *[person]* (*wait behind*) s'attarder, rester (en arrière); (*take one's time*) prendre son temps; (*dawdle*) traîner, lambiner*; *[smell, pain]* persister; *[tradition, memory]* persister, subsister; *[doubt]* subsister. **the others had gone, but he ~ed (on)** les autres étaient partis, lui restait en arrière *or* s'attardait; **after the accident he ~ed (on) for several months** après l'accident il a traîné quelques mois avant de mourir; **he always ~s behind everyone else** il est toujours derrière tout le monde, il est toujours à la traîne; **don't ~ about *or* around** ne lambine pas*, ne traîne pas; **to ~ over a meal** rester longtemps à table, manger sans se presser; **I let my eye ~ on the scene** j'ai laissé mon regard s'attarder sur la scène; **to ~ on a subject** s'attarder *or* s'étendre sur un sujet.

lingerie ['lænʒəriː] n (*NonC*) lingerie *f*.

lingering ['lɪŋgərɪŋ] adj *look* long (*f* longue), insistant; *doubt* qui subsiste (encore); *hope* faible; *death* lent.

lingo* ['lɪŋgəʊ] n, pl **~es** (*pej*) (*language*) baragouin *m*, jargon* *m*; (*jargon*) jargon (*pej*). **I had a hard time in Spain because I don't speak the ~** j'ai eu du mal en Espagne parce que je ne comprends pas leur baragouin *or* parce que je ne cause‡ pas espagnol.

lingua franca ['lɪŋgwə'fræŋkə] n, pl **linguae francae** ['lɪŋgwiː'frænsiː] *or* **lingua francas** langue *f* véhiculaire, lingua franca *f inv*.

linguist ['lɪŋgwɪst] n linguiste *mf*. **I'm no great ~** je ne suis guère doué pour les langues.

linguistic [lɪŋ'gwɪstɪk] adj (*gen*) linguistique. **~ atlas** atlas *m* linguistique; **~ borrowing** emprunt *m* linguistique; **~ geography** géographie *f* linguistique.

linguistically [lɪŋ'gwɪstɪkəlɪ] adv linguistiquement.

linguistics [lɪŋ'gwɪstɪks] 1 n (*NonC*) linguistique *f*; *see* **comparative** *etc.* 2 comp *book, degree, professor* de linguistique; *student* en linguistique.

liniment ['lɪnɪmənt] n liniment *m*.

lining ['laɪnɪŋ] n *[clothes, handbag]* doublure *f*; (*Tech*) revêtement *m*; *[brakes]* garniture *f*; *[stomach]* paroi *f*. **~ paper** papier *m* d'apprêt; (*for drawers*) papier à tapisser; *see* **silver.**

link [lɪŋk] 1 n *[chain]* maillon *m*, chaînon *m*, anneau *m*; (*connection*) lien *m*, liaison *f*; (*interrelation*) rapport *m*, lien; (*bonds*) lien, relation *f*. **a new rail ~** une nouvelle liaison ferroviaire; **there must be a ~ between the 2 phenomena** il doit y avoir un lien *or* un rapport entre les 2 phénomènes; **he served as ~ between management and workers** il a servi de lien *or* d'intermédiaire entre la direction et les ouvriers; **cultural ~s** liens culturels, relations culturelles; **~s of friendship** liens d'amitié; **he broke off all ~s with his friends** il a cessé toutes relations avec ses amis, il a rompu les liens qui l'unissaient à ses amis; *see* **cuff, missing.**

2 comp ▶**linking consonant** (*Phon*) consonne *f* de liaison ▶**linking verb** (*Ling*) verbe copulatif ▶**linkman** (*TV, Rad*) présentateur-réalisateur *m* ▶**link-up** (*gen*) lien *m*, rapport *m*; (*Rad, TV: connection*) liaison *f*; (*Rad, TV: programme*) émission *f* duplex; (*Space*) jonction *f*; **there is no apparent link-up between the 2 cases** il n'y a pas de rapport apparent *or* de lien apparent entre les 2 affaires; **is there any link-up between our company and theirs?** y a-t-il un lien entre notre compagnie et la leur?

3 vt a (*connect*) relier; (*fig*) lier. **~ed by rail/by telephone** reliés par (la) voie ferrée/par téléphone; **this is closely ~ed to our sales figures** ceci est étroitement lié à nos chiffres de vente.

b (*join*) lier, unir, joindre; *spacecraft* opérer l'arrimage de. **to ~ arms** se donner le bras; **~ed (together) in friendship** liés d'amitié; **the 2 companies are now ~ed (together)** les 2 compagnies sont maintenant liées *or* associées.

▶**link together** 1 vi s'unir, se rejoindre. 2 vt sep *two objects* unir, joindre; (*by means of a third*) relier; *see also* **link 3b.**

▶**link up** 1 vi *[persons]* se rejoindre; *[firms, organizations etc]* s'associer; *[spacecraft]* opérer l'arrimage; *[roads, railway lines]* se rejoindre, se réunir, se rencontrer. **they linked up with the other group** ils ont rejoint l'autre groupe. 2 vt sep a (*Rad, Telec, TV*) relier, assurer la liaison entre. b *spacecraft* opérer l'arrimage de. 3 **link-up** n *see* **link 2.**

linkage ['lɪŋkɪdʒ] n a (*tie*) lien *m*, relation *f*. b (*Tech*) tringlerie *f*, transmission *f* par tringlerie. c (*Bio*) linkage *m*.

links [lɪŋks] npl (terrain *m* de) golf *m*, links *mpl*.

linnet ['lɪnɪt] n linotte *f*.

lino ['laɪnəʊ] n (*Brit* *) (abbr of **linoleum**) lino *m*. **~ cut** gravure *f* sur linoléum.

linoleum [lɪ'nəʊlɪəm] n linoléum *m*.

Linotype ['laɪnəʊtaɪp] n ® linotype *f* ®.

linseed ['lɪnsiːd] n (*NonC*) graines *fpl* de lin. **~ oil** huile *f* de lin.

lint [lɪnt] n (*NonC*) a (*Med*) tissu ouaté (*pour pansements*). **a small piece of ~** une compresse, un petit pansement ouaté. b (*US: fluff*) peluches *fpl*.

lintel ['lɪntl] n linteau *m*.

Linus ['laɪnəs] n (*esp US*) **~ blanket*** couverture *f* sécurisante (*pour jeune enfant*).

lion ['laɪən] 1 n lion *m*; (*fig: person*) personnage *m* en vue, célébrité *f*. (*Astrol, Astron*) **the L~** le Lion; (*fig*) **to get *or* take the ~'s share** se tailler la part du lion; (*fig*) **to put one's head in the ~'s mouth** se jeter *or* se précipiter dans la gueule du loup; *see* **beard, mountain, Richard.** 2 comp ▶**lion cub** lionceau *m* ▶**lion-hearted** d'un courage de lion ▶**lion-hunter:** (*fig*) **she is a lion-hunter** elle cherche toujours à avoir des célébrités comme invités ▶**lion-tamer** dompteur *m*, -euse *f* de lions, belluaire *m*.

lioness ['laɪənɪs] n lionne *f*.

lionize ['laɪənaɪz] vt *person* faire fête à, fêter comme une célébrité.

lip [lɪp] 1 n (*Anat*) (*gen*) lèvre *f*; *[dog etc]* babine *f*; *[jug]* bec *m*; *[cup, saucer]* rebord *m*; *[crater]* bord *m*; *[wound]* bord, lèvre; (**: insolence*) culot* *m*, insolences *fpl*. (*fig*) **on everyone's ~s** dans toutes les bouches, sur toutes les lèvres; **none of your ~!*** ne fais pas l'insolent! *or* le répondeur!*; *see* **bite, button, stiff** *etc*.

2 comp ►**lip gloss** brillant *m* à lèvres ►**lipread** lire sur les lèvres ►**lip-reading** lecture *f* sur les lèvres ►**lip salve** (*Brit*) pommade *f* rosat *or* pour les lèvres ►**lip service**: **he pays lip service to socialism but ...** à l'écouter on dirait qu'il est socialiste mais ...; **he only pays lip service to socialism** il n'est socialiste qu'en paroles; **that was merely lip service on his part** il ne l'a dit que pour la forme, il l'a dit du bout des lèvres ►**lipstick** (*NonC: substance*) rouge *m* à lèvres; (*stick*) bâton *m* *or* tube *m* de rouge à lèvres.

lipase ['laɪpeɪs] n lipase *f*.

lipid ['laɪpɪd] n lipide *m*.

liposuction ['lɪpəʊ,sʌkʃən] n lipo-aspiration *f*, liposuccion *f*.

-lipped [lɪpt] adj *ending in comps*: **dry-lipped** aux lèvres sèches; *see* **thick** *etc*.

lip-sync(h) ['lɪp,sɪŋk] 1 vi chanter en play-back. 2 n play-back *m*.

liquefaction [,lɪkwɪ'fækʃən] n liquéfaction *f*.

liquefy ['lɪkwɪfaɪ] 1 vt liquéfier. **liquefied natural gaz** gaz *m* naturel liquéfié. 2 vi se liquéfier.

liqueur [lɪ'kjʊəʳ] 1 n liqueur *f*. 2 comp ►**liqueur brandy** fine (champagne) *f* ►**liqueur chocolates** chocolats *mpl* à la liqueur ►**liqueur glass** verre *m* à liqueur.

liquid ['lɪkwɪd] 1 adj a (*not solid etc*) *substance* liquide; *container* pour (les) liquides. **~ air/oxygen** air *m*/oxygène *m* liquide; **~ ammonia** ammoniaque *m* (liquide); (*Comput*) **~ crystal** cristal *m* liquide; **~ crystal display** affichage *m* à cristaux liquides; **~ diet** régime *m* (exclusivement) liquide; (*hum*) **to have a ~ lunch** boire de l'alcool en guise de déjeuner; **~ measure** mesure *f* de capacité pour les liquides; (*for corrections*) **L~ paper** ® correcteur *m* liquide; (*Pharm*) **~ paraffin** huile *f* de paraffine *or* de vaseline; **~ petroleum gas** GPL *m*, gaz de pétrole liquéfié.

b (*fig*) *eyes, sky* limpide, clair; *sound, voice* limpide, harmonieux; (*Phon*) liquide. (*Fin*) **~ assets** liquidités *fpl*, disponibilités *fpl*.

2 n (*fluid*) liquide *m*; (*Ling*) liquide *f*.

liquidate ['lɪkwɪdeɪt] vt a (*Fin, Jur*) liquider. (*Jur*) **~d damages** dommages-intérêts *mpl* préalablement fixés (par les parties). b (**: kill*) liquider*.

liquidation [,lɪkwɪ'deɪʃən] n (*Fin, Jur, also **) liquidation *f*; *[debt]* remboursement *m*. **to go into ~** déposer son bilan.

liquidator ['lɪkwɪ,deɪtəʳ] n (*Jur*) ≈ liquidateur *m*.

liquidity [lɪ'kwɪdɪtɪ] 1 n (*Econ*) liquidité *f*; (*Fin*) disponibilités *fpl* de trésorerie. 2 comp ►**liquidity cushion** (*Fin*) volant *m* de trésorerie.

liquidize ['lɪkwɪdaɪz] vt liquéfier; (*Culin*) passer au mixer (*or* mixeur).

liquidizer ['lɪkwɪdaɪzəʳ] n (*Culin*) mixer *or* mixeur *m*.

liquor ['lɪkəʳ] n (*alcohol*) spiritueux *m*, alcool *m*; (*Culin*) liquide *m*. **to be the worse for ~** être soûl *or* ivre; (*US*) **~ store** magasin *m* de vins et spiritueux; *see* **hard**.

►**liquor up‡** (*US*) 1 vi se pinter‡. 2 vt sep faire trop boire, soûler*.

liquorice ['lɪkərɪs] (*Brit*) 1 n (*Bot*) réglisse *f*; (*sweet*) réglisse *m*. 2 comp ►**liquorice allsorts** (*gen Brit*) bonbons assortis au réglisse ►**liquorice stick/root** bâton *m*/bois *m* de réglisse.

lira ['lɪərə] n, pl **lire** ['lɪərɪ] lire *f*.

Lisbon ['lɪzbən] n Lisbonne.

lisle [laɪl] n (*also* **~ thread**) fil *m* d'Écosse.

lisp [lɪsp] 1 vi zézayer, zozoter*. 2 vt (*also* **~ out**) dire en zézayant. **"please don't say that," she ~ed coyly** "s'il vous plaît ne dites pas cela," dit-elle en faisant des manières. 3 n zézaiement *m*. **... she said with a ~** ... dit-elle en zézayant; **to speak with** *or* **have a ~** zézayer, zozoter*, avoir un cheveu sur la langue*.

lissome ['lɪsəm] adj souple, agile.

list¹ [lɪst] 1 n liste *f*; (*Comm*) catalogue *m*. **your name isn't on the ~** votre nom ne figure pas *or* n'est pas couché (*frm*) sur la liste; **you can take me off the ~** vous pouvez me rayer de la liste; **you're (at the) top/bottom of the ~** vous êtes en tête/en fin *or* en queue de liste; *see* **active, civil, danger** *etc*.

2 comp ►**list price** (*Comm*) prix *m* de catalogue.

3 vt (*make list of*) faire *or* dresser la liste de; (*write down*) inscrire; (*produce list of: gen, also Comput*) lister; (*enumerate*) énumérer. **your name isn't ~ed** votre nom n'est pas inscrit, votre nom n'est pas (porté) sur la liste; (*Comm*) **it isn't ~ed** cela ne figure pas au catalogue; **an airgun is ~ed as a weapon** un fusil à air comprimé est classé *or* catalogué parmi les armes; **"airgun" is ~ed under "air"** "airgun" se trouve sous "air"; (*St Ex*) **the shares are ~ed at 85 francs** les actions sont cotées à 85 F; (*St Ex*) **~ed company** société *f* cotée en Bourse; (*St Ex*) **~ed securities** valeurs *fpl* inscrites *or* admises à la cote officielle, valeurs cotées en Bourse; **~ed on the stock exchange** inscrit à la cote; (*Brit*) **~ed building** monument classé *or* historique.

list² [lɪst] 1 vi donner de la bande, gîter. **the ship is ~ing badly** le bateau gîte dangereusement; **to ~ to port** gîter *or* donner de la bande sur bâbord. 2 n inclinaison *f*. **to have a ~** gîter; **to have a ~ of 20°** gîter de 20°, donner 20° de gîte *or* de bande.

listen ['lɪsn] 1 vi a écouter. **~ to me** écoute-moi (*see also* **b**); **~!** écoute!; **you never ~ to a word I say!** tu n'écoutes jamais ce que je dis!; **to ~ to the radio** écouter la radio; **you are ~ing to the BBC** vous êtes à l'écoute de la BBC; **I love ~ing to the rain** j'aime écouter la pluie (tomber); **to ~ for** *voice, remark, sign* guetter; *footsteps* guetter le bruit de; **~ for the telephone while I'm out** surveille le téléphone pendant que je suis sorti; **hush, I'm ~ing for the phone** chut! j'essaie d'entendre si le téléphone ne sonne pas; **he was ~ing for his father's return** il écoutait si son père ne rentrait pas; *see* **half**.

b (*heed*) écouter. **~ to your father** écoute ton père; (*as threat*) **~ to me!** écoute-moi bien!; **~*, I can't stop to talk now but ...** écoute, je n'ai pas le temps de parler tout de suite mais ...; **he wouldn't ~ to reason** il n'a pas voulu entendre raison.

2 n: **to have a ~*** écouter (*to sth* qch).

►**listen in** vi a (*Rad*) être à l'écoute, écouter. b (*eavesdrop*) écouter. **to listen in on sth** *or* **to sth** (*secretly*) écouter qch secrètement; **I should like to listen in to your discussion** j'aimerais assister à votre discussion.

►**listen out for** vt fus *voice, remark, sign* guetter; *footsteps* guetter le bruit de.

listener ['lɪsnəʳ] n personne *f* qui écoute; (*to speaker, radio etc*) auditeur *m*, -trice *f*. **the ~s** l'auditoire *m*, le public; **his ~s were enthralled** son auditoire était *or* son public était *or* ses auditeurs étaient sous le charme; **she's a good ~** elle sait écouter (avec patience et sympathie).

listening ['lɪsnɪŋ] n écoute *f*. (*Rad*) **goodbye and good ~!** au revoir et bonne soirée *etc* à l'écoute de nos programmes!; (*Rad*) **we don't do much ~** nous n'écoutons pas beaucoup *or* souvent la radio; (*Mil*) **~ post** poste *m* d'écoute.

listeria [lɪ'stɪərɪə] n listéria *f*.

listeriosis [lɪ,stɪərɪ'əʊsɪs] n listériose *f*.

listing ['lɪstɪŋ] n (*gen, also Comput*) listage *m*; (*St Ex*) inscription *f* à la cote officielle.

listless ['lɪstlɪs] adj (*uninterested*) indifférent; (*apathetic*) indolent, apathique, amorphe; (*without energy*) sans énergie, mou (*f* molle); *wave* indolent; *handshake* mou. **to feel ~** se sentir apathique *or* sans ressort; **the heat made him ~** la chaleur lui enlevait son énergie.

listlessly ['lɪstlɪslɪ] adv (*see* **listless**) avec indifférence; avec indolence, avec apathie; sans énergie, mollement.

listlessness ['lɪstlɪsnɪs] n (*see* **listless**) indifférence *f*; indolence *f*, apathie *f*; manque *m* d'énergie, mollesse *f*.

lists [lɪsts] npl (*Hist*) lice *f*. (*lit, fig*) **to enter the ~** entrer en lice.

lit [lɪt] 1 pret, ptp of **light¹**. 2 adj éclairé, illuminé. **the street was very badly ~** la rue était très mal éclairée; (*drunk*) **~ up*** parti*, paf‡ *inv*.

lit.¹* [lɪt] n a abbr of **literature**. b (abbr of **literary**) littér.

lit.² (abbr of **literal(ly)**) lit.

litany ['lɪtənɪ] n litanie *f*. (*Rel*) **the L~** les litanies.

litchi [,laɪ'tʃiː] n = **lychee**.

liter ['liːtəʳ] n (*US*) = **litre**.

literacy ['lɪtərəsɪ] 1 n (*ability*) fait *m* de savoir lire et écrire, degré *m* d'alphabétisation. **his ~ was not in doubt** personne ne doutait du fait qu'il savait lire et écrire; **I am beginning to doubt even his ~** je commence même à douter qu'il sache lire et écrire; **universal ~ is one of the principal aims** l'un des buts principaux est de donner à tous la capacité de lire et d'écrire; **there is a high/low degree of ~ in that country** le degré d'alphabétisation est élevé/bas dans ce pays, le taux d'analphabétisme est bas/élevé dans ce pays.

2 comp ►**literacy campaign** campagne *f* d'alphabétisation *or* contre l'illettrisme ►**literacy project, literacy scheme** projet *m* d'alphabétisation ►**literacy test** test *m* mesurant le niveau d'alphabétisation.

literal ['lɪtərəl] 1 adj a (*textual*) *translation* littéral, mot pour mot; *interpretation* au pied de la lettre; (*not fig*) *meaning* littéral, propre; (*unexaggerated*) réel, conforme à la réalité. **in the ~ sense of the word** au sens propre du terme; **it was a ~ statement of fact** c'était un simple énoncé des faits; **the drought has meant ~ starvation for millions** la sécheresse a réduit littéralement à la famine des millions de gens. b (*unimaginative*) *person* prosaïque. 2 comp ►**literal-minded** prosaïque, sans imagination ►**literal-mindedness** manque *m* d'imagination, caractère *m* prosaïque.

literally ['lɪtərəlɪ] adv a *translate* littéralement, mot à mot; *mean* littéralement, au sens propre. **he interpreted the message ~** il a interprété le message au pied de la lettre *or* dans son sens littéral; **to carry out an order ~** exécuter un ordre à la lettre; **I was exaggerating but he took it ~** j'exagérais mais il a pris tout ce que je disais au pied de la lettre; **I was joking but he took me ~** je plaisantais mais il m'a pris au sérieux; **~ (speaking)** à proprement parler.

b (*really*) réellement, bel et bien. **it's ~ true** c'est bel et bien vrai; **it had ~ ceased to exist** cela avait bel et bien *or* réellement cessé d'exister.

c (**: absolutely*) littéralement*. **the town was ~ bulging with sailors** la ville grouillait littéralement* de marins.

literary ['lɪtərərɪ] adj *history, studies, appreciation etc* littéraire. **a ~ man** (*writer etc*) un homme de lettres; **~ critic/criticism** critique *m*/critique *f* littéraire.

literate ['lɪtərɪt] adj (*able to read etc*) qui sait lire et écrire; (*educated*) instruit; (*cultured*) cultivé. **few of them are ~** peu d'entre eux savent lire et écrire; **highly ~** très instruit *or* cultivé; *see* **computer 2**.

literati [ˌlɪtə'rɑːtiː] npl gens *mpl* de lettres, lettrés *mpl*.

literature ['lɪtərɪtʃəʳ] n (*NonC*) **a** littérature *f*. **18th-century French ~** la littérature française du 18e siècle; **the ~ of ornithology** la littérature *or* la bibliographie de l'ornithologie. **b** (*brochures: about travel, school etc*) documentation *f*, brochure(s) *f(pl)*. **travel/educational ~** documentation *or* brochure(s) sur les voyages/l'éducation.

lithe [laɪð] adj *person* agile; *body, muscle* souple.

lithium ['lɪθɪəm] n lithium *m*.

lithograph ['lɪθəʊgrɑːf] **1** n lithographie *f* (*estampe*). **2** vt lithographier.

lithographer [lɪ'θɒgrəfəʳ] n lithographe *mf*.

lithographic [ˌlɪθə'græfɪk] adj lithographique.

lithography [lɪ'θɒgrəfɪ] n lithographie *f* (*procédé*).

Lithuania [ˌlɪθjʊ'eɪnɪə] n Lituanie *f*.

Lithuanian [ˌlɪθjʊ'eɪnɪən] **1** adj lituanien. **~ SSR†** RSS *f* de Lituanie†. **2** n **a** Lituanien(ne) *m(f)*. **b** (*Ling*) lituanien *m*.

litigant ['lɪtɪgənt] n (*Jur*) plaideur *m*, -euse *f*.

litigate ['lɪtɪgeɪt] **1** vi plaider. **2** vt mettre en litige, contester.

litigation [ˌlɪtɪ'geɪʃən] n litige *m*.

litigious [lɪ'tɪdʒəs] adj (*Jur*) litigieux; *person* (*given to litigation*) procédurier, chicaneur; (*argumentative etc*) chicanier.

litmus ['lɪtməs] n (*Chem*) tournesol *m*. **~ (paper)** papier *m* de tournesol; **~ test** (*lit*) réaction *f* au (papier de) tournesol; (*fig*) test *m* décisif.

litre, (*US*) **liter** ['liːtəʳ] n litre *m*. **~ bottle** (bouteille *f* d'un) litre.

litter ['lɪtəʳ] **1** n **a** (*NonC*) (*rubbish*) détritus *mpl*, (*dirtier*) ordures *fpl*; (*papers*) vieux papiers *mpl*; (*left after picnic etc*) papiers *mpl* gras. (*on basket etc*) **"~"** "papiers (S.V.P.)"; **"take your ~ home"** "ne jetez pas de papiers par *or* à terre"; **don't leave ~** ne jette pas de détritus *or* de papiers; (*on notice*) "prière de ne pas laisser de détritus".

b (*untidy mass*) fouillis *m*, désordre *m*. **in a ~** en désordre, en fouillis; **a ~ of books** un fouillis *or* un fatras de livres; (*fig*) **a ~ of caravans along the shore** des caravanes dispersées en désordre le long du rivage.

c (*Zool*) portée *f*. **10 little pigs at a ~** 10 cochonnets d'une même portée.

d (*Agr: bedding*) litière *f*.

e (*stretcher*) civière *f*; (*couch*) litière *f*.

f **cat ~** litière *f* pour chats.

2 vt **a** (*also* **~ up**) *[person] room* mettre du désordre dans, mettre en désordre; *countryside* laisser des détritus dans. **he ~ed the floor with all his football gear** il a éparpillé ses affaires de football sur le plancher; **he had ~ed papers all about the room** il avait laissé traîner des papiers dans toute la pièce.

b (*gen pass*) *[rubbish, papers]* joncher, couvrir. **the floor was ~ed with paper** des papiers jonchaient *or* couvraient le sol; **a street ~ed with broken bottles** une rue jonchée de débris de bouteilles; **~ed with mistakes** rempli *or* parsemé de fautes; **the desk was ~ed with books** le bureau était couvert *or* encombré de livres; **there were books ~ed about the room** il y avait des livres qui traînaient dans toute la pièce; **the field was ~ed with caravans*** le champ était couvert de caravanes mal rangées.

3 vi (*Zool*) mettre bas.

4 comp ► **litter-bag** sac *m* à ordures ► **litter basket, litter bin** (*in street, playground, kitchen*) boîte *f* à ordures; (*dustbin*) poubelle *f* ► **litterbug, litter-lout** (*pej*) *personne qui jette des détritus par terre;* **litterbugs should be fined** on devrait mettre à l'amende ces gens mal élevés qui jettent des détritus n'importe où; **all these litter-louts who foul up camp sites** tous ces cochons* qui jettent leurs détritus sur les terrains de camping.

little¹ ['lɪtl] adj (*small*) *house, group, gift, person* (*in height*) petit; (*short*) *stick, piece of string* petit, court; (*brief*) *period, holiday, visit* court, bref (*f* brève), petit; (*young*) *child, animal* petit, jeune; (*weak*) *voice, noise* petit, faible; *smell* petit, léger; (*small-scale*) *shopkeeper* petit; (*unimportant*) *detail, discomfort* petit, insignifiant, sans importance. **~ girl** petite fille, fillette *f*; **~ boy** petit garçon, garçonnet *m*; **my ~ brother** mon petit frère; **a ~ old woman** une petite vieille; **~ finger** petit doigt, auriculaire *m*; **~ toe** petit orteil; *[clock]* **~ hand** petite aiguille; (*Orn*) **~ auk** mergule *m* (nain); (*Orn*) **~ owl** chevêche *f*; (*Aut*) **~ end** pied *m* de bielle; **for a ~ while, for a ~ time** pendant *or* pour un petit moment; (*children*) **the ~ ones** les petits; (*lr: fairies*) **the ~ people** les fées *fpl*, les lutins *mpl*; **it's ~ things like that which impress people** ce sont des petites choses comme ça qui font bonne impression (sur les gens); **he's quite a ~ gentleman!** qu'il est bien élevé ce petit!; **he's a ~ tyrant** c'est un (vrai) petit tyran; **a tiny ~ baby** un tout petit bébé; **here's a ~ something for yourself*** voilà un petit quelque chose* pour vous; **poor ~ thing!** pauvre petit(e)!; **she's a nice ~ thing** (*of child*) c'est un beau bébé, c'est une belle enfant; (*of woman*) c'est une gentille petite; **he's got a ~ place in the country** il a une petite maison de campagne; (*small trader*) **it's always the ~ man who suffers** ce sont toujours les petits (commerçants) qui souffrent; **the ~ farmers were nearly bankrupt** les petits cultivateurs étaient au bord de la faillite; (*wife*) **the ~ woman*** ma (*etc*) petite femme*; **I know your ~ game** je connais votre petit jeu; (*pej*) **he's got a very ~ mind** il est très mesquin, il est très petit d'esprit; **all his dirty ~ jokes** toutes ses petites plaisanteries cochonnes*; *see* **bless** *etc*.

little² ['lɪtl] compar **less**, superl **least** **1** adj, pron **a** (*not much*) peu (de). **I have ~ money left** il me reste peu d'argent, il ne me reste pas beaucoup *or* il ne me reste guère d'argent; **I have very ~ money** j'ai très peu d'argent; **there is ~ hope of finding survivors** il y a peu d'espoir *or* il n'y a guère d'espoir de retrouver des survivants; **I have ~ time for reading** je n'ai pas beaucoup *or* je n'ai guère le temps de lire; **with no ~ trouble** non sans mal; **he reads ~** il lit peu, il ne lit guère; **he knows ~** il ne sait pas grand-chose; **he did ~ to help** il n'a pas fait grand-chose pour aider; **he did very ~** il a fait très peu (de chose), il n'a pas fait grand-chose; **there was ~ I (***or* **you, he** *etc***) could do** il n'y avait pas grand-chose à faire; **I got ~ out of it** je n'en ai pas tiré grand-chose; **he had ~ to say** il n'avait pas grand-chose à dire; **it says (very) ~ for him** cela n'est guère en sa faveur *or* à son honneur; **it says ~ for his honesty** cela en dit long sur son honnêteté (*iro*); **I had ~ to do with it** je n'ai pas eu grand-chose à voir là-dedans; **that has very ~ to do with it!** ça a très peu à voir (avec ça)!; **I see ~ of her nowadays** je ne la vois plus beaucoup *or* plus guère maintenant; **he had ~ or nothing to say about it** il n'avait rien ou presque rien *or* il n'avait pratiquement rien à dire là-dessus; **to make ~ of sth** (*not stress*) faire peu de cas de qch, ne pas attacher grande importance à qch; (*belittle*) rabaisser qch, déprécier qch; (*fail to understand*) ne pas comprendre grand-chose à qch.

b (*in phrases*) **as ~ as possible** le moins possible; **I need as ~ money as he does** j'ai besoin d'aussi peu d'argent que lui; **you could pay as ~ as 20 francs for that** vous pourriez ne payer que 20 F pour cela; **for as ~ as 10 francs you can buy** ... pour 10 francs au plus *or* pour la bagatelle de 10 francs, vous pouvez acheter ...; **he's got very ~ money — how ~?** il a très peu d'argent — très peu c'est-à-dire? *or* qu'entendez-vous (au juste) par très peu?; **however ~ you do** si peu que vous fassiez; **so ~ pleasure** si peu de plaisir; **so ~ of the cheese was mouldy that** ... une si petite partie du fromage était moisie que ...; **so ~ of what he says is true** il y a si peu de vrai dans ce qu'il dit; **he had eaten so ~** il avait mangé si peu; **I know too ~ about him to decide** j'en sais trop peu à son sujet pour décider; **he gave me too ~ money** il m'a donné trop peu d'argent.

c (*small amount*) **a ~ bit (of), a ~** un peu (de); **the ~** le peu (de); **I have a ~ money left** il me reste un peu d'argent; **we're having a ~ trouble** nous avons un petit ennui *or* quelques difficultés; (*Prov*) **a ~ learning is a dangerous thing** avoir de vagues connaissances est une chose dangereuse; **would you like a ~ milk in your tea?** voulez-vous un peu de *or* une goutte de lait dans votre thé?; **give me a ~** donne-m'en un peu; **I'd like a ~ of everything** je voudrais un peu de tout; **I know a ~ about stamp collecting** j'ai quelques connaissances en philatélie; **I know a ~ about what happened to him** je sais vaguement ce qui lui est arrivé; **the ~ I have seen is excellent** le peu que j'ai vu est excellent; **~ by ~** petit à petit, peu à peu; **I did what ~ I could** j'ai fait le peu que j'ai pu; (*Prov*) **every ~ helps** les petits ruisseaux font les grandes rivières (*Prov*); **it's all I can do — every ~ helps!** c'est tout ce que je peux faire — c'est toujours ça! *or* c'est toujours utile!; **stay here a ~** restez ici quelques instants *or* un petit moment; **she stayed only a ~** elle n'est restée que peu de temps *or* qu'un petit moment; **for a ~ (time** *or* **while)** pendant un petit moment, pendant quelques instants; **after a ~ (time** *or* **while)** au bout d'un petit moment *or* de quelques instants; *see* **bit² 1**.

2 adv **a** (*slightly, somewhat*) **a ~** un peu; **a ~ too big** un peu trop grand; **she is a ~ tired** elle est un peu *or* légèrement fatiguée; **he spoke a ~ harshly** il a parlé avec une certaine dureté; **a ~ more slowly** un peu plus lentement; **he was not a ~ surprised** il n'a pas été peu surpris; **a ~ later** un peu plus tard, peu de temps après; **a ~ more** un peu plus, encore un peu; **a ~ less** un peu moins; **a ~ more/less cream** un peu plus/moins de crème.

b (*hardly, scarcely, not much*) **it's ~ better now he's rewritten it** ça n'est guère mieux maintenant qu'il l'a récrit; **it's ~ short of folly** ça frise la folie; **~ more than a month ago** il y a à peine plus d'un mois; **a ~-known work by Corelli** un morceau peu connu de Corelli; **his work is ~ performed these days** on ne joue plus guère ses œuvres aujourd'hui.

c (*in phrases*) **I like him as ~ as you do** je ne l'aime guère plus que vous, je l'aime aussi peu que vous l'aimez; **I like him as ~ as I used to** je l'aime aussi peu qu'auparavant; **however ~ you like him** si peu que vous l'aimiez (*subj*); **I felt so ~ encouraged by this** je me suis senti si peu encouragé par ceci; **~ as I know him** si peu que je le connaisse.

d (*rarely*) rarement, peu souvent. **I see him/it happens very ~** je le vois/cela arrive très rarement *or* très peu souvent; **I watch television very ~ nowadays** je ne regarde presque plus *or* plus beaucoup *or* plus très souvent la télévision maintenant.

e (*+ vb: not at all*) **he ~ supposed that** ... il était loin de supposer que ...; ~ **did he know that** ... il était (bien) loin de se douter que ...; ~ **do you know!** si seulement vous saviez!, vous ne savez pas tout!

littleness [ˈlɪtlnɪs] **n** a (*in size*) petitesse *f*. b (*morally*) petitesse *f*, mesquinerie *f*.

littoral [ˈlɪtərəl] **adj, n** littoral (*m*).

liturgical [lɪˈtɜːdʒɪkəl] **adj** liturgique.

liturgy [ˈlɪtədʒɪ] **n** liturgie *f*.

livable [ˈlɪvəbl] **adj** *climate* supportable; *life, pain* supportable, tolérable; *house* habitable. **this house is not ~ (in*)** cette maison est inhabitable; **he is/is not ~ (with)*** il est facile à vivre/insupportable *or* invivable*; **her life is not ~** elle mène une vie impossible *or* insupportable.

live¹ [lɪv] 1 **vi** a (*be alive*) vivre. **he was still living when his daughter got married** il était encore en vie quand sa fille s'est mariée; **while his uncle ~d** du vivant de son oncle; **as long as I ~ I shall never leave you** je ne te quitterai pas tant que je vivrai; **I shall remember it as long as I ~** je m'en souviendrai jusqu'à mon dernier jour; **to ~ to be 90** vivre jusqu'à (l'âge de) 90 ans; **you'll ~ to be a hundred** vous serez centenaire; **he won't ~ long** (*gen*) il n'en a plus pour longtemps; *[young person]* il ne fera pas de vieux os; **she'll never ~ to see it** elle ne vivra pas assez longtemps pour le voir, elle ne sera plus là pour le voir; **she has only 6 months to ~** il ne lui reste plus que 6 mois à vivre; **he didn't ~ long after his wife died** il n'a pas survécu longtemps à sa femme; **long ~ the King!** vive le roi!; **nothing could ~ in such a storm** rien ne pourrait survivre à pareille tempête; **the doctor said she would ~** le docteur a dit qu'elle s'en sortirait; (*hum, iro*) **you'll ~!*** tu n'en mourras pas!; **this night will ~ in American history** cette nuit fera date dans l'histoire de l'Amérique; **her voice will ~ with me forever** je garderai toujours le souvenir de sa voix; **the author makes his characters ~** l'auteur fait vivre ses personnages; **let's ~ a little!*** il faut profiter de la vie!; **if you haven't been to London you haven't ~d** si tu n'es pas allé à Londres tu n'as pas encore vécu.

b (*conduct o.s.*) vivre; (*exist*) vivre, exister. **to ~ honestly** vivre honnêtement, mener une vie honnête; **to ~ in luxury** vivre dans le luxe; **to ~ in style, to ~ well, to ~ like a king** *or* **a lord** mener grand train, vivre sur un grand pied; **to ~ according to one's means** vivre selon ses moyens; **they ~d happily ever after** après cela ils vécurent toujours heureux; (*in fairy tales*) ils furent heureux et ils eurent beaucoup d'enfants; **to ~ by one's pen** vivre de sa plume; **to ~ by journalism** gagner sa vie en étant *or* comme journaliste; **to ~ by buying and selling used cars** gagner sa vie en achetant et vendant des voitures d'occasion; **to ~ by an ideal/a belief** *etc* vivre en accord avec un idéal/une croyance *etc*; **she ~s for her children** elle ne vit que pour ses enfants; **he is living for the day when he will see his son again** il ne vit que pour le jour où il reverra son fils; **I've got nothing left to ~ for** je n'ai plus de raison de vivre; **you must learn to ~ with it** il faut que tu t'y fasses *or* que tu t'en accommodes (*subj*); **he will have to ~ with that awful memory all his life** il lui faudra vivre avec cet horrible souvenir jusqu'à la fin de ses jours; (*Prov*) **~ and let ~** il faut se montrer tolérant; **you** *or* **we ~ and learn** on apprend à tout âge; *see* **hand** *etc*.

c (*reside*) vivre, habiter, résider. **to ~ in London** habiter (à) Londres, vivre à Londres; **to ~ in a flat** habiter un appartement; **where do you ~?** où habitez-vous?; **she ~s in the rue de Rivoli** elle habite rue de Rivoli; **this house isn't fit to ~ in** cette maison n'est pas habitable *or* est inhabitable; **a house fit for a queen to ~ in** une maison princière; **this is a nice place to ~ in** il fait bon vivre ici; **he's not an easy person to ~ with** il n'est pas facile à vivre; **he ~s with his mother** il vit *or* habite avec sa mère; (*in her house*) il vit chez sa mère; **he's living with Anne** (*as man and wife*) il vit avec Anne; († *or hum*) **they're living in sin** ils vivent dans le péché.

2 **vt** vivre, mener. **to ~ a healthy life** mener une vie saine; **to ~ a life of ease** avoir une vie facile; **to ~ a life of luxury/crime** vivre dans le luxe/le crime; **to ~ life to the full** vivre pleinement sa vie, profiter au maximum de la vie; **to ~ one's faith/one's socialism** *etc* vivre pleinement sa foi/son socialisme *etc*; **he just ~s* sailing/stamp collecting** *etc* il ne vit que pour la voile/pour sa collection de timbres *etc*; **to ~ a lie** vivre dans le mensonge; (*Theat, fig*) **to ~ the part** entrer dans la peau du personnage; *see* **life c**.

3 **comp** ▸**lived-in** *house, flat etc* (*lit*) habité; (*often hum*) *flat* habité; *face* marqué par le temps ▸**live-in adj** (*gen*) *housekeeper etc* à demeure; **live-in lover** petit(e) ami(e) *m(f)* avec qui l'on vit; **live-in partner** concubin(e) *m(f)* ▸**livelong: all the livelong day** tout au long du jour (*liter*), toute la journée, toute la sainte journée* (*often pej*).

▸**live down vt sep** *disgrace, scandal* faire oublier (avec le temps). **you'll never live it down!** jamais tu ne feras oublier ça!

▸**live in** 1 **vi** *[servant]* être logé et nourri; *[student, doctor]* être interne. 2 **lived-in adj** *see* **live¹ 3**. 3 **live-in adj** *see* **live¹ 3**.

▸**live off vt fus** a *fruit, rice* vivre de, se nourrir de. **to live off the land** vivre des ressources naturelles, vivre du pays. b = **live on 2c**.

▸**live on** 1 **vi** *[person]* continuer à vivre; *[tradition, memory]* rester, survivre.

2 **vt fus** a *fruit, rice* vivre de, se nourrir de. **you can't live on air*** on ne vit pas de l'air du temps; **she absolutely lives on chocolate*** elle se nourrit exclusivement de chocolat; (*fig*) **to live on hope** vivre d'espérance.

b **to live on £10,000 a year** vivre avec 10 000 livres par an; **we have just enough to live on** nous avons juste de quoi vivre; **what does he live on?** de quoi vit-il?, qu'est-ce qu'il a pour vivre?; **to live on one's salary** vivre de son salaire; **to live on one's capital** vivre de *or* manger son capital; **to live on borrowed time** être en sursis (*fig*).

c (*depend financially on*) vivre aux dépens *or* aux crochets de.

▸**live out** 1 **vi** *[servant]* ne pas être logé; *[student, doctor]* être externe. 2 **vt sep** passer. **she won't live the year out** elle ne passera pas l'année; **he lived out the war in the country** il a passé la durée de la guerre à la campagne. 3 **vt fus** (*frm*) *one's destiny*accomplir, réaliser; *one's beliefs* mettre en pratique, vivre en accord avec.

▸**live through vt fus** a (*experience*) vivre, voir. **she has lived through two world wars** elle a vu deux guerres mondiales; **the difficult years he has lived through** les années difficiles qu'il a vécues. b (*survive*) supporter, survivre à, passer. **he can't live through the winter** il ne passera pas l'hiver; **I couldn't live through another day like that** je ne pourrais pas supporter *or* passer une deuxième journée comme ça.

▸**live together vi** (*as man and wife*) vivre ensemble.

▸**live up vt sep: to live it up*** (*live in luxury*) mener la grande vie; (*have fun*) mener une vie de bâton de chaise.

▸**live up to vt fus** a (*be true to*) *one's principles* vivre en accord avec, vivre selon; *one's promises* être fidèle à, respecter.

b (*be equal to*) être *or* se montrer à la hauteur de; (*be worthy of*) répondre à, se montrer digne de. **to live up to sb's expectations** être *or* se montrer à la hauteur des espérances de qn; **the holiday didn't live up to expectations** les vacances n'ont pas été ce qu'on avait espéré; **we must try to live up to our new surroundings** nous devons essayer d'avoir un train de vie en rapport avec *or* de nous montrer dignes de notre nouveau cadre; **his brother's success will give him something to live up to** la réussite de son frère lui fera un sujet d'émulation.

live² [laɪv] 1 **adj** a *person, animal* vivant, en vie; (*fig*) dynamique. **a ~ birth** une naissance viable; (*Fishing*) **~ bait** vif *m* (*appât*); **a real ~ spaceman** un astronaute en chair et en os; (*fig*) **this is a ~ problem today** c'est un problème brûlant aujourd'hui.

b (*Rad, TV*) (transmis *or* diffusé) en direct. **that programme was ~** cette émission était (transmise *or* diffusée) en direct; **performed before a ~ audience** joué en public; **they're a great ~ act** ils font un excellent numéro sur scène.

c *coal* ardent; *ammunition, shell, cartridge* de combat; (*unexploded*) non explosé. (*Elec*) **that's ~!** c'est branché!; (*Elec*) **~ rail** rail conducteur; (*Elec*) **~ wire** fil *m* sous tension; (*fig*) **he's a ~ wire*** il a un dynamisme fou, il pète le feu*; **the switch/hair-drier was ~** l'interrupteur/le séchoir à cheveux était mal isolé (et dangereux).

2 **adv** (*Rad, TV*) en direct. (*on stage*) **to play ~** jouer sur scène; **it was broadcast ~** c'était (transmis *or* diffusé) en direct; **the match is brought to you ~ from ...** le match vous est transmis en direct depuis ...; **here, ~ from New York, is our reporter X** voici, en direct de New York, notre envoyé spécial X.

3 **comp** ▸**livestock** (*NonC*) bétail *m*, cheptel *m* ▸**live yoghurt** yaourt *m* fermenté.

liveable [ˈlɪvəbl] **adj** = **livable**.

livelihood [ˈlaɪvlɪhʊd] **n** (*NonC*) moyens *mpl* d'existence, gagne-pain *m inv*. **to earn a** *or* **one's ~** gagner sa vie; **his ~ depends on ...** son gagne-pain dépend de ...; **their principal ~ is tourism/rice** leur principale source de revenu est le tourisme/la culture du riz.

liveliness [ˈlaɪvlɪnɪs] **n** (*see* **lively**) vivacité *f*, entrain *m*, allant *m*, pétulance *f*; vie *f*; animation *f*; vigueur *f*; gaieté *f or* gaîté *f*.

lively [ˈlaɪvlɪ] **adj** *person, character* vif (*f* vive), plein d'entrain, plein d'allant, pétulant; *animal* vif, plein de vie; *imagination, colour* vif; *description, account, style* vivant; *party, discussion, conversation* animé, plein d'entrain; *performance, expression, instance, example, argument* frappant, percutant, vigoureux; *campaign* percutant, vigoureux; *tune* entraînant, allègre, gai. **he is very ~** il est plein d'entrain *or* de vie; **at a ~ pace** *or* **speed** à vive allure, à toute vitesse; **to take a ~ interest in sth** s'intéresser vivement à qch; **we had a ~ week** nous avons eu une semaine mouvementée; **we had a ~ time of it** nous avons eu des instants mouvementés; **things are getting a bit too ~** (*at party etc*) ça commence à chauffer*; (*during row etc*) ça va barder*; *see* **look 3d**.

liven [ˈlaɪvn] 1 **vt: to ~ up** *person* égayer, réjouir; *evening, discussion, party etc* animer; **a bit of paint should ~ the room up** un peu de peinture égayerait la pièce. 2 **vi: to ~ up** s'animer; **things are beginning to ~ up** (*more fun*) ça commence à s'animer; (*more trouble*) ça va barder*.

liver¹ [ˈlɪvəʳ] 1 **n** (*Anat, Culin*) foie *m* *see* **lily**. 2 **comp** ▸**liver complaint** maladie *f* de foie ▸**liver fluke** (*Vet*) douve *f* du foie ▸**liver paste** *pâte préparée au foie* ▸**liver pâté** pâté *m* de foie ▸**liver sausage** saucisse *f* au pâté de foie ▸**liverwort** (*Bot*) hépatique *f*, herbe *f* de la Trinité ▸**liverwurst** (*esp US*) = **liver sausage**.

liver² [ˈlɪvəʳ] **n** (*person*) **clean ~** vertueux *m*, -euse *f*; **fast ~** débauché(e) *m(f)*.

liveried [ˈlɪvərɪd] **adj** en livrée.

liverish* [ˈlɪvərɪʃ] **adj** a (*bilious*) qui a mal au foie. b (*irritable*) de mauvais poil*, grincheux.

Liverpudlian [ˌlɪvəˈpʌdlɪən] 1 **n: he's a ~** (*living there*) c'est un habitant de Liverpool, il habite Liverpool; (*born there*) il est originaire de Liverpool. 2 adj de Liverpool.

livery ['lɪvərɪ] 1 n a *[servant]* livrée *f*; *[company, product]* couleurs *fpl*. b **to keep a horse at ~** avoir un cheval en pension *or* en garde. 2 comp ▸**livery company** (*Brit*) corporation londonienne ▸**livery man** (*in London*) membre *m* d'une corporation; (††: *retainer*) serviteur *m* ▸**livery stable** (*boarding*) pension *f* pour chevaux; (*hiring out*) écurie *f* de louage.

lives [laɪvz] npl of **life**.

livid ['lɪvɪd] adj a (*in colour*) *complexion, scar* livide, blafard; *sky* plombé, de plomb. **he was ~ with cold** il était tout blanc de froid; **she had a ~ bruise on her forehead** elle avait une vilaine ecchymose au front. b (*furious: also* **~ with anger** *or* **rage** *or* **fury**) *person* furieux, furibond, en rage; *expression, appearance, gesture, glare* furieux, furibond.

living ['lɪvɪŋ] 1 adj *person* vivant, en vie; *language, example, faith* vivant; *coal* ardent; *water* vif (*f* vive). **~ or dead** mort ou vif; **he's the greatest ~ pianist** c'est le plus grand pianiste actuellement vivant; **there wasn't a ~ soul** il n'y avait pas âme qui vive; **a ~ skeleton** un cadavre ambulant; **"the L~ Desert"** "Le désert vivant"; **~ fossil** fossile *m* vivant; **within ~ memory** de mémoire d'homme; **a ~ death** un enfer, un calvaire; **he's the ~ image of his father*** c'est le portrait (tout craché) de son père; **the ~ rock** le roc; **carved out of the ~ rock** taillé à même le *or* dans le roc; (*fig*) **it's the ~ end*** c'est super*; *see* **daylight**.

2 n a (*means of livelihood*) vie *f*. **to earn** *or* **make a ~ by painting portraits/as an artist** gagner sa vie en peignant *or* à peindre des portraits/en tant qu'artiste; **they have to work for a ~** ils doivent travailler pour vivre; **he thinks the world owes him a ~** il croit que tout lui est dû; *see* **cost**.

b (*way of life*) vie *f*. **gracious ~** vie élégante *or* raffinée; **loose ~** vie de débauche; **~ was not easy in those days** la vie n'était pas facile en ce temps-là; *see* **standard**.

c (*Brit Rel*) cure *f*, bénéfice *m*.

3 npl: **the ~** les vivants *mpl*; *see* **land**.

4 comp ▸**living conditions** conditions *fpl* de vie ▸**living expenses** frais *mpl* de subsistance ▸**living quarters** logement(s) *m(pl)* ▸**living room** salle *f* de séjour, séjour *m*, living(-room) *m* ▸**living space** espace vital ▸**living standards** niveau *m* de vie ▸**living wage: they were asking for a living wage** ils demandaient un salaire leur permettant de vivre décemment; **£50 a week isn't a living wage** on ne peut pas vivre avec 50 livres par semaine.

Livorno [lɪ'vɔːnəʊ] n Livourne.

Livy ['lɪvɪ] n Tite-Live *m*.

Lizard ['lɪzəd] n (*Brit Geog*) **the ~** le cap Lizard.

lizard ['lɪzəd] 1 n lézard *m*; (*also* **~skin**) (peau *f* de) lézard. 2 comp *bag etc* en lézard.

llama ['lɑːmə] n lama *m* (*Zool*).

LL.B. [ˌelel'biː] n (abbr of *Legum Baccalaureus* = **Bachelor of Laws**) ≃ licence *f* de droit.

LL.D. [ˌelel'diː] n (abbr of *Legum Doctor* = **Doctor of Laws**) ≃ doctorat *m* de droit.

LM [el'em] n (abbr of **lunar module**) *see* **lunar**.

LMS [elˌem'es] n (abbr of **local management of schools**) *see* **local 1**.

LMT [elˌem'tiː] (*US*) (abbr of **local mean time**) heure locale.

LNG n (abbr of **liquefied natural gas**) *see* **liquefy**.

lo [ləʊ] excl regardez! **when ~ and behold, in he walked!** et c'est alors qu'il est entré!; **~ and behold the result!** et voilà le résultat!

loach [ləʊtʃ] n loche *f* (de rivière).

load [ləʊd] 1 n a (*thing carried*) *[person, animal, washing machine]* charge *f*; *[lorry]* chargement *m*, charge; *[ship]* cargaison *f*; (*weight*) (gros) poids *m*; (*pressure*) poids, pression *f*; (*fig*) (*burden*) fardeau *m*, charge *f*; (*mental strain*) poids. **he was carrying a heavy ~** il était lourdement chargé; **the ~ slipped off the lorry** le chargement *or* la charge a glissé du camion; **the lorry had a full ~** le camion avait un chargement complet; **the ship had a full ~** le navire avait une cargaison complète; **under (full) ~** chargé (à plein); **a ~ of coal** *[ship]* une cargaison de charbon; *[lorry]* un chargement *or* une charge de charbon; **I had 3 ~s of coal (delivered) last autumn** on m'a livré du charbon en 3 fois l'automne dernier; **tree weighed down by its ~ of fruit** arbre *m* ployant sous le poids des fruits; **supporting his brother's family was a heavy ~ for him** c'était pour lui une lourde charge (que) de faire vivre la famille de son frère; **he finds his new responsibilities a heavy ~** il trouve ses nouvelles responsabilités pesantes *or* lourdes; **to take a ~ off sb's mind** débarrasser qn de ce qui lui pèse (*fig*); **that's a ~ off my mind!** c'est un poids en moins!, quel soulagement!; *see* **bus, pay, shed²**, **work** *etc*.

b (*Constr, Elec, Tech; also of firearm*) charge *f*. (*Elec*) **the new regulations spread the ~ on the power stations more evenly** les nouveaux règlements répartissent la charge plus uniformément sur les centrales électriques.

c (* *fig*) **a ~ of** un tas de, des masses de*; **~s of** des tas de*, des masses de*; **that's a ~ of rubbish!** tout ça c'est de la blague!*; **we've got ~s of time** on a tout notre temps*, on a largement le temps; **he's got ~s of money** il est plein de fric‡; **we've got ~s (of them) at home** nous en avons (tout) plein* *or* des masses* *or* des tonnes* à la maison; **there were ~s of people** il y avait plein de monde* *or* des tas de gens* *or* des masses de gens*; **get a ~ of this!‡** (*look*) regarde un peu ça!, regarde voir!*; (*listen*) écoute un peu ça!, écoute voir!*

2 comp ▸**load-bearing** (*Constr*) *beam, structure* porteur ▸**load factor** (*Elec*) facteur *m* d'utilisation; (*Aviat*) coefficient *m* de remplissage ▸**load line** (*Naut*) ligne *f* de charge ▸**load-shedding** (*Elec*) délestage *m* ▸**loadstar** = **lodestar** (*see* **lode 2**) ▸**loadstone** = **lodestone** (*see* **lode 2**).

3 vt a *lorry, ship, washing machine etc* charger (*with* de); *person* charger; (*overwhelm*) accabler. **the branch was ~ed (down) with pears** la branche était chargée de poires, la branche ployait sous les poires; **she was ~ed (down) with shopping** elle pliait sous le poids de ses achats; **his pockets were ~ed with sweets and toys** ses poches étaient bourrées de bonbons et de jouets; **they arrived ~ed (down) with presents for us** ils sont arrivés chargés de cadeaux pour nous; **to ~ sb (down) with gifts** couvrir qn de cadeaux; **to ~ sb with honours** combler *or* couvrir qn d'honneurs; **we are ~ed (down) with debts** nous sommes couverts *or* criblés de dettes; **~ed (down) with cares** accablé de soucis; **a heart ~ed (down) with sorrow** un cœur lourd *or* accablé de chagrin; **the whole business is ~ed (down) with problems** toute cette affaire présente des monceaux de difficultés.

b *[ship etc]* **to ~ coal/grain** *etc* charger du charbon/du grain *etc*.

c *gun, camera, computer etc* charger (*with* de, avec).

d *cane etc* plomber; *dice* piper. (*lit*) **the dice were ~ed** les dés étaient pipés; (*fig*) **the dice were ~ed against him/in his favour** les cartes étaient truquées à son désavantage/à son avantage (*fig*); (*fig*) **to ~ the dice against sb** truquer les cartes pour desservir qn (*fig*); **the situation is ~ed in our favour** les faits jouent en notre faveur.

e *insurance premium* majorer.

4 vi *[lorry]* charger, prendre un chargement; *[ship]* embarquer une cargaison; *[camera, gun]* se charger; (*Comput*) se charger.

▸**load down** vt sep charger (*with* de); *see* **load 3a**.

▸**load up** 1 vi *[ship]* charger, recevoir une cargaison; *[truck]* charger, prendre un chargement; *[person]* charger, ramasser son chargement. **to load up with sth** charger qch; (*US fig*) **to load up with** *or* **on‡** *food, drink* se bourrer de*. 2 vt sep *truck, animal, person, computer* charger (*with* de, avec).

...load [ləʊd] n ending in comps: **carload, planeload;** *see* **car, plane** *etc*.

loaded ['ləʊdɪd] adj a *lorry, ship, gun, camera* chargé; *dice* pipé; *cane* plombé; *see also* **load**. b *word, statement* insidieux. **that's a ~ question!** c'est une question insidieuse!, c'est une question-piège! c (*: *rich*) friqué*, bourré de fric‡, plein aux as‡. d (‡) (*drunk*) bourré‡; (*drugged*) défoncé‡.

loader ['ləʊdəʳ] n (*person, instrument*) chargeur *m*; (*Constr*) chargeuse *f*; *see* **low¹**.

loading ['ləʊdɪŋ] 1 n chargement *m*. (*street sign*) **"no ~ or unloading"** "interdiction de charger et de décharger". 2 comp ▸**loading bay** aire *f* de chargement.

loaf¹ [ləʊf] pl **loaves** 1 n a (*also* **~ of bread**) pain *m*, (*round loaf*) miche *f* de pain. (*Prov*) **half a ~ is better than no bread** faute de grives on mange des merles (*Prov*), mieux vaut peu que pas du tout (*loc*); (*Brit*) **use your ~!‡** fais marcher tes méninges!*; *see* **cottage, sandwich, slice** *etc*. b **sugar ~** pain *m* de sucre; *see* **meat** *etc*. 2 comp ▸**loaf sugar** sucre *m* en pain ▸**loaf tin** moule *m* à pain.

loaf² [ləʊf] vi (*also* **~ about, ~ around**) fainéanter, traîner, traînasser.

loafer ['ləʊfəʳ] n a (*person*) flemmard(e)* *m(f)*, tire-au-flanc* *m inv*. b (*shoe*) mocassin *m*.

loam [ləʊm] n (*NonC*) a (*soil*) terreau *m*. b *[moulds]* terre *f* de moulage.

loamy ['ləʊmɪ] adj *soil* riche en terreau.

loan [ləʊn] 1 n a (*money*) (*lent*) prêt *m*; (*advanced*) avance *f*; (*borrowed*) emprunt *m*. **can I ask you for a ~?** pouvez-vous m'accorder un prêt?; **"~s without security"** "prêts sans garantie"; (*Banking*) **~s and deposits** emplois *mpl* et ressources *fpl*; *see* **raise**.

b prêt *m*. **this picture is on ~** *or* **is a ~ from the city museum** ce tableau est prêté par le *or* est un prêt du musée municipal; **I have a car on ~ from the company** la compagnie me prête une voiture *or* met une voiture à ma disposition; **my assistant is on ~ to another department at the moment** mon assistant prête ses services *or* est détaché à une autre division en ce moment; (*in library*) **the book is out on ~** le livre est sorti; **I have this book out on ~ from the library** j'ai emprunté ce livre à la bibliothèque; **I asked for the ~ of the lawnmower** j'ai demandé à emprunter *or* à ce qu'on me prête (*subj*) la tondeuse à gazon; **may I have the ~ of your record player?** pouvez-vous me prêter votre électrophone?; **I can give you the ~ of it for a few days** je peux vous le prêter pour quelques jours.

2 vt (*US, also Brit* *) prêter (*sth to sb* qch à qn).

3 comp ▸**loan agreement** (*Fin*) convention *f* de prêt ▸**loan capital** capital-obligations *m*, capital *m* d'emprunt ▸**loan collection** (*Art etc*) collection *f* de tableaux (*or* d'objets *etc*) prêtés ▸**loan facility** (*Fin*) prêt *m* ▸**loan fund** caisse *f* de prêt ▸**loan investment** (*Fin*) investissement *m* sous forme de prêt ▸**loan office** bureau *m* de prêt ▸**loan officer** *[bank]* gestionnaire *mf* de crédit ▸**loan shark*** (*pej*)

usurier *m* ►**loan translation** (*Ling*) calque *m* ►**loan word** (*Ling*) (mot *m* d')emprunt *m*.

loath [ləʊθ] adj: **to be (very) ~ to do sth** répugner à faire qch; **he was ~ to see her again** il n'était pas du tout disposé à la revoir; **I am ~ to add to your difficulties but ...** je ne voudrais surtout pas ajouter à vos difficultés mais ...; **nothing ~** très volontiers.

loathe [ləʊð] vt *person* détester, haïr; *thing* détester, avoir en horreur, abhorrer (*frm*). **to ~ doing sth** avoir horreur de *or* détester faire qch; **he ~s being told off** il a horreur *or* il déteste qu'on le reprenne.

loathing ['ləʊðɪŋ] n (*NonC*) dégoût *m*, répugnance *f*. **he/it fills me with ~** il/cela me répugne *or* dégoûte.

loathsome ['ləʊðsəm] adj détestable, répugnant, écœurant.

loathsomeness ['ləʊðsəmnɪs] n caractère répugnant, nature détestable *or* écœurante.

loaves [ləʊvz] npl of **loaf**.

lob [lɒb] 1 vt *stone etc* lancer (haut *or* en chandelle). (*Tennis*) **to ~ a ball** faire un lob, lober; **he ~bed the book (over) to me** il m'a lancé *or* balancé* le livre; (*Ftbl*) **to ~ the goalkeeper** lober le gardien de but. 2 vi (*Tennis*) lober, faire un lob. 3 n (*Tennis*) lob *m*.

lobby ['lɒbɪ] 1 n a (*entrance hall*) *[hotel]* hall *m*; (*smaller*) vestibule *m*, entrée *f*; *[private house]* vestibule, entrée; *[theatre]* foyer *m* (des spectateurs).

b (*Brit Parl*) (*where Members meet public*) hall *m* (*de la Chambre des communes où le public rencontre les députés*), ≃ salle *f* des pas perdus; (*where Members vote: also* **division ~**) vestibule *m* (*où les députés se répartissent pour voter*).

c (*Pol: pressure group*) groupe *m* de pression, lobby *m*. **the anti-vivisection ~** le groupe de pression *or* le lobby antivivisectionniste.

2 comp ►**lobby correspondent** (*Brit Press*) journaliste *mf* parlementaire.

3 vt (*Parl, also gen*) *person* faire pression sur, se livrer à un travail de propagande auprès de; (*esp US*) *proposal, cause* faire pression en faveur de, soutenir activement.

4 vi (*Pol*) **they are ~ing for a stricter control of firearms** ils font pression pour obtenir un contrôle plus étroit des armes à feu.

lobbyer ['lɒbɪəʳ] n (*US*) = **lobbyist**.

lobbying ['lɒbɪɪŋ] n (*Pol*) sollicitations *fpl* (*d'un groupe de pression*), pressions *fpl*.

lobbyism ['lɒbɪɪzəm] n (*US*) = **lobbying**.

lobbyist ['lɒbɪɪst] n (*Pol*) membre *m* d'un groupe de pression (*for* en faveur de); *see* **lobby**.

lobe [ləʊb] n (*Anat, Bot*) lobe *m*.

lobelia [ləʊ'biːlɪə] n lobélie *f*.

lobotomy [ləʊ'bɒtəmɪ] n lobotomie *f*.

lobster ['lɒbstəʳ] n, pl **~s** *or* **~** homard *m*. **~ nets** filets *mpl* à homards; **~ pot** casier *m* à homards.

lobule ['lɒbjuːl] n lobule *m*.

local ['ləʊkəl] 1 adj *belief, custom, saying, weather forecast, newspaper, radio* local, (*wider*) régional; *currency* du pays; *shops, library* du *or* de quartier; *wine, speciality* du pays, local; *time, train, branch, church, showers, fog* local; (*Med*) *pain* localisé. **~ anaesthetic** anesthésie *f* locale; (*Telec*) **a ~ call** une communication urbaine; **of ~ interest** d'intérêt local; **what is the ~ situation?** (*here*) quelle est la situation ici?; (*there*) quelle est la situation là-bas?; **he's a ~ man** il est du pays *or* du coin*; **the ~ doctor** (*gen*) le médecin le plus proche; (*in town*) le médecin du quartier; **it adds a bit of ~ colour** ça met un peu de couleur locale; **~ currency** monnaie *f* locale; **~ authority** (n) autorité locale; (comp) des autorités locales; **~ education authority** ≃ office régional de l'enseignement; (*Brit*) **~ management of schools** gestion *f* des établissements scolaires par les autorités locales; **~ government** administration locale; **~ government elections** élections municipales; **~ government officer** *or* **official** administrateur local, ≃ fonctionnaire *mf* (de l'administration locale); (*Comput*) **~ area network** réseau *m* local.

2 n a (**: person*) personne *f* du pays *or* du coin*. **the ~s** les gens du pays *or* du coin* *or* du cru; **he's one of the ~s** il est du pays *or* du coin*.

b (*Brit *: pub*) café *m* du coin, bistro(t)* *m* du coin.

c (*US Rail*) (train *m*) omnibus *m*.

d (*) = **local anaesthetic**; *see* **1**.

e (*US: trade union branch*) section *f* syndicale.

locale [ləʊ'kɑːl] n lieu *m*, scène *f* (*fig*), théâtre *m* (*frm*).

locality [ləʊ'kælɪtɪ] n a (*neighbourhood*) environs *mpl*, voisinage *m*; (*district*) région *f*. **in the ~** dans les environs, dans la région; **we are new to this ~** nous sommes nouveaux dans la région. b (*place, position*) lieu *m*, endroit *m*, emplacement *m*. **the ~ of the murder** le lieu *or* la scène *or* le théâtre (*frm*) du meurtre; **I don't know the ~ of the church** je ne sais pas où se trouve l'église; **she has a good/has no sense of ~** elle a/n'a pas le sens de l'orientation; *see* **bump**.

localize ['ləʊkəlaɪz] vt localiser. **~d pain** douleur localisée.

locally ['ləʊkəlɪ] adv a (*in certain areas*) localement. (*Met*) **showers ~** des averses locales, temps localement pluvieux; **onions are in short supply ~** les oignons manquent dans certaines régions; **I had it made ~** (*when I was there*) je l'ai fait faire sur place; (*around here*) je l'ai fait faire par ici; **~ appointed staff** personnel recruté localement. b (*nearby*) dans les environs *or* la région *or* le coin*; (*near here*) par ici; (*out there*) là-bas. **we deliver free ~** nous livrons gratuitement dans les environs; **you will find mushrooms ~** vous allez trouver des champignons dans la région *or* dans le coin*.

locate [ləʊ'keɪt] 1 vt a (*find*) *place, person* repérer, trouver; *noise, leak* localiser; *cause* localiser, repérer, trouver. **I can't ~ the school on this map** je n'arrive pas à repérer *or* à trouver l'école sur cette carte; **have you ~d the briefcase I left yesterday?** avez-vous retrouvé la serviette que j'ai oubliée hier?; **the doctors have ~d the cause of the pain/the source of the infection** les médecins ont localisé *or* déterminé la cause de la douleur/la source de l'infection.

b (*situate*) *factory, school etc* situer. **they decided to ~ the factory in Manchester** ils ont décidé d'implanter *or* de construire l'usine à Manchester; **where is the hospital to be ~d?** où va-t-on mettre *or* construire l'hôpital?; **the college is ~d in London** le collège est situé *or* se trouve à Londres.

c (*assume to be*) situer, placer. **many scholars ~ the Garden of Eden there** c'est là que de nombreux érudits situent *or* placent le Paradis terrestre.

d (*US: have place to live*) **to be ~d** être installé.

2 vi (*US **) s'installer.

location [ləʊ'keɪʃən] 1 n a (*position*) emplacement *m*, situation *f*. **suitable ~s for a shoe factory** emplacements convenant à une usine de chaussures. b (*Cine*) extérieur(s) *m(pl)*. **on ~** en extérieur. c (*NonC: see* **locate 1a**) repérage *m*; localisation *f*. 2 comp (*Cine*) *scene, shot* en extérieur.

locative ['lɒkətɪv] adj, n locatif (*m*) (*Ling*).

loch [lɒx] n (*Scot*) lac *m*, loch *m*. **L~ Lomond** le loch Lomond; *see* **sea**.

loci ['ləʊsaɪ] npl of **locus**.

lock[1] [lɒk] 1 n a *[door, box etc]* serrure *f*; (*on steering wheel, bicycle, motorbike*) antivol *m*. **under ~ and key** *possessions* sous clef; *prisoner* sous les verrous; **to put/keep sth under ~ and key** mettre/garder qch sous clef; **to put sb under ~ and key** enfermer qn à clef; (*prisoner*) mettre qn sous les verrous; **to keep sb under ~ and key** garder qn enfermé à clef; (*prisoner*) garder qn sous les verrous; (*US fig*) **it's a ~*** c'est dans ta poche; *see* **combination, pick** *etc*.

b *[gun]* (*safety lock*) cran *m* de sûreté; (*gunlock*) percuteur *m*. (*fig*) **he sold the factory ~, stock and barrel** il a vendu l'usine en bloc; **they rejected the proposals ~, stock and barrel** ils ont rejeté les suggestions en bloc *or* toutes les suggestions sans exception; **he has moved out ~, stock and barrel** il a déménagé en emportant tout son fourbi*.

c (*Comput*) verrouillage *m*.

d *[canal]* écluse *f*; *see* **air**.

e (*Wrestling*) immobilisation *f*. **to hold sb in a ~** immobiliser qn.

f (*Aut*) rayon *m* de braquage. **this car has a good ~** cette voiture braque bien *or* a un bon rayon de braquage; **3.5 turns from ~ to ~** 3,5 tours d'une butée à l'autre.

g (*Rugby: also* **~ forward**) (avant *m* de) deuxième ligne *m*.

2 comp ►**lockaway** (*Fin*) titre *m* à long terme ►**lock gate** porte *f* d'écluse ►**lockjaw** (*Med*) tétanos *m* ►**lock keeper** éclusier *m*, -ière *f* ►**locknut** (*washer*) contre-écrou *m*; (*self-locking*) écrou auto-bloquant ►**lockout** (*Ind*) lock-out *m inv*, grève *f* patronale ►**locksmith** serrurier *m* ►**lock-up** (*Brit: garage*) box *m*; (*Brit: shop*) boutique *f* (*sans logement*); (**: prison*) prison *f*, lieu *m* de détention provisoire, cellule *f* provisoire.

3 vt a (*fasten*) *door, suitcase, car, safe* fermer à clef, verrouiller. **behind ~ed doors** à huis clos; (*fig*) **to ~ the stable door after the horse has bolted** prendre ses précautions trop tard.

b *person* enfermer (*in* dans). **he got ~ed in the bathroom** il s'est trouvé enfermé dans la salle de bains.

c (*prevent use of*) *mechanism* bloquer; (*Comput*) verrouiller. **he ~ed the steering wheel on his car** il a bloqué la direction de sa voiture (en mettant l'antivol); (*Aut: by braking*) **to ~ the wheels** bloquer les roues.

d (*squeeze, also fig*) *person* étreindre, serrer. **she was ~ed in his arms** elle était serrée dans ses bras; **they were ~ed in a close embrace** ils étaient unis dans une étreinte passionnée; **the armies were ~ed in combat** les deux armées étaient aux prises.

4 vi a *[door]* fermer à clef.

b (*Aut*) *[wheel, steering wheel]* se bloquer.

►**lock away** 1 vt sep *object, jewels* mettre sous clef; *criminal* mettre sous les verrous; *mental patient etc* enfermer. 2 **lockaway** n *see* **lock**[1] **2**.

►**lock in** vt sep a *person, dog* enfermer (à l'intérieur). **to lock o.s. in** s'enfermer (à l'intérieur). b (*Fin*) *assets, loans* engager (à plus d'un an).

►**lock on** vi *[spacecraft]* s'arrimer (*to* à). *[radar]* **to lock on to sth** capter qch.

►**lock out** 1 vt sep a *person* (*deliberately*) mettre à la porte; (*by mistake*) enfermer dehors, laisser dehors (sans clef). **to find o.s. locked out** (*by mistake*) se trouver enfermé dehors; (*as punishment*) se trouver mis à la porte; **to lock o.s. out** s'enfermer dehors; **to lock o.s. out of one's car** fermer la voiture en laissant les clefs à l'intérieur. b (*Ind*) *workers* fermer l'usine à, lockouter. 2 **lockout** n *see* **lock**[1] **2.**

▸**lock up** 1 vi fermer à clef (toutes les portes). **will you lock up when you leave?** voulez-vous tout fermer en partant?; **to lock up for the night** tout fermer pour la nuit. 2 vt sep a *object, jewels* enfermer, mettre sous clef; *house* fermer (à clef); *criminal* mettre sous les verrous *or* en prison; *mental patient etc* enfermer. **you ought to be locked up!*** on devrait t'enfermer!, tu es bon à enfermer! b *capital, funds* immobiliser, bloquer (*in* dans). 3 **lock-up** n *see* **lock**[1] **2.**

lock[2] [lɒk] n *[hair]* mèche *f*; (*ringlet*) boucle *f*. **his ~s** sa chevelure, ses cheveux *mpl*; **her curly ~s** ses boucles.

locker ['lɒkəʳ] 1 n casier *m*, (petite) armoire *f*, (petit) placard *m*; (*at station etc: for luggage*) (casier *m* de) consigne *f* automatique. 2 comp ▸**locker-room** n vestiaire *m* ◊ adj (*fig*) *joke etc* de corps de garde, paillard.

locket ['lɒkɪt] n médaillon *m* (*bijou*).

locking ['lɒkɪŋ] 1 adj *door, container, cupboard* qui ferme à clef, verrouillable. (*Aut*) ~ **petrol cap** bouchon *m* anti-vol (*pour réservoir*). 2 n (*gen*) fermeture *f* à clef, verrouillage *m*; (*Aut*) *[door]* verrouillage *m*, condamnation *f*; (*Comput*) verrouillage; *see* **central.**

loco[1] ['ləʊkəʊ] loc adv: **in ~ parentis** en tant que substitut *or* à la place des parents.

loco[2] ['ləʊkəʊ] 1 (‡) adj toqué*, timbré*, cinglé‡. 2 comp ▸**locoweed** *plante d'Amérique qui, ingérée, provoque la paralysie et des troubles de la vision.*

locomotion [,ləʊkə'məʊʃən] n locomotion *f*.

locomotive [,ləʊkə'məʊtɪv] 1 n (*Rail*) locomotive *f*. ~ **shed** hangar *m* à locomotives. 2 adj *machine* locomotif; *muscle* locomoteur (*f* -trice).

locum ['ləʊkəm] n (*also* **locum tenens**: *esp Brit frm*) suppléant(e) *m(f)* (*de prêtre ou de médecin etc*).

locus ['lɒkəs] n, pl **loci** lieu *m*, point *m*; (*Math*) lieu géométrique.

locust ['ləʊkəst] 1 n locuste *f*, sauterelle *f*. 2 comp ▸**locust bean** caroube *f* ▸**locust tree** caroubier *m*.

locution [lə'kjuːʃən] n locution *f*.

lode [ləʊd] 1 n (*Miner*) filon *m*, veine *f*. 2 comp ▸**lodestar** (*lit*) étoile *f* polaire; (*fig*) principe directeur ▸**lodestone** magnétite *f*, aimant naturel.

lodge [lɒdʒ] 1 n (*small house in grounds*) maison *f or* pavillon *m* de gardien; (*porter's room in building*) loge *f*; (*Freemasonry*) loge; (*US Ind*) section *f* syndicale; *[beaver]* abri *m*, gîte *m*; *see* **hunting.** 2 vt a *person* loger, héberger. b *bullet* loger. c (*Admin, Jur: leave*) *money* déposer; *statement, report* présenter (*with sb* à qn), déposer (*with sb* chez qn). (*Jur*) **to ~ an appeal** interjeter appel, se pourvoir en cassation; **to ~ a complaint against** porter plainte contre; (*Jur*) **documents ~d by the parties** pièces *fpl* versées aux débats par les parties. 3 vi *[person]* être logé, être en pension (*with* chez); *[bullet]* se loger.

lodger ['lɒdʒəʳ] n (*Brit*) (*room only*) locataire *mf*; (*room and meals*) pensionnaire *mf*. **to take (in) ~s** (*room only*) louer des chambres; (*room and meals*) prendre des pensionnaires.

lodging ['lɒdʒɪŋ] 1 n a (*NonC: accommodation*) logement *m*, hébergement *m*. **they gave us a night's ~** ils nous ont logés *or* hébergés une nuit; *see* **board.** b **~s** (*room*) chambre *f*; (*flatlet*) logement *m*; **he took ~s with Mrs Smith**† (*with meals*) il a pris pension chez Mme Smith; (*without meals*) il a pris une chambre *or* un logement chez Mme Smith; **he's in ~s** il vit en meublé *or* en garni (*pej*); **to look for ~s** (*room*) chercher une chambre meublée; (*flatlet*) chercher un logement meublé; (*with meals*) chercher à prendre pension; **we took him back to his ~s** nous l'avons ramené chez lui. 2 comp ▸**lodging house** pension *f*.

loess ['ləʊɪs] n lœss *m*.

loft [lɒft] 1 n a *[house, stable, barn]* grenier *m*; *see* **hay, pigeon** *etc.* b *[church, hall]* galerie *f*; *see* **organ.** 2 vt a (*Golf*) *ball* lancer en chandelle. b (*US: send very high*) lancer très haut.

loftily ['lɒftɪlɪ] adv hautainement, avec hauteur *or* condescendance.

loftiness ['lɒftɪnɪs] n (*great height*) hauteur *f*; (*fig*) (*grandiosity*) grandeur *f*, noblesse *f*; (*haughtiness*) hauteur, condescendance *f*, dédain *m*.

lofty ['lɒftɪ] adj (*high*) *mountain, tower* haut, élevé; (*fig*) (*grandiose*) *feelings, aims, style* élevé, noble; (*haughty*) *behaviour, tone, look, remark* hautain, condescendant, dédaigneux.

log[1] [lɒg] 1 n a (*felled tree trunk*) rondin *m*; (*for fire*) bûche *f*. **he lay like a ~** il ne bougeait pas plus qu'une souche; *see* **sleep.**

b (*Naut: device*) loch *m*.

c (*also* **~book**) (*Naut*) livre *m or* journal *m* de bord; (*Aviat*) carnet *m* de vol; *[lorry driver etc]* carnet de route; (*gen*) registre *m*. **to write up** *or* **keep the ~(book)** tenir le livre de bord *or* le carnet de vol *etc;* **let's keep a ~ of everything we do today** notons *or* consignons tout ce que nous allons faire aujourd'hui.

2 comp ▸**logbook** (*Aviat, Naut etc*) *see* **1c**; (*Brit Aut*) ≃ carte grise ▸**log cabin** cabane *f* en rondins ▸**log fire** feu *m* de bois ▸**log jam** (*lit*) train *m* de flottage bloqué; (*fig*) impasse *f* (*fig*) ▸**log-rolling** (*fig*) échange *m* abusif de concessions *or* de faveurs.

3 vt a *trees* tronçonner, débiter *or* tailler en rondins.

b (*record: also* ~ **up**) (*gen*) noter, consigner, enregistrer; (*Naut*) inscrire au journal de bord *or* au livre de bord; (*Aviat*) inscrire sur le *or* au carnet de vol.

c **the ship was ~ging 18 knots** le navire filait 18 nœuds; **the plane was ~ging 300 mph** l'avion volait à *or* faisait 500 km/h.

d (*also* ~ **up**) **he has ~ged (up) 5,000 hours' flying time** il a à son actif *or* il compte 5 000 heures de vol; **we ~ged (up) 50 km that day** nous avons parcouru *or* couvert 50 km ce jour-là; **I've ~ged (up) 8 hours' work each day*** je me suis envoyé* *or* tapé* huit heures de travail par jour.

▸**log in** (*Comput*) = **log on.**

▸**log off** (*Comput*) 1 vi sortir. 2 vt sep déconnecter.

▸**log on** (*Comput*) 1 vi entrer. 2 vt sep connecter, faire entrer dans le système.

▸**log out** (*Comput*) = **log off.**

▸**log up** vt sep *see* **log**[1] **3b, 3d.**

log[2] [lɒg] n (*Math*) (abbr of **logarithm**) log* *m*. ~ **tables** tables *fpl* de logarithmes.

loganberry ['ləʊgənbərɪ] n framboise *f* de Logan.

logarithm ['lɒgərɪθəm] n logarithme *m*.

loge [ləʊʒ] n (*Theat*) loge *f*.

logger ['lɒgəʳ] n bûcheron *m*.

loggerheads ['lɒgəhedz] npl: **to be at ~ (with)** être en désaccord *or* à couteaux tirés (avec).

loggia ['lɒdʒɪə] n, pl **~s** *or* **loggie** ['lɒdʒe] loggia *f*.

logging ['lɒgɪŋ] n exploitation *f* du bois.

logic ['lɒdʒɪk] 1 n logique *f*. **I can't see the ~ of it** ça ne me paraît pas rationnel; (*Brit fig*) **to chop ~** discutailler, ergoter (*with sb* avec qn). 2 comp ▸**logic-chopping** (*Brit fig*) ergoterie *f or* ergotage *m* ▸**logic circuit** (*Comput*) circuit *m* logique.

logical ['lɒdʒɪkəl] adj (*gen*) logique. (*Philos*) ~ **positivism** positivisme *m* logique, logico-positivisme *m*; ~ **positivist** logico-positiviste *mf*; **to take sth to its ~ conclusion** amener qch à sa conclusion logique.

logically ['lɒdʒɪkəlɪ] adv logiquement.

logician [lɒ'dʒɪʃən] n logicien(ne) *m(f)*.

logistic [lɒ'dʒɪstɪk] 1 adj logistique. 2 n (*NonC*) **~s** logistique *f*.

logistical [lɒ'dʒɪstɪkəl] adj = **logistic 1.**

logistically [lɒ'dʒɪstɪkəlɪ] adv logistiquement.

logo ['ləʊgəʊ] n logo *m*.

logy* ['ləʊgɪ] adj (*US*) apathique, léthargique.

loin [lɔɪn] 1 n a **~s** (*Anat*) reins *mpl*, lombes *mpl*; (*liter*) reins; *see* **gird up.** b (*Culin*) (*gen*) filet *m*; *[veal, venison]* longe *f*; *[beef]* aloyau *m*. 2 comp ▸**loin chop** (*Culin*) côte première ▸**loin cloth** pagne *m* (*d'étoffe*).

Loire [lwar] n Loire *f*. **the ~ Valley** la vallée de la Loire; (*between Orléans and Tours*) le Val de Loire.

loiter ['lɔɪtəʳ] vi a (*also* ~ **about**) (*dawdle*) s'attarder, traîner en route; (*loaf, stand around*) traîner, flâner, musarder; (*suspiciously*) traîner d'une manière suspecte. b (*Jur*) **to ~ with intent** ≃ commettre un délit d'intention; (*Jur*) **to be charged with ~ing with intent** être accusé d'un délit d'intention.

▸**loiter away** vt sep: **to loiter away one's time/days** passer son temps/ses journées à ne rien faire.

loll [lɒl] vi *[person]* se prélasser; *[head]* pendre.

▸**loll about, loll around** vi fainéanter, flâner.

▸**loll back** vi *[person]* se prélasser; *[head]* pendre en arrière. **to loll back in an armchair** se prélasser dans un fauteuil.

▸**loll out** 1 vi *[tongue]* pendre. 2 vt sep *tongue* laisser pendre.

Lollards ['lɒlədz] npl (*Hist*) Lollards *mpl*.

lollipop ['lɒlɪpɒp] n sucette *f* (*bonbon*). (*Brit*) ~ **man***, ~ **lady*** contractuel(le) *m(f)* (*qui fait traverser la rue aux enfants*).

lollop ['lɒləp] vi (*esp Brit*) *[large dog]* galoper; *[person]* courir gauchement *or* à grandes enjambées maladroites. **to ~ in/out** *etc* entrer/sortir *etc* à grandes enjambées maladroites.

lolly ['lɒlɪ] n (*Brit*) a (*) = **lollipop;** *see* **ice.** b (‡ *NonC: money*) fric‡ *m*, pognon‡ *m*.

Lombard ['lɒmbəd] 1 n Lombard(e) *m(f)*. 2 adj lombard.

Lombardy ['lɒmbədɪ] n Lombardie *f*. ~ **poplar** peuplier *m* d'Italie.

London ['lʌndən] 1 n Londres. 2 comp *life* londonien, à Londres; *people* de Londres; *shopkeeper, taxi* londonien; *street* londonien, de Londres ▸**London Bridge** Pont *m* de Londres ▸**London pride** (*Bot*) saxifrage ombreuse, désespoir *m* des peintres.

Londoner ['lʌndənəʳ] n Londonien(ne) *m(f)*.

lone [ləʊn] adj *person* solitaire; *village, house* isolé; (*unique*) seul. (*US*) **the L~ Star State** le Texas; (*fig*) **to play a ~ hand** faire cavalier seul; (*Admin etc*) ~ **parent** parent isolé; (*fig*) **he's a ~ wolf** c'est un solitaire, c'est quelqu'un qui fait cavalier seul.

loneliness ['ləʊnlɪnɪs] n *[person]* solitude *f*, isolement *m*; *[house, road]* (*isolated position*) isolement; (*atmosphere*) solitude; *[life]* solitude.

lonely ['ləʊnlɪ] adj *person* seul, solitaire, isolé; *life, journey, job, house, road* solitaire; (*isolated*) isolé, perdu. **to feel ~** se sentir seul; **it's ~ out there** on se sent seul là-bas; **a small ~ figure on the horizon** une petite silhouette seule *or* solitaire à l'horizon; ~ **hearts' column*** petites annonces personnelles; ~ **hearts' ad*** petite annonce personnelle; ~ **hearts' club** club *m* de rencontres (pour personnes seules).

loner* ['ləʊnəʳ] n solitaire *mf*.

lonesome ['ləʊnsəm] 1 adj (*esp US*) = **lonely**. 2 n: all on my (*or* your *etc*) ~* tout seul (*f* toute seule).

long¹ [lɒŋ] 1 adj a (*in size*) *dress, hair, rope, distance, journey* long (*f* longue). how ~ is the field? quelle est la longueur du champ?; 10 metres ~ (long) de 10 mètres; to grow ~(er), to get ~er (*gen*) s'allonger; *[hair]* pousser, devenir (plus) longs; ~ trousers pantalon *m* (long); to be ~ in the leg *[person, horse]* avoir les jambes longues; *[other animal]* avoir les pattes longues; *[trousers]* être trop long; he's (a bit) ~ in the tooth* il n'est plus tout jeune, il n'est plus de la première jeunesse; (*fig*) to have a ~ arm avoir le bras long; (*fig*) the ~ arm of the law le bras de la justice, la justice toute puissante; he has a ~ reach il peut allonger le bras loin; *[boxer]* il a de l'allonge; (*fig*) to have a ~ face avoir la mine longue *or* allongée, avoir une mine de carême, faire triste mine; to make *or* pull a ~ face faire une *or* la grimace, faire une mine de carême; his face was as ~ as a fiddle il faisait une mine de dix pieds de long *or* une tête d'enterrement *or* une mine de carême; (*fig*) the biggest by a ~ chalk *or* shot de beaucoup le plus grand; (*fig*) not by a ~ chalk loin de là; (*Math*) ~ division division écrite complète (*avec indication des restes partiels*); (*Cine*) ~ shot plan général *or* d'ensemble; (*fig*) it's a ~ shot *or* chance but we might be lucky c'est très risqué mais nous aurons peut-être de la chance; (*fig*) it was just a ~ shot *or* a ~ chance c'était un coup à tenter, il y avait peu de chances pour que cela réussisse; (*fig*) ~ stop garde-fou *m* (*fig*); (*Rad*) on (the) ~ wave sur les grandes ondes; *see also* 4, *and* broad, daddy, way *etc*.

b (*in time*) *visit, wait, weekend, look, film etc* long (*f* longue); (*Ling*) *vowel* long. 6 months ~ qui dure 6 mois, de 6 mois; a ~ time longtemps; you took a ~ time to get here *or* getting here tu as mis longtemps pour *or* à venir; it took a very ~ time for this to happen ceci n'est arrivé que très longtemps après, il a fallu attendre longtemps pour que cela arrive (*subj*); it takes a ~ time for that drug to act ce médicament met du temps à agir; what a ~ time you've been! il vous en a fallu du temps!, vous y avez mis le temps!; it will be a ~ time before I see her again je ne la reverrai pas de longtemps; for a ~ time to come he will wonder ... il se demandera (pendant) longtemps ...; it'll be a ~ time before I do that again! je ne recommencerai pas de si tôt!; for a ~ time I had to stay in bed j'ai dû rester au lit longtemps; I have been learning English for a ~ time j'apprends l'anglais depuis longtemps; a ~ time ago il y a longtemps; a ~, ~ time ago il y a bien longtemps; it's a ~ time since I last saw him ça fait longtemps que je ne l'ai vu; he has not been seen for a ~ time on ne l'a pas vu depuis longtemps, cela fait longtemps *or* voilà longtemps qu'on ne l'a pas vu; for a ~ time past he has been unable to work il a longtemps été *or* voilà longtemps qu'il est hors d'état de travailler; ~ time no see!‡ tiens, un revenant!* (*fig*); at ~ last enfin; he's not ~ for this world il n'en a plus pour longtemps (à vivre); the days are getting ~er les jours rallongent; friends of ~ standing des amis de longue date; he wasn't ~ in coming il n'a pas mis longtemps pour venir; how ~ are the holidays? les vacances durent combien de temps?; (*Brit Scol, Univ*) ~ vac*, ~ vacation grandes vacances; I find the days very ~ je trouve les jours bien longs; to take a ~ look at sb regarder longuement qn; a good ~ look at the car revealed that ... un examen *or* une inspection de la voiture a révélé que ...; (*fig*) to take a ~ (hard) look at sth regarder qch bien en face; (*fig*) to take a ~ (hard) look at o.s. s'examiner honnêtement; he took a ~ drink of water il a bu une grande gorgée d'eau (*see also* 4); (*fig*) in the ~ run à la longue, finalement, en fin de compte; in the ~ term à long terme (*see also* long-term); it will be a ~ job cela demandera du temps; to take the ~ view prévoir *or* voir les choses de loin; taking the ~ view si on prévoit *or* voit les choses de loin, si on pense à l'avenir; to have a ~ memory avoir bonne mémoire, avoir de la mémoire; he's ~ on advice‡ il est toujours là pour donner des conseils, il est fort pour ce qui est de donner des conseils; he's ~ on brains‡ c'est une grosse tête‡, il en a dans la cervelle*; there are ~ odds against your doing that il y a très peu de chances pour que tu fasses cela; *see* let¹.

2 adv a depuis longtemps. this method has ~ been used in industry cette méthode est employée depuis longtemps dans l'industrie; I have ~ wished to say ... il y a longtemps que je souhaite dire ...; these are ~-needed changes ce sont des changements dont on a besoin depuis longtemps; his ~-awaited reply sa réponse (si) longtemps attendue; *see also* 4.

b (*a long time*) longtemps. ~ ago il y a longtemps; how ~ ago was it? il y a combien de temps de ça?; as ~ ago as 1930 déjà en 1930; of ~ ago d'il y a longtemps; not ~ ago il y a peu de temps, il n'y a pas longtemps; he arrived not ~ ago il est arrivé depuis peu de temps, il n'y a pas longtemps qu'il est arrivé; ~ before (adv) longtemps avant; (conj) longtemps avant que + *subj*; ~ before the war longtemps *or* bien avant la guerre; you should have done it ~ before now vous auriez dû le faire il y a longtemps; not ~ before (adv) peu de temps avant; (conj) peu de temps avant que + *subj*; before ~ (+ *future*) avant peu, dans peu de temps; (+ *past*) peu de temps après; ~ after (adv) longtemps après; (conj) longtemps après que + *indic*; not ~ since il n'y a pas longtemps; ~ since il y a longtemps; he thought of friends ~ since dead il a pensé à des amis morts depuis longtemps; how ~ is it since you saw him? cela fait combien de temps que tu ne l'as pas vu?; they didn't stay ~ ils ne sont pas restés longtemps; he hasn't been gone ~ il n'y a pas longtemps qu'il est parti; it didn't take him ~ ça ne lui a pas pris longtemps; it didn't take him ~ to realize that ... il n'a pas mis longtemps à se rendre compte que ...; have you been here/been waiting ~? il y a longtemps que vous êtes ici?/que vous attendez?; are you going away for ~? partez-vous pour longtemps?; I'm not here for ~ je ne suis pas ici pour longtemps; not for ~ pas pour (très) longtemps; not for much ~er plus pour très longtemps; he didn't live ~ after that il n'a pas longtemps survécu à ça; he hasn't ~ to live il n'(en) a plus pour longtemps à vivre; women live ~er than men les femmes vivent plus longtemps que les hommes; ~ live the King! vive le roi!; I only had ~ enough to buy a paper je n'ai eu que le temps d'acheter un journal; wait a little ~er attendez encore un peu; do we have to wait any ~er? est-ce qu'il nous faut encore attendre?; will you be ~? tu en as pour longtemps?; don't be ~ dépêche-toi, ne prends pas trop de temps; I shan't be ~ je n'en ai pas pour longtemps, je me dépêche; how ~ did they stay? combien de temps sont-ils restés?; how ~ will you be? ça va te demander combien de temps?, tu vas mettre combien de temps?; how ~ have you been learning Greek? depuis combien de temps apprenez-vous le grec?; how ~ had you been living in Paris? depuis combien de temps viviez-vous à Paris?, cela faisait combien de temps que vous viviez à Paris?; I shan't forget him as ~ as I live je ne l'oublierai pas aussi longtemps que je vivrai; stay as ~ as you like restez autant que *or* aussi longtemps que vous voulez; as ~ as the war lasted tant que dura la guerre; as ~ as the war lasts tant que la guerre durera; as ~ as necessary aussi longtemps que c'est nécessaire *or* qu'il le faut; at (the) ~est au plus.

c all night ~ toute la nuit; all summer ~ tout l'été; his whole life ~ toute sa vie, sa vie durant; so ~ as, as ~ as pourvu que + *subj*; you can borrow it so *or* as ~ as you keep it clean vous pouvez l'emprunter pourvu que vous ne le salissiez (*subj*) pas *or* à condition de ne pas le salir; so ~!* au revoir!, à bientôt!, salut!*; I can't stay any ~er, I can stay no ~er je ne peux pas rester plus longtemps; she no ~er wishes to do it elle ne veut plus le faire; he is no ~er living there il n'habite plus là; *see* last².

3 n a (*fig*) the ~ and the short of it is that ... le fin mot de l'histoire, c'est que ... .

b (*Mus, Poetry*) longue *f*.

4 comp ▸**long-acting** *drug* à action lente ▸**longboat** (grande) chaloupe *f* ▸**longbow** arc *m* (anglais) ▸**long-dated** (*Fin*) à longue échéance ▸**long-distance** *race, runner* de fond; (*Telec*) long-distance call appel *m* (à) longue distance; to call sb long-distance appeler qn à longue distance; long-distance flight vol *m* sur long parcours *or* sur long-courrier; long-distance skier fondeur *m*, -euse *f* ▸**long-drawn-out** interminable, qui traîne indéfiniment ▸**long drink** long drink *m* ▸**long-eared** aux longues oreilles ▸**long fin tuna** *or* **tunny** thon *m* blanc ▸**long-forgotten** oublié depuis longtemps ▸**long green*** (*US: money*) argent *m*, fric* *m* ▸**longhair*** (*US*) hippie *m*, chevelu* *m* ▸**long-haired** *person* aux cheveux longs; *animal* à longs poils ▸**longhand** n écriture normale *or* courante ◊ adj en écriture normale *or* courante ▸**long-haul** transport *m* à longue distance; long-haul airline/flight ligne *f*/vol *m* long-courrier ▸**long-headed** (*lit*) à tête allongée; (*fig*) avisé, perspicace, prévoyant ▸**longhorn cattle** bovins *mpl* longhorn *inv or* à longues cornes ▸**long johns*** caleçon *m* (long) ▸**long jump** (*Brit Sport*) saut *m* en longueur ▸**long jumper** sauteur *m*, -euse *f* en longueur ▸**long-lasting** durable; to be longer-lasting *or* more long-lasting durer plus longtemps ▸**long-legged** *person, horse* aux jambes longues; *other animal, insect* à longues pattes ▸**long-life** *milk* longue conservation; *batteries* longue durée ▸**long-limbed** aux membres longs ▸**long-lived** d'une grande longévité; women are longer-lived *or* more long-lived than men les femmes vivent plus longtemps que les hommes ▸**long-lost** *person* perdu de vue depuis longtemps; *thing* perdu depuis longtemps ▸**long-nosed** au nez long ▸**long play** (*US*), **long-playing record** (*Brit, US*) (disque *m*) 33 tours *m inv*, microsillon *m* ▸**long-range** *missile, rocket, gun* à longue portée; *planning etc* à long terme; long-range plane (*Mil*) avion *m* à grand rayon d'action; (*civil*) long-courrier *m*; long-range weather forecast prévisions *fpl* météorologiques à long terme ▸**long-running** *play* qui tient l'affiche depuis longtemps; *TV programme* qui est diffusé depuis longtemps; *dispute* qui dure depuis longtemps ▸**longship** *[Vikings]* drakkar *m* ▸**long-shoreman** (*US*) débardeur *m*, docker *m* ▸**long-shoring** (*US*) débardage *m* ▸**long-sighted** (*Brit*) (*lit*) hypermétrope; (*in old age*) presbyte; (*fig*) *person* prévoyant, qui voit loin; *decision* pris avec prévoyance; *attitude* prévoyant ▸**long-sightedness** (*lit*) hypermétropie *f*; (*in old age*) presbytie *f*; (*fig*) prévoyance *f* ▸**long-sleeved** à manches longues ▸**long-standing** de longue date ▸**long-stay carpark** parc *m* de stationnement ▸**long-suffering** très patient, d'une patience à toute épreuve ▸**long-tailed** à longue queue; long-tailed tit mésange *f* à longue queue ▸**long-term** *see* long-term ▸**long-time** de longue date, vieux ▸**longways** en longueur, en long; longways on dans le sens de la longueur ▸**long-winded** *person* intarissable, prolixe; *speech* interminable ▸**long-windedly** intarissablement

►**long-windedness** prolixité *f*.

long[2] [lɒŋ] **vi: to ~ to do** avoir très envie de faire, mourir d'envie de faire; **I am ~ing to see you** j'ai hâte *or* il me tarde de vous voir; **to ~ for sth** désirer (ardemment) qch, avoir très envie de qch; **the ~ed-for news** la nouvelle tant désirée; **to ~ for sb** se languir de qn; **to ~ for sb to do sth** mourir d'envie que qn fasse qch.

longevity [lɒn'dʒevɪtɪ] **n** longévité *f*.

longing ['lɒŋɪŋ] 1 **n** a (*urge*) désir *m*, envie *f* (*for sth* de qch). **to have a sudden ~ to do** avoir un désir soudain *or* une envie soudaine de faire. b (*nostalgia*) nostalgie *f*, regret *m*, désir *m*. c (*for food*) envie *f*, convoitise *f*. 2 **adj** *look* plein de désir *or* d'envie *or* de nostalgie *or* de regret *or* de convoitise.

longingly ['lɒŋɪŋlɪ] **adv** (*see* **longing**) *look, speak, think* avec désir *or* envie *or* nostalgie *or* regret *or* convoitise.

longish ['lɒŋɪʃ] **adj** assez long (*f* longue); *book, play etc* assez long, longuet* (*slightly pej*). **(for) a ~ time** assez longtemps.

longitude ['lɒŋgɪtju:d] **n** longitude *f*. **at a ~ of 48°** par 48° de longitude.

longitudinal [ˌlɒŋgɪ'tju:dɪnl] **adj** longitudinal.

longitudinally [ˌlɒŋgɪ'tju:dɪnəlɪ] **adv** longitudinalement.

long-term ['lɒŋ'tɜ:m] **adj** *loan, policy* à long terme; *view, interests, relationship* à long terme, à longue échéance. **~ car park** parc *m* de stationnement; **the ~ unemployed** les chômeurs *mpl* de longue durée; *see also* **long**[1] **1b**.

loo* [lu:] **n** (*Brit*) cabinets *mpl*, W.-C. *mpl*. **the ~'s blocked** les W.-C. *or* cabinets sont bouchés; **he's in the ~** il est au petit coin* *or* aux W.-C. *or* aux cabinets.

loofah ['lu:fəʳ] **n** (*Brit*) luffa *m or* loofa *m*.

look [lʊk] 1 **n** a **to have** *or* **take a ~ at sth** regarder qch, jeter un coup d'œil à qch, (*in order to repair it etc*) jeter un coup d'œil à qch, s'occuper de qch; **to take another** *or* **a second ~ at sth** examiner qch de plus près; **to take a good ~ at sth** regarder qch de près, examiner qch; **to take a good ~ at sb** regarder qn avec attention, observer qn; **take a good ~ at it!** *or* **him!** regarde-le bien!; **let me have a ~** faites voir, laissez-moi regarder; **let me have another ~** laissez-moi regarder encore une fois; **do you want a ~?** tu veux voir? *or* regarder? *or* jeter un coup d'œil?; **take** *or* **have a ~ at this!** regarde-moi ça!, regarde un peu ça!*; **have a ~ through the telescope** regarde dans *or* avec le télescope; **I've had a ~ inside the house** j'ai visité la maison; **to have a ~ round the house** faire un tour dans la maison; **I just want to have a ~ round** (*in town*) je veux simplement faire un tour; (*in a shop*) je ne fais que regarder; **a good long ~ at the car revealed that ...** un examen *or* une inspection de la voiture a révélé que ... .

b regard *m*. **an inquiring ~** un regard interrogateur; **with a nasty ~ in his eye** avec un regard méchant; **he gave me a furious ~** il m'a jeté un regard furieux, il m'a regardé d'un air furieux; **we got some very odd ~s** les gens nous regardaient d'un drôle d'air; **I told her what I thought and if ~s could kill* I'd be dead** je lui ai dit mon opinion et elle m'a fusillé *or* foudroyé du regard; *see* **black, dirty, long**[1] *etc*.

c (*search*) **to have a ~ for sth** chercher qch; **have another ~!** cherche encore une fois!; **I've had a good ~ for it already** je l'ai déjà cherché partout.

d (*appearance etc*) aspect *m*, air *m*, allure *f*. **he had the ~ of a sailor** il avait l'air d'un marin; **she has a ~ of her mother (about her)** elle a quelque chose de sa mère; **there was a sad ~ about him** il avait l'air plutôt triste, son allure avait quelque chose de triste; **I like the ~ of her** je lui trouve l'air sympathique *or* une bonne tête*; **I don't like the ~(s) of him** je n'aime pas son allure *or* son air, il a une tête qui ne me revient pas*; **I don't like the ~ of this at all** ça ne me plaît pas du tout, ça ne me dit rien qui vaille; **you can't go by ~s** on ne peut pas se fier aux apparences, l'habit ne fait pas le moine (*Prov*); **by the ~(s) of him** à le voir, à voir sa tête*; **by the ~(s) of it, by the ~(s) of things*** de toute apparence; **(good) ~s** beauté *f*; **she has kept her ~s** elle est restée belle; **she's losing her ~s** sa beauté se fane, elle n'est plus aussi belle qu'autrefois; **~s aren't everything** la beauté n'est pas tout; (*Fashion*) **the leather ~** la mode du cuir.

2 **comp** ►**look-alike*** sosie *m*; **a Churchill look-alike** un sosie de Churchill ►**looked-for** *result* attendu, prévu; *effect* escompté, recherché ►**look-in***: (*visit*) **to give sb a look-in** passer voir qn, faire une visite éclair *or* un saut chez qn; (*chance*) **with such competition we shan't get a look-in** avec de tels concurrents nous n'avons pas le moindre espoir *or* la moindre chance; **our team didn't have** *or* **get a look-in** notre équipe n'a jamais eu le moindre espoir *or* la moindre chance de gagner ►**look-out** *see* **look-out** ►**look-see**‡: **to have** *or* **to take a look-see** jeter un coup d'œil, donner un œil* ►**look-up** (*Comput*) **n** consultation *f* ◊ **adj** *list etc* à consulter.

3 **vi** a (*see, glance: see also* **look at**) regarder. **~ over there!** regarde là-bas! *or* par là!; **~!** regarde!; **just ~!** regarde un peu!; **~ and see if it's still there** regarde voir un peu* si c'est encore là; **let me ~** laisse-moi voir; **~ who's here!** regarde qui est là!; **~ what a mess you've made!** regarde le gâchis que tu as fait!; **~ here, we must discuss it first** écoutez, il faut d'abord en discuter; **~ here, I didn't say that at all!** dites donc, je n'ai jamais dit ça!; **to ~ the other way** (*lit*) regarder ailleurs *or* de l'autre côté; (*fig*) fermer les yeux (*fig*); **you must ~ on the bright side** il faut avoir de l'optimisme, il faut voir les bons côtés de la situation; (*Prov*) **~ before you leap** il ne faut pas se lancer à l'aveuglette *or* s'engager les yeux fermés; **to ~ about** *or* **around one** regarder autour de soi; **he ~ed around him for an ashtray** il a cherché un cendrier (des yeux); **to ~ ahead** (*in front*) regarder devant soi; (*to future*) se tourner vers l'avenir, considérer l'avenir; **~ing ahead to the future ...** si nous nous tournons vers l'avenir ...; **to ~ down one's nose at sb*** regarder qn de haut; **she ~s down her nose at suburban houses*** elle fait la moue devant *or* elle dédaigne les pavillons de banlieue; **to ~ down the list** parcourir la liste; **she ~ed into his eyes** elle a plongé son regard dans le sien; **to ~ over sb's shoulder** (*lit*) regarder par-dessus l'épaule de qn; (*fig*) surveiller qn constamment; (*fig*) **to ~ over one's shoulder** faire attention à soi; (*fig*) **he ~ed right through me** il m'a regardé sans me voir.

b *[building]* donner, regarder. **the house ~s east** la maison donne *or* regarde à l'est; **the house ~s on to the main street** la maison donne sur la grand-rue.

c (*search*) chercher, regarder. **you should have ~ed more carefully** tu aurais dû chercher plus soigneusement, tu aurais dû mieux regarder; **you can't have ~ed far** tu n'as pas dû beaucoup chercher *or* bien regarder.

d (*+ adj or noun complement: seem*) sembler, paraître, avoir l'air. **she ~s (as if she is) tired** elle semble fatiguée, elle a l'air fatigué(e), on dirait qu'elle est fatiguée; **that story ~s interesting** cette histoire a l'air intéressante *or* semble intéressante; **how pretty you ~!** que vous êtes jolie!; **he ~s older than that** il a l'air plus vieux que ça; **you ~** *or* **you're ~ing well** vous avez bonne mine; **she doesn't ~ well** elle n'a pas bonne mine, elle a mauvaise mine; **he doesn't ~ himself, he's not ~ing himself** il n'a pas l'air bien, il n'a pas l'air en forme *or* dans son assiette*; **he ~s (about) 40** il a l'air d'avoir 40 ans, on lui donnerait 40 ans; **he ~s about 75 kilos/1 metre 80** il a l'air de faire environ 75 kilos/1 mètre 80; **she ~s her age** elle fait son âge; **she doesn't ~ her age** elle ne fait pas son âge, elle porte bien son âge; **she's tired and she ~s it** elle est fatiguée et ça se voit; **he's a soldier and he ~s it** il est soldat et il en a bien l'air; **she ~s her best in blue** c'est le bleu qui lui va le mieux; **you must ~ your best for this interview** il faut que tu sois à ton avantage *or* sur ton trente et un* pour cette interview; **they made me ~ a fool** *or* **foolish** ils m'ont fait paraître ridicule, à cause d'eux j'ai eu l'air ridicule; (*fig*) **to make sb ~ small** rabaisser qn, diminuer qn; (*fig*) **it made me ~ small** j'ai eu l'air fin!* *or* malin!* (*iro*); (*fig*) **he just does it to ~ big** il fait cela uniquement pour se donner de l'importance; (*fig*) **to ~ the part** avoir le physique *or* la tête de l'emploi; **don't ~ like that!** (*sad, cross*) n'ayez pas cet air-là!, ne faites pas cette tête-là!; (*surprised*) ne faites pas des yeux comme ça!; **try to ~ as if you're glad to see them!** essaie d'avoir l'air content de les voir!; **~ alive!*** remue-toi!*; **~ lively*** *or* **~ smart*** *or* **~ snappy* (about it)!, ~ sharp about it!*** dépêche-toi!, grouille-toi!‡; **he ~s good in uniform** l'uniforme lui va bien *or* lui sied; **that dress ~s good** *or* **well on her** cette robe lui va bien; **that hat makes her ~ old** ce chapeau la vieillit; **how did she ~?, what did she ~ like?** (*health*) est-ce qu'elle avait bonne mine?; (*on hearing news etc*) quelle tête *or* quelle mine faisait-elle?; **how do I ~?** (*in these clothes*) est-ce que ça va? *or* ça ira?; (*in this new dress etc*) est-ce que ça me va?; **that ~s good** *[food]* cela a l'air bon; *[brooch, picture etc]* cela fait très bien *or* très joli; *[plan, book, idea]* ça a l'air intéressant *or* prometteur; **it doesn't ~ right** (on dirait qu')il y a quelque chose qui ne va pas; **it ~s all right to me** ça m'a l'air d'aller, je trouve que ça va, à mon avis ça va; **how does it ~ to you?** qu'en pensez-vous?, ça va à votre avis?; **it ~s promising** c'est prometteur; **it will ~ bad** cela fera mauvais effet; **it ~s good on paper** c'est *or* cela fait très bien sur le papier *or* en théorie; **it ~s as if it's going to snow** j'ai l'impression *or* on dirait qu'il va neiger; **it ~s as if he isn't coming, it doesn't ~ as if he's coming** il n'a pas l'air de venir; **it ~s to me as if he isn't coming, it doesn't ~ to me as if he's coming** j'ai l'impression qu'il ne va pas venir; **what does it ~ like?** comment est-ce?, cela ressemble à quoi?, ça a l'air de quoi?*; **what does he ~ like?** comment est-il?; **he ~s like his brother** il ressemble à son frère; **he ~s like a soldier** il a l'air d'un soldat, on dirait un soldat; (*pej*) **she ~ed like nothing on earth*** (*badly dressed*) elle avait l'air d'un épouvantail *or* de Dieu sait quoi; (*ill, depressed*) elle avait une tête épouvantable; **the picture doesn't ~ like him at all** le portrait n'est pas du tout ressemblant *or* ne lui ressemble pas du tout; **it ~s like salt** ça a l'air d'être du sel, on dirait du sel; **this ~s to me like the shop** cela m'a l'air d'être le magasin; **it ~s like rain** j'ai l'impression *or* on dirait qu'il va pleuvoir; **the rain doesn't ~ like stopping** la pluie n'a pas l'air de (vouloir) s'arrêter; **it certainly ~s like it** c'est bien probable, ça m'en a tout l'air; **the evening ~ed like being interesting** la soirée promettait d'être intéressante.

4 **vt** a regarder. **to ~ sb in the face** *or* **in the eye(s)** regarder qn en face *or* dans les yeux; **she ~ed him full in the face/straight in the eye** elle l'a regardé bien en face/droit dans les yeux; (*fig*) **I couldn't ~ him in the face** *or* **in the eye** je n'osais (*or* je n'oserais) pas le regarder en face; (*Prov*) **never ~ a gift horse in the mouth** à cheval donné on ne regarde pas la bride (*Prov*); **to ~ sb up and down** toiser qn, regarder qn de haut en bas; **to ~ daggers at sb** fusiller *or* foudroyer qn du

regard; (*liter*) **to ~ one's last on sth** jeter un ultime regard sur qch.

b (*pay attention to*) regarder, faire attention à. **~ where you're going!** regarde *or* fais attention où tu vas!; **~ what you've done now!** regarde ce que tu as fait! *or* ce que tu viens de faire!

►**look about** vi regarder autour de soi. **to look about for sb/sth** chercher qn/qch (des yeux).

►**look after** vt fus a (*take care of*) *invalid, animal, plant* s'occuper de, soigner; *one's possessions* faire attention à, prendre soin de. **she doesn't look after herself very well** elle ne se soigne pas assez, elle néglige sa santé; **look after yourself!*** fais bien attention à toi!*, prends soin de toi!; **she's quite old enough to look after herself** elle est bien assez grande pour se défendre* *or* se débrouiller* toute seule; **he certainly looks after his car** il entretient bien sa voiture; **we're well looked after here** on s'occupe bien de nous ici, on nous soigne bien ici.

b (*take responsibility for*) *child* garder, s'occuper de; *shop, business* s'occuper de; *sb's book, house, jewels* surveiller, avoir l'œil sur; (*keep temporarily*) garder (*sth for sb* qch pour qn). **to look after one's own interests** protéger ses propres intérêts.

►**look around** vi = **look about**.

►**look at** vt fus a (*observe*) *person, object* regarder. **to look hard at** *person* regarder fixement, dévisager; *thing* regarder *or* examiner de très près; **just look at this mess!** regarde un peu ce fouillis!*; **just look at you!** regarde de quoi tu as l'air!; **to look at him you would never think (that) ...** à le voir on ne penserait jamais que ...; **it isn't much to look at, it's nothing to look at** ça ne paie pas de mine.

b (*consider*) *situation, problem* considérer, voir. **that's one way of looking at it** c'est une façon de voir les choses, c'est un point de vue parmi d'autres; **that's his way of looking at things** c'est comme ça qu'il voit les choses; **it depends (on) how you look at it** tout dépend comment on voit *or* envisage la chose; **just look at him now!** regarde où il en est aujourd'hui!; **let's look at the facts** considérons les faits.

c (*fig: +neg: reject*) rejeter immédiatement. **they wouldn't look at my proposal** ils n'ont même pas pris ma proposition en considération, ils ont immédiatement rejeté ma proposition; **I wouldn't look at the job** je n'accepterais ce poste pour rien au monde; **the landlady won't look at foreigners** la propriétaire ne veut pas avoir affaire à des étrangers.

d (*check*) vérifier; (*see to*) s'occuper de. **will you look at the carburettor?** pourriez-vous vérifier le carburateur?; **I'll look at it tomorrow** je m'en occuperai demain.

►**look away** vi détourner les yeux *or* le regard (*from* de), regarder ailleurs.

►**look back** vi a regarder derrière soi. **he looked back at the church** il s'est retourné pour regarder l'église. b (*in memory*) regarder en arrière, revenir sur le passé. **to look back on sth** revoir qch en esprit, évoquer qch, penser à qch; **we can look back on 20 years of happy marriage** nous avons derrière nous 20 ans de bonheur conjugal; **after that he never looked back*** après, ça n'a fait qu'aller de mieux en mieux.

►**look down** vi baisser les yeux. **to look down at the ground** regarder à terre; **don't look down or you'll fall** ne regarde pas par terre *or* en bas, tu vas tomber; **he looked down on** *or* **at the town from the hilltop** il a regardé la ville du haut de la colline; **the castle looks down on the valley** le château domine la vallée; (*fig: show disdain for*) **to look down on sb** regarder qn de haut, mépriser qn; **to look down on an offer** faire fi d'une offre; **to look down on an attitude** mépriser une attitude.

►**look for** 1 vt fus a (*seek*) *object, work* chercher. **he goes around looking for trouble*** il cherche toujours les embêtements. b (*expect*) *praise, reward* attendre, espérer. 2 **looked-for** adj *see* **look 2**.

►**look forward to** vt fus *event, meal, trip, holiday* attendre avec impatience. **I'm looking forward to seeing you** j'attends avec impatience le plaisir de vous voir, je suis impatient de vous voir; (*in letter*) **looking forward to hearing from you** en espérant avoir bientôt une lettre de vous, dans l'attente de votre réponse (*frm*); **I look forward to the day when** j'attends avec impatience le jour où, je pense d'avance au jour où; **are you looking forward to it?** est-ce que vous êtes content à cette perspective?; **we've been looking forward to it for weeks** nous y pensons avec impatience depuis des semaines; **I'm so (much) looking forward to it** je m'en réjouis à l'avance, je m'en fais déjà une fête.

►**look in** 1 vi a (*lit*) regarder à l'intérieur. **to look in at the window** regarder par la fenêtre (*vers l'intérieur*). b (*pay visit*) passer (voir). **we looked in at Robert's** nous sommes passés chez Robert, nous avons fait un saut *or* un tour* chez Robert; **to look in on sb** passer voir qn; **the doctor will look in again tomorrow** le docteur repassera demain. c (**: watch television*) regarder la télévision. **we look in every evening** nous regardons la télé* tous les soirs. 2 **look-in** n *see* **look 2**.

►**look into** vt fus (*examine*) examiner, étudier; (*investigate*) se renseigner sur. **I shall look into it** je vais me renseigner là-dessus, je vais m'en occuper; **we must look into what happened to the money** il va falloir que nous enquêtions (*subj*) sur ce qui est arrivé à cet argent; **the complaint is being looked into** on examine la plainte; **we shall look into the question/the possibility of ...** nous allons étudier *or* examiner la question/la possibilité de ... .

►**look on** 1 vi regarder, être un spectateur (*or* une spectatrice). **they all looked on while the raiders escaped** ils se sont tous contentés de regarder *or* d'être spectateurs alors que les bandits s'enfuyaient; **he wrote the letter while I looked on** il a écrit la lettre tandis que je le regardais faire; **I've forgotten my book, may I look on with you?** j'ai oublié mon livre, puis-je suivre avec vous?

2 vt fus considérer. **to look kindly (up)on sth/sb** approuver qch/qn; **I shall look favourably on your son's application** j'examinerai d'un œil favorable la demande de votre fils; **I do not look on the matter like that** je ne vois *or* ne considère *or* n'envisage pas la chose de cette façon-là; **I look on the French as our rivals** je considère les Français comme *or* je tiens les Français pour nos rivaux.

►**look out** 1 vi a (*lit*) regarder dehors. **to look out of the window** regarder par la fenêtre.

b (*fig*) **I am looking out for a suitable house** je suis à la recherche d'une maison qui convienne, je cherche une maison qui convienne; **look out for the butcher's van and tell me when it's coming** guette la camionnette du boucher et préviens-moi; **look out for a good place to picnic** essaie de repérer un bon endroit pour le pique-nique.

c (*take care*) faire attention, prendre garde. **look out!** attention!, gare!; **I told you to look out!** je t'avais bien dit de faire attention!; **look out for sharks** soyez sur vos gardes *or* méfiez-vous, il y a peut-être des requins; **look out for ice on the road** faites attention au cas où il y aurait du verglas, méfiez-vous du verglas; **look out for the low ceiling** faites attention *or* prenez garde, le plafond est bas; **to look out for oneself** penser à ses propres intérêts.

2 vt sep (*Brit*) chercher et trouver. **I shall look out some old magazines for them** je vais essayer de leur trouver quelques vieux magazines.

3 **look-out** n, comp *see* **look-out**.

►**look over** vt sep *essay* jeter un coup d'œil à, parcourir; *book* parcourir, feuilleter; *town, building* visiter; *person* (*quickly*) jeter un coup d'œil à; (*slowly*) regarder de la tête aux pieds.

►**look round** 1 vi a regarder (autour de soi). (*in shop*) **we just want to look round** on veut seulement regarder, on ne fait que regarder; **I looked round for you after the concert** je vous ai cherché *or* j'ai essayé de vous voir après le concert; **I'm looking round for an assistant** je suis à la recherche d'un assistant, je cherche un assistant. b (*look back*) regarder derrière soi. **I looked round to see where he was** je me suis retourné pour voir où il était; **don't look round!** ne vous retournez pas! 2 vt fus *town, factory* visiter, faire le tour de.

►**look through** vt fus a (*examine*) *papers, book* examiner; (*briefly*) *papers* parcourir; *book* parcourir, feuilleter. b (*revise*) *lesson* réviser, repasser; (*reread*) *notes* revoir, relire.

►**look to** vt fus a (*attend to*) faire attention à, veiller à. **look to it that it doesn't happen again** faites attention que *or* veillez à ce que cela ne se reproduise pas; **to look to the future** regarder vers l'avenir; *see* **laurel**. b (*look after*) s'occuper de. **look to the children** occupe-toi des enfants. c **to look to sb for sth** (*gen*) compter sur qn pour qch; **I look to you for help** je compte sur votre aide; **I always look to my mother for advice** quand j'ai besoin d'un conseil je me tourne vers ma mère.

►**look up** 1 vi a regarder en haut; (*from reading etc*) lever les yeux. (*fig: respect*) **to look up to sb** respecter qn, avoir du respect pour qn.

b (*improve*) [*prospects*] s'améliorer; [*business*] reprendre; [*weather*] se lever. **things are looking up (for you)** ça va mieux *or* ça s'améliore (pour vous); **oil shares are looking up** les actions pétrolières remontent *or* sont en hausse.

2 vt sep a *person* aller *or* venir voir. **look me up the next time you are in London** venez *or* passez me voir la prochaine fois que vous serez à Londres.

b (*search*) *name, word* chercher. **to look sb up in the phone book** chercher qn dans l'annuaire (du téléphone); **to look up a name on a list** chercher un nom sur une liste; **to look up a word in the dictionary** chercher un mot dans le dictionnaire; **you'll have to look that one up** il faut que tu cherches (*subj*) (ce que cela veut dire *or* ce que c'est *etc*).

3 vt fus *reference book* consulter, chercher *or* vérifier dans.

4 **look-up** *see* **look 2**.

►**look upon** vt fus = **look on 2**.

looker [ˈlʊkəʳ] 1 n (*) **she's a good ~, she's a (real) ~** c'est une jolie fille, c'est un beau brin de fille; **he's a (good) ~** c'est un beau gars*. 2 comp ►**looker-on** spectateur *m*, -trice *f*, badaud(e) *m(f)*.

-looking [ˈlʊkɪŋ] adj ending in comps: **ugly-looking** laid (d'aspect); **sinister-looking** à l'air sinistre; *see* **good** *etc*.

looking-glass [ˈlʊkɪŋglɑːs] n glace *f*, miroir *m*.

look-out [ˈlʊkaʊt] 1 n a (*observation*) surveillance *f*, guet *m*. **to keep a ~, to be on the ~** faire le guet, guetter; **to keep a ~ for sb/sth** guetter qn/qch; **to be on the ~ for bargains** être à l'affût des bonnes affaires; **to be on the ~ for danger** être sur ses gardes à cause d'un danger éventuel; **to be on ~ (duty)** (*Mil*) être au guet; (*Naut*) être en vigie; *see* **sharp**.

b (*observer*) (*gen*) guetteur *m*; (*Mil*) homme *m* de guet, guetteur; (*Naut*) homme de veille *or* de vigie, vigie *f*.

c (*observation post*) (*gen, Mil*) poste *m* de guet; (*Naut*) vigie *f*.

d (**: esp Brit: outlook*) perspective *f*. **it's a poor ~ for cotton** les perspectives pour le coton ne sont pas brillantes; **it's a grim ~ for people like us** la situation *or* ça s'annonce mal pour les gens comme nous; **that's your ~!** cela vous regarde!, c'est votre affaire!

2 comp *tower* d'observation ▶**look-out post** (*Mil*) poste *m* de guet *or* d'observation.

loom¹ [luːm] vi (*also* ~ **up**) (*appear*) *[building, mountain]* apparaître indistinctement, se dessiner; *[figure, ship]* surgir; (*fig*) *[danger]* menacer; *[event, crisis]* être imminent. **the ship ~ed (up) out of the mist** le navire a surgi de *or* dans la brume; **the skyscraper ~ed up out of the fog** le gratte-ciel est apparu indistinctement *or* s'est dessiné dans le brouillard; **the dark mountains ~ed (up) in front of us** les sombres montagnes sont apparues *or* se sont dressées menaçantes devant nous; **the possibility of defeat ~ed (up) before him** la possibilité de la défaite s'est présentée à son esprit; **the threat of an epidemic ~ed large in their minds** la menace d'une épidémie était au premier plan de leurs préoccupations; **the exams are ~ing large*** les examens sont dangereusement proches.

loom² [luːm] n (*Tex*) métier *m* à tisser.

loon [luːn] n a (*†: *dial*) (*fool*) imbécile *m*, idiot *m*; (*good-for-nothing*) vaurien *m*. b (*US Orn*) plongeon *m* arctique, huard *m or* huart *m*.

loony‡ ['luːnɪ] 1 n timbré(e)* *m(f)*, cinglé(e)* *m(f)*. ~ **bin** maison *f* de fous, asile *m* (d'aliénés); **in the ~ bin** chez les fous. 2 adj timbré*, cinglé*.

loop [luːp] 1 n a (*in string, ribbon, writing*) boucle *f*; (*in river*) méandre *m*, boucle. **the string has a ~ in it** la ficelle fait une boucle; **to put a ~ in sth** faire une boucle à qch; *see* **knock**.

b (*Elec*) circuit fermé; (*Comput*) boucle *f*; (*Rail: also* ~ **line**) voie *f* d'évitement; (*by motorway etc*) bretelle *f*.

c (*Med: contraceptive*) **the ~** le stérilet.

d (*curtain fastener*) embrasse *f*.

2 comp ▶**loophole** (*Archit*) meurtrière *f*; (*fig: in law, argument, regulations*) point *m* faible, lacune *f*; (*fig*) **we must try to find a loophole** il faut que nous trouvions (*subj*) une échappatoire *or* une porte de sortie*.

3 vt *string etc* faire une boucle à, boucler. **he ~ed the rope round the post** il a passé la corde autour du poteau; (*Aviat*) **to ~ the loop** faire un looping, boucler la boucle.

4 vi former une boucle.

▶**loop back** 1 vi *[road, river]* former une boucle; (*Comput*) se reboucler. 2 vt sep *curtain* retenir *or* relever avec une embrasse.

▶**loop up** vt sep = **loop back 2**.

loose [luːs] 1 adj a (*not firmly attached*) *knot, shoelace* qui se défait, desserré; *screw* desserré, qui a du jeu; *stone, brick* branlant; *tooth* qui branle, qui bouge; *page from book* détaché; *hair* dénoué, flottant; *animal etc* (*free*) en liberté; (*escaped*) échappé; (*freed*) lâché. **to be coming** *or* **getting** *or* **working ~** *[knot]* se desserrer, se défaire; *[screw]* se desserrer, avoir du jeu; *[stone, brick]* branler; *[tooth]* branler, bouger; *[page]* se détacher; *[hair]* se dénouer, se défaire; **to have come ~** *[knot]* s'être défait; *[screw]* s'être desserré; *[stone, brick]* branler; *[tooth]* branler, bouger; *[page]* s'être détaché; *[hair]* s'être dénoué; *[animal etc]* **to get ~** s'échapper; **to tear (o.s.) ~** se dégager; **to tear sth ~** détacher qch (en déchirant); **to let** *or* **set** *or* **turn an animal ~** libérer *or* lâcher un animal; **to let the dogs ~ on sb** lâcher les chiens sur qn; **we can't let him ~ on that class** on ne peut pas le lâcher dans cette classe; **one of your buttons is very ~** l'un de tes boutons va tomber *or* se découd; **write it on a ~ sheet of paper** écrivez-le sur une feuille volante; (*to pupil*) écrivez-le sur une (feuille de) copie; (*on roadway*) ~ **chippings** gravillons *mpl*; (*Elec*) ~ **connection** mauvais contact; (*Brit*) *[furniture]* ~ **covers** housses *fpl*; **the reins hung ~** les rênes n'étaient pas tenues *or* tendues, les rênes étaient sur le cou; ~ **end of a rope** bout pendant *or* ballant d'une corde; (*fig*) **to be at a ~ end** ne pas trop savoir quoi faire, ne pas savoir quoi faire de sa peau*; (*fig*) **to tie up ~ ends** régler les détails qui restent; **hang** *or* **stay ~!‡** relax!*; *see* **break, cut, hell, screw** *etc*.

b (*Comm: not packed*) *biscuits, carrots etc* en vrac; *butter, cheese* au poids. **the potatoes were ~ in the bottom of the basket** les pommes de terre étaient à même au fond du panier; **just put them ~ into the basket** mettez-les à même *or* tels quels dans le panier; ~ **change** petite *or* menue monnaie.

c (*not tight*) *skin* flasque, mou (*f* molle); *coat, dress* (*not close-fitting*) vague, ample; (*not tight enough*) lâche, large; *collar* lâche. **these trousers are too ~ round the waist** ce pantalon est trop large *or* lâche à la taille; ~ **clothes are better for summer wear** l'été il vaut mieux porter des vêtements vagues *or* flottants *or* pas trop ajustés; **the rope round the dog's neck was quite ~** la corde passée au cou du chien était toute lâche; *see* **play**.

d (*pej*) *woman* facile, de mœurs légères; *morals* relâché, douteux. **to lead a ~ life** mener une vie dissolue; ~ **living** vie dissolue, débauche *f*; ~ **talk** propos grossiers.

e (*not strict*) *discipline* relâché; *reasoning, thinking* confus, vague, imprécis; *style* lâche, relâché; *translation* approximatif, assez libre; *organization* peu structuré. **a ~ interpretation of the rules** une interprétation peu rigoureuse du règlement; *see* **hang 2a**.

f (*available*) *funds* disponible, liquide.

g (*not compact*) *soil* meuble; (*fig*) *association, link* vague. **there is a ~ connection between the two theories** il y a un vague lien entre les deux théories; (*Rugby*) ~ **scrum** mêlée ouverte; **a ~ weave** un tissu lâche (*see also* **2**); (*Med*) **his bowels are ~** ses intestins sont relâchés.

2 comp ▶**loose box** (*Brit: for horses*) box *m* ▶**loose-fitting** vague, ample, qui n'est pas ajusté ▶**loose-leaf(ed)** à feuilles volantes, à feuilles *or* feuillets mobiles ▶**loose-leaf binder** classeur *m* (*dossier*) ▶**loose-limbed** agile ▶**loose-weave** *material* lâche; *curtains* en tissu lâche.

3 n *[prisoner]* **on the ~*** en cavale; **there was a crowd of kids on the ~* in the town** il y avait une bande de jeunes qui traînait dans les rues sans trop savoir quoi faire; **a gang of hooligans on the ~*** une bande de voyous déchaînés; (*Rugby*) **in the ~** dans la mêlée ouverte.

4 vt a (*undo*) défaire; (*untie*) délier, dénouer; *screw etc* desserrer; (*free*) *animal* lâcher; *prisoner* relâcher, mettre en liberté. **to ~ a boat (from its moorings)** démarrer une embarcation, larguer les amarres; **they ~d the dogs on him** ils ont lâché les chiens après *or* sur lui.

b (*also* ~ **off**) *gun* décharger (*on or at sb* sur qn); *arrow* tirer (*on or at sb* sur qn); *violence etc* déclencher (*on* contre). **they ~d (off) missiles at the invaders** ils ont fait pleuvoir des projectiles sur les envahisseurs; (*fig*) **to ~ (off) a volley of abuse at sb** déverser un torrent *or* lâcher une bordée d'injures sur qn.

▶**loose off** 1 vi (*shoot*) tirer (*at sb* sur qn). 2 vt sep = **loose 4b**.

loosely ['luːslɪ] adv a (*not tightly*) *attach, tie, hold* sans serrer; *be fixed* lâchement, sans être serré; *weave* lâchement; *associate* vaguement. **the reins hung ~** les rênes pendaient sur le cou. b (*imprecisely*) *translate* sans trop de rigueur, assez librement, approximativement. **this is ~ translated as ...** ceci est traduit approximativement *or* de façon assez libre par ...; **that word is ~ used to mean ...** on emploie ce mot de façon plutôt impropre pour dire ... .

loosen ['luːsn] 1 vt a (*slacken*) *screw, belt, knot* desserrer; *rope* détendre, relâcher; (*untie*) *knot, shoelace* défaire; (*fig*) *emotional ties* distendre; (*fig*) *laws, restrictions* assouplir. **first ~ the part then remove it gently** il faut d'abord donner du jeu à *or* ébranler la pièce puis tirer doucement; **to ~ one's grip on sth** relâcher son étreinte sur qch; (*fig*) **to ~ sb's tongue** délier la langue à qn. b (*Agr*) *soil* rendre meuble, ameublir. (*Med*) **to ~ the bowels** relâcher les intestins. 2 vi *[fastening]* se défaire; *[screw]* se desserrer, jouer; *[knot]* (*slacken*) se desserrer; (*come undone*) se défaire; *[rope]* se détendre.

▶**loosen up** 1 vi a (*limber up*) faire des exercices d'assouplissement; (*before race etc*) s'échauffer. b (*become less shy*) se dégeler, perdre sa timidité. c (*become less strict with*) **to loosen up on sb*** se montrer plus coulant* *or* moins strict envers qn. 2 vt sep: **to loosen up one's muscles** faire des exercices d'assouplissement; (*before race etc*) s'échauffer.

looseness ['luːsnɪs] n a *[knot]* desserrement *m*; *[screw, tooth]* jeu *m*; *[rope]* relâchement *m*; *[clothes]* ampleur *f*, flou *m*. **the ~ of the knot caused the accident** l'accident est arrivé parce que le nœud n'était pas assez serré. b *[translation]* imprécision *f*; *[thought, style]* manque *m* de rigueur *or* de précision. c (*immorality*) *[behaviour]* licence *f*; *[morals]* relâchement *m*. d *[soil]* ameublissement *m*. (*Med*) ~ **of the bowels** relâchement *m* des intestins.

loot [luːt] 1 n (*plunder*) butin *m*; (‡ *fig: prizes, gifts etc*) butin; (‡: *money*) pognon‡ *m*, fric‡ *m*, argent *m*. 2 vt *town* piller, mettre à sac; *shop, goods* piller. 3 vi: **to go ~ing** se livrer au pillage.

looter ['luːtəʳ] n pillard *m*.

looting ['luːtɪŋ] n pillage *m*.

lop [lɒp] vt *tree* tailler, élaguer, émonder; *branch* couper.

▶**lop off** vt sep *branch, piece* couper; *head* trancher.

lope [ləʊp] vi courir en bondissant. **to ~ along/in/out** *etc* avancer/entrer/sortir *etc* en bondissant.

lop-eared ['lɒpˌɪəd] adj aux oreilles pendantes.

lop-sided ['lɒp'saɪdɪd] adj (*not straight*) de travers, de guingois*; *smile* de travers; (*asymmetric*) disproportionné.

loquacious [lə'kweɪʃəs] adj loquace, bavard.

loquacity [lə'kwæsɪtɪ] n loquacité *f*, volubilité *f*.

lord [lɔːd] 1 n a seigneur *m*. ~ **of the manor** châtelain *m*; (*hum*) ~ **and master** seigneur et maître *m* (*hum*); (*Brit*) **L~ (John) Smith** lord (John) Smith; **the (House of) L~s** la Chambre des Lords; **my L~ Bishop of Tooting** (Monseigneur) l'évêque de Tooting; **my L~** Monsieur le baron (*or* comte *etc*); (*to judge*) Monsieur le Juge; (*to bishop*) Monseigneur, Excellence; *see* **law, live¹, sea** *etc*.

b (*Rel*) **the L~** le Seigneur; **Our L~** Notre Seigneur; **the L~ Jesus** le Seigneur Jésus; **the L~'s supper** l'Eucharistie *f*, la sainte Cène; **the L~'s prayer** le Notre-Père; **the L~'s day** le jour du Seigneur; **good L~!*** Seigneur!, mon Dieu!, bon sang!*; **oh L~!*** Seigneur!, zut!*; **L~ knows what/who** *etc* * Dieu sait quoi/qui *etc*.

2 vt (*) **to ~ it** vivre en grand seigneur, mener la grande vie; **to ~ it over sb** traiter qn avec arrogance *or* de haut.

3 comp ▶**Lord Advocate** (*Scot Jur*) ≃ Procureur *m* de la République ▶**Lord Chamberlain** (*Brit*) grand chambellan ▶**Lord Chancellor** = **Lord High Chancellor** ▶**Lord Chief Justice (of England)** (*Jur*) Président *m* de la Haute Cour de Justice ▶**Lord High Chancellor** (*Jur, Parl*) Grand Chancelier d'Angleterre ▶**Lord High**

Commissioner *représentant de la Couronne à l'Assemblée générale de l'église d'Écosse* ▸**Lord Justice of Appeal** (*Jur*) juge *m* à la Cour d'appel ▸**Lord Lieutenant** *représentant de la Couronne dans un comté* ▸**Lord Mayor** *titre du maire des principales villes anglaises et galloises* ▸**Lord of Appeal (in Ordinary)** (*Jur*) juge *m* de la Cour de cassation (*siégeant à la Chambre des Lords*) ▸**Lord President of the Council** (*Parl*) Président *m* du Conseil privé de la reine ▸**Lord Privy Seal** (*Parl*) lord *m* du Sceau privé ▸**Lord Provost** *titre du maire des principales villes écossaises* ▸**lords-and-ladies** (*flower*) pied-de-veau *m* ▸**Lord spiritual/temporal** (*Parl*) *membre ecclésiastique/laïque de la Chambre des Lords*.

lordliness ['lɔːdlɪnɪs] **n** (*see* **lordly**) noblesse *f*, majesté *f*; magnificence *f*; (*pej*) hauteur *f*, arrogance *f*, morgue *f*.

lordly ['lɔːdlɪ] **adj** (*dignified*) *bearing* noble, majestueux; (*magnificent*) *castle* seigneurial, magnifique; (*pej: arrogant*) *person, manner* hautain, arrogant, plein de morgue. ~ **contempt** mépris souverain.

lordship ['lɔːdʃɪp] **n** (*rights, property*) seigneurie *f*; (*power*) autorité *f* (*over* sur). **Your L~** Monsieur le comte (*or* le baron *etc*); (*to judge*) Monsieur le Juge; (*to bishop*) Monseigneur, Excellence.

lore [lɔːʳ] **n** (*NonC*) **a** (*traditions*) tradition(s) *f(pl)*, coutumes *fpl*, usages *mpl*; *see* **folk** *etc*. **b** (*knowledge: gen in comps*) **his bird/wood ~** sa (grande) connaissance des oiseaux/de la vie dans les forêts.

Lorenzo [lə'renzəʊ] **n** Laurent *m*. ~ **the magnificent** Laurent le Magnifique.

lorgnette [lɔː'njet] **n** (*eyeglasses*) face-à-main *m*; (*opera glasses*) lorgnette *f*, jumelles *fpl* de spectacle.

Lorraine [lɒ'reɪn] **n** Lorraine *f*. **Cross of ~** croix *f* de Lorraine.

lorry ['lɒrɪ] (*Brit*) **1 n** camion *m*, poids *m* lourd. **to transport by ~** transporter par camion, camionner; *see* **articulate**. **2 comp** ▸**lorry driver** camionneur *m*, conducteur *m* de poids lourd; (*long-distance*) routier *m* ▸**lorry load** chargement *m*.

Los Angeles [lɒs'ændʒɪ,liːz] **n** Los Angeles.

lose [luːz] **pret, ptp lost 1 vt a** *person, job, limb, game, book, key, plane, enthusiasm* perdre; (*mislay*) *glove, key etc* égarer; *opportunity* manquer, perdre. **he got lost in the wood** il s'est perdu *or* égaré dans le bois; **the key got lost during the removal** on a perdu la clef au cours du déménagement; **get lost!*** barre-toi!*, va te faire voir!*; **I lost him in the crowd** je l'ai perdu dans la foule; **I lost my father when I was 10** j'ai perdu mon père à l'âge de 10 ans; [*doctor*] **to ~ a patient** perdre un malade; **to ~ the use of an arm** perdre l'usage d'un bras; **to ~ a bet** perdre un pari; (*in business, gambling etc*) **how much did you ~?** combien avez-vous perdu?; **he lost £1,000 on that deal** il a perdu 1 000 livres dans cette affaire; **you've nothing to ~ (by it)** tu n'as rien à perdre, tu ne risques rien; (*fig*) **you've nothing to ~ by helping him** tu ne perds rien *or* tu n'as rien à perdre *or* tu ne risques rien à l'aider; (*fig*) **you can't ~!** tu ne risques rien!, ça ne peut pas ne pas marcher!; **7,000 jobs lost** 7 000 suppressions *fpl* d'emploi; **two posts have been lost** il y a eu deux suppressions de poste; **100 men were lost** 100 hommes ont péri, on a perdu 100 hommes; **20 lives were lost in the explosion** 20 personnes ont péri dans l'explosion; **the ship was lost with all hands** le navire a été perdu corps et biens; [*person*] **to be lost at sea** périr *or* être perdu en mer; **he didn't ~ a word of ...** il n'a pas perdu un mot de ...; **what he said was lost in the applause** ses paroles se sont perdues dans les applaudissements; **this was not lost on him** cela ne lui a pas échappé; **I lost his last sentence** je n'ai pas entendu sa dernière phrase; **the poem lost a lot in translation** le poème a beaucoup perdu à la traduction; (*after explanation etc*) **you've lost me there*** je ne vous suis plus, je n'y suis plus; *see also* **lost**.

b (*phrases*) **to ~ one's balance** perdre l'équilibre; (*lit, fig*) **to ~ one's bearings** être désorienté; **to ~ one's breath** perdre haleine, s'essouffler; **to have lost one's breath** être hors d'haleine, être à bout de souffle; **to ~ consciousness** perdre connaissance; **to ~ face** perdre la face; **she's lost her figure** elle s'est épaissie, elle a perdu sa ligne; (*Mil, fig*) **to ~ ground** perdre du terrain; **to ~ heart** perdre courage, se décourager; **to ~ one's heart to sb** tomber amoureux de qn; **to ~ interest in sth** se désintéresser de qch; (*Aut*) **he's lost his licence** on lui a retiré *or* il s'est fait retirer son permis de conduire; **to ~ one's life** perdre la vie, mourir; **she's losing her looks** sa beauté se fane, elle n'est plus aussi belle qu'autrefois; **to ~ patience with sb** perdre patience avec qn, s'impatienter contre qn; **to ~ one's rag*** se mettre en rogne*, piquer une rogne*; (*lit, fig*) **to ~ sight of sb/sth** perdre qn/qch de vue; **he didn't ~ any sleep over it** il n'en a pas perdu le sommeil pour autant, ça ne l'a pas empêché de dormir; **don't ~ any sleep over it!** ne vous en faites pas!, dormez sur vos deux oreilles!; **to ~ one's temper** se fâcher, se mettre en colère; **to ~ one's voice because of a cold** perdre sa voix à cause d'un rhume; **to have lost one's voice** avoir une extinction de voix, être aphone; **to ~ one's way** perdre son chemin, se perdre, s'égarer; **we mustn't ~ any time** il ne faut pas perdre de temps; **we must ~ no time in preventing this** nous devons empêcher cela au plus vite; **there's not a minute to ~** il n'y a pas une minute à perdre; *see* **cool, lost** *etc*.

c [*clock etc*] **to ~ 10 minutes a day** retarder de dix minutes par jour.

d (*get rid of*) *unwanted object* renoncer à, se débarrasser de; (*go too fast for*) *competitors, pursuers* devancer, distancer, semer. **to ~ weight** perdre du poids, maigrir; **I lost 2 kilos** j'ai maigri de *or* j'ai perdu 2 kilos; **they had to ~ 100 workers** ils ont dû licencier 100 employés; **he managed to ~ the detective who was following him** il a réussi à semer le détective qui le suivait; **try to ~ him before you come to see us*** essaie de le semer *or* le perdre en route avant de venir nous voir.

e (*cause loss of*) faire perdre, coûter. **that will ~ you your job** cela va vous faire perdre *or* vous coûter votre place; **that lost us the war/the match** cela nous a fait perdre la guerre/le match.

2 vi a [*player, team*] perdre, être perdant. (*Ftbl etc*) **they lost 6-1** ils ont perdu *or* ils se sont fait battre 6-1; **they lost to the new team** ils se sont fait battre par la nouvelle équipe; **our team is losing today** notre équipe est en train de perdre aujourd'hui; (*fig*) **he lost on the deal** il a été perdant dans l'affaire; **you can't ~*** tu n'as rien à perdre (mais tout à gagner), tu ne risques rien; (*fig*) **it ~s in translation** cela perd à la traduction; (*fig*) **the story did not ~ in the telling** l'histoire n'a rien perdu à être racontée.

b [*watch, clock*] retarder.

▸**lose out vi** être perdant. **to lose out on a deal** être perdant dans une affaire; **he lost out on it** il y a été perdant.

loser ['luːzəʳ] **n** perdant(e) *m(f)*. **good/bad ~** bon/mauvais joueur, bonne/mauvaise joueuse; **to come off the ~** être perdant; **he is the ~ by it** il y perd; **he's a born ~** il est né perdant, il est né avec la poisse*, il n'a jamais de veine*; *see* **back**.

losing ['luːzɪŋ] **1 adj** *team, number* perdant; *business, concern* mauvais. **to be on a ~ streak*** *or* **wicket** être en période de déveine*, avoir une série de pertes; (*fig*) **it's a ~ battle** c'est une bataille perdue d'avance, c'est perdu d'avance; (*fig*) **it is a ~ proposition** ce n'est pas du tout rentable. **2 n** (*money losses*) **~s** pertes *fpl*.

loss [lɒs] **1 n a** (*gen*) perte *f*; (*Insurance*) sinistre *m*. **~es amounting to £2 million** des pertes qui s'élèvent (*or* s'élevaient *etc*) à 2 millions de livres; **~ of blood** perte de sang, hémorragie *f*; **~ of heat** perte de chaleur; **there was great ~ of life** il y a eu beaucoup de victimes *or* de nombreuses victimes; **the coup succeeded without ~ of life** le coup (d'État) a réussi sans faire de victimes; (*Mil*) **to suffer heavy ~es** subir des pertes élevées *or* sévères; (*Pol : in election*) **the Labour ~es in the South** les sièges perdus par les travaillistes dans le sud, le recul des travaillistes dans le sud; **the Conservatives have suffered a number of ~es in the North** les conservateurs ont perdu un certain nombre de sièges dans le nord; **it was a comfort to her in her great ~** c'était un réconfort pour elle dans son grand malheur *or* sa grande épreuve; **his death was a great ~ to the company** sa mort a été *or* a représenté une grande perte pour la compagnie; **to suffer a ~ of face** perdre la face; **without ~ of time** sans perte *or* sans perdre de temps; **to sell at a ~** [*salesman*] vendre à perte; [*goods*] se vendre à perte; **selling at a ~** vente *f* à perte; **the car was a total ~** la voiture était bonne pour la ferraille *or* la casse, (*more frm*) le véhicule a été complètement détruit; **he's no great ~*** ce n'est pas une grande *or* une grosse perte, on peut très bien se passer de lui; *see* **cut, dead, profit** *etc*.

b to be at a ~ être perplexe *or* embarrassé; **to be at a ~ to explain sth** être incapable d'expliquer qch, être embarrassé pour expliquer qch; **we are at a ~ to know why he did it** nous ne savons absolument pas *or* il est impossible de savoir pourquoi il l'a fait; **to be at a ~ for words** (*gen*) chercher *or* ne pas trouver ses mots; **he's never at a ~ for words** il n'est jamais à court de mots; **he was at a ~ for words** il ne savait pas quoi dire, il en était bouche bée.

2 comp ▸**loss leader** (*Comm*) article *m* pilote (*vendu à perte pour attirer les clients*) ▸**loss maker** (*Comm*) (*product*) article vendu à perte; (*firm*) entreprise *f* en déficit chronique ▸**loss-making** (*Comm*) *product* vendu à perte; *firm* déficitaire ▸**loss ratio** (*Insurance*) sinistralité *f*.

lost [lɒst] **1 pret, ptp of lose**.

2 adj a (*see* **lose 1a**) perdu; égaré. **all is ~** tout est perdu; **~ cause** cause perdue; **several ~ children were reported** on a signalé plusieurs enfants qui s'étaient perdus; **the ~ generation** la génération perdue; **a ~ opportunity** une occasion manquée *or* perdue; **a ~ soul** une âme en peine; **he was wandering around like a ~ soul** il errait comme une âme en peine; **the ~ sheep** la brebis égarée; **to make up for ~ time** rattraper le temps perdu; **~ property**, (*US*) **~ and found** objets trouvés; **~ property office**, (*US*) **~-and-found department** (bureau *m* des) objets trouvés; (*Press*) **~-and-found columns** (page *f* des) objets perdus et trouvés.

b (*bewildered*) perdu, désorienté; (*uncomprehending*) perdu, perplexe. **it was too difficult for me, I was ~** c'était trop compliqué pour moi, je ne suivais plus *or* j'étais perdu *or* je n'y étais plus; **after his death I felt ~** après sa mort j'étais complètement perdu *or* désorienté *or* déboussolé*; **he had a ~ look in his eyes** *or* **a ~ expression on his face** il avait l'air complètement désorienté.

c (*dead, gone, wasted etc*) perdu. **to give sb/sth up for ~** considérer qn/qch comme perdu; **he was ~ to British science forever** ses dons ont été perdus à jamais pour la science britannique; **he is ~ to all finer feelings** tous les sentiments délicats le dépassent, dans le domaine des sentiments les finesses lui échappent; **my advice was ~ on him** il n'a pas écouté mes conseils, mes conseils ont été en pure perte; **modern**

music is ~ on me je ne comprends pas la musique moderne, la musique moderne me laisse froid; **the remark was ~ on him** il n'a pas compris la remarque.

d (*absorbed*) perdu, plongé (*in* dans), absorbé (*in* par). **to be ~ in one's reading** être plongé dans son livre, être absorbé par sa lecture; **he was ~ in thought** il était plongé dans la réflexion *or* perdu dans ses pensées *or* absorbé par ses pensées; **she is ~ to the world** elle est ailleurs, plus rien n'existe pour elle.

Lot [lɒt] **n** (*Bible*) Lot(h) *m*.

lot [lɒt] **n** a (*destiny*) sort *m*, destinée *f*, lot *m* (*liter*). **it is the common ~** c'est le sort *or* le lot commun; **the hardships that are the ~ of the poor** la dure vie qui est le partage *or* le sort *or* le lot des pauvres; **it was not his ~ to make a fortune** il n'était pas destiné à faire fortune; **her ~ (in life) had not been a happy one** elle n'avait pas eu une vie heureuse; **it fell to my ~ to break the news to her** il m'incomba de *or* il me revint de lui annoncer la nouvelle; **it fell to my ~ to be wounded early in the battle** le sort a voulu que je sois blessé au début de la bataille; **to cast in** *or* **throw in one's ~ with sb** partager (volontairement) le sort de qn, unir sa destinée à celle de qn.

b (*random selection*) tirage *m* au sort, sort *m*. **by ~** par tirage au sort; **the ~ fell on me** le sort est tombé sur moi; **to draw** *or* **cast ~s** tirer au sort.

c (*at auctions etc*) lot *m*. (*Comm*) **there are 3 further ~s of hats to be delivered** il y a encore 3 lots de chapeaux à livrer; **there was only one ~ of recruits still to arrive** il ne manquait plus qu'un lot de recrues; **he's a bad ~*** il ne vaut pas cher*, c'est un mauvais sujet; **you rotten ~!‡** vous êtes vaches!‡, vous n'êtes pas chics!*; *see* **job**.

d (*plot of land*) lot *m* (de terrain), parcelle *f*, lotissement *m*; (*film studio*) enceinte *f* des studios. **building ~** lotissement; **empty** *or* **vacant ~** terrain *m* disponible; **parking ~** parking *m*.

e **the ~** (*everything*) (le) tout; (*everyone*) tous *mpl*, toutes *fpl*; **that's the ~** c'est tout, c'est le tout, tout y est; **here are some apples, take the (whole) ~** voici des pommes, prends-les toutes; **can I have some milk? — take the ~** est-ce que je peux avoir du lait? — prends tout (ce qu'il y a); **the ~ cost £1** le tout coûtait une livre, cela coûtait une livre en tout; **big ones, little ones, the ~!** les grands, les petits, tous!; **the ~ of you** vous tous; **they went off, the whole ~ of them** ils sont tous partis, ils sont partis tous tant qu'ils étaient.

f (*large amount*) **a ~, ~s** beaucoup; **you've given me ~s** *or* **a ~** tu m'en as donné beaucoup; **a ~ of, ~s of** *butter, wine, honey* beaucoup de; *cars, dogs, flowers* beaucoup de, un tas de*; **~s of** *or* **a ~ of time/money** beaucoup de temps/d'argent, un temps/un argent fou; **there were ~s of** *or* **a ~ of people** il y avait beaucoup de monde *or* un tas* de gens; **~s of** *or* **a ~ of people think that ...** beaucoup *or* des tas* de gens pensent que ...; **what a ~ of people!** que de monde! *or* de gens!; **what a ~ of time you take to dress!** tu en mets du temps à t'habiller!; **what a ~!** quelle quantité!; **there wasn't a ~ we could do** nous ne pouvions pas faire grand-chose; **I'd give a ~ to know ...** je donnerais cher pour savoir ...; **quite a ~ of** *people, cars* un assez grand nombre de, pas mal de; *honey, cream* une assez grande quantité de, pas mal de; **such a ~ of** tellement de, tant de; **there's an awful ~ of* people/cars/cream** *etc* c'est fou* ce qu'il y a comme gens/voitures/crème *etc;* **I have an awful ~ of* things to do** j'ai énormément* de *or* un tas* de choses à faire; **~s and ~s (of)** *people, cars* des tas (de)*; *flowers, butter, honey* des masses (de)*; *milk, wine* des flots (de).

g (*adv phrase*) **a ~** (*a great deal*) beaucoup; (*often*) beaucoup, souvent; **that's ~s*** *or* **a ~ better** c'est (vraiment) beaucoup *or* (vraiment) bien mieux; **he's a ~ better** il va beaucoup *or* bien mieux; **we don't go out a ~** nous ne sortons pas beaucoup *or* pas souvent; **he cries such a ~** il pleure tellement; **he drinks an awful ~*** *or* **a tremendous ~*** il boit énormément *or* comme un trou*; **things have changed quite a ~** les choses ont beaucoup *or* pas mal* changé; **we see a ~ of her** nous la voyons souvent *or* beaucoup; **thanks a ~!*** merci beaucoup!; (*iro*) merci (bien)! (*iro*); (*iro*) **a ~ you care!*** comme si ça te faisait quelque chose!; (*iro*) **a ~ that'll help!*** comme si ça allait être utile!; *see* **fat**.

loth [ləʊθ] **adj** = **loath**.

lotion [ˈləʊʃən] **n** lotion *f*; *see* **hand** *etc*.

lotos [ˈləʊtəs] **n** = **lotus**.

lottery [ˈlɒtərɪ] **n** (*lit, fig*) loterie *f*. **~ ticket** billet *m* de loterie.

lotto [ˈlɒtəʊ] **n** loto *m*.

lotus [ˈləʊtəs] **n** lotus *m*. (*Yoga*) **the ~ position** la position du lotus; (*Myth*) **~-eater** mangeur *m*, -euse *f* de lotus, lotophage *m*.

loud [laʊd] 1 **adj** a (*noisy*) *voice* fort, sonore, grand; *laugh* grand, bruyant, sonore; *noise, cry* sonore, grand; *music* bruyant, sonore; *thunder* fracassant; *applause* vif (*f* vive); *protests* vigoureux; (*pej*) *behaviour* tapageur. **the radio/orchestra/brass section is too ~** la radio/l'orchestre/les cuivres joue(nt) trop fort; **the music is too ~** la musique est trop bruyante; **in a ~ voice** d'une voix forte; **... he said in a ~ whisper ...** chuchota-t-il bruyamment; **to be ~ in one's support/condemnation of sth** soutenir/condamner qch avec force *or* virulence; (*Mus*) **~ pedal** pédale forte.

b (*pej: gaudy*) *colour* voyant, criard; *clothes* voyant, tapageur.

2 **adv** *speak etc* fort, haut. **turn the radio up a little ~er** mets la radio un peu plus fort, augmente le volume; **out ~** tout haut; (*Telec*) **I am reading** *or* **receiving you ~ and clear** je vous reçois cinq sur cinq; (*fig*) **the president's message was received ~ and clear** le message du président a été reçu cinq sur cinq; **we could hear it ~ and clear** nous l'entendions clairement.

3 **comp** ▸**loudhailer** (*Brit*) porte-voix *m inv*, mégaphone *m* ▸**loudmouth*** (*pej*) grande gueule‡ ▸**loud-mouthed** (*pej*) braillard, fort en gueule‡ ▸**loudspeaker** (*for PA system, musical instruments*) haut-parleur *m*, enceinte *f*; *[stereo]* baffle *m*, enceinte *f*.

loudly [ˈlaʊdlɪ] **adv** a *shout, speak* fort, d'une voix forte; *laugh* bruyamment; *proclaim* vigoureusement; *knock* fort, bruyamment. **don't say it too ~** ne le dites pas trop haut *or* trop fort. b (*pej*) *dress* d'une façon voyante *or* tapageuse.

loudness [ˈlaʊdnɪs] **n** *[voice, tone, music, thunder]* force *f*; *[applause]* bruit *m*; *[protests]* vigueur *f*.

Louis [ˈluːɪ] **n** Louis *m*. **~ the Fourteenth** Louis Quatorze.

louis [ˈluːɪ] **n, pl inv** louis *m* (d'or).

Louisiana [luːˌiːzɪˈænə] **n** Louisiane *f*. **in ~** en Louisiane.

lounge [laʊndʒ] 1 **n** (*esp Brit*) *[house, hotel]* salon *m*; *see* **airport, arrival, departure, sun, television** *etc*. 2 **comp** ▸**lounge bar** *[pub]* ≃ salle *f* de café; *[hotel]* ≃ (salle de) bar *m* ▸**lounge jacket** (*US*) veste *f* d'intérieur *or* d'appartement ▸**lounge suit** (*Brit*) complet(-veston) *m*; (*US*) pyjama *m* d'intérieur (de femme); (*Brit: on invitation*) **"lounge suit"** "tenue de ville". 3 **vi** (*recline*) (*on bed, chair*) se prélasser; (*sprawl*) être allongé paresseusement; (*stroll*) flâner; (*idle*) paresser, être oisif. **to ~ against a wall** s'appuyer paresseusement contre un mur; **we spent a week lounging in Biarritz** nous avons passé une semaine à flâner *or* à nous reposer à Biarritz.

▸**lounge about, lounge around** **vi** paresser, flâner, flemmarder*.

▸**lounge back** **vi: to lounge back in a chair** se prélasser dans un fauteuil.

lounger [ˈlaʊndʒəʳ] **n** a (*sun-bed etc*) lit *m* de plage. b (*pej: person*) fainéant(e) *m(f)*, flemmard(e)* *m(f)*.

louse [laʊs] **n, pl lice** a (*insect*) pou *m*. b (‡ *pej: person*) salaud‡ *m*, (peau *f* de) vache‡ *f* (*"louse" dans ce sens est utilisé au singulier seulement*).

▸**louse up‡** **vt sep** *deal, event* bousiller*, foutre en l'air‡.

lousy [ˈlaʊzɪ] **adj** a (*lit*) pouilleux.

b (‡: *terrible*) *play, book, car* moche*. **it's ~ weather** il fait un temps dégueulasse‡; **we had a ~ weekend** nous avons passé un week-end infect *or* dégueulasse‡; **I'm ~ at maths** je suis complètement bouché* en maths; **he's a ~ teacher** il est nul *or* zéro* comme prof; **a ~ trick** un tour de cochon*, une crasse*, une vacherie‡; **I feel ~** je suis mal fichu* *or* mal foutu‡; **I've got a ~ headache** j'ai un sacré* mal de tête, j'ai vachement‡ mal à la tête; **a few ~ quid‡** quelques malheureuses livres.

c (‡) **~ with** plein de, bourré de; **the town is ~ with tourists** la ville est bourrée *or* grouille de touristes; **he is ~ with money** il est bourré de fric‡, il est plein aux as‡.

lout [laʊt] **n** rustre *m*, butor *m*; *see* **litter**.

loutish [ˈlaʊtɪʃ] **adj** *manners* de rustre, de butor. **his ~ behaviour** la grossièreté de sa conduite.

louver (*US*), **louvre** [ˈluːvəʳ] **n** (*in roof*) lucarne *f*; (*on window*) persienne *f*, jalousie *f*. **louvered** (*US*) *or* **louvred door** porte *f* à claire-voie.

lovable [ˈlʌvəbl] **adj** *person* très sympathique; *child, animal* adorable.

love [lʌv] 1 **n** a (*for person*) amour *m* (*of* de, pour; *for* pour). **her ~ for** *or* **of her children** son amour pour ses enfants, l'amour qu'elle porte (*or* portait *etc*) à ses enfants; **her children's ~ (for her)** l'amour que lui portent (*or* portaient *etc*) ses enfants; **I feel no ~ for** *or* **towards him any longer** je n'éprouve plus d'amour pour lui; **they are in ~ (with each other)** ils s'aiment; **she's in ~** elle est amoureuse; **to be/fall in ~ with** être/tomber amoureux de; **it was ~ at first sight** ça a été le coup de foudre; **to make ~** faire l'amour (*with* avec; *to* à); **he was the ~ of her life** c'était l'homme de sa vie; **he thought of his first ~** il pensait à son premier amour (*see also* **1b**); (*fig*) **there's no ~ lost between them** ils ne peuvent pas se sentir*; **for the ~ of God** pour l'amour de Dieu; (*: *indignantly*) pour l'amour du Ciel!, bon sang!*; **for the ~ of Mike*** pour l'amour du Ciel; **to marry for ~** faire un mariage d'amour; **for ~ of her son, out of ~ for her son** par amour pour son fils; **don't give me any money, I'm doing it for ~** ne me donnez pas d'argent, je le fais gratuitement *or* pour l'amour de l'art; **I won't do it for ~ nor money** je ne le ferai pour rien au monde, je ne le ferai ni pour or ni pour argent (*frm*); **it wasn't to be had for ~ nor money** c'était introuvable, on ne pouvait se le procurer à aucun prix; **give her my ~** dis-lui bien des choses de ma part, (*stronger*) embrasse-la pour moi; **he sends (you) his ~** il t'envoie ses amitiés, (*stronger*) il t'embrasse; (*in letter*) **(with) ~ (from) Jim** affectueusement, Jim; **all my ~, Jim** bises, Jim; **~ and kisses** bisous, grosses bises; (*Brit*) **thanks ~*** (*to woman*) merci madame, merci ma jolie* *or* ma chérie*; (*to man*) merci monsieur; (*to child*) merci mon petit *or* mon chou*; **yes (my) ~** oui mon amour; **he's a little ~!** qu'il est mignon!, c'est un amour!; *see* **brotherly, labour, lady** *etc*.

b (*for country, music, horses*) amour *m* (*of* de, *for* pour), (*stronger*) passion *f* (*of* de, *for* pour). **the theatre was her great ~** le théâtre était sa grande passion; **his first ~ was football** sa première passion a été le football; **he studies history for the ~ of it** il étudie l'histoire pour son *or* le plaisir.

c (*Tennis etc*) rien *m*, zéro *m*. **~ 30** rien à 30, zéro 30.

2 **vt** a *spouse, child* aimer; *relative, friend* aimer (beaucoup). **~ thy neighbour as thyself** tu aimeras ton prochain comme toi-même; **he didn't just like her, he LOVED her** il ne l'aimait pas d'amitié, mais d'amour; **she ~d him dearly** elle l'aimait tendrement; **I must ~ you and leave you*** malheureusement, il faut que je vous (*or* te) quitte; (*counting etc*) **she ~s me, she ~s me not** elle m'aime, un peu, beaucoup, passionnément, à la folie, pas du tout; (*loc*) **~ me, ~ my dog** qui m'aime aime mon chien.

b *music, food, activity, place* aimer (beaucoup), (*stronger*) adorer. **to ~ to do** *or* **doing sth** aimer (beaucoup) *or* adorer faire qch; **she ~s riding** elle aime *or* adore monter à cheval, elle est passionnée d'équitation; **I'd ~ to come** j'aimerais beaucoup venir, je serais enchanté *or* ravi de venir, cela me ferait très plaisir de venir; **I'd ~ to!** je ne demande pas mieux!, cela me fera(it) très plaisir!; **I'd ~ to but unfortunately ...** cela me ferait très plaisir mais malheureusement ... .

3 **comp** ►**love affair** liaison *f* (amoureuse) ►**love apple** (†: *tomato*) pomme *f* d'amour (†) ►**lovebirds** (*birds*) perruches *fpl* inséparables; (*fig: people*) **the lovebirds** les tourtereaux *mpl* (*fig*) ►**lovebite** suçon *m* ►**love child** enfant *mf* de l'amour, enfant illégitime *or* naturel(le) ►**love feast** (*among early Christians*) agape *f*; (*banquet*) banquet *m*; (*iro*) agapes *fpl* ►**love game** (*Tennis*) jeu blanc ►**love-hate relationship** rapport *m* ambigu; **they have a love-hate relationship** ils s'aiment et se détestent à la fois ►**love-in** love-in *m inv* ►**love-in-a-mist** (*Bot*) nigelle *f* de Damas ►**love-knot** lacs *mpl* d'amour ►**love letter** lettre *f* d'amour, billet *m* doux (*often hum*) ►**love life***: **how's your love life (these days)?** comment vont les amours?; **his love life is bothering him** il a des problèmes de cœur *or* sentimentaux ►**lovemaking** amour *m* physique, rapports *mpl* sexuels ►**love match** mariage *m* d'amour ►**love nest** nid *m* d'amoureux *or* d'amour ►**love scene** (*Theat*) scène *f* d'amour ►**love seat** causeuse *f* ►**lovesick** amoureux, qui languit d'amour ►**lovesong** chanson *f* d'amour ►**love story** histoire *f* d'amour ►**love token** gage *m* d'amour.

loveless ['lʌvlɪs] **adj** *life, future, marriage* sans amour; *person* qui n'est pas aimé (*or* qui n'est pas capable d'aimer).

loveliness ['lʌvlɪnɪs] **n** beauté *f*, charme *m*.

lovelorn ['lʌv,lɔːn] **adj** († *or hum*) qui languit d'amour.

lovely ['lʌvlɪ] 1 **adj** (*pretty*) *girl, flower, hat, house, view, voice* (très) joli, ravissant; *baby* mignon, joli; (*pleasant*) *girl, house, sense of humour, suggestion, view* charmant; *meal, evening, party* charmant, agréable; *voice* agréable; *night, sunshine, weather* beau (*f* belle); *holiday* (très) bon (*f* bonne), excellent, formidable*; *story* joli, charmant; *idea, suggestion* merveilleux, charmant; *smell* bon, agréable; *food* bon. **she's a ~ person** c'est une personne charmante *or* très agréable, elle est charmante; **she has a ~ nature** elle a vraiment bon caractère; **this dress looks ~ on you** cette robe vous va vraiment bien *or* vous va à merveille; **we had a ~ time** nous nous sommes bien amusés, nous avons passé un moment *or* une semaine *etc* excellent(e) *or* très agréable; **I hope you have a ~ time** j'espère que vous vous amuserez bien; **it's been ~ to see** *or* **seeing you** j'ai été ravi *or* vraiment content de vous voir, ça m'a fait vraiment plaisir de vous voir; **all this ~ money** tout ce bel argent; **this cloth feels ~** ce drap est très agréable au toucher; **it felt ~ to be warm again** c'était bien agréable d'avoir chaud de nouveau; **~ and cool/warm** *etc* délicieusement *or* bien frais/chaud *etc*; **we're ~ and early*** c'est bien, on est en avance.

2 **n** (*: *girl*) belle fille, beau brin de fille, mignonne *f*. **my ~** ma jolie, ma mignonne.

lover ['lʌvəʳ] 1 **n** a amant *m*; (†: *suitor*) amoureux *m*. **~s' vows** promesses *fpl* d'amoureux; **they are ~s** ils ont une liaison, ils couchent* ensemble; **they have been ~s for 2 years** leur liaison dure depuis 2 ans; **she took a ~** elle a pris un amant; **Casanova was a great ~** Casanova fut un grand séducteur.

b *[hobby, wine etc]* amateur *m*. **he's a ~ of good food** il est grand amateur de bonne cuisine, il aime beaucoup la bonne cuisine; **he's a great ~ of Brahms** *or* **a great Brahms ~** c'est un fervent de Brahms, il aime beaucoup (la musique de) Brahms; **art/theatre ~** amateur d'art/de théâtre; **music ~** amateur de musique, mélomane *mf*; **he's a nature ~** il aime la nature, c'est un amoureux de la nature; **football ~s everywhere** tous les amateurs *or* passionnés de football.

2 **comp** ►**lover boy*** (*hum or iro*) (*male idol*) apollon* *m*; (*womanizer*) don Juan *m*, homme *m* à femmes, tombeur* *m*.

lovey-dovey* ['lʌvɪ'dʌvɪ] **adj** (*hum*) (trop) tendre.

loving ['lʌvɪŋ] **adj** (*affectionate*) affectueux; (*tender*) tendre; (*dutiful*) *wife, son* aimant, bon (*f* bonne). **~ kindness** bonté *f*, charité *f*; **~ cup** coupe *f* de l'amitié.

-loving ['lʌvɪŋ] **adj ending in comps**: **art-loving** qui aime l'art, qui est amateur d'art; **money-loving** qui aime l'argent, avare.

lovingly ['lʌvɪŋlɪ] **adv** affectueusement, tendrement, (*stronger*) avec amour.

low[1] [ləʊ] 1 **adj** a *wall* bas (*f* basse), peu élevé; *shelf, seat, ceiling, level, tide* bas. (*Met*) **~ cloud** nuages bas; **the sun is ~ in the sky** le soleil est bas dans le ciel *or* bas sur l'horizon; **dress with a ~ neck** robe décolletée; (*Boxing*) **~ blow** coup bas; (*Geog*) **the L~ Countries** les Pays-Bas; **fog on ~ ground** brouillard *m* à basse altitude; **the ~ ground near the sea** les basses terres près de la mer; **the house/town is on low ground** la maison/ville est bâtie dans une dépression; **the river is very ~ just now** la rivière est très basse en ce moment; **at ~ tide** à marée basse; **~ water** marée basse, basses eaux; (*fig*) *[of sb's career]* **the ~ point** le nadir; **to make a ~ bow** saluer *or* s'incliner bien bas; *see also* **4** *and* **ebb, lower**[1].

b *voice* (*soft*) bas (*f* basse); (*deep*) bas, profond; (*Mus*) *note* bas. **in a ~ voice** (*softly*) à voix basse; (*in deep tones*) d'une voix basse *or* profonde; **a ~ murmur** un murmure sourd *or* étouffé; **they were talking in a ~ murmur** ils chuchotaient le plus bas possible; **he gave a ~ groan** il a gémi faiblement, il a poussé un faible gémissement; *[radio etc]* **it's a bit ~** on n'entend pas, ça n'est pas assez fort, c'est trop bas; *see also* **4**.

c *wage, rate* bas (*f* basse), faible; *price* bas, modéré, modique; (*Scol*) *mark* bas, faible; *latitude, number*, (*Elec*) *frequency* bas; (*Chem, Phys*) *density* faible; (*Aut*) *compression* faible, bas; *temperature* bas, peu élevé; *speed* petit, faible; *lights* faible, bas; *visibility* mauvais, limité; *standard* bas, faible; *quality* inférieur (*f* -eure). **a ~ card** une basse carte; (*Cards*) **a ~ diamond** un petit carreau; (*Comm*) **at the ~est price** au meilleur prix; (*Aut*) **in ~ (gear)** en première ou seconde (vitesse); (*Math*) **~est common denominator** plus petit commun dénominateur *m*; (*fig*) **teachers have to go at the pace of the ~est common denominator** les professeurs doivent suivre le rythme des éléments les moins doués; (*Math*) **~est common multiple** plus petit commun multiple; (*Culin*) **at** *or* **on a ~ heat** à feu doux; **cook in a ~ oven** faire cuire au four à feu doux; **the fire is getting ~ /is ~** le feu baisse/est bas; **it has never fallen below £100/20** *etc* **at the ~est** cela n'est jamais tombé à moins de 100 livres/20 *etc*; **activity is at its ~est in the summer** c'est en été que l'activité est particulièrement réduite; **the temperature is in the ~ thirties** les températures sont comprises entre 30 et 35 degrés; **people of ~ intelligence** les gens de faible intelligence; **people of ~ income** les gens aux faibles revenus; **supplies are getting ~** les provisions baissent; (*Comm etc*) **their stock of soap was very ~** leur stock de savon était presque épuisé; **~ in nitrogen/fat** contenant peu d'azote/de matières grasses; **they were ~ on water** ils étaient à court d'eau; **we're a bit ~ on petrol** nous n'avons plus *or* il ne nous reste plus beaucoup d'essence; **I'm ~ on funds** je suis à court (d'argent); **to have a ~ opinion of sb** ne pas avoir bonne opinion de qn, avoir (une) piètre opinion de qn; **to have a ~ opinion of sth** ne pas avoir bonne opinion de qch; *see also* **4** *and* **lower**[1], **profile** *etc*.

d (*feeble*) *person* faible, affaibli; *health* mauvais; (*depressed*) déprimé, démoralisé, cafardeux*. **to be in ~ spirits, to be** *or* **feel ~** être déprimé *or* démoralisé, ne pas avoir le moral*, avoir le cafard*; **the patient is very ~** le malade est bien bas; *see also* **4**.

e (*Bio, Zool: primitive*) inférieur (*f* -eure), peu évolué. **the ~ forms of life** les formes de vie inférieures *or* les moins évoluées.

f (*humble*) *rank, origin* bas (*f* basse); (*vulgar*) *company* mauvais, bas; *character* grossier, bas; *taste* mauvais; *café etc* de bas étage; (*shameful*) *behaviour* ignoble, vil (*f* vile), odieux. **the ~est of the ~** le dernier des derniers; **that's a ~ trick** c'est un sale tour*; **with ~ cunning** avec une ruse ignoble; *see also* **4** *and* **lower**[1].

2 **adv** a (*in low position*) *aim, fly* bas. **to bow ~** s'incliner profondément, saluer bien bas; **a dress cut ~ in the back** une robe très décolletée dans le dos; **she is rather ~ down in that chair** elle est bien bas dans ce fauteuil, elle est assise bien bas; **~er down the wall/the page** plus bas sur le mur/la page; **~er down the hill** plus bas sur la colline, en contrebas; **the plane came down ~ over the town** l'avion est descendu et a survolé la ville à basse altitude; **the plane flew ~ over the town** l'avion a survolé la ville à basse altitude; *see* **lay**[1], **lie**[1].

b (*fig*) **to turn the heating/lights/music/radio (down) ~** baisser le chauffage/l'éclairage/la musique/la radio; **the fire was burning ~** le feu était bas; **supplies are running ~** les provisions baissent; (*St Ex*) **to buy ~** acheter quand le cours est bas; (*Cards*) **to play ~** jouer une basse carte; **to fall** *or* **sink ~** tomber bien bas; **I wouldn't stoop so ~ as to do that** je ne m'abaisserais pas jusqu'à faire cela; **to speak ~** parler à voix basse *or* doucement; **to sing ~** chanter bas; **the song is pitched too ~ for me** le ton de cette chanson est trop bas pour moi; (*in singing*) **I can't get as ~ as that** ma voix ne descend pas si bas que cela.

3 **n** a (*Met*) dépression *f*.

b (*Aut*) = **low gear**; *see* **1c**.

c (*low point: esp Fin*) niveau *m* bas, point *m* bas. **prices/temperatures have reached a new ~** *or* **an all-time ~** les prix/les températures n'ont jamais été aussi bas(ses) *or* ne sont jamais tombé(e)s aussi bas; **this is really a new ~ in vulgarity** cela bat tous les records de vulgarité; **the pound has sunk** *or* **fallen to a new ~** la livre a atteint son niveau le plus bas.

4 **comp** ►**low-alcohol** *lager, wine, beer* à faible teneur d'alcool, peu alcoolisé ►**low-angle shot** (*Phot*) contre-plongée *f* ►**lowborn** de basse origine *or* extraction ►**lowboy** (*US*) commode *f* basse ►**low-brow** **n** personne peu intellectuelle *or* sans prétentions intellectuelles ◊ **adj** *person* terre à terre *inv*, peu intellectuel; *book, film* sans prétentions

intellectuelles ► **low-budget** *film, project* à petit budget; *car etc* pour les petits budgets ► **low-calorie** *food, diet* à basses calories, hypocalorique ► **Low Church** Basse Église (*Anglicane*) ► **low-cost** adj (à) bon marché; **low-cost housing** (*NonC*) habitations *fpl* à loyer modéré, H.L.M. *mpl* ► **low-cut** (*Dress*) décolleté ► **low-down** *see* **low-down** ► **low-fat** *diet* pauvre en matières grasses; *milk, cheese etc* allégé ► **low-flying** adj volant à basse altitude ► **low flying** n (*NonC*) vol(s) *m(pl)* à basse altitude ► **Low German** bas allemand *m* ► **low-grade** de qualité *or* de catégorie inférieure; **low-grade mental defective** débile *mf* mental(e) ► **low-heeled** à talon(s) plat(s), plat ► **low-key** adj modéré; **it was a low-key operation** l'opération a été conduite de façon très discrète; **to keep sth low-key** faire qch de façon discrète ► **Low Latin** bas latin *m* ► **low-level** adj (*gen*) bas (*f* basse); *job* subalterne; *talks, discussions* à bas niveau; (*Aviat*) **low-level flying** vol *m* *or* navigation *f* à basse altitude; (*Comput*) **low-level language** langage *m* de bas niveau; (*Nuclear Ind*) **low-level waste** déchets *mpl* de faible activité ► **lowlife***: **his lowlife friends** ses amis pas très catholiques* ► **low-loader** (*Aut*) semi-remorque *f* à plate-forme surbaissée; (*Rail*) wagon *m* (de marchandises) à plate-forme surbaissée ► **low-lying** à basse altitude ► **Low Mass** (*Rel*) messe *f* basse ► **low-minded** d'esprit vulgaire ► **low-necked** décolleté ► **low-paid** *job* mal payé, qui paie mal; *worker* mal payé, qui ne gagne pas beaucoup; **the low-paid (workers)** les petits salaires, les petits salariés (*see also* **lower[1] 2**) ► **low-pitched** *ball* bas (*f* basse); *sound* bas, grave ► **low-pressure** à *or* de basse pression ► **low-priced** à bas prix, (à) bon marché *inv* ► **low-principled** sans grands principes ► **low-profile** (*gen*) au profil bas; (*Aut*) **low-profile tyre** pneu *m* taille basse ► **low-quality** *goods* de qualité inférieure ► **low-rise** (*Archit*) à *or* de hauteur limitée, bas (*f* basse) ► **low season** n basse *or* morte saison *f* ◊ adj *rates, holiday* pendant la basse *or* morte saison ► **low-spirited** déprimé, démoralisé ► **Low Sunday** dimanche *m* de Quasimodo ► **low-tech** *machinery, design* sommaire ► **low-tension** à basse tension ► **low vowel** (*Ling*) voyelle basse ► **low-water mark** (*lit*) laisse *f* de basse mer; (*fig*) **their morale had reached low-water mark** leur moral était on ne peut plus bas, ils avaient le moral à zéro*; **sales had reached low-water mark** les ventes n'avaient jamais été aussi mauvaises; *see also* **lower[1]**.

low[2] [ləʊ] vi *[cattle]* meugler, beugler, mugir.

low-down* ['ləʊdaʊn] 1 adj (*mean*) *action* bas (*f* basse), honteux, méprisable; *person* méprisable, vil (*f* vile); (*spiteful*) mesquin. **a ~ trick** un sale tour*. 2 n: **to get the ~ on sb/sth** se tuyauter* sur qn/qch, se renseigner sur qn/qch; **to give sb the ~ on sth** tuyauter* qn sur qch, mettre qn au courant *or* au parfum‡ de qch.

lower[1] ['ləʊəʳ] compar of **low[1]** 1 adj inférieur (*f* -eure). (*Typ*) **~ case** bas *m* de casse; **~-class** de la classe inférieure; **~ middle class** (n) petite bourgeoisie; (adj) petit bourgeois; **the ~ classes** (*socially*) les classes inférieures; (*Scol: also* **the ~ school**) le premier cycle; **the ~ income groups** les économiquement faibles *mpl*; (*Naut*) **~ deck** pont inférieur; (*personnel*) gradés *mpl* et matelots *mpl*; (*Parl*) **the L~ House** (*gen*) la Chambre basse; (*Brit*) la Chambre basse, la Chambre des communes; **~ jaw** mâchoire inférieure; **the ~ valley of the Rhine** la vallée inférieure du Rhin; **~ vertebrates** vertébrés inférieurs; *see also* **low[1]** *and* **second[1]** *etc.*

2 adv: **the ~ paid** la tranche inférieure des salariés *or* du salariat.

lower[2] ['ləʊəʳ] 1 vt a *blind, window, construction* baisser, abaisser; *sail, flag* abaisser, amener; *boat, lifeboat* mettre *or* amener à la mer. **to ~ the boats** mettre les embarcations à la mer; **to ~ sb/sth on a rope** (faire) descendre qn/descendre qch au bout d'une corde; **to ~ one's guard** (*Boxing*) baisser sa garde; (*fig*) ne plus être sur ses gardes; (*fig*) **to ~ the boom on sb** serrer la vis* à qn.

b (*fig*) *pressure, heating, price, voice* baisser. (*Med*) **to ~ sb's resistance** diminuer la résistance de qn; **to ~ sb's morale** démoraliser qn, saper le moral de qn; **~ your voice!** baisse la voix!, (parle) moins fort!; **he ~ed his voice to a whisper** il a baissé la voix jusqu'à en chuchoter, il s'est mis à chuchoter; **to ~ o.s. to do sth** s'abaisser à faire qch; **I refuse to ~ myself** je refuse de m'abaisser *or* de m'avilir ainsi.

2 vi (*lit*) baisser; *[pressure, price etc]* baisser, diminuer.

lower[3] ['laʊəʳ] vi *[sky]* se couvrir, s'assombrir; *[clouds]* être menaçant; *[person]* prendre un air sombre *or* menaçant. **to ~ at sb** jeter un regard menaçant à qn, regarder qn de travers.

lowering[1] ['ləʊərɪŋ] 1 n a *[window, flag]* abaissement *m*; *[boat]* mise *f* à la mer. b *[temperature]* baisse *f*, abaissement *m*; *[price, value]* baisse, diminution *f*; *[pressure]* baisse; (*Med*) *[resistance]* diminution. **the ~ of morale** la baisse du moral, la démoralisation. 2 adj abaissant, dégradant, humiliant.

lowering[2] ['laʊərɪŋ] adj *look, sky* sombre, menaçant.

lowing ['ləʊɪŋ] n *[cattle]* meuglement *m*, beuglement *m*, mugissement *m*.

lowland ['ləʊlənd] 1 n plaine *f*. **the L~s (of Scotland)** la Basse Écosse, les Basses-Terres (d'Écosse). 2 adj (*Ling*) **L~ Scots** = **Lallans**.

lowlander ['ləʊləndəʳ] n (*gen*) habitant(e) *m(f)* de la (*or* des) plaine(s). (*in Scotland*) **L~** habitant(e) de la Basse-Écosse.

lowliness ['ləʊlɪnɪs] n humilité *f*.

lowly ['ləʊlɪ] adj (*humble*) humble, modeste; (*lowborn*) d'origine modeste.

lowness ['ləʊnɪs] n (*in height*) manque *m* de hauteur; *[price, wages]* modicité *f*; *[temperature]* peu *m* d'élévation. **the ~ of the ceiling made him stoop** la maison était si basse de plafond qu'il a dû se baisser.

lox [lɒks] n (*US*) saumon *m* fumé.

loyal ['lɔɪəl] adj (*faithful*) *friend, supporter* loyal, fidèle (*to* envers); *servant* fidèle, dévoué, loyal†; (*respectful*) *subject* loyal. (*Brit*) **the ~ toast** le toast (porté) au souverain; **he has been ~ to me** il a été loyal envers moi, il m'a été fidèle.

loyalist ['lɔɪəlɪst] adj, n loyaliste *(mf)*.

loyally ['lɔɪəlɪ] adv fidèlement, loyalement, avec loyauté.

loyalty ['lɔɪəltɪ] n (*see* **loyal**) loyauté *f*, fidélité *f* (*to* envers), dévouement *m* (*to* pour). **his ~ is not in question** (*to person*) sa loyauté n'est pas en doute; (*to cause, institution*) son loyalisme n'est pas en doute; **a man of fierce loyalties** un homme d'une loyauté à toute épreuve *or* d'une loyauté absolue.

lozenge ['lɒzɪndʒ] n a (*Med*) pastille *f*; *see* **cough**. b (*Her, Math*) losange *m*.

LP [el'piː] n (*Mus*) (abbr of **long-playing (record)**) 33 tours *m*, microsillon *m*.

LPN [elpiː'en] n (*US Med*) (abbr of **Licensed Practical Nurse**) *see* **license**.

LRAM [elɑːreɪ'em] n (*Brit*) (abbr of **Licenciate of the Royal Academy of Music**) *diplôme d'un des Conservatoires de Musique*.

LRCP [elɑːsiː'piː] n (*Brit*) (abbr of **Licentiate of the Royal College of Physicians**) ≃ agrégation *f* de médecine.

LRCS [elɑːsiː'es] n (*Brit*) (abbr of **Licentiate of the Royal College of Surgeons**) ≃ agrégation *f* de médecine (opératoire).

LSAT [eleseɪ'tiː] n (*US Univ*) (abbr of **Law School Admission Test**) *examen d'entrée à une faculté de droit*.

LSD [eles'diː] n (*Drugs*) (abbr of **lysergic acid diethylamide**) LSD *m* (*drogue*).

L.S.D. [eles'diː] n (*Brit* †) (abbr of **librae, solidi, denarii** = *pounds, shillings and pence*) *ancien système monétaire britannique*.

L.S.E. [ˌeles'iː] n (*Brit*) abbr of **London School of Economics**.

LT [el'tiː] (*Elec*) (abbr of **low tension**) *see* **low[1] 4**.

Lt. (abbr of **Lieutenant**) (*on envelope etc*) **~ J. Smith** Lieutenant J. Smith; **~-Col.** abbr of **Lieutenant-Colonel**; **~-Gen.** abbr of **Lieutenant-General**.

Ltd (*Brit Comm etc*) (abbr of **Limited (Liability)**) **Smith & Co. Ltd** Smith & Cie S.A. *or* (*Can*) Ltée.

lubricant ['luːbrɪkənt] adj, n lubrifiant *(m)*.

lubricate ['luːbrɪkeɪt] vt lubrifier; (*Aut*) graisser. **lubricating oil** huile *f* (de graissage), lubrifiant *m*.

lubricated‡ ['luːbrɪkeɪtɪd] adj (*drunk*) paf‡ *inv*, beurré‡.

lubrication [ˌluːbrɪ'keɪʃən] n lubrification *f*; (*Aut*) graissage *m*.

lubricator ['luːbrɪkeɪtəʳ] n (*person, device*) graisseur *m*.

lubricity [luː'brɪsɪtɪ] n a (*slipperiness*) caractère glissant. b (*lewdness*) lubricité *f*.

lucerne [luː'sɜːn] n (*esp Brit*) luzerne *f*.

lucid ['luːsɪd] adj a (*understandable*) *style, explanation* lucide. b (*sane*) lucide. **~ interval** intervalle *m* lucide *or* de lucidité. c (*bright*) brillant, clair, lumineux.

lucidity [luː'sɪdɪtɪ] n (*see* **lucid**) lucidité *f*; clarté *f*, luminosité *f*.

lucidly ['luːsɪdlɪ] adv *explain, argue* lucidement, clairement.

Lucifer ['luːsɪfəʳ] n a Lucifer *m*. b (††) **l~** allumette *f*.

luck [lʌk] n a (*chance, fortune*) chance *f*, hasard *m*. **good ~** (bonne) chance, bonheur *m*, veine* *f*, pot* *m*; **bad ~** malchance *f*, malheur *m*, déveine* *f*; **to bring (sb) good/bad** *or* **ill ~** porter bonheur/malheur (à qn); **it brought us nothing but bad ~** cela ne nous a vraiment pas porté chance; **good ~!** bonne chance!; **bad** *or* **hard ~!** pas *or* manque de chance!, manque de pot!*, pas de veine!*; **better ~ next time!** ça ira mieux la prochaine fois!; **any ~?*** (*gen*) ça a marché*?; (*did you find it?*) tu as trouvé*?; **no ~?*** (*gen*) ça n'a pas marché*?; (*didn't you find it?*) tu n'as pas trouvé*?; **worse ~** malheureusement; **to have the good/bad ~ to do sth** avoir la chance *or* la bonne fortune/la malchance *or* la mauvaise fortune de faire qch; **~ favoured him, ~ was with him, ~ was on his side** la fortune lui souriait, il était favorisé par la fortune *or* le destin; **as ~ would have it** comme par hasard; (*fig*) **it's the ~ of the draw** c'est une question de chance; **it's good/bad ~ to see a black cat** cela porte bonheur/malheur de voir un chat noir; **(it's) just my ~!** c'est bien ma chance! *or* ma veine!*; **it was just his ~ to meet the boss** par malchance *or* par malheur il a rencontré le patron, il a eu la malchance *or* la déveine* de rencontrer le patron; **to be down on one's ~** (*be unlucky*) avoir la déveine* *or* la poisse*; (*go through bad patch*) traverser une mauvaise passe; *see* **beginner, chance, push** *etc.*

b (*good fortune*) (bonne) chance *f*, bonheur *m*, veine* *f*, pot* *m*. **you're in ~, your ~'s in** tu as de la chance *or* de la veine* *or* du pot*; **you're out of ~, your ~'s out** tu n'as pas de chance *or* de veine* *or* de pot*; **that's a bit of ~!** quelle chance!, quelle veine!*, coup de pot!*; **he had the ~ to meet her in the street** il a eu la chance de la rencontrer dans la rue; **here's (wishing you) ~!** bonne chance!; (*drinking: also* **good ~!**) à votre santé!; **no such ~!*** ç'aurait été trop beau! *or* trop de chance!, penses-tu!; **with any ~ ...** avec un peu de chance *or* de veine* ...; **to keep a horseshoe for ~** avoir un fer à cheval comme porte-bonheur; (*iro*) **and the best of (British) ~!*** je vous (*or* leur *etc*) souhaite bien du plaisir!* (*iro*); **he's got the ~ of the devil*, he's got the devil's own ~*** il a une veine de pendu*.

▸**luck out*** vi (*US*) avoir de la veine* *or* du pot*.

luckily ['lʌkɪlɪ] adv heureusement, par bonheur. ~ **for me ...** heureusement pour moi ... .

luckless ['lʌklɪs] adj *person* malchanceux, qui n'a pas de chance; *event, action* malencontreux; *day* fatal.

lucky ['lʌkɪ] adj *person* qui a de la chance, favorisé par la chance *or* la fortune, veinard*; *day* de chance, de veine*, faste; *shot, guess, coincidence* heureux; *horseshoe, charm* porte-bonheur *inv*. **you are ~ to be alive** tu as de la chance *or* de la veine* de t'en sortir vivant; **he was ~ enough to get a seat** il a eu la chance *or* la veine* de trouver une place; **you'll be ~ to get £5 for that** tu auras de la chance si tu en tires 5 livres; **we were ~ with the weather** on a eu de la chance — il faisait beau *or* il n'a pas fait trop mauvais temps; **~ you!** (*in admiration*) veinard!*, tu en as de la chance! *or* de la veine!*; (*iro*) tu es verni!*; **(you) ~ thing*** *or* **dog!‡** veinard!*; **(he is a) ~ thing*** *or* **dog!‡** le veinard!*; **it was ~ for him that he got out of the way** heureusement (pour lui) qu'il s'est écarté; **it was ~ you got here in time** heureusement que vous êtes arrivé à temps; **you'll be ~!*** tu peux toujours y croire!*; **I should be so ~!*** tu parles!*, ce serait trop beau!*, penses-tu!*; **how ~!** quelle chance!; **we had a ~ escape** nous l'avons échappé belle; **to have a ~ break*** avoir un coup de veine*; (*Brit: at fair etc*) **~ dip** pêche miraculeuse; (*Brit fig*) **it's a ~ dip** c'est une loterie, c'est une question de chance; **~ number** chiffre *m* porte-bonheur; *see* **star**[1], **third** *etc*.

lucrative ['lu:krətɪv] adj *business* lucratif, rentable; *employment* lucratif, qui paie bien, bien rémunéré.

lucre ['lu:kəʳ] n (*NonC: pej: gain*) lucre *m*. (* *hum: money*) **(filthy) ~** fric‡ *m*, pognon‡ *m*.

Lucretia [lu:'kri:ʃɪə] n Lucrèce *f*.

Lucretius [lu:'kri:ʃɪəs] n Lucrèce *m*.

Lucy ['lu:sɪ] n Lucie *f*.

Luddite ['lʌdaɪt] adj, n luddite (*mf*).

ludicrous ['lu:dɪkrəs] adj ridicule, risible.

ludicrously ['lu:dɪkrəslɪ] adv ridiculement, risiblement.

ludo ['lu:dəʊ] n (*Brit*) jeu *m* des petits chevaux.

luff [lʌf] (*Naut*) 1 n aulof(f)ée *f*. 2 vi lofer, venir au lof.

luffa ['lʌfə] n = **loofah**.

lug[1] [lʌg] 1 n (*Constr*) tenon *m*; *[dish, saucepan etc]* oreille *f* (*d'une casserole etc*). 2 comp ▸**lughole‡** (*Brit: ear*) oreille *f*.

lug[2] [lʌg] vt traîner, tirer. **to ~ sth up/down** monter/descendre qch en le traînant; **to ~ sth out** traîner qch dehors; **why are you ~ging that parcel around?** pourquoi est-ce que tu trimbales* ce paquet?; (*fig*) **they ~ged* him off to the theatre** ils l'ont traîné *or* embarqué* au théâtre (malgré lui).

luggage ['lʌgɪdʒ] 1 n (*NonC*) bagages *mpl*. (*Rail*) **~ in advance** bagages non accompagnés; *see* **hand, left**[1], **piece**. 2 comp ▸**luggage boot** (*Brit Aut*) coffre *m* ▸**luggage carrier** porte-bagages *m inv* ▸**luggage handler** (*at airport etc*) bagagiste *m* ▸**luggage insurance** assurance-bagages *f* ▸**luggage label** étiquette *f* à bagages ▸**luggage locker** (casier *m* de) consigne *f* automatique ▸**luggage rack** (*Rail*) porte-bagages *m inv*, filet *m*; (*Aut*) galerie *f* ▸**luggage van** (*esp Brit Rail*) fourgon *m* (à bagages).

lugger ['lʌgəʳ] n lougre *m*.

lugubrious [lʊ'gu:brɪəs] adj lugubre.

lugubriously [lʊ'gu:brɪəslɪ] adv lugubrement.

Luke [lu:k] n Luc *m*.

lukewarm ['lu:kwɔ:m] adj (*lit*) tiède; (*fig*) tiède, peu enthousiaste.

lull [lʌl] 1 n *[storm]* accalmie *f*; *[hostilities, shooting]* arrêt *m*; *[conversation]* arrêt, pause *f*. 2 vt *person, fear* apaiser, calmer. **to ~ a child to sleep** endormir un enfant en le berçant; (*fig*) **to be ~ed into a false sense of security** s'endormir dans une fausse sécurité.

lullaby ['lʌləbaɪ] n berceuse *f*. **~ my baby** dors (mon) bébé, dors.

lulu* ['lu:lu:] n (*esp US*) **it's a ~!** c'est super!*; (*iro*) c'est pas de la tarte!‡

lumbago [lʌm'beɪgəʊ] n lumbago *m*.

lumbar ['lʌmbəʳ] adj lombaire. **~ puncture** ponction *f* lombaire; **in the ~ region** dans la région lombaire.

lumber[1] ['lʌmbəʳ] 1 n (*NonC*) a (*wood*) bois *m* de charpente.

b (*junk*) bric-à-brac *m inv*.

2 vt a *room* encombrer. **~ all those books together in the corner** entassez *or* empilez tous ces livres dans le coin.

b (*US Forestry*) (*fell*) abattre; (*saw up*) débiter.

c (*Brit *: burden*) **to ~ sb with sth** coller* *or* flanquer* qch à qn; **he got ~ed with the job of making the list** il s'est tapé* *or* appuyé* *or* farci‡ le boulot de dresser la liste; **I got ~ed with the girl for the evening** j'ai dû me coltiner* *or* m'appuyer* la fille toute la soirée; **now (that) we're ~ed with it ...** maintenant qu'on a ça sur les bras ... *or* qu'on nous a collé* ça ... .

3 comp ▸**lumberjack** bûcheron *m* ▸**lumber jacket** blouson *m* ▸**lumberman** = **lumberjack** ▸**lumber mill** scierie *f* ▸**lumber room** (*Brit*) (cabinet *m* de) débarras *m* ▸**lumber yard** chantier *m* de scierie.

lumber[2] ['lʌmbəʳ] vi (*also* **~ about, ~ along**) *[person, animal]* marcher pesamment; *[vehicle]* rouler pesamment. *[person]* **to ~ in/out** *etc* entrer/sortir *etc* d'un pas pesant *or* lourd.

lumbering[1] ['lʌmbərɪŋ] n (*US*) débit *m or* débitage *m or* tronçonnage *m* de bois.

lumbering[2] ['lʌmbərɪŋ] adj *step* lourd, pesant; *person* mal dégrossi.

luminary ['lu:mɪnərɪ] n (*star*) astre *m*, corps *m* céleste; (*fig: person*) lumière *f*, sommité *f*.

luminescence [ˌlu:mɪ'nesns] n luminescence *f*.

luminosity [ˌlu:mɪ'nɒsɪtɪ] n luminosité *f*.

luminous ['lu:mɪnəs] adj lumineux. **my watch is ~** le cadran de ma montre est lumineux.

lumme‡ ['lʌmɪ] excl (*Brit*) = **lummy‡**.

lummox ['lʌməks] n (*US*) lourdaud(e) *m(f)*.

lummy‡ ['lʌmɪ] excl (*Brit*) ça alors!, sapristi!*

lump[1] [lʌmp] 1 n a (*piece*) morceau *m*, (*larger*) gros morceau, masse *f*; *[metal, rock, stone]* morceau, masse; *[coal, cheese, sugar]* morceau; *[clay, earth]* motte *f*; (*in sauce etc*) grumeau *m*. **after the explosion there were large ~s of rock everywhere** après l'explosion il y avait de gros éclats de pierre partout.

b (*Med*) grosseur *f*; (*swelling*) protubérance *f*; (*from bump etc*) bosse *f*. (*fig*) **to have a ~ in one's throat** avoir une boule dans la gorge, avoir la gorge serrée.

c (* *pej: person*) lourdaud(e) *m(f)*, empoté(e)* *m(f)*. **fat ~!** gros lourdaud!, espèce d'empoté(e)!*

d (*Brit: in building trade*) **the ~** ouvriers *mpl* du bâtiment non-syndiqués.

2 comp ▸**lumpfish** lump *m or* lompe *m*; **lumpfish roe** œufs *mpl* de lump ▸**lumpsucker** lump *m or* lompe *m* ▸**lump sugar** sucre *m* en morceaux ▸**lump sum** (*Fin etc*) montant *m* forfaitaire; (*payment*) paiement *m* unique; **he was working for a lump sum** il travaillait à forfait; (*Insurance etc*) **to pay a lump sum** verser un capital.

3 vt (*also* **~ together**) *books, objects* réunir, mettre en tas; *persons* réunir; *subjects* réunir, considérer en bloc.

▸**lump together** 1 vi (*) **if we lumped together we could buy a car** si nous nous y mettions à plusieurs, nous pourrions acheter une voiture.

2 vt sep réunir; (*fig*) *people, cases* mettre dans la même catégorie *or* dans le même sac* (*pej*), considérer en bloc; *see also* **lump**[1] **3**.

lump[2]* [lʌmp] vt (*Brit: endure*) **you'll just have to ~ it** il faut bien que tu encaisses* (*subj*) sans rien dire; *see* **like**[2].

lumpectomy [lʌm'pektəmɪ] n ablation *f* d'une (*or* de) tumeur(s) mammaire(s).

lumpen ['lʌmpən] adj a **~ proletariat** sous-prolétariat *m*. b (*) stupide.

lumpish ['lʌmpɪʃ] adj a (*) (*clumsy*) gauche, maladroit, pataud; (*stupid*) idiot, godiche*. b (*shapeless*) *mass, piece* informe.

lumpy ['lʌmpɪ] adj *gravy* grumeleux, qui a des grumeaux; *bed* défoncé, bosselé.

lunacy ['lu:nəsɪ] n (*Med*) aliénation mentale, folie *f*, démence *f*; (*Jur*) démence; (*fig*) folie, démence. **that's sheer ~!** c'est de la pure folie!, c'est démentiel! *or* de la démence!

lunar ['lu:nəʳ] adj *month, rock* lunaire; *eclipse* de lune. (*Space*) **in ~ orbit** en orbite lunaire *or* autour de la lune; (*Space*) **~ module** module *m* lunaire; (*Space*) **~ landing** alunissage *m*.

lunatic ['lu:nətɪk] 1 n (*Med*) fou *m*, folle *f*, aliéné(e) *m(f)*, dément(e) *m(f)*; (*Jur*) dément(e); (*fig*) fou, folle, cinglé(e)* *m(f)*. **he's a ~!** il est fou à lier!, il est cinglé!* 2 adj (*Med*) *person* fou (*f* folle), dément; (*fig*) fou, dément, cinglé*; *idea, action* (*crazy*) absurde, extravagant, démentiel; (*stupid*) stupide, idiot. **~ asylum** asile *m* d'aliénés; **the ~ fringe** les enragés* *mpl*, les extrémistes *mpl* fanatiques.

lunch [lʌntʃ] 1 n déjeuner *m*. **light/quick ~** déjeuner léger/rapide; **we're having pork for ~** nous allons manger *or* nous avons du porc pour déjeuner *or* à midi; **to have ~** déjeuner; **he is at ~** (*away from office etc*) il est parti déjeuner; (*Brit: having lunch*) il est en train de déjeuner; **come to** *or* **for ~ on Sunday** venez déjeuner dimanche; **we had him to ~ yesterday** il est venu déjeuner (chez nous) hier; *see* **school, out 1a, working** *etc*.

2 vi déjeuner. **we ~ed on** *or* **off sandwiches** nous avons déjeuné de sandwiches, nous avons eu des sandwiches pour déjeuner.

3 vt *person* offrir un déjeuner à.

4 comp ▸**lunch basket, lunchbox** panier-repas *m* ▸**lunch break** pause *f* de midi, heure *f* du déjeuner ▸**lunch hour, lunchtime: it's his lunch hour** *or* **lunchtime just now** c'est l'heure à laquelle il déjeune, c'est l'heure de son déjeuner; **it's lunchtime** c'est l'heure de déjeuner; **during one's lunch hour, at lunchtime** à l'heure du déjeuner.

luncheon ['lʌntʃən] 1 n déjeuner *m* (*gén de cérémonie*). 2 comp ▸**luncheon basket** panier-repas *m* ▸**luncheon meat** (sorte *f* de) mortadelle *f* ▸**luncheon voucher** (*Brit*) chèque-repas *m*, ticket-repas *m*.

lung [lʌŋ] 1 n poumon *m*. (*fig*) **at the top of one's ~s** à pleins poumons, à tue-tête; *see* **iron**. 2 comp *disease, infection* pulmonaire ▸**lung cancer** cancer *m* du poumon ▸**lung specialist** pneumologue *mf* ▸**lung transplant** greffe *f* du poumon.

lunge [lʌndʒ] 1 n a (*thrust*) (brusque) coup *m or* mouvement *m* en avant; (*Fencing*) botte *f*. b (*also* **~ rein**) longe *f*. 2 vi a (*also* **~**

forward) faire un mouvement brusque en avant; (*Fencing*) se fendre. b **to ~ at sb** envoyer *or* assener un coup à qn; (*Fencing*) porter *or* allonger une botte à qn. 3 **vt** *horse* mener à la longe.
lunula ['lu:njʊlə] **n, pl lunulae** ['lu:njʊ,li:] (*Anat*) lunule *f*.
lupin ['lu:pɪn] **n** lupin *m*.
lurch[1] [lɜ:tʃ] 1 **n** *[person]* écart *m* brusque, vacillement *m*; *[car, ship]* embardée *f*. **to give a ~** *[car, ship]* faire une embardée; *[person]* vaciller, tituber. 2 **vi** *[person]* vaciller, tituber; *[car, ship]* faire une embardée. *[person]* **to ~ in/out/along** *etc* entrer/sortir/avancer *etc* en titubant; **the car ~ed along** la voiture avançait en faisant des embardées.
lurch[2] [lɜ:tʃ] **n: to leave sb in the ~** faire faux bond à qn, planter là qn*, laisser qn le bec dans l'eau.
lure [ljʊəʳ] 1 **n** a (*NonC*) (*charm: of sea, travel etc*) attrait *m*, charme *m*; (*false attraction*) appât *m*, piège *m*, leurre *m*. b (*decoy*) leurre *m*. 2 **vt** tromper, attirer *or* persuader par la ruse. **to ~ sb into a trap** attirer qn dans un piège; **to ~ sb into a house** attirer qn dans une maison (par la ruse); **to ~ sb in/out** *etc* persuader qn par la ruse d'entrer/de sortir *etc*.
►**lure away** **vt sep: to lure sb away from the house** éloigner qn *or* faire sortir qn de la maison par la ruse; **to lure sb away from the path of duty** détourner qn de son devoir par la ruse.
►**lure on** **vt sep** entraîner par la ruse, séduire.
lurex ['lʊəreks] **n** lurex *m*.
lurid ['ljʊərɪd] **adj** a (*gruesome*) *details* affreux, atroce; *account, tale* effrayant, terrifiant; *crime* horrible, épouvantable; (*sensational*) *account, tale* à sensation. **a ~ description of the riot** une terrible *or* une saisissante description de l'émeute; **he gave us a ~ description of what lunch was like*** il nous a fait une description pittoresque *or* haute en couleur du déjeuner. b (*fiery*) *colour* feu *inv*, sanglant; *sky, sunset* empourpré, sanglant; (*pej: colour scheme etc*) criard, voyant. c (*ghastly in colour*) criard; *light* surnaturel.
lurk [lɜ:k] **vi** *[person]* se cacher (*dans un but malveillant*), se tapir; *[danger]* menacer; *[doubt]* persister. **he was ~ing behind the bush** il se cachait *or* il était tapi derrière le buisson; **there's someone ~ing (about) in the garden** quelqu'un rôde dans le jardin, il y a un rôdeur dans le jardin.
lurking ['lɜ:kɪŋ] **adj** *fear, doubt* vague. **a ~ idea** une idée de derrière la tête.
luscious ['lʌʃəs] **adj** *food* succulent; (* *fig*) *blonde* appétissant, affriolant.
lush [lʌʃ] 1 **adj** a *vegetation* luxuriant; *plant* plein de sève; *pasture* riche. b (*: *opulent*) *house, surroundings* luxueux. 2 **n** (‡: *alcoholic*) alcoolo* *m*, poivrot(e)* *m(f)*.
lushness ['lʌʃnɪs] **n** a *[vegetation]* luxuriance *f*. b (*opulence*) luxe *m*.
lust [lʌst] **n** (*sexual*) désir *m* (sexuel); (*Rel: one of the 7 sins*) luxure *f*; (*for fame, power etc*) soif *f* (*for* de). **the ~ for life** la soif *or* la rage de vivre.
►**lust after, lust for** **vt fus** *woman* désirer, convoiter; *revenge, power* avoir soif de; *riches* convoiter.
luster ['lʌstəʳ] **n** (*US*) = **lustre**.
lustful ['lʌstfʊl] **adj** (*sexually*) lascif, luxurieux; (*greedy*) avide (*of* de).
lustfully ['lʌstfəlɪ] **adv** (*see* **lustful**) lascivement; avidement.
lustfulness ['lʌstfʊlnɪs] **n** lubricité *f*, lasciveté *f*.
lustre, (*US*) **luster** ['lʌstəʳ] **n** (*gloss*) lustre *m*, brillant *m*; (*substance*) lustre; (*fig: renown*) éclat *m*. **~ware** poterie mordorée.
lustreless ['lʌstəlɪs] **adj** terne; *look, eyes* terne, vitreux.
lustrous ['lʌstrəs] **adj** (*shining*) *material* lustré, brillant; *eyes* brillant; *pearls* chatoyant; (*fig: splendid*) splendide, magnifique.
lusty ['lʌstɪ] **adj** (*healthy*) *person, infant* vigoureux, robuste; (*hearty*) *cheer, voice* vigoureux, vif (*f* vive).
lute [lu:t] **n** luth *m*.
Lutetia [lu:'ti:ʃə] **n** Lutèce *f*.
lutetium [lʊ'ti:ʃɪəm] **n** lutétium *m*.
Luther ['lu:θəʳ] **n** Luther *m*.
Lutheran ['lu:θərən] 1 **n** Luthérien(ne) *m(f)*. 2 **adj** luthérien.
Lutheranism ['lu:θərənɪzəm] **n** luthéranisme *m*.
luv* [lʌv] = **love**.
Luxembourg ['lʌksəmbɜ:g] **n** Luxembourg *m*. **the Grand Duchy of ~** le Grand-Duché de Luxembourg; **the ~ Embassy, the Embassy of ~** l'ambassade luxembourgeoise.
Luxor ['lʌksɔ:ʳ] **n** Louxor.
luxuriance [lʌg'zjʊərɪəns] **n** (*see* **luxuriant**) luxuriance *f*; exubérance *f*; richesse *f*, fertilité *f*; surabondance *f*.
luxuriant [lʌg'zjʊərɪənt] **adj** *vegetation, hair* luxuriant, exubérant; *beard* exubérant; *soil, country, valley* riche, fertile; *crops* surabondant; *style, imagery* luxuriant.
luxuriantly [lʌg'zjʊərɪəntlɪ] **adv** de façon exubérante; avec abondance.
luxuriate [lʌg'zjʊərɪeɪt] **vi** a (*revel*) **to ~ in** s'abandonner *or* se livrer avec délices à. b (*grow profusely*) pousser avec exubérance *or* à profusion.
luxurious [lʌg'zjʊərɪəs] **adj** *hotel, surroundings* luxueux, somptueux; *tastes* de luxe.
luxuriously [lʌg'zjʊərɪəslɪ] **adv** *furnish, decorate* luxueusement; *live* dans le luxe; *yawn, stretch* voluptueusement.
luxuriousness [lʌg'zjʊərɪəsnɪs] **n** *[hotel etc]* luxe *m*, somptuosité *f*. **the ~ of his tastes** ses goûts de luxe *or* pour le grand luxe.
luxury ['lʌkʃərɪ] 1 **n** a (*NonC*) luxe *m*. **to live in ~** vivre dans le luxe; *see* **lap**[1]. b (*object, commodity etc*) luxe *m*. **beef is becoming a ~** le bœuf devient un (produit de) luxe; **it's quite a ~ for me to go to the theatre** c'est du luxe pour moi que d'aller au théâtre; **what a ~ to have a bath at last!*** quel luxe *or* quelle volupté que de pouvoir enfin prendre un bain! 2 **comp** *goods* de luxe; *flat, hotel* de grand luxe, de grand standing.
LV (**abbr of luncheon voucher**) *see* **luncheon 2**.
LW (*Rad*) (**abbr of long wave**) G.O. *fpl*.
lycanthropy [laɪ'kænθrəpɪ] **n** lycanthropie *f*.
lyceum [laɪ'si:əm] **n** ≃ maison *f* de la culture.
lychee ['laɪtʃi:] **n** litchi *or* letchi *m*.
lychgate ['lɪtʃgeɪt] **n** = **lichgate**.
Lycra ['laɪkrə] ® 1 **n** Lycra *m* ®. 2 **comp** en Lycra.
lye [laɪ] **n** lessive *f* (*substance*).
lying[1] ['laɪɪŋ] 1 **n** (*NonC*) mensonge(s) *m(pl)*. **~ will get you nowhere** ça ne te servira à rien de mentir. 2 **adj** *person* menteur; *statement, story* mensonger, faux (*f* fausse).
lying[2] ['laɪɪŋ] 1 **n** *[body]* **~ in state** exposition *f* (solennelle). 2 **comp** ►**lying-in** (*Med:* †) (**pl ~s-~**) accouchement *m*, couches *fpl* ►**lying-in ward** salle *f* de travail *or* d'accouchement.
lymph [lɪmf] **n** (*Anat*) lymphe *f*. **~ gland** ganglion *m* lymphatique.
lymphatic [lɪm'fætɪk] **adj** lymphatique.
lymphocyte ['lɪmfəʊ,saɪt] **n** lymphocyte *m*.
lymphoid ['lɪmfɔɪd] **adj** lymphoïde.
lymphosarcoma [,lɪmfəʊsɑ:'kəʊmə] **n** lymphosarcome *m*.
lynch [lɪntʃ] **vt** lyncher. **~ law** loi *f* de lynch.
lynching ['lɪntʃɪŋ] **n** (*action, result*) lynchage *m*.
lynchpin ['lɪntʃpɪn] **n** = **linchpin**
lynx [lɪŋks] **n, pl ~es** *or* **~** lynx *m inv*. **~-eyed** aux yeux de lynx.
Lyons ['laɪənz] **n** Lyon.
lyophilize [laɪ'ɒfɪ,laɪz] **vt** lyophiliser.
lyre ['laɪəʳ] **n** lyre *f*. **~bird** oiseau-lyre *m*, ménure *m*.
lyric ['lɪrɪk] 1 **n** a (*poem*) poème *m* lyrique. b (*words of song*) **~s** paroles *fpl*. 2 **adj** *poem, poet* lyrique. 3 **comp** ►**lyric-writer** parolier *m*, -ière *f*.
lyrical ['lɪrɪkəl] **adj** a (*Poetry*) lyrique. b (*: *enthusiastic*) lyrique, passionné, enthousiaste. **he got** *or* **waxed ~ about Louis Armstrong** il est devenu lyrique quand il a parlé de Louis Armstrong.
lyrically ['lɪrɪkəlɪ] **adv** (*Poetry*) lyriquement, avec lyrisme; (*enthusiastically*) avec lyrisme, avec enthousiasme.
lyricism ['lɪrɪsɪzəm] **n** lyrisme *m*.
lyricist ['lɪrɪsɪst] **n** (*poet*) poète *m* lyrique; (*song-writer*) parolier *m*, -ière *f*.

M

M, m [em] n a (*letter*) M, m *m or f*. **M for Mike, M for Mother** ≃ M comme Marcel. b (*Brit Aut*) (**abbr of motorway**) **on the M6** sur l'autoroute M6, ≃ sur l'A6. c **abbr of million(s)**. d (**abbr of medium**) *taille de vêtement*. e (**abbr of metre(s)**) m. f **abbr of mile(s)**.
MA [ˌem'eɪ] a (*Brit Univ*) (**abbr of Master of Arts**) **to have an ~ in French** avoir une maîtrise de français; *see* **master**. b (*US Post*) **abbr of Massachusetts**.
M.A. [ˌem'eɪ] (*US*) (**abbr of Military Academy**) *see* **military**.
ma‡ [mɑː] n maman *f*. (*pej*) **M~ Smith** la mère Smith.
ma'am [mæm] n (**abbr of madam**) (*gen*) madame *f*, mademoiselle *f*; (*to royalty*) madame.
mac [mæk] n a (*Brit* *) (**abbr of mackintosh**) imperméable *m*, imper* *m*. b (‡: *form of address*) **hurry up M~!** hé! dépêchez-vous!; (*to friend*) dépêche-toi mon vieux! *or* mon pote!‡.
macabre [mə'kɑːbrə] adj macabre.
macadam [mə'kædəm] 1 n macadam *m*; *see* **tar**[1]. 2 comp *surface* en macadam; *road* macadamisé.
macadamize [mə'kædəmaɪz] vt macadamiser.
macaroni [ˌmækə'rəʊnɪ] n, pl **~s** *or* **~es** macaroni(s) *m(pl)*. **~ cheese** macaroni au gratin.
macaronic [ˌmækə'rɒnɪk] 1 adj macaronique. 2 n vers *m* macaronique.
macaroon [ˌmækə'ruːn] n macaron *m*.
macaw [mə'kɔː] n ara *m*.
Mace [meɪs] ® 1 n (*gas*) gaz *m* incapacitant, mace *m*. 2 vt attaquer au gaz incapacitant *or* au mace.
mace[1] [meɪs] n (*NonC: spice*) macis *m*.
mace[2] [meɪs] n (*weapon*) massue *f*; (*ceremonial staff*) masse *f*. **~bearer** massier *m*.
Macedonia [ˌmæsɪ'dəʊnɪə] n Macédoine *f*.
Macedonian [ˌmæsɪ'dəʊnɪən] 1 n Macédonien(ne) *m(f)*. 2 adj macédonien.
macerate ['mæsəreɪt] vti macérer.
Mach [mæk] n (*Aviat: also* **~ number**) (nombre *m* de) Mach *m*. **to fly at ~ 2** voler à Mach 2.
machete [mə'ʃetɪ] n machette *f*.
Machiavelli [ˌmækɪə'velɪ] n Machiavel *m*.
Machiavellian [ˌmækɪə'velɪən] adj machiavélique.
machination [ˌmækɪ'neɪʃən] n machination *f*, intrigue *f*, manœuvre *f*.
machine [mə'ʃiːn] 1 n a (*gen, Tech, Theat*) machine *f*. **adding/translating** *etc* **~** machine à calculer/à traduire *etc; see* **knitting, washing** *etc*.
b (*plane*) appareil *m*; (*car, cycle*) machine *f*; *see* **flying**.
c (*fig*) machine *f*, appareil *m*, organisation *f*. **the ~ of government** la machine politique *or* de l'État; **the military ~** la machine *or* l'appareil militaire *or* de l'armée.
d (*US Pol*) **the democratic ~** la machine administrative *or* l'appareil *m* du parti démocrate; *see* **party**.
e (*pej: person*) machine *f*, automate *m*.
2 vt (*Tech*) façonner à la machine, usiner; (*Sewing*) coudre à la machine, piquer (à la machine).
3 comp (*gen*) de la machine, des machines; (*Comput*) machine ▸**machine age** siècle *m* de la machine *or* des machines ▸**machine-assisted translation** traduction *f* assistée par ordinateur ▸**machine code** (*Comput*) code *m* machine ▸**machine error** erreur *f* machine ▸**machine gun** n mitrailleuse *f* ▸**machine-gun** vt mitrailler ▸**machine gunner** mitrailleur *m* ▸**machine-gunning** mitraillage *m* ▸**machine intelligence** intelligence *f* artificielle ▸**machine language** langage-machine *m* ▸**machine-made** fait à la machine ▸**machine operator** (*Ind*) opérateur *m*, -trice *f* (sur machines); (*Comput*) opérateur *m*, -trice *f* ▸**machine-readable** (*Comput*) exploitable par une machine; **in machine-readable form** sous (une) forme exploitable par une machine ▸**machine shop** atelier *m* d'usinage ▸**machine-stitch** vt piquer à la machine ▸**machine stitch** n point *m* (de piqûre) à la machine ▸**machine time** temps *m* d'opération (d'une machine) ▸**machine tool** machine-outil *f*; **machine-tool operator** opérateur *m* sur machine-outil, usineur *m* ▸**machine translation** traduction *f* automatique.
machinery [mə'ʃiːnərɪ] n (*NonC*) (*machines collectively*) machinerie *f*, machines *fpl*; (*parts of machine*) mécanisme *m*, rouages *mpl*. **a piece of ~** un mécanisme; (*fig*) **the ~ of government** les rouages de l'État; (*fig Pol etc*) **we need the ~ to introduce these reforms** nous avons besoin de rouages qui nous permettent (*subj*) d'introduire ces réformes.
machinist [mə'ʃiːnɪst] n machiniste *mf*, opérateur *m*, -trice *f* (sur machine); (*on sewing, knitting machines*) mécanicienne *f*.
machismo [mæ'tʃiːzməʊ] n (*NonC*) machisme *m*, phallocratie *f*.
macho ['mætʃəʊ] 1 n macho *m*, phallocrate *m*. 2 adj macho *inv*.
mackerel ['mækrəl] 1 n, pl **~** *or* **~s** maquereau *m*. 2 comp ▸**mackerel sky** ciel pommelé.
Mackinaw ['mækɪˌnɔː] n (*US*) (*also* **~ coat**) grosse veste *f* de laine à carreaux; (*also* **~ blanket**) grosse couverture *f* de laine à carreaux.
mackintosh ['mækɪntɒʃ] n imperméable *m*.
macramé [mə'krɑːmɪ] 1 n macramé *m*. 2 comp *plant holder etc* en macramé.
macro ['mækrəʊ] n (*Comput*) **abbr of macro-instruction**.
macro... ['mækrəʊ] pref macro..., *e.g.* **~molecule** macromolécule *f*; *see* **macrobiotic** *etc*.
macrobiotic [ˌmækrəʊbaɪ'ɒtɪk] adj macrobiotique.
macrobiotics [ˌmækrəʊbaɪ'ɒtɪks] n (*NonC*) macrobiotique *f*.
macrocosm ['mækrəʊkɒzəm] n macrocosme *m*.
macroeconomics [ˌmækrəʊˌiːkə'nɒmɪks] n (*NonC*) macro-économie *f*.
macro-instruction [ˌmækrəʊɪn'strʌkʃən] n macro-instruction *f*.
macrolinguistics [ˌmækrəʊlɪŋ'gwɪstɪks] n (*NonC*) macrolinguistique *f*.
macromarketing [ˌmækrəʊ'mɑːkɪtɪŋ] n macromarketing *m*.
macron ['mækrɒn] n macron *m*.
macrophotography [ˌmækrəʊfə'tɒgrəfɪ] n macrophotographie *f*.
macroscopic [ˌmækrə'skɒpɪk] adj macroscopique.
mad [mæd] 1 adj a (*deranged*) fou (*f* folle), dément, cinglé‡, dingue‡; *bull* furieux; *dog* enragé; (*rash*) *person* fou, insensé; *hope, plan* insensé; *race, gallop* effréné. **to go ~** devenir fou; (*fig*) **this is idealism gone ~** c'est de l'idéalisme qui dépasse les bornes *or* (*stronger*) qui vire à la folie; **to drive sb ~** (*lit*) rendre qn fou (*see also* **1(b)**); (*exasperate*) exaspérer qn, rendre qn malade* (*fig*); **he is as ~ as a hatter** *or* **as a March hare** il travaille du chapeau‡, il a un grain*, il a le timbre fêlé*; **(stark) raving ~, stark staring ~** fou à lier *or* à enfermer; **~ with grief** fou de douleur; **that was a ~ thing to do** il fallait être fou pour faire cela; **what a ~ idea!** c'est une idée insensée!; **you're ~ to think of it!** tu es fou d'y songer!; **are you ~?** ça ne va pas?* (*iro*); **you must be ~!** ça ne va pas, non!* (*iro*); **to run like ~*** courir comme un dératé *or* un perdu; **to shout like ~*** crier à tue-tête *or* comme un forcené; **to be working like ~*** travailler d'arrache-pied; **this plant grows like ~*** cette plante pousse comme du chiendent; **we had a ~ dash for the bus** nous avons dû foncer* pour attraper le bus; **I'm in a ~ rush** c'est une vraie course contre la montre.
b (*: *angry*) furieux. **to be ~ at** *or* **with sb** être furieux contre qn; **to get ~ at** *or* **with sb** s'emporter contre qn; **don't get ~ with** *or* **at me!** ne te fâche pas contre moi!; **he makes me ~!** ce qu'il peut m'agacer! *or* m'énerver!; **to drive sb ~** faire enrager qn, mettre qn en fureur; **he was ~ at me for spilling the tea** il était furieux contre moi pour avoir renversé le thé; **he's hopping** *or* **spitting ~** il est fou furieux; (*US*) **~ as a hornet*** furibard*; **he was really ~ about the mistake** l'erreur l'avait vraiment mis hors de lui (*see also* **1c**).
c (*: *enthusiastic: also* **~ keen**) **to go ~ on sth** (*overdo it*) y aller trop fort sur; (*become enthusiastic*) devenir dingue* de; **~ on** *or* **about** fou (*f* folle) de, entiché de*, mordu de*; **to be ~ on** *or* **about sb** être engoué (*fig*) de qn; (*in love*) être fou *or* toqué* de qn; **I'm ~ on** *or*

about you je suis follement amoureux de vous; **I'm not ~ on** *or* **about him** (*not in love*) ce n'est pas la passion, on ne peut pas dire que je sois folle de lui; (*not enthusiastic, impressed*) il ne m'emballe pas*; **to be ~ on** *or* **about swimming** être un enragé *or* un mordu* de la natation; **I'm not ~ about it**ça ne m'emballe pas*, ça ne me remplit pas d'enthousiasme.

d (*: *excited*) **the audience** *etc* **went ~** la folie a gagné le public *etc;* **the dog went ~ when he saw his master** le chien est devenu comme fou quand il a vu son maître; **I went ~ and finished everything in an hour** sur un coup de tête *or* de folie, j'ai tout fini en une heure.

2 **adv** *only in* **~ keen** *see* **1(c)**.

3 **comp** ►**madcap adj, n** écervelé(e) *m(f)* ►**mad cow disease** maladie *f* des vaches folles ►**madhouse** (*lit, also * fig*) maison *f* de fous ►**madman** fou *m*, aliéné *m* ►**mad money***: (*US*) **this is my mad money** cet argent-là, c'est pour me faire des folies ►**madwoman** folle *f*, aliénée *f*.

Madagascan [ˌmædəˈgæskən] 1 **adj** malgache. 2 **n** (*person*) Malgache *mf*.

Madagascar [ˌmædəˈgæskəʳ] **n: (Democratic Republic of) ~** (République *f* démocratique de) Madagascar; **in ~** à Madagascar.

madam [ˈmædəm] **n** a madame *f*; (*unmarried*) mademoiselle *f*. (*in letters*) **Dear M~** Madame; Mademoiselle; (*frm*) **M~ Chairman** Madame la Présidente. b mijaurée *f*, pimbêche *f*. **she's a little ~** c'est une petite pimbêche *or* mijaurée. c (*brothelkeeper*) sous-maîtresse *f*, tenancière *f* de maison close.

madden [ˈmædn] **vt** rendre fou (*f* folle); (*infuriate*) exaspérer. **~ed by pain** fou de douleur, exaspéré par la souffrance.

maddening [ˈmædnɪŋ] **adj** exaspérant, à rendre fou, rageant*.

maddeningly [ˈmædnɪŋlɪ] **adv** à un degré exaspérant, à vous rendre fou. **he is ~ well-organized** il est exaspérant d'organisation; **~ slow** d'une lenteur exaspérante.

made [meɪd] 1 **pret, ptp of make**. 2 **comp** ►**made-to-measure** (*Brit*) fait sur mesure ►**made-to-order** fait sur commande ►**made-up** *story* inventé, factice; (*pej*) faux (*f* fausse); *face* maquillé; *eyes, nails* fait; **she is too made-up** elle est trop fardée.

Madeira [məˈdɪərə] 1 **n** (*Geog*) (île *f* de) Madère *f*; (*wine*) (vin *m* de) madère *m*. 2 **comp** ►**Madeira cake** (sorte *f* de) quatre-quarts *m* ►**Madeira sauce** sauce *f* madère.

Madison Avenue [ˈmædɪsənˈævənjuː] **n** le monde de la publicité (*aux USA*).

madly [ˈmædlɪ] **adv** a (*lit, also * fig*) *behave* comme un fou; *interest, excite* follement; *love sb* à la folie. **to be ~ in love with sb** être éperdument amoureux de qn; **he's ~ interested in sport, he's ~ keen on sport** il est fou *or* passionné *or* mordu* de sport; **I ~ offered to help her** j'ai eu la folie de lui offrir mon aide. b (*: *hurriedly*) désespérément, avec acharnement. **I was ~ trying to open it** j'essayais désespérément de l'ouvrir; **we were ~ rushing for the train** c'était la course pour attraper le train.

madness [ˈmædnɪs] **n** (*Med*) folie *f*, démence *f*, aliénation *f* (mentale); (*in animals*) rage *f*; (*rashness*) folie, démence. **it is sheer ~ to say so** c'est de la pure folie *or* de la démence de le dire; **what ~!** c'est de la pure folie!, il faut être fou!

Madonna [məˈdɒnə] **n** (*Rel*) Madone *f*; (*fig*) madone *f*. **m~ lily** lis *m* blanc.

Madras [məˈdrɑːs] **n**Madras. **m~ (cotton)** madras *m*.

Madrid [məˈdrɪd] **n** Madrid.

madrigal [ˈmædrɪgəl] **n** madrigal *m*.

maelstrom [ˈmeɪlstrəʊm] **n** (*lit, fig*) tourbillon *m*, maelstrom *m*.

maestro [ˈmaɪstrəʊ] **n, pl ~s** *or* **maestri** [ˈmaɪstrɪ] maestro *m*.

Mae West* [ˌmeɪˈwest] **n** gilet *m* de sauvetage (gonflable).

MAFF **n** (*Brit*) (**abbr of Ministry of Agriculture, Fisheries and Food**) ministère *m* de l'Agriculture, de la Pêche et de l'Alimentation.

mafia [ˈmæfɪə] **n** maf(f)ia *f*.

mafioso [ˌmæfɪˈəʊsəʊ] **n** maf(f)ioso *m*.

mag* [mæg] 1 **n** (**abbr of magazine a**) revue *f*, périodique *m*, magazine *m*. 2 **adj** (**abbr of magnetic**) (*Comput*) **~ tape** bande *f* magnétique.

magazine [ˌmægəˈziːn] **n** a (*Press*) revue *f*, magazine *m*, périodique *m*; (*Rad, TV: also* **~ programme**) magazine. b (*Mil: store*) magasin *m* (du corps). c (*in gun*) (*compartment*) magasin *m*; (*cartridges*) chargeur *m*; (*in slide projector etc*) magasin.

Magellan [məˈgelən] **n** Magellan *m*. **~ Strait** détroit *m* de Magellan.

magenta [məˈdʒentə] 1 **n** magenta *m*. 2 **adj** magenta *inv*.

Maggie [ˈmægɪ] **n** (**dim of Margaret**) Maguy *f*.

Maggiore [ˌmædʒɪˈɔːrɪ] **n: Lake ~** le lac Majeur.

maggot [ˈmægət] **n** ver *m*, asticot *m*.

maggoty [ˈmægətɪ] **adj** *fruit* véreux.

Maghreb [ˈmʌgrəb] **n** Maghreb *m*.

Magi [ˈmeɪdʒaɪ] **npl** (rois *mpl*) mages *mpl*.

magic [ˈmædʒɪk] 1 **n** (*NonC*) magie *f*, enchantement *m*. **as if by ~, like ~** comme par enchantement *or* magie; **the ~ of that moment** la magie de cet instant. 2 **adj** (*lit*) magique, enchanté; (*fig*) surnaturel, merveilleux, prodigieux; *beauty* enchanteur (*f* -teresse). **(it's) ~!*** (c'est) super* *or* génial!*; **~ carpet** tapis *m* volant; **the M~ Flute** la Flûte enchantée; **~ lantern** lanterne *f* magique; **~ spell** sort *m*, sortilège *m*; **~ square** carré *m* magique; **to say the ~ word** prononcer la formule magique.

magical [ˈmædʒɪkəl] **adj** magique.

magically [ˈmædʒɪkəlɪ] **adv** magiquement; (*fig*) comme par enchantement *or* magie.

magician [məˈdʒɪʃən] **n** magicien(ne) *m(f)*; (*Theat etc*) illusionniste *mf*.

magisterial [ˌmædʒɪsˈtɪərɪəl] **adj** (*lit*) de magistrat; (*fig*) magistral, formidable.

magistracy [ˈmædʒɪstrəsɪ] **n** (*NonC*) magistrature *f*.

magistrate [ˈmædʒɪstreɪt] **n** magistrat *m*, juge *m*. **~s' court** ≃ tribunal *m* d'instance.

magma [ˈmægmə] **n, pl ~s** *or* **magmata** [ˈmægmətə] magma *m*.

Magna C(h)arta [ˌmægnəˈkɑːtə] **n** (*Brit Hist*) Grande Charte.

magnanimity [ˌmægnəˈnɪmɪtɪ] **n** magnanimité *f*.

magnanimous [mægˈnænɪməs] **adj** magnanime.

magnanimously [mægˈnænɪməslɪ] **adv** magnanimement.

magnate [ˈmægneɪt] **n** magnat *m*, roi *m*. **industrial/financial ~** magnat de l'industrie/de la finance; **oil ~** roi du pétrole.

magnesia [mægˈniːʃə] **n** magnésie *f*; *see* **milk**.

magnesium [mægˈniːzɪəm] **n** magnésium *m*.

magnet [ˈmægnɪt] **n** (*lit, fig*) aimant *m*.

magnetic [mægˈnetɪk] **adj** (*lit, fig*) magnétique. **~ card reader** lecteur *m* de cartes magnétiques; **~ disk** disque *m* magnétique; **~ field** champ *m* magnétique; **~ needle** aiguille *f* aimantée; **the ~ north** le nord magnétique; **~ storm** orage *m* magnétique; (*on credit card etc*) **~ strip(e)** piste *f* magnétique; **~ tape** bande *f* magnétique.

magnetically [mægˈnetɪkəlɪ] **adv** magnétiquement.

magnetism [ˈmægnɪtɪzəm] **n** (*lit, fig*) magnétisme *m*.

magnetize [ˈmægnɪtaɪz] **vt** (*lit*) aimanter, magnétiser; (*fig*) magnétiser.

magneto [mægˈniːtəʊ] **n** magnéto *f*.

magneto... [mægˈniːtəʊ] **pref** magnéto... .

magnetometer [ˌmægnɪˈtɒmɪtəʳ] **n** magnétomètre *m*.

magnetosphere [mægˈniːtəʊˌsfɪəʳ] **n** magnétosphère *f*.

Magnificat [mægˈnɪfɪˌkæt] **n** (*Rel*) Magnificat *m inv*.

magnification [ˌmægnɪfɪˈkeɪʃən] **n** (*see* **magnify**) grossissement *m*; amplification *f*; exagération *f*; (*Rel*) glorification *f*.

magnificence [mægˈnɪfɪsəns] **n** magnificence *f*, splendeur *f*, somptuosité *f*.

magnificent [mægˈnɪfɪsənt] **adj** magnifique, splendide, superbe; (*sumptuous*) somptueux.

magnificently [mægˈnɪfɪsəntlɪ] **adv** magnifiquement.

magnify [ˈmægnɪfaɪ] **vt** a *image* grossir; *sound* amplifier; *incident etc* exagérer, grossir. **to ~ sth 4 times** grossir qch 4 fois; **~ing glass** loupe *f*, verre *m* grossissant. b (*Rel: praise*) glorifier.

magnitude [ˈmægnɪtjuːd] **n** ampleur *f*; (*Astron*) magnitude *f*. (*fig*) **of the first ~** de première grandeur.

magnolia [mægˈnəʊlɪə] **n** (*also* **~ tree**) magnolia *m*, magnolier *m*. (*US*) **the M~ State** le Mississippi.

magnox [ˈmægnɒks] **n** magnox *m*. **~ reactor** réacteur *m* au magnox.

magnum [ˈmægnəm] 1 **n, pl ~s** magnum *m*. 2 **comp** ►**magnum opus** (*Art, Literat, fig*) œuvre maîtresse.

magpie [ˈmægpaɪ] **n** (*Orn*) pie *f*; (*petty thief*) chapardeur *m*, -euse *f*. **to chatter like a ~** jacasser comme une pie, être un vrai moulin à paroles*; (*fig : collects everything*) **he's a real ~** c'est un vrai chiffonnier, il ne jette rien.

Magyar [ˈmægjɑːʳ] 1 **adj** magyar. 2 **n** Magyar(e) *m(f)*.

maharaja(h) [ˌmɑːhəˈrɑːdʒə] **n** mahara(d)jah *m*.

maharanee, maharani [ˌmɑːhəˈrɑːniː] **n** maharani *f*.

maharishi [ˌmɑːhɑːˈriːʃɪ] **n** maharishi *m*.

mahatma [məˈhɑːtmə] **n** mahatma *m*.

mahjong(g) [ˌmɑːˈdʒɒŋ] **n** ma(h)-jong *m*.

mahogany [məˈhɒgənɪ] 1 **n** acajou *m*. 2 **comp** (*made of* ~) en acajou; (*~-coloured*) acajou *inv*.

Mahomet [məˈhɒmɪt] **n** Mahomet *m*.

Mahometan [məˈhɒmɪtən] 1 **adj** musulman, mahométan. 2 **n** Mahométan(e) *m(f)*.

Mahometanism [məˈhɒmɪtənɪzəm] **n** mahométisme *m*.

mahout [məˈhaʊt] **n** cornac *m*.

maid [meɪd] 1 **n** a (*servant*) domestique *f*; (*in hotel*) femme *f* de chambre; *see* **bar¹, house, lady** *etc*. b (††) (*young girl*) jeune fille *f*; (*virgin*) vierge *f*. (*pej*) **old ~** vieille fille; (*Hist*) **the M~ (of Orleans)** la Pucelle (d'Orléans). 2 **comp** ►**maid-of-all-work** bonne *f* à tout faire ►**maid of honour** demoiselle *f* d'honneur ►**maidservant††** servante *f*.

maiden [ˈmeɪdn] 1 **n** (*liter*) (*girl*) jeune fille *f*; (*virgin*) vierge *f*. 2 **comp** *flight, voyage* premier (*before noun*), inaugural ►**maiden aunt** tante *f* célibataire, tante vieille fille (*pej*) ►**maidenhair (fern)** capillaire *m*, cheveu *m* de Vénus ►**maidenhead** (*Anat*) hymen *m*; (*state*) virginité *f* ►**maiden lady** demoiselle *f* ►**maiden name** nom *m* de jeune fille ►**maiden speech** (*Parl*) premier discours (*d'un député etc*).

maidenhood [ˈmeɪdnhʊd] **n** virginité *f*.

maidenly [ˈmeɪdnlɪ] **adj** de jeune fille, virginal, modeste.

mail[1] [meɪl] 1 n (NonC) poste f; (letters, Comput) courrier m. by ~ par la poste; here's your ~ voici votre courrier; see first-class etc.
2 vt (esp US) envoyer or expédier (par la poste), poster.
3 comp ►**mailbag** sac postal ►**mailboat** paquebot(-poste) m ►**mail bomb** (US) colis m piégé ►**mailbox** (US, Comput) boîte f aux lettres ►**mail car** (US Rail) wagon-poste m ►**mail carrier** (US) facteur m, préposé(e) m(f) ►**mail coach** (Rail) wagon-poste m; (horse-drawn) malle-poste f ►**Mailgram** ® (US) télégramme m distribué avec le courrier ►**mail(ing) clerk** (employé(e) m(f)) préposé(e) m(f) au courrier ►**mailing list** (Comm) liste f d'adresses ►**mailman** (pl -men) (US) facteur m, préposé m ►**mail-merge** (Comput) publipostage m ►**mail-order** vente f par correspondance; we got it by mail-order nous l'avons acheté par correspondance; mail-order catalogue catalogue m de vente par correspondance; mail-order firm, mail-order house maison f de vente par correspondance ►**mail shot** mailing m, publipostage m ►**mail slot** (US) entrée f des lettres ►**mail train** train-poste m ►**mail truck** (US) voiture f or fourgon m des postes ►**mail van** (Brit) (Aut) voiture f or fourgon m des postes; (Rail) wagon-poste m.

mail[2] [meɪl] n (NonC) mailles fpl. coat of ~ cotte f de mailles; (fig) the ~ed fist la manière forte; see chain.

mailing ['meɪlɪŋ] n publipostage m, mailing m. ~ list fichier m or liste f d'adresses.

maim [meɪm] vt estropier, mutiler. to be ~ed for life être estropié pour la vie or à vie.

Main [meɪn] n Main m.

main [meɪn] 1 adj a feature, idea, objective principal, premier, essentiel; door, entrance, shop principal; pipe, beam maître (f maîtresse). the ~ body of the army/the crowd le gros de l'armée/de la foule; one of his ~ ideas was ... une de ses principales idées or idées maîtresses consistait à ...; (Ling) ~ clause proposition principale; my ~ idea was to establish ... mon idée directrice était d'établir ...; the ~ point of his speech le point fondamental de son discours; the ~ point or the ~ object or the ~ objective of the meeting l'objet principal or le premier objectif de la réunion; the ~ thing is to keep quiet l'essentiel est de se taire; the ~ thing to remember is ... ce qu'il ne faut surtout pas oublier c'est ...; to have an eye to the ~ chance être opportuniste, tirer profit de toutes les situations; see also 3 and drag j, eye, issue etc.
b by ~ force de vive force.
2 n a (principal pipe, wire) canalisation or conduite maîtresse. (electricity) ~ conducteur principal; (gas) ~ (in street) conduite principale; (in house) conduite de gaz; ~ (sewer) (égout m) collecteur m; (water) ~ (in street or house) conduite d'eau de la ville; the water in this tap comes from the ~s l'eau de ce robinet vient directement de la conduite; (Elec) the ~s le secteur; connected to the ~s branché sur (le) secteur; this radio works by battery or from the ~s ce poste de radio marche sur piles ou sur (le) secteur; to turn off the electricity/gas/water at the ~(s) couper le courant/le gaz/l'eau au compteur.
b in the ~ dans l'ensemble, en général, en gros; see might[2].
c (liter: sea) the ~ l'océan m, le (grand) large; see Spanish.
3 comp ►**main beam** (Archit) poutre f maîtresse ►**main bearing** (Aut etc) palier m ►**mainbrace** (Naut) bras m (de grand-vergue) (see splice 1) ►**main clause** (Gram) proposition principale ►**main course** (Culin) plat principal ►**main deck** (Naut) pont principal ►**main door (flat)** (Brit) appartement m avec porte d'entrée particulière sur la rue ►**mainframe (computer)** (central computer) unité f centrale, processeur m central; (large computer) gros ordinateur m ►**mainland** continent m (opposé à une île); the mainland of Greece, the Greek mainland la Grèce continentale ►**mainline** (Drugs sl: inject heroin etc) vi se shooter ◊ vt to mainline heroin se shooter à l'héroïne ►**main line** (Rail) grande ligne, voie principale; main-line station/train gare f/train m de grande ligne ►**mainliner** (Drugs sl) personne f qui se pique (dans la veine), piquouseur‡ m, -euse‡ f ►**mainmast** (Naut) grand mât ►**main memory** (Comput) mémoire f centrale ►**main office** (Comm etc) bureau principal; [political party, newspaper, agency etc] siège m (social) ►**main road** grande route f, route à grande circulation; the main road la grand-route; it is one of the main roads into Edinburgh c'est une des grandes voies d'accès à Édimbourg ►**mainsail** (Naut) grand-voile f ►**main sheet** (Naut) écoute f de (la) grand-voile ►**mainspring** [clock etc] ressort principal; (fig) mobile principal ►**mains set** [radio, tape recorder etc] poste-secteur m ►**mains supply**: to be on the mains supply (for electricity/gas/water) être raccordé au réseau (de distribution) d'électricité/de gaz/d'eau ►**mainstay** (Naut) étai m (de grand mât); (fig) soutien m, point m d'appui; he was the mainstay of the organization c'était lui le pilier or le pivot de l'organisation ►**mainstream** etc see mainstream etc ►**main street** grand-rue f, rue principale ►**mains water** eau f de la ville.

Maine [meɪn] n Maine m. in ~ dans le Maine.

mainly ['meɪnlɪ] adv principalement, en grande partie; (especially) surtout.

mainstream ['meɪnstriːm] 1 n [politics etc] courant m dominant. 2 adj dans la ligne du courant dominant. ~ jazz jazz m classique, middle jazz m. 3 vt (US: Scol) intégrer dans la vie scolaire normale.

mainstreaming ['meɪnstriːmɪŋ] n (US) intégration f (d'enfants retardés ou surdoués) dans la vie scolaire normale.

maintain [meɪn'teɪn] vt a (continue) order, progress maintenir; silence garder; radio silence maintenir; friendship, correspondence entretenir; attitude, advantage conserver, garder; war continuer, soutenir; cause, rights, one's strength soutenir. he ~ed his opposition to il continua à s'opposer à; if the improvement is ~ed si l'on (or s'il etc) continue à faire des progrès, si l'amélioration se maintient. b (support) army etc entretenir; family, wife, child subvenir aux besoins de, entretenir. c (keep up) road, building, car, machine entretenir. d (assert) opinion, fact soutenir, maintenir. I ~ that je soutiens or je maintiens que.

maintenance ['meɪntɪnəns] 1 n a (NonC) [order etc] maintien m; [army, family] entretien m; [road, building, car, machine] entretien, maintenance f (Tech). car ~ entretien des voitures.
b (Jur) obligation f or pension f alimentaire, aliments mpl. he pays £50 per week ~ il verse une pension alimentaire de 50 livres par semaine.
2 comp ►**maintenance allowance** [student] bourse f (d'études); [worker away from home] indemnité f (pour frais) de déplacement ►**maintenance contract** contrat m d'entretien ►**maintenance costs** frais mpl d'entretien ►**maintenance crew** équipe f d'entretien ►**maintenance grant** = maintenance allowance ►**maintenance man** (Tech etc) employé chargé de l'entretien ►**maintenance order** (Jur) (décision f en matière d')obligation f alimentaire.

maisonette [ˌmeɪzə'net] n (esp Brit) (appartement m en) duplex m.

maître d'hôtel [ˌmetrədəʊ'tel] n, pl maîtres d'hôtel (US also maître d'* ['metrəˌdiː]) maître m d'hôtel.

maize [meɪz] n (Brit) maïs m. ~ field champ m de maïs.

Maj. (abbr of Major) (on envelope) ~ J. Smith Monsieur le Major J. Smith.

majestic [mə'dʒestɪk] adj majestueux, auguste.

majestically [mə'dʒestɪkəlɪ] adv majestueusement.

majesty ['mædʒɪstɪ] n majesté f. His M~ the King Sa Majesté le Roi; Your M~ Votre Majesté; (Brit) His or Her M~'s Government le gouvernement britannique; (Brit) on His or Her M~'s service au service du gouvernement britannique; (Brit) His or Her M~'s Stationery Office ≃ l'Imprimerie nationale; see ship.

major ['meɪdʒəʳ] 1 adj (gen, Jur, Mus, Philos etc) majeur. of ~ importance d'une importance majeure or exceptionnelle; of ~ interest d'intérêt majeur; (Mus) ~ key ton majeur; in the ~ key en majeur; for the ~ part en grande partie; the ~ portion la majeure partie; (Med) ~ operation opération f majeure, grosse opération; ~ repairs grosses réparations fpl; ~ road route f principale or à priorité; it was a ~ success cela a eu un succès considérable; (Cards) ~ suit majeure f; (Brit Scol) Smith M~ Smith aîné.
2 comp ►**major-general** (Brit, US Mil) général m de division; (US Air Force) général m de division aérienne ►**major league** (US Sport) première division f.
3 n a (Mil, also US Air Force) commandant m; (cavalry) chef m d'escadron; (infantry) chef de bataillon.
b (Jur) majeur(e) m(f).
c (Univ) matière principale.
d (esp US Univ) music/psychology etc ~ étudiant(e) m(f) en musique/psychologie etc.
4 vi (US Univ) to ~ in chemistry se spécialiser en chimie.

Majorca [mə'jɔːkə] n Majorque f. in ~ à Majorque.

Majorcan [mə'jɔːkən] 1 adj majorquin. 2 n Majorquin(e) m(f).

majordomo [ˌmeɪdʒə'dəʊməʊ] n majordome m.

majorette [ˌmeɪdʒə'ret] n majorette f.

majority [mə'dʒɒrɪtɪ] 1 n a (greater part) majorité f. to be in the ~ être majoritaire or en majorité; elected by a ~ of 9 élu avec une majorité de 9 voix; a four-fifths ~ une majorité des quatre cinquièmes; in the ~ of cases dans la majorité or la plupart des cas; the ~ of people think that la plupart or la majorité des gens pensent que; the vast ~ of them believe dans leur immense majorité ils croient; see silent. b (in age) majorité f. to reach one's ~ atteindre sa majorité.
2 comp (Pol) government, rule majoritaire ►**majority opinion** (US Jur) arrêt m rendu à la majorité des juges ►**majority verdict** (Jur) verdict m majoritaire or rendu à la majorité.

make [meɪk] pret, ptp made 1 vt a (gen: create, produce, form) bed, bread, clothes, coffee, fire, noise, peace, remark, one's will etc faire; building construire; toys, tools faire, fabriquer; pot, model faire, façonner; speech faire, prononcer; mistake faire, commettre; payment faire, effectuer (Comm); (Sport etc) points, score marquer. God made Man Dieu a créé l'homme; made in France (gen) fabriqué en France; (on label) "made in France"; watch made of gold montre en or; you were made for me tu es fait pour moi; (fig) to show what one is made of donner sa mesure; this car wasn't made to carry 8 people cette voiture n'est pas faite pour transporter 8 personnes; I'm not made for running* je ne suis pas fait pour la course à pied or pour courir; he's as clever as they ~'em* or as they're made* il est malin comme pas un*; to ~ an attempt to do essayer de faire, faire une tentative or un essai pour faire; to ~ a bow to sb faire un salut à qn, saluer qn; to ~ a case for sth apporter des arguments en faveur de qch; to ~ a start on

sth commencer qch, se mettre à qch; **to ~ a day of it** s'organiser *or* se faire une sortie; **to ~ a night of it** s'organiser *or* se faire une petite soirée; *see* **difference, offer, promise** *etc.*

b (*cause to be*) rendre; faire. **to ~ sb sad** rendre qn triste, attrister qn; **to ~ o.s. useful/ill** *etc* se rendre utile/malade *etc;* **to ~ o.s. understood** se faire comprendre; **that smell ~s me hungry** cette odeur me donne faim; **~ yourself comfortable** mettez-vous à l'aise; **~ yourself at home** faites comme chez vous; **to ~ sth ready** préparer qch; **to ~ sth yellow** jaunir qch; **to ~ sb king** faire qn roi; **he made John his assistant** il a pris Jean comme assistant, il a fait de Jean son assistant; **this actor ~s the hero a tragic figure** cet acteur fait du héros un personnage tragique; **he made her his wife** il en a fait sa femme, il l'a épousée; **I'll ~ a tennis player (out) of him yet!*** il n'est pas dit que je n'en ferai pas un joueur de tennis!; **to ~ a friend of sb** se faire un ami de qn; **I ~ it a rule to rise early** je me fais une règle de me lever tôt; **to ~ sth into something else** transformer qch en quelque chose d'autre; **let's ~ it 5 o'clock/£3** si on disait 5 heures/3 livres; **I'm coming tomorrow — ~ it the afternoon** je viendrai demain — oui, mais dans l'après-midi *or* plutôt dans l'après-midi; *see* **best, habit, little^2** *etc.*

c (*force, oblige*) faire; (*stronger*) obliger, forcer. **to ~ sb do sth** faire faire qch à qn, obliger *or* forcer qn à faire qch; **I was made to speak** on m'a fait prendre la parole; (*stronger*) on m'a obligé *or* forcé à parler; **what made you believe that ...?** qu'est-ce qui vous a fait croire que ...?; **what ~s you do that?** qu'est-ce qui te fait faire ça?; **I don't know what ~s him do it** je ne sais pas ce qui le pousse à le faire; **you can't ~ me!** tu ne peux pas m'y forcer! *or* obliger!; **to ~ sb laugh** faire rire qn; **the author ~s him die in the last chapter** l'auteur le fait mourir au dernier chapitre; **the children were making believe they were on a boat** les enfants faisaient semblant *or* jouaient à faire semblant d'être sur un bateau; **let's ~ believe we're on a desert island** on serait sur une île déserte (*see* **4**); **to ~ do with sth/sb, to ~ sth/sb do** (*be satisfied*) se contenter *or* s'arranger de qch/qn; (*manage*) se débrouiller avec qch/qn, se tirer d'affaire avec qch/qn; **to ~ do as best one can** s'arranger *or* se débrouiller de son mieux; (*fig*) **she had to ~ do and mend for many years** elle a dû se débrouiller pendant des années avec ce qu'elle avait; *see* **shift** *etc.*

d (*earn etc*) *money [person]* (se) faire, gagner; *[business deal etc]* rapporter; *profits* faire. **he ~s £400 a week** il se fait 400 livres par semaine; **how much do you ~?** combien gagnez-vous?; **to ~ a fortune** faire fortune; **I ~ a living (by) teaching music** je gagne ma vie en donnant des leçons de musique; **the deal made him £500** cette affaire lui a rapporté 500 livres; **what did you ~ by** *or* **on it?** qu'est-ce que ça t'a rapporté?; **how much do you stand to ~?** combien pensez-vous y gagner?; **he ~s a bit on the side** il se fait des (petits) à-côtés; *see* **profit** *etc.*

e (*equal; constitute; complete*) **2 and 2 ~ 4** 2 et 2 font *or* égalent 4; **100 centimetres ~ one metre** 100 centimètres font *or* égalent un mètre; **that ~s 20** ça fait 20; (*in shop etc*) **how much does that ~ (altogether)?** combien cela fait-il?, combien ça fait (en tout)?; **to ~ a quorum** atteindre le quorum; **these books ~ a set** ces livres forment une collection; **it made a nice surprise** cela nous (*or* lui *etc*) a fait une bonne surprise; **partridges ~ good eating** les perdreaux sont très bons à manger; **they ~ good cooking apples** ce sont *or* elles font de bonnes pommes à cuire; **it ~s pleasant reading** c'est d'une lecture agréable, c'est agréable à lire; **this cloth will ~ a dress** ce tissu va me (*or* te *etc*) faire une robe; **they ~ a handsome pair** ils forment un beau couple; **he made a good husband** il s'est montré bon mari; **she made him a good wife** elle a été une bonne épouse pour lui; **he'll ~ a good footballer** il fera un bon joueur de football; **"man" ~s "men" in the plural** "man" fait "men" au pluriel; **I made one of their group** j'ai fait partie de leur groupe; **will you ~ one of us?** voulez-vous vous joindre à nous? *or* être des nôtres?; (*Cards etc*) **to ~ a fourth** faire le quatrième; **that ~s the third time I've rung him** ça fait la troisième fois *or* trois fois que je lui téléphone.

f (*reach, attain*) *destination* arriver à, se rendre à; (*catch*) *train etc* attraper, avoir. **will we ~ (it to) Paris before lunch?** est-ce que nous arriverons à Paris avant le déjeuner?; (*Naut*) **to ~ port** arriver au port; **do you think he'll ~ (it to) university?** croyez-vous qu'il arrivera à entrer à la faculté?; **the novel made the bestseller list** le roman a figuré sur la liste des best-sellers, le roman a réussi à se placer sur la liste des best-sellers; **he made (it into) the first team** il a été sélectionné pour la première équipe, il a réussi à être sélectionné dans la première équipe; **he made the list of ...*** son nom a figuré sur la liste de ...; **to ~ it** (*arrive*) arriver; (*achieve sth*) parvenir à qch; (*succeed*) réussir, y parvenir, y arriver; **eventually we made it** au bout du compte nous y sommes parvenus *or* arrivés; **you'll never ~ it!** vous n'y arriverez jamais! *or* ne réussirez jamais!; **he made it just in time** il est arrivé juste à temps; **can you ~ it by 3 o'clock?** est-ce que tu peux y être pour 3 heures?; **to ~ 100 km/h** faire 100 km/h, faire du cent*; (*Naut*) **to ~ 10 knots** filer 10 nœuds; **we made 100 km in one hour** nous avons fait 100 km en une heure; **we made good time** (*gen*) nous avons bien marché; (*in vehicle*) nous avons fait une bonne moyenne, nous avons bien roulé *or* bien marché*; **we made poor time** nous n'avons pas été très rapides; **he made it* with the in-crowd*** il a réussi à se faire accepter par les gens branchés*; (*have intercourse with*) **to ~ it with a girl‡** s'envoyer‡ *or* se taper‡ une fille; **they're making it‡ (together)** ils couchent* (ensemble).

g (*reckon, estimate; consider, believe*) **what time do you ~ it?** quelle heure as-tu?, quelle heure (est-ce que) tu as?; **I ~ the total 70 francs** selon mes calculs cela fait 70 F; **how many do you ~ it?** combien tu en comptes?; **I ~ it 100 km from here to Paris** selon moi *or* d'après moi il y a 100 km d'ici à Paris; **what did you ~ of the film?** comment avez-vous compris ce film?; **what do you ~ of him?** qu'est-ce que tu penses de lui?; **I don't know what to ~ of it all** je ne sais pas quoi penser de tout ça; **I can't ~ anything of this letter, I can ~ nothing of this letter** je ne comprends rien à cette lettre.

h (*Cards*) **to ~ the cards** battre les cartes; **to ~ a trick** faire un pli; **he made 10 and lost 3 (tricks)** il en a fait 10 et en a perdu 3; (*Bridge*) **to bid and ~ 3 hearts** demander et faire 3 cœurs, faire 3 cœurs demandés; **he managed to ~ his queen of diamonds** il a réussi à faire sa dame de carreau.

i (*secure success or future of*) **this business has made him** cette affaire a fait sa fortune *or* son succès; **that film made her** ce film l'a consacrée; **he was made for life** son avenir était assuré; **you're made!*** pas de soucis à vous faire pour votre avenir!; **he's got it made‡** il n'a pas à s'en faire, pour lui c'est du tout cuit*; **to ~ or break sb** assurer ou briser la carrière de qn; **his visit made my day!*** sa visite a transformé ma journée!; (*iro*) il ne manquait plus que sa visite pour compléter ma journée!; *see* **mar.**

2 **vi** a **to ~ sure of sth** s'assurer de qch; **to ~ so bold as to suggest** se permettre de suggérer; *see* **free, good, merry** *etc.*

b **he made as if to strike me** il leva la main comme pour me frapper, il fit mine de me frapper; **the child made as if to cry** l'enfant a fait mine de pleurer; **she made (as if) to touch the book** elle a avancé la main vers le livre; **he was making like* he didn't have any money** il prétendait ne pas avoir d'argent, il faisait celui qui n'avait pas d'argent.

c (*go*) aller, se diriger. **they made after him** ils se sont mis à sa poursuite; **he made at me** *or* **for me with a knife** il s'est jeté sur moi avec un couteau; **to ~ for** aller vers, se diriger vers; *[ship etc]* faire route pour (*see also* **2(d)**); **to ~ for home** rentrer, prendre le chemin du retour; *see also* **make off.**

d *[facts, evidence]* **to ~ in sb's favour/against sb** militer en faveur de qn/contre qn; **this will ~ against your chances of success** cela va nuire à vos chances de succès; **to ~ for sth** (*tend to result in*) tendre à qch; (*contribute to*) contribuer à qch; (*conduce to*) être favorable à qch, être à l'avantage de qch.

e *[tide, flood]* monter.

3 **n** a (*Comm*) (*brand*) marque *f*; (*manufacture*) fabrication *f*. **it's a good ~** c'est une bonne marque; **French ~ of car** marque française de voiture; **car of French ~** voiture *f* de construction française; **what ~ of car have you got?** qu'est-ce que vous avez comme (marque de) voiture?; **these are our own ~** ceux-ci sont fabriqués par nous *or* sont faits maison; **its my own ~** je l'ai fait moi-même.

b (*pej*) **he's on the ~*** (*wants success*) c'est le succès qui l'intéresse; (*wants money*) il cherche à se remplir les poches; (*wants sth specific*) il pense à ses intérêts d'abord; (*sexually*) il lui fait du plat‡; (*US*) **it's on the ~*** ça a du succès.

4 **comp ▸make-believe: to play at make-believe** jouer à faire semblant; **the land of make-believe** le pays des chimères; **don't worry, it's just make-believe** ne vous en faites pas, c'est pour faire semblant; **his story is pure make-believe** son histoire est de l'invention pure *or* (de la) pure fantaisie; **they were on a make-believe island** ils jouaient à faire semblant d'être sur une île; **the child made a make-believe boat out of the chair** l'enfant faisait comme si la chaise était un bateau **▸make-fast** (*US*) point *m* d'amarre **▸makeover** (*Fashion*) changement *m* de look* *or* de style **▸makeshift n** expédient *m*, moyen *m* de fortune ◊ **adj** de fortune **▸make-up** *see* **make-up ▸makeweight** (*lit*) complément *m* de poids; (** fig: person*) bouche-trou *m*.

▸make away vi = **make off.**

▸make away with vt fus (*murder*) supprimer. **to make away with o.s.** se supprimer.

▸make off vi se sauver, filer*, décamper*. **to make off with sth** filer avec qch.

▸make out 1 **vi** (*) a (*get on*) se débrouiller; (*do well*) se tirer bien d'affaire, réussir. **how are you making out?** comment ça va?, comment vous débrouillez-vous?; **we're making out** ça va, on se débrouille; **we're just making out** on fait aller*; **the firm is making out all right** l'affaire marche bien; **he's making out very well in London** il se débrouille très bien à Londres; **I've got enough to make out** j'ai assez pour vivre, je me débrouille.

b (*US*) **to make out‡** se peloter‡; **to make out with sb** peloter‡ qn.

2 **vt sep** a (*draw up, write*) *list, account* faire, dresser; *cheque* faire; *will, document* faire, rédiger, écrire. **to make out a bill** faire une facture; **cheques made out to ...** chèques libellés à l'ordre *or* au nom de ...; **whom do I make it out to?** je le fais à l'ordre de qui?, c'est à quel ordre?; **he made out a good case for not doing it** il a présenté de bons arguments pour ne pas le faire.

b (*see, distinguish*) *object, person* discerner, reconnaître, distinguer; (*decipher*) *handwriting* déchiffrer; (*understand*) *ideas, reasons, sb's motives* comprendre, discerner. **I couldn't make out where the road was in the fog** je n'arrivais pas à voir où était la route dans le brouillard; **I can't make it out at all** je n'y comprends rien; **how do you make that out?** qu'est-ce qui vous fait penser cela?; **I can't make out what he wants/why he is here** je n'arrive pas à voir *or* comprendre ce qu'il veut/pourquoi il est ici.

c (*claim, pretend*) prétendre (*that* que); (*imply*) faire paraître. **the play makes her out to be naïve** la pièce la fait passer pour naïve; **they made him out to be a fool** ils ont dit que c'était un imbécile; **you make him out to be better than he is** vous le faites paraître mieux qu'il n'est; **he made himself out to be a doctor, he made out that he was a doctor** il se faisait passer pour (un) médecin, il prétendait être médecin; **he's not as stupid as he makes (himself) out** il n'est pas aussi stupide qu'il le prétend; **he isn't as rich as people make out** il n'est pas aussi riche que les gens le prétendent.

►**make over** 1 **vt sep** a (*assign*) *money, land* céder, transférer (*to* à). b (*remake*) *dress, coat* refaire, reprendre. **she made his jacket over to fit his son** elle a repris sa veste pour (qu'elle aille à) son fils. 2 **makeover** n *see* **make 4**.

►**make up** 1 **vi** a (*make friends again*) se réconcilier, se raccommoder*.

b (*apply cosmetics*) se maquiller, se farder; (*Theat*) se maquiller, se grimer.

2 **vt sep** a (*invent*) *story, excuse, explanation* inventer, fabriquer. **you're making it up!** tu l'inventes (de toutes pièces)!

b (*put together*) *packet, parcel* faire; *dress, salad etc* assembler; *medicine, lotion, solution* faire, préparer; *list* faire, dresser. **to make sth up into a bundle** faire un paquet de qch; **to make up a collection of** faire une collection de; (*Typ*) **to make up a book** mettre un livre en pages; (*Pharm*) **to make up a prescription** exécuter *or* préparer une ordonnance; **she made up a bed for him on the sofa** elle lui a fait *or* préparé un lit sur le canapé; **have you made up the beds?** as-tu fait les lits?; **customers' accounts are made up monthly** les relevés de compte des clients sont établis chaque mois; **I've made up an outline of what we ought to do** j'ai établi les grandes lignes de ce que nous devons faire; **they make up clothes as well as sell material** ils vendent du tissu et font aussi la confection; **"customers' own material made up"** "travail à façon"; *see* **mind** *etc*.

c (*counterbalance; replace*) compenser; *loss, deficit* combler, suppléer à; *sum of money, numbers, quantity, total* compléter. (*money*) **to make up the difference** mettre la différence; **he made it up to £100** il a complété les 100 livres; **to make up lost time** rattraper le temps perdu; (*lit, fig*) **to make up lost ground** regagner le terrain perdu.

d (*compensate for*) **to make sth up to sb, to make it up to sb for sth** compenser qn pour qch.

e (*settle*) *dispute, difference of opinion* mettre fin à. **to make up a quarrel, to make it up** se réconcilier, se raccommoder*; **let's make it up** faisons la paix.

f (*apply cosmetics to*) *person, face* maquiller, farder; (*Theat*) maquiller, grimer. **to make o.s. up, to make up one's face** se maquiller, se farder; (*Theat*) se maquiller, se grimer.

g (*compose, form*) former, composer; (*represent*) représenter. **these parts make up the whole** ces parties forment *or* composent le tout; **the group was made up of 6 teachers** le groupe était fait *or* formé *or* composé de 6 professeurs; **how many people make up the team?** combien y a-t-il de personnes dans l'équipe?; **they make up 6% of ...** ils représentent 6 % de ... .

3 **make-up** n, comp *see* **make-up**.

4 **made-up** adj *see* **made 2**.

►**make up for** vt fus compenser. **I'll make up for all you've suffered** je vous compenserai pour ce que vous avez souffert; **to make up for lost time** récupérer *or* rattraper *or* regagner le temps perdu; **he tried to make up for all the trouble he'd caused** il essaya de se faire pardonner les ennuis qu'il avait causés; **she said that nothing would make up for her husband's death** elle dit que rien ne compenserait la mort de son mari; **he has made up for last year's losses** il a rattrapé les pertes de l'année dernière; **he made up for all the mistakes he'd made** il s'est rattrapé pour toutes les erreurs qu'il avait commises.

►**make up on** vt fus (*catch up with: gen, Sport*) rattraper.

►**make up to*** vt fus (*curry favour with*) faire des avances à, essayer de se faire bien voir par; (*flatter*) flatter.

maker ['meɪkəʳ] n a (*in comps: manufacturer*) **-maker** (*gen*) fabricant(e) *m(f)* de ..., *e.g.* **tyre/furniture-maker** fabricant de pneus/de meubles; **film-maker** cinéaste *mf*; *see also* **watch** *etc*. b (*in comps: device*) *e.g.* **coffee-maker** cafetière *f* électrique; **yoghourt-maker** yaourtière *f*. c (*Rel*) **our M~** le Créateur; (*hum*) **he's gone to meet his M~** il est allé ad patres (*hum*).

make-up ['meɪkʌp] 1 n a (*NonC: nature etc*) *[object, group etc]* constitution *f*; *[person]* tempérament *m*, caractère *m*. b (*NonC: cosmetics*) maquillage *m*, fard *m*. **she wears too much ~** elle se maquille trop, elle est trop fardée. c (*US * Scol etc*) examen *m* de rattrapage. 2 **comp** ►**make-up artist** maquilleur *m*, -euse *f* ►**make-up bag** trousse *f* de maquillage ►**make-up base** base *f* (de maquillage) ►**make-up case** nécessaire *m or* boîte *f* de maquillage ►**make-up class** (*US Scol*) cours *m* de rattrapage ►**make-up girl** maquilleuse *f* ►**make-up man** maquilleur *m* ►**make-up remover** démaquillant *m*.

making ['meɪkɪŋ] n a (*NonC*) (*Comm, gen*) fabrication *f*; *[dress]* façon *f*, confection *f*; *[machines]* fabrication, construction *f*; *[food]* confection. **in the ~** en formation, en gestation; **it's still in the ~** c'est encore en cours de développement *or* en chantier; **it's history in the ~** c'est l'histoire en train de se faire; **it's civil war in the ~** c'est la guerre civile qui se prépare; **all his troubles are of his own ~** tous ses ennuis sont de sa faute; **he wrote a book on the ~ of the film** il a écrit un livre sur la genèse du film; **the ~ of the film took 3 months** le tournage du film a duré 3 mois; **it was the ~ of him** (*gen*) c'est ce qui a formé son caractère; (*made him successful*) son succès est parti de là.

b **~s** éléments essentiels; **we have the ~s of a library** nous avons les éléments nécessaires pour constituer une bibliothèque; **he has the ~s of a footballer** il a l'étoffe d'un joueur de football; **the situation has the ~s of a civil war** cette situation laisse présager une guerre civile.

Malachi ['mælə,kaɪ] n Malachie *m*.

malachite ['mælə,kaɪt] n malachite *f*.

maladjusted [,mælə'dʒʌstɪd] adj (*Psych etc*) inadapté; (*Tech*) mal ajusté, mal réglé.

maladjustment [,mælə'dʒʌsmənt] n (*Psych*) inadaptation *f*, déséquilibre *m*; (*Tech*) dérèglement *m*, mauvais ajustement.

maladministration ['mæləd,mɪnɪs'treɪʃən] n mauvaise gestion.

maladroit [,mælə'drɔɪt] adj maladroit.

maladroitly [,mælə'drɔɪtlɪ] adv maladroitement.

maladroitness [,mælə'drɔɪtnɪs] n maladresse *f*.

malady ['mælədɪ] n maladie *f*, mal *m*.

Malagasy ['mælə'gɑːzɪ] 1 n a Malgache *mf*. b (*Ling*) malgache *m*. 2 adj (*Hist*) malgache. **the ~ Republic** la République malgache.

malapropism ['mælæprɒpɪzəm] n impropriété *f* (de langage).

malaria [mə'lɛərɪə] n malaria *f*, paludisme *m*.

malarial [mə'lɛərɪəl] adj *fever* paludéen; *mosquito* de la malaria, du paludisme.

Malawi [mə'lɑːwɪ] n Malawi *m*.

Malawian [mə'lɑːwɪən] 1 n Malawien(-ienne) *m(f)*. 2 adj malawien.

Malay [mə'leɪ] 1 adj malais. **the ~ archipelago** l'archipel *m* malais. 2 n a Malais(e) *m(f)*. b (*Ling*) malais *m*.

Malaya [mə'leɪə] n Malaisie *f*.

Malayan [mə'leɪən] = **Malay**.

Malaysia [mə'leɪzɪə] n Malaisie *f*.

Malaysian [mə'leɪzɪən] 1 n Malais(e) *m(f)*. 2 adj malais.

malcontent ['mælkən,tent] adj, n mécontent(e) *m(f)*.

Maldives ['mɔːldaɪvz] npl Maldives *fpl*.

male [meɪl] 1 adj (*Anat, Bio, Bot, Tech etc*) mâle; (*fig: manly*) mâle, viril (*f* virile). **~ child** enfant mâle; **~ sex** sexe masculin; **~-voice choir** chœur *m* d'hommes, chœur de voix mâles; *see* **chauvinist, menopause, model** *etc*. 2 n mâle *m*.

malediction [,mælɪ'dɪkʃən] n malédiction *f*.

malefactor ['mælɪfæktəʳ] n malfaiteur *m*, -trice *f*.

malevolence [mə'levələns] n malveillance *f* (*towards* envers).

malevolent [mə'levələnt] adj malveillant.

malevolently [mə'levələntlɪ] adv avec malveillance.

malformation [,mælfɔː'meɪʃən] n malformation *f*, difformité *f*.

malformed [,mæl'fɔːmd] adj mal formé, difforme.

malfunction [,mæl'fʌŋkʃən] 1 n mauvais fonctionnement *m*, défaillance *f*. 2 vi mal fonctionner.

Mali ['mɑːlɪ] n Mali *m*.

Malian ['mɑːlɪən] 1 n Malien(ne) *m(f)*. 2 adj malien.

malice ['mælɪs] n malice *f*, méchanceté *f*; (*stronger*) malveillance *f*. **to bear sb ~** vouloir du mal à qn; (*Jur*) **with ~ aforethought** avec préméditation, avec intention criminelle *or* délictueuse.

malicious [mə'lɪʃəs] adj méchant; (*stronger*) malveillant; (*Jur*) délictueux, criminel. (*Jur*) **~ damage** dommage causé avec intention de nuire.

maliciously [mə'lɪʃəslɪ] adv avec méchanceté; (*stronger*) avec malveillance; (*Jur*) avec préméditation, avec intention criminelle *or* délictueuse.

malign [mə'laɪn] 1 adj pernicieux, nuisible. 2 vt calomnier, diffamer. **you ~ me** vous me calomniez.

malignancy [mə'lɪgnənsɪ] n malveillance *f*, malfaisance *f*; (*Med*) malignité *f*.

malignant [mə'lɪgnənt] adj *person* malfaisant, malveillant; *look, intention* malveillant; *action, effect* malfaisant; (*Med*) malin (*f* -igne).

malignity [mə'lɪgnɪtɪ] n = **malignancy**.

malinger [mə'lɪŋgəʳ] vi faire le (*or* la) malade.

malingerer [mə'lɪŋgərəʳ] n faux malade *m*, fausse malade *f*; (*Admin, Mil etc*) simulateur *m*, -trice *f*. **he's a ~** il se fait passer pour malade.

mall [mɔːl] n a (*gen*) allée *f*, mail *m*. b (*US*) (*pedestrianised street*) rue *f* piétonnière; (*also* **shopping ~**) centre *m* commercial.

mallard ['mæləd] n, pl **~(s)** colvert *m*.

malleability [,mælɪə'bɪlɪtɪ] n malléabilité *f*.

malleable ['mælɪəbl] adj malléable.

mallet ['mælɪt] n (*all senses*) maillet *m*.
malleus ['mælɪəs] n, pl **mallei** ['mælɪ,aɪ] marteau *m*.
mallow ['mæləʊ] n (*Bot*) mauve *f*; *see* **marsh**.
malnutrition [,mælnjʊ'trɪʃən] n sous-alimentation *f*, insuffisance *f* alimentaire.
malodorous [mæl'əʊdərəs] adj malodorant.
malpractice [,mæl'præktɪs] n (*wrongdoing*) faute professionnelle; (*neglect of duty*) négligence *or* incurie professionnelle.
malt [mɔ:lt] 1 n malt *m*. 2 comp *vinegar* de malt ►**malted milk** lait malté ►**malt extract** extrait *m* de malt ►**malt liquor** (*US*) bière *f* ►**malt whisky** (*Brit*) (whisky *m*) pur malt.
Malta ['mɔ:ltə] n Malte *f*. **in ~** à Malte.
maltase ['mɔ:lteɪz] n maltase *f*.
Maltese [,mɔ:l'ti:z] 1 adj maltais. **~ cross** croix *f* de Malte; **~ fever** fièvre *f* de Malte. 2 n a (pl inv) (*person*) Maltais(e) *m(f)*. b (*Ling*) maltais *m*.
Malthus ['mælθəs] n Malthus *m*.
malthusianism [mæl'θju:zɪə,nɪzəm] n malthusianisme *m*.
maltreat [,mæl'tri:t] vt maltraiter, malmener.
maltreatment [,mæl'tri:tmənt] n mauvais traitement.
mam‡ [mæm] n (*Brit*) maman *f*.
mam(m)a [mə'mɑ:] n mère *f*, maman *f*. (*pej*) **he's a ~'s boy** c'est un fils à sa mère (*pej*).
mammal ['mæməl] n mammifère *m*.
mammalian [mæ'meɪlɪən] adj mammifère.
mammary ['mæmərɪ] adj mammaire.
mammography [mæ'mɒgrəfɪ] n mammographie *f*.
Mammon ['mæmən] n le dieu Argent, le Veau d'or (*fig*).
mammoth ['mæməθ] 1 n mammouth *m*. 2 adj géant, monstre, énorme.
mammy ['mæmɪ] n a (*) maman *f*. b (*US: Black nurse*) nourrice noire.
man [mæn], pl **men** 1 n a (*gen*) homme *m*; (*servant*) domestique *m*, valet *m*; (*in factory etc*) ouvrier *m*; (*in office, shop etc*) employé *m*; (*Mil*) homme (de troupe), soldat *m*; (*Naut*) homme (d'équipage), matelot *m*; (*Sport: player*) joueur *m*, équipier *m*; (*husband*) homme, type* *m*. **men and women** les hommes et les femmes; **he's a nice ~** c'est un homme très agréable, il est sympathique; **an old ~** un vieillard; **a blind ~** un aveugle; **I don't like the ~** je n'aime pas ce type*; **the ~'s an idiot** c'est *or* ce type* est un imbécile; **that ~ Smith** ce (type*) Smith; (*Police etc* †) **the ~ Jones** le sieur *or* le nommé Jones; **men's room** toilettes *fpl* pour hommes; **the ~ in the moon** *le visage que l'on peut imaginer en regardant la lune;* **as one ~** comme un seul homme; **they're communists to a ~** *or* **to the last ~** ils sont tous communistes sans exception; **they fought to the last ~** ils se sont battus jusqu'au dernier; **every ~ jack of them** tous autant qu'ils sont, tous sans exception; **he's been with this firm ~ and boy for 30 years** cela fait 30 ans qu'il est entré tout jeune encore dans la maison; (*liter*) **to grow to ~'s estate** atteindre sa maturité; **officers and men** (*Aviat, Mil*) officiers et soldats, officiers et hommes de troupe; (*Naut*) officiers et matelots; **the corporal and his men** le caporal et ses hommes; **the employers and the men** les patrons et les ouvriers; **~ and wife** mari et femme; **to live as ~ and wife** vivre maritalement; **her ~*** son homme, son type*; **my old ~*** (*father*) mon paternel*; (*husband*) mon homme*; **her young ~**† son amoureux†, son futur (*hum*); **it will make a ~ of him** cela en fera un homme; **be a ~!** sois un homme!; **he took it like a ~** il a pris ça vaillamment; **he was ~ enough to apologize** il a eu le courage de s'excuser; **if you're looking for someone to help you, then I'm your ~** si vous cherchez quelqu'un pour vous aider, je suis votre homme; **he's his own ~ again** (*not subordinate to anyone*) il est de nouveau son propre maître; (*in control of his emotions etc*) il est de nouveau maître de lui; *see* **best**.
b (*sort, type*) **I'm not a drinking ~** je ne bois pas (beaucoup); **he's not a football ~** ce n'est pas un amateur de football; **I'm a whisky ~ myself** moi, je préfère le whisky; **he's a man's ~** c'est un homme qui est plus à l'aise avec les hommes; **he's a Leeds ~** (*native*) il est *or* vient de Leeds; (*football supporter*) il supporte Leeds; **it's got to be a local ~** il faut que ce soit un homme du pays (*or* de la ville *or* du quartier *etc*); **he's not the ~ to fail** il n'est pas homme à échouer; **he's not the ~ for that** il n'est pas fait pour cela; **he's the ~ for the job** c'est l'homme qu'il (nous *or* leur *etc*) faut pour ce travail; **a medical ~** un docteur; **the ~ in the street** l'homme de la rue; **a ~ of God** un homme de Dieu; **a ~ of the world** un homme d'expérience; **a ~ of letters** un homme de lettres; **a ~ about town** un homme du monde; **the ~ of the hour** *or* **the moment** le héros du jour, l'homme qui tient la vedette; *see* **destiny, idea, property** *etc*.
c (in comps) *e.g.* **the ice-cream ~** le marchand de glaces; **the TV ~** l'installateur (*or* le dépanneur) de télé; **the gas ~** l'employé du gaz; (*Brit Aut*) **it's the green/red ~** le feu pour les piétons est au vert/au rouge; *see* **repair** *etc*.
d (*NonC: humanity in general*) **M~** l'homme *m*; (*Prov*) **M~ proposes, God disposes** l'homme propose et Dieu dispose (*Prov*).
e (*person*) homme *m*. **all men must die** tous les hommes sont mortels, nous sommes tous mortels; **men say that ...** on dit que ..., certains disent que ...; **any ~ would have done the same** n'importe qui aurait fait de même; **no ~ could blame him** personne ne pouvait le blâmer; **what else could a ~ do?** qu'est-ce qu'on aurait pu faire d'autre?
f (*in direct address*) **hurry up, ~!*** dépêchez-vous!; (*to friend etc*) dépêche-toi mon vieux!*; **~*, was I terrified!** ouais*, j'étais terrifié!; **look here young ~!** dites donc jeune homme!; **(my) little ~!** mon grand!; **old ~** mon vieux*; **my (good) ~** mon brave; **good ~!** bravo!
g (*Chess*) pièce *f*; (*Draughts*) pion *m*.
h (*US*) **the M~**‡ (*white ~*) le blanc; (*boss*) le patron; (*police*) les flics* *mpl*.
2 comp ►**man-at-arms** (pl **men-~-~**) homme *m* d'armes, cuirassier *m* ►**man-child** (*liter*) enfant *m* mâle ►**man-day** (*Comm, Ind etc*) jour-homme *m*, jour *m* de main-d'œuvre ►**man-eater** (*animal*) mangeur *m* d'hommes; (*person*) cannibale *m*, anthropophage *m*; (*fig, hum: woman*) dévoreuse *f* d'hommes, mante *f* religieuse ►**man-eating** *animal* mangeur d'hommes; *tribe etc* anthropophage ►**man Friday** (*lit*) Vendredi m; (*fig*) fidèle serviteur *m* ►**manful** *see* **manful** ►**manfully** *see* **manfully** ►**manhandle** *see* **manhandle** ►**man-hater:** *[woman]* **to be a man-hater** avoir les hommes en horreur ►**manhole** bouche *f* d'égout, trou *m* (d'homme), regard *m*; **manhole cover** plaque *f* d'égout ►**manhood** *see* **manhood** ►**man-hour** (*Comm, Ind etc*) heure-homme *f*, heure *f* de travail, heure de main-d'œuvre ►**manhunt** chasse *f* à l'homme ►**mankind** (*NonC*) (*the human race*) l'homme *m*, le genre humain; (*the male sex*) les hommes ►**manlike** *form, figure* à l'aspect humain; *qualities* humain, d'homme; (*pej*) *woman* hommasse (*pej*) ►**manliness** *see* **manliness** ►**manly** *see* **manly** ►**man-made** *fibre, fabric* synthétique; *lake, barrier* artificiel ►**man management: he's not very good at man management** il ne sait pas très bien manier son personnel; **man management is an important skill** il faut bien savoir manier le personnel ►**man-of-war, man-o'-war** (pl **men-~-~**) (*Naut*) vaisseau *m* *or* navire *m* *or* bâtiment *m* de guerre (*see* **Portuguese**) ►**manpower** *see* **manpower** ►**manservant** (pl **menservants**) valet *m* de chambre ►**man-sized** (* *fig*) grand, de taille, de grande personne* ►**manslaughter** (*Jur*) homicide *m* (par imprudence) ►**man-to-man** adj, adv d'homme à homme ►**mantrap** piège *m* à hommes.
3 vt a (*provide staff for*) assurer une permanence à; (*work at*) être de service à. **they haven't enough staff to ~ the office every day** ils n'ont pas assez de personnel pour assurer une permanence au bureau tous les jours; **who will ~ the enquiry desk?** qui sera de service aux renseignements?; **the telephone is ~ned twelve hours per day** il y a une permanence téléphonique douze heures par jour.
b (*Mil*) **to ~ a ship** (*gen*) équiper un navire en personnel; **the ship was ~ned mainly by Chinese** l'équipage était composé principalement de Chinois; **the troops who ~ned the look-out posts** les troupes qui étaient de service aux postes d'observation; **the soldiers manning the fortress** les soldats qui étaient en garnison dans la forteresse; (*Naut*) **to ~ the boats** armer les bateaux; (*Mil*) **to ~ the guns** servir les canons; **to ~ the pumps** armer les pompes.
manacle ['mænəkl] 1 n: **~s** menottes *fpl*. 2 vt mettre les menottes à. **~d** les menottes aux poignets.
manage ['mænɪdʒ] 1 vt a (*direct*) *business, estate, theatre, restaurant, hotel, shop* gérer; *institution, organization* administrer, diriger, mener; *farm* exploiter; (*pej*) *election etc* truquer. **~d economy** économie *f* dirigée.
b (*handle, deal with*) *boat, vehicle* manœuvrer, manier; *tool* manier; *animal, person* se faire écouter de, savoir s'y prendre avec. **you ~d the situation very well** tu as très bien arrangé les choses, tu t'en es très bien tiré.
c (*succeed, contrive*) **to ~ to do** réussir *or* arriver *or* parvenir à faire, trouver moyen de faire, s'arranger pour faire; **how did you ~ to do it?** comment t'y es-tu pris *or* t'es-tu arrangé pour le faire?; **how did you ~ not to spill it?** comment as-tu fait pour ne pas le renverser?; **he ~d not to get his feet wet** il a réussi à ne pas se mouiller les pieds; (*iro*) **he ~d to annoy everybody** il a trouvé le moyen de mécontenter tout le monde; **you'll ~ it next time!** tu y arriveras *or* parviendras la prochaine fois!; **will you come? — I can't ~ (it) just now** tu vas venir? — je ne peux pas pour l'instant.
d (*~ to do, pay, eat etc*) **how much will you give? — I can ~ 50 francs** combien allez-vous donner? — je peux aller jusqu'à 50 F *or* je peux (y) mettre 50 F; **surely you could ~ another biscuit?** tu mangerais *or* mangeras bien encore un autre biscuit?; **I couldn't ~ another thing!*** je n'en peux plus!; **can you ~ the suitcases?** pouvez-vous porter les valises?; **can you ~ 8 o'clock?** 8 heures, ça vous convient?; **can you ~ 2 more in the car?** peux-tu encore en prendre 2 *or* as-tu de la place pour 2 de plus dans la voiture?
2 vi a (*succeed etc*) **can you ~?** tu y arrives?; **thanks, I can ~** merci, ça va; **I can ~ without him** je peux me passer de lui.
b (*financially etc*) se débrouiller. **she ~s on her pension/on £40 a week** elle se débrouille avec seulement sa pension/avec seulement 40 livres par semaine; **how will you ~?** comment allez-vous faire? *or* vous débrouiller?
manageable ['mænɪdʒəbl] adj *vehicle, boat* facile à manœuvrer, manœuvrable, maniable; *person, child, animal* docile, maniable; *size,*

proportions, amount maniable. ~ **hair** cheveux *mpl* faciles à coiffer *or* souples; **the situation is** ~ la situation ne présente pas de problèmes insolubles.

management ['mænɪdʒmənt] 1 n a (*NonC*) *[company, estate, theatre]* gestion *f*; *[institution, organization]* administration *f*, direction *f*; *[farm]* exploitation *f*. **his skilful** ~ **of his staff** l'habileté avec laquelle il dirige son personnel; (*Comm*) **"under new** ~**"** "changement de direction (*or* de propriétaire)".

b (*collective: people*) *[business, firm]* cadres *mpl*, direction *f*, administration *f*; *[hotel, shop, cinema, theatre]* direction. *[factory, company]* **the** ~ **and the workers** les cadres et les ouvriers; (*Ind*) ~ **and labour** *or* **unions** les partenaires *mpl* sociaux; **he's (one of the)** ~ **now** il fait partie des cadres maintenant; **"the** ~ **regrets ..."** "la direction regrette ...".

2 comp ▸**management accounting** comptabilité *f* de gestion ▸**management buyout** rachat *m* d'une entreprise par ses cadres ou sa direction ▸**management chart** organigramme *m* ▸**management committee** comité *m* de direction ▸**management company** société *f* de gestion ▸**management consultancy** (*business*) cabinet *m* de conseils; (*advice*) conseils *mpl* en gestion d'entreprise ▸**management consultant** conseiller *m* de *or* en gestion (d'entreprise) ▸**management game** jeu *m* d'entreprise ▸**management information system** système *m* intégré de gestion ▸**management selection procedures** (formalités *fpl* de) sélection *f* des cadres ▸**management studies** (*Educ*) (études *fpl* de) gestion *f* ▸**management style** mode *m* de gestion ▸**management trainee** cadre *m* stagiaire.

manager ['mænɪdʒəʳ] n *[company, business]* directeur *m*, administrateur *m*; *[theatre, cinema]* directeur; *[restaurant, hotel, shop]* gérant *m*; *[farm]* exploitant *m*; *[actor, singer, boxer, football team etc]* manager *m*; (*Fin*) chef *m* de file. (*Brit*) **(school)** ~ ≃ membre *m* du conseil d'établissement; **general** ~ directeur général; **to be a good** ~ (*gen*) être bien organisé, avoir le sens de l'organisation; (*in family budgeting*) bien gérer le budget familial; *see* **business, sale** *etc*.

manageress [ˌmænɪdʒə'res] n *[hotel, café, shop]* gérante *f*; *[theatre, cinema]* directrice *f*.

managerial [ˌmænə'dʒɪərɪəl] adj directorial. **the** ~ **class** la classe des cadres, les cadres *mpl*; **at** ~ **level** au niveau de la direction *or* directorial; ~ **skills** compétences *fpl* de gestion.

managing ['mænɪdʒɪŋ] 1 adj (*Brit*) (*bossy*) autoritaire. 2 comp ▸**managing bank** banque *f* chef de file ▸**managing director** (*Brit*) directeur *m* général, P.D.G. *m* ▸**managing editor** directeur *m* de la rédaction.

manatee [ˌmænə'tiː] n lamantin *m*.

Manchu [mæn'tʃuː] 1 n a (*person*) Mandchou(e) *m(f)*. b (*language*) mandchou *m*. 2 adj mandchou.

Manchuria [mæn'tʃʊərɪə] n Mandchourie *f*.

Manchurian [mæn'tʃʊərɪən] 1 adj mandchou. 2 n Mandchou(e) *m(f)*.

Mancunian [mæŋ'kjuːnɪən] 1 adj de (la ville de) Manchester. 2 n habitant(e) *m(f) or* natif *m*, -ive *f* de Manchester.

mandala ['mændələ] n mandala *m*.

mandarin ['mændərɪn] n a (*person: lit, fig*) mandarin *m*. b (*Ling*) **M~ (Chinese)** mandarin *m*. c (*also* ~ **orange**) mandarine *f*; (*tree*) mandarinier *m*. d (*duck*) canard *m* mandarin.

mandate ['mændeɪt] 1 n (*authority*) mandat *m*; (*country*) pays *m* sous mandat. **under French** ~ sous mandat français; (*Parl*) **we have a** ~ **to do this** nous avons reçu le mandat de faire cela. 2 vt (*Jur etc*) (*give authority to*) donner mandat (*sb to do* à qn pour faire); (*make obligatory*) rendre obligatoire; (*entail*) *[act, decision]* entraîner, comporter; *territory* mettre sous le mandat (*to* de).

mandatory ['mændətərɪ] adj a (*obligatory*) *[payment, retirement]* obligatoire. (*Jur*) ~ **provisions** dispositions *fpl* impératives; **it is** ~ **upon him to do so** il a l'obligation formelle de le faire. b *functions, powers* mandataire. c (*Pol*) *state* mandataire.

mandible ['mændɪbl] n *[bird, insect]* mandibule *f*; *[mammal, fish]* mâchoire *f* (inférieure).

mandolin(e) ['mændəlɪn] n mandoline *f*.

mandrake ['mændreɪk] n mandragore *f*.

mandrill ['mændrɪl] n mandrill *m*.

mane [meɪn] n (*lit, fig*) crinière *f*.

maneuver [mə'nuːvəʳ] *etc* (*US*) = **manoeuvre** *etc*.

manful ['mænfʊl] adj vaillant.

manfully ['mænfəlɪ] adv vaillamment.

manganese [ˌmæŋgə'niːz] 1 n manganèse *m*. 2 comp ▸**manganese bronze** bronze *m* au manganèse ▸**manganese oxide** oxyde *m* de manganèse ▸**manganese steel** acier *m* au manganèse.

mange [meɪndʒ] n gale *f*.

mangel(-wurzel) ['mæŋgl(ˌwɜːzl)] n betterave fourragère.

manger ['meɪndʒəʳ] n (*Agr*) mangeoire *f*; (*Rel*) crèche *f*; *see* **dog**.

mangetout ['mɒnʒ'tuː] n, pl inv (*also* ~ **pea**) mange-tout *m inv*.

mangle¹ ['mæŋgl] 1 n (*for wringing*) essoreuse *f* à rouleaux; (*for smoothing*) calandre *f*. 2 vt essorer; calandrer.

mangle² ['mæŋgl] vt (*also* ~ **up**) *object, body* déchirer, mutiler; (*fig*) *text* mutiler; *quotation* estropier; *message* estropier, mutiler.

mango ['mæŋgəʊ] n, pl ~**(e)s** (*fruit*) mangue *f*; (*tree*) manguier *m*. ~ **chutney** condiment *m* à la mangue.

mangold(-wurzel) ['mæŋgəld(ˌwɜːzl)] n = **mangel(-wurzel)**.

mangosteen ['mæŋgəˌstiːn] n mangoustan *m*.

mangrove ['mæŋgrəʊv] n palétuvier *m*, manglier *m*. ~ **swamp** mangrove *f*.

mangy ['meɪndʒɪ] adj *animal* galeux; (*) *room, hat* pelé, miteux; *act* minable, moche*. **what a** ~ **trick!*** quel sale coup!*

manhandle ['mænˌhændl] vt (*treat roughly*) maltraiter, malmener, traiter sans ménagement; (*esp Brit: move by hand*) *goods etc* manutentionner.

Manhattan [mæn'hætən] n (*US*) a (*place*) Manhattan. b (*drink*) manhattan *m* (*cocktail de whisky et de vermouth doux*).

manhood ['mænhʊd] n a (*age, state*) âge *m* d'homme, âge viril. **to reach** ~ atteindre l'âge d'homme; **during his early** ~ quand il était jeune homme. b (*manliness*) virilité *f*, caractère viril. c (*collective n*) **Scotland's** *or* **Scottish** ~ tous les hommes d'Écosse.

mania ['meɪnɪə] n (*Psych*) manie *f*, penchant *m* morbide; (*) manie, passion *f*. **persecution** ~ manie *or* folie *f* de la persécution; **to have a** ~ **for (doing) sth*** avoir la manie de (faire) qch.

...mania ['meɪnɪə] suf ...manie *f*.

maniac ['meɪnɪæk] 1 n (*Psych*) maniaque *mf*; (*) fou *m*, folle *f*; (*Jur*) dément(e) *m(f)*. **these football** ~**s*** ces mordus* *mpl or* toqués* *mpl* du football; **he drives like a** ~***** il conduit comme un fou; **he's a** ~**!*** il est fou à lier!, il est bon à enfermer! 2 adj maniaque, fou (*f* folle), dément.

maniacal [mə'naɪəkəl] adj (*Psych*) maniaque; (*fig*) fou (*f* folle).

maniacally [mə'naɪəkəlɪ] adv de manière folle. **he laughed** ~ il avait un rire de fou.

manic ['mænɪk] 1 adj (*Psych*) maniaque. 2 comp ▸**manic depression** psychose *f* maniaco-dépressive, cyclothymie *f* ▸**manic-depressive** adj, n maniaque (*mf*) dépressif (*f* -ive), cyclothymique (*mf*).

manich(a)ean [ˌmænɪ'kiːən] adj, n manichéen(ne) *m(f)*. **the** ~ **heresy** l'hérésie *f* manichéenne.

Manich(a)eism ['mænɪkiːˌɪzəm] n manichéisme *m*.

manicure ['mænɪˌkjʊəʳ] 1 n (*act*) soin *m* des mains; (*person*) manucure *mf*. 2 vt *person* faire les mains *or* les ongles à; *sb's nails* faire. **to** ~ **one's nails** se faire les ongles. 3 comp ▸**manicure case** trousse *f* à ongles *or* de manucure ▸**manicure scissors** ciseaux *mpl* de manucure *or* à ongles ▸**manicure set** = **manicure case**.

manicurist ['mænɪˌkjʊərɪst] n manucure *mf*.

manifest ['mænɪfest] 1 adj manifeste, clair, évident. (*US Hist*) **M~ Destiny** destinée *f* manifeste (*inévitable expansion territoriale des États-Unis*). 2 vt manifester. 3 n (*Aviat, Naut*) manifeste *m*.

manifestation [ˌmænɪfes'teɪʃən] n manifestation *f*.

manifestly ['mænɪfestlɪ] adv manifestement.

manifesto [ˌmænɪ'festəʊ] n, pl ~**(e)s** (*Pol etc*) manifeste *m*.

manifold ['mænɪfəʊld] 1 adj *collection* divers, varié; *duties* multiple, nombreux. ~ **wisdom** sagesse infinie. 2 n (*Aut etc*) **inlet/exhaust** ~ collecteur *m or* tubulure *f* d'admission/d'échappement.

Manila [mə'nɪlə] n Manille, Manila.

mani(l)la [mə'nɪlə] n: ~ **envelope** enveloppe *f* en papier kraft; ~ **paper** papier *m* kraft.

manioc ['mænɪɒk] n manioc *m*.

manipulate [mə'nɪpjʊleɪt] vt a *tool etc* manipuler, manœuvrer; *vehicle* manœuvrer; *person* manœuvrer. b (*pej*) *facts, figures, accounts* tripoter, trafiquer*. **to** ~ **a situation** faire son jeu des circonstances.

manipulation [məˌnɪpjʊ'leɪʃən] n (*NonC: see* **manipulate**) manipulation *f*; manœuvre *f*; (*pej*) tripotage *m*.

manipulative [mə'nɪpjʊlətɪv] adj manipulateur (*f* -trice).

manipulator [mə'nɪpjʊleɪtəʳ] n manipulateur *m*, -trice *f*.

Manitoba [ˌmænɪ'təʊbə] n Manitoba *m*.

manliness ['mænlɪnɪs] n virilité *f*, caractère viril.

manly ['mænlɪ] adj viril (*f* virile), mâle.

manna ['mænə] n manne *f*. ~ **from heaven** manne tombée du ciel *or* providentielle.

mannequin ['mænɪkɪn] n mannequin *m*.

manner ['mænəʳ] n a (*mode, way*) manière *f*, façon *f*. **the** ~ **in which he did it** la manière *or* façon dont il l'a fait; **in such a** ~ **that** de telle sorte que + *indic* (*actual result*) *or* + *subj* (*intended result*); **in this** ~, (*frm*) **after this** ~ de cette manière *or* façon; **in** *or* **after the** ~ **of Van Gogh** à la manière de Van Gogh; **in the same** ~, (*frm*) **in like** ~ de la même manière; **in a (certain)** ~ en quelque sorte; **in such a** ~ **as to force ...** de façon à forcer ...; **in a** ~ **of speaking** pour ainsi dire; **it's a** ~ **of speaking** c'est une façon de parler; ~ **of payment** mode *m* de paiement; **(as) to the** ~ **born** comme s'il (*or* elle *etc*) avait cela dans le sang.

b (*behaviour, attitude*) façon *f* de se conduire *or* de se comporter, attitude *f*, comportement *m*. **his** ~ **to his mother** son attitude envers sa mère, sa manière de se conduire avec sa mère; **I don't like his** ~ je n'aime pas son attitude; **there's something odd about his** ~ il y a quelque chose de bizarre dans son comportement.

c (*social behaviour*) ~**s** manières *fpl*; **good** ~**s** bonnes manières, savoir-vivre *m*; **bad** ~**s** mauvaises manières; **it's good/bad** ~**s (to do)**

cela se fait/ne se fait pas (de faire); **he has no ~s, his ~s are terrible** il ne sait pas se conduire, il a de très mauvaises manières, il n'a aucun savoir-vivre; (*to child*) **aren't you forgetting your ~s?** est-ce que c'est comme ça qu'on se tient?; **road ~s** politesse routière *or* au volant.
d (*social customs*) ~s mœurs *fpl*, usages *mpl*; **novel of ~s** roman *m* de mœurs; *see* **comedy**.
e (*class, sort, type*) sorte *f*, genre *m*. **all ~ of birds** toutes sortes d'oiseaux; **no ~ of doubt** aucun doute; *see* **mean²**.

mannered ['mænəd] **adj** *person, style, book etc* maniéré, affecté.

-mannered ['mænəd] **adj ending in comps: well-mannered** bien élevé; **rough-mannered** brusque, aux manières rudes; *see* **bad** *etc*.

mannerism ['mænərɪzəm] **n** a (*habit, trick of speech etc*) trait particulier; (*pej*) tic *m*, manie *f*. b (*NonC: Art, Literat etc*) maniérisme *m*.

mannerist ['mænərɪst] **adj, n** maniériste *(mf)*.

mannerliness ['mænəlɪnɪs] **n** politesse *f*, courtoisie *f*, savoir-vivre *m*.

mannerly ['mænəlɪ] **adj** poli, bien élevé, courtois.

man(n)ikin ['mænɪkɪn] **n** a (*dwarf etc*) homoncule *m*, nabot *m*. b (*Art, Dressmaking*) mannequin *m* (*objet*).

manning ['mænɪŋ] **n** (*Mil*) armement *m*; (*Ind*) effectifs *mpl*. **~ levels** niveau *m* des effectifs.

mannish ['mænɪʃ] **adj** *woman* masculin, hommasse (*pej*); *style, clothes* masculin.

mannishly ['mænɪʃlɪ] **adv** de façon masculine.

manoeuvrability, (*US*) **maneuverability** [mə,nu:vrə'bɪlɪtɪ] **n** manœuvrabilité *f*, maniabilité *f*.

manoeuvrable, (*US*) **maneuverable** [mə'nu:vrəbl] **adj** manœuvrable, maniable, facile à manœuvrer.

manoeuvre, (*US*) **maneuver** [mə'nu:vəʳ] 1 **n** (*all senses*) manœuvre *f*. (*Mil etc*) **to be on ~s** faire des *or* être en manœuvres; (*fig*) **it doesn't leave much room for ~** cela ne laisse pas une grande marge de manœuvre.
2 **vt** (*all senses*) manœuvrer. **they ~d the gun into position** ils ont manœuvré le canon pour le mettre en position; **they ~d the enemy away from the city** leur manœuvre a réussi à éloigner l'ennemi de la ville; **he ~d the car through the gate** il a pu à force de manœuvres faire passer la voiture par le portail; **to ~ sth out/in/through** *etc* faire sortir/entrer/traverser *etc* qch en manœuvrant; **to ~ sb into doing sth** manœuvrer qn pour qu'il fasse qch; **can you ~ him into another job?** pouvez-vous user de votre influence pour lui faire changer son emploi?
3 **vi** (*all senses*) manœuvrer.

manoeuvring [mə'nu:vərɪŋ] **n** (*pej*) magouille* *f*.

manometer [mæ'nɒmɪtəʳ] **n** manomètre *m*.

manor ['mænəʳ] **n** a (*also* **~ house**) manoir *m*, gentilhommière *f*. b (*Hist: estate*) domaine seigneurial; *see* **lord**. c (*Brit: Police etc sl*) fief *m*.

manorial [mə'nɔ:rɪəl] **adj** seigneurial.

manpower ['mæn,paʊəʳ] 1 **n** (*NonC*) a (*men available*) (*gen, Ind*) main-d'œuvre *f*; (*Mil etc*) effectifs *mpl*. b (*physical exertion*) force *f* physique. **he did it by sheer ~** il l'a fait uniquement par la force. 2 **comp ►Manpower Services Commission** (†: *Brit*) ≃ Agence nationale pour l'emploi.

manse [mæns] **n** presbytère *m* (*d'un pasteur presbytérien*).

mansion ['mænʃən] **n** (*in town*) hôtel particulier; (*in country*) château *m*, manoir *m*. **the M~ House** *la résidence officielle du Lord Mayor de Londres*.

mansuetude ['mænswɪtju:d] **n** mansuétude *f*, douceur *f*.

mantel ['mæntl] **n** a (*also* **~piece, ~shelf**) (dessus *m or* tablette *f* de) cheminée *f*. b (*structure round fireplace*) manteau *m*, chambranle *m* (de cheminée).

mantes ['mænti:z] **npl of mantis**

mantilla [mæn'tɪlə] **n** mantille *f*.

mantis ['mæntɪs] **n, pl ~es** *or* **mantes** mante *f*; *see* **praying**.

mantle ['mæntl] 1 **n** a (†: *cloak*) cape *f*; *[lady]* mante *f*. (*liter*) **~ of snow** manteau *m* de neige. b *[gas lamp]* manchon *m*; *see* **gas**. c (*Geol: of earth*) manteau *m*. 2 **vt** (*liter*) (re)couvrir.

mantra ['mæntrə] **n** (*also* **~ word**) mantra *m*.

manual ['mænjʊəl] 1 **adj** *labour, skill, controls* manuel. **~ worker** travailleur manuel. 2 **n** a (*book*) manuel *m*. b *[organ]* clavier *m*.

manually ['mænjʊəlɪ] **adv** à la main, manuellement.

manufacture [,mænjʊ'fæktʃəʳ] 1 **n** a (*NonC*) fabrication *f*; *[clothes]* confection *f*. b **~s** produits manufacturés. 2 **vt** fabriquer; *clothes* confectionner; (*fig*) *story, excuse* fabriquer. **~d goods** produits manufacturés.

manufacturer [,mænjʊ'fæktʃərəʳ] **n** fabricant *m*. **~s' recommended price** prix *m* public.

manufacturing [,mænjʊ'fæktʃərɪŋ] 1 **n** fabrication *f*. 2 **adj** *town etc* industriel; *industry* de fabrication manufacturière.

manure [mə'njʊəʳ] 1 **n** (*NonC*) (*farmyard ~*) fumier *m*; (*artificial ~*) engrais *m*. **liquid ~** (*organic*) purin *m*, lisier *m*; (*artificial*) engrais *m* liquide; *see* **horse**. 2 **comp ►manure heap** (tas *m* de) fumier *m*. 3 **vt** fumer; répandre des engrais sur.

manuscript ['mænjʊskrɪpt] 1 **n** manuscrit *m*. **in ~** (*not yet printed*) sous forme de manuscrit; (*handwritten*) écrit à la main. 2 **adj** manuscrit, écrit à la main.

Manx [mæŋks] 1 **adj** de l'île de Man. **~ cat** chat *m* de l'île de Man; **~man** natif *m or* habitant *m* de l'île de Man. 2 **n** a **the ~** les habitants *mpl or* les natifs *mpl* de l'île de Man. b (*Ling*) mannois *m*.

many ['menɪ] 1 **adj, pron, compar more, superl most** a beaucoup (de), un grand nombre (de). **~ books** beaucoup de livres, un grand nombre de livres, de nombreux livres; **very ~ books** un très grand nombre de livres, de très nombreux livres; **~ of those books** un grand nombre de ces livres; **~ of them** un grand nombre d'entre eux, beaucoup d'entre eux; **a good ~ of those books** (un) bon nombre de ces livres; **~ people** beaucoup de gens *or* de monde, bien des gens; **~ came** beaucoup sont venus; **~ believe that to be true** bien des gens croient que c'est vrai; **the ~** (*the masses*) la multitude, la foule; **the ~ who admire him** le grand nombre de gens qui l'admirent; **~ times** bien des fois; **~ a time, ~'s the time*** maintes fois, souvent; **before ~ days** avant qu'il soit longtemps, avant peu de jours; **I've lived here for ~ years** j'habite ici depuis des années *or* depuis (bien) longtemps; **he lived there for ~ years** il vécut là de nombreuses années *or* de longues années; **people of ~ kinds** des gens de toutes sortes; **a good** *or* **great ~ things** pas mal de choses*; **in ~ cases** dans bien des cas, dans de nombreux cas; **~ a man would be grateful** il y en a plus d'un qui serait reconnaissant; **a woman of ~ moods** une femme d'humeur changeante; **a man of ~ parts** un homme qui a des talents très divers; **~ happy returns (of the day)!** bon *or* joyeux anniversaire!
b (*in phrases*) **I have as ~ books as you** j'ai autant de livres que vous; **I have as ~ as you** j'en ai autant que vous; **as ~ as wish to come** tous ceux qui désirent venir; **as ~ as 100 people are expected** on attend jusqu'à 100 personnes; **there were as ~ again outside the hall** il y en avait encore autant dehors que dans la salle; **how ~?** combien?; **how ~ people?** combien de gens?; **how ~ there are!** qu'ils sont nombreux!; **however ~ books you have** quel que soit le nombre de livres que vous ayez; **however ~ there may be** quel que soit leur nombre; **so ~ have said it** il y en a tant qui l'ont dit; **I've got so ~ already (that ...)** j'en ai déjà tant (que ...); **there were so ~ (that ...)** il y en avait tant (que ...); **so ~ dresses** tant de robes; **ever so ~ times** je ne sais combien de fois; **they ran away like so ~ sheep** ils se sont sauvés comme un troupeau de moutons; **he did not say that in so ~ words** il n'a pas dit cela explicitement; **there were too ~** il y en avait trop; **too ~ cakes** trop de gâteaux; **3 too ~** 3 de trop; **20 would not be too ~** il n'y en aurait pas trop de 20; (*fig*) **he's had one too ~*** il a bu un coup de trop; **I've got too ~ already** j'en ai déjà trop; **there are too ~ of you** vous êtes trop nombreux; **too ~ of these books** trop de ces livres; **I've told too ~ of the children** j'ai mis trop d'enfants au courant; **too ~ of us know that ...** nous sommes trop (nombreux) à savoir que ... .
2 **comp ►many-coloured,** (*liter*) **many-hued** multicolore **►many-sided** *object* qui a de nombreux côtés; (*fig*) *person* aux intérêts (*or* talents) variés *or* multiples; *problem* complexe, qui a de nombreuses facettes.

Mao (Tse Tung) ['maʊ(tseɪ'tʊŋ)] **n** Mao (Tsê-Tung) *m*.

Maoism ['maʊɪzəm] **n** maoïsme *m*.

Maoist ['maʊɪst] **adj, n** maoïste *(mf)*.

Maori ['maʊrɪ] 1 **adj** maori. 2 **n** a Maori(e) *m(f)*. b (*Ling*) maori *m*.

map [mæp] 1 **n** (*gen*) carte *f*; *[town, bus, tube, subway]* plan *m*. **geological/historical/linguistic ~** carte géologique/historique/linguistique; **~ of France** carte de la France; **~ of Paris/the Underground** plan *m* de Paris/du métro; (*fig*) **this will put Tooting on the ~** cela fera connaître Tooting, cela mettra Tooting en vedette; (*fig*) **the whole town was wiped off the ~** la ville entière fut rayée de la carte; (*fig*) **off the ~*** (*distant*) à l'autre bout du monde; (*unimportant*) perdu; *see* **relief**.
2 **comp ►mapmaker** cartographe *mf* **►mapmaking** cartographie *f* **►mapping** (*Maths*) fonction *f*; (*Comput*) mappage *m*; **mapping pen** plume *f* de dessinateur *or* à dessin.
3 **vt** *country, district etc* faire *or* dresser la carte (*or* le plan) de; *route* tracer.

►map out vt sep *route, plans* tracer; *book, essay* établir les grandes lignes de; *one's time, career, day* organiser; *strategy, plan* élaborer. **he hasn't yet mapped out what he will do** il n'a pas encore de plan précis de ce qu'il va faire.

maple ['meɪpl] 1 **n** érable *m*. 2 **comp ►maple leaf/sugar/syrup** feuille *f*/sucre *m*/sirop *m* d'érable.

mar [mɑ:ʳ] **vt** gâter, gâcher. **to make or ~ sth** assurer le succès ou l'échec de qch.

Mar. **abbr of March.**

maraschino [,mærəs'ki:nəʊ] **n** marasquin *m*. **~ cherries** cerises *fpl* au marasquin.

marathon ['mærəθən] 1 **n** a (*Sport, fig*) marathon *m*. b **M~** Marathon *m*. 2 **adj** a (*Sport*) *runner* de marathon. b (*fig: very long*) *meeting, discussion* marathon *inv*. **a ~ session** une séance-marathon.

maraud [mə'rɔ:d] **vi** marauder, être en maraude. **to go ~ing** aller à la maraude.

marauder [mə'rɔ:dəʳ] **n** maraudeur *m*, -euse *f*.

marauding [mə'rɔ:dɪŋ] 1 **adj** maraudeur, en maraude. 2 **n** maraude *f*.

marble ['mɑːbl] 1 n a marbre *m*. **the Elgin ~s** *partie de la frise du Parthénon conservée au British Museum*. b (*toy*) bille *f*. **to play ~s** jouer aux billes; (*fig*) **to lose one's ~s*** perdre la boule*. 2 comp *staircase, statue* de *or* en marbre; *industry* marbrier ▸**marble cake** gâteau *m* marbré ▸**marble quarry** marbrière *f*. 3 vt marbrer.

March [mɑːtʃ] n mars *m*; *see* **mad**; *for phrases see* **September**.

march¹ [mɑːtʃ] 1 n a (*Mil etc*) marche *f*. **on the ~** en marche; **quick/slow ~** marche rapide/lente; **a day's ~** une journée de marche; **a 10-km ~, a ~ of 10 km** une marche de 10 km; **the ~ on Rome** la marche sur Rome; (*fig*) **~ of time/progress** la marche du temps/progrès; *see* **forced, route, steal** *etc*.

b (*demonstration*) défilé *m*, manifestation *f* (*against* contre, *for* pour).

c (*Mus*) marche *f*; *see* **dead**.

2 comp ▸**march-past** (*Mil etc*) défilé *m*.

3 vi a (*Mil etc*) marcher au pas. **to ~ into battle** marcher au combat; **the army ~ed in/out/through** *etc* l'armée entra/sortit/traversa *etc* (au pas); **to ~ past** défiler; **to ~ past sb** défiler devant qn; **~!** marche!; *see* **forward, quick** *etc*.

b (*gen*) **to ~ in/out/up** *etc* entrer/sortir/monter *etc* (*briskly*) d'un pas énergique *or* (*angrily*) d'un air furieux; **he ~ed up to me** il s'est approché de moi d'un air décidé; **to ~ up and down the room** faire les cent pas dans la pièce, arpenter la pièce.

c (*demonstrate*) manifester (*against* contre, *for* pour).

4 vt a (*Mil*) faire marcher (au pas). **to ~ troops in/out** *etc* faire entrer/faire sortir *etc* des troupes (au pas).

b (*fig*) **to ~ sb in/out/away** faire entrer/faire sortir/emmener qn tambour battant; **to ~ sb off to prison** embarquer qn en prison*.

march² [mɑːtʃ] n (*gen pl*) **~es** (*border*) frontière *f*; (*borderlands*) marche *f*.

marcher ['mɑːtʃəʳ] n (*in demo etc*) manifestant(e) *m(f)*.

marching ['mɑːtʃɪŋ] 1 n marche *f*. 2 comp ▸**marching band** (*US*) orchestre *m* d'école (avec majorettes) ▸**marching orders** (*Mil*) feuille *f* de route; (*fig*) **to give sb his marching orders*** flanquer* qn à la porte, envoyer promener qn; (*fig*) **to get one's marching orders*** se faire mettre à la porte ▸**marching song** chanson *f* de route.

marchioness ['mɑːʃənɪs] n marquise *f* (*personne*).

Marco Polo ['mɑːkəʊ'pəʊləʊ] n Marco Polo *m*.

Marcus Aurelius ['mɑːkəsɔː'riːlɪəs] n Marc Aurèle *m*.

Mardi Gras ['mɑːdɪ'grɑː] n (*US*) mardi gras *m inv*, carnaval *m*.

mare [mɛəʳ] n jument *f*. (*fig*) **his discovery turned out to be a ~'s nest** sa découverte s'est révélée très décevante.

marg* [mɑːdʒ] n (*Brit*) (abbr of **margarine**) margarine *f*.

Margaret ['mɑːgərɪt] n Marguerite *f*.

margarine [ˌmɑːdʒə'riːn] n margarine *f*. **whipped** *or* **soft ~** margarine ultra-légère.

marge* [mɑːdʒ] n (*Brit*) abbr of **margarine**.

margin ['mɑːdʒɪn] n *[book, page]* marge *f*; *[river, lake]* bord *m*; *[wood]* lisière *f*; (*fig: Comm, Econ, gen*) marge. **notes in the ~** notes en marge *or* marginales; **do not write in the ~** n'écrivez pas dans la marge; (*Typ*) **wide/narrow ~** grande/petite marge; (*fig*) **to win by a wide/narrow ~** gagner de loin/de peu; **elected by a narrow ~** élu de justesse *or* avec peu de voix de majorité; **on the ~(s) of society** en marge de la société; **to allow a ~ for** laisser une marge pour; **to allow for a ~ of error** prévoir une marge d'erreur; **~ of profit** marge (bénéficiaire); **~ of safety** marge de sécurité.

marginal ['mɑːdʒɪnl] 1 adj *comments, benefit, profit, business* marginal; *ability* moyen; *importance* secondaire; *writer, artist etc* secondaire; *existence* précaire; *land* de faible rendement. **a ~ case** un cas limite; (*Parl*) **~ seat** siège disputé. 2 n (*Parl*) siège disputé.

marginalize ['mɑːdʒɪnəlaɪz] vt marginaliser.

marginally ['mɑːdʒɪnəlɪ] adv très légèrement, de très peu.

marguerita [ˌmɑːgə'riːtə] n (*US*) cocktail *m* (*à base de téquila*).

marguerite [ˌmɑːgə'riːt] n marguerite *f*.

Maria [mə'raɪə] n Marie *f*; *see* **black**.

marigold ['mærɪgəʊld] n (*Bot*) souci *m*.

marihuana, marijuana [ˌmærɪ'hwɑːnə] n marihuana *f or* marijuana *f*.

marina [mə'riːnə] n marina *f*.

marinade [ˌmærɪ'neɪd] 1 n marinade *f*. 2 vt mariner.

marinate ['mærɪneɪt] vt mariner.

marine [mə'riːn] 1 adj (*in the sea*) *plant, animal* marin; (*from the sea*) *products* de mer; (*by the sea*) *vegetation, forces, stores* maritime. **~ biologist** océanographe *mf* biologiste; **~ biology** océanographie *f* biologique; **~ engineer** ingénieur *m* du génie maritime; **~ engineering** génie *m* maritime; **~ insurance** assurance *f* maritime; **~ life** vie marine; **~ science** sciences *fpl* marines *or* de la mer; **~ underwriter** assureur *m* maritime. 2 n a (*Naut*) **mercantile ~, merchant ~** marine marchande. b (*Mil*) fusilier marin. **M~s** (*Brit*) fusiliers marins; (*US*) marines *mpl* (américains); (*US*) **the M~ Corps** les Marines *mpl*; (*fig*) **tell that to the ~s!** à d'autres!

mariner ['mærɪnəʳ] n (*liter*) marin *m*. **~'s compass** boussole *f*, compas *m*; *see* **master**.

Mariolatry [ˌmɛərɪ'ɒlətrɪ] n (*Rel*) vénération excessive de la Vierge.

Mariology [ˌmɛərɪ'ɒlədʒɪ] n mariologie *f*.

marionette [ˌmærɪə'net] n marionnette *f*.

marital ['mærɪtl] adj a *problems* matrimonial; *happiness* conjugal. (*Jur*) **~ relations** rapports conjugaux; (*Admin*) **~ status** situation *f* de famille. b (*concerning husband*) marital.

maritime ['mærɪtaɪm] adj maritime. **~ law** droit *m* maritime; (*Can*) **the M~ provinces** les provinces *fpl* maritimes, l'Acadie *f*.

marjoram ['mɑːdʒərəm] n marjolaine *f*.

Mark [mɑːk] n Marc *m*. **~ Antony** Marc-Antoine *m*.

mark¹ [mɑːk] n (*currency*) mark *m*; (††: *weight*) marc *m*.

mark² [mɑːk] 1 n a (*written symbol on paper, cloth etc*) marque *f*, signe *m*; (*as signature*) marque, signe, croix *f*; (*on animal, body etc*) tache *f*, marque; (*print etc*) empreinte *f*; (*Comm: label*) marque, étiquette *f*; (*stain*) marque, tache, trace *f*. **I have made a ~ on the pages I want to keep** j'ai marqué les pages que je veux garder; (*as signature*) **to make one's ~** faire une marque *or* une croix; (*fig*) **to make one's ~ as a poet** se faire un nom en tant que poète, s'imposer comme poète; (*fig*) **he has certainly made his ~** il s'est certainement imposé; **the ~s of his shoes in the soil** l'empreinte de ses souliers dans la terre; **without a ~ on his body** sans trace de coups *or* de blessures sur le corps; **the ~ on this farmer's cattle** la marque (au fer rouge) sur le bétail de ce fermier; (*fig*) **to leave one's ~ on sth** laisser son empreinte sur qch; (*fig*) **it is the ~ of a good teacher** c'est le signe d'un bon professeur; **the ~s of violence were visible everywhere** les marques *or* traces de violence étaient visibles partout; **it bears the ~(s) of genius** cela porte la marque *or* l'empreinte du génie; **as a ~ of my gratitude** en témoignage de ma gratitude; **as a ~ of respect** en signe de respect; **as a ~ of our disapproval** pour marquer notre désapprobation; **printer's ~** marque de l'imprimeur; **punctuation ~** signe de ponctuation; **that will leave a ~** cela laissera une marque; **this ~ won't come out** cette marque *or* tache ne partira pas; **finger ~** marque *or* trace de doigt; (*Econ*) **the number of those out of work has fallen below the 2 million ~** le chiffre des chômeurs est descendu en dessous de la barre des 2 millions; *see* **foot, hall, trade** *etc*.

b (*Scol*) note *f*; point *m*. **good/bad ~** bonne/mauvaise note; **the ~ is out of 20** c'est une note sur 20; **you need 50 ~s to pass** il faut avoir 50 points pour être reçu; **to fail by 2 ~s** échouer à 2 points; **she got a good ~** *or* **good ~s in French** elle a eu une bonne note en français; (*Brit Scol*) **~s for effort/conduct** *etc* note d'application/de conduite *etc*; (*fig*) **you get no ~s at all as a cook** tu mérites (un) zéro comme cuisinière; (*fig*) **(I give him) full ~s for trying!** il faut le féliciter d'avoir essayé!; (*fig iro*) **there are no ~s for guessing his name** il n'y a pas besoin d'être un génie pour savoir de qui je parle.

c (*Sport etc: target*) but *m*, cible *f*. **to hit the ~** (*lit*) atteindre *or* toucher le but; (*fig*) mettre le doigt dessus*; (*lit*) **to miss the ~** manquer le but; (*fig*) **to miss the ~, to be wide of the ~** *or* **(way) off the ~** *or* **far from the ~** être loin de la vérité; **it's right on the ~** c'est absolument exact; (*fig*) **that's beside the ~** c'est à côté de la question; *[forecast, estimate]* **it's way off the ~** c'est complètement à côté de la plaque*; (*pej*) **he's an easy ~** il se fait avoir* facilement.

d (*Sport*) ligne *f* de départ; (*Rugby*) arrêt *m* de volée. **on your ~s! get set! go!** à vos marques! prêts! partez!; (*lit, fig*) **to get off the ~** démarrer; (*fig*) **to be quick off the ~** (*quick on the uptake*) avoir l'esprit vif; (*quick reactions*) avoir des réactions rapides; (*fig*) **to be quick off the ~ in doing sth** ne pas perdre de temps pour faire qch; (*fig*) **I don't feel up to the ~** je ne suis pas dans mon assiette, je ne suis pas en forme; **he is not up to the ~ for this job** il n'est pas à la hauteur de ce travail; **this work is hardly up to the ~** cet ouvrage laisse beaucoup à désirer; **to come up to the ~** répondre à l'attente; *see* **overstep**.

e (*Mil, Tech: model, type*) **M~** série *f*; **Concorde M~ 1** Concorde première série.

f (*Culin: oven temperature*) **(gas) ~ 1** thermostat *m* 1.

2 comp ▸**markdown** (*Comm*) remise *f*, réduction *f* ▸**mark reader** *or* **scanner** lecteur *m* de marques ▸**mark reading** *or* **scanning** lecture *f* de marques ▸**marksman** *see* **marksman** ▸**mark-up** (*Comm*) (*increase*) hausse *f*, majoration *f* de prix; **mark-up on a bill** majoration sur une facture; **there's a 50% mark-up on this product** ils ont une marge *or* ils font un bénéfice de 50 % sur ce produit.

3 vt a (*make a ~ on*) marquer, mettre une marque à *or* sur; *paragraph, item, linen, suitcase* marquer; (*stain*) tacher, marquer. **to ~ the cards** maquiller *or* marquer les cartes; **to ~ a shirt with one's name** marquer son nom sur une chemise; **I hope your dress isn't ~ed** j'espère que ta robe n'est pas tachée; **the accident ~ed him for life** l'accident l'a marqué pour la vie; **suffering had ~ed him** la douleur l'avait marqué; **a bird ~ed with red** un oiseau tacheté de rouge.

b (*indicate*) marquer; *price etc* marquer, indiquer; (*St Ex*) coter; (*Sport*) *score* marquer. **X ~s the spot** l'endroit est marqué d'une croix; **this flag ~s the frontier** ce drapeau marque la frontière; **it ~s a change of policy** cela indique un changement de politique; **in order to ~ the occasion** pour marquer l'occasion; **this ~s him as a future manager** ceci fait présager pour lui une carrière de cadre; **his reign was ~ed by civil wars** son règne fut marqué par des guerres civiles; **to ~ time** (*Mil*) marquer le pas; (*fig: wait*) faire du sur place, piétiner; (*by choice,* *before doing sth*) attendre son heure; *see also* **marked.**

c (*Scol etc*) *essay, exam* corriger, noter; *candidate* noter, donner une note à. **to ~ sth right/wrong** marquer qch juste/faux.

d (*note, pay attention to*) noter, faire attention à; (*Sport*) *opposing player* marquer. **~ my words!** écoutez-moi bien!, notez bien ce que je vous dis!; **~ you, he may have been right** remarquez qu'il avait peut-être raison; **~ him well†** observez-le bien.

4 **vi: this material ~s easily/will not ~** tout marque *or* se voit/rien ne se voit sur ce tissu.

►**mark down** 1 **vt sep** a (*write down*) inscrire, noter. b (*reduce*) *price* baisser; *goods* démarquer, baisser le prix de; (*Scol*) *exercise, pupil* baisser la note de. **all these items have been marked down for the sales** tous ces articles ont été démarqués pour les soldes; (*St Ex*) **to be marked down** s'inscrire en baisse, reculer. c (*single out*) *person* désigner, prévoir (*for* pour). 2 **markdown n** *see* **mark² 2.**

►**mark off vt sep** a (*separate*) séparer, distinguer (*from* de). b (*Surv etc*) (*divide by boundary*) délimiter; *distance* mesurer; *road, boundary* tracer. c *items on list etc* cocher. **he marked the names off as the people went in** il cochait les noms (sur la liste) à mesure que les gens entraient.

►**mark out vt sep** a *zone etc* délimiter, tracer les limites de; (*with stakes etc*) jalonner; *field* borner. **to mark out a tennis court** tracer les lignes d'un (court de) tennis; **the road is marked out with flags** la route est balisée de drapeaux. b (*single out*) désigner, distinguer. **to mark sb out for promotion** désigner qn pour l'avancement; **he was marked out long ago for that job** il y a longtemps qu'on l'avait prévu pour ce poste; **his red hair marked him out from the others** ses cheveux roux le distinguaient des autres.

►**mark up** 1 **vt sep** a (*on board, wall etc*) *price, score* marquer. b (*Comm: put a price on*) indiquer *or* marquer le prix de. **these items have not been marked up** le prix n'est pas marqué sur ces articles. c (*increase*) *price* hausser, augmenter, majorer; *goods* majorer le prix de. **all these chairs have been marked up** toutes ces chaises ont augmenté; (*St Ex*) **to be marked up** s'inscrire en hausse, avancer. 2 **mark-up n** *see* **mark² 2.**

marked [mɑːkt] **adj** a (*noticeable etc*) *difference, accent, bias* marqué, prononcé; *improvement, increase* sensible, manifeste. **it is becoming more ~** cela s'accentue; **he is a ~ man** (*Police etc*) c'est un homme marqué, c'est un suspect; (* *hum*) on l'a à l'œil*. b (*Ling*) marqué. **~ form** forme *f* marquée; **to be ~ for number/gender** porter la marque du nombre/du genre. c (*St Ex*) **~ shares** actions *fpl* estampillées.

markedly ['mɑːkɪdlɪ] **adv** (*see* **marked**) d'une façon marquée *or* prononcée; sensiblement, visiblement, manifestement.

marker ['mɑːkəʳ] **n** a (*pen*) marqueur *m* indélébile; (*tool: laundry ~ etc*) marquoir *m*. b (*flag, stake*) marque *f*, jalon *m*; (*light etc*) balise *f*. c (*bookmark*) signet *m*. d (*Sport etc*) (*person*) marqueur *m*, -euse *f*. (*Ftbl*) **to shake off one's ~** se démarquer. e (*Scol: person*) correcteur *m*. f (*Ling*) marqueur *m*.

market ['mɑːkɪt] 1 **n** a (*trade; place; also St Ex*) marché *m*. **to go to ~** aller au marché; **the wholesale ~** le marché de gros; **cattle ~** marché *or* foire *f* aux bestiaux; **the sugar ~, the ~ in sugar** le marché du *or* des sucre(s); **the world coffee ~** le marché mondial du *or* des café(s); **free ~** marché libre; (*St Ex*) **a dull/lively ~** un marché lourd/actif; (*St Ex*) **the ~ is rising/falling** les cours *mpl* sont en hausse/en baisse; (*St Ex*) **the company intends to go to the ~** la société pense s'introduire en Bourse; *see* **black, buyer, common** *etc.*

b (*fig*) marché *m*, débouché *m*, clientèle *f*. **to have a good ~ for sth** avoir une grosse demande pour qch; **to find a ready ~ for sth** trouver facilement un marché *or* des débouchés pour qch; **there is a (ready) ~ for small cars** les petites voitures se vendent bien *or* sont d'une vente facile; **there's no ~ for pink socks** les chaussettes roses ne se vendent pas; **this appeals to the French ~** cela plaît à la clientèle française, cela se vend bien en France; **home/overseas/world ~** marché intérieur/d'outre-mer/mondial; **to be in the ~ for sth** être acheteur de qch; **to put sth/to be on the ~** mettre qch/être en vente *or* dans le commerce *or* sur le marché; **it's the dearest car on the ~** c'est la voiture la plus chère sur le marché; **on the open ~** en vente libre; **the company hopes to go to the ~** la société espère être introduite en Bourse; *see* **flood** *etc.*

2 **comp** ►**market analysis** analyse *f* de marché ►**market cross** croix *f* sur la place du marché ►**market day** jour *m* de *or* du marché; (*St Ex*) jour *m* de bourse ►**market economy** économie *f* de marché ►**market forces** forces *fpl* du marché ►**market garden** (*Brit*) jardin maraîcher ►**market gardener** (*Brit*) maraîcher *m*, -ère *f* ►**market gardening** (*Brit*) culture maraîchère ►**market leader** leader *m* du marché ►**market opportunity** créneau *m* ►**market place** (*lit*) place *f* du marché; **in the market place** (*lit*) au marché; (*fig: Econ*) sur le marché ►**market price** (*Comm*) prix marchand *or* du marché; **at market price** au cours, au prix courant; (*St Ex*) **market prices** cours *m* du marché ►**market rates** taux *m* du cours libre ►**market research** étude *f* de marché (*in* de); **to do some market research to find out ...** faire une étude de marché pour découvrir ...; **market research institute** *or* **organization** institut *m* de marketing ►**market researcher** enquêteur *m* (*f* -euse) marketing *or* commercial(e) ►**market share** part *f* du marché ►**market square** place *f* du marché ►**market trends** (*St Ex*) tendances *fpl* du marché ►**market value** valeur marchande.

3 **vt** (*sell*) vendre; (*launch*) lancer sur le marché; (*find outlet for*) trouver un *or* des débouché(s) pour.

4 **vi** (*esp US: also* **to go ~ing**) aller faire des commissions.

marketability [ˌmɑːkɪtə'bɪlɪtɪ] **n** possibilité *f* de commercialisation.

marketable ['mɑːkɪtəbl] **adj** vendable; (*goods*) commercialisable; (*securities*) négociable. **very ~** de bonne vente.

marketeer [ˌmɑːkə'tɪəʳ] **n** a *see* **black.** b (*Brit Pol*) **(pro-)M~s** ceux qui sont en faveur du Marché Commun; **anti-M~s** ceux qui s'opposent au Marché Commun.

marketing ['mɑːkɪtɪŋ] 1 **n** *[product, goods]* commercialisation *f*, marketing *m*; (*field of activity*) marketing, marchéage *m*, mercatique *f*; (*department*) service *m* du marketing, département *m* marketing. 2 **comp** *concept, plan* de commercialisation ►**marketing arrangement** accord *m* de commercialisation ►**marketing department** service *m* du marketing, département *m* marketing ►**marketing intelligence** informations *fpl* commerciales ►**marketing manager** directeur *m*, -trice *f* du marketing ►**marketing mix** marketing mix *m*, plan *m* de marchéage ►**marketing people: one of our marketing people** l'un de nos commerciaux ►**marketing strategy** stratégie *f* marketing.

marking ['mɑːkɪŋ] 1 **n** a (*NonC*) *[animals, trees, goods]* marquage *m*. b (*Brit Scol*) (*gen*) correction *f* (des copies); (*actual giving of marks*) attribution *f* de notes, notation *f*; (*marks given*) notes *fpl*. c *[animal]* marques *fpl*, taches *fpl*. **the ~s on the road** la signalisation horizontale. d (*Ftbl*) marquage *m* (d'un joueur). 2 **comp** ►**marking ink** encre *f* à marquer ►**marking scheme** barème *m*.

marksman ['mɑːksmən] **n, pl marksmen** ['mɑːksmən] bon tireur, tireur d'élite.

marksmanship ['mɑːksmənʃɪp] **n** adresse *f* au tir.

marl [mɑːl] (*Geol*) 1 **n** marne *f*. 2 **vt** marner.

marlin ['mɑːlɪn] **n, pl ~** *or* **~s** (*fish*) marlin *m*, makaire *m*.

marlin(e) ['mɑːlɪn] **n** (*Naut*) lusin *m*. **~spike** épissoir *m*.

marly ['mɑːlɪ] **adj** marneux.

marmalade ['mɑːməleɪd] **n** confiture *f or* marmelade *f* d'oranges (*or* de citrons *etc*). **~ orange** orange amère, bigarade *f*.

Marmara, Marmora ['mɑːmərə] **n: Sea of ~** mer *f* de Marmara.

marmoreal [mɑː'mɔːrɪəl] **adj** (*liter*) marmoréen.

marmoset ['mɑːməʊzet] **n** ouistiti *m*.

marmot ['mɑːmət] **n** marmotte *f*.

maroon¹ [mə'ruːn] **adj** (*colour*) bordeaux *inv*.

maroon² [mə'ruːn] **n** (*firework; signal*) pétard *m*; (*signal*) fusée *f* de détresse.

maroon³ [mə'ruːn] **vt** *castaway* abandonner (sur une île *or* une côte déserte); (*fig*) *[sea, traffic, strike etc]* bloquer. (*fig*) **to be ~ed** être *or* se sentir abandonné *or* délaissé *or* perdu.

marquee [mɑː'kiː] **n** a (*esp Brit*) (*tent*) grande tente; (*in circus*) chapiteau *m*. b (*awning*) auvent *m*; *[theatre, cinema]* marquise *f*, fronton *m*.

Marquesas Islands [mɑː'keɪsæs'aɪləndz] **npl** îles *fpl* Marquises.

marquess ['mɑːkwɪs] **n** marquis *m*.

marquetry ['mɑːkɪtrɪ] 1 **n** marqueterie *f*. 2 **comp** *table etc* de *or* en marqueterie.

marquis ['mɑːkwɪs] **n = marquess.**

Marrakesh, Marrakech [mə'rækeʃ, mærə'keʃ] **n** Marrakech.

marriage ['mærɪdʒ] 1 **n** mariage *m*; (*fig*) mariage, alliance *f*. **to give in ~** donner en mariage; **to take in ~** (*gen*) épouser; (*actual wording of service*) prendre comme époux (*or* épouse); **civil ~** mariage civil; **~ of convenience** mariage de convenance; **aunt by ~** tante par alliance; **they are related by ~** ils sont parents par alliance; *see* **offer, shot** *etc.*

2 **comp** ►**marriage bed** lit conjugal ►**marriage bonds** liens conjugaux ►**marriage broker** agent matrimonial ►**marriage bureau** agence matrimoniale ►**marriage ceremony** mariage *m*; (*Rel*) bénédiction nuptiale ►**marriage certificate** extrait *m* d'acte de mariage ►**marriage customs** traditions *fpl* de mariage ►**marriage guidance** consultation conjugale ►**marriage guidance counsellor** conseiller *m*, -ère *f* conjugal(e) ►**marriage licence** certificat *m* de publication des bans ►**marriage lines** (*Brit*) = **marriage certificate** ►**marriage partner** conjoint(e) *m(f)*, époux *m*, épouse *f* ►**marriage rate** taux *m* de nuptialité ►**marriage settlement** ≃ constitution *f* de rente sur la tête de l'épouse survivante ►**marriage vows** vœux *mpl* de mariage.

marriageable ['mærɪdʒəbl] **adj** mariable, nubile. **of ~ age** en âge de se marier; **he's very ~** c'est un très bon parti.

married ['mærɪd] **adj** *man, woman* marié; *life, love* conjugal. **he is a ~ man** il est marié; **~ couple** couple *m* (marié), ménage *m*; **the newly ~ couple** les (nouveaux) mariés; **~ name** nom *m* de femme mariée; (*Mil etc*) **~ quarters** appartements *mpl* pour familles; (*fig*) **he's ~ to his work** il fait passer son travail avant tout, il n'existe que pour son travail; *see also* **marry.**

marrow ['mærəʊ] **n** a *[bone]* moelle *f*; (*fig*) essence *f*, moelle. **~bone** os *m* à moelle; **to be chilled** *or* **frozen to the ~** être gelé jusqu'à la moelle des os. b (*Brit: vegetable*) courge *f*. **baby ~** courgette *f*.

marry ['mærɪ] 1 **vt** a (*take in marriage*) épouser, se marier avec. **will**

you ~ me? veux-tu *or* voulez-vous m'épouser?; **to get** *or* **be married** se marier; **they've been married for 10 years** ils sont mariés depuis 10 ans; **to ~ money** faire un mariage d'argent. b (*give or join in marriage*) marier. **he has 3 daughters to ~ (off)** il a 3 filles à marier; **she married (off) her daughter to a lawyer** elle a marié sa fille avec *or* à un avocat. 2 **vi** se marier. **to ~ into a family** s'allier à une famille par le mariage, s'apparenter à une famille; **to ~ beneath o.s.** se mésallier; **to ~ again** se remarier.
▶**marry off vt sep** *[parent etc]* marier; **see marry 1b.**
▶**marry up vt sep** *[pattern etc]* faire coïncider.
Mars [mɑːz] **n** (*Myth*) Mars *m*; (*Astron*) Mars *f*.
Marseillaise [ˌmɑːsəˈleɪz] **n** Marseillaise *f*.
Marseilles [mɑːˈseɪlz] **n** Marseille.
marsh [mɑːʃ] 1 **n** marais *m*, marécage *m*; **see salt.** 2 **comp** ▶**marsh fever** paludisme *m* ▶**marsh gas** gaz *m* des marais ▶**marshland** marécage *m*, marais *m*, région marécageuse ▶**marshmallow** (*Bot*) guimauve *f*; (*sweet*) (pâte *f* de) guimauve *f* ▶**marsh marigold** souci *m* d'eau ▶**marsh warbler** rousserolle *f* verderolle.
marshal [ˈmɑːʃəl] 1 **n** a (*Mil etc*) maréchal *m*. (*Brit*) **M~ of the Royal Air Force** *maréchal de la RAF;* **see air, field.** b (*Brit: at demonstrations, sports meeting etc*) membre *m* du service d'ordre. c (*US*) (*in police/fire department*) ≃ capitaine *m* de gendarmerie/des pompiers; (*law officer*) marshal *m* (*magistrat et officier de police fédérale*). d (*Brit: at Court etc*) chef *m* du protocole. 2 **vt** *troops* rassembler; *crowd, traffic* canaliser; (*Rail*) *wagons* trier; (*fig*) *facts, one's wits, evidence* rassembler. **the police ~led the procession into the town** la police a fait entrer le cortège en bon ordre dans la ville.
marshalling [ˈmɑːʃəlɪŋ] **n** a *[crowd, demonstrators]* maintien *m* de l'ordre (*of* parmi). b (*Rail*) triage *m*. **~ yard** gare *f or* centre *m* de triage.
marshy [ˈmɑːʃɪ] **adj** marécageux.
marsupial [mɑːˈsuːpɪəl] **adj, n** marsupial *(m)*.
mart [mɑːt] **n** (*trade centre*) centre commercial; (*market*) marché *m*; (*auction room*) salle *f* des ventes; **see property.**
marten [ˈmɑːtɪn] **n, pl ~s** *or* **~** martre *f or* marte *f*.
Martha [ˈmɑːθə] **n** Marthe *f*.
martial [ˈmɑːʃəl] **adj** *bearing* martial; *music, speech* martial, guerrier. **~ art** art *m* martial; **~ law** loi martiale.
Martian [ˈmɑːʃən] 1 **n** Martien(-ienne) *m(f)*. 2 **adj** martien.
martin [ˈmɑːtɪn] **n** (*Orn*) **house ~** hirondelle *f* de fenêtre; **sand ~** hirondelle de rivage.
martinet [ˌmɑːtɪˈnet] **n: to be a ~** être impitoyable *or* intraitable en matière de discipline.
martini [mɑːˈtiːnɪ] **n** ® martini *m* ®; (*US: cocktail*) martini américain (*gin avec du vermouth sec*). **sweet ~** martini doux.
Martinique [ˌmɑːtɪˈniːk] **n** Martinique *f*. **in ~** à la Martinique.
Martinmas [ˈmɑːtɪnməs] **n** la Saint-Martin.
martyr [ˈmɑːtəʳ] 1 **n** (*Rel, fig*) martyr(e) *m(f)* (*to* de). **a ~'s crown** la couronne du martyre; **he is a ~ to migraine** ses graines lui font souffrir le martyre; (*fig*) **to make a ~ of o.s.** jouer les martyrs; **don't be such a ~!** cesse de jouer les martyrs! 2 **vt** (*Rel, fig*) martyriser.
martyrdom [ˈmɑːtədəm] **n** (*NonC*) (*Rel*) martyre *m*; (*fig*) martyre, calvaire *m*, supplice(s) *m(pl)*.
martyrize [ˈmɑːtɪraɪz] **vt** (*Rel, fig*) martyriser.
marvel [ˈmɑːvəl] 1 **n** merveille *f*, prodige *m*, miracle *m*. **the ~s of modern science** les prodiges de la science moderne; **his work is a ~ of patience** son œuvre est une merveille de patience; **if he gets there it will be a ~** ce sera (un) miracle s'il y arrive; **she's a ~** elle est merveilleuse, c'est une perle; **it's a ~ to me how he does it** je ne sais vraiment pas comment il peut le faire; **it's a ~ to me that** cela me paraît un miracle que + *subj*, je n'en reviens pas que + *subj*; **it's a ~ that** c'est un miracle que + *subj*; **see work.** 2 **vi** s'émerveiller, s'étonner (*at* de). 3 **vt** s'étonner (*that* de ce que + *indic or subj*).
marvellous, (*US*) **marvelous** [ˈmɑːvələs] **adj** (*astonishing*) merveilleux, étonnant, extraordinaire; (*miraculous*) miraculeux; (*excellent*) merveilleux, magnifique, formidable*, sensationnel*. (*iro*) **isn't it ~!** ce n'est pas extraordinaire, ça?* (*iro*).
marvellously, (*US*) **marvelously** [ˈmɑːvələslɪ] **adv** merveilleusement, à merveille.
Marxian [ˈmɑːksɪən] **adj** marxien.
Marxism [ˈmɑːksɪzəm] **n** marxisme *m*. **~-Leninism** marxisme-léninisme *m*.
Marxist [ˈmɑːksɪst] **adj, n** marxiste *(mf)*. **with ~ tendencies** marxisant; **~-Leninist** (**adj, n**) marxiste-léniniste *(mf)*.
Mary [ˈmɛərɪ] **n** Marie *f*. **~ Magdalene** Marie-Madeleine; **~ Queen of Scots, ~ Stuart** Marie Stuart (reine d'Écosse); (*Drugs sl*) **~ Jane** marie-jeanne *f*, marijuana *f*; **see bloody.**
Maryland [ˈmɛərɪlænd] **n** Maryland *m*. **in ~** dans le Maryland.
marzipan [ˈmɑːzɪˌpæn] 1 **n** pâte *f* d'amandes, massepain *m*. 2 **comp** *sweet etc* à la pâte d'amandes.
masc. **abbr of masculine.**
mascara [mæsˈkɑːrə] **n** mascara *m*.
mascot [ˈmæskət] **n** mascotte *f*.
masculine [ˈmæskjʊlɪn] 1 **adj** *sex, voice, courage* masculin, mâle; *woman* masculin, hommasse (*pej*); *gender, rhyme* masculin. **this word is ~** ce mot est (du) masculin. 2 **n** (*Gram*) masculin *m*. **in the ~** au masculin.
masculinity [ˌmæskjʊˈlɪnɪtɪ] **n** masculinité *f*.
maser [ˈmeɪzəʳ] **n** maser *m*.
MASH [mæʃ] **n** (*US*) (**abbr of mobile army surgical hospital**) unité *f* chirurgicale mobile de campagne.
mash [mæʃ] 1 **n** (*for horses*) mash *m*; (*for pigs, hens etc*) pâtée *f*; (*Brit Culin: potatoes*) purée *f* (de pommes de terre); (*Brewing*) pâte *f*; (*soft mixture*) bouillie *f*; (*pulp*) pulpe *f*. 2 **vt** a (*crush: also ~ up*) écraser, broyer; (*Culin*) *potatoes* faire en purée, faire une purée de; (*injure, damage*) écraser. **~ed potatoes** purée *f* (de pommes de terre). b (*Brewing*) brasser.
masher [ˈmæʃəʳ] **n** (*Tech*) broyeur *m*; (*in kitchen*) presse-purée *m inv*.
mashie [ˈmæʃɪ] **n** (*Golf*) mashie *m*.
mask [mɑːsk] 1 **n** (*gen*) masque *m*; (*for eyes, in silk or velvet*) masque, loup *m*; (*Comput*) masque de saisie; **see death, gas, iron** *etc.* 2 **vt** a *person, face* masquer. **~ed ball** bal masqué. b (*hide*) *house, object* masquer, cacher; *truth, motives* masquer, cacher, dissimuler, voiler; *taste, smell* masquer, recouvrir. c (*during painting, spraying*) **~ing tape** papier-cache adhésif. 3 **vi** *[surgeon etc]* se masquer.
masochism [ˈmæsəʊkɪzəm] **n** masochisme *m*.
masochist [ˈmæsəʊkɪst] **n** masochiste *mf*.
masochistic [ˌmæsəʊˈkɪstɪk] **adj** masochiste.
mason [ˈmeɪsn] **n** a (*stoneworker*) maçon *m*; **see monumental.** b (*free~*) (franc-)maçon *m*. c (*US*) **M~ jar** bocal *m* à conserves (étanche).
masonic [məˈsɒnɪk] **adj** (franc-)maçonnique.
Masonite [ˈmeɪsənaɪt] **n** ® (*US*) aggloméré *m*.
masonry [ˈmeɪsənrɪ] **n** (*NonC*) a (*stonework*) maçonnerie *f*. b (*free~*) (franc-)maçonnerie *f*.
masque [mɑːsk] **n** (*Theat*) mascarade *f*, comédie-masque *f*.
masquerade [ˌmæskəˈreɪd] 1 **n** (*lit, fig*) mascarade *f*. 2 **vi: to ~ as** se faire passer pour.
mass¹ [mæs] 1 **n** a (*NonC: bulk, size; also Art, Phys*) masse *f*.
b *[matter, dough, rocks, air, snow, water etc]* masse *f*. **a ~ of daisies** une multitude de pâquerettes; **the garden was a (solid) ~ of colour** le jardin n'était qu'une masse de couleurs; **he was a ~ of bruises** il était couvert de bleus; **in the ~** dans l'ensemble; **the great ~ of people** la (grande) masse des gens, la (grande) majorité des gens; **~es of*** des masses de*, des tas de*.
c (*people*) **the ~(es)** la masse, le peuple, les masses (populaires); **Shakespeare for the ~es** Shakespeare à l'usage des masses.
2 **adj** a (*involving many people*) *support, unemployment, opposition, destruction* massif, généralisé; *rally, marathon* monstre; (*all at the same time*) *resignations, desertions, sackings* en masse; (*as opposed to individual*) *hysteria, hypnosis* collectif. **~ funeral** obsèques collectives; **~ grave** charnier *m*; **~ mailing** publipostage *m*; **~ marketing** grande distribution; **~ meeting** grand rassemblement, meeting *m* monstre; **~ murder(s)** tuerie(s) *f(pl)*; **~ murderer** boucher *m*.
b (*for the masses*) *culture, civilization, movement, magazine,* (*Comput*) *memory* de masse; (*relating to the masses*) *psychology, education* des masses. **~ media** (mass-)médias *mpl*, moyens *mpl* de diffusion de l'information.
c (*Ling*) **~ noun** nom *m* massif.
3 **comp** ▶**mass cult*** (*US*) culture *f* populaire *or* pour les masses ▶**mass-market** grand public ▶**mass-produce** (*Ind*) fabriquer en série ▶**mass production** production *f or* fabrication *f* en série.
4 **vt: ~ed bands/troops** fanfares/troupes regroupées.
5 **vi** *[troops, people]* se masser; *[clouds]* s'amonceler.
mass² [mæs] **n** (*Rel, Mus*) messe *f*. **to say ~** dire la messe; **to go to ~** aller à la messe; **see black** *etc.*
Mass. (*US*) **abbr of Massachusetts.**
Massachusetts [ˌmæsəˈtʃuːsɪts] **n** Massachusetts *m*. **in ~** dans le Massachusetts.
massacre [ˈmæsəkəʳ] 1 **n** (*lit, fig*) massacre *m*. **a ~ on the roads** une hécatombe sur les routes. 2 **vt** (*lit, fig*) massacrer.
massage [ˈmæsɑːʒ] 1 **n** massage *m*. **~ parlour** institut *m* de massage (spécialisé); (*euph*) massage thaïlandais. 2 **vt** masser; (*fig*) *figures* manipuler.
masseur [mæˈsɜːʳ] **n** masseur *m*.
masseuse [mæˈsɜːz] **n** masseuse *f*.
massicot [ˈmæsɪkɒt] **n** massicot *m*.
massif [mæˈsiːf] **n** massif *m*. **M~ Central** Massif *m* central.
massive [ˈmæsɪv] **adj** *rock, building, attack, dose, contribution, increase* massif; *suitcase, parcel, error, change* énorme; *majority* énorme, écrasant; *features* épais (*f* -aisse), lourd; *sound* retentissant.
massively [ˈmæsɪvlɪ] **adv** massivement.
massiveness [ˈmæsɪvnɪs] **n** aspect *or* caractère massif.
mast¹ [mɑːst] 1 **n** (*on ship, also flagpole*) mât *m*; (*for radio*) pylône *m*. **the ~s of a ship** la mâture d'un navire; (*Naut*) **to sail before the ~** servir comme simple matelot. 2 **comp** ▶**masthead** *[ship]* tête *f* de mât; *[newspaper]* encadré *m* administratif.
mast² [mɑːst] **n** (*Agr*) **see beech.**

mastectomy [mæ'stektəmɪ] n mastectomie *f*.

-masted ['mɑːstɪd] adj *ending in comps:* **3-masted** à 3 mâts.

master ['mɑːstəʳ] 1 n a *[household, institution, animal]* maître *m*. **the ~ of the house** le maître de maison; **to be ~ in one's own house** être maître chez soi; **the ~ is not at home†** Monsieur n'est pas là; (*Prov*) **like ~ like man** tel maître tel valet (*Prov*); (*Art : pictures*) **old ~s** tableaux *mpl* de maître; **I am the ~ now** c'est moi qui commande *or* qui donne les ordres maintenant; (*fig*) **he has met his ~** il a trouvé son maître; **to be one's own ~** être son (propre) maître; **to be ~ of o.s./of the situation** être maître de soi/de la situation; **to be (the) ~ of one's fate** disposer de *or* être maître de sa destinée; **he is a ~ of the violin** c'est un maître du violon; (*Rel*) **the M~** Jésus-Christ, le Christ; *see* **old, past** *etc*.

b (*teacher*) (*in secondary school*) professeur *m*; (*in primary school*) instituteur *m*, maître *m*. **music ~** (*in school*) professeur de musique; (*private tutor*) professeur *or* maître de musique; *see* **fencing** *etc*.

c (*Naut*) *[ship]* capitaine *m*; *[liner]* (capitaine) commandant *m*; *[fishing boat]* patron *m*.

d (*Univ*) **M~ of Arts/Science** *etc* titulaire *mf* d'une maîtrise ès lettres/sciences *etc;* **a ~'s (degree)** une maîtrise; (*US*) **~'s essay** *or* **paper** *or* **thesis** mémoire *m* (de maîtrise).

e (*Brit Univ*) *[Oxford etc college]* ≃ directeur *m*, principal *m*.

f (*Brit : title for boys*) monsieur *m*.

g (*Brit Jur*) **M~ of the Rolls** premier président *m* de la Cour de cassation.

h = **master tape, master disk;** *see* **2**.

i (*Golf*) **the (US) M~s** les Masters *mpl*.

2 comp *scheme, idea* directeur (*f* -trice), maître (*f* maîtresse), principal; *beam* maître; *control, cylinder, switch* principal ►**master-at-arms** (pl ~s-~-~) (*Naut*) capitaine *m* d'armes ►**master baker** maître *m* boulanger ►**master bedroom** chambre principale ►**master builder** entrepreneur *m* (de bâtiments) ►**master butcher** maître *m* boucher ►**master card** (*lit, fig*) carte maîtresse ►**master chief petty officer** (*US Naut*) major *m* ►**master class** cours *m* de (grand) maître ►**master copy** original *m* ►**master cylinder** (*Aut*) maître cylindre *m* ►**master disk** (*Comput*) disque *m* d'exploitation ►**master file** (*Comput*) fichier *m* maître ►**masterful** *see* **masterful** ►**masterfully** *see* **masterfully** ►**master hand** (*expert*) maître *m*, expert *m*; (*skill*) main *f* de maître; **to be a master hand at (doing) sth** être maître dans l'art de (faire) qch ►**master key** passe-partout *m inv* ►**masterly** *see* **masterly** ►**master mariner** (*Naut*) (*foreign-going*) ≃ capitaine *m* au long cours; (*home trade*) ≃ capitaine de la marine marchande ►**mastermind** n (*genius*) intelligence *f or* esprit *m* supérieur(e), cerveau *m*; (*of plan, crime etc*) cerveau ◊ vt *operation etc* diriger, organiser ►**master of ceremonies** maître *m* des cérémonies; (*TV etc*) animateur *m*, meneur *m* de jeu ►**master of (fox)hounds** grand veneur ►**masterpiece** chef-d'œuvre *m* ►**master plan** plan *m* directeur ►**master print** (*Cine*) copie *f* étalon ►**master race** race *f* supérieure ►**master sergeant** (*US*) adjudant *m*; (*US Aviat*) ≃ sergent-chef *m* ►**"The Mastersingers (of Nuremberg)"** "les Maîtres chanteurs *mpl* (de Nuremberg)" ►**master stroke** coup magistral *or* de maître ►**master tape** bande *f* maîtresse, bande-souche *f*.

3 vt a *person, animal, emotion* maîtriser, dompter, mater; *one's defects* surmonter; *difficulty* venir à bout de, surmonter; *situation* se rendre maître de.

b (*understand*) *theory* saisir. **to have ~ed sth** posséder qch à fond.

c (*learn*) *subject, skill, craft* apprendre (à fond). **he has ~ed Greek** il connaît *or* possède le grec à fond; **he'll never ~ the violin** il ne saura jamais bien jouer du violon; **he has ~ed the trumpet** il est devenu très bon trompettiste *or* un trompettiste accompli; **it's so difficult that I'll never ~ it** c'est si difficile que je n'y parviendrai jamais.

masterful ['mɑːstəfʊl] adj a (*imperious*) dominateur (*f* -trice), autoritaire, impérieux. b (*expert*) magistral.

masterfully ['mɑːstəfəlɪ] adv a (*imperiously*) *act, decide* en maître, avec autorité, impérieusement; *speak, announce* d'un ton décisif, sur un ton d'autorité. b (*expertly*) magistralement, de main de maître.

masterly ['mɑːstəlɪ] adj magistral. **in a ~ way** magistralement.

mastery ['mɑːstərɪ] n (*gen*) maîtrise *f* (*of* de). **to gain ~ over** *person* avoir le dessus sur, l'emporter sur; *animal* dompter, mater; *nation, country* s'assurer la domination de; *the seas* s'assurer la maîtrise de.

mastic ['mæstɪk] n (*resin, adhesive*) mastic *m*.

masticate ['mæstɪkeɪt] vti mastiquer, mâcher.

mastiff ['mæstɪf] n mastiff *m*.

mastitis [mæ'staɪtɪs] n mastite *f*.

mastodon ['mæstədɒn] n mastodonte *m* (*lit*).

mastoid ['mæstɔɪd] 1 adj mastoïde. 2 n (*bone*) apophyse *f* mastoïde; (*Med *: inflammation*) mastoïdite *f*.

mastoiditis [ˌmæstɔɪ'daɪtɪs] n mastoïdite *f*.

masturbate ['mæstəbeɪt] 1 vi se masturber. 2 vt masturber.

masturbation [ˌmæstə'beɪʃən] n masturbation *f*.

MAT [ˌemeɪ'tiː] n (abbr of **machine-assisted translation**) TAO *f*.

mat¹ [mæt] 1 n a (*for floors etc*) (petit) tapis *m*, carpette *f*; (*of straw etc*) natte *f*; (*at door*) paillasson *m*, tapis-brosse *m*, essuie-pieds *m inv*; (*in car, gymnasium*) tapis. (*fig*) **to have sb on the ~*** passer un savon à qn*; **a ~ of hair** des cheveux emmêlés; *see* **rush²** *etc*. b (*on table*) (*heat-resistant*) dessous-de-plat *m inv*; (*decorative*) set *m* (de table); (*embroidered linen*) napperon *m*; *see* **drip, place** *etc*. 2 vi a *[hair etc]* s'emmêler; *see* **matted**. b *[woollens]* (se) feutrer.

mat² [mæt] adj = **matt**.

matador ['mætədɔːʳ] n matador *m*.

match¹ [mætʃ] 1 n allumette *f*. **box/book of ~es** boîte *f*/pochette *f* d'allumettes; **have you got a ~?** avez-vous une allumette? *or* du feu?; **to strike** *or* **light a ~** gratter *or* frotter *or* faire craquer une allumette; **to put** *or* **set a ~ to sth** mettre le feu à qch; *see* **safety**. 2 comp ►**matchbox** boîte *f* à allumettes ►**matchstick** allumette *f* ►**matchwood** bois *m* d'allumettes; **to smash sth to matchwood** réduire qch en miettes, pulvériser qch.

match² [mætʃ] 1 n a (*Sport*) match *m*; (*game*) partie *f*. **to play a ~ against sb** disputer un match contre qn, jouer contre qn; **international ~** match international, rencontre internationale; **~ abandoned** match suspendu; *see* **away, home, return** *etc*.

b (*equal*) égal(e) *m(f)*. **to meet one's ~ (in sb)** trouver à qui parler (avec qn), avoir affaire à forte partie (avec qn); **he's a ~ for anybody** il est de taille à faire face à n'importe qui; **he's no ~ for Paul** il n'est pas de taille à lutter contre Paul, il ne fait pas le poids* contre Paul; **he was more than a ~ for Paul** Paul n'était pas à sa mesure *or* ne faisait pas le poids contre lui.

c *[clothes, colours etc]* **to be a good ~** aller bien ensemble, s'assortir bien; **I'm looking for a ~ for these curtains** je cherche quelque chose pour aller avec ces rideaux.

d (*marriage*) mariage *m*. **he's a good ~** c'est un bon parti; **they're a good ~** ils sont bien assortis; **they made a ~ of it** ils se sont mariés.

e (*comparison* adéquation *f*. **a poor ~ between our resources and our objectives** un manque d'adéquation entre nos ressources et nos objectifs.

2 comp ►**matchless** *see* **matchless** ►**matchmaker** marieur *m*, -euse *f*; **she is a great matchmaker, she's always matchmaking** c'est une marieuse enragée*, elle veut toujours marier les gens ►**match point** (*Tennis*) balle *f* de match.

3 vt a (*be equal etc to: also* **~ up to**) égaler, être l'égal de. **his essay didn't ~ (up to) Paul's in originality** sa dissertation n'égalait pas *or* ne valait pas celle de Paul en originalité; **she doesn't ~ (up to) her sister in intelligence** elle n'a pas l'intelligence de sa sœur; **the result didn't ~ (up to) our hopes** le résultat a déçu nos espérances.

b (*produce equal to*) **to ~ sb's offer/proposal** faire une offre/une proposition équivalente à celle de qn; **I can ~ any offer** je peux offrir autant que n'importe qui; **to ~ sb's price/terms** offrir le même prix/des conditions aussi favorables que qn; **this is ~ed only by ...** cela n'a d'égal que ... .

c *[clothes, colours etc]* s'assortir à, aller bien avec. **his tie doesn't ~ his shirt** sa cravate ne va pas avec *or* n'est pas assortie à sa chemise; **his looks ~ his character** son physique va de pair avec *or* s'accorde avec sa personnalité.

d (*find similar piece etc to: also* **~ up**) **can you ~ (up) this material?** (*exactly same*) avez-vous du tissu identique à celui-ci?; (*going well with*) avez-vous du tissu assorti à celui-ci?

e (*pair off*) **to ~ sb against sb** opposer qn à qn; **she ~ed her wits against his strength** elle opposait son intelligence à sa force; **evenly ~ed** de force égale; **they are well ~ed** *[opponents]* ils sont de force égale; *[married couple etc]* ils sont bien assortis.

4 vi *[colours, materials]* être bien assortis, aller bien ensemble; *[cups]* être appareillés; *[gloves, socks]* s'apparier, faire la paire; *[two identical objects]* se faire pendant(s). **with (a) skirt to ~** avec (une) jupe assortie.

►**match up** 1 vi *[colours etc]* s'harmoniser, aller bien ensemble, être assortis. 2 vt sep = **match 3d**.

►**match up to** vt fus = **match 3a**.

matching ['mætʃɪŋ] adj a *garment, material etc* assorti. **with ~ skirt** avec jupe assortie. b (*US*) **~ funds** subvention *f* égale à la somme versée par le récipiendaire.

matchless ['mætʃlɪs] adj sans égal, sans pareil, incomparable.

mate¹ [meɪt] 1 n a (*at work*) camarade *mf* (de travail); (**: friend*) copain* *m*, copine* *f*, camarade. **hey, ~!‡** eh, mon vieux!*; *see* **class, play, work** *etc*. b (*assistant*) aide *mf*. **plumber's ~** aide-plombier *m*. c (*animal*) mâle *m*, femelle *f*; (** hum: spouse*) époux *m*, épouse *f*. d (*Brit Merchant Navy*) ≃ second *m* (capitaine *m*); (*US Naut*) maître *m* (dans la marine); *see* **first**. 2 vt accoupler (*with* à). 3 vi s'accoupler (*with* à, avec).

mate² [meɪt] (*Chess*) 1 n mat *m*; *see* **check², stalemate**. 2 vt mettre échec et mat, mater.

material [mə'tɪərɪəl] 1 adj a *force, success, object, world, benefits, goods* matériel; *comforts, well-being, needs, pleasures* matériel, physique. **from a ~ point of view** du point de vue matériel; **~ possessions** biens matériels, possessions *fpl*.

b (*important*) essentiel, important; (*relevant*) qui importe (*to* à), qui présente de l'intérêt (*to* pour); (*Jur*) *fact, evidence* pertinent; *witness* direct.

2 n a (*gen: substance*) substance *f*, matière *f*. **chemical/dangerous**

~s substances *or* matières chimiques/dangereuses; *see* **waste**.
b (*cloth, fabric*) (*gen*) tissu *m*, étoffe *f*. **dress ~** tissu pour robes.
c (*esp Ind: substances from which product is made*) matériau *m*. **building ~s** matériaux de construction; *see* **raw**.
d (*what is needed for sth*) (*gen*) matériel *m*. **the desk held all his writing ~s** le bureau contenait tout son matériel nécessaire pour écrire; **have you got any writing ~s?** avez-vous de quoi écrire?; **reading ~** (*gen*) de quoi lire, de la lecture; (*for studies*) des ouvrages *mpl* (et des articles *mpl*) à consulter; **play ~s** le matériel pour le jeu.
e (*NonC: facts, data needed for sth*) matériaux *mpl*. **they had all the ~ required for a biography** ils avaient tous les matériaux *or* toutes les données nécessaires pour une biographie; **I had all the ~ I needed for my article** j'avais tout ce qu'il me fallait pour mon article; **the amount of ~ to be examined** la quantité de matériaux *or* de documents à examiner; **all the background ~** toute la documentation d'appui.
f (*NonC: sth written/sung/composed etc*) **all his ~ is original** tout ce qu'il écrit (*or* chante *etc*) est original; **she has written some very funny ~** elle a écrit des choses très amusantes; **we cannot publish this ~** nous ne pouvons pas publier ce genre de choses; **video ~** enregistrements *mpl* vidéo, vidéos *fpl*; **30% of the programme was recorded ~** 30 % de l'émission avait été enregistrée à l'avance; **it's splendid ~!** c'est formidable!; **it's splendid ~ but ...** le contenu est formidable mais ... .
g (*sth written etc for a specific purpose*) **~(s)** matériel *m*; (*Comm*) **publicity ~** matériel de publicité *or* promotionnel; (*Scol etc*) **teaching** *or* **course ~(s)** matériel pédagogique; **reference ~** ouvrages *mpl* de référence.
h (*fig*) **he's officer ~** il a l'étoffe d'un officier; **he's not university ~** il n'est pas de calibre universitaire, il n'est pas capable d'entreprendre des études supérieures.

materialism [məˈtɪərɪəlɪzəm] n matérialisme *m*.

materialist [məˈtɪərɪəlɪst] adj, n matérialiste *(mf)*.

materialistic [məˌtɪərɪəˈlɪstɪk] adj matérialiste.

materialize [məˈtɪərɪəlaɪz] 1 vi a *[plan, wish]* se matérialiser, se réaliser; *[offer, loan etc]* se concrétiser, se matérialiser; *[idea]* prendre forme. **the promised cash didn't ~** l'argent promis ne s'est pas concrétisé *or* matérialisé; **at last the bus ~d*** le bus a enfin fait son apparition *or* est enfin arrivé. b (*Spiritualism etc*) prendre une forme matérielle, se matérialiser. 2 vt matérialiser, concrétiser.

materially [məˈtɪərɪəlɪ] adv réellement; (*Philos*) matériellement, essentiellement.

maternal [məˈtɜːnəl] adj maternel. (*Psych*) **~ deprivation** carence maternelle.

maternity [məˈtɜːnɪtɪ] 1 n maternité *f*. 2 comp *services etc* obstétrique; *clothes* de grossesse ▸**maternity benefit** (*Brit*) ≃ allocation *f* de maternité ▸**maternity home, maternity hospital** maternité *f*; (*private*) clinique *f* d'accouchement, clinique obstétrique ▸**maternity leave** congé *m* de maternité ▸**maternity ward** (service *m* de) maternité *f*.

matey* [ˈmeɪtɪ] adj (*Brit*) familier, copain-copain‡ (*f inv*). **he's very ~ with everyone** il est très copain* avec tout le monde.

math* [mæθ] n (*US*) (abbr of **mathematics**) math(s)* *fpl*.

mathematical [ˌmæθəˈmætɪkəl] adj *process etc* mathématique. **I'm not ~, I haven't got a ~ mind** je n'ai pas le sens des mathématiques, je ne suis pas (un) matheux*; **he's a ~ genius** c'est un mathématicien de génie.

mathematically [ˌmæθəˈmætɪkəlɪ] adv mathématiquement.

mathematician [ˌmæθəməˈtɪʃən] n mathématicien(ne) *m(f)*.

mathematics [ˌmæθəˈmætɪks] n mathématiques *fpl*. **I don't understand the ~ of it** je ne vois pas comment on arrive à ce chiffre *or* à ce résultat.

Mat(h)ilda [məˈtɪldə] n Mathilde *f*.

maths* [mæθs] n (abbr of **mathematics**) math(s)* *fpl*.

matinée [ˈmætɪneɪ] 1 n (*Theat*) matinée *f*. 2 comp ▸**matinée coat** (*Brit*) veste *f* (de bébé) ▸**matinée idol** (*Theat*) idole *f* du public féminin.

mating [ˈmeɪtɪŋ] 1 n *[animals]* accouplement *m*. 2 comp ▸**mating call** appel *m* du mâle ▸**mating season** saison *f* des amours.

matins [ˈmætɪnz] n sg or pl = **mattins**.

matri... [ˈmeɪtrɪ] pref matri... .

matriarch [ˈmeɪtrɪɑːk] n matrone *f*, femme *f* chef de tribu *or* de famille.

matriarchal [ˌmeɪtrɪˈɑːkl] adj matriarcal.

matriarchy [ˈmeɪtrɪɑːkɪ] n matriarcat *m*.

matric [məˈtrɪk] n (*Brit Scol sl:*††) abbr of **matriculation 1b**.

matricide [ˈmeɪtrɪsaɪd] n (*crime*) matricide *m*; (*person*) matricide *mf*.

matriculate [məˈtrɪkjʊleɪt] vi s'inscrire, se faire immatriculer; (*Brit Scol* ††) *être reçu à l'examen de "matriculation"*.

matriculation [məˌtrɪkjʊˈleɪʃən] 1 n a (*Univ*) inscription *f*, immatriculation *f*. b (*Brit Scol* ††) *examen donnant droit à l'inscription universitaire*. 2 comp (*Univ*) *card, fee* d'inscription.

matrimonial [ˌmætrɪˈməʊnɪəl] adj matrimonial, conjugal.

matrimony [ˈmætrɪmənɪ] n (*NonC*) mariage *m*; *see* **holy**.

matrix [ˈmeɪtrɪks] n, pl **~s** *or* **matrices** [ˈmeɪtrɪˌsiːz] matrice *f*.

matron [ˈmeɪtrən] 1 n a matrone *f*, mère *f* de famille. b *[hospital]* surveillante *f* générale; (*in school*) infirmière *f*; *[orphanage, old people's home etc]* directrice *f*. **yes ~** oui madame (*or* mademoiselle). 2 comp ▸**matron of honour** dame *f* d'honneur.

matronly [ˈmeɪtrənlɪ] adj de matrone. **she was a ~ person** elle faisait très digne *or* matrone (*pej*).

matt [mæt] adj mat. **paint with a ~ finish** peinture mate.

matted [ˈmætɪd] adj *hair* emmêlé; *weeds* enchevêtré; *cloth, sweater* feutré.

matter [ˈmætəʳ] 1 n a (*NonC*) (*physical substance*) matière *f*, substance *f*; (*Philos, Phys*) matière; (*Typ*) matière, copie *f*; (*Med: pus*) pus *m*. **vegetable/inanimate ~** matière végétale/inanimée; **colouring ~** substance colorante; **reading ~** choses *fpl* à lire, de quoi lire; **advertising ~** publicité *f*, réclames *fpl*; *see* **grey, mind** *etc*.
b (*NonC: content*) *[book etc]* fond *m*, contenu *m*. **~ and form** le fond et la forme; **the ~ of his essay was good but the style poor** le contenu de sa dissertation était bon mais le style laissait à désirer.
c (*affair, concern, business*) affaire *f*, question *f*, sujet *m*, matière *f*. **the ~ in hand** l'affaire en question; **business ~s** (questions d')affaires *fpl*; (*Admin: in agenda*) **~s arising** questions *fpl* en suspens; **there's the ~ of my expenses** il y a la question de mes frais; **that's quite another ~, that's another ~ altogether, that's a very different ~** c'est tout autre chose, ça c'est une autre affaire; **it's a ~ of life and death** c'est une question de vie ou de mort; **they agreed to let the ~ rest** ils ont convenu d'en rester là; **that will only make ~s worse** cela ne fera qu'aggraver la situation; **then to make ~s worse he ...** puis pour ne rien arranger *or* qui pis est, il ...; **in this ~** à cet égard; **the ~ is closed** l'affaire est close, c'est une affaire classée; **it is a ~ of great concern to us** c'est une source de profonde inquiétude pour nous; **it's not a laughing ~** il n'y a pas de quoi rire; **it's a small ~ which we shan't discuss now** c'est une question insignifiante *or* une bagatelle dont nous ne discuterons pas maintenant; **there's the small ~ of that £200 I lent you** il y a la petite question *or* le petit problème des 200 livres que je vous ai prêtées; **it will be no easy ~** cela ne sera pas facile; **in the ~ of** en matière de, en *or* pour ce qui concerne; **it's a ~ of habit/opinion** c'est (une) question *or* (une) affaire d'habitude/d'opinion; **in all ~s of education** pour tout ce qui touche à *or* concerne l'éducation; **as ~s stand** en l'état actuel des choses; **let's see how ~s stand** voyons où en sont les choses; **for that ~** d'ailleurs; **as a ~ of course** automatiquement, tout naturellement; **as a ~ of fact** à vrai dire, en réalité, en fait (*see also* **2**); **it took a ~ of days (to do it)** cela a été l'affaire de quelques jours (pour le faire); **in a ~ of 10 minutes** en l'espace de 10 minutes; *see* **mince, time 1c**.
d (*importance*) **no ~!** peu importe!, tant pis!; (*liter*) **what ~?** qu'importe?; **what ~ if ...** qu'importe si ...; **it is of no ~** *or* (*frm*) **it makes no ~ whether ...** peu importe si ...; **it is (of) no great ~** c'est peu de chose, cela n'a pas grande importance; **get one, no ~ how** débrouille-toi (comme tu veux) pour en trouver un; **it must be done, no ~ how** cela doit être fait par n'importe quel moyen; **ring me no ~ how late** téléphonez-moi même tard *or* à n'importe quelle heure; **no ~ how you use it** peu importe comment vous l'utilisez; **no ~ when he comes** quelle que soit l'heure (*or* quel que soit le jour *or* quelle que soit la date) de son arrivée, quelle que soit l'heure *etc* à laquelle il arrive (*subj*); **no ~ how big it is** quelque *or* si grand qu'il soit; **no ~ what he says** quoi qu'il dise; **no ~ where/who** où/qui que ce soit.
e (*NonC: difficulty, problem*) **is anything the ~?** quelque chose ne va pas?; **what's the ~?** qu'est-ce qu'il y a?, qu'y a-t-il?; **what's the ~ with him?** qu'est-ce qu'il a?, qu'est-ce qui lui prend?; **what's the ~ with your hand?** qu'est-ce que vous avez à la main?; **what's the ~ with my hat?** qu'est-ce qu'il a, mon chapeau?*; **what's the ~ with trying to help him?** quel inconvénient *or* quelle objection y a-t-il à ce qu'on l'aide (*subj*)?; **there's something the ~ with my arm** j'ai quelque chose au bras; **there's something the ~ with the engine** il y a quelque chose qui cloche* *or* qui ne va pas dans le moteur; **as if nothing was the ~** comme si de rien n'était; **nothing's the ~*** il n'y a rien; **there's nothing the ~ with me!** moi, je vais tout à fait bien!; **there's nothing the ~ with the car** la voiture marche très bien; **there's nothing the ~ with that idea** il n'y a rien à redire à cette idée.
2 comp ▸**matter-of-fact** *tone, voice* neutre; *style* prosaïque; *attitude, person* terre à terre *or* terre-à-terre; *assessment, account* neutre, qui se limite aux faits; **in a very matter-of-fact way** sans avoir l'air de rien.
3 vi importer (*to* à). **it doesn't ~** cela n'a pas d'importance, cela ne fait rien; **it doesn't ~ whether** peu importe que + *subj*, cela ne fait rien si, peu importe si; **it doesn't ~ who/where** *etc* peu importe qui/où *etc*; **what does it ~?** qu'est-ce que cela peut faire?; **what does it ~ to you (if ...)?** qu'est-ce que cela peut bien vous faire (si ...)?, que vous importe (*frm*) (si ...)?; **why should it ~ to me?** pourquoi est-ce que cela me ferait quelque chose?; **it ~s little** cela importe peu, peu importe; **some things ~ more than others** il y a des choses qui importent plus que d'autres; **nothing else ~s** le reste n'a aucune importance; **I shouldn't let what he says ~** je ne m'en ferais pas pour ce qu'il dit*.

Matterhorn [ˈmætəhɔːn] n: **the ~** le (mont) Cervin.

Matthew [ˈmæθjuː] n Matthieu *m*.

matting [ˈmætɪŋ] n (*NonC*) sparterie *f*, pièces *fpl* de natte; *see* **rush**[2] *etc.*

mattins [ˈmætɪnz] n sg *or* pl (*Rel*) matines *fpl*.

mattock [ˈmætək] n pioche *f*.

mattress [ˈmætrɪs] n matelas *m*. ~ **cover** (*gen*) protège-matelas *m*; (*waterproof*) alèse *f*; (*soft and warm*) molleton *m*.

maturation [ˌmætjʊəˈreɪʃən] n (*frm*) maturation *f*.

mature [məˈtjʊəʳ] 1 adj *age, reflection, plan* mûr; *person* (*gen*) mûr, (*Psych*) mature; *wine* qui est arrivé à maturité; *cheese* fait; (*Fin*) *bill* échu. **he's got much more** ~ **since then** il a beaucoup mûri depuis; (*Univ*) ~ **student** (*gen*) étudiant(e) *m(f)* plus âgé(e) que la moyenne; (*Brit Admin*) étudiant(e) de plus de 26 ans (*ou de 21 ans dans certains cas*). 2 vt faire mûrir. 3 vi *[person]* mûrir; *[wine, cheese]* se faire; (*Fin*) venir à échéance, échoir.

maturity [məˈtjʊərɪtɪ] n maturité *f*. (*Fin*) **date of** ~ échéance *f*.

maudlin [ˈmɔːdlɪn] adj larmoyant.

maul [mɔːl] 1 vt *[tiger etc]* mutiler, lacérer, (*to death*) déchiqueter; *[person]* malmener, brutaliser; (*fig*) *author, book etc* éreinter, malmener. 2 n (*Rugby*) maul *m*. 3 comp ►**maulstick** appui-main *m*.

maunder [ˈmɔːndəʳ] vi (*talk*) divaguer; (*move*) errer; (*act*) agir de façon incohérente.

Maundy [ˈmɔːndɪ] n: ~ **Thursday** le jeudi saint; (*Brit*) ~ **money** aumône royale du jeudi saint.

Mauritania [ˌmɔːrɪˈteɪnɪə] n Mauritanie *f*.

Mauritanian [ˌmɔːrɪˈteɪnɪən] 1 n Mauritanien(ne) *m(f)*. 2 adj mauritanien.

Mauritian [məˈrɪʃən] 1 n Mauricien(ne) *m(f)*. 2 adj mauricien.

Mauritius [məˈrɪʃəs] n (l'île *f*) Maurice *f*. **in** ~ à (l'île) Maurice.

mausoleum [ˌmɔːsəˈlɪəm] n, pl ~**s** *or* **mausolea** [ˌmɔːsəˈlɪə] mausolée *m*.

mauve [məʊv] adj, n mauve (*m*).

maverick [ˈmævərɪk] 1 n (*calf*) veau non marqué; (*fig: person*) dissident(e) *m(f)*, non-conformiste *mf*, franc-tireur *m* (*fig*). 2 adj dissident, non-conformiste.

maw [mɔː] n *[cow]* caillette *f*; *[bird]* jabot *m*; (*fig*) gueule *f*.

mawkish [ˈmɔːkɪʃ] adj (*sentimental*) d'une sentimentalité excessive *or* exagérée; (*insipid*) insipide, fade; (*nauseating*) écœurant.

mawkishness [ˈmɔːkɪʃnɪs] n (*see* **mawkish**) sentimentalité excessive *or* exagérée; insipidité *f*, fadeur *f*; caractère écœurant.

maxi* [ˈmæksɪ] n (*coat/skirt*) (manteau *m*/jupe *f*) maxi *m*. ~ **single** disque *m* double durée.

maxilla [mækˈsɪlə] n, pl **maxillae** [mækˈsɪliː] (*Anat*) maxillaire *m*.

maxillary [mækˈsɪlərɪ] adj (*Anat*) maxillaire.

maxim [ˈmæksɪm] n maxime *f*.

maxima [ˈmæksɪmə] npl of **maximum**.

maximization [ˌmæksɪmaɪˈzeɪʃən] n maximalisation *f*, maximisation *f*. ~ **of profits** maximalisation *or* maximisation des bénéfices.

maximize [ˈmæksɪmaɪz] vt maximiser, porter au maximum. **to** ~ **the advantages of sth** tirer le maximum de qch.

maximum [ˈmæksɪməm] 1 n, pl ~**s** *or* **maxima** [ˈmæksɪmə] maximum *m*. **a** ~ **of £8** un maximum de 8 livres, 8 livres au maximum; **at the** ~ au maximum. 2 adj maximum (*f inv or* maxima). ~ **prices** prix *mpl* maximums *or* maxima; **maximum security jail** *or* **prison** prison *f* avec système de sécurité renforcée (*see also* **security**); (*Aut etc*) ~ **speed** (*highest permitted*) vitesse *f* limite *or* maximum; (*highest possible*) plafond *m*; (*on truck*) ~ **load** charge *f* limite; ~ **temperatures** températures maximales. 3 adv (au) maximum. **twice a week** ~ deux fois par semaine (au) maximum.

may[1] [meɪ] modal aux vb (pret and cond **might**) a (*indicating possibility*) **he may arrive** il arrivera peut-être, il peut arriver; **he might arrive** il se peut qu'il arrive (*subj*), il pourrait arriver; **I said that he might arrive** j'ai dit qu'il arriverait peut-être; **you may** *or* **might be making a big mistake** tu fais peut-être *or* tu es peut-être en train de faire une grosse erreur; **might they have left already?** se peut-il qu'ils soient déjà partis?; **I might have left it behind** il se peut que je l'aie oublié, je l'ai peut-être bien oublié; **you might have killed me!** tu aurais pu me tuer!; **I might have known** j'aurais dû m'en douter; **that's as may be but,** (*frm*) **that may well be but** peut-être bien *or* c'est bien possible mais; **as soon as may be** aussitôt que possible; (*frm*) **be that as it may** quoi qu'il en soit; **one might well ask whether ...** on est en droit de demander si ...; **what might your name be?** (*abrupt*) et vous, comment vous appelez-vous?; (*polite*) puis-je savoir votre nom?; **who might you be?** qui êtes-vous sans indiscrétion?; **how old might he be, I wonder?** je me demande quel âge il peut bien avoir.

b (*indicating permission*) **may I have a word with you? — yes, you may** puis-je vous parler un instant? — (mais) oui, bien sûr; **may I help you?** puis-je *or* est-ce que je peux vous aider?; (*in shop*) vous désirez (quelque chose)?; **might I see it?** est-ce que je pourrais le voir?, vous permettez que je le voie?; **might I suggest that ...?** puis-je me permettre de suggérer que ...?; **if I may say so** si je puis me permettre; **may I tell her now? — you may** *or* **might as well** est-ce que je peux le lui dire maintenant? — après tout pourquoi pas?; **may I sit here?** vous permettez que je m'assoie ici?; **may I?** vous permettez?; **you may go now** (*permission; also polite order*) vous pouvez partir; (*to subordinate*) vous pouvez disposer; **he said I might leave** il a dit que je pouvais partir, il m'a permis de partir.

c (*indicating suggestion: with "might" only*) (*polite*) **you might try writing to him** tu pourrais toujours lui écrire; **you might give me a lift home if you've got time** tu pourrais peut-être me ramener si tu as le temps; **mightn't it be an idea to go and see him?** on ferait (*or* tu ferais *etc*) peut-être bien d'aller le voir?; (*abrupt*) **you might have told me you weren't coming!** tu aurais (tout de même) pu me prévenir que tu ne viendrais pas!; **you might at least say "thank you"** tu pourrais au moins dire "merci".

d (*phrases*) **one might as well say £5 million** autant dire 5 millions de livres; **we might as well not buy that newspaper at all since no one ever reads it** je me demande bien pourquoi nous achetons ce journal puisque personne ne le lit; **I may** *or* **might as well tell you all about it** après tout je peux bien vous le raconter, je ferais aussi bien de tout vous dire; **you may** *or* **might as well leave now as wait any longer** vous feriez aussi bien de partir tout de suite plutôt que d'attendre encore; **they might (just) as well not have gone** ils auraient tout aussi bien pu ne pas y aller, ce n'était pas la peine qu'ils y aillent; **she blushed, as well she might!** elle a rougi, et pour cause!

e (*frm, liter: in exclamations expressing wishes, hopes etc*) **may God bless you!** (que) Dieu vous bénisse!; **may he rest in peace** qu'il repose (*subj*) en paix; **o might I see her but once again!** oh que je puisse la revoir ne fût-ce qu'une fois!; **much good may it do you!** grand bien vous fasse!

f (*frm, liter: subj use*) **O Lord, grant that we may always obey** Seigneur, accorde-nous *or* donne-nous de toujours obéir; **lest he may** *or* **might be anxious** de crainte qu'il n'éprouve (*subj*) de l'anxiété; **in order that they may** *or* **might know** afin qu'ils sachent.

may[2] [meɪ] 1 n a (*month*) **M**~ mai *m*; **the merry month of M**~ le joli mois de mai; *for other phrases see* **September**. b (*hawthorn*) aubépine *f*. 2 comp *branch etc* d'aubépine ►**May beetle** hanneton *m* ►**May Day** le Premier Mai (*fête du Travail*) ►**mayday** *see* **mayday** ►**mayfly** éphémère *m* ►**maypole** mât enrubanné (*autour duquel on danse*), ≃ mai *m* ►**May queen** reine *f* de mai ►**may tree** (*Brit*) aubépine *f*.

Mayan [ˈmaɪən] (*S America*) 1 adj maya. 2 n a Maya *mf*. b (*Ling*) maya *m*.

maybe [ˈmeɪbiː] adv peut-être. ~ **he'll be there** peut-être qu'il sera là, peut-être sera-t-il là, il sera peut-être là.

mayday [ˈmeɪdeɪ] n (*Aviat, Naut*) mayday *m*, S.O.S. *m*.

Mayfair [ˈmeɪˈfɛəʳ] n (*Brit*) Mayfair (*le quartier le plus chic de Londres*).

mayhem [ˈmeɪhem] n a (*Jur* †† *or US*) mutilation *f* du corps humain. b (*havoc*) grabuge* *m*; (*destruction*) destruction *f*.

mayn't [meɪnt] = **may not**; *see* **may**[1].

mayo* [ˈmeɪəʊ] n (*US*) (abbr of **mayonnaise**) mayonnaise *f*.

mayonnaise [ˌmeɪəˈneɪz] n mayonnaise *f*.

mayor [mɛəʳ] n maire *m*. **Mr/Madam M**~ Monsieur/Madame le maire; *see* **lord**.

mayoralty [ˈmɛərəltɪ] n mandat *m* de maire.

mayoress [ˈmɛəres] n femme *f* (*or* fille *f etc*) du maire; *see* **lady**.

maze [meɪz] n labyrinthe *m*, dédale *m*. (*fig*) **a** ~ **of little streets** un labyrinthe *or* un dédale de ruelles; **to be in a** ~ être complètement désorienté.

mazuma‡ [məˈzuːmə] n (*US: money*) fric *m*‡, pognon‡ *m*.

MB [emˈbiː] n (*Comput*) (abbr of **megabyte**) Mo.

MBA [ˈembiːˈeɪ] n (*Univ*) (abbr of **Master of Business Administration**) *maîtrise de gestion.*

MBBS, MBChB (*Univ*) abbr of **Bachelor of Medicine and Surgery**.

M.B.E. [embiːˈiː] n (*Brit*) (abbr of **Member of the Order of the British Empire**) *titre honorifique.*

M.C. [emˈsiː] n a (abbr of **Master of Ceremonies**) *see* **master**. b (*US*) (abbr of **Member of Congress**) ≃ député *m*. c (*Mil*) (abbr of **Military Cross**) ≃ Croix *f* de la valeur militaire.

McCarthyisme [məˈkɑːθɪˌɪzəm] n (*US Pol*) maccarthysme *m*.

MCP‡ [ˌemsiːˈpiː] n (abbr of **male chauvinist pig**) *see* **chauvinist**.

M.D. [ˌemˈdiː] n a (*Univ*) (abbr of **Doctor of Medicine**) ≃ docteur *m* en médecine. b (*US* *) **the MD** le médecin. c (abbr of **Managing Director**) P.-D.G. *m*. d **MD** (*US*) abbr of **Maryland**.

Md. (*US*) abbr of **Maryland**.

MDT [ˌemdiːˈtiː] (*US*) (abbr of **Mountain Daylight Time**) *see* **mountain**.

ME [ˌemˈiː] n a (*Med*) (abbr of **myalgic encephalomyelitis**) SFC *m*, syndrome *m* de la fatigue chronique. b (*US*) abbr of **Maine**.

me[1] [miː] pers pron a (*direct*) (*unstressed*) me; (*before vowel*) m'; (*stressed*) moi. **he can see** ~ il me voit; **he saw** ~ il m'a vu; **you saw me!** vous m'avez vu, moi! b (*indirect*) me, moi; (*before vowel*) m'. **he gave** ~ **the book** il me donna *or* m'a donné le livre; **give it to** ~ donnez-le-moi; **he was speaking to** ~ il me parlait. c (*after prep etc*) moi. **without** ~ sans moi; **I'll take it with** ~ je l'emporterai avec moi; **it's** ~ c'est moi; **it's** ~ **he's speaking to** c'est à moi qu'il parle; **you're smaller than** ~ tu es plus petit que moi; **if you were** ~ ... à ma place ...; **poor (little)** ~!* pauvre de moi!; **dear** ~!* mon Dieu!, oh là là!*

me[2] [miː] n (*Mus*) mi *m*.

Me. (*US*) **abbr of Maine.**

mead¹ [mi:d] **n** (*drink*) hydromel *m*.

mead² [mi:d] **n** (*liter: meadow*) pré *m*, prairie *f*.

meadow ['medəʊ] 1 **n** pré *m*, prairie *f*; *see* **water.** 2 **comp ▸meadowsweet** reine *f* des prés.

meagre, (*US*) **meager** ['mi:gəʳ] 1 **adj** (*all senses*) maigre (*before noun*). 2 **n** maigre *m*.

meal¹ [mi:l] 1 **n** repas *m*. **to have a ~** prendre un repas, manger; **to have** *or* **get a good ~** bien manger; **come and have a ~** venez manger, venez déjeuner (*or* dîner); **to have one ~ a day** manger une fois par jour; **we had a ~ at the Procope** nous avons déjeuné (*or* dîné) au Procope; **midday ~** déjeuner *m*; **evening ~** dîner *m*; **that was a lovely ~!** nous avons très bien déjeuné (*or* dîné); **he made a ~ of bread and cheese** il a déjeuné (*or* dîné) de pain et de fromage; (*fig*) **to make a ~ of sth*** faire tout un plat de qch*; *see* **square** *etc.*

2 **comp ▸meals on wheels** *repas livrés à domicile aux personnes âgées ou handicapées* **▸meal ticket** (*lit*) ticket *m or* coupon *m* de repas; (* *fig: job, person etc*) gagne-pain *m inv*; **(don't forget) she's your meal ticket** (n'oublie pas que) sans elle tu crèverais de faim **▸mealtime** heure *f* du repas; **at mealtimes** aux heures des repas.

meal² [mi:l] **n** (*NonC: flour etc*) farine *f* (*d'avoine, de seigle, de maïs etc*); *see* **oat, wheat** *etc.*

mealies ['mi:lɪz] **npl** maïs *m*.

mealy ['mi:lɪ] 1 **adj** *substance, mixture, potato* farineux; *complexion* blême. 2 **comp ▸mealy-mouthed: to be mealy-mouthed** ne pas s'exprimer franchement, tourner autour du pot.

mean¹ [mi:n] **pret, ptp meant vt** a (*signify*) vouloir dire, signifier; (*imply*) vouloir dire. **what does "media" ~?, what is meant by "media"?** que veut dire *or* que signifie "media"?; **"homely" ~s something different in America** "homely" a un sens différent en Amérique; **what do you ~ (by that)?** que voulez-vous dire (par là)?, qu'entendez-vous par là?; **is he honest? — how** *or* **what do you ~, honest?** est-il honnête? — que voulez-vous dire *or* qu'entendez-vous par "honnête"?; **you don't really ~ that?** vous n'êtes pas sérieux?, vous plaisantez?; **I really ~ it** je ne plaisante pas, je suis sérieux; **he said it as if he meant it** il a dit cela d'un air sérieux *or* sans avoir l'air de plaisanter; **I always ~ what I say** quand je dis quelque chose c'est que je le pense; **see what I ~?** tu vois ce que je veux dire?; **this is John — I ~ Jim** voici John — pardon (je veux dire) Jim; **the name ~s nothing to me** ce nom ne me dit rien; **the play didn't ~ a thing to her** la pièce n'avait aucun sens pour elle; **what does this ~?** qu'est-ce que cela signifie? *or* veut dire?; **it ~s he won't be coming** cela veut dire qu'il ne viendra pas; **this ~s war** c'est la guerre à coup sûr; **it ~s trouble** cela nous annonce des ennuis; **it will ~ a lot of expense** cela entraînera beaucoup de dépenses; **catching the train ~s getting up early** pour avoir ce train il faut se lever tôt; **a pound ~s a lot to him** une livre représente une grosse somme pour lui; **holidays don't ~ much to me** les vacances comptent peu pour moi; **I can't tell you what your gift has meant to me!** je ne saurais vous dire à quel point votre cadeau m'a touché!; **don't I ~ anything to you at all?** je ne suis donc rien pour toi?; **what it ~s to be free!** quelle belle chose que la liberté!; **money doesn't ~ happiness** l'argent ne fait pas le bonheur; **I ~, it's not difficult** ce n'est pas difficile, je veux dire; *see* **know 1, world 1b.**

b (*intend, purpose*) avoir l'intention, se proposer (*to do* de faire), compter, vouloir (*to do* faire); (*intend, destine*) *gift etc* destiner (*for* à); *remark* adresser (*for* à). **I meant to come yesterday** j'avais l'intention de *or* je voulais *or* je me proposais de venir hier; **what does he ~ to do now?** que compte-t-il faire maintenant?; **I didn't ~ to break it** je n'ai pas fait exprès de le casser, je ne l'ai pas cassé exprès; **I didn't ~ to!** je ne l'ai pas fait exprès! *or* de propos délibéré!; **I touched it without ~ing to** je l'ai touché sans le vouloir; **I ~ to succeed** j'ai bien l'intention de réussir; **despite what he says I ~ to go** je partirai quoi qu'il dise; **I ~ you to leave,** (*US*) **I ~ for you to leave** je veux que vous partiez (*subj*); **I'm sure he didn't ~ it** je suis sûr que ce n'était pas intentionnel *or* délibéré; **he didn't ~ anything by it** il l'a fait (*or* dit *etc*) sans penser à mal; **I meant it as a joke** j'ai dit (*or* fait) cela par plaisanterie *or* pour rire; **we were meant to arrive at 6** nous étions censés arriver *or* nous devions arriver à 6 heures; **she ~s well** ce qu'elle fait (*or* dit *etc*) part d'un bon sentiment, elle est pleine de bonnes intentions; **he ~s trouble** il cherche la bagarre; **he looks as if he ~s trouble** il a une mine qui n'annonce rien qui vaille *oror* de bon; **do you ~ me?** (*are you speaking to me*) c'est à moi que vous parlez?; (*are you speaking about me*) c'est de moi que vous parlez?; **he meant you when he said ...** c'est vous qu'il visait *or* c'est à vous qu'il faisait allusion lorsqu'il disait ...; **I meant the book for Paul** je destinais le livre à Paul; **that book is meant for children** ce livre est destiné aux enfants *or* est à l'intention des enfants; **perhaps you're not meant to be a doctor** peut-être n'êtes-vous pas fait pour être médecin; **it was meant to be** le destin en avait décidé ainsi; **this cupboard was never meant to be** *or* **meant for a larder** ce placard n'a jamais été conçu pour servir de garde-manger *or* n'a jamais été censé être un garde-manger; **this portrait is meant to be Anne** ce portrait est censé être celui d'Anne *or* représenter Anne; *see* **business, harm, offence** *etc.*

c (*modal usage in pass*) **it's meant to be good** (*considered to be*) on dit que c'est bien; (*supposed to be*) c'est censé être bien.

mean² [mi:n] 1 **n** a (*middle term*) milieu *m*, moyen terme; (*Math*) moyenne *f*. **the golden** *or* **happy ~** le juste milieu; *see* **geometric.**

b (*method, way*) **~s** moyen(s) *m(pl)*; **to find the ~s to do** *or* **of doing** trouver le(s) moyen(s) de faire; **to find (a) ~s of doing** trouver moyen de faire; **the only ~s of contacting him is ...** le seul moyen de le joindre, c'est ...; **there's no ~s of getting in** il n'y a pas moyen d'y entrer; **he has been the ~s of my success** c'est grâce à lui que j'ai réussi; **the ~s to an end** le moyen d'arriver à ses fins; (*Rel*) **the ~s of salvation** les voies *fpl* du salut; **come in by all ~s!** je vous en prie, entrez!; **by all ~s!** mais certainement!, bien sûr!; **by all manner of ~s** par tous les moyens; **by any (manner of) ~s** n'importe comment, à n'importe quel prix; **by no (manner of) ~s** nullement, pas du tout, pas le moins du monde; **she is by no ~s stupid** elle est loin d'être stupide; **by some ~s or (an)other** d'une façon ou d'une autre; **by this ~s** de cette façon; *see also* **1c** *and* **means, fair¹** *etc.*

c **by ~s of** (*gen*) au moyen de; **by ~s of a penknife/binoculars** au moyen d'un *or* à l'aide d'un canif/au moyen des *or* à l'aide des jumelles; **by ~s of his brother** avec l'aide de *or* par l'intermédiaire de *or* par l'entremise de son frère; **by ~s of the telephone/a ballot** par le moyen du téléphone/d'un scrutin; **he taught English by ~s of play** il enseignait l'anglais par le jeu *or* par le biais du jeu; **by ~s of hard work** à force de travail.

2 **adj** *distance, temperature, price* moyen. (*Phys*) **~ life** vie *f* moyenne.

mean³ [mi:n] **adj** a (*Brit: stingy*) avare, mesquin, chiche, radin*. **~ with one's time/money** avare de son temps/argent; **don't be so ~!** ne sois pas si radin!*

b (*unpleasant, unkind*) *person, behaviour* mesquin, méchant. **a ~ trick** un sale tour, une crasse*; **you ~ thing!*** chameau!*; (*to a child*) méchant!; **you were ~ to me** tu n'as vraiment pas été chic* *or* sympa* avec moi, tu as été plutôt rosse *or* chameau* avec moi; **that was ~ of them** c'était bien mesquin de leur part, ce n'était pas chic* de leur part; **to feel ~ about sth*** avoir un peu honte de qch, ne pas être très fier de qch.

c (*US *: vicious*) *horse, dog etc* méchant, vicieux; *person* sadique, salaud‡.

d (*inferior, poor*) *appearance, existence* misérable, minable. **the ~est citizen** le dernier des citoyens; **the ~est intelligence** l'esprit le plus borné; **he is no ~ scholar** c'est un savant d'envergure; **he's no ~ singer** c'est un chanteur de talent; **it was no ~ feat** cela a été un veritable exploit, ce n'a pas été un mince exploit; **to have no ~ opinion of o.s.** avoir une (très) haute opinion de soi-même.

e (‡: *excellent*) terrible*, formidable.

meander [mɪ'ændəʳ] 1 **vi** a *[river]* faire des méandres, serpenter. b *[person]* errer, vagabonder. **she ~ed in** elle entra sans se presser. 2 **n** méandre *m*, détour *m*, sinuosité *f*.

meandering [mɪ'ændərɪŋ] **adj** *road, river* sinueux, qui serpente; *speech, writing* décousu.

meanie* ['mi:nɪ] **n** a (*Brit: stingy person*) radin(e)* *m(f)*, pingre *m*. b (*US: unpleasant person*) sale type *m*, mégère *f*.

meaning ['mi:nɪŋ] 1 **n** *[word]* sens *m*, signification *f*; *[phrase, action]* signification; (*Ling*) signification *f*. **with a double ~** à double sens; **literal ~** sens propre *or* littéral; **what is the ~ of this word?** quel est le sens de ce mot?, que signifie ce mot?; (*fig*) **he doesn't know the ~ of the word "fear"** il ne sait ce que le mot "peur" veut dire, il ignore le sens du mot "peur"; **she doesn't know the ~ of love/kindness** elle ne sait pas ce qu'est l'amour/la gentillesse; (*in anger, disapproval etc*) **what is the ~ of this?** qu'est-ce que cela signifie?; (*Jur*) **within the ~ of this Act** au sens de la présente loi; **you haven't got my ~** vous m'avez mal compris; **look/gesture full of ~** regard/geste significatif *or* éloquent; **"really?" he said with ~** son "vraiment?" fut significatif *or* éloquent.

2 **adj** *look etc* significatif, éloquent, expressif, qui en dit long; *see* **well.**

meaningful ['mi:nɪŋfʊl] **adj** a *look* qui en dit long, éloquent, expressif; *sourire* qui en dit long. b *talks, discussions, relationship* sérieux. c (*Ling*) *phrase* sémantique.

meaningfully ['mi:nɪŋfəlɪ] **adv** *explain* de façon intelligible; *say* d'un ton qui en dit long; *spend time* utilement. **he looked/smiled at her ~** il lui jeta un regard/fit un sourire qui en disait long.

meaningless ['mi:nɪŋlɪs] **adj** *word, action* dénué de sens, sans signification; *waste, suffering* insensé.

meanly ['mi:nlɪ] **adv** (*stingily*) chichement, mesquinement; (*nastily*) méchamment.

meanness ['mi:nnɪs] **n** (*see* **mean³**) avarice *f*, mesquinerie *f*; méchanceté *f*, manque *m* de cœur; pauvreté *f*.

means [mi:nz] 1 **npl** (*wealth*) moyens *mpl*, ressources *fpl*. **he is a man of ~** il a une belle fortune *or* de gros moyens*; **to live within/beyond one's ~** vivre selon ses moyens/au-dessus de ses moyens; **private ~** fortune personnelle; **slender ~** ressources très modestes; *see also* **mean² 1c.** 2 **comp ▸means test** (*Admin*) **n** examen *m* des ressources (*d'une personne qui demande une aide pécuniaire de l'État*) ◊ **vt: to means-test sb** examiner les ressources de qn (*avant d'accorder certaines* *prestations sociales*); **the grant is not means-tested** cette allocation ne dépend pas des ressources familiales (*or* personnelles).

meant [ment] pret, ptp of **mean1**.

meantime ['mi:ntaɪm] adv, **meanwhile** ['mi:nwaɪl] adv: **(in the)** ~ en attendant, pendant ce temps, dans l'intervalle.

meany* ['mi:nɪ] = **meanie***

measles ['mi:zlz] n rougeole *f*; *see* **German**.

measly* ['mi:zlɪ] adj minable, misérable, piètre (*before noun*).

measurable ['meʒərəbl] adj mesurable.

measure ['meʒər] 1 n a (*system, unit*) mesure *f*; (*fig*) mesure; *[alcohol]* dose *f*. **to give good** *or* **full** ~ faire bonne mesure *or* bon poids; **to give short** ~ voler *or* rogner sur la quantité *or* sur le poids; (*fig*) **for good** ~ pour faire bonne mesure, pour la bonne mesure; **suit made to** ~ complet fait sur mesure; **10 ~s of wheat** 10 mesures de blé; **liquid** ~ mesure de capacité pour les liquides; **a pint** ~ ≃ une mesure d'un demi-litre; (*Brit Math*) **greatest common** ~ le plus grand commun diviseur; **happiness beyond** ~ bonheur sans bornes; **in some** ~ dans une certaine mesure, jusqu'à un certain point; **in great** *or* **large** ~ dans une large mesure, en grande partie; **I've got his** ~ je sais ce qu'il vaut; (*fig*) **it had a** ~ **of success** cela a eu un certain succès; *see* **standard, tape** *etc*.

b (*sth for measuring*) (*ruler*) règle *f*; (*folding*) mètre *m* pliant; (*tape*) mètre à ruban; (*jug/glass*) pot *m*/verre *m* gradué; (*post*) toise *f*. (*fig*) **this exam is just a ~ of how you're getting on** cet examen sert simplement à évaluer votre progression.

c (*step*) mesure *f*, démarche *f*; (*Parl*) (*bill*) projet *m* de loi; (*act*) loi *f*. **strong/drastic ~s** mesures énergiques/draconiennes; **to take ~s against** prendre des mesures contre.

d (*Mus, Poetry etc*) mesure *f*.

2 vt (*lit*) *child, length, time* mesurer; (*fig*) *strength, courage* mesurer, estimer, évaluer, jauger; *success, performance* évaluer, juger. **to ~ the height of sth** mesurer *or* prendre la hauteur de qch; **to be ~d for a dress** faire prendre ses mesures pour une robe; **what does it ~?** quelles sont ses dimensions?; **the room ~s 4 metres across** la pièce a *or* fait *or* mesure 4 mètres de large; **the carpet ~s 3 metres by 2** le tapis fait *or* mesure 3 mètres sur 2; (*fig*) **to be ~d against** être comparé avec *or* à; **(fig) to ~ one's strength against sb** se mesurer à qn; (*fig: fall*) **to ~ one's length** tomber *or* s'étaler* de tout son long.

►**measure off** vt sep *lengths of fabric etc* mesurer.

►**measure out** vt sep a *ingredients, piece of ground* mesurer. b (*issue*) distribuer.

►**measure up** vt sep *wood* mesurer; (*fig*) *sb's intentions* jauger; *person* évaluer, jauger.

►**measure up to** vt fus *task* être au niveau de, être à la hauteur de; *person* être l'égal de.

measured ['meʒəd] adj *time, distance* mesuré; (*fig*) *words, language, statement* modéré, mesuré, circonspect; *tone* mesuré, avisé, modéré; *verse* mesuré, rythmique. (*Sport etc*) **over a ~ kilometre** sur un kilomètre exactement, sur une distance d'un kilomètre; **with ~ steps** à pas comptés *or* mesurés.

measureless ['meʒəlɪs] adj *power etc* incommensurable, infini, immense, sans bornes; *wrath* démesuré.

measurement ['meʒəmənt] n a (*dimensions: gen pl*) ~s mesures *fpl*, dimensions *fpl*; *[piece of furniture etc]* encombrement *m* au sol; **to take the ~s of a room** prendre les mesures d'une pièce; **what are your ~s?** quelles sont vos mesures? b (*NonC*) mesurage *m*. c *[freight]* cubage *m*. **to pay by ~ for freight** payer la cargaison au cubage.

measuring ['meʒərɪŋ] 1 n (*NonC*) mesurage *m*, mesure *f*. 2 comp ►**measuring chain** chaîne *f* d'arpenteur ►**measuring device** appareil *m* de mesure *or* de contrôle ►**measuring glass/jug** verre *m*/pot *m* gradué ►**measuring rod** règle *f*, mètre *m* ►**measuring tape** mètre *m* à ruban.

meat [mi:t] 1 n viande *f*; (*fig*) substance *f*; (††: *food*) nourriture *f*, aliment *m*. **cold ~** viande froide; **cold ~ platter** assiette *f* anglaise; **remove the ~ from the bone** ôter la chair de l'os; (*fig*) **there's not much ~ in his book** son livre n'a pas beaucoup de substance; (*lit*) **~ and drink** de quoi manger et boire; (*fig*) **this is ~ and drink to them** c'est une aubaine pour eux; (*US fig*) **that's my ~!**‡ ça me botte vachement!‡; (*Prov*) **one man's ~ is another man's poison** ce qui guérit l'un tue l'autre.

2 comp ►**meat axe** (*Brit*), **meat ax** (*US*) couperet *m* ►**meatball** boulette *f* de viande ►**meat cleaver** = **meat ax(e)** ►**meat diet** régime carné ►**meat-eater** (*animal*) carnivore *m*; **he's a big meat-eater** c'est un gros mangeur de viande ►**meat-eating** carnivore ►**meat extract** concentré *m* de viande ►**meathead**‡ (*US*) andouille‡ *f*, imbécile *mf* ►**meat hook** crochet *m* de boucherie, allonge *f* ►**meatless** *see* **meatless** ►**meat loaf** pain *m* de viande ►**meat pie** pâté *m* en croûte ►**meat safe** (*Brit*) garde-manger *m inv*.

meatless ['mi:tlɪs] adj sans viande, maigre.

meatus [mɪ'eɪtəs] n, pl ~ *or* ~es (*Anat*) conduit *m*.

meaty ['mi:tɪ] adj *flavour* de viande; (*fig*) *argument, book* étoffé, substantiel.

Mecca ['mekə] n (*Geog*) la Mecque. (*fig*) **a ~** la Mecque (*for* de).

Meccano [mɪ'kɑ:nəʊ] n ® (*Brit*) Meccano *m* ®.

mechanic [mɪ'kænɪk] n mécanicien *m*. **motor ~** mécanicien garagiste.

mechanical [mɪ'kænɪkəl] adj *power, process* mécanique; (*fig*) *action, reply* machinal, automatique, mécanique. **~ drawing** dessin *m* à l'échelle; **~ engineer** ingénieur mécanicien; **~ engineering** génie *m* mécanique.

mechanically [mɪ'kænɪkəlɪ] adv mécaniquement; (*fig*) machinalement, mécaniquement.

mechanics [mɪ'kænɪks] 1 n (*NonC: science*) mécanique *f*. 2 npl (*technical aspect*) mécanisme *m*, processus *m*; (*mechanism; working parts*) mécanisme, mécanique *f*. (*fig*) **the ~ of running an office** le processus *or* l'aspect *m* pratique de la gestion d'un bureau.

mechanism ['mekənɪzəm] n (*all senses*) mécanisme *m*. **defence ~** mécanisme de défense; *see* **safety** *etc*.

mechanistic [ˌmekə'nɪstɪk] adj mécaniste.

mechanization [ˌmekənaɪ'zeɪʃən] n mécanisation *f*.

mechanize ['mekənaɪz] vt *process, production* mécaniser; *army* motoriser. **~d industry** industrie mécanisée; **~d troops** troupes motorisées.

Med* [med] n a (*abbr of* **Mediterranean Sea**) **the ~** la Méditerranée. b (*abbr of* **Mediterranean region**) région *f* méditerranéenne.

M.Ed. [ˌem'ed] n (*Univ*) (*abbr of* **Master of Education**) ≃ CAPES.

medal ['medl] n (*Mil, Sport, gen*) médaille *f*. **swimming ~** médaille de natation; (*US: Congressional*) **M~ of Honor** Médaille *f* d'honneur (*la plus haute décoration militaire*).

medalist ['medəlɪst] n (*US*) = **medallist**.

medallion [mɪ'dæljən] n (*gen, Archit*) médaillon *m*.

medallist, (*US*) **medalist** ['medəlɪst] n: **he's a gold/silver ~** il a eu la médaille d'or/d'argent; **the 3 ~s on the podium** les 3 médaillés *or* vainqueurs sur le podium.

meddle ['medl] vi a (*interfere*) se mêler, s'occuper (*in* de), s'ingérer (*in* dans) (*frm*). **stop meddling!** cesse de t'occuper *or* de te mêler de ce qui ne te regarde pas! b (*tamper*) toucher (*with* à).

meddler ['medlər] n a (*busybody*) mouche *f* du coche, fâcheux *m*, -euse *f*. **he's a dreadful ~** il est toujours à fourrer son nez partout. b (*touching things*) touche-à-tout *m inv*.

meddlesome ['medlsəm] adj, **meddling** ['medlɪŋ] adj a (*interfering*) qui fourre son nez partout, indiscret (*f* -ète). b (*touching*) qui touche à tout.

medevac ['medɪˌvæk] n (*helicopter*) hélicoptère *m* sanitaire de l'armée.

media ['mi:dɪə] 1 npl of **medium** (*souvent employé au sg*) **the ~** (*Press, Rad, TV*) (les journalistes *mpl* et reporters *mpl* de) la presse écrite et parlée, les médias *mpl*; (*means of communication*) les médias, les moyens *mpl* de diffusion de l'information. **he claimed the ~ were all against him** il prétendait qu'il avait tous les médias contre lui; **I heard it on the ~*** je l'ai entendu à la radio (*or* à la télé); **the ~ were waiting for him at the airport*** les journalistes et les photographes l'attendaient à l'aéroport.

2 comp *attention, reaction* des médias; *event, coverage* médiatique ►**media man** (*Press, Rad, TV*) journaliste *m*, reporter *m*; (*Publicity*) publicitaire *m* ►**media person** (*Press, Rad, TV*) journaliste *mf*; (*Publicity*) publicitaire *mf* ►**media-shy** adj qui n'aime pas être interviewé ►**media star** vedette *f* des médias ►**media studies** (*Univ etc*) études *fpl* des médias.

mediaeval [ˌmedɪ'i:vəl] adj médiéval, du moyen âge; *streets, aspect, charm* moyenâgeux (*also pej*).

mediaevalism [ˌmedɪ'i:vəlɪzəm] n médiévisme *m*.

mediaevalist [ˌmedɪ'i:vəlɪst] n médiéviste *mf*.

medial ['mi:dɪəl] 1 adj a (*middle*) (*gen*) médian; (*Phon*) médial, médian. b (*average*) moyen. 2 n (*Phon*) médiale *f*.

median ['mi:dɪən] 1 adj médian. **~ income** revenu *m* moyen. 2 n a (*Math, Statistics*) médiane *f*. b (*US Aut: also* **~ strip**) bande médiane.

mediant ['mi:dɪənt] n médiante *f*.

mediate ['mi:dɪeɪt] 1 vi servir d'intermédiaire (*between* entre, *in* dans). 2 vt a (*arbitrate*) *peace, settlement* obtenir par médiation; *dispute* se faire le médiateur de. b (*frm, lit: change*) modifier (légèrement). 3 ['mi:dɪɪt] adj médiat.

mediating ['mi:dɪeɪtɪŋ] adj médiateur (*f* -trice).

mediation [ˌmi:dɪ'eɪʃən] n médiation *f*, intervention *f*, entremise *f*.

mediator ['mi:dɪeɪtər] n médiateur *m*, -trice *f*.

Medibank ['medɪbæŋk] n *Sécurité sociale australienne*.

medic* ['medɪk] n (*abbr of* **medical**) (*student*) carabin* *m*; (*doctor*) toubib* *m*.

Medicaid ['medɪˌkeɪd] n (*US Med*) assistance médicale aux indigents.

medical ['medɪkəl] 1 adj *subject, certificate, treatment* médical. **~ board** commission médicale, conseil *m* de santé; (*Mil*) conseil de révision; **~ care** soins médicaux; **~ examination** = **medical 2**; (*US Med*) **~ examiner** médecin *m* légiste; **~ insurance** assurance *f* maladie; **~ jurisprudence** médecine légale; (*US*) **~ librarian** bibliothécaire *mf* médical(e); **~ man*** médecin *m*; **~ officer** (*Ind*) médecin *m* du travail; (*Mil*) médecin-major *m* (*or* -colonel *etc*); **M~ Officer of Health** directeur *m* de la santé publique; **~ practitioner** médecin *m* (de médecine générale), généraliste *mf*; **the ~ profession** (*career*) la carrière médicale; (*personnel*) le corps médical; (*Univ*) **~ school** école *f* *or* faculté *f* de médecine; (*Brit*) ~ **social worker** assistant(e) *m(f)* social(e) (dans un hôpital); ~ **student** étudiant(e) *m(f)* en médecine; ~ **studies** études *fpl* de médecine *or* médicales; ~ **technician** technicien *m*, -ienne *f* de laboratoire; ~ **unit/ward** service *m*/salle *f* de médecine générale.

2 n (*also* ~ **examination**) (*in hospital, school, army etc*) visite médicale; (*private*) examen médical.

medically ['medɪkəlɪ] adv médicalement. **to be ~ examined** subir un examen médical.

medicament [me'dɪkəmənt] n médicament *m*.

Medicare ['medɪkɛəʳ] n (*US*) assistance médicale aux personnes âgées.

medicate ['medɪkeɪt] vt *patient* traiter avec des médicaments; *substance* ajouter une substance médicinale à.

medicated ['medɪkeɪtɪd] adj (*gen*) médical; *shampoo* médical, traitant; *soap* médical, médicamenteux.

medication [ˌmedɪ'keɪʃən] n médication *f*.

Medici ['medɪtʃɪ] npl Médicis.

medicinal [me'dɪsɪnl] adj médicinal. ~ **herbs** herbes médicinales, simples *mpl*.

medicinally [me'dɪsɪnəlɪ] adv par médicaments.

medicine ['medsn, 'medɪsn] 1 n a (*NonC: science*) médecine *f*. **to study ~** faire (sa) médecine; (*Univ*) **Doctor of M~** docteur *m* en médecine; *see* **forensic** *etc*.

b (*drug etc*) médicament *m*. **he takes too many ~s** il prend *or* absorbe trop de médicaments, il se drogue* trop; **it's a very good ~ for colds** c'est un remède souverain contre les rhumes; **to take one's ~** (*lit*) prendre son médicament; (*fig*) avaler la pilule; **let's give him a taste** *or* **dose of his own ~** on va lui rendre la monnaie de sa pièce; *see* **patent**.

2 comp ►**medicine ball** medecine-ball *m* ►**medicine box** pharmacie *f* (portative) ►**medicine cabinet** (armoire *f* à) pharmacie *f* ►**medicine chest** (*box*) pharmacie *f* (portative); (*cupboard*) (armoire *f* à) pharmacie ►**medicine cupboard** = **medicine cabinet** ►**medicine man** sorcier *m*.

medico* ['medɪkəʊ] n = **medic**.

medieval *etc* = **mediaeval** *etc*.

Medina [me'diːnə] n Médine (*ville sainte de l'Islam*).

mediocre [ˌmiːdɪ'əʊkəʳ] adj médiocre.

mediocrity [ˌmiːdɪ'ɒkrɪtɪ] n médiocrité *f*.

meditate ['medɪteɪt] 1 vt méditer (*sth* qch, *doing* de faire). 2 vi méditer (*on, about* sur), réfléchir (*on, about* à).

meditation [ˌmedɪ'teɪʃən] n méditation *f*, réflexion *f* (*on, about* sur). **the fruit of long ~** le fruit de longues méditations; (*Literat etc*) **~s** méditations (*on* sur).

meditative ['medɪtətɪv] adj méditatif.

meditatively ['medɪtətɪvlɪ] adv d'un air méditatif.

Mediterranean [ˌmedɪtə'reɪnɪən] adj (*gen*) méditerranéen. **the ~ type** le type latin; **the ~ (Sea)** la (mer) Méditerranée.

medium ['miːdɪəm] 1 n, pl **media** a (*Bio, Chem, gen*), milieu *m*; (*fig*) moyen *m*, véhicule *m*. (*fig*) **through the ~ of the press** par voie de presse; **advertising ~** organe *m* de publicité; **artist's ~** moyens d'expression d'un artiste; **language is the ~ of thought** le langage est le véhicule de la pensée; **television is the best ~ for this type of humour** c'est à la télévision que ce genre d'humour passe le mieux, c'est la télévision qui est le meilleur véhicule pour ce genre d'humour; *see* **culture**.

b (*mean*) milieu *m*. **the happy ~** le juste milieu.

c (pl **mediums**: *Spiritualism*) médium *m*.

2 adj (*gen*) moyen; *pen* à pointe moyenne. (*on garment labels*) "~" "moyen"; *see also* **3**.

3 comp ►**medium close shot** (*Cine*) plan *m* américain ►**medium-dry** *wine, champagne* demi-sec ►**medium-fine pen** stylo *m* à pointe moyenne ►**medium-priced** à un (*or* des) prix économique(s) ►**medium range missile** fusée *f* à moyenne portée ►**medium rare** (*of steaks*) à point ►**medium-sized** de grandeur *or* de taille moyenne ►**medium-term** adj à moyen terme ►**medium-wave** (*Rad*) adj sur ondes moyennes; **on medium wave, on the medium wavelength** sur les ondes moyennes.

medlar ['medləʳ] n (*fruit*) nèfle *f*; (*also* ~ **tree**) néflier *m*.

medley ['medlɪ] n mélange *m*; (*Mus*) pot-pourri *m*. (*Sport*) **400 metres ~** le 4 x cent mètres quatre nages.

medulla [me'dʌlə] n, pl **~s** *or* **medullae** [me'dʌliː] (*Anat*) moelle *f*; (*part of brain*) bulbe rachidien.

Medusa [mɪ'djuːzə] n la Méduse.

meek [miːk] adj doux (*f* douce), humble. ~ **and mild** doux comme un agneau.

meekly ['miːklɪ] adv avec douceur, humblement.

meekness ['miːknɪs] n douceur *f*, humilité *f*.

meerschaum ['mɪəʃəm] n (*pipe*) pipe *f* en écume (de mer); (*clay*) écume *f* de mer.

meet¹ [miːt] pret, ptp **met** 1 vt a *person* (*by chance*) rencontrer, tomber sur; (*coming in opposite direction*) croiser; (*by arrangement*) retrouver, rejoindre, revoir; (*go/come to ~*) (aller/venir) chercher, (aller/venir) attendre. **to arrange to ~ sb at 3 o'clock** donner rendez-vous à qn pour 3 heures; **I am ~ing the chairman at the airport** j'irai attendre le président à l'aéroport; **I am being met at the airport** on doit venir m'attendre à l'aéroport; **I'll ~ you outside the cinema** je te *or* on se retrouve devant le cinéma; **don't bother to ~ me** ne prenez pas la peine de venir me chercher; **he went out to ~ them** il s'est avancé à leur rencontre, il est allé au-devant d'eux; **she came down the steps to ~ me** elle a descendu les escaliers et est venue *or* pour venir à ma rencontre; **candidates will be required to ~ the committee** les candidats devront se présenter devant les membres du comité; *see* **halfway, match²** *etc*.

b *[river, sea]* rencontrer. **the car will ~ the train** la voiture attendra *or* sera là à l'arrivée du train; **the bus for Aix ~s the 10 o'clock train** l'autobus d'Aix assure la correspondance avec le train de 10 heures.

c (*get to know*) rencontrer, faire la connaissance de, connaître. **~ Mr Jones** je vous présente M. Jones; **I am very pleased to ~ you** enchanté de faire votre connaissance; **glad** *or* **pleased to ~ you!** enchanté!

d (*encounter*) *opponent, opposing team, obstacle* rencontrer; (*face*) *enemy, danger* faire face à, affronter; (*in duel*) se battre avec. **he met his death** *or* **his end in 1880** il trouva la mort en 1880; **to ~ death calmly** affronter la mort avec calme *or* sérénité; **this met no response** cela n'a provoqué aucune réponse *or* réaction; *see* **halfway**.

e (*satisfy etc*) *expenses, bill* régler, payer; *responsibilities, debt* faire face à, s'acquitter de; *deficit* combler; *goal, aim* atteindre; *demand, need, want* satisfaire, répondre à; *condition, stipulation* remplir; *charge, objection* réfuter; (*Comm*) *orders* satisfaire, assurer. **to ~ the cost of sth** prendre en charge les frais de qch; **he offered to ~ the full cost of the repairs** il a proposé de payer la totalité des réparations; **this will ~ the case** ceci fera l'affaire; **to ~ payments** faire face à ses obligations financières; **to ~ the payments on a washing machine** payer les traites d'une machine à laver; (*Comm etc*) **this ~s our requirements** cela correspond à nos besoins; (*Comm etc*) **it did not ~ our expectations** nous n'en avons pas été satisfaits.

f **the sound which met his ears** le bruit qui frappa ses oreilles; **the sight which met my eye(s)** le spectacle qui me frappa les yeux *or* qui s'offrit à mes yeux; **I met his eye** mon regard rencontra le sien, nos regards se croisèrent; **I dared not** *or* **couldn't ~ her eye** je n'osais pas la regarder en face; **there's more to this than ~s the eye** (*sth suspicious*) on ne voit pas *or* on ne connaît pas les dessous de cette affaire; (*more difficult than it seems*) c'est moins simple que cela n'en a l'air.

2 vi a *[people]* (*by chance*) se rencontrer; (*by arrangement*) se retrouver, se rejoindre, se revoir; (*more than once*) se voir; (*get to know each other*) se rencontrer, se connaître, faire connaissance. **to ~ again** se revoir; **until we ~ again!** au revoir!, à la prochaine fois!; **keep it until we ~ again** *or* **until we next ~** garde-le jusqu'à la prochaine fois; **have you met before?** vous vous connaissez déjà?, vous vous êtes déjà rencontrés?; **they arranged to ~ at 10 o'clock** ils se sont donné rendez-vous pour 10 heures.

b *[Parliament etc]* se réunir, tenir séance; *[committee, society etc]* se réunir, s'assembler. **the class ~s in the art room** le cours a lieu dans la salle de dessin.

c *[armies]* se rencontrer, s'affronter; *[opposing teams]* se rencontrer.

d *[lines, roads etc]* (*join*) se rencontrer; (*cross*) se croiser; *[rivers]* se rencontrer, confluer. **our eyes met** nos regards se croisèrent; *see* **end**.

3 n a (*Hunting*) rendez-vous *m* (de chasse); (*huntsmen*) chasse *f*.

b (*US Sport etc*) réunion *f*, meeting *m*.

►**meet up** vi (*by chance*) se rencontrer; (*by arrangement*) se retrouver, se rejoindre, se revoir. **to meet up with sb** rencontrer *or* rejoindre *or* retrouver *or* revoir qn; **this road meets up with the M1** cette route rejoint la M1.

►**meet with** vt fus a *difficulties, resistance, obstacles* rencontrer; *refusal, losses, storm, gale* essuyer; *welcome, reception* recevoir. **he met with an accident** il lui est arrivé un accident; **to meet with failure** essuyer un (*or* des) échec(s); **to meet with success** obtenir *or* remporter un (*or* des) succès; **we met with great kindness** on nous a traités avec une grande gentillesse; **this suggestion was met with angry protests** de vives protestations ont accueilli la suggestion. b (*US*) *person* (*by chance*) rencontrer, tomber sur; (*coming in opposite direction*) croiser; (*by arrangement*) retrouver, rejoindre, revoir.

meet² [miːt] adj († *or liter: suitable*) convenable, séant†.

meeting ['miːtɪŋ] 1 n a *[group of people, political party, club etc]* réunion *f*; (*large, formal*) assemblée *f*; (*Pol, Sport*) meeting *m*. **business ~** réunion d'affaires *or* de travail; **he's in a ~** il est en conférence; **I've got ~s all afternoon** je suis pris par des réunions tout l'après-midi; **to hold a ~** tenir une assemblée *or* une réunion *or* un meeting; **to call a ~ of shareholders** convoquer les actionnaires; **to call a ~ to discuss sth** convoquer une réunion pour débattre qch; **to address a ~** prendre la parole à une réunion (*or* un meeting); *see* **annual, mass¹, open** *etc*.

b (*between individuals*) rencontre *f*; (*arranged*) rendez-vous *m*; (*formal*) entrevue *f*. **the minister had a ~ with the ambassador** le ministre s'est entretenu avec l'ambassadeur, le ministre a eu une entrevue avec l'ambassadeur; (*fig: agreement*) **it was a ~ of minds** il y avait entre eux une entente profonde.

c (*Quakers*) culte *m*. **to go to ~** aller au culte.

2 comp ▸**(Quakers') meeting house** temple *m* ▸**meeting place** lieu *m* de réunion.

mega... ['megə] pref méga...; *film etc* méga-. **megastar** mégastar *f*.

megabuck* ['megə,bʌk] (*US*) n million *m* de dollars. (*fig*) **~s** des sommes effarantes*; **it's worth ~s** ça vaut la peau des fesses*.

megabyte ['megə,baɪt] n (*Comput*) Méga-octet *m*, Mo *m*.

megacycle ['megə,saɪkl] n mégacycle *m*.

megadeath ['megə,deθ] n million *m* de morts.

megahertz ['megə,hɜːts] n mégahertz *m*.

megalith ['megəlɪθ] n mégalithe *m*.

megalithic [,megə'lɪθɪk] adj mégalithique.

megalomania [,megələʊ'meɪnɪə] n mégalomanie *f*.

megalomaniac [,megələʊ'meɪnɪæk] adj, n mégalomane (*mf*).

megalopolis [,megə'lɒpəlɪs] n mégalopole *f*.

megaphone ['megəfəʊn] n porte-voix *m inv*.

megaton ['megətʌn] n mégatonne *f*. a **5-~ bomb** une bombe de 5 mégatonnes.

megavolt ['megəvɒlt] n mégavolt *m*.

megawatt ['megəwɒt] n mégawatt *m*.

megillah‡ [mə'gɪlə] n (*US*) grand laïus *m*, longues explications *fpl*. **the whole ~** tout le tremblement*.

meiosis [maɪ'əʊsɪs] n, pl **meioses** [maɪ'əʊ,siːz] (*Bio*) méiose *f*; (*Literat*) litote *f*.

Mekong [,miː'kɒŋ] n Mékong *m*. **~ Delta** delta *m* du Mékong.

melamine ['meləmiːn] 1 n mélamine *f*. 2 comp *cup, surface* de *or* en mélamine ▸**melamine-coated, melamine-faced** mélaminé.

melancholia [,melən'kəʊlɪə] n (*Psych*) mélancolie *f*.

melancholic [,melən'kɒlɪk] adj (*gen, Psych*) mélancolique.

melancholically [,melən'kɒlɪklɪ] adv mélancoliquement.

melancholy ['melənkəlɪ] 1 n (*NonC*) mélancolie *f*. 2 adj *person, look* mélancolique; *news, duty, event* triste, attristant.

Melanesia [,melə'niːzɪə] n Mélanésie *f*.

Melanesian [,melə'niːzɪən] 1 adj mélanésien. 2 n a Mélanésien(ne) *m(f)*. b (*Ling*) mélanésien *m*.

melanic [mə'lænɪk] adj mélanique.

melanin ['melənɪn] n mélanine *f*.

melanism ['melənɪzəm] n mélanisme *m*.

melanoma [,melə'nəʊmə] n, pl **~s** *or* **melanomata** [,melə'nəʊmətə] (*Med*) mélanome *m*.

Melba toast ['melbə'təʊst] n (*Culin*) biscotte *f* très fine.

Melbourne ['melbən] n Melbourne.

mellifluous [me'lɪfluəs] adj mélodieux, doux (*f* douce) (à l'oreille).

mellow ['meləʊ] 1 adj a *fruit* bien mûr, fondant; *wine* moelleux, velouté; *colour, light* doux, velouté; *earth, soil* meuble, riche; *voice, tone* moelleux, harmonieux, mélodieux; *building, stone* patiné (par l'âge); *person* mûri et tranquille; *character* mûri par l'expérience. **to grow ~** mûrir, s'adoucir.

b (*fig *: slightly drunk*) pompette, éméché.

c (*US*) **that's ~*** c'est idéal, c'est juste ce qu'il faut (*or* fallait).

2 vt *fruit* (faire) mûrir; *wine* rendre moelleux, donner du velouté *or* du moelleux à; *voice, sound* adoucir, rendre plus moelleux; *colour* fondre, velouter; *person, character* adoucir, arrondir les angles de (*fig*). **the years have ~ed him** les angles de son caractère se sont arrondis avec l'âge, il s'est adouci avec les années.

3 vi *[fruit]* mûrir; *[wine]* se velouter; *[colour]* se velouter, se patiner; *[voice]* prendre du moelleux, se velouter; *[person, character]* s'adoucir.

mellowing ['meləʊɪŋ] 1 n *[fruit, wine]* maturation *f*; *[voice, colours, person, attitude]* adoucissement *m*. 2 adj *effect etc* adoucissant.

mellowness ['meləʊnɪs] n *[fruit]* douceur *f* (fondante); *[wine]* moelleux *m*, velouté *m*; *[colour]* douceur, velouté; *[voice, tone]* timbre moelleux *or* velouté; *[building]* patine *f*; *[light, character, attitude]* douceur.

melodic [mɪ'lɒdɪk] adj mélodique.

melodious [mɪ'ləʊdɪəs] adj mélodieux.

melodiously [mɪ'ləʊdɪəslɪ] adv mélodieusement.

melodrama ['meləʊ,drɑːmə] n (*lit, fig*) mélodrame *m*, mélo* *m* (*pej*).

melodramatic [,meləʊdrə'mætɪk] adj mélodramatique.

melodramatically [,meləʊdrə'mætɪkəlɪ] adv d'un air *or* d'une façon mélodramatique.

melody ['melədɪ] n mélodie *f*.

melon ['melən] n melon *m*. (*US fig*) **to cut a ~*** se partager les profits *or* le gâteau; *see* **water**.

melt [melt] 1 vi a *[ice, butter, metal]* fondre; *[solid in liquid]* fondre, se dissoudre. **these cakes ~ in the mouth** ces pâtisseries fondent dans la bouche; (*fig*) **he looks as if butter wouldn't ~ in his mouth** on lui donnerait le bon Dieu sans confession*; *see also* **melting**.

b (*fig*) *[colours, sounds]* se fondre, s'estomper (*into* dans); *[person]* se laisser attendrir; *[anger]* tomber; *[resolution, determination]* fléchir, fondre. **to ~ into tears** fondre en larmes; **her heart ~ed with pity** son cœur s'est fondu de pitié; **night ~ed into day** la nuit a fait insensiblement place au jour; **one colour ~ed into another** les couleurs se fondaient les unes dans les autres; **the thief ~ed into the crowd** le voleur s'est fondu *or* a disparu dans la foule.

c (**: be too hot*) **to be ~ing** fondre, être en nage.

2 vt *ice, butter* (faire) fondre; *metal* fondre. (*fig*) **to ~ sb's heart** attendrir *or* émouvoir (le cœur de) qn; (*Culin*) **~ed butter** beurre fondu; *see also* **melting**.

3 comp ▸**meltdown** (*Nuclear Physics*) fusion *f* (du cœur d'un réacteur nucléaire).

▸**melt away** vi a *[ice etc]* fondre complètement, disparaître. b (*fig*) *[money, savings]* fondre; *[anger]* se dissiper, tomber; *[confidence]* disparaître; *[fog]* se dissiper; *[crowd]* se disperser; *[person]* se volatiliser, s'évaporer*, s'envoler*.

▸**melt down** 1 vt sep fondre; *scrap iron, coins* remettre à la fonte. 2 **meltdown** n *see* **melt 3**.

melting ['meltɪŋ] 1 adj *snow* fondant; (*fig*) *voice, look* attendri; *words* attendrissant. 2 n *[snow]* fonte *f*; *[metal]* fusion *f*, fonte. 3 comp ▸**melting point** point *m* de fusion ▸**melting pot**: (*fig*) **the country was a melting pot of many nationalities** le pays était le creuset de bien des nationalités; **the scheme was back in the melting pot again** le projet a été remis en question une fois de plus; **it's still all in the melting pot** c'est encore en pleine discussion *or* au stade des discussions.

member ['membəʳ] 1 n a *[society, political party etc]* membre *m*, adhérent(e) *m(f)*; *[family, tribe]* membre. (*on notice etc*) **"~s only"** "réservé aux adhérents"; **a ~ of the audience** un membre de l'assistance, l'un des assistants; (*hearer*) un auditeur; (*spectator*) un spectateur; (*US Pol*) **M~ of Congress** membre du Congrès; **a ~ of the congress** un(e) congressiste; **they treated her like a ~ of the family** ils l'ont traitée comme si elle faisait partie *or* était de la famille; (*Brit Pol*) **M~ of Parliament** ≃ député *m*; **the M~ (of Parliament) for Woodford** le député de Woodford; (*Brit*) **M~ of the European Parliament** Membre *m* du Parlement Européen; **a ~ of the public** un simple particulier, une simple particulière, un(e) simple citoyen(ne); *[firm, organisation]* **a ~ of the staff** un(e) employé(e); (*Scol, Univ*) **a ~ of staff** un professeur; *see* **full, honorary, private** *etc*.

b (*Anat, Bot, Math etc*) membre *m*. (*Anat*) **(male) ~** membre (viril).

2 comp ▸**member nations** *or* **countries** *or* **states** États *mpl or* pays *mpl* membres.

membership ['membəʃɪp] 1 n a (*state*) adhésion *f*. **Britain's ~ of the Common Market** l'adhésion de la Grande-Bretagne au Marché Commun; **when I applied for ~ of the club** quand j'ai fait ma demande d'adhésion au club; **he has given up his ~ of the party** il a rendu sa carte du parti; **~ carries certain privileges** l'adhésion donne droit à certains privilèges, les membres jouissent de certains privilèges.

b (*number of members*) **this society has a ~ of over 800** cette société a plus de 800 membres.

2 comp ▸**membership card** carte *f* d'adhérent *or* de membre ▸**membership fee** cotisation *f*, droits *mpl* d'inscription ▸**membership qualifications** conditions *fpl* d'éligibilité.

membrane ['membreɪn] n membrane *f*.

membranous [mem'breɪnəs] adj membraneux.

memento [mə'mentəʊ] n, pl **~s** *or* **~es** (*keepsake*) souvenir *m*; (*note, mark etc*) mémento *m*; (*scar*) souvenir. **as a ~ of** en souvenir de.

memo ['meməʊ] 1 n (abbr of **memorandum**) note *f* (de service). 2 comp ▸**memo pad** bloc-notes *m*.

memoir ['memwɑːʳ] n (*essay*) mémoire *m*, étude *f* (*on* sur); (*short biography*) notice *f* biographique. **~s** (*autobiographical*) mémoires; *[learned society]* actes *mpl*.

memorabilia [,memərə'bɪlɪə] n souvenirs *mpl* (*objets*).

memorable ['memərəbl] adj mémorable.

memorably ['memərəblɪ] adv mémorablement.

memorandum [,memə'rændəm] n, pl **~s** *or* **memoranda** [,memə'rændə] a (*reminder, note*) note *f*. **to make a ~ of sth** prendre note de qch, noter qch. b (*communication within company etc*) note *f* (de service). **he sent a ~ round about the drop in sales** il a fait circuler une note *or* il a fait passer une circulaire à propos de la baisse des ventes. c (*Diplomacy*) mémorandum *m*. d (*Jur*) sommaire *m* des statuts (d'un contrat). (*Jur*) **~ of agreement** protocole *m* d'accord.

memorial [mɪ'mɔːrɪəl] 1 adj *plaque* commémoratif. (*US*) **M~ Day** le jour des morts au champ d'honneur (*dernier lundi de mai*); (*US : cemetery*) **~ park** cimetière *m*; **~ service** ≃ messe *f* de souvenir. 2 n a (*sth serving as reminder*) **this scholarship is a ~ to John F. Kennedy** cette bourse d'études est en mémoire de John F. Kennedy. b (*monument*) monument *m* (commémoratif), mémorial *m*; (*over grave*) monument (funéraire). **a ~ to the victims** un monument aux victimes. c (*also* **war ~**) monument *m* aux morts. d (*Hist: chronicles*) **~s** chroniques *fpl*, mémoires *mpl*, mémorial *m*. e (*Admin etc: petition*) pétition *f*, requête *f* (officielle).

memorize ['meməraɪz] vt *facts, figures, names* mémoriser, retenir; *poem, speech* apprendre par cœur.

memory ['memərɪ] 1 n a (*faculty; also Comput*) mémoire *f*. **to have a good/bad ~** avoir (une) bonne/mauvaise mémoire; **to have a ~ for faces** avoir la mémoire des visages, être physionomiste; **to play/quote from ~** jouer/citer de mémoire; **to commit to ~** *poem* apprendre par cœur; *facts, figures* mémoriser, retenir; **to the best of my ~** autant que

je m'en souvienne; **loss of ~** perte *f* de mémoire; (*Med*) amnésie *f*; (*Comput*) **additional** *or* **back-up ~** mémoire auxiliaire; *see* **living.**
b (*recollection*) souvenir *m*. **childhood memories** souvenirs d'enfance; **"Memories of a country childhood"** "Souvenirs d'une enfance à la campagne"; **the ~ of the accident remained with him all his life** il a conservé toute sa vie le souvenir de l'accident, le souvenir de l'accident est resté gravé dans sa mémoire toute sa vie; **to keep sb's ~ alive** *or* **green** garder vivant le souvenir de qn, entretenir la mémoire de qn; **in ~ of** en souvenir de, à la mémoire de; **sacred to the ~ of** à la mémoire de; **of blessed ~** de glorieuse mémoire.
2 comp ▸**memory capacity** (*Comput*) capacité *f* de mémoire ▸**memory chip** (*Comput*) puce *f* mémoire ▸**memory lane**: (*fig*) **it was a trip down memory lane** c'était un retour en arrière *or* un retour aux sources ▸**memory typewriter** machine *f* à écrire à mémoire.

memsahib ['mem,sɑ:*h*ɪb] **n** Madame *f* (*aux Indes*).

men [men] 1 **npl of man.** (*hum*) **that'll separate the ~ from the boys** cela fera la différence (entre les hommes et les mauviettes*). 2 **comp** ▸**the menfolk*** les hommes *mpl* ▸**men's room** toilettes *fpl* pour hommes ▸**menswear** (*Comm*) (*clothing*) habillement masculin; (*department*) rayon *m* hommes; *see also* **man.**

menace ['menɪs] 1 **n** menace *f*. **he drives so badly he's a ~ to the public** il conduit si mal qu'il est un danger public; **that child/dog/motorbike is a ~*** cet enfant/ce chien/cette motocyclette est une plaie*. 2 **vt** menacer.

menacing ['menɪsɪŋ] **adj** menaçant.

menacingly ['menɪsɪŋlɪ] **adv** *act* d'un air menaçant; *say* d'un ton menaçant.

ménage [me'nɑ:ʒ] **n** (*often pej*) ménage *m*. **~ à trois** ménage à trois.

menagerie [mɪ'nædʒərɪ] **n** ménagerie *f*.

Menai [,menaɪ] **n**: **~ Strait** détroit *m* de Menai.

mend [mend] 1 **vt** a (*repair*) *clothes etc* raccommoder; *watch, wall, vehicle, shoes etc* réparer; (*darn*) *sock, stocking* repriser; *laddered stocking* remmailler; *see* **fence, invisibly.** b (*fig*) *mistake etc* corriger, rectifier, réparer. **that won't ~ matters** cela ne va pas arranger les choses; **to ~ one's ways, to ~ one's manners** s'amender; *see* **least.** 2 **vi** a (*darn etc*) faire le raccommodage. b (*) = **to be on the ~;** *see* **3b.** 3 **n** a (*on clothes*) raccommodage *m*; (*patch*) pièce *f*; (*darn*) reprise *f*. b **to be on the ~** *[invalid]* être en voie de guérison, aller mieux; *[business, sales]* prendre une meilleure tournure, reprendre, s'améliorer; *[conditions, situation, weather]* s'améliorer.

mendacious [men'deɪʃəs] **adj** *report* mensonger, fallacieux; *person* menteur.

mendacity [men'dæsɪtɪ] **n** a (*NonC*) (*habit*) fausseté *f*, habitude *f* de mentir; (*tendency*) propension *f* au mensonge; *[report]* caractère mensonger. b (*lie*) mensonge *m*.

mendelevium [,mendɪ'li:vɪəm] **n** mendélévium *m*.

Mendelian [men'di:lɪən] **adj** mendélien.

Mendelism ['mendəlɪzəm] **n** mendélisme *m*.

mendicancy ['mendɪkənsɪ] **n** mendicité *f*.

mendicant ['mendɪkənt] **adj, n** mendiant(e) *m(f)*.

mendicity [men'dɪsɪtɪ] **n** mendicité *f*.

mending ['mendɪŋ] **n** (*act*) raccommodage *m*; (*clothes to be mended*) vêtements *mpl* à raccommoder; *see* **invisible.**

Menelaus [,menɪ'leəs] **n** Ménélas *m*.

menhir ['menhɪər] **n** menhir *m*.

menial ['mi:nɪəl] 1 **adj** *person* servile; *task* de domestique, inférieur; *position* subalterne. 2 **n** domestique *mf*, laquais *m* (*pej*).

meninges [mɪ'nɪndʒi:s] **npl** méninges *fpl*.

meningitis [,menɪn'dʒaɪtɪs] **n** méningite *f*.

meniscus [mɪ'nɪskəs] **n, pl ~es** *or* **menisci** [mɪ'nɪsaɪ] ménisque *m*.

menopausal ['menəʊpɔ:zəl] **adj** *symptom* dû (*f* due) à la ménopause; *woman* à la ménopause.

menopause ['menəʊpɔ:z] **n** ménopause *f*. **the male ~** andropause *f*.

Menorca [mɪ'nɔ:kə] **n** Minorque *f*. **in ~** à Minorque.

menorrhagia [,menɔ:'reɪdʒɪə] **n** ménorragie *f*.

mensch [menʃ] **n** (*US* *) (*man*) type *m or* (*woman*) fille *f* vraiment bien.

menses ['mensi:z] **npl** menstrues *fpl*.

Menshevik ['menʃɪvɪk] **n, adj** menchevik *(m)*.

menstrual ['menstrʊəl] **adj** menstruel.

menstruate ['menstrʊeɪt] **vi** avoir ses règles.

menstruation [,menstrʊ'eɪʃən] **n** menstruation *f*.

mensuration [,mensjʊə'reɪʃən] **n** (*also Math*) mesurage *m*.

mental ['mentl] **adj** a *ability, process* mental, intellectuel; *illness* mental. **~ age** âge mental; **~ block** blocage *m*; (*Psych*) **~ defective** débile *mf* mental(e); (*Psych*) **~ deficiency** débilité *or* déficience mentale *or* intellectuelle; (*US Med*) **~ healing** thérapeutique *f* par la suggestion; **~ hospital, ~ institution, ~ home** hôpital *m or* clinique *f* psychiatrique; **~ illness** maladie *f* mentale; **~ patient** malade *mf* mental(e); **~ powers** facultés intellectuelles; (*Psych*) **~ retardation** déficience *f* intellectuelle, arriération mentale; **~ strain** (*tension*) tension nerveuse; (*overwork*) surmenage *m* (intellectuel); **she's been under a great deal of ~ strain** ses nerfs ont été mis à rude épreuve.
b *calculation* mental, de tête; *prayer* intérieur. **~ arithmetic** calcul mental; **to make a ~ note of sth** noter qch (en passant), retenir qch; **he made a ~ note to do it** il prit note mentalement de le faire; **to have ~ reservations about sth** avoir des doutes sur qch.
c (* *Brit: mad*) fou (*f* folle), malade*, timbré*.

mentality [men'tælɪtɪ] **n** mentalité *f*.

mentally ['mentəlɪ] **adv** *calculate, formulate* mentalement. (*Psych*) **~ defective** mentalement déficient; **~ disturbed** déséquilibré; **~ disabled, ~ handicapped** handicapé(e) *m(f)* mental(e); **~ ill** atteint de maladie mentale; **a ~ ill person** un(e) malade mental(e); (*Psych*) **~ retarded** intellectuellement déficient, (mentalement) arriéré; (*Psych*) **~ subnormal** débile *m(f)* léger (*f* -ère).

menthol ['menθɒl] **n** menthol *m*. **~ cigarettes** cigarettes mentholées.

mentholated ['menθəleɪtɪd] **adj** mentholé.

mention ['menʃən] 1 **vt** (*gen*) mentionner, faire mention de, signaler; *dates, figures* citer. **he ~ed to me that you were coming** il m'a mentionné votre venue *or* que vous alliez venir; **I'll ~ it to him** je lui en toucherai un mot, je le lui signalerai; **I've never heard him ~ his father** je ne l'ai jamais entendu parler de son père; **to ~ sb in one's will** coucher qn sur son testament; **he didn't ~ the accident** il n'a pas fait mention de l'accident, il n'a pas soufflé mot de l'accident; **just ~ my name** dites que c'est de ma part; **he ~ed several names** il a cité plusieurs noms; **without ~ing any names** sans nommer *or* citer personne; **I ~ this fact only because ...** je relève ce fait uniquement parce que ...; **they are too numerous to ~** ils sont trop nombreux pour qu'on les mentionne (*subj*) *or* cite (*subj*) (tous); **don't ~ it!** il n'y a pas de quoi!, de rien!*, je vous en prie!; **I need hardly ~ that ...** il va sans dire que ...; **it must be ~ed that ...** il faut signaler que ...; **not to ~ ..., without ~ing ...** sans compter ...; **it is not worth ~ing** cela ne vaut pas la peine d'en parler; **I have no jazz records worth ~ing** je n'ai pour ainsi dire pas de disques de jazz; *see* **dispatch.**
2 **n** mention *f*. **to make ~ of** faire mention de, signaler; **honourable ~** mention honorable; **it got a ~ in the news** on en a parlé *or* on l'a mentionné aux informations.

mentor ['mentɔ:r] **n** mentor *m*.

menu ['menju:] 1 **n** (*in restaurant etc*) menu *m*; (*printed, written*) menu, carte *f*. **on the ~** au menu; *see* **fixed.** 2 **comp** (*Comput*) menu *m* ▸**menu-driven** dirigé *or* piloté par menu.

meow [mi:'aʊ] = **miaow.**

MEP [,emi:'pi:] **n** (*Brit*) (**abbr of Member of the European Parliament**) membre *m or* député *m* du Parlement européen.

Mephistopheles [,mefɪs'tɒfɪli:z] **n** Méphistophélès *m*.

mephistophelian [,mefɪstə'fi:lɪən] **adj** méphistophélique.

mercantile ['mɜ:kəntaɪl] **adj** a *navy, vessel* marchand; *affairs* commercial; *nation* commerçant; *firm, establishment* de commerce; (*pej*) *person, attitude* mercantile. **~ law** droit commercial; **~ marine** marine marchande. b (*Econ*) mercantile.

mercantilism ['mɜ:kəntɪlɪzəm] **n** (*Econ, also pej*) mercantilisme *m*.

mercantilist ['mɜ:kəntɪlɪst] **adj, n** (*Econ*) mercantiliste *(m)*.

Mercator [mɜ:'keɪtər] **n**: **~ projection** projection *f* de Mercator.

mercenary ['mɜ:sɪnərɪ] 1 **adj** a (*pej*) *person, attitude* intéressé, mercenaire. b (*Mil*) mercenaire. 2 **n** (*Mil*) mercenaire *m*.

mercer ['mɜ:sər] **n** (*Brit*) marchand *m* de tissus.

merchandise ['mɜ:tʃəndaɪz] 1 **n** (*NonC*) marchandises *fpl*. 2 **vi** commercer, faire du commerce. 3 **vt** promouvoir la vente de.

merchandizer ['mɜ:tʃəndaɪzər] **n** spécialiste *mf* des techniques marchandes, merchandiser *m*.

merchandizing ['mɜ:tʃəndaɪzɪŋ] **n** techniques marchandes, merchandising *m*.

merchant ['mɜ:tʃənt] 1 **n** (*trader, dealer*) négociant *m*; (*wholesaler*) marchand *m* en gros, grossiste *m*; (*retailer*) marchand au détail, détaillant *m*; (*shopkeeper*) commerçant *m*. **"The M~ of Venice"** "le Marchand de Venise"; **builders'/plumbers' ~** fournisseur *m* de *or* en matériaux de construction/en sanitaires; *see* **coal, speed, wine** *etc*.
2 **comp** ▸**merchant bank** (*Brit Fin*) banque *f* de commerce *or* d'affaires, banque *f* d'acceptation ▸**merchantman** (*Naut*) = **merchant ship** ▸**merchant navy** (*Brit*), **merchant marine** (*US*) marine marchande ▸**merchant seaman** marin *m* de la marine marchande ▸**merchant ship** navire marchand *or* de commerce ▸**merchant shipping** (*NonC*) navires marchands ▸**merchant vessel** vaisseau marchand *or* de commerce.

merchantability [,mɜ:tʃəntə'bɪlɪtɪ] **n** (*Comm*) valeur *f* commerciale; (*Jur*) qualité *f* loyale et marchande.

merchantable ['mɜ:tʃəntəbl] **adj** (*Comm*) commercialisable, vendable; (*Jur*) de qualité loyale et marchande.

merciful ['mɜ:sɪfʊl] **adj** miséricordieux (*to, towards* pour), clément (*to, towards* envers). **his death was a ~ release** sa mort a été une délivrance.

mercifully ['mɜ:sɪfəlɪ] **adv** a *judge, act* miséricordieusement, avec clémence. b (*fortunately*) **~ it didn't rain** Dieu merci *or* par bonheur il n'a pas plu.

merciless ['mɜ:sɪlɪs] **adj** *person, judgment* impitoyable, implacable, sans pitié; *rain, storm, heat* implacable, impitoyable.

mercilessly ['mɜ:sɪlɪslɪ] **adv** (*see* **merciless**) impitoyablement, implacablement, sans pitié.

mercurial [mɜːˈkjʊərɪəl] **adj** (*Chem*) mercuriel; (*changeable*) d'humeur inégale *or* changeante; (*lively*) vif (*f* vive), plein d'entrain.

mercury [ˈmɜːkjʊrɪ] **n** a (*Chem*) mercure *m*. b **M~** (*Myth*) Mercure *m*; (*Astron*) Mercure *f*.

mercy [ˈmɜːsɪ] 1 **n** a pitié *f*, indulgence *f*; (*Rel*) miséricorde *f*. **without ~** sans pitié; **for ~'s sake** par pitié; **God in his ~** Dieu en sa miséricorde; **no ~ was shown to the revolutionaries** les révolutionnaires furent impitoyablement traités *or* traités sans merci; **to have ~ on sb** avoir pitié de qn; **to beg for ~** demander grâce; **to show ~ towards** *or* **to sb** montrer de l'indulgence pour *or* envers qn; (*Jur*) **with a recommendation to ~** ≃ avec avis en faveur d'une commutation de peine; **to throw o.s. on sb's ~** s'en remettre à la merci de qn; **at the ~ of sb/the weather** *etc* à la merci de qn/du temps *etc*; (*iro*) **to leave sb to the tender ~** *or* **mercies of** abandonner qn aux bons soins (*iro*) *or* au bon vouloir (*iro*) de; (*excl*) **~ (me)!*** Seigneur!, miséricorde!; *see* **errand**.

b (*piece of good fortune*) **to be thankful for small mercies** être reconnaissant du peu qui s'offre; **it's a ~ that** heureusement que + *indic*, c'est une chance que + *subj*; **his death was a ~** sa mort a été une délivrance.

2 **comp** *flight, journey* de secours, d'urgence (humanitaire) ►**mercy killing** euthanasie *f*.

mere[1] [mɪəʳ] **n** étang *m*, (petit) lac *m*.

mere[2] [mɪəʳ] **adj** simple, pur, seul (*all before noun*). **he's a ~ child** ce n'est qu'un enfant; **he's a ~ clerk** c'est un simple employé de bureau, il n'est qu'employé de bureau; **by a ~ chance** par pur hasard; **the ~ sight of him makes me shiver** sa seule vue me fait frissonner, rien qu'à le voir je frissonne; **they quarrelled over a ~ nothing** ils se sont disputés pour une vétille; **he's a ~ nobody** il est moins que rien; **it's a ~ kilometre away** ce n'est qu'à un kilomètre (de distance).

merely [ˈmɪəlɪ] **adv** purement, simplement, seulement. **I ~ said that she was coming** j'ai tout simplement dit *or* je n'ai fait que dire qu'elle arrivait; **he ~ nodded** il se contenta de faire un signe de tête; **he's ~ a clerk** il n'est qu'employé de bureau; **I did it ~ to please her** je ne l'ai fait que pour lui faire plaisir; **~ to look at him makes me shiver** rien que de le regarder me fait frissonner; **it's ~ a formality** ce n'est qu'une formalité, c'est une simple formalité; **it's not ~ broken, it's ruined** ce n'est pas seulement cassé, c'est fichu*.

meretricious [ˌmerɪˈtrɪʃəs] **adj** *charm, attraction* factice; *style* plein d'artifices, ampoulé; *jewellery, decoration* clinquant.

merge [mɜːdʒ] 1 **vi** a *[colours, shapes]* se mêler (*into, with* à), se fondre (*into, with* dans); *[sounds]* se mêler (*into, with* à), se perdre (*into, with* dans); *[roads]* se rencontrer (*with* avec), se joindre (*with* à); *[river]* confluer (*with* avec). (*also fig*) **to ~ into** *darkness, background etc* se fondre dans.

b (*Comm, Fin*) fusionner (*with* avec).

2 **vt** a unifier. **the states were ~d (into one) in 1976** les États se sont unifiés en 1976, l'unification des États s'est réalisée en 1976.

b (*Comm, Fin*) fusionner, amalgamer; (*Comput*) fusionner. **the firms were ~d** les entreprises ont fusioné; **they decided to ~ the companies into a single unit** ils décidèrent d'amalgamer *or* de fusionner les compagnies.

merger [ˈmɜːdʒəʳ] **n** (*Comm, Fin*) fusion *f*, fusionnement *m*.

meridian [məˈrɪdɪən] 1 **n** (*Astron, Geog*) méridien *m*; (*fig*) apogée *m*, zénith *m*. 2 **adj** méridien.

meridional [məˈrɪdɪənl] 1 **adj** méridional. 2 **n** Méridional(e) *m(f)*.

meringue [məˈræŋ] **n** meringue *f*.

merino [məˈriːnəʊ] **n** mérinos *m*.

merit [ˈmerɪt] 1 **n** mérite *m*, valeur *f*. **people of ~** gens de valeur *or* de mérite; **work of great ~** travail *m* de grande valeur; **the great ~ of this scheme** le grand mérite de ce projet; **there is little ~ in doing so** il y a peu de mérite à le faire; **to treat sb according to his ~s** traiter qn selon ses mérites; **to decide a case on its ~s** décider d'un cas en toute objectivité; **they went into the ~s of the new plan** ils ont discuté le pour et le contre de ce nouveau projet.

2 **comp** ►**merit list** (*Scol etc*) tableau *m* d'honneur; **to get one's name on the merit list** être inscrit au tableau d'honneur ►**merit system** (*US Admin*) système *m* de recrutement et de promotion par voie de concours.

3 **vt** mériter. **this ~s fuller discussion** ceci mérite plus ample discussion *or* d'être plus amplement discuté.

meritocracy [ˌmerɪˈtɒkrəsɪ] **n** méritocratie *f*.

meritocrat [ˈmerɪtəʊkræt] **n** membre *m* de la méritocratie.

meritocratic [ˌmerɪtəʊˈkrætɪk] **adj** méritocratique.

meritorious [ˌmerɪˈtɔːrɪəs] **adj** *person* méritant; *work, deed* méritoire.

meritoriously [ˌmerɪˈtɔːrɪəslɪ] **adv** d'une façon méritoire.

merlin [ˈmɜːlɪn] **n** (*Orn*) émerillon *m*.

mermaid [ˈmɜːmeɪd] **n** (*Myth*) sirène *f*.

merman [ˈmɜːmæn] **n** (*Myth*) triton *m*.

Merovingian [ˌmerəʊˈvɪndʒɪən] 1 **adj** mérovingien. 2 **n** Mérovingien(ne) *m(f)*.

merrily [ˈmerɪlɪ] **adv** joyeusement, gaiement *or* gaîment.

merriment [ˈmerɪmənt] **n** (*NonC*) gaieté *f or* gaîté *f*, joie *f*; (*laughter*) hilarité *f*. **this remark caused a lot of ~** cette remarque a provoqué l'hilarité générale.

merry [ˈmerɪ] 1 **adj** a gai, joyeux. **to make ~**† s'amuser, se divertir; **M~ Christmas!** Joyeux Noël!; **M~ England** l'Angleterre du bon vieux temps; **Robin Hood and his ~ men** Robin des Bois et ses joyeux lurons; *see* **may**[2], **more** *etc*. b (*: *tipsy*) éméché, pompette*. **to grow** *or* **get ~** se griser; **he's getting ~** il a un verre dans le nez*. 2 **comp** ►**merry-go-round** (*in fairground*) manège *m* (*de chevaux de bois etc*); (*fig*) tourbillon *m* ►**merrymaker** fêtard *m* ►**merrymaking** (*NonC*) réjouissances *fpl*.

mesa [ˈmeɪsə] **n** (*US*) mesa *f*, plateau *m*.

mescaline [ˈmeskəlɪn] **n** mescaline *f*.

mesh [meʃ] 1 **n** a *[net, sieve etc]* (*space*) maille *f*; (*fig*) (*network*) réseau *m*, rets *mpl*; (*snare*) rets, filets *mpl*. **netting with 5-cm ~** filet à mailles de 5 cm; **~es** (*threads*) mailles *fpl*; *[spider's web]* fils *mpl*, toile *f*; (*fig*) **trapped in the ~ of circumstances** pris dans l'engrenage des circonstances; (*fig*) **caught in the ~es of the law** pris dans les mailles de la justice; **the ~(es) of intrigue** le réseau d'intrigues; *see* **micro...** .

b (*NonC*) (*fabric*) tissu *m* à mailles. **nylon ~** tulle *m* de nylon; **wire ~** treillis *m*, grillage *m*; **a belt of fine gold ~** une ceinture tressée de fils d'or.

c *[gears etc]* engrenage *m*. **in ~** en prise.

2 **comp** ►**mesh bag** filet *m* (à provisions) ►**mesh stockings** (*non-run*) bas *mpl* indémaillables; (*in cabaret, circus etc*) bas *mpl* filet.

3 **vi** *[wheels, gears]* s'engrener; *[dates, plans]* concorder, cadrer; (*fig*) *[two people, their characters etc]* avoir des affinités.

4 **vt** *fish etc* prendre au filet.

meshug(g)a, meshuggah [mɪˈʃʊɡə] **adj** (*US*) cinglé*, maboul‡.

mesmeric [mezˈmerɪk] **adj** hypnotique, magnétique.

mesmerism [ˈmezmərɪzəm] **n** mesmérisme *m*.

mesmerize [ˈmezməraɪz] **vt** hypnotiser, magnétiser; *[snake]* fasciner. (*fig*) **I was ~d** je ne pouvais pas détourner mon regard, j'étais comme hypnotisé.

mesomorph [ˈmesəʊˌmɔːf] **n** mesomorphe *mf*.

meson [ˈmiːzɒn] **n** (*Phys*) méson *m*.

Mesopotamia [ˌmesəpəˈteɪmɪə] **n** Mésopotamie *f*.

Mesozoic [ˌmesəʊˈzəʊɪk] **adj, n** mésozoïque (*m*).

mess [mes] 1 **n** a (*confusion of objects etc*) désordre *m*, pagaïe* *f or* pagaille* *f*, fouillis* *m*, fatras *m*; (*dirt*) saleté *f*; (*muddle*) gâchis *m*; (*fig*) gâchis, pétrin *m*, cafouillage* *m*, cafouillis* *m*. **what a ~ the children have made!** quel désordre *or* gâchis les enfants ont fait!, les enfants ont mis un beau désordre!; **what a ~ your room is in!** quel fouillis* *or* quelle pagaïe* il y a dans ta chambre!; **get this ~ cleared up at once!** range-moi ce fouillis* tout de suite!; **the house was in a terrible ~** (*untidy*) la maison était dans un désordre épouvantable; (*dirty*) la maison était d'une saleté épouvantable; (*after warfare etc*) la maison était dans un triste état *or* un état épouvantable; **his shirt was in a ~** sa chemise était dans un triste état; **the toys were in a ~** les jouets étaient en pagaïe* *or* en désordre; **they left everything in a ~** ils ont tout laissé en pagaïe* *or* en désordre; **this page is (in) a ~, rewrite it** cette page est un vrai torchon, recopiez-la; (*after fight, accident etc*) **his face was in a dreadful ~** il avait le visage dans un état épouvantable; **you look a ~, you're a ~** tu n'es pas présentable; **he's a ~*** (*psychologically*) il est complètement déboussolé*; (*US: no use*) il n'est bon à rien; **she made a ~ of her new skirt** (*dirty*) elle a sali *or* tout taché sa jupe neuve; (*tear*) elle a déchiré sa jupe neuve; **the dog has made a ~ of the flowerbeds** le chien a saccagé les plates-bandes; **your boots have made an awful ~ on the carpet** tu as fait des saletés sur le tapis avec tes bottes; **the cat has made a ~ in the kitchen** le chat a fait des saletés dans la cuisine; (*fig*) **to make a ~ of** *essay, sewing, one's life, career* gâcher; **to make a ~ of things*** tout bousiller*, tout gâcher; (* *fig: difficulties*) **to be/get (o.s.) in a ~** être/se mettre dans de beaux draps *or* dans le pétrin; **his life is in a ~** sa vie est un vrai gâchis; **to get (o.s.) out of a ~** se sortir d'un mauvais pas, se dépatouiller*; **to get sb out of a ~** sortir qn d'un mauvais pas; **what a ~ it all is!** quel pétrin!, quel gâchis!; (*fig*) **the result is a political/legal** *etc* **~** politiquement/juridiquement *etc* on aboutit à un vrai gâchis.

b (*Mil*) (*place*) mess *m*, cantine *f*, popote* *f*; (*Naut*) carré *m*, gamelle *f*; (*food*) ordinaire *m*, gamelle; (*members*) mess.

c (*animal food*) pâtée *f*; (††: *dish*) mets *m*, plat *m*. (*Bible*) **a ~ of pottage** un plat de lentilles.

2 **comp** ►**mess deck** (*Naut*) poste *m* d'équipage ►**mess dress** (*Mil etc*) tenue *f* de soirée ►**mess gear*** (*Brit*) = **mess dress** ►**mess hall** (*US*) = **mess room** ►**mess jacket** (*Mil etc*) veston *m* de tenue de soirée; *[civilian waiter]* veste courte ►**mess kit** (*US*) gamelle *f*; (*Brit* *) tenue *f* de soirée ►**mess mate** (*Naut*) camarade *m* de plat ►**mess room** (*Mil*) (salle *f* de) mess *m*; (*Naut*) carré *m* ►**mess tin** (*Mil*) gamelle *f* ►**mess-up*** (*Brit*) gâchis *m*.

3 **vt** salir, souiller. (*fig*) **no ~ing!*** sans blague*!

4 **vi** (*Mil etc*) manger au mess, manger en commun (*with* avec).

►**mess about, mess around** 1 **vi** a (*in water, mud*) patouiller*, (*with feet*) patauger, (*with hands*) faire l'imbécile.

b (*) (*waste time*) gaspiller *or* perdre son temps; (*dawdle*) lambiner*, lanterner. **he was messing about with his friends** il traînait *or* (se) baguenaudait avec ses copains; **what were you doing? — just**

messing about que faisais-tu? — rien de particulier *or* de spécial; **I love messing about in boats** j'aime (m'amuser à) faire de la voile.
2 **vt sep** (**: disturb, upset*) (*Brit*) *person* créer des complications à, embêter*; *plans, arrangements* chambarder*, chambouler*. **stop messing me about** arrête de me traiter par-dessus la jambe* comme ça.
▸**mess about with*, mess around with*** **vt fus** a (*fiddle with*) *pen, ornament etc* faire l'imbécile avec. b (*amuse o.s. with*) **they were messing about with a ball** ils s'amusaient à taper *or* ils tapaient dans un ballon. c = **mess about 2.** d *boyfriend etc* s'amuser avec. e (*sexually*) peloter*.
▸**mess together** **vi** (*Mil etc*) manger ensemble au mess; (**gen*) faire popote* ensemble.
▸**mess up** 1 **vt sep** *clothes* salir, gâcher; *room* mettre en désordre, semer la pagaïe (*or* la pagaille) dans*; *hair* ébouriffer; *task, situation, plans, life etc* gâcher. **to mess sb's hair up** décoiffer qn; **that's messed everything up!** cela a tout gâché!; (*fig*) **to mess sb up*** (*psychologically*) perturber *or* traumatiser qn; (*US: beat up*) abîmer le portrait de qn. 2 **mess-up*** **n** *see* **mess 2.**
▸**mess with*** **vt fus** (*esp US*) *people* se frotter à*; *drugs, drinks etc* toucher* à. (*threatening*) **if you mess with me ...** si tu me fais perdre mon temps ... .

message ['mesɪdʒ] 1 **n** a (*communication: by speech, writing, signals etc, also Comput*) message *m*. **telephone ~** message téléphonique; **to leave a ~ (for sb)** laisser un mot (pour *or* à qn); **would you give him this ~?** voudriez-vous lui faire cette commission?
b (*official or diplomatic etc communication*) message *m*. **the President's ~ to Congress** le message du Président au Congrès.
c [*prophet, writer, artist, book etc*] message *m*. **to get the ~*** comprendre, saisir*, piger‡.
d (*Scot: errand*) course *f*, commission *f*. **to go on a ~ for sb** faire une course pour qn; **to go for** *or* **get the ~s** faire les courses *or* les commissions.
2 **comp** ▸**message bag** (*Scot*) sac *m* à provisions ▸**message-boy** garçon *m* de courses ▸**message switching** (*Comput*) commutation *f* des messages.

messaging ['mesɪdʒɪŋ] **n** (*Comput*) messagerie *f*.

messenger ['mesɪndʒəʳ] 1 **n** messager *m*, -ère *f*; (*in office*) commissionnaire *m*, coursier *m*; (*in hotel etc*) chasseur *m*, coursier; (*Post*) (petit) télégraphiste *m*; *see* **king** *etc.* 2 **comp** ▸**messenger boy** garçon *m* de courses.

Messiah [mɪ'saɪə] **n** Messie *m*.

messiah [mɪ'saɪə] **n** messie *m*.

messianic [ˌmesɪ'ænɪk] **adj** messianique.

messily ['mesɪlɪ] **adv** (*fig*) **the divorce ended ~** le divorce s'est mal terminé.

Messrs ['mesəz] **npl** (*Brit*) (**abbr of Messieurs**) messieurs *mpl* (**abbr** MM.). **~ Smith & Co** MM. Smith & Cie.

messy ['mesɪ] **adj** *clothes, room* (*dirty*) sale, malpropre; (*untidy*) en désordre, désordonné; *hair* en désordre, ébouriffé; *text, page* sale; *job* salissant; (*) *situation* embrouillé, compliqué. **what a ~ business!*** (*dirty, muddy etc*) c'est salissant!, on s'en met partout!; (*fig: confused*) quelle salade!*, quel embrouillamini*!; (*fig: hurtful: of divorce etc*) quelle sale affaire!

mestizo [mɪ'stiːzəʊ] **n, pl ~s** *or* **~es** (*US*) métis(se) *m(f)* (*né d'un parent espagnol ou portugais et d'un parent indien*).

met[1] [met] **pret, ptp of meet**[1].

met[2] [met] **adj** (*Brit*) (**abbr of meteorological**) météo *inv*. **the M~ Office** ≃ l'O.N.M. *m*; **~ report** bulletin *m* (de la) météo*.

meta... ['metə] **pref** mét(a)... .

metabolic [ˌmetə'bɒlɪk] **adj** métabolique.

metabolically [ˌmetə'bɒlɪklɪ] **adv** métaboliquement.

metabolism [me'tæbəlɪzəm] **n** métabolisme *m*.

metabolize [me'tæbəlaɪz] **vt** transformer par le métabolisme.

metacarpal [ˌmetə'kɑːpl] **adj, n** métacarpien *(m)*.

metacarpus [ˌmetə'kɑːpəs] **n** métacarpe *m*.

metal ['metl] 1 **n** a (*Miner*) métal *m*. b (*Brit*) (*also* **road ~**) empierrement *m*, cailloutis *m*; (*for railway*) ballast *m*. c (*Brit Rail*) **~s** rails *mpl*. d (*Glassware*) pâte *f* de verre. e (*Typ*) (*composed type*) caractère *m*; (*also* **type ~**) plomb *m*. f = **mettle.** 2 **comp** de métal, en métal ▸**metal detector** détecteur *m* de métaux ▸**metal polish** produit *m* d'entretien (*pour métaux*) ▸**metalwork** (*articles*) ferronnerie *f*; (*craft: also* **metalworking**) travail *m* des métaux ▸**metalworker** ferronnier *m*, (*Ind*) (ouvrier *m*) métallurgiste *m*. 3 **vt** a (*cover with metal*) métalliser. b (*Brit*) *road* empierrer, caillouter.

metalanguage ['metəlæŋgwɪdʒ] **n** métalangue *f*, métalangage *m*.

metalinguistic [ˌmetəlɪŋ'gwɪstɪk] **adj** métalinguistique.

metalinguistics [ˌmetəlɪŋ'gwɪstɪks] **n** (*NonC*) métalinguistique *f*.

metallic [mɪ'tælɪk] **adj** métallique.

metallurgic(al) [ˌmetə'lɜːdʒɪk(əl)] **adj** métallurgique.

metallurgist [me'tælədʒɪst] **n** métallurgiste *m*.

metallurgy [me'tælədʒɪ] **n** métallurgie *f*.

metamorphic [ˌmetə'mɔːfɪk] **adj** métamorphique.

metamorphism [ˌmetə'mɔːfɪzəm] **n** a (*Geol*) metamorphisme *m*. b (*metamorphosis*) métamorphose *f*.

metamorphose [ˌmetə'mɔːfəʊz] 1 **vt** métamorphoser, transformer (*into* en). 2 **vi** se métamorphoser (*into* en).

metamorphosis [ˌmetə'mɔːfəsɪs] **n, pl metamorphoses** [ˌmetə'mɔːfəˌsiːz] métamorphose *f*.

metamorphous [ˌmetə'mɔːfəs] **adj** = **metamorphic.**

metaphor ['metəfəʳ] **n** métaphore *f*, image *f*; *see* **mixed.**

metaphorical [ˌmetə'fɒrɪkəl] **adj** métaphorique.

metaphorically [ˌmetə'fɒrɪkəlɪ] **adv** métaphoriquement.

metaphysical [ˌmetə'fɪzɪkəl] **adj** (*gen*) métaphysique. (*Brit Liter*) **the M~ poets** les poètes métaphysiques.

metaphysics [ˌmetə'fɪzɪks] **n** (*NonC*) métaphysique *f*.

metastasis [mɪ'tæstəsɪs] **n, pl metastases** [mɪ'tæstəˌsiːz] métastase *f*.

metatarsal [ˌmetə'tɑːsl] **adj, n** métatarsien *(m)*.

metatarsus [ˌmetə'tɑːsəs] **n, pl metatarsi** [ˌmetə'tɑːsaɪ] métatarse *m*.

metathesis [me'tæθəsɪs] **n, pl metatheses** [me'tæθəˌsiːz] métathèse *f*.

metazoan [ˌmetə'zəʊən] **n, adj** métazoaire *(m)*.

mete [miːt] **vt: to ~ out** *punishment* infliger, donner; *reward* décerner; **to ~ justice** rendre la justice.

meteor ['miːtɪəʳ] 1 **n** météore *m*. 2 **comp** ▸**meteor crater** cratère *m* météorique ▸**meteor shower** pluie *f* d'étoiles filantes.

meteoric [ˌmiːtɪ'ɒrɪk] **adj** a météorique; (*fig*) brillant et rapide, fulgurant. **his ~ rise in the firm** sa montée en flèche dans l'entreprise. b (*of the weather*) météorologique.

meteorite ['miːtɪəraɪt] **n** météorite *m or f*.

meteorological [ˌmiːtɪərə'lɒdʒɪkəl] **adj** météorologique. (*Brit*) **M~ Office** ≃ Office national météorologique, O.N.M. *m*.

meteorologically [ˌmiːtɪərə'lɒdʒɪklɪ] **adv** météorologiquement.

meteorologist [ˌmiːtɪə'rɒlədʒɪst] **n** météorologue *mf*, météorologiste *mf*.

meteorology [ˌmiːtɪə'rɒlədʒɪ] **n** météorologie *f*.

meter ['miːtəʳ] 1 **n** a (*gen: measuring device*) compteur *m*. **electricity/gas/water ~** compteur d'électricité/à gaz/à eau; **to turn water/gas/electricity off at the ~** fermer l'eau/le gaz/l'électricité au compteur; *see* **light**[1] *etc.* b (*also* **parking ~**) parcmètre *m*. c (*US*) = **metre.** 2 **comp** ▸**meter maid** (*Aut*) contractuelle *f* ▸**meter reader** releveur *m* de compteurs.

meterage ['miːtərɪdʒ] **n** métrage *m*.

methadone ['meθəˌdəʊn] **n** méthadone *f*.

methane ['miːθeɪn] **n** (*also* **~ gas**) méthane *m*.

method ['meθəd] 1 **n** a (*NonC: orderliness*) méthode *f*, ordre *m*. **lack of ~** manque *m* de méthode; **there's ~ in his madness** sa folie ne manque pas d'une certaine logique. b (*manner, fashion*) méthode *f*, manière *f*, façon *f*. **modern ~s of teaching languages** méthodes modernes d'enseignement des langues; **his ~ of working** sa méthode de travail; **there are several ~s of doing this** il y a plusieurs manières *or* façons de faire cela; (*Scol etc*) **~ of assessment** modalités *fpl* de contrôle. c (*Cine, Theat*) **the M~** le système *or* la méthode de Stanislavski. 2 **comp** ▸**method actor** *or* **actress** (*Cine, Theat*) adepte *mf* du système *or* de la méthode de Stanislavski.

methodical [mɪ'θɒdɪkəl] **adj** méthodique.

methodically [mɪ'θɒdɪkəlɪ] **adv** méthodiquement.

Methodism ['meθədɪzəm] **n** méthodisme *m*.

Methodist ['meθədɪst] **adj, n** méthodiste *(mf)*.

methodological [ˌmeθədə'lɒdʒɪkəl] **adj** méthodologique.

methodologically [ˌmeθədə'lɒdɪkəlɪ] **adv** méthodologiquement.

methodology [ˌmeθə'dɒlədʒɪ] **n** méthodologie *f*.

meths* [meθs] (*Brit*) 1 **n abbr of methylated spirit(s).** 2 **comp** ▸**meths drinker*** alcoolique *mf* (qui se soûle à l'alcool à brûler).

Methuselah [mə'θuːzələ] **n** Mathusalem *m*; *see* **old.**

methyl ['meθɪl] **n** méthyle *m*. **~ acetate/bromide/chloride** acétate *m*/bromure *m*/chlorure *m* de méthyle.

methylated ['meθɪleɪtɪd] **adj:** (*Brit*) **~ spirit(s)** alcool *m* à brûler *or* dénaturé.

methylene ['meθɪliːn] **n** méthylène *m*.

meticulous [mɪ'tɪkjʊləs] **adj** méticuleux.

meticulously [mɪ'tɪkjʊləslɪ] **adv** méticuleusement. **~ clean** d'une propreté méticuleuse.

meticulousness [mɪ'tɪkjʊləsnɪs] **n** soin méticuleux.

métier ['meɪtɪeɪ] **n** (*trade etc*) métier *m*; (*one's particular work etc*) partie *f*, rayon* *m*, domaine *m*; (*strong point*) point fort.

metonymy [mɪ'tɒnɪmɪ] **n** métonymie *f*.

metre ['miːtəʳ] **n** (*measure, Poetry*) mètre *m*; (*Mus*) mesure *f*.

metric ['metrɪk] **adj** métrique. **~ system** système *m* métrique; **to go ~*** adopter le système métrique.

metrical ['metrɪkəl] **adj** métrique (*also Mus*). **~ psalm** psaume *m* versifié.

metricate ['metrɪˌkeɪt] **vt** convertir au système métrique.

metrication [ˌmetrɪ'keɪʃən] **n** conversion *f* au *or* adoption *f* du système métrique.

metrics ['metrɪks] **n** (*NonC*) métrique *f*.

metro ['metrəʊ] **n** métro *m*.

metrological [ˌmetrə'lɒdʒɪkəl] **adj** métrologique.

metrology [mɪ'trɒlədʒɪ] **n** métrologie *f*.

metronome ['metrənəʊm] n métronome *m*.
metropolis [mɪ'trɒpəlɪs] n, pl ~es métropole *f* (*ville*).
metropolitan [,metrə'pɒlɪtən] 1 adj (*Geog, Rel*) métropolitain. (*Brit*) M~ Police police *f* de Londres. 2 n (*Rel*) métropolitain *m*; (*in Orthodox Church*) métropolite *m*.
mettle ['metl] n *[person]* courage *m*, ardeur *f*, fougue *f*; *[horse]* fougue. to be on one's ~ être prêt à donner le meilleur de soi-même, être d'attaque, être sur le qui-vive; to prove *or* show one's ~ montrer de quoi on est capable, faire ses preuves.
mettlesome ['metlsəm] adj ardent, fougueux.
mew [mju:] *[cat etc]* 1 n (*also* mewing) miaulement *m*. 2 vi miauler.
mews [mju:z] (*Brit*) 1 npl (*souvent employé comme sg*) a (*small street*) ruelle *f*, venelle *f*. b (††: *stables*) écuries *fpl*. 2 comp ►**mews flat** petit appartement assez chic (*aménagé dans le local d'une ancienne écurie, remise etc*).
Mexican ['meksɪkən] 1 adj mexicain. ~ jumping bean fève *f* sauteuse; (*US fig*) ~ standoff impasse *f*; ~ wave *vague déferlante dans un stade produite par les spectateurs se levant tour à tour*. 2 n Mexicain(e) *m(f)*.
Mexico ['meksɪkəʊ] n Mexique *m*. ~ City Mexico.
mezcaline ['mezkəlɪn] n = mescaline.
mezzanine ['mezəni:n] n a (*floor*) mezzanine *f*, entresol *m*. b (*Theat*) (*Brit*) dessous *m* de scène; (*US*) mezzanine *f*, corbeille *f*.
mezzo-soprano [,metsəʊsə'prɑ:nəʊ] n (*voice*) mezzo-soprano *m*; (*singer*) mezzo(-soprano) *f*.
mezzotint ['metsəʊtɪnt] n mezzo-tinto *m inv*.
MF [em'ef] n (abbr of medium frequency) F.M. *f*.
M.F.A. [,emef'eɪ] n (*US Univ*) (abbr of Master of Fine Arts) *diplôme des beaux-arts*.
MFH [,emef'eɪtʃ] n (*Brit*) (abbr of Master of Foxhounds) *see* master.
mfrs. (*Comm*) abbr of manufacturers.
mg n (abbr of milligram(s)) mg.
Mgr. a abbr of Monseigneur *or* Monsignor. b abbr of manager.
M.H.R. [,emeɪtʃ'ɑ:ʳ] n (*US*) (abbr of Member of the House of Representatives) ≃ député *m*.
MHz (*Rad etc*) (abbr of megahertz) MHz.
MI n a (*US Post*) abbr of Michigan. b (abbr of machine intelligence) IA *f*.
mi [mi:] n (*Mus*) mi *m*.
MI5 [,emaɪ'faɪv] n (*Brit*) (abbr of Military Intelligence 5) ≃ D.S.T. *f*.
MI6 [,emaɪ'sɪks] n (*Brit*) (abbr of Military Intelligence 6) ≃ D.G.S.E. *f*.
MIA [,emaɪ'eɪ] (*Mil*) (abbr of missing in action) *see* missing.
miaow [mi:'aʊ] 1 n miaulement *m*, miaou *m*. ~! miaou! 2 vi miauler.
miasma [mɪ'æzmə] n, pl ~s *or* miasmata [mɪ'æzmətə] miasme *m*.
mica ['maɪkə] 1 n mica *m*. 2 comp ►**mica-schist** schiste *m* lustré.
mice [maɪs] npl of mouse.
Mich (*US*) abbr of Michigan.
Michael ['maɪkl] n Michel *m*.
Michaelmas ['mɪklməs] 1 n (*also* ~ Day) la Saint-Michel. 2 comp ►**Michaelmas daisy** aster *m* d'automne ►**Michaelmas term** (*Brit: Jur, Univ*) trimestre *m* d'automne.
Michelangelo [,maɪkəl'ændʒɪləʊ] n Michel-Ange *m*.
Michigan ['mɪʃɪgən] n Michigan *m*. in ~ dans le Michigan; Lake ~ le lac Michigan.
Mick [mɪk] n a (*name*) (dim of Michael). b (*pej* ‡) Irlandais *m*.
Mickey ['mɪkɪ] 1 n (*name*) (dim of Michael). 2 comp ►**Mickey Finn** boisson *f* droguée ►**Mickey Mouse** n (*cartoon character*) Mickey *m* ◊ adj (*: *pej: also* mickey-mouse*) *car, penknife, regulations* à la noix*; *job, courses* pas sérieux, enfantin; *degree* sans valeur, à la noix.
mickey ['mɪkɪ] 1 n (*Brit*) to take the ~‡ out of sb se payer la tête de qn; he's always taking the ~‡ il n'arrête pas de se payer la tête des gens. 2 comp ►**mickey finn** = Mickey Finn; *see* Mickey 2 ►**mickey-mouse** *see* Mickey 2.
micro ['maɪkrəʊ] n (abbr of microcomputer) micro-ordinateur *m*.
micro... ['maɪkrəʊ] pref micro... .
microanalysis [,maɪkrəʊə'nælɪsɪs] n micro-analyse *f*.
microanalytical [,maɪkrəʊ,ænə'lɪtɪkl] adj micro-analytique.
microbe ['maɪkrəʊb] n microbe *m*.
microbial [maɪ'krəʊbɪəl], **microbian** [maɪ'krəʊbɪən], **microbic** [maɪ'krəʊbɪk] adj microbien.
microbiological [,maɪkrəʊbaɪəʊ'lɒdʒɪkəl] adj microbiologique.
microbiologist [,maɪkrəʊbaɪ'ɒlədʒɪst] n microbiologiste *mf*.
microbiology [,maɪkrəʊbaɪ'ɒlədʒɪ] n microbiologie *f*.
microbus ['maɪkrəʊ,bʌs] n (*US Aut*) microbus *m*.
microcapsule ['maɪkrəʊ,kæpsjʊl] n microcapsule *f*.
microcephalic [,maɪkrəʊsɪ'fælɪk] adj microcéphale.
microcephaly [,maɪkrəʊ'sefəlɪ] n microcéphalie *f*.
microchip ['maɪkrəʊ,tʃɪp] n puce *f* (électronique).
microcircuit ['maɪkrəʊ,sɜ:kɪt] n microcircuit *m*.
microcircuitry ['maɪkrəʊ'sɜ:kətrɪ] n microcircuit *m*.
microclimate ['maɪkrəʊklaɪmɪt] n microclimat *m*.
micrococcus [,maɪkrəʊ'kɒkəs] n microcoque.
microcomputer ['maɪkrəʊkəm'pju:təʳ] n micro-ordinateur *m*.
microcomputing ['maɪkrəʊkəm'pju:tɪŋ] n micro-informatique *f*.
microcopy ['maɪkrəʊ,kɒpɪ] 1 n microcopie *f*. 2 vt microcopier.
microcorneal lens ['maɪkrəʊ'kɔ:nɪəl'lenz] n lentille *f* micro-cornéenne.
microcosm ['maɪkrəʊ,kɒzəm] n microcosme *m*. in ~ en microcosme.
microcosmic ['maɪkrəʊ'kɒzmɪk] adj microcosmique.
microcrystal [,maɪkrəʊ'krɪstəl] n microcristal.
microcrystalline ['maɪkrəʊ'krɪstə,laɪn] adj microcristallin.
microculture ['maɪkrəʊ,kʌltʃəʳ] n micro-culture *f*.
microdissection ['maɪkrəʊdɪ'sekʃən] n microdissection *f*.
microdot ['maɪkrəʊ,dɒt] n micro-image-point *m*.
microdrive ['maɪkrəʊ,draɪv] n unité *f* de microdisquette.
microeconomic ['maɪkrəʊ,i:kə'nɒmɪk] adj micro-économique.
microeconomics ['maɪkrəʊ,i:kə'nɒmɪks] n (*NonC*) micro-économie *f*.
microelectrode ['maɪkrəʊɪ'lektrəʊd] n micro-électrode *f*.
microelectronic ['maɪkrəʊɪlek'trɒnɪk] adj micro(-)électronique.
microelectronically ['maɪkrəʊɪlek'trɒnɪklɪ] adv micro(-)électroniquement.
microelectronics ['maɪkrəʊɪlek'trɒnɪks] n (*NonC*) micro(-)électronique *f*.
microenvironment ['maɪkrəʊɪn'vaɪərənmənt] n micro-environnement *m*.
microfauna ['maɪkrəʊ,fɔ:nə] n microfaune *f*.
microfiche ['maɪkrəʊ,fi:ʃ] n microfiche *f*. ~ reader microlecteur *m* (pour microfiches).
microfilm ['maɪkrəʊ,fɪlm] 1 n microfilm *m*. ~ reader microlecteur *m*. 2 vt microfilmer.
microflora ['maɪkrəʊ,flɔ:rə] n microflore *f*.
microform ['maɪkrəʊ,fɔ:m] n microforme *f*.
microgram ['maɪkrəʊ,græm] n microgramme *m*.
micrographic [,maɪkrəʊ'græfɪk] adj micrographique.
micrographically [,maɪkrəʊ'græfɪklɪ] adv micrographiquement.
micrographics [,maɪkrəʊ'græfɪks] n (*NonC*) micrographie *f*.
micrography [maɪ'krɒgrəfɪ] n micrographie *f*.
microgroove ['maɪkrəʊ,gru:v] n microsillon *m*.
microhabitat ['maɪkrəʊ'hæbɪtæt] n microhabitat *m*.
microimage ['maɪkrəʊ,ɪmɪdʒ] n microimage *f*.
microlight ['maɪkrəʊ,laɪt] n (*Aviat*) ULM *m*, ultra-léger-motorisé *m*.
microlinguistics ['maɪkrəʊlɪŋ'gwɪstɪks] n (*NonC*) microlinguistique *f*.
microlitre, (*US*) **microliter** ['maɪkrəʊ'li:təʳ] n microlitre *m*.
micromesh ['maɪkrəʊmeʃ] n: ~ stockings bas *mpl* super-fins.
micrometeorite ['maɪkrəʊ'mi:tɪə,raɪt] n micrométéorite *f*.
micrometeorologist ['maɪkrəʊmi:tɪə'rɒlədʒɪst] n micrométéorologue *mf*.
micrometeorology ['maɪkrəʊmi:tɪə'rɒlədʒɪ] n micrométéorologie *f*.
micrometer [maɪ'krɒmɪtəʳ] n micromètre *m*.
micrometry [maɪ'krɒmɪtrɪ] n micrométrie *f*.
microminiature [,maɪkrəʊ'mɪnɪtʃəʳ] n microminiature *f*.
microminiaturization ['maɪkrəʊ,mɪnɪtʃəraɪ'zeɪʃən] n microminiaturisation *f*.
microminiaturize ['maɪkrəʊ'mɪnɪtʃəraɪz] vt microminiaturiser.
micron ['maɪkrɒn] n, pl ~s *or* micra ['maɪkrə] micron *m*.
microorganism ['maɪkrəʊ'ɔ:gə,nɪzəm] n micro-organisme *m*.
microphone ['maɪkrə,fəʊn] n microphone *m*.
microphotograph ['maɪkrəʊ'fəʊtə,grɑ:f] 1 n microphotographie *f*. 2 vt microphotographier.
microphotographic ['maɪkrəʊ,fəʊtə'græfɪk] adj microphotographique.
microphotography ['maɪkrəʊfə'tɒgrəfɪ] n microphotographie *f*.
microphotometer ['maɪkrəʊfə'tɒmɪtəʳ] n microphotomètre *m*.
microphotometric ['maɪkrəʊfəʊtə'metrɪk] adj microphométrique.
microphotometry ['maɪkrəʊfə'tɒmɪtrɪ] n microphotométrie *f*.
microphysical ['maɪkrəʊ'fɪzɪkəl] adj microphysique.
microphysicist ['maɪkrəʊ'fɪzɪsɪst] n microphysicien(ne) *m(f)*.
microphysics ['maɪkrəʊ,fɪzɪks] n (*NonC*) microphysique.
microprism ['maɪkrəʊ,prɪzəm] n microprisme *m*.
microprobe ['maɪkrəʊ,prəʊb] n microsonde *f*.
microprocessor [,maɪkrəʊ'prəʊsesəʳ] n microprocesseur *m*.
microprogram ['maɪkrəʊ,prəʊgræm] n microprogramme *m*.
microprogramming ['maɪkrəʊ,prəʊgræmɪŋ] n (*Comput*) microprogrammation *f*.
microreader ['maɪkrəʊ,ri:dəʳ] n microliseuse *f*, microlecteur *m*.
microreproduction ['maɪkrəʊ,ri:prə'dʌkʃən] n microreproduction *f*.
microscope ['maɪkrəskəʊp] n microscope *m*. under the ~ au microscope.
microscopic [,maɪkrə'skɒpɪk] adj *detail, mark* microscopique; *examination* microscopique, au microscope. ~ section coupe *f* histologique.
microscopical [,maɪkrə'skɒpɪkəl] = microscopic.
microscopically [,maɪkrə'skɒpɪkəlɪ] adv au microscope. ~ small extrêmement petit.
microscopy [maɪ'krɒskəpɪ] n microscopie *f*.
microsecond ['maɪkrəʊ,sekənd] n microseconde *f*.
microstructural [,maɪkrəʊ'strʌktʃərəl] adj microstructural.
microstructure ['maɪkrəʊ,strʌktʃəʳ] n microstructure *f*.

microsurgery [ˈmaɪkrəʊˌsɜːdʒərɪ] n microchirurgie *f*.
microsurgical [ˌmaɪkrəʊˈsɜːdʒɪkəl] adj microchirurgical.
microtechnic, microtechnique [ˌmaɪkrəʊtekˈniːk] n microtechnique *f*.
microtransmitter [ˌmaɪkrəʊtrænzˈmɪtəʳ] n micro-émetteur *m*.
microvolt [ˈmaɪkrəʊˌvəʊlt] n microvolt *m*.
microwatt [ˈmaɪkrəʊˌwɒt] n microwatt *m*.
microwave [ˈmaɪkrəʊˌweɪv] 1 n micro-onde *f*. ~ **(oven)** four *m* à micro-ondes, micro-ondes* *m*; ~ **spectroscopy** spectroscopie *f* à ondes courtes. 2 vt faire cuire au micro-ondes*.
micturate [ˈmɪktjʊəreɪt] vi uriner.
micturition [ˌmɪktjʊəˈrɪʃən] n miction *f*.
mid[1] [mɪd] pref: ~ **May** la mi-mai; **in** ~ **May** à la mi-mai, au milieu (du mois) de mai; **in** ~ **morning** au milieu de la matinée; ~**-morning coffee break** pause café *f* du matin; **in** ~ **course** à mi-course; **in** ~ **ocean** en plein océan, au milieu de l'océan; **in** ~ **Atlantic** en plein Atlantique, au milieu de l'Atlantique; **a** ~**-Channel collision** une collision au milieu de la Manche; **in** ~ **discussion*** *etc* au beau milieu de la discussion *etc; see* **midday, midstream, mid-Victorian** *etc*.
mid[2] [mɪd] prep (*liter*) = **amid**.
midair [ˌmɪdˈɛəʳ] 1 n: **in** ~ (*lit*) en plein ciel; (*fig*) **to leave sth in** ~ laisser qch en suspens. 2 adj *collision etc* en plein ciel.
Midas [ˈmaɪdəs] n Midas *m*. (*fig*) **to have the** ~ **touch** avoir le don de tout transformer en or.
mid-Atlantic [ˌmɪdətˈlæntɪk] adj *accent* mi-britannique, mi-américain.
midbrain [ˈmɪdˌbreɪn] n mésencéphale *m*.
midday [ˌmɪdˈdeɪ] 1 n midi *m*. **at** ~ à midi. 2 [ˈmɪddeɪ] comp *sun, heat* de midi.
midden [ˈmɪdn] n (*dunghill*) fumier *m*; (*refuse-heap*) tas *m* d'ordures. **this place is (like) a** ~**!*** c'est une vraie écurie! *or* porcherie!, on se croirait dans une écurie! *or* porcherie!
middie [ˈmɪdɪ] n = **middy**.
middle [ˈmɪdl] 1 adj *chair, period etc* du milieu. (*fig*) **to take the** ~ **course** choisir le moyen terme *or* la solution intermédiaire; **these grapes are of** ~ **quality** ces raisins sont de qualité moyenne; **a man of** ~ **size** un homme de taille moyenne; **the** ~ **child** le moyen *or* la moyenne; *see also* **3**.
2 n a milieu *m*. **in the** ~ **of the room** au milieu de la pièce; **in the very** ~ **(of), right in the** ~ **(of)** au beau milieu (de); **the shot hit him in the** ~ **of his chest** le coup de feu l'a atteint en pleine poitrine; **in the** ~ **of the morning/year/century** au milieu de la matinée/de l'année/du siècle; **in the** ~ **of June** au milieu (du mois) de juin, à la mi-juin; **it's in the** ~ **of nowhere*** c'est en plein bled* *or* en pleine brousse*; **a village in the** ~ **of nowhere*** un petit trou perdu*; **I was in the** ~ **of my work** j'étais en plein travail; **I'm in the** ~ **of reading it** je suis justement en train de le lire; *see* **split**.
b (*: *waist*) taille *f*. **he wore it round his** ~ il le portait à la taille *or* autour de la taille; **in the water up to his** ~ dans l'eau jusqu'à mi-corps *or* la ceinture *or* la taille.
3 comp ▸**middle age** ≃ la cinquantaine; **he's reached middle age** il a près de la cinquantaine; **during his middle age** quand il n'était (déjà) plus jeune ▸**middle-aged** *person* d'un certain âge, entre deux âges; *outlook, attitude* vieux jeu *inv* ▸**the Middle Ages** le moyen âge ▸**Middle America** (*fig*) l'Amérique moyenne ▸**middlebrow*** n personne *f* sans grandes prétentions intellectuelles ◊ adj intellectuellement moyen ▸**middle C** (*Mus*) do *m* du milieu du piano ▸**middle-class** bourgeois; **the middle class(es)** les classes moyennes, la classe moyenne, la bourgeoisie ▸**middle distance: in the middle distance** (*Art etc*) au second plan; (*gen*) à mi-distance ▸**middle-distance runner/race** (*Sport*) coureur *m*, -euse *f*/course *f* de demi-fond ▸**middle ear** (*Anat*) oreille moyenne ▸**Middle East** Moyen-Orient *m* ▸**Middle Eastern** du Moyen-Orient ▸**Middle English** (*Ling*) moyen anglais ▸**middle finger** médius *m*, majeur *m* ▸**middle-grade manager** (*US*) cadre *m* moyen ▸**Middle French** (*Ling*) moyen français ▸**middle ground** terrain *m* d'entente ▸**Middle High German** (*Ling*) moyen haut allemand *m* ▸**the Middle Kingdom** (*Hist*) *[Egypt]* le Moyen Empire; *[China]* l'Empire du Milieu ▸**middleman** (*gen*) intermédiaire *m*; (*Comm*) intermédiaire, revendeur *m* ▸**middle management** cadres *mpl* moyens ▸**middle manager** cadre *m* moyen ▸**middlemost** = **midmost** ▸**middle name** deuxième nom *m*; (*Brit* * *fig*) **his middle name is Scrooge** il pourrait aussi bien s'appeler Harpagon ▸**middle-of-the-road** (*fig*) *politics, approach, group* modéré, centriste; *solution* moyen, du juste milieu; *music, fashion* neutre, sans excès ▸**middle-of-the-roader**, (*US*) **middle-roader** modéré(e) *m(f)*, centriste *mf*, partisan(e) *m(f)* du juste milieu ▸**middle school** ≃ premier cycle du secondaire ▸**middle-sized** *tree, building* de grandeur moyenne; *parcel* de grosseur moyenne; *person* de taille moyenne ▸**middle voice** (*Ling*) voix moyenne ▸**middleweight** (*Boxing*) n poids moyen ◊ adj *championship, boxer* de poids moyen ▸**Middle West** (*US*) Middle West *m*, grandes plaines *fpl* de l'intérieur des États-Unis.
middling [ˈmɪdlɪŋ] 1 adj *performance, result* moyen, passable. **of** ~ **size** de grandeur moyenne; **business is** ~ les affaires vont comme ci comme ça *or* ne vont ni bien ni mal; **how are you? —** ~* comment ça va? — moyennement *or* comme ci comme ça. 2 adv (*) assez, moyennement. ~ **well** assez bien; ~ **big** assez grand.
Middx abbr of **Middlesex**.
middy* [ˈmɪdɪ] n (*Naut*) (abbr of **midshipman**) midship* *m*.
midfield [ˈmɪdˌfiːld] n (*Ftbl*) milieu *m* de terrain.
midge [mɪdʒ] n moucheron *m*.
midget [ˈmɪdʒɪt] 1 n nain(e) *m(f)*; (*fig*) puce *f*. 2 adj minuscule.
midi [ˈmɪdɪ] 1 n (*skirt*) jupe *f* mi-longue. 2 adj (*hi-fi*) ~ **system** chaîne *f* (hi-fi) midi.
midland [ˈmɪdlənd] 1 n (*Brit Geog*) **the M**~**s** les comtés *mpl* du centre de l'Angleterre. 2 comp du centre (du pays) ▸**midland regions** régions *fpl* centrales ▸**Midland town** (*Brit*) ville *f* du centre de l'Angleterre.
midlife [ˈmɪdˌlaɪf] 1 adj de la quarantaine. ~ **crisis** crise *f* de la quarantaine. 2 adv autour de la quarantaine. 3 n: **in** ~ autour de la quarantaine.
midmost [ˈmɪdməʊst] adj le plus proche du milieu *or* centre.
midnight [ˈmɪdnaɪt] 1 n minuit *m*. **at** ~ à minuit. 2 comp de minuit ▸**midnight blue** n, **midnight-blue** adj bleu *m* nuit ▸**midnight oil: to burn the midnight oil** travailler (*or* lire *etc*) fort avant dans la nuit; **his essay smells of the midnight oil*** on dirait qu'il a passé la moitié de la nuit sur sa dissertation ▸**midnight sun** soleil *m* de minuit.
midpoint [ˈmɪdpɔɪnt] n milieu *m*.
midriff [ˈmɪdrɪf] n (*diaphragm*) diaphragme *m*; (*stomach*) estomac *m*; *[dress]* taille *f*. **dress with a bare** ~ robe découpée à la taille, robe (deux-pièces) laissant la taille nue.
mid-sentence [ˌmɪdˈsentəns] n: **in** ~ au beau milieu d'une phrase.
midshipman [ˈmɪdʃɪpmən] n (*Naut*) midshipman *m*, ≃ enseigne *m* de vaisseau de deuxième classe, aspirant *m*.
midships [ˈmɪdʃɪps] adv = **amidships**.
midsize [ˈmɪdˌsaɪz] adj de taille moyenne.
midst [mɪdst] 1 n: **in the** ~ **of** (*in the middle of*) au milieu de; (*surrounded by*) entouré de; (*among*) parmi; (*during*) pendant, au cours de, au milieu de; **in our** ~ parmi nous; (*liter*) **in the** ~ **of plenty** dans l'abondance; **in the** ~ **of life** au milieu de la vie; **I was in the** ~ **of saying*** j'étais en train de dire. 2 prep (*liter*) = **amidst**.
midstream [ˈmɪdˈstriːm] n: **in** ~ (*lit*) au milieu du courant; (*fig*) en plein milieu; (*when speaking*) au beau milieu d'une phrase.
midsummer [ˈmɪdˌsʌməʳ] 1 n (*height of summer*) milieu *m or* cœur *m* de l'été; (*solstice*) solstice *m* d'été. **in** ~ au cœur de l'été, en plein été; **at** ~ à la Saint-Jean. 2 comp *heat, weather, storm etc* estival, de plein été ▸**Midsummer Day** la Saint-Jean ▸**midsummer madness** (*fig*) pure démence ▸**"A Midsummer Night's Dream"** "le Songe d'une nuit d'été".
midterm [ˈmɪdˈtɜːm] 1 n a le milieu du trimestre. b (*also* ~ **holiday**) ≃ vacances *fpl* de (la) Toussaint (*or* de février *or* de Pentecôte). 2 comp ▸**midterm elections** ≃ élections *fpl* législatives (*intervenant au milieu du mandat présidentiel*) ▸**midterm exams** examens *mpl* de milieu de trimestre.
mid-Victorian [ˈmɪdvɪkˈtɔːrɪən] adj (*Brit*) du milieu de l'époque victorienne.
midway [ˌmɪdˈweɪ] 1 adj *place* (situé) à mi-chemin. 2 adv *stop, pause* à mi-chemin, à mi-route. ~ **between** à mi-chemin entre. 3 n (*US* = *in fair*) (centre *m* de la) fête foraine.
midweek [ˌmɪdˈwiːk] 1 adj du milieu de la semaine. (*Rail*) ~ **return (ticket)** (billet *m*) aller et retour *m* de milieu de semaine. 2 adv vers le milieu de la semaine.
Midwest [ˌmɪdˈwest] n (*US*) (les grandes plaines du) Middle West *m or* Midwest *m*.
Midwestern [ˌmɪdˈwestən] adj (*US*) du Middle West, du Midwest.
midwife [ˈmɪdwaɪf] n sage-femme *f*.
midwifery [ˈmɪdwɪfərɪ] n (*NonC*) obstétrique *f*.
midwinter [ˌmɪdˈwɪntəʳ] 1 n (*heart of winter*) milieu *m or* fort *m* de l'hiver; (*solstice*) solstice *m* d'hiver. **in** ~ au cœur de l'hiver, en plein hiver; **at** ~ au solstice d'hiver. 2 comp *cold, snow, temperature* hivernal, de plein hiver.
mien [miːn] n (*frm, liter*) contenance *f*, air *m*, mine *f*.
miff‡ [mɪf] 1 n (*quarrel*) fâcherie *f*; (*sulks*) bouderie *f*. 2 vt fâcher, mettre en boule*. **to be** ~**ed about** *or* **at sth** être fâché *or* vexé de qch.
might[1] [maɪt] 1 modal aux vb *see* **may**[1]. 2 comp ▸**might-have-been** ce qui aurait pu être, espoir déçu, vœu non comblé; (*person*) raté(e) *m(f)*, fruit sec.
might[2] [maɪt] n (*NonC*) puissance *f*, force(s) *f(pl)*. (*Prov*) ~ **is right** la force prime le droit; **with** ~ **and main, with all one's** ~ de toutes ses forces.
mightily [ˈmaɪtɪlɪ] adv (*powerfully*) puissamment, vigoureusement; (*†: *very*) rudement*, bigrement*.
mightiness [ˈmaɪtɪnɪs] n puissance *f*, pouvoir *m*, grandeur *f*.
mightn't [ˈmaɪtnt] = **might not**; *see* **may**[1].
mighty [ˈmaɪtɪ] 1 adj a *nation, king* puissant; *achievement* formidable, considérable; *ocean* vaste et puissant; *mountain, tree* imposant, majestueux; *see* **high**. b (*) sacré* (*before noun*). **he was in a** ~ **rage** il était sacrément* en colère; **there was a** ~ **row about it** cela a provoqué une sacrée bagarre* *or* un sacré chambard‡. 2 adv (*) rudement*, sacrément*, bigrement*, bougrement‡. **you think yourself**

~ clever! tu te crois très fin! *or* malin!; **I'm ~ sorry that ...** je regrette rudement* *or* sacrément* que ...; **you've got to be ~ careful** il faut faire rudement* *or* sacrément* attention.

mignonette [ˌmɪnjəˈnet] n réséda *m*.

migraine [ˈmiːgreɪn] n (*Med*) migraine *f*. **it gives me a ~** ça me donne la migraine.

migrant [ˈmaɪgrənt] 1 adj *bird, animal* migrateur (*f* -trice); *tribe* nomade, migrateur. **~ worker** (*Ind*) travailleur *m* itinérant; (*foreign*) travailleur étranger *or* immigré; (*Agr*) (travailleur) saisonnier *m*; (*Ind*) **~ labour** main-d'œuvre itinérante (*or* saisonnière *or* étrangère). 2 n a (*bird, animal*) migrateur *m*; (*person*) nomade *mf*. b = **~ worker**; *see* **1**.

migrate [maɪˈgreɪt] vi migrer.

migration [maɪˈgreɪʃən] n migration *f*.

migratory [maɪˈgreɪtərɪ] adj *bird, tribe* migrateur (*f* -trice); *movement, journey* migratoire.

mikado [mɪˈkɑːdəʊ] n mikado *m*.

Mike [maɪk] n a (dim of **Michael**). b **for the love of ~*** pour l'amour du ciel.

mike* [maɪk] n (abbr of **microphone**) micro *m*.

milady† [mɪˈleɪdɪ] n madame la comtesse *etc*.

Milan [mɪˈlæn] n Milan.

Milanese [ˌmɪləˈniːz] adj (*gen, also Culin*) milanais.

milch [mɪltʃ] adj: **~ cow** vache laitière.

mild [maɪld] 1 adj *person* doux (*f* douce), peu *or* pas sévère; *voice, temper* doux; *reproach, punishment* léger; *exercise, effect, protest* modéré; *climate* doux, tempéré; *winter* doux, clément; *breeze* doux, faible; *flavour, cheese, soap, shampoo, tobacco* doux; *beer* léger; *sauce* peu épicé *or* relevé; *medicine* bénin (*f* -igne), anodin; *illness* bénin. **it's ~ today** il fait doux aujourd'hui; (*Met*) **a ~ spell** (*gen*) une période clémente; (*after frost*) un redoux; **he had a ~ form of polio** il a eu la poliomyélite sous une forme bénigne *or* atténuée; **a ~ sedative** un sédatif léger; (*Brit*) **~ ale** *bière anglaise pas très forte*; (*Culin*) **a ~ curry** un curry pas trop fort *or* pimenté. 2 n (*Brit: beer*) *bière anglaise pas très forte*.

mildew [ˈmɪldjuː] 1 n (*NonC*) (*gen*) moisissure *f*; (*on wheat, roses etc*) rouille *f*; (*on vine*) mildiou *m*. 2 vt *plant* piquer de rouille; *vine* frapper de mildiou; *paper, cloth* piquer (d'humidité). 3 vi *[roses, wheat etc]* se rouiller; *[vine]* devenir mildiousé, être attaqué par le mildiou; *[paper, cloth]* se piquer.

mildewed [ˈmɪlˌdjuːd] adj (*gen*) moisi; *cloth, paper* piqué (par l'humidité); *wheat, roses* piqué de rouille; *vine* mildiousé.

mildly [ˈmaɪldlɪ] adv doucement, avec douceur; (*Med*) bénignement, légèrement. **he's not very clever to put it ~*** pour ne pas dire plus, il n'est pas très intelligent; **that's putting it ~!*** c'est le moins qu'on puisse (en) dire!, c'est un euphémisme!

mild-mannered [ˌmaɪldˈmænəd] adj: **to be ~** avoir un tempérament doux, être d'une disposition douce.

mildness [ˈmaɪldnɪs] n (*see* **mild**) douceur *f*; clémence *f*; bénignité *f*; modération *f*; légèreté *f*; saveur peu relevée.

mile [maɪl] 1 n mile *m or* mille *m* (= *1.609,33 m*). **a 50-~ journey** ≃ un trajet de 80 km; (*Aut*) **30 ~s per gallon** ≃ 8 litres aux cent (km); **50 ~s per hour** ≃ 80 kilomètres à l'heure; **there was nothing but sand for ~s and ~s** il n'y avait que du sable sur des kilomètres (et des kilomètres); (*fig*) **not a hundred ~s from here** sans aller chercher bien loin; **we've walked (for) ~s!** on a marché pendant des kilomètres!, on a fait des kilomètres!; **they live ~s away** ils habitent à cent lieues d'ici; **you could see/smell it a ~ off** ça se voyait/se sentait d'une lieue; **you were ~s off (the) target*** vous n'étiez pas près de toucher la cible, vous étiez bien loin du but; **he's ~s* bigger than you** il est bien plus grand que toi; **she's ~s better than I am at maths*** elle est bien plus calée que moi en maths*. 2 comp ►**milepost** ≃ poteau *m* kilométrique ►**milestone** (*lit*) borne *f* (milliaire), ≃ borne kilométrique; (*fig: in life, career etc*) jalon *m*, événement marquant *or* déterminant.

mileage [ˈmaɪlɪdʒ] 1 n (*Aut etc*) (*distance covered*) distance *f or* parcours *m* en milles, ≃ kilométrage *m*; (*distance per gallon etc*) ≃ consommation *f* (de carburant) aux cent (km). **the indicator showed a very low ~** le compteur marquait peu de kilomètres; **the car had a low ~** la voiture avait peu roulé *or* avait peu de kilomètres; **what ~ has this car done?** quel est le kilométrage de cette voiture?, combien de kilomètres a cette voiture?; **for a car of that size the ~ was very good** pour une voiture aussi puissante elle consommait peu; **you'll get a better ~ from this car** vous consommerez moins (d'essence) avec cette voiture; (*fig*) **he got a lot of ~ out of it** (*of idea, story, event*) il en a tiré le maximum; (*of coat, gadget etc*) ça lui a fait de l'usage; **there's still some ~ left in it** *[idea etc]* on peut encore en tirer quelque chose; *[coat etc]* ça peut encore faire de l'usage; *see* **gas**. 2 comp ►**mileage allowance** (*Admin etc*) ≃ indemnité *f* kilométrique ►**mileage indicator** (*Aut*) ≃ compteur *m* kilométrique.

mileometer [maɪˈlɒmɪtəʳ] n = **milometer**.

milieu [ˈmiːljɜː] n, pl **~s** milieu *m* (social).

militant [ˈmɪlɪtənt] adj, n (*all senses*) militant(e) *m(f)*.

militarily [ˌmɪlɪˈtərɪlɪ] adv militairement.

militarism [ˈmɪlɪtərɪzəm] n militarisme *m*.

militarist [ˈmɪlɪtərɪst] adj, n militariste *(mf)*.

militaristic [ˌmɪlɪtəˈrɪstɪk] adj militariste.

militarize [ˈmɪlɪtəraɪz] vt militariser.

military [ˈmɪlɪtərɪ] 1 adj *government, life, uniform* militaire; *family* de militaires. (*US*) **~ academy** (*Scol*) prytanée *m* militaire; (*Univ*) École *f* (spéciale) militaire; **of ~ age** d'âge à faire son service (militaire *or* national); **~ attaché** attaché *m* militaire; **~ band** musique *f* militaire; **~ police** police *f* militaire; **~ policeman** agent *m* de la police militaire; **~ superiority** supériorité *f* militaire; **~ training** préparation *f* militaire; **to do one's ~ service** faire son service (militaire *or* national). 2 collective n: **the ~** l'armée *f*, le(s) militaire(s) *m(pl)*. 3 comp ►**military-industrial complex** complexe *m* militaro-industriel.

militate [ˈmɪlɪteɪt] vi militer (*against* contre, *for, in favour of* pour).

militia [mɪˈlɪʃə] 1 collective n (*gen*) milice(s) *f(pl)*. (*US*) **the ~** la réserve (territoriale); *see* **state**. 2 comp ►**militiaman** milicien *m*.

milk [mɪlk] 1 n lait *m*. **coconut ~** lait de coco; (*fig*) **the ~ of human kindness** le lait de la tendresse humaine; (*fig*) **a land flowing with ~ and honey** un pays de cocagne; (*hum*) **he came home with the ~*** il est rentré avec le jour *or* à potron-minet*; *see* **condense, cry, skim** *etc*.

2 vt a *cow* traire.

b (*fig: extract*) dépouiller (*of* de), exploiter. **his son ~ed him of all his savings** son fils l'a dépouillé de toutes ses économies; **it ~ed (him of) his strength** cela a sapé *or* miné ses forces; **to ~ sb of ideas/information** soutirer des idées/des renseignements à qn; **to ~ sb dry** exploiter qn à fond, épuiser les forces créatrices de qn.

3 vi: **to go ~ing** (s'en) aller traire ses vaches.

4 comp ►**milk-and-water** (*fig pej*) dilué, insipide ►**milk bar** milk-bar *m* ►**milk can** boîte *f* à lait, pot *m* à lait; (*larger*) bidon *m* à lait ►**milk chocolate** chocolat *m* au lait ►**milk churn** bidon *m* à lait ►**milk diet** régime lacté ►**milk duct** (*Anat*) vaisseau *m* galactophore ►**milk fever** fièvre *f* lactée ►**milk float** (*Brit*) voiture *f* de laitier ►**milk gland** (*Anat*) glande *f* galactogène ►**milk jug** (petit) pot *m* à lait ►**milkmaid** trayeuse *f* ►**milkman** laitier *m* ►**milk of magnesia** lait *m* de magnésie, magnésie hydratée ►**milk pan** petite casserole *f* pour le lait ►**milk powder** lait *m* en poudre ►**milk products** produits laitiers ►**milk pudding** entremets *m* au lait ►**milk round** (*Brit*) tournée *f* (du laitier); (*Univ*) tournée *f* de recrutement dans les universités; *[child etc]* **to do a milk round** livrer le lait ►**milk run*** (*Aviat*) vol *m* sans accroc ►**milk saucepan** petite casserole *f* pour le lait ►**milk shake** milk-shake *m*, lait frappé parfumé ►**milksop*** (*pej*) chiffe molle* (*fig*), lavette* *f* (*fig*), mollusque* *m* (*fig*) ►**milk tooth** dent *f* de lait ►**the milk train** (*fig*) le tout premier train (de très bonne heure) ►**milkweed** (*Bot*) laiteron *m* ►**milk-white** (*liter*) d'une blancheur de lait, blanc (*f* blanche) comme le *or* du lait.

milking [ˈmɪlkɪŋ] 1 n traite *f*. 2 comp *pail, stool* à traire ►**milking machine** trayeuse *f* (mécanique) ►**milking time** l'heure *f* de la traite.

milky [ˈmɪlkɪ] adj (*lit*) *diet, product* lacté; (*fig: in colour etc*) laiteux. **~ coffee/tea** café *m*/thé *m* au lait; **I like my coffee ~** j'aime le café avec beaucoup de lait; **a ~ drink** une boisson à base de lait; (*Astron*) **M~ Way** Voie lactée.

mill [mɪl] 1 n a (*wind ~ or water ~*) moulin *m*; (*Ind: for grain*) minoterie *f*; (*small: for coffee etc*) moulin. **wind~** moulin à vent; **pepper-~** moulin à poivre; (*fig*) **to go through the ~** passer par de dures épreuves, en voir de dures*; (*fig*) **to put sb through the ~** mettre qn à l'épreuve, en faire voir de dures à qn*; *see* **coffee, run** *etc*. b (*factory*) usine *f*, fabrique *f*; (*spinning ~*) filature *f*; (*weaving ~*) tissage *m*; (*steel ~*) aciérie *f*. **paper ~** (usine *f* de) papeterie *f*; **cotton ~** filature de coton; *see* **saw¹** *etc*.

2 comp ►**millboard** carton *m* pâte ►**mill girl** (*Ind*) ouvrière *f* des tissages *or* des filatures ►**millhand** (*Ind*) = **mill worker** ►**mill owner** (*Ind*) industriel *m* (du textile) ►**millpond** bief *m or* retenue *f* d'un moulin; **the sea was like a millpond** la mer était d'huile, la mer était (comme) un lac ►**mill race** bief *m* d'amont *or* de moulin ►**millstone** (*lit*) meule *f*; (*fig*) **it's a millstone round his neck** c'est un boulet qu'il traîne avec lui ►**mill stream** courant *m* du bief ►**mill wheel** roue *f* d'un moulin ►**mill worker** (*Ind*) ouvrier *m*, -ière *f* des filatures (*or* tissages *or* aciéries) ►**millwright** constructeur *m or* installateur *m* de moulins.

3 vt a *flour, coffee, pepper* moudre; *vegetables* broyer.

b (*Tech*) *screw, nut* moleter; *wheel, edge of coin* créneler. *[coin]* **~ed edge** crénelage *m*, grènetis *m*.

4 vi *[crowd etc]* **to ~ round sth** grouiller autour de qch.

►**mill about, mill around** vi *[crowd]* grouiller, fourmiller; *[cattle etc]* tourner sur place *or* en rond.

millenary [mɪˈlenərɪ] adj, n, **millennial** [mɪˈlenɪəl] adj, n millénaire *(m)*.

millennium [mɪˈlenɪəm] n, pl **~s** *or* **millennia** [mɪˈlenɪə] millénaire *m*. (*Rel, also fig*) **the ~** le millénium.

millepede [ˈmɪlɪpiːd] n = **millipede**.

miller [ˈmɪləʳ] n meunier *m*; (*Ind: large-scale*) minotier *m*.

millet [ˈmɪlɪt] n (*NonC*) millet *m*.

milli... [ˈmɪlɪ] pref milli... .

milliard [ˈmɪlɪɑːd] n *(Brit)* milliard *m*.

millibar [ˈmɪlɪbɑːʳ] n millibar *m*.

milligram(me) [ˈmɪlɪɡræm] n milligramme *m*.

millilitre, *(US)* **milliliter** [ˈmɪlɪˌliːtəʳ] n millilitre *m*.

millimetre, *(US)* **millimeter** [ˈmɪlɪˌmiːtəʳ] n millimètre *m*.

milliner [ˈmɪlɪnəʳ] n modiste *f*, chapelier *m*, -ière *f*.

millinery [ˈmɪlɪnərɪ] n *(NonC)* modes *fpl*, chapellerie féminine.

milling [ˈmɪlɪŋ] 1 n *(NonC)* *[flour etc]* moulure *f*; *[screw etc]* moletage *m*; *[coin]* crénelage *m*. 2 adj: **the ~ crowd** la foule grouillante *or* en remous.

million [ˈmɪljən] n, pl **~s** *or* **~** million *m*. **a ~ men** un million d'hommes; **he's one in a ~*** c'est la crème des hommes *or* la perle des hommes; **it's a chance** *(etc)* **in a ~** c'est une occasion *(etc)* unique; *(fig)* **~s of*** des milliers de; **thanks a ~!*** merci mille fois!; *(US)* **to feel like a ~ (dollars)*** se sentir dans une forme époustouflante*.

millionaire [ˌmɪljəˈnɛəʳ] n millionnaire *m*, ≃ milliardaire *m*.

millionth [ˈmɪljənθ] 1 adj millionième. 2 n millionième *mf*; *(fraction)* millionième *m*.

millipede [ˈmɪlɪpiːd] n mille-pattes *m inv*.

millisecond [ˈmɪlɪˌsekənd] n milliseconde *f*.

Mills bomb [ˈmɪlzˌbɒm] n grenade *f* à main.

milometer [maɪˈlɒmɪtəʳ] n *(Brit)* compteur *m* de milles, ≃ compteur kilométrique.

milord [mɪˈlɔːd] n milord *m*.

milt [mɪlt] n laitance *f*, laite *f*.

mime [maɪm] 1 n *(Theat)* *(skill, classical play)* mime *m*; *(actor)* mime *m*; *(modern play)* mimodrame *m*; *(fig: gestures etc)* mimique *f*. 2 vti mimer. **to ~ to a tape** *(sing etc)* chanter *etc* en playback.

mimeo [ˈmɪmɪəʊ] (abbr of **mimeograph**) 1 n Ronéo *f* ®. 2 vt ronéoter*.

mimeograph [ˈmɪmɪəɡrɑːf] ® 1 n *(machine)* machine *f* à ronéotyper; *(copy)* Ronéo *f* ®. 2 vt ronéotyper, ronéoter*.

mimic [ˈmɪmɪk] 1 n imitateur *m*, -trice *f*; *(burlesquing)* imitateur, -trice, singe *m*. 2 adj a *(imitating)* imitateur *(f* -trice), singe. b *(sham)* factice, simulé. **~ battle** bataille simulée. 3 vt *(copy)* imiter; *(burlesque)* imiter, singer, contrefaire.

mimicry [ˈmɪmɪkrɪ] n *(NonC)* imitation *f*; *(Zool: also* **protective ~***)* mimétisme *m*.

mimosa [mɪˈməʊzə] n mimosa *m*.

Min. *(Brit)* abbr of **Ministry**.

min. a (abbr of **minute**[1]) mn, min. b (abbr of **minimum**) min.

mina [ˈmaɪnə] = **mynah**

minaret [ˈmɪnəret] n minaret *m*.

minatory [ˈmɪnətərɪ] adj comminatoire, menaçant.

mince [mɪns] 1 n *(Brit Culin)* bifteck haché, hachis *m* de viande.

2 comp ▶**mincemeat** *(Culin)* *(Brit)* *hachis de fruits secs, de pommes et de graisse, imbibé de cognac*; *(US)* = **mince 1**; *(fig)* **to make mincemeat of** *opponent, enemy* battre à plate(s) couture(s)*, pulvériser; *theories, arguments* pulvériser ▶**mince pie** *(Culin)* tartelette *f* de Noël (au mincemeat).

3 vt a *(Brit)* *meat, vegetables* hacher. **~d beef** bœuf *m* haché.

b *(fig)* **he didn't ~ (his) words, he didn't ~ matters** il n'a pas mâché ses mots, il n'y est pas allé par quatre chemins; **he didn't ~ matters with me** il ne m'a pas mâché ses mots, il n'a pas pris de gants pour me le dire, il m'a parlé sans ambages; **not to ~ matters she just wasn't good enough** pour parler carrément *or* sans ambages elle n'était pas à la hauteur.

4 vi *(in talking)* parler du bout des lèvres; *(in walking)* marcher à petits pas maniérés. **to ~ in/out** entrer/sortir à petits pas maniérés.

▶**mince up** vt sep *(Culin etc)* hacher.

mincer [ˈmɪnsəʳ] n hachoir *m* *(appareil)*.

mincing [ˈmɪnsɪŋ] 1 adj affecté, minaudier. **with ~ steps** à petits pas maniérés. 2 comp ▶**mincing machine** hachoir *m*.

mincingly [ˈmɪnsɪŋlɪ] adv d'une manière affectée, en minaudant.

mind [maɪnd] 1 n a esprit *m*; *(intellect)* esprit, intelligence *f*; *(as opposed to matter)* esprit; *(sanity)* raison *f*; *(memory)* souvenir *m*, mémoire *f*; *(opinion)* avis *m*, idée *f*; *(intention)* intention *f*. **it's all in the ~** tout ça, c'est dans la tête* (que ça se passe); **in one's ~'s eye** en imagination; **his ~ is going** il n'a plus tout à fait sa tête, il baisse; **his ~ went blank** il a eu un trou *or* un passage à vide, ça a été le vide complet dans sa tête; **I'm not clear in my own ~ about it** je ne sais pas qu'en penser moi-même; **to have a closed ~ (on/about sth)** avoir des idées *or* opinions arrêtées (sur/au sujet de qch); **to be easy in one's ~** avoir l'esprit tranquille; **to be uneasy in one's ~ (about sth)** avoir des doutes (sur qch), être inquiet *(f* -ète) (au sujet de qch); **he is one of the great ~s of the century** c'est un des (grands) cerveaux du siècle; *(Prov)* **great ~s think alike** les grands esprits se rencontrent; **it was a case of ~ over matter** c'était la victoire de l'esprit sur la matière; **of sound ~** sain d'esprit; **of unsound ~** ne jouissant plus de toutes ses facultés (mentales); **to be in one's right ~** avoir toute sa raison *or* sa tête; **nobody in their right ~ would do that** aucun être sensé ne ferait cela; **to be out of one's (right) ~** ne plus avoir toute sa raison *or* sa tête; **you must be out of your ~!*** ça va pas!*; **he went out of his ~** il a perdu la tête *or* la raison; **with one ~** comme un seul homme; **they were of one** *or* **like ~** *or* **the same ~** ils étaient d'accord *or* du même avis; **to be in two ~s about sth/about doing** se tâter *(fig)* *or* être irrésolu pour ce qui est de qch/de faire; **I'm still of the same ~** je n'ai pas changé d'avis; **I was of the same ~ as my brother** j'étais du même avis que mon frère, je partageais l'opinion de mon frère; **what's on your ~?** qu'est-ce qui vous préoccupe? *or* vous tracasse? *(see also* **1b**); **that's a load** *or* **a weight off my ~** c'est un gros souci de moins, cela m'ôte un poids; **I was of a ~** *or* **it was in my ~ to go and see him** je pensais aller le voir; **to my ~** à mon avis; **nothing is further from my ~!** (bien) loin de moi cette pensée!; **nothing was further from my ~ than going to see her** (bien) loin de moi la pensée d'aller la voir, je n'avais nullement l'intention d'aller la voir; *see* **change 3a, cross 4a, frame, sight, state** *etc*.

b *(in verbal phrases)* **to bear sth in ~** *(take account of)* tenir compte de qch; *(remember)* ne pas oublier qch; **I'll bear you in ~** je songerai *or* penserai à vous; **bear it in ~!** songez-y bien!; **to bring one's ~ to bear on sth** porter *or* concentrer son attention sur qch, appliquer son esprit à l'étude de qch; **to bring** *or* **call sth to ~** rappeler qch, évoquer qch; **to come** *or* **spring to ~** venir à l'esprit; **it came (in)to** *or* **entered my ~ that ...** il m'est venu à l'esprit que ..., l'idée m'est venue que ...; **you must get it into your ~ that ...** tu dois te mettre en tête *or* dans la tête que ...; **I can't get it out of my ~** je ne peux m'empêcher d'y penser; **to give one's ~ to sth** appliquer son esprit à qch, se concentrer sur qch; **he can't give his whole ~ to his work** il n'arrive pas à se concentrer sur son travail; **it went quite** *or* **right** *or* **clean* out of my ~** je l'ai complètement oublié, cela m'est complètement sorti de la tête*; **you can do it if you have a ~ (to)** vous pouvez le faire si vous le voulez *or* désirez vraiment; **I have no ~ to offend him** je n'ai aucune envie de l'offenser; **to have (it) in ~ to do** avoir dans l'idée de faire; **to have a ~ of one's own** *[person]* avoir ses idées; *[machine]* avoir des caprices; **I've a good ~ to do it*** j'ai bien envie de le faire, je crois bien que je vais le faire; **I've half a ~ to do it*** j'ai presque envie de le faire, ça me tente de le faire; **have you (got) anything particular in ~?** avez-vous quelque chose de particulier dans l'idée?; **whom have you in ~ for the job?** à qui songez-vous *or* qui avez-vous en vue pour le poste?; **to have sth on one's ~** avoir l'esprit préoccupé de qch; **to have something at the back of one's ~** *(gen)* avoir une idée dans la tête; *(pej: scheming etc)* avoir une idée derrière la tête; **at the back of my ~ I had the feeling that ...** au fond de moi j'avais le sentiment que ...; **to keep sth in ~** ne pas oublier qch; **to have one's ~ on sth** être préoccupé par qch; **to have one's ~ on sth else** avoir la tête* autre part; **to keep one's ~ on sth** se concentrer sur qch; **to know one's own ~** avoir des idées bien arrêtées, savoir ce que l'on veut; **to let one's ~ run on sth** se laisser aller à penser à qch, laisser ses pensées s'attarder sur qch; **to let one's ~ wander** laisser flotter ses pensées *or* son attention; **to make up one's ~ to do sth** prendre la décision *or* décider de faire qch; **we can't make up our ~s about the house** nous ne savons à quoi nous résoudre *or* nous ne savons quelle décision prendre pour la maison; **I can't make up my ~ about him** *(form opinion of)* je ne sais que penser de lui; *(decide about)* je n'arrive pas à me décider sur son compte; *(liter)* **to pass out of ~** tomber dans l'oubli; **that puts me in ~ of ...** cela me rappelle ...; **you can put that right out of your ~!** tu peux te dépêcher d'oublier tout ça!; **try to put it out of your ~** essayez de ne plus y penser; **to put** *or* **set one's ~ to a problem** s'attaquer à un problème; **you can do it if you put** *or* **set your ~ to it** tu peux le faire si tu t'y appliques; **to read sb's ~, to see into sb's ~** lire (jusqu'au fond de) la pensée de qn; **to set one's ~ on (doing) sth** vouloir fermement (faire) qch; **to set** *or* **put sb's ~ at ease** *or* **rest** rassurer qn; **to stick in one's ~** rester gravé dans sa mémoire; **this will take her ~ off her troubles** cela lui changera les idées, cela la distraira de ses ennuis; **the noise takes my ~ off my work** le bruit m'empêche de me concentrer sur mon travail; *see* **cross, improve, piece, slip, speak** *etc*.

2 comp ▶**mind-bender*** *(US)* révélation *f* ▶**mind-bending*, mind-blowing*** *drug* hallucinogène; *experience, news, scene* hallucinant ▶**mind-boggling*** époustouflant*, ahurissant ▶**mind-expanding** *drug etc* hallucinogène ▶**mindful** *see* **mindful** ▶**mind-numbing, mind-numbingly boring** ennuyeux à mourir ▶**mind reader** *(lit)* liseur *m*, -euse *f* de pensées; *(fig)* **he's a mind reader!** il lit dans la pensée des gens!; **I'm not a mind reader!*** je ne suis pas devin!* ▶**mind reading** divination *f* par télépathie ▶**mind-set** *(esp US)* tournure *f* d'esprit, mentalité *f*.

3 vt a *(pay attention to)* faire *or* prêter attention à; *(beware of)* prendre garde à; *(US: listen to)* écouter. **never ~!** *(don't worry)* ne t'en fais pas!, ne t'inquiète pas!; *(it makes no odds)* ça ne fait rien!, peu importe!; **never you ~!*** occupe-toi de tes affaires!*; **never ~ that now!** *(soothingly)* n'y pense plus (maintenant)!; *(irritably)* tu ne vas pas m'ennuyer avec ça maintenant!; **never ~ him!** ne t'occupe pas de lui!, ignore-le!; **he can't walk, never ~ run** il ne peut pas marcher, encore moins courir; *(iro)* **don't ~ me!*** ne vous gênez surtout pas (pour moi)!* *(iro)*; **never ~ the expense!** tant pis pour le prix!, ne regarde pas à la dépense!; **~ your language** *or* **tongue/your manners!** surveille ton langage/tes manières!; **to ~ one's Ps and Qs** faire attention à ce que l'on fait *or* à ce que l'on dit, se surveiller; **~ how you go*** prends bien soin de toi; **~ what I say!** écoute bien ce que je te

dis!, fais bien attention à ce que je te dis!; ~ **what you're doing!** (fais) attention à ce que tu fais!; ~ **the step!** attention *or* gare à la marche!; ~ **your head!** attention *or* gare à votre tête!; ~ **your backs!** gare à vous!, dégagez!*; ~ **yourself!**, ~ **your eye!**‡ prends garde!, fais gaffe!‡; ~ **you don't fall!** prenez garde de ne pas tomber!; ~ **you tell her!** ne manquez pas de le lui dire!; ~ **and come to see us!*** n'oublie pas de venir nous voir!; **be there at 10, ~*** tâche d'être là à 10 heures; ~ **you, I didn't know he was going to Paris** remarquez, je ne savais pas qu'il allait à Paris; ~ **you, it isn't easy** ce n'est pas facile, vous savez *or* je vous assure; ~ **you, he could be right** *or* **he could be right, ~*** peut-être qu'il a raison après tout; **I sold the car for £1500 and ~ you I had had it 4 years** j'ai vendu la voiture 1.500 livres et avec ça* *or* remarque, je l'avais gardée 4 ans; *see* **business**.

b (*object to*) **do you ~ if I take this book? — I don't ~ at all** cela ne vous fait rien *or* ça ne vous ennuie pas que je prenne ce livre? — mais non, je vous en prie!; **which do you want? — I don't ~** lequel voulez-vous? — ça m'est égal; **did you ~ my** *or* **me* telling you that?** auriez-vous préféré que je ne vous le dise pas?; **did she ~ (it) when he got married?** a-t-elle été malheureuse quand il s'est marié?; **if you don't ~** si cela ne vous fait rien; (*iro: indignantly*) non, mais!; **if you don't ~ my** *or* **me* saying** si je puis me permettre; **I don't ~ going with you** je veux bien vous accompagner; **I don't ~ the cold** je ne crains pas le froid; **I don't ~ country life but I prefer the town** vivre à la campagne ne me déplaît pas, mais je préfère la ville; **would you ~ opening the door?** cela vous ennuierait d'ouvrir la porte?; **would you ~ coming with me?** cela vous dérangerait de m'accompagner?; (*abruptly*) je vous prie de m'accompagner; **do you ~ the noise?** le bruit vous gêne-t-il?; **I don't ~ what people say** je me moque du qu'en-dira-t-on; **I don't ~ him but I hate her!** lui passe encore, mais elle je la déteste!; **cigarette? — I don't ~ (if I do)*** une cigarette? — c'est pas de refus!*; **I wouldn't ~ a cup of coffee** une tasse de café ne serait pas de refus*, je prendrais bien une tasse de café.

c (*take charge of*) *children* garder, surveiller, prendre soin de; *animals* garder; *shop, business* garder, tenir. (*fig*) **to ~ the shop*** *or* (*US*) **the store*** veiller au grain.

d (‡ *or dial: remember*) se souvenir de, se rappeler.

►**mind out*** vi faire attention, faire gaffe‡. **mind out!** attention!; **mind out of the way!** ôtez-vous de là!, dégagez!*; **mind out or you'll break it** faites attention de ne pas le casser.

minded ['maɪndɪd] adj: **if you are so ~** si le cœur vous en dit, si vous y êtes disposé; ~ **to do sth** disposé *or* enclin à faire qch.

-minded ['maɪndɪd] adj ending in comps a qui est ... d'esprit, *e.g.* **feeble-minded** faible d'esprit; *see* **high-, strong-minded** *etc.* b qui s'intéresse à ..., *e.g.* **business-minded** qui a le sens des affaires; **he's become very ecology-minded** il est très sensibilisé sur l'écologie maintenant; **an industrially-minded nation** une nation orientée vers l'industrie, une nation aux options industrielles; **a romantically-minded girl** une jeune fille aux idées romantiques; *see* **family, like**[1] *etc.*

minder ['maɪndə^r] n a (*also* **baby-~, child-~**) gardienne *f.* b (*: *bodyguard etc*) ange *m* gardien (*fig*).

mindful ['maɪndfʊl] adj: ~ **of** attentif à, soucieux de; **be ~ of what I said** songez à ce que j'ai dit.

mindless ['maɪndlɪs] adj a (*stupid*) stupide, idiot. b (*unmindful*) ~ **of** oublieux de, indifférent à, inattentif à.

mine[1] [maɪn] 1 poss pron le mien, la mienne, les mien(ne)s. **this pencil is ~** ce crayon est le mien *or* à moi; **this poem is ~** ce poème est de moi; (*frm*) **will you be ~?** voulez-vous m'épouser?; **the house became ~** la maison est devenue (la) mienne; **no advice of ~ could prevent him** aucun conseil de ma part ne pouvait l'empêcher; **no it's ~** non, c'est à moi *or* le mien; **which dress do you prefer, hers or ~?** quelle robe préférez-vous, la sienne ou la mienne?; **a friend of ~** un de mes amis, un ami à moi; **it's no fault of ~** ce n'est pas (de) ma faute; **what is ~ is yours** ce qui est à moi est à toi, ce qui m'appartient t'appartient; (*frm*) **it is not ~ to decide** ce n'est pas à moi de décider, il ne m'appartient pas de décider; ~ **is a specialized department** ma section est une section spécialisée.

2 poss adj (†† *or liter*) mon, ma, mes; *see* **host**[1].

mine[2] [maɪn] 1 n a (*Min*) mine *f.* **coal~** mine de charbon; **to go down the ~s** travailler *or* descendre à la mine; **to work a ~** exploiter une mine; (*fig*) **a real ~ of information** une véritable mine *or* une source inépuisable de renseignements.

b (*Mil, Naut etc*) mine *f.* **to lay a ~** mouiller *or* poser une mine; **to clear a beach of ~s** déminer une plage; *see* **land** *etc.*

2 vt a (*Min*) *coal, ore* extraire.

b (*Mil, Naut etc*) *sea, beach* miner, semer de mines; *ship, tank* miner.

3 vi exploiter un gisement. **to ~ for coal** extraire du charbon, exploiter une mine (de charbon).

4 comp ►**mine-clearing** (*Mil, Naut*) déminage *m* ►**mine detector** (*Mil*) détecteur *m* de mines ►**mine disposal** (*Mil*) déminage *m* ►**minefield** (*Mil, Naut*) champ *m* de mines; (*fig*) **it's a legal/political minefield** c'est un sac d'embrouilles* juridiques/politiques ►**mine-hunter** (*Naut*) chasseur *m* de mines ►**minelayer** (*Naut*) mouilleur *m* de mines ►**minelaying** (*Naut*) mouillage *m* de mines ►**mineshaft** (*Min*) puits *m* de mine ►**minesweeper** (*Naut*) dragueur *m* de mines ►**mine-sweeping** (*Naut*) dragage *m* de mines, déminage *m.*

miner ['maɪnə^r] n mineur *m.* **the ~s' strike** la grève des mineurs; **~'s lamp** lampe *f* de mineur.

mineral ['mɪnərəl] 1 n a (*Geol*) minéral *m.* b (*Brit: soft drinks*) **~s** boissons *fpl* gazeuses. 2 adj minéral. **the ~ kingdom** le règne minéral; ~ **oil** (*Brit*) huile *f* minérale; (*US*) huile de paraffine; ~ **rights** droits *mpl* miniers; ~ **water** (*natural*) eau *f* minérale; (*Brit: soft drink*) boisson *f* gazeuse.

mineralogical [ˌmɪnərəˈlɒdʒɪkl] adj minéralogique.

mineralogist [ˌmɪnəˈrælədʒɪst] n minéralogiste *mf.*

mineralogy [ˌmɪnəˈrælədʒɪ] n minéralogie *f.*

Minerva [mɪˈnɜːvə] n Minerve *f.*

minestrone [ˌmɪnɪˈstrəʊnɪ] n minestrone *m.*

mingle ['mɪŋgl] 1 vt mêler (*with* à), mélanger, confondre (*with* avec). 2 vi se mêler, se mélanger; (*become indistinguishable*) se confondre (*with* avec). **to ~ with the crowd** se mêler à la foule; **he ~s with all sorts of people** il fraye avec toutes sortes de gens.

mingy* ['mɪndʒɪ] adj *person* radin*, pingre; (*Brit*) *amount, share* misérable.

Mini ['mɪnɪ] n ® (*car*) Mini (Cooper) *f* ®.

mini* ['mɪnɪ] 1 n (*fashion*) mini *f.* 2 adj (*hi-fi*) ~ **system** chaîne *f* (hi-fi) mini.

mini... ['mɪnɪ] pref mini... . **he's a kind of ~-dictator*** c'est une sorte de mini-dictateur.

miniature ['mɪnɪtʃə^r] 1 n (*also Art*) miniature *f.* (*lit, fig*) **in ~** en miniature. 2 adj (en) miniature; *dog* nain; (*tiny*) minuscule. **her doll had a ~ handbag** sa poupée avait un sac à main minuscule; ~ **bottle of whisky** mini-bouteille *f* de whisky; ~ **camera** appareil *m* de petit format; ~ **golf** golf-miniature *m*; ~ **poodle** caniche *m* nain; ~ **railway** chemin de fer *m* miniature; ~ **submarine** sous-marin *m* de poche.

miniaturization [ˌmɪnɪtʃəraɪˈzeɪʃən] n miniaturisation *f.*

miniaturize ['mɪnɪtʃəraɪz] vt miniaturiser.

miniboom ['mɪnɪˌbuːm] n miniboom *m*, période *f* de relative prospérité.

minibudget ['mɪnɪˌbʌdʒɪt] n (*Pol*) collectif *m* budgétaire.

minibus ['mɪnɪˌbʌs] n minibus *m.*

minicab ['mɪnɪˌkæb] n (*Brit*) taxi *m* (*qu'il faut commander par téléphone*).

minicalculator ['mɪnɪ'kælkjʊˌleɪtə^r] n calculette *f*, calculatrice *f* de poche.

minicar ['mɪnɪˌkɑː^r] n toute petite voiture *f.*

minicomputer ['mɪnɪkəm'pjuːtə^r] n mini-ordinateur *m.*

mini-course ['mɪnɪˌkɔːs] n (*US Scol*) cours *m* extra-scolaire.

minidress ['mɪnɪˌdres] n minirobe *f.*

minim ['mɪnɪm] n a (*Brit Mus*) blanche *f.* ~ **rest** demi-pause *f.* b (*Measure*) (= 0,5 ml) ≃ goutte *f.*

minima ['mɪnɪmə] npl of **minimum**.

minimal ['mɪnɪml] adj minimal. **M~ Art** Minimal Art *m*; (*Ling*) ~ **free form** forme *f* libre minimale; (*Phon*) ~ **pair** paire *f* minimale.

minimalism ['mɪnɪməlɪzəm] n (*Art etc*) minimalisme *m.*

minimalist ['mɪnɪməlɪst] adj, n (*Art etc*) minimaliste *mf.*

minimally ['mɪnɪməlɪ] adv *differ, improve, move* imperceptiblement.

minimarket ['mɪnɪˌmɑːkɪt], **minimart** ['mɪnɪˌmɑːt] n supérette *f*, mini-libre-service *m.*

minimize ['mɪnɪmaɪz] vt a (*reduce to minimum*) *amount, risk* réduire au minimum. b (*estimate at lowest*) *losses etc* minimiser, réduire. c (*devalue, decry*) *sb's contribution, help* minimiser, réduire l'importance de.

minimum ['mɪnɪməm] 1 n, pl **~s** *or* **minima** minimum *m.* **to reduce to a** *or* **the ~** réduire au minimum; **keep interruptions to a** *or* **the ~** limitez les interruptions autant que possible; **a ~ of £100** un minimum de 100 livres; **with a ~ of commonsense one could ...** avec un minimum de bon sens *or* le moindre bon sens on pourrait ... . 2 adj *age, price* minimum (*f inv or* minima, *pl* minimums *or* minima). (*Econ, Ind*) ~ **wage** S.M.I.C. *m*, salaire *m* minimum (interprofessionnel de croissance). 3 adv (au) minimum. **10 times ~** dix fois (au) minimum. 4 comp ►**minimum iron fabric** tissu *m* ne demandant qu'un repassage minimum ►**minimum lending rate** (*Econ*) taux *m* de crédit minimum.

mining ['maɪnɪŋ] 1 n (*NonC*) a (*Min*) exploitation *f* minière. b (*Mil, Naut*) pose *f or* mouillage *m* de mines. 2 comp *village, company, industry, rights* minier ►**mining area** région (d'industrie) minière ►**mining engineer** ingénieur *m* des mines ►**mining engineering** (*US Univ*) ≃ études *fpl* à l'école des mines ►**mining family: he comes from a mining family** il est d'une famille de mineurs.

minion ['mɪnjən] n (*servant*) laquais *m*, serviteur *m*, larbin *m*; (*favourite*) favori(te) *m(f).* (*hum, iro*) **~s of the law** serviteurs de la loi.

minipill ['mɪnɪpɪl] n mini-pillule *f.*

miniscule ['mɪnɪˌskjuːl] adj = **minuscule**.

mini-ski ['mɪnɪˌskiː] n (*Ski*) mini-ski *m.*

miniskirt ['mɪnɪˌskɜːt] n minijupe *f.*

minister ['mɪnɪstə^r] 1 n a (*Brit: Diplomacy, Parl, Pol*) ministre *m.* **M~ of State** (*Brit Parl*) ≃ secrétaire *m* d'État; (*gen*) ministre; **M~ of**

Health ministre de la Santé; ~ **plenipotentiary** ministre plénipotentiaire; ~ **resident** ministre résident; *see* **defence, foreign** *etc.* **b** (*Rel: also* ~ **of religion**) pasteur *m*, ministre *m*. **2** vi (*frm*) **to** ~ **to sb's needs** pourvoir aux besoins de qn; **to** ~ **to sb** donner ses soins à qn; (*Rel*) **to** ~ **to a parish** desservir une paroisse; (*fig*) **~ing angel** ange *m* de bonté.

ministerial [ˌmɪnɪs'tɪərɪəl] adj **a** (*Parl*) *decision, crisis* ministériel. **the** ~ **benches** le banc des ministres. **b** (*Rel*) de ministre, sacerdotal.

ministration [ˌmɪnɪs'treɪʃən] n **a** (*services, help*) ~s soins *mpl*. **b** (*Rel*) ministère *m*.

ministry ['mɪnɪstrɪ] n **a** (*government department*) ministère *m*. **M~ of Health** ministère de la Santé; (*Parl*) **to form a** ~ former un ministère *or* un gouvernement; **the coalition** ~ **lasted 2 years** le ministère de coalition a duré 2 ans. **b** (*period of office*) ministère *m*. **c** (*body of clergy*) **the** ~ le saint ministère; **to go into** *or* **enter the** ~ devenir *or* se faire pasteur *or* ministre.

minium ['mɪnɪəm] n minium *m*.

miniver ['mɪnɪvəʳ] n menu-vair *m*.

mink [mɪŋk] **1** n, pl ~ *or* ~s (*animal, fur*) vison *m*. **2** comp *coat etc* de vison.

minke ['mɪŋkɪ] n: ~ **(whale)** baleine *f* minke.

Minn. (*US*) abbr of **Minnesota**.

minneola [ˌmɪnɪ'əʊlə] n minnéola *m*.

Minnesota [ˌmɪnɪ'səʊtə] n Minnesota *m*. **in** ~ dans le Minnesota.

minnow ['mɪnəʊ] n, pl ~ *or* ~s vairon *m*; (*any small fish*) fretin *m*; (*fig: unimportant person*) menu fretin (*sg or collective*).

Minoan [mɪ'nəʊən] adj minoen.

minor ['maɪnəʳ] **1** adj (*Jur, Mus, Philos, Rel*) mineur; *detail, expenses, repairs* petit, menu; *importance, interest, position, role* secondaire. ~ **poet** poète mineur; ~ **problem/worry** problème/souci mineur; (*Mus*) **G** ~ sol mineur; (*Mus*) ~ **key** ton mineur; **in the** ~ **key** en mineur; (*Jur*) ~ **offence** ≃ contravention *f* de simple police; (*Med*) ~ **operation** opération *f* bénigne; (*Theat, fig*) **to play a** ~ **part** jouer un rôle accessoire *or* un petit rôle; ~ **planet** petite planète, astéroïde *m*; (*Cards*) ~ **suit** (couleur *f*) mineure *f*; (*Brit Scol*) **Smith** ~ Smith junior. **2** n **a** (*Jur*) mineur(e) *m(f)*. **b** (*US Univ*) matière *f* secondaire. **3** vi (*US Univ*) **to** ~ **in chemistry** étudier la chimie comme matière secondaire *or* sous-dominante.

Minorca [mɪ'nɔːkə] n Minorque *f*. **in** ~ à Minorque.

minority [maɪ'nɒrɪtɪ] **1** n (*also Jur*) minorité *f*. **in a** *or* **the** ~ en minorité; **you are in a** ~ **of one** vous êtes le seul à penser ainsi, personne ne partage vos vues *or* votre opinion. **2** comp *party, opinion, government* minoritaire ►**minority president** (*US Pol*) *président gouvernant avec un Congrès où les membres du parti adverse sont majoritaires* ►**minority programme** (*Rad, TV*) émission *f* à l'intention d'un auditoire restreint ►**minority report** (*Admin*) rapport *m* soumis par un groupe minoritaire.

Minos ['maɪnɒs] n Minos *m*.

Minotaur ['maɪnətɔːʳ] n Minotaure *m*.

minster ['mɪnstəʳ] n cathédrale *f*; *[monastery]* église *f* abbatiale. **York M~** cathédrale de York.

minstrel ['mɪnstrəl] n (*Hist etc*) ménestrel *m*, trouvère *m*, troubadour *m*. (*Archit*) ~ **gallery** tribune *f* des musiciens; (*Theat*) ~ **show** spectacle *m* de chanteurs et musiciens blancs déguisés en noirs.

minstrelsy ['mɪnstrəlsɪ] n (*NonC*) (*art*) art *m* du ménestrel *or* trouvère *or* troubadour; (*songs*) chants *mpl*.

mint¹ [mɪnt] **1** n (*also Brit:* **Royal M~**) Monnaie *f*, hôtel *m* des monnaies; (*fig: large sum*) une *or* des somme(s) folle(s). **he made a** ~ **of money** *or* **a** ~* **in oil** il a fait fortune dans le pétrole. **2** comp ►**mint condition**: **in mint condition** à l'état (de) neuf, en parfaite condition ►**mint stamp** (*Philat*) timbre *m* non oblitéré. **3** vt *coins* battre; *gold* monnayer (*into* pour obtenir); (*fig*) *word, expression* forger, inventer. (*fig*) **he** ~**s money** il fait des affaires d'or, il ramasse l'argent à la pelle.

mint² [mɪnt] **1** n (*Bot, Culin*) menthe *f*; (*sweet*) bonbon *m* à la menthe. **2** comp *chocolate, sauce* à la menthe ►**mint julep** (*US*) whisky *etc* glacé à la menthe.

minuet [ˌmɪnjʊ'et] n menuet *m*.

minus ['maɪnəs] **1** prep **a** (*Math etc*) moins. **5** ~ **3 equals 2** 5 moins 3 égale(nt) 2; (*Scol etc*) **A/B** *etc* ~ *une note un peu en dessous de A/B etc.* **b** (*: *without*) sans, avec ... en moins *or* de moins. **he arrived** ~ **his coat** il est arrivé sans son manteau; **they found his wallet** ~ **the money** ils ont retrouvé son portefeuille avec l'argent en moins; ~ **a finger** avec un doigt en *or* de moins. **2** comp ►**minus quantity** (*Math*) quantité négative; (*: *fig*) quantité négligeable ►**minus sign** (*Math*) moins *m*. **3** n (*Math*) (*sign*) moins *m*; (*amount*) quantité *f* négative. (*fig: of situation etc*) **the** ~**es** les côtés *mpl* négatifs.

minuscule ['mɪnəˌskjuːl] adj minuscule.

minute¹ ['mɪnɪt] **1** n **a** (*of time*) minute *f*; (*fig*) minute, instant *m*, moment *m*. **it is 20** ~**s past 2** il est 2 heures 20 (minutes); **at 4 o'clock to the** ~ à 4 heures pile *or* tapant(es); **we got the train without a** ~ **to spare** une minute de plus et nous manquions le train; **I'll do it in a** ~ je le ferai dans une minute; **I'll do it the** ~ **he comes** je le ferai dès qu'il arrivera; **do it this** ~! fais-le tout de suite! *or* à la minute!; **he went out this (very)** ~ il vient tout juste de sortir; **at any** ~ à tout moment, d'une minute *or* d'un instant à l'autre; **any** ~ **now** d'une minute à l'autre; **I've just this** ~ **heard of it** je viens de l'apprendre à la minute; **at the last** ~ à la dernière minute; **to leave things till the last** ~ tout faire à la dernière minute; **I shan't be a** ~ j'en ai pour deux secondes; **it won't take five** ~**s** ce sera fait en un rien de temps; **it's a few** ~**s' walk from the station** c'est tout près de la gare, c'est à quelques minutes à pied de la gare; **wait a** ~, **just a** ~ attendez une minute *or* un instant *or* un moment; (*indignantly*) minute!; **half a** ~! une petite minute!; **up to the** ~ *equipment* dernier modèle *inv*; *fashion* dernier cri *inv*; *news* de (la) dernière heure; **there's one born every** ~**!*** il faut vraiment le faire! **b** (*Geog, Math: part of degree*) minute *f*. **c** (*official record*) compte rendu *m*, procès-verbal *m*; (*Comm etc: memorandum*) note *f*, circulaire *f*. **to take the** ~**s of a meeting** rédiger le procès-verbal *or* le compte rendu d'une réunion; **who will take the** ~**s?** qui sera le rapporteur de la réunion? **2** comp ►**minute book** (*Admin, Comm etc*) registre *m* des délibérations ►**minute hand** *[clock etc]* grande aiguille ►**minute steak** (*Culin*) entrecôte *f* minute. **3** vt **a** (*note etc*) *fact, detail* prendre note de; *meeting* rédiger le compte rendu de, dresser le procès-verbal de. **b** (*send* ~ *to*) *person* faire passer une note à (*about* au sujet de).

minute² [maɪ'njuːt] adj (*tiny*) *particles, amount* minuscule, infime, infinitésimal; *change, differences* minime, infime; (*detailed*) *report, examination, description* minutieux, détaillé. **in** ~ **detail** par le menu; **the** ~**st details** les moindres détails.

minutely [maɪ'njuːtlɪ] adv *describe, examine* minutieusement, dans les moindres détails; *change, differ* très peu. **a** ~ **detailed account** un compte rendu extrêmement détaillé *or* circonstancié; **anything** ~ **resembling a fish** quelque chose ayant très vaguement l'apparence d'un poisson.

minutiae [mɪ'njuːʃɪiː] npl menus détails *mpl*, minuties *fpl*, vétilles *fpl* (*pej*).

minx [mɪŋks] n (petite) espiègle *f*, friponne *f*.

Miocene ['maɪəˌsiːn] adj, n miocène *(m)*.

MIPS, mips [mɪps] n (**abbr of millions of instructions per second**) millions *mpl* d'instructions par seconde.

miracle ['mɪrəkl] **1** n miracle *m*; (*fig*) miracle, prodige *m*, merveille *f*. **by a** ~, **by some** ~ par miracle; **it is a** ~ **of ingenuity** c'est un miracle *or* un prodige *or* une merveille d'ingéniosité; **it is a** ~ **that ...** c'est miracle que ... + *subj*; **it will be a** ~ **if ...** ce sera (un) miracle si ... . **2** comp ►**miracle cure, miracle drug** remède-miracle *m* ►**miracle-man** homme-miracle *m* ►**miracle play** (*Rel, Theat*) miracle *m*.

miraculous [mɪ'rækjʊləs] adj (*lit*) miraculeux; (*fig*) miraculeux, prodigieux, merveilleux.

miraculously [mɪ'rækjʊləslɪ] adv (*lit, fig*) miraculeusement, par miracle.

mirage ['mɪrɑːʒ] n (*lit, fig*) mirage *m*.

mire ['maɪəʳ] n (*liter*) (*mud*) fange *f* (*liter*), bourbe *f*, boue *f*; (*swampy ground*) bourbier *m*. (*fig*) **to drag sb's name through the** ~ traîner (le nom de) qn dans la fange *or* la boue.

mirror ['mɪrəʳ] **1** n miroir *m*, glace *f*; (*Aut*) rétroviseur *m*; (*fig*) miroir. **hand** ~ glace à main; **pocket** ~ miroir de poche; **to look at o.s. in the** ~ se regarder dans le miroir *or* dans la glace; (*fig*) **it holds a** ~ **(up) to ...** cela reflète ... . **2** comp ►**mirror image** image inversée ►**mirror writing** écriture *f* inversée. **3** vt (*lit, fig*) refléter. (*lit, fig*) **to be** ~**ed in** se refléter dans.

mirth [mɜːθ] n (*NonC*) hilarité *f*, gaieté *f or* gaîté *f*, rires *mpl*. **this remark caused some** ~ cette remarque a déclenché des rires *or* une certaine hilarité.

mirthful ['mɜːθfʊl] adj gai, joyeux.

mirthless ['mɜːθlɪs] adj sans gaieté, triste.

MIRV [mɜːv] abbr of **Multiple Independently Targeted Re-entry Vehicle**.

miry ['maɪərɪ] adj (*liter*) fangeux (*liter*), bourbeux.

MIS [ˌemaɪ'es] n (**abbr of management information system**) SIG *m*.

misadventure [ˌmɪsəd'ventʃəʳ] n mésaventure *f*; (*less serious*) contretemps *m*. (*Jur*) **death by** ~ mort accidentelle.

misalignment [mɪsə'laɪnmənt] n mauvais alignement *m*. **the dollar** ~ le mauvais alignement du dollar.

misalliance [ˌmɪsə'laɪəns] n mésalliance *f*.

misanthrope ['mɪzənθrəʊp] n misanthrope *mf*.

misanthropic [ˌmɪzən'θrɒpɪk] adj *person* misanthrope; *mood* misanthropique.

misanthropist [mɪ'zænθrəpɪst] n misanthrope *mf*.

misanthropy [mɪ'zænθrəpɪ] n misanthropie *f*.

misapplication [ˌmɪsæplɪ'keɪʃən] n *[knowledge]* usage *m* impropre; *[funds]* détournement *m*.

misapply ['mɪsə'plaɪ] vt *discovery, knowledge* mal employer, mal appliquer; *abilities, intelligence* mal employer, mal diriger; *money, funds* détourner.

misapprehend ['mɪsˌæprɪ'hend] vt mal comprendre, se faire une idée fausse de *or* sur, se méprendre sur.

misapprehension ['mɪs,æprɪ'henʃən] n erreur *f*, malentendu *m*, méprise *f*. **there seems to be some ~** il semble y avoir erreur *or* malentendu *or* méprise; **he's (labouring) under a ~** il n'a pas bien compris, il se fait une idée fausse.
misappropriate ['mɪsə'prəʊprɪeɪt] vt *money, funds* détourner.
misappropriation ['mɪsə,prəʊprɪ'eɪʃən] n détournement *m*.
misbegotten ['mɪsbɪ'gɒtn] adj (*lit: liter*) illégitime, bâtard; (*fig*) *plan, scheme* mal conçu, malencontreux.
misbehave ['mɪsbɪ'heɪv] vi se conduire mal; *[child]* ne pas être sage, se tenir mal.
misbehaviour, (*US*) **misbehavior** ['mɪsbɪ'heɪvjəʳ] n *[person, child]* mauvaise conduite *or* tenue; (*stronger*) inconduite *f*.
misbelief ['mɪsbɪ'li:f] n (*Rel*) croyance fausse.
misbeliever ['mɪsbɪ'li:vəʳ] n (*Rel*) mécréant(e) *m(f)*, infidèle *mf*.
miscalculate ['mɪs'kælkjʊleɪt] 1 vt mal calculer. 2 vi (*fig*) se tromper.
miscalculation ['mɪs,kælkjʊ'leɪʃən] n (*lit, fig*) erreur *f* de calcul, mauvais calcul *m*.
miscall ['mɪs'kɔ:l] vt mal nommer, appeler à tort.
miscarriage ['mɪs'kærɪdʒ] n a *[plan etc]* insuccès *m*, échec *m*; *[letter, goods]* perte *f*, égarement *m*. **~ of justice** erreur *f* judiciaire. b (*Med*) fausse couche. **to have a ~** faire une fausse couche.
miscarry [,mɪs'kærɪ] vi a *[plan, scheme]* échouer, avorter, mal tourner; *[letter, goods]* s'égarer, ne pas arriver à destination. b (*Med*) faire une fausse couche.
miscast ['mɪs'kɑ:st] pret, ptp **miscast** vt (*Cine, Theat etc*) *play* donner une mauvaise distribution à. **he was ~** on n'aurait jamais dû lui donner *or* attribuer ce rôle.
miscegenation [,mɪsɪdʒɪ'neɪʃən] n croisement *m* entre races (*humaines*).
miscellaneous [,mɪsɪ'leɪnɪəs] adj *objects, collection* varié, divers, disparate (*pej*). **~ conversation** conversation *f* sur des sujets divers *or* à bâtons rompus; **~ expenses** frais *mpl* divers; **~ items** (*Comm*) articles divers; (*Press*) faits divers; (*on agenda*) "~" "divers".
miscellany [mɪ'selənɪ] n *[objects etc]* collection *f*; (*Literat*) recueil *m*, sélection *f*, choix *m*, anthologie *f*; (*Rad, TV*) sélection, choix. (*Literat*) **miscellanies** miscellanées *fpl*, (volume *m* de) mélanges *mpl*.
mischance [,mɪs'tʃɑ:ns] n mésaventure *f*, malchance *f*. **by (a) ~** par malheur.
mischief ['mɪstʃɪf] 1 n a (*roguishness*) malice *f*, espièglerie *f*; (*naughtiness*) sottises *fpl*, polissonnerie *f*; (*maliciousness*) méchanceté *f*. **he's up to (some) ~** *[child]* il (nous) prépare une *or* quelque sottise; *[adult]* (*in fun*) il (nous) prépare quelque farce *or* niche; (*from malice*) il médite un mauvais tour *or* coup; **he's always up to some ~** il trouve toujours une sottise *or* niche à faire; *[child only]* **to get into ~** faire des sottises, faire des siennes; **to keep sb out of ~** empêcher qn de faire des sottises *or* des bêtises, garder qn sur le droit chemin (*hum*); **the children managed to keep out of ~** les enfants sont arrivés à ne pas faire de sottises, les enfants ont même été sages; **he means ~** *[child]* il va sûrement faire une sottise; *[adult]* (*in fun*) il va sûrement faire une farce; (*from malice*) il est mal intentionné; **out of sheer ~** (*for fun*) par pure espièglerie; (*from malice*) par pure méchanceté; **full of ~** espiègle, plein de malice; **bubbling over with ~** pétillant de malice; **to make ~ (for sb)** créer des ennuis (à qn); **to make ~ between 2 people** semer la zizanie *or* la discorde entre 2 personnes.
b (**: child*) polisson(ne) *m(f)*, petit(e) vilain(e) *m(f)*.
c (*NonC: injury, damage*) (*physical*) mal *m*; (*mental etc*) tort *m*; (*to ship, building etc*) dommage *m*, dégât(s) *m(pl)*. **to do sb a ~** (*physically*) faire mal à qn, blesser qn; (*mentally etc*) faire du tort à qn; **to do o.s. a ~** (*physically*) se faire mal, se blesser; (*mentally etc*) se faire du tort.
2 comp ▸**mischief-maker** semeur *m*, -euse *f or* brandon *m* de discorde; (*esp gossip*) mauvaise langue *f*.
mischievous ['mɪstʃɪvəs] adj a (*playful, naughty*) *child, kitten* espiègle, malicieux, coquin; *adult* farceur; *glance etc* malicieux, espiègle. **he's as ~ as a monkey** c'est un vrai petit diable. b (*harmful*) *person* méchant, malveillant; *attempt, report, rumour* malveillant, malin (*f* -igne).
mischievously ['mɪstʃɪvəslɪ] adv a (*naughtily etc*) malicieusement, par espièglerie. b (*harmfully*) méchamment, avec malveillance.
mischievousness ['mɪstʃɪvəsnɪs] n (*roguishness*) malice *f*, espièglerie *f*; (*naughtiness*) polissonnerie *f*.
misconceive ['mɪskən'si:v] 1 vt mal comprendre, mal interpréter. 2 vi se tromper, se méprendre (*of* sur).
misconceived [,mɪskən'si:vd] adj *plan, decision* peu judicieux.
misconception ['mɪskən'sepʃən] n (*wrong idea/opinion*) idée *f*/opinion *f* fausse; (*misunderstanding*) malentendu *m*, méprise *f*.
misconduct [,mɪs'kɒndʌkt] 1 n a (*bad behaviour*) inconduite *f*; (*Jur: sexual*) adultère *m*. b (*bad management*) *[business etc]* mauvaise administration *f or* gestion *f*. 2 [,mɪskən'dʌkt] vt *business* mal diriger, mal gérer, mal administrer. **to ~ o.s.**† se conduire mal.
misconstruction ['mɪskən'strʌkʃən] n fausse interprétation *f*. **words open to ~** mots qui prêtent à méprise *or* contresens.
misconstrue ['mɪskən'stru:] vt *acts, words* mal interpréter.
miscount ['mɪs'kaʊnt] 1 n (*gen*) mécompte *m*; (*Pol: during election*) erreur *f* dans le compte des suffrages exprimés. 2 vti mal compter.
miscreant ['mɪskrɪənt] n († *or liter*) scélérat(e) *m(f)*, gredin(e) *m(f)*.
misdeal ['mɪs'di:l] (vb: pret, ptp **misdealt**) (*Cards*) 1 n maldonne *f*. 2 vti: **to ~ (the cards)** faire maldonne.
misdeed ['mɪs'di:d] n méfait *m*, mauvaise action; (*stronger*) crime *m*.
misdemeanour, (*US*) **misdemeanor** [,mɪsdɪ'mi:nəʳ] n incartade *f*, écart *m* de conduite; (*more serious*) méfait *m*; (*Brit Jur*) infraction *f*, contravention *f*; (*US Jur*) délit *m*.
misdescribe [,mɪsdɪ'skraɪb] vt *goods for sale* décrire de façon mensongère.
misdirect ['mɪsdɪ'rekt] vt *letter etc* mal adresser; *person* mal renseigner, fourvoyer; *blow, efforts* mal diriger, mal orienter; *operation, scheme* mener mal. (*Jur*) **to ~ the jury** mal instruire le jury.
misdirection ['mɪsdɪ'rekʃən] n *[letter etc]* erreur *f* d'adresse *or* d'acheminement; *[blow, efforts]* mauvaise orientation; *[operation, scheme]* mauvaise conduite.
miser ['maɪzəʳ] n avare *mf*, grippe-sou *m*.
miserable ['mɪzərəbl] adj a (*unhappy*) *person, life, look* malheureux, triste; (*deplorable*) *sight, failure* pitoyable, lamentable. **to feel ~** (*unhappy*) avoir le cafard* *or* des idées noires; (*unwell*) être *or* se sentir mal fichu*; **to make sb ~** peiner *or* chagriner qn; (*stronger*) affliger qn; **to make sb's life ~** *[person]* faire *or* mener la vie dure à qn; *[arthritis etc]* gâcher la vie de qn; **don't look so ~!** ne fais pas cette tête d'enterrement!
b (*filthy, wretched*) misérable, miteux, minable. **they were living in ~ conditions** ils vivaient dans des conditions misérables *or* dans la misère.
c (**: unpleasant*) *climate, weather* maussade; (*stronger*) détestable, sale* (*before noun*). **what a ~ day!, what ~ weather!** quel temps maussade!; (*stronger*) quel sale temps!*
d (*contemptible*) *meal, gift* méchant (*before noun*), misérable, piteux; *amount, offer* dérisoire; *salary* dérisoire, de misère. **a ~ 50 francs** une misérable *or* malheureuse somme de 50 F.
miserably ['mɪzərəblɪ] adv *live* misérablement, pauvrement; *look, smile, answer* pitoyablement; *pay* misérablement, chichement; *fail* lamentablement, pitoyablement. **~ small** ridiculement petit; **it was raining ~** une pluie maussade tombait; **they played ~*** ils ont joué minablement*, ils ont été minables*.
misère [mɪ'zɛəʳ] n (*Cards*) misère *f*.
miserliness ['maɪzəlɪnɪs] n avarice *f*.
miserly ['maɪzəlɪ] adj *person* avare, pingre, radin*; (*sum*) dérisoire, misérable.
misery ['mɪzərɪ] 1 n a (*unhappiness*) tristesse *f*, douleur *f*; (*suffering*) souffrances *fpl*, supplice *m*; (*wretchedness*) misère *f*, détresse *f*. **the miseries of mankind** la misère de l'homme; **a life of ~** une vie de misère; **to make sb's life a ~** *[person]* faire *or* mener la vie dure à qn; *[arthritis etc]* gâcher la vie de qn; **to put an animal out of its ~** achever un animal; **put him out of his ~* and tell him the results** abrégez son supplice et donnez-lui les résultats.
b (**: gloomy person*) (*child*) pleurnicheur *m*, -euse *f*; (*adult*) grincheux *m*, -euse *f*, rabat-joie *m inv*. **what a ~ you are!** quel grincheux tu fais!, ce que tu peux être pleurnicheur! *or* grincheux! *or* rabat-joie!
2 comp ▸**misery-guts** râleur* *m*, -euse* *f*, rabat-joie *m inv*.
misfire ['mɪs'faɪəʳ] vi *[gun]* faire long feu, rater; *[plan]* rater, foirer*; *[joke]* manquer son but, foirer*; *[car engine]* avoir des ratés.
misfit ['mɪsfɪt] n (*Dress*) vêtement *m* mal réussi *or* qui ne va pas bien; (*fig: person*) inadapté(e) *m(f)*. **he's always been a ~ here** il ne s'est jamais intégré ici, il n'a jamais su s'adapter ici; *see* **social**.
misfortune [mɪs'fɔ:tʃən] n (*single event*) malheur *m*; (*NonC: bad luck*) malchance *f*, infortune *f* (*liter*). (*loc*) **~s never come singly** un malheur n'arrive jamais seul; **~ dogs his footsteps** il joue de malchance; **companion in ~** compagnon *m or* compagne *f* d'infortune; **it is his ~ that he is deaf** pour son malheur il est sourd; **I had the ~ to meet him** par malheur *or* par malchance *or* pour mon malheur je l'ai rencontré; **that's YOUR ~!*** tant pis pour toi!
misgiving [mɪs'gɪvɪŋ] n crainte(s) *f(pl)*, doute(s) *m(pl)*, appréhension *f*. **not without some ~(s)** non sans crainte *or* appréhension *or* inquiétude; **I had ~s about the scheme** j'avais des doutes quant au projet.
misgovern ['mɪs'gʌvən] vti mal gouverner, mal administrer.
misgovernment ['mɪs'gʌvənmənt] n mauvais gouvernement, mauvaise administration.
misguided ['mɪs'gaɪdɪd] adj *person* abusé, malavisé (*liter*); *attempt* malencontreux; *decision, conduct, action* peu judicieux.
misguidedly ['mɪs'gaɪdɪdlɪ] adv malencontreusement, peu judicieusement, à mauvais escient.
mishandle ['mɪs'hændl] vt a (*treat roughly*) *object* manier *or* manipuler sans précaution. b (*mismanage*) *person* mal prendre, mal s'y prendre avec; *problem* mal traiter. **he ~d the whole situation** il a totalement manqué de sagacité *or* de finesse, il a été tout à fait maladroit.
mishap ['mɪshæp] n mésaventure *f*. **slight ~** contretemps *m*, anicroche* *f*; **without ~** sans encombre; **he had a ~** il lui est arrivé une (petite) mésaventure.

mishear ['mɪs'hɪəʳ] pret, ptp misheard vt mal entendre.
mishit ['mɪs'hɪt] 1 n coup *m* manqué. 2 vt *ball* mal jouer.
mishmash* ['mɪʃmæʃ] n méli-mélo* *m*.
misinform ['mɪsɪn'fɔːm] vt mal renseigner.
misinformation [ˌmɪsɪnfə'meɪʃən] n désinformation *f*.
misinterpret ['mɪsɪn'tɜːprɪt] vt mal interpréter, prendre à contresens.
misinterpretation ['mɪsɪnˌtɜːprɪ'teɪʃən] n interprétation erronée (*of* de), contresens *m*. **open to ~** qui prête à contresens.
misjudge ['mɪs'dʒʌdʒ] vt *amount, numbers, time* mal évaluer; (*underestimate*) sous-estimer; *person* méjuger, se méprendre sur le compte de.
misjudg(e)ment [ˌmɪs'dʒʌdʒmənt] n (*see* **misjudge**) mauvaise évaluation *f*; sous-estimation *f*.
mislay [ˌmɪs'leɪ] pret, ptp mislaid vt égarer.
mislead [ˌmɪs'liːd] pret, ptp misled vt (*accidentally*) induire en erreur, tromper; (*deliberately*) tromper, égarer, fourvoyer.
misleading [ˌmɪs'liːdɪŋ] adj trompeur. **~ advertising** publicité *f* mensongère.
mislike†† [mɪs'laɪk] vt ne pas aimer, détester.
mismanage ['mɪs'mænɪdʒ] vt *business, estate, shop* mal gérer, gérer en dépit du bon sens; *institution, organization* mal administrer. **the whole situation has been ~d** toute l'affaire a été traitée avec maladresse, on s'y est mal pris.
mismanagement ['mɪs'mænɪdʒmənt] n mauvaise gestion *f* or administration *f*.
mismatch [mɪs'mætʃ] n *[objects]* disparité *f*; *[colours, styles]* dissonance *f*.
mismatched [mɪs'mætʃt] adj *people, things* mal assortis.
misname ['mɪs'neɪm] vt donner un nom inexact *or* impropre à, mal nommer.
misnomer ['mɪs'nəʊməʳ] n nom *m* mal approprié. **that is a ~** c'est un nom vraiment mal approprié, c'est se moquer du monde* que de l'appeler (*or* les appeler *etc*) ainsi.
misogamist [mɪ'sɒgəmɪst] n misogame *mf*.
misogamy [mɪ'sɒgəmɪ] n misogamie *f*.
misogynist [mɪ'sɒdʒɪnɪst] n misogyne *mf*.
misogyny [mɪ'sɒdʒɪnɪ] n misogynie *f*.
misplace ['mɪs'pleɪs] vt a *object, word* mal placer, ne pas mettre où il faudrait; *affection, trust* mal placer. b (*lose*) égarer.
misplaced ['mɪs'pleɪst] adj *remark, humour* déplacé, hors de propos.
misprint ['mɪsprɪnt] 1 n faute *f* d'impression *or* typographique, coquille *f*. 2 [ˌmɪs'prɪnt] vt imprimer mal *or* incorrectement.
mispronounce ['mɪsprə'naʊns] vt prononcer de travers, estropier, écorcher.
mispronunciation ['mɪsprəˌnʌnsɪ'eɪʃən] n prononciation incorrecte (*of* de), faute(s) *f(pl)* de prononciation.
misquotation ['mɪskwəʊ'teɪʃən] n citation inexacte.
misquote ['mɪs'kwəʊt] vt citer faussement *or* inexactement. **he was ~d in the press as having said ...** les journalistes lui ont incorrectement fait dire que ...; **he said that he had been ~d** il a dit qu'on avait déformé ses propos.
misread ['mɪs'riːd] pret, ptp misread ['mɪs'red] vt (*lit*) *word* mal lire; (*fig: misinterpret*) *sb's reply, signs etc* mal interpréter, se tromper sur. **he misread "cat" as "rat"** il s'est trompé et a lu "rat" au lieu de "chat"; (*fig*) **he misread the statements as promises of ...** il s'est mépris sur les déclarations en y voyant des promesses de ..., il a interprété les déclarations à tort comme signifiant des promesses de ...; (*fig*) **he misread the whole situation** il a interprété la situation de façon tout à fait incorrecte.
misrepresent ['mɪsˌreprɪ'zent] vt *facts* dénaturer, déformer; *person* présenter sous un faux jour, donner une impression incorrecte de. **he was ~ed in the press** ce qu'on a dit de lui dans les journaux est faux *or* incorrect.
misrepresentation ['mɪsˌreprɪzen'teɪʃən] n déformation *f*, présentation déformée.
misrule ['mɪs'ruːl] 1 n (*bad government*) mauvaise administration; (*disorder etc*) désordre *m*, anarchie *f*. 2 vt gouverner mal.
miss¹ [mɪs] 1 n a (*shot etc*) coup manqué *or* raté; (**: omission*) manque *m*, lacune *f*; (**: mistake*) erreur *f*, faute *f*; (*failure*) four *m*, bide* *m* (*fig*). (*Prov*) **a ~ is as good as a mile** rater c'est rater (même de justesse); **to give a concert/lecture** *etc* **a ~*** s'abstenir d'assister à *or* ne pas aller à un concert/une conférence *etc*; **to give Paris/the Louvre** *etc* **a ~*** ne pas aller à Paris/au Louvre *etc*; **I'll give the wine a ~ this evening*** je m'abstiendrai de boire du vin *or* je me passerai de vin ce soir; **I'll give my evening class a ~ this week*** tant pis pour mon cours du soir cette semaine; **oh give it a ~!*** ça suffit!, en voilà assez!, arrête!; **they voted the record a ~*** le disque a été jugé minable*; *see* **hit, near** *etc*.

b (*Med* *) (abbr of **miscarriage b**) fausse couche *f*.

2 vt a (*fail to hit*) *target, goal* manquer, rater, louper*. **the shot just ~ed me** la balle m'a manqué de justesse *or* d'un cheveu; **the plane just ~ed the tower** l'avion a failli toucher la tour.

b (*fail to find, catch, use etc*) *vocation, opportunity, appointment, train, person to be met, cue, road, turning* manquer, rater; *house, thing looked out for, solution* ne pas trouver, ne pas voir; *meal* sauter; *class, lecture* manquer, sécher (*Scol sl*). (*iro*) **you haven't ~ed much!** vous n'avez pas manqué *or* perdu grand-chose!; **we ~ed the tide** nous avons manqué la marée; (*fig*) **to ~ the boat*** *or* **the bus*** louper le coche* (*fig*); **to ~ one's cue** (*Theat*) manquer sa réplique; (*fig*) rater l'occasion, manquer le coche*; **to ~ one's footing** glisser; **she doesn't ~ a trick*** rien ne lui échappe; **to ~ one's way** perdre son chemin, s'égarer; **you can't ~ our house** vous trouverez tout de suite notre maison; **you mustn't ~ (seeing) this film** ne manquez pas (de voir) *or* ne ratez pas ce film, c'est un film à ne pas manquer *or* rater; **don't ~ the Louvre** ne manquez pas d'aller au Louvre; **if we go that way we shall ~ Bourges** si nous prenons cette route nous ne verrons pas Bourges; **I ~ed him at the station by 5 minutes** je l'ai manqué *or* raté de 5 minutes à la gare.

c *remark, joke, meaning* (*not hear*) manquer, ne pas entendre; (*not understand*) ne pas comprendre, ne pas saisir. **I ~ed what you said** je n'ai pas entendu ce que vous avez dit; **I ~ed that** je n'ai pas entendu, je n'ai pas compris; **I ~ed the point of that joke** je n'ai pas compris ce que ça avait de drôle, je n'ai pas saisi l'astuce; **you've ~ed the whole point!** vous n'avez rien compris!, vous avez laissé passer l'essentiel!

d (*escape, avoid*) *accident, bad weather* échapper à. **he narrowly ~ed being killed** il a manqué *or* il a bien failli se (faire) tuer, il l'a échappé belle.

e (*long for*) *person* regretter (l'absence de). **I do ~ Paris** Paris me manque beaucoup; **we ~ you very much** nous regrettons beaucoup ton absence, tu nous manques beaucoup; **are you ~ing me?** est-ce que je te manque?; **they're ~ing one another** ils se manquent l'un à l'autre; **he will be greatly ~ed** on le regrettera beaucoup; **he won't be ~ed** personne ne le regrettera; **I ~ the old trams** je regrette les vieux trams; **I ~ the sunshine/the freedom** le soleil/la liberté me manque.

f (*notice loss of*) *money, valuables* remarquer l'absence *or* la disparition de. **I suddenly ~ed my wallet** tout d'un coup je me suis aperçu que je n'avais plus mon portefeuille; **I'm ~ing 8 dollars*** il me manque 8 dollars, j'avais 8 dollars de plus; **here's your hat back — I hadn't even ~ed it!** je vous rends votre chapeau — je ne m'étais même pas aperçu *or* n'avais même pas remarqué que je ne l'avais plus!; **you can keep that pen, I shan't ~ it** vous pouvez garder ce stylo, il ne me fera pas défaut.

3 vi a *[shot, person]* manquer son coup, rater. (*fig*) **you can't ~!** vous ne pouvez pas ne pas réussir!

b **to be ~ing** faire défaut, avoir disparu; **there is one plate ~ing, one plate is ~ing** il manque une assiette; **how many are ~ing?** combien en manque-t-il?; **there's nothing ~ing** il ne manque rien, tout y est; **one of our aircraft is ~ing** un de nos avions n'est pas rentré; *see also* **missing**.

►**miss out** vt sep a (*accidentally*) *name, word, line of verse, page* passer, sauter, oublier; (*in distributing sth*) *person* sauter, oublier. b (*on purpose*) *course at meal* ne pas prendre, sauter; *name on list* omettre; *word, line of verse, page* laisser de côté, sauter; *concert, lecture, museum* ne pas aller à; (*in distributing sth*) *person* omettre.

►**miss out on*** vt fus a (*fail to benefit*) *opportunity, bargain* laisser passer, louper*, ne pas profiter de; *one's share* ne pas recevoir, perdre. **he missed out on several good deals** il a raté *or* loupé* plusieurs occasions de faire une bonne affaire. b (*come off badly*) **he missed out on the deal** il n'a pas obtenu tout ce qu'il aurait pu de l'affaire; **make sure you don't miss out on anything** vérifie que tu reçois ton dû.

miss² [mɪs] n a Mademoiselle *f*. **M~ Smith** Mademoiselle Smith, Mlle Smith; († *or frm*) **the M~es Smith** les demoiselles *fpl* Smith; (*on letter*) Mesdemoiselles Smith; (*in letter*) **Dear M~ Smith** Chère Mademoiselle; **yes M~ Smith** oui Mademoiselle; **yes ~*** oui Mademoiselle *or* mam'selle*; **M~ France 1988** Miss France 1988. b (**: often hum*) petite *or* jeune fille. **the modern ~** la jeune fille moderne; **she's a cheeky little ~** c'est une petite effrontée.
Miss. (*US*) abbr of **Mississippi**.
missal ['mɪsəl] n missel *m*.
misshapen [mɪs'ʃeɪpən] adj *object, body, limbs* difforme, contrefait.
missile ['mɪsaɪl] 1 n (*Mil*) missile *m*; (*stone etc thrown*) projectile *m*; *see* **ballistic, ground¹, guided** *etc*. 2 comp ►**missile base** base *f* de missiles (*or* fusées) ►**missile launcher** lance-missiles *m inv*.
missing ['mɪsɪŋ] adj a *person* absent, disparu; *object* (*lost*) perdu, égaré; (*left out*) manquant. (*Admin, Police etc*) **~ person** personne *f* absente (*Jur*); **M~ Persons Bureau** ≃ brigade *f* de recherche dans l'intérêt des familles; **~ persons file** fichier *m* des personnes recherchées; **the 3 ~ students are safe** les 3 étudiants dont on était sans nouvelles sont sains et saufs; **fill in the ~ words** complétez les phrases suivantes, donnez les mots qui manquent; (*fig*) **the ~ link** (*gen*) le maillon qui manque à la chaîne; (*between ape and man*) le chaînon manquant.

b (*Mil*) disparu. **~ in action** (adj) porté disparu; (n) soldat *m* (*etc*) porté disparu; **~ believed killed** disparu présumé tué; **to be reported ~** être porté disparu.
mission ['mɪʃən] 1 n (*all senses*) mission *f*. (*Rel*) **foreign ~s** missions étrangères; **to send sb on a ~ to sb** envoyer qn en mission auprès de qn; **his ~ in life is to help others** il s'est donné pour mission

d'aider autrui. 2 comp ▶**mission control** (*Space etc*) centre *m* de contrôle ▶**mission controller** ingénieur *m* du centre de contrôle; *see* **trade**.

missionary ['mɪʃənrɪ] 1 n missionnaire *mf*. 2 comp *work, duties* missionnaire; *society* de missionnaires ▶**missionary position*** (*sex*) position *f* du missionnaire.

missis‡ ['mɪsɪz] n (*wife*) **the/my** ~ la/ma bourgeoise‡; (*boss*) **the** ~ la patronne‡; **hey** ~! dites m'dame! *or* ma petite dame!*

Mississippi [,mɪsɪ'sɪpɪ] n (*state, river*) Mississippi *m*. **in** ~ dans le Mississippi.

missive ['mɪsɪv] n missive *f*.

Missouri [mɪ'zʊərɪ] n (*state, river*) Missouri *m*. **in** ~ dans le Missouri; (*US fig*) **I'm from** ~* je veux des preuves.

misspell ['mɪs'spel] pret, ptp **misspelled** *or* **misspelt** vt mal écrire, mal orthographier.

misspelling ['mɪs'spelɪŋ] n faute *f* d'orthographe.

misspend [mɪs'spend] pret, ptp **misspent** vt *money* dépenser à tort et à travers, gaspiller; *time, strength, talents* mal employer, gaspiller. **misspent youth** folle jeunesse.

misstate ['mɪs'steɪt] vt rapporter incorrectement.

misstatement ['mɪs'steɪtmənt] n rapport inexact.

missus‡ ['mɪsɪz] n = **missis**‡.

missy*† ['mɪsɪ] n ma petite demoiselle*.

mist [mɪst] 1 n (*Met*) brume *f*; (*on glass*) buée *f*; (*before eyes*) brouillard *m*; *[perfume, dust etc]* nuage *m*; *[ignorance, tears]* voile *m*. **morning/sea** ~ brume matinale/de mer; (*fig liter*) **lost in the** ~**s of time** perdu dans la nuit des temps; *see* **Scotch** *etc*. 2 vt (*also* ~ **over**, ~ **up**) *mirror, windscreen, eyes* embuer. 3 vi (*also* ~ **over**, ~ **up**) *[scene, landscape, view]* se couvrir de brume, devenir brumeux; *[mirror, windscreen, eyes]* s'embuer.

mistakable [mɪs'teɪkəbl] adj facile à confondre (*with, for* avec).

mistake [mɪs'teɪk] (vb: pret **mistook**, ptp **mistaken**) 1 n erreur *f*, faute *f*; (*misunderstanding*) méprise *f*. **to make a** ~ **in a dictation/problem** faire une faute dans une dictée/une erreur dans un problème; **I made a** ~ **about the book/about him** je me suis trompé sur le livre/sur son compte; **I made a** ~ **about** *or* **over the road to take/about** *or* **over the dates** je me suis trompé de route/de dates, j'ai fait une erreur en ce qui concerne la route qu'il fallait prendre/les dates; **make no** ~ **about it** ne vous y trompez pas; **you're making a big** ~ tu fais une grave *or* lourde erreur; **to make the** ~ **of doing** avoir le tort de faire, commettre l'erreur de faire; **by** ~ par erreur; (*carelessly*) par inadvertance, par mégarde; **I took his umbrella in** ~ **for mine** j'ai pris son parapluie par erreur *or* en croyant prendre le mien; **there must be some** ~ il doit y avoir erreur; **there must be** *or* **let there be no** ~ **about it** qu'on ne s'y méprenne pas *or* trompe (*subj*) pas; **that's a surprise and no** ~! décidément c'est une surprise!, pour une surprise c'est une surprise!; **she told him what she thought about it and no** ~ elle lui a dit son opinion sans y aller par quatre chemins; **my** ~! c'est (de) ma faute!, mea-culpa!

2 vt *meaning* mal comprendre, mal interpréter; *intentions* se méprendre sur; *time, road* se tromper de. **there's no mistaking her voice** il est impossible de ne pas reconnaître sa voix; **there's no mistaking that** ... il est indubitable que ...; **there's no mistaking it, he** ... il ne faut pas s'y tromper, il ...; **to** ~ **A for B** prendre A pour B, confondre A avec B; *see also* **mistaken**.

mistaken [mɪs'teɪkən] 1 ptp of **mistake**. 2 adj *idea, opinion* erroné, faux (*f* fausse); *conclusion* erroné, mal fondé; *generosity* mal placé. *[person]* **to be** ~ faire erreur (*about* en ce qui concerne), se tromper (*about* sur); **if I'm not** ~ sauf erreur, si je ne me trompe; **that's just where you're** ~! c'est ce qui vous trompe!, c'est en quoi vous faites erreur!; **in the** ~ **belief that** ... croyant à tort que ...; *see* **identity**.

mistakenly [mɪs'teɪkənlɪ] adv (*in error*) par erreur; (*carelessly*) par inadvertance, par mégarde. **they were** ~ **considered to be members of the Communist Party** on avait commis l'erreur de croire qu'ils appartenaient au parti communiste.

mister ['mɪstəʳ] n a (*souvent abrégé en* **Mr**) monsieur *m*. **Mr Smith** Monsieur Smith, M. Smith; **yes Mr Smith** oui Monsieur; **Mr Chairman** monsieur le président; (*fig*) **M~ Big*** le caïd‡, le gros bonnet*; (*fig*) **M~ Right*** le mari idéal; (*US pej*) **M~ Charlie*** sale* Blanc *m*. b (‡) **hey** ~! eh, dites donc!

mistime ['mɪs'taɪm] vt a (*pick wrong time for*) *arrival, intervention* faire *etc* au mauvais moment *or* à contretemps; *act, blow* mal calculer. **to** ~ **one's arrival** (*arrive inopportunely*) arriver à contretemps; ~**d remark** remarque inopportune; **he** ~**d it** il a choisi le mauvais moment. b (*count badly*) mal calculer. **to** ~ **one's arrival** (*miscalculate time*) se tromper sur *or* mal calculer son (heure d')arrivée.

mistiming [,mɪs'taɪmɪŋ] n: **the** ~ **of his arrival** son arrivée malencontreuse; **the** ~ **of the attack** le moment malencontreusement choisi pour l'attaque.

mistiness ['mɪstɪnɪs] n *[morning etc]* bruine *f*, état brumeux; (*on windscreen etc*) condensation *f*.

mistlethrush ['mɪslθrʌʃ] n draine *f or* drenne *f*.

mistletoe ['mɪsltəʊ] n (*NonC*) gui *m*.

mistook [mɪs'tʊk] pret of **mistake**.

mistranslate ['mɪstrænz'leɪt] vt mal traduire, faire un (*or* des) contresens en traduisant.

mistranslation ['mɪstrænz'leɪʃən] n a erreur *f* de traduction, contresens *m*. b (*NonC*) *[text etc]* mauvaise traduction, traduction inexacte.

mistreat [,mɪs'triːt] vt maltraiter.

mistreatment [,mɪs'triːtmənt] n mauvais traitement *m*.

mistress ['mɪstrɪs] n a *[household, institution etc]* (*also fig*) maîtresse *f*. (*to servant*) **is your** ~ *or* **the** ~ **at home?** Madame est-elle là?; (*fig*) **to be** ~ **of oneself** être maîtresse de soi; **to be one's own** ~ être sa propre maîtresse, être indépendante. b (*Brit: teacher*) (*in primary school*) maîtresse *f*, institutrice *f*; (*in secondary school*) professeur *m*. **the English** ~ le professeur d'anglais; **they have a** ~ **for geography** ils ont un professeur femme en géographie. c (*lover; also*††: *sweetheart*) maîtresse *f*, amante†† *f*. d ['mɪsɪz] (*term of address: abrév* **Mrs** *sauf* †† *et dial*) madame *f*. **Mrs Smith** Madame Smith, Mme Smith; **yes Mrs Smith** oui Madame.

mistrial [,mɪs'traɪəl] n (*Brit, US: Jur*) procès *m* entaché d'un vice de procédure; (*US only*) procès ajourné pour défaut d'unanimité dans le jury.

mistrust ['mɪs'trʌst] 1 n méfiance *f*, défiance *f* (*of* à l'égard de). 2 vt *person, sb's motives, suggestion* se méfier de, se défier de (*liter*); *abilities* douter de, ne pas avoir confiance en.

mistrustful [mɪs'trʌstfʊl] adj méfiant, défiant (*of* à l'égard de).

mistrustfully [mɪs'trʌstfəlɪ] adv avec méfiance; *look, say* d'un air méfiant.

misty ['mɪstɪ] 1 adj *weather* brumeux; *day* de brume, brumeux; *mirror, windscreen* embué; (*fig*) *eyes, look* embrumé, embué; (*fig*) *outline, recollection, idea* nébuleux, flou. ~ **blue/grey/green** bleu/gris/vert vaporeux *or* fondu. 2 comp ▶**misty-eyed** (*near tears*) qui a les yeux voilés de larmes; (*fig: sentimental*) qui a la larme à l'œil.

misunderstand ['mɪsʌndə'stænd] pret, ptp **misunderstood** vt *words, action, reason* mal comprendre, comprendre de travers, mal interpréter. **you** ~ **me** vous m'avez mal compris, ce n'est pas ce que j'ai voulu dire; **she was misunderstood all her life** toute sa vie elle est restée incomprise *or* méconnue.

misunderstanding ['mɪsʌndə'stændɪŋ] n erreur *f*, méprise *f*; (*disagreement*) malentendu *m*, mésentente *f*. **there must be some** ~ il doit y avoir méprise *or* une erreur; **they had a slight** ~ il y a eu une légère mésentente entre eux.

misunderstood ['mɪsʌndə'stʊd] pret, ptp of **misunderstand**.

misuse ['mɪs'juːs] 1 n *[power, authority]* abus *m*; *[word, tool]* usage *m* impropre *or* abusif; *[money, resources, energies, one's time]* mauvais emploi. (*Jur*) ~ **of funds** détournement *m* de fonds. 2 ['mɪs'juːz] vt *power, authority* abuser de; *word, tool* employer improprement *or* abusivement; *money, resources, energies, one's time* mal employer; *funds* détourner.

MIT ['em,aɪ'tiː] n (*US Univ*) abbr of **Massachusetts Institute of Technology**.

mite [maɪt] n a (††: *coin*) denier *m*; (*as contribution*) obole *f*. **the widow's** ~ le denier de la veuve; **he gave his** ~ **to the collection** il a apporté son obole à la souscription. b (*small amount*) grain *m*, brin *m*, atome *m*, parcelle *f*, tantinet *m*. **there's not a** ~ **of bread left** il ne reste plus une miette de pain; **not a** ~ **of truth** pas une parcelle *or* un atome de vérité; **a** ~ **of consolation** une toute petite consolation; **well, just a** ~ **then** bon, mais alors un tantinet seulement; **we were a** ~ **surprised*** nous avons été un tantinet *or* un rien surpris. c (*small child*) petit(e) *m(f)*. **poor little** ~ (le) pauvre petit. d (*Zool*) mite *f*. **cheese** ~ mite de fromage.

miter ['maɪtəʳ] n, vt (*US*) = **mitre**.

Mithraic [mɪθ'reɪɪk] adj mithriaque.

Mithras ['mɪθræs] n Mithra *m*.

mitigate ['mɪtɪgeɪt] vt *punishment, sentence* atténuer, réduire, mitiger; *suffering, sorrow* adoucir, alléger, atténuer; *effect, evil* atténuer, mitiger. **mitigating circumstances** circonstances atténuantes.

mitigation [,mɪtɪ'geɪʃən] n (*see* **mitigate**) atténuation *f*, réduction *f*, mitigation *f*; adoucissement *m*, allégement *m*.

mitral ['maɪtrəl] adj mitral. ~ **valve** valvule *f* mitrale.

mitre, (*US*) **miter** ['maɪtəʳ] 1 n (*Rel*) mitre *f*; (*Carpentry*) onglet *m*. 2 vt (*Carpentry*) (*join*) *frame etc* assembler à *or* en onglet; (*cut*) *corner, end* tailler à onglet. 3 comp ▶**mitre box** (*Carpentry*) boîte *f* à onglets ▶**mitre joint** (assemblage *m* à) onglet *m*.

mitt [mɪt] n a = **mitten**. b (*Baseball: catcher's* ~) gant *m* de baseball. c (‡: *hand*) patte* *f*, patoche‡ *f*.

mitten ['mɪtn] n (*with cut-off fingers*) mitaine *f*; (*with no separate fingers*) moufle *f*; (*Boxing* *) gant *m*, mitaine*.

mix [mɪks] 1 n *[cement, concrete etc]* mélange *m*, mortier *m*; *[metals]* alliage *m*, amalgame *m*; (*Culin*) *[ingredients]* mélange; (*commercially prepared*) préparation *f*. **a packet of cake** ~ un paquet de préparation pour gâteau.

2 comp ▶**mix-up** confusion *f*; **there was a mix-up over tickets** il y a eu confusion en ce qui concerne les billets; **we got in a mix-up over the dates** nous nous sommes embrouillés dans les dates; **he got into a mix-up with the police** il a eu un démêlé avec la police.

3 vt *liquids, ingredients, colours* mélanger (*with* avec, à); *small objects* mêler, mélanger (*with* avec, à); *metals* allier, amalgamer; *cement, mortar* malaxer; *cake, sauce* préparer, faire; *cocktails etc* préparer; *salad* remuer, retourner. **to ~ one thing with another** mélanger une chose à une autre *or* avec une autre *or* et une autre; **to ~ to a smooth paste** battre pour obtenir une pâte homogène; **~ the eggs into the sugar** incorporez les œufs au sucre; **he ~ed the drinks** il a préparé les boissons; **can I ~ you a drink?** je vous sers un cocktail?; **never ~ your drinks!** évitez toujours les mélanges!; **to ~ business and *or* with pleasure** combiner les affaires et le plaisir; **to ~ one's metaphors** faire des métaphores incohérentes; (*Brit fig*) **to ~ it*** (*cause trouble*) causer des ennuis; (*quarrel, fight*) se bagarrer*; *see also* **mixed.**

4 vi (*see* 3) se mélanger, se mêler; s'amalgamer; s'allier. **oil and water don't ~** (*lit*) l'huile est insoluble dans l'eau; (*fig*) l'huile et l'eau sont deux choses complètement différentes; **these colours just don't ~** ces couleurs ne s'harmonisent pas *or* ne vont pas bien ensemble; **he ~es with all kinds of people** il fraye avec *or* il fréquente toutes sortes de gens; **he doesn't ~ well** il est peu sociable; **these groups of children just won't ~** ces groupes d'enfants ne fraternisent pas.

►**mix in** 1 vi: **he doesn't want to mix in** il préfère rester à l'écart; **you must try to mix in** il faut essayer de vous mêler un peu aux autres. 2 vt sep: **mix in the eggs (with)** incorporez les œufs (à).

►**mix round** vt sep mélanger, remuer.

►**mix together** vt sep mélanger, amalgamer.

►**mix up** 1 vt sep a (*prepare*) *drink, medicine* mélanger, préparer.

b (*put in disorder*) *documents, garments* mêler, mélanger.

c (*confuse*) *two objects, two people* confondre. **to mix sth/sb up with sth/sb else** confondre qch/qn avec qch/qn d'autre.

d **to mix sb up in sth** impliquer qn dans qch; **to be/get mixed up in an affair** être/se trouver mêlé à une affaire; **don't get mixed up in it!** restez à l'écart!; **he is/he has got mixed up with a lot of criminals** il fréquente/il s'est mis à fréquenter un tas de malfaiteurs*; (*US*) **to mix it up*** (*cause trouble*) causer des ennuis; (*quarrel, fight*) se bagarrer*.

e (*muddle*) *person* embrouiller. **to be mixed up** *[person]* être (tout) désorienté *or* déboussolé*; *[account, facts]* être embrouillé *or* confus; **I am all mixed up about it** je ne sais plus où j'en suis, je ne m'y reconnais plus; **you've got me all mixed up** vous m'avez embrouillé.

2 **mix-up** n *see* **mix 2.**

3 **mixed-up** adj *see* **mixed 2.**

mixed [mɪkst] 1 adj *marriage, school* mixte; *race* métissé; *biscuits, nuts* assortis. **the weather was ~** le temps était inégal *or* variable; (*fig*) **it's a ~ bag*** il y a un peu de tout; **it's a ~ blessing** c'est une bonne chose qui a son mauvais côté, c'est un avantage incertain; **man/woman of ~ blood** un/une sang-mêlé; **in ~ company** en présence d'hommes et de femmes; (*Tennis*) **~ doubles** double *m* mixte; (*Pol Econ*) **~ economy** économie *f* mixte; **~ farming** polyculture *f*; **~ feelings** sentiments *mpl* contraires *or* contradictoires; **she had ~ feelings about it** elle était partagée à ce sujet; **she agreed with ~ feelings** elle a consenti sans enthousiasme; (*Brit*) **~ grill** assortiment *m* de grillades, mixed grill *m*; **~ metaphor** métaphore incohérente; **~ motives** intentions qui ne sont pas entièrement pures; **to meet with a ~ reception** recevoir un accueil mitigé.

2 comp ►**mixed-ability group/teaching** (*Scol*) classe *f*/ enseignement *m* sans groupes de niveaux ►**mixed-up** *person* désorienté, déboussolé*; *report etc* embrouillé, confus; **he's a mixed-up kid*** c'est un gosse* qui a des problèmes.

mixer ['mɪksəʳ] 1 n a (*Culin*) **hand ~** batteur *m* à main; **electric ~** batteur électrique, mixer *m*, mixeur *m*. b *[cement, mortar etc]* malaxeur *m*; *[industrial liquids]* agitateur *m*. **cement ~** bétonnière *f*, malaxeur à béton. c (*Cine etc: also* **sound ~**) (*person*) ingénieur *m* du son; (*machine*) mélangeur *m* du son. d **he's a good ~** il est très sociable *or* liant. e (*US: social gathering*) soirée-rencontre *f*, réunion-rencontre *f*. f (*Brit *: troublemaker*) fauteur *m* de troubles. g (*drink*) boisson *f* gazeuse (*servant à couper un alcool*). 2 comp ►**mixer tap** (*Brit*) (robinet *m*) mélangeur *m*.

mixing ['mɪksɪŋ] 1 n (*see* **mix 3**) mélange *m*; préparation *f*; incorporation *f*; alliage *m*; malaxage *m*; (*Cine etc: also* **sound ~**) mixage *m*. 2 comp ►**mixing bowl** (*Culin*) grand bol (de cuisine) ►**mixing faucet** (*US*) (robinet *m*) mélangeur *m*.

mixture ['mɪkstʃəʳ] n mélange *m*; (*Med*) préparation *f*, mixture *f*. **the family is an odd ~** cette famille est un mélange bizarre *or* curieux; (*fig*) **it's just the ~ as before** c'est toujours la même chose, il n'y a rien de nouveau; *see* **cough.**

miz(z)en ['mɪzn] n (*Naut*) artimon *m*. **~mast** mât *m* d'artimon.

mizzle ['mɪzl] (* *or dial*) 1 vi bruiner. 2 n bruine *f*.

Mk. abbr of **mark**[1].

ml n (abbr of **millilitre(s)**) ml.

M.Litt. ['em'lɪt] n (abbr of **Master of Literature** *or* **Master of Letters**) ≃ doctorat *m* de troisième cycle.

MLR [ˌem,el'ɑːʳ] n (abbr of **minimum lending rate**) *see* **minimum 3.**

M.L.S. [ˌem,el'es] n (*US Univ*) (abbr of **Master of Library Science**) *diplôme supérieur de bibliothécaire.*

Mm [əm] excl Mmm.

mm (abbr of **millimetre(s)**) mm.

MMC ['em,em'siː] n (abbr of **Monopolies and Mergers Commission**) *see* **monopoly.**

M.M.E. ['em,em'iː] n (*US Univ*) a abbr of **Master of Mechanical Engineering.** b abbr of **Master of Mining Engineering.**

MN ['em'en] n a (*Brit*) (abbr of **Merchant Navy**) *see* **merchant.** b (*US Post*) abbr of **Minnesota.**

mnemonic [nɪ'mɒnɪk] adj, n mnémotechnique (*f*), mnémonique (*f*).

mnemonics [nɪ'mɒnɪks] n (*NonC*) mnémotechnique *f*.

M.O. ['em'əʊ] n a (abbr of **medical officer**) *see* **medical.** b (*US Post*) abbr of **Missouri.** c (*: *esp US*) (abbr of **modus operandi**) méthode *f*, truc* *m*.

Mo. (*US*) abbr of **Missouri.**

m.o. ['em'əʊ] n (abbr of **money order**) *see* **money.**

mo'* [məʊ] n (abbr of **moment** a) moment *m*, instant *m*. **half a ~!, just a ~!** un instant!; (*interrupting*) minute!*

moan [məʊn] 1 n (*groan: also of wind etc*) gémissement *m*, plainte *f*; (*: *complaint*) plainte, récrimination *f*. 2 vi (*groan*) gémir, pousser des gémissements, geindre; *[wind etc]* gémir; (*: *complain*) maugréer, rouspéter*, râler*. 3 vt dire en gémissant.

moaner* ['məʊnəʳ] n rouspéteur* *m*, -euse* *f*, râleur* *m*, -euse *f*.

moaning ['məʊnɪŋ] 1 n gémissements *mpl*, plainte(s) *f(pl)*; (*: *complaints*) plaintes, jérémiades *fpl*. 2 adj gémissant; (*: *complaining*) rouspéteur*, râleur*.

moat [məʊt] n douves *fpl*, fossés *mpl*.

moated ['məʊtɪd] adj *castle etc* entouré de douves *or* de fossés.

mob [mɒb] 1 n a *[people]* foule *f*, masse *f*, (*disorderly*) cohue *f*. († *pej: the common people*) **the ~** la populace; **a ~ of soldiers/supporters** une cohue de soldats/de supporters; **the embassy was burnt by the ~** les émeutiers ont brûlé l'ambassade; **they went in a ~ to the town hall** ils se rendirent en masse *or* en foule à la mairie; **a whole ~ of cars*** toute une cohue de voitures.

b (*) bande *f*, clique *f* (*pej*). **Paul and his ~** Paul et sa bande, Paul et sa clique (*pej*); **I had nothing to do with that ~** je n'avais rien à voir avec cette clique.

c *[criminals, bandits etc]* gang *m*.

2 comp ►**mob oratory** éloquence *f* démagogique ►**mob rule** (*pej*) la loi de la populace *or* de la rue.

3 vt *person* assaillir, faire foule autour de; *place* assiéger. **the shops were ~bed*** les magasins étaient pris d'assaut *or* assiégés.

mobcap ['mɒbkæp] n charlotte *f* (*bonnet*).

mobile ['məʊbaɪl] 1 adj (*gen, also Sociol*) mobile; *features, face* mobile, expressif. (*fig*) **I'm not ~ this week*** je n'ai pas de voiture *or* je ne suis pas motorisé* cette semaine; **~ canteen** (cuisine) roulante *f*; **~ data system** système *m* de données mobile; **~ home** grande caravane *f* (*utilisée comme domicile*); **~ library** bibliobus *m*; **~ phone** téléphone *m* portatif; **~ police support** renforts *mpl* mobiles de police; **~ police unit** unité *f* mobile de police; (*Rad, TV*) **~ studio** car *m* de reportage; *see* **shop, upwardly.** 2 n (*Art*) mobile *m*.

mobility [məʊ'bɪlɪtɪ] n mobilité *f*. **~ allowance** allocation *f or* indemnité *f* de transport (*pour handicapés*); *see* **upward.**

mobilization [ˌməʊbɪlaɪ'zeɪʃən] n (*all senses*) mobilisation *f*.

mobilize ['məʊbɪlaɪz] vti (*gen, also Mil*) mobiliser. **to ~ sb into doing** mobiliser qn pour faire; **they were ~d into a group which ...** on les a mobilisés pour constituer un groupe qui ... .

mobster ['mɒbstəʳ] n membre *m* du milieu, truand *m*, gangster *m*.

moccasin ['mɒkəsɪn] n mocassin *m*.

mocha ['mɒkə] n moka *m*.

mock [mɒk] 1 n a **to make a ~ of sth/sb** tourner qch/qn en ridicule.

b (*: *Brit Scol*) **~s** examens *mpl* blancs.

2 adj a (*imitation*) *leather etc* faux (*f* fausse) (*before noun*), imitation *inv* (*before noun*), simili- *inv*. **~ turtle soup** consommé *m* à la tête de veau.

b (*pretended*) *anger, modesty* simulé, feint. **a ~ battle/trial** un simulacre de bataille/de procès; (*Scol etc*) **~ examination** examen blanc.

c (*Literat*) burlesque; *see also* **3.**

3 comp ►**mock-heroic** (*gen*) burlesque; (*Literat*) héroï-comique, burlesque ►**mock orange** (*Bot*) seringa *m* ►**mock-serious** à demi sérieux ►**mock-up** maquette *f*.

4 vt a (*ridicule*) ridiculiser; (*scoff at*) se moquer de, railler; (*mimic, burlesque*) singer, parodier.

b (*liter: defy*) *sb's plans, attempts* narguer.

5 vi se moquer (*at* de).

►**mock up** 1 vt sep faire la maquette de. 2 **mock-up** n *see* **mock 3.**

mocker ['mɒkəʳ] n moqueur *m*, -euse *f*.

mockers‡ ['mɒkəz] npl: **to put the ~ on sth** ficher qch en l'air‡.

mockery ['mɒkərɪ] n (*mocking*) moquerie *f*, raillerie *f*; (*person, thing*) sujet *m* de moquerie *or* de raillerie, objet *m* de risée; (*travesty*) parodie *f*, travestissement *m*, caricature *f*. **to make a ~ of sb/sth** tourner qn/qch en dérision, bafouer qn/qch; **he had to put up with a lot of ~** il a dû endurer beaucoup de railleries *or* de persiflages; **it is a ~ of justice** c'est une parodie de (la) justice, c'est un travestissement de la justice; **a ~ of a trial** une parodie *or* une caricature de procès; **what a ~ it was!**

c'était grotesque!

mocking ['mɒkɪŋ] 1 n (*NonC*) moquerie *f*, raillerie *f*. 2 adj *person, smile, voice* moqueur, railleur; (*malicious*) narquois.

mockingbird ['mɒkɪŋˌbɜːd] n moqueur *m* (*oiseau*).

mockingly ['mɒkɪŋlɪ] adv *say* d'un ton moqueur *or* railleur *or* narquois, par moquerie *or* dérision; *smile* d'une façon moqueuse *or* narquoise.

mod[1] [mɒd] (abbr of **modern**) 1 adj a (*‡*†) *person* dans le vent*; *clothes* à la mode. b (*) ~ **cons** = **modern conveniences**; *see* **modern 1**. 2 n (*Brit*) (*in 1980's*) *garçon ou fille bon genre mais sans classe;* (*in 1960's*) *jeune personne faisant partie d'une bande circulant en scooter (opposée aux blousons noirs).*

mod[2] [mɒd] n (*Scot*) concours *m* de musique et de poésie (*en gaélique*).

M.O.D. [ˌeməʊ'diː] n (*Brit*) (abbr of **Ministry of Defence**) *see* **defence**.

modal ['məʊdl] adj (*Ling, Mus etc*) modal. ~ **verb** auxiliaire *m* modal.

modality [məʊ'dælɪtɪ] n modalité *f*.

mode [məʊd] n a (*way, manner*) mode *m*, façon *f*, manière *f*. ~ **of life** façon *or* manière de vivre, mode *m* de vie. b (*Comput, Ling, Mus, Philos etc*) mode *m*. (*Comput*) **in interactive** *etc* ~ en mode conversationnel *etc;* **to have one's calculator in the wrong** ~ faire marcher son calculateur dans le mauvais mode.

model ['mɒdl] 1 n a (*small-scale representation*) *[boat etc]* modèle *m* (réduit); (*Archit, Tech, Town Planning etc*) maquette *f*; *see* **scale**[1] *etc*.

b (*standard, example*) modèle *m*, exemple *m*. **he was a ~ of discretion** c'était un modèle de discrétion; **on the ~ of** sur le modèle de, à l'image de; **to take sb/sth as one's ~** prendre modèle *or* prendre exemple sur qn/qch; **to hold sb out** *or* **up as a ~** citer *or* donner qn en exemple.

c (*person*) (*Art, Phot, Sculp etc*) modèle *m*; (*Fashion*) mannequin *m*. **male ~** mannequin masculin.

d (*Comm*) modèle *m*. (*garments, hats*) **the latest ~s** les derniers modèles; (*Aut*) **a 1978 ~** un modèle 1978; (*Aut*) **sports ~** modèle sport; **4-door ~** version *f* 4 portes; **factory ~** modèle de fabrique.

e (*Ling*) modèle *m*.

2 adj a (*designed as a ~*) (*gen*) modèle; *prison, school etc* modèle, -pilote. ~ **factory** usine *f* modèle, usine-pilote *f*.

b (*exemplary*) *behaviour, conditions, pupil* modèle, exemplaire.

c (*small-scale*) *train, plane, car etc* modèle réduit *inv*; *railway, village* en miniature.

3 vt a (*make ~ of*) modeler (*in* en).

b **to ~ sth on sth else** modeler qch sur qch d'autre; **to ~ o.s. on sb** se modeler sur qn, prendre modèle *or* exemple sur qn.

c (*Fashion*) **to ~ clothes** être mannequin, présenter les modèles de collection; **she was ~ling swimwear** elle présentait les modèles de maillots de bain.

4 vi (*Art, Phot, Sculp*) poser (*for* pour); (*Fashion*) être mannequin (*for* chez).

modeller, (*US*) **modeler** ['mɒdləʳ] n modeleur *m*, -euse *f*.

modelling, (*US*) **modeling** ['mɒdlɪŋ] n (*Art etc*) modelage *m*. **she does ~** (*fashion*) elle travaille comme mannequin; (*for artist*) elle travaille comme modèle; ~ **clay** pâte *f* à modeler.

modem ['məʊdem] n (*Comput*) modem *m*.

Modena ['mɔːdena] n Modène.

moderate ['mɒdərɪt] 1 adj *opinions, demands, behaviour* modéré (*also Pol*); *person* modéré (*in* dans); *price, income, amount, size, appetite* modéré, raisonnable, moyen; *heat* modéré; *climate* tempéré; *language, terms* mesuré; *talent, capabilities* modéré, moyen, ordinaire; *results* passable, modéré, moyen. **he was ~ in his demands** ses exigences étaient raisonnables *or* n'avaient rien d'excessif.

2 comp ▸**moderate-sized** de grandeur *or* de grosseur *or* de taille moyenne.

3 n (*esp Pol*) modéré(e) *m(f)*.

4 ['mɒdəreɪt] vt a (*restrain, diminish*) modérer. **moderating influence** influence modératrice.

b (*preside over*) présider.

5 vi *[storm, wind etc]* se modérer, s'apaiser, se calmer.

moderately ['mɒdərɪtlɪ] adv *act, react* avec modération; *eat, drink, exercise* modérément; *pleased etc* plus ou moins, raisonnablement; *quickly, expensive, difficult* relativement. **this book is ~ priced** ce livre est d'un prix raisonnable; ~ **good** assez bon.

moderation [ˌmɒdə'reɪʃən] n (*NonC*) modération *f*, mesure *f*. **in ~** (*gen*) *eat, drink, exercise* avec modération, modérément; **it's all right in ~** c'est très bien à petites doses *or* à condition de ne pas en abuser; **with ~** avec mesure *or* modération; **to advise ~ in drinking** conseiller la modération dans le boire, conseiller de boire modérément *or* avec modération.

moderator ['mɒdəreɪtəʳ] n a (*Rel*) **M~** président *m* (*de l'Assemblée générale de l'Église presbytérienne*). b (*in assembly, council, discussion*) président(e) *m(f)*. c (*Brit Univ: examiner*) examinateur *m*, -trice *f*. d (*Phys, Tech*) modérateur *m*.

modern ['mɒdən] 1 adj moderne. **house with all ~ conveniences** maison *f* tout confort; **it has all ~ conveniences** il y a tout le confort (moderne); ~ **languages** langues vivantes; **in ~ times** dans les temps modernes, à l'époque moderne; **~-day** des temps modernes. 2 n (*artist, poet etc*) moderne *mf*.

modernism ['mɒdənɪzəm] n a (*NonC: Art, Rel*) modernisme *m*. b (*word*) néologisme *m*.

modernist ['mɒdənɪst] adj, n moderniste (*mf*).

modernistic [ˌmɒdə'nɪstɪk] adj moderniste.

modernity [mɒ'dɜːnɪtɪ] n modernité *f*.

modernization [ˌmɒdənaɪ'zeɪʃən] n modernisation *f*.

modernize ['mɒdənaɪz] 1 vt moderniser. 2 vi se moderniser.

modest ['mɒdɪst] adj a (*not boastful*) modeste, effacé, réservé; (†: *chaste*) pudique, modeste. **to be ~ about one's achievements** ne pas se faire gloire de ses réussites *or* exploits; **don't be so ~!** ne fais pas le modeste!, tu es trop modeste! b (*fairly small, simple*) *success, achievement, amount, origin* modeste; *demands, needs* modeste, très modéré; *wage, price, sum* (*moderate*) modeste, (*very small*) modique. **he was ~ in his demands** ses exigences étaient modestes *or* très modérées, il n'était vraiment pas exigeant; **a ~ little house** une modeste maisonnette, une maisonnette sans prétention(s).

modestly ['mɒdɪstlɪ] adv a (*without boasting*) modestement, avec modestie; (†: *chastely*) modestement, pudiquement, avec pudeur. b (*simply*) modestement, simplement, sans prétention(s).

modesty ['mɒdɪstɪ] n a (*gen*) modestie *f*; (†: *chasteness*) pudeur *f*, modestie. **false ~** fausse modestie; **may I say with all due ~ ...** soit dit en toute modestie ... . b *[request etc]* modération *f*; *[sum of money, price]* modicité *f*.

modicum ['mɒdɪkəm] n: **a ~ of** un minimum de.

modifiable ['mɒdɪfaɪəbl] adj modifiable.

modification [ˌmɒdɪfɪ'keɪʃən] n modification *f* (*to, in* à). **to make ~s (in** *or* **to)** faire *or* apporter des modifications (à).

modifier ['mɒdɪfaɪəʳ] n modificateur *m*; (*Gram*) modificatif *m*.

modify ['mɒdɪfaɪ] vt a (*change*) *plans, design* modifier, apporter des modifications à; *customs, society* transformer, modifier; (*Gram*) modifier. b (*make less strong*) modérer. **he'll have to ~ his demands** il faudra qu'il modère (*subj*) ses exigences *or* qu'il en rabatte; **he modified his statement** il modéra les termes de sa déclaration.

modifying ['mɒdɪfaɪɪŋ] 1 n modification *f*. 2 adj *note, term* modificatif (*also Gram*); *factor* modifiant.

modish ['məʊdɪʃ] adj à la mode, mode *inv*.

modishly ['məʊdɪʃlɪ] adv à la mode.

modiste [məʊ'diːst] n modiste *f*.

Mods* [mɒdz] n (*Oxford Univ*) (abbr of **moderations**) *premier examen (pour le grade de bachelier ès arts).*

modular ['mɒdjʊləʳ] adj (*gen*) modulaire; *furniture* modulaire, à éléments (composables). (*Univ*) ~ **degree** licence *f* modulaire, ≃ licence à U.V.; (*US*) ~ **scheduling** emploi *m* du temps avec autorisation de sortie en dehors des cours; **a six-week ~ course** des cours bloqués sur six semaines.

modulate ['mɒdjʊleɪt] 1 vt (*all senses*) moduler. 2 vi (*Mus*) moduler.

modulation [ˌmɒdjʊ'leɪʃən] n modulation *f*. **amplitude ~** modulation d'amplitude; **frequency ~** modulation de fréquence.

module ['mɒdjuːl] n (*gen*) module *m*; (*Univ*) module *m*, ≃ unité *f* de valeur, U.V. *f*. (*US*) ~ **learning** enseignement *m* par groupes de niveaux; *see* **lunar**.

modulus ['mɒdjʊləs] n, pl **moduli** ['mɒdjʊˌlaɪ] (*Math, Phys*) module *m*, coefficient *m*.

modus ['məʊdəs] n: ~ **operandi** modus operandi *m inv*; ~ **vivendi** modus vivendi *m inv*.

moggie*, **moggy*** ['mɒgɪ] n (*Brit: cat*) minou *m*.

mogul ['məʊgəl] 1 adj: **M~** des Mog(h)ols. 2 n a **M~** Mog(h)ol *m*. b (*fig: powerful person*) nabab *m*. **a ~ of the film industry** un nabab du cinéma. c (*Ski*) bosse *f*.

M.O.H. [ˌeməʊ'eɪtʃ] n (*Brit*) (abbr of **Medical Officer of Health**) *see* **medical**.

mohair ['məʊhɛəʳ] 1 n mohair *m*. 2 comp en *or* de mohair.

Mohammed [məʊ'hæmed] n Mohammed *m*, Mahomet *m*.

Mohammedan [məʊ'hæmɪdən] 1 adj mahométan, musulman. 2 n Mahométan(e) *m(f)*.

Mohammedanism [məʊ'hæmɪdənɪzəm] n Mahométisme *m*.

Mohican ['məʊhɪkən] n, pl **~s** *or* **~** (*also* **~ Indian**) Mohican *mf*; **m~ (hairdo)** iroquoise *f*.

moire [mwɑː] n moire *f*.

moiré ['mwɑːreɪ] adj, n moiré(e) (*m(f)*).

moist [mɔɪst] adj *hand, atmosphere* moite; *climate, wind, surface* humide; *heat* moite, humide; *cake* moelleux. **eyes ~ with tears** des yeux humides *or* mouillés de larmes.

moisten ['mɔɪsn] 1 vt humecter, mouiller légèrement; (*Culin*) mouiller légèrement. **to ~ one's lips** s'humecter les lèvres. 2 vi devenir humide *or* moite.

moistness ['mɔɪstnɪs] n (*see* **moist**) moiteur *f*, humidité *f*.

moisture ['mɔɪstʃəʳ] n (*on grass etc*) humidité *f*; (*on glass etc*) buée *f*.

moisturize ['mɔɪstʃəraɪz] vt *air, atmosphere* humidifier; *skin* hydrater.

moisturizer ['mɔɪstʃəraɪzəʳ] n (*for skin*) crème *f* *or* lait *m* hydratant(e).

moke‡ [məʊk] n (*Brit*) bourricot *m*, baudet *m*.

molar [ˈməʊləʳ] 1 n (*tooth*) molaire *f*. 2 adj (*Dentistry, Phys*) molaire.
molasses [məʊˈlæsɪz] n (*NonC*) mélasse *f*. (*US*) **to be as slow as ~ in winter*** être lent comme une tortue.
mold [məʊld] *etc* (*US*) = **mould** *etc*.
Moldavia [mɒlˈdeɪvɪə] n Moldavie *f*.
Moldavian [mɒlˈdeɪvɪən] 1 n Moldavien(ne) *m(f)*. 2 adj moldavien. **~ SSR** RSS *f* de Moldavie.
mole¹ [məʊl] 1 n (*Zool*) taupe *f* (*also fig: spy*).
2 comp ▸**mole-catcher** taupier *m* ▸**molehill** taupinière *f* (*see* **mountain 1**) ▸**moleskin** n (*lit*) (peau *f* de) taupe *f*; (*Brit Tex*) velours *m* de coton ◊ adj de *or* en (peau de) taupe; de *or* en velours de coton.
mole² [məʊl] n (*on skin*) grain *m* de beauté.
mole³ [məʊl] n (*breakwater*) môle *m*, digue *f*.
molecular [məʊˈlekjʊləʳ] adj moléculaire.
molecule [ˈmɒlɪkjuːl] n molécule *f*.
molest [məʊˈlest] vt (*trouble*) importuner, tracasser; (*harm*) molester, rudoyer, brutaliser; (*Jur: sexually*) attenter à la pudeur de; *[dog]* s'attaquer à.
molestation [ˌməʊlesˈteɪʃən] n (*see* **molest**) tracasserie(s) *f(pl)*; brutalités *fpl*; attentat *m* à la pudeur.
molester [məʊˈlestəʳ] n satyre *m*.
moll* [mɒl] n (*pej*) nana⁑ *f* (de gangster).
mollify [ˈmɒlɪfaɪ] vt apaiser, calmer. **~ing remarks** propos lénifiants.
mollusc, (*US*) **mollusk** [ˈmɒləsk] n mollusque *m*.
Mollybolt [ˈmɒlɪbəʊlt] n ® (*US*) cheville *f* (*Menuiserie*).
mollycoddle [ˈmɒlɪkɒdl] vt (*gen*) élever dans du coton, chouchouter*, dorloter; *pupil* materner.
mollycoddling [ˈmɒlɪkɒdlɪŋ] n (*pej*) chouchoutage *m*; maternage *m*.
Molotov [ˈmɒlətɒf] n: **~ cocktail** cocktail *m* Molotov.
molt [məʊlt] (*US*) = **moult**.
molten [ˈməʊltən] adj *metal, glass* en fusion, fondu.
Moluccan [məʊˈlʌkən] n *see* **south**.
molybdenum [mɒˈlɪbdɪnəm] n molybdène *m*.
mom* [mɒm] n (*US*) maman *f*. **~ and pop store*** petite boutique familiale, petit commerce.
moment [ˈməʊmənt] n a moment *m*, instant *m*. **man of the ~** homme *m* du moment; **the psychological ~** le moment psychologique; **wait a ~!, just a ~!, one ~!, half a ~!*** (attendez) un instant! *or* une minute!; (*objecting to sth*) minute!, pas si vite!*; **I shan't be a ~, I'll just** *or* **only be a ~** j'en ai pour un instant; **a ~ ago** il y a un instant; **a ~ later** un instant plus tard; **that very ~** à cet instant *or* ce moment précis; **the ~ he arrives** dès *or* aussitôt qu'il arrivera; **the ~ he arrived** dès *or* aussitôt qu'il arriva, dès son arrivée; **do it this ~!** fais-le à l'instant! *or* sur-le-champ!; **I've just this ~ heard of it** je viens de l'apprendre à l'instant (même); **it won't take a ~** c'est l'affaire d'un instant; **at the (present) ~, at this ~ in time** en ce moment (même), à l'heure qu'il est; **at that ~** à ce moment(-là); **(at) any ~** d'un moment *or* instant à l'autre; **at every ~** à chaque instant, à tout moment; **at the right ~** au bon moment, à point nommé; **at the last ~** au dernier moment; **to leave things till the last ~** attendre le dernier moment; **for a ~** un instant; **for a brief ~** l'espace d'un instant; **not for a ~!** jamais de la vie!; **I don't think for a** *or* **one ~ (that) he believed my story** je ne crois *or* pense pas un (seul) instant qu'il ait cru mon histoire; **for the ~** pour le moment; **from the ~ I saw him** dès l'instant où je l'ai vu; **from that ~** dès ce moment, dès cet instant; **I'll come in a ~** j'arrive dans un instant; **it was all over in a ~** tout s'est passé en un instant *or* en un clin d'œil *or* en un tournemain; **the ~ of truth** la minute *or* l'heure *f* de vérité; (*fig*) **he has his ~s** il a ses bons côtés; **it has its ~s** ça contient de bonnes choses; *see* **spur**.
b (†: *importance*) importance *f*. **of little ~** de peu d'importance; **of (great) ~** de grande *or* haute importance.
c (*Tech*) moment *m*. **~ of inertia** moment d'inertie.
momentarily [ˈməʊməntərɪlɪ] adv (*briefly*) momentanément; (*at any moment*) d'un moment à l'autre; (*US: instantly*) immédiatement, sans attendre.
momentary [ˈməʊməntərɪ] adj (*brief*) momentané, passager; (*liter: constant*) constant, continuel. **after a ~ silence** après un moment de silence.
momentous [məʊˈmentəs] adj très important, considérable, capital.
momentousness [məʊˈmentəsnɪs] n (*NonC*) importance capitale, portée *f*.
momentum [məʊˈmentəm] n, pl **~s** *or* **momenta** [məʊˈmentə] (*gen*) vitesse *f* (acquise); (*Phys etc*) moment *m* (*des quantités de mouvement*); *[political movement etc]* dynamisme *m*. **to gather ~** *[spacecraft, car etc]* prendre de la vitesse; (*fig*) gagner du terrain; (*Aut, Space etc, also fig*) **to lose ~** être en perte de vitesse; *[politician, party etc]* **to have ~** avoir le vent en poupe; **the Reagan ~** la dynamique *or* l'effet *m* Reagan.
momma* [ˈmɒmə] n (*US*) = **mom***.
mommy* [ˈmɒmɪ] n (*US*) = **mom***.
Mon. abbr of **Monday**.
Monacan [mɒˈnɑːkən] 1 adj monégasque. 2 n Monégasque *mf*.
Monaco [ˈmɒnəkəʊ] n Monaco *m*. **in ~** à Monaco.
monad [ˈmɒnæd] n (*Chem, Philos*) monade *f*.
Mona Lisa [ˈməʊnəˈliːzə] n la Joconde.
monarch [ˈmɒnək] n (*lit, fig*) monarque *m*.
monarchic(al) [mɒˈnɑːkɪk(əl)] adj monarchique.
monarchism [ˈmɒnəkɪzəm] n monarchisme *m*.
monarchist [ˈmɒnəkɪst] adj, n monarchiste *(mf)*.
monarchy [ˈmɒnəkɪ] n monarchie *f*.
monastery [ˈmɒnəstərɪ] n monastère *m*.
monastic [məˈnæstɪk] adj *life* monastique, monacal; *vows, architecture* monastique.
monasticism [məˈnæstɪsɪzəm] n monachisme *m*.
monaural [ˌmɒnˈɔːrəl] adj *instrument* monophonique, monaural; *hearing* monauriculaire.
Monday [ˈmʌndɪ] 1 n lundi *m*; *for phrases see* **Saturday**; *see also* **Easter, Whit** *etc*. 2 comp ▸**Monday-morning**: (*fig*) **that Monday-morning feeling** la déprime* du lundi matin; (*US fig*) **Monday-morning quarterback*** spécialiste *mf* du je-vous-l'avais-bien-dit.
Monegasque [mɒnəˈgæsk] 1 n Monégasque *mf*. 2 adj monégasque.
monetarism [ˈmʌnɪtərɪzəm] n monétarisme *m*.
monetarist [ˈmʌnɪtərɪst] adj, n monétariste *(mf)*.
monetary [ˈmʌnɪtərɪ] adj monétaire; **~ school** école *f* monétaire *or* monétariste; *see* **international**.
money [ˈmʌnɪ] 1 n a (*NonC*) argent *m*; (*Fin*) monnaie *f*. **French ~** argent français; **paper ~** papier-monnaie *m*, monnaie de papier (*often pej*); (*Prov*) **~ is the root of all evil** l'argent est la racine de tous les maux; **lack of ~** manque *m* d'argent; **your ~ or your life!** la bourse ou la vie!; (*Brit*) **it's ~ for jam*** *or* **for old rope*** c'est de l'argent vite gagné *or* gagné sans peine, c'est être payé à ne rien faire; **to make ~** *[person]* gagner de l'argent; *[business etc]* rapporter, être lucratif (*see also* **1b**); **he made his ~ by dealing in cotton** il s'est enrichi avec le coton; **to come into ~** (*by inheritance*) hériter (d'une somme d'argent); (*gen*) recevoir une somme d'argent; **I paid** *or* **gave good ~ for it** ça m'a coûté de l'argent; **he's earning good ~** il gagne bien sa vie (*see also* **1b**); **he's earning big ~** il gagne gros; **that's big ~** c'est une grosse somme; **the deal involves big ~** de grosses sommes sont en jeu dans cette transaction (*see also* **1b**); **he gets his ~ on Fridays** il touche son argent *or* sa paie le vendredi, il est payé le vendredi; **when do I get my ~?** quand est-ce que j'aurai mon argent?; (*lit, fig*) **to get one's ~'s worth** en avoir pour son argent; **to get one's ~ back** se faire rembourser; (*with difficulty*) récupérer son argent; **I want my ~ back!** remboursez!; **to put ~ into sth** placer son argent dans qch; **is there ~ in it?** est-ce que ça rapporte?, est-ce que c'est lucratif?; **it's a bargain for the ~!** à ce prix-là c'est une occasion!; **it was ~ well spent** j'ai (*or* nous avons *etc*) fait une bonne affaire; *see* **big, coin, counterfeit, ready** *etc*.
b (*fig phrases*) **that's the one for my ~!** c'est juste ce qu'il me faut!; **that's the team for my ~** je serais prêt à parier pour cette équipe; **for my ~ we should do it now** à mon avis nous devrions le faire maintenant; **he's made of ~*, he's rolling in ~*, he has pots of ~*** il est cousu d'or, il roule sur l'or*; **he's got ~ to burn** il a de l'argent à ne savoir qu'en faire *or* à jeter par la fenêtre; **we're in the ~ now!*** nous roulons sur l'or* maintenant; **he's in the big ~*** il récolte un fric fou⁑; (*Prov*) **~ makes ~** l'argent va où est l'argent; (*Prov*) **~ talks** l'argent est roi; (*loc*) **~ doesn't grow on trees** l'argent ne tombe pas du ciel; **to put one's ~ where one's mouth is** joindre l'acte à la parole (en deboursant une somme d'argent); **to throw** *or* **send good ~ after bad** s'enfoncer dans une mauvaise affaire; (*loc*) **bad ~ drives out good** des capitaux douteux font fuir les investissements sains; **this ~ burns a hole in his pocket** il brûle de dépenser cet argent; **~ runs through his fingers like water** l'argent lui fond dans les mains; (*US fig*) **it's ~ from home*** c'est du tout cuit*; *see* **even²**.
c (*Jur*) **~s, monies** sommes *fpl* d'argent; **~s paid out** versements *mpl*; **~s received** recettes *fpl*, rentrées *fpl*; **public ~s** deniers publics.
2 comp *difficulties, problems, questions* d'argent, financier ▸**moneybag** sac *m* d'argent; **he's a moneybags⁑** il est plein aux as⁑ ▸**moneybox** tirelire *f* ▸**moneychanger** (*person*) changeur *m*; (*change machine*) distributeur *m* de monnaie ▸**money expert** expert *m* en matières financières ▸**moneygrubber** (*pej*) grippe-sou *m* ▸**moneygrubbing** (*pej*) n thésaurisation *f*, rapacité *f* ◊ adj rapace, grippe-sou *inv* ▸**moneylender** prêteur *m*, -euse *f* sur gages ▸**moneylending** n prêt *m* à intérêt ◊ adj prêteur ▸**money-loser** affaire infructueuse *or* qui perd de l'argent ▸**moneymaker** affaire lucrative ▸**moneymaking** n acquisition *f* d'argent ◊ adj lucratif, qui rapporte ▸**moneyman*** (*US*) financier *m* ▸**money market** (*Econ*) marché *m* monétaire ▸**money matters** questions *fpl* d'argent *or* financières ▸**money order** mandat *m* postal, mandat-poste *m* ▸**money spider*** araignée *f* porte-bonheur *inv* ▸**money spinner** (*Brit*) mine *f* d'or (*fig*) ▸**money supply** (*Econ*) masse *f* monétaire.
moneyed [ˈmʌnɪd] adj riche, cossu, argenté*. **the ~ classes** les classes possédantes, les nantis *mpl*.
moneywort [ˈmʌnɪwɜːt] n (*Bot*) souci *m* d'eau, lysimaque *f*.
...monger [ˈmʌŋgəʳ] suf marchand *m* de ...; *see* **fish, scandal, war** *etc*.
Mongol [ˈmɒŋgəl] 1 adj a (*Geog, Ling*) mongol. b (⁑ *pej Med* †)

m~ mongolien. 2 n a Mongol(e) *m(f)*. b (*Ling*) mongol *m*. c (‡ *pej Med* †) m~ mongolien(ne) *m(f)*.

Mongolia [mɒŋ'gəʊlɪə] n Mongolie *f*.

Mongolian [mɒŋ'gəʊlɪən] 1 n Mongol(e) *m(f)*. 2 adj mongol. **the ~ People's Republic** la République populaire mongole.

mongolism‡ ['mɒŋgəlɪzəm] n (*pej, Med* †) mongolisme *m*.

Mongoloid ['mɒŋgəˌlɔɪd] adj, n = **Mongol 1a, 2a, 2c**.

mongoose ['mɒŋguːs] n, pl ~s (*Zool*) mangouste *f*.

mongrel ['mʌŋgrəl] 1 n (*dog*) (chien *m*) bâtard *m*; (*animal, plant*) hybride *m*, métis(se) *m(f)*. 2 adj hybride, bâtard, (de race) indéfinissable.

Monica ['mɒnɪkə] n Monique *f*.

monied ['mʌnɪd] adj = **moneyed**.

monies ['mʌnɪz] npl of **money**; *see* **money 1c**.

moniker‡ ['mɒnɪkə^r] n (*name*) nom *m*; (*nickname*) surnom *m*.

monitor ['mɒnɪtə^r] 1 n a (*device : Comput, Med, Tech, TV etc*) moniteur *m*. **heart rate ~** moniteur cardiaque. b (*person : Rad*) rédacteur *m*, -trice *f* d'un service d'écoute. c (*Scol*) ≃ chef *m* de classe. 2 vt a *[person] pupil, work, progress, system* suivre de près; *equipment etc* contrôler (les performances de); *[machine]* contrôler. **a nurse/a machine ~s the patient's progress** une infirmière suit de près *or* surveille/une machine contrôle l'évolution de l'état du malade; **to ~ the situation** surveiller l'évolution des choses. b (*Rad*) *foreign broadcasts, station* être à l'écoute de.

monitoring ['mɒnɪtərɪŋ] n a (*gen*) (*by person*) surveillance *f*; (*by machine*) contrôle *m*; (*Med, Tech*) monitorage *m*; (*Univ, Scol*) contrôle continu (des connaissances). b (*Rad*) (service *m* d')écoute *f*.

monitory ['mɒnɪtərɪ] adj monitoire, d'avertissement, d'admonition.

monk [mʌŋk] 1 n moine *m*, religieux *m*. 2 comp ▸**monkfish** (*angler fish*) lotte *f*; (*angel fish*) ange *m* de mer ▸**monk's hood** (*Bot*) aconit *m*.

monkey ['mʌŋkɪ] 1 n singe *m*; (*fig: child*) galopin(e) *m(f)*, polisson(ne) *m(f)*; (*Brit: £500*‡) cinq cents livres. **female ~** guenon *f*; **to make a ~ out of sb** tourner qn en ridicule; (*US: Drugs sl*) **to have a ~ on one's back** être esclave de la drogue.

2 comp ▸**monkey bars** (*for climbing on*) cage *f* à poules ▸**monkey business*** (*fig*) (*dishonest*) quelque chose de louche, combine(s) *f(pl)*; (*mischievous*) singeries *fpl*; **no monkey business now!*** pas de blagues!* ▸**monkey house** maison *f* des singes, singerie *f* ▸**monkey jacket** (*Naut*) vareuse ajustée ▸**monkey nut** (*Brit*) cacahouète *f or* cacahuète *f* ▸**monkey puzzle** (*Bot: tree*) araucaria *m* ▸**monkey tricks*** (*fig*) = **monkey business*** ▸**monkey wrench** clef anglaise *or* à molette; (*US fig*) **to throw a monkey wrench into the works*** flanquer la pagaille*.

▸**monkey about***, **monkey around*** vi a (*waste time*) perdre son temps. **stop monkeying about and get on with your work** cesse de perdre ton temps et fais ton travail. b (*play the fool*) faire l'idiot *or* l'imbécile. **to monkey about with sth** tripoter qch, faire l'imbécile avec qch.

monkish ['mʌŋkɪʃ] adj de moine.

mono ['mɒnəʊ] 1 adj (abbr of **monophonic**) mono* *inv*, monophonique, monaural. 2 n a **recorded in ~** enregistré en monophonie. b (*~ record*) disque *m* mono.

mono... ['mɒnəʊ] pref mon(o)... .

monobasic [mɒnəʊ'beɪsɪk] adj monobasique.

monochromatic [mɒnəʊkrəʊ'mætɪk] adj monochromatique.

monochrome ['mɒnəkrəʊm] 1 n (*gen, also Art*) camaïeu *m*; (*Phot, TV*) noir et blanc *m*. **landscape in ~** paysage *m* en camaïeu. 2 adj (*gen*) monochrome; (*Art*) en camaïeu; (*Phot, TV*) en noir et blanc.

monocle ['mɒnəkl] n monocle *m*.

monocoque ['mɒnəkɒk] adj (*Aut*) monocoque.

monocracy [mɒ'nɒkrəsɪ] n monocratie *f*.

monocrat ['mɒnəkræt] n monocrate *m*.

monocratic [mɒnə'krætɪk] adj monocratique.

monocular [mɒ'nɒkjʊlə^r] adj monoculaire.

monoculture ['mɒnəʊkʌltʃə^r] n monoculture *f*.

monocyte ['mɒnəʊsaɪt] n monocyte *m*.

monody ['mɒnədɪ] n monodie *f*.

monogamist [mɒ'nɒgəmɪst] n monogame *mf*.

monogamous [mɒ'nɒgəməs] adj monogame.

monogamy [mɒ'nɒgəmɪ] n monogamie *f*.

monogenetic [mɒnəʊdʒɪ'netɪk] adj monogénétique.

monogram ['mɒnəgræm] 1 n monogramme *m*. 2 vt marquer de son (*etc*) monogramme *or* de son (*etc*) chiffre.

monogrammed ['mɒnəgræmd] adj portant un (*or* son *etc*) monogramme, à son (*etc*) chiffre.

monograph ['mɒnəgræf] n monographie *f*.

monogynous [mɒ'nɒdʒɪnəs] adj monogame.

monogyny [mɒ'nɒdʒɪnɪ] n monogamie *f*.

monohull ['mɒnəʊhʌl] adj monocoque (*Naut*).

monokini ['mɒnəʊkiːnɪ] n monokini *m*.

monolingual [ˌmɒnəʊ'lɪŋgwəl] adj monolingue.

monolith ['mɒnəlɪθ] n monolithe *m*.

monolithic [ˌmɒnə'lɪθɪk] adj (*Archeol*) monolithe; (*fig*) *society, party* monolithique.

monologist ['mɒnəˌlɒgɪst] n monologueur *m*.

monologue, (*US also*) **monolog** ['mɒnəlɒg] n monologue *m*.

monomania [ˌmɒnəʊ'meɪnɪə] n monomanie *f*.

monomaniac [mɒnəʊ'meɪnɪæk] n, adj monomane, monomaniaque.

monometallism [ˌmɒnəʊ'metəlɪzəm] n monométallisme *m*.

monometer [mɒ'nɒmɪtə^r] n monomètre *m*.

monomial [mɒ'nəʊmɪəl] (*Math*) 1 n monôme *m*. 2 adj de *or* en monôme.

monomorphic [mɒnəʊ'mɔːfɪk] adj monomorphe.

monomorphism [mɒnəʊ'mɔːfɪzəm] n monomorphisme *m*.

mononuclear [mɒnəʊ'njuːklɪə^r] adj mononucléaire.

mononucleosis [ˌmɒnəʊnjuːklɪ'əʊsɪs] n mononucléose *f*.

monophonic [ˌmɒnəʊ'fɒnɪk] adj monophonique, monaural.

monophony [mɒ'nɒfənɪ] n monophonie *f*.

monophthong ['mɒnəfθɒŋ] n monophthongue *f*.

monoplane ['mɒnəʊpleɪn] n monoplan *m*.

monopolist [mə'nɒpəlɪst] n monopoliste *mf*.

monopolistic [mənɒpə'lɪstɪk] adj monopolistique.

monopolization [mənɒpəlaɪ'zeɪʃən] n monopolisation *f*.

monopolize [mə'nɒpəlaɪz] vt (*Comm*) monopoliser, avoir le monopole de; (*fig*) monopoliser, accaparer.

monopoly [mə'nɒpəlɪ] n a monopole *m* (*of, in* de). (*Brit*) **Monopolies and Mergers Commission** Commission *f* d'enquête sur les monopoles, Commission *f* de la concurrence. b (*game*) M~ ® Monopoly *m* ®.

monorail ['mɒnəʊreɪl] n monorail *m*.

monoski ['mɒnəʊˌskiː] n monoski *m*.

monosodium glutamate [mɒnəʊ'səʊdɪəm'gluːtəmeɪt] n glutamate *m* (de sodium).

monosyllabic ['mɒnəʊsɪ'læbɪk] adj *word* monosyllabe; *language, reply* monosyllabique. **he was ~** il a parlé par monosyllabes.

monosyllable ['mɒnəˌsɪləbl] n monosyllabe *m*. **to answer in ~s** répondre par monosyllabes.

monotheism ['mɒnəʊˌθiːɪzəm] n monothéisme *m*.

monotheist ['mɒnəʊˌθiːɪst] n monothéiste *mf*.

monotheistic [ˌmɒnəʊθiː'ɪstɪk] adj monothéiste.

monotone ['mɒnətəʊn] n (*voice/tone etc*) voix *f*/ton *m etc* monocorde. **to speak in a ~** parler sur un ton monocorde.

monotonous [mə'nɒtənəs] adj *music, routine, regularity* monotone; *landscape, scenery* monotone, uniforme; *voice* monotone, monocorde.

monotonously [mə'nɒtənəslɪ] adv de manière monotone. **~ reliable/punctual** d'une fiabilité/ponctualité monotone *or* ennuyeuse.

monotony [mə'nɒtənɪ] n monotonie *f*.

monotype ['mɒnəʊtaɪp] n (*Art, Engraving*) monotype *m*. (*Typ: machine*) M~ Monotype *f* ®.

monoxide [mɒ'nɒksaɪd] n protoxyde *m*.

Monroe doctrine [mən'rəʊ'dɒktrɪn] n doctrine *f* de Monroe.

monseigneur [ˌmɒnsen'jɜːr] n monseigneur *m*.

monsignor [mɒn'siːnjə^r] n, pl ~s *or* ~i (*Rel*) monsignor *m*.

monsoon [mɒn'suːn] n mousson *f*. **the ~ season** la mousson d'été.

mons pubis ['mɒnz'pjuːbɪs] n, pl **montes pubis** ['mɒntiːz'pjuːbɪs] pénil *m*, mont *m* de Vénus.

monster ['mɒnstə^r] 1 n (*all senses*) monstre *m*. 2 adj colossal, monstre*.

monstrance ['mɒnstrəns] n ostensoir *m*.

monstrosity [mɒn'strɒsɪtɪ] n a (*NonC*) monstruosité *f*, atrocité *f*. b (*thing*) monstruosité *f*, chose monstrueuse; (*person*) monstre *m* de laideur.

monstrous ['mɒnstrəs] adj a (*huge*) *animal, fish, building* colossal, énorme, gigantesque. b (*atrocious*) *crime, behaviour* monstrueux, abominable. **it is quite ~ that ...** il est monstrueux *or* scandaleux que ... + *subj*.

monstrously ['mɒnstrəslɪ] adv monstrueusement.

Mont. (*US*) abbr of **Montana**.

montage [mɒn'tɑːʒ] n (*Cine, Phot*) montage *m*.

Montana [mɒn'tænə] n Montana *m*. **in ~** dans le Montana.

Mont Blanc [mɔ̃ blɑ̃] n mont *m* Blanc.

Monte Carlo ['mɒntɪ'kɑːləʊ] n Monte-Carlo.

Montenegrin [ˌmɒntɪ'niːgrɪn] 1 adj monténégrin. 2 n (*person*) Monténégrin(e) *m(f)*.

Montenegro [ˌmɒntɪ'niːgrəʊ] n Monténégro *m*.

Montezuma [mɒntɪ'zuːmə] n Montezuma *m*. (*fig*) **~'s revenge*** maladie *f* du touriste, turista‡ *f*, diarrhée *f*.

month [mʌnθ] n mois *m*. **it went on for ~s** cela a duré des mois (et des mois); **in the ~ of May** au mois de mai, en mai; **to be paid by the ~** être payé au mois *or* mensualisé; **every ~** *happen* tous les mois; *pay* mensuellement; **which day of the ~ is it?** le combien sommes-nous?; **at the end of this ~** à la fin du *or* de ce mois; (*Comm*) **at the end of the current ~** fin courant*; **he owes his landlady two ~s' rent** il doit deux mois à sa propriétaire; **six ~s pregnant** enceinte de six mois; **he'll never do it in a ~ of Sundays*** il le fera la semaine des quatre jeudis* *or* à la saint-glinglin*; *see* **calendar, lunar** *etc*.

monthly ['mʌnθlɪ] 1 adj *publication* mensuel. **~ instalment, ~ payment**

mensualité *f*; (*Admin*) ~ **paid staff** employés *mpl* mensualisés; (*Med*) ~ **period** règles *fpl*; ~ **salary** salaire mensuel, mensualité *f*; ~ **ticket** carte *f* (d'abonnement) mensuelle. 2 n (*Press*) revue *or* publication mensuelle. 3 adv *pay* au mois, mensuellement; *happen* tous les mois.

Montreal [ˌmɒntrɪˈɔːl] n Montréal.

monument [ˈmɒnjʊmənt] n (*all senses*) monument *m* (*to* à).

monumental [ˌmɒnjʊˈmentl] adj (*all senses*) monumental. ~ **mason** marbrier *m*.

monumentally [ˌmɒnjʊˈmentəlɪ] adv *dull, popular etc* extrêmement. ~ **important** d'une importance capitale *or* monumentale.

moo [muː] 1 n meuglement *m*, beuglement *m*, mugissement *m*. ~! meu!; **silly** ~‡ pauvre cloche*. 2 vi meugler, beugler, mugir.

mooch‡ [muːtʃ] 1 vt (*US: cadge*) **to** ~ **sth from sb** taper qn de qch‡. 2 vi: **to** ~ **in/out** *etc* entrer/sortir *etc* en traînant.

►**mooch about‡, mooch around‡** vi traînasser, flemmarder*.

mood [muːd] 1 n a humeur *f*, disposition *f*. **to be in a good/bad** ~ être de bonne/mauvaise humeur, être de bon/mauvais poil*; **to be in a nasty** *or* **an ugly** ~ *[person]* être d'une humeur massacrante *or* exécrable; *[crowd]* être menaçant; **to be in a forgiving** ~ être en veine de générosité *or* d'indulgence; **I'm in the** ~ **for dancing** je danserais volontiers, j'ai envie de danser; **I'm not in the** ~ *or* **I'm in no** ~ **for laughing** je ne suis pas d'humeur à rire, je n'ai aucune envie de rire; **I'm in no** ~ **to listen to him** je ne suis pas d'humeur à l'écouter; **are you in the** ~ **for chess?** une partie d'échecs ça vous dit?; **he plays well when he's in the** ~ quand il est d'humeur *or* quand ça lui chante* il joue bien; **I'm not in the** ~ ça ne me dit rien; **as the** ~ **takes him** selon son humeur, comme ça lui chante*; **that depends on his** ~ cela dépend de son humeur; **he's in one of his** ~**s** il est encore mal luné; **she has** ~**s** elle a des sautes d'humeur; **the** ~ **of the meeting** l'état *m* d'esprit de l'assemblée.
b (*Ling, Mus*) mode *m*.
2 comp ►**mood music** musique *f* d'ambiance.

moodily [ˈmuːdɪlɪ] adv (*bad-temperedly*) *reply* d'un ton maussade, maussadement; (*gloomily*) *stare* d'un air morose.

moodiness [ˈmuːdɪnɪs] n (*sulkiness*) humeur *f* maussade; (*changeability*) humeur changeante.

moody [ˈmuːdɪ] adj (*variable*) d'humeur changeante, lunatique; (*sulky*) maussade, de mauvaise humeur, mal luné.

moola(h)‡ [ˈmuːlɑː] n (*US: money*) pèze‡ *m*, fric‡ *m*.

moon [muːn] 1 n lune *f*. **full/new** ~ pleine/nouvelle lune; **there was no** ~ c'était une nuit sans lune; **there was a** ~ **that night** il y avait *or* il faisait clair de lune cette nuit-là; **by the light of the** ~ à la clarté de la lune, au clair de (la) lune; **the** ~**s of Jupiter** les lunes de Jupiter; (*hum*) **many** ~**s ago** il y a de cela bien longtemps; (*fig*) **to ask** *or* **cry for the** ~ demander la lune; (*fig*) **he's over the** ~* **(about it)** il (en) est ravi, il est aux anges; *see* **blue, land, man** *etc*.
2 comp ►**moonbeam** rayon *m* de lune ►**moonboots** après-ski(s) *mpl* (*en nylon*), moonboots *mpl* ►**moon buggy** jeep *f* lunaire ►**mooncraft** (*Space*) module *m* lunaire ►**moonfaced** (*pej*) aux joues toutes rondes, joufflu ►**moon landing** alunissage *m* ►**moonless** *see* **moonless** ►**moonlight(ing)** *see* **moonlight(ing)** ►**moonlit** éclairé par la lune ►**moonlit night** nuit *f* de lune ►**moonrise** lever *m* de (la) lune ►**moon rock** roche *f* lunaire ►**moonrover** = **moon buggy** ►**moonscape** sol *m or* paysage *m* lunaire ►**moonshine*** (*fig*) (*nonsense*) balivernes *fpl*, fadaises *fpl*, sornettes *fpl*; (*US: illegal spirits*) alcool *m* de contrebande ►**moonshiner** (*US*) (*distiller*) bouilleur *m* de cru clandestin; (*smuggler*) contrebandier *m* d'alcool ►**moonshining** (*US*) distillation clandestine ►**moonship** (*Space*) module *m* lunaire ►**moon shot** (*Space*) tir *m* lunaire ►**moonstone** pierre *f* de lune ►**moonstruck** (*fig*) dans la lune ►**moon walk** marche *f* lunaire.
3 vi (‡: *exhibit buttocks*) montrer son derrière.

►**moon about, moon around** vi musarder en rêvassant.

►**moon over** vt fus: **to moon over sb** soupirer pour qn.

Moonie [ˈmuːnɪ] n mooniste *mf*, adepte *mf* de la secte Moon.

moonless [ˈmuːnlɪs] adj sans lune.

moonlight [ˈmuːnlaɪt] 1 n clair *m* de lune. **by** ~ au clair de (la) lune. 2 comp *walk, encounter* au clair de lune ►**to do a moonlight flit** (*Brit fig*) déménager à la cloche de bois ►**moonlight night** nuit *f* de lune. 3 vi (*: *work extra*) faire du travail noir, travailler au noir.

moonlighting* [ˈmuːnlaɪtɪŋ] n (*NonC*) travail noir.

Moor [mʊəʳ] n Maure *m or* More *m*, Mauresque *f or* Moresque *f*.

moor¹ [mʊəʳ] 1 n lande *f*. 2 comp ►**moorhen** poule *f* d'eau ►**moorland** lande *f*; (*boggy*) terrain tourbeux.

moor² [mʊəʳ] 1 vt *ship* amarrer. 2 vi mouiller.

mooring [ˈmʊərɪŋ] n (*Naut*) (*place*) mouillage *m*; (*ropes etc*) amarres *fpl*. **at her** ~**s** sur ses amarres; ~ **buoy** coffre *m* (d'amarrage), bouée *f* de corps-mort.

Moorish [ˈmʊərɪʃ] adj maure (*f inv or* mauresque) *or* more (*f inv or* moresque).

moose [muːs] n, pl inv (*in Canada*) orignac *m or* orignal *m*; (*in Europe*) élan *m*.

moot [muːt] 1 adj *question* discutable, controversé. **it's a** ~ **point** c'est discutable; (*Jur*) ~ **case** cas *m* hypothétique *or* sans intérêt pratique, hypothèse *f* d'école; (*US*) ~ **court** *tribunal fictif permettant aux étudiants de s'exercer*. 2 vt *question* soulever, mettre sur le tapis. **it has been** ~**ed that** ... on a suggéré que ... .

mop [mɒp] 1 n (*for floor*) balai *m* laveur; (*Naut*) faubert *m*; (*for dishes*) lavette *f* (à vaisselle); (*fig: also* ~ **of hair**) tignasse *f*. ~ **of curls** toison bouclée. 2 comp ►**mopboard** (*US*) plinthe *f* ►**mopping-up operation,** (*also US*) **mop-up** (*Mil*) (opération *f* de) nettoyage *m*. 3 vt *floor, surface* essuyer. **to** ~ **one's brow** s'éponger le front; (*fig*) **to** ~ **the floor with sb*** battre qn à plate(s) couture(s).

►**mop down** vt sep passer un coup de balai à.

►**mop up** 1 vt sep a *liquid* éponger; *floor, surface* essuyer. b (*fig*) *profits* rafler, absorber. c (*Mil*) *terrain* nettoyer; *remnants of enemy* éliminer. d (‡: *drink*) siffler*. 2 **mopping-up** adj *see* **mop 2**.

mope [məʊp] vi se morfondre, avoir le cafard* *or* des idées noires. **she** ~**d about it all day** toute la journée elle a broyé du noir en y pensant.

►**mope about, mope around** vi passer son temps à se morfondre, traîner son ennui.

moped [ˈməʊped] n (*Brit*) vélomoteur *m*, mobylette *f* ®.

moppet* [ˈmɒpɪt] n chéri(e) *m(f)*.

moquette [mɒˈket] n moquette *f* (*étoffe*).

moraine [mɒˈreɪn] n moraine *f*.

moral [ˈmɒrəl] 1 adj (*all senses*) moral. **it is a** ~ **certainty** c'est une certitude morale; **to be under** *or* **have a** ~ **obligation to do** être moralement obligé de faire, être dans l'obligation morale de faire; ~ **support** soutien moral; **I'm going along as** ~ **support for him** j'y vais pour le soutenir moralement; (*US Pol*) **the M~ Majority** les néo-conservateurs *mpl* (américains); ~ **philosopher** moraliste *mf*; ~ **philosophy** la morale, l'éthique *f*; (*Rel*) **M~ Rearmament** Réarmement *m* moral; **to raise** ~ **standards** relever le niveau moral; ~ **standards are falling** la moralité décline, le sens moral se perd, on perd le sens des valeurs; ~ **suasion** pression morale.
2 n a *[story]* morale *f*. **to point the** ~ faire ressortir la morale.
b *[person, act, attitude]* ~**s** moralité *f*; **of loose** ~**s** d'une moralité relâchée; **he has no** ~**s** il est sans moralité.

morale [mɒˈrɑːl] n (*NonC*) moral *m*. **high** ~ bon moral; **his** ~ **was very low** il avait le moral très bas *or* à zéro; **to raise sb's** ~ remonter le moral à qn; **to lower** *or* **undermine sb's** ~ démoraliser qn.

moralist [ˈmɒrəlɪst] n moraliste *mf*.

moralistic [mɒrəˈlɪstɪk] adj moralisateur (*f* -trice).

morality [məˈrælɪtɪ] n a (*NonC*) moralité *f*. b (*Theat: also* ~ **play**) moralité *f*.

moralize [ˈmɒrəlaɪz] 1 vi moraliser (*about* sur), faire le moraliste. 2 vt moraliser, faire la morale à.

moralizing [ˈmɒrəlaɪzɪŋ] 1 adj moralisateur (*f* -trice). 2 n leçons *fpl* de morale.

morally [ˈmɒrəlɪ] adv *act* moralement. ~ **certain** moralement certain; ~ **speaking** du point de vue de la morale, moralement parlant; ~ **wrong** immoral, contraire à la morale.

morass [məˈræs] n marais *m*, marécage *m*. (*fig*) **a** ~ **of problems** des problèmes à ne plus s'y retrouver *or* à ne plus s'en sortir; **a** ~ **of figures** un fatras de chiffres; **a** ~ **of paperwork** de la paperasserie, un monceau de paperasserie.

moratorium [ˌmɒrəˈtɔːrɪəm] n, pl ~**s** *or* **moratoria** [ˌmɒrəˈtɔːrɪə] moratoire *m*, moratorium *m*.

Moravian [məˈreɪvɪən] 1 n Morave *mf*. 2 adj morave. **the** ~ **Church** l'Église *f* morave.

moray eel [mɒˈreɪˈiːl] n murène *f*.

morbid [ˈmɔːbɪd] adj a *interest, curiosity, imagination* morbide, malsain; *details* morbide, horrifiant; *fear, dislike* maladif; (*gloomy*) lugubre. **don't be so** ~! ne te complais pas dans ces pensées! *or* ces idées! b (*Med*) *growth* morbide; *anatomy* pathologique.

morbidity [mɔːˈbɪdɪtɪ] n (*see* **morbid**) a morbidité *f*; état maladif; (*gloom*) abattement maladif, neurasthénie *f*. b (*Med*) morbidité *f*.

morbidly [ˈmɔːbɪdlɪ] adv (*abnormally*) d'une façon morbide *or* malsaine *or* maladive; (*gloomily*) sombrement, sinistrement. ~ **obsessed by** morbidement *or* maladivement obsédé *or* hanté par.

morbidness [ˈmɔːbɪdnɪs] n = **morbidity**.

mordacious [mɔːˈdeɪʃəs] adj mordant, caustique.

mordacity [mɔːˈdæsɪtɪ] n mordacité *f* (*liter*), causticité *f*.

mordant [ˈmɔːdənt] adj mordant, caustique.

mordent [ˈmɔːdənt] n (*Mus*) **(lower)** ~ mordant *m*, pincé *m*; **upper** *or* **inverted** ~ pincé renversé.

more [mɔːʳ] compar of **many, much** 1 adj, pron (*greater in number etc*) plus (de), davantage (de); (*additional*) encore (de); (*other*) d'autres. **I've got** ~ **money/books than you** j'ai plus d'argent/de livres que vous; **he's got** ~ **than you** il en a plus que vous; ~ **people than seats/than usual/than we expected** plus de gens que de places/que de coutume/que prévu *or* que nous ne l'escomptions; **many came but** ~ **stayed away** beaucoup de gens sont venus mais davantage *or* un plus grand nombre se sont abstenus; **many** ~ *or* **a lot** ~ **books/time** beaucoup plus de livres/de temps; **I need a lot** ~ il m'en faut beaucoup plus *or* bien davantage; **I need a few** ~ **books** il me faut encore quelques livres *or* quelques livres de plus; **some were talking and a few** ~ **were reading** il y en avait qui parlaient et d'autres qui lisaient; **a little** ~ un peu plus (de); **several** ~ **days** quelques jours de plus, encore quelques jours; **I'd**

like (some) ~ meat je voudrais encore de la viande; there's no ~ meat il n'y a plus de viande; is there (any) ~ wine? y a-t-il encore du vin?, est-ce qu'il reste du vin?; have some ~ ice cream reprenez de la glace; has she any ~ children? a-t-elle d'autres enfants?; no ~ shouting! assez de cris!, arrêtez de crier!; I've got no ~, I haven't any ~ je n'en ai plus, il ne m'en reste plus; I've no ~ time je n'ai plus le temps; he can't afford ~ than a small house il ne peut se payer qu'une petite maison; I shan't say any ~, I shall say no ~ je n'en dirai pas davantage; (*threat*) tenez-le-vous pour dit; it cost ~ than I expected c'était plus cher que je ne l'escomptais; have you heard any ~ about him? avez-vous d'autres nouvelles de lui?; one pound is ~ than 50p une livre est plus que 50 pence; ~ than half the audience plus de la moitié de l'assistance *or* des auditeurs; not ~ than a kilo pas plus d'un kilo; ~ than 20 came plus de 20 personnes sont venues; no ~ than a dozen une douzaine au plus; ~ than enough plus que suffisant, amplement *or* bien suffisant; I've got ~ like these j'en ai d'autres comme ça, j'en ai encore comme ça; (*fig*) you couldn't ask for ~ on ne peut guère en demander plus *or* davantage; we must see ~ of her il faut que nous la voyions (*subj*) davantage *or* plus souvent; I want to know ~ about it je veux en savoir plus long, je veux en savoir davantage; there's ~ where that came from ce n'est qu'un début; (*loc*) the ~ the merrier plus on est de fous plus on rit (*Prov*); and what's ~ ... et qui plus est ...; his speech, of which ~ later son discours, sur lequel nous reviendrons; let's say no ~ about it n'en parlons plus; I shall have ~ to say about that je reviendrai sur ce sujet (plus tard), ce n'est pas tout sur ce sujet; I've nothing ~ to say je n'ai rien à ajouter; nothing ~ rien de plus; something ~ autre chose, quelque chose d'autre *or* de plus; *see* meet[1] 1e.

2 adv a (*forming compar of adjs and advs*) plus. ~ difficult plus difficile; ~ easily plus facilement; ~ and ~ difficult de plus en plus difficile; even ~ difficult encore plus difficile.

b *exercise, sleep etc* plus, davantage. you must rest ~ vous devez vous reposer davantage; he talks ~ than I do il parle plus *or* davantage que moi; she talks even ~ than he does elle parle encore plus *or* davantage que lui; he sleeps ~ and ~ il dort de plus en plus; I like apples ~ than oranges je préfère les pommes aux oranges.

c (*in phrases*) ~ amused than annoyed plus amusé que fâché; he was ~ frightened than hurt il a eu plus de peur que de mal; each ~ beautiful than the next *or* the other tous plus beaux les uns que les autres; it's ~ a short story than a novel c'est une nouvelle plus qu'un roman; he's no ~ a duke than I am il n'est pas plus duc que moi; he could no ~ pay me than fly in the air* il ne pourrait pas plus me payer que devenir pape*; no *or* nothing ~ than rien (de plus) que; not much ~ than ne guère que; ~ or less plus ou moins; no ~ and no less, neither ~ nor less (than) ni plus ni moins (que); it will ~ than cover the cost cela couvrira largement *or* amplement les frais; the house is ~ than half built la maison est plus qu'à moitié bâtie; I had ~ than kept my promise j'avais fait plus que tenir ma promesse; I can't bear him! — no ~ can I! je ne peux pas le souffrir! — ni moi non plus!; I shan't go there again! — no ~† you shall je ne veux pas y retourner! — c'est entendu.

d (*the* ~) the ~ you rest the quicker you'll get better plus vous vous reposerez plus vous vous rétablirez rapidement; the ~ I think of it the ~ ashamed I feel plus j'y pense plus j'ai honte; (the) ~'s the pity! c'est d'autant plus dommage!, c'est bien dommage!; (the) ~ fool you to go! tu es d'autant plus idiot d'y aller!; he is all the ~ happy il est d'autant plus heureux (*as* que); (all) the ~ so as *or* because ... d'autant plus que ... .

e (*again etc*) I won't do it any ~ je ne le ferai plus; don't do it any ~! ne recommence pas!; he doesn't live here any ~ il n'habite plus ici; I can't stay any ~ je ne peux pas rester plus longtemps *or* davantage; (*liter*) we shall see him no ~ nous ne le reverrons jamais plus *or* plus jamais; (*liter*) he is no ~ il n'est plus; once ~ une fois de plus, encore une fois; only once ~ une dernière fois; (*liter*) never ~ (ne ...) plus jamais, (ne ...) jamais plus.

moreish* ['mɔːrɪʃ] adj: these cakes are very ~* ces gâteaux ont un goût de revenez-y*.

moreover [mɔː'rəʊvəʳ] adv (*further*) de plus, en outre; (*besides*) d'ailleurs, du reste.

mores ['mɔːreɪz] npl mœurs *fpl*.

morganatic [ˌmɔːgə'nætɪk] adj morganatique.

morganatically [ˌmɔːgə'nætɪkəlɪ] adv morganatiquement.

morgue [mɔːg] n (*mortuary*) morgue *f*; (**: of newspaper*) archives *fpl* (*d'un journal*).

MORI ['mɒrɪ] n (abbr of Market and Opinion Research Institute) ~ poll sondage *m* de l'opinion publique.

moribund ['mɒrɪbʌnd] adj moribond.

Mormon ['mɔːmən] 1 n mormon(e) *m(f)*. 2 adj mormon.

Mormonism ['mɔːmənɪzəm] n mormonisme *m*.

morn [mɔːn] n (*liter*) (*morning*) matin *m*; (*dawn*) aube *f*.

morning ['mɔːnɪŋ] 1 n matin *m*; matinée *f*. good ~! (*hallo*) bonjour!; (*goodbye*) au revoir!; he came in the ~ il est arrivé dans la matinée; I'll do it in the ~ je le ferai le matin *or* dans la matinée; (*tomorrow*) je le ferai demain matin; it happened first thing in the ~ c'est arrivé tout au début de la matinée; I'll do it first thing in the ~ je le ferai demain à la première heure; I work in the ~(s) je travaille le matin; she's working ~s *or* she's on ~s* this week elle travaille le matin, cette semaine; a ~'s work une matinée de travail; she's got the ~ off elle a congé ce matin; I have a ~ off every week j'ai un matin *or* une matinée de libre par semaine; during (the course of) the ~ pendant la matinée; I was busy all (the) ~ j'ai été occupé toute la matinée; on the ~ of January 23rd le 23 janvier au matin, le matin du 23 janvier; what a beautiful ~! quelle belle matinée!; at 7 (o'clock) in the ~ à 7 heures du matin; in the early ~ au (petit) matin; to get up very early in the ~ se lever de très bonne heure *or* très tôt (le matin), se lever de bon *or* de grand matin; this ~ ce matin; tomorrow ~ demain matin; the ~ before la veille au matin; yesterday ~ hier matin; the next *or* following ~, the ~ after le lendemain matin; the ~ after (the night before)* un lendemain de cuite*; every Sunday ~ tous les dimanches matin; one summer ~ (par) un matin d'été; *see* Monday *etc*.

2 adj *walk, swim* matinal, du matin. a ~ train un train le matin *or* dans la matinée; the ~ train le train du matin.

3 comp ►morning-after pill (*contraceptive*) pilule *f* du lendemain ►morning coat jaquette *f* ►morning coffee pause-café *f* (dans la matinée); we have morning coffee together nous prenons un café ensemble le matin ►morning dress jaquette *f* et pantalon rayé, habit *m*, frac *m* ►morning-glory (*Bot*) belle-de-jour *f* ►morning paper journal *m* (du matin) ►morning prayer(s) prière(s) *f(pl)* du matin ►morning room† petit salon *m* (*conçu pour recevoir le soleil le matin*) ►morning service office *m* du matin ►morning sickness nausée *f* (du matin), nausées matinales ►morning star étoile *f* du matin ►morning watch (*Naut*) premier quart du jour.

Moroccan [mə'rɒkən] 1 adj marocain. 2 n Marocain(e) *m(f)*.

Morocco [mə'rɒkəʊ] n a Maroc *m*. b m~ (leather) maroquin *m*; m~-bound relié en maroquin.

moron ['mɔːrɒn] n (*gen*) idiot(e) *m(f)*, crétin(e) *m(f)*, minus (habens)* *m inv*; (*Med*) débile *m* léger, débile *f* légère. he's a ~!* c'est un débile* *or* un crétin!, il est taré!

moronic [mə'rɒnɪk] adj crétin, idiot.

morose [mə'rəʊs] adj (*gloomy*) morose, sombre; (*sullen*) maussade, renfrogné.

morosely [mə'rəʊslɪ] adv d'un air morose, sombrement.

morph [mɔːf] n (*Ling*) morphe *m*.

morpheme ['mɔːfiːm] n morphème *m*.

morphemics [mɔː'fiːmɪks] n (*NonC*) morphématique *f*.

Morpheus ['mɔːfɪəs] n Morphée *m*; *see* arm[1].

morphia ['mɔːfɪə] = morphine.

morphine ['mɔːfiːn] n morphine *f*. ~ addict morphinomane *mf*; ~ addiction morphinomanie *f*.

morphological [ˌmɔːfə'lɒdʒɪkəl] adj morphologique.

morphologically [ˌmɔːfə'lɒdʒɪkəlɪ] adv morphologiquement.

morphologist [mɔː'fɒlədʒɪst] n morphologue *mf*.

morphology [mɔː'fɒlədʒɪ] n morphologie *f*.

morphophonemics [ˌmɔːfəʊfəʊ'niːmɪks] n (*NonC*) morphophonémique *f*.

morphophonology [ˌmɔːfəʊfə'nɒlədʒɪ] n morphophonologie *f*.

morphosyntax [ˌmɔːfəʊ'sɪntæks] n morphosyntaxe *m*.

morris ['mɒrɪs] n (*Brit: in comps*) ~ dance (*type de*) *danse folklorique anglaise;* ~ dancers, ~ men *danseurs folkloriques;* ~ dancing *danses folkloriques.*

morrow ['mɒrəʊ] n (†† *or liter*) (*morning*) matin *m*; (*next day*) lendemain *m*.

Morse [mɔːs] 1 n (*also* ~ code) morse *m*. 2 comp ►Morse alphabet alphabet *m* morse ►Morse signals signaux *mpl* en morse.

morsel ['mɔːsl] n (*gen*) (petit) bout *m*. she ate only a ~ of fish elle n'a mangé qu'une bouchée de poisson; choice ~ morceau *m* de choix.

mortadella [ˌmɔːtə'delə] n mortadelle *f*.

mortal ['mɔːtl] 1 adj *life, hatred, enemy, fear* mortel; *injury* mortel, fatal. ~ combat combat *m* à mort; ~ remains dépouille mortelle; ~ sin péché mortel; it's no ~ good to him* cela ne lui sert strictement à rien. 2 n mortel(le) *m(f)*.

mortality [mɔː'tælɪtɪ] n mortalité *f*. infant ~ (taux *m* de) mortalité infantile.

mortally ['mɔːtəlɪ] adv (*lit, fig*) mortellement.

mortar ['mɔːtəʳ] 1 n (*Constr, Mil, Pharm*) mortier *m*. 2 comp ►mortarboard mortier *m* (*coiffure universitaire*).

mortgage ['mɔːgɪdʒ] 1 n (*in house buying etc*) emprunt-logement *m*; (*second loan etc*) hypothèque *f*. to take out *or* raise a ~ obtenir un emprunt-logement (*on, for* pour); prendre une hypothèque; to pay off *or* clear a ~ rembourser un emprunt-logement; purger une hypothèque. 2 vt *house, one's future* hypothéquer. 3 comp ►mortgage broker courtier *m* en prêts hypothécaires ►mortgage rate taux *m* d'emprunt hypothécaire.

mortgageable ['mɔːgədʒɪbl] adj hypothécable.

mortgagee [ˌmɔːgə'dʒiː] n créancier *m*, -ière *f* hypothécaire.

mortgagor [ˌmɔːgə'dʒɔːʳ] n débiteur *m*, -trice *f* hypothécaire.

mortice ['mɔːtɪs] n = mortise.

mortician [mɔː'tɪʃən] n (*US*) entrepreneur *m* de pompes funèbres.

mortification [ˌmɔːtɪfɪˈkeɪʃən] n mortification *f* (*also Rel*), humiliation *f*.
mortify [ˈmɔːtɪfaɪ] vt mortifier (*also Rel*), humilier. **I was mortified to learn that** ... j'ai été mortifié d'apprendre que ...; (*Rel*) **to ~ the flesh** se mortifier, mortifier sa chair.
mortifying [ˈmɔːtɪfaɪɪŋ] adj mortifiant, humiliant.
mortise [ˈmɔːtɪs] n mortaise *f*. **~ lock** serrure encastrée.
mortuary [ˈmɔːtjʊərɪ] 1 n morgue *f*, dépôt *m* mortuaire. 2 adj mortuaire.
Mosaic [məʊˈzeɪɪk] adj (*Bible Hist*) mosaïque, de Moïse.
mosaic [məʊˈzeɪɪk] 1 n mosaïque *f*. 2 comp en mosaïque.
Moscow [ˈmɒskəʊ] n Moscou. **the ~ team** l'équipe *f* moscovite.
Moselle [məʊˈzel] n a (*Geog*) Moselle *f*. b (*wine*) (vin *m* de) Moselle *m*.
Moses [ˈməʊzɪz] 1 n Moïse *m*. **Holy ~!*** mince alors!* 2 comp ▸**Moses basket** moïse *m*.
mosey‡ [ˈməʊzɪ] 1 vi (*US*) **to ~ along** (se) baguenauder*, aller *or* marcher sans (trop) se presser; **they ~ed over to Joe's** ils sont allés jusque chez Joe (sans (trop) se presser); **I'll just ~ on down** je vais descendre (sans me presser *or* en prenant mon temps), je vais descendre faire un tour. 2 n: **to have a ~ round somewhere** faire une balade* *or* un tour quelque part.
Moslem [ˈmɒzləm] = **Muslim**.
mosque [mɒsk] n mosquée *f*.
mosquito [mɒsˈkiːtəʊ] 1 n, pl **~(e)s** moustique *m*. 2 comp ▸**mosquito bite** piqûre *f* de moustique ▸**mosquito net** moustiquaire *f* ▸**mosquito netting** mousseline *f or* gaze *f* pour moustiquaire.
moss [mɒs] 1 n mousse *f* (*Bot*); *see* **rolling**. 2 comp ▸**mossback*** (*US fig*) conservateur *m* à tout crin ▸**moss green** adj vert mousse *inv* ◊ n vert *m* mousse ▸**moss rose** rose moussue ▸**moss stitch** (*Knitting*) point *m* de riz.
mossy [ˈmɒsɪ] adj (*gen*) moussu. **~ green** (adj) vert mousse *inv*; (n) vert *m* mousse.
most [məʊst] superl of **many, much** 1 adj, pron a (*greatest in amount etc*) le plus (de), la plus grande quantité (de), le plus grand nombre (de). **he earns (the) ~ money** c'est lui qui gagne le plus d'argent; **I've got (the) ~ records** c'est moi qui ai le plus (grand nombre) de disques; **(the) ~** le plus, le maximum; **who has got (the) ~?** qui en a le plus?; **do the ~ you can** fais-en le plus que tu pourras; **at (the) ~, at the very ~** au maximum, (tout) au plus; **to make the ~ of** *one's time* ne pas perdre, bien employer; *respite, opportunity, sunshine, sb's absence* profiter (au maximum) de; *one's talents, business offer, money* tirer le meilleur parti de; *one's resources, remaining food* utiliser au mieux, faire durer; **make the ~ of it!** profitez-en bien!, tâchez de bien en profiter!; **he certainly made the ~ of the story** il a vraiment exploité cette histoire à fond; **to make the ~ of o.s.** se faire valoir, se mettre en valeur; **they're the ~!**‡ ils sont champions!*

b (*largest part*) la plus grande partie (de), la majeure *or* la meilleure partie (de); (*greatest number*) la majorité (de), la plupart (de). **~ (of the) people/books** *etc* la plupart *or* la majorité des gens/des livres *etc*; **~ honey is expensive** le miel en général coûte cher, la plupart des marques de miel coûtent cher; **~ of the butter** presque tout le beurre; **~ of the money** la plus grande *or* la majeure partie de l'argent, presque tout l'argent; **~ of it** presque tout; **~ of them** la plupart d'entre eux; **~ of the day** la plus grande *or* la majeure partie de la journée; **~ of the time** la plupart du temps; **for the ~ part** pour la plupart, en général; **in ~ cases** dans la plupart *or* la majorité des cas.

2 adv a (*forming superl of adjs and advs*) le plus. **the ~ intelligent boy** le garçon le plus intelligent; **the ~ beautiful woman of all** la plus belle femme *or* la femme la plus belle de toutes; **~ easily** le plus facilement.

b *work, sleep etc* le plus. **he talked ~** c'est lui qui a le plus parlé *or* parlé le plus; **what he wants ~ (of all)** ce qu'il désire le plus *or* par-dessus tout *or* avant tout; **the book he wanted ~ (of all)** le livre qu'il voulait le plus *or* entre tous; **that's what annoyed me ~ (of all)** c'est ce qui m'a contrarié le plus *or* par-dessus tout.

c (*very*) bien, très, fort. **~ likely** très probablement; **a ~ delightful day** une journée on ne peut plus agréable *or* des plus agréables *or* bien agréable; **you are ~ kind** vous êtes (vraiment) très aimable; **it's a ~ useful gadget** c'est un gadget des plus utiles *or* tout ce qu'il y a de plus utile; **the M~ High** le Très-Haut; **M~ Reverend** révérendissime.

d (*US *: almost*) presque.
...most [məʊst] suf le plus, *e.g.* **northern~** le plus au nord; *see* **foremost, inner** *etc*.
mostly [ˈməʊstlɪ] adv (*chiefly*) principalement, surtout; (*almost all*) pour la plupart; (*most often*) le plus souvent, la plupart du temps, en général. **it is ~ water** c'est presque entièrement composé d'eau; **they're ~ women** ce sont surtout des femmes, pour la plupart ce sont des femmes; **~ because** principalement *or* surtout parce que; **it's ~ raining there** il y pleut la plupart du temps *or* presque constamment; **he ~ comes on Mondays** en général il vient le lundi.
MOT [eməʊˈtiː] n (*Brit*) a (abbr of **Ministry of Transport**) *see* **transport**. b (*Aut: also* **~ test**) *contrôle périodique obligatoire des véhicules*. **the car has passed/failed its ~ (test)** la voiture a obtenu/n'a pas obtenu le certificat de contrôle; **it's got an ~ (certificate) till April** le certificat de contrôle est valable jusqu'en avril.
mote [məʊt] n atome *m*; *[dust]* grain *m*. (*Bible*) **the ~ in thy brother's eye** la paille dans l'œil du frère.
motel [məʊˈtel] n motel *m*.
motet [məʊˈtet] n motet *m*.
moth [mɒθ] 1 n papillon *m* de nuit, phalène *m or f*; (*in clothes*) mite *f*. 2 comp ▸**mothball** boule *f* de naphtaline; (*fig*) **in mothballs*** *object* en conserve (*hum*); *ship, plan* en réserve ▸**moth-eaten** mangé aux mites, mité; (** fig*) mangé aux mites*; **to become moth-eaten** se miter ▸**moth-hole** trou *m* de mite ▸**mothproof** adj traité à l'antimite ◊ vt traiter à l'antimite.
mother [ˈmʌðəʳ] 1 n a (*lit, fig*) mère *f*. **she was (like) a ~ to me** elle était une vraie mère pour moi; (*Rel*) **the Reverend M~** la Révérende Mère; **every ~'s son of them*** **was there** ils étaient là tous tant qu'ils étaient; *see* **foster, house, necessity** *etc*.

b († *or liter*) **old M~ Jones** la mère Jones; *see also* **3**.

c (*US* ‡) = **motherfucker**‡.

2 vt (*act as ~ to*) servir de mère à, entourer de soins maternels; (*indulge, protect*) dorloter, chouchouter; (*Psych*) materner; (††: *give birth to*) donner naissance à. **she always ~s her lodgers** elle est une vraie mère pour ses locataires.

3 comp ▸**motherboard** (*Comput*) carte *f* mère ▸**Mother Church**: **our Mother Church** notre sainte mère l'Église ▸**mother country** mère patrie *f* ▸**mothercraft** puériculture *f* ▸**motherfucker**‡ (*esp US*) connard‡ *m*, couillon‡ *m*, connasse‡ *f* ▸**motherfucking**‡: (*esp US*) **that motherfucking car!** cette putain de bagnole!‡; **get your motherfucking ass in gear!** magne-toi le cul!‡; **you motherfucking son-of-a-bitch!** espèce de fils de pute!‡ ▸**Mother Goose** ma Mère l'Oye ▸**mother hen** mère poule *f* ▸**mother-in-law** (pl **~s-~-~**) belle-mère *f* ▸**motherland** patrie *f* ▸**mother love** amour maternel ▸**mother-naked** tout nu, nu comme un ver ▸**Mother Nature** Dame Nature *f* ▸**Mother of God** Marie, mère de Dieu ▸**mother-of-pearl** nacre *f* (de perle) ▸**mother-of-thousands** (*Bot*) chlorophytum *m* ▸**Mother's Day** la fête des Mères ▸**mother's help**, (*US*) **mother's helper** aide maternelle ▸**mother ship** (*Naut*) ravitailleur *m* ▸**Mother Superior** (pl **~ ~s** *or* **~s ~**) (*Rel*) Mère *f* supérieure ▸**mother-to-be** future maman ▸**mother tongue** langue maternelle ▸**mother wit** bon sens inné.
motherhood [ˈmʌðəhʊd] n maternité *f*.
mothering [ˈmʌðərɪŋ] n soins maternels, amour maternel; (*Psych, fig: in teaching etc*) maternage *m*. **he needs ~** il a besoin d'une mère qui s'occupe de lui *or* de la tendresse d'une mère; (*Brit*) **M~ Sunday** la fête des Mères.
motherless [ˈmʌðəlɪs] adj orphelin de mère, sans mère.
motherly [ˈmʌðəlɪ] adj maternel.
motif [məʊˈtiːf] n (*Art, Mus*) motif *m*.
motion [ˈməʊʃən] 1 n a (*NonC*) mouvement *m*, marche *f*. **perpetual ~** mouvement perpétuel; **to be in ~** *[vehicle]* être en marche; *[machine]* être en mouvement *or* en marche; **to set in ~** *machine* mettre en mouvement *or* en marche; *vehicle* mettre en marche; (*fig*) *process etc* mettre en branle; (*fig*) **to put** *or* **set the wheels in ~** (*process etc*) lancer le processus, mettre les choses en branle; **the ~ of the car made him ill** le mouvement de la voiture l'a rendu malade.

b (*gesture etc*) mouvement *m*, geste *m*. **he made a ~ to close the door** il a esquissé le geste d'aller fermer la porte; (*fig*) **to go through the ~s of doing sth** (*mechanically*) faire qch machinalement *or* en ayant l'esprit ailleurs; (*insincerely*) faire mine *or* semblant de faire qch.

c (*at meeting etc*) motion *f*; (*Parl*) proposition *f*. **~ carried/rejected** motion adoptée/rejetée; (*Admin, Jur*) **meeting convened of its own ~** réunion convoquée d'office.

d (*bowel ~*) selles *fpl*. **to have** *or* **pass a ~** aller à la selle.

e *[watch]* mouvement *m*.

f (*Mus*) mouvement *m*.

2 comp ▸**motionless** *see* **motionless** ▸**motion picture** (*Cine*) film *m* (de cinéma); **motion-picture camera** caméra *f*; **the motion-picture industry** l'industrie *f* cinématographique, le cinéma ▸**motion sickness** mal *m* des transports ▸**motion study** (*Ind etc*) étude *f* des cadences.

3 vti: **to ~ (to) sb to do** faire signe à qn de faire; **he ~ed me in/out/to a chair** il m'a fait signe d'entrer/de sortir/de m'asseoir, il m'a invité d'un geste à entrer/à sortir/à m'asseoir.
motionless [ˈməʊʃənlɪs] adj immobile, sans mouvement. **he stood there ~** il se tenait là immobile *or* sans bouger.
motivate [ˈməʊtɪveɪt] vt *act, decision* motiver; *person* pousser, inciter (*to do* à faire).
motivated [ˈməʊtɪveɪtɪd] adj *personne* motivé. **highly/politically ~** très motivé/motivé au plan politique *or* politiquement.
motivation [ˌməʊtɪˈveɪʃən] n motivation *f*. **he lacks ~** il n'est pas assez motivé (*to do* pour faire); **~(al) research** études *fpl* de motivation.
motive [ˈməʊtɪv] 1 n a motif *m*, intention *f*, raison *f*; (*Jur*) mobile *m*. **I did it from the best ~s** je l'ai fait avec les meilleures intentions *or* avec les motifs les plus louables; **his ~ for saying that** la raison pour

laquelle il a dit cela; **he had no ~ for killing her** il l'a tuée sans raison(s) *or* sans mobile; **what was the ~ for the murder?** quel était le mobile du meurtre?; **the only suspect with a ~** le seul suspect à avoir un mobile; *see* **profit, ulterior.** b = **motif.** 2 adj moteur (*f* -trice). ~ **power** force motrice.

motiveless ['məʊtɪvlɪs] adj *act, crime* immotivé, gratuit.

motley ['mɒtlɪ] 1 adj (*many-coloured*) bigarré, bariolé; (*mixed*) bigarré, hétéroclite. **a ~ collection of ...** une collection hétéroclite de ...; **they were a ~ crew** ils formaient une bande hétéroclite *or* curieusement assortie. 2 n (*garment*) habit bigarré (*du bouffon*).

motocross ['məʊtəkrɒs] n moto-cross *m*.

motor ['məʊtəʳ] 1 n a (*engine*) moteur *m*.
b (*Brit Aut* *) = ~**car**; *see* **2.**
2 comp *accident* de voiture, d'auto ▸**motor-assisted** à moteur ▸**motorbike** moto *f* ▸**motorboat** canot *m* automobile ▸**motor bus**† autobus *m* ▸**motorcade** *see* **motorcade** ▸**motorcar** (*Brit*) auto(mobile) *f*, voiture *f* ▸**motor coach** car *m* ▸**motorcycle** moto *f*, motocyclette *f*; **motorcycle club** club *m* de moto; **motorcycle combination** (motocyclette *f* à) side-car *m*; **motorcycle engine** moteur *m* de moto; **motorcycle gang** bande *m* de motards* ▸**motorcycling** motocyclisme *m* ▸**motorcyclist** motocycliste *mf* ▸**motor drive** (*Tech*) entraînement *m* par moteur ▸**motor-driven** à entraînement par moteur ▸**motor home** (*US*) camping-car *m*, autocaravane *f* ▸**motor industry** industrie *f* automobile, (industrie de) l'automobile *f* ▸**motor insurance** assurance-automobile *f* ▸**motor launch** (*Naut*) vedette *f* ▸**motor lorry** (*Brit*) = **motor truck** ▸**motorman** (*US*) conducteur *m* (*d'un train etc électrique*) ▸**motor mechanic** mécanicien *m* garagiste ▸**motor mower** tondeuse *f* (à gazon) à moteur ▸**motor neuron disease** (*Med*) sclérose *f* latérale amyotrophique ▸**motor oil** huile *f* (de graissage) ▸**motor racing** (*NonC*) course *f* automobile ▸**motor road** route ouverte à la circulation automobile ▸**motor scooter** scooter *m* ▸**motor ship** = **motor vessel** ▸**motor show** exposition *f* d'autos; (*Brit*) **the Motor Show** le Salon de l'automobile ▸**motor torpedo boat** vedette *f* lance-torpilles ▸**the motor trade** (le secteur de) l'automobile *f* ▸**motor truck** camion *m* (automobile) ▸**motor vehicle** véhicule *m* automobile ▸**motor vessel** (*Naut*) navire *m* à moteur (diesel), motorship *m* ▸**motorway** (*Brit Aut*) n autoroute *f* ◊ adj *bridge, exit, junction* d'autoroute.
3 adj *muscle, nerve* moteur (*f* -trice); *see also* **2.**
4 vi (†) aller en auto. **to go ~ing** faire de l'auto; **to ~ away/back** *etc* partir/revenir *etc* en auto.
5 vt (*Brit* †) conduire en auto. **to ~ sb away/back** *etc* emmener/ramener *etc* qn en auto.

motorail ['məʊtəreɪl] n train *m* auto-couchettes.

motorcade ['məʊtəkeɪd] n (*US*) cortège *m* d'automobiles.

-motored ['məʊtəd] adj ending in comps: **four-motored** quadrimoteur (*f* -trice).

motoring ['məʊtərɪŋ] 1 n les promenades *fpl* en automobile. 2 comp *accident* de voiture, d'auto; *holiday* en voiture, en auto ▸**motoring correspondent** (*Brit Press*) chroniqueur *m* automobile ▸**motoring magazine** (*Press*) revue *f* automobile ▸**motoring public** automobilistes *mpl* ▸**motoring school** auto-école *f*.

motorist ['məʊtərɪst] n (*Brit*) automobiliste *mf*.

motorization [ˌməʊtəraɪ'zeɪʃən] n motorisation *f*.

motorize ['məʊtəraɪz] vt (*esp Mil*) motoriser. **~d bicycle** *or* **bike*** cyclomoteur *m*.

Motown ['məʊtaʊn] n (*US*) a *surnom de Detroit.* b (*Mus*) Motown *m*.

mottle ['mɒtl] vt tacheter, moucheter, marbrer (*with* de).

mottled ['mɒtld] adj tacheté; (*different colours*) bigarré; *horse* moucheté, pommelé; *skin* marbré; *sky* pommelé; *material* chiné; *porcelain* truité. ~ **complexion** teint brouillé.

motto ['mɒtəʊ] n, pl ~**es** *or* ~**s** a *[family, school etc]* devise *f*. b (*in cracker*) (*riddle*) devinette *f*; (*joke*) blague *f*. c (*Mus*) ~ **theme** leitmotiv *m*.

mould¹, (*US*) **mold¹** [məʊld] 1 n (*Art, Culin, Metal, Tech etc*) (*container, core, frame*) moule *m*; (*model for design*) modèle *m*, gabarit *m*. **to cast metal in a ~** couler *or* jeter du métal dans un moule; **to cast a figure in a ~** jeter une figure en moule, mouler une figure; (*fig*) **cast in a heroic ~** de la trempe des héros; (*fig*) **cast in the same ~** fait sur *or* coulé dans le même moule; (*fig*) **men of his ~** des hommes de sa trempe *or* de son calibre*; (*Culin*) **rice ~** gâteau *m* de riz. 2 vt (*cast*) *metals* fondre, mouler; *plaster, clay* mouler; (*fashion*) *figure etc* modeler (*in, out of* en); (*fig*) *sb's character, public opinion etc* former, façonner.

mould², (*US*) **mold²** [məʊld] 1 n (*fungus*) moisissure *f*. 2 vi moisir.

mould³, (*US*) **mold³** [məʊld] n (*soil*) humus *m*, terreau *m*; *see* **leaf.**

moulder, (*US*) **molder** ['məʊldəʳ] vi (*gen*) moisir; (*also* ~ **away**) *[building]* tomber en poussière, se désagréger; (* *fig*) *[person, object]* moisir.

moulding, (*US*) **molding** ['məʊldɪŋ] n a (*NonC: see* **mould¹ 2**) (*gen*) moulage *m*; *[metal]* coulée *f*; *[statue]* coulage *m*; (*fig*) formation *f*, modelage *m*. b (*Archit: ornament*) moulure *f*; (*Aut*) baguette *f*.

mouldy, (*US*) **moldy** ['məʊldɪ] adj a (*lit*) moisi. **to go ~** moisir; **to smell ~** sentir le moisi. b (*: *fig*) minable*. (*fig*) **all he gave me was a ~ £5*** il s'est tout juste fendu* d'un malheureux billet de 5 livres.

moult, (*US*) **molt** [məʊlt] 1 n mue *f*. 2 vi *[bird]* muer; *[dog, cat]* perdre ses poils. 3 vt *feathers, hair* perdre.

mound [maʊnd] n a *[earth]* (*natural*) tertre *m*, butte *f*, monticule *m*; (*artificial*) levée *f* de terre, remblai *m*; (*Archeol*) tertre artificiel, mound *m*; (*burial* ~) tumulus *m*. b (*pile*) tas *m*, monceau *m*.

mount [maʊnt] 1 n a (*liter*) mont *m*, montagne *f*. **M~ Carmel** le mont Carmel; **M~ Everest** le mont Everest; **the M~ of Olives** le mont des Oliviers; **the Sermon on the M~** le Sermon sur la Montagne.
b (*horse*) monture *f*.
c (*support*) *[machine]* support *m*; *[jewel, lens, specimen]* monture *f*; *[microscope slide]* lame *f*; *[transparency]* cadre *m* (en carton *or* en plastique); *[painting, photo]* carton *m* de montage; *[stamp in album]* charnière *f*.
2 vt a (*climb on or up*) *hill, stairs* monter, (*with effort*) gravir; *horse* monter (sur), enfourcher; *cycle* monter sur, enfourcher; *ladder* monter à *or* sur; *platform, throne* monter sur. **the car ~ed the pavement** l'auto est montée sur le trottoir.
b *[stallion etc]* monter.
c *machine, specimen, jewel* monter (*on, in* sur); *map* monter, entoiler; *picture, photo* monter *or* coller sur carton; *exhibit* fixer sur un support; *gun* mettre en position. **to ~ stamps in an album** coller *or* mettre des timbres dans un album; (*Phot*) **~ing press** colleuse *f*.
d *play, demonstration, plot, campaign, rescue operation etc* monter. (*Mil*) **to ~ guard** monter la garde (*on* sur; *over* auprès de); **to ~ an offensive** monter une attaque.
e (*provide with horse*) monter; *see* **mounted.**
3 vi a *[prices, temperature]* monter, augmenter.
b (*get on horse*) se mettre en selle.
c (*fig*) **the blood ~ed to his cheeks** le sang lui monta au visage.

▸**mount up** vi (*increase*) monter, s'élever; (*accumulate*) s'accumuler. **it all mounts up** tout cela finit par chiffrer.

mountain ['maʊntɪn] 1 n montagne *f*; (*fig*) montagne, monceau *m*, tas *m*. **to go to/live in the ~s** aller à/habiter la montagne; (*fig*) **to make a ~ out of a molehill** (se) faire une montagne d'un rien; (*Econ*) **beef/butter ~** montagne de bœuf/de beurre; (*fig*) **a ~ of dirty washing** un monceau de linge sale; **a ~ of work** un travail fou *or* monstre.
2 comp *tribe, people* montagnard; *animal, plant* de(s) montagne(s); *air* de la montagne; *path, scenery, shoes, chalet* de montagne ▸**mountain ash** sorbier *m* (d'Amérique) ▸**moutain bike** vélo *m* tout terrain, VTT *m* ▸**mountain cat** puma *m*, couguar *m or* cougouar *m* ▸**mountain chain** chaîne *f* de montagnes ▸**mountain climber** grimpeur *m*, alpiniste *mf* ▸**Mountain Daylight Time** (*US*) heure *f* d'été des Montagnes Rocheuses ▸**mountain dew*** whisky *m* (*gén illicitement distillé*) ▸**mountain guide** (*Climbing*) guide *m* de montagne ▸**mountain lion** (*US*) = **mountain cat** ▸**mountain range** chaîne *f* de montagnes ▸**mountain sickness** mal *m* des montagnes ▸**mountainside** flanc *m or* versant *m* d'une montagne ▸**Mountain Standard Time** (*US*) heure *f* d'hiver des Montagnes Rocheuses ▸**the Mountain State** (*US*) la Virginie Occidentale ▸**Mountain Time** (*US*) heure *f* des Montagnes Rocheuses ▸**mountain top** sommet *m* de la (*or* d'une) montagne, cime *f*.

mountaineer [ˌmaʊntɪ'nɪəʳ] 1 n alpiniste *mf*. 2 vi faire de l'alpinisme.

mountaineering [ˌmaʊntɪ'nɪərɪŋ] n alpinisme *m*.

mountainous ['maʊntɪnəs] adj *country* montagneux; (*fig*) gigantesque, énorme.

mountebank ['maʊntɪbæŋk] n charlatan *m*, imposteur *m*.

mounted ['maʊntɪd] adj *troops* monté, à cheval. ~ **police** police montée; ~ **policeman** membre *m* de la police montée.

Mountie* ['maʊntɪ] n membre *m* de la police montée (canadienne). **the ~s** la police montée (canadienne), la Gendarmerie (royale) (*Can*), la G.R.C. (*Can*).

mourn [mɔːn] 1 vi pleurer. **to ~ for sb** pleurer (la mort de) qn; **to ~ for sth** pleurer la perte (*or* la disparition *etc*) de qch; **it's no good ~ing over it** rien ne sert de se lamenter à ce sujet. 2 vt *person* pleurer (la mort de); *sth gone* pleurer la perte de; *sth sad* pleurer, se lamenter sur.

mourner ['mɔːnəʳ] n parent(e) *m(f) or* allié(e) *m(f) or* ami(e) *m(f)* du défunt. **the ~s** le convoi *or* le cortège funèbre; **to be the chief ~** mener le deuil.

mournful ['mɔːnfʊl] adj *person* mélancolique, triste; (*stronger*) affligé, éploré; *tone, sound, occasion* lugubre, funèbre. **what a ~ expression!** quelle tête *or* mine d'enterrement!

mournfully ['mɔːnfəlɪ] adv lugubrement, mélancoliquement.

mournfulness ['mɔːnfʊlnɪs] n tristesse *f*, air *m or* aspect *m* lugubre *or* désolé.

mourning ['mɔːnɪŋ] 1 n deuil *m*; (*clothes*) vêtements *mpl* de deuil. **in deep ~** en grand deuil; **to be in ~ (for sb)** porter le deuil (de qn), être en deuil (de qn); **to go into/come out of ~** prendre/ quitter le deuil. 2 comp *clothes* de deuil ▸**mourning band** crêpe *m*.

mouse [maʊs] 1 n, pl **mice** a souris *f*; (*fig*) timide *mf*, souris; *see*

field, white. b (*Comput*) souris *f.* 2 **adj** = **mousy.** 3 **comp** ▸**mousehole** trou *m* de souris ▸**mousetrap** souricière *f*; (*pej*) **mousetrap (cheese)*** fromage *m* ordinaire. 4 **vi** chasser les souris.

mouser ['maʊsər] **n** souricier *m.*

mousey ['maʊsɪ] **adj** = **mousy.**

moussaka [mʊ'sɑːkə] **n** moussaka *f.*

mousse [muːs] **n** (*Culin*) mousse *f.* **chocolate** ~ mousse au chocolat; (*for hair*) **(styling)** ~ mousse coiffante *or* de coiffage.

moustache [məs'tɑːʃ] **n** moustache(s) *f(pl).* **man with a** ~ homme moustachu *or* à moustache.

moustachio [məs'tɑːʃɪəʊ] **n** moustache *f* à la gauloise.

moustachioed [məs'tɑːʃɪəʊd] **adj** moustachu.

mousy ['maʊsɪ] **adj** *smell etc* de souris; (*fig*) *person, character* timide, effacé. ~ **hair** cheveux *mpl* châtain clair (sans éclat).

mouth [maʊθ] 1 **n, pl mouths** [maʊðz] a *[person, horse, sheep, cow etc]* bouche *f*; *[dog, cat, lion, tiger etc]* gueule *f.* (*Pharm*) **to be taken by** ~ à prendre par voie orale; **with one's** ~ **wide open** bouche bée, bouche béante; **she didn't dare open her** ~ elle n'a pas osé ouvrir la bouche *or* dire un mot; **he never opened his** ~ **all evening** il n'a pas ouvert la bouche *or* il n'a pas desserré les dents de la soirée; **he didn't open his** ~ **about it, he kept his** ~ **shut about it** il n'en a pas soufflé mot, il est resté bouche cousue sur la question; **keep your** ~ **shut about this!** n'en parle à personne!, garde-le pour toi!, bouche cousue!; **shut your** ~!⁑ ferme-la!⁑, boucle-la!⁑; (*fig*) **to shut** *or* **close sb's** ~ **(for him)*, to stop sb's** ~ (*silence*) fermer la bouche à qn*; (*kill*) supprimer qn; **(you've got a) big** ~!⁑ tu ne pouvais pas la fermer!⁑; **he's a big** ~ c'est un fort en gueule⁑, c'est une grande gueule⁑; **it makes my** ~ **water** cela me fait venir l'eau à la bouche; *see* **down[1], heart, word** *etc.*

b *[river]* embouchure *f*; *[bag]* ouverture *f*; *[hole, cave, harbour etc]* entrée *f*; *[bottle]* goulot *m*; *[cannon, gun]* bouche *f*, gueule *f*; *[well]* trou *m*; *[volcano]* bouche; *[letterbox]* ouverture, fente *f.*

2 **comp** ▸**mouthful** *see* **mouthful** ▸**mouthorgan** harmonica *m* ▸**mouthpiece** *[musical instrument]* bec *m*, embouchure *f*; *[telephone]* microphone *m*; (*fig: spokesman*) porte-parole *m inv* ▸**mouth-to-mouth (resuscitation)** bouche à bouche *m inv* ▸**mouth ulcer** aphte *m* ▸**mouthwash** eau *f* dentifrice, élixir *m* dentaire; (*for gargling*) gargarisme *m* ▸**mouth-watering** appétissant, alléchant.

3 [maʊð] **vt** a (*soundlessly: gen*) dire silencieusement *or* sans un son; (*during spoken voice-over*) faire semblant de prononcer; (*during singing*) faire semblant de chanter.

b (*insincerely*) **to** ~ **promises/apologies** *etc* faire des promesses/des excuses *etc* du bout des lèvres.

4 **vi: to** ~ **at sth** faire la moue en entendant (*or* en voyant) qch.

▸**mouth off**⁑ **vi** (*US*) (*talk boastfully*) en avoir plein la bouche* (*about* de); (*talk nonsense*) débiter des sottises* (*about* au sujet de); (*talk insolently*) parler insolemment.

-mouthed [maʊðd] **adj ending in comps, e.g. wide-mouthed** *person* qui a une grande bouche; *river* à l'embouchure large; *cave* avec une vaste entrée; *bottle* au large goulot; *bag* large du haut; *see* **loud, mealy** *etc.*

mouthful ['maʊθfʊl] **n** *[food]* bouchée *f.* ~ **of tea/wine** (grande) gorgée *f* de thé/de vin; **he swallowed it at one** ~ il n'en a fait qu'une bouchée *or* gorgée; (*fig*) **it's a real** ~ **of a name!*** quel nom à coucher dehors!, quel nom! on en a plein la bouche!; (*fig*) **you said a** ~!* c'est vraiment le cas de le dire, ça tu peux le dire!; (*fig*) **to give sb a** ~* passer un savon* à qn, enguirlander* qn.

movable ['muːvəbl] 1 **adj** mobile. (*Rel*) ~ **feast** fête *f* mobile; (*fig*) **it's a** ~ **feast** il n'y a pas de date fixe. 2 **npl** (*Jur*) ~**s** effets mobiliers, biens *mpl* meubles.

move [muːv] 1 **n** a mouvement *m.* **to be always on the** ~ *[gipsies etc]* se déplacer continuellement, être toujours par monts et par vaux; *[military or diplomatic personnel etc]* être toujours en déplacement; *[child, animal]* ne jamais rester en place; (*: *be busy*) ne jamais (s')arrêter; **the circus is on the** ~ **again** le cirque a repris la route; *[troops, army]* **to be on the** ~ être en marche *or* en mouvement; (*moving around*) **he's on the** ~ **the whole time** il se déplace constamment, il est sans arrêt en déplacement; **the police were after him and he had to stay on the** ~ recherché par la police, il était obligé de se déplacer *or* de déménager constamment; (*fig*) **it is a country on the** ~ c'est un pays en marche; **it was midnight and no one had made a** ~ il était minuit et personne n'avait manifesté l'intention *or* fait mine de partir; **it's time we made a** ~ (*that we left*) il est temps que nous partions; (*acted, did sth*) il est temps que nous fassions quelque chose; **he made a** ~ **towards the door** il esquissa un mouvement vers la porte; **get a** ~ **on!*** remue-toi!*, grouille-toi!⁑

b (*change of house*) déménagement *m*; (*change of job*) changement *m* d'emploi. **he made a** ~ **to Paris** il est parti s'installer à Paris; **it's our third** ~ **in 2 years** c'est notre troisième déménagement en 2 ans; **it's time he had a** ~ il a besoin de changer d'air *or* d'horizon.

c (*Chess, Draughts etc*) *[chessman etc]* coup *m*; (*player's turn*) tour *m*; (*fig*) pas *m*, démarche *f*, manœuvre *f*, mesure *f.* **knight's** ~ marche *f* du cavalier; **that was a silly** ~ (*in game*) ça c'était un coup stupide; (*fig*) c'était une démarche *or* une manœuvre stupide; **it's your** ~ c'est à vous de jouer; **to have the first** ~ avoir le trait, jouer en premier; (*fig*) **he knows every** ~ **in the game** il connaît toutes les astuces; **one false** ~ **and he's ruined** un faux pas et il est ruiné; **his first** ~ **after his election was to announce ...** son premier acte après son élection fut d'annoncer ...; **what's our** *or* **the next** ~? et maintenant qu'est-ce qu'on fait?; **it's a** ~ **in the right direction** c'est un pas dans la bonne direction; **let him make the first** ~ laisse-lui faire les premiers pas; **we must watch his every** ~ il nous faut surveiller tous ses faits et gestes; **without making the least** ~ **to do so** sans manifester la moindre intention de le faire; **there was a** ~ **to defeat the proposal** il y a eu une tentative pour faire échec à la proposition.

d (*Climbing*) (*step etc*) pas *m*; (*section of pitch*) passage *m.*

2 **vt** a (*change position of*) *object, furniture* changer de place, déplacer, bouger*; *limbs* remuer, mouvoir; *troops, animals* transporter. **you've** ~**d the stick!** tu as bougé le bâton!; **he hadn't** ~**d his chair** il n'avait pas déplacé sa chaise *or* changé sa chaise de place; ~ **your chair nearer the fire** approchez votre chaise du feu; ~ **your books over here** mets tes livres par ici; **can you** ~ **your fingers?** pouvez-vous remuer *or* mouvoir vos doigts?; **he** ~**d his family out of the war zone** il a évacué sa famille hors de la zone de guerre; **they** ~**d the crowd off the grass** ils ont fait partir la foule de sur la pelouse; ~ **your arm off my book** ôte ton bras de sur mon livre; (*Brit*) **to** ~ **house** déménager; **to** ~ **one's job** changer d'emploi; **his firm want to** ~ **him** son entreprise veut l'envoyer ailleurs; **he's asked to be** ~**d to London/to a new department/to an easier job** il a demandé à être muté à Londres/affecté à une autre section/affecté à un emploi plus facile; (*fig*) **to** ~ **heaven and earth to do sth** remuer ciel et terre pour faire qch, se mettre en quatre pour faire qch; (*Chess*) **to** ~ **a piece** jouer une pièce; (*fig*) **he didn't** ~ **a muscle** il n'a pas levé le petit doigt (*to help etc* pour aider *etc*); (*didn't flinch*) il n'a pas bronché, il n'a pas sourcillé; (*fig*) **to** ~ **sth (forward/back)** *event, date* avancer/reculer qch; (*Comm*) **we must try to** ~ **this old stock** nous devons essayer d'écouler ce vieux stock.

b (*remove*) *stain, mark* enlever, faire partir.

c (*set in motion*) **the wind** ~**s the leaves** le vent agite *or* fait remuer les feuilles; (*Med*) **to** ~ **one's bowels** aller à la selle.

d (*fig*) pousser, inciter (*sb to do* qn à faire). **I am** ~**d to ask why ...** je suis incité à demander pourquoi ...; **if I feel** ~**d to do it,** (*hum*) **if the spirit** ~**s me** si le cœur m'en dit; **he won't be** ~**d** il est inébranlable; **even this did not** ~ **him** même ceci n'a pas réussi à l'ébranler.

e (*emotionally*) émouvoir. **she's easily** ~**d** elle s'émeut facilement; **this did not** ~ **him** ceci n'a pas réussi à l'émouvoir, ceci l'a trouvé impassible; **to** ~ **sb to tears** émouvoir qn jusqu'aux larmes; **to** ~ **sb to laughter** faire rire qn; **to** ~ **sb to anger** mettre qn en colère; **to** ~ **sb to pity** attendrir qn.

f (*Admin, Parl etc*) proposer. **to** ~ **a resolution** proposer une motion; **to** ~ **that sth be done** proposer que qch soit fait; **he** ~**d the adjournment of the meeting** *or* **that the meeting be adjourned** il a proposé que la séance soit levée.

3 **vi** a *[person, animal]* (*stir*) bouger, remuer; (*go*) aller, se déplacer; *[limb]* bouger, remuer, se mouvoir; *[lips, trees, leaves, curtains, door]* bouger, remuer; *[clouds]* passer, avancer; *[vehicle, ship, plane, procession]* aller, passer; *[troops, army]* se déplacer. **don't** ~! ne bougez pas!; **he** ~**d slowly towards the door** il se dirigea lentement vers la porte; **let's** ~ **into the garden** passons dans le jardin; **she** ~**s well** elle a une démarche aisée; **troops are moving near the frontier** il y a des mouvements de troupes près de la frontière; **they** ~**d rapidly across the lawn** ils ont traversé la pelouse rapidement; **the procession** ~**d slowly out of sight** petit à petit la procession a disparu; **the car** ~**d round the corner** la voiture a tourné au coin de la rue; **I saw something moving over there** j'ai vu quelque chose bouger là-bas; **I'll not** ~ **from here** je ne bougerai pas d'ici; **keep moving!** (*to keep warm etc*) ne restez pas sans bouger!; (*pass along etc*) circulez!; **he has** ~**d into another class** il est passé dans une autre classe; (*fig*) **to** ~ **in high society** fréquenter la haute société; **to** ~ **freely** *[piece of machinery]* jouer librement; *[people, cars]* circuler aisément; *[traffic]* être fluide; **to keep the traffic moving** assurer la circulation ininterrompue des véhicules; **the car in front isn't moving** la voiture devant nous est à l'arrêt; **do not get out while the bus is moving** ne descendez pas de l'autobus en marche, attendez l'arrêt complet de l'autobus pour descendre; **the coach was moving at 30 km/h** le car faisait 30 km/h *or* roulait à 30 (km) à l'heure; **he was certainly moving!** il ne traînait pas!, il gazait!*; **that horse can certainly** ~ quand il s'agit de foncer ce cheval se défend!*; (*Comm*) **these goods** ~ **very fast** ces marchandises se vendent très rapidement; (*Comm*) **these toys won't** ~ ces jouets ne se vendent pas; **you can't** ~ **for books in that room*** on ne peut plus se retourner dans cette pièce tellement il y a de livres.

b (*depart*) **it's time we were moving** il est temps que nous partions (*subj*), il est temps de partir; **let's** ~! partons!, en route!

c (~ *house etc*) *[person, family]* déménager; *[office, shop, business]* être transféré. **to** ~ **to a bigger house** aller habiter une maison plus grande, emménager dans une maison plus grande; **to** ~ **to the country** aller habiter (à) la campagne, aller s'installer à la campagne.

d (*progress*) *[plans, talks etc]* progresser, avancer. **things are moving at last!** enfin ça avance! *or* ça progresse!; **he got things moving** avec lui ça a bien démarré *or* c'est bien parti.

e (*act, take steps*) agir. **the government won't ~ until ...** le gouvernement ne bougera pas *or* ne fera rien tant que ...; **we must ~ first** nous devons prendre l'initiative; **we'll have to ~ quickly if we want to avoid ...** il nous faudra agir sans tarder si nous voulons éviter ...; **the committee ~d to stop the abuse** le comité a pris des mesures pour mettre fin aux abus.

f (*in games*) *[player]* jouer; *[chesspiece]* marcher. **it's you to ~** (c'est) votre tour de jouer; (*Chess*) **white ~s** les blancs jouent; (*Chess*) **the knight ~s like this** le cavalier marche *or* se déplace comme cela.

►**move about** 1 vi (*fidget*) remuer; (*travel*) voyager. **he can move about only with difficulty** il ne se déplace qu'avec peine; **stop moving about!** tiens-toi tranquille!; (*change residence*) **we've moved about a good deal** nous ne sommes jamais restés longtemps au même endroit. 2 vt sep *object, furniture, employee* déplacer.

►**move along** 1 vi *[people or vehicles in line]* avancer, circuler. **move along there!** *[bus conductor]* avancez vers l'intérieur!; *[policeman]* circulez!; (*on bench etc*) **can you move along a few places?** pouvez-vous vous pousser un peu? 2 vt sep *crowd* faire circuler, faire avancer; *animals* faire avancer.

►**move around** = **move about.**

►**move away** 1 vi a (*depart*) partir, s'éloigner (*from* de). b (*move house*) déménager. **they've moved away from here** ils n'habitent plus par ici. 2 vt sep *person, object* éloigner, écarter (*from* de).

►**move back** 1 vi a (*withdraw*) reculer, se retirer. b (*to original position*) retourner, revenir. **he moved back to the desk** il retourna au bureau. c (*move house*) **they've moved back to London** ils sont retournés *or* revenus habiter (à) Londres. 2 vt sep a *person, crowd, animals* faire reculer; *troops* replier; *object, furniture* reculer. b (*to original position*) *person* faire revenir *or* retourner; *object* remettre. **his firm moved him back to London** son entreprise l'a fait revenir *or* retourner à Londres; **move the table back to where it was before** remets la table là où elle était.

►**move down** 1 vi a *[person, object, lift]* descendre. **he moved down from the top floor** il est descendu du dernier étage; (*on bench etc*) **can you move down a few places?** pouvez-vous vous pousser un peu? b (*Sport: in league*) reculer. (*Scol*) **he has had to move down one class** il a dû descendre d'une classe. 2 vt sep a *person* faire descendre; *object* descendre. b (*demote*) *pupil* faire descendre (dans une classe inférieure); *employee* rétrograder.

►**move forward** 1 vi *[person, animal, vehicle]* avancer; *[troops]* se porter en avant. 2 vt sep *person, vehicle* faire avancer; *troops* porter en avant; *object, chair* avancer.

►**move in** 1 vi a (*approach*) *[police etc]* avancer, intervenir. b (*to a house*) emménager. 2 vt sep *person* faire entrer; *furniture etc* rentrer, mettre *or* remettre à l'intérieur; (*on removal day*) installer.

►**move in on*** vt fus (*advance on: Mil etc*) marcher sur, avancer sur; *[police]* faire une descente* dans; *[gangsters]* s'intéresser à; (*attempt takeover of*) *firm* essayer de mettre la main* sur. **to move in on sb for the night*** se faire héberger par qn pour la nuit.

►**move off** 1 vi *[person]* s'en aller, s'éloigner, partir; *[car]* démarrer; *[train, army, procession]* s'ébranler, partir. 2 vt sep *object* enlever.

►**move on** 1 vi *[person, vehicle]* avancer; (*after stopping*) se remettre en route; *[time]* passer, s'écouler. **the gipsies moved on to another site** les bohémiens sont allés s'installer plus loin; *[policeman etc]* **move on please!** circulez s'il vous plaît!; **and now we move on to a later episode** et maintenant nous passons à un épisode ultérieur. 2 vt sep *person, onlookers* faire circuler; *hands of clock* avancer.

►**move out** 1 vi (*of house, office, room etc*) déménager. **to move out of a flat** déménager d'un appartement, quitter un appartement. 2 vt sep *person, animal* faire sortir; *troops* retirer, dégager; *object, furniture* sortir; (*on removal day*) déménager.

►**move over** 1 vi s'écarter, se déplacer, se pousser. **move over!** pousse-toi!; (*leave job*) **he moved over to give the young woman a chance** il a (volontairement) quitté son poste pour laisser une chance à la jeune femme; (*change over*) **to move over to sth new** adopter qch de nouveau. 2 vt sep déplacer, écarter.

►**move up** 1 vi a *[person, flag etc]* monter. **can you move up a few seats?** pouvez-vous vous pousser un peu?; **I want to move up nearer the platform** je veux m'approcher de l'estrade. b *[employee]* avoir de l'avancement; (*Sport: in league*) avancer. *[pupil]* **to move up a class** passer dans la classe supérieure. 2 vt sep a *person* faire monter; *object* monter. b (*promote*) *employee* donner de l'avancement à; *pupil* faire passer dans une classe supérieure.

moveable ['mu:vəbl] adj = **movable.**

movement ['mu:vmənt] n a (*act*) *[person, troops, army, population, vehicles, goods, capital]* mouvement *m*; (*gesture*) mouvement, geste *m*; (*St Ex: activity*) activité *f* (*in* dans); (*St Ex: price changes*) mouvement. **he lay without ~** il était étendu sans mouvement; **upward/downward ~ of the hand** mouvement ascendant/descendant de la main; **troop ~s** mouvements de troupes; **upward ~ in the price of butter** hausse *f* du prix du beurre; (*fig*) **there has been little ~ in the political situation** la situation politique demeure à peu près inchangée; **the film lacks ~** le film manque de mouvement, le rythme du film est trop lent; **there was a ~ towards the exit** il y eut un mouvement vers la sortie, on se dirigea vers la sortie; (*fig*) **there has been some ~ towards fewer customs restrictions** on va *or* s'aiguille vers une réduction des restrictions douanières; **to study sb's ~s** épier les allées et venues de qn; **the police are watching his ~s** la police a l'œil sur tous ses déplacements; **~ of traffic** circulation *f*.

b (*Pol etc*) mouvement *m*. **the Women's Liberation M~** le mouvement de libération de la femme.

c (*Mus*) mouvement *m*. **in 4 ~s** en 4 mouvements.

d (*Tech*) *[machine, clock, watch etc]* mouvement *m*.

e (*Med: also* **bowel ~**) selles *fpl*. **to have a ~** aller à la selle.

mover ['mu:vəʳ] n a (*Admin, Parl etc: of motion*) motionnaire *mf*, auteur *m* d'une motion; *see* **prime 1a.** b (*US*) déménageur *m*. c **she's a lovely ~*** elle a une chouette façon de danser (*or* de marcher *etc*)*.

movie ['mu:vɪ] (*esp US*) 1 n film *m* (*de cinéma*). **the ~s*** le cinéma, le ciné*, le cinoche*; **to go to the ~s*** aller au cinéma *or* au ciné*. 2 comp ►**movie actor/actress** acteur *m*/actrice *f* de cinéma ►**movie camera** caméra *f* ►**moviegoer** (*gen*) amateur *m* de cinéma, cinéphile *mf*; **I'm an occasional moviegoer** je vais de temps en temps au cinéma ►**movie-going** la fréquentation des salles de cinéma ►**movie house** cinéma *m* (*salle*) ►**the movie industry** l'industrie *f* cinématographique, le cinéma ►**movieland*** le (monde du) cinéma ►**movie maker** (*US*) cinéaste *m* ►**movie star** star *f or* vedette *f* (*de cinéma*) ►**movie theater** (*US*) cinéma *m* (*salle*).

moving ['mu:vɪŋ] adj a *vehicle* en marche; *object, crowd* en mouvement; *power* moteur (*f* -trice). (*in machine*) **~ part** pièce *f* mobile; (*Jur*) **the ~ party** la partie demanderesse; (*Cine*) **~ picture** film *m* (*de cinéma*); **~ pavement,** (*US*) **~ sidewalk** trottoir roulant; **~ staircase** escalier *m* mécanique *or* roulant; **he was the ~ force** *or* **spirit in the whole affair** il était l'âme *f* de toute l'affaire; **~ target** cible mouvante; **~ walkway** trottoir roulant. b (*touching*) *sight, plea* émouvant, touchant.

movingly ['mu:vɪŋlɪ] adv d'une manière émouvante *or* touchante.

mow [məʊ] pret **mowed,** ptp **mowed** *or* **mown** vt *corn* faucher. **to ~ the lawn** tondre le gazon.

►**mow down** vt sep (*fig*) *people, troops* faucher.

mower ['məʊəʳ] n a (*person*) faucheur *m*, -euse *f*. b (*machine*) (*Agr*) faucheuse *f*; (*lawn~*) tondeuse *f* (à gazon); *see* **motor.**

mowing ['məʊɪŋ] n (*Agr*) fauchage *m*. **~ machine** (*Agr*) faucheuse *f*; (*in garden*) tondeuse *f* (à gazon).

mown [məʊn] ptp of **mow.**

Mozambican [məʊzəm'bi:kən] 1 adj mozambicain. 2 n Mozambicain(e) *m(f)*.

Mozambique [məʊzəm'bi:k] n Mozambique *m*.

Mozart ['məʊtsɑ:t] n Mozart *m*.

Mozartian [məʊ'tsɑ:tɪən] adj mozartien.

mozzarella [mɒtsə'relə] n (*cheese*) mozzarella *f*.

MP [em'pi:] n a (*Brit*) (abbr of **Member of Parliament**) *see* **member.** b (abbr of **Military Police**) *see* **military.** c (*Can*) (abbr of **Mounted Police**) *see* **mounted.**

mpg [ˌempi:'dʒi:] n (abbr of **miles per gallon**) *see* **mile.**

mph [ˌempi:'aɪtʃ] n (abbr of **miles per hour**) ≃ km/h.

M.Phil. [ˌem'fɪl] n (*Univ*) (abbr of **Master of Philosophy**) ≃ DEA *m*.

MPS [ˌempi:'es] n (*Brit*) (abbr of **Member of the Pharmaceutical Society**) *diplôme de pharmacie.*

Mr ['mɪstəʳ] n, pl **Messrs** ['mesəz] M., Monsieur; *see* **mister.**

MRC [ˌemɑ:'si:] n (*Brit*) (abbr of **Medical Research Council**) *Conseil supérieur de la recherche médicale.*

MRCP [ˌemɑ:si:'pi:] n (*Brit*) (abbr of **Member of the Royal College of Physicians**) *diplôme supérieur de médecine générale.*

MRCS [ˌemɑ:si:'es] n (*Brit*) (abbr of **Member of the Royal College of Surgeons**) *diplôme supérieur de chirurgie.*

MRCVS [ˌemɑ:si:vi:'es] n (*Brit*) (abbr of **Member of the Royal College of Veterinary Surgeons**) *diplôme de médecine vétérinaire.*

MRP n (abbr of **manufacturers' recommended price**) *see* **manufacturer.**

Mrs ['mɪsɪz] n, pl inv Mme, Madame.

MS [ˌem'es] n a (*also* **ms**) abbr of **manuscript.** b (abbr of **multiple sclerosis**) *see* **multiple.** c (*US Post*) abbr of **Mississippi.** d (*US Univ*) (abbr of **Master of Science**) *maîtrise de sciences.*

Ms [mɪz, məz] n (*titre utilisé pour éviter la distinction entre Madame et Mademoiselle*) ≃ Mme.

MSA [ˌemes'eɪ] n (*US Univ*) (abbr of **Master of Science in Agriculture**) *diplôme d'ingénieur agronome.*

MSC n (†: *Brit*) (abbr of **Manpower Services Commission**) *see* **manpower.**

MSc [ˌemes'si:] n (*Brit Univ*) (abbr of **Master of Science**) **to have an ~ in Biology** avoir une maîtrise de biologie; *see* **master.**

Msgr abbr of **monsignor.**

MST (*US*) (abbr of **Mountain Standard Time**) *see* **mountain.**

MT [em'ti:] n a (abbr of **machine translation**) *see* **machine.** b (*US*) abbr of **Montana.** c (*US*) (abbr of **Mountain Time**) *see* **mountain.**

Mt (*Geog*) (abbr of **Mount**) Mt. **Mt Everest** l'Everest *m*.

mth abbr of **month.**

much [mʌtʃ] compar **more,** superl **most** 1 adj, pron a (*a great deal, a lot*) beaucoup (de). ~ **money** beaucoup d'argent; **he hasn't (very) ~ time** il n'a pas beaucoup de temps; ~ **trouble** beaucoup d'ennuis, bien des ennuis; (*fig*) **it's a bit ~!*** c'est un peu fort!; **I haven't got ~ left** il ne m'en reste pas beaucoup *or* pas grand-chose; **does it cost ~?** est-ce que ça coûte cher?; ~ **of the town/night** une bonne partie de la ville/de la nuit; ~ **of what you say** une bonne partie de ce que vous dites; **he hadn't ~ to say about it** il n'avait pas grand-chose à dire à ce sujet; **there's not ~ anyone can do about it** personne n'y peut grand-chose; **we don't see ~ of each other** nous ne nous voyons guère *or* pas souvent; **I haven't heard ~ of him lately** je n'ai pas eu beaucoup de nouvelles de lui ces derniers temps; **we have ~ to be thankful for** nous avons tout lieu d'être reconnaissants; (*iro*) ~ **you know about it!** comme si tu t'y connaissais!, comme si tu y connaissais quelque chose!; **it isn't up to ~*** ça ne vaut pas grand-chose, ce n'est pas fameux; **he's not ~ to look at** il ne paie pas de mine; **he is not ~ of a writer** il n'est pas extraordinaire comme écrivain, comme écrivain il y a mieux; **I'm not ~ of a drinker*** je ne bois pas beaucoup; **it wasn't ~ of an evening** ce n'était pas une soirée très réussie; **he didn't think ~ of that** cela ne lui a pas dit grand-chose; **I don't think ~ of that film** à mon avis ce film ne vaut pas grand-chose, je ne trouve pas ce film bien fameux; **there isn't ~ to choose between them** ils se valent plus ou moins; (*in choice, competition etc*) **there isn't ~ in it** ça se vaut, c'est kif-kif*; (*in race etc*) **there wasn't ~ in it** il a (*or* elle a *etc*) gagné de justesse; **to make ~ of sb** faire grand cas de qn; **he made ~ of the fact that ...** il a fait grand cas du fait que ..., il a attaché beaucoup d'importance au fait que ...; **I couldn't make ~ of what he was saying** je n'ai pas bien compris *or* saisi ce qu'il disait.

b (*in phrases*) **as ~ time as ...** autant de temps que ...; **as ~ as possible** autant que possible; **I've got as ~ as you** j'en ai autant que vous; **take as ~ as you can** prenez-en autant que vous pouvez; **as ~ again** encore autant; **twice as ~** deux fois autant *or* plus; **twice as ~ money** deux fois plus *or* deux fois autant d'argent; **half as ~ again** la moitié en plus; **it's as ~ as he can do to stand up** c'est tout juste s'il peut se lever; **you could pay as ~ as 200 francs for that** vous pourriez payer jusqu'à 200 F pour cela *or* payer ça jusqu'à 200 F; **there was as ~ as 4 kg of butter** il y avait bien *or* jusqu'à 4 kg de beurre; **I thought as ~!** c'est bien ce que je pensais!, je m'y attendais!; **that's what he meant, and he said as ~ later** c'est ce qu'il a voulu dire, et c'est là pratiquement ce qu'il a dit plus tard; **as ~ as to say** comme pour dire; **how ~?** combien?; **how ~ does it cost?** combien cela coûte-t-il?, qu'est-ce que cela coûte?; **how ~ money have you got?** combien d'argent as-tu?, qu'est-ce que tu as comme argent?; **however ~ you protest** vous avez beau protester; **so ~ pleasure** tant de plaisir; **so ~ of the cheese was mouldy that ...** une si grande partie du fromage était moisie que ..., comme presque tout le fromage était moisi ...; **I've read so ~** *or* **this ~** *or* **that ~** j'en ai lu (tout) ça; **so ~ of what he says is untrue** il y a tellement *or* tant de mensonges dans ce qu'il dit; **he'd drunk so ~ that ...** il avait tellement *or* tant bu que ...; **I haven't so ~ as a penny on me** je n'ai pas un sou sur moi; **without so ~ as a word** sans même (dire) un mot; **so ~ for that!** (*resignedly*) tant pis!; (*and now for the next*) et d'une!*; **so ~ for his help!** voilà ce qu'il *or* c'est ça qu'il appelle aider!; **so ~ for his promises!** voilà ce qui reste de ses promesses!, voilà ce que valaient ses promesses!; **he beat me by so ~** *or* **by this ~** il m'a battu de ça; **this** *or* **that ~ bread** ça de pain; **I'd like about this** *or* **that ~** j'en voudrais comme ça; **I know this ~** je sais tout au moins ceci; **this ~ is true** il y a ceci de vrai; **too ~ sugar** trop de sucre; **I've eaten too ~** j'ai trop mangé; **that's too ~!** (*lit*) c'est trop!; (*fig: protesting*) (ça) c'est trop fort!; (*: *fig: admiring*) **(it's) too ~!** c'est dingue*!; **£500 is too ~** 500 livres c'est trop; (*fig*) **that was too ~ for me** c'en était trop pour moi; **he was too ~ for his opponent** il était trop fort pour son adversaire; **the child was too ~ for his grandparents** l'enfant était trop fatigant pour ses grands-parents; **this work is too ~ for me** ce travail est trop fatigant *or* difficile pour moi; (*: *disapproving*) **that film was really too ~** *or* **a bit ~ for me** pour moi ce film dépassait vraiment les bornes; **he made too ~ of it** il y a attaché trop d'importance, il en a fait trop de cas.

2 **adv** a (*with vb*) beaucoup, fort, très; (*with compar and superl*) beaucoup. **thank you very ~** merci beaucoup, merci bien; (*frm*) **he ~ regrets** il regrette vivement; (*frm*) **you are ~ to be envied** vous êtes fort digne d'envie; (*frm*) **he was ~ surprised** il fut fort *or* bien surpris; **it doesn't ~ matter** cela ne fait pas grand-chose, cela n'a pas beaucoup d'importance; **she doesn't go out ~** elle ne sort pas beaucoup *or* pas souvent; **are you going? — not ~!⁑** tu y vas? — mon œil!⁑; ~ **bigger** beaucoup plus grand; ~ **more easily** beaucoup plus facilement; **he's not ~ bigger than you** il n'est guère plus grand que vous; ~ **the cleverest** de beaucoup *or* de loin le plus intelligent.

b (*in phrases*) **I like you as ~ as him** je vous aime autant que lui; **I don't like him as ~ as I used to** je ne l'aime pas autant qu'auparavant; **I love him as ~ as ever** je l'aime toujours autant; **I don't like it as ~ as all that, I don't like it all that ~** je ne l'aime pas tant que ça; **however ~ you like him** quelle que soit votre affection pour lui; **the problem is not so ~ one of money as of staff** il ne s'agit pas tant d'un problème d'argent que d'un problème de personnel; **she wasn't so ~ helping as hindering** elle gênait plus qu'elle n'aidait; **I liked the film so ~ that I went back again** j'ai tellement *or* tant aimé le film que je suis retourné le voir; **I felt so ~ encouraged by this** je me suis senti tellement encouragé par ceci; **so ~ the less to do** autant de moins à faire; **so ~ so that ...** à tel point que ...; **it's that ~ too long** c'est trop long de (tout) ça; **he talks too ~** il parle trop; **did you like the film? — not too ~** le film vous a plu? — pas trop; **he didn't even smile, ~ less speak** il n'a même pas souri et encore moins parlé; **I don't know him, ~ less his father** lui, je ne le connais pas, et son père encore moins; **(very** *or* **pretty) ~ the same** presque le même (*as* que); **it is ~ as it was then** ce n'est guère différent de ce que c'était à l'époque; **they are (very** *or* **pretty) ~ of an age** ils sont à peu près du même âge; ~ **as** *or* ~ **though I would like to go** bien que je désire (*subj*) beaucoup y aller, malgré tout mon désir d'y aller; ~ **as I like you** en dépit de *or* malgré *or* quelle que soit mon affection pour vous; ~ **as she protested** en dépit de *or* malgré ses protestations; ~ **as I dislike doing this** si peu que j'aime (*subj*) faire ceci; ~ **to my amazement** à ma grande *or* profonde stupéfaction.

muchness* [ˈmʌtʃnɪs] **n**: **they're much of a ~** c'est blanc bonnet et bonnet blanc.

mucilage [ˈmjuːsɪlɪdʒ] **n** mucilage *m*.

muck [mʌk] 1 **n** (*NonC*) (*manure*) fumier *m*; (*mud*) boue *f*, gadoue *f*; (*dirt*) saletés *fpl*; (*fig*) (*dirty talk*) ordure(s) *f(pl)*, saleté(s) *f(pl)*, cochonnerie(s) *f(pl)*; (*scandal*) scandale *m*. **dog ~** crotte *f* de chien; **that article is just ~** cet article est une ordure; (*bungle*) **to make a ~ of sth⁑** gâcher *or* saloper⁑ qch; **she thinks she is Lady M~*** ce qu'elle peut se croire!* 2 **comp** ►**muck heap** tas *m* de fumier *or* d'ordures ►**muckraker** (*fig*) déterreur *m* de scandales ►**muckraking** mise *f* au jour de scandales ►**muck-up⁑** (*bungle*) gâchis *m*.

►**muck about, muck around** (*Brit*) 1 **vi** (*) a (*spend time aimlessly*) traîner, perdre son temps. **stop mucking about and get on with your work** cesse de perdre ton temps et fais ton travail; **he enjoys mucking about in the garden** il aime bricoler dans le jardin.

b (*play the fool*) faire l'idiot *or* l'imbécile. **he will muck about with my watch!** il faut toujours qu'il joue (*subj*) avec *or* qu'il tripote (*subj*) ma montre, il ne peut pas laisser ma montre tranquille; **he keeps mucking about with matters he doesn't understand** il n'arrête pas de fourrer son nez dans des choses qui le dépassent.

2 **vt sep** (⁑) *person* créer des complications *or* des embarras à.

►**muck in⁑ vi** (*Brit*) (*share money etc*) faire bourse commune (*with* avec); (*share room*) crécher⁑ (*with* avec). **everyone mucks in here** tout le monde met la main à la pâte* ici; **come on, muck in!** allons, donne un coup de main! *or* mets la main à la pâte!*

►**muck out vt sep** *stable* nettoyer, curer.

►**muck up⁑** (*Brit*) 1 **vt sep** a (*ruin*) *task, plans, deal, life* gâcher; *car, machine* bousiller*. b (*untidy*) *room* semer la pagaïe dans; (*dirty*) *room, clothes* salir. 2 **muck-up n** *see* **muck 2**.

muckiness [ˈmʌkɪnɪs] **n** saleté *f*, malpropreté *f*.

mucky [ˈmʌkɪ] **adj** (*muddy*) boueux, bourbeux; (*filthy*) sale, crotté. **what ~ weather!*** quel sale temps!; **you ~ pup!⁑** petit goret!

mucous [ˈmjuːkəs] **adj** muqueux. ~ **membrane** (membrane *f*) muqueuse *f*.

mucus [ˈmjuːkəs] **n** mucus *m*, mucosités *fpl*.

mud [mʌd] 1 **n** boue *f*, gadoue *f*; (*in river, sea*) boue, vase *f*; (*in swamp*) bourbe *f*. **car stuck in the ~** voiture embourbée; (*fig*) **to drag sb's name in** *or* **through the ~** traîner qn dans la boue; (*fig*) **to throw** *or* **sling ~ at sb** couvrir qn de boue; (*hum*) **here's ~ in your eye!⁑** à la tienne Étienne!* (*hum*); *see* **clear, name, stick**. 2 **comp** ►**mudbank** banc *m* de vase ►**mudbath** bain *m* de boue ►**mud flap** (*Aut*) (*gen*) pare-boue *m inv*; *[truck]* bavette *f* ►**mud flat(s)** laisse *f* de vase ►**mudguard** (*Brit Aut etc*) garde-boue *m inv* ►**mud hut** hutte *f* de terre ►**mudlark†** gamin(e) *m(f)* des rues ►**mudpack** masque *m* de beauté ►**mud pie** pâté *m* (de terre) ►**mud-slinging** (*NonC*) médisance *f*, dénigrement *m*.

muddle [ˈmʌdl] 1 **n** (*disorder*) désordre *m*, fouillis *m*, pagaïe *f or* pagaille *f*; (*perplexity*) perplexité *f*, confusion *f*; (*mix-up*) confusion, embrouillamini* *m*. **what a ~!** (*disorder*) quel fouillis!; (*mix-up*) quel embrouillamini!*; **to be in a ~** *[room, books, clothes]* être en désordre *or* en pagaïe, être sens dessus dessous; *[person]* ne plus s'y retrouver (*over sth* dans qch); *[ideas]* être brouillé *or* embrouillé *or* confus; *[plans, arrangements]* être confus *or* incertain *or* sens dessus dessous; **to get into a ~** *[ideas]* se brouiller, s'embrouiller; *[person]* s'embrouiller (*over sth* dans qch, au sujet de qch); **the books have got into a ~** les livres sont en désordre; **there's been a ~ over the seats** il y a eu confusion en ce qui concerne les places.

2 **comp** ►**muddle-headed** *person* aux idées confuses, brouillon; *plan, ideas* confus ►**muddle-up** confusion *f*, embrouillamini* *m*.

3 **vt** (*also* ~ **up**) a **to ~ (up) A and B, to ~ (up) A with B** confondre A avec B.

b (*perplex*) *person* embrouiller; *sb's ideas* brouiller, embrouiller. **he was ~d by the whisky** le whisky lui avait brouillé l'esprit; **to get ~d (up)** s'embrouiller, se brouiller; **to be ~d (up)** être embrouillé.

c *facts, story, details* brouiller, embrouiller. **~d** confus.

►**muddle along vi** se débrouiller tant bien que mal.

►**muddle on vi** essayer de se débrouiller tant bien que mal.

►**muddle through** vi se tirer d'affaire *or* s'en sortir tant bien que mal. **I expect we'll muddle through** je suppose que nous nous en sortirons d'une façon ou d'une autre.
►**muddle up** 1 vt sep = **muddle 3.** 2 **muddle-up** n *see* **muddle 2.**
muddler [ˈmʌdləʳ] n esprit brouillon (*personne*).
muddy [ˈmʌdɪ] 1 adj *road* boueux, bourbeux; *water* boueux; *river* vaseux, boueux; *clothes, shoes, hands* crotté, couvert de boue; (*fig*) *light* grisâtre, terne; *liquid* trouble; *complexion* terreux, brouillé; *ideas* brouillé, confus. ~ **brown** brun terne *inv or* terreux *inv*. 2 vt *hands, clothes, shoes* crotter, salir; *road* rendre boueux; *water, river* troubler.
mudflat [ˈmʌdflæt] n *see* **mud 2.**
muesli [ˈmjuːzlɪ] n muesli *m or* müsli *m*.
muezzin [muːˈezɪn] n muezzin *m*.
muff [mʌf] 1 n (*Dress, Tech*) manchon *m*. 2 vt (*) rater, louper*; (*Sport*) *ball, shot* rater, louper*; *chance, opportunity* rater, laisser passer. (*Theat*) **to ~ one's lines** se tromper dans son texte; **to ~ it*** rater son coup. 3 vi (*) rater son coup.
muffin [ˈmʌfɪn] n (*Brit*) muffin *m* (*petit pain rond et plat*); (*US*) *petit gâteau au chocolat ou aux fruits*.
muffle [ˈmʌfl] vt a *sound, noise* assourdir, étouffer, amortir; *noisy thing, bell, drum* assourdir. **to ~ the oars** assourdir les avirons; **in a ~d voice** d'une voix sourde *or* voilée *or* étouffée. b (*also* ~ **up**: *wrap up*) *object* envelopper; *person* emmitoufler. **~d (up) in a blanket** enveloppé *or* emmitouflé *or* enroulé dans une couverture; **to ~ o.s. (up)** s'emmitoufler; **he was all ~d up** il était emmitouflé des pieds à la tête.
►**muffle up** 1 vi s'emmitoufler. 2 vt sep = **muffle b.**
muffler [ˈmʌfləʳ] n a (*scarf*) cache-nez *m inv*, cache-col *m inv*. b (*US Aut*) silencieux *m*.
mufti [ˈmʌftɪ] n a (*Brit Dress*) tenue civile. **in ~** en civil, en pékin (*Mil sl*). b (*Muslim*) mufti *m or* muphti *m*.
mug [mʌg] 1 n a (*gen*) chope *f*; (*without handle*) timbale *f*, gobelet *m*. (*amount*) **a ~ of coffee** *etc* un grand café *etc*. b (*‡: face*) bouille* *f*, bille‡ *f*. **ugly ~** sale gueule *f*. c (*Brit ‡: fool*) andouille‡ *f*, poire* *f*, nigaud(e) *m(f)*. **what sort of a ~ do you take me for?** tu me prends pour une andouille?‡; **they're looking for a ~ to help** ils cherchent une bonne poire* pour aider; **it's a ~'s game** on se fait toujours avoir*. 2 comp ►**mug shot‡** (*Police*) photo *f* de criminel (*dans les archives de la police*); (*gen*) photo *f* d'identité. 3 vt (*assault*) agresser.
►**mug up*** 1 vt sep a (*Brit : swot up*) bûcher*, potasser*, piocher*. b (*US*) **to mug it up‡** faire des grimaces. 2 vi (*Brit*) **to mug up for an exam** bûcher* pour un examen.
mugger [ˈmʌgəʳ] n agresseur *m*.
mugging [ˈmʌgɪŋ] n agression *f*.
muggins‡ [ˈmʌgɪnz] n (*Brit*) idiot(e) *m(f)*, niais(e) *m(f)*. (*oneself*) ~ **had to pay for it** c'est encore ma pomme‡ qui a payé.
muggy [ˈmʌgɪ] adj *room* qui sent le renfermé; *climate, weather* mou (*f* molle). **it's ~ today** il fait lourd aujourd'hui.
mugwump [ˈmʌgwʌmp] n (*US Pol*) non-inscrit *m*, indépendant *m*.
mujaheddin, mujahedeen [ˌmuːdʒəhəˈdiːn] npl: **the ~** les moudjahiddin *mpl*.
mulatto [mjuːˈlætəʊ] 1 n, pl **~s** *or* **~es** mulâtre(sse) *m(f)*. 2 adj mulâtre (*f inv*).
mulberry [ˈmʌlbərɪ] n (*fruit*) mûre *f*; (*also* ~ **tree**) mûrier *m*.
mulch [mʌltʃ] 1 n paillis *m*. 2 vt pailler (*des semis etc*).
mulct [mʌlkt] 1 n (*fine*) amende *f*. 2 vt a (*fine*) frapper d'une amende. b (*by fraud etc*) **to ~ sb of sth, to ~ sth from sb** extorquer qch à qn.
mule¹ [mjuːl] 1 n a mulet *m*; (*female*) mule *f*; (*fig: person*) mule. **obstinate** *or* **stubborn as a ~** têtu comme une mule *or* un mulet. b (*Spinning*) renvideur *m*. 2 comp ►**mule driver,** (*US*) **mule skinner*** muletier *m*, -ière *f* ►**mule track** chemin *m* muletier.
mule² [mjuːl] n (*slipper*) mule *f*.
muleteer [ˌmjuːlɪˈtɪəʳ] n muletier *m*, -ière *f*.
mulish [ˈmjuːlɪʃ] adj *look, air* buté, têtu; *person* entêté *or* têtu (comme un mulet).
mulishness [ˈmjuːlɪʃnɪs] n entêtement *m*.
mull [mʌl] vt *wine, ale* chauffer et épicer. **(a glass of) ~ed wine** (un) vin chaud.
►**mull over** vt sep ruminer, retourner dans sa tête, réfléchir à.
mullah [ˈmʌlə] n mollah *m*.
mullet [ˈmʌlɪt] n: **grey ~** mulet *m*; **red ~** rouget *m*.
mulligan stew‡ [ˈmʌlɪgən stjuː] n (*US*) ragoût grossier.
mulligatawny [ˌmʌlɪgəˈtɔːnɪ] n soupe *f* au curry.
mullion [ˈmʌlɪən] n meneau *m*. **~ed window** fenêtre *f* à meneaux.
multi... [ˈmʌltɪ] pref multi..., (*often translated by "plusieurs"*) *e.g.* **~-family accommodation** résidence *f* pour *or* destinée à plusieurs familles; **~-journey ticket** abonnement *m* (pour un nombre déterminé de trajets); **~-person vehicle** véhicule *m* pour plusieurs personnes; **~-stage rocket** fusée *f* à plusieurs étages.
multi-access [ˌmʌltɪˈækses] n (*Comput*) multivoie *f*. ~ **system** système *m* à multivoie.
multicellular [ˌmʌltɪˈseljʊləʳ] adj multicellulaire.
multichannel [ˌmʌltɪˈtʃænl] adj: ~ **TV** télévision *f* à canaux multiples.
multicoloured, (*US*) **multicolored** [ˈmʌltɪˌkʌləd] adj multicolore.
multicultural [ˌmʌltɪˈkʌltʃərəl] adj multiculturel.
multiculturalism [ˌmʌltɪˈkʌltʃərəlɪzəm] n multiculturalisme *m*.
multidimensional [ˌmʌltɪdaɪˈmenʃənl] adj multidimensionnel.
multidirectional [ˌmʌltɪdɪˈrekʃənl] adj multidirectionnel.
multidisciplinary [ˌmʌltɪˈdɪsɪplɪnərɪ] adj pluridisciplinaire, multidisciplinaire. ~ **system** pluridisciplinarité *f*.
multifaceted [ˌmʌltɪˈfæsɪtɪd] adj (*fig*) qui présente de nombreux aspects.
multifarious [ˌmʌltɪˈfɛərɪəs] adj très varié, divers.
multiflora [ˌmʌltɪˈflɔːrə] adj *rose etc* multiflore.
multiform [ˈmʌltɪfɔːm] adj multiforme.
multi-function [ˈmʌltɪˈfʌŋkʃən] adj multifonctionnel, polyvalent.
multigym [ˈmʌltɪˌdʒɪm] n banc *m* de musculation.
multihull [ˈmʌltɪhʌl] n multicoque *m*.
multilateral [ˌmʌltɪˈlætərəl] adj multilatéral.
multi-level [ˈmʌltɪˈlevl] adj (*US*) à plusieurs niveaux.
multilingual [ˌmʌltɪˈlɪŋgwəl] adj multilingue, plurilingue.
multilingualism [ˌmʌltɪˈlɪŋgwəlɪzəm] n multilinguisme *m*, plurilinguisme *m*.
multi-media [ˌmʌltɪˈmiːdɪə] adj multimédia.
multimillionaire [ˌmʌltɪˌmɪljəˈnɛəʳ] n multimillionnaire *mf*, multimilliardaire *mf*.
multi-million pound [ˌmʌltɪˈmɪljənˌpaʊnd] adj *deal etc* portant sur plusieurs millions de livres.
multi-nation [ˈmʌltɪˈneɪʃən] adj *treaty, agreement* multinational.
multinational [ˌmʌltɪˈnæʃənl] 1 n multinationale *f*. 2 adj multinational.
multipack [ˈmʌltɪpæk] n pack *m*.
multiparous [mʌlˈtɪpərəs] adj multipare.
multipartite [ˌmʌltɪˈpɑːtaɪt] adj divisé en plusieurs parties.
multi-party [ˌmʌltɪˈpɑːtɪ] adj (*Pol*) pluripartite.
multiple [ˈmʌltɪpl] 1 n (*Math*) multiple *m*; *see* **low¹**. 2 adj multiple. (*Aut*) ~ **crash** carambolage *m*; ~ **ownership** multipropriété *f*; (*Psych*) ~ **personality** dédoublement *m* de la personnalité; (*Med*) ~ **sclerosis** sclérose *f* en plaques; (*Brit*) ~ **store** grand magasin à succursales multiples. 3 comp ►**multiple choice** (**exam** *or* **test**) (*Scol, Univ*) QCM *m*, questionnaire *m* à choix multiple ►**multiple choice question** question *f* à choix multiple ►**multiple-risk insurance** assurance *f* multirisque.
multiplex [ˈmʌltɪpleks] 1 adj multiplex. ~ **(cinema)** (cinéma *m*) multisalles *m*. 2 n multiplex *m*. 3 vt communiquer en multiplex.
multiplexer [ˈmʌltɪpleksəʳ] n multiplexeur *m*.
multiplexing [ˈmʌltɪpleksɪŋ] n multiplexage *m*.
multipliable [ˈmʌltɪˌplaɪəbl] adj, **multiplicable** [ˈmʌltɪˌplɪkəbl] adj multipliable.
multiplicand [ˌmʌltɪplɪˈkænd] n multiplicande *m*.
multiplication [ˌmʌltɪplɪˈkeɪʃən] 1 n multiplication *f*. 2 comp ►**multiplication sign** signe *m* de multiplication ►**multiplication tables** tables *fpl* de multiplication.
multiplicative [ˈmʌltɪplɪˌkeɪtɪv] adj (*Math, Gram*) multiplicatif.
multiplicity [ˌmʌltɪˈplɪsɪtɪ] n multiplicité *f*.
multiplier [ˈmʌltɪplaɪəʳ] 1 n multiplicateur *m*. 2 comp ►**multiplier effect** effet *m* multiplicateur.
multiply [ˈmʌltɪplaɪ] 1 vt multiplier (*by* par). 2 vi se multiplier.
multiplying [ˈmʌltɪplaɪɪŋ] adj multiplicateur (*f* -trice), multiplicatif.
multipolar [ˈmʌltɪˈpəʊləʳ] adj multipolaire.
multiprocessing [ˌmʌltɪˈprəʊsesɪŋ] n (*Comput*) multitraitement *m*.
multiprocessor [ˌmʌltɪˈprəʊsesəʳ] n (*Comput*) multicalculateur *m*.
multiprogramming [ˌmʌltɪˈprəʊgræmɪŋ] n (*Comput*) multiprogrammation *f*.
multipurpose [ˌmʌltɪˈpɜːpəs] adj polyvalent, à usages multiples.
multiracial [ˌmʌltɪˈreɪʃəl] adj multiracial.
multirisk [ˌmʌltɪˈrɪsk] adj (*Insurance*) multirisque.
multisensory [ˌmʌltɪˈsensərɪ] adj multisensoriel.
multistandard [ˌmʌltɪˈstændəd] adj *TV set, video etc* multistandard *inv*.
multistorey [ˌmʌltɪˈstɔːrɪ], **multistoreyed,** (*US*) **multistoried** [ˌmʌltɪˈstɔːrɪd] adj à étages. ~ **car park** parking *m* à étages *or* à niveaux multiples.
multitasking [ˌmʌltɪˈtɑːskɪŋ] n (*Comput*) traitement *m* multitâche.
multitrack [ˌmʌltɪˈtræk] adj à plusieurs pistes.
multitude [ˈmʌltɪtjuːd] n multitude *f*. **the ~** la multitude, la foule; **for a ~ of reasons** pour une multitude *or* une multiplicité *or* une foule de raisons; **that covers** *or* **hides a ~ of sins** c'est un véritable cache-misère.
multitudinous [ˌmʌltɪˈtjuːdɪnəs] adj innombrable.
multiuser [ˌmʌltɪˈjuːzəʳ] adj (*Comput*) ~ **system** configuration *f* multiposte.
multivalence [ˌmʌltɪˈveɪləns] n polyvalence *f*.
multivalent [ˌmʌltɪˈveɪlənt] adj polyvalent.
multivitamin [ˌmʌltɪˈvɪtəmɪn] n complexe *m* vitaminé.
mum¹* [mʌm] n (*Brit: mother*) maman *f*.
mum² [mʌm] adj: **to keep ~ (about sth)** ne pas piper mot (de qch), ne pas souffler mot (de qch); **~'s the word!** motus!, bouche cousue!
mum³ [mʌm] n (**abbr of chrysanthemum**) **~s** chrysanthèmes *mpl*.

mumble [ˈmʌmbl] 1 vi marmotter. **stop mumbling!** arrête de marmotter! *or* de parler entre tes dents! 2 vt marmonner, marmotter. **to ~ one's words** manger ses mots; **to ~ an answer** répondre entre ses dents, marmonner une réponse. 3 n marmonnement *m*, marmottement *m*. **he said in a ~** dit-il entre ses dents.

mumbo jumbo [ˌmʌmbəʊˈdʒʌmbəʊ] n (*nonsense*) baragouin* *m*, charabia* *m*; (*pretentious words*) jargon obscur; (*pretentious ceremony etc*) tralala* *m*, salamalecs* *mpl*.

mummer [ˈmʌməʳ] n (*Theat*) mime *mf*.

mummery [ˈmʌmərɪ] n (*Theat, fig*) momerie *f*.

mummification [ˌmʌmɪfɪˈkeɪʃən] n momification *f*.

mummify [ˈmʌmɪfaɪ] vt momifier.

mummy[1] [ˈmʌmɪ] n (*embalmed*) momie *f*.

mummy[2]* [ˈmʌmɪ] n (*Brit: mother*) maman *f*. (*pej*) **~'s boy** fils *m* à sa mère.

mump [mʌmp] vi grogner, grommeler.

mumps [mʌmps] n (*NonC*) oreillons *mpl*.

munch [mʌntʃ] vti (*gen*) croquer; (*chew noisily*) mastiquer bruyamment. **to ~ (away) on** *or* **at sth** dévorer qch à belles dents.

munchies⁑ [ˈmʌntʃɪz] npl (*US*) a (*snack*) quelque chose à grignoter. b (*be hungry*) **to have the ~** avoir un creux.

mundane [ˌmʌnˈdeɪn] adj (*ordinary*) banal, quelconque; (*worldly*) de ce monde, terrestre (*fig*).

mung bean [ˈmʌŋbiːn] n haricot *m* mung.

Munich [ˈmjuːnɪk] n Munich.

municipal [mjuːˈnɪsɪpəl] adj (*gen*) municipal. (*US Jur*) **~ court** tribunal *m* d'instance.

municipality [mjuːˌnɪsɪˈpælɪtɪ] n municipalité *f*.

munificence [mjuːˈnɪfɪsns] n munificence *f*.

munificent [mjuːˈnɪfɪsnt] adj munificent.

muniments [ˈmjuːnɪmənts] npl (*Jur*) titres *mpl* (*concernant la propriété d'un bien-fonds*).

munitions [mjuːˈnɪʃənz] 1 npl munitions *fpl*. 2 comp ▸**munitions dump** entrepôt *m* de munitions ▸**munitions factory** usine *f* de munitions.

mural [ˈmjʊərəl] 1 adj mural. 2 n peinture murale.

murder [ˈmɜːdəʳ] 1 n a (*gen*) meurtre *m*; (*Jur*) meurtre, (*premeditated*) assassinat *m*. **4 ~s in one week** 4 meurtres en une semaine; (*excl*) **~!** au meurtre!, à l'assassin!; (*Prov*) **~ will out** tôt ou tard la vérité se fait jour; (*fig*) **he was screaming** *or* **shouting blue ~*** il criait comme un putois *or* comme si on l'écorchait; (*fig*) **she lets the children get away with ~*** elle passe tout aux enfants; (*fig*) **they get away with ~*** ils peuvent faire n'importe quoi impunément.
b (* *fig*) **the noise/heat in here is ~** le bruit/la chaleur ici est infernal(e); **did you have a good holiday? — no, it was ~** avez-vous passé de bonnes vacances? — non, des vacances tuantes *or* c'était tuant; **the roads were ~** les routes étaient un cauchemar.
2 comp ▸**murder case** (*Jur*) procès *m* en homicide; (*Police*) affaire *f* d'homicide ▸**murder hunt** opération *f* pour retrouver le (*or* un) meurtrier ▸**Murder Squad** (*Police*) ≃ brigade criminelle (de la police judiciaire) ▸**murder trial** ≃ procès *m* capital ▸**murder weapon** arme *f* du meurtre.
3 vt *person* assassiner; (*fig*) *song, music, language* massacrer; *opponent, team* battre à plates coutures, écraser. **the ~ed man** (*or* **woman** *etc*) la victime.

murderer [ˈmɜːdərəʳ] n meurtrier *m*, assassin *m*.

murderess [ˈmɜːdərɪs] n meurtrière *f*.

murderous [ˈmɜːdərəs] adj *act, rage, person, climate, road* meurtrier; (*cruel*) féroce, cruel. **a ~-looking individual** un individu à tête d'assassin; (*fig*) **this heat is ~*** cette chaleur est infernale.

murk [mɜːk] n, **murkiness** [mɜːkɪnɪs] n obscurité *f*.

murky [ˈmɜːkɪ] adj (*gen*) obscur, sombre, ténébreux; *sky* sombre; *darkness* épais (*f* -aisse); *water* trouble; *colour* terne, terreux. (*hum*) **his ~ past** son passé trouble.

murmur [ˈmɜːməʳ] 1 n murmure *m*; [*bees, traffic etc*] bourdonnement *m*; (*fig: protest*) murmure. **there wasn't a ~ in the classroom** il n'y avait pas un murmure dans la classe; **to speak in a ~** parler à voix basse, chuchoter; **a ~ of conversation** un bourdonnement de voix; **there were ~s of disagreement** il y eut des murmures de désapprobation; **he agreed without a ~** il accepta sans murmure; (*Med*) **a heart ~** un souffle au cœur. 2 vt murmurer. 3 vi [*person, stream*] murmurer; (*complain*) murmurer (*against, about* contre).

murmuring [ˈmɜːmərɪŋ] 1 n (*of people, stream; also fig: of protests*) murmures *mpl*; [*bees etc*] bourdonnement *m*. 2 adj *stream* murmurant, qui murmure.

Murphy [ˈmɜːfɪ] 1 n (*) (*US, Ir: potato*) pomme de terre *f*. 2 comp ▸**Murphy bed** (*US*) lit *m* escamotable ▸**Murphy's law*** loi *f* de la guigne* maximum.

MusBac n (abbr of **Bachelor of Music**) *diplôme d'études musicales*.

muscatel [ˌmʌskəˈtel] n (*grape, wine*) muscat *m*.

muscle [ˈmʌsl] 1 n a (*Anat*) muscle *m*. (*fig*) **put some ~ into it*** vas-y avec un peu plus de nerf* *or* de force; *see* **move**. b (*fig: power*) pouvoir effectif, impact *m*. **political ~** pouvoir politique effectif, moyens *mpl* politiques; **this union hasn't much ~** ce syndicat n'a pas beaucoup d'impact *or* de poids. 2 comp ▸**muscle-bound** (*lit*) aux muscles hypertrophiés; (*fig*) raide ▸**muscleman** (*strong man*) hercule *m*; (*gangster etc*) homme *m* de main, sbire *m*.
▸**muscle in*** vi a (*Brit: into group etc*) intervenir, s'immiscer. **to muscle in on a group/a discussion/the act** essayer de s'imposer dans un groupe/une discussion/les opérations; **stop muscling in!** occupe-toi de tes oignons!* b (*US: force one's way inside*) entrer violemment.

Muscovite [ˈmʌskəvaɪt] 1 adj moscovite. 2 n Moscovite *mf*.

muscular [ˈmʌskjʊləʳ] adj *tissue, disease* musculaire; *person, arm* musclé. **~ dystrophy** dystrophie *f* musculaire.

musculature [ˈmʌskjʊlətjʊəʳ] n musculature *f*.

MusDoc n (abbr of **Doctor of Music**) *doctorat d'études musicales*.

muse [mjuːz] 1 vi méditer (*on, about, over* sur), songer, réfléchir (*on, about, over* à). 2 vt: **"they might accept" he ~d** "il se pourrait qu'ils acceptent" dit-il d'un ton songeur *or* (*silently*) songeait-il. 3 n (*Myth, fig: also* **M~**) muse *f*.

museum [mjuːˈzɪəm] n musée *m*. **~ piece** pièce *f* de musée; (*fig*) vieillerie *f*, antiquaille *f*.

mush [mʌʃ] n (*NonC*) bouillie *f*; (*fig*) sentimentalité *f* de guimauve *or* à l'eau de rose.

mushroom [ˈmʌʃrʊm] 1 n champignon *m* (comestible). **a great ~ of smoke** un nuage de fumée en forme de champignon; **that child grows like a ~** cet enfant pousse comme un champignon; **houses sprang up like ~s** les maisons ont poussé comme des champignons.
2 comp *soup, omelette* aux champignons; *flavour* de champignons; (*colour*) *carpet etc* beige rosé *inv* ▸**mushroom cloud** champignon *m* atomique ▸**mushroom growth** poussée soudaine ▸**mushroom town** ville *f* champignon *inv*.
3 vi a (*grow quickly*) [*town etc*] pousser comme un champignon. **the village ~ed into a town** le village est rapidement devenu ville.
b (*proliferate*) proliférer, se multiplier. **shops ~ed all over the place** des magasins ont proliféré *or* se sont multipliés un peu partout.
c **a cloud of smoke went ~ing up** un nuage de fumée en forme de champignon s'est élevé dans le ciel.
d **to go ~ing** aller aux champignons.

mushrooming [ˈmʌʃrʊmɪŋ] n a (*picking mushrooms*) cueillette *f* des champignons. **I like ~** j'aime aller aux champignons. b (*fig*) (*growth: of town etc*) poussée *f* rapide; (*proliferation: of shops etc*) prolifération *f*.

mushy [ˈmʌʃɪ] adj *vegetables, food* en bouillie; *fruit* blet; *ground* spongieux; (*fig, pej*) fleur bleue *inv*, à la guimauve, à l'eau de rose. **~ peas** purée *f* de pois.

music [ˈmjuːzɪk] 1 n (*all senses*) musique *f*. **to set to ~** mettre en musique; (*fig*) **it was ~ to his ears** c'était doux à son oreille; (*Univ*) **the Faculty of M~** la faculté de musique; *see* **ear**[1], **face, pop**[2] *etc*. 2 comp *teacher, lesson, exam* de musique ▸**music box** boîte *f* à musique ▸**music case** porte-musique *m inv* ▸**music centre** (*equipment*) chaîne compacte (stéréo); (*shop*) magasin *m* de hi-fi ▸**music critic** (*Press*) critique musical ▸**music festival** festival *m* ▸**music hall** (*Brit*) n music-hall *m* ◊ adj de music-hall ▸**music lover** mélomane *mf* ▸**music paper** papier *m* à musique ▸**music stand** pupitre *m* à musique ▸**music stool** tabouret *m* de musique.

musical [ˈmjuːzɪkəl] 1 adj (*lit, fig*) *voice, sound, criticism, studies* musical. **he comes from a ~ family** il sort d'une famille musicienne; **she's very ~** (*gifted*) elle est musicienne, elle est très douée pour la musique; (*fond of it*) elle est mélomane; **~ box** boîte *f* à musique; (*game*) **~ chairs** chaises musicales; (*fig*) **they were playing at ~ chairs** ils changeaient tout le temps de place; **~ comedy** comédie musicale, opérette *f*; **~ evening** soirée musicale; **~ instrument** instrument *m* de musique. 2 n (*Cine, Theat*) comédie musicale.

musically [ˈmjuːzɪkəlɪ] adv musicalement. **~ gifted** doué pour la musique; **~ inclined** mélomane *mf*.

musician [mjuːˈzɪʃən] n musicien(-ienne) *m(f)*.

musicianship [mjuːˈzɪʃənʃɪp] n maestria *f* (de musicien), sens *m* de la musique.

musicologist [ˌmjuːzɪˈkɒlədʒɪst] n musicologue *mf*.

musicology [ˌmjuːzɪˈkɒlədʒɪ] n musicologie *f*.

musing [ˈmjuːzɪŋ] 1 adj songeur, pensif, rêveur. 2 n songerie *f*, rêverie *f*. **idle ~s** rêvasseries *fpl*.

musingly [ˈmjuːzɪŋlɪ] adv d'un air songeur *or* rêveur, pensivement.

musk [mʌsk] 1 n musc *m*. 2 comp ▸**muskmelon** cantaloup *m* ▸**musk ox** bœuf musqué ▸**muskrat** rat musqué, ondatra *m* ▸**musk rose** rose *f* muscade.

muskeg [ˈmʌskeg] n (*US: bog*) tourbière *f*.

musket [ˈmʌskɪt] n mousquet *m*.

musketeer [ˌmʌskɪˈtɪəʳ] n mousquetaire *m*.

musketry [ˈmʌskɪtrɪ] 1 n tir *m* (au fusil *etc*). 2 comp *range, training* de tir (au fusil *etc*).

musky [ˈmʌskɪ] adj musqué, de musc.

Muslim [ˈmʊzlɪm] 1 n, pl **~s** *or* **~** musulman(e) *m(f)*; *see* **black**. 2 adj musulman.

muslin [ˈmʌzlɪn] 1 n mousseline *f*. 2 comp de *or* en mousseline.

musquash [ˈmʌskwɒʃ] 1 n (*animal*) rat musqué, ondatra *m*; (*fur*) rat d'Amérique, ondatra. 2 comp *coat* d'ondatra.

muss* [mʌs] vt (*also* ~ **up**) *dress, clothes* chiffonner, froisser. **to ~ sb's hair** décoiffer qn.
mussel [ˈmʌsl] n moule *f*. ~ **bed** parc *m* à moules, moulière *f*.
must¹ [mʌst] 1 *modal aux vb* a (*indicating obligation*) **you must leave now** vous devez partir *or* il faut que vous partiez (*subj*) maintenant; († *or hum*) **I must away** je dois partir, il faut que je parte; (*on notice*) **"the windows must not be opened"** "défense d'ouvrir les fenêtres"; **I (simply *or* absolutely) MUST see him!** il faut absolument que je le voie!; **you mustn't touch it** il ne faut pas *or* tu ne dois pas y toucher, c'est défendu d'y toucher; **what must we do now?** que faut-il *or* que devons-nous faire à présent?; **why must you always be so rude?** pourquoi faut-il toujours que tu sois si grossier?; (*frm*) **you must know that ...** il faut que vous sachiez que ...; **I must ask you not to touch that** je dois vous prier *or* je vous prie de ne pas toucher à cela; (*Comm: in letters*) **we must ask you to send us ...** nous nous trouvons dans l'obligation de vous demander de nous envoyer ...; **if you MUST leave then go at once** s'il faut vraiment que vous partiez (*subj*), partez tout de suite; **(well), if I ~** (eh bien), s'il le faut vraiment; **sit down if you must** asseyez-vous si c'est indispensable *or* si vous y tenez; **if you MUST know ...** si tu tiens vraiment à le savoir ..., si tu veux vraiment le savoir ...; **I MUST say, he's very irritating** il n'y a pas à dire *or* franchement il est très agaçant; **you look well, I must say!** je dois dire que *or* vraiment tu as très bonne mine!; (*iro*) **that's brilliant, I MUST say!** pour être réussi, c'est réussi (je dois dire)! (*iro*); **well I MUST say!*** eh bien vraiment!, ça alors!*; **what must he do but bang the door just when ..., he must bang the door just when ...** il a (bien) fallu qu'il claque (*subj*) la porte juste au moment où ... .
b (*indicating certainty*) **he must be wrong** il doit se tromper, il se trompe certainement; **I realized he must be wrong** j'ai compris qu'il devait se tromper *or* qu'il se trompait certainement; **he must be clever, mustn't he?** il doit être intelligent, n'est-ce pas?; **he must be mad!** il doit être fou!, il est fou!; **is he mad? — he MUST be!** est-ce qu'il est fou? — il faut le croire! *or* sûrement!; **I must have made a mistake** j'ai dû me tromper; **you must be joking!** vous devez plaisanter!, vous plaisantez!; **you must know my aunt** vous devez connaître ma tante, vous connaissez sans doute ma tante; **that must be Paul** ça doit être Paul.
2 n (*) impératif *m*, chose *f* indispensable *or* obligatoire. **this book is a ~** c'est un livre qu'il faut absolument avoir *or* lire; **a car is a ~ in the country** une voiture est absolument indispensable à la campagne; **a ~ for all housewives!** ce que toutes les ménagères doivent posséder!, indispensable à toutes les ménagères!
must² [mʌst] n *[fruit]* moût *m*.
mustache [ˈmʌstæʃ] *etc* (*US*) = **moustache** *etc*.
mustang [ˈmʌstæŋ] n mustang *m*.
mustard [ˈmʌstəd] 1 n (*Bot, Culin*) moutarde *f*. (*US fig*) **to cut the ~‡** faire le poids, être à la hauteur; *see* **keen**.
2 adj moutarde.
3 comp ▸**mustard and cress** moutarde blanche et cresson alénois ▸**mustard bath** bain sinapisé *or* à la moutarde ▸**mustard gas** ypérite *f*, gaz *m* moutarde ▸**mustard plaster** sinapisme *m*, cataplasme sinapisé ▸**mustard pot** moutardier *m* ▸**mustard powder** farine *f* de moutarde.
muster [ˈmʌstəʳ] 1 n (*gathering*) assemblée *f*; (*Mil, Naut: also* ~ **roll**) rassemblement *m*; (*roll-call*) appel *m*. (*fig*) **to pass ~** (*gen*) (pouvoir) passer, être acceptable; **it must pass ~ with the scientists** il faut que cela soit jugé valable par les scientifiques.
2 vt a (*assemble, collect*) *helpers, number, sum* réunir; (*also* ~ **up**) *strength, courage, energy* rassembler. **he ~ed (up) the courage to say so** il prit son courage à deux mains pour le dire; **I couldn't ~ up enough energy to protest** je n'ai pas eu l'énergie de protester; **I could only ~ 50p** je n'ai pu réunir en tout et pour tout que 50 pence; **they could only ~ 5 volunteers** ils n'ont pu trouver *or* réunir que 5 volontaires; **the club can only ~ 20 members** le club ne compte que 20 membres.
b (*call roll of*) battre le rappel de.
3 vi (*gather, assemble*) se réunir, se rassembler.
mustiness [ˈmʌstɪnɪs] n (goût *m or* odeur *f* de) moisi *m*.
mustn't [ˈmʌsnt] = **must not**; *see* **must**.
musty [ˈmʌstɪ] adj *taste, smell* de moisi; *room* qui sent le moisi *or* le renfermé; (* *fig*) *ideas, methods* vieux jeu *inv*. **to grow ~** moisir; **to smell ~** *[room, air]* avoir une odeur de renfermé; *[book, clothes]* avoir une odeur de moisi *or* de vieux.
mutability [ˌmjuːtəˈbɪlɪtɪ] n mutabilité *f*.
mutable [ˈmjuːtəbl] adj muable, mutable; (*Ling*) sujet à la mutation.
mutagen [ˈmjuːtədʒən] n mutagène *m*.
mutagenic [mjuːtəˈdʒenɪk] adj mutagène.
mutant [ˈmjuːtənt] adj, n mutant (*m*).
mutate [mjuːˈteɪt] 1 vi subir une mutation. 2 vt faire subir une mutation à.
mutation [mjuːˈteɪʃən] n mutation *f*.
mutatis mutandis [muːˈtɑːtɪs muːtændɪs] adv mutatis mutandis, en opérant les changements nécessaires.
mute [mjuːt] 1 adj *person, reproach* muet. ~ **with admiration, in ~ admiration** muet d'admiration; (*Ling*) **H ~** H muet; (*Ling*) **~ "e"** "e" muet; ~ **swan** cygne *m* tuberculé *or* muet.
2 n a (*Med*) muet(te) *m(f)*; *see* **deaf**.
b (*Mus*) sourdine *f*.
3 vt a (*Mus*) mettre la sourdine à.
b *sound* assourdir, rendre moins sonore; *colour* adoucir, atténuer, assourdir.
c *feelings, emotions* affaiblir, atténuer; *enthusiasm* tempérer.
muted [ˈmjuːtɪd] adj *voice, sound* sourd, assourdi; *colour* sourd; (*Mus*) *violin* en sourdine; *criticism, protest* voilé; *feelings, emotions* affaibli, atténué; *enthusiasm* tempéré.
mutilate [ˈmjuːtɪleɪt] vt *person, limb* mutiler, estropier; *object* mutiler, dégrader; (*fig*) *text* mutiler, tronquer.
mutilation [ˌmjuːtɪˈleɪʃən] n mutilation *f*.
mutineer [ˌmjuːtɪˈnɪəʳ] n (*Mil, Naut*) mutiné *m*, mutin *m*.
mutinous [ˈmjuːtɪnəs] adj (*Mil, Naut*) *crew, troops* mutiné; (*fig*) *attitude* rebelle. **a ~ look** un regard plein de rébellion; **the children were already fairly ~** les enfants regimbaient *or* se rebiffaient* déjà.
mutiny [ˈmjuːtɪnɪ] 1 n (*Mil, Naut*) mutinerie *f*; (*fig*) révolte *f*. 2 vi se mutiner; (*fig*) se révolter.
mutt‡ [mʌt] n a (*fool*) corniaud* *m*, crétin(e)* *m(f)*, andouille‡ *f*. b (*US : dog*) clebs* *m*, corniaud *m*.
mutter [ˈmʌtəʳ] 1 n marmottement *m*, marmonnement *m*; (*grumbling*) grommellement *m*.
2 vt *threat, wish* marmotter, marmonner. **"no" he ~ed** "non" marmonna-t-il *or* dit-il entre ses dents.
3 vi marmonner, murmurer; (*grumble*) grommeler, grogner; *[thunder]* gronder.
muttering [ˈmʌtərɪŋ] n, pl ~s grommellement *m*, grognement *m*.
mutton [ˈmʌtn] 1 n (*Culin*) mouton *m*. **leg of ~** gigot *m*; **shoulder of ~** épaule *f* de mouton; (*fig, hum*) **it's ~ dressed (up) as lamb*** elle s'habille trop jeune pour son âge; *see* **dead**.
2 comp ▸**mutton chop** (*Culin*) côtelette *f* de mouton ▸**mutton chops*** (*whiskers*) (favoris *mpl* en) côtelettes *fpl* ▸**muttonhead‡** cornichon* *m*.
mutual [ˈmjuːtjʊəl] adj a (*reciprocal*) *affection, help* mutuel, réciproque; (*Comm*) mutuel. ~ **aid** entraide *f*, aide mutuelle *or* réciproque; **by ~ consent** par consentement mutuel; **the feeling is ~** c'est réciproque; ~ **insurance company** (compagnie *f* d'assurance) mutuelle *f*; (*US Fin*) ~ **fund** fonds *m* commun de placement. b (*common*) *friend, cousin, share* commun.
mutuality [ˌmjuːtjʊˈælɪtɪ] n mutualité *f*.
mutually [ˈmjuːtjʊəlɪ] adv mutuellement, réciproquement. ~ **contradictory** *or* **exclusive** qui s'excluent l'un(e) l'autre.
Muzak [ˈmjuːzæk] n ® musique *f* (d'ambiance) enregistrée.
muzzle [ˈmʌzl] 1 n *[dog, fox etc]* museau *m*; *[gun]* bouche *f*, gueule *f*; (*anti-biting device*) muselière *f*; (*fig*) muselière, bâillon *m*.
2 comp ▸**muzzle loader** arme *f* qu'on charge par le canon ▸**muzzle velocity** vitesse initiale.
3 vt *dog* museler; (*fig*) museler, bâillonner.
muzzy [ˈmʌzɪ] adj dans les vapes*, tout chose*; (*tipsy*) éméché*; *ideas* confus, nébuleux; *outline* estompé, flou. **this cold makes me feel ~** ce rhume me brouille la cervelle *or* m'abrutit.
MW n (*Rad*) (abbr of **medium wave**) P.O. *fpl*.
my [maɪ] 1 poss adj mon, ma, mes. ~ **book** mon livre; ~ **table** ma table; ~ **friend** mon ami(e); ~ **clothes** mes vêtements; **MY book** mon livre à moi; **I've broken ~ leg** je me suis cassé la jambe. 2 excl: **(oh) ~!***, ~, ~!* ça, par exemple!
myalgia [maɪˈældʒə] n myalgie *f*.
Myanmar [ˈmaɪænmɑːʳ] n Union *f* de Myanama.
mycology [maɪˈkɒlədʒɪ] n mycologie *f*.
mycosis [maɪˈkəʊsɪs] n mycose *f*.
mynah [ˈmaɪnə] n (*also* ~ **bird**) mainate *m*.
myopia [maɪˈəʊpɪə] n myopie *f*.
myopic [maɪˈɒpɪk] adj myope.
myriad [ˈmɪrɪəd] 1 n myriade *f*. 2 adj (*liter*) innombrable, sans nombre.
myrmidon [ˈmɜːmɪdən] n (*pej hum*) sbire *m*.
myrrh [mɜːʳ] n myrrhe *f*.
myrtle [ˈmɜːtl] n myrte *m*.
myself [maɪˈself] pers pron (*reflexive: direct and indirect*) me; (*emphatic*) moi-même; (*after prep*) moi. **I've hurt ~** je me suis blessé; **I said to ~** je me suis dit; **I spoke to him ~** je lui ai parlé moi-même; **people like ~** le genre de personne comme moi; **I've kept one for ~** j'en ai gardé un pour moi; **he asked me for a photo of ~** il m'a demandé une photo de moi *or* une de mes photos; **I told him ~** je le lui ai dit moi-même; **all by ~** tout seul; **I'm not ~ today** je ne suis pas dans mon état normal *or* dans mon assiette* aujourd'hui.
mysterious [mɪsˈtɪərɪəs] adj mystérieux.
mysteriously [mɪsˈtɪərɪəslɪ] adv mystérieusement.
mystery [ˈmɪstərɪ] 1 n a (*also Rel*) mystère *m*. **there's no ~ about it** ça n'a rien de mystérieux; **it's a ~ to me how he did it** je n'arrive pas à comprendre comment il l'a fait; **to make a great ~ of sth** faire grand mystère de qch.

b (*Theat:* ~ *play*) mystère *m*.
c (*Literat: also* ~ **story**) roman *m* à énigmes.
2 **comp** *ship, man* mystérieux ▸**mystery play** (*Theat*) mystère *m* ▸**mystery tour** (*in coach etc*) voyage *m* surprise (*dont on ne connaît pas la destination*).

mystic ['mɪstɪk] 1 **adj** (*Rel*) mystique; *power* occulte; *rite* ésotérique; *truth* surnaturel; *formula* magique. 2 **n** mystique *mf*.

mystical ['mɪstɪkəl] **adj** mystique.

mysticism ['mɪstɪsɪzəm] **n** mysticisme *m*.

mystification [,mɪstɪfɪ'keɪʃən] **n** (*bewildering*) mystification *f*; (*bewilderment*) perplexité *f*. **why all the ~?** pourquoi tout ce mystère?

mystify ['mɪstɪfaɪ] **vt** rendre *or* laisser perplexe; (*deliberately deceive*) mystifier.

mystique [mɪs'tiːk] **n** mystique *f*.

myth [mɪθ] **n** mythe *m*.

mythical ['mɪθɪkəl] **adj** mythique.

mythological [,mɪθə'lɒdʒɪkəl] **adj** mythologique.

mythology [mɪ'θɒlədʒɪ] **n** mythologie *f*.

myxomatosis [,mɪksəʊmə'təʊsɪs] **n** myxomatose *f*.

N

N, n [en] n a (*letter*) N, n *m*. **N for Nancy** ≃ N comme Nicolas. b (*Math*) **to the nth (power)**, (*fig*) **to the nth degree*** à la puissance n; **I told him for the nth time* to stop talking** je lui ai dit pour la énième fois de se taire; **there are n ways of doing it** il y a mille *or* des tas de* façons de le faire. c (**abbr of north**) N. d (*Elec*) (**abbr of neutral**) N.
'n'‡ [ən] conj = **and.**
n/a a (*Admin etc*) (**abbr of not applicable**) ne s'applique pas. b (*Banking*) (**abbr of no account**) pas de compte.
NAACP [enei,eisi:'pi:] n (*US*) (**abbr of National Association for the Advancement of Colored People**) *défense des droits civiques des Noirs.*
NAAFI ['næfi] n (*Brit Mil*) (**abbr of Navy, Army and Air Force Institute**) coopérative *f* militaire.
nab* [næb] vt a (*catch in wrongdoing*) pincer*, choper‡, poisser‡. b (*catch to speak to etc*) attraper, coincer*. c (*take*) *sb's pen, chair etc* accaparer.
nabob ['neibɒb] n (*lit, fig*) nabab *m*.
nacelle [næ'sel] n (*Aviat*) nacelle *f*.
nacre ['neikəʳ] n nacre *f*.
nacred ['neikəd] adj, **nacreous** ['neikriəs] adj nacré.
Naderism ['neidərizəm] n consumérisme *m*, défense *f* du consommateur.
nadir ['neidiəʳ] n (*Astron*) nadir *m*; (*fig*) point le plus bas. **in the ~ of despair** dans le plus profond désespoir; **his fortunes reached their ~ when** ... il atteignit le comble de l'infortune quand ... .
naevus, (*US*) **nevus** ['ni:vəs] n, pl **naevi**, (*US*) **nevi** ['ni:vai] nævus *m*.
naff‡ [næf] (*Brit*) adj guère sortable*.
►**naff off**‡ vi foutre le camp‡.
nag¹ [næg] 1 vt (*also* ~ **at**) *[person]* reprendre tout le temps, être toujours après*; *[doubt etc]* harceler. **he was ~ging (at) me to keep my room tidy** il me harcelait *or* m'asticotait* pour que je tienne ma chambre en ordre; **to ~ sb into doing sth** harceler qn jusqu'à ce qu'il fasse qch; **his conscience was ~ging (at) him** sa conscience le travaillait; **~ged by doubts** assailli *or* harcelé *or* poursuivi par le doute. 2 vi *[person]* (*scold*) faire des remarques continuelles; *[pain, doubts]* être harcelant. **to ~ at sb** = **to ~ sb**; *see* **1.** 3 n: **he's a dreadful ~*** (*scolding*) il n'arrête pas de faire des remarques; (*pestering*) il n'arrête pas de nous (*or le etc*) harceler.
nag²* [næg] n (*horse*) cheval *m*; (*pej*) canasson* *m* (*pej*).
Nagasaki [,nɑ:gə'sɑ:ki] n Nagasaki.
nagger ['nægəʳ] n = **nag¹ 3.**
nagging ['nægiŋ] 1 adj *person* qui n'arrête pas de faire des remarques; *pain, worry, doubt* tenace, harcelant. 2 n (*NonC*) remarques continuelles, criailleries *fpl*.
NAHT [,eneiei'tʃi:] n (*Brit*) (**abbr of National Association of Head Teachers**) *association nationale des chefs d'établissements.*
Nahum ['neihəm] n Nahum *m*.
naiad ['naiæd] n, pl **~s** *or* **~es** naïade *f*.
nail [neil] 1 n a (*Anat*) ongle *m*. **finger~** ongle (de doigt de la main); *see* **bite, toe, tooth** *etc*.
b (*Tech*) clou *m*. (*fig*) **to pay on the ~** payer rubis sur l'ongle; **he was offered the job on the ~*** on lui a offert le poste sur-le-champ *or* illico*; (*fig*) **that decision was a** *or* **another ~ in his coffin** cette décision n'a fait que le pousser davantage vers le précipice; *see* **bed, hard, hit.**
2 comp ►**nail-biting** n habitude *f* de se ronger les ongles ◊ adj *film* à suspense, angoissant, stressant; *finish, match* serré ►**nail bomb** ≃ bombe *f* de fabrication artisanale ►**nailbrush** brosse *f* à ongles ►**nail clippers** pince *f* à ongles ►**nail enamel** = **nail polish** ►**nailfile** lime *f* à ongles ►**nail lacquer, nail polish** vernis *m* à ongles ►**nail polish remover** dissolvant *m* ►**nail scissors** ciseaux *mpl* à ongles ►**nail varnish** (*Brit*) = **nail polish** ►**nail varnish remover** = **nail polish remover.**
3 vt a (*fix with ~s*) clouer. **to ~ the lid on a crate** clouer le couvercle d'une caisse; (*fig*) **to ~ one's colours to the mast** proclamer une fois pour toutes sa position; (*fig*) **to be ~ed to the spot** *or* **ground** rester cloué sur place.
b (*put ~s into*) clouter. **~ed shoes** chaussures cloutées.
c (*: *catch in crime etc*) *person* pincer*, choper‡; (*expose*) *lie* démasquer; *rumour* démentir.
d (*: *hit with shot etc*) descendre*, abattre.
►**nail down** vt sep a *lid* clouer. b (*fig*) *hesitating person* obtenir une décision de; *agreement, policy* établir, arrêter. **I nailed him down to coming at 6 o'clock** je l'ai réduit *or* contraint à accepter de venir à 6 heures.
►**nail up** vt sep a *picture etc* fixer par des clous. b *door, window* condamner (en clouant). c *box, crate* clouer. **to nail up goods in a crate** empaqueter des marchandises dans une caisse clouée.
Nairobi [nai'rəubi] n Nairobi.
naïve, naive [nai'i:v] adj naïf (*f* naïve), ingénu.
naïvely, naively [nai'i:vli] adv naïvement, ingénument.
naïveté [nai'i:vtei] n, **naïvety, naivety** [nai'i:vti] n naïveté *f*, ingénuité *f*.
naked ['neikid] adj a *person* (tout) nu; *animal* nu. **to go ~** se promener (tout) nu; *see* **stark, strip.** b *branch* dénudé, dépouillé; *countryside* pelé, dénudé; *sword* nu. **~ flame** *or* **light** flamme nue; **visible to the ~ eye** visible à l'œil nu; **you can't see it with the ~ eye** on ne peut pas le voir à l'œil nu; **the ~ truth** la vérité toute nue; **~ facts** faits bruts; **a ~ outline of the events** un aperçu des événements réduit à sa plus simple expression; **it was a ~ attempt at fraud** c'était une tentative flagrante de fraude.
nakedness ['neikidnis] n nudité *f*.
NALGO ['nælgəu] n (*Brit*) (**abbr of National and Local Government Officers Association**) *syndicat.*
namby-pamby* ['næmbi'pæmbi] 1 n gnangnan* *mf or* gnian-gnian* *mf*. 2 adj *person* gnangnan* *inv or* gnian-gnian* *inv*; *style* à l'eau de rose.
name [neim] 1 n a nom *m*. **what's your ~?** comment vous appelez-vous?, quel est votre nom?; **my ~ is Robert** je m'appelle Robert; **I'll do it or my ~'s not Robert Smith!*** je le ferai, foi de Robert Smith!; **I haven't a ha'penny** *or* **a penny to my ~*** je n'ai pas un sou vaillant, je n'ai pas le sou; **what ~ are they giving the child?** comment vont-ils appeler l'enfant?; **they married to give the child a ~** ils se sont mariés pour que l'enfant soit légitime; **what ~ shall I say?** (*Telec*) c'est de la part de qui?; (*announcing arrival*) qui dois-je annoncer?; **please fill in your ~ and address** prière d'inscrire vos nom(, prénom) et adresse; **to take sb's ~ and address** noter *or* prendre les nom(, prénom) et adresse de qn; (*Ftbl etc*) **to have one's ~ taken** recevoir un avertissement, ≃ recevoir un carton jaune; **this man, Smith by ~** *or* **by the ~ of Smith** cet homme, qui répond au nom de Smith; **we know it by** *or* **under another ~** nous le connaissons sous un autre nom; **to go by** *or* **under the ~ of** se faire appeler; **he writes under the ~ of X** il écrit sous le pseudonyme de X; **but his real ~ is Y** mais il s'appelle Y de son vrai nom, mais son vrai nom est Y; **I know him only by ~** *or* **by ~ alone** je ne le connais que de nom; **he knows all his customers by ~** il connaît tous ses clients par leur(s) nom(s); **in ~ only** de nom seulement; **to exist in ~ only** *or* **in ~ alone** n'exister que de nom; *[power, rights]* être nominal; **a marriage in ~ only** *or* **in ~ alone** un mariage (tout) nominal; **he is king in ~ only** il n'est roi que de nom, il n'a de roi que le nom; **she's the boss in all but ~** elle est le patron sans en avoir le titre; **to refer to sb by ~** désigner qn par son nom; **to name** *or* **mention no ~s, naming** *or* **mentioning no ~s** pour ne nommer personne; **to put one's ~ down for a job** poser sa candidature à un poste; **to put one's ~ down for a competition/for a class** s'inscrire à une compétition/à un cours; **I'll put my ~ down for a company car** je vais faire une demande pour avoir une voiture de fonction; (*fig*) **that's the ~ of the game** (*that's what matters*) c'est ce qui compte; (*that's how it is*) c'est toujours comme ça; **to call sb ~s** injurier qn, traiter qn de tous les noms; **~s cannot hurt me** les injures ne me touchent pas; **she was surprised to hear the**

child use those ~s elle a été surprise d'entendre l'enfant employer de si vilains mots; (*lit, fig*) **in the ~ of ...** au nom de ...; **in God's ~** pour l'amour du ciel *or* de Dieu; **in the king's ~** de par le roi; **what in the ~ of goodness*** *or* **in Heaven's*** *or* **God's‡ ~ are you doing?** pour l'amour de Dieu, qu'est-ce que vous faites?, que diable faites-vous?; **all the great** *or* **big ~s were there** tout ce qui a un nom (connu) était là; **he's one of the big ~s in show business** il est un des grands noms du monde du spectacle; *see* **first, maiden, pet¹** *etc.*

b (*reputation*) réputation *f*, renom *m*. **he has a ~ for honesty** il est réputé honnête, il a la réputation d'être honnête; **he has a ~ for carelessness** il a la réputation d'être négligent; **to protect one's (good) ~** protéger sa réputation; **this firm has a good ~** cette maison a (une) bonne réputation; **to get a bad ~** se faire une mauvaise réputation *or* un mauvais renom; **this book made his ~** ce livre l'a rendu célèbre; **to make one's ~** se faire un nom; **he made his ~ as a singer** il s'est fait un nom en tant que chanteur; **to make a ~ for o.s. (as)** se faire une réputation *or* un nom (comme *or* en tant que); **my ~ is mud* in this place** je ne suis pas en odeur de sainteté ici, je suis très mal vu ici; **if I do that my ~ will be mud* in the office** si je fais ça, c'en est fini de ma réputation *or* je peux dire adieu à ma réputation dans le bureau; *see* **dog, vain.**

2 vt a (*call by a ~, give a ~ to*) nommer, appeler, donner un nom à; *ship* baptiser; *comet, star, mountain* donner un nom à. **a person ~d Smith** un(e) nommé(e) Smith; **the child was ~d Peter** on a appelé l'enfant Pierre; **to ~ a child after** *or* **for sb** donner à un enfant le nom de qn; **the child was ~d after his father** l'enfant a reçu le nom de son père; **they ~d him Winston after Churchill** ils l'ont appelé Winston en souvenir de Churchill; **tell me how plants are ~d** expliquez-moi l'appellation des plantes.

b (*give ~ of; list*) nommer, citer (le nom de); (*designate*) nommer, désigner (par son nom *or* nominalement); (*reveal identity of*) nommer, révéler le nom de; (*fix*) *date, price* fixer. **he was ~d as chairman** il a été nommé président; **he was ~d for the chairmanship** son nom a été présenté pour la présidence; **he ~d his son (as) his heir** il a désigné son fils comme héritier; **he has been ~d as the leader of the expedition** on l'a désigné pour diriger l'expédition; **he was ~d as the thief** on l'a désigné comme étant le voleur; **he refused to ~ his accomplices** il a refusé de nommer ses complices *or* de révéler les noms de ses complices; **naming no names** pour ne nommer personne; **they have been ~d as witnesses** ils ont été cités comme témoins; **my collaborators are ~d in the preface** mes collaborateurs sont mentionnés dans l'avant-propos; **~ the presidents** donnez *or* citez le(s) nom(s) des présidents, nommez les présidents; **~ the chief works of Shakespeare** citez les principaux ouvrages de Shakespeare; **~ your price** fixez votre prix; (*wedding*) **to ~ the day** fixer la date du mariage; **you ~ it, they have it!*** tout ce que vous pouvez imaginer, ils l'ont!

3 comp ▸name-calling injures *fpl* **▸name day** fête *f* (*d'une personne*) **▸name-drop** émailler sa conversation de noms de gens en vue **▸name-dropper*: he's a dreadful name-dropper** il émaille toujours sa conversation de noms de gens en vue (*qu'il connaît*), à l'entendre il connaît la terre entière **▸name-dropping*: there was so much name-dropping in his speech** son discours était truffé de noms de gens en vue (*qu'il connaît*) **▸name part** (*Theat*) rôle *m* titulaire **▸nameplate** (*on door etc*) plaque *f*, écusson *m*; (*on manufactured goods*) plaque du fabricant *or* du constructeur **▸namesake** homonyme *m* (*personne*) **▸name tape** (ruban *m* de) noms *mpl* tissés.

-named [neɪmd] **adj ending in comps: the first-named** le premier, la première; **the last-named** ce dernier, cette dernière.

nameless [ˈneɪmlɪs] **adj a** (*unknown*) *person* sans nom, inconnu; (*anonymous*) anonyme. **a certain person who shall be** *or* **remain ~** une (certaine) personne que je ne nommerai pas; **a ~ grave** une tombe sans inscription *or* anonyme. **b** (*undefined*) *sensation, emotion, fear* indéfinissable, inexprimable; (*too hideous to name*) *vice, crime* innommable.

namely [ˈneɪmlɪ] **adv** à savoir, c'est-à-dire.

Namibia [nɑːˈmɪbɪə] **n** Namibie *f*.

Namibian [nɑːˈmɪbɪən] **1 adj** namibien. **2 n** Namibien(ne) *m(f)*.

nan¹ [nɑːn] nan *m* (*pain indien*). **~ bread** (*NonC*) nan *m*.

nan²* [næn], **nana*** [ˈnænə] **n** (*grandmother*) mamie *f*, mémé *f*.

nance‡ [næns] **n, nancy‡** [ˈnænsɪ] **n, nancy-boy‡** [ˈnænsɪbɔɪ] **n** (*Brit pej*) tante‡ *f*, tapette‡ *f*.

nankeen [nænˈkiːn] **n** (*Tex*) nankin *m*.

nanny [ˈnænɪ] **n a** (*Brit: nurse etc*) bonne *f* d'enfants, nounou* *f*, nurse *f*. **yes ~** oui nounou. **b** (**: grandmother*) mamie *f*, mémé *f*.

nanny-goat [ˈnænɪgəʊt] **n** chèvre *f*, bique* *f*, biquette* *f*.

nano... [ˈnænəʊ] **pref** nano... .

Naomi [ˈneɪəmɪ] **n** Noémi *f*.

nap¹ [næp] **1 n** (*sleep*) petit somme. **afternoon ~** sieste *f*; **to have** *or* **take a ~** faire un petit somme; (*after lunch*) faire la sieste. **2 vi** faire un (petit) somme, sommeiller. (*fig*) **to catch sb ~ping** (*unawares*) prendre qn à l'improviste *or* au dépourvu; (*in error etc*) surprendre qn en défaut.

nap² [næp] **n** (*Tex*) poil *m*. **cloth that has lost its ~** tissu râpé *or* élimé; (*on paper patterns*) **with/without ~** avec/sans sens.

nap³ [næp] **n** (*Cards*) ≃ manille *f* aux enchères.

nap⁴ [næp] **vt** (*Brit Racing*) **to ~ the winner** donner le cheval gagnant.

napalm [ˈneɪpɑːm] **1 n** napalm *m*. **2 comp ▸napalm bomb/bombing** bombe *f*/bombardement *m* au napalm. **3 vt** attaquer au napalm.

nape [neɪp] **n** nuque *f*.

naphtha [ˈnæfθə] **n** (*gen*) naphte *m*. **petroleum ~** naphta *m*.

naphthalene [ˈnæfθəliːn] **n** naphtaline *f*.

napkin [ˈnæpkɪn] **n a** serviette *f* (de table). **~ ring** rond *m* de serviette. **b** (*Brit: for babies*) couche *f*.

Naples [ˈneɪplz] **n** Naples.

Napoleon [nəˈpəʊlɪən] **n a** Napoléon *m*. **b** (*coin*) **n~** napoléon *m*. **c** (*US: pastry*) **n~** millefeuille *m*.

Napoleonic [nəˌpəʊlɪˈɒnɪk] **adj** napoléonien.

napper‡† [ˈnæpəʳ] **n** (*head*) caboche‡ *f*.

nappy [ˈnæpɪ] (*Brit*) (**abbr of napkin**) **1 n** couche *f*. **2 comp ▸nappy liner** couche *f* **▸nappy rash** érythème *m* (fessier) (*Med, frm*); (*gen*) **to have nappy rash** avoir les fesses rouges.

narc‡ [nɑːk] **n** (*US*) (**abbr of narcotics agent**) agent *m* de la brigade des stupéfiants, stupe‡ *m*.

narcissi [nɑːˈsɪsaɪ] **npl of narcissus.**

narcissism [nɑːˈsɪsɪzəm] **n** narcissisme *m*.

narcissist [ˈnɑːsɪˌsɪst] **n** narcissique *mf*.

narcissistic [ˌnɑːsɪˈsɪstɪk] **adj** narcissique.

narcissus [nɑːˈsɪsəs] **n, pl narcissi** *or* **~es a** (*flower*) narcisse *m*. **b N~** Narcisse *m*.

narcosis [nɑːˈkəʊsɪs] **n** narcose *f*.

narcotic [nɑːˈkɒtɪk] **1 adj, n** (*lit, fig*) narcotique (*m*). **2 comp ▸narcotics agent** agent *m* de la brigade des stupéfiants **▸narcotics charge: to be on a narcotics charge** être inculpé pour affaire de stupéfiants **▸Narcotics Squad** brigade *f* des stupéfiants.

narcotism [ˈnɑːkəˌtɪzəm] **n** narcotisme *m*.

narcotize [ˈnɑːkətaɪz] **vt** donner *or* administrer un narcotique à, narcotiser.

nark‡ [nɑːk] **1 vt a** (*Brit*) (*infuriate*) ficher en boule*, foutre en rogne‡; *see also* **narked. b to ~ it** arrêter (de faire qch); **~ it!** suffit!*, écrase!‡. **2 vi** (*Brit: inform police*) moucharder*. **3 n a** (*Brit: also* **copper's ~**) indic‡ *m*, mouchard* *m*. **b** (*US*) = **narc‡.**

narked‡ [nɑːkt] **adj** en boule*, en rogne*. **to get ~** se ficher en boule*, se foutre en rogne‡.

narky‡ [ˈnɑːkɪ] **adj** (*Brit*) de mauvais poil*, en boule*, en rogne*.

narrate [nəˈreɪt] **vt** raconter, narrer (*liter*).

narration [nəˈreɪʃən] **n** narration *f*.

narrative [ˈnærətɪv] **1 n a** (*story, account*) récit *m*, narration *f*, histoire *f*. **b** (*NonC*) narration *f*. **he has a gift for ~** il est doué pour la narration. **2 adj** *poem, painting* narratif; *skill* de conteur. **~ writer** narrateur *m*, -trice *f*.

narrator [nəˈreɪtəʳ] **n** narrateur *m*, -trice *f*; (*Mus*) récitant(e) *m(f)*.

narrow [ˈnærəʊ] **1 adj a** *road, path* étroit; *valley* étroit, encaissé; *passage* étranglé; *garment* étroit, étriqué; *boundary, limits* restreint, étroit. **within a ~ compass** dans d'étroites limites, dans un champ restreint; **to grow** *or* **become ~(er)** se rétrécir, se resserrer.

b (*fig*) *outlook, mind* étroit, restreint, borné; *person* aux vues étroites, à l'esprit étroit, borné; *existence* limité, circonscrit; *scrutiny* serré, poussé; *means, resources, income* limité, juste (*fig*); *majority* faible, petit; *advantage* petit. **in the ~est sense (of the word)** au sens le plus restreint (du terme); **a ~ victory** une victoire remportée de justesse; **to have a ~ escape** s'en tirer de justesse, l'échapper belle; **that was a ~ shave!*** *or* **squeak!*** on l'a échappé belle!, il était moins une!‡; (*Ling*) **~ vowel** voyelle tendue.

2 npl: ~s passage étroit; *[harbour]* passe *f*, goulet *m*; *[river]* pertuis *m*, étranglement *m*.

3 comp ▸narrow boat péniche *f* **▸narrow-gauge line, narrow-gauge track** (*Rail*) voie étroite **▸narrow-minded** *person* aux vues étroites, à l'esprit étroit, borné; *ideas, outlook* étroit, restreint, borné **▸narrow-mindedness** étroitesse *f* *or* petitesse *f* d'esprit **▸narrow-shouldered** étroit de carrure.

4 vi a *[road, path, valley]* se rétrécir. **his eyes ~ed** il plissa les yeux.

b (*fig: also* **~ down**) *[majority]* s'amenuiser, se rétrécir; *[opinions, outlook]* se restreindre. **the search has now ~ed (down) to Soho** les recherches se limitent maintenant à Soho; **the field of inquiry/the choice has ~ed (down) to 5 people** le champ d'investigation/le choix se ramène *or* se limite *or* se réduit maintenant à 5 personnes; **the question ~s (down) to this** la question se ramène *or* se réduit à ceci; **his outlook has ~ed (down) considerably since then** son horizon s'est beaucoup restreint *or* rétréci depuis lors.

5 vt (*make narrower*) *road, piece of land* rétrécir, réduire la largeur de; *skirt* rétrécir, resserrer; (*fig*) *choice* réduire, restreindre; *mind, ideas* rétrécir; *meaning, interpretation* restreindre, limiter. (*fig*) **to ~ the field (down)** restreindre le champ; **with ~ed eyes** en plissant les yeux (*de méfiance etc*).

▸narrow down 1 vi a *[road, path, valley]* se rétrécir. **b** (*fig*) = **narrow 4b. 2 vt sep** *choice* réduire, restreindre; *meaning, interpretation* restreindre, limiter; *see also* **narrow 5.**

narrowing ['nærəʊɪŋ] n (*NonC*) (*lit*) rétrécissement *m*; (*fig: reduction*) diminution *f*.

narrowly ['nærəʊlɪ] adv a (*by a small margin*) de justesse. **he ~ escaped being killed** il a bien failli être tué, il était à deux doigts d'être tué; **the bullet ~ missed him** la balle l'a raté de justesse *or* de peu. b (*strictly*) *interpret rules etc* strictement, rigoureusement, étroitement. c (*closely*) *examine* de près, minutieusement, méticuleusement.

narrowness ['nærəʊnɪs] n étroitesse *f*.

narwhal ['nɑːwəl] n narval *m*.

NAS [eneɪ'es] n (*US*) (abbr of **National Academy of Sciences**) *académie des sciences*.

NASA ['næsə] n (*US*) (abbr of **National Aeronautics and Space Administration**) N.A.S.A. *f*.

nasal ['neɪzəl] 1 adj (*Anat*) nasal; (*Ling*) *sound, vowel, pronunciation* nasal; *accent* nasillard. **to speak in a ~ voice** parler du nez, nasiller. 2 n (*Ling*) nasale *f*.

nasality [neɪ'zælɪtɪ] n nasalité *f*.

nasalization [,neɪzəlaɪ'zeɪʃən] n nasalisation *f*.

nasalize ['neɪzəlaɪz] vt nasaliser.

nasally ['neɪzəlɪ] adv *whine, complain* sur un ton nasillard. **to speak ~** parler du nez, nasiller.

nascent ['næsnt] adj naissant; (*Chem etc*) à l'état naissant.

Nassau ['næsɔː] n (*Bahamas*) Nassau.

nastily ['nɑːstɪlɪ] adv (*unpleasantly*) désagréablement; (*spitefully*) méchamment; (*obscenely*) indécemment, d'une manière obscène. **it rained quite ~** il est tombé une sale pluie.

nastiness ['nɑːstɪnɪs] n (*see* **nasty**) (*unpleasantness*) caractère *m* désagréable; (*spitefulness*) méchanceté *f*; (*indecency*) indécence *f*, obscénité *f*; (*in taste*) mauvais goût; (*in odour*) mauvaise odeur; (*dirtiness*) saleté *f*.

nasturtium [nəs'tɜːʃəm] n (*Bot*) capucine *f*. **climbing/dwarf ~** capucine grimpante/naine.

nasty ['nɑːstɪ] adj a (*unpleasant*) *person* désagréable, déplaisant (*to* envers); (*stronger*) méchant, mauvais; *remark* méchant; *moment, experience* désagréable; (*stronger*) pénible; *taste, smell* mauvais; *weather, cold, accident, wound* vilain, mauvais, sale* (*before noun*); *bend* dangereux, mauvais, sale*. **the weather turned ~** le temps s'est gâté; **to taste ~** avoir un mauvais goût; **to smell ~** sentir mauvais, avoir une mauvaise odeur; **he's a ~ piece of work*** c'est un vilain bonhomme* *or* un sale type*; **to have a ~ temper** avoir très mauvais caractère, avoir un caractère de cochon*; **a ~ job** un sale travail, un sale *or* fichu boulot*; **what a ~ man!** quel horrible bonhomme!*; **a ~ rumour** une rumeur dictée par la méchanceté; **he turned ~ when I told him that ...** il est devenu mauvais *or* méchant quand je lui ai dit que ...; **that was a ~ trick** c'était un sale tour; **to have a ~ look in one's eye** avoir l'œil mauvais *or* menaçant; **it was a ~ few moments** ce furent quelques moments très pénibles; **events took a ~ turn, the situation turned ~** la situation tourna très mal; **he had a ~ time of it!** (*short spell*) il a passé un mauvais quart d'heure!; (*longer period*) il a passé de mauvais moments; (*fig*) **what a ~ mess!** quel gâchis épouvantable! b (*indecent*) *book, story* indécent, obscène. **to have a ~ mind** avoir l'esprit mal tourné *or* malsain.

NAS/UWT [eneɪ'es,juːdʌbljʊ'tiː] (*Brit*) (abbr of **National Association of Schoolmasters/Union of Women Teachers**) *union de deux syndicats d'enseignement*.

Natal [nə'tæl] n Natal *m*.

natal ['neɪtl] adj natal. (*liter*) **~ day** jour *m* de (la) naissance; *see* **antenatal, postnatal.**

natality [nə'tælɪtɪ] n natalité *f*.

natch‡ [nætʃ] excl (abbr of **naturally**) nature‡, naturellement.

NATFHE [,eneɪ'tiː,efeɪtʃ'iː] n (*Brit*) (abbr of **National Association of Teachers in Further and Higher Education**) *syndicat enseignant*.

nation ['neɪʃən] 1 n nation *f*, peuple *m*. **the French ~** la nation française; **people of all ~s** des gens de toutes les nationalités; **the voice of the ~** la voix de la nation *or* du peuple; **in the service of the ~** au service de la nation; **the whole ~ watched while he did it** il l'a fait sous les yeux de la nation tout entière; *see* **league[1], united.** 2 comp ► **nation-state** nation *f* en tant qu'État ► **nationwide** adj *strike, protest* touchant l'ensemble du pays ◊ adv à travers tout le pays, dans l'ensemble du territoire; **there was a nationwide search for the killers** on recherchait les assassins à travers tout le pays.

national ['næʃənl] 1 adj a (*of one nation*) national. (*US Admin*) **N~ Aeronautics and Space Administration** Agence *f* nationale de l'aéronautique et de l'espace; **~ anthem** hymne national; **N~ Assembly** Assemblée *f* nationale; (*Brit Admin*) **N~ Assistance**† Sécurité sociale; (*US*) **~ bank** banque *f* fédérale; **~ costume = ~ dress;** (*Brit*) **the National Curriculum** *programme d'enseignement obligatoire dans 10 disciplines (dans les établissements secondaires d'Angleterre et du Pays de Galles)*; **~ debt** dette publique *or* nationale; **~ dress** costume national *or* du pays; (*Brit*) **N~ Economic Development Council** ≃ Agence nationale d'information économique; (*Brit*) **N~ Enterprise Board** ≃ Institut *m* de développement industriel; **N~ Executive Committee** bureau *m* exécutif *or* national; (*Brit Scol*) **N~ Extension College** ≃ Centre *m* national d'enseignement par correspondance; **~ flag** drapeau national; (*Naut*) pavillon national; (*US*) **N~ Foundation of the Arts and the Humanities** ≃ ministère *m* de la Culture; (*Brit Pol*) **N~ Front** Front *m* national; (*Brit Elec*) **~ grid** réseau *m* national; (*US*) **N~ Guard** garde nationale, (*milice fédérale formée de volontaires*); (*Brit*) **N~ Health Service** ≃ Sécurité sociale; (*Brit*) **I got it on the N~ Health*** je l'ai eu par la Sécurité sociale, ≃ ça m'a été remboursé par la Sécurité sociale; **~ holiday** fête nationale; **~ income** revenu national; (*Brit*) **N~ Insurance** ≃ Sécurité sociale; (*Brit*) **N~ Insurance benefits** prestations *fpl* de la Sécurité sociale; (*US Admin*) **N~ Labor Relations Board** *commission d'arbitrage du ministère du travail;* **N~ Liberation Front** Front *m* de Libération nationale; **~ monument** monument national; **~ park** parc national; (*Brit*) **the N~ Safety Council** la Protection civile; (*Brit*) **N~ Savings** épargne nationale; (*Brit*) **N~ Savings Bank** ≃ Caisse *f* nationale d'Épargne; (*Brit*) **N~ Savings Certificate** bon *m* d'épargne; (*US Pol*) **N~ Security Council** Conseil *m* national de sécurité; (*Brit Mil*) **(to do one's) ~ service** (faire son) service national *or* militaire; (*Brit Mil*) **~ serviceman** appelé *m*, conscrit *m*; **N~ Socialism** national-socialisme *m*; **~ status** nationalité *f*; (*Brit*) **N~ Trust** ≃ Caisse Nationale des Monuments Historiques et des Sites. b (*nationwide*) national, à l'échelon national, dans l'ensemble du pays. **on a ~ scale** à l'échelon national; **there was ~ opposition to ...** la nation (entière) s'est opposée à ...; **~ strike of miners** grève *f* des mineurs touchant l'ensemble du pays; (*Press*) **the ~ and local papers** la grande presse et la presse locale.

2 n a (*person*) ressortissant(e) *m(f)*, national(e) *m(f)*. **he's a French ~** (*in France*) il est de nationalité française; (*elsewhere*) c'est un ressortissant *or* un national français; **foreign ~s** ressortissants étrangers.

b (*Brit Racing*) **the Grand N~** le Grand National (*grande course de haies réputée pour sa difficulté*).

c (*~ newspaper*) grand journal *m*.

nationalism ['næʃnəlɪzəm] n nationalisme *m*; *see* **Scottish** *etc.*

nationalist ['næʃnəlɪst] adj, n nationaliste (*mf*). **N~ China** Chine *f* nationaliste; *see* **Scottish** *etc.*

nationalistic [,næʃnə'lɪstɪk] adj nationaliste.

nationality [,næʃə'nælɪtɪ] n nationalité *f*; *see* **dual.**

nationalization [,næʃnəlaɪ'zeɪʃən] n a (*Ind, Pol*) nationalisation *f*. b [*person*] = **naturalization a.**

nationalize ['næʃnəlaɪz] vt a (*Ind, Pol*) nationaliser. b *person* = **naturalize 1a.**

nationally ['næʃnəlɪ] adv nationalement, du point de vue national, sous l'angle national; (*Rad*) *broadcast* dans le pays tout entier. **it is ~ known/felt that ...** on sait/sent dans tout le pays que ... .

nationhood ['neɪʃənhʊd] n nationalité *f* (*existence en tant que nation*).

native ['neɪtɪv] 1 adj a *country, town* natal; *language* maternel. **~ land** pays natal, patrie *f*; (*US fig*) **~ son** enfant *m* du pays.

b (*innate*) *charm, talent, ability* inné, naturel. **~ wit** bon sens inné.

c (*indigenous*) *plant, animal* indigène; *product, resources* naturel, du pays, de la région. **plant/animal ~ to** plante *f*/animal *m* originaire de; **French ~ speaker** personne *f* dont la langue maternelle est le français *or* de langue maternelle française; (*Ling*) **you should ask a ~ speaker** il faudrait (le) demander à un locuteur natif; *see* **informant.**

d (*of the natives*) *customs, costume* du pays; *matters, rights, knowledge* du pays, des autochtones. (*US*) **N~ American (n)** Indien(ne) *m(f)* d'Amérique; (**adj**) amérindien; **Minister of N~ Affairs** ministre chargé des Affaires indigènes; **Ministry of N~ Affairs** ministère *m* des Affaires indigènes; **~ labour** main-d'œuvre *f* indigène; **~ quarter** quartier *m* indigène; **to go ~*** adopter le mode de vie indigène.

2 n a (*person*) autochtone *mf*; (*esp of colony*) indigène *mf*. **a ~ of France** un(e) Français(e) de naissance; **he is a ~ of Bourges** il est originaire de *or* natif de Bourges; **she speaks French like a ~** elle parle français comme si c'était sa langue maternelle; **the ~s** les habitants *mpl or* gens *mpl* du pays, les autochtones *mpl* (*also hum*).

b (*Bot, Zool*) indigène *mf*. **this plant/animal is a ~ of Australia** cette plante/cet animal est originaire d'Australie.

nativism ['neɪtɪ,vɪzəm] n (*US*) hostilité *f* aux immigrants.

nativity [nə'tɪvɪtɪ] 1 n a (*Rel*) **N~** Nativité *f*. b (*Astrol*) horoscope *m*. 2 comp ► **nativity play** miracle *m or* mystère *m* de la Nativité.

NATO ['neɪtəʊ] n (abbr of **North Atlantic Treaty Organization**) O.T.A.N. *f*.

NATSOPA [,næt'səʊpə] n (*Brit*) (abbr of **National Society of Operative Printers, Graphical and Media Personnel**) *syndicat*.

natter* ['nætə[r]] (*Brit*) 1 vi (*chat*) causer, bavarder; (*chatter*) bavarder, jacasser; (*continuously*) bavarder *or* jacasser sans arrêt; (*grumble*) grommeler, bougonner*. **we ~ed (away) for hours** nous avons bavardé pendant des heures; **she does ~!** elle n'arrête pas de jacasser! 2 n a (*chat*) causerie *f*, causette* *f*. **we had a good ~** nous avons bien bavardé, nous avons taillé une bonne bavette*. b (*chatterbox*) moulin *m* à paroles*.

natterer* ['nætərə[r]] n = **natter 2b.**

natty* ['nætɪ] adj a (*neat*) *dress* pimpant, coquet, chic *inv*; *person* chic *inv*, tiré à quatre épingles. b (*handy*) *tool, gadget* astucieux, bien trouvé.

natural [ˈnætʃrəl] 1 adj a (*normal*) naturel, normal. **it's only ~** c'est bien normal, c'est tout naturel; **it seems quite ~ to me** ça me semble tout à fait normal *or* naturel; **there's a perfectly ~ explanation for the sound** le bruit s'explique tout à fait naturellement; **it is ~ for this animal to hibernate** il est dans la nature de cet animal d'hiberner, il est naturel *or* normal que cet animal hiberne (*subj*); **it is ~ for you to think ..., it is ~ that you should think ...** il est naturel *or* normal *or* logique que vous pensiez (*subj*) ...; **~ break** (*in television programme*) interruption *f* normale; (*Jur*) **death from ~ causes** mort naturelle; (*Jur*) **to die of** *or* **from ~ causes** mourir de mort naturelle; **to die a ~ death** mourir de sa belle mort; (*Jur*) **for (the rest of) his ~ life** à vie; **~ size** grandeur *f* nature; (*Ind*) **to reduce the staff by ~ wastage** réduire le personnel par départs naturels.

b (*of or from nature*) naturel. **~ resources** ressources *fpl* naturelles; **her hair is a ~ blonde** ses cheveux sont naturellement blonds; **~ (child)birth** accouchement *m* sans douleur; **~ gas** gaz naturel; **~ history** histoire *f* naturelle; **~ language** langage *m* naturel; **~ law** loi *f* naturelle *or* de la nature; **~ logarithm** logarithme *m* népérien; (*Math*) **~ number** nombre naturel; **~ philosophy** physique *f*; **~ philosopher** physicien(ne) *m(f)*; **~ science** sciences naturelles; **~ selection** sélection naturelle; **~ theology** théologie *f* naturelle, théodicée *f*.

c (*inborn*) inné, naturel. **to have a ~ talent for** avoir une facilité innée pour; **he's a ~ painter** il est né peintre, c'est un peintre né; **playing the piano comes ~* to her** elle est naturellement douée pour le piano.

d (*unaffected*) *manner* simple, naturel, sans affectation.

e (*Mus*) naturel. **B ~** si naturel; **~ horn** cor *m* d'harmonie; **~ key** ton naturel; **~ trumpet** trompette *f* naturelle.

f (††) *child* naturel.

2 n a (*Mus*) (*sign*) bécarre *m*; (*note*) note *f* naturelle.

b (**: ideal*) **he's a ~ for this part** il est fait pour ce rôle, il joue ce rôle au naturel; **did you hear her play? she's a ~!** est-ce que vous l'avez entendue jouer? C'est une pianiste (*etc*) née; (*US*) **it's a ~*** ça coule de source.

c (††*: simpleton*) idiot(e) *m(f)* (de naissance), demeuré(e) *m(f)*.

naturalism [ˈnætʃrəlɪzəm] n naturalisme *m*.

naturalist [ˈnætʃrəlɪst] adj, n naturaliste *(mf)*.

naturalistic [ˌnætʃrəˈlɪstɪk] adj naturaliste.

naturalization [ˌnætʃrəlaɪˈzeɪʃən] n a *[person]* naturalisation *f*. (*Brit*) **letters of ~, ~ papers** déclaration *f* de naturalisation. b *[plant, animal]* acclimatation *f*.

naturalize [ˈnætʃrəlaɪz] 1 vt a *person* naturaliser. **to be ~d** se faire naturaliser. b *animal, plant* acclimater; *word, sport* naturaliser. 2 vi *[plant, animal]* s'acclimater.

naturally [ˈnætʃrəlɪ] adv a (*as is normal*) naturellement; (*of course*) naturellement, bien sûr, bien entendu, comme de juste. **will you do it? — ~ not!** tu le feras? — sûrement pas! *or* bien sûr que non!

b (*by nature*) de nature, par tempérament. **he is ~ lazy** il est paresseux de nature *or* par tempérament; **a ~ optimistic person** un(e) optimiste né(e); **her hair is ~ curly** elle frise naturellement; **it comes ~ to him to do this** il fait cela tout naturellement; **playing the piano comes ~ to her** elle a un don (naturel) pour le piano; **this chemical reaction occurs ~ in volcanoes** cette réaction chimique se produit spontanément dans les volcans.

c (*unaffectedly*) *accept, behave, laugh* simplement, sans affectation, avec naturel. **she said it quite ~** elle l'a dit avec un grand naturel.

naturalness [ˈnætʃrəlnɪs] n (*natural appearance, behaviour etc*) naturel *m*; (*simplicity*) simplicité *f*.

nature [ˈneɪtʃəʳ] 1 n a (*NonC: often* **N~**) nature *f*. **he loves ~** il aime la nature; **the laws of ~** les lois *fpl* de la nature; **~ versus nurture** l'inné et l'acquis; **let ~ take its course** laissez faire la nature; **a freak of ~** un caprice de la nature; **to paint from ~** peindre d'après nature; **against ~** contre nature; **~ abhors a vacuum** la nature a horreur du vide; (*hum*) **in a state of ~** à l'état naturel, dans le costume d'Adam*; **to go back** *or* **return to ~** *[person]* retourner à la nature; *[land]* retourner à l'état de nature; **return to ~** *[garden, land]* retour *m* à l'état de nature; *[person]* retour *m* à la nature; *see* **mother**.

b (*character etc*) *[person, animal]* nature *f*, naturel *m*, tempérament *m*, caractère *m*. **by ~** de nature, par tempérament (*see also* **c**); **he has a nice ~** il a un naturel *or* un tempérament *or* un caractère facile, il est d'un naturel facile, c'est une bonne nature; **she hid a loving ~ under ...** elle cachait une nature aimante *or* un caractère aimant sous ...; **the ~ of birds is to fly, it is in the ~ of birds to fly** il est de *or* dans la nature des oiseaux de voler; **it is not in his ~ to lie** il n'est pas de *or* dans sa nature de mentir; **that's very much in his ~** c'est tout à fait dans sa nature; *see* **good, better 1, human, second¹** *etc*.

c (*essential quality*) nature *f*, essence *f*. **the ~ of the soil** la nature du sol; **it is in the ~ of things** il est dans l'ordre des choses, il est de *or* dans la nature des choses; **the true ~ of things** l'essence des choses; **in the ~ of this case it is clear that ...** vu la nature de ce cas il est clair que ...; **cash is, by its (very) ~, easy to steal** l'argent est, par nature *or* de par sa nature, facile à voler.

d (*type, sort*) espèce *f*, genre *m*, sorte *f*, nature *f*. **things of this ~** les choses de cette nature *or* de ce genre; **his comment was in the ~ of a compliment** sa remarque était en quelque sorte un compliment; **invitation in the ~ of a threat** invitation qui tient de la menace; **something in the ~ of an apology** une sorte d'excuse, une vague excuse; **ceremonies of a religious/solemn** *etc* **~** cérémonies *fpl* religieuses/solennelles *etc*.

2 comp ▸**nature conservancy** protection *f* de la nature ▸**Nature Conservancy Board** (*Brit*) ≃ Direction Générale de la Protection de la Nature et de l'Environnement ▸**nature cure** (*Med*) naturisme *m* ▸**nature lover** amoureux *m*, -euse *f* de la nature ▸**nature reserve** réserve naturelle ▸**nature study** histoire naturelle; (*Scol*) sciences naturelles ▸**nature trail** itinéraire *m* aménagé pour amateurs de la nature ▸**nature worship** adoration *f* de la nature.

-natured [ˈneɪtʃəd] adj ending in comps de nature. **jealous-natured** jaloux de nature, d'un naturel jaloux; *see* **good, ill**.

naturism [ˈneɪtʃərɪzəm] n naturisme *m*.

naturist [ˈneɪtʃərɪst] n naturiste *mf*.

naught [nɔːt] n a (*Math*) zéro *m*. (*Brit*) **~s and crosses** ≃ morpion *m* (*jeu*). b († *or liter: nothing*) rien *m*. **to bring to ~** faire échouer, faire avorter; **to come to ~** échouer, n'aboutir à rien; **to care ~ for, to set at ~** ne faire aucun cas de, ne tenir aucun compte de.

naughtily [ˈnɔːtɪlɪ] adv *say, remark* avec malice. **to behave ~** se conduire mal; *[child]* être vilain.

naughtiness [ˈnɔːtɪnɪs] n a *[child etc]* désobéissance *f*, mauvaise conduite. **a piece of ~** une désobéissance. b *[story, joke, play]* grivoiserie *f*.

naughty [ˈnɔːtɪ] adj a méchant, vilain, pas sage. **a ~ child** un vilain *or* méchant (enfant), un enfant pas sage; **that was a ~ thing to do!** ce n'est pas beau ce que tu as fait! b *joke, story* grivois, risqué, leste. **the N~ Nineties** ≃ la Belle Époque; **~ word** vilain mot.

nausea [ˈnɔːsɪə] n (*Med*) nausée *f*; (*fig*) dégoût *m*, écœurement *m*. (*Med*) **a feeling of ~** un haut-le-cœur, un mal au cœur, une envie de vomir.

nauseate [ˈnɔːsɪeɪt] vt (*Med, fig*) écœurer.

nauseating [ˈnɔːsɪeɪtɪŋ] adj (*Med*) écœurant, qui soulève le cœur; (*fig*) écœurant, dégoûtant.

nauseatingly [ˈnɔːsɪeɪtɪŋlɪ] adv (*Med, fig*) d'une façon dégoûtante *or* écœurante.

nauseous [ˈnɔːsɪəs] adj (*Med*) écœurant, qui soulève le cœur; (*fig*) dégoûtant, écœurant. (*Med*) **to feel ~** avoir mal au cœur, avoir envie de vomir.

nautical [ˈnɔːtɪkəl] adj nautique, naval. **~ almanac** almanach *m* nautique; **~ matters** questions navales; **~ mile** mille marin *or* nautique; **~ term** terme *m* nautique *or* de marine *or* de navigation; **the music has a slight ~ flavour** la musique évoque un peu la mer.

nautilus [ˈnɔːtɪləs] n, pl **~es** *or* **nautili** [ˈnɔːtɪˌlaɪ] (*Zool*) nautile *m*.

Navaho [ˈnævəhəʊ] n (*also* **~ Indian**) Navaho *mf or* Navajo *mf*.

naval [ˈneɪvəl] adj *battle, strength* naval; *affairs, matters* de la marine. (*Mil*) **~ air station** station *f* aéronavale; **~ architect** ingénieur *m* du génie maritime *or* des constructions navales; **~ architecture** construction navale; **~ aviation** aéronavale *f*; **~ barracks** caserne *f* maritime; **~ base** base navale, port *m* de guerre; **~ college** école navale; **~ dockyard** arsenal *m* (maritime); **~ forces** marine *f* de guerre, marine militaire; **~ hospital** hôpital *m* maritime; **~ officer** officier *m* de marine; **one of the great ~ powers** l'une des grandes puissances maritimes; **~ station = ~ base; ~ stores** entrepôts *mpl* maritimes; **~ warfare** combat naval.

Navarre [nəˈvɑːʳ] n Navarre *f*.

nave¹ [neɪv] n *[church]* nef *f*.

nave² [neɪv] n *[wheel]* moyeu *m*. (*Aut*) **~ plate** enjoliveur *m*.

navel [ˈneɪvəl] 1 n (*Anat*) nombril *m*, ombilic *m*. 2 comp ▸**navel orange** (orange *f*) navel *f*.

navigable [ˈnævɪgəbl] adj a *river, channel* navigable. b *missile, balloon, airship* dirigeable.

navigate [ˈnævɪgeɪt] 1 vi naviguer. (*in car*) **you drive, I'll ~** tu prends le volant, moi je lis la carte (*or* le plan). 2 vt a (*plot course of*) **to ~ a ship** (*or* **a plane** *or* **a car** *etc*) naviguer. b (*steer*) *dinghy* être à la barre de; *steamer etc* gouverner; *aircraft* piloter; *missile* diriger. **he ~d the ship through the dangerous channel** il a dirigé le navire dans le dangereux chenal. c (*sail*) *seas, ocean* naviguer sur. d (*fig*) *stairs etc* franchir avec difficulté. **he ~d his way through to the bar** il s'est frayé un chemin jusqu'au bar; **he ~d the maze of back streets** il a réussi à retrouver son chemin dans le dédale des petites rues.

navigation [ˌnævɪˈgeɪʃən] 1 n navigation *f*; *see* **coastal** *etc*. 2 comp ▸**navigation laws** code *m* maritime ▸**navigation lights** feux *mpl* de bord.

navigator [ˈnævɪgeɪtəʳ] n a (*Aut, Aviat, Naut*) navigateur *m*. b (*sailor-explorer*) navigateur *m*, marin *m*.

navvy [ˈnævɪ] n (*Brit*) terrassier *m*.

navy [ˈneɪvɪ] 1 n marine *f* (militaire *or* de guerre). **he's in the ~** il est dans la marine, il est marin; (*US*) **Department of the N~, N~ Department** ministère *m* de la Marine; **Secretary for the N~** ministre *m* de la Marine; **to serve in the ~** servir dans la marine; *see* **merchant, royal**. 2 comp ▸**navy(-blue)** bleu marine *inv* ▸**Navy Register** (*US*) liste navale ▸**navy yard** (*US*) arsenal *m* (maritime).

nay [neɪ] (†† *or liter*) **1** particle non. **do not say me ~** ne me dites pas non; *see* **yea. 2** adv (et) même, voire. **surprised, ~ astonished** surpris et même abasourdi; **for months, ~ for years ...** pendant des mois, voire des années ... .
Nazareth ['næzərɪθ] n Nazareth.
Nazi ['nɑːtsɪ] **1** n Nazi(e) *m(f)*. **2** adj nazi.
Nazism ['nɑːtsɪzəm] n nazisme *m*.
NB [en'biː] (abbr of **nota bene**) N.B.
NBA [ˌenbiː'eɪ] n **a** (*US*) (abbr of **National Basketball Association**) *association nationale de basket-ball.* **b** (*Brit*) (abbr of **Net Book Agreement**) *see* **net² 1.**
N.B.C. [ˌenbiː'siː] n (*US*) (abbr of **National Broadcasting Company**) NBC *f* (*chaîne de télévision américaine*).
NC a (*Comm etc*) (abbr of **no charge**) gratuit. **b** (*US*) abbr of **North Carolina.**
N.C.B. [ˌensiː'biː] n (*Brit*) (abbr of **National Coal Board**) Charbonnages *mpl* de Grande-Bretagne.
N.C.C.L. [ˌensiːsiː'el] n (*Brit*) (abbr of **National Council for Civil Liberties**) ≃ ligue *f* des droits de l'homme.
N.C.O. [ˌensiː'əʊ] n (*Mil*) (abbr of **non-commissioned officer**) sous-officier *m*.
ND (*US*) abbr of **North Dakota.**
NDP [ˌendiː'piː] n (abbr of **net domestic product**) *see* **net² 1.**
NE (*US*) abbr of **Nebraska.**
Neanderthal [nɪ'ændətɑːl] **1** n (*Geog*) Néandert(h)al *m*. **2** adj néandert(h)alien. **~ man** homme *m* de Néandert(h)al.
neap [niːp] n (*also* **~tide**) marée *f* de morte-eau. **~(tide) season** époque *f* des mortes-eaux.
Neapolitan [nɪə'pɒlɪtən] **1** adj napolitain. **a ~ ice (cream)** une tranche napolitaine. **2** n Napolitain(e) *m(f)*.
near [nɪəʳ] **1** adv **a** (*in space*) près, à proximité; (*in time*) près, proche. **he lives quite ~** il habite tout près *or* tout à côté; **~ at hand** *object* tout près, à proximité, à portée de la main; *event* tout proche; *place* non loin, dans le voisinage; **to draw** *or* **come ~ (to)** s'approcher (de); **to draw** *or* **come ~er (to)** s'approcher davantage (de); **to draw** *or* **bring sth ~er** rapprocher qch; **it was drawing** *or* **getting ~ to Christmas, Christmas was drawing** *or* **getting ~** on était à l'approche *or* aux approches de Noël, Noël approchait; **it was ~ to 6 o'clock** il était près de *or* presque 6 heures; **~ to where I had seen him** près de l'endroit où je l'avais vu; **she was ~ to tears** elle était au bord des larmes.
b (*gen* **~ly**: *in degree*) presque. **this train is nowhere ~ full** ce train est loin d'être plein, il s'en faut de beaucoup que ce train (ne) soit plein.
c (*close*) **as ~ as I can judge** autant que je puisse juger; **the more you look at this portrait, the ~er it resembles him** plus on regarde ce portrait, plus il lui ressemble; **you won't get any ~er than that to what you want** vous ne trouverez pas mieux; **that's ~ enough*** ça pourra aller; **there were 60 people, ~ enough*** il y avait 60 personnes à peu près *or* grosso modo; **as ~ as dammit*** ou presque, ou c'est tout comme*.
d (*Naut*) près du vent, en serrant le vent. **as ~ as she can** au plus près.
2 prep **a** (*in space*) près de, auprès de, dans le voisinage de; (*in time*) près de, vers. **~ here/there** près d'ici/de là; **~ the church** près de l'église, dans le voisinage de l'église; **he was standing ~ the table** il se tenait auprès de *or* près de la table; **regions ~ the Equator** les régions avoisinant l'équateur; **stay ~ me** restez près de moi; **don't come ~ me** ne vous approchez pas de moi; **the sun was ~ setting** le soleil était près de se coucher; (*liter*) **the evening was drawing ~ its close** la soirée tirait à sa fin; **the passage is ~ the end of the book** le passage se trouve vers la fin du livre; **her birthday is ~ mine** son anniversaire est proche du mien; (*fig*) **the steak is so tough the knife won't go ~ it*** le bifteck est si dur que le couteau n'arrive pas à l'entamer*; (*fig*) **he won't go ~ anything illegal** il ne se risquera jamais à faire quoi que ce soit d'illégal.
b (*on the point of*) près de, sur le point de. **~ tears** au bord des larmes; **~ death** près de *or* sur le point de mourir; **he was very ~ refusing** il était sur le point de *or* à deux doigts de refuser.
c (*on the same level, in the same degree*) au niveau de, près de. **to be ~ sth** se rapprocher de qch; (*fig*) ressembler à qch; **French is ~er Latin than English is** le français ressemble plus au latin *or* est plus près du latin que l'anglais; **it's the same thing** *or* **~ it** c'est la même chose ou presque *or* ou à peu près; **it's as ~ snowing as makes no difference** il neige ou peu s'en faut; **nobody comes anywhere ~ him at swimming** il n'y a personne à son niveau pour la natation, personne ne lui arrive à la cheville en natation; **that's ~er it, that's ~er the thing*** voilà qui est mieux; *see* **nowhere.**
3 adj **a** (*close in space*) *building, town, tree* proche, voisin; *neighbour* proche. **to get a ~ view of sth** examiner qch de près; **these glasses make things look ~er** ces lunettes rapprochent les objets; (*Math*) **to the ~est decimal place** à la plus proche décimale près; **to the ~est pound** à une livre près; **the ~est way** la route la plus courte *or* la plus directe; **this is very ~ work** ce travail est très minutieux *or* délicat; *see also* **5.**
b (*close in time*) proche, prochain, rapproché. **the hour is ~ (when)** l'heure est proche (où); **in the ~ future** dans un proche avenir, dans un avenir prochain; **these events are still very ~** ces événements sont encore très proches *or* très rapprochés de nous.
c (*fig*) *relative, relationship* proche; *friend* cher, intime; *friendship* intime; *guess* près de la vérité, à peu près juste; *resemblance* assez exact; *portrait* ressemblant; *race, contest* disputé, serré; *result* serré. **my ~est and dearest*** mes proches (parents), ceux qui me touchent de près; **a very ~ concern of mine** une chose qui me touche de très près; **the ~est equivalent** ce qui s'en rapproche le plus; **a ~ miss** (*Aviat*) une quasi-collision; (*Mil*) *[shot]* tir *m* très près du but; **that was a ~ miss** *or* **a ~ thing** (*gen*) il s'en est fallu de peu *or* d'un cheveu; *[shot]* c'est passé très près; *[election, race etc result]* **it was a ~ thing** ça a été très juste; **we had a ~ miss with that truck** on a frôlé l'accident *or* on l'a échappé belle avec ce camion; **the translation is fairly ~** la traduction est assez fidèle; **that's the ~est thing to a compliment** ça pourrait passer pour un compliment, de sa *etc* part c'est un compliment; *see also* **5,** *and* **offer** *etc.*
d = **nearside.**
e (*: *mean*) radin*, pingre.
4 vt *place* approcher de; *person* approcher, s'approcher de. (*liter*) **to be ~ing one's end** toucher à *or* être près de sa fin; **to be ~ing one's goal** toucher au but; **my book is ~ing completion** mon livre est près d'être achevé; **the book is ~ing publication** le livre approche de sa date de publication; **the country is ~ing disaster** le pays est au bord de la catastrophe.
5 comp ▸ **near beer** (*US*) bière légère ▸ **nearby** adv près, tout près, à proximité ◊ adj proche, avoisinant, tout près de là (*or* d'ici) ▸ **near-death experience** expérience *f* au-delà du corps ▸ **the Near East** le Proche-Orient ▸ **near gold** similor *m* ▸ **near money** (*Fin*) quasi-monnaie *f* ▸ **near-nudity** nudité presque totale, quasi-nudité ▸ **nearside** *see* **nearside** ▸ **near-sighted**: (*US*) **to be near-sighted** être myope, avoir la vue basse ▸ **near-sightedness** myopie *f* ▸ **near silk** soie artificielle.
nearly ['nɪəlɪ] adv **a** (*almost*) presque, à peu près, près de. **it's ~ complete** c'est presque terminé; **~ black** presque noir; **I've ~ finished** j'ai presque fini; **we are ~ there** nous sommes presque arrivés; **it's ~ 2 o'clock** il est près de *or* presque 2 heures; **it's ~ time to go** il est presque l'heure de partir; **she is ~ 60** elle a près de 60 ans, elle va sur ses 60 ans; **their marks are ~ the same** leurs notes sont à peu près les mêmes; **~ all my money** presque tout mon argent, la presque totalité de mon argent; **he ~ laughed** il a failli rire; **I very ~ lost my place** j'ai bien failli perdre ma place; **she was ~ crying** elle était sur le point de pleurer, elle était au bord des larmes; **it's the same or very ~ so** c'est la même chose ou presque.
b not ~ loin de; **she is not ~ so old as you** elle est loin d'être aussi âgée que vous; **that's not ~ enough** c'est loin d'être suffisant; **it's not ~ good enough** c'est loin d'être satisfaisant.
c (*closely*) près, de près. **this concerns me very ~** cela me touche de très près.
nearness ['nɪənɪs] n **a** (*in time, place*) proximité *f*; *[relationship]* intimité *f*; *[translation]* fidélité *f*; *[resemblance]* exactitude *f*. **b** (*meanness*) parcimonie *f*, radinerie* *f*.
nearside ['nɪəˌsaɪd] (*Aut, Horseriding etc*) **1** n (*in Britain*) côté *m* gauche; (*in France, US etc*) côté droit. **2** adj (*in Britain*) de gauche; (*in France, US etc*) de droite.
neat [niːt] adj **a** (*clean and tidy*) *person, clothes* soigné, propre, net (*f* nette); *sb's appearance, garden, sewing, stitches* soigné, net; *house, room* net, ordonné, bien tenu. **her hair is always very ~** elle est toujours bien coiffée; **~ as a new pin** *child* propre comme un sou neuf; *house* qui brille comme un sou neuf; **he is a ~ worker** il est soigneux dans son travail; **his work is very ~** son travail est très soigné; **his desk is always very ~** son bureau est toujours bien rangé; **~ handwriting** une écriture nette; **she is very ~ in her dress** elle est très soignée dans sa mise, elle s'habille de façon très soignée; **a ~ little suit** un petit tailleur de coupe nette.
b (*pleasing to eye*) **~ ankles** chevilles fines; **~ legs** jambes bien faites; **she has a ~ figure** elle est bien faite, elle a une jolie ligne; **a ~ little horse** un beau petit cheval; **a ~ little car** une belle *or* jolie petite voiture.
c (*skilful*) *phrase, style* élégant, net (*f* nette); *solution* élégant; *plan* habile, ingénieux; (*: *wonderful*) très bien, sensass‡ *inv*. **a ~ little speech** un petit discours bien tourné; **that's ~!** c'est du beau travail!, c'est du beau boulot!*; **to make a ~ job of sth** bien faire qch, réussir qch; **he's very ~ with his hands** il est très adroit, il est très habile (de ses mains).
d (*Brit: undiluted*) *spirits* pur, sans eau, sec. **he drinks his whisky/brandy ~** il prend son whisky/son cognac sec *or* sans eau; **he had a glass of ~ whisky** il a pris un verre de whisky pur *or* sec; **I'll take it ~** je le prendrai sec.
neaten ['niːtn] vt *dress* ajuster; *desk* ranger. **to ~ one's hair** se recoiffer.
'neath [niːθ] prep (*liter*) = **beneath 1.**
neatly ['niːtlɪ] adv **a** (*tidily*) avec ordre, d'une manière ordonnée *or*

soignée; *dress* avec soin; *write* proprement. **to put sth away ~** ranger qch avec soin. b (*skilfully*) habilement, adroitement. **he avoided the question very ~** il a éludé la question très habilement *or* adroitement; **~ put** joliment dit; **a ~ turned sentence** une phrase bien tournée *or* joliment tournée; **you got out of that very ~** vous vous en êtes adroitement *or* très bien tiré.

neatness ['ni:tnɪs] n a (*tidiness*) *[person, clothes]* netteté *f*, propreté *f*; *[house, room]* netteté, belle ordonnance; *[garden, sewing, stitches]* netteté. **the ~ of her work/appearance** son travail/sa tenue soigné(e), le soin qu'elle apporte à son travail/sa tenue. b *[ankles]* finesse *f*; *[legs, figure]* finesse, galbe *m*. c (*skilfulness*) adresse *f*, habileté *f*, dextérité *f*; *[style etc]* adresse.

N.E.B. [ˌeni:'bi:] n a (*Brit*) (abbr of **National Enterprise Board**) *see* **national**. b (abbr of **New English Bible**) *see* **new**[3].

nebbish‡ ['nebɪʃ] 1 adj (*US*) empoté*. **your ~ brother** ton empoté de frère. 2 n ballot* *m*, empoté(e) *m(f)*.

Nebraska [nɪ'bræskə] n Nebraska *m*. **in ~** dans le Nebraska.

Nebuchadnezzar [ˌnebjʊkəd'nezəʳ] n Nabuchodonosor *m*.

nebula ['nebjʊlə] n, pl **~s** *or* **nebulae** ['nebjʊli:] nébuleuse *f*.

nebulous ['nebjʊləs] adj (*Astron*) nébuleux; (*fig*) nébuleux, vague, flou.

NEC [ˌeni:'si:] n (abbr of **National Executive Committee**) *see* **national**.

necessarily ['nesɪsərɪlɪ] adv nécessairement, forcément, inévitablement. **they must ~ leave tomorrow** ils devront nécessairement *or* inévitablement partir demain; **this is not ~ the case** ce n'est pas forcément *or* nécessairement le cas; **you don't ~ have to believe it** vous n'êtes pas forcé *or* obligé de le croire.

necessary ['nesɪsərɪ] 1 adj a (*essential*) nécessaire, essentiel (*to, for* à). **it is ~ to do** il faut faire, il est nécessaire de faire; **it is ~ for him to be there** il faut qu'il soit là, il est nécessaire *or* essentiel qu'il soit là; **it is ~ that ...** il faut que ... + *subj*, il est nécessaire que ... + *subj*; **if ~** s'il le faut, en cas de besoin, au besoin, si besoin est; **where ~** au besoin; **only when ~** seulement quand c'est vraiment nécessaire; **to do everything ~** *or* **what is ~ (for)** faire tout ce qu'il faut (pour), faire le nécessaire (pour); **to make the ~ arrangements (for sth to be done)** prendre les dispositions nécessaires *or* faire le nécessaire (pour que qch se fasse); **to make it ~ for sb to do** mettre qn dans la nécessité de faire; **to do more than is ~** faire plus qu'il ne faut, faire plus que le nécessaire; **don't do any more than is ~** n'en faites pas plus qu'il ne faut *or* qu'il n'est nécessaire; **to do no more than is ~** ne faire que le nécessaire; **good food is ~ to health** une bonne alimentation est nécessaire *or* essentielle à la santé; **all the ~ qualifications for this job** toutes les qualités requises pour (obtenir) ce poste; **the law was clearly ~** la loi était de toute évidence nécessaire.
b (*unavoidable*) *corollary* nécessaire; *result* inévitable. **a ~ evil** un mal nécessaire.
2 n a **to do the ~*** faire le nécessaire.
b (*money*) **the ~*** le fric‡, les fonds *mpl*.
c (*Jur: necessities*) **necessaries** nécessaire *m*.

necessitate [nɪ'sesɪteɪt] vt nécessiter, rendre nécessaire. **the situation ~d his immediate return** la situation l'a obligé à revenir immédiatement, la situation a nécessité son retour immédiat.

necessitous [nɪ'sesɪtəs] adj nécessiteux. **in ~ circumstances** dans le besoin, dans la nécessité.

necessity [nɪ'sesɪtɪ] n a (*NonC: compelling circumstances*) nécessité *f*; (*need, compulsion*) besoin *m*, nécessité. **to be under the ~ of doing** être dans la nécessité de faire; **from** *or* **out of ~** par nécessité, par la force des choses; **of ~** de (toute) nécessité, nécessairement, inévitablement; (*Prov*) **~ knows no law** nécessité fait loi (*Prov*); (*Prov*) **~ is the mother of invention** de la nécessité naît l'invention, la nécessité rend ingénieux; **case of absolute ~** cas *m* de force majeure; **there is no ~ for you to do that** vous n'avez pas besoin de faire cela, il n'est pas nécessaire que vous fassiez cela; **in case of ~** au besoin, en cas de besoin; **the ~ of doing** le besoin *or* la nécessité de faire; **she realized the ~ of going to see him** elle a compris qu'il était nécessaire d'aller le voir, elle a compris la nécessité dans laquelle elle se trouvait d'aller le voir; **he did not realize the ~ for a quick decision** il ne s'est pas rendu compte qu'il fallait très vite prendre une décision; **is there any ~?** est-ce nécessaire?; **there's no ~ for tears/apologies** vous n'avez pas besoin de pleurer/de vous excuser; *see* **virtue**.
b (*NonC: poverty*) besoin *m*, dénuement *m*, nécessité *f*.
c (*necessary object etc*) chose nécessaire *or* essentielle. **the bare necessities of life** les choses nécessaires *or* essentielles à la vie; **a dishwasher is a ~ nowadays** un lave-vaisselle est une chose essentielle *or* indispensable de nos jours.

neck [nek] 1 n a cou *m*; *[horse etc]* encolure *f*. **to have a sore ~** avoir mal au cou; (*fig*) **to risk one's ~** risquer sa vie *or* sa peau*; (*fig*) **to save one's ~** sauver sa peau*; **to fall on sb's ~, to fling one's arms round sb's ~** se jeter *or* sauter au cou de qn; (*Racing*) **to win by a ~** gagner d'une encolure; **to be up to one's ~ in work** avoir du travail par-dessus la tête*; **to be up to one's ~ in a crime** être totalement impliqué dans un crime; **he's up to his ~ in it*** il est dans le bain* jusqu'au cou; (*fig*) **he got it in the ~‡** il en a pris pour son compte *or* grade*, il a dérouillé‡; **to stick** *or* **shoot one's ~ out*** se mouiller‡, s'avancer (*fig*), prendre un *or* des risque(s); **I don't want (to have) him (hanging) round my ~*** je ne veux pas l'avoir sur le dos (*fig*); **to throw sb out ~ and crop** jeter qn dehors sans appel; (*Brit*) **it's ~ or nothing*** il faut jouer le tout pour le tout; **~ of mutton** collet *m* *or* collier *m* de mouton; **~ of beef** collier *m* de bœuf; (*Culin*) **best end of ~** côtelettes premières; *see* **break, breathe, pain, stiff** *etc*.
b *[dress, shirt etc]* encolure *f*. **high ~** col montant; **square ~** décolleté *m* *or* encolure *f* carré(e); **dress with a low ~** robe décolletée; **shirt with a 38 cm ~** chemise qui fait 38 cm d'encolure *or* de tour de cou; *see* **polo, roll** *etc*.
c *[bottle]* col *m*, goulot *m*; *[vase]* col; *[tooth, screw]* collet *m*; *[land]* isthme *m*; *[guitar, violin]* manche *m*. (*fig*) **in our ~ of the woods** dans nos parages, de par chez nous, dans notre coin; *see* **bottle**.
d (*Brit* ‡: *impertinence*) toupet* *m*, culot‡ *m*.
2 vi (‡) se peloter*. **to ~ with sb** peloter qn.
3 comp ► **neck and neck** à égalité ► **neckband** (*part of garment*) col *m*; (*ribbon etc worn on neck*) tour *m* du cou ► **necklace** *see* **necklace** ► **neckline** encolure *f*; **plunging neckline** décolleté *or* décolletage plongeant ► **neckshot** ≃ balle *f* dans la nuque ► **necktie** (*esp US*) cravate *f*.

-necked [nekt] adj ending in comps *see* **low**[1] **4, round 5, stiff 2** *etc*.

neckerchief ['nekətʃi:f] n (*scarf*) foulard *m*, tour *m* de cou; (*on dress*) fichu *m*.

necking‡ ['nekɪŋ] n pelotage‡ *m*.

necklace ['neklɪs] 1 n collier *m*; (*long*) sautoir *m*. **ruby/pearl ~** collier de rubis/de perles; **diamond ~** collier *m* *or* rivière *f* de diamants.
2 vt (*: *kill with burning tyre*) faire subir le supplice du collier à. 3 comp ► **necklace-killing, necklacing** supplice *m* du collier.

necklet ['neklɪt] n collier *m*; (*fur*) collet *m* (en fourrure).

necrological [ˌnekrəʊ'lɒdʒɪkəl] adj nécrologique.

necrologist [ne'krɒlədʒɪst] n nécrologue *m*.

necrology [ne'krɒlədʒɪ] n nécrologie *f*.

necromancer ['nekrəʊmænsəʳ] n nécromancien(ne) *m(f)*.

necromancy ['nekrəʊmænsɪ] n nécromancie *f*.

necrophile ['nekrəʊˌfaɪl] n nécrophile *mf*.

necrophilia [ˌnekrəʊ'fɪlɪə] n, **necrophilism** [ne'krɒfɪlɪzəm] n nécrophilie *f*.

necrophiliac [ˌnekrəʊ'fɪlɪˌæk] n nécrophile *mf*.

necrophilic [ˌnekrəʊ'fɪlɪk] adj nécrophile.

necrophobe ['nekrəʊˌfəʊb] n nécrophobe *mf*.

necrophobia [ˌnekrəʊ'fəʊbɪə] n nécrophobie *f*.

necrophobic [ˌnekrəʊ'fəʊbɪk] adj nécrophobe.

necropolis [ne'krɒpəlɪs] n, pl **~es** *or* **necropoleis** [ne'krɒpəˌleɪs] nécropole *f*.

necrosis [ne'krəʊsɪs] n nécrose *f*.

nectar ['nektəʳ] n nectar *m*.

nectarine ['nektərɪn] n (*fruit*) brugnon *m*, nectarine *f*; (*tree*) brugnonier *m*.

ned‡ [ned] n (*esp Scot*) voyou *m*, vandale *m*, casseur *m*, blouson *m* noir, hooligan *m*.

NEDC [ˌeni:di:'si:] n (*Brit*) (abbr of **National Economic Development Council**) *see* **national**.

Neddy* ['nedɪ] n (*Brit*) (abbr of **National Economic Development Council**) *see* **national**.

née [neɪ] adj née. **Mrs Smith, ~ Jones** Mme Smith, née Jones.

need [ni:d] 1 n a (*NonC: necessity, obligation*) besoin *m*. **if ~ be** si besoin est, s'il le faut; **in case of ~** en cas de besoin; **there is no ~ for tears** vous n'avez pas besoin de pleurer; **there's no ~ to hurry** on n'a pas besoin de se presser; **no ~ to worry!** pas besoin de s'en faire!*; **no ~ to tell him** pas besoin de lui dire; **there's no ~ for you to come, you have no ~ to come** vous n'êtes pas obligé de venir; **to have no ~ to do sth** ne pas avoir besoin de *or* ne pas être obligé de *or* ne pas avoir à faire qch; **I can't see the ~ for it** je n'en vois pas la nécessité.
b (*NonC*) (*want, lack*) besoin *m*; (*poverty*) besoin, indigence *f*, dénuement *m*, gêne *f*. **there is much ~ of food** il y a un grand besoin de vivres; **when the ~ arises** quand le besoin se présente *or* s'en fait sentir; **to have ~ of, to be in ~ of** avoir besoin de; **to be badly** *or* **greatly in ~ of** avoir grand besoin de; **I have no ~ of advice** je n'ai pas *or* aucun besoin de conseils; **I'm in ~ of a drink** il me faut à boire; **the house is in ~ of repainting** la maison a besoin d'être repeinte; **those most in ~ of help** ceux qui ont le plus besoin de secours; **to be in ~** être dans le besoin; **his ~ is great** son dénuement est grand; **your ~ is greater than mine** vous êtes plus dans le besoin que moi; (* *hum*) vous en avez plus besoin que moi; *see* **serve**.
c (*NonC: misfortune*) adversité *f*, difficulté *f*. **in times of ~** aux heures *or* aux moments difficiles; **do not fail me in my hour of ~** ne m'abandonnez pas dans l'adversité; *see* **friend**.
d (*thing needed*) besoin *m*. **to supply sb's ~s** subvenir aux besoins de qn; **his ~s are few** il a peu de besoins; **give me a list of your ~s** donnez-moi une liste de ce dont vous avez besoin *or* de ce qu'il vous faut; **the greatest ~s of industry** ce dont l'industrie a le plus besoin.
2 vt a (*require*) *[person, thing]* avoir besoin de. **they ~ one another** ils ont besoin l'un de l'autre; **I ~ money** j'ai besoin d'argent, il me faut de l'argent; **I ~ more money** il me faut davantage d'argent; **I ~ it** j'en

ai besoin, il me le faut; **do you ~ more time?** avez-vous besoin qu'on vous accorde (*subj*) plus de *or* davantage de temps?; **have you got all that you ~?** vous avez tout ce qu'il vous faut?; **it's just what I ~ed** c'est tout à fait ce qu'il me fallait; **I ~ 2 more to complete the series** il m'en faut encore 2 pour compléter la série; **he ~ed no second invitation** il n'a pas eu besoin qu'on lui répète (*subj*) l'invitation; **the house ~s repainting** *or* **to be repainted** la maison a besoin d'être repeinte; **her hair ~s brushing** *or* **to be brushed** ses cheveux ont besoin d'un coup de brosse; **a visa is ~ed** il faut un visa; **a much ~ed holiday** des vacances dont on a (*or* j'ai *etc*) grand besoin; **I gave it a much ~ed wash** je l'ai lavé, ce dont il avait grand besoin; **it ~ed a war to alter that** il a fallu une guerre pour changer ça; **it** *or* **he doesn't ~ me to tell him** il n'a pas besoin que je le lui dise; **she ~s watching** *or* **to be watched** elle a besoin d'être surveillée; **he ~s to have everything explained to him in detail** il faut tout lui expliquer en détail; **you will hardly ~ to be reminded that** ... vous n'avez sûrement pas besoin qu'on (*or* que je *etc*) vous rappelle (*subj*) que ...; **you only ~ed to ask** tu n'avais qu'à demander; (*fig*) **who ~s it?*** on s'en fiche*!; (*fig*) **who ~s politicians (anyway)?*** (de toutes façons) les hommes politiques, à quoi ça sert?* *or* qu'est-ce qu'on en a à faire?*; *see* **hole**.

b (*demand*) demander, nécessiter, exiger. **this book ~s careful reading** ce livre demande à être lu attentivement *or* nécessite une lecture attentive; **this coat ~s to be cleaned regularly** ce manteau doit être nettoyé régulièrement; **this plant ~s care** cette plante exige qu'on en prenne soin; **the situation ~s detailed consideration** la situation doit être considérée dans le détail; **this will ~ some explaining** il va falloir fournir de sérieuses explications là-dessus; **it shouldn't ~ a famine to make us realize that** ... nous ne devrions pas avoir besoin d'une famine pour nous apercevoir que ... .

3 **modal auxiliary vb** (*ne s'emploie qu'à la forme interrogative, négative et avec "hardly", "scarcely" etc: les formes du type "no one needs to do" sont moins littéraires que celles du type "no one need do"*) a (*indicating obligation*) **need he go?, does he need to go?** a-t-il besoin *or* est-il obligé d'y aller?, faut-il qu'il y aille?; **you needn't wait** vous n'avez pas besoin *or* vous n'êtes pas obligé d'attendre; **you needn't bother to write to me** ce n'est pas la peine *or* ne vous donnez pas la peine de m'écrire; **I told her she needn't reply** *or* **she didn't need to reply** je lui ai dit qu'elle n'était pas obligée *or* forcée de répondre; **we needn't have hurried** ce n'était pas la peine de nous presser; **need I finish the book now?** faut-il que je termine (*subj*) le livre maintenant?; **need we go into all this now?** est-il nécessaire de *or* faut-il discuter de tout cela maintenant?; **I need hardly say that** ... je n'ai guère besoin de dire que ..., inutile de dire que ...; **need I say more?** ai-je besoin d'en dire plus (long)?; **you needn't say any more** inutile d'en dire plus (long); **there need be no questions asked** si on fait attention personne ne demandera rien; **no one need go** *or* **needs to go hungry nowadays** de nos jours personne n'est obligé d'avoir *or* n'est condamné à avoir faim; **why need you always remind me of that?, why do you always need to remind me of that?** pourquoi faut-il toujours que tu me rappelles (*subj*) cela?

b (*indicating logical necessity*) **need that be true?** est-ce nécessairement vrai?; **that needn't be the case** ce n'est pas nécessairement *or* forcément le cas; **it need not follow that they are all affected** il ne s'ensuit pas nécessairement *or* forcément qu'ils soient tous affectés.

needful ['ni:dfʊl] 1 **adj** nécessaire. **to do what is ~** faire ce qui est nécessaire, faire le nécessaire; **as much as is ~** autant qu'il en faut. 2 **n** a **to do the ~*** faire ce qu'il faut. b (‡: *money*) **the ~** le fric‡, les fonds *mpl*.

neediness ['ni:dɪnɪs] **n** indigence *f*, dénuement *m*, nécessité *f*.

needle ['ni:dl] 1 **n** a (*most senses*) aiguille *f*. **knitting/darning** *etc* **~** aiguille à tricoter/à repriser *etc*; **record-player ~** saphir *m* de tourne-disque; **gramophone ~** aiguille de phonographe; (*Bot*) **pine ~** aiguille de pin; (*fig*) **to look for a ~ in a haystack** chercher une aiguille dans une botte de foin; (*Drugs sl*) **to be on the ~** être héroïnomane, se shooter‡ à l'héroïne; *see* **pin, sharp** *etc*.

b (*Brit fig*) **he gives me the ~‡** (*tease*) il me charrie‡; (*annoy*) il me tape sur les nerfs* *or* sur le système*; **to get the ~‡** se ficher en boule‡.

2 **vt** a (*) (*annoy*) asticoter, agacer; (*sting*) piquer *or* toucher au vif; (*nag*) harceler. **she was ~d into replying sharply** touchée au vif *or* agacée elle a répondu avec brusquerie.

b (*US*) **to ~ a drink‡** corser une boisson.

3 **comp** ▸ **needle book, needle case** porte-aiguilles *m inv* ▸ **needlecord** velours *m* mille-raies ▸ **needlecraft** travaux *mpl* d'aiguille ▸ **needlepoint** tapisserie *f* à l'aiguille ▸ **needle sharp** (*fig*) (*alert*) malin (*f* -igne) comme un singe; (*penetrating*) perspicace ▸ **needlestick injury** (*Med*) *blessure accidentelle causée par une piqûre de seringue à injection* ▸ **needlewoman**: **she is a good needlewoman** elle coud bien ▸ **needlework** (*gen*) travaux *mpl* d'aiguille; (*mending etc; also Scol*) couture *f*; **bring your needlework with you** apportez votre ouvrage.

needless ['ni:dlɪs] **adj** *expense, inconvenience* inutile, superflu; *action* inutile, qui ne sert à rien; *remark* déplacé. **~ to say, it then began to rain** inutile de dire que la pluie s'est mise alors à tomber.

needlessly ['ni:dlɪslɪ] **adv** inutilement. **you're worrying quite ~** vous vous inquiétez tout à fait inutilement *or* sans raison.

needlessness ['ni:dlɪsnɪs] **n** inutilité *f*; *[remark]* inopportunité *f*.

needn't ['ni:dnt] = **need not**; *see* **need 3**.

needs [ni:dz] **adv** (*ne s'emploie qu'avec "must"*) absolument, de toute nécessité. **I must ~ leave tomorrow** il me faut absolument partir demain, je dois de toute nécessité partir demain; **if ~ must** s'il le faut absolument, si c'est absolument nécessaire; (*Prov*) **~ must when the devil drives** nécessité fait loi (*Prov*).

needy ['ni:dɪ] 1 **adj** *person* nécessiteux, indigent. **in ~ circumstances** dans le besoin, dans l'indigence. 2 **n**: **the ~** les nécessiteux *mpl*, les indigents *mpl*.

ne'er [nɛəʳ] 1 **adv** (*liter*) = **never 1.** 2 **comp** ▸ **ne'er-do-well** **n** bon(ne) *m(f)* *or* propre *mf* à rien ◊ **adj** bon *or* propre à rien ▸ **ne'ertheless** (*liter*) = **nevertheless**.

nefarious [nɪ'fɛərɪəs] **adj** abominable, infâme, vil (*f* vile) (*liter*).

nefariousness [nɪ'fɛərɪəsnɪs] **n** scélératesse *f*.

neg. (**abbr of negative**) nég.

negate [nɪ'geɪt] **vt** (*frm*) (*nullify*) annuler; (*deny truth of*) nier la vérité de; (*deny existence of*) nier (l'existence de). **this ~d all the good that we had achieved** cela a réduit à rien tout le bien que nous avions fait.

negation [nɪ'geɪʃən] **n** (*all senses*) négation *f*.

negative ['negətɪv] 1 **adj** (*all senses*) négatif. **he's very ~ about it** il a une attitude très négative sur cette question; (*Fin*) **~ (income) tax** impôt *m* négatif; (*Ling*) **~ particle** particule négative; (*Math*) **~ sign** signe *m* moins.

2 **n** a réponse négative. **his answer was a curt ~** il a répondu par un non fort sec; **the answer was in the ~** la réponse était négative; **to answer in the ~** répondre négativement *or* par la négative, faire une réponse négative; (*as answer*) **"~"** (*gen*) "non"; (*computer voice*) "réponse négative".

b (*Ling*) négation *f*. **double ~** double négation; **two ~s make a positive** deux négations équivalent à une affirmation; **in(to) the ~** à la forme négative.

c (*Phot*) négatif *m*, cliché *m*.

d (*Elec*) (pôle *m*) négatif *m*.

3 **vt** a (*veto*) *plan* rejeter, s'opposer à, repousser. **the amendment was ~d** l'amendement fut repoussé.

b (*contradict, refute*) *statement* contredire, réfuter.

c (*nullify*) *effect* neutraliser.

negatively ['negətɪvlɪ] **adv** négativement.

Negev ['negev] **n**: **~ Desert** désert *m* du Néguev.

neglect [nɪ'glekt] 1 **vt** *child* négliger, laisser à l'abandon, délaisser; *animal, invalid* négliger, ne pas s'occuper de; *one's wife, one's friends* négliger, délaisser; *garden* laisser à l'abandon, ne pas s'occuper de, ne prendre aucun soin de; *house, car, machinery* ne pas s'occuper de, ne prendre aucun soin de; *rule, law* ne tenir aucun compte de, ne faire aucun cas de; *duty, obligation* manquer à, négliger, oublier; *business, work, hobby* négliger, délaisser, se désintéresser de; *opportunity* laisser échapper, négliger; *promise* manquer à, ne pas tenir; *one's health* négliger; *advice* négliger, ne tenir aucun compte de, ne faire aucun cas de. **to ~ o.s., to ~ one's appearance** *or* **person** se négliger; **to ~ to do** négliger *or* omettre de faire; *see also* **neglected**.

2 **n** (*NonC*) *[person]* manque *m* de soins *or* d'égards *or* d'attention (*of* envers); *[duty, obligation]* manquement *m* (*of* à); *[work]* manque *m* d'intérêt *m* (*of* pour). **~ of one's appearance** manque de soins apportés à son apparence; **his ~ of his promise** son manquement à sa promesse, le fait de ne pas tenir sa promesse; **his ~ of his house/garden/car** le fait qu'il ne s'occupe pas de sa maison/de son jardin/de sa voiture; **the garden was in a state of ~** le jardin était mal tenu *or* était à l'abandon; **children left in utter ~** enfants laissés complètement à l'abandon; **the fire happened through ~** l'incendie est dû à la négligence.

neglected [nɪ'glektɪd] **adj** *appearance* négligé, peu soigné; *wife, family* abandonné, délaissé; *house* mal tenu; *garden* mal tenu, laissé à l'abandon. **to feel ~** se sentir abandonné *or* délaissé *or* oublié; **this district of the town is very ~** ce quartier de la ville est laissé complètement à l'abandon.

neglectful [nɪ'glektfʊl] **adj** négligent. **to be ~ of** négliger.

neglectfully [nɪ'glektfəlɪ] **adv** avec négligence.

négligé, negligee ['neglɪʒeɪ] **n** négligé *m*, déshabillé *m*.

negligence ['neglɪdʒəns] **n** (*NonC*) négligence *f*, manque *m* de soins *or* de précautions. **through ~** par négligence; (*Rel*) **sin of ~** faute *f* *or* péché *m* d'omission; *see* **contributory**.

negligent ['neglɪdʒənt] **adj** a (*neglectful*) négligent. **to be ~ of one's duties** être oublieux de *or* négliger ses devoirs; **he was ~ in his work** il négligeait son travail. b (*offhand*) *gesture, look* négligent. **with a ~ air** d'un air négligent *or* détaché.

negligently ['neglɪdʒəntlɪ] **adv** a (*offhandedly*) négligemment, avec insouciance. b (*carelessly*) *omit* par négligence; *behave* avec négligence.

negligible ['neglɪdʒəbl] **adj** négligeable.

negotiable [nɪ'gəʊʃɪəbl] **adj** a (*Fin*) négociable. **~ securities** fonds *mpl* négociables; **not ~** non négociable. b *salary, conditions* négociable, à débattre. c *road* praticable; *mountain, obstacle* franchissable; *river* (*can be sailed*) navigable, (*can be crossed*) franchissable.

negotiant [nɪˈgəʊʃɪənt] n négociateur *m*, -trice *f*.

negotiate [nɪˈgəʊʃɪeɪt] 1 vt a *sale, loan, settlement, salary* négocier. b *obstacle, hill* franchir; *river* (*sail on*) naviguer, (*cross*) franchir, traverser; *rapids, falls* franchir; *bend in road* prendre, négocier; *difficulty* surmonter, franchir. c *bill, cheque, bond* négocier. 2 vi négocier, traiter (*with sb for sth* avec qn pour obtenir qch). **they are negotiating for more pay** ils sont en pourparler(s) *or* ils ont entamé des négociations pour obtenir des augmentations.

negotiation [nɪ,gəʊʃɪˈeɪʃən] n (*discussion*) négociation *f*, pourparler *m*. **to begin ~s with** engager *or* entamer des négociations *or* des pourparlers avec; **to be in ~ with** être en pourparler(s) avec; **~s are proceeding** des négociations *or* des pourparlers sont en cours.

negotiator [nɪˈgəʊʃɪeɪtəʳ] n négociateur *m*, -trice *f*.

Negress [ˈniːgres] n Noire *f*.

Negro [ˈniːgrəʊ] 1 adj nègre; *see* **spiritual**. 2 n, pl ~es Noir *m*.

negroid [ˈniːgrɔɪd] adj négroïde.

Nehemiah [,niːɪˈmaɪə] n Néhémie *m*.

neigh [neɪ] 1 vi hennir. 2 n hennissement *m*.

neighbour, (*US*) **neighbor** [ˈneɪbəʳ] 1 n voisin(e) *m(f)*; (*Bible etc*) prochain(e) *m(f)*. **she is my ~** c'est ma voisine; **she is a good ~** c'est une bonne voisine; **Britain's nearest ~ is France** la France est la plus proche voisine de la Grande-Bretagne; *see* **next door**. 2 comp ▸**Good Neighbor Policy** (*US Pol*) politique *f* de bon voisinage ▸**neighbor states** (*US*) états voisins. 3 vi (*US*) **to ~ with sb** se montrer bon voisin envers qn.

neighbourhood, (*US*) **neighborhood** [ˈneɪbəhʊd] 1 n (*district*) voisinage *m*, quartier *m*; (*area nearby*) voisinage, alentours *mpl*, environs *mpl*. **all the children of the ~** tous les enfants du voisinage *or* du quartier; **it's not a nice ~** ce n'est pas un quartier bien; **the whole ~ knows him** tout le voisinage *or* le quartier le connaît; **the soil in this ~ is very rich** la terre de cette région est très riche; **the cinema is in his ~** le cinéma est près de *or* à proximité de chez lui; **in the ~ of the church** aux alentours de *or* aux environs de l'église, dans le voisinage de l'église; **(something) in the ~ of £100** dans les 100 livres, environ 100 livres, à peu près 100 livres; **anyone in the ~ of the crime** toute personne se trouvant dans les parages du crime.

2 comp *doctor, shops* du *or* de quartier ▸**neighbourhood dentist:** (*fig, often iro*) **our** (*or* **your**) **friendly neighbourhood dentist** *etc* le (cher) dentiste *etc* du coin ▸**neighbourhood TV** télévision locale ▸**neighbourhood watch** *système de surveillance assuré par les habitants d'un quartier*.

neighbouring, (*US*) **neighboring** [ˈneɪbərɪŋ] adj avoisinant, voisin.

neighbourliness, (*US*) **neighborliness** [ˈneɪbəlɪnɪs] n: **(good) ~** rapports *mpl* de bon voisinage.

neighbourly, (*US*) **neighborly** [ˈneɪbəlɪ] adj *person* bon voisin, amical, obligeant; *feelings* de bon voisin, amical; *action* de bon voisin. **they are ~ people** ils sont bons voisins; **to behave in a ~ way** agir en bon voisin; **~ relations** rapports *mpl* de bon voisinage.

neighing [ˈneɪɪŋ] 1 n hennissement(s) *m(pl)*. 2 adj hennissant.

neither [ˈnaɪðəʳ, ˈniːðəʳ] 1 adv ni. **~ ... nor** ni ... ni (+ ne *before vb*); **~ you nor I know** ni vous ni moi ne (le) savons; **the book is ~ good nor bad** le livre n'est ni bon ni mauvais; **I've seen ~ him nor her** je n'ai vu ni lui ni elle; **he can ~ read nor write** il ne sait ni lire ni écrire; **he ~ knows nor cares** il ne le sait pas et ne s'en soucie point; (*fig*) **that's ~ here nor there** ce n'est pas la question, cela n'a rien à voir (avec la question).

2 conj a ne ... non plus, (et ...) non plus, ni. **if you don't go, ~ shall I** si tu n'y vas pas je n'irai pas non plus; **I'm not going — ~ am I** je n'y vais pas — (et) moi non plus *or* ni moi *or* ni moi non plus†; **he didn't do it — ~ did his brother** ce n'est pas lui qui l'a fait — son frère non plus *or* ni son frère.

b (*liter: moreover ... not*) d'ailleurs ... ne ... pas. **I can't go, ~ do I want to** je ne peux pas y aller et d'ailleurs je ne le veux pas.

3 adj: **~ story is true** ni l'une ni l'autre des deux histoires n'est vraie, aucune des deux histoires n'est vraie; **in ~ way** ni d'une manière ni de l'autre; **in ~ case** ni dans un cas ni dans l'autre.

4 pron aucun(e) *m(f)*, ni l'un(e) ni l'autre (+ ne *before vb*). **~ of them knows** ni l'un ni l'autre ne le sait, ils ne le savent ni l'un ni l'autre; **I know ~ of them** je ne (les) connais ni l'un ni l'autre; **which (of the two) do you prefer? — ~** lequel (des deux) préférez-vous? — ni l'un ni l'autre.

Nelly [ˈnelɪ] n (**dim of Helen, Ellen**) Hélène *f*, Éléonore *f*. **not on your ~!**‡ jamais de la vie!

nelson [ˈnelsən] n (*Wrestling*) **full ~** nelson *m*; **half-~** clef *f* du cou; (*fig*) **to put a half-~ on sb*** attraper qn (*pour l'empêcher de faire qch*).

nem. con. (**abbr of nemine contradicente = no one contradicting**) à l'unanimité.

nemesia [nɪˈmiːʒə] n némésia *m* (*fleur*).

Nemesis [ˈnemɪsɪs] n a (*Myth*) Némésis *f*. b (*also* **n~**) némésis *f*, instrument *m* de vengeance. **it's ~** c'est un juste retour des choses; (*esp US*) **she's my ~** je suis vaincu d'avance avec elle.

neo... [ˈniːəʊ] pref néo-.

Neocene [ˈniːə,siːn] n néogène *m*.

neoclassical [,niːəʊˈklæsɪkəl] adj néo-classique.

neoclassicism [,niːəʊˈklæsɪ,sɪzəm] n néo-classicisme *m*.

neocolonialism [,niːəʊkəˈləʊnɪəlɪzəm] n néo-colonialisme *m*.

neodymium [,niːəʊˈdɪmɪəm] n néodyme *m*.

neofascism [,niːəʊˈfæʃɪzəm] n néo-fascisme *m*.

neofascist [,niːəʊˈfæʃɪst] adj, n néo-fasciste (*mf*).

Neogene [ˈniːə,dʒiːn] n néogène *m*.

neolith [ˈniːəlɪθ] n (*Archaeol*) pierre *f* polie.

neolithic [,niːəʊˈlɪθɪk] adj néolithique. **~ age** âge *m* néolithique *or* de la pierre polie.

neological [,nɪəˈlɒdʒɪkəl] adj néologique.

neologism [nɪˈɒlə,dʒɪzəm] n néologisme *m*.

neologize [nɪˈɒlədʒaɪz] vi faire un (*or* des) néologisme(s).

neology [nɪˈɒlədʒɪ] n = **neologism**.

neomycin [,niːəʊˈmaɪsɪn] n néomycine *f*.

neon [ˈniːɒn] 1 n (gaz *m*) néon *m*. 2 comp *lamp, lighting* au néon ▸**neon sign** enseigne *f* (lumineuse) au néon.

neonatal [,niːəʊˈneɪtəl] adj néonatal.

neonate [ˈniːəʊ,neɪt] n nouveau-né *m*.

neonazi [,niːəʊˈnɑːtsɪ] adj, n néo-nazi(e) *(m(f))*.

neophyte [ˈniːəʊ,faɪt] n néophyte *mf*.

neoplasm [ˈniːəʊ,plæzəm] n néoplasme *m*.

Neo-Platonic, *also* **neoplatonic** [,niːəʊpləˈtɒnɪk] adj néo-platonicien.

Neo-Platonism, *also* **neoplatonism** [,niːəʊˈpleɪtə,nɪzəm] n néo-platonisme *m*.

Neo-Platonist, *also* **neoplatonist** [,niːəʊˈpleɪtə,nɪst] n néo-platonicien(ne) *m(f)*.

Neozoic [,niːəʊˈzəʊɪk] adj néozoïque.

Nepal [nɪˈpɔːl] n Népal *m*.

Nepalese [,nepɔːˈliːz], **Nepali** [nɪˈpɔːlɪ] 1 adj népalais. 2 n a (pl inv) Népalais(e) *m(f)*. b (*Ling*) népalais *m*.

nephew [ˈnevjuː], (*esp US*) [ˈnefjuː] n neveu *m*.

nephralgia [nɪˈfrældʒɪə] n néphralgie *f*.

nephrectomy [nɪˈfrektəmɪ] n néphrectomie *f*.

nephritic [neˈfrɪtɪk] adj néphrétique.

nephritis [neˈfraɪtɪs] n néphrite *f*.

nephrology [nɪˈfrɒlədʒɪ] n néphrologie *f*.

nephrosis [nɪˈfrəʊsɪs] n néphrose *f*.

nephrotomy [nɪˈfrɒtəmɪ] n néphrotomie *f*.

nepotism [ˈnepətɪzəm] n népotisme *m*.

Neptune [ˈneptjuːn] n (*Myth*) Neptune *m*; (*Astron*) Neptune *f*.

neptunium [nepˈtjuːnɪəm] n neptunium *m*.

nerd‡ [nɜːd] n ballot* *m*, pauvre mec‡ *m*.

nereid [ˈnɪərɪɪd] n (*Myth, Zool*) néréide *f*.

Nero [ˈnɪərəʊ] n Néron *m*.

nerve [nɜːv] 1 n a (*Anat, Dentistry*) nerf *m*; (*Bot*) nervure *f*. **to kill the ~ of a tooth** dévitaliser une dent.

b (*fig*) **~s** nerfs *mpl*, nervosité *f*; **her ~s are bad** elle est très nerveuse; **she suffers from ~s** elle a les nerfs fragiles; (*before performance*) **to have a fit** *or* **an attack of ~s** avoir le trac*; **it's only ~s** c'est de la nervosité; **to be all ~s, to be a bundle of ~s** être un paquet de nerfs; **he was in a state of ~s, his ~s were on edge** il était sur les nerfs, il avait les nerfs tendus *or* à vif; **he/that noise gets on my ~s** il/ce bruit me porte *or* me tape sur les nerfs* *or* sur le système*; **to live on one's ~s** vivre sur les nerfs; **to have ~s of steel** *or* **of iron** avoir les nerfs très solides *or* à toute épreuve; **war of ~s** guerre *f* des nerfs; *see* **strain¹**.

c (*NonC: fig*) (*courage*) courage *m*; (*self-confidence*) assurance *f*, confiance *f* en soi(-même). **it was a test of ~ and stamina** c'était une épreuve de sang-froid et d'endurance; **try to keep your ~** essayez de conserver votre sang-froid; **after the accident he never got his ~ back** *or* **never regained his ~** après l'accident il n'a jamais retrouvé sa confiance en lui-même; **I haven't the ~ to do that** je n'ai pas le courage *or* le cran* de faire ça (*see also* **1d**); **his ~ failed him, he lost his ~** il s'est dégonflé*.

d (*: *cheek*) toupet* *m*, culot‡ *m*. **you've got a ~!** tu es gonflé!*, tu as du culot!‡ *or* du toupet!*; (*Brit*) **you've got a bloody‡ ~!** tu charries!‡; **what a ~!, of all the ~!, the ~ of it!** quel culot!‡, quel toupet!*, en voilà un culot!‡ *or* un toupet!*; **he had the ~ to say that ...** il a eu le culot‡ *or* le toupet* de dire que ... .

2 vt: **to ~ sb to do** donner à qn le courage *or* l'assurance de faire; **to ~ o.s. to do** prendre son courage à deux mains *or* s'armer de courage pour faire; **I can't ~ myself to do it** je n'ai pas le courage de le faire.

3 comp ▸**nerve cell** cellule nerveuse ▸**nerve centre** (*Anat*) centre nerveux; (*fig*) centre *m* d'opérations (*fig*) ▸**nerve ending** terminaison nerveuse ▸**nerve gas** gaz *m* neuroplégique ▸**nerve-racking** angoissant, très éprouvant pour les nerfs ▸**nerve specialist** neurologue *mf*.

nerveless [ˈnɜːvlɪs] adj a (*Anat*) sans nerfs; (*Bot*) sans nervures. (*fig*) **it fell from his ~ grasp** sa main, inerte, l'a lâché. b (*fig: calm, collected*) maître (*f* maîtresse) de soi, (plein) de sang-froid.

nervelessness [ˈnɜːvlɪsnɪs] n (*fig: feebleness*) inertie *f*, manque *m* de vigueur *or* d'énergie; (*calmness*) sang-froid *m*.

nerviness* [ˈnɜːvɪnɪs] n a énervement *m*, nervosité *f*. b (*US: cheek*) culot‡ *m*, toupet* *m*.

nervous [ˈnɜːvəs] adj a (*Anat*) nerveux. **to have a ~ breakdown** avoir *or* faire* une dépression nerveuse; **~ disease** maladie nerveuse; **full of ~ energy** plein de vitalité *or* d'énergie; **~ exhaustion** fatigue nerveuse, (*serious*) surmenage mental; **~ system** système nerveux; **~ tension** tension nerveuse.
b (*easily excited*) nerveux, excitable; (*tense*) nerveux, tendu; (*apprehensive*) inquiet (*f* -ète), intimidé, troublé. **in a ~ state** très agité; **to feel ~** (*gen*) se sentir mal à l'aise; (*shy*) se sentir tout intimidé; (*tense*) avoir les nerfs en boule *or* à fleur de peau *or* à vif; (*before performance etc*) avoir le trac*; **he makes me (feel) ~** (*fearful*) il m'intimide; (*unsure of myself*) il me fait perdre mes moyens; (*tense*) il m'énerve; **I was ~ about him** *or* **on his account** j'avais peur *or* j'étais inquiet pour lui; **I'm rather ~ about diving** j'ai un peu peur de plonger, j'ai une certaine appréhension à plonger; **don't be ~, it'll be all right** n'aie pas peur *or* ne t'inquiète pas, tout se passera bien; **he's a ~ wreck*** il est à bout de nerfs; (*US*) **~ Nellie‡** timoré(e) *m(f)*, trouillard(e)‡ *m(f)*.

nervously [ˈnɜːvəslɪ] adv (*tensely*) nerveusement; (*apprehensively*) avec inquiétude.

nervousness [ˈnɜːvəsnɪs] n a (*excitement*) nervosité *f*, état nerveux, état d'agitation; (*apprehension*) crainte *f*, trac* *m*. b [*style etc*] nervosité *f*.

nervy* [ˈnɜːvɪ] adj a (*Brit: tense*) énervé, irrité. **to be in a ~ state** avoir les nerfs en boule *or* à fleur de peau *or* à vif. b (*US: cheeky*) effronté, qui a du toupet* *or* du culot‡.

...ness [nɪs] suf: **greatness** grandeur *f*; **selfishness** égoïsme *m*; **weariness** lassitude *f*.

nest [nest] 1 n a [*birds, mice, turtles, ants etc*] nid *m*; (*contents*) nichée *f*. (*lit, fig*) **to leave the ~** quitter le nid; *see* **hornet**. b (*fig*) nid *m*. **~ of brigands/machine guns** nid de brigands/mitrailleuses. c [*boxes etc*] jeu *m*. **~ of tables** table *f* gigogne. 2 vi a [*bird etc*] (se) nicher, faire son nid. b **to go (bird) ~ing** aller dénicher les oiseaux *or* les œufs. c [*boxes etc*] s'emboîter. 3 comp ►**nest egg** (*fig*) pécule *m*.

nested [ˈnestɪd] adj *tables* gigognes; (*Gram*) emboîté.

nesting [ˈnestɪŋ] n [*birds*] nidification *f*; (*Gram*) emboîtement *m*. **~ box** nichoir *m*.

nestle [ˈnesl] vi [*person*] se blottir, se pelotonner (*up to, against* contre); [*house etc*] se nicher. **to ~ down in bed** se pelotonner dans son lit; **to ~ against sb's shoulder** se blottir contre l'épaule de qn; **a house nestling among the trees** une maison nichée parmi les arbres *or* blottie dans la verdure.

nestling [ˈnes/lɪŋ] n oisillon *m*.

net[1] [net] 1 n a (*gen, Ftbl, Tennis etc; also fig*) filet *m*. (*fig*) **to walk into the ~** donner *or* tomber dans le panneau; (*fig*) **to be caught in the ~** être pris au piège *or* au filet; (*fig*) **to slip through the ~** passer à travers les mailles du filet; (*fig*) **to cast one's ~ wider** élargir son horizon *or* ses perspectives; **hair~** résille *f*, filet à cheveux; (*Tennis*) **to come up to the ~** monter au filet; (*Ftbl etc*) **the ball's in the ~!** c'est un but!; *see* **butterfly, mosquito, safety** *etc*.
b (*NonC: Tex*) tulle *m*, voile *m*.
2 vt a *fish, game* prendre au filet. (*fig*) **the police ~ted several wanted men** la police a ramassé dans ses filets plusieurs des hommes qu'elle recherchait.
b *river* tendre des filets dans; *fruit bushes* poser un filet sur.
c (*Sport*) **to ~ the ball** envoyer la balle dans le filet; **to ~ a goal** marquer un but.
3 comp ►**netball** (*Brit*) netball *m* ►**net call judge** (*Tennis*) juge *m* de filet ►**net curtains** voilage *m*, (*half-length*) brise-bise *m inv* ►**net fishing** pêche *f* au filet ►**net play** (*Tennis etc*) jeu *m* au filet ►**network** *see* **network**.

net[2] [net] 1 adj *price, income, weight* net. (*Brit*) **N~ Book Agreement** *accord de maintien des prix publics des livres (entre les éditeurs et les librairies)*; **~ loss** perte sèche; **~ profit** bénéfice net; **~ domestic product** produit *m* intérieur net; **~ national product** produit *m* national net; (*Fin*) **~ present value** valeur *f* actuelle nette; (*Fin*) **~ realizable value** valeur *f* nette réalisable; **the ~ result is that ...** ce qui en résulte est que ...; **the price is £15 ~** le prix est de 15 livres net; **"terms strictly ~"** "prix nets". 2 vt [*business deal etc*] rapporter *or* produire net; [*person*] gagner *or* toucher net.

nether [ˈneðəʳ] 1 adj († *or liter*) bas (*f* basse), inférieur (*f* -eure). **~ regions, ~ world** enfers *mpl*. 2 comp ►**nethermost** le plus bas, le plus profond; **in the nethermost parts of the earth** dans les profondeurs de la terre.

Netherlander [ˈneðəˌlændəʳ] n Néerlandais(e) *m(f)*.

Netherlands [ˈneðələndz] 1 npl: **the ~** les Pays-Bas *mpl*; **in the ~** aux Pays-Bas. 2 adj néerlandais.

nett [net] = **net**[2].

netting [ˈnetɪŋ] n (*NonC*) a (*nets*) filets *mpl*; (*mesh*) mailles *fpl*; (*for fence etc*) treillis *m* métallique; (*Tex*) voile *m*, tulle *m* (*pour rideaux*); *see* **mosquito, wire** *etc*. b (*net-making*) fabrication *f* de filets. c (*action*) (*Fishing*) pêche *f* au filet; (*for catching game etc*) pose *f* de filets.

nettle [ˈnetl] 1 n (*Bot*) ortie *f*. **stinging ~** ortie brûlante *or* romaine; **dead ~** ortie blanche; (*fig*) **to seize** *or* **grasp the ~** prendre le taureau par les cornes. 2 vt (*fig*) agacer, irriter, faire monter la moutarde au nez de. **he was ~d into replying sharply** agacé, il a répondu avec brusquerie. 3 comp ►**nettlerash** urticaire *f* ►**nettle sting** piqûre *f* d'ortie.

nettlesome [ˈnetlsəm] adj (*annoying*) irritant; (*touchy*) susceptible.

network [ˈnetwɜːk] 1 n (*gen, also Comput, Elec, Rad, TV*) réseau *m*. **rail ~** réseau ferré *or* ferroviaire *or* de chemin de fer; **road ~** réseau *or* système routier; **~ of narrow streets** lacis *m or* enchevêtrement *m* de ruelles; **~ of veins** réseau *or* lacis de veines; **~ of spies/contacts/salesmen** réseau d'espions/de relations/de représentants de commerce; **~ of lies** tissu *m* de mensonges; (*Rad, TV*) **the programme went out over the whole ~** le programme a été diffusé sur l'ensemble du réseau; (*TV*) **the ~s** les chaînes; *see* **old**. 2 vt (*Rad, TV*) diffuser sur l'ensemble du réseau; (*Comput*) interconnecter.

networking [ˈnetˌwɜːkɪŋ] n (*Comm*) maillage *m* de réseau; (*Comput*) gestion *f* de réseau.

neural [ˈnjʊərəl] adj neural.

neuralgia [njʊˈrældʒə] n névralgie *f*.

neuralgic [njʊˈrældʒɪk] adj névralgique.

neurasthenia [ˌnjʊərəsˈθiːnɪə] n neurasthénie *f*.

neurasthenic [ˌnjʊərəsˈθenɪk] adj, n neurasthénique *(mf)*.

neuritis [njʊəˈraɪtɪs] n névrite *f*.

neuro... [ˈnjʊərəʊ] pref neuro..., névro... .

neurogenic [ˌnjʊərəʊˈdʒenɪk] adj neurogène.

neurological [ˌnjʊərəˈlɒdʒɪkəl] adj neurologique.

neurologist [njʊəˈrɒlədʒɪst] n neurologue *mf*.

neurology [njʊəˈrɒlədʒɪ] n neurologie *f*.

neuroma [njʊˈrəʊmə] n, pl **~s** *or* **neuromata** [njʊˈrəʊmətə] névrome *m*, neurome *m*.

neuromuscular [ˌnjʊərəʊˈmʌskjʊləʳ] adj neuromusculaire.

neuron [ˈnjʊərɒn] n neurone *m*.

neuropath [ˈnjʊərəpæθ] n névropathe *mf*.

neuropathic [njʊərəˈpæθɪk] adj névropathique.

neuropathology [ˌnjʊərəʊpəˈθɒlədʒɪ] n neuropathologie *f*.

neuropathy [njʊˈrɒpəθɪ] n névropathie *f*.

neurophysiological [ˌnjʊərəʊˌfɪzɪəˈlɒdʒɪkəl] adj neurophysiologique.

neurophysiologist [ˌnjʊərəʊˌfɪzɪˈɒlədʒɪst] n neurophysiologiste *mf*.

neurophysiology [ˌnjʊərəʊˌfɪzɪˈɒlədʒɪ] n neurophysiologie *f*.

neuropsychiatric [ˌnjʊərəʊˌsaɪkɪˈætrɪk] adj neuropsychiatrique.

neuropsychiatrist [ˌnjʊərəʊsaɪˈkaɪətrɪst] n neuropsychiatre *mf*.

neuropsychiatry [ˌnjʊərəʊsaɪˈkaɪətrɪ] n neuropsychiatrie *f*.

neurosis [njʊˈrəʊsɪs] n, pl **neuroses** [njʊˈrəʊsiːz] névrose *f*.

neurosurgeon [ˌnjʊərəʊˈsɜːdʒən] n neurochirurgien(ne) *m(f)*.

neurosurgery [ˌnjʊərəʊˈsɜːdʒərɪ] n neurochirurgie *f*.

neurosurgical [ˌnjʊərəʊˈsɜːdʒɪkəl] adj neurochirurgique.

neurotic [njʊˈrɒtɪk] 1 adj *person* névrosé; *disease, disturbance* névrotique. (*fig*) **she's getting quite ~ about slimming** son désir de maigrir prend des proportions de névrose; **he's getting ~ about the whole business** il fait une véritable maladie de toute cette histoire, ça devient une obsession chez lui. 2 n névrosé(e) *m(f)*, névropathe *mf*.

neurotically [njʊˈrɒtɪkəlɪ] adv de façon obsessionnelle, jusqu'à la névrose.

neuroticism [njʊˈrɒtɪsɪzəm] n tendances *fpl* à la névrose.

neurotomy [njʊˈrɒtəmɪ] n neurotomie *f*.

neurotransmitter [ˌnjʊərəʊtrænzˈmɪtəʳ] n neurotransmetteur *m*.

neurovascular [ˈnjʊrəʊˈvæskʊləʳ] adj neurovasculaire.

neuter [ˈnjuːtəʳ] 1 adj a neutre. b (*Bot, Zool*) neutre; (*Zool: castrated*) châtré. 2 n a (*Gram*) neutre *m*. **in the ~** au neutre. b (*Zool*) animal châtré. 3 vt (*Vet*) châtrer.

neutral [ˈnjuːtrəl] 1 adj (*all senses, also Phon*) neutre. **to remain ~** garder la neutralité, rester neutre; (*Pol*) **the ~ powers** les puissances *fpl* neutres; **~ policy** politique *f* neutraliste *or* de neutralité. 2 n a (*Pol*) habitant(e) *m(f)* d'un pays neutre. b (*Aut*) point mort. **to put the gear in ~** mettre l'embrayage au point mort; **the car** *or* **the engine was in ~** la voiture était au point mort.

neutralism [ˈnjuːtrəlɪzəm] n neutralisme *m*.

neutralist [ˈnjuːtrəlɪst] adj, n neutraliste *(mf)*.

neutrality [njuːˈtrælɪtɪ] n (*gen, Chem, Pol etc*) neutralité *f*; *see* **armed**.

neutralization [ˌnjuːtrəlaɪˈzeɪʃən] n neutralisation *f*.

neutralize [ˈnjuːtrəlaɪz] vt neutraliser.

neutrino [njuːˈtriːnəʊ] n neutrino *m*.

neutron [ˈnjuːtrɒn] n neutron *m*. **~ bomb** bombe *f* à neutrons; **~ number** nombre *m* de neutrons; **~ star** étoile *f* à neutrons.

Nevada [nɪˈvɑːdə] n Nevada *m*. **in ~** dans le Nevada.

never [ˈnevəʳ] 1 adv a (ne ...) jamais. **I ~ eat it** je n'en mange jamais; **I have ~ seen him** je ne l'ai jamais vu; **I've ~ seen him before** je ne l'ai jamais vu (jusqu'à aujourd'hui); **I'd ~ seen him before** je ne l'avais jamais vu auparavant; **~ before had there been such a disaster** jamais on n'avait connu tel désastre; **he will ~ come back** il ne reviendra jamais *or* plus (jamais); **~ again!** jamais plus!, plus jamais!; ~

say that again ne répète jamais ça; **we shall ~ see her again** on ne la reverra (plus) jamais; **I have ~ yet been able to find ...** je n'ai encore jamais pu trouver ..., jusqu'ici je n'ai jamais pu trouver ...; **~ in all my life** jamais de ma vie; **I ~ heard such a thing!** (de ma vie) je n'ai jamais entendu une telle histoire!; *see* **now**.

b (*emphatic*) **that will ~ do!** c'est inadmissible!; **I ~ slept a wink** je n'ai pas fermé l'œil; **he ~ so much as smiled** il n'a pas même souri; **he ~ said a word,** (*liter*) **he said ~ a word** il n'a pas dit le moindre mot, il n'a pas soufflé mot; **~ a one** pas un seul; **~ was a child more loved** jamais enfant ne fut plus aimé; **(surely) you've ~ left it behind!*** ne me dites pas que vous l'avez oublié!; **I've left it behind! — ~!** je l'ai oublié! — ça n'est pas vrai! *or* pas possible!; **you must ~ ever come here again*** tu ne dois jamais plus revenir ici; **well I ~ (did)!*** (ça) par exemple!, pas possible!, mince alors!*; **~ mind!** ça ne fait rien!, ne vous en faites pas!; **~ fear!** n'ayez pas peur!, soyez tranquille!

2 **comp** ►**never-ending** qui n'en finit plus, sans fin, interminable ►**never-failing** *method* infaillible; *source, spring* inépuisable, intarissable ►**nevermore** ne ... plus jamais, ne ... jamais plus; **nevermore!** jamais plus!, plus jamais! ►**never-never:** (*Brit*) **to buy on the never-never*** acheter à crédit *or* à tempérament; **never-never land** pays *m* imaginaire *or* de légende *or* de cocagne ►**never-outs** (*Comm*) articles *mpl* toujours en stock ►**nevertheless** *see* **nevertheless** ►**never-to-be-forgotten** inoubliable, qu'on n'oubliera jamais.

nevertheless [ˌnevəðəˈles] **adv** néanmoins, toutefois, quand même, (et) pourtant, cependant, malgré tout. **it is ~ true that ...** il est néanmoins *or* toutefois *or* quand même *or* pourtant *or* cependant *or* malgré tout vrai que ...; **I shall go ~** j'irai quand même *or* malgré tout, et pourtant j'irai; **he is ~ my brother** c'est quand même mon frère, malgré tout c'est mon frère; **she has had no news, (yet) ~ she goes on hoping** elle n'a pas reçu de nouvelles, et pourtant *or* et malgré tout elle continue à espérer.

nevus [ˈniːvəs] **n** (*US*) = **naevus.**

new [njuː] 1 **adj** a (*not previously known etc*) nouveau (*before vowel* nouvel, *f* nouvelle); (*brand-new*) neuf (*f* neuve); (*different*) nouveau, autre. **I've got a ~ car** (*different*) j'ai une nouvelle *or* une autre voiture; (*brand-new*) j'ai une voiture neuve; **he has written a ~ book/article** il a écrit un nouveau livre/un nouvel article; **this is X's ~ book** c'est le nouveau *or* dernier livre de X; **I've got a ~ library book** j'ai emprunté un nouveau livre à la bibliothèque; **~ potatoes** pommes (de terre) nouvelles; **~ carrots** carottes *fpl* de primeur *or* nouvelles; **there are several ~ plays on in London** on donne plusieurs nouvelles pièces à Londres; **~ fashion** dernière *or* nouvelle mode; **~ theory/invention** nouvelle théorie/invention; **the ~ moon** la nouvelle lune; **there's a ~ moon tonight** c'est la nouvelle lune ce soir; **I need a ~ notebook** il me faut un nouveau carnet *or* un carnet neuf; **don't get your ~ shoes wet** ne mouille pas tes chaussures neuves; **dressed in ~ clothes** vêtu *or* habillé de neuf; **as good as ~** comme neuf, à l'état de neuf; **he made the bike as good as ~** il a remis le vélo à neuf; **"as ~"** "état neuf"; **I don't like all these ~ paintings** je n'aime pas tous ces tableaux modernes; **I've got several ~ ideas** j'ai plusieurs idées nouvelles *or* neuves; **this idea is not ~** ce n'est pas une idée nouvelle *or* neuve; **the ~ nations** les pays neufs; **a ~ town** une ville nouvelle; **this is a completely ~ subject** c'est un sujet tout à fait neuf; **this sort of work is ~ to me** ce genre de travail est (quelque chose de) nouveau pour moi; **I'm ~ to this kind of work** je n'ai jamais fait ce genre de travail, je suis novice dans ce genre de travail; **he came ~ to the firm last year** il est arrivé dans la compagnie l'an dernier; **he's ~ to the trade** il est nouveau *or* novice dans le métier; **he's quite ~ to the town** il est tout nouvellement arrivé dans la ville; **the ~ people at number 5** les nouveaux habitants du *or* au 5; **~ recruit** nouvelle recrue, bleu* *m*; **the ~ students** les nouveaux *mpl*, les nouvelles *fpl*; (*Scol*) **a ~ boy** un nouveau; (*Scol*) **a ~ girl** une nouvelle; **she's ~, poor thing** elle est nouvelle, la pauvre; **are you ~ here?** (*gen*) vous venez d'arriver ici?; (*in school, firm etc*) vous êtes nouveau ici?; **the ~ woman** la femme moderne; **the ~ diplomacy** la diplomatie nouvelle manière *or* moderne; **~ style** nouveau style (*see also* **3**); (*Pol*) **the N~ Left** la nouvelle gauche (des années 60); **the ~ rich** les nouveaux riches; **bring me a ~ glass for this one is dirty** apportez-moi un autre verre car celui-ci est sale; **there was a ~ waiter today** il y avait un autre *or* un nouveau serveur aujourd'hui; (*fig*) **he's a ~ man since he remarried** il est transformé depuis qu'il s'est remarié (*see also* **3**); (*Prov*) **there's nothing ~ under the sun** il n'y a rien de nouveau sous le soleil (*Prov*); **that's nothing ~!** ce *or* ça n'est pas nouveau!, il n'y a rien de neuf là-dedans!; **that's a ~ one on me!*** première nouvelle!*, on en apprend tous les jours! (*iro*); **that's something ~!** ça c'est nouveau!; **what's ~?*** quoi de neuf?; *see also* **3** *and* **brand, broom, leaf, split** *etc*.

b (*fresh*) *bread* frais (*f* fraîche); *milk* frais, fraîchement trait; *cheese* frais, pas (encore) fait; *wine* nouveau (*f* nouvelle), jeune.

2 **adv** (*gen in comps*) frais, nouvellement, récemment. **he's ~ out of college** il est frais émoulu du collège, il sort tout juste du collège; *see* **3**.

3 **comp** ►**New Age n** nouvel âge *m*, New Age *m* ◊ **adj** nouvel âge *inv*, New Age *inv* ►**newborn** nouveau-né(e) *m(f)*; **the newborn** les nouveaux-nés *mpl* ►**new-built** nouvellement construit, tout neuf (*f* toute neuve) ►**New Brunswick** New Brunswick *m* ►**New Caledonia** Nouvelle-Calédonie *f* ►**New Canadian** Néo-Canadien(ne) *m(f)* ►**newcomer** nouveau venu *m*, nouvelle venue *f*, nouvel(le) arrivé(e) *m(f)*, nouvel(le) arrivant(e) *m(f)*; **they are newcomers to this town** ce sont des nouveaux venus dans cette ville ►**New Delhi** New Delhi ►**New England** Nouvelle-Angleterre *f* ►**New English Bible** *nouvelle traduction anglaise de la Bible* ►**new-fangled** (*pej*) trop moderne, nouveau genre ►**new-found** *happiness etc* de fraîche date ►**Newfoundland** *see* **Newfoundland** ►**New Guinea** Nouvelle-Guinée *f* ►**New Hampshire** New Hampshire *m*; **in New Hampshire** dans le New Hampshire ►**New Hebrides** Nouvelles-Hébrides *fpl* ►**New Jersey** New Jersey *m*; **in New Jersey** dans le New Jersey ►**New Jerusalem** Nouvelle Jérusalem *f* ►**new-laid egg** œuf *m* du jour *or* tout frais (pondu) ►**New Latin** latin *m* moderne ►**new look** new-look *m* ►**new-look adj** new-look *inv* ►**New Man** ≃ homme *m* actuel *or* idéal *or* parfait, ≃ homme *m* au foyer (*qui partage les taches ménagères, s'occupe des enfants etc*) ►**new maths** mathématiques *fpl or* maths* *fpl* modernes ►**New Mexico** Nouveau-Mexique *m*; **to New Mexico** au Nouveau-Mexique; **in New Mexico** dans le Nouveau-Mexique ►**new-mown** *grass* frais coupé; *hay* frais fauché ►**New Orleans** la Nouvelle-Orléans ►**new product development** (*Comm*) développement *m* de nouveaux produits ►**New Scotland Yard** Scotland Yard *m* (≃ *le Quai des Orfèvres*) ►**New South Wales** Nouvelle-Galles *f* du Sud ►**newspeak** novlangue *m* ►**new(-style):** **the new(-style) calendar** le nouveau calendrier, le calendrier grégorien ►**New Testament** Nouveau Testament ►**New Wave adj** *film* de la Nouvelle vague; *music* de la New Wave ◊ **n** (*Cine*) Nouvelle Vague *f*; (*Mus*) New Wave *f* ►**the New World** le Nouveau Monde; (*Mus*) **the New World Symphony, the Symphony from the New World** la Symphonie du Nouveau Monde ►**New Year** *see* **New Year** ►**New York n** (*state*) (état *m* de) New York *m*; (*city*) New York ◊ **adj** new-yorkais; **in New York (State)** dans l'État de New York ►**New Yorker** New-Yorkais(e) *m(f)* ►**New Zealand n** Nouvelle-Zélande *f* ◊ **adj** néo-zélandais ►**New Zealander** Néo-Zélandais(e) *m(f)*.

newel [ˈnjuːəl] **n** noyau *m* (d'escalier).

Newfoundland [ˈnjuːfən*d*lənd] 1 **n** Terre-Neuve *f*. 2 **adj** terre-neuvien. **~ dog** chien *m* de Terre-Neuve, terre-neuve *m inv*; **~ fisherman** terre-neuvas *m*.

Newfoundlander [njuːˈfaʊndləndəʳ] **n** habitant(e) *m(f)* de Terre-Neuve, Terre-Neuvien(ne) *m(f)*.

newish [ˈnjuːɪʃ] **adj** assez neuf (*f* neuve), assez nouveau (*f* nouvelle).

newly [ˈnjuːlɪ] 1 **adv** nouvellement, récemment, fraîchement. **~ arrived** nouvellement *or* récemment *or* fraîchement arrivé; **~ shaved** rasé de frais; **the ~-elected members** les membres nouvellement élus, les nouveaux élus; **~-formed friendship** amitié *f* de fraîche date; **~-found happiness** bonheur tout neuf; **her ~-awakened curiosity** sa curiosité récemment éveillée; **~ rich** nouveau riche; **~ made** neuf (*f* neuve), nouveau (*f* nouvelle), de fabrication toute récente; **a ~-dug grave** une tombe fraîchement creusée *or* ouverte. 2 **comp** ►**newly-weds** jeunes *or* nouveaux mariés *mpl*.

newness [ˈnjuːnɪs] **n** *[fashion, ideas etc]* nouveauté *f*; *[clothes etc]* état *m* (de) neuf; *[person]* inexpérience *f*; *[bread]* fraîcheur *f*; *[cheese]* manque *m* de maturité; *[wine]* jeunesse *f*.

news [njuːz] 1 **n** (*NonC*) a nouvelle(s) *f(pl)*. **a piece** *or* **an item of ~** (*gen*) une nouvelle; (*Press*) une information; **have you heard the ~?** vous connaissez la nouvelle?; **have you heard the ~ about John?** vous savez ce qui est arrivé à Jean?; **have you any ~ of him?** avez-vous de ses nouvelles?; **I have no ~ of her** je n'ai pas de ses nouvelles, je n'ai pas de nouvelles d'elle; **do let me have your ~** surtout donnez-moi de vos nouvelles; **what's your ~?** quoi de neuf *or* de nouveau (chez vous)?; **is there any ~?** y a-t-il du nouveau?; **I've got ~ for you!** j'ai du nouveau à vous annoncer!; **this is ~ to me!** première nouvelle!*, on en apprend tous les jours! (*iro*); **it will be ~ to him that we are here** ça va le surprendre de nous savoir ici; **good ~** bonnes nouvelles; **bad** *or* **sad ~** mauvaises *or* tristes nouvelles; **he's/it's bad ~*** on a toujours des ennuis avec lui/ça; **to make ~** faire parler de soi; **she/it made ~** on a parlé d'elle/on en a parlé dans le journal; (*loc*) **bad ~ travels fast** les malheurs s'apprennent vite; **no ~ is good ~!** pas de nouvelles, bonnes nouvelles! (*loc*); **when the ~ broke** quand on a su la nouvelle; **"dog bites man" isn't ~** "un homme mordu par un chien" n'est pas (ce qu'on peut appeler) une nouvelle; (*fig*) **he's in the ~ again** le voilà qui refait parler de lui; *see* **break**.

b (*Press, Rad, TV*) informations *fpl*; (*Cine, TV*) actualités *fpl*. **I missed the ~ (broadcast** *or* **bulletin)** j'ai raté les informations *or* le bulletin d'informations *or* les actualités; **official ~** communiqué officiel; **financial/sporting** *etc* **~** chronique *or* rubrique financière/sportive *etc*; (*Press*) **"N~ in Brief"** "Nouvelles brèves"; (*name of paper*) **"Birmingham N~"** "Nouvelles de Birmingham".

2 **comp** ►**news agency** agence *f* de presse ►**newsagent** (*Brit*) marchand(e) *m(f)* de *or* dépositaire *mf* de journaux ►**newsagent's (shop)** (*Brit*) maison *f* de la presse ►**news analyst** (*US: Rad, TV*) commentateur *m* ►**news blackout** blackout *m* ►**newsboard** (*US*) carton *m* gris ►**newsboy** vendeur *m or* crieur *m* de journaux ►**newsbreak** (*US*) nouvelle *f* digne d'intérêt ►**news bulletin,** (*US*) **news-**

cast (*Rad*) (bulletin *m* d')informations *fpl*; (*TV*) actualités *fpl* (télévisées) ▸ **newscaster** (*Rad, TV*) présentateur *m*, -trice *f* ▸ **newsclip** (*US Press*) coupure *f* de journal ▸ **news conference** conférence *f* de presse ▸ **newsdealer** (*US*) = **newsagent** ▸ **news desk** service *m* des informations ▸ **news editor** rédacteur *m* ▸ **news film** film *m* d'actualités ▸ **news flash** flash *m* (d'information) ▸ **newshawk** = **newshound** ▸ **news headlines** titres *mpl* de l'actualité ▸ **newshound** reporter *m*; (*pej*) **there was a crowd of newshounds around him** il y avait une meute de journalistes acharnés après lui ▸ **news item** (*Press etc*) information *f* ▸ **newsletter** bulletin *m* (*de société, de compagnie etc*) ▸ **news magazine** magazine *m* d'actualités ▸ **newsmaker** (*US*) (*event*) sujet *m* d'actualité; (*person*) vedette *f* de l'actualité ▸ **newsman** journaliste *m* ▸ **newsmonger** (*pej*) colporteur *m*, -euse *f* de ragots *or* de potins ▸ **newspaper** *see* **newspaper** ▸ **news photographer** reporter *m* photographe ▸ **news pictures** reportage *m* photographique ▸ **newsprint** (*NonC*) papier *m* de journal, papier journal ▸ **newsreader** (*Brit: Rad, TV*) présentateur *m*, -trice *f* ▸ **newsreel** actualités *fpl* (filmées) ▸ **newsroom** (*Press*) salle *f* de rédaction; (*Rad, TV*) studio *m* ▸ **news service** agence *f* de presse ▸ **news sheet** feuille *f* d'informations ▸ **news stand** (*US*) kiosque *m* (à journaux) ▸ **news theatre** cinéma *m or* salle *f* d'actualités ▸ **news value: to have news value** présenter un intérêt pour le public ▸ **newsvendor** vendeur *m* de journaux ▸ **news weekly** hebdomadaire *m* d'actualités ▸ **newsworthy: to be newsworthy** valoir la peine d'être publié.

newspaper ['nju:z,peɪpəʳ] 1 n journal *m*; (*minor*) feuille *f*. **daily ~** (journal) quotidien *m*; **weekly ~** (journal) hebdomadaire *m*; **he works on a ~** il travaille pour un journal. 2 comp ▸ **newspaper advertising** publicité-presse *f* ▸ **newspaper clippings, newspaper cuttings** coupures *fpl* de journaux *or* de presse ▸ **newspaperman** journaliste *m* ▸ **newspaper office** (bureaux *mpl* de la) rédaction *f* ▸ **newspaper photographer** reporter *m* photographe ▸ **newspaper report** reportage *m* ▸ **newspaperwoman** journaliste *f*.

newsy* ['nju:zɪ] adj a (*full of news*) plein de nouvelles. b (*US*) = **newsworthy**.

newt [nju:t] n triton *m*.

newton ['nju:tən] n newton *m*.

Newtonian [nju:'təʊnɪən] adj newtonien.

New Year ['nju:'jɪəʳ] 1 n nouvel an, nouvelle année. **to bring in** *or* **see in the ~** faire le réveillon (de la Saint-Sylvestre *or* du jour de l'an), réveillonner (à la Saint-Sylvestre); **Happy ~!** bonne année!; **to wish sb a happy ~** souhaiter une *or* la bonne année à qn. 2 comp ▸ **New Year gift** étrennes *fpl* ▸ **New Year resolution** résolution *f* de nouvel an ▸ **New Year's Day** jour *m or* premier *m* de l'an, nouvel an ▸ **New Year's Eve** la Saint-Sylvestre; *see* **honour**.

next [nekst] 1 adj a (*in time*) (*in future*) prochain; (*in past*) suivant. **come back ~ week/month** revenez la semaine prochaine/le mois prochain; **he came back the ~ week** il revint la semaine suivante *or* d'après; **he came back the ~ day** il revint le lendemain *or* le jour suivant *or* le jour d'après; **the ~ day but one** le surlendemain; **during the ~ 5 days he did not go out** il n'est pas sorti pendant les 5 jours suivants *or* qui ont suivi; **I will finish this in the ~ 5 days** je finirai ceci dans les 5 jours qui viennent *or* à venir; **the ~ morning** le lendemain matin; **(the) ~ time I see him** la prochaine fois que je le verrai; **the ~ time I saw him** la première fois où *or* que je l'ai revu, quand je l'ai revu; **I'll come back ~ week and the ~ again** je reviendrai la semaine prochaine et la suivante; **this time ~ week** d'ici huit jours; **the ~ moment** l'instant d'après; **from one moment to the ~** d'un moment à l'autre; **the year after ~** dans deux ans.

b (*in series, list etc*) (*following*) *page, case* suivant; (*which is to come*) prochain. **he got off at the ~ stop** il est descendu à l'arrêt suivant; **you get off at the ~ stop** vous descendez au prochain arrêt; **who's ~?** à qui le tour?, c'est à qui?; **you're ~** c'est votre tour, c'est à vous (maintenant); **~ please!** au suivant!; **I was the ~ person** *or* **I was ~ to speak** ce fut ensuite à mon tour de parler (*see also* **4a**); **I'll ask the very ~ person I see** je vais demander à la première personne que je verrai; **in the ~ place** ensuite; **on the ~ page** à la page suivante; **"continued in the ~ column"** "voir colonne ci-contre"; **the ~ thing to do is ...** la première chose à faire maintenant est de ...; **he saw that the ~ thing to do was ...** il vit que ce qu'il devait faire ensuite (c')était ...; **the ~ thing (I knew), he had gone*** ensuite, tout ce que je sais, c'est qu'il n'était plus là; **I'll try the ~ size** je vais essayer la taille au-dessus; **the ~ size down** la taille au-dessous.

c (*immediately adjacent*) *house, street, room* d'à côté, à côté, voisin.

2 adv a ensuite, après; la prochaine fois. **~ we had lunch** ensuite *or* après nous avons déjeuné; **what shall we do ~?** qu'allons-nous faire maintenant?; **when ~ you come to see us** la prochaine fois que vous viendrez nous voir; **when I ~ saw him** quand je l'ai revu (la fois suivante); **when shall we meet ~?** quand nous reverrons-nous?; **a new dress! what ~?** une nouvelle robe! et puis quoi encore?

b **the ~ best thing would be to speak to his brother** à défaut le mieux serait de parler à son frère; **she's my ~ best friend** à part une autre c'est ma meilleure amie; **this is my ~ oldest daughter after Mary** c'est la plus âgée de mes filles après Marie; **she's the ~ youngest** elle suit (par ordre d'âge); **who's the ~ tallest boy?** qui est le plus grand après?; **I come ~ after you** (*in shop etc*) je viens après vous.

c **~ to** (*beside*) auprès de, à côté de; (*almost*) presque; **his room is ~ (to) mine** sa chambre est à côté de *or* contiguë à *or* attenante à la mienne; **the church stands ~ (to) the school** l'église est à côté de l'école; **he was sitting ~ (to) me** il était assis à côté de moi *or* auprès de moi; **to wear wool ~ (to) the skin** porter de la laine sur la peau *or* à même la peau; **the thing ~ (to) my heart** la chose qui me tient le plus à cœur; **~ to France, what country do you like best?** après la France, quel est votre pays préféré?; (*US*) **to get ~ to sb**⁑ se mettre bien* avec qn; **the ~ to last row** l'avant-dernier *or* le pénultième rang; **he was ~ to last** il était avant-dernier; **~ to nothing** presque rien; **I got it for ~ to nothing** je l'ai payé trois fois rien; **~ to nobody** presque personne; **there's ~ to no news** il n'y a presque rien de neuf; **the ~ to top/bottom shelf** le deuxième rayon (en partant) du haut/du bas.

3 prep (*Brit*) près de, auprès de, à côté de; *see* **2c**.

4 n a prochain(e) *m(f)*. **the ~ to speak is Paul** c'est Paul qui parle ensuite, c'est Paul qui est le prochain à parler; **the ~ to arrive was Robert** c'est Robert qui est arrivé ensuite *or* le suivant; (*baby*) **I hope my ~* will be a boy** j'espère que mon prochain (enfant) sera un garçon.

b **to be continued in our ~** suite au prochain numéro.

5 comp ▸ **next door** *see* **next door** ▸ **"next-of-kin"** (*on forms etc*) "nom et prénom de votre plus proche parent"; **who is your next-of-kin?** qui est votre plus proche parent?; **the police will inform the next-of-kin** la police préviendra la famille.

next door ['neks'dɔ:ʳ] 1 n la maison d'à côté. **it's the man from ~** c'est le monsieur d'à côté *or* qui habite à côté.

2 adv a **they live ~ to us** ils habitent à côté de chez nous, ils habitent la maison voisine (de la nôtre); **we live ~ to each other** nous habitons porte à porte; **the boy/girl ~** le garçon/la fille d'à côté *or* qui habite à côté; **despite her wealth she's just like the girl ~** malgré sa fortune elle est restée très simple; **the people/house ~** les gens/la maison d'à côté; **at the table ~***à la table d'à côté.

b (*fig*) **that is ~ to madness** cela frise la folie; **if he isn't mad he's ~ to it** s'il n'est pas fou il s'en faut de peu *or* c'est tout comme*; **we were ~ to being ruined** nous avons été au bord de la ruine, nous avons frôlé la ruine.

3 **next-door** adj: **next-door house** maison voisine *or* d'à côté; **next-door neighbour** voisin(e) *m(f)* (d'à côté).

nexus ['neksəs] n, pl inv connection *f*, liaison *f*, lien *m*.

NF [en'ef] n (*Brit Pol*) (abbr of **National Front**) *see* **national**.

n/f (*Banking*) (abbr of **no funds**) défaut de provision.

NFL [enef'el] n (*US*) (abbr of **National Football League**) Fédération *f* américaine de football.

N.F.U. [enef'ju:] n (*Brit*) (abbr of **National Farmers' Union**) *syndicat*.

NG [en'dʒi:] n (*US*) (abbr of **National Guard**) *see* **national**.

N.G.A. [,endʒi:'eɪ] n (*Brit*) (abbr of **National Graphical Association**) *syndicat*.

NGO [,endʒi:'əʊ] n abbr of **non-governmental organization**.

NH (*US*) abbr of **New Hampshire**.

NHL [,enaɪtʃ'el] n (*US*) (abbr of **National Hockey League**) Fédération américaine de hockey sur glace.

N.H.S. [,eneɪtʃ'es] n (*Brit*) (abbr of **National Health Service**) *see* **national**.

N.I. a (*Brit Post*) (abbr of **Northern Ireland**) *see* **northern**. b (*Brit*) (abbr of **National Insurance**) *see* **national**.

niacin ['naɪəsɪn] n acide *m* nicotinique.

Niagara [naɪ'ægrə] n Niagara *m*. **~ Falls** les chutes *fpl* du Niagara.

nib [nɪb] n a *[pen]* (bec *m* de) plume *f*. **fine ~** plume fine *or* à bec fin; **broad ~** grosse plume, plume à gros bec. b *[tool]* pointe *f*.

-nibbed [nɪbd] adj ending in comps: **fine-nibbed** à plume fine; **gold-nibbed** à plume en or.

nibble ['nɪbl] 1 vti (*gen*) grignoter, mordiller; *[sheep, goats etc]* brouter; *[fish]* mordre, mordiller. (*fig*) **to ~ (at) an offer** se montrer tenté par une offre; **to ~ (at) one's food** chipoter; **she was nibbling (at) some chocolate** elle grignotait un morceau de chocolat. 2 n a (*Fishing*) touche *f*. b (⁑) **I feel like a ~** je grignoterais bien quelque chose.

nibs [nɪbz] n (*hum*) **his ~**⁑ Son Altesse (*iro*), sézigue*.

NICAM ['naɪkæm] (abbr of **near-instantaneous companded audio multiplex**) NICAM.

Nicaragua [,nɪkə'rægjʊə] n Nicaragua *m*.

Nicaraguan [,nɪkə'rægjʊən] 1 adj nicaraguayen. 2 n Nicaraguayen(ne) *m(f)*.

nice [naɪs] 1 adj a (*pleasant*) *person* agréable, aimable, gentil, charmant, sympathique, sympa* *inv*; *holiday, weather* beau (*f* belle), agréable; *dress, smile, voice* joli, charmant; *view, visit* charmant, agréable; *meal* bon, délicieux; *smell, taste* bon, agréable; (*iro*) joli, beau. **that's a ~ ring/photo** elle est jolie *or* belle, cette bague/photo; **what a ~ face she's got** quel joli *or* charmant visage elle a; **how ~ you look!** vous êtes vraiment bien!; **Barcombe's a ~ place** Barcombe est un coin agréable; **Paris is a ~ place** Paris est un endroit agréable; **be ~ to him** soyez gentil *or* aimable avec lui; **that wasn't ~ of you** vous n'avez pas été gentil *or* aimable; **we had a ~ evening** nous avons passé une bonne soirée *or* une soirée agréable; **they had a ~ time** ils se sont bien amusés; **to say ~ things** dire des choses aimables *or* gentilles, dire des gentillesses; **how ~ of you to ...** comme c'est gentil *or* aimable à vous de ...; **it's ~ here** on est bien ici; (*lit, iro*) **~ one!*** bien joué!*, bravo!, félicitations!; (*iro*) **here's a ~ state of affairs!** (eh bien) voilà du joli!; (*iro*) **you're in a ~ mess** vous voilà dans un beau *or* joli pétrin, vous voilà dans de beaux *or* jolis draps; (*iro*) **that's a ~ way to talk!** c'est du joli ce que vous dites là!

b (*intensive*) **~ and warm** bien chaud; **~ and easy** très facile, tout à fait facile; **~ and sweet** bien sucré; **to have a ~ cold drink** boire quelque chose de bien frais; **he gets ~ long holidays** ce qui est bien c'est qu'il a de longues vacances.

c (*respectable, refined*) convenable, bien *inv*, comme il faut. **not ~** peu convenable, pas beau* (*f* belle); **she's a ~ girl** c'est une jeune fille (très) bien *or* très comme il faut*; **our neighbours are not very ~ people** nos voisins ne sont pas des gens très bien; **the play/film/book was not very ~** la pièce/le film/le livre n'était pas très convenable.

d (*hard to please*) *person* difficile, méticuleux; (*tricky*) *job, task* délicat; (*subtle*) *distinction, shade of meaning* délicat, subtil (*f* subtile). **she's not very ~ in her methods** elle n'a pas beaucoup de scrupules quant à ses méthodes; **to be ~ about one's food** être difficile *or* exigeant pour *or* sur la nourriture; **~ point** point délicat, question délicate *or* subtile; **he has a ~ taste in ...** il a un goût fin *or* raffiné en ... .

2 comp ▸**nice-looking** joli, beau (*f* belle); **he's nice-looking** il est joli garçon *or* beau garçon.

nicely ['naɪslɪ] adv a (*kindly*) gentiment, aimablement; (*pleasantly*) agréablement, joliment, bien. **a ~ situated house** une maison bien *or* agréablement située; **we are ~ placed to judge what has been going on** nous sommes parfaitement bien placés pour juger de ce qui s'est passé; **~ done** bien fait; **that will do ~** cela fera très bien l'affaire; **he's doing very ~ (for himself)** il s'en sort* *or* se débrouille* très bien; **~, thank you** très bien merci; **the child behaved very ~** l'enfant s'est très bien conduit *or* a été très gentil. b (*carefully*) minutieusement; (*exactly*) exactement.

Nicene ['naɪsiːn] adj: **the ~ Creed** le Credo *or* le symbole de Nicée.

niceness ['naɪsnɪs] n a (*pleasantness*) *[person]* gentillesse *f*, amabilité *f*; *[place, thing]* agrément *m*, caractère *m* agréable. b (*fastidiousness*) délicatesse *f*; (*punctiliousness*) caractère *or* côté méticuleux; *[distinction, taste etc]* subtilité *f*, finesse *f*; *[experiment, point etc]* délicatesse.

nicety ['naɪsɪtɪ] n a (*of one's judgment*) exactitude *f*, justesse *f*, précision *f*. **a point of great ~** une question très délicate *or* subtile; **to a ~** à la perfection, exactement, à point. b **niceties** (*subtleties*) finesses *fpl*; (*refinements*) raffinements *mpl*.

niche [niːʃ] n (*Archit*) niche *f*; (*Comm*) créneau *m*. (*fig*) **he found his ~ (in life)** il a trouvé sa voie (dans la vie); (*Comm*) **~ marketing** marketing *m* du créneau.

Nicholas ['nɪkələs] n Nicolas *m*.

Nick [nɪk] n (**dim of Nicholas**) **Old ~** le diable, le malin.

nick [nɪk] 1 n a (*in wood*) encoche *f*; (*in blade, dish*) ébréchure *f*; (*on face, skin*) entaille *f*, coupure *f*. (*fig*) **in the ~ of time** juste à temps.

b (*Brit: Prison etc sl*) taule‡ *f or* tôle‡ *f*. **to be in the ~** être en taule‡, faire de la taule‡.

c (*Brit* ‡: *condition*) état *m*, condition *f*. **in good ~**‡ en bon état, en bonne condition, impec‡; **in terrible ~** en très mauvais état, nase‡.

2 vt a *plank, stick* entailler, faire une *or* des encoche(s) sur; *blade, dish* ébrécher; *cards* biseauter. **he ~ed his chin while shaving** il s'est fait une entaille *or* une coupure au menton en se rasant.

b (*Brit* ‡: *arrest*) pincer*, choper‡. **to get ~ed** se faire pincer* *or* choper‡.

c (*Brit* ‡: *steal*) piquer‡, faucher‡, barboter‡.

d (*US*) **how much did they ~ you for that suit?**‡ tu t'es fait avoir* de combien pour *or* sur ce costume?

nickel ['nɪkl] 1 n a (*NonC*) nickel *m*. b (*Can, US: coin*) pièce *f* de cinq cents. 2 comp ▸**nickel-in-the-slot machine** (*US* †) appareil *m* à sous ▸**nickel-plated** nickelé ▸**nickel silver** argentan *m*, maillechort *m*. 3 vt nickeler.

nickelodeon [ˌnɪkə'ləʊdɪən] n (*US*) (*cinema*) cinéma *m* à cinq sous; (*jukebox*) juke-box *m*.

nicker ['nɪkəʳ] 1 vi a *[horse]* hennir doucement. b (*snigger*) ricaner. 2 n, pl inv (*Brit* ‡) livre *f* (sterling).

nickname ['nɪkneɪm] 1 n surnom *m*; (*esp humorous or malicious*) sobriquet *m*; (*short form of name*) diminutif *m*. 2 vt surnommer, donner un sobriquet à. **John, ~d "Taffy"** John, surnommé "Taffy"; **they ~d their teacher "Goggles"** ils ont surnommé leur professeur "Carreaux"; ils ont donné à leur professeur le sobriquet (de) "Carreaux".

Nicodemus [ˌnɪkə'diːmʊs] n Nicodème *m*.

Nicosia [nɪkə'siːə] n Nicosie.

nicotiana [nɪˌkəʊʃɪ'ɑːnə] n nicotiana *m*.

nicotine ['nɪkətiːn] 1 n nicotine *f*. 2 comp ▸**nicotine poisoning** nicotinisme *m* ▸**nicotine-stained** jauni *or* taché de nicotine.

nicotinic [nɪkə'tɪnɪk] adj: **~ acid** acide *m* nicotinique.

nicotinism ['nɪkətiːˌnɪzəm] n nicotinisme *m*, tabagisme *m*.

niece [niːs] n nièce *f*.

Nielsen rating ['niːlsənreɪtɪŋ] n (*TV*) ≃ Audimat ® *m*.

Nietzschean ['niːtʃɪən] adj nietzschéen, de Nietzsche.

niff‡ [nɪf] n (*Brit*) puanteur *f*. **what a ~!** ce que ça cocotte!‡ *or* schlingue!‡

niffy‡ ['nɪfɪ] adj (*Brit*) puant. **it's ~ in here** ça pue *or* cocotte‡ ici!

nifty‡ ['nɪftɪ] adj (*stylish*) coquet, pimpant, chic *inv*; (*clever*) dégourdi, débrouillard; (*skilful*) habile; (*US: great*) formidable, terrible*. **that's a ~ car** voilà une (petite) voiture qui a de la classe; **that was a ~ piece of work** ça a été vite fait; **you'd better be ~ about it!** il faudrait faire vite!

Niger ['naɪdʒəʳ] 1 n (*country, river*) Niger *m*. 2 comp nigérien; *ambassador etc* de la république du Niger.

Nigeria [naɪ'dʒɪərɪə] n Nigéria *m*.

Nigerian [naɪ'dʒɪərɪən] 1 n Nigérian(e) *m(f)*. 2 adj nigérian.

niggardliness ['nɪgədlɪnɪs] n avarice *f*, pingrerie *f*.

niggardly ['nɪgədlɪ] 1 adj *person* chiche, pingre, avare; *amount, portion* mesquin, piètre. 2 adv chichement, mesquinement, parcimonieusement.

nigger ['nɪgəʳ] 1 n (*‡ pej*) nègre *m*, négresse *f*. (*Brit fig*) **there's a ~ in the woodpile** il se trame quelque chose, il y a anguille sous roche; (*Brit fig*) **to be the ~ in the woodpile** faire le trouble-fête. 2 comp ▸**nigger brown** (*Brit*) tête de nègre *inv*.

niggle ['nɪgl] 1 vi *[person]* (*go into detail*) couper les cheveux en quatre; (*find fault*) trouver toujours à redire. 2 vt: **his conscience was niggling him** sa conscience le travaillait.

niggling ['nɪglɪŋ] 1 adj *person* tatillon; *details* insignifiant. **a ~ doubt** un petit doute insinuant; **a ~ little pain** une petite douleur persistante. 2 n (*NonC*) chicanerie *f*.

nigh [naɪ] (*liter*) = **near 1, 2, 3**.

night [naɪt] 1 n a nuit *f*. **at ~, in the ~** la nuit; **by ~, in the ~** de nuit; **last ~** hier soir, la nuit dernière, cette nuit; **tomorrow ~** demain soir; **the ~ before** la veille au soir; **the ~ before last** avant-hier soir; **in the ~, during the ~** pendant la nuit; **Monday ~** lundi soir, la nuit de lundi à mardi; **6 o'clock at ~** 6 heures du soir; **far into the ~** jusqu'à une heure avancée de la nuit, (très) tard dans la nuit; **to spend the ~** passer la nuit; **to have a good/bad ~** bien/mal dormir, passer une bonne/mauvaise nuit; **I've had several bad ~s in a row** j'ai mal dormi plusieurs nuits de suite; **~ and day** nuit et jour; **~ after ~** des nuits durant; **all ~ (long)** toute la nuit; **to sit up all ~ talking** passer la nuit (entière) à bavarder; **to have a ~ out** sortir le soir; **the maid's ~ out** le soir de sortie de la bonne; **let's make a ~ of it** (*gen*) autant y passer la soirée *or* nuit; (*in entertainment etc*) il est trop tôt pour aller se coucher; **he's on ~s this week** il est de nuit cette semaine; **to have an early ~** aller se coucher tôt; **I've had too many late ~s** je me suis couché tard trop souvent; **she's used to late ~s** elle a l'habitude de se coucher tard; **he needs a ~'s sleep** il a besoin d'une bonne nuit de sommeil; **a ~'s lodging** un toit *or* un gîte pour la nuit; *see* **Arabian, good** *etc*.

b (*NonC: darkness*) nuit *f*, obscurité *f*, ténèbres *fpl* (*liter*). **~ is falling** la nuit *or* le soir tombe; **he went out into the ~** il partit dans la nuit *or* les ténèbres (*liter*); **he's afraid of the ~** il a peur du noir.

c (*Theat*) soirée *f*, représentation *f*. **the last 3 ~s of ...** les 3 dernières (représentations) de ...; **Mozart ~** soirée (consacrée à) Mozart; *see* **first** *etc*.

2 adv: **to work ~s** être (au poste) de nuit; (*US*) **I can't sleep ~s** je ne peux pas dormir la nuit.

3 comp *clothes, flight* de nuit ▸**night-bird** (*lit*) oiseau *m* nocturne; (*fig*) couche-tard *mf inv*, noctambule *mf* (*hum*) ▸**night-blind** héméralope ▸**night blindness** héméralopie *f* ▸**nightcap** (*hat*) bonnet *m* de nuit; (*drink*) boisson *f* (*gén alcoolisée, prise avant le coucher*); **would you like a nightcap?** voulez-vous boire quelque chose avant de vous coucher? ▸**nightclothes** vêtements *mpl* de nuit ▸**nightclub** boîte *f* de nuit, night-club *m* ▸**nightclubber**: **he's a real nightclubber** il passe sa vie dans les boîtes de nuit ▸**nightclubbing** sortir en boîte de nuit ▸**nightdress** chemise *f* de nuit (*de femme*) ▸**night editor** (*Press*) secrétaire *mf* de rédaction de nuit ▸**nightfall** tombée *f* du jour *or* de la nuit; **at nightfall** au tomber du jour, à la nuit tombante ▸**night-fighter** (*Aviat*) chasseur *m* de nuit ▸**nightgown** chemise *f* de nuit (*de femme*) ▸**nighthawk** (*bird*) engoulevent *m* (d'Amérique); (*US fig: person*) couche-tard *mf inv* ▸**nightjar** engoulevent *m* (d'Europe) ▸**night letter** (*US*) télégramme-lettre *m* de nuit ▸**nightlife** vie *f* nocturne ▸**night light** (*child's*) veilleuse *f*; (*Naut*) feu *m* de position ▸**nightlong** (*gen*) de toute une nuit; **a nightlong wait** une nuit d'attente ▸**nightmare** (*lit, fig*) cauchemar *m*; **the very thought was a nightmare to me** rien qu'à y penser j'en avais des cauchemars ▸**nightmarish** de cauchemar, cauchemardesque ▸**night-night*** (*goodnight*) bonne nuit ▸**night nurse** infirmier *m*, -ière *f* de nuit ▸**night owl*** (*fig*) couche-tard *mf inv*, noctambule *mf* (*hum*) ▸**night porter** gardien *m* de nuit, concierge *mf* de service la nuit ▸**night safe** coffre *m* de nuit ▸**night school** cours *mpl* du soir ▸**nightshade** = **nightshade** ▸**nightshift** (*workers*) équipe *f* de nuit; (*work*) poste *m* de nuit; **to be** *or* **to work on night shift** être (au poste) de nuit ▸**nightshirt** chemise *f* de nuit (*d'homme*) ▸**the night sky** (*gen*) le ciel la nuit; (*liter*) la voûte céleste ▸**night soil** fumier *m* (*déjections humaines*) ▸**nightspot*** = **nightclub** ▸**night stand** (*US*) table *f* de nuit ▸**night stick**

(*US Police*) matraque *f* (d'agent de police) ▸**night storage**: **night storage heater/heating** radiateur *m*/chauffage *m* par accumulation (*fonctionnant au tarif de nuit*) ▸**night table** (*US*) table *f* de nuit ▸**night-time** (*NonC*) nuit *f*; **at night-time** la nuit; **in the night-time** pendant la nuit, de nuit ▸**night watch** (*activity, period of time*) veille *f* *or* garde *f* de nuit; (*group of guards*) équipe *f* des veilleurs *or* gardiens de nuit; (*one man*) = **night watchman** ▸**night watchman** veilleur *m* *or* gardien *m* de nuit ▸**nightwear** (*NonC*) vêtements *mpl* de nuit ▸**night work** travail *m* de nuit.

nightie* ['naɪtɪ] **n** chemise *f* de nuit (*de femme*).

nightingale ['naɪtɪŋgeɪl] **n** rossignol *m*.

nightly ['naɪtlɪ] 1 **adj** (*every night*) de tous les soirs, de toutes les nuits. (*Theat*) ~ **performance** représentation *f* (de) tous les soirs. 2 **adv** tous les soirs, chaque soir, chaque nuit. (*Theat*) **performances ~** représentations tous les soirs; **twice ~** deux fois par soirée *or* nuit.

nightshade ['naɪtʃeɪd] **n**: **black ~** morelle noire; **deadly ~** belladone *f*; **woody ~** douce-amère *f*.

nihilism ['naɪɪlɪzəm] **n** nihilisme *m*.

nihilist ['naɪɪlɪst] **n** nihiliste *mf*.

nihilistic [,naɪɪ'lɪstɪk] **adj** nihiliste.

nil [nɪl] **n** rien *m*; (*Brit: in form-filling etc*) néant *m*; (*Brit Sport*) zéro *m*.

Nile [naɪl] **n** Nil *m*. (*Hist*) **the Battle of the ~** la bataille d'Aboukir.

nimbi ['nɪmbaɪ] **npl of nimbus**.

nimble ['nɪmbl] 1 **adj** *person, fingers* agile, leste, preste; *mind* vif, prompt. **you have to be fairly ~ to get over this hedge** il faut être assez agile *or* leste pour passer par-dessus cette haie; *[old person]* **she is still ~** elle est encore alerte. 2 **comp** ▸**nimble-fingered/-footed** aux doigts/pieds agiles *or* lestes *or* prestes ▸**nimble-minded, nimble-witted** à l'esprit vif *or* prompt.

nimbleness ['nɪmblnɪs] **n** *[person, fingers]* agilité *f*; *[limbs etc]* agilité, souplesse *f*; *[mind]* vivacité *f*.

nimbly ['nɪmblɪ] **adv** agilement, lestement, prestement.

nimbostratus [,nɪmbəʊ'streɪtəs] **n, pl nimbostrati** [,nɪmbəʊ'streɪtaɪ] nimbostratus *m*.

nimbus ['nɪmbəs] **n, pl nimbi** *or* **~es** a (*halo*) nimbe *m*, halo *m*. b (*cloud*) nimbus *m*.

nincompoop* ['nɪŋkəmpu:p] **n** cornichon* *m*, serin(e)* *m(f)*, gourde* *f*.

nine [naɪn] 1 **adj** neuf *inv*. **~ times out of ten** neuf fois sur dix; (*fig*) **he's got ~ lives** il a l'âme chevillée au corps; **a ~ days' wonder** la merveille d'un jour; **a ~-hole golf course** un (parcours de) neuf trous.

2 **n** neuf *m inv*. (*fig*) **dressed (up) to the ~s** en grand tralala, sur son trente et un; *for other phrases see* **six**.

3 **pron** neuf *mfpl*. **there are ~** il y en a neuf.

4 **comp** ▸**ninepins** (jeu *m* de) quilles *fpl*; **they went down like ninepins** ils sont tombés comme des mouches ▸**nine-to-five***: **nine-to-five job** travail *m* de bureau routinier; **he's got a nine-to-five mentality** *or* **attitude** ce n'est pas lui qui travaillerait après cinq heures *or* en dehors des heures du bureau ▸**nine-to-fiver*** (employé(e) *m(f)*) gratte-papier *m*.

nineteen ['naɪn'ti:n] 1 **adj** dix-neuf *inv*. 2 **n** dix-neuf *m inv*. (*Brit fig*) **he talks ~ to the dozen*** c'est un vrai moulin à paroles *or* une vraie pie; **they were talking ~ to the dozen** ils jacassaient à qui mieux mieux; *for other phrases see* **six**.

nineteenth ['naɪn'ti:nθ] 1 **adj** dix-neuvième. (*Golf hum*) **the ~ (hole)** le bar, la buvette. 2 **n** dix-neuvième *mf*; (*fraction*) dix-neuvième *m*; *for other phrases see* **sixth**.

ninetieth ['naɪntɪɪθ] 1 **adj** quatre-vingt-dixième. 2 **n** quatre-vingt-dixième *mf*; (*fraction*) quatre-vingt-dixième *m*.

ninety ['naɪntɪ] 1 **adj** quatre-vingt-dix *inv*. 2 **n** quatre-vingt-dix *m inv*. **~-one** quatre-vingt-onze; **~-nine** quatre-vingt-dix-neuf; **~-nine times out of a hundred** quatre-vingt dix-neuf fois sur cent; **to be in one's nineties** être nonagénaire, avoir passé quatre-vingt-dix ans; (*at doctor's*) **"say ~-nine!"** = "dites trente-trois!"; *see* **naughty**; *for other phrases see* **sixty**.

ninny* ['nɪnɪ] **n** cornichon* *m*, serin(e)* *m(f)*, gourde* *f*.

ninth [naɪnθ] 1 **adj** neuvième. 2 **n** neuvième *mf*; (*fraction*) neuvième *m*; *for phrases see* **sixth**.

niobium [naɪ'əʊbɪəm] **n** niobium *m*.

Nip [nɪp] **n** (**abbr of Nipponese**: *pej*) Nippon *m*, -one *or* -onne *f*, Jap* *m* (*pej*).

nip[1] [nɪp] 1 **n** (*pinch*) pinçon *m*; (*bite*) morsure *f*. **the dog gave him a ~** le chien lui a donné un (petit) coup de dent; (*US*) **~ and tuck*** serré, au quart de poil près*; **there's a ~ in the air today** ça pince aujourd'hui, l'air est piquant aujourd'hui.

2 **vt** a (*pinch*) pincer; (*bite*) donner un (petit) coup de dent à; *[cold, frost]* *plants* brûler; (*prune*) *bud, shoot* pincer; (*fig*) *plan, ambition* faire échec à. **I've ~ped my finger** je me suis pincé le doigt; (*fig*) **to ~ in the bud** faire avorter, tuer *or* écraser dans l'œuf; **the cold air ~ped our faces** l'air froid nous piquait *or* pinçait le *or* au visage; **all the plants had been ~ped by the frost** toutes les plantes avaient été brûlées par la gelée.

b (*‡: steal*) piquer‡, faucher‡.

3 **vi** (*Brit **) **to ~ up/down/out** *etc* monter/descendre/sortir *etc* en courant *or* d'un pas allègre; **he ~ped into the café** il a fait un saut au café.

▸**nip along*** **vi** (*Brit*) *[person]* aller d'un bon pas; *[car]* filer. **nip along to Anne's house** cours vite *or* fais un saut chez Anne.

▸**nip in*** 1 **vi** (*Brit*) entrer en courant; entrer un instant. **I've just nipped in for a minute** je ne fais qu'entrer et sortir; **to nip in and out of the traffic** se faufiler entre les voitures. 2 **vt sep** (*Sewing*) faire une (*or* des) pince(s) à. **dress nipped in at the waist** robe *f* pincée à la taille.

▸**nip off** 1 **vi** (*Brit **) filer*, se sauver*. 2 **vt sep** *bud, shoot* pincer; *top of sth* couper.

nip[2] [nɪp] **n** (*drink*) goutte *f*, petit verre. **to take a ~** boire une goutte *or* un petit verre; **have a ~ of whisky!** une goutte de whisky?

nipper ['nɪpə^r] **n** a (*Brit ‡*) gosse* *mf*, mioche* *mf*. b **(pair of) ~s** pince *f*, tenaille(s) *f(pl)*. c (*Zool*) pince *f*.

nipple ['nɪpl] **n** (*Anat*) mamelon *m*, bout *m* de sein; *[baby's bottle]* tétine *f*; (*Geog*) mamelon; (*for grease etc*) graisseur *m*.

Nippon ['nɪpɒn] **n** (*Japan*) Nippon *m*.

Nipponese [,nɪpə'ni:z] 1 **adj** nippon (*f* -one *or* -onne). 2 **n** Nippon *m*, Nippone *f* *or* Nipponne *f*.

nippy* ['nɪpɪ] **adj** a (*Brit*) alerte, vif, preste. **be ~ about it!** fais vite!, grouille-toi!‡ b (*sharp, cold*) *wind* coupant, cuisant, âpre. **it's ~ today** ça pince aujourd'hui, l'air est piquant aujourd'hui. c *flavour* fort, piquant.

NIREX ['naɪreks] (**abbr of Nuclear Industry Radioactive Waste Executive**) *see* **nuclear**.

nirvana [nɪə'vɑ:nə] **n** nirvana *m*.

Nisei ['ni:seɪ] **n, pl inv** *or* **~s** (*US*) *Américain(e) né(e) d'immigrants japonais*.

nisi ['naɪsaɪ] **adj** *see* **decree 1**.

Nissen hut ['nɪsn,hʌt] **n** hutte préfabriquée (*en tôle, en forme de tunnel*).

nit [nɪt] 1 **n** a (*louse*) lente *f*. b (*Brit ‡: fool*) crétin(e)* *m(f)*. 2 **comp** ▸**nit-picker*** tatillon *m*, -onne *f* ▸**nit-picking***: **he's always nit-picking** il est très tatillon, il trouve toujours à redire.

niter ['naɪtə^r] **n** (*US*) = **nitre**.

nitrate ['naɪtreɪt] **n** nitrate *m*, azotate *m*.

nitration [naɪ'treɪʃən] **n** nitration *f*.

nitre, (*US*) **niter** ['naɪtə^r] **n** nitre *m*, salpêtre *m*.

nitric ['naɪtrɪk] **adj** nitrique, azotique. **~ acid** acide *m* nitrique *or* azotique; **~ oxide** oxyde *m* azotique *or* nitrique, bioxyde *m* d'azote, nitrosyle *m*.

nitrite ['naɪtraɪt] **n** nitrite *m*.

nitrogen ['naɪtrədʒən] **n** azote *m*. **~ cycle** cycle *m* de l'azote; **~ dioxide** dioxyde *m* d'azote; **~ gas** (gaz *m*) azote.

nitrogenous [naɪ'trɒdʒɪnəs] **adj** azoté.

nitroglycerin(e) ['naɪtrəʊ'glɪsəri:n] **n** nitroglycérine *f*.

nitrous ['naɪtrəs] **adj** nitreux, azoteux, d'azote. **~ acid** acide azoteux *or* nitreux; **~ oxide** oxyde azoteux *or* nitreux, protoxyde *m* d'azote.

nitty-gritty* ['nɪtɪ'grɪtɪ] **n**: **let's get down to the ~** venons-en au fond du problème *or* aux choses sérieuses (*hum*); **the ~ of life** les dures réalités de la vie (*hum*).

nitwit* ['nɪtwɪt] **n** imbécile *mf*, nigaud(e)* *m(f)*.

nix [nɪks] 1 **n** (*: *nothing*) rien *m*, que dalle‡, peau *f* de balle‡. 2 **vt** (*US*) mettre son veto à.

nixie mail* ['nɪksɪmeɪl] **n** (*US*) *courrier difficile à faire parvenir en raison d'une adresse illisible, incomplète etc*.

N.J. (*US*) **abbr of New Jersey**.

N.L.F. [,enel'ef] **n** (**abbr of National Liberation Front**) F.L.N. *m*.

N.M. (*US*) **abbr of New Mexico**.

NMR [,enem'ɑ:^r] **n** (**abbr of nuclear magnetic resonance**) RMN *f*.

no [nəʊ] 1 **particle** non. **oh ~!** mais non!; **to say/answer ~** dire/répondre non; **the answer is ~** la réponse est non *or* négative; **I won't take ~ for an answer** (il n'est) pas question de me dire non; **I wouldn't do it, ~ not for £1000** je ne le ferais pas, même pas pour 1000 livres.

2 **n, pl ~es** non *m inv*. **the ~es have it** les non l'emportent, les voix contre l'emportent; **there were 7 ~es** il y avait 7 non *or* 7 voix contre; *see* **ay(e)**.

3 **adj** a (*not any*) aucun, nul (*f* nulle), pas de, point de (*all used with ne*). **she had ~ coat** elle n'avait pas de manteau; **I have ~ idea** je n'ai aucune idée; **I have ~ more money** je n'ai plus d'argent; **~ man could do more** aucun homme *or* personne *or* nul ne pourrait faire davantage; **~ one man could do it** aucun homme ne pourrait le faire (à lui) seul; **~ two men would agree on this** il n'y a pas deux hommes qui seraient d'accord là-dessus; **~ two are alike** il n'y en a pas deux les mêmes; **~ other man** nul autre, personne d'autre; **~ sensible man would have done that** aucun homme de bon sens n'aurait fait ça, un homme de bon sens n'aurait pas fait ça; **~ Frenchman would say that** aucun Français ne dirait ça, un Français ne dirait pas ça; **there's ~ whisky like Scotch whisky** il n'y a pas de meilleur whisky que le whisky écossais; **there's ~ Catholic like a converted Catholic** il n'y a pas plus catholique qu'un catholique converti; **it's of ~ interest** c'est sans intérêt; **a man of ~ intelligence** un homme sans intelligence, un homme dénué d'intelligence; **~ go!*** pas moyen!, pas mèche!*; **it's ~ go* trying to get him to help us** pas moyen d'obtenir qu'il nous aide (*subj*)

(*see also* **5**); **it's ~ good waiting for him** cela ne sert à rien *or* ce n'est pas la peine de l'attendre; **it's ~ wonder** (ce n'est) pas étonnant (*that* que + *subj or* si + *indic*); **~ wonder!** pas étonnant!*

b (*emphatic*) peu, pas de, nullement. **by ~ means** aucunement, nullement, pas du tout; **he's ~ friend of mine** il n'est pas de mes amis; **he's ~ genius** ce n'est certes pas un génie, il n'a rien d'un génie; **this is ~ place for children** ce n'est pas un endroit pour les enfants; **in ~ time** en un rien de temps; **it's ~ small matter** ce n'est pas rien, ce n'est pas une petite affaire; **headache or ~ headache* — you'll have to do it** migraine ou pas (migraine) – tu devras le faire*; **theirs is ~ easy task** ils n'ont pas la tâche facile, leur tâche n'est pas (du tout) facile; **there's ~ such thing** cela n'existe pas; *see* **end, mistake** *etc.*

c (*forbidding*) **~ smoking** défense de fumer; **~ entry, ~ admittance** entrée interdite, défense d'entrer; **~ parking** stationnement interdit; **~ surrender!** on ne se rend pas!; **~ nonsense!** pas d'histoires!, pas de blagues!*

d (*with gerund*) **there's ~ saying what he'll do next** impossible de dire ce qu'il fera après; **there's ~ pleasing him** (quoi qu'on fasse) il n'est jamais satisfait.

4 **adv** a non. **whether he comes or ~** qu'il vienne ou non; **hungry or ~ you'll eat it** que tu aies faim ou non, tu le mangeras.

b (*with compar*) ne ... pas, ne ... plus. **the invalid is ~ better** le malade ne va pas mieux; **I can go ~ farther** je ne peux pas aller plus loin, je n'en peux plus; **I can bear it ~ longer** je ne peux plus le supporter; **she took ~ less than 4 weeks to do it** il ne lui a pas fallu moins de 4 semaines pour le faire; **she came herself, ~ less!** elle est venue en personne, voyez-vous ça! (*iro*).

5 **comp** ▸**no-account*** (*US*) **adj, n** bon(ne) (*mf*) à rien ▸**no ball** (*Cricket*) balle *f* nulle ▸**nobody** *see* **nobody** ▸**no-claim(s) bonus** bonus *m* ▸**no-fault divorce** (*US Jur*) ≃ divorce *m* par consentement mutuel (*sans torts prononcés*) ▸**no-fault insurance** (*US Jur*) assurance *f* automobile à remboursement automatique ▸**no-frills** avec service (réduit au strict) minimum *or* simplifié ▸**no-go: it's no-go*** (*US*) ça ne marche pas; (*Brit Mil*) **no-go area** zone interdite (*à la police et à l'armée*) ▸**no-good*** **adj** nul (*f* nulle), propre *or* bon (*f* bonne) à rien ◊ **n** propre *mf* à rien ▸**no-hoper*** raté(e) *m(f)*, nullard(e)* *m(f)*, zéro* *m* ▸**nohow*** aucunement, en aucune façon ▸**no jump** (*Sport*) saut *m* annulé ▸**no-knock raid** (*US*) perquisition-surprise *f* ▸**no-man's-land** (*Mil*) no man's land *m*; (*wasteland*) terrain *m* vague; (*indefinite area*) zone mal définie ▸**no-no***: (*esp US*) **it's a no-no** c'est absolument interdit ▸**no-nonsense adj** *approach, attitude* éminemment sensé *or* raisonnable, plein de bon sens ▸**no one** = **nobody 1** ▸**no sale** (*Comm*) non-vente *f* ▸**no-show** (*esp US*) (*on plane/at show*) passager *m*/spectateur *m etc* qui ne se présente pas ▸**no throw** (*Sport*) lancer *m* annulé ▸**no-trump(s)** sans-atout *m inv*; **to call no-trump(s)** annoncer sans-atout; **three tricks in no-trump(s)** trois sans-atout.

no. (**abbr of number**) no.

Noah ['nəʊə] **n** Noé *m*. **~'s ark** l'arche *f* de Noé.

nob¹‡ [nɒb] **n** (*esp Brit*) aristo‡ *m*; richard‡ *m*. **the ~s** (les gens de) la haute‡, les rupins‡ *mpl*.

nob²‡ [nɒb] **n** (*head*) caboche* *f*, fiole‡ *f*.

nobble* ['nɒbl] **vt** (*Brit*) a (*bribe, corrupt*) *person* acheter, soudoyer. b (*obtain dishonestly*) *votes etc* acheter; *money* faucher‡, rafler*. c (*Racing*) *horse, dog* droguer (*pour l'empêcher de gagner*). d (*catch*) *wrongdoer* pincer‡, choper‡. **the reporters ~d him as he left his hotel** les reporters l'ont happé *or* lui ont mis la main dessus au moment où il quittait son hôtel.

Nobel [nəʊ'bel] **n**: **~ prize** prix *m* Nobel; **~ prizewinner** (lauréat(e) *m(f)* du) prix Nobel.

nobelium [nəʊ'biːlɪəm] **n** nobélium *m*.

nobility [nəʊ'bɪlɪtɪ] **n** (*NonC*) a (*nobles*) (haute) noblesse *f*. **the old ~** la noblesse d'extraction *or* d'épée, la vieille noblesse. b (*quality*) noblesse *f*. **~ of mind** grandeur *f* d'âme, magnanimité *f*.

noble ['nəʊbl] 1 **adj** a *person, appearance, matter* noble; *soul, sentiment* noble, grand; *monument, edifice* majestueux, imposant. **of ~ birth** de haute naissance, de naissance noble; **the ~ art of self-defence** le noble art, la boxe; **a ~ wine** un grand vin, un vin noble. b (*: *unselfish*) magnanime. **I was very ~ and gave her my share** dans un geste magnanime je lui ai donné ma part, je lui ai généreusement donné ma part; **don't be so ~!** ne fais pas le (*or* la) magnanime! c *metal* noble, précieux. 2 **n** noble *m*. 3 **comp** ▸**nobleman** noble *m*, aristocrate *m* ▸**noble-minded** magnanime, généreux ▸**noblewoman** aristocrate *f*, femme *f* de la noblesse, noble *f*.

nobleness ['nəʊblnɪs] **n** [*person, birth*] noblesse *f*; [*spirit, action etc*] noblesse, magnanimité *f*, générosité *f*; [*animal, statue etc*] belles proportions, noblesse de proportions; [*building etc*] majesté *f*. **~ of mind** grandeur *f* d'âme, magnanimité, générosité.

nobly ['nəʊblɪ] **adv** a (*aristocratically*) noblement. **~ born** de haute naissance. b (*magnificently*) *proportioned* majestueusement. c (*: *selflessly*) généreusement, noblement. **he ~ gave her his seat** il lui céda généreusement sa place; **you've done ~!** vous avez été magnifique!, vous avez bien mérité de la patrie! (*hum*).

nobody ['nəʊbədɪ] 1 **pron** personne, nul, aucun (+ ne *before vb*). **I saw ~** je n'ai vu personne; **~ knows** nul *or* personne ne le sait; **~ spoke to me** personne ne m'a parlé; **who saw him? — ~** qui l'a vu? – personne; **~ knows better than I** personne ne sait mieux que moi; **~ (that was) there will ever forget ...** personne parmi ceux qui étaient là n'oubliera jamais ...; **it is ~'s business** cela ne regarde personne; **like ~'s business*** *run etc* à toutes jambes, comme un dératé; *work etc* d'arrache-pied, sans désemparer; (*fig*) **he's ~'s fool** il n'est pas né d'hier, il est loin d'être un imbécile.

2 **n** nullité *f*, zéro *m*, rien *m* du tout. **he's a mere ~, he's just a ~** c'est un rien du tout; **they are nobodies** ce sont des moins que rien; **I worked with him when he was ~** j'ai travaillé avec lui alors qu'il était encore inconnu.

nocturnal [nɒk'tɜːnl] **adj** nocturne, de nuit.

nocturne ['nɒktɜːn] **n** (*Mus*) nocturne *m*.

nod [nɒd] 1 **n** a signe *m* (affirmatif) *or* inclination *f* de (la) tête. **he gave me a ~** (*gen*) il m'a fait un signe de (la) tête; (*in greeting*) il m'a salué de la tête; (*signifying "yes"*) il m'a fait signe que oui de la tête; **he rose with a ~ of agreement** il s'est levé, signifiant son accord d'un signe de (la) tête; **to answer with a ~** répondre d'un signe de (la) tête; **to get the ~*** [*project etc*] avoir le feu vert; (*Brit*) **on the ~*** *pass, approve* sans discussion, d'un commun accord; (*loc*) **a ~ is as good as a wink (to a blind man)** c'est bien *or* ça va*, on a compris.

b **the land of N~** le pays des rêves *or* des songes.

2 **vi** a (*move head*) faire un signe de (la) tête, incliner la tête; (*as sign of assent*) hocher la tête, faire signe que oui, faire un signe de tête affirmatif. **to ~ to sb** faire un signe de tête à qn; (*in greeting*) saluer qn d'un signe de tête, saluer qn de la tête; **he ~ded to me to go** de la tête il m'a fait signe de m'en aller; **we're on ~ding terms, we have a ~ding acquaintance** nous nous disons bonjour, nous nous saluons; (*fig*) **he has a ~ding acquaintance with German/this author** il connaît vaguement l'allemand/cet auteur.

b (*doze*) sommeiller, somnoler. **he was ~ding over a book** il dodelinait de la tête *or* il somnolait sur un livre; (*fig*) **to catch sb ~ding** prendre qn en défaut.

c [*flowers, plumes*] se balancer, danser; [*trees*] onduler, se balancer.

3 **vt**: **to ~ one's head** (*move head down*) faire un signe de (la) tête, incliner la tête; (*as sign of assent*) faire signe que oui, faire un signe de tête affirmatif; **to ~ one's agreement/approval** manifester son assentiment/son approbation par un *or* d'un signe de tête; **to ~ assent** faire signe que oui, manifester son assentiment par un *or* d'un signe de tête.

▸**nod off vi** s'endormir. **I nodded off for a moment** je me suis endormi un instant.

nodal ['nəʊdl] **adj** nodal.

noddle‡† ['nɒdl] **n** (*head*) caboche* *f*, fiole‡ *f*.

Noddy* ['nɒdɪ] **adj** (*Brit: very easy etc*) d'une simplicité enfantine.

node [nəʊd] **n** (*gen, Astron, Geom, Ling, Phys*) nœud *m*; (*Bot*) nœud, nodosité *f*; (*Anat*) nodus *m*, nodosité.

nodular ['nɒdjʊlər] **adj** nodulaire.

nodule ['nɒdjuːl] **n** (*Anat, Bot, Geol*) nodule *m*.

Noel ['nəʊəl] **n** Noël *m* (*prénom*).

noggin ['nɒgɪn] **n** a (*container*) (petit) pot *m*; (*amount*) quart *m* (de pinte). (*Brit: drink*) **let's have a ~** allons boire *or* prendre un pot. b (*US* ‡: *head*) caboche* *f*, tête *f*.

noise [nɔɪz] 1 **n** a (*sound*) bruit *m*, son *m*. **I heard a small ~** j'ai entendu un petit bruit; **the ~ of bells** le son des cloches; **~s in the ears** bourdonnements *mpl* (d'oreilles); **a hammering ~** un martellement; **a clanging ~** un bruit métallique; (*fig*) **to make (all) the right ~s*** se montrer complaisant; **to make reassuring/placatory ~s** tenir des propos rassurants/apaisants.

b (*loud sound*) bruit *m*, tapage *m* (*NonC*), vacarme *m* (*NonC*). **the ~ of the traffic** le bruit *or* le vacarme de la circulation; **I hate ~** j'ai horreur du bruit; **to make a ~** faire du bruit *or* du tapage *or* du vacarme; (*fig*) **the book made a lot of ~ when it came out** le livre a fait beaucoup de bruit *or* beaucoup de tapage *or* beaucoup parler de lui quand il est sorti; (*fig*) **to make a lot of ~ about sth*** faire du tapage autour de qch; **she made ~s* about wanting to go home early** elle a marmonné qu'elle voulait rentrer tôt; **stop that ~!** arrêtez(-moi) ce tapage! *or* ce vacarme! *or* ce tintamarre!; **hold your ~!**‡ ferme-la!‡; (*person*) **a big ~*** une huile*, une grosse légume*.

c (*NonC*) (*Rad, TV*) interférences *fpl*, parasites *mpl*; (*Telec*) friture *f*; (*Comput*) bruit *m*.

2 **vt**: **to ~ sth about** *or* **abroad** ébruiter qch.

3 **comp** ▸**noise abatement** lutte *f* antibruit; **noise-abatement campaign/society** campagne *f*/ligue *f* antibruit *or* pour la lutte contre le bruit ▸**noise pollution** les nuisances *fpl* sonores ▸**noise prevention** mesure *f* antibruit *or* contre le bruit.

noiseless ['nɔɪzlɪs] **adj** silencieux. **with ~ tread** à pas feutrés.

noiselessly ['nɔɪzlɪslɪ] **adv** sans bruit, en silence, silencieusement.

noiselessness ['nɔɪzlɪsnɪs] **n** silence *m*, absence *f* de bruit.

noisily ['nɔɪzɪlɪ] **adv** bruyamment.

noisiness ['nɔɪzɪnɪs] **n** caractère bruyant; [*child*] turbulence *f*.

noisome ['nɔɪsəm] **adj** (*disgusting*) repoussant, répugnant; (*smelly*) puant, fétide, infect; (*harmful*) nocif, nuisible.

noisy ['nɔɪzɪ] **adj** **a** *child etc* bruyant, tapageur; *protest, street* bruyant; *discussion, meeting, welcome* bruyant, tumultueux. *[person, machine]* **to be ~** faire du bruit *or* du tapage. **b** *colour* criard, voyant.

nomad ['nəʊmæd] **n** nomade *mf*.

nomadic [nəʊ'mædɪk] **adj** nomade.

nomadism ['nəʊmədɪzəm] **n** nomadisme *m*.

nom de plume ['nɒmdə'plu:m] **n, pl noms de plume** (*Literat*) pseudonyme *m*.

nomenclature [nəʊ'menklətʃə^r] **n** nomenclature *f*.

nominal ['nɒmɪnl] **1 adj a** (*in name only*) *ruler* de nom (seulement); *agreement, power, rights* nominal. **he was the ~ head of state** il était chef d'État de nom. **b** (*for form only*) *salary, fee* nominal, insignifiant. **a ~ amount** *or* **sum** une somme nominale *or* insignifiante; (*Jur*) **~ damages** dommages-intérêts *mpl* symboliques, ≃ franc *m* symbolique; **~ value** valeur nominale *or* fictive; **~ rent** loyer insignifiant. **c** (*Gram*) nominal. **d** (*US: Space sl*) conforme au plan prévu. **2 n** expression *f* nominale.

nominalism ['nɒmɪnəlɪzəm] **n** nominalisme *m*.

nominalist ['nɒmɪnəlɪst] **n, adj** nominaliste *(mf)*.

nominalization [,nɒmɪnəlaɪ'zeɪʃən] **n** (*Ling*) nominalisation *f*.

nominalize ['nɒmɪnəlaɪz] **vt** (*Ling*) nominaliser.

nominally ['nɒmɪnəlɪ] **adv** (*in name only*) nominalement, de nom; (*as a matter of form*) pour la forme.

nominate ['nɒmɪneɪt] **vt a** (*appoint*) nommer, désigner. **he was ~d chairman, he was ~d to the chairmanship** il a été nommé président; **~d and elected members of a committee** membres désignés et membres élus d'un comité. **b** (*propose*) proposer, présenter. **he was ~d for the presidency** il a été proposé comme candidat à la présidence; **they ~d Mr Aylwin for mayor** ils ont proposé M. Aylwin comme candidat à la mairie; **to ~ an actor for an Oscar** proposer *or* nominer un acteur pour un Oscar.

nomination [,nɒmɪ'neɪʃən] **1 n a** (*appointment*) nomination *f* (*to* à). **b** proposition *f* de candidat. **~s must be received by ...** toutes propositions de candidats doivent être reçues avant ... . **c** (*Cine: for award*) nomination *f*. **2 comp ▸nomination paper** (*Pol*) feuille *f* de candidature.

nominative ['nɒmɪnətɪv] **1 adj** (*gen*) nominatif; *ending* du nominatif. **2 n** nominatif *m*. **in the ~** au nominatif, au cas sujet.

nominator ['nɒmɪneɪtə^r] **n** présentateur *m*.

nominee [,nɒmɪ'ni:] **n** (*for post*) personne désignée *or* nommée, candidat(e) agréé(e); (*for annuity etc*) personne dénommée; (*St Ex*) mandataire *mf*. (*St Ex*) **~ company** société *f* prête-nom.

non- [nɒn] **1 pref** non-, *e.g.* **strikers and ~-strikers** grévistes et non-grévistes; **believers and ~-believers** ceux qui croient et ceux qui ne croient pas, (les) croyants et (les) non-croyants.

2 comp ▸non-absorbent non absorbant **▸non-academic** *course* orienté vers la formation professionnelle; *staff* non enseignant; *career* qui n'exige pas des études poussées **▸non-accomplishment** inaccomplissement *m*, inachèvement *m* **▸non-accountable** non responsable **▸non-achievement** manque *m* de réussite **▸non-achiever** personne *f* qui ne réussit pas **▸non-addictive** qui ne crée pas une dépendance **▸non-admission** non-admission *f* **▸non-affiliated** *business* non affilié; *industry* non confédéré **▸non-aggression** non-agression *f*; **non-aggression pact** pacte *m* de non-agression **▸non-alcoholic** non alcoolisé, sans alcool **▸non-aligned** (*Pol*) non-aligné **▸non-alignment** (*Pol*) non-alignement *m*; **non-alignment policy** politique *f* de non-alignement **▸non-appearance** (*Jur*) non-comparution *f* **▸non-arrival** non-arrivée *f* **▸non-assertive** qui manque d'assurance, qui ne se met pas en avant **▸non-attendance** absence *f* **▸non-availability** non-disponibilité *f* **▸non-available** non disponible **▸non-believer** (*Rel*) incroyant(e) *m(f)* **▸non-biological** sans enzymes **▸non-breakable** incassable **▸non-Catholic adj, n** non-catholique *(mf)* **▸non-Christian** non chrétien **▸non-classified** qui n'est pas classé secret **▸non-collegiate** *student* qui n'appartient à aucun collège (*d'une université*); **non-collegiate university** université *f* qui n'est pas divisée en collèges **▸non-com*** (**abbr of non-commissioned officer**) (*US Mil*) sous-off* *m*, gradé *m* **▸non-combatant adj, n** non-combattant *(m)* **▸non-combustible** non combustible **▸non-commercial** sans but *m* lucratif **▸non-commissioned** (*Mil*) non breveté, sans brevet; **non-commissioned officer** sous-officier *m*, gradé *m* **▸non-communicant** (*Rel*) **adj, n** non-communiant(e) *m(f)* **▸non-communication** manque *m* de communication **▸non-completion** *[work]* non-achèvement *m*; *[contract]* non-exécution *f* **▸non-compliance** refus *m* d'obéissance (*with an order* à un ordre) **▸non compos mentis** qui n'a pas toute sa raison **▸non-conductor** (*Phys*) non-conducteur *m*, mauvais conducteur; *[heat]* isolant *m*, calorifuge *m*; (*Elec*) isolant **▸nonconformism** *etc see* **nonconformism** *etc* **▸non-contagious** non contagieux (*f* -euse) **▸non-contemporary** qui n'est pas contemporain **▸non-contributory: non-contributory pension scheme** régime *m* de retraite sans retenues *or* cotisations **▸non-controversial** = **uncontroversial** **▸non-conventional** non conventionnel **▸non-cooperation** refus *m* de coopération **▸non-cooperative** qui refuse de coopérer **▸non-crush(able)** infroissable **▸non-cumulative** non cumulatif **▸non-dairy adj** *product, fat* qui n'est pas à base de lait **▸non-dazzle** anti-éblouissant **▸non-degradable** qui n'est pas biodégradable **▸non-democratic** qui n'est pas démocratique, non démocratique **▸non-destructive** (*Tech*) *testing* non destructeur **▸non-detachable** *handle etc* fixe, indémontable; *lining, hood* non détachable **▸non-directional** omnidirectionnel **▸non-directive therapy** (*Psych*) psychothérapie non directive, non-directivisme *m* **▸non-disruptive** non perturbateur **▸non-distinctive** (*Ling*) non distinctif **▸non-drinker** personne *f* qui ne boit jamais d'alcool **▸non-drip** *paint* qui ne coule pas **▸non-driver** (*Aut*) personne *f* qui n'a pas le permis de conduire **▸non-edible** incomestible **▸non-essential** non essentiel, peu important, accessoire **▸non-essentials** accessoires *mpl* **▸non-established** *church* non établi **▸non-event*** non-événement *m* **▸non-examination course** (*Scol etc*) études *fpl* non sanctionnées par un examen **▸non-executive director** administrateur *m* **▸non-existence** non-existence *f* **▸non-existent** non existant, inexistant **▸non-explosive** inexplosible **▸non-factual** qui n'est pas basé sur des faits **▸non-family n** ceux qui ne font pas partie de la famille **▸non-fat** *cooking, diet* sans corps gras *or* matière grasse; *meat* maigre **▸non-fattening** qui ne fait pas grossir **▸non-ferrous** non ferreux **▸non-fiction** littérature *f* non-romanesque; **he only reads non-fiction** il ne lit jamais de romans **▸non-finite: non-finite verb** verbe *m* au mode impersonnel; **non-finite forms** formes *fpl* des modes impersonnels **▸non-flammable** = **non-inflammable** **▸non-fulfilment** non-exécution *f*, inexécution *f* **▸non-glare** anti-éblouissant **▸non-governmental** non gouvernemental **▸non-grammatical** non grammatical **▸non grata*** non grata; **he felt rather non grata*** il avait l'impression d'être un intrus **▸non-greasy** *ointment, lotion* qui ne graisse pas; *skin, hair* qui n'est pas gras (*f* grasse) **▸non-hero** anti-héros *m* **▸non-infectious** non contagieux (*f* -euse) **▸non-inflammable** ininflammable **▸non-interference** non-intervention *f* **▸non-intervention** (*Pol etc*) non-intervention *f*, laisser-faire *m* **▸non-interventionist** (*Pol etc*) non interventionniste **▸non-intoxicating** *drink etc* non alcoolique **▸non-involvement** (*in war, conflict*) non-engagement *m*, neutralité *f*; (*in negotiations etc*) non-participation *f*; (*Psych*) détachement *m* **▸non-iron** qui ne nécessite aucun repassage; (*on label*) **"non-iron"** "ne pas repasser" **▸non-Jew** non-Juif *m* (*f* -ive) **▸non-Jewish** non juif **▸non-joiner: to be a non-joiner** préférer ne pas s'affilier à des clubs **▸non-judgmental** qui ne porte pas de jugement **▸non-laddering** = **non-run** **▸non-linear** non linéaire **▸non-linguistic** *communication etc* non verbal **▸non-literate** non lettré, qui ne possède pas de langue écrite **▸non-malignant** *tumour* bénin (*f* -igne) **▸non-manual** *workers* intellectuel **▸non-material** immatériel **▸non-member** *[club etc]* personne étrangère (au club *etc*); **open to non-members** ouvert au public **▸non-metal** (*Chem*) métalloïde *m* **▸non-metallic** (*relating to non-metals*) métalloïdique; (*not of metallic quality*) non métallique **▸non-militant** non militant **▸non-military** non militaire **▸non-negociable bill** (*Comm*) effet *m* non négociable **▸non-nuclear** *weapon* conventionnel; *country* qui ne dispose pas de la puissance nucléaire **▸non-nutritious** sans valeur nutritive **▸non-observance** non-observance *f* **▸non obst.** *see* **non obst** **▸non-operational** qui n'est pas opérationnel **▸non-partisan** impartial, sans parti pris **▸non-party** (*Pol*) *vote, decision* indépendant (de tout parti politique) **▸non-paying** *visitor etc* qui ne paie pas, admis à titre gracieux **▸non-payment** non-paiement *m* **▸non-person** (*stateless etc*) personne *f* considérée comme n'existant pas; (*pej: useless*) nullité *f* **▸non-political** apolitique **▸non-polluting** non polluant **▸non-practising** *Christian, Muslim etc* non pratiquant; *homosexual* refoulé **▸non-productive** non productif **▸non-professional adj** *player etc* amateur ◊ **n** (*Sport etc*) amateur *mf*; **non-professional conduct** manquement *m* aux devoirs de la profession **▸non-profitmaking,** (*US*) **non-profit** à but non lucratif **▸non-proliferation** non-prolifération *f*; **non-proliferation treaty** traité *m* de non-prolifération **▸non-punitive** dont l'intention n'est pas de punir **▸non-receipt** (*of letter etc*) non-réception *f* **▸non-recurring expenses** dépenses *fpl* d'équipement **▸non-refillable** *pen, bottle* sans recharge **▸non-reflective** *glass* non réfléchissant **▸non-religious** non croyant **▸non-resident** *see* **nonresident** **▸non-residential** *area* industriel; *home* de jour; *course* sans internat **▸non-returnable** *bottle etc* non consigné **▸non-run** indémaillable **▸non-runner** non-partant *m* **▸non-scheduled** *plane, flight* spécial, en dehors des services réguliers **▸nonsectarian** non confessionnel **▸non-segregated** sans ségrégation **▸non-sexist adj** qui n'est pas sexiste ◊ **n: he is a non-sexist** il n'est pas sexiste **▸non-shrink** irrétrécissable **▸non-sinkable** insubmersible **▸nonsked** *see* **nonsked** **▸non-skid** antidérapant **▸non-skilled** = **unskilled** **▸non-slip** *shoe sole, ski* antidérapant **▸non-smoker** (*person*) non-fumeur *m*, personne *f* qui ne fume pas; (*Rail*) compartiment *m* "non-fumeurs"; **he is a non-smoker** il ne fume pas **▸non-solvent** (*Chem*) non dissolvant **▸non-specialist n** (*gen*) non-spécialiste *mf*; (*Med*) généraliste *mf* ◊ **adj** *knowledge, dictionary* général **▸non-standard** (*Ling*) non conforme à la langue correcte **▸non-starter** (*horse: lit, fig*) non-partant *m*; (*worthless person*) nullité *f*; *[idea, proposal]* **it is a non-starter** c'est voué à l'échec **▸non-stick** *coating* anti-adhérent; *saucepan* qui n'attache pas **▸non-stop** *see* **non-stop** **▸non-student** non-étudiant(e) *m(f)*, personne *f* qui n'a pas le statut d'étudiant ▸**non-support** (*US Jur*) défaut *m* de pension alimentaire ▸**non-swimmer** personne *f* qui ne sait pas nager ▸**non-taxable** non imposable ▸**non-teaching staff** (*Scol etc*) personnel *m* non enseignant ▸**non-threatening** qui n'est pas menaçant ▸**non-toxic** non toxique ▸**non-transferable** *ticket, share* nominatif (*f* -ive); *pension* non réversible ▸**non U** (*Brit* *) (**abbr of non upper class**) commun ▸**non-union** (*Ind*) *workers, labour* non syndiqué ▸**non-unionized** = **non-union** ▸**non-verbal** non verbal ▸**non-viable** non-viable ▸**non-violence** non-violence *f* ▸**non-violent** non violent ▸**non-vocational** *courses* non professionnel ▸**non-voluntary** *work* rémunéré ▸**non-voter** (*US Pol*) abstentionniste *m* ▸**non-voting share** (*Fin*) action *f* sans droit de vote ▸**non-white** (*Pol etc*) **n** personne *f* de couleur ◊ **adj** de couleur ▸**non-worker** personne *f* sans emploi ▸**non-working adj** sans emploi, qui ne travaille pas ▸**non-woven** non-tissé.

nonage ['nəʊnɪdʒ] **n** (*Jur*) minorité *f*.

nonagenarian [ˌnɒnədʒɪ'nɛərɪən] **adj, n** nonagénaire *(mf)*.

nonce [nɒns] **n: for the ~** pour la circonstance, pour l'occasion; **~ word** mot créé pour l'occasion, mot de circonstance.

nonchalance ['nɒnʃələns] **n** nonchalance *f*.

nonchalant ['nɒnʃələnt] **adj** nonchalant.

nonchalantly ['nɒnʃələntlɪ] **adv** nonchalamment.

noncommittal ['nɒnkə'mɪtl] **adj** *person, attitude* réservé, qui ne se compromet pas; *statement* qui n'engage à rien, évasif. **a ~ answer** une réponse diplomatique *or* évasive *or* de Normand; **I'll be very ~** je ne m'avancerai pas, je ne m'engagerai à rien, je resterai réservé; **he was very ~ about it** il ne s'est pas prononcé là-dessus, il a fait une réponse de Normand.

noncommittally [ˌnɒnkə'mɪtəlɪ] **adv** *answer* évasivement, sans se compromettre.

nonconformism ['nɒnkən'fɔːmɪzəm] **n** (*Rel:* **N~**) non-conformisme *m*.

nonconformist ['nɒnkən'fɔːmɪst] (*Rel:* **N~**) **1 n** non-conformiste *mf*. **2 adj** non-conformiste, dissident.

Nonconformity ['nɒnkən'fɔːmɪtɪ] **n** (*Rel*) non-conformité *f*.

nondescript ['nɒndɪskrɪpt] **adj** *colour* indéfinissable; *person* sans trait distinctif, quelconque; *appearance* insignifiant, quelconque.

none [nʌn] **1 pron a** (*not one thing*) aucun(e) *m(f)* (+ *ne before verb*). **~ of the books** aucun livre, aucun des livres; **~ of this** rien de ceci; **~ of that!** pas de ça!; **I want ~ of your excuses!** vos excuses ne m'intéressent pas!; **he would have ~ of it** il ne *or* n'en voulait rien savoir; **~ at all** pas un(e) seul(e); **I need money but have ~ at all** j'ai besoin d'argent mais je n'en ai pas du tout; **~ of this money** pas un centime de cet argent; **~ of this cheese** pas un gramme de ce fromage; **~ of this milk** pas une goutte de ce lait; **~ of this land** pas un mètre carré *or* pas un pouce de ce terrain; **there's ~ left** il n'en reste plus; **is there any bread left? — ~ at all** y a-t-il encore du pain? — pas une miette; (*liter or hum*) **money have I ~** d'argent, je n'en ai point; (*liter or hum*) **traces there were ~** de traces, aucune *or* point (*liter or hum*).

b (*not one person*) personne, aucun(e) *m(f)*, nul(le) *m(f)* (*all + ne before verb*). **~ of them** aucun d'entre eux; **~ of us** aucun de nous *or* d'entre nous, personne parmi nous; **~ can tell** personne *or* nul ne peut le dire; **~ but you can do it** vous seul êtes capable de le faire; **I have told ~ but you** je ne l'ai dit à personne d'autre que vous; **~ but a fool would do it** il n'y a qu'un imbécile pour le faire; **I know, ~ better, that** ... je sais mieux que personne que ...; **their guest was ~ other than the president himself** leur invité n'était autre que le président en personne.

c (*in form-filling etc*) néant *m*.

2 adv: he's ~ the worse for it il ne s'en porte pas plus mal; **I'm ~ the worse for having eaten it** je ne me ressens pas de l'avoir mangé; **I like him ~ the worse for it** je ne l'en aime pas moins pour cela; **the house would be ~ the worse for a coat of paint** une couche de peinture ne ferait pas de mal à cette maison; **he was ~ the wiser** il n'en savait pas plus pour autant, il n'était pas plus avancé; **it's ~ too warm** il ne fait pas tellement chaud; **and ~ too soon either!** et ce n'est pas trop tôt!; **at last he arrived and ~ too soon** il arriva enfin et il était grand temps *or* ce n'était pas trop tôt; **it was ~ too easy** ce n'était pas tellement facile; **I was ~ too sure that he would come** j'étais loin d'être sûr qu'il viendrait.

3 comp ▸**nonesuch** = **nonsuch** ▸**nonetheless** = **nevertheless**.

nonentity [nɒ'nentɪtɪ] **n** personne insignifiante *or* sans intérêt. **he's a complete ~** c'est une nullité.

nonet [nɒ'net] **n** (*Mus*) nonet *m*.

nonillion [nəʊ'nɪljən] **n** (*esp Brit:* 10^{54}) nonillion *m*; (*esp US:* 10^{30}) quintillion *m*.

non obst. prep (**abbr of non obstante** = **notwithstanding**) nonobstant.

nonpareil ['nɒnpərəl] (*frm, liter*) **1 n** personne *f or* chose *f* sans pareille. **2 adj** incomparable, sans égal.

nonplus ['nɒn'plʌs] **vt** déconcerter, dérouter, rendre perplexe. **I was utterly ~sed** j'étais complètement perplexe *or* dérouté.

nonresident [nɒn'rezɪdənt] **1 adj** (*gen*) non résidant. **~ course** stage *m* sans hébergement des participants; **~ doctor** attaché(e) *m(f)* de consultations; (*US Univ Admin*) **~ student** *étudiant(e) d'une université d'État dont le domicile permanent est situé en dehors de cet État.* **2 n** non-residant(e) *m(f)*; (*Brit: in hôtel*) client(e) *m(f)* de passage (*qui n'a pas de chambre*).

nonsense ['nɒnsəns] **1 n** (*NonC*) absurdités *fpl*, inepties *fpl*, sottises *fpl*, idioties *fpl*, non-sens *m*. **to talk ~** dire *or* débiter des absurdités *or* des inepties; **that's a piece of ~!** c'est une absurdité! *or* sottise! *or* idiotie!, c'est un non-sens!; **that's (a lot of) ~!** tout ça ce sont des absurdités *or* des inepties *or* des sottises *or* des idioties; **but that's ~** mais c'est absurde; **oh, ~!** oh, ne dis pas d'absurdités! *or* de sottises! *or* d'idioties!; **all this ~ about them not being able to pay** toutes ces histoires idiotes comme quoi* *or* selon lesquelles ils seraient incapables de payer; **it is ~ to say** il est absurde *or* idiot de dire, c'est un non-sens de dire; **it's just his ~** il dit des sottises (comme d'habitude); **he will stand no ~ from anybody** il ne se laissera pas faire par qui que ce soit, il ne se laissera marcher sur les pieds par personne; **he won't stand any ~ about that** il ne plaisante pas là-dessus; **I've had enough of this ~!** j'en ai assez de ces histoires! *or* idioties!; **stop this ~!, no more of your ~!** cesse ces idioties!; **there's no ~ about him** c'est un homme très carré; **to knock the ~ out of sb*** ramener qn à la raison; **to make (a) ~ of sth** (complètement) saboter qch; *see* **stuff**.

2 comp ▸**nonsense verse** vers *mpl* amphigouriques ▸**nonsense word** mot *m* inventé de toutes pièces.

nonsensical [nɒn'sensɪkəl] **adj** *idea, action* absurde, inepte, qui n'a pas de sens; *person* absurde, idiot. **don't be so ~** ne soyez pas si absurde *or* idiot, ne dites pas tant d'absurdités *or* de sottises.

nonsensically [nɒn'sensɪkəlɪ] **adv** absurdement.

non sequitur [ˌnɒn'sekwɪtəʳ] **n: it's a ~** ça manque de suite.

nonsked* ['nɒn'sked] **n** (*US*) avion *m* spécial.

non-stop ['nɒn'stɒp] **1 adj** sans arrêt; *train* direct; *journey* sans arrêt; *flight* direct, sans escale; (*Ski*) non-stop. (*Cine, Theat etc*) **~ performance** spectacle permanent. **2 adv** *talk etc* sans arrêt; (*Ski*) non-stop. **to fly ~ from London to Chicago** faire Londres-Chicago sans escale.

nonsuch ['nʌnsʌtʃ] **n** personne *f or* chose *f* sans pareille.

nonsuit [nɒn'suːt] **1 n** (*gen*) ordonnance *f* de non-lieu; (*on the part of the plaintiff*) cessation *f* de poursuites, retrait *m* de plainte. **to direct a ~** rendre une ordonnance de non-lieu. **2 vt** débouter. **to be ~ed** être débouté (de sa demande).

noodle ['nuːdl] **n a** (*Culin*) **~s** nouilles *fpl*; **~ soup** potage *m* au vermicelle. **b** (‡) (*person*) nouille‡ *f*, nigaud(e) *m(f)*; (*head*) caboche* *f*, tête *f*.

nook [nʊk] **n** (*corner*) coin *m*, recoin *m*; (*remote spot*) retraite *f*. **~s and crannies, ~s and corners** coins et recoins; **breakfast ~** coin-repas *m*; **a shady ~** une retraite ombragée, un coin ombragé.

nookie‡, nooky‡ ['nʊkɪ] **n** (*Brit esp hum*) la fesse‡. **to have a bit of ~** avoir une partie de jambes en l'air‡, s'envoyer en l'air‡; **he/she likes his/her ~** il/elle aime bien la fesse‡ *or* s'envoyer en l'air‡.

noon [nuːn] **1 n** midi *m*. **at/about ~** à/vers midi; *see* **high**. **2 comp** ▸**noonday, noontide n** midi *m* ◊ **adj** de midi (*fig liter*) **at the noonday** *or* **noontide of his fame** au sommet de sa gloire.

noose [nuːs] **1 n** nœud coulant; (*in animal trapping*) collet *m*; *[cowboy]* lasso *m*; *[hangman]* corde *f*. (*fig*) **to put one's head in the ~, to put a ~ round one's neck** se jeter dans la gueule du loup. **2 vt a** *rope* faire un nœud coulant à. **b** (*in trapping*) prendre au collet; *[cowboy]* prendre *or* attraper au lasso.

nope‡ [nəʊp] **particle** (*US*) non.

nor [nɔːʳ] **conj a** (*following "neither"*) ni. **neither you ~ I can do it** ni vous ni moi (nous) ne pouvons le faire; **she neither eats ~ drinks** elle ne mange ni ne boit; **neither here ~ elsewhere does he stop working** ici comme ailleurs il ne cesse pas de travailler; *see* **neither**.

b (*= and not*) **I don't know, ~ do I care** je ne sais pas et d'ailleurs je m'en moque; **that's not funny, ~ is it true** ce n'est ni drôle ni vrai; **that's not funny, ~ do I believe it's true** cela n'est pas drôle et je ne crois pas non plus que ce soit vrai; **I shan't go and ~ will you** je n'irai pas et vous non plus; **I don't like him — ~ do I** je ne l'aime pas — moi non plus; **~ was this all** et ce n'était pas tout; **~ will I deny that** ... et je ne nie pas non plus que ... + *subj*; **~ was he disappointed** et il ne fut pas déçu non plus; *see* **yet**.

nor' [nɔːʳ] **adj** (*Naut: in comps*) = **north. nor'east** *etc* = **north-east** *etc; see* **north 4**.

noradrenalin(e) ['nɔːrə'drenəlɪn, -iːn] **n** noradrénaline *f*.

Nordic ['nɔːdɪk] **adj** nordique.

norm [nɔːm] **n** norme *f*.

normal ['nɔːməl] **1 adj a** *person, situation, performance* normal; *habit* ordinaire, commun. **the child is not ~** l'enfant n'est pas normal; **it is quite ~ to believe** ... il est tout à fait normal *or* naturel de croire ...; **it was quite ~ for him to object** il était tout à fait normal *or* naturel qu'il fasse des objections; **it's quite a ~ thing for children to fight** c'est une chose très normale que les enfants se battent (*subj*); **with old people this is quite ~** chez les gens âgés c'est très normal *or* commun; **beyond ~ experience** au-delà de l'expérience ordinaire; **~ working** (*Engineering, Tech*) régime *m*; (*Ind*) **the factory is back to ~ working** le travail a repris normalement à l'usine; **~ speed** vitesse *f* de régime; (*Med*) **~ temperature** température normale.

b (*Math*) normal, perpendiculaire.

c (*Chem*) neutre.
d (*US etc*) ~ **school** école normale (d'instituteurs *or* d'institutrices).
2 n a normale *f*, état normal, condition normale. **temperatures below** ~ des températures au-dessous de la normale.
b (*Math*) normale *f*, perpendiculaire *f*.

normality [nɔː'mælɪtɪ] n, (*esp US*) **normalcy** ['nɔːməlsɪ] n normalité *f*.

normalization [ˌnɔːməlaɪ'zeɪʃən] n normalisation *f*.

normalize ['nɔːməlaɪz] 1 vt normaliser, régulariser. 2 vi se normaliser, se régulariser.

normally ['nɔːməlɪ] adv (*gen*) normalement; (*usually*) normalement, en temps normal.

Norman ['nɔːmən] 1 adj normand; (*Archit*) roman. **the** ~ **Conquest** la conquête normande; (*Ling*) ~ **French** anglo-normand *m*. 2 n Normand(e) *m(f)*.

Normandy ['nɔːməndɪ] n Normandie *f*; *see* **landing**[1].

normative ['nɔːmətɪv] adj normatif.

Norse [nɔːs] 1 adj (*Hist*) nordique, scandinave. ~**man** Scandinave *m*. 2 n (*Ling*) nordique *m*, norrois *m*. **Old** ~ vieux norrois.

north [nɔːθ] 1 n nord *m*. **magnetic** ~ nord *or* pôle *m* magnétique; **to the** ~ **of** au nord de; **house facing the** ~ maison exposée au nord; *[wind]* **to veer to the** ~, **to go into the** ~ tourner au nord, anordir (*Naut*); **the wind is in the** ~ le vent est au nord; **the wind is (coming** *or* **blowing) from the** ~ le vent vient *or* souffle du nord; **to live in the** ~ habiter dans le nord; **in the** ~ **of Scotland** dans le nord de l'Écosse; (*US Hist*) **the N**~ les États *mpl* antiesclavagistes *or* du nord.
2 adj nord *inv*, au *or* du nord, septentrional. ~ **wind** vent *m* du nord, bise *f*; ~ **coast** côte *f* nord; **in** ~ **Wales/London** dans le nord du pays de Galles/de Londres; **on the** ~ **side** du côté nord; **studio with a** ~ **light** atelier *m* qui reçoit la lumière du nord; **a** ~ **aspect** une exposition au nord; **room with a** ~ **aspect** pièce exposée au nord; ~ **wall** mur exposé au nord; (*Archit*) ~ **transept/door** transept/portail nord *or* septentrional; *see also* **4**.
3 adv *go* au nord, vers le nord, en direction du nord; *lie, be* au nord (*of* de). **further** ~ plus au nord; ~ **of the island** *be, go, sail* au nord de l'île; **the town lies** ~ **of the border** la ville est située au nord de la frontière; **we drove** ~ **for 100 km** nous avons roulé pendant 100 km en direction du nord; **go** ~ **till you get to Crewe** allez en direction du nord jusqu'à Crewe; **to sail due** ~ aller droit vers le nord; (*Naut*) avoir le cap au nord; ~ **by** ~**-east** nord quart nord-est.
4 comp ►**North Africa** Afrique *f* du Nord ►**North African** adj nord-africain, d'Afrique du Nord ◊ n Africain(e) *m(f)* du Nord, Nord-Africain(e) *m(f)* ►**North America** Amérique *f* du Nord ►**North American** adj nord-américain, d'Amérique du Nord ◊ n Nord-Américain(e) *m(f)* ►**North Atlantic** l'Atlantique *m* Nord ►**North Atlantic Drift** dérive *f* nord-atlantique ►**North Atlantic Treaty Organization** Organisation *f* du Traité de l'Atlantique Nord ►**north-bound** *traffic, vehicles* (se déplaçant) en direction du nord; *carriageway* nord *inv* ►**North Carolina** Caroline *f* du Nord; **in North Carolina** en Caroline du Nord ►**the North Country** (*Brit*) le Nord de l'Angleterre ►**north-country** adj du Nord (de l'Angleterre) ►**North Dakota** Dakota *m* du Nord; **in North Dakota** dans le Dakota du Nord ►**north-east** n nord-est *m* ◊ adj (du *or* au) nord-est *inv* ◊ adv vers le nord-est ►**north-easter** vent *m* du nord-est ►**north-easterly** adj *wind, direction* du nord-est; *situation* au nord-est ◊ adv vers le nord-est ►**north-eastern** (du) nord-est *inv* ►**north-eastward(s)** vers le nord-est ►**north-facing** exposé au nord ►**North Island** *[New Zealand]* île *f* du Nord (*de la Nouvelle-Zélande*) ►**North Korea** Corée *f* du Nord ►**North Korean** adj nord-coréen ◊ n Nord-Coréen(ne) *m(f)* ►**North-lands** pays *mpl* du Nord ►**Northman** (*Hist*) Scandinave *m* ►**north-north-east** n nord-nord-est *m* ◊ adj (du *or* au) nord-nord-est *inv* ◊ adv vers le nord-nord-est ►**north-north-west** n nord-nord-ouest *m* ◊ adj (du *or* au) nord-nord-ouest *inv* ◊ adv vers le nord-nord-ouest ►**North Pole** pôle *m* Nord ►**North Sea** mer *f* du Nord ►**North Sea gas** (*Brit*) gaz naturel (de la mer du Nord) ►**North Sea oil** pétrole *m* de la mer du Nord ►**North Star** étoile *f* polaire ►**North Vietnam** Vietnam *m* du Nord ►**North Vietnamese** adj nord-vietnamien ◊ n Nord-Vietnamien(ne) *m(f)* ►**north-wall hammer** (*Climbing*) marteau-piolet *m* ►**north-west** n nord-ouest *m* ◊ adj (du *or* au) nord-ouest *inv* ◊ adv vers le nord-ouest ►**north-wester** noroît *m*, vent *m* du nord-ouest ►**north-westerly** adj *wind, direction* du nord-ouest; *situation* au nord-ouest ◊ adv vers le nord-ouest ►**north-western** nord-ouest *inv*, du nord-ouest ►**North-West Frontier** frontière *f* du Nord-Ouest ►**North-West Passage** passage *m* du Nord-Ouest ►**Northwest Territories** (*Can*) (territoires *mpl* du) Nord-Ouest *m* ►**Northwest Territory** (*US Hist*) territoire *m* du Nord-Ouest ►**north-westward(s)** vers le nord-ouest.

Northants [nɔː'θænts] (*Brit Geog*) abbr of **Northamptonshire**.

Northd (*Brit Geog*) abbr of **Northumberland**.

northerly ['nɔːðəlɪ] 1 adj *wind* du nord; *situation* au nord; *direction* vers le nord. ~ **latitudes** latitudes boréales; ~ **aspect** exposition *f* au nord; **in a** ~ **direction** en direction du nord, vers le nord. 2 adv vers le nord.

northern ['nɔːðən] 1 adj (*gen*) nord *inv*, du nord, septentrional. **the** ~ **coast** le littoral nord *or* septentrional; **house with a** ~ **outlook** maison exposée au nord; ~ **wall** mur exposé au nord; **in** ~ **Spain** dans le nord de l'Espagne; ~ **hemisphere** hémisphère nord *or* boréal; ~ **lights** aurore boréale. 2 comp ►**Northern Ireland** Irlande *f* du Nord ►**Northern Irish** adj de l'Irlande du Nord ◊ npl Irlandais *mpl* du Nord ►**northernmost** le plus au nord, à l'extrême nord ►**Northern Territory** *[Austral]* Territoire *m* du Nord.

northerner ['nɔːðənə^r] n a homme *m* *or* femme *f* du Nord, habitant(e) *m(f)* du Nord. **he is a** ~ il vient du Nord; **the** ~**s** les gens *mpl* du Nord, les septentrionaux *mpl*. b (*US Hist*) Nordiste *mf*, antiesclavagiste *mf*.

Northumbria [nɔː'θʌmbrɪə] n Northumbrie *f*.

Northumbrian [nɔː'θʌmbrɪən] 1 adj de Northumbrie. 2 n habitant(e) *m(f)* *or* natif *m*, -ive *f* de Northumbrie.

northward ['nɔːθwəd] 1 adj au nord. 2 adv (*also* ~**s**) vers le nord.

Norway ['nɔːweɪ] n Norvège *f*.

Norwegian [nɔː'wiːdʒən] 1 adj norvégien. 2 n a Norvégien(ne) *m(f)*. b (*Ling*) norvégien *m*.

nose [nəʊz] 1 n a *[person]* nez *m*; *[dog]* nez, truffe *f*. **his** ~ **was bleeding** il saignait du nez; **he has a nice** ~ il a un joli nez; **the horse won by a** ~ le cheval a gagné d'une demi-tête; **to speak through one's** ~ nasiller, parler du nez; **it was there under his very** ~ *or* **right under his** ~ **all the time** c'était là juste *or* en plein sous son nez; **she did it under his very** ~ *or* **right under his** ~ elle l'a fait à sa barbe *or* sous son nez; (*US fig*) **right on the** ~‡ en plein dans le mille; (*fig*) **his** ~ **is out of joint** il est dépité; **that put his** ~ **out of joint** ça l'a défrisé*; (*fig*) **to lead sb by the** ~ mener qn par le bout du nez; (*fig*) **to look down one's** ~ **at sb/sth** faire le nez à qn/devant qch; (*fig*) **to turn up one's** ~ faire le dégoûté (*at* devant); (*fig*) **with one's** ~ **in the air** d'un air hautain; (*fig*) **to keep one's** ~ **to the grindstone** travailler sans répit *or* relâche; (*fig*) **to keep sb's** ~ **to the grindstone** faire travailler qn sans répit *or* relâche, ne laisser aucun répit à qn; **to poke** *or* **stick one's** ~ **into sth** mettre *or* fourrer son nez dans qch; (*fig*) **to keep one's** ~ **out of sth** ne pas se mêler de qch; (*fig*) **you'd better keep your** ~ **clean*** il vaut mieux que tu te tiennes à carreau*; (*fig*) **to have one's** ~ **in a book*** avoir toujours le nez (fourré) dans un livre; (*fig*) **it gets up my** ~* ça m'horripile, ça m'exaspère; *see* **blow**[1], **end, follow, rub, thumb** *etc*.
b (*sense of smell*) odorat *m*, nez *m*. **to have a good** ~ avoir l'odorat *or* le nez fin; (*fig*) **to have a (good)** ~ **for ...** avoir du flair pour ... .
c *[wine etc]* arôme *m*, bouquet *m*.
d *[boat etc]* nez *m*; *[tool etc]* bec *m*. (*Brit*) **a line of cars** ~ **to tail** une file de voitures pare-chocs contre pare-chocs; **he put the car's** ~ **towards the town** il a tourné la voiture en direction de la ville.
2 comp ►**nosebag** musette *f* mangeoire ►**noseband** *[horse]* muserolle *f* ►**nosebleed** saignement *m* de nez; **to have a nosebleed** saigner du nez ►**nose cone** *[missile]* ogive *f* ►**nosedive** n (*Aviat*) piqué *m*; (*fig*) *[stocks, prices]* chute *f* libre, baisse *f* rapide, plongeon *m* ◊ vi *[plane]* descendre en piqué; (*fig*) *[stocks, prices]* faire un plongeon, baisser rapidement; *[sales etc]* être en chute libre ►**nose drops** gouttes nasales, gouttes pour le nez ►**nosegay** petit bouquet ►**nose job***: (*plastic surgery*) **to have a nose job** se faire rectifier le nez ►**nosepiece** (*on spectacles*) pont *m*; (*on microscope*) porte-objectifs *m* ►**nose ring** anneau *m* de nez ►**nose wheel** (*Aviat*) roue *f* avant du train d'atterrissage.
3 vt (*smell*) flairer, renifler.
4 vi *[ship, vehicle]* s'avancer avec précaution. **the ship** ~**d (her way) through the fog** le navire progressait avec précaution dans le brouillard.

►**nose about, nose around** vi fouiller, fureter, fouiner*.

►**nose at** vt *fus* flairer, renifler.

►**nose in** vi a *[car]* se glisser dans une file. b (*) *[person]* s'immiscer *or* s'insinuer (dans un groupe).

►**nose out** 1 vi *[car]* déboîter prudemment. 2 vt sep a *[dog]* flairer. b **to nose out a secret*** découvrir *or* flairer un secret; **to nose sb out*** dénicher *or* dépister qn.

-nosed [nəʊzd] adj ending in comps au nez ... . **red-nosed** au nez rouge; *see* **long**[1], **snub**[2] *etc*.

nosey* ['nəʊzɪ] adj curieux, fouinard*, fureteur. **to be** ~ mettre *or* fourrer* son nez partout; **don't be so** ~ mêlez-vous de vos affaires! *or* de ce qui vous regarde!; (*Brit pej*) **N**~ **Parker** fouinard(e)* *m(f)*.

nosh‡ [nɒʃ] 1 n a (*Brit: food*) bouffe‡ *f*. **to have some** ~ boulotter*, bouffer‡. b (*US: snack*) casse-croûte *m*. 2 comp ►**nosh-up**‡ (*Brit*) bouffe‡ *f*; **to have a nosh-up** bouffer‡, bâfrer‡. 3 vi a (*Brit: eat*) boulotter*, bouffer‡. b (*US: have a snack*) manger *or* grignoter quelque chose entre les repas.

nosily ['nəʊzɪlɪ] adv indiscrètement.

nosing ['nəʊzɪŋ] n *[stair]* rebord *m*.

nosography [nɒ'sɒgrəfɪ] n nosographie *f*.

nosological [ˌnɒsə'lɒdʒɪkəl] adj nosologique.

nosologist [nɒ'sɒlədʒɪst] n nosologiste *mf*.

nosology [nɒ'sɒlədʒɪ] n nosologie *f*.

nostalgia [nɒs'tældʒɪə] n nostalgie *f*; (*homesickness*) nostalgie, mal *m* du pays.

nostalgic [nɒs'tældʒɪk] adj nostalgique.

Nostradamus [ˌnɒstrəˈdɑːməs] n Nostradamus *m*.

nostril [ˈnɒstrəl] n *[person, dog etc]* narine *f*; *[horse etc]* naseau *m*.

nostrum [ˈnɒstrəm] n (*patent medicine, also fig*) panacée *f*, remède universel; (*quack medicine*) remède de charlatan.

nosy [ˈnəʊzɪ] adj = **nosey**.

not [nɒt] adv a (*with vb*) ne ... pas, ne ... point (*liter, also hum*). **he is ~ here** il n'est pas ici; **he has ~** *or* **hasn't come** il n'est pas venu; **he will ~** *or* **won't stay** il ne restera pas; **is it ~?, isn't it?** non?, n'est-ce pas?; **you have got it, haven't you?** vous l'avez (bien), non? *or* n'est-ce pas?; **~ only ... but also ...** non seulement ... mais également ...; **he told me ~ to come** il m'a dit de ne pas venir; **~ to mention ...** sans compter ..., pour ne pas parler de ...; **~ wanting to be heard, he removed his shoes** ne voulant pas qu'on l'entende, il ôta ses chaussures.

b (*as substitute for clause*) non. **is he coming? — I believe ~** est-ce qu'il vient? — je crois que non; **is it going to rain? — I hope ~** va-t-il pleuvoir? — j'espère que non; **it would appear ~** il semble que non; **I am going whether he comes or ~** j'y vais qu'il vienne ou non; **believe it or ~, she has gone** le croiriez-vous, elle est partie.

c (*elliptically*) **are you cold? — ~ at all** avez-vous froid? — pas du tout; **thank you very much — ~ at all** merci beaucoup — je vous en prie *or* de rien *or* il n'y a pas de quoi; **~ in the least** pas du tout, nullement; **I wish it were ~ so** je voudrais bien qu'il en soit autrement; **for the young and the ~ so young** pour les jeunes et les moins jeunes; **big, ~ to say enormous** gros pour ne pas dire énorme; **~ that I care** non pas que cela me fasse quelque chose*; **~ that I know of** pas (autant) que je sache; **~ that they haven't been useful** on ne peut pas dire qu'ils *or* ce n'est pas qu'ils n'aient pas été utiles; **will he come? — as likely as ~** est-ce qu'il viendra? — ça se peut; **as likely as ~ he'll come** il y a une chance sur deux *or* il y a des chances (pour) qu'il vienne; **why ~?** pourquoi pas?

d (*understatement*) **~ a few ...** bien des ..., pas mal de ...; **~ without reason** et pour cause, non sans raison; **~ without some regrets** non sans quelques regrets; **I shall ~ be sorry to ...** je ne serai pas mécontent de ...; **it is ~ unlikely that ...** il n'est pas du tout impossible que ...; **a ~ inconsiderable number of ...** un nombre non négligeable de ...; **~ half!**‡ tu parles!‡, et comment!‡

e (*with pron etc*) **~ I!** moi pas!, pas moi!; **~ one book** pas un livre; **~ one man knew** pas un (homme) ne savait; **~ everyone can do that** tout le monde ne peut pas faire cela; **~ any more** plus (maintenant); **~ yet** pas encore.

f (*with adj*) non, pas. **~ guilty** non coupable; **~ negotiable** non négociable.

notability [ˌnəʊtəˈbɪlɪtɪ] n a (*NonC: quality*) prééminence *f*. b (*person*) notabilité *f*, notable *m*.

notable [ˈnəʊtəbl] 1 adj *person* notable, éminent; *thing, fact* notable, remarquable. **it is ~ that ...** il est remarquable que ... + *subj*. 2 n notable *m*.

notably [ˈnəʊtəblɪ] adv a (*in particular*) notamment, particulièrement, spécialement. b (*outstandingly*) notablement, remarquablement.

notarial [nəʊˈtɛərɪəl] adj *seal* notarial; *deed* notarié; *style* de notaire.

notarize [ˈnəʊtəˌraɪz] vt (*US*) *[notary]* authentifier, certifier conforme.

notary [ˈnəʊtərɪ] n (*also ~ public*) notaire *m*. **before a ~** par-devant notaire.

notate [nəʊˈteɪt] vt (*Mus*) noter, transcrire.

notation [nəʊˈteɪʃən] n (*Mus, Ling, Math*) notation *f*.

notch [nɒtʃ] 1 n (*in wood, stick etc*) entaille *f*, encoche *f*, coche *f*; (*in belt etc*) cran *m*; (*in wheel, board etc*) dent *f*, cran; (*in saw*) dent; (*in blade*) ébréchure *f*; (*US Geog*) défilé *m*; (*Sewing*) cran. **he pulled his belt in one ~** il a resserré sa ceinture d'un cran. 2 comp ►**notchback** (*US: car*) tri-corps *f*, trois-volumes *f*. 3 vt *stick etc* encocher, cocher; *wheel etc* cranter, denteler; *blade* ébrécher; (*Sewing*) *seam* cranter.

►**notch together** vt sep (*Carpentry*) assembler à entailles.

►**notch up** vt sep *score, point etc* marquer.

note [nəʊt] 1 n a (*short record of facts etc*) note *f*. **to take** *or* **make a ~ of sth** prendre qch en note, prendre note de qch; **please make a ~ of her name** prenez note de son nom *or* notez son nom s'il vous plaît; (*fig*) **I must make a ~ to buy some more** il faut que je me souvienne d'en racheter; *[student, policeman, secretary etc]* **to take** *or* **make ~s** prendre des notes; **lecture ~s** notes de cours; **to speak from ~s** parler en consultant ses notes; **to speak without ~s** parler sans notes *or* papiers; *see* **compare**.

b (*Diplomacy*) note *f*. **diplomatic ~** note diplomatique, mémorandum *m*; **official ~ from the government** note officielle du gouvernement.

c (*short commentary*) note *f*, annotation *f*, commentaire *m*. **author's ~** note de l'auteur; **translator's ~s** (*footnotes etc*) remarques *fpl or* notes du traducteur; (*foreword*) "préface *f* du traducteur"; **"N~s on Gibbon"** "Remarques *or* Notes sur Gibbon"; **~s on a literary work** commentaire sur un ouvrage littéraire; **to put ~s into a text** annoter un texte.

d (*informal letter*) mot *m*. (*to secretary*) **take a ~ to Mr Jones** je vais vous dicter un mot pour M. Jones; **just a quick ~ to tell you ...** un petit mot à la hâte *or* en vitesse pour te dire ... .

e (*Mus*) note *f*; *[piano]* touche *f*; *[bird]* note. **to give the ~** donner la note; **to hold a ~** tenir *or* prolonger une note; **to play a false ~, to sing a false ~** faire une fausse note; (*fig*) **his speech struck the right/wrong ~** son discours était bien dans la note/n'était pas dans la note.

f (*quality, tone*) note *f*, ton *m*, accent *m*. **with a ~ of anxiety in his voice** avec une note d'anxiété dans la voix; **his voice held a ~ of desperation** sa voix avait un accent de désespoir; **a ~ of nostalgia** une note *or* touche nostalgique; **a ~ of warning** un avertissement discret.

g (*Brit: also* **bank~**) billet *m* (de banque). **one-pound ~** billet d'une livre (sterling).

h (*Comm*) effet *m*, billet *m*, bon *m*. **~ of hand** reconnaissance *f* (de dette); (*Fin*) **~s payable** effets *mpl* à payer; *see* **advice, promissory**.

i (*NonC: notability*) **a man of ~** un homme éminent *or* de marque; **a family of ~** une famille éminente; **all the people of ~** toutes les notabilités; **nothing of ~** rien d'important.

j (*NonC: notice*) **to take ~ of** prendre (bonne) note de, remarquer; **take ~!** prenez bonne note!; **the critics took ~ of the book** les critiques ont remarqué le livre; **they will take ~ of what you say** ils feront *or* prêteront attention à ce que vous dites; **worthy of ~** remarquable, digne d'attention.

2 comp ►**notebook** carnet *m*, calepin *m*, agenda *m*; (*Scol*) cahier *m*; *[stenographer]* bloc-notes *m* ►**note-case** (*Brit*) portefeuille *m*, porte-billets *m inv* ►**note issue** émission *f* fiduciaire ►**notepad** (*Brit*) bloc-notes *m* ►**notepaper** papier *m* à lettres ►**noteworthiness** importance *f* ►**noteworthy** notable, remarquable, digne d'attention; **it is noteworthy that ...** il convient de noter que ... .

3 vt a (*Admin, Jur etc*) noter, prendre acte de, prendre (bonne) note de. **to ~ a fact** prendre acte d'un fait; (*Jur*) **"which fact is duly ~d"** "dont acte"; **we have ~d your remarks** nous avons pris (bonne) note de vos remarques.

b notice) remarquer, constater. **to ~ an error** relever une faute; **~ that the matter is not closed yet** notez *or* remarquez bien que l'affaire n'est pas encore close; **she ~d that his hands were dirty** elle remarqua qu'il avait les mains sales; **she ~d that they hadn't arrived** elle constata qu'ils n'étaient pas arrivés.

c (*also ~ down*) noter, inscrire, écrire. **let me ~ it (down)** laissez-moi le noter *or* l'écrire; **to ~ (down) sb's remarks** noter les remarques de qn; **to ~ (down) an appointment in one's diary** noter *or* inscrire un rendez-vous dans son agenda.

►**note down** vt sep = **note 3c**.

noted [ˈnəʊtɪd] adj *person* éminent, illustre, célèbre; *thing, fact* réputé, célèbre. **to be ~ for one's generosity** être (bien) connu pour sa générosité, avoir une réputation de générosité; (*iro*) **he's not ~ for his broad-mindedness** il n'est pas connu pour la largeur de ses vues; **a town ~ for its beauty** une ville connue *or* célèbre pour sa beauté; **a place ~ for its wine** un endroit célèbre *or* réputé pour son vin.

nothing [ˈnʌθɪŋ] 1 n a rien *m* (+ *ne before vb*). **I saw ~** je n'ai rien vu; **~ happened** il n'est rien arrivé, il ne s'est rien passé; **to eat ~** ne rien manger; **~ to eat/read** rien à manger/à lire; **he's had ~ to eat yet** il n'a pas encore mangé; **he's eaten ~ yet** il n'a encore rien mangé; **~ could be easier** rien de plus simple; **~ pleases him** rien ne le satisfait, il n'est jamais content; **there is ~ that pleases him** il n'y a rien qui lui plaise.

b (+ *adj*) rien de. **~ new/interesting** *etc* rien de nouveau/d'intéressant *etc*.

c (*in phrases*) **he's five foot ~** il ne fait qu'un mètre cinquante; **~ on earth** rien au monde; **you look like ~ on earth*** tu as l'air de je ne sais quoi; **as if ~ had happened** comme si de rien n'était; **fit for ~** propre *or* bon (*f* bonne) à rien; **to say ~ of ...** sans parler de ...; **I can do ~ (about it)** je n'y peux rien; **he is ~ if not polite** il est avant tout poli; **for ~** (*in vain*) en vain, inutilement; (*without payment*) pour rien, gratuitement; (*for no reason*) sans raison; **he was working for ~** il travaillait gratuitement *or* sans se faire payer *or* bénévolement; **he got ~ out of it** il n'en a rien retiré, il n'y a rien gagné; **all his fame was as ~, all his fame stood** *or* **counted for ~** toute sa gloire ne comptait pour rien; (*hum*) **I'm not Scottish for ~*** ce n'est pas pour rien que je suis Écossais; **~ of the kind!** absolument pas!, (mais) pas du tout!; **to think ~ of doing sth** (*do as matter of course*) trouver naturel de faire qch, n'attacher aucune importance à faire qch; (*do unscrupulously*) n'avoir aucun scrupule à faire qch; **think ~ of it!** mais je vous en prie!, mais pas du tout!; **don't apologize, it's ~** ne vous excusez pas, ce n'est rien; **that is ~ to you** (*it's easy for you*) pour vous ce n'est rien; (*it's not your business*) cela ne vous regarde pas; **she is** *or* **means ~ to him** elle n'est rien pour lui; **it's ~** *or* **it means ~ to me whether he comes or not** il m'est indifférent qu'il vienne ou non; **as a secretary she is ~ to** *or* **compared with her sister** comme secrétaire elle ne vaut pas sa sœur; **I can make ~ of it** je n'y comprends rien; **to have ~ on** (*be naked*) être nu; **I have ~ on (for) this evening** je ne suis pas pris ce soir, je n'ai rien (de prévu) ce soir; **the police have ~ on him** la police n'a rien pu retenir contre lui; (*fig: isn't as good as*) **he has ~ on her*** il ne lui arrive pas à la cheville; **there's ~ in it** (*not interesting*) c'est sans intérêt; (*not true*) ce n'est absolument pas vrai; **there's ~ in these rumours** il n'y a rien de vrai *or* pas un grain de vérité dans ces rumeurs; **there's ~ in it for us** nous n'avons rien à y gagner; **there's ~ to it*** c'est facile (comme tout*); **I love swimming, there's ~ like it!**

j'adore la natation, il n'y a rien de tel! *or* de mieux!; **there's ~ like exercise for keeping one fit** il n'y a rien de tel que l'exercice pour garder la forme, rien ne vaut l'exercice pour rester en forme; (*Prov*) **~ venture ~ gain** *or* **have** *or* **win** qui ne risque rien n'a rien (*Prov*); **you get ~ for ~** on n'a rien pour rien; **to come to ~** ne pas aboutir, ne rien donner, faire fiasco; **to reduce to ~** réduire à néant *or* à rien; **~ much** pas grand-chose; **~ but** rien que; **he does ~ but eat** il ne fait que manger; **I get ~ but complaints all day** je n'entends que des plaintes à longueur de journée; (*Brit*) **there's ~ for it but to go** il n'y a qu'à *or* il ne nous reste qu'à partir; **~ less than** rien moins que; **~ more** rien de plus; **~ else** rien d'autre; **there's ~ else for it** c'est inévitable; **we could do ~ else** (*nothing more*) nous ne pouvions rien faire de plus; (*no other thing*) nous ne pouvions rien faire d'autre; **that has ~ to do with us** nous n'avons rien à voir là-dedans; **I've got ~ to do with it** je n'y suis pour rien; **have ~ to do with it!** ne vous en mêlez pas!; **that has ~ to do with it** cela n'a rien à voir, cela n'entre pas en ligne de compte; **there is ~ to laugh at** il n'y a pas de quoi rire; **he had ~ to say for himself** (*no explanation*) il se trouvait sans excuse; (*no conversation*) il n'avait pas de conversation; **I have ~ against him/the idea** je n'ai rien contre lui/cette idée; **there was ~ doing* at the club so I went home** il ne se passait rien d'intéressant au club, alors je suis rentré; **~ doing!*** (*refusing*) pas question!; (*reporting lack of success*) pas moyen!; (*very quickly*) **in ~ flat*** en un rien de temps, en cinq sec‡; (*US*) **you don't know from ~‡** tu ne sais foutrement‡ rien; *see* **flat¹, money 1a, something 1, wrong.**

d (*Math*) zéro *m*.

e (*NonC: nothingness*) néant *m*, rien *m*.

f (*person*) zéro *m*, nullité *f*; (*thing*) vétille *f*, rien *m*. **it's a mere ~ compared with what he spent last year** ça n'est rien *or* c'est une paille* en comparaison de ce qu'il a dépensé l'an dernier; **to say sweet ~s to sb** conter fleurette à qn; **he's just a ~** c'est une nullité *or* un zéro.

2 **adv** aucunement, nullement, pas du tout. **~ less than** rien moins que; **he is ~ the worse for it** il ne s'en porte pas plus mal; **it was ~ like as big as we thought** c'était loin d'être aussi grand qu'on avait cru; **~ daunted, he ...** nullement *or* aucunement découragé, il ..., sans se (laisser) démonter, il ...; *see* **loath.**

3 **adj** (*US* ‡: *pej*) minable, de rien du tout.

nothingness [ˈnʌθɪŋnɪs] **n** (*NonC*) néant *m*.

notice [ˈnəʊtɪs] 1 **n** a (*NonC*) (*warning, intimation*) avis *m*, notification *f*; (*Jur: official personal communication*) mise *f* en demeure; (*period*) délai *m*. **~ is hereby given that ...** il est porté à la connaissance du public par la présente que ...; **advance** *or* **previous ~** préavis *m*; **final ~** dernier avertissement; **~ to pay** avis d'avoir à payer; (*Comm*) **~ of receipt** avis de réception; (*Jur*) **~ to appear** assignation *f*; (*Jur, Fin*) **~ of calls** (avis *m* d') appel *m* de fonds; (*Jur*) **~ of termination** avis *m* de clôture (d'une procédure); (*to tenant etc*) **~ to quit** congé *m*; **to give ~ to** (*to tenant*) donner congé à; (*to landlord etc*) donner un préavis de départ à (*see also* **lb**); **he gave her ~ to do ...** il l'a avisée qu'elle devait faire ...; **to give sb ~ that ...**, (*frm*) **to serve ~ on sb that ...** aviser qn que ..., faire savoir à qn que ...; **to give ~ that ...** faire savoir que ...; (*Admin etc: officially*) donner acte que ... (*Admin*); **to give ~ of sth** annoncer qch; **to give sb ~ of sth** avertir *or* prévenir qn de qch; (*Admin etc: officially*) donner acte à qn de qch; **I must have (some) ~ of what you intend to do** il faut que je sois prévenu *or* avisé à l'avance de ce que vous avez l'intention de faire; **we require 6 days' ~** nous demandons un préavis de 6 jours; **you must give me at least a week's ~ if you want to do ...** il faut me prévenir *or* m'avertir au moins une semaine à l'avance si vous voulez faire ...; **we had no ~ (of it)** nous n'(en) avons pas été prévenus à l'avance, nous n'avons pas eu de préavis (à ce sujet); (*Admin frm*) **without (previous) ~** sans préavis, sans avis préalable; **he did it without any ~** *or* **with no ~** il l'a fait sans en aviser personne; **it happened without ~** c'est arrivé sans que rien ne le laisse prévoir; **until further ~** jusqu'à nouvel ordre; **you must be ready to leave at very short ~** il faut que vous soyez prêt à partir dans les plus brefs délais; **he rang me up at short ~** il m'a téléphoné à la dernière minute *or* peu de temps à l'avance; (*Fin*) **at short ~** à court terme; **at a moment's ~** sur-le-champ, immédiatement; **at 3 days' ~** dans un délai de 3 jours.

b (*NonC: end of work contract*) (*by employer*) congé *m*; (*by employee*) démission *f*. **to give sb ~ of dismissal** (*employee*) licencier qn, renvoyer qn; (*servant etc*) donner son congé à qn, congédier qn; **to give ~, to give in** *or* **hand in one's ~** *[professional or office worker]* donner sa démission; *[servant]* donner ses huit jours; **he was dismissed without (any) ~** *or* **with no ~** il a été renvoyé sans préavis; **to get one's ~** recevoir son licenciement *or* son congé; **he's under ~ (to leave)** il a reçu son congé; **a week's ~** une semaine de préavis, un préavis d'une semaine.

c (*announcement*) avis *m*, annonce *f*; (*esp in newspaper*) entrefilet *m*, notice *f*; (*poster*) affiche *f*, placard *m*; (*sign*) pancarte *f*, écriteau *m*. **public ~** avis au public; **to put a ~ in the paper** mettre *or* faire insérer une annonce *or* un entrefilet dans le journal; (*Press*) **birth/marriage/death ~** annonce de naissance/mariage/décès; **I saw a ~ in the paper about the concert** j'ai vu une annonce *or* un entrefilet *or* une notice dans le journal à propos du concert; **the ~ says "keep out"** la pancarte *or* l'écriteau porte l'inscription "défense d'entrer"; **the ~ of the meeting was published in ...** l'annonce de la réunion *or* la notice annonçant la réunion a été publiée dans ... .

d (*review*) *[book, film, play etc]* compte rendu *m*, critique *f*. **the book/film/play got good ~s** le livre/le film/la pièce a eu de bonnes critiques.

e (*NonC*) **to take ~ of sb/sth** tenir compte de qn/qch, faire *or* prêter attention à qn/qch; **to take no ~ of sb/sth** ne tenir aucun compte de qn/qch, ne pas faire attention à qn/qch; **take no ~!** ne faites pas attention!; **he took no ~ of her remarks** il n'a absolument pas tenu compte de ses remarques; **he took no ~ of her** il n'a absolument pas fait attention à elle, il l'a complètement ignorée; **a lot of ~ he takes of me!** pour lui c'est comme si je n'existais pas!; **I wasn't taking much ~ at the time** je ne faisais pas très attention à ce moment-là; **it escaped his ~ that ...** il ne s'est pas aperçu que ..., il n'a pas remarqué que ...; **it has attracted a lot of ~** cela a suscité un grand intérêt; **to attract ~** se faire remarquer, s'afficher (*pej*); **to avoid ~** (essayer de) passer inaperçu; **to bring to sb's ~** faire observer *or* faire remarquer à qn, porter à la connaissance de qn; **it came to his ~ that ...** il s'est aperçu que ..., son attention a été attirée sur le fait que ...; **it has come** *or* **it has been brought to my ~ that ...** il a été porté à ma connaissance que ..., il m'a été signalé que ...; **that is beneath my ~** c'est indigne de mon attention; *see* **sit up, slip.**

2 **vt** a (*perceive*) s'apercevoir de, remarquer; (*heed*) faire attention à. **I ~d a tear in his coat** j'ai remarqué un accroc dans son manteau; **when he ~d me he called out to me** quand il m'a vu *or* s'est aperçu que j'étais là il m'a appelé; **to ~ a mistake** remarquer une *or* s'apercevoir d'une faute; **without my noticing it** sans que je le remarque (*subj*) *or* m'en aperçoive, sans que j'y fasse attention; **I'm afraid I didn't ~** malheureusement je n'ai pas remarqué; **I never ~ such things** je ne remarque jamais ces choses-là, je ne fais jamais attention à ces choses-là; **I ~d her hesitating** j'ai remarqué *or* je me suis aperçu qu'elle hésitait; **I ~ you have a new dress** je vois que vous avez une nouvelle robe; **so I've ~d!** en effet je m'en suis aperçu.

b (*review*) *book, film, play* faire le compte rendu *or* la critique de.

3 **comp ▸notice board** (*Brit*) (*printed or painted sign*) écriteau *m*, pancarte *f*; (*for holding announcements*) panneau *m* d'affichage.

noticeable [ˈnəʊtɪsəbl] **adj** (*perceptible*) perceptible, visible; (*obvious*) évident, net (*f* nette), clair. **it isn't really ~** ça ne se voit pas vraiment; **his lack of enthusiasm was very ~** son manque d'enthousiasme était très visible *or* perceptible; **she was ~ on account of her large hat** elle se faisait remarquer par son énorme chapeau; **it is ~ that ...** il est évident *or* net *or* clair que ... .

noticeably [ˈnəʊtɪsəblɪ] **adv** sensiblement, perceptiblement, nettement, visiblement.

notifiable [ˈnəʊtɪfaɪəbl] **adj** (*Admin etc*) *disease* à déclarer obligatoirement. **all changes of address are ~ immediately** tout changement d'adresse doit être signalé immédiatement aux autorités.

notification [ˌnəʊtɪfɪˈkeɪʃən] **n** avis *m*, annonce *f*, notification *f*; *[marriage, engagement]* annonce; *[birth, death]* déclaration *f*. (*Press*) **"please accept this as the only ~"** "le présent avis tient lieu de faire-part".

notify [ˈnəʊtɪfaɪ] **vt**: **to ~ sth to sb** signaler *or* notifier qch à qn; **to ~ sb of sth** aviser *or* avertir qn de qch; **any change of address must be notified** tout changement d'adresse doit être signalé *or* notifié; **you will be notified later of the result** on vous communiquera le résultat ultérieurement *or* plus tard.

notion [ˈnəʊʃən] **n** a (*thought, project*) idée *f*. **brilliant ~** idée géniale *or* de génie; **what a ~!** quelle idée!, en voilà une idée!; **what a funny ~!** quelle drôle d'idée!; **I can't bear the ~ (of it)** je n'ose pas y penser; **he has** *or* **gets some wonderful ~s** il a de merveilleuses idées; **I've got a ~ for a play** j'ai l'idée d'une pièce; **I hit (up)on** *or* **suddenly had the ~ of going to see her** tout à coup l'idée m'est venue d'aller la voir; **that ~ never entered my head** cette idée ne m'est jamais venue, je n'y ai jamais pensé; **he got the ~ (into his head)** *or* **he somehow got hold of the ~ that she wouldn't help him** il s'est mis en tête (l'idée) qu'elle ne l'aiderait pas; **where did you get the ~** *or* **what gave you the ~ that I couldn't come?** où as-tu pris l'idée que *or* qu'est-ce qui t'a fait penser que je ne pourrais pas venir?; **to put ~s into sb's head, to give sb ~s** mettre *or* fourrer* des idées dans la tête de qn; **that gave me the ~ of inviting her** cela m'a donné l'idée de l'inviter.

b (*opinion*) idée *f*, opinion *f*; (*way of thinking*) conception *f*, façon *f* de penser. **he has some odd ~s** il a de drôles d'idées; **she has some odd ~s about how to bring up children** elle a de drôles d'idées sur la façon d'élever les enfants; **according to his ~** selon sa façon de penser; **if that's your ~ of fun ...** si c'est ça que tu appelles t'amuser ...; **it wasn't my ~ of a holiday** ce n'était pas ce que j'appelle des vacances.

c (*vague knowledge*) idée *f*, notion *f*. **I've got some ~ of physics** j'ai quelques notions de physique; **have you any ~ of what he meant to do?** avez-vous la moindre idée de ce qu'il voulait faire?; **I haven't the least** *or* **slightest** *or* **foggiest* ~** je n'en ai pas la moindre idée; **I have a ~ that he was going to Paris** j'ai idée *or* j'ai dans l'idée qu'il allait à Paris; **I had no ~ they knew each other** je n'avais aucune idée *or* j'ignorais absolument qu'ils se connaissaient; **he has no ~ of time** il n'a pas la notion du temps; **can you give me a rough ~ of how many you**

want? pouvez-vous m'indiquer en gros combien vous en voulez? **d** (*US: ribbons, thread etc*) **~s** (articles *mpl* de) mercerie *f*.

notional ['nəʊʃənl] **adj** **a** (*not real*) imaginaire, irréel. **b** (*Ling*) **~ grammar** grammaire notionnelle; **~ word** mot plein. **c** (*Philos*) notionnel, conceptuel. **d** (*US: whimsical*) *person* capricieux, fantasque.

notoriety [ˌnəʊtə'raɪətɪ] **n** **a** (*NonC*) (triste) notoriété *f*, triste réputation *f*. **b** (*person*) individu *m* au nom tristement célèbre.

notorious [nəʊ'tɔːrɪəs] **adj** *event, act* d'une triste notoriété; *crime* notoire, célèbre; *liar, thief, criminal* notoire; *place* mal famé. **a ~ woman** une femme de mauvaise réputation; **the ~ case of ...** le cas tristement célèbre de ...; **he is ~ for his dishonesty** il est d'une malhonnêteté notoire; **he is ~ for this** tout le monde sait ça de lui; **the ~ Richard Thomas** Richard Thomas de triste renom; **it is ~ that ...** c'est un fait notoire que ..., il est de notoriété publique que ... .

notoriously [nəʊ'tɔːrɪəslɪ] **adv** notoirement. **~ cruel/inefficient** d'une cruauté/d'une incompétence notoire; **it is ~ difficult to do that** il est notoire qu'il est difficile de faire cela, il est notoirement difficile de faire cela.

Notts. [nɒts] (*Brit Geog*) **abbr of Nottinghamshire**.

notwithstanding [ˌnɒtwɪθ'stændɪŋ] **1 prep** malgré, en dépit de. **2 adv** néanmoins, malgré tout, quand même, tout de même, pourtant. **3 conj** (*gen* **~ that**) quoique + *subj*, bien que + *subj*.

nougat ['nuːgɑː, 'nʌgət] **n** nougat *m*.

nought [nɔːt] **n = naught**.

noun [naʊn] **1 n** nom *m*, substantif *m*. **2 comp ▸noun clause** proposition substantive **▸noun phrase** syntagme *m* nominal.

nourish ['nʌrɪʃ] **vt** *person* nourrir (*with* de); *leather etc* entretenir; (*fig*) *hopes etc* nourrir, entretenir; *see* **ill, under, well**[2].

nourishing ['nʌrɪʃɪŋ] **adj** nourrissant, nutritif.

nourishment ['nʌrɪʃmənt] **n** (*NonC: food*) nourriture *f*, aliments *mpl*. **he has taken (some) ~** il s'est (un peu) alimenté.

nous* [naʊs] **n** (*Brit: NonC*) bon sens. **he's got a lot of ~** il a du plomb dans la cervelle*.

Nov. **abbr of November**.

nova ['nəʊvə] **n, pl ~s** *or* **novae** ['nəʊviː] nova *f*.

Nova Scotia ['nəʊvə'skəʊʃə] **n** Nouvelle-Écosse *f*.

Nova Scotian ['nəʊvə'skəʊʃən] **1 adj** néo-écossais. **2 n** Néo-écossais(e) *m(f)*.

novel ['nɒvəl] **1 n** (*Literat*) roman *m*. **2 adj** nouveau (*f* nouvelle) (*after n*), original, inédit. **this is something ~** voici quelque chose d'original *or* d'inédit.

novelette [ˌnɒvə'let] **n** (*Literat*) nouvelle *f*; (*slightly pej*) roman *m* à bon marché, roman à deux sous; (*love story*) (petit) roman à l'eau de rose.

novelettish [ˌnɒvə'letɪʃ] **adj** (*pej*) de roman à deux sous; (*sentimental*) à l'eau de rose.

novelist ['nɒvəlɪst] **n** romancier *m*, -ière *f*.

novella [nəʊ'velə] **n, pl ~s** *or* **novelle** [nəʊ'veleɪ] roman *m* court.

novelty ['nɒvəltɪ] **n** **a** (*NonC*) (*newness*) nouveauté *f*; (*unusualness*) étrangeté *f*. **once the ~ has worn off** une fois passée la nouveauté. **b** (*idea, thing*) innovation *f*. **it was quite a ~** c'était une innovation *or* du nouveau *or* de l'inédit. **c** (*Comm*) (article *m* de) nouveauté *f*, fantaisie *f*.

November [nəʊ'vembəʳ] **n** novembre *m*; *for phrases see* **September**.

novena [nəʊ'viːnə] **n, pl novenae** [nəʊ'viːniː] neuvaine *f*.

novice ['nɒvɪs] **n** novice *mf*, apprenti(e) *m(f)*, débutant(e) *m(f)*; (*Rel*) novice. **to be a ~ at sth** être novice en qch; **he's a ~ in politics, he's a political ~** c'est un novice *or* débutant en politique; **he's no ~** il n'est pas novice, il n'en est pas à son coup d'essai.

noviciate, novitiate [nəʊ'vɪʃɪɪt] **n** (*Rel*) (*period*) (temps *m* du) noviciat *m*; (*place*) maison *f* des novices, noviciat; (*fig*) noviciat, apprentissage *m*.

Novocain(e) ['nəʊvəʊkeɪn] **n** ® novocaïne *f* ®.

NOW [naʊ] (*US*) (**abbr of National Organization for Women**) *organisation féministe*.

now [naʊ] **1 adv** **a** (*gen*) maintenant; (*these days*) actuellement, en ce moment, à présent; (*at that time*) alors, à ce moment-là; (*in these circumstances*) maintenant, dans ces circonstances. **what are you doing ~?** qu'est-ce que tu fais maintenant *or* en ce moment *or* actuellement *or* à présent?; **I am doing it right ~** je suis (justement) en train de le faire, je le fais à l'instant même; **he ~ understood why she had left him** alors il comprit *or* il comprit alors pourquoi elle l'avait quitté; **how can I believe you ~?** comment puis-je te croire maintenant? *or* dans ces circonstances?; **~ is the time to do it** c'est le moment de le faire; **~ is the best time to go to Scotland** c'est maintenant le meilleur moment pour aller en Écosse; **apples are in season just ~** c'est la saison des pommes maintenant *or* à présent *or* en ce moment; **I saw him come in just ~** je l'ai vu arriver à l'instant, je viens de le voir arriver; **I'll do it just ~** *or* **right ~** je vais le faire dès maintenant *or* à l'instant; **I must be off ~** sur ce *or* maintenant il faut que je me sauve (*subj*); **they won't be long ~** ils ne vont plus tarder (maintenant); **~ I'm ready** maintenant *or* à présent je suis prêt; **~ for the question of your expenses** et maintenant en ce qui concerne la question de vos dépenses *or* frais; **here and ~** sur-le-champ; **(every) ~ and again, (every) ~ and then** de temps en temps, de temps à autre, par moments; **it's ~ or never!** c'est le moment ou jamais!; **even ~ there's time to change your mind** il est encore temps (maintenant) de changer d'avis; **people do that even ~** les gens font ça encore aujourd'hui *or* maintenant; **even ~ we have no rifles** encore actuellement *or* à l'heure actuelle nous n'avons pas de fusils.

b (*with prep*) **you should have done that before ~** vous auriez déjà dû l'avoir fait; **before ~ people thought that ...** auparavant les gens pensaient que ...; **you should have finished long before ~** il y a longtemps que vous auriez dû avoir fini; **long before ~ it was realized that ...** il y a longtemps déjà on comprenait que ...; **between ~ and next Tuesday** d'ici (à) mardi prochain; **they should have arrived by ~** ils devraient être déjà arrivés, ils devraient être arrivés à l'heure qu'il est; **haven't you finished by ~?** vous n'avez toujours pas fini?, vous n'avez pas encore fini?; **by ~ it was clear that ...** déjà à ce moment-là il était évident que ...; **that will do for ~** ça ira pour l'instant *or* pour le moment; **from ~ on(wards)** (*with present tense*) à partir de maintenant; (*with future tense*) à partir de maintenant, dorénavant, désormais; (*with past tense*) dès lors, dès ce moment-là; **(in) 3 weeks from ~** d'ici (à) 3 semaines; **from ~ until then** d'ici là; **till ~, until ~, up to ~** (*till this moment*) jusqu'à présent, jusqu'ici; (*till that moment*) jusque-là.

c (*showing alternation*) **~ walking, ~ running** tantôt (en) marchant, tantôt (en) courant; **~ here, ~ there** tantôt par ici, tantôt par là.

d (*without temporal force*) **~!** bon!, alors!, bon alors!; **~, ~!** allons, allons!; (*warning*) **~, Simon!** allons, Simon!; **come ~!** allons!; **well, ~!** eh bien!; **~ then, let's start!** bon, commençons!; **~ then, what's all this?** alors *or* allons, qu'est-ce que c'est que ça?; **~, they had been looking for him all morning** or, ils avaient passé toute la matinée à sa recherche; **~, he was a fisherman** or, il était pêcheur; **~ do be quiet for a minute** allons, taisez-vous une minute.

2 conj maintenant que, à présent que. **~ (that) you've seen him** maintenant que *or* à présent que vous l'avez vu.

3 adj **a** (*esp US: present*) actuel. **the ~ president** le président actuel.

b (**‡**: *exciting and new*) *clothes* du dernier cri; (*interested in new things*) *people* branché, dans le vent.

4 n *see* **here**.

nowadays ['naʊədeɪz] **adv** aujourd'hui, de nos jours, actuellement.

noway(s) ['nəʊweɪ(z)] **adv** (*US*) aucunement, nullement, en aucune façon.

nowhere ['nəʊwɛəʳ] **adv** **a** nulle part. **he went ~** il n'est allé nulle part; **~ in Europe** nulle part en Europe; **it's ~ you'll ever find it** c'est dans un endroit où tu ne le trouveras jamais; **it's ~ you know** ce n'est pas un endroit que tu connais; **where are you going? — ~ special** où vas-tu? — nulle part en particulier; **~ else** nulle part ailleurs; **she was ~ to be found** elle était introuvable; **she is ~ to be seen** on ne la voit *or* trouve nulle part; **without me you would be ~** sans moi tu ne serais rien; **they appeared from ~** *or* **out of ~** ils sont apparus *or* se sont pointés* comme par miracle; **he seemed to come from ~** on aurait dit qu'il était tombé du ciel; **they came up from ~ and won the championship** ils sont revenus de loin pour gagner le championnat; **the rest of the runners came ~** les autres concurrents sont arrivés (bien) loin derrière; **lying will get you ~** tu ne gagneras rien à mentir, ça ne te servira à rien de mentir; **we're getting ~ (fast)*, this is getting us ~** ça ne nous mène strictement à rien; *see* **get 2**.

b **his house is ~ near the church** sa maison n'est pas du tout vers l'église; **she is ~ near as clever as he is** il s'en faut de beaucoup qu'elle soit aussi intelligente que lui; **you are ~ near the truth** vous êtes à mille lieues de la vérité; **you're ~ near it!, you're ~ near right!** tu n'y es pas du tout!; **£10 is ~ near enough** 10 livres sont (très) loin du compte; *see also* **near 1b**.

nowise ['nəʊwaɪz] **adv** (*US*) = **noway(s)**.

nowt [naʊt] **n** (*Brit dial*) = **nothing**.

noxious ['nɒkʃəs] **adj** *fumes, gas* délétère, nocif; *substance, habit, influence* nocif. **to have a ~ effect on** avoir un effet nocif sur.

nozzle ['nɒzl] **n** **a** *[hose etc]* ajutage *m*, jet *m*; *[syringe]* canule *f*; (*for icing*) douille *f*; *[bellows]* bec *m*; *[vacuum cleaner]* suceur *m*; *[flamethrower]* ajutage. **b** (**‡**: *nose*) pif**‡** *m*, blair**‡** *m*.

NPD [ˌenpiː'diː] **n** (*Comm*) (**abbr of new product development**) *see* **new 3**.

NPV [ˌenpiː'viː] **n** (*Fin*) (**abbr of net present value**) VAN *f*.

nr **prep abbr of near**.

NRV [ˌenɑːʳ'viː] **n** (*Fin*) (**abbr of net realizable value**) *see* **net**[2] **1**.

NSB [ˌenes'biː] **n** (*Brit*) **abbr of National Savings Bank**.

N.S.C. [ˌenes'siː] **n** **a** (*US*) (**abbr of National Security Council**) *see* **national**. **b** (*Brit*) (**abbr of National Safety Council**) *see* **national**.

N.S.P.C.C. [ˌenes,piː'siː'siː] **n** (*Brit*) (**abbr of National Society for the Prevention of Cruelty to Children**) *société pour la protection de l'enfance*.

N.S.W. (*Geog*) (**abbr of New South Wales**) *see* **new**.

N.T. **a** (*Bible*) (**abbr of New Testament**) *see* **new**. **b** (*Brit*) (**abbr of National Trust**) *see* **national**.

nth [enθ] **adj** *see* **N b**.

NUAAW (*Brit*) **n** (**abbr of National Union of Agricultural and Allied

Workers) *syndicat*.

nuance ['nju:ɑ̃:ns] **n** nuance *f*.

nub [nʌb] **n** (*small lump*) petit morceau. (*fig*) **the ~ of the matter** le cœur *or* le noyau *or* l'essentiel *m* de l'affaire.

Nubia ['nju:bɪə] **n** Nubie *f*.

Nubian ['nju:bɪən] 1 **adj** nubien. 2 **n** Nubien(ne) *m(f)*.

nubile ['nju:baɪl] **adj** nubile.

nubility [nju:'bɪlɪtɪ] **n** nubilité *f*.

nuclear ['nju:klɪəʳ] 1 **adj** a (*Phys*) *charge, energy, medicine* nucléaire; *war, missile, weapon* nucléaire, atomique. **~ deterrent** force *f* de dissuasion nucléaire; **~ disarmament** désarmement *m* nucléaire; **~ fission** fission *f* nucléaire; **~ fuel** combustible *m* nucléaire; **~ fusion** fusion *f* nucléaire; **N~ Industry Radioactive Waste Executive** *organisme de décision en matière de politique concernant les déchets radioactifs*; **~ magnetic resonance** résonance *f* magnétique nucléaire; **~ physicist** physicien(ne) *m(f)* atomiste; **~ physics** physique *f* nucléaire; **~ power station** centrale *f* nucléaire; **~ powers** puissances *fpl* nucléaires; **~ reaction** réaction *f* nucléaire; **~ reactor** réacteur *m* nucléaire; **~ reprocessing plant** usine *f* de retraitement des déchets nucléaires; **~ (-powered) submarine** sous-marin *m* atomique; **~ scientist** (savant *m*) atomiste *m*; **~ test(ing)** essai *m or* expérience *f* nucléaire; **~ warhead** ogive *f or* tête *f* nucléaire; **~ waste** déchets *mpl* nucléaires; **~ winter** hiver *m* nucléaire.

b (*Soc*) **~ family** famille *f* nucléaire.

2 **comp** ►**nuclear-free** où le nucléaire est interdit ►**nuclear-powered** *submarine* nucléaire.

nuclei ['nju:klɪaɪ] **npl of nucleus**.

nucleic ['nju:klɪɪk] **adj**: **~ acid** acide *m* nucléique.

nucleo... ['nju:klɪəʊ] **pref** nucléo... .

nucleus ['nju:klɪəs] **n, pl nuclei** *or* **~es** (*Astron, Phys, Ling*) noyau *m*; (*Bio*) [*cell*] nucléus *m*. **atomic ~** noyau atomique; (*fig*) **the ~ of a library/university/crew** les éléments *mpl* de base d'une bibliothèque/ d'une université/d'un équipage; **the ~ of the affair** le noyau *or* le fond de l'affaire.

nude [nju:d] 1 **adj** nu. (*Art*) **~ figures, ~ studies** nus *mpl*. 2 **n** a (*Art*) nu(e) *m(f)*, figure nue, nudité *f*. **a Goya ~** un nu de Goya; *see* **frontal**. b **the ~** le nu; **in the ~** nu.

nudge [nʌdʒ] 1 **vt** pousser du coude, donner un (petit) coup de coude à. (*fig*) **to ~ sb's memory** rafraîchir la mémoire à qn. 2 **n** coup *m* de coude.

►**nudge up vt sep** *prices* augmenter *or* relever légèrement, donner un coup de pouce à.

nudie⁑ ['nju:dɪ] **n**: **~ magazine** revue *f* porno*.

nudism ['nju:dɪzəm] **n** nudisme *m*.

nudist ['nju:dɪst] **adj, n** nudiste (*mf*). **~ colony/camp** colonie *f*/camp *m* de nudistes.

nudity ['nju:dɪtɪ] **n** nudité *f*.

nudnik⁑ ['n(j)ʊdnɪk] **n** (*US*) casse-pieds *mf inv*.

nugatory ['nju:gətərɪ] **adj** (*frm*) (*worthless*) futile, sans valeur; (*trivial*) insignifiant; (*ineffectual*) inefficace, inopérant; (*not valid*) non valable.

nugget ['nʌgɪt] **n** pépite *f*. **gold ~** pépite d'or.

NUGMW **n** (**abbr of National Union of General and Municipal Workers**) *syndicat*.

nuisance ['nju:sns] 1 **n** a (*thing, event*) ennui *m*, embêtement* *m*. **what a ~ he is not coming** que c'est ennuyeux *or* comme c'est embêtant* qu'il ne vienne pas; **it's a ~ having to shave** c'est assommant* d'avoir à se raser; **the ~ of having to shave each morning** l'embêtement* d'avoir à se raser tous les matins; **this wind is a ~** ce vent est bien embêtant* *or* gênant; **this hat is a ~** ce chapeau m'embête*; **what a ~!** quelle barbe!*, quelle plaie!*; **these mosquitoes are a ~** ces moustiques sont une plaie* *or* sont assommants*.

b (*person*) peste *f*, fléau *m*. **that child is a perfect ~** cet enfant est une vraie peste *or* un vrai fléau; **what a ~ you are!** ce que tu peux être empoisonnant!*; **you're being a ~** tu nous embêtes*, tu nous casses les pieds*; **to make a ~ of o.s.** embêter le monde*, être une peste *or* un fléau; **he's really a public ~*, he's public ~ number one*** c'est une calamité publique*, il empoisonne le monde*; *see also* **1c**.

c (*Jur*) infraction *f* simple, dommage *m* simple. **for causing a public ~** pour dommage simple à autrui; **"commit no ~"** (*no litter*) "défense de déposer des ordures"; (*do not urinate*) "défense d'uriner".

2 **comp** ►**nuisance call** appel *m* anonyme ►**nuisance caller** auteur *m* d'un appel anonyme ►**nuisance value: it has a certain nuisance value** cela sert à gêner *or* embêter* le monde.

N.U.J. [ˌenju:'dʒeɪ] **n** (*Brit*) (**abbr of National Union of Journalists**) *syndicat*.

nuke* [nju:k] 1 **vt** (*attack*) *city* lancer une bombe atomique sur; *nation, enemy* lancer une attaque nucléaire contre; (*destroy*) détruire à l'arme atomique *or* nucléaire. 2 **n** a (*weapon*) arme *f* atomique *or* nucléaire. (*: *slogan*) **"no ~s!"** "à bas les armes nucléaires!". b (*US: power station*) centrale *f* nucléaire.

null [nʌl] **adj** a (*Jur*) *act, decree* nul (*f* nulle), invalide; *legacy* caduc (*f* -uque). **~ and void** nul et non avenu; **to render ~** annuler, infirmer, invalider. b (*ineffectual*) *thing* inefficace, inopérant, sans effet; *person* insignifiant.

nullification [ˌnʌlɪfɪ'keɪʃən] **n** a infirmation *f*, invalidation *f*. b (*US Hist*) invalidation *f* par un État d'une loi fédérale.

nullify ['nʌlɪfaɪ] **vt** infirmer, invalider.

nullity ['nʌlɪtɪ] 1 **n** (*NonC: Jur*) [*act, decree*] nullité *f*, invalidité *f*; [*legacy*] caducité *f*. 2 **comp** ►**nullity suit** (*Jur*) demande *f* en nullité de mariage.

N.U.M. [ˌenju:'em] **n** (*Brit*) (**abbr of National Union of Mineworkers**) *syndicat*.

numb [nʌm] 1 **adj** engourdi, gourd; (*fig*) paralysé. **hands ~ with cold** mains engourdies par le froid; **my fingers have gone ~** mes doigts se sont engourdis; **to be ~ with fright** être paralysé par la peur, être transi *or* glacé de peur; **after she heard the news she felt ~** après avoir appris la nouvelle, elle s'est sentie inerte. 2 **comp** ►**numbhead**⁑ (*US*), **numbskull** imbécile *mf*, gourde⁑ *f*. 3 **vt** engourdir; (*fig*) [*fear etc*] transir, glacer. **~ed with grief** muet (*f* muette) *or* figé de douleur; **~ed with fear** paralysé par la peur, transi *or* glacé de peur; **it ~s the pain** cela endort la douleur.

number ['nʌmbəʳ] 1 **n** a (*gen*) nombre *m*; (*actual figure: when written etc*) chiffre *m*. **even/odd/whole/cardinal/ordinal ~** nombre pair/ impair/entier/cardinal/ordinal; (*Bible*) (**the Book of**) **N~s** les Nombres; **to paint by ~s** peindre selon des indications chiffrées; (*fig*) **to do sth by ~s** *or* (*US*) **by the ~s** faire qch mécaniquement *or* bêtement; (*US fig: bet*) **to play the ~s*** faire des paris clandestins, jouer à une loterie clandestine; *see* **lucky, round**.

b (*quantity, amount*) nombre *m*, quantité *f*. **a ~ of people** un certain nombre de gens, plusieurs personnes; **(large) ~s of people** (un grand) nombre de gens, un nombre assez important de gens, de nombreuses personnes; **a great ~ of books/chairs** une grande quantité de livres/chaises; **in a small ~ of cases** dans un petit nombre de cas; **on a ~ of occasions** à plusieurs occasions, à maintes occasions; **there were a ~ of faults in the machine** la machine avait un (certain) nombre de défauts; **there are a ~ of things which ...** il y a un certain nombre de choses *or* pas mal* de choses qui ...; **a fair ~** un assez grand nombre, un nombre assez important; **boys and girls in equal ~s** garçons et filles en nombre égal; **~s being equal** à nombre égal; **10 in ~** au nombre de 10; **they were 10 in ~** ils étaient (au nombre de) 10; **to the ~ of some 200** au nombre de 200 environ; **few in ~, in small ~s** en petit nombre; **many in ~, in large ~s** en grand nombre; **to swell the ~ of** grossir le nombre de; **he was brought in to swell the ~s** on l'a amené pour grossir l'effectif; **without** *or* **beyond ~** innombrable, sans nombre; **times without ~** à maintes reprises, mille et mille fois; **any ~ can play** le nombre de joueurs est illimité; **there were any ~ of cards in the box** il y avait une quantité *or* un tas* de cartes dans la boîte; **I've told you any ~ of times** je ne sais pas combien de fois je te l'ai dit; **they are found in ~s in Africa** on les trouve en grand nombre en Afrique; **they came in their ~s** ils sont venus en grand nombre; **there were flies in such ~s that ...** les mouches étaient en si grand nombre que ...; **the power of ~s** le pouvoir du nombre; **to win by force of ~s** *or* **by sheer ~s** l'emporter par le nombre *or* par la force du nombre; **one of their ~** un d'entre eux; **one of our ~** un des nôtres; **he was of our ~** il était des nôtres, il était avec nous.

c (*in series: of page, house etc; also Telec*) numéro *m*. (*Telec*) **wrong ~** faux numéro; **at ~ 4** au (numéro) 4; (*Brit Pol*) **N~ 10** 10 Downing Street (*résidence du Premier ministre*); **reference ~** numéro de référence; (*Aut, Mil*) **(registration) ~** (numéro d')immatriculation *f*, numéro minéralogique; **to take a car's ~** relever le numéro d'une voiture; (*fig*) **I've got his ~!*** je le connais, lui! (*pej*); **their ~ came up*** ça a été leur tour d'y passer*, il a fallu qu'ils y passent* aussi; **his ~'s up*** il est fichu*, son compte est bon; **that bullet had his ~ on it!*** (il était dit que) cette balle était pour lui!; **~ one*** (*myself*) moi, bibi⁑, ma pomme⁑, mézigue⁑; **he only thinks of ~ one*** il ne pense qu'à lui *or* à sézigue⁑ *or* à sa pomme⁑; **to take care of** *or* **look after ~ one*** penser avant tout à son propre intérêt; **the ~ one English player** le meilleur *or* premier joueur anglais; **he's the ~ one there** c'est lui qui dirige tout là-dedans; **he's my ~ two*** il est mon second; *see* **opposite**.

d (*model, issue*) [*manufactured goods, clothes, car*] modèle *m*; [*newspaper, journal*] numéro *m*. (*Press*) **the January ~** le numéro de janvier; **this car's a nice little ~*** c'est une chouette* petite voiture; **this wine is a nice little ~*** c'est un bon petit vin; (*dress*) **a little ~ in black** une petite robe noire (toute simple); **she's a pretty little ~*** c'est une jolie fille, c'est une belle nénette⁑; *see* **back**.

e [*music hall, circus*] numéro *m*; [*pianist, dance band*] morceau *m*; [*singer*] chanson *f*; [*dancer*] danse *f*. **there were several dance ~s on the programme** le programme comprenait plusieurs numéros de danse; [*singer*] **my next ~ will be ...** je vais maintenant chanter ... .

f (*NonC: Gram etc*) nombre *m*. **~ is one of the basic concepts** le nombre est un des concepts de base; (*Gram*) **to agree in ~** s'accorder en nombre.

g (*Mus*) rythme *m*. **~s** (*Poetry*) vers *mpl*, poésie *f*; (*Mus*) mesures *fpl*.

2 **comp** ►**number-cruncher*** (*machine*) calculatrice *f*; **he's the number-cruncher*** c'est le comptable, c'est le préposé aux chiffres (*hum*) ►**number-crunching*** calcul *m* ►**number plate** (*Brit Aut*)

plaque *f* minéralogique *or* d'immatriculation *or* de police; **a car with French number plates** une voiture immatriculée en France ▶**number theory** théorie *f* des nombres.

3 vt a (*give a number to*) numéroter. **they are ~ed from 1 to 10** ils sont numérotés de 1 à 10; **the houses are not ~ed** les maisons n'ont pas de numéro; **~ed (bank) account** compte *m* (en banque) numéroté.

b (*include*) compter, comprendre. **the library ~s 30,000 volumes** la bibliothèque compte *or* comporte 30 000 volumes; **I ~ him among my friends** je le compte parmi mes amis; **to be ~ed with the heroes** compter au nombre des *or* parmi les héros.

c (*amount to*) compter. **the crew ~s 50 men** l'équipage compte 50 hommes; **they ~ed 700** leur nombre s'élevait *or* se montait à 700, ils étaient au nombre de 700.

d (*count*) compter. (*fig*) **his days were ~ed** ses jours étaient comptés; **your chances of trying again are ~ed** il ne te reste plus beaucoup d'occasions de tenter ta chance; **he was ~ing the hours till the attack began** il comptait les heures qui le séparaient de l'assaut.

4 vi (*Mil etc: also* **~ off**) **to ~ (off)** se numéroter (*from the right* en partant de la droite).

numbering ['nʌmbərɪŋ] 1 n (*NonC*) *[houses, seats etc]* numérotage *m*. 2 comp ▶**numbering machine** numéroteur *m*.

numberless ['nʌmbəlɪs] adj innombrable, sans nombre.

numbly ['nʌmlɪ] adv (*fig*) avec hébétement, d'un air hébété.

numbness ['nʌmnɪs] n *[hand, finger, senses]* engourdissement *m*; *[mind]* torpeur *f*, engourdissement.

numerable ['njuːmərəbl] adj nombrable, dénombrable.

numeracy ['njuːmərəsɪ] n (*NonC*) notions *fpl* de calcul, capacités *fpl* au calcul.

numeral ['njuːmərəl] 1 n chiffre *m*, nombre *m*. **Arabic/Roman ~** chiffre arabe/romain. 2 adj numéral.

numerate ['njuːmərɪt] adj qui a le sens de l'arithmétique. **he is hardly ~** il sait à peine compter.

numeration [ˌnjuːmə'reɪʃən] n (*Math*) numération *f*.

numerator ['njuːməreɪtə^r] n (*Math*) numérateur *m*; (*instrument*) numéroteur *m*.

numerical [njuː'merɪkəl] adj numérique. **in ~ order** dans l'ordre numérique.

numerically [njuː'merɪkəlɪ] adv numériquement. **~ superior to the enemy** supérieur en nombre *or* numériquement supérieur à l'ennemi.

numerological [ˌnjuːmərə'lɒdʒɪkəl] adj numérologique.

numerology [ˌnjuːmə'rɒlədʒɪ] n numérologie *f*.

numerous ['njuːmərəs] adj nombreux. **a ~ family** une famille nombreuse; **in ~ cases** dans de nombreux cas, dans beaucoup de cas.

numinous ['njuːmɪnəs] adj numineux.

numismatic [ˌnjuːmɪz'mætɪk] adj numismatique.

numismatics [ˌnjuːmɪz'mætɪks] n (*NonC*) numismatique *f*.

numismatist [njuː'mɪzmətɪst] n numismate *mf*.

numskull ['nʌmskʌl] n imbécile *mf*, gourde⁑ *f*.

nun [nʌn] n religieuse *f*, bonne sœur*. **to become a ~** entrer en religion, prendre le voile.

nunciature ['nʌnʃɪətjʊə^r] n nonciature *f*.

nuncio ['nʌnʃɪəʊ] n nonce *m*; *see* **papal**.

nunnery† ['nʌnərɪ] n couvent *m*.

NUPE ['njuːpɪ] (*Brit*) (abbr of **National Union of Public Employees**) *syndicat*.

nuptial ['nʌpʃəl] (*liter or hum*) 1 adj nuptial. **the ~ day** le jour des noces. 2 npl: **~s** noce *f*.

N.U.R. [ˌenjuː'ɑː^r] n (*Brit*) (abbr of **National Union of Railwaymen**) *syndicat*.

nurd⁑ [nɜːd] n = **nerd**.

nurse [nɜːs] 1 n a (*in hospital*) infirmière *f*; (*at home*) infirmière, garde-malade *f*. **male ~** infirmier *m*, garde-malade *m*; (*US Med*) **~'s aide** aide-soignant(e) *m(f)*; (*US Med*) **~s' station** bureau *m* des infirmières; **the ~s' dispute/strike** les revendications *fpl*/la grève *f* du personnel soignant; *see* **night**.

b (*children's* ~) nurse *f*, bonne *f* d'enfants. **yes ~** oui nounou.

c (*wet-~*) nourrice *f*.

2 comp ▶**nursemaid** bonne *f* d'enfants.

3 vt a (*Med*) soigner; (*US: suckle*) nourrir, allaiter; (*Brit: cradle in arms*) bercer (dans ses bras). **she ~d him through pneumonia** elle l'a soigné pendant sa pneumonie; **she ~d him back to health** il a guéri grâce à ses soins; **to ~ a cold** soigner un rhume.

b (*fig*) *plant* soigner; *hope, one's wrath etc* nourrir, entretenir; *plan, plot* mijoter, couver; *horse, car engine* ménager; *a fire* entretenir. **to ~ one's pride** s'apitoyer sur son sort; (*Brit Pol*) **to ~ a constituency** soigner les électeurs; **he was nursing the contact till he needed it** il cultivait cette relation pour s'en servir quand il en aurait besoin; **to ~ the business along** (essayer de) maintenir la compagnie à flot; **to ~ a drink all evening** faire durer un verre toute la soirée.

nurseling ['nɜːslɪŋ] n = **nursling**.

nursery ['nɜːsərɪ] 1 n a (*room*) nursery *f*, chambre *f* d'enfants. **day ~** nursery; **night ~** chambre des enfants *or* d'enfants.

b (*institution*) (*daytime only*) crèche *f*, garderie *f*; (*daytime or residential*) pouponnière *f*.

c (*Agr*) pépinière *f*.

d (*fig*) pépinière *f*. **this town is the ~ of the province's cultural life** cette ville est la pépinière de la vie culturelle de la province.

2 comp ▶**nursery education** enseignement *m* de la maternelle ▶**nurseryman** pépiniériste *m* ▶**nursery nurse** puéricultrice *f* ▶**nursery rhyme** comptine *f* ▶**nursery school** (*state-run*) école *f* maternelle; (*gen private*) jardin *m* d'enfants; **nursery-school teacher** (*state-run*) institutrice *f* de maternelle; (*private*) jardinière *f* d'enfants ▶**nursery slopes** (*Brit: Ski*) pentes *fpl or* pistes *fpl* pour débutants.

nursing ['nɜːsɪŋ] 1 adj a allaitant. **~ mother** mère *f* qui allaite; (*in stations etc*) **room for ~ mothers** salle réservée aux mères qui allaitent.

b *[hospital]* **the ~ staff** le personnel soignant *or* infirmier, les infirmières *fpl*.

2 n (*suckling*) allaitement *m*; (*care of invalids*) soins *mpl*; (*profession of nurse*) profession *f* d'infirmière. **she's going in for ~** elle va être infirmière.

3 comp ▶**nursing auxiliary** (*Brit*) aide soignante ▶**nursing home** (*esp Brit: for medical, surgical cases*) clinique *f*, polyclinique *f*; (*for mental cases, disabled etc*) maison *f* de santé; (*for convalescence/rest cure*) maison de convalescence/de repos; (*US: for old people*) maison de retraite ▶**nursing officer** (*Brit Med*) surveillant(e) *m(f)* général(e) ▶**nursing orderly** (*Brit Mil*) infirmier *m* (militaire) ▶**nursing sister** (*Brit Med*) infirmière *f* chef ▶**nursing studies** études *fpl* d'infirmière *or* d'infirmier.

nursling ['nɜːslɪŋ] n nourrisson(ne) *m(f)*.

nurture ['nɜːtʃə^r] 1 n (*frm: lit, fig*) nourriture *f*; *see* **nature 1a.** 2 vt (*lit, fig*) (*rear*) élever, éduquer; (*feed*) nourrir (*on* de).

N.U.S. [ˌenjuː'es] n (*Brit*) (abbr of **National Union of Students** *and* **National Union of Seamen**) *syndicats*.

nut [nʌt] 1 n a (*Bot*) *terme générique pour fruits à écale* (*no generic term in French*). **do you like ~s?** est-ce que vous aimez les noisettes (*or* les noix *etc*)?; **this chocolate has got ~s in it** c'est du chocolat aux noisettes (*or* aux amandes *etc*); **a bag of mixed ~s** un sachet de noisettes, cacahuètes, amandes *etc* panachées; **~s and raisins** mendiants *mpl*; (*fig*) **he's a tough ~** c'est un dur à cuire*; (*fig*) **a hard ~ to crack** (*problem*) un problème difficile à résoudre; (*person*) un(e) dur(e) à cuire*; **he can't paint for ~s**⁑ il peint comme un pied⁑; *see* **beech, nuts, pistachio** *etc*.

b (*Tech*) écrou *m*; (*Climbing*) coinceur *m*. (*fig*) **the ~s and bolts of** ... les détails *mpl* pratiques de ... (*see also* **2**).

c **(coal) ~s, ~ coal** noix *fpl*, tête(s)-de-moineau *f(pl) or* tête(s) de moineau *f(pl)*; **anthracite ~s** noix *or* tête(s)-de-moineau d'anthracite.

d (*Culin*) *see* **ginger**.

e (⁑: *head*) caboche* *f*. **use your ~!** réfléchis donc un peu!, creuse-toi un peu les méninges!⁑; **to be off one's ~** être tombé sur la tête*, être cinglé*; **you must be off your ~!** mais ça (ne) va plus!*, mais tu es tombé sur la tête!*; **to go off one's ~** perdre la boule⁑; (*Brit*) **to do one's ~** piquer une crise*, se mettre dans tous ses états.

f (⁑: *mad person*) **he's a real ~** c'est un fou, il est cinglé* *or* toqué*.

g (⁑: *enthusiast*) **a movie/football ~**⁑ un(e) cinglé(e)* du cinéma/football.

h (*excl*) **~s!*** des clous!⁑; **~s to you!*** va te faire fiche!*

i (⁑⁑: *testicles*) **~s** couilles⁑⁑ *fpl*, roubignoles⁑⁑ *fpl*.

2 comp (*Culin*) *cutlet, rissoles, roast etc* à base de cacahuètes (*or* noisettes *etc*) hachées ▶**nuts-and-bolts*** adj (*fig: practical*) avant tout pratique; **nuts-and-bolts education** enseignement *m* axé sur les matières fondamentales ▶**nut-brown** *eyes* noisette *inv*; *complexion* brun; *hair* châtain ▶**nutcase**⁑ dingue* *mf*, cinglé(e)* *m(f)*; **he's a nutcase** il est bon à enfermer*, il est dingue* ▶**nut chocolate** chocolat *m* aux amandes (*or* aux noisettes *etc*) ▶**nutcracker chin** menton *m* en galoche *or* en casse-noisette ▶**nutcracker(s)** casse-noix *m inv*, casse-noisette(s) *m* ▶**The Nutcracker** (*Mus*) Casse-noisette ▶**nuthatch** (*Orn*) sittelle *f*, grimpereau *m* ▶**nuthouse**⁑ (*Brit*) asile *m* (d'aliénés), maison *f* de fous *or* de dingues*; **he's in the nuthouse** il est chez les dingues* ▶**nutmeg** (*nut*) (noix *f*) muscade *f*; (*tree*) muscadier *m*; **nutmeg-grater** râpe *f* à muscade; (*US*) **the Nutmeg State** le Connecticut ▶**nutshell** coquille *f* de noix *or* noisette *etc*; (*fig*) **in a nutshell** ... en un mot ..., bref ...; (*fig*) **to put the matter in a nutshell** résumer l'affaire en un mot.

N.U.T. [ˌenjuː'tiː] n (*Brit*) (abbr of **National Union of Teachers**) *syndicat*.

nutrient ['njuːtrɪənt] 1 adj nutritif. 2 n substance nutritive, élément nutritif.

nutriment ['njuːtrɪmənt] n nourriture *f*, éléments *mpl* nourrissants *or* nutritifs, aliments *mpl*.

nutrition [njuː'trɪʃən] n nutrition *f*, alimentation *f*.

nutritional [njuː'trɪʃənl] adj alimentaire.

nutritionist [njuː'trɪʃənɪst] n nutritionniste *mf*.

nutritious [njuː'trɪʃəs] adj nutritif, nourrissant.

nutritiousness [njuː'trɪʃəsnɪs] n caractère *m* nutritif.

nutritive ['njuːtrɪtɪv] adj = **nutritious**.

nuts⁑ [nʌts] adj dingue*, cinglé*, toqué*. **he's ~** il est dingue* *or* cinglé*, il est bon à enfermer*; **to go ~** perdre la boule*; **to be ~ about sb/sth** être dingue* de qn/qch.

nutter‡ ['nʌtəʳ] n (*Brit*) cinglé(e)* *m(f)*, dingue* *mf*.
nutty ['nʌtɪ] adj **a** (*see* **nut**) *chocolate etc* aux noisettes (*or* amandes *or* noix *etc*); *flavour* au goût de noisette *etc*, à la noisette *etc*. **b** (*Brit: coal*) ~ **slack** charbonnaille *f*. **c** (‡: *mad*) cinglé*, dingue*. ~ **as a fruitcake** complètement dingue*.
nuzzle ['nʌzl] vi *[pig]* fouiller du groin, fouiner. **the dog ~d up to my leg** le chien est venu fourrer son nez contre ma jambe.
NV (*US*) abbr of **Nevada**.
NY [en'waɪ] n (*US*) abbr of **New York**.
Nyasaland [nɪ'æsə,lænd] n Nyas(s)aland *m*.
NYC [enwaɪ'siː] n (*US*) abbr of **New York City**.
nylon ['naɪlɒn] **1** n **a** (*NonC*) nylon *m*. **b** = ~ **stocking;** *see* **2**. **2** comp de *or* en nylon ► **nylon stockings** bas *mpl* nylon.
nymph [nɪmf] n nymphe *f*; (*water* ~) naïade *f*; (*wood* ~) (hama)dryade *f*; (*sea* ~) néréide *f*; (*mountain* ~) oréade *f*.
nymphet [nɪm'fet] n nymphette *f*.
nympho‡ ['nɪmfəʊ] adj, n (abbr of **nymphomaniac**) nymphomane *(f)*.
nymphomania [,nɪmfəʊ'meɪnɪə] n nymphomanie *f*.
nymphomaniac [,nɪmfəʊ'meɪnɪæk] adj, n nymphomane *(f)*.
NYSE ['enwaɪes'iː] n (*US*) (abbr of **New York Stock Exchange**) *Bourse de New York*.
NZ, N. Zeal. (abbr of **New Zealand**) *see* **new 3**.

O

O, o¹ [əʊ] 1 n a (*letter*) O, o *m*. **O for Orange** ≃ O comme Oscar; *see also* **OK.** b (*number: Telec etc*) zéro *m*. 2 comp ▸**O Grade**† (*Scot Scol*) = **O level** ▸**O level**† (*Brit Scol*) (*gen*) ≃ brevet *m*; **to do an O level**† **in French** passer l'épreuve de français au brevet ▸**O-shaped** en forme de O *or* de cercle.
o² [əʊ] excl (*liter*) ô.
o' [əʊ] prep (abbr of **of**) de; *see* **o'clock** *etc*.
oaf [əʊf] n (*awkward*) balourd(e)* *m(f)*; (*bad-mannered*) malotru(e) *m(f)*, mufle *m*.
oafish ['əʊfɪʃ] adj *person* mufle; *behaviour* de mufle, de malotru.
oak [əʊk] 1 n chêne *m*. **light/dark ~** chêne clair/foncé. 2 comp (*made of ~*) de *or* en (bois de) chêne; (*~-coloured*) (couleur) chêne *inv* ▸**oak apple** noix *f* de galle, galle *f* du chêne ▸**oak leaf cluster** (*US*) ≃ barrette *f* (*portée sur le ruban d'une médaille*) ▸**oakwood** (*forest*) chênaie *f*, bois *m* de chênes; (*NonC: material*) (bois *m* de) chêne *m*.
oaken ['əʊkən] adj de *or* en (bois de) chêne.
oakum ['əʊkəm] n étoupe *f*. **to pick ~** faire de l'étoupe.
O & M [əʊənd'em] (abbr of **organization and method**) *see* **organization 2.**
O.A.P. [ˌəʊeɪ'piː] (*Brit*) (abbr of **old age pension** *or* **pensioner**) *see* **old 2.**
oar [ɔːʳ] 1 n a aviron *m*, rame *f*. **he always puts** *or* **pushes** *or* **sticks** *or* **shoves his ~ in** il faut toujours qu'il s'en mêle (*subj*) *or* qu'il y mette son grain de sel; *see* **rest, ship** *etc*. b (*person*) rameur *m*, -euse *f*. 2 comp ▸**oarlock** dame *f* (de nage), tolet *m* ▸**oarsman** rameur *m*; (*Naut, also Sport*) nageur *m* ▸**oarsmanship** (*art of rowing*) art *m* de ramer; (*skill as rower*) qualités *fpl* de rameur ▸**oarswoman** rameuse *f*; (*Sport*) nageuse *f*.
-oared [ɔːd] adj ending in comps: **four-oared** à quatre rames *or* avirons.
oasis [əʊ'eɪsɪs] n, pl **oases** [əʊ'eɪsiːz] (*lit, fig*) oasis *f*. **an ~ of peace** un havre *or* une oasis de paix.
oast [əʊst] n four *m* à (sécher le) houblon. **~-house** sécherie *f or* séchoir *m* à houblon.
oat [əʊt] 1 n (*plant, food*) **~s** avoine *f* (*NonC*); **to be off one's ~s**⁑ avoir perdu l'appétit; (*Brit*) **to get one's ~s**⁑ tirer son coup⁑; *see* **rolled, wild** *etc*. 2 comp ▸**oatcake** biscuit *m or* galette *f* d'avoine ▸**oatmeal** n (*NonC*) (*cereal*) flocons *mpl* d'avoine; (*US: porridge*) bouillie *f* d'avoine, porridge *m* ◊ comp (*colour*) *dress etc* beige, grège.
oath [əʊθ] pl **~s** [əʊðz] 1 n a (*Jur etc*) serment *m*. (*Jur*) **to take the ~** prêter serment; **he took** *or* **swore an ~ to avenge himself** il fit (le) serment *or* il jura de se venger; (*Jur*) **on** *or* **under ~** sous serment; (*Jur*) **witness on** *or* **under ~** témoin assermenté; (*Jur*) **to put sb on** *or* **under ~, to administer the ~ to sb** faire prêter serment à qn; (*Jur*) **to put sb on** *or* **under ~ to do sth** faire promettre à qn sous serment de faire qch; **he swore on his ~ that he had never been there** il jura n'y avoir jamais été *or* qu'il n'y avait jamais été; **on my ~!, I'll take my ~ on it!** je vous le jure!; *see* **allegiance.**
b (*bad language*) juron *m*. **to let out** *or* **utter an ~** lâcher *or* pousser un juron.
2 comp ▸**oath-taking** (*Jur etc*) prestation *f* de serment.
O.A.U. [əʊeɪ'juː] n (abbr of **Organization of African Unity**) O.U.A. *f*.
Obadiah [ˌəʊbə'daɪə] n Abdias *m*.
obbligato [ˌɒblɪ'gɑːtəʊ] (*Mus*) 1 adj obligé. 2 n, pl **~s** *or* **obbligati** [ˌɒblɪ'gɑːtiː] partie obligée.
obduracy ['ɒbdjʊrəsɪ] n (*see* **obdurate**) obstination *f*, opiniâtreté *f*; inflexibilité *f*; dureté *f*; impénitence *f*.
obdurate ['ɒbdjʊrɪt] adj (*stubborn*) obstiné, opiniâtre; (*unyielding*) inflexible; (*hard-hearted*) endurci; (*unrepentant*) impénitent.
O.B.E. [əʊbiː'iː] n (abbr of **Officer of the Order of the British Empire**) *titre honorifique*.
obedience [ə'biːdɪəns] n (*NonC*) obéissance *f*, soumission *f* (*to* à), obédience *f* (*liter*); (*Rel*) obédience (*to* à). **in ~ to the law/his orders** conformément à la loi/ses ordres; (*frm*) **to owe ~ to sb** devoir obéissance *or* obédience (*liter*) à qn; **to show ~ to sb/sth** obéir à qn/qch; **to compel ~ from sb** se faire obéir par qn; **he commands ~** il sait se faire obéir; *see* **blind.**
obedient [ə'biːdɪənt] adj *person, child* obéissant; *dog etc* obéissant, docile; (*submissive*) docile, soumis. **to be ~ to sb/sth** obéir à qn/qch, être *or* se montrer obéissant envers qn/à qch; (*frm: in letters*) **your ~ servant** ≃ je vous prie d'agréer Monsieur (*or* Madame *etc*) l'expression de ma considération distinguée.
obediently [ə'biːdɪəntlɪ] adv docilement; d'une manière soumise, avec soumission. **he ~ sat down** il s'est assis docilement; **she smiled ~** elle a souri d'un air soumis.
obeisance [əʊ'beɪsəns] n (*frm*) a (*NonC: homage*) hommage *m*. b (*bow*) révérence *f*, salut cérémonieux.
obelisk ['ɒbɪlɪsk] n a (*Archit*) obélisque *m*. b (*Typ*: †) obel *m or* obèle *m*.
obese [əʊ'biːs] adj obèse.
obeseness [əʊ'biːsnɪs] n, **obesity** [əʊ'biːsɪtɪ] n obésité *f*.
obey [ə'beɪ] 1 vt *person, instinct, order* obéir à; *the law* se conformer à, obéir à; *instructions* se conformer à, observer; (*Jur*) *summons, order* obtempérer à. **the machine was no longer ~ing the controls** la machine ne répondait plus aux commandes. 2 vi obéir.
obfuscate ['ɒbfəskeɪt] vt (*frm*) *mind, judgment* obscurcir; *person* dérouter, déconcerter.
obfuscation [ˌɒbfə'skeɪʃən] n obscurcissement *m*.
obituary [ə'bɪtjʊərɪ] 1 n (*also* **~ notice**) notice *f* nécrologique, nécrologie *f*. 2 adj *announcement* nécrologique. **~ column** nécrologie *f*, rubrique *f* nécrologique, carnet *m* de deuil.
object ['ɒbdʒɪkt] 1 n a (*thing in general*) objet *m*, chose *f*; (*pej: thing*) bizarrerie *f*; (*pej: person*) personne *f* ridicule. **~ of pity/ridicule** objet de pitié/de risée; **the ~ of one's love** l'objet aimé.
b (*Gram*) complément *m* (d'objet). **direct/indirect ~** complément (d'objet) direct/indirect.
c (*aim*) but *m*, objectif *m*, objet *m*, fin *f*; (*Philos*) objet. **he has no ~ in life** il n'a aucun but dans la vie; **with this ~ (in view** *or* **in mind)** dans ce but, à cette fin; **with the ~ of doing** dans le but de faire; **with the sole ~ of doing** à seule fin *or* dans le seul but de faire; **what ~ is there in** *or* **what's the ~ of doing that?** à quoi bon faire cela?; **money is no ~** le prix est sans importance; **"distance no ~"** "toutes distances"; *see* **defeat.**
d **~ of virtu** objet *m* d'art, curiosité *f*.
2 comp ▸**object clause** (*Gram*) proposition *f* complément d'objet, complétive *f* d'objet ▸**object language** (*Ling*) langage-objet *m* ▸**object lesson**: (*fig*) **it was an object lesson in good manners** c'était une démonstration de bonnes manières; **it was an object lesson in how not to drive a car** c'était une illustration de ce que l'on ne doit pas faire au volant.
3 [əb'dʒekt] vi élever une objection (*to sb/sth* contre qn/qch), trouver à redire (*to sth* à qch). **I ~ to that remark** je désapprouve tout à fait cette remarque; (*frm*) je proteste *or* je m'élève contre cette remarque; **I ~ to your rudeness** votre grossièreté est inadmissible; (*excl*) **I ~!** je proteste!, je regrette!; **I ~ most strongly!** je proteste catégoriquement! *or* énergiquement!; **if you don't ~** si vous n'y voyez pas d'inconvénient *or* d'objection; **I shall not come if you ~** je ne viendrai pas si vous vous y opposez *or* si vous y voyez une objection *or* si vous y voyez un inconvénient; **he didn't ~ when ...** il n'a élevé *or* formulé aucune objection quand ...; **he ~s to her drinking** il désapprouve qu'elle boive; **do you ~ to my smoking?** cela vous ennuie que je fume? (*subj*), est-ce que cela vous gêne si je fume?; **she ~s to all this noise** elle ne peut tolérer tout ce bruit; **I don't ~ to helping you** je veux bien vous aider; **to ~ to sb** élever des objections contre qn; **I would ~ to Paul but not to Robert as chairman** je serais contre Paul mais je n'ai rien contre Robert comme président; **they ~ed to him because he was too young** on lui a objecté son jeune âge; (*Jur*) **to ~ to a witness** récuser un témoin; **I wouldn't ~ to a bite to eat*** je mangerais bien un morceau.
4 [əb'dʒekt] vt: **to ~ that** objecter que, faire valoir que.
objection [əb'dʒekʃən] n objection *f*; (*drawback*) inconvénient *m*,

obstacle *m*. **I have no ~(s)** je n'ai pas d'objection, je ne m'y oppose pas; **if you have no ~(s)** si cela ne vous fait rien, si vous n'y voyez pas d'inconvénient *or* d'objection; **I have no ~ to him** je n'ai rien contre lui, je ne trouve rien à redire sur son compte; **I have a strong ~ to dogs in shops** je ne supporte pas les chiens dans les magasins; **have you any ~ to my smoking?** cela ne vous ennuie pas que je fume? (*subj*), est-ce que cela vous gêne si je fume?; **I have no ~ to the idea/to his leaving** je ne vois pas d'objection *or* je ne m'oppose pas à cette idée/à ce qu'il parte; **there is no ~ to our leaving** il n'y a pas d'obstacle *or* d'inconvénient à ce que nous partions (*subj*); **to make** *or* **raise an ~** soulever *or* élever *or* formuler une objection; (*Jur*) **to make ~ to an argument** récuser un argument; (*excl*) ~! (*Jur*) objection!; (*gen*) je proteste!; (*Jur*) ~ **overruled!** objection rejetée!

objectionable [əb'dʒekʃnəbl] **adj** **a** (*disagreeable*) *person, behaviour* extrêmement désagréable, insupportable; *smell* nauséabond; *remark* désobligeant, choquant; *language* grossier, choquant. **b** (*open to objection*) *conduct* répréhensible, blâmable, condamnable; *proposal* inadmissible, inacceptable.

objective [əb'dʒektɪv] **1 adj a** (*impartial*) objectif, impartial (*about* en ce qui concerne); (*Philos*) objectif. (*Press etc*) **he is very ~ in his reporting** ses reportages sont très objectifs *or* impartiaux. **b** (*Gram*) *case* accusatif; *pronoun* complément d'objet; *genitive* objectif. ~ **case** (cas *m*) accusatif *m*, cas régime. **2 n a** (*gen, also Phot*) objectif *m*. **to reach** *or* **attain one's ~** atteindre le but qu'on s'était fixé *or* son objectif. **b** (*Gram*) accusatif *m*.

objectively [əb'dʒektɪvlɪ] **adv** (*gen*) objectivement, impartialement, sans parti pris; (*Gram, Philos*) objectivement.

objectivism [əb'dʒektɪvɪzəm] **n** objectivisme *m*.

objectivity [ˌɒbdʒɪk'tɪvɪtɪ] **n** objectivité *f*, impartialité *f*.

objector [əb'dʒektəʳ] **n** opposant(e) *m(f)*. **the ~s to this scheme** ceux qui s'opposent à ce projet; *see* **conscientious.**

objet ['ɔbʒɛ] **n**: ~ **d'art (pl ~s d'art)** objet **m** d'art; ~ **de vertu (pl ~s de vertu)** objet d'art, curiosité *f*.

objurgate ['ɒbdʒɜːgeɪt] **vt** (*frm*) réprimander; (*stronger*) accabler de reproches.

objurgation [ˌɒbdʒɜː'geɪʃən] **n** (*frm*) objurgation *f*, réprimande *f*.

oblate ['ɒbleɪt] **1 n** (*Rel*) oblat(e) *m(f)*. **2 adj** (*Geom*) aplati aux pôles.

oblation [əʊ'bleɪʃən] **n** (*Rel*) (*act*) oblation *f*; (*offering: also ~s*) oblats *mpl*.

obligate ['ɒblɪgeɪt] **vt** obliger, contraindre (*sb to do* qn à faire). **to be ~d to do** être obligé de *or* contraint à faire.

obligation [ˌɒblɪ'geɪʃən] **n a** (*compulsion, duty etc*) obligation *f*, devoir *m*, engagement *m*. **to be under an ~ to do** être tenu de faire, être dans l'obligation de faire; **I'm under no ~ to do it** rien ne m'oblige à le faire; **to put** *or* **lay an ~ on sb to do, to put** *or* **lay sb under an ~ to do** mettre qn dans l'obligation de faire; **it is your ~ to see that ...** il est de votre devoir de veiller à ce que ... + *subj*; (*in advert*) **"without ~"** "sans engagement"; **"no ~ to buy"** (*in advert*) "aucune obligation d'achat"; (*in shop*) "entrée libre".

b (*debt etc*) devoir *m*, dette *f* (de reconnaissance). **to meet one's ~s** faire honneur à *or* satisfaire à ses obligations *or* ses engagements; **to fail to meet one's ~s** manquer à ses obligations *or* à ses engagements; **to be under an ~ to sb** devoir de la reconnaissance à qn; **to be under an ~ to sb for sth** être redevable à qn de qch; **to lay** *or* **put sb under an ~** créer une obligation à qn; **to repay an ~** acquitter une dette de reconnaissance.

obligatory [ɒ'blɪgətərɪ] **adj** (*compulsory*) obligatoire; (*imposed by custom*) de rigueur. **to make it ~ for sb to do** imposer à qn l'obligation de faire.

oblige [ə'blaɪdʒ] **vt a** (*compel*) obliger, forcer, astreindre, contraindre (*sb to do* qn à faire). **to be ~d to do** être obligé *or* forcé de faire, être astreint *or* contraint à faire, devoir faire.

b (*do a favour to*) rendre service à, obliger. **he did it to ~ us** il l'a fait par gentillesse pour nous *or* pour nous rendre service; **she is always ready** *or* **willing to ~** elle est toujours prête à rendre service *or* toujours très obligeante; **anything to ~!*** toujours prêt à rendre service!; **he asked for more time and they ~d by delaying their departure** il a demandé un délai et ils se sont pliés à ses désirs en retardant leur départ; (*frm*) **can you ~ me with a pen?** auriez-vous l'amabilité *or* l'obligeance de me prêter un stylo?; (*frm*) **~ me by leaving the room** faites-moi le plaisir de quitter la pièce; (*Comm*) **a prompt answer will ~** une réponse rapide nous obligerait; **to be ~d to sb for sth** être reconnaissant *or* savoir gré à qn de qch; **I am much ~d to you** je vous remercie infiniment; **I would be ~d if you could help** je vous saurais gré de votre aide; **thanks, I'd be ~d** merci, ce serait très gentil (de votre part); **much ~d!** merci beaucoup!, merci mille fois!

obligee [ˌɒblɪ'dʒiː] **n** (*Jur*) obligataire *m*, créancier *m*.

obliging [ə'blaɪdʒɪŋ] **adj** obligeant, serviable, complaisant. **it is very ~ of them** c'est très gentil *or* aimable de leur part.

obligingly [ə'blaɪdʒɪŋlɪ] **adv** obligeamment, aimablement. **the books which you ~ gave me** les livres que vous avez eu l'obligeance *or* l'amabilité de me donner.

obligor [ˌɒblɪ'gɔːʳ] **n** (*Jur*) obligé *m*.

oblique [ə'bliːk] **1 adj** (*Geom, gen*) oblique; *look* en biais, oblique; *allusion, reference, style* indirect; *route, method* indirect, détourné. (*Gram*) ~ **case** cas *m* oblique. **2 n** (*Anat*) oblique *m*; (*Brit Typ: also* ~ **stroke**) trait *m* oblique, oblique *f*.

obliquely [ə'bliːklɪ] **adv** obliquement, en oblique, de *or* en biais; (*fig*) indirectement. **the car was hit ~ by the lorry** la voiture a été prise en écharpe par le camion.

obliqueness [ə'bliːknɪs] **n**, **obliquity** [ə'blɪkwɪtɪ] **n** (*see* **oblique**) obliquité *f*; caractère détourné *or* indirect.

obliterate [ə'blɪtəreɪt] **vt** (*erase*) effacer, enlever; (*cross out*) rayer, raturer; (*by progressive wear*) effacer, oblitérer†; *memory, impressions* effacer, oblitérer (*liter*); *the past* faire table rase de; (*Post*) *stamp* oblitérer.

obliteration [əˌblɪtə'reɪʃən] **n** (*see* **obliterate**) effacement *m*; rature *f*; (*Post*) oblitération *f*.

oblivion [ə'blɪvɪən] **n** (état *m* d')oubli *m*. **to sink** *or* **fall into ~** tomber dans l'oubli.

oblivious [ə'blɪvɪəs] **adj** (*forgetful*) oublieux (*to, of* de); (*unaware*) inconscient (*to, of* de).

oblong ['ɒblɒŋ] **1 adj** (*rectangular*) oblong (*f* oblongue); (*elongated*) allongé. ~ **dish** plat *m* rectangulaire. **2 n** rectangle *m*.

obloquy ['ɒbləkwɪ] **n** opprobre *m*.

obnoxious [əb'nɒkʃəs] **adj** *person* odieux, infect; *child, dog* détestable, insupportable; *smell* nauséabond; *behaviour* odieux, abominable.

oboe ['əʊbəʊ] **n** hautbois *m*. ~ **d'amore** hautbois d'amour.

oboist ['əʊbəʊɪst] **n** hautboïste *mf*.

obscene [əb'siːn] **adj** *gesture, language, phone call etc* obscène; *prices, salary* révoltant, monstrueux. **an ~ difference between rich and poor** un écart monstrueux entre les riches et les pauvres; (*Jur*) ~ **publication** publication *f* obscène.

obscenely [əb'siːnlɪ] **adv** d'une manière obscène; (*hum*) *fat etc* monstrueusement. **to talk ~** dire des obscénités; ~ **rich** d'une richesse écœurante.

obscenity [əb'senɪtɪ] **n** (*gen, also Jur*) obscénité *f*; (*moral outrage*) infamie *f*. **the ~ laws** les lois *fpl* sur l'obscénité.

obscurantism [ˌɒbskjʊə'ræntɪzəm] **n** obscurantisme *m*.

obscurantist [ˌɒbskjʊə'ræntɪst] **adj, n** obscurantiste (*mf*).

obscure [əb'skjʊəʳ] **1 adj** (*dark*) obscur, sombre; (*fig*) *book, reason, origin, birth* obscur; *poem, style* obscur, abscons (*liter*); *feeling, memory* indistinct, vague; *life, village, poet* obscur, inconnu, ignoré. **2 vt** (*darken*) obscurcir, assombrir; (*hide*) *sun* voiler, cacher, éclipser; *view* cacher, masquer; (*fig*) *argument, idea* rendre obscur, embrouiller, obscurcir; *mind* obscurcir, obnubiler. **to ~ the issue** embrouiller la question.

obscurely [əb'skjʊəlɪ] **adv** obscurément.

obscurity [əb'skjʊərɪtɪ] **n** (*darkness*) obscurité *f*, ténèbres *fpl* (*liter*); (*fig*) obscurité.

obsequies ['ɒbsɪkwɪz] **npl** (*frm*) obsèques *fpl*, funérailles *fpl*.

obsequious [əb'siːkwɪəs] **adj** obséquieux, servile (*to, towards* devant).

obsequiously [əb'siːkwɪəslɪ] **adv** obséquieusement.

obsequiousness [əb'siːkwɪəsnɪs] **n** obséquiosité *f*, servilité *f*.

observable [əb'zɜːvəbl] **adj** (*visible*) observable, visible, perceptible; (*appreciable*) notable, appréciable. **as is ~ in rabbits** ainsi qu'on peut l'observer chez les lapins.

observably [əb'zɜːvəblɪ] **adv** (*visibly*) visiblement.

observance [əb'zɜːvəns] **n a** (*NonC*) *[rule]* observation *f*; *[rite, custom, Sabbath]* observance *f*; *[anniversary]* célébration *f*. **b** (*rule, practice, custom*) observance *f*. **religious ~s** observances religieuses.

observant [əb'zɜːvənt] **adj** *person, mind* observateur (*f* -trice), perspicace. **the child is very ~** cet enfant est très observateur *or* fait preuve d'un grand don d'observation.

observation [ˌɒbzə'veɪʃən] **1 n a** (*NonC*) observation *f*, surveillance *f*. **to keep sb under ~** (*Med*) garder qn en observation; (*Police etc*) surveiller qn; **to be under ~** (*Med*) être en observation; (*Police etc*) être sous surveillance; (*Police etc*) **he came under ~ when ...** on s'est mis à le surveiller quand ...; **he kept the valley under ~** il surveillait la vallée; ~ **of birds/bats** observation des oiseaux/des chauves-souris; **his powers of ~** ses facultés *fpl* d'observation; *see* **escape.**

b (*remark*) observation *f*, remarque *f*. **his ~s on "Hamlet"** ses réflexions *fpl* sur "Hamlet".

2 comp ►observation balloon ballon *m* d'observation *or* d'aérostation **►observation car** (*Rail*) wagon *m or* voiture *f* panoramique **►observation post** (*Mil*) poste *m* d'observation, observatoire *m* **►observation satellite** satellite *m* d'observation **►observation tower** mirador *m* **►observation ward** (*Med*) salle *f* des malades en observation.

observational [ˌɒbzə'veɪʃənl] **adj** *abilities, faculties* d'observation.

observatory [əb'zɜːvətrɪ] **n** observatoire *m*.

observe [əb'zɜːv] **vt a** (*obey etc*) *rule, custom* observer, se conformer à, respecter; *anniversary* célébrer; (*the Sabbath*) observer; *silence* garder, observer. (*Jur*) **failure to ~ the law** inobservation *f* de la loi.

b (*take note of*) observer, remarquer; (*study*) observer. **to ~ sth closely** observer qch attentivement, scruter qch; **I'm only here to ~** je suis seulement là en tant qu'observateur.

c (*say, remark*) (faire) remarquer, faire observer. **he ~d that it was cold** il a fait observer *or* remarquer qu'il faisait froid; **as I was about to ~** comme j'allais le dire *or* le faire remarquer; **I ~d to him that ...** je lui ai fait remarquer *or* observer que ...; **"he has gone" she ~d** "il est parti" dit-elle *or* remarqua-t-elle; **as Eliot ~d** comme l'a remarqué *or* relevé Eliot.

observer [əbˈzɜːvəʳ] **n** a (*person watching*) observateur *m*, -trice *f*, spectateur *m*, -trice *f*. **the ~ may note ...** les observateurs *or* spectateurs remarqueront ... . b (*official: at meeting etc*) observateur *m*, -trice *f*. **Third World ~s at the talks** les observateurs du Tiers Monde présents aux entretiens. c (*Pol etc: analyst, commentator*) spécialiste *mf*, expert *m*. **an ~ of Soviet politics** un spécialiste de la politique soviétique.

obsess [əbˈses] **vt** obséder, hanter. **~ed by** obsédé *or* hanté par.

obsession [əbˈseʃən] **n** (*state*) obsession *f*; (*fixed idea*) obsession, idée *f* fixe; (*of sth unpleasant*) hantise *f*. **he's got an ~ with sport, sport is an ~ with him** le sport c'est son idée fixe, le sport tient de l'obsession chez lui; **he has an ~ about cleanliness** c'est un obsédé de la propreté, il a l'obsession de la propreté; **his ~ with her** la manière dont elle l'obsède; **his ~ with death** son obsession *or* sa hantise de la mort.

obsessional [əbˈseʃənl] **adj** = **obsessive**.

obsessive [əbˈsesɪv] **adj** (*gen, also Psych*) obsessionnel; *memory, thought* obsédant.

obsessively [əbˈsesɪvlɪ] **adv** d'une manière obsédante. **~ keen to get married** obsédé par le désir de se marier; **~ anxious not to be seen** ayant la hantise d'être vu.

obsidian [ɒbˈsɪdɪən] **n** obsidienne *f*.

obsolescence [ˌɒbsəˈlesns] **n** *[machinery]* obsolescence *f*; *[goods, words]* vieillissement *m*; (*Bio*) atrophie *f*, myopathie *f*. (*Insurance*) **~ clause** clause *f* de vétusté; (*Comm*) **planned** *or* **built-in ~** obsolescence calculée.

obsolescent [ˌɒbsəˈlesnt] **adj** *machinery* obsolescent; *word* vieilli, qui tombe en désuétude; (*Bio*) *organ* en voie d'atrophie.

obsolete [ˈɒbsəliːt] **adj** *passport, ticket* périmé; *goods* vieux (*f* vieille); *machine, tool* vieux, dépassé; *attitude, idea, process, custom* dépassé, démodé, (*stronger*) désuet (*f*- uète), suranné; *law* caduc (*f* -uque), tombé en désuétude; (*Ling*) *word* obsolète, vieilli; (*Bio*) atrophié; (*Rel*) *practices* obsolète.

obstacle [ˈɒbstəkl] 1 **n** obstacle *m*; (*fig*) obstacle, empêchement *m* (*to* à). **to be an ~ to sth** faire obstacle à qch, entraver qch, être un obstacle à qch; **agriculture is the main ~ in the negotiations** l'agriculture constitue la pierre d'achoppement des négociations; **to put an ~ in the way of sth/in sb's way** faire obstacle à qch/qn. 2 **comp** ►**obstacle course** parcours *m* du combattant ►**obstacle race** (*Sport*) course *f* d'obstacles.

obstetric(al) [ɒbˈstetrɪk(əl)] **adj** *techniques etc* obstétrical; *clinic* obstétrique.

obstetrician [ˌɒbstəˈtrɪʃən] **n** obstétricien(ne) *m(f)*, (médecin *m*) accoucheur *m*.

obstetrics [ɒbˈstetrɪks] **n** (*NonC*) obstétrique *f*.

obstinacy [ˈɒbstɪnəsɪ] **n** obstination *f*, entêtement *m*, opiniâtreté *f* (*in doing* à faire); *[illness]* persistance *f*; *[resistance]* obstination, persévérance *f*, détermination *f*.

obstinate [ˈɒbstɪnɪt] **adj** *person* obstiné, têtu, entêté, opiniâtre (*about, over* en ce qui concerne); *effort, work, resistance* obstiné, acharné; *pain, illness* persistant; *fever* rebelle; *fight* acharné. **to be as ~ as a mule** être têtu comme une mule *or* comme une bourrique*, avoir une tête de mule* *or* de cochon*; **he's very ~ about it** il n'en démord pas.

obstinately [ˈɒbstɪnɪtlɪ] **adv** obstinément, opiniâtrement; *struggle* avec acharnement. **to refuse ~** refuser obstinément, s'obstiner à refuser; **he ~ insisted on leaving** il a absolument tenu à partir; **he tried ~ to do it by himself** il s'est obstiné *or* entêté à le faire tout seul.

obstreperous [əbˈstrepərəs] **adj** (*noisy*) bruyant, tapageur; (*unruly*) turbulent, chahuteur; (*rebellious*) récalcitrant, rebelle, rouspéteur*. **the crowd grew ~** la foule s'est mise à protester bruyamment *or* à rouspéter* bruyamment.

obstreperously [əbˈstrepərəslɪ] **adv** (*noisily*) bruyamment, tapageusement; (*rebelliously*) avec force protestations, en rouspétant*.

obstruct [əbˈstrʌkt] 1 **vt** a (*block*) *road* encombrer, obstruer (*with* de), barrer, boucher (*with* avec); *pipe* boucher (*with* avec, *by* par), engorger; *artery* obstruer, oblitérer; *view* boucher, cacher. b (*halt*) *traffic* bloquer; *progress* arrêter, enrayer. c (*hinder*) *progress, traffic* entraver, gêner; *plan* entraver, faire obstacle à; *person* gêner, entraver; (*Sport*) *player* faire obstruction à. (*Pol*) **to ~ (the passage of) a bill** faire de l'obstruction parlementaire; (*Jur*) **to ~ a policeman in the execution of his duty** gêner *or* entraver un agent de police dans l'exercice de ses fonctions. 2 **vi** (*Sport*) faire de l'obstruction.

obstruction [əbˈstrʌkʃən] **n** a (*NonC: act, state: see* **obstruct 1**) encombrement *m*, obstruction *f*; engorgement *m*; arrêt *m*. (*Jur*) **he was charged with ~ of the police in the course of their duties** ≃ il a été inculpé d'avoir refusé d'aider les policiers dans l'exercice de leurs fonctions. b (*sth which obstructs*) (*to road, passage, plan, progress, view*) obstacle *m*; (*to pipe*) bouchon *m*; (*to artery*) caillot *m*. (*Jur etc*) **to cause an ~** (*gen*) encombrer *or* obstruer la voie publique; (*Aut*) bloquer la circulation, provoquer un embouteillage. c (*Sport*) obstruction *f*.

obstructionism [əbˈstrʌkʃənɪzəm] **n** obstructionnisme *m*.

obstructionist [əbˈstrʌkʃənɪst] **adj, n** obstructionniste (*mf*). **to adopt ~ tactics** faire de l'obstruction, pratiquer l'obstruction.

obstructive [əbˈstrʌktɪv] **adj** a (*gen*) qui se met en travers, qui dresse des obstacles; *measures, policy, tactics* d'obstruction, obstructionniste; *person, behaviour* obstructionniste, qui fait de l'obstruction. **you're being ~** vous ne pensez qu'à mettre des bâtons dans les roues. b (*Med*) obstructif, obstruant.

obstructiveness [əbˈstrʌktɪvnɪs] **n** tendance *f* à dresser des obstacles *or* à faire obstacle.

obtain [əbˈteɪn] 1 **vt** (*gen*) obtenir; *goods* procurer (*for sb* à qn); (*for o.s.*) se procurer; *information, job, money* obtenir, (se) procurer; *votes* obtenir, recueillir; *prize* obtenir, remporter; (*Fin*) *shares* acquérir. **this gas is ~ed from coal** on obtient ce gaz à partir du charbon; **these goods may be ~ed from any large store** on peut se procurer ces articles dans tous les grands magasins. 2 **vi** (*frm*) *[rule, custom etc]* avoir cours, être en vigueur; *[fashion]* être en vogue; *[method]* être courant.

obtainable [əbˈteɪnəbl] **adj** qu'on peut obtenir *or* se procurer. **where is that book ~?** où peut-on se procurer *or* trouver *or* acheter ce livre?; **"~ at all good chemists"** "en vente dans toutes les bonnes pharmacies".

obtrude [əbˈtruːd] 1 **vt** imposer (*sth on sb* qch à qn). 2 **vi** *[person]* s'imposer, imposer sa présence. **the author's opinions do not ~** l'auteur n'impose pas ses opinions.

obtrusion [əbˈtruːʒən] **n** intrusion *f*.

obtrusive [əbˈtruːsɪv] **adj** *person, presence* importun, indiscret (*f* -ète); *opinions* ostentatoire, affiché; *smell* pénétrant; *film music* gênant, agaçant; *memory* obsédant; *building, decor etc* trop en évidence, qui accroche *or* qui heurte le regard.

obtrusively [əbˈtruːsɪvlɪ] **adv** importunément, avec indiscrétion.

obtuse [əbˈtjuːs] **adj** (*blunt*) obtus; (*Geom*) obtus; *person* obtus, borné. **you're just being ~!** tu fais exprès de ne pas comprendre!

obtuseness [əbˈtjuːsnɪs] **n** stupidité *f*.

obverse [ˈɒbvɜːs] 1 **n** *[coin]* face *f*, côté *m* face; *[statement, truth]* contrepartie *f*, contre-pied *m*. 2 **adj** a *side of coin etc* de face, qui fait face; (*fig*) correspondant, faisant contrepartie. b (*in shape*) *leaf* renversé, plus large au sommet qu'à la base.

obviate [ˈɒbvɪeɪt] **vt** *difficulty* obvier à, parer à; *necessity* parer à; *danger, objection* prévenir.

obvious [ˈɒbvɪəs] 1 **adj** évident, manifeste. **it's an ~ fact, it's quite ~** c'est bien évident, c'est l'évidence même; **it's ~ that** il est évident que, il est de toute évidence que; **it's the ~ thing to do** c'est la chose à faire, cela s'impose; **the ~ thing to do is to leave** la chose à faire c'est évidemment de partir; **that's the ~ one to choose** c'est bien évidemment celui-là qu'il faut choisir; **~ statement** truisme *m*, lapalissade *f*; **with ~ shyness** avec une timidité évidente *or* visible; **his ~ good faith** sa bonne foi évidente *or* incontestable; **we must not be too ~ about it** il va falloir ne pas trop montrer notre jeu.

2 **n**: **you are merely stating the ~** il n'y a rien de nouveau dans ce que vous dites, vous enfoncez une porte ouverte.

obviously [ˈɒbvɪəslɪ] **adv** (*clearly*) manifestement; (*of course*) évidemment, bien sûr. **it's ~ true** c'est de toute évidence vrai; **he was ~ not drunk** il était évident qu'il n'était pas ivre; **he was not ~ drunk** il n'était pas visiblement ivre; **~!** bien sûr!, évidemment!; **~ not!** bien sûr que non!

O.C. [ˈəʊˈsiː] **n abbr of Officer Commanding.**

ocarina [ˌɒkəˈriːnə] **n** ocarina *m*.

Occam [ˈɒkəm] **n** Occam *m*. **~'s razor** le rasoir d'Occam.

occasion [əˈkeɪʒən] 1 **n** a (*juncture; suitable time*) occasion *f*, circonstance *f*. **on the ~ of** à l'occasion de; **(on) the first ~ (that) it happened** la première fois que cela s'est passé; **on that ~** à cette occasion, cette fois-là; **on several ~s** à plusieurs occasions *or* reprises; **on rare ~s** en de rares occasions; **on just such an ~** dans une occasion tout à fait semblable; **on great ~s** dans les grandes occasions *or* circonstances; **on a previous** *or* **former ~** précédemment; **I'll do it on the first possible ~** je le ferai à la première occasion (possible) *or* dès que l'occasion se présentera; **(up)on ~, on ~s** à l'occasion, quand l'occasion se présente (*or* se présentait *etc*); **should the ~ arise** le cas échéant; **should the ~ so demand** si les circonstances l'exigent; **as the ~ requires** selon le cas; **he has had few ~s to speak Italian** il n'a pas eu souvent l'occasion de parler italien; **he took (the) ~ to say ...** il en a profité pour dire ...; **he was waiting for a suitable ~ to apologize** il attendait une occasion *or* circonstance favorable pour présenter ses excuses; **this would be a good ~ to try it out** c'est l'occasion tout indiquée pour l'essayer; **to rise to** *or* **be equal to the ~** se montrer *or* être à la hauteur des circonstances *or* de la situation.

b (*event, function*) événement *m*. **a big ~** un grand événement; **it was quite an ~** cela n'a pas été une petite affaire *or* un petit événement; **play/music written for the ~** pièce spécialement écrite/musique spécialement composée pour l'occasion.

c (*reason*) motif *m*, occasion *f*. **there is no ~ for alarm** *or* **to be**

alarmed il n'y a pas lieu de s'alarmer, il n'y a pas de quoi s'alarmer; **there was no ~ for it** ce n'était pas nécessaire; **I have no ~ for complaint** je n'ai pas sujet de me plaindre, je n'ai aucun motif de plainte; **you had no ~ to say that** vous n'aviez aucune raison de dire cela; **I had ~ to reprimand him** j'ai eu l'occasion de *or* j'ai eu à le réprimander.

d (*frm*) **to go about one's lawful ~s** vaquer à ses occupations.

2 vt occasionner, causer.

occasional [əˈkeɪʒənl] adj a *event* qui a lieu de temps en temps *or* de temps à autre; *visits* espacés; *rain, showers* intermittent. **we have an ~ visitor** il nous arrive d'avoir quelqu'un (de temps en temps); **we're just ~ visitors** nous ne venons ici qu'occasionnellement; **they had passed an ~ car on the road** ils avaient croisé quelques rares voitures; **~ table** table volante; (*esp round*) guéridon *m*. b *verses, music* de circonstance.

occasionally [əˈkeɪʒnəlɪ] adv de temps en temps, de temps à autre, quelquefois, parfois. **very ~** à intervalles très espacés; **only very ~** très peu souvent, rarement, presque jamais.

occident [ˈɒksɪdənt] n (*liter*) occident *m*, couchant *m*. **the O~** l'Occident *m*.

occidental [ˌɒksɪˈdentl] adj (*liter*) occidental.

occipita [ɒkˈsɪpɪtə] npl of **occiput**.

occipital [ɒkˈsɪpɪtəl] adj occipital.

occiput [ˈɒksɪpʌt] n, pl ~s *or* **occipita** occiput *m*.

occlude [ɒˈkluːd] 1 vt (*all senses*) occlure. (*Met*) **~d front** front occlus. 2 vi (*Dentistry*) s'emboîter.

occlusion [ɒˈkluːʒən] n (*all senses*) occlusion *f*.

occlusive [ɒˈkluːsɪv] 1 adj (*also Ling*) occlusif. 2 n (*Phon*) (consonne *f*) occlusive *f*.

occult [ɒˈkʌlt] 1 adj occulte. 2 n: **the ~** le surnaturel; **to study the ~** étudier les sciences occultes.

occultism [ˈɒkəltɪzəm] n occultisme *m*.

occupancy [ˈɒkjʊpənsɪ] n occupation *f* (*d'une maison etc*).

occupant [ˈɒkjʊpənt] n *[house]* occupant(e) *m(f)*, habitant(e) *m(f)*, (*tenant*) locataire *mf*; *[land, vehicle etc]* occupant(e); *[job, post]* titulaire *mf*.

occupation [ˌɒkjʊˈpeɪʃən] 1 n a (*NonC*) *[house etc]* occupation *f*; (*Jur*) prise *f* de possession. **unfit for ~** impropre à l'habitation; **the house is ready for ~** la maison est prête à être habitée; **we found them already in ~** nous les avons trouvés déjà installés.

b (*NonC: Mil etc*) occupation *f*. **army of ~** armée *f* d'occupation; **under military ~** sous occupation militaire; **during the O~** pendant *or* sous l'Occupation.

c (*trade*) métier *m*; (*profession*) profession *f*; (*work*) emploi *m*, travail *m*; (*activity, pastime*) occupation *f*. **he is a plumber by ~** il est plombier de son métier; **he needs some ~ for his spare time** il lui faut une occupation *or* de quoi occuper ses loisirs; **his only ~ was helping his father** sa seule occupation était *or* il avait pour seule occupation d'aider son père.

2 comp *troops* d'occupation.

occupational [ˌɒkjʊˈpeɪʃənl] adj qui a rapport au métier *or* à la profession. (*Jur*) **~ activity** activité professionnelle; **~ disease** maladie *f* du travail; **~ hazard** *[job]* risque *m* professionnel *or* du métier; *[skiing, sailing etc]* risque encouru par ceux qui font du ski/de la voile *etc*; **~ psychologist** psychologue *mf* du travail; **~ psychology** psychologie *f* du travail; **~ therapist** ergothérapeute *mf*; **~ therapy** thérapeutique occupationnelle, ergothérapie *f*.

occupied [ˈɒkjʊpaɪd] adj *toilet* occupé; *see* **occupy**.

occupier [ˈɒkjʊpaɪəʳ] n *[house]* occupant(e) *m(f)*, habitant(e) *m(f)*, (*tenant*) locataire *mf*; *[land]* occupant(e); *see* **owner**.

occupy [ˈɒkjʊpaɪ] vt a *house* occuper, habiter, résider dans; *room, chair* occuper; *post, position* remplir, occuper. b *[troops, demonstrators]* occuper. (*Mil*) **occupied territory** territoire occupé. c *space* occuper, tenir; *time* occuper, prendre. d *attention, mind, person* occuper. **occupied with the thought of** absorbé par la pensée de; **to be occupied in** *or* **with doing** être occupé à faire; **to ~ o.s.** *or* **one's time (with** *or* **by doing)** s'occuper (à faire); **how do you keep occupied all day?** qu'est-ce que vous trouvez à faire toute la journée?; **to keep one's mind occupied** s'occuper l'esprit.

occur [əˈkɜːʳ] vi a *[event]* avoir lieu, arriver, survenir, se produire; *[word, error]* se rencontrer, se trouver; *[difficulty, opportunity]* se présenter; *[change]* s'opérer; *[disease]* se produire, se rencontrer; *[plant etc]* se trouver. **don't let it ~ again!** que cela ne se reproduise plus! *or* ne se répète (*subj*) pas!; **if a vacancy ~s** en cas de poste vacant; **should the case ~** le cas échéant.

b (*come to mind*) se présenter *or* venir à l'esprit (*to sb* de qn). **an idea ~red to me** une idée m'est venue; **it ~s to me that he is wrong** il me vient à l'esprit qu'il a tort, l'idée me vient qu'il a tort; **it ~red to me that we could ...** j'ai pensé *or* je me suis dit que nous pourrions ...; **it didn't ~ to him to refuse** il n'a pas eu l'idée de refuser; **the thought would never ~ to me** ça ne me viendrait jamais à l'idée *or* à l'esprit; **did it never ~ to you to ask?** il ne t'est jamais venu à l'esprit de demander?, tu n'as jamais eu l'idée de demander?

occurrence [əˈkʌrəns] n a (*event*) événement *m*, circonstance *f*. **an everyday ~** un fait journalier; **this is a common ~** ceci arrive *or* se produit souvent. b fait *m* de se produire *or* d'arriver. *[plant etc]* **its ~ in the south is well-known** son existence est bien constatée dans le sud; **to be of frequent ~** se produire *or* arriver souvent.

ocean [ˈəʊʃən] 1 n (*lit, fig*) océan *m*. (*fig*) **~s of*** énormément de*. 2 comp *climate, region* océanique; *cruise* sur l'océan ▶**ocean bed** fond sous-marin ▶**ocean-going** de haute mer; **ocean-going ship** (navire *m*) long-courrier *m*, navire de haute mer ▶**ocean liner** paquebot *m* ▶**the Ocean State** (*US*) le Rhode Island.

oceanarium [ˌəʊʃəˈnɛərɪəm] n, pl ~s *or* **oceanaria** [ˌəʊʃəˈnɛərɪə] parc *m* océanographique, océanarium *m*.

Oceania [ˌəʊʃɪˈeɪnɪə] n Océanie *f*.

Oceanian [ˌəʊʃɪˈeɪnɪən] 1 adj océanien. 2 n Océanien(ne) *m(f)*.

oceanic [ˌəʊʃɪˈænɪk] adj *current* océanique, pélagique; *fauna* pélagique.

oceanographer [ˌəʊʃəˈnɒgrəfəʳ] n océanographe *mf*.

oceanographic [ˌəʊʃənəˈgræfɪk] adj océanographique.

oceanography [ˌəʊʃəˈnɒgrəfɪ] n océanographie *f*.

ocelot [ˈəʊsɪlɒt] n ocelot *m*.

och [ɒx] excl (*Scot*) oh.

ochre, (*US*) **ocher** [ˈəʊkəʳ] n (*substance*) ocre *f*; (*colour*) ocre *m*.

ochreous [ˈəʊkrɪəs] adj ocreux.

o'clock [əˈklɒk] adv: **it is one ~** il est une heure; **what ~ is it?** quelle heure est-il?; **at 5 ~** à 5 heures; **at exactly 9 ~** à 9 heures précises *or* justes; **at twelve ~** (*midday*) à midi; (*midnight*) à minuit; **the six ~ (bus/train** *etc*) le bus/train de six heures; (*Aviat, Mil: direction*) **aircraft approaching at 5 ~** avion *m* à 5 heures.

OCR [ˈəʊˌsiːˈɑːʳ] (*Comput*) (abbr of **optical character reader, optical character recognition**) *see* **optical**.

Oct. abbr of **October**.

octagon [ˈɒktəgən] n octogone *m*.

octagonal [ɒkˈtægənl] adj octogonal.

octahedron [ˈɒktəˈhiːdrən] n, pl ~s *or* **octahedra** [ˈɒktəˈhiːdrə] octaèdre *m*.

octal [ˈɒktəl] n, adj (*Comput*) **~ (notation)** octal *(m)*.

octane [ˈɒkteɪn] 1 n octane *m*. **high-~ petrol** carburant *m* à indice d'octane élevé. 2 comp d'octane ▶**octane number** indice *m* d'octane ▶**octane rating** = **octane number**.

octave [ˈɒktɪv] n (*gen, Mus, Rel, Fencing*) octave *f*; (*Poetry*) huitain *m*.

octavo [ɒkˈteɪvəʊ] n, pl ~s in-octavo *m*.

octet [ɒkˈtet] n (*Mus*) octuor *m*; (*Poetry*) huitain *m*.

octillion [ɒkˈtɪljən] n (*Brit etc*) 10^{48}; (*US, France*) 10^{27}.

October [ɒkˈtəʊbəʳ] n octobre *m*. (*Russian Hist*) **the ~ Revolution** la Révolution d'octobre; *for other phrases see* **September**.

octogenarian [ˌɒktəʊdʒɪˈnɛərɪən] adj, n, pl ~s *or* **octogenaries** [ˌɒktəʊdʒɪˈnɛəriːz] octogénaire *(mf)*.

octopus [ˈɒktəpəs] pl ~es 1 n (*Zool*) pieuvre *f*, poulpe *m*; (*Brit Aut: for luggage etc*) pieuvre, fixe-bagages *m inv*. 2 comp *organization* ramifié, à ramifications (multiples).

octoroon [ˌɒktəˈruːn] n octavon(ne) *m(f)*.

octosyllabic [ˈɒktəʊsɪˈlæbɪk] 1 adj octosyllabique. 2 n octosyllabe *m*, vers *m* octosyllabique.

octosyllable [ˈɒktəʊˈsɪləbl] n (*line*) octosyllabe *m*, vers *m* octosyllabique; (*word*) mot *m* octosyllabique.

ocular [ˈɒkjʊləʳ] adj, n oculaire *(m)*.

oculist [ˈɒkjʊlɪst] n oculiste *mf*.

OD‡ [əʊˈdiː] (*US*) (abbr of **overdose**) 1 n surdose *f*. 2 vi (*Drugs*) prendre une surdose; (*fig*) se gorger.

odalisque [ˈəʊdəlɪsk] n odalisque *f*.

odd [ɒd] 1 adj a (*strange*) bizarre, étrange, singulier, curieux. **(how) ~!** bizarre!, étrange!, curieux!; **how ~ that we should meet him** comme c'est curieux que nous l'ayons rencontré; **what an ~ thing for him to do!** c'est curieux *or* bizarre qu'il ait fait cela!; **he says some very ~ things** il dit de drôles de choses parfois; **the ~ thing about it is** ce qui est bizarre *or* étrange à ce sujet c'est, le plus curieux de l'affaire c'est; **he's got rather ~ lately** il est bizarre depuis quelque temps.

b (*Math*) *number* impair.

c (*extra, left over*) qui reste(nt); (*from pair*) *shoe, sock* dépareillé; (*from set*) dépareillé. **I've got it all but the ~ penny** il me manque un penny pour avoir le compte; **£5 and some ~ pennies** 5 livres et quelques pennies; **any ~ piece of wood** un morceau de bois quelconque; **any ~ piece of bread you can spare** n'importe quel morceau de pain dont vous n'ayez pas besoin; **an ~ scrap of paper** un bout de papier; **a few ~ hats** deux ou trois chapeaux; (*Brit*) **this is an ~ size that we don't stock** c'est une taille peu courante que nous n'avons pas (en stock); **to be the ~ one over** être en surnombre; **the ~ man out, the ~ one out** l'exception *f*; *see also* **2** *and* **odds**.

d (*and a few more*) **60-~** 60 et quelques; **forty-~ years** une quarantaine d'années, quarante et quelques années; **£20-~** 20 et quelques livres, 20 livres et quelques.

e (*occasional, not regular*) **in ~ moments he ...** à ses moments perdus il ...; **at ~ times** de temps en temps; **in ~ corners all over the house** dans les coins et recoins de la maison; **~ jobs** travaux divers (*see also* **2**); **I did a lot of ~ jobs before becoming an actor** j'ai fait beaucoup de petits boulots* *or* j'ai touché un peu à tout avant d'être acteur; **to do ~ jobs about the house** (*housework*) faire des travaux domestiques divers; (*do-it-yourself*) bricoler dans la maison; **he does ~ jobs around the garden** il fait de petits travaux de jardinage; **I've got one or two ~ jobs for you (to do)** j'ai deux ou trois choses *or* bricoles* à te faire faire; **I don't grudge her the ~ meal (or two)** je ne lui fais pas grief d'un repas par-ci par-là; **he has written the ~ article** il a écrit un ou deux articles; **I get the ~ letter from him** de temps en temps je reçois une lettre de lui; **there will be sunshine everywhere apart from the ~ shower** il y aura du soleil partout avec malgré tout quelques rares averses.

2 comp ▸**oddball*** (*esp US*) n excentrique *mf* ◊ adj rare, excentrique ▸**oddbod*** drôle *m* d'oiseau* ▸**odd-jobber, odd-job man** homme *m* à tout faire ▸**odd-looking** à l'air bizarre ▸**odd lot** (*St Ex*) lot *m* fractionné.

oddity ['ɒdɪtɪ] n a (*strangeness*) = **oddness.** b (*odd person*) personne *f* bizarre, excentrique *mf*; (*odd thing*) curiosité *f*; (*odd trait*) singularité *f*. **he's a real ~** il a vraiment un genre très spécial; **one of the oddities of the situation** un des aspects insolites de la situation.

oddly ['ɒdlɪ] adv singulièrement, bizarrement, curieusement; de façon étrange *or* bizarre. **~ enough she was at home** chose curieuse *or* singulière elle était chez elle; **she was ~ attractive** elle avait un charme insolite.

oddment ['ɒdmənt] n (*Brit Comm*) fin *f* de série; (*one of a pair or collection*) article dépareillé; *[cloth]* coupon *m*.

oddness ['ɒdnɪs] n (*NonC*) bizarrerie *f*, étrangeté *f*, singularité *f*.

odds [ɒdz] 1 npl a (*Betting*) cote *f*. **he gave him ~ of 5 to 1 (for Jupiter)** il lui a donné une cote de 5 contre 1 (sur Jupiter); **he gave him ~ of 5 to 1 that he would fail his exams** il lui a parié à 5 contre 1 qu'il échouerait à ses examens; **I got good/short/long ~** on m'a donné une bonne/faible/forte cote; **the ~ on** *or* **against a horse** la cote d'un cheval; **the ~ are 7 to 2 against Lucifer** Lucifer est à 7 contre 2, la cote de Lucifer est de 7 contre 2; **the ~ are 6 to 4 on** la cote est à 4 contre 6; **the ~ are 6 to 4 against** la cote est à 6 contre 4; **what ~ will you give me?** quelle est votre cote?; (*fig*) **the ~ are 10 to 1 in favour of his** *or* **him* going** il y a 9 chances sur 10 (pour) qu'il y aille; (*Brit: fig*) **over the ~** plus que nécessaire; **I got £2 over the ~ for it** on me l'a payé 2 livres de plus que je ne demandais (*or* ne m'y attendais *etc*).

b (*fig: balance of advantage*) chances *fpl* (*for* pour, *against* contre), avantage *m*. **all the ~ are against you** nous n'avez pratiquement aucune chance d'y arriver, c'est pratiquement perdu d'avance; **the ~ are against his** *or* **him* coming** il est pratiquement certain qu'il ne viendra pas, il y a gros à parier qu'il ne viendra pas, il y a peu de chances qu'il vienne; **the ~ against another attack are very high** une nouvelle attaque est hautement improbable; **the ~ are on him coming** *or* **that he will come** il y a gros à parier qu'il viendra, il y a de fortes chances (pour) qu'il vienne; **the ~ are even that he will come** il y a cinquante pour cent de chances qu'il vienne; **to fight against heavy** *or* **great ~** avoir affaire à plus fort que soi, combattre *or* lutter contre des forces supérieures; **he managed to succeed against overwhelming ~** *or* **against all the ~** il a réussi alors que tout était contre lui; **the ~ are too great** le succès est trop improbable; **by all the ~** (*unquestionably*) sans aucun doute; (*judging from past experience*) à en juger par l'expérience, d'après ce que l'on sait; *see* **stack 2d.**

c (*difference*) **it makes no ~** cela n'a pas d'importance, ça ne fait rien*; **it makes no ~ to me** ça m'est complètement égal, ça ne me fait rien, je m'en moque, je m'en fiche*; **what's the ~?*** qu'est-ce que ça fait?, qu'est-ce que ça peut bien faire?

d **to be at ~ (with sb over sth)** être en désaccord (avec qn sur qch); **his pompous tone was at ~ with the vulgar language he used** son ton pompeux contrastait avec le langage vulgaire qu'il employait; **to set 2 people at ~** brouiller 2 personnes, semer la discorde entre 2 personnes.

2 comp ▸**odds and ends** (*gen*) des petites choses qui restent; *[cloth]* bouts *mpl*; *[food]* restes *mpl*; **there were a few odds and ends lying about the house** quelques objets traînaient çà et là dans la maison; (*fig*) **we still have a few odds and ends to settle** il nous reste encore quelques points à régler ▸**odds-on:** (*Racing*) **odds-on favourite** grand favori *m*; (*fig*) **he's the odds-on favourite for the job** c'est le grand favori pour le poste; **it's odds-on that he'll come** il y a toutes les chances qu'il vienne, il y a gros à parier qu'il viendra.

ode [əʊd] n ode *f* (*to* à, *on* sur).

odious ['əʊdɪəs] adj détestable, odieux.

odiously ['əʊdɪəslɪ] adv odieusement.

odiousness ['əʊdɪəsnɪs] n caractère *m* détestable *or* odieux.

odium ['əʊdɪəm] n (*NonC*) réprobation *f* générale, anathème *m*.

odometer [ɒ'dɒmɪtəʳ] n (*US*) odomètre *m*.

odont(o)... [ɒ'dɒnt(əʊ)] pref odont(o)... .

odontological [ɒ,dɒntə'lɒdʒɪkəl] adj odontologique.

odontologist [,ɒdɒn'tɒlədʒɪst] n odontologiste *mf*.

odontology [,ɒdɒn'tɒlədʒɪ] n odontologie *f*.

odor ['əʊdəʳ] n (*US*) = **odour.**

odoriferous [,əʊdə'rɪfərəs] adj odoriférant, parfumé.

odorless ['əʊdəlɪs] adj (*US*) = **odourless.**

odorous ['əʊdərəs] adj (*liter*) odorant, parfumé.

odour, (*US*) **odor** ['əʊdəʳ] n odeur *f*; (*pleasant*) odeur (agréable), parfum *m*; (*unpleasant*) (mauvaise) odeur; (*fig*) trace *f*, parfum (*liter*). (*fig*) **to be in good/bad ~ with sb** être/ne pas être en faveur auprès de qn, être bien/mal vu de qn; **~ of sanctity** odeur de sainteté.

odourless, (*US*) **odorless** ['əʊdəlɪs] adj inodore.

Odysseus [ə'diːsɪəs] n Odusseus *m*.

Odyssey ['ɒdɪsɪ] n (*Myth*) Odyssée *f*. (*gen*) **o~** odyssée *f*.

OE n (*Ling*) (abbr of **Old English**) *see* **old.**

OECD ['əʊ,iːsiː'diː] n (abbr of **Organization for Economic Cooperation and Development**) O.C.D.E. *f*.

oecology [ɪ'kɒlədʒɪ] *etc* = **ecology** *etc*.

oecumenical [,iːkjʊː'menɪkəl] *etc* = **ecumenical** *etc*.

oedema [ɪ'diːmə] n, pl **~ta** [ɪ'diːmətə] (*Brit*) œdème *m*.

Oedipal ['iːdɪpəl] adj œdipien.

Oedipus ['iːdɪpəs] n Œdipe *m*. (*Psych*) **~ complex** complexe *m* d'Œdipe.

oenological [,iːnə'lɒdʒɪkəl] adj œnologique.

oenologist [iː'nɒlədʒɪst] n œnologue *mf*.

oenology [iː'nɒlədʒɪ] n œnologie *f*.

o'er ['əʊəʳ] (*liter*) = **over.**

oesophagus [iː'sɒfəgəs] n = **esophagus.**

oestrogen ['iːstrəʊdʒən] n œstrogène *m*.

oestrone ['iːstrəʊn] n folliculine *f*.

oestrous ['iːstrəs] adj œstral. **~ cycle** cycle *m* œstral.

oestrus ['iːstrəs] n œstrus *m*.

œuvre ['ɜːvrə] n œuvre *f*.

of [ɒv,əv] prep a (*possession*) de. **the wife ~ the doctor** la femme du médecin; **a painting ~ the queen's** un tableau de la reine *or* qui appartient à la reine; **a friend ~ ours** un de nos amis; **that funny nose ~ hers** son drôle de nez, ce drôle de nez qu'elle a; **~ it** en; **the tip ~ it is broken** le bout en est cassé.

b (*objective genitive*) de, pour; (*subjective*) de. **his love ~ his father** son amour pour son père, l'amour qu'il porte (*or* portait *etc*) à son père; **love ~ money** amour de l'argent; **a painting ~ the queen** un tableau de la reine *or* qui représente la reine; **a leader ~ men** un meneur d'hommes; **writer ~ legal articles** auteur d'articles de droit.

c (*partitive*) de; entre. **the whole ~ the house** toute la maison; **how much ~ this do you want?** combien *or* quelle quantité en voulez-vous?; **there were 6 ~ us** nous étions 6; **he asked the six ~ us to lunch** il nous a invités tous les six à déjeuner; **~ the ten only one was absent** sur les dix un seul était absent; **he is not one ~ us** il n'est pas des nôtres; **the 2nd ~ June** le 2 juin; **today ~ all days** ce jour entre tous; **you ~ all people ought to know** vous devriez le savoir mieux que personne; (*liter*) **he is the bravest ~ the brave** c'est un brave entre les braves; **the quality ~ (all) qualities** la qualité qui domine toutes les autres; (*liter*) **he drank ~ the wine** il but du vin; *see* **best, first, most, some** *etc*.

d (*concerning, in respect of*) de. **what do you think ~ him?** que pensez-vous de lui?; **what ~ it?** et alors?; **hard ~ hearing** dur d'oreille; **20 years ~ age** âgé de 20 ans; *see* **bachelor, capable, warn** *etc*.

e (*separation in space or time*) de. **south ~ Paris** au sud de Paris; **within a month/a kilometre ~** à moins d'un mois/d'un kilomètre de; (*US*) **a quarter ~ 6** 6 heures moins le quart.

f (*origin*) de. **~ noble birth** de naissance noble; **~ royal origin** d'origine royale; **a book ~ Dante's** un livre de Dante.

g (*cause*) de. **to die ~ hunger** mourir de faim; **because ~** à cause de; **it did not happen ~ itself** ce n'est pas arrivé tout seul; **for fear ~** de peur de; *see* **ashamed, choice, necessity** *etc*.

h (*with certain verbs*) **it tastes ~ garlic** cela a un goût d'ail; *see* **smell** *etc*.

i (*deprivation, riddance*) de. **to get rid ~** se débarrasser de; **loss ~ appetite** perte d'appétit; **cured ~** guéri de; *see* **free, irrespective, short** *etc*.

j (*material*) de, en. **dress (made) ~ wool** robe en *or* de laine.

k (*descriptive*) de. **house ~ 10 rooms** maison de 10 pièces; **man ~ courage** homme courageux; **girl ~ 10** petite fille de 10 ans; **question ~ no importance** question sans importance; **the city ~ Paris** la ville de Paris; **town ~ narrow streets** ville aux rues étroites; **fruit ~ his own growing** fruits qu'il a cultivés lui-même; **that idiot ~ a doctor** cet imbécile de docteur; **he has a real palace ~ a house** c'est un véritable palais que sa maison; *see* **extraction, make, name** *etc*.

l (*agent etc*) de. **beloved ~ all** bien-aimé de tous; **it was horrid ~ him to say so** c'était méchant de sa part (que) de dire cela; *see* **kind** *etc*.

m (*in temporal phrases*) **~ late** depuis quelque temps; (*liter*) **it was often fine ~ a morning** il faisait souvent beau le matin; *see* **old** *etc*.

off [ɒf] (*phr vb elem*) 1 prep a (*gen*) de *or etc*. **he fell/jumped ~ the wall** il est tombé/a sauté du mur; **he fell ~ it** il (en) est tombé; **he took the book ~ the table** il a pris le livre sur la table; **there are 2 buttons ~ my coat** il manque 2 boutons à mon manteau; **the lid was ~ the tin** le couvercle de la boîte n'était pas mis, on avait ôté le couvercle de la boîte; **the lid was ~ it** il n'y avait pas de couvercle; **they eat ~ chipped plates** ils mangent dans des assiettes ébréchées; **they dined ~ a chicken** ils ont dîné d'un poulet; **he cut a slice ~ the cake** il a coupé une tranche du gâteau; **I'll take something ~ the price for you** je vais vous faire une réduction *or* une remise (sur le prix); *see* **get off, keep off, road** *etc*.

b (*distant from*) de. **he was a yard ~ me** il était à un mètre de moi; **he ran towards the car and was 5 yards ~ it when** ... il a couru vers la voiture et en était à 5 mètres quand ...; **height ~ the ground** hauteur (à partir) du sol; **street (leading) ~ the square** rue qui part de la place; **house ~ the main road** maison à l'écart de la grand-route; (*Naut*) ~ **Portland Bill** au large de Portland Bill.

c **I'm** *or* **I have gone ~ sausages*** je n'aime plus les saucisses; **I'm ~ smoking*** je ne fume plus; **he's ~ meat*** il ne mange plus de viande; **I've gone ~ him*, I'm ~ him*** je ne l'aime plus; *see* **duty, food, work** *etc*.

2 adv a (*distance*) **the house is 5 km ~** la maison est à 5 km; **it fell not 50 metres ~** c'est tombé à moins de 50 mètres; **some way ~** à quelque distance (*from* de); **my holiday is a week ~** je serai *or* suis en vacances dans une semaine, mes vacances sont dans une semaine; (*Theat*) **noises/voices ~** bruits/voix dans les coulisses; *see* **far, keep off, ward off** *etc*.

b (*departure*) **to be ~** partir, s'en aller; **~ with you!, ~ you go!** va-t-en!, sauve-toi!*, file!*; **I must be ~, it's time I was ~** je dois m'en aller *or* filer* *or* me sauver*; (*Sport*) **they're ~!** et les voilà partis!; **where are you ~ to?** où allez-vous?; **we're ~ to France today** nous partons pour la France aujourd'hui; **I'm ~ fishing** je vais à la pêche; **he's ~ fishing** (*going*) il va à la pêche; (*gone*) il est (parti) à la pêche; **he's gone ~ to school** il est parti à l'école; **he's ~ on his favourite subject** le voilà lancé sur son sujet favori; *see* **go off, run off** *etc*.

c (*absence*) **to take a day ~** prendre un jour de congé; **I've got this afternoon ~** j'ai congé cet après-midi; **he gets two days ~ each week** il a deux jours de congé *or* de libre(s) par semaine; **he gets one week ~ a month** il a une semaine de congé par mois.

d (*removal*) **he had his coat ~** il avait enlevé son manteau; **with his hat ~** sans chapeau; **~ with those socks!** enlève tes chaussettes!; **~ with his head!** qu'on lui coupe (*subj*) la tête!; **hands ~!** ne touchez pas!, bas les pattes*; **the lid was ~** le couvercle n'était pas mis; **the handle is ~** *or* **has come ~** la poignée s'est détachée; **there are two buttons ~** il manque deux boutons; (*Comm*) **10% ~** 10% de remise *or* de réduction *or* de rabais; **I'll give you 10% ~** je vais vous faire une remise *or* une réduction *or* un rabais de 10%; *see* **help, take off** *etc*.

e (*phrases*) **~ and on, on and ~** de temps à autre, par intervalles, par intermittence; **right ~*, straight ~*** tout de suite, à l'instant, sur-le-champ.

3 adj a (*absence*) **he's ~ on Tuesdays** il n'est pas là le mardi; **she's ~ at 4 o'clock** elle termine à 4 heures, elle est libre à 4 heures; (*US*) **an ~ day** un jour de congé (*see also* **3e**); **to be ~ sick** (*gen*) être absent pour cause de maladie; **he is ~ sick** (il n'est pas là,) il est malade; **he's been ~ for 3 weeks** cela fait 3 semaines qu'il est absent; *see* **day, time** *etc*.

b (*not functioning*) **to be ~** *[brake]* être desserré; *[machine, light]* être éteint; *[engine, gas at main, electricity, water]* être coupé; *[tap, gas tap]* être fermé; (*at cooker etc*) **the gas is ~** le gaz est fermé; **the light/TV/radio is ~** la lumière/la télé/la radio est éteinte; **the tap is ~** le robinet est fermé; **the switch was in the ~ position** le bouton était sur la position "fermé".

c (*cancelled etc*) **the play is ~** (*cancelled*) la pièce est annulée *or* n'aura pas lieu; (*no longer running*) la pièce a quitté l'affiche *or* n'est plus à l'affiche; **the party is ~** (*cancelled*) la soirée est annulée; (*postponed*) la soirée est remise; **their engagement is ~** ils ont rompu leurs fiançailles; (*in restaurant etc*) **the cutlets are ~** il n'y a plus de côtelettes.

d (*Brit: stale etc*) **to be ~** *[meat]* être mauvais *or* avancé *or* avarié; *[milk]* être tourné; *[butter]* être rance; *[cheese]* être trop fait.

e (*unsatisfactory etc*) **it was a bit ~*, him leaving like that** c'était plutôt moche* *or* ce n'était pas très bien de sa part de partir comme ça; **that's a bit ~!*** ce n'est pas très sympa!*; **I thought his performance was a bit ~** je ne l'ai pas trouvé très bon; **he was having an ~ day** il n'était pas en forme *or* en train ce jour-là (*see also* **3a**).

f (*unwell*) **to be feeling slightly** *or* **a bit ~*** ne pas se sentir dans son assiette*.

g (*circumstances*) **they are badly ~** (*financially*) ils sont dans la gêne; **we're badly ~ for sugar** nous sommes à court de sucre; **how are you ~ for bread?** qu'est-ce que vous avez comme pain?, qu'est-ce qu'il vous reste comme pain?; **he is better ~ where he is** il est mieux là où il est.

h **I came on the ~ chance of seeing her** je suis venu avec l'espoir de la voir; **he bought it on the ~ chance that it would come in useful** il l'a acheté pour le cas où cela pourrait servir; **I did it on the ~ chance*** je l'ai fait à tout hasard *or* au cas où*; (*US Pol*) ~ **year** *année sans élections importantes*.

i (*Brit*) = **offside 2a**.

4 n (**: beginning*) **from the ~*** dès le départ.

5 vi (*‡: esp US: leave*) ficher le camp*.

6 vt (*‡: US: kill*) buter‡, tuer.

7 comp ▸**off-Broadway** (*US Theat*) expérimental, hors Broadway ▸**off-camera** (*TV, Cine*) hors champ ▸**off-campus** (*US Univ*) en dehors de l'université *or* du campus ▸**off-centre** (*gen*) désaxé, déséquilibré, décentré; *construction* en porte-à-faux; (*fig*) *assessment etc* pas tout à fait exact ▸**off-chance** *see* **off 3h** ▸**off-colour:** (*Brit*) **he's off-colour today** il est mal fichu* *or* il n'est pas dans son assiette* aujourd'hui; **an off-colour* story** une histoire osée *or* scabreuse ▸**offcut** *[fabric]* chute *f*; *[wood]* copeau *m* ▸**off-glide** (*Phon*) métastase *f* ▸**off-key** (*Mus*) adj faux (*f* fausse) ◊ adv faux ▸**off-label store** (*US*) magasin *m* de dégriffés ▸**off-licence** (*Brit*) (*shop*) magasin *m* de vins et spiritueux; (*permit*) licence *f* (*permettant la vente de boissons alcoolisées à emporter*) ▸**off-limits:** (*US Mil*) **off-limits to troops** interdit au personnel militaire ▸**off-line** (*Comput*) adj autonome ◊ adv *[computer]* **to go off-line** se mettre en mode autonome; **to put the printer off-line** déconnecter l'imprimante ▸**off-load** vt *goods* décharger, débarquer; *passengers* débarquer; *task* passer (*on or onto sb* à qn) ▸**off-off-Broadway** (*US Theat*) d'avant-garde, résolument expérimental ▸**off-peak** *see* **off-peak** ▸**off-piste** adj, adv (*Ski*) hors-piste ▸**off-putting** (*Brit*) *task* rebutant; *food* peu ragoûtant; *person, manner,* rébarbatif, peu engageant ▸**off-sales** (*Brit*) (*sales*) vente *f* de boissons alcoolisées (à emporter); (*shop*) ≃ marchand *m* de vins; (*counter*) comptoir *m* des vins et spiritueux ▸**off-season** adj hors-saison ◊ n morte-saison *f*; **in the off-season** à la morte-saison ▸**off-street parking** stationnement *m* hors de la voie publique ▸**off-the-cuff** adj *remark* impromptu; *speech* impromptu, au pied levé (*see also* **cuff**) ▸**off-the-job training** *see* **job 1b** ▸**off-the-peg** (*Brit*) de confection (*see also* **peg**) ▸**off-the-rack** (*US*) = **off-the-peg** (*see also* **rack**) ▸**off-the-record** adj (*unofficial*) sans caractère officiel; (*secret*) confidentiel (*see also* **record**) ▸**off-the-shelf** (*Econ*) *goods, item* immédiatement disponible; *purchase* direct dans le commerce (*see also* **shelf**) ▸**off-the-wall*** (*US*) bizarre, dingue* ▸**off-white** adj blanc cassé *inv*; *see also* **offbeat, offhand, offset, offshore** *etc*.

offal ['ɒfəl] n (*NonC*) (*Culin*) abats *mpl* (*de boucherie*); (*garbage*) déchets *mpl*, ordures *fpl*, détritus *mpl*.

offbeat ['ɒfbi:t] 1 adj a (*gen*) *clothes, person, behaviour* excentrique, original. b (*Mus*) à temps faible. 2 n (*Mus*) temps *m* faible.

offence, (*US*) **offense** [ə'fens] n a (*Jur*) délit *m* (*against* contre), infraction *f* (*against* à), violation *f* (*against* de); (*Rel etc: sin*) offense *f*, péché *m*. (*Jur etc*) **it is an ~ to do that** il est contraire à la loi *or* il est illégal de faire cela; **first ~** premier délit; **further ~** récidive *f*; **political ~** délit *or* crime politique; **capital ~** crime capital; **to commit an ~** commettre un délit, commettre une infraction (à la loi); **~ against common decency** outrage *m* aux bonnes mœurs; **he was charged with an ~ against** ... il a été inculpé d'avoir enfreint ...; **~ against God** offense faite à Dieu; (*fig*) **it is an ~ to the eye** cela choque *or* offense la vue; *see* **indictable** *etc*.

b (*NonC: hurting of sb's feelings*) **to give** *or* **cause ~ to sb** blesser *or* froisser *or* offenser qn; **to take ~ (at)** se vexer (de), se froisser (de), s'offenser (de), s'offusquer (de); **no ~ taken!** il n'y a pas de mal, il n'y a pas d'offense (*fig*); **no ~ meant!** je ne voulais pas vous blesser *or* froisser; **no ~ meant but** ... soit dit sans offense ... .

c (*NonC: Mil: as opposed to defence*) attaque *f*. (*US Sport*) **the ~** les attaquants *mpl*; *see* **weapon**.

offend [ə'fend] 1 vt *person* blesser, froisser, offenser; *ears, eyes* offusquer, choquer; *reason* choquer, heurter, outrager. **to be** *or* **become ~ed (at)** se vexer (de), se froisser (de), s'offenser (de), s'offusquer (de), se formaliser (de); **she was ~ed by** *or* **at my remark** mon observation l'a blessée *or* froissée *or* offensée; **you mustn't be ~ed** *or* **don't be ~ed if I say** ... sans vouloir vous vexer, je dois dire ...; **it ~s my sense of justice** cela va à l'encontre de *or* cela choque mon sens de la justice. 2 vi (*Jur etc*) commettre un délit *or* une infraction. (*gen*) **he promised not to ~ again** il a promis de ne pas recommencer.

▸**offend against** vt *fus law, rule* enfreindre, violer; *good taste* offenser; *common sense* aller à l'encontre de, être une insulte *or* un outrage à.

offender [ə'fendə^r] n a (*lawbreaker*) délinquant(e) *m(f)*; (*against traffic regulations etc*) contrevenant(e) *m(f)*. (*Jur*) **first ~** délinquant(e) primaire; **previous ~** récidiviste *mf*; **persistent** *or* **habitual ~** récidiviste *mf* (invétéré(e)); **~s against the parking regulations** les contrevenants (aux règlements du stationnement); **who left this book here? — I was the ~** qui a laissé ce livre ici? — c'est moi le (*or* la) coupable. b (*insulter*) offenseur *m*; (*aggressor*) agresseur *m*.

offending [ə'fendɪŋ] adj (*often hum*) **the ~ word/object** *etc* le mot/ l'objet *etc* incriminé.

offense [ə'fens] n (*US*) = **offence**.

offensive [ə'fensɪv] 1 adj a (*shocking*) offensant, choquant; (*hurtful*) blessant; (*disgusting*) repoussant; (*insulting*) grossier, injurieux; (*rude, unpleasant*) déplaisant. **to be ~ to sb** insulter *or* injurier qn; **~ language** propos choquants, grossièretés *fpl*; **they found his behaviour very ~** sa conduite les a profondément choqués. b (*Mil etc*) *action, tactics* offensif. (*Jur*) **~ weapon** arme offensive. 2 n (*Mil: action, state*) offensive *f*. **to be on the ~** être en position d'attaque, avoir pris l'offensive; **to go over to/take the ~** passer à/prendre l'offensive; (*fig: Comm etc*) **a sales/an advertising ~** une offensive commerciale/ publicitaire; *see* **peace**.

offensively [ə'fensɪvlɪ] adv (*see* **offensive 1a**) *behave* d'une manière offensante (*etc*); *say* d'une manière blessante *or* injurieuse, désagréablement.

offer ['ɒfə^r] 1 n (*also Comm*) offre *f* (*of* de, *for* pour, *to do* de faire), proposition *f* (*of* de); (*of marriage*) demande *f* (en mariage). **to make a**

peace ~ faire une proposition *or* offre de paix; **make me an** ~! faites-moi une proposition! *or* offre!; **I'm open to** ~**s** je suis disposé *or* prêt à recevoir des offres; **it's my best** ~ c'est mon dernier mot; ~**s over/around £90,000** offres au-dessus/autour de 90.000 livres; (*in advertisement*) **£5 or near(est)** ~ 5 livres à débattre; **he's had a good** ~ **for the house** on lui a fait une offre avantageuse *or* une proposition intéressante pour la maison; (*lit, fig*) **he made me an** ~ **I couldn't refuse** il m'a fait une offre que je ne pouvais pas refuser; (*Comm*) **this brand is on** ~ cette marque est en promotion *or* en (vente-)réclame; (*Comm*) **"on** ~ **this week", "this week's special** ~**"** "article(s) en promotion cette semaine"; (*Fin*) ~ **of cover** promesse *f* de garantie; (*St Ex*) ~ **price** prix *m* d'émission.

2 **vt** a *job, gift, prayers, entertainment, food, friendship etc* offrir (*to* à); *help, money* proposer (*to* à), offrir (*to* à). **to** ~ **to do** offrir *or* proposer de faire; **he** ~**ed me a sweet** il m'a offert un bonbon; **she** ~**ed me her house for the week** elle m'a proposé sa maison *or* elle a mis sa maison à ma disposition pour la semaine; **to** ~ **o.s. for a mission** être volontaire *or* se proposer pour exécuter une mission; **to have a lot to** ~ avoir beaucoup à offrir; (*Rel*) **to** ~ **a sacrifice** offrir un sacrifice, faire l'offrande d'un sacrifice; (*Mil*) **to** ~ **one's flank to the enemy** présenter le flanc à l'ennemi.

b (*fig*) *apology, difficulty, opportunity, view* offrir, présenter; *remark, opinion* proposer, suggérer, émettre; *see* **resistance**.

3 **vi** *[opportunity etc]* s'offrir, se présenter.

►**offer up vt sep** (*liter*) *prayers* offrir; *sacrifice etc* offrir, faire l'offrande de.

offeree [ɒfəˈriː] **n** (*Jur, Fin*) destinataire *m* de l'offre.

offering [ˈɒfərɪŋ] **n** (*act; also thing offered*) offre *f*, don *m*, offrande *f*; (*Rel*) offrande, sacrifice *m*; *see* **burnt, peace, thank** *etc*.

offeror [ˈɒfərəʳ] **n** (*Jur, Fin*) auteur *m* de l'offre, offrant *m*.

offertory [ˈɒfətərɪ] **n** (*Rel*) (*part of service*) offertoire *m*, oblation *f*; (*collection*) quête *f*. ~ **box** tronc *m*.

offhand [ɒfˈhænd] 1 **adj** (*also* **offhanded**) a (*casual*) *manner* dégagé, désinvolte; *person* sans-gêne *inv*; *behaviour* sans-gêne *inv*, cavalier, désinvolte; *tone* cavalier, désinvolte. b (*curt*) brusque. 2 **adv** spontanément. **I can't say** ~ je ne peux pas vous le dire sur-le-champ *or* comme ça*.

offhanded [ˈɒfˈhændɪd] **adj** = **offhand 1**.

offhandedly [ˈɒfˈhændɪdlɪ] **adv** (*casually*) avec désinvolture, avec sans-gêne, cavalièrement; (*curtly*) avec brusquerie.

offhandedness [ˈɒfˈhændɪdnɪs] **n** (*casualness*) désinvolture *f*, sans-gêne *m*; (*curtness*) brusquerie *f*.

office [ˈɒfɪs] 1 **n** a (*place, room*) bureau *m*; (*part of organization*) service *m*. **lawyer's** ~ étude *f* de notaire; (*US*) **doctor's** ~ cabinet *m* (médical); **our London** ~ notre siège *or* notre bureau de Londres; **the sales** ~ le service des ventes; **he works in an** ~ il travaille dans un bureau, il est employé de bureau; (*esp Brit*) *[house etc]* **"usual** ~**s"** "cuisine, sanitaires"; *see* **box office, foreign, head, home, newspaper** *etc*.

b (*function*) charge *f*, fonction *f*, poste *m*; (*duty*) fonctions, devoir *m*. (*frm*) **it is my** ~ **to ensure ...** j'ai charge d'assurer ..., il m'incombe d'assurer ...; **he performs the** ~ **of treasurer** il fait fonction de trésorier; **to be in** ~, **to hold** ~ *[mayor, chairman]* occuper sa charge, remplir sa fonction, être en fonction; *[minister]* détenir *or* avoir un portefeuille; *[political party]* être au pouvoir *or* au gouvernement; **to take** ~ *[chairman, mayor, minister]* entrer en fonction; *[political party]* arriver au *or* prendre le pouvoir; **he took** ~ **as prime minister in January** il est entré dans ses fonctions de premier ministre au mois de janvier; **to go out of** ~ *[mayor, chairman]* quitter ses fonctions; *[minister]* quitter le ministère, abandonner *or* perdre son portefeuille; *[political party]* perdre le pouvoir; **public** ~ fonctions officielles; *see* **jack, sweep**.

c ~**s** offices *mpl*, service(s) *m(pl)*, aide *f*; **through his good** ~**s** par ses bons offices; **through the** ~**s of** par l'entremise de; **to offer one's good** ~**s** offrir ses bons offices.

d (*Rel*) office *m*. **O**~ **for the dead** office funèbre *or* des morts; *see* **divine**[1] *etc*.

2 **comp** *staff, furniture, work* de bureau ►**office attorney** (*US*) avocat *m* (*qui prépare les dossiers*) ►**office automation** bureautique *f* ►**office bearer** *[club, society]* membre *m* du bureau *or* comité directeur ►**office block** (*Brit*) immeuble *m* de bureaux ►**office boy** garçon *m* de bureau ►**office building** = **office block** ►**office holder** = **office bearer** ►**office hours** heures *fpl* de bureau; **to work office hours** avoir des heures de bureau ►**office job: he's got an office job** il travaille dans un bureau ►**office junior** employé(e) *m(f)* de bureau ►**office manager** directeur *m* de bureau ►**Office of Fair Trading** ≃ Direction *f* Générale de la Concurrence, de la Consommation et de la Répression des Fraudes ►**office party** fête *f* au bureau ►**office politics** (*pej*) intrigues *fpl or* manigances *fpl* de bureau ►**office space: "office space to let"** "bureaux *mpl* à louer"; **100 m² of office space** 100 m² de bureaux ►**office-worker** employé(e) *m(f)* de bureau.

officer [ˈɒfɪsəʳ] 1 **n** a (*Aviat, Mil, Naut*) officier *m*. ~**s' mess** mess *m*; (*Mil*) ~ **of the day** officier *or* service *m* de jour; (*Naut*) ~ **of the watch** officier de quart; (*Brit Mil*) **O**~**'s Training Corps** corps *m* volontaire de formation d'officiers; *see* **commission, man, petty** *etc*.

b (*official*) *[company, institution, organization, club]* membre *m* du bureau *or* comité directeur. (*Admin, Jur*) **the Committee shall elect its** ~**s** le comité désigne son bureau; (*Jur*) **duly authorized** ~ représentant *m* dûment habilité; *see* **local**.

c **police** ~ policier *m*; (*frm*) ~ **of the law** fonctionnaire *m* de (la) police (*frm*); **the** ~ **in charge of the inquiry** l'inspecteur chargé *or* le fonctionnaire de police chargé de l'enquête; (*to policeman*) **yes** ~ oui monsieur l'agent.

2 **vt** (*Mil etc*) (*command*) commander; (*provide with* ~*s*) pourvoir d'officiers *or* de cadres.

official [əˈfɪʃəl] 1 **adj** (*gen*) officiel; *language, style* administratif; *uniform* réglementaire. **it's not yet** ~ ce n'est pas encore officiel; **through** ~ **channels** par voie hiérarchique; (*Brit Fin*) **O**~ **Receiver** séquestre *m*, syndic *m* de faillite; (*Brit*) **the O**~ **Secrets Act** *loi relative aux secrets d'État*; **"for** ~ **use only"** "réservé à l'administration".

2 **n** (*gen, Sport etc: person in authority*) officiel *m*; *[civil service]* fonctionnaire *mf*; *[railways, post office etc]* employé(e) *m(f)*. **the** ~ **in charge of ...** le (*or* la) responsable de ...; **town hall** ~ employé(e) de mairie; **local government** ~ ≃ fonctionnaire (de l'administration locale); **government** ~ fonctionnaire (de l'Administration); **an** ~ **of the Ministry** un représentant *or* personnage officiel du ministère; *see* **elect**.

officialdom [əˈfɪʃəldəm] **n** (*NonC*) administration *f*, bureaucratie *f* (*also pej*).

officialese [əˌfɪʃəˈliːz] **n** (*NonC: pej*) jargon administratif.

officially [əˈfɪʃəlɪ] **adv** a (*gen*) officiellement; *announce, appoint, recognize* officiellement, à titre officiel. (*Post*) **"may be opened** ~**"** "peut être ouvert d'office". b (*in theory*) en théorie, en principe. ~, **he shouldn't do that** en théorie *or* en principe, il ne devrait pas faire cela.

officiate [əˈfɪʃɪeɪt] **vi** a (*Rel*) officier. **to** ~ **at a wedding** célébrer un mariage. b assister en sa capacité officielle (*at* à). **to** ~ **as** remplir *or* exercer les fonctions de.

officious [əˈfɪʃəs] **adj** *person, behaviour* trop empressé, trop zélé. **to be** ~ faire l'officieux *or* l'empressé.

officiously [əˈfɪʃəslɪ] **adv** avec un empressement *or* un zèle excessif.

officiousness [əˈfɪʃəsnɪs] **n** excès *m* d'empressement.

offing [ˈɒfɪŋ] **n: in the** ~ (*Naut*) au large; (*fig*) en vue, en perspective.

off-peak [ɒfˈpiːk] (*Brit*) 1 **adj** (*gen*) *train, journey* aux heures creuses. (*Elec*) ~ **charges** tarif réduit (aux heures creuses); (*Elec*) ~ **heating** chauffage *m* par accumulation (*ne consommant d'électricité qu'aux heures creuses*); (*Comm, Rail, Traffic etc*) ~ **hours** heures *fpl* creuses; (*Rail etc*) ~ **ticket** billet au tarif réduit heures creuses. 2 **adv** aux heures creuses.

offprint [ˈɒfprɪnt] **n** (*Typ*) tirage *m or* tiré *m* à part. (*gen*) **I'll send you an** ~ **of my article** je vous enverrai une copie de mon article.

offset [ˈɒfset] (**vb: pret, ptp offset**) 1 **n** a (*counterbalancing factor*) compensation *f*. **as an** ~ **to sth** pour compenser qch.

b (*Typ*) (*process*) offset *m*; (*smudge etc*) maculage *m*.

c (*Bot*) rejeton *m*; (*in pipe etc*) coude *m*, courbure *f*.

2 **comp** ►**offset lithography** (*Typ*) = **offset printing** ►**offset paper** papier *m* offset ►**offset press** presse *f* offset ►**offset printing** offset *m*.

3 **vt** a (*counteract, compensate for*) contrebalancer, compenser. **loans can be** ~ **against corporation tax** les emprunts peuvent venir en déduction de l'impôt sur les sociétés.

b (*weigh up*) **to** ~ **one factor against another** mettre en balance deux facteurs.

c (*Typ*) (*print*) imprimer en offset; (*smudge*) maculer.

offshoot [ˈɒfʃuːt] **n** *[plant, tree]* rejeton *m*; *[organization]* ramification *f*, antenne *f*; *[scheme, discussion, action]* conséquence *f*. **a firm with many** ~**s** une société aux nombreuses ramifications.

offshore [ɒfˈʃɔːʳ] 1 **adj** *breeze* de terre; *island* proche du littoral; *waters* côtier, proche du littoral; *fishing* côtier; *funds* extraterritorial, offshore. ~ **drilling** forage *m* offshore *or* en mer *or* marin; (*Comm*) ~ **orders** commandes *fpl* d'outre-mer; ~ **worker/living conditions** ouvrier *m* travaillant/conditions *fpl* de vie sur une plateforme offshore. 2 **adv** *be, go, fish* en mer.

offside [ˈɒfˈsaɪd] 1 **n** a (*Aut etc*) (*in Britain*) côté *m* droit; (*in France, US etc*) côté *m* gauche. b (*Sport*) hors-jeu *m inv*. 2 **adj** a (*Aut etc*) (*in Britain*) de droite; (*in France, US etc*) de gauche. b (*Sport*) **to be** ~ être hors jeu; **the** ~ **rule** la règle du hors-jeu.

offspring [ˈɒfsprɪŋ] **n** (**pl inv**) progéniture *f* (*NonC*); (*fig*) fruit *m*, résultat *m*. (*hum*) **how are your** ~**?*** comment va votre progéniture?*, comment vont vos rejetons?*

offstage [ˈɒfˈsteɪdʒ] **adv, adj** (*Theat*) dans les coulisses.

oft [ɒft] **adv** (*liter*) maintes fois, souvent. **many a time and** ~ maintes et maintes fois; ~**-times**†† souventes fois††.

often [ˈɒfən, ˈɒftən] **adv** souvent, fréquemment, à maintes reprises. **very** ~ très souvent, bien des fois; **as** ~ **as he did it** toutes les fois qu'il l'a fait; **as** ~ **as not, more** ~ **than not** la plupart du temps, le plus souvent; **so** ~ si souvent, tant de fois; **every so** ~ (*in time*) de temps en temps, de temps à autre, parfois; (*in spacing, distance etc*) çà et là; **too** ~ trop souvent; **once too** ~ une fois de trop; **it cannot be said too** ~ **that ...** on ne dira *or* répétera jamais assez que ...; **how** ~ **have you seen her?** combien de fois l'avez-vous vue?; **how** ~ **do the boats leave?**

les bateaux partent tous les combien?

ogival [əʊ'dʒaɪvəl] adj ogival, en ogive.

ogive ['əʊdʒaɪv] n ogive *f* (*Archit*).

ogle ['əʊgl] vt reluquer*, lorgner.

ogre ['əʊgə^r] n ogre *m*.

ogress ['əʊgrɪs] n ogresse *f*.

OH (*US*) abbr of **Ohio**.

oh [əʊ] excl a ô!, oh!, ah! ~ **dear!** oh là là!, (oh) mon Dieu!; ~ **what a waste of time!** ah, quelle perte de temps!; ~ **for some fresh air!** si seulement on pouvait avoir un peu d'air frais!; ~ **to be in France!** que ne suis-je en France!; ~ **really?** non, c'est vrai?; **he's going with her — ~ is he!** il y va avec elle — (*surprise*) tiens, tiens!, vraiment! *or* (*interest or acceptance*) ah bon! *or* (*disapproval*) je vois! *or* (*denial*) on verra!; ~ **no you don't! — ~ yes I do!** ah mais non! — ah mais si! *or* oh que si!; ~, **just a minute** ... euh, une minute ... . b (*cry of pain*) aïe!

Ohio [əʊ'haɪəʊ] n Ohio *m*. **in** ~ dans l'Ohio.

ohm [əʊm] n ohm *m*.

OHMS [əʊeɪtʃem'es] (*Brit*) (abbr of **On His** *or* **Her Majesty's Service**) *see* **majesty**.

oi(c)k‡ [ɔɪk] n (*Brit*) péquenaud‡ *m*.

oil [ɔɪl] 1 n a (*NonC: Geol, Ind etc*) pétrole *m*. **to find** *or* **strike** ~ trouver du pétrole; (*fig*) **to pour ~ on troubled waters** ramener le calme; *see* **crude**.

b (*Art, Aut, Culin, Pharm etc*) huile *f*. **fried in ~** frit à l'huile; **painted in ~s** peint à l'huile; (*Culin*) ~ **and vinegar (dressing)** vinaigrette *f*; ~ **of cloves** essence *f* de girofle; (*Aut*) **to check the ~** vérifier le niveau d'huile; (*Aut*) **to change the ~** faire la vidange; **to paint in ~s** faire de la peinture à l'huile; **an ~ by Picasso** une huile de Picasso; *see* **hair, midnight**.

2 vt *machine* graisser, lubrifier. (*fig*) **to ~ the wheels** *or* **works** mettre de l'huile dans les rouages; (*fig*) **to be well ~ed**‡ être beurré‡, être paf‡ *inv*; *see also* **oiled**, *and* **palm**[1].

3 comp *industry, shares* pétrolier; *prices, king, magnate, millionaire* du pétrole; *deposit* pétrolifère ▸ **oil-based paint** peinture *f* glycérophtalique ▸ **oil-burning** *lamp* à pétrole, à huile; *stove* (*paraffin*) à pétrole, (*fuel oil*) à mazout; *boiler* à mazout ▸ **oilcake** tourteau *m* (*pour bétail*) ▸ **oilcan** (*for lubricating*) burette *f* d'huile *or* de graissage; (*for storage*) bidon *m* d'huile ▸ **oil change** (*Aut*) vidange *f* ▸ **oilcloth** toile cirée ▸ **oil colour** peinture *f* à l'huile ▸ **oil-cooled** refroidi par l'huile ▸ **oil deposits** gisements *mpl* de pétrole ▸ **oil drill** trépan *m* ▸ **oil drum** bidon *m* à pétrole ▸ **oilfield** gisement *m* pétrolier *or* de pétrole, champ *m* pétrolifère ▸ **oil filter** (*Aut*) filtre *m* à huile ▸ **oil find** (*Geol*) découverte *f* de pétrole ▸ **oil-fired** *boiler* à mazout; *central heating* au mazout ▸ **oil gauge** jauge *f* de niveau d'huile *or* de pression d'huile ▸ **oil industry** industrie *f* du pétrole, secteur *m* pétrolier ▸ **oil installation** installation pétrolière ▸ **oil lamp** lampe *f* à huile *or* à pétrole ▸ **oil level** (*Aut etc*) niveau *m* d'huile ▸ **oil men** pétroliers *mpl* ▸ **oil paint** peinture *f* à l'huile; (*Art*) couleur *f* à l'huile ▸ **oil painting** (*picture, occupation*) peinture *f* à l'huile; (*fig*) **she's no oil painting*** ce n'est vraiment pas une beauté ▸ **oilpan** (*US Aut*) carter *m* ▸ **oilpaper** papier huilé ▸ **oil pipeline** oléoduc *m*, pipe-line *m* ▸ **oil pollution** pollution *f* due aux hydrocarbures ▸ **oil pressure** pression *f* d'huile ▸ **oil producers, oil-producing countries** pays *mpl* producteurs de pétrole ▸ **oil refinery** raffinerie *f* (de pétrole) ▸ **oil rig** (*land*) derrick *m*; (*sea*) plate-forme pétrolière ▸ **oil sheik** émir *m* du pétrole ▸ **oilskin** n toile cirée ◊ adj en toile cirée ▸ **oilskin(s)** (*Brit: clothes*) ciré *m* ▸ **oil slick** nappe *f* de pétrole; (*on beach*) marée noire ▸ **oil spill** (*Shipping, Road Transport etc*) déversement *m* accidentel de pétrole ▸ **oilstone** pierre *f* à l'huile ▸ **oil storage tank** (*Ind*) réservoir *m* de stockage de pétrole; (*for central heating*) cuve *f* à mazout ▸ **oil stove** (*paraffin*) poêle *m* à pétrole; (*fuel oil*) poêle à mazout ▸ **oil tank** (*Ind*) réservoir *m* de stockage de pétrole; (*for central heating*) cuve *f* à mazout ▸ **oil tanker** (*ship*) pétrolier *m*, tanker *m*; (*truck*) camion-citerne *m* (à pétrole) ▸ **oil terminal** port *m* d'arrivée *or* de départ pour le pétrole ▸ **oil well** puits *m* de pétrole.

oiled [ɔɪld] adj a *cloth, paper* huilé. b (‡: *drunk: also* **well** ~) beurré‡, soûl*.

oiler ['ɔɪlə^r] n a (*ship*) pétrolier *m*; (*can*) burette *f* à huile *or* de graissage; (*person*) graisseur *m*. b (*US: clothes*) ~**s** (pl) ciré *m*.

oiliness ['ɔɪlɪnɪs] n *[liquid, consistency, stain]* aspect huileux; *[cooking, food]* aspect gras; (*fig pej*) *[manners, tone etc]* onctuosité *f*.

oily ['ɔɪlɪ] adj *liquid, consistency* huileux; *stain* d'huile; *rag, clothes, hands* graisseux; *cooking, food* gras (*f* grasse); (*fig pej*) *manners, tone* onctueux, mielleux.

oink [ɔɪŋk] 1 vi *[pig]* grogner. 2 n grognement *m*.

ointment ['ɔɪntmənt] n onguent *m*, pommade *f*.

OK[1] (*US*) abbr of **Oklahoma**.

OK[2]* ['əʊ'keɪ] (vb: pret, ptp **OK'd**) 1 excl d'accord!, O.K.! (*don't fuss*) ~, ~! ça va, ça va!; ~, **the next subject on the agenda is** ... bien, le prochain point à l'ordre du jour est ... .

2 adj a (*agreed*) parfait, très bien; (*in order*) en règle; (*on draft etc as approval*) (lu et) approuvé. **I'm coming too, ~?** je viens aussi, d'accord?; **leave me alone, ~?** tu me laisses tranquille, compris?*

b (*acceptable*) **it's ~ by me!** *or* **with me!** (je suis) d'accord!, ça me va!, OK!*; **is it ~ with you if I come too?** ça ne vous ennuie pas que je vous accompagne? (*subj*); **this car is ~ but I prefer the other one** cette voiture n'est pas mal mais je préfère l'autre; **it's the ~ thing to do these days** c'est ce qui se fait de nos jours.

c (*no problem*) **everything's ~** tout va bien; **it's ~ (, it's not your fault)** ce n'est pas grave (, ce n'est pas votre faute); **can I help? — it's ~, I've solved the problem** puis-je vous aider? — ça va, j'ai résolu le problème; **thanks! — that's ~** merci! — de rien *or* je vous en prie.

d (*undamaged, in good health*) **are you ~?** (*gen*) tu vas bien?; (*more concerned*) tu n'as rien?; **I'm ~** (*gen*) je vais bien, ça va (bien); (*after accident*) je n'ai rien; **he's ~, he's only bruised** il n'a rien de grave, seulement quelques bleus; **the car is ~** (*undamaged*) la voiture est intacte *or* n'a rien; (*repaired, functioning*) la voiture marche *or* est en bon état.

e (*likeable*) **he's ~** *or* **he's an ~ guy** c'est un type bien*.

f (*well provided for*) **another drink? — no thanks, I'm ~ (for now)** un autre verre? — non merci, ça va (pour le moment); **are you ~ for cash/work** *etc?* question argent/travail *etc*, ça va? *or* tu n'as pas de problème?

3 adv (*recovering from illness, operation*) **she's doing ~** elle va bien; (*socially, financially, in career*) **she's doing ~ (for herself)** elle se débrouille *or* se défend bien.

4 vt (*gen*) approuver; *document, draft* (*lit*) parafer *or* parapher; *plan* donner le feu vert à, approuver; (*fig*) approuver.

5 n: **to give the** *or* **one's ~** (*gen*) donner son accord *or* approbation (*to* à); **to give the** *or* **one's ~ to a plan** donner le feu vert à un projet.

okapi [əʊ'kɑːpɪ] n, pl ~s *or* ~ okapi *m*.

okay* ['əʊ'keɪ] = **OK**[2]*.

okey-doke(y)‡ ['əʊkɪ'dəʊk(ɪ)] excl d'ac*, OK*.

Okie ['əʊkiː] n (*US*) travailleur *m* agricole migrant.

Oklahoma [əʊklə'həʊmə] n Oklahoma *m*. **in** ~ dans l'Oklahoma.

okra ['əʊkrə] n gombo *m*, okra *m*.

old [əʊld] 1 adj a (*aged; not young*) vieux (*before vowel* vieil, *f* vieille), âgé. **an ~ man** un vieil homme, un vieillard, un vieux († *or slightly pej*); **an ~ lady** (*gen*) une vieille dame; (*specifically unmarried*) une vieille demoiselle; **an ~ woman** une vieille femme, une vieille († *or slightly pej*); (*pej*) **he's a real ~ woman** il a des manies de petite vieille; **a poor ~ man** un pauvre vieillard, un pauvre vieux; ~ **people,** ~ **folk,** ~ **folks*** personnes âgées, vieux *mpl*, vieillards *mpl*, vieilles gens; ~ **people's home,** ~ **folks' home** hospice *m* (de vieillards); (*private or specific groups*) maison *f* de retraite; **he's as ~ as Methuselah** il est vieux comme Mathusalem; **to have an ~ head on young shoulders** être mûr pour son âge, faire preuve d'une maturité précoce; ~ **for his age** *or* **for his years** mûr pour son âge; **to be/grow ~ before one's time** être vieux/vieillir avant l'âge; **to grow** *or* **get ~(er)** vieillir, se faire vieux; **he's getting ~** il vieillit, il se fait vieux, il prend de l'âge; **in his ~ age he** ... sur ses vieux jours *or* dans sa vieillesse il ... (*see also* **2**); **that dress is too ~ for you** cette robe fait trop vieux pour toi; ~ **Mr Smith** le vieux M. Smith; ~ **Smith*,** ~ **man Smith**‡ le vieux Smith, le (vieux) père Smith*; *see also* **2** *and* **fogey, ripe, salt** *etc*.

b (* *fig*) ~ **Paul here** ce bon vieux Paul; **he's a good ~ dog** c'est un brave (vieux) chien; **you ~ scoundrel!** sacré vieux!; **I say, ~ man** *or* ~ **fellow** *or* ~ **chap** *or* ~ **boy** dites donc mon vieux*; **my** *or* **the ~ man**‡ (*husband*) le patron‡; (*father*) le *or* mon paternel‡, le *or* mon vieux‡; (*boss*) **the ~ man** le patron; **my** *or* **the ~ woman**‡ *or* **lady**‡ (*wife*) la patronne‡, ma bourgeoise*; (*mother*) la *or* ma mater‡, la *or* ma vieille‡; *see* **Harry** *etc*.

c (*of specified age*) **how ~ are you?** quel âge avez-vous?; **he is 10 years ~** il a 10 ans, il est âgé de 10 ans; **at 10 years ~** à (l'âge de) 10 ans; **a 6-year-~ boy, a boy (of) 6 years ~** un garçon de 6 ans; **a 3-year-~** (*child*) un(e) enfant de 3 ans; (*horse*) un (cheval de) 3 ans; **for 10 to 15-year-~s** (*gen*) pour les dix-quinze ans; (*Admin, Demography*) pour la tranche des dix-quinze ans; **the firm is 80 years ~** la compagnie a 80 ans; **he is ~ enough to dress himself** il est assez grand pour s'habiller tout seul; **they are ~ enough to vote** ils sont en âge de *or* d'âge à voter; **you're ~ enough to know better!** à ton âge tu devrais avoir plus de bon sens!; **too ~ for that sort of work** trop âgé pour ce genre de travail; **I didn't know he was as ~ as that** je ne savais pas qu'il avait cet âge-là; **if I live to be as ~ as that** si je vis jusqu'à cet âge-là; (*to child*) **when you're ~er** quand tu seras plus grand; **if I were ~er** si j'étais plus âgé; **if I were 10 years ~er** si j'avais 10 ans de plus; **he is ~er than you** il est plus âgé que toi; **he's 6 years ~er than you** il a 6 ans de plus que toi; **~er brother/son** frère/fils aîné; **his ~est son** son fils aîné; **she's the ~est** elle est *or* c'est elle la plus âgée, elle est l'aînée; **the ~er generation** la génération antérieure *or* précédente; **~er people** les personnes *fpl* d'un certain âge.

d (*not new*) *gold, clothes, custom, carrots, bread, moon* vieux (*before vowel* vieil, *f* vieille); *building, furniture, debt* vieux, ancien (*after noun*); (*of long standing*) vieux, ancien (*after noun*), établi (depuis longtemps). **an ~ staircase** un vieil escalier, un escalier ancien; ~ **wine** vin vieux; **that's an ~ one!** *[story etc]* elle n'est pas nouvelle!, elle est connue!; *[trick etc]* ce n'est pas nouveau!; **as ~ as the hills** vieux comme le monde *or* comme les chemins; **it's as ~ as**

Adam c'est vieux comme le monde, ça remonte au déluge; **the ~ part of Nice** le vieux Nice; **we're ~ friends** nous sommes de vieux amis *or* des amis de longue date; **an ~ family** une vieille famille, une famille de vieille souche; *see also* **2** *and* **brigade, hand, lag³, school¹** *etc.*

e (*former*) *school, mayor, home* ancien (*before noun*). (*Brit Scol*) **~ boy** ancien élève (*see also* **2**); (*Brit Scol*) **~ girl** ancienne élève; **in the ~ days** dans le temps, autrefois, jadis; **they chatted about ~ times** ils ont causé du passé; **just like ~ times!** comme dans le passé!; **in the good ~ days** *or* **times** dans le bon vieux temps; **those were the good ~ days** c'était vraiment le bon temps; **this is the ~ way of doing it** on s'y prenait comme cela autrefois; (*Mil*) **~ campaigner** vétéran *m*; *see also* **2** *and* **school¹, soldier** *etc.*

f (**: as intensifier*) **any ~ how/where** *etc* n'importe comment/où *etc;* **any ~ thing** n'importe quoi; **we had a great ~ time** on s'est vraiment bien amusé; (*fig*) **it's the same ~ story** c'est toujours la même histoire; **it isn't (just) any ~ painting, it's a Rembrandt** ce n'est pas un tableau quelconque, c'est un Rembrandt.

2 **comp** ►**old age** vieillesse *f*; **in his old age** dans sa vieillesse, sur ses vieux jours; **old age pension** pension *f* vieillesse (*de la Sécurité sociale*); (*Brit*) **old age pensioner** retraité(e) *m(f)* ►**Old Bailey** (*Brit Jur*) *cour f d'assises de Londres* ►(**the**) **Old Bill‡** (*Brit*) les poulets‡ *mpl*, la rousse *f* (*arg Crime*) ►**the old boy network*** (*Brit*) *le réseau de relations des anciens élèves des écoles privées;* **he heard of it through the old boy network** il en a entendu parler par ses relations ►**old-clothes dealer** fripier *m*, -ière *f* ►**the old country** la mère patrie ►**the Old Dominion** (*US*) la Virginie ►**Old English** (*Ling*) vieil anglais; **Old English sheepdog** ≃ briard *m* ►**old-established** ancien (*after noun*), établi (depuis longtemps) ►**old-fashioned** *see* **old-fashioned** ►**Old French** (*Ling*) ancien *or* vieux français ►**Old Glory** (*US*) la Bannière étoilée (*drapeau des États-Unis*) ►**old gold** (*colour*) vieil or *inv* ►**old guard** *see* **guard 1b** ►**old hat** (*fig*) *see* **hat 1** ►**oldish** *see* **oldish** ►**old-line** (*Pol etc*) ultra(-conservateur (*f* -trice)), ultra-traditionaliste ►**old-looking** qui a l'air vieux ►**old maid** (*pej*) vieille fille ►**old-maidish** (*pej*) *habits* de vieille fille; *person* maniaque (comme une vieille fille) ►**Old Man River** (*US*) le Mississippi ►**old master** (*Art*) (*artist*) grand peintre, grand maître (de la peinture); (*painting*) tableau *m* de maître ►**old money** (*US*) vieilles fortunes ►**old school tie** (*Brit*) (*lit*) cravate *f* aux couleurs de son ancienne école; (*fig*) favoritisme *m* de clan; (*fig*) **it's the old school tie** c'est l'art de faire marcher ses relations ►**the Old South** (*US Hist*) le sud d'autrefois (*d'avant la guerre de Sécession*) ►**old stager** vétéran *m*, vieux routier ►**oldster** *see* **oldster** ►**old-style** à l'ancienne (mode); **old-style calendar** calendrier julien, vieux calendrier ►**Old Testament** Ancien Testament ►**old-time** du temps jadis, (*older*) ancien (*before noun*); **old-time dancing** danses d'autrefois ►**old-timer*** vieillard *m*, ancien *m*; (*as term of address*) le vieux, l'ancien ►**old wives' tale** conte *m* de bonne femme ►**old-womanish** (*pej*) *person* qui a des manies de petite vieille; *behaviour, remark* de petite vieille ►**the Old World** l'ancien monde ►**old-world** *see* **old-world**.

3 **n: (in days) of ~** autrefois, (au temps) jadis; **the men of ~** les hommes d'antan (*liter*) *or* de jadis; **I know him of ~** je le connais depuis longtemps.

4 **npl: the ~** les vieux *mpl*, les vieillards *mpl*, les vieilles gens; **it will appeal to ~ and young (alike)** cela plaira aux vieux comme aux jeunes, cela plaira à tous les âges.

olden ['əʊldən] **adj** (*liter*) vieux (*before vowel* vieil, *f* vieille), d'autrefois, de jadis. **in ~ times** *or* **days** (au temps) jadis, autrefois; **city of ~ times** ville *f* antique.

olde-worlde ['əʊldɪ'wɜːldɪ] **adj** (*hum or pej*) a = **old-world.** b (*pseudo*) vieillot (*f* -otte), faussement ancien (*after noun*).

old-fashioned ['əʊld'fæʃnd] 1 **adj** a (*old, from past times*) *attitude, idea, outlook* ancien (*after noun*), d'autrefois; *clothes, furniture, tools* à l'ancienne mode, d'autrefois. **in the ~ way** à la manière ancienne; (*fig*) **she is a good ~ kind of teacher** c'est un professeur de la vieille école *or* comme on n'en trouve plus; (*fig*) **good ~ discipline** la bonne (vieille) discipline d'autrefois; (*fig*) **to give sb/sth an ~ look*** regarder qn/qch de travers.

b (*out-of-date*) démodé, passé de mode, suranné; *person, attitude* vieux jeu *inv*. **I may be ~, but ...** vous allez me dire que je suis vieux jeu, mais ..., je suis peut-être vieux jeu mais ... .

2 **n** (*US: cocktail*) old-fashioned *m* (*cocktail à base de whisky*).

oldie* ['əʊldɪ] **n** (*film, song*) vieux succès*; (*person*) croulant(e)* *m(f)*; (*joke*) bonne vieille blague* *f*; *see* **golden.**

oldish ['əʊldɪʃ] **adj** (*see* **old**) assez vieux (*before vowel* vieil, *f* vieille), assez ancien (**after noun**).

oldster* ['əʊldstəʳ] **n** (*US*) ancien *m*, vieillard *m*.

old-world ['əʊld'wɜːld] **adj** *village, cottage* très vieux (*f* vieille) et pittoresque; *charm* suranné, désuet (*f* -ète); (*from past times*) d'antan, d'autrefois; (*outdated*) démodé, suranné, désuet. **with ~ lettering** avec une inscription archaïque; **an ~ interior** un intérieur de style antique; **Stratford is very ~** Stratford fait très petite ville d'antan.

ole‡ [əʊl] **adj** (*esp US: often hum*) = **old.**

oleaginous [ˌəʊlɪ'ædʒɪnəs] **adj** oléagineux.

oleander [ˌəʊlɪ'ændəʳ] **n** laurier-rose *m*.

olefine ['əʊlɪfiːn] **n** oléfine *f*.

oleo* ['əʊlɪəʊ] **n** (*US*) **abbr of oleomargarine.**

oleo... ['əʊlɪəʊ] **pref** olé(i)..., olé(o)... .

oleomargarine ['əʊlɪəʊ'mɑːdʒəriːn] **n** (*US*) margarine *f*.

olfactory [ɒl'fæktərɪ] **adj** olfactif.

oligarchic(al) [ˌɒlɪ'gɑːkɪk(əl)] **adj** oligarchique.

oligarchy ['ɒlɪgɑːkɪ] **n** oligarchie *f*.

Oligocene ['ɒlɪgəʊsiːn] **adj, n** oligocène (*m*).

oligopoly [ˌɒlɪ'gɒpəlɪ] **n** oligopole *m*.

olive ['ɒlɪv] 1 **n** olive *f*; (*also* **~ tree**) olivier *m*; (*also* **~ wood**) (bois *m* d')olivier; (*colour*) (vert *m*) olive *m*; *see* **mount** *etc.* 2 **adj** (*also* **~-coloured**) *paint, cloth* (vert) olive *inv*; *complexion, skin* olivâtre. 3 **comp** ►**olive branch:** (*fig*) **to hold out the olive branch to sb** se présenter à qn le rameau d'olivier à la main ►**olive drab** (*US*) **adj** gris-vert (olive) *inv* ◊ **n** toile *f* de couleur gris-vert (olive) (*utilisée pour les uniformes de l'armée des U.S.A.*) ►**olive-green adj** vert olive *inv* ◊ **n** vert *m* olive ►**olive grove** olivaie *f or* oliveraie *f* ►**olive oil** huile *f* d'olive.

Oliver ['ɒlɪvəʳ] **n** Olivier *m*.

Olympia [ə'lɪmpɪə] **n** a (*in Greece*) Olympie *f*. b (*Brit*) *nom du palais des expositions de Londres*.

Olympiad [əʊ'lɪmpɪæd] **n** olympiade *f*.

Olympian [əʊ'lɪmpɪən] 1 **adj** (*Myth, fig*) olympien. 2 **n** (*Myth*) dieu *m* de l'Olympe, Olympien *m*; (*US Sport*) athlète *mf* olympique.

Olympic [əʊ'lɪmpɪk] 1 **adj** *champion, medal, stadium* olympique. **~ flame** flambeau *m or* flamme *f* olympique; **~ Games** Jeux *mpl* olympiques; **~ torch** flambeau *m or* torche *f* olympique. 2 **n: the ~s** les Jeux *mpl* olympiques.

Olympus [əʊ'lɪmpəs] **n** (*Geog, Myth also* **Mount ~**) le mont Olympe, l'Olympe *m*.

OM [əʊ'em] (*Brit*) (**abbr of Order of Merit**) *see* **order.**

Oman [əʊ'mɑːn] **n: (the Sultanate of) ~** (le Sultanat d')Oman *m*.

Omani [əʊ'mɑːnɪ] 1 **n** Omanais(e) *m(f)*. 2 **adj** omanais.

Omar Khayyám ['əʊmɑːkaɪ'ɑːm] **n** Omar Khayam *m*.

ombudsman ['ɒmbʊdzmən] **n** médiateur *m* (*Admin*), protecteur *m* du citoyen (*Can*).

omega ['əʊmɪgə] **n** oméga *m*.

omelet(te) ['ɒmlɪt] **n** omelette *f*. **cheese ~** omelette au fromage; (*Prov*) **you can't make an ~ without breaking eggs** on ne fait pas d'omelette sans casser les œufs (*Prov*).

omen ['əʊmən] 1 **n** présage *m*, augure *m*, auspice *m*. **it is a good ~ that ...** il est de bon augure *or* c'est un bon présage que ... + *subj*; **of ill** *or* **bad ~** de mauvais augure *or* présage; *see* **bird.** 2 **vt** présager, augurer.

omentum [əʊ'mentəm] **n, pl omenta** [əʊ'mentə] épiploon *m*. **lesser/greater ~** petit/grand épiploon.

ominous ['ɒmɪnəs] **adj** *event, appearance* de mauvais augure, de sinistre présage; *look, tone, cloud, voice* menaçant; *sound* sinistre; *sign* (très) inquiétant, alarmant. **the silence was ~** le silence ne présageait rien de bon, (*stronger*) le silence était lourd de menaces; **that's ~!** c'est de bien mauvais augure!

ominously ['ɒmɪnəslɪ] **adv** (*gen*) *change, approach etc* sinistrement; (*threateningly*) *speak, say* d'un ton menaçant. **he was ~ silent** son silence ne présageait rien de bon; **it was ~ similar to ...** cela ressemblait de façon fort inquiétante à ... *or* dangereusement à ...; **it's ~ like ...** j'ai bien peur que ce soit ... .

omission [əʊ'mɪʃən] **n** (*thing omitted*) omission *f*, lacune *f*; (*Typ: word(s) omitted*) bourdon *m*; (*act of omitting*) omission, oubli *m*. **it was an ~ on my part** c'est un oubli de ma part; *see* **sin.**

omit [əʊ'mɪt] **vt** (*accidentally*) omettre, oublier (*to do* de faire); (*deliberately*) omettre, négliger (*to do* de faire). **to ~ any reference to sth** passer qch sous silence.

omni... ['ɒmnɪ] **pref** omni... .

omnibus ['ɒmnɪbəs] 1 **n** a (*†: bus*) omnibus† *m*. b (*book*) recueil *m*. 2 **adj** *device* à usage multiple. (*US Pol*) **~ bill** projet *m* de loi qui comprend plusieurs mesures; **~ edition** (*Publishing*) gros recueil *m*; (*TV, Rad*) *récapitulation des épisodes de la semaine/du mois etc.*

omnidirectional [ˌɒmnɪdɪ'rekʃənl] **adj** omnidirectionnel.

omnipotence [ɒm'nɪpətəns] **n** omnipotence *f*, toute-puissance *f*.

omnipotent [ɒm'nɪpətənt] 1 **adj** omnipotent, tout-puissant. 2 **n: the O~** le Tout-Puissant.

omnipresence ['ɒmnɪ'prezəns] **n** omniprésence *f*.

omnipresent ['ɒmnɪ'prezənt] **adj** omniprésent.

omniscience [ɒm'nɪsɪəns] **n** omniscience *f*.

omniscient [ɒm'nɪsɪənt] **adj** omniscient.

omnivore ['ɒmnɪvɔːʳ] **n** omnivore *m*.

omnivorous [ɒm'nɪvərəs] **adj** omnivore; (*fig*) *reader* insatiable.

on [ɒn] (*phr vb elem*) 1 **adv** a (*indicating idea of covering*) **he had his coat ~** il avait mis son manteau; **~ with your pyjamas!** allez, mets ton pyjama!; **she had nothing ~** elle était toute nue (*see also* **1d**); **what had he got ~?** qu'est-ce qu'il portait?; **the lid is ~** le couvercle est mis; **it was not ~ properly** cela avait été mal mis; *see* **glove, put on, shoe, try on** *etc.*

b (*indicating forward movement*) **~!** en avant!; **he put/threw it ~ to the table** il l'a mis/jeté sur la table; **he climbed (up) ~ to the wall** il a grimpé sur le mur; **from that time ~** à partir de ce moment-là; **it was getting ~ for 2 o'clock** il n'était pas loin de 2 heures; **it was well ~ in the night** la nuit était bien avancée, il était tard dans la nuit; **well ~ in September** bien avant dans le mois de septembre; **it was well ~ into September** septembre était déjà bien avancé; *see* **broadside, farther, pass on, year** *etc.*

c (*indicating continuation*) **go ~ with your work** continuez votre travail; **let's drive ~ a bit** continuons un peu (*en voiture*); **and so ~** et ainsi de suite; **life must go ~** la vie continue; **they talked ~ and ~ for hours** ils ont parlé sans discontinuer *or* sans arrêt pendant des heures; *see* **keep on, off, read on, show** *etc.*

d (*phrases*) **I've nothing ~ this evening** (*I'm free*) je ne suis pas pris *or* je n'ai rien ce soir (*see also* **1a**); **he's got a lot ~ now** il est très pris en ce moment; **he is always ~ at me*** il est toujours après moi*; **I don't know what you're ~ about*** je ne vois pas ce que tu veux dire, je ne comprends pas ce que tu racontes*; **I'll get ~ to him tomorrow** je vais me mettre en rapport avec lui demain; **he's been ~ to me about the broken window** il m'a déjà parlé du carreau cassé; **I've been ~ to him on the phone** je lui ai parlé *or* je l'ai eu au téléphone; **I'm ~ to something** je suis sur une piste intéressante; **the police are ~ to him** la police est sur sa piste; **he was ~ to it at last** (*had found it*) il l'avait enfin trouvé *or* découvert; (*had understood*) il l'avait enfin compris *or* saisi; **he's ~ to a good thing** il a trouvé un filon*; **she's ~ to the fact that we met yesterday** elle sait que nous nous sommes vus hier.

2 **prep** a (*gen*) sur; (*indicating position, direction*) sur, à *etc* . **~ the table** sur la table; **~ an island** sur une île; **~ the island of ...** dans l'île de ...; (*with names of islands*) **~ Rockall/Elba** *etc* à Rockall/Elbe *etc;* **~ the continent of ...** sur le continent de ...; **~ the high seas** en haute *or* pleine mer; **with sandals ~ her feet** des sandales aux pieds; **with a coat ~ his arm** un manteau sur le bras; **with a ring ~ her finger** une bague au doigt; **the ring ~ her finger** la bague qu'elle avait au doigt; **the finger with the ring ~ it** le doigt avec la bague; **look at the book — there's a fly ~ it** regarde le livre — il y a une mouche dessus; **I have no money ~ me** je n'ai pas d'argent sur moi; **they advanced ~ the fort** ils avancèrent sur le fort; **he turned his back ~ us** il nous a tourné le dos; **~ the right** à droite; **~ the blackboard/wall/ceiling** au tableau/mur/plafond; **he hung his hat ~ the nail** il a suspendu son chapeau au clou; **house ~ the main road** maison sur la grand-route *or* au bord de la grand-route; **~ the road/motorway/pavement** sur la route/l'autoroute/le trottoir; (*US*) **I live ~ Main Street** j'habite Main Street; **a house ~ North Street** une maison dans North Street.

b (*fig*) **he swore it ~ the Bible** il l'a juré sur la Bible; **an attack ~ the government** une attaque contre le gouvernement; **let's have a drink ~ it** on va boire un coup* pour fêter ça; **they shook hands ~ it** ils se sont serré la main en signe d'accord; **he was travelling ~ a passport/a ticket which ...** il voyageait avec un passeport/un billet qui ...; **he's got nothing ~ Paul*** (*not as good as*) Paul pourrait lui en remontrer n'importe quand; (*no hold over*) il n'a pas barre *or* de prise sur Paul.

c (*Mus*) **he played it ~ the violin** *etc*/**~ his violin** *etc* il l'a joué au violon *etc*/sur son violon *etc;* **he played ~ the violin** *etc* il jouait du violon *etc;* **with Louis Armstrong ~ the trumpet** avec Louis Armstrong à la trompette.

d (*Rad, TV*) (*gen*) à; (*+ name of channel*) sur. **~ Radio 3/Channel 4** *etc* sur Radio 3/Channel 4 *etc;* **~ the radio/TV** à la radio/la télé*; **~ the BBC** à la BBC; **you're ~ the air** vous êtes en direct.

e (*indicating source of energy*) à. **the heating works ~ oil** le chauffage marche au mazout; **the car runs ~ diesel** la voiture marche au gazole.

f (*indicating source of funds etc*) **he's ~ £9,000 a year** il gagne 9 000 livres par an; **a student ~ a grant** un (étudiant) boursier; **to be ~ a grant** avoir une bourse; **to be ~ the dole/sick pay** *etc* percevoir *or* toucher* les allocations chômage/maladie *etc;* **customer ~ a tight budget** client au budget très limité.

g (*taking, using etc*) **to be ~ pills** prendre des pillules; **to be ~ drugs** se droguer; **he's ~ heroin** il se drogue à l'héroïne; **I'm back ~ cigarettes** je me suis remis à fumer; **he's ~ a special diet** il suit un régime (spécial); **the doctor put her ~ antibiotics** le médecin l'a mise sous *or* aux antibiotiques.

h (*indicating means of travel*) **~ the train/bus/plane** dans le train/l'autobus/l'avion; **~ the boat** dans *or* sur le bateau; **I left my handbag ~ it** j'y ai laissé mon sac; *see* **foot, horse** *etc.*

i (*in expressions of time*) **~ Sunday** dimanche; **~ Sundays** le dimanche; **~ December 1st** le 1er décembre; **~ the evening of December 3rd** le 3 décembre au soir; **~ or about the 20th** vers le 20; **~ or before November 9th** le 9 novembre au plus tard; **~ and after the 20th** à partir *or* à dater du 20; **~ Easter Day** le jour de Pâques; **it's just ~ 5 o'clock** il est bientôt *or* il va être 5 heures; *see* **clear, day, occasion** *etc.*

j (*at the time etc of*) **~ my arrival home** à mon arrivée chez moi; **~ the death of his son** à la mort de son fils; **~ my refusal to go away** lorsque j'ai refusé de partir; **~ hearing this** en entendant cela; *see* **application, production, receipt** *etc.*

k (*about, concerning*) sur, de. **he lectures ~ Dante** il fait un cours sur Dante; **a book ~ grammar** un livre de grammaire; (*in library etc*) **what have you got ~ the Ancient Greeks?** qu'avez-vous sur les anciens Grecs?; **an essay ~ this subject** une dissertation sur ce sujet; **he spoke ~ atomic energy** il a parlé de l'énergie atomique; **have you heard him ~ V.A.T.?** vous l'avez entendu parler de la T.V.A.?; **we've read Jones ~ Marx** nous avons lu ce que Jones a écrit sur Marx; **a decision ~ this project** une décision concernant ce projet; *see* **congratulate, keen**[1] *etc.*

l (*indicating membership*) **to be ~ the team/committee** faire partie de l'équipe/du comité, être (membre) de l'équipe/du comité; **he is ~ the "Evening News"** il est *or* travaille à l'"Evening News"; *see* **side, staff** *etc.*

m (*engaged upon*) **he's ~ a course** il suit un cours; (*away from office, home etc*) il fait un stage; **I'm ~ a new project** je travaille à un nouveau projet; **he was away ~ an errand** il était parti faire une course; **we're ~ irregular verbs** nous en sommes aux verbes irréguliers; **while we're ~ the subject** pendant que nous y sommes; *see* **business, holiday, tour** *etc.*

n (*at the expense of*) **we had a drink ~ the house** nous avons bu un verre aux frais du patron *or* de la maison; **this round's ~ me** c'est ma tournée, c'est moi qui paie cette tournée; **have the ticket ~ me** je vous paie le billet.

o (*as against*) **prices are up/down ~ last year's** les prix sont en hausse/en baisse par rapport à *or* sur (ceux de) l'année dernière.

p (*Sport etc: in scoring*) avec. **Smith is second ~ 21, but Jones is top ~ 23** Smith est second avec 21, mais Jones le bat avec 23 points.

3 **adj** a (*functioning, operative*) **to be ~** *[machine, engine]* être en marche; *[light]* être allumé; *[radio, TV]* être allumé *or* branché, marcher; *[brakes]* être serré *or* mis; *[electrical apparatus, gas at main, electricity, water]* être branché; *[water tap, gas tap]* être ouvert. (*at cooker etc: burning*) **the gas is still ~** le gaz est encore allumé; **leave the tap ~** laisse le robinet ouvert; **don't leave the lights ~ in the kitchen** ne laisse pas la cuisine allumée; **the "~" switch** la commande *or* le bouton "marche"; **switch in the "~" position** bouton *m* en position de marche *or* sur la position "ouvert".

b (*taking place etc*) *[meeting, programme, concert]* **to be ~** être en train *or* en cours; **while the meeting** *etc* **was ~** pendant la réunion *etc;* **the show is ~ already** le spectacle a déjà commencé; *[play, concert etc]* **it's still ~** ce n'est pas fini, ça dure encore; **their engagement is ~ again** ils sont à nouveau fiancés.

c (*being presented etc*) **it's ~ in London** *[play]* cela se joue *or* cela se donne *or* cela est à l'affiche à Londres; *[film]* cela passe *or* cela est à l'affiche à Londres; **it's ~ at the Odeon** *[play]* cela se donne à l'Odéon; *[film]* cela passe à l'Odéon; *[play, film]* **it's still ~** cela se donne *or* se joue toujours; **what's ~?** (*Cine, Theat etc*) qu'est-ce qu'on joue?; (*Rad/TV: what is there?*) qu'est-ce qu'il y a à la radio/à la télé?; (*Rad, TV*) **"Dynasty"/Dirk Bogarde is ~ tonight** il y a "Dynastie"/Dirk Bogarde ce soir; (*Rad, TV, Theat*) **you're ~ now!** à vous (maintenant)!; **you're ~ in 5 minutes** c'est à vous dans 5 minutes.

d (*on duty*) **I'm ~ every Saturday** je travaille tous les samedis; **which doctor is ~ today?** quel médecin est de garde aujourd'hui?; **she's not ~ till 6 o'clock** elle n'arrive qu'à 6 heures.

e (*available: in restaurant etc*) **are the cutlets still ~?** y a-t-il encore des côtelettes?

f (*satisfactory etc*) **it's not ~*** (*behaviour etc*) cela ne se fait pas; (*refusing*) (il n'en est) pas question!; **it wasn't one of his ~ days*** il n'était pas en forme *or* en train ce jour-là.

g (*indicating agreement*) **you're ~!*** d'accord!, ça marche!; **we're going out — are you ~?*** nous sortons — vous venez (avec nous)?

4 **comp** ►**on-campus** **adj** (*US Univ*) sur le campus, à l'université ►**on-costs** (*Brit Comm*) frais *mpl* généraux ►**on-glide** (*Phon*) catastase *f* ►**on-line** (*Comput*) en ligne ►**on-off: on-off switch** commande *f* marche-arrêt; *[relationship, plan etc]* **it's an on-off affair*** c'est une affaire en dents de scie ►**onside:** (*Ftbl etc*) **to be onside** ne pas être hors-jeu ►**on-site** **adj** sur place ►**on-the-job** **adj** *see* **job 1b**; *see also* **oncoming, onlooker, onslaught** *etc.*

onanism ['əʊnənɪzəm] **n** onanisme *m.*

ONC [əʊen'siː] **n** (*Brit Educ*) (**abbr of Ordinary National Certificate**) *see* **ordinary.**

once [wʌns] 1 **adv** a (*on one occasion*) une fois. **only ~, ~ only** une seule fois; **~ before** une fois déjà; **~ again, ~ more** encore une fois, une fois de plus; **~ (and) for all** une fois pour toutes, une bonne fois, définitivement; **~ a week** tous les huit jours, une fois par semaine; **~ a month** une fois par mois; **~ and again, ~ in a while, ~ in a way** de temps en temps, de temps à autre; **more than ~** plus d'une fois, à plusieurs reprises, plusieurs fois; **~ or twice** une fois ou deux, une ou deux fois; **for ~** pour une fois; **(just) this ~** (juste) pour cette fois(-ci), (juste) pour une fois; **not ~, never ~** pas une seule fois; **~, long ago ...** une fois *or* un jour, il y a bien longtemps (de cela) ...; **I ~ saw him go in there** une fois je l'ai vu entrer là-bas; **~ punished, he ...** une fois puni, il ...; **if ~ you begin to hesitate** si jamais vous commencez à hésiter; **~ is enough** une fois suffit, une fois c'est suffisant; **~ a journalist always a journalist** qui a été journaliste le reste toute sa vie; *see* **thief, every b** *etc.*

b (*formerly*) jadis, autrefois, une fois, à un moment donné. **he was ~ famous** il était jadis *or* autrefois *or* à un moment donné bien connu;

~ **upon a time there was a prince** il y avait une fois *or* il était une fois un prince; **a ~ powerful nation** une nation puissante dans le passé, une nation jadis *or* autrefois puissante.

c **at ~** (*immediately*) tout de suite, immédiatement; (*simultaneously*) à la fois, d'un seul coup; **all at ~** (*suddenly*) tout à coup, tout d'un coup, soudain, soudainement; (*simultaneously*) à la fois.

2 **conj** une fois que. **~ she'd seen him she left** l'ayant vu *or* après l'avoir vu *or* une fois qu'elle l'eut vu elle s'en alla; **~ you give him the chance** si jamais on lui en donne l'occasion.

3 **comp** ►**once-over**‡: (*quick look*) **to give sb the once-over** jauger qn d'un coup d'œil; **to give sth the once-over** vérifier qch très rapidement *or* d'un coup d'œil; (*quick clean*) **I gave the room the once-over with the duster** j'ai donné *or* passé un coup (de chiffon) à la pièce.

oncologist [ɒŋ'kɒlədʒɪst] **n** oncologiste *mf*.

oncology [ɒŋ'kɒlədʒɪ] **n** oncologie *f*.

oncoming ['ɒnkʌmɪŋ] 1 **adj** *car etc* qui approche, qui arrive, venant en sens inverse; *danger* imminent. 2 **n** *[winter etc]* approche *f*, arrivée *f*.

OND [əʊen'diː] **n** (*Brit Educ*) (**abbr of Ordinary National Diploma**) *see* **ordinary**.

one [wʌn] 1 **adj** a (*numerical*) un, une. **~ woman out of** *or* **in two** une femme sur deux; **~ or two people** une ou deux personnes; **~ girl was pretty, the other was ugly** une des filles était jolie, l'autre était laide; **~ hundred and twenty** cent vingt; **God is ~** Dieu est un; **that's ~ way of doing it** c'est une façon (entre autres) de le faire, on peut aussi le faire comme ça; **she is ~ (year old)** elle a un an; **it's ~ o'clock** il est une heure; **for ~ thing I've got no money** d'abord *or* pour commencer je n'ai pas d'argent; **as ~ man** comme un seul homme; **as ~ woman** toutes ensemble; **with ~ voice** d'une seule voix.

b (*indefinite*) un, une. **~ day** un jour; **~ Sunday morning** un (certain) dimanche matin; **~ hot summer afternoon she went ...** par un chaud après-midi d'été elle partit ...; **~ moment she's laughing, the next she's in tears** une minute elle rit, l'autre elle pleure.

c (*sole*) (un(e)) seul(e), unique. **the ~ man who could do it** le seul qui pourrait *or* puisse le faire; **no ~ man could do it** un homme ne pourrait pas le faire (à lui) seul; **my ~ and only pleasure** mon seul et unique plaisir; **the ~ and only Charlie Chaplin!** le seul, l'unique Charlot!

d (*same*) (le/la) même, identique. **they all went in the ~ car** ils sont tous partis dans la même voiture; **they are ~ (and the same) person** ils sont une seule et même personne; **it's ~ and the same thing** c'est exactement la même chose.

2 **n** a (*numeral*) un(e) *m(f)*. **~, two, three** un(e), deux, trois; **twenty-~** vingt et un; **there are three ~s in her phone number** il y a trois uns dans son numéro de téléphone; **~ of them** (*people*) l'un d'eux, l'une d'elles; (*things*) (l')un, (l')une; **any ~ of them** (*people*) n'importe lequel d'entre eux, n'importe laquelle d'entre elles; (*things*) n'importe lequel, n'importe laquelle; **the last but ~** l'avant-dernier *m*, -ière *f*; **chapter ~** chapitre un; (*Comm*) **price of ~** prix à la pièce; **these items are sold in ~s** ces articles se vendent à la pièce.

b (*phrases*) **I for ~ don't believe it** pour ma part je ne le crois pas; **who doesn't agree? — I for ~!** qui n'est pas d'accord? — moi par exemple! *or* pour commencer!; **never (a) ~** pas un (seul); **~ by ~** un à un, un par un; **by** *or* **in ~s and twos** par petits groupes; **~ after the other** l'un après l'autre; **~ and all** tous tant qu'ils étaient, tous sans exception; **it's all ~** c'est tout un; **it's all ~ to me** cela m'est égal *or* indifférent; (*Brit* ††) **~ and sixpence** un shilling et six pence; **he's president and secretary (all) in ~** il est à la fois président et secrétaire; **it's made all in ~** c'est fait d'une seule pièce *or* tout d'une pièce; **to be** *or* **have/go** *or* **get ~ up (on sb)*** avoir/prendre l'avantage (sur qn) (*see also* 4); **to go ~ better than sb** faire mieux que qn; **he's had ~ too many*** il a bu un coup de trop*; *see* **number, road** *etc*.

3 **pron** a (*indefinite*) un(e) *m(f)*. **would you like ~?** en voulez-vous (un)?; **have you got ~?** en avez-vous (un)?; **the problem is ~ of money** c'est une question d'argent; **~ of these days** un de ces jours; **he's ~ of my best friends** c'est un de mes meilleurs amis; **she's ~ of the family** elle fait partie de la famille; **he's ~ of us** il est des nôtres; **the book is ~ which** *or* **that I've never read** c'est un livre que je n'ai jamais lu; **he's a teacher and I want to be ~ too** il est professeur et je veux l'être aussi; **every ~ of the boys/books** tous les garçons/les livres sans exception; **you can't have ~ without the other** on ne peut avoir l'un sans l'autre; **sit in ~ or other of the chairs** asseyez-vous sur l'une des chaises; *see* **anyone, no, someone** *etc*.

b (*specific*) **this ~** celui-ci, celle-ci; **these ~s*** ceux-ci, celles-ci; **that ~** celui-là, celle-là; **those ~s*** ceux-là, celles-là; **the ~ who** *or* **that** celui qui, celle qui; **the ~ whom** *or* **that** celui que, celle que; **the ~ that** *or* **which is lying on the table** celui *or* celle qui se trouve sur la table; **the ~ on the floor** celui *or* celle qui est par terre; **here's my brother's ~*** voici celui *or* celle de mon frère; **he's the ~ with brown hair** c'est celui qui a les cheveux bruns; **which is the ~ you want?** lequel voulez-vous?; **which ~?** lequel?, laquelle?; **which ~s?*** lesquels?, lesquelles?; **he hit her ~ on the nose*** il lui a flanqué un coup sur le nez*; **I want the red ~/the grey ~s** je veux le rouge/les gris; **this grey ~ will do** ce gris-ci fera l'affaire; **mine's a better ~** le mien *or* la mienne est meilleur(e); **you've taken the wrong ~** vous n'avez pas pris le bon; **that's a difficult ~!** ça c'est difficile!; *see* **eye, quick** *etc*.

c (*personal*) **they thought of the absent ~** ils ont pensé à l'absent; **the little ~s** les petits; **my dearest ~** mon chéri, ma chérie; **our dear ~s** ceux qui nous sont chers; († *or frm*) **~ John Smith** un certain *or* un nommé John Smith; **he's a clever ~** c'est un malin; (*say, sing*) **as ~** en chœur; **for ~ who claims to know the language, he ...** pour quelqu'un qui prétend connaître la langue, il ...; **he looked like ~ who had seen a ghost** il avait l'air de quelqu'un qui aurait vu un fantôme; **to ~ who can read between the lines** à celui qui sait lire entre les lignes; **he's never** *or* **not ~ to agree to that sort of thing** il n'est pas de ceux qui acceptent ce genre de choses; **he's a great ~ for chess** c'est un mordu* des échecs; **I'm not ~** *or* **much of a ~* for sweets** je ne suis pas (grand) amateur de bonbons; **you are a ~!**‡ tu en as de bonnes!*; *see* **fine 1**.

d **~ another** = **each other**; *see* **each 2c**.

e (*impersonal*) (*nominative*) on; (*accusative, dative*) vous. **~ must try to remember** on doit *or* il faut se souvenir; **it tires ~ too much** cela (vous) fatigue trop; **~ likes to see ~'s friends happy** on aime voir ses amis heureux, on aime que ses amis soient heureux.

4 **comp** ►**one-...** d'un/une (seul(e)) ..., à un/une seul(e) ..., à ... unique ►**one-acter*, one-act play** pièce *f* en un (seul) acte ►**one-armed** manchot; **one-arm(ed) bandit*** machine *f* à sous, ≈ jackpot *m* ►**one-eyed** *person* borgne; (*Zool*) uniocúlé ►**one-handed** **adj** *person* manchot, qui a une (seule) main; *tool* utilisable d'une (seule) main ◊ **adv** d'une (seule) main ►**one-horse* place** *or* **town** bled* *m*, trou* *m* ►**one-legged** unijambiste ►**one-line message** message *m* d'une (seule) ligne ►**one-liner** (*joke*) (bon) mot *m*, plaisanterie *f* express ►**one-man** *see* **one-man** ►**one-night stand** (*Theat*) soirée *f or* représentation *f* unique; (*sex*) amour *m* de rencontre, liaison *f* sans lendemain ►**one-off*** (*Brit*) **adj** *see* **one-off*** ►**one-one, one-on-one** (*US*) = **one-to-one** ►**one-owner** (*Aut etc*) qui n'a eu qu'un propriétaire ►**one-parent family** famille *f* monoparentale ►**one-party system** (*Pol*) système *m* à parti unique ►**one-piece** (*Dress*) **adj** une pièce *inv*, d'une seule pièce ◊ **n** vêtement *m* une pièce; **one-piece swimsuit** maillot *m* une pièce ►**one-reeler** (*US Cine*) court-métrage *m*, film d'une bobine ►**one-room(ed) apartment** *or* **flat** studio *m*, appartement *m* d'une pièce ►**oneself** *see* **oneself** ►**one-shot*** (*US*) = **one-off*** ►**one-sided** *decision* unilatéral; *contest, game* inégal; *judgment, account* partial; *bargain, contract* inéquitable ►**one-sidedness** (*see* **one-sided**) caractère *m* unilatéral; inégalité *f*; partialité *f*; caractère *m* inéquitable ►**"one-size"** (*Comm*) "taille unique" ►**one-stop shopping** *concentration des achats sur un seul point de vente* ►**one-time** ancien (*before noun*) ►**one-to-one** (*Brit*) *see* **one-to-one** ►**one-track** (*Rail*) à voie unique; (*fig*) **to have a one-track mind** n'avoir qu'une idée en tête, avoir une idée fixe ►**one-up***: (*US*) **to one-up sb** marquer un point sur qn ►**one-upmanship*** (*hum*) art *m* de faire mieux que les autres ►**one-way** *street* à sens unique; *traffic* en sens unique; *transaction* unilatéral; (*Comm*) *bottle* non consigné; (*Rail etc*) *ticket* simple; *mirror* sans tain; (*fig*) *friendship, emotion etc* non partagé; **one-way trip** (voyage *m*) aller *m* ►**one-woman** *business, office* que fait marcher une seule femme; **one-woman show** (*Art*) exposition *f* consacrée à une seule artiste; (*Rad, Theat, TV*) one woman show *m*; **he's a one-woman man** c'est l'homme d'une seule femme, c'est un homme qui n'aimera jamais qu'une seule femme.

one-man ['wʌn'mæn] **adj** *job* fait *or* à faire par un seul homme, pour lequel un seul homme suffit; *business, office* que fait marcher un seul homme; *woman, dog etc* qui n'aime qu'un seul homme. (*Mus, also fig*) **~ band** homme-orchestre *m*; **~ show** (*Art etc*) exposition consacrée à un seul artiste; (*Rad, Theat, TV*) one man show *m*; (*fig*) **this business is a ~ band*** *or* **show*** un seul homme fait marcher toute l'affaire.

oneness ['wʌnnɪs] **n** unité *f*; (*sameness*) identité *f*; (*agreement*) accord *m*, entente *f*.

one-off* ['wʌnɒf] 1 **adj** *object, building* unique; *event* exceptionnel. 2 **n**: **it's a ~** *[object, ornament, building]* il n'y en a qu'un comme ça; *[TV programme etc]* ça ne fait pas partie d'une série; *[event]* ça ne va pas se reproduire *or* se répéter.

onerous ['ɒnərəs] **adj** *task* pénible; *responsibility* lourd.

oneself [wʌn'self] **pron** se, soi-même; (*after prep*) soi(-même); (*emphatic*) soi-même. **to hurt ~** se blesser; **to speak to ~** se parler (à soi-même); **to be sure of ~** être sûr de soi(-même); **one must do it ~** il faut le faire soi-même; **(all) by ~** (tout) seul; **to have sth (all) to ~** avoir qch pour soi (tout) seul.

one-to-one [wʌntə'wʌn] 1 **adj** *comparison, relationship* univoque; *meeting, discussion* seul à seul, en tête-à-tête, face à face. **~ fight** combat seul à seul; **~ tuition** leçons *fpl* particulières; **on a ~ basis** *discuss etc* seul à seul, en tête-à-tête, face à face; **to teach sb on a ~ basis** donner des leçons particulières à qn; **a ~ session** (*gen*) une réunion seul à seul *or* en tête-à-tête; (*Psych*) un face à face. 2 **adv** *compare* individuellement; *discuss* seul à seul, face à face.

ongoing ['ɒngəʊɪŋ] **adj**: (*gen*) *investigation, project* en cours. **they have an ~ relationship** ils ont des relations suivies.

onion ['ʌnjən] 1 **n** oignon *m*. (*Brit*) **to know one's ~s*** connaître son affaire, s'y connaître; *see* **cocktail, spring** *etc*. 2 **comp** *soup* à l'oignon;

skin d'oignon; *stew* aux oignons ▸**onion dome** (*Archit*) dôme bulbeux ▸**onion johnny** vendeur *m* d'oignons (ambulant) ▸**onion-shaped** bulbeux ▸**onionskin** pelure *f* d'oignon.

onlooker ['ɒnlʊkəʳ] n: **the ~s** les spectateurs *mpl*, l'assistance *f*.

only ['əʊnlɪ] 1 adj seul, unique. ~ **child** enfant *mf* unique; **you're the ~ one to think of that** vous êtes le seul à y avoir pensé, vous seul y avez pensé; **I'm tired!** — **you're not the ~ one!*** je suis fatigué! — vous n'êtes pas le seul! *or* il n'y a pas que vous!; **it's the ~ one left** c'est le seul qui reste (*subj*); **he is not the ~ one here** il n'est pas le seul ici, il n'y a pas que lui ici; **the ~ book he has** le seul livre qu'il ait; **his ~ friend was his dog** son chien était son seul ami; **his ~ answer was to shake his head** pour toute réponse il a hoché la tête de droite à gauche; **your ~ hope is to find another one** votre unique espoir est d'en trouver un autre; **the ~ thing is that it's too late** seulement *or* malheureusement il est trop tard; **that's the ~ way to do it** c'est la seule façon de le faire, on ne peut pas le faire autrement; *see* **one, pebble** *etc*.

2 adv seulement, ne ... que. **he's ~ 10** il n'a que 10 ans, il a seulement 10 ans; **there are ~ two people who know that** il n'y a que deux personnes qui savent *or* sachent cela; ~ **Paul can wait** Paul seul peut attendre, il n'y a que Paul qui puisse attendre; **he can ~ wait** il ne peut qu'attendre; **God ~ knows!** Dieu seul le sait!; **I can ~ say how sorry I am** tout ce que je peux dire c'est combien je suis désolé; **that ~ makes matters worse** cela ne fait qu'empirer les choses; **it's ~ that I thought he might ...** c'est que, simplement, je pensais qu'il pourrait ...; **I will ~ say that ...** je me bornerai à dire *or* je dirai simplement que ...; ~ **time will tell** c'est l'avenir qui le dira; **it will ~ take a minute** ça ne prendra qu'une minute; **I'm ~ the secretary** je ne suis que le secrétaire; **a ticket for one person** ~ un billet pour une seule personne; **"ladies ~"** "réservé aux dames"; **I ~ looked at it** je n'ai fait que le regarder; **you've ~ to ask** vous n'avez qu'à demander; ~ **think of the situation!** imaginez un peu la situation!; ~ **to think of it** rien que d'y penser; **he was ~ too pleased to come** il n'a été que trop content de venir, il ne demandait pas mieux que de venir; **it's ~ too true** ce n'est que trop vrai; **not ~ A but also B** non seulement A mais aussi B; **not ~ was it dark, but it was also foggy** non seulement il faisait noir, mais il y avait aussi du brouillard; ~ **yesterday** hier encore, pas plus tard qu'hier; **it seems like ~ yesterday** il semble que c'était hier; **he has ~ just arrived** il vient tout juste d'arriver; **but I've ~ just bought it!** mais je viens seulement de l'acheter!; **I caught the train but ~ just** j'ai eu le train mais (c'était) de justesse.

3 conj seulement, mais. **I would buy it, ~ it's too dear** je l'achèterais bien, seulement *or* mais il est trop cher; **he would come too, ~ he's ill** il viendrait bien aussi, si ce n'est qu'il est malade *or* seulement il est malade; **if ~** si seulement; ~ **if** seulement si.

o.n.o. [əʊen'əʊ] (abbr of **or near(est) offer**) *see* **offer**.

onomasiology [ˌɒnəʊˌmeɪsɪ'ɒlədʒɪ] n a (*Ling*) onomasiologie *f*. b = **onomastics**.

onomastic [ˌɒnə'mæstɪk] adj onomastique.

onomastics [ɒnə'mæstɪks] n (*NonC*) onomastique *f*.

onomatopoeia [ˌɒnəʊmætəʊ'piːə] n onomatopée *f*.

onomatopoeic [ˌɒnəʊmætəʊ'piːɪk] adj, **onomatopoetic** [ˌɒnəʊmætəʊpəʊ'etɪk] adj onomatopéique.

onrush ['ɒnrʌʃ] n *[people]* ruée *f*; *[water]* torrent *m*.

onset ['ɒnset] n a (*attack*) attaque *f*, assaut *m*. b (*beginning: of illness, winter etc*) début *m*, commencement *m*. **at the ~** d'emblée.

onshore ['ɒn'ʃɔːʳ] adj *wind* de mer, du large.

onslaught ['ɒnslɔːt] n attaque *f*, assaut *m*, charge *f*. (*fig*) **he made a furious ~ on the chairman** il s'en prit violemment au président.

Ontario [ɒn'teərɪəʊ] n Ontario *m*. **Lake ~** le lac Ontario.

onto ['ɒntʊ] prep = **on to**; *see* **on 1b, 1d**.

ontogenesis [ˌɒntə'dʒenɪsɪs] n ontogénèse *f*.

ontogeny [ɒn'tɒdʒənɪ] n ontogénie *f*.

ontological [ˌɒntə'lɒdʒɪkəl] adj ontologique.

ontology [ɒn'tɒlədʒɪ] n ontologie *f*.

onus ['əʊnəs] n, pl ~es responsabilité *f*, charge *f*, obligation *f*. **the ~ of proof rests with him** il a la charge de (le) prouver, c'est à lui de faire la preuve; **the ~ is on him to do it** il lui incombe de le faire; **the ~ is on the manufacturers** c'est la responsabilité des fabricants.

onward ['ɒnwəd] (*phr vb elem*) 1 adv en avant, plus loin. (*excl*) ~! en avant!; **to walk ~** avancer; **from this time ~** désormais, dorénavant; **from today ~** à partir d'aujourd'hui, désormais, dorénavant. 2 adj *step, march* en avant.

onwards ['ɒnwədz] adv = **onward 1**.

onyx ['ɒnɪks] 1 n onyx *m*. 2 comp en onyx, d'onyx.

oodles‡ ['uːdlz] npl un tas*, des masses* *fpl*, des quantités *fpl*.

ooh* [uː] 1 excl oh! 2 vi: **to ~ and aah*** pousser des oh! et des ah!

oohing* ['uːɪŋ] n: **there was a lot of ~ and aahing*** on entendait fuser des oh! et des ah!

oolite ['əʊəlaɪt] n oolithe *m*.

oolitic [ˌəʊə'lɪtɪk] adj oolithique.

oompah ['uːmpɑː] n flonflon *m*.

oomph‡ [ʊmf] n (*energy*) dynamisme *m*. (*sex appeal*) **to have ~** avoir du chien*.

oophorectomy [ˌəʊəfə'rektəmɪ] n ovariectomie *f*.

oophoritis [ˌəʊəfə'raɪtɪs] n ovarite *f*.

oops* [ʊps] excl houp! **~-a-daisy!** hop-là!

oosphere ['əʊəsfɪəʳ] n oosphère *f*.

oospore ['əʊəspɔːʳ] n oospore *f*.

ooze [uːz] 1 n vase *f*, limon *m*, boue *f*. 2 vi *[water, pus, walls etc]* suinter; *[resin, gum]* exsuder. 3 vt: **his wounds ~d pus** le pus suintait de ses blessures; (*fig pej*) **she was oozing charm/complacency** le charme/la suffisance lui sortait par tous les pores.

▸**ooze away** vi *[liquids]* s'en aller, suinter; *[strength, courage, enthusiasm]* disparaître, se dérober. **his strength** *etc* **was oozing away** ses forces *etc* l'abandonnaient.

▸**ooze out** vi *[liquids]* sortir, suinter.

op[1]* [ɒp] n (*Med, Mil*) (abbr of **operation**) *see* **operation 1b, 1c**.

op[2] [ɒp] adj (*in comps*) ~ **art** op art *m*; ~ **artist** artiste *mf* op art.

op. (abbr of **opus**) op.

opacity [əʊ'pæsɪtɪ] n opacité *f*; (*fig*) obscurité *f*.

opal ['əʊpəl] 1 n opale *f*. 2 comp *ring, necklace* d'opale; (*also* **opal-coloured**) opalin.

opalescence [ˌəʊpə'lesns] n opalescence *f*.

opalescent [ˌəʊpə'lesnt] adj opalescent, opalin.

opaque [əʊ'peɪk] adj *substance, darkness* opaque; (*fig*) (*unclear*) obscur; (*stupid*) stupide, obtus. ~ **projector** épiscope *m*.

op. cit. (abbr of **opere citato**) op. cit.

OPEC ['əʊpek] n (abbr of **Organization of Petroleum-Exporting Countries**) O.P.E.P. *f*.

Op-Ed ['ɒp'ed] n, adj (*US Press*) (abbr of **opposite editorial**) ~ **(page)** *page contenant les chroniques et commentaires (en face des éditoriaux)*.

open ['əʊpən] 1 adj a (*not closed*) *door, box, envelope, book, handbag, parcel, grave, wound, eyes, flower etc* ouvert; *bottle, jar* ouvert, débouché; *map, newspaper* ouvert, déplié; *shirt, coat, collar* ouvert, déboutonné. **wide ~** grand ouvert; **the door was slightly ~** la porte était entrouverte *or* entrebâillée; (*fig*) **he is** *or* **his thoughts are** *or* **his mind is an ~ book** ses pensées sont un véritable livre ouvert, on peut lire en lui comme dans un livre; **a dress ~ at the neck** une robe à col ouvert *or* échancrée (à l'encolure); (*Brit Banking*) ~ **cheque** chèque ouvert *or* non barré; (*Ling*) ~ **vowel** voyelle ouverte; (*Mus*) ~ **string** corde *f* à vide; (*Elec*) ~ **circuit** circuit ouvert; **to welcome sb/sth with ~ arms** accueillir qn/qch à bras ouverts; **the window flew ~** la fenêtre s'ouvrit brusquement; (*Econ*) ~ **door** (*see* **2**); *see* **break, cut, eye, mouth** *etc*.

b *shop, museum* ouvert. **our grocer is ~ on Mondays** notre épicier ouvre *or* est ouvert le lundi; **gardens ~ to the public** jardins ouverts au public; *see* **throw**.

c *river, water, canal* (*not obstructed*) ouvert à la navigation, (*not frozen*) non gelé; *road, corridor* dégagé; *pipe* ouvert, non bouché; (*Med*) *bowels* relâché; *pores* dilaté. **road ~ to traffic** route ouverte à la circulation; **the way to Paris lay ~** la route de Paris était libre; **the road to anarchy lay wide ~** on allait tout droit à l'anarchie; **the ~ road** la grand-route.

d (*not enclosed*) *car, carriage* découvert, décapoté; *boat* ouvert, non ponté; *drain, sewer* à ciel ouvert. ~ **sandwich** canapé *m* (froid); **the ~ air** le plein air (*see also* **2**); **in the ~ air** *live, walk, eat* au grand air, en plein air; *sleep* à la belle étoile; *swimming pool* à ciel ouvert, en plein air; ~ **market** (*in town etc*) marché *m* en plein air (*see also* **1e**); **in ~ country** en rase campagne, en plein champ; **when you reach ~ country** *or* ~ **ground** quand vous gagnerez la campagne; **patch of ~ ground** (*between trees*) clairière *f*; (*in town*) terrain *m* vague; **beyond the woods he found the ~ fields** au-delà des bois il trouva les champs qui s'étendaient; **the ~ sea** la haute mer, le large; **on the ~ sea(s)** en haute mer, au large, de par les mers (*liter*); ~ **space** espace *m* libre; **the (wide) ~ spaces** les grands espaces vides; ~ **station** gare *f* avec accès libre aux quais; ~ **view** *or* **aspect** vue dégagée.

e (*fig: unrestricted*) *meeting, trial, discussion* public (*f* -ique); *competition* ouvert à tous, open *inv*; *economy* ouvert. (*US Univ*) ~ **admission** *or* **enrollment** admission *f* à l'Université sans baccalauréat; ~ **cheque** chèque *m* non barré; (*US Scol*) ~ **classroom** classe *f* primaire à activités libres; ~ **marriage** mariage *m* libre; (*Fin, Comm*) ~ **company** société *f* anonyme; (*Jur*) **in ~ court** en audience publique; (*Brit*) ~ **day** journée *f* portes ouvertes *or* du public; (*fig*) **to keep ~ house** tenir table ouverte; (*US Admin*) ~ **housing** politique *f* immobilière sans restrictions raciales; ~ **letter** lettre *f* ouverte; (*Econ*) ~ **market** marché *m* libre; (*US Pol*) ~ **primary** élection *f* primaire ouverte aux non-inscrits d'un parti; ~ **prison** prison *f* ouverte; (*Scol etc*) ~ **scholarship** *bourse décernée par un concours ouvert à tous*; (*Hunting*) ~ **season** saison *f* de la chasse; (*Ind*) ~ **shop** atelier *m* ouvert aux non-syndiqués; (*US Med*) ~ **staff hospital** *hôpital où tout médecin peut envoyer et traiter ses propres malades*; (*Golf*) ~ **(tournament)** tournoi *m* open; (*Brit*) **the O~ University** ≃ Centre *m* national d'Enseignement par Correspondance, C.N.E.C. *m*; (*Brit*) **an O~ University course** un cours universitaire par correspondance.

f (*exposed*) *coast etc* ouvert, exposé. **(wide) ~ to the winds/the elements** exposé à tous les vents/aux éléments; (*Mil, Pol*) ~ **city** ville ouverte; (*Mil, fig*) ~ **to attack** exposé à l'attaque; ~ **to persuasion** accessible *or* ouvert à la persuasion; **I'm ~ to advice** je me laisserais volontiers conseiller; **I'm ~ to correction, but I believe he said** ... dites-moi si je me trompe, mais je crois qu'il a dit ..., si je ne me trompe (*frm*), il a dit ...; **the decision is ~ to criticism** cette décision prête le flanc à la critique; **it is ~ to improvement** ça peut être amélioré; **it is ~ to doubt whether** ... on peut douter que ... + *subj*; **it is ~ to question** *or* **debate if** *or* **whether** ... reste à savoir si ...; *see* **lay[1], offer** *etc*.

g (*available*) **membership is not ~ to women** les femmes ne peuvent pas être membres; **the course is not ~ to schoolchildren** ce cours n'est pas ouvert aux lycéens, les lycéens ne peuvent pas choisir ce cours; **it is ~ to you to refuse** libre à vous de refuser, vous pouvez parfaitement refuser; **several methods/choices were ~ to them** plusieurs méthodes/choix s'offraient *or* se présentaient à eux; **this post is still ~** ce poste est encore vacant.

h (*frank*) *person, character, face, manner* ouvert, franc (*f* franche); (*declared*) *enemy* déclaré; *admiration, envy* manifeste; *campaign* ouvert; *attempt* non dissimulé, patent; *scandal* public (*f* -ique). **in ~ revolt (against)** en rébellion ouverte (contre); **~ secret** secret *m* de Polichinelle; **it's an ~ secret that** ... ce n'est un secret pour personne que ...; **he was not very ~ with us** il ne nous a pas tout dit, il nous a parlé avec réticence.

i (*undecided*) *question* non résolu, non tranché. **the race was still wide ~** l'issue de la course était encore indécise; **it's an ~ question whether he will come** on ne sait pas s'il viendra; **it's an ~ question whether he would have come if** ... on ne saura jamais s'il serait venu si ...; **they left the matter ~** ils n'ont pas tranché la question, ils ont laissé la question en suspens; **let's leave the date/arrangements ~** n'arrêtons pas *or* ne précisons pas la date/les dispositions; **to keep an ~ mind on sth** réserver son jugement *or* son opinion sur qch (*see also* **2**); **I've got an ~ mind about it** je n'ai pas encore formé d'opinion à ce sujet (*see also* **2**); (*Jur*) **~ verdict** verdict *m* de décès sans cause déterminée; **~ ticket** billet *m* open; *see* **option** *etc*.

2 **comp** ►**open-air** *games, activities* de plein air; *swimming pool, market, meeting* en plein air, à ciel ouvert; **open-air theatre** théâtre *m* de verdure; (*Med*) **open-air treatment** cure *f* d'air ►**open-and-shut:** (*fig*) **it's an open-and-shut case** c'est un cas transparent ►**open-cast** (*Brit*), **open-cut** (*US*) (*Min*) à ciel ouvert ►**open door** (*Econ*) **n** politique *f* d'ouverture ◊ **adj** *policy, approach etc* d'ouverture ►**open-end** (*US*), **open-ended** *box, tube* à deux ouvertures; *discussion, meeting* sans limite de durée; *ticket* sans réservation de retour; *offer, contract* flexible; *question* ouvert ►**open-eyed** (*lit*) les yeux ouverts; (*in surprise, wonder*) les yeux écarquillés; **in open-eyed astonishment** béant d'étonnement ►**open-faced sandwich** (*US*) canapé *m* (froid) ►**open-handed: to be open-handed** être généreux, avoir le cœur sur la main ►**open-hearted** franc (*f* franche), sincère ►**open-heart surgery** (*Med*) chirurgie *f* à cœur ouvert ►**open-minded** à l'esprit ouvert *or* large, sans parti pris, sans préjugés ►**open-mindedness** ouverture *f or* largesse *f* d'esprit ►**open-mouthed adj, adv** (*fig*) bouche bée; **in open-mouthed admiration** béant *or* béat d'admiration ►**open-necked** à col ouvert, échancré ►**open-plan** (*Archit*) *design* qui élimine les cloisons; *house, school* à aire ouverte, non cloisonné; **open-plan office** bureau *m* paysager ►**openwork n** (*Sewing*) (a)jours *mpl*; (*Archit*) claire-voie *f*, ajours ◊ **comp** *stockings etc* ajouré, à jour; (*Archit*) à claire-voie; *see* **reel**.

3 **n** a **to be out in the ~** (*out of doors*) être dehors *or* en plein air; (*in the country*) être au grand air *or* en plein champ; **to sleep in the ~** dormir à la belle étoile; **to come out into the ~** (*lit*) sortir au grand jour *or* en plein jour; (*fig*) se faire jour, se manifester; **he came (out) into the ~ about what had been going on** il a dévoilé *or* révélé ce qui s'était passé; **why don't you come into the ~ about it?** pourquoi n'en parlez-vous pas franchement?, pourquoi ne le dites-vous pas ouvertement?; **to bring a dispute (out) into the ~** divulguer une querelle.

b (*Golf, Tennis*) **the O~** l'open *m*, le tournoi open; **the French O~** le tournoi de Roland Garros; **the California O~** l'Open de Californie.

4 **vt** a *door, box, book, shop, grave, eyes* ouvrir; *letter, envelope* ouvrir, décacheter; *parcel* ouvrir, défaire; *bottle, jar* ouvrir, déboucher; *jacket, coat, collar* ouvrir, déboutonner; *map, newspaper* ouvrir, déplier; (*Elec*) *circuit* ouvrir; (*Med*) *abscess* ouvrir; *bowels* relâcher; *pores* dilater; *wound* (r)ouvrir; *legs* écarter; (*fig*) *horizon, career, one's heart etc* ouvrir. **to ~ wide** ouvrir tout grand; **to ~ slightly** *door, window* entrebâiller, entrouvrir; *eyes* entrouvrir; **to ~ again** rouvrir; *see* **eye, mouth** *etc*.

b (*drive*) *passage, road* ouvrir, pratiquer, frayer; *hole* percer.

c (*begin*) *meeting, account, debate,* (*Jur*) *case, trial* ouvrir; *conversation* entamer, engager; *negotiations* ouvrir, engager; (*inaugurate*) *exhibition, new hospital, factory* ouvrir, inaugurer; (*found*) *institution, school, business* ouvrir, fonder. **the Queen ~ed Parliament** la reine a ouvert la session parlementaire; (*Mil*) **to ~ fire (at** *or* **on)** ouvrir le feu (sur); (*Bridge*) **to ~ the bidding** ouvrir (les enchères); (*Ftbl*) **to ~ the scoring** ouvrir la marque.

5 **vi** a *[door]* (s')ouvrir; *[book, eyes]* s'ouvrir; *[flower]* s'ouvrir, s'épanouir, éclore; *[shop, museum, bank etc]* ouvrir; *[gulf, crevasse]* s'ouvrir, se former. **this door never ~s** cette porte n'ouvre jamais; **the door ~ed** la porte s'est ouverte; **the door ~ed slightly** la porte s'est entrouverte *or* s'est entrebâillée; **to ~ again** se rouvrir; **door that ~s on to the garden** porte qui donne sur le jardin; **the kitchen ~s into the dining room** la cuisine donne sur la salle à manger; **the two rooms ~ into one another** les deux pièces communiquent *or* se commandent; **~ sesame!** sésame ouvre-toi!; (*mouth*) **~ wide!** ouvrez grand!

b (*begin*) *[class, debate, meeting, play, book]* s'ouvrir, commencer (*with* par); (*Bridge*) ouvrir. **he ~ed with a warning about inflation** il commença par donner un avertissement sur l'inflation; (*Cine*) **it will ~ next week in London** il sera la semaine prochaine sur les écrans londoniens; **the play ~s** *or* **they ~ next week** la première a lieu la semaine prochaine; (*Bridge*) **to ~ (with) 2 hearts** ouvrir de 2 cœurs.

►**open out** 1 **vi** a *[flower]* s'ouvrir, s'épanouir, éclore; *[view, countryside]* s'ouvrir; (*fig*) *[person]* (*become less shy etc*) s'ouvrir; *[company, business]* étendre le champ de ses activités; *[team, player etc]* s'affirmer. b (*widen*) *[passage, tunnel, street]* s'élargir. **to open out on to** déboucher sur. 2 **vt sep** ouvrir; *map, newspaper* ouvrir, déplier; (*fig*) *business* développer.

►**open up** 1 **vi** a *[shop, business, new career, opportunity]* s'ouvrir.

b (*Mil etc: start shooting*) ouvrir le feu, se mettre à tirer.

c *[flower]* s'ouvrir, s'épanouir, éclore.

d (*fig*) s'ouvrir (*to sb* à qn, *about sth* de qch). **I couldn't get him to open up at all** je ne suis pas arrivé à le faire parler *or* s'épancher; **we got him to open up about his plans** il a fini par nous communiquer ses projets.

e (*Sport*) *[match]* s'animer.

2 **vt sep** a *box, suitcase, parcel* ouvrir, défaire; *map, newspaper* ouvrir, déplier; *jacket, coat* ouvrir, déboutonner; *abscess, wound* ouvrir. **the owner opened up the shop for the police** le propriétaire a ouvert le magasin spécialement pour la police; **to open up again** rouvrir.

b (*start*) *business, branch etc* ouvrir.

c *oilfield, mine* ouvrir, commencer l'exploitation de; *route* ouvrir; *road through jungle etc* frayer, ouvrir (*through* à travers); *virgin country* rendre accessible; (*Econ*) *remote area* désenclaver; *blocked road* dégager; *blocked pipe* déboucher; (*fig*) *prospects, vistas, possibility* découvrir, révéler; *horizons, career* ouvrir. **to open up a country for trade** ouvrir un pays au commerce; **to open up a country for development** développer le potentiel d'un pays; **to open up a new market for one's products** établir de nouveaux débouchés pour ses produits.

opener [ˈəʊpnəʳ] **n** a (*surtout dans les composés*) *personne ou dispositif qui ouvre*; *see* **bottle, eye, tin** *etc*. b (*Theat*) (*artiste*) artiste *mf* en lever de rideau; (*act*) lever *m* de rideau. c (*Bridge*) ouvreur *m*. d (*fig*) **for ~s*** pour commencer, tout d'abord.

opening [ˈəʊpnɪŋ] 1 **n** a ouverture *f*; (*in wall*) brèche *f*; *[door, window]* embrasure *f*; (*in trees*) échappée *f*, trouée *f*; (*in forest, roof*) percée *f*; (*in clouds*) éclaircie *f*; *[tunnel]* entrée *f*, ouverture, début *m*.

b (*beginning*) *[meeting, debate, play, speech]* ouverture *f*, début *m*, commencement *m*; *[negotiations]* ouverture, amorce *f*.

c (*NonC: act of ~*) *[door, road, letter]* ouverture *f*; *[shooting, war]* déclenchement *m*; *[flower]* épanouissement *m*, éclosion *f*; (*Jur*) exposition *f* des faits; (*Cards, Chess*) ouverture; *[ceremony, exhibition]* inauguration *f*. (*Brit*) **O~ of Parliament** ouverture de la session parlementaire.

d (*opportunity*) occasion *f* (*to do* de faire, pour faire); (*trade outlet*) débouché *m* (*for* pour). **to give one's opponent/the enemy an ~** prêter le flanc à son adversaire/à l'ennemi.

e (*work: gen*) débouché *m*; (*specific job, or work in specific firm*) poste *m* (*with* chez; *as an engineer etc* d'ingénieur *etc*).

2 **adj** *ceremony, speech* d'inauguration, inaugural; *remark* préliminaire; (*St Ex*) *price* d'ouverture. **~ gambit** (*Chess*) gambit *m*; (*fig*) manœuvre *f or* ruse *f* (stratégique); **~ hours** heures *fpl* d'ouverture; **~ lines** *[play]* premières répliques *fpl*; *[poème]* premiers vers *mpl*; **~ night** (*Theat*) première *f*; *[festival etc]* soirée *f* d'ouverture; **~ shot** (*in battle etc*) premier coup *m* de feu; (*fig: of campaign etc*) coup *m* d'envoi; (*Brit*) **~ time** l'heure *f* d'ouverture (*des pubs*).

openly [ˈəʊpənlɪ] **adv** (*frankly*) ouvertement, franchement; (*publicly*) publiquement.

openness [ˈəʊpnnɪs] **n** a (*candour*) franchise *f*. **~ of mind** largeur *f* d'esprit. b *[land, countryside]* aspect découvert *or* exposé.

opera [ˈɒpərə] 1 **n** a opéra *m*. **~ bouffe** opéra bouffe; *see* **comic, grand, light[2]**. b **pl of opus.** 2 **comp** ►**opera glasses** jumelles *fpl* de théâtre, lorgnette *f* ►**opera-goer** amateur *m* d'opéra ►**opera hat** (chapeau *m*) claque *m*, gibus *m* ►**opera house** (théâtre *m* de l')opéra *m* ►**opera-lover** amateur *m* d'opéra ►**opera singer** chanteur *m*, -euse *f* d'opéra.

operable [ˈɒpərəbl] **adj** opérable.

operand [ˈɒpərænd] **n** (*Comput*) opérande *m*.

operate [ˈɒpəreɪt] 1 **vi** a *[machine, vehicle]* marcher, fonctionner (*by electricity etc* à l'électricité *etc*); *[system, sb's mind]* fonctionner; *[law]* jouer. **several factors ~d to produce this situation** plusieurs facteurs ont joué pour produire cette situation.

b *[drug, medicine, propaganda]* opérer, faire effet (*on, upon* sur).

c *[fleet, regiment, thief etc]* opérer; (*St Ex*) faire des opérations (de bourse), spéculer. **they can't ~ efficiently on so little money** le manque d'argent les empêche d'opérer *or* de procéder avec efficacité.

d (*Med*) opérer (*on sb for sth* qn de qch). **he ~d/was ~d on for appendicitis** il a opéré/a été opéré de l'appendicite; **to ~ on sb's eyes** opérer qn aux *or* des yeux, opérer les yeux de qn; **he has still not been ~d on** il n'a pas encore été opéré, il n'a pas encore subi l'opération.

2 **vt** a *[person] machine, tool, vehicle, switchboard, telephone, brakes etc* faire marcher, faire fonctionner. **a machine ~d by electricity** une machine qui marche à l'électricité; **this switch ~s a fan** ce bouton commande *or* actionne un ventilateur; (*fig*) **such a law will ~ considerable changes** une telle loi opérera des changements considérables.

b *business, factory* diriger, gérer; *coalmine, oil well, canal, quarry* exploiter, faire valoir.

c *system* opérer, pratiquer. **he has ~d several clever swindles** il a réalisé plusieurs belles escroqueries.

operatic [ˌɒpəˈrætɪk] 1 **adj** d'opéra. 2 **n: (amateur) ~s** opéra *m* d'amateurs.

operating [ˈɒpəreɪtɪŋ] **adj** a (*Comm, Ind*) *profit, deficit, expenses etc* d'exploitation. **~ cash** trésorerie *f* d'exploitation; **~ cycle** cycle *m* d'exploitation; **~ instructions** mode *f or* notice *f* d'emploi. b (*Med*) **~ table** table *f* d'opération, billard* *m*; (*Brit*) **~ theatre,** (*US*) **~ room** salle *f* d'opération. c (*Comput*) **~ system** système *m* d'exploitation.

operation [ˌɒpəˈreɪʃən] 1 **n** a (*NonC*) *[machine, vehicle]* marche *f*, fonctionnement *m*; *[mind, digestion]* fonctionnement; *[drug etc]* action *f*, effet *m* (*on* sur); *[business]* gestion *f*; *[mine, oil well, quarry, canal]* exploitation *f*; *[system]* application *f*. **in full ~** *machine* fonctionnant à plein (rendement); *business, factory etc* en pleine activité; *mine etc* en pleine exploitation; *law* pleinement en vigueur; **to be in ~** *[machine]* être en service; *[business etc]* fonctionner; *[mine etc]* être en exploitation; *[law, system]* être en vigueur; **to come into ~** *[law, system]* entrer en vigueur; *[machine]* entrer en service; *[business]* se mettre à fonctionner; **to put into ~** *machine* mettre en service; *law* mettre *or* faire entrer en vigueur; *plan* mettre en application.

b (*gen, Comm, Fin, Ind, Math, Mil, Pol etc*) opération *f*. **that was an expensive ~** l'opération a été coûteuse; (*Comm, Ind*) **our ~s in Egypt** (*trading company*) nos opérations *or* nos activités en Égypte; (*oil, mining*) nos opérations *or* nos exploitations en Égypte; **rebuilding ~s began at once** les opérations de reconstruction ont commencé immédiatement; (*Mil*) **O~ Overlord** Opération Overlord.

c (*Med*) opération *f*, intervention (chirurgicale). **to have an ~** se faire opérer (*for* de); **a lung ~** une opération au poumon; **to perform an ~ on sb (for sth)** opérer qn (de qch).

2 **comp** ▶**operation code** (*Comput*) code *m* d'opération ▶**operations research** recherche *f* opérationnelle ▶**operations room** (*Mil, Police*) centre *m* d'opérations.

operational [ˌɒpəˈreɪʃənl] **adj** a *base, research, unit, soldiers, dangers* opérationnel; (*Ind, Comm*) *cost, expenses, profit etc* d'exploitation. (*Police etc*) **on ~ duties** en service; **~ research = operations research;** (*Fin, Econ*) **~ strategy** stratégie *f* d'intervention. b (*ready for use*) *machine, vehicle* en état de marche *or* de fonctionnement, opérationnel; *system etc* opérationnel. **when the service is fully ~** quand le service sera pleinement opérationnel *or* à même de fonctionner à plein.

operative [ˈɒpərətɪv] 1 **adj** a *law, measure, system* en vigueur. **to become ~** entrer en vigueur; **the ~ word** le mot qui compte, le mot clé; (*Jur*) **the ~ part of the text** le dispositif. b (*Med*) opératoire. 2 **n** (*worker*) ouvrier *m*, -ière *f*; (*machine operator*) opérateur *m*, -trice *f*; (*detective*) détective *m* (privé); (*spy*) espion(ne) *m(f)*; (*secret agent*) agent secret; (*US Pol: campaign worker*) membre *m* de l'état-major (*d'un candidat*). **the steel ~s** la main-d'œuvre des aciéries.

operator [ˈɒpəreɪtəʳ] **n** a (*person*) *[machine, computer etc]* opérateur *m*, -trice *f*; (*Cine*) opérateur, -trice (de prise de vues); *[telephones]* téléphoniste *mf*, standardiste *mf*; (*Telegraphy*) radio *m*; *[business, factory]* dirigeant(e) *m(f)*, directeur *m*, -trice *f*. **tour ~** organisateur *m*, -trice *f* de voyages; **~s in this section of the industry** ceux qui travaillent dans ce secteur de l'industrie; (*criminal*) **a big-time ~** un escroc d'envergure; (*pej*) **he is a smooth ~*** c'est quelqu'un qui sait y faire*. b (*Math*) opérateur *m*.

operetta [ˌɒpəˈretə] **n** opérette *f*.

ophthalmia [ɒfˈθælmɪə] **n** ophtalmie *f*.

ophthalmic [ɒfˈθælmɪk] **adj** *nerve, vein* ophtalmique; *clinic, surgeon, surgery* ophtalmologique.

ophthalmologist [ˌɒfθælˈmɒlədʒɪst] **n** ophtalmologiste *mf*, ophtalmologue *mf*.

ophthalmology [ˌɒfθælˈmɒlədʒɪ] **n** ophtalmologie *f*.

ophthalmoscope [ɒfˈθælməskəʊp] **n** ophtalmoscope *m*.

ophthalmoscopy [ˌɒfθælˈmɒskəpɪ] **n** ophtalmoscopie *f*.

opiate [ˈəʊpɪɪt] 1 **n** opiat *m*; (*fig*) soporifique *m*. 2 **adj** opiacé.

opine [əʊˈpaɪn] **vt** (*think*) être d'avis (*that* que); (*say*) émettre l'avis (*that* que).

opinion [əˈpɪnjən] 1 **n** (*point of view*) avis *m*, opinion *f*; (*belief*) opinion, conviction *f*; (*judgment*) opinion, jugement *m*, appréciation *f*; (*professional advice*) avis. **in my ~** à mon avis, pour moi, d'après moi; **in the ~ of** d'après, selon; **that's my ~ for what it's worth** c'est mon humble avis; **it's a matter of ~ whether ...** c'est (une) affaire d'opinion pour ce qui est de savoir si ...; **I'm entirely of your ~** je suis tout à fait de votre avis *or* opinion, je partage tout à fait votre opinion; **to be of the ~ that** être d'avis que, estimer que; **political ~s** opinions politiques; **to have a good *or* high ~ of sb/sth** avoir bonne opinion de qn/qch, estimer qn/qch; **what is your ~ of this book?** que pensez-vous de ce livre?; **I haven't much of an ~ of him, I've got a low ~ *or* no ~ of him** j'ai mauvaise opinion *or* une piètre opinion de lui; (*Jur*) **to take counsel's ~** consulter un avocat; (*Jur*) **~ of the court** jugement rendu par le tribunal; (*Med*) **to take a second ~** consulter un autre médecin, prendre l'avis d'un autre médecin; *see* **legal, public, strong.**

2 **comp** ▶**opinion poll** sondage *m* d'opinion.

opinionated [əˈpɪnjəneɪtɪd] **adj** arrêté dans ses opinions, dogmatique.

opium [ˈəʊpɪəm] 1 **n** opium *m*. 2 **comp** ▶**opium addict** opiomane *mf* ▶**opium den** fumerie *f* d'opium.

opossum [əˈpɒsəm] **n, pl ~s *or* ~** opossum *m*, sarigue *f*.

opponent [əˈpəʊnənt] **n** (*Mil, Sport*) adversaire *mf*; (*in election*) adversaire *mf*, rival(e) *m(f)*; (*in discussion, debate*) antagoniste *mf*; (*of government, ideas etc*) adversaire, opposant(e) *m(f)* (*of* de). **he has always been an ~ of nationalization** il a toujours été contre les nationalisations, il s'est toujours opposé aux nationalisations.

opportune [ˈɒpətjuːn] **adj** *time* opportun, propice, convenable; *action, event, remark* à propos, opportun. **you have come at an ~ moment** vous arrivez à point (nommé) *or* à propos.

opportunely [ˈɒpətjuːnlɪ] **adv** opportunément, au moment opportun, à propos.

opportuneness [ˌɒpəˈtjuːnnɪs] **n** opportunité *f*.

opportunism [ˌɒpəˈtjuːnɪzəm] **n** opportunisme *m*.

opportunist [ˌɒpəˈtjuːnɪst] **adj, n** opportuniste (*mf*).

opportunistic [ˌɒpətjuːˈnɪstɪk] **adj** opportuniste.

opportunity [ˌɒpəˈtjuːnɪtɪ] **n** occasion *f*. **to have the *or* an ~ to do *or* of doing** avoir l'occasion de faire; **to take the ~ of doing *or* to do** profiter de l'occasion pour faire; **you really missed your ~ there!** tu as vraiment laissé passer ta chance! *or* l'occasion!; **at the first *or* earliest ~** à la première occasion, dès que l'occasion se présentera; **when the ~ occurs** à l'occasion; **if the ~ should occur *or* arise** si l'occasion se présente; **if you get the ~** si vous en avez l'occasion; **equality of ~** chances égales, égalité *f* de chances; **to make the most of one's opportunities** profiter pleinement de ses chances; **this job offers great opportunities** ce poste offre d'excellentes perspectives d'avenir; *see* **every a.**

oppose [əˈpəʊz] **vt** a *person, argument, opinion* s'opposer à, combattre; *sb's will, desires, suggestion* s'opposer à, faire opposition à; *decision, plan* s'opposer à, mettre opposition à, contrecarrer, contrarier; *motion, resolution* (*Pol*) faire opposition à; (*in debate*) parler contre. **he ~s our coming** il s'oppose à ce que nous venions (*subj*); **but he ~d it** mais il s'y est opposé. b (*set against*) opposer (*sth to sth else* qch à qch d'autre).

opposed [əˈpəʊzd] **adj** opposé, hostile (*to* à). **to be ~ to sth** être opposé *or* hostile à qch, s'opposer à qch; **I'm ~ to your marrying him** je m'oppose à ce que vous l'épousiez (*subj*); **as ~ to** par opposition à; **as ~ to that, there is the question of ...** par contre, il y a la question de ... .

opposing [əˈpəʊzɪŋ] **adj** *army* opposé; *minority* opposant; (*Jur*) adverse. (*Sport*) **~ team** adversaire(s) *m(pl)*; **the ~ votes** les voix "contre".

opposite [ˈɒpəzɪt] 1 **adj** *house etc* d'en face; *bank, side, end* opposé, autre; *direction, pole* opposé; (*fig*) *attitude, point of view* opposé, contraire. **"see map on ~ page"** "voir plan ci-contre"; **the ~ sex** l'autre sexe *m*; **we take the ~ view (to his)** nous pensons le contraire (de ce qu'il pense), notre opinion est diamétralement opposée (à la sienne); **his ~ number** son homologue *mf*.

2 **adv** (d')en face. **the house ~** la maison d'en face; **the house is immediately *or* directly ~** la maison est directement en face; **~ to** en face de.

3 **prep** en face de. **the house is ~ the church** la maison est en face de l'église; **the house and the church are ~ one another** la maison et l'église sont en vis-à-vis; **they sat ~ one another** ils étaient assis face à face *or* en vis-à-vis; **they live ~ us** ils habitent en face de chez nous; (*Cine, Theat etc*) **to play ~ sb** partager la vedette avec qn; (*Naut*) **~ Calais** à la hauteur de Calais.

4 **n** opposé *m*, contraire *m*, inverse *m*. **quite the ~!** au contraire!; **he told me just the ~ *or* the exact ~** il m'a dit exactement l'inverse *or* le contraire *or* l'opposé; **he says the ~ of everything I say** il prend le contre-pied de tout ce que je dis.

opposition [ˌɒpəˈzɪʃən] 1 **n** a opposition *f* (*also Astron, Pol*). **his ~ to the scheme** son opposition au projet; **in ~ (to)** en opposition (avec); (*Pol*) **the party in ~** le parti de l'opposition; (*Pol*) **to be in ~** être dans l'opposition; (*Pol*) **the leader of the O~** le chef de l'opposition; **the ~*** (*opposing team, rival political faction*) l'adversaire *m*; (*business competitors*) la concurrence.

b (*Mil etc*) opposition *f*, résistance *f*. **they put up *or* offered considerable ~** ils opposèrent une vive résistance; **the army met with little or no ~** l'armée a rencontré peu sinon point de résistance.

2 **comp** ▶**Opposition** (*Pol*) *speaker, member, motion, party* de l'opposition; **the Opposition benches** les bancs *mpl* de l'opposition

►**opposition hold** (*Climbing*) opposition *f*.

oppress [ə'pres] **vt** a (*Mil, Pol etc*) opprimer. b *[anxiety, heat etc]* oppresser, accabler.

oppression [ə'preʃən] **n** (*all senses*) oppression *f*.

oppressive [ə'presɪv] **adj** a (*Mil, Pol etc*) *régime, government* tyrannique; *law, tax, measure* oppressif. b *anxiety, suffering* accablant; *heat* accablant, étouffant; *weather* lourd; (*fig*) *atmosphere, room* oppressant.

oppressively [ə'presɪvlɪ] **adv** (*see* **oppressive**) a d'une manière oppressive; (*Mil, Pol etc*) tyranniquement. b d'une manière accablante. **it was ~ hot** il faisait une chaleur accablante *or* étouffante.

oppressor [ə'presəʳ] **n** oppresseur *m*.

opprobrious [ə'prəʊbrɪəs] **adj** (*frm*) chargé d'opprobre.

opprobrium [ə'prəʊbrɪəm] **n** opprobre *m*.

opt [ɒpt] **vi: to ~ for sth** opter pour qch; **to ~ to do** choisir de faire.

►**opt in vi** choisir de participer (*to* à).

►**opt out vi** choisir de ne pas participer (*of* à); (*Soc*) s'évader de *or* rejeter la société (de consommation); (*Brit: pension*) choisir une caisse de retraite privée (*par opposition au système de la Sécurité Sociale*). **he opted out of going** il a choisi de ne pas y aller; **you can always opt out** tu peux toujours abandonner *or* te retirer *or* te récuser.

optative ['ɒptətɪv] **adj, n** optatif (*m*).

optic ['ɒptɪk] 1 **adj** optique. 2 **n** (*NonC*) **~s** optique *f*.

optical ['ɒptɪkəl] **adj** *glass, lens* optique (*also Comput*); *instrument* d'optique. **~ brightener** agent *m* éclaircissant; (*Comput*) **~ character reader, ~ scanner** lecteur *m* optique; **~ character recognition, ~ scanning** lecture *f* optique; **~ disk** disque *m* optique; **~ fibre** fibre *f* optique; **~ illusion** illusion *f* d'optique.

optician [ɒp'tɪʃən] **n** opticien(ne) *m(f)*.

optima ['ɒptɪmə] **npl of optimum.**

optimal ['ɒptɪml] **adj** optimal.

optimism ['ɒptɪmɪzəm] **n** optimisme *m*.

optimist ['ɒptɪmɪst] **n** optimiste *mf*.

optimistic [ˌɒptɪ'mɪstɪk] **adj** optimiste.

optimistically [ˌɒptɪ'mɪstɪklɪ] **adv** avec optimisme, d'une manière optimiste.

optimization [ˌɒptɪmaɪ'zeɪʃən] **n** optimisation *f*.

optimize ['ɒptɪmaɪz] **vt** optimiser, optimaliser.

optimum ['ɒptɪməm] 1 **adj** optimum. **~ conditions** conditions *fpl* optimums *or* optima. 2 **n, pl ~s** *or* **optima** optimum *m*.

option ['ɒpʃən] **n** a (*gen*) choix *m*, option *f*; (*Comm, Fin*) option (*on* sur). **to take up the ~** lever l'option; **at the ~ of the purchaser** au gré de l'acheteur; (*Comm, Fin*) **~ taker** optant *m*; (*Jur*) **the buyer shall have the ~ to decide** l'acheteur aura la faculté de décider; (*Jur*) **6 months with/without the ~ of a fine** 6 mois avec/sans substitution d'amende; **I have no ~** je n'ai pas le choix; **he had no ~ but to come** il n'a pas pu faire autrement que de venir; **you have the ~ of remaining here** vous pouvez rester ici si vous voulez; **it's left to your ~** c'est à vous de choisir *or* de décider; (*fig*) **he left** *or* **kept his ~s open** il n'a pas voulu s'engager (irrévocablement).

b (*Brit Scol : subject/course etc*) (matière *f*/cours *m etc* à) option *f*. **programme offering ~s** programme *m* optionnel.

optional ['ɒpʃənl] **adj** (*gen, Scol etc*) facultatif; (*Comm*) *car accessories etc* en option, optionnel. **"dress ~"** "la tenue de soirée n'est pas de rigueur"; **the sun roof is an ~ extra** le toit ouvrant est en supplément.

optometrist [ɒp'tɒmətrɪst] **n** optométriste *mf*.

opulence ['ɒpjʊləns] **n** (*NonC: see* **opulent**) opulence *f*, richesse(s) *f(pl)*; abondance *f*; luxuriance *f*.

opulent ['ɒpjʊlənt] **adj** *person, life* opulent, riche; *hair* abondant; *vegetation* abondant, luxuriant.

opulently ['ɒpjʊləntlɪ] **adv** *furnish etc* avec opulence; *live* dans l'opulence.

opus ['əʊpəs] **n, pl ~es** *or* **opera** opus *m*; *see* **magnum**.

opuscule [ɒ'pʌskjuːl] **n** opuscule *m*.

OR (*US*) **abbr of Oregon.**

or [ɔːʳ] **conj** ou (bien); (*with neg*) ni. **red ~ black?** rouge ou noir?; **~ else** ou bien; **do it ~ else!*** fais-le, sinon (tu vas voir)!; **without tears ~ sighs** sans larmes ni soupirs; **he could not read ~ write** il ne savait ni lire ni écrire; **an hour ~ so** environ *or* à peu près une heure; **botany, ~ the science of plants** la botanique, ou la science des plantes *or* autrement dit la science des plantes; *see* **either**.

oracle ['ɒrəkl] **n** (*Hist, fig*) oracle *m*. (*fig*) **he managed to work the ~ and got 3 days' leave** il s'est mystérieusement débrouillé pour obtenir 3 jours de congé.

oracular [ɒ'rækjʊləʳ] **adj** (*lit, fig*) d'oracle; (*mysterious*) sibyllin (*liter*).

oral ['ɔːrəl] 1 **adj** a *examination, teaching methods* oral; *testimony, message, account* oral, verbal. b (*Anat*) *cavity* buccal, oral; (*Pharm etc*) *dose* par voie orale. 2 **n** (examen *m*) oral *m*, épreuve orale. 3 **comp** ►**oral examiner** (*Scol etc*) examinateur *m*, -trice *f* à l'oral ►**oral history** la tradition orale ►**oral hygiene** hygiène *f* buccale *or* bucco-dentaire ►**oral hygienist** hygiéniste *mf* dentaire ►**oral sex** rapports *mpl* sexuels buccaux, relations *fpl* sexuelles bucco-génitales (SPEC); (*fellatio*) fellation *f*; (*cunnilingus*) cunnilingus *m* ►**oral society** société *f* à tradition orale ►**oral tradition** la tradition orale ►**oral vowel** (*Ling*) voyelle *f* orale.

orally ['ɔːrəlɪ] **adv** *testify, communicate* oralement, de vive voix; (*Pharm*) par voie orale.

orange ['ɒrɪndʒ] 1 **n** (*fruit, drink*) orange *f*; (*also* **~ tree**) oranger *m*; (*colour*) orange *m*, orangé *m*. **"~s and lemons"** *chanson et jeu d'enfants; see* **blood** *etc*.

2 **adj** (*colour*) orangé, orange *inv*; (*taste*) *drink, flavour* d'orange; *liqueur* à l'orange.

3 **comp** ►**orange blossom** fleur(s) *f(pl)* d'oranger ►**Orange Day** (*Ir*) le 12 juillet (*procession annuelle des orangistes de l'Irlande du Nord*) ►**Orange Free State** État *m* libre d'Orange ►**orange grove** orangeraie *f* ►**orange juice** jus *m* d'orange ►**Orangeman** (*Ir*) orangiste *m* ►**orange marmalade** confiture *f* d'oranges ►**orange peel** (*gen*) peau *f or* écorce *f* d'orange; (*Culin*) zeste *m* d'orange ►**orange squash** ≈ orangeade *f* ►**orange stick** bâtonnet *m* (*pour manucure etc*) ►**orange tree** oranger *m* ►**orangewood** (bois *m* d')oranger *m*.

orangeade ['ɒrɪndʒ'eɪd] **n** orangeade *f*.

orangery ['ɒrɪndʒərɪ] **n** orangerie *f*.

orangey ['ɒrɪndʒɪ] **adj** orangé.

orang-outang [ɔːˌræŋuː'tæŋ], **orang-utan** [ɔːˌræŋuː'tæn] **n** orang-outan(g) *m*.

orate [ɒ'reɪt] **vi** discourir, faire un discours; (*speechify*) pérorer.

oration [ɔː'reɪʃən] **n** discours solennel; *see* **funeral**.

orator ['ɒrətəʳ] **n** orateur *m*, -trice *f*.

oratorical [ˌɒrə'tɒrɪkəl] **adj** oratoire.

oratorio [ˌɒrə'tɔːrɪəʊ] **n, pl ~s** oratorio *m*.

oratory[1] ['ɒrətərɪ] **n** (*art*) art *m* oratoire; (*what is said*) éloquence *f*, rhétorique *f*. **brilliant piece of ~** brillant discours.

oratory[2] ['ɒrətərɪ] **n** (*Rel*) oratoire *m*.

orb [ɔːb] **n** a (*sphere*) globe *m*, sphère *f*; (*in regalia*) globe. b (*liter: eye*) œil *m*. c (*liter: celestial body*) orbe *m*.

orbit ['ɔːbɪt] 1 **n** (*Anat, Astron*) orbite *f*. **to be in/go into/put into ~ (around)** être/entrer/mettre en *or* sur orbite (autour de); (*fig*) **that doesn't come within my ~** ceci n'est pas de mon domaine *or* de mon rayon; **countries within the communist ~** pays dans l'orbite communiste. 2 **vt** graviter autour de, décrire une *or* des orbite(s) autour de. 3 **vi** orbiter, être *or* rester en *or* sur orbite (*round* autour de).

orbital ['ɔːbɪtl] **adj** (*Astron*) orbital; (*Anat*) orbitaire; *road* périphérique.

Orcadian [ɔː'keɪdɪən] 1 **adj** des (îles) Orcades. 2 **n** habitant(e) *m(f)* des (îles) Orcades.

orchard ['ɔːtʃəd] **n** verger *m*. **cherry ~** champ *m* de cerisiers, cerisaie *f*.

orchestra ['ɔːkɪstrə] 1 **n** a (*Mus*) orchestre *m*; *see* **leader, string** *etc*. b (*US Theat*) (fauteuils *mpl* d')orchestre *m*. 2 **comp** ►**orchestra pit** (*Theat*) fosse *f* d'orchestre ►**orchestra stalls** (fauteuils *mpl* d')orchestre *m*.

orchestral [ɔː'kestrəl] **adj** *music, style* orchestral; *concert* symphonique.

orchestrate ['ɔːkɪstreɪt] **vt** orchestrer.

orchestration [ˌɔːkɪs'treɪʃən] **n** orchestration *f*, instrumentation *f*.

orchid ['ɔːkɪd] **n** orchidée *f*. **wild ~** orchis *m*.

orchis ['ɔːkɪs] **n** orchis *m*.

ordain [ɔː'deɪn] **vt** a *[God, fate]* décréter (*that* que); *[law]* décréter (*that* que), prescrire (*that* que + *subj*); *[judge]* ordonner (*that* que + *subj*). **it was ~ed that he should die young** il était destiné à mourir jeune, le sort *or* le destin a voulu qu'il meure jeune. b (*Rel*) *priest* ordonner. **he was ~ed (priest)** il a reçu l'ordination, il a été ordonné prêtre.

ordeal [ɔː'diːl] **n** a supplice *m*, rude épreuve *f*. **they suffered terrible ~s** ils sont passés par *or* ils ont subi d'atroces épreuves; **speaking in public was an ~ for him** il était au supplice quand il devait parler en public, parler en public le mettait au supplice. b (*Hist Jur*) ordalie *f*. **~ by fire** épreuve *f* du feu.

order ['ɔːdəʳ] 1 **n** a (*NonC: disposition, sequence*) ordre *m*. **word ~** ordre des mots; **in alphabetical ~** dans l'ordre alphabétique; **what ~ should these cards be in?** dans quel ordre ces cartes devraient-elles être?; **in ~ of merit** par ordre de mérite; (*Theat*) **in ~ of appearance** par ordre *or* dans l'ordre d'entrée en scène; **to be in ~** être en ordre (*see also* **1d**); **the cards were out of ~** les cartes n'étaient pas en ordre; **to put in(to) ~** mettre en ordre, agencer, classer; *[papers etc]* **to get out of ~** se déclasser; **it is in the ~ of things** c'est dans l'ordre des choses; **the old ~ is changing** l'ancien état de choses change; *see* **battle, close[1]** *etc*.

b (*NonC: good ~*) ordre *m*. **he's got no sense of ~** il n'a aucun (sens de l')ordre; **in ~** *room etc* en ordre; *passport, documents* en règle; **to put one's room/one's affairs in ~** mettre de l'ordre dans sa chambre/ses affaires, mettre sa chambre/ses affaires en ordre; (*US*) **in short ~** sans délai, tout de suite; **machine out of ~** *or* **not in (working** *or* **running) ~** machine en panne *or* détraquée; **in good ~** en bon état; (*Telec*) **the line is out of ~** la ligne est en dérangement; **to be in running** *or* **working ~** marcher bien, être en bon état *or* en état de marche.

c **in ~ to do** pour faire, afin de faire; **in ~ that** afin que + *subj*, pour que + *subj*.

d (*correct procedure: also Parl*) ordre *m*. (*Parl*) ~, ~! à l'ordre!; (*Parl etc*) **to call sb to ~** rappeler qn à l'ordre; (*Parl etc*) **(on a) point of ~** (sur une) question de droit *or* de forme, (sur un) point de droit *or* de procédure; (*gen: of action, request etc*) **to be in ~** être dans les règles; **that's quite in ~** je n'y vois aucune objection; **is it in ~ to do that?** est-il permis de faire cela?; **would it be in ~ for me to speak to her?** serait-il approprié que je lui parle? (*subj*); **it's quite in ~ for him to do that** rien ne s'oppose à ce qu'il fasse ça; (*hum*) **a drink seems in ~** un verre (de quelque chose) me semble tout indiqué; **such behaviour is out of ~** cette conduite n'est pas de mise.

e (*peace, control*) ordre *m*. **to keep ~** *[police etc]* faire régner l'ordre, maintenir l'ordre; *[teacher]* faire régner la discipline; **she can't keep her class in ~** elle n'arrive pas à tenir sa classe; **keep your dog in ~!** surveillez *or* tenez votre chien!; *see* **law** *etc*.

f (*Bio*) ordre *m*; (*social position*) classe *f*; (*kind*) ordre, sorte *f*, genre *m*. (*social rank*) **the lower/higher ~s** les classes inférieures/supérieures; (*fig*) **of a high ~** de premier ordre; **~ of magnitude** ordre de grandeur; (*Brit*) **something of** *or* **in the ~ of 3 000 francs**, (*US*) **something on the ~ of 3 000 francs** quelque chose de l'ordre de 3 000 francs.

g (*Archit*) ordre *m*.

h (*society, association etc*) ordre *m*; (*fig: medal*) décoration *f*, insigne *m*. **Benedictine O~** ordre des bénédictins; (*Brit*) **the O~ of the Bath** l'ordre du Bain; (*Brit*) **the O~ of Merit** l'ordre *m* du mérite; *see* **boot[1]**, **garter** *etc*.

i (*Rel*) **(holy) ~s** ordres *mpl* (majeurs); **to be in/take (holy) ~s** être/entrer dans les ordres.

j (*command*) ordre *m*, commandement *m*, consigne *f* (*Mil*). **sealed ~s** instructions secrètes; **to obey ~s** obéir aux ordres, (*Mil*) observer *or* respecter la consigne; **to give sb ~s to do sth** ordonner à qn de faire qch; **you can't give me ~s!**, **I don't take ~s from you!** je ne suis pas à vos ordres!, ce n'est pas à vous de me donner des ordres!; **I don't take ~s from anyone** je n'ai d'ordres à recevoir de personne; **~s are ~s** la consigne c'est la consigne, les ordres sont les ordres; **that's an ~!** c'est un ordre!; **he gave the ~ for it to be done** il ordonna qu'on le fasse, il a donné (l')ordre de le faire; **on the ~s of** sur l'ordre de; **by ~ of** par ordre de; **to be under the ~s of** être sous les ordres de; **to be under ~s to do** avoir (reçu l')ordre de faire; **sorry, I'm under ~s** désolé, j'ai (reçu) des ordres; **till further ~s** jusqu'à nouvel ordre; **~ of the day** ordre du jour; (*fig*) **strikes were the ~ of the day** les grèves étaient à l'ordre du jour; (*Brit Parl*) **O~ in Council** ordonnance prise en Conseil privé, ≃ décret-loi *m*; (*Jur*) **judge's ~** ordonnance *f*; (*Jur*) **~ of bankruptcy** déclaration *f* de faillite; (*Jur*) **~ of the Court** injonction *f* de la cour; **deportation ~** arrêté *m* d'expulsion; *see* **marching, starter, tall** *etc*.

k (*Comm*) commande *f*. **made to ~** fait sur commande; **to give an ~ to sb (for sth)**, **to place an ~ with sb (for sth)** passer une commande (de qch) à qn; **we have received your ~ for ...** nous avons bien reçu votre commande de ...; **we have the shelves on ~ for you** vos étagères sont commandées; (*Comm, fig*) **to do sth to ~** faire qch sur commande; (*in café etc*) **an ~ of French fries** une portion de frites; *see* **repeat, rush[1]** *etc*.

l (*warrant, permit*) permis *m*. **~ to view** permis de visiter.

m (*Fin etc: money ~*) mandat *m*. **pay to the ~ of** payer à l'ordre de; **pay X or ~** payez X ou à son ordre; *see* **banker, postal** *etc*.

2 **comp** ►**order book** (*Comm, Ind*) carnet *m* de commandes; (*Ind*) **the company's order books were full** les carnets de commandes de la compagnie étaient complets ►**order form** (*Comm*) billet *m or* bon *m* de commande ►**order mark** (*Brit Scol*) avertissement *m* ►**Order of Service** (*Rel*) ordre *m* de cérémonie ►**order paper** (*Brit Parl*) ordre *m* du jour.

3 **vt** a (*command*) ordonner (*sb to do* à qn de faire, *that* que + *subj*), donner l'ordre (*that* que + *subj*). **he was ~ed to be quiet** on lui ordonna de se taire; **to ~ sb in/out/up** *etc* ordonner à qn d'entrer/de sortir/de monter *etc*; **to ~ a player off** renvoyer un joueur; **to ~ a regiment abroad** envoyer un régiment à l'étranger; **the regiment was ~ed to Berlin** le régiment a reçu l'ordre d'aller à Berlin.

b (*Comm*) *goods, meal* commander; *taxi* faire venir.

c (*put in ~*) *one's affairs etc* organiser, régler.

4 **vi** (*in restaurant etc*) passer sa commande.

►**order about, order around** **vt sep** commander. **he likes ordering people about** il aime commander les gens, il aime donner des ordres à droite et à gauche; **I won't be ordered about by him!** je ne suis pas à ses ordres!

ordered ['ɔːdɪd] **adj** (*also* **well ~**) = **orderly**.

ordering ['ɔːdərɪŋ] **n** (*Comm*) passation *f* de commandes.

orderliness ['ɔːdəlɪnɪs] **n** (habitudes *fpl* d')ordre *m*.

orderly ['ɔːdəlɪ] 1 **adj** *room* ordonné, en ordre; *mind* méthodique; *life* rangé, réglé; *person* qui a de l'ordre *or* de la méthode; *crowd* discipliné. **in an ~ way** avec ordre, méthodiquement, d'une façon disciplinée. 2 **n** a (*Mil*) planton *m*, ordonnance *f*. b (*Med*) garçon *m* de salle; *see* **nursing**. 3 **comp** ►**orderly officer** (*Mil*) officier *m* de service *or* de semaine ►**orderly room** (*Mil*) salle *f* de rapport.

ordinal ['ɔːdɪnl] 1 **adj** *number* ordinal. 2 **n** (nombre *m*) ordinal *m*.

ordinance ['ɔːdɪnəns] **n** ordonnance *f*, arrêté *m*.

ordinand ['ɔːdɪnænd] **n** ordinand *m*.

ordinarily ['ɔːdnrɪlɪ] **adv** ordinairement, d'habitude, normalement, d'ordinaire, généralement. **more than ~ polite** d'une politesse qui sort de l'ordinaire.

ordinary ['ɔːdnrɪ] 1 **adj** a (*usual*) ordinaire, normal, habituel, courant. **in the ~ way**, **in the ~ course of events** en temps normal, dans des circonstances normales; **in ~ use** d'usage *or* d'emploi courant; **for all ~ purposes** pour l'usage courant; **my ~ grocer's** mon épicerie habituelle; **it's not what you would call an ~ present** c'est vraiment un cadeau peu ordinaire *or* peu banal.

b (*not outstanding*) ordinaire, comme les autres; (*average*) *intelligence, knowledge, reader etc* moyen. **I'm just an ~ fellow** je suis un homme comme les autres; **~ people** gens *mpl* ordinaires *or* comme les autres.

c (*pej*) *person, meal etc* ordinaire, quelconque, médiocre.

d († *Brit Scol*) **O~ level**, († *Scot*) **O~ grade** ≃ première partie *f* du bac; (*Brit Educ*) **O~ National Certificate** ≃ brevet *m* de technicien; (*Brit Univ*) **~ degree** ≃ licence *f* libre; (*Brit Educ*) **O~ National Diploma** ≃ brevet *m* de technicien supérieur; (*Brit Navy*) **~ seaman** matelot *m* breveté; (*St Ex*) **~ share** action *f* ordinaire.

2 **n** a ordinaire *m*. **out of the ~** hors du commun, exceptionnel, qui sort de l'ordinaire; **above the ~** au-dessus du commun *or* de l'ordinaire.

b (*Rel*) **the ~ of the mass** l'ordinaire *m* de la messe.

ordination [ˌɔːdɪ'neɪʃən] **n** (*Rel*) ordination *f*.

ordnance ['ɔːdnəns] (*Mil*) 1 **n** (*guns*) (pièces *fpl* d')artillerie *f*; (*unit*) service *m* du matériel et des dépôts. 2 **comp** ►**Ordnance Corps** Service *m* du matériel ►**ordnance factory** usine *f* d'artillerie ►**Ordnance Survey** (*Brit*) service *m* cartographique de l'État; (*Brit*) **Ordnance Survey map** ≃ carte *f* d'État-Major.

Ordovician [ˌɔːdəʊ'vɪʃɪən] **adj** ordovicien.

ordure ['ɔːdjʊəʳ] **n** ordure *f*.

ore [ɔːʳ] **n** minerai *m*. **iron ~** minerai de fer.

oregano [ˌɒrɪ'gɑːnəʊ] **n** origan *m*.

Oregon ['ɒrɪgən] **n** Oregon *m*. **in ~** dans l'Oregon.

oreo ['əʊrɪəʊ] **n** (*US*) a (*food*) *gâteau sec au chocolat fourré à la vanille*. b (*‡: fig: person*) Noir(e) *m(f)* qui imite les Blancs.

Orestes [ɒ'restiːz] **n** Oreste *m*.

organ ['ɔːgən] 1 **n** a (*Mus*) orgue *m*, orgues *fpl*. **grand ~** grandes orgues; *see* **barrel, mouth** *etc*. b (*Press: mouthpiece*) organe *m*, porte-parole *m inv*. c (*Anat*) organe *m*. **vocal ~s**, **~s of speech** organes vocaux, appareil vocal; **sexual ~s** organes génitaux *or* sexuels; **male ~** sexe *m* masculin. d (*fig: instrument*) organe *m*. **the chief ~ of the administration** l'organe principal de l'administration. 2 **comp** ►**organ bank** (*Med*) banque *f* d'organes ►**organ-builder** facteur *m* d'orgue ►**organ-grinder** joueur *m*, -euse *f* d'orgue de Barbarie ►**organ loft** tribune *f* d'orgue ►**organ pipe** tuyau *m* d'orgue ►**organ screen** jubé *m* ►**organ stop** jeu *m* d'orgue.

organdie, (*US*) **organdy** ['ɔːgəndɪ] 1 **n** organdi *m*. 2 **comp** en organdi, d'organdi.

organic [ɔː'gænɪk] **adj** a (*gen*) *disease, life, substance, chemistry, law* organique; *part* fondamental. **~ being** être organisé; **~ whole** tout *m* systématique. b (*free of chemicals*) *food, product* naturel; *vegetables* biologique, cultivé sans engrais chimiques ni insecticides. **~ farming** agriculture *f* biologique, culture *f* sans engrais chimiques ni insecticides; **~ restaurant** restaurant *m* diététique.

organically [ɔː'gænɪkəlɪ] **adv** (*Bio, Physiol etc*) organiquement; (*basically*) foncièrement, fondamentalement.

organism ['ɔːgənɪzəm] **n** organisme *m* (*Bio*).

organist ['ɔːgənɪst] **n** organiste *mf*. **~ at X cathedral** titulaire *mf* des (grandes) orgues de *or* organiste à la cathédrale de X.

organization [ˌɔːgənaɪ'zeɪʃən] 1 **n** a (*gen*) organisation *f*; (*statutory body*) organisme *m*, organisation; (*society*) organisation, association *f*. **youth ~** organisation *or* organisme de jeunesse; **she belongs to several ~s** elle est membre de plusieurs organisations *or* associations; **a charitable ~** une œuvre *or* une fondation charitable; *see* **travel**.

b (*executives etc*) *[business firm, political party]* cadres *mpl*.

c (*NonC*) organisation *f*. **his work lacks ~** son travail manque d'organisation.

2 **comp** ►**organization and method** (*Comm, Admin*) organisation *f* et méthode *f* ►**organization chart** organigramme *m* ►**organization expenses** (*Fin*) frais *mpl* de premier établissement ►**organization man** (*pej*) cadre *m* qui s'identifie complètement à sa firme.

organizational [ˌɔːgənaɪ'zeɪʃənl] **adj** (*gen*) organisationnel. (*Jur, Comm*) **~ change** mutation *f* des structures.

organize ['ɔːgənaɪz] 1 **vt** a (*gen*) *meeting, scheme, course, club, visit* organiser (*for sb* pour qn). **they ~d (things) for me to go to London** ils ont fait le nécessaire pour que je me rende à Londres; **can you ~* some food for us?** est-ce que vous pouvez nous organiser de quoi manger? *or* nous arranger une collation?; **can you ~ the food for us?** est-ce que vous pouvez vous occuper de la nourriture?; **she's always**

organizing people elle n'arrête pas de dire aux gens ce qu'ils doivent faire; **to get ~d** s'organiser; *see also* **organized.** b (*Ind: into trade union*) syndiquer; *see also* **organized.** 2 vi (*Ind*) se syndiquer.

organized ['ɔːgənaɪzd] adj a *resistance, society, tour* organisé. ~ **labour** main-d'œuvre syndiquée *or* organisée en syndicats; ~ **crime** le grand banditisme. b (*methodical*) *approach etc* méthodique; *person* organisé. **he's not very** ~ il n'est pas très organisé, il ne sait pas s'organiser.

organizer ['ɔːgənaɪzəʳ] n a *[event, activity]* organisateur *m*, -trice *f*. **the ~s apologize for ...** les organisateurs vous prient de les excuser pour ... . b **to be a good/bad** ~ être un bon/mauvais organisateur. c (*for holding things*) vide-poches *m inv*.

organizing ['ɔːgənaɪzɪŋ] 1 n *[event, activity etc]* organisation *f*. **she loves** ~ elle adore organiser. 2 adj a *group, committee* (qui est) chargé de l'organisation. b (*bossy*) *person* qui n'arrête pas de dire aux autres ce qu'ils doivent faire.

organo... ['ɔːgənəʊ] pref organo... .

organza [ɔː'gænzə] n organza *m*.

orgasm ['ɔːgæzəm] n orgasme *m*.

orgasmic [ɔː'gæzmɪk] adj (*lit, Med*) orgastique, orgasmique; (**: fig*) orgasmique.

orgiastic [ˌɔːdʒɪ'æstɪk] adj orgiaque.

orgy ['ɔːdʒɪ] n (*lit, fig*) orgie *f*.

oriel ['ɔːrɪəl] n (*also* ~ **window**) (fenêtre *f* en) oriel *m*.

orient ['ɔːrɪənt] 1 n (*liter*) orient *m*, levant *m*. **the O~** l'Orient. 2 vt (*lit, fig*) orienter; *see* **oriented.**

oriental [ˌɔːrɪ'entəl] 1 adj *peoples, civilization* oriental; *carpet* d'Orient. 2 n: O~ Oriental(e) *m(f)*.

orientate ['ɔːrɪənteɪt] vt (*lit, fig*) orienter.

orientated ['ɔːrɪənteɪtɪd] adj = **oriented.**

orientation [ˌɔːrɪən'teɪʃən] n (*gen*) orientation *f*. (*US Univ*) ~ **week** semaine *f* d'accueil des étudiants.

oriented ['ɔːrɪəntɪd] adj (*often in comps*) **defence-~ budget** budget qui favorise la défense; **profit-~ economy** économie axée sur le profit; **socially ~ government spending** dépenses publiques axées sur le social; **industry-~ research** recherche conçue en fonction des besoins de l'industrie; **user-/pupil-** *etc* ~ adapté aux besoins de *or* spécialement conçu pour l'usager/l'élève *etc*; **politically** ~ orienté (politiquement *or* idéologiquement); ~ **to** *or* **towards** (*giving priority to, influenced by*) axé sur; (*specially for needs of*) conçu pour, adapté aux besoins de.

orienteering [ˌɔːrɪən'tɪərɪŋ] n (*Sport*) exercice *m* d'orientation sur le terrain.

orifice ['ɒrɪfɪs] n orifice *m*.

origami [ˌɒrɪ'gɑːmɪ] n origami *m*.

origan ['ɒrɪgən] n origan *m*.

origin ['ɒrɪdʒɪn] n (*parentage, source*) origine *f*; *[manufactured goods etc]* origine, provenance *f*. **the ~ of this lies in ...** l'origine en est ...; **to have humble ~s, to be of humble** ~ être d'origine modeste; **his family had its ~ in France** sa famille était originaire de France; **country of** ~ pays *m* d'origine.

original [ə'rɪdʒɪnl] 1 adj a (*first, earliest*) *sin* originel; *inhabitant, member* originel, premier, originaire; *purpose, suggestion, meaning* originel, initial, premier; *shape, colour* primitif; *edition* original, princeps *inv*. **he's an ~ thinker, he's got an ~ mind** c'est un esprit novateur; (*Fin, Comm*) ~ **cost** coût *m* d'acquisition; (*US Jur*) ~ **jurisdiction** juridiction *f* de première instance.
b (*not copied etc*) *painting, idea, writer* original; *play* inédit, original.
c (*unconventional*) *character, person* singulier, original, excentrique.
2 n a *[painting, language, document]* original *m*. **to read Dante in the** ~ lire Dante dans le texte.
b (*person*) original(e) *m(f)*, phénomène* *m*.

originality [əˌrɪdʒɪ'nælɪtɪ] n originalité *f*.

originally [ə'rɪdʒənəlɪ] adv a (*in the beginning*) originairement, à l'origine; (*at first*) originellement. b (*not copying*) originalement, d'une manière originale.

originate [ə'rɪdʒɪneɪt] 1 vt *[person]* être l'auteur de, être à l'origine de; *[event etc]* donner naissance à, produire, créer. **originating bank** banque *f* d'origine. 2 vi: **to ~ from** *[person]* être originaire de; *[goods]* provenir de; *[suggestion, idea]* **to ~ from sb** émaner de qn; *[stream, custom etc]* **to ~ in** prendre naissance *or* sa source dans.

origination fee [əˌrɪdʒɪ'neɪʃən'fiː] n frais *mpl* de constitution de dossier.

originator [ə'rɪdʒɪneɪtəʳ] n auteur *m*, créateur *m*, -trice *f*; *[plan etc]* initiateur *m*, -trice *f*.

oriole ['ɔːrɪəʊl] n loriot *m*; *see* **golden.**

Orion [ə'raɪən] n (*Astron*) Orion *f*; (*Myth*) Orion *m*.

Orkney Islands ['ɔːknɪˌaɪləndz] npl, **Orkneys** ['ɔːknɪz] npl Orcades *fpl*.

Orlon ['ɔːlɒn] ® 1 n Orlon *m* ®. 2 comp en Orlon.

ormer ['ɔːməʳ] n (*Zool*) ormeau *m*.

ormolu ['ɔːməʊluː] 1 n similor *m*, chrysocale *m*. 2 comp en similor, en chrysocale.

ornament ['ɔːnəmənt] 1 n a (*on building, ceiling, dress etc*) ornement *m*; (*vase etc*) objet décoratif, bibelot *m*; (*fig, liter: person, quality*) ornement (*fig, liter*). **a row of ~s on the shelf** une rangée de bibelots sur l'étagère. b (*NonC: Archit, Dress etc*) ornement *m*. **rich in** ~ richement orné. c (*Mus*) ornement *m*. 2 ['ɔːnəment] vt *style* orner, embellir (*with* de); *room, building, ceiling* décorer, ornementer (*with* de); *dress* agrémenter, orner (*with* de).

ornamental [ˌɔːnə'mentl] adj ornemental; *garden, lake* d'agrément; *design* décoratif.

ornamentation [ˌɔːnəmen'teɪʃən] n ornementation *f*, décoration *f*.

ornate [ɔː'neɪt] adj *vase* très orné; *style* très orné, fleuri.

ornately [ɔː'neɪtlɪ] adv *decorate, design* avec une profusion d'ornements; *write etc* dans un style très orné, dans un style très fleuri.

ornery* ['ɔːnərɪ] adj (*US*) (*nasty*) méchant; (*obstinate*) entêté, têtu comme un âne; (*base*) vil (*f* vile).

ornithological [ˌɔːnɪθə'lɒdʒɪkəl] adj ornithologique.

ornithologist [ˌɔːnɪ'θɒlədʒɪst] n ornithologiste *mf*, ornithologue *mf*.

ornithology [ˌɔːnɪ'θɒlədʒɪ] n ornithologie *f*.

orogeny [ɒ'rɒdʒɪnɪ] n orogénie *f*, orogénèse *f*.

orphan ['ɔːfən] 1 n orphelin(e) *m(f)*. 2 adj orphelin. 3 vt: **to be ~ed** devenir orphelin(e); **the children were ~ed by the accident** les enfants ont perdu leurs parents dans l'accident.

orphanage ['ɔːfənɪdʒ] n orphelinat *m*.

Orpheus ['ɔːfjuːs] n Orphée *m*. (*Mus*) ~ **in the Underworld** Orphée aux Enfers.

ortho... ['ɔːθəʊ] pref orth(o)... .

orthodontics [ˌɔːθəʊ'dɒntɪks] n (*NonC*) orthodontie *f*.

orthodontist [ˌɔːθəʊ'dɒntɪst] n orthodontiste *mf*.

orthodox ['ɔːθədɒks] adj (*Rel, also fig*) orthodoxe. **the O~ (Eastern) Church, the Greek O~ Church** l'Église *f* orthodoxe grecque.

orthodoxy ['ɔːθədɒksɪ] n orthodoxie *f*.

orthogonal [ɔː'θɒgənl] adj orthogonal.

orthographic(al) [ˌɔːθə'græfɪk(əl)] adj orthographique.

orthography [ɔː'θɒgrəfɪ] n orthographe *f*.

orthopaedic, (*US*) **orthopedic** [ˌɔːθəʊ'piːdɪk] adj orthopédique. ~ **surgeon** orthopédiste *mf*, chirurgien(ne) *m(f)* orthopédiste; ~ **surgery** chirurgie *f* orthopédique; ~ **bed** lit *m* très ferme (*pour la colonne vertébrale*).

orthopaedics, (*US*) **orthopedics** [ˌɔːθəʊ'piːdɪks] n (*NonC*) orthopédie *f*.

orthopaedist, (*US*) **orthopedist** [ˌɔːθəʊ'piːdɪst] n orthopédiste *mf*.

orthopaedy, (*US*) **orthopedy** ['ɔːθəʊpiːdɪ] n = **orthopaedics.**

ortolan ['ɔːtələn] n ortolan *m*.

Orwellian [ɔː'welɪən] adj (*Literat etc*) d'Orwell.

oryx ['ɒrɪks] n, pl **~es** *or* ~ oryx *m*.

OS [əʊ'es] abbr a (*Brit Naut*) (abbr of **Ordinary Seaman**) *see* **ordinary.** b (*Brit*) (abbr of **Ordnance Survey**) *see* **ordnance.** c abbr of **outsize.**

Oscar ['ɒskəʳ] n (*Cine*) oscar *m*. **~-winning** qui a remporté un oscar (*or* des oscars).

oscillate ['ɒsɪleɪt] 1 vi (*gen, Elec, Phys etc*) osciller; (*fig*) *[ideas, opinions]* fluctuer, varier; *[person]* osciller, balancer (*between* entre). 2 vt faire osciller.

oscillation [ˌɒsɪ'leɪʃən] n oscillation *f*.

oscillator ['ɒsɪleɪtəʳ] n oscillateur *m*.

oscillatory [ˌɒsɪ'leɪtərɪ] adj oscillatoire.

os coxae [ɒs'kɒksiː] n os *m* iliaque *or* coxal.

osculate ['ɒskjʊleɪt] (*hum*) 1 vi s'embrasser. 2 vt embrasser.

osier ['əʊʒəʳ] 1 n osier *m*. 2 comp *branch* d'osier; *basket* en osier, d'osier.

Osiris [əʊ'saɪrɪs] n Osiris *m*.

Oslo ['ɒzləʊ] n Oslo.

osmium ['ɒzmɪəm] n osmium *m*.

osmosis [ɒz'məʊsɪs] n (*Phys, fig*) osmose *f*. **by** ~ par osmose.

osmotic [ɒz'mɒtɪk] adj osmotique.

osprey ['ɒspreɪ] n (*Orn*) balbuzard *m* (pêcheur); (*on hat*) aigrette *f*.

osseous ['ɒsɪəs] adj a (*Anat, Zool*) osseux. b = **ossiferous.**

ossicle ['ɒsɪkl] n osselet *m*.

ossiferous [ɒ'sɪfərəs] adj ossifère.

ossification [ˌɒsɪfɪ'keɪʃən] n ossification *f*.

ossify ['ɒsɪfaɪ] (*lit, fig*) 1 vt ossifier. 2 vi s'ossifier.

ossuary ['ɒsjʊərɪ] n ossuaire *m*.

Ostend [ɒs'tend] n Ostende.

ostensible [ɒs'tensəbl] adj prétendu, feint, apparent.

ostensibly [ɒs'tensəblɪ] adv officiellement, en apparence. **he was ~ a student** il était soi-disant *or* c'était officiellement un étudiant, il était censé être étudiant; **he went out, ~ to telephone** il est sorti sous prétexte de téléphoner.

ostensive [ɒ'stensɪv] adj a (*Ling etc*) ostensif. b = **ostensible.**

ostentation [ˌɒsten'teɪʃən] n (*NonC*) ostentation *f*, étalage *m*, parade *f*.

ostentatious [ˌɒsten'teɪʃəs] adj *surroundings* prétentieux, plein d'ostentation; *person, manner* prétentieux, ostentatoire (*liter*); *dislike, concern, attempt* exagéré, ostentatoire (*liter*).

ostentatiously [ˌɒsten'teɪʃəslɪ] adv *decorate* avec ostentation; *try* d'une manière exagérée *or* ostentatoire.

osteo... ['ɒstɪəʊ] pref ostéo... .

osteoarthritis [ˈɒstɪəʊɑːˈθraɪtɪs] n ostéoarthrite *f*.
osteoblast [ˈɒstɪəʊblɑːst] n ostéoblaste *m*.
osteogenesis [ˌɒstɪəʊˈdʒenɪsɪs] n ostéogénèse *f*, ostéogénie *f*.
osteology [ˌɒstɪˈɒlədʒɪ] n ostéologie *f*.
osteomalacia [ˌɒstɪəʊməˈleɪʃɪə] n ostéomalacie *f*.
osteomyelitis [ˌɒstɪəʊmaɪɪˈlaɪtɪs] n ostéomyélite *f*.
osteopath [ˈɒstɪəpæθ] n ostéopathe *mf*.
osteopathy [ˌɒstɪˈɒpəθɪ] n ostéopathie *f*.
osteophyte [ˈɒstɪəfaɪt] n ostéophyte *m*.
osteoplasty [ˈɒstɪəplæstɪ] n ostéoplastie *f*.
osteoporosis [ˌɒstɪəʊpɔːˈrəʊsɪs] n ostéoporose *f*.
osteotomy [ˈɒstɪˈɒtəmɪ] n ostéotomie *f*.
ostler†† [ˈɒsləʳ] n (*esp Brit*) valet *m* d'écurie.
ostracism [ˈɒstrəsɪzəm] n ostracisme *m*.
ostracize [ˈɒstrəsaɪz] vt frapper d'ostracisme, mettre au ban de la société, mettre en quarantaine.
ostrich [ˈɒstrɪtʃ] n, pl ~es *or* ~ autruche *f*.
OT [əʊˈtiː] a (*Bible*) (abbr of **Old Testament**) *see* **old**. b (*Med*) (abbr of **occupational therapy**) *see* **occupational**.
OTC [ˌəʊtiːˈsiː] n (*Brit Mil*) (abbr of **Officers' Training Corps**) *see* **officer 1a**.
OTE [ˌəʊtiːˈiː] (abbr of **on target earnings**) *see* **target**.
other [ˈʌðəʳ] 1 adj autre. **the ~ one** l'autre *mf*; **the ~ 5** les 5 autres; **~ people have done it** d'autres l'ont fait; **~ people's property** la propriété d'autrui; **it always happens to ~ people** ça arrive toujours aux autres; (*fig*) **the ~ world** l'au-delà *m*, l'autre monde *m* (*see also* **4**); **the ~ day/week** l'autre jour/semaine; **come back some ~ day** revenez un autre jour; (*Mil: esp Brit*) **~ ranks** ≃ sous-officiers *mpl* et soldats *mpl*; **I wouldn't wish him ~ than he is** je ne le voudrais pas autre qu'il est, je ne souhaiterais pas qu'il soit différent; **some writer or ~ said that ...** je ne sais quel écrivain a dit que ..., un écrivain, je ne sais plus lequel, a dit que ...; **some fool or ~** un idiot quelconque; **there must be some ~ way of doing it** on doit pouvoir le faire d'une autre manière; *see* **every, hand, time, word** *etc*.
2 pron autre *mf*. **and these 5 ~s** et ces 5 autres; **there are some ~s** il y en a d'autres; **several ~s have mentioned it** plusieurs autres l'ont mentionné; **one after the ~** l'un après l'autre; **~s have spoken of him** il y en a d'autres qui ont parlé de lui; **he doesn't like hurting ~s** il n'aime pas faire de mal aux autres *or* à autrui; **some like flying, ~s prefer the train** les uns aiment prendre l'avion, les autres préfèrent le train; **some do, ~s don't** il y en a qui le font, d'autres qui ne le font pas; **one or ~ of them will come** il y en aura bien un qui viendra; **somebody or ~ suggested that ...** je ne sais qui a suggéré que ..., quelqu'un, je ne sais qui, a suggéré que ...; **that man of all ~s** cet homme entre tous; **you and no ~** vous et personne d'autre; **no ~ than** nul autre que; *see* **each, none**.
3 adv autrement. **he could not have acted ~ than he did** il n'aurait pas pu agir autrement; **I've never seen her ~ than with her husband** je ne l'ai jamais vue (autrement) qu'avec son mari; **I couldn't do ~ than come, I could do no *or* nothing ~ than come** je ne pouvais faire autrement que de venir, je ne pouvais que venir; **no one ~ than a member of the family** nul autre qu'un membre de la famille; *see* **somehow** *etc*.
4 comp ►**other-directed** (*US Psych*) conformiste ►**otherworldly** *attitude* détaché des contingences (de ce monde); *person* qui n'a pas les pieds sur terre.
otherwise [ˈʌðəwaɪz] 1 adv a (*in another way*) autrement, différemment, d'une autre manière. **I could not do ~ than agree** je ne pouvais faire autrement que de consentir; **it cannot be ~** il ne peut en être autrement; **until proved ~** jusqu'à preuve du contraire; **he was ~ engaged** il était occupé à (faire) autre chose; **except where ~ stated** sauf indication contraire; **whether sold or ~** vendu ou non; (*frm*) **should it be ~** dans le cas contraire; **Montgomery ~ (known as) Monty** Montgomery autrement (dit *or* appelé) Monty.
b (*in other respects*) autrement, à part cela. **~ it's a very good car** autrement *or* à part ça c'est une excellente voiture; **an ~ excellent essay** une dissertation par ailleurs excellente.
2 conj autrement, sans quoi, sans cela, sinon.
otiose [ˈəʊʃɪəʊs] adj (*frm*) (*idle*) oisif; (*useless*) oiseux, inutile, vain.
otitis [əʊˈtaɪtɪs] n otite *f*.
OTT* [ˌəʊtiːˈtiː] (abbr of **over the top**) *see* **top 1a**.
Ottawa [ˈɒtəwə] n (*city*) Ottawa; (*river*) Ottawa *f*, Outaouais *m*.
otter [ˈɒtəʳ] n, pl ~s *or* ~ loutre *f*; *see* **sea**.
Otto [ˈɒtəʊ] n Othon *m or* Otton *m*.
Ottoman [ˈɒtəmən] 1 adj ottoman. 2 n Ottoman(e) *m(f)*.
ottoman [ˈɒtəmən] n, pl ~s ottomane *f*.
OU [əʊˈjuː] (*Brit Educ*) (abbr of **Open University**) *see* **open**.
ouch [aʊtʃ] excl aïe!
ought¹ [ɔːt] pret ought modal aux vb a (*indicating obligation, advisability, desirability*) **I ought to do it** je devrais le faire, il faudrait *or* il faut que je le fasse; **I really ought to go and see him** je devrais bien aller le voir; **he thought he ought to tell you** il a pensé qu'il devait vous le dire; **if they behave as they ought** s'ils se conduisent comme ils le doivent, s'ils se conduisent correctement; **this ought to have been finished long ago** cela aurait dû être terminé il y a longtemps; **oughtn't you to have left by now?** est-ce que vous n'auriez pas dû déjà être parti?
b (*indicating probability*) **they ought to be arriving soon** ils devraient bientôt arriver; **he ought to have got there by now I expect** je pense qu'il est arrivé *or* qu'il a dû arriver (à l'heure qu'il est); **that ought to do** ça devrait aller; **that ought to be very enjoyable** cela devrait être très agréable.
ought² [ɔːt] n = **aught**.
ouija [ˈwiːdʒə] n: **~ board** oui-ja *m inv*.
ounce [aʊns] n once *f* (= *28,35 grammes*); (*fig: of truth etc*) grain *m*, once, gramme *m*.
our [ˈaʊəʳ] poss adj notre, *pl* nos. **~ book** notre livre *m*; **~ table** notre table *f*; **~ clothes** nos vêtements *mpl*; (*Rel*) **O~ Father/Lady** Notre Père *m*/Dame *f*; (*emph*) **OUR car** notre voiture à nous.
ours [ˈaʊəz] poss pron le nôtre, la nôtre, les nôtres. **this car is ~** cette voiture est à nous *or* nous appartient *or* est la nôtre; **a friend of ~** un de nos amis (à nous), un ami à nous*; **I think it's one of ~** je crois que c'est un des nôtres; **your house is better than ~** votre maison est mieux que la nôtre; **it's no fault of ~** ce n'est pas de notre faute (à nous); (*pej*) **that car of ~** notre fichue* voiture; **that stupid son of ~** notre idiot de fils; **the house became ~** la maison est devenue la nôtre; **no advice of ~ could prevent him** aucun conseil de notre part ne pouvait l'empêcher; (*frm*) **it is not ~ to decide** ce n'est pas à nous de décider, il ne nous appartient pas de décider; **~ is a specialized department** notre section est une section spécialisée.
ourself [ˌaʊəˈself] pers pron (*frm, liter: of royal or editorial "we"*) nous-même.
ourselves [ˌaʊəˈselvz] pers pron (*reflexive: direct and indirect*) nous; (*emphatic*) nous-mêmes; (*after prep*) nous. **we enjoyed ~** nous nous sommes bien amusés; **we said to ~** nous nous sommes dit, on s'est dit*; **we saw it ~** nous l'avons vu nous-mêmes; **we've kept 3 for ~** nous nous en sommes réservé 3; **people like ~** des gens comme nous; **we were talking amongst ~** nous discutions entre nous; **(all) by ~** tout seuls, toutes seules.
oust [aʊst] vt évincer (*sb from sth* qn de qch). **they ~ed him from the chairmanship** ils l'ont évincé de la présidence, ils l'ont forcé à démissionner; **X soon ~ed Y as the teenagers' idol** X a bientôt supplanté Y comme idole des jeunes.
out [aʊt] (*phr vb elem*) 1 adv a (*away, not inside etc*) dehors. **he's ~ in the garden** il est dans le jardin; **Paul is ~** Paul est sorti *or* n'est pas là; **he's ~ to dinner** il est sorti dîner; (*fig hum*) **he's ~ to lunch**‡ il n'est vraiment pas dans le coup; (*crazy*) il est timbré‡; **he's ~ a good deal** il sort beaucoup, il n'est pas souvent chez lui; (*in library*) **that book is ~** ce livre est sorti; **he's ~ fishing** il est (parti) à la pêche; **you should be ~ and about!** vous devriez être dehors!, ne restez donc pas enfermé!; **to be ~ and about again** être de nouveau sur pied; **to go ~** sortir; **get ~!** sortez!, dehors!; **~ you go!** sortez!, décampez!, filez!*; **can you find your own way ~?** pouvez-vous trouver la sortie *or* la porte tout seul?; (*above exit*) "~" "sortie"; **to lunch ~** déjeuner dehors *or* en ville; **to have a day ~** sortir pour la journée; **it's her evening ~** c'est sa soirée de sortie; **let's have a night ~ tonight** si on sortait ce soir?; **~ there** là-bas; **look ~ there** regardez là-bas *or* dehors, regardez là-bas dehors; **~ here** ici; **come in! — no, I like it ~ here** rentrez! — non, je suis bien dehors; **when he was ~ in Iran** lorsqu'il était en Iran; **he went ~ to China** il est parti pour la *or* en Chine; **the voyage ~** l'aller *m*; **to be ~ at sea** être en mer *or* au large; **the current carried him ~ (to sea)** le courant l'a entraîné vers le large; **the boat was 10 km ~ (to sea)** le bateau était à 10 km du rivage; **5 days ~ from Liverpool** à 5 jours (de voyage) de Liverpool; (*Sport*) **the ball is ~** le ballon est sorti; (*Tennis*) "~!" "out!", "dehors!"; *see* **come out, run out, throw out** *etc*.
b (*loudly, clearly*) **~ loud** tout haut, à haute voix; **~ with it!** vas-y, parle!, dis-le donc!, accouche!‡; **I couldn't get his name ~** je ne suis pas arrivé à prononcer *or* à sortir* son nom; *see* **shout out, speak out** *etc*.
c (*fig*) **the roses are ~** les roses sont ouvertes *or* épanouies, les rosiers sont en fleur(s); **the trees were ~** (*in leaf*) les arbres étaient verts; (*in flower*) les arbres étaient en fleur(s); **the sun was ~** il faisait (du) soleil; **the moon was ~** la lune s'était levée, il y avait clair de lune; **the stars were ~** les étoiles brillaient; **the secret is ~** le secret est connu (maintenant), le secret n'en est plus un; **wait till the news gets ~!** attends que la nouvelle soit ébruitée!; **his book is ~** son livre vient de paraître; **the tide is ~** la marée est basse; **there's a warrant ~ for his arrest** un mandat d'arrêt a été délivré contre lui; **the steelworkers are ~ (on strike)** les ouvriers des aciéries sont en grève *or* ont débrayé*; **long skirts are ~** les jupes longues sont démodées *or* ne se font plus; **the socialists are ~** les socialistes ne sont plus au pouvoir; **these trousers are ~ at the knees, the knees are ~ on these trousers** ce pantalon est troué aux genoux; (*unconscious*) **he was ~ for 10 minutes** il est resté évanoui *or* sans connaissance pendant 10 minutes; **3 gins and he's ~ cold*** 3 gins et il n'y a plus personne, 3 gins et il a son compte; **he was ~ (for the count)** (*Boxing*) il était K.-O.; (*drunk, exhausted*) il avait son compte; **before the month was (*or* is) ~** avant la fin du mois; (*in cards, games etc*) **you're ~** tu es éliminé; *see* **come out, have out, knock out** *etc*.

d (*extinguished*) *[light, fire, gas etc]* **to be ~** être éteint; **"lights ~ at 10 p.m."** "extinction des feux à 22 heures"; *see* **blow out, burn out, go out, put out** *etc.*

e (*wrong, incorrect*) **he was ~ in his calculations, his calculations were ~** il s'est trompé dans ses calculs *or* ses comptes; **you were ~ by 20 cm, you were 20 cm ~** vous vous êtes trompé *or* vous avez fait une erreur de 20 cm; **you're not far ~** tu ne te trompes pas de beaucoup, tu n'es pas loin du compte, tu n'es pas tombé loin*; **my watch is 10 minutes ~** (*fast*) ma montre avance de 10 minutes; (*slow*) ma montre retarde de 10 minutes.

f (*indicating purpose etc*) **to be ~ to do sth** être résolu à faire qch; **she was just ~ for a good time** elle ne voulait que s'amuser; **he's ~ for trouble** il cherche les ennuis; **he's ~ for all he can get** toutes les chances de s'enrichir sont bonnes pour lui; **she's ~ for** *or* **to get a husband** elle fait la chasse au mari, elle veut à tout prix se marier; **they were ~ to get him** ils avaient résolu sa perte; **to be ~ to find sth** chercher qch.

g (*phrases*) **to be worn ~** *or* **tired ~** *or* **all ~*** être épuisé *or* éreinté *or* à bout de forces; **the car was going all ~** *or* **flat ~** la voiture fonçait *or* allait à toute vitesse; **he was going all ~ to pass the exam** il travaillait d'arrache-pied *or* sans désemparer pour réussir à l'examen; (*unequivocally*) **right ~, straight ~, ~ straight*** franchement, sans détours, sans ambages; **it's the best car ~*** c'est la meilleure voiture qu'il y ait; **it's the biggest swindle ~*** c'est l'escroquerie de l'année; **he's the best footballer ~*** c'est le meilleur joueur de football du moment; **she was ~ and away the youngest** elle était de beaucoup *or* de loin la plus jeune.

2 **out of** *prep* a (*outside*) en dehors de, hors de. **he lives ~ of town** il habite en dehors de la ville; **he is ~ of town this week** il n'est pas en ville cette semaine; **they were 100 km ~ of Paris** ils étaient à 100 km de Paris; **fish cannot live ~ of water** les poissons ne peuvent vivre hors de l'eau; **to go ~ of the room** sortir de la pièce; **he went ~ of the door** il sortit (par la porte); **come ~ of there!** sortez de là!; **let's get ~ of here!** ne restons pas ici!, partons!; **he jumped ~ of bed** il sauta du lit; **~ of the window** par la fenêtre; **(get) ~ of my** *or* **the way!** écartez-vous!, poussez-vous (*see also* **5**); **you're well ~ of it** c'est une chance *or* c'est aussi bien que vous ne soyez pas *or* plus concerné *or* dans le coup*; **to feel ~ of it** se sentir en marge, se sentir de trop *or* en trop; **Paul looks rather ~ of it** Paul n'a pas l'air d'être dans le coup*; **get ~ of it!** (*: *go away*) sortez-vous de là!*; (‡: *I don't believe you*) tu charries!‡; **~ of danger** hors de danger; *see* **bound[1], place, sight, way** *etc.*

b (*cause, motive*) par. **~ of curiosity/necessity** *etc* par curiosité/nécessité *etc.*

c (*origin, source*) de; dans. **one chapter ~ of a novel** un chapitre d'un roman; **like a princess ~ of a fairy tale** comme une princesse sortie d'un conte de fée; **he read to her ~ of a book by Balzac** il lui a lu un extrait d'un livre de Balzac; **a box made ~ of onyx** une boîte en onyx; **he made the table ~ of a crate** il a fait la table avec une caisse; **carved ~ of wood** sculpté dans le bois; **to drink ~ of a glass** boire dans un verre; **they ate ~ of the same plate** ils mangeaient dans la même assiette; **to take sth ~ of a drawer** prendre qch dans un tiroir; **he copied the poem ~ of a book** il a copié le poème dans un livre; **it was like something ~ of a nightmare** on aurait dit un cauchemar, c'était comme dans un cauchemar; **she looks like something ~ of "Madame Butterfly"** on dirait qu'elle est sortie tout droit de "Madame Butterfly"; (*Horse-racing*) **Lexicon by Hercules ~ of Alphabet** Lexicon issu d'Hercule et d'Alphabet.

d (*from among*) sur. **in 9 cases ~ of 10** dans 9 cas sur 10; **one ~ of (every) 5 smokers** un fumeur sur 5.

e (*without*) sans, démuni de. **to be ~ of money** être sans *or* démuni d'argent; **we were ~ of bread** nous n'avions plus de pain; **~ of work** sans emploi, en chômage; *see* **mind, print, stock** *etc.*

3 *n* a (*) (*pretext*) excuse *f*, échappatoire *m*; (*solution*) solution *f*.

b (*US* ‡) **on the ~s with sb**‡ en bisbille* avec qn, brouillé avec qn.

c *see* **in 4a**.

4 *adj* (*in office*) **~-tray** courrier *m* départ.

5 *comp* ▸ **out-of-bounds** *place* interdit; (*US Sport*) *ball* hors jeu ▸ **out-of-date** *passport, ticket* périmé; *custom* suranné, désuet (*f* -ète); *clothes* démodé; *theory, concept* périmé, démodé; *word* vieilli ▸ **out-of-doors** = **outdoors** ▸ **out-of-pocket expenses** débours *mpl*, frais *mpl* ▸ **out-of-sight**‡ (*US fig*) formidable, terrible* ▸ **out-of-(the)-body experience** *expérience au-delà des limites du corps* ▸ **out-of-the-ordinary** *theory, approach, film, book* insolite, inclassable ▸ **out-of-the-way** (*remote*) *spot* écarté, peu fréquenté, perdu; (*unusual*) = **out-of-the-ordinary** ▸ **out-of-this-world*** (*fig*) sensationnel*, fantastique*; *see also* **out-and-out, output, outright** *etc.*

6 *vt* (*esp US: expose as a homosexual*) révéler l'homosexualité de.

outage ['aʊtɪdʒ] *n* a (*break in functioning: esp US*) interruption *f* de service; (*Elec*) coupure *f* de courant. b (*amount removed: gen*) quantité *f* enlevée; (*Cine: cut from film*) film *m* (*rejeté au montage*); (*amount lost: gen*) quantité *f* perdue; (*Comm: during transport*) déchet *m* de route *or* de freinte.

out-and-out ['aʊtəndaʊt] *adj* *believer, revolutionary, reactionary* à tous crins, à tout crin; *fool, liar, crook* fieffé, consommé, achevé; *defeat* total, écrasant; *victory, success* éclatant, retentissant.

out-and-outer* [aʊtən'daʊtər] *n* (*esp US*) jusqu'au-boutiste *mf*.

outasite‡ [aʊtə'saɪt] *adj* (*US* = *"out of sight"*) formidable, terrible*.

outback ['aʊtbæk] *n* (*Australia*) intérieur *m* du pays (*plus ou moins inculte*); (*gen*) campagne isolée *or* presque déserte, cambrousse* *f*.

outbid [aʊt'bɪd] *pret* **outbade** *or* **outbid**, *ptp* **outbidden** *or* **outbid** 1 *vt* enchérir sur. 2 *vi* surenchérir.

outbidding [aʊt'bɪdɪŋ] *n* (*Fin*) surenchères *fpl*.

outboard ['aʊtbɔːd] *adj, n*: **~ (motor)** (moteur *m*) hors-bord (*m*).

outbound ['aʊtbaʊnd] *adj* *passengers, train* en partance.

outbox [aʊt'bɒks] *vt* boxer mieux que.

outbreak ['aʊtbreɪk] *n* *[war, fighting etc]* début *m*, déclenchement *m*; *[violence]* éruption *f*; *[emotion]* débordement *m*; *[anger etc]* explosion *f*, bouffée *f*, accès *m*; *[fever, disease]* accès; *[spots]* éruption, poussée *f*; *[demonstrations]* vague *f*; *[revolt]* déclenchement *m*. **at the ~ of the disease** lorsque la maladie se déclara; **at the ~ of war** lorsque la guerre éclata; **the ~ of hostilities** l'ouverture *f* des hostilités.

outbuilding ['aʊtbɪldɪŋ] *n* dépendance *f*; (*separate*) appentis *m*, remise *f*. **the ~s** les communs *mpl*, les dépendances *fpl*.

outburst ['aʊtbɜːst] *n* *[person]* emportement *m* passager; *[anger]* explosion *f*, bouffée *f*, accès *m*; *[energy]* accès. **he was ashamed of his ~** il avait honte de l'éclat *or* de la scène qu'il venait de faire.

outcast ['aʊtkɑːst] *n* exilé(e) *m(f)*, proscrit(e) *m(f)*, banni(e) *m(f)*. **social ~** paria *m*, réprouvé(e) *m(f)*.

outclass [aʊt'klɑːs] *vt* (*gen*) surclasser, surpasser; (*Sport*) surclasser.

outcome ['aʊtkʌm] *n* *[meeting, work, discussion]* issue *f*, aboutissement *m*, résultat *m*; *[decision etc]* conséquence *f*.

outcrop ['aʊtkrɒp] (*Geol*) 1 *n* affleurement *m*. 2 [aʊt'krɒp] *vi* affleurer.

outcry ['aʊtkraɪ] *n* tollé *m* (général), huées *fpl*, protestations *fpl*. **to raise an ~ about sth** crier haro sur qch, ameuter l'opinion sur qch; **there was a general ~ against ...** un tollé général s'éleva contre ... .

outdated [aʊt'deɪtɪd] *adj* *custom* suranné, désuet (*f* -ète); *clothes* démodé; *theory, concept* périmé, démodé; *word* vieilli.

outdistance [aʊt'dɪstəns] *vt* distancer.

outdo [aʊt'duː] *pret* **outdid** [aʊt'dɪd], *ptp* **outdone** [aʊt'dʌn] *vt* surpasser, l'emporter sur, (r)enchérir sur (*sb in sth* qn en qch). **but he was not to be outdone** mais il ne serait pas dit qu'il serait vaincu *or* battu, mais il refusait de s'avouer vaincu *or* battu; **and I, not to be outdone, said that ...** et moi, pour ne pas être en reste, je dis que ... .

outdoor ['aʊtdɔːr] *adj* *activity, games* de plein air; *swimming pool* en plein air, à ciel ouvert. **~ centre** centre *m* aéré; **~ clothes** vêtements chauds (*or* imperméables *etc*); **to lead an ~ life** vivre au grand air; **he likes the ~ life** il aime la vie au grand air *or* en plein air.

outdoors ['aʊt'dɔːz] 1 *adv* (*also* **out-of-doors**) *stay, play* dehors; *live* au grand air; *sleep* dehors, à la belle étoile. 2 *n*: **the great ~** le grand air.

outer ['aʊtər] 1 *adj* *door, wrapping* extérieur (*f* -eure). **~ garments** vêtements *mpl* de dessus; **~ harbour** avant-port *m*; **~ space** espace *m* (cosmique *or* intersidéral), cosmos *m*; **the ~ suburbs** la grande banlieue. 2 *comp* ▸ **Outer Mongolia**† Mongolie-Extérieure *f* ▸ **outermost** (*furthest out*) le plus à l'extérieur, le plus en dehors; (*most isolated*) le plus écarté; **outermost parts of the earth** extrémités *fpl* de la terre.

outface [aʊt'feɪs] *vt* (*stare out*) dévisager; (*fig*) faire perdre contenance à.

outfall ['aʊtfɔːl] *n* *[river]* embouchure *f*; *[sewer]* déversoir *m*.

outfield ['aʊtfiːld] *n* (*Baseball, Cricket*) champ *m* *or* terrain *m* extérieur.

outfit ['aʊtfɪt] 1 *n* a (*clothes and equipment*) équipement *m*, attirail* *m*; (*tools*) matériel *m*, outillage *m*. **camping ~** matériel *or* équipement *or* attirail* de camping; **he wants a Red Indian ~ for Christmas** il veut une panoplie d'Indien pour Noël; **puncture repair ~** trousse *f* de réparation (de pneus).

b (*set of clothes*) tenue *f*. **travelling/skiing ~** tenue *f* de voyage/de ski; **she's got a new spring ~** elle a une nouvelle toilette de demi-saison; **did you see the ~ she was wearing?** (*in admiration*) avez-vous remarqué sa toilette?; (*pej*) avez-vous remarqué son accoutrement *or* comment elle était accoutrée?

c (*: *organization etc*) équipe* *f*. **he's not in our ~** il n'est pas de chez nous, il n'est pas un des nôtres; **when I joined this ~** quand je me suis retrouvé avec cette bande*.

2 *vt* équiper.

outfitter ['aʊtfɪtər] *n* (*Brit: also* **gents' ~**) spécialiste *mf* de confection (pour) hommes. **(gents') ~'s** maison *f* d'habillement *or* de confection pour hommes; **sports ~'s** maison de sports.

outflank [aʊt'flæŋk] *vt* (*Mil*) déborder; (*fig*) déjouer les manœuvres de.

outflow ['aʊtfləʊ] *n* *[water]* écoulement *m*, débit *m*; *[emigrants etc]* exode *m*; *[capital]* exode *m*, sortie(s) *f(pl)*.

outfox [aʊt'fɒks] *vt* se montrer plus malin (*f* -igne) que.

out-front* [aʊt'frʌnt] *adj* (*US: frank*) ouvert, droit.

outgeneral [aʊt'dʒenərəl] *vt* (*Mil*) surpasser en tactique.

outgoing ['aʊtgəʊɪŋ] 1 *adj* a *tenant, president* sortant; *train, boat, plane, mail* en partance; *tide* descendant. b (*extrovert*) *person,* *personality* ouvert. 2 npl (*Brit*) ~s dépenses *fpl*, débours *mpl*.

outgrow [aʊt'grəʊ] pret **outgrew** [aʊt'gruː], ptp **outgrown** [aʊt'grəʊn] vt *clothes* devenir trop grand pour; (*fig*) *hobby, sport* ne plus s'intéresser à (qch) en grandissant; *habit, defect* perdre *or* se défaire de (qch) en prenant de l'âge; *friends* se détacher de (qn) en grandissant; *opinion, way of life* abandonner en prenant de l'âge. **we've ~n all that now** nous avons dépassé ce stade, nous n'en sommes plus là.

outgrowth ['aʊtgrəʊθ] n (*Geol*) excroissance *f*; (*fig*) développement *m*, conséquence *f*.

outguess [aʊt'ges] vt (*esp US*) devancer, se montrer plus rapide que.

out-Herod [aʊt'herəd] vt: **to ~ Herod** dépasser Hérode en cruauté (*or* violence *or* extravagance *etc*).

outhouse ['aʊthaʊs] n a appentis *m*, remise *f*. (*gen*) **the ~s** les communs *mpl*, les dépendances *fpl*. b (*US: outdoor lavatory*) cabinets *mpl* extérieurs.

outing ['aʊtɪŋ] n sortie *f*, excursion *f*. **the school ~** la sortie annuelle de l'école; **the annual ~ to Blackpool** l'excursion annuelle à Blackpool; **let's go for an ~ tomorrow** faisons une sortie demain; **to go for an ~ in the car** partir faire une randonnée *or* un tour en voiture; **a birthday ~ to the theatre** une sortie au théâtre pour (fêter) un anniversaire.

outlandish [aʊt'lændɪʃ] adj exotique; (*pej*) étrange, bizarre, (*stronger*) barbare.

outlast [aʊt'lɑːst] vt survivre à.

outlaw ['aʊtlɔː] 1 n hors-la-loi *m*. 2 vt *person* mettre hors la loi; *activity, organisation* proscrire, déclarer illégal.

outlay ['aʊtleɪ] n (*expenses*) frais *mpl*, dépenses *fpl*, débours *mpl*; (*investment*) mise *f* de fonds. **national ~ on education** dépenses nationales pour l'éducation.

outlet ['aʊtlet] 1 n (*for water etc*) issue *f*, sortie *f*; (*US Elec*) prise *f* de courant; *[lake]* dégorgeoir *m*, déversoir *m*; *[river, stream]* embouchure *f*; *[tunnel]* sortie; (*fig*) (*for talents etc*) débouché *m*; (*for energy, emotions*) exutoire *m* (*for* à); (*Comm*) débouché; *see* **retail**. 2 comp (*Tech*) *pipe* d'échappement, d'écoulement; *valve* d'échappement.

outline ['aʊtlaɪn] 1 n a *[object]* contour *m*, configuration *f*; *[building, tree etc]* profil *m*, silhouette *f*; *[face]* profil; (*shorthand*) sténogramme *m*. **he drew the ~ of the house** il traça le contour de la maison; **to draw sth in ~** dessiner qch au trait; (*Art*) **rough ~** premier jet, ébauche *f*.

b (*plan, summary*) plan *m*; (*less exact*) esquisse *f*, idée *f*. (*main features*) **~s** grandes lignes, grands traits; **rough ~ of an article** canevas *m* d'un article; **to give the broad *or* main *or* general ~s of sth** décrire *or* esquisser qch à grands traits; **in broad ~ the plan is as follows** dans ses grandes lignes *or* en gros, le plan est le suivant; **I'll give you a quick ~ of what we mean to do** je vous donnerai un aperçu de ce que nous avons l'intention de faire; (*as title*) **"O~s of Botany"** "Éléments *mpl* de Botanique".

2 comp ▸ **outline drawing** dessin *m* au trait ▸ **outline map** tracé *m* des contours (d'un pays), carte muette ▸ **outline planning permission** (*Brit: for building*) avant-projet *m* (*valorisant le terrain*) ▸ **outline specifications** (*Comm*) devis *m* préliminaire.

3 vt a délinéer, tracer le contour de. **she ~d her eyes with a dark pencil** elle a souligné *or* dessiné le contour de ses yeux avec un crayon foncé; **the mountain was ~d against the sky** la montagne se profilait *or* se dessinait *or* se découpait sur le ciel.

b (*summarize*) *theory, plan, idea* exposer à grands traits *or* dans ses lignes générales, exposer les grandes lignes de; *book, event* faire un bref compte rendu de; *facts, details* passer brièvement en revue. **to ~ the situation** brosser un tableau *or* donner un aperçu de la situation.

outlive [aʊt'lɪv] vt a (*survive*) *person, era, war etc* survivre à. **he ~d her by 10 years** il lui a survécu de 10 ans; *[person, object, scheme]* **to have ~d one's (*or* its) usefulness** avoir fait son temps, ne plus servir à rien. b (*live down*) *disgrace etc* survivre à.

outlook ['aʊtlʊk] n a (*view*) vue *f* (*on, over* sur), perspective *f* (*on, over* de); (*fig: prospect*) perspective (d'avenir), horizon *m* (*fig*). **the ~ for June is wet** on annonce *or* prévoit de la pluie pour juin; **the economic ~** les perspectives *or* les horizons économiques; **the ~ for the wheat crop is good** la récolte de blé s'annonce bonne; **the ~ (for us) is rather rosy*** les choses se présentent *or* s'annoncent assez bien (pour nous); **it's a grim *or* bleak ~** l'horizon est sombre *or* bouché, les perspectives sont fort sombres.

b (*point of view*) attitude *f* (*on* à l'égard de), point *m* de vue (*on* sur), conception *f* (*on* de). **he has a pessimistic ~** il voit les choses en noir.

outlying ['aʊtlaɪɪŋ] adj (*peripheral*) périphérique, excentrique; (*remote*) écarté, isolé. **the ~ suburbs** la grande banlieue.

outmanoeuvre, (*US*) **outmaneuver** [ˌaʊtmə'nuːvəʳ] vt (*Mil*) dominer en manœuvrant plus habilement; (*gen*) se montrer plus habile que; (*get sb to do sth*) manipuler. **domestic car manufacturers are ~d by foreign competitors** les constructeurs automobiles du pays sont surclassés par leurs concurrents étrangers.

outmoded [aʊt'məʊdɪd] adj *custom* suranné, désuet (*f* -ète); *clothes* démodé; *theory, concept* périmé, démodé; *word* vieilli.

outnumber [aʊt'nʌmbəʳ] vt surpasser en nombre, être plus nombreux que. **we were ~ed five to one** ils étaient cinq fois plus nombreux que nous.

out-of-towner* [ˌaʊtəv'taʊnəʳ] n (*US*) étranger *m*, -ère *f* à la ville.

outpace [aʊt'peɪs] vt devancer, distancer.

outpatient ['aʊtpeɪʃənt] n malade *mf* en consultation externe. **~s (clinic *or* department)** service *m* de consultation externe.

outperform [ˌaʊtpə'fɔːm] vt *[person, machine, company]* être plus performant que; *[product]* donner de meilleurs résultats que; (*Fin, St Ex*) *[shares etc]* réaliser mieux que. **this car ~s its competitors on every score** cette voiture l'emporte sur ses concurrentes sur tous les plans.

outplay [aʊt'pleɪ] vt (*Sport*) dominer par son jeu.

outpoint [aʊt'pɔɪnt] vt (*gen*) l'emporter sur; (*in game*) avoir plus de points que.

outpost ['aʊtpəʊst] n (*Mil*) avant-poste *m*; *[firm, organization]* antenne *f*; (*fig*) avant-poste.

outpourings ['aʊtpɔːrɪŋz] npl (*fig*) épanchement(s) *m(pl)*, effusion(s) *f(pl)*.

output ['aʊtpʊt] (vb: pret, ptp **output**) 1 n a *[factory, mine, oilfield, writer]* production *f*; (*Agr*) *[land]* rendement *m*, production; *[machine, factory worker]* rendement. **~ fell/rose** le rendement *or* la production a diminué/augmenté; **this factory has an ~ of 600 radios per day** cette usine débite 600 radios par jour; (*Ind, Econ*) **gross ~** production brute.

b (*Comput*) sortie *f*, restitution *f*; (*also* **~ data**) données *fpl* de sortie.

c (*Elec*) puissance fournie *or* de sortie.

2 comp ▸ **output device** (*Comput*) unité *f* périphérique de sortie.

3 vt a (*Comput*) sortir (*to a printer* sur une imprimante).

b *[factory etc]* sortir, débiter.

4 vi (*Comput*) sortir les données *or* les informations (*to a printer* sur une imprimante).

outrage ['aʊtreɪdʒ] 1 n a (*act, event*) atrocité *f*; (*during riot etc*) acte *m* de violence; (*public scandal*) scandale *m*. **the prisoners suffered ~s at the hands of ...** les prisonniers ont été atrocement maltraités par ...; **it's an ~ against humanity** c'est un crime contre l'humanité; **an ~ against justice** un outrage à la justice; **several ~s occurred *or* were committed in the course of the night** plusieurs actes de violence ont été commis au cours de la nuit; **bomb ~** attentat *m* au plastic *or* à la bombe; **it's an ~!** c'est un scandale!

b (*emotion*) (sentiment *m* d')intense indignation *f*.

2 vt [aʊt'reɪdʒ] *morals, sense of decency* outrager, faire outrage à.

outraged ['aʊtreɪdʒd] adj *person* hors de soi, outré; *letter, tone* indigné; *dignity, pride* offensé. **to be ~ by *or* at sth** trouver qch monstrueux, être outré de *or* par qch.

outrageous [aʊt'reɪdʒəs] adj *crime, suffering* atroce, terrible, monstrueux; *conduct, action* scandaleux, monstrueux; *remark* outrageant, injurieux, (*weaker*) choquant; *sense of humour* outré, scabreux; *price* scandaleux*, exorbitant; *hat, fashion* impossible, extravagant. **it's ~!** c'est un scandale!, cela dépasse les bornes! *or* la mesure!; **it's absolutely ~ that ...** il est absolument monstrueux *or* scandaleux que ... + *subj*; **he's ~!** il dépasse les bornes!, il est impossible!

outrageously [aʊt'reɪdʒəslɪ] adv *suffer* atrocement, terriblement; *behave, speak* outrageusement, scandaleusement, (*weaker*) de façon choquante; *lie* outrageusement, effrontément; *dress* de manière ridicule *or* grotesque. **it is ~ expensive** c'est atrocement cher.

outrank [aʊt'ræŋk] vt (*Mil*) avoir un grade supérieur à.

outré ['uːtreɪ] adj outré, outrancier, qui dépasse la mesure *or* les bornes.

outrider ['aʊtˌraɪdəʳ] n (*on horseback*) cavalier *m*; (*on motorcycle*) motocycliste *mf*, motard* *m* (*faisant partie d'une escorte*). **there were 4 ~s** il y avait une escorte de 4 motocyclistes (*or* cavaliers *etc*).

outrigger ['aʊtˌrɪgəʳ] n (*Naut: all senses*) outrigger *m*.

outright [aʊt'raɪt] 1 adv (*completely*) *own* entièrement, complètement; *kill* sur le coup; *reject, refuse, deny* catégoriquement; (*forthrightly*) *say, tell* carrément, (tout) net, franchement. **the bullet killed him ~** la balle l'a tué net *or* sur le coup; **to buy sth ~** (*buy and pay immediately*) acheter qch au comptant; (*buy all of sth*) acheter qch en bloc; **he won the prize ~** il a été le gagnant incontesté du prix; **to laugh ~ at sth** rire franchement *or* ouvertement de qch.

2 ['aʊtraɪt] adj (*complete*) complet (*f* -ète), total, absolu; *sale* (*paying immediately*) au comptant; (*selling all of sth*) en bloc; *selfishness, arrogance* pur; *denial, refusal, rejection* catégorique; *explanation* franc (*f* franche); *supporter* inconditionnel. **to be an ~ opponent of sth** s'opposer totalement à qch; **the ~ winner** le gagnant incontesté.

outrival [ˌaʊt'raɪvəl] vt surpasser.

outrun [aʊt'rʌn] pret, ptp **outrun** vt *opponent, pursuer etc* distancer; (*fig*) *resources, abilities* excéder, dépasser.

outsell [ˌaʊt'sel] vt *[company]* obtenir de meilleurs résultats que; *[product]* mieux se vendre que.

outset ['aʊtset] n début *m*, commencement *m*.

outshine [aʊt'ʃaɪn] pret, ptp **outshone** vt (*fig*) éclipser, surpasser.

outside ['aʊt'saɪd] (*phr vb elem*) 1 adv (au) dehors, à l'extérieur. **go and play ~** va jouer dehors; (*Cine etc*) **we must shoot this scene ~** cette scène doit être tournée en extérieur; **the box was clean ~ but dirty inside** la boîte était propre à l'extérieur *or* au dehors mais sale à l'intérieur; (*lit, fig*) **seen from ~** vu du dehors *or* de l'extérieur; **he left**

the car ~ il a laissé la voiture dans la rue; (*at night*) il a laissé la voiture passer la nuit dehors*; **there's a man ~ asking for Paul** il y a un homme dehors qui demande Paul; **to go ~** sortir; (*on bus*) **to ride ~**† voyager sur l'impériale.

2 prep (*also* **~ of***) a (*lit*) à l'extérieur de, hors de. **~ the house** dehors, à l'extérieur de la maison, hors de la maison; **he was waiting ~ the door** il attendait à la porte; **don't go ~ the garden** ne sors pas du jardin; **the ball landed ~ this line** la balle a atterri de l'autre côté de cette ligne; **~ the harbour** au large du port.

b (*fig: beyond, apart from*) en dehors de. **~ the question** en dehors du problème; **~ the festival proper** en dehors du *or* en marge du vrai festival; **it's ~ the normal range** ceci sort de la gamme normale; **it's ~ our scheme** ça ne fait pas partie de notre projet; **that is ~ the committee's terms of reference** ceci n'est pas de la compétence de la commission; **she doesn't see anyone ~ her immediate family** elle ne voit personne en dehors de *or* hors ses proches parents.

3 n *[house, car, object]* extérieur *m*, dehors *m*; (*appearance*) aspect extérieur, apparence *f*; (*fig*) (monde *m*) extérieur. **on the ~ of** sur l'extérieur de; (*beyond*) à l'extérieur de, hors de, en dehors de; **he opened the door from the ~** il a ouvert la porte du dehors; **there's no window on to the ~** il n'y a pas de fenêtre qui donne sur l'extérieur; **the box was dirty on the ~** la boîte était sale à l'extérieur; **the ~ of the box was dirty** l'extérieur *or* le dehors de la boîte était sale; **~ in = inside out** (*see* **inside 3b**;) (*lit, fig*) **to look at sth from the ~** regarder qch de l'extérieur *or* du dehors; (*fig*) **(judging) from the ~** à en juger par les apparences; **he passed the car on the ~** (*in Britain*) il a doublé la voiture sur la droite; (*in US, Europe etc*) il a doublé la voiture sur la gauche; **at the (very) ~** (tout) au plus, au maximum.

4 adj a (*lit*) *measurements, repairs, aerial* extérieur (*f* -eure). (*in bus, plane etc*) **would you like an ~ seat or an inside one?** voulez-vous une place côté couloir ou côté fenêtre?; (*Aut*) **the ~ lane** (*in Britain*) la voie de droite; (*in US, Europe etc*) la voie de gauche; (*Rad, TV*) **~ broadcast** émission réalisée à l'extérieur; (*Rad, TV*) **~ broadcasting van** *or* **unit** car *m* de reportage; (*Telec*) **~ call/line** appel *m*/ligne *f* extérieur(e).

b (*fig*) *world, help, influence* extérieur (*f* -eure); (*maximum*) *price, figure, amount* maximum, le plus haut *or* élevé. **to get an ~ opinion** demander l'avis d'une personne indépendante *or* non intéressée; (*Scol, Univ*) **~ examiner** examinateur *m*, -trice *f* (venu(e)) de l'extérieur; (*hobbies etc*) **~ interests** passe-temps *mpl inv*; (*fig*) **there is an ~ possibility that he will come** il n'est pas impossible qu'il vienne; (*fig*) **he has an ~ chance of succeeding** il a une très faible chance de réussir.

5 comp ▸ **outside-left/-right** (*Ftbl*) ailier gauche/droit.

outsider [aʊt'saɪdəʳ] n a (*stranger*) étranger *m*, -ère *f*. **we don't want some ~ coming in and telling us what to do** nous ne voulons pas que quelqu'un d'étranger *or* du dehors *or* d'inconnu vienne nous dire ce qu'il faut faire; (*pej*) **he is an ~** il n'est pas des nôtres. b (*horse or person unlikely to win*) outsider *m*.

outsize ['aʊtsaɪz] adj (*gen*) énorme, colossal, gigantesque; *clothes* grande taille *inv*. (*Aut*) **~ load** convoi *m* exceptionnel; **~ shop** magasin *m* spécialisé dans les grandes tailles, magasin spécial grandes tailles.

outskirts ['aʊtskɜːts] npl *[town]* faubourgs *mpl*, banlieue *f*, approches *fpl*; *[forest]* orée *f*, lisière *f*, bord *m*.

outsmart* [aʊt'smɑːt] vt être *or* se montrer plus malin (*f* -igne) que.

outsourcing ['aʊtsɔːsɪŋ] n (*Ind*) approvisionnement *m* à l'extérieur. **the ~ of components** la délocalisation de la fabrication de composants.

outspend [aʊt'spend] pret, ptp **outspent** vt: **to ~ sb** dépenser plus que qn.

outspoken [aʊt'spəʊkən] adj *person, answer* franc (*f* franche), carré. **to be ~** avoir son franc-parler, ne pas mâcher ses mots.

outspokenly [aʊt'spəʊkənlɪ] adv franchement, carrément.

outspokenness [aʊt'spəʊkənnɪs] n franc-parler *m*, franchise *f*.

outspread ['aʊt'spred] adj: **~ wings** ailes *fpl* déployées.

outstanding [aʊt'stændɪŋ] 1 adj a (*exceptional*) *person* éminent, remarquable, exceptionnel; *talent, beauty* remarquable, exceptionnel, hors ligne; *detail, event* marquant, frappant, mémorable; *feature* dominant; *interest, importance* exceptionnel. b (*unfinished etc*) *business* en suspens, en souffrance, non encore réglé; *account* arriéré, impayé; *debt* impayé; *interest* à échoir; *problem* non résolu. **a lot of work is still ~** beaucoup de travail reste à faire; (*Fin, Comm*) **~ amount** montant *m* dû; (*Jur, Fin*) **~ share** action *f* en circulation; (*Jur, Fin*) **~ claims** sinistres *mpl* en cours; (*Banking*) **~ item** suspens *m*. 2 n (*Banking*) encours *m*.

outstandingly [aʊt'stændɪŋlɪ] adv remarquablement, exceptionnellement, éminemment.

outstare [ˌaʊt'stɛəʳ] vt = **stare out**.

outstation ['aʊtsteɪʃən] n (*in remote area*) poste *m* éloigné; (*Comput*) poste *m* terminal.

outstay [aʊt'steɪ] vt *person* rester plus longtemps que. **I hope I have not ~ed my welcome** j'espère que je n'ai pas abusé de votre hospitalité; (*fig*) **I know when I've ~ed my welcome** je sais reconnaître quand je deviens indésirable.

outstretched ['aʊtstretʃt] adj *body, leg* étendu; *arm* tendu; *wings* déployé. **to welcome sb with ~ arms** accueillir qn à bras ouverts.

outstrip [aʊt'strɪp] vt (*Sport, fig*) devancer.

outturn ['aʊttɜːn] n (*US*) *[factory]* production *f*; *[machine, worker]* rendement *m*.

outvote [aʊt'vəʊt] vt *person* mettre en minorité, battre. **his project was ~d** son projet a été rejeté à la majorité des voix *or* n'a pas obtenu la majorité.

outward ['aʊtwəd] 1 adv vers l'extérieur. (*Naut*) **~ bound (for/from)** en partance (pour/de). 2 adj *movement* vers l'extérieur; *ship, freight* en partance; (*fig*) *appearance etc* extérieur (*f* -eure). **~ journey** (voyage *m* d')aller *m*; **with an ~ show of pleasure** en faisant mine d'être ravi.

outwardly ['aʊtwədlɪ] adv à l'extérieur, extérieurement, du *or* au dehors; (*apparently*) en apparence. **he was ~ pleased but inwardly furious** il avait l'air content *or* il faisait mine d'être content mais il était secrètement furieux.

outwards ['aʊtwədz] adv = **outward 1**.

outweigh [aʊt'weɪ] vt (*be more important than*) (*gen*) l'emporter sur; *[figures, balance etc]* dépasser; (*compensate for*) compenser.

outwit [aʊt'wɪt] vt (*gen*) se montrer plus malin (*f* -igne) *or* spirituel que; *pursuer* dépister, semer*.

outwith [ˌaʊt'wɪθ] prep (*Scot*) = **outside 2b**.

outwork ['aʊtwɜːk] n travail *m* (fait) à domicile.

outworker ['aʊtwɜːkəʳ] n travailleur *m*, -euse *f* à domicile, ouvrier *m*, -ière *f* à domicile.

outworn [aʊt'wɔːn] adj *clothes* usé; *custom, doctrine* périmé, dépassé; *subject,* (*Ling*) *expression* rebattu, usé.

ouzo ['uːzəʊ] n ouzo *m*.

ova ['əʊvə] npl of **ovum**.

oval ['əʊvəl] 1 adj (en) ovale. 2 n ovale *m*.

ovarian [əʊ'vɛərɪən] adj ovarien.

ovariectomy [əʊˌvɛərɪ'ektəmɪ] n ovariectomie *f*.

ovariotomy [əʊˌvɛərɪ'ɒtəmɪ] n ovariotomie *f*.

ovaritis [əʊvə'raɪtɪs] n ovarite *f*.

ovary ['əʊvərɪ] n (*Anat, Bot*) ovaire *m*.

ovate ['əʊveɪt] adj ové.

ovation [əʊ'veɪʃən] n ovation *f*, acclamations *fpl*. **to give sb an ~** ovationner qn, faire une ovation à qn; *see* **standing**.

oven ['ʌvn] 1 n (*Culin*) four *m*; (*Tech*) four, étuve *f*. (*Culin*) **in the ~** au four; **in a hot ~** à four vif *or* chaud; **in a cool** *or* **slow ~** à four doux; **this room/Tangiers is (like) an ~** cette pièce/Tanger est une fournaise *or* une étuve; *see* **Dutch, gas** *etc*. 2 comp ▸ **oven glove** (*Brit*) gant isolant ▸ **ovenproof** allant au four ▸ **oven-ready** prêt à cuire ▸ **ovenware** (*NonC*) plats *mpl* allant au four.

over ['əʊvəʳ] (*phr vb elem*) 1 adv a (*above*) (par-)dessus. **this one goes ~ and that one under** celui-ci passe par-dessus *or* se met dessus et celui-là dessous; **we often see jets fly ~** nous voyons souvent des avions à réaction passer dans le ciel; **the ball went ~ into the field** le ballon est passé par-dessus la haie (*or* le mur *etc*) et il est tombé dans le champ; **children of 8 and ~** enfants à partir de 8 ans, enfants de 8 ans remplis (*Admin*); **if it is 2 metres or ~, then ...** si ça fait 2 mètres ou plus, alors ...; *see* **boil over** *etc*.

b (*across*) **~ here** ici; **~ there** là-bas; **he has gone ~ to Belgium** il est parti en Belgique; **~ in France** là-bas en France; **they're ~ from Canada** ils arrivent du Canada; **he drove us ~ to the other side of town** il nous a conduits de l'autre côté de la ville; (*Telec etc*) **~ (to you)!** à vous!; (*Telec*) **~ and out!** terminé!; (*Rad, TV*) **and now ~ to our Birmingham studio** et maintenant nous passons l'antenne à notre studio de Birmingham; **they swam ~ to us** ils sont venus vers nous (à la nage); **he went ~ to his mother's** il est passé chez sa mère; **let's ask Paul ~** si on invitait Paul à venir nous voir; **I'll be ~ at 7 o'clock** je serai là *or* je passerai à 7 heures; **we had them ~ last week** ils sont venus chez nous la semaine dernière; **when you're next ~ this way** la prochaine fois que vous passerez par ici; **they were ~ for the day** ils sont venus passer la journée; (*fig*) **he went ~ to the enemy** il est passé à l'ennemi; (*fig*) **I've gone ~ to a new brand of coffee** j'ai changé de marque de café; **~ against the wall** là-bas contre le mur; **yes, but ~ against that ...** oui, mais en contrepartie ... *or* par contre ...; *see* **cross over, hand over, win over** *etc*.

c (*everywhere*) partout. **the world ~** dans le monde entier, aux quatre coins du monde; **I looked for you all ~** je vous ai cherché partout; **they searched the house ~** ils ont cherché dans toute la maison; **covered all ~ with dust** tout couvert de poussière; **she was flour all ~, she was all ~ flour*** elle était couverte de farine, elle avait de la farine partout; **embroidered all ~** tout brodé; **he was trembling all ~** il tremblait de tous ses membres; (*fig*) **that's him all ~!** c'est bien de lui!, on le reconnaît bien là!; *see* **look over, read over** *etc*.

d (*down, round, sideways etc*) **he hit her and ~ she went** il l'a frappée et elle a basculé; **he turned the watch ~ and ~** il a retourné la montre dans tous les sens; **to turn ~ in bed** se retourner dans son lit; *see* **bend over, fall over, knock over** *etc*.

e (*again*) encore (une fois). **~ and ~ (again)** à maintes reprises, maintes et maintes fois; **he makes the same mistake ~ and ~ (again)** il n'arrête pas de faire la même erreur; **you'll have to do it ~** il faut que tu le refasses, il te faudra le refaire; **he did it 5 times ~** il l'a fait 5 fois de suite; **start all ~ (again)** recommencez au début *or* à partir du début, reprenez au commencement; **he had to count them ~ (again)** il a dû les recompter.

f (*finished*) fini. **the rain is ~** la pluie s'est arrêtée, il a cessé de pleuvoir; **the danger was ~** le danger était passé; **autumn/the war/the meeting was just ~** l'automne/la guerre/la réunion venait de finir *or* de s'achever; **after the war is ~** quand la guerre sera finie; **when this is all ~** quand tout cela sera fini *or* terminé; **it's all ~!** c'est fini!; **it's all ~ between us** tout est fini entre nous; **it's all ~ with him** (*he's finished*) il est tout à fait fini *or* fichu*, c'en est fait de lui; (*we're through*) nous avons rompu; **(all) ~ and done with** fini et bien fini.

g (*too*) trop, très. **he was not ~ pleased with himself** il n'était pas trop content de lui; **I'm not ~ glad to see him again** le revoir ne m'enchante guère; **there's not ~ much** il n'y en a pas tant que cela; **she's not ~ strong** elle n'est pas trop *or* tellement solide; **you haven't done it ~ well** vous ne l'avez pas trop *or* très bien fait; *see also* **3**.

h (*remaining*) en plus. **if there is any meat (left) ~** s'il reste de la viande; **there's nothing ~** il ne reste plus rien; **there are 3 ~** il en reste 3; **there were 2 apples each and one ~** il y avait 2 pommes pour chacun et une en plus; **four into twenty-nine goes seven and one ~** vingt-neuf divisé par quatre fait sept et il reste un; **I've got one card ~** il me reste une carte, j'ai une carte en trop; **6 metres and a bit ~** un peu plus de 6 mètres; *see* **leave over** *etc*.

2 **prep** a (*on top of*) sur, par-dessus. **he spread the blanket ~ the bed** il a étendu la couverture sur le lit; **~ it** dessus; **I spilled coffee ~ it** j'ai renversé du café dessus; **with his hat ~ one ear** le chapeau sur l'oreille; **tie a piece of paper ~ (the top of) the jar** couvrez le pot avec un morceau de papier et attachez; **she put on a cardigan ~ her blouse** elle a mis un gilet par-dessus son corsage; *see* **fall, trip** *etc*.

b (*above*) au-dessus de. **there was a lamp ~ the table** il y avait une lampe au-dessus de la table; **the water came ~ his knees** l'eau lui arrivait au-dessus du genou, l'eau lui recouvrait les genoux.

c (*across*) par-dessus; de l'autre côté de. **the house ~ the way** *or* **the road** la maison d'en face; **there is a café ~ the road** il y a un café en face; **the bridge ~ the river** le pont qui traverse la rivière; **it's just ~ the river** c'est juste de l'autre côté de la rivière; (*liter*) **from ~ the seas** de par delà les mers; **tourists from ~ the Atlantic/the Channel** touristes *mpl* d'outre-Atlantique/d'outre-Manche; **the noise came from ~ the wall** le bruit venait de l'autre côté du mur; **to look ~ the wall** regarder par-dessus le mur; **he looked ~ my shoulder** il a regardé par-dessus mon épaule; **to jump ~ a wall** sauter un mur; **he escaped ~ the border** il s'est enfui au-delà de la frontière; *see* **climb, leap** *etc*.

d (*during*) **~ the summer** au cours de l'été, pendant l'été; **~ Christmas** au cours des fêtes *or* pendant les fêtes de Noël; **he stayed ~ Christmas with us** il a passé Noël chez nous; **may I stay ~ Friday?** puis-je rester jusqu'à vendredi soir (*or* samedi)?; **~ a period of** sur une période de; **their visits were spread ~ several months** leurs visites se sont échelonnées sur une période de plusieurs mois; **~ the last few years** pendant les *or* au cours des quelques dernières années.

e (*fig*) **they were sitting ~ the fire** ils étaient assis tout près du feu; **they talked ~ a cup of coffee** ils ont bavardé (tout) en prenant *or* buvant une tasse de café; **~ the phone** au téléphone; **~ the radio** à la radio; **how long will you be ~ it?** combien de temps cela te prendra-t-il?; **he'll be a long time ~ that letter** cette lettre va lui prendre longtemps; **to be ~ sth** s'être remis de qch; **to get ~ sth** *see* **get over 2b**; **he ruled ~ the English** il a régné sur les Anglais; **you have an advantage ~ me** vous avez un avantage sur moi; **a sudden change came ~ him** il changea soudain; **what came ~ you?** qu'est-ce qui t'a pris?; **he's ~ me in the firm** il est au-dessus de moi dans la compagnie; **to pause ~ a difficulty** marquer un temps d'arrêt sur un point difficile; **they fell out ~ money** ils se sont brouillés pour une question d'argent; **an increase of 5% ~ last year's total** une augmentation de 5% par rapport au total de l'année dernière; **~ and above what he has already done for us** sans compter *or* en plus de ce qu'il a déjà fait pour nous; **yes, but ~ and above that** ... oui, mais en outre *or* par-dessus le marché ...; **Celtic were all ~ Rangers*** le Celtic a complètement dominé *or* baladé* les Rangers; **they were all ~ each other*** ils étaient pendus collés l'un à l'autre; **she was all ~ me* in her efforts to make me stay with her** elle était aux petits soins pour moi dans l'espoir de me convaincre de rester avec elle; **they were all ~ him* when he told them the news** quand il leur a annoncé la nouvelle, ils lui ont fait fête; *see* **look over, think over** *etc*.

f (*everywhere in*) **it was raining ~ Paris** il pleuvait sur Paris; **it snowed all ~ the country** il a neigé sur tout le pays; **all ~ France** partout en France; **all ~ the world** dans le monde entier, aux quatre coins du monde; **I'll show you ~ the house** je vais vous faire visiter la maison.

g (*more than*) plus de, au-dessus de. **they stayed for ~ 3 hours** ils sont restés plus de 3 heures; **she is ~ sixty** elle a plus de soixante ans, elle a passé la soixantaine; **over-18s/-21s** *etc* les plus de 18/21 *etc* ans; **women ~ 21** les femmes de plus de 21 ans; **candidates must be ~ 28 years** les candidats doivent avoir plus de 28 ans, les candidats doivent avoir 28 ans accomplis *or* révolus (*Admin, frm*); **the boat is ~ 10 metres long** le bateau a plus de 10 mètres de long; **well ~ 200** bien plus de 200; **all numbers ~ 20** tous les chiffres au-dessus de 20.

3 **pref** sur..., *e.g.* **overabundant** surabondant, trop abondant; **overabundance** surabondance *f*; *see* **overact, overdraw** *etc*.

4 **n** (*Cricket*) série *f* de six balles *or* lancées.

overact [əʊvər'ækt] **vi** (*Theat*) charger son rôle, en faire trop*.

overactive [əʊvər'æktɪv] **adj** trop actif. (*Med*) **to have an ~ thyroid** souffrir d'hyperthyroïdie *f*.

overage ['əʊvərɪdʒ] **n** (*US Comm*) excédent *m* (*de marchandises etc*).

overall [ˌəʊvər'ɔːl] 1 **adv** *view, survey, grasp* en général; *measure, paint, decorate* d'un bout à l'autre, de bout en bout. (*Sport*) **he came first ~** il a gagné le combiné. 2 ['əʊvərɔːl] **adj** *study, survey* global, d'ensemble; *width, length* total, hors tout; (*total*) total, complet (*f* -ète). (*Aut*) **~ measurements** encombrement *m*; (*Sport*) **~ placings** le classement général, le combiné. 3 ['əʊvərɔːl] **n** (*Brit*) (*woman's*) blouse *f*; (*child's*) tablier *m*, blouse; (*painter's*) blouse, sarrau *m*. (*Ind etc*) **~s** salopette *f*, combinaison *f*, bleus *mpl* (de travail).

overanxious [əʊvər'æŋkʃəs] **adj** (*worried*) trop inquiet (*f* -ète), trop anxieux; (*zealous*) trop zélé. **I'm not ~ to go** je n'ai pas trop *or* tellement envie d'y aller, je ne suis pas trop pressé d'y aller.

overarm ['əʊvərɑːm] **adv** *throw, serve* par en-dessus.

overate [əʊvər'eɪt] **pret of overeat**.

overawe [əʊvər'ɔː] **vt** *[person]* intimider, impressionner; *[sight etc]* impressionner.

overbade [əʊvə'beɪd] **pret of overbid**.

overbalance [ˌəʊvə'bæləns] 1 **vi** *[person]* perdre l'équilibre, basculer; *[object]* se renverser, basculer. 2 **vt** *object, boat* (faire) basculer, renverser; *person* faire perdre l'équilibre à.

overbearing [əʊvə'bɛərɪŋ] **adj** autoritaire, impérieux, arrogant.

overbid [əʊvə'bɪd] **pret overbid** *or* **overbade, ptp overbid** *or* **overbidden** (*at auction*) 1 **vt** enchérir sur. 2 **vi** surenchérir.

overblown [əʊvə'bləʊn] **adj** *flower* trop ouvert; *woman* plantureux; *style* ampoulé.

overboard ['əʊvəbɔːd] **adv** (*Naut*) *jump, fall, push* à la mer; *cast* par-dessus bord. **man ~!** un homme à la mer!; (*lit, fig*) **to throw ~** jeter par-dessus bord; **the crate was washed ~** la caisse a été entraînée par-dessus bord par une lame; (*fig*) **to go ~*** (*go too far*) en faire trop; **to go ~* for sth/sb** s'enthousiasmer *or* s'emballer* pour qch/qn; (*to excess*) s'enticher de qch/qn.

overbold [əʊvə'bəʊld] **adj** *person, remark* impudent; *action* trop audacieux.

overbook [əʊvə'bʊk] **vti** *[hotel, airline]* surréserver.

overbooking [əʊvə'bʊkɪŋ] **n** *[hotel, flight]* surréservation *f*, surbooking *m*.

overburden [əʊvə'bɜːdn] **vt** (*lit*) surcharger; (*fig*) surcharger, accabler (*with* de).

overburdened [əʊvə'bɜːdnd] **adj** surchargé.

overcast ['əʊvəˌkɑːst] (*vb*: **pret, ptp overcast**) 1 **adj** *sky* couvert, sombre; *weather* couvert, bouché. (*Met*) **to grow ~** se couvrir. 2 **n** (*Brit Sewing*) point *m* de surjet. 3 [ˌəʊvə'kɑːst] **vt** (*Brit Sewing*) coudre à points de surjet.

overcautious [əʊvə'kɔːʃəs] **adj** trop prudent, trop circonspect.

overcautiously [əʊvə'kɔːʃəslɪ] **adv** avec un excès de prudence *or* de circonspection.

overcautiousness [əʊvə'kɔːʃəsnɪs] **n** excès *m* de prudence *or* de circonspection.

overcharge [ˌəʊvə'tʃɑːdʒ] 1 **vt** a **to ~ sb for sth** faire payer qch trop cher à qn, faire payer un prix excessif à qn pour qch, (*in selling*) vendre qch trop cher à qn; **you were ~d** vous avez payé un prix excessif, vous avez été estampé*. b *electric circuit* surcharger. (*fig*) **speech ~d with emotion** discours débordant *or* excessivement empreint d'émotion. 2 **vi** demander un prix excessif, estamper* le client.

overcoat ['əʊvəkəʊt] **n** (*gen*) manteau *m*; (*men's*) pardessus *m*; (*soldier's*) capote *f*; (*sailor's*) caban *m*.

overcome [ˌəʊvə'kʌm] **pret overcame, ptp overcome vt** *enemy* vaincre, triompher de; *temptation* surmonter; *difficulty, obstacle* venir à bout de, franchir, surmonter; *one's rage, disgust, dislike etc* maîtriser, dominer; *opposition* triompher de. **we shall ~!** nous vaincrons!; **to be ~ by temptation/remorse/grief** succomber à la tentation/au remords/à la douleur; **sleep overcame him** il a succombé au sommeil; **~ with fear** paralysé par la peur, transi de peur; **~ with cold** transi (de froid); **she was quite ~** elle fut saisie, elle resta muette de saisissement.

overcommit [ˌəʊvəkə'mɪt] **vt**: **to be ~ted** (*financially*) avoir des charges financières excessives; (*too much work*) s'être engagé à faire trop de travail.

overcompensate [əʊvə'kɒmpənseɪt] **vi** (*Psych*) surcompenser (*for sth* qch).

overcompensation [ˌəʊvəˌkɒmpən'seɪʃən] **n** (*Psych*) surcompensation *f* (*for* de).

overcompress [əʊvəkəm'pres] **vt** surcomprimer.

overconfidence [əʊvə'kɒnfɪdəns] **n** (*assurance*) suffisance *f*, présomption *f*; (*trust*) confiance *f* aveugle (*in* en).

overconfident [əʊvə'kɒnfɪdənt] **adj** (*assured*) suffisant, présomptueux; (*trusting*) trop confiant (*in* en).

overconsumption [ˌəʊvəkən'sʌmpʃən] **n** (*Comm, Econ*) surconsommation *f*.

overcook [əʊvə'kʊk] vt trop (faire) cuire.
overcritical [əʊvə'krɪtɪkəl] adj trop critique.
overcrowded [əʊvə'kraʊdɪd] adj *room* bondé, comble; *bus* bondé; *house, town* surpeuplé; (*Scol*) *class* surchargé, pléthorique; *shelf* surchargé, encombré (*with* de). **room ~ with furniture** pièce encombrée (de meubles).
overcrowding [əʊvə'kraʊdɪŋ] n (*in housing etc*) surpeuplement *m*, entassement *m*; (*in classroom*) effectif(s) *m(pl)* surchargé(s); (*in bus etc*) encombrement *m*; (*in town, district*) surpeuplement, surpopulation *f*.
overdependence [ˌəʊvədɪ'pendəns] n dépendance excessive (*on* envers, à l'égard de).
overdependent [ˌəʊvədɪ'pendənt] adj trop dépendant (*on* de).
overdevelop [ˌəʊvədɪ'veləp] vt (*Econ*) surdévelopper.
overdeveloped [əʊvədɪ'veləpt] adj (*gen, also Phot*) trop développé; (*Econ*) surdéveloppé.
overdevelopment [ˌəʊvədɪ'veləpmənt] n (*Econ*) surdéveloppement *m*.
overdo [ˌəʊvə'du:] pret **overdid** [ˌəʊvə'dɪd], ptp **overdone** vt a (*exaggerate*) *attitude, accent* exagérer, outrer; *concern, interest* exagérer; (*eat or drink to excess*) prendre *or* consommer trop de. **don't ~ the smoking/the drink** ne fume/bois pas trop; **to ~ it, to ~ things** (*exaggerate*) exagérer; (*in description, sentiment etc*) dépasser la mesure, forcer la note*; (*go too far*) exagérer, pousser*; (*work etc too hard*) s'éreinter, se surmener, s'épuiser; **she rather overdoes the scent** elle se met un peu trop de parfum, elle y va un peu fort* avec le parfum; **she rather overdoes the loving wife*** elle fait un peu trop la petite épouse dévouée.
b (*overcook*) trop cuire, faire cuire trop longtemps.
overdone [ˌəʊvə'dʌn] 1 ptp of **overdo**. 2 adj (*exaggerated*) exagéré, excessif, outré; (*overcooked*) trop cuit.
overdose ['əʊvədəʊs] 1 n (*gen*) dose *f* excessive *or* massive *or* trop forte, surdose *f* (*of* de); (*suicide bid*) dose excessive (*etc*), overdose *f*. (*attempt suicide etc*) **to take an ~** prendre une dose massive de sédatifs (*or* barbituriques *or* drogue *etc*); **she died from an ~** elle est morte d'avoir absorbé une dose massive de barbituriques (*etc*), elle est morte d'une overdose. 2 [əʊvə'dəʊs] vi (*gen, also in suicide bid*) prendre une dose excessive (*on* de).
overdraft ['əʊvədrɑ:ft] (*Banking*) 1 n découvert *m*. **I've got an ~** mon compte est à découvert, j'ai un découvert à la banque. 2 comp ▸**overdraft facility** découvert *m* autorisé, autorisation *f* de découvert ▸**overdraft interest** intérêts *mpl* débiteurs.
overdraw [əʊvə'drɔ:] pret **overdrew**, ptp **overdrawn** (*Banking*) 1 vi mettre son compte à découvert, dépasser son crédit. 2 vt *one's account* mettre à découvert.
overdrawn [əʊvə'drɔ:n] 1 ptp of **overdraw**. 2 adj *account* à découvert. **I'm ~ *or* my account is ~ by £50** j'ai un découvert de 50 livres.
overdress ['əʊvədres] 1 n robe-chasuble *f*. 2 [əʊvə'dres] vi (*also* **to be ~ed**) s'habiller avec trop de recherche.
overdrive ['əʊvədraɪv] n (*Aut*) (vitesse *f*) surmultipliée *f*. (*Aut*) **in ~** en surmultipliée; (*fig*) **to go into ~*** mettre les bouchées doubles.
overdue [ˌəʊvə'dju:] adj *train, bus* en retard; *reform* qui tarde (à être réalisé); *acknowledgement, recognition, apology* tardif; *account* arriéré, impayé, en souffrance. **the plane is 20 minutes ~** l'avion a 20 minutes de retard; **that change is long ~** ce changement se fait attendre depuis longtemps; **she's (a week) ~** (*menstrual period*) elle est en retard (d'une semaine); (*baby*) elle a dépassé le terme (d'une semaine), elle aurait déjà dû accoucher (il y a une semaine); **the baby is (a week) ~** l'enfant aurait déjà dû naître (il y a une semaine); **my books are (a week) ~** je suis en retard (d'une semaine) pour rendre mes livres.
overeager [əʊvər'i:gə^r] adj (*gen*) trop zélé, trop empressé. **he was not ~ to leave** il n'avait pas une envie folle de partir, il n'était pas trop pressé de partir.
overeat [əʊvər'i:t] pret **overate**, ptp **overeaten** vi (*on one occasion*) trop manger; (*regularly*) trop manger, se suralimenter.
overeating [əʊvər'i:tɪŋ] n excès *mpl* de table.
overelaborate [ˌəʊvərɪ'læbərɪt] adj *design, plan* trop compliqué; *style* trop travaillé, contourné, tarabiscoté; *excuse* contourné; *dress* trop recherché.
overemphasize [əʊvər'emfəsaɪz] vt donner trop d'importance à.
overemphatic [ˌəʊvərɪm'fætɪk] adj trop catégorique.
overemployment [ˌəʊvərɪm'plɔɪmənt] n suremploi *m*.
overenthusiastic [ˌəʊvərɪnˌθu:zɪ'æstɪk] adj trop enthousiaste.
overenthusiastically [ˌəʊvərɪnˌθu:zɪ'æstɪkəlɪ] adv avec trop d'enthousiasme.
overestimate [əʊvər'estɪmeɪt] vt *price, costs, importance* surestimer; *strength* trop présumer de; *danger* exagérer.
overexcite [əʊvərɪk'saɪt] vt surexciter.
overexcited [əʊvərɪk'saɪtɪd] adj surexcité. **to get ~** (*gen*) se mettre dans un état de surexcitation, devenir surexcité; **don't get ~** ne vous excitez pas!
overexcitement [əʊvərɪk'saɪtmənt] n surexcitation *f*.
overexert [əʊvərɪg'zɜ:t] vt: **to ~ o.s.** se surmener, s'éreinter.
overexertion [əʊvərɪg'zɜ:ʃən] n surmenage *m*.
overexpose [əʊvərɪks'pəʊz] vt (*Phot*) surexposer.
overexposure [əʊvərɪks'pəʊʒə^r] n (*Phot, also fig*) surexposition *f*.
overfamiliar [əʊvəfə'mɪljə^r] adj trop familier.
overfed [əʊvə'fed] pret, ptp of **overfeed**.
overfeed [əʊvə'fi:d] 1 vt pret, ptp **overfed** suralimenter, donner trop à manger à. 2 vi se suralimenter, trop manger.
overfeeding [əʊvə'fi:dɪŋ] n suralimentation *f*.
overflew [əʊvə'flu:] pret of **overfly**.
overflow ['əʊvəfləʊ] 1 n a (*pipe, outlet*) *[bath, sink etc]* trop-plein *m*; *[canal, reservoir etc]* déversoir *m*, dégorgeoir *m*.
b (*flooding*) inondation *f*; (*excess liquid*) débordement *m*, trop-plein *m*.
c (*excess*) *[people, population]* excédent *m*; *[objects]* excédent, surplus *m*.
2 [ˌəʊvə'fləʊ] vt *container* déborder de. **the river has ~ed its banks** la rivière a débordé *or* est sortie de son lit.
3 [ˌəʊvə'fləʊ] vi a *[liquid, river etc]* déborder; (*fig*) *[people, objects]* déborder. **to fill a cup to ~ing** remplir une tasse à ras bords; **the river ~ed into the fields** la rivière a inondé les champs; **the crowd ~ed into the next room** la foule a débordé dans la pièce voisine.
b *[container]* déborder (*with* de); *[room, vehicle]* regorger (*with* de). **full to ~ing** *cup, jug* plein à ras bords *or* à déborder; *room, vehicle* plein à craquer.
c (*fig: be full of*) déborder, regorger (*with* de), abonder (*with* en). **his heart was ~ing with love** son cœur débordait d'amour; **the town was ~ing with visitors** la ville regorgeait de visiteurs; **he ~ed with suggestions** il abondait en suggestions.
4 ['əʊvəˌfləʊ] comp *pipe* d'écoulement.
overflown [əʊvə'fləʊn] ptp of **overfly**.
overfly [əʊvə'flaɪ] pret **overflew**, ptp **overflown** vt survoler.
overfull [əʊvə'fʊl] adj trop plein (*of* de).
overgenerous [əʊvə'dʒenərəs] adj *person* prodigue (*with* de); *amount, helping* excessif.
overgrown ['əʊvə'grəʊn] adj a **the path is ~ (with grass)** le chemin est envahi par l'herbe; **~ with weeds** recouvert de mauvaises herbes, envahi par les mauvaises herbes; **wall ~ with ivy/moss** mur recouvert *or* tapissé de lierre/de mousse; **the garden is quite ~** le jardin est une vraie forêt vierge *or* est complètement envahi (par la végétation). b *child* qui a trop grandi, qui a grandi trop vite. **he's just an ~ schoolboy** il a gardé une mentalité d'écolier.
overhand ['əʊvəhænd] (*US*) 1 adv a (*Sport etc*) *throw, serve* par en-dessus. b (*Sewing*) à points de surjet. 2 vt (*Sewing*) coudre à points de surjet.
overhang [ˌəʊvə'hæŋ] pret, ptp **overhung** ['əʊvə'hʌŋ] 1 vt *[rocks, balcony]* surplomber, faire saillie au-dessus de; *[mist, smoke]* planer sur; *[danger etc]* menacer. 2 vi *[cliff, balcony]* faire saillie, être en surplomb. 3 ['əʊvəˌhæŋ] n *[cliff, rock, balcony, building]* surplomb *m*.
overhanging [ˌəʊvə'hæŋɪŋ] adj *cliff, balcony, wall* en saillie, en surplomb.
overhastily [ˌəʊvə'heɪstɪlɪ] adv trop hâtivement, de façon trop précipitée.
overhasty [ˌəʊvə'heɪstɪ] adj trop précipité *or* hâtif. **to be ~ in doing sth** faire qch de façon trop précipitée; **he was ~ in his condemnation of ...** il a été trop hâtif en condamnant ... .
overhaul ['əʊvəhɔ:l] 1 n *[vehicle, machine]* révision *f*; *[ship]* radoub *m*; (*fig*) *[system, programme]* refonte *f*, remaniement *m*. 2 [ˌəʊvə'hɔ:l] vt a (*check, repair*) *vehicle, machine* réviser; *ship* radouber; (*fig*) *system, programme* refondre, remanier. b (*catch up with*) rattraper, gagner de vitesse; (*overtake*) dépasser.
overhead [ˌəʊvə'hed] 1 adv (*up above*) au-dessus (de nos têtes *etc*); (*in the sky*) dans le ciel; (*on the floor above*) (à l'étage) au-dessus, en haut. 2 ['əʊvəhed] adj a *wires, cables, railway* aérien. **~ lighting** éclairage vertical; **~ projector** rétroprojecteur *m*; **~ projection** rétroprojection *f*; (*Aut*) **~ valve** soupape *f* en tête. b (*Comm*) **~ charges *or* costs *or* expenses** frais généraux. 3 ['əʊvəhed] n (*US*) **~**, (*Brit*) **~s** frais généraux.
overhear [ˌəʊvə'hɪə^r] pret, ptp **overheard** [ˌəʊvə'hɜ:d] vt (*accidentally*) surprendre, entendre par hasard; (*deliberately*) entendre. **he was overheard to say that ...** on lui a entendu dire *or* on l'a surpris à dire que ...; **I overheard your conversation** j'ai entendu votre conversation malgré moi, j'ai surpris votre conversation.
overheat [əʊvə'hi:t] 1 vt surchauffer. 2 vi (*gen*) devenir surchauffé; *[engine, brakes]* chauffer.
overheated [əʊvə'hi:tɪd] adj *room* surchauffé; *brakes, engine* qui chauffe; *economy* en état de surchauffe. *[person, animal]* **to get ~** avoir trop chaud.
overheating [ˌəʊvə'hi:tɪŋ] n (*Econ*) surchauffe *f*.
overindulge [əʊvərɪn'dʌldʒ] 1 vi (*gen*) abuser (*in* de). **I rather ~d last night** je me suis laissé aller à faire des excès hier soir. 2 vt *person* trop gâter, satisfaire tous les caprices de; *passion, appetite* céder trop facilement à.
overindulgence [əʊvərɪn'dʌldʒəns] n indulgence *f* excessive (*of/towards sb* des/envers les caprices de qn); abus *m* (*in sth* de qch).
overindulgent [əʊvərɪn'dʌldʒənt] adj trop indulgent (*to, towards*

envers).
overinvestment [əʊvərɪn'vestmənt] **n** (*Econ*) surinvestissement *m*.
overjoyed [,əʊvə'dʒɔɪd] **adj** ravi, enchanté (*at, by* de; *to do* de faire; *that* que + *subj*), transporté de joie (*at, by* par). **I was ~ to see you** j'étais ravi *or* enchanté de vous voir; **she was ~ at the news** la nouvelle l'a transportée de joie *or* l'a mise au comble de la joie.
overkill ['əʊvəkɪl] **n** (*Mil*) (capacité *f* de) surextermination *f*. (*fig*) **that was a massive ~!*** c'était bien plus qu'il n'en fallait!
overladen [əʊvə'leɪdn] **adj** (*gen, also Elec*) surchargé.
overlaid [əʊvə'leɪd] **pret, ptp of overlay**.
overland ['əʊvəlænd] **1 adv** par voie de terre. **2 adj**: **the ~ route** l'itinéraire *m* par voie de terre (*to* pour aller à).
overlap ['əʊvəlæp] **1 n** empiètement *m*, chevauchement *m*; *[tiles]* embronchement *m*. **2** [,əʊvə'læp] **vi** (*also* **~ each other**) se recouvrir partiellement; *[teeth, boards]* se chevaucher; *[tiles]* se chevaucher, s'imbriquer (les uns dans les autres); (*fig*) se chevaucher. **his work and ours ~** son travail et le nôtre se chevauchent, son travail empiète sur le nôtre; **our holidays ~** nos vacances coïncident en partie *or* (se) chevauchent. **3** [,əʊvə'læp] **vt** *tiles, slates* enchevaucher, embroncher; *edges* dépasser, déborder de; (*fig*) empiéter sur. **to ~ each other** *see* **2**.
overlay [,əʊvə'leɪ] **pret, ptp overlaid 1 vt** (re)couvrir (*with* de). **2** ['əʊvə,leɪ] **n** revêtement *m*.
overleaf ['əʊvəli:f] **adv** au verso, au dos (de la page).
overload ['əʊvə,ləʊd] **1 n** surcharge *f*. **2** [,əʊvə'ləʊd] **vt** *circuit, truck, animal* surcharger (*with* de); *engine* surmener.
overlook [,əʊvə'lʊk] **vt a** (*have a view over*) *[house, balcony etc]* donner sur, avoir vue sur; *[window, door]* s'ouvrir sur, donner sur; *[castle etc]* dominer. **our garden is not ~ed** les voisins n'ont pas vue sur notre jardin, personne ne voit dans *or* n'a vue sur notre jardin.
b (*miss*) *fact, detail* oublier, laisser échapper; *problem, difficulty* oublier, négliger. **I ~ed that** j'ai oublié cela, cela m'a échappé; **it is easy to ~ the fact that ...** on oublie facilement que ...; **this plant is so small that it is easily ~ed** cette plante est si petite qu'il est facile de ne pas la remarquer.
c (*wink at, ignore*) *mistake etc* laisser passer, passer sur, fermer les yeux sur. **we'll ~ it this time** nous passerons là-dessus cette fois-ci, nous fermerons les yeux (pour) cette fois.
d (*supervise*) surveiller.
overlord ['əʊvəlɔ:d] **n** (*Hist*) suzerain *m*; (*leader*) chef *m* suprême. (*fig*) **the steel/coal** *etc* **~** le grand patron de la sidérurgie/des charbonnages *etc*.
overly ['əʊvəlɪ] **adv** trop.
overmanned [əʊvə'mænd] **adj** *industry etc* aux effectifs pléthoriques. **the firm is ~** la société souffre d'effectifs pléthoriques.
overmanning [əʊvə'mænɪŋ] **n** sureffectifs *mpl*, effectifs *mpl* pléthoriques.
overmuch [əʊvə'mʌtʃ] **1 adv** trop, excessivement, à l'excès. **2 adj** trop de, excessif.
overnice [əʊvə'naɪs] **adj** *person* trop pointilleux, trop scrupuleux; *distinction* trop subtil.
overnight [,əʊvə'naɪt] **1 adv** (*during the night*) (pendant) la nuit; (*until next day*) jusqu'au lendemain; (*fig: suddenly*) du jour au lendemain. **to stay ~ with sb** passer la nuit chez qn; **we drove ~** nous avons roulé toute la nuit; **will it keep ~?** est-ce que cela se gardera jusqu'à demain?; **the town had changed ~** la ville avait changé du jour au lendemain. **2** ['əʊvə,naɪt] **adj** *stay* d'une nuit; *journey* de nuit; (*fig: sudden*) soudain. **~ bag** nécessaire *m* de voyage; (*fig*) **there had been an ~ change of plans** depuis la veille au soir *or* en une nuit un changement de projets était intervenu.
overpaid [əʊvə'peɪd] **pret, ptp of overpay**.
overparticular [,əʊvəpə'tɪkjʊlə^r] **adj** *person* trop pointilleux, trop scrupuleux; *examination* trop minutieux. **not to be ~ about discipline/principles** ne pas être à cheval sur la discipline/les principes; (*don't care either way*) **I'm not ~ (about it)** ça m'est égal, je ne suis pas maniaque (sur ce point).
overpass ['əʊvəpɑ:s] **n** (*Aut*) (*gen*) pont *m* autoroutier; (*at flyover*) autopont *m*.
overpay [əʊvə'peɪ] **pret, ptp overpaid vt** *person, job* trop payer, surpayer. **he was overpaid by £5** on lui a payé 5 livres de trop.
overpayment [əʊvə'peɪmənt] **n a ~ (of wages)** surpaye *f*, rémunération *f* excessive. **b ~ (of tax)** trop-perçu *m*; **refund of ~** remboursement *m* du trop-perçu.
overplay [əʊvə'pleɪ] **vt** (*fig*) **to ~ one's hand** trop présumer de sa situation.
overpopulated [əʊvə'pɒpjʊleɪtɪd] **adj** surpeuplé.
overpopulation [əʊvəpɒpjʊ'leɪʃən] **n** surpopulation *f* (*in* dans), surpeuplement *m* (*of* de).
overpower [,əʊvə'paʊə^r] **vt** (*defeat*) vaincre, subjuguer; (*subdue physically*) dominer, maîtriser; (*fig: overwhelm*) accabler, terrasser.
overpowering [,əʊvə'paʊərɪŋ] **adj** *strength, forces* irrésistible, écrasant; *passion* irrésistible; *smell* suffocant; *heat* accablant, suffocant. **I had an ~ desire to tell him everything** j'éprouvais une envie irrésistible de tout lui dire.
overpraise [əʊvə'preɪz] **vt** faire des éloges excessifs de.
overprescribe [əʊvəprɪs'kraɪb] (*Pharm, Med*) **1 vi** prescrire trop de médicaments. **2 vt** prescrire en trop grande quantité.
overprice [əʊvə'praɪs] **vt** *goods* vendre trop cher, demander un prix excessif pour.
overpriced [əʊvə'praɪst] **adj** (*gen*) excessivement cher. **it's ~** c'est trop cher pour ce que c'est.
overprint [əʊvə'prɪnt] (*Typ*) **1 vt** surcharger. **to ~ a new price on an old price, to ~ an old price with a new price** imprimer un nouveau prix sur un vieux prix. **2** ['əʊvəprɪnt] **n** surcharge *f*.
overproduce [əʊvəprə'dju:s] **vt** (*Ind*) surproduire.
overproduction [əʊvəprə'dʌkʃən] **n** (*Ind*) surproduction *f*.
overprotect [əʊvəprə'tekt] **vt** *child* protéger excessivement, surprotéger.
overprotective [əʊvəprə'tektɪv] **adj** protecteur (*f* -trice) à l'excès.
overqualified [əʊvə'kwɒlɪfaɪd] **adj** trop qualifié.
overrate [əʊvə'reɪt] **vt** surévaluer, faire trop de cas de.
overrated [əʊvə'reɪtɪd] **adj** (*gen*) surfait, qui ne mérite pas sa réputation.
overreach [əʊvə'ri:tʃ] **1 vt**: **to ~ o.s.** (vouloir) trop entreprendre. **2 vi** *[person]* tendre le bras trop loin; (*fig*) aller trop loin.
overreact [,əʊvəri:'ækt] **vi** (*also Psych*) réagir de manière exagérée *or* excessive. **observers considered that the government had ~ed** les observateurs ont trouvé excessive la réaction gouvernementale; **she's always ~ing** elle exagère toujours, elle dramatise toujours tout.
overreaction [,əʊvəri:'ækʃən] **n** réaction exagérée *or* excessive *or* disproportionnée.
overreliance [,əʊvərɪ'laɪəns] **n** (*dependence*) dépendance *f* excessive (*on* vis-à-vis de); (*trust*) confiance *f* excessive (*on* en).
override [,əʊvə'raɪd] **pret overrode** [,əʊvə'rəʊd], **ptp overridden** [,əʊvə'rɪdn] **vt** *law, duty, sb's rights* fouler aux pieds; *order, instructions* outrepasser; *decision* annuler, casser; *opinion, objection, protests, sb's wishes, claims* passer outre à, ne pas tenir compte de; *person* passer outre aux désirs de. **this fact ~s all others** ce fait l'emporte sur tous les autres; **this ~s what we decided before** ceci annule ce que nous avions décidé auparavant.
overrider ['əʊvəraɪdə^r] **n** (*Aut: of bumper*) tampon *m* (de pare-choc).
overriding [,əʊvə'raɪdɪŋ] **adj** *importance* primordial; *factor, item* prépondérant; (*Jur*) *act, clause* dérogatoire. **his ~ desire was to leave as soon as possible** il était dominé par le désir de partir le plus vite possible.
overripe [əʊvə'raɪp] **adj** *fruit* trop mûr, blet (*f* blette); *cheese* trop fait.
overrule [,əʊvə'ru:l] **vt** *judgment, decision* annuler, casser; *claim, objection* rejeter. **he was ~d by the chairman** la décision du président a prévalu contre lui; *see* **objection**.
overrun [,əʊvə'rʌn] **pret overran** [,əʊvə'ræn], **ptp overrun 1 vt a** *[rats, weeds]* envahir, infester; *[troops, army]* se rendre maître de, occuper. **the town is overrun with tourists** la ville est envahie par les touristes *or* de touristes. **b** *line, edge etc* dépasser, aller au-delà de. (*Rail*) **to ~ a signal** brûler un signal; **the train overran the platform** le train s'est arrêté au-delà du quai; **to ~ one's time** *see* **2**. **2 vi** (*also* **~ one's time**) *[speaker]* dépasser le temps alloué (*by 10 minutes* de 10 minutes); *[programme, concert etc]* dépasser l'heure prévue (*by 10 minutes* de 10 minutes).
oversaw [əʊvə'sɔ:] **pret of oversee**.
overscrupulous [əʊvə'skru:pjʊləs] **adj** trop pointilleux, trop scrupuleux.
overseas ['əʊvə'si:z] **1 adv** outre-mer; (*abroad*) à l'étranger. **he's just back from ~** il revient ces jours-ci d'outre-mer *or* de l'étranger; **visitors from ~** visiteurs *mpl* (venus) d'outre-mer, étrangers *mpl*. **2 adj** *colony, market* d'outre-mer; *trade* extérieur (*f* -eure); *visitor* (venu) d'outre-mer, étranger; *aid* aux pays étrangers. (*Admin, Ind etc*) **he got an ~ posting** il a été détaché à l'étranger *or* outre-mer; (*Brit*) **Minister/Ministry of O~ Development** ≃ ministre *m*/ministère *m* de la Coopération; (*US*) **~ cap** calot *m*, bonnet *m* de police.
oversee [əʊvə'si:] **pret oversaw, ptp overseen vt** surveiller.
overseer ['əʊvəsi:ə^r] **n** (*in factory, on roadworks etc*) contremaître *m*, chef *m* d'équipe; (*in coalmine*) porion *m*; *[prisoners, slaves]* surveillant(e) *m(f)*.
oversell [əʊvə'sel] **pret, ptp oversold vt** (*fig*) faire trop valoir, mettre trop en avant. (*lit*) **the match/show was oversold** on a vendu plus de billets qu'il n'y avait de places pour le match/le spectacle.
oversensitive [əʊvə'sensɪtɪv] **adj** trop sensible, trop susceptible.
oversew [əʊvə'səʊ] **pret oversewed, ptp oversewed** *or* **oversewn vt** coudre à points de surjet.
oversexed* [əʊvə'sekst] **adj**: **he's ~** il ne pense qu'à ça*.
overshadow [əʊvə'ʃædəʊ] **vt** *[leaves etc]* ombrager; *[clouds]* obscurcir; (*fig*) *person, sb's achievements* éclipser.
overshoe ['əʊvəʃu:] **n** (*gen*) galoche *f*; (*of rubber*) caoutchouc *m*.
overshoot [,əʊvə'ʃu:t] **pret, ptp overshot** [,əʊvə'ʃɒt] **vt** dépasser, aller au-delà de. (*lit, fig*) **to ~ the mark** dépasser le but; **the plane overshot the runway** l'avion a dépassé la piste d'atterrissage.
oversight ['əʊvəsaɪt] **n a** (*omission*) omission *f*, oubli *m*. **by** *or* **through an ~** par mégarde, par inadvertance, par négligence; **it was an ~** c'était une erreur. **b** (*supervision*) surveillance *f*. **under the ~ of**

sous la surveillance de.

oversimplification [ˌəʊvəˌsɪmplɪfɪˈkeɪʃən] **n** simplification *f* excessive.

oversimplify [əʊvəˈsɪmplɪfaɪ] **vt** trop simplifier, simplifier à l'extrême.

oversize(d) [əʊvəˈsaɪz(d)] **adj** **a** (*too big*) trop grand; (*Scol*) *class* trop nombreux, pléthorique; *family* trop nombreux. **b** (*huge*) gigantesque, énorme.

oversleep [əʊvəˈsliːp] **pret, ptp overslept** [ˌəʊvəˈslept] **vi** dormir trop longtemps, se réveiller (trop) tard, ne pas se réveiller à temps.

oversold [əʊvəˈsəʊld] **pret, ptp of oversell.**

overspend [əʊvəˈspend] **pret, ptp overspent vt** *allowance, resources* dépenser au-dessus de *or* au-delà de. **to ~ by £10** dépenser 10 livres de trop.

overspending [əʊvəˈspendɪŋ] **n** (*gen*) dépenses *fpl* excessives; (*Econ, Admin etc*) dépassements *mpl* de crédits, dépassements budgétaires.

overspill [ˈəʊvəspɪl] (*Brit*) **1 n** excédent *m* de population. **the London ~** l'excédent de la population de Londres. **2 comp ▸ overspill town** ≃ ville *f* satellite.

overstaffed [əʊvəˈstɑːft] **adj** (*gen*) aux effectifs pléthoriques. **this office is ~** il y a un excédent de personnel dans ce service.

overstaffing [əʊvəˈstɑːfɪŋ] **n** effectifs *mpl* pléthoriques, sureffectifs *mpl*.

overstate [əʊvəˈsteɪt] **vt** exagérer.

overstatement [əʊvəˈsteɪtmənt] **n** exagération *f*.

overstay [əʊvəˈsteɪ] **vt: to ~ one's leave** (*Mil*) excéder la durée fixée de sa permission; (*gen*) excéder la durée fixée de son congé; **I hope I have not ~ed my welcome** j'espère que je n'ai pas abusé de votre hospitalité; (*fig*) **I know when I've ~ed my welcome** je sais reconnaître quand je deviens indésirable.

oversteer [ˌəʊvəˈstɪəʳ] **vi** trop braquer.

overstep [ˌəʊvəˈstep] **vt** *limits* dépasser, outrepasser. **to ~ one's authority** excéder *or* outrepasser son pouvoir; (*fig*) **to ~ the line** *or* **mark** exagérer (*fig*), dépasser la mesure.

overstocked [əʊvəˈstɒkt] **adj** *market* encombré (*with* de); *shop* approvisionné *or* fourni à l'excès (*with* en); *pond, river* surchargé de poissons; *farm* qui a un excès de cheptel.

overstrain [əʊvəˈstreɪn] **vt** *person* surmener; *heart* fatiguer; *strength* abuser de; *horse, metal* forcer; *resources, reserves* user avec excès. **to ~ o.s.** se surmener.

overstrung [əʊvəˈstrʌŋ] **adj** *piano* à cordes croisées.

overstuffed [əʊvəˈstʌft] **adj** *chair* rembourré.

oversubscribed [əʊvəsəbˈskraɪbd] **adj** (*St Ex*) sursouscrit. (*gen*) **this outing was ~** il y a eu trop d'inscriptions pour cette sortie.

overt [əʊˈvɜːt] **adj** déclaré, non déguisé.

overtake [ˌəʊvəˈteɪk] **pret overtook** [ˌəʊvəˈtʊk], **ptp overtaken** [ˌəʊvəˈteɪkən] **vt** (*catch up*) rattraper, rejoindre; (*Brit: pass*) *car* doubler, dépasser; *competitor, runner* devancer, dépasser; *[storm, night]* surprendre; *[fate]* s'abattre sur, frapper. **~n by fear** frappé d'effroi; **to be ~n by events** être dépassé par les événements; (*Brit Aut*) **"no overtaking"** "défense de doubler".

overtax [əʊvəˈtæks] **vt** **a** *sb's strength, patience* abuser de; *person* surmener. **to ~ one's strength** abuser de ses forces, se surmener. **b** (*Fin*) surimposer.

overthrow [ˌəʊvəˈθrəʊ] **pret overthrew** [ˌəʊvəˈθruː], **ptp overthrown** [ˌəʊvəˈθrəʊn] **1 vt** *enemy, country, empire* vaincre (définitivement); *dictator, government, system* renverser. **2** [ˈəʊvəθrəʊ] **n** *[enemy etc]* défaite *f*; *[empire, government etc]* chute *f*, renversement *m*.

overtime [ˈəʊvətaɪm] **1 n** **a** (*at work*) heures *fpl* supplémentaires. **I am on ~, I'm doing** *or* **working ~** je fais des heures supplémentaires; **£300 per week with ~** 300 livres par semaine heures supplémentaires comprises; **to work ~** faire des heures supplémentaires; (*fig*) **his conscience was working ~** sa conscience le travaillait sérieusement*; (*fig*) **we shall have to work ~ to regain the advantage we have lost** il nous faudra mettre les bouchées doubles pour reprendre l'avantage perdu. **b** (*US Sport*) prolongation *f*. **2 comp ▸ overtime pay** (rémunération *f* pour) heures *fpl* supplémentaires **▸ overtime work(ing)** heures *fpl* supplémentaires.

overtly [əʊˈvɜːtlɪ] **adv** ouvertement.

overtone [ˈəʊvətəʊn] **n** (*Mus*) harmonique *m or f*; (*fig*) note *f*, accent *m*, sous-entendu *m*. **there were ~s** *or* **there was an ~ of hostility in his voice** on sentait une note *or* des accents d'hostilité dans sa voix; **to have political ~s** *[speech]* avoir des sous-entendus politiques; *[visit]* avoir des implications politiques.

overtrick [ˈəʊvətrɪk] **n** (*Bridge*) levée *f* de mieux.

overtrump [əʊvəˈtrʌmp] **vt** (*Cards*) surcouper.

overture [ˈəʊvətjʊəʳ] **n** (*Mus*) ouverture *f*; (*fig*) ouverture, avance *f*. **The 1812 O~** l'Ouverture solennelle; **to make ~s to sb** faire des ouvertures à qn; **peace ~s** ouvertures de paix; **friendly ~s** avances amicales.

overturn [ˌəʊvəˈtɜːn] **1 vt** *car, chair* renverser; *boat* faire chavirer *or* capoter; (*fig*) *government, plans* renverser; (*fig*) *decision, judgement*annuler. **2 vi** *[chair]* se renverser; *[car, plane]* se retourner, capoter; *[railway coach]* se retourner, verser; *[boat]* chavirer, capoter.

overtype [əʊvəˈtaɪp] **vt** taper par-dessus.

overuse [əʊvəˈjuːz] **vt** abuser de.

overvalue [əʊvəˈvæljuː] **vt** (*gen*) surestimer; (*Econ*) *currency* surévaluer.

overview [ˈəʊvəvjuː] **n** (*lit*) vue *f* d'ensemble, panorama *m*; (*fig: of situation etc*) vue d'ensemble.

overweening [ˌəʊvəˈwiːnɪŋ] **adj** *person* outrecuidant; *pride, ambition, self-confidence* démesuré.

overweight [ˌəʊvəˈweɪt] **1 adj: to be ~** *[person]* peser trop, être trop gros, avoir des kilos en trop; *[suitcase etc]* peser trop lourd, être en excès du poids réglementaire; **your luggage is ~** vous avez un excédent de bagages; **to be 5 kilos ~** peser 5 kilos de trop. **2** [ˈəʊvəˌweɪt] **n** poids *m* en excès; *[person]* embonpoint *m*.

overwhelm [ˌəʊvəˈwelm] **vt** *[flood, waves, sea]* submerger, engloutir; *[earth, lava, avalanche]* engloutir, ensevelir; *one's enemy, opponent, other team* écraser; *[emotions]* accabler, submerger; *[misfortunes]* atterrer, accabler; *[shame, praise, kindness]* confondre, rendre confus. **to ~ sb with questions** accabler qn de questions; **to ~ sb with favours** combler qn de faveurs; **I am ~ed by his kindness** je suis tout confus de sa bonté; **to be ~ed (with joy)** être au comble de la joie; **to be ~ed (with grief)** être accablé (par la douleur); **to be ~ed with work** être débordé *or* accablé *or* submergé de travail; **we have been ~ed with offers of help** nous avons été submergés *or* inondés d'offres d'aide; **Venice quite ~ed me** Venise m'a bouleversé.

overwhelming [ˌəʊvəˈwelmɪŋ] **adj** *victory, majority, defeat* écrasant; *desire, power, pressure* irrésistible; *misfortune, sorrow, heat* accablant; *bad news* affligeant, atterrant; *good news* extrêmement réjouissant; *welcome, reception* extrêmement chaleureux. **one's ~ impression is of heat** l'impression dominante est celle de la chaleur, on est avant tout saisi par la chaleur.

overwhelmingly [ˌəʊvəˈwelmɪŋlɪ] **adv** *win, defeat* d'une manière écrasante *or* accablante; *vote, accept, reject* en masse. **he was ~ polite** il était d'une politesse embarrassante.

overwork [ˌəʊvəˈwɜːk] **1 n** surmenage *m*. **to be ill from ~** être malade d'avoir trop travaillé *or* de s'être surmené. **2 vt** *person* surmener, surcharger de travail; *horse* forcer; *word, concept* utiliser de façon excessive, mettre à toutes les sauces*. **to ~ o.s.** se surmener; (*iro*) **he did not ~ himself** il ne s'est pas fatigué *or* foulé* *or* cassé*. **3 vi** trop travailler, se surmener.

overwrite [ˌəʊvəˈraɪt] **vt** (*Comput*) écraser, recouvrir.

overwrought [əʊvəˈrɔːt] **adj** excédé, à bout.

overzealous [əʊvəˈzeləs] **adj** trop zélé. **to be ~** faire du zèle, faire de l'excès de zèle.

Ovid [ˈɒvɪd] **n** Ovide *m*.

oviduct [ˈəʊvɪdʌkt] **n** oviducte *m*.

oviform [ˈəʊvɪfɔːm] **adj** oviforme.

ovine [ˈəʊvaɪn] **adj** ovin.

oviparous [əʊˈvɪpərəs] **adj** ovipare.

ovoid [ˈəʊvɔɪd] **1 adj** ovoïde. **2 n** forme *f* ovoïde.

ovulate [ˈɒvjʊleɪt] **vi** ovuler.

ovulation [ˌɒvjʊˈleɪʃən] **n** ovulation *f*.

ovule [ˈɒvjuːl] **n** (*Bot, Zool*) ovule *m*.

ovum [ˈəʊvəm] **n, pl ova** (*Bio*) ovule *m*.

ow [aʊ] **excl = ouch.**

owe [əʊ] **vt** **a** *money etc* devoir (*to sb* à qn). **he ~s me £5** il me doit 5 livres; **I'll ~ it to you** je vous le devrai; **I still ~ him for the meal** je lui dois toujours le (prix du) repas; **I ~ you a lunch** je vous dois un déjeuner.

b (*fig*) *respect, obedience, one's life etc* devoir (*to sb* à qn). **to ~ sb a grudge** garder rancune à qn, en vouloir à qn (*for* de); **I ~ you thanks for ...** je ne vous ai pas encore remercié pour ... (*or* de ...); **you ~ him nothing** vous ne lui devez rien, vous ne lui êtes redevable de rien; **he ~s his talent to his father** il tient son talent de son père; **he ~s his failure to his own carelessness** il doit son échec à sa propre négligence; (*frm*) **to what do I ~ the honour of ...?** qu'est-ce qui me vaut l'honneur de ...? (*frm*); **they ~ it to you that they succeeded** ils vous doivent leur succès *or* d'avoir réussi, c'est grâce à vous qu'ils ont réussi; **I ~ it to him to do that** je lui dois (bien) de faire cela; **you ~ it to yourself to make a success of it** vous vous devez de réussir.

owing [ˈəʊɪŋ] **1 adj** dû. **the amount ~ on the house** ce qui reste dû sur le prix de la maison; **a lot of money is ~ to me** on me doit beaucoup d'argent; **the money still ~ to me** la somme qu'on me doit encore, la somme qui m'est redue (*Comm*). **2 owing to prep** à cause de, par suite de, en raison de, vu.

owl [aʊl] **n** hibou *m*, chouette *f*. (*fig: person*) **a wise old ~** un vieux hibou; *see* **barn** *etc*.

owlet [ˈaʊlɪt] **n** jeune hibou *m or* chouette *f*.

owlish [ˈaʊlɪʃ] **adj** *appearance* de hibou. **he gave me an ~ stare** il m'a regardé fixement comme un hibou.

owlishly [ˈaʊlɪʃlɪ] **adv** *look, stare* (fixement) comme un hibou.

own [əʊn] **1 adj** propre (*before n*). **his ~ car** sa propre voiture, sa voiture à lui; **this is my ~ book** ce livre est à moi *or* m'appartient; **it's my very ~ book** c'est mon livre à moi; **I saw it with my ~ eyes** je l'ai vu de mes propres yeux; **but your ~ brother said so** mais votre propre frère l'a dit; **all my ~ work!** c'est moi qui ai fait tout (le travail) moi-même!; **it was his ~ idea** c'était son idée à lui, l'idée venait de lui; **he does his ~ cooking** il fait sa cuisine lui-même; **the house has its ~ garage** la maison a son garage particulier; **my ~ one** mon chéri, ma chérie; (*in house-selling*) **"~ garden"** "jardin privatif"; **~ goal** (*Ftbl*) but *m* (*marqué contre son propre camp*); (*fig*) *action qui se retourne contre soi;* **he scored an ~ goal** (*Ftbl*) il a marqué un but contre son propre camp; (*fig*) il a ramassé une pelle*, ça a fait boomerang*; (*fig*) **to do one's ~ thing*** s'éclater‡, prendre son pied‡; *see* **accord, sake[1], sweet, thing** *etc.*

2 comp ▸**own-brand, own-label:** (*Comm*) **their own-brand** *or* **own-label peas** *etc* leur propre marque *f* de petits pois *etc.*

3 pron a **that's my ~** c'est à moi, c'est le mien; **those are his ~** ceux-là sont à lui, ceux-là sont les siens; **my time is my ~** je suis maître *or* libre de mon temps; **it's all my ~** c'est tout à moi; **a style all his ~** un style bien à lui; **it has a charm all (of) its ~** *or* **of its ~** cela possède un charme tout particulier *or* qui lui est propre; **for reasons of his ~** pour des raisons qui lui étaient propres *or* particulières, pour des raisons personnelles; **a copy of your ~** votre propre exemplaire; **can I have it for my very ~?** puis-je l'avoir pour moi tout seul?; **it's my very ~** c'est à moi tout seul; **a house of your very ~** une maison bien à vous; **she wants a room of her ~** elle veut sa propre chambre *or* sa chambre à elle; **I have money of my ~** j'ai de l'argent à moi *or* des ressources personnelles; **he gave me one of his ~** il m'a donné un des siens, il m'en a donné un qui lui appartenait; **she made the role her ~** elle est désormais à jamais indissociable du personnage.

b (*phrases*) **to be on one's ~** être tout seul; **to look after one's ~** s'occuper des siens; **did you do it (all) on your ~?** est-ce que vous l'avez fait tout seul? *or* sans aucune aide?; **if I can get him on his ~** si je réussis à le voir seul à seul; **each to his ~** chacun ses goûts; (*fig*) **you're on your ~ now!** à toi de jouer (maintenant)!; **he's got nothing to call his ~** *or* **nothing that he can call his ~** il n'a rien à lui, il n'a rien qui lui appartienne réellement; **I'm so busy I can scarcely call my time my ~** je suis si pris que je n'ai pas de temps à moi; (*fig*) **to come into one's ~** réaliser sa destinée, trouver sa justification; **to get one's ~ back (on sb for sth)** prendre sa revanche (sur qn de qch); *see* **hold 3b.**

4 vt a (*possess*) (*gen*) posséder; (*more formally, also Admin: sth imposing or expensive*) être (le *or* la) propriétaire de. **he ~s 2 tractors** il possède 2 tracteurs; **he ~s 3 houses/3 newspapers** il est le propriétaire de 3 maisons/3 journaux; **who ~s this pen/house/paper?** à qui appartient ce stylo/cette maison/ce journal?; **he looks as if he ~s the place*** on dirait qu'il est chez lui.

b (*acknowledge*) avouer, reconnaître (*that* que). **I ~ it** je le reconnais, je l'avoue; **he ~ed his mistake** il a reconnu *or* avoué son erreur; **he ~ed himself defeated** il s'est avoué vaincu; **he ~ed the child as his** il a reconnu l'enfant.

5 vi: **to ~ to a mistake** avouer *or* reconnaître avoir commis une erreur; **he ~ed to debts of £750** il a avoué *or* reconnu avoir 750 livres de dettes; **he ~ed to having done it** il a avoué l'avoir fait *or* qu'il l'avait fait.

▸**own up** vi avouer, confesser, faire des aveux. **to own up to sth** admettre qch; **he owned up to having stolen it** il a avoué *or* confessé l'avoir volé *or* qu'il l'avait volé; **come on, own up!** allons, avoue!

owner ['əʊnər] 1 n (*gen*) propriétaire *mf*; (*Jur: in house-building*) maître *m* d'ouvrage. **as ~s of this dictionary know, ...** comme les possesseurs de ce dictionnaire le savent, ...; **will the ~ of the dictionary which was left in the office please ...** le propriétaire du dictionnaire trouvé au bureau est prié de ...; **all dog ~s will agree that ...** tous ceux qui ont un chien conviendront que ...; **who is the ~ of this book?** à qui appartient ce livre?; **he is the proud ~ of ...** il est l'heureux propriétaire de ...; **the ~ of car number ...** le propriétaire de la voiture immatriculée ...; (*Comm*) **at ~'s risk** aux risques du client; *see* **land** *etc.*

2 comp ▸**owner-driver** conducteur *m* propriétaire ▸**owner-occupied house** maison occupée par son propriétaire ▸**owner-occupier** occupant *m* propriétaire.

ownerless ['əʊnəlɪs] adj sans propriétaire.

ownership ['əʊnəʃɪp] n possession *f*. (*Comm*) **"under new ~"** "changement de propriétaire"; **under his ~ business looked up** lui propriétaire, le commerce a repris; **his ~ of the vehicle was not in dispute** on ne lui contestait pas la propriété du véhicule; **to establish ~ of the estate** faire établir un droit de propriété au domaine.

ownsome* ['əʊnsəm] n, **owny-o** ['əʊnɪəʊ] n (*hum*) **on one's ~** tout seul.

owt [aʊt] n (*Brit dial*) quelque chose.

ox [ɒks] pl **oxen** 1 n bœuf *m*. **as strong as an ~** fort comme un bœuf; (*pej*) **he's a big ~*** c'est un gros balourd. 2 comp ▸**oxblood** (*colour*) rouge foncé (*m*) *inv* ▸**oxbow** (*in river*) méandre *m*; **oxbow lake** bras mort ▸**oxcart** char *m* à bœufs ▸**oxeye daisy** marguerite *f* ▸**oxhide** cuir *m* de bœuf ▸**oxtail** queue *f* de bœuf; **oxtail soup** soupe *f* à la queue de bœuf.

oxalic [ɒk'sælɪk] adj oxalique.

Oxbridge ['ɒksbrɪdʒ] (*Brit*) 1 n *l'université d'Oxford ou de Cambridge (ou les deux).* 2 comp *education* à l'université d'Oxford ou de Cambridge; *accent, attitude* typique des universitaires *or* des anciens d'Oxford ou de Cambridge.

oxen ['ɒksən] npl of **ox.**

Oxfam ['ɒksfæm] (*Brit*) (abbr of **Oxford Committee for Famine Relief**) *œuvre de secours contre la faim.*

Oxford ['ɒksfəd] n Oxford. (*Rel: Brit*) **the ~ Movement** le Mouvement d'Oxford.

oxidase ['ɒksɪdeɪs] n oxydase *f*.

oxidation [,ɒksɪ'deɪʃən] n (*Chem*) oxydation *f*, combustion *f*; (*Metal*) calcination *f*.

oxide ['ɒksaɪd] n oxyde *m*.

oxidize ['ɒksɪdaɪz] 1 vt oxyder. 2 vi s'oxyder.

Oxon. ['ɒksən] (*Brit*) (abbr of **Oxoniensis**) d'Oxford.

Oxonian [ɒk'səʊnɪən] 1 adj oxonien, oxfordien. 2 n Oxonien(ne) *m(f)*, Oxfordien(ne) *m(f)*.

oxter ['ɒkstər] n (*Scot*) aisselle *f*.

oxyacetylene ['ɒksɪə'setɪliːn] adj oxyacétylénique. **~ burner** *or* **lamp** *or* **torch** chalumeau *m* oxyacétylénique; **~ welding** soudure *f* (au chalumeau) oxyacétylénique.

oxygen ['ɒksɪdʒən] 1 n oxygène *m*. 2 comp ▸**oxygen bottle, oxygen cylinder** bouteille *f* d'oxygène ▸**oxygen mask** masque *m* à oxygène ▸**oxygen tank** ballon *m* d'oxygène ▸**oxygen tent** tente *f* à oxygène.

oxygenate ['ɒksɪdʒəneɪt] vt oxygéner.

oxygenation [,ɒksɪdʒə'neɪʃən] n oxygénation *f*.

oxymoron [,ɒksɪ'mɔːrɒn] n, pl **oxymora** [,ɒksɪ'mɔːrə] oxymore *m*.

oyez [əʊ'jez] excl oyez! (*cri du crieur public ou d'un huissier*).

oyster ['ɔɪstər] 1 n huître *f*. (*fig*) **the world is his ~** le monde est à lui; (*fig*) **to shut up like an ~*** (en) rester muet comme une carpe. 2 comp *industry* ostréicole, huîtrier; *knife* à huître ▸**oyster bed** banc *m* d'huîtres, huîtrière *f* ▸**oystercatcher** (*Orn*) huîtrier *m* ▸**oyster cracker** (*US Culin*) petit biscuit salé ▸**oyster farm** huîtrière *f*, parc *m* à huîtres ▸**oyster shell** écaille *f* *or* coquille *f* d'huître ▸**oyster stew** (*US Culin*) soupe *f* aux huîtres.

Oz‡ [ɒz] abbr of **Australia.**

oz abbr of **ounce(s).**

ozone ['əʊzəʊn] 1 n a (*Chem*) ozone *m*. b (*: *invigorating air*) air frais *m*. 2 comp ▸**ozone depletion** diminution *f* de la couche d'ozone ▸**ozone friendly** qui n'attaque pas *or* qui préserve la couche d'ozone ▸**ozone hole** trou *m* d'ozone ▸**ozone layer** couche *f* d'ozone ▸**ozone safe** sans danger pour la couche d'ozone.

ozonosphere [əʊ'zəʊnə,sfɪə] n couche *f* d'ozone.

P

P, p [piː] n a (*letter*) P, p *m*. **to mind** *or* **watch one's Ps and Qs*** faire attention à ce que l'on fait *or* à ce que l'on dit, se surveiller; **P for Peter** P comme Pierre. b (**abbr of penny** *or* **pence**) penny *m*, pence *mpl*. c (**abbr of page**) p. d **p and p** (**abbr of post(age) and packing**) frais *mpl* de port et d'emballage.

P abbr of parking.

P. abbr of President, Prince.

PA [piːˈeɪ] a (**abbr of personal assistant**) *see* **personal.** b (**abbr of public-address system**: *also* ~ **system**) système *m* de sonorisation, sono* *f*. **it was announced over the** ~ **that ...** on a annoncé par haut-parleurs que ... . c (*US Mail*) **abbr of Pennsylvania.**

Pa. (*US*) **abbr of Pennsylvania.**

p.a. (**abbr of per annum**) par an.

pa* [pɑː] n papa *m*.

pabulum [ˈpæbjʊləm] n a (*US: nonsense*) niaiseries *fpl*. b (*rare*) (*food*) aliment *m* semi-liquide.

pace¹ [peɪs] 1 n a (*measure*) pas *m*. **20 ~s away** à 20 pas.

b (*speed*) pas *m*, allure *f*. **to go at a quick** *or* **good** *or* **smart** ~ aller d'un bon pas *or* à vive allure; **to go at a slow** ~ aller à pas lents *or* lentement *or* à (une) petite allure; **at a walking** ~ au pas; **to quicken one's** ~ hâter *or* presser le pas; **to set the** ~ (*Sport*) mener le train, donner l'allure; (*fig*) donner le ton; **to keep** ~ **with sb** (*lit*) aller à la même allure que qn; (*fig*) marcher de pair avec qn; **to do sth at one's own** ~ faire qch à son rythme; (*fig*) **he can't keep** ~ **with things** il est dépassé par les événements; (*fig*) **he can't stand** *or* **stay the** ~ il ne peut pas tenir le rythme.

c **to put a horse through its ~s** faire parader un cheval; (*fig*) **to put sb through his ~s** mettre qn à l'épreuve, voir ce dont qn est capable.

2 comp ▸**pacemaker** (*Med*) stimulateur *m* (cardiaque); (*Sport*) meneur *m*, -euse *f* (de train) ▸**pacesetter** (*Sport, fig*) meneur *m*, -euse *f* (de train).

3 vi marcher à pas mesurés. **to ~ up and down** faire les cent pas, marcher de long en large.

4 vt a *room, street* arpenter.

b (*Sport*) *runner* régler l'allure de.

▸**pace out** vt sep *distance* mesurer au pas.

pace² [ˈpeɪsɪ] prep: ~ **your advisers** n'en déplaise à vos conseillers.

pacer [ˈpeɪsəʳ] n (*US Sport*) meneur *m*, -euse *f* (de train).

pachyderm [ˈpækɪdɜːm] n pachyderme *m*.

pacific [pəˈsɪfɪk] adj, n pacifique. **the P~ (Ocean)** le Pacifique, l'océan *m* Pacifique; **P~ Islands** îles *fpl* du Pacifique; (*US*) **P~ Daylight Time** heure *f* d'été du Pacifique; (*US*) **P~ Standard Time** heure (normale) du Pacifique.

pacifically [pəˈsɪfɪkəlɪ] adv pacifiquement.

pacification [ˌpæsɪfɪˈkeɪʃən] n (*see* **pacify**) apaisement *m*; pacification *f*.

pacifier [ˈpæsɪfaɪəʳ] n a (*US: dummy-teat*) tétine *f*, sucette *f*. b (*person*) pacificateur *m*, -trice *f*.

pacifism [ˈpæsɪfɪzəm] n pacifisme *m*.

pacifist [ˈpæsɪfɪst] adj, n pacifiste (*mf*).

pacify [ˈpæsɪfaɪ] vt *person, fears* calmer, apaiser; *country, creditors* pacifier.

pack [pæk] 1 n a *[goods, cotton]* balle *f*; *[pedlar]* ballot *m*; *[pack animal]* bât *m*; (*Mil*) sac *m* (d'ordonnance); (*rucksack*) sac *m* à dos.

b (*group*) *[hounds]* meute *f*; *[wolves, thieves]* bande *f*; *[brownies, cubs]* meute *f*; *[runners etc]* peloton *m*. ~ **of fools*** tas* *m* *or* bande* *f* d'imbéciles; ~ **of lies** tissu *m* de mensonges.

c *[cards]* jeu *m*.

d (*Comm*) paquet *m*. (*US*) ~ **of cigarettes** paquet de cigarettes; *see* **economy.**

e (*Rugby*) (*forwards*) pack *m*; (*scrum*) mêlée *f*.

f (*Med*) **cold/wet** ~ compresse froide/humide.

2 comp ▸**pack animal** bête *f* de somme ▸**packhorse** cheval *m* de charge ▸**pack ice** banquise *f*, pack *m* ▸**packsaddle** bât *m* ▸**pack trail** sentier *m* muletier.

3 vt a (*put into box etc*) empaqueter, emballer; (*put into suitcase etc*) mettre dans une valise *etc*, emballer; (*Comm*) *goods etc* emballer; *wool* mettre en balles. (*Comm*) **they come ~ed in dozens** on les reçoit par paquets de douze; **to ~ a vase in straw** envelopper un vase dans de la paille.

b (*fill tightly*) *trunk, suitcase* faire; *box* remplir (*with* de); (*fig*) *mind, memory* bourrer (*with* de). **to ~ one's case** faire sa valise; **to ~ one's bags** (*lit*) faire ses bagages *or* ses valises; (*fig*) plier bagage, faire ses paquets *or* son baluchon*; **to ~ one's things** faire ses bagages; (*fig*) **they ~ed the hall to see him** ils se pressaient dans la salle pour le voir; (*Theat*) *[player, play]* **to ~ the house** faire salle comble; (*fig*) **to ~ a room with furniture** bourrer une pièce de meubles; *see also* **packed.**

c (*crush together*) *earth, objects* tasser (*into* dans); (*Ski*) *snow* damer; *people* entasser (*into* dans); *see also* **packed.**

d (*pej*) **to ~ a jury** composer un jury favorable.

e (*contain: power etc*) *[boxer, fighter]* **he ~s a good punch, he ~s quite a wallop*** il a un sacré* punch; (*US*) **to ~ a gun**⁑ porter un revolver; **this machine ~s enough power to ...** cette machine a assez de puissance pour ... .

4 vi a (*do one's luggage*) faire ses bagages *or* sa valise; *see* **send.**

b **these books ~ easily into that box** ces livres tiennent bien dans cette boîte.

c *[people]* se serrer, s'entasser. **they ~ed into the hall to see him** ils se pressaient dans la salle pour le voir; **the crowd ~ed round him** la foule se pressait autour de lui.

▸**pack away** vt sep ranger.

▸**pack in**⁑ 1 vi (*fig*) *[car, watch etc]* tomber en panne. 2 vt sep *person, job* plaquer⁑. **pack it in!** laisse tomber!*, écrase!⁑; **let's pack it in for the day** assez *or* on arrête pour aujourd'hui; (*fig: of film etc*) **it's packing them in*** ça attire les foules.

▸**pack off*** vt sep (*dismiss*) envoyer promener*. **to pack a child off to bed** envoyer un enfant au lit; **they packed John off to London** ils ont expédié* Jean à Londres.

▸**pack up** 1 vi a (*do one's luggage*) faire sa valise *or* ses bagages. b (*: *give up and go*) plier bagage. c (*Brit *: break down, stop working*) tomber en panne, rendre l'âme (*hum*). 2 vt sep a *clothes, belongings* mettre dans une valise; *object, book* emballer, empaqueter. **he packed up his bits and pieces** il a rassemblé ses affaires; *see* **bag.** b (⁑: *give up*) *work, school* laisser tomber*. **pack it up now!** laisse tomber!*, arrête!

package [ˈpækɪdʒ] 1 n a (*parcel*) paquet *m*, colis *m*.

b (*fig: group*) (*items for sale*) marché *m* global; (*contract*) contrat *m* global; (*purchase*) achat *m* forfaitaire; (*also* ~ **tour**) voyage *m* organisé *or* à forfait; (*Comput*) progiciel *m*. (*Admin, Jur etc*) ~ **of measures** ensemble *m* *or* série *f* *or* train *m* de mesures; (*Comput*) **payroll/inventory/management** ~ progiciel de paie/de stock *or* inventaire/de gestion; (*fig*) **I'd rather look at it as a** ~ je préfère considérer cela comme un tout; (*fig*) **I'd like one person to do it all as a** ~ je préfère qu'une seule personne s'occupe de tout.

2 comp ▸**package deal** marché global; (*contract*) contrat global; (*purchase*) achat *m* forfaitaire ▸**package holiday** vacances organisées, voyage *m* à prix forfaitaire ▸**package policy** (*Insurance*) police *f* multirisque ▸**package store** (*US*) magasin *m* de vins et de spiritueux (à emporter) ▸**package tour** voyage organisé.

3 vt (*Comm*) emballer.

packager [ˈpækɪdʒəʳ] n (*Publishing*) sous-traitant *m*.

packaging [ˈpækɪdʒɪŋ] n (*Comm*) *[goods]* conditionnement *m*; (*wrapping materials*) emballage *m*; (*Publishing*) sous-traitance *f*.

packed [pækt] 1 adj a *room* (*with people*) comble, bondé; (*with furniture etc*) bourré (*with* de); *bus* bondé; (*Brit: also* ~ **out**) *theatre, hall* comble. **the bus was ~ (with people)** l'autobus était bondé; **the lecture was** ~ il y avait foule à la conférence; (*fig*) ~ **like sardines**

serrés comme des sardines. b (*with luggage ready*) **I'm ~ and ready to leave** j'ai fait mes bagages et je suis prêt(e) (à partir). c **~ lunch** repas *m* froid, panier-repas *m*. 2 **-packed** adj ending in comps: **a fun-packed holiday** des vacances pleines de distractions; **a thrill-packed evening** une soirée pleine de *or* riche en péripéties; *see* **action** *etc*.

packer ['pækəʳ] n a (*person*) emballeur *m*, -euse *f*. b (*device*) emballeuse *f*.

packet ['pækɪt] n a (*parcel*) paquet *m*, colis *m*; *[needles, sweets]* sachet *m*; *[cigarettes, seeds]* paquet; (*paper bag*) pochette *f*. **that must have cost a ~!*** cela a dû coûter les yeux de la tête! b (*Naut: also* **~ boat**) paquebot *m*, malle *f*. **the Dover ~** la malle de Douvres.

packing ['pækɪŋ] 1 n a (*gen, Comm*) emballage *m*; *[parcel]* emballage, empaquetage *m*. **to do one's ~** faire sa valise *or* ses bagages; (*Comm*) **meat ~** conserverie *f* de viande (*industrie*). b (*act of filling*) *[space]* remplissage *m*. c (*Tech*) *[piston, joint]* garniture *f*. d (*material used*) (fournitures *fpl or* matériaux *mpl* pour) emballage *m*; (*Tech*) (matière *f* pour) garnitures *fpl*. 2 comp ►**packing case** caisse *f* d'emballage ►**packing density** (*Comput*) densité *f* d'implantation.

pact [pækt] n pacte *m*, traité *m*. **France made a ~ with England** la France conclut *or* signa un pacte avec l'Angleterre; **they made a ~ not to tell their mother** ils se sont mis d'accord pour n'en rien dire à leur mère.

pad [pæd] 1 n a (*to prevent friction, damage*) coussinet *m*; (*Tech*) tampon *m* (amortisseur).
b (*Ftbl*) protège-cheville *m inv*; (*Hockey etc*) jambière *f*; (*Fencing*) plastron *m*.
c (*block of paper*) bloc *m*; (*writing ~*) bloc (de papier à lettres); (*note~*) bloc-notes *m*; *see* **blotting**.
d (*for inking*) tampon encreur.
e *[rabbit]* patte *f*; *[cat, dog]* coussin charnu.
f (*fig*) **the ~ of footsteps** des pas feutrés.
g (*Space: also* **launching ~**) rampe *f* (de lancement).
h *[water lily]* feuille *f* de nénuphar.
i (*: *sanitary towel*) serviette *f* hygiénique.
j (‡) (*bed*) pieu‡ *m*; (*room*) piaule* *f*.
k (*US*) *[policeman]* **to be on the ~‡** toucher des pots-de-vin, palper*.
2 vi aller à pas feutrés. **to ~ along** marcher à pas de loup *or* à pas feutrés; **to ~ about** aller et venir à pas de loup *or* à pas feutrés.
3 vt a *cushion, shoulders* rembourrer; *clothing* matelasser, ouatiner; *furniture, door* matelasser, capitonner. **to ~ with cotton wool** ouater.
b (*fig: also* **~ out**) *speech* délayer. **he ~ded his essay (out) a good deal** il y a beaucoup de délayage *or* de remplissage dans sa dissertation, il a bien allongé la sauce* dans sa dissertation.

►**pad out** vt sep a *clothes, shoulders* rembourrer. b (*fig*) *expense account etc* gonfler. c *meal* rendre plus copieux (*with potatoes*) en ajoutant des pommes de terre; *see also* **pad 3b**.

padded ['pædɪd] adj *garment* matelassé, ouatiné; *bedhead etc* capitonné, matelassé; *envelope* rembourré. **~ shoulders** épaules rembourrées; **~ cell** cellule matelassée, cabanon *m*; **~ bag** enveloppe matelassée.

padding ['pædɪŋ] n a (*action*) rembourrage *m*. b (*material*) bourre *f*, ouate *f*; (*fig: in book, speech*) délayage *m*, remplissage *m*. (*fig: starchy food*) **I've added rice for ~** j'ai ajouté du riz pour que ce soit plus copieux.

paddle ['pædl] 1 n a *[canoe]* pagaie *f*; *[waterwheel]* aube *f*, palette *f*.
b **the child went for a ~** l'enfant est allé barboter *or* faire trempette.
c (*US: table tennis bat*) raquette *f* de ping-pong.
2 comp ►**paddle boat**, (*Brit*) **paddle steamer** bateau *m* à aubes *or* à roues ►**paddle wheel** roue *f* à aubes *or* à palettes ►**paddling pool** (*Brit*) pataugeoire *f*.
3 vt a **to ~ a canoe** pagayer; (*fig*) **to ~ one's own canoe** se débrouiller tout seul, diriger seul sa barque.
b (*US: spank*) donner une fessée à.
4 vi a (*walk*) (*in water*) barboter, faire trempette; (*in mud*) patauger.
b (*in canoe*) **to ~ up/down the river** remonter/descendre la rivière en pagayant; **to ~ along the river** pagayer le long de la rivière.

►**paddle along** vi pagayer.

paddock ['pædək] n enclos *m* (*pour chevaux*); (*Racing*) paddock *m*.

Paddy ['pædɪ] n (dim of **Patrick**) (*surnom des Irlandais*).

paddy[1] ['pædɪ] n paddy *m*, riz non décortiqué. **~ field** rizière *f*.

paddy[2]* ['pædɪ] n (*anger*) rogne* *f*. **to be in a ~** être en rogne*.

paddy waggon‡ ['pædɪ,wægən] n (*US*) panier *m* à salade*.

padlock ['pædlɒk] 1 n *[door, chain]* cadenas *m*; *[cycle]* antivol *m*. 2 vt *door* cadenasser; *cycle* mettre un antivol à.

padre ['pɑːdrɪ] n a (*Mil, Naut etc*) aumônier *m*. b (*: *clergyman*) (*Catholic*) curé *m*, prêtre *m*; (*Protestant*) pasteur *m*.

Padua ['pædʒʊə] n Padoue.

paean ['piːən] n péan *m*. **~s of praise** des louanges *fpl*, un dithyrambe.

paederast ['pedəræst] n = **pederast**.

paediatric [,piːdɪ'ætrɪk] adj *department* de pédiatrie; *illness, medicine, surgery* infantile. **~ nurse** puéricultrice *f*; **~ nursing** puériculture *f*.

paediatrician [,piːdɪə'trɪʃən] n pédiatre *mf*.

paediatrics [,piːdɪ'ætrɪks] n (*NonC*) pédiatrie *f*.

paedophile ['piːdəʊfaɪl] n pédophile *m*.

paedophilia [,piːdəʊ'fɪlɪə] n pédophilie *f*.

paedophiliac [,piːdəʊ'fɪlɪæk] adj pédophile.

paella [paɪ'elə] n paella *f*.

pagan ['peɪgən] adj, n (*lit, fig*) païen(ne) *m(f)*.

paganism ['peɪgənɪzəm] n paganisme *m*.

page[1] [peɪdʒ] 1 n (*lit, fig*) page *f*. **on ~ 10** (à la) page 10; **continued on ~ 20** suite (en) page 20; (*fig: Brit*) **~ three** la page des pin up; (*Typ*) **~ proofs** épreuves *fpl* en pages. 2 vt *book* paginer; *printed sheets* mettre en pages.

page[2] [peɪdʒ] 1 n a (*also* **~boy**) (*in hotel*) groom *m*, chasseur *m*; (*at court*) page *m*. b (*US: Congress*) jeune huissier *m*. 2 vt (*call for*) *person* faire appeler; *[person calling]* appeler. **they're paging Mr Smith** on appelle M. Smith.

pageant ['pædʒənt] n (*historical*) spectacle *m or* reconstitution *f* historique; (*fig*) spectacle pompeux, pompe *f*. **air ~** fête *f* de l'air.

pageantry ['pædʒəntrɪ] n apparat *m*, pompe *f*.

pageboy ['peɪdʒ,bɔɪ] n a (*also* **~ hairstyle**) (coupe *f* au) carré *m*. b = **page**[2] **1a**.

pager ['peɪdʒəʳ] n bip* *m*, Alphapage *m* ®.

paginate ['pædʒɪneɪt] vt paginer.

pagination [,pædʒɪ'neɪʃən] n pagination *f*.

paging ['peɪdʒɪŋ] n (*Comput, also in book*) pagination *f*.

pagoda [pə'gəʊdə] n pagode *f*.

pah† [pæ] excl pouah!

paid [peɪd] 1 pret, ptp of **pay**. 2 adj *staff* rémunéré; *holidays* payé. **~ gunman** tueur *m* à gages; **a ~ hack** un nègre (*fig*). 3 comp ►**paid-in** (*Fin*) *moneys* encaissé ►**paid-up** libéré; **paid-up member** membre *m* qui a payé sa cotisation; **fully/partly paid-up shares** actions *fpl* entièrement/non entièrement libérées *see also* **pay**.

pail [peɪl] n seau *m*. **~(ful) of water** seau d'eau.

paillasse ['pælɪæs] n paillasse *f*.

pain [peɪn] 1 n a (*NonC*) (*physical*) douleur *f*, souffrance *f*; (*mental*) peine *f*, (*stronger*) douleur, souffrance. **to be in (great) ~** souffrir (beaucoup); **to cause ~ to** (*physically*) faire mal à, faire souffrir; (*mentally*) faire de la peine à, peiner, affliger; **cry of ~** cri *m* de douleur.
b (*localized*) douleur *f*. **I have a ~ in my shoulder** j'ai une douleur à l'épaule, j'ai mal à l'épaule, mon épaule me fait mal; **to have rheumatic ~s** souffrir de rhumatismes; **where have you got a ~?** où as-tu mal?
c (*nuisance*) **to be a (real) ~*** être enquiquinant* *or* embêtant*; **to give sb a ~ in the neck*** enquiquiner* qn; **he is a ~ in the neck*** il est enquiquinant* *or* casse-pieds; (*Brit*) **he is a ~ in the arse***‡, (*esp* US*) **he is a ~ in the ass***‡ c'est un emmerdeur‡ fini.
d (*trouble*) **~s** peine *f*; **to take ~s** *or* **to be at ~s** *or* **to go to great ~s (not) to do sth** se donner beaucoup de mal pour (ne pas) faire qch; **to take ~s over sth** se donner beaucoup de mal pour (faire) qch; **to spare no ~s** ne pas ménager ses efforts (*to do* pour faire).
e (*††: punishment*) peine *f*, punition *f*. (*frm*) **on ~ of death** sous peine de mort.
2 comp ►**painkiller** calmant *m*, analgésique *m* ►**painkilling** calmant, analgésique.
3 vt faire de la peine à, peiner, (*stronger*) faire souffrir.

pained [peɪnd] adj *smile, expression, voice* peiné, froissé.

painful ['peɪnfʊl] adj a (*causing physical pain*) *wound etc* douloureux. **my hand is ~** j'ai mal à la main. b (*distressing*) *sight, duty* pénible. **it is ~ to see her now** maintenant elle fait peine à voir. c (*laborious*) *climb, task* pénible, difficile.

painfully ['peɪnfəlɪ] adv *throb* douloureusement; *walk* péniblement, avec difficulté; *sensitive, embarrassed etc* terriblement. **it was ~ clear that ...** il n'était que trop évident que ...; **he was ~ shy/slow** *etc* sa timidité/sa lenteur *etc* faisait peine à voir, il était terriblement timide/lent *etc*.

painless ['peɪnlɪs] adj *operation* indolore, sans douleur; (*fig*) *experience* inoffensif, bénin (*f* -igne). (*fig*) **it's a ~ way of learning Chinese** de cette façon, on peut apprendre le chinois sans (se donner de) mal; **the exam was fairly ~*** l'examen n'avait rien de bien méchant*.

painlessly ['peɪnlɪslɪ] adv (*lit*) sans douleur; (*: *easily*) sans peine, sans difficulté.

painstaking ['peɪnz,teɪkɪŋ] adj *work* soigné; *person* assidu, appliqué, soigneux.

painstakingly ['peɪnz,teɪkɪŋlɪ] adv assidûment, avec soin, laborieusement.

paint [peɪnt] 1 n a (*NonC*) peinture *f*; *see* **coat, wet**.
b **~s** couleurs *fpl*; **box of ~s** boîte *f* de couleurs.
c (*pej: make-up*) peinture *f* (*pej*); *see* **grease**.
2 comp ►**paintbox** boîte *f* de couleurs ►**paintbrush** (*Art*) pinceau *m*; (*for decorating*) brosse *f*, pinceau *m* ►**paint gun** pistolet *m* à peinture ►**painted lady** (*butterfly*) vanesse *f see also* **painted** ►**paintpot** pot *m* de peinture (*lit*) ►**paint remover** décapant *m* (pour peinture) ►**paint roller** rouleau *m* à peinture ►**paint spray** pulvérisateur *m* (de peinture); (*Aut: for repairs*) bombe *f* de peinture *or*

de laque ►**paint-stripper** (*chemical*) décapant *m*; (*tool*) racloir *m* ►**paintwork** peintures *fpl*.

3 **vt** a *wall etc* peindre, couvrir de peinture. **to ~ a wall red** peindre un mur en rouge; **to ~ sth again** repeindre qch; **to ~ one's nails** se vernir les ongles; (*fig*) **to ~ the town red** faire la noce*, faire la bringue*.

b (*Art*) *picture, portrait* peindre; (*fig: describe*) dépeindre, décrire. (*Theat*) **to ~ the scenery** brosser les décors; (*fig*) **he ~ed the situation in very black colours** il brossa un tableau très sombre de la situation.

c (*Med*) *throat, wound* badigeonner.

4 **vi** (*Art*) peindre, faire de la peinture. **to ~ in oils** peindre à l'huile, faire de la peinture à l'huile; **to ~ in watercolours** faire de l'aquarelle.

►**paint in** **vt sep** peindre.

►**paint out** **vt sep** faire disparaître sous une couche de peinture.

►**paint over** **vt sep** *slogan, graffiti* couvrir de peinture.

painted ['peɪntɪd] **adj** a *wall, furniture, room* peint. (*pej*) **~ lady** *or* **woman** femme *f* trop fardée, ≃ cocotte *f*.

painter¹ ['peɪntəʳ] **n** a (*Art*) peintre *m*. **portrait ~** portraitiste *mf*; *see* **landscape**. b (*also* **house~**) peintre *m* (en bâtiments). **~ and decorator** peintre décorateur.

painter² ['peɪntəʳ] **n** (*Naut*) amarre *f*.

painting ['peɪntɪŋ] **n** a (*NonC*) (*Art*) peinture *f*; [*buildings*] décoration *f*; (*fig: description*) peinture, description *f*. **~ in oils** peinture à l'huile; **to study ~** étudier la peinture; **he does a bit of ~** il fait un peu de peinture, il fait de la barbouille*. b (*picture*) tableau *m*, toile *f*.

pair [pɛəʳ] 1 **n** a (*two*) [*shoes etc*] paire *f*. **these gloves make** *or* **are a ~** ces gants font la paire; **a ~ of pyjamas** un pyjama; **a ~ of trousers** un pantalon; **a ~ of scissors** une paire de ciseaux; **I have only one ~ of hands!** je ne peux pas tout faire à la fois!; **a beautiful ~ of legs** de belles jambes; **in ~s** (*two together: work etc*) à deux; (*by twos: enter etc*) par deux.

b (*man and wife*) couple *m*. **the happy ~** l'heureux couple.

c (*pej: two people*) paire *f*.

d [*animals*] paire *f*; (*mated*) couple *m*; *see* **carriage**.

e (*Brit Parl*) *un de deux députés de partis opposés qui se sont entendus pour s'absenter lors d'un vote*.

f **~s champions/skaters** champions *mpl*/patineurs *mpl* par couple;**~s championship/tournament** championnat *m*/tournoi *m* en double.

2 **comp** ►**pair-bond(ing)** (*Zool etc*) union *f* monogame.

3 **vt** a *socks* appareiller.

b *animals* accoupler, apparier.

4 **vi** a [*glove etc*] faire la paire (*with* avec).

b [*animals*] s'accoupler, s'apparier.

►**pair off** 1 **vi** a [*people*] s'arranger deux par deux. b (*Brit Parl*) *s'entendre avec un adversaire pour s'absenter lors d'un vote*. 2 **vt sep** mettre par paires. **John was paired off with her at the dance** on lui a attribué Jean comme cavalier.

►**pair up** **vi** [*people*] se mettre à deux. **he paired up with his friend for the race** il s'est mis avec son ami pour la course.

paisley ['peɪzlɪ] 1 **n** (*fabric*) lainage *m* à motif cachemire; (*design: also* **~ pattern**) motif *m* *or* dessin *m* cachemire. 2 **comp** ►**paisley shawl** châle *m* cachemire.

pajamas [pə'dʒɑːməz] **npl** (*US*) = **pyjamas**.

Paki‡ ['pækɪ] (*Brit pej*) (**abbr of Pakistani**) **the ~ shop*** *or* **the ~'s** ≃ l'arabe du coin*; **he's a ~-basher**‡ il s'attaque aux Pakistanais; **~-bashing**‡ chasse *f* aux Pakistanais, ≃ ratonnade‡ *f*.

Pakistan [ˌpɑːkɪs'tɑːn] **n** Pakistan *m*.

Pakistani [ˌpɑːkɪs'tɑːnɪ] 1 **adj** pakistanais. 2 **n** Pakistanais(e) *m(f)*.

PAL [pæl] **n** (*TV*) (**abbr of phase alternation line**) PAL *m*.

pal* [pæl] **n** copain* *m*, copine* *f*; (*: *form of address*) mon vieux*. **they're great ~s** ils sont très copains*, ce sont de grands copains*.

►**pal up**‡ **vi** devenir copain(s)* (*or* copine(s)*) (*with* avec).

palace ['pælɪs] **n** palais *m*. (*Queen, her entourage*) **the P~** le Palais (de Buckingham); **bishop's ~** évêché *m*, palais épiscopal; **royal ~** palais royal; (*fig*) **~ revolution** révolution *f* de palais.

paladin ['pælədɪn] **n** paladin *m*.

palaeo... ['pælɪəʊ] **pref** = **paleo...**.

Palaeozoic [ˌpælɪəʊ'zəʊɪk] **adj, n** (*Geol*) paléozoïque (*m*).

palais ['pæleɪ] **n** (*Brit: also* **~ de danse**†) dancing *m*, salle *f* de danse *or* de bal.

palatable ['pælətəbl] **adj** *food* agréable au goût; (*fig: fact etc*) acceptable.

palatal ['pælətl] 1 **adj** palatal. (*Ling*) **~ l** l mouillé. 2 **n** palatale *f*.

palatalize ['pælətəlaɪz] **vt** palataliser, mouiller.

palate ['pælɪt] **n** (*Anat, also fig*) palais *m*; *see* **hard, soft**.

palatial [pə'leɪʃəl] **adj** grandiose, magnifique, comme un palais. **this hotel is ~** cet hôtel est un palace; **the house is ~** la maison est un palais.

palatinate [pə'lætɪnɪt] **n** palatinat *m*.

palaver [pə'lɑːvəʳ] 1 **n** a (*parley*) palabre *f*. b (*) (*idle talk*) palabres *mpl or fpl*; (*fuss*) histoire *f*, affaire *f*. **what a ~!** quelle histoire pour si peu! 2 **vi** palabrer.

pale¹ [peɪl] 1 **adj** *face, person* (*naturally*) pâle; (*from sickness, fear*) blême; *colour* pâle; *dawn, moonlight* blafard. **to grow ~** pâlir; **~ blue eyes** yeux *mpl* bleu pâle; (*Brit*) **~ ale** pale-ale *m* (*sorte de bière blonde légère*). 2 **comp** ►**paleface** visage pâle *mf* ►**pale-faced** (*not tanned*) au teint pâle; (*from sickness, fear etc*) blême ►**pale-skinned** à la peau claire. 3 **vi** [*person*] pâlir, devenir blême. (*fig*) **it ~s into insignificance beside ...** cela perd toute importance *or* cela n'a rien d'important comparé à ...; (*fig*) **it ~s in comparison with ...** cela ne souffre pas la comparaison avec ... .

pale² [peɪl] **n** (*stake*) pieu *m*. **quite beyond the ~** *person* (*politically etc*) à mettre à l'index; (*socially*) infréquentable; *behaviour* inacceptable.

paleness ['peɪlnɪs] **n** pâleur *f*.

paleo... ['pælɪəʊ] **pref** palé(o)... .

paleographer [ˌpælɪ'ɒgrəfəʳ] **n** paléographe *mf*.

paleography [ˌpælɪ'ɒgrəfɪ] **n** paléographie *f*.

paleolithic [ˌpælɪəʊ'lɪθɪk] **adj** paléolithique. **the ~ age** l'âge *m* paléolithique *or* de la pierre taillée.

paleontology [ˌpælɪɒn'tɒlədʒɪ] **n** paléontologie *f*.

Palermo [pə'lɛəməʊ] **n** Palerme.

Palestine ['pælɪstaɪn] **n** Palestine *f*.

Palestinian [ˌpæləs'tɪnɪən] 1 **adj** palestinien. 2 **n** Palestinien(ne) *m(f)*.

palette ['pælɪt] **n** palette *f*. **~ knife** (*Art*) couteau *m* (à palette); (*for cakes*) pelle *f* (à tarte); (*for cooking*) spatule *f*.

palfrey ['pɔːlfrɪ] **n** palefroi *m*.

palimony* ['pælɪmənɪ] **n** pension *f* alimentaire versée à celle (*or* à celui) avec qui on vivait maritalement.

palimpsest ['pælɪmpsest] **n** palimpseste *m*.

palindrome ['pælɪndrəʊm] **n** palindrome *m*.

paling ['peɪlɪŋ] **n** (*fence*) palissade *f*; (*stake*) palis *m*.

palisade [ˌpælɪ'seɪd] **n** a palissade *f*. b (*US Geol*) ligne *f* de falaises abruptes.

pall¹ [pɔːl] **vi** perdre son charme (*on sb* pour qn). **it never ~s on you** on ne s'en lasse jamais; **his speech ~ed on the audience** son discours a fini par lasser l'auditoire.

pall² [pɔːl] **n** drap *m* mortuaire; (*Rel*) pallium *m*; (*fig*) [*smoke*] voile *m*; [*snow*] manteau *m*. **to be a ~bearer** porter le cercueil.

Palladian [pə'leɪdɪən] **adj** (*Archit*) palladien.

palladium [pə'leɪdɪəm] **n** (*Chem*) palladium *m*.

pallet ['pælɪt] 1 **n** a (*mattress*) paillasse *f*; (*bed*) grabat *m*. b (*for handling goods*) palette *f*. c = **palette**. 2 **comp** ►**pallet loader** palettiseur *m* ►**pallet truck** transpalette *f*.

palletization [ˌpælɪtaɪ'zeɪʃən] **n** palettisation *f*.

palletize ['pælɪtaɪz] **vt** palettiser.

palliasse ['pælɪæs] **n** = **paillasse**.

palliate ['pælɪeɪt] **vt** (*Med, fig*) pallier. **palliating circumstances** circonstances atténuantes.

palliative ['pælɪətɪv] **adj, n** palliatif (*m*).

pallid ['pælɪd] **adj** *person, complexion* pâle, blême, blafard; *light* blafard; (*fig*) *attempt* faible.

pallidness ['pælɪdnɪs] **n**, **pallor** ['pæləʳ] **n** pâleur *f*; [*face*] teint blafard, pâleur.

pally* ['pælɪ] **adj** (très) copain (*f* copine)* (*with* avec).

palm¹ [pɑːm] 1 **n** [*hand*] paume *f*. (*fig*) **to have sb in the ~ of one's hand** tenir qn, faire de qn ce qu'on veut; (*fig*) **to grease** *or* **oil sb's ~** graisser la patte* à qn. 2 **vt** (*conceal*) cacher au creux de la main; (*pick up*) subtiliser, escamoter.

►**palm off** **vt sep** *sth worthless* refiler* (*on, onto* à).

palm² [pɑːm] 1 **n** (*also* **~ tree**) palmier *m*; (*branch*) palme *f*; (*Rel*) rameau *m*; (*Rel: straw cross*) rameaux. (*fig*) **to carry off the ~** remporter la palme. 2 **comp** ►**palm court** (*Brit*) *music, orchestra etc* ≃ de thé dansant ►**palm grove** palmeraie *f* ►**Palm Sunday** (dimanche *m or* fête *f* des) Rameaux *mpl*.

palmate ['pælmeɪt] **adj** (*Bot, Zool*) palmé.

palmetto [pæl'metəʊ] **n**, **pl ~s** *or* **~es** palmier *m* nain. (*US*) **the P~ State** la Caroline du Sud.

palmist ['pɑːmɪst] **n** chiromancien(ne) *m(f)*.

palmistry ['pɑːmɪstrɪ] **n** chiromancie *f*.

palmy ['pɑːmɪ] **adj** (*fig*) heureux; *era* florissant, glorieux.

palomino [ˌpælə'miːnəʊ] **n**, **pl ~s** (*US*) alezan *m* doré à crins blancs.

palooka‡ [pə'luːkə] **n** (*US: pej*) pauvre type* *m*, type* fini.

palpable ['pælpəbəl] **adj** (*lit*) palpable; (*fig*) *error* évident, manifeste.

palpably ['pælpəblɪ] **adv** manifestement, d'une façon évidente.

palpitate ['pælpɪteɪt] **vi** palpiter.

palpitating ['pælpɪteɪtɪŋ] **adj** palpitant.

palpitation [ˌpælpɪ'teɪʃən] **n** palpitation *f*.

palsied ['pɔːlzɪd] **adj** (*paralyzed*) paralysé, paralytique; (*trembling*) tremblotant.

palsy ['pɔːlzɪ] **n** (*Med*) (*trembling*) paralysie agitante; (*paralysis*) paralysie.

paltry ['pɔːltrɪ] **adj** a (*tiny, insignificant*) *amount* misérable, dérisoire. b (*petty*) *behaviour* mesquin; *excuse* piètre.

paludism ['pæljʊdɪzəm] **n** paludisme *m*.

pampas ['pæmpəs] **npl** pampa(s) *f(pl)*. **~ grass** herbe *f* des pampas.

pamper ['pæmpəʳ] **vt** choyer, dorloter, gâter. **to ~ o.s.** se dorloter.

pamphlet ['pæmflɪt] **n** brochure *f*; (*Literat*) opuscule *m*; (*scurrilous* *tract*) pamphlet *m.*

pamphleteer [ˌpæmflɪˈtɪəʳ] n auteur *m* de brochures *or* d'opuscules; *[tracts]* pamphlétaire *mf.*

Pan [pæn] n Pan *m.*

pan¹ [pæn] 1 n a (*Culin*) casserole *f*, poêlon *m.* **frying ~** poêle *f*; **roasting ~** plat *m* à rôtir; *see* **pot.** b *[scales]* plateau *m*, bassin *m*; *[lavatory]* cuvette *f*; (*Miner*) batée *f*. (*fig*) **to go down the ~‡** tomber à l'eau*; *see* **brain, flash, salt.** c (*US* ‡: *face*) binette‡ *f*, bille *f* (de clown)‡; *see* **dead.** 2 comp ▸**pandrop** *see* **pandrop** ▸**pan-fry** (*US*) faire sauter ▸**panhandle** *see* **panhandle** ▸**pan scrubber** tampon *m* à récurer, éponge *f* métallique. 3 vt a *sand* laver à la batée. b (*: *criticize harshly*) *film, book* éreinter, démolir. 4 vi: **to ~ for gold** laver le sable aurifère (*à la batée pour en extraire de l'or*).

▸**pan out*** vi (*turn out*) tourner, se passer; (*turn out well*) bien tourner, bien se goupiller*. **it all panned out in the long run** ça s'est (bien) goupillé* en fin de compte; **events didn't pan out as he'd hoped** les événements n'ont pas tourné comme il l'avait espéré.

pan² [pæn] 1 vi (*Cine, TV*) *[camera]* faire un panoramique, panoramiquer. 2 vt: **to ~ the camera** panoramiquer.

pan... [pæn] pref pan... .

panacea [ˌpænəˈsɪə] n panacée *f.*

panache [pəˈnæʃ] n panache *m.*

Pan-African [ˈpænˈæfrɪkən] adj panafricain.

Pan-Africanism [ˈpænˈæfrɪkənɪzəm] n panafricanisme *m.*

Panama [ˈpænəˌmɑː] n Panama *m.* **~ Canal** canal *m* de Panama; **p~ (hat)** panama *m.*

Panamanian [ˌpænəˈmeɪnɪən] 1 adj panaméen. 2 n Panaméen(ne) *m(f).*

Pan-American [ˈpænəˈmerɪkən] adj panaméricain. **~ Highway** route panaméricaine; **~ Union** Union panaméricaine.

Pan-Americanism [ˈpænəˈmerɪkənɪzəm] n panaméricanisme *m.*

Pan-Asian [ˈpænˈeɪʃən] adj panasiatique.

Pan-Asianism [ˈpænˈeɪʃənɪzəm] n panasiatisme *m.*

pancake [ˈpænkeɪk] 1 n a (*Culin*) crêpe *f.* **as flat as a ~** plat comme une galette. b (*Aviat: also* **~ landing**) atterrissage *m* à plat. 2 comp ▸**pancake coil** (*Elec*) galette *f* ▸**Pancake Day** mardi gras ▸**pancake (make-up)** maquillage *m* compact ▸**Pancake Tuesday** = **Pancake Day.** 3 vi (*Aviat*) se plaquer, atterrir à plat.

panchromatic [ˈpænkrəʊˈmætɪk] adj panchromatique.

pancreas [ˈpæŋkrɪəs] n pancréas *m.*

pancreatic [ˌpæŋkrɪˈætɪk] adj pancréatique.

panda [ˈpændə] n panda *m.* (*Brit*) **~ car** ≃ voiture *f* pie *inv* (*de la police*).

pandemic [pænˈdemɪk] 1 adj universel. 2 n pandémie *f.*

pandemonium [ˌpændɪˈməʊnɪəm] n tohu-bohu *m*, chahut *m* (monstre). **it's sheer ~!** c'est un véritable charivari!, quel tohu-bohu!

pander [ˈpændəʳ] vi: **to ~ to** *person* se prêter aux exigences de; *whims, desires* se plier à; *tastes, weaknesses* flatter bassement.

p & h [ˌpiːəndeɪtʃ] n (*US*) (abbr of **postage and handling**) port et manutention.

P & L (*Comm*) (abbr of **profit and loss**) *see* **profit.**

p & p [ˌpiːəndˈpiː] n abbr of **postage and packing.**

Pandora [pænˈdɔːrə] n Pandore *f.* **~'s box** boîte *f* de Pandore.

pandrop [ˈpændrɒp] n grosse pastille *f* de menthe.

pane [peɪn] n vitre *f*, carreau *m.*

panegyric [ˌpænɪˈdʒɪrɪk] adj, n panégyrique (*m*).

panel [ˈpænəl] 1 n a *[door, wall]* panneau *m*; *[ceiling]* caisson *m.*

b (*Aut, Aviat: also* **instrument ~**) tableau *m* de bord.

c (*Dress*) pan *m.*

d (*Jur*) (*list*) liste *f* (des jurés); (*jury*) jury *m.* (*Admin, Scol etc*) **~ of examiners** jury (d'examinateurs).

e (*also* **interviewing ~**) jury *m* d'entretien.

f (*Brit Med*) **to be on a doctor's ~** être inscrit sur le registre d'un médecin conventionné.

g (*Rad, TV etc: group of speakers*) (*gen*) invités *mpl*; (*for debate*) invités, experts *mpl*, tribune *f*; (*for game*) jury *m.*

h (*in inquiry*) commission *f* d'enquête; (*committee*) comité *m*; (*of negotiators etc*) table ronde.

2 comp ▸**panel-beater** (*Aut*) tôlier *m* ▸**panel-beating** tôlerie *f* ▸**panel discussion** (*Rad, TV etc*) réunion-débat *f* ▸**panel doctor** médecin conventionné ▸**panel game** (*Rad/TV*) jeu radiophonique/télévisé (*avec des équipes d'invités*) ▸**panel patient** malade *mf* assuré(e) social(e) ▸**panel pin** pointe *f* ▸**panel truck** *or* **van** *or* **wagon** (*US Aut*) camionnette *f.*

3 vt *surface* plaquer; *room, wall* recouvrir de panneaux *or* de boiseries, lambrisser. **~led door** porte *f* à panneaux; **oak-~led** lambrissé de chêne, garni de boiseries de chêne.

panelling, (*US*) **paneling** [ˈpænəlɪŋ] n (*NonC*) panneaux *mpl*, lambris *m*, boiseries *fpl.*

panellist, (*US*) **panelist** [ˈpænəlɪst] n a (*Rad, TV etc: see* **panel 1f**) *invité(e) m(f), expert m*; membre *m* d'une tribune *or* d'un jury. b (*member of commission etc: see* **panel 1g**) membre *m* de la commission d'enquête (*or* du comité *etc*).

Pan-European [ˈpænˌjʊərəˈpiːən] adj paneuropéen.

pang [pæŋ] n serrement *m or* pincement *m* de cœur. **~s of death** affres *fpl or* angoisses *fpl* de la mort; **~ of conscience** remords *mpl* de conscience; **~ of jealousy/remorse** affres de la jalousie/du remords; **he saw her go without a ~** il l'a vue partir sans regret, cela ne lui a fait ni chaud ni froid* de la voir partir; **to feel the ~s of hunger** commencer à ressentir des tiraillements d'estomac.

panhandle [ˈpænhændl] 1 n a (*lit*) manche *m* (de casserole). b (*US: strip of land*) bande *f* de terre. **the Texas ~** la partie septentrionale du Texas; (*US*) **the P~ State** la Virginie occidentale. 2 vi (*US* ‡: *beg*) faire la manche‡. 3 vt (*US* ‡: *beg from*) mendigoter‡ auprès de.

panhandler‡ [ˈpænhændləʳ] n (*US: beggar*) mendiant(e) *m(f).*

panic [ˈpænɪk] 1 n (*NonC*) panique *f*, terreur *f*, affolement *m.* **to throw a crowd into a ~** semer la panique dans une foule; **to get into a ~** s'affoler, paniquer*; **to throw sb into a ~** affoler *or* paniquer* qn; **(there's) no ~*, it can wait** pas de panique* *or* il n'y a pas le feu*, ça peut attendre.

2 comp *fear* panique; *decision* de panique ▸**panic button*** (*fig*) signal *m* d'alarme; (*fig*) **to hit** *or* **push the panic button** paniquer* ▸**panic buying** achats *mpl* en catastrophe *or* de précaution ▸**panic stations***: **it was panic stations** ça a été la panique générale* ▸**panic-stricken** *person, crowd* affolé, pris de panique; *look* affolé.

3 vi s'affoler, être pris de panique, paniquer*. **don't ~!*** pas d'affolement!

4 vt *crowd* jeter *or* semer la panique dans; *person* affoler. **she was ~ked into burning the letter** affolée elle brûla la lettre.

panicky [ˈpænɪkɪ] adj *report, newspaper* alarmiste; *decision, action* de panique; *person* qui s'affole facilement, paniquard*.

panjandrum [pænˈdʒændrəm] n grand ponte*, gros bonnet*, gros manitou*.

pannier [ˈpænɪəʳ] n panier *m*, corbeille *f*; *[pack animal]* panier de bât; (*on motorcycle etc: also* **~ bag**) sacoche *f.*

panoply [ˈpænəplɪ] n panoplie *f.*

panorama [ˌpænəˈrɑːmə] n panorama *m.*

panoramic [ˌpænəˈræmɪk] adj panoramique. (*Cine*) **~ screen** écran *m* panoramique; **~ view** vue *f* panoramique.

panpipes [ˈpænˌpaɪps] npl flûte *f* de pan.

pansy [ˈpænzɪ] n a (*Bot*) pensée *f.* b (‡ *pej*) tante‡ *f*, tapette‡ *f.*

pant [pænt] 1 vi a (*gasp*) *[person]* haleter; *[animal]* battre du flanc, haleter. **to ~ for breath** chercher (à reprendre) son souffle; **the boy/the dog ~ed along after him** le garçon/le chien s'essoufflait à sa suite; **he ~ed up the hill** il grimpa la colline en haletant. b (*throb*) *[heart]* palpiter. 2 vt (*also* **~ out**) *words, phrases* dire d'une voix haletante, dire en haletant. 3 n (*see* 1) halètement *m*; palpitation *f.*

▸**pant after** vt fus (*liter*) *knowledge etc* aspirer à.

▸**pant for** vt fus a (*liter*) = **pant after.** b (‡) *cigarette, drink* mourir d'envie de.

pantaloon [ˌpæntəˈluːn] n a **(pair of) ~s** culotte *f.* b (*Theat*) **P~** Pantalon *m.*

pantechnicon [pænˈteknɪkən] n (*Brit: van*) grand camion de déménagement; (*warehouse*) entrepôt *m* (*pour meubles*).

pantheism [ˈpænθɪˌɪzəm] n panthéisme *m.*

pantheist [ˈpænθɪˌɪst] n panthéiste *mf.*

pantheistic [ˌpænθɪˈɪstɪk] adj panthéiste.

pantheon [ˈpænθɪən] n panthéon *m.*

panther [ˈpænθəʳ] n, pl **~s** *or* **~** panthère *f*; *see* **black.**

panties* [ˈpæntɪz] npl slip *m* (*de femme*).

pantihose [ˈpæntɪˌhəʊz] npl (*esp US*) **(pair of) ~** collant *m.*

pantile [ˈpænˌtaɪl] n tuile *f* imbriquée.

panting [ˈpæntɪŋ] n *[person, animal]* essoufflement *m*, halètement *m*; *[heart]* palpitation *f.*

pantograph [ˈpæntəgrɑːf] n (*Rail, Tech*) pantographe *m.*

pantomime [ˈpæntəmaɪm] n a (*Brit Theat: show*) spectacle *m* de Noël (*tiré d'un conte de fée*). b (*mime*) pantomime *f*, mime *m.* **in ~** en mimant. c (*fig pej: fuss*) comédie *f* (*fig pej*).

pantry [ˈpæntrɪ] n (*in hotel, mansion*) office *f*; (*in house*) garde-manger *m inv.*

pants [pænts] npl a (*Brit: underwear*) (*for women*) culotte *f*, slip *m*; (*for men*) caleçon *m*, slip. b (*US, and Brit *: trousers*) pantalon *m.* **short ~** culottes *fpl* courtes; **long ~** pantalon *m* (long); **she's the one who wears the ~*** c'est elle qui porte la culotte*; **to catch sb with his ~ down*** prendre qn au dépourvu.

pantsuit [ˈpæntsuːt] n (*esp US*) tailleur-pantalon *m.*

panty [ˈpæntɪ] in comps: **panty girdle** gaine-culotte *f.*

pantyhose [ˈpæntɪˌhəʊz] n = **pantihose.**

panzer [ˈpænzəʳ] n panzer *m.* **~ division** division blindée (allemande).

Pap [pæp] n = **Papanicolaou.**

pap¹ [pæp] n (*Culin*) bouillie *f*; (*fig pej*) niaiseries *fpl.*

pap²†† [pæp] n (*breast*) mamelon *m.*

papa [pəˈpɑː] n papa *m.*

papacy [ˈpeɪpəsɪ] n papauté *f.*

papadum [ˈpæpədəm] n poppadum *m.*

papal [ˈpeɪpəl] adj papal; *bull, legate, election* du Pape. **~ cross** croix *f* papale; **~ infallibility** infaillibilité pontificale; **~ nuncio** nonce *m* du

Pape; **P~ States** États *mpl* pontificaux *or* de l'Église.

Papanicolaou [ˌpæpəˈnɪkəluː] **n**: ~ **test** *or* **smear** test *m* de Papanicolaou.

paparazzo [ˌpæpəˈrætsəʊ] **n, pl paparazzi** [ˌpæpəˈrætsiː] paparazzi *m inv*.

papaya [pəˈpaɪə] **n** (*fruit*) papaye *f*; (*tree*) papayer *m*.

paper [ˈpeɪpəʳ] **1** **n** **a** (*NonC*) papier *m*. **a piece of** ~ (*odd bit*) un bout *or* un morceau de papier; (*sheet*) une feuille de papier; (*document etc*) un papier; **old** ~ paperasses *fpl*; (*frm*) **to commit to** ~ coucher (par écrit); **to put sth down on** ~ mettre qch par écrit; **it's a good plan on** ~ c'est un bon plan sur le papier; *see* **brown, carbon, rice** *etc*.

b (*newspaper*) journal *m*. **to write for the ~s** faire du journalisme; **it was in the ~s yesterday** c'était dans les journaux hier; **I saw it in the** ~ je l'ai vu dans le journal; *see* **illustrate** *etc*.

c (*document: gen pl*) ~**s** pièces *fpl*, documents *mpl*, papiers *mpl*; **show me your (identity) ~s** montrez-moi vos papiers (d'identité); (*Mil*) **(call-up)** ~**s** ordre *m* d'appel; **ship's ~s** papiers de bord; **voting** ~ bulletin *m* de vote.

d (*Scol, Univ*) (*set of exam questions*) épreuve *f* (écrite); (*student's written answers*) copie *f*. **geography** ~ épreuve de géographie; **she did a good** ~ **in French** elle a rendu une bonne copie de français.

e (*scholarly work*) (*printed*) article *m*; (*spoken*) communication *f*; (*in seminar: by student etc*) exposé *m*. **to write a** ~ **on** écrire un article sur; **to give** *or* **read a** ~ **on** faire une communication *or* un exposé sur.

f (*government publication*) livre *m*; *see* **white, green** *etc*.

g (*wall~*) papier *m* peint.

h (*Comm*) effet *m*. **commercial** ~ effet de commerce.

i (*US: Black sl: money*) fric*.

2 **comp** *doll, towel* en papier, de papier; (*fig pej*) *diploma etc* sans valeur, bidon* *inv*; *profits* sur le papier, théorique ►**paperback** livre broché, (*cheaper*) livre de poche; **paperback(ed) edition** édition brochée *or* de poche; **it exists in paperback** ça existe en (édition de) poche ►**paper bag** sac *m* en papier, (*small*) pochette *f* ►**paperbound** = **paperbacked** ►**paperboy** (*delivering*) (petit) livreur *m* de journaux; (*selling*) vendeur *m* de journaux ►**paper chain** chaîne *f* de papier ►**paper chase** rallye-papier *m* ►**paperclip** trombone *m*; (*staple*) agrafe *f*; (*bulldog clip*) pince *f* ►**paper cup** gobelet *m* en carton ►**paper currency** billets *mpl* (de banque) ►**paper dart** avion *m* en papier ►**paper fastener** attache *f* métallique (*à tête*); (*clip*) trombone *m* ►**paper handkerchief** mouchoir *m* en papier ►**paperhanger** (*Brit: decorator*) peintre-tapissier *m*; (*US* *: *crook*) passeur *m* de faux billets (*or* de chèques falsifiés) ►**paper industry** industrie *f* du papier ►**paper knife** coupe-papier *m inv* ►**paper lantern** lampion *m* ►**paper loss** (*Fin*) perte *f* comptable ►**paper mill** (usine *f* de) papeterie *f* ►**paper money** papier-monnaie *m* ►**paper qualifications** diplômes *mpl* ►**paper round** tournée *f* de distribution des journaux ►**paper shop*** marchand *m* de journaux ►**paper-shredder** destructeur *m* (de documents) ►**paper tape** (*Comput*) bande *f* perforée, ruban *m* perforé ►**paper tiger** tigre *m* de papier ►**paperweight** presse-papiers *m inv* ►**paperwork** (*gen*) écritures *fpl*; (*pej*) paperasserie *f*; **we need two more people to deal with the paperwork** il nous faut deux personnes de plus pour les écritures; **there's far too much paperwork** il y a beaucoup trop de paperasseries; **he brings home paperwork every night** il rapporte du travail à la maison tous les soirs.

3 **vt** **a** *room, walls* tapisser. (*fig*) **they ~ed the walls of the cafe with notices about ...** ils ont tapissé *or* complètement recouvert le mur du café d'affiches concernant ... .

b (*US fig: fill theatre*) **to** ~ **the house*** remplir la salle d'invités.

►**paper over** **vt fus** *crack in wall etc* recouvrir de papier; (*fig*) *differences, disagreements* passer sur. (*fig*) **to paper over the cracks** dissimuler les problèmes.

paperless [ˈpeɪpəlɪs] **adj** sans papier. **the** ~ **society** la société informatique *or* sans papier.

papery [ˈpeɪpərɪ] **adj** (*gen*) (fin) comme du papier; *skin* parcheminé.

papier-mâché [ˌpæpjeɪˈmæʃeɪ] **n** papier *m* mâché.

papilla [pəˈpɪlə] **n, pl ~e** [pəˈpɪliː] papille *f*.

papist [ˈpeɪpɪst] (*pej*) **1** **n** papiste *mf* (*pej*). **2** **adj** de(s) papiste(s) (*pej*).

papistry [ˈpeɪpɪstrɪ] **n** (*pej*) papisme *m* (*pej*).

papoose [pəˈpuːs] **n** bébé *m* peau-rouge.

pappus [ˈpæpəs] **n** aigrette *f* (*Bot*).

paprika [ˈpæprɪkə] **n** paprika *m*.

Papuan [ˈpæpjʊən] **1** **adj** papou. **2** **n** **a** Papou(e) *m(f)*. **b** (*Ling*) papou *m*.

Papua New Guinea [ˈpæpjʊənjuːˌgɪnɪ] **1** **n** Papouasie-Nouvelle-Guinée *f*. **2** **adj** papouan-néo-guinéen.

Papua-New-Guinean [ˈpæpjʊənjuːˌgɪnɪən] **n** Papouan-Néo-Guinéen(enne) *m(f)*.

papyrus [pəˈpaɪərəs] **n, pl ~es** *or* **papyri** [pəˈpaɪəraɪ] papyrus *m inv*.

par[1] [pɑːʳ] **1** **n** **a** (*equality of value*) égalité *f*, pair *m*; (*Fin*) [*currency*] pair. **to be on a** ~ **with** aller de pair avec, être l'égal de, être au niveau de; (*Fin*) **above/below** ~ au-dessus/au-dessous du pair; (*Fin*) **at** ~ au pair. **b** (*average*) moyenne *f*. **his work isn't up to** ~ *or* **is below** *or* **under** ~ son travail n'est pas satisfaisant; (*fig*) **to feel below** *or* **under** ~, **not to feel up to** ~ ne pas se sentir en forme. **c** (*Golf*) par *m*, normale *f* du parcours. (*Golf*) ~ **3/4** *etc* par 3/4 *etc*; (*fig*) **that's** ~ **for the course** c'est typique, il fallait (*or* faut *etc*) s'y attendre. **2** **comp** ►**par value** (*Fin*) montant nominal.

par[2]* [pɑːʳ] **n** (*Press*) **abbr of paragraph**.

para[1]* [ˈpærə] **n abbr of paragraph 1a**.

para[2]* [ˈpærə] **n** (*Mil*) (**abbr of parachutist**) **the ~s** les paras* *mpl*; **he's in the ~s** il est para*.

para... [ˈpærə] **pref** para... .

parable [ˈpærəbl] **n** parabole *f*. **in ~s** par paraboles.

parabola [pəˈræbələ] **n** parabole *f* (*Math*).

parabolic [ˌpærəˈbɒlɪk] **adj** parabolique.

paraboloid [pəˈræbəlɔɪd] **n** paraboloïde *m*.

Paracelsus [pærəˈselsəs] **n** Paracelse *m*.

paracetamol [pærəˈsiːtəmɒl] **n** paracétamol *m*.

parachute [ˈpærəʃuːt] **1** **n** parachute *m*. **2** **comp** *cords* de parachute ►**parachute drop** parachutage *m* ►**parachute jump** saut *m* en parachute ►**parachute landing** = **parachute drop** ►**parachute regiment** régiment *m* de parachutistes. **3** **vi** descendre en parachute. (*Sport*) **to go parachuting** faire du parachutisme. **4** **vt** parachuter.

parachutist [ˈpærəʃuːtɪst] **n** parachutiste *mf*.

Paraclete [ˈpærəkliːt] **n**: **the** ~ le Paraclet.

parade [pəˈreɪd] **1** **n** **a** (*Mil*) (*procession*) défilé *m*; (*ceremony*) parade *f*, revue *f*. **to be on** ~ (*drilling*) être à l'exercice; (*for review*) défiler. **b** **fashion** ~ présentation *f* de collections; **mannequin** ~ défilé *m* de mannequins. **c** (*fig: exhibition*) étalage *m*. **to make a** ~ **of one's wealth** faire étalage de sa richesse. **d** (*road*) boulevard *m* (*souvent au bord de la mer*). **e** (*Mil: also* ~ **ground**) terrain *m* de manœuvres. **2** **vt** *troops* faire défiler; (*fig: display*) faire étalage de, afficher. **3** **vi** (*Mil etc*) défiler.

►**parade about***, **parade around*** **vi** se balader*, circuler*. **don't parade about with nothing on!** ne te promène pas *or* ne te balade* pas tout nu!

paradigm [ˈpærədaɪm] **n** (*Ling etc*) paradigme *m*.

paradigmatic [ˌpærədɪgˈmætɪk] **adj** (*Ling etc*) paradigmatique.

paradisaic [ˌpærədɪˈseɪɪk] = **paradisiacal**.

paradise [ˈpærədaɪs] **n** paradis *m*. (*fig*) **earthly** ~ paradis terrestre; (*fig*) **it's a nature-lover's** *etc* ~ c'est un paradis pour les amoureux de la nature *etc*; **bird of** ~ oiseau *m* de paradis; *see* **fool[1]**.

paradisiacal [ˌpærədɪˈsaɪəkəl] **adj** paradisiaque.

paradox [ˈpærədɒks] **n** paradoxe *m*.

paradoxical [ˌpærəˈdɒksɪkəl] **adj** paradoxal.

paradoxically [ˌpærəˈdɒksɪkəlɪ] **adv** paradoxalement.

paraffin [ˈpærəfɪn] **1** **n** (*Chem*) paraffine *f*. (*Brit: fuel*) ~ **(oil)** pétrole *m* (lampant); (*Med*) **liquid** ~ huile *f* de paraffine. **2** **comp** ►**paraffin heater** radiateur *m* à pétrole ►**paraffin lamp** lampe *f* à pétrole ►**paraffin wax** paraffine *f*.

paragon [ˈpærəgən] **n** (*gen: of politeness etc*) modèle *m*, parangon *m*; (*also:* ~ **of virtue**) modèle *or* parangon de vertu.

paragraph [ˈpærəgrɑːf] **1** **n** **a** paragraphe *m*, alinéa m. **"new ~"** "à la ligne"; **to begin a new** ~ aller à la ligne. **b** (*newspaper item*) entrefilet *m*. **2** **comp** ►**paragraph mark** (*Typ*) pied *m* de mouche. **3** **vt** diviser en paragraphes *or* en alinéas.

Paraguay [ˈpærəgwaɪ] **n** Paraguay *m*.

Paraguayan [ˌpærəˈgwaɪən] **1** **adj** paraguayen. **2** **n** Paraguayen(enne) *m(f)*.

parakeet [ˈpærəkiːt] **n** perruche *f* (ondulée).

paralanguage [ˈpærəˌlæŋgwɪdʒ] **n** (*Phon*) paralangage *m*.

paralinguistic [ˈpærəˌlɪŋgwɪstɪk] **adj** (*Phon*) paralinguistique.

parallactic [ˌpærəˈlæktɪk] **adj** parallactique.

parallax [ˈpærəlæks] **n** parallaxe *f*.

parallel [ˈpærəlel] **1** **adj** **a** (*Math etc*) parallèle (*with, to* à). **the road runs** ~ **to the railway** la route est parallèle à la voie de chemin de fer; ~ **bars** barres *fpl* parallèles.

b (*fig*) analogue, parallèle (*with, to* à).

c (*Ski*) parallèle. ~ **turn** virage *m* parallèle.

2 **adv** parallèlement (*to* à).

3 **comp** ►**parallel-park** **vi** (*Aut*) faire un créneau.

4 **n** **a** (*Geog*) parallèle *m*.

b (*Math*) (ligne *f*) parallèle *f*.

c (*fig*) parallèle *m*, comparaison *f*. **to draw a** ~ **between** établir *or* faire un parallèle entre; **he/she is without** ~ il/elle est sans pareil(le); **to happen** *etc* **in** ~ **with sth** arriver *etc* parallèlement à *or* en parallèle avec.

5 **vt** (*Math*) être parallèle à; (*fig*) (*find equivalent to*) trouver un équivalent à; (*be equivalent to*) être équivalent à.

parallelepiped [ˌpærəˌleləˈpaɪped] **n** parallélépipède *m*.

parallelism [ˈpærəlelɪzəm] **n** (*Math, fig*) parallélisme *m*.

parallelogram [ˌpærəˈleləʊgræm] **n** parallélogramme *m*.

paralysis [pəˈræləsɪs] **n, pl paralyses** [pəˈræləsiːz] **a** (*Med*) paralysie *f*. **partial/total/general** ~ paralysie partielle/complète *or* totale/générale; *see* **creeping, infantile**. **b** (*fig*) [*traffic etc*] immobilisation *f*.

paralytic [ˌpærəˈlɪtɪk] **1** **adj** **a** (*Med*) paralytique. **b** (*Brit* *: *drunk*)

ivre mort. 2 n paralytique *mf*.
paralyzation [ˌpærəlaɪˈzeɪʃən] n immobilisation *f*.
paralyze [ˈpærəlaɪz] vt (*Med*) paralyser; (*fig*) *person* paralyser, pétrifier, méduser; *traffic, communications* paralyser. **his arm is ~d** il est paralysé du bras; **~d with fear** paralysé *or* transi de peur; **paralyzing cold** froid paralysant; **paralyzing fear/loneliness** peur/solitude pétrifiante.
paralyzer [ˈpærəlaɪzəʳ] n (*US: spray*) aérosol *m* défensif.
paramedic [ˌpærəˈmedɪk] n auxiliaire *mf* médical(e).
paramedical [ˌpærəˈmedɪkəl] adj paramédical.
parament [ˈpærəmənt] n, pl **~s** *or* **~a** [ˌpærəˈmentə] parement *m*.
parameter [pəˈræmɪtəʳ] n (*Math*) paramètre *m*. (*fig*) **the ~s of the event** les caractéristiques *fpl or* les données *fpl* de l'événement; **within its own narrow ~s** dans ses étroites limites; **it can be evaluated along different ~s** on peut l'évaluer selon différents critères; **the ~s of their energy policy** les grandes lignes *or* les orientations principales de leur politique énergétique.
parametric [ˌpærəˈmetrɪk] adj paramétrique.
paramilitary [ˌpærəˈmɪlɪtərɪ] 1 adj paramilitaire. 2 n a (*organisation*) **the ~** les organisations *fpl* paramilitaires. b (*member*) membre *m* d'une force paramilitaire.
paramnesia [ˌpæræmˈniːzɪə] n paramnésie *f*.
paramount [ˈpærəmaʊnt] 1 adj (*gen*) suprême; *chief* souverain. **of ~ importance** d'une suprême importance; **your health is ~** ta santé est ce qui compte le plus. 2 n chef *m* suprême.
paramour [ˈpærəmʊəʳ] n amant *m*; maîtresse *f*.
paranoia [ˌpærəˈnɔɪə] n paranoïa *f*.
paranoiac, paranoic [ˌpærəˈnɔɪɪk] adj, n paranoïaque *(mf)*.
paranoid [ˈpærənɔɪd] 1 adj paranoïde. 2 n paranoïaque *mf*.
paranoidal [ˌpærəˈnɔɪdl] adj paranoïde.
paranormal [ˌpærəˈnɔːməl] adj paranormal.
parapet [ˈpærəpɪt] n a *[bridge etc]* parapet *m*, garde-fou *m*. b (*Mil*) parapet *m*.
paraph [ˈpærəf] n parafe *m or* paraphe *m*.
paraphernalia [ˌpærəfəˈneɪlɪə] n sg or pl (*belongings, also for hobbies, sports etc*) attirail *m*; (*bits and pieces*) bazar* *m*.
paraphrase [ˈpærəfreɪz] 1 n paraphrase *f*. 2 vt paraphraser.
paraphrastic [ˌpærəˈfræstɪk] adj paraphrastique.
paraplegia [ˌpærəˈpliːdʒə] n paraplégie *f*.
paraplegic [ˌpærəˈpliːdʒɪk] 1 adj (*gen*) paraplégique; *games* pour les paraplégiques. 2 n paraplégique *mf*.
parapolice [ˌpærəpəˈliːs] n police *f* parallèle.
paraprofessional [ˌpærəprəˈfeʃənl] adj, n paraprofessionnel(le) *(mf)*.
parapsychological [ˌpærəsaɪkəˈlɒdʒɪkəl] adj parapsychique.
parapsychologist [ˌpærəsaɪˈkɒlədʒɪst] n parapsychologue *mf*.
parapsychology [ˌpærəsaɪˈkɒlədʒɪ] n métapsychologie *f*.
paras* [ˈpærəz] npl (abbr of **paratroops**) paras* *mpl*.
parascending [ˈpærəsendɪŋ] (*Sport*) 1 n parachutisme *m* ascensionnel. 2 vi: **to go ~** faire du parachute ascensionnel.
parasite [ˈpærəˌsaɪt] n (*Bot, Zool, fig*) parasite *m*.
parasitic(al) [ˌpærəˈsɪtɪk(əl)] adj a (*lit, fig*) parasite (*on* de). b (*Med*) *disease* parasitaire.
parasiticidal [ˌpærəˌsɪtɪˈsaɪdl] adj parasiticide.
parasiticide [ˌpærəˈsɪtɪsaɪd] n parasiticide *m*.
parasitism [ˈpærəsɪtɪzəm] n parasitisme *m*.
parasitologist [ˌpærəsaɪˈtɒlədʒɪst] n parasitologue *mf*.
parasitology [ˌpærəsɪˈtɒlədʒɪ] n parasitologie *f*.
parasitosis [ˌpærəsɪˈtəʊsɪs] n parasitose *f*.
parasol [ˈpærəˌsɒl] n ombrelle *f*; (*over table etc*) parasol *m*.
parasympathetic [ˌpærəˌsɪmpəˈθetɪk] adj parasympathique. **~ nervous system** système *m* parasympathique.
parataxis [ˌpærəˈtæksɪs] n parataxe *f*.
parathyroid [ˌpærəˈθaɪrɔɪd] 1 adj parathyroïdien. **~ gland** parathyroïde *f*. 2 n parathyroïde *f*.
paratrooper [ˈpærətruːpəʳ] n parachutiste *m* (*soldat*).
paratroops [ˈpærətruːps] npl (unités *fpl* de) parachutistes *mpl* (*soldats*).
paratyphoid [ˈpærəˈtaɪfɔɪd] 1 adj paratyphique. **~ fever** paratyphoïde *f*. 2 n paratyphoïde *f*.
parboil [ˈpɑːbɔɪl] vt (*Culin*) faire bouillir *or* faire cuire à demi.
parcel [ˈpɑːsəl] 1 n a (*package*) colis *m*, paquet *m*. b (*portion*) *[land]* parcelle *f*; *[shares]* paquet *m*; *[goods]* lot *m*; *see* **part**. c (*fig*) **~ of lies** tas *m or* tissu *m* de mensonges; **~ of liars/of fools** tas* *or* bande* *f* de menteurs/de sots. 2 comp ▶**parcel bomb** paquet piégé ▶**parcel net** filet *m* à bagages ▶**parcel office** bureau *m* de messageries ▶**parcel post** service *m* de colis postaux, service de messageries; **to send sth by parcel post** envoyer qch par colis postal. 3 vt (*also* **~ up**) *object, purchases* emballer, empaqueter, faire un paquet de.
▶**parcel out** vt sep distribuer; *inheritance* partager; *land* lotir.
parch [pɑːtʃ] vt a *crops, land* dessécher, brûler. b *person* altérer. **to be ~ed with thirst** avoir une soif dévorante; **to be ~ed** mourir de soif*. c (*toast*) griller légèrement.
parchment [ˈpɑːtʃmənt] n parchemin *m*. **~-like** parcheminé; **~ paper** papier-parchemin *m*.

pardner* [ˈpɑːdnəʳ] n (*US*) camarade *m*. **so long, ~!** au revoir, mon pote!*
pardon [ˈpɑːdən] 1 n a (*NonC*) pardon *m*; *see* **beg**. b (*Rel*) indulgence *f*. c (*Jur: also* **free ~**) grâce *f*. **letter of ~** lettre *f* de grâce; **general ~** amnistie *f*. 2 vt a *mistake, person* pardonner. **to ~ sb for sth** pardonner qch à qn; **to ~ sb for doing** pardonner à qn d'avoir fait; **~ me for troubling you** pardonnez-moi de vous déranger; (*iro*) **~ me for breathing/speaking/living!*** excuse-moi de respirer/de parler/de vivre!; (*hum*) **~ my French!*** pardonnez-moi l'expression; **if you'll ~ the expression** si vous me permettez *or* si vous pardonnez l'expression. b (*Jur*) (*see* **1c**) gracier; amnistier. 3 excl (*apologizing*) pardon!, excusez-moi!; (*not hearing*) (*US also* **~ me**) comment?, vous dites?
pardonable [ˈpɑːdnəbl] adj *mistake* pardonnable; (*Jur*) graciable.
pardonably [ˈpɑːdnəblɪ] adv de façon bien excusable *or* bien pardonnable.
pare [pɛəʳ] vt a *fruit* peler, éplucher; *nails* rogner, couper. b (*reduce: also* **~ down**) *expenses* réduire.
parent [ˈpɛərənt] 1 n père *m or* mère *f*. **his ~s** ses parents *mpl*, son père et sa mère, ses père et mère; (*Scol*) **~s' evening** réunion *f* d'information avec les parents (d'élèves). 2 comp *interest, involvement etc* parental, des parents ▶**parent animals, parent birds** *etc* parents *mpl* ▶**parent company** (*Comm, Fin*) maison *f or* société *f* mère ▶**parent power** (*Scol*) pouvoir *m* parental ▶**parent-teacher association** (*Scol*) association *f* des parents d'élèves et des professeurs ▶**parent tree** souche *f*.
parentage [ˈpɛərəntɪdʒ] n naissance *f*, lignée *f*, origine *f*. **of unknown ~** de parents inconnus.
parental [pəˈrentl] adj des parents, parental (*frm*); *involvement, cooperation etc* parental. **to have ~ rights over a child** (*gen*) avoir autorité parentale sur un enfant; (*Jur*) avoir la tutelle d'un enfant.
parenthesis [pəˈrenθɪsɪs] n, pl **parentheses** [pəˈrenθɪsiːz] parenthèse *f*. **in ~** entre parenthèses.
parenthetic(al) [ˌpærənˈθetɪk(əl)] adj (placé) entre parenthèses.
parenthetically [ˌpærənˈθetɪkəlɪ] adv par parenthèse, entre parenthèses.
parenthood [ˈpɛərənthʊd] n condition *f* de parent(s), paternité *f or* maternité *f*. **the joys of ~** les joies de la paternité *or* de la maternité.
parenting [ˈpɛərəntɪŋ] n: **~ is a full-time occupation** élever un enfant est un travail à plein temps.
parer [ˈpɛərəʳ] n épluche-légumes *m inv*.
pariah [pəˈraɪə] n paria *m*.
parietal [pəˈraɪɪtl] 1 adj pariétal. 2 n a (*Anat*) pariétal *m*. b npl (*US Univ*) **~s** heures *fpl* de visite (du sexe opposé dans les chambres d'étudiants).
paring [ˈpɛərɪŋ] n a (*see* **pare**) action *f* d'éplucher *or* de peler *etc*. **~ knife** couteau *m* à éplucher; *see* **cheese**. b **~s** *[fruit, vegetable]* épluchures *fpl*, pelures *fpl*; *[nails]* rognures *fpl*; *[metal]* cisaille *f*.
pari passu [ˈpærɪˈpæsuː] adv (*liter*) de pair.
Paris [ˈpærɪs] n Paris; *see* **plaster**.
parish [ˈpærɪʃ] 1 n (*Rel*) paroisse *f*; (*Brit: civil*) commune *f*; (*US: in Louisiana*) ≃ comté *m*. 2 comp ▶**parish church** église paroissiale ▶**parish council** (*Rel*) conseil *m* paroissial; (*civil*) ≃ conseil municipal ▶**parish hall** salle paroissiale *or* municipale ▶**parish priest** (*Catholic*) curé *m*; (*Protestant*) pasteur *m* ▶**parish-pump** (*Brit: pej*) *subject* d'intérêt purement local; *point of view* borné; **parish-pump mentality/politics** esprit *m*/politique *f* de clocher ▶**parish register** registre paroissial ▶**parish school**† école communale.
parishioner [pəˈrɪʃənəʳ] n paroissien(-ienne) *m(f)*.
Parisian [pəˈrɪzɪən] 1 adj *district, theatre, street* parisien, de Paris; *habit, personality, society* parisien; *life* à Paris, des Parisiens. 2 n Parisien(-ienne) *m(f)*.
parity [ˈpærɪtɪ] n a (*gen*) égalité *f*, parité *f*; (*in arms race*) équilibre *m*. (*in wage negotiations*) **~ with the teachers** *etc* la parité avec les (salaires des) professeurs *etc*. b (*Fin*) parité *f*. **exchange at ~** change *m* au pair *or* à (la) parité. c (*US Agric*) taux *m* de parité.
park [pɑːk] 1 n (*public*) jardin public, parc *m*; *[country house]* parc; *see* **car, national, safari** *etc*.
2 comp ▶**park-and-ride** *possibilité pour les banlieusards de laisser leur voiture dans une gare et de continuer le trajet en ville par le métro etc* ▶**park keeper** gardien *m* de parc ▶**parkland** bois *mpl* ▶**park-ride** = **park-and-ride** ▶**parkway** (*US*) route *f* à paysage aménagé.
3 vt a *car etc* garer, parquer. **he was ~ed near the theatre** il était garé *or* parqué près du théâtre; **to ~ the car** garer la voiture, se garer; **don't ~ the car in the street** ne laisse pas la voiture dans la rue; **a line of ~ed cars** une rangée de voitures en stationnement.
b (*: *leave*) *person, object* laisser, abandonner. **to ~* a child with sb** laisser un enfant chez qn.
4 vi stationner, se garer. **I was ~ing when I caught sight of him** j'étais en train de me garer quand je l'aperçus; **do not ~ here** ne stationnez pas ici.
parka [ˈpɑːkə] n parka *m*.
parkin [ˈpɑːkɪn] n gâteau *m* à l'avoine et au gingembre.
parking [ˈpɑːkɪŋ] 1 n stationnement *m*. **"~"** "parking",

"stationnement autorisé"; **"no ~"** "défense de stationner", "stationnement interdit"; **~ is very difficult** il est très difficile de trouver à se garer.

2 comp **►parking attendant** gardien *m* de parking, gardien de parc de stationnement **►parking bay** lieu *m* de stationnement (autorisé) **►parking brake** (*US*) frein *m* à main **►parking lights** feux *mpl* de position **►parking lot** (*US*) parking *m*, parc *m* de stationnement **►parking meter** parcomètre *m* **►parking place, parking space** lieu *m or* créneau *m* de stationnement; **I couldn't find a parking place** je n'ai pas pu trouver à me garer **►parking ticket** P.-V.* *m*, procès-verbal *m*, papillon* *m*.

Parkinson ['pɑːkɪnsən] n: **~'s disease** la maladie de Parkinson; **~'s law** le postulat de Parkinson (*selon lequel toute tâche finit par occuper le temps disponible*).

parkinsonism ['pɑːkɪnsənɪzəm] n parkinsonisme *m*.

parky* ['pɑːkɪ] adj (*Brit*) **it's ~** il fait frisquet*.

parlance ['pɑːləns] n langage *m*, parler *m*. **in common ~** en langage courant *or* ordinaire *or* de tous les jours; **in medical/legal** *etc* **~** en langage médical/juridique *etc*, en termes médicaux/juridiques *etc*.

parlay ['pɑːlɪ] (*US*) 1 vt (*Betting*) réemployer (*les gains d'un précédent pari et le pari originel*); (*fig*) *talent, inheritance* faire fructifier. 2 vi (*fig*) faire fructifier de l'argent.

parley ['pɑːlɪ] 1 n conférence *f*, pourparlers *mpl*; (*Mil*) pourparlers. 2 vi (*also Mil*) parlementer (*with* avec); (*more formally*) entrer *or* être en pourparlers (*with* avec).

parliament ['pɑːləmənt] n a (*Brit*) **P~** (*institution*) Parlement *m*, Chambres *fpl*; (*building*) Parlement; (*Hist*) Parlement; **in P~** au Parlement; **to go into** *or* **enter P~** se faire élire député, entrer au Parlement; *see* **house, member.** b parlement *m*.

parliamentarian [ˌpɑːləmen'teərɪən] 1 n a (*Brit Parl: MP*) parlementaire *mf*, membre *m* du Parlement. b (*Brit Hist*) parlementaire *mf*. c (*US: expert*) fonctionnaire *mf* spécialiste des questions de procédure. 2 adj (*Brit Hist*) parlementaire.

parliamentary [ˌpɑːlə'mentərɪ] adj *business, language, behaviour* parlementaire. **~ agent** agent *m* parlementaire; (*Brit*) **P~ Commissioner** médiateur *m*; **~ election** élection *f* législative; **~ government** gouvernement *m* parlementaire; **~ privilege** immunité *f* parlementaire; (*Brit*) **~ private secretary** *parlementaire attaché à un ministre (assurant la liaison avec les autres parlementaires)*; (*Brit*) **~ secretary** (parlementaire *mf* faisant fonction de) sous-secrétaire *m* d'État.

parlour, (*US*) **parlor** ['pɑːləʳ] 1 n (*in house:* †) petit salon; (*in convent*) parloir *m*; (*in bar:* †) arrière-salle *f*; *see* **beauty, funeral.** 2 comp **►parlor car** (*US Rail*) voiture-salon *f* **►parlour game** jeu *m* de salon *or* de société **►parlourmaid** femme *f* de chambre (*chez des particuliers*).

parlous ['pɑːləs] adj (*liter, frm,* †) précaire, périlleux, alarmant.

Parma ['pɑːmə] n Parme. **~ ham** jambon *m* de Parme; **~ violet** violette *f* de Parme.

Parmesan [ˌpɑːmɪ'zæn] n (*cheese*) parmesan *m*.

Parnassian [pɑː'næsɪən] adj parnassien.

Parnassus [pɑː'næsəs] n Parnasse *m*. **(Mount) ~** le mont Parnasse.

parochial [pə'rəʊkɪəl] adj (*Rel*) paroissial; (*fig pej*) de clocher. (*US*) **~ school** école *f* catholique.

parochialism [pə'rəʊkɪəlɪzəm] n esprit *m* de clocher.

parodist ['pærədɪst] n parodiste *mf*.

parody ['pærədɪ] 1 n (*lit, fig*) parodie *f*. 2 vt parodier.

parole [pə'rəʊl] 1 n a (*Mil etc*) parole *f* d'honneur; (*Jur*) liberté *f* conditionnelle. **on ~** (*Mil*) sur parole; (*Jur*) en liberté conditionnelle; (*Jur*) **to release sb on ~** mettre qn en liberté conditionnelle; (*Jur*) **to break ~** se rendre coupable d'un délit entraînant la révocation de sa mise en liberté conditionnelle. b [pæ'rɒl] (*Ling*) parole *f*. 2 vt *prisoner* mettre en liberté conditionnelle. 3 comp **►parole board** (*Brit*) ≃ juge *m* de l'application des peines **►parole officer** (*US*) contrôleur *m* judiciaire.

paroquet ['pærəkɪt] n = **parakeet.**

paroxysm ['pærəksɪzəm] n (*Med*) paroxysme *m*; (*fig*) *[grief, pain]* paroxysme; *[anger]* accès *m*. **in a ~ of delight** dans un transport de joie; **~ of tears/laughter** crise *f* de larmes/de fou rire.

parquet ['pɑːkeɪ] 1 n a (*also* **~ flooring**) parquet *m*. b (*US Theat*) parterre *m*. 2 vt parqueter.

parquetry ['pɑːkɪtrɪ] n parquetage *m*, parqueterie *f*.

parricidal ['pærɪsaɪdl] adj parricide.

parricide ['pærɪsaɪd] n (*act*) parricide *m*; (*person*) parricide *mf*.

parrot ['pærət] 1 n (*Orn*) perroquet *m*, perruche *f*; (*fig*) perroquet. (*Brit hum*) **he was sick as a ~**‡ il en était malade. 2 comp **►parrot disease** psittacose *f* **►parrot fashion** comme un perroquet **►parrot fever** = **parrot disease** **►parrot fish** poisson-perroquet *m*.

parry ['pærɪ] 1 vt *blow* parer, détourner; *question* éluder; *attack* parer; *difficulty* tourner, éviter. 2 n (*Fencing*) parade *f*.

parse [pɑːz] vt faire l'analyse grammaticale de.

parsec ['pɑːsek] n parsec *m*.

Parsee ['pɑːsiː] adj, n parsi(e) *m(f)*.

parser ['pɑːzəʳ] n (*Comput*) analyseur *m* syntaxique.

parsimonious [ˌpɑːsɪ'məʊnɪəs] adj parcimonieux.

parsimoniously [ˌpɑːsɪ'məʊnɪəslɪ] adv avec parcimonie, parcimonieusement.

parsimony ['pɑːsɪmənɪ] n parcimonie *f*.

parsing ['pɑːzɪŋ] n (*Ling, Scol*) analyse *f* grammaticale.

parsley ['pɑːslɪ] n persil *m*. **~ sauce** sauce persillée.

parsnip ['pɑːsnɪp] n panais *m*.

parson ['pɑːsn] n (*Church of England etc*) pasteur *m*; (*clergyman in general*) prêtre *m*, ecclésiastique *m*. (*Culin*) **~'s nose** croupion *m*.

parsonage ['pɑːsənɪdʒ] n presbytère *m*.

part [pɑːt] 1 n a (*section, division*) partie *f*. **only (a) ~ of the play is good** il n'y a qu'une partie de la pièce qui soit bonne; **the play is good in ~s, ~s of the play are good** il y a de bons passages dans la pièce; **in ~** en partie, partiellement; **for the most ~** dans l'ensemble; **to be ~ and parcel of** faire partie (intégrante) de; **a penny is the hundredth ~ of £1** un penny est le centième de une livre; (*liter*) **a man of ~s** un homme très doué; **the funny ~ of it is that ...** le plus drôle dans l'histoire c'est que ...; *see* **moving, private.**

b *[book, play]* partie *f*; (*Publishing: instalment*) livraison *f*, fascicule *m*; (*Press, Rad, TV: of serial*) épisode *m*. **a six-~ serial, a serial in six ~s** un feuilleton en six épisodes.

c (*Tech*) pièce *f*. **spare ~** pièce (de rechange), pièce détachée.

d (*esp Culin*) mesure *f*. **three ~s water to one ~ milk** trois mesures d'eau pour une mesure de lait.

e (*Gram*) *[verb]* **principal ~s** temps principaux; **~s of speech** parties *fpl* du discours, catégories grammaticales; **what ~ of speech is "of"?** à quelle catégorie grammaticale est-ce que "of" appartient?

f (*share*) participation *f*, rôle *m*; (*Cine, Theat*) rôle. **he had a large ~ in the organization of ...** il a joué un grand rôle dans l'organisation de ...; **she had some ~ in it** elle y était pour quelque chose; **we all have our ~ to play** nous avons tous notre rôle à jouer; **to take ~ in** participer à; **I'll have** *or* **I want no ~ in it, I don't want any ~ of it** je ne veux pas m'en mêler; *see* **act, play.**

g (*side, behalf*) parti *m*, part *f*. **to take sb's ~ (in a quarrel)** prendre le parti de qn *or* prendre parti pour qn (dans une dispute); **for my ~** pour ma part, quant à moi; **an error on the ~ of his secretary** une erreur de la part de sa secrétaire; **to take sth in good ~** prendre qch du bon côté.

h (*Mus*) partie *f*; *[song, fugue]* voix *f*; (*sheet of music*) partition *f*. **the violin ~** la partie de violon; **two-~ song** chant *m* à deux voix.

i (*region*) **in these ~s** dans cette région, dans ce coin*; **in this ~ of the world** dans ce coin*, par ici; **in my ~ of the world** dans mon pays, chez moi; **in foreign ~s** à l'étranger.

j (*US*) *[hair]* raie *f*.

2 comp **►part exchange** (*Brit*) reprise *f* en compte; (*Brit*) **to take a car** *etc* **in part exchange** reprendre une voiture *etc* en compte **►part owner** copropriétaire *mf* **►part payment** (*exchange*) règlement partiel; (*deposit*) arrhes *fpl* **►part song** chant *m* à plusieurs voix *or* polyphonique **►part-time** *see* **part-time** **►part-timer** travailleur *m*, -euse *f or* employé(e) *m(f)* à temps partiel **►part way: part way along/through/there** à mi-chemin **►part work** (*Brit*) fascicule *m*.

3 adv en partie. **she is ~ French** elle est en partie française.

4 vt a *crowd* ouvrir un passage dans; *people, boxers* séparer. **they were ~ed during the war years** ils sont restés séparés pendant toute la guerre.

b **to ~ one's hair** se faire une raie; **his hair was ~ed at the side** il portait une raie sur le côté.

c **to ~ company with** (*leave*) fausser compagnie à, quitter; (*disagree*) ne plus être d'accord avec; **they ~ed company** (*lit*) ils se quittèrent; (*fig*) ils se trouvèrent en désaccord; (*hum*) **the trailer ~ed company with the car** la remorque a faussé compagnie à la voiture.

5 vi (*gen: take leave of each other*) se quitter; (*break up: of couple*) se séparer; *[crowd]* s'ouvrir; *[boxers etc]* se séparer; *[rope]* se rompre. **to ~ from sb** quitter qn; (*permanently*) se séparer de qn; **to ~ with** *money* débourser; *possessions* se défaire de, renoncer à; *employee etc* se séparer de.

partake [pɑː'teɪk] pret **partook** [pɑː'tʊk] ptp **partaken** [pɑː'teɪkən] vi (*frm*) **to ~ in** prendre part à, participer à; **to ~ of** *meal, refreshment* prendre; (*fig*) tenir de, avoir quelque chose de.

parthenogenesis ['pɑːθɪnəʊ'dʒenɪsɪs] n parthénogénèse *f*.

parthenogenetic [ˌpɑːθɪnəʊdʒɪ'netɪk] adj parthénogénétique.

parthenogenetically [ˌpɑːθɪnəʊdʒɪ'netɪkəlɪ] adv parthénogénétiquement.

Parthenon ['pɑːθənɒn] n Parthénon *m*.

Parthian ['pɑːθɪən] adj: **~ shot** flèche *f* du Parthe.

partial ['pɑːʃəl] adj a (*in part*) *success, eclipse* partiel. b (*biased*) partial (*to, towards* envers), injuste. (*: *like*) **to be ~ to sth** avoir un faible pour qch; **to be ~ to doing** avoir un penchant à faire.

partiality [ˌpɑːʃɪ'ælɪtɪ] n a (*bias*) partialité *f* (*for* pour; *towards* envers), préjugé *m* (favorable) (*for* pour; *to* en faveur de), favoritisme *m*. b (*liking*) prédilection *f*, penchant *m*, faible *m* (*for* pour).

partially ['pɑːʃəlɪ] adv a (*partly*) en partie, partiellement. **the ~-sighted** les mal-voyants *mpl*. b (*with bias*) avec partialité, partialement.

participant [pɑːˈtɪsɪpənt] n participant(e) *m(f)* (*in* à).

participate [pɑːˈtɪsɪpeɪt] vi participer, prendre part (*in* à).

participation [pɑːˌtɪsɪˈpeɪʃən] n participation *f* (*in* à).

participatory [pɑːˈtɪsɪˌpeɪtərɪ] adj participatif.

participial [ˌpɑːtɪˈsɪpɪəl] adj participial.

participle [ˈpɑːtɪsɪpl] n participe *m*. **past/present ~** participe passé/présent.

particle [ˈpɑːtɪkl] n particule *f*, parcelle *f*; *[dust, flour etc]* grain *m*; *[metal]* paillette *f*; (*Ling, Phys*) particule; (*fig*) brin *m*, grain. **a ~ of truth/of sense** un grain de vérité/de bon sens; **not a ~ of evidence** pas l'ombre d'une preuve, pas la moindre preuve; (*Phys*) **~ accelerator** accélérateur *m* de particules; **~ physics** physique *f* des particules élémentaires.

parti-coloured, (*US*) **parti-colored** [ˈpɑːtɪˌkʌləd] adj bariolé.

particular [pəˈtɪkjʊləʳ] 1 adj a (*distinct from others*) particulier, distinct des autres; (*characteristic*) particulier; (*personal*) personnel. **in this ~ case** dans ce cas particulier; **for no ~ reason** sans raison précise *or* bien définie; **that ~ brand** cette marque-là (et non pas une autre); **his ~ chair** son fauteuil à lui; **her ~ type of humour** son genre particulier d'humour, son humour personnel; **my ~ choice** mon choix personnel.

b (*outstanding*) particulier, spécial. **nothing ~ happened** rien de particulier *or* de spécial n'est arrivé; **he took ~ care over it** il y a mis un soin particulier; **to pay ~ attention to sth** faire bien attention à qch; **a ~ friend of his** un de ses meilleurs amis, un de ses amis intimes; **she didn't say anything ~** elle n'a rien dit de spécial.

c (*having high standards*) minutieux, méticuleux; (*over cleanliness*) méticuleux; (*hard to please*) pointilleux, difficile, exigeant. **she is ~ about whom she talks to** elle ne parle pas à n'importe qui; **he is ~ about his food** il est difficile pour la nourriture; **which do you want? — I'm not ~** lequel voulez-vous? — cela m'est égal *or* je n'ai pas de préférence.

d (*very exact*) *account* détaillé, circonstancié.

2 n a **in ~** en particulier, notamment; **anything/anybody in ~** quelque chose/quelqu'un en particulier; **nothing/nobody in ~** rien/personne en *or* de particulier.

b (*detail*) détail *m*. **in every ~** en tout point; **he is wrong in one ~** il se trompe sur un point; **~s** (*information*) détails, renseignements *mpl*; (*description*) description *f*; *[person]* (*description*) signalement *m*; (*name, address etc*) nom *m* et adresse *f*, coordonnées *fpl*; (*for official document etc*) caractéristiques *fpl* signalétiques; **full ~s** tous les détails, tous les renseignements; **for further ~s apply to ...** pour plus amples renseignements s'adresser à ... .

particularity [pəˌtɪkjʊˈlærɪtɪ] n particularité *f*.

particularize [pəˈtɪkjʊləraɪz] 1 vt particulariser, spécifier, détailler, préciser. 2 vi spécifier, préciser.

particularly [pəˈtɪkjʊləlɪ] adv (*in particular*) en particulier, particulièrement, spécialement; (*notably*) notamment, particulièrement; (*very carefully*) méticuleusement, avec grand soin.

parting [ˈpɑːtɪŋ] 1 n a séparation *f*; *[waters]* partage *m*. (*lit, fig*) **the ~ of the ways** la croisée des chemins. b (*Brit*) *[hair]* raie *f*; *[mane]* épi *m*. 2 adj *gift* d'adieu. **~ words** paroles *fpl* d'adieu; (*fig*) **~ shot** flèche *f* du Parthe.

partisan [ˌpɑːtɪˈzæn] 1 n (*supporter; fighter*) partisan *m*. 2 adj: **~ politics** politique partisane; (*Pol etc*) **~ spirit** esprit *m* de parti; (*Mil*) **~ warfare** guerre *f* de partisans.

partisanship [ˌpɑːtɪˈzænʃɪp] n esprit *m* de parti, partialité *f*; (*membership*) appartenance *f* à un parti.

partita [pɑːˈtiːtə] n, pl **~s** *or* **partite** [pɑːˈtiːteɪ] (*Mus*) partita *f*.

partition [pɑːˈtɪʃən] 1 n a (*also* **~ wall**) cloison *f*. **glass ~** cloison vitrée. b (*dividing*) *[property]* division *f*; *[country]* partition *f*, partage *m*, démembrement *m*; *[estate]* morcellement *m*. 2 vt *property* diviser, partager; *country* partager, démembrer; *estate* morceler; *room* cloisonner.

▶**partition off** vt sep *room, part of room* cloisonner.

partitive [ˈpɑːtɪtɪv] adj, n partitif (*m*).

partly [ˈpɑːtlɪ] adv partiellement, en partie. **~ blue, ~ green** moitié bleu, moitié vert.

partner [ˈpɑːtnəʳ] 1 n a (*gen*) partenaire *mf*; (*Comm, Fin, Jur, Med etc*) associé(e) *m(f)*. **our European ~s** nos partenaires européens *or* du Marché commun; **senior ~** associé principal; **junior ~** associé adjoint; (*fig*) **~s in crime** associés *or* complices *mpl* dans le crime; *see* **sleeping, trading**.

b (*Sport*) partenaire *mf*; (*co-driver*) coéquipier *m*, -ière *f*; (*Dancing*) cavalier *m*, -ière *f*. **take your ~s for a waltz** choisissez vos partenaires pour la valse.

c (*in marriage*) époux *m*, épouse *f*, conjoint(e) *m(f)*; (*cohabiting*) concubin(e) *m(f)*, partenaire *mf*; (*in sex*) partenaire. **bring your ~ along** venez avec un(e) ami(e).

2 vt (*Comm, Fin etc*) être l'associé (de), s'associer à; (*Sport*) être le partenaire de, être le coéquipier de; (*Dancing*) être le cavalier (*or* la cavalière) de.

partnership [ˈpɑːtnəʃɪp] n (*gen*) association *f*; (*Comm, Fin, Jur*) ≃ société *f* en nom collectif. (*Comm, Fin*) **limited ~** (société *f* en) commandite *f*; **to be in ~** être en association (*with* avec), être associé; **to enter** *or* **go into ~** s'associer (*with* à, avec); **to take sb into ~** prendre qn comme associé; **a doctors' ~** un cabinet de groupe (*médical*), une association de médecins; *see* **general**.

partridge [ˈpɑːtrɪdʒ] n, pl **~s** *or* **~** perdrix *f*; (*young bird, also Culin*) perdreau *m*.

part-time [ˈpɑːtˈtaɪm] 1 adj a *job, employment* à temps partiel; (*half-time*) à mi-temps. **to do ~ work** travailler à temps partiel *or* à mi-temps. b *employee, staff* (qui travaille) à temps partiel, à mi-temps. 2 n (*Ind*) **to be on ~*** être en chômage partiel. 3 adv à temps partiel.

parturition [ˌpɑːtjʊəˈrɪʃən] n parturition *f*.

party [ˈpɑːtɪ] 1 n a (*Pol etc*) parti *m*. **political/Conservative/Labour ~** parti politique/conservateur/travailliste.

b (*group*) *[travellers]* groupe *m*, troupe* *f*; *[workmen]* équipe *f*, brigade *f*; (*Mil*) détachement *m*, escouade *f*. (*lit, fig*) **advance ~** éclaireurs *mpl*; **rescue ~** équipe de secours.

c (*Jur etc*) partie *f*. **all parties concerned** tous les intéressés; **to be ~ to a suit** être en cause; **to become a ~ to a contract** signer un contrat; **third ~** tierce personne, tiers *m* (*see also* **third**); **~ aggrieved** partie lésée, victime *f*; **innocent ~** innocent(e) *m(f)*; (*fig*) **I will not be (a) ~ to any dishonesty** je ne me ferai le (*or* la) complice d'aucune malhonnêteté; (*fig*) **to be a ~ to a crime** être complice d'un crime; *see* **guilty, moving, prevailing**.

d (*celebration*) petite fête *f*; (*in the evening*) soirée *f*; (*formal*) réception *f*. **to give a ~** donner une petite réception, inviter des amis; (*more formally*) donner une réception *or* une soirée; **birthday ~** fête *f* d'anniversaire; **dinner ~** dîner *m*; **evening ~** soirée *f*; **private ~** réunion *m* intime; **tea ~: to invite sb to a tea ~** inviter qn à prendre le thé; (*fig*) **let's keep the ~ clean*** pas d'inconvenances!, un peu de tenue!; *see* **bottle, Christmas**.

e (‡ *hum: person*) individu *m*.

f (*Telec*) correspondant *m*. **your ~ is on the line** votre correspondant est en ligne.

2 comp *politics, leader* de parti, du parti; *disputes* de partis ▶**party dress** robe habillée; (*evening dress*) toilette *f* de soirée ▶**partygoer** (*gen*) habitué(e) *m(f)* des réceptions; (*on specific occasion*) invité(e) *m(f)* ▶**party line** (*Pol*) politique *f or* ligne *f* du parti; (*Telec*) ligne commune à deux abonnés; (*Pol*) **to follow the party line** suivre la ligne du parti, être dans la ligne du parti (*see also* **toe**) ▶**party list** *système de vote sur liste politique et non sur candidat* ▶**party manners***: **his party manners were terrible** sa façon de se tenir en société était abominable; **the children were on their party manners** les enfants ont été d'une tenue exemplaire ▶**party machine** (*Pol*) machine *f or* administration *f* du parti ▶**party plan** vente *f* par réunions ▶**party political**: (*Rad, TV*) **party political broadcast** *émission réservée à un parti politique,* ≃ *"tribune libre"*; **this is not a party political question** ce n'est pas une question qui relève de la ligne du parti ▶**party politics** politique *f* de parti(s) ▶**party pooper*** rabat-joie *m inv*, trouble-fête *mf inv* ▶**party spirit** (*Pol*) esprit *m* de parti; (*: *gaiety*) entrain *m* ▶**party wall** mur mitoyen.

3 vi (* *US: go out*) sortir, aller danser; (*go to parties*) courir les réceptions.

partying* [ˈpɑːtɪɪŋ] n: **I'm not a great one for ~** je n'aime pas beaucoup courir de soirée en soirée.

PASCAL, Pascal [pæsˈkæl] n Pascal *m*.

paschal [ˈpɑːskəl] adj (*Rel*) pascal. **the P~ Lamb** l'agneau pascal.

pasha [ˈpæʃə] n pacha *m*.

pass [pɑːs] 1 n a (*permit*) *[journalist, worker etc]* coupe-file *m inv*, laissez-passer *m inv*; (*Rail etc*) carte *f* d'abonnement; (*Theat*) billet *m* de faveur; (*to museum etc*) laissez-passer *m*; (*Naut*) lettre *f* de mer; (*Mil etc: safe conduct*) sauf-conduit *m*.

b (*in mountains*) col *m*, défilé *m*; *see* **sell**.

c (*in exam*) moyenne *f*, mention *f* passable. **did you get a ~?** avez-vous eu la moyenne?, avez-vous été reçu?; **to get a ~ in history** être reçu en histoire.

d (*NonC: situation*) situation *f*, état *m*. (*iro*) **things have come to a pretty ~!** voilà à quoi on en est arrivé!; **to bring sb to a pretty ~** mettre qn dans de beaux draps; **things have reached such a ~ that ...** les choses en sont arrivées à un tel point que ... .

e (*Ftbl etc*) passe *f*; (*Fencing*) botte *f*, attaque *f*. **to make a ~* at a woman** faire du plat* à une femme.

f *[conjuror]* passe *f*.

2 comp ▶**passbook** livret *m* (bancaire) ▶**pass degree** (*Univ*) ≃ licence *f* libre ▶**passkey** passe-partout *m inv*, passe *m* ▶**pass mark** (*Scol, Univ*) moyenne *f*; **to get a passmark** avoir la moyenne ▶**pass-through** (*US*) passe-plat *m* ▶**password** mot *m* de passe.

3 vi a (*come, go*) passer (*through* par); *[procession]* défiler; (*Aut: overtake*) dépasser, doubler. **to let sb ~** laisser passer qn; **to ~ down the street** descendre la rue; **~ down the bus please!** avançons s'il vous plaît!; **to ~ behind/in front of** passer derrière/devant; **to ~ into oblivion** tomber dans l'oubli; **to ~ out of sight** disparaître; **letters ~ed between them** ils ont échangé des lettres.

b *[time]* (se) passer, s'écouler. **the afternoon ~ed pleasantly** l'après-midi a passé *or* s'est passé(e) agréablement; **how time ~es!** que le temps passe vite!

c (*esp Chem: change*) se transformer (*into* en).

d (*esp Jur: transfer*) passer, être transmis. **the estate ~ed to my brother** la propriété est revenue à mon frère.

e (*also* ~ **away**) *[memory, opportunity]* s'effacer, disparaître; *[pain]* passer.

f (*in exam*) être reçu (*in* en).

g (*take place*) se passer, avoir lieu. **all that ~ed between them** tout ce qui s'est passé entre eux; (*liter, frm*) **to bring sth to ~** accomplir qch, réaliser qch; (*liter*) **it came to ~ that** il advint que.

h (*be accepted*) *[coins]* avoir cours; *[behaviour]* convenir, être acceptable; *[project]* passer. **to ~ under the name of** être connu sous le nom de; **he tried to ~ for a doctor** il a essayé de se faire passer pour (un) médecin; **what ~es for a hat these days** ce qui de nos jours passe pour un chapeau; **she would ~ for 20** on lui donnerait 20 ans; **will this do? — oh it'll ~** est-ce que ceci convient? — oh ça peut aller; **let it ~!** (*of insult*) laisse tomber!*; (*of error*) laisse courir!*; **he let it ~** il l'a laissé passer, il ne l'a pas relevé; **he couldn't let it ~** il ne pouvait pas laisser passer ça comme ça.

i (*Cards*) passer. **(I) ~!** (*games*) (je) passe!; (*fig*) aucune idée.

j (*Sport*) faire une passe.

4 **vt** a (*go past*) *building* passer devant; *person* croiser, rencontrer; *barrier, frontier, customs* passer; (*Aut: overtake*) dépasser, doubler; (*go beyond: also Sport*) dépasser. **when you have ~ed the town hall** quand vous serez passé devant *or* quand vous aurez dépassé la mairie; **they ~ed each other on the way** ils se sont croisés en chemin; (*frm*) **no remark ~ed his lips** il ne souffla *or* ne dit pas mot.

b (*get through*) *exam* être reçu à *or* admis à, réussir. **the film ~ed the censors** le film a reçu le visa de la censure; *see* **muster**.

c *time* passer. **just to ~ the time** pour passer le temps, histoire de passer le temps*; **to ~ the evening reading** passer la soirée à lire; *see* **time**.

d (*hand over*) (faire) passer. **please ~ the salt** faites passer le sel s'il vous plaît; **~ me the box** passez-moi la boîte; **to ~ a dish round the table** faire passer un plat autour de la table; **the telegram was ~ed round the room** on fit passer le télégramme dans la salle; **to ~ sth down the line** faire passer qch (de main en main); **~ the word that it's time to go** faites passer la consigne que c'est l'heure de partir; **to play at ~-the-parcel** ≃ jouer au furet; *see* **buck**.

e (*on phone*) passer.

f (*accept, allow*) *candidate* recevoir, admettre; (*Parl*) *bill* voter, faire passer. **the censors ~ed/haven't ~ed the film** le film a été autorisé/interdit par la censure; (*Scol, Univ*) **they didn't ~ him** ils l'ont refusé *or* recalé*; **the doctor ~ed him fit for work** le docteur l'a déclaré en état de reprendre le travail; (*Typ*) **to ~ the proofs (for press)** donner le bon à tirer.

g (*utter*) *comment* faire; *opinion* émettre, formuler. **to ~ remarks about sb/sth** faire des observations sur qn/qch; (*Jur, fig*) **to ~ judgment** prononcer *or* rendre un jugement (*on* sur); (*Jur*) **to ~ sentence** prononcer une condamnation (*on sb* contre qn); *see also* **sentence**.

h (*move*) passer. **he ~ed his hand over his brow** il s'est passé la main sur le front; **he ~ed his handkerchief over his face** il a passé son mouchoir sur son visage; **to ~ a rope through a ring** passer une corde dans un anneau; **to ~ a cloth over a table** donner *or* passer un coup de chiffon à une table; **to ~ a knife through sth** enfoncer un couteau dans qch; (*Culin*) **to ~ sth through a sieve** passer qch (au tamis); (*Mil, fig*) **to ~ in review** passer en revue.

i (*Sport*) *ball* passer.

j *forged money* (faire) passer, écouler; *stolen goods* faire passer.

k (*surpass*) **to ~ comprehension** dépasser l'entendement; **to ~ belief** être incroyable.

l (*Med*) **to ~ blood** avoir du sang dans les urines; **to ~ a stone** évacuer un calcul; **to ~ water** uriner.

►**pass along** 1 **vi** passer, circuler, passer son chemin. 2 **vt sep** a (*lit*) *object, book etc* faire passer (de main en main). b = **pass on 2b**.

►**pass away** **vi** a (*euph: die*) mourir, s'éteindre (*euph*), décéder (*frm*). b = **pass 3e**.

►**pass back** **vt sep** *object* rendre, retourner. (*Rad, TV*) **I will now pass you back to the studio** je vais rendre l'antenne au studio.

►**pass by** 1 **vi** passer (à côté); *[procession]* défiler. **I saw him passing by** je l'ai vu passer. 2 **vt sep** ne pas faire attention à, négliger, ignorer. **life has passed me by** je n'ai pas vraiment vécu.

►**pass down** 1 **vi** *[inheritance etc]* être transmis, revenir (*to* à). 2 **vt sep** transmettre. **to pass sth down (in a family)** transmettre qch par héritage (dans une famille); **passed down from father to son** transmis de père en fils.

►**pass in** **vt sep** (faire) passer. **to pass a parcel in through a window** (faire) passer un colis par une fenêtre.

►**pass off** 1 **vi** a (*subside*) *[faintness etc]* passer, se dissiper. b (*take place*) *[events]* se passer, se dérouler, s'accomplir. **everything passed off smoothly** tout s'est passé sans accroc. 2 **vt sep** a faire passer, faire prendre. **to pass someone/something off as someone/something else** faire passer une personne/une chose pour une autre; **to pass o.s. off as a doctor** se faire passer pour (un) médecin. b **to pass sth off on sb** repasser *or* refiler* qch à qn.

►**pass on** 1 **vi** a (*euph: die*) s'éteindre (*euph*), mourir. b (*continue one's way*) passer son chemin, ne pas s'arrêter. (*fig*) **to pass on to a new subject** passer à un nouveau sujet. 2 **vt sep** (*hand on*) *object* faire passer (*to* à); *news* faire circuler, faire savoir; *message* transmettre. **take it and pass it on** prenez et faites passer; **to pass on old clothes to sb** repasser de vieux vêtements à qn; **you've passed your cold on to me** tu m'as passé ton rhume; **to pass on a tax to the consumer** répercuter un impôt sur le consommateur.

►**pass out** 1 **vi** a (*faint*) s'évanouir, perdre connaissance, tomber dans les pommes*; (*from drink*) tomber ivre mort; (*fall asleep*) s'endormir comme une masse. **he passed out on us** il nous a fait le coup de tomber dans les pommes* (*or* de tomber ivre mort *or* de s'endormir comme une masse). b (*US Scol*) **to pass out of high school** terminer ses études secondaires. 2 **vt sep** *leaflets etc* distribuer.

►**pass over** 1 **vi** (*euph*) = **pass on 1a**. 2 **vt sep** a (*neglect*) omettre, négliger, ignorer. **to pass over Paul in favour of Robert** donner la préférence à Robert au détriment de Paul; **he was passed over in favour of his brother** on lui a préféré son frère. 3 **vt fus** (*ignore*) passer sous silence, ne pas relever.

►**pass round** **vt sep** *bottle* faire passer; *sweets, leaflets* distribuer. (*fig*) **to pass round the hat** faire la quête.

►**pass through** 1 **vi** passer. **I can't stop — I'm only passing through** je ne peux pas rester — je ne fais que passer. 2 **vt fus** a *hardships* subir, endurer. b (*travel through*) traverser.

►**pass up** **vt sep** a (*lit*) passer. b (*: *forego*) *chance, opportunity* laisser passer.

passable ['pɑːsəbl] **adj** a (*tolerable*) passable, assez bon. b *road* praticable, carrossable; *river* franchissable.

passably ['pɑːsəblɪ] **adv** passablement, assez.

passage ['pæsɪdʒ] 1 **n** a (*passing*) (*lit*) passage *m*; *[bill, law]* adoption *f*; (*fig*) passage, transition *f* (*from* ... *to* de ... à). **with the ~ of time he understood** avec le temps il finit par comprendre; (*fig, liter*) **~ of** *or* **at arms** passe *f* d'armes; *see* **bird, rite**. b (*Naut*) voyage *m*, traversée *f*. c (*way through: also* **~way**) passage *m*. **to force a ~ through** se frayer un passage *or* un chemin (à travers); **to leave a ~** laisser un passage, laisser le passage libre. d (*also* **~way**) (*indoors*) couloir *m*, corridor *m*; (*outdoors*) ruelle *f*, passage *m*. e (*Mus*) passage *m*; *[text]* passage. (*Literat*) **selected ~s** morceaux choisis. 2 **comp** ►**passageway** = **passage 1c, 1d**.

passé ['pæseɪ] **adj** *play, book, person* vieux jeu *inv*, démodé, dépassé*; *woman* défraîchi, fané.

passel ['pæsəl] **n** (*US*) **a ~ of** ... une ribambelle de ..., un tas* de ... .

passenger ['pæsndʒəʳ] 1 **n** (*in train*) voyageur *m*, -euse *f*; (*in boat, plane, car*) passager *m*, -ère *f*. (*fig pej*) **he's just a ~** il n'est vraiment qu'un poids mort. 2 **comp** ►**passenger car** (*US*) = **passenger coach** ►**passenger cell** (*Aut*) habitacle *m* ►**passenger coach** (*Rail*) voiture *f* *or* wagon *m* de vogageurs ►**passenger list** (*Aviat, Naut*) liste *f* des passagers ►**passenger mile** (*Aviat*) ≃ kilomètre-passager *m*; (*Rail etc*) ≃ kilomètre-voyageur *m*, voyageur *m* kilométrique ►**passenger seat** (*Aut*) siège *m* du passager *or* de passagers ►**passenger (service) enquiries** (*Aviat, Rail*) renseignements *mpl* ►**passenger station** (*Rail*) gare *f* de voyageurs ►**passenger train** train *m* de voyageurs.

passe-partout ['pæspɑːtuː] **n** a (*master key*) passe-partout *m inv* (*clef*), passe *m*. b (*Art*) **~ (frame)** (encadrement *m* en) sous-verre *m*.

passer-by ['pɑːsə'baɪ] **n, pl ~s-by** passant(e) *m(f)*.

passim ['pæsɪm] **adv** passim.

passing ['pɑːsɪŋ] 1 **adj** (*lit*) *person, car* qui passe (*or* passait *etc*); (*fig: brief*) éphémère, passager. **~ desire** désir fugitif; **with each ~ day/year** de jour/année en jour/année; **~ remark** remarque *f* en passant; (*Mus*) **~ note** note *f* de passage; (*Tennis*) **~ shot** passing-shot *m*, tir *m* passant. 2 **adv** (†† *or liter*) extrêmement. **~ fair** de toute beauté. 3 **n** a *[time]* écoulement *m*; *[train, car]* passage *m*; (*Aut: overtaking*) dépassement *m*. **with the ~ of time** avec le temps; **in ~** en passant. b (*euph: death*) mort *f*, trépas *m* (*liter*). **~ bell** glas *m*. 4 **comp** ►**passing-out parade** (*Mil*) défilé *m* de promotion ►**passing place** (*in road*) aire *f* de croisement.

passion ['pæʃən] 1 **n** a (*love*) passion *f*, amour *m*; (*fig*) passion (*for* de). **to have a ~ for music** avoir la passion de la musique; **ruling ~** passion dominante. b (*burst of anger*) colère *f*, emportement *m*. **fit of ~** accès *m* de colère; **to be in a ~** être furieux; *see* **fly³**. c (*strong emotion*) passion *f*, émotion violente. d (*Rel, Mus*) **P~** Passion *f*; **the St John/St Matthew P~** la Passion selon saint Jean/saint Matthieu. 2 **comp** ►**passionflower** (*Bot*) passiflore *f* ►**passion fruit** (*Bot*) fruit *m* de la passion ►**Passion play** (*Rel*) mystère *m* de la Passion ►**Passion Sunday** (*Rel*) dimanche *m* de la Passion ►**Passion Week** (*Rel*) semaine *f* de la Passion.

passionate ['pæʃənɪt] **adj** *person, plea, love, embrace* passionné; *speech* véhément.

passionately ['pæʃənɪtlɪ] **adv** passionnément. **to be ~ fond of sth/sb** adorer qch/qn.

passionless ['pæʃənlɪs] adj sans passion, détaché.

passive ['pæsɪv] 1 adj a (*motionless*) passif, inactif, inerte; (*resigned*) passif, soumis. (*Pol*) ~ **resistance** résistance passive; (*Pol*) ~ **disobedience** désobéissance passive; ~ **smoking** tabagisme *m* passif; ~ **balance of trade** balance *f* commerciale déficitaire; (*Aut*) ~ **restraint** dispositif *m* de sécurité passive. b (*Gram*) passif. 2 n (*Gram*) passif *m*. **in the** ~ au passif.

passively ['pæsɪvlɪ] adv passivement; (*Gram*) au passif.

passiveness ['pæsɪvnɪs] n, **passivity** [pæ'sɪvɪtɪ] n passivité *f*.

Passover ['pɑːsəʊvəʳ] n pâque *f* (des Juifs).

passport ['pɑːspɔːt] n passeport *m*. **no-~ day trip to France** une journée en France sans passeport; ~ **control** contrôle *m* des passeports; ~ **section** service *m* des passeports; (*Brit*) **visitor's** *or* **short-term** ~ passeport *m* temporaire; (*fig*) ~ **to success** clef *f* de la réussite.

past [pɑːst] 1 n a passé *m*. **in the** ~ dans le temps, dans le passé, autrefois; **as in the** ~ comme par le passé; **she lives in the** ~ elle vit dans le passé; **it's a thing of the** ~ cela ne se fait plus, cela n'existe plus, c'est du passé, c'est de l'histoire ancienne; **domestic servants are a thing of the** ~ les domestiques, cela n'existe plus; **I thought you'd quarrelled? — that's a thing of the** ~ je croyais que vous étiez fâchés? — c'est de l'histoire ancienne; **do you know his** ~? vous connaissez son passé?; **a woman with a** ~ une femme au passé chargé.

b (*Gram*) passé *m*. **in the** ~ au passé; ~ **definite** passé simple, passé défini, prétérit *m*.

2 adj a passé. **for some time** ~ depuis quelque temps; **in times** ~ autrefois, (au temps) jadis; **in** ~ **centuries** pendant les siècles passés; **the** ~ **week** la semaine dernière *or* passée; **the** ~ **few days** ces derniers jours; **all that is now** ~ tout cela c'est du passé; ~ **president** ancien président; (*fig*) **to be a** ~ **master of sth** être expert en qch; **to be a** ~ **master at doing sth** avoir l'art de faire qch.

b (*Gram*) (*gen*) passé; *verb* au passé; *form, ending* du passé. ~ **perfect** plus-que-parfait *m*; **in the** ~ **tense** au passé; ~ **participle** participe passé.

3 prep a (*beyond in time*) plus de. **it is** ~ **11 o'clock** il est plus de 11 heures, il est 11 heures passées; (*Brit*) **half** ~ **3** 3 heures et demie; **quarter** ~ **3** 3 heures et quart; **at 20** ~ **3** à 3 heures 20; (*Brit*) **the train goes at 5** ~* le train part à 5*; **she is** ~ **60** elle a plus de 60 ans, elle a 60 ans passés, elle a dépassé la soixantaine.

b (*beyond in space*) au delà de, plus loin que. ~ **it** au delà, plus loin; **just** ~ **the post office** un peu plus loin que la poste, juste après la poste.

c (*in front of*) devant. **he goes** ~ **the house every day** tous les jours il passe devant la maison; **he rushed** ~ **me** il est passé devant moi *or* (*overtook*) m'a dépassé à toute allure.

d (*beyond limits of*) au delà de. ~ **endurance** insupportable; **it is** ~ **all understanding** cela dépasse l'entendement; **that is** ~ **all belief** cela n'est pas croyable, c'est incroyable; **I'm** ~ **caring** je ne m'en fais plus, j'ai cessé de m'en faire; **he is** ~ **praying for** on ne peut plus rien pour lui; **he is** ~ **work** il n'est plus en état de travailler; **he's a bit** ~ **it now*** il n'est plus dans la course*; **that cake is** ~ **its best** ce gâteau n'est plus si bon; **I wouldn't put it** ~ **her to have done it** je la croirais bien capable de l'avoir fait, cela ne m'étonnerait pas d'elle qu'elle l'ait fait; **I wouldn't put it** ~ **him** cela ne m'étonnerait pas de lui, il en est bien capable.

4 adv (phr vb elem) auprès, devant. **to go** *or* **walk** ~ passer; *see* **march**[1] *etc*.

pasta ['pæstə] n (*Culin: NonC*) pâtes *fpl*.

paste [peɪst] 1 n a (*Culin*) (*pastry, dough*) pâte *f*; [*meat etc*] pâté *m*. **liver** ~ pâté *or* crème *f* de foie; **tomato** ~ concentré *m or* purée *f* de tomate; **almond** ~ pâte d'amandes. b (*gen comp*) pâte *f*. **tooth~** pâte dentifrice, dentifrice *m*. c (*glue*) colle *f* (de pâte). d (*jewellery*) strass *m*. 2 comp *jewellery* en strass ►**pasteboard** carton *m*; (*US: pastry board*) planche *f* à pâtisserie ►**paste-up** collage *m*. 3 vt a coller; *wallpaper* enduire de colle. **to** ~ **photos into an album** coller des photos dans un album; **he** ~**d the pages together** il a collé les pages ensemble. b (*‡: thrash*) flanquer une raclée à*.

►**paste up** 1 vt sep *notice, list* afficher; *photos etc* coller. 2 **paste-up** n *see* **paste 2**.

pastel ['pæstəl] n (crayon *m*) pastel *m*. ~ **(drawing)** (dessin *m* au) pastel; ~ **(colour** *or* **shade)** ton *m* pastel *inv*.

pastern ['pæstən] n paturon *m*.

pasteurization [ˌpæstəraɪ'zeɪʃən] n pasteurisation *f*.

pasteurize ['pæstəraɪz] vt pasteuriser.

pasteurized ['pæstəraɪzd] adj pasteurisé.

pastiche [pæs'tiːʃ] n pastiche *m*.

pastille ['pæstɪl] n pastille *f*.

pastime ['pɑːstaɪm] n passe-temps *m inv*, divertissement *m*, distraction *f*.

pasting‡ ['peɪstɪŋ] n (*thrashing*) raclée* *f*. **to give sb a** ~ flanquer une raclée à qn*.

pastor ['pɑːstəʳ] n pasteur *m*.

pastoral ['pɑːstərəl] 1 adj a (*rural*) pastoral, champêtre; (*Agr*) de pâture; (*Literat etc*) pastoral. ~ **land** pâturages *mpl*. b (*Rel*) pastoral. ~ **letter** lettre *f* pastorale. c (*Educ, Sociol etc*) qui concerne la santé physique et morale de l'individu. **in a** ~ **capacity** dans un rôle de conseiller; (*Educ*) ~ **care system** tutorat *m*. 2 n (*Literat, Rel*) pastorale *f*.

pastrami [pə'strɑːmɪ] n *bœuf fumé très épicé*.

pastry ['peɪstrɪ] 1 n a (*NonC*) pâte *f*; *see* **puff, short**. b (*cake*) pâtisserie *f*. 2 comp ►**pastryboard** planche *f* à pâtisserie ►**pastrybrush** pinceau *m* à pâtisserie ►**pastrycase** croûte *f*; **in a pastrycase** en croûte ►**pastrycook** pâtissier *m*, -ière *f*.

pasturage ['pɑːstjʊrɪdʒ] n pâturage *m*.

pasture ['pɑːstʃəʳ] 1 n (*Agr*) (lieu *m* de) pâture *f*, pré *m*, pâturage *m*. **to put out to** ~ (*lit*) mettre au pré *or* au pâturage; (*fig*) mettre à la retraite; (*fig*) **to move on to** ~**s new** *or* **greener** ~**s** changer d'horizons. 2 vi paître. 3 vt faire paître, pacager. 4 comp ►**pasture land** herbage *m*, pâturage(s) *m(pl)*.

pasty ['peɪstɪ] 1 adj pâteux; (*pej*) *face, complexion* terreux. (*pej*) ~-**faced** au teint terreux *or* de papier mâché*. 2 ['pæstɪ] n (*Brit Culin*) petit pâté *m*, feuilleté *m*.

Pat [pæt] n a (dim of **Patrick** *or* **Patricia**). b *au masculin, surnom des Irlandais*.

pat[1] [pæt] 1 vt *ball etc* taper, tapoter, donner une tape à; *animal* flatter de la main, caresser. **to** ~ **sb on the back** (*lit*) tapoter qn dans le dos; (*fig*) complimenter qn, congratuler qn; **he** ~**ted my hand** il me tapota la main. 2 n a (*tap*) coup léger, petite tape; (*on animal*) caresse *f*. **to give sb a** ~ **on the back** (*lit*) tapoter qn dans le dos; (*fig*) complimenter qn, congratuler qn; **he deserves a** ~ **on the back for that** cela mérite qu'on lui fasse un petit compliment; **to give o.s. a** ~ **on the back** se congratuler, s'applaudir. b ~ **of butter** noix *f* de beurre; (*larger*) motte *f* de beurre.

pat[2] [pæt] 1 adv a (*exactly suitable*) à propos, à point. **to answer** ~ (*immediately*) répondre sur-le-champ; (*with repartee*) répondre du tac au tac. b (*perfectly*) *learn* par cœur. **to know sth off** ~ savoir qch sur le bout du doigt. c (*firm, unmoving*) *remain* inflexible. (*US*) **to stand** ~* ne rien faire, refuser de bouger. 2 adj *example, answer* tout prêt. **he had his explanation** ~ il avait son explication toute prête.

Patagonia [ˌpætə'gəʊnɪə] n Patagonie *f*.

Patagonian [ˌpætə'gəʊnɪən] 1 adj patagonien. 2 n Patagonien(-ienne) *m(f)*.

patch [pætʃ] 1 n a (*for clothes*) pièce *f*; (*for inner tube, airbed*) rustine *f*; (*over eye*) cache *m*; (*cosmetic: on face*) mouche *f*.

b (*small area*) [*colour*] tache *f*; [*sky*] morceau *m*, échappée *f*, pan *m*; [*land*] parcelle *f*; [*vegetables*] carré *m*; [*ice*] plaque *f*; [*mist*] nappe *f*; [*water*] flaque *f*; (*on dog's back etc*) tache. **a damp** ~ **on the wall** une tache d'humidité *or* une plaque humide sur le mur.

c (*fig*) **he isn't a** ~ **on his brother*** son frère pourrait lui en remontrer n'importe quand, (*stronger*) il n'arrive pas à la cheville de son frère; **to strike a bad** ~ être dans la déveine*; **a bad** *or* **sticky*** ~ un moment difficile; **good in** ~**es** bon par moments.

d (*Comput*) correction *f* (de programme).

e (*Brit*) [*policeman, social worker*] secteur *m*. **they're off my** ~ **now** ils ont quitté mon secteur.

2 comp ►**patch pocket** poche rapportée ►**patch test** (*Med*) test *m* cutané ►**patchwork** *see* **patchwork**.

3 vt *clothes* rapiécer; *tyre* réparer, poser une rustine à.

►**patch together** vt sep *garment* rapiécer; (*hum*) *old car etc* retaper*.

►**patch up** vt sep *clothes* rapiécer, rapetasser*; *machine* rafistoler*; (*) *injured person* rafistoler*. **to patch up a quarrel** se raccommoder.

patchwork ['pætʃwɜːk] 1 n (*lit, fig*) patchwork *m*. 2 comp *quilt* en patchwork; *landscape* bigarré; (*pej: lacking in unity*) fait de pièces et de morceaux, disparate.

patchy ['pætʃɪ] adj (*lit; also fig pej*) inégal.

pate [peɪt] n tête *f*. **a bald** ~ un crâne chauve.

patella [pə'telə] n, pl ~**e** [pə'teliː] rotule *f*.

paten ['pætən] n patène *f*.

patent ['peɪtənt] 1 adj a (*obvious*) *fact, dishonesty* patent, manifeste, évident.

b *invention* breveté. ~ **medicine** spécialité *f* pharmaceutique; **letters** ~ lettres patentes.

c (*also* ~ **leather**) cuir *m* verni; ~ **(leather) shoes** souliers vernis *or* en cuir verni.

2 n (*licence*) brevet *m* d'invention; (*invention*) invention brevetée. **to take out a** ~ prendre un brevet; ~**(s) applied for** demande *f* de brevet déposée; ~ **pending** brevet en cours d'homologation; **to come out of** *or* (*US*) **to come off** ~ tomber dans le domaine public.

3 comp ►**Patent and Trademark Office** (*US*) = **Patent Office** ►**patent attorney** (*Jur*) conseil *m* en propriété industrielle ►**patent engineer** conseil *m* en brevets d'invention ►**patent leather** *see* **1c** ►**Patent Office** (*Brit*) ≃ Institut *m* national de la propriété industrielle ►**patent right** droit *m* exclusif d'exploitation ►**Patent Rolls** (*Brit*) registre *m* des brevets d'invention ►**patent still** alambic *m* breveté.

4 vt faire breveter.

patentable ['peɪtəntəbl] adj (*Jur etc*) brevetable.

patentee [ˌpeɪtən'tiː] n breveté *m*.

patently ['peɪtəntlɪ] adv manifestement, clairement.

patentor ['peɪtəntəʳ] n (*Jur etc*) personne *f or* organisme *m* délivrant un (*or* le) brevet d'invention.
pater* ['peɪtəʳ] n (*esp Brit*) pater* *m*, paternel* *m*.
paterfamilias [ˌpeɪtəfə'mɪlɪˌæs] n, pl **patresfamilias** [ˌpɑːtreɪzfə'mɪlɪˌæs] pater familias *m*.
paternal [pə'tɜːnl] adj paternel.
paternalism [pə'tɜːnəlɪzəm] n paternalisme *m*.
paternalist [pə'tɜːnəlɪst] adj paternaliste.
paternalistic [pətɜːnə'lɪstɪk] adj (trop) paternaliste.
paternally [pə'tɜːnəlɪ] adv paternellement.
paternity [pə'tɜːnɪtɪ] 1 n (*lit, fig*) paternité *f*. 2 comp ►**paternity leave** congé *m* parental (*pour le père*) ►**paternity order** (*Jur*) reconnaissance *f* de paternité judiciaire ►**paternity suit** (*Jur*) action *f* en recherche de paternité.
paternoster [ˌpætə'nɒstəʳ] n a (*Rel*) Pater *m* (noster). **The P~** le Paternoster. b (*elevator*) paternoster *m*.
path¹ [pɑːθ] 1 n a (*also* **~way**) (*in woods etc*) sentier *m*, chemin *m*; (*in garden*) allée *f*; (*also* **foot ~**: *beside road*) sentier (pour les piétons); (*fig*) sentier, chemin, voie *f*. **to clear a ~ through the woods** ouvrir un sentier *or* un chemin dans les bois; (*fig*) **to beat a ~ to sb's door** accourir en foule chez qn; (*fig*) **the ~ to success** le chemin du succès; *see* **cross, primrose** *etc*. b *[river]* cours *m*; *[sun]* route *f*; *[bullet, missile, spacecraft, planet]* trajectoire *f*. 2 comp ►**pathfinder** (*gen*) pionnier *m*, éclaireur *m*; (*Aviat*) avion *m* éclaireur.
path²* [pɑːθ] n (abbr of **pathology**) ~ **lab** laboratoire *m or* labo* *m* d'analyses.
Pathan [pə'tɑːn] 1 adj pathan. 2 n Pathan(e) *m(f)*.
pathetic [pə'θetɪk] adj a *sight, grief* pitoyable, navrant. ~ **attempt** tentative désespérée; **it was ~ to see it** cela faisait peine à voir, c'était un spectacle navrant. b (*) *person, piece of work, performance* pitoyable, minable. c (*Literat*) ~ **fallacy** action *f* de prêter à la nature des sentiments humains.
pathetically [pə'θetɪklɪ] adv pitoyablement. ~ **thin** d'une maigreur pitoyable; **she was ~ glad to find him** son plaisir à le retrouver vous serrait le cœur.
pathogenic [ˌpæθə'dʒenɪk] adj pathogène.
pathological [ˌpæθə'lɒdʒɪkəl] adj pathologique.
pathologist [pə'θɒlədʒɪst] n pathologiste *mf*.
pathology [pə'θɒlədʒɪ] n pathologie *f*.
pathos ['peɪθɒs] n pathétique *m*. **the ~ of the situation** ce que la situation a (*or* avait *etc*) de pathétique; **told with great ~** raconté d'une façon très émouvante *or* très pathétique.
patience ['peɪʃəns] n a patience *f*. **to have ~** prendre patience, patienter; **to lose ~** perdre patience (*with sb* avec qn), s'impatienter (*with sb* contre qn); **I am out of ~, my ~ is exhausted** ma patience est à bout, je suis à bout de patience; **I have no ~ with these people** ces gens m'exaspèrent; *see* **possess, tax, try** *etc*. b (*Brit Cards*) réussite *f*. **to play ~** faire des réussites.
patient ['peɪʃənt] 1 adj patient, endurant. **(you must) be ~!** patientez!, (un peu de) patience!*; **he's been ~ long enough** il a assez patienté *or* attendu, sa patience a des limites. 2 n (*gen*) malade *mf*; *[dentist etc]* patient(e) *m(f)*; (*post-operative*) opéré(e) *m(f)*. **a doctor's ~s** (*undergoing treatment*) les patients *or* les malades d'un médecin; (*on his list*) les clients *mpl* d'un médecin; *see* **in, out**.
patiently ['peɪʃəntlɪ] adv patiemment, avec patience.
patina ['pætɪnə] n patine *f*.
patio ['pætɪəʊ] n patio *m*.
Patna ['pætnə] n Patna. ~ **rice** *espèce de riz à grain long*.
patois ['pætwɑː] n, pl ~ patois *m*.
pat. pend. abbr of **patent pending**.
patriarch ['peɪtrɪɑːk] n patriarche *m*.
patriarchal [ˌpeɪtrɪ'ɑːkəl] adj patriarcal.
patriarchy [ˌpeɪtrɪ'ɑːkɪ] n patriarcat *m*, gouvernement patriarcal.
Patricia [pə'trɪʃə] n Patricia *f*.
patrician [pə'trɪʃən] adj, n patricien(-ienne) *m(f)*.
patricide ['peɪtrəsaɪd] n (*crime*) patricide *m*; (*person*) patricide *mf*.
Patrick ['pætrɪk] n Patrice *m*, Patrick *m*.
patrimony ['pætrɪmənɪ] n a patrimoine *m*, héritage *m*. b (*Rel*) biens-fonds *mpl* (*d'une église*).
patriot ['peɪtrɪət] n patriote *mf*.
patriotic [ˌpætrɪ'ɒtɪk] adj *deed, speech* patriotique; *person* patriote. (*Pol*) **the P~ Front** le Front patriote.
patriotically [ˌpætrɪ'ɒtɪkəlɪ] adv patriotiquement, en patriote.
patriotism ['pætrɪətɪzəm] n patriotisme *m*.
patrol [pə'trəʊl] 1 n a (*NonC*) patrouille *f*. **to go on ~** aller en patrouille, faire une ronde; **to be on ~** être de patrouille.
b (*group of troops, police, scouts etc*) patrouille *f*; (*ship, aircraft on ~*) patrouilleur *m*; *see* **border, immigration, customs**.
2 comp *helicopter, vehicle* de patrouille ►**patrolboat** patrouilleur *m* ►**patrol car** (*Police*) voiture *f* de police ►**patrol leader** (*Mil, Scouting*) chef *m* de patrouille ►**patrolman** *see* **patrolman** ►**patrol wagon** (*US*) voiture *f or* fourgon *m* cellulaire.
3 vt *[police, troops etc] district, town, streets* patrouiller dans, faire une patrouille dans.
4 vi *[troops, police]* patrouiller, faire une patrouille. (*fig: walk about*) **to ~ up and down** faire les cent pas.
patrolman [pə'trəʊlmən] n a (*US*) agent *m* de police, gardien *m* de la paix. b (*Aut*) agent *m* de la sécurité routière.
patron ['peɪtrən] n a *[artist]* protecteur *m*, -trice *f*; *[a charity]* patron(ne) *m(f)*; (*also* **~ saint**) saint(e) patron(ne) *m(f)*. **~ of the arts** protecteur des arts, mécène *m*. b *[hotel, shop]* client(e) *m(f)*; *[theatre]* habitué(e) *m(f)*. **our ~s** (*Comm*) notre clientèle *f*; (*Theat*) notre public *m*.
patronage ['pætrənɪdʒ] n a *[artist etc]* patronage *m*, appui *m*. **under the ~ of** sous le patronage de, sous les auspices de; **~ of the arts** mécénat *m*, protection *f* des arts. b (*Comm*) clientèle *f*, pratique *f*. c (*Rel*) droit *m* de disposer d'un bénéfice; (*Pol*) droit de présentation. d (*Pol pej*) népotisme *m*; (*US*) nomination *f* d'amis politiques à des postes de responsabilité. (*US*) **to give out ~ jobs** nommer ses amis politiques à des postes de responsabilité, attribuer des postes aux petits copains*.
patronize ['pætrənaɪz] vt a (*pej*) traiter avec condescendance. b (*Comm*) *shop, firm* donner *or* accorder sa clientèle à, se fournir chez; *dress shop* s'habiller chez; *bar, cinema, club* fréquenter.
patronizing ['pætrənaɪzɪŋ] adj *person* condescendant; *look, tone, smile, manner* condescendant, de condescendance.
patronizingly ['pætrənaɪzɪŋlɪ] adv d'un air *or* d'un ton condescendant.
patronymic [ˌpætrə'nɪmɪk] 1 n patronyme *m*, nom *m* patronymique. 2 adj patronymique.
patsy* ['pætsɪ] n (*US*) pigeon* *m*, gogo* *m*, victime *f*.
patter¹ ['pætəʳ] 1 n *[comedian, conjurer]* bavardage *m*, baratin* *m*; *[salesman etc]* boniment *m*, baratin*; (*jargon*) jargon *m*. 2 vi (*also* **~ away, ~ on**) jacasser, baratiner*.
patter² ['pætəʳ] 1 n *[rain, hail]* crépitement *m*, bruit *m*. **a ~ of footsteps** un petit bruit de pas pressés; (*hum*) **we'll soon be hearing the ~ of tiny feet** on attend un heureux événement; (*Mus*) **~ song** ≃ ritournelle *f*. 2 vi *[footsteps]* trottiner; *[rain]* frapper, battre (*on* contre); *[hail]* crépiter.
►**patter about, patter around** vi trottiner çà et là.
pattern ['pætən] 1 n a (*design: on material, wallpaper etc*) dessin(s) *m(pl)*, motif *m*. **the ~ on a tyre** les sculptures *fpl* d'un pneu; **floral ~** motif de fleurs *or* floral.
b (*style*) modèle *m*, style *m*. **various ~s of cutlery** différents modèles de couverts; **dresses of different ~s** des robes de styles différents.
c (*Sewing: also* **paper ~**) patron *m*; (*Knitting etc*) modèle *m*.
d (*fig: model*) exemple *m*, modèle *m*. (*fig*) **~ of living** mode *m* de vie; **on the ~ of** sur le modèle de; **it set a ~ for other meetings** cela a institué une marche à suivre pour les autres séances.
e (*standard, regular way of acting etc*) **behaviour ~s of teenagers** les types *mpl* de comportement chez les adolescents; **it followed the usual ~** *[meeting, interview]* cela s'est déroulé selon la formule habituelle; *[crime, epidemic]* cela s'est passé selon le scénario habituel; *[timetable, schedule]* cela suivait le schéma habituel; **I began to notice a ~ in their behaviour/reactions** *etc* j'ai commencé à remarquer que certaines caractéristiques se dégageaient de leur conduite/de leurs réactions *etc*; **traffic ~** orientation *f or* sens *m* de la circulation; **to be part of a ~** faire partie d'un tout; (*Econ*) **~ of trade** structure *f or* physionomie *f* des échanges.
f (*sample*) *[material etc]* échantillon *m*.
g (*Ling*) modèle *m*; *[sentence]* structure *f*. **on the ~ of** sur le modèle de.
2 comp ►**pattern book** *[material, wallpaper etc]* liasse *f or* album *m* d'échantillons; (*Sewing*) catalogue *m or* album *m* de modes ►**pattern maker** (*Metal*) modeleur *m*.
3 vt a modeler (*on* sur).
b (*decorate*) orner de motifs.
patterned ['pætənd] adj *material, fabric, china* à motifs.
patterning ['pætənɪŋ] n a (*learning behaviour*) calcage *m* des conventions sociales; (*Psych: therapy*) thérapie *f* physique pour enfants débiles mentaux (*qui consiste à répéter les premiers mouvements de l'enfance*). b (*markings*) marquage *m*.
patty ['pætɪ] 1 n petit pâté *m*. 2 comp ►**patty pan** petit moule ►**patty shell** croûte *f* feuilletée.
paucity ['pɔːsɪtɪ] n *[crops, coal, oil]* pénurie *f*; *[money]* manque *m*; *[news, supplies, water]* disette *f*; *[ideas]* indigence *f*, disette.
Paul [pɔːl] n Paul *m*.
Pauline¹ ['pɔːliːn] n (*name*) Pauline *f*.
Pauline² ['pɔːlaɪn] adj (*Rel*) paulinien.
paulownia [pɔː'ləʊnɪə] n paulownia *m*.
paunch [pɔːntʃ] n *[person]* ventre *m*, panse *f*, bedaine* *f*; *[ruminants]* panse.
pauper ['pɔːpəʳ] n indigent(e) *m(f)*, pauvre *m*, -esse *f*. **~'s grave** fosse commune.
pause [pɔːz] 1 n a (*temporary halt*) pause *f*, arrêt *m*. **to give ~ to sb** faire hésiter qn, donner à réfléchir à qn; **a ~ in the conversation** un petit *or* bref silence (dans la conversation); **after a ~ he added ...** après une pause, il ajouta ...; **there was a ~ for discussion/for refreshments** on

s'arrêta pour discuter/pour prendre des rafraîchissements.
b (*Mus*) (*rest*) repos *m*, silence *m*; (*sign*) point *m* d'orgue, silence; (*Poetry*) césure *f*.
2 vi a (*stop*) faire une pause, marquer un temps d'arrêt, s'arrêter un instant. **to ~ for breath** s'arrêter pour reprendre haleine.
b (*hesitate*) hésiter. **it made him ~ (for thought)** cela lui a donné à réfléchir.
c (*linger over*) s'arrêter (*on* sur).

pavane [pə'vɑːn] n pavane *f*.

pave [peɪv] vt *street* paver; *yard* carreler, paver. **~d with gold** pavé d'or; (*fig*) **to ~ the way (for)** frayer *or* ouvrir la voie (à), préparer le chemin (pour).

pavement ['peɪvmənt] 1 n a (*Brit*) trottoir *m*. b (*road surface*) (*of stone, wood*) pavé *m*, pavage *m*; (*stone slabs*) dallage *m*; (*ornate*) pavement *m*. c (*US: roadway*) chaussée *f*. 2 comp ▸**pavement artist** artiste *mf* des rues (*qui dessine à la craie à même le trottoir*).

pavilion [pə'vɪlɪən] n (*tent, building*) pavillon *m* (*tente, construction*).

paving ['peɪvɪŋ] 1 n a (*material; stone*) pavé *m*; (*flagstones*) dalles *fpl*; (*tiles*) carreaux *mpl*. b (*paved ground*) pavage *m*; dallage *m*; carrelage *m*; *see* **crazy**. 2 comp ▸**paving stone** pavé *m*.

Pavlovian [pæv'ləʊvɪən] adj pavlovien.

paw [pɔː] 1 n a *[animal]* patte *f*. b (*‡: hand*) patte* *f*. **keep your ~s off!** bas les pattes!* 2 vt a *[animal]* donner un coup de patte à. *[horse]* **to ~ the ground** piaffer. b (*‡: pej*) *[person]* tripoter*; (*amorously: also* **~ about**) tripoter*, peloter‡.

pawky ['pɔːkɪ] adj (*Scot*) narquois.

pawl [pɔːl] n cliquet *m*.

pawn¹ [pɔːn] n (*Chess*) pion *m*. (*fig*) **to be sb's ~** être le jouet de qn, se laisser manœuvrer par qn; (*fig*) **he is a mere ~ (in the game)** il n'est qu'un pion sur l'échiquier.

pawn² [pɔːn] 1 vt *one's watch etc* mettre en gage *or* au mont-de-piété, mettre au clou*. 2 n a (*thing pledged*) gage *m*, nantissement *m*. b (*NonC*) **in ~** en gage, au mont-de-piété, au clou*; **to get sth out of ~** dégager qch du mont-de-piété. 3 comp ▸**pawnbroker** prêteur *m*, -euse *f* sur gages; **pawnbroker's** = **pawnshop** ▸**pawnshop** bureau *m* de prêteur sur gages, mont-de-piété *m* ▸**pawn ticket** reconnaissance *f* (du mont-de-piété) (*de dépôt de gage*).

pawpaw ['pɔːpɔː] n papaye *f*.

pax [pæks] n a (*Brit Scol sl*) pouce! b (*Rel*) paix *f*.

pay [peɪ] (vb: pret, ptp **paid**) 1 n (*gen*) salaire *m*; *[manual worker]* paie *f or* paye *f*; *[office worker]* appointements *mpl*; *[civil servant]* traitement *m*; *[servant]* gages *mpl*; (*Mil, Naut*) solde *f*, paie. **in the ~ of** à la solde de, aux gages de; **the ~'s not very good** ce n'est pas très bien payé; **holidays with ~** congés payés; *see* **equal, half, take 2** *etc*.
2 comp *dispute, negotiation* salarial ▸**pay as you earn** (*Brit*), **pay-as-you-go** (*US*) retenue *f* à la source de l'impôt sur le revenu ▸**payback** *see* **payback** ▸**pay-bed** (*Brit*) place *f* réservée aux malades privés ▸**Pay Board** Commission *f* des salaires ▸**pay-cable channel** (*TV*) réseau *m* câblé payant ▸**pay check** (*US*), **pay cheque** (*Brit*) salaire *m*, paie *f or* paye *f* ▸**pay day** jour *m* de paie ▸**pay desk** caisse *f*; (*Theat*) caisse, guichet *m* ▸**pay dirt** (*Min*) (gisement *m* d')alluvions *fpl* exploitables; (*US*) **to hit** *or* **strike pay dirt*** trouver un (bon) filon* ▸**pay increase** = **pay rise** ▸**pay(ing)-in slip, pay(ing)-in voucher** (*Banking*) bordereau *m* de versement ▸**payload** (*weight carried*) (*by aircraft*) emport *m*; (*by rocket, missile*) poids *m* utile en charge; (*explosive energy: of warhead, bomb load*) puissance *f*; (*Naut: of cargo*) charge payante ▸**paymaster** (*gen*) intendant *m*, caissier *m*, payeur *m*; (*Naut*) commissaire *m*; (*Mil*) trésorier *m*; (*Brit*) **Paymaster General** *trésorier-payeur de l'Échiquier* ▸**payoff** *[person]* remboursement *m* (total); *[debt etc]* règlement *m* (total); (*: *reward*) récompense *f*; (*: *bribe*) pot-de-vin *m*; (*: *outcome*) résultat final; (*: *climax*) comble *m*, bouquet* *m*; **payoff table** matrice *f* des gains ▸**pay packet** (*Brit*) enveloppe *f* de paie; (*fig*) paie *f* ▸**pay phone** téléphone public, cabine *f* téléphonique ▸**pay rise** augmentation *f* de salaire ▸**payslip** feuille *f or* bulletin *m* de paie ▸**pay station** (*US*) cabine *f* téléphonique, téléphone public ▸**pay structure** (*Ind*) hiérarchisation *f* des salaires ▸**pay-TV** télévision *f* payante.
3 vt a *person* payer (*to do* à faire, *for doing* pour faire); *tradesman, bill, fee* payer, régler; *instalments, money* payer; *deposit* verser; *debt* acquitter, s'acquitter de, régler; *loan* rembourser; (*Fin*) *interest* rapporter; (*Fin*) *dividend* distribuer. **to ~ sb £10** payer 10 livres à qn; **he paid them for the book** il leur a payé le livre; **he paid them £10 for the ticket** il leur a payé le billet 10 livres; **he paid £10 for the ticket** il a payé le billet 10 livres; **he paid a lot for his suit** son costume lui a coûté cher, il a payé son costume très cher; **he paid me for my trouble** il m'a dédommagé de mes peines; **I don't ~ you to ask questions** je ne vous paie pas pour poser des questions; **we're not paid for that** on n'est pas payé pour cela, on n'est pas payé pour‡; **that's what you're paid for** c'est pour cela qu'on vous paie; **they ~ good wages** ils paient bien; **I get paid on Fridays** on me paie *or* je touche ma paie le vendredi; **I get paid on a monthly basis** *or* **by the month** je suis mensualisé; **to ~ cash (down)** payer comptant; (*Prov*) **he who ~s the piper calls the tune** qui paie les violons choisit la musique; (*fig*) **to ~ the penalty** subir *or* payer les conséquences; (*fig*) **to ~ the price of** payer le prix de; (*Fin*) **shares that ~ 5%** des actions qui rapportent 5 %; (*Banking*) **to ~ money into an account** verser de l'argent à un compte; (*fig*) **his generosity paid dividends** sa générosité porta ses fruits; (*US*) **he's paid his dues** (*for achievement*) il en a bavé*; (*for crime, error*) il a payé sa dette (*fig*); (*fig*) **the business is ~ing its way now** l'affaire couvre ses frais maintenant; **he likes to ~ his (own) way** il aime payer sa part *or* son écot; **this country must ~ its way** ce pays doit être économiquement indépendant; (*fig*) **to put paid to sb's plans** mettre les projets de qn par terre; **I'll soon put paid to him!*** j'aurai vite fait de l'envoyer promener!* *or* de lui régler son compte!; *see* **rob**.
b (*fig: be profitable to*) rapporter à. **it would ~ him to employ an accountant** il aurait avantage à *or* cela lui rapporterait d'employer un comptable; **it will ~ you to be nice to him** vous gagnerez à *or* vous avez intérêt à être aimable avec lui; **it won't ~ him to tell the truth** il ne gagnera rien à dire la vérité; **it doesn't ~ to be polite these days** on ne gagne rien à *or* on n'a pas intérêt à *or* cela ne paie pas d'être poli de nos jours; **... but it paid him in the long run** ... mais il y a gagné en fin de compte.
c **to ~ attention** *or* **heed to** faire attention à, prêter attention à; **~ no heed to it!** il ne faut pas y faire attention; **to ~ compliments to** faire des compliments à; **to ~ court to†** faire la cour à; **to ~ homage to** rendre hommage à; **to ~ the last honours to, to ~ one's last respects to** rendre un dernier hommage à; **to ~ sb a visit** rendre visite à qn; **we paid a visit to Paris on our way south** nous avons fait un petit tour à Paris en descendant vers le sud; (*euph*) **to ~ a visit*** *or* **a call*** aller au petit coin*.
4 vi a payer. **to ~ for the meal** payer le repas; **his job ~s well** son travail rapporte *or* paie bien; (*fig*) **he paid dearly for it** il l'a payé cher (*fig*); **to ~ through the nose for sth*** payer le prix fort pour qch; **we'll have to ~ through the nose for it*** cela va nous coûter les yeux de la tête*; **to ~ over the odds for sth** payer qch un prix fou*; (*fig*) **you'll ~ for this!** vous (me) le payerez!; (*fig*) **I'll make him ~ for that** je lui ferai payer cela; (*fig*) **he's had to ~ for it** (*for achievement*) il en a bavé*; (*for error, crime*) il a payé sa dette (*fig*); (*on bus*) **"~ on entry"** "paiement à l'entrée"; *see* **cash, instalment, nail** *etc*.
b (*be profitable*) être avantageux, rapporter un profit *or* un bénéfice. **we need to sell 600 copies to make it ~** nous devons vendre 600 exemplaires pour faire un bénéfice *or* pour que ce soit rentable; **does it ~?** est-ce que ça paie?, c'est payant?, c'est rentable?; **this business doesn't ~** cette affaire n'est pas rentable; **it ~s to advertise** la publicité rapporte; **it doesn't ~ to tell lies** cela ne sert à rien de mentir, mentir ne sert à rien; **crime doesn't ~** le crime ne paie pas.

▸**pay away** vt sep a (*Naut*) *rope* laisser filer. b *money* dépenser.

▸**pay back** 1 vt sep a *stolen money* rendre, restituer; *loan* rembourser; *person* rembourser. **I paid my brother back the £10 I owed him** j'ai remboursé à mon frère les 10 livres que je lui devais. b (*fig*) (*get even with*) **to pay sb back for doing sth** faire payer à qn qch qu'il a fait; **I'll pay you back for that!** je vous le revaudrai! 2 **payback** n *see* **payback**.

▸**pay down** vt sep: **he paid £10 down** (*whole amount in cash*) il paya 10 livres comptant; (*as deposit*) il versa un acompte de 10 livres.

▸**pay in** vt sep verser (*to* à). **to pay in money at the bank** verser de l'argent à son compte (bancaire); **to pay a sum in to an account** verser une somme à un compte; **to pay in a cheque** verser un chèque.

▸**pay off** 1 vi *[trick, scheme etc]* être payant; *[decision]* être valable *or* payant. **his patience paid off in the long run** finalement il a été récompensé de sa patience. 2 vt sep a *debts* régler, acquitter, s'acquitter de; *creditor* rembourser. (*fig*) **to pay off an old score** régler un vieux compte; (*fig*) **to pay off a grudge against sb** prendre sa revanche sur qn. b (*discharge*) *worker, staff* licencier; *servant* donner son compte à, congédier; (*Naut*) *crew* débarquer. 3 **payoff** n *see* **pay 2**.

▸**pay out** vt sep a *rope* laisser filer. b *money* (*spend*) débourser, dépenser; *[cashier etc]* payer. c (*fig*) **I paid him out for reporting me to the boss** il m'a dénoncé au patron mais je le lui ai fait payer; **I'll pay him out for that!** je lui ferai payer ça!, je le lui revaudrai!

▸**pay up** 1 vi payer. **pay up!** payez! 2 vt sep *amount* payer, verser; *debts, arrears* régler, s'acquitter de. **the instalments will be paid up over 2 years** les versements vont s'échelonner sur 2 ans; *see* **paid**.

payable ['peɪəbəl] adj a (*due, owed*) payable (*in/over 3 months* dans/en 3 mois). (*Comm, Fin, Jur*) **~ when due** payable à l'échéance; **~ to bearer/on demand/at sight** payable au porteur/sur présentation/à vue; **to make a cheque ~ to sb** faire un chèque à l'ordre de qn. b (*profitable*) rentable, payant. **it's not a ~ proposition** ce n'est pas (une proposition) rentable, ce n'est pas payant.

payback ['peɪ,bæk] n *[investment]* retour *m*, bénéfice *m*; *[debt]* remboursement *m*.

PAYE [,piːeɪwaɪ'iː] (*Brit*) (abbr of **Pay As You Earn**) *see* **pay 2**.

payee [peɪ'iː] n *[cheque]* bénéficiaire *mf*; *[postal order]* destinataire *mf*, bénéficiaire.

payer ['peɪəʳ] n celui qui paie; *[cheque]* tireur *m*, -euse *f*. **he's a slow** *or* **bad ~** c'est un mauvais payeur.

paying ['peɪɪŋ] 1 adj a (*who pays*) payant. **~ guest** pensionnaire *mf*, hôte payant. b (*profitable*) *business* rémunérateur (*f* -trice), qui rapporte, rentable; *scheme* rentable. **it's not a ~ proposition** ce n'est pas (une proposition) rentable. 2 n *[debt]* règlement *m*, acquittement *m*; *[creditor]* remboursement *m*; *[money]* paiement *m*, versement *m*. 3 comp ▸**paying-in book** carnet *m* de bons de versement ▸**paying-in slip** bon *m* de versement.

payment ['peɪmənt] n a (*see* **pay**) paiement *m*; versement *m*; règlement *m*; acquittement *m*; remboursement *m*. **on ~ of £50** moyennant (la somme de) 50 livres; **as** *or* **in ~ for the item you sold me** en règlement de l'article que vous m'avez vendu; **as** *or* **in ~ for the sum I owe you** en remboursement de la somme que je vous dois; **as** *or* **in ~ for your help** en paiement de l'aide que vous m'avez apportée; **method of ~** mode *m* de règlement; **without ~** à titre gracieux; **cash ~** (*not credit*) paiement comptant; (*in cash*) paiement en liquide; **~ in kind** paiement en nature; **~ in full** règlement complet; **~ by instalments** paiement par traites *or* à tempérament; **~ by results** prime *f* au rendement; **in monthly ~s of £10** payable en mensualités de 10 livres *or* en versements de 10 livres par mois; **to make a ~** faire *or* effectuer un paiement; **~ of interest** service *m* d'intérêt; **to present sth for ~** présenter qch pour paiement; *see* **down¹, easy, stop** *etc*.
b (*reward*) récompense *f*. **as ~ for** en récompense de.

payola* [peɪ'əʊlə] n (*NonC: US*) pots-de-vin *mpl*.

payroll ['peɪˌrəʊl] n (*Ind*) (*list*) registre *m* du personnel; (*money*) paie *f* (de tout le personnel), (*more formally*) traitements *mpl* et salaires *mpl*; (*all the employees*) ensemble *m* du personnel. **~ tax** taxe *f* sur les traitements et salaires; **the factory has 60 people on the ~** *or* **a ~ of 60** l'usine a 60 membres de personnel *or* un personnel de 60; **to be on a firm's ~** être employé par une société.

P.B.S. [ˌpiːbiː'es] n (*US*) abbr of **Public Broadcasting Service**.

PC [piː'siː] n a (abbr of **personal computer**) P.C. *m*. b (abbr of **Police Constable**) *see* **police**. c (abbr of **Privy Councillor**) *see* **privy**. d (*) (abbr of **politically correct**) *see* **politically**.

pc [piː'siː] n abbr of **postcard**.

p.c. abbr of **per cent**.

p/c n a (abbr of **prices current**) prix *mpl* courants. b (abbr of **petty cash**) *see* **petty**.

PCB [ˌpiːsiː'biː] n (abbr of **polychlorinated biphenyl**) PCB *m*.

PD [ˌpiː'diː] n (*US*) (abbr of **police department**) *see* **police 2**.

pd (abbr of **paid**) payé.

pdq* [piːdiː'kjuː] adv (abbr of **pretty damn quick**) en vitesse*.

PDT [piːdiː'tiː] (abbr of **Pacific Daylight Time**) *see* **Pacific**.

PE [piː'iː] (abbr of **physical education**) *see* **physical**.

pea [piː] 1 n (*Bot, Culin*) pois *m*. **garden** *or* **green ~s** petits pois; **processed ~s** ≃ petits pois en boîte; (*fig*) **they are as like as two ~s (in a pod)** ils se ressemblent comme deux gouttes d'eau; *see* **shell, split, sweet** *etc*. 2 comp ▸**peagreen** vert pomme *inv* ▸**pea jacket** (*Naut*) caban *m* ▸**peapod** cosse *f* de pois ▸**peashooter** sarbacane *f* ▸**pea soup** soupe *f* aux pois; (*from split peas*) soupe aux pois cassés ▸**peasouper*** brouillard *m* à couper au couteau*, purée *f* de pois.

peace [piːs] 1 n a (*NonC*) (*not war*) paix *f*; (*treaty*) (traité *m* de) paix. **to be at ~** être en paix; **to come in ~** venir en ami(s); **to live in** *or* **at ~ with** vivre en paix avec; **to make ~** faire la paix; **to make ~ with** signer *or* conclure la paix avec; (*fig*) **to make one's ~ with** se réconcilier avec; **after a long (period of) ~ war broke out** après une longue période de paix la guerre éclata.
b (*calm*) paix *f*, tranquillité *f*, calme *m*. **to be at ~ with oneself** avoir la conscience tranquille *or* en paix; **to live at ~ with the world** avoir une vie paisible; **to be at ~ with the world** ne pas avoir le moindre souci; **~ of mind** tranquillité d'esprit; **to disturb sb's ~ of mind** troubler l'esprit de qn; **leave him in ~** laisse-le tranquille, fiche-lui la paix*; **to sleep in ~** dormir tranquille; **he gives them no ~** il ne les laisse pas en paix; **anything for the sake of ~ and quiet** n'importe quoi pour avoir la paix; **to hold** *or* **keep one's ~** garder le silence, se taire; *see* **rest**.
c (*Jur etc: civil order*) paix *f*, ordre public. **to disturb** *or* **break the ~** troubler *or* violer l'ordre public; **to keep the ~** *[citizen]* ne pas troubler l'ordre public; *[police]* veiller à l'ordre public; (*fig: stop disagreement*) maintenir le calme *or* la paix; **you two try to keep the ~!** essayez de ne pas vous disputer, vous deux!; *see* **breach, justice**.
2 comp (*Pol*) *poster, march, meeting, demonstration* pour la paix ▸**peace campaign** campagne *f* pour la paix *or* pour le désarmement nucléaire ▸**peace campaigner** militant(e) *m(f)* pour la paix *or* pour le désarmement nucléaire ▸**peace conference** conférence *f* de paix ▸**peace initiative** initiative *f* de paix ▸**peacekeeper** *see* **peacekeeper** ▸**Peace Corps** (*US*) (organisation américaine de) Coopération *f* (*pour l'aide aux pays en voie de développement*) ▸**peacekeeping force** *see* **peacekeeping** ▸**peace lobby** lobby *m* pour la paix *or* pour le désarmement nucléaire ▸**peace-loving** pacifique ▸**peacemaker** pacificateur *m*, -trice *f*, conciliateur *m*, -trice *f*; (*esp international politics*) artisan *m* de la paix ▸**Peace Movement** Mouvement *m* pour la paix *or* pour le désarmement nucléaire ▸**peace offensive** offensive *f* de paix ▸**peace offering** (*Rel: sacrifice*) offrande *f* propitiatoire; (*fig*) cadeau *m or* gage *m* de réconciliation ▸**peace pipe** calumet *m* de la paix ▸**peace studies** (*Educ*) études *fpl* sur la paix ▸**peace talks** pourparlers *mpl* de paix ▸**in peacetime** en temps de paix ▸**peace treaty** (traité *m* de) paix *f*.

peaceable ['piːsəbl] adj paisible, pacifique.

peaceably ['piːsəblɪ] adv paisiblement, pacifiquement.

peaceful ['piːsfʊl] adj a (*quiet: not violent*) *reign, period* paisible; *life, place, sleep* paisible, tranquille; *meeting* calme; *demonstration* non-violent. **~ coexistence** coexistence *f* pacifique. b (*for peacetime*) pacifique. **the ~ uses of atomic energy** l'utilisation pacifique de l'énergie nucléaire. c (*not quarrelsome*) *person, disposition* pacifique, paisible.

peacefully ['piːsfəlɪ] adv *demonstrate, reign* paisiblement; *work, lie, sleep* paisiblement, tranquillement. **the demonstration passed off ~** la manifestation s'est déroulée dans le calme *or* paisiblement.

peacefulness ['piːsfʊlnɪs] n paix *f*, tranquillité *f*, calme *m*.

peacekeeper ['piːskiːpəʳ] n (*Mil*) soldat *m* de la paix.

peacekeeping ['piːskiːpɪŋ] 1 n pacification *f*. 2 comp *operation, policy* de pacification ▸**peacekeeping force** (*Mil*) forces *fpl* de maintien de la paix.

peach¹ [piːtʃ] 1 n a pêche *f*; (*also* **~ tree**) pêcher *m*. b (*) **she's a ~!** elle est jolie comme un cœur!*; (*Sport*) **that was a ~ of a shot!** quel beau coup!; **what a ~ of a car!** quelle voiture sensationnelle!*; **what a ~ of a dress!** quel amour* de robe! 2 adj (couleur) pêche *inv*. 3 comp ▸**peaches and cream complexion** teint *m* de lis et de rose ▸**peach blossom** fleur *f* de pêcher ▸**peach melba** pêche melba *f* ▸**the Peach State** (*US*) la Géorgie ▸**peach stone** noyau *m* de pêche.

peach² [piːtʃ] vti (*Prison sl*) **to ~ (on) sb** moucharder qn*.

peacock ['piːkɒk] n, pl **~s** *or* **~** paon *m*. **~ blue** (*n*) bleu paon; **~-blue** (*adj*) bleu paon *inv*; **~ butterfly** paon de jour; *see* **proud**.

peahen ['piːhen] n paonne *f*.

peak [piːk] 1 n *[mountain]* pic *m*, cime *f*, sommet *m*; (*mountain itself*) pic; *[roof etc]* arête *f*, faîte *m*; *[cap]* visière *f*; (*on graph*) sommet; (*fig*) *[career]* sommet, apogée *m*. **when the Empire was at its ~** quand l'Empire était à son apogée; (*Comm*) **when demand was at its ~** quand la demande était à son maximum; **business was at its ~ in 1970** les affaires ont atteint un point culminant en 1970; **at the ~ of his fame** à l'apogée *or* au sommet de sa gloire; **discontent reached its ~** le mécontentement était à son comble; **traffic reaches its ~ about 5** la circulation est à son maximum (d'intensité) vers 17 heures, l'heure de pointe (de la circulation) est vers 17 heures; *see* **off, widow**.
2 comp ▸**peak demand** (*Comm*) demande *f* maximum *or* record *inv*; (*Elec*) période *f* de consommation de pointe ▸**a peak experience** (*fig*) une expérience de l'ineffable, un summum ▸**peak hours** (*for shops*) heures *fpl* d'affluence; (*for traffic*) heures d'affluence *or* de pointe ▸**peak listening time** (*Rad*) heures *fpl* de grande écoute ▸**peak load** (*Elec etc*) charge *f* maximum ▸**peak period** (*for shops, business*) période *f* de pointe; (*for traffic*) période d'affluence *or* de pointe ▸**peak production** (*Ind*) production *f* maximum ▸**peak season** pleine saison ▸**peak traffic** circulation *f* aux heures d'affluence *or* de pointe ▸**peak viewing (time)** (*TV*) heures *fpl* de grande écoute ▸**peak year** année *f* record *inv*.
3 vi (*also* **~ out**) *[sales, demand etc]* atteindre un niveau maximum *or* record.

peaked [piːkt] adj *cap* à visière; *roof* pointu.

peaky ['piːkɪ] adj fatigué. **to look ~** avoir les traits un peu tirés, ne pas avoir l'air très en forme*; **to feel ~** ne pas se sentir très en forme*, se sentir mal fichu*.

peal [piːl] 1 n: **~ of bells** (*sound*) sonnerie *f* de cloches, carillon *m*; (*set*) carillon; **~ of thunder** coup *m* de tonnerre; **the ~s of the organ** le ronflement de l'orgue; **~ of laughter** éclat *m* de rire; **to go (off) into ~s of laughter** rire aux éclats *or* à gorge déployée. 2 vi (*also* **~ out**) *[bells]* carillonner; *[thunder]* gronder; *[organ]* ronfler; *[laughter]* éclater. 3 vt *bells* sonner (à toute volée).

peanut ['piːnʌt] 1 n (*nut*) cacahouète *f or* cacahuète *f*; (*plant*) arachide *f*. **£300 is ~s for him*** pour lui 300 livres représentent une bagatelle; **what you're offering is just ~s*** ce que vous offrez est une bagatelle *or* est trois fois rien; **to work for ~s*** travailler pour trois fois rien. 2 comp ▸**peanut butter** beurre *m* de cacahouètes ▸**peanut gallery*** (*US*) poulailler* *m* (*dans un théâtre*) ▸**peanut oil** huile *f* d'arachide.

pear [pɛəʳ] n poire *f*; (*also* **~ tree**) poirier *m*. **~-shaped** en forme de poire, piriforme; *see* **prickly**.

pearl [pɜːl] 1 n perle *f*. **(mother of) ~** nacre *f*; **real/cultured ~s** perles fines/de culture; (*fig*) **~s of wisdom** trésors *mpl* de sagesse; (*liter*) **a ~ among women** la perle des femmes; (*fig*) **to cast ~s before swine** jeter des perles aux pourceaux, donner de la confiture aux cochons; *see* **seed, string** *etc*.
2 comp ▸**pearl barley** orge perlé ▸**pearl button** bouton *m* de nacre ▸**pearl diver** pêcheur *m*, -euse *f* de perles ▸**pearl diving** pêche *f* des perles ▸**pearl grey** gris perle *inv* ▸**pearl-handled** *knife* à manche de nacre; *revolver* à crosse de nacre ▸**pearl necklace** collier *m* de perles ▸**pearl oyster** huître perlière.
3 vi a *[water]* perler, former des gouttelettes.
b (*dive for* **~s**) pêcher les perles.

pearly ['pɜːlɪ] adj (*made of pearl*) en *or* de nacre; (*in colour*) nacré. (*hum*) **the P~ Gates** les portes *fpl* du Paradis; (*Brit*) **~ king, ~ queen** *marchand(e) des quatre saisons de Londres qui porte des vêtements* *couverts de boutons de nacre;* ~ **teeth** dents nacrées *or* de perle.

peasant [ˈpezənt] 1 n paysan(ne) *m(f)*; *(pej)* paysan, péquenaud(e)* *m(f)*, rustre *m*. **the ~s** *(Hist, Soc)* les paysans; *(Econ: small farmers)* les agriculteurs *mpl*, les ruraux *mpl*. 2 adj *crafts, life* rural, paysan. ~ **farmer** petit propriétaire paysan; ~ **farming** petite propriété paysanne.

peasantry [ˈpezəntrɪ] n: **the** ~ la paysannerie, les paysans *mpl*; *(countrymen)* les campagnards *mpl*.

pease [pi:z] adj: ~ **pudding** purée *f* de pois cassés.

peat [pi:t] n *(NonC)* tourbe *f*; *(one piece)* motte *f* de tourbe. **to dig** *or* **cut** ~ extraire de la tourbe; ~ **bog** tourbière *f*; *(Hort)* ~ **pot** pot *m or* godet *m* de tourbe.

peaty [ˈpi:tɪ] adj *soil* tourbeux; *smell* de tourbe.

pebble [ˈpebl] 1 n a *(stone)* caillou *m*; *(on beach)* galet *m*. *(fig)* **he's not the only** ~ **on the beach** il n'est pas unique au monde, il n'y a pas que lui. b *(Opt)* lentille *f* en cristal de roche. 2 comp ▸**pebbledash** n crépi *m* moucheté ◊ vt recouvrir d'un crépi moucheté ▸**pebbleweave (cloth)** *(Tex)* granité *m*.

pebbly [ˈpeblɪ] adj *surface, road* caillouteux. ~ **beach** plage *f* de galets.

pecan [pɪˈkæn] n *(nut)* (noix *f*) pacane *f*; *(tree)* pacanier *m*.

peccadillo [ˌpekəˈdɪləʊ] n, pl **~s** *or* **~es** peccadille *f*, vétille *f*.

peccary [ˈpekərɪ] n, pl ~ *or* **peccaries** pécari *m*.

peck¹ [pek] 1 n a *[bird]* coup *m* de bec.

b *(hasty kiss)* bise *f*. **to give sb a ~ on the cheek** donner à qn une bise sur la joue.

2 vt *[bird] object, ground* becqueter, picoter; *food* picorer; *person, attacker* donner un coup de bec à. **to ~ a hole in sth** faire un trou dans qch à (force de) coups de bec; **the bird ~ed his eyes out** l'oiseau lui a crevé les yeux à coups de bec.

3 vi: **the bird ~ed at him furiously** l'oiseau lui donnait des coups de bec furieux; **the bird ~ed at the bread** l'oiseau picora le pain; *[person]* **to ~ at one's food** manger du bout des dents, chipoter*; **~ing order**, *(US)* ~ **order** *[birds]* ordre *m* hiérarchique; *(fig)* hiérarchie *f*, ordre *m* des préséances.

peck² [pek] n *(Measure)* picotin *m*. **a ~ of troubles** bien des ennuis.

pecker [ˈpekəʳ] n a *(Brit)* **to keep one's ~ up*** garder le moral. b (*‡*: US: penis*) quéquette* *f*, verge *f*.

peckish* [ˈpekɪʃ] adj qui a de l'appétit, qui a envie de manger. **I'm feeling** ~ j'ai la dent*, je mangerais bien un morceau.

pecs* [peks] npl pectoraux *mpl*.

pectin [ˈpektɪn] n pectine *f*.

pectoral [ˈpektərəl] 1 adj pectoral. 2 n a *(muscles)* **~s** pectoraux *mpl*. b pectoral *m* *(ornement)*.

peculate [ˈpekjʊleɪt] vi détourner des fonds (publics).

peculation [ˌpekjʊˈleɪʃən] n détournement *m* de fonds (publics), péculat *m*.

peculiar [pɪˈkju:lɪəʳ] adj a *(odd)* bizarre, curieux, étrange. **to feel** ~ se sentir bizarre; **a most ~ flavour** un goût très curieux *or* bizarre; **he's rather** ~ il est un peu bizarre, il est plutôt excentrique; **it's really most** ~**!** c'est vraiment très bizarre! *or* curieux! *or* étrange!

b *(special)* particulier, spécial. **a matter of ~ importance** une question d'une importance particulière.

c *(belonging exclusively)* particulier. **the ~ properties of this drug** les propriétés particulières de ce médicament; **the region has its ~ dialect** cette région a son dialecte particulier *or* son propre dialecte; ~ **to** particulier à, propre à; **an animal ~ to Africa** un animal qui n'existe qu'en Afrique; **it is a phrase ~ to him** c'est une expression qui lui est particulière *or* propre.

peculiarity [pɪˌkju:lɪˈærɪtɪ] n a *(distinctive feature)* particularité *f*, trait distinctif. **it has the ~ that ...** cela a *or* présente la particularité de ... + *infin*; *(on passport etc)* **"special peculiarities"** "signes particuliers". b *(oddity)* bizarrerie *f*, singularité *f* *(liter)*. **she's got her little peculiarities** elle a ses petites manies; **there is some ~ which I cannot define** il y a quelque chose d'étrange *or* de bizarre que je n'arrive pas à définir.

peculiarly [pɪˈkju:lɪəlɪ] adv a *(specially)* particulièrement. b *(oddly)* étrangement, singulièrement.

pecuniary [pɪˈkju:nɪərɪ] adj pécuniaire, financier. ~ **difficulties** ennuis *mpl* d'argent, embarras *mpl* pécuniaires.

pedagogic(al) [ˌpedəˈgɒdʒɪk(əl)] adj pédagogique.

pedagogically [ˌpedəˈgɒdʒɪkəlɪ] adv pédagogiquement.

pedagogue [ˈpedəgɒg] n pédagogue *mf*.

pedagogy [ˈpedəgɒgɪ] n pédagogie *f*.

pedal [ˈpedl] 1 n a *(for foot)* pédale *f*. *[piano]* **loud** ~ pédale forte *or* de droite; **soft** ~ pédale douce *or* sourde *or* de gauche; *see* **clutch** *etc*. b *(Mus)* basse *m* continue. 2 comp ▸**pedal bicycle** bicyclette *f* à pédales ▸**pedal bin** poubelle *f* à pédale ▸**pedalboat** pédalo *m* ▸**pedalcar** voiture *f* à pédales ▸**pedal cycle** bicyclette *f* à pédales ▸**pedal cyclist** cycliste *mf* ▸**pedal pushers** (pantalon *m*) corsaire *m*. 3 vi *[cyclist]* pédaler. **he ~led through the town** il a traversé la ville (à bicyclette); *see* **soft**. 4 vt *machine, cycle* appuyer sur la *or* les pédale(s) de.

pedalo [ˈpedələʊ] n, pl **~s** *or* **~es** pédalo *m*.

pedant [ˈpedənt] n pédant(e) *m(f)*.

pedantic [pɪˈdæntɪk] adj pédant, pédantesque *(liter)*.

pedantically [pɪˈdæntɪkəlɪ] adv de façon pédante, avec pédantisme.

pedantry [ˈpedəntrɪ] n pédantisme *m*, pédanterie *f* *(liter)*.

peddle [ˈpedl] 1 vi faire du colportage. 2 vt *goods* colporter; *(fig pej) gossip* colporter, répandre; *ideas* propager; *drugs* faire le trafic de.

peddler [ˈpedləʳ] n a *(esp US)* = **pedlar**. b *[drugs]* revendeur *m*, -euse *f*.

pederast [ˈpedəræst] n pédéraste *m*.

pederasty [ˈpedəræstɪ] n pédérastie *f*.

pedestal [ˈpedɪstl] 1 n piédestal *m*, socle *m*; *(fig)* piédestal. *(fig)* **to put** *or* **set sb on a** ~ mettre qn sur un piédestal. 2 comp ▸**pedestal basin** lavabo *m* sur pied ▸**pedestal desk** bureau *m* ministre *inv* ▸**pedestal table** guéridon *m*.

pedestrian [pɪˈdestrɪən] 1 n piéton *m*. 2 adj *style, speech* prosaïque, plat, terre à terre *inv*; *exercise, activity* (qui se fait) à pied, pédestre. 3 comp ▸**pedestrian crossing** *(Brit)* passage *m* pour piétons, passage clouté ▸**pedestrian precinct** *(Brit)* zone piétonnière ▸**pedestrian traffic** piétons *mpl*; **pedestrian traffic is increasing here** les piétons deviennent de plus en plus nombreux ici; **"pedestrian traffic only"** "réservé aux piétons".

pedestrianization [pɪˌdestrɪənaɪˈzeɪʃən] n transformation *f* en zone piétonnière *(of* de), création *f* d'une *or* de zone(s) piétonnière(s).

pedestrianize [pɪˈdestrɪəˌnaɪz] vt *area* transformer en zone piétonnière.

pediatric *etc* = **paediatric** *etc*.

pedicab [ˈpedɪkæb] n cyclo-pousse *m* (à deux places).

pedicure [ˈpedɪkjʊəʳ] n a *(treatment)* pédicurie *f*, podologie *f*, soins *mpl* du pied *or* des pieds *(donnés par un pédicure)*. **to have a** ~ se faire soigner les pieds *(par un pédicure)*. b *(chiropodist)* pédicure *mf*.

pedigree [ˈpedɪgri:] 1 n a *(lineage) [animal]* pedigree *m*; *[person]* ascendance *f*, lignée *f*. **to be proud of one's** ~ être fier de son ascendance *or* de sa lignée. b *(tree) [person, animal]* arbre *m* généalogique. c *(document) [dogs, horses etc]* pedigree *m*; *[person]* pièce *f or* document *m* généalogique. 2 comp *dog, cattle* de (pure) race.

pediment [ˈpedɪmənt] n fronton *m*.

pedlar [ˈpedləʳ] n *(door to door)* colporteur *m*; *(in street)* camelot *m*.

pedological [ˌpi:dəˈlɒdʒɪkl] adj pédologique.

pedologist [pɪˈdɒlədʒɪst] n pédologue *mf*.

pedology [pɪˈdɒlədʒɪ] n pédologie *f*.

pedometer [pɪˈdɒmɪtəʳ] n podomètre *m*.

pedophile *etc* = **paedophile** *etc*.

pee‡ [pi:] 1 vi pisser‡, faire pipi*. 2 n pisse‡ *f*, pipi* *m*.

peek [pi:k] 1 n coup *m* d'œil (furtif). **to take a ~ at** jeter un coup d'œil (furtif) à *or* sur; **~-a-boo!** coucou!; *(US)* **~-a-boo* blouse** corsage *m* semi-transparent. 2 vi jeter un coup d'œil (furtif) *(at* sur, à).

peel [pi:l] 1 n *[apple, potato]* pelure *f*, épluchure *f*; *[orange]* écorce *f*, peau *m*; *(Culin, also in drink)* zeste *m*; *(also* **candied** ~*)* écorce confite. 2 vt *fruit* peler, éplucher; *potato* éplucher; *stick* écorcer; *shrimps* décortiquer, éplucher. **to keep one's eyes ~ed‡** ouvrir l'œil*, faire gaffe‡; **keep your eyes ~ed for a signpost!‡** ouvre l'œil* et tâche d'apercevoir un panneau! 3 vi *[fruit]* se peler; *[paint]* s'écailler; *[skin, part of body]* peler.

▸**peel away** 1 vi *[skin]* peler; *(Med)* se desquamer; *[paint]* s'écailler; *[wallpaper]* se décoller. 2 vt sep *rind, skin* peler; *film, covering* détacher, décoller.

▸**peel back** vt sep *film, covering* détacher, décoller.

▸**peel off** 1 vi a = **peel away 1**. b *(leave formation, group etc) [plane]* s'écarter de la formation; *[motorcyclists etc]* se détacher du groupe *(or* du cortège *etc)* en virant. **to peel off from** s'écarter de; se détacher en virant de. 2 vt sep a = **peel away 2**. b *(fig)* **to peel off one's clothes*** enlever ses vêtements, se déshabiller.

peeler [ˈpi:ləʳ] n a *(gadget)* (couteau-)éplucheur *m*; *(electric)* éplucheur électrique. b *(Brit ††: policeman)* sergent *m* de ville. c (*‡ US: stripper*) strip-teaseuse *f*.

peelie-wally‡ [ˈpi:lɪˈwælɪ] adj *(Scot)* chétif, souffreteux.

peeling [ˈpi:lɪŋ] 1 n a *[face etc] (Med)* desquamation *f*; *(cosmetic trade)* peeling *m*. b **~s** *[fruit, vegetables]* pelures *fpl*, épluchures *fpl*. 2 adj *skin* qui pèle; *wallpaper* qui se décolle; *paint* qui s'écaille.

peep¹ [pi:p] 1 n a coup *m* d'œil, regard furtif. **have a ~!** jette un coup d'œil!, regarde vite!; **to have** *or* **take a ~ at sth** jeter un coup d'œil à *or* sur qch, regarder qch furtivement *or* à la dérobée; **she had a ~ at her present** elle a jeté un (petit) coup d'œil à son cadeau; **to get** *or* **have a ~ at the exam papers** jeter un (petit) coup d'œil discret sur les sujets d'examen.

b *[gas]* veilleuse *f*, (toute) petite flamme. **a ~ of light showed through the curtains** un rayon de lumière filtrait entre les rideaux.

2 comp ▸**peep-bo!** coucou! ▸**peephole** *(gen)* trou *m* (pour épier); *(in front door etc)* judas *m* ▸**Peeping Tom** voyeur *m* ▸**peep show** *(box)* visionneuse *f*; *(pictures)* vues *fpl* stéréoscopiques; *(fig)* spectacle osé *or* risqué ▸**peeptoe sandal/shoe** sandale *f*/chaussure *f* à bout découpé.

3 vi jeter un coup d'œil, regarder furtivement. **to ~ at sth** jeter un coup d'œil à qch, regarder qch furtivement; **she ~ed into the box** elle

a jeté un coup d'œil *or* elle a regardé furtivement à l'intérieur de la boîte; **he was ~ing at us from behind a tree** il nous regardait furtivement *or* à la dérobée de derrière un arbre; **to ~ over a wall** regarder furtivement par-dessus un mur, passer la tête par-dessus un mur; **to ~ through a window** regarder furtivement *or* jeter un coup d'œil par la fenêtre; **I'll just go and ~ down the stairs** je vais seulement jeter un coup d'œil dans l'escalier.

►**peep out** 1 vi *[person]* se montrer, apparaître. **she was peeping out from behind the curtains** elle passait le nez de derrière les rideaux; **the sun peeped out from behind the clouds** le soleil s'est montré entre les nuages. 2 vt: **she peeped her head out** elle a passé la tête.

peep[2] [piːp] 1 n *[bird]* pépiement *m*, piaulement *m*; *[mouse]* petit cri aigu. **one ~ out of you and I'll send you to bed!**⁑ si tu ouvres la bouche je t'envoie te coucher! 2 vi *[bird]* pépier, piauler; *[mouse]* pousser de petits cris aigus.

peepers⁑ ['piːpəz] npl quinquets⁑ *mpl*.

peer[1] [pɪəʳ] vi (*look*) **to ~ at sb** regarder qn; (*inquiringly*) regarder qn d'un air interrogateur; (*doubtfully*) regarder qn d'un air dubitatif; (*anxiously*) regarder qn d'un air inquiet; (*short-sightedly*) regarder qn avec des yeux de myope; **to ~ at a book/photograph** scruter (du regard) *or* regarder attentivement un livre/une photographie; **she ~ed into the room** elle regarda dans la pièce d'un air interrogateur *or* dubitatif *etc;* **to ~ out of the window/over the wall** regarder par la fenêtre/par-dessus le mur d'un air interrogateur *etc;* **to ~ into sb's face** regarder qn d'un air interrogateur *etc,* dévisager qn; **she ~ed around over her spectacles** elle regarda autour d'elle par-dessus ses lunettes.

peer[2] [pɪəʳ] 1 n a (*social equal*) pair *m*. **tried/accepted by his ~s** jugé/accepté par ses pairs. b (*liter: in achievement etc*) égal(e) *m(f)*. **it will not be easy to find her ~** il sera difficile de trouver son égale *or* sa pareille; **as a musician he has no ~** comme musicien il est hors pair *or* il n'a pas son pareil. c (*noble: also* **~ of the realm,** pl **~s of the realm**) pair *m* (du royaume); *see* **life.** 2 comp ►**peer group** (*Sociol*) pairs *mpl* ►**peer pressure** pression *f* exercée par l'entourage *or* par les autres.

peerage ['pɪərɪdʒ] n (*rank*) pairie *f*; (*collective: the peers*) pairs *mpl*, noblesse *f*; (*list of peers*) nobiliaire *m*. **to inherit a ~** hériter d'une pairie; **to be given a ~** être anobli; *see* **life.**

peeress ['pɪərɪs] n pairesse *f*.

peerless ['pɪəlɪs] adj hors pair, sans pareil, sans égal.

peeve* [piːv] 1 vt mettre en rogne*. 2 n: **pet ~** bête *f* noire (*fig*).

peeved* [piːvd] adj fâché, irrité, en rogne*.

peevish ['piːvɪʃ] adj grincheux, maussade; *child* grognon, de mauvaise humeur.

peevishly ['piːvɪʃlɪ] adv maussadement, avec maussaderie, avec (mauvaise) humeur.

peevishness ['piːvɪʃnɪs] n maussaderie *f*, mauvaise humeur.

peewee* ['piːwiː] (*US*) 1 adj minuscule. 2 n (*child*) petit bout *m* de chou*, enfant *m* haut comme trois pommes*.

peewit ['piːwɪt] n vanneau *m*.

peg [peg] 1 n a (*wooden*) cheville *f*; (*metal*) fiche *f*; (*for coat, hat*) patère *f*; (*tent ~*) piquet *m*; (*Climbing*) piton *m*; *[violin]* cheville; *[cask]* fausset *m*; (*Croquet*) piquet; (*fig*) prétexte *m*, excuse *f*. (*Brit*) **clothes ~** pince *f* à linge; (*Brit*) **to buy a dress off the ~** acheter une robe de prêt-à-porter *or* de confection; **I bought this off the ~** c'est du prêt-à-porter, j'ai acheté ça tout fait (*see also* **off**); (*Climbing*) **to use ~s** pitonner; (*fig*) **to take sb down a ~ (or two)** remettre qn à sa place, rabattre *or* rabaisser le caquet à qn; (*fig*) **a ~ to hang a complaint on** un prétexte de plainte, un prétexte *or* une excuse pour se plaindre; *see* **level, square.**

b (*Brit*) **a ~ of whisky** un whisky-soda.

2 comp ►**pegboard** panneau alvéolé ►**pegleg**⁑ jambe *f* de bois, pilon *m* ►**peg pants** (*US*) ≃ pantalon *m* fuseau.

3 vt a (*gen*) fixer à l'aide de fiches (*or* de piquets *etc*); (*Tech*) cheviller. **to ~ clothes (out) on the line** étendre du linge sur la corde (à l'aide de pinces).

b (*Econ*) *prices, wages* stabiliser, bloquer. **to ~ prices** *etc* **to sth** lier les prix *etc* à qch.

c (*Climbing*) pitonner.

►**peg away**⁑ vi bosser⁑. **he is pegging away at his maths** il pioche* ses maths.

►**peg down** vt sep a *tent* fixer avec des piquets. b (*fig*) **I pegged him down to saying how much he wanted for it/to £10 an hour** j'ai réussi à le décider à fixer son prix/à accepter 10 livres de l'heure.

►**peg out** 1 vi (⁑: *die*) casser sa pipe*, clamser⁑, crever⁑. 2 vt sep *piece of land* piqueter, délimiter; *see also* **peg 3a.**

Pegasus ['pegəsəs] n Pégase *m*.

pejoration [ˌpiːdʒə'reɪʃən] n péjoration *f*.

pejorative [pɪ'dʒɒrətɪv] adj péjoratif.

peke* [piːk] n abbr of **pekin(g)ese.**

Pekin [piː'kɪn] n, **Peking** [piː'kɪŋ] n Pékin.

Pekin(g)ese [ˌpiːkɪ'niːz] n pékinois *m* (*chien*).

Pekinologist [ˌpiːkə'nɒlədʒɪst] n sinologue *mf* (*Pol*).

pekoe ['piːkəʊ] n (thé *m*) pekoe *m*.

pelagic [pɪ'lædʒɪk] adj pélagique.

pelargonium [ˌpelə'gəʊnɪəm] n pélargonium *m*.

pelf [pelf] n (*pej*) lucre *m* (*pej*), richesses *fpl*.

pelican ['pelɪkən] 1 n pélican *m*. 2 comp ►**pelican crossing** (*Brit*) passage *m* pour piétons (*commandé par des feux de circulation*).

pellagra [pə'leɪgrə] n pellagre *f*.

pellet ['pelɪt] n *[paper, bread]* boulette *f*; (*for gun*) (grain *m* de) plomb *m*; (*Med*) pilule *f*; *[owl etc]* boulette (de résidus regorgés); *[chemicals]* pastille *f*.

pell-mell ['pel'mel] adv pêle-mêle, en désordre, en vrac.

pellucid [pe'luːsɪd] adj pellucide (*liter*), transparent; (*fig*) *style* clair, limpide; *mind* lucide, clair.

pelmet ['pelmɪt] n (*wooden*) lambrequin *m*; (*cloth*) cantonnière *f*.

Peloponnese [ˌpeləpə'niːs] n: **the ~** le Péloponnèse.

Peloponnesian [ˌpeləpə'niːʃən] adj péloponnésien. **the ~ War** la guerre du Péloponnèse.

pelota [pɪ'ləʊtə] n pelote *f* basque.

pelt[1] [pelt] 1 vt bombarder, cribler (*with* de). **to ~ sb with stones** lancer une volée *or* une grêle de pierres à qn; **to ~ sb with arrows** cribler qn de flèches; **to ~ sb with tomatoes** bombarder qn de tomates. 2 vi a **the rain is** *or* **it's ~ing (down)*, it's ~ing with rain*** il tombe des cordes*, il pleut à torrents *or* à seaux; **~ing rain** pluie battante. b (*: run*) courir à toutes jambes, galoper*. **to ~ down the street** descendre la rue au grand galop *or* à fond de train *or* à toute blinde⁑. 3 n: **(at) full ~** à toute vitesse, à fond de train.

pelt[2] [pelt] n (*skin*) peau *f*; (*fur*) fourrure *f*.

pelvic ['pelvɪk] adj pelvien. **~ floor** plancher *m* pelvien; **~ girdle** ceinture *f* pelvienne.

pelvis ['pelvɪs] n, pl **~es** *or* **pelves** ['pelviːz] bassin *m*, pelvis *m*.

pem(m)ican ['pemɪkən] n pemmican *m*.

pen[1] [pen] 1 n plume *f*; (*ball-point*) stylo *m* à bille; (*felt-tip*) (crayon *m*) feutre *m*; (*fountain ~*) stylo. **he's usually too lazy to put ~ to paper** il est généralement trop paresseux pour prendre la plume *or* pour écrire; **don't put ~ to paper till you're quite sure** ne faites rien par écrit avant d'être certain; **to run** *or* **put one's ~ through sth** barrer *or* rayer qch (d'un trait de plume); **to live by one's ~** vivre de sa plume; *see* **quill** *etc.*

2 comp ►**pen-and-ink drawing** dessin *m* à la plume ►**pen friend** (*Brit*) correspondant(e) *m(f)* ►**penholder** porte-plume *m inv* ►**penknife** canif *m* ►**penmanship** calligraphie *f* ►**pen name** pseudonyme *m* (littéraire) ►**pen nib** bec *m* de plume ►**pen pal** = **pen friend** ►**penpusher** (*pej*) gratte-papier* *m inv*, rond-de-cuir* *m* ►**penpushing** (travail *m* d')écritures *fpl* ►**penwiper** essuie-plume *m inv*.

3 vt *letter* écrire; *article* rédiger.

pen[2] [pen] (vb: pret **penned,** ptp **penned** *or* **pent**) 1 n *[animals]* parc *m*, enclos *m*; (*also* **play~**) parc (d'enfant); (*also* **submarine ~**) abri *m* de sous-marins. 2 vt (*also* **~ in, ~ up**) *animals* parquer; *people* enfermer, parquer (*pej*).

pen[3] [pen] n (*Orn*) cygne *m* femelle.

pen[4]⁑ [pen] n (*US*) (abbr of **penitentiary** a) taule⁑ *f or* tôle⁑ *f*, trou⁑ *m*.

penal ['piːnl] adj *law, clause* pénal; *offence* punissable. **~ code** code pénal; **~ colony, ~ settlement** colonie *f* pénitentiaire; (*Jur*) **~ servitude (for life)** travaux forcés (à perpétuité).

penalization [ˌpiːnəlaɪ'zeɪʃən] n sanction *f*, pénalité *f*; (*Sport*) pénalisation *f*.

penalize ['piːnəlaɪz] vt a (*punish*) *person* pénaliser, infliger une pénalité à; *action, mistake* pénaliser; (*Sport*) *player, competitor* pénaliser, infliger une pénalisation à. **he was ~d for refusing** il a été pénalisé pour son refus; (*Sport*) **to be ~d for a foul** être pénalisé *or* recevoir une pénalisation pour une infraction. b (*handicap*) handicaper, désavantager. **he was greatly ~d by his deafness** il était sérieusement handicapé par sa surdité; **the rail strike ~s those who haven't got a car** la grève des chemins de fer touche les gens qui n'ont pas de voiture.

penalty ['penəltɪ] 1 n (*punishment*) pénalité *f*, peine *f*; (*fine*) amende *f*; (*Sport*) pénalisation *f*; (*Ftbl etc*) penalty *m*. **"~ for breaking these rules: £10"** "pénalité pour infraction au règlement: 10 livres"; **the ~ for this crime is 10 years' imprisonment** pour ce crime la peine est 10 ans de réclusion; **on ~ of** sous peine de; **under ~ of death** sous peine de mort; **the ~ for not doing this is ...** si on ne fait pas cela la pénalité est ...; (*fig*) **to pay the ~** supporter les conséquences; (*fig*) **to pay the ~ of wealth** payer la rançon de la fortune; (*in games*) **a 5-point ~ for a wrong answer** une pénalisation *or* une amende de 5 points pour chaque erreur.

2 comp ►**penalty area, penalty box** (*Ftbl*) surface *f* de réparation ►**penalty clause** (*Jur*) clause *f* pénale ►**penalty goal** (*Rugby etc*) but *m* sur pénalité ►**penalty kick** (*Ftbl*) penalty *m*; (*Rugby*) coup *m* de pied de pénalité ►**penalty spot** (*Ftbl*) point *m* de réparation.

penance ['penəns] n (*Rel, fig*) pénitence *f* (*for* de, pour). **to do ~ for** faire pénitence de *or* pour.

pence [pens] n a pl of **penny.** b **one ~*** un penny.

penchant ['pɑ̃ːʃɑ̃ːŋ] n penchant *m* (*for* pour), inclination *f* (*for* pour).

pencil ['pensl] 1 n a crayon *m*. **to write/draw in ~** écrire/dessiner au crayon; **coloured ~** crayon de couleur; **(eyebrow) ~** crayon à sourcils; *see* **indelible, lead[2], propel** *etc.* b (*fig*) **a ~ of light shone from his torch**

sa lampe (de poche) projetait un pinceau lumineux. 2 comp *note, line, mark* au crayon ▸**pencil box** plumier *m* ▸**pencil case** trousse *f* (d'écolier) ▸**pencil drawing** dessin *m* au crayon, crayonnage *m* ▸**pencil pusher*** (*US pej*) gratte-papier* *m inv*, rond-de-cuir *m* ▸**pencil rubber** gomme *f* (à crayon) ▸**pencil sharpener** taille-crayon *m*. 3 vt *note* crayonner, écrire au crayon. **to ~ one's eyebrows** se faire les sourcils (au crayon).

▸**pencil in** vt sep (*lit*) *note* crayonner, écrire au crayon; (*fig*) *date* marquer comme possibilité. (*fig*) **I've pencilled you in for Thursday** j'ai marqué ton nom provisoirement pour jeudi.

pendant ['pendənt] n (*on necklace*) pendentif *m*; (*earring*) pendant *m* (d'oreille); (*ceiling lamp*) lustre *m*; (*on chandelier etc*) pendeloque *f*.

pendency ['pendənsɪ] n (*Jur*) **during the ~ of the action** en cours d'instance.

pending ['pendɪŋ] 1 adj *business, question* pendant, en suspens, en souffrance; (*Jur*) *case* pendant, en instance. **the ~ tray** le casier des affaires en souffrance; **other matters ~ will be dealt with next week** les affaires en suspens seront réglées la semaine prochaine. 2 prep en attendant.

pendulous ['pendjʊləs] adj a (*hanging*) *lips, cheeks, nest* pendant; *flowers* pendant, qui retombe. b (*swinging*) *movement* de balancement, oscillant.

pendulum ['pendjʊləm] n a (*gen*) pendule *m*; *[clock]* balancier *m*. (*fig*) **the swing of the ~ will bring the socialists back to power** le mouvement du pendule ramènera les socialistes au pouvoir. b (*Climbing*) pendule *m*.

Penelope [pə'neləpɪ] n Pénélope *f*.

peneplain, peneplane ['pi:nɪpleɪn] n pénéplaine *f*.

penetrable ['penɪtrəbl] adj pénétrable.

penetrate ['penɪtreɪt] 1 vt pénétrer (dans). **the bullet ~d his heart** la balle lui a pénétré le cœur *or* lui est entrée dans le cœur; **to ~ a forest** pénétrer dans *or* entrer dans une forêt; **to ~ enemy territory** pénétrer en *or* entrer en territoire ennemi; **the car's lights ~d the darkness** les phares de la voiture perçaient l'obscurité; **the sound ~d the thick walls** le bruit passait par l'épaisseur des murs; **to ~ a mystery/sb's mind** pénétrer *or* comprendre un mystère/les pensées de qn; **to ~ sb's disguise** percer le déguisement de qn; **to ~ sb's plans** pénétrer *or* découvrir les plans de qn; (*Pol*) **subversive elements have ~d the party** des éléments subversifs se sont infiltrés dans le parti; (*Comm*) **they managed to ~ the sugar market** ils ont réussi à s'infiltrer dans le marché du sucre.

2 vi: **to ~ (into)** *[person, flames]* pénétrer (dans); *[light, water]* pénétrer (dans), filtrer (dans); **to ~ through** traverser; **the sound ~d into the deepest dungeons** le bruit parvenait *or* arrivait jusqu'aux cachots les plus éloignés.

penetrating ['penɪtreɪtɪŋ] adj a *wind, rain* pénétrant; *cold* pénétrant, mordant; *sound, voice, look* pénétrant, perçant. b (*acute, discerning*) *mind, remark* pénétrant, perspicace; *person, assessment* clairvoyant, perspicace, intelligent.

penetratingly ['penɪtreɪtɪŋlɪ] adv a *speak, shriek* d'une voix perçante. b *assess, observe* avec pénétration, avec perspicacité, avec intelligence.

penetration [,penɪ'treɪʃən] n (*NonC*) pénétration *f* (*also Comm: of markets*); (*discernment*) pénétration *f*, perspicacité *f*.

penetrative ['penɪtrətɪv] adj pénétrant.

penguin ['peŋgwɪn] n (*Orn*) manchot *m*; (*general incorrect usage*) pingouin *m*.

penicillin [,penɪ'sɪlɪn] n pénicilline *f*.

penile ['pi:naɪl] adj pénien.

peninsula [pɪ'nɪnsjʊlə] n péninsule *f*.

peninsular [pɪ'nɪnsjʊlə^r] adj péninsulaire. **the P~ War** la guerre (*napoléonienne*) d'Espagne.

penis ['pi:nɪs] n, pl **~es** *or* **penes** ['pi:ni:z] pénis *m*. (*Psych*) **~ envy** revendication subconsciente du phallus.

penitence ['penɪtəns] n pénitence *f*, repentir *m*.

penitent ['penɪtənt] adj, n pénitent(e) *m(f)*.

penitential [,penɪ'tenʃəl] 1 adj contrit. (*Rel*) **~ psalm** psaume *m* de la pénitence *or* pénitentiel. 2 n (*code*) pénitentiel *m*.

penitentiary [,penɪ'tenʃərɪ] n a (*US: prison: also* **state ~**) prison *f*, (maison *f*) centrale *f*. b (*Rel*) (*cleric*) pénitencier *m*; (*tribunal*) pénitencerie *f*.

penitently ['penɪtəntlɪ] adv d'un air *or* d'un ton contrit.

pennant ['penənt] n (*Sport etc, also on car, bicycle*) fanion *m*; (*Naut*) flamme *f*, guidon *m*.

penniless ['penɪlɪs] adj sans le sou, sans ressources. **he's quite ~** il n'a pas le sou, il est sans le sou *or* sans ressources; **she was left ~** elle s'est retrouvée sans le sou *or* sans ressources.

Pennine ['penaɪn] n: **the ~s, the ~ Range** les Pennines *fpl*, la chaîne Pennine.

pennon ['penən] n flamme *f*, banderole *f*; (*Naut*) flamme, guidon *m*.

Pennsylvania [,pensɪl'veɪnɪə] n Pennsylvanie *f*. **in ~** en Pennsylvanie; **~ Dutch** (*people*) Allemands *mpl* de Pennsylvanie; (*language*) dialecte *m* des Allemands de Pennsylvanie.

penny ['penɪ] 1 n, pl **pence** (*valeur*), **pennies** (*pièces*) penny *m* (*avant 1971, douzième du shilling; depuis 1971, centième de la livre*). **one old/new ~** un ancien/un nouveau penny; **it costs 5 pence** cela coûte 5 pence; **I have 5 pennies** j'ai 5 pennies, j'ai 5 pièces de un penny; **one ~ in the pound** ≃ un centime le franc; (*fig*) **they are two** *or* **ten a ~** on en trouve partout; (*fig*) **nobody was a ~ the worse** personne n'en a souffert, cela n'a fait de tort à personne; (*fig*) **he is not a ~ the wiser (for it)** il n'en sait pas plus long qu'avant, il n'est pas plus avancé*; **he made** *or* **earned a quick ~ or two** il s'est vite fait un peu d'argent; **he hasn't a ~ (to his name), he hasn't got two pennies to rub together** il est sans le sou, il n'a pas un sou vaillant, il n'a pas le sou *or* un radis‡; **he didn't get a ~** il n'a pas eu un sou; **(a) ~ for your thoughts!** à quoi pensez-vous?; **the ~ has dropped!*** il a (*or* j'ai *etc*) enfin pigé!‡, ça y est!*, ça a fait tilt!*; (*fig*) **he keeps turning up like a bad ~** pas moyen de se débarrasser de lui; (*Prov*) **a ~ saved is a ~ gained** un sou est un sou; (*Prov*) **in for a ~ in for a pound** (au point où on en est) autant faire les choses jusqu'au bout; (*Prov*) **take care of the pennies and the pounds will take care of themselves** les petits ruisseaux font les grandes rivières (*Prov*), il n'y a pas de petites économies; *see* **honest, pretty, spend** *etc*.

2 comp *book, pencil* de deux sous ▸**penny-a-liner*** pigiste *mf*, journaliste *mf* à la pige *or* à deux sous la ligne ▸**penny arcade** (*US*) salle *f* de jeux (*avec jeux électroniques*) ▸**penny-dreadful** (*Brit*) (pl **~-~s**) roman *m* à deux sous, (petit) roman à sensation ▸**penny farthing (bicycle)** (*Brit*) bicycle *m* ▸**penny-in-the-slot machine** (*for amusements*) machine *f* à sous; (*for selling*) distributeur *m* automatique ▸**penny-pinching** n économies *fpl* de bouts de chandelle ◊ adj *person* qui fait des économies de bouts de chandelle ▸**pennyweight** un gramme et demi ▸**penny whistle** flûteau *m* ▸**penny-wise**: (*Prov*) **to be penny-wise and pound-foolish** économiser un franc et en prodiguer mille ▸**pennyworth**: **I want a pennyworth of sweets** je voudrais pour un penny de bonbons.

penologist [pi:'nɒlədʒɪst] n pénologiste *mf*, pénologue *mf*.

penology [pi:'nɒlədʒɪ] n pénologie *f*.

pension ['penʃən] 1 n a (*state payment*) pension *f*. **(old age) ~** pension vieillesse (de la Sécurité sociale); **retirement ~** (pension de) retraite *f*; **war/widow's/disablement ~** pension de guerre/de veuve/d'invalidité; *see* **eligible**.

b (*Ind: from company etc*) retraite *f*. **he retired at 60 but got no ~** il s'est retiré à 60 ans mais n'a pas touché de retraite; **it is possible to retire on a ~ at 55** il est possible de toucher une retraite à partir de 55 ans.

c (*to artist, former servant etc*) pension *f*.

2 comp ▸**pension book** livret *m* de retraite ▸**pension fund** fonds *m* vieillesse, assurance *f* vieillesse ▸**pension scheme** (*Ind*) caisse *f* de retraite.

3 vt pensionner, attribuer une pension à.

▸**pension off** vt sep mettre à la retraite.

pensionable ['penʃnəbl] adj *post* qui donne droit à une pension. **to be of ~ age** avoir (atteint) l'âge de la retraite.

pensioner ['penʃənə^r] n (*also* **old age ~**) retraité(e) *m(f)*; (*any kind of pension*) pensionné(e) *m(f)*; (*also* **war ~**) militaire retraité, (*disabled*) invalide *m* de guerre.

pensive ['pensɪv] adj *person, look* pensif, songeur; *music etc* méditatif.

pensively ['pensɪvlɪ] adv pensivement, d'un air *or* d'un ton pensif *or* songeur.

pent [pent] 1 ptp of **pen²**. 2 adj (*liter*) emprisonné. 3 comp ▸**pent-up** *emotions, rage* refoulé, réprimé; *energy* refoulé, contenu; **she was very pent-up** elle était très tendue *or* sur les nerfs.

pentacle ['pentəkl] n pentacle *m*.

pentagon ['pentəgən] n pentagone *m*. (*US*) **the P~** le Pentagone.

pentagonal [pen'tægənl] adj pentagonal.

pentagram ['pentəgræm] n pentacle *m*.

pentahedron [,pentə'hi:drən] n, pl **~s** *or* **pentahedra** [,pentə'hi:drə] pentaèdre *m*.

pentameter [pen'tæmɪtə^r] n pentamètre *m*; *see* **iambic**.

Pentateuch ['pentətju:k] n Pentateuque *m*.

pentathlon [pen'tæθlən] n (*also* **modern ~**) pentathlon *m*.

pentatonic [,pentə'tɒnɪk] adj pentatonique.

Pentecost ['pentɪkɒst] n Pentecôte *f*.

Pentecostal [,pentɪ'kɒstl] adj de (la) Pentecôte; (*church, beliefs*) pentecôtiste.

Pentecostalism [,pentɪ'kɒstlɪzəm] n Pentecôtisme *m*.

Pentecostalist [,pentɪ'kɒstlɪst] 1 n Pentecôtiste *mf*. 2 adj pentecôtiste.

penthouse ['penthaʊs] n a (*also* **~ flat** *or* **apartment**) appartement *m* de grand standing (*construit sur le toit d'un immeuble*). b (*Archit*) auvent *m*, abri extérieur. **~ roof** appentis *m*, toit *m* en auvent.

penultimate [pɪ'nʌltɪmɪt] 1 adj avant-dernier, pénultième. 2 n (*Ling*) pénultième *f*, avant-dernière syllabe.

penumbra [pɪ'nʌmbrə] n, pl **~s** *or* **penumbrae** [pɪ'nʌmbri:] (*Astron*) pénombre *f*.

penurious [pɪ'njʊərɪəs] adj (*poor*) indigent, misérable; (*stingy*) parcimonieux, ladre; (*yielding little*) qui rend peu.

penury ['penjʊrɪ] n misère *f*, indigence *f*.

peon ['pi:ən] n (*in India*) péon *m*, fantassin *m*; (*in South America*) péon, journalier *m*.

peony (rose) ['pɪənɪ('rəʊz)] n pivoine *f*.

people ['pi:pl] 1 n a (*pl: persons*) gens *pl* (*preceding adj usu fem*), personnes *fpl*. **old ~** les personnes âgées, les vieilles gens, les vieux *mpl*; **young ~** les jeunes gens *mpl*, les jeunes *mpl*, la jeunesse; **clever ~** les gens intelligents; **all these good ~** toutes ces bonnes gens, tous ces braves gens; **old ~ are often lonely** les vieilles gens sont souvent très seuls; **all the old experienced ~** toutes ces vieilles gens pleins d'expérience; **~ are more important than animals** les gens *or* les êtres humains sont plus importants que les animaux; **a lot of ~** beaucoup de gens *or* de monde, un tas de gens*; **what a lot of ~!** que de monde!; **the place was full of ~** il y avait beaucoup de monde, il y avait un monde fou*; **several ~ said ...** plusieurs personnes ont dit ...; (*in suggesting sth*) **some ~ might prefer to wait** il y a peut-être des personnes *or* des gens qui préféreraient attendre; **how many ~?** combien de personnes?; **there were several English ~ in the hotel** il y avait plusieurs Anglais à l'hôtel; **they're strange ~** ce sont de drôles de gens; **I like the ~ in the hotel** j'aime les gens à l'hôtel; **what do you ~ think?** qu'est-ce que vous en pensez, vous (tous)? *or* vous autres?; *see* **little¹, other.**
b (*pl: in general*) **what will ~ think?** qu'est-ce que vont penser les gens?, que va-t-on penser?; **~ say ...** on dit ...; **don't tell ~ about that!** n'allez pas raconter ça (aux gens)!; **~ get worried when they see that** on s'inquiète quand on voit cela, les gens s'inquiètent quand ils voient cela; **~ quarrel a lot here** on se dispute beaucoup ici.
c (*pl: inhabitants*) *[a country]* peuple *m*, nation *f*, population *f*; *[district, town]* habitants *mpl*, population. **country ~** les gens de la campagne, les populations rurales; **town ~** les habitants des villes, les citadins *mpl*; **Liverpool ~ are friendly** à Liverpool les gens sont gentils, les habitants de Liverpool sont gentils; **the ~ of France** les Français *mpl*; **English ~ often say ...** les Anglais disent souvent ... .
d (*pl: Pol*) **the ~** le peuple; **government by the ~** gouvernement *m* par le peuple; **the king and his ~** le roi et ses sujets *or* son peuple; **~ of the Republic!** citoyens!; **the ~ at large** le grand public; **the minister must tell the ~ the truth** le ministre doit dire la vérité au pays; **man of the ~** homme *m* du peuple; **the ~'s army** l'armée *f* populaire; **~'s democracy** démocratie *f* populaire; (*in country's name*) **P~'s Democratic Republic** République *f* populaire; **the ~'s war** la guerre du peuple; (*US*) **~'s park** jardin *m* public (*à usage non réglementé par le gouvernement*); *see* **common.**
e (*sg: nation, race etc*) peuple *m*, nation *f*, race *f*. **the Jewish ~** la race juive, les Juifs *mpl*; **the ~s of the East** les nations de l'Orient, les Orientaux *mpl*.
f (*pl: *: family*) famille *f*, parents *mpl*. **I am writing to my ~*** j'écris à ma famille; **how are your ~?*** comment va votre famille?, comment ça va chez vous?*
g (*pl:*: in comps*) **the marketing ~** les gens du marketing; **the TV ~** les gens de la télé.
2 vt peupler (*with* de).

PEP [pep] n (*Brit Fin*) (abbr of **personal equity plan**) ≃ CEA *m*.

pep* [pep] 1 n (*NonC*) entrain *m*, dynamisme *m*, allant *m*. **full of ~** très dynamique, plein d'entrain *or* d'allant. 2 comp ►**pep pill*** excitant *m*, stimulant *m* ►**pep rally** (*US Scol*) *réunion des élèves avant un match interscolaire, pour encourager leur équipe* ►**pep talk*** laïus* *m* d'encouragement.

►**pep up*** 1 vi *[person]* s'animer, être ragaillardi; *[business, trade]* reprendre, remonter. 2 vt sep *person* remonter le moral à, ragaillardir; *party, conversation* animer; *drink, plot* corser.

peplos, peplus ['pepləs] n, pl **~es** péplum *m*.

pepper ['pepəʳ] 1 n a (*spice*) poivre *m*. **white/black ~** poivre blanc/gris; *see* **cayenne** *etc*.
b (*vegetable*) poivron *m*. **red/green ~** poivron rouge/vert.
2 comp ►**pepper-and-salt** *cloth* marengo *inv*; *beard, hair* poivre et sel *inv* ►**peppercorn** grain *m* de poivre; (*Brit*) **peppercorn rent** loyer nominal ►**pepper gas** gaz *m* poivre ►**pepper mill** moulin *m* à poivre ►**peppermint** (*sweet*) pastille *f* de menthe; (*plant*) menthe poivrée; **peppermint(-flavoured)** à la menthe ►**pepperpot, pepper shaker** poivrier *m*, poivrière *f*.
3 vt a (*Culin*) poivrer.
b (*fig*) **to ~ a speech with quotations** émailler *or* truffer un discours de citations; **to ~ sb with shot** cribler qn de plombs; **to ~ sb with questions** assaillir *or* bombarder qn de questions.

pepperoni [ˌpepə'rəʊnɪ] n *saucisson sec de porc et de bœuf très poivré*.

peppery ['pepərɪ] adj *food, taste* poivré; (*fig*) *person* irascible, emporté; *speech* irrité.

peppy* ['pepɪ] adj (*US*) *person* (*energetic*) énergique; (*lively*) plein d'entrain; *car* nerveux.

pepsin ['pepsɪn] n pepsine *f*.

peptic ['peptɪk] adj digestif. (*Med*) **~ ulcer** ulcère *m* de l'estomac; **he has a ~ ulcer** il a un ulcère à l'estomac.

peptone ['peptəʊn] n peptone *f*.

per [pɜːʳ] prep a par. **~ annum** par an; **~ capita** par personne; (*Econ*) **~ capita income** revenu *m* par habitant; **~ cent** pour cent; **a 10 ~ cent discount/increase** un rabais/une augmentation de 10 pour cent; **~ diem, ~ day** par jour; (*US*) **a ~ diem of 100 dollars** une indemnité journalière de 100 dollars; **30 miles ~ gallon** ≃ 8 litres aux cent (km); **~ head** par tête, par personne; **~ head of population** par habitant; **to drive at 100 km ~ hour** rouler à 100 (km) à l'heure; **she is paid 85 francs ~ hour** on la paie 85 F (de) l'heure; **30 francs ~ kilo** 30 F le kilo; **4 hours ~ person** 4 heures par personne.
b (*Comm*) **~ post** par la poste; **as ~ invoice** suivant facture; **as ~ normal*** *or* **usual*** comme d'habitude; (*also Jur*) **per pro** (abbr of **per procurationem** = **by proxy**) p.p.

peradventure [ˌpərəd'ventʃəʳ] adv (*liter*) par hasard, d'aventure (*liter*).

perambulate [pə'ræmbjʊleɪt] 1 vt parcourir (*un terrain, surtout en vue de l'inspecter*). 2 vi marcher, faire les cent pas.

perambulation [pəˌræmbjʊ'leɪʃən] n marche *f*, promenade(s) *f(pl)*, déambulation *f*.

perambulator ['præmbjʊleɪtəʳ] n (*Brit: †, frm*) voiture *f* d'enfant, landau *m*.

perborate [pə'bɔːreɪt] n perborate *m*.

perceive [pə'siːv] vt a (*see, hear*) *sound, light* percevoir. b (*notice*) remarquer, apercevoir; (*realize*) s'apercevoir de. **he ~d that ...** il a remarqué *or* s'est aperçu que ... . c (*understand*) *implication, meaning* percevoir, comprendre, saisir.

percentage [pə'sentɪdʒ] 1 n a pourcentage *m*. **the figure is expressed as a ~** le chiffre donné est un pourcentage; **a high ~ were girls** les filles constituaient un fort pourcentage. b (*profit*) pourcentage *m*. **to get a ~ on sth** recevoir *or* toucher un pourcentage sur qch; (*fig*) **there's no ~ in doing that** on ne gagne rien à faire cela, il n'y a aucun avantage à faire cela. 2 comp ►**percentage distribution** (*Econ*) ventilation *f* en pourcentage.

percentile [pə'sentaɪl] n centile *m*. **~ ranking** classement *m* par pourcentage.

perceptible [pə'septəbl] adj *sound, movement* perceptible; *difference, increase* perceptible, sensible, appréciable.

perceptibly [pə'septɪblɪ] adv *move* d'une manière perceptible; *change, increase* sensiblement.

perception [pə'sepʃən] n a *[sound, sight etc]* perception *f*. **one's powers of ~ decrease with age** la faculté de perception diminue avec l'âge. b (*sensitiveness*) sensibilité *f*, intuition *f*; (*insight*) perspicacité *f*, pénétration *f*. c (*Psych*) perception *f*. d *[rents, taxes, profits]* perception *f*.

perceptive [pə'septɪv] adj *faculty* percepteur (*f* -trice), de (la) perception; *analysis, assessment* pénétrant; *person* perspicace. **how very ~ of you!** vous êtes très perspicace!

perceptively [pə'septɪvlɪ] adv avec perspicacité.

perceptiveness [pə'septɪvnɪs] = **perception b.**

perch¹ [pɜːtʃ] n, pl **~** *or* **~es** (*fish*) perche *f*.

perch² [pɜːtʃ] 1 n a *[bird]* perchoir *m*, juchoir *m*. (*fig*) **to knock sb off his ~** faire dégringoler qn de son perchoir*. b (*measure*) perche *f*.
2 vi *[bird]* (se) percher; *[person]* se percher, se jucher. **we ~ed in a tree to see the procession** nous nous sommes perchés dans un arbre pour voir le défilé; **she ~ed on the arm of my chair** elle se percha *or* se jucha sur le bras de mon fauteuil. 3 vt percher, jucher. **to ~ a vase on a pedestal** percher *or* jucher un vase sur un piédestal; **we ~ed the child on the wall** nous avons perché *or* juché l'enfant sur le mur; **a chalet ~ed on (top of) a mountain** un chalet perché *or* juché sur le sommet d'une montagne.

perchance [pə'tʃɑːns] adv (*liter*) (*by chance*) par hasard, d'aventure (*liter*); (*perhaps*) peut-être.

percipient [pə'sɪpɪənt] 1 adj *faculty* percepteur (*f* -trice); *person* fin, perspicace; *choice* éclairé. 2 n personne *f* qui perçoit.

percolate ['pɜːkəleɪt] 1 vt *coffee* faire dans une cafetière électrique *or* à pression. **I am going to ~ the coffee** je vais passer le café; **I don't like ~d coffee** je n'aime pas le café fait dans une cafetière à pression. 2 vi *[coffee, water]* passer (*through* par). (*fig*) **the news ~d through from the front** la nouvelle a filtré du front.

percolator ['pɜːkəleɪtəʳ] n cafetière *f* à pression; (*in café*) percolateur *m*. **electric ~** cafetière électrique.

percussion [pə'kʌʃən] 1 n a (*impact; noise*) percussion *f*, choc *m*. b (*Mus*) percussion *f*, batterie *f*. 2 comp ►**percussion bullet** balle explosive ►**percussion cap** capsule fulminante ►**percussion drill** perceuse *f* à percussion ►**percussion instrument** (*Mus*) instrument *m* à *or* de percussion.

percussive [pə'kʌsɪv] adj percutant.

perdition [pə'dɪʃən] n perdition *f*, ruine *f*, perte *f*; (*Rel*) perdition, damnation *f*.

peregrination [ˌperɪgrɪ'neɪʃən] n (*†, frm*) pérégrination *f*. **~s** voyage *m*, pérégrinations.

peregrine ['perɪgrɪn] adj: **~ falcon** faucon *m* pèlerin.

peremptorily [pə'remptərɪlɪ] adv péremptoirement, d'un ton *or* d'une manière péremptoire, impérieusement.

peremptory [pə'remptərɪ] adj *instruction, order* péremptoire, formel; *argument* décisif, sans réplique; *tone* tranchant, péremptoire.

perennial [pəˈrenɪəl] 1 adj (*long lasting, enduring*) perpétuel, éternel; (*perpetual, recurrent*) perpétuel, continuel; *plant* vivace. 2 n plante *f* vivace; *see* **hardy**.

perennially [pəˈrenɪəlɪ] adv (*everlastingly*) éternellement; (*continually*) perpétuellement, continuellement.

perestroika [perəˈstrɔɪkə] n perestroïka *f*.

perfect [ˈpɜːfɪkt] 1 adj a *person, work of art, meal, weather, crime* parfait; *love* parfait, idéal; *harmony* parfait, complet (*f* -ète), total; *wife, hostess, teacher etc* parfait, exemplaire, modèle. **no one is ~** personne n'est parfait, la perfection n'est pas de ce monde; **his English is ~** son anglais est parfait *or* impeccable; **his Spanish is far from ~** son espagnol est loin d'être parfait *or* laisse beaucoup à désirer; **it was the ~ moment to speak to him about it** c'était le moment idéal *or* le meilleur moment possible pour lui en parler; (*Mus*) **~ pitch** l'oreille absolue; (*Gram*) **~ tense** parfait *m*; *see* **word**.
b (*emphatic*) véritable, parfait. **he's a ~ gentleman** c'est le parfait gentleman; **he's a ~ stranger** personne ne le connaît; **he's a ~ stranger to me** il m'est complètement inconnu; **I am a ~ stranger here** je ne connais absolument personne ici; **a ~ pest** un véritable fléau; **a ~ fool** un parfait imbécile, un imbécile fini.
2 n (*Gram*) parfait *m*. **in the ~** au parfait.
3 [pəˈfekt] vt *work of art* achever, parachever, parfaire; *skill, technique* mettre au point. **to ~ one's French** parfaire ses connaissances de français.

perfectibility [pəˌfektɪˈbɪlɪtɪ] n perfectibilité *f*.

perfectible [pəˈfektɪbl] adj perfectible.

perfection [pəˈfekʃən] n (*completion*) achèvement *m*; (*faultlessness*) perfection *f*; (*perfecting*) perfectionnement *m*. **to ~** à la perfection.

perfectionism [pəˈfekʃənɪzəm] n perfectionnisme *m*.

perfectionist [pəˈfekʃənɪst] adj, n perfectionniste (*mf*).

perfective [pəˈfektɪv] (*Gram*) 1 adj perfectif. 2 n (*aspect*) aspect perfectif; (*verb*) verbe perfectif.

perfectly [ˈpɜːfɪktlɪ] adv parfaitement.

perfidious [pɜːˈfɪdɪəs] adj perfide, traître (*f* traîtresse).

perfidiously [pɜːˈfɪdɪəslɪ] adv perfidement, traîtreusement; *act* en traître, perfidement.

perfidy [ˈpɜːfɪdɪ] n perfidie *f*.

perforate [ˈpɜːfəreɪt] vt *paper, metal* perforer, percer; *ticket* perforer, poinçonner. (*Comput*) **~d tape** bande *f* perforée; **"tear along the ~d line"** "détachez suivant le pointillé".

perforation [ˌpɜːfəˈreɪʃən] n perforation *f*.

perforce [pəˈfɔːs] adv forcément, nécessairement.

perform [pəˈfɔːm] 1 vt a *task* exécuter, accomplir; *duty* remplir, accomplir, s'acquitter de; *function* remplir; *miracle* accomplir; *rite* célébrer; (*Jur*) *contract* exécuter. **to ~ an operation** (*gen*) accomplir *or* exécuter une opération; (*Med*) pratiquer une opération, opérer.
b (*Theat etc*) *play* jouer, représenter, donner; *ballet, opera* donner; *symphony* exécuter, jouer. **to ~ a part** (*in play*) jouer *or* tenir un rôle; (*in ballet*) danser un rôle; (*in opera*) chanter un rôle; **to ~ a solo/acrobatics** exécuter un solo/un numéro d'acrobatie.
2 vi a (*gen*) donner une *or* des représentation(s); *[actor]* jouer; *[singer]* chanter; *[dancer]* danser; *[acrobat, trained animal]* exécuter un *or* des numéro(s). **to ~ on the violin** jouer du violon, exécuter un morceau au violon; **he ~ed brilliantly as Hamlet** il a brillamment joué *or* interprété Hamlet; (*Theat*) **when we ~ed in Edinburgh** quand nous avons donné une *or* des représentation(s) à Édimbourg, quand nous avons joué à Édimbourg; **the elephants ~ed well** les éléphants ont bien exécuté leur numéro (*see also* **performing**).
b *[machine, vehicle]* marcher, fonctionner. **the car is not ~ing properly** la voiture ne marche pas bien.
c (*Econ: see* **performance 1d**) *to ~ well/badly* avoir de bons/mauvais résultats; avoir de bonnes/mauvaises performances.

performance [pəˈfɔːməns] n a (*session, presentation*) (*Theat*) représentation *f*; (*Cine*) séance *f*; *[opera, ballet, circus]* représentation, spectacle *m*; *[concert]* séance, audition *f*. (*Theat*) **2 ~s nightly** 2 représentations chaque soir; **"no ~ tonight"** "ce soir relâche"; (*Theat etc*) **the late ~** la dernière représentation *or* séance de la journée; (*Theat etc*) **first ~** première *f* (représentation); **the play had 300 ~s** la pièce a eu 300 représentations; (*Cine*) **continuous ~** spectacle permanent.
b *[actor, singer, dancer]* interprétation *f*; *[musician]* interprétation, exécution *f*; *[acrobat]* numéro *m*; *[racehorse, athlete etc]* performance *f*; (*fig*) *[speaker, politician]* prestation *f*; (*Scol*) performances *fpl*. (*Sport*) **after several poor ~s he finally managed to ...** après plusieurs performances médiocres il a enfin réussi à ...; (*Sport*) **the team's ~ left much to be desired** la performance de l'équipe a beaucoup laissé à désirer; **his ~ of Bach was outstanding** son interprétation de Bach était tout à fait remarquable; **the pianist gave a splendid ~** le pianiste a joué de façon remarquable; **I didn't like her ~ of Giselle** je n'ai pas aimé son interprétation de Giselle; (*Scol*) **her ~ in the exam/in French** ses performances à l'examen/en français.
c *[machine]* fonctionnement *m*; *[vehicle]* performance *f*. **the machine has given a consistently fine ~** le fonctionnement de la machine s'est révélé uniformément excellent; *see* **high**.
d (*Econ*) *[the economy]* résultats *mpl*, comportement *m*; *[industry, factory]* performances *fpl*, rendement *m*; *[business, financial organization]* résultats, performances; *[theatre, hotel etc]* résultats. (*in*) **~ bond** garantie *f* de bonne fin *or* de bonne exécution.
e (*NonC: see* **perform 1a**) exécution *f*; accomplissement *m*; célébration *f*. **in the ~ of his duties** dans l'exercice de ses fonctions.
f (*Ling*) performance *f*.
g (**: fuss*) affaire *f*, histoire* *f*. **it was a whole ~ to get her to agree to see him!** ça a été toute une affaire *or* toute une histoire* pour la décider à le voir!; **what a ~!** quelle affaire!, quelle histoire!*; **it's such a ~ getting ready that it's hardly worth while going for a picnic** c'est une telle affaire *or* une telle histoire* de tout préparer que ça ne vaut guère la peine d'aller pique-niquer.

performative [pəˈfɔːmətɪv] adj, n: **~ (verb)** (verbe *m*) performatif *m*.

performer [pəˈfɔːməʳ] n (*Theat*) (*gen*) artiste *mf*; (*actor*) interprète *mf*, acteur *m*, -trice *f*; (*pianist etc*) exécutant(e) *m(f)*, interprète; (*dancer*) interprète.

performing [pəˈfɔːmɪŋ] adj *arts, artists* du spectacle, de représentation. (*in circus etc*) **~ seals/dogs** *etc* phoques/chiens *etc* savants.

perfume [ˈpɜːfjuːm] 1 n parfum *m*. 2 [pəˈfjuːm] vt parfumer.

perfumery [pəˈfjuːmərɪ] n parfumerie *f*.

perfunctorily [pəˈfʌŋktərɪlɪ] adv *bow, greet* négligemment; *answer, agree* sans conviction, pour la forme; *perform* avec négligence, sommairement, par-dessous la jambe.

perfunctory [pəˈfʌŋktərɪ] adj *nod, bow, greeting* négligent, pour la forme; *agreement* superficiel, fait pour la forme.

pergola [ˈpɜːgələ] n pergola *f*.

perhaps [pəˈhæps, præps] adv peut-être. **~ so/not** peut-être que oui/que non; **~ he will come** peut-être viendra-t-il, il viendra peut-être, peut-être qu'il viendra.

perianth [ˈperɪænθ] n (*Bot*) périanthe *m*.

pericardium [ˌperɪˈkɑːdɪəm] n, pl **pericardia** [ˌperɪˈkɑːdɪə] péricarde *m*.

pericarp [ˈperɪkɑːp] n (*Bot*) péricarpe *m*.

peridot [ˈperɪdɒt] n péridot *m*.

perigee [ˈperɪdʒiː] n périgée *m*.

periglacial [ˌperɪˈgleɪʃəl] adj périglaciaire.

peril [ˈperɪl] n péril *m*, danger *m*. **in ~ of** en danger de; **at the ~ of** au péril de; **at your ~** à vos risques et périls; (*Insurance*) **insured ~** risque *m* assuré.

perilous [ˈperɪləs] adj périlleux, dangereux.

perilously [ˈperɪləslɪ] adv périlleusement, dangereusement. **they were ~ near disaster/death** *etc* ils frôlaient la catastrophe/la mort *etc*.

perimeter [pəˈrɪmɪtəʳ] n périmètre *m*. **~ fence** *or* **wire** périmètre *m* enclos, clôture *f* d'enceinte.

perinatal [ˌperɪˈneɪtl] adj périnatal.

perineal [ˌperɪˈniːəl] adj périnéal.

perineum [ˌperɪˈniːəm] n, pl **perinea** [ˌperɪˈniːə] périnée *m*.

period [ˈpɪərɪəd] 1 n a (*epoch*) période *f*, époque *f*; (*Geol*) période; (*stage: in career, development etc*) époque, moment *m*; (*length of time*) période. **the classical ~** la période classique; **costumes/furniture of the ~** costumes/meubles de l'époque; **Picasso's blue ~** la période bleue de Picasso; **the ~ from 1600 to 1750** la période allant de 1600 à 1750; **the post-war ~** (la période de) l'après-guerre *m*; **during the whole ~ of the negotiations** pendant toute la période *or* durée des négociations; **at a later ~** plus tard; **at that ~ in** *or* **of his life** à cette époque *or* à ce moment de sa vie; **a ~ of social upheaval** une période *or* une époque de bouleversements sociaux; **he had several ~s of illness** il a été malade à plusieurs reprises; (*Astron*) **~ of revolution** *or* **rotation** période de rotation; (*Med*) **incubation ~** période d'incubation; **the holiday ~** la période des vacances; (*Met*) **bright/rainy ~s** périodes ensoleillées/de pluie; **in the ~ of a year** en l'espace d'une année; **it must be done within a 3-month ~** il faut le faire dans un délai de 3 mois; *see* **safe**.
b (*Scol etc: lesson*) ≃ (heure *f* de) cours *m* (*de 45 minutes*). **2 geography ~s** 2 cours *or* leçons de géographie.
c (*in punctuation: full stop*) point *m*. (*impressive sentences*) **~s** périodes *fpl*, phrases bien tournées.
d (*menstruation: also* **monthly ~**) règles *fpl*.
2 comp ▸**period costume, period dress** costume *m* de l'époque ▸**period furniture** (*genuine*) meuble *m* d'époque; (*copy*) meuble de style ancien ▸**period piece** (*fig*) curiosité *f*.

periodic [ˌpɪərɪˈɒdɪk] adj périodique. **~ table** classification *f* périodique des éléments.

periodical [ˌpɪərɪˈɒdɪkəl] 1 adj périodique. 2 n (journal *m*) périodique *m*, publication *f* périodique.

periodically [ˌpɪərɪˈɒdɪkəlɪ] adv périodiquement.

periodicity [ˌpɪərɪəˈdɪsɪtɪ] n périodicité *f*.

periosteum [ˌperɪˈɒstɪəm] n, pl **periostea** [ˌperɪˈɒstɪə] périoste *m*.

peripatetic [ˌperɪpəˈtetɪk] adj (*itinerant*) ambulant; (*Brit*) *teacher* qui exerce sur plusieurs établissements; (*Philos*) péripatétique.

peripheral [pəˈrɪfərəl] 1 adj périphérique (*all senses*). 2 n (*Comput*) périphérique *m*.

periphery [pəˈrɪfərɪ] n périphérie *f*.

periphrasis [pəˈrɪfrəsɪs] n, pl **periphrases** [pəˈrɪfrəsiːz] périphrase *f*, circonlocution *f*.

periscope ['perɪskəʊp] n périscope *m.*

perish ['perɪʃ] 1 vi a (*die*) périr, mourir. **we shall do it or ~ in the attempt!** nous réussirons ou nous y laisserons la vie!; (*hum*) **~ the thought!** jamais de la vie!, loin de moi cette pensée! (*hum*). b *[rubber, material, leather]* se détériorer, s'abîmer; *[foods etc]* (*be spoilt*) se détériorer, s'abîmer; (*be lost*) être détruit, être perdu. 2 vt *rubber, foods etc* abîmer, détériorer.

perishable ['perɪʃəbl] 1 adj périssable. 2 n: **~s** denrées *fpl* périssables.

perished ['perɪʃt] adj a *rubber* détérioré, abîmé. b (**: cold*) **to be ~*** être frigorifié*, crever* de froid.

perisher‡ ['perɪʃəʳ] n (*Brit*) enquiquineur* *m*, -euse* *f*. **little ~!** (espèce *f* de) petit poison!*

perishing ['perɪʃɪŋ] adj a très froid. **outside in the ~ cold** dehors dans le froid glacial *or* intense; **it was ~*** il faisait un froid de loup *or* de canard*; *[person]* **to be ~*** être frigorifié*, crever* de froid; *see* **perish**. b (*Brit ‡*) sacré* (*before noun*), fichu* (*before noun*), foutu‡ (*before noun*). **it's a ~ nuisance!** c'est vraiment enquiquinant!*

perishingly* ['perɪʃɪŋlɪ] adv (*Brit*) **~ cold** terriblement froid.

peristalsis [,perɪ'stælsɪs] n, pl **peristalses** [,perɪ'stælsi:z] péristaltisme *m.*

peristyle ['perɪstaɪl] n péristyle *m.*

peritoneum [,perɪtə'ni:əm] n, pl **~s** *or* **peritonea** [,perɪtə'ni:ə] péritoine *m.*

peritonitis [,perɪtə'naɪtɪs] n péritonite *f.*

periwig ['perɪwɪg] n perruque *f.*

periwinkle ['perɪ,wɪŋkl] n (*Bot*) pervenche *f*; (*Zool*) bigorneau *m.*

perjure ['pɜ:dʒəʳ] vt: **to ~ o.s.** se parjurer, (*Jur*) faire un faux serment; (*Jur*) **~d evidence** faux serment, faux témoignage (volontaire).

perjurer ['pɜ:dʒərəʳ] n parjure *mf.*

perjury ['pɜ:dʒərɪ] n parjure *m*; (*Jur*) faux serment. **to commit ~** se parjurer; (*Jur*) faire un faux serment.

perk¹ [pɜ:k] 1 vi: **to ~ up** (*cheer up*) se ragaillardir; (*after illness*) se remonter, se retaper*; (*show interest*) s'animer, dresser l'oreille. 2 vt: **to ~ sb up** ragaillardir qn, retaper qn*; **to ~ o.s. up** se faire beau; (*lit, fig*) **to ~ one's ears up** dresser l'oreille; **to ~ one's head up** relever *or* dresser la tête.

perk²* [pɜ:k] n (*Brit: gen pl*) à-côté *m*, avantage *m* accessoire. **~s** gratte* *f*, petits bénéfices *or* bénefs‡.

perk³* [pɜ:k] vi (abbr of **percolate**) *[coffee]* passer.

perkily ['pɜ:kɪlɪ] adv (*see* **perky**) d'un air *or* d'un ton guilleret; vivement, avec entrain; avec désinvolture.

perkiness ['pɜ:kɪnɪs] n (*see* **perky**) gaieté *f*; entrain *m*; désinvolture *f.*

perky ['pɜ:kɪ] adj (*gay*) guilleret, gai; (*lively*) vif, éveillé, plein d'entrain; (*cheeky*) désinvolte, effronté.

perm¹ [pɜ:m] 1 n (abbr of **permanent 3**) permanente *f*. **to have a ~** se faire faire une permanente. 2 vt: **to ~ sb's hair** faire une permanente à qn; **to have one's hair ~ed** se faire faire une permanente.

perm²* [pɜ:m] n abbr of **permutation**.

permafrost ['pɜ:məfrɒst] n permafrost *m*, pergélisol *m.*

permanence ['pɜ:mənəns] n permanence *f.*

permanency ['pɜ:mənənsɪ] n a (*NonC*) permanence *f*, stabilité *f*. b (*job*) emploi permanent, poste *m* fixe.

permanent ['pɜ:mənənt] 1 adj permanent. **we cannot make any ~ arrangements** nous ne pouvons pas prendre de dispositions permanentes *or* fixes; **I'm not ~ here** je ne suis pas ici à titre définitif; **~ address** résidence *f or* adresse *f* fixe; (*Brit Admin*) **P~ Undersecretary** ≃ secrétaire général (de ministère); **appointment to the ~ staff** nomination *f* à titre définitif; **~ wave** permanente *f*; (*Brit Rail*) **~ way** voie ferrée. 2 comp ▸ **permanent-press** adj *trousers* à pli permanent; *skirt* indéplissable. 3 n (*for hair*) permanente *f.*

permanently ['pɜ:mənəntlɪ] adv en permanence, de façon permanente, à titre définitif. **he was ~ appointed last September** en septembre dernier il a été nommé à titre définitif.

permanganate [pɜ:'mæŋgənɪt] n permanganate *m.*

permeability [,pɜ:mɪə'bɪlɪtɪ] n perméabilité *f.*

permeable ['pɜ:mɪəbl] adj perméable, pénétrable.

permeate ['pɜ:mɪeɪt] 1 vt *[liquid]* pénétrer, filtrer à travers; *[ideas]* pénétrer dans *or* parmi, se répandre dans *or* parmi. (*lit, fig*) **~d with** saturé de, imprégné de. 2 vi (*pass through*) pénétrer, s'infiltrer; (*fig: spread*) se répandre, pénétrer.

Permian ['pɜ:mɪən] adj (*Geol*) *period* permien.

permissible [pə'mɪsɪbl] adj (*permitted*) *action etc* permis; (*unobjectionable*) *behaviour, attitude* acceptable. **it is ~ to refuse** il est permis de refuser; **would it be ~ to say that ...?** serait-il acceptable de dire que ...?; **the degree of ~ error is 2%** la marge d'erreur acceptable *or* tolérable est de 2%.

permission [pə'mɪʃən] n permission *f*; (*official*) autorisation *f*. **without ~** sans permission, sans autorisation; **with your ~** avec votre permission; **"by kind ~ of"** "avec l'aimable consentement de"; **no ~ is needed** il n'est pas nécessaire d'avoir une autorisation; **she gave ~ for her daughter's marriage** elle a consenti au mariage de sa fille; **she gave her daughter ~ to marry** elle a autorisé sa fille à se marier; **~ is required in writing from the committee** il est nécessaire d'obtenir l'autorisation écrite du comité; **to ask ~ to do sth** demander la permission *or* l'autorisation de faire qch; **who gave you ~ to do that?** qui vous a autorisé à *or* qui vous a permis de faire cela?; **you have my ~ to do that** je vous permets de *or* vous autorise à faire cela, je vous accorde la permission *or* l'autorisation de faire cela.

permissive [pə'mɪsɪv] adj a (*tolerant*) *person, parent* permissif. **the ~ society** la société permissive. b (*optional*) facultatif.

permissively [pə'mɪsɪvlɪ] adv de façon permissive.

permissiveness [pə'mɪsɪvnɪs] n permissivité *f.*

permit ['pɜ:mɪt] 1 n autorisation écrite; (*for specific activity*) permis *m*; (*for entry*) laissez-passer *m inv*; (*for goods at Customs*) passavant *m*. **building ~** permis de bâtir *or* de construire; **fishing ~** permis *or* licence *f* de pêche; **residence ~** permis de séjour; **you need a ~ to go into the laboratory** pour entrer dans le laboratoire il vous faut une autorisation écrite *or* un laissez-passer; **please show your ~ at the gate** prière de montrer son laissez-passer à l'entrée; *see* **entry** *etc.*

2 [pə'mɪt] vt (*gen*) permettre (*sb to do* à qn de faire); (*more formally*) autoriser (*sb to do* qn à faire). **he was ~ted to leave** on lui a permis de partir, on l'a autorisé à partir; **is it ~ted to smoke?** est-il permis de fumer?; **it is not ~ted to smoke** il n'est pas permis *or* il est interdit de fumer; **we could never ~ it to happen** nous ne pourrions jamais permettre que cela se produise, nous ne pourrions jamais laisser cela se produire; **I won't ~ it** je ne le permettrai pas; **her mother will not ~ her to sell the house** sa mère ne lui permet pas de *or* ne l'autorise pas à vendre la maison; **her mother will never ~ the sale of the house** sa mère n'autorisera jamais la vente de la maison; **the law ~s the sale of this substance** la loi autorise la vente de cette substance; **the vent ~s the escape of gas** l'orifice permet l'échappement du gaz.

3 [pə'mɪt] vi: **to ~ of sth** permettre qch; **it does not ~ of doubt** cela ne permet pas le moindre doute; **weather ~ting** si le temps le permet.

permutation [,pɜ:mjʊ'teɪʃən] n permutation *f.*

permute [pə'mju:t] vt permuter.

pernicious [pɜ:'nɪʃəs] adj (*gen, also Med*) pernicieux. **~ anaemia** anémie pernicieuse.

perniciously [pɜ:'nɪʃəslɪ] adv pernicieusement.

pernickety* [pə'nɪkɪtɪ] adj (*stickler for detail*) pointilleux, formaliste; (*hard to please*) difficile; *job* délicat, minutieux. **he's very ~** il est très pointilleux, il cherche toujours la petite bête, il est très difficile; **he's very ~ about what he wears/about his food** il est très difficile pour ses vêtements/pour sa nourriture.

peroration [,perə'reɪʃən] n péroraison *f.*

peroxide [pə'rɒksaɪd] n (*Chem*) peroxyde *m*; (*for hair*) eau *f* oxygénée. **~ blonde*** blonde décolorée *or* oxygénée*; *see* **hydrogen**.

perpendicular [,pɜ:pən'dɪkjʊləʳ] 1 adj (*also Archit, Math*) perpendiculaire (*to* à); *cliff, slope* à pic. (*Archit*) **~ Gothic** gothique perpendiculaire anglais. 2 n perpendiculaire *f*. **to be out of ~** être hors d'aplomb, sortir de la perpendiculaire.

perpendicularly [,pɜ:pən'dɪkjʊləlɪ] adv perpendiculairement.

perpetrate ['pɜ:pɪtreɪt] vt *crime* perpétrer, commettre; *blunder, hoax* faire.

perpetration [,pɜ:pɪ'treɪʃən] n perpétration *f.*

perpetrator ['pɜ:pɪtreɪtəʳ] n auteur *m* (*d'un crime etc*). **~ of a crime** auteur d'un crime, coupable *mf*, criminel(le) *m(f).*

perpetual [pə'petjʊəl] adj *movement, calendar, rain, sunshine, flower* perpétuel; *nuisance, worry* perpétuel, constant; *noise, questions* perpétuel, continuel; *snows* éternel. **a ~ stream of visitors** un flot continu *or* perpétuel *or* ininterrompu de visiteurs; **he's a ~ nuisance** il ne cesse d'enquiquiner* le monde.

perpetually [pə'petjʊəlɪ] adv perpétuellement, continuellement, sans cesse.

perpetuate [pə'petjʊeɪt] vt perpétuer.

perpetuation [pə,petjʊ'eɪʃən] n perpétuation *f.*

perpetuity [,pɜ:pɪ'tju:ɪtɪ] n perpétuité . **in** *or* **for ~** à perpétuité.

perplex [pə'pleks] vt a (*puzzle*) plonger dans la perplexité, rendre perplexe. **I was ~ed by his refusal to help** son refus d'aider m'a rendu perplexe. b (*complicate*) *matter, question* compliquer, embrouiller. **to ~ the issue** compliquer *or* embrouiller la question.

perplexed [pə'plekst] adj *person* embarrassé, perplexe; *tone, glance* perplexe. **I'm ~** je suis perplexe, je ne sais pas trop quoi faire; **to look ~** avoir l'air perplexe *or* embarrassé.

perplexedly [pə'pleksɪdlɪ] adv avec perplexité, d'un air *or* d'un ton perplexe, d'un air embarrassé.

perplexing [pə'pleksɪŋ] adj *matter, question* embarrassant, compliqué; *situation* embarrassant, confus.

perplexity [pə'pleksɪtɪ] n (*bewilderment*) embarras *m*, perplexité *f*; (*complexity*) complexité *f.*

perquisite ['pɜ:kwɪzɪt] n à-côté *m*; (*in money*) à-côté, gratification *f.*

perry ['perɪ] n poiré *m.*

persecute ['pɜ:sɪkju:t] vt (*harass, oppress*) *minorities etc* persécuter; (*annoy*) harceler (*with* de), tourmenter, persécuter.

persecution [,pɜ:sɪ'kju:ʃən] n persécution *f*. **he has got a ~ mania** *or* **complex** il a la manie *or* la folie de la persécution.

persecutor ['pɜːsɪkjuːtəʳ] n persécuteur *m*, -trice *f*.
Persephone [pə'sefənɪ] n Perséphone *f*.
Perseus ['pɜːsjuːs] n Persée *m*.
perseverance [ˌpɜːsɪ'vɪərəns] n persévérance *f*, ténacité *f*. **by sheer ~** à force de persévérance *or* de persévérer.
persevere [ˌpɜːsɪ'vɪəʳ] vi persévérer (*in sth* dans qch), persister (*in sth* dans qch, *at doing sth* à faire qch).
persevering [ˌpɜːsɪ'vɪərɪŋ] adj (*determined*) persévérant, obstiné; (*hard-working*) assidu.
perseveringly [ˌpɜːsɪ'vɪərɪŋlɪ] adv (*see* **persevering**) avec persévérance, avec obstination; assidûment, avec assiduité.
Persia ['pɜːʃə] n Perse *f*.
Persian ['pɜːʃən] 1 adj (*Antiquity*) perse; (*from 7th century onward*) persan. **~ carpet** tapis *m* de Perse; **~ cat** chat persan; **~ Gulf** golfe *m* Persique; **~ lamb** astrakan *m*, agneau rasé. 2 n a Persan(e) *m(f)*; (*Hist*) Perse *mf*. b (*Ling*) persan *m*.
persiflage [ˌpɜːsɪ'flɑːʒ] n persiflage *m*, ironie *f*, raillerie *f*.
persimmon [pɜː'sɪmən] n (*tree*) plaqueminier *m* de Virginie *or* du Japon, kaki *m*; (*fruit*) kaki *m*.
persist [pə'sɪst] vi *[person]* persister, s'obstiner (*in sth* dans qch, *in doing* à faire); *[pain, opinion]* persister.
persistence [pə'sɪstəns] n, **persistency** [pə'sɪstənsɪ] n (*NonC*) *[person]* (*perseverance*) persistance *f*, persévérance *f*; (*obstinacy*) persistance, obstination *f*; *[pain]* persistance. **his ~ in talking** sa persistance *or* son obstination à parler; **as a reward for her ~** pour la récompenser de sa persistance *or* de sa persévérance.
persistent [pə'sɪstənt] adj *person* (*persevering*) persévérant; (*obstinate*) obstiné; *smell, chemical substance* persistant; *warnings, complaints, interruptions* continuel, répété; *noise, nuisance* continuel, incessant; *pain, fever, cough* persistant, tenace; *fears, doubts* continuel, tenace. (*Jur*) **~ offender** multi-récidiviste *mf*.
persistently [pə'sɪstəntlɪ] adv (*constantly*) constamment; (*obstinately*) avec persistance, obstinément. **he ~ refused to help us** il refusait obstinément *or* il persistait à refuser de nous aider.
persnickety* [pə'snɪkɪtɪ] adj a = **pernickety**. b (*snobbish*) snob *inv*.
person ['pɜːsn] n a personne *f*, individu *m* (*often pej*); (*Jur*) personne. **I know no such ~** (*no one of that name*) je ne connais personne de ce nom; (*no one like that*) je ne connais personne de ce genre; **in ~** en personne; **give it to him in ~** remettez-le-lui en mains propres; **in the ~ of** dans *or* en la personne de; **a certain ~ who shall be nameless** une certaine personne qui restera anonyme *or* qu'il vaut mieux ne pas nommer; (*Telec*) **a ~ to ~ call** une communication (téléphonique) avec préavis; (*Police etc*) **he had a knife on his ~** il avait un couteau sur lui; (*Jur*) **acting with ~ or ~s unknown** (agissant) de concert *or* en complicité avec un ou des tiers non-identifiés; *see* **displaced, per, private** *etc*.
b (*Gram*) personne *f*. **in the first ~ singular** à la première personne du singulier.
persona [pɜː'səʊnə] n, pl **~e** [pɜː'səʊniː] (*Liter, Psych etc*) personnage *m*. **~ grata/non grata** persona grata/non grata.
personable ['pɜːsnəbl] adj qui présente bien, de belle prestance.
personage ['pɜːsnɪdʒ] n (*Theat, gen*) personnage *m*.
personal ['pɜːsnl] 1 adj (*private*) *opinion, matter* personnel; (*individual*) *style* personnel, particulier; *liberty etc* personnel, individuel; (*for one's own use*) *luggage, belongings* personnel; (*to do with the body*) *habits* intime; (*in person*) *call, visit* personnel; *application* (fait) en personne; (*Gram*) personnel; (*slightly pej*) *remark, question* indiscret (*f* -ète). **my ~ belief is ...** personnellement *or* pour ma part *or* en ce qui me concerne je crois ...; **I have no ~ knowledge of this** personnellement *or* moi-même je ne sais rien à ce sujet; **a letter marked "~"** une lettre marquée "personnelle"; **his ~ interests were at stake** ses intérêts personnels *or* particuliers étaient en jeu; **the conversation/argument grew ~** la conversation/la discussion prit un ton *or* un tour personnel; **don't be ~!** ne sois pas si indiscret!, ne fais pas de remarques désobligeantes!; **don't let's get ~!** abstenons-nous de remarques désobligeantes!; (*Tax*) **~ allowance** abattement *m* personnel; **his ~ appearance leaves much to be desired** son apparence (personnelle) *or* sa tenue laisse beaucoup à désirer; **to make a ~ appearance** apparaître en personne; **~ assistant** secrétaire *mf* particulier(ière); (*Sport*) **~ best** record *m* personnel; **~ cleanliness** hygiène *f* intime; (*Brit Telec*) **~ call** (*person to person*) communication *f* (téléphonique) avec préavis; (*private*) appel *m* personnel; (*Brit Univ*) **to have a ~ chair** être professeur à titre personnel; (*Press*) **~ column** annonces personnelles; **~ computer** ordinateur *m* individuel *or* personnel; **~ details** (*name, address etc*) coordonnées* *fpl*; **~ effects** effets personnels; (*Jur*) **~ estate, ~ property** biens personnels; **do me a ~ favour and ...** rendez-moi service *or* faites-moi plaisir et ...; **~ friend** ami(e) *m(f)* intime; **~ identification number** code *m* personnel; **~ insurance** assurance *f* personnelle; **~ accident insurance** assurance *f* individuelle contre les accidents; **his ~ life** sa vie privée; **~ organiser** agenda *m* (personnel) (*style Filofax*); (*electronic*) agenda électronique; (*Gram*) **~ pronoun** pronom *m* personnel; **~ stationery** papier *m* à lettres à en-tête personnel; **~ stereo** baladeur *m*, Walkman *m* ®; **to give sth the ~ touch** ajouter une note personnelle *or* originale à qch; **~ tuition** cours *mpl* particuliers (*in* de).
2 n (*US Press*) (*article*) entrefilet *m* mondain; (*ad*) petite annonce *f* personnelle.
personality [ˌpɜːsə'nælɪtɪ] 1 n a (*NonC: also Psych*) personnalité *f*. **you must allow him to express his ~** vous devez lui permettre d'exprimer sa personnalité; **he has a pleasant/strong ~** il a une personnalité sympathique/forte; **he has a lot of ~** il a beaucoup de personnalité; **the house seemed to have a ~ of its own** la maison semblait avoir un caractère bien à elle; *see* **dual, split**.
b (*celebrity*) personnalité *f*, personnage connu; (*high-ranking person*) notabilité *f*. **~ cult** culte *m* de la personnalité; **a well-known television ~** une vedette de la télévision *or* du petit écran.
c **to indulge in personalities** faire des personnalités, faire des remarques désobligeantes; **let's keep personalities out of this** ne faisons pas de personnalités, abstenons-nous de remarques désobligeantes.
2 comp (*gen, Psych*) *problems* de personnalité ▸**personality test** test *m* de personnalité, test projectif.
personalize ['pɜːsənəˌlaɪz] vt personnaliser.
personalized ['pɜːsənəˌlaɪzd] adj personnalisé.
personally ['pɜːsnəlɪ] adv a (*in person*) en personne. **I spoke to him ~** je lui ai parlé en personne; **hand it over to him ~** remettez-le-lui en mains propres; **I am ~ responsible for ...** je suis personnellement responsable de ... .
b (*for my etc part*) personnellement, quant à moi (*or* toi *etc*), pour ma (*or* ta *etc*) part. **~ I believe that it is possible** personnellement *or* pour ma part je crois que c'est possible; **others may refuse but ~ I am willing to help you** d'autres refuseront peut-être, mais pour ma part *or* mais personnellement *or* quant à moi je suis prêt à vous aider.
c **don't take it ~!** ne croyez pas que vous soyez personnellement visé!; **I like him ~ but not as an employer** je l'aime en tant que personne mais pas en tant que patron.
personalty ['pɜːsnltɪ] n (*Jur*) biens personnels.
personate ['pɜːsəneɪt] vt a (*Theat*) jouer le rôle de. b (*personify*) personnifier; (*impersonate*) se faire passer pour.
personification [pɜːˌsɒnɪfɪ'keɪʃən] n (*all senses*) personnification *f*. **he is the ~ of good taste** il est la personnification *or* l'incarnation *f* du bon goût, il est le bon goût personnifié.
personify [pɜː'sɒnɪfaɪ] vt personnifier. **she's kindness personified** c'est la bonté personnifiée *or* en personne; **he's fascism personified** il est le fascisme personnifié.
personnel [ˌpɜːsə'nel] 1 n personnel *m*. 2 comp ▸**personnel agency** agence *f* pour l'emploi, bureau *m* de placement ▸**personnel carrier** (*Mil*) véhicule *m* transport de troupes ▸**personnel department** service *m* du personnel ▸**personnel management** gestion *f* *or* direction *f* de *or* du personnel ▸**personnel manager** chef *m* du personnel ▸**personnel officer** cadre *m* *or* attaché *m* de gestion du personnel, responsable *mf* du personnel.
perspective [pə'spektɪv] n a (*Archit, Art, Surv, gen*) perspective *f*; (*fig*) optique *f*. (*Art*) **in/out of ~** en perspective/qui ne respecte pas la perspective; (*Art*) **he has no sense of ~** il n'a aucun sens de la perspective; (*fig*) **to see sth in its true ~** voir qch dans son contexte; **let's get this into ~** ne perdons pas le sens des proportions; (*fig*) **in historical ~** dans une perspective historique. b (*prospect*) perspective *f*. **we have the ~ of much unemployment ahead** nous avons devant nous la perspective d'un chômage considérable; **they had in ~ a great industrial expansion** ils avaient une grande expansion industrielle en perspective.
perspex ['pɜːspeks] n ® (*esp Brit*) plexiglas *m* ®.
perspicacious [ˌpɜːspɪ'keɪʃəs] adj *person* perspicace; *analysis* pénétrant.
perspicacity [ˌpɜːspɪ'kæsɪtɪ] n perspicacité *f*, clairvoyance *f*.
perspicuity [ˌpɜːspɪ'kjuːɪtɪ] n a = **perspicacity**. b *[explanation, statement]* clarté *f*, netteté *f*.
perspicuous [ˌpə'spɪkjʊəs] adj clair, net.
perspiration [ˌpɜːspə'reɪʃən] n transpiration *f*, sueur *f*. **bathed in ~, dripping with ~** en nage, tout en sueur; **beads of ~** gouttes *fpl* de sueur *or* de transpiration.
perspire [pəs'paɪəʳ] vi transpirer. **he was perspiring profusely** il était en sueur *or* en nage, il transpirait abondamment.
persuadable [pə'sweɪdəbl] adj qui peut être persuadé.
persuade [pə'sweɪd] vt persuader (*sb of sth* qn de qch, *sb that* qn que), convaincre (*sb of sth* qn de qch). **to ~ sb to do** persuader qn de faire, amener *or* décider qn à faire; **to ~ sb not to do** persuader qn de ne pas faire, dissuader qn de faire; **I wanted to help but they ~d me not to** je voulais aider mais on m'en a dissuadé; **they ~d me that I ought to see him** ils m'ont persuadé que je devais le voir; **to ~ sb of the truth of a theory** convaincre qn de la vérité d'une théorie; **she is easily ~d** elle se laisse facilement persuader *or* convaincre; **it doesn't take much to ~ him** il n'en faut pas beaucoup pour le persuader *or* le convaincre; **I am (quite) ~d that he is wrong** je suis (tout à fait) persuadé qu'il a tort.
persuasion [pə'sweɪʒən] n a (*NonC*) persuasion *f*. **a little gentle ~ will get him to help** si nous le persuadons en douceur il nous aidera; **he needed a lot of ~** il a fallu beaucoup de persuasion pour le convaincre;

I don't need much ~ to stop working il n'en faut pas beaucoup pour me persuader de m'arrêter de travailler.

b (*frm: conviction*) persuasion *f*, conviction *f*. **it is my ~ that** ... je suis persuadé que ... .

c (*Rel*) religion *f*, confession *f*. **people of all ~s** des gens de toutes les religions *or* confessions; **I am not of that ~ myself** personnellement je ne partage pas cette croyance; **the Mahometan ~** la religion mahométane; **and others of that ~** et d'autres de la même confession.

persuasive [pə'sweɪsɪv] **adj** *person, voice* persuasif; *evidence, argument* convaincant.

persuasively [pə'sweɪsɪvlɪ] **adv** *speak* d'un ton persuasif; *smile* d'une manière persuasive.

persuasiveness [pə'sweɪsɪvnɪs] **n** pouvoir *m or* force *f* de persuasion.

pert [pɜːt] **adj** coquin, hardi. **a ~ little hat** un petit chapeau coquin.

pertain [pɜː'teɪn] **vi** a (*relate*) se rapporter, avoir rapport, se rattacher (*to* à). **documents ~ing to the case** documents se rapportant à *or* relatifs à l'affaire. b (*Jur etc*) *[land]* appartenir (*to* à).

pertinacious [ˌpɜːtɪ'neɪʃəs] **adj** (*stubborn*) entêté, obstiné; (*in opinions etc*) opiniâtre.

pertinaciously [ˌpɜːtɪ'neɪʃəslɪ] **adv** (*see* **pertinacious**) avec entêtement, obstinément; opiniâtrement.

pertinacity [ˌpɜːtɪ'næsɪtɪ] **n** (*see* **pertinacious**) entêtement *m*, obstination *f*; opiniâtreté *f*.

pertinence ['pɜːtɪnəns] **n** justesse *f*, à-propos *m*, pertinence *f*; (*Ling*) pertinence.

pertinent ['pɜːtɪnənt] **adj** *answer, remark* pertinent, approprié, judicieux; (*Ling*) pertinent. **~ to** approprié à, qui a rapport à.

pertinently ['pɜːtɪnəntlɪ] **adv** pertinemment, avec justesse, à propos.

pertly ['pɜːtlɪ] **adv** avec effronterie, avec impertinence.

pertness ['pɜːtnɪs] **n** effronterie *f*, impertinence *f*.

perturb [pə'tɜːb] **vt** perturber, inquiéter, agiter.

perturbation [ˌpɜːtɜː'beɪʃən] **n** (*NonC*) perturbation *f*, inquiétude *f*, agitation *f*.

perturbed [pə'tɜːbd] **adj** perturbé, inquiet (*f* -ète). **I was ~ to hear that** ... j'ai appris avec inquiétude que ... .

perturbing [pə'tɜːbɪŋ] **adj** troublant, inquiétant.

pertussis [pə'tʌsɪs] **n** coqueluche *f*.

Peru [pə'ruː] **n** Pérou *m*.

Perugia [pə'ruːdʒə] **n** Pérouse.

perusal [pə'ruːzəl] **n** lecture *f*; (*thorough*) lecture attentive.

peruse [pə'ruːz] **vt** lire; (*thoroughly*) lire attentivement.

Peruvian [pə'ruːvɪən] 1 **adj** péruvien. 2 **n** Péruvien(ne) *m(f)*.

perv‡ [pɜːv] **n abbr of pervert**.

pervade [pɜː'veɪd] **vt** *[smell]* se répandre dans; *[influence]* s'étendre dans; *[ideas]* s'insinuer dans, pénétrer dans; *[gloom]* envahir. **the feeling/the atmosphere ~s the whole book** ce sentiment/cette atmosphère se retrouve dans tout le livre.

pervasive [pɜː'veɪsɪv] **adj** *smell, ideas* pénétrant; *gloom* envahissant; *influence* qui se fait sentir un peu partout.

perverse [pə'vɜːs] **adj** (*wicked*) pervers, mauvais; (*stubborn*) obstiné, têtu, entêté; (*contrary*) contrariant. **driven by a ~ desire to hurt himself** poussé par un désir pervers de se faire souffrir; **how ~ of him!** qu'il est contrariant!, quel esprit de contradiction!

perversely [pə'vɜːslɪ] **adv** (*wickedly*) avec perversité, par pure méchanceté; (*stubbornly*) par pur entêtement; (*contrarily*) par esprit de contradiction.

perverseness [pə'vɜːsnɪs] **n** = **perversity**.

perversion [pə'vɜːʃən] **n** (*also Psych*) perversion *f*; *[facts]* déformation *f*, travestissement *m*. **sexual ~s** perversions sexuelles; (*Med etc*) **~ of a function** perversion *or* altération *f* d'une fonction; **a ~ of justice** (*gen*) un travestissement de la justice; (*Jur*) un déni de justice; **a ~ of truth** un travestissement de la vérité.

perversity [pə'vɜːsɪtɪ] **n** (*wickedness*) perversité *f*, méchanceté *f*; (*stubbornness*) obstination *f*, entêtement *m*; (*contrariness*) caractère contrariant, esprit *m* de contradiction.

pervert [pə'vɜːt] 1 **vt** *person* pervertir, dépraver; (*Psych*) pervertir; (*Rel*) détourner de ses croyances; *habits etc* dénaturer, dépraver; *fact* fausser, travestir; *sb's words* dénaturer, déformer; *justice, truth* travestir. **to ~ the course of justice** égarer la justice en subornant un témoin. 2 ['pɜːvɜːt] **n** a (*Psych: also* **sexual ~**) perverti(e) *m(f)* sexuel(le). b (*Rel: pej*) apostat *m*.

perverted [pə'vɜːtɪd] **adj** pervers.

pervious ['pɜːvɪəs] **adj** perméable, pénétrable; (*fig*) accessible (*to* à).

peseta [pə'setə] **n** peseta *f*.

pesky* ['peskɪ] **adj** (*US*) sale* (*before noun*), empoisonnant*.

peso ['peɪsəʊ] **n** (*money*) peso *m*.

pessary ['pesərɪ] **n** pessaire *m*.

pessimism ['pesɪmɪzəm] **n** pessimisme *m*.

pessimist ['pesɪmɪst] **n** pessimiste *mf*.

pessimistic [ˌpesɪ'mɪstɪk] **adj** pessimiste (*about* au sujet de, sur). **I'm very ~ about it** je suis très pessimiste à ce sujet *or* là-dessus; **I feel** *or* **I am fairly ~ about his coming** je n'ai pas grand espoir qu'il vienne.

pessimistically [ˌpesɪ'mɪstɪkəlɪ] **adv** avec pessimisme, d'un ton *or* d'un air pessimiste.

pest [pest] 1 **n** a (*insect*) insecte *m* nuisible; (*animal*) animal *m* nuisible. **rabbits are (officially) a ~ in Australia** en Australie les lapins sont classés comme animaux nuisibles *or* parmi les bêtes nuisibles. b (*person*) casse-pieds* *mf inv*, empoisonneur* *m*, -euse* *f*. **what a ~ that meeting is!** quelle barbe* cette réunion!; **it's a ~ having to go** c'est embêtant* *or* barbant* d'avoir à y aller; **you're a perfect ~!** tu n'es qu'un empoisonneur public!*, si tu savais ce que tu es embêtant!*

2 **comp** ► **pest control** (*insects*) lutte *f* contre les insectes; (*rats*) dératisation *f*; (*Admin*) **pest control officer** agent préposé à la lutte antiparasitaire.

pester ['pestəʳ] **vt** importuner, harceler. **to ~ sb with questions** harceler qn de questions; **he ~ed me to go to the cinema with him but I refused** il m'a harcelé *or* il m'a cassé les pieds* pour que j'aille au cinéma avec lui mais j'ai refusé; **he ~ed me to go to the cinema with him and I went, he went on ~ing me until I went to the cinema with him** il n'a eu de cesse que j'aille au cinéma avec lui, il m'a tellement cassé les pieds* que je suis allé au cinéma avec lui; **she has been ~ing me for an answer** elle n'arrête pas de me réclamer une réponse; **he ~ed his father into lending him the car** à force d'insister auprès de son père il a fini par se faire prêter la voiture; **he ~s the life out of me*** il me casse les pieds*; **stop ~ing me** laisse-moi tranquille, fiche-moi la paix*; **stop ~ing me about your bike** fiche-moi la paix* avec ton vélo; **is this man ~ing you?** est-ce que cet homme vous importune?

pesticidal [ˌpestɪ'saɪdl] **adj** pesticide.

pesticide ['pestɪsaɪd] **n** (*gen*) pesticide *m*.

pestiferous [pes'tɪfərəs] = **pestilent**.

pestilence ['pestɪləns] **n** peste *f* (*also fig*).

pestilent ['pestɪlənt] **adj**, **pestilential** [ˌpestɪ'lenʃəl] **adj** (*causing disease*) pestilentiel; (*pernicious*) nuisible; (**: annoying*) fichu* (*before noun*), sacré‡ (*before noun*).

pestle ['pesl] **n** pilon *m*.

pesto ['pestəʊ] **n** pesto *m*.

pet¹ [pet] 1 **n** a (*animal*) animal familier *or* de compagnie. **we have 6 ~s** nous avons 6 animaux chez nous *or* à la maison; **he hasn't got any ~s** il n'a pas d'animaux chez lui; **she keeps a goldfish as a ~** en fait d'animal elle a un poisson rouge; **"no ~s allowed"** "les animaux sont interdits".

b (**: favourite*) chouchou(te)* *m(f)*. **the teacher's ~** le chouchou* du professeur; **to make a ~ of sb** chouchouter qn*.

c (*) **be a ~** sois un chou*, sois gentil; **he's rather a ~** c'est un chou*, il est adorable; **come here (my) ~** viens ici mon chou* *or* mon lapin*.

2 **comp** ► **pet food** aliments *mpl* pour animaux ► **petnapping*** (*US*) vol *m* d'animaux familiers (*pour les revendre aux laboratoires*) ► **pet shop** boutique *f* d'animaux.

3 **adj** a *lion, snake* apprivoisé. **he's got a ~ rabbit** il a un lapin (apprivoisé).

b (*favourite*) favori (*f* -ite). **his ~ theme** son thème favori; **~ aversion***, **~ hate*** bête noire; **~ name** petit nom (d'amitié); **~ subject** marotte *f*, dada* *m*; **it's his ~ subject** c'est sa marotte, c'est son dada*; **once he gets on his ~ subject** ... quand il enfourche son cheval de bataille ... *or* son dada favori* ... .

4 **vt** (*indulge*) chouchouter*; (*fondle*) câliner; (**: sexually*) caresser, peloter‡.

5 **vi** (**: sexually*) se caresser, se peloter‡.

pet²* [pet] **n**: **to be in a ~** être d'une humeur de dogue, être de mauvais poil*, être en rogne*.

petal ['petl] **n** pétale *m*. **~-shaped** en forme de pétale.

petard [pɪ'tɑːd] **n** pétard *m*; *see* **hoist**.

Pete [piːt] **n** (**dim of Peter**) **for ~'s sake!*** mais enfin!, bon sang!*

Peter ['piːtəʳ] **n** Pierre *m*. (*Rel*) **~'s pence** denier *m* de saint-Pierre; *see* **blue, rob**.

peter¹ ['piːtəʳ] **vi**: **to ~ out** *[supplies]* s'épuiser; *[stream, conversation]* tarir; *[plans]* tomber à l'eau; *[story, plot, play, book]* tourner court; *[fire, flame]* mourir; *[road]* se perdre.

peter²‡‡ ['piːtəʳ] **n** (*US: penis*) bite *f*‡‡.

petit ['petɪ] **adj** (*US*) **~ jury** jury *m* (dans un procès).

petit-four ['petɪ'fɔːʳ] **n** petit-four *m*.

petite [pə'tiːt] **adj** *woman* menue.

petition [pə'tɪʃən] 1 **n** a (*list of signatures*) pétition *f*. **to get up a ~ for/against sth** organiser une pétition en faveur de/contre qch.

b (*prayer*) prière *f*; (*request*) requête *f*, supplique *f*.

c (*Jur*) requête *f*, pétition *f*. **~ for divorce** demande *f* en divorce; **right of ~** droit *m* de pétition; *see* **file²**.

2 **vt** a adresser une pétition à, pétitionner. **they ~ed the king for the release of the prisoner** ils adressèrent une pétition au roi pour demander la libération du prisonnier.

b (*beg*) implorer, prier (*sb to do* qn de faire).

c (*Jur*) **to ~ the court** adresser *or* présenter une pétition en justice.

3 **vi** adresser une pétition, pétitionner. (*Jur*) **to ~ for divorce** faire une demande en divorce.

petitioner [pə'tɪʃnəʳ] **n** pétitionnaire *mf*; (*Jur*) requérant(e) *m(f)*, pétitionnaire; (*in divorce*) demandeur *m*, -eresse *f* (en divorce).

Petrarch ['petrɑːk] **n** Pétrarque *m*.

petrel ['petrəl] n pétrel *m*; *see* **stormy**.
Petri ['pi:trɪ] n: ~ **dish** boîte *f* de Petri.
petrifaction [ˌpetrɪ'fækʃən] n (*lit, fig*) pétrification *f*.
petrified ['petrɪfaɪd] adj (*lit*) pétrifié; (*fig: also* ~ **with fear**) pétrifié de peur, paralysé de peur, cloué (sur place) de peur. **I was absolutely** ~! j'étais terrifié!, j'étais pétrifié de peur!
petrify ['petrɪfaɪ] 1 vt (*lit*) pétrifier; (*fig*) pétrifier *or* paralyser de peur, clouer (sur place) de peur. 2 vi se pétrifier (*lit*).
petro... ['petrəʊ] pref pétro... .
petrochemical [ˌpetrəʊ'kemɪkəl] 1 n produit *m* pétrochimique 2 adj pétrochimique.
petrocurrency ['petrəʊˌkʌrənsɪ] n pétro-devise *f*.
petrodollar ['petrəʊˌdɒlər] n petrodollar *m*.
petrographic(al) [ˌpetrə'græfɪk(əl)] adj pétrographique.
petrography [pe'trɒgrəfɪ] n pétrographie *f*.
petrol ['petrəl] (*Brit*) 1 n essence *f*. **high-octane** ~ supercarburant *m*, super* *m*; **2-star** ~ essence *f* ordinaire; **3-star** *or* **4-star** ~ super* *m*; **this car is heavy on** ~ cette voiture consomme beaucoup (d'essence); **we've run out of** ~ *[driver]* nous sommes en panne d'essence; *[garage owner]* nous n'avons plus d'essence; *see* **star**.
2 comp ►**petrol bomb** cocktail *m* Molotov ►**petrol can** bidon *m* à essence ►**petrol-driven** à essence ►**petrol engine** moteur *m* à essence ►**petrol (filler) cap** bouchon *m* de réservoir d'essence ►**petrol gauge** jauge *f* d'essence ►**petrol pump** pompe *f* à essence ►**petrol rationing** rationnement *m* d'essence ►**petrol station** station-service *f*, station *f or* poste *m* d'essence ►**petrol tank** réservoir *m* (d'essence) ►**petrol tanker** (*ship*) pétrolier *m*, tanker *m*; (*lorry*) camion-citerne *m* (*transportant de l'essence*).
petroleum [pɪ'trəʊlɪəm] n pétrole *m*. ~ **jelly** vaseline *f*.
petroliferous [ˌpetrə'lɪfərəs] adj pétrolifère.
petrology [pe'trɒlədʒɪ] n pétrologie *f*.
petro-politics [ˌpetrəʊ'pɒlɪtɪks] npl politique *f* menée des pays de l'OPEP.
petrosterling ['petrəʊˌstɜ:lɪŋ] n pétro-sterling *m*.
petticoat ['petɪkəʊt] n (*underskirt*) jupon *m*; (*slip*) combinaison *f*. **the rustle of** ~**s** le bruissement *or* le froufrou des jupons.
pettifogging ['petɪfɒgɪŋ] adj a (*insignificant*) *details* insignifiant; *objections* chicanier. b (*slightly dishonest*) *person* plutôt louche; *dealings* plutôt douteux, plutôt louche.
pettily ['petɪlɪ] adv avec mesquinerie, de façon mesquine.
pettiness ['petɪnɪs] n (*NonC: see* **petty b, c**) insignifiance *f*, manque *m* d'importance; mesquinerie *f*, petitesse *f*; méchanceté *f*, malveillance *f*; caractère pointilleux; manie *f* de critiquer; intolérance *f*, étroitesse *f*.
petting* ['petɪŋ] n (*NonC*) caresses *fpl*, pelotage‡ *m*. **heavy** ~ pelotage poussé‡.
pettish ['petɪʃ] adj *person* de mauvaise humeur, irritable; *remark* maussade; *child* grognon.
pettishly ['petɪʃlɪ] adv avec mauvaise humeur, d'un air *or* d'un ton maussade.
petty ['petɪ] adj a (*on a small scale*) *farmer, shopkeeper* petit. (*Brit*) ~ **cash** petite caisse *f*, caisse *f* de dépenses courantes; ~ **criminal** petit malfaiteur *m*, malfaiteur à la petite semaine; ~ **expenses** menues dépenses; (*Jur*) ~ **larceny** larcin *m*; ~ **official** fonctionnaire *mf* subalterne, petit fonctionnaire; (*Brit Jur*) **P**~ **Sessions** sessions *fpl* des juges de paix.
b (*trivial*) *detail, complaint* petit, insignifiant, sans importance. ~ **annoyances** désagréments mineurs, tracasseries *fpl*; ~ **regulations** règlement tracassier.
c (*small-minded*) mesquin, petit; (*spiteful*) méchant, mauvais, malveillant; (*preoccupied with detail*) (trop) pointilleux; (*fault-finding*) critique; (*intolerant*) intolérant, étroit. ~**-minded** mesquin.
d (*Naut*) ~ **officer** ≃ maître *m*; (*US Navy*) ~ **officer third class** quartier-maître *m* de première classe.
petulance ['petjʊləns] n (*see* **petulant**) irritabilité *f*, irascibilité *f*; mauvaise humeur *f*.
petulant ['petjʊlənt] adj *character* irritable, irascible; (*on one occasion*) irrité; *expression, gesture* irrité. **in a** ~ **mood** de mauvaise humeur; ~ **behaviour** irritabilité *f*, irascibilité *f*; (*on one occasion*) mauvaise humeur *f*.
petulantly ['petjʊləntlɪ] adv *speak* d'un ton irrité, avec irritation, avec humeur; *behave* avec mauvaise humeur.
petunia [pɪ'tju:nɪə] n pétunia *m*.
pew [pju:] n (*Rel*) banc *m* (d'église); (*) siège *m*. (*hum*) **take a** ~* prenez donc un siège.
pewter ['pju:tər] n (*NonC*) étain *m*. **to collect** ~ collectionner les étains; ~ **pot** pot *m* en *or* d'étain.
PFC [pi:ef'si:] n (*US Mil*) (abbr of **Private First Class**) *see* **private**.
pfennig ['fenɪg] n pfennig *m*.
PFLP [pi:efel'pi:] n (abbr of **Popular Front for the Liberation of Palestine**) F.P.L.P. *m*.
PG [pi:'dʒi:] (*Cine*) (*film censor's rating*) (abbr of **Parental Guidance**) *pour enfants accompagnés d'un adulte*.
P.G. (abbr of **paying guest**) *see* **paying**.
PH [pi:'eɪtʃ] (*US Mil*) (abbr of **Purple Heart**) *see* **purple**.
pH [pi:'eɪtʃ] n pH *m*.
Phaedra ['fi:drə] n Phèdre *f*.
phaeton ['feɪtən] n phaéton *m*.
phagocyte ['fægəˌsaɪt] n phagocyte *m*.
phagocytosis [ˌfægəsaɪ'təʊsɪs] n phagocytose *f*.
phalangeal [fə'lændʒɪəl] adj phalangien.
phalanstery ['fælənstərɪ] n phalanstère *m*.
phalanx ['fælæŋks] n, pl **phalanges** ['fælændʒi:z] (*gen, Mil, Hist:* pl also ~**es**; *Anat*) phalange *f*.
phalarope ['fæləˌrəʊp] n phalarope *m*.
phalli ['fælaɪ] npl of **phallus**.
phallic ['fælɪk] adj phallique. ~ **symbol** symbole *m* phallique.
phallus ['fæləs] n, pl ~**es** *or* **phalli** phallus *m*.
phantasm ['fæntæzəm] n fantasme *m*.
phantasmagoria [ˌfæntæzmə'gɔ:rɪə] n fantasmagorie *f*.
phantasmagoric(al) [ˌfæntæzmə'gɒrɪk(əl)] adj fantasmagorique.
phantasmal [fæn'tæzməl] adj fantomatique.
phantasy ['fæntəzɪ] n = **fantasy**.
phantom ['fæntəm] 1 n (*ghost*) fantôme *m*; (*vision*) fantasme *m*. 2 adj -fantôme (*also hum*). ~ **pregnancy** grossesse *f* nerveuse; (*hum*) **the** ~ **pencil thief strikes again!** le voleur de crayons fantôme a encore frappé!
Pharaoh ['fɛərəʊ] n pharaon *m*; (*as name*) Pharaon *m*.
Pharisaic(al) [ˌfærɪ'seɪɪk(əl)] adj pharisaïque.
Pharisee ['færɪsi:] n Pharisien(ne) *m(f)*.
pharmaceutical [ˌfɑ:mə'sju:tɪkəl] 1 adj pharmaceutique. 2 npl: ~**s** médicaments *mpl*, produits pharmaceutiques.
pharmacist ['fɑ:məsɪst] n pharmacien(ne) *m(f)*.
pharmacological [ˌfɑ:məkə'lɒdʒɪkəl] adj pharmacologique.
pharmacology [ˌfɑ:mə'kɒlədʒɪ] n pharmacologie *f*.
pharmacopoeia [ˌfɑ:məkə'pi:ə] n pharmacopée *f*, Codex *m*.
pharmacy ['fɑ:məsɪ] n pharmacie *f*.
pharynges [fæ'rɪndʒi:z] npl of **pharynx**.
pharyngitis [ˌfærɪn'dʒaɪtɪs] n pharyngite *f*, angine *f*. **to have** ~ avoir la pharyngite, avoir une angine.
pharynx ['færɪŋks] n, pl ~**es** *or* **pharynges** pharynx *m*.
phase [feɪz] 1 n (*stage in process*) phase *f*, période *f*; (*aspect, side*) aspect *m*; (*Astron, Chem, Elec, Phys etc*) phase. **the adolescent** ~ **in the development of the individual** la période *or* la phase de l'adolescence dans le développement de l'individu; **every child goes through a difficult** ~ tout enfant passe par une période difficile; **it's just a** ~ **(he's going through)** ça lui passera; **a critical** ~ **in the negotiations** une phase *or* une période *or* un stade critique des négociations; **the first** ~ **of the work** la première tranche des travaux; **the** ~**s of a disease** les phases d'une maladie; **the** ~**s of the moon** les phases de la lune; (*Elec, fig*) **in** ~ en phase; (*Elec, fig*) **out of** ~ déphasé.
2 comp ►**phase-out** suppression *f* progressive.
3 vt *innovations, developments* introduire graduellement; *execution of plan* procéder par étapes à. **they** ~**d the modernization of the factory** on a procédé par étapes à la modernisation de l'usine; **the modernization of the factory was** ~**d over 3 years** la modernisation de l'usine s'est effectuée en 3 ans par étapes; **the changes were** ~**d carefully so as to avoid unemployment** on a pris soin d'introduire les changements graduellement afin d'éviter le chômage; **we must** ~ **the various processes so as to lose as little time as possible** nous devons arranger *or* organiser les diverses opérations de façon à perdre le moins de temps possible; ~**d changes** changements organisés de façon progressive; **a** ~**d withdrawal of troops** un retrait progressif des troupes.
►**phase in** vt sep *new machinery, measures etc* introduire progressivement *or* graduellement.
►**phase out** 1 vt sep *machinery* retirer progressivement; *jobs* supprimer graduellement; *techniques, differences* éliminer progressivement. 2 **phase-out** n *see* **phase 2**.
phatic ['fætɪk] adj phatique.
Ph.D. [pi:eɪtʃ'di:] n (*Univ*) (abbr of **Doctor of Philosophy**) (*qualification*) doctorat *m*; (*person*) ≃ titulaire *m* d'un doctorat (d'état). **to have a** ~ **in ...** avoir un doctorat de ... .
pheasant ['feznt] n faisan *m*; (*hen* ~) faisane *f*; (*young* ~) faisandeau *m*.
phenobarbitone ['fi:nəʊ'bɑ:bɪtəʊn] n phénobarbital *m*.
phenol ['fi:nɒl] n phénol *m*.
phenomena [fɪ'nɒmɪnə] npl of **phenomenon**.
phenomenal [fɪ'nɒmɪnl] adj (*lit, fig*) phénoménal.
phenomenally [fɪ'nɒmɪnəlɪ] adv phénoménalement.
phenomenological [fənɒmənə'lɒdʒɪkəl] adj phénoménologique.
phenomenologist [fənɒmə'nɒlədʒɪst] n phénoménologue *mf*.
phenomenology [fənɒmə'nɒlədʒɪ] n phénoménologie *f*.
phenomenon [fɪ'nɒmɪnən] n, pl ~**s** *or* **phenomena** (*lit, fig*) phénomène *m*.
pheromone ['ferəˌməʊn] n phéromone *f*.
phew [fju:] excl (*from disgust*) pouah!; (*surprise*) oh!; (*relief*) ouf!; (*heat*) pfff!
Phi Beta Kappa ['faɪ'beɪtə'kæpə] n (*US Univ*) *association d'anciens étudiants très brillants*.

phial ['faɪəl] n fiole *f*.

Philadelphia [ˌfɪlə'delfɪə] n Philadelphie.

philander [fɪ'lændəʳ] vi courir après les femmes, faire la cour aux femmes.

philanderer [fɪ'lændərəʳ] n coureur *m* (de jupons), don Juan *m*.

philandering [fɪ'lændərɪŋ] n flirts *mpl*, liaisons *fpl*.

philanthropic [ˌfɪlən'θrɒpɪk] adj philanthropique.

philanthropist [fɪ'lænθrəpɪst] n philanthrope *mf*.

philanthropy [fɪ'lænθrəpɪ] n philanthropie *f*.

philatelic [ˌfɪlə'telɪk] adj philatélique.

philatelist [fɪ'lætəlɪst] n philatéliste *mf*.

philately [fɪ'lætəlɪ] n philatélie *f*.

...phile [faɪl] suf ...phile. **franco~** (adj, n) francophile *(mf)*.

Philemon [faɪ'li:mɒn] n Philémon *m*.

philharmonic [ˌfɪlɑ:'mɒnɪk] adj philharmonique.

philhellene [fɪl'heli:n] n, adj philhellène *(mf)*.

philhellenic [ˌfɪlhe'li:nɪk] adj philhellène.

philhellenism [fɪl'helɪnɪzəm] n philhellénisme *m*.

...philia ['fɪlɪə] suf ...philie *f*. **franco~** francophilie *f*.

Philip ['fɪlɪp] n Philippe *m*.

Philippi ['fɪlɪpaɪ] n Philippes.

Philippians [fɪ'lɪpɪəns] npl Philippiens *mpl*.

philippic [fɪ'lɪpɪk] n (*liter*) philippique *f*.

Philippine ['fɪlɪpi:n] adj, n: **the ~ Islands, the ~s** les Philippines *fpl*.

philistine ['fɪlɪstaɪn] 1 adj (*fig*) béotien. **P~** philistin. 2 n (*fig*) **(P)~** philistin *m*, béotien(ne) *m(f)*; (*Bible etc*) **P~** Philistin *m*.

Philistinism ['fɪlɪstɪnɪzəm] n philistinisme *m*.

Phillips ['fɪlɪps] n ® **~ screw** vis *f* cruciforme; **~ screwdriver** tournevis *m* cruciforme.

philodendron [ˌfɪlə'dendrən] n, pl **~s** *or* **philodendra** [ˌfɪlə'dendrə] philodendron *m*.

philological [ˌfɪlə'lɒdʒɪkəl] adj philologique.

philologist [fɪ'lɒlədʒɪst] n philologue *mf*.

philology [fɪ'lɒlədʒɪ] n philologie *f*.

philosopher [fɪ'lɒsəfəʳ] n philosophe *mf*. (*fig*) **he is something of a ~** il est du genre philosophe; **~'s stone** pierre philosophale.

philosophic(al) [ˌfɪlə'sɒfɪk(əl)] adj a *subject, debate* philosophique. b (*fig: calm, resigned*) philosophe, calme, résigné. **in a ~ tone** d'un ton philosophe; **I felt fairly ~ about it all** j'ai pris tout cela assez philosophiquement *or* avec une certaine philosophie.

philosophically [ˌfɪlə'sɒfɪkəlɪ] adv philosophiquement, avec philosophie.

philosophize [fɪ'lɒsəfaɪz] vi philosopher (*about, on* sur).

philosophy [fɪ'lɒsəfɪ] n philosophie *f*. **Aristotle's ~** la philosophie d'Aristote; **his ~ of life** sa philosophie, sa conception de la vie; *see* **moral, natural**.

philtre, (*US*) **philter** ['fɪltəʳ] n philtre *m*.

phiz‡ [fɪz] n, **phizog**‡ [fɪ'zɒg] n (abbr of **physiognomy**) binette‡ *f*, bouille‡ *f*.

phlebitis [flɪ'baɪtɪs] n phlébite *f*.

phlebology [flɪ'bɒlədʒɪ] n phlébologie *f*.

phlebotomist [flɪ'bɒtəmɪst] n phlébotomiste *mf*.

phlebotomy [flɪ'bɒtəmɪ] n phlébotomie *f*.

phlegm [flem] n flegme *m*.

phlegmatic [fleg'mætɪk] adj flegmatique.

phlegmatically [fleg'mætɪkəlɪ] adv flegmatiquement, avec flegme.

phlox [flɒks] n, pl **~** *or* **~es** phlox *m inv*.

Phnom-Penh ['nɒm'pen] n Phnom-Penh.

...phobe [fəʊb] suf ...phobe. **franco~** (adj, n) francophobe *(mf)*.

phobia ['fəʊbɪə] n phobie *f*. **I've got a ~ about ...** j'ai la phobie des (*or* du *etc*) ... .

...phobia ['fəʊbɪə] suf ...phobie *f*. **anglo~** anglophobie *f*.

phobic ['fəʊbɪk] adj, n phobique *(mf)*.

phoenix ['fi:nɪks] n phénix *m*.

phonatory ['fəʊnətərɪ] adj phonateur (*f* -trice), phonatoire.

phone[1] [fəʊn] abbr of **telephone**. 1 n téléphone *m*. **on** *or* **over the ~** (*gen*) au téléphone; **I'm on the ~** (*subscriber*) j'ai le téléphone; (*speaking*) je suis au téléphone; **to have sb on the ~** avoir qn au bout du fil*. 2 comp ▸**phone book** annuaire *m* ▸**phone box** cabine *f* téléphonique ▸**phone call** coup *m* de fil *or* de téléphone ▸**phonecard** (*Brit Telec*) télécarte *f* ▸**phone-in (programme)** (*Rad*) programme *m* à ligne ouverte ▸**phone number** numéro *m* de téléphone. 3 vt (*also* **~ up**) téléphoner à, passer un coup de fil à*. 4 vi téléphoner.

phone[2] [fəʊn] n (*Ling*) phone *m*.

phoneme ['fəʊni:m] n phonème *m*.

phonemic [fəʊ'ni:mɪk] adj phonémique.

phonemics [fəʊ'ni:mɪks] n phonémique *f*, phonématique *f*.

phonetic [fəʊ'netɪk] adj phonétique. **the ~ alphabet** l'alphabet *m* phonétique; **~ law** loi *f* phonétique.

phonetically [fəʊ'netɪkəlɪ] adv phonétiquement.

phonetician [ˌfəʊnɪ'tɪʃən] n phonéticien(ne) *m(f)*.

phonetics [fəʊ'netɪks] n (*NonC: subject, study*) phonétique *f*; (*symbols*) transcription *f* phonétique. **articulatory/acoustic/auditory ~** phonétique *f* articulatoire/acoustique/auditoire; **the ~ are wrong** la transcription phonétique est fausse.

phoney* ['fəʊnɪ] 1 adj *name* faux (*f* fausse); *jewels* en toc*; *emotion* factice, simulé; *excuse, story, report* bidon* *inv*, à la noix*; *person* pas franc, poseur. (*in 1939*) **the ~ war*** la drôle de guerre; **this diamond is ~** ce diamant c'est du toc*; **apparently he was a ~ doctor** il paraît que c'était un charlatan *or* un médecin marron; **a ~ company** une société bidon*; **it sounds ~** cela a l'air d'être de la frime* *or* de la blague*. 2 n (*person*) charlatan *m*, poseur *m*, faux jeton* *m*. **that diamond is a ~** ce diamant est du toc*.

phonic ['fɒnɪk] adj phonique.

phono... ['fəʊnəʊ] pref phono... .

phonograph ['fəʊnəgrɑ:f] n (*US, also Brit* †) électrophone *m*, phonographe† *m*.

phonological [ˌfəʊnə'lɒdʒɪkəl] adj phonologique.

phonologically [ˌfəʊnə'lɒdʒɪklɪ] adv phonologiquement.

phonologist [fə'nɒlədʒɪst] n phonologue *mf*.

phonology [fəʊ'nɒlədʒɪ] n phonologie *f*.

phony* ['fəʊnɪ] = **phoney***.

phooey* ['fu:ɪ] excl (*US*) (*scorn*) peuh!, pfft!; (*disappointment*) zut alors!

phosgene ['fɒzdʒi:n] n phosgène *m*.

phosphate ['fɒsfeɪt] n (*Chem*) phosphate *m*. (*Agr*) **~s** phosphates, engrais phosphatés.

phosphene ['fɒsfi:n] n phosphène *m*.

phosphide ['fɒsfaɪd] n phosphure *m*.

phosphine ['fɒsfi:n] n phosphine *f*.

phosphoresce [ˌfɒsfə'res] vi être phosphorescent.

phosphorescence [ˌfɒsfə'resns] n phosphorescence *f*.

phosphorescent [ˌfɒsfə'resnt] adj phosphorescent.

phosphoric [fɒs'fɒrɪk] adj phosphorique.

phosphorous ['fɒsfərəs] adj phosphoreux.

phosphorus ['fɒsfərəs] n phosphore *m*.

photo ['fəʊtəʊ] 1 n, pl **~s** (abbr of **photograph**) photo *f*; *for phrases see* **photograph**. 2 comp ▸**photo album** album *m* de photos ▸**photo finish** (*Sport*) photo-finish *f* ▸**photo opportunity: it is a great photo opportunity** il y a de bonnes photos à prendre.

photo... ['fəʊtəʊ] pref photo... .

photocall ['fəʊtəʊˌkɒl] n (*Brit Press*) séance *f* de photos pour la presse.

photocell ['fəʊtəʊˌsel] n photocellule *f*.

photochemistry [ˌfəʊtəʊ'kemɪstrɪ] n photochimie *f*.

photochemical [ˌfəʊtəʊ'kemɪkəl] adj photochimique.

photocompose [ˌfəʊtəʊkəm'pəʊz] vt photocomposer.

photocomposer [ˌfəʊtəʊkəm'pəʊzəʳ] n photocomposeuse *f*.

photocomposition [ˌfəʊtəʊkɒmpə'zɪʃən] n photocomposition *f*.

photoconductive [ˌfəʊtəʊkən'dʌktɪv] adj photoconducteur (*f* -trice).

photocopier ['fəʊtəʊˌkɒpɪəʳ] n photocopieur *m*, photocopieuse *f*.

photocopy ['fəʊtəʊˌkɒpɪ] 1 n photocopie *f*. 2 vt photocopier.

photocurrent ['fəʊtəʊˌkʌrənt] n photocourant *m*.

photodisintegration [ˌfəʊtəʊdɪˌsɪntɪ'greɪʃən] n photodissociation *f*.

photodisk ['fəʊtəʊˌdɪsk] n (*Comput*) photodisque *m*.

photoelasticity [ˌfəʊtəʊɪlæ'stɪsɪtɪ] n photoelastimétrie *f*.

photoelectric(al) [ˌfəʊtəʊɪ'lektrɪk(əl)] adj photo-électrique. **~ cell** cellule *f* photo-eléctrique.

photoelectricity [ˌfəʊtəʊɪlek'trɪsɪtɪ] n photoélectricité *f*.

photoelectron [ˌfəʊtəʊɪ'lektrɒn] n photo(-)électron *m*.

photoengrave [ˌfəʊtəʊɪn'greɪv] vt photograver.

photoengraving [ˌfəʊtəʊɪn'greɪvɪŋ] n photogravure *f*.

Photofit ['fəʊtəʊˌfɪt] ® 1 n (*picture*) portrait-robot *m*. 2 comp ▸**Photofit picture** portrait-robot *m*.

photoflash ['fəʊtəʊˌflæʃ] n flash *m*.

photoflood ['fəʊtəʊˌflʌd] n projecteur *m*.

photogenic [ˌfəʊtə'dʒenɪk] adj photogénique.

photogeology [ˌfəʊtəʊdʒɪ'ɒlədʒɪ] n photo-géologie *f*.

photograph ['fəʊtəgræf] 1 n photo(graphie) *f*. **to take a ~ of sb/sth** prendre une photo de qn/qch, prendre qn/qch en photo; **he takes good ~s** il fait de bonnes photos; **he takes a good ~*** (*is photogenic*) il est photogénique, il est bien en photo*; **in** *or* **on the ~** sur la photo; *see* **aerial, colour**. 2 comp ▸**photograph album** album *m* de photos *or* de photographies. 3 vt photographier, prendre en photo. 4 vi: **to ~ well** être photogénique, être bien en photo*.

photographer [fə'tɒgrəfəʳ] n (*also Press etc*) photographe *mf*. **press ~** photographe *mf* de la presse, reporter *m* photographe; **street ~** photostoppeur *m*; **he's a keen ~** il est passionné de photo.

photographic [ˌfəʊtə'græfɪk] adj photographique. **~ library** photothèque *f*; **~ memory** mémoire *f* photographique.

photographically [ˌfəʊtə'græfɪkəlɪ] adv photographiquement.

photography [fə'tɒgrəfɪ] n (*NonC*) photographie *f* (*NonC*); *see* **colour, trick**.

photogravure [ˌfəʊtəʊgrə'vjʊəʳ] n photogravure *f*, héliogravure *f*.

photojournalism [ˌfəʊtəʊ'dʒɜ:nəlɪzəm] n photoreportage *m*.

photojournalist [ˌfəʊtəʊ'dʒɜ:nəlɪst] n journaliste-photographe *mf*.

photokinesis [ˌfəʊtəʊkɪ'ni:sɪs] n photokinésie *f*.

photokinetic [ˌfəʊtəʊkɪ'netɪk] adj photokinétique.

photolitho [ˌfəʊtəʊ'laɪθəʊ] n (abbr of **photolithography**) photolithogra-

phie *f*.
photolithograph [ˌfəʊtəʊˈlɪθəˌgrɑːf] **n** gravure *f* photolithographique.
photolithography [ˌfəʊtəʊlɪˈθɒgrəfɪ] **n** photolithographie *f*.
photolysis [fəʊˈtɒlɪsɪs] **n** photolyse *f*.
photomachine [ˌfəʊtəʊməˈʃiːn] **n** photomaton *m*.
photomap [ˈfəʊtəʊˌmæp] **n** photoplan *m*.
photomechanical [ˌfəʊtəʊmɪˈkænɪkl] **adj** photomécanique.
photometer [fəʊˈtɒmɪtəʳ] **n** photomètre *m*.
photometric [ˌfəʊtəˈmetrɪk] **adj** photométrique.
photometry [fəʊˈtɒmɪtrɪ] **n** photométrie *f*.
photomontage [ˌfəʊtəʊmɒnˈtɑːʒ] **n** photomontage *m*.
photomultiplier [ˌfəʊtəʊˈmʌltɪˌplaɪəʳ] **n** photomultiplicateur *m*.
photon [ˈfəʊtɒn] **n** photon *m*.
photo-offset [ˈfəʊtəʊˈɒfˌset] **n** (*Typ*) offset *m* (*processus*).
photoperiod [ˌfəʊtəʊˈpɪərɪəd] **n** photopériode *f*.
photoperiodic [ˌfəʊtəʊˌpɪərɪˈɒdɪk] **adj** photopériodique.
photoperiodism [ˌfəʊtəʊˈpɪərɪədɪzəm] **n** photopériodisme *m*.
photophobia [ˌfəʊtəʊˈfəʊbɪə] **n** photophobie *f*.
photorealism [ˌfəʊtəʊˈrɪəˌlɪzəm] **n** photoréalisme *m*.
photoreconnaissance [ˌfəʊtəʊrɪˈkɒnɪsəns] **n** reconnaissance *f* photographique.
photosensitive [ˌfəʊtəʊˈsensɪtɪv] **adj** photosensible.
photosensitivity [ˌfəʊtəʊsensɪˈtɪvɪtɪ] **n** photosensibilité *f*.
photosensitize [ˌfəʊtəʊˈsensɪˌtaɪz] **vt** photosensibiliser.
photosensor [ˈfəʊtəʊˌsensəʳ] **n** dispositif *m* photosensible.
photoset [ˈfəʊtəʊˌset] **vt** photocomposer.
Photostat [ˈfəʊtəʊˌstæt] ® **1 n** photostat *m*. **2 vt** photocopier.
photosynthesis [ˌfəʊtəʊˈsɪnθɪsɪs] **n** photosynthèse *f*.
photosynthesize [ˌfəʊtəʊˈsɪnθɪˌsaɪz] **vt** photosynthétiser.
photosynthetic [ˌfəʊtəʊsɪnˈθetɪk] **adj** photosynthétique.
photosynthetically [ˌfəʊtəʊsɪnˈθetɪklɪ] **adv** photosynthétiquement.
phototelegram [ˌfəʊtəʊˈteleˌgræm] **n** phototélégramme *m*.
phototelegraphy [ˌfəʊtəʊtɪˈlegrəfɪ] **n** phototélégraphie *f*.
phototropic [ˌfəʊtəʊˈtrɒpɪk] **adj** phototropique.
phototropism [ˌfəʊtəʊˈtrɒpɪzəm] **n** phototropisme *m*.
phototype [ˈfəʊtəʊˌtaɪp] **n** (*process*) phototypie *f*.
phototypesetting [ˌfəʊtəʊˈtaɪpˌsetɪŋ] **n** (*US Typ*) photocomposition *f*.
phototypography [ˌfəʊtəʊtaɪˈpɒgrəfɪ] **n** phototypographie *f*.
phrasal [ˈfreɪzəl] **adj** syntagmatique. ~ **verb** verbe *m* à particule.
phrase [freɪz] **1 n a** (*saying*) expression *f*. **as the ~ is** *or* **goes** comme on dit, selon l'expression consacrée; **... to use Mrs Thatcher's ~ ...** comme dirait Mme Thatcher; **in Marx's famous ~ ...** pour reprendre la célèbre *or* classique phrase de Marx ...; **that's exactly the ~ I'm looking for** voilà exactement l'expression que je cherche; *see* **set**.
b (*Ling: gen*) locution *f*; (*Transformational Gram*) syntagme *m*. **noun/verb ~** syntagme nominal/verbal.
c (*Mus*) phrase *f*.
2 vt a *thought* exprimer; *letter* rédiger. **a neatly ~d letter** une lettre bien tournée; **can we ~ it differently?** pouvons-nous l'exprimer différemment? *or* en d'autres termes?
b (*Mus*) phraser.
3 comp ▸phrasebook recueil *m* d'expressions **▸phrase marker** (*Ling*) marqueur *m* syntagmatique **▸phrase structure** (*Ling*) **n** structure *f* syntagmatique ◊ **adj** *rule, grammar* de structure syntagmatique.
phraseology [ˌfreɪzɪˈɒlədʒɪ] **n** phraséologie *f*.
phrasing [ˈfreɪzɪŋ] **n a** *[ideas]* expression *f*; *[text]* rédaction *f*, phraséologie *f*. **the ~ is unfortunate** les termes sont mal choisis.
b (*Mus*) phrasé *m*.
phrenetic [frɪˈnetɪk] = **frenetic**.
phrenic [ˈfrenɪk] **adj** (*Anat*) phrénique.
phrenologist [frɪˈnɒlədʒɪst] **n** phrénologue *mf*, phrénologiste *mf*.
phrenology [frɪˈnɒlədʒɪ] **n** phrénologie *f*.
phthisiology [ˌθaɪsɪˈɒlədʒɪ] **n** phtisiologie *f*.
phthisis [ˈθaɪsɪs] **n** phtisie *f*.
phut‡ [fʌt] **adv**: **to go ~** *[machine, object]* péter‡, rendre l'âme*; *[scheme, plan]* tomber à l'eau.
phycology [faɪˈkɒlədʒɪ] **n** phycologie *f*.
phyla [ˈfaɪlə] **npl of phylum**.
phylactery [fɪˈlæktərɪ] **n** phylactère *m*.
phylactic [fɪˈlæktɪk] **adj** phylactique.
phyletic [faɪˈletɪk] **adj** phylogénique.
phylloxera [ˌfɪlɒkˈsɪərə] **n** phylloxéra *m*.
phylogenesis [ˌfaɪləʊˈdʒenɪsɪs] **n** phylogénèse *f*.
phylogenetic [ˌfaɪləʊdʒɪˈnetɪk] **adj** phylogénique.
phylum [ˈfaɪləm] **n, pl phyla** phylum *m*.
physic [ˈfɪzɪk] **n a** (*NonC*) **~s** physique *f*; **experimental ~s** physique expérimentale; *see* **atomic, nuclear** *etc*. **b** (††) médicament *m*.
physical [ˈfɪzɪkəl] **1 adj a** (*of the body*) physique. **~ cruelty** brutalité *f*, sévices *mpl*; **~ culture** culture *f* physique; **~ education** éducation *f* physique; **~ examination, ~ check-up** examen médical, bilan *m* de santé, check-up* *m inv*; **~ exercise** exercice *m* physique; **~ exercises, (*Brit*) ~ jerks*** exercices *mpl* d'assouplissement, gymnastique *f*; **~ handicap** handicap *m* physique; **it's a ~ impossibility for him to get there on time** il lui est physiquement *or* matériellement impossible d'arriver là-bas à l'heure; (*US Med*) **~ therapist** physiothérapeute *mf*, ≃ kinésithérapeute *mf*; **~ therapy** physiothérapie *f*, ≃ kinésithérapie *f*; **to have ~ therapy** faire de la rééducation; **~ training** éducation *f* physique.
b *geography, properties, sciences* physique; *world, universe, object* matériel.
c (*) *person* qui aime les contacts physiques.
2 n (*) examen médical, bilan *m* de santé, check-up* *m inv*. **to go for a ~** aller passer une visite médicale.
physically [ˈfɪzɪkəlɪ] **adv** physiquement. **he is ~ handicapped** c'est un handicapé physique.
physician [fɪˈzɪʃən] **n** médecin *m*.
physicist [ˈfɪzɪsɪst] **n** physicien(ne) *m(f)*. **experimental/theoretical** *etc* **~** physicien(ne) de physique expérimentale/théorique *etc*; *see* **atomic** *etc*.
physio* [ˈfɪzɪəʊ] **n a abbr of physiotherapy**. **b abbr of physiotherapist**.
physio... [ˈfɪzɪəʊ] **pref** physio... .
physiognomy [ˌfɪzɪˈɒnəmɪ] **n** (*gen*) physionomie *f*; (* *hum: face*) bobine‡ *f*, bouille‡ *f*.
physiological [ˌfɪzɪəˈlɒdʒɪkəl] **adj** physiologique.
physiologist [ˌfɪzɪˈɒlədʒɪst] **n** physiologiste *mf*.
physiology [ˌfɪzɪˈɒlədʒɪ] **n** physiologie *f*.
physiotherapist [ˌfɪzɪəˈθerəpɪst] **n** physiothérapeute *mf*, ≃ kinésithérapeute *mf*.
physiotherapy [ˌfɪzɪəˈθerəpɪ] **n** physiothérapie *f*, ≃ kinésithérapie *f*.
physique [fɪˈziːk] **n** (*strength, health etc*) constitution *f*; (*appearance*) physique *m*. **he has a fine/poor ~** il a une bonne/mauvaise constitution.
phytogeography [ˌfaɪtəʊdʒɪˈɒgrəfɪ] **n** phytogéographie *f*.
phytology [faɪˈtɒlədʒɪ] **n** phytobiologie *f*.
phytopathology [ˌfaɪtəʊpəˈθɒlədʒɪ] **n** phytopathologie *f*.
phytoplankton [ˌfaɪtəˈplæŋktən] **n** phytoplancton *m*.
pi[1]* [paɪ] **adj** (*Brit: pej*) (**abbr of pious**) *person* satisfait de soi, suffisant; *expression* suffisant, béat.
pi[2] [paɪ] **n, pl ~s** (*Math*) pi *m*.
pianissimo [pɪəˈnɪsɪˌməʊ] **adj, adv** pianissimo.
pianist [ˈpɪənɪst] **n** pianiste *mf*.
piano [ˈpjɑːnəʊ] **1 n, pl ~s** piano *m*; *see* **baby, grand, upright** *etc*.
2 comp ▸piano-accordion accordéon *m* à clavier **▸piano concerto** concerto *m* pour piano **▸piano duet** morceau *m* pour quatre mains **▸piano lesson** leçon *f* de piano **▸piano music: I love piano music** j'aime (écouter) le piano; **I'd like some piano music** je voudrais de la musique pour piano **▸piano organ** piano *m* mécanique **▸piano piece** morceau *m* pour piano **▸piano stool** tabouret *m* de piano **▸piano teacher** professeur *m* de piano **▸piano tuner** accordeur *m* (de piano).
3 adv (*Mus*) piano.
pianoforte [ˌpjɑːnəʊˈfɔːtɪ] **n** (*frm*) = **piano 1**.
pianola [pɪəˈnəʊlə] **n** ® piano *m* mécanique, pianola *m* ®.
piazza [pɪˈætsə] **n a** (*square*) place *f*, piazza *f*. **b** (*US*) véranda *f*.
pibroch [ˈpiːbrɒx] **n** pibrock *m*.
pica [ˈpaɪkə] **n** (*Typ*) douze *m*, cicéro *m*.
picador [ˈpɪkədɔːʳ] **n** picador *m*.
Picardy [ˈpɪkədɪ] **n** Picardie *f*.
picaresque [ˌpɪkəˈresk] **adj** picaresque.
picayune* [ˌpɪkəˈjuːn] **adj** insignifiant, mesquin.
piccalilli [ˈpɪkəˌlɪlɪ] **n** (espèce *f* de) pickles *mpl*.
piccaninny [ˈpɪkəˌnɪnɪ] **n** négrillon(ne) *m(f)*.
piccolo [ˈpɪkələʊ] **n, pl ~s** piccolo *m*.
pick [pɪk] **1 n a** *tool* pioche *f*, pic *m*; (*Climbing: ice ~*) piolet *m*; *[mason]* smille *f*; *[miner]* rivelaine *f*; *see* **ice, tooth**.
b (*choice*) choix *m*. **to take one's ~** faire son choix; **to have one's ~ of sth** avoir le choix de qch; **take your ~** choisissez, vous avez le choix, à votre choix; **whose ~ is it now?** à qui de choisir?; **the ~ of the bunch** le meilleur de tous; (*TV etc*) **~ of the pops** palmarès *m* de la chanson, hit-parade *m*.
2 comp ▸pickax *US*, **pickaxe n** pic *m*, pioche *f* ◊ **vt** creuser (*or* défoncer) avec un pic *or* une pioche, piocher **▸picklock** (*key*) crochet *m*, rossignol *m*; (*thief*) crocheteur *m* **▸pick-me-up*** (*Brit*) remontant *m* **▸pickpocket** pickpocket *m*, voleur *m* à la tire **▸pickup** *see* **pickup**.
3 vt a (*choose*) choisir. **you can ~ whichever you like** vous pouvez choisir celui que vous voulez; (*Sport*) **to ~ (the) sides** former *or* sélectionner les équipes; (*Racing*) **he ~ed the winner** il a pronostiqué le (cheval) gagnant; (*Racing*) **I'm not very good at ~ing the winner** je ne suis pas très doué pour choisir le gagnant; (*fig*) **they certainly ~ed a winner in Colin Smith** avec Colin Smith ils ont vraiment tiré le bon numéro; **to ~ one's way through/among** avancer avec précaution à travers/parmi; **to ~ a fight with sb** (*physical*) chercher la bagarre* *or* chercher à se bagarrer* avec qn; (*words: also* **to ~ a quarrel with sb**) chercher noise à qn, provoquer une querelle avec qn.
b (*gather*) *fruit, flower* cueillir. (*at fruit farm*) "**~ your own**" "cueillette à la ferme".
c (*take out, remove*) *spot, scab* gratter, écorcher. **to ~ one's nose** se mettre les doigts dans le nez; **to ~ a splinter from one's hand** s'enlever une écharde de la main; **to ~ the bones of a chicken** sucer les os d'un poulet; **the dog was ~ing the bone** le chien rongeait l'os; **to ~ one's teeth** se curer les dents; **you've ~ed a hole in your jersey** à force de

tirailler tu as fait un trou à ton pull; (*fig*) **to ~ holes in an argument** relever les défauts *or* les failles d'un raisonnement; **he's always ~ing holes in everything** il trouve toujours à redire; **to ~ sb's brains** faire appel aux lumières de qn; **I want to ~ your brains** j'ai besoin de vos lumières; **to ~ a lock** crocheter une serrure; **to ~ pockets** pratiquer le vol à la tire; **I've had my pocket ~ed** on m'a fait les poches; *see also* **bone.**

4 **vi: to ~ and choose** faire le (*or* la) difficile; **I like to ~ and choose** j'aime bien prendre mon temps pour choisir; **to ~ at one's food** manger du bout des dents, chipoter*, pignocher*; **the bird ~ed at the bread** l'oiseau picorait le pain; **don't ~ at that spot** ne gratte pas ce bouton.

►**pick at vt fus** (*US* *) = **pick on a.**

►**pick off vt sep** a *paint* gratter, enlever; *flower, leaf* cueillir, enlever. b (*shoot*) abattre (*après avoir visé soigneusement*). **he picked off the sentry** il a visé soigneusement et a abattu la sentinelle; **he picked off the 3 sentries** il a abattu les 3 sentinelles l'une après l'autre.

►**pick on vt fus** a (**: nag at, harass*) harceler. **to pick on sb** harceler qn, être toujours sur le dos de qn*; **he is always picking on Robert** il est toujours sur le dos de Robert*, c'est toujours après Robert qu'il rouspète* *or* qu'il en a*; **stop picking on me!** fiche-moi la paix!*, arrête de rouspéter après moi!* b (*single out*) choisir, désigner. **the teacher picked on him to collect the books** le professeur le choisit *or* le désigna pour ramasser les livres; **why pick on me? all the rest did the same** pourquoi t'en (*or* s'en) prendre à moi? les autres ont fait la même chose.

►**pick out vt sep** a (*choose*) choisir, désigner. **pick out two or three you would like to keep** choisissez-en deux ou trois que vous aimeriez garder; **she picked 2 apples out of the basket** elle choisit 2 pommes dans le panier; **he had already picked out his successor** il avait déjà choisi son successeur.

b (*distinguish*) distinguer; (*in identification parade*) identifier. **I couldn't pick out anyone I knew in the crowd** je ne pouvais repérer *or* distinguer personne de ma connaissance dans la foule; **can you pick out the melody in this passage?** pouvez-vous distinguer la mélodie dans ce passage?; **can you pick me out in this photo?** pouvez-vous me reconnaître sur cette photo?

c **to pick out a tune on the piano** retrouver un air au piano.

d (*highlight*) **to pick out a colour** rehausser *or* mettre en valeur une couleur; **letters picked out in gold on a black background** lettres rehaussées d'or sur fond noir.

►**pick over vt sep** *collection of fruit, goods etc* trier, examiner (pour choisir). **to pick some books over** examiner quelques livres; **he picked the rags over** il tria les chiffons; **she was picking over the shirts in the sale** elle examinait les chemises en solde les unes après les autres.

►**pick through vt fus** = **pick over.**

►**pick up** 1 **vi** a (*improve*) *[conditions, programme, weather]* s'améliorer; *[prices, wages]* remonter; *[trade, business]* reprendre; *[invalid]* se rétablir, se remettre. **business has picked up recently** les affaires ont repris récemment; (*Comm, Fin*) **the market will pick up soon** le marché va bientôt remonter; (*Sport*) **the team is picking up now** l'équipe est en progrès maintenant; (*Rad, TV etc*) **the sound picked up towards the end** le son s'améliora vers la fin; **things are picking up a bit*** ça commence à aller mieux.

b (*put on speed*) *[vehicle]* prendre de la vitesse. **the car picked up once we got out of town** dès la sortie de la ville la voiture prit de la vitesse.

c (**: continue*) continuer, reprendre. **after dinner we picked up where we'd left off** après le dîner nous avons repris la conversation (*or* le travail *etc*) où nous l'avions laissé(e).

2 **vt sep** a (*lift*) *sth dropped, book, clothes etc* ramasser. (*after fall*) **to pick o.s. up** se relever, se remettre sur pieds; **he picked up the child** (*gen*) il a pris l'enfant dans ses bras; (*after fall*) il a relevé l'enfant; **he picked up the telephone and dialled a number** il a décroché le téléphone et a composé un numéro; **pick up all your clothes before you go out!** ramasse tous tes vêtements avant de sortir!; **to pick up the pieces** (*lit*) ramasser les morceaux; (*fig*) sauver ce qu'on peut et recommencer, recoller les morceaux.

b (*collect*) (passer) prendre. **can you pick up my coat from the cleaners?** pourrais-tu (passer) prendre mon manteau chez le teinturier?; **I'll pick up the books next week** je passerai prendre les livres la semaine prochaine; **I'll pick you up at 6 o'clock** je passerai vous prendre à 6 heures, je viendrai vous chercher à 6 heures.

c (*Aut: give lift to*) *passenger, hitchhiker* prendre. **I'll pick you up at the shop** je vous prendrai devant le magasin.

d (*pej*) ramasser. **he picked up a girl at the cinema** il a ramassé une fille au cinéma.

e (*buy, obtain*) découvrir, dénicher. **to pick up a bargain at a jumble sale** trouver une occasion dans une vente (de charité); **where did you pick up that record?** où avez-vous déniché ce disque?; **it's a book you can pick up anywhere** c'est un livre que l'on trouve partout.

f (*acquire, learn*) *language etc* apprendre; *habit* prendre. **he picked up French very quickly** il n'a pas mis longtemps à apprendre le français; **I've picked up a bit of German** j'ai appris quelques mots d'allemand; **you'll soon pick it up again** vous vous y remettrez vite; **to pick up an accent** prendre un accent; **to pick up bad habits** prendre de mauvaises habitudes; **I picked up a bit of news about him today** j'ai appris quelque chose sur lui aujourd'hui; **see what you can pick up about their export scheme** essayez d'avoir des renseignements *or* des tuyaux* sur leur plan d'exportations; **our agents have picked up something about it** nos agents ont appris *or* découvert quelque chose là-dessus.

g (*Rad, Telec*) *station, programme, message* capter.

h (*rescue*) recueillir; (*from sea*) recueillir, repêcher; **the helicopter/lifeboat picked up 10 survivors** l'hélicoptère/le canot de sauvetage a recueilli 10 survivants.

i (*catch, arrest*) *wanted man* arrêter, cueillir*, pincer*. **they picked him up for questioning** on l'a arrêté pour l'interroger.

j (*focus on*) *[lights, camera]* saisir dans le champ. **we picked up a rabbit in the car headlights** nous avons aperçu un lapin dans la lumière des phares; **the cameras picked him up as he left the hall** en sortant du hall il est entré dans le champ des caméras; **the papers picked up the story** les journaux se sont emparés de l'affaire.

k *sb's error etc* relever, ne pas laisser passer. **he picked up 10 misprints** il a relevé 10 fautes d'impression; **he picked up every mistake** il n'a pas laissé passer une seule erreur.

l (*reprimand*) faire une remarque *or* une observation à, reprendre. **to pick sb up for having made a mistake** reprendre qn pour une faute.

m *[car, boat]* **to pick up speed** prendre de la vitesse; (*Sport*) **he managed to pick up a few points in the later events** il a réussi à gagner *or* rattraper quelques points dans les épreuves suivantes.

n (*‡: steal*) faucher*, piquer‡.

3 **vt fus** a (*detect*) *smell, sound* percevoir, détecter.

b (*) (*earn*) gagner, toucher*. (*pay*) **to pick up the bill** *or* **tab** payer la note *or* l'addition.

4 **pickup** *see* **pickup.**

5 **pick-me-up*** **n** *see* **pick 2.**

pickaback [ˈpɪkəbæk] = **piggyback 1, 2, 3a.**

pickaninny [ˈpɪkə,nɪnɪ] = **piccaninny.**

picked [pɪkt] **adj** (*also* **hand-~**) *goods, objects* sélectionné; *men* trié sur le volet. **a group of (hand-)~ soldiers** un groupe de soldats d'élite *or* de soldats triés sur le volet.

picker [ˈpɪkəʳ] **n (gen in comp)** cueilleur *m*, -euse *f*. **apple-~** cueilleur, -euse de pommes.

picket [ˈpɪkɪt] 1 **n** a (*Ind: also* **strike-~**) piquet *m* de grève; (*at civil demonstrations*) piquet *m* (de manifestants); (*group of soldiers*) détachement *m* (de soldats); (*sentry*) factionnaire *m*. **fire ~** piquet *m* d'incendie. b (*stake*) pieu *m*, piquet *m*. 2 **comp** ►**picket duty:** (*Ind*) **to be on picket duty** faire partie d'un piquet de grève ►**picket line** piquet *m* de grève; **to cross a picket line** traverser un piquet de grève. 3 **vt** a (*Ind*) **to ~ a factory** mettre un piquet de grève aux portes d'une usine; **the demonstrators ~ed the embassy** les manifestants ont formé un cordon devant l'ambassade. b *field* clôturer. 4 **vi** *[strikers]* organiser un piquet de grève.

picketing [ˈpɪkɪtɪŋ] **n** piquets *mpl* de grève. **there was no ~** il n'y a pas eu de piquet de grève; *see* **secondary.**

picking [ˈpɪkɪŋ] **n** a *[object from group]* choix *m*; *[candidate, leader]* choix, sélection *f*; *[fruit, vegetables]* cueillette *f*; *[lock]* crochetage *m*; (*careful choosing*) triage *m*. b **~s** (*of food*) restes *mpl*, débris *mpl*. c (*fig: profits etc*) **there are rich ~s** ça peut rapporter gros.

pickle [ˈpɪkl] 1 **n** a (*NonC: Culin*) (*brine*) saumure *f*; (*wine, spices*) marinade *f*; (*vinegar*) vinaigre *m*. **~(s)** pickles *mpl*, petits légumes macérés dans du vinaigre. b (*) **to be in a (pretty** *or* **fine) ~** être dans de beaux draps, être dans le pétrin; **I'm in rather a ~** je suis plutôt dans le pétrin. 2 **vt** (*see* **1a**) conserver dans de la saumure *or* dans du vinaigre. **pickling onions** oignons-grelots *mpl*.

pickled [ˈpɪkld] **adj** a *cucumber etc* conservé *or* macéré dans du vinaigre. b (*‡: drunk*) bourré‡, ivre.

pickup [ˈpɪkʌp] 1 **n** a *[record-player]* pick-up *m inv*, lecteur *m*.

b (*Aut: passenger*) passager *m*, -ère *f* ramassé(e) en route. **the bus made 3 ~s** l'autobus s'est arrêté 3 fois pour prendre *or* laisser monter des passagers.

c (**: casual lover*) partenaire *mf* de rencontre.

d (*collection*) **he made a ~** *[truck driver]* il s'est arrêté pour prendre quelque chose; *[drug runner, spy]* il est allé chercher quelque chose; **~ point** (*for people*) point *m* de rendez-vous; (*for goods*) point de collecte.

e (*Aut: acceleration*) reprise(s) *f(pl)*.

f (*recovery*) (*Med*) rétablissement *m*; (*in trade etc*) reprise *f* (d'activité).

g (**: pick-me-up*) remontant *m*.

h = **pickup truck;** *see* **2.**

2 **comp** ►**pickup truck,** (*Brit*) **pickup van** camionnette *f* (découverte).

3 **adj** (*Sport*) *game* impromptu, improvisé. **~ side** équipe *f* de fortune.

picky* [ˈpɪkɪ] **adj** difficile (à satisfaire).

picnic [ˈpɪknɪk] **(vb: pret, ptp picnicked)** 1 **n** pique-nique *m*. (*fig*) **it's no ~*** ça n'est pas une partie de plaisir*, c'est pas de la tarte‡. 2 **comp**

▸**picnic basket** panier *m* à pique-nique ▸**picnic ham** (*US*) ≃ jambonneau *m* ▸**picnic hamper** = **picnic basket.** 3 **vi** pique-niquer, faire un pique-nique.

picnicker ['pɪknɪkəʳ] **n** pique-niqueur *m*, -euse *f*.

pics‡ [pɪks] **npl abbr of pictures.** a (*films*) ciné* *m*. b (*photos*) photos *fpl*.

Pict [pɪkt] **n** Picte *mf*.

Pictish ['pɪktɪʃ] **adj** picte.

pictogram ['pɪktəˌgræm] **n** pictogramme *m*.

pictograph ['pɪktəgrɑːf] **n** a (*record, chart etc*) pictogramme *m*. b (*Ling*) (*symbol*) idéogramme *m*; (*writing*) idéographie *f*.

pictorial [pɪk'tɔːrɪəl] 1 **adj** *magazine, calendar* illustré; *record* en images; *work* pictural; *masterpiece* pictural, de peinture. 2 **n** illustré *m*.

pictorially [pɪk'tɔːrɪəlɪ] **adv** en images, au moyen d'images, à l'aide d'images.

picture ['pɪktʃəʳ] 1 **n** a (*gen*) image *f*; (*illustration*) image, illustration *f*; (*photograph*) photo(graphie) *f*; (*TV*) image; (*painting*) tableau *m*, peinture *f*; (*portrait*) portrait *m*; (*engraving*) gravure *f*; (*reproduction*) reproduction *f*; (*drawing*) dessin *m*. **~s made by reflections in the water** images produites par les reflets sur l'eau; **I took a good ~ of him** j'ai pris une bonne photo de lui; **I must get a ~ of that fountain!** je veux absolument prendre une vue de *or* photographier cette fontaine!; (*fig*) **every ~ tells a story** cela se passe de commentaire; (*TV*) **we have the sound but no ~** nous avons le son mais pas l'image; **to paint a ~** faire un tableau; **to draw a ~** faire un dessin; **to paint/draw a ~ of sth** peindre/dessiner qch; *see* **pretty**.

b (*Cine*) film *m*. **they made a ~ about it** on en a fait *or* tiré un film; (*esp Brit*) **to go to the ~s** aller au cinéma, aller voir un film; (*esp Brit*) **what's on at the ~s?** qu'est-ce qu'on donne au cinéma?; **there's a good ~ on this week** on donne *or* on passe un bon film cette semaine; *see* **motion** *etc*.

c (*fig*) (*spoken*) description *f*, tableau *m*, image *f*; (*mental image*) image, représentation *f*. **he gave us a ~ of the scenes at the front line** il nous présenta un tableau de *or* nous décrivit la situation au front; **his ~ of ancient Greece** le tableau *or* l'image qu'il présente (*or* présentait *etc*) de la Grèce antique; **he painted a black ~ of the future** il nous peignit un sombre tableau de l'avenir; **I have a clear ~ of him as he was when I saw him last** je le revois clairement *or* je me souviens très bien de lui tel qu'il était la dernière fois que je l'ai vu; **I have no very clear ~ of the room** je ne me représente pas très bien la pièce; **these figures give the general ~** ces chiffres donnent un tableau général de la situation; **do you get the ~?*** tu vois la situation?, tu vois le tableau?*, tu piges?‡; **OK, I get the ~*** ça va, je pige‡.

d (*fig phrases*) **she was a ~ in her new dress** elle était ravissante dans sa nouvelle robe; **the garden is a ~ in June** le jardin est magnifique en juin; **he is** *or* **looks the** *or* **a ~ of health/happiness** il respire la santé/le bonheur; **he is** *or* **looks the ~ of misery** c'est la tristesse incarnée; **you're the ~ of your mother!** vous êtes (tout) le portrait de votre mère!; (*fig*) **the other side of the ~** le revers de la médaille; **his face was a ~!*** son expression en disait long!, si vous aviez vu sa tête!*; **to be/put sb/keep sb in the ~** être/mettre qn/tenir qn au courant; **to be pushed** *or* **left out of the ~** être mis sur la touche, être éliminé de la scène.

2 **comp** ▸**picture book** livre *m* d'images ▸**picture card** (*Cards*) figure *f* ▸**picture frame** cadre *m* ▸**picture-framer** encadreur *m* ▸**picture-framing** encadrement *m* ▸**picture gallery** (*public*) musée *m* (de peinture); (*private*) galerie *f* (de peinture) ▸**picturegoer** cinéphile *mf*, habitué(e) *m(f)* du cinéma, amateur *m* de cinéma ▸**picture hat** capeline *f* ▸**picture house**† cinéma *m* ▸**picture postcard** carte postale (illustrée) ▸**picture rail** cimaise *f* ▸**picture tube** (*TV*) tube-image *m* ▸**picture window** fenêtre *f* panoramique ▸**picture writing** écriture *f* pictographique.

3 **vt** a (*imagine*) s'imaginer, se représenter. **just ~ yourself lying on the beach** imaginez-vous étendu sur la plage; **~ yourself as a father** imaginez-vous dans le rôle de père.

b (*describe*) dépeindre, décrire, représenter.

c (*by drawing etc*) représenter.

picturesque [ˌpɪktʃə'resk] **adj** pittoresque.

picturesquely [ˌpɪktʃə'resklɪ] **adv** d'une manière pittoresque, avec pittoresque.

picturesqueness [ˌpɪktʃə'resknɪs] **n** pittoresque *m*.

piddle‡ ['pɪdl] **vi** faire pipi*.

piddling* ['pɪdlɪŋ] **adj** (*insignificant*) insignifiant, futile; (*small*) négligeable, de rien.

pidgin ['pɪdʒɪn] **n** a (*also:* **~ English**) pidgin(-english) *m*; (*other languages*) ≃ sabir *m*. b (*) *see* **pigeon 1b**.

pie [paɪ] 1 **n** *[fruit, fish, meat with gravy etc]* tourte *f*; *[compact filling]* pâté *m* en croûte. **apple ~** tourte aux pommes; **rabbit/chicken ~** tourte au lapin/au poulet; **pork ~** pâté de porc en croûte; **it's ~ in the sky*** ce sont des promesses en l'air *or* de belles promesses (*iro*); (*fig*) **they want a piece of the ~** ils veulent leur part du gâteau; (*US fig*) **that's ~ to him**‡ pour lui, c'est du gâteau*; *see* **finger, humble, mud** *etc*. 2 **comp** ▸**pie chart** (*Math*) graphique *m* circulaire, camembert* *m* ▸**piecrust** croûte *f* de *or* pour pâté ▸**pie dish** plat *m* allant au four, terrine *f* ▸**pie-eyed**‡ beurré‡, bourré‡, rond* ▸**pie plate** moule *m* à tarte, tourtière *f*.

piebald ['paɪbɔːld] 1 **adj** *horse* pie *inv*. 2 **n** cheval *m or* jument *f* pie.

piece [piːs] 1 **n** a morceau *m*; *[cloth, chocolate, glass, paper]* morceau, bout *m*; *[bread, cake]* morceau, tranche *f*; *[wood]* bout, morceau, (*large*) pièce *f*; *[ribbon, string]* bout; (*broken or detached part*) morceau, fragment *m*; (*Comm, Ind*) pièce; (*item, section, also Chess*) pièce; (*Draughts*) pion *m*. **a ~ of silk/wood/paper** *etc* un morceau de soie/de bois/de papier *etc*; **a ~ of sarcasm/irony** un sarcasme/une ironie; **a ~ of land** (*for agriculture*) une pièce *or* parcelle de terre; (*for building*) un lotissement; **a ~ of meat** un morceau *or* une pièce de viande; (*left over*) un morceau *or* un bout de viande; **I bought a nice ~ of beef** j'ai acheté un beau morceau de bœuf; **a sizeable ~ of beef** une belle pièce de bœuf; **I've got a ~ of grit in my eye** j'ai une poussière *or* une escarbille dans l'œil; **a ~ of advice** un conseil; **a ~ of carelessness** de la négligence; **it's a ~ of folly** c'est de la folie; **a ~ of furniture** un meuble; **a ~ of information** un renseignement; **by a ~ of luck** par (un coup de) chance; **a ~ of news** une nouvelle; **a good ~ of work** du bon travail; **read me a ~ out of "Ivanhoe"** lisez-moi un passage *or* un extrait d'"Ivanhoé"; **there's a ~ in the newspaper about ...** on parle dans le journal de ...; **it is made (all) in one ~** c'est fait d'une seule pièce *or* tout d'une pièce; **we got back in one ~*** nous sommes rentrés sains et saufs; **the vase is still in one ~** le vase ne s'est pas cassé *or* est intact; **he had a nasty fall but he's still in one ~*** il a fait une mauvaise chute mais il est entier* *or* indemne; **the back is (all) of a ~ with the seat** le dossier et le siège sont d'un seul tenant; **it is (all) of a ~ with what he said before** cela s'accorde tout à fait avec ce qu'il a dit auparavant; **to give sb a ~ of one's mind*** dire ses quatre vérités à qn*, dire son fait à qn; **he got a ~ of my mind** je lui ai dit son fait, il a eu de mes nouvelles*; (*Comm*) **sold by the ~** vendu à la pièce *or* au détail; (*Ind*) **paid by the ~** payé à la pièce; **a 5-franc ~** une pièce de 5 F; **~ of eight** dollar espagnol; **a 30-~ tea set** un service à thé de 30 pièces; (*Mus*) **10-~ band** orchestre *m* de 10 exécutants; **3 ~s of luggage** 3 valises *fpl* (*or* sacs *mpl etc*); **how many ~s of luggage have you got?** qu'est-ce que vous avez comme bagages?; **to say one's ~** dire ce qu'on a à dire; **~ by ~** pièce à pièce, morceau par morceau; *[jigsaw, game]* **there's a ~ missing** il y a une pièce qui manque; **to put** *or* **fit together the ~s of a mystery** résoudre un mystère en rassemblant les éléments; *see* **bit**[2]**, museum, paper, set** *etc*.

b (*phrases*) **in ~s** (*broken*) en pièces, en morceaux, en fragments; (*not yet assembled*) *furniture etc* en pièces détachées; **it just came to ~s** c'est parti en morceaux *or* en pièces détachées (*hum*); **it fell to ~s** c'est tombé en morceaux; **the chair comes to ~s if you unscrew the screws** la chaise se démonte si on desserre les vis; (*fig*) **to go to ~s*** *[person]* (*collapse*) s'effondrer; (*emotionally*) lâcher pied (*fig*), perdre les pédales*; *[team etc]* se désintégrer; **to take sth to ~s** démonter qch, désassembler qch; **it takes to ~s** c'est démontable; **to cut** *or* **hack sth to ~s** couper *or* mettre qch en pièces; **to smash sth to ~s** briser qch en mille morceaux, mettre qch en miettes; **the boat was smashed to ~s** le bateau vola en éclats; *see* **pull, tear**[1] *etc*.

c (*Mus*) morceau *m*; (*poem*) poème *m*, (pièce *f* de) vers *mpl*. **piano ~** morceau pour piano; **a ~ by Grieg** un morceau de Grieg; **a ~ of poetry** un poème, une poésie, une pièce de vers (*liter*).

d (*firearm*) fusil *m*; (*cannon*) pièce *f* (d'artillerie).

e (‡: *girl*) **she's a nice ~** c'est un beau brin de fille.

2 **comp** ▸**piece rate** (*Ind*) tarif *m* à la pièce ▸**piecework** (*Ind*) travail *m* à la pièce *or* aux pièces; **to be on piecework, to do piecework** travailler à la pièce ▸**pieceworker** ouvrier *m*, -ière *f* payé(e) à la pièce.

▸**piece together** **vt sep** *broken object* rassembler; *jigsaw* assembler; (*fig*) *story* reconstituer; (*fig*) *facts* rassembler, faire concorder. **I managed to piece together what had happened from what he said** à partir de ce qu'il a dit, j'ai réussi à reconstituer les événements.

piecemeal ['piːsmiːl] 1 **adv** (*bit by bit*) *tell, explain, recount* par bribes; *construct* petit à petit, par bouts; (*haphazardly*) sans plan *or* système véritable, au coup par coup. **he tossed the books ~ into the box** il jeta les livres en vrac dans la caisse.

2 **adj** (*see* **1**) raconté par bribes; fait petit à petit, fait par bouts; peu systématique, peu ordonné. **he gave me a ~ account/description of it** il m'en a donné par bribes un compte rendu/une description; **the construction was ~** la construction a été réalisée petit à petit *or* par étapes; **this essay is ~** cette dissertation est décousue *or* manque de plan; **a ~ argument** un raisonnement bancal *or* peu systématique *or* qui manque de rigueur.

pied [paɪd] **adj** bariolé, bigarré, panaché; *animal* pie *inv*. **the P~ Piper** le joueur de flûte d'Hameln.

pied-à-terre [ˌpjeɪtɑː'tɛəʳ] **n, pl ~s-~-~** [ˌpjeɪtɑː'tɛəʳ] pied-à-terre *m inv*.

Piedmont ['piːdmɒnt] **n** a (*Geog*) Piémont *m*. b (*Geol*) **p~** piémont *m*; **p~ glacier** glacier *m* de piémont.

pier [pɪəʳ] 1 **n** a (*with amusements etc*) jetée *f* (*promenade*); (*landing stage*) appontement *m*, embarcadère *m*; (*breakwater*) brise-lames *m*; (*in airport*) jetée d'embarquement (*or* de débarquement).

b (*Archit*) (*column*) pilier *m*, colonne *f*; *[bridge]* pile *f*; (*brickwork*) pied-droit *m or* piédroit *m*. 2 **comp** ►**pier glass** (glace *f* de) trumeau *m* ►**pierhead** musoir *m*.

pierce [pɪəs] **vt** a (*make hole in, go through*) percer, transpercer. **to have one's ears ~d** se faire percer les oreilles; **~d earrings, earrings for ~d ears** boucles *fpl* d'oreilles pour oreilles percées; **the arrow ~d his armour** la flèche transperça son armure; **the bullet ~d his arm** la balle lui transperça le bras. b *[sound]* percer; *[cold, wind]* transpercer. (*liter*) **the words ~d his heart** ces paroles lui percèrent le cœur.

piercing ['pɪəsɪŋ] **adj** *sound, voice* aigu (*f* -guë), perçant; *look* perçant; *cold, wind* glacial, pénétrant.

piercingly ['pɪəsɪŋlɪ] **adv** *look* d'un œil perçant; *scream* d'une voix perçante. ~ **cold wind** vent d'un froid pénétrant, vent glacial.

pierrot ['pɪərəʊ] **n** pierrot *m*.

pietism ['paɪɪˌtɪzəm] **n** piétisme *m*.

pietist ['paɪɪtɪst] **adj, n** piétiste *(mf)*.

piety ['paɪətɪ] **n** piété *f*.

piezoelectric [paɪˌiːzəʊɪ'lektrɪk] **adj** piézoélectrique.

piezoelectricity [paɪˌiːzəʊɪlek'trɪsɪtɪ] **n** piézo-électricité *f*.

piezometer [ˌpaɪɪ'zɒmɪtəʳ] **n** piézomètre *m*.

piffle* ['pɪfl] **n** balivernes *fpl*, fadaises *fpl*.

piffling ['pɪflɪŋ] **adj** (*trivial*) futile, frivole; (*worthless*) insignifiant.

pig [pɪg] 1 **n** a cochon *m*, porc *m*. (*fig*) **to buy a ~ in a poke** acheter chat en poche; **~s might fly!*** ce n'est pas demain la veille*, c'est (*or* ce sera *etc*) le jour où les poules auront des dents!*; (*Brit*) **to make a ~'s ear* of sth** cochonner qch*; (*US fig*) **in a ~'s eye!⁑** jamais de la vie!, mon œil!*; **they were living like ~s** ils vivaient comme des porcs *or* dans une (vraie) porcherie; (*fig*) **it was a ~* to do** c'était vachement* difficile à faire; *see* **Guinea, suck** *etc*.

b (* *pej: person*) cochon* *m*, sale type* *m*. **to make a ~ of o.s.** manger comme un goinfre, se goinfrer*; **you ~!*** (*mean*) espèce de chameau!*; (*dirty*) espèce de cochon!*; (*greedy*) espèce de goinfre!

c (⁑ *pej: policeman*) flicard* *m*. **the ~s** la flicaille⁑.

d (*slut*) (*dirty*) souillon *f*; (*promiscuous*) salope⁑* *f*.

2 **comp** ►**pig breeding** élevage porcin ►**pig ignorant⁑** d'une ignorance crasse ►**pig industry** industrie porcine ►**pig in the middle** (*game*) ballon *m* prisonnier; (*fig*) **he's the pig in the middle** il est pris entre deux feux ►**pig iron** saumon *m* de fonte ►**pig Latin** ≃ javanais *m* (*argot*) ►**pigman** porcher *m* ►**pigpen** porcherie *f* ►**pigskin** (*leather*) peau *f* de porc; (*US Ftbl*) ballon *m* (*de football américain*) ►**pigsty** (*Brit: lit, fig*) porcherie *f*; **your room is like a pigsty!** ta chambre est une vraie porcherie! ►**pig-swill** pâtée *f* pour les porcs ►**pigtail** *[hair]* natte *f*.

3 **vi** *[sow]* mettre bas, cochonner.

4 **vt**: **to ~ o.s.*** se goinfrer (*on* de); **to ~ it⁑** vivre comme un cochon* (*or* des cochons).

►**pig out*** **vi** (*eat greedily*) s'en mettre plein derrière la cravate*.

pigeon ['pɪdʒən] 1 **n** a (*also Culin*) pigeon *m*. **wood-~** ramier *m*; *see* **carrier, clay, homing** *etc*. b (*) affaire *f*. **that's not my ~** ça n'est pas mes oignons*; **that's your ~** c'est toi que ça regarde, c'est tes oignons*. 2 **comp** ►**pigeon-chested** à la poitrine bombée *or* renflée ►**pigeon-fancier** colombophile *mf* ►**pigeonhole** *see* **pigeonhole** ►**pigeon house, pigeon loft** pigeonnier *m* ►**pigeon post**: **by pigeon post** par pigeon voyageur ►**pigeon shooting** tir *m* aux pigeons ►**pigeon-toed**: **to be pigeon-toed** avoir *or* marcher les pieds tournés en dedans.

pigeonhole ['pɪdʒɪnˌhəʊl] 1 **n** (*in desk*) case *f*, casier *m*; (*on wall etc*) casier. 2 **vt** a (*store away papers*) classer, ranger. b (*shelve*) *project, problem* enterrer provisoirement. (*US Pol*) **to ~ a bill** enterrer un projet de loi. c (*classify*) *person* étiqueter, cataloguer, classer (*as* comme).

piggery ['pɪgərɪ] **n** porcherie *f*.

piggish* ['pɪgɪʃ] **adj** (*pej*) (*in manners*) sale, grossier; (*greedy*) goinfre; (*stubborn*) têtu.

piggy ['pɪgɪ] 1 **n** (*child language*) cochon *m*. 2 **adj** *eyes* porcin, comme un cochon. 3 **comp** ►**piggyback** *see* **piggyback** ►**piggybank** tirelire *f* (*souvent en forme de cochon*) ►**piggy in the middle** = **pig in the middle** (*see* **pig 2**).

piggyback ['pɪgɪˌbæk] 1 **adv** *ride, be carried* sur le dos. (*fig*) **the shuttle rides ~ on the rocket** la navette est placée sur le dos de la fusée. 2 **adj** *ride etc* sur le dos. 3 **n** a **to give sb a ~** porter qn sur son dos; **give me a ~, Daddy!** fais-moi faire un tour (à dada) sur ton dos, Papa! b (*US Rail*) ferroutage *m*. 4 **vt** a (*carry on one's back*) porter sur son dos. b (*US Rail*) ferrouter. c (*fig*) *plan etc* englober, couvrir. 5 **vi** *[plan, expenditure etc]* être couvert, être pris en charge.

pigheaded ['pɪg'hedɪd] **adj** (*pej*) entêté, obstiné, têtu.

pigheadedly ['pɪg'hedɪdlɪ] **adv** (*pej*) obstinément, avec entêtement.

pigheadedness ['pɪg'hedɪdnɪs] **n** (*pej*) entêtement *m*, obstination *f*.

piglet ['pɪglɪt] **n** porcelet *m*, petit cochon.

pigment ['pɪgmənt] **n** pigment *m*.

pigmentation [ˌpɪgmən'teɪʃən] **n** pigmentation *f*.

pigmented [pɪg'mentɪd] **adj** pigmenté.

pigmy ['pɪgmɪ] = **pygmy**.

pike¹ [paɪk] **n** (*spear*) pique *f*.

pike² [paɪk] 1 **n, pl ~ or ~s** (*fish*) brochet *m*. 2 **comp** ►**pikeperch** (**pl ~ or ~es**) sandre *m*.

pike³ [paɪk] = **turnpike**; *see* **turn 2**.

pike⁴ [paɪk] **n** (*Brit dial: peak*) pic *m*.

piker⁑ ['paɪkəʳ] **n** (*US*) (*small gambler*) thunard⁑ *m*; (*small speculator*) boursicoteur *m*, -euse *f*; (*stingy person*) pingre *mf*; (*contemptible person*) minable *mf*.

pikestaff ['paɪkstɑːf] *see* **plain**.

pilaf(f) ['pɪlæf] **n** pilaf *m*.

pilaster [pɪ'læstəʳ] **n** pilastre *m*.

Pilate ['paɪlət] **n**: **Pontius ~** Ponce Pilate *m*.

pilau [pɪ'laʊ] **n** = **pilaff**.

pilchard ['pɪltʃəd] **n** pilchard *m*, sardine *f*.

pile¹ [paɪl] 1 **n** a (*Constr etc*) pieu *m* de fondation; (*in water*) pilotis *m*; *[bridge]* pile *f*. b (*pointed stake*) pieu *m*. 2 **comp** ►**pile driver** sonnette *f* ►**pile dwelling** (*Hist*) maison *f* sur pilotis. 3 **vt** *land* enfoncer des pieux *or* des pilotis dans.

pile² [paɪl] 1 **n** a (*heap*) *[bricks, books etc]* pile *f*; (*less tidy*) tas *m*. **his clothes lay in a ~** ses vêtements étaient en tas; **the linen was in a neat ~** le linge était rangé en une pile bien nette; **to make a ~ of books, to put books in a ~** empiler des livres, mettre des livres en tas *or* en pile; (*fig*) **to be at the top/bottom of the ~** être en haut/en bas de l'échelle (*fig*).

b (*: *fortune*) fortune *f*. **to make one's ~** faire son beurre*, faire fortune; **he made a ~ on this deal** il a ramassé un joli paquet* avec cette affaire.

c (*) **~s of, a ~ of** *butter, honey* beaucoup de, des masses de*; *cars, flowers* beaucoup de, un tas de*; **to have a ~ of** *or* **~s of money** avoir beaucoup d'argent *or* un argent fou *or* plein d'argent*.

d (*Phys*) pile *f*; *see* **atomic**.

e (*liter: imposing building*) édifice *m*. **the Louvre, that impressive ~** le Louvre, cet édifice impressionnant.

f (*Med*) **~s** hémorroïdes *fpl*.

2 **comp** ►**pileup** (*Aut*) carambolage *m*; **there was a 10-car pileup on the motorway** 10 voitures se sont carambolées sur l'autoroute.

3 **vt** a (*also* **~ up**) empiler, entasser. **he ~d the books (up) one on top of the other** il a empilé les livres les uns sur les autres; **don't ~ them (up) too high** ne les empile pas trop haut; **a table ~d (high) with books** une table couverte de piles de livres; **to ~ coal on the fire, to ~ the fire up with coal** empiler du charbon sur le feu.

b **he ~d the books into the box** il a empilé *or* entassé les livres dans la caisse; **I ~d the children into the car*** j'ai entassé *or* enfourné* les enfants dans la voiture.

4 **vi** (*) **we all ~d into the car** nous nous sommes tous entassés *or* empilés* dans la voiture; **we ~d off the train** nous sommes descendus du train en nous bousculant; **they ~d through the door** ils sont entrés *or* sortis en se bousculant.

►**pile in*** **vi** *[people]* s'entasser, s'empiler*. **the taxi/car arrived and we all piled in** le taxi/la voiture est arrivé(e) et nous nous sommes tous entassés *or* empilés* dedans; **pile in, all of you!** empilez-vous* là-dedans!

►**pile off*** **vi** *[people]* descendre en désordre.

►**pile on⁑** 1 **vt sep**: **to pile it on** exagérer, en rajouter, en remettre*; **he does tend to pile it on** il a tendance à en remettre *or* à en rajouter*; **stop piling it on** arrête de forcer la dose!*, n'en rajoute pas!; **to pile on the agony** dramatiser, faire du mélo*. 2 **vi**: **the bus/train arrived and we all piled on** l'autobus/le train est arrivé et nous nous sommes tous entassés *or* empilés* dedans.

►**pile out*** **vi** sortir en désordre *or* en se bousculant.

►**pile up** 1 **vi** a *[snow etc]* s'amonceler; *[reasons etc]* s'amonceler, s'accumuler; *[work, business]* s'accumuler. **he had to let the work pile up while his colleague was away** pendant que son collègue était parti il a dû laisser le travail s'accumuler *or* il a dû accumuler du travail en retard; **the evidence piled up against him** les preuves s'amoncelaient *or* s'accumulaient contre lui.

b (*: *crash*) **the car piled up against the wall** la voiture est rentrée* dans le mur *or* s'est écrasée contre le mur *or* a tamponné le mur; **the ship piled up on the rocks** le bateau s'est fracassé sur les rochers.

2 **vt sep** a (*lit*) *see* **pile² 3a**.

b *evidence* accumuler, amonceler; *reasons* accumuler.

c (*: *crash*) **he piled up the car/the motorbike last night** hier soir il a bousillé* la voiture/la moto.

3 **pileup n** *see* **pile² 2**.

pile³ [paɪl] **n** (*Tex*) poils *mpl*. **the ~ of a carpet** les poils d'un tapis; **carpet with a deep ~** tapis de haute laine.

pilfer ['pɪlfəʳ] 1 **vt** chaparder*. 2 **vi** se livrer au chapardage*.

pilferage ['pɪlfərɪdʒ] **n** chapardage *m*, coulage *m*.

pilferer ['pɪlfərəʳ] **n** chapardeur* *m*, -euse* *f*.

pilfering ['pɪlfərɪŋ] **n** chapardage* *m*.

pilgrim ['pɪlgrɪm] **n** pèlerin *m*. **the ~s to Lourdes** les pèlerins de Lourdes; (*Hist*) **the P~ Fathers** les (Pères) Pèlerins; **"P~'s Progress"** "Le Voyage du Pèlerin".

pilgrimage ['pɪlgrɪmɪdʒ] **n** pèlerinage *m*. **to make a ~, to go on a ~** faire un pèlerinage.

pill [pɪl] 1 n a (*Med, fig*) pilule *f*. (*fig*) to sugar *or* sweeten the ~ dorer la pilule (*for sb* à qn); *see* bitter. b (*also* birth ~) pilule *f*. to be on the ~ prendre la pilule. 2 comp ▸**pillbox** (*Med*) boîte *f* à pilules; (*Mil*) casemate *f*, blockhaus *m inv*; (*hat*) toque *f*.

pillage [ˈpɪlɪdʒ] 1 n pillage *m*, saccage *m*. 2 vt piller, saccager, mettre à sac. 3 vi se livrer au pillage *or* au saccage.

pillar [ˈpɪləʳ] 1 n (*Archit*) pilier *m*, colonne *f*; (*Min, also Climbing*) pilier; (*fig*) *[fire, smoke]* colonne; (*fig: support*) pilier, soutien *m*. he was pushed around from ~ to post on se le renvoyait de l'un à l'autre; after giving up his job he went from ~ to post until ... après avoir quitté son emploi il a erré à droite et à gauche jusqu'au jour où ...; ~ of water trombe *f* d'eau; ~ of salt statue *f* de sel; ~ of the Church pilier de l'Église; he was a ~ of strength il a vraiment été d'un grand soutien; (*Geog*) the P~s of Hercules les Colonnes d'Hercule. 2 comp ▸**pillar-box** (*Brit*) boîte *f* aux *or* à lettres; pillar-box red rouge sang *inv*.

pillion [ˈpɪljən] 1 n *[motorcycle]* siège *m* arrière, tan-sad *m*; *[horse]* selle *f* de derrière. ~ passenger passager *m* de derrière. 2 adv: to ride ~ (*on horse*) monter en croupe; (*on motorcycle*) monter derrière.

pillock‡ [ˈpɪlək] n (*Brit*) con‡ *m*.

pillory [ˈpɪlərɪ] 1 n pilori *m*. 2 vt (*Hist, fig*) mettre au pilori.

pillow [ˈpɪləʊ] 1 n a oreiller *m*. he rested his head on a ~ of moss il reposa sa tête sur un coussin de mousse. b (*Tech: also* lace ~) carreau *m* (de dentellière). 2 comp ▸**pillowcase** taie *f* d'oreiller ▸**pillow fight** bataille *f* d'oreillers *or* de polochons* ▸**pillow slip** = pillowcase ▸**pillowtalk** confidences *fpl* sur l'oreiller; *see* lace. 3 vt *head* reposer. she ~ed her head on my shoulder elle reposa *or* appuya la tête sur mon épaule; she ~ed her head in her arms elle a reposé sa tête sur ses bras.

pilot [ˈpaɪlət] 1 n (*Aviat, Naut*) pilote *m*. co-~ copilote *m*; *see* automatic.

2 adj *project etc* -pilote. ~ scheme projet-pilote *m*, projet expérimental.

3 comp ▸**pilot boat** bateau-pilote *m* ▸**pilot film** (*TV*) film-pilote *m* ▸**pilot-fish** poisson-pilote *m* ▸**pilot house** poste *m* de pilotage ▸**pilot jacket** blouson *m* d'aviateur ▸**pilot jet, pilot light** veilleuse *f* (*de cuisinière, de chauffe-eau etc*) ▸**pilot officer** sous-lieutenant *m* (de l'armée de l'air) ▸**pilot production, pilot series** (*Ind*) pré-série *f*.

4 vt (*Aviat, Naut*) piloter. he ~ed us through the crowd il nous a guidés *or* pilotés à travers la foule; he ~ed the country through the difficult post-war period il a guidé *or* dirigé le pays à travers les difficultés de l'après-guerre; (*Parl*) to ~ a bill through the House assurer le passage d'un projet de loi.

Pils [pɪls, pɪlz] n bière *f* pils.

pimento [pɪˈmentəʊ] n, pl ~s piment *m*.

pimp [pɪmp] 1 n souteneur *m*, maquereau‡ *m*, marlou *m*‡. 2 vi être souteneur, faire le maquereau‡.

pimpernel [ˈpɪmpənel] n mouron *m*; *see* scarlet.

pimple [ˈpɪmpl] n bouton *m* (*Med*). to come out in ~s avoir une poussée de boutons.

pimply [ˈpɪmplɪ] adj *face, person* boutonneux.

PIN [pɪn] n (abbr of personal identification number) ~ (number) code *m* confidentiel *or* personnel.

pin [pɪn] 1 n a (*Sewing: also for hair, tie etc*) épingle *f*; (*Brit: also* drawing ~) punaise *f*; (*badge*) badge *m*. (hat)~ épingle à chapeau; the room was like *or* was as neat as a new ~ la pièce était impeccable; he was as neat as a new ~ (*clean*) il était propre comme un sou neuf*; (*tidy*) il était tiré à quatre épingles; you could have heard a ~ drop on aurait entendu voler une mouche; I've got ~s and needles (in my foot) j'ai des fourmis (au pied); (*fig*) to be on ~s être sur des charbons ardents; for two ~s I'd smack his face* pour un peu je lui donnerais une gifle; *see* rolling, safety *etc*.

b (*Tech*) goupille *f*, goujon *m*; *[hand grenade]* goupille; *[pulley]* essieu *m*; (*Elec*) fiche *f or* broche *f* (de prise de courant); (*Med: in limb*) broche. (*Elec*) 3-~ plug prise *f* à 3 fiches *or* broches.

c (*Bowling*) quille *f*; (*Golf*) drapeau *m* de trou.

d (‡: *leg*) ~s guibolles‡ *fpl or* guiboles‡ *fpl*, quilles‡ *fpl*, pattes *fpl*; he's not very steady on his ~s il a les guibolles‡ en coton, il ne tient pas sur ses guibolles‡ *or* sur ses pattes.

2 comp ▸**pinball** flipper *m*; pinball machine flipper *m* ▸**pincushion** pelote *f* à épingles ▸**pinhead** (*lit*) tête *f* d'épingle; (‡ *pej: idiot*) imbécile *mf*, andouille‡ *f* ▸**pinhole** trou *m* d'épingle; (*Phot*) sténopé *m* ▸**pin money*** argent *m* de poche ▸**pinpoint** n (*lit*) pointe *f* d'épingle ◊ vt *place* localiser avec précision; *problem* mettre le doigt sur, définir ▸**pinprick** (*lit*) piqûre *f* d'épingle; (*fig: annoyance*) coup *m* d'épingle ▸**pinstripe** rayure très fine; black material with a white pinstripe tissu noir finement rayé de blanc; pinstripe suit costume rayé ▸**pin table** = pinball machine ▸**pinup (girl)*** pin-up *f inv*.

3 vt a (*put pin in*) *dress* épingler; *papers* (*together*) attacher *or* réunir *or* assembler avec une épingle; (*to wall etc*) attacher avec une punaise. he ~ned the medal to his uniform il a épinglé la médaille sur son uniforme; he ~ned the calendar on the wall il a accroché *or* fixé le calendrier au mur (avec une punaise).

b (*fig*) his arms were ~ned to his sides il avait les bras collés au corps; to ~ sb against a wall clouer qn à un mur, immobiliser qn contre un mur; the fallen tree ~ned him against the house l'arbre abattu le cloua *or* le coinça *or* l'immobilisa contre la maison; the battalion was ~ned (down) against the river le bataillon était bloqué sur la berge du fleuve; to ~ one's hopes on sth mettre tous ses espoirs dans qch; you can't ~ it *or* the blame on me* tu ne peux pas me mettre ça sur le dos; they tried to ~ the crime on him* ils ont essayé de lui mettre le crime sur le dos *or* de lui coller* la responsabilité du crime.

c (*Tech*) cheviller, goupiller.

d (*US: as sign of love*) to ~ a girl* offrir à une jeune fille son insigne de confrérie en gage d'affection.

▸**pin back** vt sep (*lit*) retenir (avec une épingle). (*fig*) to pin sb's ears back* (*startle*) faire dresser l'oreille à qn; (*US: scold*) passer un savon* à qn; (*US: beat up*) ficher une raclée à qn; pin back your ears* ouvre grand les oreilles.

▸**pin down** vt sep a (*secure*) attacher *or* fixer avec une épingle *or* une punaise. b (*trap*) immobiliser, coincer. to be pinned down by a fallen tree être immobilisé par *or* coincé sous un arbre tombé. c (*fig*) to pin sb down to a promise obliger qn à tenir sa promesse; I can't manage to pin him down je n'arrive pas à le coincer* (*fig*); see if you can pin him down to naming a price essaie de lui faire dire un prix; there's something wrong but I can't pin it down il y a quelque chose qui ne va pas mais je n'arrive pas à définir exactement ce que c'est *or* à mettre le doigt dessus.

▸**pin on** vt sep attacher avec une punaise *or* une épingle, épingler.

▸**pin together** vt sep épingler.

▸**pin up** 1 vt sep *notice* fixer (au mur) avec une punaise, punaiser, afficher; *hem* épingler; *hair* épingler, relever avec des épingles. 2 **pinup** n, adj *see* pin 2.

pinafore [ˈpɪnəfɔːʳ] n (*apron*) tablier *m*; (*overall*) blouse *f* (*de travail*). ~ dress robe-chasuble *f*.

pincer [ˈpɪnsəʳ] n a *[crab]* pince *f*. ~ movement (*fig, Mil*) mouvement *m* de tenailles. b (*tool*) ~s tenailles *fpl*.

pinch [pɪntʃ] 1 n a (*action*) pincement *m*; (*mark*) pinçon *m*. to give sb a ~ (on the arm) pincer qn (au bras); (*fig*) people are beginning to feel the ~ les gens commencent à être serrés *or* à être à court; (*fig*) at a ~, (*US*) in a ~ à la limite, à la rigueur; it'll do at a ~ cela fera l'affaire à la rigueur *or* faute de mieux; when it comes to the ~ au moment critique.

b *[salt]* pincée *f*; *[snuff]* prise *f*. (*fig*) to take sth with a ~ of salt ne pas prendre qch pour argent comptant *or* au pied de la lettre.

2 comp ▸**pinch-hit** *see* pinch-hit ▸**pinchpenny** adj grippe-sou.

3 vt a pincer; *[shoes]* serrer. he ~ed her arm il lui a pincé le bras, il l'a pincée au bras.

b (*: *steal*) piquer*, faucher*; (*hum, or child's language*) chiper. I had my car ~ed on m'a fauché* *or* piqué* ma voiture; he ~ed that idea from Shaw il a chipé* *or* piqué* cette idée à Shaw; Robert ~ed John's girlfriend Robert a piqué* sa petite amie à Jean.

c (‡: *arrest*) pincer*. to get ~ed se faire pincer*; they ~ed him with the jewels on him on l'a pincé* *or* piqué‡ en possession des bijoux; he got ~ed for speeding il s'est fait pincer* pour excès de vitesse.

4 vi a *[shoe]* être étroit, serrer. (*fig*) that's where the shoe ~es c'est là que le bât blesse.

b to ~ and scrape rogner sur tout, se serrer la ceinture*.

▸**pinch back, pinch off** vt sep *bud* épincer, pincer.

pinchbeck [ˈpɪntʃbek] 1 n a (*metal*) chrysocale *m*, similor *m*. b (*sth sham*) toc *m*. 2 adj a (*lit*) en chrysocale, en similor. b (*sham*) en toc, de pacotille.

pinched [ˈpɪntʃt] adj a (*drawn*) to look ~ avoir les traits tirés; to look ~ with cold/with hunger avoir l'air transi de froid/ tenaillé par la faim. b ~ for money à court d'argent; ~ for space à l'étroit.

pinch-hit [ˈpɪntʃhɪt] vi (*US Baseball*) jouer en remplaçant. (*US fig*) to ~ for sb assurer le remplacement de qn au pied levé.

pinch-hitter [ˈpɪntʃˌhɪtəʳ] n remplaçant *m*, substitut *m*.

Pindar [ˈpɪndəʳ] n Pindare *m*.

Pindaric [pɪnˈdærɪk] adj pindarique.

pindling* [ˈpɪndlɪŋ] adj (*US*) chétif, malingre.

pine¹ [paɪn] 1 n (*also* ~ tree) pin *m*. 2 comp ▸**pine cone** pomme *f* de pin ▸**pine grove** pinède *f* ▸**pine kernel** pigne *f*, pignon *m* ▸**pine marten** martre *f* ▸**pine needle** aiguille *f* de pin ▸**pine nut** = pine kernel ▸**the Pine Tree State** (*US*) le Maine ▸**pinewood** (*grove*) bois *m* de pins, pinède *f*; (*NonC: material*) bois de pin, pin *m*.

pine² [paɪn] vi a (*long*) to ~ for sth soupirer après qch (*liter*), désirer ardemment *or* vivement qch; to ~ for one's family s'ennuyer de sa famille, désirer ardemment retrouver sa famille; after 6 months in London she began to ~ for home après 6 mois passés à Londres elle ne pensait qu'à *or* aspirait à *or* désirait ardemment rentrer chez elle; exiles pining for home des exilés qui ont la nostalgie du pays natal. b (*be sad*) languir, dépérir.

▸**pine away** vi languir, dépérir.

pineal [ˈpɪnɪəl] adj: ~ body *or* gland glande *f* pinéale, épiphyse *f*.

pineapple [ˈpaɪnˌæpl] 1 n ananas *m*. 2 comp *flavour, ice cream* aux ananas ▸**pineapple juice** jus *m* d'ananas.

ping [pɪŋ] 1 n bruit *m* métallique; *[bell, clock]* tintement *m*; (*US Aut*) cliquettement *m*. 2 vi faire un bruit métallique; *[bell, clock]* tinter; (*US Aut*) cliqueter. 3 comp ►**Ping-Pong** ® ping-pong *m*; **Ping-Pong ball** balle *f* de ping-pong; **Ping-Pong player** pongiste *mf*.

pinging [pɪŋɪŋ] n (*US Aut*) cliquettement *m*.

pinion[1] ['pɪnjən] 1 n *[bird]* aileron *m*. 2 vt a *person* lier. **to ~ sb's arms** lier les bras à qn; **he was ~ed against the wall** il était cloué au mur, il était coincé contre le mur. b *bird* rogner les ailes à.

pinion[2] ['pɪnjən] n (*Tech*) pignon *m*. **~ wheel** roue *f* à pignon; *see* **rack**[1].

pink[1] [pɪŋk] 1 n a (*colour*) rose *m*. (*fig*) **to be in the ~** se porter comme un charme; **in the ~ of condition** en excellente *or* pleine forme; (*fig*) **to see ~ elephants** avoir des visions hallucinatoires (*dues à l'alcool*); *see* **hunting, salmon.**

b (*Bot*) œillet *m*, mignardise *f*.

2 adj *cheek, clothes, paper* rose; (*Pol*) gauchisant. **the petals turn ~** les pétales rosissent; **she turned ~ with pleasure** elle rosit *or* rougit de plaisir; **he turned ~ with embarrassment** il rougit de confusion; *see* **strike, tickle.**

3 comp ►**pink eye** (*Med*) conjonctivite aiguë contagieuse ►**pink gin** cocktail *m* de gin et d'angusture ►**pink lady** (*cocktail*) *cocktail à base de gin, cognac, jus de citron et grenadine* ►**pink slip*** (*US: terminating employment*) lettre *f* de licenciement.

pink[2] [pɪŋk] vt a (*Sewing*) denteler. **~ing shears** *or* **scissors** ciseaux *mpl* à denteler. b (*put holes in*) perforer. c (*pierce*) percer.

pink[3] [pɪŋk] vi (*Brit*) *[car engine etc]* cliqueter.

pinkie ['pɪŋkɪ] n petit doigt, auriculaire *m*.

pinking ['pɪŋkɪŋ] n (*Brit Aut*) cliquettement *m*.

pinkish ['pɪŋkɪʃ] adj rosâtre, rosé; (*Pol*) gauchisant. **~ brown** brun *m* rosâtre; **~ red** rouge *m* tirant sur le rose.

pinko* ['pɪŋkəʊ] adj, n, pl ~s *or* ~es (*Pol: pej*) gauchisant(e) *m(f)*.

pinnace ['pɪnɪs] n chaloupe *f*, grand canot.

pinnacle ['pɪnəkl] n (*Archit*) pinacle *m*; (*mountain peak*) pic *m*, cime *f*; (*Climbing*) gendarme *m*; (*fig*) apogée *m*, sommet *m*, pinacle.

pinny‡ ['pɪnɪ] n (abbr of **pinafore**) tablier *m*.

Pinocchio [pɪ'nəʊkjəʊ] n Pinocchio *m*.

pinochle ['piːnʌkəl] n (*US*) (sorte *f* de) belote *f*.

pint [paɪnt] 1 n a pinte *f*, ≃ demi-litre *m* (*Brit = 0,57 litre; US = 0,47 litre*). b (*Brit *: beer*) ≃ demi *m* (de bière). **let's go for a ~** allons boire un demi *or* prendre un pot*; **he had a few ~s** il a bu quelques demis; **he likes his ~** il aime son verre de bière. 2 comp ►**pint-size(d)*** minuscule.

pinta* ['paɪntə] n (abbr of **pint of milk**: *terme publicitaire*) ≃ demi-litre *m* de lait.

pioneer [,paɪə'nɪəʳ] 1 n (*gen*) pionnier *m*; (*early settler*) pionnier, colon *m*; (*Mil*) pionnier, sapeur *m*; (*explorer*) explorateur *m*, -trice *f*; *[scheme, science, method]* pionnier, promoteur *m*, -trice *f*. **he was one of the ~s in this field** il a été l'un des pionniers *or* novateurs *or* précurseurs dans ce domaine; **he was a ~ in the study of bats** il a été un pionnier de l'étude des chauves-souris, il a été l'un des premiers à étudier les chauves-souris; **one of the ~s of aviation/scientific research** l'un des pionniers de l'aviation/de la recherche scientifique.

2 vt: **to ~ the study of sth** être l'un des premiers (*or* l'une des premières) à étudier qch; **she ~ed research in this field** elle fut à l'avant-garde de la recherche dans ce domaine, elle ouvrit la voie dans ce domaine; **he ~ed the use of this drug** il a été l'un des premiers à utiliser ce médicament, il a lancé l'usage de ce médicament; *see also* **pioneering.**

3 comp *research, study* complètement nouveau ►**pioneer work**: **he did pioneer work in the development of ...** il a été le premier à développer ... .

pioneering [,paɪə'nɪərɪŋ] adj *work, research, study* complètement nouveau *or* original.

pious ['paɪəs] adj *person, deed* pieux. **a ~ deed** une action pieuse, une œuvre pie; (*iro*) **~ hope** pieux espoir.

piously ['paɪəslɪ] adv avec piété, pieusement.

pip[1] [pɪp] 1 n a *[fruit]* pépin *m*. b *[card, dice]* point *m*. c (*Brit Mil *: on uniform*) ≃ galon *m*. d (*Telec*) top *m*. **the ~s** le bip-bip; **at the third ~ it will be 6.49 and 20 seconds** au troisième top il sera exactement 6 heures 49 minutes 20 secondes; **put more money in when you hear the ~s** introduisez des pièces supplémentaires quand vous entendrez le bip-bip. e (*Radar*) spot *m*. 2 comp ►**pipsqueak*** foutriquet *m*.

pip[2] [pɪp] n (*Vet*) pépie *f*. (*Brit fig*) **he gives me the ~*** il me hérisse le poil*.

pip[3]* [pɪp] vt a (*hit*) atteindre d'une balle. b **to ~ sb (to the post)** coiffer qn (au poteau); **to be ~ped at the post** se faire coiffer au poteau, se faire battre *or* griller* de justesse. c (*fail*) **to be ~ped at the post** se faire recaler* *or* coller*.

pipe [paɪp] 1 n a (*for water, gas*) tuyau *m*, conduit *m*, conduite *f*; (*smaller*) tube *m*. **to lay water ~s** poser des conduites d'eau *or* une canalisation d'eau; *see* **drain, wind**[1].

b (*Mus*) pipeau *m*, chalumeau *m*; *[organ]* tuyau *m*; (*boatswain's*) sifflet *m*. (*bagpipes*) **~s** cornemuse *f*; **~s of Pan** flûte *f* de Pan.

c (*sound*) *[bird]* chant *m*.

d (*for smoking*) pipe *f*. **he smokes a ~** il fume la pipe; **he smoked a ~ before he left** il fuma une pipe avant de partir; **to fill a ~** bourrer une pipe; **~ of peace** calumet *m* de (la) paix; **a ~(ful) of tobacco** une pipe de tabac; **put that in your ~ and smoke it!*** si ça ne te plaît pas c'est le même prix!*, mets ça dans ta poche et ton mouchoir pardessus!

2 comp ►**pipeclay** terre *f* de pipe ►**pipe cleaner** cure-pipe *m* ►**pipe dream** château *m* en Espagne (*fig*) ►**pipefitter** tuyauteur *m* ►**pipeline** *see* **pipeline** ►**pipe organ** grandes orgues ►**pipe rack** porte-pipes *m inv* ►**pipe smoker** fumeur *m* de pipe ►**pipe tobacco** tabac *m* à pipe.

3 vt a (*Agr, Comm etc*) *liquid* transporter *or* acheminer par tuyau *or* conduite *or* canalisation *etc*. **water is ~d to the farm** l'eau est amenée jusqu'à la ferme par une canalisation; **to ~ oil across the desert** transporter du pétrole à travers le désert par pipeline *or* oléoduc; **to ~ oil into a tank** verser *or* faire passer du pétrole dans un réservoir à l'aide d'un tuyau; **~d music** musique *f* de fond enregistrée.

b (*Mus*) *tune* jouer (sur un pipeau *etc*); (*Naut*) *order* siffler. **to ~ all hands on deck** rassembler l'équipage sur le pont (au son du sifflet); **to ~ sb in/out** saluer l'arrivée/le départ de qn (au son du sifflet); **the commander was ~d aboard** le commandant a reçu les honneurs du sifflet en montant à bord.

c (*Sewing*) passepoiler, garnir d'un passepoil. **~d with blue** passepoilé de bleu, garni d'un passepoil bleu.

d (*Culin*) **to ~ icing/cream** *etc* **on a cake** décorer un gâteau de fondant/de crème fouettée *etc* (à l'aide d'une douille).

e (*say*) dire d'une voix flûtée; (*sing*) chanter d'une voix flûtée.

4 vi a (*Mus*) jouer du pipeau *or* du chalumeau *or* de la flûte *or* de la cornemuse.

b (*Naut*) donner un coup de sifflet.

►**pipe down**‡ vi mettre la sourdine*, se taire. **(do) pipe down!** un peu de calme!, mets-y une sourdine!*, baisse un peu le ton!*

►**pipe up*** vi se faire entendre.

pipeline ['paɪp,laɪn] n (*gen*) pipeline *m*; *[oil]* oléoduc *m*; *[natural gas]* gazoduc *m*; *[milk]* lactoduc *m*. **it's in the ~** (*gen*) ça doit venir (*or* sortir) bientôt; *[project, contract, agreement]* c'est en cours de réalisation; (*Ind*) **there's a new model in the ~** on est en train de développer un nouveau modèle; (*Comm*) **the goods you ordered are in the ~** les marchandises que vous avez commandées sont en route; **they have got a pay increase in the ~** ils doivent recevoir une augmentation de salaire.

piper ['paɪpəʳ] n joueur *m*, -euse *f* de pipeau *or* de chalumeau; (*bagpiper*) cornemuseur *m*; *see* **pay.**

pipette [pɪ'pet] n pipette *f*.

piping ['paɪpɪŋ] 1 n (*NonC*) a (*in house*) tuyauterie *f*, canalisation *f*, conduites *fpl*. b (*Mus*) son *m* du pipeau *or* du chalumeau *or* de la cornemuse. c (*Sewing*) passepoil *m*. **~ cord** ganse *f*. d (*on cake etc*) décorations (appliquées) à la douille. 2 adj *voice, tone* flûté. 3 adv: **~ hot** tout chaud, tout bouillant.

pipit ['pɪpɪt] n (*Orn*) pipit *m*.

pipkin ['pɪpkɪn] n poêlon *m* (en terre).

pippin ['pɪpɪn] n (pomme *f*) reinette *f*.

piquancy ['piːkənsɪ] n (*flavour*) goût piquant; *[story]* sel *m*, piquant *m*.

piquant ['piːkənt] adj *flavour, story* piquant.

piquantly ['piːkəntlɪ] adv d'une manière piquante.

pique [piːk] 1 vt a *person* dépiter, irriter, froisser. b *sb's curiosity, interest* piquer, exciter. 2 n ressentiment *m*, dépit *m*. **in a fit of ~** dans un accès de dépit.

piquet [pɪ'ket] n piquet *m* (*jeu de cartes*).

piracy ['paɪərəsɪ] n (*NonC*) piraterie *f*; (*fig*) *[book, film, tape, video]* piratage *m*; *[idea]* pillage *m*, vol *m*; (*Comm*) contrefaçon *f*. **a tale of ~** une histoire de pirates.

piranha [pɪ'rɑːnjə] n piranha *m or* piraya *m*.

pirate ['paɪərɪt] 1 n a (*Hist*) pirate *m*, corsaire *m*, flibustier *m*. b (*Comm*) (*gen*) contrefacteur *m*; *[book, tape, film, video]* pirate *m*; *[ideas]* voleur *m*, -euse *f*. 2 comp *flag, ship* de pirates ►**pirate copy** copie *f* pirate ►**pirate radio** radio *f or* émetteur *m* pirate. 3 vt *book, tape, film, video* pirater; *product* contrefaire; *invention, idea* s'approprier, piller, voler.

pirated ['paɪərɪtɪd] adj (*Comm*) contrefait. **~ edition** édition pirate.

piratical [paɪ'rætɪkəl] adj (*see* **pirate**) de pirate; de contrefacteur.

pirating ['paɪərɪtɪŋ] n *[book, tape, film, video]* piratage *m*.

pirouette [,pɪrʊ'et] 1 n pirouette *f*. 2 vi faire la pirouette, pirouetter.

Pisa ['piːzə] n Pise.

Piscean ['paɪsɪən] n: **to be a ~** être (des) Poissons.

Pisces ['paɪsiːz] n (*Astron*) les Poissons *mpl*. (*Astron*) **I'm (a) ~** je suis (des) Poissons.

piss** [pɪs] 1 n pisse** *f*. **it's ~ easy** *or* **a piece of ~** c'est fastoche‡. 2 vi pisser‡. (*fig: raining*) **it's ~ing down** il pleut comme vache qui pisse‡. 3 comp ►**piss artist**** soûlographe* *mf* ►**piss easy**** *see* **1** ►**piss-poor**** nullard*, minable* ►**piss-up**** soûlerie *f*, beuverie* *f*.

►**piss about, piss around**** 1 vi (*waste time*) glandouiller‡. **to piss around with sth** déconner‡ avec qch; **to piss around with sb** se foutre

de la gueule de qn** 2 vt (*Brit*) *person* se foutre de la gueule de**.
►**piss off**** 1 vi foutre le camp*. **piss off!** fous(-moi) le camp!* 2 vt: **I'm pissed off** j'en ai marre*, j'en ai ras le bol*.
pissed** [pɪst] adj a (*Brit: drunk*) bituré*, bourré*, blindé*. **to get ~** se soûler la gueule*; **~ as a newt, ~ out of one's mind** complètement bituré* *or* rétamé*. b (*US*) = **pissed off;** *see* **piss off 2.**
pistachio [pɪsˈtɑːʃɪəʊ] n, pl ~s a (*nut*) pistache *f*; (*tree*) pistachier *m*. **~-flavoured ice cream** glace *f* à la pistache. b (*colour*) (vert *m*) pistache *m inv*.
piste [piːst] n (*Ski*) piste *f*.
pisted [ˈpiːstɪd] adj (*Ski*) **it's well ~ down** c'est bien damé.
pistil [ˈpɪstɪl] n pistil *m*.
pistol [ˈpɪstl] 1 n pistolet *m*; (*Sport: starter's ~*) pistolet (de starter). 2 comp ►**pistol point:** at **pistol point** sous la menace du pistolet ► **pistol shot** coup *m* de pistolet ►**pistol-whip** (*US*) vt frapper avec un pistolet (au visage).
piston [ˈpɪstən] 1 n piston *m* (*lit*). 2 comp ►**piston engine** moteur *m* à pistons ►**piston-engined** à moteur à pistons ►**piston pin** (*US*) goupille *f* ►**piston ring** segment *m* (de pistons) ►**piston rod** tige *f* de piston.
pit¹ [pɪt] 1 n a (*large hole*) trou *m*; (*on moon's surface etc*) cratère *m*, dépression *f*; (*also* **coal~**) mine *f*, puits *m* de mine; (*as game trap etc*) trappe *f*, fosse *f*; (*quarry*) carrière *f*; (*in garage*) fosse; (*in motor racing*) stand *m*. **chalk~** carrière à chaux; (*Min*) **to go down the ~** (*gen*) descendre au fond de la mine; (*start work there*) aller travailler à la mine; **he works in the ~s** il travaille à la mine; **the men in the ~s** les mineurs *mpl* (de fond); (*fig: hell*) **the ~** l'enfer *m*.
b (*small depression*) (*in metal, glass*) petit trou; (*on face*) (petite) marque *f or* cicatrice *f*.
c (*Anat*) creux *m*. **the ball hit him in the ~ of his stomach/back** la balle l'a touché au creux de l'estomac/des reins; *see* **arm¹**.
d (*Brit Theat*) (fauteuils *mpl* d')orchestre *m*; (*for cock fighting*) arène *f*; (*US St Ex*) parquet *m* de la Bourse. (*US St Ex*) **the wheat ~** la Bourse du blé.
e (*fig: awful*): **it's the ~s!*** c'est merdique!*
2 comp ►**pithead** (*Min*) carreau *m* de la mine; (*Min*) **pithead ballot** référendum *m* des mineurs des houillères ►**pit pony** (*Min*) cheval *m* de mine ►**pit prop** (*Min*) poteau *m or* étai *m* de mine ►**pit stop** (*in motor racing*) arrêt *m* au stand ►**pit worker** (*Min*) mineur *m* de fond.
3 vt a opposer (*sb against sb* qn à qn). **to ~ o.s. against sb** se mesurer avec *or* à qn; **to be ~ted against sb** avoir qn comme *or* pour adversaire; **to ~ one's wits against** jouer au plus fin avec, se mesurer avec.
b *metal* trouer, piqueter; *face, skin* grêler, marquer. **a car ~ted with rust** une voiture piquée de rouille; **his face was ~ted with pockmarks** son visage était grêlé par la petite vérole; **the ~ted surface of the glass** la surface piquetée du verre.
pit² [pɪt] 1 n (*fruit-stone*) noyau *m*. 2 vt dénoyauter. **~ted prunes/cherries** *etc* pruneaux *mpl*/cerises *fpl etc* dénoyauté(e)s.
pitapat [ˈpɪtəˈpæt] adv: **to go ~** *[feet]* trottiner; *[heart]* palpiter, battre; *[rain]* crépiter.
pitch¹ [pɪtʃ] 1 n a (*throw*) acte *m* de lancer, lancement *m*. **the ball went full ~ over the fence** le ballon a volé par-dessus la barrière.
b (*degree*) degré *m*, point *m*; *[voice]* hauteur *f*. (*fig*) **at its (highest) ~** à son comble; **excitement was at fever ~** l'excitation allait jusqu'à la fièvre; **things have reached such a ~ that ...** les choses en sont arrivées à un point tel que ... .
c (*Mus*) ton *m*; (*Phon*) hauteur *f*. **to give the ~** donner le ton; *see* **concert, perfect.**
d (*Brit Sport: ground*) terrain *m*. **football/cricket** *etc* **~** terrain de football/de cricket *etc*.
e (*Brit*) *[trader]* place *f* (habituelle); *see* **queer.**
f (*sales talk*) baratin* *m* publicitaire, boniment *m*. **to make a ~* for** (*support*) *plan, suggestion, sb's point of view* parler en faveur de; (*approach sexually*) faire des avances à; *see* **sales.**
g *[roof]* degré *m* de pente.
h (*movement of boat*) tangage *m*.
i (*Aviat, Naut*) *[propeller]* pas *m*. **variable ~ propeller** hélice *f* à pas variable.
j (*Climbing*) longueur *f* (de corde).
2 comp ►**pitch-and-putt** (*Golf*) pitch-and-putt *m* (*genre de golf limité à deux clubs*) ►**pitch-and-toss** *sorte de jeu de pile ou face* ►**pitchfork** n fourche *f* (à foin) ◊ vt (*Agr*) fourcher, lancer avec une fourche; (*fig*) **I was pitchforked into it** j'ai dû le faire du jour au lendemain ►**pitchman*** (*US*) (*street seller*) camelot *m*; (*TV*) présentateur *m* de produits ►**pitch pipe** (*Mus*) diapason *m* (*en forme de sifflet*).
3 vt a (*throw*) *ball* (*also Baseball*) lancer; *object* jeter, lancer; (*Agr*) *hay* lancer avec une fourche; (*discard*) jeter, bazarder*. **~ it over here!** jette-le *or* lance-le par ici!; **he was ~ed off his horse** il a été jeté à bas de son cheval, il a été désarçonné; **the horse ~ed him off** le cheval l'a jeté à bas *or* à terre; **to ~ over/through/under** *etc* lancer *or* jeter par-dessus/à travers/par-dessous *etc*; (*US*) **~ it!*** balance-le!*, jette-le!
b (*Mus*) *note* donner; *melody* donner le ton de *or* à. **she can't ~ a note properly** elle ne sait pas trouver la note juste (*lit*); **I'll ~ you a note** je vous donne une note pour commencer; **to ~ the voice higher/lower** hausser/baisser le ton de la voix; **this song is ~ed too low** cette chanson est dans un ton trop bas; **to ~ one's aspirations too high** aspirer *or* viser trop haut, placer ses aspirations trop haut; **it is ~ed in rather high-flown terms** c'est exprimé en des termes assez ronflants; **the speech must be ~ed at the right level for the audience** le ton du discours doit être adapté au public; (*fig*) **you're ~ing it a bit high!** *or* **strong!** tu exagères un peu!, tu y vas un peu fort!; **he ~ed me a story about*** ... il m'a débité *or* m'a sorti* une histoire sur ... .
c (*set up*) **to ~ a tent** dresser une tente; **to ~ camp** établir un camp.
d (**: Comm: promote*) *product* promouvoir, faire du battage pour.
4 vi a (*fall*) tomber; (*be jerked*) être projeté; *[ball]* rebondir, tomber. **she slipped and ~ed forward** elle a glissé et est tombée le nez en avant *or* et a piqué du nez; **he ~ed forward as the bus stopped** il a été projeté en avant quand l'autobus s'est arrêté; **to ~ into the lake** tomber la tête la première dans le lac; **to ~ off a horse** tomber de cheval; **the aircraft ~ed into the sea** l'avion a plongé dans la mer; **he ~ed over** il est tombé; **he ~ed over backwards** il est tombé à la renverse; **the ball ~ed (down) at his feet** la balle est tombée *or* rebondi à ses pieds.
b (*Naut*) tanguer. **the ship ~ed and tossed** le navire tanguait.
c (*Baseball*) lancer la balle. (*US fig*) **he's in there ~ing*** il est solide au poste.
►**pitch in*** vi s'atteler *or* s'attaquer au boulot*, s'y coller*. **they all pitched in to help him** ils s'y sont tous mis *or* collés* pour l'aider; **come on, pitch in all of you!** allez, mettez-vous-y *or* collez-vous-y* tous!
►**pitch into*** vt fus a (*attack*) tomber sur; (*abuse*) tomber sur, taper sur*, éreinter*. b s'attaquer à. **they pitched into the work** ils se sont attaqués *or* collés* au travail; **they pitched into the meal** ils se sont attaqués au repas, ils y sont allés d'un bon coup de fourchette.
►**pitch out** vt sep (*get rid of*) *person* expulser, éjecter*, vider*; *thing* jeter, bazarder*. **the car overturned and the driver was pitched out** la voiture a fait un tonneau et le conducteur a été éjecté.
►**pitch (up)on** vt fus arrêter son choix sur.
pitch² [pɪtʃ] 1 n (*tar*) poix *f*, brai *m*. **mineral ~** asphalte minéral, bitume *m*. 2 comp ►**pitch-black** (*gen*) noir comme poix, noir ébène *inv*; **it's pitch-black outside** il fait noir comme dans un four dehors ►**pitch blackness** noir *m* absolu *or* complet ►**pitchblende** pechblende *f* ►**pitch-dark: it's pitch-dark** il fait noir comme dans un four; **it's a pitch-dark night** il fait nuit noire ►**pitch darkness** = **pitch blackness** ►**pitch pine** pitchpin *m*. 3 vt brayer, enduire de poix *or* de brai.
pitched [pɪtʃt] adj: **~ battle** (*Mil*) bataille rangée; (*fig*) véritable bataille.
pitcher¹ [ˈpɪtʃəʳ] n cruche *f*; (*bigger*) broc *m*.
pitcher² [ˈpɪtʃəʳ] n (*Baseball*) lanceur *m*.
piteous [ˈpɪtɪəs] adj pitoyable. **a ~ sight** un spectacle pitoyable *or* à faire pitié.
piteously [ˈpɪtɪəslɪ] adv pitoyablement.
pitfall [ˈpɪtfɔːl] n (*lit*) trappe *f*, piège *m*; (*fig*) piège, embûche *f*. **the ~s of English** les pièges de l'anglais; (*fig*) **there are many ~s ahead** de nombreuses embûches nous (*or* les *etc*) guettent.
pith [pɪθ] n a *[bone, plant]* moelle *f*; *[orange]* peau blanche. **~ helmet** casque colonial. b (*fig*) (*essence*) essence *f*, moelle *f* (*fig*); (*force*) force *f*, vigueur *f*.
pithecanthropine [ˌpɪθɪˈkænθrəʊˌpaɪn] 1 adj pithécanthropien. 2 n pithécanthrope *m*.
pithecanthropus [ˌpɪθɪkænˈθrəʊpəs] n, pl **pithecanthropi** [ˌpɪθɪkænˈθrəʊˌpaɪ] pithécanthrope *m*.
pithiness [ˈpɪθɪnɪs] n *[style]* vigueur *f*, concision *f*.
pithy [ˈpɪθɪ] adj (*forceful*) nerveux, vigoureux; (*terse*) concis; (*pointed*) savoureux, piquant. **a ~ saying** une remarque piquante.
pitiable [ˈpɪtɪəbl] adj *hovel* pitoyable; *income* misérable, de misère; *appearance* piteux, minable; *attempt* piteux. **a ~ situation** une situation pitoyable *or* navrante.
pitiably [ˈpɪtɪəblɪ] adv pitoyablement.
pitiful [ˈpɪtɪfʊl] adj a (*touching*) *appearance, sight, cripple* pitoyable. b (*deplorable*) *cowardice* lamentable, déplorable. **his ~ efforts to speak French** ses lamentables efforts pour parler français.
pitifully [ˈpɪtɪfəlɪ] adv (*pathetically*) pitoyablement, à faire pitié; (*contemptibly*) lamentablement. **he was ~ thin** il était maigre à faire pitié; **a ~ bad play** une pièce lamentable.
pitiless [ˈpɪtɪlɪs] adj sans pitié, impitoyable.
pitilessly [ˈpɪtɪlɪslɪ] adv sans pitié, impitoyablement.
piton [ˈpiːtɒn] n (*Climbing*) piton *m*.
pitta [ˈpɪtə] adj: **~ bread** pain *m* grec (*plat et de forme ovale*).
pittance [ˈpɪtəns] n (*gen*) somme *f* dérisoire; (*income*) maigre revenu *m*; (*wage*) salaire *m* de misère. **she's living on a ~** elle n'a presque rien pour vivre; **they're offering a mere ~** ils offrent un salaire de misère.
pitter-patter [ˈpɪtəˈpætəʳ] 1 adv = **pitapat.** 2 n = **patter² 1.**
pituitary [pɪˈtjuːɪtərɪ] adj pituitaire. **~ gland** glande *f* pituitaire, hypo-

physe *f*.

pity ['pɪtɪ] 1 n a pitié *f*, compassion *f*. **for ~'s sake** par pitié, de grâce; **to have ~ on sb** avoir pitié de qn; **have ~ on him!** ayez pitié de lui!; **to take ~ on sb** avoir pitié de qn, prendre qn en pitié; **to feel ~ for sb** avoir pitié de qn, s'apitoyer sur qn; **to move sb to ~** exciter la compassion de qn, apitoyer qn; **out of ~ (for him)** par pitié (pour lui).

b (*misfortune*) dommage *m*. **it is a ~/a great ~** c'est dommage/bien dommage; **it is a thousand pities that ...** il est mille fois *or* extrêmement dommage que ... + *subj*; **it's a ~ (that) you can't come** il est *or* quel dommage que vous ne puissiez (pas) venir; **what a ~!** quel dommage!; **(the) more's the ~!** c'est bien dommage!, c'est d'autant plus dommage!; **the ~ of it is that ...** le plus malheureux c'est que ... .

2 vt plaindre, s'apitoyer sur, avoir pitié de. **he is to be pitied** il est à plaindre.

pitying ['pɪtɪɪŋ] adj compatissant, plein de pitié.

pityingly ['pɪtɪɪŋlɪ] adv avec compassion, avec pitié.

Pius ['paɪəs] n Pie *m*.

pivot ['pɪvət] 1 n (*Mil, Tech, fig*) pivot *m*. **~ joint** diarthrose *f* rotatoire. 2 vt (*turn*) faire pivoter; (*mount on ~*) monter sur pivot. **he ~ed it on his hand** il l'a fait pivoter *or* tourner sur sa main. 3 vi (*Tech*) pivoter, tourner. **she ~ed round and round** elle tournoyait sans s'arrêter; **he ~ed on his heel** il a tourné sur ses talons; **his whole argument ~s on this point** son argument repose entièrement sur ce point.

pivotal ['pɪvətl] 1 adj essentiel, central. 2 n (*St Ex*) **~s** valeurs *fpl* essentielles *or* clef.

pix* [pɪks] npl (abbr of **pictures**) (*films*) ciné* *m*; (*photos*) photos *fpl*.

pixel ['pɪksəl] n pixel *m*.

pixie ['pɪksɪ] n lutin *m*, fée *f*. **~ hat, ~ hood** bonnet *m* pointu.

pixilated* ['pɪksɪ,leɪtɪd] adj farfelu.

pizano* [pɪ'zænəʊ] n (*US*) copain *m*.

pizza ['piːtsə] n pizza *f*.

piz(z)azz* [pɪ'zæz] n (*US*) (*gen*) énergie *f*, vigueur *f*; (*in car*) allure *f*; (*pej: garishness*) tape-à-l'œil *m*.

pizzeria [,piːtsə'riːə] n pizzeria *f*.

pizzicato [,pɪtsɪ'kɑːtəʊ] adj, adv pizzicato.

Pl. abbr of Place.

placard ['plækɑːd] 1 n (*gen*) affiche *f*, placard *m*; (*at demo etc*) pancarte *f*. 2 vt *wall* placarder; *announcement* afficher. **the town is ~ed with slogans** la ville est placardée de slogans.

placate [plə'keɪt] vt calmer, apaiser.

placating [plə'keɪtɪŋ], **placatory** [plə'keɪtərɪ] adj apaisant.

place [pleɪs] 1 n a (*gen*) endroit *m*, lieu *m* (*gen frm*). **to take ~** avoir lieu; **this is the ~** c'est ici, voici l'endroit; **we came to a ~ where ...** nous sommes arrivés à un endroit où ...; **any ~ will do** n'importe où fera l'affaire; (*US*) **I couldn't find it any ~** je n'ai pu le trouver nulle part; (*US*) **some ~** quelque part; (*US*) **it must be some ~ in the house** ça doit être quelque part dans la maison; (*US*) **some ~ else*** quelque part ailleurs; (*US*) **no ~** nulle part; **he was in another ~ altogether** il était dans un tout autre endroit *or* un tout autre lieu; **this is no ~ for children** cela n'est pas un endroit (convenable) pour des enfants; **can't you find a better ~ to sit down?** est-ce que tu ne pourrais pas trouver un meilleur *or* un autre endroit où t'asseoir?; **it's not a very nice ~ here for a picnic** ça n'est pas un bien joli endroit pour pique-niquer; **this is no ~** *or* **this isn't the ~ to start an argument** nous ne pouvons pas commencer à discuter ici, ce n'est pas un lieu pour discuter; **from ~ to ~** d'un endroit à l'autre, de lieu en lieu; **he went from ~ to ~ looking for her** il la chercha de ville en ville (*or* de village en village *etc*); **she moved around the room from ~ to ~** elle allait d'un coin de la pièce à un autre *or* de-ci de-là dans la pièce; **his clothes were all over the ~** ses vêtements traînaient partout; **I've looked for him all over the ~** je l'ai cherché partout; (*fig*) **to scream the ~ down** hurler, pousser des hurlements; **to find/lose one's ~ in a book** trouver/perdre sa page dans un livre (*see also* **1h**); **to laugh at the right ~** rire quand il faut, rire au bon endroit *or* moment; (*travel*) **to go ~s*** voyager, voir du pays; **we like to go ~s* at weekends** nous aimons faire un tour *or* bouger* pendant les week-ends; (*make good*) **he'll go ~s* all right!** il ira loin!, il fera son chemin!; **he's going ~s*** il fait son chemin; (*make progress*) **we're going ~s* at last** nous avançons enfin (*fig*), ça démarre* (*fig*); **I can't be in two ~s at once!*** je ne peux pas être dans deux endroits (différents) à la fois!

b (*specific spot*) lieu *m*, endroit *m*. **~ of amusement/ birth/death/ residence/work** lieu de distraction(s)/de naissance/de décès/de résidence/de travail; **~ of refuge** (lieu de) refuge *m*; **he is at his ~ of business** il est à son lieu de travail; **this building is a ~ of business** cet immeuble est occupé par des locaux commerciaux; (*Jur*) **fixed ~ of business** établissement *m* stable; **~ of worship** édifice religieux, lieu de culte; **the time and ~ of the crime** l'heure et le lieu du crime; **do you remember the ~ where we met?** te souviens-tu de l'endroit où nous nous sommes rencontrés?; (*Phon*) **~ of articulation** lieu *or* point *m* d'articulation; *see* **fortify, market, watering** *etc*.

c (*district, area*) endroit *m*, coin *m*; (*building*) endroit, bâtiment *m*, immeuble *m*; (*town*) endroit, ville *f*; (*village*) endroit, village *m*, localité *f*. **it's a small ~** (*village*) c'est un petit village; (*house*) c'est une petite maison; **it's just a little country ~** ce n'est qu'un petit village de campagne; **he has a ~ in the country** il a une maison *or* une résidence à la campagne; **the house is a vast great ~** la maison est immense; **the town is such a big ~ now that ...** la ville s'est tellement agrandie *or* étendue que ...; **we tried to find a native of the ~** nous avons essayé de trouver quelqu'un (qui soit originaire) du coin; **the train doesn't stop at that ~ any more** le train ne s'arrête plus là *or* à cet endroit; **his family is growing, he needs a bigger ~** sa famille s'agrandit, il lui faut quelque chose de plus grand *or* une maison plus grande; **his business is growing, he needs a bigger ~** son affaire s'agrandit, il lui faut quelque chose de plus grand *or* des locaux plus étendus; **we were at Anne's ~*** nous étions chez Anne; **come over to our ~*** venez à la maison *or* chez nous.

d (*in street names*) ≃ rue *f*. **Washington P~** rue de Washington.

e (*seat*) place *f*; (*at table*) place, couvert *m*. **a theatre with 2,000 ~s** un théâtre de 2.000 places; **are there any ~s left?** est-ce qu'il reste des places?; **keep a ~ for me** gardez-moi une place; (*in restaurant, theatre etc*) **is this ~ taken?** est-ce que cette place est prise? *or* occupée?; **to lay** *or* **set an extra ~ (at table)** mettre un couvert supplémentaire; *see* **change**.

f (*position, situation; circumstance; function*) place *f*; [*star, planet*] position *f*. **in ~ of** à la place de, au lieu de; **to take the ~ of sb/sth** remplacer qn/qch; **to take** *or* **fill sb's ~** remplacer qn; **out of ~** *object* déplacé; *remark* (*inopportune*) hors de propos, (*improper*) déplacé; **it looks out of ~ there** ça n'a pas l'air à sa place là-bas; **I feel rather out of ~ here** je ne me sens pas à ma place ici; **in ~** *object* à sa place; *remark* à propos; **put the book back in its ~** remets le livre à sa place; **it wasn't in its ~** ça n'était pas à sa place, ça avait été déplacé; **a ~ for everything and everything in its ~** une place pour chaque chose et chaque chose à sa place; (*Scol etc*) **he was not in his ~** il n'était pas à sa place (*lit*); (*fig*) **to put sb in his ~** remettre qn à sa place, reprendre qn; **that certainly put him in his ~!** ça l'a bien remis à sa place!; **to go back** *or* **fall back into ~** se remettre en place; (*fig*) **to fall** *or* **fit** *or* **click into ~** devenir clair; (*Scol*) **go back to your ~s** retournez à *or* reprenez vos places; **take your ~s for a quadrille** mettez-vous à *or* prenez vos places pour un quadrille; **(if I were) in your ~ ...** (si j'étais) à votre place ...; **to know one's ~** savoir se tenir à sa place; **it's not your ~ to criticize** ce n'est pas à vous de critiquer; **it's my ~ to tell him** c'est à moi de le lui dire; **can you find a ~ for this vase?** pouvez-vous trouver une place *or* un endroit où mettre ce vase?; **to give ~ to** céder la place à; **there's a ~ in this town for a good administrator** cette ville a besoin d'un bon administrateur, il manque à cette ville un bon administrateur.

g (*job, position, post, vacancy*) place *f*, situation *f*, poste *m*. **~s for 500 workers** des places *or* de l'emploi pour 500 ouvriers; **we have a ~ for a typist** nous avons une place pour une dactylo; **we have a ~ for a teacher** nous avons un poste pour un professeur; **he's looking for a ~ in publishing** il cherche une situation dans l'édition; **we will try to find a ~ for him** on va essayer de lui trouver une place *or* une situation, on va essayer de le caser* quelque part; **the school will offer 10 ~s next term** l'école disposera de 10 places le trimestre prochain; **this school must have a further 80 ~s** cette école a besoin de 80 places supplémentaires; (*Univ etc*) **I have got a ~ on the sociology course** j'ai été admis à faire sociologie.

h (*rank*) rang *m*, place *f*; (*in series*) place; (*in exam results*) place. **in the first ~** en premier lieu, premièrement, primo; **in the second ~** en second lieu, deuxièmement; **in the next ~** ensuite; **in the last ~** enfin; (*Math*) **to 5 decimal ~s, to 5 ~s of decimals** jusqu'à la 5e décimale; **Paul won the race with Robert in second ~** Paul a gagné la course et Robert s'est placé *or* a terminé second; **Robert took second ~ in the race** Robert a été second dans la course; (*Ftbl etc*) **the team was in third ~** l'équipe était placée troisième *or* était en troisième position; (*Brit Scol*) **~ in class** (*gen*) classement *m*, place; (*Brit*) **to get** *or* **take a high/low ~ in class** avoir un bon/mauvais classement, avoir une bonne/mauvaise place en classe; **he took second ~ in history/in the history exam** il a été deuxième en histoire/à l'examen d'histoire; (*Scol*) **he took first ~ in class last year** l'année dernière il a été (le) premier de sa classe; (*Racing*) **to back a horse for a ~** jouer un cheval placé; **to keep/lose one's ~ in the queue** garder/perdre sa place dans la queue; **people in high ~s** les gens haut placés *or* en haut lieu.

i (*Brit Parl*) **the other ~** l'autre Chambre (*utilisé par les députés de la Chambre des communes pour parler de la Chambre des Lords et inversement*).

2 comp ▸**place card** carte *f* marque-place ▸**place kick** (*Rugby*) coup de pied placé ▸**place mat** set *m*, napperon individuel ▸**place-name** nom *m* de lieu; (*as study, as group*) **place-names** toponymie *f* ▸**place setting** couvert *m*.

3 vt a (*put*) placer, mettre; *restrictions* imposer. **~ it on the table** mets-le *or* place-le *or* pose-le sur la table; **the picture is ~d rather high up** le tableau est placé un peu trop haut; **to ~ an advertisement in the paper** placer *or* mettre *or* passer une annonce dans le journal; **she ~d the matter in the hands of her solicitor** elle remit l'affaire entre les mains de son avocat; **to ~ the responsibility on sb** rendre qn responsable; **to ~ confidence in sb/sth** placer sa confiance en qn/qch; **to ~ trust in sb** faire confiance à qn; **he ~s good health among his greatest assets** il considère *or* place une robuste santé parmi ses meilleurs atouts.

b (*situate: gen pass*) placer, situer. **the house is well ~d** la maison est bien située; **he ~d his house high on the hill** il fit construire sa maison près du sommet de la colline; **the shop is awkwardly ~d** le magasin est mal situé *or* mal placé; **the town is ~d in the valley** la ville est située dans la vallée; (*Mil etc*) **they were well ~d to attack** ils étaient en bonne position *or* bien placés pour attaquer; (*fig*) **I am rather awkwardly ~d at the moment** je me trouve dans une situation assez délicate en ce moment; **he is well ~d to decide** il est bien placé pour décider; **we are better ~d than we were a month ago** notre situation est meilleure qu'il y a un mois.

c (*in exam*) placer, classer; (*in race*) placer. **he was ~d first in French** il s'est placé *or* classé premier en français; **he was ~d first in the race** il s'est placé premier dans la course; **he wasn't ~d in the race** il n'a pas été placé dans la course; **my horse wasn't ~d** mon cheval n'a pas été placé; (*Ftbl etc*) **our team is well ~d in the league** notre équipe a une bonne position dans le classement.

d (*Fin*) *money* placer, investir. **to ~ money at interest** placer de l'argent à intérêt; (*Comm*) **he ~d an order for wood with that firm** il a passé une commande de bois à cette firme; **to ~ a bet with sb** placer un pari chez qn; **to ~ a contract for machinery with a firm** passer un contrat d'achat avec une firme pour de l'outillage; (*Comm*) **these goods are difficult to ~** ces marchandises sont difficiles à placer; (*Comm*) **we are trying to ~ our surplus butter production** nous essayons de placer *or* d'écouler le surplus de notre production de beurre; **to ~ a book with a publisher** faire accepter un livre par un éditeur.

e (*appoint; find a job for*) placer, trouver une place *or* un emploi pour. **they ~d him in the accounts department** on l'a mis *or* placé à la comptabilité; **the agency is trying to ~ him with a building firm** l'agence essaie de lui trouver une place *or* de le placer dans une entreprise de construction.

f (*find home for*) placer.

g (*remember; identify*) se rappeler, se remettre. **I just can't ~ him at all** je n'arrive absolument pas à me le remettre *or* à le situer; **he ~d her at once** il la reconnut aussitôt, il se la rappela immédiatement; **to ~ a face** remettre un visage; **to ~ an accent** situer *or* reconnaître un accent.

4 vi (*US Racing*) être placé.

placebo [plə'siːbəʊ] n, pl ~s *or* ~es (*Med, fig*) placebo *m*.

placement ['pleɪsmənt] 1 n (*Fin*) placement *m*, investissement *m*; (*Univ etc: during studies*) stage *m*. 2 comp ▸**placement office** (*US Univ*) (*for career guidance*) centre *m* d'orientation; (*for jobs*) bureau *m* de placement pour étudiants ▸**placement test** (*US Scol etc*) examen *m* de niveau.

placenta [plə'sentə] n, pl ~s *or* **placentae** [plə'sentiː] placenta *m*.

placer ['pleɪsəʳ] n (*US Geol*) sable *m or* gravier *m* aurifère.

placid ['plæsɪd] adj *person, smile* placide, calme, serein; *waters* tranquille, calme.

placidity [plə'sɪdɪtɪ] n placidité *f*, calme *m*, tranquillité *f*.

placidly ['plæsɪdlɪ] adv avec placidité, avec calme, placidement.

placing ['pleɪsɪŋ] n [*money, funds*] placement *m*, investissement *m*; [*ball, players*] position *f*.

placket ['plækɪt] n double patte *f*.

plagal ['pleɪgəl] adj (*Mus*) plagal.

plagiarism ['pleɪdʒjərɪzəm] n plagiat *m*, démarquage *m*.

plagiarist ['pleɪdʒjərɪst] n plagiaire *mf*, démarqueur *m*, -euse *f*.

plagiarize ['pleɪdʒjəraɪz] vt plagier, démarquer.

plague [pleɪg] 1 n (*Med*) peste *f*; (*fig*) (*nuisance*) fléau *m*; (*annoying person*) plaie *f*. **to avoid/hate like the ~** fuir/haïr comme la peste; **what a ~ he is!*** c'est une vraie plaie!; *see* **bubonic** *etc*.

2 comp ▸**plague-ridden, plague-stricken** *region, household* frappé de la peste; *person* pestiféré.

3 vt [*person, fear etc*] tourmenter, harceler, tracasser. **to ~ sb with questions** harceler qn de questions; **they ~d me to tell them ...** ils m'ont cassé les pieds* pour que je leur dise ...; **~d with** (*doubts, fears, remorse*) rongé par; **we were ~d with mosquitoes** les moustiques nous ont rendu la vie impossible; **the place was ~d with flies** le coin était infesté de mouches; **to ~ the life out of sb** rendre la vie impossible à qn.

plaguey*†† ['pleɪgɪ] adj fâcheux, assommant.

plaice [pleɪs] n, pl ~ *or* ~s carrelet *m*, plie *f*.

plaid [plæd] 1 n (*NonC: cloth, pattern*) tissu écossais; (*over shoulder*) plaid *m*. 2 adj (en tissu) écossais.

plain [pleɪn] 1 adj a (*obvious*) clair, évident. **the path is quite ~** la voie est clairement tracée; **in ~ view** à la vue de tous; **it must be ~ to everyone that ...** il doit être clair pour tout le monde que ..., il ne doit échapper à personne que ...; **it's as ~ as a pikestaff** *or* **as the nose on your face*** c'est clair comme le jour *or* comme de l'eau de roche; **a ~ case of jealousy** un cas manifeste *or* évident de jalousie; **I must make it ~ that ...** vous devez bien comprendre que ...; **he made his feelings ~** il ne cacha pas ce qu'il ressentait *or* pensait; **to make sth ~ to sb** faire comprendre qch à qn.

b (*unambiguous*) clair, franc (*f* franche); *statement, assessment* clair. **~ talk, ~ speaking** (*gen*) propos *mpl* sans équivoque; **I like ~ speaking** j'aime le franc-parler *or* la franchise; **to be a ~ speaker** avoir son franc-parler; **to use ~ language** parler sans ambages, appeler les choses par leur nom; **in ~ words** *or* **in ~ English, I think you made a mistake** je vous le dis *or* pour vous le dire carrément, je pense que vous vous êtes trompé; **I explained it all in ~ words** *or* **in ~ English** j'ai tout expliqué très clairement; **I gave him a ~ answer** je lui ai répondu carrément *or* sans détours *or* sans ambages; **~ dealing(s)** procédés *mpl* honnêtes; **the ~ truth of the matter is (that)** ... à dire vrai ..., à la vérité ...; **let me be quite ~ with you** je serai franc avec vous; **do I make myself ~ ?** est-ce que je me fais bien comprendre?

c (*sheer, utter*) pur, tout pur, pur et simple. **it's ~ folly** *or* **madness** c'est pure folie, c'est de la folie toute pure.

d (*simple; unadorned*) *dress, style, diet, food* simple; (*in one colour*) *fabric, suit, colour* uni. **~ living** mode *m* de vie tout simple *or* sans luxe. **~ cooking** cuisine *f* bourgeoise; **~ cook** cuisinière *f*; **I'm a ~ man** je suis un homme tout simple, je ne suis pas un homme compliqué; **they used to be called ~ Smith** dans le temps ils s'appelaient Smith tout court; (*Knitting*) **~ stitch** maille *f* à l'endroit; (*Knitting*) **one ~, one purl** une maille à l'endroit, une maille à l'envers; **a row of ~, a ~ row** un rang à l'endroit; **~ chocolate** chocolat *m* amer *or* noir *or* à croquer; **to send under ~ cover** envoyer sous pli discret; **~ flour** farine *f* (sans levure); **~ paper** (*not lined*) papier *m* uni; (*fig*) **it's ~ sailing from now on** maintenant ça va aller comme sur des roulettes.

e (*not pretty*) sans beauté, quelconque, ordinaire (*pej*). **she's very ~** elle a un visage ingrat, elle n'a rien d'une beauté; **she's rather a ~ Jane*** ce n'est pas une Vénus.

2 adv a (*clearly*) **I told him quite ~ what I thought of him** je lui ai dit franchement *or* carrément *or* sans ambages ce que je pensais de lui; **I can't put it ~er than this** je ne peux pas m'exprimer plus clairement que cela *or* en termes plus explicites.

b (**: in truth*) tout bonnement. **she's just ~ shy** elle est tout bonnement timide; **it's just ~ wrong** c'est tout simplement faux.

3 n plaine *f*. (*US*) **the (Great) P~s** les Prairies *fpl*, la Grande Prairie.

4 comp ▸**plain chant** plain-chant *m* ▸**plain clothes: in plain clothes** en civil; **a plain-clothes (police)man** un policier en civil; (*Police*) **plain-clothes officers** personnel *m* en civil ▸**plainsman** habitant *m* de la plaine ▸**plainsong** = **plain chant** ▸**plain-spoken** qui a son franc-parler, qui appelle les choses par leur nom.

plainly ['pleɪnlɪ] adv a (*obviously*) clairement, manifestement; (*unambiguously*) carrément, sans détours. **there has ~ been a mistake** il y a eu manifestement erreur, il est clair qu'il y a eu erreur; **he explained it ~** il l'a expliqué clairement *or* en termes clairs; **I can see the answer ~** la réponse saute aux yeux; **I remember it ~** je m'en souviens distinctement *or* clairement; **to speak ~ to sb** parler à qn sans détours *or* sans ambages. b (*simply*) *dress* simplement, sobrement, sans recherche.

plainness ['pleɪnnɪs] n (*simplicity*) simplicité *f*, sobriété *f*; (*lack of beauty*) manque *m* de beauté.

plaintiff ['pleɪntɪf] n (*Jur*) demandeur *m*, -eresse *f*, plaignant(e) *m(f)*.

plaintive ['pleɪntɪv] adj *voice* plaintif.

plaintively ['pleɪntɪvlɪ] adv plaintivement, d'un ton plaintif.

plait [plæt] 1 n [*hair*] natte *f*, tresse *f*. **she wears her hair in ~s** elle porte des tresses. 2 vt *hair, string* natter, tresser; *basket, wicker* tresser; *straw* ourdir.

plan [plæn] 1 n a (*drawing, map*) [*building, estate, district etc*] plan *m*; *see* **seating**.

b (*Econ, Pol, gen: project*) plan *m*, projet *m*. **~ of action** plan d'action; **~ of campaign** plan de campagne; (*Pol*) **five-year ~** plan de cinq ans, plan quinquennal; **development ~** plan *or* projet de développement; **to draw up a ~** dresser un plan; **everything is going according to ~** tout se passe selon les prévisions *or* comme prévu; **to make ~s** faire des projets; **to upset** *or* **spoil sb's ~s** déranger les projets de qn; **to change one's ~s** changer d'idée, prendre d'autres dispositions; **the best ~ would be to leave tomorrow** le mieux serait de partir demain; **the ~ is to come back here after the show** notre idée est *or* nous prévoyons de revenir ici après le spectacle; **what ~s have you for the holiday/for your son?** quels sont vos projets pour les vacances/pour votre fils?; **I haven't any particular ~s** je n'ai aucun projet précis; **have you got any ~s for tonight?** est-ce que vous avez prévu quelque chose pour ce soir?

2 vt a (*esp Econ, Pol, Ind, Comm*) *research, project, enterprise* (*devise and work out*) élaborer, préparer; (*devise and schedule*) planifier. **to ~ the future of an industry** planifier l'avenir d'une industrie; *see also* **planned** *and* **obsolescence** *etc*.

b (*make plans for*) *house, estate, garden etc* concevoir, dresser les plans de; *programme, holiday, journey, crime* préparer à l'avance, organiser; *essay* faire le plan de; (*Mil*) *campaign, attack* organiser. **who ~ned the house/garden?** qui a dressé les plans de la maison/du jardin?; **well-~ned house** maison bien conçue; **they ~ned the attack together** ils ont concerté l'attaque; **he has got it all ~ned** il a tout prévu, il a pensé à tout; **that wasn't ~ned** cela n'était pas prévu; **we shall go on as ~ned** nous continuerons comme prévu; **couples can now ~ their families** les couples peuvent maintenant fixer le rythme des naissances dans leur foyer; *see also* **planned**.

c (*intend*) *visit, holiday* projeter. **to ~ to do, to ~ on doing** projeter de *or* se proposer de *or* avoir l'intention de faire, former *or* concevoir le projet de faire (*frm*); **how long do you ~ to be away for?** combien de temps avez-vous l'intention de vous absenter? *or* pensez-vous être absent?; **will you stay for a while? — I wasn't ~ning to** resterez-vous un peu? — ce n'était pas dans mes intentions.

3 vi faire des projets. **one has to ~ months ahead** il faut s'y prendre des mois à l'avance; **we are ~ning for the future/the holidays** *etc* nous faisons des projets *or* nous prenons nos dispositions pour l'avenir/les vacances *etc;* **we didn't ~ for such a large number of visitors** nous n'avions pas prévu un si grand nombre de visiteurs.

►**plan out** vt sep préparer *or* organiser dans tous les détails.

planchette [plɑːn'ʃet] n planchette *f* (*spiritisme*).

plane¹ [pleɪn] n (abbr of **aeroplane** *or* **airplane**) avion *m*. **by ~** par avion; **~loads of tourists** des cargaisons de touristes.

plane² [pleɪn] (*Carpentry*) 1 n rabot *m*. 2 vt (*also* **~ down**) raboter.

plane³ [pleɪn] n (*also* **~ tree**) platane *m*.

plane⁴ [pleɪn] 1 n (*Archit, Art, Math etc*) plan *m*; (*fig*) plan, niveau *m*. **horizontal ~** plan horizontal; (*fig*) **on the same ~ as** sur le même plan que, au même niveau que; **he seems to exist on another ~ altogether** il semble vivre dans un autre monde *or* un autre univers. 2 adj plan, uni, plat; (*Math*) plan. **~ geometry** géométrie plane.

plane⁵ [pleɪn] vi *[bird, glider, boat]* planer; *[car]* faire de l'aquaplanage.

►**plane down** vi *[bird, glider]* descendre en vol plané.

planet ['plænɪt] n planète *f*.

planetarium [ˌplænɪ'tɛərɪəm] n, pl **~s** *or* **planetaria** [ˌplænɪ'tɛərɪə] planétarium *m*.

planetary ['plænɪtərɪ] adj planétaire.

planetology [ˌplænɪ'tɒlədʒɪ] n planétologie *f*.

plangent ['plændʒənt] adj (*liter*) retentissant.

planisphere ['plænɪsfɪəʳ] n *[world]* planisphère *m*; *[stars]* planisphère céleste.

plank [plæŋk] 1 n planche *f*; (*fig Pol*) article *m* *or* point *m* (d'un programme politique *or* électoral); *see* **walk.** 2 vt (*: *also* **~ down**) déposer brusquement, planter.

planking ['plæŋkɪŋ] n (*NonC*) planchéiage *m*; (*Naut*) planches *fpl*, bordages *mpl*, revêtement *m*.

plankton ['plæŋktən] n plancton *m*.

planned ['plænd] adj a (*Econ, Pol, Ind, Comm*) planifié. **~ economy** économie planifiée; **~ parenthood** contrôle *m* *or* régulation *f* des naissances. b *crime etc* prémédité. **the murder was ~** le meurtre était prémédité. c (*proposed*) prévu.

planner ['plænəʳ] n (*Econ*) planificateur *m*, -trice *f*; *see* **town.**

planning ['plænɪŋ] 1 n a (*Ind, Econ, Pol, Comm: see* **plan 2a**) élaboration *f*; planification *f*. **the ~ of the project took 3 years** l'élaboration du projet a duré 3 ans; **department of ~** service *m* de (la) planification; **skilled in ~** qui a le sens de la planification.

b (*organizing*) organisation *f*. **we must do some ~ for the holidays** il faut dresser des plans pour les vacances; *see* **family, town.**

2 comp ►**planning board, planning committee** (*Econ, Ind*) service *m* *or* bureau *m* de planification; (*in local government*) ≈ service *m* de l'urbanisme ►**planning permission** permis *m* de construire ►**planning stage: it's still at the planning stage** c'est encore à l'état d'ébauche.

plant [plɑːnt] 1 n a (*Bot*) plante *f*.

b (*Ind, Tech*) (*NonC: machinery, equipment*) matériel *m*, biens *mpl* d'équipement; (*fixed*) installation *f*; (*NonC: equipment and buildings*) bâtiments *mpl* et matériel; (*factory*) usine *f*, fabrique *f*. **the heating ~** l'installation de chauffage; **he had to hire the ~ to do it** il a dû louer le matériel *or* l'équipement pour le faire; **heavy ~** engins *mpl*; **"heavy ~ crossing"** "sortie d'engins"; **a steel ~** une aciérie; *see* **nuclear.**

c (*: *frame-up*) coup monté; (*person put into suspect organization*) agent *m* infiltré.

2 comp ►**plant breeder** obtenteur *m* de nouveauté(s) végétale(s), phytogénéticien(ne) *m(f)* ►**plant-hire firm** (*Ind, Tech*) entreprise *f* de location de matériel ►**the plant kingdom** (*Bot*) le règne végétal ►**plant life** flore *f* ►**plant louse** puceron *m* ►**plant pot** pot *m* (de fleurs).

3 vt a *seeds, plants, bulbs* planter; *field etc* planter (*with* en). **a field ~ed with wheat** un champ planté de *or* en blé.

b (*place*) *flag, stick etc* planter, enfoncer; *box, chair, suitcase etc* planter, camper; *people, colonists etc* établir, installer; *spy, informer* infiltrer; *blow* appliquer, envoyer, flanquer*; *kiss* planter; *idea* implanter (*in sb's head* dans la tête de qn). **he ~ed himself in the middle of the road** il se planta *or* se campa au milieu de la route; (*fig*) **to ~ a revolver on sb** cacher un revolver sur qn (pour le faire incriminer).

►**plant down** vt sep planter, camper.

►**plant out** vt sep *seedlings* repiquer.

Plantagenet [plæn'tædʒɪnɪt] n Plantagenêt.

plantain ['plæntɪn] n a (*plant*) plantain *m*. b (*fruit*) banane *f* plantain.

plantar ['plæntəʳ] adj plantaire.

plantation [plæn'teɪʃən] n (*all senses*) plantation *f*. **coffee/rubber ~** plantation de café/de caoutchouc.

planter ['plɑːntəʳ] n (*person*) planteur *m*; (*machine*) planteuse *f*; (*plant pot*) pot *m*; (*bigger, decorative*) jardinière *f*. **coffee/rubber ~** planteur de café/de caoutchouc.

planting ['plɑːntɪŋ] n plantations *fpl*. **autumn ~** les plantations d'automne.

plaque [plæk] n (*gen*) plaque *f*; (*on teeth*) plaque *f* dentaire.

plash [plæʃ] 1 n *[waves]* clapotis *m*, clapotement *m*; *[object falling into water]* floc *m*. 2 vi clapoter; faire floc *or* flac.

plasm ['plæzəm] n protoplasme *m*.

plasma ['plæzmə] n plasma *m*; *see* **blood.**

plaster ['plɑːstəʳ] 1 n a (*Constr*) plâtre *m*.

b (*Med: NonC: for broken bones*) plâtre *m*. **~ of Paris** plâtre de moulage; **he had his leg in ~** il avait la jambe dans le plâtre *or* la jambe plâtrée.

c (*Brit Med: also* **adhesive** *or* **sticking ~**) sparadrap *m*. **a (piece of) ~** un pansement adhésif; *see* **mustard.**

2 comp *mould etc* de *or* en plâtre ►**plasterboard** (*NonC*) Placoplâtre ® *f* ►**plaster cast** (*Med*) plâtre *m*; (*Sculp*) moule *m* (en plâtre) ►**plaster work** (*NonC: Constr*) plâtre(s) *m(pl)*.

3 vt a (*Constr, Med*) plâtrer; (*fig: cover*) couvrir (*with* de). (*fig*) **~ed with** couvert de; **to ~ a wall with posters, to ~ posters on** *or* **over a wall** couvrir *or* tapisser un mur d'affiches; **the story was ~ed all over the front page/all over the newspapers** l'histoire était placardée sur toute la première page/s'étalait à la une de tous les journaux; **his fringe was ~ed to his forehead** sa frange était plaquée sur son front.

b (*Mil *: with bombs, shells*) pilonner; (‡: *bash up*) tabasser‡, battre comme plâtre*.

►**plaster down** vt: **to plaster one's hair down** se plaquer les cheveux.

►**plaster on*** vt sep *butter, hair cream, make-up etc* étaler *or* mettre une couche épaisse de.

►**plaster over, plaster up** vt sep *crack, hole* boucher.

plastered ['plɑːstəd] adj (‡: *drunk*) beurré‡, bourré‡.

plasterer ['plɑːstərəʳ] n plâtrier *m*.

plastering ['plɑːstərɪŋ] n (*Constr*) plâtrage *m*.

plastic ['plæstɪk] 1 n (*substance*) plastique *m*, matière *f* plastique; (*: *credit cards*) = **plastic money. ~s** matières *fpl* plastiques.

2 adj a (*made of ~*) *toy, box, dish* en (matière) plastique. **~ bag** sac *m* en plastique; **~ bullet** balle *f* de plastique; **~ foam** mousse *f* de plastique; (*fig*) **~ money** carte(s) *f(pl)* de crédit, monnaie *f* électronique.

b (*explosive*) **~ bomb** bombe *f* au plastic; **~ bomb attack** attentat *m* au plastic, plasticage *m*; **~ explosive** plastic *m*.

c (*: *fig, pej*) *food, coffee etc* synthétique.

d (*Art*) plastique; (*flexible*) plastique, malléable. **~ surgeon** spécialiste *mf* de chirurgie esthétique; **~ surgery** chirurgie *f* esthétique.

3 comp ►**plastics industry** industrie *f* (des) plastique(s).

plasticated ['plæstɪˌkeɪtɪd] adj (*lit*) plastifié; (*fig*) synthétique, artificiel.

plasticine ['plæstɪsiːn] n ® (*NonC*) pâte *f* à modeler.

plasticity [plæs'tɪsɪtɪ] n plasticité *f*.

Plate [pleɪt] n: **the River ~** le Rio de la Plata.

plate [pleɪt] 1 n a assiette *f*; (*platter*) plat *m*; (*in church*) plateau *m* de quête. **a ~ of soup** une assiette de soupe; (*fig*) **he wants to be handed everything on a ~** il voudrait qu'on lui apporte (*subj*) tout sur un plateau *or* sur un plat d'argent; (*fig*) **to have a lot on one's ~*** avoir du pain sur la planche; (*fig*) **he's got too much on his ~ already*** il ne sait déjà plus où donner de la tête; *see* **dinner, soup, tea** *etc.*

b (*NonC*) (*gold dishes*) orfèvrerie *f*, vaisselle *f* d'or; (*silver dishes*) argenterie *f*, vaisselle d'argent.

c (*flat metal*) plaque *f*; (*metal coating*) placage *m*; (*metal thus coated*) plaqué *m*. **it's not silver, it's only ~** ce n'est pas de l'argent massif, ce n'est que du plaqué.

d (*on wall, door; in battery, armour*) plaque *f*; (*Aut: pressure ~*) plateau *m* d'embrayage; (*Aut: number ~*) plaque d'immatriculation, plaque minéralogique; *see* **clutch, hot, number.**

e (*Geol: of earth*) plaque *f*.

f (*Phot*) plaque *f*; (*Typ*) cliché *m*; (*for engraving*) planche *f*; (*illustration: in book*) gravure *f*. (*in book*) **full-page ~** gravure hors-texte, planche; *see* **fashion.**

g (*Dentistry*) dentier *m*.

h (*Racing: prize, race*) coupe *f*.

i (*Sci*) (*for microscope*) lamelle *f*.

2 comp ►**plate armour** (*NonC*) blindage *m* ►**plate glass** (*NonC*) verre *m* à vitre très épais, verre double *or* triple; **plate-glass window** baie vitrée ►**platelayer** (*Brit Rail*) poseur *m* de rails ►**plate rack** (*for drying*) égouttoir *m*; (*for storing*) range-assiettes *m inv* ►**plate tectonics** (*Geol*) tectonique *f* des plaques ►**plate warmer** chauffe-assiettes *m inv*.

3 vt a (*with metal*) plaquer; (*with gold*) dorer; (*with silver*) argenter; (*with nickel*) nickeler; *see* **armour** *etc.*

b *ship etc* blinder.

plateau ['plætəʊ] 1 n, pl **~s** *or* **~x** ['plætəʊz] (*Geog*) plateau *m*; (*fig*) palier *m*. 2 vi atteindre un palier, se stabiliser.

plateful ['pleɪtfʊl] n assiettée *f*, assiette *f*.

platelet ['pleɪtlɪt] n plaquette *f*.

platen ['plætən] n *[printing press]* platine *f*; *[typewriter]* rouleau *m*.

platform ['plætfɔːm] 1 n a *(on oil rig, bus (Brit), scales, in scaffolding etc)* plate-forme *f*; *(for band, in hall)* estrade *f*; *(at meeting etc)* tribune *f*; *(Brit Rail)* quai *m*; *(fig Pol)* plate-forme (électorale). *(Brit Rail)* ~ **(number) six** quai (numéro) six; **he was on the ~ at the last meeting** il était sur l'estrade *or* il était à la tribune (d'honneur) lors de la dernière réunion; *see* **diving.** b *(shoes)* ~* = **platform soles***; *see* **2.** 2 comp ▸**the platform party** *(at meeting)* la tribune ▸**platform scales** (balance *f* à) bascule *f* ▸**platform(-soled) shoes, platform soles*** chaussures *fpl* à semelles compensées ▸**platform ticket** *(Brit Rail)* billet *m* de quai.

plating ['pleɪtɪŋ] n *(see* **plate 3***)* placage *m*; dorage *m*, dorure *f*; argentage *m*, argenture *f*; nickelage *m*; blindage *m*; *see* **armour** *etc.*

platinum ['plætɪnəm] 1 n *(NonC)* platine *m*. 2 comp *jewellery* en *or* de platine ▸**platinum blonde** *(colour)* blonde *f* platinée; **she's/he's a platinum blonde/blond** elle/il est blonde/blond platine; **platinum blond(e) hair** cheveux *mpl* platinés *or* blond platiné ▸**platinum disc** *(award)* disque *m* de platine.

platitude ['plætɪtjuːd] n platitude *f*, lieu commun.

platitudinize [,plætɪ'tjuːdɪnaɪz] vi débiter des platitudes *or* des lieux communs.

platitudinous [,plætɪ'tjuːdɪnəs] adj banal, d'une grande platitude, rebattu.

Plato ['pleɪtəʊ] n Platon *m*.

Platonic [plə'tɒnɪk] adj a *philosophy* platonicien. b p~ *relationship, love* platonique.

Platonism ['pleɪtənɪzəm] n platonisme *m*.

Platonist ['pleɪtənɪst] adj, n platonicien(ne) *m(f)*.

platoon [plə'tuːn] n *(Mil)* section *f*; *[policemen, firemen etc]* peloton *m*. *(US Mil)* ~ **sergeant** adjudant *m*.

platter ['plætə^r] n a *(dish)* plat *m*. *(US fig: easily)* **on a ~*** sur un plateau (d'argent). b *(US* ‡*: record)* disque *m*.

platypus ['plætɪpəs] n ornithorynque *m*.

plaudits ['plɔːdɪts] npl applaudissements *mpl*, acclamations *fpl*, ovations *fpl*.

plausibility [,plɔːzə'bɪlɪtɪ] n *[argument, excuse]* plausibilité *f*. **his ~** le fait qu'il est *(or* était *etc)* si convaincant.

plausible ['plɔːzəbl] adj *argument, excuse* plausible, vraisemblable; *person* convaincant.

plausibly ['plɔːzəblɪ] adv plausiblement, d'une manière plausible *or* convaincante.

play [pleɪ] 1 n a *(NonC: amusement)* jeu *m*, divertissement *m*, amusement *m*. **the children were at ~** les enfants jouaient *or* s'amusaient; **to say sth in ~** dire qch par jeu *or* par plaisanterie; **a ~ on words** un jeu de mots, un calembour; *(fig)* **the ~ of light on water** le jeu de la lumière sur l'eau; *see* **child.**

b *(Sport)* jeu *m*. **there was some good ~ in the second half** il y a eu du beau jeu à la deuxième mi-temps; **that was a clever piece of ~** c'était finement *or* astucieusement joué; **ball in/out of ~** ballon *or* balle en/hors jeu; **~ starts at 11 o'clock** le(s) match(s) commence(nt) à 11 heures; *(fig)* **to make a ~ for sth** tout faire pour avoir *or* obtenir qch; **he made a ~ for her** il lui a fait des avances; *(fig)* **to bring** *or* **call sth into ~** mettre *or* faire entrer qch en jeu; *(fig)* **to come into ~** entrer en jeu; *(fig)* **to make great ~ with sth** faire grand cas de qch, faire tout un plat* de qch; *see* **fair¹, foul** *etc.*

c *(NonC: Tech etc: movement, scope)* jeu *m*. **there's too much ~ in the clutch** il y a trop de jeu dans l'embrayage; *(fig)* **to give full** *or* **free ~ to one's imagination/emotions** donner libre cours à son imagination/à ses émotions; *(fig)* **to give no ~ to sth** ne pas laisser de place à qch.

d *(Theat)* pièce *f* (de théâtre). **the ~s of Molière** les pièces *or* le théâtre de Molière; **radio ~** pièce radiophonique; **television ~** dramatique *f*; **to go to (see) a ~** aller au théâtre, aller voir une pièce; **I've seen the film, but I haven't seen the ~** je l'ai vu au cinéma, mais pas au théâtre *or* à la scène, j'ai vu le film, mais pas la pièce; **the ~ ends at 10.30** la représentation se termine à 10h 30; **he's in a ~ by Pinter** il joue dans une pièce de Pinter.

e *(interaction) [passions, personalities etc]* jeu *m*; *[factors]* concours *m*.

2 comp ▸**playact** jouer la comédie, faire du théâtre ▸**playacting:** *(fig)* **it's only playacting** c'est de la (pure) comédie *or* du cinéma* ▸**playactor:** *(fig)* **he's a playactor** il est comédien, il joue continuellement la comédie ▸**playback** *(Sound Recording)* lecture *f* ▸**playbill** affiche *f* (de théâtre); *(US Theat)* **Playbill** ® programme *m* ▸**play box** coffre *m* à jouets ▸**playboy** playboy *m* ▸**play-by-play** *account etc (Sport)* suivi; *(fig)* circonstancié ▸**play clothes** vêtements *mpl* qui ne craignent rien *(pour jouer)* ▸**playfellow**† = **playmate** ▸**playgoer** amateur *m* de théâtre; **he is a regular playgoer** il va régulièrement au théâtre ▸**playground** cour *f* de récréation ▸**playgroup** ≈ garderie *f* ▸**playhouse** *(Theat)* théâtre *m*; *(for children)* maison *f* (pliante) ▸**playmate** (petit(e)) camarade *mf*, (petit) copain *m*, (petite) copine *f* ▸**play-off** *(Sport) (after a tie)* belle *f*; *(US: for championship)* finale *f* de coupe *or* de championnat ▸**playpen** parc *m* (pour petits enfants) ▸**play reading** lecture *f* d'une pièce (de théâtre) ▸**playroom** salle *f* de jeux *(pour enfants)* ▸**playschool** = **playgroup** ▸**plaything** *(lit, fig)* jouet *m* ▸**playtime** *(Scol)* récréation *f* ▸**playwright** dramaturge *m*, auteur *m* dramatique.

3 vt a *game, cards* jouer à; *card, chesspiece* jouer; *opponent, opposing team* jouer contre. **to ~ football/bridge/chess** jouer au football/au bridge/aux échecs; **will you ~ tennis with me?** voulez-vous faire une partie de tennis avec moi?; *(Sport)* **15 ~s 12** 15 à 12; **I'll ~ you for the drinks** jouons la tournée; **England are ~ing Scotland on Saturday** l'Angleterre joue contre *or* rencontre l'Écosse samedi; **England will be ~ing Smith (in the team)** l'Angleterre a sélectionné Smith (pour l'équipe); **to ~ a match against sb** disputer un match avec qn; **the match will be ~ed on Saturday** le match aura lieu samedi; **to ~ centre-forward** *etc* jouer avant-centre *etc;* **to ~ the game** *(Sport etc)* jouer franc jeu, jouer selon les règles; *(fig)* jouer le jeu, être loyal; **don't ~ games with me!** ne me faites pas marcher!, ne vous moquez pas de moi!; *(fig)* **he's ~ing a safe game** il ne prend pas de risques; *(fig)* **to ~ (it) safe** ne prendre aucun risque; **the boys were ~ing soldiers** les garçons jouaient aux soldats; *(Ftbl)* **to ~ the ball** jouer le ballon; *(Tennis)* **he ~ed the ball into the net** il mit *or* envoya la balle dans le filet; *(fig)* **to ~ ball with sb** coopérer avec qn; **he won't ~ ball** il refuse de jouer le jeu; *(Cards)* **to ~ hearts/trumps** jouer cœur/atout; **he ~ed a heart** il a joué (un) cœur; **he ~ed his ace** *(lit)* il a joué son as; *(fig)* il a joué sa carte maîtresse; *(fig)* **to ~ one's cards well** *or* **right** bien jouer son jeu; **to ~ a fish** fatiguer un poisson; *(St Ex)* **to ~ the market** jouer à la Bourse; *(fig)* **to ~ the field*** jouer sur plusieurs tableaux; *(fig)* **to ~ both ends against the middle*** jouer les uns contre les autres; *(fig)* **to ~ it cool*** garder son sang-froid, ne pas s'énerver; **to ~ a joke** *or* **trick on sb** jouer un tour à qn, faire une farce à qn; **my eyesight is ~ing tricks with** *or* **on me** ma vue me joue des tours; **his memory is ~ing him tricks** sa mémoire lui joue des tours; *(liter)* **to ~ sb false, to ~ false with sb** agir déloyalement avec qn; *see* **cat, Harry, truant, waiting** *etc.*

b *(Theat etc) part* jouer, interpréter; *play* jouer, présenter, donner. **they ~ed it as a comedy** ils en ont donné une interprétation comique, ils l'ont joué en comédie; **we ~ed Brighton last week** nous avons joué à Brighton la semaine dernière; **let's ~ it for laughs*** jouons-le en farce; **he ~ed (the part of) Macbeth** il a joué *or* il a incarné Macbeth; **he ~ed Macbeth as a well-meaning fool** il a fait de Macbeth un sot plein de bonnes intentions; **what did you ~ in "Macbeth"?** quel rôle jouiez-vous *or* interprétiez-vous dans "Macbeth"?; *(lit, fig)* **to ~ one's part well** bien jouer; *(fig)* **he was only ~ing a part** il jouait la comédie; *(fig)* **to ~ a part in sth** *[person]* prendre part à qch, contribuer à qch; *[quality, object]* contribuer à qch; *(fig)* **he ~ed no part in it** il n'y était pour rien; **to ~ the fool** faire l'imbécile; **it ~ed the devil*** *or* **merry hell* with our plans** ça a chamboulé* *or* flanqué en l'air* nos projets.

c *(Mus) instrument* jouer de; *note, tune, concerto* jouer; *record* passer, jouer*. **to ~ the piano** jouer du piano; **they were ~ing Beethoven** ils jouaient du Beethoven; **piece to be ~ed on two pianos** morceau exécuté *or* se jouant sur deux pianos; *see* **ear¹, second¹.**

d *(direct) hose, searchlight* diriger *(on, onto* sur*)*. **they ~ed the searchlights over the front of the building** ils ont promené les projecteurs sur la façade du bâtiment.

4 vi a *(gen, Cards, Sport etc)* jouer; *[lambs etc]* s'ébattre, folâtrer. **to ~ at chess** jouer aux échecs; **it's you** *or* **your turn to ~** c'est votre tour de jouer; **is Paul coming out to ~?** est-ce que Paul vient jouer? *or* s'amuser?; **what are you doing? — just ~ing** que faites-vous? — rien, on s'amuse; **there was music ~ing** il y avait de la musique; *(fig)* **he just ~s at being a soldier** il ne prend pas au sérieux son métier de soldat; **the boys were ~ing at soldiers** les garçons jouaient aux soldats; **the little girl was ~ing at being a lady** la petite fille jouait à la dame; **they were ~ing with a gun** ils jouaient avec un fusil; *(Golf)* **he ~ed into the trees** il envoya sa balle dans les arbres; **to ~ for money/matches** jouer de l'argent/des allumettes; *(lit, fig)* **to ~ for high stakes** jouer gros jeu; **to ~ fair** *(Sport etc)* jouer franc jeu, jouer selon les règles; *(fig)* jouer le jeu, être loyal.

b *(fig)* **to ~ with** *object, pencil etc* jouer avec; **to ~ with o.s.*** se masturber; **to ~ with fire/words** jouer avec le feu/les mots; **to ~ for time** essayer de gagner du temps; **how much time/money do we have to ~ with?*** combien de temps/d'argent avons-nous?; **to ~ hard to get*** se faire désirer; **to ~ fast and loose with sb** se jouer de qn, traiter qn à la légère; **to ~ into sb's hands** faire le jeu de qn, se faire avoir* par qn; **it's not a question to be ~ed with** ce n'est pas une question qui se traite à la légère; **he's not a man to be ~ed with** ce n'est pas un homme avec qui plaisanter; **he's just ~ing with you** il vous fait marcher; **to ~ with an idea** caresser une idée.

c *[light, fountain]* jouer *(on* sur*)*. **a smile ~ed on** *or* **over his lips** un sourire s'ébauchait sur ses lèvres.

d *(Mus) [person, organ, orchestra]* jouer. **to ~ on the piano** jouer du piano; **will you ~ for us?** *(perform)* voulez-vous nous jouer quelque chose *or* nous faire un peu de musique?; *(accompany)* voulez-vous nous accompagner?; *see* **ear¹.**

e *(Theat etc)* jouer. **he ~ed in a film with Greta Garbo** il a joué dans un film avec Greta Garbo; **we have ~ed all over the South** nous avons fait une tournée dans le sud; *(fig)* **to ~ dead** faire le mort; *see* **gallery.**

►**play about** vi a *[children etc]* jouer, s'amuser. b (*toy, fiddle*) jouer, s'amuser (*with* avec). (*to make sth work etc*) **to play about with sth** tourner qch dans tous les sens; **he was playing about with the gun when it went off** il s'amusait avec *or* il jouait avec *or* il tripotait le fusil quand le coup est parti; **stop playing about with that watch** arrête de tripoter cette montre, laisse cette montre tranquille; **he's just playing about with you*** il vous fait marcher.

►**play along** 1 vi (*fig*) **to play along with sb** entrer dans le jeu de qn. 2 vt sep (*fig*) **to play sb along** tenir qn en haleine.

►**play around** vi a **to play around with an idea** retourner une idée dans sa tête. b (*: *sleep around*) coucher à droite et à gauche. c = **play about**.

►**play back** 1 vt sep *tape* (ré)écouter, repasser. 2 **play back** n *see* **play 2**.

►**play down** vt sep *decision, effect* minimiser; *situation, attitude* dédramatiser; *opinion, dissent* mettre une sourdine à; *language* atténuer; *policy* mettre en sourdine.

►**play in** vt sep a (*fig*) **to play o.s. in** prendre la température* (*fig*), se faire la main*. b **the band played the procession in** le défilé entra aux sons de la fanfare.

►**play off** 1 vt sep a **to play off A against B** monter A contre B (pour en tirer profit). b (*Sport*) **to play a match off** jouer la belle. 2 **play-off** n *see* **play 2**.

►**play on** vt fus *sb's emotions, credulity, good nature* jouer sur, miser sur. **to play on words** jouer sur les mots, faire des calembours; **the noise began to play on her nerves** le bruit commençait à l'agacer *or* à lui taper sur les nerfs*.

►**play out** vt sep a **the band played the procession out** le défilé sortit aux sons de la fanfare. b **to be played out*** *[person]* être épuisé *or* éreinté* *or* vanné*; *[argument]* être périmé, avoir fait son temps. c *fantasies, roles, scenes* jouer.

►**play over, play through** vt sep *piece of music* jouer.

►**play up** 1 vi a (*Sport*) bien jouer. **play up!** allez-y!
b (*Brit* *: *give trouble*) **the engine is playing up** le moteur fait des siennes *or* ne tourne pas rond; **his rheumatism/his leg is playing up** son rhumatisme/sa jambe le tracasse; **the children have been playing up all day** les enfants ont été insupportables *or* ont fait des leurs toute la journée.
c (*: *curry favour with*) **to play up to sb** chercher à se faire bien voir de qn, faire de la lèche à qn‡.
2 vt sep a **his rheumatism/his leg is playing him up** son rhumatisme/sa jambe le tracasse; **that boy plays his father up** ce garçon en fait voir à son père.
b (*magnify importance of*) insister sur (l'importance de).

►**play upon** vt fus = **play on**.

player ['pleɪəʳ] 1 n a (*Sport*) joueur *m*, -euse *f*. **football ~** joueur de football; **he's a very good ~** il joue très bien, c'est un excellent joueur. b (*Theat*) acteur *m*, -trice *f*. c (*Mus*) musicien(ne) *m(f)*, exécutant(e) *m(f)*. **flute ~** joueur *m*, -euse *f* de flûte, flûtiste *mf*; **he's a good ~** c'est un bon musicien, il joue bien. 2 comp ► **player piano** piano *m* mécanique.

playful ['pleɪfʊl] adj *mood, tone, remark* badin, enjoué; *person* enjoué, taquin; *child, puppy etc* espiègle. **he's only being ~** il fait ça pour s'amuser, c'est de l'espièglerie.

playfully ['pleɪfəlɪ] adv *remark, say, joke* en badinant, d'un ton enjoué; *nudge, tickle* d'un air taquin, par espièglerie.

playfulness ['pleɪfʊlnɪs] n (*gen*) caractère *m* badin *or* enjoué; *[person]* enjouement *m*; *[child, puppy etc]* espièglerie *f*.

playing ['pleɪɪŋ] 1 n (*NonC*) a (*Sport*) jeu *m*. **there was some good ~ in the second half** il y a eu du beau jeu à la deuxième mi-temps. b (*Mus*) **the orchestra's ~ of the symphony was uninspired** l'orchestre manquait d'inspiration dans l'interprétation de la symphonie; **there was some fine ~ in the violin concerto** il y a eu des passages bien joués dans le concerto pour violon. 2 comp ► **playing card** carte *f* à jouer ► **playing field** terrain *m* de jeu *or* de sport.

playlet ['pleɪlət] n courte pièce *f* (de théâtre).

plaza ['plɑːzə] n (*US*) a (*public square*) (grand-)place *f*. b (*motorway services*) aire *f* de service (*sur une autoroute*); (*toll*) péage *m* (d'autoroute). c (*for parking etc*) aire *f* de stationnement.

PLC, plc [piːel'siː] (*Brit*) (abbr of **public limited company**) **Smith & Co. ~** Smith et Cie. SARL.

plea [pliː] 1 n a (*excuse*) excuse *f*; (*claim*) allégation *f*. **on the ~ of** en alléguant, en invoquant; **on the ~ that** en alléguant *or* en invoquant que. b (*Jur*) (*allegation*) argument *m* (*that* selon lequel); (*answer, defence*) défense *f* (*that* selon laquelle). **to put forward** *or* **make a ~ of self-defence** plaider la légitime défense; **to enter a ~ of guilty/not guilty** plaider coupable/non coupable. c (*entreaty*) appel *m* (*for* à), supplication *f*. **to make a ~ for mercy** implorer la clémence. 2 comp ► **plea bargaining** (*Jur*) *négociations entre le procureur et l'avocat de la défense, incluant parfois le juge, pour réduire la gravité des charges*.

pleached ['pliːtʃd] adj *tree* taillé.

plead [pliːd] pret, ptp **pleaded** *or* (*: *esp US*) **pled** 1 vi a **to ~ with sb to do** supplier *or* implorer qn de faire; **he ~ed for help** il a imploré *or* supplié qu'on l'aide (*subj*); **he ~ed with them for help** il a imploré leur aide; **to ~ for mercy** implorer la clémence; **he ~ed for mercy for his brother** (*begged*) il a imploré la clémence pour son frère; (*spoke eloquently*) il a plaidé la clémence envers son frère; **to ~ for a scheme/programme** *etc* plaider pour un projet/un programme *etc*.
b (*Jur*) plaider (*for* pour, en faveur de, *against* contre). **to ~ guilty/not guilty** plaider coupable/non coupable; **how do you ~?** plaidez-vous coupable ou non coupable?
2 vt a (*Jur etc: argue*) plaider. (*Jur*) **to ~ sb's case**, (*fig*) **to ~ sb's cause** plaider la cause de qn (*Jur, fig*).
b (*give as excuse*) alléguer, invoquer; (*Jur*) plaider. **to ~ ignorance** alléguer *or* invoquer son ignorance; **he ~ed unemployment as a reason for ...** il invoqua *or* il allégua le chômage pour expliquer ...; (*Jur*) **to ~ insanity** plaider la démence; *see* **fifth**.

pleading ['pliːdɪŋ] 1 n a prières *fpl* (*for sb* en faveur de qn), intercession *f* (*liter*). b (*Jur*) plaidoirie *f*, plaidoyer *m*. c (*Jur*) **~s** conclusions *fpl* (*des parties*); *see* **delivery**. 2 adj implorant, suppliant.

pleadingly ['pliːdɪŋlɪ] adv d'un air *or* d'un ton suppliant *or* implorant.

pleasant ['pleznt] adj *person* (*attractive*) sympathique, agréable, charmant; (*polite*) aimable; *house, town* agréable, attrayant, plaisant; *smell, taste* agréable, bon (*f* bonne); *style* agréable; *weather, summer* agréable, beau (*f* belle); *surprise* agréable, heureux, bon. **they had a ~ time** ils ont passé un bon moment, ils se sont bien amusés; **they spent a ~ afternoon** ils ont passé un bon *or* un agréable après-midi; **it's very ~ here** on est bien ici, il fait bon ici; **Barcombe is a ~ place** Barcombe est un coin agréable *or* un joli coin; **he was** *or* **he made himself very ~ to us** il s'est montré très aimable *or* charmant avec nous; **~ dreams!** fais de beaux rêves!

pleasantly ['plezntlɪ] adv *behave, smile, answer* aimablement. **~ surprised** agréablement surpris; **the garden was ~ laid out** le jardin était agréablement *or* plaisamment arrangé; **it was ~ warm** il faisait une chaleur agréable.

pleasantness ['plezntnɪs] n *[person, manner, welcome]* amabilité *f*; *[place, house]* agrément *m*, attrait *m*, charme *m*.

pleasantry ['plezntrɪ] n (*joke*) plaisanterie *f*. (*polite remarks*) **pleasantries** civilités *fpl*, propos *mpl* aimables.

please [pliːz] 1 adv s'il vous plaît, s'il te plaît. **yes ~** oui s'il vous (*or* te) plaît; **~ come in, come in ~** entrez, je vous prie; (*frm*) **~ be seated** veuillez vous asseoir (*frm*); **~ do not smoke** (*notice*) prière de ne pas fumer; (*spoken*) ne fumez pas s'il vous plaît, je vous prie de ne pas fumer; **~ let me know if I can help you** ne manquez pas de me faire savoir si je peux vous aider; **may I smoke? — ~ do!** je peux fumer? — faites donc! *or* je vous en prie! *or* mais bien sûr!; **shall I tell him? — ~ do!** je le lui dis? — mais oui dites-le-lui *or* mais oui bien sûr *or* mais oui allez-y*; (*excl*) **~!** (*entreating*) s'il vous plaît!; (*protesting*) (ah non!) je vous en prie! *or* s'il vous plaît!; **~ don't!** ne faites pas ça s'il vous plaît!; (*in prayer*) **~ let him be all right** mon Dieu, faites qu'il ne lui soit rien arrivé.
2 vi a (*think fit*) **I shall do as I ~** je ferai comme il me plaira *or* comme je veux; **do as you ~!** faites comme vous voulez *or* comme bon vous semble; **as you ~!** comme vous voulez!, à votre guise!; **you may take as many as you ~** vous pouvez en prendre autant qu'il vous plaira; **if you ~** s'il vous plaît; (*iro*) **he wanted £50 if you ~!** il voulait 50 livres, rien que ça! *or* s'il vous plaît!
b plaire, faire plaisir. (*esp Comm*) **our aim is to ~** nous ne cherchons qu'à satisfaire; **he is very anxious to ~** il est très désireux de plaire; **a gift that is sure to ~** un cadeau qui ne peut que faire plaisir *or* que plaire.
3 vt a (*give pleasure to*) plaire à, faire plaisir à; (*satisfy*) satisfaire, contenter. **the gift ~d him** le cadeau lui a plu *or* lui a fait plaisir; **I did it just to ~ you** je ne l'ai fait que pour te faire plaisir; **that will ~ him** ça va lui faire plaisir, il va être content; **he is easily ~d/hard to ~** il est facile/difficile à contenter *or* à satisfaire; **there's no pleasing him** il n'y a jamais moyen de le contenter *or* de le satisfaire; (*loc*) **you can't ~ all (of) the people all (of) the time** on ne saurait contenter tout le monde; **music that ~s the ear** musique plaisante à l'oreille *or* qui flatte l'oreille; (*frm*) **it ~d him to refuse permission ...** il lui a plu de ne pas consentir ..., il a trouvé bon de ne pas consentir ... .
b **to ~ oneself** faire comme on veut; **~ yourself!** comme vous voulez!, à votre guise!; **you must ~ yourself whether you do it or not** c'est à vous de décider si vous voulez le faire ou non; (*liter*) **~ God he comes!** plaise à Dieu qu'il vienne!

pleased [pliːzd] adj content, heureux (*with* de). **as ~ as Punch** heureux comme un roi, aux anges; **he looked very ~ at the news** la nouvelle a eu l'air de lui faire grand plaisir; **he was ~ to hear that ...** il a été heureux *or* content d'apprendre que ...; **~ to meet you!*** enchanté!; **I am ~ that you can come** je suis heureux *or* content que vous puissiez venir; (*frm*) **we are ~ to inform you that ...** nous avons l'honneur de *or* (*less frm*) le plaisir de vous informer que ...; **to be ~ with o.s./sb/sth** être content de soi/qn/qch; **they were anything but ~ with the decision** la décision était loin de leur faire plaisir; *see* **graciously**.

pleasing ['pliːzɪŋ] adj *personality* sympathique, aimable, plaisant; *sight, news, results, effect* plaisant, qui fait plaisir. **it was very ~ to him** cela lui a fait grand plaisir.

pleasingly ['pli:zɪŋlɪ] adv agréablement.
pleasurable ['pleʒərəbl] adj (très) agréable.
pleasurably ['pleʒərəblɪ] adv (très) agréablement.
pleasure ['pleʒəʳ] 1 n a (*satisfaction*) plaisir *m*. **with** ~ (*with enjoyment*) *listen etc* avec plaisir; (*willingly*) *do, agree, help* avec plaisir, volontiers; **one of my greatest ~s** un de mes plus grands plaisirs, une de mes plus grandes joies; **it's a ~!, my ~!, the ~ is mine!** je vous en prie!; **it's a ~ to see you** quel plaisir de vous voir!; **it has been a ~ to talk to you** j'ai eu beaucoup de plaisir à parler avec vous; **it gave me much ~ to hear that ...** cela m'a fait grand plaisir d'apprendre que ...; **if it gives you any ~** si ça peut vous faire plaisir; (*frm: at dance*) **may I have the ~?** voulez-vous m'accorder cette danse?; (*frm*) **may we have the ~ of your company at dinner?** voulez-vous nous faire le plaisir de dîner avec nous?; (*frm*) **I have ~ in accepting ...** j'ai l'honneur d'accepter ...; (*frm*) **Mrs A requests the ~ of Mr B's company at dinner** Mme A prie M. B de lui faire l'honneur de venir dîner; (*frm*) **Mr. and Mrs. A. request the ~ of the company of X at the marriage of their daughter ...** M. et Mme A. seraient très honorés de la présence de X au mariage de leur fille ...; **he finds** *or* **takes great ~ in chess** il trouve *or* prend beaucoup de plaisir aux échecs; **what ~ can you find in doing that?** quel plaisir pouvez-vous trouver à faire cela?; **to take great ~ in doing** éprouver *or* avoir *or* prendre *or* trouver beaucoup de plaisir à faire; (*pej*) se complaire à faire; **they took great ~ in his success** ils se sont réjouis de son succès; **it takes all the ~ out of it** ça vous gâche le plaisir; **has he gone to Paris on business or for ~?** est-il allé à Paris pour affaires ou pour son plaisir?; **a life of ~** une vie de plaisirs; *see* **business**.
b (*NonC: will, desire*) bon plaisir, volonté *f*. **at ~** à volonté; **at your ~** à votre gré; (*Jur*) **during the Queen's ~** aussi longtemps qu'il plaira à Sa Majesté, pendant le bon plaisir de la reine; (*Comm*) **we await your ~** nous sommes à votre entière disposition.
2 comp ►**pleasure boat** bateau *m* de plaisance ►**pleasure craft** (*collective*) bateaux *mpl* de plaisance ►**pleasure cruise** croisière *f*, (*short*) promenade *f* en mer *or* en bateau ►**pleasure-loving** qui aime le(s) plaisir(s) ►**the pleasure principle** (*Psych*) le principe de la recherche du plaisir ►**pleasure-seeker** hédoniste *mf* ►**pleasure-seeking** adj hédoniste ►**pleasure steamer** vapeur *m* de plaisance ►**pleasure trip** excursion *f*.
pleat [pli:t] 1 n pli *m*. 2 vt plisser.
pleb* [pleb] n (*pej*) plébéien(ne) *m(f)*, roturier *m*, -ière *f*. **the ~s** le commun (des mortels).
plebe* [pli:b] n (*US*) élève *m* de première année (*d'une école militaire ou navale*).
plebeian [plɪ'bi:ən] adj, n plébéien(ne) *m(f)*.
plebiscite ['plebɪsɪt] n plébiscite *m*. **to hold a ~** faire un plébiscite.
plectra ['plektrə] npl of **plectron** *and* **plectrum**.
plectron ['plektrən], **plectrum** ['plektrəm] n, pl **~s** *or* **plectra** plectre *m*.
pled* [pled] (*esp US*) pret, ptp of **plead**.
pledge [pledʒ] 1 n a (*security, token; also in pawnshop*) gage *m*. **as a ~ of his love** en gage *or* témoignage de son amour.
b (*promise*) promesse *f*, engagement *m*; (*agreement*) pacte *m*. **I give you this ~** je vous fais cette promesse; **he made a ~ of secrecy** il a promis de *or* il s'est engagé à garder le secret; **to be under a ~ of secrecy** avoir promis de ne rien dire; **it was told me under a ~ of secrecy** on me l'a raconté contre la promesse de ne rien en dire; **the government did not honour its ~ to cut taxes** le gouvernement n'a pas honoré son engagement *or* n'a pas tenu sa promesse de réduire les impôts; **a ~ on pay rises** un engagement concernant les augmentations de salaires; **the countries signed a ~ to help each other** les pays ont signé un pacte d'aide mutuelle; (*fig*) **to sign** *or* **take the ~** faire vœu de tempérance.
c (*US Univ*) (*promise*) *promesse f d'entrer dans une confrérie*; (*student*) *étudiant(e) m(f) qui accomplit une période d'essai avant d'entrer dans une confrérie*.
d (*toast*) toast *m* (*to* à).
2 vt a (*pawn*) engager, mettre en gage.
b (*promise*) *one's help, support, allegiance* promettre. **to ~ (o.s.) to do** (*gen*) promettre de faire, s'engager à faire; (*solemnly*) faire vœu de faire; **to ~ sb to secrecy** faire promettre le secret à qn; **he is ~d to secrecy** il a promis de garder le secret; **to ~ one's word (that)** donner sa parole (que).
c (*US Univ: into fraternity*) coopter. **to be ~d to a fraternity** *accomplir une période d'essai avant d'entrer dans une confrérie*.
d (*toast*) boire à la santé de.
Pleiades ['plaɪədi:z] npl Pléiades *fpl*.
Pleistocene ['plaɪstəsi:n] adj, n pléistocène (*m*).
plena ['plenə] npl of **plenum**.
plenary ['pli:nərɪ] 1 adj *power* absolu; *assembly* plénier; (*Rel*) plénier. **(in) ~ session** (en) séance plénière; **~ meeting** réunion plénière, plenum *m*. 2 n (~ *session*) séance plénière, plenum *m*.
plenipotentiary [,plenɪpə'tenʃərɪ] adj, n plénipotentiaire (*mf*). **ambassador** ~ ambassadeur *m* plénipotentiaire.
plenitude ['plenɪtju:d] n plénitude *f*.
plenteous ['plentɪəs] adj, **plentiful** ['plentɪfʊl] adj *harvest, food* abondant; *meal, amount* copieux. **a ~ supply of** une abondance *or* une profusion de; **eggs are ~ just now** il y a (une) abondance d'œufs en ce moment.
plentifully ['plentɪfəlɪ] adv abondamment, copieusement.
plenty ['plentɪ] 1 n a abondance *f*. **it grows here in ~** cela pousse en abondance *or* à foison ici; **he had friends in ~** il ne manquait pas d'amis; **to live in ~** vivre dans l'abondance; **land of ~** pays *m* de cocagne; *see* **horn**.
b **~ of** (bien) assez de; **I've got ~** j'en ai bien assez; **he's got ~ of friends** il ne manque pas d'amis; **to see ~ of sb*** voir qn très souvent; **he's got ~ of money** il n'est pas pauvre; **10 is ~** 10 suffisent (largement *or* amplement); **that's ~** ça suffit (amplement); **there's ~ to go on** nous avons toutes les données nécessaires pour le moment.
2 adj (‡ *or dial*) = **~ of**; *see* **1b**.
3 adv (‡) assez. **it's ~ big enough!** c'est bien assez grand!; (*US*) **it sure rained ~!** qu'est-ce qu'il est tombé!*
plenum ['pli:nəm] n, pl **~s** *or* **plena** plenum *m*, réunion *f* plénière.
pleonasm ['pli:ənæzəm] n pléonasme *m*.
pleonastic [pli:ə'næstɪk] adj pléonastique.
plethora ['pleθərə] n pléthore *f*, surabondance *f* (*of* de); (*Med*) pléthore.
plethoric [ple'θɒrɪk] adj pléthorique.
pleura ['plʊərə] n, pl **~e** ['plʊəri:] plèvre *f*.
pleurisy ['plʊərɪsɪ] n (*NonC*) pleurésie *f*. **to have ~** avoir une pleurésie.
pleuritic [plʊə'rɪtɪk] adj pleurétique.
Plexiglass ['pleksɪglɑ:s] n ® Plexiglas ® *m*.
plexus ['pleksəs] n, pl **~es** *or* ~ plexus *m*; *see* **solar**.
pliability [,plaɪə'bɪlɪtɪ] n (*see* **pliable**) flexibilité *f*; souplesse *f*, docilité *f*, malléabilité *f*.
pliable ['plaɪəbl] adj, **pliant** ['plaɪənt] adj *substance* flexible; *character, person* souple, docile, malléable.
pliers ['plaɪəz] npl (*also* **pair of ~**) pince(s) *f(pl)*, tenaille(s) *f(pl)*.
plight[1] [plaɪt] n situation *f* critique, état *m* critique. **the country's economic ~** la crise *or* les difficultés *fpl* économique(s) du pays; **in a sad** *or* **sorry ~** dans un triste état; **what a dreadful ~ (to be in)!** quelles circonstances désespérées!, quelle situation lamentable!
plight[2] [plaɪt] vt (*liter*, ††) **to ~ one's word** engager sa parole; (†† *or hum*) **to ~ one's troth** engager sa foi†, se fiancer.
plimsoll ['plɪmsəl] 1 n (*Brit*) (chaussure *f* de) tennis *m*. 2 comp ►**Plimsoll line, Plimsoll mark** (*Naut*) ligne *f* de flottaison en charge.
plink [plɪŋk] (*US*) 1 vi a (*sound*) tinter. b (*shoot*) canarder*. 2 vt a (*sound*) faire tinter. b (*shoot at*) canarder*.
plinth [plɪnθ] n *[column, pedestal]* plinthe *f*; *[statue, record player]* socle *m*.
Pliny ['plɪnɪ] n Pline *m*.
Pliocene ['plaɪəʊsi:n] adj, n pliocène (*m*).
PLO [pi:el'əʊ] n (abbr of **Palestine Liberation Organization**) O.L.P. *f*.
plod [plɒd] 1 n: **they went at a steady ~** ils cheminaient d'un pas égal; **the slow ~ of the horses on the cobbles** le lent martellement des sabots sur les pavés.
2 vi a (*also* **~ along**) cheminer, avancer d'un pas lent *or* égal *or* lourd. **to ~ in/out** *etc* entrer/sortir *etc* d'un pas lent *or* égal *or* lourd.
b (*fig: work*) bosser‡, bûcher*. **he was ~ding through his maths** il faisait méthodiquement son devoir de maths, il bûchait* ses maths; **I'm ~ding through that book** je lis ce livre mais c'est laborieux; **you'll have to ~ through it** il faudra (faire l'effort de) persévérer jusqu'au bout.
3 vt: **we ~ded the road for another hour** nous avons poursuivi notre lente marche pendant une heure.
►**plod along** vi *see* **plod 2a**.
►**plod on** vi (*lit*) continuer *or* poursuivre son chemin; (*fig*) persévérer *or* progresser (laborieusement).
plodder ['plɒdəʳ] n travailleur *m*, -euse *f* assidu(e), bûcheur* *m*, -euse *f*.
plodding ['plɒdɪŋ] adj *step* lourd, pesant; *student, worker* bûcheur.
plonk [plɒŋk] 1 n a (*sound*) plouf *m*, floc *m*. b (*Brit *: cheap wine*) vin *m* ordinaire, pinard‡ *m*. 2 adv (*) **it fell ~ in the middle of the table** c'est tombé au beau milieu de la table. 3 vt (*also* **~ down**) poser (bruyamment). **he ~ed the book (down) on to the table** il a posé (bruyamment) *or* a flanqué* le livre sur la table; **he ~ed himself (down) into the chair** il s'est laissé tomber dans le fauteuil.
plonker‡ ['plɒnkəʳ] n imbécile* *m*, con‡ *m*.
plop [plɒp] 1 n ploc *m*, floc *m*. 2 adv: **it went ~ into the water** c'est tombé dans l'eau (en faisant ploc *or* floc). 3 vi *[stone]* faire ploc *or* floc; *[single drop]* faire floc; *[raindrops]* faire flic flac.
plosive ['pləʊsɪv] (*Ling*) 1 adj occlusif. 2 n consonne *f* occlusive.
plot [plɒt] 1 n a (*of ground*) (lot *m* de) terrain *m*, lotissement *m*. **~ of grass** gazon *m*; **building ~** terrain à bâtir; **the vegetable ~** le coin des légumes.
b (*plan, conspiracy*) complot *m*, conspiration *f* (*against* contre, *to do* pour faire).
c (*Literat, Theat*) intrigue *f*, action *f*. (*fig*) **the ~ thickens** l'affaire

or l'histoire se corse.

2 vt a (*mark out: also* ~ **out**) (*Aviat, Naut etc*) *course, route* déterminer; *graph, curve, diagram* tracer point par point; *progress, development* faire le graphique de; *boundary, piece of land* relever. (*Naut*) **to ~ one's position on the map** pointer la carte.

b *sb's death, ruin etc* comploter. **to ~ to do** comploter de faire.

3 vi (*conspire*) comploter, conspirer (*against* contre).

plotter[1] ['plɒtəʳ] n conspirateur *m*, -trice *f*; (*against the government*) conjuré(e) *m(f)*.

plotter[2] ['plɒtəʳ] n (*Comput*) traceur *m* (de courbes).

plotting ['plɒtɪŋ] 1 n (*NonC*) complots *mpl*, conspirations *fpl*. 2 comp ►**plotting board, plotting table** (*Comput*) table *f* traçante.

plotz‡ [plɒts] vi (*US*) se casser la gueule‡, échouer dans les grandes largeurs*.

plotzed‡ [plɒtst] adj (*US*) (*drunk*) bourré‡, ivre.

plough, (US) plow [plaʊ] 1 n (*Agr*) charrue *f*. (*Astron*) **the P~** la Grande Ourse, le Grand Chariot; *see* **snow** *etc*.

2 comp ►**plough horse** cheval *m* de labour ►**ploughland** terre *f* de labour, terre arable ►**ploughman** laboureur *m* ►**ploughman's lunch** ≃ sandwich *m* au fromage ►**ploughshare** soc *m* (de charrue).

3 vt a (*Agr*) *field* labourer; *furrow* creuser, tracer. **to ~ money into sth** investir gros dans qch; (*fig*) **to ~ one's way** *see* **4b**.

b (*Brit* *†: *fail*) *candidate* recaler*, coller*.

4 vi a (*Agr*) labourer.

b (*fig: also* ~ **one's** *or* **its way**) **to ~ through the mud/snow** avancer péniblement dans la boue/la neige; **the ship ~ed through the heavy swell** le navire avançait en luttant contre la forte houle; **the lorry ~ed into the wall** le camion est allé se jeter contre le mur; **the car ~ed through the fence** la voiture a défoncé la barrière; **to ~ through a book** lire un livre d'une manière laborieuse; **he was ~ing through his maths** il faisait méthodiquement son devoir de maths, il bûchait* ses maths.

►**plough back** 1 vt sep *profits* réinvestir, reverser (*into* dans). 2 **ploughing back** n *see* **ploughing**.

►**plough in, plough under** vt sep *crops, grass* recouvrir *or* enterrer en labourant; *path, right of way* labourer (pour faire disparaître).

►**plough up** vt sep a *field, bushes, path, right of way* labourer. b (*fig*) **the tanks ploughed up the field** les tanks ont labouré *or* défoncé le champ; **the train ploughed up the track for 40 metres** le train a labouré *or* défoncé la voie sur 40 mètres.

ploughing ['plaʊɪŋ] n (*NonC*) labour *m*; *[field etc]* labourage *m*. (*fig*) **the ~ back of profits** le réinvestissement des bénéfices.

plover ['plʌvəʳ] n pluvier *m*.

plow [plaʊ] (*US*) = **plough**.

ploy* [plɔɪ] n stratagème *m*, truc* *m* (*to do* pour faire).

PLR [piːel'ɑːʳ] (abbr of **public lending right**) *see* **public**.

pluck [plʌk] 1 n a (*NonC: courage*) courage *m*, cran* *m*. b (*NonC: Culin*) fressure *f*. c (*tug*) petit coup. 2 vt *fruit, flower* cueillir; (*Mus*) *strings* pincer; *guitar* pincer les cordes de; (*Culin*) *bird* plumer. **to ~ one's eyebrows** s'épiler les sourcils; (*fig*) **it's an idea** *etc* **I ~ed out of the air** c'est une idée *etc* que j'ai eue comme ça* *or* qui m'est venue.

►**pluck at** vt fus: **to pluck at sb's sleeve** tirer qn doucement par la manche.

►**pluck off** vt sep *feathers* arracher; *fluff etc* détacher, enlever.

►**pluck out** vt sep arracher.

►**pluck up** vt sep a *weed* arracher, extirper. b **to pluck up courage** prendre son courage à deux mains; **he plucked up (the) courage to tell her** il a (enfin) trouvé le courage de *or* il s'est (enfin) décidé à le lui dire.

pluckily ['plʌkɪlɪ] adv avec cran*, courageusement.

pluckiness ['plʌkɪnɪs] n (*NonC*) courage *m*, cran* *m*.

plucky ['plʌkɪ] adj courageux, qui a du cran* *or* de l'estomac.

plug [plʌg] 1 n a (*for draining*) *[bath, basin]* bonde *f*, vidange *f*; *[barrel]* bonde; (*to stop a leak*) tampon *m*; (*stopper*) bouchon *m*; (*Geol: in volcano*) culot *m*. **a ~ of cotton wool** un tampon de coton; **to put in/pull out the ~** mettre/enlever *or* ôter la bonde; (*in lavatory*) **to pull the ~** tirer la chasse d'eau; (*fig*) **to pull the ~ on**‡ *patient* débrancher; *accomplice, wrongdoer* exposer; *project etc* laisser tomber*; *see* **ear**[1].

b (*Elec*) (*on flex, apparatus*) prise *f* (de courant) (*mâle*); (*wall* ~) prise (de courant) (*femelle*); *[switchboard]* fiche *f*; (*Aut: sparking* ~) bougie *f*; *see* **amp, fused, pin**.

c (*US: fire* ~) bouche *f* d'incendie.

d (*: *publicity*) coup *m* de pouce (publicitaire), réclame *f or* publicité *f* (clandestine *or* indirecte). **to give sth/sb a ~, to put in a ~ for sth/sb** donner un coup de pouce (publicitaire) à qch/qn, faire de la réclame *or* de la publicité indirecte pour qch/qn.

e (*US: tobacco*) (*for smoking*) carotte *f*; (*for chewing*) chique *f*.

2 comp ►**plug hat** (*US*) (chapeau *m* en) tuyau *m* de poêle ►**plughole** trou *m* (d'écoulement *or* de vidange), bonde *f*, vidange *f*; **it went down the plughole** (*lit*) il est tombé dans le trou (du lavabo *or* de l'évier *etc*); (*fig*) *[idea, project]* c'est tombé à l'eau ►**plug-in** (*Elec*) qui se branche sur le secteur; **plug-in telephone** téléphone *m* à fiche ►**plug-ugly*** (*US*) dur *m*, brute *f*.

3 vt a (*also* ~ **up**) *hole, crack* boucher, obturer; *barrel, jar* boucher; *leak* colmater, (*on boat*) aveugler; *tooth* obturer (*with* avec). (*fig*) **to ~ the gap in the tax laws** mettre fin aux échappatoires en matière de fiscalité; (*fig*) **to ~ the drain on gold reserves** arrêter l'hémorragie *or* la fuite des réserves d'or.

b **to ~ sth into a hole** enfoncer qch dans un trou; **~ the TV into the wall** branchez le téléviseur (sur le secteur).

c (*: *publicize*) (*on one occasion*) faire de la réclame *or* de la publicité pour; (*repeatedly*) matraquer*.

d (‡) (*shoot*) flinguer‡, ficher* *or* flanquer* une balle dans la peau à; (*punch*) ficher* *or* flanquer* un *or* des coup(s) de poing à.

►**plug away*** vi bosser‡, travailler dur (*at doing* pour faire). **he was plugging away at his maths** il faisait méthodiquement son devoir de maths, il bûchait* ses maths.

►**plug in** 1 vi se brancher. **the TV plugs in over there** la télé se branche là-bas; **does your radio plug in?** est-ce que votre radio peut se brancher sur le secteur? 2 vt sep *lead, apparatus* brancher. 3 **plug-in** adj *see* **plug 2**.

►**plug into*** vt fus (*esp US*) *ideas etc* se brancher à l'écoute de*.

►**plug up** vt sep = **plug 3a**.

plum [plʌm] 1 n a (*fruit*) prune *f*; (*also* ~ **tree**) prunier *m*. b (* *fig*) (*choice thing*) meilleur morceau (*fig*), meilleure part (*fig*); (*choice job*) boulot* *m* en or. 2 adj a (*also* **~-coloured**) prune *inv*, lie-de-vin *inv*. b (*: *best, choice*) de choix, le plus chouette*. **he got the ~ job** c'est lui qui a décroché le meilleur travail *or* le travail le plus chouette*; **he has a ~ job** il a un boulot* en or. 3 comp ►**plumcake** (plum-)cake *m* ►**plum duff, plum pudding** (plum-)pudding *m*.

plumage ['pluːmɪdʒ] n plumage *m*.

plumb [plʌm] 1 n plomb *m*. **out of ~** hors d'aplomb. 2 comp ►**plumbline** fil *m* à plomb; (*Naut*) sonde *f*. 3 adj vertical, à plomb, d'aplomb. 4 adv a en plein, exactement. **~ in the middle of** en plein milieu de, au beau milieu de. b (*US* *) complètement, absolument, tout à fait. 5 vt sonder. **to ~ the depths** (*lit*) sonder les profondeurs; (*fig*) toucher le fond (du désespoir).

►**plumb in** vt sep *washing machine etc* faire le raccordement de.

plumbago [plʌm'beɪgəʊ] n, pl **~s** a (*graphite*) plombagine *f*. b (*Bot*) plumbago *m*.

plumber ['plʌməʳ] n a plombier *m*. (*US: device*) **~'s helper** (déboucheir *m* à) ventouse *f*. b (*US* ‡) agent *m* de surveillance gouvernementale, plombier* *m*.

plumbic ['plʌmbɪk] adj plombifère.

plumbing ['plʌmɪŋ] n (*trade*) (travail *m* de) plomberie *f*; (*system*) plomberie, tuyauterie *f*.

plume [pluːm] 1 n (*large feather*) plume *f* (*d'autruche etc*); (*cluster of feathers*) plumes; (*on hat, helmet*) plumet *m*, (*larger*) panache *m*; (*fig: of smoke*) panache. (*fig*) **in borrowed ~s** paré d'atours d'emprunt, paré des plumes du paon (*fig*). 2 vt *[bird] wing, feather* lisser. **the bird was pluming itself** l'oiseau se lissait les plumes; (*fig*) **to ~ o.s. on sth** se targuer de qch.

plumed [pluːmd] adj (*see* **plume**) à plumet, empanaché.

plummet ['plʌmɪt] 1 n plomb *m*. 2 vi *[aircraft, bird]* plonger, descendre *or* tomber à pic; *[temperature]* baisser *or* descendre brusquement; *[price, sales, popularity, amount]* dégringoler; *[spirits, morale]* tomber à zéro.

plummy* ['plʌmɪ] adj a *accent, voice* (exagérément) aristocratique. b (*desirable*) recherché. **~ job** (bonne) planque* *f* (*fig*), sinécure *f*. c (*colour*) prune *inv*, lie-de-vin *inv*.

plump[1] [plʌmp] 1 adj *person* grassouillet, empâté; *child, hand* potelé; *cheek, face* rebondi, plein; *arm, leg* dodu, potelé; *chicken* dodu, charnu; *cushion* rebondi, bien rembourré. 2 vt *poultry* engraisser; (*also* ~ **up**) *pillow* tapoter, faire bouffer.

►**plump out** vi devenir rondelet, grossir.

plump[2] [plʌmp] 1 vt (*drop*) laisser tomber lourdement, flanquer*. 2 vi tomber lourdement. 3 adv a en plein, exactement. **~ in the middle of** en plein milieu de, au beau milieu de. b (*in plain words*) carrément, sans mâcher ses mots.

►**plump down** 1 vi s'affaler. 2 vt sep laisser tomber lourdement. **to plump o.s. down on the sofa** s'affaler sur le sofa.

►**plump for** vt fus fixer son choix sur, se décider pour, jeter son dévolu sur.

plumpness ['plʌmpnɪs] n *[person]* rondeur *f*, embonpoint *m*.

plunder ['plʌndəʳ] 1 n (*NonC*) (*act*) pillage *m*; (*loot*) butin *m*. 2 vt piller.

plunderer ['plʌndərəʳ] n pillard *m*.

plundering ['plʌndərɪŋ] 1 n (*NonC*) pillage *m*. 2 adj pillard.

plunge [plʌndʒ] 1 n *[bird, diver, goalkeeper]* plongeon *m*; (*quick bathe*) (petit) plongeon; (*steep fall*) chute *f*; (*fig: fall*) chute, dégringolade* *f* (*in prices* de *or* des prix); (*Fin: rash investment*) spéculation hasardeuse (*on* sur). **to take a ~** *[diver etc]* plonger; *[bather]* faire un (petit) plongeon; *[shares, prices etc]* dégringoler*; **his ~ into debt** son endettement soudain; (*fig*) **to take the ~** se jeter à l'eau, franchir *or* sauter le pas.

2 vt *hand, knife, dagger* plonger, enfoncer (*into* dans); (*into water*) plonger (*into* dans); (*fig*) plonger (*into war/darkness/despair etc* dans la guerre/les ténèbres/le désespoir *etc*).

3 vi a (*dive*) *[diver, goalkeeper, penguin, submarine]* plonger (*into* dans, *from* de); *[horse]* piquer une tête, piquer du nez; *[ship]* piquer de l'avant *or* du nez; *[road, cliff]* plonger (*into* dans); (*fig*) *[person]* se jeter, se lancer (*into* dans). **he ~d into the argument** il s'est lancé dans la discussion; (*fig*) **the stream/road ~d down the mountainside** le ruisseau/la route dévalait le flanc de la colline; **the neckline ~s at the back** le décolleté est plongeant dans le dos.

b (*fall*) *[person]* tomber, faire une chute (*from* de); *[vehicle]* dégringoler, tomber (*from* de); *[prices etc]* dégringoler, tomber. **he ~d to his death** il a fait une chute mortelle; **the plane ~d to the ground/into the sea** l'avion s'est écrasé au sol/s'est abîmé dans la mer; **the car ~d over the cliff** la voiture a plongé par-dessus la falaise; **the truck ~d across the road** le camion a fait une embardée en travers de la route.

c (*rush*) se jeter, se lancer, se précipiter. **to ~ in/out/across** *etc* entrer/sortir/traverser *etc* précipitamment *or* à toute allure *or* en quatrième vitesse*; **he ~d down the stairs** il a dégringolé *or* a dévalé l'escalier quatre à quatre; **he ~d through the hedge** il a piqué brusquement *or* s'est jeté au travers de la haie.

d (*) (*gamble*) jouer gros jeu, flamber; (*St Ex: speculate*) spéculer imprudemment. **he ~d and bought a car** il a sauté le pas et s'est offert une voiture.

►**plunge in** 1 vi *[diver etc]* plonger; (*fig: into work etc*) s'y mettre de grand cœur; *see* **deep**. 2 vt sep (y) plonger.

plunger [ˈplʌndʒəʳ] n a (*piston*) piston *m*; (*for blocked pipe*) (déboucheoir *m* à) ventouse *f*. b (*gambler*) flambeur *m*; (*St Ex*) (spéculateur *m*) risque-tout *m inv*.

plunging [ˈplʌndʒɪŋ] 1 n (*action*) plongement *m*; *[diver etc]* plongées *fpl*; *[boat]* tangage *m*. 2 adj: ~ **neckline** décolleté plongeant.

plunk [plʌŋk] = **plonk 1a, 2, 3.**

pluperfect [ˈpluːˈpɜːfɪkt] n plus-que-parfait *m*.

plural [ˈplʊərəl] 1 adj a (*Gram*) *form, number, ending, person* pluriel, du pluriel; *verb, noun* au pluriel. b *vote* plural. c *society* pluriel, diversifié. 2 n (*Gram*) pluriel *m*. **in the ~** au pluriel.

pluralism [ˈplʊərəlɪzəm] n (*Philos*) pluralisme *m*; (*Rel*) cumul *m*.

pluralist [ˈplʊərəlɪst] adj, n pluraliste (*mf*).

pluralistic [ˌplʊərəˈlɪstɪk] adj pluraliste.

plurality [ˌplʊəˈrælɪtɪ] n a pluralité *f*; *[benefices etc]* cumul *m*. b (*US Pol*) majorité relative. **a ~ of 5,000 votes** 5.000 voix *fpl* d'avance sur le candidat classé second.

plus [plʌs] 1 prep plus. **3 ~ 4** 3 plus *or* et 4; **~ what I've done already** plus ce que j'ai déjà fait; (*Bridge etc*) **we are ~ 5** nous menons par 5 points.

2 adj a (*Elec, Math*) positif. (*lit*) **on the ~ side of the account** à l'actif du compte; (*fig*) **on the ~ side of the account we have his support** l'aspect positif, c'est que nous avons son appui; (*fig*) **a ~ factor** un atout.

b **10-~ hours a week** un minimum de 10 heures *or* plus de 10 heures par semaine; (*Scol etc*) **beta** ~ bêta plus; **we've sold 100 ~** nous en avons vendu 100 et quelques *or* plus de 100.

3 n (*Math: sign*) (signe *m*) plus *m*; (*fig: extra advantage*) avantage additionnel, atout *m*. (*of situation etc*) **the ~es** les côtés positifs.

4 comp ►**plus fours** culotte *f* de golf ►**plus sign** (*Math*) signe *m* plus.

plush [plʌʃ] 1 n (*Tex*) peluche *f*. 2 adj (*made of ~*) de *or* en peluche; (*~-like*) pelucheux; (*: *sumptuous*) rupin‡, somptueux.

plushy* [ˈplʌʃɪ] adj rupin‡, somptueux.

Plutarch [ˈpluːtɑːk] n Plutarque *m*.

Pluto [ˈpluːtəʊ] n (*Astron*) Pluton *f*; (*Myth*) Pluton *m*.

plutocracy [ˌpluːˈtɒkrəsɪ] n ploutocratie *f*.

plutocrat [ˈpluːtəʊkræt] n ploutocrate *m*.

plutocratic [ˌpluːtəʊˈkrætɪk] adj ploutocratique.

plutonium [pluːˈtəʊnɪəm] n plutonium *m*.

pluviometer [ˌpluːvɪˈɒmɪtəʳ] n pluviomètre *m*.

ply¹ [plaɪ] 1 n a *[wood]* feuille *f*, épaisseur *f*; *[wool]* fil *m*, brin *m*; *[rope]* toron *m*, brin. b (comp ending) **four-~ rope** corde *f* quatre fils; **four-~ wood** contreplaqué *m* quatre épaisseurs; **three-~ (wool)** laine *f* trois fils; **two-~ tissues/napkins** mouchoirs *mpl*/serviettes *fpl* en papier double épaisseur. 2 comp ►**plywood** contre-plaqué *m*.

ply² [plaɪ] 1 vt a *needle, tool* manier, jouer (habilement) de; *oar* manier; *[ship] river* naviguer sur, voguer sur (*liter*). **they plied their oars** ils faisaient force de rames; **to ~ one's trade (as)** exercer son métier (de). b **to ~ sb with questions** presser qn de questions; **to ~ sb for information** demander continuellement des renseignements à qn; **he plied them with drink** il ne cessait de remplir leur verre. 2 vi *[ship, coach etc]* **to ~ between** faire la navette entre; **to ~ for hire** faire un service de taxi.

PM [piːˈem] n (*Brit*) abbr of **Prime Minister**.

p.m. [ˈpiːˈem] (abbr of **post meridiem**) de l'après-midi. **3 p.m.** 3 h de l'après-midi; **10 p.m.** 10 h du soir.

PMG [piːemˈdʒiː] n a (*Brit*) (abbr of **Paymaster General**) *see* **pay**. b (abbr of **Postmaster General**) *see* **post³**.

PMT [ˌpiːemˈtiː] n abbr of **premenstrual tension.**

pneumatic [njuːˈmætɪk] adj pneumatique. **~ drill** marteau-piqueur *m*; **~ tyre** pneu *m*.

pneumatically [njuːˈmætɪkəlɪ] adv pneumatiquement.

pneumoconiosis [ˌnjuːməʊˌkəʊnɪˈəʊsɪs] (*Med*) n pneumoconiose *f*.

pneumonia [njuːˈməʊnɪə] n (*NonC: Med*) pneumonie *f*, fluxion *f* de poitrine.

pneumonologist [ˌnjuːməˈnɒlədʒɪst] n pneumologue *mf*.

pneumonology [ˌnjuːməˈnɒlədʒɪ] n pneumologie *f*.

Po [pəʊ] n (*river*) Pô *m*.

po‡ [pəʊ] (*Brit*) 1 n pot *m* (de chambre). 2 comp ►**po-faced‡** à l'air pincé.

P.O. [piːˈəʊ] n a (abbr of **post office**) ~ **Box 24** B.P. *f* 24. b (abbr of **Petty Officer**) *see* **petty**. c (abbr of **Pilot Officer**) *see* **pilot**.

p.o. [piːˈəʊ] (abbr of **postal order**) *see* **postal**.

poach¹ [pəʊtʃ] vt (*Culin*) pocher. **~ed eggs** œufs pochés.

poach² [pəʊtʃ] 1 vt *game* braconner, chasser illégalement; *fish* braconner, pêcher illégalement; (*fig*) *employee* débaucher. 2 vi braconner. **to ~ for salmon** *etc* braconner du saumon *etc*; (*lit, fig*) **to ~ on sb's preserves** *or* **territory** braconner sur les terres de qn; (*fig*) **stop ~ing!*** (*in tennis*) arrête de me chiper la balle!*; (*in work*) arrête de marcher sur mes plates-bandes!*

poacher¹ [ˈpəʊtʃəʳ] n (*for eggs*) pocheuse *f*.

poacher² [ˈpəʊtʃəʳ] n (*of game etc*) braconnier *m*.

poaching [ˈpəʊtʃɪŋ] n braconnage *m*.

pock [pɒk] 1 n (*Med*) pustule *f* de petite vérole. 2 comp ►**pockmark** marque *f* de petite vérole ►**pockmarked** *face* grêlé; *surface* criblé de (petits) trous.

pocket [ˈpɒkɪt] 1 n a (*in garment, suitcase, file, book cover*) poche *f*. **with his hands in his ~s** les mains dans les poches; **in his trouser ~** dans sa poche de pantalon; **to go through sb's ~s** faire les poches à qn; (*fig*) **he is always putting his hand in his ~** il n'arrête pas de débourser; **he had to put his hand in his ~ and pay their bills** il a dû payer leurs factures de sa poche; (*fig*) **the deal put £100 in his ~** l'affaire lui a rapporté 100 livres; **it is a drain on his ~** ça grève son budget; **that will hurt his ~** ça fera mal à son porte-monnaie; (*fig*) **to have sb in one's ~** avoir qn dans sa manche *or* dans sa poche; **to live in each other's** *or* **one another's ~s** vivre les uns sur les autres; **he has the game in his ~** il a le jeu dans sa poche; **to fill** *or* **line one's ~s** se remplir les poches; **to be in ~** avoir une marge de bénéfice; **to be out of ~** en être de sa poche; **out-of-~** *see* **out 5**; **I was £5 in/out of ~** j'avais fait un bénéfice/essuyé une perte de 5 livres; **it left me £5 in/out of ~** ça m'a rapporté/coûté 5 livres.

b (*fig*) poche *f*; (*Aviat: air ~*) trou *m* d'air; (*Billiards*) blouse *f*. **~ of gas/pus/resistance** poche de gaz/de pus/de résistance; **~ of infection** foyer *m* de contagion; **there are still some ~s of unemployment** il reste quelques petites zones de chômage.

2 comp *flask, torch, dictionary, edition etc* de poche ►**pocket battleship** cuirassé *m* de poche ►**pocket billiards** (*US*) billard *m* à blouses ►**pocketbook** *see* **pocketbook** ►**pocket calculator** calculatrice *f* de poche, calculette *f* ►**pocket-handkerchief** n mouchoir *m* de poche; (*adj: fig*) grand comme un mouchoir de poche ►**pocketknife** couteau *m* de poche, canif *m* ►**pocket money** (*Brit*) argent *m* de poche ►**pocket-size(d)** (*lit*) de poche; (*fig*) *house, garden etc* tout petit ►**pocket veto** (*US Pol*) veto suspensif indirect.

3 vt a (*lit*) empocher, mettre dans sa poche. (*fig*) **to ~ one's pride** *etc* mettre son amour-propre *etc* dans sa poche.

b (*: *steal*) empocher, barboter*.

c (*US Pol*) **to ~ a bill** mettre un veto suspensif à un projet de loi.

pocketbook [ˈpɒkɪtˌbʊk] n a (*Brit: wallet*) portefeuille *m*. b (*notebook*) calepin *m*, carnet *m*. c (*US: also* **pocket book**) livre *m* de poche.

pocketful [ˈpɒkɪtfʊl] n, pl **~s** poche pleine. **~s of** plein de, un paquet* de.

pod [pɒd] n a *[bean, pea etc]* cosse *f*. (*fig*) **to be in ~**‡ être enceinte. b (*Space*) nacelle *f*.

podgy* [ˈpɒdʒɪ] adj rondelet.

podia [ˈpəʊdɪə] npl of **podium**.

podiatrist [pɒˈdiːətrɪst] n (*US*) pédicure *mf*, podologue *mf*.

podiatry [pɒˈdiːətrɪ] n (*US*) (*science*) podologie *f*; (*treatment*) soins *mpl* du pied, traitement *m* des maladies du pied.

podium [ˈpəʊdɪəm] n, pl **podia** podium *m*.

Podunk [ˈpəʊdʌŋk] n (*US*) petit village perdu, ≃ Trifouilly-les-Oies.

POE (abbr of **port of embarkation**) *see* **port**.

poem [ˈpəʊɪm] n poème *m*. **the ~s of Keats** les poèmes *or* les poésies *fpl* de Keats.

poet [ˈpəʊɪt] n poète *m*. (*Brit*) **~ laureate** (*pl* **~s laureate**) poète lauréat.

poetaster [ˌpəʊɪˈtæstəʳ] n mauvais poète, rimailleur *m*.

poetess [ˈpəʊɪtes] n poétesse *f*.

poetic [pəʊˈetɪk] 1 adj poétique. **~ licence** licence *f* poétique; **it's ~ justice** il y a une justice immanente. 2 n: **~s** poétique *f*.

poetical [pəʊˈetɪkəl] adj poétique.

poetically [pəʊˈetɪkəlɪ] adv poétiquement.

poeticize [pəʊˈetɪsaɪz] vt poétiser.

poetry [ˈpəʊɪtrɪ] 1 n (*NonC: lit, fig*) poésie *f*. **the ~ of Keats** la poésie de Keats; **he writes ~** il écrit des poèmes, il fait des vers *or* de la

poésie. 2 comp ▸**poetry reading** lecture *f* de poèmes.
pogo-stick ['pəʊgəʊ,stɪk] n échasse *f* sauteuse.
pogrom ['pɒgrəm] 1 n pogrom *m*. 2 vt massacrer (au cours d'un pogrom).
poignancy ['pɔɪnjənsɪ] n (*see* **poignant**) caractère poignant, intensité *f*.
poignant ['pɔɪnjənt] adj *emotion, grief* poignant, intense, vif (*f* vive); *look, entreaty* poignant.
poignantly ['pɔɪnjəntlɪ] adv *feel* d'une manière poignante, intensément, vivement; *look, entreat* d'une manière poignante.
poinsettia [pɔɪn'setɪə] n poinsettia *m*.
point [pɔɪnt] 1 n a (*sharp end: gen: of pencil, needle, knife, jaw, bow etc*) pointe *f*; (*Climbing*) pointe (de crampon); (*Aut*) vis *f* platinée. **knife with a sharp ~** couteau très pointu; **to put a ~ on a pencil** tailler un crayon (en pointe); (*fig*) **not to put too fine a ~ on it** pour ne pas y aller par quatre chemins, pour dire les choses comme elles sont; **star with 5 ~s** étoile à 5 branches; **stag with 8 ~s** cerf (de) 8 cors; (*Ballet*) **to be** *or* **dance on ~s** faire des pointes; **at the ~ of a sword** à la pointe de l'épée; **at the ~ of a revolver** sous la menace du revolver; *see* **gun, pistol** *etc*.

b (*dot*) (*Geom, Typ*) point *m*; (*Math: decimal ~*) virgule *f* (décimale). **3 ~ 6 (3.6)** 3 virgule 6 (3,6); (*Geom*) **~ A** le point A; *see* **2**.

c (*position*) (*on scale*) point *m*; (*in space*) point, endroit *m*; (*in time*) point, moment *m*. **~ of the compass** aire *f* de vent; **the (thirty-two) ~s of the compass** la rose des vents; **from all ~s (of the compass)** de toutes parts, de tous côtés; **all ~s east** toute ville (*or* escale *etc*) à l'est; **the train stops at Slough, and all ~s west** le train s'arrête à Slough et dans toutes les gares à l'ouest de Slough; **~ of departure** point de départ; **~ of entry (into a country)** point d'arrivée (dans un pays); (*fig*) **high ~** *[career, meeting etc]* point culminant, summum *m*; **the high ~ of the evening** le clou de la soirée; **low ~** point *or* niveau *m* le plus bas; (*fig*) **there was no ~ of contact between them** il n'y avait aucun point de contact *or* point commun entre eux; **~ of view** point de vue; **from that/my ~ of view** de ce/mon point de vue; **from the social ~ of view** du point de vue social; **the highest ~ in the district** le point culminant de la région; **at that ~ in the road** à cet endroit de la route; **at the ~ where the road forks** là où la route bifurque; *[pipe etc]* **outlet ~** point de sortie; **boiling/freezing ~** point d'ébullition/de congélation; **the bag was full to bursting ~** le sac était plein à craquer; **from that ~ onwards** (*in space*) à partir de là; (*in time*) à partir de ce moment, désormais; **at this** *or* **that ~** (*in space*) là, à cet endroit; (*in time*) à cet instant précis, à ce moment-là; **at this ~ in time** à l'heure qu'il est, en ce moment.

d (*in phrases*) **to be on the ~ of doing** être sur le point de faire; **he had reached the ~ of resigning** il en était au point de donner sa démission; (*lit, fig*) **he had reached the ~ of no return** il avait atteint le point de non-retour; (*fig*) **up to a ~** jusqu'à un certain point, dans une certaine mesure; **on** *or* **at the ~ of death** à l'article de la mort; **when it comes to the ~** en fin de compte, quand tout est dit (*see also* **1g**); **when it came to the ~ of paying** quand le moment de payer est arrivé; **severe to the ~ of cruelty** sévère au point d'être cruel; **they provoked him to the ~ of losing his temper** *or* **to the ~ where he lost his temper** ils l'ont provoqué au point de le mettre hors de lui; *see* **focal, high, low, turning** *etc*.

e (*counting unit: Scol, Sport, St Ex; also on scale*) point *m*; (*on thermometer*) degré *m*. (*Boxing*) **on ~s** aux points; **the cost-of-living index went up 2 ~s** l'indice du coût de la vie a augmenté de 2 points; (*St Ex*) **to rise** *or* **gain 3 ~s** gagner 3 points, enregistrer une hausse de 3 points; (*Typ*) **8-~ type** caractères *mpl* de 8 points; *see* **brownie, score**.

f (*idea, subject, item, detail*) point *m*. **the ~ at issue** notre (*or* leur *etc*) propos, la question qui nous (*or* les *etc*) concerne; **~ of interest/of no importance** point intéressant/sans importance; **just as a ~ of interest, did you ...?** à titre d'information *or* juste pour savoir, est-ce que vous ...?; **on this ~ we are agreed** sur ce point *or* là-dessus nous sommes d'accord, c'est un point acquis; **on all ~s** en tous points; **12-~ plan** plan *m* en 12 points; **it's a ~ of detail** c'est un point de détail; **on a ~ of principle** sur une question de principe; **a ~ of law** un point de droit; **it was a ~ of honour with him never to refuse** il se faisait un point d'honneur de ne jamais refuser, il mettait son point d'honneur à ne jamais refuser; **in ~ of fact** en fait, à vrai dire; **the main ~s to remember** les principaux points à ne pas oublier; **~ by ~** point par point (*see also* **2**); **he made the ~ that ...** il fit remarquer que ...; **he made a good ~ when he said that ...** il a fait une remarque pertinente *or* judicieuse en disant que ...; **I'd like to make a ~ if I may** j'aurais une remarque à faire si vous le permettez; **you've made your ~!** (*had your say*) vous avez dit ce que vous aviez à dire!; (*convinced me*) vous m'avez convaincu!; **I take your ~** je vois ce que vous voulez dire *or* où vous voulez en venir (*about* en ce qui concerne); **~ taken!** très juste!; **you have a ~ there!** c'est juste!, il y a du vrai dans ce que vous dites!; **to carry** *or* **gain** *or* **win one's ~** avoir gain de cause; **he gave me a few ~s on what to do** il m'a donné quelques conseils *or* il m'a donné quelques tuyaux* *or* il m'a tuyauté* sur ce que je devais faire; *see* **case[1], moot, order** *etc*.

g (*important part, main idea etc*) *[argument etc]* (point *m*) essentiel *m*; *[joke etc]* astuce *f*, sel *m*, piquant *m*; (*meaning, purpose*) intérêt *m*, sens *m*. **there's no ~ in waiting** cela ne sert à rien d'attendre; **what's the ~ of** *or* **in waiting?** à quoi bon attendre?; **what's the ~?** à quoi bon?; **I don't see any ~ in doing that** je ne vois aucun intérêt *or* sens à faire cela; **there's little ~ in saying ...** cela ne sert pas à grand-chose de dire ...; **there's some** *or* **a ~ in it** ce n'est pas sans raison; **what was the ~ of his visit?** quel était le sens de *or* à quoi rimait sa visite?; **the ~ is that you had promised it for today!** le fait est que *or* c'est que vous l'aviez promis pour aujourd'hui!; **the whole ~ was to have it today** tout l'intérêt était de l'avoir aujourd'hui; **that's the (whole) ~!, that's just the ~!** justement!, c'est justement de cela qu'il s'agit!; **that's not the ~** il ne s'agit pas de cela, là n'est pas la question; **that is beside the ~** c'est à côté de la question, cela n'a rien à voir; **that is hardly the ~!** comme s'il s'agissait de cela!; **off the ~** hors de propos; **(very much) to the ~** (très) pertinent; **the ~ of this story is that ...** là où je veux (*or* il veut *etc*) en venir avec cette histoire, c'est que ...; **a long story that seemed to have no ~ at all** une longue histoire sans rime ni raison; **to see** *or* **get the ~** comprendre, piger‡; **you get the ~?** vous saisissez?*; **to come to the ~** (en) venir au fait; **get** *or* **come to the ~!** au fait!, venez-en à l'essentiel!, abrégez!*; **let's get back to the ~** revenons à ce qui nous préoccupe *or* à ce qui nous intéresse *or* à nos moutons; **to keep** *or* **stick to the ~** rester dans le sujet; **to make a ~ of doing, to make it a ~ to do sth** ne pas manquer de faire; **the news gave ~ to his arguments** les nouvelles ont souligné la pertinence de ses arguments; **his remarks lack ~** ses remarques ne sont pas très pertinentes; *see* **miss** *etc*.

h (*characteristic*) *[horse etc]* caractéristique *f*. **good ~s** qualités *fpl*; **bad ~s** défauts *mpl*; **it is not his strong ~** ce n'est pas son fort; **he has his ~s** il a ses bons côtés, il n'est pas sans qualités; **the ~s to look for when buying a car** les détails *mpl* que vous devez prendre en considération lors de l'achat d'une voiture.

i (*Geog*) pointe *f*, promontoire *m*, cap *m*.

j (*Brit Rail*) **~s** aiguilles *fpl*.

k (*Brit Elec: also* **power ~**) prise *f* (de courant) (*femelle*).

2 comp ▸**point-blank** *see* **point-blank** ▸**point-by-point** méthodique ▸**point duty**: (*Brit: Police etc*) **to be on point duty** diriger la circulation ▸**point of reference** point *m* de référence ▸**point of sale** point *m* de vente ▸**point-of-sale**: **point-of-sale advertising** publicité *f* sur le lieu de vente, PLV *f*; **point-of-sale material** matériel *m* PLV; **point-of-sale terminal** terminal *m* point de vente ▸**points decision** (*Boxing*) décision *f* aux points ▸**pointsman** (*Rail*) aiguilleur *m* ▸**points system** système *m* des points ▸**points win** victoire *f* aux points ▸**point-to-point (race)** (*Racing*) *course de chevaux dans laquelle la liberté est laissée au cavalier de choisir son parcours d'un point à un autre* ▸**.22 (point two two) rifle** vingt-deux long rifle *m*.

3 vt a (*aim, direct*) *telescope, hosepipe etc* pointer, braquer, diriger (*on* sur). **to ~ a gun at sb** braquer un revolver sur qn; **he ~ed his stick towards the house** il a tendu *or* pointé son bâton vers la maison; **to ~ sb in the direction of** diriger qn vers; **she ~ed him in the right direction** elle l'a envoyé dans la bonne direction; **he ~ed the boat towards the harbour** il a mis le cap sur le port; **he ~ed the car towards the town** il a tourné la voiture en direction de la ville; **he ~ed his finger at me** il a pointé *or* tendu son doigt vers moi, il m'a montré du doigt; *see also* **finger**.

b (*mark, show*) montrer, indiquer. **the signs ~ the way to London** les panneaux de signalisation indiquent *or* montrent la direction de Londres; (*fig*) **it ~s the way to closer cooperation** cela montre la voie pour *or* ouvre la voie à une plus grande coopération; (*fig*) **to ~ the moral** souligner *or* faire ressortir la morale.

c (*sharpen*) *pencil, stick* tailler (en pointe); *tool* aiguiser, affûter.

d (*Constr*) *wall* jointoyer (*with* de).

e (*punctuate*) ponctuer; *Hebrew, Arabic etc* mettre les points-voyelles à; *psalm* marquer de points.

f (*Dancing*) *toe(s)* pointer.

4 vi a *[person]* montrer *or* indiquer du doigt. **it's rude to ~** ce n'est pas poli de montrer du doigt; **to ~ at** *or* **towards sth/sb** montrer *or* indiquer *or* désigner qch/qn du doigt; **he ~ed at the house with his stick** il montra *or* indiqua la maison avec sa canne; (*fig*) **I want to ~ to one or two facts** je veux attirer votre attention sur un ou deux faits; (*fig*) **all the evidence ~s to him** *or* **to his guilt** tous les témoignages l'accusent; **everything ~s to a brilliant career for him** tout annonce *or* indique qu'il aura une brillante carrière; **it all ~s to the fact that ...** tout laisse à penser que ...; **everything ~s to murder/suicide** tout laisse à penser qu'il s'agit d'un meurtre/d'un suicide; (*fig*) **everything ~s that way** tout nous amène à cette conclusion.

b *[signpost]* indiquer la direction (*towards* de); *[gun]* être braqué (*at* sur); *[vehicle etc]* être dirigé, être tourné (*towards* vers). **the needle is ~ing north** l'aiguille indique le nord; **the hour hand is ~ing to 4** la petite aiguille indique 4 heures; **the car isn't ~ing in the right direction** la voiture n'est pas tournée dans la bonne direction *or* dans le bon sens.

c (*Dancing*) pointer.

d *[dog]* tomber en arrêt.

▸**point out** vt sep a (*show*) *person, object, place* montrer, indiquer, désigner. b (*mention*) signaler, faire remarquer (*sth to sb* qch à qn, *that* que). **to point sth out to sb** signaler qch à qn, attirer l'attention de qn sur qch; **he pointed out to me that I was wrong** il m'a signalé *or* il m'a fait remarquer que j'avais tort; **I should point out that ...** je dois vous dire *or* signaler que ... .

►**point up** vt sep faire ressortir, mettre en évidence, souligner. **to point up a story** illustrer une histoire.

point-blank ['pɔɪnt'blæŋk] 1 adj *shot* à bout portant; (*fig*) *refusal* net (*f* nette), catégorique; *request* de but en blanc, à brûle-pourpoint. **at ~ range** à bout portant. 2 adv *fire, shoot* à bout portant; (*fig*) *refuse* tout net, catégoriquement; *request, demand* de but en blanc, à brûle-pourpoint.

pointed ['pɔɪntɪd] adj a *knife, stick, pencil, roof, chin, nose* pointu; *beard* en pointe; (*Archit*) *window, arch* en ogive. **the ~ end** le bout pointu. b (*fig*) *remark* lourd de sens, plein de sous-entendus. **her rather ~ silence** son silence lourd de sens *or* significatif.

pointedly ['pɔɪntɪdlɪ] adv *reply* d'une manière significative. **... she said ~ ...** dit-elle avec intention *or* d'un ton plein de sous-entendus; **rather ~ she refused to comment** sa façon de se refuser à tout commentaire disait bien ce qu'elle voulait dire.

pointer ['pɔɪntəʳ] n a (*stick*) baguette *f*; (*on scale*) (*indicator*) index *m*, (*needle*) aiguille *f*; (*on screen: arrow*) flèche lumineuse. b (*clue, indication*) indice *m* (*to* de); (*piece of advice*) conseil *m*, tuyau* *m*. **he gave me some ~s on what to do*** il m'a donné quelques conseils (pratiques) *or* indications *fpl or* tuyaux* sur ce que je devais faire; **there is at present no ~ to the outcome** rien ne permet de présumer *or* de conjecturer l'issue pour le moment; **they are looking for ~s on how the situation will develop** ils cherchent des indices permettant d'établir comment la situation va évoluer; **his remarks are a possible ~ to a solution** ses remarques pourraient bien laisser entrevoir une solution. c (*dog*) chien *m* d'arrêt.

pointillism ['pwæntɪlɪzəm] n pointillisme *m*.

pointing ['pɔɪntɪŋ] n (*Constr*) jointoiement *m*.

pointless ['pɔɪntlɪs] adj *attempt, task* inutile, vain, futile; *murder* gratuit; *suffering* inutile, vain, injustifié; *explanation, joke, story* sans rime ni raison, qui ne rime à rien. **it is ~ to complain** il ne sert à rien de se plaindre, c'est peine perdue que de se plaindre; **life seemed ~ to her** la vie lui paraissait dénuée de sens.

pointlessly ['pɔɪntlɪslɪ] adv *try, work, suffer* inutilement, vainement; *kill* gratuitement, sans raison.

pointlessness ['pɔɪntlɪsnɪs] n (*see* **pointless**) inutilité *f*; futilité *f*; gratuité *f*.

poise [pɔɪz] 1 n (*balance*) équilibre *m*; (*carriage*) maintien *m*; *[head, body etc]* port *m*; (*fig*) (*composure etc*) calme *m*, sang-froid *m*; (*self-confidence*) (calme) assurance *f*; (*grace*) grâce *f*. **they walked with books on their heads to improve their ~** elles marchaient en portant des livres sur la tête pour perfectionner leur maintien *or* pour avoir un meilleur port; **a woman of great ~** une femme pleine de grâce *or* empreinte d'une tranquille assurance; **he is young and lacks ~** il est jeune et manque d'assurance *or* d'aisance.
2 vt (*balance*) mettre en équilibre; (*hold balanced*) tenir en équilibre, maintenir en équilibre. **she ~d her pen** *or* **held her pen ~d over her notebook** elle tenait son stylo suspendu au-dessus du bloc-notes (, prête à écrire); **he ~d himself on his toes** il s'est tenu sur la pointe des pieds (sans bouger); **to be ~d** (*balanced*) être en équilibre; (*held, hanging*) être suspendu immobile; (*hovering*) être immobile *or* suspendu (en l'air); **the diver was ~d at the edge of the pool** le plongeur se tenait sur le rebord de la piscine prêt à plonger; **the tiger was ~d ready to spring** le tigre se tenait (immobile) prêt à bondir; **~d (ready) to attack/for the attack** (tout) prêt à attaquer/pour l'attaque; (*fig*) **~d on the brink of success/ruin** au bord de la réussite/de la ruine; **to be ~d between life and death** être entre la vie et la mort.

poison ['pɔɪzn] 1 n (*lit, fig*) poison *m*; *[snake]* venin *m*. **to take ~** s'empoisonner; **to die of ~** mourir empoisonné; (*fig: offering drink*) **what's your ~?**‡ tu te soûles‡ à quoi?; *see* **hate, rat**.
2 comp ►**poison fang** dent venimeuse ►**poison gas** gaz toxique *or* asphyxiant ►**poison gland** glande *f* à venin ►**poison ivy** (*Bot*) sumac vénéneux ►**poison-pen letter** lettre *f* anonyme venimeuse.
3 vt *[person] person, food, well, arrow* empoisonner; *[noxious substance] person* empoisonner, intoxiquer; *rivers etc* empoisonner. **a ~ed foot/finger** *etc* un pied/doigt *etc* infecté; **the drugs are ~ing his system** les drogues l'intoxiquent; (*fig*) **it is ~ing their friendship** cela empoisonne *or* gâche *or* gâte leur amitié; **to ~ sb's mind** (*corrupt*) corrompre qn; (*instil doubts*) faire douter qn; **he ~ed her mind against her husband** il l'a fait douter de son mari.

poisoner ['pɔɪznəʳ] n empoisonneur *m*, -euse *f* (*lit*).

poisoning ['pɔɪznɪŋ] n (*see* **poison 3**) empoisonnement *m*; intoxication *f*. **to die of ~** mourir empoisonné; **arsenic ~** empoisonnement à l'arsenic; *see* **food, lead²**.

poisonous ['pɔɪznəs] adj *snake* venimeux; *plant* vénéneux; *gas, fumes* toxique, asphyxiant; *substance* toxique; (*fig*) *propaganda, rumours, doctrine* pernicieux, diabolique. **he is quite ~*** il est absolument ignoble; **this coffee is ~*** ce café est infect.

poke¹ [pəʊk] n (*dial, esp Scot*) sac *m*; *see* **pig**.

poke² [pəʊk] 1 n (*push*) poussée *f*; (*jab*) (petit) coup *m* (*de coude, de canne, avec le doigt etc*); (*US *: punch*) coup de poing. **to give the fire a ~** donner un coup de tisonnier au feu; **to give sb a ~ in the ribs** enfoncer son coude (*or* son doigt *etc*) dans les côtes de qn, pousser qn dans les côtes avec son coude (*or* son doigt *etc*), pousser qn du coude; **I got a ~ in the eye from his umbrella** j'ai reçu son parapluie dans l'œil; **he gave the ground a ~ with his stick** il a enfoncé sa canne dans le sol.
2 vt a (*jab with elbow, finger, stick etc*) pousser, donner un coup de coude (*or* de canne *or* avec le doigt) à; (*US *: punch*) donner un coup de poing à; (*thrust*) *stick, finger etc* enfoncer (*into* dans, *through* à travers); *rag etc* fourrer (*into* dans). **to ~ the fire** tisonner le feu; **he ~d me with his umbrella** il m'a donné un petit coup de parapluie, il m'a poussé avec son parapluie; **he ~d his finger in her eye** il lui a mis le doigt dans l'œil; **he ~d the ground with his stick, he ~d his stick into the ground** il a enfoncé sa canne dans le sol; **he ~d me in the ribs** il m'a enfoncé son coude (*or* son doigt *etc*) dans les côtes, il m'a poussé dans les côtes avec son coude (*or* son doigt), il m'a poussé du coude; (*US*) **he ~d me one in the stomach*** il m'a envoyé son poing dans l'estomac; **he ~d his finger at me** il pointa son index vers moi; **he ~d his finger up his nose** il s'est fourré le doigt dans le nez; **to ~ one's head out of the window** passer la tête hors de *or* par la fenêtre; **to ~ a hole in sth (with one's finger/stick** *etc*) faire un trou dans qch *or* percer qch (avec le doigt/sa canne *etc*); *see* **fun, nose**. b (*Brit* **: *sexually*) faire l'amour avec, tringler**.
3 vi a (*also* **~ out**) *[elbows, stomach, stick]* sortir, dépasser (*from, through* de). b **he ~d at me with his finger** il pointa son index vers moi; **he ~d at the suitcase with his stick** il poussa la valise avec sa canne; **the children were poking at their food** les enfants chipotaient (en mangeant); (*fig*) **to ~ into sth*** fourrer le nez dans qch, fourgonner dans qch.

►**poke about, poke around** vi a (*lit*) fourrager; fureter. **to poke about in a drawer/a dustbin** fourrager dans un tiroir/une poubelle; **I spent the morning poking about in antique shops** j'ai passé la matinée à fureter dans les magasins d'antiquités. b (*pej*) fouiner. **he was poking about in my study** il fouinait dans mon bureau.

►**poke in** vt sep *head* passer (à l'intérieur); *stick etc* enfoncer; *rag* fourrer. (*fig*) **to poke one's nose in*** fourrer son nez dans les affaires des autres, se mêler de ce qui ne vous regarde pas.

►**poke out** 1 vi a = **poke 3a**. b (*bulge*) *[stomach, chest, bottom]* être protubérant *or* proéminent. 2 vt sep a sortir. **the tortoise poked its head out** la tortue a sorti la tête. b (*remove etc*) faire partir, déloger. **he poked the ants out with a stick** il a délogé les fourmis avec un bâton; **to poke sb's eye out** crever l'œil à qn.

poker¹ ['pəʊkəʳ] n (*for fire etc*) tisonnier *m*. (*NonC*) **~ work** (*craft*) pyrogravure *f*; (*objects*) pyrogravures *fpl*; *see* **stiff**.

poker² ['pəʊkəʳ] 1 n (*Cards*) poker *m*. 2 comp ►**poker-face** visage *m* impassible ►**poker-faced** au visage impassible.

pokey‡ ['pəʊkɪ] n (*US: jail*) trou* *m*, taule‡ *f*.

poky ['pəʊkɪ] adj (*pej*) *house, room* exigu (*f* -guë) et sombre.

pol* [pɒl] n (*US*) (abbr of **politician**) homme *m or* personnalité *f* politique.

Polack‡ ['pəʊlæk] n (*pej*) Polaque *mf*, Polonais(e) *m(f)*.

Poland ['pəʊlənd] n Pologne *f*.

polar ['pəʊləʳ] adj (*Elec, Geog*) polaire. **~ bear** ours blanc; **P~ Circle** cercle *m* polaire; **~ front** front *m* polaire; **~ lights** aurore *f* polaire *or* boréale.

polarimeter [,pəʊlə'rɪmɪtəʳ] n polarimètre *m*.

polariscope [pəʊ'lærɪskəʊp] n polariscope *m*.

polarity [pəʊ'lærɪtɪ] n polarité *f*.

polarization [,pəʊləraɪ'zeɪʃən] n (*lit, fig*) polarisation *f*.

polarize ['pəʊləraɪz] vt (*lit, fig*) polariser.

Polaroid ['pəʊlərɔɪd] ® 1 adj polaroïd ® *inv*. 2 n (*also* **~ camera**) (appareil *m*) Polaroïd *m*; (*also* **~ print**) photo *f* polaroïd. (*also* **~ sunglasses**) **~s** lunettes *fpl* de soleil à verres polaroïd.

Pole [pəʊl] n Polonais(e) *m(f)*.

pole¹ [pəʊl] 1 n a (*rod*) perche *f*; (*fixed*) poteau *m*, mât *m*; (*flag~, tent ~; also in gymnastics, for climbing*) mât; (*telegraph ~*) poteau télégraphique; (*curtain ~*) tringle *f*; (*barber's ~*) enseigne *f* de coiffeur; (*in fire station*) perche *f*; (*for vaulting, punting*) perche. **their only weapons were wooden ~s** leurs seules armes étaient des perches *or* de longs bâtons; (*fig*) **to be up the ~*** (*mistaken*) se gourer‡, se tromper; (*mad*) dérailler* (*fig*); (*fig: mad*) **to send** *or* **drive sb up the ~*** rendre qn fou (*f* folle), faire perdre la tête à qn; *see* **greasy, ski** *etc*. b (*Ski*) (*ski stick*) bâton *m*; (*marking run*) piquet *m*. c (*††: measure*) = 5,029 mètres.
2 comp ►**poleax(e)** *see* **poleax(e)** ►**pole jump, pole vault** (*Sport*) n saut *m* à la perche ►**pole-vault** vi sauter à la perche ►**pole jumper, pole vaulter** sauteur *m*, -euse *f* à la perche, perchiste *mf* ►**pole jumping, pole vaulting** saut *m* à la perche.
3 vt *punt etc* faire avancer (à l'aide d'une perche).

pole² [pəʊl] 1 n (*Elec, Geog*) pôle *m*. **North/South P~** pôle Nord/Sud; **from ~ to ~** d'un pôle à l'autre; (*fig*) **they are ~s apart** ils sont aux antipodes (l'un de l'autre). 2 comp ►**the Pole Star** L'Etoile *f* polaire.

poleax(e) ['pəʊlæks] 1 n (*weapon*) hache *f* d'armes; *[butcher etc]* merlin *m*. 2 vt *cattle etc* abattre, assommer; (*fig*) *person* terrasser.

polecat ['pəʊlkæt] **n, pl ~s** *or* **~** putois *m*.

pol. econ. (**abbr of political economy**) *see* **political**.

polemic [pɒ'lemɪk] 1 **adj** polémique. 2 **n** (*argument*) polémique *f*. **~s** polémique (*NonC*).

polemical [pɒ'lemɪkəl] **adj** polémique.

police [pə'liːs] 1 **n** (*NonC*) a (*organization*) ≃ police *f* (*under Ministry of the Interior: gen in towns*); gendarmerie *f* (*under Ministry of War: throughout France*). (*collective*) **the ~** la police, les gendarmes *mpl*; **to join the ~** entrer dans la police, se faire policier *or* gendarme; **he is in the ~, he is a member of the ~** il est dans *or* de la police, il est policier, il est gendarme; **extra ~ were called in** on a fait venir des renforts de police; **the ~ are on his track** la police est sur sa piste, les gendarmes sont sur sa piste; **river/railway ~** police fluviale/des chemins de fer; *see* **mounted** *etc*.

b (*US Mil*) corvée *f* (militaire) de rangement et de nettoyage.

2 **comp** (*gen*) de la police; *leave, vehicle, members* de la police *or* de la gendarmerie; *campaign, control, inquiry* policier, de la police *or* de la gendarmerie; *sergeant etc* de police; *harassment* par la police ►**police academy** école *f* de police ►**police car** voiture *f* de police ►**police chief** (*Brit*) ≃ préfet *m* (de police); (*US*) ≃ (commissaire *m*) divisionnaire *m* ►**Police Complaints Board** ≃ inspection *f* générale des services ►**police constable** *see* **constable** ►**police court** tribunal *m* de police ►**police custody** *see* **custody** ►**police department** (*US*) service *m* de police ►**police dog** (*gen*) chien *m* policier; (*US: alsatian*) berger *m* allemand ►**police escort** escorte policière ►**the police force** la police, les gendarmes *mpl*, les forces *fpl* de l'ordre; **member of the police force** policier *m*; **to join the police force** entrer dans la police ►**police headquarters** administration *f* centrale, siège *m* central ►**police intervention** intervention *f* de la police ►**policeman** *see* **policeman** ►**police office** gendarmerie *f* (*bureaux*) ►**police officer** policier *m*, fonctionnaire *m* de la police; **to become a police officer** entrer dans la police ►**police presence** présence *f* policière ►**police protection** protection *f* de la police ►**police record: to have a police record** avoir un casier judiciaire; **he hasn't a police record** il a un casier judiciaire vierge ►**the police service** (*the police, collectively*) la police ►**police state** état policier ►**police station** poste *m* *or* commissariat *m* de police, gendarmerie *f* ►**police wagon** (*US*) voiture *f* *or* fourgon *m* cellulaire ►**policewoman** femme *f* policier, femme *f* agent (de police) ►**police work** le métier de policier.

3 **vt** a (*lit: with policemen*) **it was decided to ~ the streets** on a décidé d'envoyer des agents de police (*or* des gendarmes) pour maintenir l'ordre dans les rues.

b *[vigilantes, volunteers etc] district, road, football match etc* faire la police dans (*or* à, sur *etc*); (*Mil*) *frontier, territory* contrôler, maintenir la paix dans (*or* à, sur *etc*); (*fig*) *agreements, controls* veiller à l'application de; *prices etc* contrôler. **the border is ~d by U.N. patrols** la frontière est sous la surveillance des patrouilles de l'O.N.U.

c (*US: keep clean*) nettoyer.

policeman [pə'liːsmən] **n, pl -men** (*in town*) agent *m* de police, gardien *m* de la paix; (*in country*) gendarme *m*. **to become a ~** entrer dans la police; **I knew he was a ~** je savais qu'il était de la police.

policing [pə'liːsɪŋ] **n** maintien *m* de l'ordre.

policy[1] ['pɒlɪsɪ] 1 **n** a (*aims, principles etc*) (*Pol*) politique *f*; *[newspaper, company, organisation]* politique (générale), ligne *f* (d'action); (*course of action*) règle *f*. **the government's policies** la politique du gouvernement; (*Pol*) **foreign/economic/social ~** politique étrangère/économique/sociale; **what is the company ~ on this matter?** quelle est la ligne suivie par la compagnie à ce sujet?; **the paper followed a ~ of attacking the Church** le journal attaquait systématiquement l'Église; **the Ruritanian ~ of expelling its critics** la politique d'expulsion pratiquée par les Ruritaniens à l'encontre de leurs critiques, la politique des Ruritaniens consistant à expulser ceux qui les critiquent; **nationalization is a matter of ~ for the party** les nationalisations sont une question de principe pour le parti; **it has always been our ~ to deliver goods free** nous avons toujours eu pour règle de livrer les marchandises franco de port; **my ~ has always been to wait and see** j'ai toujours eu pour règle d'attendre et de voir venir; **it would be good/bad ~ to do that** ce serait une bonne/mauvaise politique que de faire cela; **complete frankness is the best ~** la franchise totale est la meilleure politique; *see* **honesty**.

b (*NonC: prudence*) (bonne) politique *f*. **it would not be ~ to refuse** il ne serait pas politique de refuser.

2 **comp** (*gen*) *discussions etc* de politique générale ►**policy committee** comité *m* directeur ►**policy decision** décision *f* de principe ►**policy maker** (*within organization, firm etc*) décideur *m*; (*for political party etc*) responsable *m* politique ►**policy matter** question *f* de politique générale *or* de principe ►**policy paper** document *m* de politique générale ►**policy statement: to make a policy statement** faire une déclaration de principe.

policy[2] ['pɒlɪsɪ] **n** (*Insurance*) police *f* (d'assurance). **to take out a ~** souscrire à une police d'assurance; **~holder** assuré(e) *m(f)*, détenteur *m*, -trice *f* d'une police.

polio ['pəʊlɪəʊ] **n** (**abbr of poliomyelitis**) polio *f*. **~ victim** polio *mf*.

poliomyelitis ['pəʊlɪəʊmaɪə'laɪtɪs] **n** poliomyélite *f*.

Polish ['pəʊlɪʃ] 1 **adj** polonais. 2 **n** (*Ling*) polonais *m*.

polish ['pɒlɪʃ] 1 **n** a (*substance*) (*for shoes*) cirage *m*, crème *f* (à chaussures); (*for floor, furniture*) encaustique *f*, cire *f*; (*for nails*) vernis *m* (à ongles). **metal ~** produit *m* d'entretien pour les métaux.

b (*act*) **to give sth a ~** faire briller qch; **my shoes need a ~** mes chaussures ont besoin d'être cirées.

c (*shine*) poli *m*, éclat *m*, brillant *m*; (*fig: refinement*) *[person]* raffinement *m*; *[style, work, performance]* perfection *f*, élégance *f*. **high ~** lustre *m*; **to put a ~ on sth** faire briller qch; **the buttons have lost their ~** les boutons ont perdu leur éclat *or* leur brillant.

2 **vt** (*also* **~ up**) *stones, glass* polir; *shoes* cirer; *floor, furniture* cirer, astiquer, faire briller; *car* astiquer, briquer; *pans, metal* fourbir, astiquer, faire briller; *leather* lustrer; (*fig*) *person* parfaire l'éducation de; *manners* affiner; *style, language* polir, châtier. **to ~ (up) one's French** perfectionner *or* travailler son français; **the style needs ~ing** le style manque de poli *or* laisse à désirer *or* aurait besoin d'être plus soigné; *see also* **polished**.

►**polish off** **vt sep** *food, drink* finir; *work, correspondence* expédier; *competitor, enemy* régler son compte à, en finir avec; (*‡: kill*) liquider*, nettoyer‡. **he polished off the meal** il a tout mangé jusqu'à la dernière miette.

►**polish up** **vt sep** = **polish 2**.

polished ['pɒlɪʃt] **adj** *surface* poli, brillant; *floor, shoes* ciré, brillant; *leather* lustré; *silver, ornaments* brillant, fourbi, astiqué; *stone, glass* poli; (*fig*) *person* qui a de l'éducation *or* du savoir-vivre; *manners* raffiné; *style* poli, châtié; *performer* accompli; *performance* impeccable.

polisher ['pɒlɪʃər] **n** (*person*) polisseur *m*, -euse *f*; (*machine: gen*) polissoir *m*; (*for floors*) cireuse *f*; (*for pebbles etc*) polisseuse *f*.

Politburo ['pɒlɪtbjʊərəʊ] **n** Politburo *m*.

polite [pə'laɪt] **adj** *person, remark* poli. **to be ~ to sb** être poli *or* correct avec *or* envers *or* à l'égard de qn; **when I said it was not his best work I was being ~** c'est par pure politesse que j'ai dit que ce n'était pas sa meilleure œuvre, en disant que ce n'est pas sa meilleure œuvre j'ai voulu être poli; **be ~ about his car!** ne dis pas de mal de sa voiture!; **in ~ society** dans la bonne société.

politely [pə'laɪtlɪ] **adv** poliment, avec politesse.

politeness [pə'laɪtnɪs] **n** politesse *f*. **to do sth out of ~** faire qch par politesse.

politic ['pɒlɪtɪk] 1 **adj** politique, diplomatique. **he thought** *or* **deemed it ~ to refuse** il a jugé politique de refuser; *see* **body**. 2 **n: ~s** politique *f*; **to talk ~s** parler politique; **to go into ~s** choisir *or* embrasser une carrière politique, se lancer dans la politique; **foreign ~s** politique étrangère; *see* **party**.

political [pə'lɪtɪkəl] **adj** (*all senses*) politique. **~ economy/geography** économie *f*/géographie *f* politique; **~ science** sciences *fpl* politiques; **~ scientist** spécialiste *mf* des sciences politiques; (*US*) **~ action committee** comité *m* de soutien (*d'un candidat*); **to ask for ~ asylum** demander le droit d'asile (politique); **~ analyst** *or* **expert** *or* **commentator** politologue *mf*; (*US*) **~ convention** convention *f* politique; **he's a ~ animal** il a la politique dans le sang; *see* **party, protest**.

politically [pə'lɪtɪkəlɪ] 1 **adv** politiquement. **~ correct** politiquement correct. 2 **comp** ►**politically-minded, politically-orientated** qui s'intéresse à la politique.

politician [ˌpɒlɪ'tɪʃən] **n** homme *m* politique, femme *f* politique, politicien(ne) *m(f)* (*pej*).

politicization [pəlɪtɪsaɪ'zeɪʃən] **n** politisation *f*.

politicize [pə'lɪtɪsaɪz] **vt** politiser.

politicking ['pɒlɪtɪkɪŋ] **n** (*pej*) politique *f* politicienne.

politico* [pə'lɪtɪkəʊ] **n, pl ~s** (*pej: politician*) politicard *m*. (*very political person*) **he's a real ~** il est vraiment très politisé.

politico... [pə'lɪtɪkəʊ] **pref** politico... .

polity ['pɒlɪtɪ] **n** (*system of government*) régime *m*, administration *f* politique; (*government organization*) constitution *f* politique; (*the State*) État *m*.

polka ['pɒlkə] **n, pl ~s** polka *f*. **~ dot** pois *m* (*sur tissu*).

poll [pəʊl] 1 **n** a (*vote in general*) vote *m*; (*voting at election*) scrutin *m*; (*election*) élection(s) *f(pl)*; (*list of voters*) liste électorale; (*voting place*) bureau *m* de vote; (*votes cast*) voix *fpl*, suffrages *mpl*. **to take a ~ on sth** procéder à un vote sur *or* au sujet de qch; **the result of the ~** le résultat de l'élection *or* du scrutin; **on the eve of the ~** à la veille de l'élection *or* du scrutin; **people under 18 are excluded from the ~** les jeunes de moins de 18 ans n'ont pas le droit de vote *or* ne peuvent pas voter; **to go to the ~s** aller aux urnes; **a crushing defeat at the ~s** une écrasante défaite aux élections; **to head the ~** arriver en tête de scrutin, avoir la majorité des suffrages; **there was an 84% ~, there was an 84% turnout at the ~s** 84% des inscrits ont voté, la participation électorale était de (l'ordre de) 84%; **the ~ was heavy/light** *or* **low** la participation électorale était importante *or* forte/faible; **he got 20% of the ~** il a obtenu 20% des suffrages exprimés; **he achieved a ~ of 5,000 votes** il a obtenu 5.000 voix; *see* **standing**.

b (*opinion survey*) sondage *m*. **(public) opinion ~** sondage d'opinion; **to take a ~** sonder l'opinion (*of* de); *see* **Gallup**.

c (*††: head*) chef† *m*.

2 **comp** ►**poll taker** (*US*) sondeur *m* ►**poll tax** (*gen*) capitation *f*; (*Brit*) ≃ impôts *mpl* locaux.

3 vt a *votes* obtenir; *people* sonder, interroger. **they ~ed the students to find out whether ...** ils ont sondé l'opinion des étudiants pour savoir si ...; **40% of those ~ed supported the government** 40% de ceux qui ont participé au sondage *or* 40% des personnes interrogées étaient pour le gouvernement.
b *cattle* décorner; *tree* étêter, écimer.
4 vi a **the party will ~ badly/heavily in Scotland** le parti obtiendra peu de/beaucoup de voix *or* de suffrages en Écosse.
b (*vote*) voter.

pollack ['pɒlək] n, pl ~s *or* ~ lieu *m* jaune.

pollard ['pɒləd] 1 n (*animal*) animal *m* sans cornes; (*tree*) têtard *m*, arbre étêté *or* écimé. 2 vt *animal* décorner; *tree* étêter, écimer.

pollen ['pɒlən] n pollen *m*. ~ **count** taux *m* de pollen.

pollinate ['pɒlɪneɪt] vt féconder (avec du pollen).

pollination [,pɒlɪ'neɪʃən] n pollinisation *f*, fécondation *f*.

polling ['pəʊlɪŋ] 1 n élections *fpl*. ~ **is on Thursday** les élections ont lieu jeudi, on vote jeudi; ~ **was heavy** il y a eu une forte participation électorale, le nombre des votants a été élevé. 2 comp ►**polling booth** isoloir *m* ►**polling day** jour *m* des élections ►**polling place** (*US*), **polling station** (*Brit*) bureau *m* de vote.

pollock ['pɒlək] n = **pollack**.

pollster ['pəʊlstəʳ] n sondeur *m*, enquêteur *m*, -euse *f*.

pollutant [pə'lu:tənt] n polluant *m*.

pollute [pə'lu:t] vt polluer; (*fig*) contaminer; (*corrupt*) corrompre; (*desecrate*) profaner, polluer (*liter*). **the river was ~d with chemicals** la rivière était polluée par des produits chimiques.

polluter [pə'lu:təʳ] n pollueur *m*, -euse *f*.

pollution [pə'lu:ʃən] n (*see* **pollute**) pollution *f*; contamination *f*; profanation *f*. **air** ~ pollution de l'air.

Pollyanna [pɒlɪ'ænə] n (*US*) optimiste *m(f)* béat(e).

polo ['pəʊləʊ] 1 n polo *m*; *see* **water**. 2 comp ►**poloneck** n col roulé ◊ adj à col roulé ►**polo shirt** polo *m*, chemise *f* polo ►**polo stick** maillet *m* (de polo).

polonaise [,pɒlə'neɪz] n (*Mus, Dance*) polonaise *f*.

polonium [pə'ləʊnɪəm] n polonium *m*.

poltergeist ['pɔ:ltəgaɪst] n esprit frappeur.

poltroon† [pɒl'tru:n] n poltron *m*.

poly* ['pɒlɪ] n (abbr of **polytechnic**) ≃ IUT *m*.

poly... ['pɒlɪ] pref poly... .

polyandrous [,pɒlɪ'ændrəs] adj polyandre.

polyandry ['pɒlɪændrɪ] n polyandrie *f*.

polyanthus [,pɒlɪ'ænθəs] n primevère *f* (multiflore).

polyarchy ['pɒlɪ,ɑ:kɪ] n polyarchie *f*.

polychlorinated biphenyl [,pɒlɪ'klɔ:rɪneɪtɪdbaɪ'fenəl] n polychlorobiphényle *m*.

polychromatic [,pɒlɪkrəʊ'mætɪk] adj polychrome.

polychrome ['pɒlɪkrəʊm] 1 adj polychrome. 2 n statue *f* (*or* tableau *m etc*) polychrome.

polyclinic ['pɒlɪklɪnɪk] n polyclinique *f*.

polycotton ['pɒlɪ'kɒtən] n polyester *m* et coton *m*.

polyester [,pɒlɪ'estəʳ] 1 n polyester *m*. 2 comp de *or* en polyester.

polyethylene [,pɒlɪ'eθəli:n] n (*US*) polyéthylène *m*, polythène *m*.

polygamist [pɒ'lɪgəmɪst] n polygame *mf*.

polygamous [pɒ'lɪgəməs] adj polygame.

polygamy [pɒ'lɪgəmɪ] n polygamie *f*.

polygenesis [,pɒlɪ'dʒenɪsɪs] n polygénisme *m*.

polygenetic [,pɒlɪdʒɪ'netɪk] adj polygénétique.

polyglot ['pɒlɪglɒt] adj, n polyglotte (*mf*).

polygon ['pɒlɪgən] n polygone *m*.

polygonal [pɒ'lɪgənl] adj polygonal.

polygraph ['pɒlɪgrɑ:f] n détecteur *m* de mensonges.

polyhedra [,pɒlɪ'hi:drə] npl of **polyhedron**.

polyhedral [,pɒlɪ'hi:drəl] adj polyédrique.

polyhedron [,pɒlɪ'hi:drən] n, pl ~s *or* **polyhedra** polyèdre *m*.

polymath ['pɒlɪmæθ] n esprit *m* universel.

polymer ['pɒlɪməʳ] n polymère *m*.

polymerization ['pɒlɪməraɪ'zeɪʃən] n polymérisation *f*.

polymorphism [,pɒlɪ'mɔ:fɪzəm] n polymorphisme *m*, polymorphie *f*.

polymorphous [,pɒlɪ'mɔ:fəs] adj polymorphe.

Polynesia [,pɒlɪ'ni:zɪə] n Polynésie *f*.

Polynesian [,pɒlɪ'ni:zɪən] 1 adj polynésien. 2 n a Polynésien(ne) *m(f)*. b (*Ling*) polynésien *m*.

polynomial [,pɒlɪ'nəʊmɪəl] adj, n polynôme (*m*).

polyp ['pɒlɪp] n (*Zool, Med*) polype *m*.

polyphase ['pɒlɪfeɪz] adj polyphasé.

polyphonic [,pɒlɪ'fɒnɪk] adj polyphonique.

polyphony [pə'lɪfənɪ] n polyphonie *f*.

polypi ['pɒlɪpaɪ] npl of **polypus**.

polypropylene [,pɒlɪ'prɒpɪli:n] n polypropylène *m*.

polypus ['pɒlɪpəs] n, pl **polypi** (*Med*) polype *m*.

polysemic [,pɒlɪ'si:mɪk] adj polysémique.

polysemous [pɒ'lɪsəməs] adj polysémique.

polysemy [pɒ'lɪsəmɪ] n polysémie *f*.

polystyrene [,pɒlɪ'staɪri:n] 1 n polystyrène *m*. **expanded** ~ polystyrène expansé. 2 comp ►**polystyrene cement** colle *f* polystyrène ►**polystyrene chips** billes *fpl* (de) polystyrène.

polysyllabic ['pɒlɪsɪ'læbɪk] adj polysyllabe, polysyllabique.

polysyllable ['pɒlɪ,sɪləbl] n polysyllabe *m*, mot *m* polysyllabique.

polytechnic [,pɒlɪ'teknɪk] n (*Brit*) ≃ IUT *m*, Institut *m* Universitaire de Technologie.

polytheism ['pɒlɪθi:ɪzəm] n polythéisme *m*.

polytheistic [,pɒlɪθi:'ɪstɪk] adj polythéiste.

polythene ['pɒlɪθi:n] n (*Brit*) polyéthylène *m*, polythène *m*. ~ **bag** sac *m* en plastique *or* polyéthylène.

polyunsaturated [,pɒlɪʌn'sætʃʊ,reɪtɪd] adj polyinsaturé.

polyurethane [,pɒlɪ'jʊərɪθeɪn] n polyuréthane *m*.

polyvalent [pə'lɪvələnt] adj polyvalent.

polyvinyl ['pɒlɪvaɪnl] n polyvinyl *m*.

pom [pɒm] = **pommy**.

pomade [pə'mɑ:d] 1 n pommade *f*. 2 vt pommader.

pomander [pəʊ'mændəʳ] n (*china*) diffuseur *m* de parfum.

pomegranate ['pɒmə,grænɪt] n (*fruit*) grenade *f*; (*tree*) grenadier *m*.

pomelo ['pɒmɪləʊ] n, pl ~s pomelo *m*.

Pomeranian [,pɒmə'reɪnɪən] n (*dog*) loulou *m* (de Poméranie).

pommel ['pʌml] 1 n pommeau *m*. 2 comp ►**pommel horse** cheval *m* d'arçons. 3 vt = **pummel**.

pommy⁑ ['pɒmɪ] (*Austral pej*) 1 n Anglais(e) *m(f)*, ≃ rosbif *m* (*pej*). 2 adj anglais.

pomp [pɒmp] n pompe *f*, faste *m*, apparat *m*. ~ **and circumstance** grand apparat, pompes (*liter*); **with great** ~ en grande pompe.

Pompadour ['pɒmpə,dʊəʳ] n (*US: hairstyle*) banane *f* (*coiffure*).

Pompeii [pɒm'peɪɪ] n Pompéi.

Pompey ['pɒmpɪ] n Pompée *m*.

pompom ['pɒmpɒm] n a (*bobble*) pompon *m*. b (*Mil*) canon-mitrailleuse *m* (de D.C.A.).

pompon ['pɒmpɒn] n a (*bobble*) pompon *m*. b (*Bot*) ~ **dahlia/rose** dahlia *m*/rose *f* pompon.

pomposity [pɒm'pɒsɪtɪ] n (*pej*) manières pompeuses, air *or* ton pompeux, solennité *f*.

pompous ['pɒmpəs] adj (*pej*) *person* pompeux, solennel, plein de son importance; *remark, speech, tone, voice* pompeux, pontifiant, solennel; *style* pompeux, ampoulé.

pompously ['pɒmpəslɪ] adv (*pej*) pompeusement, d'un ton *or* d'un air pompeux.

ponce⁑ [pɒns] (*Brit*) 1 n a (*pimp*) maquereau⁑ *m*, souteneur *m*. b (*homosexual*) pédé⁑ *m*. 2 vi faire le maquereau⁑, être souteneur.
►**ponce about**⁑, **ponce around**⁑ vi se pavaner.

poncho ['pɒntʃəʊ] n, pl ~s poncho *m*.

pond [pɒnd] 1 n étang *m*; (*stagnant*) mare *f*; (*artificial*) bassin *m*; *see* **fish, mill** *etc*. 2 comp ►**pondlife** vie animale des eaux stagnantes ►**pondweed** épi *m* d'eau, potamot *m*.

ponder ['pɒndəʳ] 1 vt considérer, peser, réfléchir à *or* sur. 2 vi méditer (*over, on* sur), réfléchir (*over, on* à, sur).

ponderable ['pɒndərəbl] adj pondérable.

ponderous ['pɒndərəs] adj *movement, object* lourd, pesant; *style, joke* lourd; *speech, tone, voice* pesant et solennel.

ponderously ['pɒndərəslɪ] adv *move* pesamment; *write* avec lourdeur; *say, declaim* d'une voix pesante et solennelle.

pone [pəʊn] n (*US*) pain *m* de maïs.

pong⁑ [pɒŋ] (*Brit*) 1 n mauvaise odeur, (*stronger*) puanteur *f*. **what a ~ in here!** ça pue ici! 2 vi puer.

pons Varolii [pɒnzvə'rəʊlɪaɪ] n pont *m* de Varole, protubérance *f* annulaire.

pontiff ['pɒntɪf] n (*Rel*) (*dignitary*) pontife *m*; (*pope*) souverain pontife, pontife romain.

pontifical [pɒn'tɪfɪkəl] adj (*Rel*) pontifical; (*fig*) pontifiant.

pontificate [pɒn'tɪfɪkɪt] 1 n (*Rel*) pontificat *m*. 2 [pɒn'tɪfɪkeɪt] vi (*fig*) pontifier (*about* au sujet de, sur).

Pontius Pilate ['pɒnʃəs'paɪlət] n Ponce Pilate *m*.

pontoon [pɒn'tu:n] 1 n a (*gen*) ponton *m*; (*on aircraft*) flotteur *m*. b (*Brit Cards*) vingt-et-un *m*. 2 comp ►**pontoon bridge** pont flottant.

pony ['pəʊnɪ] 1 n poney *m*; (*Brit* ⁑) 25 livres; (*US Scol* ⁑: *crib*) traduc* *f*, corrigé *m* (*utilisé illicitement*). 2 comp ►**pony express** (*US Hist*) messageries *fpl* rapides par relais de cavaliers ►**ponytail** queue *f* de cheval; **hair in a ponytail** cheveux *mpl* en queue de cheval ►**pony trekking** randonnée *f* équestre *or* à cheval.

pooch⁑ [pu:tʃ] n cabot⁑ *m*, clebs⁑ *m*.

poodle ['pu:dl] n caniche *m*; (*fig: servile person*) chien *m*.

poof [pʊf] 1 n (*Brit pej:* ⁑) tante⁑ *f*, tapette⁑ *f*. 2 excl hop!

poofter⁑ ['pʊftəʳ] n (*Brit pej*) = **poof**.

poofy⁑ ['pʊfɪ] adj (*Brit pej*) efféminé, du genre tapette⁑. **it's ~** ça fait fille.

pooh [pu:] 1 excl bah!, peuh! 2 n (*Brit baby talk*) **to do a ~*** faire caca*. 3 vi (*Brit baby talk*) faire caca*. 4 comp ►**pooh-pooh**: **to pooh-pooh sth** faire fi de qch, dédaigner qch.

pool[1] [pu:l] n a (*puddle*) [*water, rain*] flaque *f* (d'eau); [*spilt liquid*] flaque, (*larger*) mare *f*; (*fig*) [*light from lamp, spot, flood*] rond *m*; [*sun-*

light] flaque; *[shadow]* zone *f*. **lying in a ~ of blood** étendu dans une mare de sang; **in a ~ of light** dans une flaque *or* un rond de lumière.
b (*pond*) (*natural*) étang *m*; (*artificial*) bassin *m*, pièce *f* d'eau; (*in river*) plan *m* d'eau; (*water hole*) point *m* d'eau; (*swimming ~*) piscine *f*; *see* **paddle**.

pool² [pu:l] 1 n a (*money*) (*Cards etc: stake*) poule *f*, cagnotte *f*; (*gen: common fund*) cagnotte.
b (*fig*) (*of things owned in common*) fonds *m* commun; (*reserve, source*) *[ideas, experience, ability]* réservoir *m*; *[advisers, experts]* équipe *f*. **a ~ of vehicles** un parc de voitures; **(typing) ~** bureau *m* des dactylos, pool *m*, dactylo *f*; **genetic ~** pool *m* génétique.
c (*Econ: consortium*) pool *m*; (*US: monopoly trust*) trust *m*. **the coal and steel ~** le pool du charbon et de l'acier.
d **the ~s** = **the football ~s**; *see* **football**.
e (*US: billiards*) billard américain. **to shoot ~** jouer au billard américain.
2 comp ▸**poolroom** (*Billiards*) (salle *f* de) billard *m* ▸**pool table** billard *m* (*table*).
3 vt *money, resources, objects* mettre en commun; *knowledge, efforts* unir.

poop¹ [pu:p] n (*Naut*) poupe *f*. **~ deck** dunette *f*.

poop²‡ [pu:p] n (*excrement*) crotte *f*.

poop³* [pu:p] n (*US*) (*information*) tuyau* *m*, bon renseignement *m*.

pooped‡ [pu:pt] adj (*exhausted*) pompé‡, crevé*, à plat*.

pooper-scooper* ['pu:pə'sku:pəʳ] n ramasse-crottes *m*.

poor [pʊəʳ] 1 adj a (*not rich*) *person, family, nation* pauvre. **as ~ as a church-mouse** pauvre comme un rat *or* comme Job; **how ~ is he really?** jusqu'à quel point est-il pauvre?; **to become ~er** s'appauvrir; **in ~ circumstances** dans le besoin, dans la gêne; (*fig: lacking*) **~ in mineral resources** pauvre en minerais; *see also* **3**, *and* **white** *etc*.
b (*inferior*) *amount, sales, harvest, output* maigre, médiocre; *work, worker, soldier, film, result, food, holiday, summer* médiocre, piètre (*before n*); *effort* insuffisant; *light* faible; *sight* faible, mauvais; *soil* pauvre, peu productif; *cards* médiocre. (*Scol etc: as mark*) "~" "faible", "médiocre"; **he has a ~ chance of success** il a peu de chances de réussir; **to have ~ hearing** être dur d'oreille; **he has a ~ memory** il n'a pas bonne mémoire; **to be in ~ health** ne pas être en bonne santé, être en mauvaise santé; **a ~ meal of bread and water** un maigre *or* piètre repas de pain et d'eau; **it was a ~ evening** ça n'a pas été une soirée réussie, la soirée n'a pas été une réussite; **he showed a ~ grasp of the facts** il a manifesté un manque de compréhension des faits; (*iro*) **in my ~ opinion** à mon humble avis; **to be ~ at (doing) sth, to be a ~ hand at (doing) sth** ne pas être doué pour (faire) qch; **this sparkling wine is just a ~ relation of champagne** ce vin pétillant n'est qu'une pâle imitation de champagne; **I'm a ~ sailor** je n'ai pas le pied marin; **he is a ~ traveller** il supporte mal les voyages; **he's a ~ loser** il est mauvais perdant; *see* **second¹**, **show** *etc*.
c (*pitiable*) pauvre. **~ little boy** pauvre petit garçon; **she's all alone, ~ woman** elle est toute seule, la pauvre; **~ Smith, he lost his money** ce pauvre Smith, il a perdu son argent; **~ things*, they look cold** les pauvres, ils ont l'air d'avoir froid; **you ~ old thing!*** mon pauvre vieux!, ma pauvre vieille!; **it's a ~ thing** *or* **a ~ show when ...** c'est malheureux que ... + *subj*.
2 npl: **the ~** les pauvres *mpl*.
3 comp ▸**poorbox** (*Rel*) tronc *m* des pauvres ▸**poor boy** (*US Culin*) grand sandwich *m* mixte ▸**poorhouse** (*Hist*) hospice *m* (des pauvres) ▸**poor law** (*Hist*) assistance *f* publique; (*Hist*) **the poor laws** les lois *fpl* sur l'assistance publique ▸**poor-mouth***: (*US*) **to poor-mouth sb/sth** parler en termes désobligeants de qn/qch ▸**poor-spirited** timoré, pusillanime ▸**poor White** (*esp US, South Africa pej*) petit Blanc *m*.

poorly ['pʊəlɪ] 1 adj souffrant, malade. 2 adv *live, dress* pauvrement; *perform, work, write, explain, swim, eat* médiocrement, mal. **~ lit/paid** *etc* mal éclairé/payé *etc*; **to be ~ off** être pauvre.

poorness ['pʊənɪs] n (*lack of wealth*) pauvreté *f*; (*badness*) pauvreté, mauvaise qualité, médiocrité *f*.

poovy‡ ['pu:vɪ] = **poofy**.

pop¹ [pɒp] 1 n a (*sound*) *[cork etc]* pan *m*; *[press stud etc]* bruit sec. (*excl*) **~!** pan!; **to go ~** faire pan.
b (**NonC: drink*) boisson gazeuse.
2 comp ▸**popcorn** pop-corn *m* ▸**popeyed** les yeux écarquillés, ébahi ▸**popgun** pistolet *m* à bouchon ▸**pop quiz** (*US Scol*) interrogation *f* écrite impromptue ▸**pop-up book** livre *m* animé ▸**pop-up toaster** grille-pain *m inv* (*électrique*).
3 vt a *balloon* crever; *cork* faire sauter; *corn* faire éclater; *press stud* fermer.
b (*put*) passer; mettre, fourrer; jeter. **to ~ one's head round the door/out of the window** passer brusquement la tête par la porte/par la fenêtre; **to ~ sth into the oven** passer *or* mettre qch au four; **he ~ped it into his mouth** il l'a fourré *or* l'a mis dans sa bouche; **to ~ pills*** se bourrer* de médicaments; **could you ~ this letter into the postbox?** pourriez-vous jeter *or* mettre cette lettre à la boîte?; (*fig*) **to ~ the question** faire sa demande (en mariage).
c (‡†: *pawn*) mettre au clou*.
4 vi a *[balloon]* crever; *[cork]* sauter; *[corn]* éclater; *[press stud, buttons etc]* sauter. **my ears ~ped** mes oreilles se sont brusquement débouchées; **his eyes ~ped** il a écarquillé les yeux, il a ouvert des yeux ronds *or* de grands yeux; **his eyes were ~ping out of his head** les yeux lui sortaient de la tête, il avait les yeux exorbités.
b (*go*) **I ~ped over** (*or* **round** *or* **across** *or* **out) to the grocer's** j'ai fait un saut à l'épicerie; **he ~ped into a café** il est entré dans un café en vitesse.

▸**pop back** 1 vi revenir, retourner (en vitesse *or* pour un instant). 2 vt sep *lid etc* remettre, replacer.

▸**pop in** vi entrer en passant, ne faire que passer. **I popped in to say hullo to them** je suis entré (en passant) leur dire bonjour; **she kept popping in and out** elle n'a pas cessé d'entrer et de sortir.

▸**pop off** vi a (*leave*) partir. **they popped off to Spain for a few days** ils sont partis passer quelques jours en Espagne, ils ont filé* pour quelques jours en Espagne. b (‡: *die*) mourir (subitement), claquer*. c (*US* ‡: *shout*) donner de la gueule‡.

▸**pop on*** vt sep a (*switch on*) allumer, mettre en marche. **to pop the kettle on** ≃ mettre de l'eau à chauffer. b *clothes, shirt etc* enfiler.

▸**pop out** vi *[person]* sortir; *[cork]* sauter. **the rabbit popped out of its burrow** le lapin a détalé de son terrier.

▸**pop round** vi passer, faire un saut. **pop round anytime** passe n'importe quand; *see also* **pop 4b**.

▸**pop up** vi (*from water, above wall etc*) surgir. **he popped up unexpectedly in Tangiers** il a réapparu inopinément à Tanger.

pop² [pɒp] abbr of **popular**. 1 adj *music, song, singer, concert* pop *inv*. **~ art** le pop'art. 2 n (musique *f*) pop *m*. **it's top of the ~s just now** c'est en tête du hit-parade *or* du Top 50 en ce moment.

pop³* [pɒp] n (*esp US*) papa *m*. (*to old man*) **yes ~(s)** oui grand-père*, oui pépé*.

pope [pəʊp] n pape *m*. **P~ Pius II** le pape Pie II; (*Cards*) **~ Joan** le nain jaune.

popemobile* ['pəʊpməbi:l] n *voiture blindée utilisée lors des "bains de foule" du pape*.

popery ['pəʊpərɪ] n (*pej*) papisme *m* (*pej*). **no ~!** à bas le pape!

popinjay† ['pɒpɪndʒeɪ] n fat *m*, freluquet *m*.

popish ['pəʊpɪʃ] adj (*pej*) papiste (*pej*).

poplar ['pɒpləʳ] n peuplier *m*.

poplin ['pɒplɪn] 1 n popeline *f*. 2 comp de *or* en popeline.

poppadum ['pɒpədəm] n poppadum *m*.

popper ['pɒpəʳ] n a (*Brit *: press stud*) pression *f*, bouton-pression *m*. b (*Drugs sl*) popper *m*.

poppet* ['pɒpɪt] n (*Brit*) **yes, (my) ~** oui, mon petit chou*; **she's a ~** elle est à croquer, c'est un amour.

poppy ['pɒpɪ] 1 n a (*flower*) pavot *m*; (*growing wild*) coquelicot *m*. b (*Brit: symbolic buttonhole*) coquelicot *m* (*artificiel vendu au bénéfice des mutilés de guerre*). 2 adj (*colour*) ponceau *inv*. 3 comp ▸**Poppy Day** (*Brit: see* **1b**) anniversaire *m* de l'armistice ▸**poppy seed** graine *f* de pavot.

poppycock*† ['pɒpɪkɒk] n (*NonC*) balivernes *fpl*, fariboles *fpl*. **~!** balivernes!

Popsicle ['pɒpsɪkl] n ® (*US*) glace *f* à l'eau (*tenue par deux bâtonnets*).

popsy†‡ ['pɒpsɪ] n (*Brit*) souris‡ *f*, fille *f*.

populace ['pɒpjʊlɪs] n peuple *m*, foule *f*, populace *f* (*pej*).

popular ['pɒpjʊləʳ] adj a (*well-liked*) *person, decision, book, sport* populaire; (*fashionable*) *style, model* à la mode, en vogue. **he is ~ with his colleagues** ses collègues l'aiment beaucoup, il jouit d'une grande popularité auprès de ses collègues; **he is ~ with the girls** il a du succès *or* il a la cote* auprès des filles; **I'm not very ~ with the boss just now*** je ne suis pas très bien vu du patron *or* je n'ai pas la cote* auprès du patron en ce moment; (*Comm*) **this is a very ~ colour** cette couleur se vend beaucoup; **it is ~ to despise politicians** mépriser les hommes politiques est à la mode.
b (*of, for, by the people*) *music, concert* populaire; *lecture, journal* de vulgarisation; *government, opinion, discontent* populaire, du peuple; *mistake, habit, practice* populaire, courant. **~ etymology** étymologie *f* populaire; (*Pol*) **~ front** front *m* populaire; **at ~ prices** à la portée de toutes les bourses; **by ~ request** à la demande générale; (*US Pol*) **~ vote** vote *m* populaire.

popularist ['pɒpjʊlərɪst] adj populaire, qui s'adresse au peuple.

popularity [,pɒpjʊ'lærɪtɪ] n popularité *f* (*with* auprès de, *among* parmi). **to grow in ~** être de plus en plus populaire, acquérir une popularité de plus en plus grande; **to decline in ~** être de moins en moins populaire, perdre de sa popularité; **it enjoyed a certain ~** cela a joui d'une certaine popularité *or* faveur.

popularization ['pɒpjʊlərаɪ'zeɪʃən] n a (*NonC: see* **popularize**) popularisation *f*, vulgarisation *f*. b (*popularized work*) œuvre *f or* ouvrage *m* de vulgarisation.

popularize ['pɒpjʊləraɪz] vt *sport, music, fashion, product* populariser, rendre populaire; *science, ideas* vulgariser.

popularizer ['pɒpjʊləraɪzəʳ] n *[sport, fashion]* promoteur *m*, -trice *f*; *[science, ideas]* vulgarisateur *m*, -trice *f*. **he was the ~ of the new-style bicycle** c'est lui qui a popularisé *or* rendu populaire le nouveau modèle de bicyclette.

popularly ['pɒpjʊləlɪ] adv: ~ **known as** ... communément connu *or* connu de tous sous le nom de ...; **it is ~ supposed that** ... il est communément *or* généralement présumé que ..., on croit généralement que ...; **he is ~ believed to be rich** il passe communément *or* généralement pour être riche.

populate ['pɒpjʊleɪt] vt peupler. **densely/sparsely ~d** très/peu peuplé, à forte/faible densité de population.

population [,pɒpjʊ'leɪʃən] 1 n population *f*. **a fall/rise in (the) ~** une diminution/un accroissement de la population; **the ~ of the town is 15,000** la population de la ville est de *or* la ville a une population de 15.000 habitants; **the working ~** la population active. 2 comp *increase* de la population, démographique ▸**population explosion** explosion *f* démographique ▸**population figures** démographie *f* ▸**population planning** planification *f* démographique.

populism ['pɒpjʊlɪzəm] n populisme *m*.

populist ['pɒpjʊlɪst] adj, n populiste *(mf)*.

populous ['pɒpjʊləs] adj populeux, très peuplé, à forte densité de population.

porcelain ['pɔːsəlɪn] 1 n (*NonC: substance, objects*) porcelaine *f*. **a piece of ~** une porcelaine. 2 comp *dish* de *or* en porcelaine; *clay, glaze* à porcelaine ▸**porcelain ware** (*NonC*) vaisselle *f* en *or* de porcelaine.

porch [pɔːtʃ] n *[house, church]* porche *m*; *[hotel]* marquise *f*; (*also* **sun ~**) véranda *f*.

porcine ['pɔːsaɪn] adj (*frm*) porcin, de porc.

porcupine ['pɔːkjʊpaɪn] 1 n porc-épic *m*; *see* **prickly**. 2 comp ▸**porcupine fish** poisson-globe *m*.

pore[1] [pɔːʳ] n (*in skin*) pore *m*.

pore[2] [pɔːʳ] vi: **to ~ over** *book* être absorbé dans; *letter, map* étudier de près; *problem* méditer longuement; **he was poring over the book** il était plongé dans *or* absorbé par le livre.

pork [pɔːk] (*Culin*) 1 n porc *m*. 2 comp *chop etc* de porc ▸**pork barrel*** n (*US Pol*) travaux *mpl* publics (*or* programme *m* de recherche *etc*) entrepris à des fins électorales ◊ adj *project etc* subventionné (à des fins électorales); (*US Pol*) **pork barrel law*** *loi destinée à avantager une région particulière sous prétexte de législation générale* ▸**pork butcher** ≃ charcutier *m* ▸**porkpie** ≃ pâté *m* en croûte; **porkpie hat** (chapeau *m*) feutre rond ▸**pork sausage** saucisse *f* (de porc) ▸**pork scratchings** *amuse-gueules de couennes de porc frites*.

porker ['pɔːkəʳ] n porc *m* à l'engrais, goret *m*.

porky* ['pɔːkɪ] adj (*pej*) gras comme un porc, bouffi.

porn* [pɔːn] n (*NonC*) (abbr of **pornography**) porno* *m*. **it's just ~** c'est porno (adj inv); **~ shop** boutique *f* porno; *see* **hard, soft.**

pornographic [,pɔːnə'græfɪk] adj pornographique.

pornography [pɔː'nɒgrəfɪ] n pornographie *f*.

porosity [pɔː'rɒsɪtɪ] n porosité *f*.

porous ['pɔːrəs] adj poreux, perméable.

porousness ['pɔːrəsnɪs] n porosité *f*.

porphyry ['pɔːfɪrɪ] n porphyre *m*.

porpoise ['pɔːpəs] n, pl ~ *or* ~s marsouin *m* (*Zool*).

porridge ['pɒrɪdʒ] n a porridge *m*, bouillie *f* de flocons d'avoine. **~ oats** flocons *mpl* d'avoine. b (*Brit: Prison sl*) **to do ~** faire de la taule‡.

porringer† ['pɒrɪndʒəʳ] n bol *m*, écuelle *f*.

port[1] [pɔːt] 1 n (*harbour, town*) port *m*. (*Naut*) **~ of call** (port d')escale *f*; (*fig*) **I've only one more ~ of call** il ne me reste plus qu'une course à faire; **~ of despatch** *or* (*US*) **shipment** port d'expédition; **~ of embarkation** port d'embarquement; **~ of entry** port de débarquement *or* d'arrivée; **naval/fishing ~** port militaire/de pêche; **to come into ~** entrer dans le port; **they put into ~ at Dieppe** ils ont relâché dans le port de Dieppe; **to leave ~** appareiller, lever l'ancre; (*loc*) **any ~ in a storm** nécessité n'a pas de loi (*Prov*); *see* **sea, trading** *etc*.
2 comp *facilities, security* portuaire, du port ▸**port authorities** autorités *fpl* portuaires ▸**port dues** droits *mpl* de port.

port[2] [pɔːt] n (*opening*) (*Aviat, Naut: also* **~ hole**) hublot *m*; (*Naut: for guns, cargo*) sabord *m*; (*Comput*) port *m*, porte *f* (d'accès), point *m* d'accès.

port[3] [pɔːt] (*Naut: left*) 1 n (*also* **~ side**) bâbord *m*. **to ~** à bâbord; **land to ~!** terre par bâbord! 2 adj *guns, lights* de bâbord. 3 vt: **to ~ the helm** mettre la barre à bâbord.

port[4] [pɔːt] n (*wine*) porto *m*.

portability [pɔːtə'bɪlɪtɪ] n (*esp Comput*) portabilité *f*; *[software]* transférabilité *f*.

portable ['pɔːtəbl] 1 adj (*gen*) portatif; *computer* portable; *software* transférable. **~ pension** pension *f* transférable. 2 n modèle portatif; (*computer*) portable *m*.

portage ['pɔːtɪdʒ] n (*action, route*) portage *m*; (*cost*) frais *mpl* de portage.

Portakabin ['pɔːtəkæbɪn] n ® (*gen*) bâtiment *m* préfabriqué; (*extension to office etc*) petite annexe préfabriquée; (*works office etc*) baraque *f* de chantier.

portal ['pɔːtl] 1 n portail *m*. 2 adj: **~ vein** veine *f* porte.

portcullis [pɔːt'kʌlɪs] n herse *f* (*de château fort*).

portend [pɔː'tend] vt présager, laisser pressentir, laisser augurer, annoncer.

portent ['pɔːtent] n prodige *m*, présage *m*. **of evil ~** de mauvais présage.

portentous [pɔː'tentəs] adj (*ominous*) de mauvais présage, de mauvais augure, sinistre; (*marvellous*) prodigieux, extraordinaire; (*grave*) solennel, grave; (*pej: pompous*) pompeux, pontifiant.

portentously [pɔː'tentəslɪ] adv *say* d'un air *or* d'un ton solennel *or* grave *or* pompeux (*pej*) *or* pontifiant (*pej*).

porter ['pɔːtəʳ] 1 n a (*for luggage: in station, hotel etc, on climb or expedition*) porteur *m*. b (*US Rail: attendant*) employé(e) *m(f)* des wagons-lits. c (*Brit: doorkeeper*) *[private housing]* concierge *mf*; *[public building]* portier *m*, gardien(ne) *m(f)*; (*Univ*) appariteur *m*. **~'s lodge** loge *f* du *or* de la concierge *etc*. d (*beer*) porter *m*, bière brune. 2 comp ▸**porterhouse (steak)** ≃ chateaubriand *m*.

porterage ['pɔːtərɪdʒ] n (*act*) portage *m*; (*cost*) frais *mpl* de portage.

portfolio [pɔːt'fəʊlɪəʊ] n, pl ~s a (*Pol: object, also post*) portefeuille *m*. **minister without ~** ministre *m* sans portefeuille. b *[shares]* portefeuille *m*. **~ manager** portefeuilliste *mf*. c *[artist]* portfolio *m*.

portico ['pɔːtɪkəʊ] n, pl ~es *or* ~s portique *m*.

portion ['pɔːʃən] 1 n (*part, percentage*) portion *f*, partie *f*; *[train, ticket etc]* partie; (*share*) portion, (quote-)part *f*; *[estate, inheritance etc]* portion, part; (*of food: helping*) portion; (†: *also* **marriage ~**) dot *f*; (*liter: fate*) sort *m*, destin *m*. 2 vt (*also* **~ out**) répartir (*among, between* entre).

portliness ['pɔːtlɪnɪs] n embonpoint *m*, corpulence *f*.

portly ['pɔːtlɪ] adj corpulent.

portmanteau [pɔːt'mæntəʊ] n, pl ~s *or* ~x [pɔːt'mæntəʊz] grosse valise (*de cuir*). (*Ling*) **~ word** mot-valise *m*.

portrait ['pɔːtrɪt] 1 n (*Art, gen*) portrait *m*. **to paint sb's ~** peindre (le portrait de) qn. 2 comp ▸**portrait gallery** galerie *f* de portraits ▸**portrait lens** (*Phot*) bonnette *f* ▸**portrait mode:** (*Comput*) **to output sth in portrait mode** imprimer qch à la française *or* au format portrait ▸**portrait painter** portraitiste *mf*.

portraitist ['pɔːtrɪtɪst] n portraitiste *mf*.

portraiture ['pɔːtrɪtʃəʳ] n (*NonC*) (*art*) art *m* du portrait; (*portrait*) portrait; (*collectively*) portraits.

portray [pɔː'treɪ] vt *[painter]* peindre, faire le portrait de; *[painting]* représenter. **he ~ed him as an embittered man** *[painter]* il l'a peint *or* il en a fait le portrait sous les traits d'un homme aigri; *[writer, speaker, actor]* il en a fait un homme aigri.

portrayal [pɔː'treɪəl] n (*see* **portray**) peinture *f*, portrait *m*; représentation *f*.

Portugal ['pɔːtjʊgəl] n Portugal *m*.

Portuguese [,pɔːtjʊ'giːz] 1 adj portugais. 2 n a (pl inv) Portugais(e) *m(f)*. b (*Ling*) portugais *m*. 3 comp ▸**Portuguese man-of-war** galère *f* (*Zool*).

POS [,piːəʊ'es] n (abbr of **point of sale**) PLV *m*.

pose [pəʊz] 1 n (*body position*) pose *f*, attitude *f*; (*Art*) pose; (*fig*) pose; (*pej*) pose, attitude, affectation *f*. **to strike a ~** poser (pour la galerie); **it's only a ~** c'est de la pose, c'est pure affectation, ce n'est qu'une attitude. 2 vi (*Art, Phot*) poser (*for* pour, *as* en); (*pej: attitudinize*) se donner des airs, frimer*. **to ~ as a doctor** se faire passer pour un docteur. 3 vt a *artist's model* faire prendre une pose à; *person* faire poser. b *problem, question* poser; *difficulties* créer; *argument, claim* présenter, formuler.

Poseidon [pɒ'saɪdən] n Poséidon *m*.

poser ['pəʊzəʳ] n a (*person*) poseur *m*, -euse *f* (*pej*). b (*problem, question*) question *f* difficile. **that's a ~!** ça c'est difficile, ça c'est un vrai casse-tête.

poseur [pəʊ'zɜːʳ] n (*pej*) poseur *m*, -euse *f* (*pej*).

posh [pɒʃ] 1 adj (*: *often pej*) *person* chic *inv*, snob (*f inv*), rupin‡; *accent* distingué, de la haute‡; *house, neighbourhood, hotel* chic, rupin‡; *car, school* chic, de riches, de rupins‡; *clothes* chic, élégant. **~ people** les snob(s) *mpl*, les gens chic, les gens bien, les rupins‡; **a ~ wedding** un grand mariage, un mariage à grand tralala*; **he was looking very ~** il faisait très chic, il s'était mis sur son trente et un. 2 adv (‡ *pej*) **to talk ~** parler comme les gens bien *or* la haute ‡.

▸**posh up**‡ vt sep *house* embellir; (*clean up*) briquer; *child* pomponner, bichonner. **to posh o.s. up** se pomponner; **he was all poshed up** il était sur son trente et un, il était bien sapé‡.

posidrive ['pɒzɪ,draɪv] adj ® **~ screw/~ screwdriver** vis/tourne-vis *m* cruciforme.

posit ['pɒzɪt] vt avancer, énoncer, poser en principe.

position [pə'zɪʃən] 1 n a (*place, location*) *[person, object]* position *f* (*also Geog, Math, Mil, Mus, Naut, Phys etc*), place *f*; *[house, shop, town]* emplacement *m*, situation *f*; *[gun]* emplacement. **in(to) ~** en place, en position; **to change the ~ of sth** changer qch de place; **to take up (one's) ~** prendre position *or* place; **to get o.s. into ~** se placer; **to be in a good ~** être bien placé (*see also* **1d**); (*Mil etc*) **the enemy ~s** les positions de l'ennemi; (*Sport*) **what ~ do you play (in)?** à quelle place jouez-vous?; (*lit, fig*) **to jockey** *or* **jostle** *or* **manoeuvre for ~** manœuvrer pour se placer avantageusement; (*in post office, bank*) **"~ closed"** "guichet fermé".
b (*attitude, angle: also Art, Ballet*) position *f*. **in a horizontal ~** en position horizontale; **in an uncomfortable ~** dans une position

incommode; **to change (one's) ~** changer de position.

c (*in class, league*) position *f*, place *f*; (*socially*) position, condition *f*; (*job*) poste *m*, emploi *m*, situation *f*. **he finished in 3rd ~** il est arrivé en 3e position *or* place; **her ~ in class was 4th** elle était la 4e de sa classe; **his ~ in society** sa position dans la société; **a man of ~** un homme de condition; **a man in his ~ should not ...** un homme dans sa position *or* de sa condition ne devrait pas ... (*see also* **1d**); **his ~ in the government** son poste *or* sa fonction dans le gouvernement; **a high ~ in the Ministry** une haute fonction au ministère; **a ~ of trust** un poste de confiance.

d (*fig: situation, circumstances*) situation *f*, place *f*. **to be in a ~ to do sth** être en position *or* en mesure de faire qch; **he is in a good/bad ~ to judge** il est bien/mal placé pour juger; **he is in no ~ to decide** il n'est pas en position *or* en mesure de décider; **put yourself in my ~** mettez-vous à ma place; **a man in his ~ cannot expect mercy** un homme dans sa situation ne peut s'attendre à la clémence; **what's the ~ on deliveries/sales?** où en sont les livraisons/ventes?, quel est l'état des livraisons/ventes?; **what would you do in my ~?** que feriez-vous à ma place?; **our ~ is desperate** notre situation est désespérée; **the economic ~** la situation économique, la conjoncture; **to be in a good/bad ~** être dans une bonne/mauvaise situation; **we were in a false/an awkward ~** nous étions dans une situation fausse/délicate.

e (*fig: point of view, opinion*) position *f*, opinion *f*. **you must make your ~ clear** vous devez dire franchement quelle est votre position, vous devez donner votre opinion; **his ~ on foreign aid** sa position sur la question de l'aide aux pays en voie de développement; **to take up a ~ on sth** prendre position sur qch; **he took up the ~ that ...** il a adopté le point de vue selon lequel ... .

2 **vt** a (*adjust angle of*) *light, microscope, camera* mettre en position.

b (*put in place*) *gun, chair, camera* mettre en place, placer; *house, school* situer, placer; *guards, policemen* placer, poster; *army, ship* mettre en position; (*Marketing*) *product* positionner. **he ~ed each item with great care** il a très soigneusement disposé chaque article; **to ~ o.s.** se mettre, se placer; **the company is well ~ed to sell a million cars this year** la compagnie est bien placée pour vendre un million de voitures cette année.

c (*find ~ of*) déterminer la position de.

positive ['pɒzɪtɪv] 1 **adj** a (*not negative: also Elec, Gram, Math, Phot, Typ*) positif; *test, result, reaction* positif; (*affirmative: Ling etc*) affirmatif; (*constructive*) *suggestion* positif, concret (*f* -ète); *attitude, criticism* positif. (*Brit*) **~ discrimination** mesures *fpl* anti-discriminatoires en faveur des minorités; **~ vetting** enquête *f* de sécurité (*of sb* sur qn); **a policy of ~ vetting** une politique d'enquêtes de sécurité; **they need some ~ help** ils ont besoin d'une aide concrète *or* effective; **we need some ~ thinking** ce qu'il nous faut, c'est quelque chose de positif *or* constructif; **think ~!** soyez positif!; **he's very ~ about it** il a une attitude très positive à ce sujet.

b (*definite, indisputable*) *order, rule, instruction* catégorique, formel; *fact* indéniable, irréfutable; *change, increase, improvement* réel, tangible. **~ proof, proof ~** preuve formelle; **there is ~ evidence that ...** il y a des preuves indéniables du fait que ...; **~ progress has been made** un réel progrès *or* un progrès tangible a été fait; **he has made a ~ contribution to the scheme** il a apporté une contribution effective au projet, il a contribué de manière effective au projet; **it is a ~ pleasure to do it** c'est un vrai plaisir que de faire ça; **it's a ~ miracle*** c'est pur miracle; **he's a ~ genius*** c'est un vrai *or* véritable génie; **he's a ~ fool*** il est complètement idiot *or* stupide, c'est un idiot fini.

c (*sure, certain*) *person* sûr, certain (*about, on, of* de). **are you quite ~?** en êtes-vous bien sûr? *or* certain?; **I'm absolutely ~ I put it back** je mettrais ma main au feu que je l'ai remis à sa place; **... he said in a ~ tone of voice ...** dit-il d'un ton très assuré; **to my ~ knowledge he did not see it** je sais sans l'ombre d'un doute qu'il ne l'a pas vu; **she is a very ~ person** elle est très résolue *or* tranchante, elle sait ce qu'elle veut.

2 **n** (*Elec*) pôle positif; (*Gram*) affirmatif *m*; (*Math*) nombre positif, quantité positive; (*Phot*) épreuve positive, positif. (*Ling*) **in the ~** à l'affirmatif.

positively ['pɒzɪtɪvlɪ] **adv** (*definitely, indisputably*) indéniablement, irréfutablement; (*categorically*) formellement, catégoriquement; (*affirmatively*) affirmativement; (*with certainty*) de façon certaine *or* sûre; (*emphatically*) positivement; (*absolutely*) complètement, absolument. **he was ~ rude to me** il a été positivement grossier avec moi; **he's ~ mad** il est complètement fou; (*constructively*) **to think ~** penser de façon positive *or* constructive.

positivism ['pɒzɪtɪvɪzəm] **n** positivisme *m*.

positivist ['pɒzɪtɪvɪst] **adj, n** positiviste *(mf)*.

positron ['pɒzɪtrɒn] **n** positon *m*, positron *m*.

posse ['pɒsɪ] **n** (*also fig hum*) petite troupe, détachement *m*.

possess [pə'zes] **vt** a (*own, have*) *property, qualities* posséder, avoir; *documents, money, proof* posséder, avoir, être en possession de. **all I ~** tout ce que je possède; **it ~es several advantages** cela présente plusieurs avantages; **to ~ o.s. of sth** s'emparer de qch; **to be ~ed of** posséder, avoir; **to ~ one's soul** *or* **o.s. in patience** s'armer de patience.

b *[demon, rage]* posséder; (*fig: obsess*) posséder, obséder. **like one ~ed** comme un possédé; **he was ~ed by the devil** il était possédé du démon; **~ed with** *or* **by jealousy** obsédé *or* dévoré par la jalousie, en proie à la jalousie; **one single aim ~ed him** il n'avait qu'un seul but en tête; **what can have ~ed him to say that?** qu'est-ce qui l'a pris de dire ça!*

possession [pə'zeʃən] **n** a (*NonC: act, state*) possession *f*; (*Jur: occupancy*) jouissance *f*. **in ~ of** en possession de; **to have ~ of** posséder, avoir la jouissance de; **to have in one's ~** avoir en sa possession; **to get ~ of** acquérir, obtenir; (*by force*) s'emparer de; (*improperly*) s'approprier; (*Rugby*) **to get ~ of the ball** s'emparer du ballon; **to come into ~ of** entrer en possession de; **he was in full ~ of his senses** il était en pleine possession de ses facultés, il avait le plein usage de ses facultés; **to come into sb's ~** tomber en la possession de qn; **according to the information in my ~** selon les renseignements dont je dispose; **to take ~ of** prendre possession de; (*improperly*) s'approprier; (*confiscate*) confisquer; (*Jur*) **to take ~** prendre possession; (*Jur*) **to be in ~** occuper les lieux; (*Jur etc*) **a house with vacant ~** une maison avec jouissance immédiate; (*Prov*) **~ is nine points** *or* **tenths of the law** ≃ (en fait de meubles) possession vaut titre.

b (*object*) possession *f*, bien *m*; (*territory*) possession.

possessive [pə'zesɪv] 1 **adj** a *person, nature, attitude, love* possessif. **to be ~ about sth** ne pas vouloir partager qch; **to be ~ towards** *or* **with sb** être possessif avec *or* à l'égard de qn; **an over~ mother** une mère abusive. b (*Gram*) possessif. 2 **n** (*Gram*) possessif *m*. **in the ~** au possessif.

possessively [pə'zesɪvlɪ] **adv** d'une façon possessive.

possessiveness [pə'zesɪvnɪs] **n** (*NonC*) possessivité *f*.

possessor [pə'zesəʳ] **n** possesseur *m*; (*owner*) propriétaire *mf*. **to be the ~ of** être possesseur de, posséder; **he was the proud ~ of** il était l'heureux propriétaire de.

possibility [,pɒsə'bɪlɪtɪ] **n** a (*NonC*) possibilité *f*. **within the bounds of ~** dans l'ordre des choses possibles, dans la limite du possible; **if by any ~ ...** si par impossible ..., si par hasard ...; **there is some ~/not much ~ of success** il y a quelques chances/peu de chances de succès; **there is no ~ of my leaving** il n'est pas possible que je parte; **there is some ~** *or* **a ~ that I might come** il est possible que je puisse venir, il n'est pas impossible que je vienne; **it's a distinct ~** c'est bien possible.

b (*possible event*) possibilité *f*, éventualité *f*. **to foresee all the possibilities** envisager toutes les possibilités *or* éventualités; **we must allow for the ~ that he may refuse** nous devons nous préparer à *or* nous devons envisager l'éventualité de son refus; **he is a ~ for the job** c'est un candidat possible *or* acceptable.

c (*promise, potential*) **the firm saw good possibilities for expansion** la compagnie voyait de bonnes possibilités d'expansion; **the scheme/the job has real possibilities** c'est un projet/un emploi qui offre toutes sortes de possibilités; **it's got possibilities** c'est possible, c'est à voir *or* à étudier.

possible ['pɒsəbl] 1 **adj** a possible; *event, reaction, victory, loss* possible, éventuel. **it's just ~** ce n'est pas impossible; **it's not ~!** ce n'est pas possible!, pas possible!*; **it is ~ that** il se peut que + *subj*, il est possible que + *subj*; **it's just ~ that** il n'est pas impossible que + *subj*, il y a une chance que + *subj*; **it's ~ to do so** il est possible de le faire, c'est faisable; **it is ~ for him to leave** il lui est possible de partir; **to make sth ~** rendre qch possible; **he made it ~ for me to go to Spain** il a rendu possible mon voyage en Espagne; **if (at all) ~** si possible; **he visits her whenever ~** il va la voir aussi souvent que possible *or* chaque fois qu'il le peut; **whenever** *or* **wherever ~, we try to ...** dans la mesure du possible, nous essayons de ...; **as far as ~** dans la mesure du possible; **as much as ~** autant que possible; **he did as much as ~** il a fait tout ce qu'il pouvait; **as soon as ~** dès que possible, aussitôt que possible; **as quickly as ~** le plus vite possible; **the best ~ result** le meilleur résultat possible; **one ~ result** un résultat possible *or* éventuel; **what ~ interest can you have in it?** qu'est-ce qui peut bien vous intéresser là-dedans?; **there is no ~ excuse for his behaviour** sa conduite n'a aucune excuse *or* est tout à fait inexcusable.

b (*perhaps acceptable*) *candidate, successor* possible, acceptable. **a ~ solution** une solution possible *or* à envisager; **it is a ~ solution to the problem** ce pourrait être une manière de résoudre le problème.

2 **n** a **the art of the ~** l'art *m* du possible.

b (*) **that idea is a ~** c'est une idée à suivre *or* à approfondir *or* à voir, c'est une possibilité; **a list of ~s for the job** une liste de personnes susceptibles d'être retenues pour ce poste; **he's a ~ for the match on Saturday** c'est un joueur éventuel pour le match de samedi; (*Sport*) **the P~s versus the Probables** la sélection B contre la sélection A.

possibly ['pɒsəblɪ] **adv** a (*with "can" etc*) **as often as I ~ can** aussi souvent qu'il m'est (*or* me sera) matériellement possible (de le faire); **he did all he ~ could to help them** il a fait tout son possible pour les aider; **if I ~ can** si cela m'est (le moins du monde) possible, dans la mesure du possible; **I cannot ~ come** il m'est absolument impossible de venir; **you can't ~ do that!** tu ne peux absolument pas faire ça!; **how can I ~ allow it?** comment puis-je en toute conscience le permettre?; **it can't ~ be true!** ça ne se peut pas!, ce n'est pas vrai!

b (*perhaps*) peut-être. **~ they've gone already** ils sont peut-être déjà partis, peut-être qu'ils sont déjà partis, il se peut qu'ils soient déjà partis; **(yes)** ~ peut-être bien; ~ **not** peut-être pas.

possum ['pɒsəm] n (*) (abbr of **opossum**) opossum *m*. (*fig*) **to play ~*** faire le mort.

POST n (abbr of **point-of-sale terminal**) see **point 2**.

post¹ [pəʊst] 1 n (*of wood, metal*) poteau *m*; (*stake*) pieu *m*; (*for door etc: upright*) montant *m*; (*goal* ~) poteau (de but). (*Sport*) **starting/finishing** or **winning** ~ poteau de départ/d'arrivée; (*fig*) **to be left at the** ~ manquer le départ, rester sur la touche; (*Sport, fig*) **to be beaten at the** ~ être battu or coiffé sur le poteau; see **deaf, gate, lamp** etc. 2 vt a (*also* ~ **up**) *notice, list* afficher. "~ **no bills**" "défense d'afficher". b (*announce*) *results* annoncer. **to ~ a ship/a soldier missing** porter un navire/un soldat disparu. c **to ~ a wall with advertisements** poser or coller des affiches publicitaires sur un mur.

post² [pəʊst] 1 n a (*Mil, gen*) poste *m*. **at one's ~** à son poste; see **forward, last** etc. b (*esp Can, US: trading* ~) comptoir *m*. c (*situation, job*) poste *m*, situation *f*; (*in civil service, government etc*) poste. **a ~ as a manager** un poste or une situation de directeur. 2 comp ▸**post exchange** (*US Mil*) magasin *m* de l'armée. 3 vt a (*also Mil: position*) *sentry, guard* poster. **they ~ed a man by the stairs** ils ont posté un homme près de l'escalier. b (*esp Brit: send, assign*) (*Mil*) affecter (*to* à); (*Admin, Comm*) affecter, nommer (*to* à). c (*US Jur*) **to ~ bail** déposer une caution; **to ~ the collateral required** fournir les garanties.

post³ [pəʊst] (*esp Brit*) 1 n a (*NonC*) poste *f*; (*letters*) courrier *m*. **by ~** par la poste; **by return (of) ~** par retour du courrier; **by first-/second-class ~** ≃ tarif normal/réduit; **your receipt is in the ~** votre reçu est déjà posté; **I'll put it in the ~ today** je le posterai aujourd'hui; **it went first ~ this morning** c'est parti ce matin par le premier courrier; **to catch/miss the ~** avoir/manquer la levée; **take this to the ~** allez poster ceci, portez ceci à la poste or à la boîte*; **drop it in the ~ on your way** mettez-le à la boîte en route; **the ~ was lifted** or **collected at 8 o'clock** la levée a eu lieu à 8 heures; **has the ~ been** or **come yet?** le courrier est-il arrivé?, le facteur est-il passé?; **the ~ is late** le courrier a du retard; **is there any ~ for me?** est-ce que j'ai du courrier?, y a-t-il une lettre pour moi?; (*cost*) ~ **and packing** frais *mpl* de port et d'emballage; (*Brit*) **Minister/Ministry of P~s and Telecommunications** ministre *m*/ministère *m* des Postes et (des) Télécommunications; see **registered** etc.

b (*Hist: riders etc*) poste *f*; see **general**.

2 comp ▸**postbag** (*Brit*) sac postal; **we've had a good postbag on this*** nous avons reçu beaucoup de courrier à ce sujet ▸**postbox** (*esp Brit*) boîte *f* aux lettres ▸**postcard** carte postale ▸**post chaise** (*Hist*) chaise *f* de poste ▸**postcode** code postal ▸**post-free** franco, franc de port, en franchise ▸**posthaste** see **posthaste** ▸**post horn** (*Mus*) cornet *m* de poste or de postillon ▸**postman** facteur *m*, préposé *m* (*Admin*); (*game*) **postman's knock** ≃ le mariage chinois ▸**postmark** n cachet *m* de la poste ◊ vt tamponner, timbrer; **date as postmark** pour la date se référer au cachet de la poste; **letter with a French postmark** lettre timbrée de France; **it is postmarked Paris** il y a "Paris" sur le cachet ▸**postmaster** receveur *m* des postes ▸**Postmaster General** (*Brit*) (pl ~s ~) ministre *m* des Postes et Télécommunications ▸**postmistress** receveuse *f* des postes ▸**post office** see **post office** ▸**post-paid** port payé ▸**postwoman** factrice *f*, préposée *f*.

3 vt a (*send by* ~) envoyer or expédier par la poste; (*Brit: put in mailbox*) mettre à la poste, poster, mettre à la boîte*. ~ **early for Christmas** n'attendez pas la dernière minute pour poster vos cartes et colis de Noël.

b (*Book-keeping: also* ~ **up**) *transaction* inscrire. **to ~ an entry to the ledger** passer une écriture dans le registre; **to ~ (up) a ledger** tenir un registre à jour; (*fig*) **to keep sb ~ed** tenir qn au courant.

4 vi (*Hist: travel by stages*) voyager par la poste, prendre le courrier; (††: *hasten*) courir la poste, faire diligence.

▸**post on** vt sep *letter, parcel* faire suivre.

▸**post up** vt sep = **post³ 3b**.

post... [pəʊst] pref post... . ~**glacial** postglaciaire; ~**-1950** (adj) postérieur (*f* -eure) à (l'année) 1950, d'après 1950; (adv) après 1950; see **postdate, post-impressionism** etc.

postage ['pəʊstɪdʒ] 1 n (*NonC*) tarifs postaux or d'affranchissement. **what is the ~ to Canada?** quels sont les tarifs d'affranchissement or les tarifs postaux pour le Canada?; (*in account etc*) ~: **£2** frais *mpl* de port: 2 livres; ~ **due 20p** surtaxe 20 pence; (*Comm*) ~ **and packing** frais de port et d'emballage. 2 comp ▸**postage meter** (*US*) machine *f* à affranchir (les lettres) ▸**postage rates** tarifs postaux ▸**postage stamp** timbre-poste *m*.

postal ['pəʊstəl] adj *code, zone* postal; *application* par la poste. (*US*) ~ **card** carte *f* postale; ~ **charges**, ~ **rates** tarifs postaux; ~ **dispute** conflit *m* (des employés) des postes; ~ **district** district *m* postal; ~ **order** mandat(-poste) *m*, mandat postal (*for 100 francs* de 100 F); **the ~ services** les services postaux; **2-tier ~ service** courrier *m* à 2 vitesses; ~ **strike** grève *f* des employés des postes; ~ **vote** (*paper*) bulletin *m* de vote par correspondance; (*system*) vote *m* par correspondance; ~ **worker** employé(e) *m(f)* des postes, postier *m*, -ière *f*.

postcoital ['pəʊst'kɔɪtəl] adj (d')après l'amour.

postdate ['pəʊst'deɪt] vt postdater.

postdoctoral [pəʊst'dɒktərəl] adj (*Univ*) *research, studies etc* après le doctorat. ~ **fellow** chercheur *m* qui a son doctorat; ~ **fellowship** poste *m* de chercheur (qui a son doctorat).

poster ['pəʊstəʳ] n affiche *f*; (*decorative*) poster *m*. ~ **paint** gouache *f*.

poste restante ['pəʊst'restɑ̃:nt] n, adv (*esp Brit*) poste restante.

posterior [pɒs'tɪərɪəʳ] 1 adj postérieur (*f* -eure) (*to* à). 2 n (* *hum*) derrière *m*, postérieur* *m*.

posterity [pɒs'terɪtɪ] n postérité *f*. **to go down to ~ as sth/for sth** entrer dans la postérité en tant que qch/pour qch.

postern ['pɒstən] n poterne *f*.

postfeminist [ˌpəʊst'femɪnɪst] adj, n post-féministe *(mf)*.

postgrad* ['pəʊst'græd] n, adj (abbr of **postgraduate**) see **postgraduate**.

postgraduate ['pəʊst'grædjʊɪt] 1 adj *studies, course, grant* ≃ de troisième cycle (universitaire). ~ **diploma** diplôme décerné après la licence (*maîtrise etc*). 2 n (*also* ~ **student**) étudiant(e) *m(f)* de troisième cycle.

posthaste ['pəʊst'heɪst] adv à toute allure.

posthumous ['pɒstjʊməs] adj posthume.

posthumously ['pɒstjʊməslɪ] adv *publish, appear* après la mort de l'auteur, après sa (*etc*) mort; *award* à titre posthume.

postiche [pɒs'ti:ʃ] n, adj postiche *(m)*.

postil(l)ion [pəs'tɪlɪən] n postillon *m*.

postimpressionism ['pəʊstɪm'preʃənɪzəm] n post-impressionnisme *m*.

postimpressionist ['pəʊstɪm'preʃənɪst] adj, n post-impressionniste *(mf)*.

postindustrial [ˌpəʊstɪn'dʌstrɪəl] adj post(-)industriel.

posting ['pəʊstɪŋ] n a (*NonC: sending by post*) expédition *f* or envoi *m* par la poste. b (*Brit: assignment*) affectation *f*, mutation *f*. **he got a ~ to Paris** il a été affecté or nommé à Paris, il s'est fait muter à Paris. c (*Accounting*) *[entry]* passation *f*. ~ **error** erreur *f* d'écriture.

postmodern [ˌpəʊst'mɒdən] adj postmoderne.

postmodernism [ˌpəʊst'mɒdənɪzəm] n postmodernisme *m*.

postmodernist [ˌpəʊst'mɒdənɪst] adj, n postmoderniste *(mf)*.

post-mortem ['pəʊst'mɔ:təm] 1 adj: ~ **examination** autopsie *f*. 2 n (*Med, also fig*) autopsie *f*. **to hold a ~** faire une autopsie; **to carry out a ~ on** faire l'autopsie de, autopsier.

postnatal ['pəʊst'neɪtl] adj post-natal. (*Med*) ~ **ward** salle *f* de suites de couches.

post office ['pəʊst,ɒfɪs] n (*place*) (bureau *m* de) poste *f*; (*organization*) administration *f* des postes, service *m* des postes. **he works** or **he is in the ~** il est postier, il est employé des postes; **the main ~** la grande poste; **P~ O~ Box No. 24** boîte postale no. 24; (*US*) **P~ O~ Department** ministère *m* des Postes et Télécommunications; **he has £100 in ~ ~ savings** or **in the P~ O~ Savings Bank** ≃ il a 100 livres sur son livret de Caisse d'Épargne, il a 100 livres à la Caisse (Nationale) d'Épargne; ~ ~ **worker** employé(e) *m(f)* des postes, postier *m*, -ière *f*; see **general**.

postoperative [pəʊst'ɒprətɪv] adj post-opératoire.

postpone [pəʊst'pəʊn] vt renvoyer (à plus tard), remettre, ajourner, reporter (*for* de, *until* à).

postponement [pəʊst'pəʊnmənt] n ajournement *m*, renvoi *m* (à plus tard), remise *f* à plus tard.

postposition ['pəʊstpə'zɪʃən] n postposition *f*.

postpositive [pəʊst'pɒzɪtɪv] 1 adj postpositif. 2 n postposition *f*.

postprandial ['pəʊst'prændɪəl] adj (*liter or hum*) (d')après le repas.

postproduction [ˌpəʊstprə'dʌkʃən] 1 n travail *m* postérieur à la production. 2 comp *cost etc* qui suit la production.

postscript ['pəʊsskrɪpt] n (*to letter: abbr* **P.S.**) post-scriptum *m inv* (*abbr* **P.-S.** *m*); (*to book*) postface *f*. (*fig*) **I'd like to add a ~ to what you have said** je voudrais ajouter un mot à ce que vous avez dit.

poststructuralism [ˌpəʊst'strʌktʃərəlɪzəm] n poststructuralisme *m*.

poststructuralist [ˌpəʊst'strʌktʃərəlɪst] adj, n poststructuraliste *(mf)*.

postsynchronization [pəʊst,sɪŋkrənaɪ'zeɪʃən] n postsynchronisation *f*.

postsynchronize [pəʊst'sɪŋkrə,naɪz] vt postsynchroniser.

post-tertiary [pəʊst'tɜ:ʃərɪ] adj (*Geol*) ~ **period** ère *f* post-tertiaire.

post-traumatic stress disorder [ˌpəʊsttrɔ:'mætɪk'stresdɪs'ɔ:dəʳ] n névrose *f* traumatique or d'effroi.

postulant ['pɒstjʊlənt] n (*Rel*) postulant(e) *m(f)*.

postulate ['pɒstjʊlɪt] 1 n postulat *m*. 2 ['pɒstjʊleɪt] vt poser comme principe; (*Philos*) postuler.

posture ['pɒstʃəʳ] 1 n posture *f*, position *f*, (*fig*) attitude *f*, position. **his ~ is very bad** il se tient très mal. 2 vi (*pej*) poser, prendre des attitudes.

posturing ['pɒstjərɪŋ] n pose *f*, affectation *f*.

postviral syndrome [ˌpəʊst,vaɪərəl'sɪndrəʊm] n syndrome *m* grippal.

postvocalic [pəʊstvəʊ'kælɪk] adj (*Phon*) postvocalique.

postwar ['pəʊst'wɔ:ʳ] adj de l'après-guerre. (*Brit Fin*) ~ **credits** *crédits gouvernementaux résultant d'une réduction dans l'abattement fiscal pendant la seconde guerre mondiale;* **the ~ period, the ~ years** l'après-guerre *m*.

posy ['pəʊzɪ] n petit bouquet (de fleurs).

pot¹ [pɒt] 1 n a (*for flowers, jam, dry goods etc*) pot *m*; (†: *for beer*) chope *f*; (*piece of pottery*) poterie *f*; (*for cooking*) marmite *f*, pot†; (*saucepan*) casserole *f*; (*tea~*) théière *f*; (*coffee~*) cafetière *f*; (*potful*) marmite, pot, casserole; (*chamber~*) pot (de chambre), vase *m* de nuit. **jam ~** pot à confiture; **~ of jam** pot de confiture; **~s and pans** casseroles, batterie *f* de cuisine; (*making tea*) **and one for the ~** et une cuillerée pour la théière; (*Prov*) **it's the ~ calling the kettle black** c'est la poêle qui se moque du chaudron; (*fig*) **he can just keep the ~ boiling** il arrive tout juste à faire bouillir la marmite, il arrive à peine à joindre les deux bouts; (*in game etc*) **keep the ~ boiling!** allez-y!, à votre tour!; *see* **flower** *etc.*

b (* *fig*) (*prize*) coupe *f*; (*large stomach*) brioche* *f*, bedaine* *f*; (*kitty*) cagnotte *f*. (*important person*) **a big ~*** une huile*, une grosse légume*; **to have ~s of money*** avoir un argent fou, rouler sur l'or; **to have ~s of time*** avoir tout son temps; **to go to ~*** *[person]* se laisser complètement aller; *[business]* aller à la dérive; *[plans]* aller à vau-l'eau; **to have gone to ~*** être fichu*.

c (*Billiards, Snooker*) **what a ~!** quel coup!; **if he gets** *or* **sinks this ~ he's won** s'il met cette boule, il a gagné.

2 comp ▸**potbellied** (*from overeating*) ventru, bedonnant*; (*from malnutrition*) au ventre ballonné; *vase, stove* ventru, renflé ▸**potbelly** (*from overeating*) gros ventre, bedaine* *f*; (*from malnutrition*) ventre ballonné ▸**potboiler** (*fig pej*) œuvre *f* alimentaire ▸**pot-bound**: **this plant is pot-bound** cette plante est (trop) à l'étroit dans son pot ▸**pot cheese** (*US*) ≃ fromage *m* blanc (égoutté *or* maigre) ▸**potherbs** herbes potagères ▸**pothole** (*in road*) nid *m* de poule, fondrière *f*; (*underground*) caverne *f*, (*larger*) grotte *f*, gouffre *m* ▸**potholer** spéléologue *mf*, spéléo* *mf* ▸**potholing** spéléologie *f*; **to go potholing** faire de la spéléologie ▸**pothook** (*lit*) crémaillère *f*; (*Handwriting*) boucle *f* ▸**pothunter*** chasseur acharné de trophées ▸**potluck**: (*fig*) **to take potluck** (*at meal*) manger à la fortune du pot; (*gen*) prendre ce qu'il y a, s'en remettre au sort ▸**potman** (*Brit*) laveur *m* de verres (*dans un pub*) ▸**potpie** (*US*) tourte *f* à la viande ▸**pot plant** (*Brit*) = **potted plant** ▸**potpourri** *see* **potpourri** ▸**pot roast** (*Culin*) n rôti braisé, rôti à la cocotte ▸**pot-roast** vt faire braiser, faire cuire à la cocotte ▸**pot scourer, pot scrubber** tampon *m* à récurer ▸**potsherd** (*Archeol*) tesson *m* (de poterie) ▸**potshot**: **to take a potshot at sth** tirer qch à vue de nez *or* au pifomètre* ▸**pot-trained** *child* propre.

3 vt a *plant, jam etc* mettre en pot; *see also* **potted**.

b (*Billiards, Snooker*) mettre.

c (*: *shoot*) *duck, pheasant* abattre, descendre*.

d (*) *baby* mettre sur le pot.

4 vi a (*make pottery*) faire de la poterie.

b (*shoot*) **to ~ at sth** tirer qch, canarder qch.

pot²‡ [pɒt] 1 n (*cannabis*) marie-jeanne* *f*, marijuana *f*; (*hashish*) hasch* *m*. 2 comp ▸**pothead** (*Drugs sl*) drogué(e) *m(f)* à la marijuana (*or* au hasch*) ▸**pot party** (*Drugs sl*) séance *f* de hasch*.

potable [ˈpəʊtəbl] adj potable (*lit*).

potash [ˈpɒtæʃ] n (carbonate *m* de) potasse *f*.

potassium [pəˈtæsɪəm] 1 n potassium *m*. 2 comp de potassium.

potation [pəʊˈteɪʃən] n (*gen pl*) libation *f*.

potato [pəˈteɪtəʊ] pl **~es** 1 n pomme *f* de terre. **sweet ~** patate *f* (douce); **is there any ~ left?** est-ce qu'il reste des pommes de terre?; (*fig, esp US*) **it's small ~es*** c'est de la petite bière*; *see* **fry²**, **hot**, **mash** *etc.*

2 comp *field, salad* de pommes de terre ▸**potato beetle** doryphore *m* ▸**potato blight** maladie *f* des pommes de terre ▸**potato bug** = **potato beetle** ▸**potato cake** croquette *f* de pommes de terre ▸**potato chips** (*US*), **potato crisps** (*Brit*) pommes *fpl* chips ▸**potato-masher** presse-purée *m inv* ▸**potato omelette** omelette aux pommes de terre *or* parmentière ▸**potato-peeler** couteau *m* éplucheur, épluche-légumes *m inv* ▸**potato soup** soupe *f* de pommes de terre, potage parmentier ▸**potato topping**: **with a potato topping** recouvert de pommes de terre au gratin.

poteen [pɒˈtiːn, pɒˈtʃiːn] n (*Ir*) whisky *m* (illicite).

potency [ˈpəʊtənsɪ] n, pl **potencies** *or* **potences** a *[remedy, drug, charm, argument]* puissance *f*, force *f*; *[drink]* forte teneur en alcool. b *[male]* virilité *f*.

potent [ˈpəʊtənt] adj a *remedy, drug, charm* puissant; *drink* fort; *argument, reason* convaincant, puissant. b *male* viril.

potentate [ˈpəʊtənteɪt] n potentat *m*.

potential [pəʊˈtenʃəl] 1 adj *energy, resources* potentiel; *sales, uses* possible, éventuel; *earnings* éventuel; *success, danger, enemy* potentiel, en puissance; *meaning, value* virtuel; (*Gram*) potentiel. **he is a ~ prime minister** c'est un premier ministre en puissance.

2 n (*NonC*) a (*Elec, Gram, Math, Phys etc*) potentiel *m*. **military ~** potentiel militaire.

b (*fig: promise, possibilities*) possibilités *fpl*. **the ~ of a discovery/of a new country** les possibilités d'"une découverte/d'un pays neuf; **to have ~** *[person, company, business]* être prometteur, avoir de l'avenir; *[scheme, plan, job]* être prometteur, offrir toutes sortes de possibilités; *[building, land, area]* (*gen*) offrir toutes sortes de possibilités; **area with ~ as** zone *f* convertible *or* aménageable en; **to have the ~ to do** être tout à fait capable de faire; **he's got ~ as a footballer** il a de l'avenir en tant que footballeur, c'est un footballeur prometteur; (*Scol*) **he's got ~ in maths** il a des aptitudes en maths; **to have great ~** être très prometteur, promettre beaucoup; **he hasn't yet realized his full ~** il n'a pas encore donné toute sa mesure.

potentiality [pəʊˌtenʃɪˈælɪtɪ] n potentialité *f*. **potentialities** = **potential 2b**.

potentially [pəʊˈtenʃəlɪ] adv *useful etc* potentiellement. **this is ~ one of the key issues** ceci pourrait bien constituer une des questions les plus importantes; **it's ~ dangerous** ça pourrait bien être dangereux, c'est potentiellement dangereux.

potful [ˈpɒtfʊl] n *[rice, stew]* casserole *f*; *[jam]* pot *m*.

pother [ˈpɒðəʳ] n (*NonC*) (*fuss*) agitation *f*; (*noise*) vacarme *m*, tapage *m*.

potion [ˈpəʊʃən] n (*medicine*) potion *f*; (*magic drink*) philtre *m*, breuvage *m* magique. **love ~** philtre (d'amour).

potlatch [ˈpɒtˌlætʃ] n (*US*) fête où l'on échange des cadeaux.

potpourri [pəʊˈpʊrɪ] n, pl **~s** *[flowers]* fleurs séchées; (*fig, Literat, Mus*) pot-pourri *m*.

potted [ˈpɒtɪd] adj: **~ meat** *rillettes de viande;* **~ plant** plante *f* verte, plante d'appartement; **~ shrimps** *crevettes conservées dans du beurre fondu;* (*fig*) **a ~ version of "Ivanhoe"** un abrégé *or* un condensé d'"Ivanhoé"; **he gave me a ~ account of what had happened** il m'a raconté en deux mots ce qui était arrivé, il m'a fait un bref résumé de ce qui était arrivé.

potter¹ [ˈpɒtəʳ] vi mener sa petite vie tranquille, bricoler*. **to ~ round the house** suivre son petit traintrain* *or* faire des petits travaux dans la maison; **to ~ round the shops** faire les magasins sans se presser.

▸**potter about** vi suivre son petit traintrain*, bricoler*.

▸**potter along** vi aller son petit bonhomme de chemin, poursuivre sa route sans se presser. **we potter along** nous continuons notre traintrain*.

▸**potter around, potter away** vi = **potter about**.

potter² [ˈpɒtəʳ] n potier *f*. **~'s clay** *or* **earth** argile *f* *or* terre *f* à *or* de potier; (*US: cemetery*) **~'s field** cimetière *m* des pauvres; **~'s wheel** tour *m* de potier.

pottery [ˈpɒtərɪ] 1 n a (*NonC*) (*craft, occupation*) poterie *f*; (*objects*) poteries, vaisselle *f* (*NonC*) de terre; (*glazed*) faïencerie *f* (*NonC*); (*ceramics*) céramiques *fpl*. **a piece of ~** une poterie; **Etruscan ~** poterie(s) étrusque(s). b (*place*) poterie *f*. (*Brit Geog*) **the Potteries** la région des Poteries (*dans le Staffordshire*). 2 comp *jug, dish* de *or* en terre, de *or* en céramique, de *or* en faïence.

potting compost [ˈpɒtɪŋˈkɒmpɒst] n terreau *m*.

potting shed [ˈpɒtɪŋˈʃed] n abri *m* de jardin.

potty¹* [ˈpɒtɪ] n pot *m* (de bébé). (*Brit*) **to ~-train** apprendre à devenir propre; (*Brit*) **~-trained** propre; (*Brit*) **~-training** apprentissage *m* de la propreté.

potty²* [ˈpɒtɪ] adj (*Brit*) a *person* toqué*, dingue*; *idea* farfelu. **to be ~ about sb/sth** être toqué de qn/qch*; **it's driving me ~** ça me rend dingue*. b (*slightly pej*) **a ~ little house** une maison de rien du tout.

pouch [paʊtʃ] n petit sac; (*for money*) bourse *f*; (*for ammunition*) étui *m*; (*for cartridges*) giberne *f*; (*for tobacco*) blague *f*; (*US Diplomacy*) valise *f* (diplomatique); *[kangaroo etc]* poche *f* (ventrale); (*under eye*) poche.

pouf(fe) [puːf] n a (*stool*) pouf *m*. b (*Brit* ‡) = **poof**.

poulterer [ˈpəʊltərəʳ] n marchand *m* de volailles, volailler *m*.

poultice [ˈpəʊltɪs] 1 n cataplasme *m*. 2 vt mettre un cataplasme à.

poultry [ˈpəʊltrɪ] 1 n (*NonC*) volaille *f* (*NonC*), volailles. 2 comp ▸**poultry dealer** volailler *m* ▸**poultry farm** exploitation *f* pour l'élevage de la volaille, élevage *m* de volaille(s) ▸**poultry farmer** volailleur *m*, -euse *f* ▸**poultry farming** (*NonC*) élevage *m* de volaille(s), aviculture *f*.

pounce [paʊns] 1 n bond *m*, attaque subite. 2 vi bondir, sauter. **to ~ on** *prey etc* bondir sur, sauter sur; *book, small object* se précipiter sur; (*fig*) *idea, suggestion* sauter sur.

pound¹ [paʊnd] 1 n a (*weight*) livre *f* (= *453,6 grammes*). **sold by the ~** vendu à la livre; **30p a ~** 30 pence la livre; (*fig*) **to demand one's ~ of flesh** exiger son dû impitoyablement. b (*money*) livre *f*. **~ sterling** livre sterling; **10 ~s sterling** 10 livres sterling; *see* **penny**. 2 comp ▸**pound cake** quatre-quarts *m inv* ▸**pound coin/note** pièce *f*/billet *m* d'une livre.

pound² [paʊnd] 1 vt *drugs, spices, nuts, rice etc* piler; *meat* attendrir; *dough* battre, taper sur; *rocks* concasser; *earth, paving slabs* pilonner; *[guns, bombs, shells]* pilonner, marteler. **to ~ sth to a pulp/to pieces** réduire *or* mettre qch en bouillie/en miettes; **to ~ sth to a powder** pulvériser qch, réduire *or* mettre qch en poudre; **the guns ~ed the walls to pieces** les canons ont pulvérisé les murs; **the bombs ~ed the city to rubble** les bombes n'ont laissé que des décombres dans la ville; **the artillery ~ed the enemy line** l'artillerie a pilonné *or* martelé la ligne ennemie; **the waves ~ed the boat to pieces** les vagues ont mis le bateau en miettes; **the sea was ~ing the boat** la mer battait sans arrêt contre le bateau; **to ~ sb (with one's fists)** bourrer qn de coups; **he ~ed the door (with his fists) in a fury** furieux, il a martelé la porte (à coups de poing) *or* il a tambouriné contre la porte; **he ~ed the stake into the ground with a rock** il a enfoncé le pieu dans le sol à l'aide d'une grosse pierre; (*fig*) **I tried to ~ some sense into his head** j'ai essayé de faire entrer *or* d'enfoncer un peu de bon sens dans son crâne; **she was ~ing the dough vigorously** elle battait la pâte énergiquement à coups de poing; **he was ~ing the piano** il tapait (comme un sourd) sur le piano, il jouait comme un forcené; **he was ~ing the typewriter all evening** il n'a pas arrêté de taper sur sa machine toute la soirée; **to ~ the beat** *[policeman]* faire sa ronde; (*fig: be ordinary policeman*) être simple agent; (*US fig = seek work*) battre le pavé (pour chercher du travail).

2 **vi** a *[heart]* battre fort, (*with fear*) battre la chamade; *[sea, waves]* battre (*on, against* contre). **he ~ed at** *or* **on the door** il martela la porte (à coups de poing), il frappa de grands coups à la porte; **he ~ed on the table** il donna de grands coups sur la table, il frappa du poing sur la table; **he was ~ing on the piano** il tapait (comme un sourd) sur le piano, il jouait comme un forcené; **the drums were ~ing** les tambours battaient, on entendait battre le(s) tambour(s).

b (*move heavily*) **to ~ in/out** *etc* (*heavily*) entrer/sortir *etc* en martelant le pavé (*or* le plancher); (*at a run*) entrer/sortir *etc* en courant bruyamment; **he was ~ing up and down his room** il arpentait sa chambre à pas lourds.

▸**pound away** **vi: to pound away at** *or* **on the piano** taper à tours de bras sur le piano, jouer comme un forcené; **he was pounding away at** *or* **on the typewriter all evening** il a tapé sur sa machine à tours de bras toute la soirée.

▸**pound down** **vt sep** *drugs, spices, nuts* piler; *rocks* concasser; *earth, paving slabs* pilonner. **to pound sth down to a pulp** réduire *or* mettre qch en bouillie; **to pound sth down to a powder** pulvériser qch, réduire *or* mettre qch en poudre.

▸**pound out** **vt sep: to pound out a tune on the piano** marteler un air au piano; **to pound out a letter on the typewriter** taper énergiquement une lettre à la machine.

▸**pound up** **vt sep** *drugs, spices, nuts* piler; *rocks* concasser; *earth, paving slabs* pilonner.

pound[3] [paʊnd] **n** (*for dogs, cars*) fourrière *f*.

poundage [ˈpaʊndɪdʒ] **n** a (*tax/commission*) impôt *m*/commission *f* de tant par livre (*sterling ou de poids*). b (*weight*) poids *m* (en livres).

-pounder [ˈpaʊndəʳ] **n ending in comps:** (*gun*) **thirty-pounder** pièce *f or* canon *m* de trente; (*fish*) **three-pounder** poisson *m* de trois livres.

pounding [ˈpaʊndɪŋ] **n** a (*see* **pound**[2]) pilage *m*; pilonnage *m*; concassage *m*. b *[guns etc]* pilonnage *m*; *[heart]* battement *m* frénétique; *[sea, waves]* coups *mpl* de boutoir; *[feet, hooves etc]* martellement *m*. **the boat took a ~ from the waves** le bateau a été battu par les vagues; **the city took a ~** la ville a été pilonnée; (*fig*) **our team took a ~ on Saturday*** notre équipe s'est fait battre à plate(s) couture(s) samedi.

pour [pɔːʳ] 1 **vt** *liquid* verser. **she ~ed him a cup of tea** elle lui a versé *or* servi une tasse de thé; **~ yourself some tea** prenez du thé, servez-vous *or* versez-vous du thé; **shall I ~ the tea?** je sers le thé?; **he ~ed me a drink** il m'a versé *or* servi à boire; **she ~ed the water off the carrots** elle a vidé l'eau des carottes; **to ~ metal/wax into a mould** couler du métal/de la cire; (*fig*) **to ~ money into a scheme** investir énormément d'argent dans un projet; **to ~ scorn on sb/sth** dénigrer qn/qch; **she looked as if she had been ~ed into her dress*** elle était *or* semblait moulée dans sa robe; (*US: fig*) **to ~ it on*** y mettre le paquet*, foncer*; *see* **oil, water.**

2 **vi** a *[water, blood etc]* couler à flots, se déverser, ruisseler (*from* de). **water came ~ing into the room** l'eau se déversa *or* entra à flots dans la pièce; **water was ~ing down the walls** l'eau ruisselait le long des murs; **smoke was ~ing from the chimney** des nuages de fumée s'échappaient de la cheminée; **sunshine ~ed into the room** le soleil entrait à flots dans la pièce; **the sweat ~ed off him** il ruisselait de sueur; (*fig*) **goods are ~ing out of the factories** les usines déversent des quantités de marchandises.

b **it is ~ing (with rain), it's ~ing buckets*** il pleut à verse *or* à flots *or* à torrents *or* à seaux; **it ~ed for 4 days** il n'a pas arrêté de pleuvoir à torrents pendant 4 jours; *see* **rain.**

c *[people, cars, animals]* affluer. **to ~ in/out** entrer/sortir en grand nombre *or* en masse; **tourists are ~ing into London** les touristes affluent à Londres.

d **this saucepan does not ~ well** cette casserole verse mal.

e (*US: act as hostess*) jouer le rôle de maîtresse de maison.

▸**pour away** **vt sep** *dregs etc* vider.

▸**pour down** **vi: the rain** *or* **it was pouring down** il pleuvait à verse *or* à flots *or* à torrents.

▸**pour forth** **vt sep = pour out 2b.**

▸**pour in** 1 **vi** *[water, sunshine, rain]* entrer (à flots); *[people, cars, animals]* arriver de toutes parts *or* en masse. **complaints/letters poured in** il y a eu un déluge *or* une avalanche de réclamations/de lettres.

2 **vt sep** *liquid* verser. (*fig*) **they poured in capital** ils y ont investi d'énormes capitaux.

▸**pour off** **vt sep** *liquid* vider.

▸**pour out** 1 **vi** *[water]* sortir à flots; *[people, cars, animals]* sortir en masse. **the words came pouring out** ce fut une cascade *or* un flot de paroles; **shall I pour out?** je sers?

2 **vt sep** a *tea, coffee, drinks* verser, servir (*for sb* à qn); *dregs, unwanted liquid* vider. **the factory pours out hundreds of cars a day** l'usine sort des centaines de voitures chaque jour; **the country is pouring out money on such projects** le pays engloutit des sommes folles dans de tels projets.

b (*fig*) *anger, emotion* donner libre cours à; *troubles* épancher; *complaint* déverser. **to pour out one's heart to sb** s'épancher avec qn, épancher son cœur avec qn; **he poured out his story to me** il m'a raconté *or* sorti* son histoire d'un seul jet.

pouring [ˈpɔːrɪŋ] **adj** a (*also of ~* **consistency**) *sauce etc* liquide. b **(in) the ~ rain** (sous) la pluie torrentielle *or* battante; **a ~ wet day** une journée de pluie torrentielle.

pout [paʊt] 1 **n** moue *f*. **... she said with a ~** ... dit-elle en faisant la moue. 2 **vi** faire la moue. 3 **vt: to ~ one's lips** faire la moue; **"no" she ~ed** "non" dit-elle en faisant la moue.

poverty [ˈpɒvətɪ] 1 **n** pauvreté *f*. **to live in ~** vivre dans le besoin *or* dans la gêne; **to live in extreme ~** vivre dans la misère *or* l'indigence *f or* le dénuement; **~ of ideas** pauvreté *or* manque *m or* indigence d'idées; **~ of resources** manque de ressources.

2 **comp** ▸**poverty level, poverty line: at/below/above poverty level** *or* **the poverty line** sur le/en dessous du/au-dessus du seuil de pauvreté ▸**poverty-stricken** (*lit*) *person, family* dans le dénuement; *district* miséreux, misérable; *conditions* misérable; (*hard up*) **I'm poverty-stricken** je suis fauché* (comme les blés), je suis sans le sou ▸**the poverty trap** (*Brit*) le dilemme du plafond de ressources (*dont le dépassement supprime les prestations sociales*).

pow* [paʊ] **excl** bang*.

P.O.W. [ˈpiːˌəʊˈdʌbljuː] (*Mil*) (**abbr of prisoner of war**) *see* **prisoner.**

powder [ˈpaʊdəʳ] 1 **n** (*all senses*) poudre *f*. **gun~** poudre à canon; **face ~** poudre de riz; (*Culin*) **milk ~** lait *m* en poudre; **to reduce sth to a ~** pulvériser qch, réduire qch en poudre; **in the form of a ~** en poudre; (*fig*) **to keep one's ~ dry** être paré; (*US*) **to take a ~*** prendre la poudre d'escampette*, décamper; *see* **baking, talcum** *etc*.

2 **comp** ▸**powder blue** bleu *m* pastel *inv*; **powder-blue dress** robe *f* bleu pastel ▸**powder burn** brûlure *f* (superficielle) causée par la poudre ▸**powder compact** poudrier *m* ▸**powder form: in powder form** en poudre ▸**powder keg** (*lit*) baril *m* de poudre; (*fig*) poudrière *f* ▸**powder magazine** poudrière *f* ▸**powder puff** houppette *f*, (*big, fluffy*) houppe *f* ▸**powder room** toilettes *fpl* (pour dames).

3 **vt** a *chalk, rocks* réduire en poudre, pulvériser; *milk, eggs* réduire en poudre. **~ed milk** lait *m* en poudre; (*US*) **~ed sugar** sucre *m* glace.

b *face, body* poudrer; (*Culin*) *cake etc* saupoudrer (*with* de). **to ~ one's nose** (*lit*) se mettre de la poudre; (** euph*) (aller) se refaire une beauté (*euph*); **trees ~ed with snow** arbres saupoudrés de neige; (*fig*) **nose ~ed with freckles** nez couvert de taches de rousseur.

powdering [ˈpaʊdərɪŋ] **n: a ~ of snow** une mince pellicule de neige; **a ~ of sugar** un saupoudrage de sucre.

powdery [ˈpaʊdərɪ] **adj** *substance, snow* poudreux; *stone etc* friable; *surface* couvert de poudre.

power [ˈpaʊəʳ] 1 **n** a (*ability, capacity*) pouvoir *m*, capacité *f*; (*faculty*) faculté *f*. **it is not (with)in my ~ to help you** il n'est pas en mon pouvoir de vous aider; **he did everything** *or* **all in his ~ to help us** il a fait tout son possible *or* tout ce qui était en son pouvoir pour nous aider; **it is quite beyond her ~ to save him** elle est tout à fait impuissante à le sauver, il n'est pas en son pouvoir de le sauver; **mental ~s** facultés mentales; **the ~ of movement/of hearing** la faculté de se mouvoir/d'entendre; **he lost the ~ of speech** il a perdu (l'usage de) la parole; **his ~s are failing with age** ses facultés déclinent *or* baissent avec l'âge; **his ~s of persuasion** son pouvoir *or* sa force de persuasion; **his ~s of resistance** sa capacité de résistance; **his ~s of imagination** sa faculté d'imagination; **the body's recuperative ~** la puissance de récupération de l'organisme, la capacité *or* la faculté régénératrice du corps; *see* **height,** *and also* **1c.**

b (*force*) *[person, blow, sun, explosion]* puissance *f*, force *f*; (*Ling: of grammar*) puissance. **the ~ of love/thought** la toute-puissance de l'amour/de la pensée; **sea/air ~** puissance navale/aérienne; **more ~ to your elbow!** tous mes vœux de réussite.

c (*authority*) pouvoir *m* (*also Pol*), autorité *f*. **the ~ of the President/the police/the army** l'autorité *or* le pouvoir du Président/de la police/de l'armée; **student/pupil** *etc* **~** le pouvoir des étudiants/lycéens *etc;* **absolute ~** pouvoir absolu; **he has the ~ to act** il a le pouvoir d'agir; **they have no ~ in economic matters** ils n'ont aucune autorité en matière économique; **that does not fall within my ~(s), that is beyond** *or* **outside my ~(s)** ceci n'est pas *or* ne relève pas de ma compétence; **he exceeded his ~s** il a outrepassé *or* excédé ses pouvoirs; **at the height of his ~** à l'apogée de son pouvoir; **to have the ~ of life and death over sb** avoir droit de vie et de mort sur qn; **the ~ of veto** le droit de veto; **~ of attorney** procuration *f*, pouvoir *m*; (*Pol*) **in ~** au pouvoir; **to come to ~** accéder au pouvoir; **to have ~ over sb** avoir autorité sur qn; **to have sb in one's ~** avoir qn en son pouvoir; **to fall into sb's ~** tomber au pouvoir de qn.

d (*fig*) **they are the real ~ in the government** ce sont eux qui détiennent le pouvoir réel dans le gouvernement; (*fig*) **the ~ behind**

the throne l'éminence grise, celui (*or* celle) qui tire les ficelles; **the Church is no longer the ~ it was** l'Église n'est plus la puissance qu'elle était; **he is a ~ in the university** il est très influent à l'université; **he is a ~ in the land** c'est un homme très puissant *or* très influent; **the ~s of darkness/evil** les forces *fpl* des ténèbres/du mal; **the ~s that be** les autorités constituées; *see* **above**.

e (*nation*) puissance *f*. **the nuclear/world ~s** les puissances nucléaires/mondiales; **one of the great naval ~s** une des grandes puissances navales.

f *[engine, telescope etc]* puissance *f*; (*Elec, Phys, Tech etc*) puissance, force *f*; (*energy*) énergie *f*; (*Opt*) puissance; (*output*) rendement *m*; (*electricity*) électricité *f*, courant *m*. **it works by nuclear ~** ça marche *or* fonctionne à l'énergie nucléaire; (*Elec*) **they cut off the ~** ils ont coupé le courant; (*Elec*) **our consumption of ~ has risen** notre consommation d'électricité a augmenté; **a low-~ microscope** un microscope de faible puissance; **magnifying ~** grossissement *m*; **engines at half ~** moteurs à mi-régime; **the ship returned to port under her own ~** le navire est rentré au port par ses propres moyens; *see* **horse** *etc*.

g (*Math*) puissance *f*. **5 to the ~ of 3** 5 puissance 3; **to the nth ~** (à la) puissance n.

h (*) **a ~ of** un tas* de, énormément de; **it did me a ~ of good** ça m'a fait un bien immense, ça m'a rudement* fait du bien; **he made a ~ of money** il a gagné un argent fou.

2 **comp** *saw, loom, lathe* mécanique; (*Aut*) *brakes etc* assisté; (*Ind*) *strike, dispute* des travailleurs des centrales (*électriques*) ►**power-assisted** assisté ►**power base** (*Pol*) base *f* politique, support *m* politique ►**powerboat** hors-bord *m inv* ►**power broker** (*US Pol*) éminence *f* grise ►**power cable** (*Elec*) câble *m* électrique ►**power cut** (*Brit Elec*) coupure *f* de courant ►**power dive** (*Aviat*) descente *f* en piqué ►**power dressing** *mise élégante et assurée des femmes cadres* ►**power-driven** à moteur; (*Elec*) électrique ►**power elite** élite *f* au pouvoir ►**power game** (*Brit*) lutte *f* pour le pouvoir ►**powerhouse** (*lit*) centrale *f* électrique; (*fig*) personne *f or* groupe *m* très dynamique; (*fig*) **a powerhouse of new ideas** une mine d'idées nouvelles ►**power line** (*Elec*) ligne *f* à haute tension ►**power pack** bloc *m* d'alimentation (électrique) ►**power plant** (*US*) (*building*) centrale *f* (electrique); (*in vehicle etc*) groupe *m* moteur ►**power point** (*Brit Elec*) prise *f* de courant ►**power politics** politique *f* de la force armée ►**power sharing** (*Pol*) le partage du pouvoir ►**power station** (*Elec*) centrale *f* (électrique) ►**power steering** (*Aut*) direction *f* assistée ►**power structure** (*Pol*) (*way power is held*) répartition *f* des pouvoirs; (*those with power*) ceux *mpl* qui détiennent le pouvoir ►**power tool** outil *m* éléctrique ►**power workers** (*Ind*) travailleurs *mpl* des centrales (*électriques*).

3 **vt** (*gen pass*) faire marcher, faire fonctionner, actionner; (*propel*) propulser. **~ed by nuclear energy** qui marche *or* fonctionne à l'énergie nucléaire; **~ed by jet engines** propulsé par des moteurs à réaction.

-powered ['paʊəd] **adj ending in comps: nuclear-powered** qui marche *or* fonctionne à l'énergie nucléaire; *see* **high** *etc*.

powerful ['paʊəfʊl] **adj** (*all senses, also Gram*) puissant. **he gave a ~ performance in "Hamlet"** il a donné une représentation puissante *or* émouvante dans "Hamlet"; **a ~ lot of*** beaucoup de, un tas de*.

powerfully ['paʊəfəlɪ] **adv** *hit, strike* avec force; *affect* fortement; *write etc* puissamment; *smell* fortement. **to be ~ built** avoir une carrure puissante.

powerless ['paʊəlɪs] **adj** impuissant. **he is ~ to help you** il est dans l'impossibilité de vous aider, il est impuissant à vous aider; **they are ~ in the matter** ceci n'est pas de leur compétence, ils n'ont aucun pouvoir en la matière.

powerlessly ['paʊəlɪslɪ] **adv: I looked on ~** j'ai regardé faire, impuissant, j'étais un spectateur impuissant.

powerlessness ['paʊəlɪsnɪs] **n** impuissance *f*.

powwow ['paʊwaʊ] 1 **n** assemblée *f* (*de Peaux-Rouges*); (* *fig*) tête-à-tête *m inv*. 2 **vi** (* *fig*) s'entretenir, palabrer (*pej*).

pox [pɒks] **n** (*gen:*†) variole *f*, petite vérole; (*: *syphilis*) vérole** *f*. **a ~ on ...!**† maudit soit ...!; *see* **chicken, cow**[1] *etc*.

poxy** ['pɒksɪ] **adj** merdique**.

p.p.[1] ['piː'piː] **abbr of per procurationem = by proxy.** 1 **prep** p.p. 2 **vt: to ~ a letter (for sb)** signer une lettre pour qn.

p.p.[2] a **abbr of parcel post.** b **abbr of post paid.**

PPE ['piː,piː'iː] (*Univ*) **abbr of philosophy, politics and economics.**

ppm abbr of parts per million.

PPS ['piː,piː'es] **n** (*Brit Parl*) (**abbr of Parliamentary Private Secretary**) *see* **parliamentary.**

PQ (*Can Post*) **abbr of Province of Quebec.**

PR[1] [piː'ɑːʳ] **n** (**abbr of public relations**) *see* **public.**

PR[2] [piː'ɑːʳ] (*US Post*) **abbr of Puerto Rico.**

PR[3] **n** (**abbr of proportional representation**) R.P. *f*.

Pr. abbr of Prince.

practicability [,præktɪkə'bɪlɪtɪ] **n** *[road, path]* praticabilité *f*; *[scheme, suggestion]* praticabilité, possibilité *f* de réalisation. **to doubt the ~ of a scheme** douter qu'un projet soit réalisable.

practicable ['præktɪkəbl] **adj** *scheme, solution, suggestion* praticable, réalisable, exécutable; *road* praticable.

practical ['præktɪkəl] 1 **adj** (*all senses*) pratique. **~ joke** farce *f*; (*US*) **~ nurse** infirmier *m*, -ière *f* auxiliaire, aide-soignant(e) *m(f)*; **he's very ~** il a beaucoup de sens pratique, c'est un homme très pratique; **it's a ~ certainty** c'est une quasi-certitude. 2 **n** (*exam*) épreuve *f* pratique; (*lesson*) travaux *mpl* pratiques.

practicality [,præktɪ'kælɪtɪ] **n** a (*NonC*) *[person]* sens *m or* esprit *m* pratique; *[scheme, suggestion]* aspect *m* pratique. **to doubt the ~ of a scheme** douter qu'un projet soit viable *or* réalisable (dans la pratique). b **practicalities** détails *mpl* pratiques.

practically ['præktɪklɪ] **adv** (*in a practical way*) d'une manière pratique; *say, suggest* d'une manière pragmatique; (*in practice*) dans la pratique, en fait; (*almost*) presque, pratiquement.

practicalness ['præktɪkəlnɪs] = **practicality a.**

practice ['præktɪs] 1 **n** a (*habits, usage*) pratique *f*, coutume *f*, usage *m*. **to make a ~ of doing, to make it a ~ to do** avoir l'habitude *or* se faire une habitude de faire; **it is not my ~ to do so** il n'est pas dans mes habitudes de le faire; **as is my (usual) ~** comme je fais d'habitude; **it's common ~** c'est courant; *see* **restrictive, sharp** *etc*.

b (*exercises*) exercices *mpl*; (*training*) entraînement *m*; (*rehearsal*) répétition *f*. **have you done your ~ today?** tu as fait tes exercices *or* tu t'es exercé aujourd'hui?; **he does 6 hours' piano ~ a day** il s'exerce au *or* il travaille le piano (pendant) 6 heures par jour, il fait 6 heures de piano par jour; **it takes years of ~** il faut de longues années d'entraînement, il faut s'exercer pendant des années; **I need more ~** je manque d'entraînement, je ne me suis pas assez exercé; **in ~** bien entraîné *or* exercé; **out of ~** rouillé (*fig*); (*Prov*) **~ makes perfect** c'est en forgeant qu'on devient forgeron (*Prov*); *see* **target.**

c (*NonC: as opposed to theory*) pratique *f*. **in(to) ~** en pratique; **to put into ~** mettre en pratique.

d (*profession: of law, medicine etc*) exercice *m*; (*business, clients*) clientèle *f*, cabinet *m*. **to go into ~** *or* **to set up in ~ as a doctor/lawyer** s'installer *or* s'établir docteur/avocat; **he is in ~ in Valence** il exerce à Valence; **he has a large ~** il a une nombreuse clientèle, il a un cabinet important; *see* **general.**

2 **comp** *flight, run* d'entraînement ►**practice exam, practice test** (*Scol etc*) examen *m* blanc.

3 **vti** (*US*) = **practise.**

practise, (*US*) **practice** ['præktɪs] 1 **vt** a (*put into practice*) *charity, self-denial, one's religion* pratiquer; *method* employer, appliquer. **to ~ medicine/law** exercer la médecine *or* la profession de médecin/la profession d'avocat; (*loc*) **to ~ what one preaches** mettre en pratique ce que l'on prêche, prêcher par l'exemple *or* d'exemple.

b (*exercise in*) (*Sport*) s'entraîner à; *violin etc* s'exercer à, travailler; *song, chorus, recitation* travailler. **she was practising her scales** elle faisait ses gammes; **to ~ doing** s'entraîner *or* s'exercer à faire; **I'm practising my German on him** je m'exerce à parler allemand avec lui; *see also* **practised.**

2 **vi** a (*Mus*) s'exercer; (*Sport*) s'entraîner; *[beginner]* faire des exercices. **to ~ on the piano** s'exercer au piano, travailler le piano; **he ~s for 2 hours every day** il fait 2 heures d'entraînement *or* d'exercices par jour.

b *[doctor, lawyer]* exercer. **to ~ as a doctor/lawyer** exercer la médecine *or* la profession de médecin/la profession d'avocat.

practised, (*US*) **practiced** ['præktɪst] **adj** *teacher, nurse, soldier* expérimenté, chevronné; *eye, ear* exercé; *movement* expert; *performance* accompli.

practising, (*US*) **practicing** ['præktɪsɪŋ] **adj** *doctor* exerçant; *lawyer* en exercice; *Catholic, Buddhist* pratiquant. **a ~ Christian** un (chrétien) pratiquant; **he is not a ~ homosexual** son homosexualité demeure à l'état latent.

practitioner [præk'tɪʃənəʳ] **n** (*of an art*) praticien *m*, -ienne *f*; (*Med: also* **medical ~**) médecin *m*; *see* **general** *etc*.

praesidium [prɪ'sɪdɪəm] **n** præsidium *m*.

praetorian [prɪ'tɔːrɪən] **adj** prétorien.

pragmatic [præg'mætɪk] 1 **adj** a (*Philos, gen*) pragmatique. b (*dogmatic*) dogmatique, positif; (*officious*) officieux. 2 **n** (*NonC*) **~s** la pragmatique.

pragmatical [præg'mætɪkl] = **pragmatic 1b.**

pragmatically [præg'mætɪklɪ] **adv** d'une manière pragmatique, avec pragmatisme.

pragmatism ['prægmətɪzəm] **n** (*see* **pragmatic**) pragmatisme *m*; dogmatisme *m*; caractère officieux.

pragmatist ['prægmətɪst] **adj, n** pragmatiste *(mf)*.

Prague [prɑːg] **n** Prague.

prairie ['prɛərɪ] 1 **n** plaine *f* (herbeuse). (*US*) **the ~(s)** la Grande Prairie, les Prairies. 2 **comp** ►**prairie cocktail** (*US*) = **prairie oyster** ►**prairie dog** (*US*) chien *m* de prairie, cynomys *m* ►**prairie oyster** (*US*) œuf *m* cru assaisonné et bu dans de l'alcool (*remède contre la gueule de bois*) ►**Prairie Provinces** (*Can*) Provinces *fpl* des Prairies ►**prairie schooner** (*US*) grand chariot *m* bâché (des pionniers américains) ►**the Prairie State** (*US*) l'Illinois *m* ►**prairie wolf** (*US*) coyote *m*.

praise [preɪz] 1 **n** a éloge(s) *m(pl)*, louange(s) *f(pl)*. **in ~ of** à la louange de; **to speak** (*or* **write** *etc*) **in ~ of sb/sth** faire l'éloge de qn/qch; **it is beyond ~** c'est au-dessus de tout éloge; **I have nothing but ~ for what he has done** je ne peux que le louer de ce qu'il a fait; **I have nothing but ~ for him** je n'ai qu'à me louer *or* me féliciter de lui; **all ~ to him for speaking out!** je lui tire mon chapeau d'avoir dit ce qu'il pensait; **he was loud** *or* **warm in his ~(s) of ...** il n'a pas tari d'éloges sur ..., il a chanté les louanges de ...; *see* **sing** *etc*.

b (*Rel*) **a hymn of ~** un cantique; **~ be to God!** Dieu soit loué!; **~ be!*** Dieu merci!

2 **comp ▸praiseworthy** *see* **praiseworthy**.

3 **vt** a *person, action, sb's courage etc* louer, faire l'éloge de. **to ~ sb for sth/for doing** louer qn de *or* pour qch/d'avoir fait; **to ~ sb to the skies** porter qn aux nues, chanter les louanges de qn.

b (*Rel*) louer, glorifier.

▸praise up vt sep chanter les louanges de.

praiseworthily ['preɪz,wɜːðɪlɪ] **adv** d'une manière louable *or* méritoire.

praiseworthiness ['preɪz,wɜːðɪnɪs] **n** mérite *m*.

praiseworthy ['preɪz,wɜːðɪ] **adj** *person* digne d'éloges; *cause, attempt* digne d'éloges, louable, méritoire.

pram [præm] **n** (*Brit*) voiture *f* d'enfant, landau *m*. (*Brit*) **~ park** emplacement *m* réservé aux voitures d'enfants.

prance [prɑːns] **vi** *[horse, dancer etc]* caracoler. **the horse was prancing about** le cheval caracolait; **she was prancing* around** *or* **about with nothing on** elle se baladait* toute nue; **to ~ in/out** *etc [horse]* entrer/sortir en caracolant; *[person]* (*arrogantly*) entrer/sortir en se pavanant; (*gaily*) entrer/sortir allègrement.

prang‡† [præŋ] **vt** (*Brit*) (*crash*) *plane, car* bousiller*; (*bomb*) pilonner.

prank [præŋk] **n** (*escapade*) frasque *f*, fredaine *f*, équipée *f*; (*joke*) farce *f*, tour *m*, niche *f*. **a childish ~** une gaminerie; **to play a ~ on sb** jouer un tour à qn, faire une farce *or* une niche à qn.

prankster† ['præŋkstəʳ] **n** farceur *m*, -euse *f*.

praseodymium [,preɪzɪəʊ'dɪmɪəm] **n** praséodyme *m*.

prat‡ [præt] **n** imbécile *mf*, andouille *f*.

pratfall‡ ['præt,fɔːl] **n** (*US*) chute *f* sur le derrière.

prate [preɪt] **vi** jaser, babiller (*pej*). **to ~ on about sth** parler à n'en plus finir de qch.

prattle ['prætl] 1 **vi** *[one person]* jaser, babiller (*pej*); *[several people]* papoter, jacasser; *[child]* babiller, gazouiller. **to ~ on about sth** parler à n'en plus finir de qch; **he ~s on and on** c'est un vrai moulin à paroles. 2 **n** *[one person]* bavardage *m*, babil *m* (*pej*), babillage *m* (*pej*); *[several people]* jacasserie *f*, papotage *m*; *[child]* babil, babillage.

prawn [prɔːn] **n** crevette *f* rose, bouquet *m*. **~ cocktail** salade *f* *or* mayonnaise *f* de crevettes; **~ cracker** beignet *m* de crevette; *see* **Dublin**.

pray [preɪ] 1 **vi** a prier. **they ~ed to God to help them** ils prièrent Dieu de les secourir; **he ~ed to be released from his suffering** il pria le ciel de mettre fin à ses souffrances; **to ~ for sb/sb's soul/one's country** *etc* prier pour qn/l'âme de qn/son pays *etc*; **he ~ed for forgiveness** il pria Dieu de lui pardonner; **to ~ for rain** prier pour qu'il pleuve, faire des prières pour la pluie; (*fig*) **we're ~ing for fine weather** nous faisons des prières pour qu'il fasse beau; **he's past ~ing for*** il est perdu, (*also hum*) c'est un cas désespéré.

b (†, *liter*) **~ be seated** veuillez vous asseoir, asseyez-vous je vous prie; (*iro*) **what good is that, ~?** à quoi cela peut-il bien servir, je vous le demande?

2 **vt** (†, *liter*) prier (*sb to do* qn de faire, *that* que + *subj*). **they ~ed God to help him** ils prièrent Dieu de lui venir en aide; **I ~ you** je vous (en) prie.

prayer [preəʳ] 1 **n** a (*Rel*) prière *f* (*also NonC*). **to be at ~** *or* **at one's ~s** être en prière; **he was kneeling in ~** il priait à genoux; **to say one's ~s** faire sa prière; **they said a ~ for him** ils ont fait *or* dit une prière pour lui, ils ont prié pour lui; (*as service*) **~s** office *m*; (*US*) **he didn't have a ~*** il n'avait pas la moindre chance; *see* **common, evening, lord** *etc*.

b (*liter*) **it is our earnest ~ that ...** nous espérons de tout cœur que ... .

2 **comp ▸prayer beads** chapelet *m* **▸prayer book** livre *m* de messe; **the Prayer Book** le rituel de l'Église anglicane **▸prayer mat** tapis *m* de prière **▸prayer meeting** réunion *f* de prière **▸prayer rug** tapis *m* de prière **▸prayer wheel** moulin *m* à prières.

praying ['preɪɪŋ] 1 **n** (*NonC*) prière(s) *f(pl)*. 2 **adj** en prière. (*Zool*) **~ mantis** mante religieuse.

pre... [priː] **pref** pré... . **~glacial** préglaciaire; **~-1950** **(adj)** antérieur (*f* -eure) à (l'année) 1950, d'avant 1950; **(adv)** avant 1950; *see* **predate, prerecord** *etc*.

preach [priːtʃ] 1 **vi** (*Rel*) prêcher (*also fig pej*), évangéliser; (*in church*) prêcher. **to ~ to sb** prêcher qn; (*fig pej*) **to ~ to** *or* **at sb** prêcher *or* sermonner qn; (*fig*) **you are ~ing to the converted** vous prêchez un converti; *see* **practise**. 2 **vt** *religion, the Gospel, crusade, doctrine* prêcher; (*fig*) *patience* prêcher, préconiser, prôner; *advantage* prôner. **to ~ a sermon** prêcher, faire un sermon.

preacher ['priːtʃəʳ] **n** prédicateur *m*; (*US: clergyman*) pasteur *m*.

preachify* ['priːtʃɪfaɪ] **vi** (*pej*) prêcher, faire la morale.

preaching ['priːtʃɪŋ] **n** (*NonC*) prédication *f*, sermon *m*; (*fig pej*) prêchi-prêcha* (*pej*).

preachy* ['priːtʃɪ] **adj** (*pej*) prêcheur, sermonneur.

preamble [priː'æmbl] **n** préambule *m*; (*in book*) préface *f*.

preamplifier [,priː'æmplɪfaɪəʳ] **n** préamplificateur *m*, préampli* *m*.

prearrange ['priːə'reɪndʒ] **vt** arranger *or* organiser *or* fixer à l'avance *or* au préalable.

prebend ['prebənd] **n** prébende *f*.

prebendary ['prebəndərɪ] **n** prébendier *m*.

precancerous ['prɪ'kænsərəs] **adj** précancéreux.

precarious [prɪ'kɛərɪəs] **adj** précaire.

precariously [prɪ'kɛərɪəslɪ] **adv** précairement.

precast ['priː'kɑːst] **adj**: **~ concrete** béton précontraint.

precaution [prɪ'kɔːʃən] **n** précaution *f* (*against* contre). **as a ~** par précaution; **to take ~s** prendre ses précautions; **to take the ~ of doing** prendre la précaution de faire.

precautionary [prɪ'kɔːʃənərɪ] **adj** de précaution, préventif. **as a ~ measure** par mesure de précaution.

precede [prɪ'siːd] **vt** (*in space, time*) précéder; (*in rank*) avoir la préséance sur. **the week preceding his death** la semaine qui a précédé sa mort, la semaine avant sa mort.

precedence ['presɪdəns] **n** (*in rank*) préséance *f*; (*in importance*) priorité *f*. **to have** *or* **take ~ over sb** avoir la préséance *or* le pas sur qn; **this question must take ~ over the others** ce problème a la priorité sur les autres, ce problème passe en priorité *or* est prioritaire.

precedent ['presɪdənt] **n** précédent *m*. **without ~** sans précédent; **to act as** *or* **form a ~** constituer un précédent; **to set** *or* **create a ~** créer un précédent.

preceding [prɪ'siːdɪŋ] **adj** précédent. **the ~ day** le jour précédent, la veille.

precentor [prɪ'sentəʳ] **n** premier chantre, maître *m* de chapelle.

precept ['priːsept] **n** précepte *m*.

preceptor [prɪ'septəʳ] **n** précepteur *m*, -trice *f*.

pre-Christian [priː'krɪstʃən] **adj** préchrétien.

precinct ['priːsɪŋkt] 1 **n** a (*round cathedral etc*) enceinte *f*; (*boundary*) pourtour *m*. (*fig*) **within the ~s of** dans les limites de; (*neighbourhood*) **the ~s** les alentours *mpl*, les environs *mpl*; *see* **pedestrian, shopping**.

b (*US Police*) circonscription administrative; (*US Pol*) circonscription électorale, arrondissement *m*.

2 **comp ▸precinct captain** (*US*) (*Pol*) responsable *mf* politique de quartier; (*Police*) = commissaire *m* (de police) de quartier **▸precinct cop** (*US*) flic* *m*, agent *m* **▸precinct police** (*US Police*) police *f* de quartier **▸precinct station** (*US Police*) poste *m* de police de quartier, commissariat *m* de quartier **▸precinct worker** (*US Pol*) *militant(e) politique à l'échelon du quartier*.

preciosity [,presɪ'ɒsɪtɪ] **n** préciosité *f*.

precious ['preʃəs] 1 **adj** a *metal, person, moment* précieux; *object, book, possession* précieux, de valeur; (* *iro*) chéri, cher (*f* chère). **~ stone** pierre précieuse; **don't waste ~ time arguing** ne perds pas un temps précieux à discuter; **this book is very ~ to me** ce livre a une très grande valeur pour moi, je tiens énormément à ce livre; **he is very ~ to me** il m'est très précieux; (*iro*) **your ~ son*** ton fils chéri *or* adoré, ton cher fils; (*iro*) **your ~ car** ta voiture chérie, ta chère voiture.

b *style, language* précieux, affecté. c (*) **a ~ liar** un beau *or* joli *or* fameux menteur. 2 **adv** (*) **~ few, ~ little** très *or* fort *or* bien peu.

3 **n**: **(my) ~!** mon trésor!

precipice ['presɪpɪs] **n** (*gen*) à-pic *m inv*. **to fall over a ~** tomber dans un précipice.

precipitance [prɪ'sɪpɪtəns] **n**, **precipitancy** [prɪ'sɪpɪtənsɪ] **n** précipitation *f*.

precipitant [prɪ'sɪpɪtənt] 1 **adj** = **precipitate 4**. 2 **n** (*Chem*) précipitant *m*.

precipitate [prɪ'sɪpɪteɪt] 1 **vt** a (*hasten*) *event, crisis* hâter, précipiter; (*hurl*) *person* précipiter (*into* dans). b (*Chem*) précipiter; (*Met*) condenser. 2 **vi** (*Chem*) (se) précipiter; (*Met*) se condenser. 3 **n** (*Chem*) précipité *m*. 4 [prɪ'sɪpɪtɪt] **adj** irréfléchi, hâtif.

precipitately [prɪ'sɪpɪtɪtlɪ] **adv** précipitamment, avec précipitation, à la hâte.

precipitation [prɪ,sɪpɪ'teɪʃən] **n** précipitation *f* (*also Chem, Met*).

precipitous [prɪ'sɪpɪtəs] **adj** a escarpé, abrupt, à pic. b = **precipitate 4**.

precipitously [prɪ'sɪpɪtəslɪ] **adv** à pic, abruptement.

précis ['preɪsiː] 1 **n, pl précis** ['preɪsiːz] résumé *m*, précis *m*. 2 **vt** faire un résumé *or* précis de.

precise [prɪ'saɪs] **adj** a *details, instructions, description* précis; *measurement, meaning, account* précis, exact. **be (more) ~!** soyez (plus) précis *or* explicite!, précisez!; **there were 8 to be ~** il y en avait 8 pour être exact *or* précis; **it was the ~ amount I needed** c'était exactement la quantité (*or* somme) qu'il me fallait; **he gave me that ~ book** c'est ce livre même qu'il m'a donné; **at that ~ moment** à ce moment précis *or* même.

b (*meticulous*) *movement* précis; *person, manner* méticuleux, minutieux; (*pej: over-~*) pointilleux, maniaque. **he is a very ~ worker** c'est un travailleur très méticuleux *or* minutieux, il est extrêmement méticuleux dans son travail; **in that ~ voice of hers** de sa façon de parler si nette.

precisely [prɪ'saɪslɪ] **adv** *explain, instruct, describe, recount, use instrument* avec précision; (*exactly*) précisément, exactement. ... **he said very ~** ... dit-il d'une voix très nette *or* en détachant nettement les syllabes; **at 10 o'clock ~** à 10 heures précises *or* sonnantes; **you have ~ 2 minutes to get out** vous avez très précisément *or* exactement 2 minutes pour sortir; **he said ~ nothing** il n'a absolument rien dit; **what ~ does he do for a living?** que fait-il au juste pour gagner sa vie?; ~! justement!, précisément!, exactement!

preciseness [prɪ'saɪsnɪs] = **precision 1**.

precision [prɪ'sɪʒən] 1 **n** (*see* **precise**) précision *f*; exactitude *f*; minutie *f*. 2 **comp** *instrument, tool* de précision ▸**precision bombing** bombardement *m* de précision ▸**precision-made** de haute précision.

preclude [prɪ'klu:d] **vt** *doubt* écarter, dissiper; *misunderstanding* prévenir; *possibility* exclure. **to be ~d from doing** être empêché *or* dans l'impossibilité de faire; **that ~s his leaving** cela le met dans l'impossibilité de partir.

precocious [prɪ'kəʊʃəs] **adj** précoce.

precociously [prɪ'kəʊʃəslɪ] **adv** précocement, avec précocité.

precociousness [prɪ'kəʊʃəsnɪs] **n**, **precocity** [prə'kɒsɪtɪ] **n** précocité *f*.

precognition [,pri:kɒg'nɪʃən] **n** préconnaissance *f*.

precombustion ['pri:kəm'bʌstʃən] **n** précombustion *f*.

preconceived ['pri:kən'si:vd] **adj**: **~ idea** idée préconçue.

preconception ['pri:kən'sepʃən] **n** idée préconçue, préconception *f*.

preconcerted ['pri:kən'sɜ:tɪd] **adj** arrêté *or* concerté d'avance *or* au préalable.

precondition ['pri:kən'dɪʃən] 1 **n** condition nécessaire *or* requise, condition sine qua non. 2 **vt** conditionner (*sb to do* qn à faire).

precook ['pri:'ku:k] **vt** faire cuire à l'avance.

precooked ['pri:'ku:kt] **adj** précuit.

precool ['pri:'ku:l] **vt** refroidir d'avance.

precursor [pri:'kɜ:sə[r]] **n** (*person, thing*) précurseur *m*; (*event*) annonce *f*, signe avant-coureur.

precursory [prɪ'kɜ:sərɪ] **adj** *remark* préliminaire; *taste, glimpse* annonciateur (*f* -trice).

predaceous, predacious [prɪ'deɪʃəs] = **predatory**.

predate ['pri:'deɪt] **vt** a (*put earlier date on*) *cheque, document* antidater. b (*come before in time*) *event* précéder, avoir lieu avant, venir avant; *document* être antérieur (*f* -eure) à, précéder.

predator ['predətə[r]] **n** prédateur *m*, rapace *m*.

predatory ['predətərɪ] **adj** *animal, bird, insect* de proie, prédateur, rapace; *habits* de prédateur(s); *person* rapace; *armies* pillard; *look* vorace, avide.

predecease ['pri:dɪ'si:s] **vt** prédécéder.

predecessor ['pri:dɪsesə[r]] **n** prédécesseur *m*.

predestination [pri:,destɪ'neɪʃən] **n** prédestination *f*.

predestine [pri:'destɪn] **vt** (*also Rel*) prédestiner (*to* à; *to do* à faire).

predetermination ['pri:dɪ,tɜ:mɪ'neɪʃən] **n** détermination antérieure; (*Philos, Rel*) prédétermination *f*.

predetermine ['pri:dɪ'tɜ:mɪn] **vt** déterminer *or* arrêter au préalable *or* d'avance; (*Philos, Rel*) prédéterminer.

predeterminer [,pri:dɪ'tɜ:mɪnə[r]] **n** (*Gram*) prédéterminant *m*, préarticle *m*.

predicable ['predɪkəbl] **adj, n** (*Philos*) prédicable (*m*).

predicament [prɪ'dɪkəmənt] **n** situation difficile *or* fâcheuse. **I'm in a real ~!** (*puzzled*) je ne sais vraiment pas que faire!; (*in a fix*) me voilà dans de beaux draps!

predicate ['predɪkeɪt] 1 **vt** a (*affirm, also Philos*) affirmer (*that* que). b (*imply*) *existence of sth etc* impliquer, supposer. c (*base*) *statement, belief, argument* baser, fonder (*on, upon* sur). **this is ~d on the fact that** ... ceci est fondé *or* basé sur le fait que ... . 2 ['predɪkɪt] **n** (*Gram*) prédicat *m*; (*Philos*) prédicat, attribut *m*. 3 ['predɪkɪt] **adj** (*Gram*) prédicatif; (*Philos*) attributif.

predicative [prɪ'dɪkətɪv] **adj** prédicatif.

predicatively [prɪ'dɪkətɪvlɪ] **adv** (*Gram*) en tant que prédicat.

predict [prɪ'dɪkt] **vt** prédire, prévoir.

predictability [prɪdɪktə'bɪlɪtɪ] **n** prévisibilité *f*.

predictable [prɪ'dɪktəbl] **adj** prévisible; *person, book, behaviour* sans surprise. **his reaction was very ~** sa réaction était tout à fait prévisible *or* était facile à prévoir, il a réagi comme on pouvait le prévoir.

predictably [prɪ'dɪktəblɪ] **adv** d'une manière prévisible. **~, he did not appear** comme on pouvait le prévoir, *or* comme il fallait s'y attendre, il ne s'est pas montré.

prediction [prɪ'dɪkʃən] **n** prédiction *f*.

predictive [prɪ'dɪktɪv] **adj** prophétique.

predigested [,pri:daɪ'dʒestɪd] **adj** prédigéré.

predilection [,pri:dɪ'lekʃən] **n** prédilection *f*. **to have a ~ for sth** avoir une prédilection *or* une préférence marquée pour qch, affectionner qch.

predispose ['pri:dɪs'pəʊz] **vt** prédisposer (*to or towards sth* à qch; *to do(ing)* à faire).

predisposition ['pri:,dɪspə'zɪʃən] **n** prédisposition *f* (*to* à).

predominance [prɪ'dɒmɪnəns] **n** prédominance *f*.

predominant [prɪ'dɒmɪnənt] **adj** prédominant.

predominantly [prɪ'dɒmɪnəntlɪ] **adv** principalement, surtout. **they are ~ French** il y a une prédominance de Français parmi eux, ce sont principalement *or* surtout des Français.

predominate [prɪ'dɒmɪneɪt] **vi** prédominer (*over* sur), prévaloir.

preemie* ['pri:mɪ] **n** (*US Med*) prématuré(e) *m(f)*.

pre-eminence [pri:'emɪnəns] **n** prééminence *f*.

pre-eminent [pri:'emɪnənt] **adj** prééminent.

pre-eminently [pri:'emɪnəntlɪ] **adv** avant tout.

pre-empt [pri:'empt] **vt** a *sb's decision, action* anticiper, devancer; *sb's statement* empiéter sur. **he ~ed control of the negotiations** il a pris unilatéralement *or* il s'est adjugé la direction des négociations. b *painting, land* acquérir par (droit de) préemption.

pre-emption [pri:'empʃən] **n** (droit *m* de) préemption *f*.

pre-emptive [pri:'emptɪv] **adj** *right* de préemption; *attack, strike* préventif. (*Bridge*) **~ bid** (demande *f* de) barrage *m*.

preen [pri:n] 1 **vt** *feathers, tail* lisser. **the bird was ~ing itself** l'oiseau se lissait les plumes; **she was ~ing herself in front of the mirror** elle se pomponnait *or* s'arrangeait complaisamment devant la glace; (*liter*) **to ~ o.s. on sth/on doing** s'enorgueillir de qch/de faire. 2 **vi** *[oiseau]* se lisser les plumes; *[person]* se pomponner.

pre-establish ['pri:ɪs'tæblɪʃ] **vt** préétablir.

pre-exist ['pri:ɪg'zɪst] 1 **vi** préexister. 2 **vt** préexister à.

pre-existence ['pri:ɪg'zɪstəns] **n** préexistence *f*.

pre-existent ['pri:ɪg'zɪstənt] **adj** préexistant.

prefab* ['pri:fæb] **n** (**abbr of prefabricated building**) maison (*or* salle de classe *etc*) préfabriquée.

prefabricate [,pri:'fæbrɪkeɪt] **vt** préfabriquer.

preface ['prefɪs] 1 **n** (*to book*) préface *f*, avant-propos *m inv*; (*to speech*) introduction *f*, exorde *m*, préambule *m*. 2 **vt** *book* faire précéder (*by* de). **he ~d his speech by asking for volunteers** en guise d'introduction à son discours il a demandé des volontaires; **he ~d this by saying** ... en avant-propos il a dit ..., il a commencé par dire ... .

prefaded [,pri:'feɪdɪd] **adj** *jeans etc* délavé.

prefatory ['prefətərɪ] **adj** *remarks* préliminaire; *page* liminaire.

prefect ['pri:fekt] **n** (*French Admin*) préfet *m*; (*Brit Scol*) *élève des grandes classes chargé(e) de la discipline.*

prefecture ['pri:fektjʊə[r]] **n** préfecture *f*.

prefer [prɪ'fɜ:[r]] **vt** a préférer. **to ~ A to B** préférer A à B, aimer mieux A que B; **to ~ doing** *or* **to do** aimer mieux *or* préférer faire; **I ~ to take the train rather than go by car, I ~ taking the train to going by car** j'aime mieux *or* je préfère prendre le train que d'aller en voiture; **I ~ you to leave at once** je préfère *or* j'aime mieux que vous partiez (*subj*) tout de suite; **I would ~ not to (do it)** je préférerais *or* j'aimerais mieux ne pas le faire; **I much ~ Scotland** je préfère de beaucoup l'Écosse, j'aime beaucoup mieux l'Écosse; (*of envelope etc*) **Post Office ~red size** format recommandé *or* approuvé par le service des Postes; (*US Fin*) **~red stock** = **preference shares** (*see* **preference 2**). b (*Jur*) *charge* porter; *action* intenter; *request* formuler; *petition* adresser; *argument, reason* présenter. **to ~ a complaint against sb** déposer une plainte *or* porter plainte contre qn. c (*esp Rel: promote*) élever (*to* à).

preferable ['prefərəbl] **adj** préférable (*to sth* à qch). **it is ~ to refuse** il est préférable de refuser, il vaut mieux refuser.

preferably ['prefərəblɪ] **adv** de préférence.

preference ['prefərəns] 1 **n** (*liking*) préférence *f* (*for* pour); (*priority: also Econ*) priorité *f* (*over* sur), préférence. **what is your ~?** que préférez-vous?; **in ~ to + n** de préférence à, plutôt que; **in ~ to doing** plutôt que de faire; **to give A ~ (over B)** accorder *or* donner la préférence à A (plutôt qu'à B); **I have no strong ~** je n'ai pas vraiment de préférence. 2 **comp** ▸**preference shares, preference stock** (*Brit Fin*) actions privilégiées *or* de priorité.

preferential [prefə'renʃəl] **adj** *tariff, terms* préférentiel; *treatment* de faveur; *trade, ballot, voting* préférentiel.

preferentially [prefə'renʃəlɪ] **adv** *treat* de façon privilégiée.

preferment [prɪ'fɜ:mənt] **n** (*esp Rel*) avancement *m*, élévation *f* (*to* à).

prefiguration [,pri:fɪgə'reɪʃən] **n** préfiguration *f*.

prefigure [pri:'fɪgə[r]] **vt** (*foreshadow*) préfigurer; (*imagine*) se figurer d'avance.

prefix ['pri:fɪks] 1 **n** préfixe *m*. 2 **vt** préfixer.

preflight ['pri:'flaɪt] **adj** d'avant le décollage.

preform ['pri:'fɔ:m] **vt** préformer.

preformation ['pri:fɔ:'meɪʃən] **n** préformation *f*.

prefrontal [,pri:'frʌntl] **adj** préfrontal.

preggers* ['pregəz] **adj** (*Brit: pregnant*) **to be ~** attendre un gosse*.

pregnancy ['pregnənsɪ] **n** *[woman]* grossesse *f*; *[animal]* gestation *f*. **~ test** test *m* de grossesse.

pregnant ['pregnənt] **adj** *woman* enceinte; *animal* pleine, gravide; (*fig*) *pause, silence* lourd de sens; *idea* fécond. **3 months ~** enceinte de 3 mois; (*fig*) **~ with** gros (*f* grosse) de, riche de.

preheat ['pri:'hi:t] **vt** chauffer à l'avance. **~ed oven** four chaud.

prehensile [prɪ'hensaɪl] **adj** préhensile.

prehistoric ['pri:hɪs'tɒrɪk] **adj** préhistorique.

prehistory ['pri:'hɪstərɪ] **n** préhistoire *f*.

pre-ignition [ˈpriːɪgˈnɪʃən] n auto-allumage *m*.
pre-industrial [priːɪnˈdʌstrɪəl] adj préindustriel.
prejudge [ˈpriːˈdʒʌdʒ] vt *question* préjuger de; *person* condamner *or* juger d'avance.
prejudice [ˈpredʒʊdɪs] 1 n a préjugé *m*, prévention *f*; (*NonC*) préjugés, prévention(s). **he found a lot of ~ in that country** il a trouvé beaucoup de préjugés *or* de prévention(s) dans ce pays; **racial ~** préjugés raciaux; **to have a ~ against/in favour of** avoir un préjugé *or* des préjugés *or* une prévention *or* des préventions contre/en faveur de; **he is quite without ~ in this matter** il est sans parti pris dans cette affaire. b (*esp Jur: detriment*) préjudice *m*. **to the ~ of** au préjudice de; **without ~ (to)** sans préjudice (de). 2 vt a *person* prévenir (*against* contre, *in favour of* en faveur de); *see also* **prejudiced**. b (*also Jur*) *claim, chance* porter préjudice à.
prejudiced [ˈpredʒʊdɪst] adj *person* plein de préjugés *or* de prévention(s); *idea, opinion* préconçu, partial. **he is ~/not ~ in that matter** il est de parti pris/sans parti pris dans cette affaire; **to be ~ against** avoir un (*or* des) préjugé(s) contre.
prejudicial [ˌpredʒʊˈdɪʃəl] adj préjudiciable, nuisible (*to* à). **to be ~ to** nuire à.
prelacy [ˈpreləsɪ] n (*office*) prélature *f*; (*prelates collectively*) prélats *mpl*.
prelate [ˈprelɪt] n prélat *m*.
pre-law [ˌpriːˈlɔː] adj, n (*US Univ*) ~ **(program)** enseignement *m* préparatoire aux études de droit.
prelim* [ˈpriːlɪm] n (abbr of **preliminary**) (*Univ*) examen *m* préliminaire; (*Sport*) (épreuve *f*) éliminatoire *f*.
preliminary [prɪˈlɪmɪnərɪ] 1 adj *exam, inquiry, report, remark* préliminaire; *stage* premier, initial. (*Constr etc*) ~ **estimate** devis *m* estimatif; (*Brit Jur*) ~ **hearing** audience *f* préliminaire. 2 n: **preliminaries** préliminaires *mpl*; **as a ~** en guise de préliminaire, au préalable.
prelude [ˈpreljuːd] 1 n (*Mus, gen*) prélude *m* (*to* de). 2 vt préluder à.
premarital [ˈpriːˈmærɪtl] adj avant le mariage.
premature [ˈpremətʃʊəʳ] adj *decision etc* prématuré; *birth* prématuré, avant terme. ~ **baby** (enfant) prématuré(e) *m(f)*, enfant né(e) avant terme; **you are a little ~** vous anticipez un peu.
prematurely [ˈpremətʃʊəlɪ] adv *arrive, decide, age* prématurément; *be born* avant terme. ~ **bald/lined** chauve/ridé avant l'âge; **he was ~ grey** il avait blanchi avant l'âge *or* prématurément.
pre-med* [priːˈmed] 1 n a (*Brit*) (abbr of **premedication**) prémédication *f*. b (*US*) = ~ **program**; *see* **2**. 2 adj (*US*) (abbr of **premedical**) ~ **program** enseignement *m* préparatoire aux études de médecine; ~ **student** étudiant(e) *m(f)* en année préparatoire de médecine.
premedication [ˌpriːmedɪˈkeɪʃən] n prémédication *f*.
premeditate [priːˈmedɪteɪt] vt préméditer.
premeditation [priːˌmedɪˈteɪʃən] n préméditation *f*.
premenstrual [priːˈmenstrʊəl] adj prémenstruel. ~ **tension** syndrome *m* prémenstruel.
premier [ˈpremɪəʳ] 1 adj premier, primordial. 2 n (*Pol*) (*Prime Minister*) Premier ministre; (*President*) chef *m* de l'État.
première [ˈpremɪɛəʳ] (*Cine, Theat*) 1 n première *f*. **the film had its London ~ last night** la première londonienne du film a eu lieu hier soir. 2 vt donner la première de. **the film was ~d in Paris** la première du film a eu lieu à Paris.
premiership [ˈpremɪəʃɪp] n (*Pol*) [*Prime Minister*] fonction *f* de Premier ministre; [*President*] fonction de chef d'État. **during his ~** sous son ministère, pendant qu'il était Premier ministre; **he was aiming at the ~** il aspirait à être Premier ministre.
premise [ˈpremɪs] 1 n a (*Philos, gen: hypothesis*) prémisse *f*. **on the ~ that** en partant du principe que, si l'on pose en principe que. b (*property*) **~s** locaux *mpl*, lieux *mpl*; **business ~s** locaux commerciaux; **on the ~s** sur les lieux, sur place; **off the ~s** à l'extérieur, hors des lieux; **to see sb off the ~s** escorter qn jusqu'à sa sortie des lieux; **get off the ~s** videz *or* évacuez les lieux. 2 vt (*frm*) **to be ~d on** être fondé *or* basé sur.
premiss [ˈpremɪs] n = **premise 1a**.
premium [ˈpriːmɪəm] 1 n a (*gen, Comm, Fin, Insurance*) prime *f*; (*Jur: paid on lease*) reprise *f*. (*St Ex*) **to sell sth at a ~** vendre qch à prime; (*Comm, fig*) **to be at a ~** faire prime; **to set *or* put *or* place a (high) ~ on** [*person*] faire grand cas de; [*situation, event*] donner beaucoup d'importance à, mettre l'accent sur. b (*US: gasoline*) super(carburant) *m*. 2 comp ▶**premium bond** (*Brit*) bon *m* à lots ▶**premium fuel** (*Brit*), **premium gasoline** (*US*) super(carburant) *m* ▶**premium price** prix *m* fort.
premolar [priːˈməʊləʳ] n prémolaire *f*.
premonition [ˌpriːməˈnɪʃən] n prémonition *f*, pressentiment *m*. **to have a ~ that** avoir le pressentiment que, pressentir que.
premonitory [prɪˈmɒnɪtərɪ] adj prémonitoire, précurseur.
prenatal [ˈpriːˈneɪtl] adj prénatal.
prenuptial [ˌpriːˈnʌpʃəl] adj prénuptial.
preoccupation [priːˌɒkjʊˈpeɪʃən] n préoccupation *f*. **his greatest ~ was discovering the facts** sa préoccupation majeure était de découvrir les faits; **his ~ with money** son obsession *f* de l'argent; **his ~ with finishing the book stopped him from ...** il était tellement préoccupé de l'idée de terminer le livre qu'il n'a pas ... .
preoccupy [priːˈɒkjʊpaɪ] vt *person, mind* préoccuper. **to be preoccupied** être préoccupé (*by, with* de).
pre-op* [ˈpriːˈɒp] adj: ~ **medication** prémédication *f*, médication *f* préopératoire.
preordain [ˌpriːɔːˈdeɪn] vt ordonner *or* régler d'avance; (*Philos, Rel*) préordonner.
preordained [ˌpriːɔˈdeɪnd] adj prédestiné.
prep* [prep] 1 n abbr of **preparation**. a (*Brit Scol*) (*work*) devoirs *mpl*, préparation *f*; (*period*) étude *f* (surveillée). b (*US Med*) préparation *f* (*d'un(e) malade*). 2 adj (*Brit*) ~ **school** = **preparatory school**; *see* **preparatory**. 3 vi (*US* *) a **to ~* for sth** se préparer pour qch. b (*US Scol*) entrer en classe préparatoire (pour l'université). 4 vt (*US*) **to ~ o.s.** se préparer.
prepack [ˈpriːˈpæk] vt, **prepackage** [ˈpriːˈpækɪdʒ] vt (*Comm*) préconditionner.
prepaid [ˈpriːˈpeɪd] adj (*gen*) payé (d'avance). (*Comm*) **carriage ~** port payé; **reply ~** réponse payée; (*Fin etc*) ~ **expenses** compte *m* de régularisation de l'actif; (*US Med*) ~ **health care** médecine *f* prépayée.
preparation [ˌprepəˈreɪʃən] n a (*NonC: act*) préparation *f*; (*Culin, Pharm etc: thing prepared*) préparation. **~s** préparatifs *mpl*; **the country's ~s for war** les préparatifs de guerre du pays; **to make ~s for sth** prendre ses dispositions pour qch, faire les préparatifs de qch; [*book, film etc*] **to be in ~** être en préparation; **in ~ for** en vue de; **Latin is a good ~ for Greek** le latin prépare bien au grec, le latin est une bonne formation pour le grec. b (*NonC: Scol*) (*work*) devoirs *mpl*, préparation *f*; (*period*) étude *f*.
preparatory [prɪˈpærətərɪ] adj *work* préparatoire; *measure, step* préliminaire, préalable. ~ **school** (*Brit*) école primaire privée; (*US*) lycée privé; ~ **to** avant, préalablement à, en vue de; ~ **to sth/to doing** en vue de qch/de faire, avant qch/de faire.
prepare [prɪˈpɛəʳ] 1 vt *plan, speech, lesson, work, medicine, sauce* préparer; *meal, dish* préparer, apprêter; *surprise* préparer, ménager (*for sb* à qn); *room, equipment* préparer (*for* pour); *person* préparer (*for an exam* à un examen, *for an operation* pour une opération). **to ~ sb for a shock/for bad news** préparer qn à un choc/à une mauvaise nouvelle; ~ **yourself for a shock!** prépare-toi à (recevoir) un choc!, tiens-toi bien!; **to ~ o.s. for** = **to ~ for** (*see* **2**); **to ~ the way/ground for sth** préparer la voie/le terrain pour qch; *see also* **prepared**.
2 vi: **to ~ for** (*make arrangements*) *journey, sb's arrival, event* faire des préparatifs pour, prendre ses dispositions pour; (*prepare o.s. for*) *storm, flood, meeting, discussion* se préparer pour; *war* se préparer à; *examination* préparer; **to ~ to do sth** s'apprêter *or* se préparer à faire qch.
prepared [prɪˈpɛəd] adj *person, army, country* prêt; *statement, answer* préparé à l'avance; (*Culin*) *sauce, soup* tout prêt. **be ~!** soyez sur le qui-vive!; **be ~ for bad news** préparez-vous à une mauvaise nouvelle; **I am ~ for anything** (*can cope with anything*) j'ai tout prévu, je suis paré; (*won't be surprised at anything*) je m'attends à tout; **to be ~ to do sth** être prêt *or* disposé à faire qch.
preparedness [prɪˈpɛərɪdnɪs] n état *m* de préparation. (*Mil*) **state of ~** état d'alerte préventive.
prepay [ˈpriːˈpeɪ] pret, ptp **prepaid** vt payer d'avance; *see also* **prepaid**.
prepayment [ˈpriːˈpeɪmənt] n paiement *m* d'avance.
preponderance [prɪˈpɒndərəns] n (*in numbers*) supériorité *f* numérique; (*in influence, weight*) prépondérance *f* (*over* sur).
preponderant [prɪˈpɒndərənt] adj prépondérant.
preponderantly [prɪˈpɒndərəntlɪ] adv surtout, en majorité.
preponderate [prɪˈpɒndəreɪt] vi l'emporter (*over* sur), être prépondérant.
preposition [ˌprepəˈzɪʃən] n préposition *f*.
prepositional [ˌprepəˈzɪʃənl] adj *phrase* prépositif, prépositionnel; *use* prépositionnel.
prepositionally [ˌprepəˈzɪʃənəlɪ] adv prépositivement.
prepossess [ˌpriːpəˈzes] vt (*preoccupy*) préoccuper; (*bias*) prévenir, influencer; (*impress favourably*) impressionner favorablement.
prepossessing [ˌpriːpəˈzesɪŋ] adj *appearance* avenant; *personne* très bien de sa personne.
preposterous [prɪˈpɒstərəs] adj absurde, ridicule, grotesque.
preposterously [prɪˈpɒstərəslɪ] adv absurdement, ridiculement.
preposterousness [prɪˈpɒstərəsnɪs] n (*NonC*) absurdité *f*, grotesque *m*.
preppie*, preppy* [ˈprepɪ] (*US*) 1 adj bon chic bon genre*. 2 n étudiant(e) *m(f)* d'une boîte* privée.
preprepared [ˌpriːprɪˈpɛəd] adj tout prêt.
preproduction [ˌpriːprəˈdʌkʃən] 1 n travail *m* antérieur à la production. 2 comp ▶**preproduction model** prototype *m* ▶**preproduction trial** mise *f* à l'essai du prototype.
preprogrammed [priːˈprəʊgræmd] adj programmé à l'avance.
prepubescent [ˌpriːpjuːˈbesənt] adj prépubère.
prepuce [ˈpriːpjuːs] n prépuce *m*.
Pre-Raphaelite [ˈpriːˈræfəlaɪt] adj, n préraphaélite *(mf)*.

prerecord [ˈpriːrɪˈkɔːd] vt *song, programme* enregistrer à l'avance. **~ed broadcast** émission *f* en différé; **~ed cassette** cassette *f* enregistrée.

prerelease [ˈpriːrɪˈliːs] adj (*Cine*) **~ showing** avant-première *f*.

prerequisite [ˈpriːˈrekwɪzɪt] 1 n a (*gen*) condition *f* préalable. b (*US Univ*) unité *f* de valeur dont l'obtention conditionne l'inscription dans l'unité de valeur supérieure. 2 adj nécessaire au préalable, préalablement nécessaire.

prerogative [prɪˈrɒgətɪv] n prérogative *f*, privilège *m*, apanage *m*. (*Brit*) **to exercise the Royal P~** faire acte de souverain.

presage [ˈpresɪdʒ] 1 n (*omen*) présage *m*; (*foreboding*) pressentiment *m*. 2 vt présager, annoncer, laisser prévoir.

presbyopia [ˌprezbɪˈəʊpɪə] n presbytie *f*.

Presbyterian [ˌprezbɪˈtɪərɪən] adj, n presbytérien(ne) *m(f)*.

Presbyterianism [ˌprezbɪˈtɪərɪənɪzəm] n presbytérianisme *m*.

presbytery [ˈprezbɪtərɪ] n (*part of church*) chœur *m*; (*residence*) presbytère *m*; (*court*) consistoire *m*.

preschool [ˈpriːˈskuːl] adj *years, age* préscolaire; *child* d'âge préscolaire. **~ education** enseignement *m* préscolaire; **~ playgroup** ≃ garderie *f*.

preschooler [ˈpriːˈskuːləʳ] n (*US*) enfant *mf* d'âge préscolaire.

prescience [ˈpresɪəns] n prescience *f*.

prescient [ˈpresɪənt] adj prescient.

prescribe [prɪsˈkraɪb] vt (*gen, Admin, Jur, Med*) prescrire (*sth for sb* qch pour qn). **the ~d dose/form/punishment** la dose/le formulaire/la punition prescrit(e); **~d books** œuvres *fpl* (inscrites) au programme; **this diet is ~d in some cases** ce régime se prescrit dans certains cas; **to ~ for boils** faire une ordonnance pour des furoncles; **he ~d complete rest** il a prescrit *or* ordonné le repos absolu; (*fig*) **what do you ~?** que me conseillez-vous?, que me recommandez-vous?

prescription [prɪsˈkrɪpʃən] 1 n a (*NonC: gen, Admin, Jur etc*) prescription *f*. b (*Med*) ordonnance *f*. **to make out** *or* **write out a ~ for sb** rédiger *or* faire une ordonnance pour qn; **to make up** *or* (*US*) **fill a ~** exécuter une ordonnance; **it can only be obtained on ~, it's on ~ only** on ne peut l'obtenir que sur ordonnance, c'est délivré *or* vendu seulement sur ordonnance. 2 comp (*made according to ~*) prescrit; (*available only on ~*) vendu sur ordonnance seulement ▸ **prescription charges** (*Brit Med*) *somme fixe à payer lors de l'exécution de l'ordonnance*.

prescriptive [prɪsˈkrɪptɪv] adj (*giving precepts*) (*gen*) normatif; (*grammar*) normatif, puriste, de puristes; (*legalized by custom*) *rights etc* consacré par l'usage.

prescriptivism [prɪˈskrɪptɪˌvɪzəm] n (*Ling*) normativisme *m*.

presell [ˌpriːˈsel] vt vendre à l'avance.

pre-seminal [ˈpriːˈsemɪnəl] adj (*Med*) pré-séminal. (*Med*) **~ fluid** liquide *m* pré-séminal.

presence [ˈprezns] n a présence *f*. **~ of mind** présence d'esprit; **in the ~ of** en présence de; (*Jur*) par-devant; (*frm*) **your ~ is requested** vous êtes prié d'y assister; (*liter, frm*) **they were admitted to the king's ~** ils furent admis en présence du roi; **he certainly made his ~ felt*** sa présence n'est vraiment pas passée inaperçue; **a ghostly ~** une présence surnaturelle; **this country will maintain a ~ in North Africa** ce pays maintiendra une présence en Afrique du Nord; **police ~** présence *f* policière; **there was a massive police ~ at the match** il y avait un imposant service d'ordre au match.
b (*bearing etc*) présence *f*, prestance *f*, allure *f*. **to lack ~** manquer de présence; **he has a good stage ~** il a de la présence (sur scène); **a man of noble ~** un homme de belle prestance *or* de belle allure.

present [ˈpreznt] 1 adj a (*in attendance; in existence*) présent. **~ at/in** présent à/dans; **to be ~ at sth** être présent à qch, assister à qch; **those ~** les personnes présentes, ceux qui étaient là, l'assistance *f*; **who was ~?** qui était là?; **is there a doctor ~?** y a-t-il un docteur ici? *or* dans l'assistance?; **all ~ and correct!** tous présents à l'appel!; **~ company excepted** les personnes ici présentes exceptées, à l'exception des personnes ici présentes.
b (*existing now*) *state, epoch, year, circumstances, techniques, residence* présent (*after noun*), actuel; (*in question*) présent (*before noun*), en question; (*Gram*) présent (*after noun*). **her ~ husband** son mari actuel; **the ~ writer believes** l'auteur croit; **in the ~ case** dans la présente affaire, dans le cas présent *or* qui nous intéresse *or* en question; **at the ~ day** *or* **time** actuellement, à présent (*see also* **2**); **at the ~ moment** actuellement, à présent; (*more precisely*) en ce moment même; **the ~ month** le mois courant, ce mois-ci.
2 comp ▸ **present-day** adj actuel, d'aujourd'hui, contemporain, d'à présent ▸ **present perfect** (*Gram*) passé composé.
3 n a (*also Gram*) présent *m*. **up to the ~** jusqu'à présent; **for the ~** pour le moment; **at ~** actuellement, à présent, en ce moment; **as things are at ~** dans l'état actuel des choses; (*loc*) **there's no time like the ~!** il ne faut jamais remettre au lendemain ce que l'on peut faire le jour même; **to live in the ~** (*enjoy life*) vivre dans le présent; (*live from day to day*) vivre au jour le jour; (*Gram*) **in the ~** au présent.
b (*gift*) cadeau *m*. **it's for a ~** c'est pour offrir; **she gave me the book as a ~** elle m'a offert le livre; (*lit, fig*) **to make sb a ~ of sth** faire cadeau *or* don de qch à qn; *see* **birthday, Christmas** *etc*.
c (*Jur*) **by these ~s** par les présentes.
4 [prɪˈzent] vt a **to ~ sb with sth, to ~ sth to sb** (*give as gift*) offrir qch à qn, faire don *or* cadeau de qch à qn; (*hand over*) *prize, medal* remettre qch à qn; **she ~ed him with a son** elle lui a donné un fils; **we were ~ed with a fait accompli** nous nous sommes trouvés devant un fait accompli; (*Mil*) **to ~ arms** présenter les armes; **~ arms!** présentez armes!
b *tickets, documents, credentials, one's compliments, apologies* présenter (*to* à); *plan, account, proposal, report, petition* présenter, soumettre (*to* à); *complaint* déposer; *proof, evidence* apporter, fournir; (*Parl*) *bill* introduire, présenter; (*Jur etc*) *case* exposer. **to ~ o.s. at the desk/for an interview** se présenter au bureau/à une entrevue; **to ~ a cheque (for payment)** encaisser *or* présenter un chèque; **his report ~s the matter in another light** son rapport présente la question sous un autre jour, son rapport jette une lumière différente sur la question.
c (*offer, provide*) *problem* présenter, poser; *difficulties, features* présenter; *opportunity* donner. **the bay ~s a magnificent sight** la baie présente un spectacle splendide; **the opportunity ~ed itself** l'occasion s'est présentée; **to ~ the appearance of sth** avoir *or* donner (toute) l'apparence de qch; **the patrol ~ed an easy target** la patrouille offrait *or* constituait une cible facile.
d *play, concert* donner; *film* donner, passer; (*Rad, TV*) *play, programme* donner, passer; (*act as presenter of*) présenter. **we are glad to ~ ...** nous sommes heureux de vous présenter ...; **"~ing Glenda Jackson as Lady Macbeth"** "avec Glenda Jackson dans le rôle de Lady Macbeth".
e (*introduce*) présenter (*sb to sb* qn à qn). **may I ~ Miss Smith?** permettez-moi de vous présenter Mademoiselle Smith; (*Brit*) **to be ~ed (at Court)** être présenté à la Cour.

presentable [prɪˈzentəbl] adj *person, appearance, room* présentable; *clothes* présentable, mettable, sortable*. **go and make yourself (look) ~** va t'arranger un peu; **I'm not very ~** je ne suis guère présentable, je ne peux guère me montrer.

presentably [prɪˈzentəblɪ] adv *dressed* correctement.

presentation [ˌprezənˈteɪʃən] 1 n a (*NonC*) *[plan, account, proposal, report, petition, evidence]* présentation *f*, soumission *f*; *[complaint]* déposition *f*; *[parliamentary bill]* présentation, introduction *f*; *[cheque]* encaissement *m*; *[case]* exposition *f*. **his ~ of the play** (*the fact that he did it*) le fait qu'il ait donné la pièce; (*the way he did it*) sa mise en scène de la pièce; **on ~ of this ticket** sur présentation de ce billet; **the subject matter is good but the ~ is poor** le fond est bon mais la présentation laisse à désirer.
b (*physical appearance*) présentation *f*.
c (*introduction*) présentation *f*.
d (*gift*) cadeau *m*; (*ceremony*) remise *f* du cadeau (*or* de la médaille *etc*), ≃ vin *m* d'honneur. **who made the ~?** qui a remis le cadeau (*or* la médaille *etc*)?; **to make a ~ of sth to sb** remettre qch à qn.
e (*Univ etc*) exposé *m* oral.
2 comp ▸ **presentation box, presentation case** (*Comm*) coffret *m* de luxe ▸ **presentation copy** *[book]* (*for inspection, review*) spécimen *m* (gratuit), exemplaire envoyé à titre gracieux; (*from author*) exemplaire offert en hommage.

presentational [ˌprezənˈteɪʃənl] adj: **for ~ reasons** pour des raisons de présentation.

presenter [prɪˈzentəʳ] n (*Brit: Rad, TV*) présentateur *m*, -trice *f*, speaker *m*, -ine *f*.

presentiment [prɪˈzentɪmənt] n pressentiment *m*.

presently [ˈprezntlɪ] adv a (*Brit: in a little while*) tout à l'heure, bientôt; (*+ vb in past*) au bout d'un certain temps. b (*esp US: now*) à présent, en ce moment.

presentment [prɪˈzentmənt] n *[note, bill of exchange etc]* présentation *f*; (*Jur*) déclaration *f* émanant du jury.

preservation [ˌprezəˈveɪʃən] 1 n conservation *f*; (*from harm*) préservation *f*. **in good ~, in a good state of ~** en bon état de conservation. 2 comp ▸ **preservation order**: (*Brit Admin*) **to put a preservation order on a building** classer un édifice ▸ **preservation society** (*Archit etc*) association *f* pour la sauvegarde et la conservation (*des sites etc*).

preservationist [ˌprezəˈveɪʃənɪst] n (*esp US*) défenseur *m* de l'environnement.

preservative [prɪˈzɜːvətɪv] n (*Culin*) agent *m* de conservation, conservateur *m*.

preserve [prɪˈzɜːv] 1 vt a (*keep, maintain*) *building, traditions, manuscript, eyesight, position* conserver; *leather, wood* entretenir; *memory* conserver, garder; *dignity, sense of humour, reputation* garder; *peace* maintenir; *silence* observer, garder. **well-/badly-~d** en bon/mauvais état de conservation; **she is very well-~d** elle est bien conservée (pour son âge); **to ~ one's looks** conserver sa beauté; **have you ~d the original?** avez-vous gardé *or* conservé l'original?
b (*from harm etc*) préserver, garantir (*from* de), protéger (*from* contre). **may God ~ you!** Dieu vous garde!, que Dieu vous protège!; **(heaven** *or* **the saints) ~ me from that!*** le ciel m'en préserve!
c (*Culin*) *fruit etc* conserver, mettre en conserve. **~d** en conserve;

~**d food** (*in bottles, cans*) conserves *fpl*; (*frozen*) produits surgelés.
2 n a (*Culin: often pl*) (*Brit: jam*) confiture *f*; (*Brit: chutney*) condiment *m* à base de fruits; (*Brit, US: bottled fruit/vegetables*) fruits *mpl* / légumes *mpl* en conserve.
b (*Hunting*) réserve *f*. **game** ~ chasse gardée *or* interdite.
c (*fig*) chasse *f* gardée. **that's his** ~ c'est sa chasse gardée, c'est son domaine particulier.

preserver [prɪ'zɜːvəʳ] n (*person*) sauveur *m*; *see* **life**.

preserving [prɪ'zɜːvɪŋ] adj: ~ **pan** bassine *f* à confiture.

preset ['priː'set] vt pret, ptp **preset** programmer.

preshrunk ['priː'ʃrʌŋk] adj irrétrécissable.

preside [prɪ'zaɪd] vi présider. **to** ~ **at** *or* **over a meeting** présider une réunion.

presidency ['prezɪdənsɪ] n présidence *f*.

president ['prezɪdənt] 1 n (*Pol etc*) président *m*; (*US Comm*) président-directeur général, P.D.G. *m*; (*US Univ*) président *m* (d'université) *m*. (*Brit Parl*) **P~ of the Board of Trade** ≃ ministre *m* du Commerce. 2 comp ▶**president-elect** président désigné.

presidential [ˌprezɪ'denʃəl] adj a (*gen*) *decision, suite etc* présidentiel, du président. ~ **elections** élection *f* présidentielle; **his** ~ **hopes** l'espoir qu'il a de devenir président. b (*of one specific President*) *staff, envoy, representative* du Président. (*US Pol*) ~ **adviser** conseiller *m* personnel du Président.

presidentially [ˌprezɪ'denʃəlɪ] adv en tant que président.

presidium [prɪ'sɪdɪəm] = **praesidium**.

pre-soak ['priː'səʊk] vt faire tremper.

press [pres] 1 n a (*apparatus*) (*for wine, olives, cheese etc*) pressoir *m*; (*for gluing, moulding etc*) presse *f*; (*trouser* ~) presse à pantalon; (*racket* ~) presse-raquette *m inv*. **cider** ~ pressoir à cidre; **hydraulic** ~ presse hydraulique.
b (*Typ*) (*machine: also* **printing** ~) presse *f* (typographique); (*place, publishing firm*) imprimerie *f*; (*newspapers collectively*) presse. **rotary** ~ presse rotative; **at** *or* **in the** ~ sous presse; **to go to** ~ *[book etc]* être mis sous presse; *[newspaper]* aller à l'impression; **correct at time of going to** ~ correct au moment de mettre sous presse; **to set the ~es rolling** mettre les presses en marche; **to pass sth for** ~ donner le bon à tirer de qch; **the national** ~ la grande presse; **I saw it in the** ~ je l'ai lu dans la presse *or* dans les journaux; **the** ~ **reported that ...** la presse a relaté que ..., on a rapporté dans la presse que ...; **to advertise in the** ~ (*Comm*) faire de la publicité dans la presse *or* dans les journaux; (*privately*) mettre une annonce dans les journaux; **a member of the** ~ un(e) journaliste; **is the** ~ *or* **are any of the** ~ **present?** la presse est-elle représentée?; **to get a good/bad** ~ avoir bonne/mauvaise presse.
c (*pressure: with hand, instrument*) pression *f*. **he gave his trousers a** ~ il a donné un coup de fer à son pantalon; *see* **durable, permanent**.
d (*weightlifting*) développé *m*.
e (*cupboard*) armoire *f*, placard *m*.
f († *or liter: crowd*) foule *f*, presse *f* (*liter*). **he lost his hat in the** ~ **to get out** il a perdu son chapeau dans la bousculade à la sortie.
2 comp *campaign, card etc* de presse ▶**press agency** agence *f* de presse ▶**press agent** agent *m* de publicité ▶**press attaché** attaché(e) *m(f)* de presse ▶**press baron** magnat *m* de la presse ▶**press box** tribune *f* de la presse ▶**press button** bouton(-poussoir) *m* ▶**press clipping** coupure *f* de presse *or* de journal ▶**press conference** conférence *f* de presse ▶**press corps** la presse (*travaillant à un endroit donné*) ▶**press cutting** = **press clipping; press-cutting agency** argus *m* de la presse ▶**press gallery** (*esp Parl*) tribune *f* de la presse ▶**press-gang** (*Hist*) racoleurs *mpl*; (*fig*) **to press-gang sb into doing sth** faire pression sur qn *or* forcer la main à qn pour qu'il fasse qch ▶**press hold** (*Climbing*) appui *m* ▶**press lord** = **press baron** ▶**pressman** (*Brit*) journaliste *m* ▶**pressmark** (*Brit*) cote *f* (*d'un livre de bibliothèque*) ▶**press officer** attaché(e) *m(f)* de presse ▶**press photographer** photographe *mf* de (la) presse, reporter *m* photographe ▶**press release** communiqué *m* de presse ▶**press report** reportage *m* ▶**press run** (*US*) tirage *m* (d'une revue *etc*) ▶**press secretary:** (*US*) **the White House** *etc* **press secretary** le porte-parole de la Maison Blanche *etc* ▶**press stud** (*Brit*) bouton-pression *m*, pression *f* ▶**press-up** (*Gymnastics*) traction *f*; **to do press-ups** faire des tractions *or* des pompes* ▶**press view** (*Cine*) avant-première *f*.
3 vt a (*push, squeeze*) *button, knob, switch, trigger, accelerator* appuyer sur; *sb's hand etc* serrer, presser. **he ~ed his fingertips together** il a pressé les extrémités de ses doigts les unes contre les autres; **he ~ed his nose against the window** il a collé son nez à la fenêtre; (*US*) **to** ~ **the flesh**‡ serrer une multitude de mains, prendre un bain de foule; **he ~ed her to him** il la serra *or* pressa contre lui; **she ~ed the lid on to the box** elle a fait pression sur le couvercle de la boîte (pour la fermer); **as the crowd moved back he found himself ~ed (up) against a wall** comme la foule reculait il s'est trouvé acculé *or* pressé contre un mur.
b *grapes, olives, lemons, flowers* presser.
c *clothes etc* repasser, donner un coup de fer à.
d (*make by ~ing*) *object, machine part* mouler, fabriquer; *record, disk* presser.
e (*fig*) (*in battle, game*) presser, attaquer constamment; *[pursuer]* talonner, serrer de près; *[creditor]* poursuivre, harceler. **to** ~ **sb for payment/an answer** presser qn de payer/de répondre; **to be ~ed for time/money** être à court de temps/d'argent, manquer de temps/d'argent; **I am really ~ed today** je suis débordé (de travail) aujourd'hui; **to** ~ **a gift/money on sb** presser qn d'accepter *or* insister pour que qn accepte (*subj*) un cadeau/de l'argent, offrir avec insistance un cadeau/de l'argent à qn; **to** ~ **sb to do sth** presser qn de *or* pousser qn à faire qch, insister pour que qn fasse qch; **to** ~ **sb into doing sth** forcer qn à faire qch; **he didn't need much ~ing** il n'y a guère eu besoin d'insister, il ne s'est guère fait prier; **we were all ~ed into service** nous avons tous été obligés d'offrir nos services *or* de mettre la main à la pâte*; **the box was ~ed into service as a table** la caisse a fait office de table; († *or hum*) **to** ~ **one's suit** faire sa demande (en mariage); *see* **hard**.
f *attack, advantage* pousser, poursuivre; *claim, demand* renouveler, insister sur. (*Jur*) **to** ~ **charges against sb** engager des poursuites contre qn; **I shan't** ~ **the point** je n'insisterai pas.
g (*Weightlifting*) soulever.
4 vi a (*exert pressure*) (*with hand etc*) appuyer (*on* sur); *[weight, burden]* faire pression, peser (*on* sur); *[debts, troubles]* peser (*on sb* à qn). **time ~es!** le temps presse!, l'heure tourne!; (*fig*) **to** ~ **for sth** faire pression pour obtenir qch, demander instamment qch; **they are ~ing to have the road diverted** ils font pression pour (obtenir) que la route soit déviée.
b **he ~ed through the crowd** il s'est frayé un chemin dans la foule; **he ~ed in/out** *etc* il est entré/sorti *etc* en jouant des coudes; **they ~ed in/out** *etc* ils sont entrés/sortis *etc* en masse; **the people ~ed round his car** les gens se pressaient autour de sa voiture.

▶**press ahead** vi = **press on**.

▶**press back** vt sep a *crowd, enemy* refouler. b (*replace etc*) *lid* remettre en appuyant. **he pressed the box back into shape** il a redonné sa forme à la boîte d'une pression de la main.

▶**press down** 1 vi appuyer (*on* sur). 2 vt sep *knob, button, switch* appuyer sur. **she pressed the clothes down into the suitcase** elle appuya sur les vêtements pour les faire entrer dans la valise.

▶**press in** vt sep *panel etc* enfoncer.

▶**press on** vi (*in work, journey etc*) continuer. **press on!** (*don't give up*) persévérez!, n'abandonnez pas!; (*hurry up*) continuez vite!; **we've got to press on regardless!*** continuons quand même!, nous ne pouvons pas nous permettre de nous arrêter!; (*fig*) **to press on with sth** continuer résolument (à faire) qch; **they are pressing on with the nuclear agreement** ils continuent à tout faire pour que l'accord nucléaire se réalise.

▶**press out** vt sep a *juice, liquid* exprimer. b *crease, fold* aplatir; (*with iron*) aplatir au fer *or* en repassant.

pressing ['presɪŋ] 1 adj *business, problem* urgent; *danger* pressant; *invitation* instant. **he was very** ~ **and I could not refuse** il a beaucoup insisté et je n'ai pas pu refuser. 2 n *[clothes]* repassage *m*. **to send sth for** ~ faire repasser qch.

pressure ['preʃəʳ] 1 n a (*gen, Met, Phys, Tech*) pression *f*; (*Aut: tyre* ~) pression (de gonflage). **atmospheric** ~ pression atmosphérique; **water** ~ pression de l'eau; **a** ~ **of 2 kg to the square cm** une pression de 2 kg par cm²; **to exert** *or* **put** ~ **on sth** faire pression *or* exercer une pression sur qch, presser *or* appuyer sur qch; (*Tech etc*) **at full** ~ à pression maxima; (*fig*) **the factory is now working at full** ~ l'usine fonctionne maintenant à plein rendement; **he was working at high** *or* **full** ~ il travaillait à la limite de ses possibilités; *see* **blood pressure** *etc*.
b (*fig: influence, compulsion*) pression *f*, contrainte *f*. **because of parental** ~ à cause de la pression des parents, parce que les parents ont fait pression; **to put** ~ **on sb, to bring** ~ **to bear on sb** faire pression *or* exercer une pression sur qn (*to do* pour qu'il fasse); **they're putting the** ~ **on now** ils nous (*or* le *etc*) talonnent maintenant; **he was acting under** ~ **when he said ...** il agissait sous la contrainte *or* il n'agissait pas de son plein gré quand il a dit ... (*see also* **1c**); **under** ~ **from his staff** sous la pression de son personnel; **to use** ~ **to obtain a confession** user de contrainte pour obtenir une confession.
c (*fig: stress, burden*) **the** ~ **of these events/of life today** la tension créée par ces événements/par la vie d'aujourd'hui; ~ **of work prevented him from going** le travail l'a empêché d'y aller, il n'a pas pu y aller parce qu'il avait trop de travail; **he has had a lot of** ~ **on him recently, he has been under a lot of** ~ **recently** il a été débordé récemment, il a été sous pression* ces derniers temps; **I work badly under** ~ je travaille mal quand je suis sous pression*; **I can't work well under such** ~ je ne fais pas du bon travail quand je suis talonné de cette façon.
2 comp ▶**pressure cabin** (*Aviat*) cabine pressurisée *or* sous pression ▶**pressure-cook** cuire à la cocotte-minute ® *or* en autocuiseur ▶**pressure cooker** autocuiseur *m*, cocotte-minute *f* ® ▶**pressure-feed** alimentation *f* sous pression ▶**pressure gauge** manomètre *m*, jauge *f* de pression ▶**pressure group** (*fig: Pol etc*) groupe *m* de pression ▶**pressure point** (*Anat*) point *m* de compression digitale de l'artère ▶**pressure suit** (*Space etc*) scaphandre pressurisé.
3 vt: **to** ~ **sb to do** faire pression sur qn pour qu'il fasse; **to** ~ **sb**

into doing forcer qn à *or* contraindre qn de faire.

pressurization [ˌpreʃəraɪˈzeɪʃən] n pressurisation *f*, mise *f* en pression.

pressurize [ˈpreʃəraɪz] vt a *cabin, spacesuit* pressuriser. (*Aviat*) **~d cabin** cabine pressurisée *or* sous pression; **~d water reactor** réacteur *m* à eau sous pression. b (* *fig*) = **pressure 3**.

Prestel [ˈpresˌtel] n ® ≃ Télétel *m* ®.

prestidigitation [ˈprestɪˌdɪdʒɪˈteɪʃən] n prestidigitation *f*.

prestige [presˈtiːʒ] 1 n prestige *m*. 2 adj *car, production, politics etc* de prestige.

prestigious [presˈtɪdʒəs] adj prestigieux.

presto [ˈprestəʊ] adv (*Mus, gen*) presto. **hey ~!** le tour est joué!; **and hey ~! there he was** et abracadabra! il était là.

prestressed [ˈpriːˈstrest] adj précontraint. **~ concrete** (béton armé) précontraint *m*.

presumable [prɪˈzjuːməbl] adj présumable.

presumably [prɪˈzjuːməblɪ] adv vraisemblablement, probablement. **you are ~ his son** je présume *or* je suppose que vous êtes son fils.

presume [prɪˈzjuːm] 1 vt a (*suppose*) présumer (*also Jur*), supposer (*that* que); *sb's death* présumer. **every man is ~d (to be) innocent** tout homme est présumé (être) innocent; **it may be ~d that ...** on peut présumer que ...; **I ~ so** je (le) présume, je (le) suppose; **you are presuming rather a lot** vous faites pas mal de suppositions, vous présumez pas mal de choses. b (*venture, take liberty*) se permettre (*to do* de faire). 2 vi: **you ~ too much!** vous prenez bien des libertés!; **I hope I'm not presuming** je ne voudrais pas être impertinent; (*when asking a favour*) je ne voudrais pas abuser de votre gentillesse; **to ~ (up)on** abuser de.

presumption [prɪˈzʌmpʃən] n a (*supposition*) présomption *f*, supposition *f*. **the ~ is that** on présume que, on suppose que, il est à présumer que; **there is a strong ~ that** tout laisse à présumer que. b (*NonC*) présomption *f*, audace *f*, impertinence *f*. **if you'll excuse my ~** si vous me le permettez, si vous voulez bien pardonner mon audace.

presumptive [prɪˈzʌmptɪv] adj *heir* présomptif; (*Jur*) *evidence* par présomption.

presumptuous [prɪˈzʌmptjʊəs] adj *person, letter, question* présomptueux, impertinent.

presumptuously [prɪˈzʌmptjʊəslɪ] adv présomptueusement.

presumptuousness [prɪˈzʌmptjʊəsnɪs] (*NonC*) = **presumption b**.

presuppose [ˌpriːsəˈpəʊz] vt présupposer.

presupposition [ˌpriːsʌpəˈzɪʃən] n présupposition *f*.

pre-tax [ˌpriːˈtæks] adj, adv avant impôts.

pre-teen [ˌpriːˈtiːn] 1 adj préadolescent. 2 n: **the ~s** les 10 à 12 ans.

pretence, (*US*) **pretense** [prɪˈtens] n a (*pretext*) prétexte *m*, excuse *f*; (*claim*) prétention *f*; (*NonC: affectation*) prétention. **he makes no ~ to learning** il n'a pas la prétention d'être savant; **under** *or* **on the ~ of (doing) sth** sous prétexte *or* sous couleur de (faire) qch; *see* **false**. b (*make-believe*) **to make a ~ of doing** faire semblant *or* feindre de faire; **he made a ~ of friendship** il a feint l'amitié; **it's all (a) ~** tout cela est pure comédie *or* une feinte; **I'm tired of their ~ that all is well** je suis las de les voir faire comme si tout allait bien; **his ~ of sympathy did not impress me** sa feinte sympathie m'a laissé froid, ses démonstrations de feinte sympathie m'ont laissé froid.

pretend [prɪˈtend] 1 vt a (*feign*) faire semblant (*to do* de faire, *that* que); *ignorance, concern, illness* feindre, simuler. **let's ~ we're soldiers** jouons aux soldats, on va faire comme si on était des soldats*; (*pej*) **he was ~ing to be a doctor** il se faisait passer pour un médecin. b (*claim*) prétendre (*that* que). **I don't ~ to know everything about it** je ne prétends pas tout savoir là-dessus, je n'ai pas la prétention de tout savoir là-dessus.

2 vi a (*feign*) faire semblant. **the children were playing at let's ~** les enfants jouaient à faire semblant; **I was only ~ing!** c'était pour rire!, je plaisantais!; **let's stop ~ing!** assez joué la comédie!; **let's not ~ to each other** ne nous jouons pas la comédie, soyons francs l'un avec l'autre.

b (*claim*) **to ~ to sth** prétendre à qch, avoir des prétentions à qch.

3 adj (*) *money, house etc* pour (de) rire*. **it's only ~!** c'est pour rire!*

pretended [prɪˈtendɪd] adj prétendu, soi-disant *inv*.

pretender [prɪˈtendəʳ] n prétendant(e) *m(f)* (*to the throne* au trône). (*Hist*) **the Young P~** le (Jeune) Prétendant (*Charles Édouard Stuart*).

pretense [prɪˈtens] n (*US*) = **pretence**.

pretension [prɪˈtenʃən] n a (*claim: also pej*) prétention *f* (*to sth* à qch). **this work has serious literary ~s** cette œuvre peut à juste titre prétendre à *or* cette œuvre a droit à la reconnaissance littéraire; (*pej*) **he has social ~s** il a des prétentions sociales. b (*NonC: pretentiousness*) prétention *f*.

pretentious [prɪˈtenʃəs] adj prétentieux.

pretentiously [prɪˈtenʃəslɪ] adv prétentieusement.

pretentiousness [prɪˈtenʃəsnɪs] n (*NonC*) prétention *f*.

preterite [ˈpretərɪt] n prétérit *m*, passé *m* simple.

preterm [ˌpriːˈtɜːm] 1 adj *baby* prématuré. 2 adv prématurément, avant terme.

preternatural [ˌpriːtəˈnætʃrəl] adj surnaturel.

preternaturally [ˌpriːtəˈnætʃrəlɪ] adv surnaturellement.

pretext [ˈpriːtekst] n prétexte *m* (*to do* pour faire). **under** *or* **on the ~ of (doing) sth** sous prétexte de (faire) qch.

prettify [ˈprɪtɪfaɪ] vt *child* pomponner; *house, garden, dress* enjoliver. **to ~ o.s.** se faire une beauté*, se pomponner.

prettily [ˈprɪtɪlɪ] adv joliment.

pretty [ˈprɪtɪ] 1 adj a (*pleasing*) *child, flower, music etc* joli (*before noun*). **as ~ as a picture** *person* joli comme un cœur, joli à croquer; *garden etc* ravissant; **she's not just a ~ face*** elle n'a pas seulement un joli minois, elle a d'autres atouts que son joli visage; **it wasn't a ~ sight** ce n'était pas beau à voir; (*to parrot*) **~ polly!** bonjour Jacquot!; **he has a ~ wit†** il est très spirituel, il a beaucoup d'esprit.

b (*iro*) joli, beau (*f* belle). **that's a ~ state of affairs!** c'est du joli!; **you've made a ~ mess of it!** vous avez fait là de la jolie besogne!

c (*: *considerable*) *sum, price* joli, coquet. **it will cost a ~ penny** cela coûtera une jolie somme *or* une somme coquette *or* une somme rondelette.

2 adv assez. **it's ~ cold** il fait assez froid, il ne fait pas chaud; **~ well!** pas mal!; **we've ~ well finished** nous avons presque *or* pratiquement fini; **it's ~ much the same thing** c'est à peu près *or* pratiquement la même chose; **he's ~ nearly better** il est presque *or* pratiquement guéri; **to have a ~ fair idea of sth** avoir sa petite idée quant à qch; *see* **sit**.

3 comp ►**pretty-pretty*** (*pej*) un peu trop joli.

►**pretty up*** vt sep = **prettify**.

pretzel [ˈpretsl] n bretzel *m*.

prevail [prɪˈveɪl] vi a (*gain victory*) prévaloir (*against* contre, *over* sur), l'emporter, avoir l'avantage (*against* contre, *over* sur). **commonsense will ~** le bon sens prévaudra *or* s'imposera. b *[conditions, attitude, fashion]* prédominer, avoir cours, régner; *[style]* être en vogue. **the situation which now ~s** la situation actuelle. c **to ~ (up)on sb to do** décider qn à faire, persuader qn de faire; **can I ~ on you to lend me some money?** accepteriez-vous de me prêter de l'argent?

prevailing [prɪˈveɪlɪŋ] adj a *wind* dominant. b (*widespread*) *belief, opinion, attitude* courant, répandu. c (*current*) *conditions, situation, customs* (*today*) actuel; (*at that time*) à l'époque; *style, taste, prices* (*today*) actuel, du jour; (*at that time*) de l'époque, du jour. (*Econ*) **~ market rate** cours *m* du marché. d (*Jur*) **the ~ party** la partie gagnante.

prevalence [ˈprevələns] n *[illness]* fréquence *f*; *[belief, opinion, attitude]* prédominance *f*, fréquence; *[conditions, situation, customs]* caractère généralisé; *[fashion, style]* popularité *f*, vogue *f*. **I'm surprised by the ~ of that idea** je suis surpris que cette idée soit si répandue.

prevalent [ˈprevələnt] adj a (*widespread*) *belief, opinion, attitude* courant, répandu, fréquent; *illness* répandu. **that sort of thing is very ~** ce genre de chose se voit (*or* se fait) partout, ce genre de chose est très courant. b (*current*) *conditions, customs* (*today*) actuel; (*at that time*) à l'époque; (*style, taste*) (*today*) actuel, du jour; (*at that time*) de l'époque, du jour.

prevaricate [prɪˈværɪkeɪt] vi équivoquer, biaiser, tergiverser, user de faux-fuyants.

prevarication [prɪˌværɪˈkeɪʃən] n faux-fuyant(s) *m(pl)*.

prevent [prɪˈvent] vt empêcher (*sb from doing, sb's doing* qn de faire); *event, action* empêcher; *illness* prévenir; *accident, fire, war* empêcher, éviter. **nothing could ~ him** rien ne pouvait l'en empêcher; **she couldn't ~ his death** elle n'a pu empêcher qu'il ne meure *or* l'empêcher de mourir; **I couldn't ~ the door from closing** je n'ai pas pu empêcher la porte de se fermer *or* éviter que la porte ne se ferme (*subj*).

preventable [prɪˈventəbl] adj évitable.

preventative [prɪˈventətɪv] adj préventif.

prevention [prɪˈvenʃən] n (*NonC*) prévention *f*. (*Prov*) **~ is better than cure** mieux vaut prévenir que guérir; **Society for the P~ of Cruelty to Animals** Société Protectrice des Animaux; *see* **accident, fire** *etc*.

preventive [prɪˈventɪv] 1 adj *medicine, measures,* préventif. (*Jur*) **~ detention** (forte) peine *f* de prison. 2 n (*measure*) mesure préventive (*against* contre); (*medicine*) médicament préventif (*against* contre).

preverbal [ˌpriːˈvɜːbəl] adj préverbal.

preview [ˈpriːvjuː] n *[film, exhibition]* avant-première *f*; (*art exhibition*) vernissage *m*. (*fig*) **to give sb a ~ of sth** donner à qn un aperçu de qch; (*Rad, TV*) **for a ~ of today's main events over now to Jack Smith** et maintenant pour un tour d'horizon des principaux événements de la journée je passe l'antenne à Jack Smith.

previous [ˈpriːvɪəs] 1 adj a (*gen*) (*immediately before*) précédent; (*sometime before*) antérieur (*f* -eure). **the ~ letter** la précédente lettre, la lettre précédente; **a ~ letter** une lettre précédente *or* antérieure; **the ~ day** la veille; **the ~ evening** la veille au soir; **the ~ week/year** la semaine/l'année précédente; **on ~ occasions** précédemment, auparavant; **in a ~ life** dans une vie antérieure; **~ to** antérieur à; **have you made any ~ applications?** avez-vous déjà fait des demandes?; **I have a ~ engagement** je suis déjà pris; (*Comm*) **no ~ experience necessary** aucune expérience (préalable) exigée; (*Jur*) **to have no ~ convictions** avoir un casier judiciaire vierge; (*Jur*) **he has 3 ~ convictions** il a déjà 3 condamnations; **the car has had 2 ~ owners** la voiture a déjà eu 2 propriétaires.

b (*frm: hasty*) prématuré. **this seems somewhat ~** ceci semble quelque peu prématuré; **you have been rather ~ in inviting him** votre invitation est quelque peu prématurée, vous avez été bien pressé de l'inviter.

2 adv: **~ to** antérieurement à, préalablement à, avant; **~ to (his) leaving he** ... avant de partir *or* avant son départ il ...; **~ to his leaving we** ... avant son départ *or* avant qu'il ne parte nous ... .

previously ['pri:vɪəslɪ] adv (*before*) précédemment, avant, auparavant; (*in the past*) par le passé, dans le temps, jadis; (*already*) déjà.

prewar ['pri:'wɔ:ʳ] **1** adj d'avant-guerre. **2** adv avant-guerre.

prewash ['pri:wɒʃ] n prélavage *m*.

prex* [preks] n, **prexie***, **prexy*** ['preksɪ] n (*US Univ*) président *m* (d'université).

prey [preɪ] **1** n (*lit, fig*) proie *f*. **bird of ~** oiseau *m* de proie; **to be a ~ to** *nightmares, illnesses* être en proie à; **to fall (a) ~ to** devenir la proie de. **2** vi: **to ~ on** *[animal etc]* faire sa proie de; *[person]* faire sa victime de, s'attaquer (continuellement) à; *[fear, anxiety]* ronger, miner; **something is ~ing on her mind** il y a quelque chose qui la tourmente *or* la travaille*.

prezzie‡ ['prezɪ] n (abbr of **present**) cadeau *m*.

Priam ['praɪəm] n Priam *m*.

price [praɪs] **1** n **a** (*Comm etc*) (*cost*) prix *m* (*also fig*); (*estimate*) devis *m*; (*St Ex*) cours *m*. **the ~ in sterling** le prix en livres sterling; **to go up** *or* **rise in ~** augmenter; **to go down** *or* **fall in ~** baisser; **what is the ~ of this book?** combien coûte *or* vaut ce livre?, à quel prix est ce livre?; **that's my ~ - take it or leave it** c'est mon dernier prix - c'est à prendre ou à laisser; **to put a ~ on sth** fixer le prix de qch (*see also* **1b**); **we pay top ~s for gold and silver** nous achetons l'or et l'argent au prix fort; **he got a good ~ for it** il l'a vendu cher *or* à un prix élevé; (*fig*) **he paid a high** *or* **big ~ for his success** il a payé chèrement son succès; (*fig*) **it's a high** *or* **big ~ to pay for it** c'est le payer chèrement, c'est l'obtenir au prix d'un grand sacrifice, c'est consentir un grand sacrifice pour l'avoir; (*fig*) **it's a small ~ to pay for it** c'est consentir un bien petit sacrifice pour l'avoir; (*fig*) **every man has his ~** tout homme est corruptible à condition d'y mettre le prix; **I wouldn't buy it at any ~** je ne l'achèterais à aucun prix; (*fig*) **I wouldn't help him at any ~!** je ne l'aiderais à aucun prix!; **they want peace at any ~** ils veulent la paix coûte que coûte *or* à tout prix; (*fig*) **will you do it? — not at any ~!** vous allez le faire? — pour rien au monde! *or* pas question!; **you can get it but at a ~!** vous pouvez l'avoir mais cela vous coûtera cher!; (*fig*) **he's famous now but at what a ~!** il est célèbre maintenant mais à quel prix!; **he'll do it for a ~** il le fera si on y met le prix; **competitive ~** prix *m* défiant la concurrence; **the ~ is right** c'est un prix (très) correct; **ask him for a ~ for putting in a new window** demandez-lui un devis *or* combien ça coûterait *or* quel est son prix pour poser une nouvelle fenêtre; (*St Ex*) **to make a ~** fixer un cours; (*St Ex*) **market ~** cours *m* du marché; (*fig*) **there's a ~ on his head, he has got a ~ on his head** sa tête a été mise à prix; **to put a ~ on sb's head** mettre à prix la tête de qn; *see* **cheap, closing, reduced** *etc*.

b (*value*) prix *m*, valeur *f*. **to put a ~ on a jewel/picture** évaluer un bijou/un tableau; (*fig*) **I cannot put a ~ on his friendship** son amitié n'a pas de prix (pour moi), je ne saurais dire combien j'apprécie son amitié; **he sets** *or* **puts a high ~ on loyalty** il attache beaucoup de valeur *or* un grand prix à la loyauté, il fait très grand cas de la loyauté; (*fig*) **what ~* all his promises now?** que valent *or* que dites-vous de toutes ses promesses maintenant?; (*liter*) **beyond ~, without ~** qui n'a pas de prix, hors de prix, sans prix.

c (*Betting*) cote *f*. **what ~ are they giving on Black Beauty?** quelle est la cote de Black Beauty?; **what ~* he'll change his mind?** vous pariez combien qu'il va changer d'avis?

2 comp *control, index, war* des prix; *reduction, rise* de(s) prix ▸**price bracket** = **price range** ▸**Price(s) Commission** ≃ Direction *f* générale de la concurrence et de la consommation ▸**price competitiveness** compétitivité-prix *f* ▸**price cut** réduction *f*, rabais *m* ▸**price cutting** réductions *fpl* de prix ▸**price-earnings ratio** (*Jur, Fin*) bénéfice *m* net par action ▸**price escalation** flambée *f* des prix; (*Jur*) **price escalation clause** clause *f* de révision des prix ▸**price-fixing** (*by government*) contrôle *m* des prix; (*pej: by firms*) alignement *m* des prix ▸**price freeze** blocage *m* des prix ▸**price inflation** inflation *f* par les prix ▸**price limit**: **to put a price limit on sth** fixer le prix maximum de qch; **my price limit is £400** je n'irai pas au-dessus de 400 livres ▸**price list** tarif *m*, prix courant(s) ▸**price maintenance** (*gen*) vente *f* à prix imposé; *[manufacturer]* fixation *f* des prix ▸**price range** éventail *m or* gamme *f* de prix; **within my price range** dans mes prix; **in the medium price range** d'un prix modéré, dans les prix moyens ▸**price-rigging** (*pej: by firms*) alignement *m* des prix ▸**price ring** cartel *m* des prix ▸**prices and incomes policy** politique *f* des prix et des revenus ▸**prices index** (*Brit*) indice *m* des prix ▸**price support** (*US Econ*) (politique *f* de) soutien *m* des prix ▸**price tag** (*lit*) étiquette *f*; (*fig: cost*) prix *m*, coût *m*; (*fig*) **it's got a heavy price tag** le prix est très élevé, ça coûte cher; **what's the price tag on that house?** quel prix demandent-ils pour cette maison? ▸**price ticket** étiquette *f* ▸**price variation clause** (*Jur*) clause *f* de révision des prix ▸**price war** guerre *f* des prix.

3 vt (*fix ~ of*) fixer le prix de; (*mark ~ on*) marquer le prix de; (*ask ~ of*) demander le prix de, s'informer du prix de; (*fig: estimate value of*) évaluer. **it is ~d at £10** ça coûte 10 livres, ça se vend 10 livres; **it is ~d rather high** c'est plutôt cher; **it isn't ~d in the window** le prix n'est pas (marqué) en vitrine *or* à l'étalage.

▸**price down** vt sep (*Comm*) (*reduce price of*) réduire le prix de, solder; (*mark lower price on*) inscrire un prix réduit sur, changer l'étiquette de.

▸**price out** vt sep: **to price one's goods out of the market** perdre un marché à vouloir demander des prix trop élevés; **Japanese radios have priced ours out (of the market)** nos radios ne peuvent plus soutenir la concurrence des prix japonais; **the French have priced us out of that market** les bas prix pratiqués par les Français nous ont chassés de ce marché.

▸**price up** vt sep (*Comm*) (*raise price of*) augmenter; (*mark higher price on*) inscrire un prix plus élevé sur, changer l'étiquette de.

-priced [praɪst] adj ending in comps: **high-priced** coûteux, cher; *see* **low¹** *etc*.

priceless ['praɪslɪs] adj **a** *picture, jewel* qui n'a pas de prix, sans prix, hors de prix, inestimable; *friendship, contribution, gift* inestimable, très précieux. **b** (*: *amusing*) impayable*.

pricey* ['praɪsɪ] adj coûteux, cher, chérot* (*m only*).

pricing ['praɪsɪŋ] n (*setting price*) établissement *m or* détermination *f or* fixation *f* des prix; (*for service*) tarification *f*; *[stock]* évaluation *f*. **~ policy** *or* **strategy** politique *f* des prix.

prick [prɪk] **1** n **a** (*act, sensation, mark*) piqûre *f*. **to give sth a ~** piquer qch; (*fig*) **the ~s of conscience** les aiguillons *mpl* de la conscience, le remords; *see* **kick**.

b (**: *penis*) bitte** *f*.

c (**: *person*) con** *m*.

2 vt **a** *[person, thorn, pin, hypodermic]* piquer; *balloon, blister* crever; *name on list etc* piquer, pointer. **she ~ed her finger with a pin** elle s'est piqué le doigt avec une épingle; **to ~ a hole in sth** faire un trou d'épingle (*or* d'aiguille *etc*) dans qch; (*fig*) **his conscience ~ed him** il avait mauvaise conscience, il n'avait pas la conscience tranquille.

b **to ~ (up) one's ears** *[animal]* dresser les oreilles; *[person]* (*fig*) dresser *or* tendre *or* prêter l'oreille.

3 vi **a** *[thorn etc]* piquer. (*fig*) **his conscience was ~ing** il avait mauvaise conscience.

b **my eyes are ~ing** les yeux me cuisent; **my toe is ~ing** j'ai des fourmis dans l'orteil.

▸**prick out** vt sep **a** *seedlings* repiquer. **b** (*with pin etc*) *outline, design* piquer, tracer en piquant.

▸**prick up** **1** vi (*lit*) **the dog's ears pricked up** le chien a dressé l'oreille; (*fig*) **his ears pricked up** il a dressé l'oreille. **2** vt sep = **prick 2b**.

pricking ['prɪkɪŋ] n picotement *m*, sensation cuisante. (*fig*) **~s of conscience** remords *m(pl)*.

prickle ['prɪkl] **1** n **a** *[plant]* épine *f*, piquant *m*; *[hedgehog etc]* piquant. **b** (*sensation: on skin etc*) picotement *m*, sensation cuisante. **2** vt piquer. **3** vi *[skin, fingers etc]* fourmiller, picoter.

prickly ['prɪklɪ] adj *plant* épineux, hérissé; *animal* hérissé, armé de piquants; (*fig*) *person* ombrageux, irritable; *subject* épineux, délicat. **his beard was ~** sa barbe piquait; **my arm feels ~** j'ai des fourmis *or* des fourmillements dans le bras; (*fig*) **he is as ~ as a porcupine** c'est un vrai hérisson; (*Med*) **~ heat** fièvre *f* miliaire; (*Bot*) **~ pear** (*fruit*) figue *f* de Barbarie; (*tree*) figuier *m* de Barbarie.

pride [praɪd] **1** n **a** (*NonC*) (*self-respect*) orgueil *m*, amour-propre *m*; (*satisfaction*) fierté *f*; (*pej: arrogance*) orgueil, arrogance *f*, vanité *f*. **his ~ was hurt** il était blessé dans son orgueil *or* dans son amour-propre; **he has too much ~ to ask for help** il est trop fier *or* il a trop d'amour-propre pour demander de l'aide; **she has no ~** elle n'a pas d'amour-propre; **false ~** vanité; (*Prov*) **~ comes** *or* **goes before a fall** péché d'orgueil ne va pas sans danger; (*Prov*) **~ feels no pain** il faut souffrir pour être belle (*Prov*); **her son's success is a great source of ~ to her** elle s'enorgueillit *or* elle est très fière du succès de son fils; **her ~ in her family** la fierté qu'elle tire de sa famille; **he spoke of them with ~** il parla d'eux avec fierté; **to take** *or* **have (a) ~ in** *children, achievements* être très fier de; *house, car etc* prendre (grand) soin de; **she takes a ~ in her appearance** elle prend soin de sa personne; **to take (a) ~ in doing** mettre sa fierté à faire; **to take** *or* **have ~ of place** avoir la place d'honneur.

b (*object of ~*) fierté *f*. **she is her father's ~ and joy** elle est la fierté de son père.

c **a ~ of lions** une troupe de lions.

2 vt: **to ~ o.s. (up)on (doing) sth** être fier *or* s'enorgueillir de (faire) qch.

priest [pri:st] **1** n (*Christian, pagan*) prêtre *m*; (*parish ~*) curé *m*. (*collectively*) **the ~s** le clergé; *see* **assistant, high** *etc*. **2** comp ▸**priest-ridden** (*pej*) dominé par le clergé, sous la tutelle des curés (*pej*).

priestess ['pri:stɪs] n prêtresse *f*.

priesthood ['pri:sthʊd] n (*function*) prêtrise *f*, sacerdoce *m*; (*priests collectively*) clergé *m*. **to enter the ~** se faire prêtre, entrer dans les ordres.

priestly ['pri:stlɪ] adj sacerdotal, de prêtre.

prig [prɪg] n pharisien(ne) *m(f)*. **what a ~ she is!** ce qu'elle peut se prendre au sérieux!; **don't be such a ~!** ne fais pas le petit saint! (*or* la petite sainte!).

priggish ['prɪgɪʃ] adj pharisaïque, suffisant, fat (*m only*).

priggishness ['prɪgɪʃnɪs] n (*NonC*) pharisaïsme *m*, suffisance *f*, fatuité *f*.

prim [prɪm] adj *person* (*also* **~ and proper**) (*prudish*) collet monté *inv*, guindé; (*demure*) très convenable, comme il faut*; *manner, smile, look, expression* compassé, guindé, contraint; *dress, hat* très correct, très convenable; *house, garden* trop coquet *or* net *or* impeccable.

prima ballerina ['pri:mə,bæləˈri:nə] n, pl ~ ~s danseuse *f* étoile.

primacy ['praɪməsɪ] n (*supremacy*) primauté *f*; (*Rel*) primatie *f*.

prima donna ['pri:məˈdɒnə] n, pl ~ ~s (*lit*) prima donna *f inv*. (*fig*) **she's a real ~** elle se prend pour une star.

prima facie ['praɪməˈfeɪʃɪ] 1 adv à première vue, de prime abord. 2 adj (*Jur*) recevable, bien fondé; (*gen*) légitime (à première vue). **to have a ~ case** (*Jur*) avoir une affaire recevable; (*gen*) avoir raison à première vue; (*Jur*) **~ evidence** commencement *m* de preuve; **there are ~ reasons why ...** on peut a priori raisonnablement expliquer pourquoi ... .

primal ['praɪməl] adj (*first in time*) primitif, des premiers âges; (*first in importance*) principal, primordial, premier (*before n*). (*Psych*) **~ scream** cri *m* primal.

primarily ['praɪmərɪlɪ] adv (*chiefly*) essentiellement, principalement; (*originally*) primitivement, à l'origine.

primary ['praɪmərɪ] 1 adj (*first: gen, also Astron, Chem, Econ, Elec, Geol, Med etc*) primaire; (*basic*) *reason* principal, fondamental, primordial; *concern, aim* principal, premier (*before noun*). **~ cause** (*gen*) cause *f* principale; (*Philos*) cause *f* première; **~ colour** couleur *f* fondamentale; **~ education** enseignement *m* primaire; (*US Pol*) **~ election** élection *f* primaire; (*Zool*) **~ feather** rémige *f*; **of ~ importance** d'une importance primordiale, de la plus haute *or* de toute première importance; (*Econ*) **~ industries** le secteur primaire; **the ~ meaning of a word** le sens premier d'un mot; (*Econ*) **~ producer** producteur *m* du secteur primaire; (*Econ*) **~ producing country** pays *m* de production primaire; (*Econ*) **~ product** produit *m* primaire *or* de base; (*Brit*) **~ school** école *f* primaire; (*Brit*) **~ (school)teacher** instituteur *m*, -trice *f*; (*Phon*) **~ stress** accent principal; (*Gram*) **~ tense** temps primitif; (*Elec*) **~ winding** enroulement *m* primaire.

2 n (*school*) école *f* primaire; (*colour*) couleur fondamentale; (*feather*) rémige *f*; (*Elec*) enroulement *m* primaire; (*US Pol*) primaire *f*.

primate ['praɪmɪt] n a (*Rel*) primat *m*. b ['praɪmeɪt] (*Zool*) primate *m*.

prime [praɪm] 1 adj a (*first*) premier; (*principal*) *reason etc* primordial, principal, fondamental; *concern, aim* principal, premier (*before n*). (*Econ, Fin*) **~ bill** effet *m* de premier ordre; (*Comm, Econ*) **~ cost** prix *m* de revient, prix coûtant; (*Math*) **~ factor** facteur *m* premier, diviseur *m* premier; (*gen*) **a ~ factor in ...** un facteur primordial *or* fondamental dans ...; **of ~ importance** d'une importance primordiale, de la plus haute *or* de toute première importance; (*Geog*) **~ meridian** premier meridien *m*; **~ minister** *etc see* **prime minister** *etc*; **~ mover** (*Phys, Tech*) force *f* motrice; (*Philos*) premier moteur *m*, cause *f* première; (*fig: person*) instigateur *m*, -trice *f*; (*Math*) **~ number** nombre *m* premier; (*Econ, Fin*) **~ rate** taux *m* préférentiel *or* de base.

b (*excellent*) *advantage* de premier ordre; (*best*) *meat* de premier choix. **in ~ condition** *animal, athlete* en parfaite condition; *car* en excellent état; **~ cut** morceau *m* de premier choix; **a ~ example of what to avoid** un excellent exemple de ce qu'il faut éviter; **of ~ quality** de première qualité; **~ ribs** côtes premières; (*Rad, TV*) **~ time** heure(s) *f(pl)* d'écoute maximum.

c (*Math*) premier.

2 n a **in the ~ of life, in one's ~** dans *or* à la fleur de l'âge; **when the Renaissance was in its ~** quand la Renaissance était à son apogée, aux plus beaux jours de la Renaissance; **he is past his ~** il est sur le retour; (*hum*) **this grapefruit is past its ~*** ce pamplemousse n'est plus de la première fraîcheur, ce pamplemousse a vu des jours meilleurs (*hum*).

b (*Math*) nombre premier.

c (*Rel*) prime *f*.

3 vt a *gun, pump* amorcer. (*fig*) **to ~ the pump** renflouer une entreprise *or* une affaire; **to ~ sb with drink** faire boire qn (tant et plus); **he was well ~d (with drink)** il avait bu plus que de raison.

b *surface for painting* apprêter.

c (*fig*) *person* mettre au fait, mettre au courant. **they ~d him about what he should say** ils lui ont bien fait répéter ce qu'il avait à dire; **he was ~d to say that** ils lui ont fait la leçon pour qu'il dise cela; **she came well ~d for the interview** elle est arrivée à l'entrevue tout à fait préparée.

prime minister [,praɪmˈmɪnɪstəʳ] n Premier ministre *m*.

prime ministerial [,praɪmmɪnɪˈstɪərɪəl] adj de (*or* du) Premier ministre.

prime ministership [,praɪmˈmɪnɪstə,ʃɪp], **prime ministry** [,praɪmˈmɪnɪstrɪ] n ministère *m*, fonctions *fpl* de Premier ministre.

primer ['praɪməʳ] n (*textbook*) premier livre, livre élémentaire; (*reading book*) abécédaire *m*; (*paint*) apprêt *m*.

primeval [praɪˈmi:vəl] adj primitif, des premiers âges; primordial. **~ forest** forêt *f* vierge.

priming ['praɪmɪŋ] n a [*pump*] amorçage *m*; [*gun*] amorce *f*. b (*Painting*) (*substance*) couche *f* d'apprêt; (*action*) apprêt *m*.

primitive ['prɪmɪtɪv] adj, n (*all senses*) primitif (*m*).

primly ['prɪmlɪ] adv (*prudishly*) d'une manière guindée *or* compassée *or* contrainte; (*demurely*) d'un petit air sage.

primness ['prɪmnɪs] n [*person*] (*prudishness*) façons guindées *or* compassées, air *m* collet monté; (*demureness*) façons très correctes *or* très convenables; [*house, garden*] aspect trop coquet *or* impeccable; [*dress, hat*] aspect très correct.

primogeniture [,praɪməʊˈdʒenɪtʃəʳ] n (*Jur etc*) primogéniture *f*.

primordial [praɪˈmɔ:dɪəl] adj primordial.

primp [prɪmp] 1 vi se pomponner, se bichonner. 2 vt pomponner, bichonner.

primrose ['prɪmrəʊz] 1 n (*Bot*) primevère *f* (*jaune*). (*fig*) **the ~ path** le chemin *or* la voie de la facilité. 2 adj (*also* **~ yellow**) jaune pâle *inv*, (jaune) primevère *inv*.

primula ['prɪmjʊlə] n primevère *f* (*espèce*).

Primus ['praɪməs] n a ® (*also* **~ stove**) réchaud *m* de camping (à pétrole), Primus *m* ®. b (*bishop*) ≃ primat *m*.

prince [prɪns] 1 n a prince *m* (*also fig*). **P~ Charles** le prince Charles; **the P~ of Wales** le prince de Galles; **~ consort** prince consort; **~ regent** prince régent; **P~ Charming** le Prince Charmant; **the P~ of Darkness** le prince des ténèbres *or* des démons; (*fig*) **the ~s of this world** les princes de la terre, les grands *mpl* de ce monde. b (*US fig: fine man*) chic type* *m*. 2 comp ▸**Prince Edward Island** île *f* du Prince-Édouard.

princeling ['prɪnslɪŋ] n principicule *m*.

princely ['prɪnslɪ] adj (*lit, fig*) princier.

princess [prɪnˈses] n princesse *f*. **P~ Anne** la princesse Anne; **P~ Royal** Princesse Royale (*titre donné à la fille aînée du monarque*).

principal ['prɪnsɪpəl] 1 adj principal. (*Brit Theat*) **~ boy** jeune héros *m* (*rôle tenu par une actrice dans les spectacles de Noël*); (*Gram*) **~ clause** (proposition *f*) principale *f*; (*Gram*) **~ parts of a verb** temps primitifs d'un verbe; (*Mus*) **~ horn/violin** premier cor/violon; (*Brit*) **~ nursing officer** ≃ surveillant(e) *m(f)* général(e) (*dans un hôpital*).

2 n a (*Scol etc*) (*gen*) directeur *m*, -trice *f*; [*lycée*] proviseur *m*, directrice *f*; [*college*] principal(e) *m(f)*.

b (*in orchestra*) chef *m* de pupitre; (*Theat*) vedette *f*.

c (*Fin, Jur: person employing agent, lawyer etc*) mandant *m*, commettant *m*; (*Jur: chief perpetrator of a crime*) auteur *m* (d'un crime), principal responsable. (*Jur, Fin*) **~ and agent** commettant et agent.

d (*Fin: capital sum*) principal *m*, capital *m*. **~ and interest** principal *or* capital et intérêts.

principality [,prɪnsɪˈpælɪtɪ] n principauté *f*.

principally ['prɪnsɪpəlɪ] adv principalement.

principle ['prɪnsəpl] n (*all senses*) principe *m*. **to go back to first ~s** remonter jusqu'au principe; **it is based on false ~s** cela repose sur de fausses prémisses *or* de faux principes; **in ~** en principe; **on ~, as a matter of ~** par principe; **I make it a ~ never to lend money, it's against my ~s to lend money** j'ai pour principe de ne jamais prêter d'argent; **that would be totally against my ~s** cela irait à l'encontre de tous mes principes; **for the ~ of the thing*** pour le principe; **he is a man of ~(s), he has high ~s** c'est un homme qui a des principes; **all these machines work on the same ~** toutes ces machines marchent sur *or* selon le même principe.

principled ['prɪnsəpld] adj *person* qui a des principes; *behaviour* réglé par des principes.

-principled ['prɪnsəpld] adj *ending in comps see* **high, low¹**.

prink [prɪŋk] = **primp**.

print [prɪnt] 1 n a (*mark*) [*hand, foot, tyre etc*] empreinte *f*; (*finger ~*) empreinte (digitale). **a thumb/paw** *etc* **~** l'empreinte d'un pouce/d'une patte *etc*; (*Police etc*) **to take sb's ~s** prendre les empreintes de qn; *see* **finger, foot** *etc*.

b (*NonC: Typ*) (*actual letters*) caractères *mpl*; (*printed material*) texte imprimé. **in small/large ~** en petits/gros caractères; **read the small *or* fine ~ before you sign** lisez toutes les clauses avant de signer; **the ~ is poor** les caractères ne sont pas nets; **it was there in cold ~!** c'était là noir sur blanc!; **the book is out of ~ /in ~** le livre est épuisé/disponible (en librairie); **"Books in ~"** "Livres en librairie", "Catalogue courant"; **he wants to see himself in ~** il veut se faire imprimer; **I've got into ~ at last!** me voilà enfin imprimé!; **to rush into ~** se hâter *or* s'empresser de publier un ouvrage (*or* un article *etc*); **don't let that get into ~** n'allez pas imprimer *or* publier cela.

c (*Comput*) sortie *f* sur imprimante.

d (*Art: etching, woodcut etc*) estampe *f*, gravure *f*; (*Art: reproduction*) gravure; (*Phot*) épreuve *f*; (*Tex: material, design*) imprimé *m*; (*printed dress*) robe imprimée. (*Phot*) **to make a ~ from a negative** tirer une épreuve d'un cliché; **a cotton ~** une cotonnade imprimée; *see*

blue.

2 adj *dress etc* en (tissu) imprimé.

3 comp ▸**print journalism** journalisme *m* de presse écrite ▸**printmaker** graveur *m* ▸**printout** (*Comput*) listing *m* imprimé *m*; **to do a printout of sth** imprimer un relevé de qch ▸**print reporter** (*US*) journaliste *mf* de la presse écrite ▸**print shop** (*Typ*) imprimerie *f*; (*art shop*) boutique *f* d'art (*spécialisée dans la vente de reproductions, affiches etc*) ▸**print unions** (*Ind*) syndicats *mpl* des typographes.

4 vt a (*Typ*) imprimer; (*publish*) imprimer, publier. **~ed in England** imprimé en Angleterre; **the book is being ~ed just now** le livre est sous presse *or* à l'impression en ce moment; **100 copies were ~ed** cela a été tiré *or* imprimé à 100 exemplaires, on en a tiré 100 exemplaires; **they didn't dare ~ it** ils n'ont pas osé l'imprimer *or* le publier; **will you have your lectures ~ed?** publierez-vous *or* ferez-vous imprimer vos conférences?; (*lit*) **to ~ money** imprimer des billets; (*fig: Econ*) **it's a licence to ~ money** c'est donner carte blanche à l'inflation; *see also* **printed.**

b (*Tex*) imprimer; (*Phot*) tirer.

c (*write in block letters*) écrire en caractères d'imprimerie. **~ it in block capitals** écrivez-le en lettres majuscules.

d **the mark of horses' hooves ~ed in the sand** la marque de sabots de chevaux imprimée sur le sable, la trace *or* les empreintes *fpl* de sabots de chevaux sur le sable.

5 vi *[machine]* imprimer. **the book is ~ing now** le livre est à l'impression en ce moment; (*Phot*) **this negative won't ~** ce cliché ne donnera rien.

▸**print off** vt sep (*Typ*) tirer, imprimer; (*Phot*) tirer.

▸**print out** (*Comput*) 1 vt sep imprimer. 2 **printout** n *see* **print 3.**

printable ['prɪntəbl] adj imprimable. (*hum*) **what he said is just not ~** ce qu'il a dit n'est pas répétable.

printed ['prɪntɪd] adj *notice, form, cotton, design, dress* imprimé; *writing paper* à en-tête. **~ matter, ~ papers** imprimés *mpl*; **the ~ word** tout ce qui est imprimé, la chose imprimée; (*Electronics*) **~ circuit** circuit imprimé.

printer ['prɪntəʳ] n a imprimeur *m*; (*typographer*) typographe *mf*, imprimeur. **the text has gone to the ~** le texte est chez l'imprimeur; **~'s devil** apprenti imprimeur; **~'s error** faute *f* d'impression, coquille *f*; **~'s ink** encre *f* d'imprimerie; **~'s reader** correcteur *m*, -trice *f* (d'épreuves).

b (*Comput*) imprimante *f*. c (*Phot*) tireuse *f*.

printing ['prɪntɪŋ] 1 n (*Press, Tex, Typ*) impression *f*; (*Phot*) tirage *m*; (*block writing*) écriture *f* en caractères d'imprimerie. 2 comp ▸**printing frame** (*Phot*) châssis-presse *m* ▸**printing ink** encre *f* d'imprimerie ▸**printing office** imprimerie *f* ▸**printing press** presse *f* typographique ▸**printing works** imprimerie *f* (*atelier*).

prior ['praɪəʳ] 1 adj précédent, antérieur (*f* -eure); *consent* préalable. **~ to** antérieur à; **without ~ notice** sans préavis, sans avertissement préalable; **to have a ~ claim to sth** avoir droit à qch par priorité; (*US Jur*) **~ restraint** interdiction *f* judiciaire. 2 adv: **~ to** antérieurement à, préalablement à, avant; **~ to (his) leaving he ...** avant de partir *or* avant son départ il ...; **~ to his leaving we ...** avant son départ *or* avant qu'il ne parte nous ... . 3 n (*Rel*) prieur *m*.

prioress ['praɪərɪs] n prieure *f*.

priority [praɪ'ɒrɪtɪ] 1 n priorité *f*. **to have *or* take ~ (over)** avoir la priorité (sur); **housing must be given first *or* top ~** on doit donner la priorité absolue au logement; **schools were low on the list of priorities *or* the ~ list** les écoles venaient loin sur la liste des priorités *or* étaient loin de venir en priorité; **you must get your priorities right** vous devez décider de ce qui compte le plus pour vous; **to give sb (a) high/low ~** donner/ne pas donner la priorité à qn; **it is a high/low ~** c'est/ce n'est pas une priorité. 2 comp ▸**priority case** cas *m* prioritaire ▸**priority share** (*St Ex*) action *f* de priorité.

priory ['praɪərɪ] n prieuré *m*.

prise [praɪz] vt (*Brit*) **to ~ open a box** ouvrir une boîte en faisant levier, forcer une boîte; **to ~ the lid off a box** forcer le couvercle d'une boîte; (*fig*) **I ~d him out of his chair** je l'ai enfin fait décoller* de sa chaise; (*fig*) **I managed to ~ him out of the job** je suis arrivé à le faire sauter* (de son poste); (*fig*) **to ~ a secret out of sb** arracher un secret à qn.

▸**prise off** vt sep enlever en faisant levier.

▸**prise up** vt sep soulever en faisant levier.

prism ['prɪzəm] n prisme *m*; *see* **prune**[1].

prismatic [prɪz'mætɪk] adj *surface, shape, colour* prismatique (*also fig*). **~ compass** boussole *f* topographique à prismes.

prison ['prɪzn] 1 n (*place*) prison *f*; (*imprisonment*) prison, réclusion *f*. **he is in ~** il est en prison, il fait de la prison; **to put sb in ~** mettre qn en prison, incarcérer qn, emprisonner qn; **to send sb to ~** condamner qn à la prison; **to send sb to ~ for 5 years** condamner qn à 5 ans de prison; **he was in ~ for 5 years** il a fait 5 ans de prison.

2 comp *food, life, conditions* dans la (*or* les) prison(s), pénitentiaire; *system* carcéral, pénitentiaire; *organization, colony* pénitentiaire ▸**prison authorities** administration *f* pénitentiaire ▸**prison camp** camp *m* de prisonniers ▸**prison farm** ferme *f* dépendant d'une maison d'arrêt ▸**prison governor** directeur *m* de prison ▸**prison guard** (*US*) gardien(ne) *m(f)* *or* surveillant(e) *m(f)* (de prison) ▸**prison officer** gardien(ne) *m(f)* *or* surveillant(e) *m(f)* (de prison) ▸**prison population** population *f* pénitentiaire ▸**prison riot** mutinerie *f* (*dans une prison*) ▸**prison van** voiture *f* cellulaire, panier *m* à salade* ▸**prison visitor** visiteur *m*, -euse *f* de prison ▸**prison yard** cour *f* *or* préau *m* de prison.

prisoner ['prɪznəʳ] n (*gen*) prisonnier *m*, -ière *f*; (*in jail*) détenu(e) *m(f)*, prisonnier, -ière. **~ of conscience** détenu(e) *or* prisonnier(-ière) politique; **~ of war** prisonnier de guerre; (*Jur*) **~ at the bar** accusé(e) *m(f)*, inculpé(e) *m(f)*; **the enemy took him ~** il a été fait prisonnier par l'ennemi; **to hold sb ~** détenir qn, garder qn en captivité.

prissy* ['prɪsɪ] adj (*prudish*) bégueule; (*effeminate*) efféminé; (*fussy*) pointilleux.

pristine ['prɪstaɪn] adj a (*unspoiled*) parfait, virginal. b (*original*) original, d'origine.

prithee†† ['prɪðiː] excl je vous prie.

privacy ['prɪvəsɪ] 1 n intimité *f*, solitude *f*. **his desire for ~** son désir d'être seul, son désir de solitude; *[public figure etc]* son désir de préserver sa vie privée; **there is no ~ in these flats** on ne peut avoir aucune vie privée dans ces appartements; **everyone needs some ~** tout le monde a besoin de solitude *or* a besoin d'être seul de temps en temps; **they were looking for ~** ils cherchaient un coin retiré; **he told me in strictest ~** il me l'a dit dans le plus grand secret; **in the ~ of his own home** dans l'intimité de son foyer; *see* **invasion.** 2 comp ▸**Privacy Act** (*Jur*) loi *f* sur la protection de la vie privée.

private ['praɪvɪt] 1 adj a (*not public*) *conversation, meeting, interview* privé, en privé; *land, property, road* privé; (*confidential*) confidentiel, personnel, de caractère privé. **"~"** (*on door etc*) "privé", "interdit au public"; (*on envelope*) "personnelle"; **mark the letter "~"** inscrivez "personnelle" sur la lettre; **this matter is strictly ~** cette affaire est strictement confidentielle; **it's a ~ matter *or* affair** c'est une affaire privée; **he's a very ~ person** (*gen*) c'est un homme très secret *or* qui ne se confie pas; *[public figure etc]* il tient à préserver sa vie privée; (*Jur*) **~ agreement** accord *m* à l'amiable; **they have a ~ agreement to help each other** ils ont convenu (entre eux) de s'aider mutuellement, ils se sont entendus *or* se sont mis d'accord pour s'aider mutuellement; **"~ fishing"** "pêche réservée *or* gardée"; **"funeral ~"** "les obsèques auront lieu dans la plus stricte intimité"; (*Admin, Jur*) **~ hearing** audience *f* à huis clos; **~ hotel** ≃ petit hôtel; **for your ~ information** à titre confidentiel *or* officieux; **I have ~ information that ...** je sais de source privée que ...; **~ letter** lettre de caractère privé; **in (his) ~ life** dans sa vie privée, dans le privé; (*Theat etc*) **~ performance** représentation *f* à bureaux fermés; **~ place** coin retiré, petit coin tranquille; **~ property** propriété privée; (*in hotel etc*) **~ room** salon *m* réservé (*see also* **1b**); *[film]* **~ showing** séance *f* privée; (*Brit Scol*) **~ study** permanence *f*, étude *f*; (*Art etc*) **~ view** vernissage *m*; **~ wedding** mariage célébré dans l'intimité.

b (*for use of one person*) *house, lesson, room* particulier; (*personal*) *bank account, advantage* personnel. **a ~ (bank) account** un compte en banque personnel; **room with ~ bath(room)** chambre *f* avec salle de bain particulière; **in his ~ capacity** à titre personnel; **~ car** voiture de tourisme; **~ house** domicile particulier; **he has a ~ income, he has ~ means** il a une fortune personnelle; **~ joke** plaisanterie personnelle *or* pour initiés, gag *m* intime; **it is my ~ opinion that ...** pour ma part je pense que ...; (*Anat*) **~ parts** les parties *fpl* (génitales); **~ pupil** élève *mf* en leçons particulières; **for ~ reasons** pour des raisons personnelles; **~ secretary** secrétaire particulier *or* privé, secrétaire particulière *or* privée; **~ teacher, ~ tutor** (*for full education*) précepteur *m*, institutrice *f*; (*for one subject*) répétiteur *m*, -trice *f*; **he's got a ~ teacher for maths** il prend des leçons particulières en maths, il a un répétiteur en maths; **in his ~ thoughts** dans ses pensées secrètes *or* intimes; **~ tuition** leçons particulières; **for his ~ use** pour son usage personnel.

c (*not official; not state-controlled etc*) *company, institution, army* privé; *clinic, nursing home* privé, non conventionné. **~ school** école privée *or* libre; (*Econ*) **~ enterprise** entreprise privée; (*Econ, Ind*) **the ~ sector** le secteur privé; (*esp Brit Med*) **to be in ~ practice** ≃ être médecin non conventionné; (*esp Brit Med*) **~ treatment** ≃ traitement non remboursé; (*Brit Med*) **~ patient** malade *mf* privé(e); **~ patients** clientèle *f* privée; **~ health insurance** assurance *f* maladie privée; **~ pension** retraite *f* complémentaire; **~ pension scheme** plan *m* de retraite complémentaire; **~ detective, ~ investigator, ~ eye*** détective privé; **a ~ citizen, a ~ person** un particulier, un simple citoyen, une personne privée; (*Parl*) **~ member** simple député *m*; (*Parl*) **~ member's bill** proposition *f* de loi *émanant d'un simple député*.

d (*Mil*) **~ soldier** (simple) soldat *m*, soldat de deuxième classe.

2 n a (*Mil*) (simple) soldat *m*, soldat de première classe. **P~ Martin** le soldat Martin; **P~ Martin!** soldat Martin!; (*US*) **~ 1st class** ≃ caporal *m*; (*US Mil*) **~ E.2** soldat *m* de 1ère classe; (*US Mil*) **~ E.1** soldat *m* de 2ème classe.

b **in ~ = privately a** *and* **b.**

c (†, *hum*) **~s*** les parties *fpl* (génitales).

privateer [ˌpraɪvə'tɪəʳ] n (*man, ship*) corsaire *m*.

privately ['praɪvɪtlɪ] adv a (*secretly, personally*) dans son for intérieur. **~ he believes that ...** dans son for intérieur il croit que ...; **~ he was against the scheme** intérieurement *or* secrètement il était opposé au projet.

b (*not publicly*) **may I speak to you ~?** puis-je vous parler en privé?; **he told me ~ that ...** il m'a dit en confidence que ...; **he has said ~ that ...** il a dit en privé *or* en petit comité que ...; **the wedding was held ~** le mariage a eu lieu dans l'intimité; **the committee sat ~** le comité s'est réuni en séance privée *or* à huis clos.

c (*unofficially*) *write, apply, object* à titre personnel *or* privé, en tant que particulier.

d (*in private institution*) **she is having the operation ~** (*private hospital*) elle se fait opérer dans un hôpital privé; (*non-NHS surgeon*) elle se fait opérer par un chirurgien non conventionné; **he is being ~ educated** (*private school*) il fait ses études dans une institution privée; (*private tutor*) il a un précepteur.

privation [praɪ'veɪʃən] n privation *f*.

privative ['prɪvətɪv] adj, n (*also Ling*) privatif (*m*).

privatization [ˌpraɪvɪˌtaɪ'zeɪʃən] n (*Econ*) privatisation *f*.

privatize ['praɪvɪˌtaɪz] vt (*Econ*) privatiser.

privet ['prɪvɪt] n troène *m*. ~ **hedge** haie *f* de troènes.

privilege ['prɪvɪlɪdʒ] 1 n privilège *m*; (*NonC: Parl etc*) prérogative *f*, immunité *f*. **to have the ~ of doing** avoir le privilège *or* jouir du privilège de faire; **I hate ~** je déteste les privilèges. 2 vt (*pass only*) **to be ~d to do** avoir le privilège de faire; **I was ~d to meet him once** j'ai eu le privilège de le rencontrer une fois.

privileged ['prɪvɪlɪdʒd] adj *person, group, situation, position* privilégié. **a ~ few** quelques privilégiés; **the ~ few** la minorité privilégiée; **~ information** renseignements confidentiels (*obtenus dans l'exercice de ses fonctions*); *see* **under**.

privily†† ['prɪvɪlɪ] adv en secret.

privy ['prɪvɪ] 1 adj (†† *or Jur*) privé, secret (*f* -ète). ~ **to** au courant de, dans le secret de. 2 comp ►**Privy Council** (*Brit*) conseil *m* privé ►**Privy Councillor** conseiller privé ►**Privy Purse** cassette royale ►**Privy Seal** petit sceau. 3 n cabinets *mpl*, W.-C. *mpl*.

prize¹ [praɪz] 1 n a (*gen, Scol, fig*) prix *m*; (*in lottery*) lot *m*. **to win first ~** (*Scol etc*) remporter le premier prix (*in* de); (*in lottery*) gagner le gros lot; **the Nobel P~** le prix Nobel; *see* **cash** *etc*.

b (*Naut*) prise *f* de navire (*or* de cargaison).

2 adj a (*prize-winning*) primé, qui a remporté un prix. **a ~ sheep** un mouton primé; **he grows ~ onions** il cultive des oignons pour les concours agricoles.

b (*outstanding*) magnifique, remarquable. **a ~ cow** une vache magnifique; **his ~ cow** sa plus belle vache; **that's a ~ example of official stupidity!** c'est un parfait exemple de la bêtise des milieux officiels; **she is a ~ idiot*** c'est une idiote finie *or* de premier ordre.

3 comp ►**prize day** (*Scol*) distribution *f* des prix ►**prize draw** tombola *f* ►**prize fight** (*Boxing*) combat professionnel ►**prize fighter** boxeur professionnel ►**prize fighting** boxe professionnelle ►**prize-giving** (*Scol etc*) distribution *f* des prix ►**prize list** palmarès *m* ►**prize money** (*gen, Sport*) argent *m* du prix; (*Naut*) part *f* de prise ►**prize ring** (*Boxing*) ring *m* ►**prizewinner** (*Scol, gen*) lauréat(e) *m(f)*; (*in lottery*) gagnant(e) *m(f)* ►**prizewinning** *essay, novel, entry etc* primé, qui remporte le prix; *ticket* gagnant.

4 vt priser, attacher beaucoup de prix à, faire grand cas de. **to ~ sth very highly** faire très grand cas de qch, priser hautement qch; **~d possession** bien le plus précieux.

prize² [praɪz] = **prise**.

pro¹ [prəʊ] 1 pref a (*in favour of*) pro- pro...; **~-French/-European** profrançais/proeuropéen; **~-Europe** proeurope; **he was ~-Hitler** il était hitlérien, il était partisan d'Hitler; **they were ~-Moscow** ils étaient prosoviétiques. b (*acting for*) **pro...** pro-, vice-; *see* **proconsul** *etc*. 2 n: **the ~s and the cons** le pour et le contre.

pro²* [prəʊ] 1 n a (*abbr of* **professional**) (*Sport etc*) pro *mf*. (*fig*) **you can see he's a ~** on voit bien qu'on a affaire à un professionnel, on dirait qu'il a fait ça toute sa vie. b (*abbr of* **prostitute**) prostituée *f*, professionnelle *f*. 2 comp ►**pro-am** (*Golf*) (*abbr of* **professional-amateur**) pro-am *mf*; **pro-am tournament** tournoi *m* pro-am.

P.R.O. [ˌpiːɑːr'əʊ] n (*abbr of* **public relations officer**) *see* **public**.

pro-abortion [ˌprəʊə'bɔːʃən] adj en faveur de l'avortement.

pro-abortionist [ˌprəʊə'bɔːʃənɪst] n partisan(e) *m(f)* de l'avortement.

probability [ˌprɒbə'bɪlɪtɪ] n probabilité *f*. **in all ~** selon toute probabilité; **the ~ is that** il est très probable que + *indic*, il y a de grandes chances pour que + *subj*; **there is little ~ that** il est peu probable que + *subj*.

probable ['prɒbəbl] 1 adj a (*likely*) *reason, success, event, election* probable. **it is ~ that he will succeed** il est probable qu'il réussira; **it is hardly/not ~ that ...** il est peu probable/improbable que ... + *subj*. b (*credible*) vraisemblable. **his explanation did not sound very ~** son explication ne m'a pas paru très vraisemblable. 2 n: **he is one of the ~s for the job** il est un de ceux qui sont considérés très sérieusement pour le poste, il est l'un des favoris pour le poste; *see* **possible**.

probably ['prɒbəblɪ] adv probablement, vraisemblablement, selon toute probabilité. **he ~ forgot** il a probablement *or* vraisemblablement oublié, selon toute probabilité il aura oublié; **very ~, but ...** c'est bien probable *or* peut-être bien, mais ... .

probate ['prəʊbɪt] (*Jur*) 1 n homologation *f* (d'un testament). **to value sth for ~** évaluer *or* expertiser qch pour l'homologation d'un testament; **to grant/take out ~ of a will** homologuer/faire homologuer un testament. 2 comp ►**probate court** tribunal *m* des successions. 3 vt (*US*) *will* homologuer.

probation [prə'beɪʃən] 1 n a (*Jur*) ≃ mise *f* à l'épreuve; (*for minors*) mise *f* en liberté surveillée. **to be on ~** ≃ être en sursis avec mise à l'épreuve *or* en liberté surveillée; **to put sb on ~** mettre qn en sursis avec mise à l'épreuve *or* en liberté surveillée. b **he is on ~** (*employee*) il a été engagé à l'essai; (*Rel*) il est novice; (*US Educ*) il a été pris (*or* repris) à l'essai; (*US Educ*) **a semester on ~** un semestre à l'essai. 2 comp ►**probation officer** (*Jur*) contrôleur *m* judiciaire.

probationary [prə'beɪʃnərɪ] adj (*gen*) d'essai; (*Jur*) de sursis, avec mise à l'épreuve; (*Rel*) de probation, de noviciat. **for a ~ period** pendant une période d'essai; **~ period of 3 months** période *f* de 3 mois à l'essai.

probationer [prə'beɪʃnəʳ] n (*in business, factory etc*) employé(e) *m(f)* engagé(e) à l'essai; (*Brit Police*) stagiaire *mf*; (*Rel*) novice *mf*; (*Jur*) ≃ condamné(e) *m(f)* sursitaire avec mise à l'épreuve, (*minor*) délinquant(e) *m(f)* en liberté surveillée.

probe [prəʊb] 1 n (*gen, Med, Dentistry, Space*) sonde *f*; (*fig: investigation*) enquête *f* (*into* sur), investigation *f* (*into* de). (*Space*) **Venus ~** sonde *f* spatiale à destination de Vénus.

2 vt a *hole, crack* explorer, examiner; (*Med*) sonder; (*Space*) explorer. **he ~d the ground with his stick** il fouilla la terre de sa canne.

b *sb's subconscious, past, private life* sonder, explorer, chercher à découvrir; *causes, crime, sb's death* chercher à éclaircir; *mystery* approfondir.

3 vi (*gen, Med etc*) faire un examen avec une sonde, faire un sondage; (*fig: inquire*) faire des recherches, poursuivre une investigation, fouiner (*pej*). **to ~ for sth** (*gen, Med*) chercher à localiser *or* à découvrir qch; (*fig: by investigation*) rechercher qch, fouiner à la recherche de qch; **the police should have ~d more deeply** la police aurait dû pousser plus loin ses investigations; **to ~ into sth** = **to probe sth**; *see* **2b**.

probing ['prəʊbɪŋ] 1 adj *instrument* pour sonder; (*fig*) *question, study* pénétrant; *interrogation* serré; *look* inquisiteur (*f* -trice). 2 n (*gen, Med*) sondage *m*; (*fig: investigations*) investigations *fpl* (*into* de).

probity ['prəʊbɪtɪ] n probité *f*.

problem ['prɒbləm] 1 n problème *m* (*also Math*). **the housing ~** le problème *or* (*more acute*) la crise du logement; **he is a great ~ to his mother** il pose de gros problèmes à sa mère; **we've got ~s with the car** nous avons des ennuis avec la voiture; **he's got drink(ing) ~s** il a des tendances à l'alcoolisme, il est porté sur la boisson; **it's not my ~** ça ne me concerne pas; **that's no ~ to him** ça ne lui pose pas de problème, c'est simple comme tout pour lui; **that's no ~!, no ~!*** (ça ne pose) pas de problème!*; **what's the ~?** qu'est-ce qui ne va pas?; **I had no ~ in getting the money, it was no ~ to get the money** je n'ai eu aucun mal à obtenir l'argent.

2 adj a (*causing problems*) *situation* difficile; *family, group* qui pose des problèmes; *child* caractériel, difficile. (*Sociol*) **~ cases** des cas sociaux.

b (*Literat etc*) *novel, play* à thèse.

3 comp ►**problem page** (*Press*) courrier *m* du cœur ►**problem-solving** n résolution *f* de problèmes ◊ adj *technique, abilities* de résolution de problèmes.

problematic(al) [ˌprɒblɪ'mætɪk(l)] adj problématique. **it is ~ whether ...** il n'est pas du tout certain que ... + *subj*.

proboscis [prəʊ'bɒsɪs] n, pl **~es** *or* **probocides** [prəʊ'bɒsɪˌdiːz] (*Zool*) trompe *f*; (*hum: nose*) appendice *m* (*hum*).

procedural [prə'siːdjʊrəl] adj (*Admin, Insurance etc*) de procédure.

procedure [prə'siːdʒəʳ] n procédure *f*. **what is the ~?** qu'est-ce qu'on doit faire?; (*more formally*) quelle est la procédure à suivre?, comment doit-on procéder?; **the correct** *or* **normal ~ is to apply to** pour suivre la procédure normale il faut s'adresser à; (*Admin, Jur etc*) **order of ~** règles *fpl* de procédure.

proceed [prə'siːd] 1 vi a (*go*) aller, avancer, circuler. **he was ~ing along the road** il avançait sur la route; (*lit, fig*) **before we ~ any further** avant d'aller plus loin; **cars should ~ slowly** les autos devraient avancer *or* rouler lentement; **to ~ on one's way** poursuivre son chemin *or* sa route; **you must ~ cautiously** il faut avancer avec prudence; (*fig: act*) il faut agir *or* procéder avec prudence.

b (*go on*) aller, se rendre; (*fig*) passer (*to* à); (*continue*) continuer. **they then ~ed to London** ils se sont ensuite rendus à Londres; **let us ~ to the next item** passons à la question suivante; **I am not sure how to ~** je ne sais pas très bien comment m'y prendre; **to ~ to do sth** se mettre à faire qch; **they ~ed with their plan** ils ont donné suite à leur projet; (*Jur*) **they did not ~ with the charges against him** ils ont abandonné les poursuites (engagées) contre lui; **~ with your work** continuez *or* poursuivez votre travail; **please ~!** veuillez continuer *or* poursuivre; **everything is ~ing well** les choses suivent leur cours de manière satisfaisante; **it is all ~ing according to plan** tout se passe ainsi que prévu; **the discussions are ~ing normally** les discussions se poursuivent normalement; **the text ~s thus** le texte continue ainsi.

c (*originate*) **to ~ from** venir de, provenir de; (*fig*) provenir de, découler de.

d (*Jur*) **to ~ against sb** engager des poursuites contre qn.

2 vt continuer. **"well" she ~ed** "eh bien" continua-t-elle.

3 n *see* **proceeds**.

proceeding [prəˈsiːdɪŋ] n a (*course of action*) façon *f or* manière *f* d'agir. **it was a somewhat dubious ~** c'était une manière de procéder *or* une façon d'agir quelque peu douteuse; **the safest ~ would be to wait** la conduite la plus sage serait d'attendre; **there were some odd ~s** il se passait des choses bizarres, il y avait des agissements *mpl or* des menées *fpl* bizarres.

b **~s** (*manœuvres*) opérations *fpl*; (*ceremony*) cérémonie *f*; (*meeting*) séance *f*, réunion *f*; (*discussions*) débats *mpl*; **the ~s begin at 7 o'clock** la réunion *or* la séance commencera à 19 heures; **the secretary recorded all the ~s** le secrétaire a enregistré *or* consigné tous les débats.

c (*esp Jur: measures*) **~s** mesures *fpl*; **to take ~s** prendre des mesures (*in order to do* pour faire, *against sb* contre qn); (*Jur*) **to take (legal) ~s against sb** engager des poursuites contre qn, intenter un procès à qn; **legal ~s** procès *m*; *see* **divorce, commence, institute**.

d (*records*) **~s** compte rendu, rapport *m*. **it was published in the Society's ~s** cela a été publié dans les actes de la Société; (*as title*) **P~s of the Historical Society** Actes *mpl* de la Société d'histoire.

proceeds [ˈprəʊsiːdz] npl montant *m* (des recettes). (*Jur, Fin*) **~ of insurance** indemnité *f* versée par la compagnie.

process¹ [ˈprəʊses] 1 n a (*Chem, Biol, Ling, Sociol etc*) processus *m*; (*fig, Admin, Jur*) procédure *f*. **the ~ of digestion/growing up** *etc* le processus de la digestion/de la croissance *etc*; **a natural/chemical ~** un processus naturel/chimique; **the thawing/preserving** *etc* **~** le processus de décongélation/de conservation *etc*; **the legal/administrative ~ takes a year** la procédure légale/administrative prend un an; **the ~es of the law** le processus de la justice; **it's a slow** *or* **long ~** (*Chem etc*) c'est un processus lent; (*fig*) ça prend du temps; **he supervised the whole ~** il a supervisé l'opération *f* du début à la fin.

b **to be in ~** *[discussions, examinations, work]* être en cours; *[building]* être en cours *or* en voie de construction; **while work is in ~** pendant les travaux, quand le travail est en cours; **it is in (the) ~ of construction** c'est en cours *or* en voie de construction; **we are in (the) ~ of removal to Leeds** nous sommes en train de déménager pour aller à Leeds; **in the ~ of cleaning the picture, they discovered ...** au cours du nettoyage du tableau *or* pendant qu'ils nettoyaient le tableau ils ont découvert ...; **he saved the girl, but injured himself in the ~** en sauvant la fille, il s'est blessé; **in the ~ of time** avec le temps.

c (*specific method*) procédé *m*, méthode *f*. **the Bessemer ~** le procédé Bessemer; **he has devised a ~ for controlling weeds** il a mis au point un procédé *or* une méthode pour venir à bout des mauvaises herbes; **to work sth out by ~ of elimination** résoudre qch procédant par élimination.

d (*Jur*) (*action*) procès *m*; (*summons*) citation *f*, sommation *f* de comparaître. **to bring a ~ against sb** intenter un procès à qn; **to serve a ~ on sb** signifier une citation à qn; *see* **serve**.

e (*Anat, Bot, Zool*) excroissance *f*, protubérance *f*.

2 comp ▸**process control** commande *f or* régulation *f* de processus ▸**process(ed) cheese** fromage *m* fondu, crème *f* de gruyère *etc* ▸**process printing** (*Typ*) quadrichromie *f* ▸**process-server** (*Jur*) mandataire *m* habilité à recevoir les significations.

3 vt (*Ind*) *raw materials* traiter, transformer; *seeds* traiter; *food* traiter, faire subir un traitement à; (*Phot*) *film* développer; (*Comput*) *information, data* traiter; (*Comput*) *tape* faire passer en machine; (*Admin etc*) *an application, papers, records* s'occuper de. **your application will take 6 weeks to ~** l'examen de votre candidature va prendre 6 semaines; **they ~ 10,000 forms per day** 10.000 formulaires passent chaque jour entre leurs mains; (*Comm*) **in order to ~ your order** afin de donner suite à votre commande.

process² [prəˈses] vi (*Brit: go in procession*) défiler, avancer en cortège; (*Rel*) aller en procession.

processing [ˈprəʊsesɪŋ] 1 n (*NonC: see* **process¹ 3**) traitement *m*; transformation *f*; développement *m*; *see* **data, food, word** *etc*. 2 comp ▸**processing rack** cadre *m* de développement ▸**processing unit** (*Comput*) unité *f* de traitement.

procession [prəˈseʃən] n *[people, cars]* cortège *m*, défilé *m*; (*Rel*) procession *f*. **to walk in (a) ~** défiler, aller en cortège *or* en procession; *see* **funeral**.

processional [prəˈseʃənl] (*Rel*) 1 adj processionnel. 2 n hymne processionnel.

processor [ˈprəʊsesəʳ] n a (*Comput*) processeur *m*; *see* **data, word** *etc*. b = **food processor**; *see* **food**.

pro-choice [ˌprəʊˈtʃɔɪs] adj en faveur de l'avortement.

proclaim [prəˈkleɪm] vt a (*announce*) proclamer, déclarer (*that* que); *holiday* proclamer, instituer; *one's independence* proclamer; *war, peace, one's love* déclarer; *edict* promulguer. **to ~ sb king** proclamer qn roi.

b (*reveal*) démontrer, révéler. **his tone ~ed his confidence** le ton de sa voix démontrait *or* révélait sa confiance; **their expressions ~ed their guilt** la culpabilité se lisait sur leurs visages.

proclamation [ˌprɒkləˈmeɪʃən] n proclamation *f*.

proclivity [prəˈklɪvɪtɪ] n (*frm*) propension *f*, inclination *f* (*to sth* à qch, *to do* à faire).

proconsul [ˈprəʊˈkɒnsəl] n proconsul *m*.

procrastinate [prəʊˈkræstɪneɪt] vi faire traîner les choses, avoir tendance à tout remettre au lendemain.

procrastination [prəʊˌkræstɪˈneɪʃən] n procrastination *f*.

procrastinator [prəʊˌkræstɪˈneɪtəʳ] n personne *f* qui remet tout au lendemain.

procreate [ˈprəʊkrɪeɪt] vt procréer, engendrer.

procreation [ˌprəʊkrɪˈeɪʃən] n procréation *f*.

Procrustean [prəʊˈkrʌstɪən] adj de Procuste.

proctor [ˈprɒktəʳ] n a (*Jur etc*) fondé *m* de pouvoir. b (*Univ*) (*Oxford, Cambridge*) personne *f* responsable de la discipline; (*US*) surveillant(e) *m(f)* (à un examen).

procurable [prəˈkjʊərəbl] adj que l'on peut se procurer. **it is easily ~** on peut se le procurer facilement.

procuration [ˌprɒkjʊˈreɪʃən] n a (*act of procuring*) obtention *f*, acquisition *f*. b (*Jur: authority*) procuration *f*. c (*crime*) proxénétisme *m*.

procurator [ˈprɒkjʊreɪtəʳ] n (*Jur*) fondé *m* de pouvoir. (*Scot Jur*) **P~ Fiscal** ≃ procureur *m* (de la République).

procure [prəˈkjʊəʳ] 1 vt a (*obtain for o.s.*) se procurer, obtenir; *sb's release etc* obtenir. **to ~ sth for sb, to ~ sb sth** procurer qch à qn, faire obtenir qch à qn; **to ~ sb's death**† faire assassiner qn. b (*Jur*) *prostitute etc* offrir les services de, procurer. 2 vi (*Jur*) faire du proxénétisme.

procurement [prəˈkjʊəmənt] n (*gen*) obtention *f*; (*Comm, Admin, Ind*) approvisionnement *m*; (*US, esp Mil*) acquisition *f* de matériel militaire. (*Comm, Ind*) **~ department** service *m* des achats *or* de l'approvisionnement.

procurer [prəˈkjʊərəʳ] n (*Jur*) entremetteur *m*, proxénète *m*.

procuress [prəˈkjʊərɪs] n (*Jur*) entremetteuse *f*, proxénète *f*.

procuring [prəˈkjʊərɪŋ] n *[goods, objects]* obtention *f*; (*Jur*) proxénétisme *m*.

prod [prɒd] 1 n (*push*) poussée *f*; (*jab*) (petit) coup *m* (*de canne, avec le doigt etc*). **to give sb a ~** pousser qn doucement (du doigt *or* du pied *or* avec la pointe d'un bâton *etc*); (*fig*) pousser *or* aiguillonner qn; (*fig*) **he needs a ~ from time to time** il a besoin d'être poussé *or* d'être aiguillonné *or* qu'on le secoue* (*subj*) un peu de temps en temps.

2 vt pousser doucement. **to ~ sb** pousser qn doucement (du doigt *or* du pied *or* avec la pointe d'un bâton *etc*); (*fig*) pousser *or* aiguillonner qn; **he ~ded the box with his umbrella** il a poussé la boîte avec la pointe de son parapluie; **he ~ded the map with his finger** il a pointé son doigt sur la carte; **to ~ sb into doing sth** pousser *or* inciter qn à faire qch; **he needs ~ding** il a besoin d'être poussé *or* d'être aiguillonné *or* qu'on le secoue* (*subj*); **to ~ sb along/out** *etc* faire avancer/sortir *etc* qn en le poussant (du doigt *or* du pied *or* avec la pointe d'un bâton).

3 vi: **to ~ at sb/sth = to ~ sb/sth**; *see* **2**.

prodigal [ˈprɒdɪgəl] adj prodigue (*of* de). **the ~ (son)** (*Bible*) le fils prodigue; (*fig*) l'enfant *m* prodigue.

prodigality [ˌprɒdɪˈgælɪtɪ] n prodigalité *f*.

prodigally [ˈprɒdɪgəlɪ] adv avec prodigalité, prodigalement.

prodigious [prəˈdɪdʒəs] adj prodigieux, extraordinaire.

prodigiously [prəˈdɪdʒəslɪ] adv prodigieusement.

prodigy [ˈprɒdɪdʒɪ] n prodige *m*, merveille *f*. **child ~, infant ~** enfant *mf* prodige; **a ~ of learning** un puits de science.

produce [prəˈdjuːs] 1 vt a (*make, yield, manufacture*) *milk, oil, coal, ore, crops* produire; *cars, radios* produire, fabriquer; *[writer, artist, musician etc]* produire; (*Fin*) *interest, profit* rapporter; *offspring [animal]* produire, donner naissance à; *[woman]* donner naissance à. (*Fin*) **his shares ~ a yield of 7½%** ses actions rapportent 7½%; **that investment ~s no return** cet investissement ne rapporte rien; **Scotland ~s whisky** l'Écosse produit du whisky *or* est un pays producteur de whisky; **we must ~ more coal** nous devons produire plus de charbon; **coal ~s electricity** le charbon produit *or* donne de l'électricité; **he burned sticks to ~ some warmth** il a brûlé des brindilles pour faire *or* donner un peu de chaleur; **these magazines are ~d by the same firm** ces revues sont éditées par la même maison; **he ~d a masterpiece** il a produit un chef-d'œuvre; **well-~d** *book* bien présenté; *goods* bien fait (*see also* **1d**); **he has ~d a new pop record** il a sorti un nouveau disque pop.

b (*bring out, show*) *gift, handkerchief, gun* sortir (*from* de), exhiber, produire; *ticket, documents etc* produire, présenter, exhiber; *witness* produire; *proof* fournir, apporter. **he suddenly ~d a large parcel** il a soudain sorti *or* produit *or* exhibé un gros paquet; **I can't ~ £100 just like that!** je ne peux pas trouver 100 livres comme ça!; **can you ~ a box to put this in?** vous n'auriez pas une boîte (à me donner) où je puisse mettre cela?; **he ~d a sudden burst of energy** il a eu un sursaut d'énergie.

c (*cause*) *famine, deaths* causer, provoquer; *dispute, bitterness* occasionner, provoquer, causer; *results* produire, donner; *impression* faire, donner; *pleasure, interest* susciter; (*Elec*) *current* engendrer; *spark* faire jaillir. **it ~d a sensation in my finger** cela a provoqué *or* produit une sensation dans mon doigt.

d (*Theat*) mettre en scène; (*Cine*) produire; (*Rad*) *play* mettre en ondes; *programme* réaliser; (*TV*) *play, film* mettre en scène; *programme* réaliser. **well ~d** bien monté.

e (*Geom*) *line, plane* prolonger, continuer.

2 vi a *[mine, oil well, factory]* produire; *[land, trees, cows]* produire, rendre.

b (*Theat*) assurer la mise en scène; (*Cine*) assurer la production (*d'un film*); (*Rad, TV*) assurer la réalisation d'une émission.

3 ['prɒdjuːs] **n** (*NonC*) produits *mpl* (*d'alimentation*). **agricultural/garden/foreign ~** produits agricoles/maraîchers/étrangers; **"~ of France"** "produit français", "produit de France"; **we eat mostly our own ~** nous mangeons surtout nos propres produits *or* ce que nous produisons nous-mêmes.

producer [prəˈdjuːsəʳ] **1 n** (*Agr, Ind etc*) producteur *m*, -trice *f*; (*Theat, Cine, Mus*) producteur *m*, -trice *f*; (*Rad, TV*) réalisateur *m*, metteur *m* en ondes. **2 comp ►producer gas** gaz *m* fourni par gazogène **►producer goods** (*Econ*) biens *mpl* de production.

-producing [prəˈdjuːsɪŋ] **adj ending in comps** producteur (*f* -trice) de ... . **oil-producing** producteur de pétrole; **one of the most important coal-producing countries** un des plus gros pays producteurs de charbon.

product [ˈprɒdʌkt] **1 n a** (*Comm, Ind etc*) produit *m*; (*fig*) produit, résultat *m*, fruit *m*. **food ~s** produits alimentaires *or* d'alimentation, denrées *fpl* (alimentaires); **it is the ~ of his imagination** c'est le fruit de son imagination; (*fig*) **he is the ~ of our educational system** il est le produit de notre système d'enseignement; **she is the ~ of a broken home** elle est le résultat d'un foyer désuni; *see* **finished, gross, waste** *etc.* **b** (*Math*) produit *m*. **2 comp ►product acceptance** mesure *f* du succès d'un produit auprès des consommateurs **►product liability** responsabilité *f* du fabricant **►product line** gamme *f* de produits.

production [prəˈdʌkʃən] **1 n a** (*NonC: see* **produce 1a**) production *f*, fabrication *f*. **to put sth into ~** entreprendre la production *or* la fabrication de qch; **to take sth out of ~** retirer qch de la production; **the factory is in full ~** l'usine tourne à plein rendement; **car ~ has risen recently** la production automobile a récemment augmenté.

b (*NonC: showing: see* **produce 1b**) production *f*, présentation *f*. **on ~ of this ticket** sur présentation de ce billet.

c (*act of producing: see* **produce 1d**) (*Theat*) mise *f* en scène; (*Cine*) production *f*; (*Rad*) mise en ondes, réalisation *f*; (*TV*) mise en scène, réalisation. (*Theat*) **"Macbeth": a new ~ by ...** "Macbeth": une nouvelle mise en scène de ...; (*fig*) **he made a real ~ out of it*** il en a fait toute une affaire *or* tout un plat*.

d (*work produced*) (*Theat*) pièce *f*; (*Cine, Rad, TV*) production *f*; (*Art, Literat*) production, œuvre *f*.

2 comp ►production line (*Ind*) chaîne *f* de fabrication; **he works on the production line** il travaille à la chaîne; **production line work** travail *m* à la chaîne **►production manager** directeur *m* de la production.

productive [prəˈdʌktɪv] **adj** *land, imagination* fertile, fécond; *meeting, discussion, work* fructueux, fécond; (*Econ*) *employment, labour* productif; (*Ling*) productif. **to be ~ of sth** produire qch, engendrer qch, être générateur (*f* -trice) de qch; **I've had a very ~ day** j'ai eu une journée très fructueuse, j'ai bien travaillé aujourd'hui; **~ life of an asset** vie *f* utile d'un bien.

productively [prəˈdʌktɪvlɪ] **adv** efficacement, de manière rentable; *spend time* de façon productive.

productivity [ˌprɒdʌkˈtɪvɪtɪ] **1 n** (*NonC: Econ, Ind*) productivité *f*. **2 comp** *fall, increase* de productivité **►productivity agreement** (*Brit*) accord *m* de productivité **►productivity bonus** prime *f* à la productivité.

prof* [prɒf] **n** (*Univ*) (**abbr of professor**) prof* *m*, professeur *m*. (*on envelope*) **Prof. C. Smith** Monsieur C. Smith.

profanation [ˌprɒfəˈneɪʃən] **n** profanation *f*.

profane [prəˈfeɪn] **1 adj** (*secular, lay*) profane; (*pej*) *language etc* impie, sacrilège; *see* **sacred**. **2 vt** profaner.

profanity [prəˈfænɪtɪ] **n** (*NonC: see* **profane**) nature *f or* caractère *m* profane; (*pej*) impiété *f*; (*oath*) juron *m*, blasphème *m*. **he uttered a stream of profanities** il proféra un chapelet de jurons.

profess [prəˈfes] **vt a** professer, déclarer, affirmer (*that* que); *faith, religion* professer, (*publicly*) professer, faire profession de; *an opinion, respect, hatred* professer. **she ~ed total ignorance** elle a affirmé ne rien savoir du tout; **he ~ed himself satisfied** il s'est déclaré satisfait; **she ~es to be 39** elle se donne 39 ans, elle prétend avoir 39 ans; **he ~es to know all about it** il déclare *or* prétend tout savoir sur ce sujet; **I don't ~ to be an expert** je ne prétends pas être expert en la matière. **b** (*frm: have as one's profession*) **to ~ law/medicine** exercer la profession d'avocat/de médecin. **c** (*frm: Univ: teach*) professer.

professed [prəˈfest] **adj** *atheist, communist etc* déclaré; (*Rel*) *monk, nun* profès (*f* -esse).

professedly [prəˈfesɪdlɪ] **adv** de son (*or* leur *etc*) propre aveu, d'après lui (*or* eux *etc*); (*allegedly*) soi-disant, prétendument.

profession [prəˈfeʃən] **n a** (*calling*) profession *f*; (*body of people*) (membres *mpl* d'une) profession. **by ~** de son (*or* mon *etc*) métier; **the medical ~** (*calling*) la profession de médecin, la médecine; (*doctors collectively*) le corps médical, les médecins *mpl*; **the ~s** les professions *fpl* libérales; *see* **learned** *etc.* **b** (*declaration*) profession *f*, déclaration *f*. **~ of faith** profession de foi; *[monk, nun]* **to make one's ~** faire sa profession, prononcer ses vœux.

professional [prəˈfeʃənl] **1 adj a** *skill, organization, training, etiquette* professionnel. **he is a ~ man** il exerce une profession libérale; **the ~ classes** les (membres *mpl* des) professions libérales; **to take ~ advice** (*medical/legal*) consulter un médecin/un avocat; (*on practical problem*) consulter un professionnel *or* un homme de métier; **it is not ~ practice to do so** faire cela est contraire à l'usage professionnel; (*US*) **~ school** (*Univ: faculty*) faculté *f* de droit *or* de médecine; (*business school*) grande école commerciale.

b (*by profession*) *writer, politician* professionnel, de profession; *footballer, tennis player* professionnel; *diplomat, soldier* de carrière; (*fig: of high standard*) *play, piece of work* de haute qualité, excellent. **~ army** armée *f* de métier; **~ football/tennis** *etc* football/tennis *etc* professionnel; (*Sport*) **to turn** *or* **go ~** passer professionnel; **to have a very ~ attitude to one's work** prendre son travail très au sérieux; **it is well up to ~ standards** c'est d'un niveau de professionnel; (*Ftbl*) **~ foul** faute délibérée.

2 n (*all senses*) professionnel(le) *m(f)*.

professionalism [prəˈfeʃnəlɪzəm] **n** *[writer, actor etc]* professionnalisme *m*; (*Sport*) professionnalisme; *[play, piece of work]* excellence *f*, haute qualité.

professionally [prəˈfeʃnəlɪ] **adv** professionnellement, de manière professionnelle; (*Sport*) *play* en professionnel. **he is known ~ as Joe Bloggs** dans la profession *or* le métier il est connu sous le nom de Joe Bloggs; **I know him only ~** je n'ai que des rapports de travail avec lui, je ne suis en rapport avec lui que pour le travail; **I never met him ~** je n'ai jamais eu de rapports de travail avec lui; (*fig*) **he did that very ~** il a fait cela de manière très professionnelle; **to be ~ qualified** être diplômé; **he was acting ~ when he did that** il agissait dans le cadre de ses fonctions officielles *or* à titre officiel quand il a fait cela; **he had it ~ built** il l'a fait construire par un professionnel; **the play was ~ produced** la mise en scène (de la pièce) était d'un professionnel; **have you ever sung ~?** avez-vous jamais été chanteur professionnel?

professor [prəˈfesəʳ] **n a** (*Univ: Brit, US*) professeur *m* (titulaire d'une chaire); (*US: teacher*) professeur. **~ of French, French ~** professeur (de la chaire) de français; (*in letters*) **Dear P~ Smith** monsieur, (*less formally*) Cher Monsieur, (*if known to writer*) Cher Professeur; (*on envelope*) **P~ C. Smith** Monsieur C. Smith; *see* **assistant** *etc.* **b** (*US* ‡*: iro*) maestro *m*, maître *m*.

professorial [ˌprɒfəˈsɔːrɪəl] **adj** professoral.

professorship [prəˈfesəʃɪp] **n** chaire *f* (*of* de). **he has a ~** il est titulaire d'une chaire.

proffer [ˈprɒfəʳ] **vt** *object, arm* offrir, tendre; *a remark, suggestion* faire; *one's thanks, apologies* offrir, présenter. **to ~ one's hand to sb** tendre la main à qn.

proficiency [prəˈfɪʃənsɪ] **n** (grande) compétence *f* (*in* en).

proficient [prəˈfɪʃənt] **adj** (très) compétent (*in* en).

profile [ˈprəʊfaɪl] **1 n a** *[head, building, hill etc]* profil *m* (*also Archit*). **in ~** de profil. **b** (*fig: description*) *[person]* profil *m*, portrait *m*; *[situation etc]* profil *m*, esquisse *f*. **c** (*graph or table*) profil *m*. **d to keep a low ~** essayer de ne pas (trop) se faire remarquer, adopter une attitude discrète (*see also* **low**); **to keep a high ~** (*in media etc*) garder la vedette; (*be seen on streets etc*) être très en vue *or* en évidence.

2 vt a (*show in ~*) profiler (*also Archit*). **b** (*fig*) *person* établir le profil de, brosser le portrait de; *situation* établir le profil de, tracer une esquisse de.

profit [ˈprɒfɪt] **1 n** (*Comm*) profit *m*, bénéfice *m*; (*fig*) profit, avantage *m*. **~ and loss** profits et pertes (*see also* **2**); **gross/net ~** bénéfice brut/net; **to make** *or* **turn a ~** faire un bénéfice *or* des bénéfices; **to make a ~ of £100** faire un bénéfice de 100 livres (*on sth* sur qch); **to sell sth at a ~** vendre qch à profit; **to show** *or* **yield a ~** rapporter (un bénéfice); (*lit, fig*) **there's not much ~ in doing** on ne gagne pas grand-chose à faire; (*Insurance*) **with ~s policy** police *f* (d'assurance) avec participation aux bénéfices; (*fig*) **with ~** avec profit, avec fruit; (*fig*) **to turn sth to ~** mettre à profit qch, tirer parti de qch.

2 comp ►profit and loss account (*Book-keeping*) compte *m* de profits et pertes **►profit-making** rentable; **a profit-making/non-profit-making organization** une organisation à but lucratif/non lucratif **►profit margin** marge *f* bénéficiaire **►profit motive** recherche *f* du profit **►profit-seeking** à but lucratif **►profit-sharing** (*Ind*) participation *f* aux bénéfices; **profit-sharing scheme** système *m* de participation (aux bénéfices) **►profit squeeze** compression *f* des bénéfices **►profit taking** (*St Ex*) prise *f* de bénéfices, vente *f* d'actions avec bénéfice.

3 vi (*fig*) tirer un profit *or* un avantage. **to ~ by** *or* **from sth** tirer avantage *or* profit de qch, bien profiter de qch; **I can't see how he hopes to ~ (by it)** je ne vois pas ce qu'il espère en retirer *or* y gagner.

4 vt (†† *or liter*) profiter à. **it will ~ him nothing** cela ne lui profitera en rien.

profitability [ˌprɒfɪtəˈbɪlɪtɪ] **n** (*Comm etc*) rentabilité *f*; (*fig*) rentabilité, caractère profitable *or* fructueux.

profitable [ˈprɒfɪtəbl] **adj** (*Comm etc*) *deal, sale, investment* rentable, lucratif, payant; (*fig*) *scheme, agreement, contract* avantageux, rentable; *meeting, discussion, visit* fructueux, payant (*fig*), profitable. **we don't stock them any more as they were not ~** nous ne les stockons plus parce qu'ils n'étaient pas rentables; **it was a very ~ half-hour** cela a été une demi-heure très fructueuse *or* payante *or* profitable; **you would find it ~ to read this** vous trouveriez la lecture de ceci utile *or* profitable, c'est avec profit que vous liriez ceci.

profitably [ˈprɒfɪtəblɪ] **adv** *sell* à profit; *deal* avec profit; (*fig*) avec profit, avec fruit, utilement.

profiteer [ˌprɒfɪˈtɪəʳ] (*pej*) **1 n** profiteur *m* (*pej*), mercanti *m* (*pej*). **2 vi** faire des bénéfices excessifs.

profiteering [ˌprɒfɪˈtɪərɪŋ] **n** (*pej*) réalisation *f* de bénéfices excessifs.

profitless [ˈprɒfɪtlɪs] **adj** (*lit, fig*) sans profit.

profitlessly [ˈprɒfɪtlɪslɪ] **adv** (*lit, fig*) sans profit.

profligacy [ˈprɒflɪgəsɪ] **n** (*debauchery*) débauche *f*, libertinage *m*; (*extravagance*) extrême prodigalité *f*.

profligate [ˈprɒflɪgɪt] **1 adj** (*debauched*) *person, behaviour* débauché, libertin, dissolu; *life* de débauche, de libertinage; (*extravagant*) extrêmement prodigue. **2 n** débauché(e) *m(f)*, libertin(e) *m(f)*.

pro-form [ˈprəʊˌfɔːm] **n** (*Ling*) proforme *f*.

pro forma [ˈprəʊˈfɔːmə] **1 adj** pro forma *inv*. **2 n** (*also* **~ invoice**) facture *f* pro forma; (*also* **~ letter**) (formule *f* de) lettre toute faite. **3 adv** selon les règles.

profound [prəˈfaʊnd] **adj** (*all senses*) profond.

profoundly [prəˈfaʊndlɪ] **adv** profondément.

profundity [prəˈfʌndɪtɪ] **n** profondeur *f*.

profuse [prəˈfjuːs] **adj** *vegetation, bleeding* abondant; *thanks, praise, apologies* profus, multiple. **~ in** prodigue de; **to be ~ in one's thanks/excuses** se confondre en remerciements/excuses.

profusely [prəˈfjuːslɪ] **adv** *grow etc* à profusion, à foison, en abondance; *bleed, sweat* abondamment; *thank* avec effusion. **to apologize ~** se confondre en excuses; **to praise sb ~** se répandre en éloges sur qn.

profusion [prəˈfjuːʒən] **n** profusion *f*, abondance *f* (*of* de). **in ~** à profusion, à foison.

prog.* [prɒg] **n** (*Brit: TV etc*) (**abbr of programme**) émission *f*, programme *m*.

progenitor [prəʊˈdʒenɪtəʳ] **n** (*lit*) ancêtre *m*; (*fig*) auteur *m*.

progeny [ˈprɒdʒɪnɪ] **n** (*offspring*) progéniture *f*; (*descendants*) lignée *f*, descendants *mpl*.

progesterone [prəʊˈdʒestəˌrəʊn] **n** progestérone *f*.

prognathous [prɒgˈneɪθəs] **adj** prognathe.

prognosis [prɒgˈnəʊsɪs] **n, pl prognoses** [prɒgˈnəʊsiːz] pronostic *m*.

prognostic [prɒgˈnɒstɪk] **n** (*frm*) présage *m*, signe *m* avant-coureur.

prognosticate [prɒgˈnɒstɪkeɪt] **vt** pronostiquer, prédire, présager.

prognostication [prɒgˌnɒstɪˈkeɪʃən] **n** pronostic *m*.

program [ˈprəʊgræm] **1 n a** (*Comput*) programme *m*. **b** (*US*) programme *m*. **2 comp** (*Comput*) *specification, costs* du *or* d'un programme. **3 vi** (*Comput*) établir un (*or* des) programme(s). **4 vt** (*Comput*) programmer. **to ~ sth to do ...** programmer qch de façon à faire ... .

programmable [ˈprəʊgræməbl] **adj** (*Comput*) programmable.

programme [ˈprəʊgræm] (*Brit*) **1 n a** (*most senses*) programme *m*; (*Rad, TV: broadcast*) émission *f* (*on* sur; *about* au sujet de); *[course]* emploi *m* du temps; (*Rad: station*) poste *m*; (*TV: station*) chaîne *f*. **what's the ~ for today?** (*during course etc*) quel est l'emploi du temps aujourd'hui?; (*fig*) qu'est-ce qu'on fait aujourd'hui?, quel est le programme des réjouissances aujourd'hui?*; **in the ~ for the day** parmi les activités *fpl* de la journée; **what's on the ~?** qu'est-ce qu'il y a au programme?; **detoxification ~** cure *f* de détoxification; **what's on the other ~?** (*TV*) qu'y a-t-il sur l'autre chaîne?; (*Rad*) qu'y a-t-il sur l'autre poste?; (*Rad, TV*) **details of the morning's ~s** le programme de la matinée, les détails des émissions de la matinée; *see* **request** *etc*.

b (*Comput*) = **program**.

2 comp ▸programme editor (*Rad, TV*) éditorialiste *mf* **▸programme music** musique *f* à programme **▸programme notes** (*Mus*) notes *fpl* sur le programme **▸programme seller** (*Theat*) vendeur *m*, -euse *f* de programmes.

3 vt a *washing machine etc* programmer (*to do* pour faire); *problem, task* programmer; (*fig*) *person* conditionner. **~d learning** enseignement programmé; **the broadcast was ~d for Sunday evening/for 8 o'clock** l'émission était programmée pour dimanche soir/pour 8 heures; **the meeting was ~d to start at 7** le début de la réunion était prévu pour 19 heures.

b (*Comput*) = **program**.

programmer [ˈprəʊgræməʳ] **n** (*person: also* **computer ~**) programmeur *m*, -euse *f*; (*device*) programmateur *m*.

programming [ˈprəʊgræmɪŋ] **1 n** (*also* **computer ~**) programmation *f*. **2 comp** *error, language etc* de programmation.

progress [ˈprəʊgres] **1 n a** (*NonC: lit, fig*) progrès *m(pl)*. **in the name of ~** au nom du progrès; **we made slow ~ through the mud** nous avons avancé lentement dans la boue; **we are making good ~ in our search for a solution** nos travaux pour trouver une solution progressent de manière satisfaisante; **we have made little/no ~** nous n'avons guère fait de progrès/fait aucun progrès; **he is making ~** *[student etc]* il fait des progrès, il est en progrès; *[patient]* son état (de santé) s'améliore; **the ~ of events** le cours des événements; **the meeting is in ~** la réunion est en cours *or* a déjà commencé; **while the meeting was in ~** pendant que la réunion se déroulait; **the work in ~** les travaux en cours; **"silence: exam in ~"** "silence: examen"; **to be in full ~** battre son plein.

b (*††: journey*) voyage *m*; *see* **pilgrim**.

2 comp ▸progress board tableau *m* de planning **▸progress chaser** responsable *mf* du suivi (d'un projet) **▸progress chasing** suivi *m* (d'un projet) **▸progress payment** (*Fin*) acompte *m* **▸progress report** (*gen*) compte rendu *m* (*on* de); (*Med*) bulletin *m* de santé; (*Scol*) bulletin *m* scolaire; (*Admin*) état *m* périodique; **to make a progress report on** (*gen*) rendre compte de l'évolution de; (*Scol: on pupil*) rendre compte des progrès de; (*Med: on patient*) rendre compte de l'évolution de l'état de santé de; (*Admin*) dresser un état périodique de.

3 [prəˈgres] **vi** (*lit, fig*) aller, avancer (*towards* vers); *[student etc]* faire des progrès, progresser; *[patient]* aller mieux; *[search, investigations, researches, studies etc]* progresser, avancer. **matters are ~ing slowly** les choses progressent lentement; **as the game ~ed** à mesure que la partie se déroulait; **while the discussions were ~ing** pendant que les discussions se déroulaient.

progression [prəˈgreʃən] **n** (*gen, Math*) progression *f*. **by arithmetical/geometrical ~** selon une progression arithmétique/géométrique; **it's a logical ~** c'est une suite logique.

progressive [prəˈgresɪv] **1 adj a** *movement, taxation, disease, improvement* progressif; *idea, party, person, outlook* progressiste (*also Pol*); *age* de *or* du progrès. **in ~ stages** par degrés, par étapes; **~ education** éducation *f* nouvelle. **b** (*Gram, Phon*) progressif. **2 n a** (*Pol etc*) progressiste *mf*. **b** (*Gram*) temps *m* progressif.

progressively [prəˈgresɪvlɪ] **adv** progressivement, par degrés, petit à petit, graduellement.

progressiveness [prəˈgresɪvnɪs] **n** progressivité *f*.

progressivity [ˌprəʊgreˈsɪvɪtɪ] **n** progressivité *f*.

prohibit [prəˈhɪbɪt] **vt a** (*forbid*) interdire, défendre (*sb from doing* à qn de faire); (*Admin, Jur etc*) *weapons, drugs, swearing* prohiber. **smoking ~ed** défense de fumer; **feeding the animals is ~ed** il est interdit *or* défendu de donner à manger aux animaux; **pedestrians are ~ed from using this bridge** il est interdit aux piétons d'utiliser ce pont, l'usage de ce pont est interdit aux piétons. **b** (*prevent*) empêcher (*sb from doing* qn de faire). **my health ~s me from swimming** ma santé m'empêche de nager, pour des raisons de santé il m'est interdit *or* défendu de nager.

prohibition [ˌprəʊɪˈbɪʃən] **1 n** (*see* **prohibit**) prohibition *f*; interdiction *f*, défense *f*; (*esp US: against alcohol*) prohibition. **2 comp** (*US*) *laws, party* prohibitionniste.

prohibitionism [ˌprəʊɪˈbɪʃənɪzəm] **n** prohibitionnisme *m*.

prohibitionist [ˌprəʊɪˈbɪʃənɪst] **adj, n** prohibitionniste *(mf)*.

prohibitive [prəˈhɪbɪtɪv] **adj** *price, tax, laws* prohibitif.

prohibitively [prəˈhɪbɪtɪvlɪ] **adv**: **~ expensive** à un *or* des prix prohibitif(s).

prohibitory [prəˈhɪbɪtərɪ] **adj** prohibitif.

project [ˈprɒdʒekt] **1 n a** (*gen*) projet *m*; (*plan, scheme*) projet *m*, plan *m*, programme *m* (*to do, for doing* pour faire); (*undertaking*) opération *f*, entreprise *f*; (*Constr*) grands travaux *mpl*. **they are studying the ~ for the new road** ils étudient le projet de construction de la nouvelle route; **the whole ~ will cost 2 million** l'opération *or* l'entreprise tout entière coûtera 2 millions.

b (*study*) étude *f* (*on* de); (*Scol*) dossier *m* (*on* sur); (*Univ*) mémoire *m* (*on* sur).

c (*US: also* **housing ~**) cité *f*, lotissement *m*.

2 comp *budget, staff* de l'opération, de l'entreprise **▸project leader/manager** chef *m* de projet, maître *m* d'œuvre.

3 [prəˈdʒekt] **vt a** (*gen, Psych, Math*) projeter. (*Psych*) **to ~ o.s.** se projeter; **she ~ed an image of innocence** elle projetait *or* présentait l'image de l'innocence même; **in view of the ~ed contract** étant donné le projet de contrat; **to ~ quantities/costs** *etc* **from sth** prévoir la quantité/le coût *etc* à partir de qch.

b (*propel*) propulser. **to ~ a rocket into space** propulser une fusée dans l'espace.

c (*cause to jut out*) *part of building etc* projeter en avant.

4 [prəˈdʒekt] **vi a** (*jut out*) former *or* faire saillie, être en saillie, saillir. **to ~ over sth** surplomber qch; **to ~ into sth** s'avancer (en saillie) dans qch.

b (*show personality*) **how does he ~?** quelle image de lui-même présente-t-il *or* projette-t-il?, quelle impression donne-t-il?

c (*with voice: of actor, singer*) projeter sa (*or* leur *etc*) voix. **his voice ~s very well** sa voix porte vraiment bien.

projectile [prəˈdʒektaɪl] **n** projectile *m*.

projecting [prəˈdʒektɪŋ] **adj** *construction* saillant, en saillie; *tooth* qui avance.

projection [prəˈdʒekʃən] **1 n a** (*gen*) projection *f*; (*of rocket*) propulsion *f*; (*from opinion polls, sample votes etc*) prévisions *fpl* par extrapolation, projections *fpl*. **b** (*overhang*) saillie *f*, ressaut *m*. **2 comp ▸projection booth, projection room** (*Cine*) cabine *f* de

projection.
projectionist [prəˈdʒekʃənɪst] n projectionniste *mf*.
projective [prəˈdʒektɪv] adj projectif.
projector [prəˈdʒektəʳ] n (*Cine etc*) projecteur *m*.
prolactin [prəʊˈlæktɪn] n prolactine *f*.
prolapse [ˈprəʊlæps] 1 n (*gen*) descente *f* d'organe, ptose *f*, prolapsus *m*; *[womb]* descente *f* de matrice *or* de l'utérus. 2 vi descendre.
prole* [prəʊl] adj, n (*pej*) (abbr of **proletarian**) prolo* (*m*).
proletarian [ˌprəʊləˈtɛərɪən] 1 n prolétaire *mf*. 2 adj *class, party* prolétarien; *life, ways, mentality* de prolétaire.
proletarianize [ˌprəʊləˈtɛərɪənaɪz] vt prolétariser.
proletariat [ˌprəʊləˈtɛərɪət] n prolétariat *m*.
pro-life [ˌprəʊˈlaɪf] adj contre l'avortement.
proliferate [prəˈlɪfəreɪt] vi proliférer.
proliferation [prəˌlɪfəˈreɪʃən] n prolifération *f*.
proliferous [prəˈlɪfərəs] adj prolifère.
prolific [prəˈlɪfɪk] adj prolifique.
prolix [ˈprəʊlɪks] adj prolixe.
prolixity [prəʊˈlɪksɪtɪ] n prolixité *f*.
prologue [ˈprəʊlɒg] n (*Literat etc*) prologue *m* (*to* de); (*fig*) prologue (*to* à).
prolong [prəˈlɒŋ] vt prolonger. (*fig*) **I won't ~ the agony** je vais abréger tes souffrances.
prolongation [ˌprəʊlɒŋˈgeɪʃən] n (*in space*) prolongement *m*; (*in time*) prolongation *f*.
prolonged [prəˈlɒŋd] adj long, de longue durée, prolongé; (*period*) long. **~ leave of absence** congé *m* prolongé *or* de longue durée; **~ sick leave** congé *m* de longue maladie *or* de maladie prolongé; **after a ~ absence** après une longue absence *or* une absence prolongée.
prom* [prɒm] n abbr of **promenade** a (*Brit: by sea*) promenade *f*, front *m* de mer. b (*Brit*) **~s** = **promenade concerts**; *see* **promenade 2**. c (*US*) = **promenade 1c**.
promenade [ˌprɒmɪˈnɑːd] 1 n a (*walk*) promenade *f*. b (*place*) (*by sea*) promenade *f*, front *m* de mer; (*in park etc*) avenue *f*; (*in theatre, hall etc*) promenoir *m*. c (*US*) bal *m* d'étudiants (*or* de lycéens). 2 comp ▸**Promenade Concerts** (*Brit*) série *f* de concerts de musique classique (*donnés à Londres etc*) ▸**promenade deck** (*Naut*) pont *m* promenade. 3 vi (*frm: walk*) se promener. 4 vt (*frm*) *person* promener; *avenue* se promener le long de.
promenader* [ˌprɒmɪˈnɑːdəʳ] n (*Brit Mus*) auditeur *m*, -trice *f* d'un "promenade concert"; *see* **promenade**.
Prometheus [prəˈmiːθjuːs] n Prométhée *m*.
promethium [prəˈmiːθɪəm] n prométhéum *m*.
prominence [ˈprɒmɪnəns] n (*see* **prominent**) proéminence *f*, aspect saillant *or* frappant *or* marquant; importance *f*. **to bring sth/sb into ~** mettre qch/qn en vue, attirer l'attention sur qch/qn; **to come into ~** prendre de l'importance.
prominent [ˈprɒmɪnənt] adj *ridge, structure, nose* proéminent; *cheekbones* saillant; *tooth* qui avance; (*fig: striking*) *pattern, markings* frappant; *feature* marquant; (*fig: outstanding*) *person* important, bien en vue. **he is a ~ member of ...** c'est un membre important de ...; **she is ~ in London literary circles** elle est très en vue dans les cercles littéraires londoniens; **he was very ~ in ..., he played a ~ part in ...** il a joué un rôle important dans ...; **to put sth in a ~ position** mettre qch bien en vue *or* en valeur; (*fig*) **he occupies a ~ position in ...** il occupe une position importante *or* en vue dans ... .
prominently [ˈprɒmɪnəntlɪ] adv *display, place, set* bien en vue. **his name figured ~ in the case** on a beaucoup entendu parler de lui dans l'affaire.
promiscuity [ˌprɒmɪsˈkjuːɪtɪ] n a (*pej: sexual*) promiscuité sexuelle. b (*gen*) promiscuité *f*.
promiscuous [prəˈmɪskjʊəs] adj a (*pej: in sexual matters*) *person* de mœurs faciles *or* légères; *conduct* léger, libre, immoral; **he/she is very ~** il/elle change sans arrêt de partenaire, il/elle couche avec n'importe qui. b (*disorderly, mixed*) *collection, heap* confus.
promiscuously [prəˈmɪskjʊəslɪ] adv a (*pej*) *behave* immoralement. b *heap, collect* confusément.
promiscuousness [prəˈmɪskjʊəsnɪs] = **promiscuity**.
promise [ˈprɒmɪs] 1 n a (*undertaking*) promesse *f*. **~ of marriage** promesse de mariage; **under (a *or* the) ~ of** sous promesse de; **to make sb a ~** faire une promesse à qn (*to do* de faire); **is it a ~?** c'est promis?; **to keep one's ~** tenir sa promesse; **to hold *or* keep sb to his ~** contraindre qn à tenir sa promesse, faire tenir sa promesse à qn; (*dismissively*) **~s, ~s!** oh, on dit ça, on dit ça!
b (*hope*) promesse(s) *f(pl)*, espérance(s) *f(pl)*. **a young man of ~** un jeune homme plein de promesses *or* qui promet; **he shows great ~** il donne de grandes espérances; **it holds out a ~ of peace** cela promet *or* fait espérer la paix.
2 vt a promettre (*sth to sb* qch à qn, *sb to do* à qn de faire, *that* que). **I ~ (you)!** je vous le promets!; **"I will help you" she ~d** "je vous aiderai" promit-elle; **I can't ~ anything** je ne peux rien (vous) promettre; (*fig*) **to ~ sb the earth *or* the moon** promettre monts et merveilles à qn, promettre la lune à qn; **to ~ o.s. (to do) sth** se promettre (de faire) qch.
b (*fig*) promettre, annoncer. **those clouds ~ rain** ces nuages annoncent la pluie; **they ~ us rain tomorrow** ils nous ont promis *or* annoncé de la pluie pour demain; **it ~s to be hot today** il va sûrement faire chaud aujourd'hui; **this ~s to be difficult** ça promet d'être *or* ça s'annonce difficile.
c (*assure*) assurer. **he did say so, I ~ you** il l'a vraiment dit, je vous assure.
3 vi a promettre. **(will you) ~?** (c'est) promis?, juré?; **I can't ~ but I'll do my best** je ne (vous) promets rien mais je ferai de mon mieux.
b (*fig*) **to ~ well** *[person]* promettre, être plein de promesses; *[situation, event]* être plein de promesses, être prometteur; *[crop, business]* s'annoncer bien; *[first book]* promettre, être prometteur; **this doesn't ~ well** ce n'est guère prometteur, ça ne s'annonce pas bien.
promised [ˈprɒmɪst] adj promis. **the P~ Land** la Terre Promise.
promising [ˈprɒmɪsɪŋ] adj a (*encouraging*) *situation, sign* prometteur, qui promet, plein de promesses. **the future is ~** l'avenir s'annonce bien; **that's ~** c'est prometteur; (*iro*) ça promet! (*iro*); **it doesn't look very ~** ça ne semble guère prometteur; (*of scheme, plan etc*) ça m'étonnerait que ça marche (*subj*), ça ne se présente pas bien. b (*full of promise*) *person* prometteur, plein de promesses, qui promet. **we have 2 ~ candidates** nous avons 2 candidats prometteurs; **he is a ~ pianist** c'est un pianiste d'avenir.
promisingly [ˈprɒmɪsɪŋlɪ] adv d'une façon prometteuse. **it began quite ~** tout s'annonçait bien, c'était bien parti; **it's going quite ~** c'est prometteur, ça marche bien.
promissory [ˈprɒmɪsərɪ] adj: **~ note** billet *m* à ordre.
promo [ˈprəʊməʊ] n, pl **~s** a (*Comm: promotional material*) matériel *m* promotionnel. b (*US Comm*) (abbr of **promotion**) promotion *f*.
promontory [ˈprɒməntrɪ] n promontoire *m*.
promote [prəˈməʊt] vt a *person* promouvoir (*to* à). **to be ~d** être promu, monter en grade; **he was ~d (to) colonel *or* to the rank of colonel** il a été promu (au grade de) colonel; (*Ftbl etc*) **they've been ~d to the first division** ils sont montés en première division. b (*encourage*) *cause, cooperation, plan, sales, product* promouvoir; *trade* promouvoir, développer, favoriser, encourager; (*Comm*) *firm, company, business, campaign* lancer; (*Parl*) *bill* présenter.
promoter [prəˈməʊtəʳ] n *[sport]* organisateur *m*, -trice *f*; (*Comm*) *[product]* promoteur *m* de vente; *[business, company]* fondateur *m*, -trice *f*.
promotion [prəˈməʊʃən] 1 n a promotion *f*, avancement *m*. **to get ~** obtenir de l'avancement, être promu. b (*NonC: see* **promote b**) promotion *f*; développement *m*; lancement *m*; présentation *f*. **(sales) ~** promotion des ventes. c (*advertising material*) réclames *fpl*, publicité *f*. d (*US Scol*) passage *m* de classe. 2 comp ▸**promotion opportunities, promotion prospects** possibilités *fpl* d'avancement *or* de promotion.
promotional [prəˈməʊʃənl] adj (*Comm*) promotionnel, publicitaire.
prompt [prɒmpt] 1 adj a (*speedy*) *action* rapide, prompt; *delivery, reply, service* rapide. **~ payment** paiement *m* rapide; (*Comm*) paiement dans les délais; **they were ~ to offer their services** ils ont été prompts à offrir leurs services, ils ont offert leurs services sans tarder.
b (*punctual*) ponctuel, à l'heure.
2 adv ponctuellement. **at 6 o'clock ~** à 6 heures pile *or* tapantes *or* sonnantes; **I want it on May 6th ~** je le veux le 6 mai sans faute *or* au plus tard.
3 vt a *person* pousser, inciter (*to do* à faire); *protest, reaction* provoquer, entraîner, être à l'origine de. **I felt ~ed to protest** cela m'a incité à protester, je me suis senti obligé de protester; **he was ~ed by a desire to see justice done** il était animé *or* poussé par un désir de voir la justice triompher; **it ~s the thought that ...** cela incite à penser que ..., cela vous fait penser que ...; **a feeling of regret ~ed by the sight of ...** un sentiment de regret provoqué *or* déclenché par la vue de ... .
b (*Theat*) souffler.
4 n a (*Theat*) **to give sb a ~** souffler une réplique à qn.
b (*Comput: on screen*) (message *m* de) guidage *m*.
5 comp ▸**prompt box** (*Theat*) trou *m* du souffleur ▸**prompt side** (*Brit*) côté *m* cour; (*US*) côté jardin; **off prompt side** (*Brit*) côté jardin; (*US*) côté cour.
prompter [ˈprɒmptəʳ] n (*Theat*) souffleur *m*, -euse *f*.
prompting [ˈprɒmptɪŋ] n incitation *f*. **he did it at my ~** il l'a fait à mon instigation; **he did it without (any) ~** il l'a fait de son propre chef.
promptitude [ˈprɒmptɪtjuːd] n promptitude *f*, empressement *m* (*in doing* à faire); (*punctuality*) ponctualité *f*.
promptly [ˈprɒmptlɪ] adv a (*speedily*) rapidement, promptement, avec promptitude. **to pay ~** payer sans tarder; (*Comm*) payer recta *or* dans les délais. b (*punctually*) ponctuellement. **he arrived ~ at 3** il est arrivé ponctuellement à 3 heures. c (*thereupon*) là-dessus, aussi sec*. **she refused and he ~ hit her** elle a refusé et là-dessus *or* aussi sec* il l'a frappée.
promptness [ˈprɒmptnɪs] = **promptitude**.
promulgate [ˈprɒməlgeɪt] vt *law* promulguer; *idea, doctrine, creed* répandre, disséminer.
promulgation [ˌprɒməlˈgeɪʃən] n (*see* **promulgate**) promulgation *f*; dissémination *f*.

prone [prəʊn] adj a (*face down*) (couché) sur le ventre, étendu face contre terre, prostré. b (*liable*) prédisposé, enclin, sujet (*to sth* à qch, *to do* à faire).
proneness [ˈprəʊnnɪs] n tendance *f*, prédisposition *f* (*to sth* à qch, *to do* à faire).
prong [prɒŋ] n *[fork]* dent *f*; *[antler]* pointe *f*.
pronged [prɒŋd] adj à dents.
-pronged [prɒŋd] adj ending in comps: **three-pronged** *fork* à trois dents; (*Mil etc*) *attack, advance* sur trois fronts, triple.
pronominal [prəʊˈnɒmɪnl] adj pronominal.
pronoun [ˈprəʊnaʊn] n pronom *m*.
pronounce [prəˈnaʊns] 1 vt a *word etc* prononcer. **how is it ~d?** comment ça se prononce?; **the "k" in "knot" is not ~d** on ne prononce pas le "k" dans "knot", le "k" dans "knot" est muet. b déclarer, prononcer (*that* que). (*Jur*) **to ~ sentence** prononcer la sentence; **they ~d him unfit to drive** ils l'ont déclaré inapte à la conduite; **he ~d himself in favour of the suggestion** il s'est prononcé *or* il s'est déclaré en faveur de la suggestion. 2 vi se prononcer (*on* sur, *for* en faveur de, *against* contre); (*Jur*) prononcer (*for* en faveur de, *against* contre), rendre un arrêt.
pronounceable [prəˈnaʊnsəbl] adj prononçable.
pronounced [prəˈnaʊnst] adj prononcé, marqué.
pronouncement [prəˈnaʊnsmənt] n déclaration *f*.
pronto* [ˈprɒntəʊ] adv tout de suite, illico*.
pronunciation [prəˌnʌnsɪˈeɪʃən] n prononciation *f*.
proof [pruːf] 1 n a (*gen, Jur, Math etc*) preuve *f*. (*Jur etc*) **~ of identity** papiers *mpl or* pièce(s) *f(pl)* d'identité; (*Jur*) **the burden of ~ lies with the prosecution** la charge de la preuve incombe au ministère public; **by way of ~** en guise de preuve, comme preuve, pour preuve; **as (a) ~ of, in ~ of** pour preuve de; **I've got ~ that he did it** j'ai la preuve *or* je peux prouver qu'il l'a fait; **it is ~ that he is honest** c'est la preuve qu'il est honnête; (*fig*) **he showed** *or* **gave ~ of great courage** il a fait preuve *or* il a témoigné de beaucoup de courage; *see* **positive**.
b (*test*) épreuve *f*. **to put sth/sb to the ~** mettre qch/qn à l'épreuve, éprouver qch/qn; (*Prov*) **the ~ of the pudding is in the eating** c'est à l'usage que l'on peut juger de la qualité d'une chose.
c *[book, pamphlet, engraving, photograph]* épreuve *f*. **to pass the ~s** donner le bon à tirer; **to read** *or* **correct the ~s** corriger les épreuves; **the book is in ~** le livre est au stade des épreuves; *see* **galley, page**[1] *etc*.
d (*of alcohol*) teneur *f* en alcool. **this whisky is 70 ° ~** ≃ ce whisky titre 40 ° d'alcool *or* 40 ° Gay Lussac; **under/over ~** moins de/plus de la teneur normale *or* exigée en alcool.
2 comp ▸**proofread** corriger les épreuves de ▸**proofreader** correcteur *m*, -trice *f* d'épreuves *or* d'imprimerie ▸**proofreading** correction *f* des épreuves ▸**proof sheets** épreuves *fpl* ▸**proof spirit** alcool *m* à 57° ▸**proof stage: at proof stage** au stade des épreuves.
3 adj: **~ against** *bullets, time, wear, erosion* à l'épreuve de; *temptation, suggestion* insensible à.
4 vt a *fabric, anorak, tent* imperméabiliser.
b (*Typ etc*) corriger les épreuves de.
...proof [pruːf] adj endings in comps à l'épreuve de; *see* **bullet, fool**[1] *etc*.
prop[1] [prɒp] 1 n a support *m*; (*for wall, in mine, tunnel etc*) étai *m*; (*for clothes-line*) perche *f*; (*for vines, hops etc*) échalas *m*; (*for beans, peas*) rame *f*; (*for seedlings*) tuteur *m*; (*fig*) soutien *m*, appui *m* (*to, for* de). **his presence was a great ~ to her morale** elle trouvait beaucoup de réconfort dans sa présence, sa présence lui était d'un grand réconfort (moral); (*fig*) **this drug is a ~ to many people** ce médicament rend la vie supportable à beacoup de gens.
b (*Rugby*) **~ (forward)** pilier *m*.
2 vt (*also* **~ up**) (*lean*) *ladder, cycle* appuyer (*against* contre); (*support, shore up*) *tunnel, wall, building* étayer; *clothes-line, lid* caler; *vine, hops* échalasser; *beans, peas* mettre une rame à; *seedlings* mettre un tuteur à; (*fig*) *régime* maintenir; *business, company* soutenir, renflouer; *organization* soutenir, patronner; (*Fin*) *the pound* venir au secours de. **to ~ o.s. (up) against** se caler contre, s'adosser à; **he managed to ~ the box open** il réussit à maintenir la boîte ouverte.
prop[2] [prɒp] n (*Theat*) abbr of **property 1c**.
prop[3]* [prɒp] n (*Aviat*) abbr of **propeller**.
prop. (*Comm*) abbr of **proprietor**.
propaganda [ˌprɒpəˈgændə] 1 n propagande *f*. 2 comp *leaflet, campaign* de propagande.
propagandist [ˌprɒpəˈgændɪst] adj, n propagandiste *(mf)*.
propagandize [ˌprɒpəˈgændaɪz] 1 vi faire de la propagande. 2 vt *doctrine* faire de la propagande pour; *person* soumettre à la propagande, faire de la propagande à.
propagate [ˈprɒpəgeɪt] (*lit, fig*) 1 vt propager. 2 vi se propager.
propagation [ˌprɒpəˈgeɪʃən] n propagation *f*.
propane [ˈprəʊpeɪn] n propane *m*.
propel [prəˈpel] 1 vt a *vehicle, boat, machine* propulser, faire avancer. b (*push*) pousser. **to ~ sth/sb along** faire avancer qch/qn (en le poussant); **they ~led him into the room** ils l'ont poussé dans la pièce, (*more violently*) ils l'ont propulsé dans la pièce. 2 comp ▸**propelling pencil** (*Brit*) porte-mine *m inv*.
propellant [prəˈpelənt] n *[rocket]* propergol *m*, combustible *m* (pour fusée); *[aerosol]* propulseur *m*.
propellent [prəˈpelənt] 1 adj propulseur, propulsif. 2 n = **propellant**.
propeller [prəˈpeləʳ] 1 n *[plane, ship]* hélice *f*. 2 comp ▸**propeller shaft** (*Aut*) arbre *m* de transmission; (*Aviat, Naut*) arbre d'hélice.
propensity [prəˈpensɪtɪ] n propension *f*, tendance naturelle (*to, towards, for* à; *to do, for doing* à faire).
proper [ˈprɒpəʳ] 1 adj a (*appropriate, suitable, correct*) convenable, adéquat, indiqué, correct. **you'll have to put the lid on the ~ way** il faut que vous mettiez (*subj*) le couvercle comme il faut; **you'll have to apply for it (in) the ~ way** il faudra faire votre demande dans les règles; **you should be wearing ~ clothes** vous devriez porter une tenue adéquate *or* une tenue plus indiquée; **the ~ dress for the occasion** la tenue de rigueur pour l'occasion; **that is not the ~ tool for the job** ce n'est pas le bon outil *or* l'outil adéquat *or* l'outil indiqué *or* l'outil qu'il faut *or* l'outil qui convient pour ce travail; **the ~ spelling** l'orthographe correcte; **in the ~ meaning** *or* **sense of the word** au sens propre du mot; **if you had come at the ~ time** si vous étiez venu à la bonne heure *or* à l'heure dite; **2 a.m. isn't a ~ time to phone anyone** 2 heures du matin n'est pas une heure (convenable) pour téléphoner à qui que ce soit; (*Admin etc*) **you must go through the ~ channels** vous devez passer par la filière officielle; **the ~ reply would have been "no"** la réponse qui aurait convenu c'est "non"; **to make a ~ job of sth** bien réussir qch (*also iro*); **to do the ~ thing by sb** bien agir *or* agir honorablement envers qn; (*Math*) **~ fraction** fraction *f* inférieure à l'unité; (*Gram*) **~ noun** nom *m* propre; (*Rel*) **~ psalm** psaume *m* du jour; **do as you think ~** faites ce qui vous semble bon; **if you think it ~ to do so** si vous jugez bon de faire ainsi; **in a manner ~ to his position** ainsi que l'exigeait sa position; **the qualities which are ~ to this substance** les qualités propres à *or* typiques de cette substance; *see* **right** *etc*.
b (*authentic*) vrai, véritable, authentique; (*after noun: strictly speaking*) proprement dit, même. **he's not a ~ electrician** ce n'est pas un véritable électricien; **I'm not a ~ Londoner** *or* **a Londoner ~** je ne suis pas à proprement parler londonien; **outside Paris ~** en dehors de Paris même *or* de Paris proprement dit.
c (*seemly*) *person* comme il faut*, convenable*; *book, behaviour* convenable, correct. **it isn't ~ to do that** cela ne se fait pas, faire cela n'est pas correct *or* convenable; *see* **prim**.
d (*: *intensive*) **he's a ~ fool** c'est un imbécile fini; **I felt a ~ idiot** je me suis senti vraiment idiot; **he's a ~ gentleman** c'est un monsieur très comme il faut*, c'est un vrai gentleman; **he made a ~ mess of it** il (en) a fait un beau gâchis; **it's a ~ mess in there!** c'est un beau désordre *or* la pagaïe* complète là-dedans!
2 adv a (‡) *behave, talk* comme il faut.
b (*dial*) vraiment, très. **he did it ~ quick** et comment qu'il l'a fait vite‡; **it's ~ cruel!** qu'est-ce que c'est cruel!‡
3 n (*Rel: often* **P~**) propre *m*.
properly [ˈprɒpəlɪ] adv a (*appropriately, correctly*) convenablement, correctement, comme il faut. **he was not ~ dressed for the reception** il n'était pas correctement vêtu pour la réception; **use the tool ~** sers-toi de l'outil correctement *or* comme il faut; **if you can't do it ~ I'll help you** si tu n'arrives pas à le faire comme il faut je t'aiderai; **he can't speak ~** il ne peut pas parler normalement; **~ speaking** à proprement parler; **it's not ~ spelt** ce n'est pas orthographié correctement; **he very ~ refused** il a refusé et avec raison *or* à juste titre; (*Admin, Jur etc*) **he was behaving quite ~** il se conduisait d'une manière tout à fait correcte; *see also* **b**.
b (*in seemly way*) **to behave ~** se conduire convenablement *or* comme il faut; **behave/speak ~!** tiens-toi/parle comme il faut!; **he doesn't speak ~** il parle mal; **you're not even ~ dressed** tu n'es même pas vêtu comme il faut.
c (*: *completely*) vraiment. **we were ~ beaten** nous avons été battus à plate(s) couture(s); **I was ~ ashamed** j'avais vraiment *or* drôlement* honte; **I told him ~ what I thought of him** je lui ai dit carrément *or* sans mâcher mes mots ce que je pensais de lui.
propertied [ˈprɒpətɪd] adj possédant.
property [ˈprɒpətɪ] 1 n a (*NonC: possessions*) propriété *f*, biens *mpl*. **is this your ~?** est-ce que cela vous appartient?, est-ce à vous?; **it is the ~ of ...** cela appartient à ..., c'est la propriété de ...; **personal ~ must not be left in the cloakroom** il ne faut pas laisser d'effets personnels dans le vestiaire; (*Jur*) **personal ~** biens personnels *or* mobiliers; **government/company ~** propriété *f* du gouvernement/de la compagnie; (*lit*) **it is common ~** c'est la propriété de tous, ce sont des biens communs; (*fig*) **it is common ~ that ...** chacun sait que ..., il est de notoriété publique que ...; **a man** *or* **woman of ~** un homme *or* une femme qui a du bien *or* des biens; *see* **lost, real**.
b (*NonC: estate*) propriété *f*; (*lands*) terres *fpl*; (*buildings*) biens *mpl* immobiliers. **he has** *or* **owns ~ in Ireland** il a des terres (*or* des biens immobiliers) en Irlande, il est propriétaire en Irlande; **get off my ~** décampez de ma propriété *or* de mes terres.
c (*house etc*) propriété *f*. **a fine ~ with views over the lake** une belle propriété avec vue sur le lac.
d (*Chem, Phys etc: quality*) propriété *f*. **this plant has healing properties** cette plante a des propriétés *or* des vertus thérapeutiques.
e (*Theat*) accessoire *m*.

2 comp ►**property centre** (*Brit*) ≃ agence *f* immobilière ►**property developer** promoteur *m* immobilier ►**property insurance** assurance *f* habitation ►**property law** droit *m* des biens ►**property man** (*Theat*) accessoiriste *m* ►**property market, property mart** marché *m* immobilier ►**property mistress** (*Theat*) accessoiriste *f* ►**property owner** propriétaire foncier ►**property settlement** (*US Jur*) répartition *f* des biens (en cas de divorce) ►**property speculation** spéculation *f* immobilière ►**property speculator** spéculateur *m* immobilier ►**property tax** impôt foncier.

prophecy [ˈprɒfɪsɪ] n prophétie *f*.

prophesy [ˈprɒfɪsaɪ] 1 vt prédire (*that* que); *event* prédire, prophétiser. 2 vi prophétiser, faire des prophéties.

prophet [ˈprɒfɪt] n prophète *m*. **the P~ Samuel** *etc* le prophète Samuel *etc;* (*fig*) **~s of doom** prophètes de malheur.

prophetess [ˈprɒfɪtɪs] n prophétesse *f*.

prophetic(al) [prəˈfetɪk(l)] adj prophétique.

prophetically [prəˈfetɪkəlɪ] adv prophétiquement.

prophylactic [ˌprɒfɪˈlæktɪk] 1 adj prophylactique. 2 n prophylactique *m;* (*US: contraceptive*) préservatif *m*.

prophylaxis [ˌprɒfɪˈlæksɪs] n prophylaxie *f*.

propinquity [prəˈpɪŋkwɪtɪ] n (*in time, space*) proximité *f;* (*in relationship*) parenté *f* proche, consanguinité *f; [ideas etc]* ressemblance *f*, affinité *f*.

propitiate [prəˈpɪʃɪeɪt] vt *person, the gods* se concilier.

propitiation [prəˌpɪʃɪˈeɪʃən] n propitiation *f*.

propitiatory [prəˈpɪʃɪətərɪ] adj propitiatoire.

propitious [prəˈpɪʃəs] adj propice, favorable (*to* à).

propitiously [prəˈpɪʃəslɪ] adv d'une manière propice, favorablement.

proponent [prəˈpəʊnənt] n partisan(e) *m(f)*, adepte *mf* (*of* de).

proportion [prəˈpɔːʃən] 1 n a (*ratio, relationship: also Math*) proportion *f*. **the ~ of blacks to whites** la proportion *or* le pourcentage des noirs par rapport aux blancs; **in due ~** selon une proportion équitable *or* une juste proportion; **in perfect ~** parfaitement proportionné; **in ~ as** à mesure que; **add milk in ~ to the weight of flour** ajoutez du lait en proportion avec le poids de la farine; **her weight is not in ~ to her height** son poids n'est pas proportionné à sa taille; **contributions in ~ to one's earnings** contributions au prorata de *or* en proportion de ses revenus; **in ~ to what she earns, what she gives is enormous** en proportion de ce qu'elle gagne, ce qu'elle donne est énorme; (*fig*) **to see sth in ~** relativiser qch; **out of (all) ~** hors de (toute) proportion; **out of ~ to** hors de proportion avec, disproportionné à *or* avec; **he's got it out of ~** (*lit*) *[artist etc]* il n'a pas respecté les proportions, c'est mal proportionné; (*fig*) il a exagéré, c'est hors de proportion; (*lit, fig*) **he has no sense of ~** il n'a pas le sens des proportions.
b (*size*) **~s** proportions *fpl*, dimensions *fpl*.
c (*part*) part *f*, partie *f*, pourcentage *m*. **in equal ~s** à parts égales; **a certain ~ of the staff** une certaine partie *or* un certain pourcentage du personnel; **your ~ of the work** votre part du travail; **what ~ is rented?** quel est le pourcentage de ce qui est loué?
2 vt proportionner (*to* à). **well-~ed** bien proportionné.

proportional [prəˈpɔːʃənl] adj proportionnel, proportionné (*to* à), en proportion (*to* de). (*Pol*) **~ representation** représentation proportionnelle.

proportionally [prəˈpɔːʃnəlɪ] adv proportionnellement.

proportionate [prəˈpɔːʃnɪt] 1 adj = **proportional**. 2 vt = **proportion 2**.

proportionately [prəˈpɔːʃnɪtlɪ] = **proportionally**.

proposal [prəˈpəʊzl] n a (*offer*) proposition *f*, offre *f;* (*of marriage*) demande *f* en mariage, offre de mariage. b (*plan*) projet *m*, plan *m* (*for sth* de *or* pour qch; *to do* pour faire); (*suggestion*) proposition *f*, suggestion *f* (*to do* de faire). (*Jur*) **~s for the amendment of this treaty** projet *m* tendant à la révision du présent traité.

propose [prəˈpəʊz] 1 vt a (*suggest*) proposer, suggérer (*sth to sb* qch à qn; *doing* de faire; *that* que + *subj*); *measures, course of action* proposer; *plan, motion, course* proposer, présenter, soumettre; *toast* porter; *candidate* proposer. **to ~ sb's health** porter un toast à la santé de qn; **to ~ marriage to sb** faire sa demande à qn, demander qn en mariage; **he ~d Smith as** *or* **for chairman** il a proposé Smith pour la présidence. b (*have in mind*) **to ~ to do** *or* **doing** se proposer *or* avoir l'intention de faire, penser *or* compter faire. 2 vi (*offer marriage*) faire une demande en mariage, faire sa demande (*to sb* à qn).

proposed [prəˈpəʊzd] adj proposé. **your ~ solution** la solution que vous avez proposée; **a ~ nature reserve/housing scheme** un projet de réserve naturelle/de cité.

proposer [prəˈpəʊzəʳ] n (*Admin, Parl etc*) auteur *m* de la proposition; (*for club membership etc*) parrain *m*.

proposition [ˌprɒpəˈzɪʃən] 1 n a (*gen, Comm, Math, Philos etc: statement, offer*) proposition *f*. b (*affair, enterprise*) **that's quite another ~** *or* **a different ~** ça c'est une tout autre affaire; **the journey alone is quite a ~** *or* **is a big ~** rien que le voyage n'est pas une petite affaire; **it's a tough ~** c'est ardu, ça présente de grandes difficultés; **he's a tough ~*** il est coriace, il n'est pas commode; *see* **economic, paying** *etc.* c (*pej: immoral*) proposition *f* malhonnête. 2 vt faire des propositions (malhonnêtes) à.

propound [prəˈpaʊnd] vt (*put up*) *theory, idea* proposer, soumettre; *problem, question* poser; (*explain, develop*) *programme* exposer.

proprietary [prəˈpraɪətərɪ] adj a (*Comm*) *article* de marque déposée. **~ brand** (produit *m* de) marque déposée; **~ medicine** spécialité *f* pharmaceutique; **~ name** marque déposée; **~ rights** droit *m* de propriété. b *duties etc* de propriétaire. (*US Hist*) **~ colony** colonie accordée par la Couronne à une personne en pleine propriété. c (*possessive, protective*) *behaviour, attitude* possessif. d (*US Med*) **~ hospital** hôpital privé.

proprietor [prəˈpraɪətəʳ] n propriétaire *m*.

proprietorial [prəˌpraɪəˈtɔːrɪəl] adj *rights, duties* de propriétaire; *behaviour, attitude* possessif.

proprietorship [prəˈpraɪətəʃɪp] n (*right*) droit *m* de propriété. **under his ~** quand il en était (*or* sera) le propriétaire, lui (étant) propriétaire.

proprietress [prəˈpraɪətrɪs] n, **proprietrix** [prəˈpraɪətrɪks] n propriétaire *f*.

propriety [prəˈpraɪətɪ] n a (*decency*) bienséance *f*, convenance *f*, correction *f*. **to observe the proprieties** respecter *or* observer les bienséances *or* les convenances; **he threw ~ to the winds** il a envoyé promener les convenances. b (*NonC: appropriateness, correctness etc*) *[behaviour, conduct, step]* justesse *f*, rectitude *f; [phrase, expression]* justesse, correction *f*.

propulsion [prəˈpʌlʃən] n propulsion *f*.

propulsive [prəˈpʌlsɪv] adj propulsif, propulseur, de propulsion.

pro rata [ˈprəʊˈrɑːtə] 1 adv au prorata. 2 adj proportionnel.

prorate [ˈprəʊreɪt] vt (*US*) distribuer au prorata.

prorogation [ˌprəʊrəˈgeɪʃən] n prorogation *f*.

prorogue [prəˈrəʊg] vt (*esp Parl*) proroger.

prosaic [prəʊˈzeɪɪk] adj prosaïque.

prosaically [prəʊˈzeɪɪkəlɪ] adv prosaïquement.

proscenium [prəʊˈsiːnɪəm] n, pl **~s** *or* **proscenia** [prəʊˈsiːnɪə] proscenium *m*.

proscribe [prəʊˈskraɪb] vt proscrire.

proscription [prəʊˈskrɪpʃən] n proscription *f*.

prose [prəʊz] 1 n a (*NonC: Literat*) prose *f*. **in ~** en prose. b (*Scol, Univ: also* **~ translation**) thème *m*. 2 comp *poem, comedy* en prose ►**prose writer** prosateur *m*.

prosecute [ˈprɒsɪkjuːt] 1 vt a (*Jur etc*) poursuivre (en justice), engager des poursuites (judiciaires) contre. **he was ~d for speeding** il a été poursuivi pour excès de vitesse; *see* **trespasser**. b (*frm: further*) *enquiry, researches, a war* poursuivre. 2 vi a (*take legal action*) engager des poursuites judiciaires. **"we always ~"** "nous pouvons vous poursuivre en justice". b *[lawyer]* **Mr John Mortimer, prosecuting, pointed out that ...** M. John Mortimer, représentant la partie plaignante *or* (*in higher court*) le ministère public, a fait remarquer que ...; *see also* **prosecuting**.

prosecuting [ˈprɒsɪkjuːtɪŋ] adj (*Jur*) **~ attorney** avocat *m* général; **to appear as ~ counsel** représenter le ministère public.

prosecution [ˌprɒsɪˈkjuːʃən] n a (*Jur*) (*case*) accusation *f;* (*act, proceedings*) poursuites *fpl* judiciaires. **he had six ~s for theft** il a été poursuivi six fois pour vol; **you are liable to ~ if ...** vous pouvez être poursuivi si ..., vous pouvez être *or* faire l'objet de poursuites si ...; **to appear as counsel for the ~** représenter le ministère public; **witness for the ~** témoin *m* à charge; *see* **director**. b (*Jur: prosecuting lawyers*) (*side*) partie *f* plaignante; (*in higher court*) ministère public. c (*furtherance: see* **prosecute b**) poursuite *f*.

prosecutor [ˈprɒsɪkjuːtəʳ] n plaignant *m;* (*also* **public ~**) procureur *m* (de la République), ministère public.

proselyte [ˈprɒsɪlaɪt] 1 n prosélyte *mf*. 2 vti = **proselytize**.

proselytism [ˈprɒsɪlɪtɪzəm] n prosélytisme *m*.

proselytize [ˈprɒsɪlɪtaɪz] 1 vi faire du prosélytisme. 2 vt *person* convertir, faire un(e) prosélyte de.

proseminar [prəʊˈsemɪnɑːʳ] n (*US Univ*) séminaire *m* pour étudiants de troisième année.

prosodic [prəˈsɒdɪk] adj prosodique. (*Phon*) **~ feature** trait *m* prosodique.

prosody [ˈprɒsədɪ] n prosodie *f*.

prospect [ˈprɒspekt] 1 n a (*view*) vue *f*, perspective *f* (*of, from* de); (*fig*) (*outlook*) perspective; (*future*) (perspectives d')avenir *m;* (*hope*) espoir *m* (*of sth* de qch, *of doing* de faire). **this ~ cheered him up** cette perspective l'a réjoui; **to have sth in ~** avoir qch en perspective *or* en vue; **the events in ~** les événements en perspective; **there is little ~ of his coming** il y a peu de chances *or* d'espoir (pour) qu'il vienne; **he has little ~ of succeeding** il a peu de chances de réussir; **there is no ~ of that** rien ne laisse prévoir cela; **there is every ~ of success/of succeeding** tout laisse prévoir le succès/qu'on réussira; **the ~s for the harvest are good/poor** la récolte s'annonce bien/mal; **future ~s for the steel industry** les perspectives d'avenir de la sidérurgie; **what are his ~s?** quelles sont ses perspectives d'avenir?; **he has good ~s** il a de l'avenir; **he has no ~s** il n'a aucun avenir; **the job has no ~s** c'est un emploi sans avenir; **"good ~s of promotion"** "nombreuses *or* réelles possibilités de développement", "situation *f* d'avenir"; **to improve one's career ~s** améliorer ses chances de promotion *or* d'avancement; **the job offered the ~ of foreign travel** l'emploi offrait la possibilité de voyager à l'étranger.

b (*likely person, thing*) (*for marriage*) parti *m*. **he is a good ~ for the England team** c'est un bon espoir pour l'équipe anglaise; **this product is an exciting ~ for the European market** ce produit ouvre des perspectives passionnantes en ce qui concerne le marché européen; (*Comm etc*) **he seems quite a good ~** il semble prometteur; **their offer/the deal seemed quite a good ~** leur offre/l'affaire semblait prometteuse dans l'ensemble.

2 [prəs'pekt] **vi** prospecter. **to ~ for gold** *etc* prospecter pour trouver de l'or *etc*, chercher de l'or *etc*.

3 [prəs'pekt] **vt** *land, district* prospecter.

prospecting [prəs'pektɪŋ] **n** (*Min etc*) prospection *f*.

prospective [prəs'pektɪv] **adj** *son-in-law, home, legislation* futur (*before noun*); *journey* en perspective; *customer* éventuel, possible.

prospector [prəs'pektəʳ] **n** prospecteur *m*, -trice *f*. **gold ~** chercheur *m* d'or.

prospectus [prəs'pektəs] **n** prospectus *m*.

prosper ['prɒspəʳ] 1 **vi** *[person]* prospérer; *[company, enterprise]* prospérer, réussir. 2 **vt** (†, *liter*) favoriser, faire prospérer, faire réussir.

prosperity [prɒs'perɪtɪ] **n** (*NonC*) prospérité *f*.

prosperous ['prɒspərəs] **adj** *person, city, business* prospère, florissant; *period, years* prospère; *undertaking* prospère, qui réussit; *look, appearance* prospère, de prospérité; (*liter*) *wind* favorable.

prosperously ['prɒspərəslɪ] **adv** de manière prospère *or* florissante.

prostaglandin [,prɒstə'glændɪn] **n** prostaglandine *f*.

prostate ['prɒsteɪt] **n** (*also* **~ gland**) prostate *f*. **to have a ~ operation** se faire opérer de la prostate.

prosthesis [prɒs'θi:sɪs] **n, pl prostheses** [prɒs'θi:si:z] prosthèse *f or* prothèse *f*.

prosthetic [prɒs'θetɪk] **adj** prosthétique *or* prothétique.

prosthodontics [,prɒsθə'dɒntɪks] **n** prothèse *f* dentaire.

prosthodontist ['prɒsθə'dɒntɪst] **n** prothésiste *mf* dentaire.

prostitute ['prɒstɪtju:t] 1 **n** prostituée *f*. **male ~** prostitué *m*, homme *m* se livrant à la prostitution. 2 **vt** (*lit, fig*) prostituer.

prostitution [,prɒstɪ'tju:ʃən] **n** (*NonC*) prostitution *f*.

prostrate ['prɒstreɪt] 1 **adj** (*lit*) à plat ventre; (*in respect, submission*) prosterné; (*in exhaustion*) prostré; (*fig: nervously, mentally*) prostré, accablé, abattu. 2 [prɒs'treɪt] **vt** a **to ~ o.s.** se prosterner. b (*fig*) accabler. **the news ~d him** la nouvelle l'a accablé *or* abattu; **~d with grief/by the heat** accablé de chagrin/par la chaleur.

prostration [prɒs'treɪʃən] **n** (*act*) prosternation *f*, prosternement *m*; (*Rel*) prostration *f*; (*fig: nervous exhaustion*) prostration. **in a state of ~** prostré.

prosy ['prəʊzɪ] **adj** ennuyeux, insipide.

prot* [prɒt] **n** (*pej*) **abbr of Protestant.**

protactinium [,prəʊtæk'tɪnɪəm] **n** protactinium *m*.

protagonist [prəʊ'tægənɪst] **n** protagoniste *mf*.

Protagoras [prəʊ'tægəræs] **n** Protagoras *m*.

protean ['prəʊtɪən] **adj** changeant, inconstant.

protect [prə'tekt] **vt** *person, property, country, plants* protéger (*from* de, *against* contre); *interests, rights* sauvegarder; (*Econ*) *industry* protéger. **the tigress fought to ~ her cubs** la tigresse s'est battue pour défendre ses petits; **don't lie to ~ your brother** ne cherche pas à protéger ton frère en mentant.

protection [prə'tekʃən] 1 **n** a (*see* **protect**) protection *f* (*against* contre); sauvegarde *f*. **to be under sb's ~** être sous la protection *or* sous l'aile de qn; **he wore a helmet for ~ against rock falls** il portait un casque pour se protéger des *or* contre les chutes de pierres; **the Prime Minister's personal ~** la protection rapprochée du Premier ministre; **it is some ~ against the cold** cela protège (un peu) contre le froid, cela donne une certaine protection contre le froid.

b = **protection money;** *see* **2.**

2 **comp ▸protection factor** *[sun cream]* indice *m* de protection **▸protection money: he pays 200 dollars a week protection money** il paye 200 dollars par semaine pour ne pas être attaqué (*par le gang etc*); **he pays protection money to Big Joe** il verse de l'argent à Big Joe pour qu'il le laisse (*subj*) en paix **▸protection racket: he's running a protection racket** il est à la tête d'un racket, il extorque des fonds par intimidation.

protectionism [prə'tekʃənɪzəm] **n** a (*Econ*) protectionnisme *m*. b (*US: of wildlife*) défense *f* de l'environnement.

protectionist [prə'tekʃənɪst] 1 **adj** a (*Econ*) protectionniste. b (*US: of wildlife*) *measure etc* pour la défense de l'environnement. 2 **n** a (*Econ*) protectionniste *mf*. b (*US: of wildlife*) défenseur *m* de l'environnement.

protective [prə'tektɪv] **adj** *layer, attitude, gesture* protecteur (*f* -trice), de protection; *clothing, covering* de protection; (*Econ*) *tariff, duty, system* protecteur. (*Zool*) **~ colouring** *or* **coloration** mimétisme *m*, homochromie *f*; (*Jur*) **~ custody** détention préventive (*comme mesure de protection*).

protectively [prə'tektɪvlɪ] **adv** d'un geste (*or* ton *etc*) protecteur.

protectiveness [prə'tektɪvnɪs] **n** attitude *f* protectrice.

protector [prə'tektəʳ] **n** (*person*) protecteur *m*; (*object, device*) dispositif *m* de protection. (*Brit Hist*) **the (Lord) P~** le Protecteur.

protectorate [prə'tektərɪt] **n** protectorat *m* (*also Brit Hist*).

protectress [prə'tektrɪs] **n** protectrice *f*.

protégé ['prəʊtɪ,ʒeɪ, 'prɒtɪ,ʒeɪ] **n** protégé *m*.

protégée ['prəʊtɪ,ʒeɪ, 'prɒtɪ,ʒeɪ] **n** protégée *f*.

protein ['prəʊti:n] 1 **n** protéine *f*. 2 **comp** *intake, deficiency* de protéines; *foods, diet* riche en protéines **▸protein content** teneur *f* en protéines.

pro tem* ['prəʊ'tem], **pro tempore** ['prəʊ'tempərɪ] 1 **adv** temporairement. 2 **adj** temporaire.

protest ['prəʊtest] 1 **n** a (*gen*) protestation *f* (*against* contre, *about* à propos de). **to do sth under ~** faire qch en protestant *or* contre son gré; **to make a ~** protester, élever une protestation (*against* contre); **in ~** en signe de protestation (*against* contre); **political ~(s)** (*esp actions*) agitation *f* politique; (*esp argument*) contestation *f*.

b (*Fin, Jur: in case of dishonour of a bill*) protêt *m*.

2 **comp** (*Pol etc*) *meeting* de protestation **▸protest demonstration, protest march** manifestation *f*.

3 [prə'test] **vt** a protester (*that* que); *one's innocence, loyalty* protester de. **"I didn't do it" he ~ed** "ce n'est pas moi qui l'ai fait" protesta-t-il.

b (*US*) protester contre.

4 [prə'test] **vi** protester, élever une *or* des protestation(s) (*against* contre, *about* à propos de, *to sb* auprès de qn).

Protestant ['prɒtɪstənt] **adj, n** protestant(e) *m(f)*. **~ ethic** morale *f* protestante.

Protestantism ['prɒtɪstəntɪzəm] **n** protestantisme *m*.

protestation [,prɒtes'teɪʃən] **n** protestation *f*.

protester [prə'testəʳ] **n** protestataire *mf*; (*on march, in demonstration etc*) manifestant(e) *m(f)*.

proto... ['prəʊtəʊ] **pref** proto... .

protocol ['prəʊtəkɒl] **n** (*also Comput*) protocole *m*.

proton ['prəʊtɒn] **n** proton *m*.

protoplasm ['prəʊtəʊplæzəm] **n** protoplasme *m*, protoplasma *m*.

prototype ['prəʊtəʊtaɪp] **n** prototype *m*. **a prototype aircraft** le prototype d'un avion.

protract [prə'trækt] **vt** prolonger, faire durer, faire traîner.

protracted [prə'træktɪd] **adj** prolongé, très long (*f* longue).

protraction [prə'trækʃən] **n** prolongation *f*.

protractor [prə'træktəʳ] **n** (*Geom*) rapporteur *m*.

protrude [prə'tru:d] 1 **vi** *[stick, gutter, rock, shelf]* dépasser, faire saillie, avancer; *[teeth]* avancer; *[eyes]* être globuleux. 2 **vt** faire dépasser.

protruding [prə'tru:dɪŋ] **adj** *teeth* qui avance; *eyes* globuleux; *chin* saillant; *shelf, rock* en saillie.

protrusion [prə'tru:ʒən] **n** saillie *f*, avancée *f*.

protrusive [prə'tru:sɪv] = **protruding.**

protuberance [prə'tju:bərəns] **n** protubérance *f*.

protuberant [prə'tju:bərənt] **adj** protubérant.

proud [praʊd] **adj** a *person* fier (*of sb/sth* de qn/qch, *that* que + *subj*, *to do* de faire); (*arrogant*) fier, orgueilleux, hautain. **the ~ father/owner** l'heureux père/possesseur; **that's nothing to be ~ of!** il n'y a pas de quoi être fier!; **I'm not very ~ of myself** je ne suis pas très fier de moi; **as ~ as a peacock** fier comme Artaban; (*pej*) vaniteux comme un paon; **it was a ~ day for us when ...** nous avons été remplis de fierté *or* très fiers le jour où ...; *see* **possessor** *etc*.

b **my ~est possession** ce dont je suis le plus fier; **to do o.s. ~*** ne se priver de rien; **to do sb ~*** (*entertain etc*) se mettre en frais pour qn, recevoir qn comme un roi (*or* une reine); (*honour*) faire beaucoup d'honneur à qn.

c (*splendid*) *building, ship* imposant, superbe, majestueux; *stallion* fier.

d *nail, screw* qui dépasse.

proudly ['praʊdlɪ] **adv** fièrement, avec fierté; (*pej: arrogantly*) fièrement, orgueilleusement; (*splendidly*) majestueusement, superbement, de manière imposante.

provable ['pru:vəbl] **adj** démontrable, prouvable.

prove [pru:v] 1 **vt** a (*give proof of*) prouver (*also Jur*); (*show*) prouver, démontrer. **that ~s his innocence** *or* **him innocent** *or* **that he is innocent** cela prouve son innocence *or* qu'il est innocent; **you can't ~ anything against me** vous n'avez aucune preuve contre moi; **that ~d that she did it** cela prouvait bien *or* c'était bien la preuve qu'elle l'avait fait; **he ~d that she did it** il a prouvé *or* démontré qu'elle l'avait (bien) fait; **he managed to ~ it against her** il a réussi à prouver qu'elle l'avait fait *or* qu'elle était coupable; **he couldn't ~ anything against her** il n'a rien pu prouver contre elle; **the theory remains to be ~d** il reste à prouver *or* démontrer cette théorie, cette théorie n'est pas encore prouvée; **whether he was right remains to be ~d** reste à prouver *or* encore faut-il prouver qu'il avait raison; **he was ~d right** il s'est avéré qu'il avait raison, les faits lui ont donné raison; **it all goes to ~ that ...** tout cela montre bien *or* prouve que ...; **to ~ one's point** prouver ce que l'on avance (*or* a avancé *etc*); **can you ~ it?** pouvez-vous le prouver?; **that ~s it!** c'est la preuve!; **he ~d himself innocent** il a prouvé son innocence; **he ~d himself useful** il s'est révélé *or* montré utile; *see also* **proven**.

b (*test*) mettre à l'épreuve; *will* homologuer. **to ~ o.s.** faire ses preuves.

c (*Culin*) *dough* laisser lever.

d (*Jur, Fin*) **to ~ a debt** produire une dette (à la faillite).

2 **vi** a *[person]* se montrer, s'avérer, se révéler; *[fact, object]* s'avérer, se révéler. **he ~d (to be) incapable of helping us** il s'est montré *or* avéré *or* révélé incapable de nous aider; **the information ~d (to be) correct** les renseignements se sont avérés *or* révélés justes; **the money ~d to be in his pocket** l'argent s'est trouvé être dans sa poche; **it ~d very useful** cela a été *or* (*more formally*) s'est révélé très utile; **the car ~d (to be) a success** la voiture a été une réussite; **if it ~s otherwise** s'il en est autrement *or* différemment.

b (*Culin*) *[dough]* lever.

proven ['pru:vən, 'prəʊvən] 1 **ptp of prove.** 2 **adj** *formula, method* qui a fait ses preuves; *abilities* indubitable. **a ~ track record** une expérience confirmée; (*Scot Jur*) **verdict of not ~** (ordonnance *f* de) non-lieu *m* (*en l'absence de charges suffisantes*); **the case was not ~** il y a eu ordonnance de non-lieu.

provenance ['prɒvɪnəns] **n** provenance *f*.

Provençal [,prɒvɑ̃:n'sɑ:l] 1 **adj** provençal. 2 **n** a Provençal(e) *m(f)*. b (*Ling*) provençal *m*.

Provence [prɒ'vɑ̃:ns] **n** Provence *f*. **in ~** en Provence.

provender ['prɒvɪndəʳ] **n** fourrage *m*, provende *f*.

proverb ['prɒvɜ:b] **n** proverbe *m*. (*Bible*) **(the Book of) P~s** le livre des Proverbes.

proverbial [prə'vɜ:bɪəl] **adj** proverbial.

proverbially [prə'vɜ:bɪəlɪ] **adv** proverbialement.

provide [prə'vaɪd] 1 **vt** a (*supply*) fournir (*sb with sth, sth for sb* qch à qn); (*equip*) munir, pourvoir (*sb with sth* qn de qch), fournir (*sb with sth* qch à qn). **to ~ o.s. with sth** se pourvoir *or* se munir de qch, se procurer qch; **I will ~ food for everyone** c'est moi qui fournirai la nourriture pour tout le monde; **he ~d the school with a new library** il a pourvu l'école d'une nouvelle bibliothèque; **candidates must ~ their own pencils** les candidats doivent être munis de leurs propres crayons; **can you ~ a substitute?** pouvez-vous trouver un remplaçant?; **it ~s accommodation for 5 families** cela loge 5 familles; **the field ~s plenty of space for a car park** le champ offre suffisamment d'espace pour un parc à autos; **I am already ~d with all I need** je suis déjà bien pourvu, j'ai déjà tout ce qu'il me faut; **the car is ~d with a radio** la voiture est pourvue d'une radio.

b *[legislation, treaty etc]* stipuler, prévoir (*that* que). **unless otherwise ~d** sauf dispositions contraires.

2 **vi** a (*esp financially*) **to ~ for** (*gen*) pourvoir *or* subvenir aux besoins de; *family* entretenir; (*in the future*) assurer l'avenir de qn; **I'll see you well ~d for** je ferai le nécessaire pour que vous ne manquiez (*subj*) de rien; **the Lord will ~** Dieu y pourvoira.

b (*make arrangements*) **to ~ for sth** prévoir qch; *[treaty, legislation]* prévoir *or* stipuler qch; **they hadn't ~d for such a lot of spectators** le nombre de spectateurs les a pris au dépourvu; **he had ~d for any eventuality** il avait paré à toute éventualité; **to ~ against** se prémunir contre, prendre ses précautions contre.

provided [prə'vaɪdɪd] **conj: ~ (that)** pourvu que + *subj*, à condition que + *subj*, à condition de + *infin*; **you can go ~ it doesn't rain** tu peux y aller pourvu qu'il *or* à condition qu'il ne pleuve pas; **you can go ~ you pass your exam** tu peux y aller à condition de réussir ton examen; **~ you always keep it closed** pourvu que tu le gardes toujours bien fermé; (*Admin, Jur*) **~ always that** ... sous réserve que ... + *subj*.

providence ['prɒvɪdəns] **n** a (*Rel etc*) providence *f*. **P~** la Providence. b (†: *foresight*) prévoyance *f*, prudence *f*.

provident ['prɒvɪdənt] **adj** *person* prévoyant, prudent; (*Brit*) *fund, society* de prévoyance.

providential [,prɒvɪ'denʃəl] **adj** providentiel.

providentially [,prɒvɪ'denʃəlɪ] **adv** providentiellement.

providently ['prɒvɪdəntlɪ] **adv** avec prévoyance, prudemment.

provider [prə'vaɪdəʳ] **n** pourvoyeur *m*, -euse *f*; (*Comm*) fournisseur *m*, -euse *f*.

providing [prə'vaɪdɪŋ] = **provided**.

province ['prɒvɪns] **n** a province *f*. **the ~s** (*collectively*) la province; **in the ~s** en province. b (*fig*) domaine *m*, compétence *f* (*esp Admin*). **that is not my ~, it is not within my ~** cela n'est pas de mon domaine *or* de ma compétence *or* de mon ressort; **his particular ~ is housing** le logement est son domaine *or* sa spécialité. c (*Rel*) archevêché *m*.

provincial [prə'vɪnʃəl] 1 **adj** (*gen, also pej*) provincial, de province. (*Comm*) **~ branch** branche *f or* agence *f* régionale. 2 **n** provincial(e) *m(f)*.

provincialism [prə'vɪnʃəlɪzəm] **n** provincialisme *m*.

provirus ['prəʊ,vaɪrəs] **n** provirus *m*.

provision [prə'vɪʒən] 1 **n** a (*supply*) provision *f*. **to lay in** *or* **get in a ~ of coal** faire provision de charbon; (*food etc*) **~s** provisions *fpl*; **to get ~s in** faire des provisions.

b (*NonC: supplying*) *[food]* fourniture *f*, approvisionnement *m*; *[equipment]* fourniture. **the ~ of housing** le logement; **~ of food to the soldiers** approvisionnement des soldats en nourriture; (*Fin*) **~ of capital** apport *m or* fourniture de capitaux; **to make ~ for** *one's family, dependents etc* pourvoir aux besoins de, assurer l'avenir de; *journey, siege, famine* prendre des dispositions *or* des précautions pour.

c (*Admin*) (*funding*) financement *m* (*of, for* de); (*funds*) fonds *mpl*.

d (*Admin, Jur etc: stipulation*) disposition *f*, clause *f*. **according to the ~s of the treaty** selon les dispositions du traité; **it falls within the ~s of this law** cela tombe sous le coup de cette loi, c'est un cas prévu par cette loi; **~ to the contrary** clause contraire; **there is no ~ for this in the rules, the rules make no ~ for this** le règlement ne prévoit pas cela.

2 **comp** ▶**provision merchant** marchand *m* de comestibles.

3 **vt** approvisionner, ravitailler.

provisional [prə'vɪʒənl] 1 **adj** *government* provisoire; *arrangement, agreement, acceptance* à titre conditionnel; (*Admin*) *appointment* à titre provisoire; (*Jur*) provisionnel. (*Brit*) **~ driving licence** permis *m* de conduire provisoire (*obligatoire pour l'élève conducteur*). 2 **n** (*Ir Pol*) **the P~s** les Provisionals (*tendance activiste de l'IRA*).

provisionally [prə'vɪʒnəlɪ] **adv** *agree* à titre conditionnel; *appoint* à titre provisoire.

proviso [prə'vaɪzəʊ] **n, pl ~s** *or* **~es** stipulation *f*, condition *f*; (*Jur*) clause restrictive, condition formelle. **with the ~ that** à condition que + *subj*.

provisory [prə'vaɪzərɪ] **adj** = **provisional 1**.

Provo* ['prɒvəʊ] **n** (*Ir Pol*) **the ~s** les Provisionals (*tendance activiste de l'IRA*).

provocation [,prɒvə'keɪʃən] **n** provocation *f*. **under ~** en réponse à une provocation.

provocative [prə'vɒkətɪv] **adj** (*aggressive*) *gesture, remark* provocant, provocateur (*f* -trice); (*thought-provoking*) *book, title, talk* qui donne à penser, qui vise à provoquer des réactions; (*seductive*) *woman, movement, smile* provocant, aguichant. **now you're trying to be ~** là vous essayez de me (*or* le *etc*) provoquer, là vous me (*or* lui *etc*) cherchez querelle.

provocatively [prə'vɒkətɪvlɪ] **adv** (*see* **provocative**) d'un air *or* d'un ton provocant *or* provocateur; d'une manière apte à provoquer des réactions; d'un air aguichant.

provoke [prə'vəʊk] **vt** a (*rouse*) provoquer, pousser, inciter (*sb to do or into doing* qn à faire); *war, dispute, revolt* provoquer, faire naître; *reply* provoquer, susciter. **it ~d them to action** cela les a provoqués *or* incités *or* poussés à agir. b **to ~ sb, to ~ sb's anger** *or* **sb to anger** provoquer qn.

provoking [prə'vəʊkɪŋ] **adj** contrariant, agaçant; *see* **thought**.

provost ['prɒvəst] 1 **n** (*Brit Univ*) principal *m*; (*US Univ*) ≃ doyen *m*; (*Scot*) maire *m*; (*Rel*) doyen *m*; *see* **lord**. 2 **comp** ▶**provost court** (*Mil*) tribunal prévôtal ▶**provost guard** prévôté *f* ▶**provost marshal** prévôt *m*.

prow [praʊ] **n** proue *f*.

prowess ['praʊɪs] **n** prouesse *f*.

prowl [praʊl] 1 **vi** (*also* **~ about, ~ around**) rôder. 2 **n: to be on the ~** rôder. 3 **comp** ▶**prowl car** (*US Police*) voiture *f* de police.

prowler ['praʊləʳ] **n** rôdeur *m*, -euse *f*.

prowling ['praʊlɪŋ] **adj** rôdeur; *taxi* en maraude.

proximity [prɒk'sɪmɪtɪ] **n** proximité *f*. **in ~ to, in the ~ of** à proximité de; **~ fuse** fusée *f* de proximité.

proximo ['prɒksɪməʊ] **adv** (*Comm*) (du mois) prochain.

proxy ['prɒksɪ] 1 **n** (*power*) procuration *f*, pouvoir *m*, mandat *m*; (*person*) fondé(e) *m(f)* de pouvoir, mandataire *mf*. **by ~** par procuration. 2 **comp** ▶**proxy conflict** (*Mil euph*) conflit *m* par personnes interposées ▶**proxy vote** vote *m* par procuration.

PRS [pi:ɑr'es] **n** (**abbr of Performing Rights Society**) SACEM *f*.

prude [pru:d] **n** prude *f*, bégueule *f*. **he is a ~** il est prude *or* bégueule.

prudence ['pru:dəns] **n** prudence *f*, circonspection *f*.

prudent ['pru:dənt] **adj** prudent, circonspect.

prudential [pru(:)'denʃəl] **adj** prudent, de prudence.

prudently ['pru:dəntlɪ] **adv** prudemment, avec prudence.

prudery ['pru:dərɪ] **n** pruderie *f*, pudibonderie *f*.

prudish ['pru:dɪʃ] **adj** prude, pudibond, bégueule.

prudishness ['pru:dɪʃnɪs] = **prudery**.

prune[1] [pru:n] **n** (*fruit*) pruneau *m*; (*pej* ‡: *person*) repoussoir *m*. (*fig*) **~s and prisms** afféterie *f*, préciosité *f*.

prune[2] [pru:n] **vt** *tree* tailler; (*thin out*) élaguer, émonder; *bush* tailler; (*fig: also* **~ down**) *article, essay* élaguer, faire des coupures dans.

▶**prune away** **vt sep** *branches* élaguer; (*fig*) *paragraph, words* élaguer.

pruning ['pru:nɪŋ] 1 **n** (*see* **prune**[2]) taille *f*, élagage *m*, émondage *m*. 2 **comp** ▶**pruning hook** émondoir *m*, ébranchoir *m* ▶**pruning knife** serpette *f* ▶**pruning shears** cisailles *fpl*.

prurience ['prʊərɪəns] **n** lascivité *f*, luxure *f*.

prurient ['prʊərɪənt] **adj** lascif.

Prussia ['prʌʃə] **n** Prusse *f*.

Prussian ['prʌʃən] 1 **adj** prussien. **~ blue** bleu *m* de Prusse. 2 **n** Prussien(ne) *m(f)*.

prussic ['prʌsɪk] **adj: ~ acid** acide *m* prussique.

pry[1] [praɪ] **vi** fourrer son nez dans les affaires des autres, s'occuper de ce qui ne vous regarde pas. **I don't want to ~ but** ... je ne veux pas être indiscret mais ...; **stop ~ing!** occupez-vous de ce qui vous regarde!; **to**

~ **into sb's desk** fureter *or* fouiller *or* fouiner dans le bureau de qn; **to ~ into a secret** chercher à découvrir un secret.
pry² [praɪ] **vt** (*US*) = **prise**.
prying ['praɪɪŋ] **adj** fureteur, curieux, indiscret (*f* -ète).
PS [piː'es] **n** a (**abbr of postscript**) P.-S. *m*. b **abbr of private secretary**.
psalm [sɑːm] **n** psaume *m*. (*Bible*) (**the Book of**) **P~s** le livre des Psaumes.
psalmist ['sɑːmɪst] **n** psalmiste *m*.
psalmody ['sælmədɪ] **n** psalmodie *f*.
psalter ['sɔːltəʳ] **n** psautier *m*.
PSBR [ˌpiːesbiː'ɑːʳ] (*Econ*) (**abbr of public sector borrowing requirement**) *see* **public**.
psephologist [se'fɒlədʒɪst] **n** spécialiste *mf* des élections.
psephology [sə'fɒlədʒɪ] **n** étude *f* des élections.
pseud* [sjuːd] (*Brit*) 1 **n** bêcheur* *m*, -euse *f*. 2 **adj** qui manque de sincérité, artificiel.
pseudo* ['sjuːdəʊ] **adj** insincère, faux (*f* fausse).
pseudo- ['sjuːdəʊ] **pref** pseudo-. **~antique** pseudo-antique; **~autobiography** pseudo-autobiographie *f*; **~apologetically** sous couleur de s'excuser.
pseudonym ['sjuːdənɪm] **n** pseudonyme *m*.
pseudonymous [sjuː'dɒnɪməs] **adj** pseudonyme.
pshaw [pʃɔː] **excl** peuh!
psi [piːes'aɪ] **n** (**abbr of pounds per square inch**) ≃ kg/cm³.
psittacosis [ˌpsɪtə'kəʊsɪs] **n** psittacose *f*.
psoriasis [sɒ'raɪəsɪs] **n** psoriasis *m*.
PST [piːes'tiː] (*US*) (**abbr of Pacific Standard Time**) *see* **Pacific**.
PSV [pies'viː] **n** (*Aut*) (**abbr of public service vehicle**) *see* **public**.
psych* [saɪk] **vt abbr of psychoanalyse**. a (*guess, anticipate*) *sb's reactions etc* deviner, prévoir. b (*make uneasy: also* ~ **out**) intimider, déconcerter (volontairement). **that doesn't ~ me** ça ne me fait ni chaud ni froid, ça ne me panique⁑ pas. c (*prepare psychologically: also* ~ **up**) préparer (mentalement) (*for sth* à *or* pour qch; *to do* pour faire). **to get o.s. ~ed up for sth** se préparer mentalement à qch, se chauffer* pour qch; **he was all ~ed up to start, when ...** il était gonflé à bloc*, tout prêt à commencer, quand ... .
▸**psych out*** 1 **vi** (*break down*) craquer*. 2 **vt sep** a (*cause to break down*) faire craquer*. b *see* **psych b**. c (*US: analyse, work out*) piger⁑, comprendre (*that* que); *situation etc* analyser, comprendre. **to psych sb out** voir clair dans le jeu de qn; **I psyched it all out for myself** je m'y suis retrouvé tout seul.
▸**psych up*** **vt sep** *see* **psych c**.
psyche ['saɪkɪ] **n** psychisme *m*, psyché *f*.
psychedelia [ˌsaɪkə'delɪə] **npl** (*US*) (*objects*) objets *mpl* psychédéliques; (*atmosphere*) univers *m* psychédélique.
psychedelic [ˌsaɪkə'delɪk] **adj** psychédélique.
psychiatric [ˌsaɪkɪ'ætrɪk] **adj** *hospital, treatment, medicine* psychiatrique; *disease* mental.
psychiatrist [saɪ'kaɪətrɪst] **n** psychiatre *mf*.
psychiatry [saɪ'kaɪətrɪ] **n** psychiatrie *f*.
psychic ['saɪkɪk] 1 **adj** a (*supernatural*) *phenomenon* métapsychique, psychique*; (*telepathic*) télépathe. ~ **research** recherches *fpl* métapsychiques; **I'm not ~*** je ne suis pas devin. b (*Psych*) psychique. 2 **n** médium *m*.
psychical ['saɪkɪkəl] = **psychic 1**.
psycho⁑ ['saɪkəʊ] **abbr of psychopath(ic), psychotic**.
psycho... ['saɪkəʊ] **pref** psych(o) ... .
psychoanalysis [ˌsaɪkəʊə'nælɪsɪs] **n** psychanalyse *f*.
psychoanalyst [ˌsaɪkəʊ'ænəlɪst] **n** psychanalyste *mf*.
psychoanalytic(al) ['saɪkəʊˌænə'lɪtɪk(əl)] **adj** psychanalytique.
psychoanalyze [ˌsaɪkəʊ'ænəlaɪz] **vt** psychanalyser.
psychobabble* ['saɪkəʊˌbæbəl] **n** jargon *m* de psy*.
psychodrama ['saɪkəʊdrɑːmə] **n** psychodrame *m*.
psychokinesis [ˌsaɪkəʊkɪ'niːsɪs] **n** psychocinèse *f*, psychokinésie *f*.
psychokinetic [ˌsaɪkəʊkɪ'netɪk] **adj** psychocinétique.
psycholinguistic ['saɪkəʊlɪŋ'gwɪstɪk] 1 **adj** psycholinguistique. 2 **n** (*NonC*) **~s** psycholinguistique *f*.
psychological [ˌsaɪkə'lɒdʒɪkəl] **adj** *method, study, state, moment, warfare* psychologique. **it's only ~*** c'est psychique *or* psychologique.
psychologically [ˌsaɪkə'lɒdʒɪkəlɪ] **adv** psychologiquement.
psychologist [saɪ'kɒlədʒɪst] **n** psychologue *mf*; *see* **child, industrial** *etc*.
psychology [saɪ'kɒlədʒɪ] **n** psychologie *f*; *see* **child** *etc*.
psychometric ['saɪkəʊ'metrɪk] 1 **adj** psychométrique. 2 **n** (*NonC*) **~s** psychométrie *f*.
psychometry [saɪ'kɒmɪtrɪ] **n** psychométrie *f*.
psychomotor ['saɪkəʊ'məʊtəʳ] **adj** psychomoteur (*f* -trice).
psychoneurosis ['saɪkəʊnjʊə'rəʊsɪs] **n**, **pl psychoneuroses** ['saɪkəʊnjʊə'rəʊsiːz] psychonévrose *f*, psychoneurasthénie *f*.
psychoneurotic ['saɪkəʊnjʊə'rɒtɪk] **adj** psychonévrotique.
psychopath ['saɪkəʊpæθ] **n** psychopathe *mf*.
psychopathic [ˌsaɪkəʊ'pæθɪk] **adj** *person* psychopathe; *condition* psychopathique.
psychopathology ['saɪkəʊpə'θɒlədʒɪ] **n** psychopathologie *f*.
psychopharmacological ['saɪkəʊfɑːməkə'lɒdʒɪkəl] **adj** psychopharmacologique.
psychopharmacology ['saɪkəʊfɑːmə'kɒlədʒɪ] **n** psychopharmacologie *f*.
psychophysical ['saɪkəʊ'fɪzɪkəl] **adj** psychophysique.
psychophysics ['saɪkəʊ'fɪzɪks] **n** (*NonC*) psychophysique *f*.
psychophysiological ['saɪkəʊˌfɪzɪə'lɒdʒɪkəl] **adj** psychophysiologique.
psychophysiology ['saɪkəʊfɪzɪ'ɒlədʒɪ] **n** psychophysiologie *f*.
psychoprophylactic [ˌsaɪkəʊˌprɒfɪ'læktɪk] **adj** psycho-prophylactique.
psychoprophylaxis [ˌsaɪkəʊˌprɒfɪ'læksɪs] **n** psycho-prophylaxie *f*.
psychoses [saɪ'kəʊsiːz] **npl of psychosis**.
psychosexual [ˌsaɪkəʊ'seksjʊəl] **adj** psychosexuel.
psychosis [saɪ'kəʊsɪs] **n**, **pl psychoses** psychose *f*.
psychosocial ['saɪkəʊ'səʊʃəl] **adj** psychosocial.
psychosociological ['saɪkəʊˌsəʊsɪə'lɒdʒɪkəl] **adj** psychosociologique.
psychosomatic ['saɪkəʊsəʊ'mætɪk] **adj** psychosomatique.
psychosurgery ['saɪkəʊ'sɜːdʒərɪ] **n** psychochirurgie *f*.
psychotherapist ['saɪkəʊ'θerəpɪst] **n** psychothérapeute *mf*.
psychotherapy ['saɪkəʊ'θerəpɪ] **n** psychothérapie *f*.
psychotic [saɪ'kɒtɪk] **adj, n** psychotique (*mf*).
psy-war* ['saɪwɔːʳ] **n** (*US*) guerre *f* psychologique.
PT [piː'tiː] **n** (*Educ*) (**abbr of physical training**) *see* **physical**.
pt **abbr of pint(s)** *and* **point(s)**.
PTA [ˌpiːtiː'eɪ] **n** (*Scol*) (**abbr of Parent-Teacher Association**) *see* **parent**.
ptarmigan ['tɑːmɪgən] **n, pl ~s** *or* ~ lagopède *m* des Alpes.
Pte (*Mil*) (**abbr of Private**) (*on envelope*) ~ **J. Smith** le soldat J. Smith.
pterodactyl [ˌterəʊ'dæktɪl] **n** ptérodactyle *m*.
P.T.O. [ˌpiːtiː'əʊ] (**abbr of please turn over**) T.S.V.P.
Ptolemaic [ˌtɒlə'meɪɪk] **adj** ptolémaïque.
Ptolemy ['tɒləmɪ] **n** Ptolémée *m*.
ptomaine ['təʊmeɪn] **n** ptomaïne *f*. ~ **poisoning** intoxication *f* alimentaire.
ptosis ['təʊsɪs] **n, pl ptoses** ['təʊsiːz] ptose *f*.
ptyalin ['taɪəlɪn] **n** ptyaline *f*.
pub [pʌb] (*Brit*) (**abbr of public house**) 1 **n** pub *m*, ≃ bistrot* *m*. 2 **comp** ▸**pub crawl***: **to go on a pub crawl, go pub-crawling** faire la tournée des bistrots* *or* des pubs ▸**pub food, pub grub*** cuisine *f or* nourriture *f* de bistrot*; **the pub food** *or* **grub is good here** on mange bien ici ▸**pub lunch** repas *m* de bistrot*; **to go for a pub lunch** aller manger au bistrot*.
puberty ['pjuːbətɪ] **n** puberté *f*.
pubes ['pjuːbiːz] **npl of pubis**.
pubescence [pjuː'besəns] **n** pubescence *f*.
pubescent [pjuː'besənt] **adj** pubescent.
pubic ['pjuːbɪk] **adj** *region etc* pubien. ~ **hair** poils *mpl* du pubis.
pubis ['pjuːbɪs] **n, pl pubes** pubis *m*.
public ['pʌblɪk] 1 **adj** a (*gen: Admin, Econ, Fin etc*) public (*f* -ique); (*owned by the nation*) *enterprise etc* nationalisé, étatisé. ~ **analyst** analyste *mf* d'État *or* officiel(le); ~ **assistance**† assistance publique; ~ **company** société *f* anonyme par actions; *[company]* **to go** ~ s'introduire en Bourse; (*Brit*) ~ **corporation** entreprise *f* nationale; (*Econ*) **the ~ debt** la dette publique; (*US Jur*) ~ **defender** avocat *m* de l'assistance judiciaire; *[copyright]* **in the ~ domain** dans le domaine public; (*Scol etc*) ~ **examination** examen national; (*US Med*) ~ **health** médecine orientée vers l'hygiène publique; (*US*) **P~ Health Service** ≃ Direction *f* des affaires sanitaires et sociales; (*US*) ~ **housing** logements *mpl* sociaux, ≃ H.L.M. *fpl*; (*US*) ~ **housing project** cité *f* H.L.M.; ~ **law** droit public; (*Brit*) ~ **limited company** ≃ société *f* à responsabilité limitée; (*US*) ~ **medicine** = ~ **health**; (*Econ*) ~ **money** deniers publics; (*Econ*) ~ **ownership** nationalisation *f*, étatisation *f*; **under ~ ownership** nationalisé, étatisé; **to take sth into ~ ownership** nationaliser qch, étatiser qch; (*Jur*) **P~ Prosecutor** ≃ procureur *m* (de la République), ministère public; (*Jur*) **P~ Prosecutor's Office** parquet *m*; (*Econ*) **the ~ purse** le trésor public; (*Brit*) **P~ Record Office** ≃ Archives nationales; (*Econ*) **the ~ sector** le secteur public; ~ **sector borrowing** emprunts *mpl* d'État; (*US*) ~ **television** télévision éducative (non commerciale); ~ **utility** service public; ~ **welfare** assistance publique; ~ **works** travaux publics; *[company]* **to go** ~ être coté en Bourse; *see also* **2**.
b (*of, for, by everyone*) *meeting, park, indignation* public (*f*-ique). **it is a matter of ~ interest** c'est une question d'intérêt public *or* général; **he has the ~ interest at heart** il a à cœur l'intérêt *or* le bien public; **there was a ~ protest against ...** il y a eu de nombreux mouvements de protestation contre ... (*see also* **1c**); (*Scot*) **the house has two ~ rooms and three bedrooms** la maison a cinq pièces dont trois chambres; (*US TV*) ~ **access channels** chaînes *fpl* de télévision accordant du temps d'antenne à des groupements de particuliers; ~ **affairs** affaires publiques; **"this is a ~ announcement: would passengers ..."** "votre attention s'il vous plaît: les passagers sont priés de ..."; (*Brit*) ~ **bar** bar *m*; ~ **building** édifice public; (*Admin*) ~ **convenience** toilettes *fpl* (publiques); ~ **enemy** ennemi public; (*fig*) ~ **enemy number one*** ennemi public numéro un; **to be in the ~ eye** être très en vue; **to disappear from the ~ eye** disparaître des feux de l'actualité; **he's a ~ figure** c'est quelqu'un qui est très en vue, c'est une personnalité très connue; (*Brit Admin*) ~ **footpath** passage public pour piétons, sentier public; ~ **holiday** jour férié, fête légale; ~ **lavatory** toilettes *fpl*, W.C.

mpl; ~ **library** bibliothèque municipale; **a man in ~ life** un homme public; **to go into ~ life** se consacrer aux affaires publiques; **to be active in ~ life** prendre une part active aux affaires publiques; ~ **opinion** opinion publique; ~ **opinion poll** sondage *m* d'opinion publique; ~ **servant** fonctionnaire *mf*; ~ **service** service public; (*US*) ~ **service corporation** service public non nationalisé; (*Brit*) ~ **service vehicle** véhicule *m* de transport en commun; ~ **speakers know that ...** les personnes amenées à parler fréquemment en public savent que ...; **she is a good ~ speaker** elle parle bien en public; ~ **speaking** art *m* oratoire; ~ **spirit** civisme *m*, sens *m* civique (*see also* **2**); ~ **transport** transports *mpl* en commun; *see also* **2,** *and* **image, nuisance** *etc.*

c (*open to everyone, not secret*) public (*f* -ique). **to make sth ~** rendre qch public, publier qch, porter qch à la connaissance du public; **it was all quite ~** cela n'avait rien de secret, c'était tout à fait officiel; **he made a ~ protest** il a protesté publiquement; **his ~ support of the strikers** son appui déclaré *or* ouvert aux grévistes; **let's go over there, it's too ~ here** allons là-bas, c'est trop public ici.

2 comp ►**public-address system** (système *m* de) sonorisation *f* ►**public house** (*Brit*) pub *m*, ≃ café *m* ►**public lending right** (*Brit Admin*) (*droits compensant un auteur sur le prêt de ses ouvrages en bibliothèque*) ►**public relations** relations publiques; **public relations officer** responsable *mf* de relations publiques; **it's just a public relations exercise** il (*etc*) a fait ça uniquement dans le but de se faire bien voir ►**public school** (*Brit*) public school *f*, collège *m* secondaire privé; (*US*) école secondaire publique ►**public schoolboy, public schoolgirl** (*Brit*) élève *mf* d'une public school ►**public-spirited: to be public-spirited** faire preuve de civisme.

3 n public *m*. **in ~** en public; **the reading/sporting ~** les amateurs *mpl* de lecture/de sport; (*hum*) **the great British ~** les sujets *mpl* de Sa (Gracieuse) Majesté; **he couldn't disappoint his ~** il ne pouvait pas décevoir son public; *see* **general** *etc.*

publican [ˈpʌblɪkən] n a (*Brit: pub manager*) patron(ne) *m(f)* de bistrot. b (*Bible*) publicain *m*.

publication [ˌpʌblɪˈkeɪʃən] 1 n a (*NonC: act of publishing*) *[book etc]* publication *f*; (*Jur*) *[banns]* publication; *[decree]* promulgation *f*, publication. **after the ~ of the book** après la publication *or* la parution du livre; **this is not for ~** (*lit*) (*gen*) il ne faut pas publier ceci, (*by the press*) ceci ne doit pas être communiqué à la presse; (*fig*) ceci doit rester entre nous. b (*published work*) publication *f*. 2 comp ►**publication date** date *f* de parution *or* de publication.

publicist [ˈpʌblɪsɪst] n (*Jur*) spécialiste *mf* de droit public international; (*Press*) journaliste *mf*; (*Advertising*) (agent *m*) publicitaire *m*, agent de publicité.

publicity [pʌbˈlɪsɪtɪ] 1 n (*NonC*) publicité *f* (*for* pour). **can you give us some ~ for the concert?** pouvez-vous nous faire de la publicité pour le concert?; **adverse ~** contre-publicité *f*; **I keep getting ~ about the society's meetings** je reçois tout le temps des circulaires concernant les réunions de la société; **I've seen some of their ~** j'ai vu des exemples de leur publicité *or* pub*. 2 comp ►**publicity agency** agence *f* publicitaire *or* de publicité ►**publicity agent** (agent *m*) publicitaire *m*, agent de publicité; **publicity campaign** campagne *f* d'information; (*advertising*) campagne de publicité.

publicize [ˈpʌblɪsaɪz] vt a (*make public*) rendre public (*f* -ique), publier. **I don't ~ the fact, but ...** je ne le crie pas sur les toits, mais ...; **well-~d** dont on parle beaucoup (*or* dont on a beaucoup parlé *etc*) (*see also* **b**). b (*advertise*) faire de la publicité pour. **well-~d** annoncé à grand renfort de publicité.

publicly [ˈpʌblɪklɪ] adv publiquement, en public. (*Econ*) **~-owned** étatisé, nationalisé.

publish [ˈpʌblɪʃ] vt a *news* publier, faire connaître. (*Jur*) **to ~ the banns** publier les bans. b *book* publier, éditer, faire paraître, sortir; *author* éditer. *[book, author]* **to be ~ed** être publié; **"to be ~ed"** "à paraître"; **"just ~ed"** "vient de paraître"; **"~ed monthly"** "paraît tous les mois".

publisher [ˈpʌblɪʃəʳ] n éditeur *m*, -trice *f*.

publishing [ˈpʌblɪʃɪŋ] n *[book etc]* publication *f*. **he's in ~** il travaille dans l'édition; ~ **house** maison *f* d'édition.

puce [pjuːs] adj puce *inv*.

puck[1] [pʌk] n (*elf*) lutin *m*, farfadet *m*.

puck[2] [pʌk] n (*Ice Hockey*) palet *m*.

pucker [ˈpʌkəʳ] 1 vi (*also ~ up*) *[face, feature, forehead]* se plisser; (*Sewing*) goder. **she ~ed up, waiting for his kiss** elle avança les lèvres, attendant son baiser. 2 vt a (*Sewing*) froncer. b (*also ~ up*) *lips* avancer. **to ~ (up) one's brow** *or* **forehead** plisser son front. 3 n (*Sewing*) faux pli *m*.

puckish [ˈpʌkɪʃ] adj de lutin, malicieux.

pud⁑ [pʊd] n abbr of **pudding**.

pudding [ˈpʊdɪŋ] 1 n a (*cooked dessert*) **steamed ~** pudding cuit à la vapeur; **apple ~** dessert *m* aux pommes; **rice ~** riz *m* au lait; *see* **milk, proof** *etc.* b (*dessert course in meal*) dessert *m*. **what's for ~?** qu'y a-t-il comme dessert? c (*cooked meat etc dish*) pudding *m*. **steak-and-kidney ~** pudding à la viande de bœuf et aux rognons. d (*cooked sausage*) **black/white ~** boudin noir/blanc. e (*pej: fat person*) patapouf* *mf*. 2 comp ►**pudding basin** jatte *f*, bol *m* ►**pudding-face**⁑ (*fig pej*) (face *f* de) lune⁑ *f*, tête *f* de lard⁑ ►**pudding-head**⁑ (*fig pej*) empoté(e)* *m(f)* ►**pudding rice** (*Culin*) riz *m* à grains ronds ►**puddingstone** (*Geol*) poudingue *m*, conglomérat *m*.

puddle [ˈpʌdl] n flaque *f*.

pudenda [puːˈdendə] npl parties *fpl* génitales.

pudgy [ˈpʌdʒɪ] = **podgy**.

pueblo [ˈpweblәʊ] n, pl ~s (*US*) pueblo *m*, village indien du sud-ouest.

puerile [ˈpjʊəraɪl] adj puéril (*f* puérile).

puerility [pjʊəˈrɪlɪtɪ] n puérilité *f*.

puerperal [pju(ː)ˈɜːpərəl] adj puerpéral. ~ **fever** fièvre puerpérale.

Puerto Rican [ˈpwɜːtəʊˈriːkən] 1 adj portoricain. 2 n Portoricain(e) *m(f)*.

Puerto Rico [ˈpwɜːtəʊˈriːkəʊ] n Porto Rico *f*.

puff [pʌf] 1 n a *[air]* bouffée *f*, souffle *m*; (*from mouth*) souffle; *[wind, smoke]* bouffée; (*sound of engine*) teuf-teuf *m*. **our hopes vanished in a ~ of smoke** nos espoirs se sont évanouis *or* s'en sont allés en fumée; **he blew out the candles with one ~** il a éteint les bougies d'un seul souffle; **to be out of ~*** être à bout de souffle, être essoufflé; **to get one's ~* back** reprendre son souffle, reprendre haleine; **he took a ~ at his pipe/cigarette** il a tiré une bouffée de sa pipe/cigarette; **just time for a quick ~!*** juste le temps de griller* une cigarette en vitesse!

b (*powder ~*) houppe *f*, (*small*) houppette *f*; (*in dress*) bouillon *m*; (*pastry*) feuilleté *m*. **jam ~** feuilleté à la confiture.

c (**: advertisement*) réclame *f* (*NonC*), boniment *m* (*NonC*); (*written article*) papier *m*. (*Press, Rad, TV*) **he gave the record a ~** il a fait de la réclame *or* du boniment pour le disque; **there's a ~ about his new book** il y a un papier sur son nouveau livre.

d (*Brit* ⁑) = **poof**.

2 comp ►**puff adder** vipère heurtante ►**puffball** vesse-de-loup *f* ►**puffed sleeves** = **puff sleeves** ►**puff pastry,** (*US*) **puff paste** pâte feuilletée ►**puff-puff*** (*baby talk*) teuf-teuf *m* (*baby talk*) ►**puff(ed) sleeves** manches bouffantes.

3 vi (*blow*) souffler; (*pant*) haleter; *[wind]* souffler. **smoke was ~ing from the ship's funnel** des bouffées de fumée sortaient de la cheminée du navire; **he was ~ing hard** *or* **~ing like a grampus** *or* **~ing and panting** il soufflait comme un phoque *or* un bœuf; **to ~ (away) at one's pipe/cigarette** tirer des bouffées de sa pipe/cigarette; **he ~ed up to the top of the hill** soufflant et haletant il a grimpé jusqu'en haut de la colline; *[train]* **to ~ in/out** *etc* entrer/sortir *etc* en envoyant des bouffées de fumée; *see also* **puffed**.

4 vt a *[person, chimney, engine, boat]* **to ~ (out) smoke** envoyer des bouffées de fumée; **stop ~ing smoke into my face** arrête de m'envoyer ta fumée dans la figure; **he ~ed his pipe** il tirait des bouffées de sa pipe.

b *rice* faire gonfler; (*also ~ out*) *sails etc* gonfler. **to ~ (out) one's cheeks** gonfler ses joues; **to ~ out one's chest** gonfler *or* bomber sa poitrine; **the bird ~ed out** *or* **up its feathers** l'oiseau a hérissé ses plumes; **his eyes are ~ed (up)** il a les yeux gonflés *or* bouffis.

c (**: praise: also ~ up*) porter aux nues, faire mousser*.

►**puff along** vi *[person]* se déplacer en haletant; *[steam train, ship]* avancer en haletant.

►**puff away** vi *see* **puff 3**.

►**puff out** 1 vi *[sails etc]* se gonfler; *see also* **puff 3.** 2 vt sep a *see* **puff 4a, 4b, 4c.** b (*utter breathlessly*) dire en haletant *or* tout essoufflé.

►**puff up** 1 vi *[sails etc]* se gonfler; *[eye, face]* enfler. 2 vt sep (*inflate*) gonfler. (*fig*) **to be puffed up (with pride)** être bouffi d'orgueil; *see also* **puff 4b** *and* **4c**.

puffed* [pʌft] adj (*breathless: also ~ out*) à bout de souffle, haletant.

puffer [ˈpʌfəʳ] n a (*fish*) poisson-globe *m*. b (**: train*) teuf-teuf* *m*, train *m*.

puffin [ˈpʌfɪn] n macareux *m*.

puffiness [ˈpʌfɪnɪs] n (*see* **puffy**) gonflement *m*, bouffissure *f*; boursouflure *f*.

puffy [ˈpʌfɪ] adj *eye* gonflé, bouffi; *face* gonflé, bouffi, boursouflé.

pug [pʌg] 1 n carlin *m*. 2 comp ►**pug nose** nez rond retroussé ►**pug-nosed** au nez rond retroussé.

pugilism [ˈpjuːdʒɪlɪzəm] n boxe *f*.

pugilist [ˈpjuːdʒɪlɪst] n pugiliste *m*, boxeur *m*.

pugnacious [pʌgˈneɪʃəs] adj batailleur, pugnace, querelleur.

pugnaciously [pʌgˈneɪʃəslɪ] adv avec pugnacité, d'un ton querelleur.

pugnacity [pʌgˈnæsɪtɪ] n pugnacité *f*.

puke⁑ [pjuːk] 1 vi (*also ~ up*) dégueuler⁑, dégobiller⁑. (*fig*) **it makes you ~** c'est à faire vomir, c'est dégueulasse⁑. 2 vt (*also ~ up*) dégueuler⁑. 3 n a (*vomit*) dégueulis⁑ *m*. b (*US pej: person*) salaud⁑ *m*.

►**puke up**⁑ = **puke 1, 2.**

pukka* [ˈpʌkə] adj (*genuine*) vrai, authentique, véritable; (*excellent*) de premier ordre; (*socially superior*) snob *inv*. (*Brit: fig,* †) **he's a ~ sahib** c'est ce qu'on appelle un gentleman.

pulchritude [ˈpʌlkrɪtjuːd] n (*frm*) beauté *f*.

pull [pʊl] 1 n a (*act, effect*) traction *f*; *[moon]* attraction *f*; (*attraction: magnetic, fig*) (force *f* d')attraction, magnétisme *m*. **to give sth a ~, to give a ~ on** *or* **at sth** tirer (sur) qch; **one more ~ and we'll have it up** encore un coup et on l'aura; **I felt a ~ at my sleeve** j'ai senti quelqu'un qui tirait ma manche; **it was a long ~ up the hill** la montée était longue (et raide) pour aller jusqu'en haut de la colline; (*Rowing*) **it was a long ~ to the shore** il a fallu ramer longtemps pour arriver jusqu'au rivage; **the ~ of the current** la force du courant; (*fig*) **the ~ of family ties** la force des liens familiaux; (*fig*) **the ~ of the South/the sea** *etc* l'attraction *or* l'appel *m* du Sud/de la mer *etc;* (*fig*) **to have a ~ over sb** (*have advantage over*) avoir l'avantage *or* le dessus sur qn; (*have a hold over*) avoir barre sur qn; (*fig*) **to have (some) ~ with sb** avoir de l'influence auprès de qn; (*fig*) **he's got ~*** il a le bras long; *see* **leg.**

b (*at bottle, glass, drink*) lampée *f*, gorgée *f*. **he took a ~ at the bottle** il a bu une gorgée *or* lampée à même la bouteille; **he took a long ~ at his cigarette/pipe** il a tiré longuement sur sa cigarette/pipe.

c (*handle*) poignée *f;* (*cord*) cordon *m;* *see* **bell.**

d (*Typ*) épreuve *f*.

e (*Golf*) coup *m* hooké.

2 **comp ▸pull-in** (*Brit*) (*lay-by*) parking *m;* (*café*) café *m* de bord de route, routier *m* **▸pull-off** (*US*) parking *m* **▸pull-out** *see* **pull-out ▸pullover** *see* **pullover ▸pull-ring, pull-tab** (*on can*) anneau *m*, bague *f* **▸pull-up** (*Brit: by roadside*) = **pull-in;** (*Gymnastics*) traction *f* (*sur anneaux etc*).

3 **vt** a (*draw*) *cart, carriage, coach, caravan, curtains* tirer. **to ~ a door shut** tirer une porte derrière *or* après soi; **to ~ a door open** ouvrir une porte en la tirant; **~ your chair closer to the table** approchez votre chaise de la table; **he ~ed the box over to the window** il a traîné la caisse jusqu'à la fenêtre; **he ~ed her towards him** il l'attira vers lui; **she ~ed her jacket around her shoulders** elle ramena sa veste autour de ses épaules.

b (*tug*) *bell, rope* tirer; *trigger* presser; *oars* manier. **he ~s a good oar** il est bon rameur; **to ~ to pieces** *or* **to bits** (*lit*) *toy, box etc* mettre en pièces *or* en morceaux, démolir; *daisy* effeuiller; (*fig*) *argument, scheme, play, film* démolir*; (*) *person* éreinter; **to ~ sb's hair** tirer les cheveux à qn; **~ the other one (it's got bells on)!*** à d'autres!, mon œil!*; (*Horse-racing*) **to ~ a horse** retenir un cheval; (*Boxing, also fig*) **to ~ one's punches** ménager son adversaire; **he didn't ~ any punches** il n'y est pas allé de main morte, il n'a pas pris de gants; (*fig*) **to ~ one's weight** faire sa part du travail, fournir sa part d'effort; (*fig*) **to ~ rank on sb** en imposer hiérarchiquement à qn; *see* **leg, string, wire** *etc.*

c (*draw out*) *tooth* arracher, extraire; *cork, stopper* ôter, enlever, retirer; *gun, knife* tirer, sortir; *flowers* cueillir; *weeds* arracher, extirper; *beer* tirer; (*Culin*) *chicken* vider. **he ~ed a gun on me** il a (soudain) braqué un revolver sur moi; **he's ~ing pints* somewhere in London** il est barman quelque part à Londres; (*Cards*) **to ~ trumps*** faire tomber les atouts.

d (*strain, tear*) *thread* tirer; *muscle, tendon, ligament* se déchirer, se froisser, se claquer.

e (*Typ*) tirer.

f (*Golf etc*) *ball* hooker. **to ~ a shot** hooker.

g (*fig: make, do*) faire, effectuer. **the gang ~ed several bank raids/several burglaries last month** le gang a effectué plusieurs hold-up de banques/plusieurs cambriolages le mois dernier; **to ~ a trick on sb*** jouer un mauvais tour à qn; (*fig*) **to ~ a fast one*** monter une combine pour entuber⁑ les gens; **to ~ a fast one on sb*** rouler qn*, avoir qn*, entuber qn⁑; *see* **face, long[1]** *etc.*

h (*fig *: attract*) *public* attirer; *votes* ramasser.

i (⁑*: have sex with*) lever⁑, s'envoyer⁑.

4 **vi** a (*tug*) tirer (*at, on* sur). **stop ~ing!** arrêtez de tirer!; **he ~ed at her sleeve** il lui tira la manche, il la tira par la manche; **the car/the steering is ~ing to the left** la voiture/la direction tire *or* porte à gauche (*see also* **4b**); **the brakes ~ to the left** quand on freine la voiture tire à gauche *or* porte à gauche *or* est déportée sur la gauche; **the rope won't ~, it must be stuck** la corde ne vient pas, elle doit être coincée; (*fig* *) **to ~ for sb** tenir pour qn*.

b (*move*) **the coach ~ed slowly up the hill** le car a gravi lentement la colline; **the train ~ed into/out of the station** le train est entré en gare/est sorti de la gare; **he soon ~ed clear of the traffic** il a eu vite fait de laisser le gros de la circulation derrière lui; **he began to ~ ahead of his pursuers** il a commencé à prendre de l'avance sur *or* à se détacher de *or* à distancer ses poursuivants; *[car, driver]* **to ~ sharply to the left** virer brusquement à gauche; (*see also* **4a**); **the car isn't ~ing very well** la voiture manque de reprises.

c **to ~ at a cigarette/pipe** *etc* tirer sur une cigarette/pipe *etc;* **he ~ed at his whisky** il a pris une gorgée *or* une lampée de son whisky.

d (*row*) ramer (*for* vers).

▸pull about **vt sep** a *wheeled object etc* tirer derrière soi. b (*handle roughly*) *object, ornament etc* tirailler; *person* malmener.

▸pull ahead **vi** (*in race, election etc*) prendre la tête.

▸pull along **vt sep** *wheeled object etc* tirer derrière *or* après soi. **to pull o.s. along** se traîner.

▸pull apart 1 **vi: this box pulls apart** cette boîte est démontable *or* se démonte. 2 **vt sep** a (*pull to pieces*) démonter; (*break*) mettre en pièces *or* en morceaux. (*fig*) **the police pulled the whole house apart looking for drugs** la police a mis la maison sens dessus dessous en cherchant de la drogue; (*fig*) **his parents' rows were pulling him apart** les disputes de ses parents le déchiraient. b (*separate*) *dogs, adversaries* séparer; *sheets of paper etc* détacher, séparer. c (*fig: criticize*) *play, performance* éreinter; *argument, suggestion* démolir.

▸pull around **vt sep** = **pull about.**

▸pull away 1 **vi** a *[vehicle, ship]* démarrer; *[train]* démarrer, s'ébranler. **he pulled away from the kerb** il s'est éloigné du trottoir; **he began to pull away from his pursuers** il a commencé à se détacher de *or* à prendre de l'avance sur *or* à distancer ses poursuivants; **she suddenly pulled away from him** elle s'est soudain écartée de lui.

b **they were pulling away on the oars** ils faisaient force (de) rames; **they were pulling away on the rope** ils tiraient sur la corde.

2 **vt sep** (*withdraw*) retirer brusquement (*from sb* à qn); (*snatch*) ôter, arracher (*from sb* à qn, des mains de qn). **he pulled the child away from the fire** il a éloigné *or* écarté l'enfant du feu.

▸pull back 1 **vi** (*Mil, gen, fig: withdraw*) se retirer. 2 **vt sep** a (*withdraw*) *object* retirer (*from* de); *person* tirer en arrière (*from* loin de); (*Mil*) retirer, ramener à *or* vers l'arrière. **to pull back the curtains** ouvrir les rideaux. b *lever* tirer (sur).

▸pull down 1 **vi: the blind won't pull down** le store ne descend pas.

2 **vt sep** a *blind* baisser, descendre. **he pulled his opponent down (to the ground)** il a mis à terre son adversaire; **he pulled his hat down over his eyes** il ramena *or* rabattit son chapeau sur ses yeux; **pull your skirt down over your knees** ramène *or* tire ta jupe sur tes genoux; **she slipped and pulled everything down off the shelf with her** elle a glissé et entraîné dans sa chute tout ce qui était sur l'étagère.

b (*demolish*) *building* démolir, abattre; *tree* abattre. **the whole street has been pulled down** la rue a été complètement démolie; (*fig*) **to pull down the government** renverser le gouvernement.

c (*weaken, reduce*) affaiblir, abattre. **his illness has pulled him down a good deal** la maladie a sapé ses forces, la maladie l'a beaucoup affaibli *or* abattu; **his geography marks pulled him down** ses notes de géographie ont fait baisser sa moyenne *or* l'ont fait dégringoler*.

d (*US *: earn*) *[person]* gagner; *[business, shop etc]* rapporter.

▸pull in 1 **vi** (*Aut etc*) (*arrive*) arriver; (*enter*) entrer; (*stop*) s'arrêter. **when the train pulled in (at the station)** quand le train est entré en gare.

2 **vt sep** a *rope, fishing line* ramener. **to pull sb in** (*into room, car*) faire entrer qn, tirer qn à l'intérieur; (*into pool etc*) faire piquer une tête dans l'eau à qn; **pull your chair in (to the table)** rentre ta chaise (sous la table); **pull your stomach in!** rentre le ventre!; (*fig*) **that film is certainly pulling people in** sans aucun doute ce film attire les foules; *see* **belt, horn.**

b (*detain*) **the police pulled him in for questioning** la police l'a appréhendé pour l'interroger.

c (*restrain*) *horse* retenir.

d (**: earn*) *[person]* gagner; *[business, shop etc]* rapporter.

3 **pull-in n** *see* **pull 2.**

▸pull off 1 **vt sep** a (*remove*) *handle, lid, cloth* enlever, ôter; *gloves, shoes, coat, hat* enlever, ôter, retirer. b (*fig*) *plan, aim* réaliser; *deal* mener à bien, conclure; *attack, hoax* réussir. **he didn't manage to pull it off** il n'a pas réussi son coup. 2 **vi** a (*start*) *[car, bus etc]* démarrer, partir. b *[vehicle, driver]* **to pull off the road** quitter la route. 3 **pull-off n** *see* **pull 2.**

▸pull on 1 **vi: the cover pulls on** la housse s'enfile. 2 **vt sep** *gloves, coat, cover* mettre, enfiler; *shoes, hat* mettre.

▸pull out 1 **vi** a (*leave*) *[train]* s'ébranler, démarrer; *[car, ship]* démarrer; (*withdraw: lit, fig*) se retirer (*of* de). (*Aviat*) **to pull out of a dive** se redresser; **he pulled out of the deal at the last minute** il a tiré son épingle du jeu *or* il s'est retiré à la dernière minute.

b (*Aut*) déboîter, sortir de la file. **he pulled out to overtake the truck** il a déboîté pour doubler le camion.

c **the drawers pull out easily** les tiroirs coulissent bien; **the table pulls out to seat 8** avec la rallonge 8 personnes peuvent s'asseoir à la table; **the centre pages pull out** les pages du milieu sont détachables *or* se détachent.

2 **vt sep** a (*extract, remove*) *nail, hair, page* arracher; *splinter* enlever; *cork, stopper* ôter, enlever, retirer; *tooth* arracher, extraire; *weeds* arracher, extirper; *gun, knife, cigarette lighter* sortir, tirer. **he pulled a rabbit out of his hat** il a sorti *or* tiré un lapin de son chapeau; **to pull sb out of a room** faire sortir qn d'une pièce, tirer qn à l'extérieur; **they pulled him out of the wreckage alive** ils l'ont tiré *or* sorti vivant des débris; *see* **finger, stop.**

b (*withdraw*) *troops, police etc* retirer (*of* de). **the union has pulled all the workers out on strike** tous les ouvriers ont répondu à la consigne de grève donnée par le syndicat.

c (** fig: produce*) *reason, argument* sortir*, fournir, donner. (*fig*) **he pulled out one last trick** il a usé d'un dernier stratagème.

3 **pull-out adj, n** *see* **pull-out.**

▸pull over 1 **vi** (*Aut*) **he pulled over (to one side) to let the ambulance past** il s'est rangé *or* garé sur le côté pour laisser passer l'ambulance.

2 **vt sep** a **he pulled the box over to the window** il a traîné la caisse jusqu'à la fenêtre; **she pulled the chair over and stood on it** elle a tiré

la chaise à elle pour grimper dessus; **they pulled him over to the door** ils l'ont entraîné vers la porte.

b **they climbed the wall and pulled him over** ils ont grimpé sur le mur et l'ont hissé de l'autre côté.

c (*topple*) **he pulled the bookcase over on top of himself** il a entraîné la bibliothèque dans sa chute, il s'est renversé la bibliothèque dessus.

3 **pullover** n *see* **pullover**.

►**pull round** 1 vi *[unconscious person]* revenir à soi, reprendre conscience; *[sick person]* se remettre, se rétablir, s'en sortir. 2 vt sep a *chair etc* faire pivoter, tourner. **he pulled me round to face him** il m'a fait me retourner pour me forcer à lui faire face. b *unconscious person* ranimer; *sick person* tirer *or* sortir de là.

►**pull through** 1 vi a **the rope won't pull through** la corde ne passe pas. b (*fig*) (*from illness*) s'en tirer, s'en sortir; (*from difficulties*) se tirer d'affaire *or* d'embarras, s'en sortir, s'en tirer. 2 vt sep a *rope etc* (*gen*) faire passer; (*Climbing*) rappeler. b (*fig*) *person* (*from illness*) guérir, tirer *or* sortir de là, tirer d'affaire; (*from difficulties*) sortir *or* tirer d'affaire *or* d'embarras.

►**pull together** 1 vi (*on rope etc*) tirer ensemble *or* simultanément; (*row*) ramer simultanément *or* à l'unisson; (*fig: cooperate*) (s'entendre pour) faire un effort. 2 vt sep (*join*) *rope ends etc* joindre. (*fig*) **to pull o.s. together** se reprendre, se ressaisir; **pull yourself together!** ressaisis-toi!, reprends-toi!, ne te laisse pas aller!; **you need to pull the rough draft together** tu dois organiser ton brouillon.

►**pull up** 1 vi a (*stop*) *[vehicle]* s'arrêter, stopper; *[athlete, horse]* s'arrêter (net).

b (*draw level with*) **he pulled up with the leaders** il a rattrapé *or* rejoint ceux qui menaient.

2 vt sep a *object* remonter; (*haul up*) hisser; *stockings* remonter, tirer; *chair* approcher. **pull up a chair!** prends une chaise!; **when the bucket was full he pulled it up** une fois le seau plein il l'a remonté; **he leaned down from the wall and pulled the child up** il s'est penché du haut du mur et a hissé l'enfant jusqu'à lui; **he pulled me up out of the armchair** il m'a tiré *or* fait sortir du fauteuil; (*fig*) **your geography mark has pulled you up** votre note de géographie vous a remonté*; *see* **sock**[1].

b *tree etc* arracher, déraciner; *weed* arracher, extirper. (*fig*) **to pull up one's roots** larguer ses amarres (*fig*), se déraciner.

c (*halt*) *vehicle* arrêter, stopper; *horse* arrêter. **the chairman pulled the speaker up (short)** le président a coupé la parole à *or* a interrompu l'orateur; **he pulled himself up (short)** il s'arrêta net *or* pile; **the police pulled him up for speeding** la police l'a stoppé pour excès de vitesse; (*fig*) **the headmaster pulled him up for using bad language** il a été repris *or* réprimandé par le directeur pour avoir été grossier.

3 **pull-up** n *see* **pull 2**.

pullet ['pʊlɪt] n jeune poule *f*, poulette *f*.

pulley ['pʊlɪ] n poulie *f*; (*for clothes-drying*) séchoir *m* à linge (suspendu).

Pullman ['pʊlmən] n, pl ~s (*Rail*) (*also* ~ **carriage**) pullman *m*, voiture-salon *f*, wagon-salon *m*; (*sleeper: also* ~ **car**) voiture-lit *f*, wagon-lit *m*.

pull-out ['pʊlaʊt] 1 n a (*in magazine etc*) supplément *m* détachable. b *[troops]* retrait *m*. 2 adj *magazine section* détachable; *table leaf, shelf* rétractable. ~ **bed** meuble-lit *m*.

pullover ['pʊl,əʊvəʳ] n pull *m*, pullover *m*.

pullulate ['pʌljʊleɪt] vi pulluler.

pulmonary ['pʌlmənərɪ] adj pulmonaire.

pulp [pʌlp] 1 n a pulpe *f*; (*part of fruit*) pulpe, chair *f*; (*for paper*) pâte *f* à papier, pulpe (à papier). **to reduce** *or* **crush to a** ~ *wood* réduire en pâte *or* en pulpe; *fruit* réduire en pulpe *or* en purée *or* en marmelade; (*fig*) **his arm was crushed to a** ~ il a eu le bras complètement écrasé, il a eu le bras mis en bouillie *or* en marmelade*; *see* **pound**[2] *etc*. b (*pej*) (*literature*) littérature *f* à sensation. ~ **fiction/novel** romans *mpl*/roman *m* à sensation; ~ **magazine** magazine *m* à sensation, torchon* *m*. 2 comp ►**pulp cavity** (*in tooth*) cavité *f* pulpaire. 3 vt *wood, linen* réduire en pâte *or* en pulpe; *fruit* réduire en pulpe *or* en purée *or* en marmelade; *book* mettre au pilon, pilonner.

pulpit ['pʊlpɪt] n chaire *f* (*Rel*).

pulpy ['pʌlpɪ] adj *fruit* charnu, pulpeux; (*Bio*) *tissue* pulpeux.

pulsar ['pʌlsɑːʳ] n pulsar *m*.

pulsate [pʌl'seɪt] vi produire *or* émettre des pulsations; *[heart]* battre fort, palpiter; *[blood]* battre; *[music]* vibrer. **the pulsating rhythm of the drums** le battement rythmique des tambours.

pulsating [pʌl'seɪtɪŋ] adj *heart* palpitant; *music* vibrant; (*fig: exciting*) palpitant, excitant.

pulsation [pʌl'seɪʃən] n *[heart]* battement *m*, pulsation *f*; (*Elec, Phys*) pulsation.

pulse[1] [pʌls] 1 n (*Med*) pouls *m*; (*Elec, Phys, Rad*) vibration *f*; *[radar]* impulsion *f*; (*fig*) *[drums etc]* battement *m* rythmique; *[emotion]* frémissement *m*, palpitation *f*. **to take sb's** ~ prendre le pouls de qn; **an event that stirred my** ~**s** un événement qui m'a remué le cœur *or* qui m'a fait palpiter d'émotion. 2 comp ►**pulsebeat** (*Med*) (battement *m* *or* pulsation *f* de) pouls *m* ►**pulse rate** (*Med*) pouls *m*. 3 vi *[heart]* battre fort; *[blood]* battre. **it sent the blood pulsing through his veins** cela lui fouetta le sang, cela le fit palpiter d'émotion; **the life pulsing in a great city** la vie qui palpite au cœur d'une grande ville.

pulse[2] [pʌls] n (*Bot*) légume *m* à gousse; (*Culin: dried*) légume sec.

pulverization [,pʌlvəraɪ'zeɪʃən] n pulvérisation *f*.

pulverize ['pʌlvəraɪz] vt (*lit, fig*) pulvériser.

puma ['pjuːmə] n puma *m*.

pumice ['pʌmɪs] n (*also* ~ **stone**) pierre *f* ponce.

pummel ['pʌml] vt a (*in fight*) bourrer *or* rouer de coups. b (*in massage*) pétrir.

pummelling ['pʌməlɪŋ] n a (*in fight*) volée *f* de coups. **to take a** ~ (*lit*) se faire rouer de coups; (*Sport: be beaten*) se faire battre à plate(s) couture(s); (*be criticized/attacked*) se faire violemment critiquer/attaquer. b (*in massage*) pétrissage *m*.

pump[1] [pʌmp] 1 n (*all senses*) pompe *f*; *see* **parish, petrol, prime** *etc*.

2 comp ►**pump attendant** (*Brit*) pompiste *mf* ►**pump house, pumping station** station *f* d'épuisement *or* de pompage ►**pump prices:** *[petrol]* **a rise in pump prices** une hausse à la pompe ►**pump priming** (*Econ*) amorçage *m* économique, coup *m* de pouce à l'économie ►**pump room** buvette *f* (*où l'on prend les eaux dans une station thermale*) ►**pump-water** eau *f* de la pompe.

3 vt a **to** ~ **sth out of sth** pomper qch de qch; **to** ~ **sth into sth** refouler qch dans qch (au moyen d'une pompe); **to** ~ **water into sth** pomper de l'eau dans qch; **to** ~ **air into a tyre** gonfler un pneu (avec une pompe); **the water is** ~**ed up to the house** l'eau est amenée jusqu'à la maison au moyen d'une pompe; **to** ~ **oil through a pipe** faire passer *or* faire couler du pétrole dans un pipe-line (à l'aide d'une pompe); **they** ~**ed the tank dry** ils ont vidé *or* asséché le réservoir (à la pompe), ils ont pompé toute l'eau (*or* l'essence *etc*) du réservoir; (*Med*) **to** ~ **sb's stomach** faire un lavage d'estomac à qn; **the heart** ~**s the blood round the body** le cœur fait circuler le sang dans le corps; (*fig*) **they** ~**ed money into the project** ils ont injecté de plus en plus d'argent dans le projet; (*fig*) **he** ~**ed facts into their heads** il leur bourrait* la tête de faits précis; **to** ~ **sb full of lead**‡ trouer la peau‡ *or* faire la peau‡ à qn; (*Sport*) **to** ~ **iron*** faire de l'haltérophilie.

b (*fig: question*) **to** ~ **sb for sth** essayer de soutirer qch à qn; **they'll try to** ~ **you (for information)** ils essayeront de vous faire parler *or* de vous cuisiner* *or* de vous tirer les vers* du nez; **he managed to** ~ **the figures out of me** il a réussi à me soutirer *or* à me faire dire les chiffres.

c *handle etc* lever et abaisser plusieurs fois *or* continuellement. **he** ~**ed my hand vigorously** il me secoua vigoureusement la main.

4 vi *[pump, machine, person]* pomper; *[heart]* battre fort. **blood** ~**ed from the artery** le sang coulait à flots de l'artère; **the oil was** ~**ing along the pipeline** le pétrole coulait dans le pipe-line; **the piston was** ~**ing up and down** le piston montait et descendait régulièrement.

►**pump away** vi *[heart]* battre à grands coups. **he was pumping away on the lever** il faisait fonctionner *or* actionnait le levier.

►**pump in** vt sep *water, oil, gas etc* refouler (à l'aide d'une pompe). **pump some more air in** donnez plus d'air.

►**pump out** 1 vi *[blood, oil]* couler à flots (*of* de). 2 vt sep a *water, oil, gas etc* pomper, aspirer (à l'aide d'une pompe). b (*: *produce*) pondre en masse*. (*TV, Rad*) **this station pumps out music 24 hours a day** cette station balance* de la musique 24 heures par jour.

►**pump up** vt sep *tyre, airbed* gonfler; *see also* **pump 3a**.

pump[2] [pʌmp] n (*sports shoe*) (chaussure *f* de) tennis *m*; (*slip-on shoe*) chaussure *f* sans lacet; (*dancing shoe*) escarpin *m*.

pumpernickel ['pʌmpənɪkl] n pumpernickel *m*, pain *m* de seigle noir.

pumpkin ['pʌmpkɪn] n citrouille *f*; (*bigger*) potiron *m*; *[Cinderella]* citrouille. ~ **pie** tarte *f* au potiron.

pun [pʌn] 1 n calembour *m*, jeu *m* de mots. 2 vi faire un *or* des calembour(s), faire un *or* des jeu(x) de mots.

Punch [pʌntʃ] n Polichinelle *m*. ~ **and Judy Show** (théâtre *m* de) guignol *m*; *see* **pleased**.

punch[1] [pʌntʃ] 1 n a (*blow*) coup *m* de poing. **to give sb a** ~ **on the nose** donner un coup de poing sur le nez à qn; (*Boxing*) **he's got a good** ~ il a du punch; *see* **pack, pull, rabbit, ride** *etc*.

b (*NonC: fig: force*) *[person]* punch* *m*. **a phrase with more** ~ une expression plus frappante *or* plus incisive; **we need a presentation with some** ~ **to it** il nous faut une présentation énergique *or* vigoureuse; **a story with no** ~ **to it** une histoire qui manque de mordant.

c (*tool*) (*for tickets*) poinçonneuse *f*; (*for holes in paper*) perforateur *m*; (*Metalworking*) poinçonneuse, emporte-pièce *m inv*; (*for stamping design*) étampe *f*, (*smaller*) poinçon *m*; (*for driving in nails*) chasse-clou *m*.

2 comp ►**punch bag** (*lit*) sac *m* de sable, punching-bag *m*; (*fig*) souffre-douleur *m inv* ►**punchball** (*Brit*) punching-ball *m*; (*US*) *variante simplifiée du baseball, qui se joue sans batte* ►**punch card** carte perforée; **punch card system** système *m* à cartes perforées ►**punch-drunk** (*Boxing*) abruti par les coups, groggy, sonné*; (*fig*) abruti ►**punching ball** = **punchball** ►**punch-line** *[joke etc]* conclusion *f* (comique); *[speech etc]* trait final ►**punch operator** (*Comput*) mécanographe *mf* ►**punch tape** (*Comput*) bande perforée ►**punch-up*** (*Brit*) bagarre *f*; (*Brit*) **to have a punch-up*** se bagarrer*.

3 vt a (*with fist*) *person* donner un coup de poing à; *ball, door*

frapper d'un coup de poing. **to ~ sb's nose/face, ~ sb in the nose/face** donner un coup de poing sur le nez/sur la figure à qn; **to ~ sb in the stomach/in the kidneys/on the jaw** donner un coup de poing dans le ventre/dans les reins/à la mâchoire à qn; **he ~ed his fist through the glass** il a passé son poing à travers la vitre, il a brisé la vitre d'un coup de poing; **the goalkeeper ~ed the ball over the bar** d'un coup de poing le gardien de but a envoyé le ballon par-dessus la barre; **he ~ed his way through** il s'est ouvert un chemin à (force de) coups de poing *or* en frappant à droite et à gauche.

b (*US*) **to ~ cattle** conduire le bétail (à l'aiguillon).

c (*with tool*) *paper* poinçonner, perforer; *ticket* (*by hand*) poinçonner; (*automatically*) composter; *computer cards* perforer; *metal* poinçonner, découper à l'emporte-pièce; *design* estamper; *nails* enfoncer profondément (au chasse-clou). **to ~ a hole in sth** faire un trou dans qch; (*Ind*) **to ~ the time clock, to ~ one's card** pointer.

d (*with finger*) *button* taper.

4 vi frapper (dur), cogner. (*Boxing*) **he ~es well** il sait frapper.

▸**punch in** 1 vi (*Ind: on time clock*) pointer (en arrivant). 2 vt sep a *door, lid etc* ouvrir d'un coup de poing. **to punch sb's face** *or* **head in**‡ casser la gueule à qn‡. b (*key in*) *code, number etc* taper.

▸**punch out** 1 vi (*Ind: on time clock*) pointer (en partant). 2 vt sep *hole* faire au poinçon *or* à la poinçonneuse; *machine parts* découper à l'emporte-pièce; *design* estamper.

punch[2] [pʌntʃ] n (*drink*) punch *m*. **~ bowl** bol *m* à punch.

punchy* [pʌntʃɪ] adj a (*esp US: forceful*) *person* qui a du punch*, dynamique; *remark, reply* incisif, mordant. b = **punch-drunk**; *see* **punch**[1] **2**.

punctilio [pʌŋk'tɪlɪəʊ] n, pl **~s** (*frm*) (*NonC: formality*) formalisme *m*; (*point of etiquette*) point *m or* détail *m* d'étiquette.

punctilious [pʌŋk'tɪlɪəs] adj pointilleux.

punctiliously [pʌŋk'tɪlɪəslɪ] adv de façon pointilleuse.

punctual ['pʌŋktjʊəl] adj *person, train* à l'heure; *payment* ponctuel. **he is always ~** il est très ponctuel, il est toujours à l'heure; **be ~** soyez *or* arrivez à l'heure.

punctuality [,pʌŋktjʊ'ælɪtɪ] n *[person]* ponctualité *f*, exactitude *f*; *[train]* exactitude.

punctually ['pʌŋktjʊəlɪ] adv à l'heure. **the train arrived ~** le train est arrivé *or* était à l'heure; **the train arrived ~ at 7 o'clock** le train est arrivé à 7 heures pile *or* précises; **he leaves ~ at 8 every morning** il part à 8 heures précises *or* ponctuellement à 8 heures tous les matins.

punctuate ['pʌŋktjʊeɪt] vt (*lit, fig*) ponctuer (*with* de).

punctuation [,pʌŋktjʊ'eɪʃən] n ponctuation *f*. **~ mark** signe *m* de ponctuation.

puncture ['pʌŋktʃəʳ] 1 n (*in tyre*) crevaison *f*; (*in skin, paper, leather*) piqûre *f*; (*Med*) ponction *f*. (*Aut etc*) **I've got a ~** j'ai (un pneu) crevé; **they had a ~ outside Limoges** ils ont crevé près de Limoges. 2 comp ▸**puncture repair kit** trousse *f* de secours pour crevaisons. 3 vt *tyre, balloon* crever; *skin, leather, paper* piquer; (*Med*) *abscess* percer, ouvrir. 4 vi *[tyre etc]* crever.

pundit ['pʌndɪt] n (*iro*) expert *m*, pontife *m*.

pungency ['pʌndʒənsɪ] n *[smell, taste]* âcreté *f*; *[sauce]* goût piquant *or* relevé; *[remark, criticism]* mordant *m*, causticité *f*.

pungent ['pʌndʒənt] adj *smell, taste* âcre, piquant; *sauce* piquant, relevé; *remark, criticism* mordant, caustique, acerbe; *sorrow* déchirant.

pungently ['pʌndʒəntlɪ] adv *remark* d'un ton mordant *or* caustique *or* acerbe; *criticize* de façon mordante *or* caustique *or* acerbe.

Punic ['pju:nɪk] adj punique.

punish ['pʌnɪʃ] vt a *person* punir (*for sth* de qch, *for doing* pour avoir fait); *theft, fault* punir. **he was ~ed by having to clean it all up** pour le punir on lui a fait tout nettoyer, pour sa punition il a dû tout nettoyer. b (*fig*) *opponent in fight, boxer, opposing team* malmener; *engine* fatiguer; *roast beef* faire honneur à; *bottle of whisky* taper dans*. **the jockey really ~ed his horse** le jockey a vraiment forcé *or* fatigué son cheval.

punishable ['pʌnɪʃəbl] adj *offence* punissable. **~ by death** passible de la peine de mort.

punishing ['pʌnɪʃɪŋ] 1 n (*act*) punition *f*. (*fig*) *[boxer, opponent, opposing team]* **to take a ~** se faire malmener; **the roast beef/the bottle of whisky took a ~** il n'est pas resté grand-chose du rosbif/de la bouteille de whisky, le rosbif/le whisky en a pris un (vieux) coup*. 2 adj *speed, heat, game, work* épuisant, exténuant.

punishment ['pʌnɪʃmənt] n (*gen*) punition *f*; (*solemn*) châtiment *m*; (*formal: against employee, student etc*) sanctions *fpl*. **as a ~ (for)** en punition (de); **he took his ~ bravely** *or* **like a man** il a subi *or* encaissé* sa punition sans se plaindre; **to make the ~ fit the crime** adapter le châtiment au crime, proportionner la peine au délit; (*fig*) **to take a lot of ~** *[boxer, opponent in fight]* encaisser*; *[opposing team]* se faire malmener; *see* **capital, corporal**[2] *etc*.

punitive ['pju:nɪtɪv] adj *expedition* punitif; *measure* de punition. (*Jur*) **~ damages** dommages-intérêts dissuasifs (*très élevés*).

Punjab [pʌn'dʒɑ:b] n Pendjab *m*.

Punjabi [pʌn'dʒɑ:bɪ] 1 adj pendjabi. 2 n a Pendjabi *mf*. b (*Ling*) pendjabi *m*.

punk [pʌŋk] 1 n a (*music*) punk *m*; (*musician, fan*) punk *mf*. b (‡: *nonsense*) foutaises‡ *fpl*. c (*US* ‡: *beginner*) débutant *m*, novice *m*. d (*esp US* ‡: *ruffian*) sale* petit voyou *m*. 2 adj a *music, style* punk *inv*. **~ rock** le rock punk, le punk rock. b (‡: *inferior*) qui ne vaut rien, minable, de con‡. c (*US* ‡: *ill*) mal foutu‡.

punnet ['pʌnɪt] n (*Brit*) carton *m*, petit panier (*pour fraises etc*).

punster ['pʌnstəʳ] n personne *f* qui fait des calembours.

punt[1] [pʌnt] 1 n (*boat*) bachot *m or* bateau *m* à fond plat. 2 vt *boat* faire avancer à la perche; *goods* transporter en bachot. 3 vi: **to go ~ing** faire un tour de rivière, aller se promener en bachot.

punt[2] [pʌnt] (*Ftbl, Rugby*) 1 vt *ball* envoyer d'un coup de volée. 2 n coup *m* de volée.

punt[3] [pʌnt] vi (*Brit: bet*) parier.

punter ['pʌntəʳ] n a (*Brit Bookmaking*) parieur *m*, -ieuse *f*. b (*) (*prostitute's customer*) habitué* *m*; (*St Ex*) boursicoteur *m*, -euse *f*. (*customer, member of public*) **the ~(s)** le public, la clientèle.

puny ['pju:nɪ] adj *person, animal* chétif, malingre, frêle; *effort* faible, piteux.

pup [pʌp] 1 n (*dog*) chiot *m*, jeune chien(ne) *m(f)*; (*seal*) bébé-phoque *m*, jeune phoque *m*; (* *fig pej: youth*) freluquet *m*, godelureau *m*. **he's an insolent young ~** c'est un petit morveux*; *see* **sell**. 2 comp ▸**pup tent** tente individuelle. 3 vi mettre bas.

pupa ['pju:pə] n, pl **pupae** ['pju:pi:] chrysalide *f*, pupe *f*.

pupate ['pju:peɪt] vi devenir chrysalide *or* pupe.

pupil[1] ['pju:pl] 1 n (*Scol etc*) élève *mf*. 2 comp ▸**pupil nurse** (*Brit*) élève *m(f)* infirmier(-ière) (*qui suit une formation courte*) ▸**pupil power** pouvoir *m* des lycéens ▸**pupil teacher** professeur *m* stagiaire.

pupil[2] ['pju:pl] n *[eye]* pupille *f*.

puppet ['pʌpɪt] 1 n (*lit*) marionnette *f*; (*flat cutout*) pantin *m*; (*fig*) marionnette, pantin, fantoche *m*. **he was like a ~ on a string** il n'était qu'une marionnette *or* qu'un pantin dont on tire les fils; *see* **glove** *etc*. 2 comp *theatre, play* de marionnettes; (*fig, esp Pol*) *state, leader, cabinet* fantoche ▸**puppet show** (spectacle *m* de) marionnettes *fpl*.

puppeteer [pʌpɪ'tɪəʳ] n montreur *m*, -euse *f* de marionnettes, marionnettiste *mf*.

puppetry ['pʌpɪtrɪ] n art *m* des marionnettes.

puppy ['pʌpɪ] 1 n = **pup 1**. 2 comp ▸**puppy fat** rondeurs *fpl* d'adolescent(e) ▸**puppy love** premier amour (d'adolescent).

purblind ['pɜ:blaɪnd] adj (*blind*) aveugle; (*poorly sighted*) qui voit très mal, qui a une vue très faible; (*fig: stupid*) aveugle, borné, obtus.

purchase ['pɜ:tʃɪs] 1 n a (*Comm etc*) achat *m*. **to make a ~** faire un achat. b (*grip, hold*) prise *f*. **the wheels can't get a ~ on this surface** les roues n'ont pas de prise sur cette surface; **I can't get a ~ on this rock** je n'arrive pas à trouver un point d'appui *or* une prise sur ce rocher. 2 comp ▸**purchase ledger** grand livre *m* des achats ▸**purchase money, purchase price** prix *m* d'achat ▸**purchase tax** (*Brit*) taxe *f* à l'achat. 3 vt acheter (*sth from sb* qch à qn, *sth for sb* qch pour *or* à qn).

purchaser ['pɜ:tʃɪsəʳ] n acheteur *m*, -euse *f*.

purchasing ['pɜ:tʃɪsɪŋ] 1 n (*Ind, Comm etc*) achat *m*. 2 comp ▸**purchasing department** service *m* des achats *or* de l'approvisionnement ▸**purchasing officer** (*Ind, Comm etc*) acheteur *m*, -euse *f* (professionnel(le)) ▸**purchasing power** pouvoir *m* d'achat.

pure [pjʊəʳ] 1 adj (*gen*) pur. **as ~ as the driven snow** innocent comme l'enfant qui vient de naître; (*Bible*) **~ in heart** au cœur pur; **~ science** science pure; (*Genetics*) **~ line** hérédité pure; **~ alcohol** alcool absolu; **a ~ wool suit** un complet pure laine; **~ and simple** pur et simple; **it was ~ hypocrisy** c'était de la pure hypocrisie *or* de l'hypocrisie pure; **it was a ~ accident** c'était un pur accident; **a ~ waste of time** une pure *or* belle *or* vraie perte de temps; (*Phon*) **~ vowel** voyelle pure. 2 comp ▸**purebred** adj de race ◊ n animal *m* de race; (*horse*) pur-sang *m inv* ▸**pure-hearted** (au cœur) pur ▸**pure-minded** pur (d'esprit).

purée ['pjʊəreɪ] n purée *f*.

purely ['pjʊəlɪ] adv purement. **~ and simply** purement et simplement.

pureness ['pjʊənɪs] n (*NonC*) pureté *f*.

purgation [pɜ:'geɪʃən] n (*Rel*) purgation *f*, purification *f*; (*Pol*) purge *f*, épuration *f*; (*Med*) purge.

purgative ['pɜ:gətɪv] adj, n purgatif *(m)*.

purgatory ['pɜ:gətərɪ] n (*lit, fig*) purgatoire *m*. (*fig*) **it was ~** c'était un vrai purgatoire *or* supplice; **it was ~ for me** j'étais au supplice.

purge [pɜ:dʒ] 1 n (*act: gen, Med*) purge *f*; (*Pol*) purge, épuration *f*; (*medicament*) purge, purgatif *m*. **the political ~s which followed the revolution** les purges politiques qui ont *or* l'épuration politique qui a suivi la révolution; **a ~ of the dissidents** une purge des dissidents. 2 vt a (*gen*) purger (*of* de); (*Med*) *person, body* purger; (*Pol*) *state, nation, party* purger (*of* de); *traitors, bad elements* éliminer; *sins* purger, expier. b (*Jur*) *person* disculper (*of* de); *accusation* se disculper de. **to ~ an offence** purger une peine; (*US*) **to ~ one's contempt (of Congress)** purger sa contumace.

purification [,pjʊərɪfɪ'keɪʃən] n *[air, water, metal etc]* épuration *f*; *[person]* purification *f*.

purifier ['pjʊərɪfaɪəʳ] n épurateur *m*, purificateur *m*. **air ~** purificateur d'air; *see* **water** *etc*.

purify ['pjʊərɪfaɪ] vt *substance* épurer, purifier; *person* purifier.

purism ['pjʊərɪzəm] n purisme *m*.

purist ['pjʊərɪst] adj, n puriste *(mf)*.
puritan ['pjʊərɪtən] adj, n puritain(e) *m(f)*.
puritanical [,pjʊərɪ'tænɪkəl] adj puritain, de puritain.
puritanism ['pjʊərɪtənɪzəm] n puritanisme *m*.
purity ['pjʊərɪtɪ] n pureté *f*.
purl [pɜ:l] *(Knitting)* 1 n *(also ~ stitch)* maille *f* à l'envers. **a row of ~ (stitches)** un rang à l'envers; *see* **plain.** 2 adj à l'envers. 3 vt tricoter à l'envers; *see* **knit.**
purlieus ['pɜ:lju:z] npl *(frm)* alentours *mpl*, abords *mpl*, environs *mpl*.
purloin [pɜ:'lɔɪn] vt dérober.
purple ['pɜ:pl] 1 adj cramoisi, violet, pourpre. **to go ~ (in the face)** devenir cramoisi *or* pourpre; *(US Mil)* **P~ Heart** *décoration attribuée aux blessés de guerre; (Drugs sl)* **~ heart** pilule *f* du bonheur‡; *(Literat)* **~ passage** *or* **patch** morceau *m* de bravoure. 2 n *(colour)* pourpre *m*, violet *m*. *(Rel)* **the ~** la pourpre.
purplish ['pɜ:plɪʃ] adj violacé, qui tire sur le violet.
purport ['pɜ:pət] 1 n *(meaning)* signification *f*, portée *f*, teneur *f*; *(intention)* but *m*. 2 [pɜ:'pɔ:t] vt: **to ~ to be** *[person]* se présenter comme étant, se faire passer pour, se prétendre; *[book, film, statement etc]* se vouloir; **a man ~ing to come from the Ministry** un homme qui serait envoyé *or* qui se prétend envoyé par le ministère; **to ~ that ...** prétendre *or* suggérer *or* laisser entendre que ... .
purportedly [pɛ:'pɔ:tədlɪ] adv: **~ written by ...** qui aurait été écrit par ... .
purpose ['pɜ:pəs] 1 n a *(aim, intention)* but *m*, objet *m*; *(use)* usage *m*, utilité *f*. **he's a man with a ~ in life** c'est un homme qui a un but *or* un objectif dans la vie; **it's a film with a ~** c'est un film à thèse *or* qui contient un message; **what is the ~ of the meeting?** quel est le but *or* l'objet *or* l'utilité de la réunion?; **what was the ~ of his visit?** quel était le but *or* l'objet de sa visite?, dans quel but est-il venu?; **what is the ~ of this tool?** à quoi sert cet outil?; **my ~ in doing this is ...** la raison pour laquelle je fais ceci est ..., le but *or* l'objet que je me propose est ...; **for** *or* **with the ~ of doing ...** dans le but *or* l'intention de faire ..., afin de faire ...; **for this ~** dans ce but, à cet effet, à cette fin; **for my ~s** pour ce que je veux faire; **for our ~s we may disregard this** en ce qui nous concerne *or* pour ce qui nous touche nous n'avons pas besoin de tenir compte de cela; **it is adequate for the ~** cela fait l'affaire, cela atteint son but, cela remplit son objet; **for all practical ~s** en pratique; **for the ~s of the meeting** pour (les besoins de) cette réunion; *(Jur)* **for the ~s of this Act** aux fins de la presénte loi; *see* **all, intent, serve** *etc*.
b *(phrases)* **on ~** exprès, à dessein, délibérément; **he did it on ~** il l'a fait exprès *or* à dessein; **he did it on ~ to annoy me** il l'a fait exprès pour me contrarier; **to no ~** en vain, inutilement; **to no ~ at all** en pure perte; **to some ~, to good ~** utilement, à profit; **the money will be used to good ~** l'argent sera bien *or* utilement employé; **to the ~** à propos; **not to the ~** hors de propos.
c *(NonC)* **(sense of) ~** résolution *f*; **he has no sense of ~** il vit sans but, il manque de résolution; **his activities seem to lack ~** il semble agir sans but précis; **he has great strength of ~** il est très résolu *or* déterminé, il a énormément de volonté; *see* **infirm, infirmity.**
2 comp ▸**purpose-built** construit spécialement; **it was purpose-built** c'était construit spécialement.
3 vt se proposer *(to do* de faire).
purposeful ['pɜ:pəsfʊl] adj *(determined) person* résolu, déterminé, qui sait ce qu'il veut; *gesture, look* résolu, décidé; *(intentional) act* réfléchi, significatif.
purposefully ['pɜ:pəsfəlɪ] adv *move, act* dans un but précis *or* réfléchi, avec une intention bien arrêtée, délibérément.
purposefulness ['pɜ:pəsfʊlnɪs] n résolution *f*, détermination *f*, ténacité *f*.
purposeless ['pɜ:pəslɪs] adj *person* qui manque de résolution, qui n'a pas de but, qui ne sait pas ce qu'il veut; *character* indécis, irrésolu; *act* sans but *or* objet (précis), inutile.
purposely ['pɜ:pəslɪ] adv exprès, à dessein, de propos délibéré. **he made a ~ vague statement** il a fait exprès de faire une déclaration peu précise; **the government's statement was ~ vague** la déclaration du gouvernement a été délibérément vague *or* a été vague à dessein.
purr [pɜ:ʳ] 1 vi *[cat]* ronronner, faire ronron; *[person, engine, car]* ronronner. 2 vt: **"sit down, darling" she ~ed** "assieds-toi, chéri" roucoula-t-elle. 3 n *[cat]* ronronnement *m*, ronron *m*; *[engine, car]* ronronnement.
purring ['pɜ:rɪŋ] n = **purr 3.**
purse [pɜ:s] 1 n *(for coins)* porte-monnaie *m inv*, bourse *f*; *(wallet)* portefeuille *m*; *(US: handbag)* sac *m* à main; *(esp Sport: prize)* prix *m*, récompense *f*. *(fig)* **it's beyond my ~** c'est trop cher pour moi *or* pour ma bourse, c'est au-delà de mes moyens; *see* **public.** 2 comp ▸**purse-proud** fier de sa fortune ▸**purse strings:** *(fig)* **to hold/tighten the purse strings** tenir/serrer les cordons de la bourse. 3 vt: **to ~ (up) one's lips** faire la moue, pincer les lèvres.
purser ['pɜ:səʳ] n *(Naut)* commissaire *m* (du bord).
pursuance [pə'sju:əns] n *(frm)* exécution *f*. **in ~ of** dans l'exécution de.
pursuant [pə'sju:ənt] adj *(frm)* **~ to** *(following on)* suivant; *(in accordance with)* conformément à.
pursue [pə'sju:] vt a *(chase)* poursuivre; *thief, animal* poursuivre, pourchasser, *(track)* traquer; *pleasure* rechercher; *objective* poursuivre; *success, fame* rechercher, briguer; *[misfortune etc]* suivre, accompagner. **his eyes ~d me round the room** il me suivait du regard à travers la pièce; *(fig)* **he won't stop pursuing her** il n'arrête pas de la poursuivre *or* de lui courir après*. b *(carry on) studies, career* poursuivre, continuer; *profession* exercer; *course of action* suivre; *plan, theme, inquiry* poursuivre.
pursuer [pə'sju:əʳ] n poursuivant(e) *m(f)*.
pursuit [pə'sju:t] 1 n a *(chase)* poursuite *f*; *(fig: of pleasure, happiness)* poursuite, recherche *f*. **in ~ of** *thief* à la poursuite de; *happiness, success* à la poursuite de, à la recherche de; **to go in ~ of sb/sth** se mettre à la poursuite *or* à la recherche de qn/qch; **with two policemen in hot ~** avec deux agents à ses *(or* mes *etc)* trousses. b *(occupation)* occupation *f*, travail *m*, activité *f*; *(pastime)* passe-temps *m inv*. **scientific ~s** travaux *mpl or* recherches *fpl* scientifiques. 2 comp ▸**pursuit plane** avion *m* de chasse.
purulence ['pjʊərʊləns] n purulence *f*.
purulent ['pjʊərʊlənt] adj purulent.
purvey [pə'veɪ] vt *(Comm etc)* fournir *(sth to sb* qch à qn), approvisionner *(sth to sb* qn en qch).
purveyance [pə'veɪəns] n *(Comm etc)* approvisionnement *m*, fourniture *f* de provisions.
purveyor [pə'veɪəʳ] n *(Comm etc)* fournisseur *m*, -euse *f*, approvisionneur *m*, -euse *f* *(of sth* en qch, *to sb* de qn).
purview ['pɜ:vju:] n *(frm) [act, bill]* articles *mpl*; *[the law]* domaine *m*, limites *fpl*; *[inquiry]* champ *m*, limites; *[committee]* capacité *f*, compétence *f*; *[book, film]* limites, portée *f*.
pus [pʌs] n pus *m*.
push [pʊʃ] 1 n a *(shove)* poussée *f*. **with one ~** d'une (seule) poussée, en poussant une seule fois; **to give sb/sth a ~** pousser qn/qch; **the car needs a ~** il faut pousser la voiture; *(Brit fig)* **to give sb the ~‡** *[employer]* flanquer qn à la porte*; *[boyfriend, girlfriend etc]* laisser tomber qn*, plaquer qn‡; *(Brit fig)* **he got the ~‡** *(from employer)* il s'est fait flanquer à la porte*; *(from girlfriend)* elle l'a laissé tomber*, elle l'a plaqué‡; **there was a great ~ as the crowd emerged** quand la foule est sortie il y a eu une grande bousculade; *(US fig)* **when ~ comes to shove** (en mettant les choses) au pire; *see* **bell**[1] *etc*.
b *(Mil: advance)* poussée *f*, avance *f*. *(Mil)* **they made a ~ to the coast** ils ont fait une poussée *or* ils ont avancé jusqu'à la côte; **the ~ towards the cities** le mouvement des populations vers la ville.
c *(fig) (effort)* gros effort, coup *m* de collier; *(campaign)* campagne *f*. **they made a ~ to get everything finished in time** ils ont fait un gros effort *or* ils ont donné un coup de collier pour tout terminer à temps; **they were having a ~ on sales** *or* **a sales ~** ils avaient organisé une campagne de promotion des ventes; **we're having a ~ for more teachers** nous menons une campagne pour une augmentation du nombre d'enseignants; **at a ~*** au besoin, en cas de besoin, à la rigueur; **when it comes to the ~*** au moment critique *or* crucial.
d *(*NonC: drive, energy)* dynamisme *m*, initiative *f*. **he's got plenty of ~** il est très dynamique, il est plein d'initiative.
2 comp ▸**push-bike*** *(Brit)* vélo *m*, bécane* *f* ▸**push-button** *see* **push-button** ▸**pushcart** charrette *f* à bras ▸**push chair** *(Brit)* poussette *f (pour enfant)* ▸**pushover*** *see* **pushover*** ▸**pushpin** épingle *f* (à tête de couleur) ▸**push-pull circuit** *(Electronics)* push-pull *m* ▸**push rod** *(Aut)* tige *f* de culbuteur ▸**push-up** *(Gymnastics)* traction *f*, pompe* *f*; **to do push-ups** faire des tractions *or* des pompes*.
3 vt a *(shove) car, barrow, door, person* pousser; *(press) knob, button* appuyer sur, presser sur; *(prod)* pousser; *(thrust) stick, finger etc* enfoncer *(into* dans, *between* entre); *rag etc* fourrer *(into* dans). **don't ~ me!** ne (me) poussez pas!, ne (me) bousculez pas!; **to ~ sb into a room** pousser qn dans une pièce; **to ~ sb against a wall** pousser *or* presser qn contre un mur; **to ~ sb off the pavement** pousser qn du trottoir, *(by jostling)* obliger qn à descendre du trottoir (en le bousculant); **to ~ sb in/out/up** *etc* faire entrer/sortir/monter *etc* qn en le poussant *or* d'une poussée; **he ~ed him down the stairs** il l'a poussé et l'a fait tomber dans l'escalier; **they ~ed him out of the car** ils l'ont poussé hors de la voiture; **to ~ sb/sth out of the way** écarter qn/qch en poussant, pousser qn/qch à l'écart; **he ~ed the box under the table** *(moved)* il a poussé *or* fourré* la boîte sous la table; *(hid)* il a vite caché la boîte sous la table; **they ~ed the car off the road** ils ont poussé la voiture sur le bas-côté; **she ~ed the books off the table** elle a poussé *or* balayé les livres de dessus la table; **he ~ed his finger into my eye** il m'a mis le doigt dans l'œil; **he ~ed his head through the window** il a mis *or* passé la tête par la fenêtre; **he ~ed the book into my hand** il m'a fourré* le livre dans la main; **to ~ a door open/shut** ouvrir/fermer une porte en poussant *or* d'une poussée, pousser une porte (pour l'ouvrir/la fermer); **to ~ one's way through a crowd** se frayer *or* s'ouvrir un chemin dans la foule *(see also* **4b** *and* **push in 1a** *etc)*; *(fig)* **he ~ed the thought to the back of his mind** il a repoussé *or* écarté cette pensée pour le moment; *(fig)* **it ~ed the matter right out of my mind** cela m'a fait complètement oublier l'affaire; *(fig)* **he must be ~ing* 60** il ne doit pas avoir loin de 60 ans, il doit friser la soixantaine; *(fig)* **he must be ~ing* 75** il ne doit pas avoir loin de 75 ans.

b (*fig: press, advance*) *advantage* poursuivre; *claim* présenter avec insistance; *one's views* mettre en avant, imposer; *plan, method, solution* préconiser, recommander; *product* pousser la vente de, faire de la réclame pour; *candidate etc* appuyer, soutenir. **he ~ed the bill through Parliament** il a réussi à faire voter le projet de loi; **to ~ home an attack** pousser à fond une attaque; **they are going to ~ the export side of the business** ils vont donner priorité aux exportations dans leur affaire; **to ~ drugs** revendre de la drogue; **he was ~ing drugs to students** il ravitaillait les étudiants en drogue, il revendait de la drogue aux étudiants; **don't ~ your luck*** vas-y doucement!; **he's ~ing his luck*** il y va un peu fort, il charrie⁑.

c (*put pressure on*) pousser; (*force*) forcer, obliger; (*harass*) importuner, harceler. **to ~ sb for payment/for an answer** presser *or* engager qn à payer/à répondre; **to ~ o.s. hard** se mener la vie dure; **he ~es himself too hard** il exige trop de lui-même; **don't ~ him too hard** *or* **too far** ne soyez pas trop dur envers lui, ne le poussez pas à bout; **they ~ed him to the limits of his endurance** on l'a poussé jusqu'à la limite de ses forces; **stop ~ing him and let him make up his own mind** arrêtez de le harceler *or* fichez-lui la paix* et laissez-le décider tout seul; **to ~ sb to do** pousser qn à faire, insister pour que qn fasse; **to ~ sb into doing** forcer *or* obliger qn à faire; **I was ~ed into it** on m'y a poussé *or* forcé, je n'ai pas eu le choix; **he was ~ed into teaching** on l'a poussé à devenir professeur *or* à faire de l'enseignement; **to be ~ed* for time/money** être à court de temps/d'argent, manquer de temps/d'argent; **I'm really ~ed* today** je suis vraiment bousculé *or* débordé aujourd'hui; **I'm rather ~ed* for boxes just now** je n'ai pas beaucoup de boîtes en ce moment; **that's ~ing it a bit!*** (*indignantly*) c'est un peu fort!, tu y vas (*or* il y va *etc*) un peu fort!; (*not much time etc*) ça c'est un peu juste!

d (*US Golf*) **to ~ the ball** couper *or* faire dévier la balle.

4 vi a pousser; (*on bell*) appuyer (*on* sur). **you ~ and I'll pull** poussez et moi je vais tirer; (*in crowd etc*) **stop ~ing!** arrêtez de pousser!, ne bousculez pas!; "**~**" (*on door*) "poussez"; (*on bell*) "appuyez", "sonnez"; (*fig*) **he ~es too much** il se met trop en avant; (*fig*) **to ~ for better conditions/higher wages** *etc* faire pression pour obtenir de meilleures conditions/une augmentation de salaire *etc*.

b (*move: also* **~ one's way**) **they ~ed (their way) into/out of the room** ils sont entrés dans la pièce/sortis de la pièce en se frayant un passage; **he ~ed (his way) past me** il a réussi à passer *or* il m'a dépassé en me bousculant; **she ~ed (her way) through the crowd** elle s'est frayé *or* ouvert un chemin dans la foule.

c (*Mil: advance*) **to ~ into enemy territory** avancer en territoire ennemi.

►**push about** vt sep = **push around**.

►**push ahead** vi (*make progress*) avancer à grands pas. **to push ahead with** faire avancer à grands pas.

►**push along** 1 vi a (*: *leave*) filer*, se sauver*. b (*Aut etc: move quickly*) rouler bon train. **the coach was pushing along at 70** le car faisait facilement du 110 (à l'heure). 2 vt sep *person, cart, chair* pousser; (*fig: hasten*) *work* activer, accélérer.

►**push around** vt sep a *cart, toy* pousser de-ci de-là, pousser à droite et à gauche. b (* *fig: bully*) marcher sur les pieds à* (*fig*), être vache⁑ avec. **stop pushing me around!** arrête de me donner des ordres! *or* de me marcher sur les pieds!*

►**push aside** vt sep *person, chair* écarter (brusquement), pousser à l'écart; (*fig*) *objection, suggestion* écarter, rejeter.

►**push away** vt sep *person, chair, one's plate* repousser; *gift* repousser, rejeter.

►**push back** vt sep *cover, blankets, lock of hair* rejeter *or* repousser (en arrière); *curtains* ouvrir; *person, crowd, enemy* repousser, faire reculer; (*fig*) *desire, impulse* réprimer, contenir, refréner.

►**push down** 1 vi appuyer (*on* sur). 2 vt sep a *switch, lever* abaisser; *knob, button* appuyer sur; *pin, stick* enfoncer; (*knock over*) *fence, barrier, person* renverser. **he pushed the ball down off the roof** d'une poussée il a fait tomber le ballon du toit; **he pushed the books down into the box** il a entassé les livres dans la caisse. b (*fig: reduce*) *prices, inflation, value* réduire.

►**push forward** 1 vi (*also* **push one's way forward**) avancer, se frayer *or* s'ouvrir un chemin. 2 vt sep *person, box etc* pousser en avant, faire avancer. **he pushed himself forward** il s'est avancé, il s'est frayé *or* ouvert un chemin; (*fig*) il s'est mis en avant, il s'est fait valoir.

►**push in** 1 vi a (*also* **push one's way in**) s'introduire de force. b (*fig: interfere*) intervenir. **he's always pushing in where he's not wanted** il se mêle toujours de *or* il intervient toujours dans ce qui ne le regarde pas. 2 vt sep a *stick, pin, finger* enfoncer; *rag* fourrer dedans; *person* pousser dedans; *knob, button* appuyer sur. **they opened the door and pushed him in** ils ouvrirent la porte et le poussèrent dans la pièce; **they took him to the pond and pushed him in** ils l'ont conduit à l'étang et l'ont poussé dedans; *see* **oar**. b (*break*) *window, door, sides of box* enfoncer.

►**push off** 1 vi a (*Naut*) pousser au large. b (*: *leave*) filer*, se sauver*, ficher le camp*. **I must push off** il faut que je file* (*subj*) *or* que je me sauve* (*subj*); **push off!** décampez!, fichez le camp!*, filez!* c **the top just pushes off** il suffit de pousser le haut pour l'enlever. 2 vt sep a *top, lid* pousser, enlever en poussant; *vase from shelf etc* faire tomber (*from* de); *person from cliff etc* pousser, faire tomber (*from* de, du haut de). b (*Naut*) déborder.

►**push on** 1 vi (*in journey*) pousser (*to* jusqu'à), continuer son chemin; (*in work*) continuer, persévérer. **to push on with sth** continuer (à faire) qch. 2 vt sep a *lid, cover* placer *or* (re)mettre en place (en pressant *or* en appuyant). b (*fig: incite*) pousser, inciter (*sb to do* qn à faire).

►**push out** 1 vi a (*also* **push one's way out**) se frayer *or* s'ouvrir un chemin (à travers la foule). b *[roots, branches]* pousser; *[shoots]* pointer, sortir; *[birds]* sortir. 2 vt sep a *person, object* pousser dehors; *stopper* faire sortir (en poussant); (*fig*) *employee, office-holder* évincer, se débarrasser de. **to push the boat out** (*lit*) pousser au large; (*fig*) faire la fête, célébrer. b (*Bot*) *roots, shoots* produire. c (*: *produce*) *information, products etc* débiter.

►**push over** 1 vi: **he pushed (his way) over towards her** il se fraya *or* s'ouvrit un chemin vers elle. 2 vt sep a *object* pousser (*to sb* vers qn); (*over cliff, bridge etc*) pousser, faire tomber. b (*topple*) *chair, vase, person* renverser, faire tomber. 3 **pushover*** n *see* **pushover***.

►**push through** 1 vi (*also* **push one's way through**) se frayer *or* s'ouvrir un chemin. 2 vt sep a *stick, hand etc* enfoncer, (faire) passer. b (*fig*) *deal, business* conclure à la hâte; *decision* faire accepter à la hâte; (*Parl*) *bill* réussir à faire voter.

►**push to** vt sep *door* fermer (en poussant), pousser (pour fermer).

►**push up** 1 vt sep a *stick, hand, lever, switch* (re)lever; *spectacles* relever. (*fig*) **he's pushing up the daisies*** il mange les pissenlits par la racine*. b (*fig: increase*) *numbers, taxes, sales* augmenter; *prices* augmenter, faire monter; *demand, speed* augmenter, accroître; *sb's temperature, blood pressure* faire monter. **that pushes up the total to over 100** cela fait monter le total à plus de 100. 2 **push-up** n *see* **push 2**.

push-button ['pʊʃ,bʌtn] 1 n bouton *m*, poussoir *m*. 2 adj *machine etc* à commande automatique; *telephone* à touches; *factory* automatisée. **~ controls** commande *f* automatique; **~ warfare** guerre *f* presse-bouton.

pusher ['pʊʃəʳ] n a (*pej*) arriviste *mf*; *see* **pen¹** *etc*. b (*Drugs sl: also* **drug-~**) revendeur *m*, -euse *f* (de drogue), ravitailleur *m*, -euse *f* (en drogue).

pushful* ['pʊʃfʊl] adj = **pushy**.

pushfulness* ['pʊʃfʊlnɪs] n, **pushiness*** ['pʊʃɪnɪs] n (*pej*) arrivisme *m*, excès *m* d'ambition; *[manner]* arrogance *f*.

pushing ['pʊʃɪŋ] 1 adj *person* dynamique, entreprenant; (*pej*) arriviste, qui se fait valoir, qui se met trop en avant; *manner* arrogant. 2 n (*lit*) cohue *f*; (*fig: persuasion*) persuasion *f*.

Pushkin ['pʊʃkɪn] n Pouchkine *m*.

pushover* ['pʊʃəʊvəʳ] n: **it was a ~** c'était la facilité même, c'était un jeu d'enfant, c'était l'enfance de l'art; **he was a ~** (*easily beaten*) il a été battu à plate(s) couture(s), il s'est fait enfoncer*; (*easily swindled*) il s'est laissé avoir*, il a donné dans le panneau*; (*easily convinced*) il a marché* tout de suite; **he's a ~ for blondes** quand il rencontre une blonde, il ne se tient plus.

pushy* ['pʊʃɪ] adj (*pej*) *person* arriviste, qui se fait valoir, qui se met trop en avant; *manner* arrogant.

pusillanimity [,pju:sɪlə'nɪmɪtɪ] n pusillanimité *f*.

pusillanimous [,pju:sɪ'lænɪməs] adj pusillanime.

puss* [pʊs] n a (*cat*) minet *m*, -ette *f*, minou *m*. (*to cat*) ~, ~! minet, minet!, minou, minou!; **P~ in Boots** le Chat Botté. b (⁑) (*girl*) nana⁑ *f*, souris⁑ *f*; (*face*) gueule⁑ *f*; (*mouth*) margoulette⁑ *f*.

pussy* ['pʊsɪ] 1 n a minet *m*, -ette *f*, minou *m*, chat(te) *m(f)*. b (⁂) (*female genitals*) chatte⁂ *f*; (*intercourse*) baise⁂ *f*. 2 comp ►**pussycat** (*lit*) minet *m*, -ette *f*, minou *m*; (*US*) **hi, pussycat!*** bonjour, mon chou!* *or* mon ange! ►**pussyfoot*** vi marcher à pas de loup; (*fig*) ne pas se mouiller*, ménager la chèvre et le chou ►**pussyfooting** adj (*fig*) *person* qui a peur de se mouiller*; *attitude* timoré ◊ n (*also* **pussyfooting* about** *or* **around**) tergiversations *fpl* ►**pussy willow** (*Bot*) saule *m* (blanc).

pustule ['pʌstju:l] n pustule *f*.

put [pʊt] pret, ptp **put** 1 vt a (*place*) mettre; poser; placer. **~ it on the table/beside the window/over there** mettez-le *or* posez-le *or* placez-le sur la table/près de la fenêtre/là-bas; **~ it in the drawer** mettez-le *or* placez-le dans le tiroir; **to ~ sth in one's pocket/purse** *etc* mettre qch dans sa poche/son porte-monnaie *etc*; **you've ~ the picture rather high up** tu as mis *or* placé *or* accroché le tableau un peu trop haut; **he ~s sugar in his tea** il met *or* prend du sucre dans son thé; **he ~ some sugar in his tea** il a mis du sucre dans son thé, il a sucré son thé; **he ~ some more coal on the fire** il a remis *or* rajouté du charbon sur le feu; **~ the book in its proper place** (re)mets le livre à sa place; **to ~ one's arms round sb** prendre qn dans ses bras, entourer qn de ses bras; **he ~ his head through the window** il a passé la tête par la fenêtre; **he ~ his head round the door** il a passé la tête par la porte; **she ~ the shell to her ear** elle a mis le coquillage contre son oreille, elle a porté le coquillage à son oreille; **he ~ his rucksack over the fence** il a mis *or* passé son sac à dos de l'autre côté de la barrière; **they ~ a plank across the stream** ils ont mis *or* placé *or* posé une planche en travers du ruisseau; **he ~ the lid on the box** il a mis *or* placé le couvercle sur la boîte; **he ~ his hand**

over his mouth il s'est mis la main devant la bouche; (*shaking hands*) **~ it there!*** tope là!; **to ~ a spacecraft into orbit** placer un vaisseau spatial sur orbite, mettre un vaisseau spatial en orbite; **to ~ a button on a shirt** mettre *or* coudre un bouton à une chemise; **to ~ a patch on a sheet** mettre une pièce à un drap, rapiécer un drap; **to ~ a new blade on a saw** mettre *or* fixer une nouvelle lame à une scie, remplacer la lame d'une scie; **to ~ an advertisement in the paper** placer *or* mettre *or* passer une annonce dans le journal; **he ~ me on the train** il m'a mis *or* accompagné au train; **he ~ me into a non-smoker** il m'a trouvé une place dans un compartiment non-fumeurs; **to ~ sb off a train/boat** *etc* débarquer qn d'un train/d'un bateau *etc;* **to ~ sb on to/off a committee** nommer qn à/renvoyer qn d'un comité; (*fig*) **that ~ me in a mess!*** ça m'a mis *or* fourré dans le pétrin!; *for other phrases see* **bed, stay** *etc.*

b (*fig*) **~ o.s.** se mettre; **I didn't know where to ~ myself!*** je ne savais plus où me mettre!; **~ yourself in my place** mets-toi à ma place.

c (*fig*) mettre; *signature* apposer (*on, to* à); *mark* faire (*on* sur, à). **he ~ the matter in the hands of his solicitor** il a remis l'affaire entre les mains de son avocat; **to ~ one's confidence in sb/sth** placer sa confiance en qn/qch; **what value do you ~ on this?** (*lit*) à quelle valeur *or* à quel prix estimez-vous cela?; (*fig*) quelle valeur accordez-vous *or* attribuez-vous *or* attachez-vous à cela?; **he ~ all his energy into his career** il a consacré toute son énergie à sa carrière; **you get out of life what you ~ in(to it)** on ne retire de la vie que ce qu'on y met soi-même; **he has ~ a lot into his marriage** il a fait beaucoup d'efforts pour que son mariage soit une réussite; **I've ~ a lot of time and trouble into it** j'y ai consacré beaucoup de temps et d'efforts; **to ~ money into a company** placer *or* investir de l'argent dans une affaire; **he ~ all his savings into the project** il a placé *or* englouti toutes ses économies dans ce projet; **to ~ money on a horse** parier *or* miser sur un cheval; **he ~ £10 on Black Beauty** il a parié *or* misé 10 livres sur Black Beauty; **he ~s good health among his greatest assets** il estime que sa robuste santé est l'un de ses meilleurs atouts; **we should ~ happiness before** *or* **above wealth** on devrait placer le bonheur au-dessus de la richesse, on devrait préférer le bonheur à la richesse; **I ~ Milton above Tennyson** je place Milton au-dessus de Tennyson, je trouve Milton supérieur à Tennyson; **I wouldn't ~ him among the greatest poets** je ne le place *or* classe pas parmi les plus grands poètes, à mon avis ce n'est pas l'un des plus grands poètes; *for other phrases see* **blame, end, market, pay** *etc.*

d (*thrust; direct*) enfoncer. **to ~ one's fist through a window** passer le poing à travers une vitre; **to ~ one's pen through a word** rayer *or* barrer *or* biffer un mot; **to ~ a knife into sb** poignarder qn, filer* un coup de poignard à qn; **to ~ a bullet into sb** atteindre qn d'une balle, coller une balle dans la peau de qn*; **I ~ a bullet through his head** je lui ai tiré une balle dans la tête; (*Sport*) **to ~ the shot** *or* **the weight** lancer le poids; (*Naut*) **to ~ the rudder to port** mettre la barre à bâbord.

e (*cause to be, do, begin etc*) **to ~ sb in a good/bad mood** mettre qn de bonne/mauvaise humeur; **to ~ sb on a diet** mettre qn au régime; **to ~ sb to great expense** occasionner de grosses dépenses à qn; **to ~ sb to some trouble** *or* **inconvenience** déranger qn; **to ~ one's time to good use** bien employer son temps, mettre son temps à profit, faire bon usage de son temps; **they ~ him to dig(ging) the garden** ils lui ont fait bêcher le jardin, ils lui ont donné la tâche de bêcher le jardin; **I ~ him to work at once** je l'ai mis au travail aussitôt; **they had to ~ 4 men on to this job** ils ont dû employer 4 hommes à ce travail *or* pour faire ce travail; **to ~ a watch to the right time** mettre une montre à l'heure; *for other phrases see* **death, sleep, wise** *etc.*

f (*prepositional usages*) **he tried to ~ one across** *or* **over on me*** il a essayé de me faire marcher* *or* de m'avoir*; **you'll never ~ anything across** *or* **over on him*** on ne la lui fait pas, on ne peut pas le faire marcher*; **she ~ my brother against me** elle a monté mon frère contre moi; **his remarks ~ me off my food** ses remarques m'ont coupé l'appétit; **it almost ~ me off opera for good** cela a failli me dégoûter de l'opéra pour toujours; **it certainly ~ me off going to Greece** cela m'a certainement ôté l'envie d'aller en Grèce; **the noise is ~ting me off my work** le bruit me distrait de mon travail, le bruit m'empêche de me concentrer sur mon travail; **someone has been ~ over him at the office** on a placé quelqu'un au-dessus de lui au bureau; **to ~ sb through an examination** faire subir un examen à qn; **they really ~ him through it*** ils lui en ont fait voir de dures*, ils lui ont fait passer un mauvais quart d'heure; *see* **put across, put off** *etc; for other phrases see* **pace, scent, stroke** *etc.*

g (*express*) dire, exprimer. **can you ~ it another way?** pouvez-vous vous exprimer autrement?; **to ~ it bluntly** pour parler franc, sans mâcher mes mots; **as he would ~ it** selon sa formule *or* son expression, pour employer sa formule *or* son expression; **as Shakespeare ~s it** comme le dit Shakespeare; **I don't quite know how to ~ it** je ne sais pas trop comment le dire; **let me ~ it another way** si je peux m'exprimer autrement, en d'autres mots; **how shall I ~ it?** comment dire?, comment dirais-je?; **~ it so as not to offend her** présente la chose de façon à ne pas la blesser; **how will you ~ it to him?** comment vas-tu le lui dire?, comment vas-tu lui présenter la chose?; **if I may ~ it so** si je puis dire, si je peux m'exprimer ainsi; **the compliment was gracefully ~** le compliment était bien tourné; **to ~ an expression into French** traduire *or* mettre une expression en français; **how would you ~ it in French?** comment le dirais-tu en français?; **to ~ into verse** mettre en vers; *for other phrases see* **mildly, word, writing** *etc.*

h (*submit, expound*) *case, problem* exposer, présenter; *proposal, resolution* présenter, soumettre; *question* poser. **he ~ the arguments for and against the project** il a présenté les arguments pour et contre le projet; **he ~ his own side of the argument very clearly** il a présenté *or* exposé très clairement son côté de l'affaire; **I ~ it to you that ...** n'est-il pas vrai que ...?, je maintiens que ...; **it was ~ to me in no uncertain terms that I should resign** on m'a déclaré en termes très clairs que je devrais donner ma démission.

i (*estimate*) estimer, évaluer. **they ~ the loss at £10,000** on estime *or* évalue *or* chiffre la perte à 10.000 livres; **the population was ~ at 50,000** on a évalué *or* estimé le nombre d'habitants à 50.000; **what would you ~ it at?** à combien l'estimez-vous? *or* l'évaluez-vous?; **I'd ~ her** *or* **her age at 50** je lui donnerais 50 ans.

j (*St Ex: offer to sell*) *stock, security* se déclarer vendeur de.

2 vi (*Naut*) **to ~ into port** faire escale *or* relâche, entrer au *or* dans le port; **the ship ~ into Southampton** le navire est entré au *or* dans le port de Southampton; **to ~ to sea** appareiller, lever l'ancre, prendre le large.

3 comp ▸**put-down*** (*denigrating*) dénigrement *m*; (*snub*) rebuffade *f* ▸**put-in** (*Rugby*) introduction *f* ▸**put-on*** n (*pretence*) comédie *f*; (*hoax*) mystification *f*, farce *f* ◊ adj (*feigned*) affecté, feint, simulé ▸**put option** *see* 4 ▸**put-up job*** coup *m* monté ▸**put-upon***: **to be put-upon** se faire marcher sur les pieds (*fig*); **I feel put-upon** je trouve qu'on profite de moi, je me sens exploité; *see also* **put upon 1**.

4 n (*St Ex*) (*premium*) prime *f* pour livrer. **~ (option)** option *f* de vente, ou *m*, put *m*.

▸**put about** 1 vi (*Naut*) virer de bord. 2 vt sep a *rumour etc* faire courir, faire circuler. **he put it about that ...** il a fait courir *or* circuler le bruit que ... . b (†) = **put out 2g**. c (*Naut*) **to put the ship about** virer de bord.

▸**put across** vt sep a (*communicate; get accepted*) *ideas, intentions, desires* faire comprendre, faire accepter, communiquer (*to sb* à qn). **to put sth across to sb** faire comprendre *or* faire accepter qch à qn; **the play puts the message across very well** l'auteur de la pièce communique très bien son message, le message de la pièce passe la rampe; **he knows his stuff but he can't put it across** il connaît son sujet à fond mais il n'arrive pas à le faire comprendre aux autres *or* à communiquer; **he can't put himself across** il n'arrive pas à se mettre en valeur; **there was a special campaign to put the new product across to the housewife** il y a eu une campagne spéciale pour faire accepter le nouveau produit aux ménagères; **she put the song across beautifully** elle a interprété la chanson à merveille.

b (*perform successfully*) **to put a deal across** réussir une affaire, conclure un marché; **he tried to put one** *or* **it across on me*** il a essayé de me faire marcher* *or* de m'avoir*; **you'll never put one** *or* **it across on him*** on ne la lui fait pas, on ne peut pas le faire marcher*.

▸**put apart** vt sep (*fig*) **that puts him apart from the others** cela le distingue des autres.

▸**put around** vt sep = **put about 2a**.

▸**put aside** vt sep a *object* mettre à part *or* de côté; (*keep, save*) *food, money* mettre de côté, garder en réserve. **she put her book aside when I came in** elle a posé son livre quand je suis entré; **he put aside the document to read later** il a mis le document à part *or* de côté pour le lire plus tard; (*Comm*) **I have had it put aside for you** je vous l'ai fait mettre de côté. b (*fig*) *doubts, worries* écarter, éloigner de soi, chasser; *idea, hope* renoncer à, écarter.

▸**put away** vt sep a = **put aside a**. b = **put aside b**. c (*put in correct or proper place*) *clothes, toys, books* ranger. **to put the car away** rentrer la voiture, mettre la voiture au garage; (*to person with knife*) **put that knife away!** range ce couteau! d (*confine*) (*in prison*) mettre en prison, boucler*, coffrer*; (*in mental hospital*) (faire) enfermer, (faire) interner. e (*: *consume*) *food* engloutir, avaler, bâfrer*; *drink* siffler*. f = **put down k**.

▸**put back** 1 vi (*Naut*) **to put back to port** rentrer au port; **they put back to Dieppe** ils sont rentrés *or* retournés à Dieppe.

2 vt sep a (*replace*) remettre (à sa place *or* en place). **put it back on the shelf** remettez-le *or* replacez-le sur l'étagère; **put it back!** remets-le à sa place!

b (*retard*) *development, progress* retarder, freiner; *clock* retarder (*by one hour* d'une heure); *clock hands* remettre en arrière. **the disaster put the project back (by) 10 years** le désastre a retardé de 10 ans la réalisation du projet; **this will put us back 10 years** cela nous fera perdre 10 ans, cela nous ramènera où nous en étions il y a 10 ans; *see also* **clock**.

c (*postpone*) remettre (*to* à).

▸**put by** vt sep = **put aside a**.

▸**put down** 1 vi [*aircraft*] se poser, atterrir; (*on carrier*) apponter.

2 vt sep a *parcel, book* poser, déposer; *child* poser, mettre à terre (*or* sur un lit *etc*); (*Aut*) *passenger* déposer, laisser. **put it down!** pose ça!; **she put her book down and rose to her feet** elle posa son livre et

se leva; (*fig*) **I simply couldn't put that book down** je ne pouvais pas m'arracher à ce livre, j'ai dévoré ce livre; (*Aut*) **put me down at the corner here** déposez-moi *or* laissez-moi *or* débarquez-moi au coin; *see* **foot** *etc.*

b (*Aviat*) *aircraft* poser.

c *umbrella* fermer.

d (*pay*) *deposit, money* verser (*on* pour). **he put down £100 (as a deposit) on the car** il a versé 100 livres d'arrhes pour la voiture.

e *wine* mettre en cave.

f (*suppress*) *revolt* réprimer, étouffer; *custom, practice* faire cesser, abolir, supprimer. **there was a campaign to put down vandalism** il y avait une campagne pour la répression du vandalisme.

g (*fig*) *person* (*silence*) réduire au silence, faire taire; (*snub*) rabrouer; (*humiliate*) humilier, rabaisser.

h (*record*) noter, inscrire. **to put sth down in writing** *or* **on paper** coucher *or* mettre qch par écrit; (*Comm*) **put it down on my account** mettez-le *or* portez-le sur mon compte; **I have put you down as a teacher/for £10** je vous ai inscrit comme professeur/pour 10 livres; **I'll put you down for the next vacancy** je vais inscrire votre nom pour la prochaine place disponible; *see* **name** *etc.*

i (*attribute*) attribuer (*sth to sth* qch à qch). **I put it down to his stupidity** je l'attribue à sa stupidité; **the accident must be put down to negligence** l'accident doit être imputé à la négligence; **we put it all down to the fact that he was tired** nous avons attribué tout cela à sa *or* la fatigue, nous avons mis tout cela sur le compte de sa *or* la fatigue.

j (*consider, assess*) considérer (*as* comme), tenir (*as* pour), prendre (*as* pour). **I had put him down as a complete fool** je l'avais pris pour *or* je le considérais comme *or* je le tenais pour un parfait imbécile; **I'd put her down as about forty** je lui donnerais la quarantaine *or* environ quarante ans.

k (*Brit: euph: kill*) *dog, cat* faire piquer; *horse* abattre, tuer.

3 **put-down** n *see* **put 3**.

▶**put forth** vt sep (*liter*) *leaves, roots, shoots* produire; *arm, hand* tendre, avancer; (*fig*) *idea, suggestion* avancer, émettre; *effort* fournir, déployer; *news, rumour* répandre, faire circuler.

▶**put forward** vt sep a (*propose*) *theory, argument, reason* avancer, présenter; *opinion* exprimer, émettre; *plan* proposer. **he put his name forward as a candidate** il s'est porté candidat, il a posé sa candidature; **he put himself forward for the job** il s'est porté candidat au poste, il a posé sa candidature au poste; **he put Jones forward for the job** il a proposé Jones pour le poste. b (*advance*) *meeting, starting time, clock, schedule, programme* avancer (*by* de, *to, until* à).

▶**put in** 1 vi (*Naut*) faire relâche *or* escale (*at* à).

2 vt sep a (*into box, drawer, room etc*) mettre dedans *or* à l'intérieur; *plant, seeds* planter, semer. **he put his head in at the window** il a passé la tête par la fenêtre; **I've put the car in for repairs** j'ai donné la voiture à réparer; (*into luggage etc*) **have you put in the camera?** est-ce que tu as pris l'appareil photo?; *see* **appearance, oar** *etc.*

b (*insert*) *word, paragraph* insérer, introduire; *remark* ajouter, glisser; (*include: in letter, publication*) inclure. **have you put in why you are not going?** est-ce que vous avez expliqué pourquoi vous n'y allez pas?; **"but it's cold" he put in** "mais il fait froid" fit-il remarquer.

c (*enter*) *document* présenter, produire, fournir; *claim* présenter; *application* faire; *one's name* avancer, inscrire. (*Jur*) **to put in a plea** plaider; **to put in a protest** élever *or* formuler une protestation; **to put sb in for an exam** inscrire *or* présenter qn à un examen; **to put sb in for a job/promotion** proposer qn pour un poste/pour de l'avancement.

d (*install*) *political party, person* élire; *central heating, double glazing etc* faire installer.

e *time* passer. **he put in the morning writing the report** il a passé la matinée à écrire le rapport; **they put in the time playing cards** ils ont passé le temps *or* ils se sont occupés en jouant aux cartes; **we have an hour to put in before the plane leaves** nous avons une heure à perdre *or* à occuper avant le départ de l'avion; **I've put in a lot of time on it** j'y ai passé *or* consacré beaucoup de temps; **he has put in a full day's work** il a bien rempli sa journée, il a bien travaillé (aujourd'hui); **can you put in a few hours at the weekend?** pourrais-tu travailler quelques heures pendant le week-end?; **she puts in an hour a day at the piano** elle fait une heure de piano par jour.

3 **put-in** n *see* **put 3**.

▶**put in for** vt fus *job* poser sa candidature pour *or* à; *promotion, rise, new house, supplementary benefit* faire une demande de, solliciter.

▶**put off** 1 vi (*Naut*) démarrer (from de), pousser au large.

2 vt sep a (*postpone*) *departure, appointment, meeting* retarder, ajourner, repousser; *decision* remettre à plus tard, différer; *visitor* renvoyer à plus tard. **he put off writing the letter** il a remis la lettre à plus tard; **to put sth off for 10 days/until January** remettre qch de 10 jours/jusqu'à janvier; **I'm sorry to have to put you off** je suis désolé d'avoir à vous décommander (jusqu'à une autre fois), je suis désolé d'avoir à vous renvoyer à plus tard.

b (*dissuade, divert*) dissuader; (*hinder, distract*) démonter, dérouter; (*disconcert*) déconcerter, troubler. **he put her off with vague promises** il l'a dissuadée avec de vagues promesses; **he is not easily put off** il ne se laisse pas facilement démonter *or* dérouter *or* décourager; **he puts me off when he laughs like that** cela me déconcerte quand il rit de cette façon; **the colour of the drink quite put me off** la couleur de la boisson m'a plutôt dégoûté; **don't let his abruptness put you off** ne vous laissez pas troubler *or* démonter par sa brusquerie.

c *coat, hat etc* enlever, retirer; *passenger* déposer, débarquer.

d (*extinguish etc*) *light, gas* éteindre; *radio, TV, heater* fermer.

▶**put on** 1 vt sep a *coat, skirt, trousers* mettre, passer, enfiler; *gloves, socks* mettre, enfiler; *hat, glasses, lotion* mettre. **to put on one's shoes** mettre ses chaussures, se chausser; **to put on one's make-up** se maquiller.

b (*add, increase*) *pressure, speed* augmenter, accroître. **to put on weight** prendre du poids, grossir; **he put on 3 kilos** il a pris 3 kilos, il a grossi de 3 kilos; **they put on two goals in the second half** ils ont encore marqué deux buts pendant la deuxième mi-temps.

c (*assume*) *indignation* affecter, feindre, simuler; *air, accent* prendre, se donner, emprunter; (**: deceive*) *person* faire marcher*. **he's just putting it on** il fait seulement semblant, c'est un air qu'il se donne; **she really puts it on*** elle se donne des airs, c'est une poseuse *or* une crâneuse*; **you're only putting me on!*** tu me fais marcher!*; **he is always putting people on* about his rich relations** il fait toujours de l'épate* avec la richesse de sa famille.

d (*make available etc*) *concert, play, show* organiser; *film* projeter; *extra train, bus etc* mettre en service. **he put on a childish display of temper** il a manifesté sa mauvaise humeur de façon puérile; **when the veal was finished they put on beef** quand il n'y a plus eu de veau ils ont servi du bœuf; (*Telec*) **put me on to Mr Brown** passez-moi M. Brown; (*Telec*) **would you put on Mrs Smith?** je voudrais parler à Mme Smith, passez-moi Mme Smith.

e (*start functioning etc*) *light, gas* allumer; *radio, TV* ouvrir; *radiator, heater* ouvrir, allumer; *tape, CD, music* mettre. **put the kettle on** mets l'eau à chauffer; **I'll just put the soup on** je vais juste mettre la soupe à cuire (*or* chauffer); **to put the brakes on** freiner.

f (*advance*) *clock* avancer (*by* de).

g (*wager*) parier, miser, mettre (*on* sur).

h (*inform, indicate*) indiquer. **they put the police on to him** ils l'ont signalé à la police; **can you put me on to a good dentist?** pourriez-vous me donner l'adresse d'un bon dentiste? *or* m'indiquer un bon dentiste?; **Paul put us on to you** c'est Paul qui nous a dit de nous adresser à vous, c'est Paul qui nous envoie; **what put you on to it?** qu'est-ce qui vous en a donné l'idée?, qu'est-ce qui vous y a fait penser?

2 **put-on*** adj, n *see* **put 3**.

▶**put out** 1 vi (*Naut*) prendre le large. **to put out to sea** prendre le large, quitter le port; **to put out from Dieppe** quitter Dieppe.

2 vt sep a (*put outside*) *chair etc* sortir, mettre dehors; (*Baseball*) *ball* mettre hors jeu; (*get rid of*) *rubbish* sortir; (*expel*) *person* expulser (*of* de), mettre dehors; *country, organization* expulser (*of* de). **he put the rug out to dry** il a mis *or* étendu la couverture dehors pour qu'elle sèche (*subj*); **he put the cat out for the night** il a fait sortir le chat *or* il a mis le chat dehors pour la nuit; **to put sb's eyes out** crever les yeux à qn; (*fig*) **to put sth out of one's head** *or* **mind** ne plus penser à qch; *for other phrases see* **grass** *etc.*

b (*Naut*) *boat* mettre à l'eau *or* à la mer.

c (*stretch out, extend*) *arm, leg* allonger, étendre; *foot* avancer; *tongue* tirer (*at sb* à qn); *leaves, shoots, roots* produire. **to put out one's hand** tendre *or* avancer la main; (*in greeting*) tendre la main; [*car driver, traffic policeman*] tendre le bras; **to put one's head out of the window** passer la tête par la fenêtre; **the snail put out its horns** l'escargot a sorti ses cornes; *for other phrases see* **feeler** *etc.*

d (*lay out in order*) *cards* étaler; *chessmen etc* disposer; *sb's clothes* sortir; *dishes, cutlery* sortir, disposer. **you can put the papers out on the table** vous pouvez étaler les papiers sur la table.

e (*extinguish*) *light, flames, gas, cigarette* éteindre; *heater* fermer. **put the fire out** (*heater*) fermez le radiateur; (*coal etc*) éteignez le feu.

f (*disconcert*) déconcerter, dérouter (*by, about* par), interloquer; (*vex*) fâcher, contrarier, ennuyer (*by, about* par). **she looked very put out** elle avait l'air très contrariée.

g (*inconvenience*) déranger, gêner. **I don't want to put you out** je ne voudrais pas vous déranger; **don't put yourself out** ne vous dérangez pas; (*iro*) surtout ne vous gênez pas!; **she really put herself out for us** elle s'est donné beaucoup de mal pour nous, elle s'est mise en quatre *or* en frais pour nous.

h (*issue*) *news* annoncer; *report, regulations* publier; *rumour* faire courir *or* circuler; *appeal, warning* lancer; *announcement, statement* publier; *propaganda* faire; *book, edition* sortir, publier. **the government will put out a statement about it** le gouvernement va faire une déclaration *or* va publier un communiqué à ce sujet.

i (*spend*) dépenser. **they put out half a million on the project** ils ont dépensé un demi-million pour ce projet, ils ont investi un demi-million dans ce projet.

j (*lend at interest*) placer, prêter à intérêt. **he has £1,000 put out at 12%** il a placé 1.000 livres à 12%.

k *repairs, small jobs* donner au dehors; (*Ind: subcontract*) donner à un *or* des sous-traitant(s). **that shop puts out all its repair work** ce magasin donne toutes les réparations au dehors.

l (*exert*) *one's strength* déployer, user de. **they had to put out all their diplomacy to reach agreement** ils ont dû déployer *or* prodiguer tous leurs talents de diplomatie pour arriver à un accord.

m (*dislocate*) *shoulder* déboîter, disloquer, démettre; *ankle, knee, back* démettre.

►**put over** vt sep = **put across.**

►**put round** vt sep *rumour* faire courir, faire circuler.

►**put through** vt sep a (*make, complete*) *deal* conclure, mener à bien; *decision* prendre; *proposal* faire accepter, faire approuver. b (*Telec: connect*) *call* passer; *caller* brancher, mettre en communication. **I'm putting you through now** je vous mets en communication, vous êtes en ligne; **put me through to Mr Smith** passez-moi M. Smith. c (*fig*) *see* **put 1e.**

►**put together** vt sep a (*lit*) mettre ensemble. **you must not put two hamsters together in the same cage** il ne faut pas mettre deux hamsters ensemble dans une cage; **we don't want to put two men together at table** il vaut mieux ne pas placer deux hommes l'un à côté de l'autre à table; **he's worth more than the rest of the family put together** à lui tout seul il vaut largement le reste de la famille; *for other phrases see* **head, two** *etc.*

b (*assemble*) *table, bookcase, radio* assembler, monter; *jigsaw* assembler, faire; *book, story, account* composer; *facts, what happened* reconstituer; (*mend*) *broken vase etc* réparer, recoller, remettre ensemble les morceaux de. **she put together an excellent supper** elle a improvisé un délicieux dîner; (*Scol etc*) **to put together an application** constituer un dossier.

►**put up** 1 vi a (*lodge*) descendre (*at* dans); (*for one night*) passer la nuit (*at* à).

b (*Pol: offer o.s.*) se porter candidat(e) (*for* à), se présenter comme candidat(e) (*for* pour). **to put up for president** se porter candidat à la présidence, poser sa candidature à la présidence; (*Parl*) **to put up for a constituency** chercher à se faire accepter comme candidat dans une circonscription électorale; **to put up for re-election** être candidat pour un nouveau mandat.

2 vt sep a (*raise*) *hand* lever; *flag, sail* hisser; *tent* dresser; *collar, window* remonter; *umbrella* ouvrir; *notice* mettre, afficher (*on* sur); *picture* mettre, accrocher (*on* sur); *missile, rocket, space probe* lancer; *building, bridge* construire, ériger; *fence, barrier* ériger, dresser. **to put a ladder up against a wall** poser *or* dresser une échelle contre un mur; **put them up!*** (*in robbery etc*) haut les mains!; (*challenge to fight*) défends-toi!; *for other phrases see* **back, foot** *etc.*

b (*increase*) *numbers, taxes, sales* augmenter; *prices* augmenter, faire monter; *demand, speed* augmenter, accroître; *sb's temperature, blood pressure* faire monter. **that puts up the total to over 1,000** cela fait monter le total à plus de 1.000.

c (*offer*) *proposal, suggestion, idea* présenter, soumettre; *plea, prayer* offrir; *resistance* opposer, offrir; (*nominate*) proposer comme candidat (*for* à, *as* comme). **the plans were put up to the committee** les plans ont été présentés *or* soumis au comité; **the matter was put up to the board for a decision** l'affaire a été soumise au conseil d'administration pour qu'il décide (*subj*); **to put sth up for sale/auction** mettre qch en vente/aux enchères; **he was put up by his local branch** il a été présenté comme candidat par sa section locale; **they put him up for the chairmanship** on l'a présenté *or* proposé comme candidat à la présidence; **I'll put you up for the club** je vous proposerai comme membre du club; *for other phrases see* **fight, show, struggle** *etc.*

d (*provide*) *money, funds* fournir (*for* pour); *reward* offrir. **to put up money for a project** financer un projet, fournir les fonds pour un projet; **how much can you put up?** combien pouvez-vous (y) mettre?

e (*prepare, pack*) *picnic, sandwiches* préparer; (*Comm*) *order* exécuter; (*Pharm*) *prescription* préparer, exécuter. **the pills are put up in plastic tubes** les pilules sont présentées *or* emballées dans des tubes en plastique; **to put up apples for the winter** emmagasiner des pommes pour l'hiver, se constituer une réserve de pommes pour l'hiver.

f (*lodge*) loger, héberger. **I'm sorry I can't put you up** je suis désolé de ne pas pouvoir vous recevoir pour la nuit *or* vous coucher.

g (*incite*) **to put sb up to doing** pousser *or* inciter qn à faire; **someone must have put him up to it** quelqu'un a dû l'y pousser *or* l'y inciter *or* lui en donner l'idée.

h (*inform about*) **to put sb up to sth** mettre qn au courant de qch, renseigner qn sur qch; **I'll put you up to all his little tricks** je te mettrai au courant *or* je t'avertirai de tous ses petits tours; **he put her up to all the ways of avoiding tax** il l'a renseignée *or* tuyautée* sur tous les moyens d'éviter de payer des impôts.

3 **put-up** adj *see* **put 3.**

►**put upon** 1 vt fus (*gen pass*) **she is put upon** on abuse de sa gentillesse; **I won't be put upon any more!** je ne vais plus me laisser faire! *or* me laisser marcher sur les pieds! 2 **put-upon*** adj *see* **put 3.**

►**put up with** vt fus tolérer, supporter, encaisser*. **he has a lot to put up with** il a beaucoup de problèmes, il n'a pas la vie facile; **it is difficult to put up with** c'est difficile à supporter, c'est difficilement supportable.

putative ['pjuːtətɪv] adj (*frm*) putatif.

putrefaction [ˌpjuːtrɪ'fækʃən] n putréfaction *f.*

putrefy ['pjuːtrɪfaɪ] 1 vt putréfier. 2 vi se putréfier.

putrescence [pjuː'tresns] n putrescence *f.*

putrescent [pjuː'tresnt] adj putrescent, en voie de putréfaction.

putrid ['pjuːtrɪd] adj putride, pourrissant; (**fig*) dégoûtant, dégueulasse‡.

putsch [pʊtʃ] n putsch *m*, coup *m* d'État.

putt [pʌt] (*Golf*) 1 n putt *m*, coup roulé. 2 vti putter.

puttee ['pʌtiː] n, pl ~s *or* **putties** ['pʌtiːz] bande molletière.

putter[1] ['pʌtəʳ] n (*golf club*) putter *m.*

putter[2] ['pʌtəʳ] = **potter**[1].

putter[3] ['pʌtəʳ] vi [*engine, car, boat etc*] brouter.

putting ['pʌtɪŋ] 1 n putting *m.* 2 comp ►**putting green** (putting) green *m*, vert *m.*

putty ['pʌtɪ] 1 n mastic *m* (*ciment*). **she's like ~ in my hands** c'est une pâte molle entre mes mains.

2 comp ►**putty knife** couteau *m* de vitrier.

3 vt mastiquer.

put-you-up ['pʊtˌjuːʌp] n (*Brit*) canapé-lit *m*, divan *m.*

puzzle ['pʌzl] 1 n a (*mystery*) énigme *f*, mystère *m*; (*bewilderment*) perplexité *f.* **he is a real ~ to me** c'est une énigme vivante pour moi; **it is a ~ to me how he ever got the job** je n'arriverai jamais à comprendre comment il a obtenu le poste; **to be in a ~ about sth** être perplexe au sujet de qch; **I'm in a ~ about what to do** je suis dans l'incertitude *or* la perplexité, je ne sais pas quoi faire.

b (*game*) casse-tête *m inv*; (*word game*) rébus *m*; (*crossword*) mots croisés; (*jigsaw*) puzzle *m*; (*riddle*) devinette *f.*

2 comp ►**puzzle book** livre *m* de jeux.

3 vt rendre *or* laisser perplexe. **that really ~d him** ça l'a vraiment rendu *or* laissé perplexe; **I am ~d to know why** je n'arrive pas à comprendre pourquoi; **he was ~d about what to say** il ne savait pas quoi dire; **to ~ one's head** se creuser la tête.

4 vi: **to ~ over** *or* **about** *problem, mystery* essayer de résoudre; *event, sb's actions, intentions* essayer de comprendre; **I'm still puzzling over where he might have hidden it** j'en suis encore à me demander où il a bien pu le cacher.

►**puzzle out** vt sep *problem* résoudre; *mystery* éclaircir, élucider; *writing* déchiffrer; *answer, solution* trouver, découvrir; *sb's actions, attitude* comprendre. **I'm trying to puzzle out why he did it** j'essaie de comprendre *or* découvrir pourquoi il l'a fait.

puzzled ['pʌzld] adj perplexe; *see also* **puzzle.**

puzzlement ['pʌzlmənt] n (*NonC*) perplexité *f.*

puzzler ['pʌzləʳ] n (*gen*) énigme *f*; (*problem*) question *f* difficile, casse-tête *m inv.*

puzzling ['pʌzlɪŋ] adj *behaviour etc* curieux, inexplicable; *mechanism etc* mystérieux, incompréhensible.

PVC [ˌpiːviː'siː] n (*Tex*) (abbr of **polyvinyl chloride**) p.v.c. *m.*

PVS [ˌpiːviː'es] n (abbr of **postviral syndrome**) *see* **post-viral.**

PW [piː'dʌbljuː] n a (*US Mil*) (abbr of **prisoner of war**) prisonnier *m* de guerre. b (*Brit*) (abbr of **policewoman**) *see* **police.**

p.w. (abbr of **per week**) par semaine.

PWR [piːˌdʌbljuː'ɑːʳ] n (abbr of **pressurized water reactor**) *see* **pressurize.**

PX [piː'eks] n (*US Mil*) (abbr of **post exchange**) coopérative *f* militaire.

pygmy ['pɪgmɪ] 1 n (*also fig*) pygmée *m.* 2 adj (*also fig*) pygmée (*f inv*), pygméen.

pyjama [pɪ'dʒɑːmə] (*Brit*) 1 npl: ~s pyjama *m*; **a pair of ~s** un pyjama; **in (one's) ~s** en pyjama.

2 comp *jacket, trousers* de pyjama.

pylon ['paɪlən] n pylône *m.*

pylori [paɪ'lɔːraɪ] npl of **pylorus.**

pyloric [paɪ'lɔːrɪk] adj pylorique.

pylorus [paɪ'lɔːrəs] n, pl **pylori** pylore *m.*

pyorrhea [paɪə'rɪə] n pyorrhée *f* alvéolaire.

pyramid ['pɪrəmɪd] 1 n pyramide *f.*

2 comp ►**pyramid selling** vente *f* à la boule de neige *or* en cascade *or* en pyramide.

3 vt (*US Fin*) **to ~ winnings** spéculer en réinvestissant les bénéfices réalisés.

pyramidal [pɪ'ræmɪdl] adj pyramidal.

Pyramus ['pɪrəməs] n: ~ **and Thisbe** Pyrame *m* et Thisbé *f.*

pyre ['paɪəʳ] n bûcher *m* funéraire.

Pyrenean [pɪrə'niːən] adj pyrénéen, des Pyrénées.

Pyrenees [pɪrə'niːz] npl Pyrénées *fpl.*

pyrethrum [paɪ'riːθrəm] n pyrèthre *m.*

pyretic [paɪ'retɪk] adj pyrétique.

Pyrex ['paɪreks] ® 1 n Pyrex *m* ®. 2 comp *dish* en Pyrex.

pyrexia [paɪ'reksɪə] n pyrexie *f.*

pyrexic [paɪ'reksɪk] adj pyrexique.

pyrites [paɪ'raɪtiːz] n, pl ~ pyrite *f.* **iron ~** sulfure *m* de fer, fer sulfuré.

pyritic [paɪ'rɪtɪk] adj pyriteux.

pyro... ['paɪərəʊ] pref pyro ... .

pyromania [ˌpaɪərəʊ'meɪnɪə] n pyromanie *f.*

pyromaniac [ˌpaɪərəʊ'meɪnɪæk] n pyromane *mf*, incendiaire *mf.*

pyrotechnic [ˌpaɪərəʊ'teknɪk] 1 **adj** pyrotechnique. ~ **display** feu(x) *m(pl)* d'artifice. 2 **n:** ~**s** (*NonC: Phys*) pyrotechnie *f*; (*pl: fig hum*) feux *mpl* d'artifice.
Pyrrhic ['pɪrɪk] **adj:** ~ **victory** victoire *f* à la Pyrrhus, victoire coûteuse.
Pyrrhus ['pɪrəs] **n** Pyrrhus *m*.
Pythagoras [paɪ'θægərəs] **n** Pythagore *m*.
Pythagorean [paɪˌθægə'rɪən] **adj** (*gen*) pythagoricien; (*number, letter*) pythagorique.
python ['paɪθən] **n** python *m*.
pyx [pɪks] **n** (*in church*) ciboire *m*; (*for sick communions*) pyxide *f*.
pzazz⁑ [pə'zæz] **n** (*US*) = **piz(z)azz**⁑.

Q

Q, q [kjuː] n (*letter*) Q, q *m*. **Q for Queen** ≈ Q comme Quintal; *see* **P**.
Qatar [kæ'tɑːʳ] 1 n a (*country*) Qatar *m*. b (*inhabitant*) Qatarien(ne) *m(f)*. 2 adj qatarien.
Q.C. [kjuː'siː] n (*Brit Jur*) (abbr of **Queen's Counsel**) *see* **counsel 1b**.
QE2 [ˌkjuːiː'tuː] n (*Brit Naut*) (abbr of **Queen Elizabeth II**) *paquebot*.
Q.E.D. [ˌkjuːiː'diː] (*Math*) (abbr of **quod erat demonstrandum**) C.Q.F.D.
qt n abbr of **quart(s)**.
q.t. [kjuː'tiː] n (abbr of **quiet**) **on the ~*** en douce*, en cachette.
qty n abbr of **quantity**.
qua [kweɪ] adv en tant que, considéré comme, en (sa *etc*) qualité de.
quack¹ [kwæk] 1 n coin-coin *m inv* (*cri du canard*). 2 vi faire coin-coin. 3 comp ▸ **quack-quack** (*baby talk*) coin-coin *m inv*.
quack²* [kwæk] 1 n (*bogus doctor, also gen: sham*) charlatan *m*; (*hum: doctor*) toubib* *m*. 2 adj: **~ doctor** charlatan *m*.
quackery ['kwækərɪ] n (*NonC*) charlatanisme *m*.
quad¹ [kwɒd] n abbr of **quadruplet** *and* **quadrangle**.
quad²‡ [kwɒd] n = **quod‡**.
Quadragesima [kwɒdrə'dʒesɪmə] n Quadragésime *f*.
quadrangle ['kwɒdræŋgl] n (*Math*) quadrilatère *m*; (*courtyard*) cour *f* (*d'un collège etc*).
quadrangular [kwɒ'dræŋgjʊləʳ] adj quadrangulaire.
quadrant ['kwɒdrənt] n [*circle*] quadrant *m*, quart *m* de cercle.
quadraphonic [ˌkwɒdrə'fɒnɪk] adj quadriphonique, tétraphonique. **in ~ (sound)** en quadriphonie, en tétraphonie.
quadraphonics [ˌkwɒdrə'fɒnɪks] n (*NonC*) quadriphonie *f*, tétraphonie *f*.
quadraphony [kwɒd'rɒfənɪ] n = **quadraphonics**.
quadrasonic [ˌkwɒdrə'sɒnɪk] adj quadriphonique, tétraphonique.
quadrasonics [ˌkwɒdrə'sɒnɪks] n (*NonC*) quadriphonie *f*, tétraphonie *f*.
quadrat ['kwɒdrət] n quadrat *m*.
quadratic [kwɒ'drætɪk] adj (*Math*) quadratique. **~ equation** équation *f* du second degré.
quadrature ['kwɒdrətʃəʳ] n quadrature *f*.
quadrennial [ˌkwɒ'drenɪəl] adj quadriennal.
quadr(i)... [kwɒdrɪ] pref quatr(i)... .
quadriceps ['kwɒdrɪseps] n, pl **~es** *or* **~** quadriceps *m*.
quadrilateral [ˌkwɒdrɪ'lætərəl] (*Math*) 1 adj quadrilatère, quadrilatéral. 2 n quadrilatère *m*.
quadrilingual [ˌkwɒdrɪ'lɪŋgwəl] adj quadrilingue.
quadrille [kwə'drɪl] n (*Dancing*) quadrille *m*.
quadrillion [kwɒ'drɪljən] n (*Brit, France*) 10^{24}; (*US*) 10^{15}.
quadripartite [ˌkwɒdrɪ'pɑːtaɪt] adj quadriparti (*f* -e *or* -te).
quadriplegia [ˌkwɒdrɪ'pliːdʒɪə] n tétraplégie *f*, quadriplégie *f*.
quadriplegic [ˌkwɒdrɪ'pliːdʒɪk] adj, n tétraplégique (*mf*), quadriplégique (*mf*).
quadroon [kwɒ'druːn] n quarteron(ne) *m(f)*.
quadrophonic *etc* = **quadraphonic** *etc*.
quadruped ['kwɒdrʊped] adj, n quadrupède (*m*).
quadruple ['kwɒdrʊpl] 1 adj, n quadruple (*m*). 2 [kwɒ'druːpl] vti quadrupler.
quadruplet [kwɒ'druːplɪt] n quadruplé(e) *m(f)*.
quadruplicate [kwɒ'druːplɪkɪt] 1 adj quadruple. 2 n: **in ~** en quatre exemplaires.
quaff [kwɒf] vt († *or hum*) *glass* vider à longs traits; *wine* lamper.
quag [kwæg] n = **quagmire**.
quagga ['kwægə] n, pl **~s** *or* **~** couagga *m*.
quagmire ['kwægmaɪəʳ] n (*lit, fig*) bourbier *m*.
quahaug, quahog ['kwɑːhɒg] n (*US*) clam *m*.
quail¹ [kweɪl] vi [*person*] perdre courage, reculer (*before* devant). **his heart** *or* **spirit ~ed** son courage l'a trahi.
quail² [kweɪl] n, pl **~** *or* **~s** (*Orn*) caille *f*.
quaint [kweɪnt] adj (*odd*) *person, dress, attitude, idea, custom* bizarre, original; (*picturesque*) pittoresque; (*old-fashioned etc*) au charme vieillot, qui a un petit cachet vieillot *or* désuet. **a ~ little village** un petit village au charme vieillot; **a ~ custom** une coutume pittoresque; **~ old countryman** vieux paysan pittoresque.
quaintly ['kweɪntlɪ] adv (*see* **quaint**) d'une manière originale *or* bizarre *or* pittoresque.
quaintness ['kweɪntnɪs] n (*see* **quaint**) originalité *f*, bizarrerie *f*; pittoresque *m*; cachet *or* caractère vieillot.
quake [kweɪk] 1 vi [*earth*] trembler; [*person etc*] trembler, frémir (*with* de). **I was quaking** je tremblais comme une feuille. 2 n (abbr of **earthquake**) tremblement *m* de terre, séisme *m*.
Quaker ['kweɪkəʳ] 1 n quaker(esse) *m(f)*. 2 adj *community, family* de quakers; *beliefs* des quakers. **~ meeting** réunion *f* de quakers.
Quakerism ['kweɪkərɪzəm] n quakerisme *m*.
qualification [ˌkwɒlɪfɪ'keɪʃən] n a (*ability*) compétence *f* (*for* en; *to do* pour faire), aptitude *f* (*for* à), capacité *f* (*to do* pour faire). **I doubt his ~ to teach English** je doute qu'il ait les compétences requises *or* qu'il ait les capacités requises pour enseigner l'anglais; **we have never questioned his ~ for the job** nous n'avons jamais mis en doute son aptitude à remplir le poste.

b (*gen pl*) **~s** (*degrees, diplomas etc*) diplômes *mpl*, titres *mpl* (*in* de); (*for a trade etc*) qualifications *fpl* professionnelles; (*necessary conditions for a post etc*) conditions requises *or* nécessaires, conditions à remplir. **his only ~ for the job was his experience in similar work** seule son expérience dans des domaines similaires le qualifiait pour ce travail; **what are your ~s?** (*skill, degrees, experience etc*) quelle est votre formation?; (*paper ~s*) qu'est-ce que vous avez comme diplômes? *or* qualifications professionnelles?; **he has a lot of experience but no paper ~s** *or* **formal ~s** il a beaucoup d'expérience mais il n'a aucun diplôme *or* il n'a aucun titre *or* il n'a pas de qualifications professionnelles; **I have no teaching ~(s)** je n'ai pas le(s) diplôme(s) requis pour enseigner.

c (*limitation*) réserve *f*, restriction *f*, condition *f*. **to accept a plan with ~(s)** accepter un projet avec des réserves *or* avec des restrictions *or* à certaines conditions; **without ~(s)** sans réserves *or* restrictions *or* conditions.

d (*gen, Gram: qualifying*) qualification *f*.
qualified ['kwɒlɪfaɪd] adj a *person* compétent, qualifié (*for* pour, en matière de); *engineer, doctor, nurse, teacher* diplômé; *craftsman, player* qualifié. **we must find a ~ person to take charge of the project** il nous faut trouver une personne ayant la compétence voulue pour prendre la direction du projet; **he was not ~ for this job** il ne remplissait pas les conditions requises pour ce poste, il n'avait pas le(s) diplôme(s) requis *or* les titres requis *or* les qualifications professionnelles requises pour ce poste; **to be ~ to do** être qualifié *or* avoir la compétence voulue pour faire, être habilité à faire (*esp Jur*); **he is ~ to teach** il a les diplômes requis pour l'enseignement, il a qualité pour enseigner; **they are not ~ to vote** ils ne sont pas habilités à voter; **I'm not ~ to speak for her** je ne suis pas qualifié pour parler en son nom; **I don't feel ~ to judge** je ne me sens pas qualifié pour juger.

b (*modified*) *praise* mitigé; *support, acceptance, approval* conditionnel. **a ~ success** une demi-réussite.
qualifier ['kwɒlɪfaɪəʳ] n (*Gram*) qualificatif *m*, qualificateur *m*.
qualify ['kwɒlɪfaɪ] 1 vt a (*make competent*) **to ~ sb to do/for sth** (*gen*) qualifier qn pour faire/pour qch; [*experience etc*] donner à qn les compétences *or* qualités requises pour faire/pour qch; [*degree, diploma*] donner à qn les diplômes *or* titres requis pour faire/pour qch; [*trade diploma, certificates*] donner à qn les qualifications professionnelles nécessaires pour faire/pour qch; (*Jur*) **to ~ sb to do** habiliter qn à faire; **that doesn't ~ him to speak on it** cela ne lui donne pas qualité pour en parler.

b (*modify*) *attitude, praise* mitiger, tempérer, atténuer; *approval, support* mettre des réserves à; *statement, opinion* nuancer. **to ~ one's acceptance of sth** accepter qch sous réserve *or* sous condition; **I think you should ~ that remark** je pense que vous devriez nuancer cette remarque.

c (*describe*) qualifier (*as* de); (*Gram*) qualifier.

2 vi obtenir son diplôme (*or* son brevet *etc*) (*in* en). **to ~ as a doctor/a nurse/an engineer** obtenir son diplôme de docteur (en médecine)/d'infirmière/d'ingénieur; **he has qualified as a teacher** il a obtenu son diplôme de professeur; **while he was ~ing as a teacher** pendant qu'il faisait des études pour devenir professeur; **to ~ for a job** obtenir le(s) diplôme(s) *or* titre(s) nécessaire(s) pour un poste; **he doesn't ~ for that post** il n'a pas le(s) diplôme(s) *or* titre(s) nécessaire(s) pour (occuper) ce poste; **does he ~?** est-ce qu'il remplit les conditions requises?; (*Sport*) **to ~ for the final** se qualifier pour la finale; (*fig*) **he hardly qualifies as a poet** il ne mérite pas vraiment le nom de poète.

qualifying ['kwɒlɪfaɪɪŋ] adj a *mark* de passage, qui permet de passer; *examination* d'entrée; *score* qui permet de se qualifier. (*Sport*) **~ heat** éliminatoire *f*; (*Jur*) **~ period** période *f* probatoire *or* de stage; **~ round** série *f* éliminatoire; (*St Ex*) **~ shares** actions *fpl* de garantie. b (*Gram*) qualificatif.

qualitative ['kwɒlɪtətɪv] adj qualitatif.

qualitatively ['kwɒlɪtətɪvlɪ] adv qualitativement.

quality ['kwɒlɪtɪ] 1 n a (*nature, kind*) qualité *f*. **of the best ~** de première qualité, de premier ordre *or* choix; **of good** *or* **high ~** de bonne qualité, de qualité supérieure; **of poor** *or* **bad** *or* **low ~** de mauvaise qualité, de qualité inférieure; **the ~ of life** la qualité de la vie.

b (*NonC: goodness*) qualité *f*. **guarantee of ~** garantie *f* de qualité; **it's ~ rather than quantity that counts** c'est la qualité qui compte plus que la quantité; **this wine has ~** ce vin a de la qualité *or* est de qualité; **he has real ~** il a de la classe.

c (*attribute*) qualité *f*. **natural qualities** qualités naturelles; **one of his (good) qualities** une de ses qualités; **one of his bad qualities** un de ses défauts; **he has many artistic qualities** il a beaucoup de qualités *or* de dons *mpl* artistiques.

d *[voice, sound]* qualité *f*, timbre *m*.

e († *or hum: high rank*) qualité† *f*.

2 comp *car, film, product* de qualité ►**quality control** (*Ind*) contrôle *m* de qualité (*auquel on soumet les produits manufacturés*) ►**quality papers** (*Press*) journaux *mpl* sérieux.

qualm [kwɑːm] n a (*scruple*) doute *m*, scrupule *m*; (*misgiving*) appréhension *f*, inquiétude *f*. **~s of conscience** scrupules de conscience; **he did it without a ~** il l'a fait sans le moindre scrupule; **I would feel no ~s about doing that** je n'aurais pas le moindre scrupule à faire cela; **I had some ~s about his future** j'avais quelques inquiétudes sur *or* pour son avenir. b (*nausea*) malaise *m*, nausée *f*, haut-le-cœur *m inv*.

quandary ['kwɒndərɪ] n embarras *m*, dilemme *m*, difficulté *f*. **to be in a ~** être dans l'embarras, être pris dans un dilemme; **he was in a ~ about** *or* **as to** *or* **over what to do** il était bien embarrassé de savoir quoi faire; **that got him out of a ~** ça l'a sorti d'un dilemme, ça l'a tiré d'embarras.

quango ['kwæŋgəʊ] n (*Brit*) (abbr of **quasi-autonomous nongovernmental organization**) organisme *m* non-gouvernemental quasi-autonome.

quanta ['kwɒntə] npl of **quantum**.

quantifiable [ˌkwɒntɪ'faɪəbl] adj quantifiable.

quantifier ['kwɒntɪfaɪəʳ] n (*Ling, Philos*) quantificateur *m*.

quantify ['kwɒntɪfaɪ] vt déterminer la quantité de, évaluer quantitativement; (*Philos*) quantifier.

quantitative ['kwɒntɪtətɪv] adj (*Chem etc*) quantitatif; (*Ling, Poetry*) de quantité. (*Chem*) **~ analysis** analyse quantitative.

quantitatively ['kwɒntɪtətɪvlɪ] adv quantitativement.

quantity ['kwɒntɪtɪ] 1 n (*gen, Ling, Math, Poetry*) quantité *f*. **a small ~ of rice** une petite quantité de riz; **what ~ do you want?** quelle quantité (en) voulez-vous?; **in ~** en (grande) quantité; **in large quantities** en grandes quantités; **a ~ of, any ~ of, quantities of** une quantité de, (des) quantités de, un grand nombre de; *see* **quality, unknown.** 2 comp (*Comm*) *production* sur une grande échelle, en série ►**quantity mark** (*Ling, Poetry*) signe *m* de quantité ►**quantity surveying** (*Brit*) métrage *m* ►**quantity surveyor** (*Brit*) métreur *m* (vérificateur).

quantum ['kwɒntəm], pl **quanta** 1 n quantum *m*. 2 comp ►**quantum leap** (*fig*) bond *m* en avant ►**quantum mechanics** (*Phys*) mécanique *f* quantique ►**quantum number** nombre *m* quantique ►**quantum theory** théorie *f* des quanta.

quarantine ['kwɒrəntiːn] 1 n quarantaine *f* (*pour raisons sanitaires*). **in ~** en quarantaine. 2 comp *regulations, period* de quarantaine. 3 vt mettre en quarantaine.

quark [kwɑːk] n quark *m*.

quarrel ['kwɒrəl] 1 n (*dispute*) querelle *f*, dispute *f*; (*more intellectual*) différend *m*; (*breach*) brouille *f*. **I had a ~ with him yesterday** je me suis disputé *or* querellé avec lui hier; **they've had a ~** (*argued*) ils se sont disputés *or* querellés; (*fallen out*) ils se sont brouillés; **they had a sudden ~** ils ont eu un accrochage*; **the children's little ~s** les disputes *or* chamailleries* *fpl* des enfants; **the ~ between the professor and his assistant** la querelle entre le professeur et son assistant; (*longer: more formally*) la querelle qui oppose (*or* opposait *etc*) le professeur à son assistant; **to start a ~** provoquer *or* susciter une querelle *or* dispute; **to pick a ~ with sb, to try to start a ~ with sb** chercher querelle à qn; (*fig*) **I have no ~ with you** je n'ai rien contre vous; **he had no ~ with what we had done** il n'avait rien à redire à ce que nous avions fait.

2 vi (*have a dispute*) se disputer, se quereller, se chamailler* (*with sb* avec qn, *about, over* à propos de); (*break off friendship*) se brouiller (*with sb* avec qn). (*fig*) **I cannot ~ with that** je n'ai rien à redire à cela; **what he ~s with is ...** ce contre quoi il s'insurge c'est ... .

quarrelling, (*US*) **quarreling** ['kwɒrəlɪŋ] 1 n (*NonC*) disputes *fpl*, querelles *fpl*; (*petty*) chamailleries* *fpl*. 2 adj qui se disputent.

quarrelsome ['kwɒrəlsəm] adj querelleur, batailleur, chamailleur, mauvais coucheur.

quarrier ['kwɒrɪəʳ] n (ouvrier *m*) carrier *m*.

quarry¹ ['kwɒrɪ] 1 n carrière *f*; *see* **marble** *etc*. 2 comp ►**quarryman** (ouvrier *m*) carrier *m* ►**quarry tile** carreau *m* ►**quarry-tiled floor** sol carrelé. 3 vt *stone* extraire; *hillside* exploiter (*en carrière*). 4 vi exploiter une carrière. **they are ~ing for marble** ils exploitent une carrière de marbre.

►**quarry out** vt sep *block, stone* extraire.

quarry² ['kwɒrɪ] n (*animal, bird etc*) proie *f*; (*Hunting: game*) gibier *m*. **the detectives lost their ~** les policiers ont perdu la trace de celui qu'ils pourchassaient.

quart [kwɔːt] n (*measure*) ≃ litre *m* (*Brit = 1,136 litres; US = 0,946 litre*). (*fig*) **it's like trying to put a ~ into a pint pot** c'est tenter l'impossible (il n'y a vraiment pas la place).

quarter ['kwɔːtəʳ] 1 n a (*fourth part*) quart *m*. **to divide sth into ~s** diviser qch en quatre (parties égales) *or* en (quatre) quartiers; **a ~ (of a pound) of tea** un quart (de livre) de thé; **a ~ full/empty** au quart plein/vide; **it's a ~ gone already** il y en a déjà un quart de parti; **a ~ as big as** quatre fois moins grand que; **I bought it for a ~ of the price** *or* **for ~ the price** je l'ai acheté au quart du prix *or* pour le quart de son prix.

b (*in expressions of time*) quart *m* (d'heure). **a ~ of an hour** un quart d'heure; **a ~ to 7,** (*US*) **a ~ of 7** 7 heures moins le quart *or* moins un quart; **a ~ past 6,** (*US*) **a ~ after 6** 6 heures un quart *or* et quart; (*Aut*) **to drive with one's hands at a ~ to three** conduire avec les mains à neuf heures et quart; **it wasn't the ~ yet** il n'était pas encore le quart; **the clock strikes the ~s** l'horloge sonne les quarts.

c (*specific fourth parts*) *[year]* trimestre *m*; (*US and Can money*) quart *m* de dollar, vingt-cinq cents; (*Brit weight*) = *28 livres (= 12,7 kg)*; (*US weight*) = *25 livres (= 11,34 kg)*; (*Her*) quartier *m*; *[beef, apple etc]* quartier; *[moon]* quartier. **to pay by the ~** payer tous les trois mois *or* par trimestre; **a ~'s rent** un terme (de loyer); *see* **forequarters, hindquarters** *etc*.

d (*direction*) direction *f*, part *f*, côté *m*; (*compass point*) point cardinal. (*Naut*) **on the port/starboard ~** par la hanche de bâbord/tribord; **from all ~s** de toutes parts, de tous côtés; **you must report that to the proper ~** vous devez signaler cela à qui de droit; **in responsible ~s** dans les milieux autorisés.

e (*part of town*) quartier *m*. **the Latin ~** le quartier latin.

f (*lodgings*) **~s** résidence *f*, domicile *m*; (*Mil*) quartiers *mpl*, (*temporary*) cantonnement *m*; **they are living in very cramped ~s** ils sont logés très à l'étroit; *see* **married** *etc*.

g (*NonC: liter: mercy*) quartier *m* (*liter*), grâce *f*. **to give/cry ~** faire/demander quartier.

2 vt a (*divide into four*) diviser en quatre (parts égales), diviser en (quatre) quartiers; *traitor's body* écarteler; (*Her*) écarteler; *see* **hang**.

b (*lodge*) (*Mil*) *troops* caserner, (*temporarily*) cantonner; (*gen*) loger (*on* chez).

c *[dogs]* **to ~ the ground** quêter; *[police etc]* **to ~ a town in search of sb** quadriller une ville à la recherche de qn.

3 adj quart de. **the ~ part of** le quart de; **a ~ share in sth** (une part d')un quart de qch; *see also* **4**.

4 comp ►**quarterback** *see* **quarterback** ►**quarter day** (*Fin, Jur*) (jour *m* du) terme *m* ►**quarter-deck** (*Naut*) plage *f* arrière; *[sailing ship]* gaillard *m* d'arrière ►**quarter final** (*Sport*) quart *m* de finale ►**quarter-hour** (*period of time*) quart *m* d'heure; (*division of clock face*) **on the quarter-hour** tous les quarts d'heure ►**quarter light** (*Brit Aut*) déflecteur *m* ►**quartermaster** *see* **quartermaster** ►**quarter mile** (*Sport*) (course *f* d'un) quart *m* de mille ►**quarter note** (*US Mus*) noire *f* ►**quarter pound** n quart *m* de livre ►**quarter-pound** adj d'un quart de livre ►**quarter sessions** (*Jur*) (*sessions*) ≃ assises trimestrielles (de tribunal de grande instance); (*court*) ≃ tribunal *m* de grande instance (*jusqu'en 1972*) ►**quarter turn** quart *m* de tour ►**quarter window** (*US Aut*) déflecteur *m*.

quarterback ['kwɔːtəbæk] (*US*) 1 n (*Ftbl*) stratège *m* (*souvent en position d'arrière*). 2 vt a (*Ftbl*) diriger la stratégie de. b (*fig*) gérer. 3 vi (*Ftbl*) servir de stratège.

quartering ['kwɔːtərɪŋ] n (*NonC*) a division *f* en quatre; (*Her*) écartelure *f*. b (*Mil: lodging*) cantonnement *m*.

quarterly ['kwɔːtəlɪ] 1 adj *review, payment* trimestriel. 2 n (*periodical*) publication trimestrielle. 3 adv tous les trois mois; trimestriellement, (une fois) par trimestre.

quartermaster [ˈkwɔːtəˌmɑːstəʳ] 1 n a (*Mil*) intendant *m* militaire de troisième classe. b (*Naut*) maître *m* de manœuvre. 2 comp ▸**quartermaster general** (*Mil*) intendant général d'armée de première classe ▸**quartermaster sergeant** (*Mil*) intendant militaire adjoint.

quartet(te) [kwɔːˈtet] n (*classical music players*) quatuor *m*; (*jazz players*) quartette *m*; (*often hum: four people*) quatuor*.

quarto [ˈkwɔːtəʊ] 1 n in-quarto *m*. 2 adj *paper* in-quarto *inv*.

quartz [ˈkwɔːts] 1 n quartz *m*. 2 comp de *or* en quartz ▸**quartz clock/watch** pendule *f*/montre *f* à quartz ▸**quartz crystal** cristal *m* de quartz ▸**quartz(-iodine) lamp** lampe *f* à iode.

quartzite [ˈkwɔːtsaɪt] n quartzite *m*.

quasar [ˈkweɪzɑːʳ] n quasar *m*.

quash [kwɒʃ] vt *decision* casser, annuler; *verdict, judgment* infirmer, réformer, casser; *rebellion* réprimer, étouffer; *proposal, suggestion* rejeter, repousser.

quasi- [ˈkwɑːzɪ] pref (+ *n*) quasi-; (+ *adj*) quasi, presque. **~-marriage** quasi-mariage *m*; **~-revolutionary** quasi *or* presque révolutionnaire.

quatercentenary [ˌkwɒtəsenˈtiːnərɪ] n quatrième centenaire *m*.

quaternary [kwəˈtɜːnərɪ] 1 adj (*Chem, Geol, Math*) quaternaire. 2 n (*set of four*) ensemble *m* de quatre; (*number four*) quatre *m*. (*Geol*) **the Q~** le quaternaire.

quatrain [ˈkwɒtreɪn] n quatrain *m*.

quaver [ˈkweɪvəʳ] 1 n (*Mus: esp Brit: note*) croche *f*; (*gen: voice tremor*) tremblement *m*, chevrotement *m*. 2 comp ▸**quaver rest** (*Brit Mus*) demi-soupir *m*. 3 vi *[voice]* chevroter, trembloter; *[person]* chevroter, parler d'une voix chevrotante *or* tremblotante. 4 vt (*also* **~ out**) chevroter.

quavering [ˈkweɪvərɪŋ] 1 adj tremblotant, chevrotant. 2 n tremblement *m*, tremblotement *m*, chevrotement *m*.

quaveringly [ˈkweɪvərɪŋlɪ] adv d'une voix chevrotante *or* tremblotante, avec des tremblements dans la voix.

quavery [ˈkweɪvərɪ] adj = **quavering 1**.

quay [kiː] n (*Naut etc*) quai *m*. **at** *or* **alongside the ~side** à quai.

queasiness [ˈkwiːzɪnɪs] n (*NonC*) nausée *f*, malaise *m*.

queasy [ˈkwiːzɪ] adj *food* (*upsetting*) indigeste; (*nauseating*) écœurant; *stomach, digestion* délicat; *person* sujet aux nausées. **he was ~, he felt ~, his stomach was ~** il avait mal au cœur, il avait envie de vomir; (*fig*) **he's got a ~ conscience** il n'a pas la conscience tranquille.

Quebec [kwɪˈbek] 1 n a (*city*) Québec. b (*province*) (Province *f* du) Québec *m*. 2 adj québécois. (*Ling*) **~ French** québécois *m*.

Quebec(k)er [kwɪˈbekəʳ] n Québécois(e) *m(f)*.

Quebecois [kebeˈkwɑː] n, pl inv (*person*) Québécois(e) *m(f)*.

queen [kwiːn] 1 n a (*also fig*) reine *f*. **Q~ Elizabeth** la reine Élisabeth; **she was ~ to George III** elle était l'épouse de Georges III; (*iro*) **Q~ Anne's dead!*** ce n'est pas une nouvelle!, tu ne nous apprends rien! (*see also* **2**); **~ of the ball** reine du bal; *see* **beauty, Mary, may[2]** *etc*.

b (*Brit*) (*Jur*) **Q~'s Bench** cour supérieure de justice; (*Jur*) **Q ~'s Counsel** avocat *m* de la Couronne; (*Jur*) **to turn Q~'s evidence** témoigner contre ses complices; **the Q~'s highway** la voie publique; **Q~'s Messenger** courrier *m* diplomatique.

c (*ant, bee, wasp*) reine *f*; (*Chess*) dame *f*, reine; (*Cards*) dame.

d (‡ *pej: homosexual*) folle‡ *f*, tante‡ *f*.

2 comp ▸**Queen Anne** (*Brit*) *furniture etc* de l'époque de la reine Anne (*début 18e s.*) ▸**queen bee** reine *f* des abeilles; (*fig*) **she's the queen bee*** c'est elle qui commande ▸**queencake** *petit gâteau aux raisins secs en forme de cœur* ▸**queen consort** reine *f* (*épouse du roi*) ▸**queen dowager** reine douairière ▸**Queen Mother** reine mère *f*.

3 vt a (*) **to ~ it** faire la grande dame; **to ~ it over sb** prendre des airs d'impératrice avec qn.

b (*Chess*) *pawn* damer.

queenly [ˈkwiːnlɪ] adj de reine.

Queensland [ˈkwiːnzlənd] n Queensland *m*. **in ~** dans le Queensland.

queer [kwɪəʳ] 1 adj a (*odd*) étrange, bizarre, singulier. **a ~ fellow** *or* **fish** un curieux personnage *or* bonhomme, un drôle de corps*; (*pej*) **a ~ customer** un drôle d'individu *or* de type*; **~ in the head*** dérangé, toqué*; (*Brit*) **to be in Q~ Street*** se trouver dans une mauvaise passe *or* en mauvaise posture.

b (*suspicious*) suspect, louche. **there's something ~ going on** il se passe quelque chose de louche; **there's something ~ about the way he always has money** il y a quelque chose de suspect dans le fait qu'il a toujours de l'argent.

c (*Brit *: unwell*) mal fichu*, patraque*. **she suddenly felt ~** elle s'est soudain trouvée prise d'un malaise.

d (‡ *pej: homosexual*) homosexuel, pédé‡. **he's ~** c'est un pédé‡.

e (*US fig*) **to be ~ for sth‡** adorer qch, être dingue* de qch.

2 comp ▸**queer-bashing‡** chasse *f* aux pédés‡ ▸**queer-looking**: **he was a queer-looking man** il avait une drôle d'allure ▸**queer-sounding**: **it was a queer-sounding name** c'était un nom (qui avait une consonance) bizarre.

3 n (‡ *pej: homosexual*) (*male*) pédéraste *m*, pédé‡ *m*; (*female*) lesbienne *f*, gouine‡ *f*.

4 vt gâter, abîmer. (*Brit fig*) **to ~ sb's pitch** couper l'herbe sous les pieds à *or* de qn.

queerly [ˈkwɪəlɪ] adv étrangement, bizarrement, singulièrement.

queerness [ˈkwɪənɪs] n étrangeté *f*, bizarrerie *f*, singularité *f*.

quell [kwel] vt *rebellion, rage, anxieties* réprimer, étouffer. **she ~ed him with a glance** elle l'a fait rentrer sous terre d'un regard, elle l'a foudroyé du regard.

quench [kwentʃ] vt *flames, fire* éteindre; *steel etc* tremper; *hope, desire* réprimer, étouffer; *enthusiasm* refroidir. **to ~ one's thirst** se désaltérer.

quenchless [ˈkwentʃlɪs] adj (*liter*) inextinguible.

quern [kwɜːn] n moulin *m* à bras (*pour le grain*).

querulous [ˈkwerʊləs] adj *person* récriminateur (*f* -trice), bougon*, ronchonneur*; *tone* plaintif, bougon*.

querulously [ˈkwerʊləslɪ] adv en se lamentant, d'un ton plaintif *or* bougon*.

query [ˈkwɪərɪ] 1 n a (*question*) question *f*; (*doubt*) doute *m*. **readers' queries** questions des lecteurs; **this raises a ~ about the viability of the scheme** cela met en question la viabilité de ce projet. b (*Gram: question mark*) point *m* d'interrogation. c (*Comput*) **~ language** langage *m* d'interrogation. 2 vt a *statement, motive, evidence* mettre en doute *or* en question. **I ~ that!** je me permets d'en douter!; **to ~ whether** demander si, chercher à savoir si. b (*write "?" against*) *part of text* marquer d'un point d'interrogation.

quest [kwest] (*liter*) 1 n quête *f*, recherche *f*, poursuite *f* (*for* de). **in ~ of** en quête de. 2 vi **to ~ for sth** être en quête de qch; **~ing** *hand, fingers* chercheur (*f* -euse); *look, voice* interrogateur (*f* -trice).

question [ˈkwestʃən] 1 n a question *f* (*also Parl*). **to ask sb a ~, to put a ~ to sb,** (*Parl*) **to put down a ~ for sb** poser une question à qn; **what a ~ to ask!** quelle question!, belle question! (*iro*); (*prevaricating*) **that's a good ~!** voilà une bonne question, la question est pertinente; (*Gram*) **indirect** *or* **oblique ~** interrogation indirecte; **to put sth to the ~** soumettre qch au vote; *see* **leading, pop[1], sixty** *etc*.

b (*NonC: doubt*) (mise *f* en) doute *m*. **beyond (all) ~, without ~, past ~** (adj) hors de doute, incontestable; (adv) incontestablement, sans aucun doute; **there is no ~ about it** cela ne fait aucun doute; **there's no ~ that this is better** une chose est sûre, ceci est mieux; *see* **bring, call.**

c (*matter, subject*) question *f*, sujet *m*, affaire *f*. **that's the ~!** là est la question!, c'est là (toute) la question!; **that's not the ~** là n'est pas la question, il ne s'agit pas de cela; **that's another ~ altogether** ça c'est une tout autre affaire; **the person in ~** la personne en question *or* dont il s'agit; **there's some/no ~ of closing the shop** il est/il n'est pas question de fermer *or* qu'on ferme (*subj*) le magasin; **there's no ~ of that, that is out of the ~** il ne peut en être question, il n'en est pas question, il ne saurait en être question (*frm*); **the ~ is how many** la question c'est de savoir combien, il s'agit de savoir combien; (*in concluding*) reste à savoir combien; **the ~ is to decide ...** il s'agit de décider ...; (*in concluding*) reste à décider ...; **the German ~** la question allemande, le problème allemand; **it is a ~ of sincerity** c'est une question de sincérité; **it's (all) a ~ of what you want to do eventually** tout dépend de ce que tu veux faire en fin de compte; **it's an open ~ (whether)** la question reste posée (de savoir si), personne ne sait (si); **success is a ~ of time** le succès n'est qu'une affaire de temps; *see* **burning, time 1c** *etc*.

2 comp ▸**question mark** point *m* d'interrogation; (*fig*) **there is a question mark over whether he meant to do it** on ne sait pas au juste s'il avait l'intention de le faire; (*fig*) **a big question mark hangs over his future** quant à son avenir c'est un point d'interrogation ▸**questionmaster** meneur *m* de jeu; (*Rad, TV*) animateur *m* ▸**question tag** queue *f* de phrase interrogative ▸**question time** (*Brit Parl*) heure réservée aux questions orales.

3 vt a interroger, poser des questions à, questionner (*on* sur, *about* au sujet de, à propos de); (*Police*) interroger. **we ~ed him closely to find out whether** nous l'avons interrogé de près pour savoir si; **I will not be ~ed about it** je refuse d'être l'objet de questions à ce sujet.

b *motive, account, sb's honesty* mettre en doute *or* en question, douter de; *claim* contester. **to ~ whether** douter que + *subj*.

questionable [ˈkwestʃənəbl] adj *statement, figures* discutable, douteux, contestable; (*pej*) *motive etc* louche, douteux, suspect; *taste* discutable, douteux. **it is ~ whether** il est douteux *or* discutable que + *subj*.

questioner [ˈkwestʃənəʳ] n personne *f* qui pose des questions; (*interrupting*) interpellateur *m*, -trice *f*. **she looked at her ~** elle regarda la personne qui l'interrogeait.

questioning [ˈkwestʃənɪŋ] 1 adj interrogateur (*f* -trice), questionneur. **he gave me a ~ look** il m'interrogea du regard. 2 n interrogation *f*.

questionnaire [ˌkwestʃəˈnɛəʳ] n questionnaire *m*.

queue [kjuː] 1 n a (*Brit*) *[people]* queue *f*, file *f* (d'attente); *[cars]* file. **to stand in a ~, to form a ~** faire la queue; **go to the end of the ~!** prenez la queue!; **he joined the theatre ~** il s'est joint aux personnes qui faisaient la queue au théâtre; **ticket ~** queue devant les guichets; *see* **jump** *etc*. b (*pigtail*) natte *f* (*d'homme*). 2 comp ▸**queue-jump** (*Brit*) vi passer avant son tour, ne pas attendre son tour ▸**queue-jumper** resquilleur *m*, -euse *f* (*qui passe avant son tour*) ▸**queue-**

jumping resquillage *m* (*pour passer avant son tour*). 3 vi (*Brit: also* ~ **up**) *[people, cars]* faire la queue (*for* pour). **we ~d (up) for an hour** nous avons fait une heure de queue.

quibble ['kwɪbl] 1 n chicane *f*, argutie *f*. **that's just a ~** c'est couper les cheveux en quatre*. 2 vi chicaner, ergoter (*over* sur).

quibbler ['kwɪblə^r] n chicaneur *m*, -euse *f*, chicanier *m*, -ière *f*, ergoteur *m*, -euse *f*.

quibbling ['kwɪblɪŋ] 1 adj *person* ergoteur, chicaneur, chicanier; *argument* captieux, spécieux; *objection* spécieux. 2 n (*NonC*) chicanerie *f*.

quiche [ki:ʃ] n quiche *f*.

quick [kwɪk] 1 adj a (*rapid*) *pulse, train, movement, route, decision, method* rapide; *recovery, answer* prompt. **be ~!** dépêche-toi!, fais vite!; **try to be ~er next time** essaie de faire plus vite la prochaine fois; **at a ~ pace** d'un pas vif *or* rapide, d'un bon pas; (*Mil*) **~ march!** en avant, marche!; **I had a ~ chat with her** *or* **a few ~ words with her** j'ai échangé quelques mots (rapides) avec elle; **going cheap for a ~ sale** sacrifié pour vente rapide; **we had a ~ meal** nous avons mangé en vitesse *or* sur le pouce*; **to have a ~ one** (*: *drink*) prendre un pot* en vitesse; (‡: *sex*) tirer un coup en vitesse‡; **it's ~er by train** c'est plus rapide *or* ça va plus vite par le train; **he's a ~ worker** il travaille vite; (* *iro*) il ne perd pas de temps (*iro*), il va vite en besogne (*iro*); *see* **double, draw** *etc*.

b (*lively*) *mind* vif (*f* vive), rapide, éveillé, agile; *child* vif, éveillé. **he's too ~ for me** il est trop rapide pour moi, il va trop vite pour moi; **he has a ~ eye for mistakes** il repère vite les fautes; **to have a ~ ear** avoir l'oreille fine; **to have a ~ wit** avoir la repartie facile *or* de la repartie (*see also* **4**); **he was ~ to see that ...** il a tout de suite vu *or* remarqué que ...; **to be ~ to take offence** être prompt à s'offenser, s'offenser pour un rien; **to have a ~ temper** s'emporter facilement, être soupe au lait* (*see also* **4**); (*liter*) **to be ~ to anger** avoir la tête chaude, être prompt à s'emporter; **he is ~ at figures** il calcule vite.

2 n a (*Anat*) vif *m*. **to bite one's nails to the ~** se ronger les ongles jusqu'au sang; (*fig*) **to cut** *or* **sting sb to the ~** piquer *or* blesser qn au vif.

b (††, *liter*) **the ~ and the dead** les vivants *mpl* et les morts *mpl*.

3 adv (= **quickly**) **~, over here!** vite, par ici!; **as ~ as lightning** *or* **as a flash** avec la rapidité de l'éclair; *for other phrases see* **quickly**.

4 comp ►**quick-acting** *drug etc* qui agit rapidement ►**quick-assembly furniture** meubles *mpl* à monter soi-même ►**quick assets** (*Fin*) actif *m* disponible à court terme ►**quick-change artist** (*Theat*) spécialiste *mf* des transformations rapides ►**quick-fire: a series of quick-fire questions** un feu roulant de questions; **to shoot quick-fire questions at sb** mitrailler qn de questions ►**quick-firing** (*Mil*) à tir rapide ►**quick-freeze** surgeler ►**quicklime** chaux vive ►**quick money** (*Fin*) capital *m* investi réalisable sur demande ►**quicksand** sable mouvant ►**quicksands** sables mouvants; **to get stuck in quicksands** s'enliser ►**quickset hedge** haie *f* vive; (*hawthorn*) haie d'aubépine ►**quick-setting** *cement* à prise rapide; *jelly* qui prend facilement ►**quicksilver** vif-argent *m*, mercure *m* ►**quickstep** (*Dancing*) fox(-trot) *m* ►**quick-tempered: to be quick-tempered** avoir la tête chaude, être prompt à s'emporter, être soupe au lait* *inv* ►**quickthorn (hedge)** (haie *f* d')aubépine *f* ►**quick-witted** à l'esprit vif *or* délié; (*in answering*) qui a la repartie facile *or* de la repartie.

quicken ['kwɪkən] 1 vt (*lit*) accélérer, presser, hâter; (*fig*) *feelings, imagination* exciter, stimuler; *appetite* stimuler, aiguiser. **to ~ one's pace** accélérer son allure, presser le pas; (*Mus*) **to ~ the tempo** presser l'allure *or* la cadence. 2 vi *[pace, movement]* s'accélérer, devenir *or* se faire plus rapide; *[hope]* se ranimer; *[foetus]* remuer.

quickie* ['kwɪkɪ] 1 n chose faite en vitesse *or* à la hâte; (*drink*) pot* pris en vitesse; (*question*) question *f* éclair *inv*; (*sex*) coup *m* rapide*; (*Cine*) court métrage vite fait. 2 adj **~ divorce** divorce *m* à la hâte.

quickly ['kwɪklɪ] adv (*fast*) vite, rapidement; (*without delay*) promptement, sans tarder. **~!** vite!, dépêchez-vous!; **as ~ as possible** aussi vite que possible, au plus vite; **as ~ as I can** aussi vite que je peux; **the police were ~ on the spot** la police est arrivée sans tarder *or* promptement sur les lieux.

quickness ['kwɪknɪs] n vitesse *f*, rapidité *f*; *[intelligence, sight, gesture]* vivacité *f*; *[mind]* promptitude *f*, vivacité; *[pulse]* rapidité; *[hearing]* finesse *f*. **~ of temper** promptitude à s'emporter; **~ of wit** vivacité d'esprit.

quid[1]‡ [kwɪd] n (pl inv) *Brit: pound*) livre *f* (*sterling*).

quid[2] [kwɪd] n *[tobacco]* chique *f*.

quiddity ['kwɪdɪtɪ] n (*Philos*) quiddité *f*.

quid pro quo ['kwɪdprəʊ'kwəʊ] n, pl **~ ~ ~s: it's a ~ (for)** c'est en contrepartie (de), c'est à titre de réciprocité (pour).

quiescence [kwaɪ'esns] n (*see* **quiescent**) passivité *f*; tranquillité *f*; état *m* latent.

quiescent [kwɪ'esnt] adj *person* (*passive*) passif; (*quiet*) tranquille; *symptoms, disease, problem* latent. **in a ~ state** dans un état latent.

quiet ['kwaɪət] 1 adj a (*silent, not noisy, still*) *sea, street, evening, neighbour* tranquille; *person* silencieux, tranquille. **he was ~ for a long time** (*silent*) il est resté longtemps sans rien dire; (*still*) il est resté longtemps sans bouger; **you're very ~ today** tu ne dis rien *or* pas grand-chose aujourd'hui; **be ~!, keep ~!** taisez-vous!; **isn't it ~!** que c'est calme! *or* tranquille!; **it was ~ as the grave** il y avait un silence de mort; **try to be a little ~er** essayez de ne pas faire autant de bruit; **to keep** *or* **stay ~** (*still*) se tenir *or* rester tranquille; (*silent*) garder le silence; **to keep sb ~** (*still*) faire tenir qn tranquille, forcer qn à se tenir tranquille; (*silent*) faire taire qn, imposer silence à qn; **that book should keep him ~ for a while** ce livre devrait le faire se tenir tranquille un moment; **keep those bottles ~** empêchez ces bouteilles de tinter, ne faites pas de bruit avec ces bouteilles.

b (*not loud*) *music* doux (*f* douce); *voice, tone* bas (*f* basse); *foot-step, sound* léger; *cough, laugh* petit (*see also* **1e**). **keep the radio ~** baisse le volume (de la radio).

c (*subdued*) *person, face, temperament* doux (*f* douce); *dog, horse* docile; *child* calme, facile, doux; *dress, colour* sobre, discret (*f* -ète); *style* simple. **a ~ old lady** une vieille dame tranquille; **my daughter is a very ~ girl** ma fille n'est pas expansive, ma fille est une silencieuse.

d (*peaceful, calm*) calme, paisible, tranquille. **the patient had a ~ night** le malade a passé une nuit tranquille *or* paisible; **he had a ~ sleep** il a dormi tranquillement *or* paisiblement; **those were ~ times** la vie était calme en ce temps-là; (*Mil etc*) **all ~** rien de nouveau; **all ~ on the western front** à l'ouest rien de nouveau; **they lead a ~ life** ils mènent une vie tranquille; **this town is too ~ for me** cette ville est trop endormie pour moi, pour moi cette ville manque d'animation; **business is ~** les affaires sont calmes; (*St Ex*) **the market was ~** la Bourse était calme; **he went to sleep with a ~ mind** il s'endormit l'esprit tranquille.

e (*secret*) caché, dissimulé; (*private*) intime; *evening, dinner, discussion* intime; *irony* voilé, discret (*f* -ète); *resentment* sourd. **they had a ~ wedding** ils se sont mariés dans l'intimité; **the wedding was very ~** le mariage a eu lieu dans la plus stricte intimité; **I'll have a ~ word with her** je vais lui glisser discrètement un mot à l'oreille, je vais lui dire deux mots en particulier; **they had a ~ laugh over it** ils en ont ri doucement; **he said with a ~ smile** dit-il avec un petit sourire; **with ~ humour** avec une pointe d'humour; **he had a ~ dig* at his brother** il lança une pointe discrète à son frère; **he kept the whole thing ~** il n'a pas ébruité l'affaire; **keep it ~** gardez cela pour vous.

2 n (*NonC*) a (*silence*) silence *m*, tranquillité *f*. **in the ~ of the night** dans le silence de la nuit; **let's have complete ~ for a few minutes** faisons silence complet pendant quelques minutes.

b (*peace*) calme *m*, paix *f*, tranquillité *f*. **an hour of blessed ~** une heure de répit fort appréciée; **there was a period of ~ after the fighting** il y a eu une accalmie après les combats; *see* **peace**.

c (*) **on the ~** en cachette, en douce*; **to do sth on the ~** faire qch en cachette *or* en dessous; **she had a drink on the ~** elle a pris un verre en douce* *or* en suisse; **he told me on the ~** il me l'a dit en confidence.

3 vt = **quieten**.

quieten ['kwaɪətn] vt (*esp Brit*) *person, crowd, horse, suspicion* calmer, apaiser; *fear* calmer, dissiper; *pain* calmer; *conscience* tranquilliser, apaiser.

►**quiet(en) down** 1 vi s'apaiser, se calmer, s'assagir; (*after unruly youth*) se ranger. **their children have quietened down a lot** leurs enfants se sont beaucoup assagis. 2 vt sep *person, dog, horse* calmer, apaiser.

quietism ['kwaɪɪtɪzəm] n quiétisme *m*.

quietist ['kwaɪɪtɪst] adj, n quiétiste (*mf*).

quietly ['kwaɪətlɪ] adv (*silently*) silencieusement, sans (faire de) bruit; (*not loudly*) *speak, sing* doucement; (*gently*) doucement, calmement; (*discreetly*) discrètement; (*secretly*) en cachette, en douce*, secrètement. **~ dressed** habillé simplement *or* discrètement; **he was made to resign** ~ on l'a forcé à démissionner sans faire de bruit; (*not to resist arrest*) **to come** *or* **go ~** se rendre sans faire de difficultés *or* calmement; **they got married very ~** ils se sont mariés dans la plus stricte intimité.

quietness ['kwaɪətnɪs] n (*silence*) silence *m*; (*stillness*) calme *m*, tranquillité *f*, quiétude *f*; (*gentleness*) douceur *f*; (*peacefulness*) repos *m*, tranquillité, calme.

quietude ['kwaɪətju:d] n quiétude *f*.

quietus [kwaɪ'i:təs] n, pl **~es** (*Jur*) quittance *f*; (*fig*) (*release*) coup *m* de grâce (*lit, fig*); (*death*) mort *f*.

quiff [kwɪf] n (*Brit: also* **~ of hair**) (*on forehead*) mèche *f*; (*on top of head*) épi *m*; (*on top of baby's head*) coque *f*.

quill [kwɪl] n (*feather*) penne *f*; (*part of feather*) tuyau *m* de plume; (*also* **~-pen**) plume *f* d'oie; *[porcupine etc]* piquant *m*.

quilt [kwɪlt] 1 n édredon *m* (piqué), courtepointe *f*. **continental ~** couette *f*. 2 vt *eiderdown, cover* matelasser, ouater et piquer; *dressing gown* matelasser, ouatiner; *furniture, bedhead etc* capitonner.

quilted ['kwɪltɪd] adj *jacket, bed cover* matelassé; *dressing gown* matelassé, ouatiné; *bed head* capitonné.

quilting ['kwɪltɪŋ] n (*NonC*) (*process*) ouatage *m*, capitonnage *m*; (*material*) ouate *f*, matelassé *m*, ouatine *f*, capitonnage.

quin [kwɪn] n (*Brit*) abbr of **quintuplet**.

quince [kwɪns] 1 n (*fruit*) coing *m*; (*tree*) cognassier *m*. 2 comp *jam* de coings.

quincentenary [ˌkwɪnsen'ti:nərɪ] n cinquième centenaire *m*.

quinine [kwɪ'ni:n] n quinine *f*.

Quinquagesima [ˌkwɪŋkwə'dʒesɪmə] n Quinquagésime *f*.

quinquennia [kwɪŋ'kwenɪə] npl of **quinquennium**.
quinquennial [kwɪŋ'kwenɪəl] adj quinquennal.
quinquennium [kwɪŋ'kwenɪəm] n, pl **quinquennia** quinquennat *m*.
quinsy ['kwɪnzɪ] n (*Med* ††) amygdalite purulente.
quint [kwɪnt] n (*US*) abbr of **quintuplet**.
quintal ['kwɪntl] n a (*100 kg*) quintal *m*. b (*100 lb*) 100 livres *fpl* (= *45,36 kg*).
quintessence [kwɪn'tesns] n quintessence *f*.
quintessential [ˌkwɪntɪ'senʃəl] adj quintessenciel.
quintet(te) [kwɪn'tet] n quintette *m*.
quintillion [kwɪn'tɪljən] n, pl ~s or ~ (*Brit, France*) 10^{18}, (*US*) 10^{30}, quintillion *m*.
quintuple ['kwɪntjʊpl] 1 adj, n quintuple (*m*). 2 [kwɪn'tju:pl] vti quintupler.
quintuplet [kwɪn'tju:plɪt] n quintuplé(e) *m(f)*.
quip [kwɪp] 1 n raillerie *f*, quolibet *m*, mot *m* piquant. 2 vi railler, lancer des pointes. 3 vt: **"never on a Sunday" she ~ped** "jamais le dimanche" dit-elle avec piquant *or* avec esprit.
quire ['kwaɪəʳ] n a (*Bookbinding*) (*part of book*) cahier *m* (d'un livre) (*4 feuilles*). **book in ~s** livre en feuilles (détachées) *or* en cahiers. b *[paper]* ≈ main *f* (*de papier*).
quirk [kwɜ:k] n a bizarrerie *f*, excentricité *f*. **it's just one of his ~s** c'est encore une de ses excentricités; **by a ~ of fate** par un caprice du destin; **by some ~ of nature/of circumstance** par une bizarrerie de la nature/de(s) circonstance(s). b (*flourish*) (*Art, Mus*) arabesque *f*; (*in signature*) parafe *m or* paraphe *m*; (*in handwriting*) fioriture *f*.
quirky ['kwɜ:kɪ] adj capricieux, primesautier; (*strange*) étrange, original.
quirt [kwɜ:t] 1 n (*US*) cravache *f* tressée. 2 vt (*US*) cravacher.
quisling ['kwɪzlɪŋ] n collaborateur *m*, -trice *f* (*pej*), collabo* *mf*.
quit [kwɪt] pret, ptp **quit** *or* **quitted** 1 vt a (*leave*) *place, premises* quitter, s'en aller de; *person* quitter, laisser. **to give a tenant notice to ~** donner congé à un locataire.
b (*give up*) lâcher, quitter, abandonner; (*esp US: stop*) cesser, arrêter (*doing* de faire). **to ~ school** quitter l'école *or* le collège *etc*; **to ~ one's job** quitter sa place; **to ~ hold** lâcher prise; **to ~ hold of sth** lâcher qch; **to ~ work** cesser le travail; **~ fooling!** arrête de faire l'idiot!
c (*Comput*) *file, window etc* sortir de, quitter.
2 vi a (*esp US*) (*give up: in game etc*) se rendre; (*accept defeat*) abandonner la partie, renoncer; (*resign*) démissionner. **I ~!** j'arrête!, j'abandonne!; **he ~s too easily** il se laisse décourager *or* il abandonne la partie trop facilement.
b (*Comput*) sortir, quitter.
3 adj: **~ of** débarrassé de.
quite [kwaɪt] adv a (*entirely*) tout à fait, tout, complètement, entièrement. (*also iro*) **~ (so)!** exactement!; **I ~ agree with you** je suis entièrement *or* tout à fait de votre avis; **he ~ realizes that he must go** il se rend parfaitement compte qu'il doit partir; **I ~ understand** je comprends très bien; **I ~ believe it** je le crois volontiers *or* sans difficulté, je n'ai aucun mal à le croire; **I don't ~ know** je ne sais pas bien *or* trop; **I don't ~ see what he means** je ne vois pas tout à fait *or* pas trop ce qu'il veut dire; **that's ~ enough!** ça suffit comme ça!; **that's ~ enough for me** j'en ai vraiment assez; **it was ~ something*** c'était épatant* *or* formidable*; **it wasn't ~ what I wanted** ce n'était pas exactement ce que je voulais; **not ~ as many as last week** pas tout à fait autant que la semaine dernière; **that's ~ another matter** c'est une tout autre affaire; **~ 4 days ago** il y a bien 4 jours; **he was ~ right** il avait bien raison *or* tout à fait raison; **my watch is ~ right** ma montre a l'heure exacte; **~ new** tout (à fait) neuf; **he was ~ alone** il était tout seul; **she was ~ a beauty** c'était une véritable beauté; **it is ~ splendid** c'est vraiment splendide!; *see* **thing**.
b (*to some degree, moderately*) plutôt, assez. **it was ~ dark for 6 o'clock** il faisait plutôt sombre pour 6 heures; **~ a long time** assez longtemps; **~ a** *or* **some time** un bon moment, un bon bout de temps*; **~ a few people** un bon *or* assez grand nombre de gens; **your essay was ~ good** votre dissertation n'était pas mal *inv or* pas mauvaise du tout; **he is ~ a good singer** c'est un assez bon chanteur; **I ~ like this painting** j'aime assez ce tableau.
quits [kwɪts] adj quitte. **to be ~ with sb** être quitte envers qn; **now they are ~** maintenant ils sont quittes; **let's call it ~** restons-en là; **to cry ~** se déclarer quittes, déclarer match nul.
quittance ['kwɪtəns] n (*Fin etc*) quittance *f*.
quitter ['kwɪtəʳ] n (*pej*) personne *f* qui abandonne facilement la partie *or* qui se laisse rebuter par les difficultés, dégonflé(e)* *mf*.
quiver¹ ['kwɪvəʳ] 1 vi *[person]* frémir, frissonner, trembler (*with* de); *[voice]* trembler, trembloter, chevroter; *[leaves]* frémir, frissonner; *[flame]* vaciller; *[wings]* battre, palpiter; *[lips]* trembler, frémir; *[eyelids]* battre; *[flesh, heart]* frémir, palpiter; *[violin]* frémir. 2 n (*see* **1**) frémissement *m*; tremblement *m*; frisson *m*, frissonnement *m* (*liter*); vacillement *m*; battement *m*; palpitation *f*.
quiver² ['kwɪvəʳ] n (*for arrows*) carquois *m*.
qui vive [ki:'vi:v] n: **on the ~** sur le qui-vive.
Quixote ['kwɪksət] n: **Don ~** don Quichotte *m*.
quixotic [kwɪk'sɒtɪk] adj *person* (*unselfish*) chevaleresque, généreux; (*visionary*) chimérique; *plan, idea* donquichottesque. **with a ~ disregard for his own safety** avec un mépris donquichottesque pour sa propre sécurité.
quixotically [kwɪk'sɒtɪkəlɪ] adv à la (manière de) don Quichotte. **to behave ~** jouer le don Quichotte; **he volunteered ~ to go himself** en don Quichotte, il offrit d'y aller lui-même.
quixotism ['kwɪksətɪzəm] n, **quixotry** ['kwɪksətrɪ] n donquichottisme *m*.
quiz [kwɪz] 1 n, pl **~zes** a (*Rad, TV*) quiz *m*, jeu-concours *m* (radiophonique *or* télévisé); (*in magazine etc*) série *f* de questions; (*puzzle*) devinette *f*. b (*US Scol*) interrogation *f* rapide (*orale ou écrite*). 2 vt a (*gen*) interroger, questionner, presser de questions (*about* au sujet de). b (*US Scol*) interroger rapidement. 3 comp ▸**quiz kid*** (*US*) enfant *mf* prodige ▸**quizmaster** meneur *m* de jeu; (*Rad, TV*) animateur *m* ▸**quiz programme** (*Rad, TV*) quiz *m*.
quizzical ['kwɪzɪkəl] adj (*mocking, questioning*) moqueur, narquois, ironique; (*puzzled*) perplexe.
quizzically ['kwɪzɪkəlɪ] adv (*see* **quizzical**) d'un air narquois *or* ironique; d'un air perplexe.
quod‡ [kwɒd] n (*Brit*) taule‡ *f or* tôle‡ *f*, bloc* *m*. **to be in ~** être au bloc* *or* à l'ombre*, faire de la taule‡.
quoin [kwɔɪn] n (*angle*) coin *m or* angle *m* d'un mur; (*stone*) pierre *f* d'angle.
quoit [kwɔɪt] n palet *m*. **~s** jeu *m* du palet; **to play ~s** jouer au palet.
quondam ['kwɒndæm] adj (*liter*) ancien (*before n*), d'autrefois.
Quonset hut ['kwɒnsɪt'hʌt] n ® (*US*) baraque *or* hutte préfabriquée (*en tôle, cylindrique*).
quorate ['kwɔ:reɪt] adj (*Admin*) qui a le quorum, où le quorum est atteint.
Quorn [kwɔ:n] n ® *substitut de viande à partir de protéines végétales*.
quorum ['kwɔ:rəm] n quorum *m*. **we have not got a ~** nous n'avons pas de quorum, le quorum n'est pas atteint.
quota ['kwəʊtə] 1 n a (*share*) quote-part *f*, part *f*. b (*permitted amount*) *[imports, immigrants]* quota *m*, contingent *m*. 2 comp ▸**quota system** système *m* de quotas.
quotable ['kwəʊtəbl] adj (*which one may quote*) que l'on peut (*or* puisse) citer; (*worth quoting*) digne d'être cité, bon à citer; (*St Ex*) *securities* cotable.
quotation [kwəʊ'teɪʃən] 1 n a (*passage cited*) citation *f* (*from* de). b (*St Ex*) cours *m*, cote *f*; (*Comm: estimate*) devis *m* (estimatif). 2 comp ▸**quotation marks** guillemets *mpl*; **in quotation marks** entre guillemets; **to open/close the quotation marks** ouvrir/fermer les guillemets.
quote [kwəʊt] 1 vt a *author, poem, fact, text* citer; *words* rapporter, citer; *reference number etc* rappeler. **to ~ Shelley** citer Shelley; **to ~ sb as an example** citer *or* donner qn en exemple; **you can ~ me** vous pouvez me citer *or* citer ce que j'ai dit; **don't ~ me** ne dites pas que c'est moi qui vous l'ai dit; **he was ~d as saying that ...** il aurait dit que ...; **can you ~ (me) a recent instance of this?** pouvez-vous (me) citer un exemple récent de ceci?; (*Comm*) **when ordering please ~ this number** pour toute commande prière de rappeler ce numéro.
b (*Comm*) *price* indiquer, établir, spécifier; (*St Ex*) *price* coter (*at* à). **this was the best price he could ~ us** c'est le meilleur prix qu'il a pu nous faire *or* proposer; (*St Ex*) **~d company** société *f* dont les actions sont inscrites à la cote officielle, société *f* cotée en Bourse.
2 vi a (*Literat etc*) faire des citations. **to ~ from the Bible** citer la Bible.
b (*Comm*) **to ~ for a job** établir *or* faire un devis pour un travail.
3 n a (*quotation*) citation *f* (*from* de).
b (*to journalist etc: short statement*) déclaration *f*, commentaire *m*. **"give us a ~!" the pressmen cried** "faites-nous une déclaration *or* un commentaire!" ont crié les journalistes.
c (*Gramm*) **~s*** npl guillemets *mpl*; **in ~s*** entre guillemets.
d (*Comm*) (*: *estimate*) devis *m*.
4 adv (*indicating beginning of quotation*) (*in dictation*) ouvrez les guillemets; (*in lecture, report etc*) je cite.
quoth [kwəʊθ] defective vb (†† *or hum*) **~ he** fit-il, dit-il.
quotient ['kwəʊʃənt] n (*esp Math*) quotient *m*; *see* **intelligence**.
qv (abbr of **quod vide** (= *"which see"*)) ≈ voir.
QWERTY, qwerty ['kwɜ:tɪ] adj: **~ keyboard** clavier *m* qwerty.

R

R, r [ɑːʳ] n a (*letter*) R, r *m.* **the three R's** *la lecture, l'écriture et l'arithmétique (les trois bases de l'enseignement);* **R for Robert** *or* (*US*) **Roger** R comme Raoul. b (*Cine*) (**abbr of Restricted**) (*Brit*) distribution restreinte (à des clubs); (*US*) interdit aux moins de 17 ans. c (**abbr of right**) droite. d (*Geog*) **abbr of river.** e (**abbr of Réaumur**) R. f (*Brit*) (**abbr of Rex, Regina**) **George R** le roi Georges; **Elizabeth R** la reine Élisabeth.

® (**abbr of registered trademark**) ®.

R.A. [ɑːr'eɪ] n (*Brit*) (**abbr of Royal Academician**) *membre de l'Académie Royale.*

R.A.A.F. [ˌɑːreɪeɪ'ef] n **abbr of Royal Australian Air Force.**

rabbet ['ræbɪt] n feuillure *f*, rainure *f*.

rabbi ['ræbaɪ] n rabbin *m*; *see* **chief.**

Rabbinic [rə'bɪnɪk] n (*Ling*) langue *f* rabbinique.

rabbinical [rə'bɪnɪkəl] adj rabbinique.

rabbit ['ræbɪt] 1 n, pl ~ *or* ~s lapin *m*; (* *fig: Sport etc*) nullard(e)* *m(f)*. **doe** ~ lapin *f*; **wild** ~ lapin *m* de garenne; ~ **food*** herbe *f* à lapins*; *see* **Welsh** *etc.* 2 vi a (*shoot ~s*) **to go ~ing** chasser le lapin. b (*Brit *: also* ~ **on, go ~ing on**) ne pas cesser de parler (*about* de). **to** ~ **on about** s'étendre à n'en plus finir sur. 3 comp ▸**rabbit burrow, rabbit hole** terrier *m* (de lapin) ▸**rabbit ears** (*US fig: TV aerial*) antenne *f* en V d'intérieur ▸**rabbit hutch** clapier *m*, cabane *f or* cage *f* à lapins ▸**rabbit punch** (*Boxing etc*) coup *m* du lapin *or* sur la nuque ▸**rabbit warren** (*lit*) garenne *f*; (*fig: streets, corridors*) labyrinthe *m*.

rabble ['ræbl] 1 n (*disorderly crowd*) cohue *f*, foule *f* (confuse). (*pej: lower classes*) **the** ~ la populace (*pej*). 2 comp ▸**rabble-rouser** (*pej*) fomentateur *m*, -trice *f* de troubles, agitateur *m*, -trice *f* ▸**rabble-rousing** (*pej*) n incitation *f* à la révolte *or* à la violence ◊ adj qui incite à la révolte *or* à la violence, qui cherche à soulever les masses.

Rabelaisian [ˌræbə'leɪzɪən] adj rabelaisien.

rabid ['ræbɪd] adj a (*Med*) (*animal*) enragé; (*person*) atteint de la rage. b (*fanatical*) *reformer etc* forcené, enragé, fanatique; *hatred etc* farouche, féroce.

rabidly ['ræbɪdlɪ] adv farouchement, férocement, avec fanatisme, comme un(e) enragé(e).

rabies ['reɪbiːz] 1 n rage *f* (*Med*). 2 comp *virus* rabique, de la rage; *injection* contre la rage.

R.A.C. [ˌɑːreɪ'siː] n (*Brit*) (**abbr of Royal Automobile Club**) ≃ Automobile-Club *m*, Touring-Club *m*.

raccoon [rə'kuːn] 1 n, pl ~ *or* ~s raton *m* laveur. 2 comp en fourrure de raton (laveur).

race¹ [reɪs] 1 n a (*Sport etc*) course *f*. **the 100 metres** ~ la course sur *or* de 100 mètres, le 100 mètres; **horse** ~ course de chevaux; **cycle** ~ course cycliste; (*Horse-racing*) **the ~s** les courses (de chevaux); (*lit, fig*) ~ **against time** course contre la montre; *see* **arm², long¹, relay.**

b (*swift current*) (*in sea*) raz *m*; (*in stream*) courant fort; *see* **mill.**

c (*fig, liter*) *[sun, moon]* cours *m*.

2 vt a *person* faire une course avec, s'efforcer de dépasser. **I'll** ~ **you to school!** à qui arrivera le premier à l'école!; **the car was racing the train** la voiture faisait la course avec le train *or* luttait de vitesse avec le train.

b (*cause to speed*) *car* lancer (à fond). (*Aut*) **to** ~ **the engine** emballer le moteur.

c (*Sport*) *horse* faire courir. **the champion ~s Ferraris** le champion court sur Ferrari.

3 vi a (*compete*) *[racing driver, athlete, jockey etc]* courir, faire la course. **to** ~ **against sb** faire la course avec qn; (*fig*) **to** ~ **against time** *or* **the clock** courir contre la montre; *[horse owner]* **he ~s at Longchamp every week** il fait courir à Longchamp toutes les semaines.

b (*rush*) *[person]* aller *or* courir à toute allure *or* à toute vitesse. **to** ~ **in/out/across** *etc* entrer/sortir/traverser *etc* à toute allure; **to** ~ **for a taxi** courir pour avoir un taxi; **to** ~ **to the station** courir à la gare, foncer jusqu'à la gare; **to** ~ **along** filer (à toute allure); **he ~d down the street** il a descendu la rue à toute vitesse.

c *[engine]* s'emballer; *[propeller]* s'affoler; *[pulse]* être très rapide.

4 comp ▸**race card** programme *m* (des courses) ▸**racecourse** (*esp Brit*) champ *m* de courses, hippodrome *m* ▸**racegoer** turfiste *mf* ▸**racehorse** cheval *m* de course ▸**race meeting** (réunion *f* de) courses *fpl* ▸**racetrack** (*US*) champ *m* de courses; (*Brit*) piste *f* ▸**raceway** (*US*) (*for horses*) piste *f* (de champ de courses); (*for cars*) piste *f* (pour courses automobiles).

race² [reɪs] 1 n (*lit, fig*) race *f*. **the human** ~ la race *or* l'espèce humaine. 2 comp *hatred, prejudice* racial ▸**race relations** relations *fpl* inter-raciales; (*Brit*) **the Race Relations Board** *commission chargée de supprimer la discrimination raciale* ▸**race riot** émeute(s) *f(pl)* raciale(s).

raceme ['ræsiːm] n racème *m* (*rare*), grappe *f*.

racer ['reɪsəʳ] n (*person*) coureur *m*, -euse *f*; (*car, yacht*) racer m; (*horse*) cheval *m* de course; (*cycle*) vélo *m or* bicyclette *f* de course.

Rachel ['reɪtʃəl] n Rachel *f*.

rachitic [ræ'kɪtɪk] adj rachitique.

rachitis [rə'kaɪtɪs] n (*Med frm*) rachitisme *m*.

Rachmanism ['rækməˌnɪzəm] n *intimidation de locataires par des propriétaires sans scrupules (pour obtenir une expulsion).*

racial ['reɪʃəl] adj *discrimination etc* racial. ~ **minorities** minorités raciales; *see* **violence.**

racialism ['reɪʃəlɪzəm] n racisme *m*.

racialist ['reɪʃəlɪst] adj, n raciste (*mf*).

racially ['reɪʃəlɪ] adv: ~ **mixed community** communauté *f* pluriraciale; **of** ~ **mixed parentage** de parents de races différentes, métis; ~ **motivated attack/sacking** attaque *f* raciste/licenciement *m* à motivation raciste; ~ **prejudiced** ayant des préjugés racistes.

racily ['reɪsɪlɪ] adv (*saucily*) lestement; (*in a lively way*) avec verve.

raciness ['reɪsɪnɪs] n (*see* **racy**) piquant *m*.

racing ['reɪsɪŋ] 1 n: **horse-~** courses *fpl* de chevaux, hippisme *m*; **motor** ~ courses d'automobiles. 2 comp *calendar, stables* de(s) courses ▸**racing bicycle** vélo *m or* bicyclette *f* de course ▸**racing car** voiture *f* de course, racer *m* ▸**racing colours** couleurs *fpl* d'une écurie (*portées par le jockey*) ▸**racing cyclist** coureur *m*, -euse *f* cycliste ▸**racing driver** coureur *m*, -euse *f* automobile, pilote *m* de courses ▸**racing man** turfiste *m*, amateur *m* de courses ▸**racing pigeon** pigeon *m* voyageur de compétition ▸**the racing world** *[horses]* le monde hippique *or* du turf; *[cars]* le monde des courses (automobiles) ▸**racing yacht** racer *m*, yacht *m* de course.

racism ['reɪsɪzəm] n racisme *m*.

racist ['reɪsɪst] adj, n raciste (*mf*).

rack¹ [ræk] 1 n a (*for bottles, documents*) casier *m*; (*for luggage*) porte-bagages *m*; (*for dishes*) égouttoir *m*; (*for hanging tools/ties etc*) porte-outils/-cravates *etc m*; (*for vegetables*) bac(s) *m(pl)* à légumes; (*for fodder, rifles, pipes*) râtelier *m*. (*US*) **off the** ~ en confection, en prêt-à-porter (*see also* **off**); *see* **bicycle, hat, luggage, toast** *etc.*

b (*Hist*) chevalet *m*. **to put sb on the** ~ infliger *or* faire subir à qn le supplice du chevalet; (*fig*) mettre qn au supplice.

2 comp ▸**rack and pinion** (*Tech*) crémaillère *f* ▸**rack railway** chemin *m* de fer à crémaillère ▸**rack rent** loyer exorbitant.

3 vt (*Hist*) faire subir le supplice du chevalet à; (*fig*) *[pain]* torturer, tourmenter. (*fig*) **~ed by remorse** tenaillé par le remords; **to** ~ **one's brains** se creuser la tête *or* la cervelle*.

rack² [ræk] n: **to go to** ~ **and ruin** *[building]* tomber en ruine; *[business, economy]* aller à vau-l'eau; *[person, country]* aller à la ruine.

racket¹ ['rækɪt] n (*Sport*) raquette *f*. (*game*) **~s** (jeu *m* de) paume *f*; ~ **press** presse-raquette *m inv*, presse *f*.

racket² ['rækɪt] 1 n a (*noise*) *[people]* tapage *m*, raffut* *m*, boucan‡ *m*; *[machine]* vacarme *m*. **to make a** ~ faire du raffut* *or* du boucan‡ *or* du vacarme.

b (*) (*organized crime*) racket *m*; (*dishonest scheme*) escroquerie *f*. **the drugs/stolen car** ~ le trafic de la drogue/des voitures volées; **that**

firm is on to quite a ~ cette firme a trouvé une jolie combine*; **he's in on the ~** il est dans le coup*; (*fig: job etc*) **what's your ~** qu'est-ce que vous faites (dans la vie)?

c **to stand the ~**‡ (*take responsibility*) payer les pots cassés*; (*pay up*) payer, casquer ‡.

2 **vi** (†) (*make a noise*) faire du raffut* *or* du boucan‡; (*also* **~ about, ~ around:** *lead a hectic social life*) faire la bombe* *or* la bringue‡.

racketeer [ˌrækɪˈtɪəʳ] **n** racketter *m*, racketteur *m*. **drugs ~** trafiquant *m* de drogue.

racketeering [ˌrækɪˈtɪərɪŋ] **n** racket *m*. **drugs ~** trafic *m* de drogue.

racking [ˈrækɪŋ] **adj** *pain* atroce, épouvantable.

raconteur [ˌrækɒnˈtɜːʳ] **n** conteur *m*, -euse *f*.

racoon [rəˈkuːn] = **raccoon.**

racquet [ˈrækɪt] = **racket**[1].

racy [ˈreɪsɪ] **adj** **a** (*risqué*) *story* risqué, osé, piquant. **b** (*lively*) *style of writing, speaking* piquant, plein de verve. **c** *wine* qui a du caractère.

RADA [ˈrɑːdə] **n** (**abbr of Royal Academy of Dramatic Art**) ≃ Conservatoire *m* d'Art Dramatique.

radar [ˈreɪdɑːʳ] **1** **n** radar *m*. **by ~** au radar. **2** **comp** *echo, screen, station* radar *inv* ▸**radar astronomy** radarastronomie *f* ▸**radar beacon** balise *f* radar ▸**radar operator** radariste *mf* ▸**radar scanner** déchiffreur *m* de radar ▸**radar sensor** détecteur *m* (radar) ▸**radar trap** (*Aut Police*) piège *m* radar; **to get caught in a radar trap** se faire piéger par un radar.

raddle [ˈrædl] **1** **n** ocre *f* rouge. **2** **vt** passer à l'ocre; *sheep* marquer à l'ocre.

raddled [ˈrædld] **adj** *face* marqué, aux traits accusés, fripé; *person* au visage marqué, aux traits accusés.

radial [ˈreɪdɪəl] **adj** (*Med, Tech*) radial. **~ engine** moteur *m* en étoile; (*Brit*) **~ (tyre)** pneu *m* à carcasse radiale.

radiance [ˈreɪdɪəns] **n, radiancy** [ˈreɪdɪənsɪ] **n** *[sun, lights etc]* éclat *m*, rayonnement *m*, splendeur *f* (*liter*); *[face, personality, beauty]* éclat, rayonnement.

radiant [ˈreɪdɪənt] **1** **adj** *sun* radieux, rayonnant; *colour* éclatant; *person, beauty, smile* radieux. **to be ~ with joy/health** rayonner de joie/de santé; (*Phys*) **~ heat** chaleur radiante; **~ heater** radiateur *m* à foyer rayonnant; **~ heating** chauffage direct *or* par rayonnement. **2** **n** (*Phys*) point radiant; (*Math*) radian *m*; (*Astron*) (point *m*) radiant *m*.

radiantly [ˈreɪdɪəntlɪ] **adv** *shine* d'un vif éclat; *smile* d'un air radieux. **to be ~ happy** rayonner de joie.

radiate [ˈreɪdɪeɪt] **1** **vi** (*emit rays*) irradier, rayonner (*liter*); (*emit heat*) rayonner; (*Phys*) irradier; (*fig*) *[lines, roads]* rayonner (*from* de), partir du même centre. **2** **vt** *heat* émettre, dégager, répandre. (*fig*) **to ~ happiness** être rayonnant *or* rayonner de bonheur; **he ~s enthusiasm** il respire l'enthousiasme.

radiation [ˌreɪdɪˈeɪʃən] **1** **n** *[light]* irradiation *f*; *[heat]* rayonnement *m*; (*radioactivity*) radiation *f*. **2** **comp** ▸**radiation exposure** irradiation *f* ▸**radiation levels** niveaux *mpl* de radiation ▸**radiation sickness** mal *m* des rayons ▸**radiation treatment** (*Med*) radiothérapie *f*.

radiator [ˈreɪdɪeɪtəʳ] **1** **n** (*also Aut*) radiateur *m*. **2** **comp** ▸**radiator cap** (*Aut*) bouchon *m* de radiateur ▸**radiator grill** (*Aut*) calandre *f*.

radical [ˈrædɪkəl] **adj, n** (*gen, Pol, Ling, Bot, Math*) radical (*m*).

radicalism [ˈrædɪkəlɪzəm] **n** radicalisme *m*.

radicalize [ˈrædɪkəlaɪz] **vt** radicaliser.

radically [ˈrædɪkəlɪ] **adv** radicalement.

radices [ˈreɪdɪsiːz] **npl of radix.**

radicle [ˈrædɪkl] **n** (*Bot*) radicule *f*, radicelle *f*; (*Chem*) radical *m*.

radii [ˈreɪdɪaɪ] **npl of radius.**

radio [ˈreɪdɪəʊ] **1** **n** **a** (*also* **~ set**) poste *m* (de radio), radio *f*. **on the ~** à la radio; **he has got a ~** il a un poste de radio, il a la radio; **to put the ~ on/off** allumer/éteindre la radio *or* le poste; *see* **transistor.**

b (*NonC: Telec*) radio *f*, radiotélégraphie *f*. **to send a message by ~** envoyer un (message) radio; **they were communicating by ~** ils communiquaient par radio.

2 **vt** *person* appeler *or* joindre par radio; *one's position* signaler par radio. **to ~ a message** envoyer un (message) radio.

3 **vi: to ~ for help** appeler au secours par radio.

4 **comp** *talk, programme* à la radio ▸**radioactive** radioactif; **radioactive waste** déchets radioactifs ▸**radioactivity** radioactivité *f* ▸**radio alarm (clock)** radio-réveil *m* ▸**radio announcer** speaker(ine) *m(f)*, annonceur *m* ▸**radio astronomy** radioastronomie *f* ▸**radio beacon** (*Aviat, Naut*) radiophare *m*, radiobalise *f* ▸**radio beam** faisceau *m* radio *inv* ▸**radiobiology** radiobiologie *f* ▸**radio broadcast** émission *f* radiophonique ▸**radiocab** radio-taxi *m* ▸**radio car** voiture-radio *f*, voiture émettrice ▸**radiocarbon dating** datation *f* à l'analyse du carbone 14 ▸**radio cassette (recorder)** radiocassette *m* ▸**radiochemistry** radiochimie *f* ▸**radiocommunication** contact *m* radio *inv* ▸**radio compass** radiocompas *m* ▸**radio contact** = **radiocommunication** ▸**radio control** téléguidage *m* ▸**radio-controlled** téléguidé ▸**radio direction finding** radiogoniométrie *f* ▸**radioelement** radioélément *m* ▸**radio engineer** ingénieur *m* radio *inv* ▸**radio frequency** radiofréquence *f* ▸**radio galaxy** radio-galaxie *f* ▸**radio ham*** radio-amateur *m* ▸**radioisotope** radio-isotope *m* ▸**radio link** liaison *f* radio *inv* ▸**radio mast** antenne *f* (radio) ▸**radio operator** opérateur *m* (radio), radio *m* ▸**radiopager** bip* *m*, Alphapage *m* ® ▸**radiopaging** (service *m*) Alphapage *m* ®, radio-recherche *f* ▸**radio play** pièce *f* de théâtre pour la radio, audiodrame *m* ▸**radio programme** émission *f* (de radio), programme *m* radiophonique ▸**radio receiver** récepteur *m* de radio ▸**radio set** poste *m* (de radio), radio *f* ▸**radio silence** silence *m* radio *inv* ▸**radio (sono-)buoy** bouée *f* sonore ▸**radio source, radio star** radiosource *f* ▸**radio station** station *f* de radio, poste émetteur ▸**radio taxi** radio-taxi *m* ▸**radiotelegraph** **n** radiotélégramme *m*, radiogramme *m* ▸**radiotelegraphy** radiotélégraphie *f* ▸**radiotelephone** radiotéléphone *m* ▸**radiotelephony** radiotéléphonie *f* ▸**radio telescope** radiotélescope *m* ▸**radio valve** valve *f*, tube *m* à vide ▸**radio van** (*Rad, TV*) studio *m* mobile (de radiodiffusion *or* d'enregistrement) ▸**radio wave** onde hertzienne.

radiogram [ˈreɪdɪəʊgræm] **n** (*message*) radiogramme *m*, radio *m*; (*Brit: apparatus*) combiné *m* (*avec radio et pickup*).

radiograph [ˈreɪdɪəʊgrɑːf] **n** radio *f*, radiographie *f*.

radiographer [ˌreɪdɪˈɒgrəfəʳ] **n** radiologue *mf* (*technicien*).

radiography [ˌreɪdɪˈɒgrəfɪ] **n** radiographie *f*, radio *f*.

radiological [ˌreɪdɪəˈlɒdʒɪkəl] **adj** radiologique.

radiologist [ˌreɪdɪˈɒlədʒɪst] **n** radiologue *mf* (*médecin*).

radiology [ˌreɪdɪˈɒlədʒɪ] **n** radiologie *f*.

radiolysis [ˌreɪdɪˈɒlɪsɪs] **n** radiolyse *f*.

radiometer [ˌreɪdɪˈɒmɪtəʳ] **n** radiomètre *m*.

radioscopy [ˌreɪdɪˈɒskəpɪ] **n** radioscopie *f*.

radiotherapist [ˌreɪdɪəʊˈθerəpɪst] **n** radiothérapeute *mf*.

radiotherapy [ˌreɪdɪəʊˈθerəpɪ] **n** radiothérapie *f*. **to have ~ (treatment)** subir une radiothérapie.

radish [ˈrædɪʃ] **n** radis *m*.

radium [ˈreɪdɪəm] **n** radium *m*. (*Med*) **~ therapy, ~ treatment** radiumthérapie *f*, curiethérapie *f*.

radius [ˈreɪdɪəs] **n, pl ~es** *or* **radii** (*Math, fig*) rayon *m*; (*Anat*) radius *m*. **within a 6 km ~ of Paris** dans un rayon de 6 km autour de Paris.

radix [ˈreɪdɪks] **n, pl ~es** *or* **radices** (*Math*) base *f*; (*Ling*) radical *m*.

radon [ˈreɪdɒn] **n** radon *m*.

R.A.F. [ɑːreɪˈef, ræf] **n** (*Brit*) (**abbr of Royal Air Force**) RAF *f*.

raffia [ˈræfɪə] **1** **n** raphia *m*. **2** **comp** en raphia.

raffish [ˈræfɪʃ] **adj** *person* qui mène une vie dissolue *or* déréglée, libertin; *look* canaille.

raffle [ˈræfl] **1** **n** tombola *f*. **~ ticket** billet *m* de tombola. **2** **vt** mettre en tombola.

raft [rɑːft] **n** **a** (*flat structure*) radeau *m*; (*logs*) train *m* de flottage; *see* **life.** **b** (*US fig*) **a ~ of*** un tas de.

rafter [ˈrɑːftəʳ] **n** (*Archit*) chevron *m*.

rafting [ˈrɑːftɪŋ] **n** rafting *m*.

rag[1] [ræg] **1** **n** **a** lambeau *m*, loque *f*; (*for wiping etc*) chiffon *m*. **a ~ to wipe the floor** un (bout de) chiffon pour essuyer le plancher; **I haven't a ~ to wear*** je n'ai rien à me mettre sur le dos*; **to feel like a wet ~*** (*emotionally*) se sentir vidé *or* mou (*f* molle) comme une chiffe; (*physically*) se sentir ramollo* *inv*; **~s** (*for paper-making*) chiffons, peilles *fpl*; (*old clothes*) guenilles *fpl*, haillons *mpl*; **his clothes were in ~s** ses vêtements étaient en lambeaux *or* tombaient en loques; **to be (dressed) in ~s** être vêtu de guenilles *or* de haillons, être déguenillé; **in ~s and tatters** tout en loques; **to go from ~s to riches** passer de la misère à la richesse; *see* **glad.**

b (*fig: of truth, self-respect*) brin *m*; (* *pej: newspaper*) torchon* *m* (*pej*), feuille *f* de chou*.

c (‡ *US: sanitary towel*) serviette *f* hygiénique.

d (*Mus*) rag *m*.

2 **comp** ▸**ragbag** (*lit*) sac *m* à chiffons; (*Brit fig*) ramassis *m*, pot-pourri *m* ▸**rag doll** poupée *f* de chiffon ▸**rag(-and-bone) man, ragpicker** (*Brit*) chiffonnier *m* ▸**rag rug** carpette *f* faite de bouts de tissu ▸**ragtag** *see* **ragtag** ▸**ragtime** rag(-)time *m* ▸**ragtop** (*US Aut*) décapotable *f* ▸**the rag trade*** la confection ▸**ragweed** (*Bot*) ambroisie *f* ▸**ragwort** (*Bot*) jacobée *f*.

rag[2]* [ræg] (*Brit*) **1** **n** (*joke*) farce *f*, blague* *f*. **for a ~** par plaisanterie, pour s'amuser, pour blaguer*; (*Univ*) **the ~, ~ week** *la semaine où les étudiants organisent des attractions au profit d'œuvres charitables*. **2** **vt** (*tease*) taquiner, mettre en boîte*; (*play trick on*) faire une blague* à.

ragamuffin [ˈrægəˌmʌfɪn] **n** (*urchin*) galopin* *m*; (*ragged fellow*) va-nu-pieds *m inv*.

rage [reɪdʒ] **1** **n** rage *f*, fureur *f*; *[sea]* furie *f*. **to be in a ~** être furieux *or* en fureur *or* en rage; **to put sb into a ~** mettre qn en rage *or* en fureur; **to fly into a ~** entrer en fureur, se mettre en rage, sortir de ses gonds; **fit of ~** accès *m or* crise *f* de fureur *or* rage; (*fig*) **to be (all) the ~** faire fureur. **2** **vi** *[person]* être furieux (*against* contre), rager*; *[battle, fire]* faire rage; *[sea]* être démonté, être en furie; *[storm]* se déchaîner, faire rage; *[wind]* être déchaîné. (*fig*) **the fire ~d through the city** l'incendie s'est propagé dans la ville avec une violence inouïe.

ragged [ˈrægɪd] **adj** *clothes* en lambeaux, en loques; *person* déguenillé, en haillons; *animal's coat* à poil long (et broussailleux); *edge of page, rock* déchiqueté; *cuff* usé, effiloché; (*fig*) *cloud* échevelé; *performance* inégal. (*Bot*) ~ **robin** fleur *f* de coucou; (*US fig*) **on the ~ edge** (*gen*) au bord de l'abîme (*fig*); **on the ~ edge of poverty** à la limite de la misère; **to run sb ~*** éreinter qn; **to run o.s. ~*** s'éreinter, s'épuiser.

raggedly ['rægɪdlɪ] adv ~ **dressed** déguenillé; *[engine]* **to run ~** fonctionner irrégulièrement *or* par à-coups.

raging ['reɪdʒɪŋ] 1 adj *person* furieux; *thirst* ardent; *pain* atroce; *sea* démonté, en furie; *wind, storm* déchaîné. **to be in a ~ temper, to be ~ mad*** être dans une colère noire *or* une rage folle; ~ **toothache** rage *f* de dents; ~ **fever** fièvre violente *or* de cheval. 2 n *[person]* rage *f*, fureur *f*; *[elements]* déchaînement *m*. **the ~ of the sea** la mer en furie.

raglan ['ræglən] adj, n raglan *(m) inv*.

ragout ['rægu:] n ragoût *m*.

ragtag ['ræg,tæg] n: **ragtag and bobtail** racaille *f*, populace *f*.

rah* [rɑ:] (*US*) 1 excl hourra!, bravo! 2 comp ▸**rah-rah*** enthousiaste, exubérant.

raid [reɪd] 1 n (*Mil*) raid *m*, incursion *f*; (*by police*) raid *m*, descente *f*, rafle *f*; (*by bandits*) razzia *f*; (*by thieves*) hold-up *m inv*; (*Fin*) raid *m*, tentative *f* de rachat. **air ~** raid (aérien), bombardement aérien; **bank ~** hold-up *m or* braquage* *m* d'une banque. 2 vt (*Mil*) faire une incursion *or* un raid dans; (*Aviat*) bombarder, faire un raid sur; *[police]* faire une descente *or* une rafle dans; *[bandits]* razzier; *[thieves]* faire un hold-up à, braquer*; (*fig*) *orchard* marauder dans; (*hum*) *cashbox, penny bank* puiser dans; (*hum*) *larder, fridge* dévaliser, faire une descente dans*; (*Fin*) monter une OPA contre.

raider ['reɪdə^r] n (*thief*) braqueur* *m*; (*ship*) navire *m* qui accomplit un raid, raider *m*; (*plane*) bombardier *m*; (*Fin*) raider *m*. (*Mil*) **~s** commando *m*.

raiding ['reɪdɪŋ] n (*Mil*) raids *mpl*; *[police]* raids *mpl*, descentes *fpl*. ~ **party** groupe *m* d'attaque.

rail[1] [reɪl] 1 n a (*bar*) *[bridge, quay]* garde-fou *m*; *[boat]* bastingage *m*, rambarde *f*; *[balcony, terrace]* balustrade *f*; (*handrail: on wall*) main courante; (*banister*) rampe *f*; (*for carpet, curtains, spotlights etc*) tringle *f*. (*Racing*) **the horse was close to the ~s** le cheval tenait la corde; (*fence*) **~s** grille *f*, barrière *f*; *see* **altar, towel** *etc*.

b (*for train, tram*) rail *m*. **to travel by ~** voyager en train; **to send by ~** envoyer par (le) train *or* par chemin de fer; **to go off the ~s** (*lit*) *[train etc]* dérailler; (*fig*) *[person]* (*err*) s'écarter du droit chemin; (*be confused*) être déboussolé*; (*fig*) **to keep sb on the ~s** maintenir qn sur le droit chemin; *see* **live**[2].

2 comp *ticket* de chemin de fer; *journey* en chemin de fer; *dispute* des employés des chemins de fer ▸**railcar** autorail *m* ▸**railcard** carte *f* de chemin de fer (≃ *carte SNCF*); **family railcard** ≃ carte *f* couple-famille; **student's railcard** carte *f* d'étudiant ▸**railhead** tête *f* de ligne ▸**railroad** *see* **railroad** ▸**rail strike** grève *f* des employés des chemins de fer ▸**rail traffic** trafic *m* ferroviaire ▸**rail transport** transport *m* par chemin de fer *or* par train ▸**railway** *see* **railway** ▸**railworkers** employés des chemins de fer, cheminots *mpl*.

▸**rail in** vt sep clôturer, entourer d'une clôture *or* d'une barrière.

▸**rail off** vt sep fermer au moyen d'une clôture *or* d'une barrière.

rail[2] [reɪl] vi: **to ~ at** *or* **against sb** se répandre en injures contre qn.

railing ['reɪlɪŋ] n a (*rail*) *[bridge, quay]* garde-fou *m*; *[balcony, terrace]* balustrade *f*; (*on stairs*) rampe *f*; (*on wall*) main courante. b (*part of fence*) barreau *m*; (*fence: also* **~s**) grille *f*.

raillery ['reɪlərɪ] n taquinerie *f*, badinage *m*.

railroad ['reɪlrəʊd] 1 n (*US*) = **railway 1**. 2 vt a (*US*) expédier par chemin de fer *or* par rail. b (** fig*) **to ~ a bill** faire voter un projet de loi (après un débat sommaire); **to ~ sb into doing sth** forcer qn à faire qch sans qu'il ait le temps de réfléchir *or* de faire ouf*.

railway ['reɪlweɪ] 1 n a (*Brit*) (*system*) chemin *m* de fer; (*track*) voie ferrée; *see* **aerial, scenic, underground**.

b (*US: for trams etc*) rails *mpl*.

2 comp *bridge, ticket* de chemin de fer ▸**railway carriage** voiture *f*, wagon *m* ▸**railway engine** locomotive *f* ▸**railway guide** indicateur *m* des chemins de fer ▸**railway journey** voyage *m* en chemin de fer ▸**railway line** ligne *f* de chemin de fer; (*track*) voie ferrée ▸**railwayman** cheminot *m* ▸**railway network** réseau *m* ferroviaire ▸**railway porter** porteur *m* ▸**railway station** gare *f*; (*small*) station *f or* halte *f* de chemin de fer ▸**railway timetable** horaire *m* des chemins de fer, ≃ Chaix *m* ® ▸**railway workers** employés *mpl* des chemins de fer, cheminots *mpl* ▸**railway yard** dépôt *m* (d'une gare).

raiment ['reɪmənt] n (*liter*) vêtements *mpl*.

rain [reɪn] 1 n a (*Met*) pluie *f*. **it looks like ~** le temps est à la pluie; **in the ~** sous la pluie; **heavy/light ~** pluie battante/fine; **the ~'s on*** ça pleut*; **(come) ~ (hail) or shine** (*lit*) par tous les temps, qu'il pleuve ou qu'il vente; (*fig*) quoi qu'il arrive; **the ~s** la saison des pluies; *see* **right**.

b (*fig*) *[arrows, blows, bullets]* pluie *f*.

2 comp ▸**rain belt** zone *f* des pluies ▸**rainbow** *see* **rainbow** ▸**rain check*** (*US*) billet *m* pour un autre match (*or* pour un autre spectacle); (*US fig*) **to give sb a rain check** inviter qn une autre fois (à la place); (*US fig*) **I'll take a rain check** je viendrai une autre fois, ce n'est que partie remise ▸**raincoat** imperméable *m*, imper* *m* ▸**rain cloud** nuage *m* de pluie ▸**raindrop** goutte *f* de pluie ▸**rainfall** (*shower*) chute *f* de pluie; (*amount*) hauteur *f* des précipitations ▸**rainforest** (*also* **tropical rainforest**) forêt *f* tropicale humide ▸**rain gauge** pluviomètre *m* ▸**rain hood** capuchette *f* ▸**rainmaker** faiseur *m* de pluie ▸**rainmaking** adj *ceremony etc* pour faire pleuvoir ▸**rainproof** adj imperméable ◊ vt imperméabiliser ▸**rainstorm** pluie torrentielle, trombe *f* d'eau ▸**rainwater** eau *f* de pluie ▸**rainwear** (*Comm*) vêtements *mpl* de pluie, imperméables *mpl*.

3 vt *blows* faire pleuvoir.

4 vi pleuvoir. **it is ~ing** il pleut; **it is ~ing heavily** il pleut à verse; **it's ~ing cats and dogs*, it's ~ing buckets*** il pleut à seaux *or* à torrents, il pleut *or* il tombe des cordes*; (*Prov*) **it never ~s but it pours** un malheur n'arrive jamais seul.

▸**rain down** vi *[bullets, stones etc]* pleuvoir.

▸**rain off**, (*US*) **rain out** vt sep: **the match was rained off** *or* **out** le match a été annulé (*or* abandonné) à cause de la pluie.

rainbow ['reɪnbəʊ] n arc-en-ciel *m*. **of all colours of the ~** de toutes les couleurs de l'arc-en-ciel; ~ **trout** truite *f* arc-en-ciel; ~ **wrasse** girelle *f*; (*loc*) **to look for the pot of gold at the end of the ~** poursuivre un rêve impossible.

rainless ['reɪnlɪs] adj sec (*f* sèche), sans pluie.

rainy ['reɪnɪ] adj pluvieux. **the ~ season** la saison des pluies; **a ~ day** une journée pluvieuse, un jour de pluie; (*fig*) **to put something away for a ~ day** mettre de l'argent de côté, garder une poire pour la soif.

raise [reɪz] 1 vt a (*lift, cause to rise*) *arm, leg, eyes* lever; *object, weight* lever, soulever; *dust* soulever. **to ~ a blind** (re)lever un store; (*Theat*) **to ~ the curtain** lever le rideau; (*lit*) **to ~ one's eyebrows** lever les sourcils; (*in surprise*) **they ~d their eyebrows when they heard ...** ils ont eu une expression perplexe *or* l'étonnement s'est lu sur leur visage quand ils ont entendu ...; (*fig*) **that will make him ~ his eyebrows** cela le fera tiquer; (*fig*) **he didn't ~ an eyebrow** il n'a pas sourcillé *or* tiqué; **to ~ one's hat to sb** donner un coup de chapeau à qn; (*fig*) tirer son chapeau à qn*; **to ~ one's glass to sb** lever son verre à qn, boire à la santé de qn; **to ~ one's hand to sb** lever la main sur qn; **to ~ one's fist to sb** menacer qn du poing; **to ~ sb from the dead** ressusciter qn (d'entre les morts); **to ~ one's voice** (*speak louder*) hausser la voix; (*get angry*) élever la voix, hausser le ton; **not a voice was ~d in protest** personne n'a élevé la voix pour protester; **to ~ sb's spirits** remonter le moral de qn; **to ~ sb's hopes** donner à espérer à qn; **he ~d the people to revolt** il souleva le peuple; (*fig*) **to ~ the roof*** faire un boucan monstre‡; (*in protest*) rouspéter ferme*; **to ~ the level of the ground** rehausser le niveau du sol; (*Naut*) **to ~ a sunken ship** renflouer un navire coulé; *see* **tone**.

b (*increase*) *salary* augmenter, relever (*Admin*); *price* majorer, augmenter; *standard, level* élever; *age limit* reculer; *temperature* faire monter. **to ~ the school-leaving age** prolonger la scolarité obligatoire.

c (*build, erect*) *monument* élever, ériger; *building* construire, édifier, bâtir.

d (*produce*) *spirit* évoquer; *ghosts* faire apparaître; *problems, difficulties* soulever, provoquer. **to ~ a blister** provoquer une ampoule; **to ~ a laugh** provoquer le rire, faire rire; **to ~ a cheer** (*oneself*) crier, "hourra"; (*in others*) faire jaillir des hourras; **to ~ difficulties** soulever *or* faire des difficultés; **to ~ a smile** (*oneself*) ébaucher un sourire; (*in others*) faire sourire, donner à sourire; **to ~ suspicion in sb's mind** faire naître des soupçons dans l'esprit de qn; **to ~ Cain*** *or* **hell‡** (*make a noise*) faire un éclat *or* du boucan‡; (*make a fuss*) faire une scène de tous les diables*.

e (*bring to notice*) *question* soulever; *objection, protest* élever.

f (*grow, breed*) *animals, children, family* élever; *corn, wheat* cultiver, faire pousser.

g (*get together*) *army, taxes* lever; *money* se procurer. **to ~ funds for sth** (*gen*) réunir *or* rassembler *or* se procurer les fonds pour qch; *[professional fundraiser]* collecter des fonds pour qch; (*Fin, Econ*) mobiliser des fonds pour qch; **to ~ a loan** *[government etc]* lancer *or* émettre un emprunt; *[person]* emprunter; **to ~ money on sth** emprunter de l'argent sur qch; **I can't ~ the £500 I need** je n'arrive pas à me procurer les 500 livres dont j'ai besoin; *see* **mortgage**.

h (*end*) *siege, embargo* lever.

i (*Cards*) (*Poker*) faire une mise supérieure à; (*Bridge*) faire une annonce supérieure à. **I'll ~ you 6/£10** je fais une relance *or* je relance de 6/10 livres; *see* **bid**.

j (*contact*) **have you managed to ~ anyone on the radio?** avez-vous réussi à entrer en contact avec *or* à toucher quelqu'un par (la) radio?

2 n a (*US, also Brit *: payrise*) augmentation *f* (de salaire).

b (*Cards*) (*Poker*) relance *f*, mise supérieure; (*Bridge*) annonce supérieure, enchère *f*.

▸**raise up** vt sep lever, soulever. **he raised himself up on his elbow** il s'est soulevé sur son coude.

raiser ['reɪzə^r] n a (*Agr*) éleveur *m*. **cattle-/sheep-~** éleveur de bétail/de moutons. b comp ending *see* **fire, fund** *etc*.

raisin ['reɪzən] n raisin sec. ~ **bread** pain *m* aux raisins secs.

raising ['reɪzɪŋ] adj (*Culin*) ~ **agent** poudre *f* à lever.

raj [rɑ:dʒ] n empire *m* (*britannique aux Indes*).

rajah ['rɑ:dʒə] n raja(h) *m or* radja(h) *m*.

rake[1] [reɪk] 1 n (*for gardener, croupier*) râteau *m*; (*for grate*) râble *m*, ringard *m*. 2 comp ▸**rake-off*** (*pej*) pourcentage *m*, comme* *f*; **he**

gets a rake-off on each sale il prélève son pourcentage *or* sa comme* sur chaque vente. 3 vt *garden* ratisser; *hay, leaves* râteler. **to ~ a fire** tisonner un feu; **to ~ the stones off the lawn** enlever les cailloux de la pelouse (à l'aide d'un râteau); (*fig*) **to ~ one's memory** fouiller dans sa mémoire *or* dans ses souvenirs; (*fig*) **his glance ~d the crowd** il a parcouru la foule du regard; **to ~ sth with machine-gun fire** balayer qch avec une mitrailleuse. 4 vi (*fig: search*) **to ~ among** *or* **through** fouiller dans.

►**rake in*** vt sep *money* amasser. **he's just raking it in!** il remue le fric à la pelle! ‡

►**rake out** vt sep: **to rake out a fire** éteindre un feu en faisant tomber la braise.

►**rake over** vt sep *flower bed* ratisser; (*fig*) *memories* remuer.

►**rake up** vt sep *fire* attiser; *leaves* ramasser avec un râteau, ratisser; (*fig*) *grievance* rappeler. **to rake up the past** remuer le passé; **to rake up sb's past** fouiller dans le passé de qn.

rake²† [reɪk] n (*person*) roué† *m*, débauché *m*, coureur *m*.

rake³ [reɪk] 1 n (*Naut*) *[mast]* quête *f*; (*Theat*) *[stage]* pente *f*; (*Aut*) *[seat]* inclinaison *f*. 2 vi (*Naut*) être incliné; (*Theat*) être en pente.

rakish¹ ['reɪkɪʃ] adj *person* débauché, libertin; *appearance* cavalier, désinvolte. **he wore his hat at a ~ angle** il portait *or* il avait campé son chapeau sur le coin de l'œil.

rakish² ['reɪkɪʃ] adj (*Naut*) élancé, à la ligne élancée.

rakishly ['reɪkɪʃlɪ] adv *behave* en libertin, en débauché; *speak, dress* avec désinvolture.

rally¹ ['rælɪ] 1 n a *[troops]* rassemblement *m*, ralliement *m*; *[people]* rassemblement; (*Pol*) rassemblement, meeting *m*; (*Aut*) rallye *m*; (*Tennis*) échange *m*. **youth/peace ~** rassemblement de la jeunesse/en faveur de la paix; **electoral ~** meeting de campagne électorale.

b (*in health*) amélioration *f*, mieux *m*; (*St Ex*) reprise *f*.

2 vt *troops* rassembler, rallier; *supporters* rallier; *one's strength* retrouver, reprendre. **hoping to ~ opinion within the party** en espérant rallier à sa cause des membres du parti.

3 vi *[troops, people]* se rallier; *[sick person]* aller mieux, reprendre des forces *or* le dessus. **~ing point** point *m* de ralliement; (*fig*) **to ~ to a movement/to the support of sb** se rallier à un mouvement/à la cause de qn; **~ing call** *or* **cry** cri *m* de ralliement; (*Aut*) **to go ~ing** faire un *or* des rallye(s); (*St Ex*) **the market rallied** les cours ont repris.

►**rally round** 1 vi (*fig*) venir en aide. 2 vt fus: **during her husband's illness everyone rallied round her** pendant la maladie de son mari tout le monde est venu lui apporter son soutien.

rally² ['rælɪ] vt (*tease*) taquiner, se moquer (gentiment) de.

RAM [ræm] n (*Comput*) (abbr of **random access memory**) R.A.M. *m*. **~ chip** puce *f* à accès sélectif.

ram [ræm] 1 n bélier *m* (*also Astron*); (*Tech*) hie *f*, dame *f*; *[pile driver]* mouton *m*; (*for water*) bélier hydraulique; *see* **battering**.

2 comp ►**ramjet** (*Aviat*) statoréacteur *m* ►**ram raiding** *pillage de magasin en faisant éclater la vitrine avec une voiture*.

3 vt a (*push down*) enfoncer, pilonner (*Tech*), damer (*Tech*); (*pack down*) tasser (*into* dans). **he ~med his umbrella down the pipe** il a enfoncé son parapluie dans le tuyau; **he ~med the clothes into the case** il a tassé les vêtements dans la valise, il a bourré la valise de vêtements; (*Mil, Min*) **to ~ a charge home** refouler une charge; (*fig*) **to ~ home an argument** donner beaucoup de poids à un argument, corroborer un argument; (*fig*) **to ~ sth down sb's throat** rebattre les oreilles à qn de qch; (*fig*) **to ~ sth into sb's head** enfoncer *or* fourrer* qch dans la tête *or* dans le crâne de qn.

b (*crash into*) (*Naut*) heurter de l'avant *or* par l'étrave, (*in battle*) éperonner; (*Aut: deliberately or accidentally*) *another vehicle* emboutir; *post, tree* percuter (contre).

►**ram down** vt sep *earth* tasser; (*Tech*) damer; *piles* enfoncer. **his hat rammed down over his ears** le chapeau enfoncé jusqu'aux oreilles.

►**ram in** vt sep enfoncer.

Ramadan [ˌræmə'dɑːn] n ramadan *m*.

ramble ['ræmbl] 1 n randonnée *f* (pédestre), excursion *f* (à pied), balade* *f*. **to go for a ~** faire une randonnée *or* une excursion (à pied) *or* une balade*; **to go on a ~** partir en randonnée *or* en excursion. 2 vi a (*wander about*) se promener au hasard; (*also* **go rambling**) (*go on hike*) partir en randonnée *f* (pédestre), faire une excursion à pied. b (*pej: in speech: also ~* **on**) parler pour ne rien dire; *[old person]* radoter. **he ~d on for half an hour** il a discouru *or* n'a cessé de discourir pendant une demi-heure.

rambler ['ræmblər] n a (*hiker*) randonneur *m*, -euse *f*, promeneur *m*, -euse *f*. b (*also ~* **rose**) rosier grimpant.

rambling ['ræmblɪŋ] 1 adj *speech, writing* décousu; *person* qui radote; *town, building* construit au hasard *or* sans plan défini; *old house, flat* plein de coins et de recoins; *plant* grimpant. 2 n a (*incoherent speech*) divagations *fpl*, radotages *mpl*. b (*walking in country*) randonnée *f* (pédestre). **to go ~** partir en randonnée; **~ club** club *m* de randonnée (pédestre).

Ramboesque* [ˌræmbəʊ'esk] adj digne de Rambo.

rambunctious [ræm'bʌŋkʃəs] adj (*US*) = **rumbustious**.

R.A.M.C. [ˌɑːreɪem'siː] n (abbr of **Royal Army Medical Corps**) *service de santé de l'Armée*.

ramification [ˌræmɪfɪ'keɪʃən] n ramification *f*.

ramify ['ræmɪfaɪ] 1 vt ramifier. 2 vi se ramifier.

rammer ['ræmər] n (*Tech*) dame *f*, hie *f*; *[cannon]* refouloir *m*.

ramp [ræmp] n a (*slope*) rampe *f*; (*in road: for speed control*) casse-vitesse *m*; (*in garage etc*) pont *m* de graissage. (*Aviat*) **(approach** *or* **boarding) ~** passerelle *f*; (*in garage*) **hydraulic ~** pont élévateur; (*sign on road*) "~" "dénivellation". b (*Brit* ‡: *swindle*) escroquerie *f*. **it's a ~** c'est du vol.

rampage [ræm'peɪdʒ] 1 n: **to be** *or* **go on the ~** se déchaîner; (*looting etc*) se livrer au saccage. 2 vi (*also ~* **about**, **~ around**) se déchaîner.

rampancy ['ræmpənsɪ] n *[plants]* exubérance *f*; (*fig*) *[evil etc]* déchaînement *m*.

rampant ['ræmpənt] adj *plants* exubérant, luxuriant; (*Her*) rampant. (*fig*) **to be ~** *[corruption, violence]* sévir, régner; *[disease]* sévir.

rampart ['ræmpɑːt] n (*lit, fig*) rempart *m*.

rampike ['ræmpaɪk] n (*US*) arbre *m* mort (debout).

ramrod ['ræmrɒd] n *[gun]* baguette *f*; *[cannon]* refouloir *m*. **~ straight** raide *or* droit comme un piquet; *see* **stiff**.

ramshackle ['ræmˌʃækl] adj *building* délabré, branlant; *table* branlant; *machine* déglingué*. **~ old car** vieille guimbarde, vieux tacot*.

R.A.N. [ɑːreɪ'en] n abbr of **Royal Australian Navy**.

ran [ræn] pret of **run**.

ranch [rɑːntʃ] 1 n ranch *m*. 2 comp ►**ranch hand** ouvrier *m* de ranch ►**ranch(-type) house** maison *f* rustique (en rez-de-chaussée).

rancher ['rɑːntʃər] n (*US*) (*owner*) propriétaire *mf* de ranch; (*employee*) cowboy *m*.

ranching ['rɑːntʃɪŋ] n (*US*) élevage *m* en ranch.

rancid ['rænsɪd] adj rance. **to go ~** rancir; **to smell ~** sentir le rance.

rancidity [ræn'sɪdɪtɪ] n, **rancidness** ['rænsɪdnɪs] n rance *m*.

rancorous ['ræŋkərəs] adj plein de rancœur, rancunier.

rancour, (*US*) **rancor** ['ræŋkər] n rancœur *f*, rancune *f*.

rand [rænd] n, pl inv (*monetary unit*) rand *m*.

R & B [ɑːrən'biː] n (abbr of **rhythm and blues**) *see* **rhythm**.

R & D [ɑːrən'diː] n (abbr of **research and development**) R-D *f*.

random ['rændəm] 1 n: **at ~** au hasard, (*stronger*) à l'aveuglette; **chosen at ~** choisi au hasard; **to walk about at ~** se promener à l'aventure; **to hit out at ~** lancer des coups à l'aveuglette. 2 adj fait au hasard; *killings* commis au hasard. **~ bullet** balle perdue; **~ sample** échantillon prélevé au hasard; (*Comput*) **~ access** accès *m* sélectif *or* aléatoire; (*Comput*) **~ access memory** mémoire *f* vive; **~ number** nombre *m* aléatoire *or* au hasard.

randomly ['rændəmlɪ] adv au hasard. **the breakdowns occurred ~ over a period of weeks** les pannes survenaient de façon erratique pendant plusieurs semaines.

R & R [ɑːrənd'ɑːr] n (*US Mil*) (abbr of **rest and recreation**) permission *f*. **for a bit of ~*** pour se la couler douce*, pour se détendre.

randy* ['rændɪ] adj (*gen*) libidineux; (*aroused*) excité, allumé*. **to feel ~** être tout excité (*sexuellement*).

ranee ['rɑːniː] = **rani**.

rang [ræŋ] pret of **ring²**.

range [reɪndʒ] 1 n a *[mountains]* chaîne *f*; (*row*) rangée *f*, rang *m*.

b (*scope, distance covered*) *[telescope, gun, missile]* portée *f*; *[plane, ship, mooncraft]* rayon *m* d'action, autonomie *f*. **at a ~ of** à une distance de; **at long ~** à longue portée; (*Mil*) **to find the ~** régler son tir; (*lit, fig*) **to be out of ~** être hors de portée; **within (firing) ~** à portée de tir; (*fig*) **within my ~** à ma portée; **~ of vision** champ visuel; *see* **free, long¹, shooting** *etc*.

c (*extent between limits*) *[temperature]* écarts *mpl*, variations *fpl*; *[prices, salaries]* échelle *f*, éventail *m*; *[musical instrument, voice]* étendue *f*, tessiture *f*, registre *m*; (*selection*) *[colours, feelings, speeds]* gamme *f*; *[goods, patterns]* assortiment *m*, choix *m*, gamme; (*Comm*) gamme. **there will be a wide ~ of subjects** il y aura un grand choix de sujets; (*Comm*) **a car/house at the lower end of the ~** une voiture/maison bas de gamme.

d *[animal, plant]* habitat *m*, région *f*.

e (*domain, sphere*) *[activity]* champ *m*, rayon *m*; *[influence]* sphère *f*; *[knowledge]* étendue *f*, cercle *m*, champ. **the ~ of his ideas is limited** le cercle de ses idées est restreint.

f (*US: grazing land*) prairie *f*, (grand) pâturage *m*.

g (*also* **shooting ~**) (*Mil*) champ *m* de tir; (*at fair*) stand *m* (de tir); *see* **rifle²**.

h (*Surv*) direction *f*, alignement *m*. **in ~ with** dans l'alignement *or* le prolongement de.

i (*cooking stove*) fourneau *m* de cuisine.

2 vt a (*place in a row*) *objects* ranger, mettre en rang, disposer en ligne; *troops* aligner. (*fig*) **to ~ o.s. on the side of** se ranger du côté de; **they ~d themselves along the pavement to see the procession** ils se sont postés le long du trottoir pour regarder le défilé.

b (*classify*) ranger, classer (*among* parmi).

c (*roam over*) parcourir. **he ~d the whole country looking for ...** il a parcouru le pays en tous sens à la recherche de ...; **to ~ the seas** parcourir *or* sillonner les mers.

d (*direct*) *gun, telescope* braquer (*on* sur).

3 vi a (*extend*) *[discussion, quest]* s'étendre (*from ... to* de ... à,

over sur); *[results, opinions]* aller (*from* ... *to* de ... à), varier (*from* ... *to* entre ... et). **the search ~d over the whole country** les recherches se sont étendues sur tout le pays; **the numbers ~ from 10 to 20** les numéros vont de 10 à 20; **the temperature ~s from 18° to 24°** *or* **between 18° and 24°** la température varie entre 18° et 24°; (*fig*) **researches ranging over a wide field** recherches qui embrassent un large domaine.

b (*roam*) errer, vagabonder. **to ~ over the area** parcourir la région; **animals ranging through the jungle** des animaux qui rôdent dans la jungle.

c *[guns, missiles, shells]* **to ~ over** avoir une portée de, porter à.

4 **comp ►rangefinder** (*Mil, Naut, Phot*) télémètre *m*.

ranger [ˈreɪndʒəʳ] **n** a *[forest etc]* garde *m* forestier. b (*US: mounted patrolman*) gendarme *m* à cheval. (*US*) **~s** gendarmerie *f* à cheval. c **R~ (Guide)** guide *f* aînée.

Rangoon [ræŋˈguːn] **n** Rangoon.

rangy [ˈreɪndʒɪ] **adj** (*US*) grand et élancé, sans une once de graisse.

rani [ˈrɑːniː] **n** rani *f*.

rank¹ [ræŋk] 1 **n** a (*row*) rang *m*; (*Brit: also* **taxi ~**) station *f* de taxis. **the taxi at the head of the ~** le taxi en tête de file; **to break ~s** rompre les rangs; **to serve in the ~s** servir dans les rangs; (*Brit Mil*) **other ~s** les sous-officiers *mpl* et hommes *mpl* de troupe; **the ~ and file** (*Mil*) les hommes de troupe; (*fig*) la masse, le peuple; (*Pol*) **the ~ and file of the party** la base du parti; **the ~ and file workers** la base, les ouvriers *mpl*; **to rise from the ~s** sortir du rang; **to reduce to the ~s** casser; (*fig*) **they were drawn from the ~s of the unemployed** on les avait tirés des rangs des chômeurs; *see* **close²**.

b (*Mil: grade*) grade *m*, rang *m*. **to reach the ~ of general** atteindre le grade de général; *see* **pull**.

c (*class, position*) rang *m* (social), condition *f*, classe *f*. **people of all ~s** gens de toutes conditions; **a person of ~** une personne de haut rang; **a singer of the first ~** un chanteur de (tout) premier ordre; **a second-~ painter** un peintre de seconde zone *or* de deuxième ordre.

d (*Gram*) rang *m*.

e *[organ]* rang *m*.

2 **comp ►rankshifted** (*Gram*) déplacé de rang.

3 **vt** a **I ~ it as one of the best red wines** je le classe parmi les meilleurs vins rouges; **I ~ Beethoven among the great** je compte Beethoven parmi les grands; (*US Scol*) **to be ~ed high/low in class** avoir un bon/mauvais classement.

b (*US Mil*) = **outrank**.

4 **vi** *[book etc]* se classer, compter; *[person]* compter. **he ~s among my friends** il compte parmi mes amis; **to ~ above/below sb** être supérieur/inférieur à qn; **to ~ high among** occuper un rang élevé parmi; **the British team only ~ed tenth on the medals table** l'équipe britannique n'était que dixième au tableau des médaillés; **the country ~s as one of the poorest in the world** ce pays compte parmi les plus pauvres du monde; *see also* **ranking**.

rank² [ræŋk] **adj** a *plants* exubérant, luxuriant; *weeds, grass* touffu; *soil* plantureux, trop fertile, trop riche. **it is ~ with weeds** les mauvaises herbes y poussent à foison. b *smell* fétide, fort; *dustbin, drains* fétide; *fats* rance; *person* grossier, répugnant, ignoble. c (*flagrant*) *disgrace* absolu, complet (*f* -ète); *poison, traitor* véritable (*before noun*); *injustice* criant, flagrant; *insolence* caractérisé; *liar* fieffé (*before noun*); *lie* grossier, flagrant. **a ~ beginner** un pur novice, un parfait débutant; **he's a ~ outsider** il n'est vraiment pas dans la course.

ranker [ˈræŋkəʳ] **n** (*Mil*) (*soldier*) simple soldat *m*; (*officer*) officier sorti du rang.

ranking [ˈræŋkɪŋ] 1 **n** classement *m*. 2 **adj** a (*in hierarchy*) (*Mil, Admin*) **high-~**, (*US*) **~** de haut rang *or* grade; **low-~** (*Mil*) de grade inférieur; (*Admin*) au bas de l'échelle hiérarchique; (*Mil*) **the ~ officer** l'officier responsable *or* le plus haut en grade. b (*esp US: prominent*) renommé.

rankle [ˈræŋkl] **vi** rester sur le cœur, laisser une rancœur. **it ~d with him** il en était ulcéré, il l'avait sur le cœur, ça lui était resté sur l'estomac*.

rankness [ˈræŋknɪs] **n** a *[plants etc]* exubérance *f*, luxuriance *f*. b (*smell*) odeur *f* fétide; (*taste*) goût *m* rance.

ransack [ˈrænsæk] **vt** (*pillage*) *house, shop* saccager, piller; *town, region* mettre à sac; (*search*) *room, luggage, drawer* fouiller (à fond), mettre tout sens dessus dessous dans; *files, one's memory* fouiller dans (*for* pour trouver).

ransom [ˈrænsəm] 1 **n** (*lit, fig*) rançon *f*. **to hold sb to ~** mettre qn à rançon; (*fig*) exercer un chantage sur qn; (*fig*) **they are being held to ~** ils ont le couteau sur la gorge; *see* **king**. 2 **vt** racheter.

rant [rænt] **vi** a (*pej*) *[orator etc]* déclamer (de façon exagérée), parler avec emphase. b (*also* **~ on**) divaguer. **to ~ and rave** tempêter; **to ~ (and rave) at sb** tempêter *or* fulminer contre qn.

ranting [ˈræntɪŋ] 1 **n** rodomontade(s) *f(pl)*. 2 **adj** déclamatoire.

ranunculus [rəˈnʌŋkjʊləs] **n, pl ~es** *or* **ranunculi** [rəˈnʌŋkjʊˌlaɪ] renoncule *f*.

rap [ræp] 1 **n** a (*noise*) petits coups *mpl* secs; (*blow*) tape *f*. **there was a ~ at the door** on a frappé bruyamment à la porte; **to give sb a ~ on the knuckles** donner sur les doigts à qn; (*fig: rebuke*) taper sur les doigts de qn; **to take the ~*** devoir payer les pots cassés; (*US*) **to get the ~* for sth** trinquer* *or* écoper* pour qch; **I don't care a ~*** je m'en fiche* éperdument.

b (*esp US* ‡) (*criminal charge*) inculpation *f*; (*prison sentence*) condamnation *f*. **to beat the ~** échapper à une condamnation; **to hang a murder ~ on sb** faire endosser un meurtre à qn.

c (*Mus*) **~ (music)** (musique *f*) rap *m*; **~ artist** rappeur *m*, -euse *f*.

d (*US* ‡: *chat*) causette *f* *, conversation *f*.

2 **comp ►rap session*** (*US*) discussion *f* à bâtons rompus **►rap sheet** (*US: record*) casier *m* judiciaire.

3 **vt** *door* frapper bruyamment à; *table* frapper sur. **to ~ sb's knuckles, to ~ sb over the knuckles** donner sur les doigts de qn; (*fig: rebuke*) taper sur les doigts de qn.

4 **vi** a (*knock*) frapper, cogner, donner un coup sec; (*fig: rebuke*) blâmer, réprouver.

b (*US*:‡: *chat*) tailler une bavette*, bavarder.

►rap out vt sep a (*say curtly*) dire brusquement; *oath* lâcher; *order, retort* lancer. b (*Spiritualism*) *message* communiquer *or* annoncer au moyen de coups.

rapacious [rəˈpeɪʃəs] **adj** rapace, avide.

rapaciously [rəˈpeɪʃəslɪ] **adv** avec rapacité *or* avidité.

rapacity [rəˈpæsɪtɪ] **n** rapacité *f*, avidité *f*.

rape¹ [reɪp] 1 **n** (*also Jur*) viol *m*; (††: *abduction*) ravissement† *m*, rapt *m*. (*Brit*) **~ crisis centre** centre *m* d'aide aux femmes victimes de viol. 2 **vt** violer.

rape² [reɪp] **n** (*Bot*) colza *m*. **~ oil/seed** huile *f*/graine *f* de colza.

rape³ [reɪp] **n** (*grape pulp*) marc *m* de raisin; (*wine*) râpé *m*.

Raphael [ˈræfeɪəl] **n** Raphaël *m*.

rapid [ˈræpɪd] 1 **adj** *action* rapide, prompt; *river, pulse* rapide; *slope, descent* raide, rapide. (*Mil*) **~ deployment force** force *f* d'intervention; **~ eye movement sleep** phase *f* de mouvements oculaires, sommeil *m* paradoxal. (*Mil*) **~ fire** tir *m* rapide; (*fig*) **~ fire of questions** feu roulant de questions; (*US*) **~ transit** métro *m*. 2 **npl** (*in river*) **~s** rapides *mpl*.

rapidity [rəˈpɪdɪtɪ] **n** rapidité *f*.

rapidly [ˈræpɪdlɪ] **adv** rapidement.

rapier [ˈreɪpɪəʳ] 1 **n** rapière *f*. **~ thrust** (*lit*) coup *m* de pointe; (*fig*) remarque mordante. 2 **comp** (*fig*) *wit etc* mordant.

rapine [ˈræpaɪn] **n** rapine *f*.

rapist [ˈreɪpɪst] **n** (*Jur*) violeur *m*, auteur *m* d'un viol.

rapper [ˈræpəʳ] **n** (*Mus*) rappeur *m*, -euse *f*.

rapping [ˈræpɪŋ] **n** a (*noise*) coups secs et durs. b (*Mus*) rap *m*.

rapport [ræˈpɔːʳ] **n** rapport *m* (*with* avec, *between* entre). **in ~ with** en harmonie avec.

rapprochement [ræˈprɒʃmɑ̃ːŋ] **n** rapprochement *m* (*fig*).

rapscallion [ræpˈskælɪən] **n** vaurien *m*, mauvais garnement.

rapt [ræpt] **adj** *interest, attention* profond, intense; *look, smile* ravi, extasié; *welcome* enthousiaste, délirant. **~ in contemplation/in thought** plongé dans la contemplation/dans ses pensées; **~ with wonder** émerveillé.

rapture [ˈræptʃəʳ] **n** (*delight*) ravissement *m*, enchantement *m*; (*ecstasy*) extase *f*, transport *m*. **to be in ~s over** *or* **about** *object* être ravi *or* enchanté de; *person* être en extase devant; **to go into ~s over** *or* **about sth/sb** s'extasier sur qch/qn.

rapturous [ˈræptʃərəs] **adj** *exclamation* de ravissement, d'extase; *applause* frénétique, enthousiaste.

rapturously [ˈræptʃərəslɪ] **adv** *greet, listen* avec ravissement; *applaud* avec frénésie.

ra-ra [ˈrɑːrɑː] **adj: ~ skirt** jupe *f* à falbalas.

rare [rɛəʳ] **adj** *occurrence, plant* rare; *atmosphere* raréfié; (*: *excellent*) fameux*; (*underdone*) *meat* saignant. (*Chem*) **~ earth** terre *f* rare; **with very ~ exceptions** à de rares exceptions près; **it is ~ for her to come** il est rare qu'elle vienne; **to grow ~(r)** *[plants, atmosphere]* se raréfier; *[visits]* devenir plus rares *or* moins fréquents; **we had a ~ (old) time* on holiday** nous avons passé de fameuses* vacances; **a very ~ steak** un bifteck bleu; *see* **medium**.

rarebit [ˈrɛəbɪt] *see* **Welsh**.

rarefaction [ˌrɛərɪˈfækʃən] **n** raréfaction *f*.

rarefied [ˈrɛərɪfaɪd] **adj** *atmosphere* raréfié; (*fig*) trop raffiné. **to become ~** se raréfier.

rarefy [ˈrɛərɪfaɪ] 1 **vt** raréfier. 2 **vi** se raréfier.

rarely [ˈrɛəlɪ] **adv** rarement.

rareness [ˈrɛənɪs] **n** rareté *f* (*qualité*).

raring [ˈrɛərɪŋ] **adj: to be ~ to go*** être très impatient *or* mourir d'impatience de commencer, ne demander qu'à commencer; **to be ~ to do sth*** être très impatient *or* mourir d'impatience de faire qch.

rarity [ˈrɛərɪtɪ] **n** (*scarity*) rareté *f*; (*rare thing*) chose *f* rare. **rain is a ~ here** la pluie est rare ici; **to have ~ value** avoir de la valeur de par sa rareté.

rascal [ˈrɑːskəl] **n** (†: *scoundrel*) coquin *m*, vaurien *m*; (*scamp*) polisson(ne) *m(f)*, fripon(ne) *m(f)*.

rascality [rɑːsˈkælɪtɪ] **n** coquinerie *f*, friponnerie *f*.

rascally [ˈrɑːskəlɪ] **adj** *lawyer, merchant* retors; *trick* méchant, vilain, de coquin. **a ~ man** un vaurien, un coquin; **his ~ nephew** son coquin de neveu; **~ habits** habitudes *fpl* de vaurien *or* de coquin.

rash¹ [ræʃ] **n** a (*Med: gen sense*) rougeur *f*, éruption *f*; (*from food etc*) (plaques *fpl* d')urticaire *f*; (*in measles etc*) éruption, taches *fpl* rouges. **to come out** *or* **break out in a ~** avoir une éruption; *see* **heat, nettle.** b (*fig*) *[strikes, attacks etc]* éruption *f*.

rash² [ræʃ] **adj** *person* imprudent, impétueux, téméraire, qui manque de réflexion, qui agit à la légère; *promise, words, thoughts, judgment* irréfléchi, imprudent. **it was ~ of him to do that** il s'est montré très imprudent en faisant cela; **in a ~ moment** dans un moment d'impétuosité *or* d'enthousiasme.

rasher ['ræʃəʳ] **n** (*Brit*) (mince) tranche *f* (de bacon).

rashly ['ræʃlɪ] **adv** (*gen*) *behave etc* imprudemment, sans réfléchir; *offer, promise etc* dans un moment d'impétuosité *or* d'enthousiasme.

rashness ['ræʃnɪs] **n** (*see* **rash²**) imprudence *f*, impétuosité *f*, irréflexion *f*.

rasp [rɑːsp] 1 **n** (*tool*) râpe *f*; (*noise*) grincement *m*. 2 **vt** a (*Tech*) râper. b (*speak: also ~ out*) dire *or* crier d'une voix grinçante *or* âpre. 3 **vi** grincer, crisser.

raspberry ['rɑːzbərɪ] 1 **n** (*fruit*) framboise *f*. (*fig*) **to blow a ~*** faire pfft, faire un bruit de dérision; **to get a ~* from** se faire rabrouer *or* rembarrer* par. 2 **comp** *ice cream, tart* (à la) framboise *inv*; *jam* de framboise ► **raspberry bush, raspberry cane** framboisier *m*.

rasping ['rɑːspɪŋ] 1 **adj** *sound* grinçant, crissant; *voice* âpre, grinçant, rugueux. 2 **n** (*sound*) crissement *m*, grincement *m*.

Rasputin [ræ'spjuːtɪn] **n** Raspoutine *m*.

Rasta ['ræstə] **n, adj** (**abbr of Rastafarian**) rasta *(mf) inv*.

Rastafarian [ˌræstə'fɛərɪən] **n, adj** rastafari *(mf) inv*.

Rastafarianism [ˌræstə'fɛərɪənɪzəm] **n** rastafarianisme *m*.

rat [ræt] 1 **n** (*Zool*) rat *m*; (* *pej: person*) salaud‡ *m*, vache* *f*; (‡: *informer*) mouchard(e) *m(f)*; (‡: *blackleg*) jaune *m*; (*: *abandoning friends*) lâcheur* *m*, -euse* *f*. **he's a dirty ~*** c'est un salaud‡ *or* un sale individu*; **you ~!*** espèce de salaud! ‡; **~s!*** (*Brit: expressing disbelief*) mon œil!*; (*expressing irritation*) zut alors!*; *see* **smell.**

2 **comp** ► **rat-arsed*‡** bituré‡; **to get rat-arsed** se biturer‡ ► **ratbag‡** peau *f* de vache* ► **ratcatcher** chasseur *m* de rats ► **ratcatching** chasse *f* aux rats; (*extermination*) dératisation *f* ► **rat fink‡** (*US*) salaud‡ *m*, vache* *f* ► **ratline** (*Naut*) enfléchure *f* ► **rat poison** mort-aux-rats *f* ► **rat race** foire *f* d'empoigne ► **rats' tails***: (*pej*) **her hair was in rats' tails** ses cheveux étaient en queues de rat ► **rattrap** piège *m* à rats, ratière *f*.

3 **vi** a **to go ~ting** faire la chasse aux rats.

b (*) **to ~ on sb** (*desert*) lâcher qn*; (*inform on*) donner qn, moucharder qn*.

ratable ['reɪtəbl] = **rateable.**

rat-a-tat ['rætə'tæt], **rat-a-tat-tat** ['rætəˌtæt'tæt] **n** (*at door*) toc toc *m*; (*of gunfire*) ta ta ta ta *m*; (*on drum*) ran-tan-plan *m*.

ratchet ['rætʃɪt] **n** rochet *m*. **~ wheel** roue *f* à rochet.

rate¹ [reɪt] 1 **n** a (*ratio, proportion*) proportion *f*, taux *m*; (*speed*) vitesse *f*, train *m*, allure *f*. **birth/death ~** (taux *m* de) la natalité/la mortalité; **the failure/success ~ for this exam is high** il y a un pourcentage élevé d'échecs/de réussites à cet examen; **~ of consumption** taux de consommation; (*Elec, Water*) **~ of flow** débit *m* (moyen); **at the ~ of 100 litres an hour** à raison de 100 litres par heure; **at a ~ of** à une vitesse de; (*Aviat*) **~ of climb** vitesse ascensionnelle; (*Med*) **pulse ~** fréquence *f* des pulsations; **to pay sb at the ~ of £4 per hour** payer qn à raison de 4 livres de l'heure; **at a great ~, at a ~ of knots*** à toute allure, au trot*, à fond de train*; **to go at a terrific ~** aller à un train d'enfer; **if you continue at this ~** si vous continuez à ce train-là *or* de cette façon; **at his ~ of working, he'll never finish** au rythme auquel il travaille, il n'aura jamais terminé; (*fig*) **at the ~ you're going, you'll be dead before long** du train où vous allez, vous ne ferez pas de vieux os; (*fig*) **at any ~** en tout cas, de toute façon; **at that ~** à ce compte-là, dans ce cas; *see* **first-rate** *etc*.

b (*Comm, Fin*) taux *m*, cours *m*, tarif *m*. **~ of exchange** taux *or* cours du change; (*Econ*) **~ of growth, growth ~** taux *m* de croissance; **~ of interest/pay/taxation** taux d'intérêt/de rémunération/d'imposition; **postage/advertising ~s** tarifs postaux/de publicité; **insurance ~s** primes *fpl* d'assurance; **there is a reduced ~ for children** les enfants bénéficient d'un tarif réduit *or* d'une réduction; **basic salary ~** traitement *m* de base; *see* **basic.**

c (*Brit Fin: municipal tax*) **~s** impôts locaux; **~s and taxes** impôts et contributions; **a penny on/off the ~s** une augmentation/réduction d'un pour cent des impôts locaux; *see* **water.**

2 **comp** ► **rate-cap** (*Brit*) plafonner les impôts locaux de ► **rate-capping** (*Brit*) plafonnement *m* des impôts locaux ► **rate collector** receveur municipal ► **ratepayer** contribuable *mf* (*payant les impôts locaux*) ► **rate(s) office** recette municipale (*bureau*) ► **rate rebate** dégrèvement *m* (d'impôts locaux).

3 **vt** a (*estimate worth of, appraise*) évaluer (*at* à); (*fig: consider*) considérer (*as* comme). **to ~ sb/sth highly** faire grand cas de qn/qch; **how does he ~ that film?** que pense-t-il de ce film?; **I ~ him amongst my best pupils** je le considère comme un de mes meilleurs élèves, je le compte parmi mes meilleurs élèves.

b (*Local Govt*) fixer le loyer matriciel de. **house ~d at £800 per annum** ≃ maison *f* dont le loyer matriciel (*Admin*) *or* la valeur locative imposable est de 800 livres par an.

c (*deserve*) mériter. (*Scol*) **I think he ~s a pass (mark)** je crois qu'il mérite *or* vaut la moyenne.

4 **vi** (*be classed*) être classé, se classer (*as* comme).

rate² [reɪt] (*liter*) = **berate.**

rateable ['reɪtəbl] **adj** *property* imposable. **~ value** ≃ loyer matriciel (*Admin*), valeur locative imposable.

rather ['rɑːðəʳ] **adv** a (*for preference*) plutôt. **~ than wait, he went away** plutôt que d'attendre, il est parti; **I would ~ have the blue dress** je préférerais *or* j'aimerais mieux *or* je prendrais plutôt la robe bleue; **I would much ~ ...** je préférerais de beaucoup ...; **I would ~ be happy than rich** j'aimerais mieux être heureux que riche, je préfère le bonheur à la richesse; **I would ~ wait here than go** je préférerais attendre (plutôt) que de partir; **I would ~ you came yourself** je préférerais que vous veniez (*subj*) vous-même; **do you mind if I smoke? — I'd ~ you didn't** est-ce que je peux fumer? — j'aimerais autant que vous ne le fassiez pas; **I'd ~ not** je ne préfère pas*, j'aime mieux pas*; **I'd ~ not go** j'aimerais mieux ne pas y aller; **I'd ~ die!** plutôt mourir!; **~ you than me** je ne t'envie pas, je n'irai pas te disputer la place*.

b (*more accurately*) plus exactement, plutôt. **a car, or ~ an old banger** une voiture, ou plus exactement *or* ou plutôt une vieille guimbarde; **he isn't on holiday, but ~ out of work** il n'est pas en vacances, mais bien plutôt en chômage.

c (*to a considerable degree*) plutôt; (*to some extent*) un peu; (*somewhat*) quelque peu; (*fairly*) assez; (*slightly*) légèrement. **he's a ~ clever person, he's ~ a clever person** il est plutôt intelligent; **he felt ~ better** il se sentait un peu mieux; **he looked ~ silly** il a eu l'air plutôt stupide; **it's ~ more difficult than you think** c'est un peu plus difficile que vous ne croyez; **Latin is ~ too difficult for me** le latin est un peu trop difficile pour moi; **it's ~ a pity** c'est plutôt dommage; **his book is ~ good** son livre n'est pas mauvais du tout; **that costs ~ a lot** cela coûte assez cher; **I ~ think he's wrong** je crois bien *or* j'ai l'impression qu'il a tort; (*excl*) **~!*** et comment!*

ratification [ˌrætɪfɪ'keɪʃən] **n** ratification *f*.

ratify ['rætɪfaɪ] **vt** ratifier.

rating¹ ['reɪtɪŋ] **n** a (*assessment*) estimation *f*, évaluation *f*. b (*npl: TV*) **the (audience** *or* **TV) ~s** l'indice *m* d'écoute; **to have a high ~, to get good ~s** *[programme]* avoir un bon indice d'écoute, *[person]* avoir la faveur du public. c (*Brit Fin: tax on property*) montant *m* des impôts locaux. d (*placing*) classement *m*. e (*Brit Naut*) (*classification*) classe *f*; (*sailor*) marin *m*, matelot *m*. **the ~s** les matelots et gradés *mpl*.

rating² ['reɪtɪŋ] **n** réprimande *f*, semonce *f*, engueulade‡ *f*.

ratio ['reɪʃɪəʊ] **n** proportion *f*, raison *f*, rapport *m*. **in the ~ of 100 to 1** dans la proportion de 100 contre 1, dans le rapport de 100 contre *or* à 1; **inverse** *or* **indirect ~** raison inverse; **in direct ~ to** en raison directe de.

ratiocinate [rætɪ'ɒsɪneɪt] **vi** (*frm*) raisonner, ratiociner (*pej*).

ratiocination [ˌrætɪɒsɪ'neɪʃən] **n** (*frm*) raisonnement *m*, ratiocination *f* (*pej*).

ration ['ræʃən] 1 **n** (*allowance: of food, goods etc*) ration *f*. **it's off the ~*** ce n'est plus rationné; (*food*) **~s** vivres *mpl*; **to put sb on short ~s** réduire les rations de qn; *see* **iron.** 2 **comp** ► **ration book, ration card** carte *f* de rationnement. 3 **vt** *goods, food, people* rationner. **he was ~ed to 1 kg** sa ration était 1 kg.

► **ration out** **vt sep** *food etc* rationner.

rational ['ræʃənl] **adj** *creature, person* doué de raison, raisonnable; (*Med: lucid*) lucide; *faculty* rationnel; (*Math*) rationnel; *activity, thinking* rationnel, conforme à la raison; *action, argument, behaviour, person* raisonnable, sensé; *explanation* logique, raisonné; *solution* logique. **it was the only ~ thing to do** c'était la seule façon logique *or* rationnelle d'agir; **it wasn't very ~ of him to do that** il n'a pas agi de façon très logique *or* rationnelle.

rationale [ræʃə'nɑːl] **n** (*reasoning*) raisonnement *m*; (*statement*) exposé raisonné.

rationalism ['ræʃnəlɪzəm] **n** rationalisme *m*.

rationalist ['ræʃnəlɪst] **adj, n** rationaliste *(mf)*.

rationalistic [ˌræʃnə'lɪstɪk] **adj** rationaliste.

rationality [ˌræʃə'nælɪtɪ] **n** rationalité *f*.

rationalization [ˌræʃnəlaɪ'zeɪʃən] **n** rationalisation *f*.

rationalize ['ræʃnəlaɪz] 1 **vt** a *event, conduct etc* (tenter de) trouver une explication logique à; (*Psych*) justifier *or* motiver après coup. b (*organize efficiently*) *industry, production, problems* rationaliser. c (*Math*) rendre rationnel. 2 **vi** (*Psych*) chercher une justification après coup.

rationally ['ræʃnəlɪ] **adv** *behave, discuss, speak* rationnellement, raisonnablement. **~, it should be possible to do it** logiquement, il devrait être possible de le faire.

rationing ['ræʃnɪŋ] **n** rationnement *m*. **food ~** rationnement de l'alimentation.

rattan [ræ'tæn] 1 **n** rotin *m*. 2 **comp** de *or* en rotin.

rat-tat-tat ['rætə'tæt] **n** = **rat-a-tat.**

rattiness ['rætɪnɪs] **n** (*gen*) caractère grincheux. **I apologize for my ~**

yesterday je m'excuse d'avoir été grincheux hier.

rattle ['rætl] 1 n a (*sound*) [*vehicle*] bruit *m* (de ferraille), fracas *m*; [*chains, bottles, typewriter*] cliquetis *m*; [*door*] vibrations *fpl*; [*hailstones, machine gun*] crépitement *m*; [*rattlesnake*] sonnettes *fpl*; (*Med: also* **death** ~) râle *m*.

b (*baby's*) (*gen*) hochet *m*; (*strung on pram*) boulier *m* (de bébé); [*sports fan*] crécelle *f*.

2 comp ►**rattlebrained** écervelé, étourdi, sans cervelle ►**rattlesnake** serpent *m* à sonnettes, crotale *m* ►**rattletrap*** guimbarde *f*, tacot* *m*.

3 vi [*box, container, object*] faire du bruit; [*articles in box*] s'entrechoquer, bringuebaler, ballotter; [*vehicle*] faire un bruit de ferraille; [*bullets, hailstones*] crépiter; [*machinery*] cliqueter; [*window*] trembler. **to ~ at the door** cogner à la porte; **there is something rattling** il y a quelque chose qui cogne; [*vehicle*] **to ~ along/away** *etc* rouler/partir *etc* dans un bruit de ferraille.

4 vt a *box* agiter (avec bruit); *bottles, cans* faire s'entrechoquer; *dice* agiter, secouer; *keys* faire cliqueter.

b (*: *alarm*) *person* déconcerter, démonter, ébranler. **to get ~d** perdre son sang-froid, paniquer*; **don't get ~d!** pas de panique!*.

►**rattle away** vi = **rattle on**.

►**rattle down** vi [*falling stones etc*] dégringoler *or* tomber avec fracas.

►**rattle off** vt sep *poem, speech, apology* débiter à toute allure.

►**rattle on** vi parler sans arrêt (*about sth* de qch), jacasser.

►**rattle through** vt fus faire (*or* écrire *or* lire *etc*) à toute vitesse *or* au grand galop.

rattler* ['rætləʳ] n (*esp US: rattlesnake*) serpent *m* à sonnettes, crotale *m*.

rattling ['rætlıŋ] 1 n = **rattle 1a.** 2 adj bruyant. **I heard a ~ noise** j'ai entendu un cliquetis, j'ai entendu quelque chose qui cognait; **at a ~ pace** *or* **speed** à grande vitesse, à vive allure. 3 adv (*†) ~ **good** formidable*, épatant*.

ratty* ['rætı] adj (*Brit*) grincheux. **don't get ~ with me!** ne passe pas tes nerfs sur moi!*

raucous ['rɔːkəs] adj *voice* rauque; *person* braillard, tapageur; *evening* tapageur.

raucously ['rɔːkəslı] adv d'une voix rauque.

raucousness ['rɔːkəsnıs] n ton *m* rauque, raucité *f*.

raunch‡ [rɔːntʃ] n (*US*) [*story, film, song*] obscénité *f*, lubricité *f*.

raunchy‡ ['rɔːntʃı] adj (*US*) *person* libidineux, chaud lapin*; *story, film, song* obscène, cochon*, lubrique.

ravage ['rævıdʒ] 1 n [*war etc*] ravage *m*, dévastation *f*. **the ~s of time** les outrages *mpl* *or* les ravages du temps, l'injure *f* des ans. 2 vt (*ruin*) ravager, dévaster; (*plunder*) ravager, piller. **body ~d by disease** corps ravagé par la maladie.

rave [reıv] 1 vi (*be delirious*) délirer, divaguer; (*talk wildly*) divaguer, déraisonner; (*speak furiously*) s'emporter, tempêter (*at, against* contre); (*speak enthusiastically*) s'extasier (*about, over* sur), parler avec enthousiasme (*about, over* de); [*storm*] faire rage; [*wind*] être déchaîné; [*sea*] être démonté *or* en furie; *see* **rant.** 2 n (*Acid House party*) rave *f*. 3 comp ►**rave notice***, **rave review*** critique *f* dithyrambique ►**rave-up**‡: (*Brit: wild party*) **to have a rave-up** faire la foire* *or* la fête*.

ravel ['rævəl] 1 vt a (*entangle: lit, fig*) emmêler, embrouiller, enchevêtrer. b (*disentangle*) = **ravel out 2.** 2 vi (*become tangled*) s'embrouiller, s'enchevêtrer; (*fray*) s'effilocher.

►**ravel out** 1 vi s'effilocher. 2 vt sep *material* effilocher; *threads* démêler; *knitting* défaire; (*fig*) *difficulty* débrouiller; *plot* dénouer.

raven ['reıvn] 1 n corbeau *m*. 2 comp (*colour*) noir comme (du) jais *or* comme l'ébène ►**raven-haired** aux cheveux de jais.

ravening ['rævnıŋ] adj vorace, rapace.

Ravenna [rə'venə] n Ravenne.

ravenous ['rævənəs] adj *animal* vorace, rapace; *person* affamé; *appetite* vorace, féroce; *hunger* dévorant. **I'm ~*** j'ai une faim de loup, j'ai l'estomac dans les talons*.

ravenously ['rævənəslı] adv voracement. **to be ~ hungry** avoir une faim de loup, avoir l'estomac dans les talons*.

raver* ['reıvəʳ] n a (*gen, Brit*) noceur* *m* -euse *f*, fêtard(e)* *m(f)*. b (*person attending a rave*) raver* *m*.

ravine [rə'viːn] n ravin *m*.

raving ['reıvıŋ] 1 adj délirant. ~ **lunatic** fou furieux, folle furieuse; *see* **mad.** 2 n: **~(s)** délire *m*, divagations *fpl*.

ravioli [ˌrævı'əʊlı] n ravioli *mpl*.

ravish ['rævıʃ] vt a (*delight*) ravir, enchanter, transporter. b (†† *or liter*) (*rape*) violer; (*abduct*) ravir.

ravisher ['rævıʃəʳ] n ravisseur *m*.

ravishing ['rævıʃıŋ] adj *woman, sight* ravissant, enchanteur (*f* -teresse); *beauty* enchanteur.

ravishingly ['rævıʃıŋlı] adv de façon *or* de manière ravissante. **she is ~ beautiful** elle est belle à ravir, elle est d'une beauté éblouissante.

ravishment ['rævıʃmənt] n a (*delight*) enchantement *m*, ravissement *m*. b (†† *or liter*) (*rape*) viol *m*; (*abduction*) ravissement† *m*, rapt *m*.

raw [rɔː] 1 adj a (*uncooked*) *meat, food* cru; (*unprocessed*) *cloth* écru; *ore, sugar* brut; *silk* grège; *alcohol* pur; (*Comput*) *data etc* brut. ~ **colour** couleur crue; **he got** *or* **had a ~ deal*** on ne lui a vraiment pas fait de cadeaux*; **she got a ~ deal from life*** la vie ne lui a pas fait de cadeaux*; **the old get a ~ deal* nowadays** les vieux ne sont pas gâtés* de nos jours; [*cloth etc*] ~ **edge** bord coupé; ~ **material(s)** matières premières; (*US Scol etc*) ~ **score** première approximation *f* de note; ~ **spirits** alcool pur.

b (*inexperienced*) inexpérimenté, novice; *troops* non aguerri; (*uncouth*) mal dégrossi; (*coarse*) *humour, story* cru. ~ **recruit** bleu* *m*.

c (*sore*) sensible, irrité; *wound* à vif; *skin* écorché; *nerves* à fleur de peau, à vif. (*fig*) **to touch a ~ nerve** toucher un point sensible.

d *climate* froid et humide, âpre; *wind* âpre, aigre; *air* vif.

e (*frank*) *report, writing* crû, sans complaisance.

f (*pure*) (*gen*) brut; *ambition* pur.

2 n: **to get sb on the ~** toucher *or* piquer qn au vif; **life/nature in the ~** la vie/la nature telle qu'elle est; (*naked*) **in the ~*** nu, à poil*.

3 comp ►**rawboned** *person* maigre, décharné; *horse* efflanqué ►**rawhide** (*whip*) fouet *m* à lanières; (*material*) cuir brut *or* vert.

Rawlbolt ['rɔːlbəʊlt] n ® cheville *f* (pour murs *or* corps *or* matériaux creux).

Rawlplug ['rɔːlplʌg] n ® cheville *f* (*menuiserie*).

rawness ['rɔːnıs] n a **the ~ of this meat/colour** cette viande/couleur crue. b (*lack of experience*) inexpérience *f*. c (*on skin*) écorchure *f*. d [*climate*] froid *m* humide. **the ~ of the wind** l'âpreté *f* du vent, le vent aigre.

ray¹ [reı] n [*light, heat, sun etc*] rayon *m*; (*fig*) rayon, lueur *f*. ~ **of hope** lueur d'espoir; *see* **cathode, death, X-ray** *etc*.

ray² [reı] n (*fish*) raie *f*; *see* **sting.**

ray³ [reı] n (*Mus*) ré *m*.

rayon ['reıɒn] 1 n (*Tex*) rayonne *f*, soie artificielle. 2 adj en rayonne.

raze [reız] vt raser. **to ~ to the ground** *town* raser; *building* raser, abattre à ras de terre.

razor ['reızəʳ] 1 n rasoir *m*. **electric ~** rasoir électrique; (*fig*) **on** *or* **at the ~'s edge** sur la corde raide; *see* **safety** *etc*. 2 comp ►**razorbill** petit pingouin *m* ►**razor blade** lame *f* de rasoir ►**razor burn** feu *m* du rasoir ►**razor clam** (*US*) couteau *m* ►**razor cut** (*Hairdressing*) coupe *f* au rasoir ►**razor-edged** *knife etc* tranchant comme un rasoir; (*fig*) *wit* acéré ►**razor-sharp** *knife etc* tranchant comme un rasoir; (*fig*) *person, mind* délié, vif; *wit* acéré ►**razor-shell** (*Brit*) couteau *m* ►**razor-slashing** taillades *fpl* à coup de rasoir ►**razor wire** feuillard *m*.

razz‡ [ræz] vt mettre en boîte*.

razzle‡ ['ræzl] 1 n: **to go (out) on the ~** (sortir) faire la bringue‡ *or* la nouba‡. 2 comp ►**razzledazzle**‡ tape-à-l'œil* *m*.

razzmatazz* ['ræzmə'tæz] n a (*glitter*) tape-à-l'œil* *m*. b (*double talk*) propos *mpl* trompeurs.

R.C. [ɑː'siː] (*Rel*) (abbr of **Roman Catholic**) *see* **Roman.**

R.C.A.F. [ˌɑːsiːˌeı'ef] n abbr of **Royal Canadian Air Force.**

R.C.M.P. [ˌɑːsiːˌem'piː] n (abbr of **Royal Canadian Mounted Police**) *see* **royal.**

R.C.N. [ɑːˌsiː'en] n abbr of **Royal Canadian Navy.**

Rd. (*in addresses*) (abbr of **Road**) (*in town*) Rue; (*esp outside town*) Rte (de).

R.D.C. [ɑːˌdiː'siː] n (*Brit Local Govt*) (abbr of **Rural District Council**) *see* **rural.**

R.E. [ɑːr'iː] n a (*Scol*) (abbr of **religious education**) *see* **religious.** b (*Brit Mil*) (abbr of **Royal Engineers**) *génie militaire britannique*.

re¹ [reı] n (*Mus*) ré *m*.

re² [riː] prep (*Admin, Comm etc: referring to*) au sujet de, relativement à, concernant; (*Jur: also* **in ~**) en l'affaire de.

re... [riː] pref (*before consonant*) re..., ré...; (*before vowel*) r..., ré... . **to ~do** refaire; **to ~heat** réchauffer; **to ~open** rouvrir; **to ~-elect** réélire.

reach [riːtʃ] 1 n a (*accessibility*) portée *f*, atteinte *f*. **within ~** à portée; **out of ~** hors de portée *or* d'atteinte; **within sb's ~** à (la) portée de qn; **out of sb's ~** hors de (la) portée de qn; **within arm's ~** à portée de la main; **cars are within everyone's ~ nowadays** de nos jours les voitures sont à la portée de toutes les bourses *or* de tous; **out of the children's ~** hors de (la) portée des enfants; **I keep it within easy ~** *or* **within my ~** je le garde à portée de main *or* sous la main; **mountains not within easy ~** montagnes difficilement accessibles *or* d'accès difficile; **within easy ~ of the sea** à proximité de la mer, proche de la mer; **she was beyond (the) ~ of human help** elle était au-delà de tout secours humain; **beyond the ~ of the law** à l'abri de la justice; **this subject is beyond his ~** ce sujet le dépasse.

b (*length*) [*beach, river*] étendue *f*; [*canal*] bief *m*.

c (*esp Boxing*) allonge *f*. **he has a long ~** il a une bonne allonge.

2 comp ►**reach-me-down:** (*pej*) **it is a reach-me-down from my sister** c'est un vêtement qui me vient de ma sœur.

3 vt a (*get as far as*) *place* atteindre, gagner, arriver à; *age, goal, limit* atteindre; *agreement, understanding* aboutir à, arriver à; *conclusion* arriver à; *perfection* atteindre. **when we ~ed him he was dead** quand nous sommes arrivés auprès de lui, il était mort; **to ~ the terrace you have to cross the garden** pour accéder à la terrasse, il faut traverser le jardin; **I hope this letter ~es him** j'espère que cette lettre lui parviendra; **the news ~ed us too late** nous avons appris *or* reçu la

nouvelle trop tard; **to ~ page 50** arriver *or* en être à la page 50; **not a sound ~ed our ears** aucun bruit ne parvenait à nos oreilles; **you can ~ me at my hotel** vous pouvez me joindre à mon hôtel; **he is tall enough to ~ the top shelf** il est assez grand pour atteindre l'étagère d'en haut; **he ~es her shoulder** il lui arrive à l'épaule; **her dress ~es the floor** sa robe descend jusqu'à terre.

b (*get and give*) passer. **~ me (over) that book** passez-moi ce livre; **~ (over) the salt for Richard** passez le sel à Richard.

c (*US Jur: suborn*) *witness* corrompre, suborner.

4 **vi** a *[territory etc]* s'étendre; *[voice, sound]* porter (*to* jusqu'à); *see* **far.**

b (*stretch out hand: also* **~ across, ~ out, ~ over**) étendre le bras (*for sth* pour prendre qch, *to grasp etc* pour saisir *etc*). (*US*) **~ for the sky!‡** haut les mains!

►**reach back vi** (*fig*) remonter (*to* à). **to reach back to Victorian times** remonter à l'époque victorienne.

►**reach down** 1 **vi** *[clothes, curtains etc]* descendre (*to* jusqu'à). 2 **vt sep** (*from hook*) décrocher; (*from shelf*) descendre. **will you reach me down the book?** voulez-vous me descendre le livre?, voulez-vous me passer le livre qui est là-haut?

►**reach out vt sep** tendre. **he reached out his hand for the cup** il a étendu le bras pour prendre la tasse.

►**reach up vi** a lever le bras. **he reached up to get the book on the shelf** il a levé le bras pour atteindre le livre sur le rayon. b monter. **the flood water reached up to the windows** la crue (des eaux) est montée jusqu'aux fenêtres.

reachable ['ri:tʃəbl] **adj** *place* accessible; *object* accessible, à portée. **he is ~* at ...** on peut le joindre à ... .

react [ri:'ækt] **vi** a (*gen*) réagir (*against* contre, *on* sur, *to* à). b (*Phys, Chem*) réagir (*with* avec).

reaction [ri:'ækʃən] 1 **n** (*gen*) réaction *f*. **what was his ~ to your suggestion?** comment a-t-il réagi *or* quelle a été sa réaction à votre proposition?; **this decision was a ~ against violence** cette décision a été le contrecoup de la violence *or* a été la riposte à la violence *or* a été prise en réaction contre la violence; (*Pol*) **forces of ~** forces *fpl* de la réaction, forces réactionnaires; *see* **chain.** 2 **comp** ►**reaction engine** moteur *m* à réaction.

reactionary [ri:'ækʃənrɪ] **adj, n** réactionnaire (*mf*).

reactivate [ri:'æktɪveɪt] **vt** réactiver.

reactivation [ri:ˌæktɪ'veɪʃən] **n** réactivation *f*.

reactive [ri:'æktɪv] **adj** (*gen, Chem, Phys, Psych*) réactif.

reactor [ri:'æktəʳ] **n** (*Chem, Elec, Phys*) réacteur *m*; *see* **nuclear.**

read [ri:d] **pret, ptp read** [red] 1 **vt** a *book, letter etc* lire; *music, bad handwriting* déchiffrer, lire; *hieroglyphs* déchiffrer; *proofs* corriger. **to ~ sb sth, ~ sth to sb** lire qch à qn; **I read him to sleep** je lui ai fait la lecture jusqu'à ce qu'il s'endorme; **I brought you something to ~** je vous ai apporté de la lecture; **to ~ sb's lips** lire sur les lèvres de qn; (*Jur*) **to ~ the Riot Act** ≃ faire les trois sommations; (*fig*) **he read them the riot act*** ils les a tancés vertement; (*fig*) **to ~ sb a lesson*** faire la leçon à qn, sermonner qn; (*fig*) **to take sth as read** (*as self-evident*) considérer qch comme allant de soi; (*as agreed*) considérer qch comme convenu; (*Admin*) **they took the minutes as read** ils sont passés à l'ordre du jour (sans revenir sur le procès-verbal de la dernière séance); (*in errata*) **for "meet" ~ "met"** au lieu de "meet" prière de lire "met"; (*Jur: on document*) **read and approved** lu et approuvé; *see* **well.**

b (*interpret*) *dream* interpréter, expliquer; (*understand*) comprendre. **to ~ sb's hand** lire les lignes de la main de *or* à qn; **to ~ the tea leaves** *or* **the teacups** ≃ lire dans le marc de café; (*US fig*) **to ~ the wind** flairer le vent; **these words can be read in several ways** ces mots peuvent s'interpréter de plusieurs façons; (*fig*) **to ~ between the lines** lire entre les lignes; **to ~ something into a text** faire dire à un texte quelque chose qu'il ne dit pas, solliciter un texte; (*fig*) **we mustn't ~ too much into this** nous ne devons pas y attacher trop d'importance; **to ~ sb's thoughts** lire (dans) la pensée de qn; **I can ~ him like a book** je sais *or* devine toujours ce qu'il pense; **I read disappointment in his eyes** j'ai lu la déception dans ses yeux.

c (*esp Univ: study*) étudier, faire. **to ~ medicine/law** faire (des études de) médecine/droit, faire sa médecine/son droit; **he is ~ing English/geography** *etc* il fait de l'anglais/de la géographie *etc.*

d *thermometer, barometer etc* lire. **to ~ a meter** relever un compteur.

e *[instruments]* marquer, indiquer. **the thermometer ~s 37°** le thermomètre indique (une température de) 37° *or* marque 37°.

f (*Telec*) recevoir. **do you ~ me?** est-ce que vous me recevez?; (*fig*) vous me comprenez?; *see* **loud.**

g (*Comput*) lire.

2 **vi** a lire. **he can ~ and write** il sait lire et écrire; **she ~s well** elle lit bien, elle fait bien la lecture; *[learner, beginner]* elle sait bien lire; **he likes ~ing** il aime lire *or* bouquiner*, il aime la lecture; **to ~ aloud** lire à haute voix; **to ~ to oneself** lire; **do you like being read to?** aimez-vous qu'on vous fasse la lecture?; **I read about it in the paper** je l'ai lu *or* je l'ai vu dans le journal; **I've read about him** j'ai lu quelque chose à son sujet.

b **the letter ~s thus** voici ce que dit la lettre, voici comment la lettre est rédigée; **the quotation ~s as follows** voici les termes exacts de la citation; **this book ~s well/badly** ce livre se lit bien/mal; **his article ~s like an official report** le style de son article fait penser à celui d'un rapport officiel, son article a l'allure d'un rapport officiel.

c (*esp Univ: study*) étudier, faire des études. **to ~ for an examination** préparer un examen; *see* **bar¹.**

3 **n** (*) lecture *f*. **she enjoys a good ~** elle aime bien la lecture, elle aime bouquiner*; **it's a good ~** ça se lit facilement, ça se laisse bien lire; **to have a quiet/a little ~** lire *or* bouquiner* tranquillement/un peu.

4 **comp** ►**read head** (*Comput*) tête *f* de lecture ►**read-only memory** (*Comput*) mémoire *f* morte ►**read-out** (*Comput*) **n** affichage *m*, sortie *f* ►**read-write head** (*Comput*) tête *f* de lecture-écriture ►**read-write memory** (*Comput*) mémoire *f* lecture-écriture ►**read-write window** (*Comput*) fenêtre *f* d'inscription-lecture.

►**read back vt sep** *one's notes etc* relire.

►**read off vt sep** a *text* (*without pause*) lire d'un trait; (*at sight*) lire à livre ouvert. b *instrument readings* relever.

►**read on vi** continuer à lire, poursuivre sa lecture. **"now read on"** "suite du feuilleton".

►**read out** 1 **vt sep** a *text* lire à haute voix; *instrument readings* relever à haute voix. b (*Comput*) afficher, extraire, sortir. 2 **read-out n** *see* **read 4.**

►**read over vt sep** relire.

►**read through vt sep** (*rapidly*) parcourir; (*thoroughly*) lire en entier *or* d'un bout à l'autre.

►**read up vt sep** étudier, bûcher*, potasser*. **I must read up the Revolution** il faut que j'étudie (*subj*) *or* que je potasse* (*subj*) la Révolution.

►**read up on vt fus** = **read up.**

readability [ˌri:də'bɪlɪtɪ] **n** lisibilité *f*.

readable ['ri:dəbl] **adj** *handwriting etc* lisible; *book* agréable *or* facile à lire. **not very ~** difficile à lire; **it's very ~** ça se lit facilement.

readdress [ˌri:ə'dres] **vt** *letter, parcel* réadresser; (*forward*) faire suivre.

reader ['ri:dəʳ] **n** a lecteur *m*, -trice *f*. **publisher's ~** lecteur, -trice dans une maison d'édition; **he's a great ~** il aime beaucoup lire, c'est un grand liseur; *see* **lay⁴, proof** *etc.* b (*Brit Univ*) ≃ chargé(e) *m(f)* d'enseignement; (*US Univ*) directeur *m*, -trice *f* de thèse *or* d'études. c (*schoolbook*) (*to teach reading*) livre *m* de lecture; (*anthology*) recueil *m* de textes. **first French ~** recueil de textes français pour première année. d (**microfiche**) **~** lecteur *m* (de microfiche).

readership ['ri:dəʃɪp] **n** a *[newspaper, magazine]* nombre *m* de lecteurs. **this paper has a big ~/a ~ of millions** ce journal a beaucoup de lecteurs/des millions de lecteurs. b (*Brit Univ*) ≃ poste *m* (*or* fonctions *fpl*) de chargé(e) d'enseignement; (*US Univ*) fonctions (*or* responsabilités) de directeur(-trice) de thèse *or* d'études.

readily ['redɪlɪ] **adv** (*willingly*) volontiers, de bon cœur; (*easily*) facilement, aisément.

readiness ['redɪnɪs] **n** a (*preparedness*) **to be (kept) in ~** être (tenu) prêt (*for* à, pour). b (*willingness*) empressement *m*, bonne volonté *f*. **his ~ to help us** son empressement à nous aider, l'empressement qu'il a montré à nous aider.

reading ['ri:dɪŋ] 1 **n** a (*NonC*) lecture *f*; *[proofs]* correction *f*. **she likes ~** elle aime bien lire *or* la lecture; **this book is** *or* **makes very interesting ~** ce livre est très intéressant (à lire); **I'd prefer some light ~** je préférerais qch de distrayant *or* de facile à lire.

b (*recital*) (séance *f* de) lecture *f*; *see* **play, poetry.**

c (*interpretation*) interprétation *f*, explication *f*. **my ~ of the sentence** mon explication *or* interprétation de la phrase; (*Cine, Theat*) **his ~ of the part** son interprétation du rôle.

d (*variant*) variante *f*, leçon *f*.

e (*Elec, Med, Phys etc: from instrument*) **to take a ~** lire un instrument, relever les indications d'un instrument; **the ~ is ...** l'instrument indique ... .

f (*Parl*) *[bill]* discussion *f*, lecture *f*. **the House gave the bill its first ~** la Chambre a examiné le projet de loi en première lecture; **the third ~ of the bill was debated** le projet de loi a été discuté en troisième lecture.

g (*NonC: knowledge*) culture *f*, connaissances *fpl*. **of wide ~** instruit, cultivé.

2 **comp** ►**reading age:** (*Scol*) **he has a reading age of eight** il a le niveau de lecture d'un enfant de huit ans; **she has a low/advanced reading age** son niveau de lecture est bas/élevé pour son âge; **child of reading age** enfant *m* en âge de lire ►**reading book** livre *m* de lecture ►**reading desk** pupitre *m*; (*Rel*) lutrin *m* ►**reading glass** loupe *f* ►**reading glasses** lunettes *fpl* pour lire ►**reading knowledge: to have a reading knowledge of Spanish** savoir lire l'espagnol ►**reading lamp** *or* **light** (*gen*) lampe *f* de travail, lampe de bureau; (*in train, plane etc*) liseuse *f* ►**reading list** bibliographie *f*, (liste *f* d')ouvrages *mpl* recommandés ►**reading matter** choses *fpl* à lire, de quoi lire ►**reading room** salle *f* de lecture *or* de travail ►**reading speed** vitesse *f* de lecture.

readjust [ˌri:ə'dʒʌst] 1 **vt** rajuster, réarranger, réadapter; (*correct*) rectifier; *salary* rajuster; *instrument* régler (de nouveau). 2 **vi** se réadapter (*to* à).

readjustment [ˌriːəˈdʒʌstmənt] **n** réadaptation *f*; *[salary]* rajustement *m or* réajustement *m*.

ready [ˈredɪ] 1 **adj** a (*prepared*) *person, thing* prêt. **dinner is ~** le dîner est prêt; **"dinner's ~!"** "à table!"; **everything is ~ for his visit** tout est prêt pour sa visite; **~ for anything** prêt à toute éventualité; **~ to use** *or* **for use** prêt à l'usage; **to be ~ to do** être prêt à faire; **to get ~ to do** se préparer *or* s'apprêter à faire; **to get (o.s.) ~** se préparer, s'apprêter; **to be ~ with an excuse** avoir une excuse toute prête *or* en réserve; **to make** *or* **get sth ~** préparer *or* apprêter qch; (*loc*) **~ when you are*** quand vous voulez, quand tu veux*; **to be ~ and waiting** être (fin) prêt; (*Sport*) **~, steady, go!** prêts? 1-2-3 partez!; (*Naut*) **~ about!** pare à virer!; **I'm ~ for him!** je l'attends de pied ferme!; **get ~ for it!** tenez-vous prêt!; (*before momentous news etc*) tenez-vous bien!; (*Publishing*) **"now ~"** "vient de paraître"; (*Comm*) **we have the goods you ordered ~ to hand** nous tenons à votre disposition les marchandises que vous avez commandées; **~ money, ~ cash** (argent *m*) liquide *m*; **to pay in ~ cash** payer en espèces; **how much have you got in ~ money** *or* **~ cash?** combien avez-vous en liquide?

b (*willing*) prêt, disposé (*to* à); (*inclined*) enclin, porté (*to* à); (*quick*) prompt (*to do* à faire); (*about to*) sur le point, près (*to do* de faire). **he is always ~ to help** il est toujours prêt à rendre service; **I am quite ~ to see him** je suis tout à fait disposé à le voir; **don't be so ~ to criticize** ne soyez pas si prompt à critiquer; **I'm ~ to believe it** je veux bien le croire, je suis prêt à le croire; **he was ~ to cry** il était sur le point de *or* près de pleurer.

c (*wanting, needing*) **I'm ~ for bed/a break/a drink** j'irais bien me coucher/je ferais bien une pause/je prendrais bien à boire.

d (*prompt*) *reply, wit* prompt. **to have a ~ tongue** avoir la langue déliée, avoir la parole facile; *[goods]* **to have a ~ sale** se vendre facilement, être de vente courante; **~ solution** solution tout indiquée.

2 **n** a (*Mil*) **to come to the ~** apprêter l'arme; **at the ~** (*Mil*) prêt à faire feu; (*Naut*) paré à faire feu; (*fig*) tout prêt.

b (*money*) **the ~**‡ *or* **readies**‡ le fric‡.

3 **adv** (*in comps*) **ready-cooked/-furnished** *etc* tout cuit/tout meublé *etc* (d'avance).

4 **comp** ▸**ready-made** *curtains* tout fait; *clothes* de confection, prêt à porter; *solution, answer* tout prêt; **ready-made ideas** des idées banales *or* toutes faites ▸**ready-mix:** (*Culin*) **ready-mix for cakes/pancakes** *etc* préparation *f* pour gâteaux/crêpes *etc;* **she made a ready-mix cake** elle a fait un gâteau à partir d'une préparation *or* d'un sachet ▸**ready reckoner** barème *m* ▸**ready-to-serve** prêt à servir ▸**ready-to-wear** prêt à porter.

reafforestation [ˈriːəˌfɒrɪsˈteɪʃən] **n,** (*US*) **reforestation** [ˌriːfɒrɪsˈteɪʃən] **n** reboisement *m*.

reagent [riːˈeɪdʒənt] **n** (*Chem*) réactif *m*.

real [rɪəl] 1 **adj** a (*gen*) vrai (*before noun*); (*as opposed to apparent*) véritable, vrai (*before noun*), réel; *gold, jewels* vrai, véritable; *flowers, silk* naturel; (*Philos, Math*) réel. **in ~ life** dans la réalité, dans la vie réelle; **he is the ~ boss** c'est lui le véritable patron *or* le patron réel; **this is the ~ thing** ça c'est pour de vrai *or* de bon; **he has no ~ power** il n'a pas de pouvoir effectif; **what is the ~ reason?** quelle est la vraie *or* véritable raison?; **when you've tasted the ~ thing, this whisky ...** quand tu as (*or* auras) goûté du vrai whisky, celui-ci ...; **climbing this hill isn't much when you've done the ~ thing** si tu as vraiment fait de l'alpinisme, cette petite colline n'est rien du tout; **it's the ~ thing*** *or* **the ~ McCoy*** c'est de l'authentique, c'est du vrai de vrai*; **~ tennis** jeu *m* de paume; (*Brit*) **~ ale** bière *f* traditionnelle; (*Rel*) **R~ Presence** présence réelle.

b (*Jur*) **~ estate** biens fonciers *or* immeubles *or* immobiliers; (*US*) **to work in ~ estate** *or* **the ~ estate business** travailler dans l'immobilier; (*US*) **~-estate agent** agent *m* immobilier; (*US*) **~-estate developer** promoteur *m* (de construction); **~-estate office** agence immobilière; (*US*) **~-estate register** cadastre *m*; **~ property** biens *mpl* immobiliers *or* immeubles.

c (*Comput*) **~ time** temps *m* réel; **~-time computer** ordinateur *m* exploité en temps réel; **~-time processing** traitement *m* immédiat; **~-time system** système *m* temps-réel.

d (*Fin, Econ*) *value* effectif, réel. **~ cost** coût réel; **here in ~ terms is how inflation affects us** voici comment l'inflation nous touche dans la réalité *or* dans la pratique.

2 **adv** (‡) rudement*, vachement*. **we had a ~ good laugh** on a rudement bien ri*, on a vachement rigolé*, on s'est drôlement marré*.

3 **n** a **for ~*** pour de vrai*.

b (*Philos*) **the ~** le réel.

realism [ˈrɪəlɪzəm] **n** réalisme *m*.

realist [ˈrɪəlɪst] **adj, n** réaliste (*mf*).

realistic [rɪəˈlɪstɪk] **adj** réaliste.

realistically [rɪəˈlɪstɪkəlɪ] **adv** avec réalisme, d'une façon réaliste.

reality [rɪˈælɪtɪ] **n** a réalité *f*. **to bring sb back to ~** ramener qn à la réalité; **in ~** en réalité, en fait. b (*trueness to life*) réalisme *m*.

realizable [ˈrɪəlaɪzəbl] **adj** *assets, hope, plan* réalisable.

realization [ˌrɪəlaɪˈzeɪʃən] **n** a *[assets, hope, plan]* réalisation *f*. b (*awareness*) prise *f* de conscience. **the sudden ~ that ...** la découverte soudaine que ... .

realize [ˈrɪəlaɪz] **vt** a (*become aware of*) se rendre compte de, prendre conscience de; (*understand*) comprendre. **does he ~ the problems?** se rend-il compte des problèmes?; **the committee ~s the gravity of the situation** le comité a pris conscience de la gravité de la situation; **he had not fully ~d that she was dead** il n'avait pas (vraiment) réalisé qu'elle était morte; **I ~d it was raining** je me suis rendu compte qu'il pleuvait, j'ai réalisé* qu'il pleuvait; **I made her ~ that I was right** je lui ai bien fait comprendre que j'avais raison; **I ~ that ...** je me rends compte du fait que ...; **yes, I ~ that!** oui, je sais bien!, oui, je m'en rends bien compte!; **I ~d how he had done it** j'ai compris comment *or* je me suis rendu compte de la façon dont il l'avait fait; **I ~d why ...** j'ai compris pourquoi ...; **I ~ it's too late, but ...** je sais bien qu'il est trop tard, mais ... .

b *ambition, hope, plan* réaliser. **to ~ one's (full) potential** réaliser son plein potentiel; **my worst fears were ~d** mes pires craintes se sont réalisées.

c (*Fin*) *assets* réaliser; *price* atteindre; *interest* rapporter. **how much did your Rembrandt ~?, how much did you ~ on your Rembrandt?** combien votre Rembrandt vous a-t-il rapporté?

reallocate [rɪˈæləʊkeɪt] **vt** *money, tasks* réallouer, réattribuer; *time* réallouer.

reallocation [ˌriːæləˈkeɪʃən] **n** (*see* **reallocate**) réallocation *f*, réattribution *f*.

really [ˈrɪəlɪ] 1 **adv** vraiment, réellement, véritablement. **I ~ don't know what to think** je ne sais vraiment pas quoi penser; **he ~ is an idiot** c'est un véritable imbécile, il est vraiment idiot; **it won't ~ last** ça ne durera guère; **I don't REALLY like ...** je ne peux vraiment pas dire que j'aime ..., je n'aime guère ...; **you ~ MUST visit Paris** il faut absolument que vous visitiez (*subj*) Paris. 2 **excl** (*in doubt*) vraiment?, sans blague!*; (*in surprise*) c'est vrai?; (*in protest: also* **well ~!**) vraiment!, ça alors!; **not ~!** pas vraiment!; (*in disbelief*) pas possible!

realm [relm] **n** (*liter: kingdom*) royaume *m*; (*fig*) domaine *m*; *see* **coin**.

realtor [ˈrɪəltɔːʳ] **n** (*US*) agent *m* immobilier.

realty [ˈrɪəltɪ] **n** (*Jur*) biens immobiliers *or* immeubles.

ream¹ [riːm] **n** *[paper]* ≈ rame *f* (de papier). (*fig*) **he always writes ~s*** il écrit toujours des volumes *or* toute une tartine*.

ream² [riːm] **vt** (*Tech*) fraiser.

reamer [ˈriːməʳ] **n** (*Tech*) fraise *f*.

reanimate [ˌriːˈænɪmeɪt] **vt** ranimer, raviver.

reanimation [ˈriːˌænɪˈmeɪʃən] **n** (*Med*) réanimation *f*.

reap [riːp] 1 **vt** (*Agr*) moissonner, faucher; (*fig*) *profit* récolter, tirer. **to ~ the fruit of one's labours** recueillir le fruit de son labeur; (*fig*) **to ~ what one has sown** récolter ce qu'on a semé; (*fig, liter*) **they left him to ~ the bitter harvest of his corruption** ils l'ont laissé payer le prix de sa corruption; *see* **sow²**. 2 **vi** moissonner, faire la moisson.

reaper [ˈriːpəʳ] **n** (*person*) moissonneur *m*, -euse *f*; (*machine*) moissonneuse *f*. **~ and binder** moissonneuse-lieuse *f*; (*fig, liter: death*) **the (Grim) R~** la Faucheuse.

reaping [ˈriːpɪŋ] 1 **n** moisson *f*. 2 **comp** ▸**reaping hook** faucille *f* ▸**reaping machine** moissonneuse *f*.

reappear [ˌriːəˈpɪəʳ] **vi** réapparaître, reparaître.

reappearance [ˌriːəˈpɪərəns] **n** réapparition *f*.

reappoint [ˌriːəˈpɔɪnt] **vt** renommer (*to* à).

reappointment [ˌriːəˈpɔɪntmənt] **n** renouvellement *m* de nomination (*to* à).

reapportion [ˌriːəˈpɔːʃən] 1 **vt** réassigner, répartir à nouveau; (*US Pol*) redécouper, procéder à une révision du découpage électoral de. 2 **vi** (*US Pol*) subir un redécoupage électoral.

reapportionment [ˌriːəˈpɔːʃənmənt] **n** (*US Pol*) redécoupage *m* électoral.

reappraisal [ˌriːəˈpreɪzəl] **n** *[situation, problem]* réévaluation *f*, réexamen *m*; *[author, film etc]* réévaluation.

reappraise [ˌriːəˈpreɪz] **vt** réévaluer.

rear¹ [rɪəʳ] 1 **n** a (*back part*) arrière *m*, derrière *m*; (**: buttocks*) derrière*. **in** *or* **at the ~** à l'arrière; **at the ~ of** derrière, à l'arrière de; **from the ~, he looks like Chaplin** (vu) de dos, il ressemble à Charlot; **from the ~ the car looks like ...** par l'arrière *or* vue de derrière la voiture ressemble à ... .

b (*Mil*) arrière-garde *f*, arrières *mpl*; *[squad]* dernier rang; *[column]* queue *f*. **to attack an army in the ~** attaquer une armée à revers; (*also gen*) **to bring up the ~** fermer la marche.

2 **adj** de derrière, arrière *inv*. **~ bumper** pare-chocs *m* arrière; **~ door** *[house]* porte *f* de derrière; (*Aut*) portière *f* arrière; (*Aut*) **~ wheel** roue *f* arrière *or* de derrière (*see also* **3**); (*Aut*) **~ window** glace *f* arrière.

3 **comp** ▸**rear admiral** vice-amiral *m* ▸**rear-engined** (*Aut*) avec moteur *m* à l'arrière ▸**rear gunner** mitrailleur *m* arrière *inv* ▸**rear-mounted** installé à l'arrière ▸**rear projection** (*Cine*) projection *f* par transparence ▸**rear-view mirror** (*Aut*) rétroviseur *m* ▸**rear-wheel drive** (*Aut*) roues *fpl* arrière motrices.

rear² [rɪəʳ] 1 **vt** a *animals, family* élever; *plants* faire pousser, cultiver. b **to ~ one's head** relever *or* dresser la tête; **the snake ~ed**

its head le serpent s'est dressé; **violence ~s its ugly head again** la violence fait sa réapparition (dans toute son horreur), on voit poindre à nouveau l'horrible violence. c (*set up*) *monument* dresser, ériger. 2 **vi** (*also* ~ **up**) *[animal]* se cabrer; *[snake]* se dresser.

rearguard ['rɪəgɑːd] **n** (*Mil*) arrière-garde *f*. (*lit, fig*) ~ **action** combat *m* d'arrière-garde; (*fig*) **to fight a ~ action** mener un combat d'arrière-garde.

rearm [,riː'ɑːm] **vti** réarmer.

rearmament [,riː'ɑːməmənt] **n** réarmement *m*.

rearmost ['rɪəməʊst] **adj** dernier, de queue.

rearrange [,riːə'reɪndʒ] **vt** réarranger.

rearrangement [,riːə'reɪndʒmənt] **n** réarrangement *m*, nouvel arrangement.

rearward ['rɪəwəd] 1 **n** arrière *m*. 2 **adj** *part* arrière *inv*; *position* (situé) à l'arrière, de l'arrière; *movement* en arrière. 3 **adv** (*also* ~**s**) vers l'arrière, par derrière.

reason ['riːzn] 1 **n** a (*cause, justification*) *[behaviour]* raison *f*, motif *m*; *[event]* raison, cause *f*. **the ~s are ...** les raisons en sont ...; **the ~ for my lateness/why I am late is that ...** la raison de mon retard/pour laquelle je suis en retard, c'est que ...; **my ~ for going, the ~ for my going** la raison de mon départ *or* pour laquelle je pars (*or* suis parti *etc*); **I want to know the ~ why** je veux savoir (le) pourquoi; **and that's the ~ why** et voilà pourquoi, et voilà la raison; **I have (good** *or* **every) ~ to believe that ...** j'ai (tout) lieu *or* j'ai de bonnes raisons de croire que ...; **there is ~ to believe that he is dead** il y a lieu de croire qu'il est mort; **for the simple ~ that ...** pour la simple *or* bonne raison que ...; **for the very ~ that ...** précisément parce que ...; **for that very ~** pour cette raison, pour cela même; **for no ~** sans raison, sans motif; **for some ~ (or another)** pour une raison ou pour une autre; **for ~s best known to himself** pour des raisons qu'il est seul à connaître, pour des raisons connues de lui seul; **all the more ~ for doing** *or* **to do** raison de plus pour faire; **with ~** avec (juste) raison, à juste titre; **by ~ of** en raison de, à cause de; **for personal/health** *etc* **~s** pour des raisons personnelles/de santé *etc*.
b (*NonC: mental faculty*) raison *f*. **to lose one's ~** perdre la raison.
c (*NonC: common sense*) raison *f*, bon sens. **to see ~** entendre raison; **to make sb see ~** raisonner qn, faire entendre raison à qn; **he listened to ~** il s'est rendu à la raison; **he won't listen to ~** on ne peut pas lui faire entendre raison; **that stands to ~** cela va sans dire, cela va de soi; **it stands to ~ that** il va sans dire que; **I will do anything in** *or* **within ~** je ferai tout ce qu'il est raisonnablement possible de faire; *see* **rhyme**.
2 **vi** a (*think logically*) raisonner.
b (*argue*) **to ~ with sb** raisonner avec qn; **one can't ~ with her** il n'y a pas moyen de lui faire entendre raison.
3 **vt** a (*work out*) calculer (*that* que); (*argue*) soutenir (*that* que); *see also* **reasoned**.
b **to ~ sb out of his folly** ramener qn à la raison, faire renoncer qn à sa folie en le raisonnant; **to ~ sb into a sensible decision** amener qn à prendre une décision intelligente en le raisonnant.

reasonable ['riːznəbl] **adj** *person, attitude* raisonnable; *price, offer* raisonnable, honnête, correct; *essay, results* honnête, correct. (*Jur*) **~ doubt** doute bien fondé; (*Jur*) **to prove guilt beyond (a) ~ doubt** prouver la culpabilité de l'accusé avec quasi-certitude; **there is a ~ chance that ...** il y a des chances (pour) que ... + *subj*; **a ~ amount of** une certaine quantité de.

reasonableness ['riːznəblnɪs] **n** caractère *m or* nature *f* raisonnable.

reasonably ['riːznəblɪ] **adv** a (*gen*) raisonnablement. **one can ~ think that ...** il est raisonnable de penser que ...; **~ priced** à *or* d'un prix raisonnable. b (*fairly, quite*) assez, relativement.

reasoned ['riːznd] **adj** raisonné.

reasoning ['riːznɪŋ] 1 **n** raisonnement *m*, dialectique *f*. 2 **adj** *mind* doué de raison.

reassemble [,riːə'sembl] 1 **vt** *people, troops* rassembler; *tool, machine* remonter. 2 **vi** se rassembler. **school ~s on 5th September** la rentrée des classes aura lieu le 5 septembre.

reassembly [,riːə'semblɪ] **n** *[machine]* remontage *m*.

reassert [,riːə'sɜːt] **vt** réaffirmer. **to ~ o.s.** s'imposer à nouveau.

reassess [,riːə'ses] **vt** *situation* réexaminer; (*for taxation*) *person* réviser la cote de; (*Jur*) *damages* réévaluer.

reassessment [,riːə'sesmənt] **n** *[situation]* réexamen *m*; (*for taxation*) *[person]* réévaluation *f* (fiscale); (*Jur*) *[damages]* réévaluation *f*.

reassurance [,riːə'ʃʊərəns] **n** a (*emotional*) réconfort *m*. b (*factual*) assurance *f*, garantie *f*. **to seek ~ that** chercher à obtenir l'assurance *or* une garantie que.

reassure [,riːə'ʃʊəʳ] **vt** rassurer.

reassuring [,riːə'ʃʊərɪŋ] **adj** rassurant.

reassuringly [,riːə'ʃʊərɪŋlɪ] **adv** d'une manière rassurante.

reawaken [,riːə'weɪkən] 1 **vt** *person* réveiller de nouveau; *interest* réveiller de nouveau, faire renaître. 2 **vi** se réveiller de nouveau.

reawakening [,riːə'weɪknɪŋ] **n** réveil *m*; *[ideas, interest]* renaissance *f*, réveil.

Reb* [reb] **n** (*US: also* **reb***) soldat *m* confédéré.

rebarbative [rɪ'bɑːbətɪv] **adj** rébarbatif, rebutant.

rebate ['riːbeɪt] **n** (*discount*) rabais *m*, remise *f*; (*money back*) remboursement *m*; (*on tax, rates*) dégrèvement *m*; (*on rent*) réduction *f*; *see* **rate, rent, tax**.

Rebecca [rɪ'bekə] **n** Rébecca *f*.

rebel ['rebl] 1 **n** rebelle *mf*, insurgé(e) *m(f)*, révolté(e) *m(f)*; (*fig*) rebelle. 2 **adj** rebelle. 3 [rɪ'bel] **vi** a (*gen*) (*lit, fig*) se rebeller, se révolter, s'insurger (*against* contre). b (*fig*) **my stomach/feet/skin ~(s)** mon foie n'en pouvait plus/mes pieds n'en pouvaient plus/ma peau a commencé à faire une réaction.

rebellion [rɪ'beljən] **n** rébellion *f*, révolte *f*. **to rise in ~** se rebeller, se révolter.

rebellious [rɪ'beljəs] **adj** rebelle; (*fig*) *child* indocile, rebelle.

rebelliousness [rɪ'beljəsnɪs] **n** esprit *m* de rébellion, disposition *f* à la rébellion.

rebirth [,riː'bɜːθ] **n** renaissance *f*.

reboot [,riː'buːt] **vt** (*Comput*) réinitialiser, réamorcer.

rebore [,riː'bɔːʳ] (*Tech*) 1 **vt** réaléser. 2 ['riː,bɔːʳ] **n** réalésage *m*. **this engine needs a ~** ce moteur a besoin d'être réalésé.

reborn [,riː'bɔːn] **adj** réincarné. (*fig*) **to be ~ in** se réincarner dans.

rebound [rɪ'baʊnd] 1 **vi** a *[ball]* rebondir (*against* sur). (*fig*) **your violent methods will ~ (on you)** vos méthodes violentes retomberont sur vous *or* se retourneront contre vous.
b (*after setback: of firm etc*) repartir, reprendre du poil de la bête*.
2 ['riːbaʊnd] **n** *[ball]* rebond *m*; *[bullet]* ricochet *m*; *[sales, economy]* reprise *f*; (*in prices*) remontée *f* (*in* de). **to hit a ball on the ~** frapper une balle après le premier rebond; (*fig*) **to be on the ~ from a setback** *etc* (*feeling effects*) être sous le coup d'un échec (*or* d'une déception *etc*); (*recovering*) reprendre du poil de la bête* après un échec (*or* une déception *etc*); **she married Robert on the ~*** elle était encore sous le coup d'une déception (sentimentale) quand elle a épousé Robert.

rebroadcast [,riː'brɔːdkɑːst] 1 **n** retransmission *f*. 2 **vt** retransmettre.

rebuff [rɪ'bʌf] 1 **n** rebuffade *f*. **to meet with a ~** essuyer une rebuffade. 2 **vt** *person* repousser, rabrouer; *offering, suggestion* repousser.

rebuild [,riː'bɪld] **pret, ptp rebuilt vt** rebâtir, reconstruire.

rebuilding [,riː'bɪldɪŋ] **n** (*NonC*) reconstruction *f*.

rebuke [rɪ'bjuːk] 1 **n** reproche *m*, réprimande *f*, blâme *m*. 2 **vt** réprimander, faire des reproches à. **to ~ sb for sth** reprocher qch à qn; **to ~ sb for having done** reprocher à qn d'avoir fait.

rebus ['riːbəs] **n, pl ~es** rébus *m*.

rebut [rɪ'bʌt] **vt** réfuter.

rebuttal [rɪ'bʌtl] **n** réfutation *f*.

recalcitrance [rɪ'kælsɪtrəns] **n** caractère *or* esprit récalcitrant.

recalcitrant [rɪ'kælsɪtrənt] **adj** récalcitrant.

recalculate [riː'kælkjʊleɪt] **vt** (*gen*) recalculer; *risk, probability* réévaluer.

recall [rɪ'kɔːl] 1 **vt** a (*summon back*) *ambassador, library book* rappeler; (*Comm*) *faulty products* retirer de la vente; (*Fin*) *capital* faire rentrer. (*fig*) **this music ~s the past** cette musique rappelle le passé; (*lit, fig*) **to ~ sb to life** rappeler qn à la vie; **to ~ Parliament** convoquer le Parlement (en session extraordinaire). b (*remember*) se rappeler (*that* que), se souvenir de. **I cannot ~ meeting him** *or* **whether I met him** je ne me rappelle pas l'avoir rencontré. 2 **n** rappel *m* (*also Mil*). *[library]* **this book is on ~** ce livre a été rappelé; (*fig*) **beyond** *or* **past ~ (adj)** irrévocable; **(adv)** irrévocablement. 3 **comp ▸ recall slip** *[library]* fiche *f* de rappel.

recant [rɪ'kænt] 1 **vt** *statement* rétracter; *opinion* désavouer; *religious belief* abjurer. **to ~ one's opinion** se déjuger. 2 **vi** se rétracter; (*Rel*) abjurer.

recantation [,riːkæn'teɪʃən] **n** rétractation *f*, reniement *m*; (*Rel*) abjuration *f*.

recap[1]***** ['riːkæp] 1 **n** (**abbr of recapitulation**) récapitulation *f*. 2 **vti** [rɪ'kæp] (**abbr of recapitulate**) **well, to ~, ...** eh bien, en résumé ... .

recap[2] ['riːkæp] (*US*) 1 **n** (*tyre*) pneu rechapé. 2 **vt** rechaper.

recapitalization [,riːkæpɪtəlaɪ'zeɪʃən] **n** restructuration *f* financière *or* du capital.

recapitalize [,riː'kæpɪtəlaɪz] **vt** restructurer le capital de, changer la structure financière de.

recapitulate [,riːkə'pɪtjʊleɪt] 1 **vt** *argument* récapituler, faire le résumé de; *facts* reprendre. 2 **vi** récapituler, faire un résumé.

recapitulation ['riːkə,pɪtjʊ'leɪʃən] **n** récapitulation *f*.

recapture [,riː'kæptʃəʳ] 1 **vt** *animal, prisoner* reprendre, rattraper, capturer; *emotion, enthusiasm* retrouver; *[film, play, book] atmosphere, period* recréer. 2 **n** *[town, territory]* reprise *f*; *[escapee]* arrestation *f*, capture *f*; *[escaped animal]* capture.

recast [,riː'kɑːst] 1 **vt** a (*Metal*) refondre. b *play, film* changer la distribution (des rôles) de; *actor* donner un nouveau rôle à. c (*re-write*) refondre, remanier. 2 **n** (*Metal*) refonte *f*.

recce* ['rekɪ] (*Mil*) **abbr of reconnaissance, reconnoitre**.

recd (*Comm*) (**abbr of received**) reçu.

recede [rɪ'siːd] **vi** a *[tide]* descendre; (*fig*) *[coast, person]* s'éloigner; *[memories, hopes of rescue etc]* s'estomper. **to ~ into the distance** s'éloigner, disparaître dans le lointain. b *[chin, forehead]* être fuyant. **his**

hair is *or* **he is receding** son front se dégarnit; **receding chin/forehead** menton/front fuyant; **receding hairline** front dégarni. c *[price]* baisser. d *(fml)* **to ~ from** *opinion, promise* revenir sur.

receipt [rɪ'siːt] 1 n a *(NonC: esp Comm)* réception *f*. **to acknowledge ~ of** accuser réception de; **on ~ of** au reçu de, dès réception de; **I am in ~ of ...** j'ai reçu ...; **to pay on ~** payer à la réception. b *(paper)* *(for payment)* reçu *m*, quittance *f*, récépissé *m* *(for* de); *(for parcel, letter)* accusé *m* de réception. **~ book** livre *m or* carnet *m* de quittances, quittancier *m*. c *(Comm, Fin: money taken)* **~s** recette(s) *f(pl)*, rentrées *fpl*. d *(Culin ††)* = **recipe**. 2 vt *bill* acquitter.

receivable [rɪ'siːvəbl] 1 adj recevable. 2 n *(Fin)* **~s** créances *fpl* (recouvrables).

receive [rɪ'siːv] 1 vt a *(get) letter, present* recevoir; *money, salary* recevoir, toucher; *punch* encaisser*; *refusal, setback* essuyer; *(Jur) stolen goods* recéler *or* receler; *(Med) care* recevoir; *(Med) treatment* subir. *(Jur)* **to ~ 2 years** *or* **2 years' imprisonment** être condamné à 2 ans de prison; **we ~d nothing but abuse** nous n'avons reçu que des insultes; *(Comm)* **we ~d your request yesterday** votre demande nous est parvenue hier; *(Comm)* **~d with thanks** pour acquit.
b *(welcome)* recevoir, accueillir. **to ~ sb with open arms** recevoir qn à bras ouverts; **his suggestion was well/not well ~d** sa suggestion a reçu un accueil favorable/défavorable; *(Rel)* **to be ~d into the Church** être reçu dans l'Église.
c *(Rad, TV) transmissions* capter, recevoir. **are you receiving me?** me recevez-vous?; *see* **loud**.
2 vi a recevoir. **Mrs X ~s on Mondays** Mme X reçoit le lundi.
b *(Jur)* être coupable de recel.

received [rɪ'siːvd] adj *opinion* reçu, admis. *(Brit Ling)* **~ pronunciation** prononciation *f* standard *(de l'anglais)*.

receiver [rɪ'siːvəʳ] n a receveur *m*, -euse *f*; *[letter]* destinataire *mf*; *[goods]* consignataire *mf*, réceptionnaire *mf*; *[stolen property]* receleur *m*, -euse *f*. b *(Fin, Jur)* ≈ administrateur *m* provisoire. **official ~** *(in bankruptcy)* séquestre *m*, syndic *m* de faillite, administrateur *m* judiciaire (en matière de faillite); **to call in the (official) ~** placer la société sous administration judiciaire. c *[telephone]* récepteur *m*, combiné *m*. **to lift the ~** décrocher; **to put down** *or* **replace the ~** raccrocher; **~ rest** commutateur *m*. d *(radio set)* (poste *m*) récepteur *m*.

receivership [rɪ'siːvəʃɪp] n *(Fin)* **the company has gone into ~** la société a été placée sous administration judiciaire.

receiving [rɪ'siːvɪŋ] 1 adj récepteur (*f* -trice), de réception. *(fig)* **to be on the ~ end* of a gift** recevoir un cadeau; **he blew his top and I was on the ~ end*** il s'est mis dans une colère noire, et c'est moi qui ai écopé* *or* qui en ai fait les frais*; *(Rad)* **~ set** poste récepteur. 2 n *[stolen goods]* recel *m*.

recension [rɪ'senʃən] n a *(NonC)* révision *f*. b *(text)* texte révisé.

recent ['riːsnt] adj *arrival, event, invention* récent; *development* nouveau (*f* nouvelle); *acquaintance etc* de fraîche date, nouveau. **in ~ years** ces dernières années.

recently ['riːsntlɪ] adv récemment, dernièrement. **as ~ as** pas plus tard que; **until (quite) ~** jusqu'à ces derniers temps.

receptacle [rɪ'septəkl] n récipient *m*; *(fig)* réceptacle *m*.

reception [rɪ'sepʃən] 1 n a *(NonC)* réception *f*. b *(ceremony)* réception *f*. c *(welcome)* réception *f*, accueil *m*. **to get a favourable ~** être bien accueilli *or* reçu; **to give sb a warm/chilly ~** faire un accueil chaleureux/froid à qn. d *(Rad, TV)* réception *f*. e *(in hotel)* réception *f*. **at ~** à la réception. 2 comp ►**reception centre** centre *m* d'accueil ►**reception class** *(Brit Scol)* cours *m* préparatoire ►**reception clerk** *(Brit)* réceptionniste *mf* ►**reception committee** *(lit, fig)* comité *m* d'accueil ►**reception (desk)** (bureau *m* de) réception *f* ►**reception room** *(in public building)* salle *f* de réception; *(in house)* pièce *f* commune, salon *m*.

receptionist [rɪ'sepʃənɪst] n réceptionniste *mf*.

receptive [rɪ'septɪv] adj réceptif *(to* à).

receptiveness [rɪ'septɪvnɪs] n, **receptivity** [ˌriːsep'tɪvɪtɪ] n réceptivité *f*.

receptor [rɪ'septəʳ] n *(Physiol, Rad)* récepteur *m*.

recess [rɪ'ses] 1 n a *(holidays)* *(Jur)* vacances *fpl* (judiciaires); *(Parl)* vacances (parlementaires). *(Parl)* **in ~** en vacances.
b *(short break)* *(US Jur)* suspension *f* d'audience; *(Scol, esp US)* récréation *f*. *(US Jur)* **the court is in ~** l'audience est suspendue.
c *(alcove)* renfoncement *m*; *[bed]* alcôve *f*; *[door, window]* embrasure *f*; *[statue]* niche *f*.
d *(secret place)* recoin *m*; *(fig: depths)* recoin, repli *m*. **in the ~es of his mind** dans les recoins de son esprit.
2 comp ►**recess appointment** *(US Pol)* *nomination effectuée par le chef de l'exécutif pendant les vacances parlementaires*.
3 vt *(make an alcove in)* pratiquer un renfoncement dans; *(put in alcove) bed etc* mettre dans un renfoncement.
4 vi *(US Jur, Parl)* suspendre les séances, être en vacances.

recessed ['rɪsesd] adj *doorway, cupboard* en retrait.

recession [rɪ'seʃən] n a *(NonC)* recul *m*, régression *f*. b *(Econ)* récession *f*.

recessional [rɪ'seʃənl] *(Rel)* 1 n hymne *m* de sortie du clergé. 2 adj de sortie.

recessionary [rɪ'seʃənərɪ] adj *factors etc* de récession.

recessive [rɪ'sesɪv] adj rétrograde; *(Genetics)* récessif.

recharge ['riː'tʃɑːdʒ] 1 vt *battery, gun* recharger. *(fig)* **to ~ one's batteries** recharger ses batteries* *or* ses accus*. 2 vi *[battery]* se recharger.

rechargeable [rɪ'tʃɑːdʒəbl] adj *battery* rechargeable.

recidivism [rɪ'sɪdɪvɪzəm] n récidive *f*.

recidivist [rɪ'sɪdɪvɪst] adj, n récidiviste *(mf)*.

recipe ['resɪpɪ] n *(Culin, Pharm)* recette *f*. *(Culin)* **~ book** livre *m* de cuisine *or* de recettes *(fig)*; **~ for happiness/good skin** *etc* recette *f* de *or* secret *m* du bonheur/secret *m* d'une belle peau; **what is your ~ for success?** quelle est votre recette pour réussir?; **lifting restrictions would be a ~ for disaster/anarchy/chaos** la levée des restrictions, c'est le meilleur moyen de s'attirer de gros ennuis/de tomber dans l'anarchie/de tomber dans le chaos.

recipient [rɪ'sɪpɪənt] n *(gen)* personne *f* qui reçoit *(or* a reçu *etc)*; *(Post: of letter)* destinataire *mf*; *[cheque]* bénéficiaire *mf*; *[award, decoration]* récipiendaire *m*; *(Jur)* donataire *mf*.

reciprocal [rɪ'sɪprəkəl] 1 adj *(mutual)* réciproque, mutuel; *(Gram)* réciproque; *(Math)* réciproque, inverse. 2 n *(Math)* réciproque *f*.

reciprocally [rɪ'sɪprəkəlɪ] adv réciproquement, mutuellement; *(Math)* inversement.

reciprocate [rɪ'sɪprəkeɪt] 1 vt a *smiles, wishes* rendre; *help* donner *or* offrir en retour; *kindness* retourner. b *(Tech)* donner un mouvement alternatif à. 2 vi a faire la même chose en retour, s'empresser d'en faire autant. **he insulted me and I ~d** il m'a injurié, et je lui ai rendu la pareille; **he called me a fool and I ~d** il m'a traité d'imbécile et je lui ai retourné le compliment. b *(Tech)* avoir un mouvement alternatif *or* de va-et-vient. **reciprocating engine** moteur alternatif; **reciprocating device** dispositif *m* de va-et-vient.

reciprocation [rɪˌsɪprə'keɪʃən] n a *[help, kindness]* échange *m*. b *(Tech)* alternance *f*, va-et-vient *m inv*.

reciprocity [ˌresɪ'prɒsɪtɪ] n réciprocité *f*.

recital [rɪ'saɪtl] n a *(account)* récit *m*, compte rendu *m*, narration *f*; *[details]* énumération *f*. b *[poetry]* récitation *f*, récital *m*; *[music]* récital. c *(Jur: in contract)* **~s** préambule *m*.

recitation [ˌresɪ'teɪʃən] n récitation *f*.

recitative [ˌresɪtə'tiːv] n récitatif *m*.

recite [rɪ'saɪt] 1 vt a *poetry* réciter, déclamer. b *facts* exposer; *details* énumérer. 2 vi réciter, déclamer.

reckless ['reklɪs] adj *(heedless)* insouciant; *(rash)* imprudent, téméraire, casse-cou* *inv*. *(Aut)* **~ driving** conduite imprudente; **~ driver** automobiliste *mf* imprudent(e).

recklessly ['reklɪslɪ] adv *(see* **reckless**) avec insouciance; imprudemment.

recklessness ['reklɪsnɪs] n *(see* **reckless**) insouciance *f*; imprudence *f*; manque *m* de prudence; témérité *f*.

reckon ['rekən] 1 vt a *(calculate) time, numbers, points* compter; *cost, surface* calculer.
b *(judge)* considérer, estimer. **I ~ him among my friends** je le compte parmi *or* au nombre de mes amis; **Mrs X is ~ed (to be) a beautiful woman** Mme X est considérée comme une femme très belle.
c (*) *(think)* penser, croire; *(estimate)* estimer, juger; *(suppose)* supposer, imaginer. **I ~ we can start** je pense qu'on peut commencer; **I ~ he must be about forty** j'estime qu'il a *or* je lui donnerais la quarantaine; **about thirty, I ~** une trentaine, à mon avis.
2 vi a calculer, compter. **~ing from tomorrow** en comptant à partir de demain, à compter de demain.
b *(fig)* **you can ~ on 30** tu peux compter sur 30; **I was ~ing on doing that tomorrow** j'avais prévu faire *or* je pensais faire ça demain; **I wasn't ~ing on having to do that** je ne m'attendais pas à devoir faire ça; **they ~ to sell most of them abroad** ils comptent en vendre la majorité à l'étranger; **you'll have to ~ with 6 more** il faudra compter avec 6 de plus; **you'll have to ~ with an objection from them** il faut s'attendre à une objection de leur part; **he's a person to be ~ed with** c'est une personne avec laquelle il faut compter; **if you insult him you'll have to ~ with the whole family** si vous l'insultez, vous aurez affaire à toute la famille; **he was ~ing without his secretary** il avait compté sans sa secrétaire; **he ~ed without the fact that ...** il n'avait pas prévu que ..., il n'avait pas tenu compte du fait que ... .

►**reckon up** vt sep *(gen)* calculer; *(add)* ajouter, additionner.

reckoner ['rekənəʳ] *see* **ready**.

reckoning ['reknɪŋ] n a *(Math etc)* *(evaluation)* compte *m*; *(calculation)* calcul *m*. **to be out in one's ~** s'être trompé dans ses calculs. b *(Comm)* règlement *m* de compte(s) *(lit)*; *[hotel]* note *f*; *[restaurant]* addition *f*. *(Rel)* **the day of ~** le jour du Jugement; *(fig)* **the day of ~ can't be far away** un de ces jours ça va lui *etc* retomber dessus. c *(judgment)* estimation *f*. **to the best of my ~** (pour) autant que je puisse en juger; **in your ~** d'après vous, à votre avis. d *(Naut)* estime *f*; *see* **dead**.

reclaim [rɪ'kleɪm] 1 vt *land (gen)* reconquérir; *(from forest, bush)* défricher; *(from sea)* assainir, assécher, conquérir par assèchement; *(with manure etc)* amender, bonifier; *by-product* récupérer; *(demand* *back*) réclamer (*sth from sb* qch à qn). 2 n: **past** *or* **beyond** ~ perdu à tout jamais; **he is beyond** ~ il ne se corrigera jamais.

reclaimable [rɪ'kleɪməbl] adj *land* amendable; *by-products* récupérable.

reclamation [,reklə'meɪʃən] n (*see* **reclaim**) reconquête *f*; assainissement *m*; défrichement *m*; assèchement *m*; amendement *m*; récupération *f*; réclamation *f*.

reclassify [,riː'klæsɪfaɪ] vt reclasser, reclassifier.

recline [rɪ'klaɪn] 1 vt *head, arm* reposer, appuyer. 2 vi *[person]* être couché, être allongé, être étendu. **she was reclining in the armchair** elle était allongée *or* étendue sur le fauteuil; **reclining in his bath** étendu *or* allongé dans son bain; **the seat ~s** le siège est inclinable, le dossier (du siège) est réglable.

reclining [rɪ'klaɪnɪŋ] adj: ~ **chair** chaise longue; *[coach, plane, car]* ~ **seat** siège *m* inclinable *or* à dossier réglable.

recluse [rɪ'kluːs] n reclus(e) *m(f)*, solitaire *mf*.

reclusive [rɪ'kluːsɪv] adj solitaire.

recognition [,rekəg'nɪʃən] n a (*gen, Pol: acknowledgement*) reconnaissance *f*. **in ~ of** en reconnaissance de.

b (*fame etc*) **he seeks** ~ il désire que ses mérites (*or* talents *etc*) soient reconnus; **this brought him ~ at last** c'est ce qui lui a enfin permis d'être reconnu; **his exploits have gained world-wide** ~ ses exploits ont été reconnus dans le monde entier; **to receive no** ~ passer inaperçu.

c (*identification*) reconnaissance *f*; (*Aviat*) identification *f*. **he has changed beyond** *or* **out of all** ~ il est devenu méconnaissable; **he has changed it beyond** *or* **out of all** ~ il l'a rendu méconnaissable; **to improve beyond** *or* **out of (all)** ~ s'améliorer jusqu'à en être méconnaissable.

d (*Comput*) reconnaissance *f*. **speech** ~ reconnaissance de la parole.

recognizable ['rekəgnaɪzəbl] adj reconnaissable.

recognizably [,rekəg'naɪzəblɪ] adv: **it is ~ different/better** *etc* on voit bien que c'est différent/meilleur *etc*.

recognizance [rɪ'kɒgnɪzəns] n (*Jur*) engagement *m*; (*sum of money*) caution *f* (personnelle). **to enter into ~s (for sb)** donner *or* fournir *or* se porter caution (pour qn); **bail in his own ~ of £1000** mise en liberté (provisoire) sous caution personnelle de 1 000 livres.

recognize ['rekəgnaɪz] vt a (*gen*) reconnaître (*by* à, *as* comme étant, *that* que). b (*US*) *[chairman of meeting]* donner la parole à.

recognized ['rekəgnaɪzd] adj a reconnu, admis, reçu. **a ~ fact** un fait reconnu *or* indiscuté. b (*Comm*) attitré.

recoil [rɪ'kɔɪl] 1 vi a *[person]* reculer, avoir un mouvement de recul (*from* devant). **to ~ in disgust** reculer de dégoût; **to ~ from doing** reculer devant l'idée de faire, se refuser à faire. b *[gun]* reculer; *[spring]* se détendre; (*fig*) *[actions etc]* retomber (*on* sur). 2 n *[gun]* recul *m*; *[spring]* détente *f*; (*fig*) dégoût *m* (*from* pour, de), horreur *f* (*from* de), répugnance *f* (*from* pour).

recollect [,rekə'lekt] 1 vt se rappeler, se souvenir de. **to ~ o.s.** se recueillir. 2 vi se souvenir. **as far as I ~** autant que je m'en souvienne.

recollection [,rekə'lekʃən] n souvenir *m*. **to the best of my ~, within my** ~ autant que je m'en souvienne; **his ~ of it is vague** il ne s'en souvient que vaguement; **I have some ~ of it** j'en ai un vague souvenir; **I have no ~ of it** je ne m'en souviens pas, je n'en ai aucun souvenir.

recommence [,riːkə'mens] vti recommencer (*doing* à faire).

recommend [,rekə'mend] vt a (*speak good of*) recommander. **to ~ sb for a job** recommander qn pour un emploi, appuyer la candidature de qn; **it is to be ~ed** c'est à conseiller; **it is not to be ~ed** c'est à déconseiller.

b (*advise*) recommander, conseiller (*sb to do* à qn de faire). **what do you ~ for curing a cough?** que recommandez-vous pour guérir une toux?; **he was ~ed to accept** on lui a recommandé *or* conseillé d'accepter; (*Comm*) **~ed retail price** prix *m* conseillé.

c (*make acceptable*) prévenir en faveur de, rendre acceptable. **she has a lot to ~ her** elle a beaucoup de qualités en sa faveur, il y a beaucoup à dire en sa faveur; **she has little to ~ her** elle n'a pas grand-chose pour elle.

d (*commit*) *child, one's soul* recommander, confier (*to* à).

recommendable [,rekə'mendəbl] adj recommandable. **it is not ~** c'est à déconseiller.

recommendation [,rekəmen'deɪʃən] n recommandation *f*. **on the ~ of** sur la recommandation de.

recommendatory [,rekə'mendətərɪ] adj de recommandation.

recommittal [,riːkə'mɪtl] n (*US Parl*) renvoi *m* en commission (*d'un projet de loi*).

recompense ['rekəmpens] 1 n a (*reward*) récompense *f*. **in ~ for** en récompense de. b (*Jur: for damage*) dédommagement *m*, compensation *f*. 2 vt a (*reward*) récompenser (*for* de). b (*Jur etc: repay*) *person* dédommager; *damage, loss* compenser, réparer.

recompose [,riːkəm'pəʊz] vt a (*rewrite*) recomposer. b (*calm*) **to ~ o.s.** se ressaisir, retrouver son calme *or* son sang-froid.

reconcilable ['rekənsaɪləbl] adj *ideas, opinions* conciliable, compatible (*with* avec).

reconcile ['rekənsaɪl] vt *person* réconcilier (*to* avec); *argument, dispute* arranger; *two facts or ideas* concilier, accorder (*with* avec, *and* et). **they became ~d** ils se sont réconciliés; **to ~ o.s. to sth** se résigner à qch, se faire à qch; **what ~d him to it was ...** ce qui le lui a fait accepter, c'était ... .

reconciliation [,rekənsɪlɪ'eɪʃən] n *[persons]* réconciliation *f*; *[opinions, principles]* conciliation *f*.

recondite [rɪ'kɒndaɪt] adj abstrus, obscur.

recondition [,riːkən'dɪʃən] vt remettre à neuf *or* en état, rénover; *machine* réviser. (*Aut*) **~ed engine** moteur remis à neuf *or* révisé.

reconnaissance [rɪ'kɒnɪsəns] n (*Aviat, Mil*) reconnaissance *f*. ~ **flight/patrol** vol *m*/patrouille *f* de reconnaissance.

reconnoitre, (*US*) **reconnoiter** [,rekə'nɔɪtəʳ] (*Aviat, Mil*) 1 vt *region* reconnaître. 2 vi faire une reconnaissance.

reconnoitring [,rekə'nɔɪtərɪŋ] n (*Mil etc*) reconnaissance *f*.

reconquer [,riː'kɒŋkəʳ] vt reconquérir.

reconquest [,riː'kɒŋkwest] n reconquête *f*.

reconsider [,riːkən'sɪdəʳ] 1 vt *decision, opinion* reconsidérer; *judgment* réviser. **won't you ~ it?** est-ce que vous seriez prêt à reconsidérer la question? 2 vi (*gen*) reconsidérer la question; (*and change mind*) changer d'avis.

reconsideration ['riːkən,sɪdə'reɪʃən] n remise *f* en cause, nouvel examen.

reconstitute [,riː'kɒnstɪtjuːt] vt reconstituer.

reconstitution ['riː,kɒnstɪ'tjuːʃən] n reconstitution *f*.

reconstruct [,riːkən'strʌkt] vt *building* reconstruire, rebâtir; *crime* reconstituer; *policy, system* reconstruire.

reconstruction [,riːkən'strʌkʃən] n *[building, policy, system]* reconstruction *f*; *[crime]* reconstitution *f*. (*US Hist*) **The R~** la Reconstruction de l'Union (*après 1865*).

reconvene [,riːkən'viːn] 1 vt reconvoquer. 2 vi *[committee, jury etc]* se réunir *or* s'assembler de nouveau; *[meeting]* reprendre. **we will ~ at 10 o'clock** la réunion (*or* l'audience *etc*) reprendra à 10 heures.

record [rɪ'kɔːd] 1 vt a (*register*) *facts, story* enregistrer; *protest, disapproval* prendre acte de; *event etc* (*in journal, log*) noter; (*describe*) décrire. **to ~ the proceedings of a meeting** tenir le procès-verbal d'une assemblée; (*Parl*) **to ~ one's vote** voter; **his speech as ~ed in the newspapers** ... son discours, tel que le rapportent les journaux ...; **history/the author ~s that** ... l'histoire/l'auteur rapporte que ...; **it's not ~ed anywhere** ce n'est pas attesté; **to ~ the population** recenser la population.

b *[thermometer etc]* enregistrer, marquer.

c *speech, music* enregistrer. **to ~ on tape** enregistrer sur bande; **to ~ on video** magnétoscoper; (*Telec*) **this is a ~ed message** ceci est *or* vous écoutez un message enregistré; *see* **tape**.

2 vi enregistrer. **he is ~ing at 5 o'clock** il enregistre à 5 heures; **his voice does not ~ well** sa voix ne se prête pas bien à l'enregistrement.

3 ['rekɔːd] n a (*account, report*) rapport *m*, récit *m*; (*of attendance*) registre *m*; (*of act, decision*) minute *f*; (*of evidence, meeting*) procès-verbal *m*; (*official report*) rapport officiel; (*Jur*) enregistrement *m*; (*historical report*) document *m*. **the society's ~s** les actes *mpl* de la société; **(public) ~s** archives *fpl*, annales *fpl*; **to make** *or* **keep a ~ of** noter, consigner; (*fig*) **it is on ~ that** ... c'est un fait établi *or* il est établi que ...; **there is no similar example on ~** aucun exemple semblable n'est attesté; **to go/be on ~ as saying that** ... déclarer/avoir déclaré publiquement que ...; **to put on ~** consigner, mentionner (par écrit); **the highest temperatures on ~** les plus fortes températures enregistrées; **there is no ~ of his having said it** il n'est noté *or* consigné nulle part qu'il l'ait dit; **there is no ~ of it in history** l'histoire n'en fait pas mention; **to put** *or* **set the ~ straight** mettre les choses au clair, dissiper toute confusion possible; **just to put** *or* **set the ~ straight, let me point out that** ... pour qu'il n'y ait aucune confusion possible, disons bien que ...; (*fig*) **for the ~, they refuse** ... il faut noter *or* signaler qu'ils refusent ...; **this is strictly off the ~*** ceci est à titre (purement) confidentiel *or* officieux, ceci doit rester strictement entre nous; **the interview was off the ~*** l'interview n'était pas officielle; **off the ~*, he did come!** (*gen*) entre nous, il est venu!; (*to reporter*) vous ne me citerez pas, hein, mais il est venu; (*Press etc*) **on the ~, he admitted that** ... dans ses déclarations officielles, il a avoué que ...; (*fig*) **this statue is a ~ of a past civilization** cette statue est la marque d'une civilisation passée.

b (*case history*) dossier *m*; (*card*) fiche *f*. (*Mil*) **service ~** états *mpl* de service; (*Jur*) **(police) ~** casier *m* judiciaire; **~ of previous convictions** dossier du prévenu; (*Jur, Police*) **he's got a clean ~, he hasn't got a ~*** il a un casier (judiciaire) vierge; **he's got a long ~** il a un casier judiciaire chargé; **France's splendid ~** les succès glorieux de la France; **his past ~** sa conduite passée; **his war ~** son passé militaire; (*Scol*) **his attendance ~ is bad** il a été souvent absent; **to have a good ~ at school** avoir un bon dossier scolaire; **this airline has a good safety ~** cette compagnie aérienne a une bonne tradition de sécurité; **he left a splendid ~ of achievements** il avait à son compte de magnifiques réussites; *see* **police, track** *etc*.

c (*Comput*) article *m*.

d (*recording*) *[voice etc]* enregistrement *m*.

e (*also* **gramophone ~**) disque *m*. **to make** *or* **cut a ~** graver un disque.

f (*Sport, fig*) record *m*. **to beat** *or* **break the ~** battre le record; **to hold the ~** détenir le record; **long-jump ~** record du saut en longueur; *see* **world** *etc*.

g *[seismograph etc]* courbe enregistrée.

4 **comp** *amount, attendance, result* record *inv* ▸**record album** (*Mus*) album *m* de disques ▸**record breaker** (*Sport*) personne *f* (*or* performance *f*) qui bat le(s) record(s) ▸**record-breaking** (*Sport, fig*) qui bat tous les records ▸**record cabinet** casier *m* à disques, discothèque *f* ▸**record card** fiche *f* ▸**record changer** changeur *m* de disques automatique ▸**record company** maison *f* de disques ▸**record dealer** disquaire *mf* ▸**record holder** (*Sport*) détenteur *m*, -trice *f* du record ▸**record library** discothèque *f* (*collection*) ▸**record player** tourne-disque *m*, électrophone *m* ▸**record producer** producteur *m* de disques ▸**record programme** (*Rad*) programme *m* de disques ▸**record time: to do sth in record time** faire qch en un temps record ▸**record token** bon-cadeau *m* (négociable contre un disque), chèque-disque *m*.

recorded [rɪ'kɔːdɪd] **adj** a *music* enregistré; (*Rad, TV*) *programme* enregistré à l'avance, transmis en différé. (*Brit Post*) **to send by ~ delivery** ≃ envoyer en recommandé *or* avec avis de réception. b *fact, occurrence* attesté, noté.

recorder [rɪ'kɔːdər] **n** a *[official facts]* archiviste *mf*; (*registrar*) greffier *m*. b (*Brit Jur*) ≃ avocat nommé à la fonction de juge; (*US Jur*) ≃ juge suppléant. c *[sounds]* (*apparatus*) appareil *m* enregistreur; (*tape ~*) magnétophone *m*; (*cassette ~*) magnétophone à cassettes; *see* **video**. d (*person*) artiste *mf* qui enregistre. e (*Mus*) flûte *f* à bec. **descant/treble/tenor/bass ~** flûte *f* à bec soprano/alto/ténor/basse.

recording [rɪ'kɔːdɪŋ] 1 **n** *[sound, facts]* enregistrement *m*. (*Rad*) **"this programme is a ~"** "ce programme est enregistré". 2 **adj** a (*Admin etc*) *official* chargé du recensement. (*Rel*) **the R~ Angel** l'ange qui tient le grand livre des bienfaits et des méfaits. b *artist* qui enregistre; *apparatus* enregistreur. **~ equipment** matériel *m* d'enregistrement; (*Mus*) **~ session** séance *f* d'enregistrement; (*Mus*) **~ studio** studio *m* d'enregistrement; **~ tape** bande *f or* ruban *m* magnétique; (*Rad, TV*) **~ van** car *m* de reportage.

recount [rɪ'kaʊnt] **vt** (*relate*) raconter, narrer.

re-count [ˌriː'kaʊnt] 1 **vt** recompter, compter de nouveau. 2 ['riːkaʊnt] **n** *[votes]* deuxième compte *m* (des suffrages exprimés).

recoup [rɪ'kuːp] 1 **vt** a (*make good*) *losses* récupérer. **to ~ costs** *[person]* rentrer dans ses fonds; *[earnings]* couvrir les frais; *[course of action]* permettre de couvrir les frais. b (*reimburse*) dédommager (*for* de). **to ~ o.s.** se dédommager, se rattraper. c (*Jur*) déduire, défalquer. 2 **vi** récupérer ses pertes.

recourse [rɪ'kɔːs] **n** recours *m* (*to* à). **to have ~ to** avoir recours à, recourir à.

recover [rɪ'kʌvər] 1 **vt** *sth lost, one's appetite, reason, balance* retrouver; *sth lent* reprendre (*from sb* à qn), récupérer; *lost territory* regagner, reconquérir; *sth floating* repêcher; *space capsule, wreck* récupérer; (*Ind etc*) *materials* récupérer; (*Fin*) *debt* recouvrer, récupérer; *goods, property* rentrer en possession de. **to ~ one's breath** reprendre haleine *or* sa respiration; *[invalid]* **to ~ one's strength** reprendre des forces; **to ~ consciousness** revenir à soi, reprendre connaissance; **to ~ one's sight/health** retrouver *or* recouvrer la vue/la santé; **to ~ land from the sea** conquérir du terrain sur la mer; (*fig*) **to ~ lost ground** se rattraper; **to ~ o.s.** *or* **one's composure** se ressaisir, se reprendre; **to ~ expenses** rentrer dans ses frais, récupérer ses débours; **to ~ one's losses** réparer ses pertes; (*Jur*) **to ~ damages** obtenir des dommages-intérêts.

2 **vi** a (*after shock, accident etc*) se remettre (*from* de); (*from illness*) guérir, se rétablir (*from* de); (*regain consciousness*) revenir à soi, reprendre connaissance; (*after error*) se ressaisir; *[the economy, the dollar]* se rétablir, se redresser; *[stock market]* reprendre; *[shares]* remonter. **she has completely ~ed** elle est tout à fait rétablie.

b (*Jur*) obtenir gain de cause. **right to ~** droit *m* de reprise.

re-cover [ˌriː'kʌvər] **vt** couvrir de nouveau, recouvrir; *chair, umbrella* recouvrir.

recoverable [rɪ'kʌvərəbl] **adj** (*Fin*) récupérable, recouvrable; *losses* réparable.

recovered [rɪ'kʌvəd] **adj** (*Med: better*) rétabli.

recovery [rɪ'kʌvərɪ] 1 **n** a (*see* **recover 1**) récupération *f*; recouvrement *m*; reconquête *f*; (*Jur: of damages*) obtention *f*.

b (*see* **recover 2a**) guérison *f*; rétablissement *m*; redressement *m*; reprise *f*; remontée *f*. **to be on the road** *or* **way to ~** *[patient]* être en voie de guérison; *[economy, country]* se redresser; **he is making a good ~** il est en bonne voie de guérison; **best wishes for a speedy ~** tous nos vœux de prompt rétablissement; **past ~** *sick person* dans un état désespéré; *situation* sans remède, irrémédiable; (*Sport*) **to make a ~** se ressaisir.

2 **comp** ▸**recovery operation** (*Space*) opération *f* de récupération (d'un vaisseau spatial *etc*) ▸**recovery room** (*Med*) salle *f* de réveil ▸**recovery ship** (*Space, Naut*) navire *m* de récupération ▸**recovery vehicle** (*Aut*) dépanneuse *f* ▸**recovery vessel** (*Space, Naut*) = **recovery ship**.

recreant ['rekrɪənt] **adj, n** (*liter*) lâche (*m*), traître(sse) *m(f)*.

recreate [ˌriːkrɪ'eɪt] **vt** recréer.

recreation [ˌrekrɪ'eɪʃən] 1 **n** a (*NonC*) récréation *f*, détente *f*, délassement *m*. **for ~ I go fishing** je vais à la pêche pour me détendre. b (*Scol*) récréation *f*, récré* *f*. 2 **comp** ▸**recreation ground** terrain *m* de jeux ▸**recreation room** salle *f* de récréation.

recreational [ˌrekrɪ'eɪʃənəl] **adj** *facilities* de récréation. **~ drugs** drogues *fpl* douces; (*US*) **~ vehicle** camping-car *m*.

recreative ['rekrɪˌeɪtɪv] **adj** récréatif, divertissant.

recriminate [rɪ'krɪmɪneɪt] **vi** récriminer (*against* contre).

recrimination [rɪˌkrɪmɪ'neɪʃən] **n** récrimination *f*.

recriminatory [rɪ'krɪmɪneɪtərɪ] **adj** de récrimination, de protestation. **~ remark** récrimination *f*.

recrudesce [ˌriːkruː'des] **vi** être en recrudescence.

recrudescence [ˌriːkruː'desns] **n** recrudescence *f*.

recrudescent [ˌriːkruː'desnt] **adj** recrudescent.

recruit [rɪ'kruːt] 1 **n** (*Mil, fig*) recrue *f*. **the party gained ~s from the middle classes** le parti faisait des recrues dans la bourgeoisie; *see* **raw** *etc*. 2 **vt** *member, soldier, staff* recruter. **the party was ~ed from the middle classes** le parti se recrutait dans la bourgeoisie; **he ~ed me to help** il m'a embauché* pour aider.

recruiting [rɪ'kruːtɪŋ] 1 **n** recrutement *m*. 2 **comp** ▸**recruiting office** (*Mil*) bureau *m* de recrutement ▸**recruiting officer** recruteur *m*.

recruitment [rɪ'kruːtmənt] **n** recrutement *m*. **~ agency** agence *f* de recrutement; **~ consultant** conseil *m* en recrutement.

recta ['rektə] **npl of rectum**.

rectal ['rektəl] **adj** rectal.

rectangle ['rekˌtæŋgl] **n** rectangle *m*.

rectangular [rek'tæŋgjʊlər] **adj** rectangulaire.

rectifiable ['rektɪfaɪəbl] **adj** rectifiable.

rectification [ˌrektɪfɪ'keɪʃən] **n** (*Chem, Math, gen*) rectification *f*; (*Elec*) redressement *m*.

rectifier ['rektɪfaɪər] **n** (*Elec*) redresseur *m*.

rectify ['rektɪfaɪ] **vt** a *error* rectifier, corriger. **to ~ an omission** réparer une négligence *or* un oubli. b (*Chem, Math*) rectifier. c (*Elec*) redresser.

rectilineal [ˌrektɪ'lɪnɪəl] **adj**, **rectilinear** [ˌrektɪ'lɪnɪər] **adj** rectiligne.

rectitude ['rektɪtjuːd] **n** rectitude *f*.

rector ['rektər] **n** a (*Rel*) pasteur *m* (*anglican*). b (*Scot*) (*Scol*) proviseur *m* (de lycée); (*Univ*) ≃ recteur *m*.

rectorship ['rektəʃɪp] **n** (*Scot*) (*Scol*) provisorat *m*; (*Univ*) ≃ rectorat *m*.

rectory ['rektərɪ] **n** presbytère *m* (*anglican*).

rectum ['rektəm] **n, pl ~s** *or* **recta** rectum *m*.

recumbent [rɪ'kʌmbənt] **adj** couché, étendu. (*Art*) **~ figure** (*gen*) figure *f* couchée *or* étendue; (*on tombs*) gisant *m*.

recuperate [rɪ'kuːpəreɪt] 1 **vi** (*Med*) se rétablir, se remettre, récupérer. 2 **vt** *object* récupérer; *losses* réparer.

recuperation [rɪˌkuːpə'reɪʃən] **n** (*Med*) rétablissement *m*; *[materials etc]* récupération *f*.

recuperative [rɪ'kuːpərətɪv] **adj** régénérateur (*f* -trice). **he has amazing ~ powers** il a des pouvoirs étonnants de récupération, il récupère à une vitesse étonnante.

recur [rɪ'kɜːr] **vi** a (*happen again*) *[error, event]* se reproduire; *[idea, theme]* se retrouver, revenir; *[illness, infection]* réapparaître; *[opportunity, problem]* se représenter. b (*come to mind again*) revenir à la mémoire (*to sb* de qn). c (*Math*) se reproduire périodiquement.

recurrence [rɪ'kʌrəns] **n** *[error, event, idea, theme]* répétition *f*; *[headaches, symptoms]* réapparition *f*; *[opportunity, problem]* réapparition, retour *m*. **a ~ of the illness** un nouvel accès de la maladie, une rechute; **let there be no ~ of this** que ceci ne se reproduise plus.

recurrent [rɪ'kʌrənt] **adj** a fréquent, périodique, qui revient souvent. (*Comm*) **~ expenses** frais généraux. b (*Anat*) récurrent.

recurring [rɪ'kɜːrɪŋ] **adj** a (*Math*) périodique. **~ decimal** fraction *f* périodique. b *event* qui se reproduit régulièrement; *complaints* régulier, périodique; *illness* chronique.

recursion [rɪ'kɜːʃən] **n** (*Math, Gram*) récursion *f*.

recursive [rɪ'kɜːsɪv] **adj** (*Gram*) récursif.

recursively [rɪ'kɜːsɪvlɪ] **adv** de façon récursive.

recursiveness [rɪ'kɜːsɪvnɪs] **n** récursivité *f*.

recusant ['rekjʊzənt] **adj** (*Rel*) réfractaire.

recyclable [ˌriː'saɪkləbl] **adj** (*see* **recycle**) recyclable; retraitable.

recycle [ˌriː'saɪkl] **vt** (*gen*) recycler; *waste water* retraiter; (*Ind*) *revenue* réinvestir. **~d paper** papier *m* recyclé.

recycling [ˌriː'saɪklɪŋ] **n** (*see* **recycle**) recyclage *m*; retraitement *m*. **~ plant** centre *m* de recyclage; centre *m* de retraitement.

red [red] 1 **adj** a (*in colour*) (*gen*) *flag, wine, meat, sky, blood, apple etc* rouge; *hair* roux (*f* rousse); *lips* vermeil. **~ with anger** rouge de colère; **~ as a beetroot** rouge comme une pivoine *or* un coquelicot *or* une tomate; (*lit*) **he was rather ~ in the face** il était rougeaud, il avait le teint rouge; (*fig*) **was I ~ in the face!*, was my face ~!*, did I have a ~ face!*** j'étais rouge de confusion, j'étais très embarrassé; **to go** *or* **turn ~ (with embarrassment)** rougir (d'embarras); **to see ~** voir rouge, se fâcher tout rouge; **it's like a ~ rag to a bull** c'est comme le rouge pour les taureaux; **that is like a ~ rag to him** il voit rouge quand on lui parle de cela (*or* quand on lui montre cela *etc*); (*US*) **it's not worth a ~ cent*** ça ne vaut pas un sou *or* un rond*; (*fig*) **to roll out the ~ carpet for sb** recevoir qn en grande pompe, se mettre en frais pour recevoir qn; (*Rel: cardinal's*) **~ hat** chapeau *m* de cardinal; (*US*) **to go into ~ ink*** *[company]* être en déficit; *[individual]* se mettre à découvert; **~ light** (*lit*) feu *m* rouge; (*fig*) **to see the ~ light** se rendre compte du danger; (*fig*) **he got the ~ light on the project** son projet n'a pas eu le feu vert, on a mis le veto à son projet; (*Aut*) **to go through the ~ light** passer au rouge, brûler un feu rouge; (*loc*) **~ sky at night, shepherd's delight** un ciel rouge le soir, c'est signe de beau temps, ≃ ciel rouge au soir, blanc au matin, c'est la journée du pélerin (*loc*); (*loc*) **~ sky in the morning, shepherd's warning** un ciel rouge le matin, c'est signe de mauvais temps; *see also* **3**, *and* **man, paint** *etc.*

b (*Pol*) rouge. **the R~ Army** l'Armée rouge; **the R~ Army Faction** Fraction *f* de l'Armée Rouge; **R~ China** Chine *f* communiste; (*in the USSR*) **the R~ Guard** la garde rouge; (*in China*) **the R~ Guards** les gardes *mpl* rouges.

2 n a (*colour*) rouge *m*; (**: wine*) rouge *m*.

b (*Pol: person*) rouge *mf*, communiste *mf*. **he sees ~s under the bed** il voit des communistes partout.

c (*Billiards*) bille *f* rouge; (*Roulette*) rouge *m*.

d (*fig*) **to be in the ~*** *[individual]* être à découvert; *[company]* être en déficit; **to get out of the ~** ne plus être à découvert, combler le déficit; **to be £100 in the ~** avoir un découvert *or* un déficit de 100 livres.

e (*US Hist: Indians*) **the R~s** les Peaux-Rouges *mpl*.

3 comp ►**red admiral (butterfly)** vulcain *m* ►**red alert** alerte maximale; (*Mil*) **to be on red alert** être en état d'alerte maximale ►**red-blooded** vigoureux ►**redbreast** rouge-gorge *m* ►**red-breasted merganser** harle *m* huppé ►**red-brick** en briques rouges; (*Brit*) **red-brick university** université *f* de fondation assez récente ►**red cap** (*Brit Mil **) policier *m* militaire; (*US Rail*) porteur *m* ►**red card** (*Ftbl*) carton *m* rouge ►**red-carpet treatment** accueil *m* princier *or* somptueux ►**redcoat** (*Brit Hist*) soldat anglais; (*Brit: in holiday camp*) animateur *m*, -trice *f* ►**Red Crescent** Croissant *m* Rouge ►**Red Cross (Society)** Croix-Rouge *f* ►**redcurrant** groseille *f* (rouge) ►**red deer** cerf commun ►**red duster*** (*Naut*) = **red ensign** ►**red ensign** (*Naut*) pavillon *m* de la marine marchande (britannique) ►**red eye** (*Phot*) (effet *m* d')yeux *mpl* rouges ►**red-eye** (*US*) mauvais whisky *m* ►**red-eyed** aux yeux rouges ►**red-faced** (*lit*) rougeaud, rubicond; (*fig*) gêné, rouge de confusion ►**Red Flag** drapeau *m* rouge ►**red grouse** grouse *f*, lagopède *m* d'Écosse ►**red-handed: to be caught red-handed** être pris en flagrant délit *or* la main dans le sac ►**red-haired, red-headed** roux (*f* rousse) ►**redhead** roux *m*, rousse *f*, rouquin(e) *m(f)* ►**red heat: to raise iron to red heat** chauffer le fer au rouge ►**red herring** (*lit*) hareng saur; (*fig*) **that's a red herring** c'est pour brouiller les pistes, c'est une diversion ►**red-hot** adj (*lit*) chauffé au rouge, brûlant; (*fig: enthusiastic*) ardent, enthousiaste; (*fig: up to the moment*) *news, information* tout chaud ◊ n (*US Culin **) hot-dog *m* ►**Red Indian** Peau-Rouge *mf* ►**red lead** minium *m* ►**red-letter day** jour *m* mémorable, jour à marquer d'une pierre blanche ►**red light** *see* **1; red-light district** quartier *m* des prostituées ►**redline** (*US Fin*) discriminer (financièrement) à l'encontre de ►**red man** (*US*) Indien *m* (aux USA); (*Brit*) (*at pedestrian crossing*) **it's the red man** c'est rouge (pour les piétons) ►**red mullet** rouget-barbet *m* ►**redneck*** (*esp US*) rustre *m*, péquenaud *m* ►**red pepper** poivron *m* rouge ►**Red Riding Hood** (*also* **Little Red Riding Hood**) le Petit Chaperon Rouge ►**red salmon** saumon *m* rouge ►**Red Sea** (*Geog*) mer *f* Rouge; **red sea bream** daurade *f* (*or* dorade *f*) rose ►**red shank** chevalier *m* gambette ►**redskin** Peau-Rouge *mf* ►**red snapper** vivaneau *m* (*Can*) ►**Red Square** (*in Moscow*) la place Rouge ►**red squirrel** écureuil *m* ►**redstart** (*Orn*) rouge-queue *m* ►**red tape** (*fig*) paperasserie *f*, bureaucratie *f* tatillonne, chinoiseries administratives ►**redwing** (*Orn*) mauvis *m* ►**redwood** (*Bot*) séquoia *m*.

redact [rɪ'dækt] vt (*draw up*) rédiger; (*edit*) éditer.

redaction [rɪ'dækʃən] n (*see* **redact**) rédaction *f*; édition *f*.

redden ['redn] 1 vt rendre rouge, rougir. 2 vi *[person]* rougir; *[foliage]* roussir, devenir roux.

reddish ['redɪʃ] adj rougeâtre. **~ hair** cheveux qui tirent vers *or* sur le roux.

redecorate [ˌriː'dekəreɪt] 1 vt *room, house* refaire, repeindre, retapisser. 2 vi refaire les peintures *or* les papiers peints.

redecoration [riːˌdekə'reɪʃən] n remise *f* à neuf des peintures, remplacement *m* des papiers peints.

redeem [rɪ'diːm] vt (*buy back*) racheter; (*from pawn*) dégager; (*Fin*) *debt* amortir, rembourser; *bill* honorer; *mortgage* purger; *insurance policy* encaissable; (*Comm*) *coupon, token* échanger (*for* contre); (*US*) *banknote* convertir en espèces; *promise* tenir; *obligation* s'acquitter de, satisfaire à; (*Rel*) *sinner* racheter, rédimer, sauver; (*compensate for*) *failing* racheter, compenser; *fault* réparer. **to ~ o.s.** *or* **one's honour** se racheter.

redeemable [rɪ'diːməbl] adj rachetable; *debt* amortissable; *bill* remboursable; *mortgage* remboursable, amortissable; *insurance policy* encaissable; (*from pawn*) qui peut être dégagé.

Redeemer [rɪ'diːmə^r] n (*Rel*) Rédempteur *m*.

redeeming [rɪ'diːmɪŋ] adj *quality* qui rachète les défauts. **it's a bad newspaper and its only ~ feature is that it is politically unbiased** c'est un mauvais journal qui ne se rachète que par son objectivité en politique *or* dont le seul bon côté est son objectivité en politique.

redefine [ˌriːdɪ'faɪn] vt (*gen*) redéfinir. **to ~ the problem** modifier les données du problème.

redemption [rɪ'dempʃən] n (*see* **redeem**) rachat *m*; dégagement *m*; amortissement *m*; remboursement *m*; purge *f*; (*Rel*) rédemption *f*. (*fig*) **beyond** *or* **past ~** *object* irréparable; *situation* irrémédiable; *person* qui ne peut plus être sauvé.

redemptive [rɪ'demptɪv] adj rédempteur (*f* -trice).

redeploy [ˌriːdɪ'plɔɪ] vt *troops* redéployer; *workers, staff* reconvertir; (*Econ*) *sector etc* redéployer.

redeployment [ˌriːdɪ'plɔɪmənt] n (*see* **redeploy**) redéploiement *m*; reconversion *f*.

redesign [ˌriːdɪ'zaɪn] vt reconcevoir.

redevelop [ˌriːdɪ'veləp] vt *area* rénover, réaménager.

redevelopment [ˌriːdɪ'veləpmənt] n *[area]* rénovation *f*, réaménagement *m*. **~ area** zone *f* de rénovation *or* de réaménagement.

redial [ˌriː'daɪəl] (*Telec*) 1 vt recomposer. 2 vi recomposer le numéro. 3 ['riːdaɪəl] n: **(automatic) ~ facility** rappel *m* du dernier numéro composé; **~ (button)** ≃ touche *f* bis.

redid [ˌriː'dɪd] pret of **redo**.

redirect [ˌriːdaɪ'rekt] vt *letter, parcel* faire suivre, réadresser; *funds, resources* réallouer; *traffic* dévier. **to ~ one's energies** réorienter *or* rediriger son énergie (*towards* vers).

rediscover [ˌriːdɪs'kʌvə^r] vt redécouvrir.

redistribute [ˌriːdɪs'trɪbjuːt] vt redistribuer.

redistrict [ˌriː'dɪstrɪkt] 1 vt (*US Pol, Admin*) soumettre à un redécoupage électoral (*or* administratif). 2 vi (*US Pol, Admin*) se soumettre à un redécoupage électoral (*or* administratif).

redistricting [ˌriː'dɪstrɪktɪŋ] n (*US Pol, Admin*) redécoupage électoral (*or* administratif).

redness ['rednɪs] n rougeur *f*; *[hair]* rousseur *f*.

redo [ˌriː'duː] pret **redid**, ptp **redone** vt refaire.

redolence ['redəʊləns] n parfum *m*, odeur *f* agréable.

redolent ['redəʊlənt] adj odorant, parfumé. **~ of lavender** qui sent la lavande; (*fig*) **~ of** qui évoque *or* suggère, évocateur (*f* -trice) de.

redone [ˌriː'dʌn] ptp of **redo**.

redouble [ˌriː'dʌbl] 1 vt a redoubler. **to ~ one's efforts** redoubler ses efforts *or* d'efforts. b (*Bridge*) surcontrer. 2 vi redoubler. 3 n (*Bridge*) surcontre *m*.

redoubt [rɪ'daʊt] n (*Mil*) redoute *f*.

redoubtable [rɪ'daʊtəbl] adj redoutable, formidable.

redound [rɪ'daʊnd] vi contribuer (*to* à). **to ~ upon** retomber sur; **to ~ to sb's credit** être (tout) à l'honneur de qn.

redraft [ˌriː'drɑːft] vt rédiger de nouveau.

redress [rɪ'dres] 1 vt *wrong, errors* redresser, réparer; *situation* redresser. **to ~ the balance** redresser *or* rétablir l'équilibre; **to ~ a grievance** réparer un tort. 2 n (*see* **1**) redressement *m*, réparation *f* (*also Jur*). **to seek ~ for** demander réparation de; **you have no ~** vous ne pouvez pas obtenir réparation.

reduce [rɪ'djuːs] 1 vt a (*lessen*) réduire (*to* à; *by sth* de qch), diminuer; (*shorten*) raccourcir; (*weaken*) affaiblir; (*lower*) abaisser, ravaler; *drawing, plan* réduire; *expenses* réduire, restreindre; *price* baisser, diminuer; (*Med*) *swelling* résorber, résoudre; *temperature* faire descendre, abaisser; (*Culin*) *sauce* faire réduire; (*Ind*) *output* ralentir; (*Mil etc: in rank*) rétrograder, réduire à un grade inférieur. (*Mil*) **to ~ to the ranks** casser; **to ~ unemployment** réduire le chômage; (*gradually*) résorber le chômage; (*Aut*) **to ~ speed** diminuer la vitesse, ralentir; **"~ speed now"** "ralentir"; (*Jur*) **to ~ a prisoner's sentence** réduire la peine d'un prisonnier; (*Comput*) **~d instruction set computer** ordinateur *m* à jeu d'instructions réduit; (*Comput*) **~d instruction set computing** traitement *m* avec jeu d'instructions réduit.

b (*Chem, Math, fig*) réduire (*to* en, à). **to ~ sth to a powder/to pieces/to ashes** réduire qch en poudre/en morceaux/en cendres; **to ~ an argument to its simplest form** réduire un raisonnement à sa plus simple expression, simplifier un raisonnement au maximum; **it has been ~d to nothing** cela a été réduit à zéro; **he's ~d to a skeleton** il n'est plus qu'un squelette ambulant; **to ~ sb to silence/obedience/despair** réduire qn au silence/à l'obéissance/au désespoir; **to ~ sb to begging/to slavery** réduire qn à la mendicité/en esclavage; **to be ~d to begging** être réduit *or* contraint à mendier; **to ~ sb to submission** soumettre qn; **to ~ sb to tears** faire pleurer qn; (*Admin, Jur*) **to ~ to writing** consigner par écrit.

2 vi (*slim*) maigrir. **to be reducing** être au régime.

reduced [rɪ'djuːst] adj réduit. **to buy at a ~ price** *rail, theatre ticket* acheter à prix réduit; *goods in shops* acheter au rabais *or* en solde; (*Comm*) **~ goods** soldes *mpl*; **it was ~, I couldn't resist (buying) it** c'était soldé *or* en solde, je n'ai pas pu y résister; (*on ticket*) **"~"** "prix réduit"; **on a ~ scale** à échelle réduite; (*fig*) sur une petite échelle, en petit; **in ~ circumstances** dans la gêne.

reducer [rɪˈdjuːsəʳ] n (*slimming device*) appareil *m* d'amaigrissement; (*Phot*) réducteur *m*.

reducible [rɪˈdjuːsəbl] adj réductible.

reductio ad absurdum [rɪˈdʌktɪəʊˌædəbˈsɜːdəm] n réduction *f* à l'absurde.

reduction [rɪˈdʌkʃən] n (*gen, Chem, Math etc*) réduction *f*; (*in length*) raccourcissement *m*; (*in width*) diminution *f*; *[expenses, staff]* réduction, compression *f*; *[prices, wages]* diminution, réduction, baisse *f*; *[temperature]* baisse; (*Elec: of voltage*) diminution; (*Jur: of sentence*) réduction, modération *f*; (*Med: of swelling*) résorption *f*, résolution *f*; (*Phot*) réduction *f*; (*Tech*) démultiplication *f*. (*Comm*) **to make a ~ on an article** faire une remise sur un article; (*Comm*) **this is a ~** c'est un rabais; **to sell sth at a ~** vendre qch au rabais; **~ for cash** escompte *m* au comptant; **~ of taxes** dégrèvement *m* d'impôts; **~ of speed** ralentissement *m*; (*Mil etc*) **~ in strength** réduction *or* diminution des effectifs; **~ in rank** rétrogradation *f*.

reductionism [rɪˈdʌkʃəˌnɪzəm] n a (*pej*) approche réductrice. b (*Philos*) réductionnisme *m*.

reductionist [rɪˈdʌkʃənɪst] 2 adj a (*pej*) réducteur. b (*Philos*) réductionniste. 2 n a (*pej*) personne *f* aux vues réductrices. b (*Philos*) réductionniste *mf*.

redundance [rɪˈdʌndəns] = **redundancy 1b, 1c**.

redundancy [rɪˈdʌndənsɪ] 1 n a (*Ind*) licenciement *m* (économique), mise *f* au *or* en chômage (technique). **it caused a lot of redundancies** cela a causé de nombreux licenciements *or* la mise au chômage de nombreux employés *or* beaucoup de chômage technique; **he feared ~** il redoutait d'être licencié *or* mis au chômage; **he went in the last round of redundancies** il a perdu son emploi lors de la dernière série de licenciements, il fait partie de la dernière charrette*; **compulsory ~** licenciement *m* sec; **voluntary ~** départ *m* volontaire.
b (*gen*) excès *m*, superfluité *f*, surabondance *f*.
c (*Literat*) redondance *f*, pléonasme *m*, tautologie *f*.
2 comp ►**redundancy payment** *or* **money** (*Brit Ind*) indemnité *f* de licenciement.

redundant [rɪˈdʌndənt] adj *object, example, detail* superflu; *style, word* redondant; (*Brit*) *person, helper, worker* en surnombre; (*Brit Ind: out of work*) au chômage (technique), qui a été licencié (pour raisons économiques). (*Brit Ind*) **to be made ~, to become ~** être licencié, être mis en chômage (technique); **he found himself ~** il s'est retrouvé au chômage.

reduplicate [rɪˈdjuːplɪkeɪt] 1 vt redoubler; (*Ling*) rédupliquer. 2 [rɪˈdjuːplɪkɪt] adj redoublé; rédupliqué.

reduplication [rɪˌdjuːplɪˈkeɪʃən] n redoublement *m*; (*Ling*) réduplication *f*.

reduplicative [rɪˈdjuːplɪkətɪv] adj (*Ling*) réduplicatif.

re-echo [riːˈekəʊ] 1 vi retentir, résonner (de nouveau *or* plusieurs fois). 2 vt répéter, renvoyer en écho.

reed [riːd] 1 n (*Bot*) roseau *m*; *[wind instrument]* anche *f*; (*liter: pipe*) chalumeau *m*, pipeau *m*. (*Mus*) **the ~s** les instruments *mpl* à anche; *see* **broken**. 2 comp *basket etc* de *or* en roseau(x) ►**reed bunting** (*Orn*) bruant *m* des roseaux ►**reed instrument** (*Mus*) instrument *m* à anche ►**reed stop** (*Mus*) jeu *m* d'anches *or* à anches.

re-educate [ˌriːˈedjʊkeɪt] vt rééduquer.

re-education [ˈriːˌedjʊˈkeɪʃən] n rééducation *f*.

reedy [ˈriːdɪ] adj *field, area* couvert de roseaux; (*fig*) *instrument, sound* nasillard, aigu (*f* -guë); *voice* flûté, ténu.

reef¹ [riːf] n a récif *m*, écueil *m*; (*fig*) écueil. **coral ~** récif de corail. b (*Min*) reef *m*, veine *f*, filon *m*.

reef² [riːf] 1 n (*Naut*) ris *m*. 2 vt (*Naut*) *sail* prendre un ris dans. 3 comp ►**reef knot** nœud *m* plat.

reefer [ˈriːfəʳ] n a (*jacket*) caban *m*. b (‡) joint‡ *m*, cigarette *f* de marijuana. c (*US* ‡: *truck etc*) camion *m* (*or* wagon *m*) frigorifique.

reek [riːk] 1 n puanteur *f*, relent *m*. 2 vi a (*smell*) puer, empester, sentir mauvais. **to ~ of sth** puer *or* empester qch. b (*Scot*) *[chimney]* fumer.

reel [riːl] 1 n a *[thread etc]* bobine *f*; (*Fishing*) moulinet *m*; (*Cine*) *[film]* bande *f*; (*Tech*) dévidoir *m*, touret *m*, bobine. (*US fig*) **off the ~*** d'une seule traite, d'affilée; *see* **inertia** *etc*.
b (*dance*) reel *m*, quadrille *m* écossais.
2 comp ►**reel holder** porte-bobines *m inv* ►**reel-to-reel** adj à bobines.
3 vt (*Tech*) *thread* bobiner.
4 vi chanceler, vaciller; *[drunken man]* tituber. **he ~ed back from the edge of the cliff** il s'est écarté en chancelant du bord de la falaise; **he went ~ing down the street** il a descendu la rue en vacillant *or* titubant; **the blow made him ~** le coup l'a fait chanceler, il a chancelé sous le coup; (*fig*) **the street ~ed before her eyes** la rue a vacillé *or* chaviré autour d'elle; (*fig*) **my head is ~ing** la tête me tourne; (*fig*) **the news made him** *or* **his mind ~** la nouvelle l'a ébranlé *or* bouleversé; (*fig*) **I ~ed at the very thought** cette pensée m'a donné le vertige.

►**reel in** vt sep (*Fishing, Naut*) ramener, remonter.

►**reel off** vt sep *verses, list* débiter; *thread* dévider.

►**reel up** vt sep enrouler.

re-elect [ˌriːɪˈlekt] vt réélire.

re-election [ˌriːɪˈlekʃən] n (*Pol*) **to stand** *or* **run** *or* **offer o.s. for ~**, (*US*) **face ~** se représenter.

re-embark [ˌriːɪmˈbɑːk] vti rembarquer.

re-embarkation [ˈriːˌembɑːˈkeɪʃən] n rembarquement *m*.

re-emerge [ˌriːɪˈmɜːdʒ] vi *[object, swimmer]* ressurgir; *[facts]* ressortir.

re-employ [ˌriːɪmˈplɔɪ] vt réembaucher.

re-enact [ˌriːɪˈnækt] vt a (*Jur*) remettre en vigueur. b *scene, crime* reconstituer, reproduire.

re-enactment [ˌriːɪˈnæktmənt] n *[law etc]* remise *f* en vigueur; *[crime]* reconstitution *f*.

re-engage [ˌriːɪnˈgeɪdʒ] vt *employee* rengager, réembaucher (*Ind*); (*Tech*) rengrener. (*Aut*) **to ~ the clutch** rembrayer.

re-engagement [ˌriːɪnˈgeɪdʒmənt] n (*see* **re-engage**) rengagement *m*, réembauchage *m* (*Ind*); rengrènement *m*.

re-enlist [ˌriːɪnˈlɪst] 1 vi se rengager. 2 vt rengager.

re-enter [ˌriːˈentəʳ] 1 vi a rentrer. b **to ~ for an exam** se représenter à *or* se réinscrire pour un examen. 2 vt rentrer dans. (*Space*) **to ~ the atmosphere** rentrer dans l'atmosphère.

re-entry [ˌriːˈentrɪ] n (*also Space*) rentrée *f*. (*Space*) **~ point** point *m* de rentrée; **~ permit** permis *m* de ré-entrée (*dans un pays où l'on voyage avec un visa*).

re-erect [ˌriːɪˈrekt] vt *building, bridge* reconstruire; *scaffolding, toy* remonter.

re-establish [ˌriːɪsˈtæblɪʃ] vt *order* rétablir; *person* réhabiliter; *custom* restaurer.

re-establishment [ˌriːɪsˈtæblɪʃmənt] n (*see* **re-establish**) rétablissement *m*; réhabilitation *f*; restauration *f*.

re-evaluate [ˌriːɪˈvæljʊeɪt] vt réévaluer.

reeve¹ [riːv] n (*Hist*) premier magistrat; (*Can*) président *m* du conseil municipal.

reeve² [riːv] vt (*Naut*) *rope* passer dans un anneau *or* une poulie, capeler; *shoal* passer au travers de.

re-examination [ˈriːɪgˌzæmɪˈneɪʃən] n nouvel examen; (*Jur: of witness*) nouvel interrogatoire.

re-examine [ˌriːɪgˈzæmɪn] vt examiner de nouveau; (*Jur*) *witness* interroger de nouveau.

re-export [ˌriːɪkˈspɔːt] 1 vt réexporter. 2 [ˌriːˈekspɔːt] n réexportation *f*.

ref¹ (*Comm*) (abbr of **with reference to**) *see* **reference**.

ref²* [ref] n (*Sport*) (abbr of **referee**) arbitre *m*.

refection [rɪˈfekʃən] n (*light meal*) collation *f*, repas léger; (*refreshment*) rafraîchissements *mpl*.

refectory [rɪˈfektərɪ] n réfectoire *m*. **~ table** table *f* de réfectoire.

refer [rɪˈfɜːʳ] 1 vt a (*pass*) *matter, question, file* soumettre (*to* à). **the problem was ~red to the U.N.** le problème a été soumis *or* renvoyé à l'O.N.U.; **the dispute was ~red to arbitration** le litige a été soumis à l'arbitrage; **it was ~red to us for (a) decision** on nous a demandé de prendre une décision là-dessus; **I have to ~ it to my boss** je dois le soumettre à *or* en parler à mon patron; **I ~red him to the manager** je lui ai dit de s'adresser au gérant, je l'ai renvoyé au gérant; **the doctor ~red me to a specialist** le docteur m'a adressé à un spécialiste; **to ~ sb to the article on ...** renvoyer qn à l'article sur ..., prier qn de se reporter *or* se référer à l'article sur ...; **"the reader is ~red to page 10"** "prière de se reporter *or* se référer à la page 10"; (*Banking*) **to ~ a cheque to drawer** refuser d'honorer un chèque; (*Med*) **~red pain** douleur *f* irradiée.
b (*Jur*) *accused* déférer.
c (*Univ*) *student* refuser. **his thesis has been ~red** on lui a demandé de revoir *or* de reprendre sa thèse.
d (*liter, frm: ascribe*) attribuer (*to* à); (*relate*) rattacher (*to* à).
2 vi a (*allude*) (*directly*) parler (*to* de), faire référence (*to* à); (*indirectly*) faire allusion (*to* à). **I am not ~ring to you** je ne parle pas de vous; **we shall not ~ to it again** nous n'en reparlerons pas, nous n'en parlerons plus; **he never ~s to that evening** il ne parle jamais de ce soir-là; **what can he be ~ring to?** de quoi parle-t-il?, à quoi peut-il bien faire allusion?; **he ~red to her as his assistant** il l'a appelée son assistante; (*Comm*) **~ring to your letter** (comme) suite *or* en réponse à votre lettre.
b (*apply*) s'appliquer (*to* à). **does that remark ~ to me?** est-ce que cette remarque s'applique à moi?; **this ~s to you all** cela vous concerne tous.
c (*consult*) se référer, se reporter (*to sth* à qch). **to ~ to one's notes** consulter ses notes, se référer *or* se reporter à ses notes; **"please ~ to section 3"** "prière de se reporter *or* se référer à la section 3"; **you must ~ to the original** vous devez vous référer *or* vous reporter à l'original; **he ~red to the manager** il a consulté le gérant, il en a référé au gérant.

►**refer back** vt sep *decision* remettre (à plus tard), ajourner. **to refer sth back to sb** consulter qn sur *or* au sujet de qch.

referable [rɪˈfɜːrəbl] adj attribuable (*to* à).

referee [ˌrefəˈriː] 1 n a (*Sport, also fig*) arbitre *m*. b (*Brit: giving a reference*) répondant(e) *m(f)*. **to act as** *or* **be ~ for sb** fournir des références *or* une attestation à qn; **to give sb as a ~** donner qn en référence; **may I give your name as a ~** puis-je donner votre nom en référence. 2 **vt** (*Sport, fig*) arbitrer. 3 **vi** (*Sport, fig*) servir d'arbitre, être arbitre.

reference ['refrəns] 1 **n** a (*NonC*) référence *f* (*to* à); *[question for judgment]* renvoi *m*; *[committee, tribunal]* compétence *f*. **outside the ~ of** hors de la compétence de; *see* **term**.

b (*allusion*) (*direct*) mention *f* (*to* de); (*indirect*) allusion *f* (*to* à). **a ~ was made to his illness** on a fait allusion à *or* on a fait mention de *or* on a parlé de sa maladie; **in** *or* **with ~ to** quant à, en ce qui concerne; (*Comm*) (comme) suite à; **without ~ to** sans tenir compte de, sans égard pour.

c (*testimonial*) **~(s)** références *fpl*; **to give sb a good ~** *or* **good ~s** fournir de bonnes références à qn; **a banker's ~** des références bancaires; **I've been asked for a ~ for him** on m'a demandé de fournir des renseignements sur lui.

d = **referee 1b**.

e (*in book, article: note redirecting reader*) renvoi *m*, référence *f*; (*on map*) coordonnées *fpl*; (*Comm: on letter*) référence. **please quote this ~** prière de rappeler cette référence; *see* **cross**.

f (*connection*) rapport *m* (*to* avec). **this has no ~ to ...** cela n'a aucun rapport avec ... .

g (*Ling*) référence *f*.

2 **comp** ►**reference book** ouvrage *m* de référence *or* à consulter ►**reference library** bibliothèque *f* d'ouvrages à consulter ►**reference mark** renvoi *m* ►**reference number** (*Comm*) numéro *m* de référence ►**reference point** point *m* de référence ►**reference strip** (*Phot*) bande *f* étalon.

3 **vt** a *quotation* référencer; *book* fournir les références de.

b (*refer to*) faire référence à.

referendum [ˌrefə'rendəm] **n, pl ~s** *or* **referenda** [ˌrefə'rendə] référendum *m*. **to hold a ~** organiser un référendum; **a ~ will be held** un référendum aura lieu.

referent ['refərənt] **n** référent *m*.

referential [ˌrefə'renʃəl] **adj** référentiel.

referral [rɪ'fɜːrəl] **n** (*see* **refer 1**) soumission *f*; (*Jur*) traduction *f*. (*Med*) **she got a ~ to a specialist** elle a été adressée à un spécialiste.

refill [ˌriː'fɪl] 1 **vt** *glass, bottle* remplir à nouveau; *pen, lighter* recharger. 2 ['riːfɪl] **n** (*gen*) recharge *f*; (*cartridge*) cartouche *f*; *[propelling pencil]* mine *f* de rechange; *[notebook]* feuilles *fpl* de rechange. (*of drink*) **would you like a ~*?** encore un verre (*or* une tasse)?

refine [rɪ'faɪn] 1 **vt** *ore* affiner; *oil* épurer; *crude oil, sugar* raffiner; *language* châtier; *manners* réformer; *taste* affiner; (*fig*) *essay etc* peaufiner*. 2 **vi**: **to ~ upon sth** raffiner sur qch.

refined [rɪ'faɪnd] **adj** a *crude oil, sugar* raffiné; *ore* affiné, pur; *oil* épuré. b *person* raffiné, cultivé; *style, taste* raffiné, fin.

refinement [rɪ'faɪnmənt] **n** a (*NonC: refining*) *[crude oil, sugar]* raffinage *m*; *[ore]* affinage *m*; *[oil]* épuration *f*. b (*NonC*) *[person]* raffinement *m*, délicatesse *f*; *[language, style]* raffinement, subtilité *f*, recherche *f*. c (*improvement: in technique, machine etc*) perfectionnement *m* (*in* de). (*fig*) **that is a ~ of cruelty** c'est la cruauté raffinée.

refiner [rɪ'faɪnəʳ] **n** *[crude oil, sugar]* raffineur *m*; *[metals]* affineur *m*; *[oil]* épureur *m*.

refinery [rɪ'faɪnərɪ] **n** *[crude oil, sugar]* raffinerie *f*; *[metals]* affinerie *f*.

refit [ˌriː'fɪt] 1 **vt** (*gen, ship etc*) remettre en état, réparer; *factory* équiper de nouveau, renouveler l'équipement de. 2 **vi** *[ship]* être réparé, être remis en état. 3 ['riːfɪt] **n** (*Naut*) réparation *f*, remise *f* en état, refonte *f*; *[factory]* nouvel équipement. **~ yard** chantier *m* de réarmement.

refitting [ˌriː'fɪtɪŋ] **n**, **refitment** [ˌriː'fɪtmənt] **n = refit 3**.

reflate [ˌriː'fleɪt] **vt** (*Econ*) relancer.

reflation [riː'fleɪʃən] **n** (*Econ*) relance *f*.

reflationary [riː'fleɪʃnərɪ] **adj** (*Econ*) de relance.

reflect [rɪ'flekt] 1 **vt** a (*throw back*) *heat, sound* renvoyer; *light, image* refléter; *[mirror]* réfléchir; (*fig*) (*gen*) refléter; *credit, discredit* faire rejaillir, faire retomber (*on* sur). **the moon is ~ed in the lake** la lune se reflète dans le lac; **I saw him ~ed in the mirror** j'ai vu son image dans le miroir *or* réfléchie par le miroir; **he saw himself ~ed in the mirror** le miroir a réfléchi *or* lui a renvoyé son image; **~ing prism** prisme réflecteur; (*fig*) **he basked** *or* **bathed in the ~ed glory of his friend's success** il se chauffait aux rayons de la gloire de son ami; **the many difficulties are ~ed in his report** son rapport reflète les nombreuses difficultés; **his music ~s his love for her** sa musique reflète *or* exprime *or* traduit son amour pour elle.

b (*think*) se dire, penser, se faire la réflexion (*that* que).

2 **vi** (*meditate*) réfléchir, méditer (*on* sur), penser (*on* à).

►**reflect (up)on** **vt fus** (*discredit*) *person* faire tort à; *reputation* nuire à, porter atteinte à; *motives, reasons* discréditer.

reflectingly [rɪ'flektɪŋlɪ] **adv = reflectively**.

reflection [rɪ'flekʃən] **n** a (*NonC: reflecting*) *[light, heat, sound]* réflexion *f*.

b (*image: in mirror etc*) reflet *m*, image *f*. **to see one's ~ in a mirror** voir son reflet dans un miroir; (*fig*) **a pale ~ of former glory** un pâle reflet de la gloire passée.

c (*NonC: consideration*) réflexion *f*. **on ~** (toute) réflexion faite, à la réflexion; **on serious ~** après mûre réflexion; **he did it without sufficient ~** il l'a fait sans avoir suffisamment réfléchi.

d (*thoughts, comments*) **~s** pensées *fpl*, réflexions *fpl*, remarques *fpl* (*on, upon* sur).

e (*adverse criticism*) critique *f* (*on* de), réflexion désobligeante (*on* sur); (*on sb's honour*) atteinte *f* (*on* à). **this is a ~ on your motives** cela fait douter de vos motifs; **this is no ~ on ...** cela ne porte pas atteinte à ... .

reflective [rɪ'flektɪv] **adj** a (*Phys etc*) *surface* réfléchissant, réflecteur (*f* -trice); *light* réfléchi. b *faculty, powers* de réflexion; *person* réfléchi. c (*indicative*): **~ of** qui reflète, révélateur (*f* -trice) de. d (*Gram*) = **reflexive**.

reflectively [rɪ'flektɪvlɪ] **adv** d'un air *or* d'un ton réfléchi *or* pensif, avec réflexion.

reflectiveness [rɪ'flektɪvnɪs] **n** caractère réfléchi.

reflector [rɪ'flektəʳ] **n** (*gen*) réflecteur *m*; (*Aut*) réflecteur, cataphote *m*.

reflex ['riːfleks] 1 **adj** (*Physiol, Psych, fig*) réflexe; (*Math*) *angle* rentrant; (*Phys*) réfléchi. (*Phot*) **~ (camera)** (appareil *m*) reflex *m*. 2 **n** réflexe *m*; *see* **condition**.

reflexion [rɪ'flekʃən] = **reflection**.

reflexive [rɪ'fleksɪv] (*Gram*) 1 **adj** réfléchi. 2 **n** verbe réfléchi.

reflexively [rɪ'fleksɪvlɪ] **adv** (*Gram*) au sens réfléchi, à la forme réfléchie.

reflexology [ˌriːflek'sɒlədʒɪ] **n** réflexologie *f*.

refloat [ˌriː'fləʊt] 1 **vt** *ship, business etc* renflouer, remettre à flot. 2 **vi** être renfloué, être remis à flot.

reflux ['riːflʌks] **n** reflux *m*.

reforestation [ˌriːfɒrɪs'teɪʃən] (*US*) **n = reafforestation**.

reform [rɪ'fɔːm] 1 **n** réforme *f*; *see* **land**. 2 **comp** *measures etc* de réforme ►**Reform Judaism** judaïsme *m* non orthodoxe ►**the Reform Laws** (*Brit Hist*) les lois *fpl* de réforme parlementaire ►**reform school** (*US*) maison *f* de redressement. 3 **vt** *law* réformer; *institutions, services* réformer, faire des réformes dans; *conduct* corriger; *person* faire prendre de meilleures habitudes à. **to ~ spelling** faire une réforme de *or* réformer l'orthographe. 4 **vi** *[person]* se réformer, se corriger, s'amender.

re-form [ˌriː'fɔːm] 1 **vt** a (*form again*) reformer, rendre sa première forme à; (*Mil*) *ranks* reformer; *troops* rallier, remettre en rangs. b (*give new form to*) donner une nouvelle forme à. 2 **vi** se reformer; (*Mil*) se reformer, se remettre en rangs, reprendre sa formation.

reformable [rɪ'fɔːməbl] **adj** réformable.

reformat [ˌriː'fɔːmæt] **vt** (*Comput*) reformater.

reformation [ˌrefə'meɪʃən] **n** (*NonC*) *[church, spelling, conduct]* réforme *f*; *[person]* retour *m* à une vie honnête *or* à une conduite meilleure. (*Hist*) **the R~** la Réforme, la Réformation.

reformative [rɪ'fɔːmətɪv] **adj** de réforme, réformateur (*f* -trice).

reformatory [rɪ'fɔːmətərɪ] **n** (*Brit* ††) maison *f* de correction *or* de redressement; (*US Jur*) centre *m* d'éducation surveillée.

reformed [rɪ'fɔːmd] **adj** a *behaviour, person* amendé. (*hum*) **he's a ~ character*** il s'est rangé *or* assagi. b (*Admin*) *spelling etc* réformé. c (*Rel*) *church* réformé; *Jew* non orthodoxe.

reformer [rɪ'fɔːməʳ] **n** réformateur *m*, -trice *f*.

reformist [rɪ'fɔːmɪst] **adj, n** réformiste (*mf*).

reformulate [riː'fɔːmjʊˌleɪt] **vt** reformuler.

refract [rɪ'frækt] **vt** réfracter.

refracting [rɪ'fræktɪŋ] **adj** (*Phys*) réfringent. **~ angle** angle *m* de réfringence; **~ telescope** lunette *f* d'approche.

refraction [rɪ'frækʃən] **n** réfraction *f*.

refractive [rɪ'fræktɪv] **adj** réfractif, réfringent. **~ index** indice *m* de réfraction.

refractometer [ˌriːfræk'tɒmɪtəʳ] **n** réfractomètre *m*.

refractor [rɪ'fræktəʳ] **n** a (*Phys*) milieu réfringent, dispositif *m* de réfraction. b (*telescope*) lunette *f* d'approche.

refractory [rɪ'fræktərɪ] **adj** *person* réfractaire, rebelle, insoumis; *disease* rebelle, opiniâtre; (*Chem, Miner*) réfractaire.

refrain[1] [rɪ'freɪn] **vi** se retenir, s'abstenir (*from doing* de faire). **he ~ed from comment** il s'est abstenu de tout commentaire; **they ~ed from measures leading to ...** ils se sont abstenus de toute mesure menant à ...; **I couldn't ~ from laughing** je n'ai pas pu m'empêcher de rire; **please ~ from smoking** (*on notice*) prière de ne pas fumer; (*spoken*) ayez l'obligeance de ne pas fumer.

refrain[2] [rɪ'freɪn] **n** (*Mus, Poetry, fig*) refrain *m*.

refrangible [rɪ'frændʒəbl] **adj** réfrangible.

refresh [rɪ'freʃ] **vt** *[drink, bath]* rafraîchir; *[food]* revigorer, redonner des forces à; *[sleep, rest etc]* délasser, détendre. **to ~ o.s.** (*with drink*) se rafraîchir; (*with food*) se restaurer; (*with sleep*) se reposer, se délasser; **to ~ one's memory** se rafraîchir la mémoire; **to ~ one's memory about sth** se remettre qch en mémoire; **let me ~ your memory!** je vais vous rafraîchir la mémoire!*; **to feel ~ed** se sentir revigoré.

refresher [rɪ'freʃəʳ] 1 **n** a *drink etc* boisson *f etc* pour se rafraîchir. b (*Jur*) honoraires *mpl* supplémentaires. 2 **comp** ►**refresher course** (*Univ etc*) cours *m* de recyclage.

refreshing [rɪˈfreʃɪŋ] adj *fruit, drink* rafraîchissant; *sleep* reposant, réparateur (*f* -trice); *sight, news* réconfortant; *change* agréable; *idea, approach, point of view* nouveau (*f* nouvelle), original, intéressant.
refreshingly [rɪˈfreʃɪŋlɪ] adv *different, frank* agréablement. ~ **new** frais et nouveau (*f* fraîche et nouvelle).
refreshment [rɪˈfreʃmənt] 1 n a *[mind, body]* repos *m*, délassement *m*. b (*food, drink*) (**light**) ~**s** rafraîchissements *mpl*; (*place*) ~**s** = ~ **room** (*see 2*). 2 comp ▸**refreshment bar** buvette *f* ▸**refreshment room** (*Rail*) buffet *m* ▸**refreshment stall** = **refreshment bar**.
refrigerant [rɪˈfrɪdʒərənt] adj, n réfrigérant (*m*); (*Med*) fébrifuge (*m*).
refrigerate [rɪˈfrɪdʒəreɪt] vt réfrigérer; (*in cold room etc*) frigorifier.
refrigeration [rɪˌfrɪdʒəˈreɪʃən] n réfrigération *f*; frigorification *f*.
refrigerator [rɪˈfrɪdʒəreɪtəʳ] 1 n (*cabinet*) réfrigérateur *m*, frigidaire *m* ®, frigo* *m*; (*room*) chambre *f* frigorifique; (*apparatus*) condenseur *m*. 2 comp *truck etc* frigorifique.
refrigeratory [rɪˈfrɪdʒərətərɪ] adj, n (*Chem*) réfrigérant (*m*).
refringent [rɪˈfrɪndʒənt] adj réfringent.
refuel [ˌriːˈfjʊəl] 1 vi se ravitailler en carburant *or* en combustible. 2 vt ravitailler.
refuelling [ˌriːˈfjʊəlɪŋ] n ravitaillement *m* (en carburant *or* en combustible). (*Aviat*) ~ **stop** escale *f* technique.
refuge [ˈrefjuːdʒ] n (*lit, fig*) refuge *m*, abri *m* (*from* contre); (*for climbers, pedestrians etc*) refuge. **place of** ~ asile *m*; **to seek** ~ chercher refuge *or* asile; (*lit, fig*) **to take** ~ **in** se réfugier dans; **to take** ~ **in lying** se réfugier dans les mensonges; **God is my** ~ Dieu est mon refuge.
refugee [ˌrefjʊˈdʒiː] n réfugié(e) *m(f)*. ~ **camp** camp *m* de réfugiés.
refulgence [rɪˈfʌldʒəns] n (*liter*) splendeur *f*, éclat *m*.
refulgent [rɪˈfʌldʒənt] adj (*liter*) resplendissant, éclatant.
refund [rɪˈfʌnd] 1 vt a rembourser (*to sb* à qn). **to** ~ **sb's expenses** rembourser qn de ses frais *or* dépenses; **to** ~ **postage** rembourser les frais de port. b (*Fin*) *excess payments* ristourner. 2 [ˈriːfʌnd] n remboursement *m*; (*Fin*) ristourne *f*. **tax** ~ bonification *f* de trop-perçu; **to get a** ~ se faire rembourser.
refundable [rɪˈfʌndəbl] adj remboursable.
refurbish [ˌriːˈfɜːbɪʃ] vt *building* réaménager, remettre à neuf; *furniture* remettre à neuf.
refurbishment [ˌriːˈfɜːbɪʃmənt] n remise *f* à neuf.
refurnish [ˌriːˈfɜːnɪʃ] vt remeubler.
refusal [rɪˈfjuːzəl] n refus *m* (*to do* de faire). (*Jur*) ~ **of justice** déni *m* de justice; **to get a** ~, **to meet with a** ~ se heurter à *or* essuyer un refus; **to give a flat** ~ refuser net; (*Equitation*) **3** ~**s** 3 refus; **to give** *or* **offer sb first** ~ **of sth** accorder à qn l'option sur qch; **to have (the) first** ~ **of sth** recevoir la première offre de qch, avoir le droit de préemption sur qch.
refuse[1] [rɪˈfjuːz] 1 vt (*gen*) refuser (*sb sth* qch à qn, *to do* de faire), se refuser (*to do* à faire); *offer, invitation* refuser, décliner; *request* refuser, rejeter, repousser. **I absolutely** ~ **to do it** je me refuse catégoriquement à le faire; **to be** ~**d** essuyer un refus; **to be** ~**d sth** se voir refuser qch; **they were** ~**d permission to leave** on leur a refusé *or* ils se sont vu refuser la permission de partir; **she** ~**d him** elle l'a rejeté; **she** ~**d his proposal** elle a rejeté son offre de mariage; *[horse]* **to** ~ **a fence** refuser l'obstacle. 2 vi refuser, opposer un refus; *[horse]* refuser l'obstacle.
refuse[2] [ˈrefjuːs] 1 n détritus *mpl*, ordures *fpl*; (*industrial or food waste*) déchets *mpl*. **household** ~ ordures ménagères; **garden** ~ détritus de jardin. 2 comp ▸**refuse bin** poubelle *f*, boîte *f* à ordures ▸**refuse chute** (*at dump*) dépotoir *m*; (*in building*) vide-ordures *m inv* ▸**refuse collection** ramassage *m* d'ordures ▸**refuse collector** éboueur *m* ▸**refuse destructor** incinérateur *m* (d'ordures) ▸**refuse disposal** traitement *m* des ordures; **refuse disposal service** service *m* de voirie; **refuse disposal unit** broyeur *m* d'ordures ▸**refuse dump** (*public*) décharge *f* (publique), dépotoir *m*; (*in garden*) monceau *m* de détritus ▸**refuse lorry** voiture *f* d'éboueurs.
refus(e)nik [rɪˈfjuːznɪk] n (*Pol*) refuznik *mf*.
refutable [rɪˈfjuːtəbl] adj réfutable.
refutation [ˌrefjʊˈteɪʃən] n réfutation *f*.
refute [rɪˈfjuːt] vt réfuter.
regain [rɪˈgeɪn] vt regagner; *health, one's sight* recouvrer; *territory* reconquérir; (*liter: arrive back at*) regagner. **to** ~ **one's strength** récupérer (ses forces); **to** ~ **consciousness** revenir à soi, reprendre connaissance; **to** ~ **lost time** regagner *or* rattraper le temps perdu; **to** ~ **one's footing** reprendre pied; **to** ~ **possession (of)** rentrer en possession (de).
regal [ˈriːgəl] adj royal; (*fig*) majestueux.
regale [rɪˈgeɪl] vt régaler (*sb with sth* qn de qch).
regalia [rɪˈgeɪlɪə] n *[monarch]* prérogatives *fpl* royales; (*insignia*) insignes royaux; *[Freemasons etc]* insignes. (*hum*) **she was in full** ~ elle était dans ses plus beaux atours *or* en grand tra-la-la*.
regally [ˈriːgəlɪ] adv (*lit, fig*) royalement.
regard [rɪˈgɑːd] 1 vt a (*look at*) regarder, observer, considérer; (*consider*) considérer, regarder (*as* comme), tenir (*as* pour). **to** ~ **with favour/horror** regarder d'un œil favorable/avec horreur; **we** ~ **it as worth doing** à notre avis ça vaut la peine de le faire; **we don't** ~ **it as necessary** nous ne le considérons pas comme nécessaire; (*frm*) **I** ~ **him highly** je le tiens en grande estime; **without** ~**ing his wishes** sans tenir compte de ses souhaits.
b (*concern*) concerner, regarder. **as** ~**s** ... pour *or* en ce qui concerne ..., pour ce qui regarde ... .
2 n a (*attention, concern*) attention *f*, considération *f*. **to pay** ~ **to, to have** ~ **for** tenir compte de; **to have** *or* **show little** ~ **for** faire peu de cas de; **to have** *or* **show no** ~ **for** ne faire aucun cas de; **without** ~ **to** *or* **for** sans égard pour; **out of** ~ **for** par égard pour; **having** ~ **to** si l'on tient compte de; **in this** *or* **that** ~ à cet égard, sous ce rapport; **with** *or* **in** ~ **to** pour *or* en ce qui concerne, quant à, relativement à.
b (*NonC: esteem*) respect *m*, estime *f*, considération *f*. (*frm*) **to hold sb/sth in high** ~ tenir qn/qch en haute estime; **to hold sb/sth in low** ~ tenir qn/qch en piètre estime; **to have a great** ~ **for sb** avoir beaucoup d'estime pour qn.
c (*in messages*) **give him my** ~**s** transmettez-lui mon bon *or* meilleur souvenir; **Paul sends his kind** ~**s** Paul vous envoie son bon souvenir; (*as letter-ending*) (**kindest**) ~**s** meilleurs souvenirs.
d (*liter: look*) regard *m*.
regardful [rɪˈgɑːdfʊl] adj: ~ **of** *feelings, duty* attentif à; *interests* soucieux de, soigneux de.
regarding [rɪˈgɑːdɪŋ] prep pour *or* en ce qui concerne, quant à, relativement à.
regardless [rɪˈgɑːdlɪs] 1 adj: ~ **of** *sb's feelings, fate* indifférent à; *future, danger* insouciant de; *sb's troubles* inattentif à; ~ **of consequences** sans se soucier des conséquences; ~ **of expense** *or* **cost** sans regarder à la dépense; ~ **of rank** sans distinction de rang. 2 adv (*) quand même. **he did it** ~ il l'a fait quand même.
regatta [rɪˈgætə] n (*one event*) régate *f*; (*regular event*) régates *fpl*. **to take part in a** ~ régater, prendre part à une régate.
regency [ˈriːdʒənsɪ] 1 n régence *f*. 2 comp ▸**Regency** *furniture, style* Régence (*anglaise*) *inv* (*1810-1820*).
regenerate [rɪˈdʒenəreɪt] 1 vt régénérer. 2 vi se régénérer. 3 [rɪˈdʒenərɪt] adj régénéré.
regeneration [rɪˌdʒenəˈreɪʃən] n régénération *f*.
regenerative [rɪˈdʒenərətɪv] adj régénérateur (*f* -trice).
regent [ˈriːdʒənt] n régent(e) *m(f)*; (*US Univ*) membre *m* du conseil d'université. **prince** ~ prince régent.
reggae [ˈregeɪ] n reggae *m*.
regicide [ˈredʒɪsaɪd] n (*person*) régicide *mf*; (*act*) régicide *m*.
régime [reɪˈʒiːm] n régime *m* (*politique etc*).
regimen [ˈredʒɪmen] n (*frm*) régime *m* (*médical*).
regiment [ˈredʒɪmənt] 1 n (*Mil, fig*) régiment *m*. 2 [ˈredʒɪment] vt (*fig*) imposer une discipline trop stricte à, enrégimenter.
regimental [ˌredʒɪˈmentl] 1 adj (*Mil*) *insignia, car* régimentaire; *traditions* du régiment. ~ **band** musique *f* du régiment; (*Mil*) ~ **sergeant-major** ≃ adjudant-chef *m*. 2 n (*Mil*) ~**s** uniforme *m*; **in full** ~**s** en grand uniforme, en grande tenue.
regimentation [ˌredʒɪmenˈteɪʃən] n (*pej*) discipline excessive.
regimented [ˈredʒɪmentɪd] adj *way of life, institution* enrégimenté. **they are too** ~ **at that college** la discipline est trop stricte dans ce collège.
region [ˈriːdʒən] n (*all senses*) région *f*. (*fig*) **the lower** ~**s** les enfers *mpl*; **in the** ~ **of 5 kg/10 francs** environ *or* dans les 5 kg/1 F, aux alentours de 5 kg/10 F.
regional [ˈriːdʒənl] adj régional. (*Admin, Ind*) ~ **development** ≃ aménagement *m* du territoire, action *f* régionale; (*Scot*) ~ **council** ≃ conseil *m* général.
regionalism [ˈriːdʒənəlɪzəm] n régionalisme *m*.
regionalist [ˈriːdʒənəlɪst] adj, n régionaliste (*mf*).
register [ˈredʒɪstəʳ] 1 n a (*gen*) registre *m*; (*of members etc*) liste *f*. (*Scol: also* **attendance** ~) registre *m* d'absences; **electoral** ~ liste électorale; ~ **of births, marriages and deaths** registre d'état civil.
b (*Tech: gauge of speed, numbers etc*) compteur *m*, enregistreur *m*; *see* **cash**.
c *[voice, organ etc]* registre *m*.
d (*Ling*) registre *m*. **it's the wrong** ~ ce n'est pas le bon registre.
e (*Typ*) registre *m*.
f (*US: air vent*) registre *m*.
g (*US: cash register*) caisse *f* (enregistreuse).
2 comp ▸**register ton** (*Naut*) tonneau *m* (de jauge).
3 vt a (*record formally*) *fact, figure* enregistrer; *birth, death, marriage* déclarer; *vehicle* (faire) immatriculer. **to** ~ **a trademark** déposer une marque de fabrique; **he is** ~**ed as disabled** il est officiellement reconnu comme handicapé; **he** ~**ed his disapproval by refusing** ... il a manifesté sa désapprobation en refusant ...; **to** ~ **a protest** protester; *see also* **registered**.
b (*take note of*) *fact* enregistrer; (*: *realize*) se rendre compte de, réaliser*. **I** ~**ed the fact that he had gone** je me suis rendu compte *or* j'ai réalisé* qu'il était parti.
c (*indicate*) *[machines] speed, quantity* indiquer, marquer; *rainfall* enregistrer; *temperature* marquer; *[face, expression] happiness, sorrow* exprimer, refléter. **he** ~**ed surprise** son visage *or* il a exprimé l'étonnement, il a paru étonné; **he** ~**ed no emotion** il n'a pas exprimé

d'émotion, il n'a pas paru ému.

d (*Post*) *letter* recommander; (*Rail*) *luggage* (faire) enregistrer. **to ~ one's luggage through to London** (faire) enregistrer ses bagages jusqu'à Londres; *see also* **registered**.

e (*Tech*) *parts* faire coïncider; (*Typ*) mettre en registre.

4 vi a (*on electoral list etc*) se faire inscrire, s'inscrire; (*in hotel*) s'inscrire sur *or* signer le registre. **to ~ with a doctor** se faire inscrire comme patient chez un médecin; **to ~ with the police** se déclarer à la police; **to ~ for military service** se faire recenser, se faire porter sur les tableaux de recensement; **to ~ for a course/for French literature** s'inscrire à un cours/en littérature française.

b (*Tech*) *[two parts of machine]* coïncider exactement; (*Typ*) être en registre.

c (*: *be understood*) être compris, pénétrer. **it hasn't ~ed (with him)** cela n'a pas encore pénétré, il n'a pas saisi, il n'a pas pigé‡; **her death hadn't ~ed with him** il n'avait pas vraiment réalisé qu'elle était morte.

registered ['redʒɪstəd] adj a *student, voter* inscrit; *vehicle* immatriculé; (*Brit Admin*) *nursing home, playgroup, charity* agréé par l'État, reconnu par les autorités. **~ charity** œuvre *f* de bienfaisance reconnue d'utilité publique; **~ company** société inscrite au tribunal de commerce; (*Brit*) **R~ General Nurse** ≃ infirmière *f* diplomée; **~ name** nom déposé; (*US*) **~ nurse** infirmière diplômée d'État; (*Fin*) **~ share** action *f* nominative; **~ shareholder** ≃ actionnaire inscrit; **~ stocks** actions *or* valeurs nominatives, titres nominatifs; **~ trademark** marque déposée; *see* **state**. b (*Post*) *letter* recommandé; (*Rail*) *luggage* enregistré. **by ~ post** par envoi recommandé.

registrar [ˌredʒɪ'strɑːʳ] n a (*Brit Admin*) officier *m* de l'état civil. **~'s office** bureau *m* de l'état civil; **to be married by the ~** se marier civilement *or* à la mairie. b (*Univ*) (*Brit*) secrétaire *m* (général); (*US*) chef *m* du service des inscriptions. c (*Brit Med*) chef *m* de clinique. d (*Jur*) (*in court*) greffier *m*. (*Fin*) **(companies')** ~ conservateur *m* (du registre des sociétés).

registration [ˌredʒɪ'streɪʃən] 1 n a (*gen*: *see* **register**) enregistrement *m*, inscription *f*; *[trademark]* dépôt *m*. b (*Post*) *[letter]* recommandation *f*; (*Rail*) *[luggage]* enregistrement *m*. c (*Brit Scol*: *also* **~ period**) l'appel *m*. 2 comp ▸ **registration document** (*Brit Aut*) ≃ carte grise ▸ **registration car**: (*Brit*) **an E** *etc* **registration car** un modèle de 1968 *etc* ▸ **registration fee** (*Post*) taxe *f* de recommandation; (*Rail*: *for luggage*) frais *mpl* d'enregistrement; (*Univ*) droits *mpl* d'inscription ▸ **registration number** (*Brit Aut*) numéro *m* minéralogique *or* d'immatriculation; **car (with) registration number K971 VBW** voiture immatriculée K971 VBW.

registry ['redʒɪstrɪ] 1 n (*act*) enregistrement *m*, inscription *f*; (*office*) (*gen*) bureau *m* de l'enregistrement; (*Brit Admin*) bureau de l'état civil; (*Naut*) certificat *m* d'immatriculation. (*Naut*) **port of ~** port *m* d'attache. 2 comp ▸ **registry office** (*Brit*) bureau *m* de l'état civil; **to get married in a registry office** se marier civilement *or* à la mairie.

regius ['riːdʒəs] adj (*Brit Univ*) **~ professor** professeur *m* (*titulaire d'une chaire de fondation royale*).

regnal ['regnl] adj: **~ year** année *f* du règne.

regnant ['regnənt] adj régnant. **queen ~** reine *f* régnante.

regorge [rɪ'gɔːdʒ] 1 vt vomir, régurgiter. 2 vi refluer.

regress [rɪ'gres] 1 vi a (*Bio, Psych, fig*) régresser (*to* au stade de), rétrograder. b (*move backwards*) retourner en arrière, reculer. 2 ['riːgres] n = **regression**.

regression [rɪ'greʃən] n (*lit*) retour *m* en arrière, recul *m*; (*Bio, Psych, fig*) régression *f*.

regressive [rɪ'gresɪv] adj régressif. **~ tax** impôt *m* dégressif, taxe *f* dégressive.

regret [rɪ'gret] 1 vt regretter (*doing, to do* de faire; *that* que + *subj*); *mistake, words, event* regretter, être désolé *or* navré de; *one's youth, lost opportunity* regretter. **I ~ to say that** ... j'ai le regret de dire que ...; **he is very ill, I ~ to say** il est très malade, hélas *or* je regrette de le dire; **we ~ to hear that** ... nous sommes désolés d'apprendre que ...; **we ~ that it was not possible to** ... (*gen*) nous sommes désolés de n'avoir pu ...; (*Comm*) nous sommes au regret de vous informer qu'il n'a pas été possible de ...; **it is to be ~ted that** ... il est regrettable que ... + *subj*; **you won't ~ it!** vous ne le regretterez pas!; (*frm*) **the President ~s he cannot see you today** le Président est au regret *or* exprime ses regrets de ne pouvoir vous recevoir aujourd'hui; **he is much ~ted** on le regrette beaucoup.

2 n regret *m* (*for* de). **much to my ~** à mon grand regret; **I have no ~s** je ne regrette rien, je n'ai aucun regret; **to do sth with ~** (*sadly*) faire qch avec regret; (*against one's wishes*) faire qch à regret *or* à contrecœur; **to send ~s** envoyer ses regrets; **please give her my ~s that I cannot come** dites-lui, s'il vous plaît, combien je regrette de ne pouvoir venir.

regretful [rɪ'gretfʊl] adj *person* plein de regrets; *look, attitude* de regret.

regretfully [rɪ'gretfəlɪ] adv (*sadly*) avec regret; (*unwillingly*) à regret, à contrecœur.

regrettable [rɪ'gretəbl] adj regrettable, fâcheux. **it is ~ that** il est à regretter *or* regrettable *or* fâcheux que + *subj*.

regrettably [rɪ'gretəblɪ] adv *late, poor* fâcheusement. **~, he refused** malheureusement, il a refusé.

regroup [ˌriː'gruːp] 1 vt regrouper. 2 vi se regrouper; (*fig*) se ressaisir.

regrouping [ˌriː'gruːpɪŋ] n regroupement *m*.

regs‡ [regz] npl (abbr of **regulations**) règlement *m*.

Regt. abbr of **Regiment**.

regular ['regjʊləʳ] 1 adj a (*symmetrical*) régulier, symétrique; (*Math*) *figure* régulier; (*even*) *surface* uni. **~ features** traits réguliers, visage régulier.

b (*recurring at even intervals*) *pulse, breathing, footsteps, reminders, periods* régulier. **at ~ intervals** à intervalles réguliers; **there is a ~ bus service to town** il y a un service régulier d'autobus allant en ville; **to be ~ in one's habits** être régulier dans ses habitudes; **~ way of life** vie régulière *or* réglée; **to keep ~ hours** mener une vie réglée; **he is as ~ as clockwork** il est très ponctuel, il est réglé comme une horloge; **his visits are as ~ as clockwork** ses visites sont très régulières, ses visites sont réglées comme du papier à musique*; **he has no ~ employment** il est sans emploi régulier; (*Med*) **~ bowel movements** selles régulières.

c (*habitual*) habituel, normal, ordinaire; (*Comm*) *size* ordinaire, standard *inv*; *price* normal, courant; *listener, reader* fidèle. **the ~ staff** le personnel permanent; **our ~ cleaning woman** notre femme de ménage habituelle; **my ~ dentist** mon dentiste habituel; **my ~ doctor** mon médecin traitant; **his ~ time for getting up** l'heure à laquelle il se lève habituellement *or* normalement; (*US*) **~ gas** essence *f* (ordinaire).

d (*permissible, accepted*) *action, procedure* régulier, en règle. **to make ~** régulariser; **it is quite ~ to apply in person** il est tout à fait normal *or* régulier de faire sa demande en personne.

e (*Mil*) (*not conscripted*) *soldier, army* de métier; *officer* de carrière; (*not territorial*) d'active. **the ~ police force** la police de métier.

f (*Ling*) régulier.

g (*Rel*) **~ clergy** clergé régulier.

h (*) vrai, véritable. **he's a ~ idiot** c'est un imbécile fini; (*US*) **~ guy** chic type* *m*.

2 n a (*Mil*) soldat *m* de métier; (*police officer*) policier *m* (de métier).

b (*habitual customer etc*) habitué(e) *m(f)*, bon(ne) client(e) *m(f)*. (*Rad, TV*) **he's one of the ~s on that programme** il participe *or* prend part régulièrement à ce programme.

c (*Rel*) régulier *m*, religieux *m*.

d (*US*: *gas*) essence *f* (ordinaire), ordinaire *m*.

regularity [ˌregjʊ'lærɪtɪ] n régularité *f*.

regularize ['regjʊləraɪz] vt régulariser.

regularly ['regjʊləlɪ] adv régulièrement.

regulate ['regjʊleɪt] vt a (*control systematically*) *amount, flow* régler; *expenditure* régler, calculer. **to ~ one's life by** se régler sur; **a well-~d life** une vie bien réglée. b *machine* régler, ajuster.

regulation [ˌregjʊ'leɪʃən] 1 n (*rule*) règlement *m*; (*Admin*) règlement, arrêté *m*. **against ~s** contraire au règlement; *see* **fire, safety**. 2 comp *style, size* réglementaire ▸ **regulation boots** (*Mil*) brodequins *mpl* d'ordonnance ▸ **regulation dress** (*Mil*) tenue *f* réglementaire.

regulative ['regjʊlətɪv] adj régulateur (*f* -trice).

regulator ['regjʊleɪtəʳ] n (*person*) régulateur *m*, -trice *f*; (*instrument*) régulateur *m*. **acidity ~** correcteur *m* d'acidité.

Regulo ['regjʊləʊ] n ®: **~ (mark) 6** *etc* thermostat 6 *etc*.

regurgitate [rɪ'gɜːdʒɪteɪt] 1 vt *[person]* régurgiter, rendre; *[drainpipe etc]* dégorger. 2 vi refluer.

regurgitation [rɪˌgɜːdʒɪ'teɪʃən] n régurgitation *f*.

rehab‡ ['riːhæb] n (*US*) *[drug user, alcoholic]* abbr of **rehabilitation**.

rehabilitate [ˌriːə'bɪlɪteɪt] vt *the disabled* (*to everyday life*) rééduquer; (*to work*) réadapter; *refugees* réadapter; *demobilized troops* réintégrer (dans la vie civile); *ex-prisoner* réinsérer; *drug user, alcoholic* désintoxiquer; *disgraced person, sb's memory* réhabiliter.

rehabilitation ['riːəˌbɪlɪ'teɪʃən] n (*see* **rehabilitate**) rééducation *f*; réadaptation *f*; réintégration *f* (dans la vie civile); réinsertion *f*; désintoxication *f*; réhabilitation *f*. (*Admin*) **~ centre** centre *m* de réadaptation.

rehash [ˌriː'hæʃ] 1 vt *literary material etc* remanier, réarranger. 2 ['riːhæʃ] n réchauffé *m*, resucée* *f*.

rehearsal [rɪ'hɜːsəl] n a (*Theat*) répétition *f*. **this play is in ~** on répète cette pièce; *see* **dress**. b (*NonC*) *[facts etc]* énumération *f*, récit détaillé.

rehearse [rɪ'hɜːs] vt (*Theat*) répéter; (*gen*) *facts, grievances* réciter, énumérer, raconter en détail. **to ~ what one is going to say** préparer ce qu'on va dire; **well ~d** *play etc* répété avec soin; *actor* qui a soigneusement répété son texte; (*fig*) *intervention, protest etc* soigneusement étudié.

reheat [ˌriː'hiːt] vt réchauffer.

rehouse [ˌriː'haʊz] vt reloger.

reign [reɪn] 1 n (*lit, fig*) règne *m*. **in the ~ of** sous le règne de; (*Hist*) **the R~ of Terror** la Terreur; (*fig*) **~ of terror** régime *m* de terreur. 2 vi (*lit, fig*) régner (*over* sur). **silence ~s** le silence règne; **to ~ supreme** *[monarch etc]* régner en *or* être le maître absolu; *[champion etc]* être sans rival; *[justice, peace]* régner en souverain(e).

reigning ['reɪnɪŋ] adj *monarch* régnant; *king, queen* présent, actuel (*before noun*); *champion* actuel; (*fig*) *attitude* regnant, en vogue.

reimburse [ˌriːɪm'bɜːs] vt rembourser (*sb for sth* qch à qn, qn de qch). **to ~ sb (for) his expenses** rembourser qn de ses dépenses.

reimbursement [ˌriːɪm'bɜːsmənt] n remboursement *m*.

reimpose [ˌriːɪm'pəʊz] vt réimposer.

rein [reɪn] n (*often pl: lit, fig*) rêne *f*; *[horse in harness]* guide *f*. *[child]* **~s** rênes; (*lit, fig*) **to hold the ~s** tenir les rênes; (*lit, fig*) **to keep a ~ on** tenir en bride; (*lit, fig*) **to keep a tight ~ on** *person* tenir la bride haute *or* serrée à; *expenses* surveiller étroitement; (*fig*) **to give (a) free ~ to** *anger, passions, one's imagination* donner libre cours à.

►**rein back** 1 vt sep *horse* faire reculer. 2 vi reculer.

►**rein in** 1 vi (*fig*) ralentir. 2 vt sep *horse* serrer la bride à, ramener au pas; (*fig*) *passions* contenir, maîtriser.

►**rein up** vi s'arrêter.

reincarnate [ˌriːɪn'kɑːneɪt] 1 vt réincarner. 2 adj réincarné.

reincarnation [ˌriːɪnkɑː'neɪʃən] n réincarnation *f*.

reindeer ['reɪndɪəʳ] n, pl ~ *or* ~s renne *m*.

reinforce [ˌriːɪn'fɔːs] vt (*Mil*) renforcer; (*gen*) *wall, bridge, heel* renforcer; *beam* armer, renforcer; *one's demands etc* appuyer. **~d concrete** béton armé.

reinforcement [ˌriːɪn'fɔːsmənt] 1 n a (*action*) renforcement *m*; (*thing*) renfort *m*. b (*Mil: action*) renforcement *m*. (*also fig*) **~s** renforts *mpl*. 2 comp *troops, supplies* de renfort.

reinsert [ˌriːɪn'sɜːt] vt réinsérer.

reinstate [ˌriːɪn'steɪt] vt *employee* réintégrer, rétablir dans ses fonctions; *text* rétablir (*in* dans).

reinstatement [ˌriːɪn'steɪtmənt] n réintégration *f*, rétablissement *m*.

reinstitute [ˌriː'ɪnstɪtjuːt] vt rétablir.

reinstitution [ˌriːɪnstɪ'tjuːʃən] n rétablissement *m*.

reinsurance [ˌriːɪn'ʃʊərəns] n réassurance *f*; *[underwriter etc, against possible losses]* contre-assurance *f*.

reinsure [ˌriːɪn'ʃʊəʳ] vt (*see* **reinsurance**) réassurer; contracter une contre-assurance sur.

reintegrate [ˌriː'ɪntɪgreɪt] vt réintégrer.

reintegration [ˌriːɪntɪ'greɪʃən] n réintégration *f*.

reinvest [ˌriːɪn'vest] vt (*Fin*) réinvestir.

reinvestment [ˌriːɪn'vestmənt] n (*Fin*) nouveau placement, nouvel investissement.

reinvigorate [ˌriːɪn'vɪgəreɪt] vt revigorer.

reissue [ˌriː'ɪʃjuː] 1 vt *book* donner une nouvelle édition de, rééditer; *film* ressortir, redistribuer. 2 n (*act*) réédition *f*; redistribution *f*. **it is a ~** *[book]* il a été réédité; *[film]* il est ressorti.

reiterate [riː'ɪtəreɪt] vt réitérer, répéter.

reiteration [riːˌɪtə'reɪʃən] n réitération *f*, répétition *f*.

reiterative [riː'ɪtərətɪv] adj réitératif.

reject [rɪ'dʒekt] 1 vt a (*gen*) rejeter, repousser; *damaged goods etc* *[customer, shopkeeper]* refuser; *[maker, producer]* mettre au rebut; *suitor* repousser, éconduire; *candidate, manuscript* refuser; *offer, proposal, application* rejeter; *plea, advances* repousser; *possibility* rejeter, repousser; *coins [machine]* refuser. b (*Med*) *[body] medicament, transplant* rejeter. c (*Comput*) rejeter. 2 ['riːdʒekt] n a (*Comm*) pièce *f or* article *m* de rebut; *see* **export**. b (*Comput*) rejet *m*. 3 ['riːdʒekt] comp (*Comm, Ind*) *goods* de rebut ► **reject shop** boutique *f* (d'articles) de second choix.

rejection [rɪ'dʒekʃən] 1 n refus *m*; rejet *m*; (*Med*) rejet *m*. 2 comp ► **rejection slip** (*Publishing*) lettre *f* de refus.

rejig* [riː'dʒɪg], (*US*) **rejigger*** [riː'dʒɪgəʳ] vt réorganiser, réarranger.

rejoice [rɪ'dʒɔɪs] 1 vt réjouir, ravir, enchanter. (*frm, liter*) **it ~d his heart to see ...** il s'est félicité du fond du cœur de voir ... . 2 vi se réjouir, être ravi, être enchanté (*at, over* de). **to ~ in sth** jouir de qch, posséder qch; (*hum, iro*) **he ~s in the name of Marmaduke** il a le privilège de s'appeler Marmaduke (*iro*).

rejoicing [rɪ'dʒɔɪsɪŋ] n a (*NonC*) réjouissance *f*, jubilation *f*. b **~s** réjouissances *fpl*, fête *f*.

rejoin[1] [ˌriː'dʒɔɪn] 1 vt *person, army* rejoindre. (*Naut*) **to ~ ship** rallier le bord; **the road ~s the motorway** la route rejoint l'autoroute. 2 vi se rejoindre.

rejoin[2] [rɪ'dʒɔɪn] vi (*reply*) répliquer, répondre.

rejoinder [rɪ'dʒɔɪndəʳ] n réplique *f*, repartie *f*, riposte *f*; (*Jur*) réplique *f*, réponse *f* à une réplique.

rejuvenate [rɪ'dʒuːvɪneɪt] vti rajeunir.

rejuvenating [rɪ'dʒuːvɪneɪtɪŋ] adj rajeunissant.

rejuvenation [rɪˌdʒuːvɪ'neɪʃən] n rajeunissement *m*.

rekindle [ˌriː'kɪndl] 1 vt *fire* rallumer, attiser; (*fig*) *hope, enthusiasm* ranimer, raviver. 2 vi se rallumer; se ranimer.

relapse [rɪ'læps] 1 n (*Med, fig*) rechute *f*. **to have a ~** avoir *or* faire une rechute, rechuter. 2 vi (*gen*) retomber (*into* dans); *[invalid]* rechuter.

relate [rɪ'leɪt] 1 vt a (*recount*) *story* raconter, relater, faire le récit de; *details* rapporter. **strange to ~ ...** chose curieuse (à dire) ... . b (*associate*) établir un rapport entre, rapprocher; *breeds* apparenter; (*to a category*) rattacher, lier. **it is often difficult to ~ the cause to the effect** il est souvent difficile d'établir un rapport de cause à effet *or* d'établir un lien entre la cause et l'effet *or* de rattacher l'effet à la cause.

2 vi a (*refer*) se rapporter, toucher (*to* à).

b (*Psych*) **to ~ to sb** (*form relationship*) établir des rapports avec qn; (*maintain relationship*) entretenir des rapports avec qn; **how do you ~ to your parents?** quels rapports entretenez-vous avec vos parents?; **he doesn't ~ to other people** il n'a pas le sens des contacts; **women ~ more to this than men** les femmes se sentent plus concernées par ça que les hommes; **I can ~ to that*** je comprends ça.

related [rɪ'leɪtɪd] 1 adj a (*in family*) apparenté, allié (*to* à), parent (*to* de). **she is ~ to us** elle est notre parente; **to be closely/distantly ~** être proche parent/parent éloigné; **~ by marriage to** parent par alliance de, allié à.

b (*connected*) (*Chem*) apparenté; (*Philos*) connexe; (*Mus*) relatif. **French is ~ to Spanish** le français est parent de l'espagnol; **geometry and other ~ subjects** la géométrie et les sujets connexes *or* qui s'y rattachent; *[fact, incident etc]* **to be ~ to** avoir rapport à; **the facts are certainly ~** les faits sont certainement liés; **the incidents are not ~** ces incidents n'ont pas de lien entre eux *or* n'ont aucun rapport (entre eux).

2 **-related** adj ending in comps qui est lié à; **health-related problems** problèmes liés à la santé; **earnings-related pensions** retraites *fpl* ramenées au salaire.

relating [rɪ'leɪtɪŋ] adj: **~ to** concernant, relatif à.

relation [rɪ'leɪʃən] n a (*family: person*) parent(e) *m(f)*; (*kinship*) parenté *f*. **I've got some ~s coming to dinner** j'ai de la famille à dîner; **is he any ~ to you?** est-il de vos parents?; **he is no ~ (of mine *or* to me)** il n'est pas de ma famille, il n'y a aucun lien de parenté *or* aucune parenté entre nous; **what ~ is she to you?** quelle est sa parenté avec vous?

b (*relationship*) rapport *m*, relation *f*. **to bear a ~ to** avoir rapport à; **to bear no ~ to** n'avoir aucun rapport avec, être sans rapport avec; **in ~ to** par rapport à, relativement à; **~s** relations, rapports; (*personal ties*) rapports; **to have business ~s with** être en rapports *or* relations d'affaires avec; **diplomatic/friendly/international ~s** relations diplomatiques/d'amitié/internationales; **~s are rather strained** les relations *or* les rapports sont assez tendu(e)s; **sexual ~s** rapports (sexuels); *see* **public**.

c (*telling*) *[story]* récit *m*, relation *f*; *[details]* rapport *m*.

relational [rɪ'leɪʃənl] adj (*gen, Ling*) relationnel.

relationship [rɪ'leɪʃənʃɪp] n a (*family ties*) liens *mpl* de parenté. **what is your ~ to him?** quels sont les liens de parenté entre vous?, quels sont vos liens de parenté avec lui?

b (*connection*) rapport *m*; (*relations*) relations *fpl*, rapports; (*personal ties*) rapports. **to see a ~ between 2 events** voir un rapport *or* un lien entre 2 événements; **to have a ~ with sb** (*general*) avoir des relations *or* être en relations avec qn; (*sexual*) avoir une liaison avec qn; **he has a good ~ with his clients** il est en bons rapports avec ses clients; **they have a good ~** ils s'entendent bien; **friendly/business ~** relations d'amitié/d'affaires; **his ~ with his father was strained** ses rapports avec son père étaient tendus; **the ~ between mother and child** les rapports entre la mère et l'enfant.

relative ['relətɪv] 1 adj a (*comparative*) relatif; (*respective*) respectif. **happiness is ~** le bonheur est relatif; **petrol consumption is ~ to speed** la consommation d'essence est fonction de *or* relative à la vitesse; **there is a shortage of labour ~ to demand** il y a une pénurie de main d'œuvre par rapport à la demande; **to live in ~ luxury** vivre dans un luxe relatif; **the ~ merits of A and B** les mérites respectifs de A et de B; *see* **humidity**.

b (*relevant*) **~ to** relatif à, qui se rapporte à; **the documents ~ to the problem** les documents relatifs au *or* qui se rapportent au problème.

c (*Gram, Mus*) relatif. (*Gram*) **~ clause** (proposition *f*) relative *f*; (*Gram*) **~ conjunction** conjonction *f* de subordination; (*Gram*) **~ pronoun** pronom relatif; (*Mus*) **~ major/minor (key)** (ton) majeur/mineur relatif.

2 n a (*person*) parent(e) *m(f)*. **one of my ~s** un(e) parent(e) à moi, un membre de ma famille; **all my ~s came** toute ma famille est venue.

b (*Gram*) relatif *m*.

relatively ['relətɪvlɪ] adv (*see* **relative**) relativement; respectivement; (*fairly, rather*) assez. **~ speaking** relativement parlant.

relativism ['relətɪvɪzəm] n relativisme *m*.

relativist ['relətɪvɪst] adj, n relativiste (*mf*).

relativistic [ˌrelətɪ'vɪstɪk] adj relativiste.

relativity [ˌrelə'tɪvɪtɪ] n (*gen, Ling, Philos, Phys*) relativité *f*. **theory of ~** théorie *f* de la relativité.

relativization [ˌrelətɪvaɪ'zeɪʃən] n relativisation *f*.

relativize ['relətɪvaɪz] vt relativiser.

relax [rɪ'læks] 1 vt *hold, grip* relâcher, desserrer; (*Med*) *bowels* relâcher; *muscles* relâcher, décontracter, relaxer; *discipline, attention, effort* relâcher; *restrictions* modérer; *measures, tariffs* assouplir; *person,* *one's mind* détendre, délasser; *see also* **relaxed.** 2 **vi** a (*rest*) se détendre, se délasser, se relaxer. (*: *calm down*) **let's just ~!** restons calmes!, ne nous énervons pas!, du calme! b (*see* **1**) se relâcher; se desserrer; se décontracter.

relaxant [rɪ'læksənt] **n** décontractant *m*. **muscle ~** décontractant *m* musculaire.

relaxation [ˌriːlæk'seɪʃən] **n** a (*NonC*) *[muscles, discipline, attention]* relâchement *m*; *[mind]* détente *f*, relaxation *f*; *[body]* décontraction *f*, relaxation; *[restriction, measures, tariffs]* assouplissement *m*. (*Jur*) **measures of ~** mesures *fpl* d'assouplissement. b (*recreation*) détente *f*, délassement *m*; (*rest*) repos *m*. **you need some ~ after work** on a besoin d'une détente après le travail; **books are her ~** pour se délasser *or* se détendre elle lit; **the ~s of the wealthy** les distractions *fpl* des riches.

relaxed [rɪ'lækst] **adj** *discipline, effort, attention* relâché; *muscle etc* relâché, relaxé; *smile, voice, attitude* détendu. (*Med*) **~ throat** gorge irritée *or* enflammée; **to feel ~** se sentir détendu *or* décontracté; (*fig: don't feel strongly one way or other*) **I feel fairly ~ about it*** ça m'est égal, ça ne me fait ni chaud ni froid*.

relaxing [rɪ'læksɪŋ] **adj** *climate* reposant, amollissant (*pej*), débilitant (*pej*); *atmosphere, activity* délassant, relaxant, qui procure de la *or* une détente.

relay ['riːleɪ] 1 **n** a *[horses, men etc]* relais *m*. **to work in ~s** travailler par relais, se relayer. b (*Rad, TV*) émission relayée. c (*Sport*) = **relay race**; *see* **2.** d (*Elec, Phys, Tech*) relais *m*. 2 **comp** ▸**relay race** course *f* de relais ▸**relay station** (*Rad, TV*) relais *m*. 3 **vt** (*Elec, Rad, TV etc*) *programme, signal, message* relayer, retransmettre. **to ~ each other** se relayer.

re-lay [ˌriː'leɪ] **vt pret, ptp re-laid** *carpet* reposer.

release [rɪ'liːs] 1 **n** a (*NonC*) (*from captivity*) libération *f*; (*from prison*) libération, élargissement *m* (*frm*); (*Jur: from custody*) relaxe *f*; (*from obligation, responsibility*) libération; (*from service*) dispense *f*, exemption *f*; (*Comm: from customs, bond*) congé *m*. **on his ~ from prison he ...** dès sa sortie de prison, il ...; **the ~ of the prisoners by the allied forces** la libération des prisonniers par les forces alliées; **death was a happy ~ for him** pour lui la mort a été une délivrance; (*Fin, Econ, Jur*) **~ of appropriation** déblocage *m* de crédit.

b (*NonC*) (*Comm*) *[goods]* mise *f* en vente; *[news]* autorisation *f* de publier; *[film, record]* sortie *f*; *[book]* parution *f*, sortie. **this film is now on general ~** ce film n'est plus en exclusivité.

c (*Comm: sth just brought out*) **new ~** (*record*) nouveau disque *m*; (*film*) nouveau film *m*; (*book*) nouveauté *f*; (*video*) nouvelle vidéo *f*; (*CD*) nouveau (disque *m*) compact *m*; **their latest ~** leur dernier disque (*or* film *etc*); *see* **press 2.**

d (*NonC*) *[bomb]* lâchage *m*, largage *m*; (*Phot etc*) déclenchement *m*; *[brake]* dégagement *m*, desserrage *m*; *[steam]* échappement *m*. **~ valve** soupape *f* de sûreté.

e (*also* **~ switch/button**) touche *f* de déclenchement.

2 **comp** *switch, knob, catch etc* de déclenchement *or* de sortie *etc* ▸**release print** (*Cine*) copie *f* d'exploitation.

3 **vt** a (*set free*) *person* (*from prison*) libérer, relâcher (*from* de), mettre en liberté, relaxer, élargir (*Jur*); (*from chains*) libérer (*from* de); (*from rubble, wreckage*) dégager (*from* de); (*from obligation*) dégager, libérer (*from* de); (*from promise, vow*) relever (*from* de). (*Jur*) **to ~ sb on bail** mettre qn en liberté provisoire sous caution; **to ~ sb from a debt** faire la remise d'une dette à qn; **death ~d him from pain** la mort mit fin à ses souffrances; **his employer agreed to ~ him** son patron lui a permis de cesser son travail; **can you ~ him for a few hours each week?** pouvez-vous le libérer *or* le rendre disponible quelques heures par semaine?

b (*let go*) *object, sb's hand, pigeon* lâcher; *bomb* lâcher, larguer; (*Chem*) *gas* dégager. **to ~ one's grip** *or* **hold** lâcher prise; **to ~ one's hold of** *or* **one's grip on sth** lâcher qch.

c (*issue*) *book, record* sortir, faire paraître; *film* (faire) sortir; *goods* mettre en vente; (*publish, announce*) *news* autoriser la publication de; *details of sth* publier. **to ~ a statement** publier un communiqué (*about* au sujet de).

d (*Jur*) *property* céder.

e *spring, clasp, catch* faire jouer; (*Phot*) *shutter* déclencher; *handbrake* desserrer. (*Aut*) **to ~ the clutch** débrayer.

relegate ['relɪgeɪt] **vt** a (*demote*) *person* reléguer; (*Sport*) *team* reléguer (*to* à, en), déclasser. (*Ftbl*) **to be ~d** descendre en seconde *etc* division; **to ~ old furniture to the attic** reléguer de vieux meubles au grenier. b (*hand over*) *matter, question* renvoyer (*to* à), se décharger de (*to* sur).

relegation [ˌrelɪ'geɪʃən] **n** relégation *f* (*also Sport*); *[matter, question]* renvoi *m* (*to* à).

relent [rɪ'lent] **vi** s'adoucir, se laisser toucher, se laisser fléchir; (*reverse one's decision*) revenir sur une décision.

relentless [rɪ'lentlɪs] **adj** implacable, impitoyable.

relentlessly [rɪ'lentlɪslɪ] **adv** implacablement, impitoyablement.

relet [ˌriː'let] **vt** relouer.

relevance ['reləvəns] **n**, **relevancy** ['reləvənsɪ] **n** pertinence *f*, à-propos *m inv*; rapport *m* (*to* avec). **what is the ~ of your question to the problem?** quel est le rapport entre votre question et le problème?

relevant ['reləvənt] **adj** ayant rapport (*to* à); *remark, argument* pertinent (*to* à); *regulation* applicable, approprié (*to* à); *fact* significatif; *information, course, study* utile; (*Jur*) *document* justificatif. (*Jur, Fin*) **the ~ year** l'année de référence; **to be ~ to sth** avoir rapport à qch; **that is not ~** cela n'entre pas en ligne de compte, cela n'a rien à voir*; **you must refer to the ~ chapter** vous devez vous rapporter au chapitre approprié.

reliability [rɪˌlaɪə'bɪlɪtɪ] **n** *[person, character]* (esprit *m* de) sérieux *m*; *[memory, description]* sûreté *f*, précision *f*; *[device, machine]* qualité *f*, robustesse *f*, solidité *f*, fiabilité *f*.

reliable [rɪ'laɪəbl] **adj** *person* sérieux, digne de confiance, sûr; *employee* sérieux, efficace, sur qui l'on peut compter *or* se reposer; *firm, company* sérieux; *machine* bon, solide, fiable; *information* sérieux, sûr; *description, memory, account* auquel *or* à laquelle on peut se fier. **she's very ~** elle est très sérieuse, on peut toujours compter sur elle; **a ~ source of information** une source digne de foi, une source sûre; **her memory is not very ~** on ne peut pas vraiment se fier à sa mémoire.

reliably [rɪ'laɪəblɪ] **adv** *work* sérieusement. **I am ~ informed that ...** j'apprends de source sûre *or* de bonne source que ... .

reliance [rɪ'laɪəns] **n** (*trust*) confiance *f* (*on* en); (*dependence*) dépendance *f* (*on* de), besoin *m* (*on* de). **to place ~ on sb/in sth** avoir confiance en qn/en qch.

reliant [rɪ'laɪənt] **adj** (*trusting*) confiant (*on* en). (*dependent*) **~ on** dépendant de, qui compte sur, qui a besoin de; **self-~** indépendant.

relic ['relɪk] **n** relique *f* (*also Rel*). **~s** (*human remains*) dépouille *f* (mortelle); (*of the past*) reliques *fpl*, vestiges *mpl*.

relict†† ['relɪkt] **n** veuve *f*.

relief [rɪ'liːf] 1 **n** a (*from pain, anxiety, sexual frustration*) soulagement *m*. **to bring ~ to** apporter *or* procurer du soulagement à; **I felt great ~ when ...** j'ai éprouvé un grand *or* vif soulagement quand ...; **to my ~** à mon grand soulagement; **that's a ~!** ouf! je respire!, j'aime mieux ça!; **(to me) it was a ~ to find it** j'ai été soulagé de le retrouver; *see* **comic.**

b (*assistance*) secours *m*, aide *f*, assistance *f*. **to go to the ~ of** aller au secours de; **to come to the ~ of** venir en aide à; **to send ~ to** envoyer des secours à.

c (*US Admin*) aides *fpl* sociales. **to get ~, to be on ~** bénéficier d'aides sociales.

d (*Mil*) *[town]* délivrance *f*; *[guard]* relève *f*.

e (*substitute or extra worker(s)*) relève *f*.

f (*exemption*) (*Jur*) exonération *f*; (*fiscal*) dégrèvement *m*.

g (*Art, Geog*) relief *m*. **high/low ~** haut-/bas-relief; **to stand out in (bold)** *or* **(sharp)** *or* **(clear) ~ against** se détacher sur; (*lit, fig*) **to bring** *or* **throw sth into ~** mettre qch en relief, faire ressortir qch.

2 **comp** *train, coach* supplémentaire; *typist, clerk* suppléant ▸**relief agency** organisme *m* d'aide humanitaire ▸**relief fund** caisse *f* de secours ▸**relief map** carte *f* en relief ▸**relief organization** *[refugees, earthquakes etc]* société *f* de secours ▸**relief road** (*Brit*) route *f* de délestage ▸**relief supplies** secours *mpl* ▸**relief troops** relève *f*, troupes *fpl* de secours ▸**relief valve** soupape *f* de sûreté ▸**relief work** travail *m* humanitaire ▸**relief worker** représentant *m* d'un organisme humanitaire.

relieve [rɪ'liːv] **vt** a *person* soulager. **to feel/look ~d** se sentir/avoir l'air soulagé; **he was ~d to learn that ...** il a été soulagé d'apprendre que ...; **to ~ sb of a burden** soulager qn d'un fardeau; **to ~ sb of a coat/suitcase** débarrasser qn d'un manteau/d'une valise; **to ~ sb of a duty** décharger qn d'une obligation; **to ~ sb of a post,** (*Mil*) **to ~ sb of a command** relever qn de ses fonctions; **the news ~d me of anxiety** la nouvelle a dissipé mes inquiétudes; (*hum*) **a thief has ~d me of my purse** un voleur m'a soulagé de (*hum*) *or* délesté de* mon porte-monnaie.

b (*mitigate*) *anxiety, pain* soulager, alléger; *fear, boredom* dissiper; *poverty* remédier à, pallier. **to ~ sb's mind** tranquilliser (l'esprit de) qn; **to ~ one's feelings** (*sorrow*) s'épancher, décharger son cœur; (*anger*) décharger sa colère *or* sa bile; **to ~ a situation** remédier à une situation; **the black of her dress was ~d by a white collar** un col blanc égayait sa robe noire; **the new road ~s peak-hour congestion** la nouvelle route facilite la circulation aux heures de pointe; **the new road ~s congestion in the town centre** la nouvelle route décongestionne le centre de la ville; (*Med*) **to ~ congestion** décongestionner; (*euph*) **to ~ o.s.** se soulager*, faire ses besoins*.

c (*help*) secourir, aider, venir en aide à.

d (*take over from*) relayer. **Paul will ~ you at 6** Paul vous relayera à 6 heures; (*Mil*) **to ~ the guard** relever la garde.

e (*Mil*) *town* délivrer, faire lever le siège de.

relievo [rɪ'liːvəʊ] **n** (*Art*) relief *m*.

religion [rɪ'lɪdʒən] **n** (*belief*) religion *f*; (*form of worship*) culte *m*; (*item on form etc*) confession *f*. **the Christian ~** la religion chrétienne; **this new ~ already has many adherents** ce nouveau culte a déjà de nombreux adeptes; **wars of ~** guerres *fpl* de religion; (*fig*) **to make a ~ of doing** se faire une obligation (absolue) de faire; (*lit*) **it's against my ~ (to do that)** c'est contraire à ma religion (de faire cela); (*hum*) **it's against my ~ to clean windows*** je ne fais jamais les vitres, c'est contraire à ma religion (*hum*); **to enter ~** entrer en religion; **her name in ~** son nom de religion; **he's got ~*** il s'est converti.

religiosity [rɪˌlɪdʒɪ'ɒsɪtɪ] n religiosité *f*.

religious [rɪ'lɪdʒəs] 1 adj a *person, teaching, order, life, freedom* religieux; *book* de piété; *wars* de religion. **he's a ~ person** il est croyant *or* pratiquant; **he's very ~** il est très croyant *or* très pieux; (*Scol*) **~ education, ~ instruction** instruction religieuse; **~ leader** chef religieux. b (*fig: conscientious, exact*) *care* scrupuleux, religieux; *silence* religieux. 2 n (pl inv) religieux *m*, -ieuse *f*.

religiously [rɪ'lɪdʒəslɪ] adv religieusement, pieusement; (*conscientiously*) scrupuleusement.

religiousness [rɪ'lɪdʒəsnɪs] n piété *f*, dévotion *f*.

reline [ˌriː'laɪn] vt *coat, jacket* mettre une nouvelle doublure à, redoubler. (*Aut*) **to ~ the brakes** changer les garnitures de freins.

relinquish [rɪ'lɪŋkwɪʃ] vt a (*give up*) *hope, power* abandonner; *plan, right* renoncer à (*to sb* en faveur de qn); *habit* renoncer à; *post* quitter, abandonner; *goods, property etc* se dessaisir de, abandonner. b (*let go*) *object* lâcher. **to ~ one's hold on sth** lâcher qch.

relinquishment [rɪ'lɪŋkwɪʃmənt] n (*see* **relinquish**) abandon *m* (*of* de); renonciation *f* (*of* à).

reliquary ['relɪkwərɪ] n reliquaire *m*.

relish ['relɪʃ] 1 n a (*enjoyment*) goût *m* (*for* pour). **to do sth with (great) ~, to take ~ in doing sth** faire qch avec goût *or* délectation; **he ate with ~** il mangeait de bon appétit; **he rubbed his hands with ~ at the prospect of ...** il se frotta les mains de plaisir à la perpective de ... .

b (*Culin*) (*flavour*) goût *m*, saveur *f*; (*pickle: for hamburger etc*) achards *mpl*; (*seasoning*) condiment *m*, assaisonnement *m*; (*trace: of spices etc*) soupçon *m*; (*fig: charm*) attrait *m*, charme *m*. (*fig*) **it had lost all ~** cela avait perdu tout attrait.

2 vt *food, wine* savourer. **to ~ doing** se délecter à faire, trouver du plaisir à faire; **I don't ~ the idea** *or* **prospect** *or* **thought of getting up at 5** l'idée de me lever à 5 heures ne me sourit guère *or* ne me dit rien.

relive [ˌriː'lɪv] vt revivre.

reload [ˌriː'ləʊd] vt recharger.

relocate [ˌriːləʊ'keɪt] 1 vt (*gen*) installer ailleurs; (*company*) réimplanter; *worker* (*in a new place*) transférer, muter; (*in a new job*) reconvertir. 2 vi (*US: move house*) déménager, s'installer ailleurs; *[company]* se réimplanter; *[worker]* (*in a new place*) changer de lieu de travail; (*in a new job*) se reconvertir.

relocation [ˌriːləʊ'keɪʃən] n (*gen*) déménagement *m*; *[company]* réimplantation *f*, déménagement *m*; *[worker]* (*in a new place*) transfert *m*, mutation *f*; (*in a new job*) reconversion *f*; *[household]* déménagement *m*. **~ allowance** prime *f* de relogement; *[worker]* **~ expenses** frais *mpl* de déménagement.

reluctance [rɪ'lʌktəns] n a répugnance *f* (*to do* à faire). **to do sth with ~** faire qch à regret *or* à contrecœur; **to make a show of ~** se faire prier, se faire tirer l'oreille. b (*Elec*) réluctance *f*.

reluctant [rɪ'lʌktənt] adj a (*unwilling, disinclined*) *person, animal* peu disposé (*to* à), peu enthousiaste. **he is ~ to do it** il hésite *or* il rechigne *or* il est peu disposé à le faire; **the ~ soldier** le soldat malgré lui. b (*done unwillingly*) fait à regret *or* à contrecœur; *consent, praise* accordé à contrecœur.

reluctantly [rɪ'lʌktəntlɪ] adv à regret, à contrecœur, sans enthousiasme.

rely [rɪ'laɪ] vi: **to ~ (up)on sb/sth** compter sur qn/qch, avoir confiance en qn/qch, se fier à qn/qch; **she relied on the trains being on time** elle comptait *or* tablait sur le fait que les trains seraient à l'heure; **I ~ on him for my income** je dépends de lui pour mes revenus; **you can ~ upon it** vous pouvez y compter; **you can ~ on me not to say anything about it** vous pouvez compter sur moi pour ne pas en parler, comptez sur ma discrétion; **she is not to be relied upon** on ne peut pas compter sur elle; **he relies increasingly on his assistants** il se repose de plus en plus sur ses assistants; **you mustn't ~ on other people for everything** il faut se prendre en charge; (*Jur*) **to ~ on sth** invoquer qch.

REM [rem] n (abbr of **rapid eye movement**) **~ sleep** sommeil *m* paradoxal.

remain [rɪ'meɪn] vi a (*be left*) rester. **much ~s to be done** il reste beaucoup à faire; **nothing ~s to be said** il ne reste plus rien à dire; **nothing ~s but to accept** il ne reste plus qu'à accepter; **it ~s to be seen whether** ... reste à savoir si ...; **that ~s to be seen** c'est ce que nous verrons, c'est ce qu'il reste à voir; **the fact ~s that he is wrong** il n'en est pas moins vrai *or* toujours est-il qu'il a tort; **take 2 from 4, 2 ~** 4 moins 2, il reste 2.

b (*stay*) rester, demeurer. **to ~ faithful** demeurer *or* rester fidèle; **~ seated** restez assis; **to ~ out/in** *etc* rester (en) dehors/(en) dedans *etc;* **to ~ up** rester levé; **let the matter ~ as it is** laissez l'affaire comme cela; **it ~s the same** ça ne change pas; **to ~ silent** garder le silence; **it ~s unsolved** ce n'est toujours pas résolu; **if the weather ~s fine** si le temps se maintient (au beau); (*in letters*) **I ~, yours faithfully** je vous prie d'agréer *or* veuillez agréer l'expression de mes sentiments distingués.

►**remain behind** vi rester.

remainder [rɪ'meɪndəʳ] 1 n a (*sth left over*) reste *m*; (*remaining people*) autres *mfpl*; (*Math*) reste; (*Jur*) usufruit *m* avec réversibilité. **for the ~ of the week** pendant le reste *or* le restant de la semaine. b **~s** (*Comm*) (*books etc*) invendus *mpl* soldés, soldes *mpl* d'éditeur; (*clothes, articles*) fin(s) *f(pl)* de série. 2 vt *books etc* solder.

remaining [rɪ'meɪnɪŋ] adj qui reste. **I have only one ~** il ne m'en reste qu'un, je n'en ai qu'un de reste; **the ~ cakes** le reste des gâteaux, les gâteaux qui restent.

remains [rɪ'meɪnz] npl *[meal]* restes *mpl*; *[fortune, army]* débris *mpl*; *[building]* restes, vestiges *mpl*, ruines *fpl*. **literary ~** œuvres *fpl* posthumes; **his (mortal) ~** ses restes, sa dépouille mortelle; **human ~** restes humains.

remake [ˌriː'meɪk] 1 vt refaire. 2 ['riːmeɪk] n (*Cine*) remake *m*.

remand [rɪ'mɑːnd] 1 vt (*gen, Jur*) *case, accused person* déférer, renvoyer (*to* à). (*Jur*) **to ~ sb to a higher court** renvoyer qn à une instance supérieure; **to ~ in custody** mettre en détention préventive; **to ~ on bail** laisser en liberté provisoire (sous caution); **case ~ed for a week** affaire renvoyée à huitaine; *see* **further**. 2 n renvoi *m* (à une autre audience). **to be on ~** (*in custody*) être en détention préventive *or* en prévention; (*on bail*) être en liberté provisoire. 3 comp ►**remand centre** (*Brit*) centre *m* de détention préventive ►**remand home**† (*Brit*) ≃ maison *f* d'arrêt ►**remand wing** quartier *m* des détenus préventifs.

remark [rɪ'mɑːk] 1 n a (*comment*) remarque *f*, réflexion *f*, observation *f*, commentaire *m*. **to make** *or* **pass the ~ that** remarquer que, faire observer que; **I have a few ~s to make on that subject** j'ai quelques remarques *or* réflexions *or* observations à vous communiquer à ce sujet; (*pej*) **to pass ~s about sb** faire des réflexions sur qn; **~s were passed about your absence** on a fait des remarques *or* des réflexions sur votre absence.

b (*NonC*) remarque *f*, attention *f*. **worthy of ~** digne d'attention, remarquable.

2 vt a (*say*) (faire) remarquer, (faire) observer. **"I can't go" he ~ed** "je ne peux pas y aller" dit-il.

b (*notice*) remarquer, observer.

3 vi faire des remarques *or* des observations (*on* sur). **he ~ed on it to me** il m'en a fait l'observation *or* la remarque.

remarkable [rɪ'mɑːkəbl] adj remarquable (*for* par); *event* remarquable, marquant; *pupil, mind* remarquable, brillant.

remarkably [rɪ'mɑːkəblɪ] adv remarquablement.

remarriage [ˌriː'mærɪdʒ] n remariage *m*.

remarry [ˌriː'mærɪ] vi se remarier.

remaster [ˌriː'mɑːstəʳ] vt *recording* remixer. (*on record, CD etc cover*) **"digitally ~ed"** "mixage *m* numérique".

rematch ['riːˌmætʃ] 1 n (*gen*) match *m* retour; (*Boxing*) deuxième combat *m*. 2 [ˌriː'mætʃ] vt opposer à nouveau.

remediable [rɪ'miːdɪəbl] adj remédiable.

remedial [rɪ'miːdɪəl] adj *action* réparateur (*f* -trice); *measures* de redressement; *class* de rattrapage. **~ (course in) English** cours *m* de soutien *or* de rattrapage en anglais; **~ exercises** gymnastique médicale *or* corrective; **~ teaching** cours *mpl* de rattrapage; **~ treatment** traitement curatif.

remedy ['remədɪ] 1 n (*Med, fig*) remède *m* (*for* contre, à, de); (*Jur*) recours *m*. **past** *or* **beyond ~** sans remède; **we must provide a ~ for injustice** nous devons trouver un remède à l'injustice; **the ~ for boredom is work** le travail est le remède de *or* contre l'ennui; **the ~ for despair** le remède contre le désespoir. 2 vt (*Med*) remédier à; (*fig*) remédier à, porter remède à. **the situation cannot be remedied** la situation est sans remède.

remember [rɪ'membəʳ] 1 vt a (*recall*) *person, date, occasion* se souvenir de, se rappeler. **to ~ that** se rappeler que; **I ~ doing it** je me rappelle l'avoir fait *or* que je l'ai fait, je me souviens de l'avoir fait; **I ~ed to do it** j'ai pensé à le faire; **I ~ when an egg cost one penny** je me souviens de l'époque où un œuf coûtait un penny; **I cannot ~ your name** je ne me rappelle pas votre nom; **don't you ~ me?** (*face to face*) vous ne me reconnaissez pas?; (*phone*) vous ne vous souvenez pas de moi?; **I ~ your face** je me souviens de votre visage, je vous reconnais; **I don't ~ a thing about it** je n'en ai pas le moindre souvenir, je ne me souviens de rien; **I can never ~ phone numbers** je n'ai aucune mémoire pour les *or* je ne me souviens jamais des numéros de téléphone; **let us ~ that ...** n'oublions pas que ...; **here's something to ~ him by** voici un souvenir de lui; **he is ~ed as a fine violinist** il a laissé le souvenir d'un violoniste talentueux; **she will be ~ed by millions (for her honesty/for supporting this cause)** des millions de gens se souviendront d'elle (pour son honnêteté/pour son soutien à cette cause); **I can't ~ the word at the moment** le mot m'échappe pour le moment; **we can't always ~ everything** on ne peut pas toujours songer à tout; **~ where you are!** ressaisissez-vous!; **to ~ o.s.** se reprendre; **to ~ sb in one's prayers** ne pas oublier qn dans ses prières; **that's worth ~ing** c'est bon à savoir.

b (*commemorate*) *the fallen, a battle* commémorer.

c (*give good wishes to*) rappeler (*to* au bon souvenir de). **~ me to your mother** rappelez-moi au bon souvenir de votre mère; **he asks to be ~ed to you** il vous envoie son meilleur souvenir.

d (*give money or a present to*) ne pas oublier. **to ~ sb in one's will** ne pas oublier qn dans son testament.

2 **vi** se souvenir. **I can't ~** je ne me souviens pas, je ne sais plus; **as far as I ~** autant qu'il m'en souvienne; **not as far as I ~** pas à ma connaissance, pas que je m'en souvienne; **if I ~ right(ly)** si j'ai bonne mémoire, si je m'en *or* me souviens bien; **the last time we had a party, if you ~, it tooks us days to clear up** la dernière fois que nous sommes allés à une fête, je te rappelle qu'il nous a fallu des jours pour nous remettre; **he was, you ~, a great man** il était, comme vous le savez, un grand homme.

remembered [rɪ'membəd] **adj** (*liter*) *happiness etc* inscrit dans la mémoire.

remembrance [rɪ'membrəns] **n** (*memory, thing remembered*) souvenir *m*, mémoire *f*; (*act of remembering, keepsake*) souvenir. (*Brit*) **R~ Day** ≃ (le jour de) l'Armistice *m*, le 11 Novembre; **in ~ of** en souvenir de; **to the best of my ~** autant qu'il m'en souvienne; **within the ~ of man** de mémoire d'homme; **to have no ~ of** ne pas se souvenir de, n'avoir aucun souvenir de; **give my kind ~s to your sister** rappelez-moi au bon souvenir de votre sœur.

remind [rɪ'maɪnd] **vt** rappeler (*sb of sth* qch à qn, *sb that* à qn que). **you are ~ed that ...** nous vous rappelons que ...; **to ~ sb to do** faire penser à qn à faire; **must I ~ you (again)?** faut-il que je (vous) le redise? *or* le rappelle (*subj*) encore une fois?; **she ~ed him of his mother** elle lui rappelait sa mère; **that ~s me!** à propos!, j'y pense!

reminder [rɪ'maɪndəʳ] **n** (*note, knot etc*) mémento *m*, pense-bête *m*. **as a ~ that** pour (vous *or* lui *etc*) rappeler que; **his presence was a ~ of ...** sa présence rappelait ...; **a gentle ~** un rappel discret; **give him a gentle ~** rappelez-le-lui discrètement; (*Comm*) **(letter of) ~** lettre *f* de rappel; **~ advertising** publicité *f* de rappel *or* de relance.

reminisce [ˌremɪ'nɪs] **vi** évoquer *or* raconter ses souvenirs. **to ~ about sth** évoquer qch.

reminiscence [ˌremɪ'nɪsəns] **n** réminiscence *f*.

reminiscent [ˌremɪ'nɪsənt] **adj**: **~ of** qui rappelle, qui fait penser à, évocateur (*f* -trice) de; **style ~ of Shakespeare's** style qui rappelle (celui de) Shakespeare.

reminiscently [ˌremɪ'nɪsəntlɪ] **adv**: **to smile ~** sourire à un souvenir *or* à ce souvenir; **he talked ~ of the war** il rappelait ses souvenirs de (la) guerre, il évoquait des souvenirs de (la) guerre.

remiss [rɪ'mɪs] **adj** négligent, insouciant, peu zélé. **he has been ~ in not finishing his work** c'est négligent de sa part de ne pas avoir terminé son travail; **that was very ~ of you** vous vous êtes montré très négligent.

remission [rɪ'mɪʃən] **n** (*gen, Med, Rel*) rémission *f*; (*Jur*) remise *f*. **the ~ of sins** la rémission des péchés; (*Jur*) **he earned 3 years' ~ (for good conduct)** on lui a accordé 3 ans de remise (pour bonne conduite); (*Jur*) **~ from a debt** remise d'une dette; **there can be no ~ of registration fees** il ne peut y avoir de dispense *or* d'exemption des droits d'inscription.

remissness [rɪ'mɪsnɪs] **n** négligence *f*, manque *m* de zèle.

remit[1] [rɪ'mɪt] 1 **vt** a (*Rel*) *sins* pardonner, remettre; (*Jur etc*) *fee, debt, penalty* remettre. **to have part of one's sentence ~ted** bénéficier d'une remise de peine; **to ~ sb's sentence** faire bénéficier qn d'une remise de peine; **the prisoner's sentence was ~ted** on a remis la peine du détenu, le détenu a reçu une remise de peine. b (*send*) *money* envoyer, verser. c (*lessen*) relâcher, se relâcher de. d (*postpone*) différer. e (*Jur*) renvoyer (à une instance inférieure). 2 **vi** (*become less*) diminuer; *[storm]* se calmer; *[effort]* se relâcher.

remit[2] ['ri:mɪt] **n** attributions *fpl*.

remittal [rɪ'mɪtl] **n** (*Jur*) renvoi *m* (à une instance inférieure).

remittance [rɪ'mɪtəns] 1 **n** a (*of money*) (*gen*) versement *m*; (*Banking, Econ, Fin*) remise *f* de fonds; (*Comm etc: payment*) paiement *m*, règlement *m*. **enclose your ~** joignez votre règlement. b (*of documents*) remise *f*. 2 **comp** ▸**remittance advice** (*Comm*) avis *m* de versement ▸**remittance man** (*US*) *résident étranger entretenu (par ses parents etc)*.

remittee [remɪ'ti:] **n** destinataire *mf* (*d'un envoi de fonds*).

remittent [rɪ'mɪtənt] **adj** (*Med*) rémittent; (*fig*) intermittent.

remitter [rɪ'mɪtəʳ] **n** a remetteur *m*, -euse *f*; *[money]* envoyeur *m*, -euse *f*; (*Comm*) remettant *m*. b (*Jur*) renvoi *m* (à une instance inférieure).

remix ['ri:mɪks] 1 **n** (*Mus*) remix *m*. 2 [ˌri:'mɪks] **vt** (*Mus*) remixer.

remnant ['remnənt] 1 **n** (*anything remaining*) reste *m*, restant *m*; (*piece*) débris *m*, bout *m*; *[custom, splendour]* vestige *m*; *[food, fortune]* bribe *f*, débris; *[cloth]* coupon *m*. (*Comm*) **~s** soldes *mpl* (de fins de série); **the ~ of the army** ce qui restait (*or* reste) de l'armée. 2 **comp** ▸**remnant day** (*Comm*) jour *m* de soldes ▸**remnant sale** solde *m* (de coupons *or* d'invendus *or* de fins de série).

remodel [ˌri:'mɒdl] **vt** (*also Art, Tech*) remodeler; (*fig*) *society* réorganiser; *constitution* remanier.

remonstrance [rɪ'mɒnstrəns] **n** a (*NonC*) remontrance *f*. b (*protest*) protestation *f*; (*reproof*) reproche *f*.

remonstrant [rɪ'mɒnstrənt] 1 **adj** *tone* de remontrance, de protestation. 2 **n** protestataire *mf*.

remonstrate ['remənstreɪt] 1 **vi** protester (*against* contre). **to ~ with sb about sth** faire des remontrances à qn au sujet de qch. 2 **vt** faire observer *or* remarquer (*that* que) (*avec l'idée de reproche ou de contradiction*).

remorse [rɪ'mɔ:s] **n** (*NonC*) remords *m* (*at* de, *for* pour). **a feeling of ~** un remords; **without ~** sans pitié.

remorseful [rɪ'mɔ:sfʊl] **adj** plein de remords.

remorsefully [rɪ'mɔ:sfəlɪ] **adv** avec remords.

remorsefulness [rɪ'mɔ:sfʊlnɪs] **n** (*NonC*) remords *m*.

remorseless [rɪ'mɔ:slɪs] **adj** sans remords, dénué de remords; (*fig*) implacable.

remorselessly [rɪ'mɔ:slɪslɪ] **adv** sans remords; (*fig*) sans pitié, impitoyablement, implacablement.

remorselessness [rɪ'mɔ:slɪsnɪs] **n** absence *f or* manque *m* de pitié *or* de remords.

remote [rɪ'məʊt] 1 **adj** a *place* (*distant*) lointain, éloigné; (*isolated*) écarté, isolé; *past time* lointain, ancien, reculé; *future time* lointain; *person* distant, froid, réservé. **in ~ country districts** au (fin) fond de la campagne; **in the remotest parts of Africa** au fin fond de l'Afrique; **in a ~ spot** dans un lieu retiré *or* écarté *or* à l'écart; **house ~ from a main road** maison située loin *or* à l'écart d'une grand-route; **~ antiquity** antiquité reculée, haute antiquité; **in the ~ past/future** dans le passé/ l'avenir lointain; **~ ancestor/relative** ancêtre/parent éloigné; **what he said was rather ~ from the subject in hand** ce qu'il a dit était plutôt éloigné de la question; **you will find her rather ~** vous la trouverez assez distante *or* d'un abord assez difficile.

b (*slight*) vague, petit. **very ~ resemblance** ressemblance très vague *or* lointaine; **I haven't the remotest idea** je n'ai pas la moindre idée; **he hasn't a ~ chance** il n'a pas le moindre espoir; **there is a ~ possibility that he will come** il y a une petite chance qu'il vienne.

2 **comp** ▸**remote access** (*Comput*) accès *m* à distance, téléconsultation *f* ▸**remote control** télécommande *f*, commande *f* à distance ▸**remote-controlled** télécommandé ▸**remote job entry** (*Comput*) télésoumission *f* de travaux.

remotely [rɪ'məʊtlɪ] **adv** a (*distantly*) *situated* au loin, dans le lointain. **we are ~ related** nous sommes parents éloignés. b (*haughtily*) *look, speak* de façon distante, avec froideur. c (*slightly*) vaguement, faiblement. **it is ~ possible that** il est tout juste possible que + *subj*; **it doesn't ~ resemble** cela ne ressemble absolument pas à *or* pas le moins du monde à; **he isn't ~ interested** il n'est pas le moins du monde *or* absolument pas intéressé.

remoteness [rɪ'məʊtnɪs] **n** (*in space*) éloignement *m*, isolement *m*; (*in time*) éloignement. **his ~** son attitude distante *or* réservée (*from sb* envers qn); **his ~ from everyday life** son isolement de la vie ordinaire.

remould [ˌri:'məʊld] (*Brit*) 1 **vt** (*Tech*) remouler; *tyre* rechaper; (*fig*) *sb's character* corriger. 2 ['ri:məʊld] **n** (*tyre*) pneu rechapé.

remount [ˌri:'maʊnt] 1 **vt** a *horse* remonter sur; *bicycle* enfourcher de nouveau; *hill* remonter; *ladder* grimper de nouveau sur. b *picture* rentoiler; *photo* faire un nouveau montage de. 2 **vi** remonter à cheval (*or* à bicyclette).

removable [rɪ'mu:vəbl] **adj** (*detachable*) amovible, détachable; (*movable*) *object* mobile; *machine* transportable.

removal [rɪ'mu:vəl] 1 **n** enlèvement *m*; *[furniture, household]* déménagement *m*; *[abuse, evil]* suppression *f*; *[pain]* soulagement *m*; (*from a job*) (*demotion*) déplacement *m*; (*sacking*) renvoi *m*, révocation *f*; (*Med*) ablation *f*. **stain ~** détachage *m*; **after our ~** après notre changement *m* de domicile; **our ~ to this house** notre emménagement *m* dans cette maison; **our ~ from London** notre déménagement de Londres. 2 **comp** ▸**removal allowance** indemnité *f* de déménagement ▸**removal expenses** frais *mpl* de déménagement ▸**removal man** déménageur *m* ▸**removal van** (*Brit*) voiture *f or* camion *m or* fourgon *m* de déménagement.

remove [rɪ'mu:v] 1 **vt** *object* enlever (*from* de); *clothes* enlever, ôter; *furniture* enlever, *[removers]* déménager; *stain, graffiti* enlever, faire partir; *paragraph, word, item on list* rayer, barrer; *threat, tax, abuse* supprimer; *objection* réfuter; *difficulty, problem* résoudre; (*lit, fig*) *obstacle* écarter; *doubt* chasser; *suspicion, fear* dissiper; *employee* renvoyer, destituer; *official* déplacer; (**: murder*) liquider‡; (*Med*) *lung, kidney* enlever, pratiquer l'ablation de, retirer; *tumour* extirper, enlever; *splint, bandage* enlever. **~ the lid** enlevez le couvercle; **he was ~d to the cells** on l'a emmené en cellule; **to ~ sb to hospital** hospitaliser qn; **to ~ a child from school** retirer un enfant de l'école; (*Jur: in court*) **~ the prisoner!** faire sortir l'accusé!; **he ~d himself to another room** il s'est retiré dans une autre pièce; (*hum*) **I must ~ myself*** je dois filer*; **to ~ sb's name** rayer qn, radier qn; **to ~ one's make-up** se démaquiller; **make-up removing cream** crème démaquillante; **to ~ unwanted hair from the legs** épiler les jambes; (*fig*) **to be far ~d from** être loin de; **cousin once/twice ~d** cousin(e) *m(f)* au deuxième/troisième degré.

2 **vi** déménager, changer de domicile. **to ~ to London** aller habiter (à) Londres, aller s'installer à Londres.

3 **n** (*in relationship*) degré *m* de parenté. (*fig*) **to be only a few ~s from** être tout proche de; **this is but one ~ from disaster** nous frisons (*or* ils frisent *etc*) le désastre; **it's a far ~ from ...** c'est loin d'être ... .

remover [rɪ'mu:vəʳ] **n** a (*removal man*) déménageur *m*. b (*substance*) (*for varnish*) dissolvant *m*; (*for stains*) détachant *m*. **paint ~** décapant *m* (pour peintures); *see* **cuticle, hair, make-up**.

remunerate [rɪ'mju:nəreɪt] **vt** rémunérer.
remuneration [rɪ,mju:nə'reɪʃən] **n** rémunération *f* (*for* de).
remunerative [rɪ'mju:nərətɪv] **adj** rémunérateur (*f* -trice), lucratif.
renaissance [rɪ'neɪsɑ̃:ns] 1 **n** renaissance *f*. (*Hist*) **the R ~** la Renaissance. 2 **comp ►Renaissance** *art, scholar* de la Renaissance; *style, palace* Renaissance *inv*.
renal ['ri:nl] **adj** rénal. **~ failure** défaillance *or* insuffisance rénale.
rename [,ri:'neɪm] **vt** *person, street, town* rebaptiser (*fig*); (*Comput*) *file* renommer.
renascence [rɪ'næsns] = **renaissance**.
renascent [rɪ'næsnt] **adj** renaissant.
rend [rend] **pret, ptp rent vt** (*liter*) *cloth* déchirer; *armour* fendre; (*fig*) déchirer, fendre. (*lit, fig*) **to ~ sth from** arracher qch à *or* de; **country rent by civil war** pays déchiré par la guerre civile; **a cry rent the silence** un cri déchira le silence; **to ~ sb's heart** fendre le cœur à qn.
render ['rendəʳ] **vt** a (*frm: give*) *service, homage, judgment* rendre; *help* donner; *explanation* donner, fournir. **~ unto Caesar the things which are Caesar's** rendez donc *or* il faut rendre à César ce qui est de César; **to ~ thanks to sb** remercier qn; **to ~ thanks to God** rendre grâce à Dieu; **to ~ assistance** prêter assistance *or* secours; **to ~ an account of sth** rendre compte de qch.
b (*Comm*) *account* remettre, présenter. **(to) account ~ed £10** rappel de compte *or* facture de rappel — 10 livres.
c *music* interpréter; *text* rendre, traduire (*into* en).
d (*make*) rendre. **his accident ~ed him helpless** son accident l'a rendu complètement infirme.
e (*Culin*) *fat* faire fondre.
f (*Constr*) plâtrer.
►render down vt sep *fat* faire fondre.
►render up vt sep (*liter*) *fortress* rendre; *prisoner, treasure* livrer.
rendering ['rendərɪŋ] **n** *[piece of music, poem]* interprétation *f*; (*translation*) traduction *f* (into en).
rendez-vous ['rɒndɪvu:] 1 **n, pl rendez-vous** ['rɒndɪvu:z] rendez-vous *m*. 2 **vi** (*meet*) se retrouver; (*assemble*) se réunir. **to ~ with sb** rejoindre qn; (*Mil etc*) **they rendez-voused with the patrol at dawn** ils ont rejoint la patrouille à l'aube.
rendition [ren'dɪʃən] = **rendering**.
reneague [rɪ'ni:g] = **reneg(u)e**.
renegade ['renɪgeɪd] **n** renégat(e) *m(f)*.
renegotiate [,ri:nɪ'gəʊʃɪeɪt] **vt** renégocier.
reneg(u)e [rɪ'ni:g] **vi** manquer à sa parole; (*Cards*) faire une renonce. **to ~ on a promise** manquer à sa promesse.
renew [rɪ'nju:] **vt** *appointment, attack, contract, passport, promise, one's strength* renouveler; *lease* renouveler, reconduire; *supplies* remplacer, renouveler. **to ~ negotiations/discussions** reprendre des négociations/discussions; **to ~ one's subscription** renouveler son abonnement, se réabonner; **to ~ one's acquaintance with sb** renouer connaissance avec qn; *see also* **renewed**.
renewable [rɪ'nju:əbl] **adj** renouvelable.
renewal [rɪ'nju:əl] **n** (*see also* **renew**) renouvellement *m*; reconduction *f*; remplacement *m*; reprise *f*; *[strength]* regain *m*. **~ of subscription** réabonnement *m*.
renewed [rɪ'nju:d] **adj** (*gen*) accru. **with ~ vigour** avec une force accrue; **with ~ enthusiasm** avec un regain d'enthousiasme; **~ outbreaks of rioting** recrudescence *f* de troubles; **to make ~ efforts to do** redoubler d'efforts pour faire.
rennet ['renɪt] **n** (*for junket*) présure *f*.
renounce [rɪ'naʊns] 1 **vt** *liberty, opinions, ideas, title* renoncer à; *religion* abjurer; *right* renoncer à, abandonner; *treaty* dénoncer; † *friend* renier; *cause, party* renier, désavouer; *principles* répudier. 2 **vi** (*Bridge*) défausser.
renouncement [rɪ'naʊnsmənt] = **renunciation**.
renovate ['renəʊveɪt] **vt** *clothes, house* remettre à neuf, rénover; *building, painting, statue* restaurer.
renovation [,renəʊ'veɪʃən] **n** (*see* **renovate**) remise *f* à neuf, rénovation *f*; restauration *f*.
renown [rɪ'naʊn] **n** renommée *f*, renom *m*, célébrité *f*. **of high ~** de grand renom.
renowned [rɪ'naʊnd] **adj** renommé (*for* pour), célèbre (*for* par), en renom, illustre.
rent¹ [rent] 1 **n** *[house, room]* loyer *m*; *[farm]* fermage *m*; *[television etc]* (prix *m* de) location *f*. (*US*) **for ~** à louer; **quarter's ~** terme *m*; **(one week) late** *or* **behind with one's ~** en retard (d'une semaine) sur son loyer; **to pay a high/low ~ for** payer un gros/petit loyer pour; **evicted for non-payment of ~** expulsé pour non-paiement de loyer.
2 **comp ►"rent-a-bike"** *etc* (*Brit Comm*) "location de vélos" *etc* **►rent-a-car** *firm* compagnie *f* de location de voitures **►rent-a-crowd*** (*Brit*) (*gen*) agitateurs *mpl* professionnels; (*supporters: at meeting etc*) claque *f* **►rent allowance** (*Brit*) indemnité *f* or allocation *f* (de) logement **►rent-a-mob*** = **rent-a-crowd*** **►rent book** (*for accommodation*) carnet *m* de quittances de loyer **►rent boy** jeune (garçon) prostitué *m* **►rent collector** receveur *m* de loyers **►rent control** contrôle *m* des loyers **►rent-controlled** au loyer contrôlé (par le gouvernement) **►rent-free adj** exempt de loyer, gratuit ◊ **adv** sans payer de loyer **►rent rebate** réduction *f* de loyer **►rent review** (*Brit Admin*) réajustement *m* des loyers.
3 **vt** a (*take for ~*) louer, prendre en location. **we don't own it, only ~ it** nous ne sommes pas propriétaires, mais locataires seulement; **~ed accomodation/flat** *etc* logement *m*/appartement *m etc* en location.
b (*also* **~ out**) louer, donner en location.
rent² [rent] 1 **pret, ptp of rend.** 2 **n** (*tear*) *[cloth]* déchirure *f*, accroc *m*; *[rock]* fissure *f*; *[clouds]* déchirure, trouée *f*; (*fig*) *[party etc]* rupture *f*, scission *f*.
rental ['rentl] **n** (*amount paid*) *[house, land]* (montant *m* du) loyer *m*; (*esp for holiday accommodation*) prix *m* de location; *[television etc]* (prix de) location *f*; *[telephone]* abonnement *m*; (*income from rents*) revenu *m* en loyers *or* fermages. **~ car** voiture *f* de location; (*US*) **~ library** bibliothèque *f* de prêt (*payante*).
renumber [,ri:'nʌmbəʳ] **vt** numéroter de nouveau, renuméroter.
renunciation [rɪ,nʌnsɪ'eɪʃən] **n** (*see* **renounce**) renonciation *f* (*of* à); abjuration *f*; dénonciation *f*; reniement *m*, désaveu *m* (*of* de); (*Jur*) répudiation *f*.
reoccupy [,ri:'ɒkjʊpaɪ] **vt** réoccuper.
reopen [,ri:'əʊpən] 1 **vt** *box, door* rouvrir; *fight, battle, hostilities* reprendre; *debate, discussion* rouvrir. (*Jur*) **to ~ a case** rouvrir une affaire. 2 **vi** *[school]* reprendre; *[shop, theatre etc]* rouvrir; *[wound]* se rouvrir.
reopening [,ri:'əʊpnɪŋ] **n** réouverture *f*.
reorder [,ri:'ɔ:dəʳ] **vt** a *goods, supplies* commander de nouveau. b (*reorganize*) reclasser, réorganiser.
reorganization ['ri:,ɔ:gənaɪ'zeɪʃən] **n** réorganisation *f*.
reorganize [,ri:'ɔ:gənaɪz] 1 **vt** réorganiser. 2 **vi** se réorganiser.
Rep. (*US Pol*) **abbr of Representative.**
rep¹* [rep] **n abbr of repertory b.**
rep² [rep] **n** (*Tex*) reps *m*.
rep³* [rep] **n** a (*Comm*) (**abbr of representative**) représentant(e) *m(f)* (de commerce). b (*spokesperson*) porte-parole *m*.
repackage [,ri:'pækɪdʒ] **vt** *product* reconditionner; *parcel* remballer; (*fig*) *proposal, scheme* reformuler.
repaid [rɪ'peɪd] **pret, ptp of repay.**
repaint [,ri:'peɪnt] **vt** repeindre.
repair¹ [rɪ'pɛəʳ] 1 **vt** *tyre, shoes, chair* réparer; *clothes* réparer, raccommoder; *machine, watch* réparer, arranger; *roof, road* réparer, refaire; (*Naut*) *hull* radouber; (*fig*) *error, wrong* réparer, remédier à.
2 **n** a (*gen*) réparation *f*; *[clothes]* raccommodage *m*; *[shoes]* ressemelage *m*; *[roof, road]* réfection *f*; (*Naut*) *[hull]* radoub *m*. **to be under ~** être en réparation; **beyond ~** (**adj**) irréparable; (**adv**) irréparablement; **damaged** *or* **broken beyond ~** irréparable; **closed for ~s** fermé pour cause de travaux; **"road ~s"** "chantier"; **"(shoe) ~s while you wait"** "talon minute".
b (*NonC: condition*) **to be in good/bad ~** être en bon/mauvais état; **to keep in (good) ~** entretenir.
3 **comp ►repair kit** trousse *f* de réparation *or* d'outils **►repair man** réparateur *m* **►repair outfit** = **repair kit ►repair shop** atelier *m* de réparations.
repair² [rɪ'pɛəʳ] **vi** (*liter: go*) aller, se rendre.
repairable [rɪ'pɛərəbl] **adj** réparable.
repairer [rɪ'pɛərəʳ] **n** réparateur *m*, -trice *f*; *see* **clock, shoe** *etc*.
repaper [,ri:'peɪpəʳ] **vt** retapisser, refaire les papiers peints de.
reparable ['repərəbl] **adj** réparable.
reparation [,repə'reɪʃən] **n** réparation *f*. **to make ~s for** réparer (*une injure etc*).
repartee [,repɑ:'ti:] **n** repartie *f*, réplique *f*. **to be good at ~** avoir la réplique facile, avoir de la repartie.
repast [rɪ'pɑ:st] **n** (*liter*) repas *m*, banquet *m*.
repatriate [ri:'pætrɪeɪt] 1 **vt** rapatrier. 2 [ri:'pætrɪət] **n** rapatrié(e) *m(f)*.
repatriation [ri:,pætrɪ'eɪʃən] **n** rapatriement *m*.
repay [ri:'peɪ] **pret, ptp repaid vt** a (*pay back*) *money* rendre, rembourser; *person* rembourser; *debt, obligation* s'acquitter de. **if you lend me £2 I'll ~ you on Saturday** si tu me prêtes 2 livres je te les rendrai *or* je te rembourserai samedi; **to ~ sb's expenses** rembourser *or* indemniser qn de ses frais; (*fig*) **how can I ever ~ you?** comment pourrais-je (jamais) te remercier?
b (*give in return*) récompenser. **to ~ sb's kindness** payer de retour la gentillesse de qn, récompenser qn de sa gentillesse; **to ~ sb with gratitude** payer qn de gratitude; **to be repaid for one's efforts** être récompensé de ses efforts; **it ~s obstinacy** la persévérance paie *or* est payante, cela vaut la peine de persévérer.
repayable [ri:'peɪəbl] **adj** remboursable. **~ in 10 monthly instalments** remboursable en 10 mensualités.
repayment [ri:'peɪmənt] **n** *[money]* remboursement *m*; *[effort]* récompense *f*. **~s can be spread over 3 years** les remboursements peuvent s'échelonner sur 3 ans; (*Brit*) **~ mortgage** *emprunt-logement sans capital différé;* (*Fin*) **~ schedule** calendrier *m* d'amortissement.
repeal [rɪ'pi:l] 1 **vt** *law* abroger, annuler; *sentence* annuler; *decree* révoquer. 2 **n** abrogation *f*; annulation *f*; révocation *f*.

repeat [rɪ'pi:t] 1 vt (*say again*) répéter, redire, réitérer; *demand, promise* réitérer; (*Mus*) reprendre; (*recite*) *poem etc* réciter (par cœur); (*do again*) *action, attack* répéter, renouveler; *pattern, motif* répéter, reproduire; (*Comm*) *order* renouveler. (*Comm*) **this offer will never be ~ed** (c'est une) offre unique *or* exceptionnelle; **you must not ~ what I tell you** il ne faut pas répéter ce que je vous dis; **to ~ o.s.** se répéter; **to ~ one's efforts** renouveler ses efforts; (*Scol*) **to ~ a class** redoubler une classe.

2 vi a répéter. **I ~, it is impossible** je le répète, c'est impossible.

b (*Math*) se reproduire périodiquement. **0.054 ~ing** 0,054 périodique.

c (*) **radishes ~ on me** les radis me donnent des renvois*.

3 n répétition *f*; (*Mus*) reprise *f*; (*Rad, TV*) reprise *f*, rediffusion *f*. (*Mus*) **shall we play the ~?** est-ce qu'on joue les reprises?

4 comp ►**repeat mark(s)** (*Mus*) barre *f* de reprise, renvoi *m* ►**repeat order** (*Brit Comm*) commande renouvelée ►**repeat performance** (*Theat*) deuxième représentation *f*; (*fig*) **he gave a repeat performance** il a fait exactement la même chose; (*pej*) il a fait la même comédie ►**repeat sign** (*Mus*) = **repeat marks**.

repeated [rɪ'pi:tɪd] adj *requests, criticism* répété; *efforts* renouvelé.

repeatedly [rɪ'pi:tɪdlɪ] adv à maintes reprises, très souvent. **I have ~ told you** je ne cesse de vous répéter; **he had ~ proclaimed his innocence** il n'avait pas cessé de proclamer son innocence.

repeater [rɪ'pi:tə^r] 1 n a (*gun/watch/alarm clock*) fusil *m*/montre *f*/réveil *m* à répétition. b (*Math*) fraction *f* périodique. c (*US Scol*) redoublant(e) *m(f)*; (*US Jur*) récidiviste *mf*. 2 comp ►**repeater loan** (*Econ, Fin*) prêt-relais *m*.

repeating [rɪ'pi:tɪŋ] adj (*Math*) périodique.

repeg [ˌri:'peg] vt (*Econ, Fin*) ne plus faire flotter, redonner une parité fixe à.

repel [rɪ'pel] 1 vt *enemy, sb's advances, magnetic pole* repousser; (*fig: disgust*) repousser, rebuter, inspirer de la répulsion *or* de la répugnance à. (*fig*) **to be ~led by** éprouver de la répulsion pour. 2 vi [*magnetic poles*] se repousser.

repellent [rɪ'pelənt] adj repoussant, répugnant. **I find him ~** il me répugne, il me dégoûte; *see* **insect, water** *etc*.

repent [rɪ'pent] 1 vi se repentir (*of* de). 2 vt se repentir de, regretter.

repentance [rɪ'pentəns] n repentir *m*.

repentant [rɪ'pentənt] adj repentant.

repercussion [ˌri:pə'kʌʃən] n [*sounds*] répercussion *f*; [*shock*] répercussion, contrecoup *m*; (*fig*) répercussion *f*. **to have ~s on** se répercuter sur, avoir des répercussions sur *or* son contrecoup dans; **the ~(s) of this defeat** le contrecoup *or* les répercussions de cet échec; **there will be no ~s** il n'y aura pas de répercussions; **the ~ on prices of the rise in costs** la répercussion sur les prix de la hausse du coût.

repertoire ['repətwɑ:^r] n (*Theat, fig*) répertoire *m*.

repertory ['repətərɪ] a (*Theat, fig*) = **repertoire**. b (*also* **~ theatre**) théâtre *m* de répertoire. **~ company** compagnie *f or* troupe *f* (de théâtre) de répertoire; **to act in ~, to play ~** faire partie d'une troupe de répertoire; **he did 3 years in ~** il a joué pendant 3 ans dans un théâtre de répertoire.

repetition [ˌrepɪ'tɪʃən] n a (*NonC: see* **repeat 1**) répétition *f*, redite *f*, réitération *f*; récitation *f*; renouvellement *m*; reproduction *f*. b (*recurrence*) répétition *f*, retour *m*.

repetitious [ˌrepɪ'tɪʃəs] adj plein de répétitions *or* de redites.

repetitive [rɪ'petɪtɪv] adj *person* rabâcheur; *writing* plein de redites; *work* répétitif, monotone. (*Med*) **~ strain injury** microtraumatisme *m* permanent.

rephrase [ˌri:'freɪz] vt reformuler. **let me ~ that, I'll ~ that** je me reprends.

repine [rɪ'paɪn] vi se plaindre, murmurer.

replace [rɪ'pleɪs] vt a (*put back*) replacer, remettre (à sa place *or* en place), ranger. (*Telec*) **to ~ the receiver** raccrocher. b (*take the place of*) remplacer, tenir la place de. c (*provide substitute for*) remplacer (*by, with* par).

replaceable [rɪ'pleɪsəbl] adj remplaçable.

replacement [rɪ'pleɪsmənt] 1 n a (*putting back*) remise *f* en place, replacement *m*. b (*substituting*) remplacement *m*, substitution *f*; (*person*) remplaçant(e) *m(f)*; (*product*) produit *m* de remplacement. 2 comp ►**replacement engine** (*Aut*) moteur *m* de rechange; **to fit a replacement engine** faire l'échange standard du moteur ►**replacement part** (*Tech*) pièce *f* de rechange.

replant [ˌri:'plɑ:nt] vt replanter.

replay ['ri:pleɪ] (*Sport*) 1 n: **the ~ is on October 15** le match sera rejoué le 15 octobre; *see* **action, instant**. 2 [ˌri:'pleɪ] vt *match* rejouer; *cassette, video* repasser.

replenish [rɪ'plenɪʃ] vt remplir de nouveau (*with* de). **to ~ one's supplies of sth** se réapprovisionner en qch; **to ~ one's wardrobe** remonter sa garde-robe.

replenishment [rɪ'plenɪʃmənt] n remplissage *m*. **~ of supplies** réapprovisionnement *m*.

replete [rɪ'pli:t] adj rempli, plein (*with* de); (*well-fed*) *person* rassasié.

repletion [rɪ'pli:ʃən] n satiété *f*.

replica ['replɪkə] n (*gen*) copie exacte; [*painting*] réplique *f*; [*document*] fac-similé *m*, copie exacte.

replicate ['replɪˌkeɪt] 1 vt a (*reproduce*) (*gen*) reproduire; (*Bio*) se reproduire par mitose ou méiose. b (*fold back*) replier. 2 ['replɪkɪt] adj *leaf etc* replié.

replication [ˌreplɪ'keɪʃən] n (*gen*) reproduction *f*; (*Bio*) reproduction *f* par mitose ou méiose.

reply [rɪ'plaɪ] 1 n réponse *f*; (*quick*) réplique *f*; (*Jur*) réplique *f*. **in ~ (to)** en réponse (à); **he made no ~** il n'a pas répondu. 2 vti répondre; (*quickly*) répliquer. 3 comp ►**reply coupon** (*Post*) coupon-réponse *m* ►**reply paid** réponse payée.

repoint [ˌri:'pɔɪnt] vt *building etc* rejointoyer.

repointing [ˌri:'pɔɪntɪŋ] n rejointoyage *m*.

repo man* ['ri:pəʊˌmæn] (*US*) = **repossession man**.

report [rɪ'pɔ:t] 1 n a (*account, statement*) rapport *m*; [*speech*] compte rendu *m*; [*debate, meeting*] compte rendu, procès-verbal *m*; (*Press, Rad, TV*) reportage *m*; (*official*) rapport (d'enquête); (*at regular intervals: on weather, sales, etc*) bulletin *m*. **(Government) ~ on the motor industry** report *m* (parlementaire) sur l'industrie automobile; **monthly ~** bulletin mensuel; **school ~** bulletin *m* scolaire; **to make a ~ on** faire un rapport sur; (*Press, Rad, TV*) faire un reportage sur; (*Comm*) **annual ~** rapport annuel (de gestion); **chairman's ~** rapport présidentiel; (*Jur*) **law ~s** recueil *m* de jurisprudence *or* de droit; (*Jur*) **to make a ~ against** dresser un procès-verbal à; *see* **progress, weather**.

b (*rumour*) rumeur *f*. **there is a ~ that ...** le bruit court que ..., on dit que ...; **as ~ has it** selon les bruits qui courent, selon la rumeur publique; **there are ~s of rioting** il y aurait (*or* il y aurait eu) des émeutes; **the ~s of rioting have been proved ...** les allégations selon lesquelles il y aurait eu des émeutes se sont révélées ...; **to know sth only by ~** ne savoir qch que par ouï-dire; **I have heard a ~ that ...** j'ai entendu dire que ... .

c (*repute*) [*person*] réputation *f*; [*product*] renom *m*, renommée *f*. **of good ~** de bonne réputation, dont on dit du bien.

d (*explosion*) détonation *f*, explosion *f*; [*rifle, gun*] coup *m* de fusil *etc*. **with a loud ~** avec une forte détonation.

2 comp ►**report card** (*Scol*) bulletin *m* scolaire ►**report stage**: (*Brit Parl*) **the bill has reached the report stage** le rapport de la Commission du projet de loi a été présenté.

3 vt a (*give account of*) rapporter, rendre compte de; (*bring to notice esp of authorities*) signaler; (*Press, Rad, TV*) rapporter. **to ~ a speech** faire le compte rendu d'un discours; **to ~ one's findings** [*scientist etc*] rendre compte de l'état de ses recherches; [*commission*] présenter ses conclusions; **to ~ progress** (*orally*) faire un exposé de l'état de la situation; (*in writing*) dresser un état sur la situation; **only one paper ~ed his death** un seul journal a signalé *or* mentionné sa mort; **the papers ~ed the crime as solved** les journaux ont présenté le crime comme résolu; **our correspondent ~s from Rome that ...** notre correspondant à Rome nous apprend que ...; (*Press*) **~ing restrictions** l'embargo sur l'information (*fig*); **he is ~ed as having said** il aurait dit; **it is ~ed that a prisoner has escaped, a prisoner is ~ed to have escaped** un détenu se serait évadé; (*Gram*) **~ed speech** style *or* discours indirect; (*Parl*) **to ~ a bill** présenter un projet de loi; (*Parl*) **to move to ~ progress** demander la clôture des débats.

b (*announce*) déclarer, annoncer. **it is ~ed from the White House that ...** on annonce à la Maison Blanche que ... .

c (*notify authorities of*) *accident, crime, suspect* signaler; *criminal, culprit* dénoncer (*often pej*). **all accidents must be ~ed to the police** tous les accidents doivent être signalés à la police; **to ~ a theft to the police** signaler un vol à la police; **to ~ sb for bad behaviour** signaler qn pour mauvaise conduite; **to ~ sb's bad behaviour** signaler la mauvaise conduite de qn; **her colleague ~ed her to the boss out of jealousy** sa collègue l'a dénoncée au patron par jalousie.

d (*Mil, Naut*) signaler. **to ~ sb sick** signaler que qn est malade; **~ed missing** porté manquant *or* disparu; **nothing to ~** rien à signaler; **to ~ one's position** signaler *or* donner sa position.

4 vi a (*announce o.s. ready*) se présenter. **~ to the director on Monday** présentez-vous chez le directeur lundi; **to ~ for duty** se présenter au travail, prendre son service.

b (*Mil*) **to ~ to one's unit** rallier son unité; **to ~ sick** se faire porter malade.

c (*give a report*) faire un rapport (*on* sur); (*Press, Rad, TV*) faire un reportage (*on* sur). **the committee is ready to ~** le comité est prêt à faire son rapport; (*Rad, TV*) **Michael Brown ~s from Rome** de Rome, (le reportage de) Michael Brown.

d (*Admin: in hierarchy*) **he ~s to the sales manager** il est sous les ordres (directs) du directeur des ventes; **who do you ~ to?** qui est votre supérieur hiérarchique?

►**report back** vi a (*return*) (*Mil etc*) rentrer au quartier. (*gen*) **you must report back at 6 o'clock** il faut que vous soyez de retour à 6 heures. b (*give report*) donner *or* présenter son rapport (*to* à). **the committee was asked to investigate the complaint and report back to the assembly** le comité a été chargé d'examiner la plainte et de présenter son rapport à l'assemblée.

reportage [ˌrepɔ:'tɑ:ʒ] n reportage *m*.

reportedly [rɪ'pɔ:tɪdlɪ] adv: **he had ~ seen her** il l'aurait vue, il paraît

qu'il l'a vue, on dit qu'il l'a vue.
reporter [rɪ'pɔːtəʳ] n a (*Press*) journaliste *mf*; (*on the spot*) reporter *m*; (*Rad, TV*) reporter. **special** ~ envoyé(e) spécial(e) *m(f)*; (*Jur, Parl*) **~s' gallery** tribune *f* de la presse. b (*Parl: stenographer*) sténographe *mf*; (*Jur*) greffier *m*.
reporting [rɪ'pɔːtɪŋ] n (*Press, Rad, TV*) reportages *mpl*.
repose [rɪ'pəʊz] 1 n (*rest*) repos *m*; (*sleep*) sommeil *m*; (*peace*) repos, tranquillité *f*, paix *f*. **in** ~ en repos, au repos. 2 vt (*frm*) *confidence, trust* mettre, placer (*in* en). (*rest*) **to** ~ **o.s.** se reposer. 3 vi a (*rest*) se reposer; *[dead]* reposer. b (*be based*) reposer, être fondé (*on* sur).
repository [rɪ'pɒzɪtərɪ] n (*gen, also Comm*) (*warehouse*) dépôt *m*, entrepôt *m*; (*fig*) *[facts etc]* répertoire *m*, mine *f*; (*person*) dépositaire *mf* (*d'un secret etc*).
repossess [ˌriːpə'zes] vt reprendre possession de, rentrer en possession de.
repossession [ˌriːpə'zeʃən] n reprise *f* de possession. (*US* *) ~ **man** récupérateur* *m, sorte d'huissier chargé de saisir un bien non payé.*
repot [ˌriː'pɒt] vt rempoter.
repp [rep] = **rep²**.
reprehend [ˌreprɪ'hend] vt *person* réprimander; *action, behaviour* blâmer, condamner.
reprehensible [ˌreprɪ'hensɪbl] adj répréhensible, blâmable.
reprehensibly [ˌreprɪ'hensɪblɪ] adv de façon répréhensible.
reprehension [ˌreprɪ'henʃən] n (*NonC*) réprimande *f*, blâme *m*.
represent [ˌreprɪ'zent] vt a (*stand for, symbolize*) représenter. **a drawing ~ing prehistoric man** un dessin représentant *or* qui représente l'homme préhistorique; **phonetic symbols** ~ **sounds** les symboles phonétiques représentent des sons; (*fig*) **he ~s all that is best in his country's culture** il représente *or* personnifie les meilleurs aspects de la culture de son pays; **£100 doesn't** ~ **a good salary these days** 100 livres ne représentent *or* ne constituent plus un bon salaire de nos jours.
b (*declare to be*) *person, event* représenter, dépeindre, décrire (*as* comme étant); *grievance, risk etc* présenter (*as* comme étant). **he ~ed me to be a fool** *or* **as a fool** il m'a représenté *or* dépeint comme un imbécile; **I am not what you** ~ **me to be** je ne suis pas tel que vous me décrivez *or* dépeignez; **he ~s himself as a doctor** il se fait passer pour un médecin; **it is exactly as ~ed in the advertisement** cela est exactement conforme à la description de l'annonce (publicitaire); **he ~ed the risks as being slight** il a présenté les risques comme négligeables.
c (*explain*) expliquer, exposer, représenter (*liter*); (*point out*) faire remarquer, signaler. **can you** ~ **to him how much we need his help?** pouvez-vous lui expliquer *or* lui faire comprendre à quel point nous avons besoin de son aide?
d (*act or speak for*) représenter (*also Parl*); (*Jur*) représenter (en justice), postuler pour. **he ~s Bogminster in Parliament** il représente Bogminster au Parlement, il est le député de Bogminster; **the delegation ~ed the mining industry** la délégation représentait l'industrie minière; **he ~s their firm in London** il représente leur maison à Londres; **many countries were ~ed at the ceremony** de nombreux pays s'étaient fait représenter à la cérémonie; **women artists were well/strongly ~ed at the exhibition** les femmes artistes étaient bien/fortement représentées à l'exposition; **I** ~ **Mr Thomas** je viens de la part de M. Thomas.
e (*Theat*) *character* jouer (le rôle de); *part* jouer, interpréter.
f (*Jur*) (*in contracts etc*) déclarer.
re-present [ˌriːprɪ'zent] vt présenter de nouveau.
representation [ˌreprɪzen'teɪʃən] n a (*Theat, gen*) représentation *f*; *[role]* interprétation *f*. (*Parl*) **proportional** ~ représentation proportionnelle. b (*protest*) **~s** démarche *f*; **the ambassador made ~s to the government** l'ambassadeur a fait une démarche auprès du gouvernement.
representational [ˌreprɪzen'teɪʃənl] adj représentatif, qui représente; (*Painting*) figuratif.
representative [ˌreprɪ'zentətɪv] 1 adj a (*typical*) représentatif, caractéristique, typique (*of* de). **a** ~ **cross section of the public** une fraction représentative du public; **this is not a** ~ **sample** ceci ne constitue pas un échantillon représentatif. b (*Parl*) ~ **government** gouvernement représentatif. 2 n représentant(e) *m(f)*; (*Comm*) représentant (de commerce); (*US Pol*) député *m*; (*spokesperson*) porte-parole *m*; *see* **house**.
repress [rɪ'pres] vt *emotions* réprimer, contenir; *revolt* réprimer; *sneeze* étouffer; (*Psych*) refouler.
repressed [rɪ'prest] adj réprimé, contenu; (*Psych*) refoulé.
repression [rɪ'preʃən] n a répression *f*. b (*Psych*) (*voluntary*) répression *f*; (*involuntary*) refoulement *m*.
repressive [rɪ'presɪv] adj répressif. (*Pol*) ~ **measures** mesures *fpl* de répression.
reprieve [rɪ'priːv] 1 n (*Jur*) (lettres *fpl* de) grâce *f*, commutation *f* de la peine capitale; (*delay*) sursis *m*; (*fig: respite*) répit *m*, sursis, délai *m*. **they won a** ~ **for the house** ils ont obtenu un sursis pour la maison. 2 vt (*Jur*) accorder une commutation de la peine capitale à; (*delay*) surseoir à l'exécution de; (*fig*) accorder du répit à. (*fig*) **the building has been ~d for a while** le bâtiment bénéficie d'un sursis.
reprimand ['reprɪmɑːnd] 1 n (*from parents, teachers*) réprimande *f*; (*from employer*) blâme *m*. 2 vt réprimander; blâmer.
reprint [ˌriː'prɪnt] 1 vt réimprimer. **this book is being ~ed** ce livre est en réimpression. 2 vi *[book]* être en réimpression. 3 ['riːprint] n réimpression *f*. **cheap** ~ édition *f* à bon marché.
reprisal [rɪ'praɪzəl] n: **~s** représailles *fpl*; **to take ~s** user de représailles; **as a** ~ **for** en représailles de; **by way of** ~ par représailles.
repro* ['riːprəʊ] 1 n abbr of **reprographics, reprography.** 2 comp (abbr of **reproduction**) ~ **furniture** copie(s) *f(pl)* de meuble(s) ancien(s).
reproach [rɪ'prəʊtʃ] 1 n a (*rebuke*) reproche *m*. **to heap ~es on sb** accabler qn de reproches; **term of** ~ parole *f* de reproche. b (*NonC: discredit*) honte *f*, opprobre *m*. (*fig*) **to be a** ~ **to** être la honte de; **to bring** ~ **on** jeter le discrédit sur, discréditer; **above** *or* **beyond** ~ sans reproche(s), irréprochable. 2 vt faire des reproches à, reprocher à. **to** ~ **sb for sth** reprocher qch à qn; **to** ~ **sb for having done** reprocher à qn d'avoir fait; **he has nothing to** ~ **himself with** il n'a rien à se reprocher.
reproachful [rɪ'prəʊtʃfʊl] adj *look, tone, person* réprobateur (*f* -trice); *words* de reproche.
reproachfully [rɪ'prəʊtʃfəlɪ] adv avec reproche, d'un air *or* ton de reproche.
reprobate ['reprəʊbeɪt] 1 adj, n dépravé(e) *m(f)*. 2 vt réprouver.
reprobation [ˌreprəʊ'beɪʃən] n réprobation *f*.
reprocess [ˌriː'prəʊses] vt retraiter.
reprocessing [ˌriː'prəʊsesɪŋ] n retraitement *m*; *see* **nuclear**.
reproduce [ˌriːprə'djuːs] 1 vt reproduire. 2 vi se reproduire.
reproducible [ˌriːprə'djuːsɪbl] adj reproductible.
reproduction [ˌriːprə'dʌkʃən] 1 n a (*procreation*) reproduction *f*. b (*Art*) reproduction *f*. **sound** ~ reproduction sonore; **this picture is a** ~ ce tableau est une reproduction *or* une copie. 2 comp ▸**reproduction furniture** copie(s) *f(pl)* de meuble(s) ancien(s).
reproductive [ˌriːprə'dʌktɪv] adj reproducteur (*f* -trice).
reprographic [ˌriːprə'græfɪk] adj de reprographie.
reprographics [ˌriːprə'græfɪks] n, **reprography** [ˌrɪ'prɒgrəfɪ] n reprographie *f*.
re-proof [ˌriː'pruːf] vt *garment* réimperméabiliser.
reproof [rɪ'pruːf] n reproche *m*, réprimande *f*, désapprobation *f*.
reproval [rɪ'pruːvəl] n reproche *m*, blâme *m*.
reprove [rɪ'pruːv] vt *person* blâmer (*for* de), réprimander (*for* sur); *action* réprouver, condamner.
reproving [rɪ'pruːvɪŋ] adj réprobateur (*f* -trice).
reprovingly [rɪ'pruːvɪŋlɪ] adv d'un air *or* ton de reproche.
reptile ['reptaɪl] adj, n (*also fig pej*) reptile (*m*).
reptilian [rep'tɪlɪən] 1 adj (*Zool*) reptilien; (*fig pej*) reptile (*liter*), de reptile. 2 n reptile *m* (*also fig*).
republic [rɪ'pʌblɪk] n république *f*. (*US*) **the R~** les États-Unis d'Amérique.
republican [rɪ'pʌblɪkən] adj, n républicain(e) *m(f)*.
republicanism [rɪ'pʌblɪkənɪzəm] n (*gen*) républicanisme *m*. (*US*) **R~** politique *f* du parti républicain.
republication [ˌriːpʌblɪ'keɪʃən] n *[book]* réédition *f*, nouvelle édition; *[law, banns]* nouvelle publication.
republish [ˌriː'pʌblɪʃ] vt *book* rééditer; *banns* publier de nouveau.
repudiate [rɪ'pjuːdɪeɪt] vt *friend, ally* renier, désavouer; *accusation* répudier, repousser, rejeter; *[government etc] debt, treaty, obligation* refuser d'honorer. **to** ~ **one's wife** répudier sa femme.
repudiation [rɪˌpjuːdɪ'eɪʃən] n (*see* **repudiate**) reniement *m*, désaveu *m*; répudiation *f*, rejet *m*.
repugnance [rɪ'pʌgnəns] n répugnance *f*, aversion *f* (*to* pour). **he shows** ~ **to accepting charity** il répugne à accepter la charité.
repugnant [rɪ'pʌgnənt] adj répugnant, dégoûtant. **he finds her** ~ elle lui répugne; **to find sth** ~ **to do** répugner à faire qch.
repulse [rɪ'pʌls] 1 vt (*Mil*) repousser, refouler; (*fig*) *help, offer* repousser, rejeter. 2 n (*Mil*) échec *m*; (*fig*) rebuffade *f*, refus *m*. **to meet with** *or* **suffer a** ~ essuyer une rebuffade.
repulsion [rɪ'pʌlʃən] n (*also Phys*) répulsion *f*.
repulsive [rɪ'pʌlsɪv] adj répulsif, repoussant; (*Phys*) répulsif.
repulsively [rɪ'pʌlsɪvlɪ] adv d'une façon repoussante. ~ **ugly** d'une laideur repoussante.
repulsiveness [rɪ'pʌlsɪvnɪs] n aspect *or* caractère repoussant.
repurchase [ˌriː'pɜːtʃɪs] 1 n rachat *m*. 2 vt racheter.
reputable ['repjʊtəbl] adj *person* honorable, estimé, de bonne réputation; *occupation* honorable; *dealer, firm* de bonne réputation.
reputation [ˌrepjʊ'teɪʃən] n réputation *f*. **to have a good/bad** ~ avoir (une) bonne/(une) mauvaise réputation; **a good** ~ **as a singer** une bonne réputation de chanteur; **to have a** ~ **for honesty** avoir la réputation d'être honnête, être réputé pour son honnêteté; **to live up to one's** ~ soutenir sa réputation.
repute [rɪ'pjuːt] 1 n réputation *f*, renom *m*. **to know sb by** ~ connaître qn de réputation; **to be of good** ~ avoir (une) bonne réputation; **a restaurant of** ~ un restaurant réputé *or* en renom; **place of ill** ~ endroit *m* mal famé; (*euph: brothel*) **a house of ill** ~ une maison close; **to hold sb in high** ~ avoir une très haute opinion de qn. 2 vt (*pass only*) **to be**

~d rich passer pour riche; **he is ~d to be the best player** il est réputé *or* censé être le meilleur joueur.

reputed [rɪ'pjuːtɪd] **adj** réputé. (*Jur*) ~ **father** père putatif.

reputedly [rɪ'pjuːtɪdlɪ] **adv** à *or* d'après ce qu'on dit, selon la rumeur publique.

request [rɪ'kwest] **1 n a** demande *f*, requête *f*. **at sb's ~** sur *or* à la demande de qn, à la requête de qn; **by general** *or* **popular ~** à la demande générale; **on** *or* **by ~** sur demande; **to make a ~ for sth** faire une demande de qch; **to make a ~ to sb for sth** demander qch à qn; **to grant a ~** accéder à une demande *or* à une requête.
b (*Rad*) disque *m* des auditeurs *or* demandé par un auditeur. **to play a ~ for sb** faire passer un disque à l'intention de qn.
2 vt demander. **to ~ sth from sb** demander qch à qn; **to ~ sb to do** demander à qn de faire, prier qn de faire; **"you are ~ed not to smoke"** "prière de ne pas fumer"; (*Comm etc*) **as ~ed in your letter of ...** comme vous (nous) l'avez demandé dans votre lettre du ...; (*Comm etc*) **herewith, as ~ed, my cheque for £50** ci-joint, selon votre demande, un *or* mon chèque de £50; **it's all I ~ of you** c'est tout ce que je vous demande.
3 comp ►request programme (*Rad*) programme *m* des auditeurs **►request stop** (*Brit*) *[bus]* arrêt facultatif.

requiem ['rekwɪem] **n** requiem *m*. ~ **mass** messe *f* de requiem.

require [rɪ'kwaɪəʳ] **vt a** (*need*) *[person]* avoir besoin de; *[thing, action]* demander, nécessiter. **I have all I ~** j'ai tout ce qu'il me faut *or* tout ce dont j'ai besoin; **the journey will ~ 3 hours** le voyage prendra *or* demandera trois heures; **it ~s great care** cela demande *or* nécessite *or* exige beaucoup de soin; **this plant ~s frequent watering** cette plante demande à être arrosée souvent; **if ~d** au besoin, si besoin est, s'il le faut; **when (it is) ~d** quand il le faut; **what qualifications are ~d?** quels sont les diplômes nécessaires? *or* exigés?
b (*demand*) exiger; (*order*) exiger, réclamer. **to ~ sb to do** exiger de qn qu'il fasse; (*fml*) **you are ~d to present yourself here tomorrow** vous êtes prié de vous présenter ici demain; **to ~ sth of sb** exiger qch de qn; **as ~d by law** comme la loi l'exige; **we ~ two references** nous exigeons deux références.

required [rɪ'kwaɪəd] **adj** exigé, demandé, requis. **to satisfy the ~ conditions** satisfaire aux conditions requises; **by the ~ date** en temps voulu; **in the ~ time** dans les délais prescrits; **the ~ amount** la quantité voulue; (*US Scol etc*) ~ **course** matière *f* obligatoire.

requirement [rɪ'kwaɪəmənt] **n a** (*need*) exigence *f*, besoin *m*. **to meet sb's ~s** satisfaire aux exigences *or* aux besoins de qn; **there isn't enough to meet the ~** il n'y en a pas assez pour satisfaire *or* suffire à la demande. **b** (*condition*) condition *f* requise. **to fit the ~s** remplir les conditions. **c** (*US Univ*) cursus *m* obligatoire.

requisite ['rekwɪzɪt] **1 n** chose *f* nécessaire *or* requise (*for* pour). **all the ~s** tout ce qui est nécessaire; **travel/toilet ~s** accessoires *mpl* de voyage/toilette. **2 adj** requis, nécessaire.

requisition [ˌrekwɪ'zɪʃən] **1 n** demande *f*; (*gen Mil*) réquisition *f*. **to put in a ~ for** faire une demande de. **2 vt** (*gen*) faire une demande de; (*Mil*) réquisitionner.

requital [rɪ'kwaɪtl] **n** (*repayment*) récompense *f*; (*revenge*) revanche *f*.

requite [rɪ'kwaɪt] **vt a** (*repay*) *person, action* récompenser, payer (*for* de). **~d love** amour partagé. **b** (*avenge*) *action* venger; *person* se venger de.

reran [ˌriː'ræn] **pret of rerun**.

reread [ˌriː'riːd] **pret, ptp reread** [ˌriː'red] **vt** relire.

reredos ['rɪədɒs] **n** retable *m*.

reroof [ˌriː'ruːf] **vt** refaire la toiture de.

reroute [ˌriː'ruːt] **vt** *train, coach* changer l'itinéraire de, dérouter. **our train was ~d through Leeds** on a fait faire à notre train un détour par Leeds, notre train a été dérouté par Leeds.

rerun ['riːrʌn] **(vb: pret reran, ptp rerun) 1 n** *[film, tape]* reprise *f*; (*TV programme, series*) rediffusion *f*. **2** [ˌriː'rʌn] **vt** *film, tape* passer de nouveau; *race* courir de nouveau.

resale [ˌriː'seɪl] **n** (*gen*) revente *f*. **what's the ~ value?** cela se revend combien?, quelle est la valeur de rachat?; (*on package etc*) **"not for ~"** "échantillon gratuit"; (*Comm*) ~ **price maintenance** prix *m* de vente imposé.

resat [ˌriː'sæt] **pret, ptp of resit**.

reschedule [ˌriː'ʃedjuːl], (*US*) [ˌriː'skedjuːl] **vt** *meeting, visit* changer l'heure (*or* la date) de; *train service etc* changer l'horaire de; *repayments, debt* rééchelonner; *plans, course* changer le programme de.

rescind [rɪ'sɪnd] **vt** *judgment* rescinder, casser; *law* abroger; *act* révoquer; *contract* résilier, dissoudre; *decision, agreement* annuler.

rescission [rɪ'sɪʒən] **n** (*see* **rescind**) rescision *f*; abrogation *f*; révocation *f*; résiliation *f*; annulation *f*.

rescript ['riːskrɪpt] **n** (*Hist, Rel*) rescrit *m*.

rescriptions [rɪ'skrɪpʃənz] **npl** (*St Ex*) bons *mpl* du Trésor, emprunts *mpl* des collectivités publiques.

rescue ['reskjuː] **1 n** (*help*) secours *mpl*; (*saving*) sauvetage *m*; (*freeing*) délivrance *f*. ~ **was difficult** le sauvetage a été difficile; ~ **came too late** les secours sont arrivés trop tard; **to go to sb's ~** aller au secours *or* à la rescousse de qn; **to come to sb's ~** venir en aide à qn *or* à la rescousse de qn; **to the ~** à la rescousse; *see* **air**.
2 vt (*save*) sauver, secourir; (*free*) délivrer (*from* de). **you ~d me from a difficult situation** vous m'avez tiré d'une situation difficile; **the ~d were taken to hospital** les rescapés ont été emmenés à l'hôpital.
3 comp *attempt* de sauvetage **►rescue operations** opérations *fpl* de sauvetage **►rescue party** (*gen*) équipe *f* de secours; (*Ski, Climbing*) colonne *f* de secours **►rescue services** services *mpl* de secours.

rescuer ['reskjuəʳ] **n** (*see* **rescue**) sauveteur *m*; libérateur *m*, -trice *f*.

resealable [ˌriː'siːləbl] **adj** *container* refermable.

research [rɪ'sɜːtʃ] **1 n** recherche(s) *f(pl)*. **a piece of ~** un travail de recherche; **to do ~** faire des recherches *or* de la recherche; **to carry out ~ into the effects of ...** faire des recherches sur les effets de ... .
2 vi faire des recherches (*into, on* sur).
3 vt *article, book etc* faire des recherches pour *or* en vue de. **well-~ed** bien documenté.
4 comp ►research and development (*Ind etc*) recherche *f* et développement *m*, recherche-développement *f* **►research assistant, research associate** (*Univ*) ≈ étudiant(e) *m(f)* de maîtrise (*ayant statut de chercheur*) **►research establishment** centre *m* de recherches **►research fellow** (*Univ*) ≈ chercheur *m*, -euse *f* attaché(e) à l'université (*see also* **researcher**) **►research laboratory** laboratoire *m* de recherches **►research scientist** = **researcher ►research student** (*Univ*) étudiant(e) *m(f)* qui fait de la recherche, étudiant(e) *m(f)* de doctorat (*ayant statut de chercheur*) **►research work** travail *m* de recherche, recherches *fpl* **►research worker** chercheur *m*, -euse *f* (*see also* **researcher**).

researcher [rɪ'sɜːtʃəʳ] **n** chercheur *m*, -euse *f* (*NB some women researchers consider the feminine form derogatory*). **she is a ~** elle est chercheur.

reseat [ˌriː'siːt] **vt a** *person* faire changer de place à. **to ~ o.s.** se rasseoir. **b** *chair* refaire le fond de; *trousers* mettre un fond à.

resection [riː'sekʃən] **n** résection *f*.

resell [ˌriː'sel] **pret, ptp resold vt** revendre.

resemblance [rɪ'zembləns] **n** ressemblance *f*. **to bear a strong/faint ~ to** avoir une grande/vague ressemblance avec; **there's not the slightest ~ between them** il n'y a pas la moindre ressemblance entre eux, ils ne se ressemblent pas du tout; **this bears no ~ to the facts** ceci n'a aucune ressemblance avec les faits.

resemble [rɪ'zembl] **vt** *[person]* ressembler à; *[thing]* ressembler à, être semblable à. **they ~ each other** ils se ressemblent.

resent [rɪ'zent] **vt** *sb's reply, look, attitude* être contrarié par, (*stronger*) être indigné de. **I ~ that!** je vous en prie!, je proteste!; **I ~ your tone** votre ton me déplaît fortement; **he ~ed my promotion** il n'a jamais pu accepter *or* admettre ma promotion; **he ~ed having lost his job/(the fact) that I married her** il n'a jamais pu admettre *or* accepter d'avoir perdu son emploi/le fait que je l'ai épousée; **he really ~ed this** ça lui est resté en travers de la gorge*; **he may ~ my being here** il n'appréciera peut-être pas ma présence.

resentful [rɪ'zentfʊl] **adj** *person, reply* plein de ressentiment, amer. **to be ~ of sb's success** envier à qn son succès; **to feel ~ about** éprouver du ressentiment de, être froissé *or* irrité de.

resentfully [rɪ'zentfəlɪ] **adv** avec ressentiment.

resentment [rɪ'zentmənt] **n** ressentiment *m*.

reservation [ˌrezə'veɪʃən] **1 n a** réserve *f*; (*Jur*) réservation *f*. **mental ~** restriction mentale; **without ~** sans réserve, sans arrière-pensée; **with ~s** avec certaines réserves, sous réserve; **to have ~s about** avoir des doutes sur.
b (*booking*) réservation *f*, location *f*. **to make a ~ at the hotel/on the boat** réserver *or* retenir une chambre à l'hôtel/une place sur le bateau; **to have a ~** (*in train, coach, plane*) avoir une place réservée; (*in hotel*) avoir une chambre réservée; (*in restaurant*) avoir une table réservée.
c (*area of land*) réserve *f*; (*US*) réserve (indienne). (*on roadway*) **(central) ~** bande *f* médiane.
d (*Rel*) **R~ (of the Sacrament)** les Saintes Réserves.
2 comp ►reservation desk (*in airport, hotels etc*) comptoir *m* des réservations.

reserve [rɪ'zɜːv] **1 vt a** (*keep*) réserver, garder, mettre en réserve *or* de côté. **to ~ one's strength** ménager *or* garder ses forces; (*Sport*) se réserver; **to ~ the best wine for one's friends** réserver le meilleur vin pour ses amis; **to ~ judgment/one's decision** se réserver de prononcer un jugement/de prendre une décision; **to ~ the right to do** se réserver le droit de faire; **to ~ a warm welcome for sb** ménager *or* réserver un accueil chaleureux à qn; **to ~ o.s. for** se réserver pour.
b (*book in advance*) *room, seat* réserver, retenir.
2 n a (*sth stored*) réserve *f*, stock *m*. **to have great ~s of energy** avoir une grande réserve d'énergie; **cash ~** réserve de caisse; **gold ~s** réserves *fpl* d'or; **world ~s of pyrites** réserves mondiales de pyrite; **to keep** *or* **hold in ~** tenir en réserve.
b (*restriction*) réserve *f*, restriction *f*. **without ~** sans réserve, sans restriction; **with all ~** *or* **all proper ~s** sous toutes réserves.
c = ~ **price**; *see* **3**.
d (*piece of land*) réserve *f*; *see* **game**[1], **nature**.
e (*NonC: attitude*) réserve *f*, retenue *f*. **he treated me with some ~** il s'est tenu sur la réserve avec moi; **to break through sb's ~** amener

qn à se départir de sa réserve *or* retenue.
f (*Mil*) **the R~** la réserve; **the ~s** la réserve, les réservistes *mpl*.
g (*Sport*) remplaçant(e) *m(f)*.
3 **comp** *currency, fund* de réserve ► **reserve bank** (*US*) banque *f* de réserve ► **reserve list** (*Mil*) cadre *m* de réserve ► **reserve (petrol) tank** réservoir *m* (d'essence) de secours, nourrice *f* ► **reserve player** (*Sport*) remplaçant(e) *m(f)* ► **reserve price** (*Brit*) prix *m* minimum ► **reserve team** deuxième équipe *f*, équipe B.
reserved [rɪ'zɜːvd] **adj** a (*shy*) réservé, timide; (*uncommunicative*) renfermé. **he was very ~ about ...** il est resté sur la réserve quant à ... . b *room* réservé. **~ seats** places réservées. c (*Comm*) **all rights ~** tous droits de reproduction réservés; *see* **copyright**.
reservedly [rɪ'zɜːvɪdlɪ] **adv** avec réserve, avec retenue.
reservist [rɪ'zɜːvɪst] **n** (*Mil*) réserviste *m*.
reservoir ['rezəvwɑːʳ] **n** (*lit, fig*) réservoir *m*.
reset [ˌriː'set] **pret, ptp reset** 1 **vt** a *precious stone* remonter. b *clock, watch* mettre à l'heure. **to ~ the alarm** remettre l'alarme. c (*Med*) *limb* remettre. **to ~ a broken bone** réduire une fracture. d (*Typ*) recomposer. 2 **comp** ► **reset button, reset switch** (*Comput*) commande *f* de remise à zéro.
resettle [ˌriː'setl] **vt** *refugee* établir, implanter; *land* repeupler.
resettlement [ˌriː'setlmənt] **n** (*see* **resettle**) établissement *m*, implantation *f*; repeuplement *m*.
reshape [ˌriː'ʃeɪp] **vt** *dough, clay* refaçonner, modeler de nouveau; *text, policy* réorganiser.
reshuffle [ˌriː'ʃʌfl] 1 **vt** a *cards* battre de nouveau. b (*fig*) *cabinet, board of directors* remanier. 2 **n** a *[cards]* **to have a ~** rebattre. b (*in command etc*) remaniement *m*. (*Pol*) **Cabinet ~** remaniement ministériel.
reside [rɪ'zaɪd] **vi** (*lit, fig*) résider. **the power ~s in** *or* **with the President** le pouvoir est entre les mains du Président *or* réside dans le Président.
residence ['rezɪdəns] 1 **n** a (*house: frm*) résidence *f*, demeure *f*. **the President's official ~** la résidence officielle du Président.
b (*also* **university ~, hall of ~**) résidence *f* universitaire.
c (*NonC: stay*) séjour *m*, résidence *f*. **after 5 years' ~ in Britain** après avoir résidé en Grande-Bretagne pendant 5 ans; (*Admin*) **place/country of ~** lieu *m*/pays *m* de résidence; **to take up ~ in the country** élire domicile *or* s'installer à la campagne; *[monarch, governor etc]* **to be in ~** être en résidence; **the students are now in ~** les étudiants sont maintenant rentrés; **there is always a doctor in ~** il y a toujours un médecin résidant.
2 **comp** ► **residence hall** (*US Univ*) résidence *f* universitaire ► **residence permit** (*Brit*) permis *m or* carte *f* de séjour.
residency ['rezɪdənsɪ] **n** (*gen*) résidence officielle; (*US Med*) internat *m* de deuxième et de troisième années. (*Mus: regular engagement*) **they've got a ~ at Steve's Bar** ils jouent régulièrement au Steve's Bar.
resident ['rezɪdənt] 1 **n** a habitant(e) *m(f)*; (*in foreign country*) résident(e) *m(f)*; (*in street*) riverain(e) *m(f)*; (*in hostel*) pensionnaire *mf*. **"parking for ~s only"** "voie privée", "emplacement pour résidents autorisés"; **"~s only"** "interdit sauf aux riverains"; **~s' association** association *f* de riverains.
b (*US Med*) interne *mf* de deuxième et de troisième années.
2 **adj** résidant; *chaplain, tutor* à demeure. **they are ~ in France** ils résident en France; **the ~ population** la population fixe, les habitants *mpl* du pays; (*Med*) **~ physician** interne *mf*; (*US Univ*) **~ head** directeur *m*, -trice *f* d'une résidence universitaire; (*US Univ*) **~ student** *étudiant(e) d'une université d'État dont le domicile permanent est situé dans cet État*.
residential [ˌrezɪ'denʃəl] **adj** *area* résidentiel; *conditions* de résidence; *work, post* qui demande résidence. (*US*) **~ school** internat *m* (*surtout pour handicapés*); (*US*) **~ student** interne *mf* (*en général handicapé*).
residua [rɪ'zɪdjʊə] **npl of residuum**.
residual [rɪ'zɪdjʊəl] 1 **adj** restant; (*Chem*) résiduaire, résiduel. **~ unemployment** chômage *m* résiduel. 2 **n** a (*Chem*) résidu *m*; (*Math*) reste *m*. b (*royalties*) **~s** *droits versés aux acteurs et à l'auteur à l'occasion d'une rediffusion d'un programme télévisé ou d'un film*.
residuary [rɪ'zɪdjʊərɪ] **adj** restant; (*Chem*) résiduaire. (*Jur*) **~ estate** montant *m* net d'une succession; (*Jur*) **~ legatee** ≃ légataire *mf* universel(le).
residue ['rezɪdjuː] **n** reste(s) *m(pl)*; (*Chem*) résidu *m*; (*Math*) reste; (*Jur*) reliquat *m*.
residuum [rɪ'zɪdjʊəm] **n, pl residua** résidu *m*, reste *m*.
resign [rɪ'zaɪn] 1 **vt** (*give up*) se démettre de; *one's job* démissionner de; (*hand over*) céder (*to* à). **he ~ed the leadership to his colleague** il a cédé la direction à son collègue; (*Mil etc*) **to ~ one's commission** démissionner (*se dit d'un officier*); **to ~ o.s. to (doing) sth** se résigner à (faire) qch. 2 **vi** démissionner, donner sa démission (*from* de).
resignation [ˌrezɪg'neɪʃən] **n** a (*from job*) démission *f*. **to tender one's ~** donner sa démission. b (*mental state*) résignation *f*. c (*NonC*) *[a right]* abandon *m* (*of* de), renonciation *f* (*of* à).
resigned [rɪ'zaɪnd] **adj** *person, look, voice* résigné. **to become ~ to (doing) sth** se résigner à (faire) qch; **I was ~ to walking, when ...** je m'étais résigné à y aller à pied, lorsque ... .
resignedly [rɪ'zaɪnɪdlɪ] **adv** avec résignation, d'un ton *or* d'un air résigné.
resilience [rɪ'zɪlɪəns] **n** *[person, character]* élasticité *f*, ressort *m*; *[rubber]* élasticité.
resilient [rɪ'zɪlɪənt] **adj** *nature, character* qui réagit; *rubber, metal* élastique. **he's very ~** (*physically*) il a beaucoup de résistance, il récupère bien; (*mentally etc*) il a du ressort, il ne se laisse pas abattre *or* déprimer.
resin ['rezɪn] **n** résine *f*.
resinous ['rezɪnəs] **adj** résineux.
resist [rɪ'zɪst] 1 **vt** *attack, arrest* résister à, s'opposer à; *temptation* résister à; *person* repousser, résister à; *order* refuser d'obéir *or* d'obtempérer à; *change* s'opposer à. **I couldn't ~ (eating) another cake** je n'ai pas pu résister à l'envie de *or* je n'ai pas pu m'empêcher de manger encore un gâteau; **he ~s any advice** il s'oppose à *or* il est rebelle à tout conseil; **she can't ~ him** elle ne peut rien lui refuser. 2 **vi** résister, offrir de la résistance.
resistance [rɪ'zɪstəns] 1 **n** (*gen, Elec, Med, Mil, Phys*) résistance *f*. (*Hist*) **the R~** la Résistance; **to meet with ~** se heurter à une résistance; **to offer ~ to sth** résister à qch; **to put up** *or* **offer stiff ~ to sth** opposer une vive résistance à qch; **he offered no ~** il n'opposa aucune résistance (*to* à); (*Med*) **his ~ was very low** il n'offrait presque plus de résistance (au mal); *see* **line**[1], **passive**. 2 **comp** ► **resistance fighter** résistant(e) *m(f)* ► **resistance movement** résistance *f* (*mouvement*).
resistant [rɪ'zɪstənt] **adj** résistant; (*Med*) rebelle. (*of virus, strain*) **~ to** rebelle à; **~ to penicillin** pénicillo-résistant; *see* **water**.
-resistant [rɪ'zɪstənt] **adj ending in comps: disease-resistant** *plant* résistant aux maladies; **fire-resistant** *paint, cloth* ignifugé; **heat-resistant** résistant à la chaleur.
resistor [rɪ'zɪstəʳ] **n** (*Elec*) résistance *f*.
resit [ˌriː'sɪt] **pret, ptp resat** (*Brit*) 1 **vt** se représenter à, repasser. 2 **vi** se présenter à la deuxième session. 3 ['riːsɪt] **n** deuxième session *f* (*d'un examen*). **to have a ~ in law** devoir se représenter en droit.
resite [ˌriː'saɪt] **vt** *factory* réimplanter, transférer.
resold [ˌriː'səʊld] **pret, ptp of resell**.
resole [ˌriː'səʊl] **vt** ressemeler.
resolute ['rezəluːt] **adj** résolu, déterminé.
resolutely ['rezəluːtlɪ] **adv** résolument, avec détermination.
resoluteness ['rezəluːtnɪs] **n** résolution *f*, détermination *f*, fermeté *f*.
resolution [ˌrezə'luːʃən] **n** a (*decision*) résolution *f*. **to make a ~ to do** prendre la résolution de faire; **good ~s** bonnes résolutions; *see* **New Year**. b (*Admin, Pol*) résolution *f*. **to make a ~** prendre une résolution; **to adopt/reject a ~** adopter/rejeter une résolution. c (*NonC: resoluteness*) fermeté *f*, résolution *f*. **to show ~** faire preuve de fermeté, faire preuve (d'esprit) de décision. d (*NonC: solving*) *[problem, puzzle]* solution *f*. e (*NonC: Chem, Med, Mus*) résolution *f* (*into* en).
resolvable [rɪ'zɒlvəbl] **adj** résoluble.
resolve [rɪ'zɒlv] 1 **vt** a (*break up*) résoudre, réduire (*into* en). **to ~ sth into its elements** ramener *or* réduire qch à ses éléments; **water ~s itself into steam** l'eau se résout *or* se transforme en vapeur; **the meeting ~d itself into a committee** l'assemblée se constitua en commission.
b *problem, difficulty* résoudre; *doubt* dissiper.
c (*Med, Mus*) résoudre.
2 **vi** a (*decide*) résoudre, décider (*to do* de faire), se résoudre, se décider (*to do* à faire). **to ~ (up)on sth** se résoudre à qch; **to ~ that ...** décider que ...; **it has been ~d that** il a été résolu que.
b (*break up*) se résoudre (*into* en). **the question ~s into 4 points** la question se divise en 4 points.
3 **n** a (*decision*) résolution *f*, décision *f*. **to make a ~ to do** prendre la résolution de faire, résoudre de faire.
b (*NonC: resoluteness*) résolution *f*, fermeté *f*. **to do sth with ~** faire qch avec détermination.
resolved [rɪ'zɒlvd] **adj** résolu, décidé (*to do* à faire).
resonance ['rezənəns] **n** (*gen, Mus, Phon, Phys*) résonance *f*; *[voice]* résonance, sonorité *f*.
resonant ['rezənənt] **adj** (*gen, Mus, Phys*) résonant; (*Phon*) sonnant, résonant; *voice* sonore, résonant.
resonate ['rezəneɪt] **vi** a *[sound]* résonner. b **the room ~d with the sound of laughter** la pièce résonnait de rires.
resonator ['rezəneɪtəʳ] **n** résonateur *m*.
resorption [rɪ'zɔːpʃən] **n** résorption *f*.
resort [rɪ'zɔːt] 1 **n** a (*recourse*) recours *m*; (*thing, action resorted to*) ressource *f*, recours, expédient *m* (*often pej*). **without ~ to violence** sans recourir *or* avoir recours à la violence; **as a last ~, in the last ~** en dernier ressort; **it was/you were my last ~** c'était/tu étais mon dernier recours; **hiding was the only ~ left to them** se cacher était la seule ressource qui leur restait.
b (*place*) lieu *m* de séjour *or* de vacances. **coastal ~** plage *f*; **seaside/summer ~** station *f* balnéaire/estivale; **winter sports ~** station de sports d'hiver; (*fig liter*) **a ~ of thieves** un repaire de voleurs; *see* **health, holiday**.
2 **vi** avoir recours (*to sth/sb* à qch/qn), recourir (*to sth* à qch), en venir (*to doing* à faire).

resound [rɪ'zaʊnd] 1 vi retentir, résonner (*with* de). (*fig*) **his speech will ~ throughout France** son discours aura du retentissement dans toute la France. 2 vt faire retentir *or* résonner.

resounding [rɪ'zaʊndɪŋ] adj *noise, shout* sonore, retentissant; *laugh* sonore; *voice* sonore, tonitruant (*pej*); *triumph, victory* retentissant. **~ success** succès retentissant *or* fou*; **~ defeat** défaite écrasante.

resoundingly [rɪ'zaʊndɪŋlɪ] adv d'une manière retentissante. **the play was ~ successful** la pièce a eu un succès retentissant.

resource [rɪ'sɔːs] 1 n a (*wealth, supplies etc*) **~s** ressources *fpl*; **financial/mineral/natural ~s** ressources pécuniaires/en minerais/naturelles; **~s of men and materials** ressources en hommes et en matériel; (*Fin*) **the total ~s of a company** les ressources totales d'une société; (*fig*) **he has no ~s against boredom** il ne sait pas lutter *or* se défendre contre l'ennui; (*fig*) **left to his own ~s** livré à ses propres ressources *or* à lui-même.
b (*Comput*) ressources *fpl*.
c (*expedient*) ressource *f*. **as a last ~** en dernier ressort, en dernière ressource; **you are my last ~** vous êtes ma dernière ressource *or* mon dernier espoir.
2 comp ►**resource centre** (*Scol, Univ etc*) centre *m* de documentation ►**resource(s) gap** (*Econ*) déficit *m* de ressources.

resourceful [rɪ'sɔːsfʊl] adj *person* (plein) de ressources, ingénieux, débrouillard*; *scheme* ingénieux.

resourcefully [rɪ'sɔːsfəlɪ] adv d'une manière ingénieuse *or* débrouillarde*.

resourcefulness [rɪ'sɔːsfʊlnɪs] n (*NonC*) ressource *f*.

respect [rɪ'spekt] 1 n a (*NonC: esteem*) respect *m*, considération *f*, estime *f*. **to have ~ for** *person* avoir du respect pour, respecter; *the law, sb's intelligence* respecter; **I have the greatest ~ for him** j'ai infiniment de respect pour lui; **to treat with ~** traiter avec respect; **to be held in ~** être tenu en haute estime; **he can command ~** il impose le respect, il sait se faire respecter.
b (*NonC: consideration*) respect *m*, considération *f*, égard *m*. **she has no ~ for other people's feelings** elle n'a aucune considération *or* aucun respect pour les sentiments d'autrui; **out of ~ for** par respect *or* égard pour; **with (due) ~ I still think that** sans vouloir vous contredire *or* sauf votre respect je crois toujours que; (*frm*) **without ~ of persons** sans acception de personne; **without ~ to the consequences** sans tenir compte *or* se soucier des conséquences, sans s'arrêter aux conséquences.
c (*NonC: reference; aspect*) égard *m*, rapport *m*. **with ~ to** pour *or* en ce qui concerne, quant à, relativement à; **good in ~ of content** bon sous le rapport du contenu *or* quant au contenu; **in what ~?** sous quel rapport?, à quel égard?; **in some ~s** à certains égards, sous certains rapports; **in many ~s** à bien des égards; **in this ~** à cet égard, sous ce rapport; **in one ~** d'un certain côté; **in other ~s** à d'autres égards.
d (*regards*) **~s** respects *mpl*, hommages *mpl*; **to pay one's ~s to sb** présenter ses respects à qn; **give my ~s to** présentez mes respects *or* mes hommages à.
2 vt a *person, customs, sb's wishes, opinions, grief, the law* respecter. **to ~ o.s.** se respecter.
b **as ~s** quant à, en ce qui concerne.

respectability [rɪˌspektə'bɪlɪtɪ] n respectabilité *f*.

respectable [rɪ'spektəbl] adj a (*estimable*) *person* respectable, honorable, estimable; *motives* respectable, honorable; (*socially approved*) *person* respectable, convenable; *clothes, behaviour* convenable, comme il faut. **a poor but ~ woman** une femme pauvre mais tout à fait respectable; **they are very ~ people** ce sont de très braves gens; **he was outwardly ~ but ...** il avait l'apparence de la respectabilité mais ...; **in ~ society** entre gens convenables *or* comme il faut; **that's not ~** ça ne se fait pas.
b (*of some size, importance*) *size, income* considérable, respectable. **a ~ writer** un écrivain qui n'est pas sans talent; **a ~ sum** une somme respectable *or* rondelette.

respectably [rɪ'spektəblɪ] adv a *dress, behave* convenablement, correctement, comme il faut*. b (*quite well*) passablement, pas mal*.

respecter [rɪ'spektəʳ] n: **death/the law is no ~ of persons** tout le monde est égal devant la mort/la loi; **death is no ~ of wealth** les riches et les pauvres sont égaux devant la mort; **he is no ~ of persons** il ne s'en laisse imposer par personne.

respectful [rɪ'spektfʊl] adj *person, behaviour, tone* respectueux (*of* de, *towards* envers, à l'égard de).

respectfully [rɪ'spektfəlɪ] adv respectueusement, avec respect. (*in letters*) **I remain ~ yours** *or* **yours ~** je vous prie d'agréer l'expression de mes sentiments respectueux *or* (*man to woman*) de mes très respectueux hommages.

respectfulness [rɪ'spektfʊlnɪs] n respect *m*, caractère respectueux.

respecting [rɪ'spektɪŋ] prep en ce qui concerne, quant à, concernant, touchant.

respective [rɪ'spektɪv] adj respectif.

respectively [rɪ'spektɪvlɪ] adv respectivement.

respiration [ˌrespɪ'reɪʃən] n (*Bot, Med*) respiration *f*.

respirator ['respəˌreɪtəʳ] n (*Med*) respirateur *m*; (*Mil*) masque *m* à gaz.

respiratory ['respərətərɪ] adj respiratoire. (*Med*) **~ failure** arrêt *m* respiratoire; *see* **system 1a, tract¹**.

respire [rɪ'spaɪəʳ] vti respirer.

respite ['respaɪt] n répit *m*, relâche *m or f*; (*Jur*) sursis *m*. **without (a) ~** sans répit, sans relâche, sans cesse.

resplendence [rɪ'splendəns] n resplendissement *m* (*liter*); splendeur *f*.

resplendent [rɪ'splendənt] adj resplendissant.

respond [rɪ'spɒnd] vi a (*reply*) répondre (*to* à, *with* par), faire une réponse (*to* à); (*Rel*) chanter les répons. **to ~ to a toast** répondre à un toast. b (*show reaction to*) répondre (*to* à). **brakes that ~ well** freins qui répondent bien; **car that ~s well to controls** voiture qui a de bonnes réactions *or* qui répond bien aux commandes; **the patient ~ed to treatment** le malade a bien réagi au traitement; **the illness ~ed to treatment** le traitement a agi sur la maladie.

respondent [rɪ'spɒndənt] 1 n a (*Jur*) défendeur *m*, -deresse *f*. b (*in opinion poll etc*) personne interrogée, sondé *m*. 2 adj qui répond *or* réagit (*to* à).

response [rɪ'spɒns] n a (*lit, fig*) réponse *f*; (*to treatment*) réaction *f*. **in ~ to** en réponse à; **in ~ to the radio appeal, the sum of £10,000 was raised** par suite de *or* en réponse à l'appel radiodiffusé, on a recueilli la somme de 10 000 livres; **his only ~ was to nod** pour toute réponse, il a incliné la tête; **we had hoped for a bigger ~ from the public** nous n'avons pas reçu du public la réponse escomptée; (*Comput*) **~ time** temps *m* de réponse. b (*Rel*) répons *m*.

responsibility [rɪˌspɒnsə'bɪlɪtɪ] 1 n responsabilité *f*. **to lay** *or* **put** *or* **place the ~ for sth on sb** tenir qn pour responsable de qch, faire porter la responsabilité de qch à qn; **to take ~ for sth** prendre la responsabilité de qch; **"the company takes no ~ for objects left here"** ≃ "la compagnie décline toute responsabilité pour les objets en dépôt"; **to take on the ~** accepter *or* assumer la responsabilité; **the group which claimed ~ for the attack** le groupe qui a revendiqué l'attentat; **that's HIS ~** c'est à lui de s'en occuper; **it's not MY ~ to do that** ce n'est pas à moi de faire ça; **on my own ~** sous ma responsabilité; **he wants a position with more ~** il cherche un poste offrant plus de responsabilités; **he has too many responsibilities** il a *or* assume trop de responsabilités; **it is a big ~ for him** c'est une grande *or* lourde responsabilité pour lui; **it is a ~ of course** évidemment, c'est une grande responsabilité.
2 comp ►**responsibility allowance, responsibility payment** prime *f* de fonction.

responsible [rɪ'spɒnsəbl] adj a (*liable*) responsable (*for* de). **she is not ~ for her actions** elle n'est pas responsable de ses actes; **to be ~ to sb for sth** être responsable de qch envers qn *or* devant qn; **to be directly ~ to sb** relever directement de qn; **who is ~ for this mistake?** qui est l'auteur *or* le responsable de cette erreur?; **I hold you ~ for all that happened** je vous considère *or* rends responsable de tout ce qui est arrivé. b (*trustworthy*) *person* digne de confiance, sur qui on peut compter. **he has a very ~ nature** il est très sérieux, il a un grand sens des responsabilités. c *job, duty* comportant des responsabilités.

responsibly [rɪ'spɒnsəblɪ] adv avec sérieux.

responsive [rɪ'spɒnsɪv] adj *audience, class, pupil* qui réagit bien. **he is very ~** il n'est pas du tout timide *or* réservé; (*to affection*) il est très affectueux; **~ to criticism** sensible à la critique; **he wasn't very ~ when I spoke to him about it** quand je lui en ai parlé, il a été plutôt réservé *or* il n'a pas beaucoup réagi.

responsiveness [rɪ'spɒnsɪvnɪs] n (*see* **responsive**) bonne réaction (*to* à); manque *m* de réserve *or* de timidité; caractère affectueux.

respray [ˌriː'spreɪ] 1 vt *car* refaire la peinture de. 2 ['riːspreɪ] n: **the car needs a ~** il faut que je fasse refaire la peinture de la voiture.

rest [rest] 1 n a (*gen: relaxation etc*) repos *m*. **a day of ~** un jour de repos; **to need ~** avoir besoin de repos; **to need a ~** avoir besoin de se reposer; **to have a ~** se reposer; **she took** *or* **had an hour's ~** elle s'est reposée pendant une heure; **we had a couple of ~s during the walk** pendant la promenade nous nous sommes arrêtés deux fois pour nous reposer; (*loc*) **no ~ for the wicked** pas de repos pour les braves; (*US Mil: leave*) **~ and recuperation** permission *f*; **take a ~!** reposez-vous!; **to have a good night's ~** passer une bonne nuit; (*liter*) **to retire to ~** se retirer; **at ~** au repos; **to be at ~** (*peaceful*) être tranquille *or* calme; (*immobile*) rester immobile, ne pas bouger; (*euph: dead*) reposer en paix; (*lit*) **to lay to ~** porter en terre; (*fig*) **to lay** *or* **put to ~** *idea, notion* enterrer; **to set at ~** *fears, doubts* dissiper; **to put** *or* **set sb's mind at ~** tranquilliser qn, rassurer qn; **you can set** *or* **put your mind at ~** tu peux être tranquille; **to come to ~** *[ball, car etc]* s'arrêter, s'immobiliser; *[bird, insect]* se poser (*on* sur); **give it a ~!*** (*change the subject*) change de disque!*; (*stop working*) laisse tomber!*.
b (*support*) support *m*, appui *m*; *see* **arm¹, receiver** *etc*.
c (*remainder*) **the ~ of the money** le reste *or* le restant *or* ce qui reste de l'argent, l'argent qui reste; **the ~ of the boys** les garçons qui restent, les autres garçons; **I will take half of the money and you keep the ~** je prends la moitié de l'argent et tu gardes le reste *or* le restant; **I will take this book and you keep the ~** je prends ce livre et tu gardes les autres; **you go off and the ~ of us will wait here** pars, nous (autres) nous resterons ici; **he was as drunk as the ~ of them** il était aussi ivre que (tous) les autres; **all the ~ of the money** tout ce qui reste de l'argent, tout l'argent qui reste; **all the ~ of the books** tous les autres

livres; **and all the ~ (of it)*** et tout ça*, et tout ce qui s'ensuit; **for the ~** quant au reste.

d (*Mus*) pause *f*; (*Poetry*) césure *f*. (*Mus*) **crotchet** (*Brit*) *or* **quarter-note** (*US*) ~ soupir *m*.

2 comp ►**rest camp** (*Mil*) cantonnement *m* de repos ►**rest centre** centre *m* d'accueil ►**rest cure** cure *f* de repos ►**rest day** jour *m* de repos ►**rest home, rest house** maison *f* de repos ►**resting place** lieu *m* de repos; *[the dead]* dernière demeure ►**rest room** (*US*) toilettes *fpl*.

3 vi a (*repose*) se reposer; *[the dead]* reposer. **she never ~s** elle ne se repose jamais, elle ne sait pas se reposer; **you must ~ for an hour** il faut vous reposer pendant une heure; (*fig*) **he won't ~ till he finds out the truth** il n'aura de cesse qu'il ne découvre (*subj*) la vérité; (*fig*) **to ~ easy** dormir sur ses deux oreilles; **to ~ on one's oars** (*lit*) lever les avirons *or* les rames; (*fig*) prendre un repos bien mérité; (*fig*) **to ~ on one's laurels** se reposer *or* s'endormir sur ses lauriers; *[actor]* (*euph*) **to be ~ing** se trouver sans engagement; **may he ~ in peace** qu'il repose en paix; (*Agr*) **to let a field ~** laisser reposer un champ, laisser un champ en jachère; (*Jur*) **"the defence** (*or* **prosecution) ~s"** "plaise au tribunal adopter nos conclusions".

b (*remain*) rester, demeurer. **~ assured that** soyez certain *or* assuré que; **he refused to let the matter ~** il refusait d'en rester là; **the matter must not ~ there, things must not ~ like that** il n'est pas admissible que l'affaire en reste (*subj*) là; **and there the matter ~s for the moment** l'affaire en est là pour le moment; **the authority ~s with him** c'est lui qui détient l'autorité; **the decision ~s with him, it ~s with him to decide** il lui appartient de décider, c'est à lui de prendre la décision; **it doesn't ~ with me** cela ne dépend pas de moi.

c (*lean, be supported*) *[person]* s'appuyer (*on* sur, *against* contre); *[ladder]* appuyer (*on* sur, *against* contre); *[roof etc]* reposer, appuyer (*on* sur); (*fig*) *[argument, reputation, case]* reposer (*on* sur); *[eyes, gaze]* se poser, s'arrêter (*on* sur). **her elbows were ~ing on the table** elle appuyait ses coudes sur la table; (*fig*) **a heavy responsibility ~s on him** il a de lourdes responsabilités.

4 vt a faire *or* laisser reposer, donner du repos à. **to ~ o.s.** se reposer; **I am quite ~ed** je me sens tout à fait reposé; **to ~ the horses** laisser reposer les chevaux; **God ~ his soul!** que Dieu ait son âme!, paix à son âme!; (*Jur*) **to ~ one's case** conclure sa plaidoirie.

b (*lean*) poser, appuyer (*on* sur, *against* contre); (*fig: base*) *suspicions* fonder, faire reposer, baser (*on* sur). **to ~ one's hand on sb's shoulder** poser la main sur l'épaule de qn; **to ~ one's elbows on the table** appuyer *or* poser les coudes sur la table; **to ~ a ladder against a wall** appuyer une échelle contre un mur.

►**rest up*** vi se reposer.

restart [ˌriːˈstɑːt] 1 vt *work, activity* reprendre, recommencer; *engine* relancer, remettre en marche; *machine* remettre en marche. 2 vi reprendre, recommencer; *[engine, machine]* se remettre en marche.

restate [ˌriːˈsteɪt] vt *argument, reasons* répéter; *problem* énoncer de nouveau; *theory, case, one's position* exposer de nouveau.

restatement [ˌriːˈsteɪtmənt] n (*gen*) répétition *f*; *[plan, theory]* nouvel énoncé. (*Jur*) **~ of the law** réexposé *m* du droit.

restaurant [ˈrestərɔ̃ːŋ] 1 n restaurant *m*. 2 comp *food, prices* de restaurant ►**restaurant car** (*Brit Rail*) wagon-restaurant *m*.

restaurateur [ˌrestərəˈtɜːʳ] n restaurateur *m*, -trice *f*.

restful [ˈrestfʊl] adj *occupation, pastime etc* reposant, qui procure du repos; *colour* reposant; *place* paisible, tranquille, reposant. **she is very ~ to be with** elle est très reposante.

restfully [ˈrestfəlɪ] adv paisiblement, tranquillement.

restitution [ˌrestɪˈtjuːʃən] n a (*NonC*) restitution *f*. **to make ~ of sth** restituer qch; (*Jur*) **~ of conjugal rights** ordre *m* de réintégration du domicile conjugal. b (*reparation*) réparation *f*, compensation *f*, indemnité *f*.

restive [ˈrestɪv] adj *horse* rétif; *person* agité, énervé; *manner* impatient, nerveux. **to get** *or* **grow ~** *[person]* s'agiter, s'énerver; *[horse]* devenir rétif.

restiveness [ˈrestɪvnɪs] n *[horse]* état rétif; *[person]* agitation *f*, énervement *m*.

restless [ˈrestlɪs] adj *person, manner, sea* agité; *child* agité, remuant. **I had a ~ night** j'ai mal dormi; **he is ~ in his sleep** il a le sommeil agité; *[audience, class etc]* **to get ~** s'impatienter, s'agiter, donner des signes d'agitation; (*fig: unsettled*) **he is very ~ just now** il n'a pas encore trouvé sa voie, il ne sait pas quoi faire de sa peau*.

restlessly [ˈrestlɪslɪ] adv avec agitation. **to walk ~ up and down** faire nerveusement les cent pas.

restlessness [ˈrestlɪsnɪs] n *[sleep]* agitation *f*; *[manner]* agitation, nervosité *f*; *[crowd]* impatience *f*.

restock [ˌriːˈstɒk] vt *shop* réapprovisionner; *pond, river* empoissonner.

restoration [ˌrestəˈreɪʃən] n a (*NonC: return*) rétablissement *m*; (*Jur*) *[property]* restitution *f*. (*Brit Hist*) **the R~** la Restauration (*de la monarchie en 1660*); (*Brit*) **R~** *comedy, drama etc* de la Restauration. b *[text]* rétablissement *m*; *[monument, work of art]* restauration *f*.

restorative [rɪˈstɔːrətɪv] adj, n fortifiant (*m*), reconstituant (*m*).

restore [rɪˈstɔːʳ] vt a (*give or bring back*) *sth lost, borrowed, stolen* rendre, restituer (*to* à); *sb's sight etc* rendre; (*Jur*) *rights, law etc* rétablir; *confidence* redonner (*to sb* à qn, *in* dans); *order, calm* rétablir, ramener. **to ~ sb's health** rétablir la santé de qn, rendre la santé à qn; **~d to health** rétabli, guéri; **to ~ sb to life** ramener qn à la vie; **to ~ sth to its former condition** remettre qch en état; **the brandy ~d my strength** *or* **me** le cognac m'a redonné des forces; **he was ~d to them safe and sound** il leur a été rendu sain et sauf; **to ~ to the throne** replacer sur le trône; **to ~ to power** ramener au pouvoir.

b (*repair*) *building, painting, furniture etc* restaurer; *leather goods* rénover; *text* restituer, rétablir.

restorer [rɪˈstɔːrəʳ] n (*Art etc*) restaurateur *m*, -trice *f*; *see* **hair**.

restrain [rɪˈstreɪn] vt a (*prevent: gen*) retenir. **I was going to do it but he ~ed me** j'allais le faire mais il m'a retenu *or* m'en a empêché; **to ~ sb from doing** empêcher *or* retenir qn de faire. b *dangerous person etc* (*overcome*) maîtriser; (*control*) contenir; (*imprison*) interner, priver de liberté. c (*control*) *one's anger, feelings etc* contenir, réprimer, refréner. **please ~ yourself!** je vous en prie dominez-vous! d (*restrict*) *trade etc* restreindre.

restrained [rɪˈstreɪnd] adj *emotions* contenu; *tone, voice, words, manner* mesuré; *style* sobre. **he was very ~ when he heard the news** quand il a appris la nouvelle, il est resté très maître de lui-même *or* de soi.

restraint [rɪˈstreɪnt] n a (*restriction*) contrainte *f*, entrave *f*, frein *m*. **without ~** sans contrainte; (*Jur*) **to place under ~** interner; **subject to many ~s** sujet à de nombreuses contraintes. b (*NonC: moderation*) *[person]* retenue *f*; *[speech]* retenue, mesure *f*; *[style]* sobriété *f*. **to show a lack of ~** manquer de maîtrise de soi *or* de retenue; **he said with great ~ that** mesurant ses paroles, il a déclaré que. c (*act of restraining: see* **restrain b, c**) maîtrise *f*; répression *f*; domination *f*; *see* **wage**.

restrict [rɪˈstrɪkt] vt restreindre, limiter (*to* à). **visiting is ~ed to one hour per day** les visites sont limitées à une heure par jour; **to ~ sb's authority/freedom** restreindre *or* limiter l'autorité/la liberté de qn; **access ~ed to members of staff** accès interdit aux personnes étrangères à l'établissement.

restricted [rɪˈstrɪktɪd] adj *number, group, circulation, aim* restreint, limité; (*Admin, Mil*) *document* confidentiel; *point of view, horizon* étroit. **within a ~ area** dans une zone restreinte *or* limitée; (*fig*) dans certaines limites; (*Aut*) **~ area** zone à vitesse limitée; (*Ling*) **~ code** code restreint.

restriction [rɪˈstrɪkʃən] n restriction *f*, limitation *f*. **to place ~s on** apporter des restrictions à; (*Aut*) **speed ~** limitation de vitesse; (*Comm*) **price ~** contrôle *m* de prix.

restrictive [rɪˈstrɪktɪv] adj restrictif. **~ practices** (*by trade unions*) pratiques restrictives de production; (*by manufacturers*) entraves *fpl* à la libre concurrence *or* à la liberté du commerce.

re-string [ˌriːˈstrɪŋ] pret, ptp **re-strung** vt *pearls, necklace* renfiler; (*Mus*) *violin* remplacer les cordes de; (*Sport*) *racket* recorder; *bow* remplacer la corde de, remettre une corde à.

restyle [ˌriːˈstaɪl] vt *product* donner un nouveau look à. **to have one's hair ~d** changer de coiffure; **to ~ sb's hair** changer le style de la coiffure de qn.

result [rɪˈzʌlt] 1 n a résultat *m*, conséquence *f*; (*Math*) résultat. **as a ~ he failed** en conséquence il a échoué, résultat — il a échoué*; **to be the ~ of** être la conséquence de, être dû à, résulter de; **as a ~ of** (*gen*) à la suite de; (*directly because of: esp Admin*) par suite de; **he died as a ~ of his injuries** il est décédé des suites de ses blessures; **without ~** sans résultat.

b *[election, exam, race]* résultat *m*. **to demand ~s** exiger des résultats; **to get ~s*** *[person]* obtenir de bons résultats, arriver à quelque chose*; *[action]* donner de bons résultats, aboutir à quelque chose*.

2 vi a (*follow*) résulter, provenir (*from* de). **it ~s that** il s'ensuit que.

b (*finish*) **that's going to ~ badly** cela va mal se terminer.

►**result in** vt fus (*gen*) mener à, aboutir à, se terminer par; *failure, setback etc* se solder par.

resultant [rɪˈzʌltənt] 1 adj résultant, qui (en) résulte. 2 n (*Math*) résultante *f*.

resume [rɪˈzjuːm] 1 vt a (*restart etc*) *tale, account* reprendre; *activity, discussions* reprendre, recommencer; *relations* renouer. **to ~ work** reprendre le travail, se remettre au travail; **to ~ one's journey** reprendre la route, continuer son voyage; **"well" he ~d** "eh bien" reprit-il; **to ~ one's seat** se rasseoir; (*frm*) **to ~ possession of** reprendre possession de. b (*sum up*) résumer. 2 vi *[classes, work etc]* reprendre, recommencer.

résumé [ˈreɪzjuːmeɪ] n résumé *m*; (*US*) curriculum vitæ *m inv*.

resumption [rɪˈzʌmpʃən] n reprise *f*.

resurface [ˌriːˈsɜːfɪs] 1 vt *road* refaire la surface de. 2 vi *[diver, submarine]* remonter à la *or* en surface, faire surface; (*fig: reappear*) refaire surface. **she ~d* after a year of mourning** elle a recommencé à sortir après un an de deuil.

resurgence [rɪˈsɜːdʒəns] n (*gen*) réapparition *f*; (*Econ*) redémarrage *m*.

resurgent [rɪˈsɜːdʒənt] adj (*gen*) qui connaît un nouvel essor, renaissant; (*Econ*) *spending etc* en nette augmentation.

resurrect [ˌrezəˈrekt] vt ressusciter; (*fig*) *fashion, ideas* faire revivre; *memories* ressusciter, réveiller; (* *hum*) *dress, chair etc* remettre en service.
resurrection [ˌrezəˈrekʃən] n (*Rel, fig*) résurrection *f*.
resuscitate [rɪˈsʌsɪteɪt] vt (*Med*) réanimer.
resuscitation [rɪˌsʌsɪˈteɪʃən] n (*Med*) réanimation *f*.
resuscitator [rɪˈsʌsɪteɪtəʳ] n (*Med*) réanimateur *m*.
retail [ˈriːteɪl] 1 n (vente *f* au) détail *m*.
2 vt vendre au détail, détailler; (*fig*) *gossip* colporter, répandre.
3 vi *[goods]* se vendre (au détail) (*at* à).
4 adv: **to sell ~** vendre au détail.
5 comp ▸**retail banking** (*Fin*) opérations *fpl* bancaires axées sur le marché des particuliers ▸**retail business** commerce *m* de détail ▸**retail dealer** détaillant(e) *m(f)* ▸**retail outlet**: **they are looking for a retail outlet for** ... ils cherchent un débouché pour ...; **50 retail outlets** 50 points *mpl* de vente ▸**retail price** prix *m* de détail; **retail price index** ≃ indice *m* des prix de l'INSEE ▸**retail shop** (*Brit*), **retail store** (*US*) magasin *m* de détail, détaillant *m* ▸**the retail trade** (*traders*) les détaillants *mpl*; (*selling*) la vente au détail.
retailer [ˈriːteɪləʳ] n détaillant(e) *m(f)*.
retain [rɪˈteɪn] vt a (*keep*) conserver, garder; (*hold*) retenir, maintenir; *heat* conserver. **~ing wall** mur *m* de soutènement; **to ~ control (of)** garder le contrôle (de); (*Fin*) **~ed earnings** bénéfices *mpl* non distribués. b (*remember*) garder en mémoire. c (*engage*) *lawyer* retenir, engager. **~ing fee** = **retainer b**.
retainer [rɪˈteɪnəʳ] n a (†, *liter: servant*) serviteur *m*. b (*fee*) acompte *m*, avance *f* sur honoraires; (*Brit: to lawyer*) provision *f*; (*rent*) caution *f* (*versée à titre de loyer réduit par un locataire lors de son absence*). (*Brit*) **to be on a ~** être sous contrat (*garantissant une disponibilité future*).
retake [ˈriːteɪk] (vb: pret **retook**, ptp **retaken**) 1 n (*Cine*) nouvelle prise (de vues). 2 [ˌriːˈteɪk] vt a reprendre; *prisoner* reprendre, rattraper. b (*Cine*) faire une nouvelle prise.
retaliate [rɪˈtælɪeɪt] vi se venger (*against sb/sth* de qn/qch), user de représailles (*against sb* envers qn). **he ~d by breaking a window** pour se venger il a brisé une fenêtre; **he ~d by pointing out that** ... il a riposté *or* rétorqué que ..., pour sa part il a fait observer que ...; **to ~ (up)on sb** rendre la pareille à qn, user de représailles envers qn.
retaliation [rɪˌtælɪˈeɪʃən] n revanche *f*, vengeance *f*, représailles *fpl*. **in ~** par représailles; **in ~ for** pour venger, pour se venger de; **policy of ~** politique *f* de représailles.
retaliatory [rɪˈtælɪətərɪ] adj de représailles. **~ measures** (*gen, Mil*) représailles *fpl*; (*Econ*) mesures *fpl* de rétorsion.
retard [rɪˈtɑːd] 1 vt retarder; (*Aut*) *ignition* retarder. 2 n retard *m*.
retarded [rɪˈtɑːdɪd] 1 adj (*Med*) retardé, arriéré; (*pej*) demeuré*. (*Aut*) **~ ignition** retard *m* à l'allumage; (*Tech*) **~ acceleration** accélération négative; **mentally ~** attardé. 2 npl: **the (mentally) ~** les attardés *mpl* (mentaux).
retch [retʃ] 1 vi avoir des haut-le-cœur. 2 n haut-le-cœur *m inv*.
retching [ˈretʃɪŋ] n haut-le-cœur *mpl*.
retd (abbr of **retired**) en retraite.
retell [ˌriːˈtel] pret, ptp **retold** vt raconter de nouveau.
retention [rɪˈtenʃən] n conservation *f*, maintien *m*; (*Med*) rétention *f*; (*memory*) mémoire *f*.
retentive [rɪˈtentɪv] adj *memory* fidèle, sûr. **he is very ~** il a une très bonne mémoire.
retentiveness [rɪˈtentɪvnɪs] n faculté *f* de retenir, mémoire *f*.
rethink [ˌriːˈθɪŋk] pret, ptp **rethought** 1 vt repenser. 2 [ˈriːθɪŋk] n: **we'll have to have a ~** nous allons devoir y réfléchir encore un coup*.
reticence [ˈretɪsəns] n réticence *f*.
reticent [ˈretɪsənt] adj réticent, réservé. **to be ~ about** (*habitually*) ne pas parler beaucoup de; (*on one occasion*) ne pas dire grand-chose de.
reticently [ˈretɪsəntlɪ] adv avec réticence, avec réserve.
reticle [ˈretɪkl] n (*Opt*) réticule *m*.
reticulate [rɪˈtɪkjʊlɪt] adj, **reticulated** [rɪˈtɪkjʊleɪtɪd] adj réticulé.
reticule [ˈretɪkjuːl] n a = **reticle**. b (*handbag*) réticule *m*.
retina [ˈretɪnə] n, pl **~s** *or* **retinae** [ˈretɪniː] rétine *f*.
retinal [ˈretɪnl] adj rétinien.
retinue [ˈretɪnjuː] n suite *f*, escorte *f*, cortège *m*.
retire [rɪˈtaɪəʳ] 1 vi a (*withdraw*) se retirer, partir; (*Mil*) reculer, se replier. **to ~ from the room** quitter la pièce; **to ~ to the lounge** se retirer au salon, passer au salon; (*Sport*) **to ~ hurt** abandonner à la suite d'une blessure; **to ~ into o.s.** rentrer en *or* se replier sur soi-même; **to ~ from the world/from public life** se retirer du monde/de la vie publique.
b (*go to bed*) (aller) se coucher.
c (*give up one's work*) prendre sa retraite. **he ~d on a good pension** il a pris sa retraite et il touche une bonne pension; **to ~ from business** se retirer des affaires.
2 vt *worker, employee* mettre à la retraite; (*Fin*) *bond* retirer de la circulation. **to be compulsorily ~d** être mis à la retraite d'office.
retired [rɪˈtaɪəd] adj a (*no longer working*) retraité, à la retraite. **a ~ person** un(e) retraité(e); (*Mil*) **~ list** état *m* des mises à la retraite; **~ pay** pension *f* de retraite. b (*secluded*) *life, spot* retiré.
retiree [rɪtaɪˈriː] n (*US*) retraité(e) *m(f)*.
retirement [rɪˈtaɪəmənt] 1 n a (*stopping work*) retraite *f*. **~ at 60** (mise *f* à la) retraite à 60 ans; **to announce one's ~** annoncer que l'on prend sa retraite; **to come out of ~** reprendre ses activités *or* une occupation *or* du service (*après avoir pris sa retraite*); **how will you spend your ~?** qu'est-ce que vous ferez quand vous aurez pris votre retraite?; *see* **compulsory, early**.
b (*seclusion*) isolement *m*, solitude *f*. **to live in ~** vivre retiré du monde.
c (*Mil*) retraite *f*, repli *m*; (*Sport*) abandon *m*.
2 comp ▸**retirement age** âge *m* de (la) retraite ▸**retirement benefit** prime *f* de retraite ▸**retirement community** (*US*) communauté *f* de retraités ▸**retirement pay** retraite *f* ▸**retirement pension** (pension *f* de) retraite *f*; (*Mil*) solde *f* de retraite ▸**retirement relief** (*Brit*) *exonération, dont bénéficient les retraités, sur les plus-values en capital*; *see also* **pension**.
retiring [rɪˈtaɪərɪŋ] adj a (*shy*) réservé. b **~ room** cabinet particulier. c (*taking retirement*) *manager, employee etc* sur le point de prendre sa retraite. **~ age** âge *m* de (la) retraite. d (*outgoing*) *chairman, president etc* sortant.
retool [ˌriːˈtuːl] (*US*) 1 vt (*reorganize*) réorganiser, rééquiper. 2 vi se réorganiser, se rééquiper.
retort [rɪˈtɔːt] 1 n a (*answer*) réplique *f*, riposte *f*. b (*Chem*) cornue *f*. 2 vt rétorquer, riposter, répliquer (*that* que). **"not at all" he ~ed** "pas du tout" rétorqua-t-il *or* riposta-t-il *or* répliqua-t-il.
retouch [ˌriːˈtʌtʃ] vt (*Art, Phot*) retoucher.
retrace [rɪˈtreɪs] vt *developments etc* (*research into*) reconstituer; (*give account of*) retracer. **to ~ one's path** *or* **steps** revenir sur ses pas, rebrousser chemin.
retract [rɪˈtrækt] 1 vt a (*withdraw*) *offer* rétracter, retirer; *statement* rétracter, revenir sur, désavouer. b (*draw back*) *claws* rétracter, rentrer; (*Aviat*) *undercarriage* rentrer, escamoter. 2 vi a (*withdraw*) se rétracter, se désavouer. b (*draw back*) se rétracter; (*Aviat*) rentrer.
retractable [rɪˈtræktəbl] adj (*lit*) rentrant, escamotable; (*fig*) *remark* que l'on peut rétracter *or* retirer.
retraction [rɪˈtrækʃən] n *[offer]* rétraction *f*; *[declaration]* rétractation *f*, désaveu *m*; *[claws etc]* rétraction *f*; *[undercarriage]* escamotage *m*.
retrain [ˌriːˈtreɪn] 1 vt recycler, donner une nouvelle formation (professionnelle) à. 2 vi se recycler.
retraining [ˌriːˈtreɪnɪŋ] n recyclage *m*.
retransmit [ˌriːtrænzˈmɪt] vt réexpédier; (*Phys, Rad, TV*) retransmettre, rediffuser.
retread [ˌriːˈtred] (*Brit*) 1 vt *tyre* rechaper. 2 [ˈriːtred] n (*tyre*) pneu rechapé.
retreat [rɪˈtriːt] 1 n a (*gen, also Mil*) retraite *f*, repli *m*, recul *m*. **the army is in ~** l'armée bat en retraite; **to sound the ~** battre la retraite; **to make** *or* **beat a hasty ~** partir en vitesse.
b (*Econ: of currency*) repli *m*. **the pound went into ~** la livre a cédé du terrain.
c (*place*) asile *m*, refuge *m*, retraite *f* (*liter*); (*Rel*) retraite. **to go on a ~** faire une retraite; **a country ~** un endroit (*or* une maison *etc*) tranquille à la campagne.
2 vi (*Mil*) battre en retraite; (*withdraw*) se retirer (*from* de); *[flood, glacier]* reculer; *[chin, forehead]* être fuyant. **to ~ within o.s.** se replier sur soi-même; **~ing** *army, troops* en retraite; (*fig*) **to ~ from** *promise, belief etc* abandonner, se défaire de.
3 vt (*Chess*) ramener.
retrench [rɪˈtrentʃ] 1 vt restreindre, réduire; *book* faire des coupures dans. 2 vi faire des économies.
retrenchment [rɪˈtrentʃmənt] n a *[expense]* réduction *f* (des dépenses). b (*Mil*) retranchement *m*.
retrial [ˌriːˈtraɪəl] n (*Jur*) nouveau procès *m*.
retribution [ˌretrɪˈbjuːʃən] n châtiment *m*, récompense *f* (*d'une mauvaise action.*)
retributive [rɪˈtrɪbjʊtɪv] adj *person, action* vengeur (*f* -geresse); *justice* distributif.
retrievable [rɪˈtriːvəbl] adj *object, material* récupérable; *money* recouvrable; *error, loss* réparable.
retrieval [rɪˈtriːvəl] n (*see* **retrieve**) récupération *f*; recouvrement *m*; réparation *f*; (*Comput: also* **information ~**) recherche *f* documentaire, retrouve *f* de l'information. **beyond** *or* **past ~** irréparable; *see also* **information 2**.
retrieve [rɪˈtriːv] 1 vt (*recover*) *object* récupérer (*from* de); *[dog]* rapporter; (*Fin*) recouvrer; (*Comput*) retrouver; *information* rechercher et extraire; *fortune, honour, position* rétablir; (*set to rights*) *error* réparer; *situation* redresser, sauver; (*rescue*) sauver, tirer (*from* de). (*lit, fig*) **we shall ~ nothing from this disaster** nous ne sauverons *or* récupérerons rien de ce désastre. 2 vi *[dog]* rapporter.
retriever [rɪˈtriːvəʳ] n retriever *m*, chien *m* d'arrêt.
retro... [ˈretrəʊ] pref rétro... .
retroactive [ˌretrəʊˈæktɪv] adj rétroactif. **the law came into force ~ to October 1st** la loi est entrée en vigueur avec effet rétroactif à compter du 1er octobre; **~ payment** (*on salary etc*) rappel *m*.
retroactively [ˌretrəʊˈæktɪvlɪ] adv rétroactivement.

retroengine [ˈretrəʊˌendʒɪn] n fusée *f* de freinage.
retrofit [ˈretrəʊfɪt] vt (*Tech*) *machine system* réajuster, modifier.
retroflex(ed) [ˈretrəʊfleks(t)] adj (*Ling*) apical, rétroflexe.
retroflexion [ˌretrəʊˈflekʃən] n (*Med*) rétroflexion *f*.
retrograde [ˈretrəʊgreɪd] 1 adj rétrograde. 2 vi rétrograder.
retrogress [ˌretrəʊˈgres] vi rétrograder.
retrogression [ˌretrəʊˈgreʃən] n rétrogradation *f*, régression *f*.
retrogressive [ˌretrəʊˈgresɪv] adj rétrogressif, rétrograde; (*Bio*) régressif.
retropack [ˈretrəʊpæk] n système *m* de rétrofusées.
retrorocket [ˈretrəʊˌrɒkɪt] n rétrofusée *f*.
retrospect [ˈretrəʊspekt] n examen *or* coup d'œil rétrospectif. **in ~** rétrospectivement, après coup.
retrospection [ˌretrəʊˈspekʃən] n examen rétrospectif.
retrospective [ˌretrəʊˈspektɪv] 1 adj *glance, thought, wisdom* rétrospectif; (*Admin, Jur*) *pay rise, effect* rétroactif. 2 n (*Art*) rétrospective *f*.
retrospectively [ˌretrəʊˈspektɪvlɪ] adv rétrospectivement; (*Admin, Jur*) rétroactivement.
retrovirus [ˈretrəʊˌvaɪərəs] n rétrovirus *m*.
retry [ˌriːˈtraɪ] vt (*Jur*) juger de nouveau.
retune [ˌriːˈtjuːn] 1 vi (*Rad*) (*change wavelength*) se mettre à l'écoute (*to* de); (*go back*) reprendre l'écoute (*to* de). 2 vt *musical instrument* réaccorder; *engine* réviser. 3 [ˈriːtjuːn] n *[engine]* révision *f*.
return [rɪˈtɜːn] 1 vi *[person, vehicle etc]* (*come back*) revenir; (*go back*) retourner; *[property]* retourner, revenir, faire retour (*to* à); *[symptoms, doubts, fears]* réapparaître. **to ~ home** rentrer; **have they ~ed?** sont-ils revenus? *or* rentrés? *or* de retour?; **his good spirits ~ed** sa bonne humeur est revenue; **to ~ to one's work** se remettre à *or* reprendre son travail; **to ~ to school** rentrer (en classe); **to ~ to a subject/an idea** revenir à un sujet/une idée; **to ~ to what we were talking about, he ...** pour en revenir à la question, il ...; **to ~ to one's bad habits** reprendre ses mauvaises habitudes.
2 vt a (*give back*) (*gen*) rendre; *sth borrowed, stolen, lost* rendre, restituer; (*bring back*) rapporter; *goods to shop* rendre, rapporter; (*put back*) remettre; (*send back*) renvoyer, retourner; *ball, sound, light* renvoyer; *compliment, salute, blow, visit* rendre; *sb's love* répondre à. **to ~ money to sb** rembourser qn; **he ~ed the £5 to him** il lui a remboursé les 5 livres, il l'a remboursé des 5 livres; **to ~ a book to the library** rapporter *or* rendre un livre à la bibliothèque; **to ~ a book to the shelf** remettre un livre sur le rayon; **he ~ed it to his pocket** il l'a remis dans sa poche; (*on letter*) **"~ to sender"** "retour à l'envoyeur"; (*liter*) **to ~ thanks** rendre grâce, remercier; **to ~ the favour** renvoyer l'ascenseur (*fig*); **to ~ sb's favour** rendre service à qn (en retour); **I hope to ~ your kindness** j'espère pouvoir vous rendre service en retour; **his love was not ~ed** elle n'a pas répondu à son amour; **to ~ good for evil** rendre le bien pour le mal; **to ~ like for like** rendre la pareille; (*Bridge*) **to ~ hearts** rejouer du cœur, renvoyer cœur; (*Tennis*) **to ~ the ball** renvoyer la balle; **backhand well ~ed by ...** revers bien repris par ...; *see* **fire 1c**.
b (*reply*) répondre, répliquer, riposter.
c (*declare*) *income, details* déclarer. (*Jur*) **to ~ a verdict** rendre *or* prononcer un verdict; (*Jur*) **to ~ a verdict of guilty on sb** déclarer qn coupable; **to ~ a verdict of murder** conclure au meurtre.
d (*Fin*) *profit, income* rapporter, donner.
e (*Parl*) *candidate* élire. **he was ~ed by an overwhelming majority** il a été élu à *or* avec une très forte majorité.
3 n a (*coming, going back*) *[person, illness, seasons]* retour *m*. **on my ~** dès mon retour; **~ home** retour; **after their ~ to school** après la rentrée (des classes); **by ~ of post** par retour du courrier; **a ~ to one's old habits** un retour à ses vieilles habitudes; **many happy ~s (of the day)!** bon anniversaire!; *see* **point**.
b (*giving back*) retour *m*; (*sending back*) renvoi *m*; (*putting back*) remise *f* en place; *[sth lost, stolen, borrowed]* restitution *f*; *[money]* remboursement *m*; *see* **sale**.
c (*Brit: also* **~ ticket**) aller et retour *m*.
d (*recompense*) récompense *f* (*for* de), (*from land, business, mine*) rendement *m*, rapport *m*, (*from investments, shares*) rapport. **~s** (*profits*) bénéfice *m*, profit *m*; (*receipts*) rentrées *fpl*, recettes *fpl*; **small profits and quick ~s** de bas prix et un gros chiffre d'affaires; (*Fin*) **~ on capital** rapport *m* de capital; **~ on investments** rentabilité *f* des investissements; **to get a poor ~ for one's kindness** être mal récompensé *or* mal payé de sa gentillesse; **in ~** en revanche; **in ~ for** en récompense de, en échange de; *see* **diminish**.
e (*act of declaring*) *[verdict]* déclaration *f*; *[election results]* proclamation *f*; (*report*) rapport *m*, relevé *m*; (*statistics*) statistique *f*. **official ~s** statistiques officielles; **the population ~s show that ...** le recensement montre que ...; **the election ~s** les résultats *mpl* de l'élection; **tax ~** (feuille *f* de) déclaration de revenus *or* d'impôts.
f (*Parl*) *[candidate]* élection *f*.
g (*Sport*) riposte *f*; (*Tennis*) retour *m*, reprise *f*. **~ of service** retour de service.
h (*Comput etc*) **~ (key)** (touche *f*) "retour".
4 comp ▸**return fare** (*Brit*) (prix *m*) aller et retour *m* ▸**return flight** vol *m* de retour ▸**return half** *[ticket]* coupon *m* de retour ▸**return item** (*Fin*) impayé *m* ▸**returning officer** (*Pol*) président *m* du bureau de vote ▸**return journey** (voyage *m or* trajet *m* de) retour *m* ▸**return match** revanche *f*, match *m* retour ▸**return stroke** (*Tech*) course *f* retour ▸**return ticket** (*Brit*) (billet *m* d')aller et retour *m*.
returnable [rɪˈtɜːnəbl] adj que l'on doit rendre; *bottle etc* consigné. **the bottles are non-~** ça n'est pas consigné *or* repris, c'est du verre perdu.
returner [rɪˈtɜːnəʳ] n (*also* **woman ~**) *femme qui reprend un travail après avoir élevé ses enfants*.
retype [ˌriːˈtaɪp] vt retaper (à la machine).
reunification [ˌriːjuːnɪfɪˈkeɪʃən] n réunification *f*.
reunify [ˌriːˈjuːnɪfaɪ] vt réunifier.
reunion [rɪˈjuːnjən] n réunion *f*.
Réunion [riːˈjuːnjən] n: **~ (Island)** (île *f* de) la Réunion.
reunite [ˌriːjuːˈnaɪt] 1 vt réunir. **they were ~d at last** ils se sont enfin retrouvés. 2 vi se réunir.
re-up* [ˌriːˈʌp] vi (*US Mil*) rempiler*, se réengager.
re-usable [ˌriːˈjuːzəbl] adj réutilisable.
re-use [ˌriːˈjuːz] vt réutiliser.
rev [rev] 1 n (*Aut*) (abbr of **revolution**) tour *m*. **~ counter** compte-tours *m inv*; **4,000 ~s per minute** 4 000 tours minute. 2 vt: **to ~ (up) the engine** emballer le moteur. 3 vi (*also* **~ up**) *[engine]* s'emballer; *[driver]* emballer le moteur.
revaluation [ˌriːvæljʊˈeɪʃən] n (*Fin*) réévaluation *f*.
revalue [ˌriːˈvæljuː] vt (*Fin*) réévaluer.
revamp* [ˌriːˈvæmp] vt *company, department* réorganiser; *house, room, object* retaper*.
revanchism [rɪˈvæntʃɪzəm] n revanchisme *m*.
revanchist [rɪˈvæntʃɪst] n, adj revanchiste (*mf*).
Rev(d). abbr of **Reverend**.
reveal [rɪˈviːl] vt (*gen*) révéler; (*make visible*) *hidden object etc* découvrir, laisser voir; (*make known*) révéler (*that* que); *truth, facts* révéler, faire connaître; *corruption* révéler, mettre à jour. **I cannot ~ to you what he said** je ne peux pas vous révéler ce qu'il a dit; **to ~ one's identity** se faire connaître, révéler son identité; **he ~ed himself as being ...** il s'est révélé comme étant ...; **his condition ~ed itself as (being) psychological in origin** ses problèmes se sont avérés avoir une cause psychologique; **~ed religion** religion révélée.
revealing [rɪˈviːlɪŋ] adj révélateur (*f* -trice); *dress, blouse etc* (*gen*) qui ne cache pas grand chose; (*see-through*) transparent; (*low-cut*) très décolleté.
reveille [rɪˈvælɪ] n (*Mil*) réveil *m*; *see* **sound[1]**.
revel [ˈrevl] 1 vi a (*make merry*) s'amuser, se divertir; (*carouse*) faire la fête. b (*delight*) se délecter (*in sth* de qch). **to ~ in doing** se délecter à faire, prendre grand plaisir à faire. 2 n: **~s** (*entertainment*) divertissements *mpl*; (*carousing*) festivités *fpl*.
revelation [ˌrevəˈleɪʃən] n révélation *f*. (*Rel*) **(the Book of) R~** l'Apocalypse *f*.
reveller, (*US*) **reveler** [ˈrevləʳ] n fêtard *m*, joyeux convive *m*. **the ~s** les gens *mpl* de la fête, les fêtards *mpl*.
revelry [ˈrevlrɪ] n (*NonC*) festivités *fpl*.
revenge [rɪˈvendʒ] 1 n (*lit*) vengeance *f*; (*fig, Sport etc*) revanche *f*. **to take ~ on sb for sth** se venger de qch sur qn; **to get one's ~** se venger; **to do sth out of ~** faire qch par vengeance; **in ~ he killed him** pour se venger il l'a tué. 2 vt *insult, murder* venger. **to ~ o.s., to be ~d** (*gen*) se venger (*on sb* de qn, *on sb for sth* de qch sur qn); (*in sport competition etc*) prendre sa revanche (*on sb* sur qn, *for sth* de qch).
revengeful [rɪˈvendʒfʊl] adj *person* vindicatif; *act* vengeur (*f* -geresse).
revengefully [rɪˈvendʒfəlɪ] adv par (esprit de) vengeance.
revenger [rɪˈvendʒəʳ] n vengeur *m*, -geresse *f*.
revenue [ˈrevənjuː] 1 n *[state]* revenu *m*; *[individual]* revenu, rentes *fpl*; *see* **inland** *etc*. 2 comp ▸**revenue man** douanier *m* ▸**revenue officer** agent *m or* employé(e) *m(f)* des douanes ▸**revenue sharing** (*US Econ*) redistribution *f* d'une partie des impôts fédéraux aux autorités locales ▸**revenue stamp** timbre *m* fiscal.
reverberate [rɪˈvɜːbəreɪt] 1 vi *[sound]* retentir, résonner, se répercuter; *[light, heat]* se réverbérer; (*fig*) *[protests etc]* se propager. 2 vt *sound* renvoyer, répercuter; *light* réverbérer, réfléchir; *heat* réverbérer.
reverberation [rɪˌvɜːbəˈreɪʃən] n *[sound]* répercussion *f*; *[light, heat]* réverbération *f*.
reverberator [rɪˈvɜːbəreɪtəʳ] n réflecteur *m*.
revere [rɪˈvɪəʳ] vt révérer, vénérer. **~d** *leader etc* vénéré.
reverence [ˈrevərəns] 1 n a vénération *f*, respect *m* (religieux). **to have ~ for sb, to hold sb in ~** révérer qn; **to show** *or* **pay ~ to** rendre hommage à. b **your R~** ≃ mon (révérend) père, monsieur l'abbé. 2 vt révérer.
reverend [ˈrevərənd] 1 adj vénérable. **the R~ Robert Martin** (*Anglican*) le révérend Robert Martin; (*Roman Catholic*) l'abbé (Robert) Martin; (*Nonconformist*) le pasteur (Robert) Martin; **the Most R~** le Révérendissime; **the Very** *or* **Right R~ Robert Martin** (*Anglican*) le très révérend Robert Martin; (*Roman Catholic*) monseigneur Martin; **R~ Mother** révérende mère. 2 n (*) (*Roman Catholic*)

curé *m*; (*Protestant*) pasteur *m*.
reverent ['revərənt] **adj** respectueux.
reverential [ˌrevə'renʃəl] **adj** révérenciel.
reverently ['revərəntlɪ] **adv** avec respect, avec vénération.
reverie ['revərɪ] **n** rêverie *f*.
revers [rɪ'vɪəʳ] **n, pl revers** [rɪ'vɪəz] revers *m* (*d'un vêtement*).
reversal [rɪ'vɜːsəl] **n** (*turning upside down*) renversement *m*; (*switching over of 2 objects*) interversion *f*; *[opinion, view etc]* revirement *m*; (*Jur*) *[judgment]* arrêt *m* d'annulation, réforme *f*.
reverse [rɪ'vɜːs] **1 adj a** (*gen*) inverse, contraire, opposé. **~ side** *[coin, medal]* revers *m*; *[sheet of paper]* verso *m*; *[cloth]* envers *m*; *[painting]* dos *m*; **in ~ order** dans l'ordre inverse; (*Dancing*) **~ turn** renversement *m*; (*US*) **~ discrimination, ~ racism** racisme *m* à l'envers, discrimination *f* raciale en faveur des Noirs.
b (*Aut: backwards*) **~ gear** marche *f* arrière; (*Tech*) **~ motion** *or* **action** (*backwards*) mouvement renversé; (*opposite direction*) mouvement inverse; **~ turn** virage *m* en marche arrière.
2 n a (*opposite*) contraire *m*, opposé *m*, inverse *m*. **quite the ~!** tout *or* bien au contraire!; **it is quite the ~** c'est tout le contraire *or* tout l'opposé, c'est justement l'inverse; **he is the ~ of polite** il n'est rien moins que poli, c'est tout le contraire d'un homme poli; (*fig*) **in ~** dans l'ordre inverse; *see also* **2d**.
b (*back*) *[coin, medal]* revers *m*; *[sheet of paper]* verso *m*; *[cloth]* envers *m*; *[painting]* dos *m*.
c (*setback, loss*) revers *m*, échec *m*; (*defeat*) défaite *f*.
d (*Aut*) **in ~** en marche arrière; (*fig*) *[process, one's fortunes etc]* **to go into ~** renverser la vapeur.
3 vt a (*turn the other way round*) renverser, retourner; *garment* retourner; *situation* renverser, changer complètement; *photo, result* inverser. **to ~ the order of things** inverser l'ordre des choses; **to ~ one's policy** faire volte-face (*fig*); **to ~ a procedure** procéder par ordre inverse; **to ~ a trend** renverser une tendance; (*Brit Telec*) **to ~ the charges** téléphoner en P.C.V. (*see* **5**); **to ~ the position(s) of two objects** intervertir *or* inverser deux objets.
b (*cause to move backwards*) *moving belt* renverser la direction *or* la marche de; *typewriter ribbon* changer de sens. (*Tech*) **to ~ the engine** faire machine arrière; **to ~ one's car into the garage/down the hill** rentrer dans le garage/descendre la côte en marche arrière; **he ~d the car into a tree** il a heurté un arbre en faisant une marche arrière; **to ~ one's car across the road** faire une marche arrière en travers de la route.
c (*Jur: annul*) *decision, verdict* réformer, annuler; *judgment* réformer, déjuger; *sentence* révoquer, casser.
4 vi (*Brit*) (*move backwards*) *[car]* faire marche arrière; *[dancer]* renverser. (*Aut*) **to ~ into the garage/out of the driveway/down the hill** rentrer dans le garage/sortir de l'allée/descendre la côte en marche arrière; **to ~ into a tree** heurter un arbre en faisant une marche arrière; **to ~ across the road** faire une marche arrière en travers de la route; (*Aut*) **reversing lights** feux *mpl* de marche arrière, feux de recul.
5 comp ►reverse-charge call (*Brit Telec*) (appel *m* *or* communication *f* en) P.C.V. *m*, appel *m* à frais virés (*Can*).
►reverse out vt fus (*Typ*) passer du noir au blanc.
reversibility [rɪˌvɜːsɪ'bɪlɪtɪ] **n** réversibilité *f*.
reversible [rɪ'vɜːsəbl] **adj** réversible; *garment, cloth* réversible, sans envers ni endroit; *decision* révocable.
reversion [rɪ'vɜːʃən] **n a** (*return to former state*) retour *m* (*to* à); (*Bio*) réversion *f*. **~ to type** réversion au type primitif. **b** (*Jur*) réversion *f*, droit *m* de retour. **c** (*Phot*) inversion *f*.
reversionary [rɪ'vɜːʃnərɪ] **adj a** (*Jur*) de réversion, réversible. **b** (*Bio*) atavique, régressif.
revert [rɪ'vɜːt] **vi a** (*return*) revenir (*to* à); (*Jur*) revenir, retourner (*to* à); *[property]* faire retour (*to* à). **to ~ to the question** pour en revenir à la question; (*Bio*) **to ~ to type** retourner *or* revenir au type primitif; (*fig*) **he has ~ed to type** le naturel a repris le dessus. **b** (*become again*) **fields ~ing to woodland** des champs qui retournent à l'état de forêt.
review [rɪ'vjuː] **1 n a** *[situation, events, the past]* examen *m*, étude *f*, bilan *m*; *[wages, prices, contracts]* révision *f*; (*printed etc report*) rapport *m* d'enquête. *[salaries, policy]* **under ~** en cours de révision; **the agreement comes up for ~** *or* **comes under ~ next year** l'accord doit être révisé l'année prochaine; **I shall keep your case under ~** je suivrai votre cas de très près; **he gave a ~ of recent developments in photography** il passa en revue les progrès récents de la photographie.
b (*Mil, Naut: inspection*) revue *f*. **to hold a ~** passer une revue.
c (*US Scol etc: revision*) révision *f*.
d (*critical article*) *[book, film, play etc]* critique *f*, compte rendu *m*. *[book]* **~ copy** exemplaire *m* de service de presse.
e (*magazine*) revue *f*, périodique *m*.
2 vt a (*consider again*) *one's life, the past* passer en revue. **we shall ~ the situation next year** nous réexaminerons *or* reconsidérerons la situation l'année prochaine.
b *troops* passer en revue.
c (*US Scol etc*) revoir, réviser.
d *book, play, film* faire la critique de, donner *or* faire un compte rendu de.
3 comp ►review body commission *f* de révision **►review panel** jury *m* de révision.
reviewer [rɪ'vjuːəʳ] **n** critique *m*. **book/film** *etc* **~** critique littéraire/de cinéma *etc*.
revile [rɪ'vaɪl] **1 vt** injurier, insulter, vilipender. **2 vi** proférer des injures (*at, against* contre).
revise [rɪ'vaɪz] **1 vt a** (*change*) *opinion, estimate* réviser, modifier. **to ~ sth upward(s)** réviser en hausse qch. **b** (*update*) *dictionary etc* réviser, mettre à jour; (*correct*) *proof* corriger, revoir; *text* revoir, réviser, corriger. **~d edition** édition revue et corrigée; *[Bible]* **R~d Standard Version** traduction (anglaise) de la bible de 1953; (*Brit*) *[Bible]* **R~d Version** traduction (anglaise) de la Bible de 1884. **c** (*Brit: learn up*) revoir, repasser, réviser. **2 vi** réviser. **to ~ for exams** réviser *or* faire des révisions pour des examens; **to start revising** commencer à réviser *or* (à faire) ses révisions. **3 n** (*Typ*) (épreuve *f* de) mise *f* en pages, seconde épreuve.
reviser [rɪ'vaɪzəʳ] **n** réviseur *m*; *[proof]* correcteur *m*, -trice *f*.
revision [rɪ'vɪʒən] **n** révision *f*.
revisionism [rɪ'vɪʒənɪzəm] **n** révisionnisme *m*.
revisionist [rɪ'vɪʒənɪst] **adj, n** révisionniste (*mf*).
revisit [ˌriː'vɪzɪt] **vt** *place* revisiter; *person* retourner voir.
revitalize [ˌriː'vaɪtəlaɪz] **vt** (*gen*) redonner de la vitalité à, revivifier (*liter*). **to ~ the economy** relancer l'économie.
revival [rɪ'vaɪvəl] **n a** (*bringing back*) *[custom, ceremony]* reprise *f*; (*Jur*) remise *f* en vigueur. (*Hist*) **the R~ of Learning** la Renaissance. **b** (*Theat: play*) reprise *f*; (*Rel*) *[faith]* renouveau *m*, réveil *m*. **~ meeting** réunion *f* pour le renouveau de la foi.
revivalism [rɪ'vaɪvəlɪzəm] **n** (*Rel*) revivalisme *m*.
revivalist [rɪ'vaɪvəlɪst] **adj, n** revivaliste (*mf*).
revive [rɪ'vaɪv] **1 vt a** *person* (*from fainting*) ranimer; (*from near death, esp Med*) réanimer. **a glass of brandy will ~ you** un verre de cognac vous remontera *or* vous requinquera. **b** *fire, feeling, pain, memory* ranimer, raviver; *conversation* ranimer; *hope, interest* faire renaître, raviver; *trade, business* relancer, réactiver; *fashion* remettre en vogue; *law* remettre en vigueur; *custom, usage* rétablir; *play* reprendre. **to ~ sb's courage** redonner du courage à qn; **to ~ sb's spirits** remonter le moral à qn. **2 vi** *[person]* reprendre connaissance; *[hope, feelings]* renaître; *[business, trade]* reprendre.
reviver [rɪ'vaɪvəʳ] **n** (*drink*) remontant *m*.
revivify [ˌriː'vɪvɪfaɪ] **vt** revivifier (*liter*).
revocation [ˌrevə'keɪʃən] **n** *[order, promise, edict]* révocation *f*; *[law, bill]* abrogation *f*; *[licence]* retrait *m*; *[decision]* annulation *f*.
revoke [rɪ'vəʊk] **1 vt** *law* rapporter, abroger; *order, edict* révoquer; *promise* revenir sur, révoquer; *decision* revenir sur, annuler; *licence* retirer. **2 vi** (*Cards*) faire une (fausse) renonce. **3 n** (*Cards*) (fausse) renonce *f*.
revolt [rɪ'vəʊlt] **1 n** révolte *f*. **to break out in ~, to rise in ~** se révolter, se soulever; **to be in ~ (against)** se révolter *or* être révolté (contre); *see* **stir**[1]. **2 vi a** (*rebel*) se révolter, se soulever, se rebeller (*against* contre). **b** (*be disgusted*) se révolter (*at* contre), être dégoûté (*at* par). **3 vt** révolter, dégoûter, répugner. **to be ~ed by** être révolté *or* dégoûté par.
revolting [rɪ'vəʊltɪŋ] **adj** (*repulsive, disgusting*) dégoûtant, écœurant, révoltant; *sight, story, meal* dégoûtant, répugnant; (**: unpleasant*) *weather, colour* épouvantable, dégueulasse*; *dress* affreux.
revoltingly [rɪ'vəʊltɪŋlɪ] **adv** d'une manière révoltante *or* écœurante.
revolution [ˌrevə'luːʃən] **n a** (*turn*) *[planet]* révolution *f*; *[wheel]* révolution, tour *m*. **b** (*Pol etc: uprising*) révolution *f*, coup *m* d'État; (*fig*) révolution. (*Hist*) **French R~** Révolution française; **~ in farming methods** révolution dans les méthodes d'exploitation agricole; (*Hist*) **Industrial/Agricultural R~** Révolution industrielle/agricole.
revolutionary [ˌrevə'luːʃnərɪ] **adj, n** (*lit, fig*) révolutionnaire (*mf*).
revolutionize [ˌrevə'luːʃənaɪz] **vt** révolutionner, transformer radicalement.
revolve [rɪ'vɒlv] **1 vt** (*lit*) faire tourner. (*fig*) **to ~ a problem in one's mind** tourner et retourner un problème dans son esprit. **2 vi** tourner. **to ~ on an axis/around the sun** tourner sur un axe/autour du soleil; (*fig*) **the discussion ~d around two topics** la discussion tournait autour de deux sujets; (*fig*) **everything ~s around him** tout dépend de lui.
revolver [rɪ'vɒlvəʳ] **n** revolver *m*.
revolving [rɪ'vɒlvɪŋ] **adj** tournant; (*Astron*) en rotation, qui tourne; (*Tech*) rotatif, à rotation. **~ chair/bookcase** fauteuil *m*/bibliothèque *f* pivotant(e); (*US*) **~ credit** crédit *m* documentaire renouvelable; **~ door** tambour *m*; **~ light** (*gen*) feu tournant, feu à éclats; (*on police car etc*) gyrophare *m*; **~ stage** scène tournante.
revue [rɪ'vjuː] **n** (*Theat*) (*satirical*) revue *f*; (*spectacular*) revue, spectacle *m* de music-hall. **~ artist** artiste *mf* de music-hall.
revulsion [rɪ'vʌlʃən] **n a** (*disgust*) dégoût *m*, écœurement *m*, répugnance *f* (*at* devant). **b** (*sudden change*) revirement *m*; (*reaction*) réaction *f* (*against* contre).
reward [rɪ'wɔːd] **1 n** récompense *f*. **as a ~ for your honesty** en récompense de votre honnêteté; **as ~ for helping me** pour vous (*or* le *etc*) récompenser de m'avoir aidé; **1,000 francs ~** 1 000 F de

récompense; **to offer a ~** offrir une récompense. 2 **vt** récompenser (*for* de); (*with money*) récompenser, rémunérer (*for* de). **"finder will be ~ed"** "récompense à qui rapportera l'objet"; **to ~ sb with a smile** remercier qn d'un sourire; (*fig*) **to ~ attention/investigation** mériter de l'attention/des recherches.

rewarding [rɪ'wɔːdɪŋ] **adj** (*financially*) rémunérateur (*f* -trice); (*mentally, morally*) qui en vaut la peine. **this is a very ~ book** ce livre vaut la peine d'être lu; **a ~ film** un film qui vaut la peine d'être vu; **bringing up a child is exhausting but ~** élever un enfant est une occupation exténuante mais qui a sa récompense.

rewind [ˌriː'waɪnd] **pret, ptp rewound vt** (*Tex*) rebobiner; (*Cine*) rembobiner; *ribbon, tape* rembobiner; *watch* remonter.

rewinding [ˌriː'waɪndɪŋ] **n** (*see* **rewind**) rebobinage *m*; rembobinage *m*; remontage *m*.

rewire [ˌriː'waɪəʳ] **vt: to ~ a house** refaire l'installation électrique d'une maison.

reword [ˌriː'wɜːd] **vt** *paragraph, sentence* rédiger à nouveau, recomposer; *idea* exprimer en d'autres termes.

rework [ˌriː'wɜːk] **vt** retravailler.

rewound [ˌriː'waʊnd] **pret, ptp of rewind.**

rewrite [ˌriː'raɪt] **pret rewrote, ptp rewritten** 1 **vt** (*gen*) récrire; (*rework*) remanier; (*copy*) recopier. (*Gram*) **to ~ as** réécrire sous la forme de. 2 **n** (*) remaniement *m*. 3 **comp ►rewrite rule, rewriting rule** (*Gram*) règle *f* de réécriture.

rewriter [ˌriː'raɪtəʳ] **n** (*US Press*) rewriter *m*, rédacteur-réviseur *m*.

rewritten [ˌriː'rɪtn] **ptp of rewrite.**

rewrote [ˌriː'rəʊt] **pret of rewrite.**

Reykjavik ['reɪkjəviːk] **n** Reykjavik.

RGN [ˌɑːdʒiː'en] **n** (**abbr of Registered General Nurse**) *see* **registered a.**

rhapsodic [ræp'sɒdɪk] **adj** (*Mus*) r(h)apsodique; (*fig*) dithyrambique (*often iro*), élogieux.

rhapsodize ['ræpsədaɪz] **vi** s'extasier (*over, about* sur).

rhapsody ['ræpsədɪ] **n** (*Mus*) r(h)apsodie *f*; (*fig*) dithyrambe *m* (*often iro*), éloge *m* enthousiaste.

rhea ['riːə] **n** nandou *m*.

rheme [riːm] **n** rhème *m*.

Rhenish ['renɪʃ] **adj** *wine* du Rhin.

rhenium ['riːnɪəm] **n** rhénium *m*.

rheostat ['riːəʊstæt] **n** rhéostat *m*.

rhesus ['riːsəs] 1 **n** rhésus *m*. 2 **comp ►rhesus baby** enfant *m* rhésus **►rhesus factor** facteur *m* rhésus **►rhesus monkey** rhésus *m* **►rhesus negative/positive** rhésus négatif/positif.

rhetic ['riːtɪk] **adj** (*Ling*) rhétique.

rhetoric ['retərɪk] **n** rhétorique *f* (*also pej*), éloquence *f*.

rhetorical [rɪ'tɒrɪkəl] **adj** (de) rhétorique; *style* ampoulé (*pej*). **~ question** question *f* pour la forme *or* l'effet.

rhetorically [rɪ'tɒrɪkəlɪ] **adv** *speak, declaim* en orateur, en rhéteur (*pej*); *ask* pour la forme, pour l'effet.

rhetorician [ˌretə'rɪʃən] **n** rhétoricien(-ienne) *m(f)*, rhéteur *m* (*pej*).

rheumatic [ruː'mætɪk] 1 **n** (*person*) rhumatisant(e) *m(f)*. 2 **adj** rhumatismal. **~ fever** rhumatisme *m* articulaire aigu.

rheumaticky* [ruː'mætɪkɪ] **adj** *person* rhumatisant; *part of body* plein de rhumatismes.

rheumatics* [ruː'mætɪks] **npl** rhumatismes *mpl*.

rheumatism ['ruːmətɪzəm] **n** rhumatisme *m*.

rheumatoid ['ruːmətɔɪd] **adj: ~ arthritis** polyarthrite *f* chronique évolutive, rhumatisme *m* chronique polyarticulaire.

rheumatologist [ˌruːmə'tɒlədʒɪst] **n** rhumatologiste *mf*, rhumatologue *mf*.

rheumatology [ˌruːmə'tɒlədʒɪ] **n** rhumatologie *f*.

rheumy ['ruːmɪ] **adj** chassieux.

Rhine [raɪn] 1 **n** Rhin *m*. 2 **comp ►Rhineland: the Rhineland** la Rhénanie.

rhinestone ['raɪnstəʊn] **n** faux diamant *m*.

rhino* ['raɪnəʊ] **n, pl ~ or ~es abbr of rhinoceros.**

rhinoceros [raɪ'nɒsərəs] **n, pl ~ or ~es** rhinocéros *m*.

rhizome ['raɪzəʊm] **n** rhizome *m*.

Rhode Island ['rəʊd'aɪlənd] **n** Rhode Island *m*. **in ~** à Rhode Island.

Rhodes [rəʊdz] **n** (*Geog*) Rhodes *f*. **in ~** à Rhodes.

Rhodesia [rəʊ'diːʒə] **n** Rhodésie *f*.

Rhodesian [rəʊ'diːʒən] 1 **adj** rhodésien. 2 **n** Rhodésien(-ienne) *m(f)*.

rhodium ['rəʊdɪəm] **n** rhodium *m*.

rhododendron [ˌrəʊdə'dendrən] **n** rhododendron *m*.

rhomb [rɒm] **n = rhombus.**

rhombi ['rɒmbaɪ] **npl of rhombus.**

rhombic ['rɒmbɪk] **adj** rhombique.

rhomboid ['rɒmbɔɪd] 1 **n** rhomboïde *m*. 2 **adj** rhombique, rhomboïdal.

rhombus ['rɒmbəs] **n, pl ~es or rhombi** losange *m*, rhombe *m*.

Rhône [rəʊn] **n** Rhône *m*.

rhubarb ['ruːbɑːb] 1 **n a** (*Bot, Culin*) rhubarbe *f*. **b** (*Theat*) **"~, ~, ~"** ≃ brouhaha *m* (*mot employé pour constituer un murmure de fond*). **c** (*US* ‡: *quarrel*) prise *f* de bec, éclats *mpl* de voix. 2 **comp** *jam* de rhubarbe; *pie* à la rhubarbe.

rhyme [raɪm] 1 **n a** (*identical sound*) rime *f*. **for (the sake of) the ~** pour la rime; (*fig*) **without ~ or reason** sans rime ni raison; (*fig*) **there seems to be neither ~ nor reason to it** cela ne rime à rien, cela n'a ni rime ni raison.

b (*poetry*) vers *mpl*; (*a poem*) poème *m*. **in ~** en vers (rimés); **to put into ~** mettre en vers; *see* **nursery.**

2 **comp ►rhyme scheme** agencement *m* des rimes.

3 **vt** faire rimer (*with* avec).

4 **vi a** *[word]* rimer (*with* avec). **rhyming** *words, verse* qui rime; **rhyming dictionary** dictionnaire *m* des rimes; **rhyming game** jeu *m* de rimes; **rhyming slang** *argot des Cockneys qui substitue à un mot donné une locution qui rime avec ce mot.*

b (*pej: write verse*) faire de mauvais vers, rimailler (*pej*).

rhymed [raɪmd] **adj** rimé.

rhymer ['raɪməʳ] **n, rhymester** ['raɪmstəʳ] **n** (*pej*) rimailleur *m*, -euse *f* (*pej*).

rhythm ['rɪðəm] 1 **n** rythme *m*. (*Mus*) **~ and blues** rhythm and blues *m* (*combinaison de blues et de rock*). 2 **comp ►rhythm method** *[contraception]* méthode *f* des températures **►rhythm section** (*Mus*) section *f* rythmique.

rhythmic(al) ['rɪðmɪk(əl)] **adj** *movement, beat* rythmique; *music* rythmé, cadencé.

rhythmically ['rɪðmɪkəlɪ] **adv** de façon rythmée, avec rythme.

RI [ɑːr'aɪ] **n a** (**abbr of religious instruction**) *see* **religious. b** (*US*) **abbr of Rhode Island.**

rib [rɪb] 1 **n a** (*Anat, Culin*) côte *f*. **true/false ~** vraie/fausse côte; **to dig or poke sb in the ~s** pousser qn du coude; *see* **floating, stick** *etc.* **b** *[leaf, ceiling]* nervure *f*; *[ship]* membre *m*, membrure *f*; *[shell]* strie *f*; *[umbrella]* baleine *f*; *[knitting]* côte *f*. 2 **comp ►rib cage** cage *f* thoracique **►rib roast** (*Culin*) côte *f* de bœuf **►rib-tickler**† histoire *f* drôle. 3 **vt** (*: *tease*) taquiner, mettre en boîte*.

ribald ['rɪbəld] **adj** grivois, paillard. **~ joke** grivoiserie *f*, paillardise *f*.

ribaldry ['rɪbəldrɪ] **n** (*NonC*) paillardises *fpl*.

riband†† ['rɪbənd] **= ribbon;** *see* **blue.**

ribbed [rɪbd] **adj** *knitting* à *or* en côtes; *shell* strié; *ceiling* à nervures.

ribbing ['rɪbɪŋ] **n a** (*Knitting*) côtes *fpl*. **b** (*: *teasing*) **to give sb a/take a ~** taquiner qn/se faire taquiner.

ribbon ['rɪbən] 1 **n a** *[dress, hair, typewriter, decoration]* ruban *m*. **velvet ~** ruban de velours; *see* **bunch. b** (*tatters*) **in ~s** en lambeaux; **to tear sth to ~s** (*lit*) mettre qch en lambeaux; (*fig*) *play etc* éreinter. **c** (*†: *reins*) **~s** guides *fpl*. 2 **comp ►ribbon development** extension urbaine linéaire en bordure de route.

riboflavin [ˌraɪbəʊ'fleɪvɪn] **n** riboflavine *f*.

ribonucleic ['raɪbəʊnjuː'kliːɪk] **adj: ~ acid** acide *m* ribonucléique.

rice [raɪs] 1 **n** riz *m*. 2 **comp ►rice bowl** (*bowl*) bol *m* à riz; (*region*) région *f* rizicole **►ricefield** rizière *f* **►rice growing** riziculture *f* **►rice-growing** rizicole, producteur (*f* -trice) de riz **►Rice Krispies** ® grains *mpl* de riz soufflés, Rice Krispies *mpl* ® **►rice paper** papier *m* de riz **►rice pudding** riz *m* au lait **►rice wine** saké *m*.

rich [rɪtʃ] 1 **adj** *person, nation, country, countryside* riche; *profit* gros (*f* grosse); *furniture, decoration, style* riche, magnifique, luxueux; *gift, clothes, fabric, banquet* riche, somptueux; *wine* généreux; *food* riche; *soil, land* riche, fertile; *colour, sound* riche, chaud, vif; *voice* chaud, ample, étoffé; *smell* (*gen*) embaumant; *life, history, experience* riche. **to grow or get ~(er)** s'enrichir; **to make sb ~** enrichir qn; **~ in corn/minerals/vitamins** riche en maïs/minerais/vitamines; (*fig*) **~ in detail** riche en *or* qui abonde en détails; **he lives in a very ~ district** il habite un quartier très chic; **~ tea biscuit** ≃ petit-beurre *m*; (*iro*) **that's ~!*** ça c'est pas mal!* (*iro*), c'est le comble!; *see* **get, Croesus.**

2 **n a the ~** les riches *mpl*.

b ~es richesse(s) *f(pl)*.

-rich [rɪtʃ] **adj ending in comps: calcium/protein-rich** riche en calcium/protéines; **oil-rich** *nation* riche en pétrole.

Richard ['rɪtʃəd] **n** Richard *m*. **~ (the) Lionheart** Richard Cœur de Lion.

richly ['rɪtʃlɪ] **adv** *dress* richement, somptueusement; *decorate* richement, magnifiquement, luxueusement; *deserve* largement, grandement, joliment. (*lit, fig*) **he was ~ rewarded** il a été largement *or* richement récompensé; **the library is ~ provided with reference books** la bibliothèque est riche en *or* largement fournie en ouvrages de référence.

richness ['rɪtʃnɪs] **n** (*see* **rich**) richesse *f*; luxe *m*; somptuosité *f*; fertilité *f*; ampleur *f*; *[colour]* éclat *m*. **~ in oil/vitamins** richesse en pétrole/vitamines.

Richter ['rɪxtəʳ] **n: the ~ scale** l'échelle *f* de Richter.

rick¹ [rɪk] **n** (*Agr*) meule *f* (de foin *etc*).

rick² [rɪk] **= wrick.**

rickets ['rɪkɪts] **n** (*NonC*) rachitisme *m*. **to have ~** être rachitique.

rickety ['rɪkɪtɪ] **adj** (*Med*) rachitique; (*fig*) *bicycle* délabré; *furniture* bancal, boiteux, branlant; *stairs* délabré, branlant. **~ old car** vieille guimbarde* *f*, vieux tacot* *m*.

rickey ['rɪkɪ] **n** (*US*) eau *f* gazeuse sucrée au citron vert (*avec ou sans alcool*).

rickshaw ['rɪkʃɔː] **n** pousse(-pousse) *m inv*.

ricky-tick ['rɪkɪtɪk] adj démodé, rétro* *(inv)*.
ricochet ['rɪkəʃeɪ] 1 n ricochet *m*. 2 vi ricocher.
ricotta [rɪ'kɒtə] n ricotte *f*.
rictus ['rɪktəs] n, pl ~ *or* ~es rictus *m*.
rid [rɪd] pret, ptp rid *or* ridded vt (*of pests, disease*) débarrasser; (*of bandits etc*) délivrer (*of* de). **to get ~ of** (*gen*) se débarrasser de; *habit, illusion, desire, tendency* perdre, se défaire de; *fears, doubts* perdre; *spots, cold, cough, fleas, rubbish* se débarrasser de; *unwanted goods* se débarrasser de, se défaire de; (*: *sell*) fourguer*; *boyfriend, girlfriend* laisser tomber*, se débarrasser de; (*frm*) **to ~ o.s. of** = **to get ~ of; to be ~ of sb/sth** être débarrassé de qn/qch; **to get ~ of one's debts** liquider *or* régler ses dettes; **the body gets ~ of waste** l'organisme élimine les déchets.
riddance ['rɪdəns] n débarras *m*. **good ~ (to bad rubbish)!*** bon débarras!*; **it was (a) good ~!*** quel débarras!*.
ridden ['rɪdn] 1 ptp of ride. 2 adj: **~ by** tourmenté *or* hanté par; **~ by fears** hanté par la peur; **~ by remorse** tourmenté par le remords.
-ridden [,rɪdn] adj ending in comps: **disease/guilt/remorse-ridden** accablé par la maladie/la culpabilité/le remords; **angst/fear-ridden** tourmenté par l'angoisse/la peur; *see* **debt, hag** *etc*.
riddle¹ ['rɪdl] 1 n crible *m*, claie *f*. 2 vt a *coal, soil etc* cribler, passer au crible; *stove* agiter la grille de. b *person, target* cribler (*with bullets etc* de balles *etc*). **~d with holes** criblé de trous; **the council is ~d with corruption** la corruption règne au conseil; **the committee is ~d with troublemakers** le comité grouille de provocateurs.
riddle² ['rɪdl] n énigme *f*, devinette *f*; (*mystery*) énigme, mystère *m*. **to speak** *or* **talk in ~s** parler par énigmes; **to ask sb a ~** poser une devinette à qn.
ride [raɪd] (vb: pret rode, ptp ridden) 1 n a (*outing*) promenade *f*, tour *m*, balade* *f*; (*distance covered*) trajet *m*. **horse ~, ~ on horseback** (*for pleasure*) promenade *or* tour *or* balade* à cheval; (*long journey*) chevauchée *f*; **the ~ of the Valkyries** la chevauchée des Valkyries; **after a hard ~ across country** après une chevauchée pénible à travers la campagne; **he gave the child a ~ on his back** il a promené l'enfant sur son dos; **to go for a ~ in a car** faire un tour *or* une promenade en voiture, se promener en voiture; **to take sb for a ~** (*in car etc*) emmener qn en promenade; (*fig: make fool of*) faire marcher qn*, mener qn en bateau*; (*swindle*) rouler qn*, posséder qn*; (*US *: kill*) emmener qn pour l'assassiner; **he gave me a ~ into town in his car** il m'a emmené en ville dans sa voiture; **it's my first ~ in a Rolls** c'est la première fois que je me promène en Rolls *or* que je roule dans une Rolls; **I've never had a ~ in a train** je n'ai jamais pris le train; **can I have a ~ on your bike?** est-ce que je peux monter sur ton vélo?; **3 ~s on the merry-go-round** 3 tours sur le manège; **to have a ~ in a helicopter** faire un tour en hélicoptère; **we had a ~ in a taxi** nous avons pris un taxi; **it was the taxi ~ they liked best** c'est le taxi qu'ils ont préféré; **cycle/car ~** tour *or* promenade *or* balade* à bicyclette/en voiture; **coach ~** tour *or* excursion *f* en car; **it's a short taxi ~ to the airport** ce n'est pas loin en taxi jusqu'à l'aéroport; **he has a long (car/bus) ~ to work** il a un long trajet (en voiture/en autobus) jusqu'à son lieu de travail; **it's only a short ~ by bus/coach/train/car/taxi** il n'y en a pas pour longtemps par l'autobus/par l'autocar/par le train/en voiture/en taxi; **it's a 60p ~ from the station** le trajet depuis la gare coûte 60 pence; **to steal a ~** voyager sans billet *or* sans payer; *see* **joy**.
b (*path for horses*) allée cavalière.
2 vi a (*Sport etc: ride a horse*) monter à cheval, faire du cheval, monter. **can you ~?** savez-vous monter à cheval?; **she ~s a lot** elle monte beaucoup à cheval, elle fait beaucoup d'équitation; **he has ridden since childhood** il fait du cheval depuis son enfance; **she learnt to ~ on Oscar** elle a appris à monter sur Oscar; **to go riding** faire du cheval, monter (à cheval); **to ~ astride/sidesaddle** monter à califourchon/en amazone; **he ~s well** il monte bien, il est bon cavalier; **to ~ to hounds** chasser à courre, faire de la chasse à courre; **the jockey was riding just under 65 kilos** (en tenue) le jockey pesait un peu moins de 65 kilos.
b (*go on horseback/by bicycle/by motorcycle*) aller à cheval/à bicyclette/en *or* à moto. **to ~ down/away** *etc* descendre/s'éloigner *etc* à cheval (*or* à bicyclette *or* en moto *or* à moto); **he stopped then rode on** il s'est arrêté puis a repris sa route; **they had ridden all day** ils avaient passé toute la journée à cheval *or* en selle; **he rode to London** il est allé à Londres à cheval (*or* à bicyclette *etc*); **he was riding on a bicycle/a camel** il était à bicyclette/à dos de chameau; **the child was riding on his father's back** l'enfant était à cheval sur le dos de son père; **he was riding on his father's shoulders** il était (assis à califourchon) sur les épaules de son père; **the witch was riding on a broomstick** la sorcière était à cheval *or* à califourchon sur un balai; **they were riding on a bus/in a car/in a train/in a cart** ils étaient en autobus/en voiture/en train/en charrette; **they rode in a bus to ...** ils sont allés en autobus à ...; (*fig*) **to be riding for a fall** courir à un échec; (*fig*) **to ~ roughshod over** *person* passer sur le corps *or* sur le ventre* de; *objection* passer outre à; (*fig liter*) **the seagull ~s on the wind** la mouette est portée par le vent; (*fig*) **the moon was riding high in the sky** la lune voguait dans le ciel; (*fig*) **he's riding high** tout lui réussit, il est dans une bonne passe, il a le vent en poupe; *[ship]* **to ~ at anchor** être à l'ancre *or* au mouillage; (*fig, esp US*) **to ~ with the punches** encaisser*; (*fig*) **we'll just have to let the matter** *or* **to let things ~ for a while** nous allons devoir laisser l'affaire suivre son cours *or* laisser courir* pendant un certain temps; (*fig*) **she had to let things ~** elle a dû laisser courir*; *see* **shank**.
c *[horse]* **to ~ well** être une bonne monture.
d (*Tech etc*) (*overlap*) chevaucher; (*work out of place*) travailler.
3 vt a **to ~ a horse** monter à cheval; **have you ever ridden a horse?** avez-vous jamais fait du cheval?, êtes-vous jamais monté à cheval?; **I have never ridden Flash** je n'ai jamais monté Flash; **he rode Cass at Newmarket** il montait Cass à Newmarket; **he rode Buster into town** il a pris Buster pour aller en ville, il est allé en ville sur Buster; **Jason will be ridden by J. Bean** Jason sera monté par J. Bean; **who is riding Omar?** qui monte Omar?; *[jockey]* **to ~ a race** monter dans une course; **Alfie rode a good race** Alfie a fait une bonne course; **he rode his horse straight at me** il a dirigé son cheval droit sur moi; **he rode his horse up the stairs** il a fait monter l'escalier à son cheval; **he rode his horse away/back** *etc* il est parti/revenu *etc* à cheval; **he ~s his pony to school** il va à l'école à dos de poney; **have you ever ridden a donkey/camel?** êtes-vous jamais monté à dos d'âne/à dos de chameau?; **he was riding a donkey** il était à dos d'âne; **he was riding a motorbike** il était à *or* en moto; **he rode his motorbike to the station** il est allé à la gare en moto; **I have never ridden a bicycle/a motorbike** je ne suis jamais monté à bicyclette/à moto; **can I ~ your bike?** est-ce que je peux monter sur ton vélo?; **he was riding a bicycle** il était à bicyclette; **he rode his cycle into town** il est allé en ville à bicyclette; **he always ~s a bicycle** il va partout à *or* il se déplace toujours à bicyclette; **witches ~ broomsticks** les sorcières chevauchent des balais; **she was riding a broomstick** elle était à cheval *or* à califourchon sur un balai; **they had ridden 10 km** ils avaient fait 10 km à cheval (*or* à bicyclette *or* à *or* en moto); **they had ridden all the way** ils avaient fait tout le trajet *or* le voyage à cheval (*or* à bicyclette *etc*); **he rode the country looking for ...** il a parcouru tout le pays à cheval (*or* à bicyclette *etc*) à la recherche de ...; (*US*) **to ~ sb on a rail** expulser qn de la ville (en l'emmenant à califourchon sur un poteau); (*fig*) **the birds rode the wind** les oiseaux étaient portés par le vent; (*liter*) **the ship rode the waves** le bateau voguait sur les vagues; (*fig*) **he's riding (on) a wave of personal popularity** il jouit d'une poussée de sa cote de popularité personnelle.
b (*: *esp US: nag etc*) être toujours sur le dos de*, ne pas ficher la paix à* (*about* au sujet de). **don't ~ him too hard** ne soyez pas trop dur avec lui, ne le poussez pas trop loin.
►**ride about, ride around** vi se déplacer *or* aller çà et là *or* faire un tour (à cheval *or* à bicyclette *or* en voiture *etc*).
►**ride behind** vi (*on same horse*) monter en croupe; (*on motorcycle*) monter derrière *or* en croupe; (*in car*) s'asseoir *or* être assis à l'arrière.
►**ride down** vt sep a (*trample*) renverser, piétiner. b (*catch up with*) rattraper (*à cheval*).
►**ride out** 1 vi sortir (à cheval *or* à bicyclette *etc*). 2 vt sep (*fig*) surmonter. **to ride out the storm** (*Naut*) étaler la tempête; (*fig*) surmonter la crise; **to ride out a difficult time** se tirer d'une *or* surmonter une mauvaise passe; **the company managed to ride out the depression** la société a réussi à survivre à la dépression.
►**ride up** vi a *[horseman, motorcyclist etc]* arriver. b *[skirt etc]* remonter.
rider ['raɪdəʳ] n a (*person*) *[horse]* cavalier *m*, -ière *f*; *[racehorse]* jockey *m*; *[circus horse]* écuyer *m*, -ère *f*; *[bicycle]* cycliste *mf*; *[motorcycle]* motocycliste *mf*. **a good ~** un bon cavalier, une bonne cavalière; *see* **dispatch, out**. b (*addition: to document*) annexe *f*, acte *or* article additionnel; (*to bill*) clause additionnelle; (*to insurance policy, jury's verdict*) avenant *m*. **the committee added a ~ condemning ...** la commission ajouta un article *or* une annexe condamnant ... .
ridge [rɪdʒ] 1 n a (*top of a line of hills or mountains*) arête *f*, crête *f*; (*extended top of a hill*) faîte *m*; (*ledge on hillside*) corniche *f*; (*chain of hills, mountains*) chaîne *f*; (*in sea: reef*) récif *m*.
b (*in roof, on nose*) arête *f*; (*on sand*) ride *f*; (*in ploughed land*) billon *m*; (*on cliff, rockface*) strie *f*. **alveolar ~, teeth~** arcade *f* alvéolaire; (*Met*) **a ~ of high pressure** une ligne de hautes pressions; (*Agr*) **~ and furrow (formation)** crêtes *fpl* de labours.
2 comp ►**ridge piece, ridge pole** (poutre *f* de) faîte *m*, faîtage *m* ►**ridge tent** tente *f* (à toit en arête) ►**ridge tile** (tuile *f*) faîtière *f*, enfaîteau *m* ►**ridge way** chemin *m* de faîte, route *f* des crêtes.
3 vt *roof* enfaîter; *earth* billonner; *rockface* strier; *sand* rider.
ridicule ['rɪdɪkju:l] 1 n raillerie *f*, ridicule *m*. **to hold sb/sth up to ~** tourner qn/qch en ridicule *or* en dérision; **to lay o.s. open to ~** s'exposer aux railleries; **she's an object of ~** elle est un objet de risée.
2 vt ridiculiser, tourner en ridicule *or* en dérision.
ridiculous [rɪ'dɪkjʊləs] adj ridicule. **to make sth ~** ridiculiser qch; **to make o.s. (look) ~** se rendre ridicule, se ridiculiser; **to see the ~ side of sth** voir le ridicule de qch *or* le côté risible de qch; *see* **sublime**.
ridiculously [rɪ'dɪkjʊləslɪ] adv ridiculement.
ridiculousness [rɪ'dɪkjʊləsnɪs] n ridicule *m* (*état*).
riding ['raɪdɪŋ] 1 n (*horse-riding*) équitation *f*; (*horsemanship*) monte *f*. 2 comp ►**riding boots** bottes *fpl* (de cheval) ►**riding breeches** culotte *f* de cheval ►**riding crop** = **riding whip** ►**riding habit** habit *m*

or tenue *f* d'amazone ►**riding jacket** veste *f* de cheval *or* d'équitation ►**riding master** professeur *m* d'équitation ►**riding school** manège *m*, école *f* d'équitation ►**riding stable(s)** centre *m* d'équitation, manège *m* ►**riding whip** cravache *f*.

rife [raɪf] adj **a** (*widespread*) *disease, corruption* répandu. **to be ~** sévir, être répandu, régner; **rumour is ~** des bruits courent. **b** (*full of*) **~ with** (*gen*) abondant en; **a city ~ with violence** une ville où règne la violence; **the company was ~ with rumours about ...** des bruits couraient dans toute la compagnie à propos de ... .

riff [rɪf] n (*Mus*) riff *m* (*mélodie improvisée et répétée*).

riffle ['rɪfl] vt (*also* **~ through**) *pages, papers etc* feuilleter rapidement, parcourir.

riffraff ['rɪf,ræf] n racaille *f*.

rifle¹ ['raɪfl] vt *town* piller; *tomb* violer; *drawer, till* vider, dévaliser, rafler* le contenu de; *house* dévaliser, vider. **to ~ sb's pockets** (*steal from*) puiser dans les poches de qn; (*go through*) faire les poches à qn; **she ~d through the papers** elle feuilletait rapidement *or* parcourait les documents.

rifle² ['raɪfl] **1** n (*gun*) fusil *m* (rayé); (*for hunting*) carabine *f* de chasse. (*Mil*) **the R~s** ≃ les chasseurs *mpl* à pied, (le régiment de) l'infanterie légère. **2** comp ►**rifle butt** crosse *f* de fusil ►**rifleman** fusilier *m* ►**rifle range** (*outdoor*) champ *m* de tir; (*indoor*) stand *m* de tir; **within rifle range** *or* **rifle shot** à portée de fusil ►**rifle shot** coup *m* de fusil; (*marksman*) tireur *m*.

rift [rɪft] n **a** (*lit*) fente *f*, fissure *f*, crevasse *f*; (*in clouds*) éclaircie *f*, trouée *f*. (*Geol*) **~ valley** graben *m*. **b** (*fig: disagreement*) désaccord *m*; (*Pol*) (*in party*) division *f*; (*in cabinet, group*) division, désaccord. **this caused a ~ in their friendship** ceci a causé une faille dans leur amitié; **the ~ between them was widening** ils s'éloignaient de plus en plus l'un de l'autre.

rig [rɪg] **1** n **a** (*Naut*) gréement *m*. **b** (*oil* ~) (*land*) derrick *m*; (*sea: also* **floating ~**) plate-forme *f* (pétrolière) flottante. **c** (**: outfit: also* **~ out**) tenue *f*, accoutrement *m* (*pej*). **d** (*US: tractor-trailer*) semi-remorque *m*. **2** vt **a** (*Naut*) gréer. **b** (*fix dishonestly*) *election, competition, game* truquer; *prices* fixer illégalement. **it was ~ged** c'était un coup monté; (*St Ex*) **to ~ the market** manipuler le marché, provoquer une hausse *or* une baisse factice dans les cours. **3** vi (*Naut*) être gréé.

►**rig out** vt sep (*clothe*) habiller (*with* de, *as* en).

►**rig up** vt *boat* gréer; (*with mast*) mâter; *equipment* monter, installer; (*fig*) (*make hastily*) faire avec des moyens de fortune *or* avec les moyens du bord; (*arrange*) arranger.

rigger ['rɪgəʳ] n **a** (*Naut*) gréeur *m*; (*Aviat*) monteur-régleur *m*. **b** (*St Ex*) agioteur *m*, manipulateur *m*.

rigging ['rɪgɪŋ] n **a** (*Naut*) (*ropes etc*) gréement *m*; (*action*) gréage *m*. **b** (*US: clothes*) vêtements *mpl*, fringues‡ *fpl*. **c** (**: dishonest interference*) *[election, competition]* truquage *m*; *[prices]* fixation illégale; (*St Ex*) agiotage *m*, manipulation *f*.

right [raɪt] **1** adj **a** (*just, fair*) juste, équitable; (*morally good*) bien *inv*, conforme au devoir, conforme à la morale. **it isn't ~ to lie, lying isn't ~** ce n'est pas bien de mentir; **to do what is ~** faire ce qui est conforme au devoir *or* à la morale, faire ce qu'il faut, se conduire bien *or* honnêtement (*see also* **1c**); **he thought it ~ to warn me** il a cru *or* jugé bon de m'avertir; **it seemed only ~ to give him the money** il ne semblait que juste de lui donner l'argent; **it's only ~ and proper** ce n'est que justice, c'est bien le moins; **it is only ~ for her to go** *or* **that she should go** il n'est que juste qu'elle y aille; **it is only ~ to point out that ...** nous devons néanmoins signaler que ..., en toute justice il faut signaler que ...; **would it be ~ to tell him?** ferait-on bien de le lui dire?; **to do the ~ thing by sb** bien agir *or* agir honorablement envers qn.

b (*accurate*) juste, exact, conforme à la vérité. **to be ~** *[person]* avoir raison; *[answer, solution]* être juste, être exact; **you're quite ~** vous avez parfaitement raison; **how ~ you are!*** (*approvingly*) vous avez cent fois raison!; (*iro*) et comment!*; **that's ~** c'est juste, c'est exact, c'est ça*; **that can't be ~!** ça ne doit pas être ça!, ça ne doit pas être juste!; **the ~ answer** la bonne réponse; **the ~ time** (*o'clock*) l'heure exacte *or* juste (*see also* **1c**); **is the clock ~?** est-ce que la pendule est à l'heure?; **you were ~ to refuse** *or* **in refusing** vous avez bien fait de *or* vous avez eu raison de refuser; **my guess was ~** j'avais deviné juste; **I got all my sums ~ at school** j'ai réussi toutes mes opérations en classe; (*iro*) **the Chancellor didn't get his sums ~** le ministre des Finances n'est pas tombé juste dans ses calculs; **to get one's facts ~** être sûr de ce qu'on avance; **let's get it ~ this time!** essayons d'y arriver cette fois-ci!; **your opinions are ~** vos opinions sont bien fondées; **to put** *or* **set ~** *error* corriger, rectifier; *situation* redresser, rétablir; *clock* remettre à l'heure; **that can easily be put ~** on peut facilement arranger ça; **I tried to put things ~ after their quarrel** j'ai essayé d'arranger les choses *or* la situation après leur querelle; **the plumber came and put things ~** le plombier est venu et a fait la *or* les réparation(s); **to put** *or* **set sb ~** détromper qn, éclairer qn, tirer qn d'erreur; **put me ~ if I'm wrong** dites-moi si je me trompe (*see also* **1d**); *see* **all right**.

c (*correct etc*) bon (*f* bonne) (*before n*); (*best*) meilleur (*f* -eure). (*lit*) **on the ~ road** sur le bon chemin; (*fig*) **on the ~ road, on the ~ track** sur la bonne voie; **is this the ~ road for Paris?** est-ce bien la route de Paris?, est-ce que c'est la bonne route pour Paris?; **you are on the ~ train now** vous êtes dans le bon train maintenant; **what's the ~ thing to do?** quelle est la meilleure chose à faire?, qu'est ce qu'il vaut mieux faire?; **I don't know what's the ~ thing to do** je ne sais pas ce qu'il vaut mieux faire; **to come at the ~ time** arriver au bon moment, tomber bien; **to do sth at the ~ time** faire qch au bon moment *or* au moment voulu; **she wasn't wearing the ~ clothes** elle ne portait pas les vêtements appropriés *or* qui convenaient; **I haven't got the ~ papers with me** je n'ai pas les bons documents sur moi; **you must chose the ~ books for this course** il ne faut pas se tromper en choisissant les livres pour ce cours, il faut choisir les meilleurs livres pour ce cours; **to do sth the ~ way** faire qch comme il faut, s'y prendre bien; **that is the ~ way of looking at it** c'est bien ainsi qu'il faut envisager la question; **the ~ word** le mot juste; **the ~ man for the job** l'homme de la situation, l'homme qu'il faut; **Mr R~*** l'homme *m* de ma (*or* sa *etc*) vie; **it is just the ~ size** c'est exactement la taille qu'il faut; **we will do what is ~ for the country** nous ferons ce qui est dans l'intérêt du pays; **she is on the ~ side of forty** elle n'a pas encore quarante ans, elle a moins de quarante ans; **to get on the ~ side of sb*** s'insinuer dans les bonnes grâces *or* dans les petits papiers* de qn; **the ~ side of the material** l'endroit *m* du tissu; **to know the ~ people** avoir des relations utiles; **he's the ~ sort*** c'est un type bien*, c'est un chic type*; **more than is ~** plus que de raison; *see also* **noise, time, side**.

d (*well*) *person* en bonne santé, bien portant; *car, engine, machine* en état, qui marche (bien). **the medicine soon put** *or* **set him ~** le médicament l'a vite guéri; **I don't feel quite ~ today** je ne me sens pas très bien *or* pas très d'aplomb *or* pas dans mon assiette* aujourd'hui; (*Brit*) **to be as ~ as rain*** (*after illness*) se porter comme un charme; (*after fall*) être indemne; **he put the engine ~** il a remis le moteur en état; **to be in one's ~ mind** avoir toute sa raison; **he's not ~ in the head‡** il est un peu dingue‡; *see* **all right**.

e (*Math*) *angle, cone* droit. **at ~ angles** à angle droit (*to* avec), perpendiculaire (*to* à).

f (*phrases*) **~!**, (*Brit*) **~-oh!***, **~ you are!*** d'accord!, entendu!, convenu!; **~, who's next?** bon *or* bien, c'est à qui maintenant?; **that's ~!** mais oui!, c'est ça!; (*I see*) **oh ~!*** ah, d'accord!; **is that ~?** vraiment?, c'est vrai?; **~ enough!** bien sûr!, c'est vrai!, effectivement!; **it's a ~ mess in there*** c'est la pagaïe* complète là-dedans; **he's a ~ fool!*** c'est un imbécile fini!

g (*opposite of left*) droit, de droite. **~ hand** main droite (*see also* **5**); **I'd give my ~ hand** *or* **arm to know the answer** je donnerais beaucoup *or* cher* pour connaître la réponse; **on my ~ hand you see the bridge** sur ma droite vous voyez le pont; *see* **hook**.

2 adv **a** (*straight, directly*) droit, tout droit, directement; (*exactly*) tout, tout à fait. **~ in front of you** (tout) droit devant vous; **~ ahead of you** directement devant vous; **~ behind you** (*gen*) en plein derrière vous; **you'll have the wind ~ behind you** vous aurez le vent juste dans le dos; **go ~ on** continuez tout droit; **~ away, ~ off*** (*immediately*) tout de suite, sur-le-champ; (*at the first attempt*) du premier coup; **~ now** en ce moment; (*at once*) tout de suite; **~ here** ici même; **~ in the middle** au beau milieu, en plein milieu; **~ at the start** dès le (tout) début; **the blow hit me ~ on the face** j'ai reçu le coup en pleine figure.

b (*completely, all the way*) tout, tout à fait, complètement. **~ round the house** tout autour de la maison; **to fall ~ to the bottom** tomber droit au fond *or* tout au fond; (*lit, fig*) **rotten ~ through** complètement pourri; **pierced ~ through** transpercé *or* percé de part en part; **to turn ~ round** se retourner; **~ (up) against the wall** tout contre le mur; **~ at the top of the mountain** tout en haut *or* juste au sommet de la montagne; **~ at the back, ~ at the bottom** tout au fond; **push it ~ in** enfoncez-le complètement *or* jusqu'au bout; **~ on!‡** bravo!, c'est ça!; (*in race etc*) **he's ~ up there** il est en tête, il est parmi les favoris.

c (*correctly*) bien, juste, correctement; (*well*) bien, comme il faut, d'une manière satisfaisante. **to guess ~** deviner juste; **to answer ~** répondre correctement; **if I remember ~** si je me souviens bien; **you did ~ to refuse** vous avez bien fait de refuser, vous avez eu raison de refuser; **if everything goes ~** si tout va bien; **nothing goes ~ for them** rien ne leur réussit; **if I get you ~*** si je comprends bien; **I'll see you ~‡** je veillerai à ce que vous n'y perdiez (*subj*) pas, vous n'en serez pas de votre poche*; *see* **serve**.

d (*†, dial: very*) fort, très, tout à fait. (*Brit*) **the R~ Honourable** le Très Honorable; *see* **reverend**.

e (*opposite of left*) à droite. **to look ~ and left** regarder à droite et à gauche; **to be cheated ~ and left** être volé par tout le monde, être volé de tous les côtés; **there is a spot just ~ of centre** il y a une tache dans le centre-droit; **to owe money ~ and left** devoir de l'argent à tout le monde; **~, left and centre*** partout, de tous côtés; (*Mil*) **eyes ~!** tête droite!; (*Mil*) **~ about turn!** demi-tour *m* à droite!

3 n **a** (*moral*) bien *m*; (*intellectual*) vrai *m*. **he doesn't know ~ from wrong** il ne sait pas discerner le bien du mal; **to be in the ~** avoir raison, être dans le vrai.

b (*entitlement*) droit *m*. **to have a ~ to sth** avoir droit à qch; **to have a** *or* **the ~ to do** avoir le droit de faire, être en droit de faire; **he**

has no ~ to sit here il n'a pas le droit de s'asseoir là; **what ~ have you to say that?** de quel droit dites-vous cela?; **by what ~?** à quel titre?, de quel droit?; **he has no ~ to the money** il n'a pas droit à cet argent; **he is within his ~s** il est dans son (bon) droit; **by ~s** en toute justice; **by ~ of conquest** par droit de conquête, à titre de conquérant; **I know my ~s** je sais quels sont mes droits; (*Jur*) **in one's own ~** de son propre chef; **she's a good actress in her own ~** elle est elle-même une bonne actrice; **to stand on** *or* **assert one's ~s** revendiquer *or* faire valoir ses droits; **divine ~** droit divin; **women's ~s** droits de la femme; **women's ~s movement** mouvement *m* pour les droits de la femme; (*Jur*) **~ of appeal** droit d'appel; (*Jur*) **~ of user** droit d'usage; *see* **abode, civil, human, inspect.**

c (*Comm*) ~s droits *mpl*; **manufacturing/publication/reproduction ~s** droits de fabrication/publication/reproduction; **TV/film ~s** droits d'adaptation pour la télévision/le cinéma; **"all ~s reserved"** "tous droits (de reproduction) réservés"; **to have the (sole) ~s of** *or* **to sth** avoir les droits (exclusifs) pour qch.

d (*proper state*) **to put** *or* **set sth to ~s** mettre qch en ordre; (*fig*) **to put the world** *or* **things to ~s** reconstruire *or* refaire le monde; **to know the ~s and wrongs of a question** connaître tous les détails d'une question, être tout à fait au courant d'une question; **I want to know the ~s and wrongs of it first** je veux d'abord savoir qui a tort et qui a raison là-dedans.

e (*opposite of left*) droite *f*. **to drive on the ~** conduire à droite; **to keep to the ~** tenir la *or* sa droite; **on my ~** à ma droite; **on** *or* **to the ~ of the church** à droite de l'église; (*Pol*) **the R~** la droite.

f (*Boxing*) droite *f*.

4 **vt** a (*return to normal*) *car, ship* redresser. **the car ~ed itself** la voiture s'est redressée (toute seule); **the problem should ~ itself** le problème devrait s'arranger tout seul *or* se résoudre de lui-même.

b (*make amends for*) *wrong* redresser; *injustice* réparer.

5 **comp** ►**right angle** angle droit; **to be at right angles (to)** être à angle droit (de) ►**right-angled** à angle droit; **right-angled triangle** triangle *m* rectangle ►**right-hand**: **right-hand drive car** voiture *f* avec (la) conduite à droite; (*fig*) **his right-hand man** son bras droit (*personne*); **the right-hand side** le côté droit ►**right-handed** *person* droitier; *punch, throw* du droit; *screw* fileté à droite ►**right-hander** (*Sport*) coup *m* du droit; (*person*) droitier *m*, -ière *f* ►**right-minded** = **right-thinking** ►**right-of-centre** (*Pol*) (de) centre droit; *see also* **right 2e** ►**right-of-way** (*across property*) droit *m* de passage; (*Aut: priority*) priorité *f*; (*Aut*) **it's his right-of-way** c'est lui qui a priorité; **he has (the) right-of-way** il a (la) priorité ►**right-on*** politiquement correct ►**right-thinking** sensé, sain d'esprit ►**rightward(s)** à droite, vers la droite ►**right whale** (*Zool*) baleine *f* franche ►**right wing** (*Sport*) ailier droit; (*Pol*) droite *f*; **the right wing of the party** l'aile droite du parti ►**right-wing** (*Pol*) de droite; (*Pol*) **to be right-wing** être de droite ►**right-winger** (*Pol*) membre *m* de la droite; (*Sport*) ailier droit.

righteous [ˈraɪtʃəs] **adj** *person* droit, vertueux; (*in Bible*) juste; *anger, indignation* juste, justifié; *see* **self.**

righteously [ˈraɪtʃəslɪ] **adv** vertueusement.

righteousness [ˈraɪtʃəsnɪs] **n** droiture *f*, vertu *f*.

rightful [ˈraɪtfʊl] **adj** a *heir, owner* légitime. **~ claimant** ayant droit *m*. b (*fair*) *action* juste.

rightfully [ˈraɪtfəlɪ] **adv** légitimement, à juste titre.

rightism [ˈraɪtɪzəm] **n** opinions *fpl* de droite.

rightist [ˈraɪtɪst] (*Pol*) 1 **n** homme *m* *or* femme *f* de droite. 2 **adj** de droite.

rightly [ˈraɪtlɪ] **adv** a (*correctly*) bien, correctement. **I don't ~ know*** je ne sais pas très bien *or* pas au juste; **it shouldn't ~ do that** cela ne devrait vraiment pas faire ça. b (*justifiably*) avec justesse, à juste titre. **~ or wrongly** à tort ou à raison; **~ so** à juste titre, avec (juste) raison.

rigid [ˈrɪdʒɪd] **adj** (*lit*) *board, material* rigide, raide; (*fig*) *person, discipline, character* rigide, inflexible, sévère; *specifications, interpretation, principles* strict; *system* qui manque de flexibilité. **~ with fear** paralysé de peur; **he's quite ~ about it** il est inflexible là-dessus.

rigidity [rɪˈdʒɪdɪtɪ] **n** (*see* **rigid**) rigidité *f*; raideur *f*; inflexibilité *f*, sévérité *f*; caractère strict; manque *m* de flexibilité.

rigidly [ˈrɪdʒɪdlɪ] **adv** *stand etc* avec raideur, rigidement; (*fig*) *behave* inflexiblement; *define, follow rules* rigoureusement; *oppose, insist* absolument.

rigmarole [ˈrɪgmərəʊl] **n** (*speech*) galimatias *m*, discours *mpl* incohérents *or* verbeux. **to go through the whole** *or* **same ~ again** recommencer la même comédie*.

rigor [ˈrɪgəʳ] **n** (*US*) = **rigour.**

rigor mortis [ˈrɪgəˈmɔːtɪs] **n** rigidité *f* cadavérique.

rigorous [ˈrɪgərəs] **adj** rigoureux.

rigorously [ˈrɪgərəslɪ] **adv** rigoureusement, avec rigueur.

rigour, (*US*) **rigor** [ˈrɪgəʳ] **n** rigueur *f*.

rile* [raɪl] **vt** agacer, mettre en boule*.

rill [rɪl] **n** (*liter*) ruisselet *m*.

rim [rɪm] 1 **n** (*gen*) bord *m*; *[wheel]* jante *f*; *[spectacles]* monture *f*. **a ~ of dirt** *or* **a dirty ~ around the bath** une trace sale sur le bord de la baignoire. 2 **vt** border; *wheel* janter, cercler.

rimaye [rɪˈmeɪ] **n** (*Climbing*) rimaye *f*.

rime¹ [raɪm] = **rhyme.**

rime² [raɪm] **n** (*liter*) givre *m*.

rimless [ˈrɪmlɪs] **adj** *spectacles* à monture invisible, à verres non cerclés.

rind [raɪnd] 1 **n** *[orange, lemon]* peau *f*, pelure *f*, écorce *f*; (*in cooking, drink*) zeste *m*; (*larger piece*) écorce; (*peelings*) pelure; *[cheese]* croûte *f*; *[bacon]* couenne *f*. **melon ~** écorce de melon. 2 **vt** peler; enlever la croûte *or* la couenne de; écorcer.

ring¹ [rɪŋ] 1 **n** a (*gen: also for curtain, in gym etc*) anneau *m*; (*on finger*) anneau, (*with stone*) bague *f*, *[bishop]* anneau; (*on bird's foot*) bague; (*for napkin*) rond *m*; (*for swimmer*) bouée *f* de natation; (*for invalid to sit on*) rond (pour malade); *[piston]* segment *m*; *[turbine]* couronne *f*. **diamond ~** bague de diamant(s); **wedding ~** alliance *f*, anneau de mariage; (*for cooking*) **electric/gas ~** plaque *f* chauffante à l'électricité/au gaz; *see* **ear¹, key, signet** *etc*.

b (*circle*) cercle *m*, rond *m*; (*of people*) cercle; (*of smoke, in water etc*) rond; (*in treetrunk*) cercle; (*round sun, moon*) auréole *f*, halo *m*. **the ~s of Saturn** les anneaux *mpl* de Saturne; **to have ~s round the eyes** avoir les yeux cernés *or* battus; **to stand in a ~** se tenir en cercle *or* en rond, former un cercle; (*fig*) **to run** *or* **make ~s round sb*** battre qn à plate(s) couture(s), enfoncer qn*.

c (*group*) (*gen, Pol*) coterie *f*, clique *f* (*pej*); *[dealers]* groupe *m*, cartel *m*; *[gangsters]* bande *f*, gang *m*; *[spies]* réseau *m*. (*at auction*) **there is a ~ operating** il y a un système d'enchères privées.

d (*enclosure*) (*at circus*) piste *f*; (*at exhibition*) arène *f*, piste; (*Horse-racing*) enceinte *f* des bookmakers; (*Boxing*) ring *m*. (*boxing itself*) **the ~** la boxe, le ring.

2 **vt** (*surround*) entourer, encercler, cerner; (*with quoit, hoop*) jeter un anneau sur; (*put ~ on or round*) *item on list etc* entourer d'un cercle; *bird, tree* baguer; *bear, bull* mettre un anneau au nez de.

3 **comp** ►**ring-a-ring-a-roses** *ronde et jeu enfantins* ►**ring binder** classeur *m* à anneaux ►**ringbolt** (*Tech*) piton *m*; (*Naut*) anneau *m* (d'amarrage) ►**ringdove** ramier *m* ►**ring exercise** (*Gymnastics*) exercice *m* aux anneaux ►**ring-fence** *money* allouer; **to ring-fence a local authority** *obliger une municipalité à utiliser l'argent destiné à un usage particulier* ►**ring finger** annulaire *m* ►**ringleader** chef *m*, meneur *m* ►**the ringmaster** ≃ "Monsieur Loyal" ►**ring ouzel** merle *m* à plastron ►**ring-pull** (*on can*) anneau *m* (d'ouverture), bague *f*; **ring-pull can** boîte *f* avec anneau (d'ouverture) ►**ring road** (*Brit*) route *f* de ceinture; (*motorway-type*) périphérique *m* ►**ringside seat** place *f* au premier rang; (*fig*) **to have a ringside seat** être aux premières loges ►**ring spanner** clef polygonale ►**ring-tailed** à queue zébrée ►**ring-way** = **ring road** ►**ringworm** teigne *f*.

ring² [rɪŋ] (**vb: pret rang, ptp rung**) 1 **n** a (*sound*) son *m*; *[bell]* sonnerie *f*, (*lighter*) tintement *m*; *[electric bell]* retentissement *m*; *[coins]* tintement. **there was a ~ at the door** on a sonné à la porte; **to hear a ~ at the door** entendre sonner à la porte; **give 2 ~s for the maid** sonne 2 coups *or* 2 fois pour (appeler) la bonne; **his voice had an angry ~ (in it)** il y avait un accent *or* une note de colère dans sa voix; **that has the ~ of truth (to it)** ça sonne juste.

b (*Telec **) coup *m* de téléphone *or* de fil*. **to give sb a ~** donner *or* passer un coup de téléphone *or* de fil* à qn.

c **~ of bells** jeu *m* de cloches.

2 **comp** ►**ring-a-ding**‡: (*US*) **to have a ring-a-ding** faire la nouba‡, faire la bringue*.

3 **vi** a *[bell]* sonner, retentir, (*lightly*) tinter; *[alarm clock, telephone]* sonner. **the bell rang** la cloche a sonné *or* tinté, la sonnette a retenti; **the bell rang for dinner** la cloche a sonné le dîner; **to ~ for sb** sonner qn; **to ~ for sth** sonner pour demander qch; **please ~ for attention** prière de sonner; **to ~ for the lift** appeler l'ascenseur; **to ~ at the door** sonner à la porte; **you rang, sir?** Monsieur a sonné?

b (*telephone*) téléphoner.

c (*sound*) *[words]* retentir, résonner; *[voice]* vibrer; *[coin]* sonner, tinter; (*resound*) résonner, retentir; *[ears]* tinter, bourdonner. *[coin]* **to ~ false/true/hollow** sonner faux/clair/creux; (*fig*) **that ~s true** ça sonne juste; **that doesn't ~ true** ça sonne faux; **the room rang with their shouts** la pièce résonnait de leurs cris; **the town rang with his praises** la ville entière chantait ses louanges; **the news set the town ~ing** toute la ville parlait de la nouvelle, dans toute la ville il n'était bruit que de la nouvelle; **his voice rang with emotion** sa voix vibrait d'émotion; **his words still ~ in my ears** ses mots retentissent encore à mes oreilles.

4 **vt** a (*sound: gen*) sonner; *coin* faire sonner, faire tinter. **to ~ the doorbell** sonner (à la porte); **to ~ the bell** (*lit*) sonner, donner un coup de sonnette; (*handbell*) agiter la sonnette; (** fig: succeed*) décrocher la timbale*, réussir magnifiquement; **they rang the church bells** (*gen*) ils ont fait sonner les cloches; *[bellringers]* ils ont sonné les cloches; (*fig*) **his name ~s a bell*** son nom me dit quelque chose *or* me rappelle quelque chose; (*liter: lit, fig*) **to ~ the knell (of)** sonner le glas (de); **to ~ the hours** sonner les heures; *[bells]* **to ~ the changes** carillonner (*en variant l'ordre des cloches*); (*fig*) **to ~ the changes on the same speech** rabâcher le même discours avec des variantes; **to ~ the changes on an outfit/the menu** *etc* varier un ensemble/le menu *etc*.

b (*Telec: also* ~ **up**) téléphoner à, donner *or* passer un coup de téléphone *or* de fil* à.

▸**ring around** = **ring round**.

▸**ring back** (*Telec*) vi, vt sep rappeler.

▸**ring down** vt sep (*Theat*) **to ring down the curtain** (faire) baisser le rideau; (*fig*) **to ring down the curtain on sth** marquer la fin de qch.

▸**ring in** 1 vi a (*report by telephone*) téléphoner un reportage. b (*US: clock on*) pointer en arrivant. 2 vt sep: **to ring in the New Year** carillonner le Nouvel An.

▸**ring off** vi (*Telec*) raccrocher.

▸**ring out** vi a *[bell]* sonner; *[electric bell]* retentir; *[voice]* résonner; *[shot]* éclater, retentir. b (*US: clock off*) pointer en partant.

▸**ring round** 1 vi (*Telec*) donner des coups de téléphone. 2 vt fus: **I'll ring round my friends** je vais appeler (tous) mes amis.

▸**ring up** vt sep a (*Telec*) donner un coup de téléphone *or* de fil* à. b (*Theat*) **to ring up the curtain** frapper les trois coups, (sonner pour faire) lever le rideau; (*fig*) **to ring up the curtain on a new career** *etc* marquer le début d'une nouvelle carrière *etc.* c (*on cash register*) *amount* enregistrer.

ringer ['rɪŋəʳ] n a (*bell* ~) sonneur *m*, carillonneur *m*. b (*look-alike*) sosie *m*. **he is a dead ~* for the President** c'est le sosie du président.

ringing ['rɪŋɪŋ] 1 adj *bell* qui résonne *or* tinte; *voice, tone* sonore, retentissant, vibrant. (*Brit Telec*) ~ **tone** tonalité *f*. 2 n *[bell]* sonnerie *f*, son *m*, (*lighter*) tintement *m*; *[electric bell]* retentissement *m*; *[telephone]* sonnerie; (*in ears*) tintement, bourdonnement *m*.

ringlet ['rɪŋlɪt] n frisette *f*; (*long*) anglaise *f*.

rink [rɪŋk] n *[ice-hockey, ice-skating]* patinoire *f*; *[roller-skating]* skating *m*.

rinky-dink* ['rɪŋkɪ'dɪŋk] adj (*US*) (*old-fashioned; also small-time*) ringard*; (*poor quality*) de camelote*; (*broken down*) déglingué*, démoli.

rinse [rɪns] 1 n a (*act*) rinçage *m*. **give the cup a ~** rincez la tasse, passez la tasse sous le robinet. b (*for hair*) rinçage *m*. 2 vt a *clothes etc* rincer. **to ~ one's hands** se passer les mains à l'eau; **to ~ the soap off one's hands** se rincer les mains. b (*colour with a* ~) **to ~ one's hair** se faire un *or* des rinçage(s); **she ~d her hair black** elle s'est fait un rinçage noir.

▸**rinse out** vt sep a *hair tint, colour, dirt* faire partir à l'eau. b *cup* rincer. **to rinse out one's mouth** se rincer la bouche.

Rio ['riːəʊ] n: ~ (**de Janeiro**) Rio (de Janeiro); ~ **Grande** Rio Grande *m*.

riot ['raɪət] 1 n a (*uprising*) émeute *f*, violentes bagarres *fpl*; (*Jur*) actes *mpl* séditieux. **the ~s against the régime** les émeutes contre le régime; **last night's ~s** les émeutes *or* les violentes bagarres de la nuit dernière.

b (*fig*) **a ~ of colour(s)** une débauche de couleurs; **a ~ of reds and blues** une profusion de rouges et de bleus; **a ~ of flowers** une profusion de fleurs; **he's a ~** ‡ c'est un (type) rigolo*; **she is a ~**‡ elle est rigolote*; **the film is a ~**‡ (*funny*) le film est tordant*; (*successful*) le film a un succès fou*; *see* **run**.

2 comp ▸**Riot Act** (*Hist*) loi *f* contre les attroupements séditieux (*see also* **read**[1]) ▸**riot gear**: **in riot gear** casqué et portant un bouclier ▸**the riot police** la brigade anti-émeute ▸**riot shield** bouclier *m* (*utilisé par la police*) ▸**the Riot Squad** = **the riot police**.

3 vi manifester avec violence, se livrer à de violentes bagarres, (*stronger*) faire une émeute; (*Jur*) se livrer à des actes séditieux. *[mob, youths etc]* **~ing** en émeute.

rioter ['raɪətəʳ] n manifestant(e) *m(f)* (*violent*), (*stronger*) émeutier *m*, -ière *f*; (*vandalizing*) casseur *m*.

rioting ['raɪətɪŋ] n (*NonC*) émeutes *fpl*; *see also* **riot 3**.

riotous ['raɪətəs] adj a (*Jur*) *behaviour* séditieux. ~ **assembly** attroupements séditieux. b (*noisy, debauched*) tapageur. ~ **living** vie *f* de débauche, vie déréglée. c (*: *boisterous*) *laughter* exubérant; *evening* d'une gaieté bruyante; *funny* tordant*. **a ~ success** un succès fou* *or* monstre*; **we had a ~ time*** nous nous sommes bien marrés‡.

riotously ['raɪətəslɪ] adv a *behave, act* (*noisily*) de façon tapageuse; (*Jur*) de façon séditieuse. b **it was ~ funny*** c'était à se tordre*, c'était rigolo* au possible.

R.I.P. [ɑːraɪ'piː] (**abbr of rest in peace**) R.I.P.

rip [rɪp] 1 n déchirure *f*.

2 comp ▸**ripcord** poignée *f* d'ouverture (*pour parachute ou ballon*) ▸**rip-off**‡ *see* **rip-off**‡ ▸**rip-roaring*** (*gen*) d'une gaieté bruyante, exubérant; *success* monstre* ▸**ripsaw** scie *f* à refendre ▸**riptide** courant *m* de retour, contre-courant *m*, turbulence *f*.

3 vt déchirer, fendre. **to ~ open a letter** ouvrir une lettre en hâte, fendre une enveloppe; **to ~ the buttons from a shirt** arracher les boutons d'une chemise.

4 vi a *[cloth]* se déchirer, se fendre.

b (*) **the fire/explosion ~ped through the house** l'incendie a fait rage à travers la maison/l'explosion a soufflé la maison de part en part; **the jet ~ped through the sky** le jet a fendu le ciel; **the car ~s along** la voiture roule à toute vitesse *or* roule à toute biture*; *[boat, car]* **let her** *or* **it ~!** appuie!, fonce!*; **to let ~** (*gen*) laisser courir*; (*in anger*) éclater, exploser (*de colère etc*); **he let ~ a string of oaths** il a lâché un chapelet de jurons; **he let ~ at me** il m'a passé un bon savon*.

▸**rip off** 1 vt sep a (*lit*) arracher, déchirer, enlever à la hâte (*from* de). b (‡: *steal*) *object, goods* voler; (*defraud etc*) *customer* arnaquer*, filouter*; *employee* exploiter. **they're ripping you off!** c'est du vol manifeste!, c'est de l'arnaque*! 2 **rip-off**‡ *see* **rip-off**‡.

▸**rip out** vt sep arracher.

▸**rip up** vt sep déchirer.

riparian [raɪ'pɛərɪən] adj, n riverain(e) *m(f)*.

ripe [raɪp] adj *fruit* mûr; *cheese* fait; *age, judgment* mûr. **to live to a ~ old age** vivre très vieux, vivre jusqu'à un bel âge *or* un âge avancé; (*fig*) **to be ~ for** être mûr *or* bon pour; (*fig iro*) **that's ~!**‡ ça c'est pas mal!*, faut le faire!*; **he smelled rather ~*, he gave off a rather ~ smell*** il ne sentait pas la rose*; *see* **over**.

ripen ['raɪpən] 1 vt (faire) mûrir. 2 vi mûrir; *[cheese]* se faire.

ripeness ['raɪpnɪs] n maturité *f*.

rip-off‡ ['rɪpɒf] 1 n escroquerie *f*. **it's a ~!** c'est du vol manifeste!, c'est de l'arnaque*! 2 comp ▸**rip-off artist**‡ escroc *m*.

riposte [rɪ'pɒst] 1 n (*Fencing: also fig*) riposte *f*. 2 vi riposter.

ripper ['rɪpəʳ] n (*murderer*) éventreur *m*. **Jack the R~** Jack l'éventreur.

ripping‡† ['rɪpɪŋ] adj (*Brit*) épatant*, sensationnel*.

ripple ['rɪpl] 1 n a (*movement*) *[water]* ride *f*, ondulation *f*; *[crops]* ondulation. b (*noise*) *[waves]* clapotis *m*; *[voices]* murmure(s) *m(pl)*, gazouillement *m*; *[laughter]* cascade *f*. c (*ice-cream*) **chocolate/raspberry ~** *glace à la vanille avec des traînées de glace au chocolat/à la framboise*. 2 comp ▸**ripple effect** effet *m* de vague. 3 vi *[water]* se rider; *[crops, hair]* onduler; *[waves]* clapoter. 4 vt rider; faire onduler.

RISC [ɑːraɪessiː] n (*Comput*) a (**abbr of reduced instruction set computer**) *see* **reduced 1a**. b (**abbr of reduced instruction set computing**) *see* **reduced 1a**.

rise [raɪz] (vb: **pret rose, ptp risen**) 1 n a *[theatre curtain, sun]* lever *m*; (*Mus*) hausse *f*; (*increase*) (*in temperature*) élévation *f*, hausse; (*in pressure*) hausse; *[tide]* flux *m*, flot *m*; *[river]* crue *f*; (*Brit: in wages*) augmentation *f*, relèvement *m* (*Admin*); (*in prices*) hausse, augmentation, majoration *f*; (*in bank rate*) relèvement. **prices are on the ~** les prix sont en hausse; (*Brit*) *[employee]* **to ask for a ~** demander une augmentation (de salaire); **there has been a ~ in the number of people who do this** le nombre de personnes qui font cela a augmenté; (*fig*) **his meteoric ~** son ascension *f* rapide; **his ~ to power** sa montée au pouvoir; **his ~ to fame took 20 years** il a mis 20 ans à parvenir à la gloire *or* à devenir célèbre; **the ~ of Bristol/the steel industry** l'essor *m* de Bristol/de l'industrie de l'acier; **the ~ of the working classes** l'ascension du prolétariat; **the ~ and fall of an empire** l'essor et la chute d'un empire, la grandeur et la décadence d'un empire; (*fig*) **to get a ~ out of sb*** faire marcher qn*.

b (*small hill*) éminence *f*, hauteur *f*, élévation *f*; (*slope*) côte *f*, pente *f*.

c (*origin*) *[river]* source *f*; (*fig*) source, origine *f*, naissance *f*. **the river has** *or* **takes its ~ (in)** la rivière prend sa source *or* a son origine (dans); (*fig*) **to give ~ to** *trouble* causer, provoquer; *speculation, rumour* donner lieu à, engendrer; *bitterness* occasionner, causer; *fear, suspicions* donner naissance à, susciter; *pleasure, interest* susciter; *impression* faire, donner.

2 vi a (*get up*) (*from sitting, lying*) se lever, se mettre debout; (*from bed*) se lever; (*after falling*) se relever. **he ~s early/late** il se lève tôt/tard; **~ and shine!** allez, lève-toi!, debout, là-dedans!*; **he rose to go** il s'est levé pour partir; **to ~ to one's feet** se mettre debout, se lever; **to ~ on tiptoe** se mettre sur la pointe des pieds; **to ~ from (the) table** se lever de table; **he rose from his chair** il s'est levé de sa chaise; **he rose from his sickbed to go and see her** il a quitté son lit pour aller la voir; **to ~ from the dead** ressusciter (des morts); **the horse rose on its hind legs** le cheval s'est dressé (sur ses jambes de derrière) *or* s'est cabré.

b *[smoke, mist]* s'élever, monter; *[balloon]* s'élever; *[aircraft, lift]* monter; *[theatre curtain, sun, moon, wind, bread]* se lever; *[dough]* lever; *[hair]* se dresser; *[ground]* monter (en pente); *[voice]* monter, devenir plus aigu (*f* -guë); *[sea]* devenir houleux; *[water, river, tide, blood pressure, temperature, exchange rate]* monter; *[barometer]* remonter, être en hausse; *[hopes, anger]* croître, grandir; *[prices]* monter, augmenter; *[cost of living]* augmenter, être en hausse; *[stocks, shares]* monter, être en hausse. *[swimmer, object, fish]* **to ~ to the surface** remonter à la *or* en surface; **the fish are rising well** les poissons mordent bien; (*fig*) **he rose to the bait** il a mordu à l'hameçon; **he won't ~ to any of your taunts** il ne réagira à aucune de vos piques; **his eyebrows rose at the sight of her** quand il l'a vue il a levé les sourcils (d'étonnement); (*fig*) **the idea/image rose in his mind** l'idée/l'image s'est présentée à son esprit; **the mountain ~s to 3,000 metres** la montagne a une altitude de 3 000 mètres; **the mountains rising before him** les montagnes qui se dressaient *or* s'élevaient devant lui; **great cheers rose from the audience** de nombreux hourras s'élevèrent de la foule; **to ~ to the occasion** se montrer à la hauteur de la situation *or* des circonstances; **I can't ~ to £10** je ne peux pas aller jusqu'à 10 livres; **to ~ in price** augmenter (de prix); **to ~ above a certain temperature/a certain level** dépasser une température donnée/un niveau donné; **her**

spirits rose son moral a remonté; **the colour rose to her cheeks** ses joues se sont empourprées, le rouge lui est monté aux joues; *see* **challenge, gorge.**

c (*fig: in society, rank*) s'élever. **to ~ in the world** réussir, faire son chemin dans le monde; **to ~ from nothing** partir de rien; (*Mil*) **to ~ from the ranks** sortir du rang; **he rose to be President/a captain** il s'est élevé jusqu'à devenir Président/jusqu'au grade de capitaine.

d (*adjourn*) *[assembly]* clore la session; *[meeting]* lever la séance. (*Parl*) **the House rose at 2 a.m.** l'Assemblée a levé la séance à 2 heures du matin; **Parliament will ~ on Thursday next** les vacances parlementaires commenceront jeudi prochain.

e (*originate*) *[river]* prendre sa source *or* sa naissance (*in* dans).

f (*rebel: also ~* **up**) se soulever, se révolter (*against* contre). **to ~ (up) in revolt** se révolter (*against* contre); **they rose (up) in anger and assassinated the tyrant** emportés par la colère ils se sont soulevés et ont assassiné le tyran.

►**rise up** vi *[person]* se lever. **a feeling of inadequacy rose up within him** un sentiment de médiocrité montait en lui; *see also* **rise 2f.**

risen ['rɪzn] 1 ptp of **rise.** 2 adj (*Rel*) **the ~ Lord** le Christ ressuscité.

riser ['raɪzəʳ] n a (*person*) **to be an early ~** (aimer) se lever tôt, être lève-tôt *inv or* matinal; **to be a late ~** (aimer) se lever tard, être lève-tard *inv*. b *[stair]* contremarche *f*.

risibility [ˌrɪzɪ'bɪlɪtɪ] n caractère *m* drôle.

risible ['rɪzɪbl] adj risible.

rising ['raɪzɪŋ] 1 n a (*rebellion*) soulèvement *m*, insurrection *f*.

b (*NonC*) *[sun, star]* lever *m*; *[barometer]* hausse *f*; *[prices]* augmentation *f*, hausse; *[river]* crue *f*; *[person from dead]* résurrection *f*; (*Theat*) *[curtain]* lever; *[ground]* élévation *f*. **the ~ and falling of the waves** le mouvement montant et descendant des vagues, les vagues s'élevant et s'abaissant; **the ~ and falling of the boat on the water** le mouvement du bateau qui danse sur les flots.

c *[Parliament, court]* ajournement *m*, clôture *f* de séance.

2 adj a *sun* levant; *barometer, prices, temperature* en hausse; *tide* montant; *wind* qui se lève; *tone* qui monte; *anger, fury* croissant; *ground* qui monte en pente. **~ damp** humidité *f* (par capillarité).

b (*fig*) nouveau (*f* nouvelle). **the ~ sap** la sève ascendante; **a ~ young doctor** un jeune médecin d'avenir; **the ~ generation** la nouvelle génération, les jeunes *mpl*; *see also* **3.**

3 adv (*) **she's ~ six** elle va sur ses six ans; (*Brit Scol*) **the ~ fives** les enfants qui auront cinq ans dans l'année.

risk [rɪsk] 1 n a (*possible danger*) risque *m*. **to take *or* run ~s** courir des risques; **to take *or* run the ~ of doing** courir le risque de faire; **that's a ~ you'll have to take** c'est un risque à courir; **there's too much ~ involved** c'est trop risqué; **it's not worth the ~** ça ne vaut pas la peine de courir un tel risque; **there is no ~ of his coming *or* that he will come** il n'y a pas de risque qu'il vienne, il ne risque pas de venir; **you do it at your own ~** vous le faites à vos risques et périls; (*Comm*) **goods sent at sender's ~** envois faits aux risques de l'expéditeur; **at the ~ of seeming stupid** au risque de *or* quitte à paraître stupide; **at the ~ of his life** au péril de sa vie; **at ~** *person* en danger, en péril, exposé; *plan, custom* menacé; **children at ~** l'enfance *f* en danger; **some jobs are at ~** des emplois risquent d'être supprimés *or* sont menacés; *see* **occupational, owner** *etc.*

b (*Insurance*) risque *m*. **fire ~** risque d'incendie; **he is a bad accident ~** il présente des risques élevés d'accident; **he is a bad ~** on court trop de risques avec lui; *see* **security.**

2 comp ►**risk capital** capitaux *mpl* à risques ►**risk factor** facteur *m* de risque ►**risk management** gestion *f* des risques ►**risk-taking** (le fait de) prendre des risques; **he does not like risk-taking** il n'aime pas prendre des risques, il n'a pas le goût du risque.

3 vt a *life, career, future* risquer, aventurer, hasarder; *reputation, savings* risquer. **you ~ falling** vous risquez de tomber; **he ~ed life and limb to rescue the drowning child** il a risqué sa vie pour sauver l'enfant qui se noyait; *see* **neck.**

b *battle, defeat, quarrel* s'exposer aux risques de; *accident* risquer d'avoir, courir le risque de; (*venture*) *criticism, remark* risquer, aventurer, hasarder. **she won't ~ coming today** elle ne se risquera pas à venir aujourd'hui; **I'll ~ it** je vais risquer *or* tenter le coup*; **I can't ~ it** je ne peux pas prendre un tel risque.

riskiness ['rɪskɪnɪs] n (*NonC*) risques *mpl*, hasards *mpl*, aléas *mpl*.

risky ['rɪskɪ] adj *enterprise, deed* plein de risques, risqué, hasardeux; *joke, story* risqué, osé. **it's ~, it's a ~ business** c'est risqué.

risotto [rɪ'zɒtəʊ] n risotto *m*.

risqué ['riːskeɪ] adj *story, joke* risqué, osé.

rissole ['rɪsəʊl] n (*Brit*) rissole *f*.

rite [raɪt] n rite *m*. **funeral ~s** rites funèbres; **last ~s** derniers sacrements; **~ of passage** rite de passage; (*Mus*) **the R~ of Spring** le Sacre du printemps.

ritual ['rɪtjʊəl] 1 adj rituel. 2 n rituel *m*. (*fig*) **he went through the ~** il a fait les gestes rituels, il s'est conformé aux rites; **he went through the ~ of apologizing** il a fait les excuses rituelles, il s'est excusé comme de coutume.

ritualism ['rɪtjʊəlɪzəm] n ritualisme *m*.

ritualist ['rɪtjʊəlɪst] adj, n ritualiste *(mf)*.

ritualistic [ˌrɪtjʊə'lɪstɪk] adj ritualiste.

ritually ['rɪtjʊəlɪ] adv rituellement.

ritzy* ['rɪtsɪ] adj (*US*) luxueux.

rival ['raɪvəl] 1 n rival(e) *m(f)*. 2 adj *firm, enterprise* rival, concurrent; *attraction, claim* opposé, antagonique. **two ~ firms** deux entreprises rivales, deux concurrents. 3 vt (*gen*) rivaliser avec (*in* de); (*Comm*) être en concurrence avec; (*equal*) égaler (*in* en). **he can't ~ her in intelligence** il ne peut pas l'égaler en intelligence, il ne peut pas rivaliser d'intelligence avec elle; **his achievements ~ even yours** ses réussites égalent même les vôtres.

rivalry ['raɪvəlrɪ] n rivalité *f* (*with* avec, *between* entre).

rive [raɪv] pret **rived,** ptp **riven** ['rɪvən] (*liter*) 1 vt fendre. 2 vi se fendre. **riven by** fendu par; (*fig*) déchiré par.

river ['rɪvəʳ] 1 n rivière *f*, (*major*) fleuve *m* (*also fig*), (*Admin, Econ, Geog etc*) cours *m* d'eau. **down ~** en aval; **up ~** en amont; (*Brit*) **the ~ Seine,** (*US*) **the Seine ~** la Seine; (*fig*) **~s of blood** des fleuves de sang; *see* **sell.**

2 comp *police, port, system* fluvial ►**riverbank** rive *f*, berge *f*, bord *m* ►**river basin** bassin fluvial ►**riverbed** lit *m* de rivière *or* de fleuve ►**river blindness** (*Med*) cécité *f* des rivières, onchocercose *f* ►**river fish** poisson *m* d'eau douce *or* de rivière ►**river fishing** pêche fluviale *or* en eau douce ►**river head** source *f* (de rivière *or* de fleuve) ►**river horse** hippopotame *m* ►**river lamprey** lamproie *f* de rivière ►**river-mouth** bouche *f* d'une rivière *or* d'un fleuve, embouchure *f* ►**riverside** n bord *m* de l'eau (*or* de la rivière *or* du fleuve), rive *f* ◊ adj (situé) au bord de la rivière *etc;* **by the riverside** au bord de l'eau (*or* de la rivière *etc*); **along the riverside** le long de la rivière (*or* du fleuve) ►**river traffic** trafic fluvial, navigation fluviale.

riverine ['rɪvəraɪn] adj fluvial; *person* riverain.

rivet ['rɪvɪt] 1 n rivet *m*. 2 vt (*Tech*) riveter, river. (*fig*) **it ~ed our attention** ça nous a fascinés; **~ed with fear** rivé *or* cloué sur place par la peur. 3 comp ►**rivet joint** assemblage *m* par rivets.

riveter ['rɪvɪtəʳ] n (*person*) riveur *m*; (*machine*) riveuse *f*.

rivet(t)ing ['rɪvɪtɪŋ] 1 n rivetage *m*. 2 adj (*fascinating*) fascinant.

Riviera [ˌrɪvɪ'ɛərə] n: **the (French) ~** la Côte d'Azur; **the Italian ~** la Riviera (italienne).

rivulet ['rɪvjʊlɪt] n (petit) ruisseau *m*.

Riyadh [rɪ'jɑːd] n Riyad.

RL n abbr of **Rugby League.**

RN a (*Brit*) (abbr of **Royal Navy**) *see* **royal.** b (*US*) abbr of **registered nurse.**

RNA [ɑːren'eɪ] n (*Med*) (abbr of **ribonucleic acid**) A.R.N.

RNLI [ˌɑːrene'laɪ] n (abbr of **Royal National Lifeboat Institution**) ≃ Société *f* nationale de sauvetage en mer; ≃ CROSS *mpl* (centres *mpl* régionaux opérationnels de surveillance et de sauvetage).

RNR (*Brit*) (abbr of **Royal Naval Reserve**) *see* **royal.**

RNZAF abbr of **Royal New Zealand Air Force.**

RNZN abbr of **Royal New Zealand Navy.**

roach¹ [rəʊtʃ] n, pl **~** *or* **~es** (*fish*) gardon *m*.

roach² [rəʊtʃ] 1 n a (*) (abbr of **cockroach**) cafard *m*, cancrelat *m*, blatte *f*. b (*US Drugs sl*) mégot *m* de joint. 2 comp ►**roach clip** (*US Drugs sl*) pince *f* (métallique) pour joint.

road [rəʊd] 1 n a (*gen*) route *f*; (*minor*) chemin *m*; (*in town*) rue *f*; (*fig*) chemin, voie *f*. **trunk ~** (route) nationale *f*, grande route; **country ~** route de campagne, petite route, (route) départementale *f*; **"~ up"** "attention travaux"; **she lives across the ~ (from us)** elle habite en face de chez nous; **just across the ~ is a bakery** il y a une boulangerie juste en face; **my car is off the ~ just now** (*laid up*) ma voiture est sur cales pour le moment; (*being repaired*) ma voiture est en réparation; **I hope to put it back on the ~ soon** j'espère qu'elle sera bientôt en état (de rouler); **my car is (back) on the ~ again** ma voiture est à nouveau en état de marche; **this vehicle shouldn't be on the ~** on ne devrait pas laisser circuler un véhicule dans cet état; **a spot of petrol will get us on the ~ again** un peu d'essence va nous dépanner; **he is a danger on the ~** (au volant) c'est un danger public; **to take (to) the ~** prendre la route, se mettre en route; *[salesman, theatre company]* **to be on the ~** être en tournée; **we were on the ~ at 6 in the morning** nous étions sur la route à 6 heures du matin; **we've been on the ~ since this morning** nous voyageons depuis ce matin; **we were on the ~ to Paris** nous étions en route pour Paris; **is this the ~ to London? *or* the London ~?** c'est (bien) la route de Londres?; (*in towns*) **London R~** rue de Londres; **you're on the right ~** vous êtes sur la bonne route; (*fig*) vous êtes sur la bonne voie; **on the ~ to ruin/success** sur le chemin de la ruine/du succès; (*fig*) **somewhere along the ~ he changed his mind** à un moment donné *or* en cours de route* il a changé d'avis; **you're in my ~*** vous me barrez le passage, vous m'empêchez de passer, vous êtes sur *or* dans mon chemin; **(get) out of the ~!*** dégagez!; (*dial*) **any ~‡** de toute façon; **to have one for the ~*** prendre un dernier verre avant de partir, boire le coup de l'étrier; (*Naut*) **~s** rade *f*; (*Brit: car sales*) **on-the-~ price, price on the ~** prix *m* clés en mains; *see* **arterial, end 1a, hit, main, Rome** *etc.*

b (*US*) abbr of **railroad.**

2 comp ►**road accident** accident *m* de la route *or* de la circulation ►**roadbed** (*US*) *[railroad]* ballast *m*; *[road]* empierrement *m* ►**road-**

block barrage *m* routier ►**road book** guide *m* routier ►**roadbridge** pont *m* routier ►**road construction** construction *f* des routes ►**road-fund licence** (*Brit*) vignette *f* automobile ►**road gang** (*US*) équipe *f* de forçats (employés à construire des routes) ►**road haulage** transports *mpl* routiers ►**road haulier** entrepreneur *m* de transports routiers ►**roadhog** chauffard *m*, écraseur* *m*, -euse* *f* ►**roadholding** tenue *f* de route ►**roadhouse** hostellerie *f*, relais *m* ►**road hump** casse-vitesse *m* ►**roadmaking** (*NonC*) construction *f* de (la) route ►**roadman** cantonnier *m* ►**roadmap** carte routière ►**roadmender** = **roadman** ►**road metal** empierrement *m* ►**road movie** road movie *m* ►**road race** course *f* automobile (*or* cycliste) sur route ►**road racer** (*Cycling*) routier *m*, -ière *f* ►**road racing** compétition *f* automobile (*or* cycliste) sur route ►**road rider** (*Cycling*) = **road racer** ►**roadroller** rouleau *m* compresseur ►**road runner** (*US: bird*) coucou *m* terrestre (du Sud-Ouest) ►**road safety** sécurité routière ►**road sense**: **he has no road sense** *[driver]* il n'a aucune notion de la conduite; *[pedestrian]* il n'a aucune notion de la circulation; **to teach a child road sense** apprendre à un enfant à faire attention à la circulation ►**road show** (*Theat*) spectacle *m* de tournée ►**roadside** *see* **roadside** ►**roadsign** signal *m* routier, panneau *m* (de signalisation), poteau *m* indicateur; **international roadsigns** signalisation routière internationale ►**road stability** (*Aut*) tenue *f* de route ►**roadstead** (*Naut*) rade *f* ►**road surveyor** agent *m* voyer, agent des Ponts et Chaussées ►**roadsweeper** (*person*) balayeur *m*, -euse *f*; (*vehicle*) balayeuse *f* ►**road tax** (*Brit*) *taxe différentielle sur les véhicules à moteur;* (*Brit*) **road tax disc** vignette *f* automobile ►**road test** n essai *m* sur route ►**road-test**: **they are road-testing the car tomorrow** ils vont faire les essais sur route demain ►**road traffic** circulation routière ►**road transport** transports routiers ►**road-trials** (*road test*) essais *mpl* sur route; (*rally*) épreuves *fpl* sur route ►**road-user** (*gen*) usager *m* de la route; **road-user charges** taxation *f* des usagers de la route ►**roadway** chaussée *f*, (*on bridge*) tablier *m*, chaussée ►**roadworks** travaux *mpl* (d'entretien des routes) ►**roadworthy**: **a roadworthy car** une voiture en état de marche.

roadie [ˈrəʊdɪ] n (*Pop sl*) membre *m* de l'équipe d'une vedette en tournée.

roadside [ˈrəʊdsaɪd] 1 n bord *m* de la route, accotement *m*, bas-côté *m*. **along** *or* **by the ~** au bord de la route. 2 comp *inn* (situé) au bord de la route ►**roadside repairs** (*professional*) dépannage *m*; (*done alone*) réparations *fpl* de fortune.

roadster [ˈrəʊdstəʳ] n (*car*) roadster *m*; (*cycle*) bicyclette *f* routière.

roam [rəʊm] 1 vt *streets, countryside* parcourir, errer dans *or* par. **to ~ the (seven) seas** courir *or* parcourir les mers, bourlinguer; *[child, dog]* **to ~ the streets** traîner dans les rues. 2 vi errer, rôder; *[thoughts]* vagabonder. **to ~ about the house** errer dans la maison; **to ~ about the world** rouler *or* errer (de) par le monde; **to ~ about the streets** traîner dans les rues, traîner les rues (*pej*).

►**roam about, roam around** vi errer de-ci de-là; (*wider*) vagabonder, bourlinguer*, rouler sa bosse*.

roamer [ˈrəʊməʳ] n vagabond *m*.

roaming [ˈrəʊmɪŋ] 1 adj *person* errant, vagabond; *dog* errant; *thoughts* vagabond. 2 n vagabondage *m*.

roan[1] [rəʊn] adj, n (*horse*) rouan *(m)*; *see* **strawberry**.

roan[2] [rəʊn] n (*leather*) basane *f*.

roar [rɔːʳ] 1 vi *[person, crowd]* hurler, pousser de grands cris; (*with anger*) rugir; *[lion]* rugir; *[bull]* mugir, beugler; *[wind, sea]* mugir; *[thunder, gun, waterfall, storm, forest fire, engine, vehicle]* gronder; (*Aut: rev*) vrombir; *[fire in hearth]* ronfler. **to ~ with pain** hurler de douleur; **to ~ with laughter** rire à gorge déployée, éclater de rire, se tordre; **this will make you ~!*** tu vas te marrer!‡, tu vas rigoler!*; **the trucks ~ed past** les camions sont passés bruyamment à toute allure; **the car ~ed up the street** la voiture est passée dans la rue en vrombissant; **he ~ed away on his motorbike** il est parti en faisant vrombir sa moto.

2 vt a (*also* ~ **out**) *order* vociférer; *song* chanter à tue-tête, brailler, beugler*; *one's disapproval* hurler.

b (*Aut*) **to ~ the engine*** faire ronfler *or* faire vrombir le moteur.

3 n hurlement(s) *m(pl)*; rugissement *m*; mugissement *m*; beuglement *m*; grondement *m*; vrombissement *m*; ronflement *m*. **~s of laughter** de gros éclats de rire; **the ~s of the crowd** les clameurs *fpl* de la foule.

roaring [ˈrɔːrɪŋ] 1 adj (*see* **roar 1**) hurlant; rugissant; mugissant; beuglant; grondant; vrombissant; ronflant. (*in hearth*) **a ~ fire** une belle flambée; (*1920s*) **the R~ Twenties*** ≃ les années folles, ≃ les années 20; (*Geog*) **the ~ forties** les quarantièmes rugissants *mpl*; (*fig*) **~ drunk** complètement bourré* *or* noir*; **a ~ success** un succès fou* *or* monstre*; **to do a ~ trade** faire un gros commerce (*in* de), faire des affaires d'or*. 2 n = **roar 3**.

roast [rəʊst] 1 n a rôti *m*. **~ of beef** rôti de bœuf, rosbif *m*; **~ of veal/pork** *etc* rôti de veau/porc *etc*; **a slice off the ~** une tranche de *or* du rôti. b (*US: barbecue*) barbecue *m*. 2 adj *pork, veal, chicken* rôti. **~ beef** rôti *m* de bœuf, rosbif *m*; **~ potatoes** pommes *fpl* de terre rôties. 3 vt a *meat* (faire) rôtir; *chestnuts* griller, rôtir; *coffee beans* griller, torréfier; *minerals* calciner, griller. **the sun was ~ing the city** le soleil grillait la ville; **to ~ o.s. by the fire** se rôtir au coin du feu. b (*US* ‡: *criticize*) éreinter. 4 vi *[meat]* rôtir; *see also* **roasting**.

roaster [ˈrəʊstəʳ] n (*device*) rôtissoire *f*; (*bird*) poulet *m etc* à rôtir.

roasting [ˈrəʊstɪŋ] 1 n (*lit*) rôtissage *m*. (*fig*) **to give sb a ~**‡ sonner les cloches à qn*; **~ jack, ~ spit** tournebroche *m*. 2 adj a (*: *hot*) *day, weather* torride. **it's ~ in here*** on crève* (de chaleur) ici, on rôtit* ici; **I'm ~!*** je crève* (de chaleur)! b (*Culin*) *chicken etc* à rôtir.

rob [rɒb] vt *person* voler, dévaliser; *shop* dévaliser; *orchard* piller. **to ~ sb of sth** (*purse etc*) voler *or* dérober qch à qn; (*rights, privileges*) dépouiller *or* priver qn de qch; **to ~ an orchard** piller un verger; **to ~ the till** voler de l'argent dans la caisse; (*loc*) **to ~ Peter to pay Paul** déshabiller saint Pierre pour habiller saint Paul, faire un trou pour en boucher un autre; **I've been ~bed of my watch** on m'a volé ma montre; **I've been ~bed!** j'ai été volé!; **the bank was ~bed** la banque a été dévalisée, il y a eu un vol à la banque; (*Sport, games*) **we were ~bed*** on nous a volé la victoire; (*fig*) **he has been ~bed of the pleasure of seeing her** il a été privé du plaisir de la voir; **the shock ~bed him of speech** (*briefly*) le choc lui a fait perdre la parole; (*long-term*) le choc lui a ôté l'usage de la parole.

robber [ˈrɒbəʳ] 1 n bandit *m*, voleur *m*. 2 comp ►**robber baron** (*US Ind*) requin *m* de l'industrie *or* de la finance.

robbery [ˈrɒbərɪ] n vol *m*. (*Jur*) **~ with violence** vol avec voies de fait *or* coups et blessures; **highway ~** vol de grand chemin, brigandage *m*; **at that price it's sheer ~!*** à ce prix-là c'est du vol manifeste! *or* de l'escroquerie!; *see* **armed, daylight**.

robe [rəʊb] 1 n a (*garment*) robe *f* de cérémonie; (*for house wear*) peignoir *m*. **he was wearing his ~ of office** il portait la robe *or* la toge de sa charge; **ceremonial ~s** vêtements *mpl* de cérémonie; **christening ~** robe de baptême; *see* **coronation**. b (*US: rug*) couverture *f*. 2 vt revêtir (d'une robe); (*fig, liter*) parer, revêtir (*in* de). 3 vi *[judge etc]* revêtir sa robe.

Robert [ˈrɒbət] n Robert *m*.

robin [ˈrɒbɪn] n a (*in Europe: also* ~ **redbreast**) rouge-gorge *m*. b (*US*) merle *m* américain; *see* **round**.

robot [ˈrəʊbɒt] 1 n robot *m*; (*fig*) robot, automate *m*. 2 comp *worker, guidance, pilot* automatique, -robot ►**robot bomb** bombe-robot *f* ►**robot plane** avion-robot *m*, avion *m* à commande automatique.

robotics [rəʊˈbɒtɪks] n (*NonC*) robotique *f*.

robotization [ˌrəʊbɒtaɪˈzeɪʃən] n robotisation *f*.

robotize [ˈrəʊbɒtaɪz] vt robotiser.

robust [rəʊˈbʌst] adj *person* robuste, vigoureux, solide; *defence* vigoureux, énergique; *material, structure, appetite* solide; *wine* robuste; *humour, style* robuste.

robustly [rəʊˈbʌstlɪ] adv *build* solidement; (*fig*) *answer* avec vigueur.

robustness [rəʊˈbʌstnɪs] n robustesse *f*, solidité *f*, vigueur *f*.

roc [rɒk] n roc(k) *m*.

rock[1] [rɒk] 1 vt a (*swing to and fro*) *child* bercer; *cradle* balancer. **to ~ a child to sleep** endormir un enfant en le berçant; **a boat ~ed by the waves** un bateau bercé par les vagues (*see also* **1b**); **to ~ o.s. in a rocking chair** se balancer dans un fauteuil à bascule.

b (*shake*) ébranler, secouer; *ship [waves]* ballotter; *[explosion]* ébranler; (* *fig: startle*) ébranler, secouer. **town ~ed by an earthquake** ville ébranlée par un tremblement de terre; (*fig*) **country ~ed by rioting** *etc* pays ébranlé par des émeutes *etc;* (*fig*) **to ~ the boat*** jouer les trouble-fête, semer le trouble *or* la perturbation; (*fig*) **don't ~ the boat*** ne compromets pas les choses, ne fais pas l'empêcheur de danser en rond*; **that bit of news will ~ her!*** cette nouvelle va la bouleverser! *or* lui donner un sale coup!*

2 vi a (*sway gently*) *[cradle, hammock]* (se) balancer; *[person, ship]* se balancer. **he was ~ing back and forth** il se balançait d'avant en arrière.

b (*sway violently*) *[person]* chanceler; *[building]* être ébranlé *or* secoué. **the mast was ~ing in the wind** le mât oscillait sous les coups du vent; **the ground ~ed beneath our feet** le sol a tremblé sous nos pieds; **they ~ed with laughter*** ils se sont tordus *or* gondolés‡.

3 n (*also* ~ **music**) rock *m*; *see also* **5** *and* **punk**.

4 adj (*Mus*) *ballet, musical etc* rock *inv*. **~ musician** rocker *m*.

5 comp ►**rock-and-roll** rock (and roll) *m or* rock 'n' roll *m*; **to do the rock-and-roll** danser le rock (and roll).

rock[2] [rɒk] 1 n a (*substance*) (*any kind*) roche *f*; (*hard*) roc *m*; (*rock face*) rocher *m*, paroi rocheuse. **caves hewn out of the ~** des cavernes taillées dans la roche *or* le roc *or* le rocher; **hewn out of solid ~** creusé à même le roc, creusé dans le roc; (*lit, fig*) **built on ~** bâti sur le roc; **they were drilling into ~ and not clay** ils foraient la roche *or* le roc et non l'argile; **plants that grow in ~** plantes qui poussent sur la roche; **porous/volcanic** *etc* **~** roche poreuse/volcanique *etc*.

b **the study of ~s** l'étude des roches.

c (*large mass, huge boulder*) rocher *m*, roc *m* (*liter*); (*smaller*) roche *f*. **a huge ~ blocked their way** un énorme rocher leur bouchait le chemin; **the entrance was blocked by a pile of fallen ~s** l'entrée était bouchée par des éboulis de roches; (*Geog*) **the R~ (of Gibraltar)** le rocher de Gibraltar; (*fig*) **as solid as a ~** solide comme le roc; **the ship went on the ~s** le bateau est allé donner sur les rochers *or* sur les écueils; *[drink]* **on the ~s** avec des glaçons; (*fig*) **he's on the ~s**‡ il n'a pas le sou, il est à sec* *or* dans la dèche⁑; **that firm went on the ~s last year*** cette firme a fait faillite *or* est tombée en déconfiture* l'an dernier; **their marriage is on the ~s*** leur mariage est en train de craquer*; (*US*) **to be between a ~ and a hard place** être pris dans un dilemme.

d (*US: small stone*) galet *m*.

e (⁑) (*diamond*) bouchon *m* de carafe* (*hum*), diamant *m*. (*jewels*) ~s quincaillerie* *f*.

f (*Brit: sweet*) ≈ sucre *m* d'orge. (*US*) ~ **candy** ≈ sucre d'orge; **Brighton** ~ *bâton de sucre d'orge marqué au nom de Brighton.*

2 comp ▸**rock bass** achigan *m* de roche ▸**rock bun, rock cake** (*Brit*) rocher *m* (*Culin*) ▸**rock carving** sculpture *f* sur roc ▸**rock-climber** varappeur *m*, -euse *f*, rochassier *m*, -ière *f* ▸**rock-climbing** varappe *f*, escalade *f* ▸**rock crystal** cristal *m* de roche ▸**rock face** paroi rocheuse ▸**rock fall** chute *f* de pierres *or* de rochers ▸**rockfish** gobie *m*, rascasse *f*, scorpène *f* ▸**rock garden** (jardin *m* de) rocaille *f* ▸**rock-hard** (*lit*) dur comme la pierre; (*fig*) solide comme un roc ▸**rock painting** (*Art*) peinture rupestre *or* pariétale ▸**rock plant** plante *f* alpestre *or* de rocaille ▸**rock pool** mare *f* entre les rochers (*en bord de mer*) ▸**rock-ribbed** (*US fig*) inébranlable, à toute épreuve ▸**rock rose** hélianthème *m* ▸**rock salmon** (*Brit*) roussette *f* ▸**rock salt** sel *m* gemme ▸**rock-solid** (*lit, fig*) solide comme un roc.

rock-bottom ['rɒk'bɒtəm] n (*Geol*) fond rocheux. (*fig*) **this is ~*** c'est la fin de tout, c'est la catastrophe; **her spirits reached ~*** elle avait le moral au plus bas *or* à zéro*; **prices were at ~** les prix étaient tombés aux niveaux les plus bas; (*Comm*) "**~ prices**" "prix sacrifiés", "prix défiant toute concurrence".

rocker ['rɒkəʳ] n a [*cradle etc*] bascule *f*; (*chair*) fauteuil *m* à bascule. **to be off one's ~**⁑ être cinglé*, avoir le cerveau détraqué*; **to go off one's ~**⁑ perdre la boule*. b (*person*) blouson noir.

rockery ['rɒkərɪ] n (jardin *m* de) rocaille *f*.

rocket ['rɒkɪt] 1 n (*Mil*) fusée *f*, roquette *f*; (*Aviat, also firework*) fusée. **to fire** *or* **send up a ~** lancer une fusée; **distress ~** fusée *or* signal *m* de détresse; **space ~** fusée interplanétaire; (*Brit: fig*) **he's just had a ~* from the boss** le patron vient de lui passer un savon* *or* de l'enguirlander*.

2 vi [*prices*] monter en flèche. (*fig*) **to ~ to fame** devenir célèbre du jour au lendemain; **he went ~ing* past my door** il est passé en trombe devant ma porte.

3 comp ▸**rocket attack** attaque *f* à la roquette ▸**rocket base** = **rocket range** ▸**rocket gun** fusil *m* lance-fusées *inv or* lance-roquettes *inv* ▸**rocket launcher** lance-fusées *m inv*, lance-roquettes *m inv* ▸**rocket plane** avion-fusée *m* ▸**rocket-propelled** autopropulsé ▸**rocket propulsion** propulsion *f* par fusée, autopropulsion *f* ▸**rocket range** base *f* de lancement de missiles; **within rocket range** à portée de missiles ▸**rocket research** recherches aérospatiales ▸**rocket ship** navire *m* lance-fusées *inv or* lance-missiles *inv* ▸**rocket technology** fuséologie *f*.

rocketry ['rɒkɪtrɪ] n (*science*) fuséologie *f*; (*rockets collectively*) (panoplie *f* de) fusées *fpl*.

rocking ['rɒkɪŋ] 1 n balancement *m*, ballottement *m*. 2 comp ▸**rocking chair** fauteuil *m* à bascule ▸**rocking horse** cheval *m* à bascule.

rockling ['rɒklɪŋ] n, pl ~ *or* ~s loche *f* de mer.

rocky[1] ['rɒkɪ] adj (*unsteady*) *table* branlant; (* *fig*) *health* précaire, chancelant; *situation* instable, précaire; *government* branlant. **his English is rather ~*** son anglais est faiblard*; **his finances are ~*** sa situation financière est précaire.

rocky[2] ['rɒkɪ] adj *mountain, hill* rocheux; *road, path* rocailleux. (*Geog*) **the R~ Mountains, the Rockies** les (montagnes *fpl*) Rocheuses *fpl*.

rococo [rəʊ'kəʊkəʊ] 1 n rococo *m*. 2 adj rococo *inv*.

rod [rɒd] 1 n a (*wooden*) baguette *f*; (*metallic*) tringle *f*; [*machinery*] tige *f*; (*for punishment*) baguette *f*, canne *f*; (*symbol of authority*) verge *f*. **curtain/stair ~** tringle à rideaux/d'escalier; (*fig*) **to make a ~ for one's own back** se préparer *or* s'attirer des ennuis; **to rule with a ~ of iron** *country* gouverner d'une main de fer *or* avec une verge de fer (*liter*); *person, family* mener à la baguette *or* à la trique*; *see* **black, connect, piston, spare** *etc*.

b (*fishing ~*) canne *f* (à pêche). **to fish with ~ and line** pêcher à la ligne.

c (*measure*) perche *f* (= *5,03 m*).

d (*in eye*) bâtonnet *m*.

e (*US* ⁑: *gun*) flingue⁑ *m*.

f (*Aut *: hotrod*) hotrod *m*, voiture *f* gonflée.

g (**⁑: *penis*) bite**⁑ *f*.

2 comp ▸**rod bacterium** (*Med*) bâtonnet *m* ▸**rod bearing** (*Tech*) manchon *m* de bielle.

rode [rəʊd] pret of **ride**.

rodent ['rəʊdənt] 1 n rongeur (*m*). 2 adj rongeur. (*Med*) **~ cancer, ~ ulcer** cancer *m* de la peau.

rodeo ['rəʊdɪəʊ] n rodeo *m*.

rodomontade [,rɒdəmɒn'teɪd] n rodomontade *f*.

roe[1] [rəʊ] n, pl ~ *or* ~s (*species: also* ~ **deer**) chevreuil *m*. ~ **buck** chevreuil mâle; (*female*) ~ **deer** chevreuil *m* femelle, chevrette *f*.

roe[2] [rəʊ] n [*fish*] **hard** ~ œufs *mpl* de poisson; **soft** ~ laitance *f*; **herring** ~ œufs *or* laitance de hareng.

roentgen ['rɒntjən] n Roentgen *m or* Röntgen *m*.

rogation [rəʊ'geɪʃən] (*Rel*) 1 n (*gen pl*) rogations *fpl*. 2 comp ▸**Rogation Days** *les 3 jours qui précèdent l'Ascension* ▸**Rogation Sunday** dimanche *m* des Rogations ▸**Rogation-tide** période *f* des Rogations.

rogatory ['rɒgətərɪ] adj (*Jur*) rogatoire; *see* **letter**.

Roger ['rɒdʒəʳ] n Roger *m*. (*Telec*) "**r~**" "compris"; *see* **jolly**.

rogue [rəʊg] 1 n a (*scoundrel*) coquin *m*, gredin *m*; (*scamp*) polisson(ne) *m(f)*, coquin(e) *m(f)*, fripon(ne) *m(f)*. **you little ~!** petit coquin! b (*Zool*) solitaire *m*. 2 adj (*US fig: gone to the bad*) dévoyé; (*maverick*) non conformiste; *gene* aberrant. 3 comp ▸**rogue elephant** éléphant *m* solitaire ▸**rogues' gallery** (*Police*) (collection *f* de) photographies *fpl* de repris de justice; (*fig*) **they look like a rogues' gallery** ils ont des têtes de repris de justice.

roguery ['rəʊgərɪ] n (*wickedness*) coquinerie *f*, malhonnêteté *f*; (*mischief*) espièglerie *f*, friponnerie *f*, polissonnerie *f*.

roguish ['rəʊgɪʃ] adj espiègle, coquin, polisson.

roguishly ['rəʊgɪʃlɪ] adv *behave, speak* avec espièglerie, malicieusement; *look* d'un œil coquin.

roily ['rɔɪlɪ] adj *water, sea* troublé, agité; (*fig*) *person* exaspéré.

roister ['rɔɪstəʳ] vi s'amuser bruyamment.

roisterer ['rɔɪstərəʳ] n fêtard(e)* *m(f)*.

Roland ['rəʊlənd] n Roland *m*. (*loc*) **a ~ for an Oliver** un prêté pour un rendu.

role, rôle [rəʊl] 1 n (*Theat, fig*) rôle *m*; *see* **leading** *etc*. 2 comp ▸**role model** (*Psych*) modèle *m* à émuler ▸**role-play(ing)** (*Psych*) psychodrame *m*; (*Scol*) jeu *m* de rôle.

roll [rəʊl] 1 n a [*cloth, paper, netting, wire, hair etc*] rouleau *m*; [*banknotes*] liasse *f*; [*tobacco*] carotte *f*; [*butter*] coquille *f*; [*flesh, fat*] bourrelet *m*. (*Phot*) ~ **of film** (rouleau *m* de) pellicule *f*.

b (*also* **bread ~**) petit pain; *see* **sausage, Swiss** *etc*.

c (*movement*) [*ship*] roulis *m*; [*sea*] houle *f*; (*Aviat*) vol *m* en tonneau. **to walk with a ~** rouler les hanches, se dandiner *or* se balancer en marchant; **the ship gave a sudden ~** le bateau roula brusquement; **the horse was having a ~ on the grass** le cheval se roulait dans l'herbe; **to have a ~ in the hay with sb**⁑ batifoler* dans l'herbe avec qn; *see* **rock**[1].

d (*sound*) [*thunder, drums*] roulement *m*; [*organ*] ronflement *m*.

e (*list, register*) liste *f*, tableau *m*; (*for court, ship's crew etc*) rôle *m*. (*Scol*) **class ~** liste *f* (nominative) des élèves; **we have 60 pupils on our ~(s)** nous avons 60 élèves inscrits; (*Scol*) **falling ~s** diminutions *fpl* d'effectifs; **to call the ~** faire l'appel; **~ of honour** (*Mil*) liste des combattants morts pour la patrie *or* tombés au champ d'honneur; (*Scol*) tableau d'honneur; (*Jur*) **to strike sb** *or* **sb's name off the ~s** radier qn des listes *or* du tableau; *see* **electoral**.

f (*US *: prospering*) **the company is on a ~** l'entreprise prospère *or* a le vent en poupe.

2 comp ▸**rollaway bed** (*US*) lit *m* pliant (sur roulettes) ▸**rollback** (*US*) (*gen*) réduction *f*; (*Econ*) baisse *f* forcée des prix (sur ordre du gouvernement) ▸**roll bar** (*Aut*) arceau *m* de sécurité ▸**roll call** (*gen, Mil, Scol*) appel *m* ▸**roll-collar** (*Brit*) = **roll-neck** ▸**roll film** pellicule *f* (en rouleau) ▸**rollmop** (*Brit*) *see* **rollmop** ▸**roll-neck** (*Brit*) [*sweater*] col *m* roulé; **roll-neck(ed)** à col roulé ▸**roll-on** *see* **roll-on** ▸**rollover** (*Fin: of loan*) refinancement *m*; (*Fin*) **rollover project** projet-relais *m* ▸**roll-top desk** bureau *m* à cylindre.

3 vi a (*turn over*) rouler. **to ~ over and over** [*object*] rouler sur soi-même; [*person*] se rouler; **the coin ~ed under the table** la pièce a roulé sous la table; **stones ~ed down the hill** des pierres ont roulé *or* déboulé jusqu'au pied de la colline; **the car ~ed down the hill** (*brakes off*) la voiture a descendu la pente toute seule; (*over and over*) la voiture a dévalé la pente en faisant une série de tonneaux; **the lorries ~ed through the streets** les camions roulaient le long des rues; **his car ~ed to a stop** sa voiture s'arrêta doucement; **to ~ headlong down a slope** dégringoler une pente, rouler du haut en bas d'une pente; **the children were ~ing down the slope** les enfants roulaient le long de la pente; **tears were ~ing down her cheeks** les larmes roulaient sur ses joues; **the waves were ~ing on to the beach** les vagues déferlaient sur la plage; **the newspapers were ~ing off the presses** les journaux tombaient des rotatives; **the wheels kept ~ing** les roues continuaient à tourner; (*fig*) **heads will ~** il y aura des limogeages*, des têtes tomberont; (*Aut*) **we were ~ing along at 100 km/h** nous roulions à 100 (km) à l'heure; **the horse ~ed in the mud** le cheval s'est roulé *or* vautré dans la boue; (*fig*) **he's ~ing in money*** *or* **in it*** il roule sur l'or; (*fig*) **they were ~ing in the aisles*** ils se tordaient, ils se tenaient les côtes*; **she is trainer and manager ~ed into one** elle est entraîneur et manager tout à la fois *or* en même temps.

b [*ship*] rouler. **he ~ed from side to side as he walked** il se balançait en marchant; **his eyes were ~ing** ses yeux roulaient, il roulait les yeux.

c [*thunder*] gronder, rouler; [*drums, words*] rouler; [*voice*] retentir; [*organ*] rendre un son grave et prolongé; [*noises*] se répercuter.

d (*function, operate*) [*machines*] marcher, fonctionner; [*film cameras*] tourner. **cameras ~!** on tourne!; (*Theat*) **to keep the show ~ing*** s'arranger pour que le spectacle continue (*subj*); (*fig*) **you must**

keep the ball *or* **things ~ing while I'm away*** arrangez-vous pour que ça tourne (*subj*) rond *or* pour que tout marche (*subj*) pendant mon absence.

4 **vt** a *barrel, hoop, ball* (faire) rouler; *umbrella, cigarette* rouler; *pastry, dough* étendre *or* abaisser au rouleau; *metal* laminer; *lawn* rouler; *road* cylindrer. **to ~ one's eyes** rouler les yeux; **to ~ one's r's** rouler les r; **to ~ sth between one's fingers** rouler qch avec *or* entre ses doigts; **to ~ string into a ball** enrouler de la ficelle en pelote; **the hedgehog ~ed itself up into a ball** le hérisson s'est roulé en boule; **he ~ed himself in a blanket** il s'est roulé *or* enroulé dans une couverture; **they ~ed the car to the side of the road** ils ont poussé la voiture sur le bas-côté; *see also* **rolled**.

b (*US* ‡: *rob*) dévaliser.

▸**roll about** **vi** *[coins, marbles]* rouler çà et là; *[ship]* rouler; *[person, dog]* se rouler par terre.

▸**roll along** 1 **vi** a *[ball, vehicle]* rouler. b (*: *arrive*) s'amener‡, se pointer‡. 2 **vt sep** *ball* faire rouler; *car* pousser.

▸**roll around** **vi** = **roll about**.

▸**roll away** 1 **vi** *[clouds, mist, vehicle]* s'éloigner; *[ball]* rouler au loin. **the ball rolled away from me** le ballon a roulé loin de moi. 2 **vt sep** *trolley, table* éloigner, emmener.

▸**roll back** 1 **vi** *[object]* rouler en arrière; *[eyes]* chavirer. 2 **vt sep** a *object* rouler en arrière; *carpet* rouler; *sheet* enlever (en roulant). b (*fig: bring back*) ramener. **if only we could roll back the years** si seulement nous pouvions ramener le temps passé. c (*US fig: reduce*) réduire. 3 **rollback*** **n** *see* **roll 2**.

▸**roll by** **vi** *[vehicle, procession]* passer; *[clouds]* être chassé; *[time, years]* s'écouler, passer.

▸**roll down** 1 **vi** *[ball, person]* rouler de haut en bas; *[tears]* couler. 2 **vt sep** a *cart* descendre (en roulant). b (*wind down*) *car window* descendre, baisser. c *socks, sleeves* baisser; *stockings* rouler.

▸**roll in** 1 **vi** *[waves]* déferler; (*) *[letters, contributions, suggestions]* affluer; (*) *[person]* s'amener‡, se pointer‡, entrer (avec désinvolture). **he rolled in* half an hour late** il s'est amené‡ avec une demi-heure de retard; **the money keeps rolling in*** l'argent continue à affluer. 2 **vt sep** *barrel, trolley* faire entrer (en roulant).

▸**roll off** **vi** a *[vehicle, procession]* s'ébranler, se mettre en marche. b (*fall off*) dégringoler.

▸**roll on** 1 **vi** *[vehicle etc]* continuer de rouler; *[time]* s'écouler. **roll on the holidays!*** vivement les vacances!; **roll on Tuesday!*** vivement qu'on soit mardi! 2 **vt sep** *stockings* enfiler. 3 **roll-on** **n** *see* **roll-on 1**. 4 **roll-on-roll-off** **n, adj** *see* **roll-on 3**.

▸**roll out** **vt sep** a *barrel, trolley* rouler *or* pousser dehors. b *sentence, verse* débiter. c *pastry* étendre *or* abaisser au rouleau; *metal* laminer.

▸**roll over** 1 **vi** *[person, animal]* (*once*) se retourner (sur soi-même); (*several times: also* **roll over and over**) se rouler. 2 **vt sep** *person, animal, object* retourner.

▸**roll past** **vi** = **roll by**.

▸**roll up** 1 **vi** a *[animal]* se rouler (*into* en). b (*: *arrive*) arriver, s'amener‡. *[fairground]* **roll up and see the show!** approchez, venez voir le spectacle! 2 **vt sep** *cloth, paper, map* rouler. **to roll up one's sleeves** retrousser ses manches; *see also* **roll 4**.

rolled [rəʊld] **adj** a (*in a roll: also* **~ up**) *blanket etc* roulé, enroulé, en rouleau. b **~ tobacco** tabac *m* en carotte; **~ gold** plaqué *m* or; **~-gold bracelet** bracelet *m* plaqué or; **~ oats** flocons *mpl* d'avoine. c (*Phon*) roulé.

roller ['rəʊləʳ] 1 **n** a (*for pressing, smoothing*) rouleau *m*; *[pastry]* rouleau à pâtisserie; *[roads]* rouleau compresseur; *[lawn]* rouleau de jardin; *[metal]* laminoir *m*, cylindre *m* lamineur; (*Papermaking, Tex*) calandre *f*.

b (*for painting and decorating*) rouleau *m* (à peinture); (*for inking*) rouleau (encreur).

c (*for winding sth round*) rouleau *m*; *[blind]* enrouleur *m*; *[hair]* rouleau (à mise en plis). **to put one's hair in ~s** se mettre des rouleaux.

d (*for moving things*) rouleau *m*; (*wheel*) roulette *f*, galet *m*. **table on ~s** table *f* à roulettes.

e (*part of harness*) surfaix *m*.

f (*wave*) lame *f* de houle.

2 **comp** ▸**rollerball** stylo *m* à bille ▸**roller bandage** bande roulée ▸**roller blind** store *m* ▸**roller coaster** montagnes *fpl* russes ▸**roller skate** patin *m* à roulettes ▸**roller-skate** faire du patin à roulettes ▸**roller-skating** patinage *m* à roulettes ▸**roller towel** essuie-main(s) *m* à *or* en rouleau.

rollerdrome ['rəʊləˌdrəʊm] **n** (*US*) piste *f* de patin à roulettes.

rollick ['rɒlɪk] **vi** (*also* **~ about**) s'amuser bruyamment.

rollicking ['rɒlɪkɪŋ] 1 **adj** *person* d'une gaieté exubérante, joyeux; *play, farce* bouffon; *occasion* (bruyant et) joyeux. **to lead a ~ life** mener joyeuse vie *or* une vie de patachon*; **to have a ~ time** s'amuser follement *or* comme des fous; **it was a ~ party** nous nous sommes amusés comme des petits fous à la soirée. 2 **n** (*: *telling off*) savon* *m*. **to give sb a (real) ~** passer un (sacré *or* bon) savon à qn*; **to get a (real) ~** recevoir un (sacré *or* bon) savon*.

rolling ['rəʊlɪŋ] 1 **adj** *ship* qui roule; *sea* houleux; *countryside, ground* onduleux, à ondulations. (*Prov*) **a ~ stone gathers no moss** pierre qui roule n'amasse pas mousse (*Prov*); (*fig*) **he's a ~ stone** il a l'âme d'un nomade; **to have a ~ gait** *or* **walk** rouler *or* balancer les hanches, se déhancher; **~ waves** grosses vagues, lames déferlantes. 2 **comp** ▸**rolling mill** (*factory*) laminerie *f*, usine *f* de laminage; (*machine*) laminoir *m* ▸**rolling pin** rouleau *m* (à pâtisserie) ▸**rolling plan** (*Fin*) plan *m* chenille *or* glissant ▸**rolling stock** (*Rail*) matériel roulant ▸**rolling targets** (*US Econ*) objectifs *mpl* économiques révisables.

rollmop ['rəʊlmɒp] **n** (*Brit*) (*also* **~ herring**) rollmops *m*.

roll-on ['rəʊlɒn] 1 **n** (*corset*) gaine *f*. 2 **adj** *deodorant etc* à bille. 3 **comp** ▸**roll-on-roll-off** (manutention *f* par) roulage *m*; **roll-on-roll-off port** port *m* de roulage; **roll-on-roll-off ship** roulier *m*.

roly-poly ['rəʊlɪ'pəʊlɪ] 1 **adj** (*) grassouillet, boulot (*f* -otte), rondelet. 2 **n** a (*Brit: also* **~ pudding**) roulé *m* à la confiture. b (*: *plump child*) poupard *m*.

ROM [rɒm] **n** (*Comput*) (**abbr of Read-Only-Memory**) mémoire *f* morte *or* fixe.

Romagna ['romaɲa] **n** Romagne *f*.

romaine [rəʊ'meɪn] **n** (*US: also* **~ lettuce**) (laitue *f*) romaine *f*.

Roman ['rəʊmən] 1 **n** a (*person*) Romain(e) *m(f)*. (*Bible*) **the Epistle/Letter to the ~s** l'épître/la lettre aux Romains. b (*Typ*) romain *m*. 2 **adj** (*Archit, Geog, Hist, Rel, Typ*) romain. **~ candle** chandelle romaine; **~ Catholic** (**adj, n**) catholique (*mf*); **the ~ Catholic Church** l'Église catholique (et romaine); **the ~ Empire** l'Empire romain; **the ~ Emperor** l'Empereur romain (*see also* **holy**); (*Typ*) **~ letters** caractères romains; **~ nose** nez aquilin; **~ numerals** chiffres romains; (*Rel*) **the ~ Rite** le rite romain.

romance [rəʊ'mæns] 1 **n** a (*tale of chivalry*) roman *m*; (*love story/film*) roman/film *m* à l'eau de rose; (*Mus*) romance *f*; (*love affair*) idylle *f*; (*love*) amour *m*; (*NonC: charm, attraction*) charme *m*. **it's quite a ~** c'est un vrai roman; (*fig: lies*) **it's pure ~** c'est de la pure invention, c'est du roman; **their ~ lasted six months** leur idylle a duré six mois; **he was her first ~** il était son premier amoureux *or* amour; **they had a beautiful ~** ils ont vécu un beau roman (d'amour); **the ~ of the sea/of foreign lands** la poésie de la mer/des pays étrangers. b (*Ling*) **R~** roman *m*. 2 **adj** (*Ling*) **R~** roman. 3 **vi** enjoliver (à plaisir), broder (*fig*).

romancer [rəʊ'mænsəʳ] **n** conteur *m*, -euse *f*. (*fig*) **he's a ~** il enjolive toujours tout.

Romanesque [ˌrəʊmə'nesk] **adj** *architecture* roman.

Romania [rəʊ'meɪnɪə] **n** Roumanie *f*.

Romanian [rəʊ'meɪnɪən] 1 **adj** roumain. 2 **n** a (*person*) Roumain(e) *m(f)*. b (*Ling*) roumain *m*.

Romanic [rəʊ'mænɪk] **adj** *language* roman.

romanize ['rəʊmənaɪz] **vt** (*Hist*) romaniser; (*Rel*) convertir au catholicisme.

Romans(c)h [rəʊ'mænʃ] **n** romanche *m*.

romantic [rəʊ'mæntɪk] 1 **adj** *appearance, landscape, building* romantique (*also Art, Hist, Literat, Mus*); *person, film, book* romantique, sentimental (*pej*); *adventure, setting* romanesque. (*Art, Literat, Mus*) **the R~ Movement** le Mouvement romantique, le romantisme; (*Cine, Theat*) **~ lead** jeune premier *m*. 2 **n** romantique *mf*, sentimental(e) *m(f)*; (*Art, Literat, Mus*) romantique.

romantically [rəʊ'mæntɪkəlɪ] **adv** *write, describe* d'une façon romanesque; *sing, woo* en romantique. **castle ~ situated in a wood** château situé dans le cadre romantique d'un bois; **their names have been ~ linked** on leur attribue des relations amoureuses.

romanticism [rəʊ'mæntɪsɪzəm] **n** (*Art, Literat, Mus*) romantisme *m*.

romanticist [rəʊ'mæntɪsɪst] **n** (*Art, Literat, Mus*) romantique *mf*.

romanticize [rəʊ'mæntɪsaɪz] **vti** romancer.

Romany ['rɒmənɪ] 1 **n** a bohémien(-ienne) *m(f)*. b (*Ling*) romani *m*. 2 **adj** de bohémien.

Rome [rəʊm] **n** Rome. (*Prov*) **when in ~ (do as the Romans do)** à Rome il faut vivre comme les Romains; (*Prov*) **~ wasn't built in a day** Paris *or* Rome ne s'est pas fait en un jour; (*Prov*) **all roads lead to ~** tous les chemins mènent à Rome; **the Church of ~** l'Église (catholique) romaine; (*Rel*) **to go over to ~** se convertir au catholicisme.

Romeo ['rəʊmɪəʊ] **n** Roméo *m* (*also fig*).

Romish ['rəʊmɪʃ] **adj** (*pej*) catholique.

romp [rɒmp] 1 **n** jeux bruyants, ébats *mpl*. **the play was just a ~** la pièce n'était (guère) qu'une farce. 2 **vi** *[children, puppies]* jouer bruyamment, s'ébattre. **the horse ~ed home** le cheval est arrivé dans un fauteuil*; (*fig*) **to ~ through an exam** passer un examen haut la main.

rompers ['rɒmpəz] **npl** barboteuse *f* (*pour enfant*).

Romulus ['rɒmjʊləs] **n**: **~ and Remus** Romulus *m* et Rémus *m*.

Roncesvalles ['rɒnsəvælz] **n** Roncevaux.

rondeau ['rɒndəʊ] **n, pl ~x** ['rɒndəʊz], **rondel** ['rɒndl] **n** (*Mus, Poetry*) rondeau *m*.

rondo ['rɒndəʊ] **n** (*Mus*) rondeau *m*.

Roneo ['rəʊnɪəʊ] **vt** ® polycopier, ronéotyper, ronéoter.

rood [ru:d] **n** a (*Rel Archit*) crucifix *m*. **~ screen** jubé *m*. b (*Brit: measure*) quart *m* d'arpent.

roof [ru:f] 1 **n** *[building, car]* toit *m* (*also Climbing*); *[cave, tunnel]* plafond *m*; (*fig: of sky, branches*) voûte *f*. (*Anat*) **the ~ of the mouth** la voûte du palais; **without a ~ over one's head** sans abri *or* toit; **a room in the ~** une chambre sous les combles *or* sous les toits; **I couldn't live under her ~** je ne pourrais pas vivre chez elle; **to live under the same ~ as sb** vivre sous le même toit avec *or* que qn; **under one ~** (*gen*) sous le même toit; (*in shopping arcade, hypermarket etc*) réuni(s) au même endroit; (*fig*) **to go through** *or* **to hit the ~*** *[person]* exploser, piquer une crise*; *[price, claim]* devenir excessif; *see* **flat¹, raise, sunshine** *etc*.

2 comp ▸**roof garden** jardin *m* sur le toit ▸**roof light** (*gen, Aut*) plafonnier *m* ▸**roof rack** (*Brit Aut*) galerie *f* ▸**rooftop** toit *m*; (*fig*) **to shout** *or* **proclaim sth from the rooftops** crier qch sur tous les toits (*fig*).

3 vt *house* couvrir (d'un toit). **red-~ed** à toit rouge.

▸**roof in** vt sep couvrir d'un toit.

▸**roof over** vt sep recouvrir d'un toit.

roofing [ˈruːfɪŋ] n a (*on house*) toiture *f*, couverture *f*. **~ felt** couverture bitumée *or* goudronnée. b (*act*) pose *f* de la toiture *or* de la couverture.

roofless [ˈruːflɪs] adj sans toit.

rook¹ [rʊk] 1 n (*Orn*) (corbeau *m*) freux *m*. 2 vt (*‡: swindle*) rouler*, empiler*, escroquer.

rook² [rʊk] n (*Chess*) tour *f*.

rookery [ˈrʊkərɪ] n colonie *f* de freux; *[seals, penguins]* colonie; (*fig pej: overcrowded slum*) taudis surpeuplé.

rookie‡ [ˈrʊkɪ] n (*esp Mil*) bleu* *m*.

room [rʊm] 1 n a (*in house*) pièce *f*; (*large*) salle *f*; (*bedroom*) chambre *f*; (*office, study*) bureau *m*; (*in hotel*) chambre. **~s to let** chambres à louer; **~ and board** pension *f*; **his ~s** son appartement *m*; **come to my ~s for coffee** venez prendre le café chez moi; **they live in ~s** ils habitent un meublé *or* un garni (*pej*); *see* **double, lecture, roof** *etc*.

b (*NonC: space*) place *f*. **is there ~?** y a-t-il de la place?; **there is ~ for 2 people** il y a de la place pour 2 personnes; **there's no ~** il n'y a pas de place; (*fig*) **there's no ~ to swing a cat*** il n'y a pas la place de se retourner; **to take up ~/too much ~** prendre de la place/trop de place; **to make ~ for sb** faire une place pour qn; **to make ~ for sth** faire de la place pour qch; (*fig*) **there is still ~ for hope** il y a encore lieu d'espérer; **there is little ~ for hope** il ne reste pas beaucoup d'espoir; **there is no ~ for doubt** il n'y a pas de doute possible; **there is ~ for improvement in your work** votre travail laisse à désirer.

2 vi partager une chambre (*with* avec). **to ~ with a landlady** louer une chambre meublée.

3 comp ▸**room clerk** (*US*) réceptionniste *mf*, réceptionnaire *mf* ▸**room divider** meuble *m* de séparation ▸**rooming house** (*US*) maison *f* *or* immeuble *m* de rapport; **he lives in a rooming house** il habite un meublé ▸**rooming-in** (*US: in maternity wards*) *politique de garde du nouveau-né dans la chambre de la mère* ▸**roommate** camarade *mf* de chambre; (*sharing lodgings*) colocataire *mf* ▸**room service** (*on bill etc*) service *m* des chambres (d'hôtel); **ring for room service** appelez le garçon d'étage ▸**room temperature** température ambiante; **wine at room temperature** vin chambré.

-roomed [rʊmd] adj *ending in comps*: **a 6-roomed house** une maison de 6 pièces; **a two-roomed flat** un deux-pièces.

roomer [ˈrʊməʳ] n (*US*) locataire *mf*.

roomette [ruːˈmet] n (*US Rail*) compartiment *m* individuel de wagons-lits.

roomful [ˈrʊmfʊl] n pleine salle.

roominess [ˈrʊmɪnɪs] n dimensions spacieuses.

roomy [ˈrʊmɪ] adj *flat, handbag* spacieux; *garment* ample.

roost [ruːst] 1 n perchoir *m*, juchoir *m*; *see* **rule**. 2 vi (*settle*) se percher, se jucher; (*sleep*) jucher. (*fig*) **all her little schemes are coming home to ~** toutes ses petites combines vont lui retomber dessus *or* se retourner contre elle.

rooster [ˈruːstəʳ] n coq *m*.

root [ruːt] 1 n a (*gen, Bot, Math etc*) racine *f*; (*fig*) *[trouble etc]* origine *f*, cause *f*. **to pull up** *or* **out by the ~s** déraciner, extirper; (*lit, fig*) **to take ~** prendre racine; (*fig*) **to pull up one's ~s** se déraciner; **her ~s are in France** elle est restée française de cœur *or* d'esprit; **she has no ~s** c'est une déracinée; **to put down ~s in a country** s'enraciner dans un pays; (*fig*) **~ and branch** entièrement, radicalement; **the ~ of the matter** la vraie raison; **to get to the ~s of the problem** trouver la cause *or* aller au fond du problème; **that is at the ~ of ...** cela est à l'origine de ...; **what lies at the ~ of his attitude?** quelle est la raison fondamentale de son attitude?; *see* **cube, grass, square**.

b (*Ling*) (*gen*) racine *f*; (*Morphology: of verb*) radical *m*; (*Morphology: of non-verb*) base *f*.

c *[tooth]* racine *f*; *[tongue]* base *f*.

d (*Mus*) fondamentale *f*.

2 comp ▸**root beer** (*US*) *sorte de limonade à base d'extraits végétaux* ▸**root canal** *[tooth]* canal *m* des racines ▸**root cause** cause première ▸**root crops** racines *fpl* alimentaires ▸**root ginger** (racine *f* de) gingembre *m* ▸**root sign** (*Math*) radical *m* ▸**roots music** (*Mus*) (*world music*) world music *f*; (*reggae*) reggae *m* (originel) ▸**rootstock** (*Bot*) rhizome *m* ▸**root vegetable** racine *f* (comestible) ▸**root word** (*Ling*) mot souche *inv*.

3 vt (*Bot*) enraciner. (*fig*) **a deeply ~ed belief** une croyance bien enracinée; (*fig*) **to be** *or* **stand ~ed to the spot** être cloué sur place.

4 vi a *[plants etc]* s'enraciner, prendre racine.

b *[pigs]* fouiller (avec le groin).

▸**root about** vi fouiller (*among* dans, *for sth* pour trouver qch).

▸**root among** vi fouiller dans.

▸**root around** vi = **root about**.

▸**root for** vt fus (*: esp US*) *team* encourager, applaudir.

▸**root out** vt sep (*fig*) (*find*) dénicher; (*remove*) extirper.

▸**root through** vi = **root among**.

▸**root up** vt sep *plant* déraciner; *[pigs]* déterrer; (*fig*) extirper.

rootless [ˈruːtlɪs] adj (*lit, fig*) sans racine(s).

rope [rəʊp] 1 n a (*gen*) corde *f*; (*Naut*) cordage *m*; *[bell]* cordon *m*. (*fig*) **to give sb more ~** lâcher la bride à qn; **give him enough ~ and he'll hang himself** si on le laisse faire il se passera lui-même la corde au cou *or* il creusera sa propre tombe; (*Boxing etc*) **the ~s** les cordes *fpl*; **on the ~s** (*Boxing*) dans les cordes; (** fig*) *person* sur le flanc*; *business* ne battant que d'une aile*; (*fig*) **to know the ~s*** être au courant, connaître son affaire *or* les ficelles*; **to show sb the ~s*** mettre qn au courant; **to learn the ~s*** se mettre au courant; **a ~ of pearls** un collier de perles; **a ~ of onions** un chapelet d'oignons; **a ~ of hair** une torsade de cheveux; *see* **clothes, skipping, tight** *etc*.

b (*Climbing*) corde *f*; (*people on ~*) cordée *f*. **a ~ of climbers** une cordée d'alpinistes; **to put on the ~** s'encorder; **there were 3 of them on the ~** ils formaient une cordée de 3.

2 comp ▸**rope burn** brûlure *f* (*provoquée par une corde*) ▸**ropedancer** funambule *mf*, danseur *m*, -euse *f* de corde ▸**rope ladder** échelle *f* de corde ▸**rope-length** (*Climbing*) longueur *f* de corde ▸**ropemaker** cordier *m* ▸**rope trick**: **Indian rope trick** tour *m* de la corde (*prestidigitation*) ▸**ropewalker** = **ropedancer** ▸**roping-off** (*Climbing*) rappel *m*.

3 vt a *box, case* corder. **to ~ sb to a tree** lier qn à un arbre; **to ~ climbers (together)** encorder des alpinistes; (*Climbing*) **~d party** cordée *f*.

b (*US: catch*) *cattle* prendre au lasso.

▸**rope in** vt sep *area* entourer de cordes, délimiter par une corde. (*fig*) **to rope sb in*** enrôler qn, embringuer qn*; **he got himself roped in to help at the fête** il s'est laissé embringuer* pour aider à la fête; **I don't want to get roped in* for anything** je ne veux pas me laisser embringuer*.

▸**rope off** vt sep (*section off*) réserver par une corde; (*block off*) interdire l'accès de.

▸**rope up** (*Climbing*) 1 vi s'encorder. 2 vt sep encorder. **to be roped up** être encordé.

rop(e)y [ˈrəʊpɪ] adj a *liquid* visqueux. b (** fig: bad*) pas fameux, pas brillant, mal en point. **to feel a bit ~** être *or* se sentir mal en point.

RORO (abbr of **roll-on-roll-off**) *see* **roll-on**.

rosary [ˈrəʊzərɪ] n a (*Rel*) chapelet *m*; (*fifteen decades*) rosaire *m*. b (*in garden*) roseraie *f*.

rose¹ [rəʊz] pret of **rise**.

rose² [rəʊz] 1 n a (*flower*) rose *f*; (*also* **~bush, ~ tree**) rosier *m*. **wild ~** églantine *f*; (*fig*) **life isn't all ~s** le vie n'est pas une partie de plaisir; (*fig*) **it isn't all ~s** ce n'est pas tout rose; (*Prov*) **there is no ~ without a thorn** il n'y a pas de roses sans épines; (*fig*) **she's an English ~** elle est belle comme une fleur *or* fraîche comme une rose; (*fig*) **that will put ~s back in your cheeks** cela va te rendre tes belles couleurs; (*fig liter*) **under the ~** en confidence, sous le manteau; (*Brit Hist*) **the Wars of the R~s** la guerre des Deux-Roses; (*fig*) **to come up ~s‡** marcher comme sur des roulettes*; *see* **bed, Christmas, rock²**.

b *[hose, watering can]* pomme *f*; (*on hat, shoe*) rosette *f*; *[pump]* crépine *f*; (*on ceiling*) rosace *f* (de plafond); *see* **compass**.

c (*colour*) rose *m*.

2 adj rose.

3 comp *leaf, petal* de rose ▸**rosebay** laurier-rose *m* ▸**rosebed** massif *m* de rosiers ▸**rosebowl** coupe *f* à fleurs ▸**rosebud** bouton *m* de rose; **rosebud mouth** bouche *f* en cerise ▸**rose-coloured** rose, couleur de rose *inv*; (*fig*) **to see everything/life through rose-coloured spectacles** voir tout/la vie en rose ▸**rose diamond** rose *f* (*diamant*) ▸**rose garden** roseraie *f* ▸**rose grower** rosiériste *mf* ▸**rosehip** gratte-cul *m*; **rosehip syrup** sirop *m* d'églantine ▸**roselike** rosacé ▸**rosemary** *see* **rosemary** ▸**rose pink** rose, rosé ▸**rose-red** vermeil ▸**rose-tinted** = **rose-coloured** ▸**rose water** eau *f* de rose (*lit*) ▸**rose window** rosace *f*, rose *f* ▸**rosewood** n palissandre *m*, bois *m* de rose ◊ adj en bois de rose.

rosé [ˈrəʊzeɪ] n rosé *m* (*vin*).

roseate [ˈrəʊzɪɪt] adj rose.

rosemary [ˈrəʊzmərɪ] n romarin *m*.

roseola [rəʊˈzɪələ] n roséole *f*.

rosette [rəʊˈzet] n (*ribbons etc*) rosette *f*; (*Sport: as prize*) cocarde *f*; (*Archit*) rosace *f*.

Rosicrucian [ˌrəʊzɪˈkruːʃən] adj, n rosicrucien(ne) *m(f)*.

rosin [ˈrɒzɪn] n colophane *f*.

ROSPA [ˈrɒspə] n (abbr of **Royal Society for the Prevention of Accidents**)

société pour la prévention des accidents.
roster ['rɒstəʳ] n liste f, tableau m (de service); see duty.
rostrum ['rɒstrəm] n, pl ~s or rostra ['rɒstrə] tribune f; (Roman Hist) rostres mpl.
rosy ['rəʊzɪ] adj rose, rosé. ~ cheeks joues fpl roses or vermeilles (liter); to have a ~ complexion avoir les joues roses; (fig) his future looks ~ il semble avoir un brillant avenir devant lui; the situation looks ~ la situation se présente bien; to paint a ~ picture of sth dépeindre or peindre qch en rose.
rot [rɒt] 1 n (NonC) a pourriture f; (Bot, Med) carie f. (fig) he worked well at the beginning then the ~ set in* au début il travaillait bien mais par la suite il a flanché* or les problèmes ont commencé; (fig) to stop the ~ redresser la situation; see dry.
b (*: nonsense) bêtises fpl, balivernes fpl, idioties fpl. to talk ~ dire des bêtises, débiter des blagues* or des foutaises ‡; that's utter ~, that's a lot of ~ ça, c'est de la blague* or de la foutaise‡; (what) ~ quelle idiotie or blague*, c'est de la blague* or de la foutaise‡.
2 comp ▸rotgut* (pej) tord-boyaux ‡ m ▸rotproof imputrescible.
3 vi pourrir, se décomposer, se putréfier; (fig) [person] dépérir, pourrir, croupir. to ~ in jail pourrir or croupir en prison; let him ~!* qu'il aille se faire pendre!*.
4 vt (faire) pourrir.
▸**rot away** vi tomber en pourriture.
rota ['rəʊtə] n a liste f, tableau m (de service). b (Rel) R~ rote f.
Rotarian [rəʊ'tɛərɪən] adj, n rotarien (m).
rotary ['rəʊtərɪ] adj a rotatif, rotatoire. ~ cultivator motoculteur m; ~ engine moteur m rotatif; ~ (printing) press rotative f; ~ printer rotativiste m; (Phot) ~ shutter obturateur m à secteur. b R~ (Club) Rotary Club m.
rotate [rəʊ'teɪt] 1 vt (revolve) faire tourner; (on pivot) faire pivoter; (change round) crops alterner; [two people] work, jobs faire à tour de rôle. 2 vi tourner; (on pivot) pivoter; [crops] être alterné.
rotating [rəʊ'teɪtɪŋ] adj (see rotate) tournant; rotatif; pivotant; alternant.
rotation [rəʊ'teɪʃən] n (turning) rotation f; (turn) rotation, tour m. in or by ~ à tour de rôle; ~ of crops assolement m, rotation f (des cultures).
rotatory [rəʊ'teɪtərɪ] adj rotatoire.
rote [rəʊt] n: by ~ learn machinalement, sans essayer de comprendre; recite comme un perroquet; ~ learning apprentissage m par cœur.
rotisserie [rəʊ'tɪsərɪ] n (grill or oven) rôtissoire f; (fitment) tournebroche m; (restaurant) rôtisserie f.
rotogravure [ˌrəʊtəʊgrə'vjʊəʳ] n rotogravure f.
rotor ['rəʊtəʳ] 1 n (Aviat, Elec) rotor m. 2 comp ▸rotor arm (Aut) toucheau m ▸rotor blade pale f de rotor ▸rotorcraft giravion m, hélicoptère m.
rototill ['rəʊtəʊtɪl] vt (US) labourer avec un motoculteur.
Rototiller ['rəʊtəʊtɪləʳ] n ® (US) motoculteur m.
rotovate ['rəʊtəveɪt] vt labourer avec un motoculteur.
Rotovator ['rəʊtəveɪtəʳ] n ® (Brit) motoculteur m.
rotten ['rɒtn] adj a wood, vegetation, egg pourri; tooth carié, gâté; fruit gâté, pourri; (fig: corrupt) véreux, corrompu. (lit, fig) ~ to the core complètement pourri. b (*: bad) mauvais, moche*. it's ~ weather! quel temps de chien!; to feel ~* se sentir patraque* or mal fichu*; it's a ~ business c'est une sale affaire; what ~ luck! quelle guigne!*, quelle poisse!*; what a ~ trick! quel sale tour!*
rottenness ['rɒtnnɪs] n (état m de) pourriture f.
rotter*† ['rɒtəʳ] n (Brit) sale type* m, vache‡ f.
rotting ['rɒtɪŋ] adj en pourriture, qui pourrit.
Rottweiler ['rɒtˌvaɪləʳ] n Rottweiler m.
rotund [rəʊ'tʌnd] adj person replet (f -ète), rondelet; object rond, arrondi; (fig) speech, literary style emphatique, ampoulé, ronflant; voice sonore.
rotunda [rəʊ'tʌndə] n rotonde f.
rotundity [rəʊ'tʌndɪtɪ] n [person] embonpoint m, corpulence f; (fig) [style] grandiloquence f; [voice] sonorité f.
rouble, (US) **ruble** ['ru:bl] n rouble m.
roué ['ru:eɪ] n roué m, débauché m.
rouge [ru:ʒ] 1 n rouge m (à joues). 2 vt: to ~ one's cheeks se farder les joues, se mettre du rouge (à joues).
rough [rʌf] 1 adj a (uneven) ground accidenté, inégal; skin, cloth rêche, rugueux; surface rugueux; path, road raboteux, rocailleux. ~ to the touch rude or rêche or rugueux au toucher; ~ hands [peasant] mains rugueuses; [housewife] mains rêches.
b (fig) sound rude, âpre; taste âpre, âcre; voice rauque, rude; (coarse, unrefined) person, manners rude, fruste; speech rude; (harsh etc) person brutal, violent; neighbourhood mauvais; life dur, rude; tongue mauvais; tone, voice brusque. ~ handling of sth manque m de soin envers qch; a ~ sea, ~ seas mer agitée or houleuse, grosse mer; the waves were very ~ il y avait de très grosses vagues; a ~ crossing une mauvaise traversée; ~ weather gros temps, mauvais temps; (Sport etc) ~ play jeu brutal; it's a ~ game c'est un jeu brutal; ~ stuff* brutalité f (gratuite); there was a bit of ~ stuff* at the pub last night il y a eu de la bagarre or ça a bardé* hier soir au café; these boys are very ~ ces garçons sont des brutes or de petites brutes or sont très durs; a ~ customer* un dur*; to have a ~ time (of it) en voir de rudes or de dures*; to be ~ with sb, to give sb a ~ time (of it) malmener qn; (fig) être dur avec qn, en faire voir de toutes les couleurs à qn*; (fig) to make things ~ for sb* mener la vie dure à qn; (fig) they gave him a ~ ride ils lui en ont fait baver*; it is ~ on him* (in this instance) il n'a pas de veine*, c'est un coup dur* pour lui; (generally) ce n'est pas marrant‡ pour lui; (fig: ill) to feel ~* ne pas se sentir bien, être mal fichu*.
c (approximate, unfinished) plan non travaillé, ébauché; calculation, translation approximatif. ~ copy, ~ draft, (NonC) ~ work brouillon m; ~ sketch croquis m, ébauche f; ~ paper papier m de brouillon; ~ justice justice f sommaire; ~ estimate, ~ guess approximation f; at a ~ estimate or guess à vue d'œil, approximativement; in its ~ state à l'état brut; ~ diamond diamant brut; (fig) he's a ~ diamond sous ses dehors frustes c'est un brave garçon; (fig) the proposal still has ~ edges le projet est encore à l'état brut; he'll be a good salesman once we knock off the ~ edges il fera un bon vendeur lorsque nous l'aurons un peu dégrossi.
2 adv live à la dure; play brutalement. to sleep ~ coucher dehors or à la dure; (fig) to cut up ~* (angry) se mettre en rogne* or en boule*; (violent) devenir violent.
3 n a (ground) terrain accidenté or rocailleux; (Golf) rough m. (fig) to take the ~ with the smooth prendre les choses comme elles viennent.
b (draft) brouillon m, premier jet m. (unfinished) in (the) ~ brut, à l'état brut or d'ébauche.
c (*: person) voyou m.
4 comp ▸rough-and-ready method fruste, rudimentaire; work grossier, fait à la hâte; installation, equipment rudimentaire, de fortune; person sans façons ▸rough-and-tumble adj désordonné, confus ◊ n mêlée f, bagarre f; after the rough-and-tumble of his life in the navy après sa vie mouvementée de marin ▸roughcast adj, n crépi (m) ◊ vt crépir ▸rough-dry vt sécher sans repasser ▸rough-hewn dégrossi, ébauché ▸roughhouse* bagarre f ▸roughneck* voyou m, dur m à cuire* ▸rough puff pastry pâte f feuilletée (simplifiée) ▸roughrider dresseur m or dompteur m de chevaux ▸roughshod see ride 2b ▸rough-spoken au langage grossier ▸rough trade‡ partenaire m homo* des basses classes.
5 vt: to ~ it* vivre à la dure.
▸**rough out** vt sep plan, drawing ébaucher.
▸**rough up** vt sep hair ébouriffer. (fig) to rough sb up* malmener qn, (stronger) tabasser‡ qn.
roughage ['rʌfɪdʒ] n (NonC) aliments mpl de lest or de volume.
roughen ['rʌfn] 1 vt rendre rude or rugueux or rêche. 2 vi devenir rude or rugueux.
roughly ['rʌflɪ] adv a (not gently) push rudement, brutalement; play brutalement; answer, order avec brusquerie. to treat sth/sb ~ malmener qch/qn. b (not finely) make, sew grossièrement. the table is very ~ made la table est très grossière; to sketch sth ~ faire un croquis de qch. c (approximately) approximativement, en gros, à peu près. ~ speaking en gros, approximativement; it costs ~ 100 francs cela coûte environ 100 F; tell me ~ what it's all about dites-moi grosso modo or en gros de quoi il s'agit; she is ~ 40 elle a dans les or à peu près 40 ans.
roughness ['rʌfnɪs] n (see rough) inégalité f, rugosité f, rudesse f, âpreté f, violence f, brutalité f, grossièreté f, brusquerie f, dureté f, état brut; [road] inégalités fpl, mauvais état; [sea] agitation f.
roulette [ru:'let] n roulette f (jeu, cuvette); see Russian 1.
Roumania [ru:'meɪnɪə] = Romania.
Roumanian [ru:'meɪnɪən] = Romanian.
round [raʊnd] (phr vb elem) 1 adv a (around) autour. there was a wall right ~ or all ~ il y avait un mur tout autour; he went ~ by the bridge il a fait le détour or il est passé par le pont; you can't get through here, you'll have to go ~ vous ne pouvez pas passer par ici, il faut faire le tour; the long way ~ le chemin le plus long; it's a long way ~ ça fait un grand détour or un grand crochet; ~ and ~ en rond; (looking for sth) to go (or drive or ride) ~ and ~ tourner en rond; the idea was going ~ and ~ in his head il tournait et retournait l'idée dans sa tête; she ran ~ to her mother's elle a couru chez sa mère; come ~ and see me venez me voir; I asked him ~ for a drink je l'ai invité à (passer) prendre un verre chez moi; I'll be ~ at 8 o'clock je serai là à 8 heures; spring will soon be ~ again le printemps reviendra bientôt; all (the) year ~ pendant toute l'année, d'un bout à l'autre de l'année; drinks all ~!* je paie une tournée!*; (fig) taking things all ~, taken all ~ tout compte fait; see gather round, look round etc.
b ~ about see 2b.
2 prep a (of place etc) autour de. sitting ~ the table assis autour de la table; sitting ~ the fire assis au coin du feu or auprès du feu; all ~ the house tout autour de la maison; the villages ~ Lewes les villages des environs or des alentours de Lewes; she knows everybody ~ about elle connaît tout le monde dans le coin; the house is just ~ the corner la maison est au coin de la rue or juste après le coin de la rue; (fig) la maison est tout près; come and see me if you're ~ this way viens me

voir si tu passes par ici *or* si tu es dans le coin*; **to go ~ a corner** tourner un coin; (*Aut*) prendre un virage; **to go ~ an obstacle** contourner un obstacle; **to look ~ a house** visiter une maison; **to show sb ~ a town** faire visiter une ville à qn; **they went ~ the castle** ils ont visité le château; **they went ~ the cafés looking for** ... ils ont fait le tour des cafés à la recherche de ...; **she's 75 cm ~ the waist** elle fait 75 cm de tour de taille; **put a blanket ~ him** enveloppez-le d'une couverture; *see* **clock, world** *etc*.

b (*approximately: also* ~ **about**) autour de, environ. ~ **(about) 7 o'clock** autour de *or* à environ 7 heures, vers (les) 7 heures; ~ **(about) £800** 800 livres environ, dans les 800 livres, autour de 800 livres.

3 **adj** (*circular*) rond, circulaire; (*rounded*) rond, arrondi. **to have ~ shoulders** avoir le dos rond *or* voûté; (*Ling*) ~ **vowel** voyelle arrondie; **in rich ~ tones** d'une voix riche et sonore; (*Archit*) ~ **arch** (arc *m* en) plein cintre, arc roman; ~ **handwriting** écriture ronde; (*fig*) **a ~ dozen** une douzaine tout rond; ~ **figure**, ~ **number** chiffre rond; **in ~ figures that will cost 20 million** cela coûtera 20 millions en chiffres ronds *or* pour donner un chiffre rond; **at a ~ pace** à vive allure; **a (good) ~ sum** une somme rondelette *or* coquette*; **he told me in ~ terms why** ... il m'a expliqué tout net pourquoi ...; **the cost of the ~ journey** *or* **the ~ trip** le prix du voyage aller et retour; **Concorde does 3 ~ trips a week** Concorde effectue 3 rotations *fpl* par semaine; *see also* **5**.

4 **n** a (*circle etc*) rond *m*, cercle *m*; (*slice: of bread, meat*) tranche *f*. **a ~ of toast** un toast, une tranche de pain grillé.

b (*esp Brit: delivery* ~) tournée *f*. **to do** *or* **make one's ~(s)** *[watchman, policeman]* faire sa ronde *or* sa tournée; *[postman, milkman]* faire sa tournée; *[doctor]* faire ses visites; **to do** *or* **make the ~s of** faire le tour de; **he has got a paper ~** il distribue des journaux; **to go** *or* **do the ~s** *[infection, a cold etc]* faire des ravages; *[news, joke etc]* courir, circuler; **the story is going the ~s that** ... le bruit court que ..., on raconte *or* on dit que ...; **the story went the ~s of the club** l'histoire a fait le tour du club; **this coat has gone the ~s of the family*** ce manteau a fait le tour de la famille; (*fig*) **the daily ~** la routine quotidienne, le train-train quotidien; **one long ~ of pleasures** une longue suite de plaisirs.

c *[cards, golf]* partie *f*; (*Boxing*) round *m*, reprise *f*; (*Equitation*) tour *m* de piste, parcours *m*; *[competition, tournament]* partie, manche *f*; *[election]* manche; *[talks, discussions]* série *f*. (*Equitation*) **to have a clear ~** faire un tour de piste *or* un parcours sans fautes; **a new ~ of negotiations** une nouvelle série de négociations; **to pay for a ~ (of drinks)** payer une tournée*; **it's my ~** c'est ma tournée*; (*Mil*) ~ **of ammunition** cartouche *f*; **a ~ of 5 shots** une salve de 5 coups; **a ~ of applause** une salve d'applaudissements; (*Theat*) **let's have a ~ of applause for Lucy!** applaudissons Lucy!, un ban* pour Lucy!

d (*Mus*) canon *m*; (*Dancing*) ronde *f*.

e **in the ~** (*Sculp*) en ronde-bosse; (*Theat*) en rond; (*fig*) en détail.

5 **comp** ►**roundabout** *see* **roundabout** ►**round-cheeked** aux joues rondes, joufflu ►**round dance** ronde *f* ►**round-eyed** (avec) des yeux ronds, aux yeux ronds ►**round-faced** au visage rond ►**round-game** *jeu pour un nombre indéterminé de joueurs* ►**Roundhead** (*Brit Hist*) Tête ronde ►**roundhouse** (*US Rail*) rotonde *f* ►**round-necked pull-over** pullover *m* ras du cou ►**round robin** (*petition*) pétition *f* (*où les signatures sont disposées en rond*); (*esp US Sport*) *tournoi où tous les joueurs se rencontrent* ►**round-shouldered** voûté ►**roundsman** *see* **roundsman** ►**Round Table** (*Myth*) Table ronde; (*fig*) **round-table discussion** table ronde ►**round-the-clock adj** 24 heures sur 24; *see also* **clock** ►**round trip** (*US*) aller *m* et retour; **round trip ticket** billet *m* aller-retour ►**roundup** *[cattle, people]* rassemblement *m*; *[criminals, suspects]* rafle *f*; (*meeting*) séance *f* de compte rendu; (*news summary*) résumé *m* ►**roundworm** ascaride *m*.

6 **vt** a (*make round*) arrondir.

b (*Comput, Math*) *figure* arrondir. **~ing error** erreur *f* d'arrondi.

c (*go round*) *corner* tourner; *bend* prendre; (*Naut*) *cape* doubler; *obstacle* contourner.

►**round down vt sep** *prices etc* arrondir (au chiffre inférieur).

►**round off vt sep** *speech, list, series* terminer; *sentence* parachever; *debate, meeting* mettre fin à, clore; *meal* terminer, finir (*with* par). **and now, to round off, I must say** ... et maintenant, pour conclure *or* en dernier lieu, je dois dire ... .

►**round up** 1 **vt sep** a (*bring together*) *people* rassembler, réunir; *cattle* rassembler; *criminals* effectuer une rafle de, ramasser*. b *prices etc* arrondir (au chiffre supérieur). 2 **roundup n** *see* **round 5**.

►**round (up)on vt fus** (*in words*) s'en prendre à; (*in actions*) sauter sur, attaquer.

roundabout ['raʊndəbaʊt] 1 **adj** *route* détourné, indirect. **we came (by) a ~ way** nous avons fait un détour; **by ~ means** par des moyens détournés; ~ **phrase** circonlocution *f*; **what a ~ way of doing things!** quelle façon contournée *or* compliquée de faire les choses! 2 **n** (*Brit*) (*merry-go-round*) manège *m* (*dans une fête foraine*); (*at road junction*) rond-point *m* (à sens giratoire); (*on traffic sign*) sens *m* giratoire; *see* **swing**.

rounded ['raʊndɪd] **adj** *object, face* arrondi; *cheeks* rebondi, plein; (*Phon*) *vowel* arrondi; (*fig*) *sentences, style* harmonieux, élégant.

roundelay ['raʊndɪleɪ] **n** (*Mus* ††) rondeau *m*.

rounder ['raʊndəʳ] **n** (*US*) fêtard* *m*, noceur* *m*.

rounders ['raʊndəz] **n** (*Brit*) *sorte f de baseball*.

roundly ['raʊndlɪ] **adv** (*fig*) tout net, franchement, carrément, rondement.

roundness ['raʊndnɪs] **n** rondeur *f*.

roundsman ['raʊndzmən] **n, pl roundsmen** ['raʊndzmən] (*Brit*) livreur *m*. **milk ~** laitier *m*.

rouse [raʊz] 1 **vt** (*awaken*) réveiller, éveiller; (*stimulate*) activer, éveiller; *feeling* exciter, stimuler; *admiration, interest* susciter; *indignation* provoquer, soulever; *suspicions* éveiller. ~ **yourself!** secouez-vous!*; **to ~ the masses** soulever les masses; **to ~ sb to action** inciter *or* pousser qn à agir; **to ~ sb (to anger)** mettre qn en colère; **he's a terrible man when he's ~d** il est terrible quand il est en colère. 2 **vi** (*waken*) se réveiller; (*become active*) sortir de sa torpeur.

rousing ['raʊzɪŋ] **adj** *speech, sermon* vibrant, véhément; *cheers, applause* frénétique, enthousiaste; *music* entraînant.

roustabout ['raʊstəbaʊt] **n** (*US*) débardeur *m*; (*Austral*) manœuvre *m*, homme *m* à tout faire.

rout[1] [raʊt] 1 **n** a (*Mil: defeat*) déroute *f*, débâcle *f*. **to put to ~** mettre en déroute. b (††: *revels*) raout†† *m*, fête mondaine. c (*Jur: mob*) attroupement illégal. 2 **vt** (*defeat*) mettre en déroute.

rout[2] [raʊt] **vi** (*search: also ~ about*) fouiller.

►**rout out vt** (*find*) dénicher; (*force out*) déloger. **to rout sb out of bed** tirer qn de son lit.

route [ruːt] 1 **n** a (*gen, also of train, plane, ship etc*) itinéraire *m*; (*Climbing*) itinéraire, voie *f*. **shipping/air ~s** routes maritimes/aériennes; (*Aut*) **all ~s** toutes directions; **what ~ does the 39 bus take?** par où passe le 39?, quel est le trajet *or* le parcours *or* l'itinéraire du 39?; **we're on a bus ~** nous sommes sur une ligne d'autobus; **the ~ to the coast goes through** ... pour aller à la côte on passe par ...; **I know a good ~ to London** je connais un bon itinéraire pour aller à Londres; **en ~** en route (*for* pour); *see* **sea, trade**.

b (*often* [raʊt]: *Mil*) ordres *mpl* de marche, route *f* à suivre.

c (*US: often* [raʊt]: *delivery round*) tournée *f*. **he has a paper ~** il distribue des journaux.

d (*US: often* [raʊt]: *in highway names*) **R~ 39** ≃ la Nationale 39, la RN39.

2 **comp** ►**route map** (*for a journey*) croquis *m* d'itinéraire, topo* *m*; (*for trains etc*) carte *f* du réseau ►**route march** (*Mil*) marche *f* d'entraînement.

3 **vt** (*plan ~ of*) *train, coach, bus* fixer le parcours *or* l'itinéraire de. **to ~ a train through Leeds** faire passer un train par Leeds; **my luggage was ~d through Amsterdam** mes bagages ont été expédiés via Amsterdam; **they've ~d the train by Leeds** le train passe maintenant par Leeds.

routine [ruːˈtiːn] 1 **n** a routine *f*. **daily ~** (*Mil, Naut*) emploi *m* du temps; (*gen*) occupations journalières, train-train *m* de la vie quotidienne; **business** *or* **office ~** travail courant du bureau; **as a matter of ~** automatiquement, systématiquement.

b (*Theat*) numéro *m*. **dance ~** numéro de danse; (*fig*) **he gave me the old ~**‡ **about his wife not understanding him** il m'a ressorti la vieille rengaine du mari incompris, il a mis le disque* du mari incompris.

2 **adj** *procedure* d'usage; *work etc* ordinaire, habituel; (*pej*) monotone, de routine. ~ **duties** affaires *or* obligations courantes; ~ **questions** questions *fpl* de routine *or* d'usage; **we're making a few ~ enquiries** nous menons une enquête de routine; **it was quite ~** ça n'avait rien d'anormal *or* de spécial.

routinely [ruːˈtiːnlɪ] **adv** (*following a routine*) de façon routinière; (*as a matter of course*) couramment.

rove [rəʊv] 1 **vi** errer, vagabonder, rôder; *[eyes]* errer. 2 **vt** *countryside* parcourir, errer dans *or* sur; *streets* errer dans, aller au hasard dans.

rover ['rəʊvəʳ] **n** vagabond(e) *m(f)*.

roving ['rəʊvɪŋ] 1 **adj** vagabond, nomade. **he has a ~ eye** il aime reluquer* *or* lorgner les filles; ~ **life** vie *f* nomade; ~ **ambassador** ambassadeur itinérant; ~ **reporter** reporter volant; **to have a ~ commission** avoir (toute) liberté de manœuvre. 2 **n** vagabondage *m*.

row[1] [rəʊ] 1 **n** *[objects, people]* (*beside one another*) rang *m*, rangée *f*; (*behind one another*) file *f*, ligne *f*; *[seeds, plants]* rayon *m*, rang; *[houses, trees, figures]* rangée; *[cars]* file; (*Knitting*) rang. **in the front ~** au premier rang; (*Rugby*) **the front/second/back ~ (of the scrum)** la première/deuxième/troisième ligne (de mêlée); **they were sitting in a ~** ils étaient assis en rang; (*fig*) **4 failures in a ~** 4 échecs d'affilée *or* de suite *or* à la file*; (*fig*) **a hard** *or* **long ~ to hoe** une rude besogne. 2 **comp** ►**row-house:** (*US*) **they live in a row-house** leur maison est attenante aux maisons voisines.

row[2] [rəʊ] 1 **vt** *boat* faire aller à la rame *or* à l'aviron; *person, object* transporter en canot (*to* à). **to ~ sb across** faire traverser qn en canot; **to ~ a race** faire une course d'aviron; *see* **stroke**.

2 **vi** (*gen*) ramer; (*Sport*) faire de l'aviron. **to ~ away/back** s'éloigner/revenir à la rame; **he ~ed across the Atlantic** il a traversé l'Atlantique à la rame *or* à l'aviron; **to go ~ing** (*for pleasure*) canoter, faire du canotage; (*Sport*) faire de l'aviron.

3 n promenade *f* en canot. **to go for a ~** canoter, faire un tour en canot; **it will be a hard ~ upstream** ce sera dur de remonter la rivière à la rame *or* à l'aviron.

4 comp ▸**rowboat** canot *m* (à rames) ▸**rowlock** [ˈrɒlək] dame *f* de nage, tolet *m*.

row³* [raʊ] 1 n (*noise*) tapage *m*, vacarme *m*, raffut* *m*, boucan‡ *m*; (*quarrel*) querelle *f*, dispute *f*; (*scolding*) réprimande *f*, savon* *m*, engueulade‡ *f*. **to make a ~** faire du raffut* *or* du boucan‡; **what a ~!** quel boucan! ‡; **to have a ~ with sb** se disputer avec qn, s'engueuler avec qn‡; **to give sb a ~** passer un savon à qn*, sonner les cloches à qn*, engueuler qn‡; **to get (into) a ~** se faire passer un savon*, se faire laver la tête*, se faire sonner les cloches*. 2 vt passer un savon à*, sonner les cloches à*. 3 vi se quereller, se disputer, s'engueuler ‡ (*with* avec).

rowan [ˈraʊən] n (*tree*) sorbier *m* des oiseleurs; (*berry*) sorbe *f*.

rowdiness [ˈraʊdɪnɪs] n (*noise*) tapage *m*, chahut *m*; (*fighting*) bagarre* *f*.

rowdy [ˈraʊdɪ] 1 adj (*noisy*) chahuteur; (*rough*) bagarreur*. **to be ~** (*make a din*) chahuter; (*fight*) se bagarrer*. 2 n (*) bagarreur* *m*, voyou *m*. **football rowdies** voyous *mpl* qui vont aux matchs de football.

rowdyism [ˈraʊdɪɪzəm] n (*see* **rowdy**) chahut *m*; bagarre* *f*; (*at football match etc*) violence *f*.

rower [ˈrəʊəʳ] n rameur *m*, -euse *f*; (*in navy*) nageur *m*.

rowing [ˈrəʊɪŋ] 1 n (*for pleasure*) canotage *m*; (*Sport*) aviron *m*; (*in navy*) nage *f*. 2 comp ▸**rowing boat** (*Brit*) canot *m* (à rames) ▸**rowing club** cercle *m* *or* club *m* d'aviron ▸**rowing machine** rameur *m*.

royal [ˈrɔɪəl] 1 adj a *person, age, family, palace, etiquette* royal; (*fig*) royal, princier, magnifique. (*Brit*) **R~ Academy** Académie Royale; (*Brit*) **R~ Air Force** Royal Air Force *f*, armée *f* de l'air; (*Brit Pol*) **R~ assent** assentiment royal (*accordé à un projet de loi*); **~ blue** (n) **~-blue** (adj) bleu roi (*m*) *inv*; **R~ Canadian Mounted Police** Gendarmerie *f* Royale Canadienne; (*Brit*) **R~ Commission** Commission *f* extra-parlementaire; (*Brit Mil*) **R~ Engineers** génie *m*; (*Cards*) **~ flush** flush *m* royal; **Your/His R~ Highness** Votre/Son Altesse Royale; **the ~ household** la maison du roi *or* de la reine; **~ jelly** gelée *f* royale; (*Brit*) **R~ Marines** les Marines (*de la Marine anglaise*); (*Brit*) **R~ Naval Reserve** *corps de réservistes de la Marine*; (*Brit*) **R~ Navy** marine nationale; (*fig*) **the ~ road to freedom/success** *etc* la voie *or* la route royale de la liberté/du succès *etc*; (*Brit*) **R~ Society** Académie *f* des Sciences; (*Brit Police*) **R~ Ulster Constabulary** police *f* de l'Irlande du Nord; (*Brit*) **~ warrant** *autorisation que reçoit un commerçant de fournir la famille royale*; **the ~ "we"** le "nous" de majesté; (*fig*) **they gave him a ~ welcome** ils l'ont reçu de façon royale; *see* **prerogative**.

b *paper* de format grand raisin. **~ octavo** in-huit raisin.

2 n (*) personne *f* de la famille royale. **the ~s** la famille royale.

royalism [ˈrɔɪəlɪzəm] n royalisme *m*.

royalist [ˈrɔɪəlɪst] adj, n royaliste (*mf*).

royally [ˈrɔɪəlɪ] adv (*lit, fig*) royalement.

royalty [ˈrɔɪəltɪ] n a (*position, dignity, rank*) royauté *f*. b (*royal person*) membre *m* de la famille royale; (*royal persons*) (membres *mpl* de) la famille royale. c **royalties** (*from book*) redevance *f*, droits *mpl* d'auteur; (*from oil well, patent*) royalties *fpl*.

rozzer‡ [ˈrɒzəʳ] n (*Brit*) flic* *m*, poulet* *m*.

RP [ɑːˈpiː] n (*Brit Ling*) (abbr of **Received Pronunciation**) prononciation *f* standard (de l'anglais).

RPI [ɑːpiːˈaɪ] n (*Brit*) (abbr of **retail price index**) *see* **retail**.

rpm [ɑːpiːˈem] n a (abbr of **revolutions per minute**) tr/min. b (*Comm*) (abbr of **resale price maintenance**) *see* **resale**.

R.R. (*US*) abbr of **railroad**.

RRP [ˌɑːrɑːˈpiː] n (*Comm*) (abbr of **recommended retail price**) prix *m* conseillé.

R.S.A. [ɑːresˈeɪ] n a (abbr of **Royal Society of Arts**) *organisme habilité à conférer des diplômes*. b (abbr of **Royal Scottish Academy**) Académie *f* Royale d'Écosse.

RSI [ɑːresˈaɪ] n (abbr of **repetitive strain injury**) *see* **repetitive**.

R.S.M. [ɑːresˈem] n (*Mil*) (abbr of **Regimental Sergeant Major**) *see* **regimental**.

R.S.P.C.A. [ˌɑːrespiːsiːˈeɪ] n (*Brit*) (abbr of **Royal Society for the Prevention of Cruelty to Animals**) ≃ S.P.A. *f*.

RSV n (abbr of **Revised Standard Version**) *see* **revise**.

R.S.V.P. [ˌɑːresviːˈpiː] (abbr of **please reply**) RSVP.

Rt. Hon. (*Brit Pol*) (abbr of **Right Honorable**) *see* **right 2d**.

Rt. Rev. (abbr of **Right Reverend**) *see* **reverend**.

RU n abbr of **Rugby Union**.

rub [rʌb] 1 n (*on thing*) frottement *m*; (*on person*) friction *f*; (*with duster etc*) coup *m* de chiffon *or* de torchon. **to give sth a ~** (*furniture, shoes, silver*) donner un coup de chiffon *or* de torchon à qch; (*sore place, one's arms*) frotter qch; (*fig*) **there's the ~!** c'est là la difficulté!, voilà le hic!*; **the ~ is that ...** l'ennui *or* le hic*, c'est que ... .

2 comp ▸**rub-a-dub(-dub)** rataplan *m* ▸**rub-down: to give a horse a rub-down** bouchonner un cheval; **to give sb a rub-down** faire une friction à qn, frictionner qn ▸**rub-up: to give sth a rub-up** frotter *or* astiquer qch.

3 vt frotter; (*polish*) astiquer, frotter; (*Art*) *brass, inscription* prendre un frottis de. **~ yourself and you'll soon be dry** frictionne-toi *or* frotte-toi, tu seras bientôt sec; **to ~ one's nose** se frotter le nez; (*fig*) **to ~ sb's nose in sth** ne jamais laisser oublier qch à qn; **to ~ one's hands (together)** se frotter les mains; **to ~ sth dry** sécher qch en le frottant; **to ~ a hole in sth** faire un trou dans qch à force de frotter; **to ~ sth through a sieve** passer qch au tamis; **to ~ lotion into the skin** faire pénétrer de la lotion dans la peau; (*fig*) **to ~ shoulders with all sorts of people** coudoyer toutes sortes de gens; *see* **salt**.

4 vi [*thing*] frotter (*against* contre); [*person, cat*] se frotter (*against* contre).

▸**rub along*** vi faire *or* poursuivre son petit bonhomme de chemin. [*two people*] **to rub along (together)** vivre *or* s'accorder tant bien que mal; (*fig*) **he can rub along in French, he knows enough French to rub along with** il sait assez de français pour se tirer d'affaire tant bien que mal *or* pour se débrouiller.

▸**rub away** vt sep *mark* faire disparaître (en frottant), effacer. **she rubbed her tears away** elle a essuyé ses larmes (de la main).

▸**rub down** 1 vt sep *horse* bouchonner; *person* frictionner (*with* avec); *wall, paintwork* (*clean*) frotter, nettoyer du haut en bas; (*sandpaper*) poncer, polir. 2 **rub-down** n *see* **rub 2**.

▸**rub in** vt sep *oil, liniment* faire pénétrer en frottant; (*fig*) *idea* insister sur; *lesson* faire entrer (*to* à). (*fig*) **don't rub it in!*** pas besoin de me le rappeler, ne remuez pas le couteau dans la plaie; **he's always rubbing in how rich he is** il ne vous laisse jamais oublier à quel point il est riche.

▸**rub off** 1 vi [*mark*] partir, s'en aller; [*writing*] s'effacer, disparaître. **the blue will rub off on to your hands** tu vas avoir les mains toutes bleues; (*fig*) **I hope some of his politeness will rub off on to his brother*** j'espère qu'il passera un peu de sa politesse à son frère, j'espère que sa politesse déteindra un peu sur son frère. 2 vt sep *writing on blackboard* effacer; *dirt* enlever en frottant.

▸**rub on** vt sep *cream, polish etc* passer.

▸**rub out** 1 vi [*mark, writing*] s'effacer, s'en aller. **that ink won't rub out** cette encre ne s'effacera pas. 2 vt sep (*erase*) effacer; (‡: *kill*) descendre*, liquider*.

▸**rub up** 1 vi (*fig*) **to rub up against all sorts of people** côtoyer toutes sortes de gens. 2 vt sep *vase, table* frotter, astiquer. (*fig*) **to rub sb up the right way** savoir (comment) s'y prendre avec qn; (*fig*) **to rub sb up the wrong way** prendre qn à rebrousse-poil*; (*: *revise*) **to rub up one's French** dérouiller* son français. 3 **rub-up** n *see* **rub 2**.

rubato [ruːˈbɑːtəʊ] n, adv rubato (*m*).

rubber¹ [ˈrʌbəʳ] 1 n a (*material: no pl*) caoutchouc *m*. **synthetic ~** caoutchouc synthétique; (*US fig*) **to lay ~‡** (*start*) démarrer sur les chapeaux de roue; (*pass*) passer en trombe; *see* **foam** *etc*.

b (*Brit: eraser*) gomme *f*.

c (*esp US* ‡: *condom*) préservatif *m*, capote *f* anglaise.

d (*shoes*) **~s** caoutchoucs *mpl*.

2 adj *goods, clothes* de *or* en caoutchouc. **~ band** élastique *m*; **~ boots** bottes *fpl* de caoutchouc; **~ bullet** balle *f* en caoutchouc; (*US fig*) **~ check*** chèque *m* en bois* *or* sans provision; **~ ring** (*for sitting on*) rond *m* (pour malade); (*for swimming*) bouée *f* de natation; *see also* **3**.

3 comp ▸**rubber cement** mastic *m* au caoutchouc ▸**rubber-covered** sous caoutchouc ▸**rubberneck‡†** (*US*) n touriste *mf*, badaud(e) *m(f)* ◊ vi baguenauder ▸**rubber plant** caoutchouc *m* (*plante verte*) ▸**rubber plantation** plantation *f* de hévéas ▸**rubber solution** dissolution *f* ▸**rubber stamp** tampon *m* ▸**rubber-stamp*** (*lit*) tamponner; (*fig*) approuver sans discussion ▸**rubber tree** arbre *m* à gomme, hévéa *m* ▸**rubber-tyred** sur pneus.

rubber² [ˈrʌbəʳ] n (*Cards*) rob *m*, robre *m*. **to play a ~** faire un robre *or* une partie; (*Bridge*) **that's game and ~** c'est la partie.

rubberized [ˈrʌbəraɪzd] adj caoutchouté.

rubbery [ˈrʌbərɪ] adj caoutchouteux.

rubbing [ˈrʌbɪŋ] 1 n (*action*) frottement *m*, frottage *m*; (*Art*) frottis *m*, reproduction *f* par frottage; *see* **brass**. 2 comp ▸**rubbing alcohol** (*US*) alcool à 90 (degrés).

rubbish [ˈrʌbɪʃ] 1 n a (*waste material*) détritus *mpl*; (*Brit: household ~*) ordures *fpl*, immondices *fpl*; [*factory*] déchets *mpl*; [*building site*] décombres *mpl*; (*pej: worthless things*) choses *fpl* sans valeur, camelote* *f*, pacotille *f*. **household ~** ordures ménagères; **garden ~** détritus de jardin; **this shop sells a lot of ~** ce magasin ne vend que de la camelote* *or* des saletés*; **it's just ~** ça ne vaut rien (*see also* **1b**).

b (*fig: nonsense*) bêtises *fpl*, absurdités *fpl*, inepties *fpl*. **to talk ~** débiter des bêtises *or* des absurdités *or* des inepties; **(what a lot of) ~!*** quelle blague!*; **this book is ~** ce livre ne vaut strictement rien *or* est une ineptie; **that's just ~** ça ne veut rien dire, ça n'a aucun sens; **it is ~ to say that ...** c'est idiot de dire que ... .

2 comp ▸**rubbish bin** (*Brit*) poubelle *f*, boîte *f* à ordures ▸**rubbish cart** voiture *f* d'éboueurs ▸**rubbish chute** (*at dump*) dépotoir *m*; (*in building*) vide-ordures *m* *inv* ▸**rubbish collection** ramassage *m* d'ordures ▸**rubbish dump, rubbish heap** (*public*) décharge publique, dépotoir *m*; (*in garden*) monceau *m* de détritus.

3 vt (*fig *: denigrate*) débiner*.

rubbishy [ˈrʌbɪʃɪ] adj *goods* sans valeur, de pacotille; (*fig*) *book, film,*

ideas inepte, idiot, qui ne vaut rien. ~ **shoes** chaussures de mauvaise qualité; **this is ~ stuff** c'est de la camelote* *or* de la saleté*.
rubble ['rʌbl] **n** *[ruined house, bomb site, demolition site]* décombres *mpl*, (*smaller pieces*) gravats *mpl*; (*in roadbuilding*) blocaille *f*, blocage *m*. **the building was reduced to a heap of ~** il ne restait du bâtiment qu'un tas de décombres.
rube* [ru:b] **n** (*US*) péquenaud * *m*.
Rube Goldberg ['ru:b'gəʊldbɜ:g] **n** (*US*) **a ~ machine** un engin tarabiscoté (fait avec les moyens du bord).
rubella [ru:'belə] **n** rubéole *f*.
Rubicon ['ru:bɪkən] **n** Rubicon *m*. **to cross the ~** passer *or* franchir le Rubicon.
rubicund ['ru:bɪkənd] **adj** *complexion* rubicond, rougeaud.
rubidium [ru:'bɪdɪəm] **n** rubidium *m*.
ruble ['ru:bl] (*US*) = **rouble**.
rubric ['ru:brɪk] **n** rubrique *f*.
ruby ['ru:bɪ] **1 n** rubis *m*; (*colour*) couleur *f* de rubis. **2 comp** (*colour*) *wine* (couleur de) rubis *inv*; *lips* vermeil; (*made of rubies*) *necklace, ring* de rubis ▸ **ruby wedding** noces *fpl* de rubis.
R.U.C. [ɑ:ju:'si:] **n** (**abbr of Royal Ulster Constabulary**) *see* **royal**.
ruche [ru:ʃ] **n** ruche *f*.
ruck[1] [rʌk] **n** (*Racing*) peloton *m*; (*Rugby*) mêlée *f* ouverte *or* spontanée. (*fig*) **the (common) ~** les masses *fpl*, la foule, le peuple; (*fig*) **to get out of the ~** se distinguer du commun des mortels.
ruck[2] [rʌk], **ruckle** ['rʌkl] **1 n** (*crease*) faux pli, godet *m*. **2 vi** se froisser, se chiffonner. **3 vt** froisser, chiffonner.
▸**ruck up vi** *[skirt, blouse]* remonter en faisant des plis.
rucksack ['rʌksæk] **n** sac *m* à dos, sac de montagne.
ruckus* ['rʌkəs] **n, pl ~es** (*US*) chahut *m*, grabuge* *m*.
ruction* ['rʌkʃən] **n** (*gen pl*) (*rows*) disputes *fpl*, grabuge* *m*; (*riots*) troubles *mpl*, bagarres *fpl*. **there'll be ~s if you break that glass** si tu casses ce verre tu vas te faire sonner les cloches* *or* il va y avoir du grabuge*.
rudder ['rʌdə^r] **n** (*Aviat, Naut, fig*) gouvernail *m*. (*Aviat*) **vertical/horizontal ~** gouvernail de direction/de profondeur.
rudderless ['rʌdəlɪs] **adj** (*lit*) sans gouvernail, à la dérive; (*fig*) à la dérive.
ruddiness ['rʌdɪnɪs] **n** rougeur *f*, teint vif *or* coloré.
ruddy ['rʌdɪ] **adj a** *complexion* (*gen*) rubicond (*pej*), rougeaud (*pej*), coloré; (*with healthy glow*) rouge de santé; *sky, glow* rougeoyant, rougeâtre. **b** (**: Brit* **euph of bloody**) fichu*, sacré*. **he's a ~ fool** c'est un sacré* *or* fichu* imbécile; **you're a ~ nuisance** tu me casses les pieds*, tu m'enquiquines*.
rude [ru:d] **adj a** *person, speech, behaviour, reply, gesture* (*impolite*) impoli, mal élevé, (*stronger*) insolent; (*coarse*) grossier; (*improper*) inconvenant, indécent; *story* scabreux; *song* grivois; *gesture* obscène, indécent. **~ remarks** (*insults*) paroles injurieuses *or* offensantes; (*obscenities etc*) grossièretés *fpl*; **to be ~ to sb** se conduire grossièrement envers qn, être grossier *or* très impoli envers qn; **he's always ~** c'est un malappris; **would it be ~ to ask you your address?** sans indiscrétion peut-on savoir votre adresse?; **it's ~ to stare** c'est très mal élevé de dévisager les gens; **there's nothing ~ about that picture** ce tableau n'a rien d'inconvenant *or* d'indécent; **~ word** gros mot.
b (*sudden*) *shock* brusque, violent, rude. (*fig*) **to have** *or* **get a ~ awakening** être rappelé brusquement *or* brutalement à la réalité.
c (*primitive*) *way of living, peasant* primitif, rude; (*simply made*) *implement* grossier, primitif, rudimentaire.
d (*vigorous*) *strength* robuste, vigoureux. **he's in ~ health** il a une santé robuste *or* de fer.
rudely ['ru:dlɪ] **adv** (*see* **rude**) impoliment; insolemment; grossièrement; violemment, brusquement. **~-fashioned object** objet grossièrement fabriqué, objet fabriqué sans art.
rudeness ['ru:dnɪs] **n** (*see* **rude**) impolitesse *f*; insolence *f*; grossièreté *f*; violence *f*, brusquerie *f*; caractère primitif, rudesse *f*.
rudiment ['ru:dɪmənt] **n** (*Anat*) rudiment *m*. (*fig*) **~s** rudiments *mpl*, éléments *mpl*, notions *fpl* élémentaires.
rudimentary [ˌru:dɪ'mentərɪ] **adj** rudimentaire.
rue[1] [ru:] **vt** (*liter*) se repentir de, regretter amèrement.
rue[2] [ru:] **n** (*Bot*) rue *f*.
rueful ['ru:fʊl] **adj** *person* triste, chagrin; *look* triste, piteux; *situation* triste, attristant.
ruefully ['ru:fəlɪ] **adv** d'un air piteux, avec regret.
ruff[1] [rʌf] **n a** (*Dress*) collerette *f*, (*Hist*) fraise *f*; *[bird, animal]* collier *m*, collerette *f*. **b** (*Orn*) (*sandpiper*) combattant *m*; (*pigeon*) pigeon capucin.
ruff[2] [rʌf] (*Cards*) **1 n** action *f* de couper (avec un atout). **2 vti** couper (avec un atout).
ruffian ['rʌfɪən] **n** voyou *m*, brute *f*. **you little ~!*** petit polisson!
ruffianly ['rʌfɪənlɪ] **adj** *person* brutal; *behaviour* de voyou, de brute; *looks, appearance* de brigand, de voyou.
ruffle ['rʌfl] **1 n** (*on wrist*) manchette *f* (*en dentelle etc*); (*on chest*) jabot *m*; (*round neck*) fraise *f*; (*ripple: on water*) ride *f*, ondulation *f*. **2 vt a** (*disturb*) *hair, feathers* ébouriffer; *surface, water* agiter, troubler, rider; *one's clothes* déranger, froisser, chiffonner. **the bird ~d (up) its feathers** l'oiseau a hérissé ses plumes. **b** (*fig*) (*upset*) froisser; (*disturb*) troubler; (*annoy*) contrarier, irriter. **she wasn't at all ~d** elle était parfaitement calme.
Rufflette [rʌf'let] **n**: ® **~ (tape)** galon *m* fronceur, rufflette *f* ®.
rug [rʌg] **n a** (*for floor*) petit tapis; (*bedside*) descente *f* de lit, carpette *f*; (*fireside*) carpette. (*fig*) **to pull the ~ out from under sb's feet** couper l'herbe sous les pieds de qn. **b** (*woollen cover*) couverture *f*; (*in tartan*) plaid *m*; *see* **travelling**.
rugby ['rʌgbɪ] **1 n** (*also* **~ football**) rugby *m*. **2 comp** ▸**rugby league** (le) rugby *m* à treize ▸**rugby player** rugbyman *m*, joueur *m* de rugby ▸**rugby union** (le) rugby *m* à quinze.
rugged ['rʌgɪd] **adj** *country, ground, landscape* accidenté; *road* raboteux, rocailleux; *cliff, coast* déchiqueté; *mountains* aux contours déchiquetés; *bark* rugueux; *features* irrégulier, rude; *workmanship, statue* fruste; *character, manners* rude, sans raffinement; *person* bourru, rude; *determination, resistance* acharné, farouche; (**: solid*) *machine, construction* robuste, solide. **covered with ~ rocks** hérissé de rochers.
ruggedness ['rʌgɪdnɪs] **n** *[surface]* aspérité *f*, rugosité *f*; *[rock]* anfractuosités *fpl*; *[character]* rudesse *f*; *[features]* irrégularité *f*, rudesse. **the ~ of the ground** les accidents *mpl or* les aspérités du terrain.
rugger* ['rʌgə^r] **n** (*Brit*) rugby *m*.
Ruhr [rʊə^r] **n** Ruhr *f*.
ruin ['ru:ɪn] **1 n a** (*NonC*) ruine *f*; (*thing, event, person*) ruine, perte *f*. **the palace was going to ~** *or* **falling into ~** le palais tombait en ruine *or* menaçait ruine *or* se délabrait; **he was on the brink of ~, ~ stared him in the face** il était au bord de la ruine; **the ~ of my hopes** la ruine *or* la faillite de mes espérances; **drink was his ~** l'alcool a été sa perte; **it will be the ~ of him** ça sera sa ruine; **you will be the ~ of me** tu seras ma perte *or* ma ruine; *see* **rack**[3].
b (*gen pl*) *[building, hopes, beauty etc]* ruine(s) *f(pl)*. (*lit, fig*) **in ~s** en ruine; **the castle is now a ~** le château est maintenant une ruine.
2 vt *building, reputation, hopes, health, person* ruiner; *clothes* abîmer; *event, enjoyment* gâter.
ruination [ˌru:ɪ'neɪʃən] **n** ruine *f*, perte *f*. **to be the ~ of** ruiner.
ruined ['ru:ɪnd] **adj** *building* en ruine; *person* ruiné.
ruinous ['ru:ɪnəs] **adj** ruineux. **that trip proved ~ for his firm** ce voyage a entraîné la ruine de *or* a ruiné sa compagnie; **the price of butter is ~*** le prix du beurre est exorbitant *or* ruineux.
ruinously ['ru:ɪnəslɪ] **adv**: **~ expensive** ruineux.
rule [ru:l] **1 n a** (*guiding principle*) règle *f*; (*regulation*) règlement *m*; (*Gram*) règle. **the ~s of the game** la règle du jeu; **school ~s** règlement *m* intérieur (de l'école *or* du lycée *etc*); **it's against the ~s** c'est contraire à la règle *or* au règlement; **running is against the ~s, it's against the ~s to run** il est contraire à la règle *or* il n'est pas permis de courir; (*lit, fig*) **to play by the ~s** jouer suivant *or* selon les règles; **~s and regulations** statuts *mpl*; **standing ~** règlement; **it's a ~ that ...** il est de règle que ... + *subj*; **~ of the road** (*Aut*) règle générale de la circulation; (*Naut*) règles générales du trafic maritime; **to do sth by ~** faire qch selon les règles; (*Math*) **the ~ of three** la règle de trois; **a rough ~ of thumb is that it is best to ...** en règle générale il vaut mieux ...; **by ~ of thumb** à vue de nez; **golden ~** règle d'or; *see* **exception, work** *etc*.
b (*custom*) coutume *f*, habitude *f*. **ties are the ~ in this hotel** les cravates sont de règle dans cet hôtel; **bad weather is the ~ in winter** le mauvais temps est habituel *or* normal en hiver; **he makes it a ~ to get up early** il a pour règle de se lever tôt; **to make tidiness a ~** faire de l'ordre une règle; **as a ~** en règle générale, normalement, en principe.
c (*NonC: authority*) autorité *f*, empire *m*. **under British ~** sous l'autorité britannique; **under a tyrant's ~** sous l'empire *or* la domination d'un tyran; (*Pol etc*) **majority ~, the ~ of the majority** le gouvernement par la majorité; **the ~ of law** l'autorité de la loi; *see* **home**.
d (*for measuring*) règle *f* (graduée). **a foot ~** une règle d'un pied; **folding ~** mètre pliant; *see* **slide**.
e (*Rel*) règle *f*.
2 comp ▸**the rule book** le règlement; (*fig*) **to do sth by the rule book** faire qch dans les règles; (*fig*) **to throw the rule book at sb*** remettre qn à sa place, rembarrer qn*.
3 vt a *country* gouverner; (*fig*) *passions, emotion* maîtriser; *person* dominer, mener. (*fig*) **to ~ the roost** faire la loi; **he ~d the company for 30 years** il a dirigé la compagnie *or* il a été à la tête de la compagnie pendant 30 ans; **to be ~d by jealousy** être mené *or* dominé par la jalousie; **to ~ one's passions** maîtriser ses passions; **he is ~d by his wife** il est mené par sa femme; **if you would only be ~d by what I say ...** si seulement tu voulais consentir à écouter mes conseils ...; **I won't be ~d by what he wants** je ne veux pas me plier à ses volontés.
b *[judge, umpire etc]* décider, déclarer (*that* que). (*Jur*) **the judge ~d the defence out of order** le juge a déclaré non recevables les paroles de l'avocat pour la défense; **the judge ~d that the child should go to school** le juge a décidé que l'enfant irait à l'école.
c (*draw lines on*) *paper* régler, rayer; *line* tirer à la règle. **~d paper** papier réglé *or* rayé.
4 vi a (*reign*) régner (*over* sur). (*in graffiti*) **United ~ OK** United vaincra, United est le meilleur.

b **the prices ruling in Paris** les cours (pratiqués) à Paris.
c (*Jur*) statuer (*against* contre, *in favour of* en faveur de, *on* sur).

►**rule off** vt (*Comm*) *account* clore, arrêter. **to rule off a column of figures** tirer une ligne sous une colonne de chiffres.

►**rule out** vt sep *word, sentence* barrer, rayer, biffer; (*fig*) *possibility, suggestion, date, person* exclure, écarter. **the age limit rules him out** il est exclu du fait de la limite d'âge; **murder can't be ruled out** il est impossible d'écarter *or* d'exclure l'hypothèse d'un meurtre.

ruler ['ru:lər] n a (*sovereign*) souverain(e) *m(f)*; (*political leader*) chef *m* (d'État). **the country's ~s** les dirigeants *mpl* du pays. b (*for measuring*) règle *f*.

ruling ['ru:lɪŋ] 1 adj *principle* souverain; *factor, passion* dominant; *price etc* pratiqué, actuel. **the ~ class** la classe dirigeante; (*Pol*) **the ~ party** le parti au pouvoir. 2 n (*Admin, Jur*) décision *f*, jugement *m*; *[judge]* décision. **to get/give a ~** obtenir/rendre un jugement.

rum¹ [rʌm] 1 n rhum *m*. 2 comp ►**rumrunner** (*Hist*) (*person*) contrebandier *m* d'alcool; (*ship*) bateau *m* servant à la contrebande de l'alcool ►**rum-running** contrebande *f* de l'alcool ►**rum toddy** grog *m*.

rum²* [rʌm] adj (*Brit: odd*) bizarre, drôle; *idea* biscornu*.

Rumania [ru:'meɪnɪə] n (*Brit*) Roumanie *f*.

Rumanian [ru:'meɪnɪən] (*Brit*) 1 adj roumain. 2 n a (*person*) Roumain(e) *m(f)*. b (*Ling*) roumain *m*.

rumba ['rʌmbə] n rumba *f*.

rumble ['rʌmbl] 1 n a (*noise*) *[thunder, cannon]* grondement *m*; *[train, lorry]* roulement *m*, grondement; *[pipe, stomach]* gargouillement *m*, borborygme *m*.
b (‡: *fight*) bagarre *f* entre bandes de jeunes.
2 comp ►**rumble seat** strapontin *m* ►**rumble strip** (*on road*) section *f* de route avec rainurage.
3 vi *[thunder, cannon]* gronder; *[stomach, pipes]* gargouiller. *[vehicle]* **to ~ past** passer avec fracas.
4 vt a (*also* **~ out**) *comments, remarks* dire en grondant, grommeler.
b (*Brit*) (‡: *see through*) *swindle* flairer, subodorer*; *trick* piger‡; *person* voir venir; (*find out*) piger‡, découvrir (*what/why etc* ce que/pourquoi *etc*). **I soon ~d him** *or* **his game** *or* **what he was up to** j'ai tout de suite pigé sa combine!‡

rumbling ['rʌmblɪŋ] n *[thunder]* grondement *m*; *[vehicle]* roulement *m*, grondement; *[stomach, pipe]* gargouillement *m*. (*fig*) **~s of discontent** signes *mpl* de mécontentement; **tummy ~s*** gargouillis *mpl*, borborygmes *mpl*.

rumbustious [rʌm'bʌstʃəs] adj bruyant, exubérant.

ruminant ['ru:mɪnənt] adj, n ruminant (*m*).

ruminate ['ru:mɪneɪt] 1 vi (*lit, fig*) ruminer. (*fig*) **to ~ over** *or* **about** *or* **on sth** ruminer qch, retourner qch dans sa tête. 2 vt ruminer.

rumination [,ru:mɪ'neɪʃən] n (*lit, fig*) rumination *f*.

ruminative ['ru:mɪnətɪv] adj (*fig*) pensif, méditatif, réfléchi.

ruminatively ['ru:mɪnətɪvlɪ] adv pensivement.

rummage ['rʌmɪdʒ] 1 n a (*action*) **to have a good ~ round** bien fouiller partout. b (*jumble*) bric-à-brac *m*, vieilleries *fpl*, objets *mpl* divers. 2 comp ►**rummage sale** vente *f* de charité (*de bric-à-brac*).
3 vi (*also* **~ about, ~ around**) farfouiller*, fouiller (*among, in* dans, *for* pour trouver).

rummy¹* ['rʌmɪ] 1 adj = **rum²**. 2 n (*US* *: *drunk*) poivrot* *m*, ivrogne *m*.

rummy² ['rʌmɪ] n (*Cards*) rami *m*.

rumour, (*US*) **rumor** ['ru:mər] 1 n rumeur *f* (*that* selon laquelle), bruit *m* (qui court). **there is a disturbing ~ (to the effect) that** il court un bruit inquiétant selon lequel; **all these nasty ~s** toutes ces rumeurs pernicieuses; **~ has it that ...** on dit que ..., le bruit court que ...; **there is a ~ of war** le bruit court *or* on dit qu'il va y avoir la guerre. 2 vt: **it is ~ed that ...** on dit que ..., le bruit court que ...; **he is ~ed to be in London** il serait à Londres, le bruit court qu'il est à Londres; **he is ~ed to be rich** on le dit riche.

rump [rʌmp] 1 n a *[animal]* croupe *f*; *[fowl]* croupion *m*; (*Culin*) culotte *f* (de bœuf); (*) *[person]* derrière *m*, postérieur* *m*. b (*pej*) *[group, organization]* derniers vestiges *mpl*. **a ~ party/opposition** *etc* un parti/une opposition *etc* croupion; (*Brit Hist*) **the R~ Parliament** le Parlement Croupion. 2 comp ►**rumpsteak** romsteck *m or* rumsteck *m*.

rumple ['rʌmpl] vt *clothes* chiffonner, froisser, friper; *paper* froisser, chiffonner; *hair* ébouriffer.

rumpus* ['rʌmpəs] 1 n, pl **~es** chahut *m*; (*noise*) tapage *m*, boucan‡ *m*; (*quarrel*) prise *f* de bec*. **to make a ~** faire du chahut *or* du boucan; **to have a ~ with sb** se chamailler* avec qn, avoir une prise de bec avec qn*. 2 comp ►**rumpus room** (*esp US*) salle *f* de jeux.

run [rʌn] (vb: pret **ran**, ptp **run**) 1 n a (*act of running*) action *f* de courir, course *f*. **to go for a ~** faire un peu de course à pied; **to go for a 2-km ~** faire 2 km de course à pied; **at a ~** au pas de course, en courant; **to break into a ~** se mettre à courir, prendre le pas de course; **to make a ~ for it** prendre la fuite, se sauver, filer*; **to have the ~ of a place** avoir un endroit à son entière disposition; **to give sb the ~ of a place** mettre un endroit à l'entière disposition de qn; **you have the entire ~ of my garden** mon jardin est à votre entière disposition, vous pouvez aller partout *or* où bon vous semble dans mon jardin; **a criminal on the ~ (from the police)** un criminel recherché par la police; **he is still on the ~** il court encore, il est toujours en cavale; **he was on the ~ for several months** il a réussi à rester en liberté plusieurs mois, il n'a été repris qu'au bout de plusieurs mois; **to have the enemy on the ~** mettre l'ennemi en fuite; **to keep the enemy on the ~** harceler l'ennemi; **she has so much to do she's always on the ~*** elle a tant à faire qu'elle est tout le temps à courir *or* en train de courir; (*fig*) **we've given him a good ~ for his money** nous ne nous sommes pas avoués vaincus d'avance; **he's had a good ~ for his money** (*been strongly challenged*) on lui a donné du fil à retordre; (*enjoyed himself*) il en a bien profité; (*on sb's retirement, death etc*) **he's had a good ~** il a bien profité de l'existence; **to have the ~s‡** (*diarrhoea*) avoir la courante‡.
b (*outing*) tour *m*, promenade *f*, excursion *f*. **to go for a ~ in the car** faire un tour *or* une promenade en voiture; **they went for a ~ in the country** ils ont fait un tour *or* une excursion *or* une promenade à la campagne; **we had a pleasant ~ down** le voyage a été agréable; **to take a ~ up to London** faire un tour *or* une virée* à Londres, pousser une pointe jusqu'à Londres; **I'll give you a ~ up to town** je vais vous conduire *or* vous emmener en ville; *see* **trial**.
c (*distance travelled*) *[bus, train, boat, plane]* parcours *m*; *[car]* trajet *m*. **it's a 30-minute ~** il y a une demi-heure de trajet; **it's a 30-minute bus ~** il y a une demi-heure d'autobus; **it's a short car ~** le trajet n'est pas long en voiture, on n'en a pas pour longtemps en voiture; **the boat no longer does that ~** le bateau ne fait plus cette traversée, ce service n'existe plus; **on the outward ~ the ferry ...** pendant le parcours aller le ferry ...; **the ferries on the Dover-Calais ~** les ferrys sur le parcours Douvres-Calais *or* qui assurent le service Douvres-Calais; **the ships on the China ~** les paquebots qui font la Chine.
d (*series*) succession *f*, série *f*, suite *f*; (*Cards*) séquence *f*. (*Roulette*) **a ~ on the red** une série à la rouge; **the ~ of the cards** le hasard du jeu; **that fashion has had a long ~** cette mode a duré longtemps; (*Theat*) **when the London ~ was over** quand la saison à Londres *or* la série de représentations à Londres s'est terminée; (*Theat*) **the play had a long ~** la pièce a tenu longtemps l'affiche; **there was no difference in the long ~** en fin de compte il n'y a pas eu de différence; **things will sort themselves out in the long ~** les choses s'arrangeront à la longue *or* avec le temps; **in the short ~** à court terme; **to have a ~ of luck** être en veine*; **a ~ of bad luck** une période de malchance *or* de déveine*; **a ~ of misfortunes** une suite de malheurs, une série noire*.
e (*rush, great demand*) ruée *f*. (*St Ex*) **a ~ on shares** une très forte demande d'actions; (*Fin*) **there has been a ~ on the pound sterling** il y a eu une ruée sur la livre (sterling); **there was a ~ on the banks** les guichets (des banques) ont été assiégés; (*Comm*) **there has been a ~ on sugar** on s'est rué sur le sucre.
f *[tide]* poussée *f*, flux *m*.
g (*fig: trend*) *[market]* tendance *f*; *[events]* direction *f*, tendance; *[opinion]* tendance, courant *m*. **the (common) ~ of mankind** le commun des mortels; **the ordinary ~ of things** la routine, le train-train habituel; **the usual ~ of problems** tous les problèmes habituels *or* typiques, les mêmes problèmes que d'habitude; **outside the usual ~ of things** inhabituel, qui sort de l'ordinaire, hors du commun.
h (*track for sledging, skiing etc*) piste *f*, descente *f*; (*animal enclosure*) enclos *m*. **ski ~** piste de ski; *see* **chicken**.
i (*in stocking*) échelle *f*, maille filée.
j (*Mus*) roulade *f*.
k (*Typ*) tirage *m*. **a ~ of 5,000 copies** un tirage de 5 000 exemplaires.
l (*Cricket, Baseball*) point *m*, course *f*. (*Baseball*) **to make a ~** marquer un point.
m (*Ind: batch of production*) lot *m*.
n (*Mil: raid, mission*) raid *m* (aérien).
o (*Pol: bid for leadership*) candidature *f* (*for* à).
2 comp ►**runabout** (*car*) petite voiture; (*boat*) runabout *m*; (*Rail etc*) **runabout ticket** billet *m* circulaire ►**run-around**‡: **he gave me the run-around** il est resté très évasif, il m'a fait des réponses de Normand ►**runaway** *see* **runaway** ►**rundown** *see* **rundown** ►**run-flat** n (*Brit: tyre*) pneu *m* traité anti-crevaison ►**run-in** (*: *quarrel*) prise *f* de bec (*over* à propos de); (*rehearsal*) répétition *f*; (*approach*) approche *f* ►**run-off** (*Sport*) finale *f* (d'une course) ►**run-of-the-mill** moyen, banal, ordinaire ►**run-on line** (*Typ*) enjambement *m* ►**runproof, run-resist** indémaillable ►**run-through** essai *m*, répétition *f* ►**run time** (*Comput*) durée *f* d'exploitation ►**run-up** (*Sport*) course *f* d'élan; (*Brit: preparation*) période *f* préparatoire (*to* à); (*US: increase*) augmentation *f* (*in* de); **the run-up to the elections** la période qui précède les élections; **the run-up in prices** la flambée des prix ►**runway** (*Aviat*) piste *f* (d'envol *or* d'atterrissage); (*Tech*) chemin *m* de roulement, piste, rampe *f*.
3 vi a (*gen*) courir; (*hurry*) courir, se précipiter. **to ~ down/in/off** *etc* descendre/entrer/partir *etc* en courant; **she came ~ning out** elle est sortie en courant; **to ~ down a slope** descendre une pente en courant; **he is always ~ning about the streets** il court toujours dans les rues; **don't ~ across the road** ne traverse pas la rue en courant; **to ~ for all one is worth, to ~ like hell*** courir à toutes jambes; **to ~ for the bus**

courir pour attraper l'autobus; **she ran to meet him** elle a couru à sa rencontre, elle s'est précipitée au-devant de lui; **she ran to help him** elle a couru l'aider, elle a couru *or* s'est précipitée *or* a volé à son secours; **she ran over to her neighbour's** elle a couru *or* s'est précipitée chez sa voisine; **he used to ~ for his school** il a disputé des épreuves de course *or* il a couru dans les compétitions d'athlétisme pour son lycée; (*fig*) **to ~ with the hare and hunt with the hounds** ménager la chèvre et le chou; **the car ran into a tree** la voiture a heurté un arbre (*see also* **run into**); (*fig*) **to ~ behind sb** prendre un retard de plus en plus grand par rapport à qn.

b (*flee*) fuir, se sauver. **to ~ for one's life** se sauver à toutes jambes; **~ for your lives!** sauve-qui-peut!; **~ for it!** sauvez-vous!; *[fox, criminal]* **to ~ to earth** se terrer; **go on then, ~ to mummy!** c'est ça, va (te réfugier) dans les jupes de ta mère!; *see* **cut**.

c (*fig*) **the news ran like wildfire through the crowd** la nouvelle s'est répandue comme une traînée de poudre dans la foule; **a rumour ran through the school** un bruit a couru dans l'école; **this theme ~s through the whole history of art** ce thème se retrouve *or* est présent dans toute l'histoire de l'art; **asthma ~s in the family** l'asthme est héréditaire dans la famille; **it ~s in the family** ça tient *or* c'est de famille; **that tune is ~ning through my head** cet air me trotte* par la tête; **the idea ran through my head that ...** il m'est venu à l'esprit *or* à l'idée que ...; **the conversation ran on that very subject** la conversation a roulé précisément sur ce sujet; **my thoughts ran on Jenny** je pensais (toujours) à Jenny; **the order ran down the column** l'ordre a couru *or* a été transmis d'un bout de la colonne à l'autre; **laughter ran round the room** le rire a gagné toute la salle; **a ripple of fear ran through the town** la peur a gagné toute la ville; **how does the last sentence ~?** comment la dernière phrase est-elle rédigée?, rappelez-moi la dernière phrase; **so the story ~s** c'est ainsi que l'histoire est racontée; **to be ~ning scared*** avoir la frousse*; (*Pol etc*) **to ~ for President, to ~ for the Presidency** être candidat à la présidence; **he isn't ~ning this time** il n'est pas candidat cette fois-ci; **he won't ~ again** il ne se représentera plus; *see* **re-election**.

d (*become etc*) **to ~ dry** *[river]* se tarir, être à sec; *[resources etc]* s'épuiser; **my pen's ~ dry** je n'ai plus d'encre; **he ran dry of ideas** il s'est trouvé à court d'idées; **supplies are ~ning short** *or* **low** les provisions s'épuisent *or* commencent à manquer *or* tirent à leur fin; **to ~ short of sth** se trouver à court de qch, venir à manquer de qch; **to ~ riot** *[people, imagination]* être déchaîné; *[vegetation]* pousser follement; **to ~ to fat** engraisser, prendre de la graisse; **he ~s to sentiment in some of his books** dans quelques-uns de ses livres il a tendance à être sentimental *or* il donne dans le sentimental (*pej*); **to ~ wild** *[person]* faire le fou (*f* la folle)*; *[children]* être déchaîné; *[animals]* courir en liberté; *[plants, garden]* retourner à l'état sauvage; *see* **seed**.

e (*move*) filer; *[drawer, curtains]* glisser. **the rope ran through his fingers** la corde lui a filé entre les doigts; (*fig*) **money simply ~s through his fingers** l'argent lui fond entre les mains *or* lui file entre les doigts; **the bed ~s on rollers** le lit a des roulettes; **the drawer ~s smoothly** le tiroir glisse facilement; **this zip doesn't ~ well** cette fermeture éclair ne joue pas bien *or* accroche.

f (*flow*) couler; (*drip*) dégoutter; *[river, tears, tap]* couler; *[pen]* fuir, couler; *[sore, abscess]* suppurer; *[butter]* fondre; *[cheese]* couler; *[colour, dye]* s'étaler, se mélanger (à une couleur voisine), baver; (*in washing*) déteindre; *[ink]* baver, faire des bavures. **my ice cream is ~ning** ma glace fond *or* coule; **the river ~s for 30 km** la rivière a 30 km de long; **the river ~s between wooded banks** la rivière coule entre des berges boisées; **rivers ~ into the sea** les fleuves se jettent dans la mer; **the street ~s into the square** la rue débouche dans la place; **to ~ high** *[river]* être haut, couler à pleins bords; *[sea]* être gros (*f* grosse); (*fig*) **feelings were ~ning high** les passions étaient exacerbées; **prices are ~ning high** les prix sont très hauts en ce moment; **the game was ~ning against them** ils étaient en train de perdre la partie, ça allait mal pour eux; **a heavy sea was ~ning** la mer était très forte; **where the tide is ~ning strongly** là où la marée monte (*or* descend) très vite; **to leave a tap ~ning** laisser un robinet ouvert; **your bath is ~ning now** votre bain est en train de couler; **the milk ran all over the floor** le lait s'est répandu sur le sol; **the floor was ~ning with water** le plancher était inondé (d'eau); **the walls were ~ning with moisture** les murs ruisselaient d'humidité; **the streets were ~ning with blood** les rues ruisselaient de sang; **his face was ~ning with sweat** sa figure ruisselait de sueur; **tears ran down her cheeks** les larmes coulaient le long de ses joues; **his eyes are ~ning** il a les yeux qui coulent *or* pleurent; **his nose was ~ning** il avait le nez qui coulait; (*fig*) **his blood ran cold** son sang s'est glacé *or* s'est figé dans ses veines.

g (*extend, continue*) *[play]* tenir l'affiche, se jouer; *[film]* passer; *[contract]* valoir, être valide; (*Fin*) *[interest]* courir. **the play has been ~ning for a year** la pièce tient l'affiche *or* se joue depuis un an; **this contract has 10 months to ~** ce contrat expire dans 10 mois *or* vaut (encore) pour 10 mois; (*Jur*) **the two sentences to ~ concurrently/consecutively** avec/sans confusion des deux peines; (*Rad, TV*) **the programme ran for an extra 10 minutes** le programme a duré dix minutes de plus que prévu; (*TV, Rad*) **our scheduled programmes are ~ning a few minutes late/a bit over time** nos programmes auront quelques minutes de retard/un léger retard sur l'horaire prévu; **the expenditure ~s into thousands of pounds** les dépenses s'élèvent *or* se chiffrent à des milliers de livres; **the book has ~ into 3 editions** on a publié 3 éditions de ce livre; **the poem ~s (in)to several hundred lines** le poème comprend plusieurs centaines de vers; **I can't ~ to a new car** je ne peux pas m'offrir *or* me payer* une nouvelle voiture; **the funds won't ~ to a party at the end of term** les fonds ne permettent pas d'organiser une soirée à la fin du trimestre.

h (*Naut*) **to ~ before the wind** courir vent arrière; **to ~ ashore** *or* **aground** s'échouer, se jeter à la côte; **to ~ on the rocks** donner *or* se jeter sur les rochers; **to ~ into port** entrer au port; **to ~ foul of another ship** entrer en collision avec *or* aborder un autre navire; (*fig*) **to ~ foul of sb** se disputer avec qn, indisposer qn contre soi.

i *[bus, train, coach, ferryboat]* faire le service. **this train ~s between London and Manchester** ce train fait le service Londres-Manchester *or* entre Londres et Manchester; **the buses ~ once an hour** les autobus passent toutes les heures; **the buses aren't ~ning today** il n'y a pas d'autobus *or* les autobus sont supprimés aujourd'hui; **the buses are ~ning early/late/to** *or* **on time** les bus sont en avance/en retard/à l'heure; **that train doesn't ~ on Sundays** ce train est supprimé le dimanche; **there are no trains ~ning on Christmas Day** le service des trains est suspendu le jour de Noël; **there are no trains ~ning to Birmingham** il n'y a pas de trains en direction de Birmingham.

j (*function*) *[machine]* marcher, fonctionner; *[factory]* travailler, marcher; *[wheel]* tourner. **the car is ~ning smoothly** la voiture marche bien; **you mustn't leave the engine ~ning** il ne faut pas laisser tourner le moteur; **this car ~s on diesel** cette voiture marche au gas-oil; **the radio ~s off the mains/off batteries** cette radio marche sur le secteur/sur piles; (*fig*) **things are ~ning smoothly/badly for them** tout va *or* marche bien/mal pour eux.

k (*pass*) *[road, river etc]* passer (*through* à travers); *[mountain range]* s'étendre; *[plants, stems etc]* pousser. **the road ~s past our house** la route passe devant notre maison; **the road ~s right into town** la route débouche en plein centre de la ville; **the main road ~s north and south** la route principale va du nord au sud; **he has a scar ~ning across his chest** il a une cicatrice en travers de la poitrine; **a wall ~s round the garden** un mur entoure le jardin; **the river ~s through the valley** la rivière traverse la vallée.

l *[stockings]* filer; *[knitting]* se démailler.

4 vt a (*gen*) courir. **he ~s 3 km every day** il fait 3 km de course à pied tous les jours; **he ran 2 km non-stop** il a couru pendant 2 km sans s'arrêter; **he ran the distance in under half an hour** il a couvert la distance en moins d'une demi-heure; **to ~ the 100 metres** courir le 100 mètres; **to ~ a race** courir dans une épreuve, participer à une épreuve de course; **you ran a good race** vous avez fait une excellente course; **the first race will be ~ at 2 o'clock** la première épreuve se courra à 2 heures; **if I saw a ghost I'd ~ a mile*** si je voyais un fantôme je prendrais mes jambes à mon cou; **this horse will ~ the Grand Prix** ce cheval va courir (dans) le Grand Prix; **to ~ errands** *or* **messages** faire des commissions *or* des courses; *[child, dog]* **to ~ the streets** traîner dans les rues; **to ~ a blockade** forcer un blocus; (*US*) **to ~ a red** *or* **a stop-light** brûler *or* griller un feu rouge; **they ran the rapids** ils ont franchi les rapides; (*fig*) **to ~ sb close** serrer qn de près; **you're ~ning things a bit close!*** *or* **fine!*** ça va être juste!, tu calcules un peu juste!; **to let events ~ their course** laisser les événements suivre leur cours; **the disease ran its course** la maladie a suivi son cours normal *or* son évolution normale; **to ~ risks** courir des risques; **you're ~ning the risk of being arrested** *or* **of arrest** vous risquez de vous faire arrêter; **to ~ a temperature** *or* **a fever** avoir *or* faire de la température, avoir de la fièvre; **he was ~ning a high temperature** il avait une forte fièvre; **she ran the car into a tree** elle a percuté *or* heurté un arbre, elle est rentrée* dans un arbre (avec sa voiture); *see* **gauntlet**.

b (*chase, hunt*) *fox, deer* chasser; (*make run*) *person, animal* faire courir; (*Sport*) *horse* faire courir, engager; (*Pol*) *candidate* poser *or* appuyer la candidature de. **the party is ~ning 100 candidates this year** le parti présente 100 candidats (aux élections) cette année; **he ran the quotation to earth in "Hamlet"** il a fini par dénicher la citation dans "Hamlet"; **to ~ a horse in the Derby** engager *or* faire courir un cheval dans le Derby; **the sheriff ran him out of town** le shérif l'a chassé de la ville; **they ran him out of the house** ils l'ont saisi et l'ont chassé de la maison; **to ~ sb off his feet*** fatiguer *or* éreinter qn; **she is absolutely ~ off her feet*** elle est débordée, elle n'en peut plus, elle ne sait plus où donner de la tête; (*fig*) **that will ~ him into trouble** ça lui créera des ennuis; **that will ~ you into a lot of expense** ça va vous causer de grandes dépenses; **to ~ sb into debt** forcer qn à s'endetter; *see* **earth**.

c (*transport*) *person* conduire (en voiture *or* en bateau); *thing* transporter (en voiture *or* en bateau); (*smuggle*) *guns, whisky* passer en contrebande, faire la contrebande de. **he ran her home** il l'a ramenée chez elle (en voiture); **to ~ sb into town** conduire qn en ville; **I'll ~ your luggage to the station** j'emporterai vos bagages à la gare en voiture; **he was ~ning guns to the island** il faisait passer *or* passait des fusils en contrebande dans l'île.

d (*operate etc*) *machine* faire marcher, faire aller, faire fonctionner; (*Comput*) *program* exécuter. **to ~ a radio off the mains**

faire marcher une radio sur le secteur; **to ~ a machine by compressed air** actionner une machine par air comprimé, faire marcher une machine à l'air comprimé; **to ~ an engine on gas** faire fonctionner un moteur au gaz; **to ~ a lorry on diesel** faire marcher un camion au gas-oil; **I can't afford to ~ a car** je ne peux pas me permettre d'avoir une voiture; **he ~s a Rolls** il a une Rolls; **this car is very cheap to ~** cette voiture est très économique; **to ~ the car into/out of the garage** rentrer la voiture au/sortir la voiture du garage; **to ~ a boat ashore** mettre un bateau à la côte; *see* **ground**.

e (*organize, manage*) *business, company, organization, school* diriger, administrer; *shop, mine* diriger, faire marcher; *hotel, club* tenir, diriger; *newspaper* éditer, gérer, administrer; *competition* organiser; *public transport* organiser (le service de). **they ~ trains to London every hour** il y a un train pour Londres toutes les heures; **the company ~s extra buses at rush hours** la compagnie met en service des autobus supplémentaires aux heures de pointe; **the school is ~ning courses for foreign students** le collège organise des cours pour les étudiants étrangers; **he is ~ning the courses for them** il leur fait des cours; **to ~ a house** tenir une maison; **a house which is easy to ~** une maison facile à tenir *or* entretenir; **who will ~ your house now?** qui va tenir votre maison *or* votre ménage maintenant?; **I want to ~ my own life** je veux être maître de ma vie *or* de mes décisions; **she's the one who really ~s everything** en réalité c'est elle qui dirige tout *or* fait tout marcher; (*fig*) **I'm ~ning this show!*** c'est moi qui fais marcher la baraque!*; (*fig*) **he ~s the whole show*** c'est lui qui fait la loi.

f (*put, move casually or quickly*) **to ~ one's hand over sth** passer *or* promener la main sur qch; **to ~ one's fingers over the piano keys** faire glisser ses doigts sur les touches *or* sur le clavier; **to ~ one's finger down a list** suivre une liste du doigt; **to ~ one's fingers through one's hair** se passer la main dans les cheveux; **to ~ a comb through one's hair** se passer un peigne dans les cheveux, se donner un coup de peigne; **to ~ one's eye over a page** jeter un coup d'œil sur une page; **he ran the vacuum cleaner over the carpet** il a passé rapidement le tapis à l'aspirateur; **she ran her pencil through the word** elle a barré le mot d'un coup de crayon; **she ran a line of stitches along the hem** elle a fait une série de points le long de l'ourlet; **to ~ a rope through a ring** enfiler *or* faire passer une corde dans un anneau; **to ~ a piece of elastic through the waist of a dress** faire passer un élastique dans la ceinture d'une robe; **to ~ a rope round a tree** passer une corde autour d'un arbre; **to ~ a fence round a garden** entourer un jardin d'une barrière; **to ~ a pipe into a room** faire passer un tuyau *or* amener un tuyau dans une pièce.

g (*issue*) (*Press*) publier, imprimer, faire paraître; (*Cine*) présenter, donner; (*Comm*) vendre, mettre en vente. **the paper ran a series of articles on the housing situation** le journal a publié *or* fait paraître une série d'articles sur la crise du logement; **the papers ran the story on the front page** les journaux ont imprimé *or* publié l'article en première page; **the supermarket is ~ning a new line in soap powder** le supermarché est en train de lancer une nouvelle lessive.

h (*cause to flow*) faire couler. **to ~ water into a bath** faire couler de l'eau dans une baignoire; **I'll ~ you a bath** je vais te faire couler un bain; **he ~s his words together** il mange ses mots.

►**run about** 1 vi (*gen*) courir çà et là; (*looking for sb/sth, working etc*) courir dans tous les sens. **the children were running about all over the house** les enfants couraient partout dans la maison; (*fig*) **she has been running about with him for several months*** elle sort avec lui depuis plusieurs mois. 2 **runabout** n, adj *see* **run 2**.

►**run across** 1 vi traverser en courant. 2 vt fus (*meet*) *person* rencontrer par hasard, tomber sur; (*find*) *object* trouver par hasard; *quotation, reference* trouver *or* rencontrer par hasard.

►**run after** vt fus courir après. (*fig*) **she runs after everything in trousers*** elle est très coureuse; (*fig*) **I'm not going to spend my days running after you!** je ne suis pas ton valet de chambre!* *or* ta bonne!*

►**run along** vi courir; (*go away*) s'en aller. **run along!** sauvez-vous!, filez!*

►**run around** 1 vi = **run about 1.** 2 **run-around** n *see* **run 2**.

►**run at** vt fus (*attack*) se jeter *or* se précipiter sur.

►**run away** 1 vi a partir en courant; (*flee*) *[person]* se sauver, s'enfuir; (*abscond*) décamper; *[horse]* s'emballer. **to run away from home** s'enfuir (de chez soi), faire une fugue; **don't run away, I need your advice** ne te sauve pas, j'ai besoin d'un conseil; **run away and play!** va jouer (et fiche-moi la paix*)!; (*elope*) **to run away with sb** s'enfuir avec qn; **she ran away with another man** elle est partie *or* elle s'est enfuie avec un autre homme; (*steal*) **he ran away with the funds** il s'est sauvé* *or* enfui avec les fonds; (*fig*) **don't run away with the idea that** ... n'allez pas vous mettre dans la tête que ...; (*fig*) **don't let your emotions run away with you** ne te laisse pas envahir par tes émotions; (*fig*) **he lets his temper run away with him** il ne sait pas se contrôler *or* se dominer.

b *[water]* s'écouler. **he let the bath water run away** il a laissé la baignoire se vider.

2 vt sep *water* laisser s'écouler.

3 **runaway** n, adj *see* **runaway**.

►**run away with** vt fus (*use up*) *funds, money, resources* épuiser; (*Sport etc: win easily*) *race* gagner dans un fauteuil*; *prize* gagner haut la main; *see also* **run away 1a**.

►**run back** 1 vi revenir *or* retourner *or* rentrer en courant. 2 vt sep a *person* ramener (en voiture). b (*rewind*) *tape, film* rembobiner.

►**run down** 1 vi a *[person]* descendre en courant.

b *[watch etc]* s'arrêter (faute d'être remonté); *[battery]* se décharger.

2 vt sep a (*Aut*) (*knock over*) renverser; (*run over*) écraser.

b (*Naut*) *ship* heurter *or* aborder par l'avant *or* par l'étrave; (*in battle*) éperonner.

c (*limit, reduce*) *production* restreindre de plus en plus; *factory* restreindre la production de; *shop* réduire peu à peu l'ampleur de. (*Med*) **to be run down** être fatigué *or* surmené; **I feel a little run down** je me sens à plat*, je suis mal fichu*.

d (*: *disparage*) *person* décrier, dénigrer, déblatérer* contre; *thing* éreinter, démolir*; *action* critiquer, dénigrer.

e (*pursue and capture*) *criminal* découvrir la cachette de; *stag etc* mettre aux abois.

f *list, page etc* parcourir.

3 **rundown** n *see* **rundown**.

►**run in** 1 vi entrer en courant; (*: *call*) passer. **I'll run in and see you tomorrow*** je passerai vous voir demain, je ferai un saut* chez vous demain. 2 vt sep a (*Brit*) *car* roder. (*Aut*) **"running in, please pass"** "en rodage". b (*: *arrest*) emmener au poste. 3 **run-in** n *see* **run 2**.

►**run into** vt fus a (*meet*) rencontrer par hasard, tomber sur. (*fig*) **to run into difficulties** *or* **trouble** se heurter à des difficultés; **to run into danger** se trouver exposé à un danger; **to run into debt** s'endetter; **we've run into a problem** nous nous trouvons devant un problème. b (*merge, overlap*) **the colours are ~ning into each other** les couleurs déteignent les unes sur les autres; **I was so tired, my words began to run into one another** j'étais si fatigué que mes mots commençaient à s'emmêler. c (*amount to*) atteindre, s'élever à, se monter à.

►**run off** 1 vi = **run away 1.** 2 vt sep a = **run away 2.** b *poem, letter* écrire *or* rédiger en vitesse; (*Typ*) tirer. **to run off an article** écrire un article au fil de la plume; **to run off 600 copies** tirer 600 exemplaires. c (*Sport*) **to run off the heats** faire (se) disputer les éliminatoires. 3 **run-off** n *see* **run 2**.

►**run on** 1 vi a continuer de courir; (* *fig: in talking etc*) parler sans arrêt, baratiner‡. **he does run on so** c'est un vrai moulin à paroles; **she ran on at great length about her new house** elle n'arrêtait pas *or* elle n'en finissait pas de parler de sa nouvelle maison; **it ran on for 4 hours** ça a duré quatre bonnes heures. b *[letters, words]* ne pas être séparés, être liés; *[line of writing]* suivre sans alinéa; *[verse]* enjamber; *[time]* passer, s'écouler; *[disease etc]* suivre son cours. 2 vt sep *letters, words* faire suivre sans laisser d'espace; *sentences* faire suivre sans laisser d'alinéa. 3 **run-on** adj *see* **run 2**.

►**run out** 1 vi a *[person]* sortir en courant; *[rope, chain]* se dérouler; *[liquid]* couler. **the pier runs out into the sea** la jetée s'avance dans la mer. b (*come to an end*) *[lease, contract]* expirer; *[supplies]* s'épuiser, venir à manquer; *[period of time]* s'écouler, tirer à sa fin. **my patience is running out** je suis à bout de patience; **when the money runs out** quand il n'y a (*or* aura) plus d'argent, quand l'argent est (*or* sera) épuisé; (*fig*) **their luck ran out** la chance les a lâchés *or* abandonnés. 2 vt sep *rope, chain* laisser filer.

►**run out off** vt fus *supplies, money* manquer de, être à court de; *patience* être à bout de; *time* manquer de.

►**run out on*** vt fus *boyfriend, girlfriend* laisser tomber*.

►**run over** 1 vi a (*overflow*) *[liquid, container]* déborder. (*Rad, TV etc*) **the play ran over by 10 minutes** la pièce a duré dix minutes de plus que prévu; (*Rad, TV etc*) **we're running over** nous avons pris du retard.

b (*go briefly*) passer, faire un saut. **she ran over to her neighbour's** elle a fait un saut (jusque) chez sa voisine, elle est passé chez sa voisine.

2 vt fus a (*recapitulate*) *story, part in play* repasser, revoir. **I'll run over your part with you** je vous ferai répéter *or* repasser *or* revoir votre rôle; **let's just run over it again** revoyons *or* reprenons cela encore une fois.

b (*reread*) *notes* jeter un coup d'œil sur, parcourir, revoir.

3 vt sep (*Aut*) *person, animal* écraser.

►**run through** 1 vi passer *or* traverser en courant. 2 vt fus a (*use up*) *fortune* gaspiller, manger. b (*read quickly*) *notes, text* parcourir, jeter un coup d'œil sur. c (*rehearse*) *play* (faire) répéter; (*recapitulate*) résumer, reprendre. **let's run through it again** reprenons cela (encore une fois); **if I may just run through the principal points once more?** puis-je reprendre *or* rappeler *or* récapituler les points principaux? 3 vt sep a **to run sb through (with a sword)** passer une épée à travers le corps de qn. b (*Comput*) *data* passer (en revue). 4 **run-through** n *see* **run 2**.

►**run up** 1 vi monter en courant. (*fig*) **to run up against difficulties** se heurter à des difficultés. 2 vt sep a *flag* hisser. b *bill, account* laisser accumuler. **to run up a debt** s'endetter (*of* de). c (*: *sew quickly*) fabriquer*. 3 **run-up** n *see* **run 2**.

runaway [ˈrʌnəweɪ] 1 n (*gen*) fuyard *m*, fugitif *m*, -ive *f*; (*teenager, pupil etc*) fugueur *m*, -euse *f*. 2 adj *slave, person* fugitif; *horse* emballé; *car, railway truck* fou (*f* folle). ~ **wedding** mariage clandestin; **the ~ couple** le couple clandestin, les amants; (*Fin*) ~ **inflation** inflation galopante; (*fig*) ~ **success** succès *m* à tout casser*, succès monstre*; **he had a ~ victory** il a remporté une victoire haut la main.

rundown [ˈrʌndaʊn] **n** a (*gen*) réduction *f*, diminution *f*; *[industry, business]* réductions *fpl* délibérées. **there will be a ~ of staff** il y aura une réduction de personnel. b **to give sb a ~ on sth*** mettre qn au courant *or* au parfum‡ de qch.

rune [ruːn] **n** rune *f*.

rung¹ [rʌŋ] **ptp of ring²**.

rung² [rʌŋ] **n** *[ladder]* barreau *m*, échelon *m*, traverse *f*; *[chair]* bâton *m*, barreau.

runic [ˈruːnɪk] **adj** runique.

runnel [ˈrʌnl] **n** (*brook*) ruisseau *m*; (*gutter*) rigole *f*.

runner [ˈrʌnəʳ] 1 **n** a (*athlete*) coureur *m*; (*horse*) partant *m*; (*messenger*) messager *m*, courrier *m*; (*smuggler*) contrebandier *m*. (*Brit Hist*) **Bow Street R~** sergent *m* (de ville); *see* **blockade, gun.** b (*sliding part*) *[sledge]* patin *m*; *[skate]* lame *f*; *[turbine]* couronne *f* mobile; *[drawer]* coulisseau *m*; *[car seat, door etc]* glissière *f*; *[curtain]* suspendeur *m*. c (*table-~*) chemin *m* de table; (*hall carpet*) chemin de couloir; (*stair carpet*) chemin d'escalier. d (*Bot: plant*) coulant *m*, stolon *m*. 2 **comp** ►**runner bean** (*Brit*) haricot *m* à rames ►**runner-up** (**pl ~s-~**) (*Scol, Sport etc*) second(e) *m(f)*.

running [ˈrʌnɪŋ] 1 **n** a (*action: in race etc*) course *f*. **to make the ~** (*Sport*) faire le lièvre; (*fig*) (*in work*) mener la course; (*in relationship*) prendre l'initiative; **to be in the ~** avoir des chances de réussir; **to be out of the ~*** ne plus être dans la course, n'avoir aucune chance de réussir, ne plus compter; **to be in the ~ for promotion/for the job** être sur les rangs pour obtenir de l'avancement/pour avoir le poste.

b (*NonC: functioning*) *[machine]* marche *f*, fonctionnement *m*; *[train]* marche.

c (*NonC: see* **run 4e**) direction *f*; administration *f*; organisation *f*.

d (*NonC: smuggling*) contrebande *f*; *see* **gun**.

2 **adj**: ~ **jump** saut *m* avec élan; **go and take a ~ jump!**‡ va te faire cuire un œuf!‡; ~ **kick** coup de pied donné en courant; (*fig*) ~ **accompaniment** accompagnement soutenu; (*Fin*) ~ **account** compte courant (*entre banques etc*); **to have** *or* **to keep a ~ account with sb** être en compte avec qn; ~ **battle** (*lit*) *combat où l'un des adversaires est en retraite;* (*fig*) lutte continuelle; **to keep up a ~ battle** (*Aviat, Naut*) soutenir *or* appuyer la chasse; (*fig*) être en lutte continuelle (*with* avec); ~ **argument/disagreement** dispute *f* continuelle/désaccord *m* perpétuel; (*Naut*) ~ **bowline** laguis *m*; (*Rad, TV*) ~ **commentary** commentaire suivi; (*fig*) **she gave us a ~ commentary on what was going on** elle nous a fait un commentaire détaillé sur ce qui se passait; (*Mil*) ~ **fire** feu roulant; ~ **hand** écriture cursive; ~ **knot** nœud coulant; (*Sewing*) ~ **stitch** point *m* de devant; (*Typ*) ~ **title** titre courant; **a ~ stream,** ~ **water** un cours d'eau; ~ **water (in every room)** eau courante (dans toutes les chambres); ~ **sore** (*Med*) plaie *f* qui suppure; (*fig*) véritable plaie; (*Med*) ~ **cold** rhume *m* de cerveau; ~ **tap** robinet *m* qui coule.

3 **comp** ►**running board** *[car, train]* marchepied *m* ►**running costs** frais *mpl* d'exploitation; **the running costs of the car/the central heating are high** la voiture/le chauffage central revient cher ►**running mate:** (*US Pol*) **his running mate** celui (*or* celle) qu'il a choisi(e) comme candidat(e) à la vice-présidence ►**running order: in running order** en état de marche ►**running repairs** réparations *fpl* mineures ►**running shoe** chaussure *f* de course ►**running track** (*Sport*) piste *f*.

4 **adv** de suite. **4 days/times** ~ 4 jours/fois de suite.

runny [ˈrʌnɪ] **adj** *substance* liquide, qui coule, qui a tendance à couler; *omelette* baveux; *nose, eyes* qui coule.

runt [rʌnt] **n** (*animal*) avorton *m*; (*pej: person*) nabot *m*, avorton. **a little ~ of a man** un bonhomme tout riquiqui*.

rupee [ruːˈpiː] **n** roupie *f*.

rupture [ˈrʌptʃəʳ] 1 **n** (*lit, fig*) rupture *f*; (*Med *: hernia*) hernie *f*. 2 **vt** rompre. (*Med*) **to ~ o.s.** se donner une hernie; **~d appendix** appendice *m* rompu. 3 **vi** se rompre.

rural [ˈrʊərəl] **adj** *economy, population* rural; *tranquillity, scenery* rural, agreste; *life* rural, champêtre. (*Brit Rel*) ~ **dean** doyen rural; ~ **depopulation** exode rural; (*Brit*) ~ **district council** conseil *m* municipal rural.

ruse [ruːz] **n** ruse *f*, stratagème *m*.

rush¹ [rʌʃ] 1 **n** a (*rapid movement*) course précipitée, ruée *f*; *[crowd]* ruée, bousculade *f*, rush *m*; (*Mil: attack*) bond *m*, assaut *m*. **he was caught in the ~ for the door** il a été pris dans la ruée vers la porte; **it got lost in the ~** ça s'est perdu dans la bousculade *or* dans la confusion; **to make a ~ at** se précipiter sur; **there was a ~ for the empty seats** il y a eu une ruée vers les places libres, on s'est rué vers *or* sur les places libres; **gold ~** ruée vers l'or; (*Comm*) **there's a ~ on matches** on se rue sur les allumettes; **we have a ~ on in the office just now** c'est le coup de feu en ce moment au bureau; **the Christmas ~** la bousculade des fêtes de fin d'année; **we've had a ~ of orders** on nous a submergés de commandes; **a ~ of warm air** une bouffée d'air tiède; **there was a ~ of water** l'eau a jailli; **he had a ~ of blood to the head** il a eu un coup de sang.

b (*hurry*) hâte *f*. **the ~ of city life** le rythme effréné de la vie urbaine; **to be in a ~** être extrêmement pressé; **I had a ~ to get here in time** j'ai dû me dépêcher pour arriver à l'heure; **I did it in a ~** je l'ai fait à toute vitesse *or* en quatrième vitesse*; **what's all the ~?** pourquoi est-ce que c'est si pressé?; **is there any ~ for this?** est-ce que c'est pressé? *or* urgent?; **it all happened in a ~** tout est arrivé *or* tout s'est passé très vite.

c (*Cine*) (projection *f* d')essai *m*.

d (*US Drugs sl*) flash *m* (*sl*).

e (*US Univ: of fraternity etc*) campagne *f* de recrutement.

2 **comp** ►**rush hour** heures *fpl* de pointe *or* d'affluence ►**rush-hour traffic** circulation *f* des heures de pointe ►**rush job** travail *m* d'urgence; **that was a rush job** c'était fait à la va-vite* ►**rush order** (*Comm*) commande pressée *or* urgente.

3 **vi** *[person]* se précipiter, s'élancer, se ruer; *[car]* foncer. **the train went ~ing into the tunnel** le train est entré à toute vitesse dans le tunnel; **they ~ed to help her** ils se sont précipités pour l'aider; **I ~ed to her side** je me suis précipité à ses côtés; (*to offer encouragement etc*) je me suis précipité pour être avec elle; **I'm ~ing to finish it** je me presse *or* je me dépêche pour en avoir fini; **to ~ through** *book* lire à la hâte *or* en diagonale; *meal* prendre sur le pouce*; *museum* visiter au pas de course; *town* traverser à toute vitesse; *work* expédier; **to ~ in/out/back** *etc* entrer/sortir/rentrer *etc* précipitamment *or* à toute vitesse (*see also* **rush in, rush out**); **to ~ to the attack** se jeter *or* se ruer à l'attaque; **to ~ to conclusions** conclure à la légère; **the blood ~ed to his face** le sang lui est monté au visage; **memories ~ed into his mind** des souvenirs lui affluèrent à l'esprit; (*fig*) **he ~ed into marriage** il s'est marié hâtivement *or* à la hâte; **the wind ~ed through the stable** le vent s'engouffrait dans l'écurie; **a torrent of water ~ed down the slope** un véritable torrent a dévalé la pente; *see* **headlong**.

4 **vt** a (*cause to move quickly*) entraîner *or* pousser vivement. **to ~ sb to hospital** transporter qn d'urgence à l'hôpital; **they ~ed more troops to the front** ils ont envoyé *or* expédié d'urgence des troupes fraîches sur le front; **they ~ed him out of the room** ils l'ont fait sortir précipitamment *or* en toute hâte de la pièce; **I don't want to ~ you** je ne voudrais pas vous bousculer; **don't ~ me!** laissez-moi le temps de souffler!; **to be ~ed off one's feet** être débordé; **to ~ sb off his feet** ne pas laisser à qn le temps de souffler; **to ~ sb into a decision** forcer *or* obliger qn à prendre une décision à la hâte; **to ~ sb into doing sth** forcer *or* obliger qn à faire qch à la hâte; **they ~ed the bill through Parliament** ils ont fait voter la loi à la hâte.

b (*take by storm*) (*Mil*) *town, position* prendre d'assaut; *fence, barrier* franchir (sur son élan). **her admirers ~ed the stage** ses admirateurs ont envahi la scène; **the mob ~ed the line of policemen** la foule s'est élancée contre le cordon de police.

c (*do hurriedly*) *job, task* dépêcher; *order* exécuter d'urgence. (*Comm*) **"please ~ me 3 tickets"** "envoyez-moi de toute urgence 3 billets".

d (‡) (*charge*) faire payer; (*swindle*) faire payer un prix exorbitant à, estamper*. **how much were you ~ed for it?** combien on te l'a fait payer?; **you really WERE ~ed for that!** tu t'es vraiment fait estamper* pour ça!

e (*US Univ: of fraternity etc*) recruter.

►**rush about, rush around** **vi** courir çà et là.

►**rush at** **vt fus** se jeter sur, se ruer sur; *enemy* se ruer sur, fondre sur. **don't rush at the job, take it slowly** ne fais pas ça trop vite, prends ton temps.

►**rush down** **vi** *[person]* descendre précipitamment; *[stream]* dévaler.

►**rush in** **vi** (*lit*) entrer précipitamment *or* à toute vitesse; (*fig*) se précipiter (*to* pour); *see also* **rush 3**.

►**rush out** 1 **vi** sortir précipitamment *or* à toute vitesse. 2 **vt sep** (*produce quickly*) *goods* sortir rapidement. (*deliver*) **we'll rush it out to you right away** nous vous le livrerons directement dans les plus brefs délais.

►**rush through** **vt sep** (*Comm*) *order* exécuter d'urgence; *goods, supplies* envoyer *or* faire parvenir de toute urgence. **they rushed medical supplies through to him** on lui a fait parvenir des médicaments de toute urgence; *see also* **rush 3**.

►**rush up** 1 **vi** (*arrive*) accourir. 2 **vt sep** *help, reinforcements* faire parvenir *or* (faire) envoyer d'urgence (*to* à).

rush² [rʌʃ] 1 **n** (*Bot*) jonc *m*; (*for chair*) jonc, paille *f*. 2 **comp** ►**rush light** chandelle *f* à mèche de jonc ►**rush mat** ≃ tapis *m* tressé ►**rush matting** (*NonC*) ≃ tapis *m* tressé.

rushed [rʌʃt] **adj** *work* fait à la va-vite, bâclé.

rusk [rʌsk] **n** biscotte *f*.

russet [ˈrʌsɪt] 1 **n** a (*colour*) couleur *f* feuille-morte *inv*, brun roux *inv*. b (*apple*) reinette grise. 2 **adj** feuille-morte *inv*, brun roux *inv*.

Russia [ˈrʌʃə] **n** Russie *f*.

Russian [ˈrʌʃən] 1 **adj** (*gen*) russe; *teacher* de russe. (*Culin*) ~ **dressing** sauce *f* rouge relevée (*pour la salade*); **R~ salad** salade *f* russe; ~ **roulette** roulette *f* russe; ~ **S.S.R.** R.S.S. *f* de Russie. 2 **n** a Russe *mf*. b (*Ling*) russe *m*.

rust [rʌst] 1 **n** (*on metal; also Bot*) rouille *f*; (*colour*) couleur *f* rouille, roux *m*. 2 **comp** ►**rust(-coloured)** (couleur) rouille *inv*, roux (*f* rousse) ►**rustproof** *etc see* **rustproof** *etc* ►**rust-resistant** = **rustproof 1.** 3 **vt** (*lit, fig*) rouiller. 4 **vi** (*lit, fig*) se rouiller.

►**rust in vi** *[screw]* se rouiller dans son trou.

►**rust up vi** se rouiller.

rustic ['rʌstɪk] 1 **n** campagnard(e) *m(f)*, paysan(ne) *m(f)*, rustaud(e) *m(f)* (*pej*), rustre *m* (*pej*). 2 **adj** *scene* rustique, champêtre; *bench, charm, simplicity* rustique.

rusticate ['rʌstɪkeɪt] 1 **vi** habiter la campagne. 2 **vt** (*Brit Univ*) exclure (temporairement).

rustiness ['rʌstɪnɪs] **n** rouillure *f*, rouille *f*.

rustle ['rʌsl] 1 **n** *[leaves]* bruissement *m*; *[silk, skirts]* bruissement, frou-frou *m*; *[papers]* froissement *m*. 2 **vi** *[leaves, wind]* bruire; *[papers]* produire un froissement *or* un bruissement; *[clothes, skirt]* faire frou-frou. **she ~d into the room** elle est entrée en froufroutant dans la pièce; **something ~d in the cupboard** il y a eu un froissement *or* un bruissement dans le placard. 3 **vt** a *leaves* faire bruire; *paper* froisser; *programme* agiter avec un bruissement; *petticoat, skirt* faire froufrouter. b (*esp US: steal*) *cattle* voler.

►**rustle up* vt sep** se débrouiller* pour trouver (*or* faire), préparer (à la hâte). **can you rustle up a cup of coffee?** tu voudrais me (*or* nous *etc*) donner un café en vitesse?

rustler ['rʌsləʳ] **n** a (*esp US: cattle thief*) voleur *m* de bétail. b (*US *: energetic person*) type* *m* énergique *or* expéditif.

rustling ['rʌslɪŋ] **n** a (*cattle theft*) vol *m* de bétail. b = **rustle 1.**

rustproof ['rʌstpru:f] 1 **adj** *metal, alloy* inoxydable, qui ne rouille pas; *paint, treatment* antirouille, anticorrosion; *bodywork* traité contre la rouille *or* la corrosion. 2 **vt** traiter contre la rouille *or* la corrosion.

rustproofing ['rʌstpru:fɪŋ] **n** traitement *m* antirouille *or* anticorrosion.

rusty ['rʌstɪ] **adj** (*lit, fig*) rouillé. (*lit*) **to get** *or* **go ~** se rouiller; (*fig*) **my English is ~** mon anglais est un peu rouillé.

rut¹ [rʌt] (*Zool*) 1 **n** rut *m*. 2 **vi** être en rut. **~ting season** saison *f* du rut.

rut² [rʌt] 1 **n** (*in track, path*) ornière *f*; (*fig*) routine *f*, ornière. (*fig*) **to be in** *or* **to get into a ~** *[person]* suivre l'ornière, s'encroûter; *[mind]* devenir routinier; (*fig*) **to get out of the ~** sortir de l'ornière. 2 **vt** sillonner. **~ted** *road, path* défoncé.

rutabaga [ˌru:tə'beɪgə] **n** (*US*) rutabaga *m*.

Ruth [ru:θ] **n** Ruth *f*.

ruthenium [ru:'θi:nɪəm] **n** ruthénium *m*.

ruthless ['ru:θlɪs] **adj** impitoyable, cruel, sans pitié.

ruthlessly ['ru:θlɪslɪ] **adv** sans pitié, sans merci, impitoyablement.

ruthlessness ['ru:θlɪsnɪs] **n** caractère *m or* nature *f* impitoyable.

RV [ɑ:'vi:] **n** a (*Bible*) (**abbr of Revised Version**) *see* **revise.** b (*US*) (**abbr of recreational vehicle**) camping-car *m*. **~ park** terrain *m* pour camping-cars.

Rwanda [rʊ'ændə] **n** Rwanda *m*.

rye [raɪ] 1 **n** a (*grain*) seigle *m*. b (*US*) = **~ whisky, ~ bread.** 2 **comp** ►**rye bread** pain *m* de seigle ►**ryegrass** ivraie *f* vivace, ray-grass *m* ►**rye whisky** whisky *m* à base de seigle.

S

S, s [es] n a (*letter*) S, s *m*. **S for sugar** ≃ S comme Suzanne. b (**abbr of south**) S. c **S** (*Rel*) (**abbr of Saint**) St(e). d **S** (**abbr of small**) (taille *f*) S *m*.

SA [es'eɪ] n (**abbr of South America, South Africa, South Australia**) *see* **south**.

Saar [zɑːʳ] n (*river, region*) **the** ~ la Sarre.

sabbatarian [ˌsæbə'tɛərɪən] 1 n (*Christian*) partisan(e) *m(f)* de l'observance stricte du dimanche; (*Jew*) personne *f* qui observe le sabbat. 2 adj (*Jewish Rel*) de l'observance du sabbat.

Sabbath ['sæbəθ] n (*Jewish*) sabbat *m*; (†: *Sunday*) dimanche *m*. **to keep/break the** ~ observer/violer le sabbat *or* le dimanche; **(witches') s**~ sabbat.

sabbatical [sə'bætɪkəl] adj sabbatique. (*Univ*) ~ **(year)** année *f* sabbatique.

saber ['seɪbəʳ] (*US*) = **sabre**.

sable ['seɪbl] 1 n a (*Zool*) zibeline *f*, martre *f*. b (*Her*) sable *m*. 2 comp a *fur* de zibeline, de martre; *brush* en poil de martre. b (*liter: black*) noir.

sabot ['sæbəʊ] n (*all wood*) sabot *m*; (*leather etc upper*) socque *m*.

sabotage ['sæbətɑːʒ] 1 n (*NonC*) sabotage *m*. **an act of** ~ un sabotage. 2 vt (*lit, fig*) saboter.

saboteur [ˌsæbə'tɜːʳ] n saboteur *m*, -euse *f*.

sabre, (*US*) **saber** ['seɪbəʳ] 1 n sabre *m*. 2 comp ►**sabre rattling** (*fig*) bruits *mpl* de sabre (*fig*) ►**sabre-toothed tiger** smilodon *m*, machairodus *m*.

sac [sæk] n (*Anat, Bio*) sac *m*.

saccharin ['sækərɪn] n (*US*) = **saccharine 2**.

saccharine ['sækəriːn] 1 adj *drink* sacchariné; *product* à la saccharine; *pill, flavour* de saccharine; (*fig*) *smile* mielleux, douceâtre. 2 n saccharine *f*.

sacerdotal [ˌsæsə'dəʊtl] adj sacerdotal.

sachet ['sæʃeɪ] n sachet *m*; *[shampoo]* berlingot *m*.

sack¹ [sæk] 1 n a (*bag*) sac *m*. **coal**~ sac à charbon; ~ **of coal** sac de charbon; **a** ~**(ful) of potatoes** un (plein) sac de pommes de terre; **that dress makes her look like a** ~ **of potatoes** dans cette robe elle ressemble à un sac de pommes de terre.

b (*: *dismissal*) renvoi *m*. **to give sb the** ~ renvoyer qn, mettre *or* flanquer* qn à la porte, virer* qn; **to get the** ~ être renvoyé, être mis *or* flanqué* à la porte, se faire virer*.

c (‡: *bed*) pieu‡ *m*, plumard‡ *m*. **to hit the** ~‡ aller se pieuter‡.

2 comp ►**sackcloth** grosse toile d'emballage, toile à sac; (*Rel*) **sackcloth and ashes** le sac et la cendre; (*fig*) **to be in sackcloth and ashes** être contrit ►**sack dress** robe *f* sac ►**sack race** course *f* en sac.

3 vt (*: *dismiss*) *employee* renvoyer, mettre à la porte, virer*.

►**sack out**‡, **sack up**‡ vi (*US: go to bed*) aller se pieuter‡.

sack² [sæk] 1 n (*plundering*) sac *m*, pillage *m*. 2 vt *town* mettre à sac, saccager, piller.

sack³ [sæk] n (*wine*) vin *m* blanc sec.

sackbut ['sækbʌt] n (*Mus*) saquebute *f*.

sacking¹ [sækɪŋ] n a (*NonC: Tex*) grosse toile d'emballage, toile à sac. b (*: *dismissal*) (*gen*) renvoi *m*. **large scale** ~**s** renvois massifs, largage *m*.

sacking² ['sækɪŋ] n (*plundering*) sac *m*, pillage *m*.

sacra ['sækrə] npl of **sacrum**.

sacral ['seɪkrəl] adj (*Anat*) sacré.

sacrament ['sækrəmənt] n sacrement *m*. **to receive the** ~**s** communier; *see* **blessed**.

sacramental [ˌsækrə'mentl] 1 adj sacramentel. 2 n sacramental *m*.

sacred ['seɪkrɪd] adj a (*Rel*) sacré, saint; *music* sacré, religieux. **the S**~ **Heart** le Sacré-Cœur; **S**~ **History** l'Histoire sainte; **things** ~ **and profane** le sacré et le profane; ~ **writings** livres sacrés. b (*solemn*) *duty* sacré; *moment* solennel, sacré; *promise* sacré, inviolable; (*revered*) sacré. ~ **to the memory of** consacré *or* voué à la mémoire de; **the cow is a** ~ **animal in India** aux Indes la vache est un animal sacré; **to her nothing was** ~ pour elle rien n'était sacré, elle ne respectait rien; **is nothing** ~? vous ne respectez donc rien?; (*fig*) ~ **cow** chose sacro-sainte.

sacrifice ['sækrɪfaɪs] 1 n (*all senses*) sacrifice *m*. (*Rel*) **the** ~ **of the mass** le saint sacrifice (de la messe); (*fig*) **to make great** ~**s** faire *or* consentir de grands sacrifices (*for sb* pour qn, *to do* pour faire); *see* **self**. 2 vt (*all senses*) sacrifier (*to* à). **to** ~ **o.s. for sb** se sacrifier pour qn; (*in small ads etc*) **"cost £25:** ~ **for £5"*** "coût 25 livres: sacrifié à 5 livres".

sacrificial [ˌsækrɪ'fɪʃəl] adj (*gen, also Rel*) sacrificiel. **the** ~ **lamb** l'agneau *m* du sacrifice.

sacrilege ['sækrɪlɪdʒ] n (*lit, fig*) sacrilège *m*.

sacrilegious [ˌsækrɪ'lɪdʒəs] adj sacrilège.

sacrist(an) ['sækrɪst(ən)] n sacristain(e) *m(f)*, sacristine *f*.

sacristy ['sækrɪstɪ] n sacristie *f*.

sacroiliac [ˌseɪkrəʊ'ɪlɪæk] 1 adj sacro-iliaque. 2 n articulation *f* sacro-iliaque.

sacrosanct ['sækrəʊsæŋkt] adj sacro-saint.

sacrum ['sækrəm] n, pl **sacra** sacrum *m*.

SAD [sæd] n (**abbr of seasonal affective disorder**) *see* **seasonal**.

sad [sæd] adj a (*unhappy*) triste (*before n*), affligé; (*depressed*) triste, déprimé; *feeling, look* triste, de tristesse; *smile* triste. ~**-eyed** aux yeux tristes; ~**-faced** au visage triste; **to make sb** ~ attrister qn; **to grow** ~ s'attrister, devenir triste; **he eventually departed a** ~**der and (a) wiser man** finalement il partit ayant appris la dure leçon de l'expérience.

b (*deplorable*) *news, duty, occasion* triste, attristant; *loss* douloureux; *state, condition* triste; *mistake* regrettable, fâcheux. **it's a very** ~ **state of affairs** c'est un triste état de choses *or* un état de choses déplorable; **it's a** ~ **business** c'est une triste affaire, c'est une affaire lamentable; ~ **to say** ... (et) chose triste à dire ...; (*US fig*) ~ **sack*** (*gen*) empoté* *m*; (*Mil*) pauvre troufion* *m*.

sadden ['sædn] vt attrister, rendre triste, affliger.

saddening ['sædnɪŋ] adj affligeant, attristant.

saddle ['sædl] 1 n a *[horse, cycle]* selle *f*. (*lit*) **in the** ~ en selle; **he leapt into the** ~ il sauta en selle; (*fig*) **when he was in the** ~ quand c'était lui qui tenait les rênes; *see* **side** *etc*.

b *[hill]* col *m*.

c (*Culin*) ~ **of lamb** selle *f* d'agneau.

2 comp ►**saddle-backed** ensellé ►**saddlebag** *[horse]* sacoche *f* de selle; *[cycle]* sacoche de bicyclette ►**saddlebow** pommeau *m*, arçon *m* ►**saddlecloth** tapis *m* de selle ►**saddle horse** cheval *m* de selle ►**saddle joint** articulation *f* en selle ►**saddle shoes** (*US*) chaussures *fpl* basses bicolores ►**saddle-sore** meurtri à force d'être en selle ►**saddle-stitched** cousu à longs points.

3 vt a (*also* ~ **up**) *horse* seller.

b (* *fig*) **to** ~ **sb with sth** imposer qch à qn, coller qch à qn*; **I've been** ~**d with organizing the meeting** on m'a collé* l'organisation de la réunion; **we're** ~**d with it** nous voilà avec ça sur les bras.

saddler ['sædləʳ] n sellier *m*.

saddlery ['sædlərɪ] n (*articles, business*) sellerie *f*.

Sadducee ['sædjʊsiː] n Sad(d)ucéen(ne) *m(f)*.

sadism ['seɪdɪzəm] n sadisme *m*.

sadist ['seɪdɪst] adj, n sadique (*mf*).

sadistic [sə'dɪstɪk] adj sadique.

sadistically [sə'dɪstɪkəlɪ] adv sadiquement, avec sadisme.

sadly ['sædlɪ] adv (*unhappily*) *smile, speak* tristement, avec tristesse; (*regrettably*) fâcheusement. **a** ~ **incompetent teacher** un professeur fort incompétent; ~ **lacking in** ... qui manque fortement de ...; **you are** ~ **mistaken** vous vous trompez fort; **it's** ~ **in need of repair** cela a bien besoin d'être réparé.

sadness ['sædnɪs] n (*NonC*) tristesse *f*, mélancolie *f*.

sadomasochism [ˌseɪdəʊ'mæsəkɪzəm] n sadomasochisme *m*.

sadomasochist [ˌseɪdəʊ'mæsəkɪst] n sadomasochiste *mf*.

sadomasochistic [ˌseɪdəʊmæsəˈkɪstɪk] adj sadomasochiste.

s.a.e. [eseɪˈiː] n (abbr of **stamped addressed envelope**) *see* **stamp.**

safari [səˈfɑːrɪ] 1 n safari *m.* **to make a ~, to go** *or* **be on ~** faire un safari. 2 comp ▸**safari hat** chapeau *m* de brousse ▸**safari jacket** saharienne *f* ▸**safari park** réserve *f* ▸**safari shirt** saharienne *f* ▸**safari suit** ensemble *m* saharien.

safe [seɪf] 1 adj a (*not in danger*) *person* hors de danger, en sécurité. **~ and sound** sain et sauf; **to be ~ from** être à l'abri de; **all the passengers are ~** tous les passagers sont sains et saufs *or* sont hors de danger; (*fig*) **no girl is ~ with him** les filles courent toujours un risque avec lui; **you'll be quite ~ here** vous êtes en sécurité ici, vous ne courez aucun danger ici; **his life was not ~** sa vie était en danger *or* menacée; **I don't feel very ~ on this ladder** je ne me sens pas très en sécurité sur cette échelle; **I'll keep it ~ for you** je vais vous le garder en lieu sûr; **a ~ investment** un placement sûr *or* de père de famille; **your reputation is ~** votre réputation est inattaquable *or* ne craint rien; **your secret is ~ with me** avec moi votre secret ne risque rien.

b (*not dangerous*) *toy, animal* sans danger; *method, vehicle* sûr; *action* sans risque, sans danger; *structure, bridge* solide; (*secure*) *hiding place, harbour* sûr; (*prudent*) *action, choice, guess, estimate* prudent, raisonnable. (*Naut*) **a ~ anchorage** un bon mouillage; **is it ~ to come out?** est-ce qu'on peut sortir sans danger?; **it is quite ~ to go alone** on peut y aller seul sans aucun danger; **it's not ~ to go alone** il est dangereux d'y aller tout seul; **is that dog ~?** ce chien n'est pas méchant?; **that dog isn't ~ with children** il ne faut pas laisser les enfants s'approcher du chien; **the ice isn't ~** la glace n'est pas solide *or* ferme; **is the ladder ~ for the children?** est-ce que l'échelle est assez solide pour les enfants?; **this boat is not ~** *or* **not in a ~ condition** ce bateau n'est pas en état; **is the bathing/the beach ~?** la baignade/la plage n'est pas dangereuse?; **~ journey!** bon voyage!; **~ home!*** bon retour!; **in a ~ place** en lieu sûr; **in ~ hands** en mains sûres; **he's ~ in jail for the moment** pour le moment on est tranquille – il est sous les verrous; (*for spy, hunted man etc*) **~ house** lieu *m* sûr; **it's ~ as houses** (*runs no risk*) cela ne court aucun risque; (*offers no risk*) cela ne présente aucun risque; (*Med*) **the ~ period*** la période sans danger; **I'd feel ~r if we waited** je me sentirais plus en sécurité si nous attendions; **it might be ~r to wait** il vaudrait peut-être mieux attendre pour plus de sûreté; **the ~st thing (to do) would be to wait here** le plus sûr serait d'attendre ici; **(just) to be on the ~ side** par précaution, pour plus de sûreté, par acquit de conscience; **it's better to be on the ~ side and take an umbrella** pour être plus sûr il vaut mieux prendre un parapluie; **better ~ than sorry!** mieux vaut être trop prudent!; **he was a ~ choice** *or* **they chose a ~ man for headmaster** en le nommant directeur ils n'ont couru aucun risque; (*Sport*) **a ~ winner** un gagnant certain *or* assuré; **it's a ~ bet he'll win** il gagnera à coup sûr; **he's ~ for re-election** il sera réélu à coup sûr; (*Pol*) **a ~ seat** un siège assuré *or* imperdable; **it is ~ to predict ...** on peut prédire sans risque d'erreur *or* en toute tranquillité ...; *see* **play.**

2 n a (*for money, valuables*) coffre-fort *m.*

b (*for food*) garde-manger *m inv.*

3 comp ▸**safe-blower** perceur *m* de coffre-fort (*qui utilise des explosifs*) ▸**safe-breaker** perceur *m* de coffre-fort ▸**safe-conduct** (*Mil etc*) sauf-conduit *m* ▸**safe-cracker** = **safe-breaker** ▸**safe deposit** (*vault*) dépôt *m* de coffres-forts; (*also:* **safe deposit box**) coffre(-fort) *m* ▸**safeguard** *see* **safeguard** ▸**safekeeping** bonne garde, sécurité *f*; **in safekeeping** sous bonne garde, en sécurité; **I gave it to him for safekeeping, I put it in his safekeeping** je le lui ai donné à garder *or* pour qu'il le garde (*subj*); **the key is in his safekeeping** on lui a confié (la garde de) la clef ▸**safe sex** rapports *mpl* sexuels sans risque; (*specifically with condom*) rapports *mpl* sexuels protégés.

safeguard [ˈseɪfgɑːd] 1 vt sauvegarder, protéger (*against* contre). 2 n sauvegarde *f*, garantie *f* (*against* contre). **as a ~ against** comme sauvegarde contre, pour éviter; (*Jur*) **~ clause** clause *f* de sauvegarde.

safely [ˈseɪflɪ] adv (*without mishap*) sans accident; (*without risk*) sans risque, sans danger; (*without damage*) sans dommage; (*securely*) en sûreté. **to arrive ~** *[person]* bien arriver, arriver à bon port, arriver sain et sauf; *[parcel]* bien arriver, arriver à bon port; **"arrived ~"** "bien arrivé"; (*Comm*) **the consignment reached us ~** nous avons bien reçu les marchandises; **you can walk about quite ~ in this town** vous pouvez vous promener sans risque *or* sans danger dans cette ville; **he's ~ through to the semifinal** il est arrivé (sans encombre) en demi-finale; **to put sth away ~** ranger qch en lieu sûr; **we can ~ say that ...** nous pouvons dire à coup sûr *or* sans risque d'erreur que ... .

safeness [ˈseɪfnɪs] n (*freedom from danger*) sécurité *f*; *[construction, equipment]* solidité *f.*

safety [ˈseɪftɪ] 1 n a (*freedom from danger*) sécurité *f.* **in a place of ~** en lieu sûr; **to ensure sb's ~** veiller sur *or* assurer la sécurité de qn; **his ~ must be our first consideration** sa sécurité doit être notre premier souci; **this airline is very concerned over the ~ of its passengers** cette compagnie d'aviation se préoccupe beaucoup de la sécurité de ses passagers; **he reached ~ at last** il fut enfin en sûreté *or* en sécurité; **he sought ~ in flight** il chercha le salut dans la fuite; **to play for ~** ne pas prendre de risques, jouer au plus sûr; **there is ~ in numbers** plus on est nombreux moins il y a de danger; **for ~'s sake** pour plus de sûreté, par mesure de sécurité; **~ on the roads/in the factories** la sécurité sur les routes/dans les usines; **~ first!** la sécurité d'abord!; (*Aut*) soyez prudents! (*see also* **2**); *see also* **road.**

b *[construction, equipment]* solidité *f.*

2 comp ▸**safety belt** ceinture *f* de sécurité ▸**safety blade** lame *f* de sûreté ▸**safety bolt** verrou *m* de sûreté ▸**safety catch** cran *m* de sécurité ▸**safety chain** chaîne *f* de sûreté ▸**safety curtain** (*Theat*) rideau *m* de fer ▸**safety-deposit box** (*US*) coffre(-fort) *m* ▸**safety device** dispositif *m* de sécurité ▸**safety factor** facteur *m* de sécurité ▸**safety first campaign** (*gen*) campagne *f* de sécurité; (*Aut*) campagne de la prévention routière ▸**safety glass** verre *m* Sécurit ® ▸**safety lamp** lampe *f* de mineur ▸**safety lock** serrure *f* de sécurité ▸**safety margin** marge *f* de sécurité ▸**safety match** allumette *f* de sûreté *or* suédoise ▸**safety measure** mesure *f* de sécurité; **as a safety measure** pour plus de sûreté, par mesure de sécurité ▸**safety mechanism** dispositif *m* de sécurité ▸**safety net** (*lit*) filet *m* (de protection); (*fig*) filet de sécurité ▸**safety pin** (*gen*) épingle *f* de sûreté *or* de nourrice; *[hand grenade]* goupille *f* ▸**safety precaution** mesure *f* de sécurité ▸**safety razor** rasoir *m* de sûreté *or* mécanique ▸**safety regulations** règles *fpl* de sécurité ▸**safety screen** écran *m* de sécurité ▸**safety valve** (*lit, fig*) soupape *f* de sûreté ▸**safety zone** (*US Aut*) zone protégée pour piétons.

saffron [ˈsæfrən] 1 n safran *m.* 2 adj *colour* safran *inv*; *flavour* safrané. **~ rice** riz au safran *or* safrané; **~ yellow** jaune safran *inv.*

sag [sæg] 1 vi *[roof, chair]* s'affaisser; *[beam, floorboard]* s'arquer, fléchir; *[cheeks, breasts, hemline]* pendre; *[rope]* pendre au milieu, être détendu; *[gate]* être affaissé; *[prices]* fléchir, baisser. 2 n affaissement *m*, fléchissement *m*; *[prices]* fléchissement, baisse *f.*

saga [ˈsɑːgə] n (*Liter*) saga *f*; (*film, story*) aventure *f* épique; (*novel*) roman-fleuve *m.* (*fig*) **he told me the whole ~ of what had happened** il m'a raconté tout ce qui était arrivé *or* toutes les péripéties en long et en large.

sagacious [səˈgeɪʃəs] adj *person* sagace, avisé; *comment* judicieux, perspicace.

sagaciously [səˈgeɪʃəslɪ] adv avec sagacité.

sagaciousness [səˈgeɪʃəsnɪs] n, **sagacity** [səˈgæsɪtɪ] n sagacité *f.*

sage¹ [seɪdʒ] 1 n (*Bot, Culin*) sauge *f.* **~ and onion stuffing** farce *f* à l'oignon et à la sauge. 2 comp ▸**sage brush** (*US*) armoise *f*; (*US*) **the Sagebrush State** le Nevada ▸**sage green** vert cendré *inv.*

sage² [seɪdʒ] 1 adj (*wise*) sage, savant, avisé; (*solemn*) solennel, grave. 2 n sage *m.*

sagely [ˈseɪdʒlɪ] adv (*wisely*) avec sagesse; (*solemnly*) d'un air *or* d'un ton solennel.

sagging [ˈsægɪŋ] adj *ground* affaissé; *beam* arqué, fléchi; *cheek, hemline* pendant; *rope* détendu; *gate* affaissé.

Sagittarian [ˌsædʒɪˈtɛərɪən] n: **to be (a) ~** être (du) Sagittaire.

Sagittarius [ˌsædʒɪˈtɛərɪəs] n (*Astron*) le Sagittaire. **I'm ~** je suis (du) Sagittaire.

sago [ˈseɪgəʊ] 1 n sagou *m.* 2 comp ▸**sago palm** sagoutier *m* ▸**sago pudding** sagou au lait.

Sahara [səˈhɑːrə] n: **the ~ (Desert)** le (désert du) Sahara.

sahib [ˈsɑːhɪb] n (*aux Indes*) Monsieur *m*, maître *m.* **Smith S~** Monsieur Smith; *see* **pukka.**

said [sed] pret, ptp of **say.**

Saigon [saɪˈgɒn] n Saigon.

sail [seɪl] 1 n a *[boat]* voile *f.* **under ~** à la voile; **the boat has set ~** le bateau a pris la mer; *[boat]* **to set ~ for** partir à destination de; **he has set ~ for America** il est parti pour l'Amérique (en bateau); **there wasn't a ~ in sight** il n'y avait pas une seule voile en vue; *see* **hoist, wind¹** *etc.*

b (*trip*) **to go for a ~** faire un tour en bateau *or* en mer; **Spain is 2 days' ~ from here** l'Espagne est à 2 jours de mer.

c *[windmill]* aile *f.*

2 comp ▸**sailboard** planche *f* à voile ▸**sailboarder** véliplanchiste *mf* ▸**sailboarding** planche *f* à voile; **to go sailboarding** faire de la planche à voile ▸**sailboat** (*US*) bateau *m* à voiles, voilier *m* ▸**sailcloth** toile *f* à voile ▸**sail maker** voilier *m* (*personne*) ▸**sailplane** planeur *m.*

3 vi a *[boat]* **to ~ into harbour** entrer au port; **the ship ~ed into Cadiz** le bateau arriva à Cadix; **it ~ed round the cape** il doubla le cap; **to ~ at 10 knots** filer 10 nœuds; **the boat ~ed down the river** le bateau descendit la rivière; **the steamer ~s at 6 o'clock** le vapeur prend la mer *or* part à 6 heures.

b *[person]* **to ~ away/back** *etc* partir/revenir *etc* en bateau; **to ~ round the world** faire le tour du monde en bateau; **we ~ed for Australia** nous sommes partis pour l'Australie (en bateau); **we ~ed into Southampton** nous sommes entrés dans le port de Southampton; **we ~ at 6 o'clock** nous partons à 6 heures, le bateau part à 6 heures; **he ~s** *or* **goes ~ing every weekend** il fait du bateau *or* de la voile tous les week-ends; (*fig*) **he was ~ing close to** *or* **near the wind** il jouait un jeu dangereux.

c (*fig*) *[swan etc]* glisser. **clouds were ~ing across the sky** des nuages glissaient *or* couraient dans le ciel; **the book ~ed across the room and landed at her feet** le livre a volé à travers la pièce et a atterri à ses pieds; **the book ~ed out of the window** le livre est allé voler par la fenêtre; **she ~ed into the room*** elle est entrée dans la pièce toutes voiles dehors (*hum*).

4 vt a **to ~ the seas** parcourir les mers; **he ~ed the Atlantic last year** l'année dernière il a fait la traversée de *or* il a traversé l'Atlantique (en bateau).

b *boat* manœuvrer, piloter, commander. **he ~ed his boat round the cape** il a doublé le cap; **he ~s his own yacht** (*owns it*) il a son propre yacht; (*captains it*) il pilote son yacht lui-même.

►**sail into** vt fus a (‡: *scold*) passer un savon à*, laver la tête à*, voler dans les plumes à‡. b (*) **he sailed into the work** il a attaqué le travail avec entrain.

►**sail through*** 1 vi réussir haut la main. 2 vt fus: **to sail through one's degree/one's driving test** avoir sa licence/son permis de conduire haut la main.

sailing ['seɪlɪŋ] 1 n a (*NonC: activity, hobby*) (*dinghies etc*) navigation *f* à voile; (*yachts*) navigation *f* de plaisance. **a day's ~** une journée de voile *or* en mer; **his hobby is ~** son passe-temps favori est la voile; *see* **plain.** b (*departure*) départ *m*. 2 comp ►**sailing boat** (*Brit*) bateau *m* à voiles, voilier *m* ►**sailing date** date *f* de départ (d'un bateau) ►**sailing dinghy** canot *m* à voiles, dériveur *m* ►**sailing orders** instructions *fpl* pour appareiller ►**sailing ship** grand voilier *m*, navire *m* à voiles.

sailor ['seɪləʳ] 1 n (*gen*) marin *m*; (*before the mast*) matelot *m*. **to be a good/bad ~** avoir/ne pas avoir le pied marin. 2 comp ►**sailor hat** chapeau *m* de marin ►**sailor suit** costume marin.

sainfoin ['sænfɔɪn] n sainfoin *m*.

saint [seɪnt] 1 n saint(e) *m(f)*. **~'s day** fête *f* (de saint); **All S~s' (Day)** la Toussaint; **he's no ~*** ce n'est pas un petit saint.

2 comp ►**Saint Bernard** (*dog*) saint-bernard *m inv* ►**Saint Helena** (*Geog*) Sainte-Hélène *f*; **on Saint Helena** à Sainte-Hélène ►**Saint John** *etc* saint Jean *etc* ►**Saint-John's-wort** mille-pertuis *m* ►**Saint Lawrence** le Saint-Laurent; **the Saint Lawrence Seaway** la voie maritime du Saint-Laurent ►**saint-like** = **saintly** ►**Saint Lucia** (*Geog*) Sainte-Lucie *f*; **in Saint Lucia** à Sainte-Lucie ►**Saint Lucian** n Saint-Lucien(ne) *m(f)* ◊ adj saint-lucien ►**Saint Patrick's** *etc* **Day** la Saint-Patrick *etc* ►**Saint Peter's** *etc* **Church** (l'église *f*) Saint-Pierre *etc* ►**Saint Pierre and Miquelon** (*Geog*) Saint-Pierre-et-Miquelon ►**Saint Vincent and the Grenadines** (*Geog*) Saint-Vincent-et-Grenadines ►**Saint Vitus' dance** (*Med*) danse *f* de Saint-Guy.

sainted ['seɪntɪd] adj sanctifié.

sainthood ['seɪnthʊd] n sainteté *f*.

saintliness ['seɪntlɪnɪs] n sainteté *f*.

saintly ['seɪntlɪ] adj *quality* de saint; *smile* plein de bonté. **a ~ person** une sainte personne, une personne pleine de bonté.

saithe [seɪθ] (*Brit*) n lieu noir *m*, colin *m*.

sake¹ [seɪk] n: **for the ~ of sb** pour l'amour de qn, par égard pour qn; **for God's ~** pour l'amour de Dieu; **for my ~** pour moi, par égard pour moi; **for your own ~** pour ton bien; **for their ~(s)** pour eux; **do it for both our ~s** fais-le (par égard) pour nous deux; **to eat for the ~ of eating** manger pour le plaisir de manger; **for old times' ~** en souvenir du passé; **for argument's ~** à titre d'exemple; **for safety's ~** pour plus de sûreté; **art for art's ~** l'art pour l'art; **for the ~ of your career/my health** pour ta carrière/ma santé; **for the ~ of peace** pour avoir la paix; *see* **goodness, heaven, pity** *etc*.

sake² ['sɑːkɪ] n saké *m*.

sal [sæl] n sel *m*. **~ ammoniac** sel ammoniac; **~ volatile** sel volatil.

salaam [sə'lɑːm] 1 n salutation *f* (à l'orientale). 2 vi saluer (à l'orientale). 3 excl salaam.

salability [ˌseɪlə'bɪlɪtɪ] n (*US*) = **saleability**.

salable ['seɪləbl] adj (*US*) = **saleable**.

salacious [sə'leɪʃəs] adj *joke, remark* licencieux, grivois; *smile, look* lubrique.

salaciousness [sə'leɪʃəsnɪs] n grivoiserie *f*; lubricité *f*.

salad ['sæləd] 1 n salade *f*. **ham ~** jambon accompagné de salade; **tomato ~** salade de tomates; *see* **fruit, potato** *etc*. 2 comp ►**salad bowl** saladier *m* ►**salad cream** (*Brit*) (sorte *f* de) mayonnaise *f* (*en bouteille etc*) ►**salad days** (*fig*) années *fpl* de jeunesse et d'inexpérience ►**salad dish** = **salad bowl** ►**salad dressing** (*oil and vinegar*) vinaigrette *f*; (*made with egg*) mayonnaise *f* ►**salad oil** huile *f* de table ►**salad servers** couvert *m* à salade ►**salad shaker** (*basket*) panier *m* à salade; (*spinner*) essoreuse *f* (à salade).

salamander ['sæləˌmændəʳ] n (*Myth, Zool*) salamandre *f*.

salami [sə'lɑːmɪ] n salami *m*.

salaried ['sælərɪd] adj *person* qui touche un traitement *or* des appointements, mensualisé; *post* où l'on touche un traitement. (*Ind*) **~ staff** employés *mpl* touchant un traitement *or* des appointements.

salary ['sælərɪ] 1 n (*monthly, professional etc*) traitement *m*, appointements *mpl*; (*pay in general*) salaire *m*. **he couldn't do that on his ~** il ne pourrait pas faire ça avec ce qu'il gagne *or* avec son salaire; 2 comp ►**salary bracket** fourchette *f* des traitements ►**salary earner** personne *f* qui touche un traitement ►**salary range** éventail *m* des traitements ►**salary scale** échelle *f* des traitements.

sale [seɪl] 1 n a (*act*) vente *f*. **"for ~"** "à vendre"; **"not for ~"** "cet article n'est pas à vendre"; **to put up for ~** mettre en vente; **our house is up for ~** notre maison est à vendre *or* en vente; **on ~** en vente; **on ~ at all good chemists** en vente dans toutes les bonnes pharmacies; **we made a quick ~** la vente a été vite conclue; **it's going cheap for a quick ~** le prix est bas parce qu'on espère vendre vite; **he finds a ready ~ for his vegetables** il n'a aucun mal à vendre ses légumes; **his vegetables find a ready ~** ses légumes se vendent sans aucun mal; **on ~ or return (basis)** avec possibilité de reprise des invendus, avec faculté de retour; **~s are up/down** les ventes ont augmenté/baissé; **she is in ~s** elle est *or* travaille dans la vente; **~ by auction** vente publique, vente aux enchères; *see* **cash** *etc*.

b (*event: gen*) vente *f*; (*auction ~*) vente (aux enchères); (*Comm: also ~s*) soldes *mpl*. **the ~s are on** c'est la saison des soldes; **the ~ begins** *or* **the ~s begin next week** les soldes commencent la semaine prochaine; **this shop is having a ~ just now** il y a des soldes dans ce magasin en ce moment; **to put in the ~** mettre en solde, solder; **in a ~** en solde; **they are having a ~ in aid of the blind** on organise une vente (de charité) en faveur des aveugles; *see* **bring, clearance, jumble** *etc*.

2 comp ►**sale of work** vente *f* de charité ►**sale price** prix *m* de solde *or* de rabais ►**saleroom** salle *f* des ventes ►**sales assistant** (*Brit*), **sales clerk** (*US*) vendeur *m*, -euse *f* ►**sales department** service *m* des ventes ►**sales director** directeur *m*, -trice *f or* chef *m* des ventes ►**sales drive** campagne *f* de promotion des ventes ►**sales force** ensemble *m* des représentants ►**salesgirl** = **sales assistant** ►**sales leaflet** argumentaire *m* ►**salesman** (*in shop*) vendeur *m*; (*representative*) représentant *m* de commerce; **he's a good salesman** il sait vendre (*see* **door 1a** *etc*) ►**sales manager** directeur commercial ►**salesmanship** art *m* de la vente ►**sales office** bureau *m* de vente ►**salesperson** vendeur *m*, -euse *f* ►**sales pitch*** baratin* *m* publicitaire, boniment *m* ►**sales promotion** promotion *f* des ventes ►**sales resistance** réaction *f* défavorable (à la publicité), résistance *f* (de l'acheteur) ►**salesroom** (*US*) = **saleroom** ►**sales slip** (*in shops*) ticket *m* (de caisse) ►**sales talk*** baratin* *m* publicitaire, boniment *m*; (*US*) ►**sales tax** taxe *f* à l'achat ►**saleswoman** (*in shop*) vendeuse *f*; (*representative*) représentante *f* de commerce ►**sale value** valeur marchande.

saleability [ˌseɪlə'bɪlɪtɪ] n: **the ~ of electronic games was exaggerated** on a surestimé l'attrait commercial *or* les possibilités de vente des jeux électroniques.

saleable ['seɪləbl] adj vendable. **highly ~** très demandé.

Salerno [sə'lɜːnəʊ] n Salerne.

salient ['seɪlɪənt] adj, n saillant (*m*).

salina [sə'liːnə] n a (*marsh etc*) (marais *m*) salant *m*, salin *m*, saline *f*; (*saltworks*) saline(s), raffinerie *f* de sel. b (*mine*) mine *f* de sel.

saline ['seɪlaɪn] 1 adj *solution* salin. 2 n a = **salina a.** b (*Chem: solution*) solution *f* isotonique de sel(s) alcalin(s); (*Med*) purgatif salin.

salinity [sə'lɪnɪtɪ] n salinité *f*.

saliva [sə'laɪvə] n salive *f*.

salivary ['sælɪvərɪ] adj salivaire.

salivate ['sælɪveɪt] vi saliver.

salivation [ˌsælɪ'veɪʃən] n salivation *f*.

sallow¹ ['sæləʊ] adj *complexion* jaunâtre, cireux.

sallow² ['sæləʊ] n (*Bot*) saule *m*.

sallowness ['sæləʊnɪs] n teint *m* jaunâtre.

sally ['sælɪ] n a (*Mil*) sortie *f*. b (*flash of wit*) saillie *f*, boutade *f*. **to make a ~** dire une boutade.

►**sally forth, sally out** vi sortir gaiement.

Sally Army* [ˌsælɪ'ɑːmɪ] n (*Brit*) (abbr of **Salvation Army**) Armée *f* du Salut.

salmon ['sæmən] 1 n, pl **~s** *or* **~** saumon *m*; *see* **rock², smoke.** 2 comp ►**salmon fishing** pêche *f* au saumon ►**salmon pink** (rose) saumon *inv* ►**salmon steak** darne *f* de saumon ►**salmon trout** truite saumonée.

salmonella [ˌsælmə'nelə] n, pl **salmonellae** [ˌsælmə'neliː] salmonelle *f*. **~ poisoning** salmonellose *f*.

salmonellosis [ˌsælməne'ləʊsɪs] n salmonellose *f*.

Salome [sə'ləʊmɪ] n Salomé *f*.

salon ['sælɒn] n (*all senses*) salon *m*; *see* **beauty, hair.**

saloon [sə'luːn] 1 n a (*large room*) salle *f*, salon *m*; (*on ship*) salon; *see* **billiard.** b (*Brit: also ~ bar*) bar *m*; (*US: bar*) bar, saloon *m*. c (*Brit: car*) (*two-door*) coach *m*; (*four-door*) berline *f*. **5-seater ~** berline 5 places. 2 comp ►**saloon bar** (*Brit*) bar *m* ►**saloon car** (*Brit Aut*) (*two-door*) coach *m*; (*four-door*) berline *f*; (*US Rail*) wagon-salon *m*.

salsa ['sɑːlsə] n a (*Culin*) *sauce aux oignons, tomates et poivrons (spécialité portoricaine)*. b (*Mus*) salsa *f*.

salsify ['sælsɪfɪ] n salsifis *m*.

SALT [sɔːlt] (abbr of **Strategic Arms Limitation Talks**) **~ negotiations** négociations *fpl* S.A.L.T.

salt [sɔːlt] 1 n a (*NonC: Chem, Culin*) sel *m*. **kitchen/table ~** sel de cuisine/de table; **there's too much ~ in the potatoes** les pommes de terre sont trop salées; **I don't like ~ in my food** je n'aime pas manger salé; (*fig*) **to rub ~ in the wound** retourner le couteau dans la plaie;

(*fig*) **he's not worth his ~** il ne vaut pas grand-chose; (*fig*) **to take sth with a pinch** *or* **grain of ~** ne pas prendre qch au pied de la lettre; (*fig*) **the ~ of the earth** le sel de la terre; (*fig*) **to sit above/below the ~** être socialement supérieur/inférieur.

b **~s** sels *mpl*; *see* **bath, smell** *etc.*

c (*Naut*) **an old ~** un vieux loup de mer.

2 **adj** *water, butter, beef* salé; *taste* salé, de sel. **~ lake** lac *m* salé; **~ pork** petit salé *m*; (*fig*) **~ tears** larmes *fpl* amères.

3 **comp ▸salt box** (*US: house*) *maison à deux étages et à toit dissymétrique* **▸saltcellar** salière *f* **▸salt flat** salant *m* **▸salt-free** sans sel **▸salt lick** (*block of salt*) pierre *f* à lécher; (*place*) salant *m* **▸salt marsh** marais *m* salant, salin *m*, saline *f* **▸salt mine** mine *f* de sel; (*US: fig, hum*) **back to the salt mines*!** allez, il faut reprendre le collier*! **▸salt pan** puits salant **▸salt shaker** salière *f* **▸salt spoon** cuiller *f* à sel **▸salt tax** (*Hist*) gabelle *f* **▸saltwater fish** poisson *m* de mer **▸saltworks** (*NonC*) salin *m*, saline(s) *f(pl)*, raffinerie *f* de sel.

4 **vt** *meat, one's food* saler.

▸salt away vt sep *meat* saler; (*fig*) *money* mettre à gauche*.

▸salt down vt fus saler, conserver dans le sel.

saltine [sɔːl'tiːn] **n** (*US: cracker*) petit biscuit *m* salé.

saltiness ['sɔːltɪnɪs] **n** *[water]* salinité *f*; *[food]* goût salé.

salting ['sɔːltɪŋ] **n** a (*act of putting salt on*) salaison *f*. b (*place: esp Brit*) (marais *m*) salant *m*.

saltpetre, (*US*) **saltpeter** ['sɔːlt,piːtəʳ] **n** salpêtre *m*.

salty ['sɔːltɪ] **adj** *taste* salé; *deposit* saumâtre.

salubrious [sə'luːbrɪəs] **adj** salubre, sain. (*fig*) **not a very ~ district** un quartier peu recommandable.

salubrity [sə'luːbrɪtɪ] **n** salubrité *f*.

saluki [sə'luːkɪ] **n** sloughi *m* (*chien*).

salutary ['sæljʊtərɪ] **adj** salutaire.

salutation [,sæljʊ'teɪʃən] **n** salut *m*; (*exaggerated*) salutation *f*. **in ~** pour saluer.

salutatorian [sə,luːtə'tɔːrɪən] **n** (*US Scol*) deuxième *mf* de la promotion (*qui prononce un discours de fin d'année*).

salute [sə'luːt] 1 **n** (*with hand*) salut *m*; (*with guns*) salve *f*. **military ~** salut militaire; **to give (sb) a ~** faire un salut (à qn); **to return sb's ~** répondre au salut de qn; **to take the ~** passer les troupes en revue; *see* **fire, gun.** 2 **vt** (*Mil etc*) saluer (*de la main*); (*fig: acclaim*) saluer (*as* comme). **to ~ the flag** saluer le drapeau. 3 **vi** (*Mil etc*) faire un salut.

Salvador(i)an [,sælvə'dɔːr(ɪ)ən] 1 **n** Salvadorien(ne) *m(f)*. 2 **adj** salvadorien.

salvage ['sælvɪdʒ] 1 **n** (*NonC*) a (*saving*) *[ship, cargo]* sauvetage *m*; (*for re-use*) récupération *f*. b (*things saved from fire, wreck*) objets *or* biens sauvés *or* récupérés; (*things for re-use*) objets récupérables. **to collect old newspapers for ~** récupérer les vieux journaux. c (*payment*) prime *f or* indemnité *f* de sauvetage. 2 **comp** *operation, work, company, vessel* de sauvetage. 3 **vt** *ship* sauver, effectuer le sauvetage de; *material, cargo* sauver (*from* de); (*for re-use*) récupérer. (*fig*) **we'll have to ~ what we can from the situation** il nous faudra sauver ce que nous pourrons de la situation.

salvation [sæl'veɪʃən] 1 **n** (*Rel etc*) salut *m*; (*economic*) relèvement *m*. (*fig*) **work has been his ~** c'est le travail qui l'a sauvé, il a trouvé son salut dans le travail; *see* **mean²**. 2 **comp ▸Salvation Army** Armée *f* du Salut; **Salvation Army band** fanfare *f* de l'Armée du Salut.

salvationist [sæl'veɪʃənɪst] **n** salutiste *mf*.

salve¹ [sælv] 1 **n** (*lit, fig*) baume *m*. 2 **vt** soulager, calmer, apaiser. **to ~ his conscience he ...** pour être en règle avec sa conscience il ... .

salve² [sælv] **vt** (*salvage*) sauver.

salver ['sælvəʳ] **n** plateau *m* (*de métal*).

salvia ['sælvɪə] **n** sauge *f* à fleurs rouges, salvia *f*.

salvo¹ ['sælvəʊ] **n, pl ~s** *or* **~es** (*Mil*) salve *f*; *see* **fire.**

salvo² ['sælvəʊ] **n, pl ~s** (*Jur*) réserve *f*, réservation *f*.

salvor ['sælvəʳ] **n** sauveteur *m* (*en mer*).

Salzburg ['sæltsbɜːg] **n** Salzbourg.

SAM [sæm] **n** (**abbr of surface-to-air-missile**) SAM *m*.

Sam [sæm] 1 **n** (**dim of Samuel**) *see* **uncle.** 2 **comp ▸Sam Browne (belt)** ceinturon *m* et baudrier *m*.

Samaria [sə'mɛərɪə] **n** Samarie *f*.

Samaritan [sə'mærɪtən] 1 **n** Samaritain(e) *m(f)*. (*Rel*) **the Good ~** le bon Samaritain; **he was a good ~** il faisait le bon Samaritain; (*US*) **Good ~ Laws** *lois mettant un sauveteur à l'abri de poursuites judiciaires qui pourraient être engagées par le blessé;* (*organization*) **the S~s** ≃ S.O.S. Amitié. 2 **adj** samaritain.

samarium [sə'mɛərɪəm] **n** samarium *m*.

samba ['sæmbə] **n** samba *f*.

sambo** ['sæmbəʊ] **n** (*pej*) noiraud(e)‡ *m(f)*, moricaud(e)** *m(f)* (*pej*).

same [seɪm] 1 **adj** même; (*Jur: aforementioned*) susdit. **the ~ books as** *or* **that** les mêmes livres que; **the ~ day** le même jour; **the very ~ day** le jour même, exactement le même jour; **that ~ day** ce même jour, ce jour même; **in the ~ way ...** de même ...; **in the ~ way as** *or* **that** de la même façon que; **we sat at the ~ table as usual** nous nous sommes assis à notre table habituelle; **how are you? — ~ as usual!*** comment vas-tu? – comme d'habitude! *or* toujours pareil!*; **is that the ~ man (that) I saw yesterday?** est-ce bien le même homme que celui que j'ai vu hier?; **they turned out to be one and the ~ person** en fin de compte il s'agissait d'une seule et même personne; **he always says the ~ old thing** il répète toujours la même chose; **it comes to the ~ thing** cela revient au même (*see* **one**); **~ difference*** c'est la même chose, c'est du pareil au même*; **they both arrived at the ~ time** ils sont arrivés tous les deux en même temps; **don't all talk at the ~ time** ne parlez pas tous en même temps *or* à la fois; **at the ~ time we must remember that ...** en même temps il faut se rappeler que ...; **at the very ~ time as ...** au moment même *or* précis où ...; **to go the ~ way as sb** (*lit*) aller dans la même direction que qn; (*fig*) suivre les traces *or* l'exemple de qn, marcher sur les traces de qn; (*in health*) **she's much about the ~** son état est inchangé, elle est pareille*.

2 **pron** a **the ~** (*gen*) la même chose; (*specific reference*) le *or* la même; (*Jur: aforementioned*) le susdit, la susdite; **it's the ~ as ...** c'est la même chose que ...; **the film is the ~ as before** le film est le même qu'avant; **the price is the ~ as last year** c'est le même prix que l'année dernière; **we must all write the ~** il faut que nous écrivions tous la même chose; **do the ~ as your brother** fais comme ton frère; **he left and I did the ~** il est parti et j'ai fait de même *or* j'en ai fait autant; **I'll do the ~ for you** je te le rendrai *or* revaudrai; **I would do the ~ again** je recommencerais; **don't do the ~ again!** ne recommence pas!; (*in bar etc*) **(the) ~ again please** la même chose s'il vous plaît, remettez ça‡; **I don't feel the ~ about it as I did** maintenant je vois la chose différemment; **I still feel the ~ about you** mes sentiments à ton égard n'ont pas changé; **it's all** *or* **just the ~ to me** cela m'est égal; **thanks all the** *or* **just the ~** merci tout de même *or* quand même*; **all the ~** *or* **just the ~, he refused** il a refusé quand même *or* tout de même, n'empêche qu'il a refusé; **things go on just the ~** (*monotonously*) rien ne change; (*in spite of everything*) rien n'est changé, la vie continue (quand même); **it's not the ~ at all** ce n'est pas du tout la même chose, ce n'est pas du tout pareil; **it's not the ~ as before** ce n'est plus pareil, ce n'est plus comme avant; **it's the ~ everywhere** c'est partout pareil; **and the ~ to you!** à vous aussi, à vous de même; (*as retort: in quarrel etc*) et je te souhaite la pareille!; **~ here!*** moi aussi!; **it's the ~ with us** (et) nous aussi!

b (*Comm*) le *or* la même. **to repairing ~** réparation du même (*or* de la même).

3 **comp ▸same-day adj** (*Comm*) *delivery, service etc* (garanti) le même jour *or* dans la journée.

sameness ['seɪmnɪs] **n** identité *f*, similitude *f*; (*monotony*) monotonie *f*, uniformité *f*.

Samoa [sə'məʊə] **n** Samoa *m*.

Samoan [sə'məʊən] 1 **n** Samoan(e) *m(f)*. 2 **adj** samoan.

samosa [sə'məʊsə] **n, pl ~s** *or* **~** samosa *m*

samovar [,sæməʊ'vɑːʳ] **n** samovar *m*.

sampan ['sæmpæn] **n** sampan(g) *m*.

sample ['sɑːmpl] 1 **n** (*gen*) échantillon *m*; (*Med*) *[urine]* échantillon; *[blood, tissue]* prélèvement *m*. **as a ~** à titre d'échantillon; **to take a ~** prélever un échantillon, faire un prélèvement (*also Geol*); **to take a blood ~** faire une prise *or* un prélèvement de sang (*from* à); **to choose from ~s** choisir sur échantillons; (*Comm*) **all the goods are up to ~** toutes les marchandises sont d'aussi bonne qualité que les échantillons; (*Comm*) **free ~** échantillon gratuit; **a ~ of his poetry** un exemple de sa poésie; *see* **random** *etc.*

2 **comp** *bottle, cigarette, selection etc* échantillon *m*; *line, sentence etc* exemple *m* **▸sample book** (*Comm*) collection *f* d'échantillons **▸sample section: a sample section of the population** une section représentative de la population **▸sample survey** enquête *f* par sondage.

3 **vt** a *food, wine* goûter.

b (*Mus*) sampler, échantillonner.

sampler ['sɑːmpləʳ] **n** (*Sewing*) échantillon *m* de broderie; (*Mus*) sampler *m*, échantillonneur *m*.

sampling ['sɑːmplɪŋ] **n** (*gen*) prélèvement *m* d'échantillons, choix *m* d'échantillons, échantillonnage *m*; (*Mus*) sampling *m*, échantillonnage. (*Comm etc*) **~ technique** technique *f* d'échantillonnage.

Samson ['sæmsn] **n** Samson *m*.

Samuel ['sæmjʊəl] **n** Samuel *m*.

samurai ['sæmʊ,raɪ] **n, pl inv** samouraï *m*, samurai *m*. **~ sword/tradition** épée *f* de samouraï/tradition *f* samouraï; **~ warrior** (guerrier *m*) samouraï *m*; (*Fin*) **~ bond** obligation libellée en yens émise par des emprunteurs étrangers.

San Andreas [sænæn'dreɪəs] **n: ~ Fault** faille *f* de San Andreas.

sanatorium [,sænə'tɔːrɪəm] **n, pl ~s** *or* **sanatoria** [,sænə'tɔːrɪə] (*Brit*) sanatorium *m*; (*Scol*) infirmerie *f*.

Sancho Panza [,sæntʃəʊ'pænzə] **n** Sancho Pança *m*.

sancta ['sæŋktə] **npl of sanctum.**

sanctification [,sæŋktɪfɪ'keɪʃən] **n** sanctification *f*.

sanctify ['sæŋktɪfaɪ] **vt** sanctifier.

sanctimonious [,sæŋktɪ'məʊnɪəs] **adj** moralisateur (*f* -trice).

sanctimoniously [,sæŋktɪ'məʊnɪəslɪ] **adv** d'une manière moralisatrice; *speak* d'un ton moralisateur *or* prêcheur.

sanctimoniousness [,sæŋktɪ'məʊnɪəsnɪs] **n** caractère *or* ton moralisateur, attitude moralisatrice.

sanction [ˈsæŋkʃən] 1 n a (*NonC: authorization*) sanction *f*, approbation *f*. **with the ~ of sb** avec le consentement de qn; **he gave it his ~** il a donné son approbation. b (*enforcing measure*) sanction *f*. **to impose economic ~s against** prendre des sanctions économiques contre. 2 vt *law, conduct* sanctionner, approuver. **I will not ~ such a thing** je ne peux pas approuver *or* sanctionner une chose pareille; **this expression has been ~ed by usage** cette expression est consacrée par l'usage.

sanctity [ˈsæŋktɪtɪ] n *[person, behaviour]* sainteté *f*; *[oath, place]* caractère sacré; *[property, marriage]* inviolabilité *f*. **odour of ~** odeur *f* de sainteté.

sanctuary [ˈsæŋktjʊərɪ] n (*holy place*) sanctuaire *m*; (*refuge*) asile *m*; (*for wild life*) réserve *f*. **right of ~** droit *m* d'asile; **to seek ~** chercher asile; *see* **bird**.

sanctum [ˈsæŋktəm] n, pl **~s** *or* **sancta** a (*holy place*) sanctuaire *m*. b (*: *sb's study etc*) retraite *f*, tanière *f*. (*hum*) **the (inner) ~** le saint des saints (*hum*).

sand [sænd] 1 n a sable *m*. **a grain of ~** un grain de sable; **this resort has miles and miles of golden ~(s)** cette station balnéaire a des kilomètres de plages de sable doré; (*fig*) **the ~s are running out** nos instants sont comptés; **~s** *[beach]* plage *f* (de sable); *[desert]* désert *m* (de sable). b (*US* *: *courage*) cran* *m*. 2 comp ► **sandbag** *see* **sandbag** ► **sandbank** banc *m* de sable ► **sand bar** barre *f* (*de rivière*) ► **sandblast** n jet *m* de sable ◊ vt décaper à la sableuse ► **sandblaster** sableuse *f* ► **sandblasting** décapage *m* à la sableuse; **sandblasting machine = sandblaster** ► **sandblind** (*US*) qui a mauvaise vue, mal voyant ► **sandbox** (*US*) tas *m* de sable ► **sandboy: happy as a sandboy** heureux comme un poisson dans l'eau *or* comme un roi ► **sandcastle** château *m* de sable ► **sand desert** désert *m* de sable ► **sand dollar** (*US Zool*) oursin *m* plat ► **sand dune** dune *f* (de sable) ► **sand eel** anguille *f* de sable, lançon *m*, équille *f* ► **sand flea** (*beach flea*) puce *f* de mer; (*tropical*) chique *f* ► **sandfly** phlébotome *m*; (*biting midge*) simulie *f* ► **sandglass** sablier *m* ► **sandlot** (*US*) terrain *m* vague; **sandlot baseball** baseball *m* pratiqué dans les terrains vagues ► **sandman** (*fig*) marchand *m* de sable ► **sand martin** hirondelle *f* de rivage ► **sandpaper** n papier *m* de verre ◊ vt (*also* **sandpaper down**) frotter *or* poncer au papier de verre ► **sandpapering** ponçage *m* au papier de verre ► **sandpile** (*US*) tas *m* de sable ► **sandpiper** bécasseau *m* ► **sandpit** (*esp Brit*) sablonnière *f*, carrière *f* de sable; (*for children*) tas *m* de sable ► **sandshoes** (*rubber-soled*) tennis *fpl*; (*rope-soled*) espadrilles *fpl* ► **sandstone** grès *m*; **sandstone quarry** grésière *f* ► **sandstorm** tempête *f* de sable ► **sand trap** (*US Golf*) bunker *m*, obstacle *m* de sable ► **sandworm** arénicole *m* ► **sand yacht** char *m* à voile ► **sand-yachting: to go sand-yachting** faire du char à voile. 3 vt a *path* sabler, couvrir de sable; (*against ice*) sabler. b (*also* **~ down**) frotter *or* poncer au papier de verre.

sandal [ˈsændl] n sandale *f*; (*rope-soled*) espadrille *f*.

sandal(wood) [ˈsændl(wʊd)] 1 n santal *m*. 2 comp *box, perfume* de santal.

sandbag [ˈsændbæg] 1 n sac *m* de sable *or* de terre. 2 vt a (*stun*) assommer. b *wall, door, dam* renforcer avec des sacs de sable *or* de terre.

sander [ˈsændəʳ] n (*tool*) ponceuse *f*.

Sandhurst [ˈsændhɜːst] n (*Brit*) école *f* militaire, ≃ Saint-Cyr.

sanding [ˈsændɪŋ] n *[road]* sablage *m*; (*sandpapering*) ponçage *m* au papier de verre.

sandwich [ˈsænwɪdʒ] 1 n sandwich *m*. **cheese ~** sandwich au fromage; **open ~** canapé *m*. 2 comp ► **sandwich bar** boutique *f* qui ne vend que des sandwiches, sandwich bar *m* ► **sandwich board** panneau *m* publicitaire (*porté par un homme-sandwich*) ► **sandwich cake** (*Brit Culin*) gâteau *m* fourré ► **sandwich course** (*Ind*) stage *m* de formation professionnelle alterné ► **sandwich loaf** pain *m* de mie ► **sandwich man** homme-sandwich *m*. 3 vt (*also* **~ in**) *person, appointment* intercaler. **to be ~ed (between)** être pris en sandwich (entre)*.

sandy [ˈsændɪ] adj a *soil, path* sablonneux; *water, deposit* sableux; *beach* de sable. b (*colour*) couleur (de) sable *inv*. **~ hair** cheveux *mpl* blond roux.

sane [seɪn] adj *person* sain d'esprit; *judgment* sain, raisonnable, sensé. **he isn't quite ~** il n'a pas toute sa raison.

sanely [ˈseɪnlɪ] adv sainement, raisonnablement, judicieusement.

Sanforized [ˈsænfəraɪzd] adj ® irrétrécissable, qui ne rétrécit pas au lavage.

San Francisco [ˌsænfrænˈsɪskəʊ] n San Francisco.

sang [sæŋ] pret of **sing**.

sangfroid [ˈsɑ̃ːŋˈfrwɑː] n sang-froid *m*.

sangria [sæŋˈgriːə] n sangria *f*.

sanguinary [ˈsæŋgwɪnərɪ] adj *battle, struggle* sanglant; *ruler* sanguinaire, altéré de sang (*liter*).

sanguine [ˈsæŋgwɪn] adj a *person* optimiste, plein d'espoir; *temperament, outlook* optimiste; *prospect* encourageant. **we are ~ about our chances of success** nous sommes optimistes quant à nos chances de succès; **of ~ disposition** d'un naturel optimiste, porté à l'optimisme. b *complexion* sanguin, rubicond.

sanguinely [ˈsæŋgwɪnlɪ] adv avec optimisme, avec confiance.

sanguineous [sæŋˈgwɪnɪəs] adj sanguinolent.

sanitarium [ˌsænɪˈteərɪəm] n, pl **~s** *or* **sanitaria** [ˌsænɪˈteərɪə] (*esp US*) = **sanatorium**.

sanitary [ˈsænɪtərɪ] 1 adj a (*clean*) hygiénique, salubre. b *system, equipment* sanitaire. **there are poor ~ arrangements** les conditions sanitaires laissent *or* le sanitaire laisse à désirer. 2 comp ► **sanitary engineer** ingénieur *m* sanitaire ► **sanitary inspector** inspecteur *m*, -trice *f* de la Santé publique ► **sanitary napkin** (*US*), **sanitary towel** (*Brit*) serviette *f* hygiénique.

sanitation [ˌsænɪˈteɪʃən] n (*in house*) installations *fpl* sanitaires, sanitaire *m*; (*in town*) système *m* sanitaire; (*science*) hygiène publique. (*US*) **~ man** éboueur *m* (municipal).

sanitize [ˈsænɪtaɪz] vt (*lit*) assainir, désinfecter; (*fig*) assainir, expurger.

sanitized [ˈsænɪtaɪzd] adj (*fig*) *account, view of events* édulcoré, expurgé.

sanity [ˈsænɪtɪ] n *[person]* santé mentale; *[judgment, reasoning]* rectitude *f*. **he was restored to ~** il retrouva sa santé mentale *or* sa raison; **~ demands that** ... le bon sens exige que ... + *subj*; **fortunately ~ prevailed** heureusement le bon sens l'emporta.

sank [sæŋk] pret of **sink**[1].

San Marinese [ˌsænˌmærɪˈniːz] 1 n Saint-Marinais(e) *m(f)*. 2 adj saint marinais.

San Marino [ˌsænməˈriːnəʊ] n Saint-Marin *m*. **in ~** à Saint-Marin.

sansevieria [ˌsænsɪˈvɪərɪə] n sansevière *f*.

Sanskrit [ˈsænskrɪt] adj, n sanscrit *(m)*.

Santa Claus [ˌsæntəˈklɔːz] n le père Noël.

Santiago [ˌsæntɪˈɑːgəʊ] n (*also*: **~ de Chili**) Santiago (du Chili). (*Spain*) **~ de Compostela** Saint-Jacques-de-Compostelle.

Saone [soːn] n Saône *f*.

sap[1] [sæp] n (*Bot*) sève *f*.

sap[2] [sæp] 1 n (*Mil: trench*) sape *f*. 2 vt *strength, confidence* saper, miner.

sap[3]‡ [sæp] 1 n (*fool*) cruche* *f*, andouille* *f*. 2 comp ► **saphead**‡ cruche* *f*, andouille* *f*.

sapless [ˈsæplɪs] adj *plant* sans sève, desséché.

sapling [ˈsæplɪŋ] n jeune arbre *m*; (*fig*) jeune homme *m*. **~s** boisage *m*.

sapper [ˈsæpəʳ] n (*Brit Mil*) soldat *m* du génie. (*Brit Mil*) **the S~s*** le génie.

sapphic [ˈsæfɪk] adj saphique.

sapphire [ˈsæfaɪəʳ] 1 n (*jewel, gramophone needle*) saphir *m*. 2 comp *ring* de saphir(s) ► **sapphire (blue) sky** un ciel de saphir.

sappiness [ˈsæpɪnɪs] n abondance *f* de sève.

sappy[1] [ˈsæpɪ] adj *leaves* plein de sève; *wood* vert.

sappy[2]‡ [ˈsæpɪ] adj (*foolish*) cruche*.

saraband [ˈsærəbænd] n sarabande *f*.

Saracen [ˈsærəsn] 1 adj sarrasin. 2 n Sarrasin(e) *m(f)*.

Saragossa [ˌsærəˈgɒsə] n Saragosse.

Sarah [ˈsɛərə] n Sara(h) *f*.

Saranwrap [səˈrænræp] n ® (*US*) film alimentaire transparent, scellofrais ® *m*.

Saratoga [ˌsærəˈtəʊgə] n Saratoga. (*US*) **~ trunk** grosse malle à couvercle bombé.

sarcasm [ˈsɑːkæzəm] n (*NonC*) sarcasme *m*, raillerie *f*.

sarcastic [sɑːˈkæstɪk] adj sarcastique. **~ remarks** sarcasmes *mpl*.

sarcastically [sɑːˈkæstɪkəlɪ] adv avec sarcasme, railleusement, sarcastiquement.

sarcoma [sɑːˈkəʊmə] n, pl **~s** *or* **sarcomata** [sɑːˈkəʊmətə] (*Med*) sarcome *m*.

sarcomatosis [sɑːˌkəʊməˈtəʊsɪs] n sarcomatose *f*.

sarcophagus [sɑːˈkɒfəgəs] n, pl **~es** *or* **sarcophagi** [sɑːˈkɒfəgaɪ] sarcophage *m*.

sardine [sɑːˈdiːn] n, pl **~** *or* **~s** sardine *f*. **tinned** *or* (*US*) **canned ~s** sardines en boîte *or* en conserve, ≃ sardines à l'huile; *see* **pack**.

Sardinia [sɑːˈdɪnɪə] n Sardaigne *f*. **in ~** en Sardaigne.

Sardinian [sɑːˈdɪnɪən] 1 adj sarde. 2 n a Sarde *mf*. b (*Ling*) sarde *m*.

sardonic [sɑːˈdɒnɪk] adj sardonique.

sardonically [sɑːˈdɒnɪkəlɪ] adv sardoniquement.

Sargasso [sɑːˈgæsəʊ] n: **~ Sea** mer *f* des Sargasses.

sarge [sɑːdʒ] n (abbr of **sergeant**) sergent *m*.

sari [ˈsɑːrɪ] n sari *m*.

Sark [sɑːk] n (île *f* de) Sercq *m*.

sarky‡ [ˈsɑːkɪ] adj sarcastique.

sarnie* [ˈsɑːnɪ] n (*Brit*) sandwich *m*, casse dalle *m*.

sarong [səˈrɒŋ] n sarong *m*.

sarsaparilla [ˌsɑːsəpəˈrɪlə] n (*plant*) salsepareille *f*; (*drink*) boisson *f* à la salsepareille.

sartorial [sɑːˈtɔːrɪəl] adj *elegance, matters* vestimentaire. **~ art** art *m* du

tailleur.
sartorius [sɑːˈtɔːrɪəs] n, pl **sartorii** [sɑːˈtɔːrɪaɪ] (*Anat*) muscle *m* couturier.
SAS [eserˈes] n (*Brit Mil*) (abbr of **Special Air Service**) ≃ GIGN *m*.
sash¹ [sæʃ] n (*on uniform*) écharpe *f*; (*on dress etc*) large ceinture *f* à nœud.
sash² [sæʃ] 1 n *[window]* châssis *m* à guillotine. 2 comp ▸ **sash cord** corde *f* (d'une fenêtre) ▸ **sash window** fenêtre *f* à guillotine.
sashay* [sæˈʃeɪ] vi (*walk stylishly*) évoluer d'un pas léger, glisser.
Saskatchewan [ˈsæsˈkætʃɪˌwən] n (*province*) Saskatchewan *m*.
sasquatch [ˈsæskwætʃ] n *animal hypothétique des forêts du Nord-Ouest des États Unis et du Canada.*
sass‡ [sæs] (*US*) 1 n toupet* *m*, culot* *m*. 2 vt répondre d'un ton insolent à.
Sassenach [ˈsæsənæx] n (*Scot: gen pej*) *nom donné aux Anglais par les Écossais.*
sassy* [ˈsæsɪ] adj (*US*) insolent, impertinent. **don't be ~ with me** je n'aime pas qu'on (me) réponde.
sat [sæt] pret, ptp of **sit**.
Sat. abbr of **Saturday**.
Satan [ˈseɪtn] n Satan *m*; *see* **limb**.
satanic [səˈtænɪk] adj satanique, démoniaque.
satanically [səˈtænɪkəlɪ] adv d'une manière satanique.
Satanism [ˈseɪtənɪzəm] n satanisme *m*.
Satanist [ˈseɪtənɪst] 1 n sataniste *mf*. 2 adj = **satanic**.
satchel [ˈsætʃəl] n cartable *m*.
Satcom [ˈsætˌkɒm] n centre *m* de communications par satellite.
sate [seɪt] vt = **satiate**.
sateen [sæˈtiːn] 1 n satinette *f*. 2 comp en satinette.
satellite [ˈsætəlaɪt] 1 n a (*Astron, Pol, Space*) satellite *m*. **artificial ~** satellite artificiel; **communications ~** satellite de télécommunications, satellite-relais *m*. b (*US: dormitory town*) ville *f* satellite. 2 comp *town, country etc* satellite ▸ **satellite broadcasting** diffusion *f* par satellite ▸ **satellite dish (aerial)** antenne *f* parabolique ▸ **satellite killer** satellite *m* d'intervention, destructeur *m* de satellites ▸ **satellite nations** (*Pol*) nations *fpl* satellites ▸ **satellite televison** télévision *f* par satellite. 3 vt (*transmit via satellite*) transmettre par satellite.
satiate [ˈseɪʃɪeɪt] vt (*lit*) assouvir, rassasier (*with* de); (*fig*) blaser (*with* par).
satiated [ˈseɪʃɪeɪtɪd] adj (*with food*) repu, rassasié; (*with pleasures*) comblé, blasé (*pej*).
satiation [ˌseɪʃɪˈeɪʃən] n (*lit, fig*) assouvissement *m*. **to ~ (point)** (jusqu')à satiété.
satiety [səˈtaɪətɪ] n satiété *f*.
satin [ˈsætɪn] 1 n satin *m*; *see* **silk**. 2 comp *dress, slipper* en *or* de satin; *paper, finish* satiné ▸ **satin stitch** plumetis *m* ▸ **satinwood** bois *m* de citronnier.
satinette [ˌsætɪˈnet] 1 n satinette *f*. 2 comp en satinette.
satire [ˈsætaɪəʳ] n satire *f* (*on* contre).
satiric(al) [səˈtɪrɪk(əl)] adj satirique.
satirically [səˈtɪrɪkəlɪ] adv d'une manière satirique.
satirist [ˈsætərɪst] n (*writer*) écrivain *m* satirique; (*cartoonist*) caricaturiste *mf*; (*in cabaret etc*) ≃ chansonnier *m*. **he's TV's greatest ~** il n'a pas son pareil à la télévision pour la satire.
satirize [ˈsætəraɪz] vt faire la satire de.
satisfaction [ˌsætɪsˈfækʃən] n a (*pleasure*) satisfaction *f*, contentement *m* (*at* de). **to feel ~/great ~** éprouver de la satisfaction/une satisfaction profonde; **it was a great ~ to us to hear that ...** nous avons appris avec beaucoup de satisfaction que ...; **one of his greatest ~s was his son's success** le succès de son fils lui a apporté l'une de ses plus grandes satisfactions; **to note with ~** constater avec satisfaction; **to my (great) ~ he ...** à ma grande satisfaction il ...; **to everybody's ~** à la satisfaction générale; **it has not been proved to my ~** cela n'a pas été prouvé de façon à me convaincre; **has the repair been done to your ~?** est-ce que vous êtes satisfait de la réparation?; *see* **job**.
b *[demand, need]* satisfaction *f*; *[wrong]* réparation *f*, dédommagement *m*; *[appetite]* assouvissement *m*; *[debt]* règlement *m*, acquittement *m*. **to give/obtain ~** donner/obtenir satisfaction; **I demand ~** j'exige qu'on me donne (*subj*) satisfaction.
satisfactorily [ˌsætɪsˈfæktərɪlɪ] adv d'une manière satisfaisante *or* acceptable.
satisfactory [ˌsætɪsˈfæktərɪ] adj *result, report, work* satisfaisant. **to bring sth to a ~ conclusion** mener qch à bien; **his work is/isn't ~** son travail est satisfaisant/laisse à désirer; (*in commercial letters etc*) **we are sorry it was not ~** nous regrettons vivement que vous n'en soyez pas satisfait *or* que cela ne vous ait pas donné (entière) satisfaction.
satisfied [ˈsætɪsfaɪd] adj satisfait, content. **he is never ~** il n'est jamais content *or* satisfait; **he was ~ to remain ...** il a accepté de rester ..., il a trouvé suffisant de rester ...; **in a ~ voice** d'un ton satisfait *or* content; **I am not ~ with your answer** votre réponse ne me satisfait pas; (*iro*) **are you ~ now?** vous voilà satisfait!; **a ~ audience** un public satisfait; **very ~ with the results** très content des résultats; *see also* **satisfy**.
satisfy [ˈsætɪsfaɪ] 1 vt a *person* satisfaire, contenter, faire plaisir à. (*Scol, Univ*) **to ~ the examiners** être reçu (à un examen); *see also* **satisfied**. b *hunger, need, want, creditor* satisfaire; *condition* satisfaire, remplir; *objection* répondre à; *debt, obligation* s'acquitter de; (*Comm*) *demand* satisfaire à. c (*convince*) convaincre, assurer (*sb that* qn que, *of* de). **to ~ o.s. of sth** s'assurer de qch; **I am satisfied that you have done your best** je suis convaincu *or* persuadé que vous avez fait de votre mieux. 2 vi donner satisfaction.
satisfying [ˈsætɪsfaɪɪŋ] adj *report, result, experience* satisfaisant; *food* nourrissant, substantiel; *work, task* motivant.
satrap [ˈsætrəp] n satrape *m*.
satsuma [ˌsætˈsuːmə] n satsuma *f*.
saturate [ˈsætʃəreɪt] vt saturer (*with* de). (*Comm*) **to ~ the market** saturer le marché; **my shoes are ~d** mes chaussures sont trempées; **~d fat** graisse *f* saturée.
saturation [ˌsætʃəˈreɪʃən] 1 n saturation *f*. 2 comp ▸ **saturation bombing** tactique *f* de saturation (par bombardement) ▸ **saturation point** point *m* de saturation; **to reach saturation point** arriver à saturation.
Saturday [ˈsætədɪ] n samedi *m*. **on ~** samedi; **on ~s** le samedi; **next ~, ~ next** samedi prochain *or* qui vient; **last ~** samedi dernier; **the first/last ~ of the month** le premier/dernier samedi du mois; **every ~** tous les samedis, chaque samedi; **every other ~, every second ~** un samedi sur deux; **it is ~ today** nous sommes aujourd'hui samedi; **~ December 18th** samedi 18 décembre; **on ~ January 23rd** le samedi 23 janvier; **the ~ after next** samedi en huit; **a week on ~, ~ week** samedi en huit; **a fortnight on ~, ~ fortnight** samedi en quinze; **a week/fortnight past on ~** il y a huit/quinze jours samedi dernier; **the following ~** le samedi suivant; **the ~ before last** l'autre samedi; **~ morning** samedi matin; **~ afternoon** samedi après-midi; **~ evening** samedi soir; **~ night** samedi soir, (*overnight*) la nuit de samedi; (*TV*) **~ evening viewing** émissions *fpl* du samedi soir; (*Comm*) **~ closing** fermeture *f* le samedi; (*Press*) **the ~ edition** l'édition de *or* du samedi; (*US: gun*) **~ night special*** revolver *m* bon marché; *see* **holy**.
Saturn [ˈsætən] n (*Myth*) Saturne *m*; (*Astron*) Saturne *f*.
Saturnalia [ˌsætəˈneɪlɪə] n, pl ~ *or* ~s (*fig*) saturnale(s) *f(pl)*.
saturnine [ˈsætənaɪn] adj saturnien (*liter*), sombre.
satyr [ˈsætəʳ] n satyre *m*.
sauce [sɔːs] 1 n a (*Culin*) sauce *f*. **mint ~** sauce à la menthe; (*Prov*) **what's ~ for the goose is ~ for the gander** ce qui est bon pour l'un l'est pour l'autre; *see* **apple, tomato, white** *etc*. b (*‡: impudence*) toupet* *m*. **none of your ~!** (*to child*) petit(e) impertinent(e)!; (*to adult*) assez d'impertinence! c (*US: drink*) **the ~‡** l'alcool *m*; **to hit the ~‡, to be on the ~‡** picoler dur‡. 2 comp ▸ **sauceboat** saucière *f* ▸ **saucepan** casserole *f* (*see* **double 4**).
saucer [ˈsɔːsəʳ] n soucoupe *f*, sous-tasse *f*. **~-eyed, with eyes like ~s** avec des yeux comme des soucoupes; **~-shaped** en forme de soucoupe; *see* **flying**.
saucily [ˈsɔːsɪlɪ] adv *behave, speak* avec impertinence, impertinemment; *dress* avec coquetterie; *look* d'un air coquin.
sauciness [ˈsɔːsɪnɪs] n (*cheekiness*) toupet* *m*, impertinence *f*; (*smartness*) coquetterie *f*.
saucy [ˈsɔːsɪ] adj (*cheeky*) impertinent; *look* coquin; (*hat*) coquin, déluré. **hat at a ~ angle** chapeau coquettement posé sur l'oreille.
Saudi [ˈsaʊdɪ] 1 adj saoudien. 2 n Saoudien(ne) *m(f)*. 3 comp ▸ **Saudi Arabia** Arabie *f* Saoudite *or* Séoudite ▸ **Saudi Arabian** Saoudien(ne) *m(f)*.
sauerkraut [ˈsaʊəkraʊt] n (*NonC*) choucroute *f*.
Saul [sɔːl] n Saül *m*.
sauna [ˈsɔːnə] n (*also* **~ bath**) sauna *m*.
saunter [ˈsɔːntəʳ] 1 vi flâner, se balader*. **to ~ in/out/away** *etc* entrer/sortir/s'éloigner *etc* d'un pas nonchalant. 2 n balade* *f*, flânerie *f*. **to go for a ~** faire une petite promenade *or* une balade*.
saurian [ˈsɔːrɪən] adj, n saurien (*m*).
sausage [ˈsɒsɪdʒ] 1 n saucisse *f*; (*pre-cooked*) saucisson *m*. **beef/pork ~** saucisse de bœuf/de porc; (*Brit*) **not a ~‡** rien, des clous‡; *see* **cocktail, garlic, liver¹** *etc*. 2 comp ▸ **sausage dog*** teckel *m*, saucisson *m* à pattes (*hum*) ▸ **sausage machine** machine *f* à saucisses ▸ **sausage meat** chair *f* à saucisse ▸ **sausage roll** (*esp Brit*) ≃ friand *m*.
sauté [ˈsəʊteɪ] 1 vt *potatoes, meat* faire sauter. 2 adj: **~ potatoes** pommes (de terre) sautées.
savage [ˈsævɪdʒ] 1 adj a (*cruel, fierce*) *person* brutal; *dog* méchant, féroce; *attack, criticism* virulent, féroce; *look* furieux, féroce. **to have a ~ temper** être très colérique, avoir un caractère de chien*; **to deal a ~ blow (to)** frapper brutalement. b (*primitive*) *tribe, customs* primitif, sauvage, barbare. 2 n sauvage *mf*. 3 vt *[dog etc]* attaquer férocement; (*fig*) *[critics etc]* éreinter, attaquer violemment.
savagely [ˈsævɪdʒlɪ] adv sauvagement, brutalement.
savageness [ˈsævɪdʒnɪs] n, **savagery** [ˈsævɪdʒrɪ] n (*cruelty*) sauvagerie *f*, brutalité *f*, férocité *f*; (*primitiveness*) barbarie *f*.
savanna(h) [səˈvænə] n savane *f*.
savant [ˈsævənt] n érudit(e) *m(f)*, homme *m* de science, lettré(e) *m(f)*.
save¹ [seɪv] 1 vt a (*rescue*) *person, animal, jewels, building etc* sauver (*from* de); (*Rel*) *sinner* sauver, délivrer. (*Rel*) **to ~ one's soul** sauver son âme; (*fig*) **I couldn't do it to ~ my life** *or* **my soul** je ne le ferais pour rien au monde; **to ~ sb from death/drowning** *etc* sauver qn de la

mort/de la noyade *etc;* **to ~ sb from falling** empêcher qn de tomber; **to ~ sb's life** sauver la vie à *or* de qn; **to ~ sb from himself** protéger qn de *or* contre lui-même; **to ~ the situation** sauver la situation; (*fig*) **to ~ one's bacon*** se tirer du pétrin; **to ~ one's skin*** *or* **neck*** *or* **hide*** sauver sa peau*; **to ~ face** sauver la face; **God ~ the Queen!** vive la reine!; **to ~ sth from the wreck/the fire** *etc* sauver qch du naufrage/de l'incendie *etc;* (*fig*) **things look black but we must try to ~ something from the wreckage** la situation est sombre mais il faut essayer de sauver les meubles*; **to ~ a building from demolition** sauver un bâtiment de la démolition, empêcher la démolition d'un bâtiment; **they ~d the palace for posterity** on a préservé le palais pour la postérité.

b (*store away: also* ~ **up**) *money* mettre de côté; *food* mettre de côté, garder. **he has money ~d** il a de l'argent de côté; **I've ~d you a piece of cake** je t'ai gardé un morceau de gâteau; **to ~ o.s. (up) for sth** se réserver pour qch; **he was saving (up) the cherry till last** il gardait la cerise pour la bonne bouche; **I ~d your letter till the last** j'ai gardé ta lettre pour la bonne bouche; **to ~ (up) old newspapers for charity** garder les vieux journaux pour les bonnes œuvres; (*collect*) **to ~ stamps/matchboxes** *etc* collectionner les timbres/les boîtes d'allumettes *etc.*

c (*not spend, not use*) *money, labour* économiser; *time* (faire) gagner; (*avoid*) *difficulty etc* éviter, épargner (*sb sth* qch à qn). **you have ~d me a lot of trouble** vous m'avez épargné *or* évité bien des ennuis; **to ~ time let's assume that** ... pour aller plus vite *or* pour gagner du temps admettons que ... + *subj*; **this route will ~ you 10 miles** cet itinéraire vous fera gagner 10 milles; **that will ~ my going** *or* **me from going** cela m'évitera d'y aller; **think of all the money you'll ~** pensez à tout l'argent que vous économiserez *or* à toutes les économies que vous ferez; (*Comm*) **"~ 10p on this packet"** "10 pence d'économie sur ce paquet"; **you ~ £1 if you buy 3 packets** vous économisez une livre si vous achetez 3 paquets; **to ~ petrol** faire des économies d'essence, économiser l'essence; **he's saving his strength** *or* **himself for tomorrow's race** il se ménage pour la course de demain; (*Brit*) **~ as you earn** *plan d'épargne par prélèvements mensuels aux intérêts exonérés d'impôts; see* **penny, stitch.**

d (*Sport*) **to ~ a goal** empêcher de marquer, faire un blocage, sauver un but.

e (*Comput*) sauvegarder, conserver.

2 **vi** a (*also* ~ **up**) mettre de l'argent de côté, faire des économies, épargner. **to ~ (up) for the holidays/for a new bike** mettre de l'argent de côté pour les vacances/pour (acheter) un nouveau vélo.

b **to ~ on sth** économiser sur qch, faire des économies sur qch.

3 **n** a (*Sport*) arrêt *m* (du ballon), blocage *m.* **what a brilliant ~!** c'est un arrêt de toute première classe!

b (*Comput*) sauvegarde *f.*

►**save up** 1 **vi** = **save[1] 2a.** 2 **vt sep** = **save[1] 1b.**

save[2] [seɪv] **prep** sauf, à l'exception de. ~ **that** ... sauf que ..., à cette exception près que ..., à ceci près que ... .

saveloy ['sævəlɔɪ] **n** cervelas *m.*

saver ['seɪvəʳ] **n** épargnant(e) *m(f).*

Savile Row ['sævɪl'rəʊ] **n** (*Brit*) *rue de Londres où se trouvent les meilleurs tailleurs.* **a ~ suit** un costume de Savile Row.

saving ['seɪvɪŋ] 1 **n** a (*rescue*) sauvetage *m*; *[sinner]* salut *m*; *see* **face, life.**

b *[time]* économie *f*; *[money]* économie, épargne *f.* **we must make ~s** il faut économiser *or* faire des économies; **this means a great ~ of time/petrol** *etc* cela représente une grande économie de temps/d'essence *etc;* **a great ~ of money** une grande économie; **the government is trying to encourage ~(s)** le gouvernement cherche à encourager l'épargne; **small ~s** la petite épargne; **to live on one's ~s** vivre de ses économies; *see* **national, post office.**

c (*Comput*) sauvegarde *f.*

2 **comp** ►**savings account** (*Brit*) compte *m* d'épargne; (*US*) compte *m* de dépôt ►**savings and loan association** (*US*) ≃ société *f* de crédit immobilier ►**savings bank** caisse *f* d'épargne ►**savings stamp** timbre-épargne *m.*

3 **adj** (*Jur*) ~ **clause** avenant *m*; **generosity is his ~ grace** il se rachète par sa générosité; **energy** (*etc*) **-~ campaign** campagne *f* pour les économies d'énergie *etc; see* **labour** *etc.*

4 **prep** (†) sauf. ~ **your presence** sauf votre respect.

savior ['seɪvjəʳ] **n** (*US*) = **saviour.**

saviour ['seɪvjəʳ] **n** sauveur *m.* (*Rel*) **the S~** le Sauveur.

savoir-faire ['sævwɑːfɛəʳ] **n** savoir-vivre *m.*

savor ['seɪvəʳ] *etc* (*US*) = **savour** *etc.*

savory ['seɪvərɪ] 1 **n** a (*herb*) sarriette *f.* b (*US*) = **savoury 2.** 2 **adj** (*US*) = **savoury 1.**

savour, (*US*) **savor** ['seɪvəʳ] 1 **n** (*flavour*) saveur *f*, goût *m*; (*fig*) pointe *f*, trace *f*, soupçon *m.* 2 **vt** *food, drink* savourer, déguster. 3 **vi: to ~ of sth** sentir qch; **his attitude ~s of pedantry** son attitude sent le pédantisme.

savouriness, (*US*) **savoriness** ['seɪvərɪnɪs] **n** saveur *f*, succulence *f.*

savourless, (*US*) **savorless** ['seɪvəlɪs] **adj** sans saveur, sans goût, insipide, fade.

savoury, (*US*) **savory** ['seɪvərɪ] 1 **adj** a (*appetising*) *smell, taste* savoureux, appétissant. (*fig*) **not a very ~ subject** un sujet peu appétissant *or* peu ragoûtant; **not a very ~ district** un quartier peu recommandable. b (*not sweet*) *dish* salé (*par opposition à sucré*). 2 **n** (*Culin*) mets *m* non sucré, (*on toast*) canapé *m* chaud.

Savoy [sə'vɔɪ] 1 **n** Savoie *f.* 2 **adj** savoyard. (*Brit*) ~ **cabbage** chou frisé de Milan.

Savoyard [sə'vɔɪɑːd] 1 **n** Savoyard(e) *m(f).* 2 **adj** savoyard.

savvy* ['sævɪ] 1 **n** jugeote* *f*, bon sens *m.* 2 **vi** a (‡: †: *know*) **no ~** sais pas, moi*. b (*US* ‡: *understand*) piger‡, comprendre. **I can take care of myself, ~?** je me débrouille tout seul, tu piges?‡ 3 **adj** (*US* ‡) drôlement calé* (*about* en).

saw[1] [sɔː] (**vb: pret sawed, ptp sawed** *or* **sawn**) 1 **n** scie *f*; *see* **circular** *etc.*

2 **comp** ►**sawbones*†** (*pej*) chirurgien *m*, charcutier‡ *m* (*pej*) ►**sawbuck** (*US*) (*sawhorse*) chevalet *m* de scieur de bois; (‡: *$10 bill*) billet *m* de dix dollars ►**sawdust** (*NonC*) sciure *f* (de bois) ►**saw edge** lame dentée ►**saw-edged knife** couteau-scie *m* ►**sawfish** poisson *m* scie, scie *f* ►**sawhorse** chevalet *m* de scieur de bois ►**sawmill** scierie *f.* 3 **vt** scier, débiter à la scie. (*US fig*) **to ~ wood‡** (*sleep*) roupiller*; (*snore*) ronfler; *see also* **sawn.** 4 **vi: to ~ through a log** scier une bûche en deux; **to ~ through a plank/the bars of a cell** scier une planche/les barreaux d'une cellule.

►**saw away vi** (* *pej*) **to saw away at the violin** racler du violon.

►**saw off** 1 **vt sep** enlever à la scie. 2 **sawed-off adj** *see* **sawed 2** 3 **sawn-off adj** *see* **sawn 3.**

►**saw up vt sep** débiter à la scie.

saw[2] [sɔː] **n** (*saying*) dicton *m.*

saw[3] [sɔː] **pret of see[1].**

sawed [sɔːd] 1 **pret, ptp of saw[1].** 2 **comp** ►**sawed-off** (*US * pej: short*) court sur pattes*, petit; (*US*) **sawed-off shotgun** carabine *f* à canon scié.

sawn [sɔːn] 1 **ptp of saw[1].** 2 **adj** scié. ~ **timber** bois *m* de sciage. 3 **comp** ►**sawn-off shotgun** carabine *f* à canon scié.

sawyer ['sɔːjəʳ] **n** scieur *m.*

sax* [sæks] **n** (**abbr of saxophone**) saxo* *m.*

saxhorn ['sækshɔːn] **n** saxhorn *m.*

saxifrage ['sæksɪfrɪdʒ] **n** saxifrage *f.*

Saxon ['sæksn] 1 **adj** saxon. 2 **n** a Saxon(ne) *m(f).* b (*Ling*) saxon *m.*

Saxony ['sæksənɪ] **n** Saxe *f.*

saxophone ['sæksəfəʊn] **n** saxophone *m.*

saxophonist [ˌsæk'sɒfənɪst] **n** saxophoniste *mf*, saxo* *m.*

say [seɪ] **pret, ptp said** 1 **vt** a (*speak, utter, pronounce*) dire (*sth to sb* qch à qn); *lesson, poem* réciter. (*Rel*) **to ~ mass** dire *or* célébrer la messe; **to ~ a prayer** faire *or* dire une prière; **to ~ thank you** dire merci; **to ~ goodbye to sb** dire au revoir à qn; (*more formally*) faire ses adieux à qn; (*fig*) **you can ~ goodbye to peace and quiet!** tu peux dire adieu à ta tranquillité!; (*fig*) **to ~ yes/no to an invitation** accepter/refuser une invitation (*see also* **1f**); **your father said no** ton père a dit (que) non; ~ **after me** ... répétez après moi ...; **could you ~ that again?** pourriez-vous répéter ce que vous venez de dire?; **I've got nothing to ~** (*can't think of anything*) je n'ai rien à dire; (*to police, judge etc: no formal statement*) je n'ai pas de déclaration à faire; (*to press etc: no comment*) pas de commentaire, je n'ai rien à dire; **I've got nothing more to ~** je n'ai rien à ajouter; **all of that can be said in 2 sentences** tout cela tient en 2 phrases; **something was said about it** on en a parlé, il en a été question; **I should like to ~ a few words about** j'aimerais dire quelques mots au sujet de *or* à propos de; **I should like to ask Mr Smith to ~ a few words** je voudrais prier M. Smith de prendre la parole; **he said I was to give you this** il m'a dit de vous donner ceci; **he said to wait here** il a dit d'attendre ici; **to ~ one's say** dire ce qu'on a à dire (*see also* **3**); **so ~ing, he sat down** sur ces mots *or* sur ce, il s'assit; *see* **least, less** *etc.*

b (*assert, state*) dire; (*make formal statement about*) déclarer, indiquer; (*claim*) prétendre. **as I said yesterday** comme je l'ai dit hier; **as I said in my letter/on the phone** comme je vous l'ai dit dans ma lettre/au téléphone; **it ~s in the rules, the rules ~** il est dit dans le règlement; **it ~s on the radio there's going to be snow** la radio annonce de la neige; **well said!** bravo!, bien dit!; (*expressing doubt*) **that's what you ~!, so you ~!** que vous dites!*, c'est ce que vous dites!, c'est vous qui le dites!; **he got home at 6 so he ~s** il est rentré à 6 heures à ce qu'il dit *or* prétend; **it is said that** ... on dit que ...; **he is said to have an artificial leg** on dit qu'il a une jambe artificielle.

c (*suppose; think; assume; estimate*) dire, penser. **what will people ~?** qu'est-ce que les gens vont dire?; **he doesn't care what people ~** il se moque du qu'en-dira-t-on; **I ~ he should take it** je suis d'avis qu'il le prenne; **I should ~ she's intelligent** je pense qu'elle est intelligente; **I would ~ she was 50** je lui donnerais 50 ans; **what would you ~ is the population of Paris?** quelle est à votre avis *or* d'après vous la population de Paris?; **to see him you would ~ he was drunk** à le voir on dirait qu'il est ivre; **let us ~ for argument's sake that** ... mettons à titre d'exemple que ...; ~ **someone left you a fortune, what would you do with it?** si vous *or* imaginons que vous héritiez d'une fortune, qu'en feriez-vous?; *see also* **1f.**

d (*admit*) dire, reconnaître. **I must ~ (that) she's very pretty** je dois dire *or* reconnaître qu'elle est très jolie.

e (*register*) *[dial, gauge etc]* marquer, indiquer. **my watch ~s 10 o'clock** ma montre marque *or* indique 10 heures; **the thermometer ~s 30°** le thermomètre marque *or* indique 30°.

f (*in phrases*) dire. **I can't ~ I'm fond of anchovies** je ne peux pas dire que j'aime (*subj*) les anchois; **"10 o'clock" he said to himself** "10 heures" se dit-il; **would you really ~ so?** (le pensez-vous) vraiment?; **is he right? — I should ~ he is** *or* **I should ~ so** (*emphatic: expressing certainty*) est-ce qu'il a raison? — et comment! *or* pour avoir raison il a raison!; (*expressing doubt*) est-ce qu'il a raison? — il me semble *or* je pense que oui; **I should ~ he is right!** il a bien raison, c'est moi qui vous le dis!; **didn't I ~ so?** je l'avais bien dit n'est-ce pas?; **and so ~ all of us** nous sommes tous d'accord là-dessus; **to ~ nothing of ...** (+ *n*) sans parler de ...; (+ *vb*) sans parler du fait que ..., sans compter que ...; **that's ~ing a lot*** ce n'est pas peu dire; **he's cleverer than his brother but that isn't ~ing much*** *or* **a lot*** il est plus intelligent que son frère, mais ça ne veut pas dire grand-chose; **that doesn't ~ much for him** ce n'est pas à son honneur; **that doesn't ~ much for his intelligence** cela ne dénote pas beaucoup d'intelligence de sa part, cela en dit long (*iro*) sur son intelligence; **it ~s much** *or* **a lot for his courage that he stayed** il a bien prouvé son courage en restant; **his clothes ~ a lot about him** ses vêtements en disent long sur lui *or* sa personnalité; **she hasn't much to ~ for herself** elle n'a jamais grand-chose à dire; **he always has a lot to ~ for himself** il parle toujours beaucoup, il a toujours son mot à dire; **what have you (got) to ~ for yourself?** qu'avez-vous comme excuse?; **you might as well ~ the earth is flat!** autant dire que la terre est plate!; **don't ~ it's broken!*** ne me dis pas que c'est cassé!; **you can ~ THAT again!*** c'est le cas de le dire!, à qui le dites-vous!*; (*emphatic*) **you('ve) said it!*** tu l'as dit!*; (*hum*) **though I ~s‡ it as shouldn't ...** ce n'est pas à moi de dire ça mais ...; **~ no more** (= *I understand*) ça va, j'ai compris; **let's ~ no more about it!** n'en parlons plus!; **enough said!*, 'nuff said!‡** (ça) suffit!, assez parlé!, en voilà assez!; **interesting, not to ~ encouraging** intéressant, pour ne pas dire encourageant; **to ~ the least** c'est le moins qu'on puisse dire; **she was not very wise, to ~ the least** elle était pour le moins imprudente; **it wasn't a very good meal, to ~ the least of it** c'était un repas assez médiocre pour ne pas dire plus; **it goes without ~ing that ...** il va sans dire que ..., il va de soi que ...; **shall we ~ £5/Tuesday?** disons *or* mettons 5 livres/mardi?; **just ~ the word and I'll go** vous n'avez qu'un mot à dire pour que je parte; **he hadn't a good word to ~ for her** il n'a rien trouvé à dire en sa faveur; **I'll ~ this** *or* **one thing for him, he's clever** je dirai ceci en sa faveur, il est intelligent; **there's something to be said for it** cela a des mérites *or* du bon *or* des avantages; **there's something to be said for waiting** il y aurait peut-être intérêt à attendre, on ferait peut-être mieux d'attendre; **it's easier** *or* **sooner said than done!** c'est plus facile à dire qu'à faire!, facile à dire!*; **when all is said and done** tout compte fait, au bout du compte; **~ what you like** *or* **will (about him), he's not a bad chap** tu peux dire ce que tu veux (de lui), ce n'est pas un mauvais bougre; **what do you ~ to a cup of tea? — I won't ~ no (to it)*** que diriez-vous d'une tasse de thé? — j'en boirais bien une *or* ce ne serait pas de refus* *or* je ne dirais pas non; **what would you ~ to a round of golf?** si on faisait une partie de golf?; **there's no ~ing what he'll do** (il est) impossible de dire *or* on ne peut pas savoir ce qu'il fera.

2 vi dire. **so to ~** pour ainsi dire; **that is to ~** c'est-à-dire; **it is (as) one** *or* **you might ~ a new method** c'est comme qui dirait* une nouvelle méthode; **(I) ~!*** dites donc!; (*iro*) **you don't ~!*** sans blague!* (*iro*), pas possible! (*iro*); **~*, what time is it?** dites, quelle heure est-il?; **if there were, ~, 500 people** s'il y avait, mettons *or* disons, 500 personnes; (*iro*) **~s** *or* **sez you!‡** que tu dis!*; **~s who?‡, sez who?‡** ah oui? (*iro*); **as they ~** comme on dit, comme dirait l'autre*; **it seems rather rude, I must ~** cela ne me paraît guère poli, je l'avoue; (*expressing indignation*) **well, I must ~!** ça alors!*; **it's not for me to ~** (*not my responsibility*) ce n'est pas à moi de décider *or* de juger; (*not my place*) ce n'est pas à moi de le dire.

3 n: **to have one's ~** dire son mot, dire ce qu'on a à dire; **to have a ~/no ~ in the matter** avoir/ne pas avoir voix au chapitre; **to have a ~ in selecting ...** avoir son mot à dire dans la sélection de ...; **to have a strong ~ in sth** jouer un rôle déterminant dans qch; *see also* **1a**.

4 comp ► **say-so***: **on your say-so** parce que vous le dites (*or* l'aviez dit *etc*); **on his say-so** parce qu'il le dit (*or* l'a dit *etc*), sur ses dires; **it's his say-so** c'est lui qui décide, c'est à lui de dire.

SAYE [ˌeseɪwaɪˈiː] (*Brit*) (abbr of **Save As You Earn**) *see* **save 1c**.

saying [ˈseɪɪŋ] n dicton *m*, proverbe *m*, adage *m*. **as the ~ goes** comme dit le proverbe, comme on dit; **~s of the week** les mots *mpl or* les citations *fpl* de la semaine.

SBU [esbiːˈjuː] n (abbr of **strategic business unit**) *see* **strategic**.

SC (*US*) abbr of **South Carolina**.

s/c (abbr of **self-contained**) *see* **self 2**.

scab [skæb] 1 n a *[wound]* croûte *f*, escarre *f*. b (*NonC*) = **scabies**. c (‡ *pej: strikebreaker*) jaune *m* (*pej*), briseur *m* de grève. 2 vi a se cicatriser, former une croûte. b (‡ *pej: strikebreaker*) refuser de faire grève, faire le jaune.

scabbard [ˈskæbəd] n *[dagger]* gaine *f*; *[sword]* fourreau *m*.

scabby [ˈskæbɪ] adj *skin* croûteux; (*Med*) scabieux; (‡) *behaviour* moche*, méprisable.

scabies [ˈskeɪbiːz] n (*NonC: Med*) gale *f*.

scabious¹ [ˈskeɪbɪəs] adj (*Med*) scabieux.

scabious² [ˈskeɪbɪəs] n (*Bot*) scabieuse *f*.

scabrous [ˈskeɪbrəs] adj a *question, topic* scabreux, risqué. b (*Bot, Zool*) rugueux.

scads‡ [skædz] npl (*US*) **to have ~ of** avoir beaucoup de *or* plein* de.

scaffold [ˈskæfəld] n a (*gallows*) échafaud *m*. b (*Constr*) échafaudage *m*.

scaffolding [ˈskæfəldɪŋ] n (*NonC*) (*structure*) échafaudage *m*; (*material*) matériel *m* pour échafaudages.

scag‡ [skæg] n (*US Drugs sl*) héroïne *f*.

scalawag* [ˈskæləwæg] n (*US*) = **scallywag***.

scald [skɔːld] 1 vt *jar, teapot, tomatoes* échauder, ébouillanter; (*sterilize*) stériliser. **to ~ one's hand** s'ébouillanter la main; **to ~ o.s.** s'ébouillanter; (*Culin*) **to ~ the milk** chauffer le lait sans le faire bouillir. 2 n brûlure *f* (causée par l'eau *etc* bouillante).

scalding [ˈskɔːldɪŋ] adj (*also* **~ hot**) bouillant, brûlant. (*fig*) **~ tears** larmes brûlantes.

scale¹ [skeɪl] 1 n a *[thermometer, ruler]* graduation *f*, échelle *f* (graduée); *[numbers]* série *f*; *[wages]* barème *m*, échelle. **~ of charges** (*gen*) tableau *m* des tarifs; (*Econ, Fin*) barème *m* des redevances; **social ~** échelle sociale; *see* **centigrade, Fahrenheit, sliding**.

b *[map, drawing]* échelle *f*. **(drawn) to ~** à l'échelle; **drawn to a ~ of** rapporté à l'échelle de; **on a ~ of 1 cm to 5 km** à une échelle de 1 cm pour 5 km *or* de 1/500 000; **this map is not to ~** *or* **is out of ~** les distances ne sont pas respectées sur cette carte.

c (*fig*) (*scope*) échelle *f*; (*size etc*) importance *f*. **on a large ~** sur une grande échelle, en grand; **on a small ~** sur une petite échelle, en petit; **on a national ~** à l'échelle nationale; **a disaster of** *or* **on this ~** une catastrophe de cette importance.

d (*Mus*) gamme *f*. **to practise one's ~s** faire ses gammes.

2 comp ► **scale drawing** dessin *m* à l'échelle ► **scale model** modèle réduit; *see* **full-scale** *etc*.

3 vt a *wall, mountain* escalader.

b *map* dessiner à l'échelle.

► **scale back** vt sep (*US*) = **scale down**.

► **scale down** vt sep (*gen*) réduire; *salary*, (*Scol*) *marks* réduire proportionnellement; *drawing* réduire l'échelle de; *production* réduire, baisser.

► **scale up** vt sep augmenter proportionnellement.

scale² [skeɪl] 1 n *see* **scales**. 2 comp ► **scale maker** fabricant *m* de balances ► **scale pan** plateau *m* de balance. 3 vti peser.

scale³ [skeɪl] 1 n a *[fish, reptile, rust]* écaille *f*; *[skin]* squame *f*. **metal ~** écaille métallique; (*fig*) **the ~s fell from his eyes** les écailles lui sont tombées des yeux. b (*NonC*) *[water pipes, kettle]* tartre *m*, dépôt *m* calcaire; *[teeth]* tartre. 2 vt a *fish* écailler. b *teeth, kettle* détartrer.

► **scale off** vi s'en aller en écailles, s'écailler.

scales [skeɪlz] npl (*for weighing*) (*gen: in kitchen, shop*) balance *f*; (*in bathroom*) pèse-personne *m inv*, balance *f*; (*for babies*) pèse-bébé *m inv*; (*for luggage, heavy goods*) bascule *f*; (*for letters*) pèse-lettres *m inv*; (*manual, with weight on a rod*) balance romaine. **kitchen** *or* **household ~** balance de ménage; **pair of ~** balance *f* (à plateaux); (*Astrol, Astron*) **the S~** la Balance; **to turn the ~ at 80 kilos** peser 80 kilos; (*fig*) **to tip the ~** faire pencher la balance (*in sb's favour* du côté de qn; *against sb* contre qn); *see* **platform** *etc*.

scallion [ˈskælɪən] n (*gen*) oignon *m*; (*US: shallot*) échalote *f*; (*US: leek*) poireau *m*.

scallop [ˈskɒləp] 1 n a coquille *f* Saint-Jacques, pétoncle *m*. **~ shell** coquille. b (*Sewing*) **~s** festons *mpl*. 2 vt a **~ed fish/lobster** coquille *f* de poisson/de homard. b *hem etc* festonner. (*Sewing*) **~ed edge** bordure festonnée *or* à festons; (*Culin*) **to ~ (the edges of) a pie** canneler le bord d'une tourte.

scallywag* [ˈskælɪwæg] n a (*rascal*) petit(e) polisson(ne) *m(f)*. b (*US Hist*) *Sudiste républicain (après la guerre de Sécession)*.

scalp [skælp] 1 n cuir *m* chevelu; (*Indian trophy*) scalp *m*. 2 vt scalper. 3 vi (* *St Ex*) boursicoter.

scalpel [ˈskælpəl] n (*Med*) scalpel *m*; (*for paper etc*) cutter *m*.

scalper* [ˈskælpəʳ] n (*St Ex*) spéculateur *m* sur la journée.

scaly [ˈskeɪlɪ] adj *fish* écailleux; *skin* squameux; *kettle, pipe* entartré.

scam‡ [skæm] (*US*) 1 n arnaque‡ *m*, escroquerie *f*. 2 vi faire de la gratte* *or* des bénefs‡.

scamp¹* [skæmp] n (*child*) polisson(ne) *m(f)*, galopin* *m*; (*adult*) coquin(e) *m(f)*.

scamp² [skæmp] vt *one's work etc* bâcler*.

scamper [ˈskæmpəʳ] 1 n galopade *f*; *[mice]* trottinement *m*. 2 vi *[children]* galoper; *[mice]* trottiner. *[children]* **to ~ in/out** *etc* entrer/sortir *etc* en gambadant.

► **scamper about** vi *[children]* gambader; *[mice]* trottiner çà et là.

► **scamper away, scamper off** vi *[children, mice]* s'enfuir, détaler*.

scampi [ˈskæmpɪ] npl langoustines *fpl* (frites), scampi *mpl*.

scan [skæn] 1 vt a (*examine closely*) *horizon, sb's face* scruter; *crowd* fouiller du regard; *newspaper* lire attentivement (*for sth* pour y trouver qch).

b (*glance quickly over*) *horizon* promener son regard sur; *crowd* parcourir des yeux; *newspaper* parcourir rapidement, feuilleter.

c (*Comput*) scruter.

d (*Radar, TV*) balayer; (*Med*) *[machine]* balayer; *[person]* faire une scanographie de.

e (*Poetry*) scander.

2 **vi** se scander. **this line does not ~** ce vers est faux.

3 **n a** (*Rad, TV*) balayage *m*.

b (*Med*) (*scanning*) scanographie *f*, tomodensitométrie *f*; (*picture*) scanographie *f*, scanner* *m*. (*Med*) **(ultra-sound) ~** échographie *f*; **to have a ~** passer un scanner*; passer une échographie.

scandal [ˈskændl] 1 **n a** (*disgrace*) scandale *m*; (*Jur*) diffamation *f*. **to cause a ~** causer un scandale; **the groundnuts ~** le scandale des arachides; **it's a (real) ~** c'est scandaleux, c'est une honte; **it's a ~ that** ... c'est un scandale *or* une honte que ... + *subj*. b (*NonC: gossip*) médisance *f*, cancans *mpl*, ragots* *mpl*. **to talk ~** colporter des cancans *or* des ragots*; **have you heard the latest ~?** avez-vous entendu les derniers potins?*; **there's a lot of ~ going around about him** il y a beaucoup de ragots* qui circulent sur son compte. 2 **comp ►scandalmonger** mauvaise langue, colporteur *m*, -euse *f* de ragots*; (*US Press*) torchon* *m*.

scandalize [ˈskændəlaɪz] **vt** scandaliser, indigner. **to be ~d by** se scandaliser de, s'indigner de; **she was quite ~d** elle était vraiment scandalisée *or* indignée.

scandalous [ˈskændələs] **adj** *talk, behaviour* scandaleux; (*Jur*) diffamatoire. **that's a ~ price** c'est scandaleux de demander ce prix-là; **it's simply ~** c'est vraiment scandaleux, c'est un vrai scandale.

scandalously [ˈskændələslɪ] **adv** scandaleusement.

Scandinavia [ˌskændɪˈneɪvɪə] **n** Scandinavie *f*.

Scandinavian [ˌskændɪˈneɪvɪən] 1 **adj** scandinave. **~ (type *or* style) furniture** *etc* mobilier *m etc* de type scandinave, ≃ mobilier *etc* design. 2 **n** Scandinave *mf*.

scandium [ˈskændɪəm] **n** scandium *m*.

scanner [ˈskænəʳ] **n** (*Med*) tomodensitomètre *m*, scanographe *m*, scanner *m*; (*Med*) (*ultra-sound ~*) échographe *m*; (*Radar, TV*) scanner, analyseur *m* à balayage; (*graphic arts*) scanner; (*optical ~*) lecteur *m* optique.

scanning [ˈskænɪŋ] 1 **n** (*see* **scan 1d**) balayage *m*; scanographie *f*. 2 **adj**: **~ device** = œil *m* électronique; **~ electron microscope** microscope *m* électronique à balayage.

scansion [ˈskænʃən] **n** scansion *f*.

scant [skænt] **adj** peu abondant, insuffisant. **to pay ~ attention** faire à peine attention; **~ praise** éloge des plus brefs.

scantily [ˈskæntɪlɪ] **adv** insuffisamment. **~ clad** vêtu du strict minimum, en tenue légère (*hum*).

scantiness [ˈskæntɪnɪs] **n** insuffisance *f*.

scanty [ˈskæntɪ] **adj** *meal, harvest* peu abondant, insuffisant; *swimsuit* minuscule, réduit à sa plus simple expression (*hum*). **a ~ income** de maigres revenus *mpl*.

scapegoat [ˈskeɪpgəʊt] **n** bouc *m* émissaire.

scapegrace [ˈskeɪpgreɪs] **n** coquin(e) *m(f)*, vaurien(ne) *m(f)*.

scapula [ˈskæpjʊlə] **n, pl ~s *or* scapulae** [ˈskæpjʊliː] omoplate *f*.

scapular [ˈskæpjʊləʳ] **adj, n** scapulaire *(m)*.

scar¹ [skɑːʳ] 1 **n** (*mark: lit, fig*) cicatrice *f*; (*knife wound, esp on face*) balafre *f*. **it left a ~ on his face** cela a laissé une cicatrice sur son visage; (*fig*) **the quarrying left a ~ on the hillside** l'exploitation de la carrière a laissé une cicatrice sur *or* a mutilé le flanc de la colline; (*fig*) **it left a deep ~ on his mind** il en est resté profondément marqué (*fig*).

2 **comp ►Scarface** le Balafré **►scar tissue** (*Med*) tissus *mpl* cicatrisés.

3 **vt** marquer d'une cicatrice, (*with knife*) balafrer. **he was ~red with many wounds** il portait les cicatrices de nombreuses blessures; **face ~red by smallpox** figure grêlée par la petite vérole; **war-~red town** ville qui porte des cicatrices de la guerre; **walls ~red by bullets** des murs portant des traces de balles.

scar² [skɑːʳ] **n** (*crag*) rocher escarpé.

scarab [ˈskærəb] **n** (*beetle, gem*) scarabée *m*.

scarce [skɛəs] 1 **adj** *food, money* peu abondant; *copy, edition* rare. **money/corn is getting ~** l'argent/le blé se fait rare; **such people are ~** de telles gens sont rares, on ne rencontre pas souvent de telles gens; **to make o.s. ~*** s'esquiver, se sauver*. 2 **adv** (††) = **scarcely**.

scarcely [ˈskɛəslɪ] **adv** à peine. **it ~ touched him** cela l'a à peine touché; **I could ~ stand** je pouvais à peine tenir debout, j'avais de la peine *or* du mal à tenir debout; **~ anybody knows** il y a très peu de gens qui savent; **he ~ ever goes there** il n'y va presque jamais, il n'y va guère; **I ~ know what to say** je ne sais trop que dire; **I can ~ believe it** j'ai peine à *or* du mal à le croire.

scarceness [ˈskɛəsnɪs] **n**, **scarcity** [ˈskɛəsɪtɪ] **n** (*lack: of corn, money etc*) manque *m*, pénurie *f*, disette *f*; (*scarcity*) rareté *f*. **there is a ~ of good artists today** il n'y a plus guère de bons artistes; **the ~ of the metal** la rareté du métal; **scarcity value** valeur *f* de rareté.

scare [skɛəʳ] 1 **n a to give sb a ~** effrayer qn, faire peur à qn, donner la frousse à qn*; **what a ~ he gave me!** il m'a fait une de ces peurs! *or* une de ces frousses!*

b (*rumour etc*) bruit *m* alarmant *or* alarmiste. **to raise a ~** semer la panique *or* l'alarme, faire courir des bruits alarmants; **the invasion ~** les bruits alarmistes d'invasion; **bomb/gas/typhoid** *etc* **~** alerte *f* à la bombe/au gaz/à la typhoïde *etc*; **because of the war ~** à cause des rumeurs *fpl* de guerre; **there have been several war ~s this year** à plusieurs reprises cette année les gens ont craint la guerre.

2 **comp** *headlines, tactics* alarmiste **►scarecrow** (*lit, fig*) épouvantail *m* **►scarehead**‡ (*US Press*) manchette *f* à sensation **►scaremonger** alarmiste *mf* **►scaremongering** alarmisme *m* **►scare story** histoire *f* alarmante.

3 **vt** effrayer, faire peur à. **to ~ sb stiff*** faire une peur bleue à qn; **to ~ the life *or* wits out of sb** faire une peur bleue à qn; *see also* **scared, hell, living, shit.**

►scare away, scare off vt sep: **the dog scared him away** la peur du chien l'a fait fuir, il a fui par peur du chien; (*fig*) **the price scared him away** le prix lui a fait peur.

►scare up* vt sep (*US*) *food, money* arriver à trouver.

scared [skɛəd] **adj** effrayé, affolé (*of* par). **to be ~** avoir peur (*of* de); **to be ~ stiff*** avoir une peur bleue, avoir la frousse* *or* la trouille‡; **to be ~ out of one's wits*** être complètement affolé *or* paniqué*; **he's ~ to death of women*** il a une peur terrible *or* mortelle des femmes.

scaredy* [ˈskɛədɪ] **n** (*Brit: children's talk*) **~ (cat)** trouillard(e)‡ *m(f)*, poule *f* mouillée*.

scarf¹ [skɑːf] **n, pl ~s *or* scarves** écharpe *f*; (*square*) foulard *m*. **~-ring** coulant *m or* anneau *m* pour foulard; *see* **head.**

scarf²‡ [skɑːf] **vt** (*US: also* **~ down**) engloutir, s'enfiler‡.

scarify [ˈskɛərɪfaɪ] **vt** (*Agr, Med*) scarifier; (*fig*) éreinter.

scarlatina [ˌskɑːləˈtiːnə] **n** scarlatine *f*.

scarlet [ˈskɑːlɪt] 1 **adj** écarlate. **to go *or* blush ~ (with shame)** devenir rouge *or* écarlate (de honte). 2 **comp ►scarlet fever** scarlatine *f* **►scarlet pimpernel** mouron *m* rouge **►scarlet runner (bean)** haricot grimpant. 3 **n** écarlate *f*.

scarp [skɑːp] **n** escarpement *m*.

scarper‡ [ˈskɑːpəʳ] **vi** (*Brit*) ficher le camp*.

scarves [skɑːvz] **npl of scarf.**

scary* [ˈskɛərɪ] **adj** qui donne des frissons *or* la frousse*, effrayant, angoissant.

scat¹‡ [skæt] **excl** allez ouste!*

scat² [skæt] **n** (*US Jazz*) scat *m* (*style d'improvisation vocale*).

scathing [ˈskeɪðɪŋ] **adj** *remark, criticism* acerbe, caustique, cinglant. **to be ~ about sth** critiquer qch de façon cinglante; **to give sb a ~ look** jeter un regard noir à qn, foudroyer qn du regard.

scathingly [ˈskeɪðɪŋlɪ] **adv** d'une manière acerbe *or* cinglante. **to look ~ at sb** foudroyer qn du regard.

scatter [ˈskætəʳ] 1 **vt a** (*also* **~ about, ~ around**) *crumbs, papers* éparpiller; *seeds* semer à la volée; *sand, salt, sawdust* répandre. (*fig*) **to ~ sth to the four winds** semer qch aux quatre vents; **he ~ed pennies among the children** il a jeté à la volée des piécettes aux enfants; **to ~ cushions on a divan** jeter des coussins çà et là sur un divan.

b *clouds, crowd* disperser; *enemy* mettre en déroute; *light* diffuser. **my relatives are ~ed all over the country** ma famille est dispersée aux quatre coins du pays.

2 **vi** *[clouds, crowd]* se disperser. **the onlookers ~ed at the approach of the police** les badauds se sont dispersés à l'arrivée de la police.

3 **n** (*Math, Tech*) dispersion *f*. **a ~ of houses** des maisons dispersées *or* éparses; **a ~ of raindrops** quelques gouttes de pluie éparses.

4 **comp ►scatterbrain** écervelé(e) *m(f)*, hurluberlu* *m* **►scatterbrained** écervelé, hurluberlu* **►scatter cushions** petits coussins **►scatter rugs** carpettes *fpl*.

scattered [ˈskætəd] **adj** *books etc* éparpillés; *houses* dispersés, éparpillés; *population* dispersé, disséminé; *light* diffus. **the village is very ~** les maisons du village sont très dispersées; (*Met*) **~ showers** averses *fpl* intermittentes.

scattering [ˈskætərɪŋ] **n** *[clouds, crowd]* dispersion *f*; *[light]* diffusion *f*. **there was a ~ of people in the hall** il y avait quelques personnes dispersées *or* çà et là dans la salle.

scattiness* [ˈskætɪnɪs] **n** (*Brit*) (*see* **scatty***) loufoquerie* *f*, folie *f*; étourderie *f*.

scatty* [ˈskætɪ] **adj** (*Brit*) **a** (*eccentric*) loufoque*, farfelu. (*crazy*) fou (*f* folle). **to drive sb ~** rendre qn fou. **b** (*scatterbrained*) écervelé, hurluberlu*, étourdi.

scavenge [ˈskævɪndʒ] 1 **vt** *streets* enlever les ordures de; *object* récupérer. 2 **vi**: **to ~ in the dustbins for sth** faire les poubelles pour trouver qch.

scavenger [ˈskævɪndʒəʳ] 1 **n a** (*Zool*) charognard *m*. **b** (*street cleaner*) éboueur *m*. **c** (*person: on rubbish dumps, in bins etc*) pilleur *m* de poubelles. 2 **comp ►scavenger hunt** chasse *f* au trésor, rallye *m*.

scenario [sɪˈnɑːrɪəʊ] **n a** (*Cine*) scénario *m*. **b** (*fig*) (*sequence of events*) scénario *m*; (*plan of action*) plan *m* d'action, stratégie *f* (*for* pour). (*Mil, Pol, etc*) **best-/worst-case ~** meilleure/pire hypothèse *f*.

scenarist ['si:nərɪst] n scénariste *mf*.

scene [si:n] 1 n a (*Theat etc*) (*part of play*) scène *f*; (*setting*) scène, décor *m*; (*fig*) scène; (*happening*) incident *m*. **the garden ~ in "Richard II"** la scène du jardin dans "Richard II"; (*Cine, TV*) **outdoor** *or* **outside ~** extérieur *m*; **~ from a film** scène *or* séquence *f* (tirée) d'un film; **the big ~ in the film** la grande scène du film; **it was his big ~** c'était sa grande scène; **the ~ is set in Paris** la scène se passe à Paris, l'action se déroule à Paris; (*fig*) **the ~ was set for their romance** toutes les conditions étaient réunies pour leur idylle; **this set the ~ for the discussion** ceci a préparé le terrain pour les discussions; (*fig*) **now let our reporter set the ~ for you** notre reporter va maintenant vous mettre au courant de la situation; (*Theat, fig*) **behind the ~s** dans les coulisses; (*fig*) **to work behind the ~s** travailler dans l'ombre *or* dans les coulisses; **~s of violence** scènes de violence; **there were angry ~s at the meeting** des incidents violents ont eu lieu au cours de la réunion; *see* **change**.
b (*place*) lieu(x) *m(pl)*, endroit *m*. **the ~ of the crime/accident** le lieu du crime/de l'accident; (*Mil*) **~ of operations** théâtre *m* des opérations; **he needs a change of ~** il a besoin de changer d'air *or* de décor*; **they were soon on the ~** ils furent vite sur les lieux; **to appear** *or* **come on the ~** faire son apparition; **when I came on the ~** quand je suis arrivé; **he has disappeared from the political ~** il a disparu de la scène politique; **the political ~ in France** la situation politique en France; **the drug ~ in our big cities** la situation de la drogue dans nos grandes villes; (*fig*) **it's a bad ~*** c'est pas brilliant*, la situation n'est pas brillante; **it's not my ~‡** ça n'est pas mon genre, ce n'est pas mon truc*.
c (*sight, view*) spectacle *m*, vue *f*, tableau *m*. **the ~ from the top is marvellous** du sommet la vue *or* le panorama est magnifique; **the ~ spread out before you** la vue *or* le panorama qui s'offre à vous; **the hills make a lovely ~** les collines offrent un très joli spectacle *or* tableau; **picture the ~ ...** représentez-vous la scène ...; **it was a ~ of utter destruction** c'était un spectacle de destruction totale.
d (**: fuss*) scène *f*. **try not to make a ~ about it** tâche de ne pas en faire (toute) une scène *or* toute une histoire*; **to have a ~ with sb** avoir une scène avec qn; **I hate ~s** je déteste les scènes.
e (*‡: sexually*) **to have a ~ with sb** avoir une liaison avec qn.
2 comp ▶**scene change** (*Theat*) changement *m* de décor(s) ▶**scene painter** peintre *m* de décors ▶**scene shift** changement *m* de décor(s) ▶**scene shifter** machiniste *mf*.

scenery ['si:nərɪ] n a paysage *m*, vue *f*. **the ~ is very beautiful** le paysage est très beau, la vue est très belle; **mountain ~** paysage de montagnes; (*fig*) **a change of ~ will do you good** un changement d'air *or* de cadre *or* de décor* vous fera du bien. b (*Theat*) décor(s) *m(pl)*.

scenic ['si:nɪk] adj scénique. (*esp US Rail*) **~ car** voiture *f* panoramique; **~ railway** (*panoramic*) petit train (d'agrément); (*Brit: switchback*) montagnes *fpl* russes; (*US*) **~ road** route *f* touristique; **an area of great ~ beauty** une région qui offre de très beaux panoramas.

scenography [si:'nɒgrəfɪ] n scénographie *f*.

scent [sent] 1 n a (*odour*) parfum *m*, senteur *f* (*liter*).
b (*liquid perfume*) parfum *m*. **to use ~** se parfumer.
c (*animal's track*) fumet *m*; (*fig*) piste *f*, voie *f*. (*Hunting, fig*) **to lose the ~** perdre la piste; **to throw** *or* **put sb off the ~** dépister *or* déjouer qn; **to put** *or* **throw dogs off the ~** dépister les chiens, brouiller *or* faire perdre la piste aux chiens; **to be on the (right) ~** être sur la bonne piste *or* voie; **he got the ~ of something suspicious** il a flairé quelque chose de louche.
d (*sense of smell*) [*person*] odorat *m*; [*animal*] flair *m*.
2 comp ▶**scent bottle** flacon *m* à parfum ▶**scent spray** vaporisateur *m* (à parfum); (*aerosol*) atomiseur *m* (à parfum).
3 vt a (*put ~ on*) *handkerchief, air* parfumer (*with* de). **the ~ed air** l'air parfumé *or* odorant.
b (*smell*) *game* flairer; (*fig*) *danger, trouble* flairer, pressentir.

scentless ['sentlɪs] adj inodore, sans odeur.

scepter ['septəʳ] n (*US*) = **sceptre**.

sceptic, (*US*) **skeptic** ['skeptɪk] adj, n sceptique (*mf*).

sceptical, (*US*) **skeptical** ['skeptɪkəl] adj sceptique (*of, about* sur). **I'm rather ~ about it** cela me laisse sceptique.

sceptically, (*US*) **skeptically** ['skeptɪkəlɪ] adv avec scepticisme.

scepticism, (*US*) **skepticism** ['skeptɪsɪzəm] n scepticisme *m*.

sceptre, (*US*) **scepter** ['septəʳ] n sceptre *m*.

schedule ['ʃedju:l], (*US*) ['skedju:l] 1 n a [*work, duties*] programme *m*, plan *m*; [*trains etc*] horaire *m*; [*events*] calendrier *m*. **production/building** *etc* **~** prévisions *fpl or* programme pour la production/la construction *etc*; **to make out a ~** établir un programme *or* un plan *or* un horaire; **the whole ceremony went off according to ~** toute la cérémonie s'est déroulée selon le programme *or* les prévisions; (*fig*) **it all went according to ~** tout s'est passé comme prévu; **the train is on** *or* **up to ~** le train est à l'heure; **the train is behind ~** le train a du retard; **the preparations are on ~/behind ~** il n'y a pas de retard/il y a du retard dans les préparatifs; **the work is on ~** les travaux avancent selon les prévisions; **our work has fallen behind ~** nous sommes en retard dans notre travail *or* sur notre plan de travail; **the ceremony will take place on ~** la cérémonie aura lieu à l'heure prévue (*or* à la date prévue *etc*); **our ~ does not include the Louvre** notre programme ne comprend pas le Louvre; **to be ahead of ~** (*in work*) avoir de l'avance sur son programme; [*train*] avoir de l'avance; **to work to a very tight ~** avoir un programme de travail très serré.
b (*list*) [*goods, contents*] liste *f*, inventaire *m*; [*prices*] barème *m*, tarif *m*. **~ of charges** tarif *or* liste *or* barème des prix, échéancier *m*, calendrier *m* des remboursements.
c (*Jur: to contract*) annexe *f* (*to* à).
2 vt a (*gen pass*) *activity* établir le programme *or* l'horaire de. **his ~d speech** le discours qu'il doit (*or* devait *etc*) prononcer; **his ~d departure** son départ prévu; **at the ~d time/date** *etc* à l'heure/à la date *etc* prévue *or* indiquée; **~d price** prix tarifé; **as ~d** comme prévu; [*train, bus etc*] **~d service** service régulier; **~d flight** vol régulier; **this stop is not ~d** cet arrêt n'est pas indiqué dans l'horaire; **he is ~d to leave at midday** son départ est fixé pour midi; **you are ~d to speak after him** d'après le programme c'est à vous de parler après lui; **the train is ~d for 11 o'clock** *or* **to arrive at 11 o'clock** selon l'horaire le train doit arriver à 11 heures; **~d territories** zone *f* sterling.
b *object* inscrire sur une liste. (*Brit: Admin, Archit*) **~d building** bâtiment classé (*comme monument historique*).

schema ['ski:mə] n, pl **schemata** [ski:'mɑ:tə] schéma *m*.

schematic [skɪ'mætɪk] adj schématique.

schematically [skɪ'mætɪkəlɪ] adv schématiquement.

scheme [ski:m] 1 n a (*plan*) plan *m* (*to do* pour faire); (*project*) projet *m*; (*method*) procédé *m* (*for doing* pour faire). **he's got a ~ for re-using plastic bottles** il a un plan *or* un projet *or* un procédé pour réutiliser les bouteilles en plastique; **a ~ of work** un plan de travail; **profit-sharing ~** système *m* de participation (aux bénéfices); **pension ~** régime *m* de retraites; **a ~ for greater productivity** un plan destiné à augmenter la productivité; (*fig*) **main's place in the ~ of things** le rôle de l'homme dans l'ordre des choses; (*fig*) **where does he stand in the ~ of things?** quel est son rôle dans toute cette affaire?, où se situe-t-il dans tout cela?; **in my/your** *etc* **~ of things** dans ma/votre *etc* façon de voir; **the ~ for the new bridge** le projet pour le nouveau pont; **it's some crazy ~ of his** c'est une de ses idées invraisemblables; **it's not a bad ~*** ça n'est pas une mauvaise idée; *see* **supplementary**.
b (*plot*) complot *m*, machination(s) *f(pl)*; (*dishonest plan*) procédé *m* malhonnête, combine* *f*. **it's a ~ to get him out of the way** c'est un complot pour l'éliminer.
c (*arrangement*) classification *f*, arrangement *m*, combinaison *f*; *see* **colour, rhyme**.
2 vt combiner, machiner.
3 vi comploter, conspirer, intriguer (*to do* pour faire).

schemer ['ski:məʳ] n (*on small scale*) intrigant(e) *m(f)*; (*on large scale*) conspirateur *m*, -trice *f*, comploteur *m*, -euse *f*.

scheming ['ski:mɪŋ] 1 adj intrigant, rusé. 2 n machinations *fpl*, intrigues *fpl*.

scherzo ['skɜ:tsəʊ] n, pl **~s** *or* **scherzi** ['skɜ:tsi:] scherzo *m*.

schism ['sɪzəm] n schisme *m*.

schismatic [sɪz'mætɪk] adj, n schismatique (*mf*).

schist [ʃɪst] n schiste *m* cristallin.

schiz‡ [skɪts] (*US, Can*) n a (abbr of **schizophrenic**) schizo‡ *mf*. b (abbr of **schizophrenia**) schizophrénie *f*.

schizo‡ ['skɪtsəʊ] adj, n (*Brit*) (abbr of **schizophrenic**) schizo‡ (*mf*).

schizoid ['skɪtsɔɪd] adj, n schizoïde (*mf*).

schizophrenia [ˌskɪtsəʊ'fri:nɪə] n schizophrénie *f*.

schizophrenic [ˌskɪtsəʊ'frenɪk] adj, n schizophrène (*mf*).

schlemiel‡, schlemihl‡ [ʃlə'mi:l] n (*US*) pauvre bougre* *m*, minable *m*.

schlep(p)‡ [ʃlep] (*US*) 1 vi se traîner, crapahuter‡. 2 vt trimballer*, (se) coltiner*.

schlock‡ [ʃlɒk] (*US*) 1 n camelote *f*. 2 adj de camelote.

schmaltz* [ʃmɔ:lts] n (*NonC*) sentimentalisme excessif.

schmaltzy* ['ʃmɔ:ltsɪ] adj à la guimauve, à l'eau de rose.

schmo [ʃməʊ] n, pl **~es** (*US*) ballot* *m*, andouille* *f*.

schmuck‡ [ʃmʌk] n (*US*) con‡ *m*, connard‡ *m*.

schnapps [ʃnæps] n schnaps *m*.

schnook [ʃnʊk] n (*US*) ballot* *m*, pauvre type* *m*.

schnorkel ['ʃnɔ:kl] n = **snorkel**.

schnorrer‡ ['ʃnɔ:rəʳ] n (*US*) mendigot *m*, tapeur* *m*.

schnozzle‡ ['ʃnɒzl] n (*US*) gros pif* *m*, tarin* *m*.

scholar ['skɒləʳ] n a lettré(e) *m(f)*, érudit(e) *m(f)*. **a ~ and a gentleman** un homme cultivé et raffiné; **a Dickens ~** un(e) spécialiste de Dickens; **I'm not much of a ~** je ne suis pas bien savant *or* instruit.
b (*scholarship holder*) boursier *m*, -ière *f*; (*†: pupil*) écolier *m*, -ière *f*.

scholarly ['skɒləlɪ] adj *account, work, man* érudit, savant.

scholarship ['skɒləʃɪp] 1 n a érudition *f*, savoir *m*. b (*award*) bourse *f* (d'études); (*US Univ*) bourse *f* (*pour étudiant de licence*). **to win a ~ to Cambridge** obtenir une bourse pour Cambridge (*par concours*). 2 comp ▶**scholarship holder** boursier *m*, -ière *f*.

scholastic [skə'læstɪk] 1 adj *philosophy* scolastique; *work, achievement* scolaire. **the ~ profession** (*gen*) l'enseignement *m*; (*teachers collectively*) les enseignants *mpl*; **~ agency** (*teachers' employment*) bureau *m* de placement pour enseignants; (*selection of school*) *organisme* *d'orientation sur le choix d'établissement scolaire;* (*US*) ~ **aptitude test** examen *m* d'entrée à l'université. 2 n (*Philos*) scolastique *m*.

scholasticism [skəˈlæstɪsɪzəm] n scolastique *f*.

school¹ [skuːl] 1 n a (*gen*) école *f*; (*primary* ~) école; (*secondary* ~) (*gen*) lycée *m*; (*up to 16 only*) collège *m*; (*of dancing*) école, académie *f*; (*of music*) école, conservatoire *m*. ~ **of motoring** auto-école *f*; **to go to** ~ aller à l'école (*or* au collège *or* au lycée *etc*); **to leave** ~ quitter l'école *etc;* **to send a child to** ~ (*gen*) envoyer un enfant à l'école; (*Admin*) scolariser un enfant; **at** *or* **in** ~ à l'école *etc;* **we were at** ~ **together** nous étions à la même école *etc;* **he wasn't at** ~ **yesterday** il n'était pas à l'école *etc or* en classe hier, il était absent hier; **the whole** ~ **wish(es) you well** toute l'école *etc* vous souhaite du succès; **to go skiing** (*etc*) **with the** ~ ≃ partir en classe de neige (*etc*); **television** (*etc*) **for** ~**s** la télévision (*etc*) scolaire; *see* **boarding, high, old, summer** *etc*.

b (*lessons*) classe(s) *f(pl)*, (*gen secondary*) cours *mpl*. ~ **reopens in September** la rentrée scolaire *or* la rentrée des classes est en septembre; **there's no** ~ **this morning** il n'y a pas classe *or* pas de classes ce matin, il n'y a pas (de) cours ce matin.

c (*Univ*) faculté *f*, collège *m*; (*Oxford and Cambridge*) salle *f* d'examens. (*Oxford and Cambridge*) **S**~**s** les examens *mpl* (*see also* **1f**); **he's at law/medical** ~ il fait son droit/sa médecine.

d (*institute*) institut *m*. **S**~ **of Linguistics/African Studies** *etc* Institut *m or* (*smaller*) Département *m* de Linguistique/d'Études africaines *etc;* (*US*) ~ **of education** école *f* normale (primaire).

e (*fig*) école *f*. **the hard** ~ **of poverty** la dure école de la pauvreté; **he learnt that in a good** ~ il a appris cela à bonne école.

f (*Hist: scholasticism*) **the** ~**s** l'École, la scolastique.

g [*painting, philosophy etc*] école *f*. (*Art*) **the Dutch** ~ l'école hollandaise; **the Freudian** ~ l'école freudienne; **a** ~ **of thought** une école de pensée; **an aristocrat/doctor** *etc* **of the old** ~ un aristocrate/un docteur *etc* de la vieille école; **he's one of the old** ~ il est de la vieille école *or* de la vieille garde, c'est un traditionaliste.

2 comp *equipment, edition, television, doctor* scolaire ►**school-age child** enfant *mf* d'âge scolaire ►**school attendance** scolarisation *f*, scolarité *f*; **school attendance officer** fonctionnaire *mf* chargé(e) de faire respecter les règlements de la scolarisation ►**schoolbag** cartable *m* ►**schoolbook** livre *m* scolaire *or* de classe ►**schoolboy** (*see* **1**) élève *m*, écolier *m*, lycéen *m*, collégien *m* (*see also* **public**); **schoolboy slang** argot *m* des écoles *or* des lycées ►**school bus** autobus *m or* car *m* de ramassage scolaire; **school bus service** service *m* de ramassage scolaire ►**school certificate**† ≃ BEPC *m* ►**schoolchild** écolier *m*, -ière *f*, lycéen(ne) *m(f)*, collégien(ne) *m(f)* ►**school council** (*Brit, Scol*) comité *m* des délégués de classe ►**school counsellor** (*US*) conseiller *m*, -ère *f* général(e) d'éducation ►**school crossing patrol** *see* **crossing b** ►**schooldays** années *fpl* de scolarité *or* d'école; **during my schooldays** du temps où j'allais en classe ►**school district** (*US*) secteur *m* scolaire ►**school doctor** médecin *m* scolaire ►**school educational outing** = **school outing** ►**school fees** frais *mpl* de scolarité ►**schoolfellow, schoolfriend** camarade *mf* de classe ►**school fund** (*in primary schools*) coopérative *f*; (*in secondary schools*) caisse *f* de solidarité ►**schoolgirl** (*see* **1a**) élève *f*, écolière *f*, lycéenne *f*, collégienne *f*; **schoolgirl complexion** teint *m* de jeune fille; **schoolgirl crush*** béguin* *m* (*on* pour) ►**school holidays** vacances *fpl* scolaires ►**school hours**: **during school hours** pendant les heures de classe ►**schoolhouse** (*school building*) école *f*; (*for headmaster*) maison *f* du directeur ►**school inspector** (*Brit Scol*) (*secondary*) ≃ inspecteur *m*, -trice *f* d'académie; (*primary*) ≃ inspecteur *m*, -trice *f* primaire ►**school leaver** (*Brit*) jeune *mf* qui a terminé ses études secondaires ►**school-leaving age** âge *m* de fin de scolarité; **to raise the school-leaving age** prolonger la scolarité (*to* jusqu'à) ►**school librarian** (*books only*) bibliothécaire *mf* scolaire; (*books and other resources*) documentaliste *mf* scolaire ►**school life** vie *f* scolaire ►**school lunch** repas *m* scolaire *or* pris à la cantine; **he hates school lunches** il déteste manger à la cantine; **to take school lunches** manger à la cantine (*à l'école etc*) ►**schoolmarm** (*pej*) institutrice *f* ►**schoolmarmish**: (*pej*) **she is very schoolmarmish** elle fait *or* est très maîtresse d'école ►**schoolmaster** (*primary*) instituteur *m*; (*secondary*) professeur *m* ►**schoolmate** = **schoolfellow** ►**school meal** = **school lunch** ►**school medical officer** (*Brit*) médecin *m* scolaire ►**Schoolmen** (*Philos*) scolastiques *mpl* ►**schoolmistress** (*primary*) institutrice *f*; (*secondary*) professeur *m* ►**school officer** = **school attendance officer** ►**school outing** (*Brit*) sortie *f* (éducative) scolaire ►**school phobia** phobie *f* de l'école ►**school record** (*Brit*) dossier *m* d'élève *or* scolaire ►**school report** bulletin *m* (scolaire) ►**schoolroom** salle *f* de classe; **in the schoolroom** dans la (salle de) classe, en classe ►**schools inspector** = **school inspector** ►**schools medical officer** = **school medical officer** ►**school superintendent** (*US*) inspecteur *m* (responsable du bon fonctionnement des établissements scolaires) ►**schoolteacher** (*primary*) instituteur *m*, -trice *f*; (*secondary*) professeur *m* ►**schoolteaching** enseignement *m* ►**school time**: **in school time** pendant les heures de classe ►**school uniform** uniforme *m* scolaire ►**school visit** sortie *f* (éducative) scolaire ►**schoolwork** travail *m* scolaire ►**school year** année *f* scolaire.

3 vt *animal* dresser; *feelings, reactions* contrôler; *voice etc* discipliner. **to** ~ **o.s. to do** s'astreindre à faire.

school² [skuːl] n [*fish*] banc *m*.

schooling [ˈskuːlɪŋ] n a (*Scol*) instruction *f*, études *fpl*. ~ **is free** les études sont gratuites; **compulsory** ~ scolarité *f* obligatoire; ~ **is compulsory up to 16** la scolarité est obligatoire jusqu'à 16 ans; **he had very little formal** ~ il a reçu très peu d'instruction; **he lost a year's** ~ il a perdu une année (d'école). b [*horse*] dressage *m*.

schooner [ˈskuːnəʳ] n a (*Naut*) schooner *m*, goélette *f*. b (*Brit: sherry glass*) grand verre *m* (à Xérès); (*US: beer glass*) demi *m* (de bière).

schuss [ʃʊs] n (*Ski*) schuss *m*.

schwah [ʃwɑː] n (*Phon*) schwa *m*.

sciatic [saɪˈætɪk] adj sciatique.

sciatica [saɪˈætɪkə] n sciatique *f*.

science [ˈsaɪəns] 1 n a science(s) *f(pl)*. **we study** ~ **at school** nous étudions les sciences au lycée; **gardening for him is quite a** ~ pour lui le jardinage est une véritable science; (*Univ*) **the Faculty of S**~, **the S**~ **Faculty** la faculté des Sciences; (*Brit*) **Secretary (of State) for S**~, **Minister of S**~ ministre *m* de la Recherche scientifique; **Department** *or* **Ministry of S**~ ministère *m* de la Recherche scientifique; *see* **applied, natural, social** *etc*.

b (†: *knowledge*) savoir *m*, connaissances *fpl*, science *f*. **to blind sb with** ~ éblouir qn de sa science.

2 comp *equipment, subject* scientifique; *exam* de sciences ►**science fiction** n science-fiction *f* ◊ adj de science-fiction ►**science park** parc *m* scientifique ►**science teacher** professeur *m* de sciences.

scientific [ˌsaɪənˈtɪfɪk] adj *investigation, method, studies* scientifique; *gifts* pour les sciences; *instrument* de précision. ~ **farming** l'agriculture *f* scientifique; (*Brit Police*) ~ **officer** expert *m* (de la police); **he's a very** ~ **footballer** il joue au football avec science.

scientifically [ˌsaɪənˈtɪfɪkəlɪ] adv scientifiquement; *plan etc* avec science.

scientist [ˈsaɪəntɪst] n (*as career*) scientifique *mf*; (*scientific scholar*) savant *m*. **my daughter is a** ~ ma fille est une scientifique; **one of our leading** ~**s** l'un de nos plus grands savants; *see* **Christian, social** *etc*.

scientologist [ˌsaɪənˈtɒlədʒɪst] adj, n scientologue (*mf*).

scientology [ˈsaɪənˈtɒlədʒɪ] n scientologie *f*.

sci-fi* [ˈsaɪˈfaɪ] (abbr of **science-fiction**) 1 n science-fiction *f*, S.F. *f*. 2 adj de science-fiction, de S.F.

Scillies [ˈsɪlɪz] npl, **Scilly Isles** [ˈsɪlɪaɪlz] npl Sorlingues *fpl*, îles *fpl* Scilly.

scimitar [ˈsɪmɪtəʳ] n cimeterre *m*.

scintillate [ˈsɪntɪleɪt] vi [*star, jewel*] scintiller; (*fig*) [*person*] briller (*dans une conversation*), pétiller d'esprit.

scintillating [ˈsɪntɪleɪtɪŋ] adj *star* scintillant; *jewel* scintillant, étincelant; *conversation, wit, remark* brillant, pétillant, étincelant.

scion [ˈsaɪən] n (*person*) descendant(e) *m(f)*; (*Bot*) scion *m*.

Scipio [ˈsɪpɪəʊ] n Scipion *m*.

scissor [ˈsɪzəʳ] 1 n: ~**s** ciseaux *mpl*; **a pair of** ~**s** une paire de ciseaux; *see* **kitchen, nail** *etc*. 2 comp ►**scissor bill** bec *m* en ciseaux ►**scissors-and-paste job** (*lit*) montage *m* à coups de ciseaux; (*fig*) compilation *f* ►**scissors jump** (*Sport*) saut *m* en ciseaux. 3 vt (*) couper avec des ciseaux.

sclera [ˈsklɪərə] n (*Anat*) sclérotique *f*.

sclerosis [sklɪˈrəʊsɪs] n, pl **scleroses** [sklɪˈrəʊsiːz] sclérose *f*; *see* **multiple**.

sclerotic [sklɪˈrɒtɪk] adj (*Anat*) sclérotique.

SCM [essiːˈem] n (*Brit*) (abbr of **State Certified Midwife**) *see* **state**.

scoff¹ [skɒf] vi se moquer. **to** ~ **at** se moquer de, mépriser; **he was** ~**ed at by the whole town** il a été l'objet de risée de toute la ville.

scoff²* [skɒf] vti (*esp Brit*) bouffer‡.

scoffer [ˈskɒfəʳ] n moqueur *m*, -euse *f*, railleur *m*, -euse *f*.

scoffing [ˈskɒfɪŋ] 1 adj *remark, laugh* moqueur, railleur. 2 n moqueries *fpl*, railleries *fpl*.

scofflaw [ˈskɒflɔː] n (*US*) personne *f* qui se moque des lois et des règlements.

scold [skəʊld] 1 vt réprimander, attraper, passer un savon à* (*for doing* pour avoir fait); *child* gronder, attraper, tirer les oreilles à* (*for doing* pour avoir fait). **he got** ~**ed** il s'est fait attraper. 2 vi grogner, rouspéter*. 3 n (*woman*) mégère *f*, chipie *f*.

scolding [ˈskəʊldɪŋ] n gronderie *f*, réprimande *f*. **to get a** ~ **from sb** se faire gronder *or* attraper par qn; **to give sb a** ~ réprimander *or* gronder qn.

scoliosis [ˌskɒlɪˈəʊsɪs] n scoliose *f*.

scollop [ˈskɒləp] = **scallop**.

scone [skɒn] n (*Brit*) scone *m* (*sorte de petit pain au lait.*)

scoop [skuːp] 1 n a (*for flour, sugar*) pelle *f* (*à main*); (*for water*) écope *f*; (*for ice cream*) cuiller *f* à glace; (*for mashed potatoes*) cuiller à purée; [*bulldozer*] lame *f*; [*dredger*] benne *f* preneuse; (*also* ~**ful**) pelletée *f*. **at one** ~ en un seul coup de pelle; (*with hands*) d'un seul coup.

b (*Press*) reportage exclusif *or* à sensation, scoop *m*; (*Comm*) bénéfice important. **to make a** ~ (*Comm*) faire un gros bénéfice;

(*Press*) publier une information *or* une nouvelle (à sensation) en exclusivité, faire un scoop; (*Press*) **it was a ~ for the "Globe"** le "Globe" l'a publié en exclusivité, cela a été un scoop pour le "Globe".

2 **vt** (*Comm*) *market* s'emparer de; *competitor* devancer; *profit* ramasser; (*Press*) *story* publier en exclusivité; (*fig*) **to ~ the pool** tout rafler.

►**scoop out vt sep: to scoop water out of a boat** écoper un bateau; **he scooped the sand out (of the bucket)** il a vidé le sable (du seau); **he had to scoop the water out of the sink** il a dû se servir d'un récipient pour vider l'eau de l'évier; **he scooped out a hollow in the soft earth** il a creusé un trou dans la terre molle.

►**scoop up vt sep** *earth, sweets* ramasser, (*with instrument*) ramasser à la pelle. **the eagle scooped up the rabbit** l'aigle a saisi le lapin dans ses serres; **he scooped up the child and ran for his life** il a ramassé l'enfant en vitesse et s'est enfui à toutes jambes.

scoot‡ [sku:t] **vi** se sauver*, filer*. **~!** allez-vous-en!, fichez le camp!*, filez!*; **to ~ in/out** *etc* entrer/sortir *etc* rapidement *or* en coup de vent.

►**scoot away**‡, **scoot off**‡ **vi** se sauver*, filer*.

scooter ['sku:tə^r] **n** (*also* **motor ~**) scooter *m*; (*child's*) trottinette *f*.

scope [skəʊp] **n** (*opportunity: for activity, action etc*) possibilité *f*, occasion *f*; (*range*) [*law, regulation*] étendue *f*, portée *f*; (*capacity*) [*person*] compétence *f*, moyens *mpl* (intellectuels), capacité(s) *f(pl)*; [*undertaking*] envergure *f*. **a programme of considerable ~** un programme d'une envergure considérable *or* très ambitieux; **to extend the ~ of one's activities** élargir le champ de ses activités, étendre son rayon d'action; **his job gave him plenty of ~ (for his ability)** son travail lui offrait beaucoup de possibilités pour montrer ses compétences; **he wants a job with more ~** il voudrait un travail avec un champ d'activité plus varié; **it gave him full ~ to decide for himself** cela le laissait entièrement libre de *or* cela lui donnait carte blanche pour prendre les décisions lui-même; **this work is within/beyond his ~** ce travail entre dans ses compétences/dépasse ses compétences; **the subject is within/beyond the ~ of this book** le sujet entre dans les limites/dépasse les limites de ce livre; **that is within the ~ of the new regulations** ceci est prévu par le nouveau règlement.

scorbutic [skɔ:'bju:tɪk] **adj** scorbutique.

scorch [skɔ:tʃ] 1 **n** (*also* **~ mark**) brûlure légère. **there was a ~ on her dress** sa robe avait été roussie. 2 **vt** *linen* roussir, brûler légèrement; *grass* [*fire etc*] brûler; [*sun*] dessécher, roussir. **~ed earth policy** tactique *f* de la terre brûlée. 3 **vi** a roussir. b (*Brit *: drive fast*) (*also* **~ along**) [*cyclist*] pédaler à fond de train *or* comme un fou* (*or* une folle*); [*driver*] conduire à un train d'enfer; [*car*] rouler à toute vitesse; **this car can ~ from 0 - 80 mph in under 10 seconds** cette voiture peut passer de 0 à 120 km/h en moins de 10 secondes.

scorcher* ['skɔ:tʃə^r] **n** journée *f* torride. **it was a (real) ~ (of a day)** il faisait une chaleur caniculaire *or* une de ces chaleurs*.

scorching ['skɔ:tʃɪŋ] **adj** a *heat* torride; *sand* brûlant. **~ sun** soleil *m* de plomb. b (**: also* **~ hot**) *food* brûlant; *liquid* bouillant; *weather* très chaud. **it was a ~ (hot) day** il faisait une de ces chaleurs*.

score [skɔ:^r] 1 **n** a (*amount won etc*) (*Sport*) score *m*; (*Cards*) marque *f*; (*US Scol: mark*) note *f*. **to keep (the) ~** (*gen*) compter *or* marquer les points; (*Cards*) tenir la marque; (*Tennis*) tenir le score; (*Ftbl*) **there's no ~ yet** on n'a pas encore marqué (de but); **there was no ~ in the match between X and Y** X et Y ont fait match nul *or* zéro à zéro; **what's the ~?** (*Sport*) où en est le jeu? *or* la partie? *or* le match?; (** fig*) où en sommes-nous?; (*fig*) **to know the ~*** connaître le topo*, savoir de quoi il retourne; *see* **half** *etc*.

b (*debt*) compte *m*, dette *f*. (*fig*) **to settle a ~ with sb** régler son compte à qn; **he's got a ~** *or* **an old ~ to settle with him** il a un compte à régler avec lui.

c (*subject, account*) titre *m*. **on the ~ of** pour cause de, en raison de; **on more ~s than one** à plus d'un titre; **on that ~** à cet égard, sur ce chapitre, à ce titre; **on what ~?** à quel titre?; **on several ~s** à plusieurs titres.

d (*mark, cut*) (*on metal, wood*) rayure *f*; (*deeper*) entaille *f*; (*on rock*) strie *f*; (*on skin, leather*) (*accidental*) éraflure *f*; (*deliberate*) incision *f*.

e (*Mus*) (*sheets of music*) partition *f*; (*film ~*) musique *f* du film. **piano ~** partition de piano; **to follow the ~** suivre la partition; (*Cine*) **who wrote the ~?** qui est l'auteur de la musique?; *see* **vocal**.

f (*twenty*) **a ~** vingt; **a ~ of people** une vingtaine de personnes; **three ~ and ten**†† soixante-dix; (*fig*) **~s of times** trente-six fois*; **there were ~s of mistakes** il y avait un grand nombre de *or* des tas* de fautes.

2 **comp** ►**scoreboard** (*gen*) tableau *m* (d'affichage); (*Billiards*) boulier *m* ►**scorecard** [*game*] carte *f or* fiche *f* de score; (*Shooting*) carton *m*; (*Golf*) carte *f* de parcours; (*Cards*) feuille *f* de marque ►**scorekeeper** marqueur *m* ►**scoresheet** (*Games*) feuille *f* de match; (*Ftbl*) **they're ahead on the scoresheet** ils mènent à la marque.

3 **vt** a *goal, point* marquer. (*Scol etc*) **to ~ 70% (in an exam)** avoir 70 sur 100 (à un examen); **to ~ well in a test** avoir *or* obtenir un bon résultat à un test; (*Tennis*) **he went 5 games without scoring a point** il n'a pas marqué un seul point pendant 5 jeux; **they had 14 goals ~d against them** leurs adversaires ont marqué 14 buts; **to ~ a hit** (*Fencing*) toucher; (*Shooting*) viser juste; (*fig*) **to ~ a great success** *or* **a hit** remporter *or* se tailler un grand succès; **he certainly ~d a hit with her*** il a vraiment eu une touche*; (*fig, esp US*) **to ~ points** marquer des points; (*fig*) **to ~ a point (over** *or* **off sb)** prendre le dessus (sur qn), l'emporter (sur qn), marquer un point (aux dépens de qn).

b (*cut*) *stick* entailler; *rock* strier; *ground* entamer; *wood, metal* rayer; *leather, skin* inciser, (*accidentally*) érafler; (*Culin*) inciser.

c (*Mus*) (*arrange*) adapter (*for* pour); (*orchestrate*) orchestrer (*for* pour); (*US: compose*) composer. **the film was ~d by X** la musique du film a été composée par X; **it is ~d for piano and cello** c'est écrit pour piano et violoncelle.

4 **vi** a (*Sport*) [*player*] marquer un *or* des point(s); [*footballer etc*] marquer un but; (*keep the score*) marquer les points. (*Ftbl*) **they failed to ~** ils n'ont pas réussi à marquer (un but); (*fig*) **that is where he ~s** c'est là qu'il a le dessus *or* l'avantage; **to ~ over** *or* **off sb** marquer un point aux dépens de qn, damer le pion à qn; (*fig*) **that doesn't ~** ça ne compte pas.

b (‡*: succeed*) (*gen*) avoir du succès; (*have sex*) tomber une fille; (*in buying drugs*) réussir à acheter de la drogue.

►**score off, score out, score through vt sep** rayer, barrer, biffer.

►**score up vt sep** *points* marquer, faire; *debt* porter en compte, inscrire. (*fig*) **that remark will be scored up against you** on ne vous pardonnera pas cette réflexion.

scorer ['skɔ:rə^r] **n** (*keeping score*) marqueur *m*; (*also* **goal ~**) marqueur (de but).

scoring ['skɔ:rɪŋ] **n** (*NonC*) a (*Sport*) buts *mpl*; (*Cards*) points *mpl*. (*Ftbl etc*) **all the ~ was in the second half** tous les buts ont été marqués pendant la deuxième mi-temps; **"rules for ~"** "comment marquer les points"; **the rules for ~ should be changed** il faudrait changer la règle pour marquer les points. b (*cut*) incision *f*, striage *m*; (*Culin*) incision. c (*Mus*) arrangement *m*.

scorn ['skɔ:n] 1 **n** (*NonC*) mépris *m*, dédain *m*. **to be filled with ~ (for)** éprouver un grand mépris (pour), n'avoir que du mépris (pour); **to heap** *or* **pour ~ on sb/sth** couvrir qn/qch de mépris; *see* **finger, laugh**. 2 **vt** *person* mépriser; *action* dédaigner, mépriser; *advice* faire fi de, négliger; *suggestion* rejeter, passer outre à. **he ~s telling lies** *or* **to tell a lie** il ne s'abaisserait pas à mentir.

scornful ['skɔ:nfʊl] **adj** *person, look, laugh, remark* méprisant, dédaigneux. **to be ~ about sth** manifester son mépris *or* son dédain pour qch.

scornfully ['skɔ:nfəlɪ] **adv** *say, wave, point* avec mépris, avec dédain, d'un air méprisant *or* dédaigneux; *speak* d'un ton méprisant *or* dédaigneux.

Scorpio ['skɔ:pɪəʊ] **n** (*Astron*) le Scorpion. **I'm (a) ~** je suis (du) Scorpion.

scorpion ['skɔ:pɪən] **n** scorpion *m*. (*Astrol, Astron*) **the S~** le Scorpion; **~ fish** rascasse *f*.

Scorpionic [ˌskɔ:pɪ'ɒnɪk] **n: to be a ~** être (du) Scorpion.

Scot [skɒt] **n** Écossais(e) *m(f)*. **the ~s** les Écossais; *see also* **Scots**.

Scotch [skɒtʃ] 1 **n** a (*also* **~ whisky**) whisky *m*, scotch *m*. b (*abusivement pour* **Scottish** *or* **Scots**) **the ~** les Écossais *mpl*. 2 **comp** ►**Scotch broth** potage *m* (*de mouton, de légumes et d'orge*) ►**Scotch egg** (*Brit*) *œuf dur enrobé de chair à saucisse* ►**Scotch-Irish** (*US*) irlando-écossais ►**Scotch mist** bruine *f*, crachin *m* ►**Scotch pine** pin *m* sylvestre ►**Scotch tape** ® (*US*) scotch *m* ®, ruban adhésif ►**Scotch terrier** scotch-terrier *m* ►**Scotch woodcock** (*Culin*) toast *m* aux œufs brouillés aux anchois. 3 **adj** (*abusive term for* **Scottish** *or* **Scots**) écossais.

scotch [skɒtʃ] **vt** *rumour* étouffer; *plan, attempt* faire échouer; *revolt, uprising* réprimer; *claim* démentir.

scot-free ['skɒt'fri:] **adj** (*unpunished*) sans être puni; (*not paying*) sans payer, gratis; (*unhurt*) indemne.

Scotland ['skɒtlənd] **n** Écosse *f*. **Secretary of State for ~** ministre *m* pour l'Écosse; *see* **yard**².

Scots [skɒts] 1 **n** (*Ling*) écossais *m*. 2 **comp** ►**Scotsman** Écossais *m* ►**Scots pine** pine *m* sylvestre ►**Scotswoman** Écossaise *f*. 3 **adj** écossais. (*Mil*) **~ Guards** la Garde écossaise; **~ law** le droit écossais.

Scotticism ['skɒtɪsɪzəm] **n** expression écossaise.

Scottie ['skɒtɪ] **n** (**abbr of Scotch terrier**) scotch-terrier *m*.

Scottish ['skɒtɪʃ] **adj** écossais. **~ country dancing** danses folkloriques écossaises; (*Brit Pol*) **~ National Party** Parti National Écossais; **~ Nationalism** nationalisme écossais; **~ Nationalist n** nationaliste *mf* écossais(e); **adj** de *or* des nationaliste(s) écossais; **the ~ Office** le ministère des Affaires écossaises; **~ terrier** scotch-terrier *m*.

scoundrel† ['skaʊndrəl] **n** fripouille *f*, vaurien *m*, (*stronger*) crapule *f*; (*child*) coquin(e) *m(f)*, (petit) chenapan *m*. **you little ~!** (espèce de) petit coquin *or* chenapan!

scoundrelly ['skaʊndrəlɪ] **adj** de gredin, de vaurien.

scour ['skaʊə^r] 1 **vt** a *pan, sink* récurer; *metal* décaper; *table, floor* frotter; (*with water*) nettoyer à grande eau. b *channel* creuser, éroder. c (*search*) parcourir. **they ~ed the town for the murderer** ils ont parcouru toute la ville à la recherche de l'assassin; **to ~ the area/the woods/the countryside** battre le secteur/les bois/toute la région. 2 **comp** ►**scouring powder** poudre *f* à récurer.

►**scour off** vt sep enlever en frottant.
►**scour out** vt sep récurer.
scourer ['skaʊərəʳ] n (*powder*) poudre *f* à récurer; (*pad*) tampon abrasif *or* à récurer.
scourge [skɜːdʒ] 1 n (*fig*) fléau *m*; (*whip*) discipline *f*, fouet *m*. 2 vt (*fig*) châtier, être un fléau pour; (*whip*) fouetter. **to ~ o.s.** se flageller.
scouse* [skaʊs] 1 n a (*person*) (*living in Liverpool*) habitant(e) *m(f)* de Liverpool; (*born there*) originaire *mf* de Liverpool. b (*dialect*) dialecte *m* de Liverpool. 2 adj de Liverpool.
scout [skaʊt] 1 n a (*Mil*) éclaireur *m*. **he's a good ~*†** c'est un chic type*; *see* **talent**. b (*gen Catholic*) scout *m*; (*gen non-Catholic*) éclaireur *m*; *see* **cub** *etc.* c (*) **to have a ~ round** reconnaître le terrain; **have a ~ round to see if he's there** allez jeter un coup d'œil pour voir s'il est là. d (*Brit Univ*) domestique *m*. 2 comp ►**scout camp** camp *m* scout ►**scout car** (*Mil*) voiture *f* de reconnaissance ►**scoutmaster** chef *m* scout ►**scout movement** mouvement *m* scout ►**scout uniform** uniforme *m* de scout. 3 vi (*Mil*) aller en reconnaissance.
►**scout about, scout around** vi (*Mil*) aller en reconnaissance. (*fig*) **to scout about for** chercher, aller *or* être à la recherche de.
scouting ['skaʊtɪŋ] n (*NonC*) a (*youth movement*) scoutisme *m*. b (*Mil*) reconnaissance *f*.
scow [skaʊ] n chaland *m*.
scowl [skaʊl] 1 n air *m* de mauvaise humeur, mine renfrognée. **he said with a ~** dit-il en se renfrognant *or* d'un air renfrogné. 2 vi se renfrogner, faire la grimace, froncer les sourcils. **to ~ at sb/sth** jeter un regard mauvais à qn/qch; **"shut up!" he ~ed** "tais-toi!" dit-il en se renfrognant *or* l'œil mauvais.
scowling ['skaʊlɪŋ] adj *face, look* renfrogné, maussade.
scrabble ['skræbl] 1 vi (*also* **~ about, ~ around**) **to ~ in the ground for sth** gratter la terre pour trouver qch; **she ~d (about *or* around) in the sand for the keys she had dropped** elle cherchait à tâtons dans le sable les clefs qu'elle avait laissé tomber; **he ~d (about *or* around) for a pen in the drawer** il a tâtonné dans le tiroir à la recherche d'un stylo. 2 n (*game*) **S~** ® Scrabble *m* ®.
scrag [skræg] 1 n (*Brit Culin: also* **~ end**) collet *m* (de mouton). 2 vt (‡) *person* tordre le cou à*.
scragginess ['skrægɪnɪs] n [*neck, body, person*] aspect décharné, maigreur *f* squelettique; [*animal*] aspect famélique.
scraggy ['skrægɪ] adj (*Brit*) *person, animal* efflanqué, décharné; *arm* décharné. **~ cat** chat *m* famélique; **~ chicken** poulet *m* étique; **~ neck** cou *m* de poulet* (*fig*).
scram‡ [skræm] vi ficher le camp*. **~!** fiche(-moi) le camp!*; **I'd better ~** je dois filer*.
scramble ['skræmbl] 1 vi a (*clamber*) **to ~ up/down** grimper/descendre tant bien que mal; **he ~d along the cliff** il a avancé avec difficulté le long de la falaise; **they ~d over the rocks/up the cliff** en s'aidant des pieds et des mains ils ont avancé sur les rochers/escaladé la falaise; **he ~d into/out of the car** il est monté dans/est descendu de la voiture à toute vitesse, il s'est précipité dans/hors de la voiture; **he ~d down off the wall** il a dégringolé du mur; **he ~d through the hedge** il s'est frayé tant bien que mal un passage à travers la haie; **to ~ for** *coins, seats* se bousculer pour (avoir), se disputer; *jobs etc* faire des pieds et des mains pour (avoir).
b (*Brit Sport*) **to go scrambling** faire du trial.
c (*Aviat*) décoller sur alerte.
2 vt (*Culin, Telec*) brouiller. **~d eggs** œufs brouillés.
3 n a bousculade *f*, ruée *f*, curée *f*. **the ~ for seats** la ruée pour les places; **there was a ~ for seats** (*lit*) on s'est rué sur les places; (*fig*) on s'est arraché les places.
b (*also* **motorcycle ~**) (réunion *f* de) moto-cross *m*.
scrambler ['skræmbləʳ] n a (*Telec: device*) brouilleur *m*. b (*Brit*) (*motorcyclist*) trialiste *mf*.
scrambling ['skræmblɪŋ] n (*Brit Sport*) trial *m*.
scrap¹ [skræp] 1 n a (*small piece*) [*paper, cloth, bread, string*] (petit) bout *m*; [*verse, writing*] quelques lignes *fpl*; [*conversation*] bribe *f*; [*news*] fragment *m*. **~s** (*broken pieces*) débris *mpl*; (*food remnants*) restes *mpl*; (*fig*) **there isn't a ~ of evidence** il n'y a pas la moindre preuve; **it wasn't a ~ of use** cela n'a servi absolument à rien; **there wasn't a ~ of truth in it** il n'y avait pas un brin de vérité là-dedans; **not a ~** pas du tout.
b (*NonC: ~ iron*) ferraille *f*. **to collect ~** récupérer de la ferraille; **I put it out for ~** je l'ai envoyé à la ferraille; **to sell a car/ship for ~** vendre une voiture/un bateau à la casse; **what is it worth as ~?** qu'est-ce que cela vaudrait (vendu) à la casse?
2 comp ►**scrapbook** album *m* (*de coupures de journaux etc*) ►**scrap car** voiture mise à la ferraille ►**scrap dealer** marchand *m* de ferraille, ferrailleur *m* ►**scrap heap** tas *m* de ferraille; (*fig*) **to throw sth on the scrap heap** mettre qch au rebut *or* au rancart*, bazarder qch*; **to throw sb on the scrap heap*** mettre qn au rancart*; **only fit for the scrap heap*** seulement bon à mettre au rancart* ►**scrap iron** ferraille *f* ►**scrap merchant** = **scrap dealer** ►**scrap metal** = **scrap iron** ►**scrap paper** (*for scribbling on*) (papier *m* de) brouillon *m*; (*old newspapers etc*) vieux papiers *mpl* ►**scrap value**: **its scrap value is £10** (vendu) à la casse cela vaut 10 livres ►**scrap yard** chantier *m* de ferraille; (*for cars*) cimetière *m* de voitures, casse* *f*.
3 vt jeter, bazarder*; *car, ship* envoyer à la ferraille *or* à la casse; *equipment* mettre au rebut; *project* abandonner, mettre au rancart*. **let's ~ the idea** laissons tomber cette idée.
scrap²* [skræp] 1 n (*fight*) bagarre *f*. **to get into *or* have a ~** se bagarrer* (*with* avec). 2 vi se bagarrer*.
scrape [skreɪp] 1 n a (*action*) coup *m* de grattoir *or* de racloir; (*sound*) grattement *m*, raclement *m*; (*mark*) éraflure *f*, égratignure *f*. **to give sth a ~** gratter *or* racler qch; **to give one's knee a ~** s'érafler *or* s'égratigner le genou.
b [*butter etc*] lichette* *f*.
c (*: *trouble*) **to get (o.s.) into a ~** s'attirer des ennuis, se mettre dans un mauvais pas; **he's always getting into ~s** il lui arrive toujours des histoires*; **to get (o.s.) out of a ~** se tirer d'affaire *or* d'embarras *or* du pétrin; **to get sb into a ~** attirer des ennuis à qn, mettre qn dans un mauvais pas; **to get sb out of a ~** tirer qn d'affaire *or* d'embarras *or* du pétrin.
2 vt (*clean: gen*) gratter, racler; *vegetables* gratter; (*graze*) érafler, égratigner; (*just touch*) frôler, effleurer. **to ~ (the skin off) one's knees** s'érafler les genoux; **to ~ one's plate clean** tout manger, nettoyer *or* racler* son assiette; **to ~ a living** vivoter; **to ~ a violin*** racler du violon; (*Naut*) **to ~ the bottom** talonner (le fond); (*fig*) **to ~ (the bottom of) the barrel** en être réduit aux raclures (*fig*); (*Aut*) **I ~d his bumper** je lui ai frôlé *or* éraflé le pare-chocs; *see also* **scrape up**.
3 vi (*make scraping sound*) racler, gratter; (*rub*) frotter (*against* contre). **to ~ along the wall** frôler le mur; **the car ~d past the lamppost** la voiture a frôlé le réverbère; **to ~ through the doorway** réussir de justesse à passer par la porte; (*fig*) **he just ~d clear of a prison sentence** il a frisé la peine de prison, il a tout juste évité une peine de prison; **to ~ through an exam** réussir un examen de justesse; **to ~ and save** économiser sur tout; *see* **bow²**.
►**scrape along** vi: **she scraped along on £10 per week** elle vivotait avec 10 livres par semaine; **I can just scrape along in Spanish** je me débrouille en espagnol*.
►**scrape away** 1 vi (*) **to scrape away at the violin** racler du violon. 2 vt sep enlever en grattant *or* en raclant.
►**scrape off** vt sep = **scrape away 2**.
►**scrape out** vt sep *contents* enlever en grattant *or* en raclant; *pan* nettoyer en raclant, récurer.
►**scrape through** vi passer de justesse; (*fig: succeed*) réussir de justesse.
►**scrape together** vt sep a **to scrape 2 bits of metal together** frotter 2 morceaux de métal l'un contre l'autre. b *objects* rassembler, ramasser; (*fig*) *money* réunir *or* amasser à grand-peine *or* en raclant les fonds de tiroirs.
►**scrape up** vt sep *earth, pebbles* ramasser, mettre en tas; (*fig*) *money* réussir à économiser, amasser à grand-peine. **to scrape up an acquaintance with sb** réussir à faire la connaissance de qn.
scraper ['skreɪpəʳ] 1 n racloir *m*, grattoir *m*; (*at doorstep*) décrottoir *m*, gratte-pieds *m inv*. 2 comp ►**scraperboard** carte *f* à gratter.
scraping ['skreɪpɪŋ] 1 adj *noise* de grattement, de raclement. 2 n a [*butter*] mince couche *f*, lichette* *f*. **~s** [*food*] restes *mpl*; [*dirt, paint*] raclures *fpl*. b (*action*) grattement *m*, raclement *m*; *see* **bow²**.
scrappy ['skræpɪ] adj *conversation, essay* décousu; *education* incomplet (*f* -ète), présentant des lacunes. **a ~ meal** (*insubstantial*) un repas sur le pouce*; (*from left-overs*) un repas (fait) de restes.
scratch [skrætʃ] 1 n a (*mark*) (*on skin*) égratignure *f*, éraflure *f*; (*on paint*) éraflure; (*on glass, record*) rayure *f*. **they came out of it without a ~** ils s'en sont sortis indemnes *or* sans une égratignure; **it's only a ~** ce n'est qu'une égratignure.
b (*action*) grattement *m*; (*by claw*) coup *m* de griffe; (*by fingernail*) coup d'ongle. **the cat gave her a ~** le chat l'a griffée; **to have a good ~*** se gratter un bon coup*.
c (*noise*) grattement *m*, grincement *m*.
d (*Sport*) **to be on *or* start from ~** être scratch *inv*; (*fig*) **to start from ~** partir de zéro*; **we'll have to start from ~ again** il nous faudra repartir de zéro*; **he didn't come up to ~** il ne s'est pas montré à la hauteur; **my car didn't come up to ~** ma voiture n'a pas été aussi bonne qu'il l'aurait fallu; **to bring up to ~** amener au niveau voulu; **to keep sb up to ~** maintenir qn au niveau voulu.
2 comp *crew, team* de fortune, improvisé; *vote* par surprise; *golfer* scratch *inv*, de handicap zéro ►**scratch file** (*Comput*) fichier *m* de travail *or* de manœuvre ►**scratch pad** (*gen*) bloc-notes *m*; (*Comput*) zone *f* de travail ►**scratch race** course *f* scratch ►**scratch score** (*Golf*) scratch score *m* ►**scratch tape** (*Comput*) bande *f* de travail *or* de manœuvre.
3 vt a (*with nail, claw*) griffer; *varnish* érafler; *record, glass* rayer. **to ~ a hole in sth** creuser un trou en grattant qch; **he ~ed his hand on a nail** il s'est éraflé *or* écorché la main sur un clou; **he ~ed his name on the wood** il a gravé son nom dans le bois; (*fig*) **it only ~ed the surface** (*gen*) c'était (*or* c'est) très superficiel; [*report, lecture*] ça n'a fait qu'effleurer la question, c'était très superficiel; (*fig*) **to ~ a few lines** griffonner quelques mots.

b (*to relieve itch*) gratter. **to ~ o.s.** se gratter; (*lit, fig*) **to ~ one's head** se gratter la tête; (*fig*) **you ~ my back and I'll ~ yours** un petit service en vaut un autre.
c (*cancel*) *meeting* annuler; (*Comput*) effacer; (*Sport etc*) *competitor, horse* scratcher; *match, game* annuler; (*US Pol*) *candidate* rayer de la liste. (*US Pol*) **to ~ a ballot** modifier un bulletin de vote (*en rayant un nom etc*).
4 **vi** a (*with nail, claw*) griffer; (*to relieve itch*) se gratter; *[hens]* gratter le sol; *[pen]* gratter, grincer. **the dog was ~ing at the door** le chien grattait à la porte.
b (*Sport etc*) *[competitor]* se faire scratcher; *[candidate]* se désister.
►**scratch out** **vt sep** a (*from list*) rayer, effacer. b *hole* creuser en grattant. **to scratch sb's eyes out** arracher les yeux à qn.
►**scratch together** **vt sep** (*fig*) *money* réussir à amasser (en grattant les fonds de tiroirs).
►**scratch up** **vt sep** *bone* déterrer; (*fig*) *money* = **scratch together**.
scratchy ['skrætʃɪ] **adj** *surface, material* rêche, qui accroche; *pen* qui grince, qui gratte; *handwriting* en pattes de mouche; *record* rayé, éraillé.
scrawl [skrɔːl] 1 **n** a (*gen*) gribouillage *m*, griffonnage *m*. **I can't read her ~** je ne peux pas déchiffrer son gribouillage; **the word finished in a ~** le mot se terminait par un gribouillage; **her letter was just a ~** sa lettre était griffonnée. b (*brief letter, note*) mot *m* griffoné à la hâte. 2 **vt** gribouiller, griffonner. **to ~ a note to sb** griffonner un mot à qn; **there were rude words ~ed all over the wall** il y avait des mots grossiers gribouillés sur tout le mur. 3 **vi** gribouiller.
scrawny ['skrɔːnɪ] **adj** *person, animal* efflanqué, décharné; *arm* décharné. **~ cat** chat *m* famélique; **~ neck** cou *m* de poulet* (*fig*).
scream [skriːm] 1 **n** a *[pain, fear]* cri aigu *or* perçant, hurlement *m*; *[laughter]* éclat *m*. **to give a ~** pousser un cri.
b (*) **it was a ~** c'était à se tordre, c'était vraiment marrant‡; **he's a ~** il est impayable*.
2 **vi** (*also* **~ out**) *[person]* crier, pousser des cris, hurler; *[baby]* crier, brailler; *[siren, brakes, wind]* hurler. **to ~ with laughter** rire aux éclats *or* aux larmes; **to ~ with pain/with rage** hurler de douleur/de rage; **to ~ for help** crier à l'aide *or* au secours; **to ~ at sb** crier après qn.
3 **vt** (*also* **~ out**) a *abuse etc* hurler (*at* à). **"shut up" he ~ed** "taisez-vous" hurla-t-il; **to ~ o.s. hoarse** s'enrouer à force de crier, s'égosiller.
b *[headlines, posters]* annoncer en toutes lettres.
►**scream down** **vt sep**: **to scream the place down** crier comme un damné *or* sourd.
►**scream out** 1 **vi** = **scream 2**. 2 **vt sep** = **scream 3**.
screamer‡ ['skriːmə^r] **n** (*US*) a (*headline*) énorme manchette *f*. b (*joke*) histoire *f* désopilante. **he's a ~**‡ il est désopilant *or* tordant*.
screamingly* ['skriːmɪŋlɪ] **adv**: **~ funny** à mourir de rire, tordant*.
scree ['skriː] **n** éboulis *m* (*en montagne*).
screech [skriːtʃ] 1 **n** (*gen*) cri strident; (*from pain, fright, rage*) hurlement *m*; *[brakes]* grincement *m*; *[tyres]* crissement *m*; *[owl]* cri (rauque et perçant); *[siren]* hurlement. **she gave a ~ of laughter** elle est partie d'un rire perçant. 2 **comp** ►**screech owl** chouette-effraie *f*, chat-huant *m*. 3 **vi** *[person]* pousser des cris stridents, hurler; *[brakes]* grincer; *[tyres]* crisser; *[singer, owl]* crier; *[siren]* hurler. 4 **vt** crier à tue-tête.
screed [skriːd] **n** a (*discourse*) laïus* *m*, topo* *m* (*about* sur); (*letter*) longue missive *f* (*about* sur). (*fig: a lot*) **to write ~s*** écrire des volumes *or* toute une tartine*. b (*Constr*) (*depth guide strip*) guide *m*; (*levelling device*) règle *f* à araser le béton; (*NonC: surfacing material*) matériau *m* de ragréyage.
screen [skriːn] 1 **n** a (*in room*) paravent *m*; (*for fire*) écran *m* de cheminée; (*fig: of troops, trees*) rideau *m*; (*pretence*) masque *m*; *see* **safety, silk, smoke** *etc*.
b (*Cine, TV etc*) écran *m*. **to show sth on a ~** projeter qch; (*TV*) **a 50-cm ~** un écran de 50 cm; (*Cine*) **the ~** l'écran, le cinéma; (*Cine*) **the big** *or* **large ~** le grand écran; (*TV*) **the small ~** le petit écran; **to write for the ~** écrire des scénarios; *see* **panoramic, television, wide** *etc*.
c (*sieve*) crible *m*, claie *f*.
2 **comp** ►**screen actor** acteur *m* de cinéma, vedette *f* de l'écran ►**screen door** porte grillagée ►**screenplay** scénario *m* ►**screen rights** droits *mpl* d'adaptation cinématographique ►**screen test** bout *m* d'essai; **to do a screen test** tourner un bout d'essai ►**screen wash(er)** (*Brit Aut*) lave-glace(s) ►**screen writer** scénariste *mf*.
3 **vt** a (*hide*) masquer, cacher; (*protect*) faire écran à, protéger. **the trees ~ed the house** les arbres masquaient *or* cachaient la maison; **to ~ sth from sight** *or* **view** dérober *or* masquer qch aux regards; **he ~ed the book with his hand** il a caché le livre de sa main; **to ~ sth from the wind/sun** protéger qch du vent/du soleil; **to ~ one's eyes** se protéger les yeux avec la main, faire écran de sa main pour se protéger les yeux; **in order to ~ our movements from the enemy** pour cacher *or* masquer nos mouvements à l'ennemi.
b (*Cine, TV*) *film* projeter.
c (*sieve*) *coal* cribler; *candidates* (pré)selectionner, trier, filtrer. (*fig*) **to ~ sb (for a job)** passer au crible la candidature de qn; **the candidates were carefully ~ed** les candidats ont été passés au crible; (*Med*) **to ~ sb for cancer** faire subir à qn un test de dépistage du cancer.
►**screen off** **vt sep**: **the kitchen was screened off from the rest of the room** la cuisine était cachée du reste de la pièce (par un rideau *or* un paravent); **the nurses screened off his bed** les infirmières ont mis un *or* des paravent(s) autour de son lit; **the trees screened off the house from the road** les arbres cachaient la maison de la route, les arbres formaient un écran (de verdure) entre la maison et la route; **a cordon of police screened off the accident from the onlookers** les agents de police ont formé un cordon pour cacher l'accident aux badauds.
screening ['skriːnɪŋ] **n** a *[film]* projection *f*. b *[coal]* criblage *m*; (*fig*) *[person]* tri *m*, procédure *f* de sélection sur dossier; (*Med*) *[person]* test *m or* visite *f* de dépistage (*of sb* que l'on fait subir à qn).
screw [skruː] 1 **n** a vis *f*; (*action*) tour *m* de vis. (*Brit*) **a ~ of tea/sweets/tobacco** *etc* un cornet de thé/de bonbons/de tabac *etc*; (*fig*) **he's got a ~ loose*** il lui manque une case*; (*fig*) **to put the ~(s) on sb*** forcer la main à qn; *see* **thumb, tighten** *etc*.
b (*Aviat, Naut*) hélice *f*; *see* **air, twin**.
c (*Brit* †‡: *income*) salaire *m*. **he gets a good ~** son boulot paie bien‡.
d (*Prison sl: warder*) maton(ne) *m(f)* (*sl*).
e (**‡) **it was a good ~** on a bien baisé**‡; **she's a good ~** elle baise bien**‡.
2 **comp** ►**screwball**‡ **adj, n** (*US*) cinglé(e)* *m(f)*, tordu(e)‡ *m(f)* ►**screw bolt** boulon *m* à vis ►**screwdriver** (*tool*) tournevis *m*; (*drink*) vodka-orange *f* ►**screw joint** joint *m* à vis ►**screw propeller** hélice *f* ►**screw thread** filet *m* de vis ►**screw top** **n** couvercle *m* à pas de vis ►**screw-top(ped)** **adj** avec couvercle à pas de vis ►**screw-up**‡ (*fig: muddle*) pagaille *f* complète, fiasco* *m*.
3 **vt** a visser (*on* sur, *to* à), fixer avec une vis. **to ~ sth tight** visser qch à bloc; (*fig*) **to ~ one's face into a smile** grimacer un sourire; **to ~ sb's neck**‡ tordre le cou à qn*.
b (*extort*) *money* extorquer, soutirer (*out of* à); *information* arracher (*out of* à); (‡: *defraud*) *person* arnaquer‡, pigeonner‡.
c (**‡) *woman* baiser**‡.
d (‡: *in exclamations*) **~ you!** va te faire voir* *or* foutre**‡!; **~ the cost/the neighbours!** on se fout du prix/des voisins!‡
4 **vi** se visser.
►**screw around** **vi** a (‡: *waste time*) glander‡, glandouiller‡. b (**‡: *sexually*) baiser**‡ avec tout le monde, coucher à droite à gauche*.
►**screw down** 1 **vi** se visser. 2 **vt sep** visser (à fond).
►**screw off** 1 **vi** se dévisser. 2 **vt sep** dévisser.
►**screw on** 1 **vi** se visser. 2 **vt sep** visser, fixer avec des vis; *lid* visser. (*fig*) **he's got his head screwed on all right*** *or* **the right way*** il a la tête sur les épaules.
►**screw round** **vt sep** tourner, visser. (*fig*) **to screw one's head round** se dévisser la tête *or* le cou.
►**screw together** **vt sep** *two parts* fixer avec une vis. **to screw sth together** assembler qch avec des vis.
►**screw up** 1 **vt sep** a visser (à fond), resserrer (à fond). b *paper* chiffonner, froisser; *handkerchief* rouler, tortiller. **to screw up one's eyes** plisser les yeux; **to screw up one's face** faire la grimace; (*fig*) **to screw up (one's) courage** prendre son courage à deux mains* (*to do* pour faire). c (‡: *spoil*) foutre en l'air‡, bousiller*. d (‡) **to screw sb up** détraquer* *or* perturber qn; **he is screwed up** il est paumé‡. 2 **screw-up**‡ **n** *see* **screw 2**.
screwed‡ [skruːd] **adj** (*Brit*) soûl, paf‡ *inv*, bourré‡; *see also* **screw up**.
screwy‡ ['skruːɪ] **adj** (*mad*) cinglé*, tordu‡.
scribble ['skrɪbl] 1 **vi** gribouiller, griffonner. 2 **vt** gribouiller, griffonner. **to ~ a note to sb** griffonner un mot à qn; **there were comments ~d all over the page** il y avait des commentaires griffonnés *or* gribouillés sur toute la page. 3 **n** gribouillage *m*, griffonnage *m*. **I can't read her ~** je ne peux pas déchiffrer son gribouillage; **the word ended in a ~** le mot se terminait par un gribouillage; **her letter was just a ~** sa lettre était griffonnée.
►**scribble down** **vt sep** *notes* griffonner.
►**scribble out** **vt sep** a (*erase*) rayer, raturer. b *essay, draft* jeter sur le papier, ébaucher.
scribbler ['skrɪblə^r] **n** (*lit*) gribouilleur *m*, -euse *f*; (*fig: bad author*) plumitif *m*.
scribbling ['skrɪblɪŋ] **n** gribouillage *m*, gribouillis *m*. (*Brit*) **~ pad** bloc-notes *m*.
scribe [skraɪb] **n** (*all senses*) scribe *m*.
scrimmage ['skrɪmɪdʒ] **n** (*gen, Sport*) mêlée *f*.
scrimp [skrɪmp] **vi** lésiner (*on* sur), être chiche (*on* de). **to ~ and save** *or* **scrape** économiser sur tout.
scrimpy ['skrɪmpɪ] **adj** *amount, supply* microscopique; *garment* étriqué.
scrimshank ['skrɪmʃæŋk] (*Brit Mil sl*) 1 **n** = **scrimshanker**. 2 **vi** (‡) tirer au flanc*.
scrimshanker ['skrɪm,ʃæŋkə^r] **n** (*Brit Mil sl*) tire-au-flanc* *m inv*.
scrip [skrɪp] **n** (*Fin*) titre *m* provisoire (d'action).
scripholder ['skrɪphəʊldə^r] **n** (*Fin*) détenteur *m*, -trice *f* de titres (provisoires).

script [skrɪpt] 1 n a (*Cine*) scénario *m*; (*Rad, Theat, TV*) texte *m*. b (*in exam*) copie *f*; (*Jur*) document *m* original. c (*NonC*) (*handwriting*) script *m*, écriture *f* script; (*Typ*) scriptes *fpl*; see **italic**. 2 comp ► **scriptwriter** (*Cine*) scénariste *mf*. 3 vt *film* écrire le scénario de. (*Rad, TV*) ~**ed talk/discussion** *etc* conversation/discussion *etc* préparée d'avance.

scriptural ['skrɪptʃərəl] adj scriptural, biblique.

Scripture ['skrɪptʃəʳ] n (*also* **Holy** ~**(s)**) Écriture sainte, Saintes Écritures. (*Scol*) ~ **(lesson)** (cours *m* d')instruction religieuse.

scripture ['skrɪptʃəʳ] n texte *m* sacré.

scrivener†† ['skrɪvnəʳ] n (*scribe*) scribe *m*; (*notary*) notaire *m*.

scrod [skrɒd] n (*US*) jeune morue *f* or cabillaud *m* (*spécialité du Massachussetts*).

scrofula ['skrɒfjʊlə] n scrofule *f*.

scrofulous ['skrɒfjʊləs] adj scrofuleux.

scroll [skrəʊl] 1 n a [*parchment*] rouleau *m*; (*ancient book*) manuscrit *m*; see **dead**. b (*Archit*) volute *f*, spirale *f*; (*in writing*) enjolivement *m*; [*violin*] volute *f*. 2 vi (*Comput*) défiler. 3 vt (*Comput*) **to** ~ **up/down** faire remonter/descendre, faire défiler vers le haut/le bas.

Scrooge [skru:dʒ] n harpagon *m*.

scrotum ['skrəʊtəm] n, pl ~**s** or **scrota** ['skrəʊtə] scrotum *m*.

scrounge* [skraʊndʒ] 1 vt *meal, clothes etc* se faire payer (*from* or *off sb* par qn). **to** ~ **money from sb** taper qn*; **he** ~**d £5 off him** il l'a tapé de 5 livres*; **can I** ~ **your pen?** je peux te piquer ton stylo? 2 vi: **to** ~ **on sb** vivre aux crochets de qn; **he's always scrounging** c'est un parasite; (*for meals*) c'est un pique-assiette. 3 n: **to be on the** ~ **for sth** essayer d'emprunter qch; **he's always on the** ~ c'est un parasite.

scrounger* ['skraʊndʒəʳ] n parasite *m*, profiteur *m*, -euse *f*; (*for meals*) pique-assiette *mf inv*.

scrub¹ [skrʌb] 1 n nettoyage *m* à la brosse, bon nettoyage. **to give sth a good** ~ bien nettoyer qch (à la brosse or avec une brosse); **give your face a** ~! lave-toi bien la figure!; **it needs a** ~ cela a besoin d'être bien nettoyé.

2 comp ► **scrubbing brush** brosse dure ► **scrubland** brousse *f*, scrub *m* (*Tech*) ► **scrubwoman** (*US*) femme *f* de ménage.

3 vt a *floor* nettoyer or laver à la brosse; *washing* frotter; *pan* récurer. **to** ~ **one's hands** se brosser les mains, se nettoyer les mains à la brosse; **she** ~**bed the walls clean** elle a nettoyé les murs à fond.

b (*: *cancel*) *match etc* annuler. **let's** ~ **that** laissons tomber.

4 vi frotter. **she's been on her knees** ~**bing all day** elle a passé sa journée à genoux à frotter les planchers; (*fig*) **let's** ~ **round it**‡ laissons tomber*, n'en parlons plus.

►**scrub away** vt sep *dirt* enlever en frottant; *stain* faire partir (en frottant).

►**scrub down** vt sep *room, walls* nettoyer à fond or à grande eau, se livrer à un nettoyage en règle de. **to scrub oneself down** faire une toilette en règle.

►**scrub off** vt sep = **scrub away**.

►**scrub out** vt sep *name* effacer; *stain* faire partir; *pan* récurer.

►**scrub up** vi [*surgeon etc*] se brosser les mains avant d'opérer.

scrub² [skrʌb] n (*NonC: brushwood*) broussailles *fpl*.

scrubber¹ ['skrʌbəʳ] n (*also* **pan-**~) tampon *m* à récurer.

scrubber²‡ ['skrʌbəʳ] n sauteuse‡ *f*, putain‡ *f*.

scrubby ['skrʌbɪ] adj *tree* rabougri; *countryside* couvert de broussailles.

scruff [skrʌf] n a **by the** ~ **of the neck** par la peau du cou. b (*: *untidy person*) individu débraillé or peu soigné.

scruffily ['skrʌfɪlɪ] adv: ~ **dressed** débraillé.

scruffiness ['skrʌfɪnɪs] n [*person*] débraillé *m*, laisser-aller *m*; [*clothes, building*] miteux *m*.

scruffy ['skrʌfɪ] adj *person* sale et débraillé; *clothes, building* miteux; *hair* sale et mal peigné; *handwriting* peu soigné.

scrum [skrʌm] n a (*Rugby*) mêlée *f*. **to put the ball into the** ~ introduire la balle en mêlée; **loose** ~ mêlée ouverte or spontanée; (*Rugby*) ~ **half** demi *m* de mêlée. b (*fig* *: *pushing*) bousculade *f*, mêlée *f*. **there was a terrible** ~ **at the sales** il y avait une de ces bousculades aux soldes.

scrummage ['skrʌmɪdʒ] 1 n = **scrum**. 2 vi (*Rugby*) jouer en mêlée; (*fig*) se bousculer.

scrump* [skrʌmp] vt (*Brit*) *apples etc* chaparder.

scrumptious* ['skrʌmpʃəs] adj succulent, délicieux.

scrumpy ['skrʌmpɪ] n (*Brit*) cidre *m* fermier.

scrunch [skrʌntʃ] = **crunch**.

scruple ['skru:pl] 1 n scrupule *m*. **to have** ~**s about sth** avoir des scrupules au sujet de qch; **he has no** ~**s** il est sans scrupules, il est dénué de scrupules; **to have no** ~**s about doing sth** n'avoir aucun scrupule à faire qch, ne pas se faire scrupule de faire qch. 2 vi: **not to** ~ **to do** ne pas hésiter à faire, ne pas se faire scrupule de faire.

scrupulous ['skru:pjʊləs] adj *person, honesty* scrupuleux; *attention* scrupuleux, méticuleux. **he was very** ~ **about paying his debts** il payait ses dettes de façon scrupuleuse.

scrupulously ['skru:pjʊləslɪ] adv scrupuleusement, d'une manière scrupuleuse. ~ **honest** d'une honnêteté scrupuleuse; ~ **exact** exact jusqu'au scrupule; ~ **clean** d'une propreté irréprochable.

scrupulousness ['skru:pjʊləsnɪs] n (*NonC*) (*honesty*) scrupules *mpl*, esprit scrupuleux; (*exactitude*) minutie *f*.

scrutineer [ˌskru:tɪ'nɪəʳ] n (*Brit*) scrutateur *m*, -trice *f*.

scrutinize ['skru:tɪnaɪz] vt *writing, document* scruter, examiner minutieusement; *votes* pointer.

scrutiny ['skru:tɪnɪ] n a (*act of scrutinizing*) [*document, conduct*] examen minutieux or rigoureux; [*votes*] pointage *m*. b (*watchful gaze*) regard *m* insistant or scrutateur (*frm*). **to keep sb under close** ~ surveiller qn de près; **under his** ~**, she felt nervous** son regard insistant or scrutateur la mettait mal à l'aise.

SCSI ['skʌzɪ] n (*Comput*) (**abbr of small computer systems interface**) SCSI *f*.

scuba ['sku:bə] n (**abbr of self-contained underwater breathing apparatus**) scaphandre *m* autonome. ~ **diver** plongeur *m*, -euse *f*; ~ **diving** plongée *f* sous-marine (autonome).

scud [skʌd] vi (*also* ~ **along**) [*clouds, waves*] courir (à toute allure); [*boat*] filer (vent arrière). **the clouds were** ~**ding across the sky** les nuages couraient (à toute allure) dans le ciel.

scuff [skʌf] 1 vt *shoes, furniture* érafler. ~**ed shoes** chaussures éraflées; **to** ~ **one's feet** traîner les pieds. 2 vi traîner les pieds. 3 comp ► **scuff marks** (*on shoes*) éraflures *fpl*, marques *fpl* d'usure.

scuffle ['skʌfl] 1 n bagarre *f*, échauffourée *f*, rixe *f*. 2 vi se bagarrer* (*with* avec).

scull [skʌl] 1 n (*one of a pair of oars*) aviron *m* (de couple); (*single oar for stern*) godille *f*. 2 vi (*with 2 oars*) ramer (en couple); (*with single oar*) godiller. **to go** ~**ing** faire de l'aviron. 3 vt (*with 2 oars*) faire avancer à l'aviron; (*with single oar*) faire avancer à la godille.

scullery ['skʌlərɪ] n (*esp Brit*) arrière-cuisine *f*. ~ **maid** fille *f* de cuisine.

sculpt [skʌlp(t)] 1 vt sculpter (*out of* dans). 2 vi sculpter, faire de la sculpture.

sculptor ['skʌlptəʳ] n sculpteur *m*.

sculptress ['skʌlptrɪs] n femme *f* sculpteur, sculpteur *m*. **I met a** ~ j'ai rencontré une femme sculpteur; **she is a** ~ elle est sculpteur.

sculptural ['skʌlptʃərəl] adj sculptural.

sculpture ['skʌlptʃəʳ] 1 n sculpture *f*. **a (piece of)** ~ une sculpture. 2 vti sculpter.

scum [skʌm] n a (*gen*) écume *f*; (*foamy*) écume, mousse *f*; (*dirty*) couche *f* de saleté; (*on bath*) crasse *f*. **to remove the** ~ **(from)** (*foam*) écumer; (*dirt*) décrasser, nettoyer. b (*pej: people*) rebut *m*, lie *f*. **the** ~ **of the earth** le rebut du genre humain. c (‡ *pej: person*) (*also* ~**bag**‡) salaud‡ *m*, ordure‡ *f*.

scummy ['skʌmɪ] adj (*lit*) écumeux, couvert d'écume, mousseux; (‡ *pej*) de salaud‡.

scunner‡ ['skʌnəʳ] n (*esp N Engl, Scot*) **to take a** ~ **to sb/sth** prendre qn/qch en grippe, avoir qn/qch dans le nez*.

scupper ['skʌpəʳ] 1 n (*Naut*) dalot *m* or daleau *m*. 2 vt (*Brit* *) *plan, negotiations* saborder, faire capoter, saboter; *effort* saboter. **we're** ~**ed** nous sommes fichus*.

scurf [skɜ:f] n [*scalp*] pellicules *fpl* (*du cuir chevelu*); [*skin*] peau morte.

scurfy ['skɜ:fɪ] adj *scalp* pelliculeux; *skin* dartreux.

scurrility [skʌ'rɪlɪtɪ] n (*see* **scurrilous**) caractère calomnieux; caractère fielleux; virulence *f*; grossièreté *f*, vulgarité *f*.

scurrilous ['skʌrɪləs] adj (*defamatory*) calomnieux; (*vicious*) fielleux, haineux; (*bitter*) virulent; (*coarse*) grossier, vulgaire.

scurrilously ['skʌrɪləslɪ] adv (*see* **scurrilous**) calomnieusement; avec virulence; grossièrement, vulgairement.

scurry ['skʌrɪ] 1 n débandade *f*, sauve-qui-peut *m inv*. **a** ~ **of footsteps** des pas précipités. 2 vi se précipiter, filer* (à toute allure). (*fig: through work etc*) **to** ~ **through sth** faire qch à toute vitesse, expédier qch.

►**scurry away, scurry off** vi [*person*] détaler, se sauver (à toutes jambes), décamper; [*animal*] détaler.

scurvy ['skɜ:vɪ] 1 n scorbut *m*. 2 adj (†† *or liter*) bas (*f* basse), mesquin, vil (*f* vile).

scut [skʌt] n [*rabbit, deer*] queue *f*.

scutcheon ['skʌtʃən] n = **escutcheon**.

scuttle¹ ['skʌtl] n (*for coal*) seau *m* (à charbon).

scuttle² ['skʌtl] vi courir précipitamment. **to** ~ **in/out/through** *etc* entrer/sortir/traverser *etc* précipitamment.

►**scuttle away, scuttle off** vi déguerpir, filer*.

scuttle³ ['skʌtl] 1 n a (*Naut*) écoutille *f*. b (*US: in ceiling etc*) trappe *f*. 2 vt a (*Naut*) saborder. **to** ~ **one's own ship** se saborder. b (*fig*) *hopes, plans* faire échouer. 3 comp ► **scuttlebutt** (*Naut: water cask*) baril *m* d'eau douce; (*US fig: gossip*) ragots *mpl*, commérages *mpl*.

Scylla ['sɪlə] n Scylla. (*fig*) **to be between** ~ **and Charybdis** tomber de Charybde en Scylla.

scythe [saɪð] 1 n faux *f*. 2 vt faucher.

SD (*US*) abbr of **South Dakota**.

SDI [esdi:'aɪ] n (*US: Mil, Space*) (**abbr of Strategic Defense Initiative**) *see* **strategic**.

SDLP [esdi:el'pi:] n (*Irish Pol*) (**abbr of Social Democratic and Labour Party**) *see* **social**.

SDP [esdiːˈpiː] n (*Brit Pol* †) (abbr of **Social Democratic Party**) *see* **social**.

sea [siː] 1 n a (*not land*) mer *f*. **on the ~** *boat* en mer; *town* au bord de la mer; **by** *or* **beside the ~** au bord de la mer; **over** *or* **beyond the ~(s)** outre-mer; **from over** *or* **beyond the ~(s)** d'outre-mer; **to swim in the ~** nager *or* se baigner dans la mer; **to go to ~** *[boat]* prendre la mer; *[person]* devenir *or* se faire marin; **to put to ~** prendre la mer; **by ~** par mer, en bateau; (*Naut*) **service at ~** service *m* à la mer; **look out to ~** regardez au *or* vers le large; **(out) at ~** en mer; **to be swept** *or* **carried out to ~** être emporté par la mer; (*fig*) **I'm all at ~** (*in lecture, translation etc*) je nage complètement*; (*after moving house, changing jobs etc*) je suis complètement déboussolé*; **I'm all at ~ over how to answer this question** je ne sais absolument pas comment répondre à cette question; **he was all at ~ in the discussion** il était complètement perdu dans la discussion; **it left him all at ~** cela l'a complètement désorienté, cela l'a laissé extrêmement perplexe; (*fig*) **the call of the ~** l'appel *m* du large; *see* **follow, half, high** *etc*.

b (*particular area: also on moon*) mer *f*. **the S~ of Galilee** la mer de Galilée; *see* **dead, red, seven** *etc*.

c (*NonC: state of the ~*) (état *m* de la) mer *f*. **what's the ~ like?** (*for sailing*) comment est la mer?, quel est l'état de la mer?; (*for bathing*) est-ce que l'eau est bonne?; **the ~ was very rough** la mer était très houleuse *or* très mauvaise, il y avait une très grosse mer; **a rough** *or* **heavy ~** une mer houleuse; **a calm ~** une mer calme; (*Naut*) **to ship a ~** embarquer un paquet de mer.

d (*fig*) *[faces, difficulties]* océan *m*, multitude *f*; *[corn, blood]* mer *f*.

2 comp ►**sea air** air marin *or* de la mer ►**sea anchor** ancre flottante ►**sea anemone** anémone *f* de mer, actinie *f* ►**sea bathing** bains *mpl* de mer ►**sea battle** bataille navale ►**sea bed** fond *m* de la mer ►**sea bird** oiseau *m* de mer, oiseau marin ►**sea biscuit** biscuit *m* de mer ►**seaboard** littoral *m*, côte *f* ►**sea boot** botte *f* de mer *or* de marin ►**seaborne** *goods* transporté par mer; *trade* maritime ►**sea bream** daurade *f* *or* dorade *f* ►**sea breeze** brise *f* de mer *or* du large ►**sea calf** veau marin, phoque *m* ►**sea captain** capitaine *m* (de la marine marchande) ►**sea change** (*fig*) profond changement *m* ►**sea chest** (*fig*) malle-cabine *f* ►**sea coast** côte *f* ►**sea cow** vache marine ►**sea crossing** traversée *f* (par mer) ►**sea dog** (*fish*) roussette *f*, chien *m* de mer; (*seal*) phoque commun; (*sailor*) **(old) sea dog** (vieux) loup *m* de mer ►**sea eagle** aigle *m* de mer ►**sea eel** anguille *f* de mer ►**sea elephant** éléphant *m* de mer ►**seafarer** marin *m* ►**seafaring** (*also* **seafaring life**) vie *f* de marin; **seafaring man** = **seafarer** ►**sea fight** combat naval ►**sea fish** poisson *m* de mer; **sea fish farming** aquiculture *f* ►**seafood** fruits *mpl* de mer ►**sea front** bord *m* de (la) mer, front *m* de mer ►**seagirt** (*liter*) ceint par la mer ►**sea god** dieu marin ►**seagoing** (*Naut*) long-courrier; *theme, experience* maritime; **seagoing man** marin *m*; **seagoing ship** (navire *m*) long-courrier *m*, navire de mer ►**sea-green** vert glauque *inv* ►**seagull** mouette *f* ►**sea horse** hippocampe *m* ►**sea kale** chou marin, crambe *m* ►**sea lamprey** lamproie *f* de mer ►**sea lane** couloir *m* *or* voie *f* de navigation maritime ►**sea lavender** lavande *f* de mer, statice *m* ►**sea legs: to find** *or* **get one's sea legs** s'amariner, s'habituer à la mer; **he's got his sea legs** il a retrouvé le pied marin ►**sea level** niveau *m* de la mer ►**sea lift** (*Mil etc*) évacuation *f* par mer ►**sea lion** otarie *f* ►**sea loch** (*Scot*) bras *m* de mer ►**Sea Lord** (*Brit*) ≃ amiral *m* de l'état-major de la Marine; **First Sea Lord** ≃ amiral-chef *m* d'état-major de la Marine ►**seaman** *see* **seaman** ►**sea mile** mille marin ►**sea otter** loutre *f* de mer ►**sea perch** perche *f* de mer ►**seaplane** hydravion *m*; **seaplane base** hydrobase *f* ►**seaport** port *m* de mer ►**sea power** puissance navale ►**sea route** route *f* maritime ►**sea rover** (*ship*) bateau *m* pirate; (*person*) pirate *m* ►**sea salt** sel *m* de mer ►**seascape** (*view*) panorama marin; (*Art*) marine *f* ►**Sea Scout** scout marin ►**sea serpent** serpent *m* de mer ►**sea shanty** chanson *f* de marins ►**sea shell** coquillage *m* ►**seashore** rivage *m*, plage *f*, bord *m* de (la) mer; **by** *or* **on the seashore** au bord de la mer; **children playing on the seashore** enfants *mpl* qui jouent sur la plage *or* sur le rivage ►**seasick: to be seasick** avoir le mal de mer ►**seasickness** mal *m* de mer ►**seaside** *see* **seaside** ►**sea transport** transports *mpl* maritimes ►**sea trout** truite *f* de mer ►**sea urchin** oursin *m* ►**sea wall** digue *f* ►**sea water** eau *f* de mer ►**seaway** route *f* maritime ►**seaweed** algue(s) *f(pl)* ►**seaworthiness** bon état de navigabilité (*d'un navire*) (*see* **certificate a**) ►**seaworthy** en état de naviguer.

Seabee [ˈsiːˌbiː] n (*US Mil*) militaire *m* du Génie maritime.

seal[1] [siːl] 1 n phoque *m*. 2 comp ►**seal cull, seal culling** massacre *m* des bébés-phoques ►**sealskin** n peau *f* de phoque ◊ adj (en peau) de phoque. 3 vi: **to go ~ing** chasser le phoque.

seal[2] [siːl] 1 n a (*stamping device*) sceau *m*, cachet *m*; (*on document*) sceau, cachet; (*on envelope*) cachet; (*on package*) plomb *m*; (*Jur: on door etc*) scellé *m*. (*fig*) **under ~ of secrecy** sous le sceau du secret; **under the ~ of confession** dans le secret de la confession; (*Comm*) **~ of quality** label *m* de qualité; (*Jur*) **given under my hand and ~** signé et scellé par moi; **to put** *or* **set one's ~ to sth** apposer son sceau à qch; (*fig*) **to set** *or* **give one's ~ (of approval) to sth** donner son approbation à qch; (*fig*) **this set the ~ on their alliance** ceci a scellé leur alliance; *see* **privy, self** *etc*.

b (*ornamental stamp*) **Christmas ~** timbre *m* ornemental de Noël.

c (*device for sealing, also Aut*) joint *m* (d'étanchéité). **the ~ is not very good** ce n'est pas très étanche.

2 comp ►**seal ring** chevalière *f*.

3 vt a (*put ~ on*) *document* sceller, apposer un sceau sur; (*stick down*) *envelope, packet* coller, fermer; (*close with ~*) *envelope* cacheter; *package* plomber; *jar* sceller, fermer hermétiquement; *tin* souder. **~ed orders** instructions secrètes; (*fig*) **my lips are ~ed** mes lèvres sont scellées; (*Culin*) **to ~ a steak** *etc* saisir un bifteck *etc; see* **hermetically**.

b (*decide*) *fate* régler, décider (de); *bargain* conclure. **this ~ed his fate** cela a décidé (de) *or* a réglé son sort.

►**seal in** vt sep enfermer (hermétiquement). **our special process seals the flavour in** notre procédé spécial garde *or* conserve toute la saveur.

►**seal off** vt sep (*close up*) *door, room* condamner; (*forbid entry to*) *passage, road, room* interdire l'accès de; (*with troops, police etc*) *district* mettre un cordon autour de, encercler, boucler.

►**seal up** vt sep *window, door, jar* fermer hermétiquement, sceller; *tin* souder.

sealant [ˈsiːlənt] n (*device*) joint *m*; (*substance*) enduit *m* étanche.

sealer [ˈsiːləʳ] n (*person*) chasseur *m* de phoques; (*ship*) navire équipé pour la chasse au(x) phoque(s).

sealing[1] [ˈsiːlɪŋ] n chasse *f* aux phoques.

sealing[2] [ˈsiːlɪŋ] n *[document]* scellage *m*; *[letter]* cachetage *m*; *[package]* plombage *m*. **~ wax** cire *f* à cacheter.

seam [siːm] 1 n a (*in cloth, canvas*) couture *f*; (*in plastic, rubber*) couture, joint *m*; (*in planks, metal*) joint; (*in welding*) soudure *f*. **to fall** *or* **come apart at the ~s** *[garment]* se découdre; (*fig: of relationship etc*) se désagréger; *[suitcase, room]* **to be bursting at the ~s*** être plein à craquer. b (*Min*) filon *m*, veine *f*; (*Geol*) couche *f*. c (*on face*) (*wrinkle*) ride *f*; (*scar*) balafre *f*, couture *f*. 2 vt faire une couture *or* un joint à.

seaman [ˈsiːmən], pl **seamen** 1 n (*gen*) marin *m*; (*US Navy*) quartier-maître *m* de 2ème classe; *see* **able, ordinary**. 2 comp ►**seaman apprentice** (*US Navy*) matelot *m* breveté ►**seamanlike** de bon marin ►**seaman recruit** (*US Navy*) matelot *m*.

seamanship [ˈsiːmənʃɪp] n habileté *f* dans la manœuvre, qualités *fpl* de marin.

seamed [siːmd] adj *stockings, tights* à coutures. **a face ~ with wrinkles/scars** un visage sillonné de rides/couturé (de cicatrices).

seamen [ˈsiːmən] npl of **seaman**.

seamless [ˈsiːmlɪs] adj (*gen*) sans couture(s); *bra* à bonnets moulés, sans couture(s); (*fig*) sans faille.

seamstress [ˈsemstrɪs] n couturière *f*.

seamy [ˈsiːmɪ] adj *district* mal famé, louche. **the ~ side of life** le côté peu reluisant de la vie, l'envers *m* du décor (*fig*).

séance [ˈseɪɑ̃ːns] n *[spiritualists]* séance *f* de spiritisme; *[committee etc]* séance *f*, réunion *f*.

sear [sɪəʳ] 1 adj desséché, flétri. 2 vt (*wither*) *flower, grain, leaves* *[heat]* dessécher, flétrir; *[frost]* flétrir; (*burn*) brûler; (*Med: cauterize*) cautériser; (*brand*) marquer au fer rouge; (*fig: make callous*) *person, conscience, feelings* endurcir.

►**sear through** vt fus *walls, metal* traverser, percer.

search [sɜːtʃ] 1 n a (*for sth lost*) recherche(s) *f(pl)*. **in ~ of** à la recherche de; **a ~ was made for the child** on a entrepris des recherches pour retrouver l'enfant; **the ~ for the missing man** les recherches entreprises pour retrouver l'homme; **to begin a ~ for** *person* partir à la recherche de; *thing* se mettre à la recherche de; **in my ~ I found an interesting book** au cours de mes recherches j'ai découvert un livre intéressant; *see* **house**.

b *[drawer, box, pocket, district]* fouille *f*; (*Admin*) *[luggage etc]* visite *f*; (*Jur*) *[building etc]* perquisition *f*. **the ~ did not reveal anything** la fouille n'a rien donné; **his ~ of the drawer revealed nothing** il a fouillé le tiroir sans rien trouver *or* pour ne rien trouver; **the thieves' ~ of the house** la fouille de la maison par les voleurs; (*Police*) **house ~** perquisition à domicile, visite domiciliaire; (*Jur*) **right of ~** droit *m* de visite; **passengers must submit to a ~** les passagers doivent se soumettre à une fouille.

c (*Comput*) recherche *f*. **~ and replace** recherche *f* et remplacement *m*.

2 comp ►**searchlight** projecteur *m* (*pour éclairer*) ►**search party** équipe *f* *or* caravane *f* *or* expédition *f* de secours ►**search warrant** (*Jur*) mandat *m* de perquisition.

3 vt a (*hunt through*) *house, park, woods, district* fouiller; (*Jur*) *house etc* perquisitionner. **they ~ed the woods for the child** ils ont fouillé les bois *or* ils ont passé les bois au peigne fin à la recherche de l'enfant; **we have ~ed the library for it** nous l'avons cherché partout dans la bibliothèque.

b (*examine*) *pocket, drawer, suitcase* fouiller (dans) (*for* pour essayer de retrouver); *luggage* (*gen*) fouiller; (*Customs, Police etc*) visiter; *suspect* fouiller. **they ~ed him for a weapon** ils l'ont fouillé pour s'assurer qu'il n'avait pas d'arme; **~ me!*** je n'en sais rien moi!, je n'en ai pas la moindre idée!

c (*scan*) *documents, records, photograph* examiner (en détail) (*for* pour trouver). (*fig*) **he ~ed her face for some sign of affection** il a cherché sur son visage un signe d'affection; **to ~ one's conscience** sonder sa conscience; **to ~ one's memory** chercher dans *or* fouiller dans ses souvenirs.

d (*Comput*) *file* consulter. **to ~ a file for sth** rechercher qch dans un fichier.

4 **vi** a (*gen*) chercher. **to ~ after** *or* **for sth** chercher *or* rechercher qch; **to ~ through sth** fouiller qch, chercher dans qch; **they ~ed through his belongings** ils ont fouillé ses affaires.

b (*Comput*) **to ~ for** rechercher.

►**search about, search around vi: to search about for sth** chercher qch un peu partout, fouiller un peu partout pour trouver qch.

►**search out vt sep** se mettre à la recherche de, rechercher; chercher à trouver; (*and find*) découvrir.

searcher ['sɜːtʃəʳ] **n** chercheur *m*, -euse *f* (*for, after* en quête de).

searching ['sɜːtʃɪŋ] **adj** *look* pénétrant, scrutateur (*f* -trice); *examination* rigoureux, minutieux; *question* brûlant; *see* **heart**.

searchingly ['sɜːtʃɪŋlɪ] **adv** de façon pénétrante.

searing ['sɪərɪŋ] **adj** *pain* aigu (*f* -guë), fulgurant; *documentary, criticism* virulent.

seaside ['siːsaɪd] 1 **n** (*NonC*) bord *m* de la mer. **at** *or* **beside** *or* **by the ~** au bord de la mer, à la mer; **we're going to the ~** nous allons à la mer *or* au bord de la mer. 2 **comp** *town* au bord de la mer; *holiday* à la mer; *hotel* en bord de mer, sur le bord de la mer ►**seaside resort** station *f* balnéaire.

season ['siːzn] 1 **n** a (*spring, summer etc*) saison *f*. **the dry ~** la saison sèche; *see* **monsoon, rainy** *etc*.

b (*Sport, Comm, Zool, Agr, Hunting etc*) saison *f*; (*period of activity, availability etc*) saison, époque *f*, temps *m*; (*fig*) moment opportun. **to be out of/in ~** *[food]* ne pas être/être de saison; *[remark etc]* être hors de/à propos; *[animals]* (*for mating*) *[males]* ne pas être/être (en période de) rut; *[females]* ne pas être/être en chaleur; (*for hunting*) être fermé/ouvert; **to go somewhere out of/in ~** aller quelque part hors saison *or* en basse saison/en haute saison; **it isn't the ~ for lily of the valley** ce n'est pas la saison du muguet; **the Christmas ~** la période de Noël *or* des fêtes; **the (social) ~** la saison (mondaine); **the London (social) ~** la saison londonienne; **her first ~** sa première saison, ses débuts *mpl* dans le monde; **the busy ~** (*for shops etc*) la période de grande activité/la plus active; (*for hotels etc*) la pleine saison; **the hunting/fishing** *etc* **~** la saison de la chasse/de la pêche *etc;* **the football ~** la saison de football; (*Sport*) **his first ~ in the Celtic team** sa première saison dans l'équipe du Celtic; **the ~ is at its height** la saison bat son plein, c'est le plein de la saison; **the start of the ~** *[tourism, hotels etc]* le début de (la) saison; (*Shooting*) l'ouverture de la chasse; (*social*) le commencement de la saison (mondaine); **"S~'s greetings"** "Joyeux Noël et Bonne Année"; **early in the ~** (*specific*) au début de la saison; (*non-specific*) en début de saison; **late in the ~** (*specific*) à l'arrière-saison; (*non-specific*) en arrière-saison; (*Brit*) **the peak/high/low ~** la pleine/haute/basse saison; **the off-~** la morte-saison; **during the off-~** hors saison, pendant la morte saison; **a word in ~** un mot dit à propos *or* au moment opportun; (*fig*) **in (~) and out of ~** à tout bout de champ; **strawberries out of/in ~** fraises hors de/de saison; (*fig*) **in due ~** en temps utile, au moment opportun; *see* **breeding, festive, silly, tourist** *etc*.

c (*Theat*) saison *f* (théâtrale). **he did a ~ at the Old Vic** il a joué à l'Old Vic pendant une saison; **the film is here for a short ~** le film sera projeté quelques semaines; (*on notice*) **"for a ~, Laurence Olivier in "Macbeth"** "pour quelques semaines, Laurence Olivier dans "Macbeth"; (*TV*) **a ~ of Renoir (films), a Renoir ~** un cycle Renoir.

d = **~ ticket;** *see* **2**.

e (*Vet*) **in ~** en chaleur.

2 **comp** ►**season ticket** (*Rail, Theat etc*) carte *f* d'abonnement; **to take out a season ticket** prendre un abonnement, s'abonner (*for* à); **season ticket holder** abonné(e) *m(f)*.

3 **vt** a *wood* faire sécher, dessécher; *cask* abreuver; *see also* **seasoned**.

b (*Culin*) (*with condiments*) assaisonner; (*with spice*) épicer, relever. **a highly ~ed dish** un plat relevé; (*fig*) **a speech ~ed with humour** un discours assaisonné *or* pimenté d'humour.

seasonable ['siːznəbl] **adj** *weather* de saison; *advice* à propos, opportun.

seasonal ['siːzənl] **adj** (*all senses*) saisonnier. **it's very ~** c'est très saisonnier, cela dépend beaucoup de la saison; **~ worker** (ouvrier *m*, -ière *f*) saisonnier *m*, -ière *f*; (*Psych*) **~ affective disorder** *dépression due au changement des saisons*.

seasonally ['siːzənəlɪ] **adv** selon la saison. (*Statistics*) **~ adjusted** corrigé en fonction des variations saisonnières, désaisonalisé.

seasoned ['siːznd] **adj** *wood* séché, desséché; (*fig*) *worker* expérimenté; *writer, actor, footballer etc* chevronné, expérimenté; *troops* aguerri. **a ~ campaigner for civil rights** un vétéran des campagnes pour les droits civils; (*fig*) **~ campaigner** vieux routier (*fig*); **to be ~ to sth** être habitué à qch; *see also* **season**.

seasoning ['siːznɪŋ] **n** assaisonnement *m*, condiment *m*. **add ~** assaisonnez; **check the ~** vérifiez l'assaisonnement; **there's too much ~** c'est trop assaisonné; (*fig*) **with a ~ of humour** avec un grain d'humour.

seat [siːt] 1 **n** a (*chair etc*) (*gen*) siège *m*; (*in theatre, cinema*) fauteuil *m*; (*in bus, train*) banquette *f*; (*Aut*) (*individual*) siège; (*for several people*) banquette; (*on cycle*) selle *f*; *see* **back, driver, hot** *etc*.

b (*place or right to sit*) place *f*. **to take a ~** s'asseoir; **to take one's ~** prendre place (*see also* **1d**); **to keep one's ~** rester assis; **to lose one's ~** perdre sa place (*see also* **1d, 1f**); (*Cine, Theat*) **I'd like 2 ~s for ...** je voudrais 2 places pour ...; **keep a ~ for me** gardez-moi une place; **there are ~s for 70 people** il y a 70 places assises; *see* **book** *etc*.

c (*part of chair*) siège *m*; *[trousers]* fond *m*; (**: buttocks*) derrière *m*, postérieur* *m*. (*fig*) **he was flying by the ~ of his pants** il a dû faire appel à toute la présence d'esprit dont il était capable.

d (*Parl*) siège *m*. **to keep/lose one's ~** être/ne pas être réélu; (*Brit*) **to take one's ~ in the Commons/in the Lords** prendre son siège aux Communes/à la Chambre des lords, ≃ être validé comme député à l'Assemblée nationale/comme sénateur; **the socialists won/lost 10 ~s** les socialistes ont gagné/perdu 10 sièges; **they won the ~ from the Conservatives** ils ont pris le siège aux conservateurs; **a majority of 50 ~s** une majorité de 50 (députés *etc*); *see* **safe**.

e (*location, centre*) *[government]* siège *m*; *[commerce]* centre *m*; (*Med*) *[infection]* foyer *m*. **~ of learning** siège *or* haut lieu du savoir; **he has a (country) ~ in the north** il a un manoir *or* un château dans le nord.

f (*Equitation*) **to have a good ~** avoir une bonne assiette, bien se tenir en selle; **to keep one's ~** rester en selle; **to lose one's ~** être désarçonné, vider les étriers.

2 **comp** ►**seat back** dossier *m* (de chaise *etc*) ►**seat belt** (*Aut, Aviat*) ceinture *f* de sécurité ►**seatmates:** (*US*) **we were seatmates** nous étions assis l'un(e) à côté de l'autre ►**seatwork** (*US Scol*) travail *m* fait en classe; *see* **fasten**.

3 **vt** a *child* (faire) asseoir; (*at table*) *guest* placer. **to ~ o.s.** s'asseoir; **please be ~ed** veuillez vous asseoir, asseyez-vous je vous prie; **to remain ~ed** rester assis; **the waiter ~ed him at my table** le garçon l'a placé à ma table; *see* **deep**.

b (*have or find room for*) **we cannot ~ them all** nous n'avons pas assez de sièges pour tout le monde; **how many does the hall ~?** combien y a-t-il de places assises *or* à combien peut-on s'asseoir dans la salle?; **this car ~s 6 in comfort** on tient confortablement à 6 dans cette voiture; **this table ~s 8** on peut tenir à 8 à cette table, c'est une table pour 8 personnes *or* couverts.

c (*also* **re~**) *chair* refaire le siège de; *trousers* (re)mettre un fond à.

4 **vi: this skirt won't ~** cette jupe ne va pas se déformer derrière.

-seater ['siːtəʳ] **adj, n ending in comps:** (*Aut*) **a two-seater** une deux places; **two-seater car/plane** voiture *f*/avion *m* biplace *or* à deux places; **a 50-seater coach** un car de 50 places.

seating ['siːtɪŋ] 1 **n** (*NonC*) a (*act*) répartition *f or* allocation *f* des places. **is the ~ (of the guests) all right?** est-ce qu'on a bien placé les invités? b (*seats*) sièges *mpl*; (*as opposed to standing room*) places assises. **~ for 600** 600 places assises. 2 **comp** ►**seating accommodation** nombre *m* de places assises ►**seating arrangements: we must think about the seating arrangements** il faut penser à placer les gens; **what are the seating arrangements?** comment va-t-on placer les gens? ►**seating capacity** = **seating accommodation** ►**seating plan** (*at dinner*) plan *m* de table.

SEATO ['siːtəʊ] **n** (**abbr of South East Asia Treaty Organisation**) O.T.A.S.E. *f*.

seaward ['siːwəd] 1 **adj** *journey* vers le large; *breeze* de terre. 2 **adv** = **seawards**.

seawards ['siːwədz] **adv** vers le large, vers la mer.

sebaceous [sɪ'beɪʃəs] **adj** sébacé.

Sebastian [sɪ'bæstjən] **n** Sébastien *m*.

seborrhoea [ˌsebə'rɪə] **n** séborrhée *f*.

sebum ['siːbəm] **n** sébum *m*.

SEC [ˌesiː'siː] **n** (*US: abbr of* **Securities and Exchange Commission**) ≃ C.O.B. *f*.

sec* [sek] **n abbr of second²**.

SECAM ['siːˌkæm] (*TV*) (**abbr of séquentiel couleur à mémoire**) SECAM *m*.

secant ['siːkənt] 1 **n** sécante *f*. 2 **adj** sécant.

secateurs [ˌsekə'tɜːz] **npl** (*esp Brit: also* **pair of ~**) sécateur *m*.

secede [sɪ'siːd] **vi** faire sécession, se séparer (*from* de).

secession [sɪ'seʃən] **n** sécession *f*, séparation *f*.

secessionist [sɪ'seʃnɪst] **adj, n** sécessionniste *(mf)*.

seclude [sɪ'kluːd] **vt** éloigner *or* isoler (du monde).

secluded [sɪ'kluːdɪd] **adj** *house* à l'écart, (dans un endroit) retiré; *garden* isolé; *life* retiré (du monde), solitaire. **~ spot** endroit retiré.

seclusion [sɪ'kluːʒən] **n** solitude *f*. **to live in ~** vivre en solitaire, vivre retiré du monde.

second¹ ['sekənd] 1 **adj** a (*esp one of many*) deuxième; (*more often one of 2*) second. **to be ~ in the queue** être le (*or* la) deuxième dans la queue; **to be ~ in command** (*Mil*) commander en second; (*gen*) être deuxième dans la hiérarchie (*see also* **2**); (*Scol*) **he was ~ in French** il a été deuxième en français; (*fig*) **he's a ~ Beethoven** c'est un autre Beethoven; **Britain's ~ city** la deuxième ville de Grande-Bretagne; (*Brit*

Parl) **the ~ chamber** la Chambre des lords; **give him a ~ chance to show what he can do** donnez-lui encore une chance de montrer ce dont il est capable; **you won't get a ~ chance to go to Australia** vous ne retrouverez pas l'occasion d'aller en Australie, l'occasion d'aller en Australie ne se représentera pas; **would you like a ~ cup of tea?** voulez-vous encore du thé?; **would you like a ~ cup?** voulez-vous une seconde *or* autre tasse?; **he had a ~ cup of coffee** il a repris du café; **every ~ day** tous les deux jours, un jour sur deux; **every ~ Thursday** un jeudi sur deux; **on the ~ floor** (*Brit*) au deuxième (étage); (*US*) au premier (étage); (*Aut*) **~ gear** seconde *f*; (*Theat*) **the ~ house** la deuxième représentation de la journée; **~ language** seconde *or* deuxième langue *f*; (*Med*) **to ask for a ~ opinion** demander l'avis d'un autre *or* d'un deuxième médecin; (*Med*) **I'd like a ~ opinion** je voudrais consulter un deuxième *or* autre médecin, j'aimerais avoir un autre avis; (*Gram*) **in the ~ person** à la deuxième personne; (*Gram*) **~ person singular/plural** deuxième personne du singulier/pluriel; **in the ~ place** deuxièmement, (*more formally*) en second lieu; **in the first place ... in the ~ place** d'abord ... ensuite; **~ teeth** seconde dentition; **for the ~ time** pour la deuxième fois; **for the ~ and last time** pour la seconde et dernière fois; (*Mus*) **~ violin** second violon; **Charles the S~** Charles Deux, Charles II; *see also* **2** *and* **helping, look, row** *etc; for other phrases see* **sixth.**

b (*fig phrases*) **to be in one's ~ childhood** retomber en enfance; **to play ~ fiddle to sb** jouer un rôle secondaire auprès de qn, (*over longer period*) vivre dans l'ombre de qn; **it's ~ nature to him** c'est une seconde nature chez lui; **it was ~ nature for him to help his friends** aider ses amis était chez lui une seconde nature; **~ to none** sans pareil, sans rival, inégalable; **for elegance of style he is ~ to none** pour ce qui est de l'élégance du style il ne le cède à personne *or* il n'a pas son pareil; **Edinburgh is ~ only to Glasgow as a tourist attraction** Edimbourg ne le cède qu'à *or* n'est surpassé que par Glasgow comme lieu touristique; **~ self** autre soi-même *m*; **my ~ self** un(e) autre moi-même; **to have ~ sight** avoir le don de double vue; **he has a ~ string to his bow** il a plus d'une corde à son arc; **to do sth without a ~ thought** faire qch sans hésiter *or* réfléchir; **he didn't give it a ~ thought** il l'a fait sans hésiter; **I'm having ~ thoughts (about it)** je commence à avoir des doutes (là-dessus); **I've had ~ thoughts about the holiday** pour ce qui est des vacances j'ai changé d'avis; **the director has had ~ thoughts about it** le directeur est revenu sur sa première décision là-dessus; **on ~ thoughts ...** réflexion faite ..., à la réflexion ...; **to get one's ~ wind** (*lit*) retrouver son souffle; (*fig*) reprendre des forces, retrouver ses forces; *see also* **2**; *for other phrases see* **sixth.**

2 comp ▸ **second-best** *see* **second-best** ▸ **second-class** *see* **second-class** ▸ **the second coming** (*Rel*) le second avènement (du Messie) ▸ **second cousin** petit(e) cousin(e) (*issu(e) de germains*) ▸ **second-guess** (*: *esp US*) vi comprendre après coup ◊ vt *person, sb's reaction* (essayer d')anticiper ▸ **secondhand** *see* **secondhand** *and also* **second² 2** ▸ **second-in-command** (*Mil*) commandant *m* en second; (*Naut*) second *m*; (*gen*) second, adjoint *m* ▸ **second lieutenant** (*Mil etc*) sous-lieutenant *m* ▸ **second mate, second officer** (*Merchant Navy*) commandant *m* en second ▸ **second-rate** (*goods*) de qualité inférieure; (*writer, work*) médiocre, de deuxième ordre ▸ **second-rater*** médiocre *mf*, médiocrité *f* ▸ **second-story man⁑** (*US*) monte-en-l'air *m inv*.

3 adv a (*in race, exam, competition*) en seconde place *or* position. **he came** *or* **was placed ~** il s'est classé deuxième *or* second; (*at meeting, party etc*) **he arrived ~** il est arrivé le deuxième.

b = **secondly.**

c (*Rail etc*) **to travel ~** voyager en seconde.

d (+ *superl adj*) **the ~ largest/smallest book** le plus grand/petit livre sauf un.

4 n a deuxième *mf*, second(e) *m(f)*. **he came a good ~** il s'est fait battre de justesse; **he came a poor ~** il a été largement battu (en deuxième place); (*Climbing*) **~ (on the rope)** second (de cordée).

b (*Boxing*) soigneur *m*; (*in duel*) second *m*, témoin *m*. (*Boxing*) **~s out (of the ring)!** soigneurs hors du ring!

c (*Brit Univ*) ≃ licence *f* avec mention (assez) bien. **he got an upper/a lower ~** ≃ il a eu sa licence avec mention bien/assez bien; **many students get a lower ~** de nombreux étudiants sont reçus avec la mention assez bien.

d (*Aut: ~ gear*) seconde *f*. **in ~** en seconde.

e (*Comm: non perfect goods*) **~s** articles *mpl* de second choix, articles comportant un défaut.

f (*second helping*) **~s*** rabiot* *m*, rab⁑ *m*; **anyone for ~s*?** qui en reveut?, qui veut du rab⁑?

g (*Mus: interval*) seconde *f*.

5 vt a *motion* appuyer; *speaker* appuyer la motion de. **I'll ~ that** (*at meeting*) j'appuie la proposition *or* la demande; (*gen*) je suis d'accord *or* pour*.

b [sɪ'kɒnd] (*Brit: Admin, Mil*) affecter provisoirement (*to* à), détacher (*to* à). **he has been ~ed for service abroad** il est en détachement à l'étranger.

second² ['sekənd] 1 n seconde *f* (*also Geog, Math etc*); (*fig*) seconde, instant *m*. **it won't take a ~** il y en a pour une seconde *or* un instant; **at that very ~** à cet instant précis; **just a ~!, half a ~!*** un instant!, une (petite) seconde!; **I'm coming in half a ~** j'arrive tout de suite *or* dans une seconde; **I'll be with you in (just) a ~** je suis à vous dans une seconde; *see* **split.** 2 comp ▸ **second(s) hand** trotteuse *f*.

secondary ['sekəndərɪ] 1 adj (*gen*) secondaire; *meaning* secondaire, dérivé; *education* secondaire, du second degré; (*minor*) secondaire, accessoire. **of ~ importance** secondaire, peu important; (*Philos*) **~ cause** cause seconde; (*Geol*) **~ era** (ère *f*) secondaire *m*; (*Brit*) **~ modern (school)**† ≃ collège *m* d'enseignement général; (*Ind*) **~ picketing** piquets *mpl* de grève de solidarité; **~ road** route départementale *or* secondaire; (*Chem, Ind*) **~ product** sous-produit *m*; **~ stress** accent *m* secondaire.

2 n a (*Univ etc: minor subject*) matière *f* secondaire.

b (**~ school**) (*gen*) établissement *m* d'enseignement secondaire; (*up to 3rd form*) collège *m* (d'enseignement secondaire); (*from 4th form upwards*) lycée *m* citoyen(ne) *m(f)* de deuxième ordre.

second-best ['sekənd'best] 1 n: **it is the ~** (*gen*) c'est ce qu'il y a de mieux après; (*poor substitute*) c'est un pis-aller; **as a ~** faute de mieux, au pis-aller. 2 adj *jacket etc* de tous les jours. **his ~ novel** de tous ses romans celui qui vient en second du point de vue de la qualité. 3 adv: **to come off ~** perdre, se faire battre.

second-class ['sekənd'klɑːs] 1 adj (*lit*) de deuxième classe; (*Rail*) *ticket, compartment* de seconde (classe); *hotel* de seconde catégorie, de second ordre; (*pej*) *food, goods etc* de qualité inférieure. **~ citizen** citoyen(ne) *m(f)* de deuxième ordre; (*Univ*) **~ degree** = **second¹ 4c**; **~ mail** (*Brit*) courrier *m* à tarif réduit; (*US*) imprimés *mpl* périodiques; (*Brit*) **~ stamp** timbre *m* à tarif réduit; (*Rail*) **a ~ return to London** un aller et retour en seconde (classe) pour Londres; (*Rail*) **~ seat** seconde *f*. 2 adv (*Rail etc*) **to travel ~** voyager en seconde; **to send sth ~** envoyer qch en courrier ordinaire.

seconder ['sekəndəʳ] n [*motion*] personne *f* qui appuie une motion; [*candidate*] deuxième parrain *m*.

secondhand ['sekənd'hænd] 1 adj *clothes, car* d'occasion, de seconde main; (*fig*) *information, account* de seconde main. **~ bookseller** libraire *m* d'occasion, bouquiniste *mf*; **~ bookshop** librairie *f* d'occasion; **~ dealer** marchand(e) *m(f)* d'occasion; **~ smoke*** la fumée des autres. 2 adv *buy* d'occasion. **to hear sth ~** entendre dire qch, entendre qch de quelqu'un d'autre.

secondly ['sekəndlɪ] adv deuxièmement, (*more formally*) en second lieu. **firstly ... ~ ...** d'abord ... ensuite ... .

secondment [sɪ'kɒndmənt] n (*Brit*) affectation *f* provisoire, détachement *m*. **on ~** (*at home*) en détachement, détaché (*to* à); (*abroad*) en mission (*to* à).

secrecy ['siːkrəsɪ] n (*NonC*) secret *m*. **in ~** en secret, secrètement; **in strict ~** en grand secret, dans le plus grand secret; **under pledge of ~** sous le sceau du secret; **there's no ~ about it** on n'en fait pas (un) mystère; **there was an air of ~ about her** elle avait un petit air mystérieux; **I rely on your ~** je compte sur votre discrétion; **a country where ~ reigns** un pays qui a la manie du secret; *see* **swear.**

secret ['siːkrɪt] 1 n a secret *m*. **to keep a ~** garder un secret; **I told it you as a ~** je vous l'ai dit en confidence; **to let sb into the ~** mettre qn dans le secret; **to let sb into a ~** révéler *or* confier *or* dire un secret à qn; **to be in the ~** être au courant *or* dans le coup*; **there's no ~ about it** cela n'a rien de secret; **to have no ~s from sb** ne pas avoir de secrets pour qn; **he makes no ~ of the fact that** il ne cache pas que; **lovers' ~** confidence *f* d'amoureux; **the ~ of success/successful writing** le secret du succès/de la littérature à succès; **the ~ of being a good teacher is ...** pour être bon professeur le secret est ...; **the ~s of nature** les secrets *or* les mystères *mpl* de la nature; *see* **open, state** *etc.*

b (*NonC: secrecy*) **in ~** en secret, secrètement, en cachette.

2 adj a (*concealed*) *place, drawer, marriage, negotiations* secret (*f* -ète); *door, passage* secret, dérobé; (*secluded*) *place* retiré, caché. **to keep one's plans ~** ne pas révéler ses plans, cacher ses plans; **to keep sth ~ from sb** ne pas révéler *or* montrer qch à qn; **it's all highly ~** c'est tout ce qu'il y a de plus secret; **~ admirer** admirateur *m*, -trice *f* inconnu(e); **~ agent** agent secret; **~ ballot** vote *m* à bulletin secret; **~ funds** caisse *f* noire; **~ police** police secrète; **the S~ Service** (*Brit*) les services secrets; (*US*) les services chargés de la protection du président; **~ society** société secrète; *see* **top¹.**

b (*secretive*) secret (*f* -ète), dissimulé (*pej*).

secretaire [ˌsekrɪ'tɛəʳ] n secrétaire *m*.

secretarial [ˌsekrə'tɛərɪəl] adj *work* de secrétariat, de secrétaire. **~ college** école *f* de secrétariat; **~ course** études *fpl* de secrétaire; **to have a ~ job** être secrétaire.

secretariat [ˌsekrə'tɛərɪət] n secrétariat *m* (*personnel, bureau, services*).

secretary ['sekrətrɪ] 1 n a (*in office, of club etc*) secrétaire *mf*; (*also* **company ~**) secrétaire général (*d'une société*). (*Pol*) **S~ of State** (*Brit*) ministre *m* (*of, for* de); (*US*) secrétaire *m* d'État, ≃ ministre des Affaires étrangères; *see* **foreign, parliamentary, under** *etc.* b (*writing desk*) secrétaire *m*. 2 comp ▸ **secretary-general** (pl **secretaries-~**) secrétaire général.

secrete [sɪ'kriːt] vt a (*Anat, Bio, Med*) sécréter. b (*hide*) cacher.

secretion [sɪ'kriːʃən] n (*see* **secrete**) a sécrétion *f*. b action *f* de cacher.

secretive ['si:krətɪv] adj (*by nature*) secret (*f* -ète), dissimulé (*pej*), cachottier (*pej*). **to be ~ about sth** faire un secret *or* un mystère de qch, se montrer très réservé à propos de qch.

secretively ['si:krətɪvlɪ] adv d'une façon très réservée, d'une façon dissimulée (*pej*).

secretiveness ['si:krətɪvnɪs] n (*NonC*) réserve *f*, caractère dissimulé (*pej*) *or* cachottier (*pej*).

secretly ['si:krətlɪ] adv secrètement, en secret, en cachette; *believe etc* secrètement, en son for intérieur.

sect [sekt] n secte *f*.

sectarian [sek'tɛərɪən] 1 adj (*gen*) sectaire (*mf*). **~ school** école *f* confessionnelle. 2 n sectaire *mf*.

sectarianism [sek'tɛərɪənɪzəm] n sectarisme *m*.

section ['sekʃən] 1 n a *[book, law, population]* section *f*, partie *f*; *[text, document]* section, article *m*, paragraphe *m*; *[country]* partie; *[road, pipeline]* section, tronçon *m*; *[town]* quartier *m*; *[machine, furniture]* élément *m*; (*Mil*) groupe *m* (de combat). *[orchestra]* **the brass/string ~** les cuivres *mpl*/les cordes *fpl*; (*Press*) **the financial ~** la *or* les page(s) financière(s); (*Admin, Jur*) **~ 2 of the municipal by-laws** l'article 2 des arrêtés municipaux; **this bookcase comes in ~s** cette bibliothèque se vend par éléments; **there is a ~ of public opinion which maintains ...** il y a une partie *or* une section de l'opinion publique qui maintient ... .

b (*Admin, Ind*) section *f*; (*Comm*) rayon *m*; *see* **consular, passport** *etc*.

c (*Rail*) (*part of network*) canton *m* (de voie ferrée); (*US Rail*) (*extra train*) train *m* supplémentaire, train-bis *m*; (*US: in sleeping car*) compartiment-lits *m*.

d (*cut*) coupe *f*, section *f*; (*for microscope*) coupe, lamelle *f*. **longitudinal/vertical ~** coupe longitudinale/verticale; *see* **cross**.

e (*act of cutting*) section *f*, sectionnement *m*.

2 comp ▸**section hand** (*US Rail*) cantonnier *m* (des chemins de fer), agent *m* de la voie ▸**section mark** signe *m* de paragraphe.

3 vt sectionner.

▸**section off** vt sep séparer.

sectional ['sekʃənl] adj (*made of sections*) *bookcase etc* à éléments; (*representing a part*) *interests* d'un groupe; *drawing* en coupe.

sectionalism ['sekʃənəlɪzəm] n défense *f* des intérêts d'un groupe.

sector ['sektəʳ] 1 n a secteur *m*; (*Mil*) secteur, zone *f*; (*Comput*) secteur; (*fig*) secteur, domaine *m*. **private/public ~** secteur privé/public. b (*Geom*) secteur *m*; (*instrument*) compas *m* (de proportions). 2 vt sectoriser.

sectorial [sek'tɔ:rɪəl] adj sectoriel.

secular ['sekjʊləʳ] adj *authority, clergy* séculier; *teaching, school* laïque; *art, writer, music* profane. **we live in a ~ society** nous vivons dans une société qui a perdu la foi.

secularism ['sekjʊlərɪzəm] n (*policy*) laïcité *f*; (*doctrine*) laïcisme *m*.

secularization [,sekjʊləraɪ'zeɪʃən] n (*see* **secular**) sécularisation *f*; laïcisation *f*.

secularize ['sekjʊləraɪz] vt (*see* **secular**) séculariser; laïciser.

secure [sɪ'kjʊəʳ] 1 adj a (*solid, firm*) *bolt, padlock* solide; *nail, knot* solide, qui tient bien; *rope* bien attaché; *door, window* bien fermé; *structure, ladder* qui ne bouge pas, ferme; *foothold, handhold* bon, sûr. **to make ~** *rope* bien attacher; *door, window* bien fermer; *tile* bien fixer.

b (*in safe place*) en sûreté, en sécurité, en lieu sûr; *hideout, place* sûr; (*certain*) *career, future, promotion, fame* assuré. **~ from** *or* **against** à l'abri de.

c (*unworried*) tranquille, sans inquiétude. **to feel ~ about** ne pas avoir d'inquiétudes sur *or* au sujet de; **~ in the knowledge that** ayant la certitude que; **a child must be (emotionally) ~** un enfant a besoin de sécurité sur le plan affectif, un enfant a besoin d'être sécurisé.

2 vt a (*get*) *object* se procurer, obtenir; *staff, performer* engager. **to ~ sth for sb** procurer qch à qn, obtenir qch pour qn.

b (*fix*) *rope* fixer, attacher; *door, window* bien fermer; *tile* fixer; (*tie up*) *person, animal* attacher.

c (*make safe*) (*from danger*) préserver, protéger, garantir (*against, from* de); *debt, loan* garantir; *career, future* assurer.

securely [sɪ'kjʊəlɪ] adv (*see* **secure 1**) (*firmly*) solidement, bien; (*safely*) en sécurité.

Securicor [sɪ'kjʊərɪkɔ:ʳ] n ® *société de surveillance et de convoi de fonds*. **~ guard** employé *m* du service de surveillance, convoyeur *m* de fonds.

securitization [sɪ,kjʊərɪtaɪ'zeɪʃən] n (*Fin*) titrisation *f*.

securitize [sɪ'kjʊərɪtaɪz] vt *loan* titriser.

security [sɪ'kjʊərɪtɪ] 1 n a (*safety, confidence*) sécurité *f*. **in ~** en sécurité; (*Admin, Ind*) **job ~** sécurité de l'emploi; **~ of tenure** (*in one's job*) sécurité totale de l'emploi; (*Jur: of tenant*) bail assuré; (*Psych*) **a child needs ~** un enfant a besoin de sécurité sur le plan affectif, un enfant a besoin d'être sécurisé.

b (*Ind, Pol etc: against spying, escape etc*) sécurité *f*. **~ was very lax** les mesures de sécurité étaient très relâchées; *[jail]* **maximum** *or* **top** *or* **high ~ wing** quartier *m* de haute surveillance; *see also* **maximum**.

c (*Fin: for loan*) caution *f*, garantie *f*. **loans without ~** crédit *m* à découvert; **up to £1,000 without ~** jusqu'à 1.000 livres sans caution *or* sans garantie; **to stand ~ for sb** se porter garant pour *or* de qn.

d (*St Ex*) **securities** valeurs *fpl*, titres *mpl*; **government securities** fonds *mpl* d'État.

2 comp ▸**securities market** (*Fin*) marché *m* des valeurs ▸**security agreement** (*Fin*) accord *m* de sûreté ▸**security blanket** (*Psych*) objet *m* transitionnel; *[police]* dispositif *m* de sécurité ▸**Security Council** Conseil *m* de sécurité ▸**security firm** société *f* de surveillance ▸**security forces** forces *fpl* de sécurité ▸**security guard** (*gen*) garde chargé de la sécurité; (*transporting money*) convoyeur *m* de fonds ▸**security leak** fuite *f* (*de documents, de secrets etc*) ▸**security officer** (*Mil, Naut*) officier chargé de la sécurité; (*Comm, Ind*) inspecteur *m* (chargé) de la sécurité ▸**security police** services *mpl* de la sûreté ▸**security risk** *personne susceptible de compromettre la sûreté de l'État, la sécurité d'une organisation etc;* **that man is a security risk** cet homme constitue un risque *or* n'est pas sûr ▸**security vetting** enquête *f* de sécurité (*of sb* sur qn); **a policy of security vetting** une politique d'enquêtes de sécurité.

sedan [sɪ'dæn] n a (*also* **~ chair**) chaise *f* à porteurs. b (*US: car*) conduite intérieure, berline *f*.

sedate [sɪ'deɪt] 1 adj *person* posé, calme, réfléchi; *behaviour* calme, pondéré. 2 vt (*Med*) donner des sédatifs à, mettre sous sédation.

sedately [sɪ'deɪtlɪ] adv posément, calmement.

sedateness [sɪ'deɪtnɪs] n (*see* **sedate**) allure posée *or* réfléchie; calme *m*, pondération *f*.

sedation [sɪ'deɪʃən] n sédation *f*. **under ~** sous sédation, sous calmants.

sedative ['sedətɪv] adj, n calmant (*m*), sédatif (*m*).

sedentary ['sedntrɪ] adj *work* sédentaire. **~ worker** travailleur *m*, -euse *f* sédentaire.

sedge [sedʒ] n laîche *f*, carex *m*. **~ warbler** phragmite *m* des joncs, rousserolle *f*.

sediment ['sedɪmənt] n (*Geol, Med*) sédiment *m*; (*in boiler, liquids*) dépôt *m*; (*in wine*) dépôt, lie *f*.

sedimentary [,sedɪ'mentərɪ] adj sédimentaire.

sedimentation [,sedɪmen'teɪʃən] n sédimentation *f*.

sedition [sə'dɪʃən] n sédition *f*.

seditious [sə'dɪʃəs] adj séditieux.

seduce [sɪ'dju:s] vt (*also sexually*) séduire. **to ~ sb from sth** détourner qn de qch; **to ~ sb into doing sth** entraîner qn à faire qch.

seducer [sɪ'dju:səʳ] n séducteur *m*, -trice *f*.

seduction [sɪ'dʌkʃən] n séduction *f*.

seductive [sɪ'dʌktɪv] adj *person, charms* séduisant, attrayant; *smile, perfume* aguichant, séducteur (*f* -trice); *offer* alléchant.

seductively [sɪ'dʌktɪvlɪ] adv d'une manière séduisante, avec séduction.

seductiveness [sɪ'dʌktɪvnɪs] n caractère séduisant, qualité séduisante.

seductress [sɪ'dʌktrɪs] n séductrice *f*.

sedulous ['sedjʊləs] adj assidu, persévérant, attentif.

sedulously ['sedjʊləslɪ] adv assidûment, avec persévérance.

see[1] [si:] pret **saw**, ptp **seen** 1 vt a (*gen*) voir. **I can ~ him** je le vois; **I saw him read/reading the letter** je l'ai vu lire/qui lisait la lettre; **he was ~n to read the letter** on l'a vu lire la lettre; **she saw him knocked down** elle l'a vu (se faire) renverser; **there was no one at all** *or* **not a soul to be ~n** il n'y avait pas un chat* (*fig*), il n'y avait pas âme qui vive; **there was not a house to be ~n** il n'y avait pas une seule maison en vue; (*Brit*) **I could ~ him far enough!*** j'en ai (*or* avais) marre de sa tête!‡, ce qu'il peut (*or* a pu) me casser les pieds!‡; **I could ~ it** *or* **that one coming*** je le sentais venir, je m'y attendais; **to ~ fit to do** juger bon de faire; **will she come? — if she ~s fit** est-ce qu'elle viendra? — oui, si elle le juge bon; **I'll be glad to ~ the back of him*** je serai heureux de le voir partir *or* d'être débarrassé de lui; **~ page 10** voir (à la) page 10; **to ~ double** voir double; (*fig*) **to ~ red** voir rouge; **to ~ sth with one's own eyes** voir qch de ses propres yeux; **to ~ the sights** faire du tourisme, visiter la ville; **to ~ the sights of Paris** visiter (les monuments de) Paris; **we spent a few days in Paris ~ing the sights** nous avons passé quelques jours à Paris à visiter la ville; (*fig*) **to ~ stars** voir trente-six chandelles; **I must be ~ing things*** je dois avoir des visions* *or* des hallucinations; **can you ~ your way without a torch?** est-ce que vous pouvez trouver votre chemin *or* est-ce que vous y voyez assez sans lampe de poche?; (*fig*) **can you ~ your way to helping us?** est-ce que vous trouveriez (le) moyen de nous aider?; **I can't ~ my way to doing that** je ne vois pas comment je pourrais le faire; (*fig*) **he can't ~ the wood for the trees** il se perd dans les détails; **I want to ~ the world** je veux voyager; *see* **last, light, remain** *etc*.

b (*understand, conceive*) voir, comprendre, saisir. **to ~ the joke** comprendre *or* saisir la plaisanterie; **to ~ sense** entendre raison; **he won't ~ sense** il ne veut pas entendre raison, il ne veut pas comprendre; **try to make him ~ sense** essaie de lui faire entendre raison; **I can't ~ the point of it** je n'en vois pas l'intérêt *or* l'utilité; **I don't ~ the point of inviting him** je ne vois pas l'intérêt de l'inviter; **do you ~ what I mean?** voyez-vous *or* vous voyez ce que je veux dire?; **I ~ what you're getting at** je vois *or* je devine où vous voulez en venir; **I fail to ~** *or* **I can't ~ how you're going to do it** je ne vois pas du tout *or* je ne vois vraiment pas comment vous allez le faire; **the way I ~ it, as I ~ it** à mon avis, selon moi; **this is how** *or* **the way I ~ it** voici comment je vois *or* comprends la chose; **the French ~ it differently** les Français voient la chose différemment; **I don't ~ why** je ne vois pas pourquoi; **I don't ~ why not** (*granting permission*) je n'y vois aucune objection; (*not understanding sb's refusal*) je ne vois pas pourquoi.

c (*notice, learn, discover*) voir, remarquer, apprendre, découvrir. **I saw in the paper that he is gone** j'ai vu *or* lu dans le journal qu'il est parti; **I ~ they've bought a new car** je vois *or* je remarque *or* j'apprends qu'ils ont acheté une nouvelle voiture; **I ~ nothing wrong in it** je n'y trouve rien à redire; **I don't know what she ~s in him** (*what good qualities*) je ne sais pas ce qu'elle lui trouve (de bien); (*what attracts her*) je ne sais pas ce qui l'attire en lui; **~ who's at the door** allez voir qui est à la porte; **not until I ~ how many there are** pas avant de savoir *or* de voir *or* de découvrir combien il y en a; **I'll ~ what's what first** je vais d'abord voir de quoi il retourne; **I'll ~ what I can do** je verrai *or* je vais voir ce que je peux faire; **let's ~ what you're capable of** voyons (un peu) ce que vous savez faire.

d (*visit, meet, speak to*) voir; *doctor, lawyer* voir, consulter. **to go and ~ sb, to go to ~ sb** aller voir qn; **I'm ~ing the doctor tomorrow** je vais chez le docteur *or* je vois le docteur demain; **the manager wants to ~ you** le directeur veut vous voir, le directeur vous demande; **I can't ~ you today** je ne peux pas vous voir *or* recevoir aujourd'hui; **I want to ~ you about my son** je voudrais vous voir *or* vous parler au sujet de mon fils; **they ~ a lot of him** ils le voient souvent; **you must ~ less of him** il faut que vous le voyiez (*subj*) moins souvent.

e (**: phrases*) **~ you!, (I'll) be ~ing you!** à bientôt!, salut!*; **~ you later!** à tout à l'heure!; **~ you some time!** à un de ces jours!; **~ you soon!** à bientôt!; **~ you (on) Sunday** *etc* à dimanche *etc*; **~ you next week** *etc* à la semaine prochaine *etc*.

f (*experience, know*) voir, éprouver, connaître. **this hat has ~n better days** ce chapeau a connu des jours meilleurs; **I never thought we'd ~ the day when ...** je n'aurais jamais cru qu'un jour ...; **we'll never ~ his like again** nous ne verrons jamais son pareil; **1963 saw the assassination of John F. Kennedy** (l'année) 1963 a vu l'assassinat de John F. Kennedy; (*Mil*) **he saw service in Libya** il a servi en Libye, il a fait la campagne de Libye; **he has ~n service abroad** il a servi à l'étranger; **since she's started going round with that crowd she has certainly ~n life** depuis qu'elle fait partie de cette bande elle en a vu des choses; **I'm going to Australia because I want to ~ life** je pars en Australie parce que je veux voir le monde *or* rouler ma bosse*; **since becoming a social worker she's certainly ~n life** depuis qu'elle est assistante sociale elle a pu se rendre compte de ce que c'est que la vie; **I've ~n some things in my time* but ...** j'en ai vu (des choses) dans ma vie* mais ... .

g (*accompany, escort*) (re)conduire, (r)accompagner. **to ~ sb to the station** accompagner *or* conduire qn à la gare; **to ~ sb home/to the door** reconduire *or* raccompagner qn jusque chez lui/jusqu'à la porte; **the policeman saw him off the premises** l'agent l'a reconduit (jusqu'à la porte); **to ~ the children to bed** coucher les enfants; **he was so drunk we had to ~ him to bed** il était tellement ivre que nous avons dû l'aider à se coucher; *see also* **see off, see out**.

h (*allow to be*) laisser, permettre. **I couldn't ~ her left alone** je ne pouvais pas supporter *or* permettre qu'on la laisse (*subj*) toute seule.

i (*ensure*) s'assurer. **~ that he has all he needs** (*make sure*) veillez à ce qu'il ait tout ce dont il a besoin; (*check*) assurez-vous qu'il ne manque de rien; **~ that you have it ready for Monday** faites en sorte que ce soit prêt pour lundi; **I'll ~ he gets the letter** je ferai le nécessaire pour que la lettre lui parvienne, je me charge de lui faire parvenir la lettre; (*Brit*) **I'll ~ you all right**‡ (*gen*) je vais arranger ton affaire; (*bribe etc*) je te garantis que tu y trouveras ton compte; **I'll ~ you damned** *or* **in hell first!*** jamais de la vie!, il faudra que vous me passiez sur le corps d'abord; *see also* **see to**.

j (*imagine*) (s')imaginer, se représenter, voir. **I can't ~ him as Prime Minister** je ne le vois *or* ne l'imagine pas du tout en Premier ministre; **I can't ~ myself doing that** je me vois mal *or* je m'imagine mal *or* je ne me vois pas du tout faisant cela; **I can't ~ myself being elected** je ne vois pas très bien comment je pourrais être élu; **I can just ~ her!** je l'imagine tout à fait!

k (*Poker etc*) **(I'll) ~ you** je demande à vous voir, je vous vois.

2 vi a voir. **to ~ in/out/through** *etc* voir à l'intérieur/à l'extérieur/à travers *etc*; **let me ~** montre-moi, fais voir (*see also* **2d**); **~ for yourself** voyez vous-même; **as you can ~** comme vous pouvez (le) constater; **so I ~** c'est bien ce que je vois; (*in anger*) **now ~ here!** non, mais dites donc!*, écoutez-moi un peu!; **he couldn't ~ to read** il n'y voyait pas assez clair pour lire; **cats can ~ in the dark** les chats voient clair la nuit; **you can ~ for miles** on y voit à des kilomètres; *see* **eye**.

b (*find out*) voir. **I'll go and ~** je vais (aller) voir; **I'll go and ~ if dinner's ready** je vais (aller) voir si le dîner est prêt.

c (*understand*) voir, comprendre. **as far as I can ~** à ce que je vois, pour autant que je puisse en juger; **I ~!** je vois!, ah bon!; (*in explanations etc*) **... you ~ ...** voyez-vous, ... vous comprenez, ... vous voyez; **it's all over now, ~?**‡ c'est fini, compris?*; **but he's dead don't you ~?** tu ne vois pas qu'il est mort?, il est mort tu vois *or* sais bien.

d (*think, deliberate*) voir. **let me ~, let's ~** voyons (un peu); **let me ~** *or* **let's ~, what have I got to do?** voyons, qu'est-ce que j'ai à faire?; **I'll have to ~ (if ...)** je vais voir (si ...); **we'll soon ~** nous le saurons bientôt; **we'll soon ~ if ...** nous saurons bientôt, si ...; **can I go out? — we'll ~** est-ce que je peux sortir? — on va voir *or* on verra (ça).

3 comp ►**see-through** *blouse etc* transparent.

►**see about** vt fus a (*deal with*) s'occuper de. **he came to see about buying the house** il est venu voir s'il pouvait acheter la maison; **he came to see about the washing machine** il est venu au sujet de la machine à laver. b (*consider*) **to see about sth** voir si qch est possible; **may I go? — we'll see about it** est-ce que je peux y aller? — on va voir *or* on verra (ça); **he said he wouldn't do it — we'll see about that!** il a dit qu'il ne le ferait pas — c'est ce qu'on va voir!; **we must see about (getting) a new television** il va falloir songer à s'acheter une nouvelle télévision.

►**see after** vt fus s'occuper de.

►**see in** vt sep *person* faire entrer. **to see the New Year in** fêter la Nouvelle Année, faire le réveillon du Nouvel An.

►**see into** vt fus (*study, examine*) s'enquérir de, examiner. **we shall have to see into this** il va falloir examiner la question *or* se renseigner là-dessus.

►**see off** vt sep a **I saw him off at the station/airport** *etc* je l'ai accompagné au train *or* à la gare/à l'avion *or* à l'aéroport *etc*; **we'll come and see you off** on viendra vous dire au revoir (à la gare *or* à l'aéroport *or* au bateau *etc*). b (*fig *: defeat*) damer le pion à.

►**see out** vt sep a *person* reconduire *or* raccompagner à la porte. **I'll see myself out*** ne vous dérangez pas, je trouverai le chemin, pas la peine de me raccompagner!*; **he saw himself out** il est sorti sans qu'on le raccompagne (*subj*). b **this coat will have to see the winter out** il faut que ce manteau lui (*or* me *etc*) fasse l'hiver; **he was so ill we wondered whether he'd see the week out** il était si malade que nous nous demandions s'il passerait la semaine; **I saw the third act out then left** je suis resté jusqu'à la fin du troisième acte et je suis parti.

►**see over** vt fus *house, factory, gardens* visiter.

►**see through** 1 vt fus *person* ne pas se laisser tromper *or* duper par, pénétrer les intentions de, voir dans le jeu de; *behaviour, promises* ne pas se laisser tromper *or* duper par, voir clair dans. **I saw through him at once** j'ai tout de suite compris où il voulait en venir, j'ai tout de suite deviné ses intentions *or* vu son jeu. 2 vt sep (*never fus*) *project, deal* mener à bonne fin. **£10 should see you through** 10 livres devraient vous suffire; **don't worry, I'll see you through** ne vous inquiétez pas, vous pouvez compter sur moi. 3 **see-through** adj *see* **see[1] 3**.

►**see to** vt fus (*deal with*) s'occuper de, veiller à; (*mend*) réparer. **I'll see to the car** je m'occuperai de la voiture; **please see to it that ...** veillez s'il vous plaît à ce que ... + *subj*; **see to it that the door is shut** veillez à ce que la porte soit bien fermée; **the sweets didn't last long, the children saw to that!** les bonbons n'ont pas fait long feu, les enfants se sont chargés de les faire disparaître!

see[2] [si:] n *[bishop]* siège épiscopal, évêché *m*; *[archbishop]* archevêché *m*; *see* **holy**.

seed [si:d] 1 n a (*Agr, Bot etc*) graine *f*; (*collective n: for sowing*) graines *fpl*, semence *f*; (*in apple, grape etc*) pépin *m*. **to run** *or* **go to ~** *[plant etc]* monter en graine; *[person]* (*grow slovenly*) se négliger, se laisser aller; (*lose vigour*) se décatir.

b (*fig: source, origin*) germe *m*, semence *f*. **the ~s of discontent** les germes du mécontentement; **to sow ~s of doubt in sb's mind** semer le doute dans l'esprit de qn.

c (*sperm*) semence *f*, sperme *m*; (*offspring*) progéniture *f*.

d (*Tennis etc: also* **~ed player**) tête *f* de série. **first** *or* **number one ~** tête de série numéro un; **the top ~s** les premières têtes de série.

2 comp ►**seedbed** semis *m*, couche *f* ►**seed box** germoir *m* ►**seedcake** gâteau *m* au carvi ►**seed corn** blé *m* de semence ►**seeding machine** semoir *m* ►**seed merchant** grainetier *m* ►**seed money** (*Econ, Fin*) capital *m* initial, mise *f* de fonds initiale ►**seed pearls** semence *f* de perles, très petites perles ►**seed pod** tégument *m* ►**seed potato** pomme *f* de terre de semence ►**seedsman** = **seed merchant**.

3 vt a *lawn* ensemencer; *raisin, grape* épépiner. **to ~ clouds** ensemencer les nuages.

b (*Tennis*) **he was ~ed third** il était (classé) troisième tête de série; *see also* **1d**.

4 vi monter en graine.

seedily ['si:dɪlɪ] adv *dress* minablement, de façon miteuse *or* minable.

seediness ['si:dɪnɪs] n a (*shabbiness*) aspect *m* minable *or* miteux. b (**: illness*) indisposition *f*.

seedless ['si:dlɪs] adj sans pépins.

seedling ['si:dlɪŋ] n semis *m*, (jeune) plant *m*.

seedy ['si:dɪ] adj a (*shabby*) *clothes* râpé, miteux; *person, hotel* minable, miteux. b (**: ill*) **I'm feeling ~** je suis *or* je me sens mal fichu*, je me sens patraque*, je ne me sens pas dans mon assiette; **he looks rather ~** il a l'air mal fichu*.

seeing ['si:ɪŋ] 1 n vue *f*, vision *f*. (*Prov*) **~ is believing** voir c'est croire. 2 conj: **~ (that** *or* **as*)** vu que, étant donné que. 3 comp ►**Seeing Eye dog** (*US*) chien *m* d'aveugle.

seek [siːk] **pret, ptp sought** 1 **vt** a (*look for*) *object, solution, person, death* chercher; *fame, honours* rechercher, ambitionner; *happiness, peace* chercher, rechercher. **to ~ one's fortune in Canada** chercher *or* tenter fortune au Canada; **they sought shelter from the storm** ils ont cherché un abri *or* un refuge contre la tempête; **we sought shelter in the embassy/under a big tree** nous nous sommes réfugiés à l'ambassade/sous un grand arbre; **the reason is not far to ~** la raison n'est pas difficile à trouver, on n'a pas à chercher loin pour trouver la raison.
b (*ask*) demander (*from sb* à qn). **to ~ advice/help from sb** demander conseil/de l'aide à qn, chercher conseil/secours auprès de qn.
c (*frm: attempt*) chercher (*to do* à faire). **they sought to kill him** ils ont cherché à le tuer.
2 **vi: to ~ for** *or* **after sth/sb** rechercher qch/qn; **much sought after** très recherché, très demandé.
►**seek out** **vt sep** *person* aller voir, (aller) s'adresser à; *trouble etc* (re)chercher.

seeker ['siːkəʳ] **n** a (*person*) chercheur *m*, -euse *f* (*after* en quête de); *see* **self**. b (*Mil: device*) autodirecteur *m*.

seem [siːm] **vi** a sembler, paraître, avoir l'air. **he ~s honest** il semble (être) honnête, il paraît honnête, il a l'air honnête; **she ~s to know you** elle a l'air de vous connaître, elle semble vous connaître, on dirait qu'elle vous connaît; **she ~s not to want to leave** elle semble ne pas vouloir partir, on dirait qu'elle ne veut pas partir; **we ~ to have met before** il me semble *or* j'ai l'impression que nous nous sommes déjà rencontrés; **I ~ to have heard that before** il me semble avoir déjà entendu cela, il me semble que j'ai déjà entendu cela; **I can't ~ to do it** je n'arrive pas à le faire; **I ~ed to be floating** j'avais l'impression de planer; **how did she ~ to you?** comment l'as-tu trouvée?; **how does it ~ to you?** qu'en penses-tu?; **it all ~s like a dream** on croit rêver.
b (*impers vb*) paraître, sembler. (*looks to me as if*) **it ~s that** *or* **as if the government is going to fall** il semble bien que le gouvernement va tomber; (*people say*) **it ~s that the government is going to fall** il paraît que le gouvernement va tomber; **I've checked and it ~s she's right** j'ai vérifié et il semble qu'elle a raison *or* on dirait qu'elle a raison *or* elle semble avoir raison; **it ~s she's right for everybody says so** il semble bien qu'elle a raison *or* il y a de fortes chances qu'elle ait raison puisque tout le monde est d'accord là-dessus; **I've checked and it doesn't ~ she's right** *or* **it ~s she's not right** j'ai vérifié et il ne semble pas qu'elle ait raison *or* elle semble avoir tort *or* il y a de fortes chances qu'elle ait tort; **from what people say it doesn't ~ she's right** d'après ce qu'on dit elle semble avoir tort; **does it ~ that she is right?** est-ce qu'il semble qu'elle ait raison?, est-ce qu'elle semble avoir raison?; **the heat was so terrible it ~ed that the whole earth was ablaze** il faisait une chaleur si terrible qu'il semblait que la terre entière fût *or* était en feu; **it ~s to me that he refused** il me semble qu'il a refusé; **it ~s to me that we should leave at once** il me semble qu'il faudrait partir tout de suite; **it does not ~ to me that we can accept** il ne me semble pas que nous puissions accepter; **does it ~ to you as though it's going to rain?** est-ce qu'il te semble qu'il va pleuvoir?, est-ce que tu crois qu'il va pleuvoir?; **they're getting married next week – so it ~s** ils vont se marier *or* ils se marient la semaine prochaine – (à ce qu')il paraît; **it ~s not** il paraît que non; **it ~s that he died yesterday** il paraît qu'il est mort hier; **he died yesterday it ~s** il est mort hier paraît-il; **I did what ~ed best** j'ai fait ce que j'ai jugé bon; **it ~s ages since we last met** il y a des siècles* que nous ne nous sommes vus; **there ~s to be a mistake in this translation** il semble y avoir une erreur dans cette traduction; **there ~s to be a mistake, I'm the one who booked this room** il semble y avoir erreur, c'est moi qui ai retenu cette chambre.

seeming ['siːmɪŋ] **adj** apparent, soi-disant *inv*.

seemingly ['siːmɪŋlɪ] **adv** apparemment. **there has ~ been a rise in inflation** à ce qu'il paraît il y a eu une hausse de l'inflation; **he's left then? – ~** il est donc parti? – (à ce qu')il paraît *or* d'après ce qu'on dit.

seemliness ['siːmlɪnɪs] **n** *[behaviour]* bienséance *f*; *[dress]* décence *f*.

seemly ['siːmlɪ] **adj** *behaviour* convenable, bienséant; *dress* décent, correct.

seen [siːn] **ptp of see**[1].

seep [siːp] **vi** suinter, filtrer. **water was ~ing through the walls** l'eau suintait des murs *or* filtrait à travers les murs, les murs suintaient.
►**seep away** **vi** s'écouler peu à peu *or* goutte à goutte.
►**seep in** **vi** s'infiltrer.
►**seep out** **vi** suinter.

seepage ['siːpɪdʒ] **n** *[water, blood]* suintement *m*; (*from tank*) fuite *f*, déperdition *f*.

seer [sɪəʳ] **n** (*liter*) voyant(e) *m(f)*, prophète *m*, prophétesse *f*.

seersucker ['sɪəˌsʌkəʳ] **n** crépon *m* de coton.

seesaw ['siːsɔː] 1 **n** (jeu *m* de) bascule *f*. 2 **comp** ►**seesaw motion** mouvement *m* de bascule, va-et-vient *m inv*. 3 **vi** (*lit*) jouer à la bascule; (*fig*) osciller.

seethe [siːð] **vi** a *[boiling liquid etc]* bouillir, bouillonner, être en effervescence; *[sea]* bouillonner. b (*fig*) **to ~ with anger** *or* **rage** *or* **fury** bouillir de colère *or* rage *or* fureur; **he was (positively) seething*** il était furibond, il était (fou) furieux; **a country seething with discontent** un pays où le mécontentement fermente; **the crowd ~d round the film star** la foule se pressait autour de la vedette; **the streets were seething with people** les rues grouillaient de *or* foisonnaient de monde.

segment ['segmənt] 1 **n** (*gen, Anat, Geom, Ling, Zool*) segment *m*; *[orange etc]* quartier *m*, morceau *m*. 2 [seg'ment] **vt** segmenter, couper en segments. 3 [seg'ment] **vi** se segmenter.

segmental [ˌseg'mentl] **adj** (*gen*) segmentaire; (*Ling*) segmental.

segmentation [ˌsegmən'teɪʃən] **n** segmentation *f*.

segregate ['segrɪgeɪt] **vt** séparer, isoler (*from* de); (*Pol*) séparer. **to ~ the sexes** séparer les sexes; **they decided to ~ the contagious patients** ils ont décidé d'isoler les (malades) contagieux; **the political prisoners were ~d from the others** les prisonniers politiques ont été séparés *or* isolés des autres.

segregated ['segrɪgeɪtɪd] **adj** (*Pol*) *school, club, bus* où la ségrégation (raciale) est appliquée. **a ~ school system** un système d'enseignement où la ségrégation est appliquée.

segregation [ˌsegrɪ'geɪʃən] **n** (*Pol*) ségrégation *f*; *[group, person, object]* séparation *f*, isolement *m* (*from* de).

segregationist [ˌsegrɪ'geɪʃnɪst] 1 **n** ségrégationniste *mf*. 2 **adj** *riot, demonstration* ségrégationniste; *policy* de ségrégation, ségrégationniste.

Seine [seɪn] **n** Seine *f*.

seine [seɪn] **n** seine *f*.

seismic ['saɪzmɪk] **adj** sismique.

seismograph ['saɪzməgrɑːf] **n** sismographe *m*.

seismography [saɪz'mɒgrəfɪ] **n** sismographie *f*.

seismologist [saɪz'mɒlədʒɪst] **n** sismologue *mf*.

seismology [saɪz'mɒlədʒɪ] **n** sismologie *f*.

seize [siːz] 1 **vt** a (*clutch, grab*) saisir, attraper. **she ~d (hold of) his hand, she ~d him by the hand** elle lui a saisi la main; **he ~d her by the hair** il l'a empoignée par les cheveux; **to ~ sb bodily** attraper qn à bras-le-corps; **to ~ the opportunity to do** saisir l'occasion *or* sauter sur l'occasion de faire; **to be ~d with rage** avoir un accès de rage; **to be ~d with fear** être saisi de peur; **she was ~d with the desire to see him** un désir soudain de le voir s'est emparé d'elle *or* l'a saisie; **he was ~d with a bout of coughing** il a été pris d'un accès de toux, il a eu un accès de toux; *see* **bull**[1].
b (*get possession of by force*) s'emparer de, se saisir de; (*Mil*) *territory* s'emparer de; *person, gun, ship* capturer, s'emparer de. **to ~ power** s'emparer du pouvoir.
c (*Jur*) *person* arrêter, détenir; *property* saisir; *contraband* confisquer, saisir.
2 **vi** (*Tech*) se gripper.
►**seize up** **vi** (*Tech*) se gripper; (*Med*) s'ankyloser; (*fig*) *[traffic]* se paralyser, s'immobiliser.
►**seize (up)on** **vt fus** *idea, suggestion, offer, chance* saisir, sauter sur.

seizure ['siːʒəʳ] **n** a (*NonC*) *[goods, gun, property]* saisie *f*; *[city, ship]* capture *f*; *[power, territory]* prise *f*; *[criminal]* capture, arrestation *f*; (*Jur*) appréhension *f* (au corps); *[contraband]* saisie, confiscation *f*. b (*Med*) crise *f*, attaque *f*. **to have a ~** avoir une crise *or* une attaque.

seldom ['seldəm] **adv** rarement, peu souvent, ne ... guère. **he ~ worked** il travaillait rarement, il ne travaillait guère; **~ if ever** rarement pour ne pas dire jamais.

select [sɪ'lekt] 1 **vt** *team, candidate* sélectionner (*from, among* parmi); *gift, book, colour* choisir (*from, among* parmi). **to ~ a sample of** *rock* prélever un échantillon de; *colours, materials* choisir un échantillon de; **~ed poems** poèmes choisis; **~ed works** œuvres choisies; (*Comm*) **~ed fruit** fruits sélectionnés *or* de premier choix.
2 **adj** *audience* choisi, d'élite; *club* fermé; *restaurant* chic *inv*, sélect. (*Brit Parl*) **~ committee** commission *f* parlementaire (d'enquête); **a ~ few** quelques privilégiés; **a ~ group of friends** quelques amis choisis; **they formed a small ~ group** ils formaient un petit groupe fermé.
3 **comp** ►**selectman** (*US*) conseiller *m* municipal (en Nouvelle-Angleterre).

selectee [sɪlek'tiː] **n** (*US Mil*) appelé *m*.

selection [sɪ'lekʃən] 1 **n** sélection *f*, choix *m*. **to make a ~** faire une sélection *or* un choix; (*Literat, Mus*) **~s from** morceaux choisis de; *see* **natural**. 2 **comp** ►**selection committee** comité *m* de sélection.

selective [sɪ'lektɪv] **adj** *recruitment, classification* sélectif. **one must be ~** il faut savoir faire un choix; **~ breeding** élevage *m* à base de sélection; (*Scol*) (*Brit*) **~ entry**, (*US*) **~ admissions** sélection *f*; (*Brit*) **~ school** école *f or* lycée *m or* collège *m* à recrutement sélectif; (*US Mil*) **~ service** service *m* militaire obligatoire, conscription *f*; (*Ind*) **~ strike** grève *f* ponctuelle *or* limitée.

selectively [sɪ'lektɪvlɪ] **adv** *[terrorists etc]* **to strike ~** se livrer à des actions ponctuelles.

selectivity [ˌsɪlek'tɪvɪtɪ] **n** (*Elec, Rad*) sélectivité *f*; (*Scol*) sélection *f*.

selector [sɪ'lektəʳ] **n** (*person*) sélectionneur *m*, -euse *f*; (*Tech*) sélecteur *m*.

selenium [sɪ'liːnɪəm] **n** sélénium *m*.

self [self] 1 **n, pl selves** a (*also Philos, Psych*) **the ~** le moi *inv*; **the cult of ~** le culte du moi; **the conscious ~** le moi conscient; **his better ~** le meilleur de lui-même; **her real ~** son vrai moi; **my former ~** le moi *or* la personne que j'étais auparavant; **she's her old ~ again** elle est redevenue complètement elle-même; **she had no thought of ~** elle ne pensait jamais à elle-même *or* à son intérêt personnel; *see* **second**[1], **shadow**.

b (*Comm etc*) moi-même *etc*. **your good ~** vous-même; **your good selves** vous-mêmes; (*on cheque*) **pay ~** payez à l'ordre de moi-même.

2 **comp** ▸ **self-abasement** avilissement *m or* abaissement *m* de soi ▸ **self-absorbed** égocentrique ▸ **self-absorption** égocentrisme *m* ▸ **self-abuse** († *pej*) masturbation *f* ▸ **self-accusation** auto-accusation *f* ▸ **self-acting** automatique ▸ **self-addressed envelope** enveloppe *f* à mon (*or* son *etc*) nom et adresse ▸ **self-adhesive** auto-adhésif ▸ **self-adjusting** à réglage automatique ▸ **self-advertisement: to indulge in self-advertisement** faire sa propre réclame ▸ **self-aggrandizement** autoglorification *f* ▸ **self-analysis** auto-analyse *f* ▸ **self-apparent** évident, qui va (*or* allait *etc*) de soi ▸ **self-appointed: he was a self-appointed critic of** ... il a pris sur lui de critiquer ... ▸ **self-appraisal** auto-évaluation *f* ▸ **self-assertion** affirmation *f* de soi ▸ **self-assertive** très sûr de soi ▸ **self-assessment** auto-évaluation *f* ▸ **self-assurance** assurance *f*, confiance *f* en soi ▸ **self-assured** sûr de soi, plein d'assurance ▸ **self-aware: to be self-aware** avoir pris conscience de soi-même ▸ **self-awareness** (prise *f* de) conscience *f* de soi-même ▸ **self-belay, self-belaying system** (*Climbing*) auto-assurance *f* ▸ **self-betterment** amélioration *f* de soi-même *or* de sa condition ▸ **self-catering n** appartement *m etc* indépendant (avec cuisine) ◊ **adj** indépendant (avec cuisine) ▸ **self-centred,** (*US*) **self-centered** égocentrique ▸ **self-centredness,** (*US*) **self-centeredness** égocentrisme *m* ▸ **self-cleaning** *oven etc* autonettoyant ▸ **self-closing** à fermeture automatique ▸ **self-coloured,** (*US*) **self-colored** uni ▸ **self-composed** posé, calme ▸ **self-composure** calme *m*, sang-froid *m* ▸ **self-conceit** vanité *f*, suffisance *f* ▸ **self-conceited** vaniteux, suffisant ▸ **self-confessed: he is a self-confessed thief** *etc* il est voleur *etc* de son propre aveu ▸ **self-confidence** confiance *f* en soi ▸ **self-confident** sûr de soi, plein d'assurance ▸ **self-congratulation** autolouange *f* ▸ **self-congratulatory** satisfait de soi ▸ **self-conscious** (*shy*) *person, manner* emprunté, embarrassé, gauche; (*aware of oneself/itself etc*) *art, person, political movement etc* conscient (de son image); **to be self-conscious about** être gêné *or* embarrassé par ▸ **self-consciously** (*shyly*) de façon empruntée, timidement; (*deliberately*) volontairement ▸ **self-consciousness** (*shyness*) gêne *f*, timidité *f*, gaucherie *f*; (*awareness*) conscience *f* (de son image) ▸ **self-contained** *person* indépendant; (*Brit*) *flat* indépendant, avec entrée particulière ▸ **self-contempt** mépris *m* de soi ▸ **self-contradiction** contradiction *f* avec soi-même ▸ **self-contradictory** *text* contradictoire (*en soi*); *person* qui se contredit ▸ **self-control** maîtrise *f* de soi, sang-froid *m* ▸ **self-controlled** maître (*f* maîtresse) de soi ▸ **self-correcting** autocorrectif ▸ **self-critical** qui se critique; (*Pol, Rel*) qui fait son autocritique ▸ **self-criticism** critique *f* de soi; (*Pol, Rel*) autocritique *f* ▸ **self-deception** aveuglement *m* ▸ **self-defeating** *action, plan* qui va à l'encontre du but recherché ▸ **self-defence,** (*US*) **self-defense** (*skill, art*) autodéfense *f*; (*Jur*) **in self-defence** en légitime défense (*see* **noble 1a**) ▸ **self-delusion** aveuglement *m* ▸ **self-denial** abnégation *f*, sacrifice *m* de soi ▸ **self-denying** *person* qui fait preuve d'abnégation, qui se sacrifie; *decision etc* qui impose le sacrifice de ses intérêts ▸ **self-deprecating: to be self-deprecating** *[person]* se dénigrer soi-même ▸ **self-deprecatory** *thoughts* autodénigrant ▸ **self-destruct vi** (*Space etc*) s'autodétruire, se désintégrer ◊ **adj** *device, program* autodestructeur ▸ **self-destruction** autodestruction *f* ▸ **self-determination** autodétermination *f* ▸ **self-determined** déterminé par soi-même ▸ **self-determining** autodéterminant ▸ **self-discipline** autodiscipline *f* ▸ **self-disciplined** qui fait preuve d'autodiscipline ▸ **self-discovery** (*Psych*) découverte *f* de soi ▸ **self-doubt** fait *m* de douter de soi-même ▸ **self-doubting** qui doute de soi-même ▸ **self-drive (hire) car** (*Brit Aut*) voiture *f* sans chauffeur ▸ **self-drive car hire** location *f* de voitures sans chauffeur ▸ **self-educated** autodidacte ▸ **self-effacement** modestie *f*, effacement *m* ▸ **self-effacing** effacé, modeste ▸ **self-elected** (*Pol*) qui s'est élu lui-même; **he was a self-elected critic of** ... il avait pris sur lui de critiquer ... ▸ **self-employed** indépendant, qui travaille à son compte; **the self-employed** les travailleurs indépendants ▸ **self-employment: in self-employment** = **self-employed** ▸ **self-esteem** respect *m* de soi, amour-propre *m* ▸ **self-evaluation** auto-évaluation *f* ▸ **self-evident** évident, qui va de soi ▸ **self-evidently** fort *or* bien évidemment ▸ **self-examination** examen *m* de conscience ▸ **self-explanatory** qui se passe d'explication, évident (en soi) ▸ **self-expression** expression *f* (libre) ▸ **self-fertilization** autofécondation *f* ▸ **self-fertilizing** autofertile ▸ **self-filling** à remplissage automatique ▸ **self-financing n** autofinancement *m* ▸ **self-flattery** autolouange *f* ▸ **self-forgetful** désintéressé ▸ **self-forgetfulness** désintéressement *m* ▸ **self-fulfilling prophecy** prédiction *f* qui se réalise ▸ **self-glorification** autoglorification *f* ▸ **self-governing** autonome ▸ **self-government** autonomie *f* ▸ **self-hate** haine *f* de soi, fait *m* de se détester ▸ **self-hating** qui se déteste ▸ **self-hatred** = **self-hate** ▸ **self-help** (*gen*) efforts personnels, débrouillardise* *f*; (*Econ*) auto-assistance *f*; **self-help group** groupe *m* d'entraide ▸ **self-hypnosis** autohypnose *f* ▸ **self-ignite** s'enflammer spontanément ▸ **self-ignition** (*gen*) combustion *f* spontanée; (*Aut*) auto-allumage *m* ▸ **self-image** image *f* de soi-même ▸ **self-importance** suffisance *f* ▸ **self-important** suffisant, m'as-tu-vu* *inv* ▸ **self-imposed** auto-imposé, que l'on s'impose à soi-même ▸ **self-improvement** progrès *mpl* personnels ▸ **self-induced** *illness, misery, problems* que l'on a provoqué soi-même ▸ **self-indulgence** (*gen*) amour *m* de son propre confort, sybaritisme *m*; (*self-pity*) apitoiement *m* sur soi-même ▸ **self-indulgent** (*gen*) qui ne se refuse rien, sybarite; (*self-pitying*) qui s'apitoie sur son (propre) sort ▸ **self-inflicted** que l'on s'inflige à soi-même, volontaire ▸ **self-interest** intérêt *m* (personnel) ▸ **self-interested** intéressé, qui recherche son avantage personnel ▸ **self-justification** autojustification *f* ▸ **self-justifying** justificatif ▸ **self-knowledge** connaissance *f* de soi ▸ **self-levelling foot** (*on furniture*) pied *m* de nivellement, pied autoréglable ▸ **self-loader** arme *f* automatique ▸ **self-loading** *gun* automatique ▸ **self-loathing n** dégoût *m* de soi-même ◊ **adj** qui a horreur de soi-même ▸ **self-locking** à fermeture automatique ▸ **self-love** narcissisme *m*, amour *m* de soi-même ▸ **self-lubricating** autolubrifiant ▸ **self-lubrication** autolubrification *f* ▸ **self-made** qui a réussi par ses propres moyens; **self-made man** self-made man *m*, fils *m* de ses œuvres (*frm*) ▸ **self-maintenance** entretien *m* automatique ▸ **self-mastery** maîtrise *f* de soi-même ▸ **self-mockery** autodérision *f* ▸ **self-mocking** *person* moqueur à l'égard de soi-même; *humour* empreint d'autodérision ▸ **self-mockingly** par autodérision ▸ **self-motivated** très motivé (de par soi-même) ▸ **self-murder** suicide *m* ▸ **self-neglect** négligence *f* de soi ▸ **self-obsessed** obsédé par soi-même ▸ **self-obsession** obsession *f* de soi-même ▸ **self-opinionated** entêté, opiniâtre ▸ **self-ordained: he was a self-ordained critic of** ... il avait pris sur lui de critiquer ... ▸ **self-perpetuating: it's self-perpetuating** ça se perpétue indéfiniment ▸ **self-pity** apitoiement *m* sur soi-même; **full of self-pity** = **self-pitying** ▸ **self-pitying** qui s'apitoie sur son (propre) sort ▸ **self-portrait** autoportrait *m* ▸ **self-possessed** assuré, qui garde son sang-froid ▸ **self-possession** assurance *f*, sang-froid *m* ▸ **self-praise** éloge *m* de soi-même, autolouange *f* ▸ **self-preoccupied** égocentrique ▸ **self-preservation** instinct *m* de conservation ▸ **self-pride** orgueil *m* personnel ▸ **self-proclaimed: he was a self-proclaimed critic of** ... il avait pris sur lui de critiquer ... ▸ **self-propelled** autopropulsé ▸ **self-protection: from self-protection** pour sa propre protection ▸ **self-punishment** autopunition *f* ▸ **self-raising flour** (*Brit*) farine *f* pour gâteaux (*avec levure incorporée*) ▸ **self-regard** = **self-esteem** ▸ **self-regulating** autorégulateur ▸ **self-regulation** autorégulation *f* ▸ **self-regulatory** = **self-regulating** ▸ **self-reliance** indépendance *f* ▸ **self-reliant** indépendant; **to be self-reliant** ne compter que sur soi (-même) ▸ **self-renewal** renouvellement *m* automatique ▸ **self-renewing** qui se renouvelle automatiquement ▸ **self-replicating** *computer, machine etc* autoreproducteur ▸ **self-reproach** repentir *m*, remords *m* ▸ **self-reproachful** plein de reproches à l'égard de soi-même ▸ **self-respect** respect *m* de soi, dignité personnelle ▸ **self-respecting** qui se respecte; **no self-respecting teacher would agree that** ... aucun professeur qui se respecte (*subj*) ne conviendrait que ... ▸ **self-restraint** retenue *f* ▸ **self-revelation** révélation *f* de soi-même ▸ **self-ridicule** autodérision *f* ▸ **self-righteous** pharisaïque, satisfait de soi ▸ **self-righteousness** pharisaïsme *m*, satisfaction *f* de soi ▸ **self-righting** (*Naut*) inchavirable ▸ **self-rising flour** (*US*) = **self-raising flour** ▸ **self-rule** (*Pol*) autonomie *f* ▸ **self-ruling** (*Pol*) autonome ▸ **self-sacrifice** abnégation *f*, dévouement *m* ▸ **self-sacrificing** qui se sacrifie, qui a l'esprit de sacrifice ▸ **selfsame** *see* **selfsame** ▸ **self-satisfaction** contentement *m* de soi, fatuité *f* ▸ **self-satisfied** *person* content de soi, suffisant; *smile* suffisant, de satisfaction ▸ **self-sealing** *envelope* autocollant, auto-adhésif; *container* à obturation automatique ▸ **self-seeker** égoïste *mf* ▸ **self-seeking** égoïste ▸ **self-service** libre-service *m inv*; **self-service shop/restaurant** (magasin *m*/restaurant *m*) libre-service *m inv or* self-service *m inv*; **self-service garage** station *f or* poste *m* (d'essence) libre-service ▸ **self-serving** égoïste, intéressé ▸ **self-starter** (*Aut*) démarreur *m* (automatique *or* électrique); (*fig: hard-working person*) personne *f* motivée (et pleine d'initiative) ▸ **self-steering** à pilotage automatique ▸ **self-styled** soi-disant *inv*, prétendu ▸ **self-sufficiency** (*economic*) autarcie *f*; (*self-confidence*) autosuffisance *f* ▸ **self-sufficient** (*economically*) autarcique; (*self-confident*) autosuffisant ▸ **self-supporting** *person* qui subvient à ses (propres) besoins; *firm* financièrement indépendant ▸ **self-sustaining growth** (*Econ*) croissance *f* autonome ▸ **self-taught** autodidacte; **"French self-taught"** "apprenez le français tout seul" ▸ **self-timer** (*Phot*) retardateur *m* ▸ **self-torture** torture *f* délibérée de soi-même ▸ **self-treatment** (*Med*) automédication *f* ▸ **self-will** volonté *f* inébranlable ▸ **self-willed** entêté, volontaire ▸ **self-winding** (à remontage) automatique ▸ **self-worship** adulation *f* de soi-même.

selfdom ['selfdəm] **n** (*Psych*) individualité *f*.

selfhood ['selfhʊd] **n** (*Psych*) individualité *f*.

selfish ['selfɪʃ] **adj** *person, behaviour* égoïste; *motive* intéressé.

selfishly ['selfɪʃlɪ] **adv** égoïstement, en égoïste.

selfishness ['selfɪʃnɪs] **n** égoïsme *m*.

selfless ['selflɪs] **adj** désintéressé, altruiste.

selflessly ['selflɪslɪ] **adv** sans penser à soi, d'une façon désintéressée, par altruisme.

selflessness ['selflɪsnɪs] **n** désintéressement *m*, altruisme *m*.

selfsame ['selfseɪm] adj même. **this is the ~ book** c'est bien le même livre; **I reached Paris the ~ day** je suis arrivé à Paris le même jour *or* le jour même.

sell [sel] pret, ptp **sold** 1 vt a vendre. **"to be sold"** "à vendre"; **to ~ sth for 25 francs** vendre qch 25 F; **he sold it (to) me for 10 francs** il me l'a vendu 10 F; **he sold the books at 10 francs each** il a vendu les livres 10 F chaque *or* pièce; **he was selling them at** *or* **for 10 francs a dozen** il les vendait 10 F la douzaine; **do you ~ stamps?** avez-vous des timbres?; **are stamps sold here?** est-ce qu'on vend des timbres ici?; **I was sold this in Grenoble** on m'a vendu cela à Grenoble; **he's a commercial traveller who ~s shirts** c'est un voyageur de commerce qui place *or* vend des chemises; **it's not the price but the quality that ~s this item** ce n'est pas le prix mais la qualité qui fait vendre cet article; **we're finding it difficult to ~ our stock of ...** nous avons du mal à écouler notre stock de ...; (*pej*) **to ~ o.s.** se vendre (*see also* **1b**); **to ~ sb into slavery** vendre qn comme esclave; **to ~ a secret** vendre *or* trahir un secret; (*fig*) **to ~ the pass** abandonner *or* trahir la cause; (*St Ex*) **to ~ short** vendre à découvert; (*fig*) **to ~ sb short** (*cheat*) avoir qn*, posséder qn*; (*belittle*) débiner qn*; (*fig*) **to ~ sb a bill of goods*** en faire accroire à qn; **to ~ one's life dearly** vendre chèrement sa vie; **he sold his soul for political power** il a vendu son âme contre le pouvoir (politique); **I'd ~ my soul for a coat like that!*** je donnerais n'importe quoi *or* je me damnerais pour avoir un manteau comme ça!; **to ~ sb down the river** trahir qn, lâcher qn*; **to ~ sb a pup**‡ rouler qn*.
b (*: *put across*) **to ~ sb an idea** faire accepter une idée à qn; **if we can ~ coexistence to Ruritania** si nous arrivons à faire accepter le principe de la coexistence à la Ruritanie; **he doesn't ~ himself** *or* **his personality very well** il n'arrive pas à se faire valoir *or* à se mettre en valeur; **if you can ~ yourself to the voters** si vous arrivez à vous faire accepter par *or* à convaincre les électeurs; **to be sold on* an idea** *etc* être enthousiasmé *or* emballé* par une idée *etc*; **to be sold on sb*** être complètement emballé* par qn *or* entiché de qn.
c (*: *cheat, betray*) tromper, attraper, avoir*. **I've been sold!** on m'a eu!*, je me suis fait avoir!*; **to ~ sb down the river** complètement laisser tomber qn, trahir qn de belle façon.
2 vi se vendre. **these books ~ at** *or* **for 10 francs each** ces livres se vendent 10 F chaque *or* pièce; **they ~ at 10 francs a dozen** ils se vendent 10 F la douzaine; **your car should ~ for 18,000 francs** votre voiture devrait se vendre 18 000 F *or* réaliser 18 000 F; **it ~s well** cela se vend bien; **that line doesn't ~** cet article se vend mal; **the idea didn't ~** l'idée n'a pas été acceptée; *see* **cake**.
3 n a (‡) (*disappointment*) déception *f*; (*fraud*) attrape-nigaud *m*. **what a ~!** ce que je me suis (*or* tu t'es *etc*) fait avoir!*
b (*Comm*) *see* **hard, soft**.
4 comp ►**sell-by date** (*Comm*) date *f* limite de vente.

►**sell back** vt sep revendre (*à la même personne etc*).

►**sell off** vt sep *stock* liquider; *goods* solder; *shares* vendre, liquider.

►**sell out** 1 vi (*Comm*) (*sell one's business*) vendre son fonds *or* son affaire; (*sell one's stock*) liquider son stock. (*fig*) **to sell out to the enemy** passer à l'ennemi; **to sell out on sb** trahir qn, laisser tomber qn*. 2 vt sep a (*St Ex*) vendre, réaliser. b (*Comm*) vendre tout son stock de. **this item is sold out** cet article est épuisé; **we are sold out on** n'en a plus; **we are sold out of milk** on n'a plus de lait; (*Theat*) **the house was sold out** toutes les places étaient louées. 3 **sellout** n *see* **sellout**.

►**sell up** (*esp Brit*) 1 vi (*gen*) se défaire de *or* vendre toutes ses possessions; (*Comm*) vendre son fonds *or* son affaire. 2 vt sep a (*Jur*) *goods* opérer la vente forcée de, saisir; *debtor* vendre les biens de. b (*Comm*) *business* vendre, liquider.

seller ['seləʳ] n a (*in compounds*) vendeur *m*, -euse *f*, marchand(e) *m(f)*; e.g. **newspaper-~** vendeur *m*, -euse *f* de journaux; **onion-~** marchand(e) *m(f)* d'oignons; *see* **book** *etc*. b (*as opposed to buyer*) vendeur *m*. **~'s market** marché favorable au vendeur. c (*) **this book is a (good) ~** ce livre se vend bien *or* comme des petits pains*; *see* **best**.

selling ['selɪŋ] 1 n vente(s) *f(pl)*. 2 comp ►**selling point** avantage *m* *or* atout *m* intéressant pour le client ►**selling price** prix *m* de vente ►**selling rate** (*Fin*) cours *m* vendeur.

sellotape ['seləʊteɪp] (*Brit*) ® 1 n: **S~** Scotch *m* ®, ruban adhésif. 2 vt scotcher, coller avec du ruban adhésif.

sellout ['selaʊt] n a (*Cine, Theat etc*) **the play was a ~** tous les billets (pour la pièce) ont été vendus, on a joué à guichets fermés *or* à bureaux fermés. b (*betrayal*) trahison *f*, capitulation *f*. **a ~ of minority opinion** une trahison de l'opinion de la minorité; (*Pol*) **a ~ to the left** une capitulation devant la gauche.

seltzer ['seltsəʳ] n (*US: also* **~ water**) eau *f* de Seltz.

selvage, selvedge ['selvɪdʒ] n lisière *f* (*d'un tissu*).

selves [selvz] npl of **self**.

semantic [sɪ'mæntɪk] adj sémantique.

semantically [sɪ'mæntɪkəlɪ] adv du point de vue de la sémantique.

semanticist [sɪ'mæntɪsɪst] n sémanticien(ne) *m(f)*.

semantics [sɪ'mæntɪks] n (*NonC*) sémantique *f*.

semaphore ['seməfɔːʳ] 1 n a signaux *mpl* à bras. **in ~** par signaux à bras. b (*Rail*) sémaphore *m*. 2 vt transmettre par signaux à bras.

semblance ['sembləns] n semblant *m*, apparence *f*. **without a ~ of respect** sans le moindre semblant de respect; **to put on a ~ of sorrow** prétendre avoir *or* faire semblant d'avoir de la peine.

seme [siːm] n (*Ling*) sème *m*.

semen ['siːmən] n sperme *m*, semence *f*.

semester [sɪ'mestəʳ] n (*esp US*) semestre *m*.

semi ['semɪ] 1 pref a semi-, demi-, à demi; *see* **2**.
b (*not completely + adj*) plus ou moins. **it's ~ tidy** c'est plus ou moins bien rangé.
2 comp ►**semiautomatic** semi-automatique ►**semibasement** ≃ rez-de-jardin *m* ►**semibreve** (*Mus: esp Brit*) ronde *f*; (*Mus: esp Brit*) **semibreve rest** pause *f* ►**semicircle** demi-cercle *m* ►**semicircular** demi-circulaire, semi-circulaire, en demi-cercle ►**semicolon** point-virgule *m* ►**semicommercial** semi-commercial ►**semiconductor** semi-conducteur *m* ►**semiconscious** à demi conscient ►**semiconsonant** semi-consonne *f* ►**semidarkness** pénombre *f*, demi-jour *m* ►**semidesert** adj semi-désertique ►**semidetached (house)** (maison) jumelée *or* jumelle; **semidetached houses** maisons mitoyennes ►**semifinal** demi-finale *f* ►**semifinalist** (*player*) joueur *m*, -euse *f* de demi-finale; (*team*) équipe *f* jouant dans la demi-finale ►**semiliquid** semi-liquide ►**semiliterate** semi-analphabète, presque illettré ►**semimonthly** (*US Press*) bimensuel (*m*) ►**semiofficial** semi-officiel, officieux ►**semipolitical** semi-politique ►**semiprecious** semi-précieux; **semiprecious stone** pierre fine *or* semi-précieuse ►**semiprivate room** (*US Med*) chambre *f* d'hôpital à plusieurs lits ►**semiprofessional** semi-professionnel ►**semiquaver** (*Mus: esp Brit*) double croche *f* ►**semiskilled** *work* d'ouvrier spécialisé; **semiskilled worker** ouvrier *m*, -ière *f* spécialisé(e), O.S. *mf* ►**semi-skimmed** demi-écrémé ►**semisolid** semi-solide ►**semitone** demi-ton *m* ►**semitrailer** (*Aut*) semi-remorque *f* ►**semitropical** semi-tropical ►**semivowel** semi-voyelle *f*, semi-consonne *f* ►**semiweekly** (*US Press*) bihebdomadaire (*m*).
3 n a (*Brit* *) (abbr of **semidetached house**) *see* **2**.
b (*US*) (abbr of **semi-trailer**) *see* **2**.

seminal ['semɪnl] adj (*Anat*) séminal; (*fig*) qui fait école, riche et original.

seminar ['semɪnɑːʳ] n séminaire *m*, colloque *m*; (*Univ*) séminaire, séance *f* de travaux pratiques *or* de T.P.

seminarist ['semɪnərɪst] n séminariste *m*.

seminary ['semɪnərɪ] n (*priests' college*) séminaire *m*; (*school*) petit séminaire.

semiology [ˌsemɪ'ɒlədʒɪ] n sémiologie *f*.

semiotic [ˌsemɪ'ɒtɪk] adj sémiotique.

semiotics [ˌsemɪ'ɒtɪks] n (*NonC*) sémiotique *f*.

Semite ['siːmaɪt] n Sémite *mf*.

Semitic [sɪ'mɪtɪk] adj *language* sémitique; *people* sémite.

semolina [ˌsemə'liːnə] n semoule *f*. **~ (pudding)** semoule au lait.

sempiternal [ˌsempɪ'tɜːnl] adj (*liter*) éternel, perpétuel.

sempstress ['sempstrɪs] n = **seamstress**.

SEN [esiː'en] n (*Brit*) (abbr of **State Enrolled Nurse**) *see* **state**.

Sen. (*US*) abbr of **Senator**.

sen. abbr of **senior**.

senate ['senɪt] n a (*Pol*) sénat *m*. (*US, Can, Austral*) **the S~** le Sénat. b (*Univ*) conseil *m* d'université.

senator ['senɪtəʳ] n sénateur *m*.

senatorial [ˌsenə'tɔːrɪəl] adj sénatorial.

send [send] pret, ptp **sent** 1 vt a (*dispatch*) *thing* envoyer (*to sb* à qn); (*by post*) envoyer *or* expédier (par la poste). **I sent him a letter to say that ...** je lui ai envoyé *or* expédié une lettre pour lui dire que ...; **I sent the letter to him yesterday** je lui ai envoyé *or* expédié la lettre hier; **I wrote the letter but didn't ~ it (off)** j'ai écrit la lettre mais je ne l'ai pas envoyée *or* expédiée *or* mise à la poste; **to ~ good wishes** adresser *or* envoyer ses bons vœux; **Paul ~s his best wishes** Paul vous (*or* nous *etc*) envoie ses bons vœux; **~ her my regards** faites-lui mes amitiés; **to ~ help** envoyer des secours; **to ~ word that ...** faire savoir que ..., faire dire que ...; **I'll ~ a car (for you)** j'enverrai une voiture (vous chercher); **to ~ washing to the laundry** donner *or* envoyer du linge au blanchissage; **God sent a plague to punish the Egyptians** Dieu envoya *or* infligea un fléau aux Égyptiens pour les punir; **the rain has been sent to save our crops** cette pluie nous a été envoyée *or* donnée pour sauver nos récoltes; (*hum*) **these things are sent to try us!** c'est le ciel qui nous envoie ces épreuves!
b (*cause to go*) *person* envoyer. **to ~ sb for sth** envoyer qn chercher qch; **to ~ sb to do sth** envoyer qn faire qch; **I sent him (along) to see her** je l'ai envoyé la voir; **~ him (along) to see me** dis-lui de venir me voir, envoie-le-moi; **to ~ sb to bed** envoyer qn se coucher; **to ~ sb home** (*through illness*) renvoyer qn chez lui, dire à qn de rentrer chez lui; (*for misbehaviour*) renvoyer qn chez lui; (*from abroad*) rapatrier qn; (*Ind*) **to ~ workers home** mettre des employés en chômage technique; (*lit, fig*) **to ~ sb to sleep** endormir qn; **they sent him to school in London** ils l'ont envoyé *or* mis à l'école (*or* au lycée *etc*) à Londres; **I won't ~ you to school today** je ne t'envoie pas à l'école aujourd'hui, tu n'iras pas à l'école aujourd'hui; **children are sent to school at the age of 5** les enfants doivent aller à l'école à partir de 5

ans; **some children are sent to school without breakfast** il y a des enfants qui vont à l'école *or* qui partent pour l'école sans avoir pris de petit déjeuner; **he was sent to prison** on l'a envoyé en prison; **the rain sent us indoors** la pluie nous a fait rentrer; **they sent the dogs after the escaped prisoner** ils ont envoyé les chiens à la poursuite *or* à la recherche du prisonnier évadé; (*fig*) **to ~ sb packing*** *or* **about his business*** envoyer promener qn*, envoyer paître qn*, envoyer qn sur les roses*; (*fig*) **to ~ sb to Coventry** mettre qn en quarantaine, boycotter qn.

c (*propel, cause to move*) *ball* envoyer, lancer; *stone, arrow* lancer. **to ~ an astronaut/a rocket into space** lancer *or* envoyer un astronaute/une fusée dans l'espace; **he sent the ball over the trees** il a envoyé *or* lancé le ballon par-dessus les arbres; **he screwed up the paper and sent it straight into the basket** il a froissé le papier et l'a envoyé *or* l'a lancé tout droit dans la corbeille; **the explosion sent a cloud of smoke into the air** l'explosion a projeté un nuage de fumée (en l'air); (*fig*) **to ~ a shiver down sb's spine** faire passer un frisson dans le dos de qn; **the news sent a thrill through her** la nouvelle l'a électrisée; **the sight of the dog sent her running to her mother** en voyant le chien elle s'est précipitée vers sa mère; **the blow sent him sprawling** le coup l'a envoyé par terre; **he sent the plate flying** il a envoyé voler *or* valser* l'assiette; **to ~ sb flying** envoyer qn rouler à terre.

d (*+adj: cause to become*) rendre. **the noise is ~ing me mad** le bruit me rend fou.

e (*‡: make ecstatic*) emballer*, exciter, enthousiasmer. **he ~s me** je le trouve sensationnel; **this music ~s me** cette musique m'emballe* *or* me fait quelque chose.

2 vi (*frm, liter*) **they sent to ask if ...** ils envoyèrent demander si ... .

3 comp ►**send-off: they were given a warm send-off** on leur a fait des adieux chaleureux; **they gave him a big send-off** ils sont venus nombreux lui souhaiter bon voyage ►**send-up*** (*Brit*) *[person]* mise *f* en boîte*, parodie *f*; *[book]* parodie.

►**send away** 1 vi: **to send away for sth** (*order by post*) commander qch par correspondance; (*order and receive*) se faire envoyer qch. 2 vt sep a faire partir, envoyer. **to send one's children away to school** mettre ses enfants en pension. b (*dismiss*) renvoyer, congédier. **to send sb away with a flea in his ear‡** envoyer promener qn*, envoyer qn sur les roses*. c *parcel, letter, goods* envoyer, expédier; (*post*) mettre à la poste.

►**send back** vt sep *person, thing* renvoyer.

►**send down** vt sep a (*lit*) *person* faire descendre, envoyer en bas. b *prices, sb's temperature, blood pressure* faire baisser. c (*Brit Univ*) renvoyer (de l'université). d (**: jail*) envoyer en prison, coffrer.

►**send for** vt fus a *doctor, police etc* faire venir, appeler; (*send sb to get*) faire appeler, envoyer chercher. **to send for help** envoyer chercher de l'aide, se faire envoyer des secours. b (*order by post*) commander par correspondance; (*order and receive*) se faire envoyer.

►**send forth** vt sep (*liter*) *light* émettre; *leaf* produire; *smell* exhaler, répandre; *army* envoyer.

►**send in** vt sep a *person* faire entrer; *troops etc* envoyer. b *resignation* envoyer, donner; *report, entry form* envoyer, soumettre. **to send in an application** faire une demande; (*for job*) poser sa candidature; **to send in a request** envoyer *or* faire une demande; **send in your name and address if you wish to receive ...** envoyez vos nom et adresse si vous désirez recevoir ... .

►**send off** 1 vi = **send away 1**. 2 vt sep a *person* envoyer. **I sent him off to think it over/get cleaned up** *etc* je l'ai envoyé méditer là-dessus/se débarbouiller *etc*; **she sent the child off to the grocer's** elle a envoyé l'enfant chez l'épicier; **she sent him off with a flea in his ear‡** elle l'a envoyé promener*, elle l'a envoyé sur les roses*. b (*say goodbye to*) dire au revoir à. **there was a large crowd to send him off** une foule de gens était venue *or* étaient venus lui dire au revoir *or* lui souhaiter bon voyage. c *letter, parcel, goods* envoyer, expédier; (*post*) mettre à la poste. d (*Ftbl etc*) *player* renvoyer du terrain. 3 **send-off** n *see* **send 3**.

►**send on** vt sep (*Brit*) *letter* faire suivre; *luggage* (*in advance*) expédier à l'avance; (*afterwards*) faire suivre; *object left behind* renvoyer.

►**send out** 1 vi: **to send out for sth** envoyer chercher qch; **prisoners are allowed to send out for meals from a nearby café** les détenus ont le droit d'envoyer chercher leurs repas dans un café voisin.

2 vt sep a *person, dog etc* faire sortir, mettre à la porte. **she sent the children out to play** elle a envoyé les enfants jouer dehors; **I sent her out for a breath of air** je l'ai envoyée prendre l'air; **they were sent out for talking too loudly** on les a fait sortir *or* on les a mis à la porte parce qu'ils parlaient trop fort.

b (*post*) *correspondence, leaflets* envoyer (par la poste).

c *scouts, messengers, emissary* envoyer, expédier, dépêcher.

d (*emit*) *smell* répandre, exhaler; *heat* émettre, répandre; *light* diffuser, émettre; *smoke* jeter, répandre.

►**send round** vt sep a *document, bottle etc* faire circuler. b faire parvenir. **I'll send it round to you as soon as it's ready** je vous le ferai parvenir *or* porter dès que cela sera prêt. c *person* envoyer. **I sent him round to the grocer's** je l'ai envoyé chez l'épicier.

►**send up** 1 vt sep a *person, luggage* faire monter; *smoke* jeter, répandre; *aeroplane* envoyer; *spacecraft, flare* lancer; *prices* faire monter en flèche. b (*Brit *: make fun of*) *person* mettre en boîte*, charrier‡; *book* parodier. c *entry form* envoyer. d (*blow up*) faire sauter*, faire exploser. e (**: jail*) envoyer en prison, coffrer. 2 (*Brit*) **send-up*** n *see* **send 3**.

sender ['sendəʳ] n expéditeur *m*, -trice *f*, envoyeur *m*, -euse *f*; *see* **return**.

Seneca ['senɪkə] n Sénèque *m*.

Senegal [ˌsenɪ'gɔːl] n Sénégal *m*.

Senegalese ['senɪgə'liːz] 1 adj sénégalais. 2 n, pl inv Sénégalais(e) *m(f)*.

senile ['siːnaɪl] adj sénile. **~ decay** dégénérescence *f* sénile; **~ dementia** démence *f* sénile.

senility [sɪ'nɪlɪtɪ] n sénilité *f*.

senior ['siːnɪəʳ] 1 adj a (*older*) aîné, plus âgé. **he is 3 years ~ to me, he is ~ to me by 3 years** il est mon aîné de 3 ans, il est plus âgé que moi de 3 ans, il a 3 ans de plus que moi; **(Mr) Smith S~** (M.) Smith père; **Mrs Smith S~** Mme Smith mère; **~ citizen** personne âgée *or* du troisième âge; **the problem of ~ citizens** les problèmes des gens âgés *or* du troisième âge; **~ citizens' club** club *m* du troisième âge; (*Brit*) **~ school** (*oldest classes*) grandes classes; (*secondary school*) collège *m* d'enseignement secondaire; (*US*) **~ high school** ≃ lycée *m*; (*US Scol*) **~ year** (classe *f*) terminale *f*, dernière année d'études (scolaires).

b (*of higher rank*) *employee* de grade supérieur; *officer* supérieur (*f* -eure); *position, rank* supérieur, plus élevé. **he is ~ to me in the firm** (*in rank*) il est au-dessus de moi dans l'entreprise, son poste dans l'entreprise est plus élevé que le mien; (*in service*) il a plus d'ancienneté que moi dans la maison; (*Mil*) **the ~ officer** l'officier supérieur; **a ~ official** (*Civil Service*) un haut fonctionnaire; (*private firm*) un cadre supérieur *or* haut placé; (*Brit*) **~ CID officer** officier *m* de police judiciaire haut placé; **~ police officer** officier *m* de police haut placé; (*Brit Air Force*) **~ aircraftman, ~ aircraftwoman** ≃ soldat *m*; (*US Air Force*) **~ airman** caporal-chef *m*; (*US Navy*) **~ chief petty officer** premier maître *m*; **~ clerk** premier commis, commis principal; **~ executive** cadre supérieur; (*Brit Scol*) **~ master** professeur principal; (*US Air Force*) **~ master sergeant** adjudant *m*; **~ partner** associé principal; (*Brit*) **the S~ Service** la marine (de guerre).

2 n a (*in age*) aîné(e) *m(f)*. **he is my ~ by 3 years, he is 3 years my ~** (*in age*) il est mon aîné de 3 ans, il est plus âgé que moi de 3 ans; (*in service*) il a 3 ans d'ancienneté de plus que moi.

b (*US Univ*) étudiant(e) *m(f)* de licence; (*US Scol*) élève *mf* de terminale. (*Brit Scol*) **the ~s** les grand(e)s *m(f)pl*.

seniority [ˌsiːnɪ'ɒrɪtɪ] n (*in age*) priorité *f* d'âge; (*in rank*) supériorité *f*; (*in years of service*) ancienneté *f*. **promotion by ~** avancement *m* à l'ancienneté.

senna ['senə] n séné *m*. **~ pod** gousse *f* de séné.

sensation [sen'seɪʃən] n a (*NonC: feeling*) sensation *f*. **to lose all ~ in one's arm** perdre toute sensation dans le bras. b (*impression*) sensation *f*, impression *f*. **to have a dizzy ~** avoir une sensation de vertige; **I had a gliding ~** *or* **the ~ of gliding** j'avais la sensation *or* l'impression de planer. c (*excitement*) sensation *f*; (*Press*) sensation, scandale *m*. **to create** *or* **cause a ~** faire sensation; **it was a ~ in Paris** cela a fait sensation à Paris; **it's a ~!** c'est sensationnel!

sensational [sen'seɪʃənl] adj a *event* qui fait sensation, sensationnel; *fashion* qui fait sensation. **~ murder** meurtre *m* qui fait sensation. b *film, novel, newspaper* à sensation. **he gave a ~ account of the accident** il a fait un récit dramatique de l'accident. c (**: marvellous*) sensationnel*, formidable*, sensass* *inv*.

sensationalism [sen'seɪʃnəlɪzəm] n (*NonC*) a (*Press etc*) recherche *f or* exploitation *f* du sensationnel. b (*Philos*) sensualisme *m*.

sensationalist [sen'seɪʃnəlɪst] 1 n colporteur *m*, -euse *f* de nouvelles à sensation; (*writer*) auteur *m* à sensation. 2 adj à sensation.

sensationalize [sen'seɪʃnəlaɪz] vt dramatiser.

sensationally [sen'seɪʃnəlɪ] adv *report, describe* en recherchant le sensationnel. **it was ~ successful/popular** *etc* cela a connu un succès/une popularité *etc* inouï(e) *or* fantastique.

sense [sens] 1 n a (*faculty*) sens *m*. **~ of hearing** ouïe *f*; **~ of smell** odorat *m*; **~ of sight** vue *f*; **~ of taste** goût *m*; **~ of touch** toucher *m*; **to come to one's ~s** (*regain consciousness*) reprendre connaissance, revenir à soi (*see also* **1d**); *see* **sixth**.

b (*awareness*) sens *m*, sentiment *m*. **~ of colour** sens de la couleur; **~ of direction** sens de l'orientation; **~ of duty** sentiment du devoir; **~ of humour** sens de l'humour; **to lose all ~ of time** perdre toute notion de l'heure; **the ~ of my own inadequacy** le sentiment de mon impuissance; **to have no ~ of shame** ne pas savoir ce que c'est que la honte; *see* **business, road, strong**.

c (*sensation, impression*) (*physical*) sensation *f*; (*mental*) sentiment *m*. **a ~ of warmth** une sensation de chaleur; **a ~ of guilt** un sentiment de culpabilité.

d (*sanity*) **~s** raison *f*; **to take leave of one's ~s** perdre la tête *or* la raison; **to come to one's ~s** (*become reasonable*) revenir à la raison; **to bring sb to his ~s** ramener qn à la raison; **anyone in his ~s would know ...** tout homme sensé *or* tout homme jouissant de sa raison saurait ...; **no one in his ~s would do that** il faudrait être fou pour faire ça.

e (*wisdom, sound judgment; also* **common~**) bon sens, intelligence *f*. **haven't you enough ~ *or* the (good) ~ to refuse?** n'avez-vous pas assez de bon sens pour refuser?; **there is some ~ in what he says** il y a du bon sens dans ce qu'il dit; **to have more ~ than to do** avoir trop de bon sens pour faire, être trop sensé pour faire; **you should have had more ~ than to do it** vous auriez dû avoir assez de bon sens pour ne pas le faire; *see* **common**.

f (*reasonable quality*) sens *m*. **there's no ~ in (doing) that** cela n'a pas de sens, cela ne rime à rien; **what's the ~ of *or* in (doing) that?** à quoi bon (faire) cela?; *see* **see[1], sound[2], talk.**

g (*meaning*) *[word, phrase, writing, text etc]* sens *m* (*also Ling*), signification *f*. **in the literal/figurative ~** au sens propre/figuré; **in every ~ of the word** dans toute l'acception du terme; **she is in no ~ suitable for the job** elle n'est pas du tout la personne qu'il faut pour le poste; **in a ~** dans un (certain) sens, dans une certaine mesure; **in a very real ~** de fait; **to get the ~ of what sb says** saisir l'essentiel de ce que dit qn.

h (*rational meaning*) *[words, speech etc]* **to make ~** avoir du sens; *[words, speech etc]* **not to make ~** ne pas avoir de sens, être dénué de sens; **what she did makes ~** ce qu'elle a fait est logique *or* se tient; **what she did just doesn't make ~** ce qu'elle a fait n'a pas le sens commun *or* n'est pas logique *or* ne tient pas debout*; **why did she do it? — I don't know, it doesn't make ~** pourquoi est-ce qu'elle a fait ça? — je n'en sais rien, ça n'a pas le sens commun *or* ça n'est pas logique *or* ça ne tient pas debout*; **to make ~ of sth** arriver à comprendre qch, saisir la signification de qch.

i (*opinion*) **the general ~ of the meeting** l'opinion générale *or* le sentiment de ceux présents; (*US Pol*) **the ~ of the Senate** la recommendation du Sénat.

2 **comp** ►**sense organ** organe des sens *or* sensoriel.

3 **vt** (*become aware of, feel*) sentir (intuitivement), deviner, pressentir. **to ~ somebody's presence** se rendre compte d'une présence, sentir une présence; **to ~ danger** pressentir le danger; **I could ~ his eyes on me** je sentais qu'il me regardait; **one could ~ the life flowing in ...** on devinait la vie qui coulait dans ...; **I ~d his interest in what I was saying** j'ai senti *or* je me suis rendu compte que ce que je disais l'intéressait; **to ~ that one is unwelcome** sentir *or* deviner qu'on n'est pas le bienvenu; **I ~d as much** c'est bien ce que j'ai deviné *or* senti.

senseless ['sensləs] **adj** a (*stupid*) *person* insensé; *action, idea* stupide, qui n'a pas le sens commun, (*stronger*) absurde, insensé. **a ~ waste of energy resources** un gâchis insensé des ressources d'énergie; **a ~ waste of human life** des pertes insensées en vies humaines; **what a ~ thing to do! (*or* to say! *etc*)** c'est d'une stupidité sans nom!, ça n'a pas le sens commun! b (*unconscious*) sans connaissance. **to fall ~ (to the floor)** tomber sans connaissance; *see* **knock**.

senselessly ['sensləslɪ] **adv** stupidement, d'une façon insensée.

senselessness ['sensləsnɪs] **n** *[person]* manque *m* de bon sens; *[action, idea]* absurdité *f*. **the absolute ~ of the war** l'absurdité totale de la guerre.

sensibility [,sensɪ'bɪlɪtɪ] **n** a (*NonC*) sensibilité *f*. b **sensibilities** susceptibilité *f*.

sensible ['sensəbl] **adj** a (*wise, of sound judgment*) *person* sensé, raisonnable. **she's a ~ person *or* type*** elle est très raisonnable *or* sensée, elle a les deux pieds sur terre*; **try to be ~ about it** sois raisonnable; **that was ~ of you** c'était raisonnable de ta part, tu as fait preuve de bon sens.

b (*reasonable, practicable*) *act, decision, choice* sage, raisonnable; *clothes* pratique, commode. **the most ~ thing (to do) would be to see her** le plus sage *or* raisonnable serait de la voir; **~ shoes** chaussures *fpl* pratiques.

c (*perceptible*) *change, difference, rise in temperature* sensible, appréciable, assez considérable.

d (†, *frm: aware*) **I am ~ of the honour you do me** je suis sensible à *or* conscient de l'honneur que vous me faites.

sensibleness ['sensəblnɪs] **n** bon sens, jugement *m*.

sensibly ['sensəblɪ] **adv** a (*reasonably*) *act, decide* raisonnablement, sagement, judicieusement. **to be ~ dressed** porter des vêtements pratiques. b (*perceptibly*) sensiblement.

sensitive ['sensɪtɪv] 1 **adj** a *person* (*emotionally aware, responsive*) sensible; (*easily hurt*) sensible (*to* à); (*easily offended*) facilement blessé (*to* par), susceptible, ombrageux; (*easily influenced*) impressionnable, influençable. **she is ~ about her nose** elle n'aime pas qu'on lui parle (*subj*) de son nez.

b *tooth, eyes,* (*Phot*) *film* sensible (*to* à); (*Phot*) *paper* sensibilisé. **public opinion is very ~ to hints of corruption** l'opinion publique réagit vivement à tout soupçon de corruption.

c (*delicate*) *skin* délicat, sensible.

d (*difficult*) *matter, subject, topic* délicat, sensible; *situation* névralgique, délicat. **this is politically very ~** sur le plan politique ceci est très délicat; **that is a very ~ area** (*place*) c'est un point chaud; (*fig: subject matter*) c'est un domaine très délicat *or* sensible.

e (*esp US: affecting national security*) *document etc* sensible.

f (*St Ex, Comm*) *market* sensible, instable, nerveux.

2 **-sensitive adj ending in comps: heat-/light-sensitive** sensible à la chaleur/la lumière.

sensitively ['sensɪtɪvlɪ] **adv** avec sensibilité, d'une manière sensible.

sensitiveness ['sensɪtɪvnɪs] **n** (*see* **sensitive 1a**) sensibilité *f*; susceptibilité *f*.

sensitivity [,sensɪ'tɪvɪtɪ] **n** (*see* **sensitive 1a, 1b, 1c**) sensibilité *f*; susceptibilité *f*; délicatesse *f*; (*Fin, St Ex*) instabilité *f*.

sensitize ['sensɪtaɪz] **vt** (*Med, Phot*) sensibiliser.

sensor ['sensəʳ] **n** (*Tech*) détecteur *m*. **heat ~** palpeur *m*.

sensory ['sensərɪ] **adj** des sens; (*Physiol*) *organ, nerve* sensoriel.

sensual ['sensjʊəl] **adj** sensuel.

sensualism ['sensjʊəlɪzəm] **n** sensualité *f*; (*Philos*) sensualisme *m*.

sensualist ['sensjʊəlɪst] **n** personne sensuelle, voluptueux *m*, -euse *f*; (*Philos*) sensualiste *mf*.

sensuality [,sensjʊ'ælɪtɪ] **n** sensualité *f*.

sensually ['sensjʊəlɪ] **adv** sensuellement.

sensuous ['sensjʊəs] **adj** *poetry, music* voluptueux, qui fait appel aux sens, qui affecte les sens; *person, temperament* voluptueux, sensuel.

sensuously ['sensjʊəslɪ] **adv** avec volupté, voluptueusement.

sensuousness ['sensjʊəsnɪs] **n** *[poetry, music]* qualité voluptueuse *or* évocatrice; *[person, temperament]* volupté *f*.

sent [sent] **pret, ptp of send.**

sentence ['sentəns] 1 **n** a (*Gram*) phrase *f*. b (*Jur*) (*judgment*) condamnation *f*, sentence *f*; (*punishment*) peine *f*. (*lit, fig*) **to pass ~ on sb** prononcer une condamnation *or* une sentence contre qn; **~ of death** arrêt *m* de mort, condamnation à mort; **under ~ of death** condamné à mort; **he got a 5-year ~** il a été condamné à 5 ans de prison; **a long ~** une longue peine; *see* **commute, life, serve** *etc.* 2 **comp** ►**sentence structure** (*Gram*) structure *f* de la phrase. 3 **vt** prononcer une condamnation *or* une sentence contre. **to ~ sb to death/to 5 years** condamner qn à mort/à 5 ans de prison.

sententious [sen'tenʃəs] **adj** sentencieux, pompeux.

sententiously [sen'tenʃəslɪ] **adv** sentencieusement.

sententiousness [sen'tenʃəsnɪs] **n** *[speech]* ton sentencieux; *[person]* caractère sentencieux.

sentient ['senʃənt] **adj** sensible, doué de sensation.

sentiment ['sentɪmənt] **n** a (*feeling*) sentiment *m*; (*opinion*) opinion *f*, avis *m*. **my ~s towards your daughter** les sentiments que j'éprouve pour votre fille *or* que m'inspire votre fille. b (*NonC: sentimentality*) sentimentalité *f*, sentiment* *m*, sensiblerie *f* (*pej*).

sentimental [,sentɪ'mentl] **adj** *person, novel* sentimental (*also pej*). **it's of ~ value only** sa valeur est purement sentimentale; (*Literat*) **~ comedy** comédie larmoyante.

sentimentalism [,sentɪ'mentəlɪzəm] **n** sentimentalisme *m*, sensiblerie *f* (*pej*).

sentimentalist [,sentɪ'mentəlɪst] **n** sentimental(e) *m(f)*.

sentimentality [,sentɪmen'tælɪtɪ] **n** sentimentalité *f*, sensiblerie *f* (*pej*).

sentimentalize [,sentɪ'mentəlaɪz] 1 **vt** rendre sentimental. 2 **vi** faire du sentiment*.

sentimentally [,sentɪ'mentəlɪ] **adv** sentimentalement, d'une manière *or* d'une voix sentimentale.

sentinel ['sentɪnl] **n** sentinelle *f*, factionnaire *m*.

sentry ['sentrɪ] 1 **n** (*Mil etc*) sentinelle *f*, factionnaire *m*; (*fig*) sentinelle. 2 **comp** ►**sentry box** guérite *f* ►**sentry duty: to be on sentry duty** être en *or* de faction.

Seoul [səʊl] **n** Seoul.

Sep. abbr of September.

sepal ['sepəl] **n** sépale *m*.

separable ['sepərəbl] **adj** séparable.

separate ['seprət] 1 **adj** *section, piece* séparé, distinct; *treaty, peace* séparé; *career, existence* indépendant; *organization, unit* distinct, indépendant; *entrance* particulier; *occasion, day* différent; *question, issue* différent, autre. **the children have ~ rooms** les enfants ont chacun leur (propre) chambre; **Paul and his wife sleep in ~ beds/rooms** Paul et sa femme font lit/chambre à part; **they live completely ~ lives** ils mènent des vies complètement séparées; (*in restaurant etc*) **we want ~ bills** nous voudrions des additions séparées *or* chacun notre addition; **the two houses though semidetached are quite ~** les deux maisons bien que jumelées sont tout à fait indépendantes (l'une de l'autre); **I wrote it on a ~ sheet** je l'ai écrit sur une feuille séparée *or* sur une feuille à part; **take a ~ sheet for each answer** prenez une nouvelle feuille pour chaque réponse; **there will be ~ discussions on this question** cette question sera discutée à part *or* séparément; **there is a ~ department for footwear** il y a un rayon séparé *or* spécial pour les chaussures; **"with ~ toilet"** "avec W.-C. séparé"; **keep the novels ~ from the textbooks** ne mélangez pas les romans et les livres de classe; (*Can*) **~ school** école *f* *or* collège *m* privé(e); (*US Jur*) **~ opinion** avis *m* divergeant de la minorité des juges.

2 **n** (*clothes*) **~s** vêtements non coordonnés.

3 ['sepəreɪt] **vt** séparer (*from* de); (*sort out*) séparer, trier; (*divide up*) diviser; *strands* dédoubler; *milk* écrémer. **to ~ truth from error** distinguer le vrai du faux; **they are ~d but not divorced** ils sont séparés mais ils n'ont pas divorcé; *see* **sheep, wheat.**

4 ['sepəreɪt] **vi** a *[liquids]* se séparer (*from* de); *[metals etc]* se séparer, se détacher (*from* de).

b *[people]* se séparer, se quitter; *[fighters]* rompre.
c *[married couple]* se séparer; *[non-married couple]* rompre.
► **separate out** vt sep séparer, trier.
separately ['seprətlɪ] adv a (*apart*) séparément, à part. b (*one by one*) séparément, un par un, un à la fois. **these articles are sold ~** ces articles se vendent séparément.
separateness ['seprətnɪs] n séparation *f* (*from* de). **feeling of ~** sentiment *m* de séparation *or* d'être à part.
separation [ˌsepə'reɪʃən] 1 n séparation *f*; *[ore]* triage *m*; (*Pol, Rel*) scission *f*, séparation; (*after marriage*) séparation (*from* d'avec). **judicial ~** séparation de corps. 2 comp ► **separation allowance** (*Mil*) allocation *f* militaire; (*Jur: alimony*) pension *f* alimentaire.
separatism ['sepərətɪzəm] n séparatisme *m*.
separatist ['sepərətɪst] adj, n séparatiste *(mf)*.
separator ['sepəreɪtə^r] n (*all senses*) séparateur *m*.
Sephardi [se'fɑːdɪ] n, pl **Sephardim** [se'fɑːdɪm] Séfardi *mf or* Séfaraddi *mf*.
Sephardic [se'fɑːdɪk] adj séfarade.
sepia ['siːpjə] n a (*colour*) sépia *f*. **~ drawing** sépia. b (*fish*) seiche *f*.
sepoy ['siːpɔɪ] n cipaye *m*.
sepsis ['sepsɪs] n (*Med*) septicité *f*, état *m* septique.
Sept. abbr of **September**.
septa ['septə] npl of **septum**.
September [sep'tembə^r] 1 n septembre *m*, mois *m* de septembre. **the first of ~** le premier septembre; **the tenth of ~** le dix septembre; **on the tenth of ~** le dix septembre; **in ~** en septembre; **in the month of ~** au mois de septembre; **each** *or* **every ~** tous les ans *or* chaque année en septembre; **at the beginning of ~** au début (du mois) de septembre, début septembre*; **in the middle of ~, in mid ~** au milieu (du mois) de septembre, à la mi-septembre; **at the end of ~** à la fin (du mois) de septembre, fin septembre*; **during ~** pendant le mois de septembre; **there are 30 days in ~** il y a 30 jours au mois de septembre, septembre a 30 jours; **~ was cold** septembre a été froid, il a fait froid en septembre; **early in ~, in early ~** au début de septembre; **late in ~, in late ~** vers la fin de septembre; **last/next ~** septembre dernier/prochain.
2 comp ► **September holidays/rains** *etc* congés *mpl*/pluies *fpl etc* (du mois) de septembre ► **September Riots** (*Hist*) massacres *mpl* de septembre ► **September weather: it's September weather** il fait un temps de septembre.
Septembrist [sep'tembrɪst] n septembriseur *m*.
septet [sep'tet] n septuor *m*.
septic ['septɪk] adj septique; *wound* infecté. **to go** *or* **become ~** s'infecter; **~ poisoning** septicémie *f*; **~ tank** fosse *f* septique.
septicaemia, (*US*) **septicemia** [ˌseptɪ'siːmɪə] n septicémie *f*.
septuagenarian [ˌseptjʊədʒɪ'nɛərɪən] adj, n septuagénaire *(mf)*.
Septuagesima [ˌseptjʊə'dʒesɪmə] n Septuagésime *f*.
Septuagint ['septjʊədʒɪnt] n version *f* (biblique) des Septante.
septum ['septəm] n, pl **septa** (*Anat, Bot*) cloison *f*, septum *m*.
septuplet [sep'tʌplɪt] n septuplé(e) *m(f)*.
sepulchral [sɪ'pʌlkrəl] adj sépulcral; (*fig: gloomy*) funèbre, sépulcral.
sepulchre, (*US*) **sepulcher** ['sepəlkə^r] n sépulcre *m*, tombeau *m*; (*Rel*) sépulcre. (*fig*) **whited ~** hypocrite *mf*; *see* **holy**.
sequel ['siːkwəl] n a (*consequence*) suite *f*, conséquence *f*; (*to illness etc*) séquelles *fpl*. **it had a tragic ~** cela a eu des suites *or* des conséquences tragiques. b *[book, film etc]* suite *f*.
sequence ['siːkwəns] n a (*order*) ordre *m*, suite *f*. **in ~** par ordre, les uns à la suite des autres; **in historical ~** par ordre chronologique; **logical ~** ordre *or* enchaînement *m* logique. b (*series*) suite *f*, succession *f*; (*Cards*) séquence *f*. c **(film)** ~ séquence *f*; **(dance) ~** numéro *m* (de danse). d (*Mus*) séquence *f*. e (*Comput*) séquence *f*. f (*Ling: gen*) suite *f*. (*Gram*) **~ of tenses** concordance *f* des temps.
sequential [sɪ'kwenʃəl] adj a (*in regular sequence*) séquentiel. b (*following*) qui suit. **~ upon** *or* **from** qui résulte de. c (*Comput*) séquentiel. **~ access/processing** accès *m*/traitement *m* séquentiel.
sequester [sɪ'kwestə^r] vt a (*isolate*) isoler; (*shut up*) enfermer, séquestrer. **~ed** *life* isolé, retiré; *spot* retiré, peu fréquenté. b (*Jur*) *property* séquestrer. **~ed** *property* mis *or* placé sous séquestre.
sequestrate [sɪ'kwestreɪt] vt (*Jur*) a = **sequester b**. b (*confiscate*) confisquer, saisir.
sequestration [ˌsiːkwes'treɪʃən] n (*Jur*) a *[property]* séquestration *f*, mise *f* sous séquestre. b (*confiscation*) confiscation *f*, saisie *f* conservatoire.
sequin ['siːkwɪn] n paillette *f*.
sequinned, (*US*) **sequined** ['siːkwɪnd] adj pailleté, cousu de paillettes.
sequoia [sɪ'kwɔɪə] n séquoia *m*.
seraglio [se'rɑːlɪəʊ] n sérail *m*.
serape [sə'rɑːpɪ] n (*US*) poncho *m*, couverture *f* mexicaine.
seraph ['serəf] n, pl **~s** *or* (*Rel, liter etc*) **seraphim** séraphin *m*.
seraphic [sə'ræfɪk] adj (*lit, fig*) séraphique.
seraphim ['serəfɪm] npl of **seraph**.
Serb [sɜːb] 1 adj serbe. 2 n a Serbe *mf*. b (*Ling*) serbe *m*.
Serbia ['sɜːbɪə] n Serbie *f*.
Serbian ['sɜːbɪən] = **Serb**.
Serbo-Croat ['sɜːbəʊ'krəʊæt], **Serbo-Croatian** ['sɜːbəʊkrəʊ'eɪʃən] 1 adj serbo-croate. 2 n a Serbo-croate *mf*. b (*Ling*) serbo-croate *m*.
sere [sɪə^r] adj = **sear 1**.
serenade [ˌserə'neɪd] 1 n sérénade *f*. 2 vt donner une sérénade à.
serendipitous [ˌserən'dɪpɪtəs] adj (*US*) *discovery etc* heureux. **his timing was ~** il a eu la chance de bien tomber*.
serendipity [ˌserən'dɪpɪtɪ] n (*NonC: hum*) don *m* de faire par hasard des découvertes heureuses.
serene [sə'riːn] adj *person, smile* serein, tranquille, paisible; *sky* serein, clair; *sea* calme. **to become** *or* **grow ~** *[person]* redevenir serein, se rasséréner; *[sky]* redevenir serein; *[sea]* redevenir calme; **His S~ Highness** Son Altesse Sérénissime; **all ~!*** tout va bien!
serenely [sə'riːnlɪ] adv *smile etc* avec sérénité, sereinement; *say* d'un ton serein. **~ indifferent to the noise** suprêmement indifférent au bruit.
serenity [sɪ'renɪtɪ] n (*see* **serene**) sérénité *f*; calme *m*; tranquillité *f*.
serf [sɜːf] n serf *m*, serve *f*.
serfdom ['sɜːfdəm] n servage *m*.
serge [sɜːdʒ] 1 n serge *f*. 2 comp de serge ► **serge suit** complet *m* en serge; **blue serge suit** complet *m* en serge bleue.
sergeant ['sɑːdʒənt] 1 n a (*Brit: Mil, Air Force*) sergent *m*. **yes, ~** oui, chef; *see also* **2**, *and* **colour, drill²**, **flight¹** *etc*. b (*US Air Force*) caporal-chef *m*. c (*Police*) (*Brit, US*) ≃ brigadier *m*; *see* **detective**. 2 comp ► **sergeant at arms** huissier *m* d'armes ► **sergeant first class** (*US Mil*) sergent-chef *m* ► **sergeant-major** (*Mil*) (*Brit*) sergent-major *m*; (*US Mil*) adjudant-chef *m*; *see* **company, regimental**.
serial ['sɪərɪəl] 1 n a (*Rad, TV*) feuilleton *m*; (*in magazine etc: also* **~ story**) roman-feuilleton *m*, feuilleton. **television/radio ~** feuilleton à la télévision/à la radio, feuilleton télévisé/radiophonique; **13-part ~** feuilleton en 13 épisodes.
b (*publication, journal*) publication *f* périodique, périodique *m*.
2 adj a d'une série, formant une série, en série; *music* sériel. **~ number** *[goods, car engine]* numéro *m* de série; *[soldier]* (numéro) matricule *m*; *[cheque, banknote]* numéro.
b (*Comput*) *disk, transmission, processing, programming etc* série *inv*; *access* séquentiel.
c **~ rights** droits *mpl* de reproduction en feuilleton; **~ writer** feuilletoniste *mf*.
d **~ killer** meurtrier *m* tuant en série; **~ killings** meurtres *mpl* en série.
serialism ['sɪərɪəˌlɪzəm] n (*Mus*) sérialisme *m*.
serialization [ˌsɪərɪəlaɪ'zeɪʃən] n (*Press*) publication *f* en feuilleton; (*Rad, TV*) adaptation *f* en feuilleton.
serialize ['sɪərɪəlaɪz] vt (*Press*) publier en feuilleton; (*Rad, TV*) adapter en feuilleton. **it was ~d in 6 parts** cela a été publié *or* adapté en 6 épisodes; **it has been ~d in the papers** cela a paru *or* été publié en feuilleton dans les journaux.
serially ['sɪərɪəlɪ] adv a *number* en série. b **to appear/be published ~** *[story]* paraître/être publié en feuilleton; *[magazine, journal]* paraître/être publié en livraisons périodiques.
seriatim [ˌsɪərɪ'eɪtɪm] adv (*frm*) successivement, point par point.
sericulture [ˌserɪ'kʌltʃə^r] n sériciculture *f*.
series ['sɪərɪz] 1 n, pl inv a (*also Chem, Comm, Elec, Ling, Mus*) série *f*; (*succession*) série, suite *f*, succession *f*; (*Math*) série, suite. **in ~** (*also Elec*) en série; **~ of stamps/coins** *etc* série de timbres/de monnaies *etc*; **~ of colours** gamme *f or* échelle *f* de couleurs; **a ~ of volumes on this subject** une série de volumes sur ce sujet; **there has been a ~ of incidents** il y a eu une série *or* une suite *or* une succession d'incidents, il y a eu plusieurs incidents successifs; **it will be one of a ~ of measures intended to …** cette mesure entrera dans le cadre d'une série de mesures destinées à … .
b (*Rad, TV*) série *f* (d'émissions); (*set of books*) collection *f*; (*set of stamps*) série. (*Rad, TV*) **this is the last in the present ~ (of programmes)** c'est la dernière émission de cette série; (*Publishing*) **a new paperback ~** une nouvelle collection de poche; *see* **world**.
2 comp ► **series connection** (*Elec*) montage *m* en série.
serio-comic [ˌsɪərɪəʊ'kɒmɪk] adj mi-sérieux mi-comique.
serious ['sɪərɪəs] adj a (*in earnest, not frivolous*) *person, offer, suggestion, interest* sérieux, sincère; *publication, conversation, discussion, occasion* sérieux, important; *report, information, account* sérieux, sûr; *literature, music* respectable; *attitude, voice, smile, look* plein de sérieux, grave; *tone* sérieux, grave; (*unsmiling*) *person* sérieux, grave, froid; *look* grave, sévère; (*thoughtful*) sérieux, réfléchi, posé; *pupil* sérieux, appliqué. **are you ~?** (parlez-vous) sérieusement?; **I'm quite ~** je suis sérieux, je parle sérieusement, je ne plaisante pas; **to give ~ thought to sth** (*ponder*) bien réfléchir à qch; (*intend*) songer sérieusement à (faire) qch; **to be ~ about one's work** être sérieux dans son travail; **the ~ student of jazz will maintain that …** quelqu'un qui s'intéresse sérieusement au jazz affirmera que …; **marriage is a ~ business** le mariage est une affaire sérieuse; **she earns ~ money*** elle gagne un bon paquet*; **~ wine*** vin *m* décent.
b (*causing concern*) *illness, injury, mistake, situation* grave, sérieux; *damage* important, considérable; *threat* sérieux; *loss* grave, lourd. I

have ~ doubts about ... je doute sérieusement de ..., j'ai de graves doutes sur ...; **the patient's condition is ~** le patient est dans un état grave.

seriously ['sɪərɪəslɪ] adv a (*in earnest*) sérieusement, avec sérieux; (*not jokingly*) sérieusement, sans plaisanter, sans blaguer*. **he said it all quite ~** il l'a dit tout à fait sérieusement, en disant ça il ne plaisantait *or* ne blaguait* pas; **yes, but ~ ...** oui, mais sérieusement ...; **~ now ...** sérieusement ..., sans blague* ..., toute plaisanterie *or* blague* (mise) à part ...; **to take sth/sb ~** prendre qch/qn au sérieux; **to think ~ about sth** (*ponder*) bien réfléchir à qch; (*intend*) songer sérieusement à (faire) qch.
b (*dangerously*) gravement, sérieusement, dangereusement; *ill* gravement; *wounded* grièvement; *worried* sérieusement.

seriousness ['sɪərɪəsnɪs] n a *[intention, offer, suggestion, interest]* sérieux *m*, sincérité *f*; *[publication, discussion, conversation, occasion]* sérieux, importance *f*; *[report, information, account]* caractère sérieux *or* sûr; *[attitude, voice, smile, tone, look]* sérieux, gravité *f*; *[character]* sérieux, gravité, froideur *f*; (*thoughtfulness*) sérieux, caractère posé *or* réfléchi. **in all ~** sérieusement, en toute sincérité. b *[situation, illness, mistake, threat, loss, injury]* gravité *f*; *[damage]* importance *f*, ampleur *f*.

serjeant ['sɑːdʒənt] = **sergeant**.

sermon ['sɜːmən] n (*Rel*) sermon *m*; (*fig pej*) sermon, laïus* *m*. **the S~ on the Mount** le Sermon sur la Montagne; (*fig pej*) **to give sb a ~** faire un sermon à qn.

sermonize ['sɜːmənaɪz] (*fig pej*) 1 vt sermonner. 2 vi prêcher, faire des sermons.

serous ['sɪərəs] adj séreux.

seropositive [ˌsɪərəʊ'pɒzɪtɪv] adj séropositif *m*, -ive *f*.

serpent ['sɜːpənt] n (*lit, fig*) serpent *m*; *see* **sea**.

serpentine ['sɜːpəntaɪn] 1 adj *river, road* sinueux, tortueux, qui serpente; (*treacherous*) perfide; (*Zool*) de serpent. 2 n (*Miner*) serpentine *f*, ophite *m*.

SERPS [sɜːps] n (*Brit*) (abbr of **state earnings-related pension scheme**) *système de retraite calculée sur le salaire*.

serrate [se'reɪt] vt denteler, découper en dents de scie.

serrated [se'reɪtɪd] adj *edge, blade* en dents de scie; *knife* à dents de scie.

serration [se'reɪʃən] n dentelure *f*.

serried ['serɪd] adj serré. **in ~ ranks** en rangs serrés.

serum ['sɪərəm] n, pl **~s** *or* **sera** ['sɪərə] sérum *m*. **tetanus ~** sérum antitétanique.

servant ['sɜːvənt] 1 n (*in household*) domestique *mf*; (*maid*) bonne *f*; (*fig*) serviteur *m*, servante *f*. **to keep a ~** avoir un(e) domestique; **a large staff of ~s** une nombreuse domesticité; **the ~s' hall** l'office *f*; **I'm not your ~** je ne suis pas votre domestique; **the government is the ~ of the people** le gouvernement est le serviteur *or* est au service du peuple; (*frm*) **your obedient ~** ≃ je vous prie d'agréer, Monsieur (*or* Madame *etc*), l'expression de ma considération distinguée; *see* **civil, humble, man, public** *etc*. 2 comp ▸**servant girl** servante *f*, bonne *f*.

serve [sɜːv] 1 vt a (*work for*) *master, employer, family* servir, être au service de; *God, one's country* servir. **he ~d his country well** il a bien servi son pays, il a bien mérité de la patrie (*frm*); **he has ~d the firm well** il a bien servi la compagnie, il a rendu de grands services à la compagnie; **he has ~d our cause well** il a bien servi notre cause; (*fig*) **to ~ two masters** servir deux maîtres à la fois; (*Rel*) **to ~ mass** servir la messe.
b (*be used as*) *[object etc]* servir (*as* de); (*be useful to*) rendre service à, être utile à. **it ~s her as a table** ça lui sert de table; **it's not very good but it will ~ me** ça n'est pas parfait mais ça fera l'affaire; **it will ~ my** (*or* **your** *etc*) **purpose** *or* **needs** cela fera l'affaire; **it ~s its purpose** *or* **turn** cela fait l'affaire, cela suffit bien; **it ~s a variety of purposes** cela sert à divers usages; **it ~s no useful purpose** cela ne sert à rien (de spécial); **if my memory ~s me (right)** (*see also* **1c**) si j'ai bonne mémoire, si je me souviens bien; **his knowledge of history ~d him well** ses connaissances en histoire *or* d'histoire lui ont été très utiles *or* se sont avérées très utiles *or* lui ont bien servi; **that excuse won't ~ you when ...** cette excuse ne vous servira à rien quand ... .
c (*phrases*) **(it) ~s him right** c'est bien fait pour lui, il ne l'a pas volé; **(it) ~s you right for being so stupid** cela t'apprendra à être si stupide; **it would have ~d them right if they hadn't got any** ça aurait été bien fait pour eux s'ils n'en avaient pas reçu.
d (*in shop, restaurant*) servir. **to ~ sb (with) sth** servir qch à qn; **are you being ~d?** est-ce qu'on vous sert? *or* s'occupe de vous?
e *food, meal* servir (*to sb* à qn). **dinner is ~d** le dîner est servi; (*as formal announcement*) Madame est servie (*or* Monsieur est servi); **this fish should be ~d with mustard sauce** ce poisson se sert *or* se mange avec une sauce à la moutarde; (*in recipe etc*) **"~s 5"** "5 portions"; *see also* **serving** *and* **first**.
f (*with transport, church services*) desservir; (*with gas, electricity*) alimenter. **the bus ~s 6 villages** le car dessert 6 villages; **the power station ~s a large district** la centrale alimente une zone étendue.
g (*work out*) **to ~ one's apprenticeship** *or* **time (as)** faire son apprentissage (de); **he ~d (out) his term of office** il est resté à son poste jusqu'à la fin de son mandat; **to ~ one's time** (*Mil*) faire son temps de service; (*Prison*) faire son temps de prison; (*in prison*) **to ~ time** faire de la prison; **to ~ (out) a prison sentence** purger une peine (de prison); *[prisoner]* **he has ~d over 25 years altogether** en tout il a fait plus de 25 ans de prison.
h (*Jur*) **to ~ legal process** signifier *or* notifier un acte judiciaire; **to ~ notice on sb (to the effect) that ...** notifier *or* signifier à qn que ...; **to ~ a summons on sb, to ~ sb with a summons** remettre une assignation à qn; **to ~ a warrant on sb, to ~ sb with a warrant** délivrer à qn un mandat; **to ~ a writ on sb, to ~ sb with a writ** assigner qn.
i (*Tennis etc*) servir.
j *[bull, stallion etc]* servir.
2 vi a *[servant, waiter]* servir. **to ~ at table** servir à table; **is there anyone serving at this table?** est-ce que quelqu'un fait le service de cette table? *or* s'occupe du service à cette table?
b (*work, do duty*) **to ~ on a committee/jury** être membre d'un comité/d'un jury; **he has ~d for 2 years as chairman of this society** cela fait 2 ans qu'il exerce la fonction de président de cette société; *see also* **serving**.
c (*Mil*) servir. **to ~ in the army** servir dans l'armée; **he ~d in Germany** il a servi en Allemagne; **he ~d as a Sapper in the Engineers** il a servi comme simple soldat dans le génie; **to ~ under sb** servir sous (les ordres de) qn; **he ~d with my brother** mon frère et lui ont été soldats ensemble.
d (*be useful*) servir (*for, as* de), être utile. **that table is not exactly what I want but it will ~** cette table n'est pas exactement ce que je veux mais elle fera l'affaire; **it ~s to show/explain** *etc* cela sert à montrer/expliquer *etc*.
e (*Rel*) servir; (*Tennis*) servir, être au service.
3 n (*Tennis etc*) service *m*. **he has a strong ~** il a un service puissant; **it's your ~** c'est à vous de servir.

▸**serve out** vt sep a *meal, soup* servir; *rations, provisions* distribuer. b **to serve sb out (for sth)** prendre sa revanche sur qn (pour qch), payer qn de retour (pour qch). c *see* **1g**.

▸**serve up** vt sep servir, mettre sur la table.

server ['sɜːvə^r] n a (*Rel*) servant *m*; (*Tennis etc*) servant(e) *m(f)*, serveur *m*, -euse *f*. b (*tray*) plateau *m*; (*utensil*) couvert *m* à servir; *see* **salad**.

servery ['sɜːvərɪ] n (*Brit*) office *f*.

service ['sɜːvɪs] 1 n a (*NonC: act of serving: gen, domestic, Mil etc*) service *m*. (*Mil*) **to see ~ (as)** avoir du service *or* servir (comme); **this coat has seen** *or* **given good ~** ce manteau a fait de l'usage; **10 years' ~** 10 ans de service; **on Her Majesty's ~** au service de Sa Majesté; *[domestic servant]* **to be in ~** être domestique *or* en service; **to be in sb's ~** être au service de qn; **at your ~** à votre service *or* disposition; **our company is always at your ~** notre compagnie est toujours à votre service; **to be of ~ to sb** être utile à qn, rendre service à qn; **can I be of ~?** est-ce que je peux vous aider?; (*in shop*) qu'y a-t-il pour votre service?; **to bring/come into ~** mettre/entrer en service; **this machine is out of ~** cette machine est hors service; **how long has this machine been in ~?** depuis quand cette machine fonctionne-t-elle?; (*in shop, hotel etc*) **the ~ is very poor** le service est très mauvais; (*Brit: on bill*) **15% ~ included** service 15% compris; *see* **active, military**.
b (*department; system*) service *m*. **medical/public/social** *etc* **~s** services médicaux/publics/sociaux *etc*; **customs ~** (service de la) douane *f*; (*Mil*) **when I was in the S~s** quand j'étais dans l'armée (*or* la marine *or* l'aviation *etc*); (*Mil*) **the S~s were represented** il y avait des représentants (des différentes branches) des forces armées; **the train ~ to London is excellent** le service de chemin de fer pour Londres est *or* les trains pour Londres sont excellent(s); **do you know what the train ~ is (to London)?** connaissez-vous l'horaire des trains (pour Londres)?; **the number 4 bus ~** la ligne *or* le service du (numéro) 4; *see* **civil, health, postal** *etc*.
c (*help etc rendered*) service *m*. **to do sb a ~** rendre service à qn; **for ~s rendered (to)** pour services rendus (à); **they dispensed with his ~s** ils se sont passés *or* privés de ses services; **do you need the ~s of a lawyer?** avez-vous besoin (des services) d'un avocat?
d (*Rel*) (*gen*) service *m*; (*Catholic*) service, office *m*; (*Protestant*) service, culte *m*; *see* **evening, funeral** *etc*.
e (*maintenance work*) *[car etc]* révision *f*; *[household machine]* entretien *m*, service *m* après-vente. (*Aut*) **30,000-km ~** révision des 30.000 km; **to put one's car in for ~** donner sa voiture à réviser; *see* **after** *etc*.
f (*set of crockery*) service *m*. **coffee ~** service à café; *see* **dinner, tea** *etc*.
g *[motorway]* **~s** aire *f* de services.
h (*Tennis etc*) service *m*.
i (*Jur*) **~ of documents** signification *f or* notification *f* d'actes; (*Jur*) **~ of process** signification *f* d'un acte judiciaire *or* d'une citation.
2 comp ▸**service area** *[motorway]* aire *f* de services ▸**service bus** autobus *m* régulier ▸**service charge** (*Brit*) service *m* ▸**service department** (*office etc*) service *m* des réparations *or* d'entretien; (*repair shop*) atelier *m* de réparations ▸**service dress** (*Brit Mil*) tenue *f* numéro un ▸**service elevator** (*US*) = **service lift** ▸**service families** (*Mil*) familles *fpl* de militaires ▸**service flat** (*Brit*) appartement *m* avec service (*assuré par le personnel de l'immeuble*) ▸**service hatch**

passe-plat *m* ► service industries (*Econ*) services *mpl*, industries *fpl* de service ► service lift (*Brit*) (*for goods*) monte-charge *m inv*; (*for personnel*) ascenseur *m* de service ► service line (*Tennis*) ligne *f* de service ► serviceman (*Mil*) militaire *m* ► service module (*Space*) module *m* de service ► service rifle (*Mil*) fusil *m* de guerre ► service road (*Brit*) (*access road*) voie *f or* chemin *m* d'accès; (*for works traffic*) voie de service ► service sector (*Econ*) secteur *m* tertiaire ► service station (*Aut*) station-service *f*.

3 vt *car* réviser; *washing machine etc* entretenir, assurer le service après-vente de; (*Fin*) *debt* servir les intérêts de; *organization, group etc* pourvoir aux besoins de, offrir ses services à. I put my car in to be ~d j'ai donné ma voiture à réviser.

serviceable [ˈsɜːvɪsəbl] adj (*useful, practical*) *building* commode; *style, clothes* pratique, commode; (*durable*) *building* durable, solide; *clothes* solide, qui fait de l'usage; (*usable, working*) utilisable.

servicing [ˈsɜːvɪsɪŋ] n *[car]* révision *f*; *[washing machine etc]* entretien *m*.

serviette [ˌsɜːvɪˈet] n (*esp Brit*) serviette *f* (de table). ~ ring rond *m* de serviette.

servile [ˈsɜːvaɪl] adj *person, behaviour* servile, obséquieux, rampant; *flattery etc* servile.

servility [sɜːˈvɪlɪtɪ] n servilité *f*.

serving [ˈsɜːvɪŋ] 1 n a (*action*) service *m*. b (*portion*) portion *f*, part *f*. 2 adj (*in office*) the ~ chairman *etc* le président *etc* en exercice.

3 comp ► serving dish plat *m* ► serving hatch passe-plat *m*.

servitude [ˈsɜːvɪtjuːd] n servitude *f*, asservissement *m*; (*slavery*) esclavage *m*; *see* penal.

servo [ˈsɜːvəʊ] n (*abbr of* servo-mechanism, servo-motor) *see* servo-.

servo- [ˈsɜːvəʊ] pref servo... ~assisted assisté; ~control servocommande *f*; ~mechanism servomécanisme *m*; ~motor servomoteur *m*.

sesame [ˈsesəmɪ] 1 n sésame *m*; *see* open. 2 comp ► sesame oil huile *f* de sésame ► sesame seeds graines *fpl* de sésame.

sesquipedalian [ˌseskwɪpɪˈdeɪlɪən] adj polysyllabique.

session [ˈseʃən] n a (*NonC: Admin, Jur, Parl etc*) séance *f*, session *f*. to be in ~ siéger; this court is now in ~ le tribunal est en session *or* en séance, l'audience est ouverte; to go into secret ~ siéger en séance secrète *or* à huis clos; *see* quarter *etc*.

b (*gen, Admin, Jur, Parl etc: sitting*) séance *f*. 2 afternoon ~s a week 2 séances par semaine l'après-midi; I had a ~ with him yesterday nous avons travaillé ensemble *or* nous avons eu une (longue) discussion *etc* hier; he's just had a ~ with the dentist il vient d'avoir une séance chez le dentiste; we're in for a long ~ nous n'aurons pas fini de sitôt, cela menace de durer; (*Brit Scol*) the morning/afternoon ~ les cours *mpl* du matin/de l'après-midi; *see* jam², recording.

c (*Scol, Univ*) (*year*) année *f* (universitaire *or* scolaire); (*US: term*) trimestre *m* (universitaire).

set [set] (vb: pret, ptp set) 1 n a *[objects]* jeu *m*, série *f*, assortiment *m*; (*kit*) trousse *f*; *[sails, oars, keys, golf clubs, knives, spanners, needles]* jeu; *[ties, pens]* jeu, assortiment; *[chairs, coffee tables, rugs, saucepans, weights, numbers, stamps etc]* série; *[books, ornaments, toy cars]* collection *f*; *[bracelets, magazines]* collection, série; *[dishes, plates, mugs etc]* service *m*; *[tyres]* train *m*; *[jewels]* parure *f*; *[theories etc]* corps *m*, ensemble *m*. a ~ of rooms un appartement; a ~ of kitchen utensils une batterie de cuisine; I want a new ~ of buttons for my coat je veux de nouveaux boutons pour mon manteau; I bought her a ~ of hairclasps je lui ai acheté des barrettes assorties; ~ of teeth dentition *f*, denture *f*; ~ of false teeth dentier *m*; *[teeth]* top/bottom ~ appareil *m* pour la mâchoire supérieure/inférieure; a ~ of dining-room furniture un mobilier *or* un ensemble de salle à manger; he had a whole ~ of telephones on his desk il avait toute une collection *or* batterie (*hum*) de téléphones sur son bureau; in ~s of 3 par séries *or* jeux de 3; in ~s en jeux complets, en séries complètes; it makes a ~ with those over there cela forme un jeu *or* un ensemble avec les autres là-bas; I need 2 more to make up the ~ il m'en manque 2 pour avoir tout le jeu *or* toute la série; sewing ~ trousse *f* de couture; painting ~ boîte *f* de peinture; chess/draughts ~ jeu d'échecs/de dames (*objet*); *see* tea *etc*.

b (*Tennis*) set *m*. (*Tennis*) ~ to Connors set Connors.

c (*Math, Philos*) ensemble *m*.

d (*Elec*) appareil *m*; (*Rad, TV*) poste *m*; *see* head, transistor, wireless *etc*.

e (*group of people*) groupe *m*, bande *f* (*also pej*); (*larger*) cercle *m*, monde *m*, milieu *m*. the golfing ~ le monde du golf; the literary ~ le monde des lettres, les milieux littéraires; I'm not in their ~, we're not in the same ~ nous ne sommes pas du même monde *or* milieu, je n'appartiens pas à leur cercle; a ~ of thieves/gangsters *etc* une bande de voleurs/gangsters *etc*; they're just a ~ of fools! ce n'est qu'une bande d'imbéciles!; *see* jet¹ *etc*.

f (*Brit Scol*) groupe *m* de niveau.

g (*stage*) (*Cine*) plateau *m*; (*Theat etc*) scène *f*; (*scenery*) décor *m*. on (the) ~ (*Cine*) sur le plateau; (*Theat*) en scène.

h (*Mus: part of concert*) set *m*, partie *f*.

i (*Hairdressing*) mise *f* en plis. to have a ~ se faire faire une mise en plis; I like your ~ j'aime ta coiffure; *see* shampoo.

j (*NonC: position, posture, direction etc*) *[body]* position *f*, attitude *f*; *[head]* port *m*; *[shoulders]* position; *[tide, wind]* direction *f*; *[opinion, sb's mind etc]* tendance *f*. (*liter*) at ~ of sun au coucher du soleil.

k (*Hunting*) arrêt *m*; *see* dead.

l (*Horticulture*) plante *f* à repiquer. onion ~s oignons *mpl* à repiquer.

2 adj a (*unchanging*) *rule, price, time* fixe; *smile etc* figé; *purpose, dogma* fixe, (bien) déterminé; *opinion, idea* (bien) arrêté; *lunch* à prix fixe; (*prearranged*) *time, date* fixé, décidé d'avance; (*Scol etc*) *book, subject* au programme; *speech, talk* étudié, préparé d'avance; *prayer* liturgique. ~ in one's ways conservateur (*f* -trice), routinier (*f* -ière), qui tient à ses habitudes; ~ in one's opinions immuable dans ses convictions; (*Met*) ~ fair au beau fixe; (*in restaurant*) the ~ meal, the ~ menu la table d'hôte; ~ expression, ~ phrase expression *f* consacrée *or* toute faite, locution *f* figée (*frm*); ~ piece (*fireworks*) pièce *f* (de feu) d'artifice; (*Art, Literat, Mus*) morceau traditionnel; (*in music competition etc*) morceau de concours; (*Sport*) combinaison *f* calculée; (*Rugby*) ~ scrum mêlée *f* ordonnée; the fruit is ~ les fruits ont (bien) noué.

b (*determined*) résolu, déterminé; (*ready*) prêt. to be ~ (up)on sth vouloir qch à tout prix, avoir jeté son dévolu sur qch; since you are so ~ on it puisque vous y tenez tant; to be ~ on doing être résolu à faire, vouloir à tout prix faire; to be (dead) ~ against s'opposer (absolument *or* formellement) à; they're all ~! ils sont fin prêts!; to be all ~ to do être prêt pour faire; (*Sport*) on your marks, get ~, go! à vos marques, prêts, partez!; (*fig*) the scene is ~ for ... tout est prêt pour ... .

3 comp ► setback (*hitch*) contretemps *m*, (*more serious*) revers *m*, échec *m*; (*in health*) rechute *f* ► set-in sleeve manche rapportée ► set point (*Tennis*) balle *f* de set ► set square équerre *f* (à dessin) ► set theory (*Math*) théorie *f* des ensembles ► set-to* (*fight*) bagarre *f*; (*quarrel*) prise *f* de bec*; to have a set-to with sb* se bagarrer avec qn*, avoir une prise de bec avec qn* ► setup *see* setup.

4 vt a (*place, put*) *object* mettre, poser, placer; *signature etc* apposer; *sentry, guard* poster. ~ it on the table/beside the window/over there mettez-le *or* posez-le *or* placez-le sur la table/près de la fenêtre/là-bas; the house is ~ on a hill la maison est située sur une colline; his stories, ~ in the Paris of 1890 ses histoires, situées *or* qui se passent *or* qui se déroulent dans le Paris de 1890; he ~ the scheme before the committee il a présenté le projet au comité; I ~ him above Wordsworth je le place *or* mets au-dessus de Wordsworth, je le considère supérieur à Wordsworth; what value do you ~ on this? (*lit*) à quelle valeur *or* à quel prix estimez-vous cela?; (*fig*) quelle valeur accordez-vous à cela?; we must ~ the advantages against the disadvantages il faut peser le pour et le contre, il faut mettre en balance les avantages et les inconvénients; to ~ fire to sth, ~ sth on fire mettre le feu à qch; *for other phrases see* fire, foot, heart, store *etc*.

b (*arrange, adjust*) *clock, mechanism* régler; *alarm* mettre; (*on display*) *specimen, butterfly etc* monter; *eggs, hen* faire couver; *plant* repiquer; (*Typ*) *type, page* composer; (*Med*) *arm, leg* (*in plaster*) plâtrer; (*with splint*) mettre une attelle à; *fracture* réduire. he ~s his watch by the radio il règle sa montre sur la radio; ~ your watch to the right time/to 2pm mettez votre montre à l'heure/à 14 heures; have you ~ the alarm clock? est-ce que tu as mis le réveil?; I've ~ the alarm for 6 *or* to wake me at 6 j'ai mis le réveil à *or* pour 6 heures; he ~ the needle to zero il a ramené l'aiguille à zéro; (*Aviat*) he ~ the controls to automatic il a mis les commandes sur automatique; to ~ sb's hair faire une mise en plis à qn; to have one's hair ~ se faire faire une mise en plis; *for other phrases see* sail, table *etc*.

c (*fix, establish*) *date, deadline, limit* fixer. let's ~ a time for the meeting fixons l'heure de la réunion; I've ~ myself a time limit je me suis fixé une limite (de temps) *or* un délai; he ~ a new record for the 100 metres il a établi un nouveau record pour le 100 mètres; they ~ the pass mark at 10 on a fixé la moyenne à 10; *for other phrases see* course, fashion, pace *etc*.

d (*give, assign*) *task* donner; *exam, test* composer *or* choisir les questions de; *texts, books* mettre au programme; *subject* donner. I ~ them a difficult translation je leur ai donné une traduction difficile (à faire); to ~ sb a problem poser un problème à qn; Molière is not ~ this year Molière n'est pas au programme cette année; I ~ him the job of clearing up je l'ai chargé de ranger *or* du rangement; *for other phrases see* example *etc*.

e (*Brit Scol*) to ~ maths, to ~ pupils for *or* in maths répartir les élèves en groupes de niveau en maths.

f (*cause to be, do, begin etc*) to ~ a dog on sb lâcher *or* lancer un chien contre qn (*see also* set upon); they ~ the police on to him ils l'ont signalé à la police; she ~ my brother against me elle a monté mon frère contre moi; someone has been ~ over him at the office on a placé quelqu'un au-dessus de lui au bureau; to ~ sth going mettre qch en marche; the news ~ me thinking la nouvelle m'a fait réfléchir *or* m'a donné à réfléchir; that ~ him wondering whether ... cela l'a porté *or* poussé à se demander si ...; this ~ everyone laughing cela a fait rire tout le monde, à cela tout le monde s'est mis à rire; to ~ sb to do sth faire faire qch à qn, donner à qn la tâche de faire qch; I ~ him to work at once je l'ai mis au travail aussitôt; to ~ o.s. to do entreprendre de faire.

g *gem* sertir (*in* dans), enchâsser (*in* dans), monter (*in* sur). **to ~ sth with jewels** orner *or* incruster qch de pierres précieuses.

h *jelly, jam* faire prendre; *concrete* faire prendre, faire durcir; *dye, colour* fixer.

5 **vi** a *[sun, moon etc]* se coucher. **the ~ting sun** le soleil couchant.

b *[broken bone, limb]* se ressouder; *[jelly, jam]* prendre; *[glue]* durcir; *[concrete]* prendre, durcir; *[fruit]* nouer; (*fig*) *[character]* se former, s'affermir. **quick-~ting cement** ciment prompt *or* à prise rapide; **his face ~ in a hostile expression** son visage s'est figé dans une expression hostile.

c (*begin*) se mettre, commencer (*to doing* à faire). **to ~ to work** se mettre au travail, s'y mettre*.

►**set about** 1 **vt fus** a (*begin*) *task, essay* entreprendre, se mettre à. **to set about doing** se mettre à faire; **I don't know how to set about it** je ne sais pas comment m'y prendre. b (*attack*) attaquer. **they set about each other** (*blows*) ils en sont venus aux coups *or* aux mains; (*words*) ils se sont mis à se disputer. 2 **vt sep** *rumour etc* faire courir. **he set it about that ...** il a fait courir le bruit que ... .

►**set apart** **vt sep** *object etc* mettre de côté *or* à part. (*fig*) **that sets him apart from the others** cela le distingue des autres.

►**set aside** **vt sep** a (*keep, save*) mettre de côté, garder en réserve. b **she set her book aside when I came in** elle a posé son livre quand je suis entré. c (*reject, annul*) *request, objection, proposal, petition* rejeter; *decree, will* annuler; (*Jur*) *judgment* casser.

►**set back** 1 **vt sep** a (*replace*) remettre. **set it back on the shelf** remets-le sur l'étagère.

b **the house was set back from the road** la maison était (construite) en retrait de la route; **the dog set its ears back** le chien a couché les oreilles.

c (*retard*) *development, progress* retarder; *clock* retarder (*by one hour* d'une heure). **the disaster set back the project by 10 years** le désastre a retardé de 10 ans la réalisation du projet; *see* **clock**.

d (*: *cost*) coûter. **that car must have set him back a good deal** *or* **a packet**‡ cette voiture a dû lui coûter les yeux de la tête; **how much did all that set you back?** combien tu as dû cracher‡ pour tout ça?

2 **setback** **n** *see* **set 3**.

►**set by** **vt sep** = **set aside a**.

►**set down** **vt sep** a (*put down*) *object* poser, déposer; *[coach, plane, taxi etc] passenger* laisser, déposer. (*Aut*) **I'll set you down at the corner** je vais vous laisser *or* déposer au coin.

b (*Aviat*) *plane* poser.

c (*record*) noter, inscrire. **to set sth down in writing** *or* **on paper** coucher *or* mettre qch par écrit; (*Comm*) **set it down on** *or* **to my account** mettez-le *or* portez-le sur mon compte.

d (*attribute*) attribuer (*sth to sth* qch à qch). **I set it down to his stupidity** je l'attribue à sa stupidité; **the accident must be set down to negligence** l'accident doit être imputé à la négligence; **we set it all down to the fact that he was tired** nous avons expliqué tout cela par sa fatigue, nous avons attribué tout cela à sa fatigue.

e (*assess, estimate*) **I had already set him down as a liar** je le tenais déjà pour menteur, j'avais déjà constaté qu'il était menteur.

►**set forth** 1 **vi** = **set off 1**. 2 **vt sep** *idea, plan, opinion* faire connaître, exposer; *conditions, rules* inclure.

►**set in** 1 **vi** (*begin*) *[complications, difficulties]* survenir, surgir; *[disease]* se déclarer. **a reaction set in after the war** une réaction s'est amorcée après la guerre; **the rain will soon set in** il va bientôt commencer à pleuvoir; **the rain has set in for the night** il va pleuvoir toute la nuit; **the rain has really set in now!** la pluie a l'air bien installée! 2 **vt sep** (*Sewing*) *sleeve* rapporter. 3 **set-in** **adj** *see* **set 3**.

►**set off** 1 **vi** (*leave*) se mettre en route, partir, s'en aller. **to set off on a journey/an expedition** partir en voyage/en expédition; (*fig*) **he set off on a long explanation** il s'est lancé dans une longue explication.

2 **vt sep** a *bomb* faire exploser; *firework* faire partir; *mechanism, alarm, rise in inflation* déclencher. **to set sb off (laughing/crying** *etc*) faire rire/pleurer *etc* qn; **her remark set him off and she couldn't get a word in edgeways** après sa remarque il s'est lancé et elle n'a pas pu placer un mot.

b (*enhance*) *hair, eyes, picture, furnishings etc* mettre en valeur, faire valoir; *complexion, colour* rehausser, mettre en valeur.

c (*balance etc*) **to set off profits against losses** balancer les pertes et les profits, opposer les pertes aux profits; **we must set off the expenses against the profits** il faut déduire les dépenses des bénéfices; **the profit on hats will set off the loss on ties** le bénéfice sur les chapeaux compensera le déficit sur les cravates.

►**set on** **vt fus** = **set upon**.

►**set out** 1 **vi** a (*leave, depart*) se mettre en route (*for* pour), partir (*for* pour, *from* de, *in search of* à la recherche de).

b (*intend, propose*) **he set out to explain why it had happened** il a cherché à *or* s'est proposé d'expliquer pourquoi cela s'était produit; **I didn't set out to prove you were wrong** il n'était pas dans mon intention de prouver *or* mon but n'était pas de prouver que vous aviez tort; **I set out to convince him he should change his mind** j'ai entrepris de le persuader de changer d'avis; **the book sets out to show that ...** ce livre a pour objet *or* but de montrer que ... .

2 **vt sep** *books, goods* exposer; *chessmen etc on board* disposer; (*fig*) *reasons, ideas* présenter, exposer. **the conditions are set out in paragraph 3** les modalités sont indiquées *or* prévues au paragraphe 3; **it's very clearly set out here** c'est expliqué *or* exposé ici de façon très claire; **the information is well set out on the page** l'information est bien présentée sur la page.

►**set to** 1 **vi** (*start*) commencer, se mettre (*to do* à faire); (*start work*) s'y mettre*. **they set to with their fists** ils en sont venus aux coups (de poing). 2 **set-to*** **n** *see* **set 3**.

►**set up** 1 **vi** (*Comm etc*) **to set up in business as a grocer** s'établir épicier; **he set up in business in London** il a monté une affaire *or* une entreprise à Londres.

2 **vt sep** a (*place in position*) *chairs, table, stall* placer, installer; *tent* dresser; *monument, statue* ériger, dresser. (*Typ*) **to set up type** assembler les caractères, composer; **to set up camp** établir un camp.

b (*fig: start, establish*) *school, institution* fonder; *business, company, fund* créer, lancer; *tribunal, government, committee* constituer; *fashion* lancer; *irritation, quarrel* causer, provoquer, susciter; *record* établir; *theory* avancer. **to set up an inquiry** ouvrir une enquête; **to set up house** s'installer; **they set up house** *or* **home together** ils se sont mis en ménage; **to set up shop** (*Comm*) ouvrir un commerce *or* un magasin, s'établir, s'installer; (*fig*) s'établir, s'installer; **he set up shop as a grocer** il s'est établi épicier, il a ouvert une épicerie; (*fig*) **he set up shop as a doctor*** il s'est établi docteur; **to set up a yell** se mettre à hurler; **to set sb up in business** établir *or* lancer qn dans les affaires; **he's all set up now** il est bien établi *or* lancé maintenant; **I've set it all up for you** je vous ai tout installé *or* préparé.

c (*pose*) **I've never set myself up as a scholar** je n'ai jamais prétendu être savant.

d (*after illness*) remonter, rétablir, remettre sur pied.

e (*equip*) munir, approvisionner (*with* de), monter (*with* en).

f (*: *falsely incriminate*) monter un coup contre. **I've been set up** je suis victime d'un coup monté.

g (*: *lure into a trap*) piéger.

3 **setup*** **n** *see* **setup**.

4 **setting-up** **n** *see* **setting 2**.

►**set upon** **vt fus** (*attack*) (*physically*) attaquer, se jeter sur; (*verbally*) attaquer.

sett [set] **n** a (*in roadway etc*) pavé *m*. b *[badger]* terrier *m*.

settee [se'tiː] **n** canapé *m*. **~ bed** canapé-lit *m*.

setter ['setəʳ] **n** a (*dog*) setter *m*, chien *m* d'arrêt. b (*person*) *[gems]* sertisseur *m*; *see* **type** *etc*.

setting ['setɪŋ] 1 **n** a *[jewel]* monture *f*; (*fig: framework, background*) cadre *m*.

b (*Mus*) *[poem etc]* mise *f* en musique. **~ for piano** arrangement *m* pour piano.

c (*NonC*) *[sun etc]* coucher *m*; (*act of placing*) mise *f*; *[machine etc]* réglage *m*; (*Typ*) composition *f*; (*Med*) *[fracture]* réduction *f*; *[limb, bone]* pose *f* d'un plâtre *or* d'une attelle (*of* à); (*hardening*) *[jam]* épaississement *m*; *[cement]* solidification *f*, durcissement *m*; *see* **set 5a**.

d (*Brit Scol*) répartition *f* par groupes de niveaux.

2 **comp** ►**setting lotion** lotion *f* *or* fixateur *m* pour mise en plis ►**setting ring** (*Phot*) bague *f* de réglage ►**setting-up** *[institution, company etc]* création *f*, lancement *m*; (*Typ*) composition *f*; **setting-up exercises** exercices *mpl* d'assouplissement.

settle¹ ['setl] **n** banc *m* à haut dossier.

settle² ['setl] 1 **vt** a (*place carefully*) placer *or* poser délicatement; (*stop wobbling*) stabiliser; (*adjust*) ajuster. **he ~d himself into the chair** il s'est installé confortablement *or* il s'est enfoncé dans le fauteuil; **to ~ an invalid for the night** installer un malade pour la nuit; **he ~d his daughter in a flat** il a installé sa fille dans un appartement; **she ~d her gaze on the painting** son regard se posa *or* s'arrêta sur le tableau; **to get ~d** s'installer.

b (*arrange, solve etc*) *question, matter* régler, décider, trancher; *argument* régler; *conditions, terms, details* régler, décider de; *date* fixer; *difficulty* résoudre, trancher; *problem* résoudre; *affairs* régler, mettre en ordre; *debt* rembourser, s'acquitter de; *bill, account* régler. **that ~s it** (*no more problem*) comme ça le problème est réglé; (*that's made my mind up*) ça me décide; **that's ~d then?** alors c'est convenu? *or* entendu?; **nothing is ~d** rien n'est décidé; **~ it among yourselves** arrangez ça entre vous; (*Jur*) **to ~ a case out of court** régler une affaire à l'amiable; **several points remain to be ~d** il reste encore plusieurs points à régler; (*Ftbl etc*) **the result was ~d in the first half** la première mi-temps a décidé du résultat; **I'll ~ him, I'll ~ his hash**‡ je vais lui régler son compte*; *see* **score**.

c (*calm; stabilize*) *nerves* calmer; *doubts* apaiser, dissiper. **he sprinkled water on the floor to ~ the dust** il a aspergé le sol d'eau pour faire retomber la poussière; **to ~ one's stomach** *or* **digestion** calmer *or* soulager les douleurs d'estomac; (*Brit*) **the weather is ~d** le temps est au beau fixe; **a man of ~d habits** un homme aux habitudes régulières.

d (*Jur*) **to ~ sth on sb** faire don de qch à qn; (*in will*) léguer qch à qn.

e *land* (*colonize*) coloniser; (*inhabit*) peupler.

2 vi a *[bird, insect]* se poser (*on* sur); *[dust etc]* retomber; *[sediment, coffee grounds etc]* se déposer; *[building]* se tasser; *[emotions]* s'apaiser; *[conditions, situation]* redevenir normal, s'arranger, se tasser*; *[snow]* tenir, ne pas fondre. *[dust, snow]* **to ~ on sth** couvrir qch; (*fig*) **when the dust has ~d we shall be able ...** quand les choses se seront arrangées *or* tassées* nous pourrons ...; **let the grounds ~ before you pour the coffee** laissez le marc se déposer avant de verser le café; **the wind ~d in the east** le vent a définitivement tourné à l'est; **the weather has ~d** le temps s'est mis au beau fixe; **to ~ into an armchair** s'installer confortablement *or* s'enfoncer dans un fauteuil; **to ~ into one's new job** s'habituer *or* se faire à son nouvel emploi; **to ~ into a routine** adopter une routine; **to ~ into a habit** prendre une habitude *or* un pli*; **a feeling of calm/gloom ~d on him** un sentiment de calme descendit sur lui/de tristesse s'abattit sur lui; **an expression of sorrow ~d on his face** une expression de tristesse apparut sur son visage; **her eyes ~d on him** son regard s'arrêta *or* se posa sur lui; **to ~ to sth** se mettre (sérieusement) à qch, s'appliquer à qch; **I can't ~ to anything** je suis incapable de me concentrer; **let your meal ~ before you go swimming** attends d'avoir digéré avant de te baigner; (*fig*) **things are settling into shape** cela commence à prendre tournure.

b (*go to live*) s'installer, se fixer; (*as colonist*) s'établir. **he ~d in London/in France** il s'est installé *or* fixé à Londres/en France; **the Dutch ~d in South Africa** les Hollandais se sont établis en Afrique du Sud.

c **to ~ with sb for the cost of the meal** régler qn pour le prix du repas, régler le prix du repas à qn; **I'll ~ for all of us** je vais régler la note (pour tout le monde); (*Jur*) **to ~ out of court** arriver à un règlement à l'amiable; **he ~d for £200** il s'est contenté de 200 livres, il a accepté 200 livres; **they ~d on £200** ils se sont mis d'accord sur 200 livres; **will you ~ for a draw?** accepteriez-vous un match nul?; **to ~ on sth** fixer son choix sur qch, opter *or* se décider pour qch.

►**settle down** 1 vi *[person]* (*in armchair etc*) s'installer (*in* dans); (*take up one's residence etc*) s'installer, se fixer; (*become calmer*) se calmer; (*after wild youth etc*) se ranger, s'assagir; *[excitement, emotions]* s'apaiser; *[situation, conditions]* s'arranger, redevenir normal, se tasser*. **he settled down to read the document** il s'est installé pour lire tranquillement le document; **to settle down to work** se mettre (sérieusement) au travail; **he has settled down in his new job** il s'est habitué *or* adapté *or* fait à son nouvel emploi; **to settle down at school** s'habituer *or* s'adapter à l'école; **it's time he got married and settled down** il est temps qu'il se marie (*subj*) et qu'il mène (*subj*) une vie stable; **he can't settle down anywhere** il n'arrive à se fixer nulle part; **he took some time to settle down in Australia/to civilian life** il a mis du temps à s'habituer *or* à s'adapter à la vie en Australie/à la vie civile; **when things have settled down again** quand les choses se seront calmées *or* seront redevenues normales *or* se seront tassées*.

2 vt sep installer. **to settle o.s. down in an armchair** s'installer confortablement dans un fauteuil; **he settled the child down on the settee** il a installé l'enfant sur le canapé.

►**settle in** vi (*get things straight*) s'installer; (*get used to things*) s'adapter. **the house is finished and they're quite settled in** la maison est terminée et ils sont tout à fait installés; **we took some time to settle in** nous avons mis du temps à nous adapter.

►**settle up** 1 vi régler (la note). **to settle up with sb** (*financially*) régler qn; (*fig*) régler son compte à qn*; **let's settle up** faisons nos comptes. 2 vt sep *bill* régler.

settled ['setld] 1 pret, ptp of **settle**[2] 2 adj a *land, area* (*colonized*) colonisé; (*inhabited*) habité, peuplé. b (*unchanging*) *social order, life, team* établi. c (*at ease: in new job, home etc*) **to feel ~** se sentir bien établi; **to get ~** s'installer.

settlement ['setlmənt] n a (*NonC*) *[question, argument, bill, debt]* règlement *m*; *[conditions, terms, details, date]* décision *f* (*of* concernant); *[problem]* solution *f*. **in ~ of an account** pour *or* en règlement d'un compte.

b (*agreement*) accord *m*. **to reach a ~** arriver à *or* conclure un accord; (*Pol etc*) **the chances of a ~** les chances d'un accord; *see* **negotiate, wage.**

c (*Jur*) donation *f* (*on sb* en faveur de qn); (*act of settling*) constitution *f*; (*income*) rente *f*; (*dowry*) dot *f*; *see* **marriage.**

d (*colonization*) colonisation *f*; (*colony*) colonie *f*; (*village*) village *m*, hameau *m*; (*homestead*) ferme *f or* habitation *f* (isolée); *see* **penal.**

e (*for social work: also* **~ house**) centre *m* d'œuvres sociales.

f (*Constr: of building etc*) tassement *m*.

settler ['setləʳ] n colon *m*, colonisateur *m*, -trice *f*.

settlor ['setləʳ] n (*Fin, Jur*) constituant *m*.

setup ['setʌp] n a (*way sth is organised*) **what's the ~?** comment est-ce que c'est organisé? *or* que ça marche?; **it's an odd ~** c'est une drôle de situation; **I don't like that ~ at all** je n'aime pas l'allure de tout ça*; **when did he join the ~?** quand est-ce qu'il est entré là-dedans? (*or* dans l'équipe? *or* dans l'affaire?). b (*esp US* *) (*sth incriminating arranged in advance*) coup *m* monté, machination *f*; (*trap*) piège *m*.

seven ['sevn] 1 adj sept *inv*. (*liter*) **the ~ seas** toutes les mers *or* tous les océans (du globe); **the ~ deadly sins** les sept péchés capitaux; (*US Univ*) **the S~ Sisters** le groupement d'universités du nord-est réservées aux jeunes filles; **the ~-year itch*** ≃ le démon de midi (*sentiment d'insatisfaction après 7 ans de mariage*). 2 n sept *m inv*; *for other phrases see* **six.** 3 comp ►**sevenfold** adj septuple ◊ adv au septuple ►**seven-league boots** bottes *fpl* de sept lieues. 4 pron sept *mfpl*. **there are ~** il y en a sept.

seventeen ['sevn'tiːn] 1 adj dix-sept *inv*. 2 n dix-sept *m inv*.

seventeenth ['sevn'tiːnθ] 1 adj dix-septième. 2 n dix-septième *mf*; (*fraction*) dix-septième *m*; *for phrases see* **sixth.**

seventh ['sevnθ] 1 adj septième. **S~ Day Adventist** adventiste *mf* du septième jour; (*US : Baseball*) **~ inning stretch** mi-temps *f*; *see* **heaven.** 2 n a (*thing, person*) septième *mf*; (*fraction*) septième *m*; *for other phrases see* **sixth.** b (*Mus*) septième *f*.

seventieth ['sevntɪɪθ] 1 adj soixante-dixième. 2 n soixante-dixième *mf*; (*fraction*) soixante-dixième *m*.

seventy ['sevntɪ] 1 adj soixante-dix *inv*. 2 n soixante-dix *m inv*. **he's in his seventies** il est septuagénaire, il a plus de soixante-dix ans; *for other phrases see* **sixty.**

sever ['sevəʳ] 1 vt *rope etc* couper, trancher; (*fig*) *relations* rompre, cesser; *communications* interrompre. **to ~ one's connections with sb** cesser toutes relations avec qn; (*Comm*) se dissocier de qn. 2 vi *[rope etc]* se rompre, casser, céder.

severability [ˌsevərə'bɪlɪtɪ] n (*Jur*) autonomie *f* des dispositions d'un contrat.

several ['sevrəl] 1 adj a (*in number*) plusieurs. **~ times** plusieurs fois. b (*separate*) différent, divers, distinct. **they went their ~ ways** (*lit*) ils sont partis chacun de son côté; (*fig*) la vie les a séparés; *see* **joint.** 2 pron plusieurs *mfpl*. **~ of them** plusieurs d'entre eux (*or* elles); **~ of us saw the accident** plusieurs d'entre nous ont vu l'accident, nous sommes plusieurs à avoir vu l'accident; **~ of us passed the exam** nous sommes plusieurs à avoir été reçus à l'examen.

severally ['sevrəlɪ] adv séparément, individuellement.

severance ['sevərəns] 1 n séparation *f* (*from* de); *[relations]* rupture *f*; *[communications]* interruption *f*. 2 comp ►**severance motion** (*US Jur*) demande *f* de procès séparés (par des co-accusés) ►**severance pay** (*Ind*) indemnité *f* de licenciement.

severe [sɪ'vɪəʳ] adj *person* sévère (*with, on, towards* pour, envers), strict, dur (*with, on, towards* avec, envers); *look, measure, criticism, blow, reprimand* sévère; *style, clothes* sévère, austère; *punishment* dur, sévère; *examination, test* dur, difficile; *competition* serré, acharné; *climate, winter* rigoureux, rude, dur; *cold, frost* intense; *pain* vif (*before noun*), violent; *wound, defeat* grave; *illness* grave, sérieux. **~ loss** (*of life, troops*) pertes *fpl* sévères *or* lourdes; (*bereavement*) perte cruelle; (*financial*) lourde perte; **a ~ attack of toothache** une rage de dents; (*Med*) **a ~ cold** un gros rhume.

severely [sɪ'vɪəlɪ] adv *punish* durement, sévèrement; *look, speak, criticize, reprimand* sévèrement; *injure, wound* grièvement; *dress, design* sévèrement, avec austérité. **~ ill** gravement malade; (*Med*) **~ subnormal** débile profond; **~ handicapped** (*physically*) handicapé moteur; (*mentally*) débile profond; **~ tried** durement éprouvé; **to leave ~ alone** *object* ne jamais toucher à; *politics, deal* ne pas du tout se mêler de; *person* ignorer complètement.

severity [sɪ'verɪtɪ] n (*see* **severe**) sévérité *f*; gravité *f*; rigueur *f*; violence *f*; dureté *f*; austérité *f*; difficulté *f*; intensité *f*.

Seville [sə'vɪl] n Séville. (*Brit*) **~ orange** orange amère, bigarade *f*.

sew [səʊ] pret **sewed**, ptp **sewn, sewed** 1 vt coudre. **to ~ a button on sth** coudre un bouton à qch; (*if button missing*) recoudre un bouton à qch. 2 vi coudre, faire de la couture.

►**sew on** vt sep *button etc* (*gen*) coudre; (*also* **sew back on**) recoudre.

►**sew up** vt sep *tear* recoudre; *seam* faire; *sack* fermer par une couture; *wound* (re)coudre, suturer. **to sew sth up in a sack** coudre qch dans un sac; **we've got the contract all sewn up*** le contrat est dans le sac* *or* dans la poche*; **the French market is pretty well sewn up*** le marché français est pratiquement verrouillé; **they've got the match all sewn up*** ils ont le match dans leur poche*; **it's all sewn up now*** l'affaire est dans le sac*.

sewage ['sjuːɪdʒ] 1 n (*NonC*) vidanges *fpl*. 2 comp ►**sewage disposal** évacuation *f* des vidanges ►**sewage farm, sewage works** champ *m* d'épandage.

sewer ['sjʊəʳ] n égout *m*. **~ gas** gaz *m* méphitique (d'égouts); **sewer rat** rat *m* d'égout; *see* **main.**

sewerage ['sjʊərɪdʒ] n a (*disposal*) évacuation *f* des vidanges; (*system*) (système *m* d')égouts *mpl*; (*cost of service*) frais *mpl* de vidange. b = **sewage.**

sewing ['səʊɪŋ] 1 n (*NonC*) (*activity, skill*) couture *f*; (*piece of work*) ouvrage *m*. **I like ~** j'aime coudre *or* la couture; **she put her ~ down** elle a posé son ouvrage. 2 comp ►**sewing basket** boîte *f* à couture ►**sewing bee**: (*esp US*) **they have a sewing bee on Thursdays** elles se réunissent pour coudre le jeudi ►**sewing cotton** fil *m* de coton, fil à coudre ►**sewing machine** machine *f* à coudre ►**sewing silk** fil *m* de soie.

sewn [səʊn] ptp of **sew.**

sex [seks] 1 n a sexe *m*. **the gentle** *or* **weaker ~** le sexe faible; *see* **fair**[1] *etc.*

b (*NonC: sexual act*) rapports *mpl* sexuels, relations *fpl* sexuelles. **to have ~ with sb** coucher avec qn*, avoir des rapports (sexuels) avec qn; **all he ever thinks about is ~*, he's got ~ on the brain*** il ne pense qu'au sexe *or* qu'à ça*; ~ **outside marriage** relations *fpl* extra-conjugales.

2 **comp** *discrimination, education, instinct* sexuel ►**sex act** acte sexuel ►**sex appeal** sex-appeal *m* ►**sex change (operation)** (opération *f* de) changement *m* de sexe; **to have** *or* **undergo a sex change (operation)** se faire opérer pour changer de sexe ►**sex clinic** clinique *f* de sexothérapie ►**sex-crazy*: he is sex-crazy** c'est un obsédé (sexuel) ►**sex drive** = **sex urge** ►**sex fiend** satyre *m** ►**sex hormone** hormone sexuelle ►**sex hygiene** (*US*) hygiène sexuelle ►**sex kitten*** minette *f* très sexy ►**sex-linked** (*Bio*) sex-linked *inv* ►**sex-mad*** = **sex-crazy*** ►**sex maniac** obsédé(e) sexuel(le) *m(f)* ►**sex object** objet sexuel ►**sex offender** délinquant(e) sexuel(le) *m(f)* ►**sex organ** organe sexuel ►**sex pot*** fille *f or* femme *f* très sexy* ►**sex-ridden** *person* qui ramène tout au sexe; *book* farci de sexe ►**sex shop** sex-shop *m*, boutique *f* porno *inv* ►**sex-starved*** (sexuellement) frustré*, refoulé* ►**sex symbol** sex-symbol *m* ►**sex therapist** sexothérapeute *mf* ►**sex therapy** sexothérapie *f* ►**sex urge** pulsion sexuelle.

3 **vt** *chick etc* déterminer le sexe de.

sexagenarian [ˌseksədʒɪˈnɛərɪən] **adj, n** sexagénaire *(mf)*.

Sexagesima [seksəˈdʒesɪmə] **n** sexagésime *f*.

sexed [sekst] **adj** a (*Bio, Zool*) sexué. b **to be highly ~** avoir une forte libido.

sexiness [ˈseksɪnɪs] **n** (*see* **sexy**) côté *m* sexy; côté sympa*.

sexism [ˈseksɪzəm] **n** sexisme *m*.

sexist [ˈseksɪst] **adj** sexiste.

sexless [ˈsekslɪs] **adj** a (*Bio etc*) asexué. b *person* frigide.

sexologist [sekˈsɒlədʒɪst] **n** sexologue *mf*.

sexology [sekˈsɒlədʒɪ] **n** sexologie *f*.

sexploitation* [ˌseksplɔɪˈteɪʃən] **n** utilisation *f* de l'image de la femme-objet dans la publicité *etc*.

sextant [ˈsekstənt] **n** sextant *m*.

sextet [seksˈtet] **n** sextuor *m*.

sexton [ˈsekstən] **n** sacristain *m*, bedeau *m*.

sextuplet [seksˈtjuːplɪt] **n** sextuplé(e) *m(f)*.

sexual [ˈseksjʊəl] **adj** sexuel. ~ **harassment** harcèlement *m* sexuel; ~ **intercourse** rapports sexuels.

sexuality [ˌseksjʊˈælɪtɪ] **n** sexualité *f*.

sexually [ˈseksjʊəlɪ] **adv** sexuellement. ~ **attractive** physiquement *or* sexuellement attirant; ~ **transmitted disease** maladie *f* sexuellement transmissible.

sexy [ˈseksɪ] **adj** a (*sexually exciting*) sexy* *inv*. b (*: *trendy, interesting*) sympa*.

Seychelles [seɪˈʃel(z)] **npl** Seychelles *fpl*.

sez⁑ [sez] = **says** (*see* **say**). (*iro*) ~ **you!** que tu dis!*

SF [esˈef] **n** (**abbr of science fiction**) S.F. *f*.

SFA [ˌesefˈeɪ] a (**abbr of Scottish Football Association**) fédération *f* écossaise de football. b (*Brit* ⁑) (**abbr of sweet Fanny Adams**) *see* **fanny**.

sgd (**abbr of signed**) *see* **sign 3a**.

Sgt. (**abbr of Sergeant**) (*on envelopes*) **Sgt. J. Smith** le Sergent J. Smith.

shabbily [ˈʃæbɪlɪ] **adv** *dress* pauvrement; *behave, treat* mesquinement, petitement.

shabbiness [ˈʃæbɪnɪs] **n** *[dress]* aspect élimé *or* râpé; *[person]* mise *f* pauvre; *[behaviour, treatment]* mesquinerie *f*, petitesse *f*.

shabby [ˈʃæbɪ] 1 **adj** *garment* râpé, usé, élimé; *furniture* pauvre, minable; *house, district* miteux; *person* miteux, pauvrement vêtu *or* mis; *behaviour, excuse* mesquin, méprisable. **a ~ trick** un vilain tour, une mesquinerie. 2 **comp** ►**shabby-genteel** pauvre mais digne ►**shabby-looking** de pauvre apparence.

shack [ʃæk] **n** cabane *f*, hutte *f*.

►**shack up**⁑ **vi** (*live*) crécher⁑, habiter. **to shack up with sb** se coller avec qn⁑; **to shack up together** avoir un collage⁑.

shackle [ˈʃækl] 1 **n: ~s** chaînes *fpl*, fers *mpl*; (*fig*) chaînes, entraves *fpl*. 2 **vt** mettre aux fers, enchaîner; (*fig*) entraver.

shad [ʃæd] **n, pl ~** *or* **~s** alose *f*.

shade [ʃeɪd] 1 **n** a (*NonC*) ombre *f*. **in the ~ of a tree** à l'ombre *or* sous l'ombrage d'un arbre; **40° in the ~** 40° à l'ombre; (*Art*) **light and ~** les clairs *mpl* et les ombres *or* les noirs *mpl*; (*fig*) **to put sth in(to) the ~** éclipser qch, rejeter qch dans l'ombre.

b *[colour]* nuance *f*, ton *m*; *[opinion]* nuance. **several ~s darker than that** plus sombre de plusieurs tons (que cela); **several ~s of red** plusieurs nuances *or* tons de rouge; **a new ~ of lipstick** un nouveau ton *or* une nouvelle couleur de rouge à lèvres; **a ~ of meaning** une nuance (*de sens*).

c (*fig*) **a ~ of vulgarity** un soupçon de vulgarité; **there's not a ~ of difference between them** il n'y a pas la moindre différence entre eux; **a ~ bigger** un tout petit peu *or* légèrement *or* un tantinet* plus grand.

d (*lamp~*) abat-jour *m inv*; (*eye~*) visière *f*; (*US: blind*) store *m*. (*US: sunglasses*) **~s** lunettes *fpl* de soleil.

e (*liter: ghost*) ombre *f*, fantôme *m*. **~s of Sartre** voilà qui fait penser à Sartre!, ça rappelle Sartre!

2 **vt** a *[trees, parasol]* donner de l'ombre à, ombrager, abriter du soleil; *[person] one's work etc* abriter du soleil *or* de la lumière. **~d place** endroit ombragé *or* à l'ombre; **he ~d his eyes with his hands** il s'abrita les yeux de la main; **to ~ a light** voiler une lampe.

b (*also* **~ in**) *painting etc* ombrer, nuancer; (*by hatching*) *outline, drawing etc* hachurer; (*colour in*) colorer (*in* en).

c *price* baisser *or* diminuer progressivement. **prices ~d for quantities** tarif *m* dégressif pour commandes en gros; **~d charges tarif** tarif dégressif.

3 **vi** (*also* **~ off**) a se dégrader (*into* jusqu'à), se fondre (*into* en). **the red ~s (off) into pink** le rouge se fond en rose.

b *[prices]* baisser.

►**shade off** 1 **vi** = **shade 3.** 2 **vt sep** *colours etc* estomper.

shadiness [ˈʃeɪdɪnɪs] **n** (*NonC*) (*shade*) ombre *f*; (*fig*) malhonnêteté *f*, caractère suspect *or* louche.

shading [ˈʃeɪdɪŋ] **n** (*NonC*) (*in painting etc*) ombres *fpl*, noirs *mpl*; (*crosshatching*) hachure(s) *f(pl)*.

shadow [ˈʃædəʊ] 1 **n** a ombre *f*. **in the ~ of the tree** à l'ombre de l'arbre; **in the ~ of the porch** dans l'ombre du porche; **he was standing in (the) ~** il se tenait dans l'ombre; (*darkness*) **the ~s** l'obscurité *f*, les ténèbres *fpl*; **I could see his ~ on the wall** je voyais son ombre (projetée) sur le mur; (*fig*) **he's afraid of his own ~** il a peur de son ombre; **to cast a ~ over sth** (*lit*) projeter une ombre sur qch; (*fig*) assombrir qch; **without a ~ of doubt** sans l'ombre d'un doute; **not a ~ of truth** pas le moindre atome de vérité; **he's only a ~ of his former self** il n'est plus que l'ombre de lui-même; **to have (dark) ~s under one's eyes** avoir les yeux cernés, avoir des cernes *mpl* sous les yeux; **five o'clock ~** (*on chin*) la barbe du soir; *see* **wear**.

b (*fig: detective etc*) personne *f* (*or* policier *m or* détective *m etc*) qui file quelqu'un. **to put a ~ on sb** faire filer qn, faire prendre qn en filature.

c (*inseparable companion*) ombre *f*.

2 **comp** ►**shadow-box** boxer à vide ►**shadow-boxing** (*Sport*) boxe *f* à vide; (*fig*) attaque *f* de pure forme, attaque purement rituelle ►**shadow cabinet** (*Brit Parl*) cabinet *m* fantôme (*de l'opposition*) ►**shadow Foreign Secretary:** (*Brit Parl*) **he is (the) shadow Foreign Secretary** il est le porte-parole de l'opposition pour les Affaires étrangères ►**shadow play** spectacle *m* d'ombres chinoises.

3 **vt** (*follow*) filer, prendre en filature.

shadowy [ˈʃædəʊɪ] **adj** *path* ombragé; *woods* sombre, ombreux; *outline, form, idea, plan* vague, indistinct.

shady [ˈʃeɪdɪ] **adj** a *spot* ombragé. b (*dishonest etc*) *person, business* louche, véreux.

shaft [ʃɑːft] **n** a (*stem etc*) *[arrow, spear]* hampe *f*; *[tool, golf club]* manche *m*; *[feather]* tuyau *m*; *[column]* fût *m*; *[bone]* diaphyse *f*; (*on cart, carriage, plough etc*) brancard *m*; (*Aut, Tech*) arbre *m*; *see* **cam** *etc*. b (*liter: arrow*) flèche *f*. **Cupid's ~s** les flèches de Cupidon; (*fig*) **~ of light** rayon *m or* trait *m* de lumière; **~ of lightning** éclair *m*; **~ of sarcasm/wit** trait de raillerie/d'esprit. c (*vertical enclosed space*) *[mine]* puits *m*; *[lift, elevator]* cage *f*; (*for ventilation*) puits, cheminée *f*.

shag¹ [ʃæg] **n** (*tobacco*) tabac très fort.

shag² [ʃæg] **n** (*Orn*) cormoran huppé.

shag³ [ʃæg] 1 **n** (*Brit*) **to have a ~**⁑⁑ baiser⁑⁑. 2 **vt** (*Brit*⁑⁑*: have sex with*) baiser ⁑⁑. 3 **vi** a (*Brit*⁑⁑*: have sex*) baiser⁑⁑. b (*US*) **to ~ off**⁑ se tirer⁑, foutre le camp⁑.

shag⁴* [ʃæg] **vt** (*US: retrieve*) *ball* récupérer.

shag⁵ [ʃæg] **n** (*napped fabric*) laine *f* à longues mèches. **~ (pile) carpet/rug** moquette *f*/tapis *m* à longues mèches.

shagged⁑ [ʃægd] **adj** (*also* **~ out**) éreinté, crevé*.

shaggy [ˈʃægɪ] **adj** *hair, beard* hirsute; *mane* broussailleux; *eyebrows* hérissé; *animal* à longs poils rudes; *carpet, rug* à longs poils. (*fig*) **~ dog story** histoire *f* sans queue ni tête.

shagreen [ʃæˈgriːn] **n** chagrin *m* (*cuir*).

Shah [ʃɑː] **n** schah *m*.

shake [ʃeɪk] (**vb: pret shook, ptp shaken**) 1 **n** secousse *f*, ébranlement *m*; (*quiver*) tremblement *m*. **to give sth a ~** secouer qch; **with a ~ of his head** avec un hochement de tête *or* en hochant la tête en signe de refus; **with a ~ in his voice** la voix tremblante, d'une voix tremblante; **to be all of a ~*** être tout tremblant; **to have the ~s*** (*from nerves*) avoir la tremblote*; (*from drink*) trembler, être agité de tremblements; **I'll be there in a ~*** j'arrive dans un instant *or* une seconde; **in a brace of ~s*, in two ~s (of a lamb's tail)*** en un clin d'œil, en moins de deux*; **he/it is no great ~s*** il/cela ne casse rien*; **he's no great ~s* at swimming** *or* **as a swimmer** il n'est pas fameux *or* il ne casse rien* comme nageur; *see* **hand, milk** *etc*.

2 **comp** ►**shakedown** (*bed*) lit *m* de fortune; (*US* ⁑*: search*) fouille *f*; (*US* ⁑*: extortion*) extorsion *f*, chantage *m* ►**shake-out** (*US Econ*) tassement *m* ►**shake-up** grande réorganisation, grand remaniement.

3 **vt** a *duster, rug, person* secouer; *dice, bottle, medicine, cocktail* agiter; *house, windows etc* ébranler, faire trembler; (*brandish*) *stick etc* brandir. "**~ the bottle**" "agiter avant emploi"; **to ~ one's head** (*in refusal etc*) dire *or* faire non de la tête, hocher la tête en signe de refus; (*at bad news etc*) secouer la tête; **he shook his finger at me** (*playfully, warningly*) il m'a fait signe du doigt; (*threateningly*) il m'a menacé du doigt; **to ~ one's fist/stick at sb** menacer qn du poing/de sa canne; **to ~**

hands with sb, ~sb's hand serrer la main à qn; **they shook hands** ils se sont serré la main; **they shook hands on it** ils se sont serré la main en signe d'accord; (*fig*) ~ **a leg!*** remue-toi!, remue tes abattis!*; *[person, animal]* **to** ~ **o.s.** *or* **itself** se secouer; (*to remove sand, water etc*) s'ébrouer.

b **to** ~ **apples from a tree** secouer un arbre pour en faire tomber les pommes; **he shook the sand out of his shoes** il a secoué ses chaussures pour en vider le sable; **he shook 2 aspirins into his hand** il a fait tomber 2 comprimés d'aspirine dans sa main; **he shook pepper on to his steak** il a saupoudré son bifteck de poivre; **he shook himself free** il s'est libéré d'une secousse.

c (*fig: weaken, impair*) *confidence, belief, resolve* ébranler; *opinion* affecter; *health* ébranler, compromettre; *reputation* nuire à, compromettre. **even torture could not** ~ **him** même la torture ne l'a pas ébranlé.

d (*fig*) (*amaze*) stupéfier; (*disturb*) secouer, bouleverser. **this will** ~ **you!** tu vas en être soufflé!*, ça va t'en boucher un coin!‡; **4 days which shook the world** 4 jours qui ébranlèrent le monde; **he needs to be** ~**n out of his smugness** il faudrait qu'il lui arrive (*subj*) quelque chose qui lui fasse perdre de sa suffisance; *see also* **shaken**.

e (*US* *) = **shake off b**.

4 vi a *[person, hand, table]* trembler; *[building, windows, walls]* trembler, être ébranlé; *[leaves, grasses]* trembler, être agité; *[voice]* trembler, trembloter. **he was shaking with laughter, his sides were shaking** il se tordait (de rire); **to** ~ **with cold** trembler de froid, grelotter; **to** ~ **with fear** trembler de peur; (*fig*) **to** ~ **in one's shoes** avoir une peur bleue*, avoir la frousse*; **the walls shook at the sound** le bruit a ébranlé les murs.

b (~ *hands*) **they shook on the deal** ils ont scellé leur accord d'une poignée de main; **(let's)** ~ **on it!** tope là!, topez là!

►**shake down** 1 vi a (*: *settle for sleep*) se coucher, se pieuter‡. **I can shake down anywhere** je peux pioncer‡ *or* me pieuter‡ n'importe où.

b (*learn to work etc together*) **they'll be a good team once they've shaken down** ils formeront une bonne équipe quand ils se seront habitués *or* faits les uns aux autres.

c (*settle : contents of packet etc*) se tasser.

2 vt sep a **to shake down apples from a tree** faire tomber des pommes en secouant l'arbre, secouer l'arbre pour en faire tomber les pommes; **to shake down the contents of a packet** secouer un paquet pour en tasser le contenu.

b (*US* ‡) **to shake sb down for £50** soutirer *or* faire cracher‡ 50 livres à qn.

c (*US* ‡: *frisk, search*) *person* fouiller.

3 **shakedown** n *see* **shake 2**.

►**shake off** vt sep a **to shake off dust/sand/water from sth** secouer la poussière/le sable/l'eau de qch; (*fig, liter*) **he shook off the dust of that country from his feet** en quittant ce pays il secoua la poussière de ses sandales. b (*fig: get rid of*) *cold, cough* se débarrasser de; *yoke etc* se libérer de, s'affranchir de; *habit* se défaire de, perdre; *pursuer* se débarrasser de, semer*.

►**shake out** 1 vt sep a *flag, sail* déployer; *blanket* bien secouer; *bag* vider en secouant. **she picked up the bag and shook out its contents** elle a pris le sac et l'a vidé en le secouant; **she shook 50p out of her bag** elle a secoué son sac et en a fait tomber 50 pence. b (*Ind*) dégraisser. 2 **shake-out** n *see* **shake 2**.

►**shake up** 1 vt sep a *pillow, cushion* secouer, taper; *bottle, medicine* agiter. b (*fig: disturb*) bouleverser, secouer. **he was considerably shaken up by the news** il a été très secoué *or* il a été bouleversé par la nouvelle, la nouvelle lui a fait un coup*; *see also* **shook**. c (*fig: rouse, stir*) *person* secouer, secouer les puces à*; *firm, organization* réorganiser de fond en comble. 2 **shake-up** n *see* **shake 2**.

shaken ['ʃeɪkn] adj (*upset*) secoué, (*stronger*) bouleversé; (*amazed*) stupéfié.

shaker ['ʃeɪkəʳ] n (*for cocktails*) shaker *m*; (*for dice*) cornet *m*; (*for salad*) panier *m* à salade; *see* **flour** *etc*.

Shakespearean, Shakespearian [ʃeɪks'pɪərɪən] adj shakespearien.

shakily ['ʃeɪkɪlɪ] adv (*gen*) en tremblant; *walk* d'un pas mal assuré, à pas chancelants; *write* d'une main tremblante; *say, reply* d'une voix tremblante *or* chevrotante, (*nervously*) d'une voix mal assurée. **he got** ~ **to his feet** il s'est levé tout tremblant.

shakiness ['ʃeɪkɪnɪs] n (*NonC*) *[hand]* tremblement *m*; *[table etc]* manque *m* de stabilité *or* solidité; *[building]* manque de solidité; *[voice]* chevrotement *m*; (*fig*) *[position]* instabilité *f*; *[health]* faiblesse *f*; *[knowledge]* insuffisance *f*, faiblesse.

shako ['ʃækəʊ] n, pl ~**s** *or* ~**es** s(c)hako *m*.

shaky ['ʃeɪkɪ] adj *hand* tremblant, tremblotant; *voice* tremblant, chevrotant, (*nervous*) mal assuré; *writing* tremblé; *table, building* branlant, peu solide; (*fig*) *health* chancelant, faible; *business, firm, deal* à l'avenir incertain. **I feel a bit** ~ je ne me sens pas solide sur mes jambes, je me sens faible; (*fig*) **my Spanish is very** ~ mes notions d'espagnol sont chancelantes; **his memory is rather** ~ sa mémoire n'est pas très sûre, sa mémoire est assez mauvaise.

shale [ʃeɪl] n argile schisteuse, schiste argileux. ~ **oil** huile *f* de schiste.

shall [ʃæl] modal aux vb (2nd pers sg **shalt**††; neg **shall not** often abbr to **shan't**; (*see also* **should**) a (*in 1st person fut tense*) **I shall** *or* **I'll arrive on Monday** j'arriverai lundi; **we shall not** *or* **we shan't be there before 6 o'clock** nous n'y serons pas avant 6 heures; **I'll come in a minute** je vais venir *or* je viens dans un instant.

b (*in 1st person questions*) **shall I open the door?** dois-je ouvrir la porte?, voulez-vous que j'ouvre (*subj*) la porte?, j'ouvre la porte?*; **I'll buy 3, shall I?** je vais en acheter 3, n'est-ce pas? *or* d'accord?*; **let's go in, shall we?** entrons, voulez-vous?; **shall we ask him to come with us?** si on lui demandait de venir avec nous?

c (*indicating command, guarantee etc*) **it shall be done this way and no other** cela sera fait *or* doit être fait de cette façon et d'aucune autre; (*Bible*) **thou shalt not kill** tu ne tueras point; **you shall obey me** vous m'obéirez, vous devez m'obéir; **you shan't have that job!** tu n'auras pas ce poste!

shallot [ʃə'lɒt] n (*Brit*) échalote *f*.

shallow ['ʃæləʊ] 1 adj a *water, dish* peu profond. ~ **breathing** respiration superficielle. b (*fig*) *mind, character, person* superficiel, sans profondeur; *conversation* futile, superficiel. **to be** ~**-minded** manquer de profondeur d'esprit. 2 n: ~**s** bas-fond *m*, haut-fond *m*.

shallowness ['ʃæləʊnɪs] n (*lit*) manque *m* de profondeur; (*fig*) *[person]* esprit superficiel; *[character]* manque de profondeur; *[conversation]* futilité *f*; *[knowledge]* caractère superficiel.

shalt†† [ʃælt] 2nd pers sg of **shall**.

sham [ʃæm] 1 n (*pretence*) comédie *f*, feinte *f*; (*person*) imposteur *m*; (*jewellery, furniture*) imitation *f*. **this diamond is a** ~ ce diamant est faux *or* de l'imitation *or* du toc*; **the election was a** ~ l'élection n'était qu'une comédie; **his promises were a** ~ ses promesses n'étaient que du vent; **the whole organization was a** ~ l'entière organisation n'était qu'une imposture.

2 adj *jewellery* faux (*f* fausse), en toc*; *piety* feint; *title* faux; *illness* feint, simulé; *fight* simulé. ~ **Louis XVI** de l'imitation *or* du faux Louis XVI.

3 vt feindre, simuler. **to** ~ **ill** *or* **illness** feindre *or* simuler une maladie, faire semblant d'être malade; **she** ~**med dead** elle a fait la morte, elle a fait semblant d'être morte.

4 vi faire semblant, jouer la comédie. **he is only** ~**ming** il fait seulement semblant.

shaman ['ʃæmən] n chaman *m*.

shamanism ['ʃæməˌnɪzəm] n chamanisme *m*.

shamateur* ['ʃæmətəʳ] n (*Sport*) sportif *m*, -ive *f* prétendu(e) amateur (*qui se fait rémunérer*).

shamble ['ʃæmbl] vi marcher en traînant les pieds. **to** ~ **in/out/away** *etc* entrer/sortir/s'éloigner *etc* en traînant les pieds.

shambles ['ʃæmblz] n (*NonC*) (*gen : muddle*) confusion *f*, désordre *m*, pagaille* *f*; (*stronger: after battle, disaster*) scène *f* *or* spectacle *m* de dévastation. **what a** ~! quelle (belle) pagaille!*; **his room was (in) a** ~ sa chambre était sens dessus dessous *or* tout en l'air; **the match degenerated into a** ~ le match s'est terminé dans la pagaille*; **your essay is a** ~* votre dissertation est un fouillis sans nom*; **it's a bloody** ~‡ c'est complètement bordélique‡.

shambolic* [ʃæm'bɒlɪk] adj bordélique‡.

shame [ʃeɪm] 1 n a (*NonC*) (*feeling*) honte *f*, confusion *f*; (*humiliation*) honte. **to my eternal** *or* **lasting** ~ à ma très grande honte; **he hung his head in** ~ il a baissé la tête de honte *or* de confusion; **to bring** ~ **(up)on sb** être *or* faire la honte de qn, déshonorer qn; **to put sb/sth to** ~ faire honte à qn/qch; ~ **on you!** quelle honte!, c'est honteux de votre part!; **the** ~ **of it!** quelle honte!, c'est honteux!; **the** ~ **of that defeat** la honte de cette défaite, cette défaite déshonorante; **the street is the** ~ **of the town** cette rue déshonore la ville; **she has no sense of** ~ elle ne sait pas ce que c'est que la honte, elle n'a aucune pudeur; **he has lost all sense of** ~ il a perdu toute honte, il a toute honte bue (*liter*); *see* **cry, crying**.

b (*NonC*) dommage *m*. **it is a** ~ c'est dommage (*that* que + *subj*, *to do* de faire); **it's a dreadful** ~! c'est tellement dommage!; **it would be a** ~ **if he were to refuse** *or* **if he refused** il serait dommage qu'il refuse (*subj*); **what a** ~! (quel) dommage!; **what a** ~ **he isn't here** (quel) dommage qu'il ne soit pas ici.

2 vt (*bring disgrace on*) couvrir de honte, faire la honte de, déshonorer; (*make ashamed*) faire honte à, humilier, mortifier. **to** ~ **sb into doing sth** obliger qn à faire qch en lui faisant honte, piquer l'amour-propre de qn pour qu'il fasse qch; **to be** ~**d into doing sth** faire qch par amour-propre *or* pour conserver son amour-propre.

shamefaced ['ʃeɪmfeɪst] adj (*ashamed*) honteux, penaud; (*confused*) confus, timide. **he was rather** ~ **about it** il en était tout honteux *or* penaud.

shamefacedly ['ʃeɪmfeɪsɪdlɪ] adv (*see* **shamefaced**) d'un air honteux *or* penaud; avec confusion, timidement.

shamefacedness ['ʃeɪmfeɪstnɪs] n (*see* **shamefaced**) air honteux *or* penaud; confusion *f*, timidité *f*.

shameful ['ʃeɪmfʊl] adj honteux, scandaleux. **it's** ~ **to spend so much on drink** c'est une honte de tant dépenser pour la boisson.

shamefully ['ʃeɪmfəlɪ] adv *behave* honteusement; *bad, late* scandaleusement, abominablement. **he is** ~ **ignorant** il est d'une ignorance crasse, il est si ignorant que c'en est une honte.

shameless ['ʃeɪmlɪs] adj a (*unashamed*) *person* éhonté, effronté; *behaviour* effronté, impudent. **he is a ~ liar** c'est un menteur éhonté, c'est un effronté menteur, il ment sans vergogne; **he is quite ~ about it** il n'en a pas du tout honte. b (*immodest*) *person* sans pudeur, impudique; *act* impudique.

shamelessly ['ʃeɪmlɪslɪ] adv (*see* **shameless**) effrontément, sans honte, sans vergogne; sans pudeur, de façon impudique.

shamelessness ['ʃeɪmlɪsnɪs] n (*see* **shameless**) effronterie *f*, impudence *f*; impudeur *f*.

shaming ['ʃeɪmɪŋ] adj mortifiant, humiliant. **it's too ~!** quelle humiliation!

shammy* ['ʃæmɪ] n (*also* **~ leather**) peau *f* de chamois.

shampoo [ʃæm'puː] 1 n (*product, process*) shampooing *m*. **~ and set** shampooing (et) mise *f* en plis; **to give o.s. a ~** se faire un shampooing, se laver la tête; *see* **dry**. 2 vt *person* faire un shampooing à; *hair, carpet* shampouiner, shampooiner. **to have one's hair ~ed and set** se faire faire un shampooing (et) mise en plis.

shamrock ['ʃæmrɒk] n trèfle *m* (*emblème national de l'Irlande*).

shamus* ['ʃeɪməs] n (*policeman*) flic* *m*; (*detective*) détective *m* privé.

shandy ['ʃændɪ] n (*Brit*) panaché *m*.

Shanghai ['ʃæŋ'haɪ] n Shanghai.

shanghai [ʃæŋ'haɪ] vt (*Naut* ††) embarquer de force comme membre d'équipage, shangailler (*rare*). (*fig*) **to ~ sb into doing*** contraindre qn à faire.

Shangri-la ['ʃæŋrɪ'lɑː] n paradis *m* terrestre.

shank [ʃæŋk] n (*Anat*) jambe *f*; *[horse]* canon *m*; (*Culin*) jarret *m*; (*handle etc*) manche *m*. (*fig*) **to go** *or* **ride on S~s' pony** *or* **mare** aller à pied, prendre le train onze*.

shan't [ʃɑːnt] = **shall not**; *see* **shall**.

shantung [ˌʃæn'tʌŋ] n shant(o)ung *m*.

shanty[1] ['ʃæntɪ] n (*hut*) baraque *f*, cabane *f*, bicoque* *f*. **~town** bidonville *m*.

shanty[2] ['ʃæntɪ] n (*Brit*) (*also* **sea ~**) chanson *f* de marins.

SHAPE [ʃeɪp] n (abbr of **Supreme Headquarters Allied Powers Europe**) *quartier général des forces alliées de l'OTAN en Europe*.

shape [ʃeɪp] 1 n a (*form, outline*) forme *f*. **what ~ is the room?, what is the ~ of the room?** quelle est la forme de la pièce?, de quelle forme est la pièce?; **stamps of all ~s** des timbres de toutes formes; **of all ~s and sizes** de toutes les formes et de toutes les tailles; **children of all ~s and sizes** des enfants d'allures diverses; **they come in all ~s and sizes** (*lit*) il y en a de toutes sortes et de toutes les tailles; (*fig*) il y en a une variété infinie; **his nose is a funny ~** son nez a une drôle de forme; **this hat has lost its ~** ce chapeau s'est déformé; **it's like a mushroom in ~** cela a la forme d'un champignon, cela ressemble à un champignon; **it's triangular in ~** c'est en forme de triangle, c'est triangulaire; **in the ~ of a cross** en forme de croix; **a prince in the ~ of a swan** un prince sous la forme d'un cygne; **a monster in human ~** un monstre à figure humaine; **I can't stand racism in any ~ or form** je ne peux pas tolérer le racisme sous quelque forme que ce soit; (*lit, fig*) **to take the ~ of sth** prendre la forme de qch; **the news reached him in the ~ of a telegram from his brother** c'est par un télégramme de son frère qu'il a appris la nouvelle; (*fig*) **perks in the ~ of luncheon vouchers** des avantages sous la forme de chèques-restaurant; **that's the ~ of things to come** cela donne une idée de ce qui nous attend; **who knows what ~ the future will take?** qui sait comment se présentera l'avenir?; *[dress, vase, project]* **to take ~** prendre forme *or* tournure; **to be in good ~** *[person]* être en (bonne) forme; *[business etc]* marcher bien; **in poor ~** *person, business* mal en point; **he carved the wood into ~** il a façonné le bois; **he beat the silver into ~** il a façonné l'argent; (*fig*) **to knock** *or* **lick* into ~** *assistant* former, dresser*; *soldier* entraîner, dresser*; **to knock** *or* **lick* sth into ~** arranger qch, rendre qch présentable; **he managed to knock** *or* **lick* the team into ~** il a réussi à mettre l'équipe au point; **to get (o.s.) into ~** (re)trouver la forme; **to keep o.s. in good ~** rester *or* se maintenir en forme; **to get one's ideas into ~** formuler *or* préciser ses idées.

b (*human figure*) forme *f*, figure *f*; (*silhouette*) forme, silhouette *f*; (*thing dimly seen*) forme vague *or* imprécise; (*ghost etc*) fantôme *m*, apparition *f*. **a ~ loomed up out of the darkness** une forme imprécise surgit de l'obscurité.

c (*for jellies etc*) moule *m*; (*in hat-making*) forme *f*.

d (*Culin*) **rice ~** gâteau *m* de riz; **meat ~** pain *m* de viande.

2 vt *clay* façonner, modeler; *stone, wood* façonner, tailler; (*fig*) *statement, explanation* formuler. **he ~d the clay into a tree, he ~d a tree out of the clay** il a façonné l'argile en arbre; **oddly ~d** d'une forme bizarre; **a nicely ~d stone** une pierre d'une jolie forme; (*Phot*) **~d canvas** détourage *m*; **~d like a ball/a pole** *etc* en forme de boule/de piquet *etc* **to ~ sb's ideas/character** modeler *or* former les idées/le caractère de qn; **to ~ sb's life** déterminer le destin de qn; **to ~ the course of events** influencer la marche des événements.

3 vi (*fig*) prendre forme *or* tournure; *see* **shape up**.

►**shape up** vi a (*get on*) progresser. (*progress*) *[project]* prendre forme *or* tournure. **our plans are shaping up well** nos projets prennent tournure *or* s'annoncent bien *or* sont en bonne voie; **things are shaping up well** tout marche bien, on avance; **how is he shaping up?** comment s'en sort-il?*, est-ce qu'il se fait?; **he is shaping up nicely as a goalkeeper** il est en train de devenir un bon gardien de but; **shape up!*** secoue-toi un peu!*; (*US*) **shape up or ship out!*** rentre dans le rang ou fiche le camp!* b (*esp US : slim etc*) retrouver la forme.

-shaped ['ʃeɪpt] adj ending in comps en forme de. **heart-shaped** en forme de cœur; *see* **egg** *etc*.

shapeless ['ʃeɪplɪs] adj *mass, lump* informe; *dress, hat, shoes* informe, sans forme. *[clothes, shoes]* **to become ~** se déformer, s'avachir.

shapelessness ['ʃeɪplɪsnɪs] n absence *f* de forme.

shapeliness ['ʃeɪplɪnɪs] n belles proportions, beauté *f* (de forme), galbe *m*.

shapely ['ʃeɪplɪ] adj *vase, building, person* bien proportionné, beau (*f* belle). **a ~ woman** une femme bien faite *or* bien tournée *or* bien roulée*; **a ~ pair of legs** des jambes bien galbées *or* bien faites.

shard [ʃɑːd] n tesson *m* (de poterie).

share [ʃɛəʳ] 1 n a part *f*. **here's your ~** voici votre part, voici ce qui vous est dû; **my ~ is £5** (*receiving*) ma (quote-)part s'élève à *or* j'ai droit à *or* je dois recevoir 5 livres; (*paying*) ma (quote-)part s'élève à *or* je dois (payer) 5 livres; **his ~ of the inheritance** sa part *or* sa portion de l'héritage; **his ~ of** *or* **in the profits** sa part des bénéfices; **he will get a ~ of** *or* **in the profits** il aura part aux bénéfices; **he has a ~ in the business** il est l'un des associés dans cette affaire; **he has a half-~ in the firm** il possède la moitié de l'entreprise; **to have a ~ in doing sth** contribuer à faire qch; **he had some ~ in it** il y était pour quelque chose; **I had no ~ in that** je n'y étais pour rien; **to take a ~ in sth** participer à qch; **to pay one's ~** payer sa (quote-)part; **to bear one's ~ of the cost** participer aux frais; **he wants more than his ~** il veut plus qu'il ne lui est dû, il tire la couverture à lui (*fig*); **he isn't doing his ~** il ne fournit pas sa part d'efforts; **he's had more than his (fair) ~ of misfortune** il a eu plus que sa part de malheurs; **to take one's ~ of the blame** accepter sa part de responsabilité; **he does his full ~ of work** il fournit toute sa (quote-)part de travail; **they went ~s in the cost of the holiday** ils ont payé les vacances à deux (*or* trois *etc*), ils ont partagé le coût des vacances entre eux; *see* **fair**[1], **lion**.

b (*Brit St Ex*) action *f*. **he has 500 ~s in an oil company** il a 500 actions d'une compagnie de pétrole; *see* **ordinary, preference, qualifying** *etc*.

c (*Agr: plough~*) soc *m* (*de charrue*).

2 comp ►**share capital** (*Fin*) capital *m* social ►**share certificate** (*Brit Fin etc*) titre *m or* certificat *m* d'actions ►**sharecrop** (*US Agr*) vt cultiver (comme métayer) ◊ vi travailler comme métayer ►**sharecropper** (*US Agr*) métayer *m*, -ère *f* ►**sharecropping** métayage *m* ►**shareholder** (*Brit Fin etc*) actionnaire *mf* ►**share index** (*St Ex*) indice *m* de la Bourse ►**share option** (*St Ex*) *possibilité de prise de participation des employés dans leur entreprise* ►**share-out** partage *m*, distribution *f* ►**share premium** (*St Ex*) prime *f* d'émission ►**share prices** (*St Ex*) prix *mpl* des actions ►**shareware** (*Comput*) shareware *m*.

3 vt a (*gen*) partager; *room, prize* partager (*with sb* avec qn); *expenses, work* partager (*with sb* avec qn), participer à; *profits* avoir part à; *sorrow, joy* partager, prendre part à; *responsibility, blame, credit* partager. **they ~d the money (between them)** ils se sont partagé l'argent; (*in school etc*) **you can ~ Anne's book** tu peux suivre avec Anne; (*Comput*) **~d facility** installation *f* commune; (*Telec*) **~d line** ligne partagée; **they ~ certain characteristics** ils ont certaines caractéristiques en commun; **I do not ~ that view** je ne partage pas cette opinion; **I ~ your hope that ...** j'espère avec *or* comme vous que ... .

b (*also* **~ out**) partager, répartir (*among, between* entre).

4 vi partager. (*loc*) **~ and ~ alike** à chacun sa part; **to ~ in** *sorrow, joy* partager, prendre part à; *responsibility* partager; *profits* avoir part à; *expenses, work* participer à, partager.

►**share out** 1 vt sep = **share 3b**. 2 **share-out** n *see* **share 2**.

shark [ʃɑːk] n (*fish : gen*) requin *m*; (*generic name*) squale *m*; (*fig pej: sharp businessman*) requin *m*; (*swindler*) escroc *m*, aigrefin *m*. **~skin** (*Tex*) peau *f* d'ange; *see* **bask** *etc*.

sharon ['ʃærən] n (*also* **~ fruit**) charon *m or* sharon *m*.

sharp [ʃɑːp] 1 adj a *razor, knife* tranchant, bien affilé, bien aiguisé; *point* aigu (*f* -guë), acéré; *teeth* pointu; *fang* acéré; *needle, pin, nail* pointu, acéré; *pencil* bien taillé, pointu. **take a ~ knife** prenez un couteau qui coupe bien *or* bien tranchant; **the ~ edge** *[blade, knife]* le côté coupant, le (côté) tranchant; *[tin etc]* le bord tranchant *or* coupant.

b (*pointed etc*) *nose, chin* pointu; *features* anguleux; *corner, angle* aigu (*f* -guë); *bend in road* aigu, brusque. **the car made a ~ turn** la voiture a tourné brusquement.

c (*abrupt*) *descent* raide; *fall in price, change* brusque, soudain.

d (*well-defined*) *outline* net, distinct; (*TV*) *contrast, picture* net; *difference, contrast* marqué, prononcé.

e (*shrill, piercing*) *cry, voice* perçant, aigu (*f* -guë).

f (*Mus*) **C ~** do dièse; **that note was a little ~** cette note était un peu trop haute.

g (*harsh, bitter*) *wind, cold* pénétrant, vif; *frost* fort; *pain* violent, cuisant, vif; *smell, taste, cheese, sauce, perfume* piquant, âpre (*pej*), âcre (*pej*); *words, retort* cinglant, mordant; *rebuke* sévère; *tone* acerbe. **to have a ~ tongue** avoir la langue acérée.

h (*brisk etc*) *pace, quarrel* vif. **that was ~ work!** ça n'a pas traîné!*, ça n'a pas pris longtemps!, ça a été vite fait!; **look** *or* **be ~ (about it)!** fais vite!, dépêche-toi!, grouille-toi!‡

i (*acute*) *eyesight* perçant; *hearing, smell* fin; *intelligence, mind* délié, vif, pénétrant; *person* vif, malin (*f* -igne), dégourdi*; *child* vif, éveillé. **to have ~ ears** avoir l'ouïe fine; **to have ~ eyes** avoir une vue perçante; (*fig*) **he has a ~ eye for a bargain** il sait repérer *or* flairer une bonne affaire; **to keep a ~ look-out for sb/sth** guetter qn/qch avec vigilance *or* d'un œil attentif; **he is as ~ as a needle** (*clever*) il est malin comme un singe; (*missing nothing*) il est très perspicace, rien ne lui échappe.

j (*pej: unscrupulous*) *person* peu scrupuleux, malhonnête. **~ practice** procédés déloyaux *or* (*stronger*) malhonnêtes.

2 adv a (*Mus*) *sing, play* trop haut.

b (*abruptly*) *stop* brusquement, net. **turn** *or* **take ~ left** tournez à gauche à angle droit *or* tout à fait à gauche.

c (*punctually*) **at 3 o'clock ~** à 3 heures précises *or* sonnantes, à 3 heures pile.

3 n (*Mus*) dièse *m*.

4 comp ►sharp-eared (*fig*) à l'ouïe fine **►sharp-eyed** à qui rien n'échappe **►sharp-faced, sharp-featured** aux traits anguleux **►sharpshooter** tireur *m* d'élite **►sharp-sighted** = **sharp-eyed** **►sharp-tempered** coléreux, soupe au lait* *inv* **►sharp-tongued** qui a la langue acérée **►sharp-witted** à l'esprit vif *or* prompt.

sharpen ['ʃɑ:pən] **1 vt** (*often* **~ up**) **a** *blade, knife, razor, tool* aiguiser, affûter, affiler; *scissors* aiguiser; *pencil* tailler. **the cat was ~ing its claws on the chair leg** le chat aiguisait ses griffes *or* se faisait les griffes sur le pied de la chaise. **b** (*fig*) *outline,* (*TV*) *contrast, picture, focus* rendre plus net; *difference, contrast* rendre plus marqué; *appetite* aiguiser; *desire* exciter; *pain* aggraver, aviver; *feeling* aviver; *intelligence* affiner, rendre plus fin. **to ~ one's wits** se dégourdir. **c** (*esp Brit Mus*) diéser. **2 vi** *[voice]* devenir plus perçant; *[desire, pain]* s'accroître, devenir plus vif, s'aviver.

sharpener ['ʃɑ:pnəʳ] **n** (*knife ~*) (*on wall, on wheel etc*) aiguisoir *m* à couteaux, affiloir *m*; (*long, gen with handle*) fusil *m* à repasser les couteaux; (*pencil ~*) taille-crayons *m inv*.

sharpening ['ʃɑ:pnɪŋ] **n** aiguisage *m*, affilage *m*, affûtage *m*.

sharper ['ʃɑ:pəʳ] **n** escroc *m*, filou *m*, aigrefin *m*; (*card ~*) tricheur *m*, -euse *f* (*professionnel(le)*).

sharpie‡ ['ʃɑ:pɪ] **n** (*US*) (*alert person*) petit(e) futé(e) *m(f)*; (*crook*) filou *m*, escroc *m*.

sharpish ['ʃɑ:pɪʃ] **1 adj** (*quite sharp*) assez tranchant *or* aigu *or* pointu *etc; see* **sharp 1**. **2 adv** (*: *quickly*) en vitesse*.

sharply ['ʃɑ:plɪ] **adv a** (*lit*) **~ pointed** *knife, scissors* à pointe effilée *or* acérée; *nose* pointu, en quart de Brie (*hum*).

b (*abruptly*) *change, rise* brusquement, soudain; *turn* brusquement, court; *stop* brusquement, net. (*Aut*) **to corner ~** prendre un virage à la corde; **the road goes up/down ~** la route monte brusquement *or* raide/ descend brusquement *or* en pente abrupte.

c (*harshly*) *criticize, reproach* sévèrement, vivement; *observe, comment, retort* sèchement, avec brusquerie, d'un ton acerbe. **to speak ~ to sb about sth** faire des observations sévères *or* parler sans ménagements à qn au sujet de qch.

d (*distinctly*) *show up, stand out* nettement; *differ* nettement, clairement. **~ in focus** bien net; **the black contrasts ~ with the white** le noir forme un contraste très net avec le blanc.

e (*acutely, alertly*) *say, ask* vivement, avec intérêt. **he looked at me ~** il m'a regardé soudain avec intérêt.

f (*quickly*) rapidement, en vitesse*.

sharpness ['ʃɑ:pnɪs] **n a** *[razor, knife]* tranchant *m*; *[pencil, needle, nail]* pointe aiguë. **b** (*fig*) *[turn, bend]* angle *m* brusque; *[outline etc]* netteté *f*; *[pain]* violence *f*, acuité *f*; *[criticism, reproach, rebuke]* sévérité *f*, tranchant *m*; *[tone, voice]* brusquerie *f*, aigreur *f*; *[taste, smell]* piquant *m*, âcreté *f* (*pej*); *[wind, cold]* âpreté *f*. **there's a ~ in the air** il fait frais *or* frisquet*, le fond de l'air* est frais.

shat*‡ [ʃæt] **pret, ptp of shit***‡.

shatter ['ʃætəʳ] **1 vt** *window, door* fracasser (*against* contre); *health* ruiner, briser; *self-confidence* briser; *faith* détruire; (*fig*) *hopes, chances* ruiner, détruire; *career* briser. **the sound ~ed the glasses** le bruit a brisé les verres; **to ~ sb's nerves** démolir les nerfs de qn; (*fig*) **she was ~ed by his death** sa mort l'a anéantie; *see also* **shattered**. **2 vi** *[glass, windscreen, cup]* voler en éclats; *[box etc]* se fracasser (*against* contre). **3 comp ►shatterproof glass** verre *m* sécurit *inv* ®.

shattered ['ʃætəd] **adj** (*grief-stricken*) anéanti, consterné; (*aghast, overwhelmed*) bouleversé, complètement retourné; (*: *exhausted*) éreinté*.

shattering ['ʃætərɪŋ] **adj** (*fig*) *attack* destructeur (*f* -trice); *defeat* écrasant, accablant; *news* bouleversant, renversant*; *experience, disappointment* bouleversant; (*exhausting*) *day, journey* épuisant, éreintant. **this was a ~ blow to our hopes/plans** nos espoirs/nos projets ont été gravement compromis.

shave [ʃeɪv] (**vb: pret shaved, ptp shaved, shaven††**) **1 n: to give sb a ~** raser qn; **to have** *or* **give o.s. a ~** se raser, se faire la barbe; (*fig*) **to have a close** *or* **narrow ~** l'échapper belle, y échapper de justesse; **that was a close** *or* **narrow ~!** il était moins une!*, on l'a échappé belle!; *see* **after** *etc*. **2 vt** *person, face, legs etc* raser; *wood* raboter, planer; (*fig: brush against*) raser, frôler. (*fig*) **to ~ the price of sth** faire un rabais sur le prix de qch. **3 vi** se raser.

►shave off vt sep a to shave off one's beard se raser la barbe. **b the joiner shaved some of the wood off** le menuisier a enlevé un peu du bois au rabot; (*fig*) **to shave off a few pounds** faire un rabais de quelques livres.

shaven ['ʃeɪvn] **1** (††) **ptp of shave**. **2 adj** rasé; *see* **clean** *etc*.

shaver ['ʃeɪvəʳ] **n a** rasoir *m* électrique. **b (young) ~***† gosse* *m*, gamin *m*.

Shavian ['ʃeɪvɪən] **adj** à la *or* de George Bernard Shaw.

shaving ['ʃeɪvɪŋ] **1 n a** (*piece of wood, metal etc*) copeau *m*. **b** (*NonC: with razor etc*) rasage *m*. **~ is a nuisance** c'est embêtant* de se raser. **2 comp ►shaving brush** blaireau *m* **►shaving cream** crème *f* à raser **►shaving soap** savon *m* à barbe **►shaving stick** bâton *m* de savon à barbe.

shawl [ʃɔ:l] **n** châle *m*.

she [ʃi:] **1 pers pron a** (*stressed, unstressed*) elle. **~ has come** elle est venue; **here ~ is** la voici; **~ is a doctor** elle est médecin, c'est un médecin; **~ is a small woman** elle est petite; **it is ~** c'est elle; (*frm*) **if I were ~** si j'étais elle, si j'étais à sa place; **SHE didn't do it** ce n'est pas elle qui l'a fait; **younger than ~** plus jeune qu'elle; **~'s a fine boat/car** c'est un beau bateau/une belle voiture.

b (+ *rel pron*) celle. **~ who** *or* **that can ...** celle qui peut ... .

2 comp (*gen: with names of animals*) **she-** femelle (*after noun*) **►she-bear** ourse *f* **►she-cat** (*fig*) mégère *f*, furie *f* **►she-devil** (*fig*) démon *m*, furie *f* **►she-goat** chèvre *f*; *see* **wolf** *etc*.

3 n (*) femelle *f*. **it's a ~** (*animal*) c'est une femelle; (*baby*) c'est une fille.

shea ['ʃɪə] **n** karité *m*.

sheaf [ʃi:f] **n, pl sheaves** *[corn]* gerbe *f*; *[papers]* liasse *f*; *[arrows]* faisceau *m*.

shear [ʃɪəʳ] (**vb: pret sheared, ptp sheared** *or* **shorn**) **1 npl: ~s** (*Horticulture*) cisaille(s) *f(pl)*; (*Sewing, gen*) grands ciseaux; **a pair of ~s** une paire de cisailles; *see* **pruning** *etc*. **2 vt** *sheep* tondre. (*fig*) **shorn of** dépouillé de.

►shear off 1 vi *[branch etc]* partir, se détacher. **2 vt sep** *wool* tondre; *projecting part, nail* faire partir, arracher; *branch* couper, élaguer. **the ship had its bow shorn off in the collision** dans la collision l'avant du navire a été emporté.

►shear through vt fus *paper, cloth* trancher; *wood, metal* fendre; (*fig*) *the waves, the crowd* fendre.

shearer ['ʃɪərəʳ] **n** (*person*) tondeur *m*, -euse *f*; (*machine*) tondeuse *f*.

shearing ['ʃɪərɪŋ] **n** (*process*) tonte *f*. (*wool etc*) **~s** tonte.

sheath [ʃi:θ] **1 n, pl ~s** [ʃi:ðz] **a** *[dagger]* gaine *f*; *[sword]* fourreau *m*; *[scissors etc]* étui *m*; *[electric cable, flex]* gaine; (*Bio*) gaine, enveloppe *f*; (*Bot*) enveloppe; (*Brit: contraceptive*) préservatif *m*. **b** (*also* **~ dress**) fourreau *m* (*robe*). **2 comp ►sheath knife** couteau *m* à gaine.

sheathe [ʃi:ð] **vt a** *sword, dagger* rengainer; *cable* gainer; *[cat etc] claws* rentrer. **b** (*cover*) recouvrir, revêtir (*with* de).

sheaves [ʃi:vz] **npl of sheaf**.

Sheba ['ʃi:bə] **n** Saba. **the Queen of ~** la reine de Saba.

shebang* [ʃə'bæŋ] **n** (*US*) **the whole ~** toute l'affaire, tout le tremblement*.

shebeen [ʃɪ'bi:n] **n** (*Ir*) débit *m* de boissons clandestin.

shed¹ [ʃed] **n a** (*gen*) abri *m*; (*smallish*) abri, cabane *f*; (*larger*) remise *f*, resserre *f*; (*large, open-sided: Rail, Agr etc*) hangar *m*; (*lean-to*) appentis *m*. **bicycle ~** abri à vélos, remise pour les vélos; **garden ~** abri de jardin, cabane; *see* **cow, tool** *etc*. **b** (*part of factory*) atelier *m*.

shed² [ʃed] **pret, ptp shed vt a** (*lose, get rid of*) *petals, leaves, fur, horns* perdre; *shell* dépouiller; *[truck] load* déverser, perdre; (*Space: rocket, section of craft*) larguer, éjecter; *tears* verser, répandre; *coat etc* enlever, se dépouiller de (*frm*); *unwanted thing* se débarrasser de, se défaire de; *assistant, employee* se défaire de, se séparer de. *[dog, cat]* **to ~ hairs** perdre ses poils; **the snake ~s its skin** le serpent mue; **to ~ blood** (*one's own*) verser son sang; (*other people's*) faire couler le sang, verser *or* répandre le sang; **I'm trying to ~ 5 kilos** j'essaie de perdre 5 kilos; **to ~ water** ne pas laisser pénétrer l'eau.

b (*send out*) *light* répandre, diffuser; *warmth, happiness* répandre. **to ~ light on** (*lit*) éclairer; (*fig*) *sb's motives etc* jeter de la lumière sur; *problem* éclaircir; *little-known subject* éclairer.

she'd [ʃi:d] = **she had, she would;** *see* **have, would**.

sheen [ʃi:n] **n** (*on silk*) lustre *m*, luisant *m*; (*on hair*) brillant *m*, éclat *m*. **to take the ~ off sth** (*lit*) délustrer qch; (*fig*) diminuer l'éclat de qch.

sheep [ʃi:p] **1 n, pl inv** mouton *m* (*animal*); (*ewe*) brebis *f*. **they followed him like a lot of ~** ils l'ont suivi comme des moutons, ils l'ont suivi comme les moutons de Panurge; (*fig*) **to make ~'s eyes at** faire les yeux doux à; (*fig*) **we must divide** *or* **separate the ~ from the goats** il ne faut pas mélanger les torchons et les serviettes* (*fig*); *see* black, lost *etc*.

2 comp ►**sheep-dip** bain *m* parasiticide (*pour moutons*) ►**sheepdog** chien *m* de berger (*see* **trial**) ►**sheep farm** ferme *f* d'élevage de moutons ►**sheep farmer** éleveur *m* de moutons ►**sheep farming** élevage *m* de moutons ►**sheepfold** parc *m* à moutons, bergerie *f* ►**sheepherder** (*US*) berger *m*, gardien *m* de moutons ►**sheepshank** (*Naut*) jambe *f* de chien ►**sheepshearer** (*person*) tondeur *m*, -euse *f* (de moutons); (*machine*) tondeuse *f* (à moutons) ►**sheepshearing** (*NonC*) tonte *f* (des moutons) ►**sheepskin** *see* **sheepskin** ►**sheep track** piste *f* à moutons ►**sheep-worrying** harcèlement *m* des moutons (*par des chiens*).

sheepish ['ʃi:pɪʃ] adj penaud.

sheepishly ['ʃi:pɪʃlɪ] adv d'un air penaud.

sheepishness ['ʃi:pɪʃnɪs] n timidité *f*, air penaud.

sheepskin ['ʃi:pskɪn] 1 n a peau *f* de mouton. b (*US Univ *: fig*) peau *f* d'âne, diplôme *m*. 2 comp *waistcoat etc* en peau de mouton ►**sheepskin jacket** canadienne *f*.

sheer¹ [ʃɪəʳ] 1 adj a (*utter*) *chance, kindness, malice* pur; *impossibility, necessity* absolu. **it was ~ mud/rock** *etc* ce n'était que de la boue/du roc *etc;* **by (a) ~ accident** tout à fait par hasard, par pur hasard; **in ~ amazement** absolument stupéfait, bouche bée de stupéfaction; **~ carelessness** pure étourderie, étourderie pure et simple; **in ~ desperation** en désespoir de cause; **by ~ hard work** uniquement grâce au travail *or* aux efforts; **it's ~ madness** c'est de la folie pure *or* douce*; **it's ~ robbery** c'est du vol manifeste; **a ~ waste of time** une véritable perte de temps, une perte de temps absolue.

b *stockings, material* extra-fin.

c *rock, cliff* à pic, abrupt. **a ~ drop** *or* **fall** un à-pic.

2 adv à pic, abruptement.

sheer² [ʃɪəʳ] (*Naut: swerve*) 1 n embardée *f*. 2 vi faire une embardée.

►**sheer off** vi *[ship]* faire une embardée; (*gen*) changer de direction.

sheet [ʃi:t] 1 n a (*on bed*) drap *m*; (*shroud*) linceul *m*; (*dust ~*) housse *f*; (*tarpaulin*) bâche *f*; *see* **water, white** *etc*.

b (*piece*) *[plastic, rubber]* morceau *m*; *[paper, notepaper]* feuille *f*; *[iron, steel]* tôle *f*; *[glass, metal etc]* feuille, plaque *f*. **an odd** *or* **loose ~** une feuille volante; (*Comm*) **order ~** bulletin *m* de commande; **baking ~** plaque à gâteaux *or* de four; *see* **balance** *etc*.

c (*expanse: of water, snow etc*) étendue *f*. **a ~ of ice** (*large*) une plaque *or* nappe de glace; (*thin film*) une couche de glace; (*on road*) une plaque de verglas; **a ~ of flame** un rideau de flammes; **the rain came down in ~s** il pleuvait à torrents.

d (*periodical*) périodique *m*; (*newspaper*) journal *m*.

e (*Naut*) écoute *f*; *see* **main** *etc*.

2 comp ►**sheet anchor** (*Naut*) ancre *f* de veille; (*fig*) ancre de salut ►**sheet lightning** (*NonC*) éclair *m* en nappe(s) ►**sheet metal** (*NonC*) (*gen*) tôle *f*; (*US Aut*) carosserie *f*; **sheet metal (work)shop** tôlerie *f* ►**sheet music** (*NonC*) partitions *fpl*.

Sheherazade [ʃəˌherə'zɑ:də] n Schéhérazade *f*.

sheik(h) [ʃeɪk] n a cheik *m*; *see* **oil**. b (*US fig*) séducteur *m*, Roméo *m*.

sheik(h)dom ['ʃeɪkdəm] n tribu *f or* territoire *m* sous l'autorité d'un cheik.

shekel ['ʃekl] n (*modern*) shekel *m*; (*Hist: Bible etc*) sicle *m*; (*US fig *: coin*) pièce *f* de monnaie. (*fig*) **~s*** fric* *m*, sous* *mpl*; (*US fig*) **to be in the ~s**‡ être en fonds, avoir du fric*.

sheldrake ['ʃelˌdreɪk], **shelduck** ['ʃelˌdʌk] n tadorne *m* de Bellon.

shelf [ʃelf], pl **shelves** 1 n a étagère *f*, planche *f*, rayon *m*; (*in shop*) rayon; (*in oven*) plaque *f*. **a ~ of books** un rayon de livres; **a set of shelves** une étagère, un rayonnage; (*Comm*) **there are more luxury goods on the shelves nowadays** il y a plus d'articles de luxe sur les rayons *or* dans les magasins aujourd'hui; **to buy sth off the ~** acheter qch tout fait (*see also* **off**); (*fig: postpone*) **to leave sth on the ~** laisser qch de côté *or* au placard*; (*fig: woman*) **to be (left) on the ~** monter en graine (*fig*), être laissée pour compte; *see* **book** *etc*.

b (*edge*) (*in rock*) rebord *m*, saillie *f*; (*underwater*) écueil *m*; *see* **continental**.

2 comp ►**shelf life** (*Comm*) durée *f* de conservation avant vente ►**shelf mark** (*Libraries*) cote *f*.

shell [ʃel] 1 n a *[egg, nut, oyster, snail etc]* coquille *f*; *[tortoise, lobster, crab]* carapace *f*; (*on beach, in collection etc*) coquillage *m*; *[peas]* cosse *f*. (*lit, fig*) **to come out of/go back into one's ~** sortir de/rentrer dans sa coquille; (*US*) **"clam on the ~"** ≃ "dégustation de clams"; *see* **cockle** *etc*.

b *[building]* carcasse *f*; *[ship]* coque *f*. (*Culin*) **pastry ~** fond *m* de tarte.

c (*Mil*) obus *m*; (*US: cartridge*) cartouche *f*.

d (*racing boat*) outrigger *m*.

2 comp *necklace, ornament etc* de *or* en coquillages► (*Mil*) **shellfire** bombardement *m* par obus, pilonnage *m* d'artillerie ►**shellfish** pl inv (*lobster, crab*) crustacé *m*; (*mollusc*) coquillage *m*; (*pl: Culin*) fruits *mpl* de mer ►**shell game** (*US*) (*trick*) tour *m* de passe-passe (pratiqué avec des coques de noix); (*fig : fraud*) escroquerie *f* ►**shellproof** (*Mil*) blindé ►**shell shock** (*Med*) psychose *f* traumatique, commotion cérébrale (*à la suite d'éclatements d'obus*) ►**shell-shocked** (*Med*) commotionné (par des éclatements d'obus); (*fig*) abasourdi; **shell-shocked ex-serviceman** commotionné *m* de guerre ►**shellsuit** survêtement *m*.

3 vt a *peas* écosser; *nut* décortiquer, écaler; *oyster* écailler, retirer de sa coquille; *crab, prawn, shrimp, lobster* décortiquer; *see also* **shelled**.

b (*Mil*) bombarder (d'obus).

►**shell out*** 1 vi casquer‡, payer. **to shell out for sth** payer qch, casquer‡ pour qch. 2 vt sep cracher‡, aligner*.

she'll [ʃi:l] = **she will;** *see* **will**.

shellac [ʃə'læk] 1 n (*NonC*) (gomme *f*) laque *f*. 2 vt laquer; (*US fig *: beat*) battre à plates coutures.

shelled [ʃeld] adj *nut, prawn* décortiqué; *pea* écossé.

shelling ['ʃelɪŋ] n (*NonC: Mil*) bombardement *m* (par obus), pilonnage *m* d'artillerie.

shelter ['ʃeltəʳ] 1 n a (*NonC*) abri *m*, couvert *m*. **under the ~ of** sous l'abri de; **to take ~, to get under ~** se mettre à l'abri *or* à couvert; **to take ~ from/under** s'abriter de/sous; **to seek/offer ~** chercher/offrir un abri (*from* contre); **she gave him ~ for the night** elle lui a donné (un) asile pour la nuit; **we must find ~ for the night** nous devons trouver un abri pour cette nuit; (*Brit*) **S~** *organisation bénévole qui cherche à loger les sans-logis*.

b (*hut etc*) (*on mountain*) abri *m*, refuge *m*; (*for sentry*) guérite *f*; (*bus ~*) abribus *m*; (*air-raid ~*) abri.

2 vt a (*protect*) (*from wind, rain, sun, shells etc*) abriter (*from* de), protéger (*from* de, contre); (*from blame etc*) protéger (*from* de); *criminal etc* protéger; (*hide*) cacher. **~ed from the wind** à l'abri du vent; *see also* **sheltered**.

b (*give lodging to*) recueillir, donner un asile *or* le couvert à; *fugitive etc* donner asile à, recueillir.

3 vi s'abriter (*from* de, *under* sous), se mettre à l'abri *or* à couvert.

sheltered ['ʃeltəd] adj *place* abrité; (*fig*) *life* bien protégé, retiré; *conditions, environment* protégé; (*Econ*) *industry* protégé (*contre la concurrence étrangère*). (*Ind*) **~ workshop** centre *m* d'aide, atelier protégé (*réservé aux travailleurs handicapés*); (*for elderly, disabled*) **~ housing** foyers-logements *mpl* (*dans une résidence pour personnes âgées ou handicapées*); **he had a ~ childhood** son enfance s'est écoulée à l'abri des soucis, on lui a fait une enfance sans soucis.

shelve [ʃelv] 1 vt a (*fig: postpone*) *plan, project, problem* mettre en sommeil *or* en suspens. b (*lit*) *cupboard, wall* garnir de rayons *or* d'étagères. 2 vi (*slope: also ~* **down**) descendre en pente douce.

shelves [ʃelvz] npl of **shelf**.

shelving ['ʃelvɪŋ] n (*NonC*) rayonnage(s) *m(pl)*, étagères *fpl*; *[project etc]* mise *f* en sommeil *or* en suspens.

shemozzle* [ʃə'mɒzl] n (*Brit*) bagarre* *f*, chamaillerie* *f*. **there was quite a ~!** ça a bardé!‡

shenanigan(s)* [ʃə'nænɪgən(z)] n (*NonC*) (*trickery*) manigances *fpl*, entourloupettes* *fpl*; (*rowdy fun*) chahut *m*.

shepherd ['ʃepəd] 1 n a berger *m*; (*Rel*) pasteur *m*. (*Rel*) **the Good S~** le bon Pasteur. b (*also ~* **dog**) chien *m* de berger. 2 comp ►**shepherd boy** jeune pâtre *m* (*liter*), jeune berger *m* ►**shepherd's check** = **shepherd's plaid** ►**shepherd's crook** houlette *f* ►**shepherd's pie** (*esp Brit Culin*) hachis *m* Parmentier ►**shepherd's plaid** plaid noir et blanc ►**shepherd's purse** (*Bot*) bourse-à-pasteur *f*. 3 vt *sheep* garder, soigner. **the dog ~ed the flock into the field** le chien a fait entrer le troupeau dans le pré; (*fig*) **to ~ sb in** faire entrer qn; **to ~ sb out** escorter qn jusqu'à la porte; **he ~ed us round Paris** il nous a escortés *or* nous a guidés *or* nous a servi de guide dans Paris.

shepherdess ['ʃepədɪs] n bergère *f*.

sherbet ['ʃɜ:bət] n a (*Brit*) (*fruit juice*) jus *m* de fruit glacé; (*fizzy*) boisson gazeuse; (*powder*) poudre acidulée *or* de sorbet. b (*US: water ice*) sorbet *m*.

sheriff ['ʃerɪf] 1 n a (*Brit Jur*) shérif *m*. b (*US*) shérif *m*, ≃ capitaine *m* de gendarmerie. 2 comp ►**Sheriff Court** (*Scot*) ≃ tribunal *m* de grande instance; (*US*) ≃ tribunal de police.

Sherpa ['ʃɜ:pə] n, pl **~s** *or* **~** sherpa *m*.

sherry ['ʃerɪ] n xérès *m*, sherry *m*.

she's [ʃi:z] = **she is, she has;** *see* **be, have**.

Shetland ['ʃetlənd] 1 n (*also* **the ~ Islands** *or* **Isles, the ~s**) les îles *fpl* Shetland. 2 adj (*gen*) *people, customs, village* shetlandais; *sweater* en shetland. 3 comp ►**Shetland pony** poney shetlandais ►**Shetland pullover** pull-over *m* en shetland ►**Shetland wool** shetland *m*.

Shetlander ['ʃetləndəʳ] n Shetlandais(e) *m(f)*.

shew [ʃəʊ] vti = **show**.

shhh [ʃ:] excl chut!

Shiah ['ʃi:ə] 1 n a (*doctrine*) chi'isme *m*. b (*follower: also ~* **Muslim**) chi'ite *mf*. 2 adj chi'ite.

shiatsu [ˌʃi:'ætsu:] n shiatsu *m*.

shibboleth ['ʃɪbəleθ] n (*Bible*) schibboleth *m*; (*fig*) (*doctrine*) doctrine *f or* principe *m* arbitraire; (*password*) mot *m* de passe; (*characteristic*) caractéristique *f*, signe distinctif.

shield [ʃi:ld] 1 n (*gen*) bouclier *m*; (*not round*) écu *m*; (*Her*) écu, blason *m*; (*on gun*) bouclier; (*on or around machine*) écran *m* de protection, tôle protectrice; (*against radiation*) écran; (*fig*) (*safeguard*) sauvegarde *f*, bouclier (*liter*) (*against* contre); (*person*) protecteur *m*, -trice *f*. (*Space*) **thermal ~** bouclier thermique; *see* **dress, wind[1]** *etc*. 2 **vt** protéger (*from* de, contre); *fugitive, criminal* protéger, couvrir; (*Tech*) *machine operator* protéger; *gun, machine* fixer un bouclier *or* un écran de protection à. **to ~ one's eyes from the sun** se protéger les yeux du soleil; **to ~ sb with one's body** faire à qn un bouclier *or* un rempart de son corps.

shieling ['ʃiːlɪŋ] **n** (*Scot: hut etc*) petite cabane de berger.

shift [ʃɪft] 1 **n** a (*change*) changement *m* (*in* de), modification *f* (*in* de); (*Ling*) mutation *f*; (*movement: of cargo, load etc*) déplacement *m* (*in* de). **there has been a ~ in policy/attitude** la politique/l'attitude a changé; **a sudden ~ in policy/attitude** un retournement *or* un bouleversement de la politique/de l'attitude; **~ of emphasis** changement *m* d'éclairage; **a sudden ~ in the wind** une saute de vent; **he asked for a ~ to London/to another department/to an easier job** il a demandé à être muté à Londres/affecté à une autre section/affecté à un emploi plus facile; **it's time he made a ~** il est temps qu'il change (*subj*) d'horizon; *see* **scene, vowel** *etc*.

b (*Ind etc*) (*period of work*) poste *m*, période *f* de travail d'une équipe; (*people*) poste, équipe (*de relais*). **he works ~s, he's on ~s*** il travaille par roulement, il fait un travail posté; **they used to work a 10-hour ~ in that factory** ils avaient des postes de 10 heures dans cette usine; **I work an 8-hour ~** je fais les trois-huit, je fais un poste de 8 heures; **this factory operates on 3 ~s per 24-hour period** dans cette usine ils font les trois-huit *or* 3 équipes *or* 3 postes se relaient sur 24 heures; **to be on day/night ~** être (au poste) de jour/de nuit; **which ~ do you prefer?** quel poste préférez-vous?; **the next ~ were late in coming on** le poste suivant *or* l'équipe suivante était en retard pour prendre le relais *or* la relève; **they worked in ~s to release the injured man** ils se sont relayés pour (essayer de) libérer le blessé; *see* **day, night** *etc*.

c (*expedient*) expédient *m*, stratagème *m*, truc* *m*, ruse *f* (*pej*), tour *m* (*pej*). **to make ~ with sth/sb** se contenter de *or* s'accommoder de *or* se débrouiller avec qch/qn; **to make ~ without sth/sb** se passer de qch/qn, se débrouiller* sans qch/qn; **to make ~ to do** se débrouiller* pour faire; **as a last desperate ~ he ...** en désespoir de cause il ... .

d (*US Aut: gear~*) (changement *m* de) vitesse *f*.

e (*straight dress*) robe droite; (*†: woman's slip*) chemise *f*.

f (*Comput*) décalage *m*.

2 **comp** ►**shift key** [*typewriter*] touche *f* de majuscule ►**shift register** (*Comput*) registre *m* à décalage ►**shift work** (*Brit Ind etc*) travail *m* posté *or* par relais *or* par roulement; **to do shift work, to be on shift work** travailler par roulement, faire un travail posté ►**shift worker** ouvrier posté.

3 **vt** a (*move*) *object, furniture* déplacer, changer de place; *one's head, arm etc* bouger, remuer; *chair, car etc* déplacer, changer de place, bouger; (*Theat*) *scenery* changer; *screw* débloquer, faire bouger; *lid, top, cap* faire bouger; *stain* enlever, faire disparaître; *employee* (*to another town*) muter (*to* à); (*to another job, department*) affecter (*to* à); *pupil* transférer, faire passer (*to another class* dans une autre classe); (*fig*) *blame, responsibility* rejeter (*on, on to* sur). **he ~ed his chair nearer the fire** il a approché sa chaise du feu; **to ~ sth in/out/away** *etc* rentrer/sortir/écarter qch; **we couldn't ~ him (from his opinion)** nous n'avons pas réussi à le faire changer d'avis *or* à l'ébranler; **I can't ~ this cold*** je n'arrive pas à me débarrasser de ce rhume.

b (*change; exchange*) changer de. (*lit, fig*) **to ~ position** changer de position; (*US Aut*) **to ~ gears** changer de vitesse, passer les vitesses; *see* **ground[1]**.

4 **vi** a (*go*) aller; (*move house*) déménager; (*change position, stir*) [*person, animal, planet etc*] changer de place *or* de position, bouger; [*limb*] remuer, bouger; [*wind*] tourner; [*ballast, cargo, load*] se déplacer; [*opinions, ideas*] changer, se modifier; (*fig: change one's mind*) changer d'avis; [*stain*] s'en aller, disparaître. **he ~ed over to the window** il s'est approché de la fenêtre; **~ a minute to let me past** pousse-toi *or* bouge-toi* une minute pour me laisser passer; **~ off the rug** va-t-en du tapis; (*on seat etc*) **can you ~ down *or* up *or* along a little?** pourriez-vous vous pousser un peu?; **he has ~ed to London** (*gen*) il est à Londres maintenant; (*moved house*) il a déménagé à Londres; (*changed job*) il a trouvé un nouvel emploi à Londres; (*within same firm*) il a été muté à Londres; **he has ~ed into another class** il a été transféré *or* il est passé dans une autre classe; (*Theat etc*) **the scene ~s to Paris** la scène est maintenant à Paris; (*Aut*) **to ~ into second (gear)** passer la deuxième; **he won't ~** (*lit*) il ne bougera pas; (*fig : change opinion*) il est inébranlable, il ne bougera pas; **the government has not ~ed from its original position** le gouvernement n'a pas modifié sa première position; (*go fast*) **he/that car certainly ~s*** il/cette voiture ne traîne pas! *or* ne lanterne pas! *or* fonce!; (*hurry*) **come on, ~!*** allez, remue-toi!* *or* grouille-toi!‡

b **to ~ for o.s.** se débrouiller* tout seul.

►**shift about, shift around** 1 **vi** a (*move house*) déménager souvent; (*change job*) changer souvent d'emploi; (*within same firm*) être muté plusieurs fois. b (*fidget*) bouger, remuer. 2 **vt sep** *furniture etc* déplacer, changer de place.

►**shift away vi** (*move house*) déménager. **they've shifted away from here** ils n'habitent plus par ici.

►**shift back** 1 **vi** a (*move house*) **they've shifted back to London** ils sont retournés *or* revenus habiter (à) Londres. b (*withdraw*) (se) reculer. 2 **vt sep** *chair etc* reculer.

►**shift over vi** s'écarter, se déplacer, se pousser. **shift over!** pousse-toi!

shiftily ['ʃɪftɪlɪ] **adv** (*see* **shifty**) sournoisement; de façon évasive.

shiftiness ['ʃɪftɪnɪs] **n** (*see* **shifty**) manque *m* de franchise, caractère *m or* aspect *m* louche, sournoiserie *f*; caractère évasif.

shifting ['ʃɪftɪŋ] **adj** *scene, opinion* changeant; *sand* mouvant.

shiftless ['ʃɪftlɪs] **adj** (*idle*) fainéant, paresseux, flemmard*; (*unresourceful*) manquant de ressources.

shiftlessness ['ʃɪftlɪsnɪs] **n** manque *m* de ressources.

shifty ['ʃɪftɪ] **adj** *person, behaviour* louche, qui manque de franchise, sournois; *answer* évasif; *look* fuyant. **~-eyed** aux yeux fuyants.

shiitake ['ʃiːˌtækɪ] **n**: **~ mushroom** champignon *m* shiitake (*sorte de champignon japonais*).

Shiite, Shi'ite ['ʃiːaɪt] (*also* **~ Muslim**) **n, adj** chi'ite (*mf*).

shiksa, shikse(h) ['ʃɪksə] **n** (*US: often pej*) jeune fille *f* non juive.

shill [ʃɪl] **n** (*US: at fairground etc*) compère *m*.

shillelagh [ʃə'leɪlə] **n** (*Ir*) gourdin irlandais.

shilling ['ʃɪlɪŋ] **n** (*Brit*) shilling *m* (*ancienne pièce valant le vingtième de la livre*).

shilly-shally ['ʃɪlɪˌʃælɪ] 1 **vi** hésiter; (*deliberately*) tergiverser, atermoyer. **stop ~ing!** décide-toi enfin! 2 **n** = **shilly-shallying**.

shilly-shallying ['ʃɪlɪˌʃælɪɪŋ] **n** (*NonC*) hésitations *fpl*, valse-hésitation *f*; (*deliberate*) tergiversations *fpl*, atermoiements *mpl*.

shimmer ['ʃɪmər] 1 **vi** [*satin, jewels*] chatoyer; [*water, lake, heat haze, road surface*] miroiter. **the moonlight ~ed on the lake** le clair de lune se reflétait sur le lac *or* faisait miroiter le lac. 2 **n** [*satin, jewels*] chatoiement *m*; [*water, lake*] miroitement *m*.

shimmering ['ʃɪmərɪŋ] **adj**, **shimmery** ['ʃɪmərɪ] **adj** *material, jewel* chatoyant; *water, lake* miroitant. **the ~ moonlight on the lake** le clair de lune qui faisait miroiter le lac.

shimmy ['ʃɪmɪ] 1 **n** a (*US Aut*) shimmy *m*. b (*dance*) shimmy *m*. 2 **vi** (*US Aut*) avoir du shimmy.

shin [ʃɪn] 1 **n** a tibia *m*. b (*Culin*) **~ of beef** jarret *m* de bœuf. 2 **comp** ►**shinbone** tibia *m* ►**shin guard, shin pad** jambière *f*. 3 **vi**: **to ~ up a tree** grimper à un arbre; **to ~ down a tree** dégringoler lestement d'un arbre; **to ~ over a wall** escalader un mur.

►**shin down vi** dégringoler* lestement.

►**shin up vi** grimper lestement.

shindig* ['ʃɪndɪg] **n** (*dance, party etc*) fiesta *f*, soirée joyeuse.

shindy* ['ʃɪndɪ] **n** a (*brawl*) bagarre *f*; (*row, commotion*) tapage *m*, boucan* *m*. **to kick up *or* make a ~** faire du boucan*. b = **shindig**.

shine [ʃaɪn] (**vb: pret, ptp shone**) 1 **n** [*sun*] éclat *m*; [*metal*] éclat, brillant *m*; [*shoes*] brillant. **to give sth a ~** faire briller qch, faire reluire qch; **to take the ~ off** *brass, shoes* rendre mat *or* terne (*pej*); *trouser seat* délustrer; (* *fig*) *success, news* diminuer l'attrait de, faire tomber à plat; *sb else's achievement* éclipser; **the ~ on his trousers** son pantalon lustré; **to take a ~ to sb‡** se toquer de qn*; *see* **moon, rain** *etc*.

2 **vi** [*sun, stars, lamp*] briller; [*metal, shoes*] briller, reluire; (*fig: excel*) briller. **the sun is shining** il fait (du) soleil, il y a du soleil, le soleil brille; **the moon is shining** il y a clair de lune; **to ~ on sth** éclairer *or* illuminer qch; **the light was shining in my eyes** j'avais la lumière dans les yeux; **her face shone with happiness** son visage rayonnait de bonheur; **her eyes shone with pleasure/envy** ses yeux brillaient de plaisir/luisaient d'envie; (*fig*) **to ~ at football/Spanish** briller *or* faire des étincelles* au football/en espagnol.

3 **vt** a **~ your torch *or* the light over here** éclairez par ici; **he shone his torch on the car** il a braqué sa lampe de poche sur la voiture, il a éclairé la voiture.

b (*pret, ptp* **shone** *or* **shined**) *furniture, brass, shoes* faire briller, faire reluire, astiquer.

►**shine down vi** [*sun, moon, stars*] briller.

►**shine through vi** [*light etc*] passer, filtrer; (*fig*) [*courage etc*] transparaître.

►**shine up vi** (*US fig*) **to shine up to sb*** (*to girl*) faire du plat* à qn; (*to boss*) faire de la lèche* à qn.

shiner ['ʃaɪnər] **n** a (‡: *black eye*) œil poché, œil au beurre noir*. b *see* **shoe**.

shingle ['ʃɪŋgl] 1 **n** (*NonC: on beach etc*) galets *mpl*; (*NonC: on roof*) bardeaux *mpl*; (*US *: signboard*) petite enseigne (*de docteur, de notaire etc*); (*†: hairstyle*) coupe *f* à la garçonne. 2 **comp** ►**shingle beach** plage *f* de galets. 3 **vt** (†) *hair* couper à la garçonne.

shingles ['ʃɪŋglz] **n** (*NonC*) zona *m*.

shingly ['ʃɪŋglɪ] **adj** *beach* (couvert) de galets.

shininess ['ʃaɪnɪnɪs] **n** éclat *m*, brillant *m*.

shining ['ʃaɪnɪŋ] **adj** *furniture, car, floor* luisant, reluisant; (*clean*) reluisant (de propreté); (*happy*) *face* rayonnant; *eyes, hair* brillant; *example* resplendissant; *see* **improve**.

shinny ['ʃɪnɪ] **vi** = **shin 3**.

Shinto ['ʃɪntəʊ] **n** shintô *m*.

Shintoism ['ʃɪntəʊɪzəm] **n** shintoïsme *m*.

Shintoist ['ʃɪntəʊɪst] **adj, n** shintoïste *(mf)*.
shinty ['ʃɪntɪ] **n** *(Scot) sorte de hockey sur gazon.*
shiny ['ʃaɪnɪ] **adj** *surface etc* brillant; *car, furniture* brillant, reluisant; *coin, nose* brillant; *clothes* lustré.
ship [ʃɪp] 1 **n** *(gen)* bateau *m*; *(large)* navire *m*; *(vessel)* vaisseau *m*, bâtiment *m*. **His** (*or* **Her**) **Majesty's S~ Maria/Falcon** la Maria/le Falcon; (†, *liter*) **the good ~ Caradoc** la nef† Caradoc, le Caradoc; *(Hist)* **~ of the line** bâtiment de ligne; **~'s biscuit** biscuit *m* (de mer); **~'s boat** chaloupe *f*; **~'s boy** mousse *m*; **~'s company** équipage *m*, hommes *mpl* du bord; **~'s papers** papiers *mpl* de bord *or* d'un navire; *(fig)* **when my ~ comes home** quand j'aurai fait fortune; *(fig)* **he runs** *or* **keeps a tight ~** il ne plaisante pas sur l'organisation (*or* la discipline); *(fig)* **the ~ of the desert** le vaisseau du désert, le chameau; *see* **board, jump, war** *etc*.
2 **comp** ►**shipbuilder** constructeur *m* de navires ►**shipbuilding** construction navale ►**ship canal** canal *m* maritime *or* de navigation ►**ship chandler** = **ship's chandler** ►**shipload** *(lit)* charge *f*; *(fig)* grande quantité, masse* *f*; **tourists were arriving by the shipload** les touristes arrivaient par bateaux entiers ►**shipmate** camarade *m* de bord ►**shipowner** armateur *m* ►**ship's chandler** fournisseur *m* d'équipement maritime, shipchandler *m* ►**shipshape** bien rangé, en ordre; *(loc)* **all shipshape and Bristol fashion** arrangé d'une façon impeccable ►**ship-to-shore radio** liaison *f* radio avec la côte ►**shipwreck** *see* **shipwreck** ►**shipwright** *(builder)* constructeur *m* de navires; *(carpenter)* charpentier *m* (de chantier naval) ►**shipyard** chantier naval.
3 **vt** a *(transport)* transporter; *(send by ~)* expédier (par bateau); *(send by any means)* expédier. *(Comm)* **the goods were ~ped on SS Wallisdown** la marchandise a été expédiée à bord du SS Wallisdown.
b *(put or take on board) cargo* embarquer, charger; *water* embarquer. **to ~ the oars** rentrer les avirons.
►**ship off, ship out** 1 **vi** s'embarquer (*to* pour). 2 **vt sep** a *(send by ship) goods, troops etc* envoyer (par bateau *or* par mer). b (*: *send*) *goods, person* expédier*.
shipment ['ʃɪpmənt] **n** *(load)* cargaison *f*; *(act of shipping)* expédition *f (par bateau)*. *(Comm)* **ready for ~** prêt à l'expédition.
shipper ['ʃɪpər] **n** expéditeur *m*, affréteur *m*.
shipping ['ʃɪpɪŋ] 1 **n** *(NonC)* a *(ships collectively)* navires *mpl*; *(traffic)* navigation *f*. *(Rad)* **attention all ~!** avis à la navigation!; **it was a danger to ~** cela constituait un danger pour la navigation; **the canal is closed to British ~** le canal est fermé aux navires britanniques.
b *(act of loading)* chargement *m*, embarquement *m*. 2 **comp** ►**shipping agent** agent *m* maritime ►**shipping company** compagnie *f* de navigation ►**shipping lane** voie *f* de navigation ►**shipping line** = **shipping company** ►**shipping losses: shipping losses during 1944** les pertes en navires pendant 1944.
shipwreck ['ʃɪprek] 1 **n** *(event)* naufrage *m*; *(wrecked ship)* épave *f*.
2 **vt** *(lit)* faire sombrer; *(fig)* ruiner, anéantir. **to be ~ed** faire naufrage; **~ed on a desert island** *[vessel]* échoué sur une île déserte; *[person]* naufragé sur une île déserte; **a ~ed person** un(e) naufragé(e); **~ed sailor/vessel** marin/vaisseau naufragé.
shire ['ʃaɪər] **n** *(Brit)* comté *m*. **the S~s** les comtés du centre de l'Angleterre; **~ horse** shire *m*, cheval *m* de gros trait.
shirk [ʃɜːk] 1 **vt** *task, work* ne pas faire; *obligation, duty* esquiver, se dérober à; *difficulty, problem, issue* escamoter, éluder, esquiver. **to ~ doing** éviter de faire, s'arranger pour ne pas faire. 2 **vi** tirer au flanc*.
shirker ['ʃɜːkər] **n** tire-au-flanc* *mf inv*.
shirr [ʃɜːr] **vt** a *(Sewing)* froncer. b *(US Culin)* **~ed eggs** œufs *mpl* en cocotte *or* au four.
shirring ['ʃɜːrɪŋ] 1 **n** fronces *fpl*. 2 **comp** ►**shirring elastic** (fil *m*) élastique *m* à froncer, ≃ Lastex ® *m*.
shirt [ʃɜːt] 1 **n** *(man's)* chemise *f*; *(woman's)* chemisier *m*; *(footballer's etc)* maillot *m*. *(fig)* **keep your ~ on**‡ ne vous mettez pas en rogne* *or* en pétard‡; *(Betting etc)* **to put one's ~ on sth** jouer (toute) sa fortune *or* tout ce qu'on a sur qch; *(Betting etc)* **to lose one's ~** perdre (toute) sa fortune *or* tout ce qu'on a, y laisser sa chemise; *see* **boil, night, stuff** *etc*.
2 **comp** ►**shirtdress** robe *f* chemisier ►**shirt front** plastron *m* ►**shirt sleeves: in (one's) shirt sleeves** en bras *or* manches de chemise ►**shirt-tail** pan *m* de chemise; **in (one's) shirt-tails** en (pans de) chemise; *(US)* **shirt-tail* cousin** cousin(e) *m(f)* éloigné(e), cousin(e) à la mode de Bretagne ►**shirtwaist** *(US)* *(blouse)* chemisier *m*; *(dress)* robe *f* chemisier ►**shirtwaist(ed) dress, shirtwaister** robe *f* chemisier.
shirting ['ʃɜːtɪŋ] **n** *(NonC)* shirting *m*.
shirty* ['ʃɜːtɪ] **adj** *(esp Brit)* en rogne*, de mauvais poil*. **to get ~** se mettre en rogne*, prendre la mouche.
shish kebab ['ʃiːʃkə'bæb] chiche-kebab *m*.
shit*** [ʃɪt] **(vb: pret, ptp shat)** 1 **n** *(excrement)* merde*** *f*; *(fig)* connerie‡ *f*. *(excl)* **~!** merde!‡; *(fig)* **to be in the ~** être dans la merde***; **don't give me that ~!** arrête de déconner!‡; **I don't give a ~!** j'en ai rien à branler!***, je m'en contrefous!‡ *(about* de); **he's a ~** c'est un salaud‡; **to scare the ~ out of sb** flanquer une de ces trouilles*** à qn; **to beat** *or* **kick** *or* **knock the ~ out of sb** passer qn à tabac*, dérouiller qn‡; *(fig)* **then the ~ really hit the fan** alors ça a vraiment explosé*.
2 **vi** chier***.
3 **comp** ►**shit-hole***** endroit *m* de merde ►**shit-hot***** vachement bon‡ ►**shitlist***** liste *f* noire ►**shit-scared*****: **to be shit-scared** avoir une trouille bleue‡ ►**shit-stirrer***** fout-la-merde*** *mf*.
4 **vt** *(lit, fig)* **to ~ o.s.** chier dans son froc***.
shite*** [ʃaɪt] **n** *(Brit)* = **shit**.
shitless*** ['ʃɪtlɪs] **adj: to scare sb ~** flanquer une de ces trouilles*** à qn; **to be scared ~** avoir une trouille bleue‡; **to bore sb ~** casser les couilles à qn***; **to be bored ~** se faire chier***.
shitty*** ['ʃɪtɪ] **adj** dégueulasse‡, dégoûtant. **what a ~ thing to happen!** quelle vacherie!‡, quelle saloperie!‡
shiv‡ [ʃɪv] **n** *(US: knife)* surin‡ *m*, couteau *m*.
shiver[1] ['ʃɪvər] 1 **vi** *(with cold)* frissonner, trembler *(with* de); *(with fear)* frissonner, trembler, tressaillir *(with* de); *(with pleasure)* frissonner, tressaillir *(with* de); *see* **shoe**. 2 **n** *(from cold)* frisson *m*; *(from fear, pleasure)* frisson, tressaillement *m*. **it sent ~s down his spine** cela lui a donné froid dans le dos; **he gave a ~** il a frissonné, il a eu un frisson; **to give sb the ~s** donner le frisson à qn.
shiver[2] ['ʃɪvər] 1 **n** *(fragment)* éclat *m*, fragment *m*. 2 **vi** *(shatter)* voler en éclats, se fracasser. 3 **vt** fracasser.
shivery ['ʃɪvərɪ] **adj** *(from cold)* frissonnant, qui a des frissons; *(from fever)* fiévreux; *(from fear/emotion etc)* tremblant *or* frissonnant (de peur/d'émotion *etc*).
shoal[1] [ʃəʊl] **n** *[fish]* banc *m (de poissons)*. *(fig)* **they came in (their) ~s** ils sont venus en foule; **~s of*** une grande quantité de, une masse de*; **~s of applications** une avalanche de demandes.
shoal[2] [ʃəʊl] **n** *(shallows)* haut-fond *m*, bas-fond *m*; *(sandbank)* banc *m* de sable, écueil *m*.
shock[1] [ʃɒk] 1 **n** a *(impact) [collision etc]* choc *m*, heurt *m*; *[earthquake, explosion]* secousse *f*.
b *(Elec)* décharge *f* (électrique). **to get a ~** recevoir une décharge (électrique), prendre le jus*; **she got a ~ from the refrigerator, the refrigerator gave her a ~** elle a reçu une décharge en touchant le réfrigérateur.
c *(to sensibilities etc)* choc *m*, coup *m*, secousse *f*; *(feeling, emotion)* horreur *f*. **he got such a ~ when he heard that ...** cela lui a donné un tel choc *or* un tel coup *or* une telle secousse d'apprendre que ...; **he hasn't yet got over the ~ of her death** il ne s'est pas encore remis du choc que lui a causé sa mort; **the ~ killed him** le choc l'a tué; **the ~ of the election results** les résultats stupéfiants de l'élection; **their refusal came as a ~ to me** leur refus m'a stupéfié *or* ébahi; **it comes as a ~ to hear that ...** il est stupéfiant d'apprendre que ...; **you gave me a ~!** vous m'avez fait peur!; **I got such a ~!** *(at sth startling)* j'ai eu une de ces émotions!*; *(at bad news)* ça m'a bouleversé!; *(hum)* **~ horror!*** quelle horreur!; *(see also* **2**); **pale with ~** pâle de saisissement; **my feeling is one of ~ at the idea that ...** j'éprouve un sentiment d'horreur à l'idée que ..., je suis bouleversé à l'idée que ... .
d *(Med)* commotion *f*, choc *m*. **to be suffering from ~** être sous le coup du choc, être commotionné; **in a state of ~** en état de choc, commotionné; *see* **shell** *etc*.
e *(US Aut)* **~s*** amortisseurs *mpl*.
2 **comp** *(Mil etc) tactics, troops* de choc ►**shock absorber** *(Aut)* amortisseur *m* ►**shock-horror story*** histoire *f* catastrophe ►**shock-proof** *(Tech)* anti-choc *inv*; (* *fig*) *person* difficile à choquer ►**shock resistant** résistant aux chocs ►**shock therapy, shock treatment** *(Med)* (traitement *m* par) électrochoc *m* ►**shock wave** *(Phys)* onde *f* de choc.
3 **adj** (*) *result, reaction* stupéfiant.
4 **vt** *(take aback)* secouer, retourner*; *(stronger)* bouleverser; *(disgust)* dégoûter; *(scandalize)* choquer, scandaliser. **his mother's death ~ed him into going to see his father** bouleversé par la mort de sa mère il est allé voir son père; **to ~ sb out of his complacency** secouer *(fig)* qn jusqu'à ce qu'il perde sa suffisance; **he's easily ~ed** il se choque facilement *or* pour un rien.
shock[2] [ʃɒk] **n: a ~ of hair** une tignasse*.
shocked [ʃɒkt] **adj** *(taken aback)* secoué, *(stronger)* bouleversé; *(disgusted)* dégoûté; *(scandalized)* choqué; *(Med)* commotionné. **a ~ silence** un silence accablé.
shocker ['ʃɒkər] **n** a (*) **he's a ~** il est impossible *or* imbuvable*; **his essay's a ~** sa dissertation est une catastrophe*; **what a ~ of a day!** quel temps épouvantable! *or* de cochon!* b *(cheap book)* livre *m* à sensation.
shocking ['ʃɒkɪŋ] 1 **adj** a *(appalling) crime, cruelty* affreux, atroce, odieux; *news, sight* atroce, bouleversant; *(scandalizing) book, behaviour* choquant, scandaleux; *decision, waste of money* scandaleux; *price* exorbitant, scandaleux. **the film wasn't really ~** le film n'avait rien de vraiment choquant. b *(very bad) weather, results, cold, cough* affreux, terrible, épouvantable; *handwriting* épouvantable; *meal* infect. **she has ~ taste** son manque de goût est atroce. 2 **adv** (‡) terriblement, affreusement. 3 **comp** ►**shocking pink adj, n** rose *m* criard.
shockingly ['ʃɒkɪŋlɪ] **adv** *unfair, expensive, difficult* terriblement, af-

freusement; *behave* (*appallingly*) épouvantablement, de façon terrible; (*scandalously*) scandaleusement, de façon choquante; (*very badly*) très mal, odieusement; *play, act etc* de façon lamentable.

shod [ʃɒd] **pret, ptp of shoe 3.**

shoddily [ˈʃɒdɪlɪ] **adv** *made* mal, à la six-quatre-deux*; *behave* de façon mesquine.

shoddiness [ˈʃɒdɪnɪs] **n** *[work, goods]* mauvaise qualité; *[behaviour]* bassesse *f*, mesquinerie *f*.

shoddy [ˈʃɒdɪ] 1 **adj** *work* de mauvaise qualité; *goods* de mauvaise qualité, mal fait, mal fini; *behaviour* mesquin. 2 **n** (*cloth*) tissu *m* fait d'effiloché.

shoe [ʃuː] **(vb: pret, ptp shod)** 1 **n** chaussure *f*, soulier *m*; (*horse~*) fer *m* (à cheval); (*brake ~*) sabot *m* (de frein). **to have one's ~s on/off** être chaussé/déchaussé; **to put on one's ~s** mettre ses chaussures, se chausser; **to take off one's ~s** enlever ses chaussures, se déchausser; (*fig*) **to shake** *or* **shiver in one's ~s** avoir une peur bleue, (*less strong*) être dans ses petits souliers*; (*fig*) **I wouldn't like to be in his ~s** je n'aimerais pas être à sa place; (*fig*) **to step into** *or* **fill sb's ~s** succéder à qn; **he's waiting for dead men's ~s** il attend que quelqu'un meure pour prendre sa place; (*fig*) **you'll know where the ~ pinches when ...** vous vous trouverez serré *or* à court quand ...; (*fig*) **that's another pair of ~s** c'est une autre paire de manches; *see* **court** *etc*.

2 **comp** ►**shoeblack** cireur *m* de chaussures ►**shoebrush** brosse *f* à chaussures ►**shoe cream** crème *f* pour chaussures ►**shoehorn** chausse-pied *m* ►**shoelace** lacet *m* de soulier; (*fig*) **you are not fit** *or* **worthy to tie his shoelaces** vous n'êtes pas digne de délier le cordon de ses souliers ►**shoe leather** cuir *m* pour chaussures; (*fig*) **I wore out a lot of shoe leather, it cost me a lot in shoe leather** ça m'est revenu cher en chaussures, j'ai dû faire des kilomètres à pied ►**shoemaker** (*cobbler*) cordonnier *m*; (*manufacturer*) fabricant *m* de chaussures; (*shoeshop owner*) chausseur *m*; **shoemaker's shop** cordonnerie *f* ►**shoe polish** cirage *m* ►**shoe repairer** cordonnier *m*; **shoe repairer's (shop)** cordonnerie *f* ►**shoe repairing** (*NonC*) cordonnerie *f* ►**shoe repairs** réparation *f* de chaussures ►**shoeshine (boy), shoeshiner** cireur *m* de chaussures ►**shoeshop** magasin *m* de chaussures ►**shoestring** (*lit*) = **shoelace**; (*fig*) **to do sth on a shoestring** faire qch à peu de frais *or* avec peu d'argent; **they're living on a shoestring** ils sont gênés, ils doivent se serrer la ceinture*; **shoestring budget** budget *m* minime *or* infime ►**shoetree** embauchoir *m*.

3 **vt** *horse* ferrer. *[person]* **to be well/badly shod** être bien/mal chaussé; (*Prov*) **the cobbler's children are always the worst shod** ce sont les cordonniers qui sont les plus mal chaussés (*Prov*).

shone [ʃɒn] **pret, ptp of shine.**

shoo [ʃuː] 1 **excl** (*to animals*) pschtt!; (*to person*) ouste!* 2 **vt** (*also* ~ **away,** ~ **off**) chasser. 3 **comp** ►**shoo-in***: (*US*) **it's a shoo-in*** c'est du tout cuit*, c'est du gâteau*.

shook [ʃʊk] 1 **pret of shake.** 2 **comp** ►**shook up***: **to be shook up about sth** être tout remué *or* tout émotionné* à propos de qch; **a shook-up generation** une génération de paumés*.

shoot [ʃuːt] **(vb: pret, ptp shot)** 1 **n** a (*on branch etc*) pousse *f*, scion *m*, rejeton *m*; (*seedling*) pousse.

b (*chute*) glissière *f*, déversoir *m*.

c (*shooting party*) partie *f* de chasse; (*land*) (terrain *m* de) chasse *f*. (*fig*) **the whole (bang) ~**‡ (*things*) absolument tout, le tout, tout le tremblement* *or* le bataclan*; (*people*) tout le monde, tout le tremblement*.

d (*US: excl*) ~!* oh zut!*, mince!*

2 **comp** ►**shoot'em-up*** (*US Cine*) film *m* de violence ►**shoot-out*** fusillade *f* ►**shoot-the-chute** (*US*) toboggan *m* (*glissière*).

3 **vt** a *game* (*hunt*) chasser; (*kill*) abattre, tirer; *injured horse etc* abattre; *person* (*hit*) atteindre *or* (*wound*) blesser *or* (*kill*) tuer d'un coup de fusil (*or* de revolver *etc*), abattre, descendre*; (*execute*) fusiller. **to be shot in the head** être atteint *or* blessé *or* tué d'une balle dans la tête; **to be shot in the arm** recevoir une balle dans le bras, être atteint d'une balle au bras; **he had been shot through the heart** il avait reçu une balle en plein cœur; **to ~ sb dead** abattre qn; **he was shot as a spy** il a été fusillé pour espionnage; (*hum*) **people have been shot for less*** c'est se mettre la corde au cou*; (*hum*) **you'll get shot for that!*** tu vas te faire incendier pour ça!*; **to ~ from the hip** (*lit*) tirer dès qu'on a dégainé; (*fig*) (*challenging sb*) attaquer impulsivement; (*answering sb*) riposter impulsivement; (*Aut*) **to ~ the lights** griller *or* brûler le feu rouge; (*fig*) **to ~ o.s. in the foot*** mal juger son coup, ramasser une pelle*.

b (*fire*) *gun* tirer *or* lâcher un coup de (*at* sur); *arrow* décocher, lancer, tirer (*at* sur); *bullet* tirer (*at* sur); *rocket, missile* lancer (*at* sur). (*fig*) **the volcano shot lava high into the air** le volcan projetait *or* lançait de la lave dans les airs; **they shot the coal into the cellar** ils ont déversé le charbon dans la cave; **to ~ rubbish** déverser des ordures; **to ~ a goal, to ~ the ball into the net** marquer *or* shooter un but; **he shot the bolt** (*fastened*) il a mis *or* poussé le verrou; (*opened*) il a tiré le verrou; (*fig*) **he has shot his bolt** il a joué sa dernière carte, il a brûlé ses dernières cartouches; (*US fig*) **to ~ the breeze*** bavarder; (*US fig*) **to ~ the bull**‡ raconter des conneries‡; (*fig*) **to ~ a line**‡ faire de l'épate*, en mettre plein la vue*; (*Brit fig*) **to ~ a line about** ‡ raconter des histoires *or* des bobards* à propos de; (*US fig: spend all*) **to ~ the works* on sth** claquer* tout ce qu'on a pour acheter qch; **to ~ dice** jeter les dés; (*fig*) **to ~ the moon** déménager à la cloche de bois; *see* **pool**[2].

c (*direct*) *look, glance* décocher, lancer (*at* à); *[searchlight etc] beam of light* braquer (*at* sur); *[sun] ray of light* lancer, darder. **he shot a smile at her** il lui a jeté un sourire, il lui a souri rapidement; **to ~ questions at sb** bombarder *or* mitrailler qn de questions.

d (*Cine etc*) *film, scene* tourner; *subject of snapshot etc* prendre (en photo).

e *rapids* franchir, descendre; *bridge* passer rapidement sous.

f (*) (*send*) envoyer, expédier; (*give*) donner; (*throw*) jeter, flanquer*.

g (*Drugs sl*) **to ~ heroin** se shooter (*sl*) à l'héroïne.

4 **vi** a (*with gun, bow*) tirer (*at* sur); (*Sport: at target*) tirer (à la cible). (*Brit: hunt*) **to go ~ing** chasser, aller à la chasse, tirer le gibier; **to ~ to kill** tirer pour abattre; **to ~ on sight** tirer à vue; **he can't ~ straight** il tire mal *or* comme un pied*.

b (*move quickly*) *[person, car, ball etc]* **to ~ in/out/past** *etc* entrer/sortir/passer *etc* en flèche; **to ~ along** filer; **he shot to the door** il n'a fait qu'un bond jusqu'à la porte; **the car shot out of a side street** la voiture est sortie *or* a débouché à toute vitesse d'une rue transversale; **he shot across the road** il a traversé la rue comme une flèche; **the ball shot over the wall** le ballon a été projeté par-dessus le mur; **the bullet shot past his ears** la balle lui a sifflé aux oreilles; **the cat shot up the tree** le chat a grimpé à l'arbre à toute vitesse; **the pain went ~ing up his arm** la douleur au bras le lancinait, son bras l'élançait; (*in class etc*) **he has shot ahead in the last few weeks** il a fait des progrès énormes depuis quelques semaines.

c (*Ftbl etc*) shooter, tirer. **to ~ at goal** shooter, faire un shoot; (*fig: in conversation*) ~!‡ vas-y!, dis ce que tu as à dire!, dis!*

d (*Bot*) bourgeonner, pousser.

►**shoot away** 1 **vi** a (*Mil etc: fire*) continuer à tirer, tirer sans arrêt. b (*move*) partir comme une flèche, s'enfuir à toutes jambes. 2 **vt sep** = **shoot off 2b**.

►**shoot back** **vi** a (*Mil etc*) retourner le (*or* son *etc*) feu (*at* à). b (*move*) retourner *or* rentrer *or* revenir en flèche.

►**shoot down** **vt sep** a *plane* abattre, descendre. (*Aviat*) **he was shot down in flames** son avion s'est abattu en flammes; (*fig*) **to shoot down in flames*** *project* démolir; *person* descendre en flammes*. b (*kill*) *person* abattre, descendre*.

►**shoot off** 1 **vi** = **shoot away 1b.** 2 **vt sep** a *gun* décharger, faire partir. (*fig*) **he's always shooting his mouth off**‡ il faut toujours qu'il ouvre (*subj*) le bec* *or* sa grande gueule‡; **to shoot off (one's mouth) about sth**‡ raconter des histoires *or* des bobards* au sujet de qch. b **he had a leg shot off** il a eu une jambe emportée par un éclat d'obus, un éclat d'obus lui a emporté la jambe.

►**shoot out** 1 **vi** *[person, car etc]* sortir comme une flèche; *[flame, water]* jaillir. 2 **vt sep** a **to shoot out one's tongue** *[person]* tirer la langue; *[snake]* darder sa langue; **he shot out his arm and grabbed my stick** il a avancé brusquement le bras et a attrapé ma canne; **he was shot out of the car** il a été éjecté de la voiture; *see* **neck.** b **to shoot it out** avoir un règlement de compte (à coups de revolvers *or* de fusils), s'expliquer à coups de revolvers *or* de fusils. 3 **shoot-out*** **n** *see* **shoot 2.**

►**shoot up** 1 **vi** a *[flame, water]* jaillir; *[rocket, price etc]* monter en flèche. b (*grow quickly*) *[tree, plant]* pousser vite; *[child]* pousser comme un champignon. c (*Drugs sl*) se shooter (*sl*). 2 **vt sep** a (*US *: with gun*) flinguer‡, tirer sur. b (*Drugs sl*) *heroin etc* se shooter à (*sl*). 3 **shot up**‡ **adj** *see* **shot 3.**

-shooter [ˈʃuːtəʳ] **n ending in comps** *see* **pea, six** *etc*.

shooting [ˈʃuːtɪŋ] 1 **n** a (*NonC*) (*shots*) coups *mpl* de feu; (*continuous*) fusillade *f*. **I heard some ~ over there** j'ai entendu des coups de feu par là-bas; **the ~ caused 10 deaths** la fusillade a fait 10 morts.

b (*act*) (*murder*) meurtre *m* *or* assassinat *m* (avec une arme à feu); (*execution*) fusillade *f*, exécution *f*. **the ~ of a policeman in the main street** le meurtre d'un agent de police abattu dans la grand-rue.

c (*Hunting*) chasse *f*. **rabbit ~** la chasse au lapin; **there's good ~ there** il y a une bonne chasse là-bas.

d (*Cine*) *[film, scene]* tournage *m*.

2 **adj** *pain* lancinant.

3 **comp** ►**shooting brake** (*Brit Aut*) break *m* ►**shooting-down**: **the shooting-down of the diplomat** l'attentat *m* contre le diplomate; **the shooting-down of the plane (by the enemy)** la perte *or* la destruction de l'avion (abattu par l'ennemi) ►**shooting gallery** tir *m*, stand *m* (de tir) ►**shooting incident**: **there were a few shooting incidents last night** la nuit dernière il y a eu quelques échanges *mpl* de coups de feu ►**shooting match***: (*Brit fig*) **the whole shooting match** tout le bataclan*, tout le tremblement* ►**shooting party** partie *f* de chasse ►**shooting range** tir *m*, stand *m* (de tir); **within shooting range** à portée de fusil (*or* de canon *etc*) ►**shooting script** (*Cine*) découpage *m* ►**shooting star** étoile filante ►**shooting stick** canne-siège *f*.

shop [ʃɒp] 1 **n** a (*esp Brit: Comm*) magasin *m*, (*small*) boutique *f*. **wine ~** marchand *m* de vins; **at the butcher's ~** à la boucherie, chez le boucher; **"The Toy S~"** "la Maison du Jouet"; **mobile** *or* **travelling ~** épicerie *etc* roulante; **he's just gone (round) to the ~s** il est juste sorti faire des courses; **to set up ~** (*Comm*) ouvrir un commerce *or* un magasin, s'établir, s'installer; (*fig*) s'établir, s'installer; (*lit, fig*) **to shut up ~** fermer boutique; (*fig*) **you've come to the wrong ~*** tu te trompes d'adresse* (*fig*); (*fig*) **to talk ~** parler boutique *or* affaires *or* métier; (*fig*) **all over the ~*** (*everywhere*) partout; (*in confusion*) en désordre, en pagaille; *see* **back, corner, grocer** *etc.*

b (*workshop*) atelier *m.*

c (*part of factory*) atelier *m.* **assembly ~** atelier de montage; *see* **closed, machine** *etc.*

2 comp (*bought in shop*) *cakes etc* acheté dans le commerce ▸**shop assistant** (*Brit*) vendeur *m*, -euse *f*, employé(e) *m(f)* (de magasin) ▸**shopfitter** (*esp Brit*) décorateur *m* de magasin ▸**shop floor:** (*Brit Ind*) **he works on the shop floor** c'est un ouvrier; (*Brit Ind*) **the shopfloor (workers)** les ouvriers *mpl* ▸**shop front** (*Brit*) devanture *f* ▸**shopgirl** (*Brit*) vendeuse *f* ▸**shopkeeper** commerçant(e) *m(f)*, marchand(e) *m(f)*; **small shopkeeper** petit commerçant ▸**shoplift** voler à l'étalage ▸**shoplifter** voleur *m*, -euse *f* à l'étalage ▸**shoplifting** (*NonC*) vol *m* à l'étalage ▸**shopsoiled** (*Brit*) qui a fait l'étalage *or* la vitrine, défraîchi ▸**shop steward** (*Brit Ind*) délégué(e) syndical(e) *m(f)* ▸**shoptalk*** (*jargon*) jargon *m* (de métier); **I'm getting tired of shoptalk** je commence à en avoir assez de parler affaires *or* métier ▸**shopwalker†** (*Brit*) chef *m* de rayon ▸**shop window** vitrine *f* ▸**shopworn** (*US*) = **shopsoiled.**

3 vi: **to ~ at Harrods** faire ses courses *or* ses achats chez Harrods; (*sign*) **"~ at Brown's"** "achetez chez Brown"; **to go ~ping** (*locally etc*) faire les courses; (*on shopping expedition*) faire des courses, courir les magasins; **I was ~ping for a winter coat** je cherchais un manteau d'hiver.

4 vt (*‡: esp Brit: betray*) vendre, donner*.

▸**shop around** vi comparer les prix. **to shop around for sth** comparer les prix avant d'acheter qch; (*fig*) **you ought to shop around before you decide on a university** vous devriez vous renseigner à droite et à gauche avant de choisir une université.

shopper ['ʃɒpəʳ] n a (*person*) personne *f* qui fait ses courses; (*customer*) client(e) *m(f)*. b (*bag*) sac *m* (à provisions), cabas *m*; (*on wheels*) caddie *m.*

shopping ['ʃɒpɪŋ] 1 n (*NonC*) a **to do the/some ~** faire les/des courses; **~ is very tiring** faire les courses est très fatigant; **"open Thursdays for late evening ~"** "ouvert le jeudi en nocturne", "nocturne le jeudi"; *see* **mall, window** *etc.* b (*goods*) achats *mpl.* 2 comp *street, district* commerçant ▸**shopping bag** sac *m* (à provisions), cabas *m* ▸**shopping basket** panier *m* (à provisions) ▸**shopping centre, shopping complex** centre *m* commercial ▸**shopping list** liste *f* de(s) courses ▸**shopping mall** centre *m* commercial ▸**shopping precinct** zone commerciale (piétonnière) ▸**shopping trip** tournée *f* d'achats ▸**shopping trolley** caddie *m.*

shore¹ [ʃɔːʳ] 1 n [*sea*] rivage *m*, bord *m*; [*lake*] rive *f*, bord; (*coast*) côte *f*, littoral *m*; (*beach*) plage *f*. (*fig liter*) **these ~s** ces rives; (*esp Naut*) **on ~** à terre; (*Naut*) **to go on ~** débarquer. 2 comp ▸**shore leave** (*Naut*) permission *f* à terre ▸**shoreline** littoral *m* ▸**shore patrol** (*US Navy*) détachement *m* de police militaire (de la Marine) ▸**shoreward(s)** *see* **shoreward(s).**

shore² [ʃɔːʳ] 1 n (*for wall, tunnel*) étai *m*, étançon *m*; (*for tree*) étai; (*for ship*) accore *m*, étançon. 2 vt étayer, étançonner; accorer.

▸**shore up** vt sep a = **shore² 2.** b (*fig*) consolider.

shoreward ['ʃɔːwəd] adj, adv vers le rivage *or* la côte *or* la rive.

shorewards ['ʃɔːwədz] adv = **shoreward.**

shorn [ʃɔːn] ptp of **shear.**

short [ʃɔːt] 1 adj a (*gen*) court; *person* petit, de petite taille; *step, walk* petit; *visit, message, conversation* court, bref; *programme* court; (*Ling*) *vowel, syllable* bref. **the ~est route** le chemin le plus court; **the ~est distance between two points** le plus court chemin d'un point à un autre; **a ~ distance away, a ~ way off** à peu de distance, à une faible distance; **~ trousers** culottes courtes (*de petit garçon*); **he is rather ~ in the leg, he's got rather ~ legs** il est plutôt court de jambes *or* [*dog etc*] court sur pattes; **these trousers are ~ in the leg** ce pantalon est court de jambes; (*Ski*) **~ ski** ski *m* court (*see also* **2**); **one ~ year of happiness** une petite *or* brève année de bonheur; **to take a ~ holiday** prendre quelques jours de vacances; **a ~ time** *or* **while ago** il y a peu de temps; **in a ~ time** *or* **while** dans peu de temps, bientôt, sous peu; **time is getting ~** il ne reste plus beaucoup de temps; **the days are getting ~er** les jours raccourcissent; **make the skirt ~er** raccourcis la jupe; (*fig*) **the ~ answer is that he ...** tout simplement il ...; **I'd like a ~ word** *or* **a few ~ words with you** j'aimerais vous dire un mot; **~ and to the point** bref et précis; (*hum*) **that was ~ and sweet** ça n'a pas traîné (*hum*), ça a été du vite fait*; (*fig*) **to have sb by the ~ hairs‡** *or* **~ and curlies‡** tenir qn à la gorge *or* par les couilles**‡; (*lit, fig*) **~ cut** raccourci *m*; **I took a ~ cut through the fields** j'ai pris un raccourci *or* j'ai coupé *or* j'ai pris au plus court à travers champs; **you'll have to do it all with no ~ cuts** il faudra que tu fasses le tout sans rien omettre; **a ~ drink** un petit verre d'apéritif (*or* d'alcool); **~ drinks** des apéritifs, de l'alcool; (*fig*) **he got the ~ end of the stick** c'est lui qui en a pâti; **to win by a ~ head** (*Racing*) gagner d'une courte tête; (*fig*) gagner de justesse; (*Ind*) **~er hours and better pay** une réduction des heures de travail et une augmentation de salaire; **they want a ~er working week** on veut réduire la semaine de travail; **at ~ notice** dans un court *or* bref délai; **to have a ~ temper** être coléreux *or* soupe au lait *inv*; (*Ind*) **to be on ~ time, to work ~ time** être en chômage partiel (*see also* **2**); **to put sb on ~ time** mettre qn au chômage partiel; (*fig*) **to make ~ work of sth** ne pas mettre beaucoup de temps à faire qch; (*fig*) **to make ~ work of sb*** envoyer promener qn*; *see also* **2** *and* **shrift, story, term** *etc.*

b **"TV" is ~ for "television"** "TV" est l'abréviation de "television"; **Fred is ~ for Frederick** Fred est le diminutif de Frederick; **he's called Fred for ~** son diminutif est Fred.

c (*lacking etc*) **they never went ~** ils n'ont jamais manqué du nécessaire; **to be ~ of sugar** être à court de sucre, manquer de sucre; **I'm a bit ~ this month*** je suis un peu fauché* *or* à court ce mois-ci; **we're ~ of 3** il nous en manque 3, il s'en faut de 3; **we're not ~ of volunteers** nous ne manquons pas de volontaires; **he's long on muscle but a bit ~ on brains*** il a beaucoup de muscle mais pas tellement de cervelle; *see* **breath** *etc.*

d (*insufficient etc*) insuffisant, incomplet (*f* -ète). **petrol is ~** *or* **in ~ supply at the moment** on manque d'essence en ce moment; **to give sb ~ change** ne pas rendre la monnaie juste à qn, ne pas rendre assez à qn; (*deliberately*) tricher en rendant la monnaie à qn; **to give ~ weight** *or* **measure** ne pas donner le poids juste; (*deliberately*) tricher sur le poids; *see* **commons.**

e (*curt*) *reply, manner* brusque, sec (*f* sèche). **he was rather ~ with me** il m'a répondu (*or* parlé *etc*) assez sèchement *or* brusquement, il s'est montré assez sec *or* brusque à mon égard.

f (*Fin*) *bill* à courte échéance; *loan* à court terme. **~ sale** vente *f* à découvert.

2 comp ▸**short-acting** *drug* à effet rapide ▸**short back-and-sides** coupe *f* très courte derrière et sur les côtés ▸**shortbread** (*Culin*) sablé *m* ▸**shortcake:** (*US*) **strawberry** *etc* **shortcake** tarte sablée aux fraises *etc* ▸**short-change:** **to short-change sb** (*lit: in shop etc*) ne pas rendre assez à qn; (*fig*) rouler* qn ▸**short-circuit** n (*Elec*) court-circuit *m* ◊ vt (*Elec, fig: bypass*) court-circuiter; (*fig: cause to fail*) faire capoter ◊ vi se mettre en court-circuit ▸**shortcoming** défaut *m* ▸**short covering** (*St Ex*) rachat *m* pour couvrir un découvert ▸**shortcrust pastry** (*Culin*) pâte brisée ▸**short-dated** (*Fin*) à courte échéance ▸**short division** (*Math*) division *f* simple ▸**shortfall** *see* **shortfall** ▸**short-haired** *person* aux cheveux courts; *animal* à poil ras ▸**shorthand** *see* **shorthand** ▸**short-handed** à court de personnel *or* de main-d'œuvre ▸**short-haul** n [*truck*] camionnage *m* à *or* sur courte distance; [*plane*] vol *m* à *or* sur courte distance ◊ adj à courte distance ▸**shorthorn** (*Zool*) race *f* shorthorn ▸**short-life** adj (*Brit Comm*) *garment* qui n'est pas fait pour durer; *food* de conservation limitée ▸**shortlist** (*Brit*) n liste *f* de(s) candidats sélectionnés ◊ vt mettre sur la liste des candidats sélectionnés; **he was shortlisted for the post of ...** il avait été parmi les candidats sélectionnés pour le poste de ... ▸**short-lived** *animal* à la vie éphémère; *happiness* de courte durée ▸**short-order:** (*US*) **short-order cook** cuisinier *m*, -ière *f* préparant des plats rapides; (*US*) **short-order service** service *m* de plats rapides ▸**short pastry** = **shortcrust pastry** ▸**short-range** *shot, gun* de *or* à courte portée; *aircraft* à court rayon d'action; (*fig*) *plan, weather forecast* à court terme ▸**short seller** (*St Ex*) vendeur à découvert ▸**shortsheet** vt (*US*) *bed* mettre en portefeuille ▸**short sight** myopie *f* ▸**short-sighted** (*lit: esp Brit*) myope; (*fig*) *person* myope, qui manque de perspicacité; *policy, measure* qui manque de vision ▸**short-sightedness** (*lit*) myopie *f*; (*fig*) [*person*] myopie intellectuelle, manque *m* de perspicacité; [*policy, measure*] manque de vision ▸**short ski method** ski *m* évolutif ▸**short-sleeved** à manches courtes ▸**short-staffed:** **to be short-staffed** manquer de personnel, souffrir d'une pénurie de personnel ▸**shortstop** (*Baseball*) bloqueur *m* ▸**short story** nouvelle *f*; **short-story writer** nouvelliste *mf*, conteur *m*, -euse *f* ▸**short-tempered:** **to be short-tempered** (*in general*) être coléreux *or* soupe au lait* *inv*, s'emporter facilement; (*in a bad temper*) être d'humeur irritable ▸**short-term** *parking etc* de courte durée; *loan, planning, solution* à court terme; **short-term car park** parc *m* de stationnement de courte durée (*see also* **passport**) ▸**short-time working** (*Ind*) chômage partiel ▸**shortwave** (*Rad*) n ondes courtes ◊ adj *radio* à ondes courtes; *transmission* sur ondes courtes ▸**short-winded** qui manque de souffle, au souffle court.

3 adv a **to cut ~** *speech, TV etc programme* couper court à, abréger; *class, visit, holiday* écourter, abréger; *person* couper la parole à (*see also* **cut 4a**); **the ball fell ~** le ballon n'est pas tombé assez loin (*see also* **fall 2b**).

b **~ of** (*except*) sauf; (*less than*) moins de, en dessous de; (*before*) avant; **£10 ~ of what they needed** 10 livres de moins que ce dont ils ont besoin, 10 livres en dessous de ce dont ils ont besoin; **it's well ~ of the truth** c'est bien en deçà de la vérité; **a week ~ of their arrival/his birthday** *etc* une semaine avant leur arrivée/son anniversaire *etc*; **we're 3 ~** il nous en manque 3, il s'en faut de 3; **I'm £2 ~** il me manque 2 livres; **not far ~ of £100** pas loin de 100 livres, presque 100 livres; **we are £2,000 ~ of our target** il nous manque encore 2 000 livres pour arriver à la somme que nous nous sommes fixée; **he fell 10 metres ~ of the winning post** il est tombé à 10 mètres du poteau d'arrivée; **it's little ~ of suicide** c'est presque un suicide, peu s'en faut que ce ne soit un suicide; **it's little ~ of folly** cela frise la folie; **it's nothing ~ of robbery** c'est du vol ni plus ni moins; **nothing ~ of a revolution will satisfy them** seule la révolution saura les satisfaire, il ne leur faudra rien moins que la révolution pour les satisfaire; **I don't see what you can do ~ of asking him yourself** je ne vois pas ce que vous pouvez faire à moins de *or* si ce n'est lui demander vous-même; **he did everything ~ of asking her to marry him** il a tout fait sauf *or* hormis lui demander de l'épouser; **to go ~ of sth** manquer de qch, se priver de qch; **sugar is running ~** le sucre commence à manquer; **to run ~ of sth** se trouver à court de qch, venir à manquer de qch; **the car stopped ~ of the house** la voiture s'est arrêtée avant (d'arriver au niveau de) la maison; (*fig*) **I'd stop ~ of murder** je n'irais pas jusqu'au meurtre (*see also* **stop 3b**); **to take sb up ~** couper la parole à qn; **to be taken** *or* **caught ~*** être pris d'un besoin pressant; *see* **bring up, sell.**

c (*St Ex*) **to sell ~** vendre à découvert.

4 n a **in ~** (enfin) bref.

b (*) (*Cine*) court métrage *m*; (*Elec*) court-circuit *m*. (*Brit: drinks*) **~s** des apéritifs *mpl*, de l'alcool *m*; *see* **long[1]**.

c (*garment*) **(a pair of) ~s** (*gen*) un short; *[footballer etc]* une culotte; (*US : men's underwear*) un caleçon.

5 vt (*Elec*) court-circuiter.

6 vi (*Elec*) se mettre en court-circuit.

shortage ['ʃɔːtɪdʒ] n *[corn, coal, energy, cash etc]* manque *m*, pénurie *f*; *[resources]* manque, insuffisance *f*. **in times of ~** en période de pénurie; **there was no ~ of water** on ne manquait pas d'eau; **owing to the ~ of staff** à cause d'un manque de personnel; **the food ~** la disette *or* pénurie de vivres, la disette; **the housing ~** la crise du logement; **the ~ of £100 in the amount** l'absence *f* *or* le déficit de 100 livres dans la somme.

shorten ['ʃɔːtn] 1 vt *skirt, rope* raccourcir; *visit, holiday, journey* écourter; *life* abréger; *book, programme, letter* raccourcir, abréger; *syllabus* alléger; *distance, time* réduire. 2 vi *[days etc]* raccourcir. **the odds are ~ing** (*lit*) la cote s'affaiblit; (*fig*) les chances s'amenuisent *or* deviennent moindres.

shortening ['ʃɔːtnɪŋ] n (*NonC*) a (*see* **shorten**) raccourcissement *m*; abrègement *m*; allègement *m*; réduction *f*. b (*Culin*) matière grasse.

shortfall ['ʃɔːtfɔːl] n (*in payments, profits, savings etc*) montant *m* insuffisant (*in* de); (*in numbers etc*) nombre *m* insuffisant (*in* de). **~ in earnings** manque *m* à gagner; **there is a ~ of £5,000** il manque 5 000 livres; **the ~ of £5,000** les 5 000 livres qui manquent; **there is a ~ of 200 in the registrations for this course** il manque 200 inscriptions à ce cours.

shorthand ['ʃɔːthænd] (*Brit*) 1 n a (*lit*) sténographie *f*. **to take sth down in ~** prendre qch en sténo, sténographier qch. b (*fig*) (*abbreviation*) abréviation *f*; (*code of behaviour, coded message*) code *m*. (*hum*) **"motivation essential" - that's ~ for "you'll be working 24 hours a day"** "motivation essentielle" - ça revient à dire que tu vas travailler 24 heures sur 24. 2 adj (*fig: abbreviated*) *term, version, formula* abrégé. 3 comp ▸**shorthand notebook** carnet *m* de sténo ▸**shorthand notes** notes *fpl* en *or* de sténo ▸**shorthand typing** sténodactylo *f* ▸**shorthand typist** sténodactylo *mf* ▸**shorthand writer** sténo(graphe) *mf*.

shortie ['ʃɔːtɪ] n = **shorty**.

shortish ['ʃɔːtɪʃ] adj (*see* **short**) plutôt court; assez petit; assez bref.

shortly ['ʃɔːtlɪ] adv a (*soon*) bientôt, dans peu de temps; (*in a few days*) prochainement, sous peu. **~ after** peu (de temps) après; **~ before twelve** peu avant midi (*or* minuit). b (*concisely*) brièvement; (*curtly*) sèchement, brusquement.

shortness ['ʃɔːtnɪs] n a *[stick, skirt, hair, grass, arms]* peu *m* *or* manque *m* de longueur; *[person]* petite taille, petitesse *f*; *[visit, message, conversation, programme]* brièveté *f*, courte durée; *[vowel, syllable]* brévité *f*. **because of its ~** parce que c'est (*or* c'était) si court.

b (*curtness*) brusquerie *f*, sécheresse *f*.

shorty* ['ʃɔːtɪ] n courtaud(e) *m(f)*. **hey ~!** hé toi le *or* la petit(e)!

Shostakovich [ˌʃɒstəˈkəʊvɪtʃ] n Chostakovitch *m*.

shot [ʃɒt] 1 n a (*act of firing*) coup *m*, décharge *f*; (*causing wound*) coup; (*sound*) coup (de feu *or* de fusil *etc*); (*bullet*) balle *f*; (*NonC: pellets: also* **lead ~**) plomb *m*. **not a single ~ was fired** on n'a pas tiré un seul coup; **to take** *or* **have** *or* **fire a ~ at sb/sth** tirer sur qn/qch; **good ~!** (c'était) bien visé! (*see also* **1c**); **a ~ across the bows** (*Naut*) un coup de semonce; (*fig*) un avertissement; **at the first ~** du premier coup; **the first ~ killed him** la première balle l'a tué; **I've got 4 ~s left** il me reste 4 coups *or* balles; **he is a good/bad ~** il est bon/mauvais tireur; (*fig*) **big ~*** huile⁑ *f*, grosse légume⁑, gros bonnet*; (*fig*) **Parthian ~** flèche *f* du Parthe; (*fig*) **to make a ~ in the dark** tenter le coup, deviner à tout hasard; (*fig*) **that was just a ~ in the dark** c'était dit à tout hasard; **he was off like a ~** il est parti comme une flèche; **he agreed like a ~*** il y a consenti sans hésiter *or* avec empressement; **would you go? — like a ~!*** est-ce que tu irais? — sans hésiter! *or* et comment!*; *see* **crack, long[1], parting** *etc.*

b (*Space*) lancement *m*; *see* **moon, space**.

c (*Sport*) (*Ftbl, Hockey*) tir *m*; (*Golf, Tennis etc*) coup *m*; (*throw*) lancer *m*. **good ~!** (c'était) bien joué!; **a ~ at goal** un shoot, un tir au but; (*Sport*) **to put the ~** lancer le poids; *see* **call.**

d (*attempt*) essai *m*, tentative *f*, coup *m*; (*guess*) hypothèse *f*; (*turn to play*) tour *m*. **to have a ~ at (doing) sth** essayer de faire qch; **have a ~ at it!** (*try it*) tentez le coup!; (*guess*) devinez!, dites voir!*

e (*Phot*) photo(graphie) *f*; (*Cine*) prise *f* de vue(s), plan *m*.

f (*injection*) piqûre *f* (*against* contre). (*fig*) **a ~ in the arm**un coup de fouet, un stimulant.

g (*of whisky etc*) coup *m*. **put a ~ of gin in it** ajoute donc une goutte de gin.

2 comp ▸**shot angle** (*Cine, Phot*) angle *m* de prise de vue(s) ▸**shotgun** fusil *m* de chasse; (*US*) **to ride shotgun** voyager comme passager, accompagner; (*fig*) **shotgun marriage** *or* **wedding** régularisation *f* (précipitée), mariage forcé ▸**shot put** (*Sport*) lancer *m* du poids ▸**shot putter** lanceur *m*, -euse *f* de poids.

3 pret, ptp of **shoot**. **to get/be ~ of*** se débarrasser/être débarrassé de; (*exhausted*) **to be (all) ~ up⁑** être exténué *or* sur les rotules⁑.

4 adj a **~ silk** soie changeante; **~ (through) with yellow** strié de jaune.

b (*US fig *: in bad state*) *machine, plan etc* fichu*, foutu⁑.

should [ʃʊd] modal aux vb (cond of **shall**: neg **should not** abbr **shouldn't**) a (*indicating obligation, advisability, desirability*) **I should go and see her** je devrais aller la voir, il faudrait que j'aille la voir; **should I go too? — yes you should** devrais-je y aller aussi? — oui vous devriez *or* ça vaudrait mieux; **he thought he should tell you** il a pensé qu'il ferait bien de vous le dire *or* qu'il devrait vous le dire; (*frm*) **you should know that we have spoken to him** il faut que vous sachiez que nous lui avons parlé; **you should have been a teacher** vous auriez dû être professeur; **shouldn't you go and see her?** est-ce que vous ne devriez pas aller la voir?, est-ce que vous ne feriez pas bien d'aller la voir?; **everything is as it should be** tout est comme il se doit, tout est en ordre; **... which is as it should be** ... comme il se doit; **how should I know?** comment voulez-vous que je (le) sache?

b (*indicating probability*) **he should win the race** il devrait gagner la course, il va probablement gagner la course; **he should have got there by now I expect** je pense qu'il est arrivé, il a dû arriver à l'heure qu'il est; **that should be John at the door now** ça doit être Jean (qui frappe *or* qui sonne); **this should do the trick*** ça devrait faire l'affaire; **why should he suspect me?** pourquoi me soupçonnerait-il?

c (*often used to form cond tense in 1st person*) **I should** *or* **I'd go if he invited me** s'il m'invitait, j'irais; **we should have come if we had known** si nous avions su, nous serions venus; **will you come? — I should like to** est-ce que vous viendrez? — j'aimerais bien; **I shouldn't be surprised if he comes** *or* **came** *or* **were to come** ça ne m'étonnerait pas qu'il vienne; **I should think there were about 40** (je pense qu')il devait y en avoir environ 40; **was it a good film? — I should think it was!** est-ce que c'était un bon film? — je pense bien! *or* et comment!*; **he's coming to apologize — I should think so too!** il vient présenter ses excuses — j'espère bien!; **I should hope not!** il ne manquerait plus que ça!*; **I should say so!** et comment!*

d (*subj uses*) (*frm*) **it is necessary that he should be told** il faut qu'on le lui dise; (*frm*) **lest he should change his mind** de crainte qu'il ne change (*subj*) d'avis; **it is surprising that he should be so young** c'est étonnant qu'il soit si jeune; **who should come in but Paul!** et devinez qui est entré? Paul!

shoulder ['ʃəʊldə^{r}] 1 n a (*Anat, Culin, Dress etc*) épaule *f*. **to have broad ~s** (*lit*) être large d'épaules *or* de carrure; (*fig*) avoir les reins solides (*fig*); **the ~s are too wide, it's too wide across the ~s** c'est trop large d'épaules *or* de carrure; **put my jacket round your ~s** mets *or* jette ma veste sur tes épaules *or* sur ton dos; (*lit, fig*) **to cry** *or* **weep on sb's ~** pleurer sur l'épaule de qn; **she had her bag on** *or* **over one ~** elle portait son sac à l'épaule; **they stood ~ to ~** (*lit*) ils étaient coude à coude *or* côte à côte; (*fig*) ils se serraient les coudes, ils s'entraidaient, ils unissaient leurs efforts; (*fig*) **all the responsibilities had fallen on his ~s** toutes les responsabilités étaient retombées sur lui *or* sur ses épaules; (*fig*) **to put** *or* **set one's ~ to the wheel** s'atteler à la tâche; *see* **cold, head, rub, straighten, look 3a** *etc.*

b (*Brit*) *[road]* accotement *m*, bas-côté *m*; *[hill]* contrefort *m*, épaulement *m*; (*Climbing*) épaule *f*. *[road]* **hard/soft ~** accotement stabilisé/non stabilisé.

2 comp ▸**shoulder bag** sac *m* à bandoulière ▸**shoulder blade** omoplate *f*; **it hit him between the shoulder blades** cela l'a atteint en plein entre les deux épaules ▸**shoulder-high** *grass, hedge, wall* à hauteur d'épaule; **to carry sb shoulder-high** porter qn en triomphe ▸**shoulder joint** (*Anat*) articulation *f* de l'épaule ▸**shoulder-length hair** cheveux milongs *or* jusqu'aux épaules ▸**shoulder pad** épaulette *f* (*rembourrage d'épaules de vêtement*) ▸**shoulder strap** *[garment]* bretelle *f*; *[bag]* bandoulière *f*; (*Mil*) patte *f* d'épaule.

3 vt a *load, case etc* charger sur son épaule; *child etc* hisser sur ses épaules; (*fig*) *responsibility* endosser; *task* se charger de. (*Mil*) **to ~ arms** porter l'arme; **~ arms!** portez arme!

b **to ~ sb aside** *or* **out of the way** écarter qn d'un coup d'épaule; **to ~ one's way through the crowd** se frayer un chemin à travers *or* dans la foule à coups d'épaules.

shouldn't ['ʃʊdnt] = **should not**; *see* **should**.
should've ['ʃʊdv] = **should have**; *see* **should**.
shout [ʃaʊt] 1 n cri *m* (*of joy etc* de joie *etc*). **there were ~s of applause/protest/laughter** des acclamations/des protestations bruyantes/des éclats de rire ont retenti; **he gave a ~ of laughter** il a éclaté de rire; **to give sb a ~** appeler qn; **~s of "long live the queen" could be heard** on entendait crier "vive la reine"; (*Brit: in bar etc*) **it's my ~‡** c'est ma tournée*.
2 vt *order, slogan* crier. **"no" he ~ed** "non" cria-t-il; **to ~ o.s. hoarse** s'enrouer à force de crier; *see* **head**.
3 vi a crier, pousser des cris (*for joy etc* de joie *etc*). **stop ~ing, I'm not deaf!** ne crie pas comme ça, je ne suis pas sourd!; **to ~ with laughter** éclater de rire; **to ~ for help** crier *or* appeler au secours; **she ~ed for Jane to come** elle a appelé Jane en criant *or* à grands cris; **she ~ed for someone to come and help her** elle a appelé pour qu'on vienne l'aider; **he ~ed to *or* at me to throw him the rope** il m'a crié de lui lancer la corde; (*fig*) **it's nothing to ~ about*** ça n'a rien d'extraordinaire, il n'y a pas de quoi en faire un plat*.
b (*scold etc*) **to ~ at sb** engueuler‡ qn, crier après* qn.
►**shout down** vt sep a (*boo, express disagreement*) *speaker* huer. **they shouted down the proposal** ils ont rejeté la proposition avec de hauts cris. b (*shout loudly*) **to shout the place *or* house down** crier comme un damné *or* un sourd; **I thought she was going to shout the place down** elle criait tellement que j'ai crû que tout allait s'écrouler.
►**shout out** 1 vi (*gen*) pousser un cri. **to shout out to sb** interpeller qn. 2 vt sep *order* crier; *slogan* crier, lancer.
shouting ['ʃaʊtɪŋ] n (*NonC*) cris *mpl*, clameur *f*; (*noise of quarrelling*) éclats *mpl* de voix. (*fig*) **it's all over bar the ~** l'important est fait (il ne reste plus que les détails).
shove [ʃʌv] 1 n poussée *f*. **to give sb/sth a ~** pousser qn/qch; **give it a good ~** poussez-le un bon coup.
2 comp ►**shove-ha'penny** (*Brit*) jeu *m* de palet de table.
3 vt a (*push*) pousser; (*with effort*) pousser avec peine *or* effort; (*thrust*) *stick, finger etc* enfoncer (*into* dans, *between* entre); *rag* fourrer (*into* dans); (*jostle*) bousculer. **to ~ sth in/out/down** *etc* faire entrer/sortir/descendre *etc* qch en poussant; **to ~ sth/sb aside** pousser qch/qn de côté, écarter qch/qn (d'un geste); **to ~ sth into a drawer/one's pocket** fourrer qch dans un tiroir/sa poche; **stop shoving me!** arrêtez de me pousser! *or* bousculer!; **to ~ sb into a room** pousser qn dans une pièce; **to ~ sb against a wall** pousser *or* presser qn contre un mur; **to ~ sb off the pavement** pousser qn du trottoir, (*by jostling*) obliger qn à descendre du trottoir (en le bousculant); **to ~ sb/sth out of the way** écarter qn/qch en poussant, pousser qn/qch à l'écart; **he ~d the box under the table** (*moved*) il a poussé *or* fourré la boîte sous la table; (*hid*) il a vite caché la boîte sous la table; **they ~d the car off the road** ils ont poussé la voiture sur le bas-côté; **she ~d the books off the table** elle a poussé *or* balayé les livres de dessus la table; **he ~d his finger into my eye** il m'a mis le doigt dans l'œil; **he ~d his head through the window** il a mis *or* passé la tête par la fenêtre; **he ~d the book into my hand** il m'a fourré le livre dans la main; **to ~ a door open** ouvrir une porte en poussant *or* d'une poussée, pousser une porte (pour l'ouvrir); **to ~ one's way through the crowd** se frayer un chemin dans *or* à travers la foule, s'ouvrir un passage dans la foule en poussant.
b (*: *put*) mettre, poser, ficher*, flanquer*.
4 vi pousser. **stop shoving!** arrêtez de pousser!, ne bousculez pas!; **he ~d (his way) past me** il m'a dépassé en me bousculant; **two men ~d (their way) past** deux hommes sont passés en jouant des coudes *or* en bousculant les gens; **he ~d (his way) through the crowd** il s'est frayé un chemin dans *or* à travers la foule.
►**shove about, shove around** vt sep (*lit*) *object* pousser çà et là *or* dans tous les sens; *person* bousculer; (* *fig: treat high-handedly*) en prendre à son aise avec.
►**shove away** vt sep *person, object* repousser.
►**shove back** vt sep (*push back*) *person, chair* repousser; (*replace*) remettre (à sa place); (*into pocket etc*) fourrer de nouveau, remettre.
►**shove down*** vt sep *object* poser. **he shoved down a few notes before he forgot** il a griffonné *or* gribouillé quelques notes pour ne pas oublier.
►**shove off** 1 vi (*Naut*) pousser au large; (*: *leave*) ficher le camp*, filer*, se tirer‡. 2 vt sep *boat* pousser au large, déborder.
►**shove on*** vt sep a *one's coat etc* enfiler; *hat* enfoncer. b **shove on another record** mets donc un autre disque.
►**shove out** vt sep *boat* pousser au large, déborder; *person* mettre à la porte.
►**shove over** 1 vi (*: *move over*) se pousser. 2 vt sep a (*knock over*) *chair etc* renverser; *person* faire tomber (par terre). b (*over cliff etc*) pousser. c **shove it over to me*** passe-le-moi.
►**shove up*** vi = **shove over 1**.
shovel ['ʃʌvl] 1 n pelle *f*; (*mechanical*) pelleteuse *f*, pelle mécanique.
2 vt *coal, grain* pelleter; (*also* **~ out**) *snow, mud* enlever à la pelle. **to ~ earth into a pile** pelleter la terre pour en faire un tas; (*fig*) **he ~led the food into his mouth*** il fourrait* *or* enfournait* la nourriture dans sa bouche.
►**shovel up** vt sep *sth spilt etc* ramasser avec une pelle *or* à la pelle; *snow* enlever à la pelle.
shoveler ['ʃʌvələʳ] n (canard *m*) souchet *m*.
shovelful ['ʃʌvlfʊl] n pelletée *f*.
show [ʃəʊ] (*vb: pret* **showed**, *ptp* **shown** *or* **showed**) 1 n a [*hatred etc*] manifestation *f*, démonstration *f*; [*affection etc*] démonstration, témoignage *m*; (*semblance*) apparence *f*, semblant *m*; (*ostentation*) parade *f*. **there were some fine pieces on ~** quelques beaux objets étaient exposés; **an impressive ~ of strength** un impressionnant étalage de force, une impressionnante démonstration de force; **a ~ of hands** un vote à main levée; **to vote by ~ of hands** voter à main levée; **the dahlias make *or* are a splendid ~** les dahlias sont splendides (à voir) *or* offrent un spectacle splendide; **they make a great ~ of their wealth** ils font parade *or* étalage de leur richesse; **with a ~ of emotion** en affectant l'émotion, en affectant d'être ému; **they made a ~ of resistance** ils ont fait semblant de résister, ils ont offert un simulacre de résistance; **to make a ~ of doing** faire semblant *or* mine de faire; **just for ~** pour l'effet.
b (*exhibition*) (*Agr, Art, Tech etc*) exposition *f*; (*Comm*) foire *f*; (*Agr: contest*) concours *m*. **flower ~** floralies *fpl*; (*smaller*) exposition de fleurs; **dress ~** défilé *m* de couture; [*artist etc*] **he's holding his first London ~** il a sa première exposition à Londres, il expose à Londres pour la première fois; **the Boat S~** le Salon de la Navigation; *see* **dog, fashion, motor** *etc*.
c (*Theat etc*) spectacle *m*; (*variety ~*) show *m*. **there are several good ~s on in London** on donne plusieurs bons spectacles à Londres en ce moment; **I often go to a ~** je vais souvent au spectacle; **the last ~ starts at 9** (*Theat*) la dernière représentation *or* (*Cine*) la dernière séance commence à 21 heures; **there is no ~ on Sundays** (*Theat*) il n'y a pas de représentation le dimanche; (*Cine*) il n'y a pas de séance le dimanche; **on with the ~!** que la représentation commence (*subj*)! *or* continue (*subj*)!; **the ~ must go on** (*Theat, fig*) il faut continuer malgré tout; (*fig*) **let's get the ~ on the road*** il faut faire démarrer* tout ça, passons à l'action.
d (*phrases*) (*esp Brit*) **good ~!*** bravo!; **to put up a good ~** faire bonne figure, bien se défendre*; **to make a poor ~** faire triste *or* piètre figure; **it's a poor ~*** c'est lamentable, il n'y a pas de quoi être fier; **it's a poor ~* that ...** il est malheureux que ... + *subj*; **this is Paul's ~*** c'est Paul qui commande ici; **to run the ~*** faire marcher l'affaire; **to give the ~ away*** vendre la mèche*; *see* **steal** *etc*.
2 comp ►**show bill** (*Theat*) affiche *f* de spectacle ►**show biz*** = **show business** ►**showboat** (*US*) n (*lit*) bateau-théâtre *m*; (‡ *fig: person*) m'as-tu-vu(e)* *m(f)* (*pl inv*) ◊ vi crâner*, en mettre plein la vue ►**show business** le monde du spectacle, l'industrie *f* du spectacle ►**showcase** (*lit, fig*) vitrine *f*; **showcase project** opération *f* de prestige ►**showdown** épreuve *f* de force ►**show flat** (*Brit*) appartement *m* témoin ►**show girl** girl *f* ►**showground** champ *m* de foire ►**show house** (*Brit*) maison *f* témoin ►**showjumper** (*rider*) cavalier *m*, -ière *f* de concours hippique; (*horse*) cheval *m* (de saut) d'obstacles, jumpe(u)r *m* ►**show jumping** (*NonC*) concours *m* hippique, saut *m* d'obstacles, jumping *m* ►**showman, pl -men** (*in fair, circus etc*) forain *m*; (*fig*) **he's a real showman** il a vraiment le sens de la mise en scène (*fig*) ►**showmanship** art *m or* don *m or* sens *m* de la mise en scène ►**show-me* attitude** (*US*) attitude *f* sceptique ►**the Show-me State** (*US*) le Missouri ►**show-off** m'as-tu-vu(e)* *m(f)* (*pl inv*) ►**showpiece** (*of exhibition etc*) trésor *m*, joyau *m*, clou* *m*; **this vase is a real showpiece** ce vase est une pièce remarquable; **the new school is a showpiece *or* showplace** la nouvelle école est un modèle du genre ►**showplace** (*see also* **showpiece**) (*tourist attraction*) lieu *m* de grand intérêt touristique; (*US*) **showplace home** maison *f* de rêve ►**showroom** magasin *m or* salle *f* d'exposition; (*Aut*) **in showroom condition** à l'état *m* de neuf ►**show-stopper: he/it was a show-stopper*** il était/c'était le clou* du spectacle ►**show trial** (*Jur*) grand procès *m* (*souvent idéologique*) ►**show window** (*lit, fig*) vitrine *f*.
3 vt a (*display, make visible*) montrer, faire voir; *ticket, passport* montrer, présenter; (*exhibit*) *goods for sale, picture, dog* exposer. **~ it me!** faites voir!, montrez-le moi!; **we're going to ~ (you) some slides** nous allons (vous) passer *or* projeter quelques diapositives; **they ~ a film during the flight** on passe un film *or* il y a une projection de cinéma pendant le vol; **what is ~ing at that cinema/at the Odeon?** qu'est-ce qu'on donne *or* qu'est-ce qui passe dans ce cinéma/à l'Odéon?; **the film was first ~n in 1974** ce film est sorti en 1974; **it has been ~n on television** c'est passé à la télévision; (*in shop*) **what can I ~ you?** que puis-je vous montrer?, que désirez-vous voir?; **as ~n by the graph** comme le montre *or* l'indique le graphique; **as ~n in the illustration on page 4** voir l'illustration page 4; (*fig*) **there's nothing to ~ for it** on ne le dirait pas, ça ne se voit *or* ne se remarque pas; **he has nothing to ~ for it** il n'en a rien tiré, ça ne lui a rien donné *or* apporté; **he has nothing to ~ for all the effort he has put into it** les efforts qu'il y a consacrés n'ont rien donné; **I ought to ~ myself at Paul's party** il faudrait que je fasse acte de présence à la soirée de Paul; **he daren't ~ himself *or* his face there again** il n'ose plus s'y montrer *or* montrer son nez là-bas*; (*fig*) **to ~ one's hand *or* cards** dévoiler ses intentions, abattre son jeu *or* ses cartes; (*fig*) **to ~ a clean pair of heels** se sauver à toutes jambes; (*Brit fig*) **~ a leg!*** lève-toi!, debout!; (*lit, fig*) **to ~ one's teeth** montrer les

dents; (*fig*) **to ~ sb the door** mettre qn à la porte; (*fig*) **to ~ the flag** être là pour le principe, faire acte de présence.
b (*indicate*) *[dial, clock etc]* indiquer, marquer; (*gen*) montrer, indiquer. **what time does your watch ~?** quelle heure est-il à votre montre?; (*Comm, Fin*) **to ~ a loss/profit** indiquer une perte/un bénéfice; **the figures ~ a rise over last year's sales** les chiffres montrent *or* indiquent que les ventes ont augmenté par rapport à l'année dernière; **the roads are ~n in red** les routes sont marquées en rouge.
c (*demonstrate*) montrer, faire voir; (*reveal*) montrer, laisser voir; (*explain*) montrer, expliquer; (*prove*) montrer, prouver; *one's intelligence, kindness, courage, tact* montrer, faire preuve de; *one's interest, enthusiasm, surprise, agreement* montrer, manifester; *one's approval* montrer, indiquer; *one's gratitude, respect* témoigner. **to ~ loyalty** se montrer loyal (*to sb* envers qn); **that dress ~s her bra** cette robe laisse voir son soutien-gorge; **this skirt ~s the dirt** cette jupe est salissante; **it's ~ing signs of wear** cela porte des signes d'usure; **he was ~ing signs of tiredness** il montrait des signes de fatigue; **it ~ed signs of having been used** il était visible qu'on s'en était servi, manifestement on s'en était servi; **it was ~ing signs of rain** il avait l'air de vouloir pleuvoir; **to ~ fight** faire montre de combativité; **her choice of clothes ~s good taste** sa façon de s'habiller témoigne de son bon goût; **he ~ed that he was angry** il a montré *or* manifesté *or* laissé voir *or* laissé paraître sa colère; **she's beginning to ~ her age** elle commence à faire son âge; **this ~s great intelligence** cela montre *or* révèle *or* dénote beaucoup d'intelligence; **he ~ed himself (to be) a coward** il s'est montré *or* révélé lâche; **to ~ sth to be true** démontrer la vérité de qch, montrer que qch est vrai; **it all goes to ~ that ...** tout cela montre *or* prouve bien que ...; **it only** *or* **just goes to ~!*** tu m'en diras tant!*, c'est bien ça la vie!; **I ~ed him that it was impossible** je lui ai prouvé *or* démontré que c'était impossible; **he ~ed me how it works** il m'a montré *or* il m'a fait voir comment cela fonctionne; (*fig*) **I'll ~ him!*** je lui apprendrai!; **to ~ sb the way** montrer *or* indiquer le chemin à qn; **I'll ~ you the way** suivez-moi (je vais vous montrer le chemin); *see* **willing** *etc*.
d (*guide, conduct*) **to ~ sb into the room** faire entrer qn dans la pièce; **to ~ sb to his seat** placer qn; **to ~ sb to the door** reconduire qn jusqu'à la porte; **to ~ sb over** *or* **round a house** faire visiter une maison à qn.
4 vi a *[emotion]* être visible; *[stain, scar]* se voir; *[underskirt etc]* dépasser. **it doesn't ~** cela ne se voit pas, on ne dirait pas; **don't worry, it won't ~** ne t'inquiète pas, ça ne se verra pas; **his fear ~ed on his face** la peur se voyait *or* se lisait sur son visage.
b (*‡: arrive*) = **show up 1b**.

►**show about, show around** vt sep faire visiter les lieux *mpl* (*or* la ville *or* la maison *etc*) à.

►**show in** vt sep *visitor etc* faire entrer.

►**show off** 1 vi (*gen*) crâner*, poser (pour la galerie); *[child]* chercher à se rendre intéressant, faire l'intéressant. **she's always showing off** c'est une crâneuse* *or* une poseuse; **stop showing off** (*gen*) arrête de crâner* *or* d'en fiche plein la vue*; (*showing off knowledge*) arrête d'étaler ta science*. 2 vt sep a *sb's beauty, complexion etc* faire valoir, mettre en valeur. b (*pej*) *one's wealth, knowledge etc* faire parade *or* étalage de, étaler. **he wanted to show off his new car** il voulait faire admirer sa nouvelle voiture. 3 **show-off** n *see* **show 2**. 4 **showing-off** n *see* **showing 2**.

►**show out** vt sep *visitor etc* accompagner *or* reconduire (jusqu'à la porte).

►**show round** vt sep = **show about, show around**.

►**show through** vi (*be visible*) se voir au travers.

►**show up** 1 vi a (*stand out*) *[feature]* ressortir; *[mistake]* être visible *or* manifeste; *[stain]* se voir (nettement). **the tower showed up clearly against the sky** la tour se détachait nettement sur le ciel. b (**:arrive, appear*) arriver, se pointer*, s'amener*. 2 vt sep a *visitor etc* faire monter. b *fraud, impostor* démasquer, dénoncer; *flaw, defect* faire ressortir. c (*embarrass*) faire honte à (en public).

shower ['ʃaʊəʳ] 1 n a *[rain]* averse *f*; (*fig*) *[blows]* volée *f*, avalanche *f*, grêle *f*; *[sparks, stones, arrows]* pluie *f*; *[blessings]* déluge *m*; *[insults]* torrent *m*, flot *m*.
b douche *f*. **to have** *or* **take a ~** prendre une douche.
c (*Brit ‡ pej: people*) bande *f* de crétins*.
d (*before wedding etc*) **to give a ~ for sb** organiser une soirée pour donner ses cadeaux à qn.
2 comp ► **shower bath†** = **shower 1b** ► **shower cap** bonnet *m* de douche ► **showerproof** imperméable ► **shower unit** bloc-douche *m*.
3 vt (*fig*) **to ~ sb with gifts/praise, to ~ gifts/praise on sb** combler qn de cadeaux/de louanges; **to ~ blows on sb** faire pleuvoir des coups sur qn; **to ~ abuse** *or* **insults on sb** accabler *or* couvrir qn d'injures; **invitations were/advice was ~ed (up) on him** des invitations/des conseils pleuvaient sur lui.
4 vi a (*wash*) se doucher, prendre une douche.
b (*fall*) **small stones/hailstones ~ed (down) on to the car** des petites pierres/grêlons pleuvaient sur la voiture; **advice ~ed upon him** les conseils pleuvaient sur lui.

showery ['ʃaʊərɪ] adj *day* pluvieux. **it will be ~** il y aura des averses.

showing ['ʃəʊɪŋ] 1 n a *[pictures etc]* exposition *f*; *[film]* projection *f*. (*Cine*) **the first ~ is at 8 p.m.** la première séance est à 20 heures; (*Cine, TV*) **another ~ of this film** une nouvelle projection de ce film. b (*performance*) performance *f*, prestation* *f*. **on this ~ he doesn't stand much chance** si c'est là ce dont il est capable *or* à en juger d'après cette prestation*, il n'a pas de grandes chances; **he made a good ~** il s'en est bien tiré; **he made a poor ~** il ne s'est vraiment pas distingué. c **on his own ~** de son propre aveu. 2 comp ► **showing-off** (*NonC*) pose *f*, crânerie* *f*.

shown [ʃəʊn] ptp of **show**.

showy ['ʃəʊɪ] adj *garment, material, décor* qui attire l'attention, voyant (*pej*), tape-à-l'œil* *inv* (*pej*); *colour* éclatant, voyant (*pej*), criard (*pej*); (*pej*) *manner* ostentatoire, prétentieux; (*pej*) *ceremony* plein d'ostentation.

shrank [ʃræŋk] pret of **shrink**.

shrapnel ['ʃræpnl] n (*Mil*) a obus *m* à balles, shrapnel *m*. b (*NonC*) éclats *mpl* d'obus.

shred [ʃred] 1 n *[cloth, paper, skin, plastic sheeting]* lambeau *m*; (*fig*) *[truth]* parcelle *f*, grain *m*; *[commonsense]* once *f*, atome *m*, grain. **not a ~ of evidence** pas la moindre *or* plus petite preuve; **her dress hung in ~s** sa robe était en lambeaux; **without a ~ of clothing on** nu comme un ver, complètement nu; 2 vt a *paper etc* (*gen*) mettre en lambeaux, déchiqueter; (*in shredder*) détruire (par lacération), déchiqueter. b *carrots etc* râper; *cabbage, lettuce* couper en lanières.

shredder ['ʃredəʳ] n a *[food processor]* (disque-)râpeur *m*. b (*also* **paper** *or* **document ~**) destructeur *m* (de documents), déchiqueteuse *f*. **to put through the ~** détruire, déchiqueter.

shrew [ʃruː] n a (*Zool*) musaraigne *f*. b (*woman*) mégère *f*, chipie* *f*; *see* **taming**.

shrewd [ʃruːd] adj *person* (*clearsighted*) perspicace; (*cunning*) astucieux; *businessman, lawyer* habile; *assessment* perspicace; *plan* astucieux; *reasoning, action* judicieux. **I have a ~ idea that ...** je soupçonne fortement que ..., j'ai l'impression très nette que ...; **I've a ~ idea of what he will say** je vois d'ici *or* je sais d'avance ce qu'il va dire; **I can make a ~ guess at how many there were** je peux deviner à peu près combien il y en avait; **that was a ~ move** il (*or* elle) a bien manœuvré.

shrewdly ['ʃruːdlɪ] adv *assess, suspect* avec perspicacité; *reason* habilement; *guess* astucieusement.

shrewdness ['ʃruːdnɪs] n *[person]* perspicacité *f*, habileté *f*, sagacité *f*; *[assessment]* perspicacité; *[plan]* astuce *f*.

shrewish ['ʃruːɪʃ] adj acariâtre, de mégère, de chipie*.

shriek [ʃriːk] 1 n hurlement *m*, cri perçant *or* aigu. **to give a ~** pousser un hurlement *or* un cri; **~s of laughter** grands éclats de rire; **with ~s of laughter** en riant à gorge déployée. 2 vi hurler, crier (*with* de). **to ~ with laughter** rire à gorge déployée, se tordre de rire; (*fig*) **the colour simply ~s at one** cette couleur hurle *or* est vraiment criarde. 3 vt hurler, crier. **to ~ abuse at sb** hurler des injures à qn; **"no" he ~ed** "non" hurla-t-il.

shrift [ʃrɪft] n: **to give sb short ~** expédier qn sans ménagement, envoyer promener qn*; **I got short ~ from him** il m'a traité sans ménagement, il m'a envoyé promener*.

shrike [ʃraɪk] n pie-grièche *f*.

shrill [ʃrɪl] 1 adj *voice* criard, perçant, aigu (*f* -guë); *cry* perçant, aigu; *whistle, laugh, music* strident. 2 vi *[whistle etc]* retentir. 3 vt: **"stop!" she ~ed** "arrête!" cria-t-elle d'une voix perçante *or* stridente.

shrillness ['ʃrɪlnɪs] n (*NonC*) ton aigu *or* perçant.

shrilly ['ʃrɪlɪ] adv d'un ton aigu *or* perçant.

shrimp [ʃrɪmp] 1 n crevette *f*. (*fig*) **he's just a little ~** il n'est pas plus haut que trois pommes. 2 comp ► **shrimp cocktail** (*Culin*) hors-d'œuvre *m* de crevettes ► **shrimp sauce** sauce *f* crevette. 3 vi: **to go ~ing** aller pêcher la crevette.

shrine [ʃraɪn] n (*place of worship*) lieu saint, lieu de pèlerinage; (*reliquary*) châsse *f*; (*tomb*) tombeau *m*; (*fig*) haut lieu.

shrink [ʃrɪŋk] pret **shrank**, ptp **shrunk** 1 vi a (*get smaller*) *[clothes]* rétrécir; *[area]* se réduire; *[boundaries]* se resserrer; *[piece of meat]* réduire; *[body, person]* se ratatiner, rapetisser; *[wood]* se contracter; *[quantity, amount]* diminuer. (*on label*) **"will not ~"** "irrétrécissable".
b (*also* **~ away, ~ back**) reculer, se dérober (*from sth* devant qch, *from doing* devant l'idée de faire). **she shrank (away** *or* **back) from him** elle a eu un mouvement de recul; **he did not ~ from saying that ...** il n'a pas craint de dire que ... .
2 vt *wool* (faire) rétrécir; *metal* contracter.
3 n (*‡: psychiatrist*) psychiatre *mf*, psy* *mf*.
4 comp ► **shrink-wrap** vt emballer sous film plastique (par rétraction) ► **shrink-wrapped** emballé sous film plastique.

shrinkage ['ʃrɪŋkɪdʒ] n (*see* **shrink**) rétrécissement *m*; contraction *f*; diminution *f*; *[metal]* retrait *m*. **allowing for ~** compte tenu du rétrécissement.

shrinking ['ʃrɪŋkɪŋ] adj craintif. (*fig*) **~ violet** sensitive *f*, personne *f* sensible et timide.

shrive†† [ʃraɪv] pret **shrived** *or* **shrove**, ptp **shrived** *or* **shriven** vt confesser et absoudre.

shrivel ['ʃrɪvl] (*also* **~ up**) 1 vi *[apple, body]* se ratatiner; *[skin]* se rider, se flétrir; *[leaf]* se flétrir, se racornir; *[steak]* se racornir, se ratatiner. (*fig*) **her answer made him ~ (up)** sa réponse lui a donné envie de rentrer sous terre. 2 vt ratatiner; rider; flétrir; racornir.

shriven [ˈʃrɪvn] ptp of **shrive**.

shroud [ʃraʊd] 1 n a linceul *m*, suaire *m* (*liter*); (*fig*) *[mist]* voile *m*, linceul (*liter*); *[snow]* linceul (*liter*); *[mystery]* voile. b *[mast]* hauban *m*; *[parachute]* suspentes *fpl*. c (*Space: of rocket*) coiffe *f*. 2 vt *corpse* envelopper dans un linceul, ensevelir. (*fig*) **~ed in mist/snow** enseveli sous la brume/la neige, sous un linceul de brume/de neige (*liter*); **~ed in mystery** enveloppé de mystère.

shrove [ʃrəʊv] 1 pret of **shrive**. 2 comp ►**Shrovetide** les jours gras (*les trois jours précédant le Carême*) ►**Shrove Tuesday** (le) Mardi gras.

shrub [ʃrʌb] n arbrisseau *m*; (*small*) arbuste *m*; *see* **flowering**.

shrubbery [ˈʃrʌbərɪ] n (massif *m* d')arbustes *mpl*.

shrug [ʃrʌg] 1 n haussement *m* d'épaules. **to give a ~ of contempt** hausser les épaules (en signe) de mépris; **... he said with a ~ ...** dit-il en haussant les épaules *or* avec un haussement d'épaules. 2 vti: **to ~ (one's shoulders)** hausser les épaules.

►**shrug off** vt sep *suggestion, warning* dédaigner, faire fi de; *remark* ignorer, ne pas relever; *infection, a cold* se débarrasser de.

shrunk [ʃrʌŋk] ptp of **shrink**.

shrunken [ˈʃrʌŋkən] adj *person, body* ratatiné, rabougri. **~ head** tête réduite.

shtick [ʃtɪk] n (*US: Theat, also gen*) truc* *m*.

shtoom‡ [ʃtʊm] adj: **to keep ~ (about sth)** garder bouche cousue* (à propos de qch).

shuck [ʃʌk] (*US*) 1 n (*pod*) cosse *f*; *[nut]* écale *f*; *[chestnut]* bogue *f*; *[corn]* spathe *f*. 2 excl: **~s!*** mince alors!*, zut alors!* 3 vt *bean* écosser; *nut* écaler; *chestnut* éplucher; *corn* égrener. **to ~ one's clothes** se déshabiller à la va-vite.

shudder [ˈʃʌdəʳ] 1 n (*from cold*) frisson *m*; (*from horror*) frisson, frémissement *m*; *[vehicle, ship, engine]* vibration *f*, trépidation *f*. **to give a ~** *[person]* frissonner, frémir; *[vehicle, ship]* avoir une forte secousse, être ébranlé; **it gives me the ~s*** ça me donne des frissons; **he realized with a ~ that ...** il a frissonné *or* frémi, comprenant que ... .
2 vi (*from cold*) frissonner; (*from horror*) frémir, frissonner; *[engine, motor]* vibrer, trépider; *[vehicle, ship]* (*on striking sth*) avoir une forte secousse, être ébranlé; (*for mechanical reasons*) vibrer, trépider. **I ~ to think what might have happened** je frémis rien qu'à la pensée de ce qui aurait pu se produire; **what will he do next? — I ~ to think!** qu'est-ce qu'il va encore faire? — j'en frémis d'avance!

shuffle [ˈʃʌfl] 1 n a **the ~ of footsteps** le bruit d'une démarche traînante. b (*Cards*) battage *m*; (*fig*) réorganisation *f*. **give the cards a good ~** bats bien les cartes; (*Parl*) **a cabinet (re)~** un remaniement ministériel. 2 comp: **shuffleboard** jeu *m* de palets. 3 vt a **to ~ one's feet** traîner les pieds. b *cards* battre; *dominoes* mêler, brouiller; *papers* remuer, déranger. 4 vi a traîner les pieds. **to ~ in/out/along** *etc* entrer/sortir/avancer *etc* d'un pas traînant *or* en traînant les pieds. b (*Cards*) battre (les cartes).

►**shuffle off** 1 vi s'en aller *or* s'éloigner d'un pas traînant *or* en traînant les pieds. 2 vt sep *garment* enlever maladroitement; (*fig*) *responsibility* rejeter (*on to sb* sur qn), se dérober à.

►**shuffle out of** vt fus (*fig*) *duty, responsibility* se dérober à.

shufti, shufty‡ [ˈʃʌftɪ, ˈʃʊftɪ] n (*Brit*) **to have** *or* **take a ~ (at sth)** jeter un œil* *or* coup d'œil (à qch).

shun [ʃʌn] vt *place, temptation* fuir; *person, publicity* fuir, éviter; *work, obligation* éviter, esquiver. **I ~ned his company** j'ai fui sa présence; **to ~ doing** éviter de faire.

shunt [ʃʌnt] 1 vt a (*Rail*) (*direct*) aiguiller; (*divert*) dériver, détourner; (*move about*) manœuvrer; (*position*) garer. b (* *fig*) *conversation, discussion* aiguiller, détourner (*on to* sur); *person* expédier* (*to* à). (*fig*) **they ~ed the visitors to and fro between the factory and the offices*** ils ont fait faire la navette aux visiteurs entre l'usine et les bureaux; **~ that book over to me!**‡ passe-moi *or* file-moi ce bouquin!* c (*Elec*) shunter, dériver. 2 vi (* *fig*) *[person, object, document]* **to ~ (to and fro)** faire la navette (*between* entre). 3 n (*Rail*) aiguillage *m*; (*fig* *) collision *f*.

shunter [ˈʃʌntəʳ] n (*Brit Rail*) (*person*) aiguilleur *m* (de train); (*engine*) locomotive *f* de manœuvre.

shunting [ˈʃʌntɪŋ] (*Rail*) 1 n manœuvres *fpl* d'aiguillage. 2 comp ►**shunting operation** (*Brit*) opération *f* de triage ►**shunting yard** voies *fpl* de garage et de triage.

shush [ʃʊʃ] 1 excl chut! 2 vt (*) faire chut à; (*silence: also* **~ up**) faire taire.

shut [ʃʌt] pret, ptp **shut** 1 vt *eyes, door, factory, shop* fermer; *drawer* (re)fermer, repousser. **the shop is ~ now** le magasin est fermé maintenant; **the shop is ~ on Sundays** le magasin ferme *or* est fermé le dimanche; **we're ~ting the office for 2 weeks in July** nous fermons le bureau pour 2 semaines au mois de juillet; **to ~ one's finger in a drawer** se pincer *or* se prendre le doigt dans un tiroir; **to ~ sb in a room** enfermer qn dans une pièce; **~ your mouth!**‡ ferme-la!‡, boucle-la!‡; **~ your face!**‡ ta gueule!‡, la ferme!‡; *see* **door, ear**[1], **eye, open, stable**[2] *etc*.
2 vi *[door, box, lid, drawer]* se fermer, fermer; *[museum, theatre, shop]* fermer. **the door ~** la porte s'est (re)fermée; **the door ~s badly** la porte ferme mal; **the shop ~s on Sundays/at 6 o'clock** le magasin ferme le dimanche/à 18 heures.
3 comp ►**shutdown** fermeture *f* ►**shut-eye**‡: **to get a bit of shut-eye** *or* **some shut-eye** piquer un roupillon‡, dormir un peu ►**shut-in** (*esp US*) enfermé, confiné ►**shutoff (device)** interrupteur *m* automatique, dispositif *m* d'arrêt automatique ►**shut-out** (*Ind*) lock-out *m inv*; (*US Sport*) victoire éclatante (*au cours de laquelle une équipe ne marque pas de points*); **shut-out bid** (*Bridge*) (annonce *f* de) barrage *m*.

►**shut away** vt sep *person, animal* enfermer; *valuables* mettre sous clef. **he shuts himself away** il s'enferme chez lui, il vit en reclus.

►**shut down** 1 vi *[business, shop, theatre]* fermer (définitivement), fermer ses portes. 2 vt sep *lid* fermer, rabattre; *business, shop, theatre* fermer (définitivement); *machine* arrêter. 3 **shutdown** n *see* **shut 3**.

►**shut in** 1 vt sep *person, animal* enfermer; (*surround*) entourer (*with* de). **to feel shut in** se sentir enfermé *or* emprisonné (*fig*). 2 **shut-in** adj *see* **shut 3**.

►**shut off** 1 vt sep a (*stop, cut*) *electricity, gas* couper, fermer; *engine* couper; *supplies* arrêter, couper. b (*isolate*) *person* isoler, séparer (*from* de). **we're very shut off here** nous sommes coupés de tout ici *or* très isolés ici. 2 **shutoff** n, adj *see* **shut 3**.

►**shut out** 1 vt sep a **he found that they had shut him out, he found himself shut out** il a trouvé qu'il était à la porte *or* qu'il ne pouvait pas entrer; **don't shut me out, I haven't got a key** ne ferme pas la porte, je n'ai pas de clef; **I shut the cat out at night** je laisse *or* mets le chat dehors pour la nuit; **close the door and shut out the noise** ferme la porte pour qu'on n'entende pas le bruit; **he shut them out of his will** il les a exclus de son testament; **you can't shut him out of your life** tu ne peux pas l'exclure *or* le bannir de ta vie.
b (*block*) *view* boucher; *memory* chasser de son esprit.
c (*US Sport*) *opponent* bloquer.
2 **shut-out** n, adj *see* **shut 3**.

►**shut to** 1 vi *[door]* se (re)fermer. 2 vt sep (re)fermer.

►**shut up** 1 vi (*: *be quiet*) se taire. **shut up!** tais-toi!, ferme-la!‡, boucle-la!‡; **better just shut up and get on with it** mieux vaut se taire *or* ne rien dire et continuer. 2 vt sep a *factory, business, theatre, house* fermer; *see* **shop**. b *person, animal* enfermer; *valuables* mettre sous clef. **to shut sb up in prison** emprisonner qn, mettre qn en prison. c (*: *silence*) faire taire, clouer le bec à*.

shutter [ˈʃʌtəʳ] 1 n volet *m*; (*Phot*) obturateur *m*. **to put up the ~s** mettre les volets; (*Comm*) fermer (le magasin); (*fig: permanently*) fermer boutique, fermer définitivement. 2 comp ►**shutter speed** vitesse *f* d'obturation.

shuttered [ˈʃʌtəd] adj (*with closed shutters*) *window, house etc* aux volets fermés; (*fitted with shutters*) *window* avec des volets. **the windows were ~** (*closed shutters*) les fenêtres avaient leurs volets fermés; (*fitted with shutters*) les fenêtres avaient des volets.

shuttle [ˈʃʌtl] 1 n a *[loom, sewing machine]* navette *f*.
b (*plane, train etc*) navette *f*. **air ~** navette aérienne; **space ~** navette spatiale.
c (*: *shuttlecock*) volant *m* (*Badminton*).
2 comp ►**shuttlecock** volant *m* (*Badminton*) ►**shuttle diplomacy** navettes *fpl* diplomatiques ►**shuttle movement** (*Tech*) mouvement alternatif ►**shuttle service** (*Aviat, Rail etc*) (service *m* de) navette *f*.
3 vi *[person, vehicle, boat, documents]* faire la navette (*between* entre).
4 vt: **to ~ sb to and fro** envoyer qn à droite et à gauche; **he was ~d (back and forth) between the factory and the office** on l'a renvoyé de l'usine au bureau et vice versa, il a dû faire la navette entre l'usine et le bureau; **the papers were ~d (backwards and forwards) from one department to another** les documents ont été renvoyés d'un service à l'autre.

shy[1] [ʃaɪ] 1 adj *person* timide; (*reserved*) réservé; (*unsociable*) sauvage; *animal* timide, peureux; *look, smile* timide; (*self-conscious*) embarrassé, gauche. **he's a ~ person, he's ~ of people** c'est un timide, il est mal à l'aise avec les gens, il est sauvage; **he's ~ with** *or* **of women** il est timide avec les femmes *or* auprès des femmes, les femmes l'intimident; **to make sb (feel) ~** intimider qn, gêner qn, embarrasser qn; **don't be ~** ne fais pas le (*or* la) timide; **don't be ~ of telling me what you want** n'ayez pas peur de *or* n'hésitez pas à *or* ne craignez pas de me dire ce que vous voulez; **I'm rather ~ of inviting him** je n'ose guère l'inviter, j'ai un peu peur de l'inviter; (*US fig*) **he is 2 months ~ of 70** il aura 70 ans dans 2 mois; (*US fig*) **I'm $5 ~** il me manque 5 dollars; *see* **bite, fight, work** *etc*.
2 vi *[horse]* broncher (*at* devant).

►**shy away** vi (*fig*) **to shy away from doing** répugner à faire, s'effaroucher à l'idée de faire.

shy[2] [ʃaɪ] (*Brit*) 1 vt (*throw*) lancer, jeter. 2 n (*lit*) **to take** *or* **have a ~ at sth** lancer un projectile (*or* une pierre *etc*) vers qch; **"20p a ~"** "20 pence le coup"; (*fig: try*) **to have a ~ at doing** tenter de faire; *see* **coconut**.

shyly [ˈʃaɪlɪ] adv (*see* **shy**[1] **1**) timidement; avec réserve; gauchement.

shyness [ˈʃaɪnɪs] n (*see* **shy**[1] **1**) timidité *f*; réserve *f*; sauvagerie *f*;

embarras *m*, gaucherie *f*.

shyster* [ˈʃaɪstəʳ] n escroc *m*; (*specifically lawyer*) avocat véreux *or* marron.

SI [ˌesˈaɪ] n (abbr of **Système international (d'unités)**) SI *m*.

si [siː] n (*Mus*) si *m*.

Siam [saɪˈæm] n Siam *m*.

Siamese [ˌsaɪəˈmiːz] 1 adj siamois. ~ **cat** chat siamois; ~ **twins** (frères) siamois, (sœurs) siamoises. 2 n a (pl inv) Siamois(e) *m(f)*. b (*Ling*) siamois *m*.

SIB [ˌesaɪˈbiː] n (*Brit*) (abbr of **Securities and Investments Board**) ≈ COB *f*.

Siberia [saɪˈbɪərɪə] n Sibérie *f*.

Siberian [saɪˈbɪərɪən] 1 adj sibérien, de Sibérie. 2 n Sibérien(ne) *m(f)*.

sibilant [ˈsɪbɪlənt] 1 adj (*also Phon*) sifflant. 2 n (*Phon*) sifflante *f*.

sibling [ˈsɪblɪŋ] 1 n: ~**s** enfants *mfpl* de mêmes parents; **one of his ~s** l'un de ses frères et sœurs; **Paul and Lucy are ~s** Paul et Lucie sont de mêmes parents *or* sont frère et sœur. 2 comp ▸**sibling rivalry** (*Psych*) rivalité fraternelle.

sibyl [ˈsɪbɪl] n sibylle *f*.

sibylline [ˈsɪbɪlaɪn] adj sibyllin.

sic [sɪk] adv sic.

Sicilian [sɪˈsɪlɪən] 1 adj sicilien. 2 n a Sicilien(ne) *m(f)*. b (*Ling*) sicilien *m*.

Sicily [ˈsɪsɪlɪ] n Sicile *f*. **in ~** en Sicile.

sick [sɪk] 1 adj a (*ill*) *person* malade; *pallor* maladif. **he's a ~ man** c'est un malade; **he's (away *or* off) ~** (il n'est pas là,) il est malade; **to go ~** se faire porter malade; **to fall *or* take ~** tomber malade; **to be ~ of a fever**† avoir la fièvre; *see* **home, off** *etc*.

b (*Brit: nauseated, vomiting*) **to be ~** vomir; **to feel ~** avoir mal au cœur, avoir des nausées, avoir envie de vomir; **a ~ feeling** (*lit*) un haut-le-cœur; (*fig*) une (sensation d')angoisse; **melon makes me ~** le melon me fait mal au cœur *or* (*stronger*) me fait vomir (*see also* **1c**); **I get ~ in planes** j'ai mal au cœur *or* je suis malade en avion, j'ai le mal de l'air; ~ **headache** migraine *f*; *see* **sea** *etc*.

c (*fig*) *mind, imagination, fancies* malsain. ~ **humour** humour noir; ~ **joke** plaisanterie macabre *or* malsaine; ~ **comedian** comédien porté sur l'humour noir; **to be ~ at heart** avoir la mort dans l'âme; **to be ~ of sth/sb*** en avoir assez de qch/qn, en avoir marre* de qch/qn; **to be ~ and tired of sth/sb*** en avoir par-dessus la tête de qch/qn; **to be ~ to death* *or* to the (back) teeth‡ of** en avoir par-dessus la tête de, en avoir ras le bol‡ *or* plein le dos* de; **to be ~ of the sight of sth/sb*** en avoir assez *or* marre* de voir qch/qn; **it's enough to make you ~** il y a de quoi vous écœurer *or* vous rendre malade*; **it makes me ~ to think that ...** ça m'écœure *or* me dégoûte de penser que ...; **you make me ~!*** tu m'écœures!, tu me dégoûtes!; **he was really ~ at failing the exam‡** il était vraiment écœuré d'avoir échoué à l'examen; **he really looked ~‡** il avait l'air écœuré, il faisait une de ces têtes!*

2 n (*Brit *: vomit*) vomi* *m*, vomissure *f*.

3 npl: **the ~** les malades *mpl*.

4 comp ▸**sick bay** infirmerie *f* ▸**sickbed** lit *m* de malade ▸**sick benefit** (*Brit*) (prestations *fpl* de l')assurance *f* maladie ▸**sick building syndrome** *maladie dont peuvent être atteints les employés travaillant dans des bureaux climatisés* ▸**sick leave: on sick leave** en congé *m* de maladie ▸**sick list: to be on the sick list** (*Admin*) être porté malade; (*: *ill*) être malade ▸**sick-making‡** dégoûtant ▸**sick note*** (*for work*) certificat *m* médical; (*for school*) billet *m* d'excuse ▸**sick pay** indemnité *f* de maladie (*versée par l'employeur*) ▸**sick-room** (*in school etc*) infirmerie *f*; (*at home*) chambre *f* de malade.

▸**sick up*** vt sep (*Brit*) vomir, rendre.

sicken [ˈsɪkn] 1 vt rendre malade, donner mal au cœur à; (*fig*) dégoûter, écœurer. 2 vi tomber malade. *[person]* **to ~ for sth** couver qch; (*fig*) **to ~ of** se lasser de, en avoir assez de.

sickening [ˈsɪknɪŋ] adj *sight, smell* écœurant, qui soulève le cœur; (*fig*) *cruelty, crime* répugnant, ignoble; *waste* dégoûtant, révoltant; (*: *annoying*) *person, behaviour* agaçant, exaspérant.

sickeningly [ˈsɪknɪŋlɪ] adv: **it is ~ sweet** c'est tellement sucré que c'en est écœurant; ~ **polite*** d'une politesse écœurante.

sickle [ˈsɪkl] 1 n faucille *f*. 2 comp ▸**sickle-cell anaemia** (*Med*) anémie *f* à hématies falciformes, drépanocytose *f*.

sickliness [ˈsɪklɪnɪs] n *[person]* état maladif; *[cake]* goût écœurant.

sickly [ˈsɪklɪ] adj a *person* maladif, souffreteux, mal en point; *complexion* blafard, pâle; *climate* malsain; *plant* étiolé; *smile* pâle, faible; (*fig*) *business etc* mal en point. b (*Brit*) *colour, smell, cake* écœurant. ~ **sweet** douceâtre; *[person]* mielleux; **to act *or* be ~ sweet** avoir des manières doucereuses, être mielleux.

sickness [ˈsɪknɪs] 1 n (*NonC*) (*illness*) maladie *f*. **there's a lot of ~ in the village** il y a beaucoup de malades dans le village; **there's ~ on board** il y a des cas de maladie à bord; (*vomiting*) **bouts of ~** vomissements *mpl*; **mountain ~** mal *m* des montagnes; *see* **travel** *etc*. 2 comp ▸**sickness benefit** (*Brit*) (prestations *fpl* de l')assurance *f* maladie ▸**sickness insurance** assurance(-)maladie *f*.

side [saɪd] 1 n a *[person]* côté *m*; *[animal]* flanc *m*. **wounded in the ~** blessé au côté; **to sleep on one's ~** dormir sur le côté; **he had the telephone by his ~** il avait le téléphone à côté de lui *or* à portée de la main; **his assistant was at *or* by his ~** son assistant était à ses côtés; (*fig*) **she remained by his ~ through thick and thin** elle est restée à ses côtés *or* elle l'a soutenu à travers toutes leurs épreuves; ~ **by ~** (*people*) côte à côte; (*things*) l'un à côté de l'autre; (*fig: in agreement*) en parfait accord (*with* avec); (*Culin*) **a ~ of bacon** une flèche de lard; **a ~ of beef/mutton** un quartier de bœuf/mouton; *see* **split** *etc*.

b (*as opposed to top, bottom etc*) *[box, house, car, triangle etc]* côté *m*; *[ship]* flanc *m*, côté; (*of mountain: gen*) versant *m*; (*flank*) flanc *m*; (*inside*) *[cave, ditch, box]* paroi *f*. *[mountain]* **the north ~** le versant nord; **vines growing on the ~ of the hill** des vignes qui poussaient sur le flanc de la colline; **by the ~ of the church** à côté de *or* tout près de l'église; **set the box on its ~** pose la caisse sur le côté; **go round the ~ of the house** contournez la maison; **you'll find him round the ~ of the house** tournez le coin de la maison et vous le verrez; **she is like the ~ of a house‡** c'est un monument*, elle est colossale; *see* **near, off** *etc*.

c (*outer surface*) *[cube, record, coin]* côté *m*, face *f*; *[square]* côté; *[garment, cloth, slice of bread, sheet of paper]* côté; (*fig*) *[matter, problem etc]* aspect *m*; *[sb's character]* facette *f*. *[garment, cloth]* **the right ~** l'endroit *m*; **the wrong ~** l'envers *m*; *[cloth]* **right/wrong ~ out** à l'endroit/l'envers; **right/wrong ~ up** dans le bon/mauvais sens; (*on box etc*) **"this ~ up"** "haut"; **write on both ~s of the paper** écrivez des deux côtés de la feuille, écrivez recto verso; **I've written 6 ~s** j'ai écrit 6 pages; (*fig*) **the other ~ of the coin *or* picture** le revers de la médaille; (*fig*) **they are two ~s of the same coin** *[issues]* ce sont les deux facettes du même problème; *[people]* ils représentent les deux facettes de la même tendance; **there are two ~s to every quarrel** dans toute querelle il y a deux points de vue; (*fig*) **look at it from his ~ (of it)** considère cela de son point de vue; **now listen to my ~ of the story** maintenant écoute MA version des faits; **he's got a nasty ~* to him *or* to his nature** il a un côté très déplaisant, il a quelque chose de très déplaisant; *see* **bright, flip, right, wrong** *etc*.

d (*edge*) *[road, lake, river]* bord *m*; *[wood, forest]* lisière *f*, bord; *[field, estate]* bord, côté *m*. **by the ~ of the road/lake** *etc* au bord de la route/du lac *etc*.

e (*lateral part*) côté *m*. **on the other ~ of the street/room** de l'autre côté de la rue/la pièce; **he crossed to the other ~ of the room** il a traversé la pièce; **the east ~ of the town** le côté est *or* la partie est de la ville; **he is paralysed down one ~ of his face** il a un côté du visage paralysé; (*fig*) **the science ~ of the college** la section sciences du collège; (*Brit Parl*) **members on the other ~ of the House** (*the government*) les députés de la majorité; (*the opposition*) les députés de l'opposition; **from all ~s, from every ~** de tous côtés, de toutes parts; **from ~ to ~** d'un côté à l'autre; **he moved to one ~** il s'est écarté *or* poussé; **to take sb on *or* to one ~** prendre qn à part; **to put sth to *or* on one ~** mettre qch de côté; **leaving that question to one ~ for the moment** ... laissant la question de côté pour le moment ...; **it's on this ~ of London** c'est de notre côté de Londres; (*between here and London*) c'est avant Londres, c'est entre ici et Londres; (*fig*) **he's on the wrong ~ of fifty** il a passé la cinquantaine; (*fig*) **he's on the right ~ of 50** il n'a pas encore 50 ans; (*fig*) **this ~ of Christmas** avant Noël; **he makes a bit (of money) on the ~*** il se fait un peu d'argent en plus, il fait de la gratte* (*pej*); **a cousin on his mother's ~** un cousin du côté de sa mère; **my grandfather on my mother's ~** mon grand-père maternel; (*TV*) **on the other ~** sur l'autre chaîne; (*fig*) **it's on the heavy/big ~** c'est plutôt lourd/grand; *[weather]* **it's on the hot/chilly ~** il fait plutôt chaud/froid; *see* **safe, sunny** *etc*.

f (*group, team, party*) (*gen*) camp *m*, côté *m*; (*Sport*) équipe *f*; (*Pol etc*) parti *m*. **he's on our ~** il est de notre camp *or* avec nous; **God was on their ~** Dieu était avec eux; **we have time on our ~** nous avons le temps pour nous, le temps joue en notre faveur; **whose ~ are you on?** qui soutenez-vous?, qui défendez-vous?; **there are faults on both ~s** les deux côtés *or* camps ont des torts *or* sont fautifs; **with a few concessions on the government ~** avec quelques concessions de la part du gouvernement; **to take ~s (with sb)** prendre parti (pour qn); **to pick *or* choose ~s** former les camps; (*Sport*) **they've picked *or* chosen the England ~** on a sélectionné l'équipe d'Angleterre; *see* **change**.

g (*Brit *: conceit*) **he's got no ~, there's no ~ about him** il est très simple, ce n'est pas un crâneur*; **to put on ~** prendre des airs supérieurs, crâner*.

2 comp *chapel, panel, elevation, seat* latéral; (*fig*) *effect* secondaire ▸**sideboard** buffet *m* ▸**sideboards** (*Brit*), **sideburns** (*Brit, US*) pattes *fpl*, rouflaquettes* *fpl* ▸**sidecar** side-car *m* ▸**side dish** plat *m* d'accompagnement ▸**side door** entrée latérale, petite porte ▸**side drum** tambour *m* plat, caisse *f* claire ▸**side effect** effet *m* secondaire *or* indésirable ▸**side entrance** entrée latérale ▸**side face** adj, adv (*Phot*) de profil ▸**side glance** regard *m* de côté ▸**side issue** question *f* secondaire, à-côté *m* ▸**side judge** (*US Jur*) juge *m* adjoint ▸**sidekick*** (*assistant*) sous-fifre* *m*; (*friend*) copain* *m*, copine* *f* ▸**sidelight** (*Brit Aut*) feu *m* de position, veilleuse *f*; (*fig*) **it gives us a sidelight on ...** cela nous donne un aperçu de ..., cela révèle un côté *or* aspect inattendu de ... ▸**sideline** *see* **sideline** ▸**sidelong** adj oblique, de côté ◊ adv de côté, en oblique ▸**side plate** petite assiette ▸**side road** (*Brit*) petite route, route transversale; (*in town*) petite

rue, rue transversale ▸**sidesaddle: to ride sidesaddle** monter en amazone ▸**side shows** attractions *fpl* ▸**sideslip** (*Aviat*) **n** glissade *f or* glissement *m* sur l'aile ◊ **vi** glisser sur l'aile ▸**side-slipping** (*Ski*) dérapage *m* ▸**sidesman** (*Brit Rel*) adjoint *m* au bedeau ▸**side-splitting*** tordant* ▸**sidestep vt** *blow* éviter, esquiver; *question* éviter, éluder; *rules etc* ne pas tenir compte de ◊ **vi** (*lit*) faire un pas de côté; (*Ski*) monter en escalier; (*fig*) rester évasif; (*Boxing*) esquiver ▸**sidestepping** montée *f* en escalier ▸**side street** petite rue, rue transversale ▸**side stroke** (*Swimming*) nage *f* indienne ▸**sidetable** desserte *f* ▸**sidetrack** *train* dériver, dérouter; (*fig*) *person* faire dévier de son sujet; (*fig*) **to get sidetracked** s'écarter de son sujet ▸**side trim** (*Aut*) moulure *f* latérale ▸**side view** vue *f* de côté ▸**sidewalk** (*US*) trottoir *m* ▸**sideways** *see* **sideways** ▸**side-wheeler** (*US*) bateau *m* à aubes ▸**side whiskers** favoris *mpl*.

▸**side against vt fus: to side against sb** prendre parti contre qn.

▸**side with vt fus: to side with sb** se ranger du côté de qn, prendre parti pour qn, faire cause commune avec qn.

-sided ['saɪdɪd] **adj ending in comps: three-sided** à trois côtés, trilatéral; **many-sided** multilatéral; *see* **one** *etc*.

sideline ['saɪdlaɪn] **n** **a** (*Sport*) (ligne *f* de) touche *f*. **on the ~s** (*Sport*) sur la touche; (*fig*) dans les coulisses; (*fig*) **he stayed** *or* **stood on the sidelines** il n'a pas pris position, il n'est pas intervenu. **b** activité *f* (*or* travail *m etc*) secondaire. **he sells wood as a ~** il a aussi un petit commerce de bois; (*Comm*) **it's just a ~** ce n'est pas notre spécialité.

sidereal [saɪ'dɪərɪəl] **adj** sidéral.

sideways ['saɪdweɪz] **1 adj** oblique, de côté. (*fig: in hierarchy, career*) **~ move** déplacement *m* horizontal dans la hiérarchie. **2 adv** *look* de côté, obliquement; *walk* en crabe; *stand* de profil. **it goes in ~** ça rentre de côté; **car parked ~ on to the kerb** voiture garée le long du trottoir; (*fig*) (*in career*) **to move ~** se déplacer hoizontalement dans la hiérarchie.

siding ['saɪdɪŋ] **n** **a** (*Rail*) voie *f* de garage *or* d'évitement; *see* **goods**. **b** (*US: wall covering*) revêtement *m* extérieur.

sidle ['saɪdl] **vi: to ~ along** marcher de côté, avancer de biais; **to ~ in/out** *etc* entrer/sortir *etc* furtivement; **he ~d into the room** il s'est faufilé dans la pièce; **he ~d up to me** il s'est glissé vers moi.

Sidon ['saɪdən] **n** Sidon.

siege [siːdʒ] **1 n** (*Mil, fig*) siège *m*. **in a state of ~** en état de siège; **to lay ~ to a town** assiéger une ville, mettre le siège devant une ville; **to raise** *or* **lift the ~** lever le siège (*lit*). **2 comp** ▸**siege economy** économie *f* de siège ▸**siege mentality** mentalité *f* de persécuté ▸**siege warfare** guerre *f* de siège.

Siena [sɪ'enə] **n** Sienne.

Sienese [sɪə'niːz] **adj** siennois.

sienna [sɪ'enə] **n** (*earth*) terre *f* de Sienne *or* d'ombre; (*colour*) ocre brun; *see* **burnt**.

sierra [sɪ'erə] **n** sierra *f*.

Sierra Leone [sɪ'erəlɪ'əʊn] **n** Sierra Leone *f*.

Sierra Leonean [sɪ'erəlɪ'əʊnɪən] **1 n** Sierra-Léonien(ne) *m(f)*. **2 adj** sierra-léonien(ne).

siesta [sɪ'estə] **n** sieste *f*. **to have** *or* **take a ~** faire une *or* la sieste.

sieve [sɪv] **1 n** (*for coal, stones*) crible *m*; (*for sugar, flour, sand, soil*) tamis *m*; (*for wheat*) van *m*; (*for liquids*) passoire *f*. (*Culin*) **to rub** *or* **put through a ~** passer au tamis; **he's got a head** *or* **memory like a ~*** sa mémoire est une (vraie) passoire. **2 vt** *fruit, vegetables* passer; *sugar, flour, sand, soil* tamiser; *coal, stones* passer au crible, cribler.

sift [sɪft] **1 vt** **a** *flour, sugar, sand* tamiser, passer au tamis; *coal, stones* cribler, passer au crible; *wheat* vanner; (*fig*) *evidence* passer au crible *or* au tamis. **to ~ flour on to sth** saupoudrer qch de farine (au moyen d'un tamis). **b** (*also* **~ out**) *cinders etc* séparer (à l'aide d'un crible); (*fig*) *facts, truth* dégager. **2 vi** (*fig*) **to ~ through sth** passer qch en revue, examiner qch.

sifter ['sɪftəʳ] **n** (*see* **sift 1**) tamis *m*; crible *m*; (*machine*) cribleuse *f*; (*for flour, sugar*) saupoudreuse *f*.

sigh [saɪ] **1 n** soupir *m*. **to heave** *or* **give a ~** soupirer, pousser un soupir. **2 vt: "if only he had come" she ~ed** "si seulement il était venu" dit-elle en soupirant *or* soupira-t-elle. **3 vi** soupirer, pousser un soupir; *[wind]* gémir. **he ~ed with relief** il a poussé un soupir de soulagement; **to ~ for sth** soupirer après *or* pour qch; (*for sth lost*) regretter qch; **to ~ over sth** se lamenter sur qch, regretter qch.

sighing ['saɪɪŋ] **n** *[person]* soupirs *mpl*; *[wind]* gémissements *mpl*.

sight [saɪt] **1 n** **a** (*faculty; act of seeing; range of vision*) vue *f*. **to have good/poor ~** avoir une bonne/mauvaise vue; **to lose one's ~** devenir aveugle, perdre la vue; **to get back** *or* **regain one's ~** recouvrer la vue; **to know sb by ~** connaître qn de vue; **to shoot on ~** *or* **at ~** tirer à vue; **he translated it at ~** il l'a traduit à livre ouvert; **he played the music at ~** il a déchiffré le morceau de musique; **at the ~ of** à la vue de, en voyant, au spectacle de; **the train was still in ~** on voyait encore le train, le train était encore visible; **the end is (with)in ~** la fin est en vue, on entrevoit la fin; **we are within ~ of a solution** nous entrevoyons une solution; **we live within ~ of the sea** de chez nous on voit *or* aperçoit la mer; **to come into ~** apparaître; **keep the luggage in ~, keep ~ of the luggage, don't let the luggage out of your ~** ne perdez pas les bagages de vue, surveillez les bagages; **out of ~** hors de vue; **to keep out of ~ (vi)** se cacher, ne pas se montrer; **(vt)** cacher, ne pas montrer; **it is out of ~** on ne le voit pas, ce n'est pas visible, ce n'est pas à portée de vue; **he never lets it out of his ~** il le garde toujours sous les yeux; (*liter*) **out of my ~!** hors de ma vue!; **keep out of his ~!** qu'il ne te voie pas!; (*Prov*) **out of ~ out of mind** loin des yeux loin du cœur (*Prov*); **to catch ~ of** apercevoir; (*lit, fig*) **to lose ~ of sb/sth** perdre qn/qch de vue; **at first ~ it seems to be ...** à première vue *or* au premier abord cela semble être ...; **love at first ~** le coup de foudre; **it was my first ~ of Paris** c'était la première fois que je voyais Paris; **I got my first ~ of that document yesterday** j'ai vu ce document hier pour la première fois; **their first ~ of land came after 30 days at sea** la terre leur est apparue pour la première fois au bout de 30 jours en mer; **the ~ of the cathedral** la vue de la cathédrale; **I can't bear** *or* **stand the ~ of blood** je ne peux pas supporter la vue du sang; **I can't bear** *or* **stand the ~ of him, I hate the ~ of him** je ne peux pas le voir (en peinture*) *or* le sentir*; (*Comm*) **to buy/accept sth ~ unseen** acheter/accepter qch sans l'avoir examiné; (*fig liter*) **to find favour in sb's ~** trouver grâce aux yeux de qn; **all men are equal in the ~ of God** tous les hommes sont égaux devant Dieu; **in the ~ of the law** aux yeux de la loi, devant la loi; *see* **heave, second[1], short** *etc*.

b (*spectacle*) spectacle *m* (*also pej*). **the tulips are a wonderful ~** les tulipes sont magnifiques; **it is a ~ to see** *or* **a ~ to be seen** cela vaut la peine d'être vu, il faut le voir; **the Grand Canyon is one of the ~s of the world** le Grand Canyon constitue l'un des plus beaux spectacles du monde *or* est l'un des plus beaux paysages du monde; **it's one of the ~s of Paris** c'est l'une des attractions touristiques de Paris, c'est l'une des choses à voir à Paris; **it's a sad ~** c'est triste (à voir), ça fait pitié; **it's not a pretty ~** ça n'est guère joli (à voir); **it was a ~ for sore eyes** (*welcome*) c'était un spectacle à réjouir le cœur; (* *pej*) c'était à en pleurer; **his face was a ~!** (*amazed etc*) il faisait une de ces têtes!*; (*after injury etc*) il avait une tête à faire peur*; (*pej*) **I must look a ~!** je dois avoir une de ces allures!* *or* l'air de Dieu sait quoi!*; **doesn't she look a ~ in that hat!** elle a l'air d'un épouvantail avec ce chapeau!; *see* **see[1]**.

c (*on gun*) mire *f*. **to take ~** viser; **to have sth in one's ~s** avoir qch dans sa ligne de tir; (*fig*) **to have sb in one's ~s** avoir qn dans le collimateur; (*fig*) **to set one's ~s too high** viser trop haut (*fig*); **to set one's ~s on sth** viser qch, décider d'obtenir qch.

d (*phrases*) **not by a long ~** loin de là, bien au contraire; **it's a (far** *or* **long) ~ better than the other*** c'est infiniment mieux que l'autre; **he's a ~ too clever*** il est par *or* bien trop malin.

2 comp ▸**sight draft** (*Comm, Fin*) effet *m* à vue ▸**sight-read** (*Mus*) déchiffrer ▸**sight-reading** déchiffrage *m* ▸**sightseeing** tourisme *m*; **to go sightseeing, to do some sightseeing** (*gen*) faire le (*or* la) touriste, faire du tourisme; (*in town*) visiter la ville ▸**sightseer** touriste *mf*.

3 vt **a** (*see*) *land, person* apercevoir.

b **to ~ a gun** (*aim*) prendre sa visée, viser; (*adjust*) régler le viseur d'un canon.

sighted ['saɪtɪd] **1 adj** qui voit, doué de vue *or* de vision. **to be partially ~** avoir un certain degré de vision. **2 npl: the ~** les voyants *mpl* (*lit*), ceux qui voient.

-sighted ['saɪtɪd] **adj ending in comps: weak-sighted** à la vue faible; *see* **clear, short** *etc*.

sighting ['saɪtɪŋ] **n: numerous ~s of the monster have been reported** de nombreuses personnes ont déclaré avoir vu le monstre; **he has reported 6 ~s** il déclare l'avoir vu 6 fois.

sightly ['saɪtlɪ] **adj: it's not very ~** ce n'est pas beau à voir.

sign [saɪn] **1 n** **a** (*with hand etc*) signe *m*, geste *m*. **he made a ~ of recognition** il m'a (*or* lui a *etc*) fait signe qu'il me (*or* le *etc*) reconnaissait; **they communicated by ~s** ils se parlaient par signes; **to make a ~ to sb** faire signe à qn (*to do* de faire); **to make the ~ of the Cross** faire le signe de la croix (*over sb/sth* sur qn/qch); (*cross o.s.*) se signer; **he made a rude ~** il a fait un geste grossier.

b (*symbol: Astron, Ling, Math, Mus etc*) signe *m*. **the ~s of the zodiac** les signes du zodiaque; **this ~ means "do not machine-wash"** ce signe *or* ce symbole signifie "ne pas laver à la machine"; (*Astrol*) **born under the ~ of Leo** né sous le signe du Lion; (*Astrol*) **air/earth/fire/water ~** signe d'air/de terre/de feu/d'eau; *see* **minus** *etc*.

c (*indication*) signe *m*, preuve *f*, indication *f*; (*Med*) symptôme *m*; (*trace*) signe, trace *f*, marque *f*. **as a ~ of** en signe de; **it's a good/bad ~** c'est bon/mauvais signe; **all the ~s are that ...** tout laisse à penser que ...; **those clouds are a ~ of rain** ces nuages sont un signe de pluie *or* présagent la pluie; **violence is a ~ of fear** la violence est (un) signe *or* une preuve de peur, la violence dénote *or* indique *or* révèle la peur; **it's a ~ of the times** c'est un signe des temps; **it's a sure ~** c'est un signe infaillible; **at the slightest ~ of disagreement** au moindre signe de désaccord; **there is no ~ of his agreeing** rien ne laisse à penser *or* rien n'indique qu'il va accepter; **he gave no ~ of wishing to come with us** il ne donnait aucun signe de *or* il n'avait pas du tout l'air de vouloir venir avec nous; **there was no ~ of life** il n'y avait aucun signe de vie; **there's no ~ of him anywhere** on ne le trouve nulle part, il n'y a aucune trace de lui; **there's no ~ of it anywhere** c'est introuvable, je (*or* il *etc*) n'arrive pas à le (re)trouver; *see* **show**.

d (*notice*) panneau *m*; (*on inn, shop*) enseigne *f*; (*Aut: traffic warnings etc*) panneau (de signalisation); (*Aut: directions on motorways etc*) panneau (indicateur); (*writing on signpost*) direction *f*, indication *f*. (*on road*) **I can't read the ~** je n'arrive pas à lire le panneau.

2 **comp** ▸**sign language** langage *m* par signes; **to talk in sign language** parler *or* communiquer par signes ▸**signpost** *etc see* **signpost** *etc* ▸**sign writer** peintre *m* d'enseignes.

3 **vt** a *letter, document, register, visitors' book* signer. (*fig*) **it was ~ed, sealed and delivered by twelve noon** à midi, l'affaire était entièrement réglée; **to ~ one's name** signer (son nom); **he ~s himself John Smith** il signe "John Smith"; (*in letters*) **~ed John Smith** signé John Smith; *see* **pledge**.

b (*Ftbl etc*) **to ~ a player** engager un joueur.

4 **vi** a signer. **you have to ~ for the key** vous devez signer pour obtenir la clef; **he ~ed for the parcel** il a signé le reçu de livraison du paquet; (*Ftbl*) **Smith has ~ed for Celtic** Smith a signé un contrat d'engagement avec le Celtic; *see* **dot**.

b **to ~ to sb to do sth** faire signe à qn de faire qch.

▸**sign away** **vt sep: to sign away sth** signer sa renonciation à qch, signer l'abandon de son droit sur qch; (*fig*) **to sign one's life away** hypothéquer son avenir.

▸**sign in** 1 **vi** (*in factory*) pointer (*en arrivant*); (*in hotel, club etc*) signer le registre (*en arrivant*). 2 **vt sep** (*at club*) **to sign sb in** faire entrer qn en tant qu'invité (*en signant le registre*).

▸**sign off** **vi** a (*Rad, TV*) terminer l'émission. **this is Jacques Dupont signing off** c'est Jacques Dupont qui vous dit au revoir. b (*on leaving work*) pointer en partant. c (*at end of letter*) mettre un point final à sa lettre, terminer sa lettre.

▸**sign on** 1 **vi** a (*Ind etc*) (*for job*) se faire embaucher (*as* comme, en tant que); (*Mil*) s'engager (*as* comme, en tant que); (*at employment office*) pointer au chômage, ≃ pointer à l'ANPE. b (*on arrival at work*) pointer en arrivant. c (*enrol*) s'inscrire. **I've signed on for German conversation** je me suis inscrit au cours de conversation allemande. 2 **vt sep** *employee* embaucher; (*Mil*) engager.

▸**sign out** 1 **vt sep** *library book, sports equipment etc* signer pour emprunter. 2 **vi** (*in hotel, club etc*) signer le registre (*en partant*); (*in office*) pointer (*en partant*).

▸**sign over** **vt sep** céder par écrit (*to* à).

▸**sign up** 1 **vi** = **sign on 1a**. 2 **vt sep** = **sign on 2**.

signal ['sɪgnl] 1 **n** a (*gen, Ling, Naut, Psych, Rail etc*) signal *m*. **at a prearranged ~** à un signal convenu; **the ~ for departure** le signal du départ; (*Naut*) **flag ~s** signaux par pavillons; **(traffic) ~s** feux *mpl* de circulation; (*Rail*) **the ~ is at red** le signal est au rouge; (*Aut*) **I didn't see his ~** je n'ai pas vu son signal (*or* clignotant); *see* **distress, hand** *etc*.

b (*electronic impulse; message: Rad, Telec, TV*) signal *m*. **I'm getting the engaged ~** ça sonne occupé *or* pas libre; **send a ~ to HQ to the effect that ...** envoyez un signal *or* message au Q.G. pour dire que ...; (*Rad, Telec, TV*) **the ~ is very weak** le signal est très faible; (*Rad, TV*) **station ~** indicatif *m* de l'émetteur; (*Mil*) **the S~s** les Transmissions *fpl*.

2 **comp** ▸**signal book** (*Naut*) code international de signaux, livre *m* des signaux ▸**signal box** (*Rail*) cabine *f* d'aiguillage, poste *m* d'aiguillage *or* de signalisation ▸**signal flag** (*Naut*) pavillon *m* de signalisation ▸**signalman** (*Rail*) aiguilleur *m*; (*Naut*) signaleur *m*, sémaphoriste *m*.

3 **adj** *success* remarquable, insigne; *importance* capital.

4 **vt** *message* communiquer par signaux. **to ~ sb on/through** *etc* faire signe à qn d'avancer/de passer *etc;* (*Aut*) **to ~ a turn** indiquer *or* signaler un changement de direction.

5 **vi** (*gen*) faire des signaux; (*Aut*) mettre son clignotant. **to ~ to sb** faire signe à qn (*to do* de faire).

signalize ['sɪgnəlaɪz] **vt** (*mark, make notable*) marquer; (*point out*) distinguer, signaler.

signally ['sɪgnəlɪ] **adv** singulièrement, extraordinairement. **he has ~ failed to do it** il a manifestement échoué *or* bel et bien échoué dans sa tentative.

signatory ['sɪgnətərɪ] 1 **adj** signataire. 2 **n** signataire *mf* (*to* de).

signature ['sɪgnətʃəʳ] 1 **n** a signature *f*. **to set** *or* **put one's ~ to sth** apposer sa signature à qch. b (*Mus: key ~*) armature *f*. 2 **comp** ▸**signature tune** (*esp Brit*) indicatif musical.

signer ['saɪnəʳ] **n** signataire *mf*.

signet ['sɪgnɪt] **n** sceau *m*, cachet *m*. **~ ring** chevalière *f*; *see* **writer**.

significance [sɪg'nɪfɪkəns] **n** (*meaning*) signification *f*; (*importance*) *[event, speech]* importance *f*, portée *f*. **a look of deep ~** un regard lourd de sens; **what he thinks is of no ~** peu importe ce qu'il pense.

significant [sɪg'nɪfɪkənt] **adj** *achievement, increase, amount* considérable; *event* important, de grande portée; *look* significatif. **it is ~ that ...** il est significatif *or* révélateur que ...+ *subj*; (*Math*) **~ figure** chiffre *m* significatif.

significantly [sɪg'nɪfɪkəntlɪ] **adv** *smile, wink, nudge* d'une façon significative. **she looked at me ~** elle m'a jeté un regard lourd de sens; **~, he refused** fait révélateur, il a refusé; **he was ~ absent** son absence était significative; **it has improved ~** l'amélioration est considérable; **it is not ~ different** la différence est insignifiante.

signification [ˌsɪgnɪfɪ'keɪʃən] **n** signification *f*, sens *m*.

signify ['sɪgnɪfaɪ] 1 **vt** a (*mean*) signifier, vouloir dire (*that* que); (*indicate*) signifier, être (un) signe de, indiquer. **it signifies intelligence** cela indique *or* dénote *or* révèle de l'intelligence. b (*make known*) signifier, indiquer, faire comprendre (*that* que); *one's approval* signifier; *one's opinion* faire connaître. 2 **vi** avoir de l'importance. **it does not ~** cela n'a aucune importance, cela importe peu.

signing ['saɪnɪŋ] **n** a *[letter, contract, treaty etc]* signature *f*. b (*Sport*) **Clarke, their recent ~ from Manchester Utd** Clarke, leur récent transfert *or* transfuge de Manchester Utd.

signpost ['saɪnpəʊst] 1 **n** poteau *m* indicateur. 2 **vt** *direction, place* indiquer. **Lewes is ~ed at the crossroads** Lewes est indiqué au carrefour; **the road is badly ~ed** (*not indicated*) la route est mal indiquée; (*no signposts on it*) la route est mal signalisée.

signposting ['saɪnpəʊstɪŋ] **n** signalisation *f* (verticale).

Sikh [siːk] 1 **n** Sikh *mf*. 2 **adj** sikh (*f inv*).

silage ['saɪlɪdʒ] **n** (*fodder*) fourrage ensilé *or* vert; (*method*) ensilage *m*.

silence ['saɪləns] 1 **n** silence *m*. **he called for ~** il a demandé *or* réclamé le silence; **when he finished speaking, there was ~** quand il a fini de parler, le silence a régné *or* on a gardé le silence *or* personne n'a soufflé mot; **the ~ was broken by a cry** un cri a déchiré le silence; **they listened in ~** ils ont écouté en silence *or* sans rien dire; **a two minutes' ~** deux minutes de silence; **your ~ on this matter ...** le silence *or* le mutisme que vous gardez sur ce sujet ...; (*fig*) **there is ~ in official circles** dans les milieux autorisés on garde le silence; (*fig*) **to pass sth over in ~** passer qch sous silence; (*Prov*) **~ gives** *or* **means consent** qui ne dit mot consent (*Prov*); (*Prov*) **~ is golden** le silence est d'or (*Prov*); *see* **dead, radio, reduce** *etc*.

2 **vt** *person, critic, guns* réduire au silence, faire taire; *noise* étouffer; *conscience* faire taire. **to ~ criticism** faire taire les critiques, imposer silence aux critiques; **to ~ the opposition** réduire l'opposition au silence.

silencer ['saɪlənsəʳ] **n** (*on gun, (Brit) on car*) silencieux *m*.

silent ['saɪlənt] 1 **adj** *person* silencieux; (*taciturn*) silencieux, peu communicatif, taciturne; *engine, movement* silencieux; *step* silencieux, feutré; *room* silencieux, tranquille; *film, wish, reproach* muet. **it was (as) ~ as the grave** *or* **the tomb** il y avait un silence de mort; **to fall** *or* **become ~** se taire; **to keep** *or* **be ~** garder le silence, se taire; **be ~!** taisez-vous!, silence!; **to remain ~ about sth** se taire *or* garder le silence *or* ne rien dire au sujet de qch; (*Ling*) **a ~ letter** une lettre muette; **~ "h"** "h" muet; **the ~ majority** la majorité silencieuse; (*US Comm*) **~ partner** (associé *m*) commanditaire *m*; (*in road*) **~ policeman** casse-vitesse *m*; (*Pol*) **the ~ revolution** la révolution Silencieuse.

2 **n** (*Cine: gen pl*) **the ~s** les films muets, le (cinéma) muet.

silently ['saɪləntlɪ] **adv** (*noiselessly*) silencieusement, sans (faire de) bruit; (*without speaking*) silencieusement, en silence.

Silesia [saɪ'liːʃɪə] **n** Silésie *f*.

silex ['saɪleks] **n** silex *m*.

silhouette [ˌsɪluː'et] 1 **n** (*gen, Art*) silhouette *f*. **to see sth in ~** voir la silhouette de qch, voir qch en silhouette. 2 **vt: to be ~d against** se découper contre, se profiler sur, se silhouetter sur; **~d against** se découpant contre, se profilant sur, silhouetté sur.

silica ['sɪlɪkə] **n** silice *f*. **~ gel** gel *m* de silice.

silicate ['sɪlɪkɪt] **n** silicate *m*.

siliceous [sɪ'lɪʃəs] **adj** siliceux.

silicon ['sɪlɪkən] **n** silicium *m*. **~ carbide** carbure *m* de silicium; **~ chip** puce *f* électronique, pastille *f* de silicium, microplaquette *f*.

silicone ['sɪlɪkəʊn] **n** silicone *f*.

silicosis [ˌsɪlɪ'kəʊsɪs] **n** silicose *f*.

silk [sɪlk] 1 **n** a (*material*) soie *f*; (*thread*) (fil *m* de) soie. **they were all in their ~s and satins** elles étaient toutes en grande toilette; **the shelves were full of ~s and satins** les rayonnages regorgeaient de soierie et de satin; *see* **artificial, raw, sewing** *etc*.

b (*Brit Jur: barrister*) avocat *m* de la couronne. **to take ~** être nommé avocat de la couronne.

2 **comp** *blouse etc* de *or* en soie ▸**silk factory** soierie *f* (*fabrique*) ▸**silk finish: with a silk finish** *cloth* similisé, mercerisé; *paintwork* satiné ▸**silk hat** haut-de-forme *m* ▸**silk industry** soierie *f* (*industrie*) ▸**silk manufacturer** fabricant *m* en soierie; (*in Lyons*) soyeux *m* ▸**silkscreen printing** (*NonC*) sérigraphie *f* ▸**silk stocking** bas *m* de soie ▸**silk thread** fil *m* de soie, soie *f* à coudre ▸**silkworm** ver *m* à soie; **silkworm breeding** sériciculture *f*, élevage *m* des vers à soie.

silken ['sɪlkən] **adj** *dress, hair* soyeux; *skin* soyeux, satiné; *voice* doucereux. **it has a ~ sheen** cela a des reflets soyeux.

silkiness ['sɪlkɪnɪs] **n** qualité *or* douceur soyeuse, soyeux *m*.

silky ['sɪlkɪ] **adj** *hair, dress* (à l'aspect) soyeux; *voice* doucereux.

sill [sɪl] **n** *[window]* rebord *m*, appui *m*; *[door]* seuil *m*; (*Aut*) bas *m* de marche.

silliness ['sɪlɪnɪs] **n** sottise *f*, stupidité *f*, niaiserie *f*.

silly ['sɪlɪ] 1 **adj** *person* bête, idiot, sot (*f* sotte); *behaviour, answer* stupide, idiot, bête; *clothes, shoes* peu pratique, ridicule. **you ~ fool!**

espèce d'idiot(e)!, espèce d'imbécile!; **the ~ idiot!** quel(le) imbécile!; **don't be ~** ne fais pas l'idiot(e) *or* l'imbécile; **I felt ~ when he said** ... je me suis senti bête *or* ridicule quand il a dit ...; **I feel ~ in this hat** je me sens ridicule *or* je dois avoir l'air idiot avec ce chapeau; **he'll do something ~** il va faire une bêtise; **that was a ~ thing to do** c'était bête *or* idiot de faire cela; (*Press*) **the ~ season** la période creuse (*où les nouvelles manquent d'intérêt*); *see* **knock**.

2 **n** (*also* **~ billy***) idiot(e) *m(f)*. **you big ~!** espèce d'imbécile!, gros bêta (*f* grosse bêtasse)!*

silo ['saɪləʊ] **n** (*gen, Mil*) silo *m*.

silt [sɪlt] **n** (*gen*) limon *m*; (*mud*) vase *f*.

►silt up 1 **vi** (*with mud*) s'envaser; (*with sand*) s'ensabler. 2 **vt sep** *[mud]* envaser; *[sand]* ensabler; (*gen*) boucher, engorger.

silting ['sɪltɪŋ] **n** envasement *m*, ensablement *m*.

Silurian [saɪ'lʊərɪən] **adj, n** (*Geol*) silurien *(m)*.

silver ['sɪlvəʳ] 1 **n** (*NonC*) a (*metal*) argent *m*; (*~ware, cutlery etc*) argenterie *f*.

b (*money*) argent *m* (monnayé), monnaie *f* (*en pièces d'argent*). **have you got any ~? — sorry, only notes and coppers** est-ce que vous avez de la monnaie? — désolé, je n'ai que des billets ou alors de la petite monnaie; **£2 in ~** 2 livres en pièces d'argent.

2 **adj** (*made of ~*) *cutlery, jewellery etc* d'argent, en argent; (*~-coloured*) argenté; *coin* d'argent. (*at meeting etc*) **~ collection** quête *f*; **"there will be a ~ collection"** "vous êtes priés de contribuer généreusement à la quête"; (*Prov*) **every cloud has a ~ lining** à quelque chose malheur est bon (*Prov*); (*Cine*) **the ~ screen** le grand écran; (*fig*) **to have a ~ tongue** être beau parleur; (*fig*) **his ~ tongue** ses belles paroles; (*fig*) **to be born with a ~ spoon in one's mouth** naître fortuné, naître avec une cuiller d'argent dans la bouche.

3 **comp ►silver age** âge *m* d'argent **►silver birch** bouleau argenté **►silver disc** (*Brit Mus*) disque *m* d'argent **►silver fir** sapin argenté **►silverfish** poisson *m* d'argent **►silver foil** = **silver paper ►silver fox** renard argenté **►silver gilt** plaqué *m* argent **►silver-grey** argenté **►silver-haired** aux cheveux argentés **►silver jubilee** (fête *f* du) vingt-cinquième anniversaire *m* (*d'un événement*) **►silver medal** médaille *f* d'argent **►silver medallist** médaillé(e) *m(f)* d'argent **►silver paper** papier *m* d'argent *or* d'étain **►silver plate** (*NonC*) (*solid silver articles*) argenterie *f*; (*electroplate*) plaqué *m* argent **►silver-plated** argenté, plaqué argent *inv* **►silver plating** argenture *f* **►silverside** (*Brit Culin*) tranche *f* grasse **►silversmith** orfèvre *mf* **►the Silver State** (*US*) le Nevada **►silver-tongued** à la langue déliée, éloquent **►silverware** (*NonC*) argenterie *f* **►silver wedding** noces *fpl* d'argent.

4 **vt** *mirror, fork* argenter.

silvery ['sɪlvərɪ] **adj** *light, colour* argenté; *sound* argentin. **~ grey/white** gris/blanc argenté *inv*.

silviculture ['sɪlvɪˌkʌltʃəʳ] **n** sylviculture *f*.

simian ['sɪmɪən] **adj, n** simien(ne) *m(f)*.

similar ['sɪmɪləʳ] **adj** semblable (*to* à); (*less strongly*) similaire, comparable (*to* à); (*Geom*) semblable. **we have a ~ house** notre maison est presque la même *or* presque pareille; **the 2 houses are ~ in size** les 2 maisons sont de dimensions similaires *or* comparables; **the 2 houses are so ~ that** ... les 2 maisons sont si semblables que ... *or* se ressemblent à un point tel que ...; **on a ~ occasion** dans des circonstances semblables *or* similaires, en semblable occasion; **your case is ~** votre cas est semblable *or* similaire *or* analogue; **paint removers and ~ products** les décapants et produits similaires *or* voisins; **vehicles ~ to the bicycle** véhicules voisins de *or* apparentés à la bicyclette; **it is ~ in colour** ce n'est pas exactement la même couleur mais presque *or* mais c'est dans les mêmes tons; **it is ~ in colour to ruby** c'est d'une couleur semblable *or* comparable à celle du rubis.

similarity [ˌsɪmɪ'lærɪtɪ] **n** ressemblance *f* (*to* avec, *between* entre), similitude *f* (*between* entre), similarité *f* (*between* entre).

similarly ['sɪmɪləlɪ] **adv** de la même façon. **and ~,** ... et de même, ...

simile ['sɪmɪlɪ] **n** (*Literat*) comparaison *f*. **style rich in ~** style qui abonde en comparaisons.

similitude [sɪ'mɪlɪtjuːd] **n** similitude *f*, ressemblance *f*; (*Literat etc*) comparaison *f*.

simmer ['sɪməʳ] 1 **n** (*slight boil*) faible ébullition *f*. **the stew was just on the ~** le ragoût cuisait à feu doux *or* mijotait. 2 **vi** *[water]* frémir; *[vegetables]* cuire à feu doux; *[soup, stew]* cuire à feu doux, mijoter, mitonner; (*fig*) (*with excitement*) être en ébullition; (*with anticipation*) être tout excité d'avance; (*with discontent*) bouillir de mécontentement; *[revolt]* couver, fermenter; *[anger]* couver, monter. **he was ~ing (with rage)** il bouillait (de rage). 3 **vt** *water, dye* laisser frémir; *soup, stew* faire cuire à feu doux, mijoter, mitonner; *vegetables* faire cuire à feu doux.

►simmer down* **vi** (*fig*) s'apaiser, se calmer. **simmer down!** calme-toi!, un peu de calme!

simnel cake ['sɪmnlkeɪk] **n** (*Brit*) gâteau *m* aux raisins recouvert de pâte d'amandes (*généralement servi à Pâques*).

Simon ['saɪmən] **n** Simon *m*.

simonize ['saɪmənaɪz] **vt** ® lustrer, polir.

simony ['saɪmənɪ] **n** simonie *f*.

simper ['sɪmpəʳ] 1 **n** sourire affecté. **~s** minauderie(s) *f(pl)*. 2 **vti** minauder. **"yes" she ~ed** "oui" dit-elle en minaudant.

simpering ['sɪmpərɪŋ] 1 **n** minauderies *fpl*, mignardises *fpl*. 2 **adj** minaudier, affecté, mignard.

simperingly ['sɪmpərɪŋlɪ] **adv** d'une manière affectée, avec affectation.

simple ['sɪmpl] 1 **adj** a (*not compound*) *substance, machine, fracture, sentence* simple; (*Ling*) *tense* simple, non composé; *form of life* simple, élémentaire. **~ division** division *f* simple; **~ equation** équation *f* du premier degré; (*Fin, Math*) **~ interest** intérêts *mpl* simples; (*Mus*) **~ time** mesure *f* simple; *see* **pure**.

b (*uncomplicated, easy*) simple, facile; (*plain*) *furniture, way of dressing, style* simple, sans recherche; *dress* simple, sans apprêt; *attitude, answer* simple, franc (*f* franche). **it's as ~ as ABC** c'est simple comme bonjour; **it's very ~!** c'est très simple!, c'est tout ce qu'il y a de plus simple!; **it's a ~ matter to have the clock repaired** il est tout à fait simple *or* très simple de faire réparer la pendule; **it's a ~ matter of buying another key** il s'agit tout simplement d'acheter une autre clef; **the ~ life** la vie simple; **she likes the ~ life** elle aime vivre simplement *or* avec simplicité; **a ~ little black dress** une petite robe noire toute simple *or* très sobre; **he's a ~ labourer** c'est un simple ouvrier; **they're ~ people** ce sont des gens simples *or* sans façons; **I'm a ~ soul** je suis tout simple *or* sans façons (*see also* **1c**); **to make ~(r)** simplifier; **in ~ terms, in ~ English, in ~ language** pour parler simplement *or* clairement, ≃ en bon français; **the ~ fact that** ... le simple fait que ...; **the ~ truth** la vérité pure et simple; **for the ~ reason that** ... pour la seule *or* simple raison que ...; **a dangerously ~ way of** ... une façon dangereusement simpliste de ... .

c (*innocent*) simple, ingénu, naïf (*f* naïve); (*foolish*) simple, sot (*f* sotte), niais. **~ Simon** nigaud *m*, naïf *m*; **he's a ~ soul** c'est une âme simple, c'est un naïf; (*iro*) c'est une bonne âme; **he's a bit ~** il est un peu simplet *or* un peu simple d'esprit.

2 **comp ►simple-hearted** (qui a le cœur) candide, franc (*f* franche), ouvert **►simple-minded** simplet, simple d'esprit, naïf (*f* naïve) **►simple-mindedness** simplicité *f* d'esprit, naïveté *f*.

simpleton ['sɪmpltən] **n** nigaud(e) *m(f)*, niais(e) *m(f)*.

simplicity [sɪm'plɪsɪtɪ] **n** simplicité *f*. **it's ~ itself** c'est tout ce qu'il y a de plus simple, c'est la simplicité même, rien de plus simple.

simplifiable ['sɪmplɪfaɪəbl] **adj** simplifiable.

simplification [ˌsɪmplɪfɪ'keɪʃən] **n** simplification *f*.

simplify ['sɪmplɪfaɪ] **vt** simplifier.

simplistic [sɪm'plɪstɪk] **adj** simpliste.

Simplon ['sɪmplɒn] **n: ~ Pass** col *m* du Simplon.

simply ['sɪmplɪ] **adv** a *talk* simplement, avec simplicité; *live, dress* simplement, avec simplicité, sans prétention. b (*only*) simplement, seulement; (*absolutely*) absolument. **it ~ isn't possible, it is ~ impossible** c'est absolument *or* tout simplement impossible; **I ~ said that** ... j'ai simplement *or* seulement dit que ...; **she could ~ refuse** elle pourrait refuser purement et simplement; **you ~ MUST come!** il faut absolument que vous veniez! (*subj*).

simulacrum [ˌsɪmjʊ'leɪkrəm] **n, pl simulacra** [ˌsɪmjʊ'leɪkrə] simulacre *m*.

simulate ['sɪmjʊleɪt] **vt** a (*Aviat, Comput, Space, Tech etc*) simuler. b *passion, enthusiasm, grief* simuler, feindre, affecter; *illness* simuler, feindre. **~d leather** imitation *f* cuir.

simulation [ˌsɪmjʊ'leɪʃən] **n** (*gen, Comput*) simulation *f*.

simulator ['sɪmjʊleɪtəʳ] **n** (*Aut, Space*) simulateur *m*; (*Aviat: also* **flight ~**) simulateur *m* de vol.

simultaneity [ˌsɪməltə'niːɪtɪ] **n** simultanéité *f*.

simultaneous [ˌsɪməl'teɪnɪəs] **adj** *event, translation* simultané. (*Math*) **~ equations** équations équivalentes.

simultaneously [ˌsɪməl'teɪnɪəslɪ] **adv** simultanément, en même temps. **~ with** en même temps que.

sin [sɪn] 1 **n** péché *m*. **~s of omission/commission** péchés par omission/par action; **a ~ against (the law of) God** un manquement à la loi de Dieu; **it's a ~ to do that** (*Rel*) c'est un péché que de faire cela; (** fig:* † *or hum*) c'est une honte *or* un crime de faire cela; (*fig: unmarried*) **to live in ~** vivre dans le péché (*fig*) (*with sb* avec qn); *see* **seven, ugly** *etc.* 2 **comp ►sin bin** (*US*) (*Ice Hockey etc*) prison *f* **►sin tax*** (*US*) taxe *f* sur le tabac et les alcools. 3 **vi** pécher (*against* contre). (*fig*) **he was more ~ned against than ~ning** il était plus victime que coupable.

Sinai ['saɪneɪaɪ] **n** Sinaï *m*. **the ~ Desert** le désert du Sinaï; **Mount ~** le mont Sinaï.

Sinbad ['sɪnbæd] **n: ~ the Sailor** Sinbad le Marin.

since [sɪns] 1 **conj** a (*in time*) depuis que. **~ I have been here** depuis que je suis ici; **ever ~ I met him** depuis que *or* depuis le jour où je l'ai rencontré; **it's a week ~ I saw him** cela fait une semaine que je ne l'ai (pas) vu, je ne l'ai pas vu depuis une semaine; **it's ages ~ I saw you** cela fait des siècles qu'on ne s'est pas vus*.

b (*because*) puisque, comme, vu que, étant donné que. **why don't you buy it, ~ you are so rich!** achète-le donc, toi qui es si riche!

2 **adv** depuis. **he has not been here ~** il n'est pas venu depuis; **he has been my friend ever ~** il est resté mon ami depuis (ce moment-là); **a short time ~, not long ~** il y a peu de temps; **it's many years ~** il y a

bien des années de cela, cela fait bien des années.

3 **prep** depuis. ~ **arriving** *or* **his arrival** depuis son arrivée, depuis qu'il est arrivé; **I have been waiting ~ 10 o'clock** j'attends depuis 10 heures; ~ **then** depuis (lors); **ever ~ 1900 France has attempted to ...** depuis 1900 la France tente de *or* a sans cesse tenté de ...; **ever ~ then** *or* **that time she's never gone out alone** depuis ce temps-là elle ne sort plus jamais seule; **how long is it ~ the accident?** combien de temps s'est passé *or* il s'est passé combien de temps depuis l'accident?, l'accident remonte à quand?

sincere [sɪn'sɪəʳ] **adj** *person, letter, apology* sincère; *emotion, offer, attempt* sincère, réel, vrai. **it is my ~ belief that ...** je crois sincèrement que ...; **are they ~ in their desire to help us?** est-ce que leur désir de nous aider est (vraiment) sincère?

sincerely [sɪn'sɪəlɪ] **adv** sincèrement. (*letter-ending*) **Yours ~** ≃ Je vous prie d'agréer, Monsieur (*or* Madame *etc*), l'expression de mes sentiments les meilleurs; (*man to woman*) je vous prie d'agréer, Madame, mes très respectueux hommages; (*less formally*) cordialement à vous, bien à vous.

sincerity [sɪn'serɪtɪ] **n** *[person]* sincérité *f*, bonne foi; *[emotion]* sincérité. **in all ~** en toute sincérité.

sine [saɪn] **n** (*Math*) sinus *m*.

sinecure ['saɪnɪkjʊəʳ] **n** sinécure *f*.

sine qua non ['saɪnɪkweɪ'nɒn] **n** condition *f* sine qua non.

sinew ['sɪnju:] **n** (*Anat*) tendon *m*. **~s** (*muscles*) muscles *mpl*; (*strength*) force(s) *f(pl)*; (*energy*) vigueur *f*, nerf *m*; **money is the ~s of war** l'argent est le nerf de la guerre; **a man of great moral ~** un homme d'une grande force morale.

sinewy ['sɪnjʊɪ] **adj** *body* musclé, nerveux; *meat* tendineux, nerveux; *fibres* tendineux.

sinfonietta [ˌsɪnfən'jetə] **n** (*short symphony*) sinfonietta *f*; (*small symphony orchestra*) sinfonietta *m*.

sinful ['sɪnfʊl] **adj** *pleasure, desire, thought* coupable, inavouable; *act, waste* scandaleux, honteux; *town* immonde (*fig*). **~ person** pécheur *m*, -eresse *f*.

sinfully ['sɪnfəlɪ] **adv** *behave, think* d'une façon coupable; *waste etc* scandaleusement.

sinfulness ['sɪnfʊlnɪs] **n** (*NonC*) *[person]* péchés *mpl*; *[deed]* caractère coupable *or* scandaleux.

sing [sɪŋ] **pret sang, ptp sung** 1 **vt** *[person, bird]* chanter; (*fig*) *sb's beauty etc* chanter, célébrer. **she sang the child to sleep** elle a chanté jusqu'à ce que l'enfant s'endorme; **she was ~ing the child to sleep** elle chantait pour que l'enfant s'endorme; **to ~ mass** chanter la messe; **sung mass** messe chantée, grand-messe *f*; (*fig*) **to ~ another tune** déchanter, changer de ton; (*fig*) **to ~ sb's/one's own praises** chanter les louanges de qn/ses propres louanges.

2 **vi** a *[person, bird, violin]* chanter; *[ears]* bourdonner, tinter; *[wind, kettle]* siffler. **to ~ like a lark** chanter comme un rossignol; **to ~ soprano** chanter soprano; **to ~ small*** se faire tout petit, filer doux*.

b (*US* ‡) moucharder*, se mettre à table‡.

3 **comp ▸singsong: to have a singsong** chanter en chœur **▸singsong voice** voix qui psalmodie; **to repeat sth in a singsong (voice)** répéter qch sur deux tons.

▸sing out vi chanter fort; (* *fig*) crier, parler fort, se faire entendre. **if you want anything just sing out*** si vous voulez quoi que ce soit vous n'avez qu'à appeler (bien fort); **to sing out for sth*** réclamer qch à grands cris.

▸sing up vi chanter plus fort. **sing up!** plus fort!

Singapore [ˌsɪŋgə'pɔ:ʳ] **n** Singapour *m*. **in ~** à Singapour.

Singaporean [ˌsɪŋgə'pɔ:rɪən] 1 **adj** singapourien. 2 **n** Singapourien(ne) *m(f)*.

singe [sɪndʒ] 1 **vt** brûler légèrement; *cloth, clothes* roussir; *poultry* flamber. (*fig*) **to ~ one's wings** se brûler les ailes *or* les doigts. 2 **n** (*also* **~ mark**) légère brûlure; (*scorch mark on cloth*) tache *f* de roussi, roussissure *f*.

singer ['sɪŋəʳ] **n** chanteur *m*, -euse *f*; *see* **opera** *etc*.

Singhalese [ˌsɪŋgə'li:z] 1 **adj** cingalais. 2 **n** a (*pl* **~s** *or* **~**) Cingalais(e) *m(f)*. b (*Ling*) cingalais *m*.

singing ['sɪŋɪŋ] 1 **n** (*NonC*) *[person, bird, violin]* chant *m*; *[kettle, wind]* sifflement *m*; (*in ears*) bourdonnement *m*, tintement *m*. 2 **comp ▸singing lesson: to have singing lessons** prendre des leçons de chant, apprendre le chant **▸singing teacher** professeur *m* de chant **▸singing telegram** *service qui consiste à envoyer des filles chanter des compliments à des gens dont c'est l'anniversaire* **▸singing voice: to have a good singing voice** avoir de la voix, avoir une belle voix (*pour le chant*).

single ['sɪŋgl] 1 **adj** a (*only one*) seul, unique. **there was a ~ rose in the garden** il y avait une seule rose dans le jardin; **he gave her a ~ rose** il lui a donné une rose; **if there is a ~ *or* one ~ objection to this proposal** s'il y a une seule *or* la moindre objection à cette proposition; **he was the ~ survivor** il était le seul *or* l'unique survivant; **a ~ diamond** un diamant monté seul; (*as ring*) un solitaire; (*Rail*) **a ~ track** une voie unique (*see also* 3); **every ~ day** tous les jours sans exception; **not a ~ person spoke** pas une seule personne n'a parlé; **I didn't see a ~ soul** je n'ai vu personne, je n'ai pas vu âme qui vive; **I haven't a ~ moment to lose** je n'ai pas une minute à perdre; **a *or* one ~ department should deal with all of these matters** un service unique *or* un même service devrait traiter toutes ces affaires; *see also* **3**.

b (*not double etc*) *knot, flower* simple. (*Brit*) **a ~ ticket to London** un aller (simple) *or* un billet simple pour Londres; (*Brit*) **~ fare** prix *m* d'un aller (simple); **in ~ file** *stand* en *or* à la file; **a ~ whisky/gin** *etc* un whisky/gin normal, une mesure normale de whisky/gin; **~ bed** lit *m* d'une personne; **~ (bed)room** chambre *f* à un lit *or* particulière *or* pour une personne; *see also* **3** *and* **spacing**.

c (*unmarried*) célibataire. **~ people** célibataires *mpl*; (*Admin*) **~ parent** (*gen*) parent *m* isolé *or* unique; (*unmarried*) père *m or* mère *f* célibataire; **she's a ~ woman** elle est célibataire, c'est une célibataire; (*Soc*) **the ~ homeless** les gens seuls et sans abri; **the ~ state, the ~ life** le célibat.

2 **n** a (*Tennis etc: pl*) **~s** simple *m*; **ladies' ~s** simple dames.

b (*Cricket: one run*) **a ~** une seule course, un seul point; **3 ~s** 3 fois une course *or* un point.

c (*Brit Rail etc: ticket*) aller *m* (simple), billet *m* simple.

d (*in cinema, theatre*) **there are only ~s left** il ne reste que des places séparées *or* isolées.

e (*record*) **a ~** un 45 tours; **his latest ~** son dernier 45 tours.

f (*: *unmarried people*) **~s** célibataires *mfpl*; **~s bar/club** bar *m*/club *m* de rencontres pour célibataires.

g (*Brit: £1 note or coin*) billet *m or* pièce *f* d'une livre; (*esp US: $1 note*) billet *m* d'un dollar.

h (*also* **~ room**) chambre *f* simple *or* d'une personne.

i (*drink: one measure*) **make mine a ~** donnez-moi une mesure normale; **double or ~?** double ou normal?

3 **comp ▸single-barrelled** à un canon **▸single-breasted** (*Dress*) droit **▸single-celled** unicellulaire **▸single combat: in single combat** en combat singulier **▸single cream** (*Brit*) crème fraîche liquide **▸single-crop farming** monoculture *f* **▸single-decker** (*Brit*) **adj** sans impériale ◊ **n** autobus *m or* tramway *m etc* sans impériale **▸single-density** *see* **density ▸single-engined** monomoteur (*f* -trice) **▸single-entry book-keeping** comptabilité *f* en partie simple **▸single-handed adv** tout seul, sans aucune aide ◊ **adj** *achievement* fait sans aucune aide; (*Naut*) *sailing, voyage, race* en solitaire; *[person]* **to be single-handed** n'avoir aucune aide, être tout seul **▸singlehandedly** tout(e) seul(e), à lui (*etc*) tout seul **▸single honours (degree)** (*Brit Univ*) ≃ licence *f* préparée dans *or* avec une seule matière **▸single lens reflex (camera)** reflex *m* (à un objectif) **▸single malt (whisky)** single malt *m*, (whisky *m*) pur malt *m* **▸single-masted** à un mât **▸single-minded** *person* résolu, ferme; *attempt* énergique, résolu; *determination* tenace; **to be single-minded about sth** concentrer tous ses efforts sur qch; **to be single-minded in one's efforts to do sth** tout faire en vue de faire qch **▸single-mindedly** résolument **▸single-mindedness** détermination *f*, ténacité *f* **▸single-parent family** famille monoparentale **▸single-party** (*Pol*) *state, government* à parti unique **▸single-seater (aeroplane)** (*Aviat*) (avion *m*) monoplace *m* **▸single-sex school** (*Brit*) établissement *m* scolaire non mixte **▸single-sided disk** (*Comput*) disque *m* simple **▸single-track** (*Rail*) à voie unique; (*fig*) **to have a single-track mind** (*one thing at a time*) ne pouvoir se concentrer que sur une seule chose à la fois; (*obsessive idea*) n'avoir qu'une idée en tête **▸Single Transferable Vote** (*Pol*) ≃ scrutin *m* de liste à représentation proportionnelle.

▸single out vt sep (*distinguish*) distinguer; (*pick out*) choisir. **I don't want to single anyone out** je ne veux pas faire de distinctions; **he's singled out for all the nasty jobs** on le choisit pour toutes les corvées; **to single o.s. out** se singulariser.

singleness ['sɪŋglnɪs] **n**: **~ of purpose** persévérance *f*, ténacité *f*, unité *f* d'intention.

singlet ['sɪŋglɪt] **n** (*Brit*) maillot *m or* tricot *m* de corps.

singleton ['sɪŋgltən] **n** (*Cards*) singleton *m*.

singly ['sɪŋglɪ] **adv** séparément, un(e) à un(e).

singular ['sɪŋgjʊləʳ] 1 **adj** a (*Gram*) *noun, verb* au singulier, singulier; *form, ending* du singulier. **the masculine ~** le masculin singulier. b (*outstanding*) singulier, remarquable; (*unusual*) singulier, rare; (*strange*) singulier, étrange, bizarre; (*surprising*) singulier, extraordinaire, surprenant. 2 **n** (*Gram*) singulier *m*. **in the ~** au singulier.

singularity [ˌsɪŋgjʊ'lærɪtɪ] **n** singularité *f*.

singularize ['sɪŋgjʊləraɪz] **vt** singulariser.

singularly ['sɪŋgjʊləlɪ] **adv** singulièrement.

Sinhalese [ˌsɪnə'li:z] = **Singhalese**.

sinister ['sɪnɪstəʳ] **adj** a *omen, sign, silence* sinistre, funeste, de mauvais augure; *plan, plot, appearance, figure* sinistre, menaçant. b (*Her*) sénestre.

sinisterly ['sɪnɪstəlɪ] **adv** sinistrement.

sink[1] [sɪŋk] **pret sank, ptp sunk** 1 **vi** a (*go under*) *[ship]* couler, sombrer; *[person, object]* couler. **to ~ to the bottom** couler *or* aller au fond; **to ~ like a stone** couler à pic; (*fig*) **they left him to ~ or swim** ils l'ont laissé s'en sortir* *or* s'en tirer* tout seul; (*fig*) **it was ~ or swim** il fallait bien s'en sortir* *or* s'en tirer* tout seul; **~ or swim he'll have to manage by himself** il n'a qu'à se débrouiller comme il peut.

b *[ground]* s'affaisser; *[foundation, building]* s'affaisser, se tasser; *[level, river, fire]* baisser. **the land ~s towards the sea** le terrain descend en pente vers la mer; **the sun was ~ing** le soleil se couchait; **the sun sank below the horizon** le soleil a disparu *or* s'est enfoncé au-dessous de l'horizon; **to ~ out of sight** disparaître; **to ~ to one's knees** tomber à genoux; **to ~ to the ground** s'affaisser, s'écrouler; **he sank into a chair** il s'est laissé tomber *or* s'est affaissé *or* s'est effondré dans un fauteuil; **he sank into the mud up to his knees** il s'est enfoncé *or* il a enfoncé dans la boue jusqu'aux genoux; **she let her head ~ into the pillow** elle a laissé retomber sa tête sur l'oreiller; **the water slowly sank into the ground** l'eau a pénétré *or* s'est infiltrée lentement dans le sol; (*fig: dying*) **he is ~ing fast** il décline *or* il baisse rapidement.

c (*fig*) **to ~ into a deep sleep** tomber *or* sombrer dans un sommeil profond; **to ~ into despondency** tomber dans le découragement, se laisser aller au découragement; **to ~ into insignificance/poverty/despair** sombrer dans l'insignifiance/la misère/le désespoir; **he has sunk in my estimation** il a baissé dans mon estime; **his voice sank** sa voix s'est faite plus basse; **his voice sank to a whisper** il s'est mis à chuchoter, sa voix n'a plus été qu'un murmure; **his heart** *or* **his spirits sank** le découragement *or* l'accablement s'est emparé de lui, il en a eu un coup de cafard*; **his heart sank at the thought** il a eu un serrement de cœur *or* son cœur s'est serré à cette pensée, il a été pris de découragement à cette idée; **it's enough to make your heart ~** c'est à vous démoraliser *or* à vous donner le cafard*.

d *[prices, value, temperature]* tomber très bas, baisser beaucoup; *[sales, numbers]* baisser beaucoup. (*St Ex*) **the shares have sunk to 3 dollars** les actions sont tombées à 3 dollars; (*Fin*) **the pound has sunk to a new low** la livre est tombée plus bas que jamais *or* a atteint sa cote la plus basse.

2 **vt** a *ship* couler, faire sombrer; *object* faire couler (au fond); (*fig*) *theory* démolir; *business, project* ruiner, couler; *play, book* couler, démolir; (*) *person* couler, ruiner la réputation de. (*fig*) **they sank their differences** ils ont enterré *or* oublié *or* mis de côté leurs querelles; **to be sunk in thought/depression/despair** être plongé dans ses pensées/la dépression/le désespoir; **I'm sunk*** je suis fichu* *or* perdu.

b *mine, well* creuser, forer; *foundations* creuser; *pipe etc* noyer. **to ~ a post 2 metres in the ground** enfoncer un pieu 2 mètres dans le sol; **the dog sank his fangs into my leg** le chien a enfoncé *or* planté ses crocs dans ma jambe; **he sank his teeth into the sandwich** il a mordu (à belles dents) dans le sandwich; **he can ~ a glass of beer in 5 seconds*** il peut avaler *or* s'envoyer‡ une bière en 5 secondes; (*Golf*) **to ~ the ball** faire entrer la balle dans le trou; (*fig*) **to ~ a lot of money in a project** (*invest*) investir *or* placer beaucoup d'argent dans une entreprise; (*lose*) perdre *or* engloutir *or* engouffrer beaucoup d'argent dans une entreprise.

►**sink back** **vi** (se laisser) retomber, se renverser. **it sank back into the water** c'est retombé dans l'eau; **he managed to sit up but soon sank back exhausted** il a réussi à s'asseoir mais s'est bientôt laissé retomber épuisé; **he sank back into his chair** il s'est enfoncé dans son fauteuil.

►**sink down** **vi** *[building]* s'enfoncer, s'affaisser; *[post]* s'enfoncer. **to sink down into a chair** s'affaisser dans un fauteuil; **to sink down on one's knees** tomber à genoux; **he sank down (out of sight) behind the bush** il a disparu derrière le buisson.

►**sink in** **vi** a *[person, post etc]* s'enfoncer; *[water, ointment etc]* pénétrer. b (*fig*) *[explanation]* rentrer; *[remark]* faire son effet. **when the facts sank in, he ...** quand il a pleinement compris les faits, il ...; **as it hadn't really sunk in yet he ...** comme il n'arrivait pas encore à s'en rendre compte il ..., comme il ne réalisait* pas encore il ...; **my explanation took a long time to sink in** j'ai eu du mal à lui (*or* leur *etc*) faire rentrer *or* pénétrer l'explication dans la tête, il a (*or* ils ont *etc*) mis longtemps à comprendre mon explication.

sink² [sɪŋk] 1 **n** (*in kitchen*) évier *m*; (*US also in bathroom*) lavabo *m*. **double ~** évier à deux bacs; (*fig*) **a ~ of iniquity** un cloaque du *or* de vice; *see* **kitchen.** 2 **comp** ►**sink tidy** coin *m* d'évier (*ustensile ménager*) ►**sink unit** bloc-évier *m*.

sinker ['sɪŋkəʳ] **n** a (*lead*) plomb *m*; *see* **hook.** b (*US *: doughnut*) beignet *m*.

sinking ['sɪŋkɪŋ] 1 **adj**: **with ~ heart** le cœur serré; (*stronger*) la mort dans l'âme; **that ~ feeling** ce serrement de cœur; (*stronger*) ce sentiment de désastre imminent; **to have a ~ feeling** avoir un serrement de cœur; (*stronger*) avoir la mort dans l'âme; **I had a ~ feeling that he would come back again** j'avais le pénible *or* fâcheux pressentiment qu'il reviendrait. 2 **n**: **the ~ of a ship** (*accidental*) le naufrage d'un navire; (*in battle*) le torpillage d'un navire; **the submarine's ~ of the cruiser made possible ...** quand le sous-marin a coulé le croiseur cela a permis ... . 3 **comp** ►**sinking fund** (*Fin*) fonds *mpl* d'amortissement.

sinless ['sɪnlɪs] **adj** sans péché, pur, innocent.

sinner ['sɪnəʳ] **n** pécheur *m*, -eresse *f*.

Sinn Fein ['ʃɪn'feɪn] **n** Sinn Fein *m* (*mouvement politique républicain pour la réunification de l'Irlande*).

Sino- ['saɪnəʊ] **pref** sino-. **~Soviet** sino-soviétique.

Sinologist [ˌsaɪ'nɒlədʒɪst] **n** sinologue *mf*.

Sinology [ˌsaɪ'nɒlədʒɪ] **n** sinologie *f*.

Sinophobia [ˌsaɪnəʊ'fəʊbɪə] **n** sinophobie *f*.

sinuosity [ˌsɪnjʊ'ɒsɪtɪ] **n** sinuosité *f*.

sinuous ['sɪnjʊəs] **adj** (*lit, fig*) sinueux.

sinus ['saɪnəs] **n, pl ~es** sinus *m inv* (*Med*). **to have ~ trouble** avoir de la sinusite.

sinusitis [ˌsaɪnə'saɪtɪs] **n** (*NonC*) sinusite *f*. **to have ~** avoir de la sinusite.

Sioux [suː] 1 **adj** sioux *inv*. (*US*) **the ~ State** le Dakota du Nord. 2 **n** a **(pl inv)** Sioux *mf*. b (*Ling*) sioux *m*.

sip [sɪp] 1 **n** petite gorgée. **do you want a ~ of rum?** voulez-vous une goutte de rhum?; **he took a ~** il a bu une petite gorgée. 2 **vt** (*drinking a little at a time*) boire à petites gorgées *or* à petits coups; (*take a sip*) boire une petite gorgée de; (*with enjoyment*) siroter*. 3 **vi** **he ~ped at his whisky** (*drank it a little at a time*) il a bu son whisky à petites gorgées; (*took a sip*) il a bu une petite gorgée de son whisky.

siphon ['saɪfən] 1 **n** siphon *m*; *see* **soda.** 2 **vt** siphonner.

►**siphon off** **vt sep** (*lit*) siphonner; (*fig*) *people etc* mettre à part; *profits, funds* canaliser; (*illegally*) détourner.

sir [sɜːʳ] **n** monsieur *m*. **yes ~** oui, Monsieur; (*to officer: in Army, Navy, Air Force*) oui, mon commandant (*or* mon lieutenant *etc*); (*to surgeon*) oui docteur; (*emphatic*) **yes/no ~!*** ça oui/non!; (*in letter*) **Dear S~** (Cher) Monsieur; (*to newspaper editor*) **S~** Monsieur (le Directeur); (*iro*) **my dear/good ~** mon cher/bon Monsieur; (*Brit*) **S~ John Smith** sir John Smith.

sire ['saɪəʳ] 1 **n** (*Zool*) père *m*; (††: *father*) père; (††: *ancestor*) aïeul *m*. (*to king*) **yes ~** oui sire. 2 **vt** engendrer.

siree* [sɪ'riː] **n** (*US: emphatic*) **yes/no ~!** ça oui/non!

siren ['saɪərən] 1 **n** a (*device*) sirène *f*. b (*Myth*) **the S~s** les sirènes *fpl*. 2 **adj** (*liter*) *charms* séducteur (*f* -trice); *song* de sirène, enchanteur (*f* -teresse).

sirloin ['sɜːlɔɪn] **n** aloyau *m*. **a ~ steak** un bifteck dans l'aloyau *or* d'aloyau.

sirocco [sɪ'rɒkəʊ] **n** sirocco *m*.

sis‡ [sɪs] **n** (**abbr of sister**) sœurette *f*, frangine‡ *f*.

sisal ['saɪsəl] 1 **n** sisal *m*. 2 **comp** en *or* de sisal.

sissy* ['sɪsɪ] 1 **n** (*coward*) poule mouillée. (*effeminate*) **he's a bit of a ~** il est un peu efféminé, il fait un peu tapette‡. 2 **adj** efféminé. **that's ~!** ça fait fille!

sister ['sɪstəʳ] 1 **n** a sœur *f*. **her younger ~** sa (sœur) cadette, sa petite sœur; *see* **half, step** *etc*. b (*Rel*) religieuse *f*, (bonne) sœur *f*. **yes ~** oui, ma sœur; **S~ Mary Margaret** sœur Marie Marguerite; **the S~s of Charity** les sœurs de la Charité. c (*Brit Med: also* **nursing ~**) infirmière *f* chef. **yes ~** oui Madame (*or* Mademoiselle). d (*US*) **listen ~!‡** écoute ma vieille!* 2 **comp** ►**sister-in-law** (**pl ~s-~-~**) belle-sœur *f*. 3 **adj** (*with fem nouns*) sœur; (*with masc nouns*) frère. **~ organization** organisation *f* sœur (**pl** organisations sœurs); **~ country** pays *m* frère (**pl** pays frères); (*US Univ*) **~ school** université *f* de filles jumelée avec une université de garçons; **~ ship** sister-ship *m*.

sisterhood ['sɪstəhʊd] **n** (*solidarity*) solidarité *f* féminine; (*Rel*) communauté *f* (religieuse). (*group of women*) **the ~** la communauté (des femmes).

sisterly ['sɪstəlɪ] **adj** de sœur, fraternel.

Sistine ['sɪstiːn] **adj**: **the ~ Chapel** la chapelle Sixtine.

Sisyphus ['sɪsɪfəs] **n** Sisyphe *m*.

sit [sɪt] **pret, ptp sat** 1 **vi** a (*also ~ down*) s'asseoir. **to be ~ting** être assis; (*to dog*) **~!** assis!; **~ by me** assieds-toi près de moi; **he was ~ting at his desk/at table** il était (assis) à son bureau/à table; **they spent the evening ~ting at home** ils ont passé la soirée (tranquillement) à la maison; **she just ~s at home all day** elle reste chez elle toute la journée à ne rien faire; **he was ~ting over his books all evening** il a passé toute la soirée dans ses livres; **to ~ through a lecture/play** *etc* assister à une conférence/à une pièce jusqu'au bout; **don't just ~ there, do something!** ne reste pas là à ne rien faire!; **to ~ still** rester *or* se tenir tranquille, ne pas bouger; **to ~ straight** *or* **upright** se tenir droit; (*lit, fig: stay put*) **to ~ tight** ne pas bouger; (*fig*) **to be ~ting pretty*** avoir le bon filon*, tenir le bon bout*; (*fig: hum or liter*) **to ~ at sb's feet** suivre l'enseignement de qn; (*Art, Phot*) **to ~ for one's portrait** poser pour son portrait; **she sat for Picasso** elle a posé pour Picasso; **to ~ on a committee/jury** être membre *or* faire partie d'un comité/jury; (*fig*) **to ~ for an exam** passer un examen, se présenter à un examen; **he sat for Sandhurst** il s'est présenté au concours d'entrée de Sandhurst; (*Brit Parl*) **he ~s for Brighton** il est (le) député de Brighton.

b *[bird, insect]* se poser, se percher. **to be ~ting** être perché; (*on eggs*) couver; **the hen is ~ting on 12 eggs** la poule couve 12 œufs.

c *[committee, assembly etc]* être en séance; siéger. **the committee is ~ting now** le comité est en séance; **the House ~s from November to June** la Chambre siège de novembre à juin; **the House sat for 16 hours** la Chambre a été en séance pendant 16 heures.

d *[dress, coat etc]* tomber (*on sb* sur qn). **the jacket ~s badly across the shoulders** la veste tombe mal aux épaules; (*fig*) **this policy would ~ well with their allies** cette politique serait bien vue de leurs alliés; (*liter*) **it sat heavy on his conscience** cela lui pesait sur la conscience; (*liter*) **how ~s the wind?** d'où vient *or* souffle le vent?

2 vt a (*also* ~ **down**) asseoir, installer; (*invite to* ~) faire asseoir. **he sat the child (down) on his knee** il a assis *or* installé l'enfant sur ses genoux; **they sat him (down) in a chair** (*placed him in it*) ils l'ont assis *or* installé dans un fauteuil; (*invited him to sit*) ils l'ont fait asseoir dans un fauteuil.

b **to ~ a horse well/badly** monter bien/mal, avoir une bonne/ mauvaise assiette.

c (*esp Brit*) *exam* passer, se présenter à.

3 comp ►**sit-down***: **he had a 10-minute sit-down** il s'est assis 10 minutes (pour se reposer); **we had a sit-down lunch** nous avons déjeuné à table; **sit-down strike** grève *f* sur le tas ►**sit-in** *see* **sit-in** ►**sit-up** (*Gymnastics*) redressement *m* assis ►**sit-upon*** derrière *m*, fesses *fpl*.

►**sit about, sit around** vi rester assis (à ne rien faire), traîner.

►**sit back** vi: **to sit back in an armchair** s'enfoncer *or* se carrer *or* se caler dans un fauteuil; **to sit back on one's heels** s'asseoir sur les talons; **just sit back and listen to this** installe-toi bien et écoute un peu (ceci); (*fig*) **he sat back and did nothing about it** il s'est abstenu de faire quoi que ce soit, il n'a pas levé le petit doigt; (*fig*) **I can't just sit back and do nothing!** je ne peux quand même pas rester là à ne rien faire! *or* à me croiser les bras!; **the Government sat back and did nothing to help them** le gouvernement n'a pas fait le moindre geste pour les aider.

►**sit down** 1 vi s'asseoir. **to be sitting down** être assis; **he sat down to a huge dinner** il s'est attablé devant un repas gigantesque; (*fig*) **to take sth sitting down*** rester les bras croisés devant qch (*fig*); (*fig*) **to sit down under an insult** supporter une insulte sans broncher, encaisser* une insulte. 2 vt sep = **sit 2a**. 3 **sit-down*** n, adj *see* **sit 3**.

►**sit in** 1 vi a **she sat in all day waiting for him to come** elle est restée à la maison toute la journée à l'attendre, elle a passé la journée chez elle à l'attendre; **to sit in on a discussion** assister à une discussion (sans y prendre part); (*fig: replace*) **to sit in for sb** remplacer qn. b **the demonstrators sat in in the director's office** les manifestants ont occupé le bureau du directeur. 2 **sit-in** n *see* **sit-in**.

►**sit on*** vt fus (*fig*) a (*keep secret, not publish etc*) *news, facts, report* garder secret, garder le silence sur, garder sous le boisseau; (*not pass on*) *file, document* garder (pour soi), accaparer. **the committee sat on the proposals for weeks, then decided to ...** pendant des semaines, le comité ne s'est pas occupé des propositions, puis a décidé de ... . b *person* (*silence*) faire taire, fermer *or* clouer le bec à*; (*snub etc*) remettre à sa place, rabrouer, rembarrer*. **he won't be sat on** il ne se laisse pas marcher sur les pieds. c (*reject*) *idea, proposal* rejeter, repousser.

►**sit out** 1 vi (*sit outside*) (aller) s'asseoir dehors, se mettre *or* s'installer dehors. 2 vt sep a **to sit a lecture/play** *etc* **out** rester jusqu'à la fin d'une conférence/d'une pièce *etc*, assister à une conférence/à une pièce *etc* jusqu'au bout. b **she sat out the waltz** elle n'a pas dansé la valse.

►**sit up** 1 vi a (*sit upright*) se redresser, s'asseoir bien droit. **to be sitting up** être assis bien droit, se tenir droit; **he was sitting up in bed** il était assis dans son lit; **you can sit up now** vous pouvez vous asseoir maintenant; (*fig*) **to make sb sit up** secouer *or* étonner qn; (*fig*) **to sit up (and take notice)** (*gen*) se secouer, se réveiller; (*after illness*) **he began to sit up and take notice** il a commencé à reprendre intérêt à la vie *or* à refaire surface.

b (*stay up*) rester debout, ne pas se coucher. **to sit up late** se coucher tard, veiller tard; **to sit up all night** ne pas se coucher de la nuit; **don't sit up for me** couchez-vous sans m'attendre; **the nurse sat up with him** l'infirmière est restée à son chevet *or* l'a veillé.

2 vt sep *doll, child* asseoir, redresser.

3 **sit-up** n *see* **sit 3**.

►**sit upon*** 1 vt fus = **sit on***. 2 **sit-upon*** n *see* **sit 3**.

sitar [sɪ'tɑːʳ] n sitar *m*.

sitcom* ['sɪtkɒm] n (*Rad, TV*) (abbr of **situation comedy**) comédie *f* de situation.

site [saɪt] 1 n [*town, building*] emplacement *m*; (*Archeol*) site *m*; (*Constr*) chantier *m* (de construction *or* de démolition *etc*); (*Camping*) (terrain *m* de) camping *m*. **the ~ of the battle** le champ de bataille; *see* **building, launching** *etc*. 2 comp ►**site measuring** (*Jur*) métré *m* ►**Site of Specific Scientific Interest** (*Brit*) site *m* d'intérêt scientifique, ≃ réserve *f* naturelle. 3 vt *town, building, gun* placer. **they want to ~ the steelworks in that valley** on veut placer *or* construire l'aciérie dans cette vallée; **the factory is very badly ~d** l'usine est très mal située *or* placée.

sit-in ['sɪtɪn] n [*demonstrators etc*] sit-in *m*, manifestation *f* avec occupation de locaux; [*workers*] grève *f* sur le tas. **the workers held a ~** les ouvriers ont organisé une grève sur le tas; **the students held a ~ in the university offices** les étudiants ont occupé les bureaux de l'université; **the ~ at the offices** l'occupation *f* des bureaux.

siting ['saɪtɪŋ] n: **the ~ of the new town there was a mistake** c'était une erreur de bâtir *or* placer la ville nouvelle à cet endroit; **the ~ of the new factories has given rise to many objections** le choix de l'emplacement pour les nouvelles usines a soulevé de nombreuses critiques.

sitter ['sɪtəʳ] n (*Art*) modèle *m*; (*baby-~*) baby-sitter *m*; (*hen*) couveuse *f*. (*Sport*) **he missed a ~⁑** il a raté un coup enfantin; **it's a ~⁑** tu ne peux pas (*or* il ne peut pas *etc*) le rater!

sitting ['sɪtɪŋ] 1 n [*committee, assembly etc*] séance *f*; (*for portrait*) séance de pose; (*in canteen etc*) service *m*. **they served 200 people in one ~/in 2 ~s** ils ont servi 200 personnes à la fois/en 2 services; **2nd ~ for lunch** 2e service pour le déjeuner. 2 adj *committee* en séance; *official* en exercice; *game bird* posé, au repos. (*Jur*) **~ judge** juge *m* en exercice; (*Brit Parl*) **~ member** député *m* en exercice; (*Brit*) **~ tenant** locataire *mf* en possession des lieux *or* en place. 3 comp ►**sitting and standing room** places debout et assises ►**sitting duck*** (*fig*) victime *f or* cible *f* facile ►**sitting room** salon *m*.

situ ['sɪtjuː] (*frm*) **in ~** in situ, en place.

situate ['sɪtjueɪt] vt (*locate*) *building, town* placer; (*put into perspective*) *problem, event* situer. **the house is ~d in the country** la maison se trouve *or* est située à la campagne; **the shop is well ~d** le magasin est bien situé *or* bien placé; **we are rather badly ~d as there is no bus service** nous sommes assez mal situés car il n'y a pas d'autobus; (*fig*) **he is rather badly ~d at the moment** il est dans une situation assez défavorable *or* en assez mauvaise posture en ce moment; (*financially*) il est assez gêné *or* il a des ennuis d'argent en ce moment; **I am well ~d to appreciate the risks** je suis bien placé pour apprécier les risques; **how are you ~d for money?** est-ce que tu as l'argent qu'il te faut?, est-ce que tu as besoin d'argent?

situation [ˌsɪtjʊ'eɪʃən] 1 n a (*location*) [*town, building etc*] situation *f*, emplacement *m*. **the house has a fine ~** la maison est bien située.

b (*circumstances*) situation *f* (*also Literat*). **he was in a very difficult ~** il se trouvait dans une situation très difficile; **they managed to save the ~** ils ont réussi à sauver *or* redresser la situation; **the international ~** la situation internationale, la conjoncture internationale; (*jargon*) **they're in a waiting/discussion** *etc* **~** ils sont en situation d'attente/de dialogue *etc*; **in an exam ~, you must ...** à un examen, il faut ... .

c (*job*) situation *f*, emploi *m*, poste *m*. **"~s vacant/wanted"** "offres/demandes d'emploi".

2 comp ►**situation comedy** (*Theat etc*) comédie *f* de situation.

situational [ˌsɪtjʊ'eɪʃənl] adj situationnel.

six [sɪks] 1 adj six *inv*. **he is ~ (years old)** il a six ans (*see also* **3**); **he'll be ~ on Saturday** il aura six ans samedi; **he lives in number ~** il habite au (numéro) six; **~ times six** six fois six.

2 pron six *mfpl*. **there were about ~** il y en avait six environ *or* à peu près; **~ of the girls came** six des filles sont venues; **there are ~ of us** nous sommes *or* on est* six; **all ~ (of us) left** nous sommes partis tous les six; **all ~ (of them) left** tous les six sont partis, ils sont partis tous les six.

3 n a six *m inv*. **it is ~ o'clock** il est six heures; **come at ~** venez à six heures; **it struck ~** six heures ont sonné; **they are sold in ~es** c'est vendu *or* cela se vend par (lots *or* paquets de) six; **the children arrived in ~es** les enfants sont arrivés par groupes de six; **he lives at ~ Churchill Street** il habite (au) six rue Churchill; (*Cards*) **the ~ of diamonds** le six de carreaux; **two ~es are twelve** deux fois six douze; (*Brit*) **~ of the best*** six grands coups; (*fig*) **to be at ~es and sevens** [*books, house etc*] être en désordre *or* en pagaille*, être sens dessus dessous; [*person*] être tout retourné*; (*hum*) **to be ~ foot under*** manger les pissenlits par la racine*; (*fig*) **it's ~ of one and half a dozen of the other*, it's ~ and half a dozen*** c'est blanc bonnet et bonnet blanc, c'est du pareil au même*, c'est kif-kif*.

b (*Cricket*) **to hit a ~** marquer six courses *fpl or* points *mpl*; **he hit 3 ~es** il a marqué 3 fois six courses *or* points; *see* **knock**.

4 comp ►**six-cylinder** (*Aut*) adj à six cylindres ◊ n (voiture *f* à) six cylindres *f* ►**six-eight time:** (*Mus*) **in six-eight time** en mesure à six-huit ►**sixfold** adj sextuple ◊ adv au sextuple ►**six-footer*** grand *m* d'un mètre quatre-vingts ►**six-pack** pack *m* de six ►**sixpence** (*Brit*) (*coin*) (ancienne) pièce *f* de six pence; (*value*) six pence *mpl* ►**sixpenny** adj à six pence ►**six-seater** adj à six places ◊ n (*car etc*) (voiture *f etc* à) six places *f*; (*plane etc*) (avion *m etc* à) six places *m* ►**six-shooter** pistolet *m* automatique ►**six-sided** hexagonal ►**six-speed gearbox** (*Aut*) boîte *f* à six vitesses ►**six-storey** à six étages ►**six-year-old** adj *child, horse* de six ans; *house, car* vieux (*f* vieille) de six ans ◊ n (*child*) enfant (âgé) de six ans; (*horse*) cheval *m* de six ans.

sixish ['sɪksɪʃ] adj: **he is ~** il a dans les six ans, il a six ans environ; **he came at ~** il est venu vers (les) six heures.

sixteen ['sɪks'tiːn] 1 adj seize *inv*. **she was sweet ~** c'était une fraîche jeune fille (de seize ans). 2 n seize *m inv*; *for phrases see* **six**. 3 pron seize *mfpl*. **there are ~** il y en a seize.

sixteenth ['sɪks'tiːnθ] 1 adj seizième. 2 n seizième *mf*; (*fraction*) seizième *m*; *for phrases see* **sixth**.

sixth [sɪksθ] 1 adj sixième. **to be ~ in an exam/in German** être sixième à un concours/en allemand; **she was the ~ to arrive** elle est arrivée la sixième; **Charles the S~** Charles six; **the ~ of November, November the ~** le six novembre; (*fig*) **~ sense** sixième sens *m*.

2 n sixième *mf*; (*fraction*) sixième *m*; (*Mus*) sixte *f*. **he wrote the letter on the ~** il a écrit la lettre le six, sa lettre est du six; **your letter of the ~** votre lettre du six (courant); (*Brit Scol*) **the ~ = the ~ form** (*see* **4**).

3 adv a (*in race, exam, competition*) en sixième position *or* place.

he came *or* **was placed** ~ il s'est classé sixième.

b = **sixthly.**

4 **comp** ▸**sixth form** (*Brit Scol*) ≃ classes *fpl* de première et terminale; **to be in the sixth form** ≃ être en première *or* en terminale ▸**sixth-form college** *lycée n'ayant que des classes de première et de terminale* ▸**sixth-former, sixth-form pupil** ≃ élève *mf* de première *or* de terminale.

sixthly ['sɪksθlɪ] **adv** sixièmement, en sixième lieu.

sixtieth ['sɪkstɪɪθ] 1 **adj** soixantième. 2 **n** soixantième *mf*; (*fraction*) soixantième *m*.

sixty ['sɪkstɪ] 1 **adj** soixante *inv*. **he is about** ~ il a une soixantaine d'années, il a dans les soixante ans; **about** ~ **books** une soixantaine de livres.

2 **n** soixante *m inv*. **about** ~ une soixantaine, environ soixante; **to be in one's sixties** avoir entre soixante et soixante-dix ans, être sexagénaire; **he is in his early sixties** il a un peu plus de soixante ans; **he is in his late sixties** il approche de soixante-dix ans; **she's getting on** *or* **going on for** ~ elle approche de la soixantaine, elle va sur ses soixante ans; (*1960s etc*) **in the sixties** dans les années soixante; **in the early/late sixties** au début/vers la fin des années soixante; **the temperature was in the sixties** ≃ il faisait entre quinze et vingt degrés; **the numbers were in the sixties** le nombre s'élevait à plus de soixante; (*Aut*) **to do** ~* faire du soixante milles (à l'heure), ≃ faire du cent (à l'heure); *for other phrases see* **six.**

3 **pron** soixante *mfpl*. **there are** ~ il y en a soixante.

4 **comp** ▸**sixty-first** soixante et unième ▸**sixty-four (thousand) dollar question***: (*fig*) **that's the sixty-four (thousand) dollar question** c'est la question cruciale, c'est toute la question ▸**sixty-odd***: **there were sixty-odd** il y en avait soixante et quelques*, il y en avait une soixantaine; **sixty-odd books** un peu plus de soixante livres, soixante et quelques livres ▸**sixty-one** soixante et un ▸**sixty-second** soixante-deuxième ▸**sixty-two** soixante-deux.

sizable ['saɪzəbl] **adj** = **sizeable.**

sizably ['saɪzəblɪ] **adv** = **sizeably.**

size¹ [saɪz] 1 **n** (*for plaster, paper*) colle *f*; (*for cloth*) apprêt *m*. 2 **vt** encoller; apprêter.

size² [saɪz] 1 **n** a *[person, animal, sb's head, hands]* taille *f*; *[room, building]* grandeur *f*, dimensions *fpl*; *[car, chair]* dimensions; *[egg, fruit, jewel]* grosseur *f*; *[parcel]* grosseur, dimensions; *[book, photograph, sheet of paper, envelope]* taille, dimensions; (*format*) format *m*; *[sum]* montant *m*; *[estate, park, country]* étendue *f*, superficie *f*; *[problem, difficulty, obstacle]* ampleur *f*, étendue; *[operation, campaign]* ampleur, envergure *f*. *[packet, tube etc]* **the small/large** ~ le petit/grand modèle; **the** ~ **of the town** l'importance *f* de la ville; **a building of vast** ~ un bâtiment de belles dimensions; **the** ~ **of the farm** (*building*) les dimensions de la ferme; (*land*) l'étendue de la ferme; **the** ~ **of the fish you caught** la taille du poisson que tu as attrapé; **the** ~ **of the sum involved was so large that ...** la somme en question était d'une telle importance que ...; **sort them according to** ~ triez-les selon la grosseur (*or* le format *etc*); **to alter/cut/make sth to** ~ transformer/couper/faire qch sur mesure; **it's the** ~ **of a brick** c'est de la taille d'une brique; **it's the** ~ **of a walnut** c'est de la grosseur d'une noix; **it's the** ~ **of a house/elephant** c'est grand comme une maison/un éléphant; **a child of that** ~ **shouldn't be allowed to do that** un enfant de cette taille *or* de cet âge ne devrait pas avoir le droit de faire ça; **he's about your** ~ il est à peu près de la même taille que vous; (*fig*) **that's about the** ~ **of it!** c'est à peu près ça!, quelque chose dans ce genre-là!; **he cut the wood to** ~ il a coupé le bois à la dimension voulue; **they are all of a** ~ ils sont tous de la même grosseur (*or* de la même taille *etc*); *see* **cut down, shape** *etc*.

b *[coat, skirt, dress, trousers etc]* taille *f*; *[shoes, gloves]* pointure *f*; *[shirt]* encolure *f*. **what** ~ **are you?, what** ~ **do you take?** (*in dress etc*) quelle taille faites-vous?; (*in shoes, gloves*) quelle pointure faites-vous?; (*in hats*) quel est votre tour de tête?; **what** ~ **of collar?** *or* **shirt?** quelle encolure?; **I take** ~ **12** je prends du 12 *or* la taille 12; **what** ~ **of waist are you?** quel est votre tour de taille?; **hip** ~ tour *m* de hanches; **what** ~ **(of) shoes do you take?** quelle pointure faites-vous?, vous chaussez du combien?; **I take** ~ **5 (shoes)** ≃ je chausse *or* je fais du 38; **we are out of** ~ **5 (shoes)** ≃ nous n'avons plus de (chaussures en) 38; **"one** ~**"** "taille unique"; **I need a** ~ **smaller** il me faut la taille (*or* la pointure *etc*) en-dessous; **it's 2** ~**s too big for me** c'est 2 tailles au-dessus de ce qu'il me faut; **we haven't got your** ~ nous n'avons pas votre taille (*or* pointure *etc*); *see* **try.**

2 **vt** classer *or* trier selon la grosseur (*or* la dimension *or* la taille *etc*).

▸**size up vt sep** *person* juger, jauger; *situation* mesurer. **to size up the problem** mesurer l'étendue du problème; **I can't quite size him up** (*know what he is worth*) je n'arrive pas vraiment à le juger *or* à décider ce qu'il vaut; (*know what he wants*) je ne vois pas vraiment où il veut en venir.

-size [saɪz] **adj ending in comps** = **-sized.**

sizeable ['saɪzəbl] **adj** *dog, building, car, book, estate* assez grand; *egg, fruit, jewel* assez gros (*f* grosse); *sum, problem, operation* assez important, assez considérable.

sizeably ['saɪzəblɪ] **adv** considérablement, de beaucoup.

-sized [saɪzd] **adj ending in comps** (*see* **size² 1**): **medium-sized** de taille (*or* grandeur *or* grosseur *or* pointure *etc*) moyenne; *see* **life** *etc*.

sizzle ['sɪzl] 1 **vi** grésiller. 2 **n** grésillement *m*.

sizzler* ['sɪzləʳ] **n** journée *f* torride *or* caniculaire.

sizzling ['sɪzlɪŋ] 1 **adj** *fat, bacon* grésillant. **a** ~ **noise** un grésillement. 2 **adv**: ~ **hot** brûlant; **it was a** ~ **hot day*** on étouffait *or* il faisait une chaleur étouffante ce jour-là.

ska [skɑː] **n** (*Mus*) ska *m*.

skate¹ [skeɪt] **n, pl** ~ *or* ~**s** (*Brit: fish*) raie *f*.

skate² [skeɪt] 1 **n** patin *m*. (*fig*) **put** *or* **get your** ~**s on!*** dépêche-toi!, grouille-toi!*, magne-toi!‡; *see* **ice, roller.** 2 **comp** ▸**skateboard n** skateboard *m*, planche *f* à roulettes ◊ **vi** faire de la planche à roulettes ▸**skateboarder** skateur *m*, -euse *f* ▸**skateboarding** (*Sport*) skateboard *m*, planche *f* à roulettes. 3 **vi** patiner. **to go skating** (*ice*) faire du patin *or* du patinage; (*roller*) faire du patin à roulettes *or* du skating; **he** ~**d across the pond** il a traversé l'étang (en patinant *or* à patins); (*fig*) **it went skating across the room** cela a glissé à travers la pièce; *see* **ice, roller.**

▸**skate around, skate over, skate round vt fus** *problem, difficulty, objection* esquiver autant que possible.

skater ['skeɪtəʳ] **n** (*ice*) patineur *m*, -euse *f*; (*roller*) personne *f* qui fait du skating *or* du patinage à roulettes.

skating ['skeɪtɪŋ] 1 **n** (*ice*) patinage *m*; (*roller*) skating *m*, patinage à roulettes. 2 **comp** *champion, championship, display* (*ice*) de patinage; (*roller*) de skating, de patinage à roulettes ▸**skating rink** (*ice*) patinoire *f*; (*roller*) skating *m* ▸**skating turn** (*Ski*) pas *m* de patineur.

skean dhu ['skiːən'duː] **n** (*Scot*) poignard *m*.

skedaddle* [skɪ'dædl] **vi** (*run away*) décamper*, déguerpir*; (*flee in panic*) fuir en catastrophe.

skeet shooting ['skiːtˌʃuːtɪŋ] **n** skeet *m*, tir *m* au pigeon d'argile, ball-trap *m*.

skein [skeɪn] **n** *[wool etc]* écheveau *m*.

skeletal ['skelɪtl] **adj** squelettique.

skeleton ['skelɪtn] 1 **n** (*Anat*) squelette *m*; *[building, ship, model etc]* squelette, charpente *f*; *[plan, scheme, suggestion, novel etc]* schéma *m*, grandes lignes. **he was a mere** *or* **a walking** *or* **a living** ~ c'était un véritable cadavre ambulant; **he was reduced to a** ~ il n'était plus qu'un squelette, il était devenu (d'une maigreur) squelettique; **the staff was reduced to a** ~ le personnel était réduit au strict minimum; (*fig*) **the** ~ **at the feast** le *or* la trouble-fête *inv*, le rabat-joie *inv*; (*fig*) **the** ~ **in the cupboard** (*Brit*) *or* **closet** (*US*), **the family** ~ la honte cachée *or* le honteux secret de la famille.

2 **comp** *army, crew, staff* squelettique (*fig*), réduit au strict minimum ▸**skeleton key** passe *m*, passe-partout *m inv*, crochet *m*, rossignol *m* ▸**skeleton law** (*Ind*) loi-cadre *f* ▸**skeleton map** carte *f* schématique ▸**skeleton outline** *[drawing, map, plan etc]* schéma simplifié; *[proposals, report etc]* résumé *m*, grandes lignes.

skep [skep] **n** a (*beehive*) ruche *f*. b (*basket*) panier *m*.

skeptic(al) ['skeptɪk(əl)] (*US*) = **sceptic(al).**

sketch [sketʃ] 1 **n** a (*drawing*) croquis *m*, esquisse *f*; (*fig*) *[ideas, proposals etc]* résumé *m*, aperçu *m*, ébauche *f*. **a rough** ~ (*drawing*) une ébauche; (*fig*) **he gave me a (rough)** ~ **of what he planned to do** il m'a donné un aperçu de *or* il m'a dit en gros ce qu'il comptait faire.

b (*Theat*) sketch *m*, saynète *f*.

2 **comp** ▸**sketch(ing) book** carnet *m* à croquis *or* à dessins ▸**sketch(ing) pad** bloc *m* à dessins ▸**sketch map** carte faite à main levée.

3 **vi** faire des croquis *or* des esquisses. **to go** ~**ing** aller *or* partir faire des croquis.

4 **vt** *view, castle, figure* faire un croquis *or* une esquisse de, croquer, esquisser; *map* faire à main levée; (*fig*) *ideas, proposals, novel, plan* ébaucher, esquisser.

▸**sketch in vt sep** *detail in drawing* ajouter, dessiner; (*fig*) *details* ajouter; *facts* indiquer.

▸**sketch out vt sep** *plans, proposals, ideas* ébaucher, esquisser. (*lit, fig*) **to sketch out a picture of sth** ébaucher qch, dessiner les grandes lignes de qch.

sketchily ['sketʃɪlɪ] **adv** (*see* **sketchy**) incomplètement, superficiellement.

sketchy ['sketʃɪ] **adj** *answer, account* incomplet (*f* -ète), sommaire; *piece of work* incomplet, peu détaillé. **his knowledge of geography is** ~ il n'a que des connaissances superficielles *or* insuffisantes en géographie, il a de grosses lacunes en géographie.

skew [skjuː] 1 **n**: **to be on the** ~ être de travers *or* en biais *or* mal posé. 2 **adj** (*also* ~**ed**) (*squint*) de travers, oblique, de guingois*; (*slanting*) penché, de travers. 3 **adv** (*squint*) de travers, de guingois*; (*slanting*) de travers. 4 **comp** ▸**skewbald adj** fauve et blanc, pie *inv* ◊ **n** cheval *m* fauve et blanc, cheval pie *inv* ▸**skew-eyed*** qui louche, qui a un œil qui dit zut à l'autre* ▸**skew-whiff***: (*Brit*) **(on the) skew-whiff** de travers, de guingois*, de traviole‡. 5 **vi** a (*also* ~ **round**) obliquer. (*fig*) **negotiations** ~**ed off course** les négotiations ont dévié de leur but original. b (*squint*) loucher.

skewed [skjuːd] **adj** a (*squint, slanting*) = **skew 2.** b (*fig*) (*distorted*) faux (*f* fausse), erroné; (*biased*) orienté.

skewer ['skjʊəʳ] 1 n (*for roast etc*) broche *f*; (*for kebabs*) brochette *f*. 2 vt *chicken* embrocher; *pieces of meat* mettre en brochette; (*fig*) transpercer, embrocher*.

ski [skiː] 1 n, pl ~s *or* ~ ski *m* (*équipement*), planche* *f*; (*Aviat*) patin *m*; *see* **water**.
2 comp *school, clothes* de ski ►**ski binding** fixation *f* ►**skibob** skibob *m*, véloski *m* ►**ski boot** chaussure *f* de ski ►**ski bunny*** (*US: girl*) minette *f* de station de ski ►**ski instructor** moniteur *m*, -trice *f* de ski ►**skijump** (*action*) saut *m* à skis; (*place*) tremplin *m* (de ski) ►**skijumping** saut *m* à skis ►**skilift** télésiège *m*, remonte-pente *m inv*; **skilifts** (*gen*) remontées *fpl* mécaniques ►**ski-mountaineering** ski *m* de haute montagne ►**ski pants** fuseau *m* (de ski) ►**ski-pass** forfait-skieur(s) *m* ►**ski pole** = **ski stick** ►**ski-rack** (*Aut*) porte-skis *m* ►**ski resort** station *f* de ski *or* de neige, station de sports d'hiver ►**ski run** piste *f* de ski ►**ski slopes** pentes *fpl or* pistes *fpl* de ski ►**ski stick** bâton *m* de ski ►**ski-suit** combinaison *f* (de ski) ►**ski-touring** ski *m* de randonnée ►**ski tow** téléski *m*, remonte-pente *m inv* ►**ski trousers** = **ski pants** ►**ski wax** fart *m* ►**ski-wear** vêtements *mpl* de ski.
3 vi faire du ski, skier. **to go ~ing** (*as holiday*) partir aux sports d'hiver; (*go out ~ing*) (aller) faire du ski; **I like ~ing** j'aime le ski *or* faire du ski *or* skier; **to ~ down a slope** descendre une pente à *or* en skis.

skid [skɪd] 1 n a (*Aut*) dérapage *m*. **to get** *or* **go into a ~** déraper, faire un dérapage; **to get out of a ~, to correct a ~** redresser *or* contrôler un dérapage.
b (*on wheel*) cale *f*.
c (*under heavy object*) (*rollers, logs etc*) traîneau *m*. (*cause to fail*) **to put the ~s‡ on** *or* **under** *person* faire un croc-en-jambe à (*fig*); *plan etc* faire tomber à l'eau*; (*US*) **to hit the ~s*** devenir clochard(e)*.
2 comp ►**skidlid*** casque *m* (de moto) ►**skidmark** trace *f* de dérapage ►**skidpad, skidpan** piste *f or* chaussée *f or* terrain *m* de dérapages (*pour apprendre à contrôler un véhicule*) ►**skidproof** antidérapant ►**skid row** (*US*) quartier *m* de clochards, cour *f* des miracles; (*US fig*) **he's heading for skid row** il finira clochard*.
3 vi (*Aut*) déraper; [*person*] déraper, glisser. **the car ~ded to a halt** la voiture s'est arrêtée en dérapant; (*Aut*) **I ~ded into a tree** j'ai dérapé et percuté contre un arbre; **he went ~ding into the bookcase** il a glissé *or* dérapé et est allé se cogner contre la bibliothèque; **the toy ~ded across the room** le jouet a glissé jusqu'à l'autre bout de la pièce; (*US*) **prices ~ded*** les prix ont dérapé.

skier ['skiːəʳ] n skieur *m*, -euse *f*. **~s' hut** chalet-skieurs *m*.

skiff [skɪf] n skiff *m*, yole *f*.

skiing ['skiːɪŋ] 1 n (*NonC*) ski *m* (*sport*); *see* **water**. 2 comp *clothes, school* de ski ►**skiing holiday** vacances *fpl* aux sports d'hiver, vacances de neige; **to go on a skiing holiday** partir aux sports d'hiver ►**skiing instructor** moniteur *m*, -trice *f* de ski ►**skiing pants** fuseau *m* (de ski) ►**skiing resort** station *f* de ski *or* de neige, station de sports d'hiver ►**skiing trousers** = **skiing pants**.

skilful, (*US*) **skillful** ['skɪlfʊl] adj *person* habile, adroit (*at doing* à faire); *gesture, action* habile.

skilfully, (*US*) **skillfully** ['skɪlfəlɪ] adv habilement, adroitement.

skilfulness, (*US*) **skillfulness** ['skɪlfʊlnɪs] n (*NonC*) habileté *f*, adresse *f*.

skill [skɪl] n a (*NonC: competence, ability*) habileté *f*, adresse *f*; (*gen manual*) dextérité *f*; (*talent*) savoir-faire *m*, talent *m*. **the ~ of the dancers** l'adresse *or* l'habileté *or* le talent des danseurs; **the ~ of the juggler** l'adresse *or* la dextérité *or* le talent du jongleur; **his ~ at billiards** son habileté *or* son adresse au billard; **his ~ in negotiation** son savoir-faire *or* son talent *or* son habileté en matière de négociations; **his ~ in persuading them** l'habileté dont il a fait preuve en les persuadant; **lack of ~** maladresse *f*.
b (*in craft etc*) technique *f*. **~s** (*gen*) capacités *fpl*, compétences *fpl*; (*Scol : innate*) aptitudes *fpl* scolaires; (*Scol : learnt*) savoir *m*; **it's a ~ that has to be acquired** c'est une technique qui s'apprend; **we could make good use of his ~s** ses capacités *or* ses compétences nous seraient bien utiles; **what ~s do you have?** quelles sont vos compétences?; **learning a language is a question of learning new ~s** apprendre une langue consiste à acquérir de nouveaux automatismes.

skilled [skɪld] adj a *person* habile, adroit (*in, at doing* pour faire, *in or at sth* en qch); *movement, stroke* adroit. **he's a ~ driver** c'est un conducteur habile *or* adroit; **~ in diplomacy** expert en diplomatie, qui a beaucoup d'habileté *or* d'expérience en diplomatie; **~ in the art of negotiating** versé *or* maître (*f inv*) dans l'art de la négociation. b (*Ind*) *worker, engineer etc* qualifié; *work* de technicien, de spécialiste. **~ labour** main-d'œuvre qualifiée.

skillet ['skɪlɪt] n poêlon *m*.

skillful ['skɪlfʊl] adj (*US*) = **skilful**.

skillfully ['skɪlfəlɪ] adv (*US*) = **skilfully**.

skillfulness ['skɪlfʊlnɪs] n (*US*) = **skilfulness**.

skim [skɪm] 1 vt a *milk* écrémer; *soup* écumer. **to ~ the cream/scum/grease from sth** écrémer/écumer/dégraisser qch.
b [*bird etc*] **to ~ the ground/water** raser *or* effleurer *or* frôler le sol/la surface de l'eau; **to ~ a stone across the pond** faire ricocher une pierre sur l'étang.
c (*US * fig*) *one's income* ne pas déclarer en totalité au fisc.
2 vi: a **to ~ across the water/along the ground** raser l'eau/le sol; **the stone ~med across the pond** la pierre a ricoché d'un bout à l'autre de l'étang; (*fig*) **to ~ through a book** parcourir *or* feuilleter un livre; **he ~med over the difficult passages** il s'est contenté de parcourir rapidement les passages difficiles.
b (*US * fig: cheat on taxes*) frauder (le fisc).
3 comp ►**skim(med) milk** lait écrémé.

►**skim off** vt sep *cream, grease* enlever. (*fig*) **they skimmed off the brightest pupils** ils ont mis à part les élèves les plus brillants.

skimmer ['skɪməʳ] n (*Orn*) rhyncops *m*, bec-en-ciseaux *m*.

skimming ['skɪmɪŋ] n (*US *: tax fraud*) ≃ fraude *f* fiscale.

skimp [skɪmp] 1 vt *butter, cloth, paint etc* lésiner sur; *money* économiser; *praise, thanks* être chiche de; *piece of work* faire à la va-vite, bâcler*. 2 vi lésiner, économiser.

skimpily ['skɪmpɪlɪ] adv *serve, provide* avec parcimonie; *live* chichement.

skimpiness ['skɪmpɪnɪs] n [*meal, helping, allowance*] insuffisance *f*; [*dress etc*] ampleur insuffisante; [*person*] avarice *f*.

skimpy ['skɪmpɪ] adj *meal, allowance* insuffisant, maigre, chiche; *dress* étriqué, trop juste; *person* avare, radin*.

skin [skɪn] 1 n a [*person, animal*] peau *f*. **she has a good/bad ~** elle a une jolie/vilaine peau; **to wear wool next (to) the ~** porter de la laine sur la peau *or* à même la peau; **wet** *or* **soaked to the ~** trempé jusqu'aux os; **the snake casts** *or* **sheds its ~** le serpent mue; **rabbit ~** peau de lapin; (*fig*) **to be (all** *or* **only) ~ and bone** n'avoir que la peau sur les os; (*fig*) **with a whole ~** indemne, sain et sauf, sans une écorchure; (*fig*) **to escape by the ~ of one's teeth** l'échapper belle; (*fig*) **we caught the last train by the ~ of our teeth** nous avons attrapé le dernier train de justesse; (*fig*) **to have a thick ~** avoir une peau d'éléphant, être insensible; **to have a thin ~** être susceptible, avoir l'épiderme sensible; (*fig*) **to get under sb's ~*** porter *or* taper* sur les nerfs à qn; (*fig*) **I've got you under my ~*** je t'ai dans la peau‡, je suis amoureux fou (*f* amoureuse folle) de toi; (*fig*) **it's no ~ off my nose‡** (*does not hurt me*) pour ce que ça me coûte!; (*does not concern me*) ce n'est pas mon problème; *see* **pig, save¹** *etc*.
b (*fig*) [*fruit, vegetable, milk pudding, sausage, drum*] peau *f*; (*peeled*) pelure *f*; [*boat, aircraft*] revêtement *m*; (*for duplicating*) stencil *m*; (*for wine*) outre *f*. **to cook potatoes in their ~(s)** faire cuire des pommes de terre en robe des champs *or* en robe de chambre; **a banana ~** une peau de banane.
c (*Ski*) **~s** peaux *fpl* (de phoque), peluches *fpl*.
2 comp *colour, texture* de (la) peau ►**skin cancer** cancer *m* de la peau ►**skin-deep** superficiel (*see also* **beauty**); **it's only skin-deep** ça ne va pas (chercher) bien loin ►**skin disease** maladie *f* de (la) peau ►**skin diver** plongeur *m*, -euse *f* sous-marin(e) ►**skin diving** plongée sous-marine ►**skinflick‡** (*Cine*) film *m* porno* *inv* ►**skinflint** grippe-sou *m*, radin(e)* *m(f)* ►**skin game*** (*US*) escroquerie *f* ►**skin graft** greffe *f* de la peau ►**skin grafting** greffe *f or* greffage *m* de la peau ►**skinhead** (*Brit: thug*) skinhead *m*, jeune voyou *m* (aux cheveux tondus ras) ►**skin mag(azine)*** (*US*) revue *f* porno* ►**skin test** (*Med*) cuti(-réaction) *f* ►**skintight** collant, ajusté.
3 vt a *animal* dépouiller, écorcher; *fruit, vegetable* éplucher. (*fig*) **I'll ~ him alive!*** je vais l'écorcher tout vif!; **to ~ one's knee** s'érafler *or* s'écorcher le genou; (*fig*) **there are more ways than one** *or* **there is more than one way to ~ a cat** il y a plusieurs façons de plumer un canard; *see* **eye**.
b (*‡: steal from*) estamper*, plumer*.

skinful‡ ['skɪnfʊl] n: **to have (had) a ~** être bourré‡, être noir‡; **he's got a ~ of whisky** il s'est soûlé* *or* il a pris une biture‡ au whisky.

-skinned [skɪnd] adj ending in comps: **fair-skinned** à (la) peau claire; *see* **thick, thin** *etc*.

skinner ['skɪnəʳ] n peaussier *m*.

skinny ['skɪnɪ] 1 adj (*person*) maigrelet, maigrichon; (*sweater*) moulant. (*Fashion*) **the ~ look** la mode ultra-mince. 2 comp ►**skinny-dip*** (*US*) n baignade *f* à poil* ◊ vi se baigner à poil* ►**skinny-rib (sweater** *or* **jumper)*** pull-chaussette *m*.

skint‡ [skɪnt] adj (*Brit*) fauché*, sans le rond*.

skip¹ [skɪp] 1 n petit bond, petit saut. **to give a ~** faire un petit bond *or* saut.
2 comp ►**skip rope** (*US*) corde *f* à sauter.
3 vi a gambader, sautiller; (*with rope*) sauter à la corde. **to ~ with joy** sauter *or* bondir de joie; **the child ~ped in/out** *etc* l'enfant est entré/sorti *etc* en gambadant *or* en sautillant; **she ~ped lightly over the stones** elle sautait légèrement par-dessus les pierres; **he ~ped out of the way of the cycle** il a bondi pour éviter le vélo, il a évité le vélo d'un bond; (*fig*) **he ~ped over that point** il est passé sur ce point, il a sauté par-dessus *or* a glissé sur ce point; **to ~ from one subject to another** sauter d'un sujet à un autre; **the author** *or* **book ~s about a lot** l'auteur papillonne beaucoup dans ce livre.
b (*fig*) **I ~ped up to London yesterday** j'ai fait un saut à Londres hier; **he ~ped off without paying** il a décampé *or* filé* sans payer; **I ~ped round to see her** j'ai fait un saut chez elle, je suis passé la voir

en vitesse; **he ~ped across to Spain** il a fait un saut *or* une virée* en Espagne.

4 **vt** (*omit*) *chapter, page, paragraph* sauter, passer; *class, meal* sauter. **I'll ~ lunch** je vais sauter le déjeuner, je ne vais pas déjeuner, je vais me passer de déjeuner; **~ it!*** laisse tomber!*; **~ the details!** laisse tomber les détails!*, épargne-nous les détails!; **to ~ school** sécher les cours.

skip[2] [skɪp] **n** (*container*) benne *f*.

skipper [ˈskɪpəʳ] 1 **n** (*Naut*) capitaine *m*, patron *m*; (*Sport* *) capitaine, chef *m* d'équipe; (*in race*) skipper *m*. 2 **vt** (*) *boat* commander; *team* être le chef de, mener.

skipping [ˈskɪpɪŋ] **n** saut *m* à la corde. (*Brit*) **~ rope** corde *f* à sauter.

skirl [skɜːl] **n** son aigu (*de la cornemuse*).

skirmish [ˈskɜːmɪʃ] 1 **n** (*Mil*) échauffourée *f*, escarmouche *f*, accrochage *m*; (*fig*) escarmouche, accrochage*. 2 **vi** (*Mil*) s'engager dans une escarmouche. (*fig*) **to ~ with sb** avoir un accrochage* avec qn.

skirt [skɜːt] 1 **n** a (*garment*) jupe *f*; *[frock coat]* basque *f*. (*fig: girl*) **a bit of ~‡** une nana‡. b (*Tech: on machine, vehicle*) jupe *f*. c (*Culin: steak*) flanchet *m*. 2 **comp ▸skirt length** hauteur *f* de jupe. 3 **vt** (*also* **~ round**) (*go round*) contourner, longer; (*miss, avoid*) *town, obstacle* contourner, éviter; *problem, difficulty* esquiver, éluder. **the road ~s (round) the forest** la route longe *or* contourne la forêt; **we ~ed (round) Paris to the north** nous sommes passés au nord de Paris, nous avons contourné Paris par le nord; **to ~ (round) the issue (of whether ...)** esquiver *or* éluder *or* se défiler* sur la question (de savoir si ...). 4 **vi: to ~ round** *see* **3**.

skirting [ˈskɜːtɪŋ] **n** (*Brit: also* **~ board**) plinthe *f*.

skit [skɪt] **n** parodie *f* (*on* de); (*Theat*) sketch *m* satirique.

skitter [ˈskɪtəʳ] **vi: to ~ across the water/along the ground** *[bird]* voler en frôlant l'eau/le sol; *[stone]* ricocher sur l'eau/le sol.

skittish [ˈskɪtɪʃ] **adj** (*playful*) espiègle; (*coquettish*) coquet, frivole; *horse* ombrageux.

skittishly [ˈskɪtɪʃlɪ] **adv** (*see* **skittish**) avec espièglerie; en faisant la coquette; d'une manière ombrageuse.

skittle [ˈskɪtl] 1 **n** quille *f*. (*esp Brit*) **~s** (jeu *m* de) quilles; *see* **beer**. 2 **comp ▸skittle alley** piste *f* de jeu *m* de quilles, bowling *m*.

skive* [skaɪv] (*Brit*) 1 **vi** tirer au flanc*. 2 **n: to be on the ~** tirer au flanc*.

▸skive off* **vi** (*Brit*) se défiler*.

skiver* [ˈskaɪvəʳ] **n** (*Brit*) tire-au-flanc* *m inv*.

skivvy* [ˈskɪvɪ] 1 **n** a (*Brit pej: servant*) boniche *f* (*pej*), bonne *f* à tout faire. b (*US: underwear*) **skivvies*** sous-vêtements *mpl* (d'homme). 2 **vi** (*Brit*) faire la boniche.

skua [ˈskjuːə] **n** stercoraire *m*, labbe *m*.

skulduggery* [skʌlˈdʌgərɪ] **n** (*NonC*) maquignonnage *m*, trafic *m*. **a piece of ~** un maquignonnage.

skulk [skʌlk] **vi** (*also* **~ about**) rôder en se cachant, rôder furtivement. **to ~ in/away** *etc* entrer/s'éloigner *etc* furtivement.

skull [skʌl] 1 **n** crâne *m*. **~ and crossbones** (*emblem*) tête *f* de mort; (*flag*) pavillon *m* à tête de mort; **I can't get it into his (thick) ~* that ...** pas moyen de lui faire comprendre que ..., je n'arrive pas à lui faire entrer dans le crâne* que ... . 2 **comp ▸skullcap** calotte *f*.

skunk [skʌŋk] **n, pl ~** *or* **~s** (*animal*) mouffette *f*; (*fur*) sconse *m*; (* *pej: person*) mufle* *m*, canaille *f*, salaud‡ *m*.

sky [skaɪ] 1 **n** ciel *m*. **the skies** le(s) ciel(s); (*fig*) les cieux; **there was a clear blue ~** le ciel était clair et bleu; **in the ~** dans le ciel; **under the open ~** à la belle étoile; **under a blue ~, under blue skies** sous des ciels bleus, sous un ciel bleu; **the skies over** *or* **of England** les ciels d'Angleterre; **the skies of Van Gogh** les ciels de Van Gogh; **under warmer skies** sous des cieux plus cléments; **to praise sb to the skies** porter qn aux nues; (*fig*) **it came out of a clear (blue) ~** c'est arrivé de façon tout à fait inattendue, on ne s'y attendait vraiment pas; (*fig*) **the ~'s the limit*** tout est possible.

2 **comp ▸sky ad** publicité *f or* annonce *f* aérienne **▸sky blue n** bleu ciel **▸sky-blue adj** bleu ciel *inv* **▸skydive n** saut *m* (en parachute) en chute libre ◊ **vi** faire du parachutisme en chute libre **▸skydiver** parachutiste *mf* (faisant de la chute libre) **▸skydiving** parachutisme *m* (en chute libre) **▸sky-high** très haut (dans le ciel); (*fig*) extrêmement haut; **he hit the ball sky-high** il a envoyé le ballon très haut (dans le ciel); **the bridge was blown sky-high** le pont a sauté, le pont a volé en morceaux; **to blow a theory sky-high** démolir une théorie; **prices are sky-high** les prix sont exorbitants; **the crisis sent sugar prices sky-high** la crise a fait monter en flèche le prix du sucre **▸skyjack*** détourner, pirater (*un avion*) **▸skyjacker*** pirate *m* de l'air **▸skyjacking*** détournement *m* d'avion, piraterie *f* aérienne **▸Skylab** (*Space*) laboratoire *m* spatial, Skylab *m* **▸skylark n** (*bird*) alouette *f* (des champs) ◊ **vi** (*) chahuter, faire le fou (*f* la folle) **▸skylarking*** rigolade* *f*, chahut *m* **▸skylight** lucarne *f* **▸skyline** ligne *f* d'horizon; *[city]* ligne des toits; *[buildings]* profil *m*, silhouette *f* **▸sky pilot‡** (*fig*: †) aumônier *m*, curé *m* **▸skyrocket n** fusée volante *or* à baguette ◊ **vi** *[prices]* monter en flèche **▸skyscraper** gratte-ciel *m inv* **▸sky train** (*Aviat*) train *m* du ciel **▸skyway** (*Aviat**) route *or* voie aérienne; (*US Aut*) route surélevée **▸skywriting** publicité tracée (dans le ciel) par un avion.

3 **vt** *ball* envoyer très haut *or* en chandelle.

Skye [skaɪ] **n** (l'île *f* de) Skye *f*.

skyward [ˈskaɪwəd] **adj, adv** vers le ciel.

skywards [ˈskaɪwədz] **adv** vers le ciel.

slab [slæb] 1 **n** a (*large piece*) *[stone, wood, slate]* bloc *m*; (*flat*) plaque *f*; *[meat]* pièce *f*; (*smaller*) carré *m*, pavé *m*; *[cake]* pavé; (*smaller*) grosse tranche; *[chocolate]* plaque; (*smaller*) tablette *f*. b (*paving ~*) dalle *f*; (*table, surface*) (*in butcher's etc*) étal *m*; (*in mortuary*) table *f* de dissection *or* d'autopsie. 2 **comp ▸slab cake** grand cake rectangulaire.

slack [slæk] 1 **adj** a (*loose*) *rope* lâche, mal tendu; *joint, knot* desserré; *hold, grip* faible. **to be ~** *[screw etc]* avoir du jeu; *[rope etc]* avoir du mou; (*of rope etc*) **keep it ~!** laissez du mou!; (*fig*) **~ water** eau(x) morte(s) *or* dormante(s); (*between tides*) mer *f* étale, étale *m*.

b (*inactive*) *demand* faible; *market, trade* faible, stagnant. **during ~ periods** (*weeks, months etc*) pendant les jours *or* mois creux, pendant les périodes creuses; (*in the day*) aux heures creuses; **the ~ season** la morte-saison; **business is ~ this week** les affaires marchent au ralenti *or* ne vont pas fort* cette semaine.

c *person* (*lacking energy*) mou (*f* molle), indolent; (*lax*) négligent; *student* inappliqué, peu sérieux; *worker* peu sérieux, peu consciencieux. **to be ~ about one's work** négliger son travail, se relâcher dans son travail; **he has grown very ~** (*in general*) il se laisse aller; (*in work etc*) il fait preuve de mollesse dans *or* il n'est plus consciencieux dans son travail; **this pupil is very ~** cet élève est très peu sérieux *or* ne travaille pas assez *or* ne s'applique pas assez; **he is ~ in answering letters** il met longtemps à répondre aux lettres qu'il reçoit.

2 **n** a (*in rope: gen, also Climbing*) mou *m*; (*in cable*) ballant *m*; (*in joint etc*) jeu *m*. **to take up the ~ in a rope** raidir un cordage; (*fig*) **to take up the ~ in the economy** relancer les secteurs affaiblis de l'économie.

b (*Dress: pl*) **~s** pantalon *m*.

c (*coal*) poussier *m*.

3 **vi** (*) ne pas travailler comme il le faudrait.

▸slack off 1 **vi** a (*: *stop working/trying etc*) se relâcher (dans son travail/dans ses efforts *etc*). b *[business, trade, demand]* ralentir. 2 **vt sep** *rope, cable* détendre, donner du mou à.

▸slack up* **vi** ralentir (ses efforts *or* son travail).

slacken [ˈslækn] 1 **vt** (*also* **~ off**) *rope* relâcher, donner du mou à; *cable* donner du ballant à; *reins* relâcher; *screw* desserrer; *pressure etc* diminuer, réduire. **to ~ one's pace** ralentir l'allure; (*Aut*) **to ~ speed** diminuer de vitesse, ralentir. 2 **vi** (*also* **~ off**) *[rope]* se relâcher, prendre du mou; *[cable]* prendre du ballant; *[screw]* se desserrer; *[gale]* diminuer de force; *[speed]* diminuer; *[activity, business, trade]* ralentir, diminuer; *[effort, enthusiasm, pressure]* diminuer, se relâcher.

▸slacken off 1 **vi** a = **slacken 2**. b *[person]* se relâcher, se laisser aller. 2 **vt sep** = **slacken 1**.

▸slacken up vi = **slacken off 1b**.

slackening [ˈslæknɪŋ] **n** (*also* **~ off**; *see* **slacken**) ralentissement *m*; relâchement *m*; desserrement *m*; diminution *f*.

slacker* [ˈslækəʳ] **n** flemmard(e)* *m(f)*, fainéant(e) *m(f)*.

slackly [ˈslæklɪ] **adv** *hang* lâchement, mollement; (*fig*) *work* négligemment.

slackness [ˈslæknɪs] **n** *[rope etc]* manque *m* de tension; (*) *[person]* négligence *f*, laisser-aller *m*. **the ~ of trade** le ralentissement *or* la stagnation *or* (*stronger*) le marasme des affaires.

slag [slæg] 1 **n** a (*Metal*) scories *fpl*, crasses *fpl*. b (*Min*) stériles *mpl*. c (‡: *slut*) salope *f*‡. 2 **comp ▸slag heap** (*Metal*) crassier *m*; (*Min*) terril *m*.

▸slag off‡ **vt sep** (*US*) **to slag sb off‡** (*scold; insult*) engueuler‡ qn; (*speak badly of*) débiner* qn.

slain [sleɪn] (*liter*) 1 **ptp of slay**. 2 **npl** (*Mil*) **the ~** les morts, les soldats tombés au champ d'honneur.

slake [sleɪk] **vt** *lime* éteindre; *one's thirst* étancher; (*fig*) *desire for revenge etc* assouvir, satisfaire.

slalom [ˈslɑːləm] 1 **n** slalom *m*. 2 **vi** slalomer. 3 **comp ▸slalom descent** descente *f* en slalom **▸slalom racer, slalom specialist** slalomeur *m*, -euse *f*.

slam [slæm] 1 **n** a *[door]* claquement *m*. b (*Bridge*) chelem *m*. **to make a grand/little ~** faire un grand/petit chelem. 2 **vt** a *door* (faire) claquer, fermer violemment; *lid* (faire) claquer, rabattre violemment. **to ~ the door shut** claquer la porte; **she ~med the books on the table** elle a jeté brutalement *or* a flanqué* les livres sur la table; **he ~med the ball into the grandstand** d'un coup violent il a envoyé le ballon dans la tribune; (*fig*) **our team ~med yours*** notre équipe a écrasé la vôtre. b (‡) *play, singer* critiquer, éreinter*, démolir*. 3 **vi** *[door, lid]* claquer. **the door ~med shut** la porte s'est refermée en claquant.

▸slam down **vt sep** (*gen*) poser d'un geste violent, jeter brutalement, flanquer*; *lid* rabattre brutalement.

▸slam on **vt sep: to slam on the brakes** freiner à mort; (*fig: stop*) **to slam the brakes on sth*** mettre le hola à qch.

▸slam to 1 **vi** se refermer en claquant. 2 **vt sep** refermer en claquant.

slammer [ˈslæməʳ] **n** (*Prison sl*) **the ~** la taule (*sl*), la prison.

slander [ˈslɑːndəʳ] 1 **n** calomnie *f*; (*Jur*) diffamation *f*. **it's a ~ to**

suggest that ... c'est de la calomnie que de suggérer que ... . 2 vt calomnier, dire du mal de; (*Jur*) diffamer.

slanderer ['slɑ:ndərə^r] n calomniateur *m*, -trice *f*; (*Jur*) diffamateur *m*, -trice *f*.

slanderous ['slɑ:ndərəs] adj calomnieux, calomniateur (*f* -trice); (*Jur*) diffamatoire.

slanderously ['slɑ:ndərəslɪ] adv calomnieusement; (*Jur*) de façon diffamatoire.

slang [slæŋ] 1 n (*NonC*) argot *m*. **in ~** en argot; **in army/school ~** en argot militaire/d'écolier, dans l'argot des armées/des écoles; **that word is ~** c'est un mot d'argot *or* argotique, c'est un argotisme; **to talk ~** parler argot; **he uses a lot of ~** il emploie beaucoup d'argot, il s'exprime dans une langue très verte; *see* **rhyme**. 2 adj *phrase, word* d'argot, argotique. **a ~ expression** un argotisme. 3 vt (*) traiter de tous les noms. 4 comp ►**slanging match*** (*Brit*) prise *f* de bec*.

slangily* ['slæŋɪlɪ] adv: **to talk ~** parler argot, employer beaucoup d'argot.

slangy* ['slæŋɪ] adj *person* qui parle argot, qui emploie beaucoup d'argot; *style, language* argotique.

slant [slɑ:nt] 1 n a inclinaison *f*, aspect penché; (*fig: point of view*) point *m* de vue (*on* sur), angle *m*, perspective *f*. **what's his ~ on it?** quel est son point de vue sur la question?; (*fig*) **his mind has a curious ~** il a une curieuse tournure *or* forme d'esprit; **to give/get a new ~* on sth** présenter/voir qch sous un angle *or* jour nouveau.

b (*Type: also* **~ mark**) (barre *f*) oblique *f*.

2 comp ►**slant-eyed** aux yeux bridés ►**slantwise** obliquement, de biais.

3 vi *[line, handwriting]* pencher, être incliné, ne pas être droit; *[light, sunbeam]* passer obliquement.

4 vt *line, handwriting* faire pencher, incliner; (*fig*) *account, news* présenter avec parti pris. **~ed eyes** yeux *mpl* bridés; **a ~ed report** un rapport orienté *or* tendancieux.

slanting ['slɑ:ntɪŋ] adj *roof, surface* en pente, incliné; *handwriting* penché, couché; *line* penché, oblique. **~ eyes** yeux *mpl* bridés; **~ rain** pluie *f* (qui tombe en) oblique.

slanty* ['slɑ:ntɪ] adj: **~-eyed** = **slant-eyed** (*see* **slant 2**); **~ eyes** yeux *mpl* bridés.

slap [slæp] 1 n claque *f*; (*on face*) gifle *f*; (*on back*) grande tape, (*stronger*) grande claque. **a ~ on the bottom** une fessée; (*lit, fig*) **a ~ in the face** une gifle; **a ~ on the back** une grande tape *or* claque dans le dos; (*fig*) **to give s.o./to get a ~ on the wrist** taper qn/se faire taper sur les doigts.

2 comp ►**slap and tickle**‡: (*Brit*) **they were having a bit of the old slap and tickle** ils étaient en train de se peloter* ►**slap-bang***: **slap-bang into the wall** en plein *or* tout droit dans le mur; **he ran slap-bang(-wallop) into his mother** il s'est cogné en plein contre sa mère; (*fig: met*) il est tombé tout d'un coup sur sa mère, il s'est retrouvé tout d'un coup nez à nez avec sa mère ►**slapdash** adj *person* insouciant, négligent; *work* bâclé*, fait à la va-vite *or* sans soin *or* n'importe comment ◊ adv à la va-vite, sans soin, n'importe comment ►**slap-happy*** (*carelessly cheerful*) insouciant, décontracté*, relaxe*; (*US: punch-drunk*) groggy, abruti de coups ►**slapstick (comedy)** grosse farce, comédie *or* farce bouffonne ►**slap-up meal*** (*Brit*) repas *m* fameux *or* extra*.

3 adv (*) en plein, tout droit. **he ran ~ into the wall** il est rentré en plein dans *or* tout droit dans le mur; **~ in the middle** en plein *or* au beau milieu.

4 vt a (*hit*) *person* donner une tape *or* (*stronger*) claque à. **to ~ sb on the back** donner une tape *or* une claque dans le dos à qn; **to ~ a child's bottom** donner une fessée à un enfant; **to ~ sb's face** *or* **sb in the face** gifler qn; (*in amusement etc*) **to ~ one's knees** se taper sur les cuisses.

b (*put*) mettre brusquement, flanquer*; (*apply*) appliquer *or* mettre à la va-vite *or* sans soin. **he ~ped the book on the table** il a flanqué* le livre sur la table; **he ~ped a coat of paint on the wall** il a flanqué* un coup de peinture *or* il a donné un coup de pinceau au mur; **he ~ped £5 on to the price*** il a collé* 5 livres de plus sur le prix, il a gonflé son prix de 5 livres; **she ~ped some foundation on her face*** elle s'est collé du fond de teint n'importe comment *or* à la va-vite.

►**slap around** vt sep donner des tapes *or* (*stronger*) des claques à. **he slaps his wife around** il bat sa femme.

►**slap down** vt sep *object* poser brusquement *or* violemment. (*fig*) **to slap sb down*** rembarrer* qn, envoyer qn sur les roses*.

►**slap on** vt sep *paint etc* appliquer à la va-vite *or* n'importe comment; (*fig*) *tax* flanquer*, imposer brusquement. **to slap on make-up** se maquiller n'importe comment *or* à la va-vite.

slash [slæʃ] 1 n a (*cut: gen*) entaille *f*, taillade *f*; (*on face*) entaille, balafre *f*; (*Sewing: in sleeve*) crevé *m*.

b (*Typ: also* **~ mark**) (barre *f*) oblique *f*.

c (**‡**: *urinate*) **to go for a ~** aller pisser une jatte**‡** *or* un coup‡.

2 vt a (*with knife, sickle etc*) entailler, (*several cuts*) taillader; *rope* couper net, trancher; *face* balafrer; (*with whip, stick*) cingler; (*Sewing*) *sleeve* faire des crevés dans. **to ~ sb** taillader qn; **his attacker ~ed his face/his jacket** son assaillant lui a balafré le visage/a tailladé sa veste; **~ed sleeves** manches *fpl* à crevés.

b (*fig*) *prices* casser*, écraser*; *costs, expenses* réduire radicalement; *speech, text* couper *or* raccourcir radicalement. **"prices ~ed"** "prix cassés", "prix sacrifiés".

c (*: *condemn*) *book, play* éreinter*, démolir*.

3 vi: **he ~ed at me with his stick** il m'a flanqué* un *or* des coup(s) de bâton; **he ~ed at the grass with his stick** il cinglait l'herbe de sa canne.

slashing ['slæʃɪŋ] adj (*fig*) *criticism, attack* cinglant, mordant.

slat [slæt] n *[blind]* lamelle *f*; *[bed-frame]* latte *f*; *[room divider etc]* lame *f*.

slate [sleɪt] 1 n (*substance, object: Constr, Scol etc*) ardoise *f*; (*fig: Pol*) liste *f* provisoire de candidats. (*Pol*) **they've got a full ~ there** ils ont des candidats dans toutes les circonscriptions; (*Brit Comm*) **put it on the ~*** mettez-le sur mon compte, ajoutez ça sur mon ardoise*; (*fig*) **to start with a clean ~** repartir sur une bonne base; *see* **wipe**.

2 comp *deposits* d'ardoise, ardoisier; *industry* ardoisier, de l'ardoise; *roof* en ardoise, d'ardoise ►**slate-blue** adj, n bleu ardoise *(m) inv* ►**slate-coloured** ardoise *inv* ►**slate-grey** adj, n gris ardoise *(m) inv* ►**slate quarry** ardoisière *f*, carrière *f* d'ardoise.

3 vt a *roof* ardoiser.

b (*US Pol*) *candidate* proposer.

c (*Brit* *) *book, play, actor, politician* éreinter*, démolir*; (*scold*) attraper*, engueuler‡.

d (*: *destined*) **to be ~d* for sth** être désigné pour qch.

slater ['sleɪtə^r] n a (*in quarry*) ardoisier *m*; *[roof]* couvreur(-ardoisier) *m*. b (*woodlouse*) cloporte *m*.

slatted ['slætɪd] adj (*see* **slat**) fait de lamelles *or* lattes *or* lames.

slattern ['slætən] n souillon *f*.

slatternly ['slætənlɪ] adj *woman, appearance* peu soigné, négligé; *behaviour, habits* de souillon.

slaty ['sleɪtɪ] adj (*in texture*) ardoisier, semblable à l'ardoise; (*in colour*) (couleur) ardoise *inv*.

slaughter ['slɔ:tə^r] 1 n *[animals]* abattage *m*; *[people]* carnage *m*, massacre *m*, tuerie *f*. **the ~ on the roads** les hécatombes *fpl* sur la route; **there was great ~** cela a été un carnage *or* un massacre *or* une tuerie. 2 comp ►**slaughterhouse** abattoir *m*. 3 vt *animal* abattre; *person* tuer sauvagement; *people* massacrer. **our team really ~ed them*** notre équipe les a écrasés *or* massacrés*.

slaughterer ['slɔ:tərə^r] n *[animals]* tueur *m*, assommeur *m*; *[person]* meurtrier *m*; *[people]* massacreur *m*.

Slav [slɑ:v] 1 adj slave. 2 n Slave *mf*.

slave [sleɪv] 1 n (*lit, fig*) esclave *mf*. (*fig*) **to be a ~ to** être (l')esclave de; *see* **white**. 2 comp ►**slave driver** (*lit*) surveillant *m* d'esclaves; (*fig*) négrier *m*, -ière *f* ►**slave labour** (*exploitation*) exploitation *f* des esclaves; (*work*) travail fait par les esclaves; (* *fig*) travail de forçat *or* de galérien; **slave labour camp** camp *m* de travaux forcés ►**slave ship** (vaisseau *m*) négrier *m* ►**slave trade** commerce *m* des esclaves, traite *f* des noirs ►**slave trader** marchand *m* d'esclaves, négrier *m* ►**slave traffic** trafic *m* d'esclaves. 3 vi (*also* **~ away**) travailler comme un nègre, trimer. **to ~ (away) at sth/at doing** s'escrimer sur qch/à faire.

slaver[1] ['sleɪvə^r] n (*person*) marchand *m* d'esclaves, négrier *m*; (*ship*) (vaisseau *m*) négrier.

slaver[2] ['slævə^r] (*dribble*) 1 n bave *f*, salive *f*. 2 vi baver.

slavery ['sleɪvərɪ] n (*lit, fig*) esclavage *m*. **housework is nothing but ~** le ménage est un véritable esclavage *or* une perpétuelle corvée; *see* **sell**.

slavey* ['sleɪvɪ] n boniche* *f*.

Slavic ['slɑ:vɪk] adj, n slave *(m)*.

slavish ['sleɪvɪʃ] adj *subjection* d'esclave; *imitation, devotion* servile.

slavishly ['sleɪvɪʃlɪ] adv servilement.

Slavonic [slə'vɒnɪk] adj, n slave *(m)*.

slavophile ['slævəʊ,faɪl] n, adj slavophile *(mf)*.

slay [sleɪ] pret **slew**, ptp **slain** vt (*liter*) tuer. (*fig*) **he ~s me!**‡ il me fait mourir *or* crever de rire!; *see also* **slain**.

slayer ['sleɪə^r] n (*liter*) tueur *m*, -euse *f*.

SLD [esel'di:] n (*Brit*) (abbr of **Social and Liberal Democrats**) *see* **social**.

sleaze* [sli:z] n sordidité *f*. **that film is pure ~** ce film est complètement sordide.

sleaziness* ['sli:zɪnɪs] n (*see* **sleazy**) sordidité *f*, aspect *m* miteux* *or* sordide.

sleazy* ['sli:zɪ] adj *place, person* miteux*, sordide; *atmosphere* sordide.

sled [sled] n = **sledge 1**.

sledding ['sledɪŋ] n (*US*) **hard** *or* **tough ~*** période *f* (*or* tâche *f*) difficile.

sledge [sledʒ] 1 n traîneau *m*; (*child's*) luge *f*. 2 vi: **to go sledging** faire de la luge, se promener en traîneau; **to ~ down/across** *etc* descendre/traverser *etc* en luge *or* en traîneau.

sledgehammer ['sledʒ,hæmə^r] n marteau *m* de forgeron. (*fig*) **to strike sb/sth a ~ blow** assener un coup violent *or* magistral à qn/qch.

sleek [sli:k] adj *hair, fur* lisse et brillant, luisant; *cat* au poil soyeux *or* brillant; *person* (*in appearance*) (trop) soigné, bichonné; (*in manner*) onctueux; *manners* onctueux, doucereux; *car, plane* aérodynamique;

boat aux lignes pures.
▶**sleek down** vt sep: **to sleek one's hair down** se lisser les cheveux.
sleekly ['sli:klı] adv *smile, reply* doucereusement, avec onction.
sleekness ['sli:knıs] n *[hair etc]* brillant *m*, luisant *m*; *[person]* allure (trop) soignée, air bichonné; *[manner]* onctuosité *f*; *[car, plane]* ligne *f* aérodynamique; *[boat]* finesse *f or* pureté *f* (de lignes).
sleep [sli:p] (vb: pret, ptp **slept**) 1 n a sommeil *m*. **to be in a deep** *or* **sound** ~ dormir profondément; **to be in a very heavy** ~ dormir d'un sommeil de plomb; **to talk in one's** ~ parler en dormant *or* dans son sommeil; **to walk in one's** ~ marcher en dormant; **to sleep the** ~ **of the just** dormir du sommeil du juste; **overcome by** ~ ayant succombé au sommeil; **to have a** ~, **to get some** ~ dormir; (*for a short while*) faire un somme; **to get** *or* **go to** ~ s'endormir; **my leg has gone to** ~ j'ai la jambe engourdie; **I didn't get a wink of** ~ *or* **any** ~ **all night** je n'ai pas fermé l'œil de la nuit; **she sang the child to** ~ elle a chanté jusqu'à ce que l'enfant s'endorme; **to put** *or* **send sb to** ~ endormir qn; (*euph : put down*) **to put a cat to** ~ faire piquer un chat; **I need 8 hours'** ~ **a night** il me faut (mes) 8 heures de sommeil chaque nuit; **a 3-hour** ~ 3 heures de sommeil; **I haven't had enough** ~ **lately** je manque de sommeil ces temps-ci; **I had a good** ~ **last night** j'ai bien dormi la nuit dernière; **to have a good night's** ~ passer une bonne nuit; **a** ~ **will do you good** cela vous fera du bien de dormir; **let him have his** ~ **out** laisse-le dormir tant qu'il voudra; *see* **beauty, lose** *etc*.
b (**: matter in eyes*) chassie *f*.
2 comp ▶**sleep-learning** hypnopédie *f* ▶**sleepwalk** marcher en dormant; **he sleepwalks** il est somnambule ▶**sleepwalker** somnambule *mf* ▶**sleepwalking** (*NonC*) somnambulisme *m* ▶**sleepwear** (*NonC: Comm etc*) vêtements *mpl or* lingerie *f* de nuit.
3 vi a dormir. **to** ~ **tight** *or* **like a log** *or* **like a top** dormir à poings fermés *or* comme une souche *or* comme un loir; ~ **tight!** dors bien!; **to** ~ **heavily** dormir d'un sommeil de plomb; **he was** ~**ing deeply** *or* **soundly** il dormait profondément, il était profondément endormi; **to** ~ **soundly** (*without fear*) dormir sur ses deux oreilles; **to** ~ **lightly** (*regularly*) avoir le sommeil léger; (*on one occasion*) dormir d'un sommeil léger; **I didn't** ~ **a wink all night** je n'ai pas fermé l'œil de la nuit; **to** ~ **the clock round** faire le tour du cadran; (*fig*) **he was** ~**ing on his feet** il dormait debout.
b (*spend night*) coucher. **he slept in the car** il a passé la nuit *or* dormi dans la voiture; **he slept at his aunt's** il a couché chez sa tante; **he** ~**s on a hard mattress** il couche *or* dort sur un matelas dur; (*euph*) **to** ~ **with sb** coucher* avec qn.
4 vt: **the house** ~**s 8 (people)** on peut loger *or* coucher 8 personnes dans cette maison; **this room will** ~ **4 (people)** on peut coucher 4 personnes *or* coucher à 4 dans cette chambre; **the hotel** ~**s 500** l'hôtel peut loger *or* contenir 500 personnes; **can you** ~ **us all?** pouvez-vous nous coucher tous?
▶**sleep around*** vi coucher* avec n'importe qui, coucher* à droite et à gauche.
▶**sleep away** vt sep: **to sleep the morning away** passer la matinée à dormir, ne pas se réveiller de la matinée.
▶**sleep in** vi a (*lie late*) faire la grasse matinée, dormir tard; (*oversleep*) ne pas se réveiller à temps, dormir trop tard. b *[nurse, servant etc]* être logé sur place.
▶**sleep off** vt sep: **to sleep sth off** dormir pour faire passer qch, se remettre de qch en dormant; **go to bed and sleep it off** va te coucher et cela te passera en dormant; **to sleep off a hangover, to sleep it off*** dormir pour faire passer sa gueule de bois‡, cuver son vin*.
▶**sleep on** 1 vi: **he slept on till 10** il a dormi jusqu'à 10 heures, il ne s'est pas réveillé avant 10 heures; **let him sleep on for another hour** laisse-le dormir encore une heure. 2 vt fus: **to sleep on a problem/a letter/a decision** attendre le lendemain pour résoudre un problème/répondre à une lettre/prendre une décision; **let's sleep on it** nous verrons demain, la nuit porte conseil; **I'll have to sleep on it** il faut que j'attende demain pour décider.
▶**sleep out** vi a (*in open air*) coucher à la belle étoile; (*in tent*) coucher sous la tente. b *[nurse, servant etc]* ne pas être logé (sur place).
▶**sleep through** 1 vi: **I slept through till the afternoon** j'ai dormi comme une souche *or* sans me réveiller jusqu'à l'après-midi. 2 vt fus: **he slept through the storm** l'orage ne l'a pas réveillé; **he slept through the alarm clock** il n'a pas entendu son réveil (sonner).
▶**sleep together** vi (*euph*) coucher ensemble.
sleeper ['sli:pə^r] n a (*person*) dormeur *m*, -euse *f*; (*fig: spy*) espion(ne) *m(f)* en sommeil. **to be a light/heavy** ~ avoir le sommeil léger/lourd; **that child is a good** ~ cet enfant dort très bien *or* fait sa nuit sans se réveiller. b (*Brit Rail*) (*on track*) traverse *f*; (*berth*) couchette *f*; (*rail car*) voiture-lit *f*; (*train*) train-couchettes *m*. **I took a** ~ **to Marseilles** j'ai pris une couchette pour aller à Marseille, je suis allé à Marseille en couchette. c (*esp Brit: earring*) clou *m* (*boucle d'oreille*). d (*US fig: sudden success*) révélation *f*.
sleepily ['sli:pılı] adv d'un air *or* ton endormi.
sleepiness ['sli:pınıs] n *[person]* envie *f* de dormir, torpeur *f*; *[town]* somnolence *f*, torpeur.
sleeping ['sli:pıŋ] 1 adj *person* qui dort, endormi. (*Prov*) **let** ~ **dogs lie** il ne faut pas réveiller le chat qui dort (*Prov*); **the S**~ **Beauty** la Belle au bois dormant.
2 comp ▶**sleeping bag** sac *m* de couchage ▶**sleeping berth** couchette *f* ▶**sleeping car** (*Rail*) wagon-couchettes *m*, voiture-lit *f* ▶**sleeping draught** soporifique *m* ▶**sleeping partner** (*Brit Comm*) (associé *m*) commanditaire *m* ▶**sleeping pill** somnifère *m* ▶**sleeping policeman** (*in road*) casse-vitesse *m* ▶**sleeping porch** (*US*) chambre-véranda *f* ▶**sleeping quarters** chambres *fpl* (à coucher); (*in barracks*) chambrées *fpl*; (*dormitory*) dortoir *m* ▶**sleeping sickness** maladie *f* du sommeil ▶**sleeping suit** grenouillère *f* ▶**sleeping tablet** = **sleeping pill**.
sleepless ['sli:plıs] adj *person* qui ne dort pas, éveillé; (*fig: alert*) infatigable, inlassable. **to have a** ~ **night** ne pas dormir de la nuit, passer une nuit blanche; **he spent many** ~ **hours worrying about it** il a passé bien des heures sans sommeil à se faire du souci à ce sujet.
sleeplessly ['sli:plıslı] adv sans dormir.
sleeplessness ['sli:plısnıs] n insomnie *f*.
sleepy ['sli:pı] 1 adj *person* qui a envie de dormir, somnolent; (*not alert*) endormi; *voice, look, village* endormi, somnolent. **to be** *or* **feel** ~ avoir sommeil, avoir envie de dormir. 2 comp ▶**sleepyhead*** n endormi(e) *m(f)* ▶**sleepyheaded*** adj (à moitié) endormi.
sleet [sli:t] 1 n neige fondue. 2 vi: **it is** ~**ing** il tombe de la neige fondue.
sleeve [sli:v] 1 n *[garment]* manche *f*; *[record]* pochette *f*; *[cylinder etc]* chemise *f*. (*fig*) **he's always got something up his** ~ il a plus d'un tour dans son sac; **he's bound to have something up his** ~ il a certainement quelque chose en réserve, il garde certainement un atout caché; **I don't know what he's got up his** ~ je ne sais pas ce qu'il nous réserve (comme surprise); **I've got an idea up my** ~ j'ai une petite idée en réserve *or* dans la tête; *see* **heart, laugh, shirt** *etc*. 2 comp ▶**sleeveboard** jeannette *f* ▶**sleevenote** (*Brit: on record sleeve*) texte *m* (*sur pochette de disque*).
-sleeved [sli:vd] adj ending in comps: **long-sleeved** à manches longues.
sleeveless ['sli:vlıs] adj sans manches.
sleigh [sleı] 1 n traîneau *m*. 2 comp ▶**sleigh bell** grelot *m or* clochette *f* (de traîneau) ▶**sleigh ride**: **to go for a sleigh ride** faire une promenade en traîneau. 3 vi aller en traîneau.
sleight [slaıt] n: ~ **of hand** (*skill*) habileté *f*, dextérité *f*; (*trick*) tour *m* de passe-passe; **by (a)** ~ **of hand** par un tour de passe-passe.
slender ['slendə^r] adj *figure, person* svelte, mince; *stem, hand* fin; *wineglass* élancé; *neck* fin, gracieux; *waist* fin, délié; *fingers* fin, effilé; (*fig*) *hope* ténu, faible; *chance, possibility* faible; *excuse* faible, peu convaincant; *income, means* maigre, insuffisant, modeste; *knowledge, resources* maigre, limité, insuffisant. *[person]* **tall and** ~ élancé; **small and** ~ menu; **a** ~ **majority** une faible majorité.
slenderize ['slendəraız] vt (*US*) amincir.
slenderly ['slendəlı] adv: ~ **built** svelte, mince.
slenderness ['slendənıs] n (*see* **slender**) sveltesse *f*, minceur *f*; finesse *f*; faiblesse *f*; insuffisance *f*.
slept [slept] pret, ptp of **sleep**.
sleuth [slu:θ] 1 n (*dog: also* ~ **hound**) limier *m* (*chien*); (**: detective*) limier, détective *m*. 2 vi (**: also* ~ **around**) fureter, fouiner*.
slew[1] [slu:] pret of **slay**.
slew[2] [slu:] (*also* ~ **round**) 1 vi virer, pivoter; (*Naut*) virer; *[car]* déraper par l'arrière; (*right round*) faire un tête-à-queue. **the car** ~**ed (round) to a stop** la voiture s'est arrêtée après un tête-à-queue. 2 vt faire pivoter, faire virer. **he** ~**ed the car (round)** il a fait déraper la voiture par l'arrière; (*right round*) il a fait un tête-à-queue.
slew[3] [slu:] n (*US*) **a** ~ **of*** ... un tas* de ..., un grand nombre de ... .
slewed‡ [slu:d] adj (*Brit: drunk*) paf‡ *inv*, soûl*.
slice [slaıs] 1 n a *[cake, bread, meat]* tranche *f*; *[lemon, cucumber, sausage]* rondelle *f*, tranche. ~ **of bread and butter** tranche de pain beurré, tartine beurrée.
b (*fig*) (*part*) partie *f*; (*share*) part *f*. **it took quite a** ~ **of our profits** cela nous a pris une bonne partie de nos bénéfices; **a large** ~ **of the credit** une grande part du mérite; ~ **of life** tranche *f* de vie; ~ **of luck** coup *m* de chance.
c (*kitchen utensil*) spatule *f*, truelle *f*.
d (*Sport*) balle *f* coupée, slice *m*.
2 vt a *bread, cake, meat* couper (en tranches); *lemon, sausage, cucumber* couper (en rondelles); *rope etc* couper net, trancher. **to** ~ **sth thin** couper qch en tranches *or* rondelles fines; ~**d bread/a** ~**d loaf** le/un pain en tranches; **it's the best thing since** ~**d bread*** on n'a pas vu mieux depuis l'invention du fil à couper le beurre.
b (*Sport*) *ball* couper, slicer.
3 vi: **this knife won't** ~ ce couteau coupe très mal; **this bread won't** ~ ce pain se coupe très mal *or* est très difficile à couper.
▶**slice off** vt sep *piece of rope, finger etc* couper net. **to slice off a piece of sausage** couper une rondelle de saucisson; **to slice off a steak** couper *or* tailler un bifteck.
▶**slice through** vt fus *rope* couper net, trancher; (*fig*) *restrictions etc* (réussir à) passer au travers de, court-circuiter*. (*fig*) **to slice through the air/the waves** fendre l'air/les flots.
▶**slice up** vt sep couper *or* débiter en tranches *or* en rondelles.
slicer ['slaısə^r] n couteau *m* mécanique, machine *f* à couper (*la viande*

ou le pain); (*in shop etc*) coupe-jambon *m inv*.

slick [slɪk] 1 adj a *hair* lissé et brillant, luisant; *road, surface* glissant, gras (*f* grasse).

b (*pej*) *explanation* trop prompt; *excuse* facile; *style* superficiel, brillant en apparence; *manners* doucereux, mielleux; *person* (*glib*) qui a la parole facile, qui a du bagout*; (*cunning*) astucieux, rusé; *business deal* mené rondement, mené bon train. **he always has a ~ answer** il a toujours la réponse facile, il a toujours réponse à tout; **a ~ customer*** une fine mouche, un(e) fin(e) rusé(e).

2 n (*oil ~*) nappe *f* de pétrole; (*on beach*) marée noire.

3 vt: **to ~ (down) one's hair** (*with comb etc*) se lisser les cheveux; (*with hair cream*) se brillantiner les cheveux; **~ed-back hair** cheveux *mpl* lissés en arrière.

slicker* ['slɪkəʳ] n combinard(e)* *m(f)*; *see* **city**.

slickly ['slɪklɪ] adv *answer* habilement.

slickness ['slɪknɪs] n (*see* **slick**) a brillant *m*; nature glissante. b (*pej*) excès *m* de promptitude; qualité superficielle; caractère doucereux; parole *f* facile, bagout* *m*; astuce *f*, ruse *f*.

slide [slaɪd] (vb: pret, ptp **slid**) 1 n a (*action*) glissade *f*; (*land~*) glissement *m* (de terrain); (*fig: in prices, temperature etc*) baisse *f*, chute *f* (*in* de).

b (*in playground, pool etc*) toboggan *m*; (*polished ice etc*) glissoire *f*; (*for logs etc*) glissoir *m*.

c *[microscope]* porte-objet *m*; (*Phot*) diapositive *f*, diapo* *f*. **illustrated with ~s** accompagné de diapositives; **a film for ~s** une pellicule à diapositives; *see* **colour, lantern**.

d (*Tech: runner*) coulisse *f*; (*on trombone etc*) coulisse; (*Mus: between notes*) coulé *m*; (*hair ~*) barrette *f*.

2 comp ►**slide box** (*Phot*) classeur *m* pour diapositives, boîte *f* à diapositives ►**slide changer** (*Phot*) passe-vues *m* ►**slide fastener** (*Dress etc*) fermeture *f* éclair ®, fermeture à glissière ►**slide guitar** slide guitar *f* ►**slide magazine** (*Phot*) panier *m* ►**slide projector** (*Phot*) projecteur *m* de diapositives ►**slide rule** règle *f* à calcul.

3 vi a *[person, object]* glisser; (*on ice etc*) *[person]* faire des glissades, glisser. **to ~ down the bannisters** descendre en glissant sur la rampe; **to ~ down a slope** descendre une pente en glissant, glisser le long d'une pente; **the drawer ~s in and out easily** le tiroir glisse bien, le tiroir s'ouvre et se ferme facilement; **the top ought to ~ gently into place** on devrait pouvoir mettre le haut en place en le faisant glisser doucement; **the book slid off my knee** le livre a glissé de mes genoux; **to let things ~** laisser les choses aller à la dérive; **he let his studies ~** il a négligé ses études.

b (*move silently*) se glisser. **he slid into the room** il s'est glissé dans la pièce; (*fig*) **to ~ into bad habits** prendre insensiblement de mauvaises habitudes.

4 vt faire glisser, glisser. **he slid the chair across the room** il a fait glisser la chaise à travers la pièce; **he slid the packing case into a corner** il a glissé la caisse dans un coin; **he slid the photo into his pocket** il a glissé la photo dans sa poche; **to ~ the top (back) onto a box** (re)mettre le couvercle sur une boîte (en le faisant glisser); **~ the drawer into place** remets le tiroir en place; **he slid the gun out of the holster** il a sorti le revolver de l'étui.

►**slide down** vi *[person, animal, vehicle]* descendre en glissant; *[object]* glisser.

►**slide off** vi a *[top, lid etc]* s'enlever facilement *or* en glissant. b (*fig: leave quietly*) *[guest]* s'en aller discrètement, s'éclipser*; *[thief]* s'éloigner furtivement.

sliding ['slaɪdɪŋ] 1 adj *movement* glissant; *part* qui glisse, mobile; *panel, door, seat* coulissant. (*Aut*) **~ roof** toit ouvrant; (*Admin, Comm, Ind etc*) **~ scale** échelle *f* mobile; (*US*) **~ time** horaire *m* variable. 2 n glissement *m*.

slight [slaɪt] 1 adj a *person, figure* (*slim*) mince, menu; (*frail*) frêle; *framework* fragile.

b (*small*) *movement, increase, pain, difference, wind, accent* petit, léger (*before n only*); (*trivial, negligible*) *increase, difference* faible, insignifiant, négligeable; *error* petit, insignifiant, sans importance. **he showed some ~ optimism** il a fait preuve d'un peu d'optimisme; **to a ~ extent** dans une faible mesure; **not the ~est danger** pas le moindre danger; **not in the ~est** pas le moins du monde, pas du tout; **I haven't the ~est idea** je n'(en) ai pas la moindre idée; **just the ~est bit short** un tout petit peu trop court; **there's not the ~est possibility** *or* **chance of that** il n'y en a pas la moindre possibilité, c'est tout à fait impossible; **he takes offence at the ~est thing** il se pique pour un rien; **the wound is only ~** la blessure est légère *or* sans gravité.

2 vt (*ignore*) ignorer, manquer d'égards envers; (*offend*) blesser, offenser. **he felt (himself) ~ed** il s'est senti blessé *or* offensé.

3 n manque *m* d'égards, humiliation *f*, offense *f*. **this is a ~ on all of us** c'est un affront qui nous touche tous.

slighting ['slaɪtɪŋ] adj blessant, offensant, désobligeant.

slightingly ['slaɪtɪŋlɪ] adv avec peu d'égards, d'une manière blessante *or* offensante *or* désobligeante.

slightly ['slaɪtlɪ] adv a *sick, cold, better* légèrement, un peu. **I know her ~** je la connais un peu. b **~ built** mince, menu.

slightness ['slaɪtnɪs] n (*slimness*) minceur *f*; (*frailty*) fragilité *f*; *[difference, increase etc]* caractère insignifiant *or* négligeable.

slim [slɪm] 1 adj *person, figure, waist* mince, svelte; *ankle, book, volume* mince; (*fig*) *hope, chance* faible; *excuse* mince, médiocre, faible; *evidence* insuffisant, peu convaincant; *resources* maigre, insuffisant, faible. 2 vi maigrir; (*diet*) suivre un régime amaigrissant. **she's ~ming** elle essaie de maigrir, elle suit un régime pour maigrir. 3 vt (*also* **~ down**) *[diet etc]* faire maigrir; *[dress etc]* amincir. 4 n (*: *East African name for AIDS*) **S~** Sida *m*.

►**slim down** 1 vi maigrir, perdre du poids. 2 vt sep a = **slim 3.** b (*fig*) **slimmed down** *business, industry* allégé, dégraissé.

slime [slaɪm] n (*mud*) vase *f*; (*on riverbeds*) limon *m*; (*sticky substance*) dépôt visqueux *or* gluant; (*from snail*) bave *f*.

sliminess ['slaɪmɪnɪs] n (*see* **slimy**) nature vaseuse *or* limoneuse; viscosité *f*; suintement *m*; obséquiosité *f*; servilité *f*.

slimline ['slɪmlaɪn] adj léger, hypocalorique (*SPEC*); (*sugar-free*) sans sucre *inv*.

slimmer ['slɪməʳ] n personne *f* suivant un régime amaigrissant, personne au régime.

slimming ['slɪmɪŋ] 1 n fait *m* de suivre un régime amaigrissant, amaigrissement *m*. **~ can be very tiring** un régime amaigrissant peut être très fatigant, ça peut être très fatigant de se faire maigrir *or* d'être au régime. 2 adj *diet, pills* amaigrissant, pour maigrir; *food* qui ne fait pas grossir; *dress etc* amincissant.

slimness ['slɪmnɪs] n (*see* **slim**) minceur *f*, sveltesse *f*; faiblesse *f*; insuffisance *f*.

slimy ['slaɪmɪ] adj a (*gen : greasy, slippery*) *liquid, secretion, mark, deposit* visqueux, gluant; *fish, slug* visqueux; *walls* suintant. b (*of slime etc; see* **slime**) vaseux; limoneux; (*covered with slime*) couvert de vase (*or* de limon); (*muddy*) boueux. c (*fig*) *manners, smile* doucereux, obséquieux, servile; *person* rampant, servile, visqueux. **he's really ~** c'est un lécheur *or* un lèche-bottes*.

sling [slɪŋ] (vb: pret, ptp **slung**) 1 n a (*weapon*) fronde *f*; (*child's*) lance-pierre(s) *m inv*.

b (*hoist*) cordages *mpl*, courroies *fpl*; (*for oil drums etc*) courroie; (*Naut: for loads, casks, boats*) élingue *f*; (*Naut: for mast*) cravate *f*; (*for rifle*) bretelle *f*; (*Med*) écharpe *f*. **to have one's arm in a ~** avoir le bras en écharpe.

c (*Climbing*) anneau *m* (de corde); (*gear ~*) baudrier *m*.

2 comp ►**slingbacks** chaussures *fpl* ouvertes (derrière) ►**slingshot** (*US*) lance-pierre(s) *m inv*.

3 vt a (*throw*) *objects, stones* lancer, jeter (*at sb, to sb* à qn, *at sth* sur qch); *insults, accusations* lancer (*at sb* à qn).

b (*hang*) *hammock etc* suspendre; *load etc* hisser; (*Naut*) élinguer. **to ~ across one's shoulder** *rifle* mettre en bandoulière *or* à la bretelle; *satchel* mettre en bandoulière; *load, coat* jeter par derrière l'épaule; **with his rifle slung across his shoulder** avec son fusil en bandoulière *or* à la bretelle.

►**sling away*** vt sep (*get rid of*) jeter, se débarrasser de, ficher en l'air*.

►**sling out*** vt sep (*put out*) *person* flanquer* à la porte *or* dehors; *object* jeter, se débarrasser de, ficher en l'air*.

►**sling over*** vt sep (*pass*) passer, envoyer, balancer*.

►**sling up** vt sep suspendre.

slink [slɪŋk] pret, ptp **slunk** vi: **to ~ away/out** *etc* s'en aller/sortir *etc* furtivement *or* sournoisement *or* honteusement.

slinkily* ['slɪŋkɪlɪ] adv *walk* d'une démarche ondoyante *or* ondulante, avec un mouvement onduleux.

slinking ['slɪŋkɪŋ] adj furtif.

slinky* ['slɪŋkɪ] adj *woman* séduisant, provocant, aguichant; *body* sinueux, ondoyant; *walk* ondoyant, ondulant; *dress* moulant, collant.

slip [slɪp] 1 n a (*slide*) dérapage *m*; (*trip*) faux pas; (*of earth*) éboulement *m*; (*fig: mistake*) erreur *f*, bévue *f*, gaffe* *f*; (*oversight*) étourderie *f*, oubli *m*; (*moral*) écart *m*, faute légère. (*Prov*) **there's many a ~ 'twixt cup and lip** il y a loin de la coupe aux lèvres (*Prov*); **~ of the tongue, ~ of the pen** lapsus *m*; **it was a ~ of the tongue** c'était un lapsus, la langue lui a (*or* m'a *etc*) fourché; **he made several ~s** il a fait *or* commis plusieurs lapsus; **to give sb the ~** fausser compagnie à qn.

b (*pillow~*) taie *f* (d'oreiller); (*underskirt*) combinaison *f*; *see* **gym**.

c **the ~s** (*Naut*) la cale; (*Theat*) les coulisses *fpl*; (*Cricket*) *partie du terrain se trouvant diagonalement derrière le batteur;* **in the ~s** (*Naut*) sur cale; (*Theat*) dans les coulisses.

d (*plant-cutting*) bouture *f*; (*paper: in filing system*) fiche *f*. **a ~ of paper** (*small sheet*) une petite feuille *or* un bout *or* un morceau de papier; (*strip*) une bande de papier; (*fig*) **a (mere) ~ of a boy/girl** un gamin/une gamine, un jeune homme/une jeune fille gracile.

e (*NonC: Pottery*) engobe *m*.

f (*Aviat: side~*) glissade *f or* glissement *m* sur l'aile.

2 comp ►**slipcase** coffret *m* (de livres) ►**slipcover** (*esp US*) (*on book*) jaquette *f*; (*on furniture*) housse *f* ►**slipknot** nœud coulant ►**slip-on** adj facile à mettre *or* à enfiler*; **slip-ons, slip-on shoes** chaussures *fpl* sans lacets ►**slipover*** pull-over *m* sans manches, débardeur *m* ►**slip road** (*Brit*) (*to motorway*) bretelle *f* d'accès; (*bypass road*) voie *f* de déviation ►**slipshod** *person* (*in dress etc*) dé-

braillé, négligé; (*in work*) négligent; *work, style* négligé, peu soigné ►**slipslop*** (*liquor*) lavasse* *f*, bibine* *f*; (*talk, writing*) bêtises *fpl* ►**slip stitch** (*Knitting*) maille glissée ►**slipstream** (*Aviat*) sillage *m* ►**slip-up*** bévue *f*, cafouillage* *m*; **there has been a slip-up somewhere** quelqu'un a dû faire une gaffe*, quelque chose a cafouillé*, il y a eu un cafouillage*; **a slip-up in communication(s)** une défaillance *or* un cafouillage* dans les communications ►**slipway** (*Naut*) (*for building, repairing*) cale *f* (de construction); (*for launching*) cale de lancement.

3 **vi** a (*slide*) *[person, foot, hand, object]* glisser. **he ~ped on the ice** il a glissé *or* dérapé sur la glace; **my foot/hand ~ped** mon pied/ma main a glissé; (*Aut*) **the clutch ~ped** l'embrayage a patiné; **the knot has ~ped** le nœud a glissé *or* coulissé; **the fish ~ped off the hook** le poisson s'est détaché de l'hameçon; **the drawer ~s in and out easily** le tiroir glisse bien, le tiroir s'ouvre et se ferme facilement; **the top ought to ~ gently into place** on devrait pouvoir mettre le haut en place en le faisant glisser doucement; **the saw ~ped and cut my hand** la scie a glissé *or* dérapé et m'a entaillé la main; **the book ~ped out of his hand/off the table** le livre lui a glissé des doigts/a glissé de la table; **the beads ~ped through my fingers** les perles m'ont glissé entre les doigts; (*fig*) **money ~s through her fingers** l'argent lui file entre les doigts; **the thief ~ped through their fingers** le voleur leur a filé entre les doigts; **several errors had ~ped into the report** plusieurs erreurs s'étaient glissées dans le rapport; **to let an opportunity ~, to let ~ an opportunity** laisser passer *or* laisser échapper une occasion; **he let ~ an oath** il a laissé échapper un juron; **he let (it) ~ that ...** il a laissé échapper que ...; **he's ~ping*** (*getting old, less efficient*) il baisse, il n'est plus ce qu'il était, il perd les pédales*; (*making more mistakes*) il ne fait plus assez attention, il ne se concentre plus assez; *see* **net**.

b (*move quickly*) *[person]* se glisser, passer, se faufiler; *[vehicle]* se faufiler, passer. **he ~ped into/out of the room** il s'est glissé *or* coulé dans/hors de la pièce; **he ~ped through the corridors** il s'est faufilé dans les couloirs; **I'll just ~ through the garden** je vais passer par le jardin; **the motorbike ~ped through the traffic** la motocyclette s'est faufilée à travers la circulation; **he ~ped over** *or* **across the border** il se faufila de l'autre côté de la frontière; **to ~ into bed** se glisser *or* se couler dans son lit; **to ~ into a dress** *etc* se glisser dans *or* enfiler (rapidement) une robe *etc*; **to ~ out of a dress** *etc* enlever (rapidement) une robe *etc*; (*fig*) **he ~ped easily into his new role** il s'est ajusté *or* adapté *or* fait facilement à son nouveau rôle; **to ~ into bad habits** prendre insensiblement de mauvaises habitudes.

4 **vt** a (*slide*) glisser. **to ~ a coin to sb/into sb's hand** glisser une pièce à qn/dans la main de qn; **he ~ped the book back on the shelf** il a glissé *or* remis le livre à sa place sur l'étagère; **he ~ped the ring on her finger** il lui a glissé *or* passé la bague au doigt; **he ~ped the photo into his pocket** il a glissé la photo dans sa poche; **to ~ the top (back) onto a box** (re)mettre le couvercle sur une boîte (en le faisant glisser); **~ the drawer (back) into place** remets le tiroir en place; **he ~ped the gun out of its holster** il a retiré *or* sorti le revolver de son étui; (*Aut*) **to ~ the clutch** faire patiner l'embrayage; **a question on Proust was ~ped into the exam** l'épreuve a comporté une question inattendue sur Proust; (*Med*) **a ~ped disc** une hernie discale.

b (*escape*) échapper à; (*Naut*) *anchor, cable, moorings* filer. **the dog ~ped its collar** le chien s'est dégagé de son collier; **he ~ped the dog's leash** il a lâché le chien; (*Knitting*) **to ~ a stitch** glisser une maille; **that ~ped his attention** *or* **his notice** cela lui a échappé; **it ~ped his notice that ...** il ne s'est pas aperçu que ..., il n'a pas remarqué que ..., il lui a échappé que ...; **it ~ped my memory** *or* **my mind** j'avais complètement oublié cela, cela m'était complètement sorti de la tête.

►**slip along** **vi** faire un saut, passer. **he has just slipped along to the shops** il a fait un saut jusqu'aux magasins; **slip along to Mary's and ask her ...** fais un saut *or* passe chez Marie et demande-lui ... .

►**slip away** **vi** *[car, boat]* s'éloigner doucement; *[guest]* partir discrètement, s'esquiver, s'éclipser*; *[thief]* s'en aller furtivement, filer*, s'esquiver. **I slipped away for a few minutes** je me suis esquivé *or* éclipsé* pour quelques minutes; **her life was slipping away (from her)** la vie la quittait.

►**slip back** 1 **vi** *[car, boat]* revenir *or* retourner doucement; *[guest]* revenir *or* retourner discrètement; *[thief, spy]* revenir *or* retourner furtivement *or* subrepticement. **I'll just slip back and get it** je retourne le chercher. 2 **vt sep** *see* **slip 4a**.

►**slip by** **vi** = **slip past**.

►**slip down** **vi** a *[object, car]* glisser; *[person]* glisser et tomber. **I'll just slip down and get it** je descends le chercher. b *[food, drink]* descendre* tout seul.

►**slip in** 1 **vi** *[car, boat]* entrer doucement; *[person]* entrer discrètement *or* sans se faire remarquer; *[thief]* entrer furtivement *or* subrepticement; *[cat etc]* entrer inaperçu. **several errors have slipped in** plusieurs erreurs s'y sont glissées; **I'll just slip in and tell him** je vais juste entrer le lui dire; **I've only slipped in for a minute** je ne fais que passer, je ne fais qu'entrer et sortir. 2 **vt sep** *object* glisser, placer; *part, drawer* glisser à sa place; *remark, comment* glisser, placer. (*Aut*) **to slip in the clutch** embrayer.

►**slip off** 1 **vi** a = **slip away**. b *[coat, lid, cover]* glisser. 2 **vt sep** *cover, ring, bracelet, glove, shoe* enlever; *garment* enlever, ôter.

►**slip on** 1 **vt sep** *garment* passer, enfiler*; *ring, bracelet, glove* mettre, enfiler; *shoe* mettre; *lid, cover* (re)mettre, placer. 2 **slip-on** **adj** *see* **slip 2**.

►**slip out** 1 **vi** *[guest]* sortir discrètement, s'esquiver, s'éclipser*; *[thief]* sortir furtivement, filer*, s'esquiver. **I must just slip out for some cigarettes** il faut que je sorte un instant chercher des cigarettes; **she slipped out to the shops** elle a fait un saut jusqu'aux magasins; **the secret slipped out** le secret a été révélé par mégarde; **the words slipped out before he realized it** les mots lui ont échappé avant même qu'il ne s'en rende compte. 2 **vt sep** sortir doucement (*or* discrètement *etc*).

►**slip over** 1 **vi** a = **slip along**. b (*fall*) glisser et tomber. 2 **vt sep**: **to slip one over on sb*** rouler qn*; *see also* **slip 3b**. 3 **slipover*** **n** *see* **slip 2**.

►**slip past** **vi** *[person, vehicle]* passer, se faufiler. **the years slipped past** les années passèrent.

►**slip round** **vi** = **slip along**.

►**slip through** **vi** *[person]* passer quand même; *[error etc]* ne pas être remarqué.

►**slip up*** 1 **vi** (*make mistake*) gaffer*, cafouiller*, se ficher dedans*. 2 **slip-up** **n** *see* **slip 2**.

slippage ['slɪpɪdʒ] **n** (*Ind*) *[output]* dérapage *m*, baisse *f*, recul *m* (*in* de).

slipper ['slɪpəʳ] **n** pantoufle *f*, (*warmer*) chausson *m*; (*mule*) mule *f*; *see* **glass**.

slippery ['slɪpərɪ] **adj** *surface, road, stone, fish* glissant; (*fig pej*) *person* (*evasive*) fuyant, insaisissable; (*unreliable*) sur qui on ne peut pas compter. **it's ~ underfoot** le sol est glissant, on glisse en marchant; (*fig pej*) **he's as ~ as an eel** il glisse *or* il échappe comme une anguille; (*fig*) **to be on ~ ground** être sur un terrain glissant; (*fig*) **to be on a ~ slope** être sur un terrain glissant *or* une pente savonneuse*.

slippy* ['slɪpɪ] **adj** *fish, stone* glissant; *road, floor* glissant, casse-gueule‡ *inv*. (*Brit*) **look ~ (about it)!** grouille-toi!‡

slit [slɪt] (**vb: pret, ptp slit**) 1 **n** (*opening*) fente *f*; (*cut*) incision *f*; (*tear*) déchirure *f*. **to make a ~ in sth** fendre *or* inciser *or* déchirer qch; **the skirt has a ~ up the side** la jupe a une fente *or* est fendue sur le côté.

2 **adj**: **to have ~ eyes** (*nearly closed*) plisser les yeux; (*slanting*) avoir les yeux bridés.

3 **comp** ►**slit-eyed** (*eyes nearly closed*) aux yeux plissés; (*with slanting eyes*) aux yeux bridés.

4 **vt** (*make an opening in*) fendre; (*cut*) inciser, couper, faire une fente dans; (*tear*) déchirer. **to ~ sb's throat** couper *or* trancher la gorge à qn, égorger qn; **to ~ a letter open** ouvrir une lettre (*avec un objet tranchant*); **to ~ a sack open** éventrer *or* fendre un sac; **a ~ skirt** une jupe fendue.

slither ['slɪðəʳ] **vi** *[person, animal]* glisser; *[snake]* onduler. **he ~ed about on the ice** il dérapait sur la glace, il essayait de se tenir en équilibre sur la glace; **the car ~ed (about) all over the place** la voiture a dérapé dans tous les sens; **he ~ed down the slope/down the rope** il a dégringolé* la pente/le long de la corde; **the snake ~ed across the path** le serpent a traversé le sentier en ondulant.

sliver ['slɪvəʳ] **n** *[glass, wood]* éclat *m*; *[cheese, ham etc]* lamelle *f*, petit morceau.

slivovitz ['slɪvəʊvɪts] **n** (*NonC*) slivowitz *m*.

Sloane Ranger* [ˌsləʊn'reɪndʒəʳ] **n** (*Brit*) ≃ personne *f* B.C.B.G.

slob* [slɒb] **n** rustaud(e) *m(f)*, plouc‡ *mf*.

slobber ['slɒbəʳ] 1 **vi** *[person, dog etc]* baver. **to ~ over sth** (*lit*) baver sur qch; (*fig pej*) s'attendrir *or* s'extasier exagérément sur qch; **to ~ over sb** *[dog]* couvrir qn de grands coups de langue; (*fig pej : kiss etc*) *[person]* faire des mamours* à qn, donner une fricassée de museau à qn‡. 2 **n** (*NonC*) bave *f*, salive *f*; (*fig pej*) sensiblerie *f*, attendrissement exagéré.

slobbery ['slɒbərɪ] **adj** baveux.

sloe [sləʊ] 1 **n** prunelle *f*; (*bush*) prunellier *m*. 2 **comp** ►**sloe-eyed** aux yeux de biche ►**sloe gin** gin *m* à la prunelle.

slog [slɒg] 1 **n** (*work*) long travail pénible, travail de Romain* *or* de nègre*; (*effort*) gros effort. **the programme was one long ~** le programme exigeait un grand effort *or* représentait un travail de Romain*; **it was a (hard) ~ to pass the exam** il a fallu fournir un gros effort *or* travailler comme un nègre* pour réussir à l'examen; **after a long ~ he reached the top of the hill** après un gros effort il a atteint le sommet de la colline; **he found it nothing but a ~** c'était une vraie corvée pour lui.

2 **vt** *ball* donner un grand coup à; *opponent* donner un grand coup à, donner un gnon‡ à. **we left them to ~ it out** nous les avons laissé s'expliquer à coups de poing.

3 **vi** a (*work etc*) travailler très dur *or* comme un nègre*. **he ~ged (his way) through the book** il s'est forcé à lire le livre, il a poursuivi péniblement la lecture du livre.

b (*walk etc*) marcher d'un pas lourd, avancer avec obstination. **he ~ged up the hill** il a gravi la colline avec effort *or* avec obstination *or* d'un pas lourd.

►**slog along** **vi** marcher d'un pas lourd, avancer avec obstination. **we slogged along for 10 km** nous nous sommes traînés sur 10 km.

►**slog away** **vi** travailler dur *or* comme un nègre*. **to slog away at sth**

trimer* sur qch.
►slog on vi = **slog along.**
slogan [ˈsləʊgən] n slogan *m*.
slogger* [ˈslɒgəʳ] n (*hard worker*) bourreau *m* de travail, bûcheur *m*, -euse *f*, bosseur‡ *m*, -euse‡ *f*; (*Boxing*) cogneur *m*.
sloop [sluːp] n sloop *m*.
slop [slɒp] 1 n: **~s** (*dirty water*) eaux sales; (*in teacup etc*) fond *m* de tasse; (*liquid food*) (*for invalids etc*) bouillon *m*, aliment *m* liquide; (*for pigs*) pâtée *f*, soupe *f*. 2 comp **►slop basin** vide-tasses *m inv* **►slop bucket, slop pail** (*in kitchen etc*) boîte *f* à ordures, poubelle *f*; (*in bedroom*) seau *m* de toilette; (*on farm*) seau à pâtée. 3 vt *liquid* (*spill*) renverser, répandre; (*tip carelessly*) répandre (*on to* sur, *into* dans). **you've ~ped paint all over the floor** tu as éclaboussé tout le plancher de peinture. 4 vi (*also* **~ over**) *[water, tea etc]* déborder, se renverser (*into* dans, *on to* sur); *[bowl, bucket]* déborder.
►slop about, slop around 1 vi a **the water was slopping about in the bucket** l'eau clapotait dans le seau; **they were slopping about in the mud** ils pataugeaient dans la boue. b (*fig*) **she slops about in a dressing gown all day*** elle traîne *or* traînasse* toute la journée en robe de chambre. 2 vt sep renverser *or* mettre un peu partout.
►slop out vi (*Prison*) vider les seaux hygiéniques.
►slop over 1 vi = **slop 4.** 2 vt sep renverser, répandre.
slope [sləʊp] 1 n a *[roof, floor, ground, surface]* inclinaison *f*, pente *f*, déclivité *f*; *[handwriting etc]* inclinaison. **roof with a slight/steep ~** toit (qui descend) en pente douce/raide; **road with a ~ of 1 in 8** route avec une pente de 12,5%; (*Mil*) **rifle at the ~** fusil sur l'épaule.
b (*rising ground, gentle hill*) côte *f*, pente *f*; (*mountainside*) versant *m*, flanc *m*. **~ up** montée *f*; **~ down** descente *f*; **the car got stuck on a ~** la voiture est restée en panne dans une côte; **halfway up** *or* **down the ~** à mi-côte, à mi-pente; **on the ~s of Mount Etna** sur les flancs de l'Etna; **the southern ~s of the Himalayas** le versant sud de l'Himalaya; **on the (ski) ~s** sur les pistes (de ski).
2 vi *[ground, roof]* être en pente, être incliné; *[handwriting]* pencher. **the garden ~s towards the river** le jardin descend en pente vers la rivière.
3 vt incliner, pencher. (*Mil*) **to ~ arms** mettre l'arme sur l'épaule; "**~ arms!**" "portez arme!"
►slope away, slope down vi *[ground]* descendre en pente (*to* jusqu'à, *towards* vers).
►slope off* vi se sauver*, se tirer‡, se barrer‡.
►slope up vi *[road, ground]* monter.
sloping [ˈsləʊpɪŋ] adj *ground, roof etc* en pente, incliné; *handwriting etc* penché; *shoulders* tombant.
sloppily [ˈslɒpɪlɪ] adv (*carelessly*) *dress* de façon négligée, sans soin; *work* sans soin; (*sentimentally*) *talk, behave* avec sensiblerie.
sloppiness [ˈslɒpɪnɪs] n (*see* **sloppy**) état liquide *or* détrempé; manque *m* de soin; négligé *m*; sensiblerie *f*; excès *m* de sentimentalité.
sloppy [ˈslɒpɪ] 1 adj a *food* trop liquide; *ground, field* détrempé. b (*poor*) *work* peu soigné, bâclé*, saboté*; *appearance* négligé, débraillé. **~ English** anglais très relâché *or* négligé. c *garment* trop grand, mal ajusté. d (*sentimental*) *smile, look* pâmé, débordant de sensiblerie; *book, film* fadement sentimental. **don't be ~!** pas de sensiblerie! 2 comp **►sloppy Joe** (*sweater*) gros pull *m* vague; (*US: sandwich*) hamburger *m* servi en sandwich.
slosh [slɒʃ] 1 vt a (*Brit* ‡: *hit*) flanquer* un coup *or* un gnon‡ à. b (*: *spill*) renverser, répandre; (*apply lavishly*) répandre (*on to, over* sur, *into* dans). **to ~ paint on a wall** barbouiller un mur de peinture, flanquer* de la peinture sur un mur; **he ~ed water over the floor** (*deliberately*) il a répandu de l'eau par terre; (*accidentally*) il a renversé *or* fichu* de l'eau par terre. 2 vi: **water was ~ing everywhere** l'eau se répandait partout.
►slosh about*, slosh around* 1 vi = **slop about 1a.** 2 vt sep = **slop about 2.**
sloshed‡ [slɒʃt] adj (*esp Brit: drunk*) bourré‡, paf‡ *inv*, noir‡. **to get ~** se soûler la gueule‡, prendre une cuite*.
slot [slɒt] 1 n a (*slit*) fente *f*; (*groove*) rainure *f*; (*in door, for mail*) ouverture *f* pour les lettres. **to put a coin in the ~** mettre *or* introduire une pièce dans la fente.
b (*fig: space in schedule etc*) (*gen, also Rad, TV*) créneau *m*, plage *f* *or* tranche *f* horaire; (*Scol etc: in timetable*) heure *f*, plage horaire. (*Rad, TV etc*) **they are looking for something to fill the early-evening comedy ~** on cherche quelque chose pour la tranche comédie du début de soirée; (*job etc*) **who will fit this ~?** qui fera l'affaire pour ce créneau?
2 comp **►slot car** (*US*) petite voiture *f* de circuit-auto **►slot machine** (*for tickets, cigarettes etc*) distributeur *m* (automatique); (*in fair etc*) appareil *m* *or* machine *f* à sous **►slot meter** compteur *m* (de gaz *etc*) (à pièces).
3 vt: **to ~ a part into another part** emboîter *or* encastrer une pièce dans une autre pièce; (*fig*) **to ~ sth into a programme/timetable** insérer *or* faire rentrer qch dans une grille de programmes/d'horaires.
4 vi: **this part ~s into that part** cette pièce-ci s'emboîte *or* s'encastre dans celle-là; (*fig*) **the song will ~ into the programme here** on peut insérer *or* faire figurer la chanson à ce moment-là du programme.
►slot in 1 vi *[piece, part]* s'emboîter, s'encastrer; (*fig*) *[item on programme etc]* s'insérer, figurer. 2 vt sep *piece, part* emboîter, encastrer; (*fig*) *item on programme* insérer, faire figurer.
►slot together 1 vi *[pieces, parts]* s'emboîter *or* s'encastrer les un(e)s dans les autres. 2 vt sep *pieces, parts* emboîter *or* encastrer les un(e)s dans les autres.
sloth [sləʊθ] n a (*NonC*) paresse *f* (*also Rel*), fainéantise *f*, indolence *f*. b (*Zool*) paresseux *m*.
slothful [ˈsləʊθfʊl] adj paresseux, fainéant, indolent.
slothfully [ˈsləʊθfəlɪ] adv avec indolence, avec paresse.
slouch [slaʊtʃ] 1 n a **to walk with a ~** mal se tenir en marchant. b **he's no ~*** il n'est pas empoté*. 2 comp **►slouch hat** chapeau *m* (mou) à larges bords. 3 vi: **he was ~ing in a chair** il était affalé dans un fauteuil; **she always ~es** elle ne se tient jamais droite, elle est toujours avachie; **stop ~ing!** redresse-toi!, tiens-toi droit!; **he ~ed in/out** *etc* il entra/sortit *etc* en traînant les pieds, le dos voûté.
►slouch about, slouch around vi traîner à ne rien faire.
slough[1] [slaʊ] n (*swamp*) bourbier *m*, marécage *m*. (*fig*) **the S~ of Despond** l'abîme *m* du désespoir.
slough[2] [slʌf] 1 n *[snake]* dépouille *f*, mue *f*. 2 vt (*also* **~ off**) **the snake ~ed (off) its skin** le serpent a mué.
►slough off vt sep a = **slough**[2] **2.** b (*fig*) *habit etc* perdre, se débarrasser de.
Slovak [ˈsləʊvæk], **Slovakian** [sləʊˈvækɪən] 1 adj slovaque. 2 n Slovaque *mf*.
sloven [ˈslʌvn] n (*dirty*) souillon *f* (*woman only*), personne sale *or* négligée dans sa tenue; (*careless*) personne sans soin.
Slovene [ˈsləʊviːn] 1 adj slovène. 2 n a Slovène *mf*. b (*Ling*) slovène *m*.
Slovenia [sləʊˈviːnɪə] n Slovénie *f*.
Slovenian [sləʊˈviːnɪən] = **Slovene.**
slovenliness [ˈslʌvnlɪnɪs] n (*untidiness*) négligé *m*, débraillé *m*; (*carelessness*) manque *m* de soin, négligence *f*.
slovenly [ˈslʌvnlɪ] adj (*untidy*) *person, appearance* sale, négligé, débraillé; (*careless*) *work* qui manque de soin, négligé, bâclé*. **she's ~** c'est une souillon.
slow [sləʊ] 1 adj a (*gen*) *person, vehicle, movement, pulse, voice, progress* lent. **it's ~ but sure** c'est lent mais sûr, cela avance (*or* fonctionne *etc*) lentement mais sûrement; (*Aut*) **~ lane** voie *f* réservée aux véhicules lents; (*Brit*) **a ~ train** un (train) omnibus; **at a ~ speed** à petite vitesse; (*lit, fig*) **it's ~ going** on n'avance pas vite; **it's ~ work** c'est un travail qui avance lentement; **he's a ~ worker** il est lent dans son travail, il travaille lentement; **he's a ~ learner** il apprend lentement, il est lent à apprendre; **to be ~ of speech** avoir la parole lente; **he is ~ to anger** il est lent à se mettre en colère, il lui en faut beaucoup pour se mettre en colère; (*not naturally quick*) **he was ~ to understand/notice** *etc*, **he was ~ in understanding/noticing** *etc* il a été lent à comprendre/remarquer *etc*, il lui a fallu longtemps pour comprendre/remarquer *etc*; (*taking his time*) **he was ~ in deciding/acting** *etc*, **he was ~ to decide/act** *etc* il a été long à décider/agir *etc*, il a tardé à décider/agir *etc*; **he was not ~ to notice** *or* **in noticing ...** il a vite remarqué ..., il n'a pas mis longtemps à remarquer ... .
b (*fig*) *pitch, track, surface* collant, lourd; *market, trading* trop calme, stagnant; (*boring*) *party, evening* ennuyeux, qui manque d'entrain; *novel, plot, play* qui avance lentement, ennuyeux; *person* (*phlegmatic*) flegmatique, à l'allure posée; (*stupid*) lent, lourd, endormi. **my watch is ~** ma montre retarde; **my watch is 10 minutes ~** ma montre retarde de 10 minutes; **in a ~ oven** à four doux; **business is ~** les affaires stagnent; **life here is ~** la vie s'écoule lentement ici, ici on vit au ralenti.
2 adv lentement. (*Naut*) **~ astern!** (en) arrière doucement!; **to go ~** *[walker, driver, vehicle]* aller *or* avancer lentement; (*fig: be cautious*) y aller doucement; (*fig: be less active, do less*) ralentir (ses activités); (*Ind*) faire la grève perlée; *[watch etc]* prendre du retard; **to go ~er** ralentir (le pas).
3 comp **►slow-acting/-burning** *etc* à action/combustion *etc* lente; **it is slow-acting/-burning** *etc* cela agit/brûle *etc* lentement **►slow burn‡:** (*US*) **he did a slow burn** sa colère a couvé *or* monté **►slowcoach** (*Brit*) (*dawdler*) lambin(e)* *m(f)*; (*dullard*) esprit lent **►slow cooker** (*Culin*) mijoteuse *f* électrique **►slowdown** ralentissement *m*; (*US Ind*) grève perlée **►slow handclap** (*Brit: by audience*) applaudissements *mpl* lents (*pour exprimer l'exaspération, le mécontentement*) **►slow match** mèche *f* à combustion lente **►slow motion:** (*Cine etc*) **in slow motion** au ralenti; **slow-motion film/shot** *etc* (film *m*/prise *f* de vues *etc* au) ralenti *m* **►slow-moving** *person, animal* lent, aux mouvements lents; *vehicle* lent; *play* lent, dont l'action est lente **►slowpoke*** (*US*) = **slowcoach** **►slow-speaking, slow-spoken** à la parole lente, au débit lent **►slow virus** virus *m* lent **►slow-witted** lourdaud, qui a l'esprit lent *or* lourd **►slow worm** (*Zool*) orvet *m*, serpent *m* de verre.
4 vt (*also* **~ down, ~ up**) *person* (*in walk*) faire ralentir; (*in activity*) ralentir, retarder; *vehicle, machine* ralentir (la marche de); *traffic* ralentir; *horse* ralentir l'allure *or* le pas de; *progress, production, negotiations, reaction* ralentir, retarder. **his injury ~ed him down** *or* **up**

sa blessure l'a ralenti *or* l'a diminué; **all these interruptions have ~ed us down** *or* **up** toutes ces interruptions nous ont retardés.

5 **vi** (*also* ~ **down,** ~ **off,** ~ **up**) *[driver, vehicle, machine, one's reactions, production, progress]* ralentir; *[walker etc]* ralentir (le pas); *[worker]* ralentir (ses efforts). (*Aut*) **"~"** "ralentir"; (*Aut*) **a "~" signal** un signal de ralentissement; (*fig*) **you must ~ down or you will make yourself ill** il faut que vous ralentissiez (*subj*) (vos activités) sinon vous allez tomber malade; **since his retirement his life has ~ed down** depuis qu'il a pris sa retraite il vit au ralenti.

▶**slow down** 1 **vi, vt sep** = **slow 5, 4.** 2 **slowdown n** *see* **slow 3.**

▶**slow off vi** = **slow 5.**

▶**slow up vi, vt sep** = **slow 5, 4.**

slowly ['sləʊlɪ] **adv** *think, work* lentement; *walk* lentement, à pas lents; *talk* lentement, d'une voix lente; (*little by little*) peu à peu. **~ but surely** lentement mais sûrement; *[car etc]* **to go** *or* **drive** *or* **move ~** aller lentement *or* au pas; **to go** (*or* **speak** *or* **work** *or* **drive** *etc*) **more ~** ralentir.

slowness ['sləʊnɪs] **n** *[person, vehicle, movement etc]* lenteur *f*; *[pitch, track]* lourdeur *f*; *[party, evening]* manque *m* d'entrain *or* d'intérêt; *[novel, plot, play]* lenteur, manque de mouvement *or* d'action; (*lack of energy etc*) allure posée; (*stupidity*) lenteur d'esprit, stupidité *f*. **~ of mind** lenteur *or* lourdeur d'esprit; **his ~ to act** *or* **in acting** la lenteur avec laquelle *or* le retard avec lequel il a agi.

SLR [ˌesel'ɑːʳ] **n** (*Phot*) (**abbr of single lens reflex (camera)**) *see* **single 3.**

sludge [slʌdʒ] **n** (*NonC*) (*mud*) boue *f*, vase *f*, bourbe *f*; (*sediment*) boue, dépôt *m*; (*sewage*) vidanges *fpl*; (*melting snow*) neige fondante *or* fondue.

slug [slʌg] 1 **n** (*Zool*) limace *f*; (*bullet*) balle *f*; (*blow*) coup *m*; (*Min, Typ*) lingot *m*; (*esp US: metal token*) jeton *m*; (*US* ‡ *: false coin*) fausse pièce *f*, pièce *f* bidon* *inv*, faux jeton *m*. (*US*) **a ~ of whisky**‡ un peu *or* un coup* de whisky sec. 2 **vt** (**: hit*) frapper comme une brute.

▶**slug out* vt sep: to slug it out** se taper dessus* (pour régler une question).

slugfest‡ ['slʌgfest] **n** bagarre *f*, rixe *f*.

sluggard ['slʌgəd] **n** paresseux *m*, -euse *f*, indolent(e) *m(f)*, fainéant(e) *m(f)*.

sluggish ['slʌgɪʃ] **adj** *person, temperament* mou (*f* molle), léthargique, apathique; (*slow-moving*) lent; (*lazy*) paresseux; *growth, reaction, movement, circulation, digestion* lent; *liver* paresseux; *market, business* (trop) calme, stagnant. (*Aut*) **the engine is ~** le moteur manque de reprise *or* de nervosité; (*Comm*) **sales are ~** les ventes ne vont pas fort.

sluggishly ['slʌgɪʃlɪ] **adv** (*see* **sluggish**) mollement; lentement; paresseusement. (*Aut*) **the engine picks up ~** le moteur n'est pas nerveux.

sluggishness ['slʌgɪʃnɪs] **n** *[person]* mollesse *f*, léthargie *f*, lenteur *f*, apathie *f*; *[engine]* manque *m* de nervosité.

sluice [sluːs] 1 **n** a (*whole structure*) écluse *f*; (*gate: also* ~ **gate,** ~ **valve**) vanne *f*, porte *f* d'écluse; (*channel: also* ~**way**) canal *m* (à vannes); (*water held back*) eaux retenues par la vanne. b **to give sth/o.s. a ~ (down)** laver qch/se laver à grande eau. 2 **comp** ▶**sluice gate** *see* **sluice 1a** ▶**sluice valve** = **sluice gate** ▶**sluiceway** *see* **sluice 1a.** 3 **vt** (*also* ~ **down**) laver à grande eau.

slum [slʌm] 1 **n** (*house*) taudis *m*. **the ~s** les quartiers *mpl* pauvres *or* misérables, les bas quartiers; (*in suburb*) la zone.

2 **comp** ▶**slum area** quartier *m* pauvre ▶**slum clearance** aménagement *m* des quartiers insalubres; **slum clearance area** zone *f* de quartiers insalubres en voie d'aménagement; **slum clearance campaign** campagne *f* pour la démolition des taudis ▶**slum-dweller** habitant(e) *m(f)* de taudis ▶**slum dwelling** taudis *m* ▶**slumlord*** (*US pej*) marchand* *m* de sommeil.

3 **vi** (**: live cheaply: also* (*esp Brit*) **~ it**) vivre à la dure, manger de la vache enragée*. (*iro*) **we don't see you often round here — I'm ~ming (it) today!** on ne te voit pas souvent ici — aujourd'hui je m'encanaille!

4 **vt** (*) **to ~ it** *see* **3.**

slumber ['slʌmbəʳ] 1 **n** (*liter: also* ~**s**) sommeil *m* (paisible). 2 **comp** ▶**slumber wear** (*Comm*) vêtements *mpl or* lingerie *f* de nuit. 3 **vi** dormir paisiblement.

slumb(e)rous ['slʌmb(ə)rəs] **adj** (*liter*) (*drowsy*) somnolent; (*soporific*) assoupissant (*liter*).

slumgullion [slʌm'gʌljən] **n** (*US*) ragoût *m*.

slummy ['slʌmɪ] **adj** *house, district, background, kitchen, appearance* sordide, misérable. **the ~ part (of the town)** les bas quartiers, les quartiers pauvres.

slump [slʌmp] 1 **n** (*in numbers, popularity, morale etc*) forte baisse, baisse soudaine (*in* de); (*Econ*) récession *f*, crise *f* (économique *or* monétaire), marasme *m*; (*St Ex*) effondrement *m* (des cours); (*Comm: in sales etc*) crise, baisse soudaine (*in* de); (*in prices*) effondrement (*in* de). **the 1929 ~** la crise (économique) de 1929.

2 **vi** a *[popularity, morale, production, trade]* baisser brutalement; *[prices, rates]* s'effondrer. **business has ~ed** les affaires sont en baisse, c'est le marasme (économique).

b (*also* ~ **down**) s'effondrer, s'écrouler, s'affaisser (*into* dans, *onto* sur). **he lay ~ed on the floor** il gisait effondré *or* écroulé par terre; **he was ~ed over the wheel** il était affaissé sur le volant.

c (*stoop*) avoir le dos rond *or* voûté.

▶**slump back vi** *[person]* retomber en arrière.

▶**slump down vi** = **slump 2b.**

slumpflation [ˌslʌmp'fleɪʃən] **n** (*US Econ*) récession *f* avec inflation.

slung [slʌŋ] **pret, ptp of sling.**

slunk [slʌŋk] **pret, ptp of slink.**

slur [slɜːʳ] 1 **n** a (*stigma*) tache *f* (*on* sur), atteinte *f* (*on* à), insinuation *f* (*on* contre); (*insult*) insulte *f*, affront *m*. **to be a ~ on sb's reputation** porter atteinte à *or* être une tache sur la réputation de qn; **that is a ~ on him** cela porte atteinte à son intégrité; **to cast a ~ on sb** porter atteinte à la réputation de qn; **it's no ~ on him to say ...** ce n'est pas le calomnier que de dire ... .

b (*Mus*) liaison *f*.

2 **vt** (*join*) *several sounds, words* lier à tort; (*Mus*) lier; (*enunciate indistinctly*) *word etc* mal articuler, ne pas articuler. **his speech was ~red, he ~red his words** il n'arrivait pas à articuler, il n'articulait pas.

3 **vi** *[sounds etc]* être *or* devenir indistinct.

▶**slur over vt fus** *incident, mistake, differences, discrepancies* passer sous silence, glisser sur.

slurp [slɜːp] 1 **vti** boire à grand bruit. 2 **n** slurp *m*.

slurry ['slʌrɪ] **n** gadoue *f*.

slush [slʌʃ] 1 **n** (*NonC*) (*snow*) neige fondante *or* fondue; (*mud*) gadoue *f*; (*fig: sentiment*) sensiblerie *f*. 2 **comp** ▶**slush fund** fonds *mpl* secrets, caisse *f* noire.

slushy ['slʌʃɪ] **adj** (*see* **slush**) *snow* fondant, fondu; *mud* détrempé; *streets* couvert de neige fondante *or* de neige fondue *or* de gadoue; (*fig*) *novel, film* fadement sentimental, fadasse*.

slut [slʌt] **n** (*dirty*) souillon *f*; (*immoral*) fille *f* (*pej*), salope‡ *f*.

sluttish ['slʌtɪʃ] **adj** *appearance* sale, de souillon; *morals, behaviour* de salope‡. **a ~ woman** une souillon.

sly [slaɪ] 1 **adj** (*wily*) rusé; (*secretive*) dissimulé; (*underhand*) sournois; (*mischievous*) espiègle, malin (*f* -igne). **a ~ look** un regard rusé *or* sournois *or* espiègle *or* par en dessous; **he's a ~ dog*** (*wily*) c'est une fine mouche *or* un fin matois; (*not as pure as he seems*) ce n'est pas un petit saint, ce n'est pas un enfant de chœur; *see* **fox.** 2 **comp** ▶**slyboots*** malin *m*, -igne *f*. 3 **n: on the ~** en cachette, en secret, en douce*; sournoisement (*pej*).

slyly ['slaɪlɪ] **adv** *plan, act* de façon rusée *or* dissimulée, sournoisement; *say, smile, suggest* sournoisement (*pej*); (*mischievously*) avec espièglerie; (*in secret*) en cachette, en secret, en douce*.

slyness ['slaɪnɪs] **n** (*see* **sly**) ruse *f*; dissimulation *f*; sournoiserie *f*; espièglerie *f*.

smack[1] [smæk] 1 **vi** (*lit, fig*) **to ~ of sth** sentir qch. 2 **n** a (*small taste*) léger *or* petit goût; (*fig*) soupçon *m*. b (*US Drugs sl*) héroïne *f*, (poudre *f*) blanche *f* (*sl*).

smack[2] [smæk] 1 **n** (*slap*) tape *f*, (*stronger*) claque *f*; (*on face*) gifle *f*; (*sound*) bruit sec, claquement *m*; (* *fig: kiss*) gros baiser (qui claque). **he gave the ball a good ~** il a donné un grand coup dans le ballon; (*fig: esp Brit*) **it was a ~ in the eye for them*** (*snub*) c'était une gifle pour eux; (*setback*) c'était un revers pour eux; (*fig: esp Brit*) **to have a ~ at doing sth*** essayer (un coup*) de faire qch; **I'll have a ~ at it** je vais essayer, je vais tenter le coup*.

2 **vt** *person* donner une tape *or* (*stronger*) une claque à; (*on face*) gifler. **to ~ sb's face** gifler qn, donner une paire de gifles à qn; **I'll ~ your bottom!** je vais te donner la fessée!, tu vas avoir la fessée!; **he ~ed the table (with his hand)** il a frappé sur la table (de la main); **to ~ one's lips** se lécher les babines.

3 **adv** (*) en plein. **~ in the middle** en plein milieu; **he kissed her ~ on the lips** il l'a embrassée en plein sur la bouche; **he ran ~ into the tree** il est rentré en plein *or* tout droit dans l'arbre.

smack[3] [smæk] **n** (*also* **fishing ~**) smack *m or* sémaque *m*.

smacker‡ ['smækəʳ] **n** (*kiss*) gros baiser, grosse bise*; (*blow*) grand coup (retentissant); (*Brit: pound*) livre *f*; (*US: dollar*) dollar *m*.

smacking ['smækɪŋ] 1 **n** fessée *f*. **to give sb a ~** donner une *or* la fessée à qn. 2 **adj: at a ~ pace** *or* **speed** à toute vitesse, à toute allure.

small [smɔːl] 1 **adj** a *child, table, town, quantity, organization, voice* petit; *person* petit, de petite taille; *family* petit, peu nombreux; *audience, population* peu nombreux; *income, sum* petit, modeste; *stock, supply* petit, limité; *meal* petit, léger; *garden, room* petit, de dimensions modestes; (*unimportant*) *mistake, worry, difficulty* petit, insignifiant, mineur (*f* -eure); (*pej: morally mean*) *person, mind* petit, bas (*f* basse), mesquin. **a ~ waist** une taille mince *or* svelte; **the ~est details** les moindres détails; **the ~est possible of books** le moins de livres possible; **a ~ proportion of the business comes from abroad** un pourcentage limité *or* restreint des affaires vient de l'étranger; **to grow** *or* **get ~er** *[income, difficulties, population, amount, supply]* diminuer; *[town, organization]* décroître; **to make ~er** *income, amount, supply* diminuer; *organization* réduire; *garden, object, garment* rapetisser; (*Typ*) **in ~ letters** en (lettres) minuscules *fpl*; (*euph*) **the ~est room** le petit coin; **he is a ~ eater** il ne mange pas beaucoup, il a un petit appétit; **~ shopkeeper/farmer** petit commerçant/cultivateur; **he felt ~ when he was told that ...** il ne s'est pas senti fier *or* il s'est senti tout honteux quand on lui a dit que ...; **to make sb feel ~** humilier qn, rabaisser qn; *see also* **4** *and* **hour, look, print, way** *etc.*

b (*in negative sense: little or no*) **to have ~ cause** *or* **reason to do** n'avoir guère de raisons de faire; **a matter of no ~ consequence** une affaire d'une grande importance *or* qui ne manque pas d'importance; *see* **wonder** *etc.*

2 **adv**: **to cut up ~** *paper* couper en tout petits morceaux; *meat* hacher menu.

3 **n** **a** **the ~ of the back** le creux des reins.

b (*Brit: underwear: npl*) **~s*** dessous *mpl*, sous-vêtements *mpl*.

4 **comp** ►**small ads** (*Brit Press*) petites annonces ►**small-arms** (*Mil*) armes portatives, petites armes ►**small barbel** (*Zool*) barbillon *m*, colinot *m or* colineau *m* ►**small beer:** (*Brit fig*) **it is small beer** c'est de la petite bière*; **he is small beer** il ne compte pas, il est insignifiant ►**small change** petite *or* menue monnaie ►**small claims court** (*Jur*) tribunal *m* d'instance (*s'occupant d'affaires mineures*) ►**small end** (*Aut*) pied *m* de bielle ►**small fry** menu *m* fretin; **he's just small fry** c'est du menu fretin, il ne compte pas, il est insignifiant ►**smallholder** (*Brit Agr*) ≃ petit cultivateur ►**smallholding** (*Brit Agr*) ≃ petite ferme (*de moins de deux hectares*) ►**small intestine** (*Anat*) intestin *m* grêle ►**small-minded** d'esprit bas, mesquin ►**small-mindedness** petitesse *f* d'esprit, mesquinerie *f* ►**small-mouth bass** (*Zool*) achigan *m* à petite bouche ►**small potatoes** (*US*) = **small beer** ►**smallpox** variole *f*, petite vérole ►**small-scale** **adj** peu important; *undertaking* de peu d'importance, de peu d'envergure; *map* à petite échelle ►**the small screen** (*TV*) le petit écran ►**small-size(d)** petit ►**small talk** (*NonC*) papotage *m*, menus propos; **he's got plenty of small talk** il a de la conversation, il a la conversation facile ►**small-time** **adj** peu important, de troisième ordre; **a small-time crook** un escroc à la petite semaine ►**small-timer*** moins *m* que rien, individu insignifiant ►**small-town** **adj** (*pej*) provincial, qui fait province; *see* **print 1b**.

smallish ['smɔːlɪʃ] **adj** (*see* **small 1a**) plutôt *or* assez petit (*or* modeste *etc*); assez peu nombreux.

smallness ['smɔːlnɪs] **n** *[person]* petite taille; *[hand, foot, object]* petitesse *f*; *[income, sum, contribution etc]* modicité *f*; (*small-mindedness*) petitesse (d'esprit), mesquinerie *f*.

smarm* [smɑːm] **vi** (*Brit*) flatter, flagorner. **to ~ over sb** flagorner qn, lécher les bottes* à qn, passer de la pommade* à qn.

smarmy* ['smɑːmɪ] **adj** (*Brit*) *person* flagorneur, lécheur*; *words, manner* obséquieux. **he's always so ~** ce qu'il est flagorneur! *or* lèche-bottes *inv!**

smart [smɑːt] **1** **adj** **a** (*not shabby*) *person, clothes* chic *inv*, élégant, qui a de l'allure; *hotel, shop, car, house* élégant; *neighbourhood, party, dinner* élégant, chic *inv*, select (*f inv*); (*fashionable*) à la mode, dernier cri *inv*. **she was looking very ~** elle était très élégante *or* très chic, elle avait beaucoup d'allure; **the ~ set** le grand monde, le beau monde; **the Washington/London ~ set** le tout-Washington/le tout-Londres; **it's considered ~ these days to do that** de nos jours on trouve que ça fait bien *or* chic de faire ça.

b *person* (*clever*) intelligent, habile, dégourdi*; (*shrewd*) astucieux, malin (*f* -igne); (*pej*) retors, roublard*; *deed, act* intelligent, astucieux; *answer* spirituel, bien envoyé. **a ~ lad***, (*US*) **a ~ guy*** un malin, un finaud; **he's trying to be ~** il fait le malin; **he's too ~ for me** il est beaucoup trop futé pour moi; **don't get ~ with me!*** ne la ramène pas!*; **he thinks it ~ to do that** il trouve (ça) bien *or* intelligent de faire cela; **that was ~ of you!, that was ~ work!** c'était futé de ta part! (*see also* **1c**).

c (*quick*) *pace* vif, rapide; *action* prompt. **that was ~ work!** tu n'as pas (*or* il n'a pas *etc*) perdu de temps! *or* mis longtemps! *or* traîné!; **look ~ (about it)!** remue-toi!*, grouille-toi!*; **a ~ rebuke** une verte semonce.

2 **comp** ►**smart aleck***, (*US also*) **smart ass*** (*pej*) bêcheur* *m*, -euse *f*, (Monsieur *or* Madame *or* Mademoiselle) je-sais-tout* *mf inv* ►**smart card*** (*credit card*) carte *f* à mémoire ►**smart money** (*US*) réserve *f* d'argent (*destinée à faire des investissements au moment opportun*).

3 **vi** **a** *[cut, graze]* faire mal, brûler; *[iodine etc]* piquer. **my eyes were ~ing** j'avais les yeux irrités *or* qui me brûlaient *or* qui me piquaient; **the smoke made his throat ~** la fumée lui irritait la gorge, la gorge lui cuisait *or* lui brûlait à cause de la fumée.

b (*fig*) être piqué au vif. **he was ~ing under the insult** il ressentait vivement l'insulte, l'insulte l'avait piqué au vif; **you'll ~ for this!** il vous en cuira!, vous me le payerez!

4 **npl** (*US: brains*) **~s*** jugeote* *f*.

smarten ['smɑːtn] **vt** = **smarten up 2**.

►**smarten up** **1** **vi** **a** (*make o.s. tidy etc*) *[person]* devenir plus élégant *or* soigné; *[town]* devenir plus élégant *or* pimpant. **you'd better smarten up for dinner** il faut que tu t'arranges (*subj*) (un peu) *or* que tu te fasses beau (*f* belle) pour le dîner. **b** (*speed up*) *[production, pace]* s'accélérer. **2** **vt sep** **a** (*tidy up*) *person* rendre plus élégant *or* plus soigné; *child* pomponner, bichonner; *house, room, town* (bien) arranger, rendre élégant *or* pimpant. **to smarten o.s. up** se faire beau (*f* belle) *or* élégant. **b** (*speed up*) accélérer.

smartly ['smɑːtlɪ] **adv** (*elegantly*) *dress* avec beaucoup de chic *or* d'élégance *or* d'allure; (*cleverly*) *act, say* habilement, astucieusement; (*quickly*) *move* promptement, vivement; *answer* du tac au tac. **he rebuked her ~** il lui a fait un reproche cinglant *or* une verte semonce.

smartness ['smɑːtnɪs] **n** (*NonC*) (*in appearance etc*) chic *m*, élégance *f*, allure *f*; (*cleverness*) intelligence *f*, habileté *f*, astuce *f*; (*pej*) roublardise *f*; (*quickness*) promptitude *f*, rapidité *f*.

smarty* ['smɑːtɪ] **n** (*also* **~-pants***) bêcheur* *m*, -euse* *f*, (Monsieur *or* Madame *or* Mademoiselle) je-sais-tout* *mf inv*.

smash [smæʃ] **1** **n** **a** (*sound*) fracas *m*; (*blow*) coup violent; (*Tennis etc*) smash *m*. **the ~ as the car hit the lamppost** le choc quand la voiture a percuté le réverbère; **the cup fell with a ~** la tasse s'est fracassée (en tombant) par terre; **he fell and hit his head a nasty ~ on the kerb** en tombant il s'est violemment cogné la tête contre le trottoir.

b (*also* **~-up***) (*accident*) accident *m*; (*Aut, Rail: collision*) collision *f*, tamponnement *m*; (*very violent*) télescopage *m*. **car/rail ~** accident de voiture/de chemin de fer.

c (*Econ, Fin: collapse*) effondrement *m* (financier), débâcle *f* (financière); (*St Ex*) krach *m*; (*bankruptcy*) faillite *f*; (*ruin*) ruine *f*, débâcle complète.

d = **smash hit**; *see* **2**.

e **whisky/brandy ~** whisky/cognac glacé à la menthe.

2 **comp** ►**smash-and-grab (raid)** cambriolage *m* (commis en brisant une devanture); **there was a smash-and-grab (raid) at the jeweller's** des bandits ont brisé la vitrine du bijoutier et raflé les bijoux ►**smash hit***: **it was a smash hit** cela a fait un malheur*, cela a été un succès foudroyant; **it was the smash hit of the year** c'était le succès de l'année ►**smash-up*** *see* **smash 1b**.

3 **adv** (*) **to run ~ into a wall** heurter un mur de front *or* de plein fouet, rentrer en plein dans un mur; **the cup fell ~ to the ground** la tasse s'est fracassée par terre; (*Fin*) **to go ~** faire faillite.

4 **vt** **a** (*break*) casser, briser; (*shatter*) fracasser. **I've ~ed my watch** j'ai cassé ma montre; **the waves ~ed the boat on the rocks** les vagues ont fracassé le bateau contre les rochers; **to ~ sth to pieces** *or* **to bits** briser qch en mille morceaux, mettre qch en miettes; **when they ~ed the atom*** quand on a désintégré *or* fissionné l'atome; **to ~ a door open** enfoncer une porte; **he ~ed the glass with the hammer, he ~ed the hammer through the glass** il a fracassé la vitre avec le marteau; **he ~ed his fist into Paul's face** il a envoyé *or* balancé* son poing dans la figure de Paul; (*Tennis*) **to ~ the ball** faire un smash, smasher; (*Tennis*) **he ~ed the ball into the net** il a envoyé son smash dans le filet.

b (*fig*) *spy ring etc* briser, détruire; *hopes* ruiner; *enemy* écraser; *opponent* battre à plate(s) couture(s), pulvériser*. (*Sport etc*) **he ~ed* the record in the high jump** il a pulvérisé* le record du saut en hauteur.

5 **vi** **a** se briser (en mille morceaux), se fracasser. **the cup ~ed against the wall** la tasse s'est fracassée contre le mur; **the car ~ed into the tree** la voiture s'est écrasée contre l'arbre; **his fist ~ed into my face** il a envoyé *or* balancé* son poing sur ma figure, il m'a assené son poing sur la figure.

b (*Fin*) *[person, firm]* faire faillite.

►**smash down** **vt sep** *door, fence* fracasser.

►**smash in** **vt sep** *door* enfoncer. **to smash sb's face in*** casser la gueule à qn*.

►**smash up** **1** **vt sep** *room, house, shop* tout casser dans, tout démolir dans; *car* accidenter, bousiller*. **he was smashed up* in a car accident** il a été grièvement blessé *or* sérieusement amoché* dans un accident de voiture. **2** **smash-up*** **n** *see* **smash 1b**.

smashed* [smæʃt] **adj** (*drunk*) bourré*, complètement paf* (*inv*); (*drugged*) défoncé*.

smasher* ['smæʃəʳ] **n** (*esp Brit*) (*in appearance*) **he's a ~** il est vachement* beau; **she's a ~** elle est vachement* jolie *or* bien roulée*; (*in character etc*) **to be a ~** être épatant* *or* vachement chouette*; **it's a ~** c'est épatant* *or* sensationnel* *or* formidable*.

smashing* ['smæʃɪŋ] **adj** (*esp Brit*) formidable*, du tonnerre*, terrible*. **they had a ~ time** ils se sont vachement* bien *or* formidablement* bien amusés.

smattering ['smætərɪŋ] **n** connaissances vagues *or* superficielles. **a ~ of** un petit nombre de; **he has a ~ of German** il sait un peu l'allemand, il sait quelques mots d'allemand; **I've got a ~ of maths** j'ai quelques connaissances vagues *or* quelques notions en maths.

smear [smɪəʳ] **1** **n** **a** (*mark*) trace *f*, (*longer*) traînée *f*; (*stain*) (légère) tache *f*, salissure *f*. **a long ~ of ink** une traînée d'encre; **there is a ~ on this page** il y a une légère tache *or* une salissure sur cette page, cette page est tachée *or* salie.

b (*sth said or written*) diffamation *f* (*on, against* de). **this ~ on his honour/reputation** cette atteinte à son honneur/sa réputation.

c (*Med*) frottis *m*, prélèvement *m*; *see* **cervical**.

2 **comp** ►**smear campaign** campagne *f* de diffamation ►**smear tactics** méthodes *fpl* diffamatoires ►**smear test** (*Med*) frottis *m* ►**smear word**: **it is a smear word** c'est un mot diffamatoire.

3 **vt** **a** **to ~ cream on one's hands, to ~ one's hands with cream** s'enduire les mains de crème; **he ~ed his face with mud, he ~ed mud on his face** il s'est barbouillé le visage de boue; **his hands were ~ed with ink** il avait les mains barbouillées *or* tachées d'encre, il avait des traînées d'encre sur les mains; **you've ~ed it all over the place** tu en a mis partout; **he ~ed butter on the slice of bread** il a étalé du beurre sur la tranche de pain.

b *page of print* maculer; *wet paint* faire une trace *or* une marque sur; *lettering* étaler (accidentellement); (*fig*) *reputation, integrity* salir, entacher, porter atteinte à. **to ~ sb** *[story, report]* porter atteinte à la réputation de qn; *[person]* calomnier qn.

c (*US* ‡: *defeat*) battre à plates coutures.

4 vi *[ink, paint]* se salir.

smeary ['smɪərɪ] adj *face* barbouillé; *printed page* plein de macules; *window* couvert de taches *or* de traînées; *ink, paint* sali.

smell [smel] (vb: pret, ptp **smelled** *or* **smelt**) 1 n (*sense of ~*) odorat *m*; *[animal]* odorat, flair *m*; (*odour*) odeur *f*; (*stench*) mauvaise odeur. **he has a keen sense of ~** il a l'odorat très développé, il a le nez très fin; **he has no sense of ~** il n'a pas d'odorat; **the mixture has no ~** le mélange est inodore *or* n'a pas d'odeur *or* ne sent rien; **a gas with no ~** un gaz inodore *or* sans odeur; **it has a nice/nasty ~** cela sent bon/mauvais; **what a ~ in here!** que ça sent mauvais ici!, ça pue ici!; **there was a ~ of burning in the room** il y avait une odeur de brûlé dans la pièce, la pièce sentait le brûlé; **to have a ~ at sth** *[person]* sentir qch, (*more carefully*) renifler qch; *[dog etc]* flairer *or* renifler qch.

2 comp ►**smelling salts** sels *mpl*.

3 vt sentir; (*sniff at*) sentir, renifler. **he could ~ *or* he smelt something burning** il sentait que quelque chose brûlait; **he smelt the meat to see if it was bad** il a senti *or* reniflé la viande pour voir si elle était encore bonne; **the dog could ~ *or* the dog smelt the bone** le chien a flairé *or* éventé l'os; **the dog smelt the bone suspiciously** le chien a flairé *or* reniflé l'os d'un air soupçonneux; (*fig*) **I ~ a rat!** je soupçonne quelque chose!, il y a anguille sous roche, il y quelque chose de louche là-dedans *or* là-dessous; **he ~ed danger and refused to go on** il a flairé *or* deviné *or* pressenti le danger et a refusé de continuer; **I (can) ~ danger!** je pressens un danger!

4 vi a **since the accident he cannot ~** depuis l'accident il n'a plus d'odorat; **to ~ at sth** *[person]* sentir *or* renifler qch; *[dog etc]* renifler *or* flairer qch.

b **that mixture doesn't ~ (at all)** ce mélange ne sent rien *or* n'a pas (du tout) d'odeur; **this gas doesn't ~** ce gaz est inodore; **these socks ~!** ces chaussettes sentent mauvais! *or* sentent!*; (*stink*) ces chaussettes puent!; **this room ~s!** cette pièce sent mauvais! *or* pue!; **his breath ~s** il a mauvaise haleine; **that ~s like chocolate** ça sent le chocolat, on dirait du chocolat; **to ~ of onions/burning** *etc* sentir l'oignon/le brûlé *etc*; **to ~ good *or* sweet** sentir bon; **to ~ bad** sentir mauvais; **to ~ foul** empester; **it ~s delicious!** ça embaume!; **it ~s dreadful!** ça pue!; **that deal ~s a bit*** cette affaire semble plutôt louche *or* ne semble pas très catholique*; (*fig*) **that idea ~s!**‡ cette idée ne vaut rien!, c'est une idée catastrophique!*; (*fig*) **I think he ~s!**‡ je trouve que c'est un sale type!*

►**smell out** vt sep a (*discover*) *[dog etc]* découvrir en flairant *or* en reniflant; *[person]* *criminal, traitor* découvrir, dépister; *treachery, plot* découvrir. b **it's smelling the room out** ça empeste la pièce.

smelliness ['smelɪnɪs] n (*NonC*) mauvaise odeur, (*stronger*) puanteur *f*.

smelly ['smelɪ] adj a qui sent mauvais, malodorant. **to be ~** sentir mauvais, (*stronger*) puer; **it's ~ in here** ça sent mauvais ici, ça sent* ici. b (‡ *fig: unpleasant*) *person, object, idea* moche*.

smelt[1] [smelt] pret, ptp of **smell**.

smelt[2] [smelt] n, pl ~ *or* ~s (*fish*) éperlan *m*.

smelt[3] [smelt] vt *ore* fondre; *metal* extraire par fusion.

smelter ['smeltəʳ] n haut-fourneau *m*.

smelting ['smeltɪŋ] n (*see* **smelt**[3]) fonte *f*; extraction *f* par fusion. **~ furnace** haut-fourneau *m*; **~ works** fonderie *f*.

smidgen*, smidgin* ['smɪdʒən] n: **a ~ of** (*gen*) un tout petit peu de; (*of truth*) un grain *or* un brin de, une once de.

smile [smaɪl] 1 n sourire *m*. **with a ~ on his lips** le sourire aux lèvres; **... he said with a ~ ...** dit-il en souriant; **... he said with a nasty ~ ...** dit-il en souriant méchamment *or* avec un mauvais sourire; **he had a happy ~ on his face** il avait un sourire heureux, il souriait d'un air heureux; **to give sb a ~** faire *or* adresser un sourire à qn, sourire à qn; **to be all ~s** être tout souriant *or* tout sourire; **take that ~ off your face!** arrête donc de sourire comme ça!; **I'll wipe *or* knock the ~ off his face!** il verra s'il a encore envie de sourire!, je vais lui faire passer l'envie de sourire!; *see* **raise, wear, wreathe.**

2 vi sourire (*at or to sb* à qn). **to ~ to oneself** sourire intérieurement; **to ~ sadly** avoir un sourire triste, sourire tristement *or* d'un air triste; **to keep smiling** garder le sourire; **he ~d at my efforts** il a souri de mes efforts; (*fig*) **fortune ~d (up)on him** la fortune lui sourit.

3 vt: **to ~ a bitter smile** avoir un sourire amer, sourire amèrement *or* avec amertume; **to ~ one's thanks** remercier d'un sourire.

smiling ['smaɪlɪŋ] adj souriant.

smilingly ['smaɪlɪŋlɪ] adv en souriant, avec un sourire.

smirch [smɜːtʃ] 1 vt (*lit*) salir, souiller; (*fig liter*) ternir, entacher. 2 n (*lit, fig*) tache *f*.

smirk [smɜːk] 1 n (*self-satisfied smile*) petit sourire satisfait *or* suffisant; (*knowing*) petit sourire narquois; (*affected*) petit sourire affecté. 2 vi sourire d'un air satisfait *or* suffisant *or* narquois *or* affecté.

smite [smaɪt] pret **smote**, ptp **smitten** 1 vt a (†† *or liter*) (*strike*) frapper (d'un grand coup); (*punish*) châtier (*liter*); (*fig*) *[pain]* déchirer; *[one's conscience]* tourmenter; *[light]* frapper. b (*fig*) **to be smitten with** *or* **by** *remorse, desire, urge* être pris de; *terror, deafness* être frappé de; (*) *sb's beauty* être enchanté par; (*) *idea* s'enthousiasmer pour; **he was really smitten* with her** il en était vraiment toqué* *or* amoureux. 2 n coup violent.

smith [smɪθ] n (*shoes horses*) maréchal-ferrant *m*; (*forges iron*) forgeron *m*; *see* **gold, silver** *etc*.

smithereens [ˌsmɪðəˈriːnz] npl: **to smash sth to ~** briser qch en mille morceaux, faire voler qch en éclats; **it lay in ~** cela s'était brisé en mille morceaux, cela avait volé en éclats.

smithy ['smɪðɪ] n forge *f*.

smitten ['smɪtn] ptp of **smite**.

smock [smɒk] 1 n (*dress, peasant's garment etc*) blouse *f*; (*protective overall*) blouse, sarrau *m*; (*maternity top*) blouse de grossesse; (*maternity dress*) robe *f* de grossesse. 2 vt faire des smocks à.

smocking ['smɒkɪŋ] n (*NonC*) smocks *mpl*.

smog [smɒg] n brouillard dense mélangé de fumée, smog *m*. **~ mask** masque *m* antibrouillard.

smoke [sməʊk] 1 n a (*NonC*) fumée *f*. (*Prov*) **there's no ~ without fire** il n'y a pas de fumée sans feu (*Prov*); **to go up in ~** *[house etc]* brûler; *[plans, hopes etc]* partir en fumée, tomber à l'eau; (*fig*) **the ~ is beginning to clear** on commence à y voir plus clair; (*Brit*) **the (Big) S~**‡ Londres; *see* **cloud, holy, puff** *etc*.

b **to have a ~** fumer une cigarette (*or* une pipe *etc*); **have a ~!** prends une cigarette!; **I've no ~s**‡ je n'ai plus de sèches‡.

c (*Drugs sl: marijuana*) marijuana *f*.

2 comp ►**smoke bomb** obus *m* fumigène ►**smoke detector** détecteur *m* de fumée ►**smoke-dry** vt fumer ►**smoke-filled** (*during fire*) rempli de fumée; (*from smoking etc*) enfumé; (*fig*) **smoke-filled room** salle *f* de réunion très animée, P.C. de crise ►**smokeless** *see* **smokeless** ►**smoke pollution** (*Ind*) pollution *f* par les fumées; (*tobacco*) pollution par la fumée de tabac ►**smoke screen** (*Mil*) rideau *m or* écran *m* de fumée; (*fig*) paravent *m* (*fig*) ►**smoke shop** (*US*) tabac *m* ►**smoke signal** signal *m* de fumée ►**smokestack** cheminée *f* (*extérieure*); **smokestack America** l'Amérique industrielle; **smokestack industries** (*Econ*) industries traditionnelles.

3 vi a *[chimney, lamp etc]* fumer.

b *[person]* fumer. **he ~s like a chimney*** il fume comme un sapeur.

4 vt a *cigarette etc* fumer. **he ~s cigarettes/a pipe** il fume la cigarette/la pipe.

b *meat, fish, glass* fumer. **~d salmon/trout** *etc* saumon *m*/truite *f etc* fumé(e); **~d glass** verre *m* fumé; **~d-glass** *window, windscreen etc* en verre fumé; *see* **haddock** *etc*.

►**smoke out** vt sep *insects, snake etc* enfumer; (*fig*) *traitor, culprit etc* dénicher, débusquer. **it was smoking the room out** c'était en train d'enfumer la pièce.

smokeless ['sməʊklɪs] adj sans fumée. **~ fuel** combustible non polluant; **~ zone** zone *f* où l'usage de combustibles solides est réglementé (*en vue de limiter la pollution atmosphérique*).

smoker ['sməʊkəʳ] n a (*person*) fumeur *m*, -euse *f*. **he has a ~'s cough** il a une toux de fumeur; *see* **heavy.** b (*Rail*) = **smoking car** *or* **compartment**; *see* **smoking 3.**

smokey ['sməʊkɪ] = **smoky.**

smoking ['sməʊkɪŋ] 1 n tabagisme *m*. **I hate ~** (*other people*) je déteste qu'on fume, je déteste le tabagisme; (*myself*) je déteste fumer; **"no ~"** "défense de fumer"; **campaign against ~** campagne *f* contre le tabac *or* le tabagisme; **~ can damage your health** le tabac est nuisible à *or* est mauvais pour la santé; **to give up ~** arrêter de fumer.

2 adj fumant. 3 comp ►**smoking compartment,** (*US*) **smoking car** (*Rail*) wagon *m* fumeurs ►**smoking jacket** veste *f* d'intérieur *or* d'appartement ►**smoking room** fumoir *m*.

smoky ['sməʊkɪ] 1 adj *atmosphere, room* enfumé; *fire* qui fume; *flame* fumeux; *surface* sali *or* noirci par la fumée; *stain* produit *or* laissé par la fumée; *glass* fumé; (*colour: also* **~ grey, ~-coloured**) gris fumée *inv*.

2 n (*US* ‡) motard *m* (de la police routière).

smolder ['sməʊldəʳ] vi (*US*) = **smoulder.**

smoldering ['sməʊldərɪŋ] adj (*US*) = **smouldering.**

smooch* [smuːtʃ] 1 vi (*kiss*) se bécoter*; (*pet*) se peloter‡; (*dance*) se frotter l'un contre l'autre. 2 n: **to have a ~** = **smooch 1.**

smoochy* ['smuːtʃɪ] adj *record, song* langoureux, romantique.

smooth [smuːð] 1 adj a *surface* lisse, uni, égal; *road* à la surface égale *or* unie; *sea, lake* lisse, plat; *stone* lisse, poli; *fabric* lisse, soyeux; (*Aut*) *tyre* lisse, qui n'a plus de stries; *hair* lisse; *skin* lisse, satiné, doux (*f* douce); *cheek, brow* lisse, sans rides; (*hairless*) *face, chin* glabre, lisse; *paste, sauce* homogène, onctueux; *flavour, wine, whisky* moelleux; *voice, sound* doux.

b *running of machinery etc* régulier, sans secousses, sans à-coups; *takeoff* en douceur; *flight* confortable; *sea, crossing, trip* par mer calme; *breathing, heartbeat, pulse* régulier; *verse, style* coulant, harmonieux; (*fig*) *day, life* calme, paisible, sans heurts. **~ running** *[machinery]* bon fonctionnement; *[organization, business]* bonne marche (*see also* **2**); (*fig*) **to make things** *or* **the way ~ for sb** aplanir les difficultés pour qn; (*fig*) **the way is now ~** il n'y a plus d'obstacles maintenant; (*Parl*) **the bill had a ~ passage** on n'a pas fait obstacle au projet de loi.

c (*suave*) *person* doucereux, mielleux; *manners* doucereux, mielleux, onctueux (*pej*). **he's a ~ operator*** il sait s'y prendre; **he is a ~ talker** c'est un beau parleur, il parle de façon insinuante *or* un peu trop persuasive; **I didn't like his rather ~ suggestion that** ... je n'ai pas aimé la façon insinuante *or* un peu trop persuasive dont il a suggéré que ... .

2 **comp** ►**smooth-faced** au visage glabre *or* lisse; (*fig: slightly pej*) trop poli, doucereux ►**smooth-running** **adj** *engine, machinery* qui fonctionne sans à-coups *or* à un rythme uniforme, qui tourne rond*; *car* qui ne secoue pas, qui ne donne pas d'à-coups; *business, organization, scheme* qui marche bien *or* sans heurts ►**smooth-shaven** rasé de près ►**smooth-spoken, smooth-talking, smooth-tongued** enjôleur, doucereux.

3 **vt** *sheets, cloth, piece of paper, skirt* lisser, défroisser; *pillow, hair, feathers* lisser; *wood* rendre lisse, planer; *marble* rendre lisse, polir. **to ~ cream into one's skin** faire pénétrer la crème dans la peau (en massant doucement); (*fig*) **to ~ sb's way** *or* **path to the top** faciliter le chemin de qn vers le top-niveau; **to ~ the way** *or* **path of an application/request** faciliter le passage d'une candidature/demande.

►**smooth back** **vt sep** *one's hair* ramener doucement en arrière; *sheet* rabattre en lissant *or* en défroissant.

►**smooth down** **vt sep** *hair, feathers* lisser; *sheet, cover* lisser, défroisser; (*fig*) *person* calmer, apaiser.

►**smooth out** **vt sep** *material, dress* défroisser; *wrinkles, creases* faire disparaître; (*fig*) *anxieties* chasser, faire disparaître; *difficulties* aplanir, faire disparaître.

►**smooth over** **vt sep** *soil* aplanir, égaliser; *sand* égaliser, rendre lisse; *wood* rendre lisse, planer. (*fig*) **to smooth things over** arranger les choses, aplanir des difficultés.

smoothie‡ ['smu:ðɪ] **n** (*pej*) beau parleur. **to be a ~** savoir un peu trop bien y faire‡, être un peu trop poli.

smoothly ['smu:ðlɪ] **adv** (*easily*) facilement; (*gently*) doucement; *move* sans secousses, sans à-coups; *talk* doucereusement. ... **he said ~** ... dit-il sans sourciller *or* doucereusement (*pej*); **everything is going ~** il n'y a pas de difficultés, tout marche comme sur des roulettes; **the journey went off ~** le voyage s'est bien passé *or* s'est passé sans incident.

smoothness ['smu:ðnɪs] **n** (*NonC: see* **smooth**) **a** qualité *f or* aspect *m* lisse *or* uni(e) *or* égal(e) *or* poli(e); douceur *f*; moelleux *m*; aspect glabre; *[road]* surface égale *or* unie; *[sea]* calme *m*. **the ~ of the tyre caused the accident** c'est parce que le pneu était complètement lisse que l'accident est arrivé. **b** rythme régulier; douceur *f*; régularité *f*; harmonie *f*; calme *m*. **c** (*slightly pej: suaveness*) caractère doucereux *or* mielleux; *[voice]* ton doucereux *etc*.

smoothy‡ ['smu:ðɪ] **n** = **smoothie**‡.

smorgasbord ['smɔ:gəs,bɔ:d] **n** (*Culin*) smorgasbord *m*, assortiment *m or* buffet *m* scandinave.

smote [sməʊt] **pret of smite**.

smother ['smʌðəʳ] **1 vt a** (*stifle*) *person* étouffer; *flames* étouffer, éteindre; *noise* étouffer, amortir; *scandal, feelings* étouffer, cacher; *criticism, doubt, yawn* étouffer, réprimer; *one's anger* contenir, réprimer.

b (*cover*) (re)couvrir (*with* de). **she ~ed the child with kisses** elle a couvert *or* dévoré l'enfant de baisers; **books ~ed in dust** des livres enfouis sous la poussière *or* tout (re)couverts de poussière; **a child ~ed in dirt** un enfant tout sale *or* tout couvert de crasse; **a face ~ed in make-up** une figure toute emplâtrée de maquillage; **he was ~ed in blankets** il était tout emmailloté de couvertures, il était tout emmitouflé dans ses couvertures.

2 **vi** *[person]* être étouffé, mourir étouffé.

3 **comp** ►**smother-love*** (*iro*) amour maternel possessif *or* dévorant.

smoulder, (*US*) **smolder** ['sməʊldəʳ] **vi** *[fire, emotion]* couver.

smouldering, (*US*) **smoldering** ['sməʊldərɪŋ] **adj** *fire, emotion* qui couve; *ashes, rubble* fumant; *expression, look* provocant, aguichant. **his ~ hatred** la haine qui couve (*or* couvait *etc*) en lui.

smudge [smʌdʒ] **1 n** (*on paper, cloth*) (légère) tache *f*, traînée *f*; (*in text, print etc*) bavure *f*, tache. **2 vt** *face* salir; *print* maculer; *paint* faire une trace *or* une marque sur; *lettering, writing* étaler accidentellement. **3 vi** se salir; se maculer; s'étaler.

smudgy ['smʌdʒɪ] **adj** *page* sali, taché, maculé; *writing* à moitié effacé; *face* sali, taché; *eyelashes, eyebrows* épais (*f* -aisse); *outline* brouillé, estompé.

smug [smʌg] **adj** *person, smile, voice* suffisant, avantageux; *optimism, satisfaction* béat. **don't be so ~!** ne fais pas le (*or* la) suffisant(e)!, ne prends pas ton air supérieur!

smuggle ['smʌgl] **1 vt** *tobacco, drugs* faire la contrebande de, passer en contrebande *or* en fraude. **to ~ in/out** *etc contraband* faire entrer/sortir *etc; goods* faire entrer/sortir *etc* en contrebande; (*fig*) *letters etc* faire entrer/ sortir *etc* clandestinement *or* en fraude; *person, animal* faire entrer/sortir *etc* clandestinement; **to ~ sth past** *or* **through the customs** passer qch en contrebande *or* sans le déclarer à la douane; **~d goods** contrebande *f*; **~d whisky** whisky *m* de contrebande. **2 vi** faire de la contrebande.

smuggler ['smʌgləʳ] **n** contrebandier *m*, -ière *f*.

smuggling ['smʌglɪŋ] **1 n** (*NonC*) *[goods]* contrebande *f* (*action*). **2 comp** ►**smuggling ring** réseau *m* de contrebandiers.

smugly ['smʌglɪ] **adv** d'un air *or* d'un ton suffisant *or* avantageux, avec suffisance.

smugness ['smʌgnɪs] **n** *[person]* suffisance *f*; *[voice, reply]* ton suffisant *or* avantageux.

smut [smʌt] **n** (*dirt*) petite saleté; (*soot*) flocon *m* de suie; (*in eye*) escarbille *f*; (*dirty mark*) tache *f* de suie; (*Bot*) charbon *m* du blé; (*NonC: obscenity*) obscénité(s) *f(pl)*, cochonneries* *fpl*. **programme full of ~** programme cochon* *or* salé.

smuttiness ['smʌtɪnɪs] **n** (*NonC: fig*) obscénité *f*, grossièreté *f*.

smutty ['smʌtɪ] **adj** *face, object* noirci, sali, taché; (*fig*) *joke, film* cochon*, sale, grossier.

snack [snæk] **1 n a** (*gen*) casse-croûte *m inv*. **to have a ~** casser la croûte, manger (un petit) quelque chose; **~ bar** snack-bar *m*, snack *m*. **b** (*party snack*) amuse-gueule *m*. **2 vi** = **to have a snack**; *see* **1a**.

snaffle ['snæfl] **1 n** (*also* **~ bit**) mors brisé. **2 vt** (*Brit *: steal*) chiper*, faucher*.

snafu‡ [snæ'fu:] (*US*) **1 adj** en pagaille*. **2 vt** mettre la pagaille* dans.

snag [snæg] **1 n** (*hidden obstacle*) obstacle caché; (*stump of tree, tooth etc*) chicot *m*; (*tear*) (*in cloth*) accroc *m*; (*in stocking*) fil tiré; (*fig: drawback*) inconvénient *m*, obstacle, difficulté *f*, écueil *m*. **there's a ~ in it somewhere** il y a sûrement un inconvénient *or* une difficulté *or* un os* là-dedans; **to run into** *or* **hit a ~** tomber sur un os* *or* sur un bec*; **that's the ~!** voilà la difficulté! *or* l'os!* *or* le hic!*; **the ~ is that you must** ... l'embêtant* c'est que vous devez ... .

2 **vt** *cloth* faire un accroc à; *stockings, tights* déchirer, accrocher (*on sth* contre qch), tirer un fil à.

3 **vi** *[rope etc]* s'accrocher (à quelque chose); *[stockings, tights etc]* s'accrocher.

snail [sneɪl] **1 n** escargot *m*. **at a ~'s pace** *walk* comme un escargot, à un pas de tortue; (*fig*) *progress, continue* à un pas de tortue. **2 comp** ►**snail shell** coquille *f* d'escargot.

snake [sneɪk] **1 n** serpent *m*; (*fig pej: person*) traître(sse) *m(f)*, faux frère. (*fig*) **~ in the grass** (*person*) ami(e) *m(f)* perfide, traître(sse) *m(f)*; (*danger*) serpent caché sous les fleurs; (*Pol Econ*) **the S~** le serpent (monétaire); *see* **grass, water** *etc*.

2 **comp** ►**snakebite** morsure *f* de serpent ►**snake charmer** charmeur *m* de serpent ►**snake eyes** (*US* ‡*: at dice*) double un *m*, deux *m* (aux dés) ►**snake fence** (*US*) barrière *f* en zigzag, barrière pliante ►**snake oil** (*US*) (*quack remedy*) remède *m* de charlatan; (*nonsense*) inepties *fpl*, foutaises* *fpl* ►**snake pit** fosse *f* aux serpents ►**snakes and ladders** (espèce *f* de) jeu *m* de l'oie ►**snakeskin** **n** peau *f* de serpent ◊ **comp** *handbag etc* en (peau de) serpent.

3 **vi** *[road, river]* serpenter (*through* à travers). **the road ~d down the mountain** la route descendait en lacets *or* en serpentant au flanc de la montagne; **the whip ~d through the air** la lanière du fouet a fendu l'air en ondulant.

►**snake along** **vi** *[road, river]* serpenter; *[rope, lasso etc]* fendre l'air en ondulant.

snaky ['sneɪkɪ] **adj** *place* infesté de serpents; (*fig*) *road, river* sinueux; (*pej*) *person* perfide; *cunning, treachery* de vipère, perfide.

snap [snæp] **1 n a** (*noise*) *[fingers, whip, elastic]* claquement *m*; *[sth breaking]* bruit sec, craquement *m*; *[sth shutting]* bruit sec, claquement; (*action*) *[whip]* claquement; *[breaking twig etc]* rupture *or* cassure soudaine. **he closed the lid with a ~** il a refermé le couvercle avec un bruit sec *or* d'un coup sec; **with a ~ of his fingers he** ... faisant claquer ses doigts il ...; **the dog made a ~ at my leg** le chien a essayé de me mordre la jambe; (*Met*) **a cold ~** une brève vague de froid, un coup de froid; (*fig*) **put some ~ into it!** allons, un peu de nerf!* *or* de dynamisme! *or* d'énergie!; **he has plenty of ~** il a du nerf*, il est très dynamique; *see* **brandy, ginger** *etc*.

b (*also* **~shot**) photo *f* (d'amateur); (*not posed*) instantané *m*. **here are our holiday ~s** voici nos photos de vacances; **it's only a ~** ce n'est qu'une photo d'amateur.

c (*US: ~ fastener*) pression *f*, bouton-pression *m*.

d (*Brit: Cards*) (sorte *f* de jeu de) bataille *f*.

e (*US : easy*) **it's a ~*** c'est du gâteau*, c'est facile comme tout, c'est un jeu d'enfant.

2 **adj a** (*sudden*) *vote, strike* subit, décidé à l'improviste; *judgment, answer, remark* fait sans réflexion, irréfléchi. **to make a ~ decision** (se) décider tout d'un coup *or* subitement.

b (*US *: easy*) facile comme tout, facile comme pas deux*.

3 **adv: to go ~** se casser net *or* avec un bruit sec.

4 **excl** (*gen*) tiens! on est *or* fait pareil!; (*Cards*) ≃ bataille!

5 **comp** ►**snapdragon** (*Bot*) gueule-de-loup *f* ►**snap fastener** (*US: on clothes*) pression *f*, bouton-pression *m*; (*on handbag, bracelet etc*) fermoir *m* ►**snap-in, snap-on** *hood, lining* amovible (à pressions)

►**snapshot** *see* **1b.**
6 vi a (*break*) se casser net *or* avec un bruit sec.
b *[whip, elastic, rubber band]* claquer. **to ~ shut/open** se fermer/ s'ouvrir avec un bruit sec *or* avec un claquement; **the rubber band ~ped back into place** l'élastique est revenu à sa place avec un claquement.
c **to ~ at sb** *[dog]* essayer de mordre qn; *[person]* parler à qn d'un ton brusque, rembarrer* qn; **the dog ~ped at the bone** le chien a essayé de happer l'os.
7 vt a (*break*) casser net *or* avec un bruit sec.
b *whip, rubber band etc* faire claquer. **to ~ one's fingers** faire claquer ses doigts; **to ~ one's fingers at** *person* faire la nique à; (*fig*) *suggestion, danger* se moquer de; **to ~ sth open/shut** ouvrir/fermer qch d'un coup sec *or* avec un bruit sec.
c (*Phot*) prendre un instantané de.
d **"shut up!" he ~ped** "silence!" fit-il avec brusquerie *or* d'un ton brusque.
►**snap back** vi a *[elastic, rope etc]* revenir en place brusquement *or* avec un claquement. b (*fig: after illness, accident*) se remettre très vite. c (*in answering*) répondre d'un ton brusque.
►**snap off** 1 vi se casser *or* se briser net. 2 vt sep casser net. (*fig*) **to snap sb's head off** rabrouer qn, rembarrer* qn, envoyer qn au diable.
►**snap out** 1 vi (*) **to snap out of** *gloom, lethargy, self-pity* se sortir de, se tirer de, ne pas se laisser aller à; *bad temper* contrôler, dominer; **snap out of it!** (*gloom etc*) secoue-toi!*, réagis!, ne te laisse pas aller!; (*bad temper*) contrôle-toi *or* domine-toi un peu! 2 vt sep *question/order* poser/lancer d'un ton brusque *or* cassant.
►**snap up** vt sep *[dog etc]* happer, attraper. (*fig*) **to snap up a bargain** sauter sur *or* se jeter sur une occasion, faire une bonne affaire; **they are snapped up as soon as they come on the market** on se les arrache *or* on saute dessus dès qu'ils sont mis en vente.
snappish [ˈsnæpɪʃ] adj *dog* toujours prêt à mordre; *person* hargneux, cassant; *reply, tone* brusque, mordant, cassant.
snappishness [ˈsnæpɪʃnɪs] n *[person]* caractère hargneux *or* cassant, (*temporary*) brusquerie *f*, mauvaise humeur; *[voice, reply]* ton brusque *or* mordant *or* cassant.
snappy* [ˈsnæpɪ] adj a *reply* prompt, bien envoyé; *phrase, slogan* qui a du punch*. **look ~!, make it ~!** grouille-toi!*, magne-toi!⁑ b = **snappish.**
snare [snɛəʳ] 1 n piège *m*; (*fig*) piège, traquenard *m*. (*fig*) **these promises are a ~ and a delusion** ces promesses ne servent qu'à allécher *or* appâter. 2 vt (*lit, fig*) attraper, prendre au piège. 3 comp ►**snare drum** tambour *m* à timbre.
snarky⁑ [ˈsnɑːkɪ] adj désagréable, de mauvais poil*, râleur*.
snarl[1] [snɑːl] 1 n *[dog]* grondement *m* féroce. **to give a ~ of fury** *[dog]* gronder férocement; *[person]* pousser un rugissement de fureur; **... he said with a ~ ...** dit-il d'une voix rageuse *or* avec hargne. 2 vi *[dog]* gronder en montrant les dents *or* férocement; *[person]* lancer un grondement (*at sb* à qn), gronder. **when I went in the dog ~ed at me** quand je suis entré le chien a grondé en montrant les dents. 3 vt *order* lancer d'un ton hargneux *or* d'une voix rageuse. **to ~ a reply** répondre d'un ton hargneux *or* d'une voix rageuse; **"no" he ~ed** "non" dit-il avec hargne *or* d'une voix rageuse.
snarl[2] [snɑːl] 1 n (*in wool, rope, hair etc*) nœud *m*, enchevêtrement *m*. (*fig*) **a traffic ~(-up)** un embouteillage. 2 comp ►**snarl-up** *[vehicles]* embouteillage *m*; (* *fig: in plans etc*) **there's been a snarl-up*** il y a eu du cafouillage* *or* quelques anicroches. 3 vi (*also* **~ up, get ~ed up**) *[wool, rope, hair]* s'emmêler, s'enchevêtrer; *[traffic]* se bloquer; (*) *[plans, programme]* cafouiller*. 4 vt (*also* **~ up**) *wool, rope, hair* emmêler, enchevêtrer.
►**snarl up** 1 vi = **snarl**[2] **3.** 2 vt sep a = **snarl**[2] **4.** b *traffic* bloquer; (*) *plans, programme* mettre la pagaille* dans. 3 **snarl-up** n *see* **snarl**[2] **2.**
snatch [snætʃ] 1 n a (*action*) geste vif (*pour saisir quelque chose*); (*fig*) *[jewellery, wages etc]* vol *m* (à l'arraché); *[child etc]* enlèvement *m*. **there was a jewellery/wages ~ yesterday** hier des voleurs se sont emparés de bijoux/de salaires.
b (*small piece*) fragment *m*. **a ~ of music/poetry** quelques mesures *fpl*/vers *mpl*; **a ~ of conversation** des bribes *fpl* *or* un fragment de conversation; **a few ~es of Mozart** quelques mesures *or* un fragment de Mozart; **to work in ~es** travailler de façon intermittente *or* par accès *or* par à-coups.
c (*Weightlifting*) arraché *n*.
2 vt (*grab*) *object* saisir, s'emparer (brusquement) de; *a few minutes' peace, a short holiday* réussir à avoir; *opportunity* saisir, sauter sur; *kiss* voler, dérober (*from sb* à qn); *sandwich, drink* avaler à la hâte; (*steal*) voler, chiper* (*from sb* à qn), saisir; (*kidnap*) enlever. **she ~ed the book from him** elle lui a arraché le livre; **he ~ed the child from the railway line just in time** il a saisi *or* attrapé *or* empoigné l'enfant et l'a tiré hors de la voie juste à temps; **to ~ some sleep/rest** (réussir à) dormir/se reposer un peu; **to ~ a meal** déjeuner (*or* dîner) à la hâte.
3 vi: **to ~ at** *object, end of rope etc* essayer de saisir, faire un geste vif pour saisir; *opportunity, chance* saisir, sauter sur.
►**snatch away, snatch off** vt sep enlever d'un geste vif *or* brusque.
►**snatch up** vt sep *object, child* saisir, ramasser vivement.
-snatcher [ˈsnætʃəʳ] n ending in comps *see* **cradle 3** *etc.*
snatchy* [ˈsnætʃɪ] adj *work* fait par à-coups, fait de façon intermittente; *conversation* à bâtons rompus.
snazzy* [ˈsnæzɪ] adj chouette*. **a ~ suit/hotel** un chouette* complet/ hôtel, un complet/un hôtel drôlement chouette*; **a ~ new car** une nouvelle voiture drôlement chouette*; **she's a ~ dresser** elle est toujours drôlement bien sapée⁑ *or* fringuée⁑.
sneak [sniːk] (vb: pret, ptp **sneaked** *or* (*US* *) **snuck**) 1 n (*: *underhand person*) faux jeton*; (*Brit Scol: telltale*) mouchard(e)* *m(f)*, rapporteur* *m*, -euse* *f*.
2 adj *attack, visit* furtif, subreptice. **~ preview** (*Cine*) avant-première *f*; (*gen*) avant-goût *m*; **~ thief** chapardeur* *m*, -euse* *f*.
3 vi a **to ~ in/out** *etc* entrer/sortir *etc* furtivement *or* subrepticement *or* à la dérobée; **he ~ed into the house** il s'est faufilé *or* s'est glissé dans la maison; **he ~ed up on me** il s'est approché de moi sans faire de bruit.
b (*Brit Scol* *) moucharder*, cafarder* (*on sb* qn).
4 vt a **I ~ed the letter onto his desk** j'ai glissé la lettre discrètement *or* furtivement *or* en douce* sur son bureau; **he ~ed the envelope from the table** il a enlevé furtivement *or* subrepticement l'enveloppe de la table; **to ~ a look at sth** lancer un coup d'œil furtif à qch, regarder qch à la dérobée; **he was ~ing* a cigarette** il était en train de fumer en cachette.
b (*: *pilfer*) chiper*, faucher⁑, piquer⁑.
►**sneak away, sneak off** vi s'esquiver, s'éclipser*, s'en aller furtivement.
sneaker* [ˈsniːkəʳ] n (chaussure *f* de) tennis *f* *or* basket *f*.
sneaking [ˈsniːkɪŋ] adj *dislike, preference* caché, secret (*f* -ète), inavoué. **I had a ~ feeling that ...** je ne pouvais m'empêcher de penser que ..., j'avais (comme qui dirait*) l'impression que ...; **to have a ~ suspicion that ...** soupçonner secrètement *or* à part soi que ...; **I have a ~ respect for him** je ne peux pas m'empêcher de le respecter.
sneaky* [ˈsniːkɪ] adj *person, character* sournois, dissimulé; *action* sournois.
sneer [snɪəʳ] 1 vi ricaner, sourire d'un air méprisant *or* sarcastique. **to ~ at sb** se moquer de qn d'un air méprisant; **to ~ at sth** tourner qch en ridicule. 2 n (*act*) ricanement *m*; (*remark*) remarque moqueuse, sarcasme *m*, raillerie *f*. **... he said with a ~ ...** dit-il d'un ton ricaneur *or* en ricanant *or* avec un sourire de mépris.
sneerer [ˈsnɪərəʳ] n ricaneur *m*, -euse *f*, moqueur *m*, -euse *f*, persifleur *m*, -euse *f*.
sneering [ˈsnɪərɪŋ] (*see* **sneer 2**) 1 adj ricaneur; moqueur, sarcastique, railleur. 2 n (*NonC*) ricanement(s) *m(pl)*; sarcasme(s) *m(pl)*, raillerie(s) *f(pl)*.
sneeringly [ˈsnɪərɪŋlɪ] adv d'un air *or* d'un ton ricaneur, avec un ricanement; de façon sarcastique, en raillant.
sneeze [sniːz] 1 n éternuement *m*. 2 vi éternuer. (*fig*) **it is not to be ~d at** ce n'est pas à dédaigner, il ne faut pas cracher dessus*.
snick [snɪk] 1 n petite entaille, encoche *f*. 2 vt *stick etc* faire une petite entaille *or* une encoche dans, entailler légèrement, encocher; (*Sport*) *ball* juste toucher.
snicker [ˈsnɪkəʳ] 1 n a *[horse]* petit hennissement. b = **snigger 1.** 2 vi a *[horse]* hennir doucement. b = **snigger 2.**
snide [snaɪd] adj (*sarcastic*) sarcastique, narquois; (*unpleasant, suggestive*) insidieux.
sniff [snɪf] 1 n (*from cold, crying etc*) reniflement *m*. **to give a ~** renifler (une fois); (*disdainfully*) faire la grimace *or* la moue; **... he said with a ~ ...** dit-il en reniflant; (*disdainfully*) ... dit-il en faisant la grimace *or* la moue; **I got a ~ of gas** j'ai senti l'odeur du gaz; **to have *or* take a ~ at sth** *[person]* renifler qch, (*suspiciously*) flairer qch; *[dog]* renifler *or* flairer qch; **one ~ of that is enough to kill you** il suffit de respirer cela une fois pour en mourir; (*fig*) **I didn't get a ~* of the whisky** je n'ai pas eu droit à une goutte de whisky.
2 vi (*from cold, crying*) renifler; (*disdainfully*) faire la grimace *or* la moue; *[dog]* renifler. **to ~ at sth** *[dog]* renifler *or* flairer qch; *[person]* renifler qch; (*fig*) faire la grimace *or* la moue à qch; **it's not to be ~ed at** ce n'est pas à dédaigner, il ne faut pas cracher dessus*.
3 vt *[dog etc]* renifler, flairer; *[person] food, bottle* renifler, sentir l'odeur de, (*suspiciously*) flairer; *air, perfume, aroma* humer; *drug* aspirer; *smelling salts* respirer; (*Pharm*) *inhalant etc* aspirer. **to ~ glue** respirer de la colle, sniffer⁑.
sniffle [ˈsnɪfl] 1 n (*sniff*) reniflement *m*; (*slight cold*) petit rhume de cerveau. **... he said with a ~ ...** dit-il en reniflant; **to have a ~ *or* the ~s*** avoir un petit rhume, être légèrement enrhumé. 2 vi *[person, dog]* renifler; (*from catarrh etc*) avoir le nez bouché, renifler.
sniffy* [ˈsnɪfɪ] adj a (*disdainful*) dédaigneux, pimbêche (*f only*). **to be ~ about sth** faire le *or* la dégoûté(e) devant qch. b (*smelly*) qui sent plutôt mauvais, qui a une drôle d'odeur.
snifter [ˈsnɪftəʳ] n a (⁑: *drink*) petit (verre d')alcool. **to have a ~** prendre un petit verre, boire la goutte*. b (*US: glass*) verre *m* ballon.
snigger [ˈsnɪgəʳ] 1 n rire *m* en dessous; (*cynical*) ricanement *m*. 2 vi pouffer de rire; (*cynically*) ricaner. **to ~ at** *remark, question* pouffer de

rire *or* ricaner en entendant; *sb's appearance etc* se moquer de; **stop ~ing**! arrête de rire *or* de ricaner comme ça!

sniggering ['snɪgərɪŋ] (*see* **snigger**) 1 **n** rires *mpl* en dessous; ricanements *mpl*. 2 **adj** qui n'arrête pas de pouffer de rire *or* de ricaner.

snip [snɪp] 1 **n** a (*cut*) petit coup (de ciseaux *etc*), petite entaille; (*small piece*) petit bout (*d'étoffe etc*), échantillon *m*. b (*Brit* *: *bargain*) bonne affaire, (bonne) occasion *f*; (*Horse Racing*) gagnant *m* sûr. 2 **vt** couper (à petits coups de ciseaux *etc*). 3 **vi**: **to ~ at sth** donner des petits coups dans qch.

►**snip off vt sep** couper *or* enlever *or* détacher (à coups de ciseaux *etc*).

snipe [snaɪp] 1 **n, pl ~** *or* **~s** (*Orn*) bécassine *f*. 2 **vi** (*shoot*) tirer (en restant caché), canarder*. **to ~ at sb/sth** (*shoot*) canarder* qn/qch; (*fig: verbally*) critiquer qn/qch par en dessous *or* sournoisement.

sniper ['snaɪpəʳ] **n** tireur *m* isolé.

snippet ['snɪpɪt] **n** *[cloth, paper]* petit bout; *[conversation, news, information]* fragment *m*, bribes *fpl*.

snitch‡ [snɪtʃ] 1 **vi** moucharder* (*on sb* qn). 2 **vt** chiper*, chaparder*, piquer‡. 3 **n** (*nose*) pif‡ *m*; (*US: telltale*) mouchard(e)* *m(f)*, rapporteur* *m*, -euse* *f*. (*fig*) **it's a ~**! (*easy job*) c'est un jeu d'enfant!, c'est du billard!‡; (*bargain*) c'est une bonne affaire!, c'est une occasion!

snivel ['snɪvl] 1 **vi** (*whine*) pleurnicher, larmoyer; (*sniff*) renifler; (*have a runny nose*) avoir le nez qui coule, avoir la morve au nez (*pej*). 2 **n** pleurnicherie(s) *f(pl)*, larmoiement(s) *m(pl)*; reniflement(s) *m(pl)*.

sniveler ['snɪvləʳ] **n** (*US*) = **sniveller**.

sniveling ['snɪvlɪŋ] **adj** (*US*) = **snivelling**.

sniveller ['snɪvləʳ] **n** pleurnicheur *m*, -euse *f*.

snivelling ['snɪvlɪŋ] 1 **adj** pleurnicheur, larmoyant. 2 **n** pleurnicherie(s) *f(pl)*, larmoiement(s) *m(pl)*, reniflement(s) *m(pl)*.

snob [snɒb] **n** snob *mf*. **he's a terrible ~** il est terriblement snob; *[lowly placed person]* il se laisse impressionner par *or* il est à plat ventre devant les gens importants; **she's a musical ~** c'est une snob en matière de musique.

snobbery ['snɒbərɪ] **n** snobisme *m*.

snobbish ['snɒbɪʃ] **adj** snob *inv*; *lowly placed person* très impressionné par les gens importants (*or* riches *etc*); *accent, manner, district* snob *inv*.

snobbishness ['snɒbɪʃnɪs] **n** snobisme *m*.

snobby* ['snɒbɪ] **adj** snob *inv*.

snog‡ [snɒg] (*Brit*) 1 **vi** se bécoter*. 2 **n**: **to have a ~** se bécoter*.

snood [snu:d] **n** résille *f*.

snook[1] [snu:k] **n, pl ~** *or* **~s** (*fish*) brochet *m* de mer.

snook[2] [snu:k] **n** *see* **cock 2b**.

snooker ['snu:kəʳ] 1 **n** (*game*) snooker *m*, ≃ jeu *m* de billard; (*shot*) snooker *m*. 2 **vt** (*lit*) faire un snooker; (*US: hoodwink*) tromper, avoir*. (*Brit* ‡: *be in difficulty*) **to be ~ed** être coincé*, être dans une situation difficile.

snoop [snu:p] 1 **n** a **to have a ~ around** jeter un coup d'œil discret; **I had a ~ around the kitchen** j'ai fureté discrètement *or* sans être vu dans la cuisine. b = **snooper**. 2 **vi** se mêler des affaires des autres. **to ~ (around)** rôder *or* fureter *or* fouiller en essayant de passer inaperçu; **he's been ~ing (around) here again** il est revenu fourrer son nez* par ici; **to ~ on sb** surveiller qn, espionner qn; **he was ~ing into her private life** il fourrait son nez* dans *or* il se mêlait de sa vie privée.

snooper ['snu:pəʳ] **n** (*pej*) *personne qui fait une enquête furtive sur quelqu'un*. **all the ~s from the Ministry** tous les espions du ministère, tous les inspecteurs du ministère qui fourrent leur nez* partout; **he's a terrible ~** il met son nez partout.

snoot* [snu:t] **n** pif‡ *m*, nez *m*.

snooty* ['snu:tɪ] **adj** snob *inv*, prétentieux, hautain. **to be ~** se donner de grands airs.

snooze* [snu:z] 1 **n** petit somme, roupillon* *m*. **afternoon ~** sieste *f*; **to have a ~** = **to snooze**; *see* **2**. 2 **vi** sommeiller, piquer un roupillon*; faire la sieste.

snore [snɔ:ʳ] 1 **n** ronflement *m* (*d'un dormeur*). 2 **vi** ronfler.

snorer ['snɔ:rəʳ] **n** ronfleur *m*, -euse *f*.

snoring ['snɔ:rɪŋ] **n** (*NonC*) ronflement(s) *m(pl)*.

snorkel ['snɔ:kl] 1 **n** *[submarine]* schnorchel *m*; *[swimmer]* tube *m* respiratoire. 2 **vi** nager avec un tube respiratoire.

snort [snɔ:t] 1 **n** a *[person]* grognement *m*; *[horse etc]* ébrouement *m*. b (‡) = **snorter b**. c (*Drugs sl*) prise *f*. 2 **vi** a *[horse etc]* s'ébrouer; *[person]* (*angrily, contemptuously*) grogner, ronchonner; (*laughing*) s'étrangler de rire. b (*Drugs sl*) renifler *or* sniffer *or* priser de la drogue. 3 **vt** a (*say*) (*angrily etc*) grogner, dire en grognant; (*laughing*) dire en s'étranglant de rire. b (*Drugs sl*) renifler, sniffer‡, priser.

snorter‡ ['snɔ:təʳ] **n** a **a ~ of a question/problem** une question/un problème vache‡; **a ~ of a game** un match formidable*; **a ~ of a storm** une tempête terrible. b (*drink*) petit (verre d')alcool. **to have a ~** prendre un petit verre, boire la goutte*.

snot* [snɒt] **n** a (*NonC: in nose*) morve *f*. b (*: *insolent person*) morveux‡ *m*, -euse *f*.

snotty* ['snɒtɪ] 1 **adj** *nose* qui coule; *face* morveux; *child* morveux, qui a le nez qui coule. 2 **comp** ►**snotty-faced*** morveux, qui a le nez qui coule ►**snotty-nosed*** (*lit*) = **snotty-faced***; (*fig*) morveux* (*fig*). 3 **n** (*midshipman*) midshipman *m*, ≃ enseigne *m* de vaisseau de deuxième classe, aspirant *m*.

snout [snaʊt] **n** a (*gen*) museau *m*; *[pig]* museau, groin *m*; (* *pej*) *[person]* pif‡ *m*. b (*Prison sl: NonC*) tabac *m*, perlot‡ *m*.

snow [snəʊ] 1 **n** a neige *f*. **hard/soft ~** neige dure/molle; **the eternal ~s** les neiges éternelles; *see* **fall, white** *etc*.

b (*fig*) (*on TV screen*) neige *f*.

c (*Culin*) **apple** *etc* **~** purée *f* de pommes *etc* (*aux blancs d'œufs battus en neige*).

d (*Drugs sl*) (*cocaine*) neige *f* (*sl*); (*heroin*) blanche *f* (*sl*).

2 **comp** ►**snowball** *see* **snowball** ►**snow bank** talus *m* de neige, congère *f* ►**snowbelt** (*US*) régions *fpl* neigeuses ►**snow-blind**: **to be snow-blind** souffrir de *or* être atteint de la cécité des neiges ►**snow blindness** cécité *f* des neiges ►**snow blower** chasse-neige *m inv* à soufflerie, souffleuse *f* (*Can*) ►**snowboard n** surf *m* des neiges ◊ **vi** faire du surf sur neige ►**snowboarding** surf *m* sur neige ►**snowboot** (*Ski*) après-ski *m* ►**snowbound** *road, country* complètement enneigé; *village, house, person* bloqué par la neige ►**snow buggy** skidoo *m*, autoneige *f* ►**snow bunny*** (*US: girl*) minette *f* de station de ski ►**snow cap** couronne *f or* couverture *f* de neige ►**snow-capped** couronné de neige ►**snowcat** (*Aut*) autoneige *f*; (*Ski*) snowcat *m* ►**snow-clad, snow-covered** (*liter*) enneigé, enfoui sous la neige ►**snowdrift** congère *f*, amoncellement *m* de neige ►**snowdrop** (*Bot*) perce-neige *m inv* ►**snowfall** chute *f* de neige ►**snowfield** champ *m* de neige ►**snowflake** flocon *m* de neige ►**snow goose** oie *f* des neiges ►**snow job***: (*US*) **it's a snow job** c'est du baratin*; **to give sb a snow job** baratiner* qn ►**snow leopard** léopard *m* des neiges, once *f* ►**snow line** limite *f* des neiges (éternelles) ►**snowman** bonhomme *m* de neige (*see* **abominable**) ►**snowmobile** (*US*) = **snowcat** ►**snowplough,** (*US*) **snowplow** chasse-neige *m inv* (*also Ski*); (*Ski*) **snowplough (turn)** stem *m* ►**snow report** (*Met*) bulletin *m* d'enneigement ►**the Snow Queen** (*Myth*) la Reine des neiges ►**snowshoe** raquette *f* (*pour marcher sur la neige*) ►**snowslide** (*US*) avalanche *f* ►**snowstorm** tempête *f* de neige ►**snowsuit** combinaison *f or* ensemble *m* matelassé(e) ►**snow tyre** (*Brit*), **snow tire** (*US*) pneu-neige *m*, pneu clouté ►**snow-white** blanc (*f* blanche) comme neige, d'une blancheur de neige ►**Snow White (and the Seven Dwarfs)** Blanche-Neige *f* (et les sept nains).

3 **vi** neiger. **it is ~ing** il neige, il tombe de la neige.

4 **vt** (*US* ‡: *charm glibly*) avoir qn au charme*. **she ~ed**‡ **him into believing that he would win** elle a si bien su l'enjôler qu'il a cru qu'il allait gagner.

►**snow in vt** (*Brit*) (*pass only*) **to be snowed in** être bloqué par la neige.

►**snow under vt** (*fig: pass only*) **he was snowed under with work** il était complètement submergé *or* débordé de travail, il avait tellement de travail qu'il ne savait pas où donner de la tête; **to be snowed under with letters/offers** être submergé de lettres/d'offres, recevoir une avalanche de lettres/d'offres.

►**snow up vt** (*Brit*) (*pass only*) **to be snowed up** *[road]* être complètement enneigé, être bloqué par la neige; *[village, farm, person]* être bloqué par la neige.

snowball ['snəʊbɔ:l] 1 **n** boule *f* de neige. **it hasn't got a ~'s chance in hell*** ça n'a pas l'ombre d'une chance; **~(ing) effect** effet *m* boule de neige; **~ fight** bataille *f* de boules de neige. 2 **vt** lancer des boules de neige à, bombarder de boules de neige. 3 **vi** (*lit*) se lancer des *or* se bombarder de boules de neige; (*fig*) *[project etc]* faire boule de neige. (*fig*) **~ing costs** coûts qui montent en flèche; *see also* **1**.

Snowdon ['snəʊdən] **n** (*Brit*) le (mont) Snowdon.

Snowdonia [snəʊ'dəʊnɪə] **n** le massif *or* le parc national du Snowdon.

snowy ['snəʊɪ] **adj** *weather, valley, climate, region* neigeux; *countryside, hills, roof* enneigé, couvert de neige; *day etc* de neige; (*fig*) (*also* **~ white**) *linen* neigeux; *hair, beard* de neige. **it was very ~ yesterday** il a beaucoup neigé hier; **~ owl** harfang *m*.

SNP [esen'pi:] **n** (*Brit Pol*) (**abbr of Scottish National Party**) *see* **Scottish**.

Snr. (*esp US*) **abbr of senior**.

snub[1] [snʌb] 1 **n** rebuffade *f*. 2 **vt** *person* snober; *offer* repousser, rejeter. **to be ~bed** essuyer une rebuffade.

snub[2] [snʌb] **adj** *nose* retroussé, camus (*pej*). **~-nosed** au nez retroussé *or* camus (*pej*).

snuck* [snʌk] (*US*) **pret, ptp of sneak**.

snuff[1] [snʌf] 1 **n** tabac *m* à priser. **pinch of ~** prise *f*; **to take ~** priser. 2 **comp** ►**snuffbox** tabatière *f*. 3 **vti** = **sniff 2, 3**.

snuff[2] [snʌf] **vt** *candle* moucher. (*Brit euph: die*) **to ~ it**‡ mourir, claquer, casser sa pipe*.

►**snuff out** 1 **vi** (‡: *die*) mourir, casser sa pipe*. 2 **vt sep** a *candle* moucher. b *interest, hopes, enthusiasm, sb's life* mettre fin à. c (‡: *kill*) zigouiller‡.

snuffer ['snʌfəʳ] **n** (*also* **candle-~**) éteignoir *m*. **~s** mouchettes *fpl*.

snuffle ['snʌfl] 1 **n** a = **sniffle 1**. b **to speak in a ~** parler du nez *or* d'une voix nasillarde, nasiller. 2 **vi** a = **sniffle 2**. b parler (*or* chanter) d'une voix nasillarde, nasiller. 3 **vt** dire *or* prononcer d'une voix nasillarde.

snug [snʌg] 1 adj (*cosy*) *room, house* confortable, douillet; *bed* douillet; *garment* (*cosy*) douillet, moelleux et chaud; (*close-fitting*) bien ajusté; (*compact*) *boat, cottage* petit mais confortable, bien agencé; (*safe etc*) *harbour* bien abrité; *hideout* très sûr; (*fig*) *income etc* gentil, confortable. **it's a ~ fit** *[garment]* c'est bien ajusté; *[object in box etc]* cela rentre juste bien; **it's nice and ~ here** il fait bon ici; **he was ~ in bed** il était bien au chaud dans son lit; **to be as ~ as a bug in a rug*** être bien au chaud, être douillettement installé (*or* couché *etc*).
2 n (*Brit*) = **snuggery.**

snuggery ['snʌgərɪ] n (*Brit*) (*gen*) petite pièce douillette *or* confortable; (*in pub*) petite arrière-salle.

snuggle ['snʌgl] 1 vi se blottir, se pelotonner (*into sth* dans qch, *beside sb* contre qn). 2 vt *child etc* serrer *or* attirer contre soi.

►**snuggle down** vi se blottir, se pelotonner (*beside sb* contre qn); se rouler en boule. **snuggle down and go to sleep** installe-toi bien confortablement et dors.

►**snuggle together** vi se serrer *or* se blottir l'un contre l'autre.

►**snuggle up** vi se serrer, se blottir (*to sb* contre qn).

snugly ['snʌglɪ] adv chaudement, confortablement, douillettement. **~ tucked in** bien au chaud dans ses couvertures, bordé bien au chaud; **to fit ~** *[garment]* être bien ajusté; *[object in box etc]* rentrer juste bien.

so [səʊ] 1 adv a (*degree: to such an extent*) si, tellement, aussi. (*liter*) **oh ~ easy/quickly** tellement facile/rapidement; **is it really ~ tiring?** est-ce vraiment si *or* tellement fatigant?, est-ce vraiment aussi fatigant (que cela)?; **do you really need ~ long?** vous faut-il vraiment si longtemps *or* tellement de temps *or* aussi longtemps (que cela)?; **~ early** si tôt, tellement tôt, d'aussi bonne heure; **~ ... that** si *or* tellement ... que; **he was ~ clumsy (that) he broke the cup, he broke the cup he was ~ clumsy*** il était si *or* tellement maladroit qu'il a cassé la tasse; **the body was ~ burnt that it was unidentifiable** *or* **burnt as to be unidentifiable** le cadavre était brûlé à un point tel *or* à (un) tel point qu'il était impossible de l'identifier; **he ~ loves her that he would give his life for her†** il l'aime tant *or* tellement *or* à un point tel qu'il donnerait sa vie pour elle; **~ ... as to** + *infin* assez ... pour + *infin*; **he was ~ stupid as to tell her what he'd done** il a eu la stupidité de *or* il a été assez stupide pour lui raconter ce qu'il avait fait; **he was not ~ stupid as to say that to her** il n'a pas été bête au point de lui dire cela, il a eu l'intelligence de ne pas lui dire cela; (*frm*) **would you be ~ kind as to open the door?** auriez-vous l'amabilité *or* la gentillesse *or* l'obligeance d'ouvrir la porte?; **not ~ ... as** pas si *or* aussi ... que; **he is not ~ clever as his brother** il n'est pas aussi *or* si intelligent que son frère; **it's not ~ big as all that!** ce n'est pas si grand que ça!; **it's not ~ big as I thought it would be** ce n'est pas aussi grand que je le pensais *or* que je l'imaginais; **it's not nearly ~ difficult as you think** c'est loin d'être aussi difficile que vous le croyez; **it's not ~ early as you think** il n'est pas aussi *or* si tôt que vous le croyez; **he's not ~ good a teacher as his father** il n'est pas aussi bon professeur que son père, il ne vaut pas son père comme professeur; **he's not ~ stupid as he looks** il n'est pas aussi *or* si stupide qu'il en a l'air.

b (*so as to, so that ...*) **~ as to do** afin de faire, pour faire; **he hurried ~ as not to be late** il s'est dépêché pour ne pas être *or* afin de ne pas être en retard; **~ that** (*purpose*) pour + *infin*, afin de + *infin*, pour que + *subj*, afin que + *subj*; (*result*) si bien que + *indic*, de (telle) sorte que + *indic*; **I'm going early ~ that I'll get a ticket** j'y vais tôt pour obtenir *or* afin d'obtenir un billet; **I brought it ~ that you could read it** je l'ai apporté pour que *or* afin que vous le lisiez; **he arranged the timetable ~ that the afternoons were free** il a organisé l'emploi du temps de façon à laisser les après-midi libres *or* de telle sorte que les après-midi étaient libres; **he refused to move, ~ that the police had to carry him away** il a refusé de bouger, si bien que *or* de sorte que les agents ont dû l'emporter de force.

c (*very, to a great extent*) si, tellement. **I'm ~ tired!** je suis si *or* tellement fatigué!; **I'm ~ very tired!** je suis vraiment si *or* tellement fatigué!; **there's ~ much to do** il y a tellement *or* tant (de choses) à faire; **his speech was ~ much nonsense** son discours était complètement stupide; **thanks ~ much*, thanks ever ~‡** merci bien *or* beaucoup *or* mille fois; **it's not ~ very difficult!** cela n'est pas si difficile que ça!; **he who ~ loved France** lui qui aimait tant la France; *see also* **ever.**

d (*manner: thus, in this way*) ainsi, comme ceci *or* cela, de cette façon. **you should stand (just** *or* **like) ~** vous devriez vous tenir ainsi *or* comme ceci, voici comment vous devriez vous tenir; **he likes everything (to be) just ~** il aime que tout soit fait d'une certaine façon *or* fait comme ça et pas autrement*, il est très maniaque; **as A is to B ~ A is to D** C est à D ce que A est à B; **as he failed once ~ he will fail again** il échouera comme il a déjà échoué; **you don't believe me but it is ~** vous ne me croyez pas mais il en est bien ainsi; **~ it was that ...** c'est ainsi que ...; (*frm*) **~ be it** soit; **it ~ happened that ...** il s'est trouvé que ...; (*frm, Jur etc*) **~ help me God!** que Dieu me vienne en aide!

e (*unspecified amount*) **how tall is he? —** (*accompanied by gesture*) **oh, about ~ tall** quelle taille fait-il? — oh, à peu près (grand) comme ça; **~ much per head** tant par tête; **they just sat there like ~ many dummies** ils se tenaient là comme des pantins; **how long will it take? — a week or ~** combien de temps cela va-t-il prendre? — une semaine environ *or* à peu près; **twenty or ~** à peu près vingt, environ vingt, une vingtaine.

f (*used as substitute for phrase, word etc*) **~ saying ...** ce disant ..., sur ces mots ...; **~ I believe** c'est ce que je crois, c'est ce qu'il me semble; **is that ~?** pas possible?, tiens!; (*iro*) vraiment?, vous croyez?, pensez-vous!; **that is ~** c'est bien ça, c'est exact, c'est bien vrai; **if that is ~ ...** s'il en est ainsi ...; **if ~** si oui; **perhaps ~** peut-être bien (que oui), cela se peut; **just ~!, quite ~!** exactement!, tout à fait!, c'est bien ça!; **I told you ~ yesterday** je vous l'ai dit hier; **I told you ~!** je vous l'avais bien dit!; **~ it seems!** à ce qu'il paraît!; **he certainly said ~** il l'a bien dit, il a bien dit ça; **please do ~** faites-le, faites ainsi; **I think ~** je (le) crois, je (le) pense; **I hope ~** (*answering sb*) j'espère que oui; (*agreeing with sb*) je l'espère, j'espère bien; **... only more ~** ... mais encore plus; **how ~?** comment (ça se fait)?; **why ~?** pourquoi (donc)?; **he said they would be there and ~ they were** il a dit qu'ils seraient là, et en effet ils y étaient; **~ do I!, ~ have I!, ~ am I!** *etc* moi aussi!; **he's going to bed and ~ will I** il va se coucher et moi aussi *or* et je vais en faire autant; **if you do that ~ will I** si tu fais ça, j'en ferai autant; **I'm tired — ~ am I!** je suis fatigué — moi aussi! *or* et moi donc!; **he said he was French — ~ he did!** il a dit qu'il était français — mais oui (c'est vrai)! *or* en effet!; **it's raining — ~ it is!** il pleut — en effet! *or* c'est vrai!; **I want to see that film — ~ you shall!** je veux voir ce film — eh bien tu le verras!

g (*phrases*) **I didn't say that! — you did SO!*** je n'ai pas dit ça! — mais si tu l'as dit! *or* c'est pas vrai* tu l'as dit!; **~ to speak, ~ to say** pour ainsi dire; **and ~ forth, and ~ on (and ~ on** *or* **and ~ forth)** et ainsi de suite; **~ long!*** au revoir!, à bientôt!, à un de ces jours!; **I'm not going, ~ there!** je n'y vais pas, voilà!; *see* **far, many, much.**

2 conj a (*therefore*) donc, par conséquent. **he was late ~ he missed the train** il est arrivé en retard, donc il a *or* par conséquent il a *or* aussi a-t-il (*liter*) manqué le train; **the roads are busy ~ be careful** il y a beaucoup de circulation, alors fais bien attention.

b (*exclamatory*) **~ there he is!** le voilà donc!; **~ you're selling it?** alors vous le vendez?; **~ he's come at last!** il est donc enfin arrivé!; **and ~ you see ...** alors comme vous voyez ...; **I'm going home — ~?** je rentre — (bon) et alors?; **~ (what)?*** (bon) et alors?, et après?; (*dismissively*) bof.

3 comp ►**so-and-so: Mr So-and-so*** Monsieur un tel; **Mrs So-and-so*** Madame une telle; **then if so-and-so says ...** alors si quelqu'un *or* Machin Chouette* dit ...; **he's an old so-and-so*** c'est un vieux schnock‡; **if you ask me to do so-and-so** si vous me demandez de faire ci et ça ►**so-called** soi-disant *inv*, prétendu ►**so-so*** comme ci comme ça, couci-couça*; **his work is only so-so** son travail n'est pas fameux*.

s/o (*Banking*) (abbr of **standing order**) *see* **standing.**

soak [səʊk] 1 n a **to give sth a (good) ~** (bien) faire tremper qch, (bien) laisser tremper qch; **the sheets are in ~** les draps sont en train de tremper.

b (‡: *drunkard*) soûlard* *m*, poivrot‡ *m*.

2 vt a faire *or* laisser tremper (*in* dans). **to be/get ~ed to the skin** être trempé/se faire tremper jusqu'aux os *or* comme une soupe*; **to ~ o.s. in the bath** faire trempette dans la baignoire; **bread ~ed in milk** pain imbibé de lait *or* qui a trempé dans du lait; (*fig*) **he ~ed himself in the atmosphere of Paris** il s'est plongé dans l'atmosphère de Paris.

b (‡: *take money from*) (*by overcharging*) estamper*; (*by taxation*) faire payer de lourds impôts à. **the government's policy is to ~ the rich** la politique du gouvernement est de faire casquer* les riches.

3 vi a tremper (*in* dans). **to put sth in to ~** faire tremper qch, mettre qch à tremper.

b (‡: *drink*) boire comme une éponge, avoir la dalle en pente*.

4 comp ►**soak test** (*Comput*) rôdage *m*.

►**soak in** vi *[liquid]* pénétrer, s'infiltrer, être absorbé. (* *fig*) **I told him what I thought and left it to soak in** je lui ai donné mon opinion et je l'ai laissé la digérer *or* je l'ai laissé méditer dessus.

►**soak out** 1 vi *[stain etc]* partir (*au trempage*). 2 vt sep *stains* faire partir (en trempant le linge *etc*).

►**soak through** 1 vi *[liquid]* traverser, filtrer au travers, s'infiltrer. 2 vt sep: **to be soaked through** *[garment etc]* être trempé; *[person]* être trempé (jusqu'aux os).

►**soak up** vt sep (*lit, fig*) absorber.

soaking ['səʊkɪŋ] 1 n trempage *m*. **to get a ~** se faire tremper (jusqu'aux os); **to give sth a ~** faire *or* laisser tremper qch. 2 adj: **to be ~ (wet)** *[object]* être trempé; *[person]* être trempé (jusqu'aux os).

soap [səʊp] 1 n a savon *m*; (* *fig: also* **soft ~**) flatterie(s) *f(pl)*, flagornerie *f* (*pej*). (*US fig*) **no ~!‡** rien à faire!, des clous!‡; *see* **shaving, toilet** *etc*. b = **soap opera**; *see* **3.** 2 vt savonner. 3 comp ►**soapbox** (*fig*) *see* **soapbox** ►**soap bubble** bulle *f* de savon ►**soapdish** porte-savon *m* ►**soapflakes** savon *m* en paillettes, paillettes *fpl* de savon ►**soap opera** (*fig*) (*Rad, TV*) feuilleton *m* mélo* *or* à l'eau de rose ►**soap powder** lessive *f* (en poudre), poudre *f* à laver ►**soapstone** stéatite *f* ►**soapsuds** (*lather*) mousse *f* de savon; (*soapy water*) eau savonneuse.

►**soap down** vt sep savonner.

soapbox ['səʊpbɒks] 1 n a (*lit*) caisse *f* à savon; (*fig: for speaker*) tribune improvisée (*en plein air*). b (*go-cart*) auto *f* sans moteur (pour enfants), caisse *f* à savon*. 2 comp ▸**soapbox derby** course *f* en descente d'autos sans moteur (pour enfants) ▸**soapbox orator** orateur *m* de carrefour, harangueur *m*, -euse *f* de foules ▸**soapbox oratory** harangue(s) *f(pl)* de démagogue.

soapy ['səʊpɪ] adj *water* savonneux; *taste* de savon; (* *fig pej*) *person* mielleux, doucereux, lécheur*; *manner* onctueux. **that smells ~** ça sent le savon.

soar [sɔːʳ] vi (*often* ~ **up**) *[bird, aircraft]* monter (en flèche); *[ball etc]* voler (*over the wall etc* par-dessus le mur *etc*); (*fig*) *[tower, cathedral]* s'élancer (vers le ciel); *[prices, costs, profits]* monter en flèche, (*suddenly*) faire un bond; *[ambitions, hopes]* grandir démesurément; *[spirits, morale]* remonter en flèche.

▸**soar up** vi *see* **soar**.

soaring ['sɔːrɪŋ] 1 n *[bird]* essor *m*; *[plane]* envol *m*. 2 adj *spire* élancé; *price* qui monte en flèche; *ambition, pride, hopes* grandissant.

sob [sɒb] 1 n sanglot *m*. **... he said with a ~** ... dit-il en sanglotant.
2 comp ▸**sob sister*** (*US*) journaliste *f* qui se spécialise dans les histoires larmoyantes ▸**sob story*** histoire *f* mélodramatique *or* d'un pathétique facile *or* larmoyante; (*Press etc*) **the main item was a sob story* about a puppy** l'article principal était une histoire à vous fendre le cœur concernant un chiot; **he told us a sob story* about his sister's illness** il a cherché à nous apitoyer *or* à nous avoir au sentiment* en nous parlant de la maladie de sa sœur ▸**sob stuff: there's too much sob stuff* in that film** il y a trop de sensiblerie *or* de mélo* dans ce film; **he gave us a lot of sob stuff*** il nous a fait tout un baratin* larmoyant.
3 vi sangloter.
4 vt: **"no" she ~bed** "non" dit-elle en sanglotant; **to ~ o.s. to sleep** s'endormir à force de sangloter *or* en sanglotant.

▸**sob out** vt sep *story* raconter en sanglotant. (*fig*) **to sob one's heart out** pleurer à chaudes larmes *or* à gros sanglots.

s.o.b. [ˌesəʊ'biː] n (*US*) (**abbr of son of a bitch**) salaud‡ *m*, fils *m* de garce‡.

sobbing ['sɒbɪŋ] 1 n sanglots *mpl*. 2 adj sanglotant.

sober ['səʊbəʳ] 1 adj a (*moderate, sedate*) *person* sérieux, posé, sensé; *estimate, statement* modéré, mesuré; *judgment* sensé; *occasion* plein de gravité *or* de solennité; *suit, style, colour* sobre, discret (*f* -ète). **in ~ earnest** sans plaisanterie, bien sérieusement; **to be in ~ earnest** être tout à fait sérieux, ne pas plaisanter; **in ~ fact** en réalité, si l'on regarde la réalité bien en face; **the ~ truth** la vérité toute simple; **the ~ fact of the matter** les faits tels qu'ils sont; **as ~ as a judge** sérieux comme un pape* (*see also* **1b**); **to be in a ~ mood** être plein de gravité.
b (*not drunk*) **I'm perfectly ~** je n'ai vraiment pas trop bu; **he's never ~** il est toujours ivre, il ne dessoûle* pas; **he is ~ now** il est dégrisé *or* dessoûlé* maintenant; **to be as ~ as a judge, to be stone-cold ~** n'être absolument pas ivre.
2 comp ▸**sober-headed** *person* sérieux, posé, sensé; *decision* réfléchi, posé ▸**sober-minded** sérieux, sensé ▸**sober-sided** sérieux, grave, qui ne rit pas souvent ▸**sobersides*** bonnet *m* de nuit (*fig*).
3 vt a (*fig: also* ~ **down,** ~ **up**) (*calm*) calmer; (*deflate*) dégriser.
b (*also* ~ **up**: *stop being drunk*) désenivrer, dessoûler*.

▸**sober down** 1 vi (*calm down*) se calmer; (*grow sadder*) être dégrisé. 2 vt sep = **sober 3a**.

▸**sober up** 1 vi désenivrer, dessoûler*. 2 vt sep = **sober 3a, 3b**.

sobering ['səʊbərɪŋ] adj (*fig*) *experience* qui donne à réfléchir. **it is a ~ thought** cela fait réfléchir; **it had a ~ effect on him** ça lui a donné à réfléchir.

soberly ['səʊbəlɪ] adv *speak, say* avec modération *or* mesure *or* calme, d'un ton posé; *behave, act* de façon posée *or* sensée; *furnish, dress* sobrement, discrètement.

soberness ['səʊbənɪs] n, **sobriety** [səʊ'braɪətɪ] n a (*calm etc: see* **sober 1a**) sérieux *m*, caractère mesuré *or* posé *or* sensé; modération *f*, mesure *f*; gravité *f*; sobriété *f*. b (*not drunk*) **to return to ~** désenivrer, dessoûler*; **his ~ was in question** on le soupçonnait d'être ivre.

sobriquet ['səʊbrɪkeɪ] n sobriquet *m*.

soccer ['sɒkəʳ] 1 n football *m*, foot* *m*. 2 comp *match, pitch, team* de football, de foot* ▸**soccer player** footballeur *m* *or* footballer *m* ▸**soccer season** saison *f* du football *or* du foot*.

sociability [ˌsəʊʃə'bɪlɪtɪ] n sociabilité *f*.

sociable ['səʊʃəbl] adj *person* (*gregarious*) sociable, qui aime la compagnie, liant; (*friendly*) sociable, aimable; *animal* sociable; *evening, gathering* amical, agréable. **I'll have a drink just to be ~** je prendrai un verre rien que pour vous (*or* lui *etc*) faire plaisir; **I'm not feeling very ~ this evening** je n'ai pas envie de voir des gens ce soir.

sociably ['səʊʃəblɪ] adv *behave* de façon sociable, aimablement; *invite, say* amicalement.

social ['səʊʃəl] 1 adj a (*Soc etc*) *behaviour, class, relationship, customs, reforms* social. **man is a ~ animal** l'homme est un animal social *or* sociable; **a ~ outcast** une personne mise au ban de la société, un paria; *see also* **3**.
b (*in or of society*) *engagements, obligations* mondain. **~ climber** (*still climbing*) arriviste *mf*; (*arrived*) parvenu(e) *m(f)*; **~ climbing** arrivisme *m*; (*Press*) **~ column** carnet mondain, mondanités *fpl*; **to be a ~ drinker/smoker** boire/fumer seulement en société; **~ drinking** consommation *f* d'alcool en société; **his ~ equals** ses pairs *mpl*; **a (lively) ~ life** une vie sociale (très active); **we've got almost no ~ life** nous menons une vie très retirée, nous ne sortons presque jamais; **the ~ life in this town is non-existent** c'est vraiment une ville morte, il ne se passe rien dans cette ville; **how's your ~ life?*** est-ce que tu vois des amis?, est-ce que tu sors beaucoup?; **~ mobility** mobilité *f* sociale; **~ order** ordre *m* social; (*US*) **the ~ register** ≃ le bottin mondain.
c (*gregarious*) *person* sociable. **~ club** association amicale (*qui n'est pas spécialisée dans une activité précise*); **~ evening** soirée *f* de rencontre.
2 n (petite) fête *f*.
3 comp ▸**social administration** administration *f* sociale, politique *f* sociale ▸**Social and Liberal Democrats** (*Brit Pol*) parti *m* social et libéral démocrate ▸**social anthropologist** spécialiste *mf* de l'anthropologie sociale ▸**social anthropology** anthropologie sociale ▸**social benefits** prestations *fpl* sociales ▸**social contract** contrat social ▸**Social Democracy** social-démocratie *f* ▸**Social Democrat** social-démocrate *mf* ▸**Social Democratic** social-démocrate ▸**Social Democratic and Labour Party** (*Ir Pol*) parti *m* social-démocrate et travailliste ▸**Social Democratic Party**† (*Brit Pol*) parti *m* social-démocrate ▸**social disease** (*gen*) maladie *f* due à des facteurs socio-économiques; (*venereal*) maladie vénérienne ▸**social engineering** manipulation *f* des structures sociales ▸**social fund** (*Brit*) ≃ fonds *m* de solidarité ▸**social insurance** (*US*) sécurité sociale ▸**social misfit** inadapté(e) *m(f)* social(e) ▸**social science** sciences humaines; (*Univ*) **Faculty of Social Science** faculté *f* des sciences humaines ▸**social scientist** spécialiste *mf* des sciences humaines ▸**social security** n (*gen*) aide sociale; (*also* **social security benefits**) prestations *fpl* sociales; **to be on social security*** recevoir l'aide sociale; **Department of Social Security** (*Brit*) ≃ Sécurité *f* sociale ▸**Social Security Administration** (*US*) *service des pensions* ▸**social security card** (*US*) ≃ carte *f* d'assuré social ▸**social service** = **social work** ▸**social services** services *mpl* sociaux; **Secretary of State for/Department of Social Services** ministre *m*/ministère *m* des Affaires sociales ▸**social studies** sciences sociales ▸**social welfare** sécurité sociale ▸**social work** assistance sociale ▸**social worker** assistant(e) *m(f)* de service social, assistant(e) social(e).

socialism ['səʊʃəlɪzəm] n socialisme *m*.

socialist ['səʊʃəlɪst] 1 adj socialiste. (*Geog*) **the S~ Republic of ...** la République socialiste de ... . 2 n socialiste *(mf)*.

socialistic [ˌsəʊʃə'lɪstɪk] adj socialiste.

socialite ['səʊʃəlaɪt] n personnalité *f* en vue dans la haute société. **a Paris ~** un membre du Tout-Paris.

sociality [ˌsəʊʃɪ'ælɪtɪ] n socialité *f*, sociabilité *f*.

socialization [ˌsəʊʃəlaɪ'zeɪʃən] n socialisation *f* (*Pol*).

socialize ['səʊʃəlaɪz] 1 vt (*Pol, Psych*) socialiser. 2 vi (*be with people*) fréquenter des gens; (*make friends*) se faire des amis; (*chat*) s'entretenir, bavarder (*with sb* avec qn).

socializing ['səʊʃəlaɪzɪŋ] n: **he doesn't like ~** il n'aime pas fréquenter les gens; **there isn't much ~ on campus** on ne se fréquente pas beaucoup sur le campus.

socially ['səʊʃəlɪ] adv *interact, be valid* socialement; *acceptable* en société. **I know him** (*or* **her** *etc*) **~** nous nous rencontrons en société.

society [sə'saɪətɪ] 1 n a (*social community*) société *f*. **to live in ~** vivre en société; **for the good of ~** dans l'intérêt social *or* de la société *or* de la communauté; **it is a danger to ~** cela constitue un danger social, cela met la société en danger; **modern industrial societies** les sociétés industrielles modernes.
b (*NonC: high* ~) (haute) société *f*, grand monde. **polite ~** la bonne société; **the years she spent in ~** ses années de vie mondaine.
c (*NonC: company, companionship*) société *f*, compagnie *f*. **in the ~ of** dans la société de, en compagnie de; **I enjoy his ~** je me plais en sa compagnie, j'apprécie sa compagnie.
d (*organized group*) société *f*, association *f*; (*charitable* ~) œuvre *f* de charité, association de bienfaisance; (*Scol, Univ etc*) club *m*, association. **dramatic ~** club théâtral, association théâtrale; **learned ~** société savante; (*Rel*) **the S~ of Friends** la Société des Amis, les Quakers *mpl*; (*Rel*) **the S~ of Jesus** la Société de Jésus, les Jésuites *mpl*; *see* **royal** *etc*.
2 comp *correspondent, news, photographer, wedding* mondain, de la haute société ▸**society column** (*Press*) carnet mondain, mondanités *fpl*.

socio... ['səʊsɪəʊ] pref socio... . **~cultural** socioculturel; **~economic** socio-économique; **~ political** sociopolitique; *see also* **sociological** *etc*.

sociobiology [ˌsəʊsɪəʊbaɪ'ɒlədʒɪ] n sociobiologie *f*.

sociolect ['səʊsɪəʊˌlekt] n (*Ling*) sociolecte *m*.

sociolinguistic [ˌsəʊsɪəʊlɪŋ'gwɪstɪk] adj sociolinguistique.

sociolinguistics [ˌsəʊsɪəʊlɪŋ'gwɪstɪks] n (*NonC*) sociolinguistique *f*.

sociological [ˌsəʊsɪə'lɒdʒɪkəl] adj sociologique.

sociologically [ˌsəʊsɪə'lɒdʒɪkəlɪ] adv sociologiquement.

sociologist [ˌsəʊsɪ'ɒlədʒɪst] n sociologue *mf*.

sociology [ˌsəʊsɪ'ɒlədʒɪ] n sociologie *f*.

sociometry [ˌsəʊsɪˈɒmɪtrɪ] n sociométrie *f*.

sociopath [ˈsəʊsɪəʊpæθ] n inadapté(e) social(e).

sociopathic [ˌsəʊsɪəʊˈpæθɪk] adj socialement inadapté, sociopathe.

sock[1] [sɒk] n a (pl ~s) (*short stocking*) chaussette *f*, (*shorter*) socquette *f*; (*inner sole*) semelle *f* (intérieure); *[footballer etc]* bas *m*. (*Brit fig*) **to pull one's ~s* up** se secouer*, faire un effort; (*fig*) **put a ~ in it!**‡ la ferme!‡, ta gueule!‡ b (*wind~*) manche *f* à air.

sock[2]* [sɒk] 1 n (*blow*) coup *m*, beigne‡ *f*, gnon‡ *m*. **to give sb a ~ on the jaw** flanquer un coup *or* son poing sur la gueule‡ à qn. 2 vt (*strike*) flanquer une beigne‡ *or* un gnon‡ à. **~ him one!** cogne dessus!*, fous-lui une beigne!‡; **~ it to me!** vas-y envoie!*; **~ it to them!** montre-leur un peu!

sockdolager* [sɒkˈdɒlədʒəʳ] n (*US*) a (*decisive event*) coup *m* décisif. b (*great person/thing*) personne *f*/chose *f* fantastique.

socket [ˈsɒkɪt] 1 n (*gen*) cavité *f*, trou *m* (*où qch s'emboîte*); *[hipbone]* cavité articulaire; *[eye]* orbite *f*; *[tooth]* alvéole *f*; (*Elec: for light bulb*) douille *f*; (*Brit Elec: also* **wall** ~) prise *f* de courant, prise femelle; (*Carpentry*) mortaise *f*; (*in candlestick etc*) trou. **to pull sb's arm out of its ~** désarticuler *or* démettre l'épaule à qn. 2 comp ►**socket joint** (*Carpentry*) joint *m* à rotule *or* à genou; (*Anat*) énarthrose *f* ►**socket wrench** (*Tech*) clef *f* à pipe.

socko* [ˈsɒkəʊ] (*US*) 1 adj fantastique, du tonnerre. 2 n grand succès *m*.

Socrates [ˈsɒkrətiːz] n Socrate *m*.

Socratic [sɒˈkrætɪk] adj socratique.

sod[1] [sɒd] n (*NonC: turf*) gazon *m*; (*piece of turf*) motte *f* (de gazon).

sod[2]** [sɒd] (*Brit*) 1 n con** *m*, couillon** *m*; (*pej*) salaud‡ *m*, salopard‡ *m*. **the poor ~s who tried** les pauvres cons** *or* couillons** *or* bougres* qui l'ont essayé; **poor little ~!** pauvre petit bonhomme!; **he's a real ~** c'est un salaud‡ *or* un salopard‡; **~ all** que dalle‡. 2 comp ►**Sod's Law**** (*Brit*) loi *f* de l'emmerdement** maximum. 3 vt: **~ it!** merde (alors)!**; **~ him!** il m'emmerde!**, qu'il aille se faire foutre!**

►**sod off**** vi foutre le camp‡. **sod off!** fous le camp!‡, va te faire foutre!**

soda [ˈsəʊdə] 1 n a (*Chem*) soude *f*; (*also* **washing ~**, **~ crystals**) soude du commerce, cristaux *mpl* (de soude); *see* **baking, caustic** *etc*. b (*also* **~ water**) eau *f* de Seltz. **whisky and ~** whisky *m* soda *or* à l'eau de Seltz; *see* **club, ice**. c (*US: also* **~ pop**) soda *m*. 2 comp ►**soda ash** (*Chem*) soude *f* du commerce ►**soda biscuit** (*US*), **soda cracker** (*US*) biscuit *m* sec à la levure chimique ►**soda crystals** *see* **1a** ►**soda fountain** (*US*) (*siphon*) siphon *m* d'eau de Seltz; (place) buvette *f* ►**soda jerk(er)** (*US*) marchand(e) *m(f)* de soda et de glace ►**soda pop** (*US*) soda *m* ►**soda siphon** siphon *m* (d'eau de Seltz) ►**soda water** *see* **1b**.

sodality [səʊˈdælɪtɪ] n camaraderie *f*; (*association, also Rel*) confrérie *f*.

sodden [ˈsɒdn] adj *ground* détrempé; *clothes* trempé. (*fig*) **~ with drink** hébété *or* abruti par l'alcool.

sodding** [ˈsɒdɪŋ] 1 adj: **her ~ dog** son putain de chien‡, son chien à la con**; **shut the ~ door!** ferme cette putain de porte!‡; **it's a ~ disgrace!** c'est une honte, nom de Dieu!** 2 adv (*very*) **it's ~ difficult** c'est foutrement difficile‡; (*emph*) **he's ~ crazy!** il est fou, nom de Dieu!**

sodium [ˈsəʊdɪəm] 1 n sodium *m*. 2 comp ►**sodium bicarbonate** bicarbonate *m* de soude ►**sodium carbonate** carbonate *m* de sodium ►**sodium chloride** chlorure *m* de sodium ►**sodium light** lampe *f* à vapeur de sodium ►**sodium nitrate** nitrate *m* de soude ►**sodium sulfate** sulfate *m* de soude ►**sodium-vapor lamp** (*US*) = **sodium light**.

Sodom [ˈsɒdəm] n Sodome.

sodomite [ˈsɒdəmaɪt] n sodomite *m*.

sodomy [ˈsɒdəmɪ] n sodomie *f*.

sofa [ˈsəʊfə] n sofa *m*, canapé *m*. **~ bed** canapé-lit *m*.

Sofia [ˈsəʊfɪə] n Sofia.

soft [sɒft] 1 adj a (*in texture, consistency: not hard etc*) *bed, mattress, pillow* doux (*f* douce), moelleux, (*unpleasantly so*) mou (*f* molle) (*pej*); *mud, snow, clay, ground, pitch* mou; *substance* mou, malléable; *wood, stone, pencil, paste* tendre; *metal, iron* doux, tendre; *butter* mou, (r)amolli; *leather, brush, toothbrush* souple, doux; *contact lenses* souple; *collar, hat* mou; *material* doux, soyeux, satiné; *silk, hand* doux; *skin, cheek* doux, fin, satiné; *hair* soyeux; (*pej: flabby*) *person, muscle* flasque, avachi. **as ~ as butter** mou comme du beurre; **as ~ as silk/velvet** doux comme de la soie/du velours; **a ~ cheese** un fromage mou *or* à pâte molle; **to grow** *or* **get** *or* **become ~(er)** *[butter, snow, mud, ground, pitch]* devenir mou, se ramollir; *[leather]* s'assouplir; *[bed, mattress, pillow]* s'amollir, devenir plus moelleux *or* trop mou (*pej*); *[skin]* s'adoucir; *[person, body, muscle]* s'avachir, devenir flasque; **to make ~(er)** *butter, snow, clay, ground* (r)amollir; *leather* assouplir; *bed, mattress, pillow* amollir, rendre moelleux; *skin* adoucir; **this sort of life makes you ~** ce genre de vie vous (r)amollit *or* vous enlève votre énergie; (*fig*) **the brakes are ~** il y a du mou dans la pédale de freins; *see also* **3** *and* **coal, margarine, roe[2], solder** *etc*.

b (*gentle, not strong or vigorous*) *tap, touch, pressure* doux (*f* douce), léger; *breeze, day, rain, climate* doux. (*Aviat, Space*) **~ landing** atterrissage *m* en douceur; (*dial*) **~ weather** temps doux et pluvieux.

c (*not harsh*) *words, expression, look, glance* doux (*f* douce), aimable, gentil; *answer* aimable, gentil; *heart* tendre, compatissant; *life* doux, facile, tranquille; *job, option* facile; *person* indulgent (*with or on sb* envers qn). (*fig: lenient*) **to be ~*on sth/sb** se montrer indulgent *or* faire preuve d'indulgence pour qch/envers qn (*see also* **1h**); **you're too ~!** tu es trop indulgent! *or* trop bon!; **he has a ~ time of it*** il se la coule douce*; **to have a ~ spot for** avoir un faible pour; **the ~er side of his nature** le côté moins sévère *or* moins rigoureux de son tempérament; (*fig Pol*) **the ~ line** la politique du compromis.

d (*not loud*) *sound, laugh* doux (*f* douce), léger; *tone* doux; *music, voice* doux, mélodieux, harmonieux; *steps* ouaté, feutré. **in a ~ voice** d'une voix douce, doucement; **the radio/orchestra/brass section is too ~** la radio/l'orchestre/les cuivres ne joue(nt) pas assez fort; **the music is too ~** la musique n'est pas assez forte, on n'entend pas assez la musique; *see also* **3**.

e *light* doux (*f* douce), pâle; *colour* doux, pastel *inv*; *outline* doux, estompé, flou. **~ lights, ~ lighting** un éclairage doux *or* tamisé; **~ pastel shades** de doux tons pastel; (*Phot*) **~ focus** flou *m* artistique (*see also* **3**).

f (*Ling*) *consonant* doux.

g (*Fin*) *currency* faible. **the market is ~** le marché est lourd; **~ loan** prêt *m* à des conditions favorables; **~ terms** termes *mpl* favorables.

h (**: stupid*) stupide, bête, débile*. **to go ~** perdre la boule*; **he must be ~ (in the head)*** il doit être cinglé‡ *or* débile*; **he is ~ on her*** il en est toqué*.

i (**: unmanly; without stamina*) mollasson, qui manque de nerf. **he's ~** c'est une mauviette *or* un mollasson, il n'a pas de nerf.

2 adv doucement. (*excl*) **~!**†† silence!

3 comp ►**softback** (*US*) livre *m* broché, (*paperback*) livre *m* de poche ►**softball** (*US*) espèce *f* de base-ball (*joué sur un terrain plus petit avec une balle plus grande et plus molle*) ►**soft-boiled egg** œuf *m* à la coque ►**soft-bound book** livre broché, (*paperback*) livre de poche ►**soft copy** (*Comput*) présentation *f* visuelle ►**soft-core** adj légèrement porno* (*inv*) ►**soft-cover** = **softback** ►**soft currency** (*Fin*) devise *f* faible ►**soft drinks** boissons non alcoolisées ►**soft drugs** drogues douces ►**soft-focus** (*Phot*) *image, picture* (artistiquement) flou; (*Phot*) **soft-focus filter** écran *m* de flou (artistique); (*Phot*) **soft-focus lens** objectif *m* pour flou (artistique) ►**soft-footed** à la démarche légère, qui marche à pas feutrés *or* sans faire de bruit ►**soft fruit** baies *fpl* comestibles, ≃ fruits *mpl* rouges ►**soft furnishings** (*Brit Comm*) tissus *mpl* d'ameublement (*rideaux, tentures, housses etc*) ►**soft goods** (*Brit Comm*) textiles *mpl*, tissus *mpl* ►**soft-headed*** faible d'esprit, cinglé‡ ►**soft-hearted** au cœur tendre, compatissant ►**soft ice-cream** glace *f* à l'italienne ►**soft palate** (*Anat*) voile *m* du palais ►**soft pedal** n (*Mus*) pédale douce ◊ vt (*fig*) ne pas trop insister sur ►**soft porn** pornographie *f* non explicite, soft porn *m* ►**soft sell** (*Comm*) promotion (de vente) discrète; (*fig*) **he's a master of the soft sell** il est maître dans l'art de persuader discrètement les gens ►**soft-shelled** *egg, mollusc* à coquille molle; *crustacean, turtle* à carapace molle ►**soft shoulder** *[road]* accotement non stabilisé ►**soft soap** n (*lit*) savon vert; (*fig pej *: flattery*) flatterie *f*, flagornerie *f* (*pej*) ►**soft-soap*** vt (*fig pej*) flatter, passer de la pommade à, lécher les bottes à* ►**soft-spoken** à la voix douce ►**soft touch***: (*fig*) **to be a soft touch** se faire avoir* (facilement), se faire refaire* *or* rouler* ►**soft toy** (jouet *m* en) peluche *f* ►**soft verge** (*Aut*) accotement non stabilisé ►**software** (*Comput: NonC*) software* *m*, logiciel *m*; (*Comput*) **software engineer** ingénieur-conseil *m* en informatique, ingénieur *m* en logiciel; **software engineering** (*Comput*) ingénierie *f* du logiciel; (*Comput*) **software house** société *f* de services et de conseils en informatique, SSCI *f*; (*Comput*) **software package** progiciel *m* ►**soft water** eau *f* qui n'est pas calcaire, eau douce ►**softwood** bois *m* tendre ►**soft X-rays** rayons X mous; *see* **hyphen**.

soften [ˈsɒfn] 1 vt *butter, clay, ground, pitch* (r)amollir; *collar, leather* assouplir; *skin* adoucir; *sound* adoucir, atténuer, étouffer; *lights, lighting* adoucir, tamiser; *outline* adoucir, estomper, rendre flou; *colour* adoucir, atténuer; *pain, anxiety* adoucir, atténuer, soulager; *sb's anger, reaction, effect, impression* adoucir, atténuer; *resistance* amoindrir, réduire. (*fig*) **to ~ the blow** adoucir *or* amortir le choc.

2 vi *[butter, clay, ground, pitch]* devenir mou (*f* molle), se ramollir; *[collar, leather]* s'assouplir; *[skin]* s'adoucir; *[outline]* s'adoucir, devenir flou, s'estomper; *[colour]* s'adoucir, s'atténuer; *[sb's anger]* s'atténuer. **his heart ~ed at the sight of her** il s'attendrit en la voyant; **his eyes ~ed as he looked at her** son regard s'est adouci à sa vue.

►**soften up** 1 vi *[butter, clay, ground, pitch]* devenir mou (*f* molle), se ramollir; *[collar, leather]* s'assouplir; *[skin]* s'adoucir; (*grow less stern*) s'adoucir. **we must not soften up towards** *or* **on these offenders** nous ne devons pas faire preuve d'indulgence envers ces délinquants. 2 vt sep a *butter, clay, pitch, ground* (r)amollir; *collar, leather* assouplir; *skin* adoucir. b *person* attendrir; (**: by cajoling*) *customer etc* bonimenter*, baratiner*; (**: by bullying*) intimider, malmener; *resistance, opposition* réduire; (*Mil: by bombing etc*) affaiblir par bombardement intensif.

softener [ˈsɒfnəʳ] n (*water* ~) adoucisseur *m*; (*fabric* ~) produit *m* assouplissant.

softening [ˈsɒfnɪŋ] n (*see* **soften 1**) (r)amollissement *m*; assouplissement *m*; adoucissement *m*; atténuation *f*; soulagement *m*. (*Med*) ~ **of the brain** ramollissement cérébral; (*fig*) **he's got ~ of the brain*** il devient ramollo‡ *or* débile*; **there has been a ~ of their attitude** ils ont modéré leur attitude.

softie* [ˈsɒftɪ] n (*too tender-hearted*) tendre *mf*; (*no stamina etc*) mauviette *f*, mollasson(ne) *m(f)*; (*coward*) poule mouillée, dégonflé(e)* *m(f)*. **you silly ~, stop crying!** ne pleure plus grand(e) nigaud(e)!

softly [ˈsɒftlɪ] adv (*quietly*) *say, call, sing* doucement; *walk* à pas feutrés, sans (faire de) bruit; (*gently*) *touch, tap* légèrement, doucement; (*tenderly*) *smile, look* tendrement, gentiment.

softness [ˈsɒftnɪs] n (*see* **soft**) **a** *[bed, mattress, pillow]* douceur *f*, moelleux *m*, mollesse *f* (*pej*); *[mud, snow, ground, pitch, butter]* mollesse; *[substance]* mollesse, malléabilité *f*; *[leather, brush]* souplesse *f*, douceur; *[collar]* souplesse; *[material, silk, hand, skin, hair]* douceur; (*pej*) *[person, muscle]* avachissement *m*.
b *[tap, touch, pressure]* douceur *f*, légèreté *f*; *[breeze, wind, rain, climate]* douceur.
c *[words, expression, glance]* douceur *f*, amabilité *f*, gentillesse *f*; *[answer]* amabilité, gentillesse; *[life]* douceur, facilité *f*; *[job]* facilité; (*gentleness, kindness*) douceur, affabilité *f*; (*indulgence*) manque *m* de sévérité (*towards* envers).
d *[sound, tone, voice, music]* douceur *f*.
e *[light, colour]* douceur *f*; *[outline, photograph]* flou *m*.
f (*: *stupidity*) stupidité *f*, bêtise *f*.

software [ˈsɒft,wɛəʳ] n *see* **soft 3**.

softy* [ˈsɒftɪ] n = **softie***.

SOGAT [ˈsəʊgæt] n (*Brit*) (abbr of **Society of Graphical and Allied Trades**) *syndicat*.

soggy [ˈsɒgɪ] adj *ground* détrempé; *clothes* trempé; *bread* mal cuit, pâteux; *heat, atmosphere, pudding* lourd.

soh [səʊ] n (*Mus*) sol *m*.

soil¹ [sɔɪl] n sol *m*, terre *f*. **rich/chalky ~** sol *or* terre riche/calcaire; **cover it over with ~** recouvre-le de terre; (*liter*) **a man of the ~** un terrien, un homme de la terre; (*fig*) **my native ~** ma terre natale, mon pays natal; **on French ~** sur le sol français, en territoire français.

soil² [sɔɪl] **1** vt (*lit*) salir; (*fig*) *reputation, honour* souiller, salir, entacher. **this dress is easily ~ed** cette robe se salit vite *or* est salissante; **~ed linen** linge *m* sale; (*Comm*) **~ed copy/item** exemplaire/article défraîchi; *see* **shop**. **2** vi *[material, garment]* se salir, être salissant. **3** n (*excrement*) excréments *mpl*, ordures *fpl*; (*sewage*) vidange *f*. **4** comp ►**soil pipe** tuyau *m* d'écoulement; (*vertical*) tuyau de descente.

soirée [ˈswɑːreɪ] n soirée *f* (*à but culturel, souvent organisée par une association*).

sojourn [ˈsɒdʒɜːn] (*liter*) **1** n séjour *m*. **2** vi séjourner, faire un séjour.

solace [ˈsɒlɪs] (*liter*) **1** n consolation *f*, réconfort *m*. **to be a ~ to sb** être un réconfort pour qn. **2** vt *person* consoler; *pain* soulager, adoucir.

solanum [səʊˈleɪnəm] n solanacée *f*.

solar [ˈsəʊləʳ] adj *warmth, rays* du soleil, solaire; *cycle, energy, system* solaire. ~ **battery** batterie *f* solaire, photopile *f*; ~ **cell** pile *f* solaire, photopile *f*; ~ **collector** capteur *m* solaire; ~ **eclipse** éclipse *f* de soleil; ~ **flare** facule *f* solaire; ~ **furnace** four *m* solaire; ~ **heating** chauffage *m* (à l'énergie) solaire; ~ **panel** panneau *m* solaire; (*Anat*) ~ **plexus** plexus *m* solaire; ~ **power** énergie *f* solaire; ~ **wind** vent *m* solaire.

solarium [səʊˈlɛərɪəm] n, pl **~s** *or* **solaria** [səʊˈlɛərɪə] solarium *m*.

sold [səʊld] pret, ptp of **sell**.

solder [ˈsəʊldəʳ] **1** n soudure *f*. **hard ~** brasure *f*; **soft ~** claire soudure. **2** vt souder. **~ing iron** fer *m* à souder.

soldier [ˈsəʊldʒəʳ] **1** n soldat *m* (*also fig*), militaire *m*. **woman ~** femme *f* soldat; **~s and civilians** (les) militaires et (les) civils; **Montgomery was a great ~** Montgomery était un grand homme de guerre *or* un grand soldat; **he wants to be a ~** il veut se faire soldat *or* être militaire de carrière *or* entrer dans l'armée; **to play (at) ~s** (*pej*) jouer à la guerre; *[children]* jouer aux soldats; ~ **of fortune** soldat de fortune, mercenaire *m*; **old ~** vétéran *m*; (*fig*) **to come the old ~ with sb*** prendre des airs supérieurs avec qn, vouloir en imposer à qn; *see* **foot, private** *etc*.
2 comp ►**soldier ant** (fourmi *f*) soldat *m*.
3 vi servir dans l'armée, être militaire *or* soldat. **he ~ed for 10 years in the East** il a servi (dans l'armée) pendant 10 ans en Orient; **after 6 years' ~ing** après 6 ans dans l'armée; **to be tired of ~ing** en avoir assez d'être soldat *or* d'être militaire *or* d'être dans l'armée.
►**soldier on** vi (*Brit fig*) persévérer (malgré tout).

soldierly [ˈsəʊldʒəlɪ] adj (typiquement) militaire.

soldiery [ˈsəʊldʒərɪ] n (*collective*) soldats *mpl*, militaires *mpl*, soldatesque *f* (*pej*).

sole¹ [səʊl] n, pl ~ *or* **~s** (*fish*) sole *f*; *see* **lemon**.

sole² [səʊl] **1** n *[shoe, sock, stocking]* semelle *f*; *[foot]* plante *f*; *see* **inner**. **2** vt ressemeler. **to have one's shoes ~d** faire ressemeler ses chaussures; **crepe/rubber/leather-~d** avec semelles de crêpe/caoutchouc/cuir.

sole³ [səʊl] adj **a** (*only, single*) seul, unique. **the ~ reason** la seule *or* l'unique raison, la seule et unique raison; (*Comm*) ~ **trader** gérant *m* (*or* propriétaire *m*) unique. **b** (*exclusive*) *right* exclusif. **for the ~ use of ...** à l'usage exclusif de ...; (*Comm*) ~ **agent for ...**, ~ **stockist of ...** concessionnaire *mf* de ..., dépositaire exclusif (*or* dépositaire exclusive) de ...; (*Jur*) ~ **legatee** légataire universel(le).

solecism [ˈsɒləsɪzəm] n (*Ling*) solécisme *m*; (*social offence*) manque *m* de savoir-vivre, faute *f* de goût.

solei [ˈsɒlɪaɪ] npl of **soleus**.

solely [ˈsəʊllɪ] adv (*gen: only*) seulement, uniquement. **I am ~ to blame** je suis seul coupable, je suis entièrement coupable.

solemn [ˈsɒləm] adj *occasion, promise, silence, music* solennel; *duty* sacré; *plea, warning* formel, plein de solennité *or* de gravité; *person, face* sérieux, grave, solennel (*often pej*).

solemnity [səˈlemnɪtɪ] n (*see* **solemn**) solennité *f*; caractère sacré; sérieux *m*, gravité *f*. **with all ~** très solennellement; **the solemnities** les fêtes solennelles, les solennités.

solemnization [ˌsɒləmnaɪˈzeɪʃən] n *[marriage]* célébration *f*.

solemnize [ˈsɒləmnaɪz] vt *marriage* célébrer; *occasion, event* solenniser.

solemnly [ˈsɒləmlɪ] adv *swear, promise, utter* solennellement; *say, smile, nod* gravement, avec sérieux, d'un ton *or* air solennel (*often pej*). (*Jur*) **I do ~ swear to tell the truth** je jure de dire la vérité.

solenoid [ˈsəʊlənɔɪd] n (*Elec*) solénoïde *m*.

soleus [ˈsɒlɪəs] n, pl **solei** muscle *m* soléaire.

sol-fa [ˈsɒlˈfɑː] n (*also* **tonic ~**) solfège *m*.

soli [ˈsəʊliː] npl of **solo**.

solicit [səˈlɪsɪt] **1** vt solliciter (*sb for sth, sth from sb* qch de qn); *vote* solliciter, briguer; *alms* quémander. **2** vi *[prostitute]* racoler.

solicitation [səˌlɪsɪˈteɪʃən] n sollicitation *f*.

soliciting [səˈlɪsɪtɪŋ] n racolage *m*.

solicitor [səˈlɪsɪtəʳ] **1** n **a** (*Jur*) (*Brit*) (*for sales, wills etc*) ≃ notaire *m*; (*in divorce, police, court cases*) ≃ avocat *m*; (*US*) ≃ juriste *m* conseil *or* avocat conseil attaché à une municipalité *etc*. **to instruct a ~** donner ses instructions à un notaire (*or* un avocat). **b** (*US*) (*for contribution*) solliciteur *m*, -euse *f*; (*for trade*) courtier *m*, placier *m*. **2** comp ►**Solicitor General** (pl **~s ~**) (*Brit*) adjoint *m* du procureur général; (*US*) adjoint *or* substitut *m* du ministre de la Justice.

solicitous [səˈlɪsɪtəs] adj plein de sollicitude; (*anxious*) inquiet (*f* -ète), préoccupé (*for, about* de); (*eager*) désireux, avide (*of* de, *to do* de faire).

solicitously [səˈlɪsɪtəslɪ] adv avec sollicitude.

solicitude [səˈlɪsɪtjuːd] n sollicitude *f*.

solid [ˈsɒlɪd] **1** adj **a** (*not liquid or gas*) solide. **a ~ body** un corps solide; ~ **food** aliments *mpl* solides; **frozen ~** complètement gelé; **to become ~** se solidifier; **this soup is rather ~** cette soupe est un peu trop épaisse *or* n'est pas assez liquide; *see also* **3**.
b (*not hollow etc*) *ball, block, tyre* plein; *crowd etc* compact, dense; *row, line* continu, ininterrompu. **cut out of** *or* **in ~ rock** taillé à même la pierre; **6 metres of ~ rock** 6 mètres de roche massive; **of** *or* **in ~ gold/oak** en or/chêne massif; (*fig*) **the garden was a ~ mass of colour** le jardin resplendissait d'une profusion de couleurs; **a ~ stretch of yellow** une étendue de jaune uni.
c *bridge, house etc* solide; *car* solide, robuste; *reasons, scholarship, piece of work, character* solide, sérieux; *business firm* solide, sain; *vote, voters* unanime; *meal* copieux, consistant, substantiel. **he was 6 ft 6 of ~ muscle** c'était un homme de 2 mètres de haut et tout en muscles; **on ~ ground** (*lit*) sur la terre ferme; (*fig: in discussion etc*) en terrain sûr; **a man of ~ build** un homme bien bâti *or* bien charpenté; **~ (common) sense** solide *or* gros bon sens; **he is a good ~ worker** c'est un bon travailleur, c'est un travailleur sérieux; **he's a good ~ bloke*** c'est quelqu'un sur qui on peut compter, il a les reins solides (*fig*); **the square was ~ with cars*** la place était complètement embouteillée; **to be packed ~** *[case]* être plein à craquer; *[street, train, shop]* être bondé; **he was stuck ~ in the mud** il était complètement pris *or* enlisé dans la boue; **we are ~ for peace** nous sommes unanimes à vouloir la paix; **Newtown is ~ for Labour** Newtown vote massivement *or* presque à l'unanimité pour les travaillistes; (*US Pol*) **the S~ South** *états du Sud des États-Unis qui votent traditionnellement pour le parti démocrate;* **I waited a ~ hour** j'ai attendu une heure entière; **he slept 10 ~ hours** *or* **10 hours ~** il a dormi 10 heures d'affilée; **they worked for 2 ~ days** *or* **2 days ~** ils ont travaillé 2 jours sans s'arrêter *or* sans relâche; **it will take a ~ day's work** cela exigera une journée entière de travail; *see* **book**.
d (*Math*) ~ **angle** angle *m* solide *or* polyèdre; ~ **figure** solide *m*; ~ **geometry** géométrie *f* dans l'espace.
e (*US: excellent*) au poil*, formidable*.
2 n (*gen, Chem, Math, Phys*) solide *m*. (*food*) **~s** aliments *mpl* solides.
3 comp ►**solid compound** (*Ling*) composé *m* dont les termes sont graphiquement soudés ►**solid fuel** (*coal etc*) combustible *m* solide; (*for rockets etc: also* **solid propellant**) mélange *m* de comburant et de

carburant ►**solid-fuel (central) heating** chauffage central au charbon *or* à combustibles solides ►**solid propellant** *see* **solid fuel** ►**solid-state** *physics* des solides; *electronic device* à circuits intégrés ►**solid word** (*Ling*) mot *m or* lexie *f* simple.

solidarity [ˌsɒlɪˈdærɪtɪ] n (*NonC*) solidarité *f*. (*Ind*) ~ **strike** grève *f* de solidarité.

solidi [ˈsɒlɪˌdaɪ] npl of **solidus**.

solidification [səˌlɪdɪfɪˈkeɪʃən] n (*see* **solidify**) solidification *f*; congélation *f*.

solidify [səˈlɪdɪfaɪ] 1 vt *liquid, gas* solidifier; *oil* congeler. 2 vi se solidifier; se congeler.

solidity [səˈlɪdɪtɪ] n solidité *f*.

solidly [ˈsɒlɪdlɪ] adv *build etc* solidement; (*fig*) *vote* massivement, en masse, presque à l'unanimité. **they are ~ behind him** ils le soutiennent unanimement *or* à l'unanimité.

solidus [ˈsɒlɪdəs] n, pl **solidi** (*Typ*) barre *f* oblique.

soliloquize [səˈlɪləkwaɪz] vi soliloquer, monologuer. **"perhaps" he ~d** "peut-être" dit-il, se parlant à lui-même.

soliloquy [səˈlɪləkwɪ] n soliloque *m*, monologue *m*.

solipsism [ˈsəʊlɪpsɪzəm] n solipsisme *m*.

solitaire [ˌsɒlɪˈtɛəʳ] n a (*stone, board game*) solitaire *m*. b (*US Cards*) réussite *f*, patience *f*.

solitary [ˈsɒlɪtərɪ] 1 adj a (*alone*) *person, life, journey* solitaire; *hour* de solitude; *place* solitaire, retiré; (*lonely*) seul. (*Jur*) **(in) ~ confinement** (au) régime cellulaire; **to take a ~ walk** se promener tout seul *or* en solitaire. b (*only one*) seul, unique. **a ~ case of hepatitis** un seul *or* unique cas d'hépatite; **not a ~ one** pas un seul. 2 n (*) = ~ **confinement**; *see* **1a**.

solitude [ˈsɒlɪtjuːd] n solitude *f*.

solo [ˈsəʊləʊ], pl ~s *or* **soli** 1 n a (*Mus*) solo *m*. **piano ~** solo de piano. b (*Cards: also* ~ **whist**) whist-solo *m*. 2 adv *play, sing* en solo; *fly* en solitaire. 3 comp *violin etc* solo *inv*; *flight etc* en solitaire.

soloist [ˈsəʊləʊɪst] n soliste *mf*.

Solomon [ˈsɒləmən] n Salomon *m*. **the judgment of ~** le jugement de Salomon; (*Geog*) ~ **Islands** îles *fpl* Salomon; *see* **song**.

solon [ˈsəʊlən] n (*US*) législateur *m*.

solstice [ˈsɒlstɪs] n solstice *m*. **summer/winter ~** solstice d'été/d'hiver.

solubility [ˌsɒljʊˈbɪlɪtɪ] n solubilité *f*.

soluble [ˈsɒljʊbl] adj *substance* soluble; *problem* (ré)soluble.

solus [ˈsəʊləs] adj (*Publicity*) *advertisement, site, position* isolé.

solution [səˈluːʃən] n a (*to problem etc*) solution *f* (*to* de). b (*Chem*) (*act*) solution *f*, dissolution *f*; (*liquid*) solution; (*Pharm*) solution, soluté *m*. **in ~** en solution; *see* **rubber**[1].

solvable [ˈsɒlvəbl] adj (ré)soluble.

solve [sɒlv] vt *equation, difficulty* résoudre; *problem* résoudre, élucider, trouver la solution de; *crossword puzzle* réussir; *murder* élucider, trouver l'auteur de; *mystery* élucider, éclaircir, débrouiller. **to ~ a riddle** trouver la solution d'une énigme *or* d'une devinette, trouver la clef d'une énigme; **that question remains to be ~d** cette question est encore en suspens.

solvency [ˈsɒlvənsɪ] n solvabilité *f*.

solvent [ˈsɒlvənt] 1 adj (*Fin*) solvable; (*Chem*) dissolvant. 2 n (*Chem*) solvant *m*, dissolvant *m*. 3 comp ►**solvent abuse** usage *m* de solvants hallucinogènes (*colle etc*).

Solzhenitsyn [sɒlʒəˈnɪtsɪn] n Soljenitsyne *m*.

soma [ˈsəʊmə] n, pl ~s *or* **somata** (*Physiol*) soma *m*.

Somali [səʊˈmɑːlɪ] 1 adj somali, somalien. 2 n a Somali(e) *m(f)*, Somalien(ne) *m(f)*. b (*Ling*) somali *m*.

Somalia [səʊˈmɑːlɪə] n Somalie *f*.

Somaliland [səʊˈmɑːlɪlænd] n Somalie *f*.

somata [ˈsəʊmətə] npl of **soma**.

somatic [səʊˈmætɪk] adj somatique.

somato... [ˈsəʊmətəʊ] pref somato... .

sombre, (*US*) somber [ˈsɒmbəʳ] adj *colour, outlook, prediction, prospect* sombre; *mood, person* sombre, morne; *day, weather* morne, maussade.

sombrely, (*US*) somberly [ˈsɒmbəlɪ] adv sombrement.

sombreness, (*US*) somberness [ˈsɒmbənɪs] n caractère *m or* aspect *m* sombre; (*colour*) couleur *f* sombre; (*darkness*) obscurité *f*.

sombrero [sɒmˈbrɛərəʊ] n sombrero *m*.

some [sʌm] 1 adj a (*a certain amount or number of*) ~ **tea/ice/water/cakes** du thé/de la glace/de l'eau/des gâteaux; **there are ~ children outside** il y a des enfants *or* quelques enfants dehors; ~ **old shoes** de vieilles chaussures; ~ **dirty shoes** des chaussures sales; **have you got ~ money?** est-ce que tu as de l'argent?; **will you have ~ more meat?** voulez-vous encore de la viande? *or* encore un peu de viande?; **this will give you ~ idea of ...** cela vous donnera une petite idée de ... .

b (*unspecified, unknown*) quelconque, quelque (*frm*). ~ **woman was asking for her** il y avait une dame qui la demandait; **I read it in ~ book (or other)** je l'ai lu quelque part dans un livre, je l'ai lu dans un livre quelconque; **at ~ place in Africa** quelque part en Afrique; **give it to ~ child** donnez-le à un enfant *or* à quelque enfant (*frm*); ~ **day** un de ces jours, un jour ou l'autre; ~ **day next week** (dans le courant de) la semaine prochaine; ~ **other day** un autre jour; ~ **other time!** pas maintenant!; ~ **time last week** (un jour) la semaine dernière; ~ **more talented person** quelqu'un de plus doué; **there must be ~ solution** il doit bien y avoir une solution (quelconque).

c (*contrasted with others*) ~ **children like school** certains enfants aiment l'école, il y a des enfants qui aiment l'école; ~ **few people** quelques rares personnes; ~ **people say that ...** certaines personnes disent que ..., il y a des gens qui disent que ..., on dit que ...; ~ **people like spinach, others don't** certaines personnes *or* certains aiment les épinards et d'autres non, il y a des gens qui aiment les épinards et d'autres non; ~ **people just don't care** il y a des gens qui ne s'en font pas *or* qui se fichent* de tout; (*in exasperation*) ~ **people!** il y a des gens, je vous jure!; ~ **butter is salty** certains beurres sont salés, certaines sortes de beurre sont salées; **in ~ ways, he's right** dans un (certain) sens, il a raison; **in ~ way or (an)other** d'une façon ou d'une autre.

d (*a considerable amount of*) pas mal de*, certain, quelque. **it took ~ courage to refuse** il a fallu un certain courage *or* pas mal de* courage pour refuser; **he spoke at ~ length** il a parlé assez longuement *or* pas mal de* temps *or* un certain temps; ~ **distance away** à quelque distance; **I haven't seen him for ~ years** cela fait quelques *or* plusieurs années que je ne l'ai pas vu; *see* **time**.

e (*emphatic: a little*) quand même un peu. **we still have SOME money left** il nous reste quand même un peu d'argent; **the book was SOME help but not much** le livre m'a aidé un peu mais pas beaucoup; **that's SOME consolation!** c'est quand même une petite consolation!

f (*: *intensive*) **that's ~ fish!** quel poisson!, c'est un fameux* poisson!, voilà ce qu'on appelle un poisson!; **she's ~ girl!** c'est une fille formidable!* *or* sensass!*; **that was ~ film!** quel film!, c'était un film formidable.

g (* *iro*) **you're ~ help!** tu parles* d'une aide!, que tu m'aides ou non c'est du pareil au même; **I'm trying to help! — ~ help!** j'essaie de t'aider! — tu parles!* *or* tu appelles ça aider?; ~ **garage that is!** vous parlez* d'un garage!

2 pron a (*a certain number*) quelques-un(e)s *m(f)pl*, certain(e)s *m(f)pl*. ~ **went this way and others went that** il y en a qui sont partis par ici et d'autres par là; ~ **(of them) have been sold** certains (d'entre eux) ont été vendus, on en a vendu quelques-uns *or* un certain nombre; **I've still got ~ of them** j'en ai encore quelques-uns *or* plusieurs; ~ **of them were late** certains d'entre eux *or* quelques-uns d'entre eux étaient en retard; ~ **of us knew him** quelques-uns d'entre nous le connaissaient; ~ **of my friends** certains *or* quelques-uns de mes amis; **I've got ~** j'en ai (quelques-uns *or* certains *or* plusieurs).

b (*a certain amount*) **I've got ~** j'en ai; **have ~!** prenez-en!, servez-vous!; **have ~ more** reprenez-en, resservez-vous; **give me ~!** donnez-m'en!; **if you find ~ tell me** si vous en trouvez dites-le-moi; **have ~ of this cake** prenez un peu de (ce) gâteau, prenez un morceau de (ce) gâteau; ~ **(of it) has been eaten** on en a mangé (un morceau *or* une partie); ~ **of this work is good** une partie de ce travail est bonne, ce travail est bon en partie; **I liked ~ of what you said in that speech** j'ai aimé certaines parties de votre discours *or* certaines choses dans votre discours; ~ **of what you say is true** il y a du vrai dans ce que vous dites; **and then ~!*** et plus (encore)!, et pas qu'un peu!*; *see* **time**.

3 adv a (*about*) quelque, environ. **there were ~ twenty houses** il y avait quelque *or* environ vingt maisons, il y avait une vingtaine de maisons.

b (*) *sleep, speak, wait* (*a bit*) un peu; (*a lot*) beaucoup. **you'll have to run ~ to catch him** tu vas vraiment devoir courir pour le rattraper, il va falloir que tu fonces* (*subj*) pour le rattraper; **Edinburgh-London in 30 minutes, that's going ~!** Edimbourg-Londres en 30 minutes, (il) faut le faire!‡

...some [səm] n ending in comps groupe *m* de ... . **threesome** groupe de trois personnes; **we went in a threesome** nous y sommes allés à trois; *see* **four** *etc*.

somebody [ˈsʌmbədɪ] pron a (*some unspecified person*) quelqu'un. **there is ~ at the door** il y a quelqu'un à la porte; **there is ~ knocking at the door** on frappe à la porte; ~ **else** quelqu'un d'autre; **he was talking to ~ tall and dark** il parlait à quelqu'un de grand aux cheveux sombres; **we need ~ really strong to do that** il nous faut quelqu'un de vraiment fort *or* quelqu'un qui soit vraiment fort pour faire cela; **ask ~ French** demande à un Français (quelconque); **they've got ~ French staying with them** ils ont un Français *or* quelqu'un de français chez eux en ce moment; ~ **from the audience** quelqu'un dans l'auditoire *or* l'assemblée; ~ **or other** quelqu'un, je ne sais qui; (*hum*) ~ **up there loves me*/hates me*** c'est/ce n'est pas mon jour de veine*; **Mr S~-or-other** Monsieur Chose *or* Machin*; **you must have seen SOMEBODY!** tu as bien dû voir quelqu'un!

b (*important person*) personnage important. **she thinks she's ~** elle se prend pour quelqu'un, elle se croit quelqu'un; **they think they are ~ *or* somebodies** ils se prennent pour *or* ils se croient des personnages importants.

somehow [ˈsʌmhaʊ] adv a (*in some way*) d'une façon ou d'une autre, d'une manière ou d'une autre, on ne sait trop comment. **it must be done ~ (or other)** il faut que ce soit fait d'une façon *or* manière ou d'une autre; **he managed it ~** il y est arrivé tant bien que mal; **we'll**

manage ~ on se débrouillera*; **we saved him ~ or other** nous l'avons sauvé je ne sais comment; **~ or other we must find £100** d'une façon ou d'une autre nous devons nous procurer 100 livres, nous devons nous débrouiller* pour trouver 100 livres.

b (*for some reason*) pour une raison ou pour une autre. **~ he's never succeeded** pour une raison ou pour une autre *or* pour une raison quelconque *or* je ne sais pas pourquoi il n'a jamais réussi; **it seems odd ~** je ne sais pas pourquoi mais ça semble bizarre.

someone ['sʌmwʌn] pron = **somebody.**

someplace ['sʌmpleɪs] adv (*US*) = **somewhere a.**

somersault ['sʌməsɔːlt] 1 n (*on ground, also accidental*) culbute *f*, (*by child*) galipette *f*; (*in air*) saut périlleux; (*by car*) tonneau *m*. **to turn a ~** faire la culbute *or* un saut périlleux *or* un tonneau. 2 vi *[person]* faire la culbute, faire un *or* des saut(s) périlleux; *[car]* faire un *or* plusieurs tonneau(x).

something ['sʌmθɪŋ] 1 pron a quelque chose *m*. **~ moved over there** il y a quelque chose qui a bougé là-bas; **~ must have happened to him** il a dû lui arriver quelque chose; **~ unusual** quelque chose d'inhabituel; **there must be ~ wrong** il doit y avoir quelque chose qui ne va pas; **did you say ~?** pardon?, comment?, vous dites?; **I want ~ to read** je veux quelque chose à lire; **I need ~ to eat** j'ai besoin de manger quelque chose; **would you like ~ to drink?** voulez-vous boire quelque chose?; **give him ~ to drink** donnez-lui (quelque chose) à boire; **he has ~ to live for at last** il a enfin une raison de vivre; **you can't get ~ for nothing** on n'a rien pour rien; **I have ~ else to do** j'ai quelque chose d'autre à faire, j'ai autre chose à faire; **it's ~ else!*** (*incredible*) c'est quelque chose!; (*in comparison*) c'est (vraiment) autre chose!, c'est une autre paire de manches!*; **I'll have to tell him ~ or other** il faudra que je lui dise quelque chose *or* que je trouve (*subj*) quelque chose à lui dire; **he whispered ~ or other in her ear** il lui a chuchoté quelque chose *or* on ne sait quoi à l'oreille; **~ of the kind** quelque chose dans ce genre-là; **there's ~ about her** *or* **she's got ~ about her I don't like** il y a chez elle *or* en elle quelque chose que je n'aime pas; **there's ~ in what you say** il y a du vrai dans ce que vous dites; **~ tells me that ...** j'ai l'impression que ...; **here's ~ for your trouble** voici pour votre peine; **give him ~ for himself** donnez-lui la pièce* *or* un petit quelque chose; **you've got ~ there!*** là tu n'as pas tort!, c'est vrai ce que tu dis là!; (*challengingly*) **do you want to make ~ (out) of it?** tu cherches la bagarre?*; **that's (really) ~!*, that really is ~!*** c'est pas rien!*, ça se pose là!*; **she has a certain ~*** elle a un petit quelque chose, elle a un certain je ne sais quoi; **that certain ~* which makes all the difference** ce petit je ne sais quoi qui fait toute la différence; **the 4-~* train** le train de 4 heures et quelques; **it's sixty-~** c'est soixante et quelques; **he's called Paul ~** il s'appelle Paul Chose *or* Paul quelque chose; **that has ~ to do with accountancy** ça a quelque chose à voir avec la comptabilité; **he's got ~ to do with it** (*is involved*) il a quelque chose à voir là-dedans (*or* avec ça); (*is responsible*) il y est pour quelque chose; **he is ~ to do with Brown and Co.** il a quelque chose à voir avec Brown et Cie.; **he is ~ (or other) in aviation** il est quelque chose dans l'aéronautique; **I hope to see ~ of you** j'espère vous voir un peu; **it is really ~ to find good coffee nowadays** ça n'est pas rien* de trouver du bon café aujourd'hui; **he scored 300 points, and that's ~!** il a marqué 300 points et ça c'est quelque chose!* *or* et ça n'est pas rien!*; **that's always ~** c'est toujours quelque chose, c'est toujours ça, c'est mieux que rien; **he thinks himself ~*** il se croit quelque chose, il se prend pour quelqu'un.

b **or ~** ou quelque chose dans ce genre-là, ou quelque chose comme ça; **he's got flu or ~** il a la grippe ou quelque chose comme ça *or* dans ce genre-là; **do you think you're my boss or ~?** tu te prends pour mon patron ou quoi?*; **he fell off a wall or ~** il est tombé d'un mur ou quelque chose dans ce genre-là*, je crois qu'il est tombé d'un mur.

c **he is ~ of a miser** il est quelque peu *or* plutôt avare; **he is ~ of a pianist** il est assez bon pianiste, il joue assez bien du piano, il est assez doué pour le piano; **it was ~ of a failure** c'était plutôt un échec.

2 adv a **he left ~ over £5,000** il a laissé plus de 5 000 livres, il a laissé dans les 5 000 livres et plus; **~ under £10** un peu moins de 10 livres; **he won ~ like 10,000 francs** il a gagné quelque chose comme 10 000 F, il a gagné dans les 10 000 F; **it's ~ like 10 o'clock** il est 10 heures environ, il est quelque chose comme 10 heures; **it weighs ~ around 5 kilos** ça pèse 5 kilos environ, ça pèse dans les 5 kilos, ça fait quelque chose comme 5 kilos; **there were ~ like 80 people there** 80 personnes environ étaient présentes, il y avait quelque chose comme 80 personnes; **he talks ~ like his father** il parle un peu comme son père; **now that's ~ like a claret!** voilà ce que j'appelle un bordeaux!, ça au moins c'est du bordeaux!; **now that's ~ like it!*** ça au moins c'est bien! *or* c'est vraiment pas mal!*

b (**: emphatic*) **it was ~ dreadful!** c'était vraiment épouvantable!; **the weather was ~ shocking!** comme mauvais temps ça se posait là!*; **the dog was howling ~ awful** le chien hurlait que c'en était abominable*, le chien hurlait fallait voir comme‡.

sometime ['sʌmtaɪm] 1 adv a (*in past*) **~ last month** le mois dernier, au cours du mois dernier; **~ last May** au (cours du) mois de mai dernier; **it was ~ last winter** c'était durant *or* pendant *or* au cours de l'hiver dernier (je ne sais pas *or* plus exactement quand); **it was ~ before 1950** c'était avant 1950 (je ne sais pas *or* plus exactement quand).

b (*in future*) un de ces jours, un jour ou l'autre. **~ soon** bientôt, avant peu; **~ before January** d'ici janvier; **~ next year** (dans le courant de) l'année prochaine; **~ after my birthday** après mon anniversaire; **~ or (an)other it will have to be done** il faudra (bien) le faire à un moment donné *or* tôt ou tard *or* un jour ou l'autre.

2 adj a (*former*) ancien (*before noun*). (*US*) **it's a ~ thing*** cela appartient au passé.

b (*US: occasional*) intermittent.

sometimes ['sʌmtaɪmz] adv a quelquefois, parfois, de temps en temps. b **~ happy ~ sad** tantôt gai tantôt triste; **~ he agrees and ~ not** tantôt il est d'accord et tantôt non.

somewhat ['sʌmwɒt] adv quelque peu. **~ surprised** quelque peu surpris; **it was ~ of a surprise** cela m'a (*or* l'a *etc*) quelque peu surpris; **he was more than ~ proud of ...** il n'était pas peu fier de ... .

somewhere ['sʌmwɛəʳ] adv a (*in space*) quelque part. **~ else** autre part, ailleurs; **he's ~ about** il est quelque part par ici, il n'est pas loin; **~ about** *or* **around here** (quelque part) par ici, pas loin d'ici; **~ near Paris** (quelque part) pas bien loin de Paris; **~ or other** je ne sais où, quelque part; **~ (or other) in France** quelque part en France; **he's in the garden or ~** il est dans le jardin ou quelque part; **have you got ~ to stay?** avez-vous trouvé où vous loger? *or* un logement?; (*fig*) **to be getting ~** faire des progrès, avancer.

b (*approximately*) environ. **~ about 10 o'clock** vers 10 heures, à 10 heures environ *or* à peu près; **she's ~ about fifty** elle a environ cinquante ans, elle a une cinquantaine d'années, elle a dans les cinquante ans; **he paid ~ about £12** il a payé environ 12 livres *or* dans les 12 livres.

Somme [sɒm] n (*river*) Somme *f*. **Battle of the ~** bataille *f* de la Somme.

somnambulism [sɒm'næmbjʊlɪzəm] n somnambulisme *m*.

somnambulist [sɒm'næmbjʊlɪst] n somnambule *mf*.

somniferous [sɒm'nɪfərəs] adj somnifère, soporifique.

somnolence ['sɒmnələns] n somnolence *f*.

somnolent ['sɒmnələnt] adj somnolent.

son [sʌn] 1 n fils *m*. (*Rel*) **S~ of God/Man** Fils de Dieu/de l'Homme; **his ~ and heir** son héritier; (*liter*) **the ~s of men** les hommes *mpl*; **he is his father's ~** (*in looks*) c'est tout le portrait de son père; (*in character*) c'est bien le fils de son père; **I've got 3 ~s** j'ai 3 fils *or* 3 garçons; **every mother's ~ of them** tous tant qu'ils sont (*or* étaient *etc*); **come here ~!*** viens ici mon garçon! *or* mon gars!* *or* fiston!*; *see* **father** *etc.* 2 comp ►**son-in-law** (pl **~s-~-~**) gendre *m*, beau-fils *m* ►**son-of-a-bitch**‡ (pl **~s-of-bitches**) salaud‡ *m*, fils *m* de garce‡ ►**son-of-a-gun**‡ (pl **~s-of-guns**) (espèce *f* de) vieille fripouille *or* vieux coquin.

sonar ['səʊnɑːʳ] n sonar *m*.

sonata [sə'nɑːtə] n sonate *f*. **~ form** forme *f* sonate.

sonatina [ˌsɒnə'tiːnə] n sonatine *f*.

sonde [sɒnd] n (*Met, Space*) sonde *f*.

sone [səʊn] n sone *f*.

song [sɒŋ] 1 n (*ditty, ballad, folksong etc*) chanson *f*; (*more formal*) chant *m*; *[birds]* chant, ramage *m*. **festival of French ~** festival *m* de chant français *or* de la chanson française; **to burst into ~** se mettre à chanter (une chanson *or* un air), entonner une chanson *or* un air; **give us a ~** chante-nous quelque chose; **~ without words** romance *f* sans paroles; **the S~ of S~s, the S~ of Solomon** Le cantique des cantiques; (*fig*) **it was going for a ~** c'était à vendre pour presque rien *or* pour une bouchée de pain; **what a ~ and dance* there was!** ça a fait une de ces histoires!*; **there's no need to make a ~ and dance* about it** il n'y a pas de quoi en faire toute une histoire* *or* tout un plat*; (*US: excuse*) **to give sb the same old ~ and dance*** débiter les excuses habituelles à qn; *see* **marching, sing** *etc.*

2 comp ►**songbird** oiseau chanteur ►**songbook** recueil *m* de chansons ►**song cycle** cycle *m* de chansons ►**song hit** chanson *f* à succès, tube* *m* ►**song thrush** grive musicienne ►**song writer** (*words*) parolier *m*, -ière *f*, auteur *m* de chansons; (*music*) compositeur *m*, -trice *f* de chansons; (*both*) auteur-compositeur *m*.

songfest ['sɒŋfest] n (*US*) festival *m* de chansons.

songster ['sɒŋstəʳ] n (*singer*) chanteur *m*; (*bird*) oiseau chanteur.

songstress ['sɒŋstrɪs] n chanteuse *f*.

sonic ['sɒnɪk] 1 adj *speed* sonique. **~ barrier** mur *m* du son, barrière *f* sonique; **~ boom** détonation *f* supersonique, bang *m* (super)sonique; **~ depth-finder** sonde *f* à ultra-sons; **~ mine** mine *f* acoustique. 2 n (*NonC*) **~s** l'acoustique *f* (*dans le domaine transsonique*).

sonnet ['sɒnɪt] n sonnet *m*.

sonny* ['sʌnɪ] n mon (petit) gars*, fiston* *m*. **~ boy, ~ Jim** mon gars*, fiston*.

sonority [sə'nɒrɪtɪ] n sonorité *f*.

sonorous ['sɒnərəs] adj sonore.

sonorously ['sɒnərəslɪ] adv *say* d'une voix sonore.

sonorousness ['sɒnərəsnɪs] n sonorité *f*.

soon [suːn] adv a (*before long*) bientôt; (*quickly*) vite. **we shall ~ be in Paris** nous serons bientôt à Paris, nous serons à Paris dans peu de temps *or* sous peu; **you would ~ get lost** vous seriez vite perdu; **he ~**

changed his mind il a vite changé d'avis, il n'a pas mis longtemps *or* il n'a pas tardé à changer d'avis; **I'll ~ finish that!** j'aurai bientôt terminé!, j'aurai vite *or* tôt fait!; **(I'll) see you ~!** à bientôt!; **very ~** très vite, très bientôt*; **quite ~** dans assez peu de temps, assez vite; **~ afterwards** peu après; **quite ~ afterwards** assez peu de temps après; **all too ~ it was over** ce ne fut que trop vite fini; **all too ~ it was time to go** malheureusement il a bientôt fallu partir; **the holidays can't come ~ enough!** vivement les vacances!

b (*early*) tôt. **why have you come so ~?** pourquoi êtes-vous venu si tôt?; **I expected you much ~er than this** je vous attendais bien plus tôt (que cela) *or* bien avant; **I couldn't get here any ~er** je n'ai pas pu arriver plus tôt; **how ~ can you get here?** dans combien de temps au plus tôt peux-tu être ici?, quel jour (*or* à quelle heure *etc*) peux-tu venir au plus tôt?; **how ~ will it be ready?** dans combien de temps *or* quand est-ce que ce sera prêt?; **Friday is too ~** vendredi c'est trop tôt; **we were none too ~** il était temps que nous arrivions (*subj*), nous sommes arrivés juste à temps; **and none too ~ at that!** et ce n'est pas trop tôt!; **must you leave so ~?** faut-il que vous partiez (*subj*) déjà? *or* si tôt?, quel dommage que vous deviez (*subj*) partir déjà! *or* si tôt!; **so ~?** déjà?; **on Friday at the ~est** vendredi au plus tôt, pas avant vendredi; **in 5 years or at his death, whichever is the ~er** dans 5 ans ou à sa mort, s'il meurt avant 5 ans *or* si celle-ci survient avant.

c (*in phrases*) **as ~ as possible** dès que possible, aussitôt que possible; **I'll do it as ~ as I can** je le ferai dès que je le pourrai *or* aussitôt que je le pourrai *or* aussitôt que possible; **let me know as ~ as you've finished** prévenez-moi dès que *or* aussitôt que vous aurez fini; **as ~ as he spoke to her he knew ...** aussitôt qu'il lui a parlé il a su ...; **as ~ as 7 o'clock** dès 7 heures; **the ~er we get started the ~er we'll be done** plus tôt nous commencerons plus tôt nous aurons fini, plus tôt commencé plus tôt fini; **the ~er the better!** le plus tôt sera le mieux!; (*iro*) il serait grand temps!, ça ne serait pas trop tôt!; **~er or later** tôt ou tard; **no ~er had he finished than his brother arrived** à peine avait-il fini que son frère est arrivé; **no ~er said than done!** aussitôt dit aussitôt fait!; **he could (just) as ~ fly to the moon as pass that exam** il a autant de chances de réussir cet examen que d'aller sur la lune.

d (*expressing preference*) **I'd ~er you didn't tell him** je préférerais que vous ne le lui disiez (*subj*) pas; **I'd as ~ you ...** j'aimerais autant que vous ... + (*subj*); **I would ~er stay here than go** je préférerais rester ici (plutôt) que d'y aller; **I would just as ~ stay here with you** j'aimerais tout autant rester ici avec vous, cela me ferait tout autant plaisir de rester ici avec vous; **he would as ~ die as betray his friends** il préférerait mourir plutôt que de trahir ses amis; **will you go? — I'd ~er not!** *or* **I'd as ~ not!** est-ce que tu iras? — je n'y tiens pas *or* je préférerais pas*; **I'd ~er die!** plutôt mourir!; **what would you ~er do?** qu'est-ce que vous aimeriez mieux (faire)? *or* vous préféreriez (faire)?; **~er than have to speak to her, he left** plutôt que d'avoir à lui parler il est parti; **she'd marry him as ~ as not** elle l'épouserait volontiers, elle aimerait bien l'épouser; **~er you than me!*** je n'aimerais pas être à ta place, je te souhaite bien du plaisir!* (*iro*).

sooner ['su:nəʳ] 1 **compar of soon.** 2 **n** (*US*) pionnier *m* de la première heure (*dans l'Ouest des États-Unis*). 3 **comp** ▸**the Sooner State** (*US*) l'Oklahoma *m*.

soot [sʊt] **n** (*NonC*) suie *f*.

▸**soot up** 1 **vi** s'encrasser. 2 **vt sep** encrasser.

sooth [su:θ] 1 **n** (††) vérité *f*. **in ~** en vérité. 2 **comp** ▸**soothsayer** devin *m*, devineresse *f* ▸**soothsaying** divination *f*.

soothe [su:ð] **vt** *person* calmer, apaiser; *nerves, mind, pain* calmer; *anger, anxieties* apaiser; *sb's vanity* flatter. **to ~ sb's fears** apaiser les craintes de qn, tranquilliser qn.

soothing ['su:ðɪŋ] **adj** *medicine, ointment* lénitif; *tone, voice, words* apaisant; *sb's presence* rassurant, réconfortant; *hot bath* relaxant. **you need a ~ hot drink** il te faut une boisson chaude, ça te fera du bien; **she's very ~** sa présence a quelque chose de rassurant *or* de réconfortant.

soothingly ['su:ðɪŋlɪ] **adv** d'une manière apaisante; *say, whisper* d'un ton apaisant.

sooty ['sʊtɪ] **adj** *surface, hands* couvert *or* noir de suie; *mixture, dust* fuligineux. **~ black** charbonneux.

SOP [ˌesəʊpi:] **n** (**abbr of standard operating procedure**) *see* **standard 2**.

sop [sɒp] **n** a (*Culin*) pain trempé (*dans du lait, du jus de viande etc*), mouillette *f*. **he can eat only ~s** il ne peut rien manger de trop solide, il doit se nourrir d'aliments semi-liquides; (*fig*) **it's just a ~ to Cerberus** c'est simplement pour le (*or* les *etc*) ramener à de meilleures dispositions *or* pour l'amadouer (*or* les *etc* amadouer); **he gave the guard £10 as a ~** il a donné 10 livres au gardien pour s'acheter ses bons services *or* pour lui graisser la patte*; **it's a ~ to my conscience** c'est pour faire taire ma conscience; **as a ~ to his pride, I agreed** j'ai accepté pour flatter son amour-propre; **he only said that as a ~ to the unions** il a dit cela uniquement pour amadouer les syndicats.

b (**: sissy*) (*man*) poule mouillée, lavette* *f*; (*woman*) femme *f* très fleur bleue.

▸**sop up** **vt sep** *spilt liquid [sponge, rag]* absorber; *[person]* éponger (*with* avec). **he sopped up the gravy with some bread** il a saucé son assiette avec un morceau de pain.

Sophia [səʊ'faɪə] **n** Sophie *f*.

sophism ['sɒfɪzəm] **n = sophistry**.

sophist ['sɒfɪst] **n** sophiste *mf*. (*Hist Philos*) **S~s** sophistes *mpl*.

sophistical [sə'fɪstɪkəl] **adj** sophistique, captieux.

sophisticate [sə'fɪstɪkeɪt] **n** raffiné(e) *m(f)*, élégant(e) *m(f)*.

sophisticated [sə'fɪstɪkeɪtɪd] **adj** *person* (*in taste, life style*) raffiné, blasé (*pej*); (*in appearance*) élégant, sophistiqué (*slightly pej*); *mind, style, tastes* raffiné, recherché; *clothes, room* d'une élégance raffinée *or* étudiée, plein de recherche; *play, film, book* plein de complexité, avancé; *song, revue* plein de recherche; *machinery, machine, method, weapon* hautement perfectionné, sophistiqué; *philosophy* développé, avancé; *discussion* subtil (*f* subtile); *wine* élégant. **he's very ~** il est très raffiné, il a beaucoup de savoir-vivre; **he's not very ~** il est très simple; **the author's ~ approach to this problem** la façon très mûre dont l'auteur aborde ce problème; **a ~ little black dress** une petite robe noire toute simple *or* d'un style très dépouillé.

sophistication [səˌfɪstɪ'keɪʃən] **n** (*see* **sophisticated**) raffinement *m*, caractère blasé; élégance *f*, sophistication *f*; recherche *f*; complexité *f*, caractère avancé; subtilité *f*; *[machine etc]* degré *m* de perfectionnement, complexité, sophistication.

sophistry ['sɒfɪstrɪ] **n** (*NonC*) sophistique *f*. **(piece of) ~** sophisme *m*; (*Hist Philos*) **S~** sophistique *f*.

Sophocles ['sɒfəkli:z] **n** Sophocle *m*.

sophomore ['sɒfəmɔ:ʳ] **n** (*US*) étudiant(e) *m(f)* de seconde année.

sophomoric [ˌsɒfə'mɔ:rɪk] **adj** (*US pej*) aussi prétentieux qu'ignorant.

soporific [ˌsɒpə'rɪfɪk] 1 **adj** soporifique. 2 **n** somnifère *m*.

sopping ['sɒpɪŋ] **adj** (*also* **~ wet**) *clothes* tout trempé, à tordre; *person* trempé (jusqu'aux os).

soppy* ['sɒpɪ] **adj** (*Brit*) a (*sentimental*) *person* sentimental, fleur bleue *inv*; *film, book, scene* sentimental, à l'eau de rose. b (*unmanly; without stamina*) mollasson, qui manque de nerf. **he's ~** c'est une mauviette *or* un mollasson, il manque de nerf. c (*silly*) *person* bébête*; *action* bête, idiot.

soprano [sə'prɑ:nəʊ] 1 **n, pl ~s** *or* **soprani** [sə'prɑ:ni:] (*singer*) soprano *mf*; (*voice, part*) soprano *m*; *see* **boy**. 2 **adj** *voice, part* de soprano; *aria* pour soprano. **~ clef** clef *f* d'ut dernière ligne.

sorb [sɔ:b] **n** (*tree*) sorbier *m*; (*fruit*) sorbe *f*.

sorbet ['sɔ:beɪ, 'sɔ:bɪt] **n** a (*water ice*) sorbet *m*. **lemon ~** sorbet au citron. b (*US*) = **sherbet a**.

sorbic ['sɔ:bɪk] **adj**: **~ acid** acide *m* sorbique.

sorbitol ['sɔ:bɪtɒl] **n** sorbitol *m*.

sorcerer ['sɔ:sərəʳ] **n** sorcier *m*. (*Mus etc*) **The S~'s Apprentice** l'Apprenti-sorcier *m*.

sorceress ['sɔ:sərеs] **n** sorcière *f*.

sorcery ['sɔ:sərɪ] **n** sorcellerie *f*.

sordid ['sɔ:dɪd] **adj** *conditions, surroundings* sordide, misérable, repoussant; (*fig*) *behaviour, motive, method* sordide, honteux, abject; *agreement, deal* honteux, infâme; *crime, greed, gains* sordide; *film, book* sale, dégoûtant, ignoble. **a ~ little room** une petite pièce sordide *or* d'une saleté repoussante *or* qui est un véritable taudis; **in ~ poverty** dans la misère la plus noire; **it's a pretty ~ business** c'est une affaire assez sordide *or* ignoble; **I find the whole thing quite ~** je suis écœuré par cette affaire; **all the ~ details** tous les détails sordides *or* répugnants; **they had a ~ little affair** ils ont eu ensemble une misérable petite liaison.

sordidly ['sɔ:dɪdlɪ] **adv** sordidement.

sordidness ['sɔ:dɪdnɪs] **n** *[conditions, surroundings]* aspect *m* sordide, misère *f*, saleté repoussante; (*fig*) *[behaviour, motive, method]* bassesse *f*; *[agreement, deal]* caractère honteux; *[crime, greed, gains]* caractère sordide; *[film, book]* saleté.

sore [sɔ:ʳ] 1 **adj** a (*painful*) douloureux, endolori, sensible; (*inflamed*) irrité, enflammé. **his ~ leg** sa jambe douloureuse *or* endolorie *or* qui lui fait (*or* faisait *etc*) mal; **this spot is very ~** cet endroit est très sensible *or* douloureux; **ouch! that's ~!** aïe! ça me fait mal!, aïe! tu me fais mal!; **where is it ~?** où est-ce que vous avez mal?; **tell me if it's ~** dites-moi si cela vous fait mal; **I'm ~ all over** j'ai mal partout; **I have a ~ finger/foot** j'ai mal au doigt/au pied; **I have a ~ head** j'ai mal à la tête, j'ai un mal de tête; (*fig*) **it's a ~ point** c'est un point délicat; (*liter*) **to be ~ at heart** être affligé *or* désolé; *see* **bear²**, **sight**, **throat** *etc*.

b (*esp US: offended*) contrarié, vexé (*about sth* par qch), fâché (*with sb* contre qn), en rogne* (*about sth* à cause de qch, *with sb* contre qn). **he was feeling very ~ about it** il en était vraiment ulcéré, ça l'a vraiment mis en rogne*; **to get ~** râler*, être en rogne* (*about sth* à cause de qch, *with sb* contre qn), prendre la mouche; **don't get ~!** ne te vexe pas!, ne te fâche pas!, ne râle* pas!; **what are you so ~ about?** pourquoi es-tu si fâché?, qu'est-ce que tu as à râler?*

c († *or liter*) **to be in ~ need of** avoir grandement besoin de; **a ~ temptation** une tentation difficile à vaincre.

2 **comp** ▸**sorehead*** (*US*) râleur* *m*, -euse* *f*, rouspéteur* *m*, -euse* *f*.

3 **adv** († *or liter*) cruellement, péniblement. **~ distressed** cruellement affligé; **to be ~ afraid** avoir grand-peur.

4 **n** (*Med*) plaie *f*. (*fig*) **to open up old ~s** rouvrir *or* raviver d'anciennes blessures (*fig*); *see* **running**.

sorely [ˈsɔːlɪ] adv *wounded* gravement, grièvement; *missed, regretted* amèrement. **it is ~ needed** on en a grandement besoin; **he/his patience was ~ tried** il/sa patience a été soumis(e) à rude *or* cruelle épreuve; **~ tempted** fortement *or* très tenté.

soreness [ˈsɔːnɪs] n a (*Med etc*) (*painfulness*) endolorissement *m*. b (* *fig*) (*annoyance*) contrariété *f*, irritation *f*; (*bitterness*) amertume *f*; (*anger*) colère *f*, rogne* *f*.

sorghum [ˈsɔːgəm] n sorgho *m*.

soroptimist [sɒˈrɒptɪmɪst] n *membre d'une association internationale pour les femmes dans les professions libérales*.

sorority [səˈrɒrɪtɪ] n (*US Univ*) club féminin, club d'étudiantes.

sorrel [ˈsɒrəl] 1 n a (*Bot*) oseille *f*. b (*horse*) alezan clair *m*; (*colour*) roux *m*, brun rouge *m*. 2 adj *horse* alezan clair *inv*.

sorrow [ˈsɒrəʊ] 1 n peine *f*, chagrin *m*, tristesse *f*; (*stronger*) douleur *f*. **his ~ at the loss of his son** la peine *or* le chagrin *or* la douleur qu'il a éprouvé(e) à la mort de son fils; **to my (great) ~** à mon grand chagrin, à ma grande tristesse *or* douleur; **this was a great ~ to me** j'en ai eu beaucoup de peine *or* de chagrin *or* de tristesse; **he was a great ~ to her** il lui a causé beaucoup de peine *or* de chagrin; **more in ~ than in anger** avec plus de peine *or* de tristesse que de colère; **the ~s of their race** les afflictions *fpl or* les peines qui pèsent sur leur race; (*Rel*) **the Man of S~s** l'Homme de douleur; *see* **drown**.
2 vi: **to ~ over** *sb's death, loss* pleurer; *news* déplorer, se lamenter de; **she sat ~ing by the fire** elle était assise au coin du feu toute à son chagrin.

sorrowful [ˈsɒrəʊfʊl] adj *person* triste, (*stronger*) affligé; *expression, look, smile, face* triste, attristé, (*stronger*) désolé; *news* pénible, triste, affligeant; *music* triste, mélancolique.

sorrowfully [ˈsɒrəʊfəlɪ] adv tristement, avec chagrin, d'un air triste *or* désolé; *say* d'un ton triste *or* désolé.

sorrowing [ˈsɒrəʊɪŋ] adj affligé.

sorry [ˈsɒrɪ] adj a (*regretful*) désolé. **I was ~ to hear of your accident** j'étais désolé *or* très peiné *or* navré d'apprendre que vous avez eu un accident; **I am ~ I cannot come** je regrette *or* je suis désolé de ne (pas) pouvoir venir; **I am ~ she cannot come** je regrette *or* je suis désolé qu'elle ne puisse (pas) venir; **I am ~ to have to tell you that ...** je regrette d'avoir à vous dire que ...; (*frm*) **we are ~ to inform you ...** nous avons le regret de vous informer ...; **he didn't pass, I'm ~ to say** il a échoué hélas *or* malheureusement; **(I am) ~ I am late, I'm ~ to be late** excusez-moi *or* je suis désolé d'être en retard; **say you're ~!** dis *or* demande pardon!; **~!, ~ about that!*** pardon!, excusez-moi!, je suis désolé!; **I'm very** *or* **terribly ~** je suis vraiment désolé *or* navré; **awfully ~!, so ~!** oh pardon!, excusez-moi!, je suis vraiment désolé!; **will you go? — I'm ~ I can't** est-ce que tu vas y aller? — impossible hélas *or* (je suis) désolé mais je ne peux pas; **can you do it? — no, ~** est-ce que tu peux le faire? — non, désolé *or* désolé, je ne peux pas *or* malheureusement pas; **I am ~ to disturb you** je suis désolé de vous déranger, excusez-moi de vous déranger; **I am** *or* **feel ~ about all the noise yesterday** je regrette beaucoup qu'il y ait eu tellement de bruit hier; **~ about that vase!** excusez-moi pour ce vase!; **you'll be ~ for this!** vous le regretterez!, vous vous en repentirez!
b (*pitying*) **to be** *or* **feel ~ for sb** plaindre qn; **I feel so ~ for her since her husband died** elle me fait pitié depuis la mort de son mari; **I'm ~ for you but you should have known better** je suis désolé pour vous *or* je vous plains mais vous auriez dû être plus raisonnable; (*iro*) **if he can't do better than that then I'm ~ for him** s'il ne peut pas faire mieux, je regrette pour lui *or* je le plains; **there's no need to feel** *or* **be ~ for him** il est inutile de le plaindre, il n'est pas à plaindre; **to be** *or* **feel ~ for o.s.** se plaindre (de son sort), s'apitoyer sur soi-même *or* sur son propre sort; **he looked very ~ for himself** il faisait piteuse mine.
c (*woeful*) *condition* triste, déplorable, lamentable; *excuse* piètre, mauvais, lamentable. **to be in a ~ plight** être dans une triste situation, être en fâcheuse posture; **to be in a ~ state** être dans un triste état, être en piteux état; **he was a ~ figure** il faisait triste *or* piteuse figure; **a ~ sight** un triste spectacle, un spectacle désolant *or* affligeant; **it was a ~ tale of mismanagement and inefficiency** c'était une lamentable *or* déplorable histoire de mauvaise gestion et d'inefficacité.

sort [sɔːt] 1 n a (*class, variety, kind, type*) genre *m*, espèce *f*, sorte *f*; (*make*) [*car, machine, coffee etc*] marque *f*. **this ~ of book** ce genre de *or* cette espèce de *or* cette sorte de livre; **books of all ~s** des livres de tous genres *or* de toutes espèces *or* de toutes sortes; **... and all ~s of things** ... et toutes sortes de choses encore, ... et j'en passe, ... et que sais-je; **this ~ of thing(s)** ce genre de chose(s); **what ~ of flour do you want? — the ~ you gave me last time** quelle sorte *or* quelle espèce *or* quel genre de farine voulez-vous? — la même que vous m'avez donnée (*or* le même que vous m'avez donné) la dernière fois; **what ~ do you want?** vous en (*or* le *or* la *etc*) voulez de quelle sorte?; **what ~ of car is it?** quelle marque de voiture est-ce?; **what ~ of man is he?** quel genre *or* type d'homme est-ce?; **what ~ of dog is he?** qu'est-ce que c'est comme (race de) chien?; **he is not the ~ of man to refuse** ce n'est pas le genre d'homme à refuser, il n'est pas homme à refuser; **he's not that ~ of person** ce n'est pas son genre; **I'm not that ~ of girl!** ce n'est pas mon genre!, mais pour qui me prenez-vous?; **that's the ~ of person I am** c'est comme ça que je suis (fait); **what ~ of people does he think we are?** (mais enfin) pour qui nous prend-il?; **what ~ of a fool does he take me for?** (non mais*) il me prend pour un imbécile!; **what ~ of behaviour is this?** qu'est-ce que c'est que cette façon de se conduire?; **what ~ of an answer do you call that?** vous appelez ça une réponse?; **classical music is the ~ she likes most** c'est la musique classique qu'elle préfère; **and all that ~ of thing** et autres choses du même genre, et tout ça*; **you know the ~ of thing I mean** vous voyez (à peu près) ce que je veux dire; **I don't like that ~ of talk/behaviour** je n'aime pas ce genre de conversation/de conduite; **he's the ~ that will cheat** il est du genre à tricher; **I know his ~!** je connais les gens de son genre *or* espèce; **your ~* never did any good** les gens de votre genre *or* espèce ne font rien de bien; **they're not our ~*** ce ne sont pas des gens comme nous; **it's my ~* of film** c'est le genre de film que j'aime *or* qui me plaît.
b (*in phrases*) **something of the ~** quelque chose de ce genre(-là) *or* d'approchant; **this is wrong — nothing of the ~!** c'est faux — pas le moins du monde!; **I shall do nothing of the ~!** je n'en ferai rien!, certainement pas!; **I will have nothing of the ~!** je ne tolérerai pas cela!; (*pej*) **it was beef of a ~** c'était quelque chose qui pouvait passer pour du bœuf; **he is a painter of ~s** c'est un peintre si l'on peut dire; **after a ~, in some ~** dans une certaine mesure, en quelque sorte, jusqu'à un certain point; **to be out of ~s** ne pas être dans son assiette; (*Prov*) **it takes all ~s (to make a world)** il faut de tout pour faire un monde (*Prov*); (*fig*) **a good ~*** un brave garçon, un brave type*; une brave fille.
c **a ~ of** une sorte *or* espèce de, un genre de; **there was a ~ of box in the middle of the room** il y avait une sorte *or* une espèce *or* un genre de boîte au milieu de la pièce, il y avait quelque chose qui ressemblait à une boîte au milieu de la pièce; **there was a ~ of tinkling sound** il y avait une sorte *or* une espèce de bruit de grelot, on entendait quelque chose qui ressemblait à un bruit de grelot; **in a ~ of way* I'm sorry** d'une certaine façon je le regrette; **I had a ~ of fear that ..., I was ~ of* frightened that ...** j'avais comme peur que ... + ne + *subj*; **I ~ of* thought that he would come** j'avais un peu l'idée qu'il viendrait; **he was ~ of* worried-looking** il avait un peu l'air inquiet, il avait l'air comme qui dirait* inquiet; **it's ~ of* blue** c'est plutôt bleu; **aren't you pleased? — ~ of!*** tu n'es pas content? — assez! *or* ben si!*
2 comp ▸ **sort code** (*Banking*) numéro *m* d'agence ▸ **sort-out***: **to have a sort-out** faire du rangement; **I've had a sort-out of all these old newspapers** j'ai trié tous ces vieux journaux.
3 vt a (*also* **~ out**) (*classify*) *documents, stamps* classer; (*select those to keep*) *documents, clothes, apples* trier, faire le tri de; (*separate*) séparer (*from* de). **he spent the morning ~ing (out) his stamp collection** il a passé la matinée à classer *or* trier les timbres de sa collection; **to ~ things (out) into sizes** *or* **according to size** trier des objets selon leur taille; (*Cards*) **to ~ out one's cards** *or* **one's hand** arranger ses cartes, mettre de l'ordre dans ses cartes; **to ~ (out) the clothes into clean and dirty** séparer les vêtements sales des propres, mettre les vêtements sales à part; **can you ~ out the green ones and keep them aside?** pourriez-vous les trier et mettre les verts à part?
b (*Post: letters etc; Comput: data, file*) trier.
c (*Scot *: mend*) arranger. **I've ~ed your bike** j'ai arrangé ton vélo.

▸**sort out** 1 vt sep a = **sort 3a**.
b (*fig*) (*tidy*) *papers, toys, clothes* ranger, mettre de l'ordre dans; *ideas* mettre de l'ordre dans; (*solve*) *problem* régler, résoudre; *difficulties* venir à bout de; (*fix, arrange*) arranger. **I just can't sort the twins out* (one from the other)** je ne peux pas distinguer les jumeaux (l'un de l'autre); **can you sort this out for me?** est-ce que vous pourriez débrouiller ça pour moi?; **we've got it all sorted out now** nous avons réglé *or* résolu la question; **we'll soon sort it out** nous aurons vite fait d'arranger ça *or* de régler ça; **things will sort themselves out** les choses vont s'arranger d'elles-mêmes; **he was so excited I couldn't sort out what had happened** il était tellement excité que je n'ai pas pu débrouiller *or* comprendre ce qui s'était passé; **did you sort out with him when you had to be there?** est-ce que tu as décidé *or* fixé avec lui l'heure à laquelle tu dois y être?; (*Brit*) **to sort sb out*** (*by punishing, threatening etc*) régler son compte à qn*; (*get him out of difficulty etc*) tirer qn d'affaire; (*after depression, illness etc*) aider qn à reprendre pied (*fig*).
c (*explain*) **to sort sth out for sb** expliquer qch à qn.
2 **sort-out*** n *see* **sort 2**.

sorter [ˈsɔːtəʳ] n a (*person*) trieur *m*, -euse *f*. b (*machine*) (*for letters*) trieur *m*; (*for punched cards*) trieuse *f*; (*for grain*) trieur; (*for wool, coke etc*) trieur, trieuse.

sortie [ˈsɔːtɪ] n (*Aviat, Mil*) sortie *f*. **they made** *or* **flew 400 ~s** ils ont fait 400 sorties.

sorting [ˈsɔːtɪŋ] 1 n (*Comput, Post*) tri *m*. 2 comp ▸ **sorting office** (*Post*) bureau *m or* centre *m* de tri.

SOS [ˌesəʊˈes] n (*signal*) S.O.S. *m*; (*fig*) S.O.S., appel *m* au secours (*for sth* pour demander qch).

sot [sɒt] n ivrogne invétéré.

sottish [ˈsɒtɪʃ] adj abruti par l'alcool.

sotto voce [ˈsɒtəʊˈvəʊtʃɪ] adv (tout) bas, à mi-voix; (*Mus*) sotto-voce.

sou' [saʊ] adj (*Naut: in comps*) = **south**.

Soudan [suˈdɑːn] n = **Sudan**.

Soudanese [ˌsuːdəˈniːz] = **Sudanese.**

soufflé [ˈsuːfleɪ] 1 n soufflé *m*. **cheese/fish ~** soufflé au fromage/au poisson. 2 comp ▸**soufflé dish** moule *m* à soufflé ▸**soufflé omelette** omelette soufflée.

sough [saʊ] (*liter*) 1 n murmure *m* (du vent). 2 vi *[wind]* murmurer.

sought [sɔːt] pret, ptp of **seek.**

soul [səʊl] 1 n a âme *f*. **with all one's ~** de toute son âme, de tout son cœur; **All S~s' Day** le jour des Morts; **upon my ~!*†** grand Dieu!; **he cannot call his ~ his own** il ne s'appartient pas, il est complètement dominé; (*fig*) **he was the ~ of the movement** c'était lui l'âme *or* l'animateur *m or* la cheville ouvrière du mouvement; **he is the ~ of discretion** c'est la discrétion même *or* personnifiée *or* en personne; **he has no ~** il est trop terre à terre, il a trop les pieds sur terre; **it lacks ~** cela manque de sentiment; *see* **bare, body, heart, sell** *etc.*

b (*person*) âme *f*, personne *f*. **a village of 300 ~s** un village de 300 âmes *or* habitants; **the ship sank with 200 ~s** le bateau a sombré avec 200 personnes à bord; **the ship sank with all ~s** le bateau a péri corps et biens; **I didn't see a (single *or* living) ~** je n'ai vu personne, je n'ai pas vu âme qui vive; **don't tell a ~** surtout n'en soufflez mot à personne; **(you) poor ~!** mon (*or* ma) pauvre!; **he's a good ~** c'est une excellente personne, il est bien brave*; **lend me your pen, there's a good ~*** sois gentil *or* sois un ange, prête-moi ton stylo; *see* **simple** *etc.*

c (*US: esp of black Americans*) soul *m*, *façon de ressentir des Noirs.*

d (*US **) (abbr of **soul brother, soul food** *and* **soul music**) *see* **2.**

2 adj (*US: of black Americans*) (*gen*) noir, de Noirs; *hotel etc* où l'on ne pratique pas la discrimination; *radio station* émettant pour un public noir. **~ brother** frère *m* de race (*terme employé par les Noirs entre eux*); **S~ City*** Harlem; **~ food** nourriture *f* traditionnelle des Noirs du Sud; **~ music** musique *f* soul, soul *m*; **~ sister** sœur *f* de race (*terme employé par les Noirs entre eux*).

3 comp ▸**soul-destroying** (*boring*) abrutissant; (*depressing*) démoralisant ▸**soul mate*** âme *f* sœur ▸**soul-searching** introspection *f*; **after a lot of soul-searching ...** après avoir bien fait son (*or* mon *etc*) examen de conscience ... ▸**soul-stirring** très émouvant.

soulful [ˈsəʊlfʊl] adj *expression, performance, music* sentimental, attendrissant; *eyes, glance* expressif, éloquent.

soulfully [ˈsəʊlfəlɪ] adv *sing, write* de façon sentimentale *or* attendrissante; *look* d'un air expressif *or* éloquent.

soulless [ˈsəʊllɪs] adj *person* sans cœur; *cruelty* inhumain; *task* abrutissant.

sound¹ [saʊnd] 1 n (*Ling, Mus, Phys, Rad, TV etc*) son *m*; *[sea, storm, breaking glass, car brakes etc]* bruit *m*; *[sb's voice, bell, violins etc]* son. **the speed of ~** la vitesse du son; **within ~ of** à portée du son de; **to the ~(s) of the national anthem** au(x) son(s) de l'hymne national; **there was not a ~ to be heard** on n'entendait pas le moindre bruit; **without (making) a ~** sans bruit, sans faire le moindre bruit; **we heard the ~ of voices** nous avons entendu un bruit de voix; **the Glenn Miller ~** la musique de Glenn Miller; (*fig*) **I don't like the ~ of it** (*it doesn't attract me*) ça ne me dit rien, ça ne me plaît pas; (*it's worrying*) ça m'inquiète; (*fig*) **I don't like the ~ of his plans** ses projets ne me disent rien qui vaille; (*fig*) **the news has a depressing ~** les nouvelles semblent déprimantes.

2 comp *film, recording* sonore ▸**sound archives** phonothèque *f* ▸**sound barrier** mur *m* du son ▸**sound bite** phrase *f* toute faite (*pour être citée dans les médias*); **to talk in sound bites** parler en utilisant des phrases toutes faites ▸**sound board** = **sounding board** (*see* **sounding¹**) ▸**sound box** (*Mus*) caisse *f* de résonnance ▸**sound change** (*Phon*) changement *m* phonétique ▸**sound effects** (*Rad etc*) bruitage *m*; **sound effects man** (*Cine, TV, Rad*) bruiteur *m* ▸**sound engineer** (*Cine, Rad etc*) ingénieur *m* du son ▸**sound hole** (*Mus*) ouïe *f* ▸**sounding board** *see* **sounding¹** ▸**sound law** (*Phon*) loi *f* phonétique ▸**sound library** phonothèque *f* ▸**sound pollution** nuisance *f* due au bruit ▸**soundpost** (*Mus*) âme *f* ▸**sound-producing** (*Phon*) phonatoire ▸**soundproof** vt insonoriser ◊ adj insonorisé ▸**soundproofing** insonorisation *f* ▸**sound shift** (*Phon*) mutation *f* phonétique ▸**sound stage** (*Recording*) salle *f* de tournage ▸**sound system** (*Ling*) système *m* de sons; (*hi-fi*) chaîne *f* hi-fi; (*for disco, concert*) sonorisation *f*, sono* *f* ▸**soundtrack** (*Cine*) bande *f* sonore ▸**sound truck** (*US*) camionnette équipée d'un haut-parleur ▸**sound wave** (*Phys*) onde *f* sonore.

3 vi a *[bell, trumpet, voice]* sonner, retentir; *[car horn, siren, signal, order]* retentir. **footsteps/a gun ~ed a long way off** on a entendu un bruit de pas/un coup de canon dans le lointain; (*fig*) **a note of warning ~s through his writing** un avertissement retentit dans ses écrits; **it ~s better if you read it slowly** c'est *or* ça sonne mieux si vous le lisez lentement.

b (*suggest by sound*) **that instrument ~s like a flute** le son de cet instrument ressemble à celui de la flûte, on dirait le son de la flûte; **it ~s empty** (au son) on dirait que c'est vide; **a language which ~ed (to me) like Dutch** une langue qui aurait pu être *or* qui (me) semblait être du hollandais; **he ~s (like an) Australian** à l'entendre parler on dirait un Australien; **the train ~ed a long way off, it ~ed as if *or* as though the train were a long way off** le train semblait être encore bien loin; **it ~ed as if someone were coming in** on aurait dit que quelqu'un entrait; **that ~s like Paul arriving** ça doit être Paul qui arrive; **she ~s tired** elle semble fatiguée; **you ~ like your mother when you say things like that** quand tu parles comme ça, tu me rappelles ta mère *or* on croirait entendre ta mère; (*to sick person*) **you ~ terrible** (à t'entendre) tu sembles en triste état.

c (*fig: seem, appear*) sembler (être). **that ~s like an excuse** cela a l'air d'une excuse, cela ressemble à une excuse; **how does it ~ to you?** qu'en penses-tu?; **it ~s like a good idea** ça a l'air d'(être) une bonne idée, ça semble être une bonne idée; **it doesn't ~ too good** cela n'annonce rien de bon, ce n'est pas très prometteur; **it ~s as if she isn't coming** j'ai l'impression qu'elle ne viendra pas; **you don't ~ like the kind of person we need** (à en juger par ce que vous dites) vous ne semblez pas être le genre de personne qu'il nous faut.

4 vt a *bell, alarm* sonner; *trumpet, bugle* sonner de; (*Mil*) *reveille, retreat* sonner. (*Mil*) **to ~ the last post** envoyer la sonnerie aux morts; (*Aut*) **to ~ the *or* one's horn** klaxonner; (*Aut*) **~ing the horn** l'usage *m* du klaxon; (*fig*) **to ~ a (note of) warning** lancer un avertissement; **to ~ sb's praises** faire l'éloge de qn, chanter les louanges de qn.

b (*Ling*) **to ~ one's "t's** faire sonner ses "t"; **the "n" in "hymn" is not ~ed** le "n" de "hymn" ne se prononce pas.

c (*examine*) *rails, train wheels* vérifier au marteau. (*Med*) **to ~ sb's chest** ausculter qn.

▸**sound off** vi a (‡) (*proclaim one's opinions*) faire de grands laïus* (*about* sur); (*boast*) se vanter (*about* de), la ramener‡ (*about* à propos de); (*grumble*) rouspéter*, râler* (*about* à propos de). **to sound off at sb** engueuler‡ qn. b (*US Mil: number off*) se numéroter.

sound² [saʊnd] 1 adj a (*healthy; robust*) *person* en bonne santé, bien portant; *heart* solide; *constitution, teeth, lungs, fruit, tree* sain; *timber* sain, solide; *structure, floor, bridge* solide, en bon état; (*fig*) *firm, business, financial position* sain, solide; *bank, organization* solide; *alliance, investment* bon, sûr, sans danger. **the bullet struck his ~ leg** la balle a atteint sa jambe valide; **of ~ mind** sain d'esprit; **~ in body and mind** sain de corps et d'esprit; **to be ~ in wind and limb** avoir bon pied bon œil; **to be as ~ as a bell** être en parfait état; *see* **safe.**

b (*competent, judicious, sensible*) *reasoning, judgment* solide, juste, sain; *doctrine* orthodoxe, solide; *argument* solide, valable; *decision, step, advice, opinion* sensé, valable, judicieux; *case, training* solide; *rule, policy, behaviour, tactics* sensé, valable; *claim, title* valable, sérieux; *statesman, player etc* compétent. **he is a ~ worker** il sait travailler, il est compétent dans son travail; **he is a ~ socialist** c'est un bon socialiste, c'est un socialiste bon teint; **he is ~ enough on theory ...** il connaît très bien la théorie ...; **he is a ~ chap** (*sensible*) il est très sérieux *or* sensé; (*we can trust him*) c'est quelqu'un en qui on peut avoir confiance; **~ sense** bon sens, sens pratique; **that was a ~ move** c'était une action judicieuse *or* sensée.

c (*thorough*) *defeat* complet (*f* -ète), total; *sleep* profond. **a ~ thrashing** une bonne *or* belle correction; **he is a ~ sleeper** il a un bon sommeil, il dort bien.

2 adv: **to be ~ asleep** être profondément endormi, dormir à poings fermés; **to sleep ~** bien dormir.

sound³ [saʊnd] 1 n (*Med: probe*) sonde *f*. 2 comp ▸**sound(ing) line** *see* **sounding² 2.** 3 vt (*gen, Med, Naut etc*) sonder; (*fig: also* **~ out**) *person* sonder (*on, about* sur). **to ~ sb's opinions/feelings on sth** sonder qn sur ses opinions/ses sentiments à propos de qch. 4 vi sonder.

sound⁴ [saʊnd] n (*Geog*) détroit *m*, bras *m* de mer.

sounding¹ [ˈsaʊndɪŋ] 1 n a *[trumpet, bell etc]* son *m*. **the ~ of the retreat/the alarm** le signal de la retraite/de l'alerte. b (*Med*) auscultation *f*. 2 comp ▸**sounding board** (*Mus*) table *f* d'harmonie; (*behind rostrum etc*) abat-voix *m inv*; (*fig*) **he used the committee as a sounding board for his new idea** il a d'abord essayé sa nouvelle idée sur les membres du comité.

sounding² [ˈsaʊndɪŋ] 1 n (*Aviat, Naut, Space etc*) (*act*) sondage *m*. (*measurement, data*) **~s** sondages; (*lit, fig*) **to take ~s** faire des sondages. 2 comp ▸**sounding line** ligne *f* de sonde.

-sounding [ˈsaʊndɪŋ] adj ending in comps qui sonne. **foreign-sounding name** nom *m* qui a une consonnance étrangère; **strange-/respectable-sounding** qui sonne étrange/respectable *or* bien.

soundless [ˈsaʊndlɪs] adj silencieux.

soundlessly [ˈsaʊndlɪslɪ] adv sans bruit, en silence.

soundly [ˈsaʊndlɪ] adv *sleep* profondément; *advise, reason, argue* de façon sensée *or* valable, judicieusement, avec justesse *or* bon sens; *organize, manage* bien, de façon saine *or* sûre; *invest* bien, sans danger; (*Sport*) *play* de façon compétente. **~ based** *business, firm* sain, solide; *financial position* sain, solide, sans danger; **he was ~ beaten** (*defeated*) il a été complètement battu, il a été battu à plate(s) couture(s); (*thrashed*) il a reçu une bonne *or* belle correction; *see* **sleep.**

soundness [ˈsaʊndnɪs] n (*see* **sound²**) *[body]* santé *f*; *[mind]* équilibre *m*, santé; *[business]* solidité *f*; (*solvency*) solvabilité *f*; *[argument]* solidité; *[judgment]* justesse *f*; *[doctrine]* orthodoxie *f*; *[sleep]* profondeur *f*.

soup [suːp] 1 n a soupe *f*; (*thinner or sieved*) potage *m*; (*very smooth*) velouté *m*. **clear ~** potage clair; **mushroom/tomato ~** velouté de champignons/de tomates; **onion** ~ soupe à l'oignon; **vegetable** ~ soupe *or* potage aux légumes; (*fig*) **to be in the** ~* être dans le pétrin* *or* dans de beaux draps; *see* **pea** *etc*. **b** (*US* ‡: *nitroglycerine*) nitroglycérine *f*. **2** **comp** ►**soup cube** potage *m* en cube; (*stock cube*) bouillon-cube *m* ►**soup kitchen** soupe *f* populaire ►**soup plate** assiette creuse *or* à soupe ►**soupspoon** cuiller *f* à soupe ►**soup tureen** soupière *f*.

►**soup up*** **vt sep** (*Aut*) *engine* gonfler*. **he was driving a souped-up Mini** ® il conduisait une Mini ® au moteur gonflé* *or* poussé.

soupçon ['su:psɔ̃:n] **n** *[garlic, malice]* soupçon *m*, pointe *f*.

soupy ['su:pɪ] **adj** *liquid* (*thick*) épais (*f* -aisse); (*unclear*) trouble; *fog, atmosphere* épais, dense; (* *fig: sentimental*) *film, story, voice* sirupeux.

sour ['saʊəʳ] **1** **adj** *flavour, fruit, wine etc* aigre, acide, sur; *milk* tourné, aigre; *soil* trop acide; (*fig*) *person, voice* acerbe, revêche, aigre; *face* revêche, rébarbatif; *remark* aigre, acerbe. **the juice is too** ~ le jus est trop acide *or* n'est pas assez sucré; ~**(ed) cream** ≈ crème *f* aigre; **to go** *or* **turn** ~ *[milk]* tourner, devenir aigre; *[relationship, discussion]* tourner au vinaigre; *[plans]* mal tourner; **to be in a** ~ **mood** être d'humeur revêche *or* massacrante; (*fig*) **it was clearly** ~ **grapes on his part** il l'a manifestement fait (*or* dit *etc*) par dépit *or* par rancœur.

2 **comp** ►**sourdough** (*US*) levain *m* ►**sour-faced** à la mine revêche *or* rébarbative ►**sourpuss*** grincheux *m*, -euse *f*.

3 **vt** aigrir (*also fig*); *milk* faire tourner.

4 **vi** **a** (*lit*) s'aigrir; *[milk]* tourner.

b (*fig*) *[person, character]* s'aigrir; *[relations]* se dégrader; *[situation]* mal tourner, se dégrader.

5 **n: whisky** *etc* ~ cocktail *m* de whisky *etc* au citron.

source [sɔ:s] **1** **n** *[river]* source *f*; (*fig*) source, origine *f*. (*Literat etc*) ~**s** sources; **a** ~ **of heat** une source de chaleur; (*Med*) **a** ~ **of infection** un foyer d'infection; **we have other** ~**s of supply** nous avons d'autres sources d'approvisionnement, nous pouvons nous approvisionner ailleurs; **what is the** ~ **of this information?** quelle est l'origine *or* la provenance de cette nouvelle?; **I have it from a reliable** ~ **that ...** je tiens de bonne source *or* de source sûre que ...; **at** ~ à la source. **2** **comp** ►**source language** (*Ling*) langue *f* de départ; (*Comput*) langage *m* source ►**source materials** (*Literat etc*) sources *fpl* ►**source program** (*Comput*) programme *m* source.

sourcing ['sɔ:sɪŋ] **n** (*Comm*) approvisionnement *m*.

sourdine [sʊə'di:n] **n** sourdine *f*.

sourish ['saʊərɪʃ] **adj** (*lit, fig*) aigrelet.

sourly ['saʊəlɪ] **adv** aigrement, avec aigreur.

sourness ['saʊənɪs] **n** (*see* **sour 1**) aigreur *f*, acidité *f*; humeur *f or* aspect *m or* ton *m* revêche.

sousaphone ['su:zəfəʊn] **n** sousaphone *m*.

souse [saʊs] **1** **vt** **a** (*immerse*) tremper (*in* dans); (*soak*) faire *or* laisser tremper (*in* dans). **to** ~ **sth with water** inonder qch d'eau; (*fig: drunk*) ~**d**‡ rond*, noir‡. **b** (*Culin*) mariner. ~**d herrings** harengs marinés; (*rolled up*) rollmops *mpl*. **2** **n** **a** (*Culin*) marinade *f* (*à base de vinaigre*). **b** (‡: *drunkard*) poivrot* *m*, ivrogne *m*.

south [saʊθ] **1** **n** sud *m*. **to the** ~ **of** au sud de; **in the** ~ **of Scotland** dans le sud de l'Écosse; **house facing the** ~ maison exposée au sud *or* au midi; *[wind]* **to veer to the** ~, **to go into the** ~ tourner au sud; **the wind is in the** ~ le vent est au sud; **the wind is (coming** *or* **blowing) from the** ~ le vent vient *or* souffle du sud; **to live in the** ~ habiter dans le Sud; (*in France*) habiter dans le Midi; **the S**~ **of France** le Sud de la France, le Midi; (*US Hist*) **the S**~ le Sud, les États *mpl* du Sud; *see* **deep** *etc*.

2 **adj** sud *inv*, du *or* au sud. ~ **wind** vent *m* du sud; ~ **coast** côte sud *or* méridionale; **on the** ~ **side** du côté sud; **room with a** ~ **aspect** pièce exposée au sud *or* au midi; (*Archit*) ~ **transept/door** transept/portail sud *or* méridional; **in** ~ **Devon** dans le sud du Devon; **in the S**~ **Atlantic** dans l'Atlantique Sud; *see also* **4**.

3 **adv** *go* au sud, vers le sud, en direction du sud; *be, lie* au sud, dans le sud. ~ **of the island** *go, sail* au sud de l'île; *be, lie* dans le sud de l'île; **the town lies** ~ **of the border** la ville est située au sud de la frontière; **further** ~ plus au sud; **we drove** ~ **for 100 km** nous avons roulé pendant 100 km en direction du sud *or* du midi; **go** ~ **till you get to Crewe** allez en direction du sud jusqu'à Crewe; **to sail due** ~ aller droit vers le sud; (*Naut*) avoir le cap au sud; ~ **by** ~**-west** sud quart sud-ouest.

4 **comp** ►**South Africa** Afrique *f* du Sud ►**South African** **adj** sud-africain, d'Afrique du Sud ◊ **n** Sud-Africain(e) *m(f)* ►**South America** Amérique *f* du Sud ►**South American** **adj** sud-américain, d'Amérique du Sud ◊ **n** Sud-Américain(e) *m(f)* ►**South Australia** Australie-Méridionale *f* ►**southbound** *traffic, vehicles* (se déplaçant) en direction du sud; *carriageway* sud *inv* ►**South Carolina** Caroline *f* du Sud; **in South Carolina** en Caroline du Sud ►**South Dakota** Dakota *m* du Sud; **in South Dakota** dans le Dakota du Sud ►**south-east** **n** sud-est *m* ◊ **adj** (du *or* au) sud-est *inv* ◊ **adv** vers le sud-est ►**South-East Asia** le Sud-Est asiatique, l'Asie *f* du Sud-Est ►**south-easter** vent *m* du sud-est ►**south-easterly** **adj** *wind, direction* du sud-est; *situation* au sud-est ◊ **adv** vers le sud-est ►**south-eastern** (du *or* au) sud-est ►**south-eastward(s)** vers le sud-est ►**south-facing** exposé au sud *or* au midi ►**South Georgia** Géorgie *f* du Sud ►**South Moluccan** Moluque *mf* du Sud ►**the South Pacific** le Pacifique Sud ►**southpaw** (*Sport*) gaucher *m* ►**South Pole** Pôle *m* Sud, pôle austral ►**South Sea Islands** l'Océanie *f* ►**the South Seas** les Mers *fpl* du Sud ►**south-south-east** **n** sud-sud-est *m* ◊ **adj** (du *or* au) sud-sud-est *inv* ◊ **adv** vers le sud-sud-est ►**south-south-west** **n** sud-sud-ouest *m* ◊ **adj** (du *or* au) sud-sud-ouest *inv* ◊ **adv** vers le sud-sud-ouest ►**south-west** **n** sud-ouest *m* ◊ **adj** (du *or* au) sud-ouest *inv* ◊ **adv** vers le sud-ouest ►**South West Africa**† Afrique *f* du Sud-Ouest† ►**south-wester** vent *m* du sud-ouest, suroît *m* ►**south-westerly** **adj** *wind, direction* du sud-ouest; *situation* au sud-ouest ◊ **adv** vers le sud-ouest ►**south-western** (du *or* au) sud-ouest *inv* ►**south-westward(s)** vers le sud-ouest; *see* **Korea, Vietnam** *etc*.

southerly ['sʌðəlɪ] **1** **adj** *wind* du sud; *situation* au sud, au midi. **in a** ~ **direction** en direction du sud *or* du midi, vers le sud *or* le midi; ~ **latitudes** latitudes australes; ~ **aspect** exposition *f* au sud *or* au midi. **2** **adv** vers le sud.

southern ['sʌðən] **1** **adj** sud *inv*, du sud. **the** ~ **coast** la côte sud *or* méridionale; **house with a** ~ **outlook** maison exposée au sud *or* au midi; ~ **wall** mur exposé au sud *or* au midi; ~ **hemisphere** hémisphère sud *inv or* austral; **S**~ **Africa** Afrique australe; ~ **France** le Sud de la France, le Midi; **in** ~ **Spain** dans le Sud de l'Espagne, en Espagne méridionale. **2** **comp** ►**the Southern Cross** la Croix-du-Sud ►**southernmost** le plus au sud, à l'extrême sud.

southerner ['sʌðənəʳ] **n** **a** homme *m or* femme *f* du Sud, habitant(e) *m(f)* du Sud; (*in France*) Méridional(e) *m(f)*. **he is a** ~ il vient du Sud; **the** ~**s** les gens *mpl* du Sud. **b** (*US Hist*) sudiste *mf*.

southward ['saʊθwəd] **1** **adj** au sud. **2** **adv** (*also* ~**s**) vers le sud.

souvenir [ˌsu:və'nɪəʳ] **n** souvenir *m* (*objet*).

sou'wester [saʊ'westəʳ] **n** (*hat*) suroît *m*; (*wind*) = **south-wester**; *see* **south 4**.

sovereign ['sɒvrɪn] **1** **n** souverain(e) *m(f)*; (*Brit: coin*) souverain (*ancienne pièce d'or qui valait 20 shillings*). **2** **adj** *power, authority* souverain (*after noun*), suprême; *rights* de souveraineté; (*fig*) *contempt, indifference* souverain (*before noun*), absolu. (*Pol*) ~ **state** état souverain; (*fig*) ~ **remedy** remède souverain *or* infaillible.

sovereignty ['sɒvrəntɪ] **n** souveraineté *f*.

soviet† ['səʊvɪət] **1** **n** soviet *m*. **the Supreme S**~ le Soviet Suprême; (*people*) **the S**~**s** les Soviétiques *mpl*. **2** **adj** soviétique. **3** **comp** ►**Soviet Russia**† Russie *f* soviétique† ►**the Soviet Union**† l'Union *f* soviétique†.

sovietize† ['səʊvɪətaɪz] **vt** soviétiser†.

sow¹ [saʊ] **1** **n** (*pig*) truie *f*. **2** **comp** ►**sowbelly** (*US*) petit salé *m* (gras).

sow² [səʊ] **pret sowed, ptp sown** *or* **sowed** **1** **vt** *seed, grass* semer; *field* ensemencer (*with* en); (*fig*) *mines, pebbles, doubt, discord* semer. (*Prov*) ~ **the wind and reap the whirlwind** qui sème le vent récolte la tempête (*Prov*); *see* **seed, wild** *etc*. **2** **vi** semer.

sower ['səʊəʳ] **n** (*person*) semeur *m*, -euse *f*; (*machine*) semoir *m*.

sowing ['səʊɪŋ] **1** **n** **a** (*work*) semailles *fpl*; (*period, seeds*) semailles; (*young plants*) semis *mpl*. **b** (*NonC: act*) *[field]* ensemencement *m*. **the** ~ **of seeds** les semailles. **2** **comp** ►**sowing machine** semoir *m*.

sown [səʊn] **ptp of sow²**.

sox* [sɒks] **n** (*US*) **pl of sock¹ a**.

soy [sɔɪ] **n** **a** (*also* ~ **sauce**) sauce *f* au soja. **b** (*US*) = **soya**.

soya ['sɔɪə] **n** (*esp Brit: also* ~ **bean**) (*plant*) soja *m or* soya *m*; (*bean*) graine *f* de soja. ~ **flour** farine *f* de soja.

sozzled‡ ['sɒzld] **adj** paf‡ *inv*, noir‡.

spa [spɑ:] **n** **a** (*town*) station thermale, ville *f* d'eau; (*spring*) source minérale. **b** (*US: also* **health** ~) établissement *m* de cure de rajeunissement.

space [speɪs] **1** **n** **a** (*NonC: gen, Astron, Phys etc*) espace *m*. **the rocket vanished into** ~ la fusée a disparu dans l'espace; **he was staring into** ~ il regardait dans l'espace *or* dans le vide; *see* **outer**.

b (*NonC: room*) espace *m*, place *f*. **to clear (a** *or* **some)** ~ *or* **make** ~ **for sb/sth** faire de la place pour qn/qch; **to take up a lot of** ~ *[car, books, piece of furniture]* prendre une grande place *or* beaucoup de place, être encombrant; *[building]* occuper un grand espace; **the** ~ **occupied by a car/a building** l'encombrement *m* d'une voiture/d'un bâtiment; **there isn't enough** ~ **for it** il n'y a pas assez de place pour ça; **I haven't enough** ~ **to turn the car** je n'ai pas assez de place pour *or* je n'ai pas la place de tourner la voiture; **to buy** ~ **in a newspaper (for an advertisement)** acheter de l'espace (publicitaire) dans un journal.

c (*gap, empty area*) espace *m*, place *f* (*NonC*); (*Mus*) interligne *m*; (*Typ: between two words etc*) espace *m*, blanc *m*; (*Typ: blank type*) espace *f*. **in the** ~**s between the trees** (dans les espaces) entre les arbres; **a** ~ **of 10 metres between the buildings** un espace *or* un écart *or* une distance de 10 mètres entre les bâtiments; **leave a** ~ **for the name** laisse de la place *or* un espace *or* un blanc pour le nom; **in the** ~ **provided** dans la partie (*or* la case) réservée à cet effet; **in an enclosed** ~ dans un espace clos *or* fermé; **I'm looking for a** ~ **to park the car in** *or* **a parking** ~ je cherche une place (pour me garer); *see* **blank, open** *etc*.

d (*interval, period*) laps *m* de temps, période *f* (de temps), espace *m* (de temps). **after a** ~ **of 10 minutes** après un intervalle de 10 minutes;

for the ~ of a month pendant une durée *or* une période d'un mois; **a ~ of 5 years** une période de 5 ans; **in the ~ of 3 generations/one hour** en l'espace de 3 générations/d'une heure; **a short ~ of time** un court laps de temps *or* espace de temps; **for a ~** pendant un certain temps.

2 **comp** *journey, programme, research, rocket* spatial ►**the Space Age** l'ère spatiale ►**space-age** de l'ère spatiale, de l'an 2000 ►**space bar** *[typewriter, keyboard]* barre *f* d'espacement ►**space capsule** capsule spatiale ►**spacecraft** engin *or* vaisseau spatial ►**space fiction** science-fiction *f* (*sur le thème des voyages dans l'espace*) ►**space flight** (*journey*) voyage spatial *or* dans l'espace; (*NonC*) voyages *or* vols spatiaux ►**space heater** radiateur *m* ►**space helmet** casque *m* d'astronaute *or* de cosmonaute ►**space lab** laboratoire spatial ►**spaceman** astronaute *m*, cosmonaute *m* ►**space opera*** space opera *m* (*film ou série de science-fiction sur le thème des voyages dans l'espace*) ►**space plane** = **space shuttle** ►**space platform** = **space station** ►**spaceport** base *f* de lancement (d'engins spatiaux) ►**space probe** sonde spatiale ►**space-saving** qui économise *or* gagne de la place ►**spaceship** = **spacecraft** ►**space shot** (*launching*) lancement *m* d'un engin spatial; (*flight*) vol spatial ►**space shuttle** navette spatiale ►**space sickness** mal *m* de l'espace ►**space station** station orbitale *or* spatiale ►**spacesuit** scaphandre *m* de cosmonaute ►**space-time (continuum)** Espace-Temps *m* ►**space travel** voyages spatiaux *or* interplanétaires *or* dans l'espace ►**spacewalk n** marche *f* dans l'espace ◊ **vi** marcher dans l'espace ►**spacewalker** marcheur *m*, -euse *f* de l'espace ►**spaceware** (*US* *) matériel *m* aérospatial ►**spacewoman** astronaute *f*, cosmonaute *f* ►**space writer** (*Press*) journaliste *mf* payé(e) à la ligne.

3 **vt** (*also* ~ **out**) *chairs, words, visits, letters* espacer; *payments* échelonner (*over* sur). **~ the posts (out) evenly** espacez les poteaux régulièrement, plantez les poteaux à intervalles réguliers; **you'll have to ~ them further out** *or* **further apart, you'll have to ~ them out more** il faudra laisser plus d'espace entre eux *or* les espacer davantage; *[text]* **to be single-/double-~d** avoir des interlignes *mpl* simples/doubles; **to ~ type out to fill a line** espacer *or* répartir les caractères sur toute une ligne; **the houses were well ~d (out)** les maisons étaient bien *or* largement espacées; **to be ~d (out)**⁑ être défoncé⁑.

spacing [ˈspeɪsɪŋ] **n** (*esp Typ*) espacement *m*; (*between two objects*) espacement, écartement *m*, intervalle *m*; (*also* ~ **out**: *of payments, sentries*) échelonnement *m*. (*Typ*) **to type sth in single/double ~** taper qch à simple/double interligne *or* avec un interligne simple/double.

spacious [ˈspeɪʃəs] **adj** *room, car* spacieux, grand; *garden* grand, étendu; *garment* ample. **~ accommodation** logement spacieux.

spaciousness [ˈspeɪʃəsnɪs] **n** grandes dimensions, grandeur *f*.

spade [speɪd] 1 **n** a bêche *f*, pelle *f*; (*child's*) pelle. (*fig*) **to call a ~ a ~** appeler un chat un chat, ne pas avoir peur des mots. b (*Cards*) pique *m*. **the six of ~s** le six de pique; (*US fig*) **in ~s*** par excellence; *for other phrases see* **club 1b**. c (⁑ *pej*) nègre *m*, négresse *f*. 2 **comp** ►**spadework** (*fig*) gros *m* du travail.

spadeful [ˈspeɪdfʊl] **n** pelletée *f*. (*fig*) **by the ~** en grandes quantités.

spaghetti [spəˈgetɪ] 1 **n** spaghetti *mpl*. 2 **comp** ►**spaghetti junction** (*Aut*) échangeur *m* à niveaux multiples ►**spaghetti western*** (*Cine: esp US*) western-spaghetti* *m*, western italien.

Spain [speɪn] **n** Espagne *f*.

spake†† [speɪk] **pret of speak**.

Spam [spæm] **n** ® ≃ mortadelle *f*.

span¹ [spæn] 1 **n** a *[hands, arms]* envergure *f*; *[girder]* portée *f*; *[bridge]* travée *f*; *[arch]* portée, ouverture *f*; *[roof]* portée, travée; *[plane, bird]* (*also* **wing~**) envergure. **a bridge with 3 ~s** un pont à 3 travées; **single-~ bridge** pont à travée unique; **the bridge has a ~ of 120 metres** le pont a une travée *or* une portée de 120 mètres; (*fig*) **the whole ~ of world affairs** l'horizon international.

b (*in time*) espace *m* (de temps), durée *f*. **the average ~ of life** la durée moyenne de vie; (*liter*) **man's ~ is short** la vie humaine est brève; **for a brief** *or* **short ~ (of time)** pendant un bref moment, pendant un court espace de temps; *see* **life**.

c (††: *measure*) empan *m*.

d (*yoke: of oxen etc*) paire *f*.

2 **vt** a *[bridge, rope, plank etc]* *stream, ditch* enjamber, franchir, traverser; *[bridge-builder]* jeter *or* construire un pont sur. **he could ~ her waist with his hands** il pouvait lui entourer la taille de ses deux mains; (*fig*) **Christianity ~s almost 2,000 years** le christianisme embrasse presque 2 000 ans; **his life ~s almost the whole of the 18th century** sa vie couvre *or* embrasse presque tout le 18ᵉ siècle.

b (*measure*) mesurer à l'empan.

span² [spæn] **pret of spin**.

spandex [ˈspændeks] **n** (*US Tex*) fibre *f* (synthétique) élastique.

spangle [ˈspæŋgl] 1 **n** paillette *f*. **dress with ~s on it** robe pailletée *or* à paillettes. 2 **vt** orner de paillettes. (*fig*) **~d with** pailleté de; *see* **star**.

Spaniard [ˈspænjəd] **n** Espagnol(e) *m(f)*.

spaniel [ˈspænjəl] **n** épagneul *m*.

Spanish [ˈspænɪʃ] 1 **adj** *language, cooking* espagnol; *king, embassy* d'Espagne; *teacher* d'espagnol; (*Culin*) *omelette, rice* à l'espagnole. **the ~ way of life** la vie espagnole, la façon de vivre des Espagnols; **~ onion** oignon *m* d'Espagne; **the ~ people** les Espagnols *mpl*; **~ guitar** guitare *f* classique. 2 **n** a **the ~** les Espagnols *mpl*. b (*Ling*) espagnol *m*. 3 **comp** ►**Spanish America** les pays *mpl* d'Amérique du Sud de langue espagnole ►**Spanish-American** hispano-américain ►**the Spanish Armada** (*Hist*) l'Invincible Armada *f* ►**Spanish chestnut** châtaigne *f*, marron *m* ►**the Spanish Main** (*Geog*) la mer des Antilles ►**Spanish moss** (*US*) mousse *f* espagnole.

spank [spæŋk] 1 **n**: **to give sb a ~** donner un coup *or* une claque à qn sur les fesses. 2 **vt** donner une fessée à. 3 **vi** *[horse, vehicle, ship]* **to be** *or* **go ~ing along** aller *or* filer à bonne allure.

spanking [ˈspæŋkɪŋ] 1 **n** fessée *f*. **to give sb a ~** donner une fessée à qn. 2 **adj** a *breeze* fort, bon. **to go at a ~ pace** aller *or* filer à bonne allure. b (*†: *splendid*) épatant*.

spanner [ˈspænəʳ] **n** (*Brit*) clef *f or* clé *f* (à écrous). (*fig*) **to put a ~ in the works** mettre des bâtons dans les roues; **~ wrench** clef *f* à ergots.

spar¹ [spɑːʳ] **n** (*Geol*) spath *m*.

spar² [spɑːʳ] **n** (*Naut*) espar *m*.

spar³ [spɑːʳ] 1 **vi** (*Boxing*) s'entraîner (à la boxe) (*with sb* avec qn); (*rough and tumble*) se bagarrer* amicalement (*with sb* avec qn); *[two people]* échanger des coups de poing pour rire; (*fig: argue*) se disputer (*with sb* avec qn); *[two people]* se défier en paroles. 2 **comp** ►**sparring match** (*Boxing*) combat *m* d'entraînement; (*fig*) échange *m* verbal ►**sparring partner** sparring-partner *m*.

spare [spɛəʳ] 1 **adj** a dont on ne se sert pas; (*reserve*) de réserve, de rechange; (*surplus*) de *or* en trop, dont on n'a pas besoin, disponible. **take a ~ pen in case that one doesn't work** prends un stylo de réserve *or* de rechange au cas où celui-ci ne marcherait pas; **I've a ~ pen if you want it** je peux te prêter un stylo, tu peux prendre mon stylo de rechange; **have you any ~ cups?** est-ce que tu as des tasses dont tu ne te sers pas? *or* de réserve? *or* en trop?; **take some ~ clothes** prends des vêtements de rechange, prends de quoi te changer; **there are 2 going ~** il y en a 2 en trop *or* de trop *or* de reste *or* dont on peut disposer; **we've 2 ~ seats for the film** nous avons 2 places disponibles pour le film; **~ bed/(bed)room** lit *m*/chambre *f* d'ami; **~ cash** (*small amount*) argent *m* en trop *or* de reste; (*larger*) argent disponible; **I have very little ~ time** j'ai très peu de loisirs *or* de temps libre; **in my ~ time** à mes heures perdues, pendant mes moments de loisir (*see also* **2**); (*Aut, Tech*) **~ part** pièce *f* de rechange, pièce détachée (*see also* **2**); **~ tyre** (*Aut*) pneu *m* de rechange; (* *fig: fat*) bourrelet *m* (de graisse); (*Aut*) **~ wheel** roue *f* de secours.

b (*lean*) *person* maigre; *diet, meal* frugal.

c (*Brit* ⁑: *mad*) dingue*, fou (*f* folle). **to go ~** devenir dingue*, piquer une crise*; **to drive sb ~** rendre qn dingue*.

2 **comp** ►**spare-part surgery*** chirurgie *f* des greffes ►**sparerib** (*Culin*) côtelette *f* (de porc) dans l'échine ►**spare-time** (fait) à temps perdu *or* pendant les moments de loisir; **spare-time activities** (activités *fpl* de) loisirs *mpl*.

3 **n** (*part*) pièce *f* de rechange, pièce détachée; (*tyre*) pneu *m* de rechange; (*wheel*) roue *f* de secours.

4 **vt** a (*do without*) se passer de. **we can't ~ him** *or* **we can ill ~ him just now** nous ne pouvons pas nous passer de lui en ce moment; **can you ~ it?** pouvez-vous vous en passer?, vous n'en avez pas besoin?, ça ne vous dérange pas trop (de vous en passer)? (*also iro*); **can you ~ £10?** est-ce que tu as 10 livres en trop? *or* de disponibles?; **I can only ~ a few minutes, I've only a few minutes to ~** je ne dispose que de quelques minutes, je n'ai que quelques minutes de libres *or* devant moi; **I can't ~ the time (to do it)** je n'ai pas le temps (de le faire), je n'ai pas une minute (à y consacrer); **he had time to ~ so he went to the pictures** il n'était pas pressé *or* il avait du temps devant lui, alors il est allé au cinéma; **did you have a rush to get here? — no, I had time (and) to ~** est-ce que tu as dû te dépêcher pour arriver? — non, j'ai eu plus de temps qu'il ne m'en fallait; **I can only ~ an hour for my piano practice** je peux seulement consacrer une heure à *or* je ne dispose que d'une heure pour mes exercices de piano; **I can ~ you 5 minutes** je peux vous accorder *or* consacrer 5 minutes; **can you ~ me £5?** est-ce que tu peux me passer 5 livres?; **to ~ a thought for** penser à, dédier une pensée à; **there are 3 to ~** il y en a 3 de trop *or* en surplus, il y en a 3 qui ne servent pas; **I've got none** *or* **nothing to ~** j'en ai juste ce qu'il me faut, je n'en ai pas de trop; **I've enough and to ~** j'en ai plus qu'il ne m'en faut; **she had a metre to ~** elle en avait un mètre de trop *or* de plus que nécessaire; **with 2 minutes to ~** avec 2 minutes d'avance; **we did it with £5 to ~** nous l'avons fait et il nous reste encore 5 livres.

b (*show mercy to*) *person, sb's life, tree etc* épargner. (*lit, fig*) **he ~d no one** il n'a épargné personne, il n'a fait grâce à personne; **the plague ~d no one** la peste n'a épargné personne; **if I'm ~d*** si Dieu me prête vie; **to ~ sb's feelings** ménager (les sentiments de) qn; **~ my blushes!** épargnez ma modestie!, ne me faites pas rougir!

c *suffering, grief etc* éviter, épargner (*to sb* à qn). **to ~ sb embarrassment** épargner *or* éviter de l'embarras à qn; **I wanted to ~ him trouble** je voulais lui éviter de se déranger; **you could have ~d yourself the trouble** vous auriez pu vous épargner tout ce mal (*see also* **4d**); **I'll ~ you the details** je vous fais grâce des détails.

d (*refrain from using etc: gen neg*) *one's strength, efforts* ménager.

we have ~d no expense to make her stay a pleasant one nous n'avons pas reculé devant la dépense pour que son séjour soit agréable; **he ~d no expense to renovate the house** il a dépensé sans compter pour moderniser la maison; **"no expense ~d"** "sans considération de frais *or* de prix"; **he didn't ~ himself, he ~d no pains** il s'est donné beaucoup de mal; **he could have ~d his pains, he could have ~d himself the trouble** il s'est donné du mal pour rien; **~ your pains, it's too late now** pas la peine de te donner du mal, c'est trop tard maintenant; (*Prov*) **~ the rod and spoil the child** qui aime bien châtie bien (*Prov*).

sparing ['spɛərɪŋ] **adj** *amount* limité, modéré. **his ~ use of colour** la façon discrète dont il emploie les couleurs, son emploi restreint des couleurs; **~ of words/praise** avare *or* chiche de paroles/compliments; **he was ~ with** *or* **of the wine** il a ménagé le vin, il n'y est pas allé trop fort avec le vin, il a lésiné sur le vin (*pej*); **you must be more ~ of your strength** vous devez économiser *or* ménager vos forces.

sparingly ['spɛərɪŋlɪ] **adv** *eat, live* frugalement; *spend, drink, praise* avec modération; *use* avec modération, au compte-gouttes* (*fig*).

spark [spɑ:k] **1 n a** (*also Elec*) étincelle *f*; (*fig*) *[intelligence, wit, life]* étincelle; *[commonsense, interest]* lueur *f*. (*fig*) **to make the ~s fly** (*start a row*) mettre le feu aux poudres (*fig*); (*fight*) se bagarrer un bon coup*; (*fig*) **they'll strike ~s off each other** ils se stimuleront (l'un l'autre); *see* **bright. b ~s‡** (*electrician*) électricien *m*; (*radio operator*) radio *m* (de bord). **2 comp ▸spark gap** (*Elec*) écartement *m* des électrodes **▸spark(ing) plug** (*Aut*) bougie *f*. **3 vi** jeter des étincelles. **4 vt** (*also* **~ off**) *rebellion, complaints, quarrel* provoquer, déclencher; *interest, enthusiasm* susciter, éveiller (*in sb* chez qn).

sparkle ['spɑ:kl] **1 n** (*NonC*) *[stars, dew, tinsel]* scintillement *m*, étincellement *m*; *[diamond]* éclat *m*, feux *mpl*; (*in eye*) étincelle *f*, éclair *m*; (*fig*) vie *f*, éclat. **2 vi** *[glass, china, drops of water, snow etc]* étinceler, briller; *[surface of water, lake etc]* scintiller, miroiter; *[diamond]* étinceler, jeter des feux, scintiller; *[fabric]* chatoyer; *[wine]* pétiller; *[eyes]* étinceler, pétiller (*with* de); *[person]* briller; *[conversation, play, book]* étinceler, pétiller (*with* de), être brillant *or* étincelant.

sparkler ['spɑ:klə^r] **n** (*firework*) cierge *m* magique; (**‡**: *diamond*) diam‡ *m*.

sparkling ['spɑ:klɪŋ] **1 adj** (*see* **sparkle 2**) étincelant (*with* de), brillant; scintillant; miroitant; chatoyant; pétillant (*with* de); *mineral water, soft drink* pétillant, gazeux; *wine* pétillant, mousseux. (*fig*) **he was in ~ form** il était dans une forme éblouissante. **2 adv: ~ clean** étincelant de propreté.

sparrow ['spærəʊ] **1 n** moineau *m*; *see* **hedge. 2 comp ▸sparrow-grass** (*dial*) asperge(s) *f(pl)* **▸sparrowhawk** épervier *m*.

sparse [spɑ:s] **adj** clairsemé.

sparsely ['spɑ:slɪ] **adv** *wooded, furnished* peu. **~ populated** peu peuplé, qui a une population clairsemée.

Sparta ['spɑ:tə] **n** Sparte *f*.

Spartacus ['spɑ:təkəs] **n** Spartacus *m*.

Spartan ['spɑ:tən] **1 n** Spartiate *mf*. **2 adj a** (*from Sparta*) spartiate. **b** (*fig: also* **s~**) spartiate.

spasm ['spæzəm] **n** (*Med*) spasme *m*; (*fig*) accès *m* (*of* de). **a ~ of coughing** un accès *or* une quinte de toux; **to work in ~s** travailler par à-coups *or* par accès.

spasmodic [spæz'mɒdɪk] **adj** (*Med*) spasmodique; (*fig*) *work, attempt, desire* irrégulier, intermittent.

spasmodically [spæz'mɒdɪkəlɪ] **adv** *work, try* par à-coups, de façon intermittente *or* irrégulière.

spastic ['spæstɪk] **1 adj** (*Med*) *movement, colon, paralysis* spasmodique; *child etc* handicapé moteur (*f* handicapée moteur). **2 n** (*Med*) handicapé(e) *m(f)* moteur (*f inv*).

spasticity [spæs'tɪsɪtɪ] **n** (*Med*) paralysie *f* spasmodique.

spat[1] [spæt] **pret, ptp of spit**[1].

spat[2] [spæt] **n** (*gaiter*) demi-guêtre *f*.

spat[3] [spæt] **n** (*oyster*) naissain *m*.

spat[4]* [spæt] (*US: quarrel*) **1 n** prise *f* de bec*. **2 vi** avoir une prise de bec*.

spate [speɪt] **n** (*Brit: of river*) crue *f*; (*fig*) *[letters, orders etc]* avalanche *f*; *[words, abuse]* torrent *m*; *[bombings etc]* série *f*. **in ~** en crue; (*fig: talking at length*) **to be in full ~** être parti (dans son sujet); **to have a ~ of work** être débordé *or* submergé de travail; **a fresh ~ of sabotage/attacks** *etc* une recrudescence d'actes de sabotage/d'attaques *etc*.

spatial ['speɪʃəl] **adj** (*Philos, Psych*) spatial. (*Elec*) **~ frequency** fréquence *f* spatiale.

spatiotemporal ['speɪʃɪəʊ'tempərəl] **adj** spatio-temporel.

spatter ['spætə^r] **1 vt** (*accidentally*) éclabousser (*with* de); (*deliberately*) asperger (*with* de). **to ~ mud on** *or* **over a dress** éclabousser de boue une robe. **2 vi** (*splash*) gicler (*on* sur); (*sound*) crépiter (*on* sur). **3 n** (*mark*) éclaboussure(s) *f(pl)*; (*sound*) crépitement *m*.

-spattered ['spætəd] **adj ending in comps: the butcher's blood-spattered apron** le tablier éclaboussé de sang du boucher; **mud-spattered car** voiture éclaboussée de boue.

spatula ['spætjʊlə] **n** (*Culin*) spatule *f*; (*Med*) abaisse-langue *m inv*.

spavin ['spævɪn] **n** éparvin *m*.

spawn [spɔ:n] **1 n** *[fish, frog]* frai *m*, œufs *mpl*; *[mushroom]* mycélium *m*; (*pej: person*) progéniture *f* (*iro*). **2 vt** pondre; (*fig pej*) engendrer, faire naître. **3 vi** frayer; (*fig pej*) se reproduire, se multiplier.

spawning ['spɔ:nɪŋ] **n** (*NonC*) frai *m*. **~ place** frayère *f*.

spay [speɪ] **vt** *animal* enlever les ovaires de.

S.P.C.A. [espi:si:'eɪ] (*US*) (**abbr of Society for the Prevention of Cruelty to Animals**) ≃ S.P.A. *f*.

S.P.C.C. [espi:si:'si:] **n** (*US*) (**abbr of Society for the Prevention of Cruelty to Children**) *association pour la protection de l'enfance*.

speak [spi:k] **pret spoke, spake††, ptp spoken 1 vi a** (*talk*) parler (*to* à, *of, about* de); (*converse*) parler, s'entretenir (*with* avec); (*be on speaking terms*) parler, adresser la parole (*to* à); (*fig*) *[gun, trumpet etc]* retentir, se faire entendre. **to ~ in a whisper** chuchoter; **~, don't shout!** parle sans crier!; **to ~ to o.s.** parler tout seul; **I'll ~ to him about it** je vais lui en parler, je vais lui en toucher un mot *or* deux mots; **I don't know him to ~ to** je ne le connais pas assez bien pour lui parler *or* pour lui adresser la parole; **I'll never ~ to him again** je ne lui adresserai plus jamais la parole; **did you ~?*** pardon?, tu m'as parlé?, tu dis?*; **you have only to ~** tu n'as qu'un mot à dire; **so to ~** pour ainsi dire; **biologically ~ing** biologiquement parlant; **~ing personally** pour ma (*or* sa *etc*) part, personnellement; **~ing as a member of the society I ...** en tant que membre de la société je ...; (*Telec*) **who's (that) ~ing?** qui est à l'appareil?; (*passing on call*) c'est de la part de qui?; (*Telec*) **(this is) Paul ~ing** ici Paul, (c'est) Paul à l'appareil; (*Telec*) **~ing!** lui- *or* elle-même!, c'est moi-même!; *see* **action, badly, roughly** *etc*.

b (*make a speech*) parler (*on or about sth* de qch); (*begin to* ~) prendre la parole. **to ~ in public** parler en public; **he rose to ~** il s'est levé pour prendre la parole *or* pour parler; **Mr X will ~ next** ensuite c'est M. X qui prendra la parole; **the chairman asked him to ~** le président lui a donné la parole; **Mr X will now ~ on "The Incas"** M. X va maintenant (nous) parler des Incas; **it's years since he spoke in the House** cela fait des années qu'il n'a pas fait *or* prononcé de discours à l'Assemblée; **to ~ in a debate** *[proposer, seconder]* faire un discours *or* prendre la parole au cours d'un débat; (*from floor of house*) participer à un débat, intervenir dans un débat.

c (*phrases*) **to ~ for sb** (*be spokesman for*) parler pour qn *or* au nom de qn; (*give evidence for*) parler *or* témoigner en faveur de qn; **~ing for myself** personnellement, pour ma part, en ce qui me concerne; **~ for yourself!*** parle pour toi!*; **let him ~ for himself** laisse-le s'exprimer, laisse-le dire lui-même ce qu'il a à dire; **it ~s for itself** c'est évident, c'est tout ce qu'il y a de plus clair; **the facts ~ for themselves** les faits parlent d'eux-mêmes *or* se passent de commentaires; **I can ~ for** *or* **to his honesty** je peux témoigner de *or* répondre de son honnêteté; **that ~s well for his generosity** ceci montre bien *or* prouve bien qu'il est généreux; **that is already spoken for** c'est déjà réservé *or* retenu; **she is already spoken for** elle est déjà prise; **he always ~s well of her** il dit toujours du bien d'elle; **he is very well spoken of** on dit beaucoup de bien de lui; **~ing of holidays** à propos de vacances, puisqu'on parle de vacances; **he has no friends/money to ~ of** il n'a pour ainsi dire pas d'amis/d'argent; **nobody to ~ of** pour ainsi dire personne; **it's nothing to ~ of** ce n'est pas grand-chose, cela ne vaut pas la peine qu'on en parle (*subj*), c'est trois fois rien*; **there were plenty of French, not to ~ of Italians** il y avait plein de Français, sans parler des Italiens; **everything spoke of wealth** tout indiquait *or* révélait *or* dénotait la richesse; **everything spoke of fear/hatred** tout révélait *or* trahissait la peur/la haine; **you must ~ to the point** *or* **to the subject** vous devez vous en tenir au sujet; (*Parl etc*) **to ~ to a motion** soutenir une motion.

2 vt a *language* parler. **"English spoken"** "ici on parle anglais"; **French is spoken all over the world** le français se parle dans le monde entier.

b (*liter*) *a poem, one's lines, the truth* dire. **to ~ one's mind** dire ce que l'on pense; **I didn't ~ a word** je n'ai rien dit; (*fig*) **it ~s volumes for ...** cela en dit long sur ..., cela témoigne bien de ...; **her silence ~s volumes** son silence en dit long, son silence est révélateur.

3 comp ▸speakeasy* (*US*) bar clandestin (*pendant la période de prohibition*).

4 ...speak n ending in comps langage *m* de ..., jargon *m* de ..., *e.g.* **computerspeak** langage *or* jargon de l'informatique, langage *or* jargon des informaticiens.

▸speak out vi = speak up b.

▸speak up vi a (*talk loudly*) parler fort *or* haut; (*raise one's voice*) parler plus fort *or* plus haut. **speak up!** (parle) plus fort! *or* plus haut!; (*don't mumble*) parle plus clairement! **b** (*fig*) parler franchement, ne pas mâcher ses mots. **he's not afraid to speak up** il n'a pas peur de dire ce qu'il pense *or* de parler franchement, il ne mâche pas ses mots; **I think you ought to speak up** je crois que vous devriez dire franchement ce que vous pensez; **to speak up for sb** parler en faveur de qn, défendre qn; **to speak up against sth** s'élever contre qch.

speaker ['spi:kə^r] **n a** (*gen*) celui (*or* celle) qui parle; (*in dialogue, discussion*) interlocuteur *m*, -trice *f*; (*in public*) orateur *m*; (*lecturer*) conférencier *m*, -ière *f*. **he's a good/poor ~** il parle bien/mal, c'est un bon/mauvais orateur *or* conférencier; **the previous ~** la personne qui a parlé la dernière, l'orateur *or* le conférencier précédent; (*Parl*) **the S~ (of the House)** le Speaker (*Président de la Chambre des Communes en*

G.B., au Canada, ou de la Chambre des Représentants aux É.-U., en Australie et en Nouvelle-Zélande).

b **French** ~ personne *f* qui parle français; (*as native or official language*) francophone *mf*; **he is not a Welsh** ~ il ne parle pas gallois; *see* **native.**

c (*loudspeaker*) (*for PA system, musical instruments*) haut-parleur *m*, enceinte *f*; *[hi-fi]* baffle *m*, enceinte.

speaking ['spi:kɪŋ] 1 **adj** *doll etc* parlant; (*fig*) *proof* parlant, criant; *likeness* criant; *portrait* parlant, très ressemblant. **he has a pleasant** ~ **voice** il a une voix bien timbrée, il est agréable à entendre parler. 2 **n** (*skill*) art *m* de parler; *see* **public** *etc.* 3 **comp** ►**the speaking clock** (*Brit*) l'horloge *f* parlante ►**speaking terms: to be on speaking terms with sb** parler à qn, adresser la parole à qn; **they're not on speaking terms** ils ne s'adressent plus la parole, ils ne se parlent plus ►**speaking tube** tuyau *m* acoustique.

-speaking ['spi:kɪŋ] **adj ending in comps: English-speaking** (*with English as native or official language*) *person, country* anglophone; (*knowing English*) *person* parlant anglais; **slow-speaking** au débit lent, à la parole lente.

spear [spɪəʳ] 1 **n** a *[warrior, hunter]* lance *f.*

b *[broccoli, asparagus]* pointe *f.*

2 **vt** transpercer d'un coup de lance. **he** ~**ed a potato with his fork** il a piqué une pomme de terre avec sa fourchette.

3 **comp** ►**spearcarrier** (*Theat*) (*lit*) soldat *m*; (*fig*) **he started as a spearcarrier** il a commencé par être figurant ►**spearfish** (*US: also* **go spearfishing**) pratiquer la pêche sous-marine ►**spear grass** (*Brit*) chiendent *m* ►**spear gun** fusil *m* sous-marin *or* à harpon ►**spearhead n** fer *m* de lance (*also fig Mil*) ◊ **vt** *attack, offensive* être le fer de lance de; *campaign* mener ►**spearmint n** (*Bot*) menthe verte; (*: *chewing gum*) chewing-gum *m* (à la menthe) ◊ **comp** *sweet* à la menthe; *flavour* de menthe.

spec* [spek] **n** a (**abbr of speculation**) **to buy sth on** ~ risquer *or* tenter le coup* en achetant qch; **I went along on** ~ j'y suis allé à tout hasard.

b (**abbr of specification**) ~**s*** spécification *f*, caracteristiques *fpl* (techniques).

special ['speʃəl] 1 **adj** a (*specific*) *purpose, use, equipment* spécial, particulier; *notebook, box, room* spécial, réservé (à cet usage); *arrangement, order, permission, fund, edition* spécial. **are you thinking of any** ~ **date?** est-ce que tu penses à une date particulière? *or* en particulier?; **I've no** ~ **person in mind** je ne pense à personne en particulier; ~ **to that country** spécial *or* particulier *or* propre à ce pays; **by** ~ **command of** sur ordre spécial *or* exprès de; *see also* **3.**

b (*exceptional*) *attention, pleasure, effort* (tout) particulier; *favour, price, study, skill* (tout) spécial; *occasion* spécial, extraordinaire, exceptionnel; *case, circumstances* extraordinaire, exceptionnel; (*Pol etc*) *powers, legislation* extraordinaire. **take** ~ **care of it** fais-y particulièrement attention, prends-en un soin tout particulier; (*Ski*) ~ **slalom** slalom *m* spécial; **it's a** ~ **case** c'est un cas spécial *or* particulier *or* à part; **it's rather a** ~ **situation** ce n'est pas une situation ordinaire, c'est une situation plutôt exceptionnelle; **in this one** ~ **instance** dans ce cas bien particulier; **he has a** ~ **place in our affections** nous sommes tout particulièrement attachés à lui; **her** ~ **friend** sa meilleure amie, une amie qui lui est particulièrement chère *or* intime; **he's a very** ~ **person to her** il lui est tout particulièrement cher; **you're extra** ~**!*** tu es quelqu'un à part!; **this is rather a** ~ **day for me** c'est une journée particulièrement importante pour moi; **to ask for** ~ **treatment** demander à être considéré comme un cas à part; **it's a** ~ **feature of the village** c'est une caractéristique *or* une particularité du village; (*Press*) ~ **feature** article spécial; **he has his own** ~ **way with the children** il a une façon toute particulière *or* bien à lui de s'y prendre avec les enfants; **my** ~ **chair** mon fauteuil préféré, le fauteuil que je me réserve; **nothing** ~ rien de spécial *or* de particulier; **what's so** ~ **about her?** qu'est-ce qu'elle a de spécial? *or* de particulier? *or* d'extraordinaire?; *see also* **3.**

c (*Brit*) ~ **education** *or* **schooling** enseignement *m* spécialisé (*pour attardés mentaux*); (*Brit*) ~ **school** établissement *m* scolaire spécialisé; (*Brit*) ~ **school teacher** instituteur *m*, -trice *f* spécialisé(e); (*US Univ*) ~ **student** étudiant(e) *m(f)* libre (*ne préparant pas de diplôme*); (*Univ etc*) ~ **subject** option *f*; (*advanced*) sujet specialisé.

2 **n** (*train*) train *m* supplémentaire; (*newspaper*) édition spéciale; (*policeman*) auxiliaire *m* de police; (*: *Rad or TV programme*) émission spéciale. **the chef's** ~ la spécialité du chef *or* de la maison; (*on menu*) **today's** ~ le plat du jour; (*on item in shop*) **this week's** ~ l'affaire *f* de la semaine; *see* **football.**

3 **comp** ►**special agent** (*Comm etc*) concessionnaire *mf*; (*spy*) agent secret ►**Special Air Service** (*Brit Mil*) ≃ groupement *m* d'intervention de la gendarmerie nationale ►**Special Branch** (*Brit Police*) les renseignements *mpl* généraux ►**special constable** (*Brit*) auxiliaire *m* de police ►**special correspondent** (*Press, Rad, TV*) envoyé(e) *m(f)* spécial(e) ►**special delivery:** (*Post*) **by special delivery** en exprès ►**special-delivery letter** (*Post*) lettre *f* exprès ►**special effects** (*Cine etc*) effets *mpl* spéciaux ►**special handling** (*US Post*) acheminement *m* rapide ►**special interest group** (*Pol etc*) groupe *m* de pression ►**special jury** (*Jur*) jury spécial ►**special licence** (*Jur*) (*gen*) dispense spéciale; (*for marriage*) dispense de bans ►**special messenger: by special messenger** par messager spécial ►**special offer** (*Comm*) réclame *f* ►**Special Patrol Group** (*Brit Police*) ≃ brigade *f* anti-émeute.

specialism ['speʃəlɪzəm] **n** a (*subject, skill*) spécialité *f.* b (*specialization*) spécialisation *f.*

specialist ['speʃəlɪst] 1 **n** (*also Med*) spécialiste *mf* (*in* de). (*Med*) **an eye/heart** ~ un(e) ophtalmologiste/cardiologue; (*gen*) **you need a** ~ **to tell you that** seul un spécialiste *or* un expert peut vous dire cela. 2 **comp** *knowledge, dictionary* spécialisé, spécial ►**specialist teacher** (*primary*) instituteur *m*, -trice *f or* (*secondary*) professeur *m* (spécialisé(e) dans une matière) ►**specialist work: it's specialist work** cela requiert un spécialiste *or* un professionnel, un amateur ne peut pas le faire.

speciality [ˌspeʃɪ'ælɪtɪ] **n** a (*NonC: see* **special 1b**) caractère (tout) particulier *or* (tout) spécial (*or* extraordinaire *or* exceptionnel). b (*special quality or activity etc*) spécialité *f.* **to make a** ~ **of sth** se spécialiser dans qch; **his** ~ **is Medieval English** il est spécialisé dans *or* c'est un spécialiste de l'anglais du moyen-âge; **it is a** ~ **of the village** c'est une spécialité du village; **armchairs are this firm's** ~ cette firme se spécialise dans les fauteuils; **the chef's** ~ la spécialité du chef *or* de la maison.

specialization [ˌspeʃəlaɪ'zeɪʃən] **n** spécialisation *f* (*in* dans).

specialize ['speʃəlaɪz] **vi** *[student, firm, chef etc]* se spécialiser (*in* dans). (*hum*) **he** ~**s in making a fool of himself** il se fait un point de passer pour un imbécile.

specialized ['speʃəlaɪzd] **adj** *department, training* spécialisé; *tools* à usage spécial. (*Scol, Univ*) ~ **subject** option *f*; (*advanced*) sujet spécialisé; ~ **knowledge** connaissances spéciales.

specially ['speʃəlɪ] **adv** a (*especially*) spécialement, particulièrement, surtout. ~ **written for children** écrit spécialement pour les enfants; **he is** ~ **interested in Proust** il s'intéresse tout spécialement *or* tout particulièrement à Proust; **we would** ~ **like to see the orchard** nous aimerions particulièrement *or* surtout voir le verger; **a** ~ **difficult task** une tâche particulièrement difficile. b (*on purpose*) (tout) spécialement, exprès. **I had it** ~ **made** je l'ai fait faire exprès *or* tout spécialement; **I asked for it** ~ je l'ai demandé exprès *or* tout spécialement, j'avais bien dit *or* spécifié que je le voulais.

specialty ['speʃəltɪ] **n** (*US*) = **speciality b.**

specie ['spi:ʃi:] **n** (*Fin*) espèces *fpl* (monnayées).

species ['spi:ʃi:z] **n, pl inv** (*all senses*) espèce *f.*

specific [spə'sɪfɪk] 1 **adj** *statement, instruction* précis, explicite, clair; *purpose, reason, plan, meaning, case* précis, particulier, déterminé; *example* précis; (*Bio, Bot, Chem, Phys*) spécifique. **he was very** ~ **on that point** il s'est montré très explicite sur ce point; **nothing very** ~ rien de bien précis; (*Phys*) ~ **gravity** densité *f*; (*Phys*) ~ **heat** chaleur *f* spécifique; (*Bio*) ~ **name** nom *m* d'espèce. 2 **n** a (*Med*) (remède *m*) spécifique *m* (*for* de, contre); (*fig*) remède spécifique. b (*pl: details etc*) **let's get down to** ~**s** entrons dans les détails, prenons des exemples précis.

specifically [spə'sɪfɪkəlɪ] **adv** (*explicitly*) *warn, state, mention* explicitement, de façon précise; (*especially*) *intend, plan* particulièrement, expressément. **I told you quite** ~ je vous l'avais bien précisé *or* spécifié; **designed** ~ **for** conçu expressément *or* tout spécialement *or* tout particulièrement pour; **we asked for that one** ~ nous avons bien spécifié *or* précisé que nous voulions celui-là; **the law does not** ~ **refer to** ... la loi ne se rapporte pas explicitement à ... .

specification [ˌspesɪfɪ'keɪʃən] **n** a (*NonC: act of specifying*) spécification *f*, précision *f.* b (*item in contract etc*) stipulation *f*, prescription *f.* **this** ~ **was not complied with** cette stipulation *or* cette prescription n'a pas été respectée; (*for building, machine etc*) ~**s** spécification *f*, caractéristiques *fpl* (techniques); (*in contract etc*) cahier *m* des charges; *see* **outline.**

specify ['spesɪfaɪ] **vt** spécifier, préciser. **unless otherwise specified** sauf indication contraire; **not elsewhere specified** non dénommé ailleurs; **at a specified time** à un moment précis, à une heure précise.

specimen ['spesɪmɪn] 1 **n** *[rock, species, style]* spécimen *m*; *[blood, tissue]* prélèvement *m*; *[urine]* échantillon *m*; (*fig: example*) spécimen, exemple *m* (*of* de). **that trout is a fine** ~ cette truite est un magnifique spécimen *or* est magnifique; (*fig*) **an odd** ~* (*man or woman*) un drôle d'échantillon d'humanité; (*man*) un drôle de type*; (*woman*) une drôle de bonne femme*; **you're a pretty poor** ~* tu es un (*or* une) pas grand-chose*. 2 **comp** ►**specimen copy** spécimen *m* ►**specimen page** page *f* spécimen ►**specimen signature** spécimen *m* de signature.

specious ['spi:ʃəs] **adj** *logic, argument* spécieux; *beauty* illusoire, trompeur.

speciousness ['spi:ʃəsnɪs] **n** (*see* **specious**) caractère spécieux; apparence illusoire *or* trompeuse.

speck [spek] 1 **n** *[dust, soot]* grain *m*; *[dirt, mud, ink]* toute petite tache; (*on fruit, leaves, skin*) tache, tavelure *f*; (*tiny amount*) *[sugar, butter]* tout petit peu; *[truth etc]* grain, atome *m.* **it has got black** ~**s all over it** c'est entièrement couvert de toutes petites taches noires; **I've got a** ~ **in my eye** j'ai une poussière *or* une escarbille dans l'œil; **just a**

~ on the horizon/in the sky rien qu'un point noir à l'horizon/dans le ciel; **cream? — just a ~*, thanks** de la crème? — rien qu'un tout petit peu, merci. 2 **vt** (*gen pass*) tacheter, moucheter; *fruit* tacheter, taveler.

speckle ['spekl] 1 **n** tacheture *f*, moucheture *f* (*d'un animal*). 2 **vt** tacheter, moucheter.

speckled ['spekld] **adj** tacheté.

specs* [speks] **npl** a (**abbr of spectacles**) lunettes *fpl*. b *see* **spec***.

spectacle ['spektəkl] 1 **n** a (*sight*) spectacle *m* (*also pej*); (*Cine/Theat etc*) superproduction *f*, film *m*/revue *f etc* à grand spectacle. **the coronation was a great ~** le couronnement a été un spectacle somptueux; (*pej*) **to make a ~ of o.s.** se donner en spectacle. b (*Brit*) **(pair of) ~s** lunettes *fpl*. 2 **comp ►spectacle case** (*Brit*) étui *m* à lunettes.

spectacled ['spektəkld] **adj** (*also Zool*) à lunettes.

spectacular [spek'tækjʊləʳ] 1 **adj** *sight, act, results, change, fall* spectaculaire, impressionnant; *defeat, victory* spectaculaire; *view* splendide. **a ~ success** un succès fou. 2 **n** (*Cine/Theat*) superproduction *f*, film *m*/revue *f* à grand spectacle.

spectacularly [spek'tækjʊləlɪ] **adv** *crash, succeed* de manière spectaculaire. **to be ~ successful** avoir un succès spectaculaire; **~ beautiful** extraordinairement beau; **everything went ~ wrong** tout s'est extraordinairement mal passé.

spectate [spek'teɪt] **vi** (*esp US*) être présent en tant que spectateur (*or* spectatrice).

spectator [spek'teɪtəʳ] 1 **n** spectateur *m*, -trice *f*. **the ~s** les spectateurs, le public, l'assistance *f*. 2 **comp ►spectator sport: I don't like spectator sports** je n'aime pas le sport en tant que spectacle, je n'aime pas les sports auxquels on assiste sans participer; **rugby, the most exciting of spectator sports** le rugby, sport qui passionne le grand public; **it is one of the great spectator sports** c'est l'un des sports qui attirent un très grand nombre de spectateurs; **this tends to be rather a spectator sport** c'est un sport qui attire plus de spectateurs que de joueurs.

specter ['spektəʳ] **n** (*US*) = **spectre**.

spectra ['spektrə] **npl of spectrum**.

spectral ['spektrəl] **adj** (*all senses*) spectral.

spectre, (*US*) **specter** ['spektəʳ] **n** spectre *m*, fantôme *m*.

spectrogram ['spektrəʊgræm] **n** spectrogramme *m*.

spectrograph ['spektrəʊgrɑːf] **n** spectrographe *m*.

spectroscope ['spektrəʊskəʊp] **n** spectroscope *m*.

spectroscopy [spek'trɒskəpɪ] **n** spectroscopie *f*.

spectrum ['spektrəm] 1 **n, pl spectra** (*Phys*) spectre *m*; (*fig: of ideas, opinions*) gamme *f* (*fig*). (*fig*) **the political ~** l'éventail *m* politique. 2 **comp** *analysis, colours* spectral.

specula ['spekjʊlə] **npl of speculum**.

speculate ['spekjʊleɪt] **vi** a (*Philos*) spéculer (*about, on* sur); (*gen: ponder*) s'interroger (*about, on* sur, *whether* pour savoir si). **he was speculating about going** il se demandait s'il devait y aller ou non. b (*Fin*) spéculer; (*St Ex*) spéculer *or* jouer à la Bourse.

speculation [ˌspekjʊ'leɪʃən] **n** a (*NonC*) (*Philos*) spéculation *f*; (*gen: guessing*) conjecture(s) *f(pl)*, supposition(s) *f(pl)* (*about* sur). **it is the subject of much ~** cela donne lieu à bien des conjectures; **it is pure ~** ce n'est qu'une supposition; **after all the ~ about ...** après toutes ces conjectures *or* suppositions sur ... . b (*Fin, St Ex, gen*) spéculation *f* (*in, on* sur). **he bought it as a ~** il a spéculé en achetant cela; **it proved a good ~** ce fut une spéculation réussie *or* une bonne affaire; **that picture he bought was a good ~** il a fait une bonne affaire en achetant ce tableau, il a eu du nez en achetant ce tableau.

speculative ['spekjʊlətɪv] **adj** (*all senses*) spéculatif.

speculatively ['spekjʊlətɪvlɪ] **adv** (*inquiringly*) avec curiosité; (*by guesswork*) spéculativement.

speculator ['spekjʊleɪtəʳ] **n** spéculateur *m*, -trice *f*.

speculum ['spekjʊləm] **n, pl ~s** *or* **specula** *[telescope]* miroir *m*; (*Med*) spéculum *m*.

sped [sped] **pret, ptp of speed**.

speech [spiːtʃ] 1 **n** a (*NonC*) (*faculty*) parole *f*; (*enunciation*) articulation *f*, élocution *f*; (*manner of speaking*) façon *f* de parler, langage *m*; (*as opposed to writing*) parole; (*language: of district or group*) parler *m*, langage. **to lose the power of ~** perdre (l'usage de) la parole; **his ~ was very indistinct** il parlait *or* articulait très indistinctement, sa façon de parler *or* son élocution était très indistincte; (*on one occasion*) il parlait très indistinctement; **he expresses himself better in ~ than in writing** il s'exprime mieux oralement que par écrit; **the ~ of the playground is different from that of the classroom** le langage *or* le parler des enfants qui jouent diffère de celui des enfants en classe; **his ~ betrays his origins** son langage *or* sa façon de s'exprimer trahit ses origines; (*Prov*) **~ is silver but silence is golden** la parole est d'argent mais le silence est d'or (*Prov*); **free ~, freedom of ~** liberté *f* de parole *or* d'expression; *see* **figure, part** *etc*.

b (*formal address*) discours *m* (*on* sur); (*short, less formal*) speech* *m*, allocution *f*. **to make a ~** faire un discours; **~, ~!** un discours!; (*Britain and Commonwealth*) **Queen's (***or* **King's) ~** discours *m* de la Reine (*or* du Roi) (*pour l'ouverture de la saison parlementaire*); *see* **maiden** *etc*.

c (*Ling*) (*utterances*) parole *f*; (*spoken language*) langage parlé. (*Gram*) **direct/indirect ~** discours direct/indirect.

2 **comp ►speech act** (*Ling*) acte *m* de parole **►speech clinic** centre *m* d'orthophonie **►speech community** (*Ling*) communauté *f* linguistique **►speech day** (*Brit Scol etc*) distribution *f* des prix **►speech defect** troubles *mpl* du langage **►speech difficulty** défaut *m* d'élocution **►speech disorder** = **speech defect ►speech from the throne** (*Britain and Commonwealth*) *discours du monarque pour l'ouverture de la saison parlementaire* **►speech generation** (*Comput*) génération *f* de parole **►speech impediment** = **speech difficulty ►speechmaker** orateur *m* **►speechmaking** (*NonC: slightly pej*) discours *mpl*, beaux discours (*pej*) **►speech organ** (*Anat*) organe *m* de la parole **►speech recognition** (*Comput*) reconnaissance *f* de la parole **►speech sound** (*Ling*) phonème *m* **►speech synthesis** (*Comput*) synthèse *f* vocale **►speech synthesizer** (*Comput*) synthétiseur *m* de parole **►speech therapist** orthophoniste *mf*, phoniatre *mf* **►speech therapy** orthophonie *f*, phoniatrie *f* **►speech training** leçons *fpl* d'élocution **►speechwriter: his speechwriter** la personne qui écrit ses discours.

speechify ['spiːtʃɪfaɪ] **vi** (*pej*) discourir, pérorer.

speechifying ['spiːtʃɪfaɪɪŋ] **n** (*pej*) laïus* *mpl*, beaux discours.

speechless ['spiːtʃlɪs] **adj** *person* (*from surprise, shock*) muet, interloqué, tout interdit; (*from horror, anger, terror, delight*) muet. **~ with rage/shock** muet de rage/sous le choc; **it left him ~** il en est resté sans voix, il en a perdu la parole; **I'm ~!*** j'en suis sans voix!

speed [spiːd] (**vb: pret, ptp sped** *or* **speeded**) 1 **n** a (*rate of movement*) vitesse *f*; (*rapidity*) rapidité *f*; (*promptness*) promptitude *f*. **the ~ of light/sound** la vitesse de la lumière/du son; **his reading ~ is low** il lit lentement; **shorthand/typing ~s** nombre *m* de mots-minute en sténo/en dactylo; **a secretary with good ~s** une secrétaire qui a une bonne vitesse (de frappe et de sténo); (*Aut*) **what ~ were you going at?** *or* **doing?** quelle vitesse faisiez-vous?, à quelle vitesse rouliez-vous?; **at a ~ of 80 km/h** à une vitesse de 80 km/h; **at a great ~** à toute vitesse; **at (full** *or* **top) ~** *go, run, move, row* à toute vitesse *or* allure; *drive off* à toute vitesse *or* allure, sur les chapeaux de roues*; *do sth* très vite, en quatrième vitesse*; **with all possible ~** le plus vite possible; **with such ~** si vite; **to pick up** *or* **gather ~** prendre de la vitesse; *see* **air, cruise, full, high** *etc*.

b (*Aut, Tech: gear*) vitesse *f*. **4 forward ~s** 4 vitesses avant; **a 3-~ gear** une boîte à 3 vitesses.

c (*NonC: Phot*) *[film]* rapidité *f*; (*width of aperture*) degré *m* d'obturation; (*length of exposure*) durée *f* d'exposition.

d (*NonC: Drugs sl*) speed *m* (*sl*), amphétamines *fpl*.

e **good ~!††** Dieu vous garde!†

2 **comp ►speedball n** (*game*) speedball *m*; (*Drugs sl*) mélange *m* de cocaïne et d'héroïne ◊ **vi** (*Drugs sl*) s'injecter un mélange de cocaïne et d'héroïne **►speedboat** vedette *f*, (*with outboard motor*) hors-bord *m inv* **►speed bump** casse-vitesse *m* **►speed chess** blitz *m* **►speed cop*** (*Brit*) motard* *m* **►speed limit:** (*Brit*) **there's no speed limit** il n'y a pas de limitation *f* de vitesse; **the speed limit is 80 km/h** la vitesse maximale permise est 80 km/h **►speed merchant*** fou *m* de la route (*pej*), mordu(e)* *m(f)* de la vitesse **►speed reading** lecture *f* rapide **►speed restriction** (*Aut*) limitation *f* de vitesse **►speed skating** (*Sport*) patinage *m* de vitesse **►speed trap** (*Aut*) piège *m* de police pour contrôle de vitesse **►speed-up** accélération *f*; (*Ind: of production*) amélioration *f* de rendement **►speedwalk** (*US*) tapis roulant **►speedway** (*Sport: racetrack*) piste *f* de vitesse pour motos; (*US Aut: road*) voie *f* express; (*Sport: NonC*) **speedway racing** course(s) *f(pl)* de motos, épreuve(s) *f(pl)* de vitesse de motos **►speed zone** (*US*) zone *f* à vitesse limitée.

3 **vt pret, ptp sped** *or* **speeded** (*liter*) *arrow etc* lancer, décocher. **to ~ sb on his way** souhaiter bon voyage à qn; **to ~ the parting guest** précipiter *or* brusquer le départ de l'invité; **God ~ you!††** Dieu vous garde!†

4 **vi** a **pret, ptp sped** (*move fast*) *[person, vehicle, horse, boat, plane etc]* **to ~ along** aller à toute vitesse *or* à toute allure, filer comme un éclair; (*liter*) **the arrow sped from his bow** la flèche jaillit de son arc.

b **pret, ptp speeded** (*Aut: go too fast*) conduire trop vite, excéder la limitation de vitesse. **you're ~ing!** tu vas trop vite!, tu fais un *or* des excès de vitesse!

►speed along 1 **vi pret, ptp sped along** *[person, vehicle]* aller à toute allure *or* à toute vitesse, filer comme l'éclair. 2 **vt sep pret, ptp speeded along** *work, production* activer.

►speed up **pret, ptp speeded up** 1 **vi** (*gen*) aller plus vite; *[walker/worker/singer/pianist/train etc]* marcher/travailler/chanter/jouer/rouler *etc* plus vite; (*Aut*) accélérer; *[engine, machine etc]* tourner plus vite. **do speed up!** plus vite!, active!* 2 **vt sep** *machine* faire tourner plus vite; *service, work, delivery* activer, accélérer; *production* accélérer, augmenter; *person* faire aller *or* faire travailler plus vite, presser; *film* accélérer. **to speed things up** activer les choses. 3 **speed-up n** *see* **speed 2**.

speeder ['spiːdəʳ] **n** (*fast driver*) fou *m* de la vitesse; (*convicted*) automobiliste *mf* coupable d'excès de vitesse.

speedily [ˈspiːdɪlɪ] adv *progress, move, finish, work* vite, rapidement; *reply, return* promptement; (*soon*) bientôt. **as ~ as possible** le plus vite *or* rapidement possible; **he replied very ~** il a répondu très promptement, il s'est dépêché de répondre.

speediness [ˈspiːdɪnɪs] n (*see* **speedy**) rapidité *f*; promptitude *f*.

speeding [ˈspiːdɪŋ] 1 n (*Aut*) excès *m* de vitesse. 2 comp ►**speeding conviction/fine/ticket** (*Jur*) condamnation *f*/contravention *f*/p.v. *m* pour excès de vitesse.

speedometer [spɪˈdɒmɪtəʳ] n (*Aut*) compteur *m* (de vitesse), indicateur *m* de vitesse.

speedster* [ˈspiːdstəʳ] n (*Aut*) fou *m* de la route (*pej*), mordu(e)* *m(f)* de la vitesse.

speedwell [ˈspiːdwel] n (*Bot*) véronique *f*.

speedy [ˈspiːdɪ] adj *reply, recovery, service, decision* rapide, prompt; *vehicle, movement* rapide.

speleologist [ˌspiːlɪˈɒlədʒɪst] n spéléologue *mf*.

speleology [ˌspiːlɪˈɒlədʒɪ] n spéléologie *f*.

spell[1] [spel] 1 n (*magic power*) charme *m* (*also fig*), sortilège *m*; (*magic words*) formule *f* magique, incantation *f*. **an evil ~** un maléfice; **to put** *or* **cast** *or* **lay a ~ on** *or* **over sb, to put sb under a ~** jeter un sort à qn, ensorceler qn, envoûter qn; (*fig*) ensorceler qn, envoûter qn; **under a ~** ensorcelé, envoûté, sous le charme; (*fig*) **under the ~ of sb/sth, under sb's/sth's ~** ensorcelé *or* envoûté par qn/qch; **to break the ~** rompre le charme (*also fig*); (*fig*) **the ~ of the East** le charme *or* les sortilèges de l'Orient.

2 comp ►**spellbinder** (*speaker*) orateur fascinant, ensorceleur *m*, -euse *f*; **that film was a spellbinder** ce film était ensorcelant *or* était envoûtant *or* vous tenait en haleine ►**spellbinding** ensorcelant, envoûtant ►**spellbound** (*lit, fig*) ensorcelé, envoûté; (*fig*) **to hold sb spellbound** subjuguer qn, fasciner qn, tenir qn sous le charme.

spell[2] [spel] 1 n a (*period of work; turn*) tour *m*. **we each took a ~ at the wheel** nous nous sommes relayés au volant, nous avons conduit chacun à notre tour; **~ of duty** tour de service.

b (*brief period*) (courte) période *f*. (*Met*) **cold/sunny ~s** périodes de froid/ensoleillées; **for/after a ~** pendant/après un certain temps; **for a short ~** pendant un petit moment; **he has done a ~ in prison** il a été en prison pendant un certain temps, il a fait de la prison; **he's going through a bad ~** il traverse une mauvaise période, il est dans une mauvaise passe; **to have a dizzy** *or* **giddy ~** avoir un vertige.

c (*Scot, Austral, N. Z.: short rest*) petite sieste *f*.

2 vt relayer. **to ~ sb at the wheel/at the oars** relayer qn au volant/aux avirons.

spell[3] [spel] pret, ptp **spelt** *or* **spelled** 1 vt a (*in writing*) écrire, orthographier; (*aloud*) épeler. **how do you ~ it?** comment est-ce que cela s'écrit?, comment écrit-on cela?; **can you ~ it for me?** pouvez-vous me l'épeler?; **he spelt "address" with one "d"** il a écrit "address" avec un seul "d".

b *[letters]* former, donner; (*fig*) (*mean*) signifier, représenter (*for sb* pour qn); (*entail*) mener à. **d-o-g ~s "dog"** d-o-g forment *or* donnent *or* font (le mot) "dog"; (*fig*) **that would ~ ruin for him** cela signifierait *or* représenterait *or* serait la ruine pour lui; **effort ~s success** l'effort mène au succès.

2 vi épeler. **to learn to ~** apprendre à épeler, apprendre l'orthographe; **he can't ~, he ~s badly** il fait des fautes d'orthographe, il ne sait pas l'orthographe, il a une mauvaise orthographe.

►**spell out** vt sep a (*read letter by letter*) épeler; (*decipher*) déchiffrer. b (*fig*) *consequences, alternatives* expliquer bien clairement (*for sb* à qn). **let me spell it out for you** laissez-moi vous expliquer bien clairement, laissez-moi mettre les points sur les i; **do I have to spell it out for you?** faut-il que je mette les points sur les i?

spellchecker [ˈspelˌtʃekəʳ] n (*Comput*) contrôle *m* orthographiquee.

speller [ˈspeləʳ] n a *[person]* **to be a good/bad ~** savoir/ne pas savoir l'orthographe. b (*book*) livre *m* d'orthographe.

spelling [ˈspelɪŋ] 1 n orthographe *f*. **reformed ~** nouvelle orthographe. 2 comp *test, practice* d'orthographe ►**spelling bee** concours *m* d'orthographe ►**spelling book** livre *m* d'orthographe ►**spelling checker** (*Comput*) contrôle *m* orthographique ►**spelling error, spelling mistake** faute *f* d'orthographe ►**spelling pronunciation** prononciation *f* orthographique.

spelt[1] [spelt] pret, ptp of **spell[3]**.

spelt[2] [spelt] n (*Bot*) épeautre *m*.

spelunker [spɪˈlʌŋkəʳ] n (*US*) spéléologue *mf*.

spelunking [spɪˈlʌŋkɪŋ] n (*US*) spéléologie *f*.

spend [spend] pret, ptp **spent** 1 vt a *money* dépenser. **he ~s a lot (of money) on food/bus fares/clothes** *etc* il dépense beaucoup en nourriture/tickets d'autobus/vêtements *etc*; **he ~s a lot (of money) on his house/car/girlfriend** il dépense beaucoup *or* il fait de grosses dépenses pour sa maison/sa voiture/sa petite amie; **he spent a fortune on having the roof repaired** il a dépensé une somme folle *or* une fortune pour faire réparer le toit; **without ~ing a penny** *or* **a ha'penny** sans dépenser un sou, sans bourse délier; (*Brit fig euph*) **to ~ a penny*** aller au petit coin*; *see also* **money**.

b (*pass*) *holiday, evening, one's life* passer; (*devote*) *labour, care* consacrer (*on sth* à qch, *doing, in doing* à faire); *time, afternoon* passer, consacrer, employer. **to ~ time on sth** passer du temps sur qch, consacrer du temps à qch; **to ~ time (in) doing** passer *or* consacrer *or* employer du temps à faire; **he ~s his time reading** il passe son temps à lire, il consacre son temps à la lecture; **I spent 2 hours on that letter** j'ai passé 2 heures sur cette lettre, cette lettre m'a pris 2 heures; **he spent a lot of effort (in) getting it just right** il a fait beaucoup d'efforts pour que ce soit juste comme il faut.

c (*consume, exhaust*) *ammunition, provisions* épuiser. *[fury, hatred, enthusiasm]* **to be spent** être tombé; (*liter*) **the storm had spent its fury** la tempête s'était calmée; *see also* **spent**.

2 vi dépenser.

3 comp ►**spendthrift** n dépensier *m*, -ière *f*, panier percé* *m* ◊ adj *habits, attitude etc* de prodigalité; **he's a spendthrift** il est très dépensier, il jette l'argent par les fenêtres.

spender [ˈspendəʳ] n: **to be a big ~** dépenser beaucoup.

spending [ˈspendɪŋ] 1 n (*NonC*) dépenses *fpl*. **government ~** dépenses publiques. 2 comp ►**spending money** argent *m* de poche ►**spending power** pouvoir *m* d'achat ►**spending spree: to go on a spending spree** dépenser beaucoup (en une seule fois), faire des folies *or* de folles dépenses.

spent [spent] 1 pret, ptp of **spend**. 2 adj *match, cartridge etc* utilisé. **~ (nuclear) fuel** combustibles *mpl* irradiés; **that movement is a ~ force** ce mouvement n'a plus l'influence *or* le pouvoir qu'il avait; **he was quite ~** il n'en pouvait plus, il était épuisé; (*permanently*) il était fini.

sperm [spɜːm] 1 n sperme *m*. 2 comp ►**sperm bank** banque *f* de sperme ►**sperm oil** huile *f* de baleine ►**sperm whale** cachalot *m*.

spermaceti [ˌspɜːməˈsetɪ] n spermaceti *m*, blanc *m* de baleine.

spermatic [spɜːˈmætɪk] adj (*Anat*) spermatique.

spermatozoon [ˌspɜːmətəʊˈzəʊɒn] n, pl **spermatozoa** [ˌspɜːmətəʊˈzəʊə] spermatozoïde *m*.

spermicidal [ˌspɜːmɪˈsaɪdl] adj spermicide.

spermicide [ˈspɜːmɪsaɪd] n spermicide *m*.

spew [spjuː] vt (‡: *also* **~ up**) dégueuler‡, vomir; (*fig: also* **~ forth, ~ out**) *fire, lava, curses* vomir. **it makes me ~‡** ça (me) donne envie de dégueuler‡ *or* vomir, c'est dégueulasse‡.

SPG [espiːˈdʒiː] n (*Brit Police*) (abbr of **Special Patrol Group**) *see* **special**.

sphagnum [ˈsfægnəm] n sphaigne *f*.

sphere [sfɪəʳ] n (*gen, Astron, Math etc*) sphère *f*; (*fig*) sphère, domaine *m*. **the music of the ~s** la musique des sphères célestes; **~ of interest/influence** sphère d'intérêt/d'influence; **the ~ of poetry** le domaine de la poésie; **in the social ~** dans le domaine social; **distinguished in many ~s** renommé dans de nombreux domaines; **that is outside my ~** cela n'entre pas dans mes compétences; **within a limited ~** dans un cadre *or* domaine restreint.

spherical [ˈsferɪkəl] adj (*also Math*) sphérique. (*hum*) **he was perfectly ~*** il était gros comme une barrique*.

spheroid [ˈsfɪərɔɪd] 1 n sphéroïde *m*. 2 adj sphéroïdal.

sphincter [ˈsfɪŋktəʳ] n sphincter *m*.

sphinx [sfɪŋks] n, pl **~es** *or* **sphinges** [ˈsfɪndʒiːz] sphinx *m*. **the S~** le Sphinx.

spic‡ [spɪk] n (*US*) = **spick‡**.

spice [spaɪs] 1 n (*Culin*) épice *f*; (*fig*) piquant *m*, sel *m*. (*Culin*) **mixed ~(s)** épices mélangées; **~ rack** casier *m* *or* étagère *f* à épices; (*Culin*) **there's too much ~ in it** c'est trop épicé; **the papers like a story with a bit of ~ to it** les journaux aiment les nouvelles qui ont du piquant *or* qui ne manquent pas de sel; **a ~ of irony/humour** une pointe d'ironie/d'humour; **the ~ of adventure** le piment de l'aventure. 2 vt (*Culin*) épicer, relever (*with* de); (*fig*) relever, pimenter (*with* de).

spiciness [ˈspaɪsɪnɪs] n (*NonC*) *[food]* goût épicé *or* relevé; *[story]* piquant *m*.

spick‡ [spɪk] n (*US*) Latino *mf*.

spick-and-span [ˈspɪkənˈspæn] adj *room, object* impeccable, reluisant de propreté; *person* qui a l'air de sortir d'une boîte.

spicy [ˈspaɪsɪ] adj *food, flavour* épicé, relevé; (*fig*) *story, detail* piquant, salé, croustillant.

spider [ˈspaɪdəʳ] 1 n a (*Zool*) araignée *f*. b (*Aut: for luggage*) pieuvre *f* (*à bagages*). c (*US: frypan*) poêle *f* (à trépied). 2 comp ►**spider crab** araignée *f* de mer ►**spiderman** (*Constr*) ouvrier *m* travaillant sur un bâtiment élevé ►**spider plant** chlorophytum *m*, parachute *m* ►**spider's web**, (*US*) **spiderweb** toile *f* d'araignée.

spidery [ˈspaɪdərɪ] adj *shape* en forme d'araignée; *writing* tremblé.

spiel* [spiːl] 1 n laïus* *m inv*, baratin* *m*; (*Advertising etc*) boniment(s)* *m(pl)*, baratin*. 2 vi faire un laïus* *or* du boniment*, baratiner* (*about* sur).

►**spiel off*** vt sep (*US*) débiter, réciter à toute allure.

spiffing*† [ˈspɪfɪŋ] adj épatant*.

spigot [ˈspɪgət] n a (*plug for barrel*) fausset *m*. b (*Brit: part of tap*) clef *f* *or* clé *f* (*d'un robinet*); (*US: faucet*) robinet *m*.

spik‡ [spɪk] n (*US*) = **spick‡**.

spike [spaɪk] 1 n a (*sharp point*) (*wooden, metal*) pointe *f*; (*on railing*) pointe de fer, (fer *m* de) lance *f*; (*on shoe*) pointe; (*for letters, bills etc*) pique-notes *m inv*; (*nail*) gros clou à large tête; (*tool*) pointe; *[antler]* dague *f*; (*Bot*) épi *m*; (*on graph*) pointe, haut *m*.

b (*Sport: shoes*) **~s*** chaussures *fpl* à pointes.

c (*Climbing*) **rocky ~** becquet *m*.
d (*Volleyball*) smash *m*.
2 comp ▸**spike file** pique-notes *m inv* ▸**spike heels** talons *mpl* aiguilles ▸**spike lavender** (*Bot*) (lavande *f*) aspic *m*.
3 vt a (*pierce*) transpercer; (*put ~s on*) garnir de pointes *or* de clous; (*fig: frustrate*) *plan, hope* contrarier. (*Sport*) **~d shoes** chaussures *fpl* à pointes; (*fig*) **to ~ sb's guns** mettre des bâtons dans les roues à qn.
b (*) *drink* corser (*with* de). **~d coffee** café arrosé d'alcool.
c (*Press: suppress*) *article, story, quote* supprimer.
4 vi (*Volleyball*) smasher.

spikenard ['spaɪknɑːd] n (*NonC*) nard *m* (indien).

spiky ['spaɪkɪ] adj *branch, top of wall* garni *or* hérissé de pointes; *hair* en épi; (*fig: quick-tempered*) prompt à prendre la mouche, chatouilleux.

spill[1] [spɪl] (vb: pret, ptp **spilt** *or* **spilled**) 1 n a (*act of spilling*) fait *m* de renverser, renversement *m*; *see* **oil**.
b (*from horse, cycle*) chute *f*, culbute *f*; (*Aut*) accident *m*. **to have a ~** faire une chute *or* une culbute, avoir un accident.
2 comp ▸**spillover** *see* **spillover** ▸**spillway** (*US*) déversoir *m*.
3 vt *water, sand, salt* renverser, répandre; *rider, passenger* jeter à terre. **she spilt the salt** elle a renversé le sel; **she spilt wine all over the table** elle a renversé *or* répandu du vin sur toute la table; **you're ~ing water from that jug** tu laisses tomber de l'eau de cette cruche; **to ~ blood** verser *or* faire couler le sang; (*fig*) **to ~ the beans*** (*gen*) vendre la mèche (*about* à propos de); (*under interrogation*) se mettre à table‡, parler; (*US fig: talk*) **to ~ one's guts‡** (*gen*) raconter sa vie; (*under interrogation*) se mettre à table‡, parler; (*Naut*) **to ~ (wind from) a sail** étouffer une voile.
4 vi [*liquid, salt etc*] se répandre.

▸**spill out** 1 vi se répandre; (*fig*) [*people etc*] sortir en masse. **the crowd spilled out into the streets** la foule s'est déversée dans la rue. 2 vt sep *contents, sand, liquid* répandre; (*fig*) *story, truth, details* révéler, raconter (précipitamment).

▸**spill over** 1 vi [*liquids*] déborder, se répandre; (*fig*) [*population*] déborder, se déverser (*into* dans). **these problems spilled over into his private life** ces problèmes ont gagné sa vie privée. 2 **spillover** n *see* **spillover; overspill** n, adj *see* **over 3**.

spill[2] [spɪl] n (*for lighting with*) longue allumette (*de papier etc*).

spillikins ['spɪlɪkɪnz] n (*Brit*) (jeu *m* de) jonchets *mpl*, mikado *m*.

spillover ['spɪləʊvəʳ] n (*act of spilling*) fait *m* de renverser, renversement *m*; (*quantity spilt*) quantité *f* renversée; (*fig*) (*excess part*) excédent *m*; (*Econ: effect*) retombées *fpl*, effet *m* d'entraînement.

spilt [spɪlt] pret, ptp of **spill**[1].

spin [spɪn] (vb: pret **spun** *or* **span**††, ptp **spun**) 1 n a (*turning motion*) tournoiement *m*; (*Aviat*) (chute *f* en) vrille *f*. **to give a wheel a ~** faire tourner une roue; (*on washing machine*) **long/short ~** essorage complet/léger; (*Sport*) **to put a ~ on a ball** donner de l'effet à une balle; (*Aviat*) **to go into a ~** tomber en vrille *or* en vrillant; (*Aviat*) **to pull** *or* **get out of a ~** se sortir d'une (chute en) vrille; (*fig*) [*person*] **to get into a ~** s'affoler, perdre la tête, paniquer*; **everything was in such a ~** c'était la pagaille* complète; (*fig: try out*) **to give sth a ~‡** essayer qch; *see* **flat**[1] *etc*.
b (*: *ride*) petit tour, balade* *f*. **to go for a ~** faire un petit tour *or* une balade* (en voiture *or* à bicyclette *etc*).
2 comp ▸**spin-drier** = **spin dryer** ▸**spindrift** embrun(s) *m(pl)*, poudrin *m* ▸**spin-dry** essorer (à la machine) ▸**spin-dryer** (*Brit*) essoreuse *f* ▸**spin-drying** (*NonC*) essorage *m* à la machine ▸**spin-off** *see* **spin-off**.
3 vt a *wool, yarn, fibres, glass* filer (*into* en, pour en faire); *thread etc* fabriquer, produire; [*spider, silkworm*] filer, tisser; (*fig*) *story etc* inventer, fabriquer, débiter (*pej*). (*fig*) **to ~ a yarn** (*make up*) inventer *or* débiter (*pej*) une histoire; (*tell*) raconter une histoire; **he spun me a yarn about his difficulties/about having been ill** il m'a inventé *or* débité (*pej*) une longue histoire sur ses problèmes/comme quoi il avait été malade; **spun glass** verre filé; **hair like spun gold** des cheveux ressemblant à de l'or filé; **spun silk** schappe *m or f*; (*Naut*) **spun yarn** bitord *m*; *see* **fine**[2].
b *wheel, nut, revolving stand etc* faire tourner; *top* lancer, fouetter; (*Sport*) *ball* donner de l'effet à. **to ~ a coin** jouer à pile ou face.
c (*Brit*) = **spin-dry**; *see* **2**.
4 vi a [*spinner etc*] filer; [*spider*] filer *or* tisser sa toile.
b (*often ~* **round**) [*suspended object*] tourner, tournoyer, pivoter; [*top, dancer*] tourner, tournoyer; [*planet, spacecraft*] tourner (sur soi-même); [*machinery wheel*] tourner; [*car wheel*] patiner; [*aircraft*] vriller, tomber en vrillant; (*Sport*) [*ball*] tournoyer. **to ~ round and round** continuer à tourner (*or* tournoyer *etc*); **to send sth/sb ~ning** envoyer rouler qch/qn; **the disc went ~ning away over the trees** le disque s'envola en tournoyant par-dessus les arbres; **he spun round as he heard me come in** il s'est retourné vivement *or* sur ses talons en m'entendant entrer; (*fig*) **my head is ~ning (round)** j'ai la tête qui tourne; (*fig*) **the room was ~ning (round)** la chambre tournait (autour de moi *or* lui *etc*).
c (*move quickly*) [*vehicle*] **to ~** *or* **go ~ning along** rouler à toute vitesse, filer (à toute allure).
d (*Fishing*) **to ~ for trout** *etc* pêcher la truite *etc* à la cuiller.

▸**spin off** 1 vi (*arise as result of*) **to spin off from** résulter de. 2 **spin-off** *see* **spin-off**.

▸**spin out** vt sep *story, explanation* faire durer, délayer; *visit etc* faire durer; *money, food* faire durer, économiser, ménager.

▸**spin round** 1 vi *see* **spin 4b**. 2 vt sep *wheel, nut, revolving stand* faire tourner; *person* faire pivoter; *dancing partner* faire tourner *or* tournoyer.

spina bifida ['spaɪnə'bɪfɪdə] n spina-bifida *m*.

spinach ['spɪnɪdʒ] n (*plant*) épinard *m*; (*Culin*) épinards.

spinal ['spaɪnl] adj (*Anat*) *nerve, muscle* spinal; *ligament, column, disc* vertébral; *injury* à la colonne vertébrale. **~ anaesthesia** rachianesthésie *f*; **~ anaesthetic** rachianesthésique *m*; **~ cord** moelle épinière; **~ meningitis** méningite cérébro-spinale.

spindle ['spɪndl] 1 n a (*Spinning*) fuseau *m*; (*on machine*) broche *f*. b (*Tech*) [*pump*] axe *m*; [*lathe*] arbre *m*; [*valve*] tige *f*. 2 comp ▸**spindle-legged*** qui a des jambes de faucheux ▸**spindlelegs*** (*person*) faucheux *m* (*fig*) ▸**spindle-shanked*** = **spindle-legged*** ▸**spindle-shanks*** = **spindlelegs***.

spindly ['spɪndlɪ] adj *legs, arms* grêle, maigre comme une *or* des allumette(s); *person* grêle, chétif; *chair leg* grêle; *plant* étiolé.

spine [spaɪn] 1 n a (*Anat*) colonne vertébrale, épine dorsale; [*fish*] épine; [*hedgehog*] piquant *m*, épine; (*Bot*) épine, piquant; [*book*] dos *m*; [*hill etc*] crête *f*. b (*US fig: courage*) courage *m*, résolution *f*. 2 comp ▸**spine-chiller** roman *m or* film *m etc* à vous glacer le sang ▸**spine-chilling** à vous glacer le sang.

spineless ['spaɪnlɪs] adj (*Zool*) invertébré; (*fig*) mou (*f* molle), flasque (*fig*), sans caractère.

spinelessly ['spaɪnlɪslɪ] adv (*fig*) lâchement, mollement.

spinet [spɪ'net] n (*Mus*) épinette *f*.

spinnaker ['spɪnəkəʳ] n spinnaker *m*, spi *m*.

spinner ['spɪnəʳ] n (*person*) fileur *m*, -euse *f*; (*Fishing*) cuiller *f*; (*spin-dryer*) essoreuse *f*; (*revolving display stand*) tourniquet *m*. (*Baseball, Cricket*) **he sent down a ~*** il a donné de l'effet à la balle; *see* **money**.

spinneret [ˌspɪnə'ret] n (*Tex, Zool*) filière *f*.

spinney ['spɪnɪ] n (*Brit*) bosquet *m*, petit bois.

spinning ['spɪnɪŋ] 1 n (*by hand*) filage *m*; (*by machine*) filature *f*; (*Fishing*) pêche *f* à la cuiller. 2 comp ▸**spinning jenny** jenny *f* ▸**spinning machine** machine *f or* métier *m* à filer ▸**spinning mill** filature *f* ▸**spinning top** toupie *f* ▸**spinning wheel** rouet *m*.

spin-off ['spɪnɒf] n (*gen*) profit *m or* avantage *m* inattendu; (*Ind, Tech etc*) sous-produit *m*, application *f* secondaire. (*Fin*) **~ effect** retombées *fpl*, effet *m* d'entraînement; **this TV series is a ~ from the famous film** ce feuilleton télévisé est tiré *or* issu du célèbre film.

Spinoza [spɪ'nəʊzə] n Spinoza *m*.

spinster ['spɪnstəʳ] n célibataire *f* (*also Admin*), vieille fille (*pej*). **she is a ~** elle est célibataire, elle n'est pas mariée.

spiny ['spaɪnɪ] adj (*see* **spine**) épineux, couvert d'épines *or* de piquants. **~ lobster** homard *m* épineux, langouste *f*.

spiracle ['spɪrəkl] n (*airhole*) orifice *m* d'aération; [*whale etc*] évent *m*; [*insect etc*] stigmate *m*; (*Geol*) cassure *f*.

spiral ['spaɪərəl] 1 adj *curve, shell* en spirale, spiroïdal; *movement, dive, decoration* en spirale; *spring* en spirale, à boudin; *nebula, galaxy* spiral; (*Aviat*) en vrille. **~ staircase** escalier tournant *or* en colimaçon.
2 n spirale *f*. **in a ~** en spirale; (*fig*) **the wage-price ~** la montée inexorable des salaires et des prix; **the inflationary ~** la spirale inflationniste. 3 vi [*staircase, smoke*] former une spirale; [*ball, missile etc*] tourner en spirale; [*plane*] vriller; (*fig*) [*prices*] monter en flèche; [*prices and wages*] former une spirale.

▸**spiral down** vi (*Aviat*) descendre en vrille.

▸**spiral up** vi (*Aviat*) monter en vrille; [*staircase, smoke, missile*] monter en spirale; [*prices*] monter en flèche.

spirally ['spaɪərəlɪ] adv en spirale, en hélice.

spire ['spaɪəʳ] n (*Archit*) flèche *f*, aiguille *f*; [*tree, mountain*] cime *f*; [*grass, plant*] brin *m*, pousse *f*.

spirit ['spɪrɪt] 1 n a (*soul*) esprit *m*, âme *f*. **the life of the ~** la vie de l'esprit, la vie spirituelle; **he was there in ~** il était présent en esprit *or* de cœur; **the ~ is willing but the flesh is weak** l'esprit est prompt mais la chair est faible; **God is pure ~** Dieu est un pur esprit; *see* **holy, move** *etc*.
b (*supernatural being*) esprit *m*; (*ghost*) esprit, revenant *m*, fantôme *m*; (*Spiritualism*) esprit. **evil ~** esprit malin *or* du mal.
c (*person*) esprit *m*, âme *f*. **one of the greatest ~s of his day** un des plus grands esprits de son temps; **the courageous ~ who ...** l'esprit courageux *or* l'âme courageuse qui ...; **a few restless ~s** quelques mécontents; **the leading ~ in the party** l'âme du parti; *see* **kindred, moving** *etc*.
d (*attitude etc*) esprit *m*, disposition *f*; [*proposal, regulations etc*] esprit, intention *f*, but *m*. **he's got the right ~** il a la disposition *or* l'attitude qu'il faut; **in a ~ of forgiveness** dans un esprit *or* une intention de pardon; **he has great fighting ~** il ne se laisse jamais abattre; **you must take it in the ~ in which it was meant** prenez-le dans l'esprit où c'était dit *or* voulu; **to take sth in the right/wrong ~** prendre qch en bonne/mauvaise part *or* du bon/mauvais côté; **you must enter into**

the ~ of the thing il faut y participer de bon cœur; **in a ~ of revenge** par esprit de vengeance; **in a ~ of mischief** *etc* par espièglerie *etc;* **the ~, not the letter of the law** l'esprit et non la lettre de la loi; **the film is certainly in the ~ of the book** le film est certainement conforme à l'esprit du livre; **the ~ of the age** *or* **the times** l'esprit des temps *or* de l'époque; **that's the ~!** c'est ça!, voilà comment il faut réagir!, voilà l'attitude à prendre!; *see* **community, public, team** *etc.*

e (*frame of mind*) **~s** humeur *f*, état *m* d'esprit; (*morale*) moral *m*; **in good ~s** de bonne humeur; **in poor** *or* **low ~s, out of ~s** déprimé, qui n'a pas le moral; **to keep one's ~s up** ne pas se laisser abattre, garder le moral; **my ~s rose** j'ai repris courage; **to raise sb's ~s** remonter le moral à qn; *see* **animal, high** *etc.*

f (*courage*) courage *m*, caractère *m*, cran* *m*; (*energy*) énergie *f*; (*vitality*) entrain *m*. **man of ~** homme *m* énergique *or* de caractère; **he replied with ~** il a répondu courageusement *or* énergiquement *or* avec fougue; **he sang/played with ~** il a chanté/joué avec fougue *or* brio.

g (*Chem*) alcool *m*. **preserved in ~(s)** conservé dans de l'alcool; **~(s) of ammonia** sel *m* ammoniaque; **~(s) of salt** esprit-de-sel *m*; **~(s) of turpentine** (essence *f* de) térébenthine *f*; (*drink*) **~s** spiritueux *mpl*, alcool; **raw ~s** alcool pur; *see* **methylated, surgical** *etc.*

2 **comp** *lamp, stove, varnish* à alcool; (*Spiritualism*) *help, world* des esprits ►**spirit gum** colle *f* gomme ►**spirit level** niveau *m* à bulle.

3 **vt: he was ~ed out of the castle** on l'a fait sortir du château comme par enchantement *or* magie; **the documents were mysteriously ~ed off his desk** les documents ont été mystérieusement escamotés *or* subtilisés de son bureau.

►**spirit away, spirit off vt sep** *person* faire disparaître comme par enchantement; *object, document etc* escamoter, subtiliser.

spirited ['spɪrɪtɪd] **adj** *person* vif, fougueux, plein d'entrain; *horse* fougueux; *reply, speech* plein de verve, fougueux; *conversation* animé; *music* plein d'allant; *undertaking, defence* courageux, qui montre du cran*. (*Mus*) **he gave a ~ performance** il a joué avec fougue *or* avec brio; *see* **high, low[1], public** *etc.*

spiritless ['spɪrɪtlɪs] **adj** *person* sans entrain, sans énergie, sans vie; *acceptance, agreement* veule, lâche.

spiritual ['spɪrɪtjʊəl] 1 **adj** (*not material etc*) *life, power, welfare* spirituel; (*religious*) *music etc* spirituel, religieux; (*in spirit*) *heir, successor* spirituel. **he is a very ~ person** c'est vraiment une nature élevée; (*Rel*) **~ adviser** conseiller spirituel, directeur *m* de conscience; **~ home** terre *f* spirituelle; (*Brit*) **the lords ~** les lords spirituels (*évêques siégeant à la Chambre des pairs*). 2 **n** chant *m* religieux; (*also* **Negro ~**) (negro-)spiritual *m*.

spiritualism ['spɪrɪtjʊəlɪzəm] **n** (*Rel*) spiritisme *m*; (*Philos*) spiritualisme *m*.

spiritualist ['spɪrɪtjʊəlɪst] **adj, n** (*Rel*) spirite (*mf*); (*Philos*) spiritualiste (*mf*).

spirituality [ˌspɪrɪtjʊ'ælɪtɪ] **n** a (*NonC*) spiritualité *f*, qualité spirituelle. b (*Rel*) **spiritualities** biens *mpl* et bénéfices *mpl* ecclésiastiques.

spiritually ['spɪrɪtjʊəlɪ] **adv** spirituellement, en esprit.

spirituous ['spɪrɪtjʊəs] **adj** spiritueux, alcoolique. **~ liquor** spiritueux *mpl*.

spirt [spɜːt] = **spurt.**

spit[1] [spɪt] (**vb: pret, ptp spat**) 1 **n** (*spittle*) crachat *m*; (*saliva*) *[person]* salive *f*; *[animal]* bave *f*; (*Bot*) écume printanière, crachat de coucou; (*action*) crachement *m*. (*esp Mil*) **~ and polish** briquage *m*, astiquage *m*; **there was just a ~ of rain** il tombait quelques gouttes de pluie; (*fig*) **he's the dead** *or* **very ~* of his uncle** c'est le portrait craché* de son oncle, son oncle et lui se ressemblent comme deux gouttes d'eau; *see* **frog[1].**

2 **comp** ►**spitfire:** *[person]* **to be a spitfire** s'emporter pour un rien.

3 **vt** *blood, curses, flames etc* cracher.

4 **vi** *[person, cat etc]* cracher (*at sb* sur qn); *[fire, fat]* crépiter. **she spat in his face** elle lui a craché à la figure; **it was ~ting (with rain)** il tombait quelques gouttes de pluie.

►**spit out vt sep** *pip, pill* (re)cracher; *tooth, curses, information* cracher. (*fig: say it*) **spit it out!*** allons, accouche!‡ *or* vide ton sac!* (*fig*).

►**spit up vt sep** *blood etc* cracher.

spit[2] [spɪt] 1 **n** (*Culin*) broche *f*; (*Geog*) pointe *f or* langue *f* (de terre). 2 **comp** ►**spitroast** faire rôtir à la broche ►**spitroasted** (rôti) à la broche. 3 **vt** embrocher.

spit[3] [spɪt] **n** (*Horticulture*) **to dig sth 2 ~s deep** creuser qch à une profondeur de 2 fers de bêche.

spite [spaɪt] 1 **n** (*NonC*) a (*ill-feeling*) rancune *f*, dépit *m*. **out of pure ~** par pure rancune *or* malveillance; **to have a ~ against sb*** avoir une dent contre qn, en vouloir à qn. b **in ~ of** malgré, en dépit de; **in ~ of it** malgré cela, en dépit de cela; **in ~ of the fact that he has seen me** bien qu'il m'ait vu, malgré qu'il m'ait vu; **in ~ of everyone** envers et contre tous. 2 **vt** vexer, contrarier.

spiteful ['spaɪtfʊl] **adj** *person* méchant, malveillant, rancunier; *comment* malveillant; *tongue* venimeux. **a ~ remark** une méchanceté, une rosserie*.

spitefully ['spaɪtfəlɪ] **adv** par méchanceté, par rancune, par dépit.

spitefulness ['spaɪtfʊlnɪs] **n** méchanceté *f*, malveillance *f*, rancune *f*.

spitting ['spɪtɪŋ] **n: "~ prohibited"** "défense de cracher"; (*fig*) **within ~ distance*** à deux pas (*of* de); *see* **image.**

spittle ['spɪtl] **n** (*ejected*) crachat *m*; (*dribbled*) *[person]* salive *f*; *[animal]* bave *f*.

spittoon [spɪ'tuːn] **n** crachoir *m*.

spitz [spɪts] **n** loulou *m* (*chien*).

spiv* [spɪv] **n** (*Brit*) chevalier *m* d'industrie.

splash [splæʃ] 1 **n** a (*act*) éclaboussement *m*; (*sound*) floc *m*, plouf *m*; (*series of sounds*) clapotement *m*; (*mark*) éclaboussure *f*, tache *f*; (*fig: of colour*) tache. **he dived in with a ~** il a plongé dans un grand éclaboussement *or* en faisant une grande gerbe; **it made a great ~ as it hit the water** c'est tombé dans l'eau avec un gros plouf *or* en faisant une grande gerbe; (*fig*) **to make a ~*** faire sensation, faire du bruit; (*fig*) **a great ~ of publicity** un grand étalage de *or* une débauche de publicité.

b (*in drinks etc: small amount*) **a ~ of** (*gen*) un petit peu de; (*soda water*) une giclée de.

2 **comp** ►**splashback** revêtement *m* (au dessus d'un évier *etc*) ►**splashboard** (*Aut etc*) garde-boue *m inv* ►**splashdown** (*Space*) amerrissage *m* ►**splash guard** (*Aut*) garde-boue *m inv.*

3 **adv: it went ~ into the stream** c'est tombé dans l'eau (en faisant floc *or* plouf).

4 **vt** a (*gen*) éclabousser (*sth over sb/sth* qch sur qn/qch, *sb/sth with sth* qn/qch de qch). **to ~ milk on the floor** renverser du lait par terre; **he ~ed paint on the floor** il a fait des éclaboussures de peinture par terre; (*in swimming etc*) **don't ~ me!** ne m'éclabousse pas!; **to ~ one's way through a stream** traverser un ruisseau en éclaboussant *or* en pataugeant; **~ed with red/colour/light** avec des taches de rouge/de couleur/de lumière.

b (*apply hastily*) **to ~ o.s. with water, to ~ water on o.s.** s'asperger d'eau; **he ~ed paint on the wall** il a barbouillé le mur de peinture.

c (*fig*) *headlines* mettre en manchette. (*Press*) **the news was ~ed across the front page** la nouvelle a été mise en manchette, la nouvelle a fait cinq colonnes à la une.

5 **vi** a *[liquid, mud etc]* faire des éclaboussures. **the milk ~ed on** *or* **over the tablecloth** le lait a éclaboussé la nappe; **tears ~ed on to her book** les larmes s'écrasaient sur son livre.

b *[person, animal]* barboter, patauger (*in* dans). **to ~ across a stream** traverser un ruisseau en éclaboussant *or* en pataugeant; **the dog ~ed through the mud** le chien pataugeait dans la boue; **to ~ into the water** *[person]* plonger dans l'eau dans un grand éclaboussement *or* en faisant une grande gerbe; *[stone etc]* tomber dans l'eau avec un gros floc *or* plouf.

►**splash about** 1 **vi** *[person, animal]* barboter, patauger (*in* dans). 2 **vt sep** *ink, mud* faire des éclaboussures de; (*fig*) *money* faire étalage de.

►**splash down** 1 **vi** *[spacecraft]* amerrir. 2 **splashdown n** *see* **splash 2.**

►**splash out*** 1 **vi** (*spend money*) faire une folie. 2 **vt sep** *money* claquer‡, dépenser.

►**splash up** 1 **vi** gicler (*on sb* sur qn). 2 **vt sep** faire gicler.

splat [splæt] 1 **n: with a ~** avec un flac *or* floc. 2 **excl** flac!, floc!

splatter ['splætəʳ] = **spatter.**

splay [spleɪ] 1 **vt** *window frame* ébraser; *end of pipe etc* évaser; *feet, legs* tourner en dehors. 2 **vi** (*also* **~ out**) *[window frame]* s'ébraser; *[end of pipe etc]* se tourner en dehors. 3 **comp** ►**splayfeet** pieds tournés en dehors ►**splayfooted** *person* aux pieds plats; *horse* panard.

spleen [spliːn] **n** (*Anat*) rate *f*; (*fig: bad temper*) mauvaise humeur, humeur noire; (*††: melancholy*) spleen *m*. **to vent one's ~ on** décharger sa bile sur.

splendid ['splendɪd] **adj** (*imposing etc*) *ceremony, view, beauty* splendide, superbe, magnifique; (*excellent*) *holiday, result, idea* excellent, magnifique, formidable*; *teacher, mother etc* excellent. **in ~ isolation** dans un splendide isolement; **that's simply ~!** c'est parfait! *or* épatant!* *or* formidable!*

splendidly ['splendɪdlɪ] **adv** (*see* **splendid**) splendidement, superbement, magnifiquement; de façon excellente, épatamment*, formidablement*. **~ dressed** superbement *or* magnifiquement habillé; **you did ~** tu as été merveilleux *or* épatant*; **it all went ~** tout a marché comme sur des roulettes; **it's coming along ~** ça avance très bien *or* formidablement* bien.

splendiferous* [splen'dɪfərəs] **adj** magnifique, merveilleux, mirobolant*.

splendour, (US) splendor ['splendəʳ] **n** splendeur *f*, magnificence *f*, éclat *m*.

splenetic [splɪ'netɪk] **adj** (*bad-tempered*) atrabilaire, morose; (*††: melancholy*) porté au spleen.

splice [splaɪs] 1 **vt** *rope, cable* épisser; *film, tape* coller; *timbers* enter, abouter. **to ~ the mainbrace** (*Naut*) distribuer une ration de rhum; (* *fig: have a drink*) boire un coup*; (*fig*) **to get ~d‡** convoler. 2 **n** (*in rope*) épissure *f*; (*in film*) collure *f*; (*in wood*) enture *f*.

splicer ['splaɪsəʳ] **n** (*for film*) colleuse *f* (*à bandes adhésives*).

splint [splɪnt] **n** (*Med*) éclisse *f*, attelle *f*. **to put sb's arm in ~s** éclisser le bras de qn; **she had her leg in ~s** elle avait la jambe éclissée.

splinter ['splɪntəʳ] 1 n *[glass, shell, wood]* éclat *m*; *[bone]* esquille *f*; (*in one's finger etc*) écharde *f*. 2 comp ► **splinter group** groupe dissident *or* scissionniste ► **splinterproof glass** verre *m* sécurit *inv* ®. 3 vt *wood* fendre en éclats; *glass, bone* briser en éclats; (*fig*) *party etc* scinder, fragmenter. 4 vi *[wood]* se fendre en éclats; *[glass, bone]* se briser en éclats; (*fig*) *[party]* se scinder, se fragmenter.

split [splɪt] (vb: pret, ptp **split**) 1 n a (*in garment, fabric, canvas*) (*at seam*) fente *f*; (*tear*) déchirure *f*; (*in wood, rock*) crevasse *f*, fente; (*in earth's surface*) fissure *f*, crevasse, fente; (*in skin*) fissure, déchirure, (*from cold*) gerçure *f*, crevasse; (*fig: quarrel*) rupture *f*; (*Pol*) scission *f*, schisme *m*. **there was a 3-way ~ in the committee** le comité s'est trouvé divisé en 3 clans; **they did a 4-way ~ of the profits** ils ont partagé les bénéfices en 4; (*fig: share*) **I want my ~*** je veux ma part (du gâteau*); **to do the ~s** faire le grand écart.

b (*small bottle*) **soda/lemonade ~** petite bouteille d'eau gazeuse/de limonade; (*cake*) **jam/cream ~** gâteau fourré à la confiture/à la crème; (*ice cream etc*) **banana ~** banana split *m*.

2 comp ► **split-cane** n osier *m* ◊ adj en osier ► **split decision** (*Boxing etc*) décision *f* majoritaire ► **split ends** (*in hair*) fourches *fpl* ► **split infinitive** (*Gram*) *infinitif où un adverbe est intercalé entre "to" et le verbe* ► **split-level cooker** cuisinière *f* à plaques de cuisson et four indépendants ► **split-level house** maison *f* à deux niveaux ► **split mind** = **split personality** ► **split-new** tout neuf (*f* toute neuve) ► **split-off** séparation *f*, scission *f* (*from* de) ► **split peas** pois cassés ► **split-pea soup** soupe *f* de pois cassés ► **split personality** double personnalité *f* ► **split pin** (*Brit*) clavette fendue ► **split ring** anneau brisé ► **split screen** (*Cine, TV, Comput*) écran *m* divisé ► **split-screen facility** (*Comput*) écran *m* divisible en fenêtres, fonction *f* écran divisé ► **split second** fraction *f* de seconde; **in a split second** en un rien de temps ► **split-second timing** *[military operation etc]* précision *f* à la seconde près; *[actor, comedian]* sens *m* du moment ► **split-site** *school etc* dont les locaux ne sont pas regroupés ► **split ticket**: (*US Pol*) **to vote a split ticket** voter pour une liste avec panachage ► **split-up** *[engaged couple, friends]* rupture *f*; *[married couple]* séparation *f*; *[political party]* scission *f*, schisme *m*.

3 vt a (*cleave*) *wood, pole* fendre; *slate, diamond* cliver; *stones* fendre, casser; *fabric, garment* déchirer; *seam* fendre; *[lightning, frost, explosion, blow]* fendre; (*fig*) *party etc* diviser, créer une scission *or* un schisme dans. **to ~ the atom** fissionner l'atome; **to ~ sth open** ouvrir qch en le coupant en deux *or* en fendant; **he ~ his head open as he fell** il s'est fendu le crâne en tombant; **the sea had ~ the ship in two** la mer avait brisé le bateau en deux; **he ~ it in two** il l'a fendu (en deux); **he ~ it into three** il l'a coupé en trois; **~ the loaf lengthwise** fendez le pain dans le sens de la longueur; (*fig*) **to ~ hairs** couper les cheveux en quatre, chercher la petite bête, chinoiser; (*Gram*) **to ~ an infinitive** *intercaler un adverbe entre "to" et le verbe*; (*fig*) **to ~ one's sides (laughing *or* with laughter)** se tordre de rire; **this decision ~ the radical movement** cette décision a divisé le mouvement radical, cette décision a provoqué une scission *or* un schisme dans le mouvement radical; **it ~ the party down the middle** cela a littéralement divisé le parti en deux; **the voters were ~ down the middle** l'électorat était divisé *or* coupé en deux.

b (*divide, share*) *work, profits, booty, the bill* (se) partager, (se) répartir. **let's ~ a bottle of wine** si on prenait une bouteille de vin à deux (*or* trois *etc*)?; **they ~ the money 3 ways** ils ont divisé l'argent en 3; **to ~ the difference** (*lit*) partager la différence; (*fig*) couper la poire en deux; **they ~ the work/the inheritance** ils se sont partagé le travail/l'héritage.

4 vi a *[wood, pole, seam]* se fendre; *[stones]* se fendre, se casser; *[fabric, garment]* se déchirer; (*fig*) *[party, Church, government]* se diviser, se désunir. **to ~ open** se fendre; (*fig*) **my head is ~ting** j'ai atrocement mal à la tête; **the party ~ over nationalization** le parti s'est divisé sur la question des nationalisations, il y a eu une scission *or* un schisme dans le parti à propos de la question des nationalisations.

b (*divide: also* **~ up**) *[cells]* se diviser; *[people, party etc]* se diviser, se séparer. **the crowd ~ into smaller groups** la foule s'est divisée *or* séparée en petits groupes; **Latin ~ into the Romance languages** le latin s'est divisé *or* ramifié en langues romanes.

c (*Brit *: tell tales, inform*) vendre la mèche*. **to ~ on sb** donner qn, vendre qn, cafarder qn*.

d (*‡: depart*) filer*, mettre les bouts‡.

► **split off** 1 vi *[piece of wood, branch etc]* se détacher (en se fendant) (*from* de); (*fig*) *[group, department, company etc]* se séparer (*from* de). **a small group of children split off and wandered away** un petit groupe d'enfants s'est séparé des autres et est parti de son côté. 2 vt sep *branch, splinter, piece* enlever (en fendant *or* en cassant) (*from* de); (*fig*) *company, group, department* séparer (*from* de). 3 **split-off** n *see* **split 2**.

► **split up** 1 vi *[ship]* se briser; *[boulder, block of wood etc]* se fendre; (*fig*) *[meeting, crowd]* se disperser; *[party, movement]* se diviser, se scinder; *[friends]* rompre, se brouiller; *[married couple]* se séparer; *[engaged couple]* rompre.

2 vt sep *wood, stones* fendre (*into* en); *money, work* partager, répartir (*among* entre), diviser (*into* en); *compound* diviser (*into* en); *party, group, organization* diviser, scinder (*into* en); *meeting* mettre fin à; *crowd* disperser; *friends* séparer. **to split up a book into 6 chapters** diviser un livre en 6 chapitres; **we must split the work up amongst us** nous devons nous partager *or* nous répartir le travail; **you'll have to split up those two boys if you want them to do any work** il faut que vous sépariez (*subj*) ces deux garçons si vous voulez qu'ils travaillent (*subj*).

3 **split-up** n *see* **split 2**.

splitting ['splɪtɪŋ] 1 n (*see* **split 3a, 3b, 4a, 4b**) fendage *m*; clivage *m*; cassage *m*; déchirement *m*; division *f*, scission *f*, schisme *m*; partage *m*, répartition *f*; séparation *f*. **the ~ of the atom** la fission de l'atome; *see* **hair** *etc*. 2 adj: **I have a ~ headache** j'ai atrocement mal à la tête; *see* **ear**[1], **side** *etc*.

splodge [splɒdʒ], **splotch** [splɒtʃ] 1 n *[ink, paint, colour, dirt, mud]* éclaboussure *f*, tache *f*. **strawberries with a great ~ of cream** des fraises avec un monceau de crème. 2 vt *windows, dress etc* éclabousser, barbouiller (*with* de); *mud, ink etc* faire des taches *or* des éclaboussures de (*on* sur). 3 vi *[mud etc]* gicler (*on* sur).

splurge* [splɜːdʒ] 1 n (*ostentation*) tralala* *m*; (*spending spree*) folles dépenses, folie *f*. **the wedding reception was *or* made a great ~** la réception de mariage était à grand tralala*; **she went on a *or* had a ~ and bought a Rolls** elle a fait une vraie folie et s'est payé* une Rolls. 2 vi (*also* **~ out**) faire une *or* des folie(s) (*on* en achetant). 3 vt dépenser (en un seul coup) (*on sth* pour qch), engloutir (*on sth* dans qch).

splutter ['splʌtəʳ] 1 n *[person]* (*spitting*) crachotement *m*; (*stuttering*) bredouillement *m*, bafouillage* *m*; *[engine]* bafouillage*; *[fire, frying pan, fat, candle]* crépitement *m*. 2 vi *[person]* (*spit*) crachoter, crachouiller*, postillonner; (*stutter*) bredouiller, bafouiller*; *[pen]* cracher; *[engine]* bafouiller*, tousser; *[fire, frying pan, fat, candle]* crépiter. **he ~ed indignantly** il a bredouillé *or* bafouillé* d'indignation. 3 vt (*also* **~ out**) *words, excuse* bredouiller, bafouiller*.

spoil [spɔɪl] (vb: pret, ptp **spoiled** *or* **spoilt**) 1 n a (*gen pl*) **~(s)** (*booty*) butin *m*; (*fig: after business deal etc*) bénéfices *mpl*, profits *mpl*; (*US Pol*) poste *m or* avantage *m* reçu en récompense de services politiques rendus; **the ~s of war** le butin *or* les dépouilles *fpl* de la guerre; (*fig*) **he wants his share of the ~s** il veut sa part du gâteau*.

b (*NonC: from excavations etc*) déblais *mpl*.

2 comp ► **spoilsport** trouble-fête *mf inv*, rabat-joie *m inv*; **don't be such a spoilsport!** ne joue pas les trouble-fête! *or* les rabat-joie! ► **spoils system** (*US Pol*) système *m* des dépouilles (*consistant à distribuer des postes administratifs à des partisans après une victoire électorale*).

3 vt a (*damage*) *paint, dress etc* abîmer. **to ~ one's eyes** s'abîmer la vue; **fruit ~ed by insects** des fruits abîmés par les insectes; **the drought has really ~t the garden** la sécheresse a vraiment fait des dégâts dans le jardin; **to ~ a ballot paper** rendre un bulletin de vote nul.

b (*detract from*) *view, style, effect* gâter; *holiday, occasion, pleasure* gâter, gâcher. **these weeds quite ~ the garden** ces mauvaises herbes enlaidissent *or* défigurent le jardin; **his peace of mind was ~t by money worries** sa tranquillité était empoisonnée par des soucis d'argent; **to ~ one's appetite** s'enlever *or* se couper l'appétit; **if you eat that now you'll ~ your lunch** si tu manges ça maintenant tu n'auras plus d'appétit pour le déjeuner; **don't ~ your life by doing that** ne gâche pas ta vie en faisant cela; **if you tell me the ending you'll ~ the film for me** si vous me racontez la fin vous me gâcherez tout l'intérêt du film; **she ~t the meal by overcooking the meat** elle a gâté le repas en faisant trop cuire la viande; **she ~t the meal by telling him the bad news** elle a gâché le repas en lui racontant la triste nouvelle; **the weather ~ed our holiday** le temps nous a gâté *or* gâché nos vacances; (*Prov*) **to ~ the ship for a ha'p'orth of tar** faire des économies de bouts de chandelle; *see* **fun**.

c (*pamper*) *child, one's spouse, dog etc* gâter. **to ~ o.s.** se gâter soi-même, se faire plaisir; **to ~ sb rotten‡** pourrir qn; *see* **spare**.

4 vi a *[food]* s'abîmer; (*in ship's hold, warehouse, shop*) s'avarier.

b **to be ~ing for a fight** brûler de se battre, chercher la bagarre*.

spoilage ['spɔɪlɪdʒ] n (*NonC*) (*process*) détérioration *f*; (*thing, amount spoilt*) déchet(s) *m(pl)*.

spoiled [spɔɪld] = **spoilt**.

spoiler ['spɔɪləʳ] n (*Aut*) becquet *m*; (*Aviat*) aérofrein *m*.

spoilt [spɔɪlt] 1 pret, ptp of **spoil**. 2 adj a (*see* **spoil 3a, 3b**) abîmé; gâté, gâché; *ballot paper* nul. b *child etc* gâté; *desire, refusal* d'enfant gâté. **to be ~ for choice** avoir l'embarras du choix.

spoke[1] [spəʊk] 1 n *[wheel]* rayon *m*; *[ladder]* barreau *m*, échelon *m*. (*Brit fig*) **to put a ~ in sb's wheel** mettre des bâtons dans les roues à qn. 2 comp ► **spokeshave** (*Tech*) vastringue *f*.

spoke[2] [spəʊk] pret of **speak**.

spoken ['spəʊkən] 1 ptp of **speak**. 2 adj *dialogue, recitative* parlé. **the ~ language** la langue parlée; **~ French** le français parlé; *see* **well**[2] *etc*.

spokesman ['spəʊksmən] n, pl **spokesmen** ['spəʊksmən] porte-parole *m inv* (*of, for* de).

spokesperson ['spəʊks,pɜːsən] n porte-parole *m inv*.

spokeswoman ['spəʊks,wʊmən] n, pl **spokeswomen** ['spəʊks,wɪmɪn] porte-parole *m inv* (femme).

Spoleto [spəʊ'letəʊ] n Spolète.
spoliation [,spəʊlɪ'eɪʃən] n (*esp Naut*) pillage *m*, spoliation *f*.
spondaic [spɒn'deɪɪk] adj spondaïque.
spondee ['spɒndiː] n spondée *m*.
sponge [spʌndʒ] 1 n a (*Zool, gen*) éponge *f*. **to give sth a ~** donner un coup d'éponge à *or* sur qch; (*fig*) **to throw in** *or* **up the ~*** s'avouer vaincu, abandonner la partie.
b (*Culin: also* **~ cake**) gâteau *m or* biscuit *m* de Savoie.
2 comp ►**sponge bag** (*Brit*) sac *m* de toilette ►**sponge bath** toilette *f* à l'éponge ►**sponge cake** (*Culin*) see **1b** ►**sponge-down** *[person]* toilette *f* à l'éponge; *[walls]* coup *m* d'éponge ►**sponge finger** (*Culin*) boudoir *m* ►**sponge mop** balai *m* éponge ►**sponge pudding** (*Culin*) ≃ pudding *m* (*sorte de gâteau de Savoie*) ►**sponge rubber** caoutchouc *m* mousse ®.
3 vt a *face, person, carpet* éponger, essuyer *or* nettoyer à l'éponge; *wound* éponger; *liquid* éponger, étancher.
b (*: *cadge*) *meal* se faire payer* (*from or off sb* par qn). **to ~ money from sb** taper* qn; **he ~d £10 off his father** il a tapé* son père de 10 livres.
4 vi (*: *cadge*) **to ~ on sb** vivre aux crochets de qn; **he's always sponging** c'est un parasite; (*for meals*) c'est un pique-assiette.
►**sponge down** 1 vt sep *person* laver à l'éponge; *horse* éponger; *walls etc* nettoyer *or* laver *or* essuyer à l'éponge. **to sponge o.s. down** se laver à l'éponge, s'éponger. 2 **sponge-down** n see **sponge 2**.
►**sponge out** vt sep *wound* éponger; *stain, writing* effacer à l'éponge.
►**sponge up** vt sep *liquid* éponger, étancher.
sponger* ['spʌndʒəʳ] n (*pej*) parasite *m*; (*for meals*) pique-assiette *mf inv*.
sponginess ['spʌndʒɪnɪs] n spongiosité *f*.
spongy ['spʌndʒɪ] adj spongieux.
sponsor ['spɒnsəʳ] 1 n (*gen: of appeal, proposal, announcement etc*) personne *f* qui accorde son patronage, membre *m* d'un comité de patronage; (*Fin: for loan etc*) répondant(e) *m(f)*, caution *f*; (*for commercial enterprise*) promoteur *m*, parrain *m*; (*Rel: godparent*) parrain *m*, marraine *f*; (*for club membership*) parrain, marraine; (*Rad, TV: advertiser*) personne *or* organisme *m* qui assure le patronage; (*of concert, event*) personne *or* organisme qui accorde son parrainage; (*of sports event*) sponsor *m*, commanditaire *m*; (*individual: for fund-raising event*) donateur *m*, -trice *f* (*à l'occasion d'un "sponsored walk" etc*) (*see* **2**); (*US: of club*) animateur *m*, -trice *f*. (*Fin*) **to be sb's ~, to stand ~ to sb, to act as ~ for sb** être le (*or* la) répondant(e) de qn, se porter caution pour qn.
2 vt *appeal, proposal, announcement* patronner, présenter; (*Fin*) *borrower* se porter caution pour; *commercial enterprise* être le promoteur de, parrainer; (*Rel*) être le parrain (*or* la marraine) de; *club member, concert, event* parrainer; (*Rad, TV*) *programme* patronner; *sporting event* sponsoriser, être le(s) sponsor(s) *or* commanditaire(s) de; *fund-raising walker, swimmer etc* s'engager à rémunérer (en fonction de sa performance). (*in fund-raising*) **~ed walk** *etc marche etc entreprise pour procurer des donations à une œuvre de charité, les participants étant rémunérés par les donateurs en fonction de leur performance*.
-sponsored ['spɒnsəd] adj ending in comps: **government/Soviet†-sponsored** à l'initiative du gouvernement/de l'Union Soviétique†.
sponsorship ['spɒnsəʃɪp] n *[loan]* cautionnement *m*; *[child, member]* parrainage *m*; (*Rad, TV*) commande *f* publicitaire; *[appeal, announcement]* patronage *m*; (*Sport*) sponsoring *m*.
spontaneity [,spɒntə'neɪətɪ] n spontanéité *f*.
spontaneous [spɒn'teɪnɪəs] adj (*all senses*) spontané. **~ combustion** combustion vive.
spontaneously [spɒn'teɪnɪəslɪ] adv spontanément.
spoof⁑ [spuːf] 1 n (*hoax*) blague* *f*, tour *m*, canular *m*; (*parody*) parodie *f*, satire *f* (*on* de). 2 adj *announcement etc* fait par plaisanterie, prétendu (*before noun*). 3 vt *reader, listener etc* faire marcher; (*parody*) *book etc* parodier. 4 vi raconter des blagues* *or* des histoires.
spook [spuːk] 1 n a (*hum *: ghost*) apparition *f*, revenant *m*. b (*US* ⁑: *secret agent*) barbouze* *f*. 2 vt (*US*) a (*haunt*) *person, house* hanter. b (*frighten*) effrayer, faire peur à.
spooky* ['spuːkɪ] adj qui donne la chair de poule *or* le frisson, qui fait froid dans le dos.
spool [spuːl] n *[camera, film, tape, thread, typewriter ribbon]* bobine *f*; *[fishing reel]* tambour *m*; *[sewing machine, weaving machine]* canette *f*; *[wire]* rouleau *m*.
spoon [spuːn] 1 n cuiller *f or* cuillère *f*; (*spoonful*) cuiller *f*, cuillerée *f*; (*Golf*) spoon *m*, bois *m* trois; *see* **dessert, silver** *etc*. 2 comp ►**spoonbill** *see* **spoonbill** ►**spoonfeed:** (*lit*) **to spoonfeed sb** nourrir qn à la cuiller; (*fig*) **he needs to be spoonfed all the time** il faut toujours qu'on lui mâche (*subj*) le travail. 3 vt: **to ~ sth into a plate/out of a bowl** *etc* verser qch dans une assiette/enlever qch d'un bol *etc* avec une cuiller. 4 vi (*fig:* *†) flirter.
►**spoon off** vt sep *fat, cream etc* enlever avec une cuiller.
►**spoon out** vt sep (*take out*) verser avec une cuiller; (*serve out*) servir avec une cuiller.
►**spoon up** vt sep *food, soup* manger avec une cuiller; *spillage* ramasser avec une cuiller.
spoonbill ['spuːnbɪl] n spatule *f*.
spoonerism ['spuːnərɪzəm] n contrepèterie *f*.
spoonful ['spuːnfʊl] n cuillerée *f*, cuiller *f*.
spoor [spʊəʳ] n (*NonC*) *[animal]* foulées *fpl*, trace *f*, piste *f*.
sporadic [spə'rædɪk] adj sporadique. **~ fighting** engagements isolés, échauffourées *fpl*.
sporadically [spə'rædɪkəlɪ] adv sporadiquement.
spore [spɔːʳ] n spore *f*.
sporran ['spɒrən] n (*Scot*) escarcelle *f* en peau (*portée avec le kilt*).
sport [spɔːt] 1 n a sport *m*. **he is good at ~** il est doué pour le sport, il est très sportif; **he is good at several ~s** il est doué pour plusieurs sports; **outdoor/indoor ~s** sports de plein air/d'intérieur; (*meeting*) **~s** réunion sportive; **school ~s** réunion *or* compétition sportive scolaire; *see* **field** *etc*.
b (*NonC: fun, amusement*) divertissement *m*, amusement *m*; (*fig liter: plaything*) jouet *m*. **it was great ~** c'était très divertissant *or* amusant; **in ~** pour rire, pour s'amuser; **we had (some) good ~** (*gen*) nous nous sommes bien divertis *or* amusés; (*Hunting/Fishing*) nous avons fait bonne chasse/bonne pêche; (*liter*) **to make ~ of sb** se moquer de qn, tourner qn en ridicule; *see* **spoil**.
c (*: *person*) **(good) ~** chic* *or* brave type* *m*, chic* *or* brave fille *f*; **be a ~!** sois chic!*; (*Austral*) **come on, ~!** allez, mon vieux!* *or* mon pote!⁑
d (*Bio, Zool*) variété anormale.
2 comp ►**sport coat** *or* **jacket** (*US*) = **sports jacket** ►**sports** *programme, reporting, newspaper etc* de sport, sportif; *commentator, reporter, news, editor, club* sportif; *clothes* sport *inv* ►**sports car** voiture *f* de sport ►**sportscast** (*US: Rad, TV*) émission sportive ►**sportscaster** (*US: Rad, TV*) reporter sportif ►**sports coat** = **sports jacket** ►**sports day** (*Brit Scol etc*) réunion *or* compétition sportive scolaire ►**sports desk** (*Press etc*) rédaction sportive ►**sports enthusiast** = **sports fan*** ►**sports equipment** équipement *m or* matériel *m* de sport ►**sports fan*** fanatique *mf* de sport ►**sports ground** terrain *m* de sport, stade *m* ►**sports jacket** veste *f* sport *inv* ►**sportsman** sportif *m*, amateur *m* de sport; (*fig*) **he's a real sportsman** il est beau joueur, il est très sport *inv* ►**sportsmanlike** (*lit, fig*) sportif, chic* *inv* ►**sportsmanship** (*lit, fig*) sportivité *f*, esprit sportif ►**sports medicine** médecine *f* sportive ►**sports page** (*Press*) page sportive *or* des sports ►**sports shop** magasin *m* de sports ►**sportswear** (*NonC*) vêtements *mpl* de sport ►**sportswoman** sportive *f*, athlète *f* ►**sportswriter** rédacteur *m* sportif.
3 vi (*liter*) folâtrer, batifoler.
4 vt *tie, hat, beard, buttonhole* arborer, exhiber; *black eye* exhiber.
sportiness ['spɔːtɪnɪs] n (*lit, fig*) caractère *m* sportif.
sporting ['spɔːtɪŋ] adj (*lit, fig*) sportif. (*fig*) **there's a ~ chance that she will be on time** il est possible qu'elle soit à l'heure, elle a des chances d'arriver à l'heure; **that gave him a ~ chance to do ...** cela lui a donné une certaine chance de faire ...; **it's very ~ of you** c'est très chic* de votre part; (*US: brothel*) **~ house** bordel⁑ *m*.
sportingly ['spɔːtɪŋlɪ] adv (*fig*) très sportivement, avec beaucoup de sportivité.
sportive ['spɔːtɪv] adj folâtre, badin.
sporty* ['spɔːtɪ] adj (*lit*) sportif; (*fig*) chic* *inv*, sportif.
spot [spɒt] 1 n a *[blood, ink, paint]* (*mark, dot etc*) tache *f*; (*splash*) éclaboussure *f*; (*on fruit*) tache, tavelure *f*; (*polka dot*) pois *m*; (*on dice, domino*) point *m*; *[leopard etc]* tache, moucheture *f*; (*pimple*) bouton *m*; (*freckle-type*) tache (de son); (*fig: on reputation etc*) tache, souillure *f* (*on* sur). **a ~ of dirt** une tache, une salissure; **a ~ of red** une tache *or* un point rouge; **a dress with red ~s** une robe à pois rouges; **a ~ of rain** quelques gouttes *fpl* de pluie; **to have ~s before one's eyes** *or* **the eyes** voir des mouches volantes devant les yeux; **he came out in ~s** il a eu une éruption de boutons; **these ~s are measles** ce sont des taches de rougeole; (*Cards*) **the ten ~ of spades** le dix de pique; (*US: money*) **a five/ten ~**⁑ un billet de cinq/dix dollars; (*fig liter*) **without a ~ or stain** sans la moindre tache *or* souillure; *see* **beauty, knock, sun** *etc*.
b (*esp Brit: small amount*) **a ~ of** un peu de; *[whisky, coffee etc]* une goutte de; *[irony, jealousy]* une pointe de; *[truth, commonsense]* un grain de; **a ~ of sleep will do you good** cela te fera du bien de dormir un peu, un petit somme te fera du bien; **he did a ~ of work** il a travaillé un peu, il a fait quelques bricoles* *fpl*; **brandy? — just a ~** du cognac? — juste une goutte *or* un soupçon; **there's been a ~ of trouble** il y a eu un petit incident *or* un petit problème; **how about a ~ of lunch?*** et si on déjeunait?, et si on mangeait un morceau?; **we had a ~ of lunch** nous avons déjeuné légèrement, nous avons mangé un morceau; *see* **bother**.
c (*place*) endroit *m*. **show me the ~ on the map** montrez-moi l'endroit sur la carte; **a good ~ for a picnic** un bon endroit *or* coin pour un pique-nique; **it's a lovely ~!** c'est un endroit *or* un coin ravissant!; **there's a tender ~ on my arm** j'ai un point sensible au bras; **the ~ in the story where ...** l'endroit *or* le moment dans l'histoire où ...; *see* **high, hit, soft** *etc*.

d (*phrases*) **the police were on the ~ in 2 minutes** la police est arrivée sur les lieux en 2 minutes; **it's easy if you're on the ~** c'est facile si vous êtes sur place *or* si vous êtes là; **leave it to the man on the ~ to decide** laissez décider la personne qui est sur place; (*Press etc*) **our man on the ~** notre envoyé spécial; **an on-the-~ broadcast/report** une émission/un reportage sur place; **an on-the-~ enquiry** une enquête sur le terrain; **an on-the-~ fine** une amende avec paiement immédiat; **he was fined on the ~** on lui a infligé une amende sur-le-champ; **he decided on the ~** il s'est décidé sur le coup *or* sur-le-champ *or* tout de suite; **he was killed on the ~** il a été tué sur le coup; **to put sb on the ~** mettre qn en difficulté *or* dans l'embarras; **to be in a (bad *or* tight) ~*** être dans le pétrin*, être dans de beaux draps.

e (**: Rad, Theat, TV: in show*) numéro *m*; (*Rad, TV: also* **~ advertisement**) spot *m*, message *m* publicitaire. **a solo ~ in cabaret** un numéro individuel dans une revue; **he got a ~ in the Late Show** il a fait un numéro dans le Late Show; **Glo-kleen had a ~ (advertisement) before the news** Glo-kleen a fait passer un spot *or* un message publicitaire avant les informations; **there was a ~ (announcement) about the referendum** il y a eu une brève annonce au sujet du referendum.

f (**: also* **night~**) boîte *f* de nuit.

g = **spotlight.**

h (*Billiards, Snooker*) mouche *f*.

2 **comp** *transaction, goods, price* payé comptant; *count, test* intermittent, fait à l'improviste ►**spot advertisement, spot announcement** *see* **1e** ►**spot cash** argent comptant *or* liquide ►**spot check** contrôle intermittent, vérification *f* de sondage ►**spot-check** contrôler *or* vérifier de façon intermittente ►**spotlight** *see* **spotlight** ►**spot market** marché *m* au comptant *or* du disponible ►**spot-on***: (*Brit*) **what he said was spot-on** ce qu'il a dit était en plein dans le mille*; (*Brit*) **he guessed spot-on** il est tombé en plein dans le mille* ►**spot remover** détachant *m* ►**spot survey** sondage *m* ►**spot-weld vt** souder par points.

3 **vt** a (*speckle, stain*) tacher (*with* de). **a tie ~ted with fruit stains** une cravate portant des taches de fruit; *see also* **spotted.**

b (*recognize, notice*) *person, object, vehicle* apercevoir, repérer*; *mistake* trouver, remarquer, relever; *bargain, winner, sb's ability* déceler, découvrir. **can you ~ any bad apples in this tray?** est-ce que tu vois *or* tu trouves des pommes gâtées sur cette claie?

4 **vi** a *[material, garment etc]* se tacher, se salir.

b **it is ~ting (with rain)** il commence à pleuvoir, il tombe quelques gouttes de pluie.

c (*Mil etc: act as spotter*) observer.

spotless ['spɒtlɪs] **adj** impeccable *or* reluisant de propreté; (*fig*) sans tache.

spotlessly ['spɒtlɪslɪ] **adv: ~ clean** impeccable *or* reluisant de propreté.

spotlessness ['spɒtlɪsnɪs] **n** propreté *f*.

spotlight ['spɒtlaɪt] 1 **n** (*Theat: beam*) rayon *m or* feu *m* de projecteur; (*Theat: lamp*) projecteur *m*, spot *m*; (*in home*) spot; (*Aut*) phare *m* auxiliaire. **in the ~** (*Theat*) sous le feu du *or* des projecteur(s), dans le rayon du *or* des projecteur(s); (*fig*) en vedette, sous le feu des projecteurs; (*fig*) **the ~ was on him** il était en vedette; (*in the public eye*) les feux de l'actualité étaient braqués sur lui; (*Theat, fig*) **to turn the ~ on sb/sth** = **to spotlight sb/sth** (*see* **2**). 2 **vt** (*Theat*) diriger les projecteurs sur; (*fig*) *sb's success, achievements* mettre en vedette; *changes, differences, a fact* mettre en lumière.

spotlit ['spɒtlɪt] **adj** illuminé.

spotted ['spɒtɪd] **adj** *animal* tacheté, moucheté; *fabric* à pois; *fruit* taché, tavelé; (*dirty*) taché, sali. (*Culin*) **~ dick** pudding *m* aux raisins de Corinthe; **~ fever** fièvre éruptive; **~ flycatcher** gobe-mouches *m inv* gris.

spotter ['spɒtəʳ] **n** a (*Brit: as hobby*) **train/plane ~** passionné(e) *m(f)* de trains/d'avions; *see also* **spotting.** b (*Mil etc*) (*for enemy aircraft*) guetteur *m*; (*during firing*) observateur *m*. c (*US Comm **) surveillant(e) *m(f)* du personnel.

spotting ['spɒtɪŋ] **n** a repérage *m*. (*Brit*) **train/plane ~** *passe-temps consistant à identifier le plus grand nombre possible de trains/d'avions.* b (*Med*) traces *fpl* (de sang).

spotty ['spɒtɪ] **adj** a *face, skin, person* boutonneux; (*patterned*) *fabric* à pois; (*dirty*) *tie* taché, sali; *mirror* piqueté. b (*esp US: not consistent*) incomplet (*f* -ète).

spouse [spaʊz] **n** (*frm or hum*) époux *m*, épouse *f*; (*Jur*) conjoint(e) *m(f)*.

spout [spaʊt] 1 **n** *[teapot, jug, can]* bec *m*; (*for tap*) brise-jet *m inv*; *[gutter, pump etc]* dégorgeoir *m*; *[pipe]* orifice *m*; *[fountain]* jet *m*, ajutage *m*; (*stream of liquid*) jet, colonne *f*. (*Brit fig*) **to be up the ~**‡ *[plans, timetable etc]* être fichu* *or* foutu‡; *[person]* (*in trouble*) être dans un mauvais cas, être dans de beaux draps; (*pregnant*) être en cloque‡; **that's another £50 (gone) up the ~**‡ voilà encore 50 livres de foutues en l'air‡ *or* de parties en fumée; *see* **water.**

2 **vi** a *[liquid]* jaillir, sortir en jet (*from, out of* de); *[whale]* lancer un jet d'eau, souffler.

b (** fig pej: harangue*) pérorer, laïusser‡ (*about* sur).

3 **vt** (*also* **~ out**) a *liquid* faire jaillir, laisser échapper un jet de; *smoke, lava etc* lancer *or* émettre un jet de, vomir.

b (** fig*) *poem etc* débiter, déclamer. **he can ~ columns of statistics** il peut débiter *or* dévider des colonnes entières de statistiques.

sprain [spreɪn] 1 **n** entorse *f*, (*less serious*) foulure *f*. 2 **vt** *muscle, ligament* fouler, étirer. **to ~ one's ankle** se faire *or* se donner une entorse à la cheville, (*less serious*) se fouler la cheville; **to have a ~ed ankle** s'être fait une entorse à la cheville, (*less serious*) s'être foulé la cheville.

sprang [spræŋ] **pret of spring.**

sprat [spræt] **n** sprat *m*.

sprawl [sprɔːl] 1 **vi** (*also* **~ out**) (*fall*) tomber, s'étaler*; (*lie*) être affalé *or* vautré; *[handwriting]* s'étaler (dans tous les sens); *[plant]* ramper, s'étendre (*over* sur); *[town]* s'étaler (*over* dans). **he was ~ing *or* lay ~ed in an armchair** il était affalé *or* vautré dans un fauteuil; **to send sb ~ing** faire tomber qn de tout son long *or* les quatre fers en l'air, envoyer qn rouler par terre.

2 **n** (*position*) attitude affalée; *[building, town]* étendue *f*. **an ugly ~ of buildings down the valley** d'affreux bâtiments qui s'étalent dans la vallée; **London's suburban ~** l'étalement *m or* l'extension *f* de la banlieue londonienne; **the seemingly endless ~ of suburbs** l'étendue apparemment infinie des banlieues, les banlieues tentaculaires.

sprawling ['sprɔːlɪŋ] **adj** *person, position, body* affalé; *handwriting* étalé, informe; *city* tentaculaire.

spray¹ [spreɪ] 1 **n** a (*gen*) (nuage *m* de) gouttelettes *fpl*; (*from sea*) embruns *mpl*; (*from hose pipe*) pluie *f*; (*from atomizer*) spray *m*; (*from aerosol*) pulvérisation *f*. **wet with the ~ from the fountain** aspergé par le jet de la fontaine.

b (*container*) (*aerosol*) bombe *f*, aérosol *m*; (*for scent etc*) atomiseur *m*, spray *m*; (*refillable*) vaporisateur *m*; (*for lotion*) brumisateur *m*; (*larger: for garden etc*) pulvérisateur *m*. **insecticide ~** (*aerosol*) bombe (d')insecticide; (*contents*) insecticide *m* (*en bombe*); *see* **hair** *etc*.

c (*also* **~ attachment, ~ nozzle**) pomme *f*, ajutage *m*.

2 **comp** *deodorant, insecticide etc* (présenté) en bombe *etc* (*see* **1b**) ►**spray can** bombe *f etc* (*see* **1b**) ►**spray gun** pistolet *m* (*à peinture etc*) ►**spraying machine** (*Agr*) pulvérisateur *m* ►**spray-paint n** peinture *f* en bombe ◊ **vt** peindre à la bombe.

3 **vt** a *roses, garden, crops* faire des pulvérisations sur; *room* faire des pulvérisations dans; *hair* vaporiser (*with* de); (*spray-paint*) *car* peindre à la bombe. **to ~ the lawn with weedkiller** faire des pulvérisations de désherbant sur la pelouse; **they ~ed the oil slick with detergent** ils ont répandu du détergent sur la nappe de pétrole; (*fig*) **to ~ sth/sb with bullets** arroser qch/qn de balles, envoyer une grêle de balles sur qch/qn.

b *water* vaporiser, pulvériser (*on* sur); *scent* vaporiser; *insecticide, paint* pulvériser. **they ~ed foam on the flames** ils ont projeté de la neige carbonique sur les flammes.

4 **vi: it ~ed everywhere** ça a tout arrosé; **it ~ed all over the carpet** ça a arrosé tout le tapis.

►**spray out vi** *[liquid etc]* jaillir (*on to, over* sur). **water sprayed out all over them** ils ont été complètement aspergés *or* arrosés d'eau.

spray² [spreɪ] **n** *[flowers]* gerbe *f*; *[greenery]* branche *f*; (*brooch*) aigrette *f*.

sprayer ['spreɪəʳ] **n** a = **spray¹ 1b.** b (*aircraft: also* **crop-~**) avion-pulvérisateur *m*.

spread [spred] (**vb: pret, ptp spread**) 1 **n** a (*NonC*) *[fire, disease, infection]* propagation *f*, progression *f*; *[nuclear weapons]* prolifération *f*; *[idea, knowledge]* diffusion *f*, propagation. **to stop the ~ of a disease** empêcher une maladie de s'étendre, arrêter la propagation d'une maladie; **the ~ of education** le progrès de l'éducation; (*Insurance*) **the ~ of risk** la division des risques.

b (*extent, expanse*) *[wings]* envergure *f*; *[arch]* ouverture *f*, portée *f*; *[bridge]* travée *f*; *[marks, prices, ages etc]* gamme *f*, échelle *f*; *[wealth etc]* répartition *f*, distribution *f*. (*Naut*) **a ~ of canvas *or* of sail** un grand déploiement de voiles; **he's got a middle-age ~** il a pris de l'embonpoint avec l'âge.

c (*cover*) (*for table*) dessus *m or* tapis *m* de table; (*for meals*) nappe *f*; (*bed~*) dessus-de-lit *m inv*, couvre-lit *m*.

d (*Culin*) pâte *f* (à tartiner). **cheese ~** fromage *m* à tartiner; **anchovy ~** ≃ pâte d'anchois.

e (** fig: meal*) festin *m*. **what a lovely ~!** c'est un vrai festin!, comme c'est appétissant!

f (*Cards*) séquence *f*.

g (*Press, Typ*) (*two pages*) double page *f*; (*across columns*) deux (*or* trois *etc*) colonnes *fpl*.

2 **adj** (*Ling*) *vowel* non arrondi; *lips* étiré.

3 **comp** ►**spread eagle** (*Her*) aigle éployée ►**spread-eagle*** (*US*) chauvin (*employé à propos d'un Américain*); **to spread-eagle sb** envoyer rouler qn les quatre fers en l'air; **to be *or* lie spread-eagled** être étendu bras et jambes écartés, être vautré ►**spreadsheet** (*Comput*) (*chart*) tableau *m*; (*software*) tableur *m*.

4 **vt** a (*also* **~ out**) *cloth, sheet, map* étendre, étaler (*on sth* sur qch); *carpet, rug* étendre, dérouler; *wings, bird's tail, banner, sails* déployer; *net* étendre, déployer; *fingers, toes, arms, legs* écarter; *fan* ouvrir. **to ~ the table** mettre le couvert *or* la table; **the peacock ~ its tail** le paon a fait la roue; (*fig*) **to ~ one's wings** élargir ses horizons;

to ~ o.s. (*lit: also* ~ **o.s. out**) s'étaler, prendre plus de place; (*speak etc at length*) s'étendre, s'attarder (*on* sur); (*extend one's activities*) s'étendre.

b *bread etc* tartiner (*with* de); *butter, jam, glue* étaler (*on* sur); *face cream* étendre (*on* sur). ~ **both surfaces with glue,** ~ **glue on both surfaces** étalez de la colle sur les deux côtés, enduisez les deux côtés de colle; **to ~ butter on a slice of bread, to ~ a slice of bread with butter** tartiner de beurre une tranche de pain, beurrer une tartine.

c (*distribute*) *sand etc* répandre (*on, over* sur); *fertilizer* épandre, étendre (*over, on* sur); (*also* ~ **out**) *objects, cards, goods* étaler (*on* sur); *soldiers, sentries etc* disposer, échelonner (*along* le long de). **he ~ sawdust on the floor** il a répandu de la sciure sur le sol, il a couvert le sol de sciure; **he ~ his books (out) on the table** il a étalé ses livres sur la table; **there were policemen ~ (out) all over the hillside** il y avait des agents de police éparpillés *or* dispersés sur toute la colline; **the wind ~ the flames** le vent a propagé les flammes.

d (*diffuse, distribute*) *disease, infection* propager; *germs* disséminer; *wealth* distribuer; *rumours* faire courir; *news* faire circuler, communiquer; *knowledge* répandre, diffuser; *panic, fear, indignation* répandre, semer; (*in time: also* ~ **out**) *payment, studies etc* échelonner, étaler (*over* sur). **his visits were ~ (out) over 3 years** ses visites se sont échelonnées *or* étalées sur une période de 3 ans; **he ~ his degree (out) over 5 years** il a échelonné ses études de licence sur 5 ans, il a mis 5 ans à finir sa licence; **his research was ~ over many aspects of the subject** ses recherches embrassaient *or* recouvraient de nombreux aspects du sujet; **our resources are ~ very thinly** nous n'avons plus aucune marge dans l'emploi de nos ressources; (*fig*) **to ~ o.s. too thin** trop disperser ses efforts, faire trop de choses à la fois; (*fig*) **to ~ the word** (*propagate ideas*) prêcher la bonne parole; (*announce*) **to ~ the word about sth** annoncer qch.

5 **vi** a (*widen, extend further*) *[river, stain]* s'élargir, s'étaler; *[flood, oil slick, weeds, fire, infection, disease]* gagner du terrain, s'étendre; *[water]* se répandre; *[pain]* s'étendre; *[panic, indignation, news, rumour]* s'étendre, se répandre, se propager; *[knowledge]* se répandre, se disséminer, se propager. **to ~ into** *or* **over sth** *[river, flood, water, oil slick]* se répandre dans *or* sur qch; *[fire, pain]* se communiquer à qch, atteindre qch; *[weeds, panic]* envahir qch; *[disease]* atteindre qch, contaminer qch; *[news, education]* atteindre qch, se répandre dans *or* sur qch; **under the ~ing chestnut tree** sous les branches étendues du marronnier.

b (*stretch, reach: also* ~ **out**) *[lake, plain, oil slick, fire etc]* s'étendre (*over* sur). **the desert ~s (out) over 500 square miles** le désert s'étend sur *or* recouvre 500 milles carrés; **his studies ~ (out) over 4 years** ses études se sont étendues sur 4 ans *or* ont duré 4 ans.

c *[butter, paste etc]* s'étaler.

►**spread out** 1 **vi** a *[people, animals]* se disperser, s'éparpiller. **spread out!** dispersez-vous! b (*open out*) *[fan]* s'ouvrir; *[wings]* se déployer; *[valley]* s'élargir. c = **spread 5b.** 2 **vt sep**: **the valley lay spread out before him** la vallée s'étendait à ses pieds; **he was spread out on the floor** il était étendu de tout son long par terre; *see also* **spread 4a, 4c, 4d.**

spreader ['spredəʳ] **n** (*for butter etc*) couteau *m* à tartiner; (*for glue etc*) couteau à palette; (*Agr: for fertilizer*) épandeur *m*, épandeuse *f*.

spree [spriː] **n** fête *f*. **to go on** *or* **have a ~** faire la fête *or* la noce*; *see* **spending.**

sprig [sprɪg] **n** brin *m*.

sprightliness ['spraɪtlɪnɪs] **n** (*see* **sprightly**) activité *f*; vivacité *f*.

sprightly ['spraɪtlɪ] **adj** (*physically*) alerte, actif; (*mentally*) alerte, vif, fringant.

spring [sprɪŋ] (**vb: pret sprang, ptp sprung**) 1 **n** a (*leap*) bond *m*, saut *m*. **in** *or* **with** *or* **at one ~** d'un bond, d'un saut; **to give a ~** bondir, sauter.

b (*for chair, mattress, watch; also Tech*) ressort *m*. (*Aut*) **the ~s** la suspension; *see* **hair, main** *etc.*

c (*NonC: resilience*) *[mattress]* élasticité *f*; *[bow, elastic band]* détente *f*. **he had a ~ in his step** il marchait d'un pas élastique *or* souple.

d *[water]* source *f*. **hot ~** source chaude.

e (*fig*) **~s** (*cause, motive*) mobile *m*, motif *m*, cause *f*; (*origin*) source *f*, origine *f*.

f (*season*) printemps *m*. **in (the) ~** au printemps; **~ is in the air** il fait un temps printanier *or* de printemps, on sent venir le printemps.

2 **comp** *weather, day, flowers* printanier, de printemps; *mattress* à ressorts ►**spring balance** balance *f* à ressort ►**spring binder** (*file*) classeur *m* à ressort ►**spring binding** *[file etc]* reliure *f* à ressort ►**springboard** (*lit, fig*) tremplin *m* ►**spring chicken** (*Culin*) poussin *m*; (*fig*) **he/she is no spring chicken** il/elle n'est pas de toute première jeunesse ►**spring-clean n** (*NonC: also* **spring-cleaning**) grand nettoyage (de printemps) ◊ **vt** nettoyer de fond en comble ►**spring fever** malaises *mpl* des premières chaleurs ►**spring greens** (*Brit*) chou *m* précoce ►**spring gun** piège *m* à fusil ►**spring-like** printanier, de printemps ►**spring lock** serrure *f* à pompe ►**spring onion** (*Brit*) ciboule *f*, cive *f* ►**spring roll** (*Culin*) rouleau *m* de printemps ►**spring snow** (*Ski*) neige *f* de printemps ►**springtide** (*liter*) = **springtime** ►**spring tide** (*sea*) marée *f* de vive eau *or* de syzygie ►**springtime** printemps *m* ►**spring water** eau *f* de source.

3 **vi** a (*leap*) bondir, sauter. **to ~ in/out/across** *etc* entrer/sortir/traverser *etc* d'un bond; **to ~ at sth/sb** bondir *or* sauter *or* se jeter sur qch/qn; **to ~ to one's feet** se lever d'un bond.

b (*fig*) **to ~ to attention** bondir au garde-à-vous; **to ~ to sb's help** bondir *or* se précipiter à l'aide de qn; **to ~ to the rescue** se précipiter pour porter secours; **he sprang into action** il est passé à l'action; **they sprang into the public eye** ils ont tout à coup attiré l'attention du public; **to ~ into existence** apparaître du jour au lendemain; **to ~ into view** apparaître soudain, surgir; **to ~ to mind** venir *or* se présenter à l'esprit; **tears sprang to her eyes** les larmes lui sont venues aux yeux, les larmes lui sont montées aux yeux; **a denial sprang to his lips** une dénégation lui est venue *or* montée aux lèvres; **his hand sprang to his gun** il a saisi *or* attrapé son pistolet; **the door sprang open** la porte s'est brusquement ouverte; **where did you ~ from?** d'où est-ce que tu sors?; (*loc*) **hope ~s eternal** l'espoir fait vivre.

c (*originate from*) provenir, découler (*from* de). **the oak sprang from a tiny acorn** le chêne est sorti d'un tout petit gland; **all his actions ~ from the desire to ...** toutes ses actions proviennent *or* découlent de son désir de ...; **it sprang from his inability to cope with the situation** c'est venu *or* né de son incapacité à faire face à la situation.

d *[timbers etc]* (*warp*) jouer, se gondoler; (*split*) se fendre.

4 **vt** a (*leap over*) *ditch, fence etc* sauter, franchir d'un bond.

b *trap, lock* faire jouer; *mine* faire sauter. (*fig*) **to ~ a surprise on sb** surprendre qn; **to ~ a question on sb** poser une question à qn à brûle-pourpoint *or* de but en blanc; **to ~ a piece of news on sb** annoncer une nouvelle à qn de but en blanc; **he sprang the suggestion on me suddenly** il me l'a suggéré de but en blanc *or* à l'improviste; **he sprang it on me** il m'a pris de court *or* au dépourvu.

c (*put ~s in*) *mattress* pourvoir de ressorts; *car* suspendre. (*Aut*) **well-sprung** bien suspendu.

d (*Hunting*) *game* lever; (*‡ fig*) *prisoner* faire sauter le mur à, aider à faire la belle‡. **he was sprung‡ from Dartmoor** on l'a aidé à faire la cavale‡ de Dartmoor.

e *timbers, mast* (*warp*) gondoler, faire jouer; (*split*) fendre; *see* **leak.**

►**spring up vi** *[person]* se lever d'un bond *or* précipitamment; *[flowers, weeds]* surgir de terre; *[corn]* lever brusquement; *[new buildings, settlements]* surgir de terre, apparaître brusquement; *[wind, storm]* se lever brusquement; *[rumour]* naître, s'élever; *[doubt, fear]* naître, jaillir; *[friendship, alliance]* naître, s'établir; *[problem, obstacle, difficulty]* se dresser, se présenter, surgir.

springbok ['sprɪŋbɒk] **n, pl ~** *or* **~s** springbok *m*.

springe [sprɪndʒ] **n** collet *m*.

springiness ['sprɪŋɪnɪs] **n** (*see* **springy**) élasticité *f*; souplesse *f*; moelleux *m*; flexibilité *f*.

springy ['sprɪŋɪ] **adj** *rubber, mattress* élastique, souple; *carpet* moelleux; *plank* flexible, qui fait ressort; *ground, turf* souple; *step* alerte, souple.

sprinkle ['sprɪŋkl] **vt**: **to ~ sth with water, to ~ water on sth** asperger qch d'eau; **to ~ water on the garden** arroser légèrement le jardin; **a rose ~d with dew** une rose couverte de rosée; **to ~ sand on** *or* **over sth, to ~ sth with sand** répandre une légère couche de sable sur qch, couvrir qch d'une légère couche de sable; **to ~ sand/grit on the roadway** sabler/cendrer la route; (*Culin*) **to ~ sugar over a dish, to ~ a dish with sugar** saupoudrer un plat de sucre; **lawn ~d with daisies** pelouse parsemée *or* émaillée (*liter*) de pâquerettes; (*fig*) **they are ~d about here and there** ils sont éparpillés *or* disséminés ici et là.

sprinkler ['sprɪŋkləʳ] 1 **n** (*for lawn etc*) arroseur *m*; (*for sugar etc*) saupoudreuse *f*, (*larger*) saupoudroir *m*; (*in ceiling for fire-fighting*) diffuseur *m* (d'extincteur automatique d'incendie), sprinkler *m*. 2 **comp** ►**sprinkler system** (*for lawn*) combiné *m* d'arrosage; (*for fire-fighting*) installation *f* d'extinction automatique d'incendie.

sprinkling ['sprɪŋklɪŋ] **n** (*see* **sprinkle**) aspersion *f*; arrosage *m*; légère couche. **to give sth a ~ (of) = to sprinkle sth (with)** (*see* **sprinkle**); **a ~ of water** quelques gouttes *fpl* d'eau; **a ~ of sand** une légère couche de sable; (*fig*) **there was a ~ of young people** il y avait quelques jeunes (gens) çà et là; **a ~ of quotations in the text** des citations émaillant le texte.

sprint [sprɪnt] 1 **n** (*Sport*) sprint *m*. **to make a ~ for the bus** piquer* un sprint *or* foncer pour attraper l'autobus. 2 **vi** (*Sport*) sprinter; (*gen*) foncer, piquer* un sprint. **to ~ down the street** descendre la rue à toutes jambes.

sprinter ['sprɪntəʳ] **n** (*Sport*) sprinter *m*, sprinteur *m*, -euse *f*.

sprit [sprɪt] **n** (*Naut*) livarde *f*, balestron *f*.

sprite [spraɪt] **n** lutin *m*, farfadet *m*.

sprocket ['sprɒkɪt] **n** pignon *m*. **~ wheel** pignon (d'engrenage).

sprout [spraʊt] 1 **n** (*Bot*) (*on plant, branch etc*) pousse *f*; (*from bulbs, seeds*) germe *m*. **(Brussels) ~s** choux *mpl* de Bruxelles.

2 **vi** a *[bulbs, onions etc]* germer, pousser.

b (*also* ~ **up**: *grow quickly*) *[plants, crops, weeds]* bien pousser; *[child]* grandir *or* pousser vite.

c (*also* ~ **up**: *appear*) *[mushrooms etc]* pousser, apparaître, surgir; *[weeds]* surgir de terre; *[new buildings]* surgir de terre, pousser comme des champignons.

3 vt: **to ~ new leaves** pousser *or* produire de nouvelles feuilles; *[potatoes, bulbs]* **to ~ shoots** germer; **the wet weather has ~ed the barley** le temps humide a fait germer l'orge; **the deer has ~ed horns** les cornes du cerf ont poussé, le cerf a mis ses bois; **Paul has ~ed* a moustache** Paul s'est laissé pousser la moustache.

spruce[1] [spru:s] n (*also* **~ tree**) épicéa *m* spruce. (*Can*) **white/black ~** épinette blanche/noire.

spruce[2] [spru:s] adj *person* net, pimpant, soigné; *garment* net, impeccable; *house* impeccable, pimpant.

►**spruce up** vt sep *child* faire beau (*f* belle); *house* bien astiquer. **all spruced up** *person* tiré à quatre épingles, sur son trente et un; *house* bien astiqué, reluisant de propreté; **to spruce o.s. up** se faire tout beau (*f* toute belle).

sprucely ['spru:slɪ] adv: **~ dressed** tiré à quatre épingles, sur son trente et un.

spruceness ['spru:snɪs] n *[person]* élégance *f*, mise soignée; *[house]* propreté *f*.

sprung [sprʌŋ] 1 ptp of **spring**. 2 adj *seat, mattress* à ressorts.

spry [spraɪ] adj alerte, vif, plein d'entrain.

spud [spʌd] 1 n (*tool*) sarcloir *m*; (**: potato*) patate* *f*. 2 comp ►**spud-bashing** (*Mil sl*) la corvée de patates*.

spume [spju:m] n (*liter*) écume *f*.

spun [spʌn] pret, ptp of **spin**.

spunk‡ [spʌŋk] n (*NonC*) cran* *m*, courage *m*.

spunky‡ ['spʌŋkɪ] adj plein de cran*.

spur [spɜ:r] 1 n a *[horse, fighting cock; also mountain, masonry etc]* éperon *m*; *[bone]* saillie *f*; (*fig*) aiguillon *m*. **to win** *or* **gain one's ~s** (*Hist*) gagner ses éperons; (*fig*) faire ses preuves; **on the ~ of the moment** sous l'impulsion du moment, sur un coup de tête; **the ~ of hunger** l'aiguillon de la faim; **it will be a ~ to further achievements** cela nous (*or* les *etc*) poussera *or* incitera *or* encouragera à d'autres entreprises.

b (*Rail: also* **~ track**) (*siding*) voie latérale, voie de garage; (*branch*) voie de desserte, embranchement *m*.

c (*motorway etc*) embranchement *m*.

2 comp ►**spur gear** = **spur wheel** ►**spur-of-the-moment** adj fait sur l'impulsion du moment ►**spur wheel** roue *f* à dents droites.

3 vt (*also* **~ on**) *horse* éperonner; (*fig*) éperonner, aiguillonner. **he ~red his horse on** (*applied spurs once*) il a éperonné son cheval, il a donné de l'éperon à son cheval; (*sped on*) il a piqué des deux; **~red on by ambition** éperonné *or* aiguillonné par l'ambition; **to ~ sb (on) to do sth** pousser *or* encourager *or* inciter qn à faire qch; **this ~red him (on) to greater efforts** ceci l'a encouragé à redoubler d'efforts.

spurge [spɜ:dʒ] n euphorbe *f*. **~ laurel** daphné *m*.

spurious ['spjʊərɪəs] adj (*gen*) faux (*f* fausse); *document, writings* faux, apocryphe; *claim* fallacieux; *interest, affection, desire* simulé, feint.

spuriously ['spjʊərɪəslɪ] adv faussement.

spurn [spɜ:n] vt *help, offer etc* repousser *or* rejeter (avec mépris); *lover etc* éconduire.

spurt [spɜ:t] 1 n *[water, flame]* jaillissement *m*, jet *m*; *[anger, enthusiasm, energy]* sursaut *m*, regain *m*; (*burst of speed*) accélération *f*; (*fig: at work etc*) effort soudain, coup *m* de collier. (*Racing*) **final ~** emballage *m*, rush *m*; **to put on a ~** (*Sport*) démarrer, sprinter; (*in running for bus etc*) piquer* un sprint, foncer; (*fig: in work etc*) faire un soudain *or* suprême effort, donner un coup de collier; (*sporadically*) **in ~s** par à-coups.

2 vi a (*also* **~ out, ~ up**) *[water, blood]* jaillir, gicler (*from* de); *[flame]* jaillir (*from* de).

b *[runner]* piquer* un sprint, foncer; (*Sport*) démarrer, sprinter.

3 vt (*also* **~ out**) *flame, lava* lancer, vomir; *water* laisser jaillir, projeter.

sputa ['spju:tə] npl of **sputum**.

sputnik ['spʊtnɪk] n spoutnik *m*.

sputter ['spʌtər] vi, vt = **splutter 2, 3**.

sputum ['spju:təm] n, pl **sputa** crachat *m*, expectorations *fpl*.

spy [spaɪ] 1 n (*gen, Ind, Pol*) espion(ne) *m(f)*. **police ~** indicateur *m*, -trice *f* de police. 2 comp *film, story etc* d'espionnage ►**spyglass** lunette *f* d'approche ►**spyhole** petit trou, espion *m* ►**spy-in-the-sky*** (*satellite*) satellite-espion *m* ►**spy ring** réseau *m* d'espions. 3 vi (*gen*) espionner, épier; (*Ind, Pol*) faire de l'espionnage (*for a country* au service *or* au compte d'un pays). **to ~ on sb** espionner qn; **to ~ on sth** épier qch; **stop ~ing on me!** arrête de m'espionner! *or* de me surveiller!; **to ~ into sth** chercher à découvrir qch subrepticement. 4 vt (*catch sight of*) apercevoir, découvrir, remarquer. **I spied him coming** je l'ai vu qui arrivait *or* s'approchait.

►**spy out** vt sep reconnaître. (*lit, fig*) **to spy out the land** reconnaître le terrain.

spying ['spaɪɪŋ] n (*NonC*) espionnage *m*.

Sq (abbr of **Square**) *employé dans les adresses.*

sq. (abbr of **square**) carré. **4 sq. m** 4 m².

squab [skwɒb] n, pl **~s** *or* **~** a (*Orn*) pigeonneau *m*. b (*Brit Aut*) assise *f*.

squabble ['skwɒbl] 1 n querelle *f*, chamaillerie* *f*, prise *f* de bec*. 2 vi se chamailler*, se disputer, se quereller (*over sth* à propos de qch).

squabbler ['skwɒblər] n chamailleur* *m*, -euse* *f*, querelleur *m*, -euse *f*.

squabbling ['skwɒblɪŋ] n (*NonC*) chamaillerie(s)* *f(pl)*.

squad [skwɒd] 1 n *[soldiers, policemen, workmen, prisoners]* escouade *f*, groupe *m*; (*US Sport*) équipe *f*. (*Ftbl*) **the England ~** le contingent anglais; *see* **firing, flying** *etc.* 2 comp ►**squad car** (*Police*) voiture *f* de police.

squaddie, squaddy‡ ['skwɒdɪ] n (*Brit: private soldier*) deuxième classe *m inv*.

squadron ['skwɒdrən] 1 n (*Mil*) escadron *m*; (*Aviat, Naut*) escadrille *f*. 2 comp ►**squadron leader** (*Brit Aviat*) commandant *m*.

squalid ['skwɒlɪd] adj *room, conditions* misérable, sordide; *motive* vil (*f* vile), ignoble; *dispute* mesquin, sordide. **it was a ~ business** c'était une affaire ignoble *or* sordide; **they had a ~ little affair** ils ont eu une petite liaison pitoyable *or* minable*.

squall [skwɔ:l] 1 n a (*Met*) rafale *f* *or* bourrasque *f* (de pluie); (*at sea*) grain *m*. (*fig*) **there are ~s ahead** il y a de l'orage dans l'air, il va y avoir du grabuge*. b (*cry*) hurlement *m*, braillement *m*. 2 vi *[baby]* hurler, brailler.

squalling ['skwɔ:lɪŋ] adj criard, braillard*.

squally ['skwɔ:lɪ] adj *wind* qui souffle en rafales; *weather* à bourrasques, à rafales; *day* entrecoupé de bourrasques.

squalor ['skwɒlər] n (*NonC*) conditions *fpl* sordides, misère noire. **to live in ~** vivre dans des conditions sordides *or* dans la misère noire; (*pej*) vivre comme un cochon* (*or* des cochons*).

squander ['skwɒndər] vt *time, money, talents* gaspiller; *fortune, inheritance* dissiper, dilapider; *opportunity, chances* perdre.

square [skwɛər] 1 n a (*shape: also Geom, Mil*) carré *m*; *[chessboard, crossword, graph paper]* case *f*; (*~ piece*) *[fabric, chocolate, toffee etc]* carré; *[cake]* carré, part *f*; (*window pane*) carreau *m*. **to fold paper into a ~** plier une feuille de papier en carré; **divide the page into ~s** divisez la page en carrés, quadrillez la page; **she was wearing a silk (head)~** elle portait un carré *or* un foulard de soie; **linoleum with black and white ~s on it** du linoléum en damier noir et blanc *or* à carreaux noirs et blancs; **the troops were drawn up in a ~** les troupes avaient formé le carré; **form (yourselves into) a ~** placez-vous en carré, formez un carré; (*fig*) **to start again from ~ one*** repartir à zéro*, repartir de la case départ; (*fig*) **now we're back to ~ one*** nous nous retrouvons à notre point de départ, nous repartons à zéro*.

b (*in town*) place *f*; (*with gardens*) square *m*; (*esp US: block of houses*) pâté *m* de maisons; (*Mil: also* **barrack ~**) cour *f* (de caserne). **the town ~** la (grand-)place.

c (*drawing instrument*) équerre *f*. **out of ~** qui n'est pas d'équerre; **to cut sth on the ~** équarrir qch; (*fig*) **to be on the ~** *[offer, deal]* être honnête *or* régulier*; *[person]* jouer franc jeu, jouer cartes sur table; *see* **set, T** *etc.*

d (*Math*) carré *m*. **four is the ~ of two** quatre est le carré de deux.

e (** pej: conventional person*) **he's a real ~** il est vraiment vieux jeu *or* vraiment rétro*, il retarde*; **don't be such a ~!** ne sois pas si vieux jeu! *or* si rétro*!, tu retardes!*

2 adj a (*in shape*) *figure, sheet of paper, shoulders, chin, face* carré. **of ~ build** trapu, ramassé; **to cut sth ~** équarrir qch, couper qch au carré *or* à angle droit; **a ~ corner** un coin à angle droit; (*Typ*) **~ bracket** crochet *m*; (*fig*) **he is a ~ peg in a round hole** il n'est pas à son affaire, il n'est pas taillé pour cela; (*fig*) **a ~ meal** un bon repas, un repas substantiel; *see also* **3**.

b (*even, balanced*) *books, accounts, figures* en ordre. **to get one's accounts ~** mettre ses comptes en ordre, balancer ses comptes; **to get ~ with sb** (*financially*) régler ses comptes avec qn; (*fig: get even with*) régler son compte à qn, faire son affaire à qn; (*fig*) **to be all ~** être quitte; (*Sport*) être à égalité.

c (*honest*) *dealings* honnête, régulier*; (*unequivocal*) *refusal, denial* net, catégorique. **he is absolutely ~** il est l'honnêteté même, il joue franc jeu. **a ~ deal** un arrangement équitable *or* honnête; **to get** *or* **have a ~ deal** être traité équitablement; **to give sb a ~ deal** agir honnêtement avec qn; *see* **fair**[1].

d (*Math etc*) *number* carré. **6 ~ metres** 6 mètres carrés; **6 metres ~** (de) 6 mètres sur 6; **~ root** racine carrée.

e (** pej: conventional*) *person* vieux jeu *inv*, rétro* *inv*, qui retarde*; *habit* vieux jeu, rétro*.

3 adv (*at right angles*) **~ to** *or* **with** à angle droit avec, d'équerre avec; **the ship ran ~ across our bows** le navire nous a complètement coupé la route; **~ in the middle** en plein milieu; **to look sb ~ in the face** regarder qn bien en face; **he hit me ~ on the jaw** il m'a frappé en plein sur la mâchoire; *see* **fair**[1].

4 comp ►**square-bashing** (*Brit Mil sl*) exercice *m* ►**square-built** trapu ►**square-cut** coupé à angle droit, équarri ►**square dance** quadrille *m* ►**square-dancing** (*NonC*) quadrille *m* ►**square-faced** au visage carré ►**square-jawed** à la mâchoire carrée ►**square knot** (*US*) nœud plat ►**square-rigged** (*Naut*) gréé (en) carré ►**square-shouldered** aux épaules carrées, carré d'épaules ►**square-toed** *shoes* à bout carré.

5 **vt** a (*make* ~) *figure, shape* rendre carré, carrer; *stone, timber* équarrir, carrer; *corner* couper au carré *or* à angle droit. **to ~ one's shoulders** redresser les épaules; (*fig*) **to try to ~ the circle** chercher à faire la quadrature du cercle.

b (*settle etc*) *books, accounts* mettre en ordre, balancer; *debts* acquitter, régler; *creditors* régler, payer; (*reconcile*) concilier, faire cadrer (*A with B* A avec B). **to ~ one's account with sb** (*lit*) régler ses comptes avec qn; (*fig*) régler son compte à qn, faire son affaire à qn; **to ~ o.s. with sb** régler ses comptes avec qn; **I can't ~ that with what he told me yesterday** ça ne cadre pas avec ce qu'il m'a dit hier; **he managed to ~ it with his conscience** il s'est arrangé avec sa conscience; **can you ~* it with the boss?** est-ce que vous pouvez arranger ça avec le patron?; **I can ~* him** (*get him to agree*) je m'occupe de lui, je me charge de lui; (*bribe him*) je peux lui graisser la patte*.

c (*Math*) *number* carrer, élever au carré. **four ~d is sixteen** quatre au carré fait seize.

6 **vi** cadrer, correspondre, s'accorder. **that doesn't ~ with the facts** ceci ne cadre pas *or* ne s'accorde pas avec les faits, ceci ne correspond pas aux faits, ceci n'est pas en rapport avec les faits; **that ~s!** ça cadre!, ça colle!*

►**square off** 1 **vi** (*US: in quarrel etc*) se faire face; (*in fist fight etc*) se mettre en garde (*to sb* devant qn). 2 **vt sep** *paper, plan* diviser en carrés, quadriller; *wood, edges* équarrir.

►**square up** 1 **vi** a *[boxers, fighters]* se mettre en garde (*to sb* devant qn). (*fig*) **to square up to a problem** faire face à un problème. b (*pay debts*) régler ses comptes (*with sb* avec qn). 2 **vt sep** a (*make square*) *paper* couper au carré *or* à angle droit; *wood* équarrir. b *account, debts* régler, payer. **I'll square things up* for you** j'arrangerai les choses pour vous.

squarely ['skwɛəlɪ] **adv** a (*completely*) carrément. **we must face this ~** nous devons carrément y faire face; **~ in the middle** en plein milieu, carrément* au milieu; **to look sb ~ in the eyes** regarder qn droit dans les yeux. b (*honestly*) honnêtement, régulièrement*. (*fig*) **he dealt with us very ~** il a agi très honnêtement avec nous, il a été parfaitement régulier avec nous*.

squash[1] [skwɒʃ] 1 **n** a (*crowd*) cohue *f*, foule *f*; (*crush*) cohue, bousculade *f*. **a great ~ of people** une cohue, une foule; **I lost him in the ~ at the exit** je l'ai perdu dans la cohue *or* dans la bousculade à la sortie.

b (*Brit*) **lemon/orange ~** citronnade *f*/orangeade *f* (concentrée).

c (*Sport: also* **~ rackets**) squash *m*.

2 **comp** ►**squash court** (*Sport*) court *m* de squash ►**squash player** joueur *m*, -euse *f* de squash ►**squash racket** raquette *f* de squash ►**squash rackets** (*game*) *see* **squash[1] 1c**.

3 **vt** *fruit, beetle, hat, box* écraser; (*fig*) *argument* réfuter; (*snub*) *person* remettre à sa place, rabrouer, rembarrer*. **to ~ flat** *fruit, beetle* écraser, écrabouiller*; *hat, box* aplatir; **he ~ed his nose against the window** il a écrasé son nez contre la vitre; **you're ~ing me!** tu m'écrases!; **she ~ed the shoes into the suitcase** elle a réussi à faire rentrer les chaussures dans la valise; **can you ~ 2 more people in the car?** est-ce que tu peux introduire *or* faire tenir 2 personnes de plus dans la voiture?

4 **vi** a *[people]* **they ~ed into the elevator** ils se sont serrés *or* entassés dans l'ascenseur; **they ~ed through the gate** ils sont sortis (*or* entrés) en se pressant *or* s'écrasant *or* se bousculant près du portail.

b *[fruit, parcel etc]* s'écraser. **will it ~?** est-ce que cela risque de s'écraser?

►**squash in** 1 **vi** *[people]* s'empiler, s'entasser. **when the car arrived they all squashed in** quand la voiture est arrivée ils se sont tous empilés *or* entassés dedans; **can I squash in?** est-ce que je peux me trouver une petite place? 2 **vt sep** (*into box, suitcase etc*) réussir à faire rentrer.

►**squash together** 1 **vi** *[people]* se serrer (les uns contre les autres). 2 **vt sep** *objects* serrer, tasser. **we were all squashed together** nous étions très serrés *or* entassés.

►**squash up** 1 **vi** *[people]* se serrer, se pousser. **can't you squash up a bit?** pourriez-vous vous serrer *or* vous pousser un peu? 2 **vt sep** *object* écraser; *paper* chiffonner en boule.

squash[2] [skwɒʃ] **n, pl ~es** *or* **~** (*gourd*) gourde *f*; (*US: marrow*) courge *f*.

squashy ['skwɒʃɪ] **adj** *fruit* mou (*f* molle), qui s'écrase facilement; *ground* bourbeux, boueux.

squat [skwɒt] 1 **adj** *person* ramassé, courtaud; *building* écrasé, lourd; *armchair, jug etc* bas et ramassé. **a ~ parcel** un petit paquet épais *or* rebondi. 2 **vi** a (*also* **~ down**) *[person]* s'accroupir, s'asseoir sur ses talons; *[animal]* se tapir, se ramasser. **to be ~ting (down)** *[person]* être accroupi, être assis sur ses talons; *[animal]* être tapi *or* ramassé. b *[squatters]* faire du squattage. **to ~ in a house** squatter *or* squatteriser une maison. 3 **n** (*act of squatting*) squat *m*, squattage *m*; (*place*) squat. (*Gymnastics*) **~ thrust** saut *m* de main.

squatter ['skwɒtəʳ] **n** squatter *m*. **~'s rights** droit *m* de propriété par occupation du terrain.

squatting ['skwɒtɪŋ] **n** squat *m*, squattage *m*.

squaw [skwɔː] **n** squaw *f*, femme *f* peau-rouge.

squawk [skwɔːk] 1 **vi** *[hen, parrot]* pousser un *or* des gloussement(s); *[baby]* brailler; *[person]* pousser un *or* des cri(s) rauque(s); (** fig: complain*) râler*, gueuler‡. 2 **n** gloussement *m*; braillement *m*; cri *m* rauque. 3 **comp** ►**squawk box*** (*US: loudspeaker*) haut-parleur *m*.

squeak [skwiːk] 1 **n** *[hinge, wheel, pen, chalk]* grincement *m*; *[shoes]* craquement *m*; *[mouse, doll]* petit cri aigu, vagissement *m*; *[person]* petit cri aigu, glapissement *m*. **to let out** *or* **give a ~ of fright/surprise** *etc* pousser un petit cri *or* glapir de peur/de surprise *etc*; **not a ~*, mind!** pas un murmure hein!, n'en souffle pas mot!; **I don't want another ~ out of you** je ne veux plus t'entendre; *see* **narrow**. 2 **vi** *[hinge, wheel]* grincer, crier; *[pen, chalk]* grincer; *[shoe]* crier, craquer; *[mouse, doll]* vagir, pousser un *or* des petit(s) cri(s) aigu(s); *[person]* glapir. 3 **vt: "no" she ~ed** "non" glapit-elle.

squeaker ['skwiːkəʳ] **n** (*in toy etc*) sifflet *m*.

squeaky ['skwiːkɪ] **adj** *hinge, wheel, pen* grinçant; *doll* qui crie; *shoes* qui crient, qui craquent. **~-clean*** *hair* si propre que ça crisse; (*fig: very clean*) *office, home etc* ultra propre; (*fig: person: clean-living*) blanc comme neige, au-dessus de tout soupçon.

squeal [skwiːl] 1 **n** *[person, animal]* cri aigu *or* perçant; *[brakes]* grincement *m*, hurlement *m*; *[tyres]* crissement *m*. **to let out** *or* **give a ~ of pain** pousser un cri de douleur; **... he said with a ~ of laughter** ... dit-il avec un rire aigu.

2 **vi** a *[person, animal]* pousser un *or* des cri(s) aigu(s) *or* perçant(s); *[brakes]* grincer, hurler; *[tyres]* crisser. **he ~ed like a (stuck) pig** il criait comme un cochon qu'on égorge; **she tickled the child and he ~ed** elle a chatouillé l'enfant et il a poussé un petit cri.

b (*‡: inform*) vendre la mèche*. **to ~ on sb** dénoncer qn, vendre qn, donner* qn; **somebody ~ed to the police** quelqu'un les (*or* nous *etc*) a donnés* à la police.

3 **vt: "help" he ~ed** "au secours" cria-t-il d'une voix perçante.

squeamish ['skwiːmɪʃ] **adj** (*easily nauseated*) délicat, facilement dégoûté; (*queasy*) qui a mal au cœur, qui a la nausée; (*very fastidious*) facilement dégoûté; (*easily shocked*) qui s'effarouche facilement. (*lit, fig*) **I'm not ~** je ne suis pas bien délicat, je ne suis pas facilement dégoûté; **I'm too ~ to do that** je n'ose pas faire cela; **don't be so ~!** ne joue pas aux petits délicats!; **spiders make me feel ~** les araignées me dégoûtent.

squeamishness ['skwiːmɪʃnɪs] **n** (*NonC*) délicatesse exagérée; (*queasiness*) nausée *f*; (*prudishness*) pruderie *f*.

squeegee [ˌskwiː'dʒiː] **n** (*for windows etc*) raclette *f* (à bord de caoutchouc); (*mop*) balai-éponge *m*.

squeeze [skwiːz] 1 **n** a (*act, pressure*) pression *f*, compression *f*; (*NonC: in crowd*) cohue *f*, bousculade *f*. **to give sth a ~ = to squeeze sth** (*see* **3a**); **he gave her a big ~** il l'a serrée très fort dans ses bras; **a ~ of lemon** quelques gouttes *fpl* de citron; **a ~ of toothpaste** un peu de dentifrice; **there was a great** *or* **tight ~ in the bus** on était serrés comme des sardines* *or* on était affreusement tassés dans l'autobus; **it was a (tight) ~ to get through** il y avait à peine la place de passer; (*fig*) **to put the ~ on sb‡** presser qn, harceler qn.

b (*Econ: also* **credit ~**) restrictions *fpl* de crédit.

c (*Bridge*) squeeze *m* (*in clubs* à trèfle).

2 **comp** ►**squeeze bottle** (*US*) flacon *m* en plastique déformable ►**squeeze-box*** (*accordion*) accordéon *m*; (*concertina*) concertina *m*.

3 **vt** a (*press*) *handle, tube, plastic bottle, lemon* presser; *sponge, cloth* presser, tordre, comprimer; *doll, teddy bear* appuyer sur; *sb's hand, arm* serrer. **he ~d his finger in the door** il s'est pris *or* pincé le doigt dans la porte; **she ~d another jersey into the case** elle a réussi à faire rentrer un autre chandail dans la valise; (*fig*) **he ~d his victim dry*** il a saigné sa victime à blanc.

b (*extract: also* **~ out**) *water, juice, toothpaste* exprimer (*from, out of* de).

c (** fig*) *names, information, money, contribution* soutirer, arracher, extorquer (*out of* à). **you won't ~ a penny out of me for that type of thing** tu ne me feras pas lâcher* un sou pour ce genre de chose; **the government hopes to ~ more money out of the taxpayers** le gouvernement espère obtenir *or* tirer plus d'argent des contribuables.

d (*Fin*) *wages, prices* bloquer, geler.

4 **vi: he ~d past me** il s'est glissé devant moi en me poussant un peu; **he managed to ~ into the bus** il a réussi à se glisser *or* à s'introduire dans l'autobus en poussant; **they all ~d into the car** ils se sont entassés *or* empilés dans la voiture; **can you ~ underneath the fence?** est-ce que tu peux te glisser sous la barrière?; **he ~d through the crowd** il a réussi à se faufiler à travers la foule; **she ~d through the window** elle s'est glissée par la fenêtre; **the car ~d into the empty space** il y avait juste assez de place pour se garer.

►**squeeze in** 1 **vi** *[person]* trouver une petite place; *[car etc]* rentrer tout juste, avoir juste la place. **can I squeeze in?** est-ce qu'il y a une petite place pour moi? 2 **vt sep** *object into box*, (** fig*) *item on programme etc* réussir à faire rentrer, trouver une petite place pour. **can you squeeze 2 more people in?** est-ce que vous avez de la place pour 2 autres personnes?, est-ce que vous pouvez prendre 2 autres personnes?; **I can squeeze you in* tomorrow at 9** je peux vous prendre (en vitesse) demain à 9 heures.

►**squeeze past** vi *[person]* passer en se faufilant *or* en poussant; *[car]* se faufiler, se glisser.

►**squeeze through** vi *[person]* se faufiler, se frayer un chemin; *[car]* se faufiler, se glisser (*between* entre).

►**squeeze up*** vi *[person]* se serrer, se pousser.

squeezer [ˈskwiːzəʳ] n presse-fruits *m inv*. **lemon ~** presse-citron *m inv*.

squelch [skweltʃ] 1 n a bruit *m* de succion *or* de pataugeage. **I heard the ~ of his footsteps in the mud** je l'ai entendu patauger dans la boue; **the tomato fell with a ~** la tomate s'est écrasée par terre avec un bruit mat.
b (‡ *fig: crushing retort*) réplique *f* qui coupe le sifflet*.
2 vi *[mud etc]* faire un bruit de succion. *[person]* **to ~ in/out** *etc* entrer/sortir *etc* en pataugeant; **to ~ (one's way) through the mud** avancer en pataugeant dans la boue; **the water ~ed in his boots** l'eau faisait flic flac* dans ses bottes.
3 vt a (*crush underfoot*) piétiner, écraser.
b (*fig: stifle*) *enthusiasm etc* réprimer, étouffer.
c (‡: *snub*) clouer le bec à*, couper le sifflet à*.

squib [skwɪb] n pétard *m*; *see* **damp**.

squid [skwɪd] n, pl ~ *or* ~s calmar *m*, encornet *m*.

squiffy* [ˈskwɪfɪ] adj (*Brit*) éméché, pompette*.

squiggle [ˈskwɪgl] 1 n (*scrawl*) gribouillis *m*; (*wriggle*) tortillement *m*. 2 vi (*in writing etc*) gribouiller, faire des gribouillis; *[worm etc]* se tortiller.

squint [skwɪnt] 1 n (*Med*) strabisme *m*; (*sidelong look*) regard *m* de côté; (*quick glance*) coup *m* d'œil. (*Med*) **to have a ~** loucher, être atteint de strabisme; **to have** *or* **take a ~ at sth** (*obliquely*) regarder qch du coin de l'œil, lorgner qch; (*quickly*) jeter un coup d'œil à qch; **let's have a ~!*** donne voir!, montre voir!*; **have a ~* at this** jette un coup d'œil là-dessus, zieute‡ ça.
2 vi (*Med*) loucher. **he ~ed in the sunlight** il grimaçait un peu à cause du soleil; **he ~ed down the tube** il a plongé son regard dans le tube; **to ~ at sth** (*obliquely*) regarder qch du coin de l'œil, lorgner qch; (*quickly*) jeter un coup d'œil à qch; **he ~ed at me quizzically** il m'a interrogé du regard.
3 comp ►**squint-eyed** qui louche, atteint de strabisme.

squirarchy [ˈskwaɪərɑːkɪ] n = **squirearchy**.

squire [ˈskwaɪəʳ] 1 n (*landowner*) propriétaire *m* terrien, ≃ châtelain *m*; (*Hist: knight's attendant*) écuyer *m*. **the ~ told us ...** le châtelain nous a dit ...; **the ~ of Barcombe** le seigneur† *or* le châtelain de Barcombe; (*Brit*) **yes ~!‡** oui chef!* *or* patron!* 2 vt *lady* escorter, servir de cavalier à. **she was ~d by** elle était escortée par.

squirearchy [ˈskwaɪərɑːkɪ] n (*NonC*) hobereaux *mpl*, propriétaires terriens.

squirm [skwɜːm] vi a *[worm etc]* se tortiller. *[person]* **to ~ through a window** passer par une fenêtre en faisant des contorsions. b (*fig*) *[person]* (*from embarrassment*) ne pas savoir où se mettre, être au supplice; (*from distaste*) avoir un haut-le-corps. **spiders make me ~** j'ai un haut-le-corps quand je vois une araignée; **her poetry makes me ~** ses poèmes me donnent mal au cœur.

squirrel [ˈskwɪrəl] 1 n, pl ~s *or* ~ écureuil *m*. **red ~** écureuil; **grey ~** écureuil gris. 2 comp *coat etc* en petit-gris.

►**squirrel away** vt sep *nuts etc* amasser.

squirt [skwɜːt] 1 n a *[water]* jet *m*; *[detergent]* giclée *f*; *[scent]* quelques gouttes *fpl*.
b (* *pej*) (*person*) petit bout* de rien du tout, petit morveux*, petite morveuse*; (*child*) mioche* *mf*.
2 vt *water* faire jaillir, faire gicler (*at, on, onto* sur, *into* dans); *detergent* verser une giclée de; *oil* injecter; *scent* faire tomber quelques gouttes de. **he ~ed the insecticide onto the roses** il a pulvérisé de l'insecticide sur les roses; **to ~ sb with water** asperger *or* arroser qn d'eau; **to ~ scent on sb, to ~ sb with scent** asperger qn de parfum.
3 vi *[liquid]* jaillir, gicler. **the water ~ed into my eye** j'ai reçu une giclée d'eau dans l'œil; **water ~ed out of the broken pipe** l'eau jaillissait du tuyau cassé.

squirter [ˈskwɜːtəʳ] n poire *f* (en caoutchouc).

Sr (abbr of **Senior**) Sr.

SRC [esɑːˈsiː] n (*Brit*) (abbr of **Science Research Council**) ≃ CNRS *m*.

Sri Lanka [ˌsriːˈlæŋkə] n Sri Lanka *m or f*. **in ~** à Sri Lanka.

Sri Lankan [ˌsriːˈlæŋkən] 1 adj sri-lankais. 2 n Sri-Lankais(e) *m(f)*.

SRN [esɑːrˈen] n (*Brit*) (abbr of **State Registered Nurse**) *see* **state**.

SS [esˈes] n a (abbr of **steamship**) *navire de la marine marchande britannique*. **SS Charminster** le Charminster. b (abbr of **Saints**) St(e)s *m(f)pl*. c (*Nazi*) S.S. *m inv*.

S.S.A. [esesˈeɪ] n (*US*) (abbr of **Social Security Administration**) *see* **social**.

SSSI [ˌesesesˈaɪ] n (*Brit*) (abbr of **Site of Specific Scientific Interest**) *see* **site**.

St 1 n a (abbr of **Street**) rue, *e.g.* **Churchill St** rue Churchill. b (abbr of **Saint**) St(e), *e.g.* **St Peter** saint Pierre; **St Anne** sainte Anne; *see also* **2**.
2 comp ►**St John Ambulance** (*Brit*) *association bénévole de secouristes* ►**St. Lawrence (River)** (*Geog*) Saint-Laurent *m* ►**St. Lawrence Seaway** (*Geog*) voie *f* maritime du Saint-Laurent.

st (abbr of **stone(s)**) *see* **stone 1d**.

stab [stæb] 1 n a (*with dagger/knife etc*) coup *m* (de poignard/de couteau *etc*). (*fig*) **a ~ in the back** un coup bas *or* déloyal; **a ~ of pain** un élancement; **a ~ of remorse/grief** un remords/une douleur lancinant(e).
b (*: *attempt*) **to have** *or* **make a ~ at (doing) sth** s'essayer à (faire) qch; **I'll have a ~ at it** je vais tenter le coup.
2 comp ►**stab-wound** coup *m* de poignard (*or* couteau *etc*); (*mark*) trace *f* de coup de poignard (*or* couteau *etc*); **to die of stab-wounds** mourir poignardé.
3 vt (*with knife etc*) (*kill*) tuer d'un coup de *or* à coups de couteau *etc*; (*wound*) blesser d'un coup de *or* à coups de couteau *etc*; (*kill or wound with dagger*) poignarder. **to ~ sb with a knife** frapper qn d'un coup de couteau, donner un coup de couteau à qn; **to ~ sb to death** tuer qn d'un coup de *or* à coups de couteau *etc*; **he was ~bed through the heart** il a reçu un coup de couteau *etc* dans le cœur; (*lit, fig*) **to ~ sb in the back** poignarder qn dans le dos; **he ~bed his penknife into the desk** il a planté son canif dans le bureau; **he ~bed the pencil through the map** il a transpercé la carte d'un coup de crayon.
4 vi: **he ~bed at the book with his finger** il a frappé le livre du doigt.

stabbing [ˈstæbɪŋ] 1 n agression *f* (à coups de couteau *etc*). **there was another ~ last night** la nuit dernière une autre personne a été attaquée à coups de couteau *etc*. 2 adj *gesture* comme pour frapper; *sensation* lancinant. **~ pain** douleur lancinante, élancement *m*.

stabile [ˈsteɪbaɪl] n (*Art*) stabile *m*.

stability [stəˈbɪlɪtɪ] n (*see* **stable[1]**) stabilité *f*; fermeté *f*; solidité *f*; équilibre *m*.

stabilization [ˌsteɪbəlaɪˈzeɪʃən] n stabilisation *f*.

stabilize [ˈsteɪbəlaɪz] vt stabiliser.

stabilizer [ˈsteɪbəlaɪzəʳ] 1 n (*Aut, Naut, Aviat*) stabilisateur *m*. 2 comp ►**stabilizer bar** (*US Aut*) barre *f* anti-roulis, stabilisateur *m*.

stable[1] [ˈsteɪbl] adj *scaffolding, ladder* stable; (*Chem, Phys*) stable; *government* stable, durable; *job* stable, permanent; *prices* stable, (*St Ex*) ferme; *relationship, marriage* solide; *character, conviction* constant, ferme; (*Psych etc*) *person* équilibré. **he is not very ~** il n'est pas très équilibré, il est plutôt instable.

stable[2] [ˈsteɪbl] 1 n (*building*) écurie *f*; (*racehorses: also* **racing ~**) écurie (de courses). **(riding) ~(s)** centre *m* d'équitation, manège *m*; (*fig*) **another best-seller from the Collins ~** un nouveau best-seller de l'écurie Collins. 2 comp ►**stableboy** garçon *m or* valet *m* d'écurie ►**stable door**: (*Prov*) **to shut** *or* **close the stable door after the horse has bolted** *or* **has gone** prendre des précautions après coup ►**stable girl** (*Brit*) valet *m* d'écurie (*fille*) ►**stablelad** (*Brit*) lad *m* ►**stablemate** (*horse*) compagnon *m* de stalle; (*fig: person*) camarade *mf* d'études (*or* de travail *etc*). 3 vt *horse* mettre dans une *or* à l'écurie.

staccato [stəˈkɑːtəʊ] 1 adv (*Mus*) staccato. 2 adj (*Mus*) *note* piqué; (*gen*) *sounds, firing, voice, style* saccadé, coupé.

stack [stæk] 1 n a (*Agr*) meule *f*; *[rifles]* faisceau *m*; *[wood, books, papers]* tas *m*, pile *f*; (*US*) *[tickets]* carnet *m*. **~s* of** un tas* de, plein* de; **I've got ~s*** *or* **a ~* of things to do** j'ai des tas* de choses *or* plein* de choses à faire; **to have ~s* of money** rouler sur l'or, être bourré de fric‡; **we've got ~s* of time** on a tout le temps, on a plein* de temps; *see* **hay** *etc*.
b (*group of chimneys*) souche *f* de cheminée; (*on factory/boat etc*) (tuyau *m* de) cheminée *f* (*d'usine/de bateau etc*).
c (*in library, bookshop*) ~s rayons *mpl*, rayonnages *mpl*.
d (*Comput*) pile *f*.
2 vt a (*Agr*) mettre en meule; (*also* **~ up**) *books, wood* empiler, entasser; *dishes* empiler. **the table was ~ed with books** la table était couverte de piles de livres; (*US fig*) **she's (well-)~ed‡** elle est bien roulée*.
b (*supermarket shelves*) remplir. (*gen*) **she ~ed the shelf with books** elle a entassé des livres sur le rayon.
c (*hold waiting: incoming calls, applications etc*) mettre en attente; (*Aviat*) *aircraft* mettre en attente (à différentes altitudes).
d (*) (*pej*) *jury, committee etc* sélectionner avec partialité (*in favour of* pour favoriser, *against* pour défavoriser). **to ~ the cards** *or* (*US*) **the deck** tricher en battant les cartes; (*fig*) **the cards** *or* **odds are ~ed against me** les jeux sont faits d'avance contre moi, je suis défavorisé.

►**stack up** 1 vi (*US: measure, compare*) se comparer (*with, against* à). 2 vt sep (*gen*) empiler, entasser; *wheat, barrels* gerber; *see also* **stack 2a**.

stadium [ˈsteɪdɪəm] n, pl ~s *or* **stadia** [ˈsteɪdɪə] stade *m* (*sportif*).

staff[1] [stɑːf] 1 n, pl ~s (*work force*) (*Comm, Ind*) personnel *m*; (*Scol, Univ*) personnel enseignant, professeurs *mpl*; (*servants*) domestiques *mpl*; (*Mil*) état-major *m*. **a large ~** un personnel *etc* nombreux; **to be on the ~** faire partie du personnel; **we have 30 typists on the ~** notre personnel comprend 30 dactylos; **he's left our ~** il nous a quittés, il est parti, il ne fait plus partie de notre personnel; **he joined our ~ in 1974** il est entré chez nous en 1974, il a commencé à travailler chez nous en 1974; **he's ~** (*gen*) il fait partie du personnel; (*in factory offices*) c'est un employé; (*Scol, Univ*) c'est un professeur *or* un enseignant; **15 ~** (*gen*) 15 employés; (*teachers*) 15 professeurs *or* enseignants; *see* **chief, editorial**.
2 comp ►**staff canteen** (*in firm etc*) restaurant *m* d'entreprise,

cantine *f* (des employés) ►**staff college** (*Mil*) école supérieure de guerre ►**staff corporal** (*Brit*) ≃ adjudant *m* ►**staff discount** remise *f* pour le personnel ►**staff meeting** (*Scol, Univ*) conseil *m* des professeurs ►**staff nurse** (*Med*) infirmier *m*, -ière *f* ►**staff officer** (*Mil*) officier *m* d'état-major ►**staffroom** (*Scol, Univ*) salle *f* des professeurs ►**staff sergeant** (*Brit, US Army*) ≃ sergent-chef *m*; (*US Air Force*) sergent *m* ►**staff-student ratio** = **staffing ratio** (*see* **staffing 2**) ►**staff training** (*Comm, Ind etc*) formation *f* du personnel.

3 **vt** *school, hospital etc* pourvoir en personnel. **it is ~ed mainly by immigrants** le personnel se compose surtout d'immigrants; **the hotel is well-~ed** l'hôtel est pourvu d'un personnel nombreux; *see* **over, short, under** *etc*.

staff[2] [stɑːf] **n, pl staves** *or* **~s** (*liter: rod, pole*) bâton *m*, (*longer*) perche *f*; (*walking stick*) bâton; (*shepherd's*) houlette *f*; (*weapon*) bâton, gourdin *m*; (*symbol of authority*) bâton de commandement; (*Rel*) crosse *f*, bâton pastoral; (*also* **flag~**) mât *m*; (††) *[spear, lance etc]* hampe *f*; (*fig: support*) soutien *m*. **their only weapons were long staves** ils n'étaient armés que de longs bâtons; (*fig*) **a ~ for my old age** mon bâton de vieillesse; (*fig*) **bread is the ~ of life** le pain est l'aliment vital *or* le soutien de la vie.

staff[3] [stɑːf] **n, pl staves** (*Mus*) portée *f*.

staffing ['stɑːfɪŋ] 1 **n** dotation *f* en personnel. 2 **comp** *problems etc* de personnel ►**staffing officer** (*Can*) agent *m* de dotation ►**staffing ratio** (*Scol etc*) taux *m* d'encadrement; **the staffing ratio is good/bad** le taux d'encadrement est fort/faible.

Staffs [stæfs] **abbr of Staffordshire**.

stag [stæg] 1 **n** a (*deer*) cerf *m*; (*other animal*) mâle *m*. b (*Brit St Ex*) loup *m*. 2 **comp** ►**stag beetle** cerf-volant *m*, lucane *m* ►**staghound** *espèce de fox-hound* ►**stag hunt(ing)** chasse *f* au cerf. 3 **adj** a (*men only*) *event, evening* entre hommes. **~ night, ~ party** (*gen: men-only party*) soirée *f* entre hommes; (*before wedding*) enterrement *m* de la vie de garçon *or* célibataire; **he's having a ~ night** *or* **party** il enterre sa vie de garçon *or* de célibataire; **to go ~ to a party** aller à une soirée seul (*en parlant d'un homme*); (*US*) **the ~ line** le coin des hommes seuls (*dans une soirée*). b (*US *: pornographic*) *film* porno* *inv*. **~ show** spectacle *m* porno.

stage [steɪdʒ] 1 **n** a (*Theat: place*) scène *f*. (*profession etc*) **the ~** le théâtre; **on (the) ~** sur scène; **to come on ~** entrer en scène; **to go on the ~** monter sur la scène; (*fig: as career*) monter sur les planches, commencer à faire du théâtre, devenir acteur (*or* actrice); **on the ~ as in real life** au théâtre comme dans la vie ordinaire; **she has appeared on the ~** elle a fait du théâtre; **to write for the ~** écrire des pièces de théâtre; **the book was adapted for the ~** le livre a été adapté pour le théâtre *or* porté à la scène; **his play never reached the ~** sa pièce n'a jamais été jouée; (*fig*) **to hold the ~** être le point de mire, être en vedette, occuper le devant de la scène; (*fig*) **it was the ~ of a violent confrontation** cela a été le cadre *or* le théâtre (*liter*) d'une violente confrontation; *see* **down[1]** *etc*.

b (*platform: in hall etc*) estrade *f*; (*Constr: scaffolding*) échafaudage *m*; (*also* **landing ~**) débarcadère *m*; *[microscope]* platine *f*.

c (*point, section*) *[journey]* étape *f*; *[road, pipeline]* section *f*; *[rocket]* étage *m*; *[operation, process, disease]* étape, stade *m*, phase *f*. **a 4-~ rocket** une fusée à 4 étages; **the second ~ fell away** le deuxième étage s'est détaché; **a critical ~** un point *or* une phase *or* un stade critique; **the first ~ of his career** le premier échelon de sa carrière; **in ~s** par étapes, par degrés; **in** *or* **by easy ~s** *travel* par *or* à petites étapes; *study* par degrés; **by ~s** *travel* par étapes; *study* par degrés; **~ by ~** étape par étape; **the reform was carried out in ~s** la réforme a été appliquée en plusieurs étapes *or* temps; **in the early ~s** au début; **at an early ~ in its history** vers le début de son histoire; **at this ~ in the negotiations** à ce point *or* à ce stade des négociations; **what ~ is your project at?** à quel stade *or* à quel point *or* où en est votre projet?; **it has reached the ~ of being translated** c'en est au stade de la traduction, on en est à le traduire; **we have reached a ~ where ...** nous (en) sommes arrivés à un point *or* à un stade où ...; **the child has reached the talking ~** l'enfant en est au point *or* au stade où il commence à parler; **he's going through a difficult ~** il passe par une période difficile; **it's just a ~ in his development** ce n'est qu'une phase *or* un stade dans son développement; *see* **fare** *etc*.

d (*also* **~coach**) diligence *f*.

2 **comp** ►**stagecraft** (*Theat: NonC*) technique *f* de la scène ►**stage designer** décorateur *m*, -trice *f* de théâtre ►**stage direction** (*instruction*) indication *f* scénique; (*NonC: art, activity*) (art *m* de la) mise *f* en scène ►**stage director** metteur *m* en scène ►**stage door** entrée *f* des artistes ►**stage effect** effet *m* scénique ►**stage fright** trac* *m* ►**stagehand** machiniste *m* ►**stage left** côté *m* cour ►**stage-manage** *play, production* être régisseur pour; (*fig*) *event, confrontation etc* mettre en scène, orchestrer ►**stage manager** (*Theat*) régisseur *m* ►**stage name** nom *m* de théâtre ►**stage production** production *f* théâtrale ►**stage race** (*Sport*) course *f* par étapes ►**stage right** côté *m* jardin ►**stage show** = **stage production** ►**stage-struck**: **to be stage-struck** brûler d'envie de faire du théâtre ►**stage whisper** (*fig*) aparté *m*; **in a stage whisper** en aparté.

3 **vt** (*Theat*) monter, mettre en scène. (*fig*) **they ~d an accident/a reconciliation** (*organize*) ils ont organisé *or* manigancé un accident/une réconciliation; (*feign*) ils ont monté un accident/fait semblant de se réconcilier; **they ~d a demonstration** (*organize*) ils ont organisé une manifestation; (*carry out*) ils ont manifesté; **to ~ a strike** (*organize*) organiser une grève; (*go on strike*) faire la grève, se mettre en grève; **that was no accident, it was ~d** ce n'était pas un accident, c'était un coup monté; *see* **come** *etc*.

stager ['steɪdʒəʳ] **n**: **old ~** vétéran *m*, vieux routier.

stagey* ['steɪdʒɪ] **adj** (*pej*) *habits* du théâtre, de la scène; *appearance, diction, mannerisms* théâtral; *person* cabotin.

stagflation [stæg'fleɪʃən] **n** (*Econ*) stagflation *f*.

stagger ['stægəʳ] 1 **vi** chanceler, tituber. **he ~ed to the door** il est allé à la porte d'un pas chancelant *or* titubant; **to ~ along/in/out** *etc* avancer/entrer/sortir *etc* en chancelant *or* titubant; **he was ~ing about** il se déplaçait en chancelant *or* titubant, il vacillait sur ses jambes.

2 **vt** a (*amaze*) stupéfier, renverser; (*upset*) atterrer, bouleverser. **this will ~ you** tu vas trouver cela stupéfiant *or* renversant; **I was ~ed to learn** (*amazed*) j'ai été absolument stupéfait d'apprendre; (*upset*) j'ai été atterré *or* bouleversé d'apprendre.

b *spokes, objects* espacer; *visits, payments* échelonner; *holidays* étaler. **they work ~ed hours** leurs heures de travail sont étalées *or* échelonnées; (*Sport*) **~ed start** départ *m* décalé.

3 **n** allure chancelante *or* titubante. (*Vet*) **~s** vertigo *m*.

staggering ['stægərɪŋ] 1 **adj** (*fig*) *news, suggestion* renversant, bouleversant, atterrant; *amount, size* renversant, stupéfiant. (*lit, fig*) **~ blow** coup *m* de massue. 2 **n** a (*action*) démarche chancelante *or* titubante. b *[hours, visits etc]* échelonnement *m*; *[holidays]* étalement *m*.

staggeringly ['stægerɪŋlɪ] **adj**: **~ beautiful/bad** d'une beauté/nullité renversante; **~ high prices** des prix *mpl* extraordinairement élevés.

staging ['steɪdʒɪŋ] 1 **n** a (*scaffolding*) (plate-forme *f* d')échafaudage *m*. b (*Theat: of play*) mise *f* en scène. c (*Space*) largage *m* (d'un étage de fusée). 2 **comp** ►**staging post** (*Mil, also gen*) relais *m*, étape *f* de ravitaillement.

stagnancy ['stægnənsɪ] **n** stagnation *f*.

stagnant ['stægnənt] **adj** *water* stagnant; (*fig*) *business* stagnant, dans le marasme; *career* stagnant; *mind* inactif.

stagnate [stæg'neɪt] **vi** *[water]* être stagnant, croupir; (*fig*) *[business]* stagner, être dans le marasme; *[person]* stagner, croupir; *[mind]* être inactif.

stagnation [stæg'neɪʃən] **n** stagnation *f*.

stagy* ['steɪdʒɪ] **adj** = **stagey***.

staid [steɪd] **adj** *person* posé, rassis; *opinion, behaviour* pondéré; *appearance* collet monté *inv*.

staidness ['steɪdnɪs] **n** (*see* **staid**) caractère posé *or* rassis *or* pondéré; aspect *m* collet monté.

stain [steɪn] 1 **n** a (*lit, fig: mark*) tache *f* (*on* sur). **blood/grease ~** tache de sang/graisse; **without a ~ on his character** sans une tache à sa réputation. b (*colouring*) colorant *m*. **wood ~** couleur *f* pour bois. 2 **comp** ►**stain remover** détachant *m* ►**stain resistant** intachable. 3 **vt** a (*mark, soil*) tacher; (*fig*) *reputation etc* tacher, souiller, ternir. **~ed with blood** taché de sang. b (*colour*) *wood* teinter, teindre; *glass* colorer. **~ed glass** (*substance*) verre coloré; (*windows collectively*) vitraux *mpl*; **~ed-glass window** vitrail *m*, verrière *f*. 4 **vi**: **this material will ~** ce tissu se tache facilement *or* est très salissant.

(-)stained [steɪnd] **adj ending in comps**: **grease-stained** taché de graisse; **nicotine-stained** taché par la nicotine *or* le tabac; **oil-stained** taché d'huile; *see also* **blood, tear[2]**.

stainless ['steɪnlɪs] **adj** sans tache, pur. **~ steel** acier *m* inoxydable, inox *m*.

stair [stɛəʳ] 1 **n** (*step*) marche *f*; (*also* **~s, flight of ~s**) escalier *m*. **to pass sb on the ~(s)** rencontrer qn dans l'escalier; **below ~s** à l'office.

2 **comp** *carpet* d'escalier ►**staircase** escalier *m* (*see* **moving, spiral** *etc*) ►**stair rod** tringle *f* d'escalier ►**stairway** escalier *m* ►**stairwell** cage *f* d'escalier.

stake [steɪk] 1 **n** a (*for fence, tree etc*) pieu *m*, poteau *m*; (*as boundary mark*) piquet *m*, jalon *m*; (*for plant*) tuteur *m*; (*Hist*) bûcher *m*. **to die** *or* **be burnt at the ~** mourir sur le bûcher; (*US fig*) **to pull up ~s*** déménager.

b (*Betting*) enjeu *m*; (*fig: share*) intérêt *m*. (*horse-race*) **~s** course *f* de chevaux; (*Horse-Racing*) **the Newmarket ~s** le Prix de Newmarket; **to play for high ~s** (*lit*) jouer gros jeu; (*fig*) jouer gros jeu, risquer gros; **the issue at ~** ce dont il s'agit, ce qui est en jeu, ce qui se joue ici; **our future is at ~** notre avenir est en jeu, il s'agit de *or* il y va de notre avenir; **there is a lot at ~** l'enjeu est considérable, il y a gros à perdre; **there is a lot at ~ for him** il a gros à perdre; **he has got a lot at ~** il joue gros jeu, il risque gros, il a misé gros; (*fig*) **to have a ~ in sth** avoir des intérêts dans qch; **he has got a ~ in the success of the firm** il est intéressé matériellement *or* financièrement au succès de l'entreprise; **Britain has a big ~ in North Sea oil** la Grande-Bretagne a de gros investissements *or* a engagé de gros capitaux dans le pétrole de la mer du Nord.

2 **comp** ►**stakeholder** dépositaire *mf* d'enjeux ►**stakeout** (*Police*) surveillance *f*; **to be on a stakeout** effectuer une surveillance.

3 vt a *territory, area* marquer *or* délimiter (avec des piquets *etc*); *path, line* marquer, jalonner; *claim* établir. (*fig*) **to ~ one's claim to sth** revendiquer qch, établir son droit à qch.

b (*also* **~ up**) *fence* soutenir à l'aide de poteaux *or* de pieux; *plants* mettre un tuteur à, soutenir à l'aide d'un tuteur.

c (*bet*) *money, jewels etc* jouer, miser (*on* sur); (*fig*) *one's reputation, life* risquer, jouer (*on* sur). (*fig*) **he ~d everything** *or* **his all on the committee's decision** il a joué le tout pour le tout *or* il a joué son va-tout sur la décision du comité; **I'd ~ my life on it** j'en mettrais ma tête à couper.

d (*back financially*) *show, project, person* financer, soutenir financièrement.

►**stake out** 1 vt sep a *piece of land* marquer *or* délimiter (avec des piquets *etc*); *path, line* marquer, jalonner; (*fig*) *section of work, responsibilities etc* s'approprier, se réserver. (*fig*) **to stake out a position as ...** se tailler une position de ... . b (*Police*) *person, house* mettre *or* garder sous surveillance, surveiller. 2 **stakeout** n *see* **stake 2**.

stalactite ['stæləktaɪt] n stalactite *f*.

stalagmite ['stæləgmaɪt] n stalagmite *f*.

stale [steɪl] 1 adj *meat, eggs, milk* qui n'est plus frais (*f* fraîche); *cheese* desséché, dur; *bread* rassis, (*stronger*) dur; *beer* éventé, plat; *air* confiné; (*fig*) *news* déjà vieux (*f* vieille); *joke* rebattu, éculé; *writer, musician, actor* usé, qui n'a plus d'inspiration; *athlete* surentraîné. **the bread has gone ~** le pain a rassis *or* s'est rassis; **the room smells ~** cette pièce sent le renfermé; **the room smelt of ~ cigar smoke** la pièce avait une odeur de cigares refroidie; **I'm getting ~** je perds mon entrain *or* mon enthousiasme *or* mon inspiration; (*Fin*) **~ cheque** chèque *m* prescrit. 2 vi (*liter*) *[pleasures etc]* perdre de sa (*or* leur) fraîcheur *or* nouveauté.

stalemate ['steɪlmeɪt] 1 n (*Chess*) pat *m*; (*fig*) impasse *f*. **the discussions have reached ~** les discussions sont dans l'impasse; **the ~ is complete** c'est l'impasse totale; **to break the ~** sortir de l'impasse. 2 vt (*Chess*) faire pat *inv*; (*fig*) *project* contrecarrer; *adversary* paralyser, neutraliser.

stalemated ['steɪlmeɪtɪd] adj (*fig*) *discussions* au point mort, dans l'impasse; *project* au point mort; *person* coincé.

staleness ['steɪlnɪs] n (*see* **stale 1**) manque *m* de fraîcheur; dureté *f*; caractère déjà vieux (*or* rebattu *or* éculé); perte *f* d'inspiration; surentraînement *m*.

Stalin ['stɑːlɪn] n Staline *m*.

Stalinism ['stɑːlɪnɪzəm] n stalinisme *m*.

Stalinist ['stɑːlɪnɪst] 1 n Staliniste *mf*. 2 adj staliniste.

stalk[1] [stɔːk] 1 n *[plant]* tige *f*; *[fruit]* queue *f*; *[cabbage]* trognon *m*; (*Zool*) pédoncule *m*. (*fig*) **his eyes were out on ~s*** il ouvrait des yeux ronds, il écarquillait les yeux. 2 comp ►**stalk-eyed** (*Zool*) aux yeux pédonculés.

stalk[2] [stɔːk] 1 vt a *game, prey* traquer; *suspect* filer. b *[fear, disease, death]* **to ~ the streets/town** *etc* régner dans les rues/la ville *etc*. 2 vi: **to ~ in/out/off** *etc* entrer/sortir/partir *etc* d'un air digne *or* avec raideur; **he ~ed in haughtily/angrily/indignantly** il est entré d'un air arrogant/furieux/indigné. 3 comp ► **stalking-horse** (*fig*) prétexte *m*.

stall [stɔːl] 1 n a (*in stable, cowshed*) stalle *f*. (*Horse-racing*) (**starting**) **~s** stalles *fpl* de départ.

b (*in market, street, at fair*) éventaire *m*, boutique *f* (en plein air); (*in exhibition*) stand *m*. **newspaper/flower ~** kiosque *m* à journaux/de fleuriste; (*in station*) **book~** librairie *f* (*de gare*); **coffee ~** buvette *f*.

c (*Brit Theat*) (fauteuil *m* d')orchestre *m*. **the ~s** l'orchestre.

d (*in showers etc*) cabine *f*; (*in church*) stalle *f*; *see* **choir**.

e (*US: in car park*) place *f*, emplacement *m*.

f (*finger ~*) doigtier *m*.

g (*Aut*) fait *m* de caler. (*US fig*) **in a ~** grippé, qui n'avance pas.

2 comp ►**stall-fed** (*Agr*) engraissé à l'étable ►**stallholder** marchand(e) *m(f)* en plein air, marchand(e) tenant un kiosque.

3 vi a *[car, engine, driver]* caler; *[aircraft]* être en perte de vitesse, décrocher.

b (*fig*) **to ~ (for time)** essayer de gagner du temps, atermoyer; **he managed to ~ until ...** il a réussi à trouver des faux-fuyants jusqu'à ce que ...; **stop ~ing!** cesse de te dérober!

4 vt a (*Aut*) *engine, car* caler; (*Aviat*) causer une perte de vitesse *or* un décrochage à. **to be ~ed** (*Aut*) avoir calé; (*fig: of project etc*) être grippé, ne pas avancer.

b (*also* **~ off**) *person* tenir à distance. **I managed to ~ him until ...** j'ai réussi à le tenir à distance *or* à esquiver ses questions jusqu'à ce que ...; **try to ~ him (off) for a while** essaie de gagner du temps.

stallion ['stæljən] n étalon *m* (*cheval*).

stalwart ['stɔːlwət] 1 adj (*in build*) vigoureux, bien charpenté, costaud‡; (*in spirit*) vaillant, résolu, déterminé. **to be a ~ supporter of** soutenir vaillamment *or* de façon inconditionnelle. 2 n brave homme *m* (*or* femme *f*); *[party etc]* fidèle *mf*, pilier *m*.

stamen ['steɪmen] n, pl **~s** *or* **stamina** ['stæmɪnə] (*Bot*) étamine *f*.

stamina ['stæmɪnə] n (*NonC*) (*physical*) vigueur *f*, résistance *f*, endurance *f*; (*intellectual*) vigueur; (*moral*) résistance, endurance. **he's got ~** il est résistant, il a du nerf*; *see also* **stamen**.

stammer ['stæməʳ] 1 n bégaiement *m*, balbutiement *m*; (*Med*) bégaiement. **to have a ~** bégayer, être bègue. 2 vi bégayer, balbutier; (*Med*) bégayer, être bègue. 3 vt (*also* **~ out**) *name, facts* bégayer, balbutier. **to ~ (out) a reply** bégayer *or* balbutier une réponse, répondre en bégayant *or* balbutiant; **"n-not t-too m-much" he ~ed** "p-pas t-trop" bégaya-t-il.

stammerer ['stæmərəʳ] n bègue *mf*.

stammering ['stæmərɪŋ] 1 n (*NonC*) bégaiement *m*, balbutiement *m*; (*Med*) bégaiement. 2 adj *person* (*from fear, excitement*) bégayant, balbutiant; (*Med*) bègue; *answer* bégayant, hésitant.

stammeringly ['stæmərɪŋlɪ] adv en bégayant, en balbutiant.

stamp [stæmp] 1 n a timbre *m*; (*postage ~*) timbre(-poste); (*fiscal ~, revenue ~*) timbre (fiscal); (*savings ~*) timbre(-épargne); (*trading ~*) timbre(-prime). **(National) Insurance ~** cotisation *f* à la Sécurité sociale; **to put** *or* **stick a ~ on a letter** coller un timbre sur une lettre, timbrer une lettre; **used/unused ~** timbre oblitéré/non-oblitéré.

b (*implement*) (*rubber ~*) timbre *m*, tampon *m*; (*date ~*) timbre dateur; (*for metal*) étampe *f*, poinçon *m*.

c (*mark, impression*) (*on document etc*) cachet *m*; (*on metal*) empreinte *f*, poinçon *m*; (*Comm: trademark etc*) estampille *f*. **look at the date ~** regardez la date sur le cachet; **here's his address ~** voici le cachet indiquant son adresse; **it's got a receipt ~ on it** il y a un cachet accusant paiement; (*fig*) **he gave the project his ~ of approval** il a approuvé le projet; **the ~ of genius/truth** la marque *or* le sceau du génie/de la vérité; **men of his ~** des hommes de sa trempe *or* de son envergure *or* de son acabit (*pej*).

d *[foot]* (*from cold*) battement *m* de pied; (*from rage*) trépignement *m*. **with a ~ (of his foot)** en tapant du pied.

2 comp ►**Stamp Act** (*Brit Hist*) loi *f* sur le timbre ►**stamp album** album *m* de timbres(-poste) ►**stamp-book** carnet *m* de timbres(-poste) ►**stamp collecting** (*NonC*) philatélie *f* ►**stamp collection** collection *f* de timbres(-poste) ►**stamp collector** collectionneur *m*, -euse *f* de timbres(-poste), philatéliste *mf* ►**stamp dealer** marchand(e) *m(f)* de timbres(-poste) ►**stamp duty** droit *m* de timbre ►**stamping ground*** (*fig*) lieu favori, royaume *m* (*fig*) ►**stamp machine** distributeur *m* (automatique) de timbres(-poste).

3 vt a **to ~ one's foot** taper du pied; **to ~ one's feet** (*in rage*) trépigner; (*in dance*) frapper du pied; (*to keep warm*) battre la semelle; **he ~ed the peg into the ground** il a tapé du pied sur le piquet pour l'enfoncer en terre.

b (*stick a ~ on*) *letter, parcel* timbrer, affranchir; *savings book, insurance card* timbrer, apposer un *or* des timbre(s) sur; (*put fiscal ~ on*) timbrer. **this letter is not sufficiently ~ed** cette lettre n'est pas suffisamment affranchie; **I enclose a ~ed addressed envelope (for your reply)** veuillez trouver ci-joint une enveloppe affranchie pour la réponse.

c (*mark with ~*) tamponner, timbrer; *passport, document* viser; *metal* estamper, poinçonner. **to ~ a visa on a passport** apposer un visa sur un passeport; **to ~ the date on a form, to ~ a form with the date** apposer la date au tampon sur un formulaire; **he ~ed a design on the metal** il a estampillé le métal d'un motif; (*fig*) **to ~ sth on one's memory** graver qch dans sa mémoire; (*fig*) **his accent ~s him (as) a Belgian** son accent montre bien *or* indique bien qu'il est belge; (*fig*) **to ~ o.s. on sth** laisser sa marque *or* son empreinte sur qch; *see* **die[2]** *etc*.

4 vi a taper du pied; (*angrily*) taper du pied, trépigner; *[horse]* piaffer. **he ~ed on my foot** il a fait exprès de me marcher sur le pied; **he ~ed on the burning wood** il a piétiné les tisons, il a éteint les tisons du pied; (*fig*) **to ~ on a suggestion*** rejeter *or* repousser une suggestion.

b (*angrily*) **to ~ in/out** *etc* entrer/sortir *etc* en tapant du pied; **to ~ about** *or* **around** (*angrily*) marcher de long en large en tapant du pied; (*to keep warm*) marcher de long en large en battant la semelle.

►**stamp down** vt sep *peg etc* enfoncer du pied; (*fig*) *rebellion* écraser, étouffer; *protests* refouler.

►**stamp out** vt sep a *fire* piétiner, éteindre en piétinant; *cigarette* écraser sous le pied; (*fig*) *rebellion* enrayer, juguler; *custom, belief, tendency* déraciner, détruire. b *coin etc* frapper; *design* découper à l'emporte-pièce. c *rhythm* marquer en frappant du pied.

stampede [stæm'piːd] 1 n *[animals, people]* débandade *f*, fuite précipitée, sauve-qui-peut *m inv*; *[retreating troops]* débâcle *f*, déroute *f*; (*fig: rush*) ruée *f*. **there was a ~ for the door** on s'est précipité *or* rué vers la porte; **he got knocked down in the ~ for seats** il a été renversé dans la ruée vers les sièges.

2 vi *[animals, people]* s'enfuir en désordre *or* à la débandade (*from* de), fuir en désordre *or* à la débandade (*towards* vers); (*fig: rush*) se ruer (*for sth* pour obtenir qch, *for the door* vers la porte).

3 vt *animals, people* jeter la panique parmi. (*fig*) **they ~d him into agreeing** il a accepté parce qu'ils ne lui ont pas laissé le temps de la réflexion; **we mustn't let ourselves be ~d** il faut que nous prenions (*subj*) le temps de réfléchir.

stance [stæns] n (*lit, fig*) position *f*; (*Climbing*) relais *m*. (**bus**) **~** quai *m*; **to take up a ~** (*lit*) se mettre en position; (*fig*) prendre position.

stanch [stɑːntʃ] vt = **staunch[1]**.

stanchion ['stɑːnʃən] n (*as support*) étançon *m*, étai *m*; (*for cattle*) montant *m*.

stand [stænd] (**vb: pret, ptp stood**) **1 n a** (*position: lit, fig*) position *f*; (*resistance: Mil, fig*) résistance *f*, opposition *f*; (*Theat: stop, performance*) représentation *f*. **to take (up) one's ~** (*lit*) prendre place *or* position; (*fig*) adopter une attitude (*on sth* envers *or* sur qch), prendre position (*against sth* contre qch); **he took (up) his ~ beside me** (*lit*) il s'est placé *or* mis *or* posté à côté de moi, il a pris position à côté de moi; (*fig*) il m'a soutenu, il a pris la même position *or* adopté la même attitude que moi; (*fig*) **I admired the firm ~ he took on that point** j'ai admiré la fermeté de son attitude *or* de sa position sur ce point; **I make my ~ upon these principles** je fonde *or* je base mon attitude sur ces principes; (*fig*) **to make** *or* **take a ~ against sth** prendre position contre qch, s'élever contre qch, s'opposer à qch, résister à qch; (*Mil*) **they turned and made a ~** ils se sont arrêtés et ont résisté; (*Mil*) **the ~ of the Australians at Tobruk** la résistance des Australiens à Tobrouk; **Custer's last ~** la dernière bataille de Custer; *see* **hand, one** *etc*.

b (*taxi ~*) station *f* (de taxis).

c (*structure*) (*for plant, bust etc*) guéridon *m*; (*lamp~*) support *m or* pied *m* (de lampe); (*hat~*) porte-chapeaux *m inv*; (*coat~*) portemanteau *m*; (*music ~*) pupitre *m* à musique; (*Comm: for display-ing goods*) étal *m*, étalage *m*; (*newspaper ~*) kiosque *m* à journaux; (*market stall*) éventaire *m*, étal *m*; (*at exhibition, trade fair*) stand *m*; (*at fair*) baraque *f*; (*US: witness ~*) barre *f*; (*band~*) kiosque (à musique); (*Sport; also along procession route etc*) tribune *f*. (*Sport*) **I've got a ticket for the ~(s)** j'ai un billet de tribune(s), j'ai une tribune; (*esp US*) **to take the ~** venir à la barre; *see* **grand, hall, wash** *etc*.

d (*Agr*) *[wheat etc]* récolte *f* sur pied; *[trees]* bouquet *m*, groupe *m*.

e = **standstill**.

2 comp ▸**stand-alone (computer) system** (*Comput*) système *m* (informatique) autonome *or* indépendant ▸**stand-by** *see* **stand-by** ▸**stand-in** remplaçant(e) *m(f)*, vacataire *mf*; (*Cine*) doublure *f* ▸**stand-offish** *see* **stand-offish** ▸**standpat*** (*US: esp Pol*) immobiliste ▸**standpipe** colonne *f* d'alimentation ▸**standpoint** (*lit, fig*) point *m* de vue ▸**standstill** *see* **standstill** ▸**stand-to** (*Mil*) alerte *f* ▸**stand-up** *see* **stand-up**.

3 vt a (*place*) *object* mettre, poser (*on* sur). **he stood the child on the chair** il a mis l'enfant debout sur la chaise; **to ~ sth (up) against a wall** dresser *or* mettre *or* placer qch contre le mur; **to ~ sth on its end** faire tenir qch debout.

b (*tolerate*) *heat, pain* supporter; *insolence, attitude* supporter, tolérer. **I can't ~ it any longer** (*pain etc*) je ne peux plus le supporter; (*boredom etc*) j'en ai assez, j'en ai plein le dos*, j'en ai par-dessus la tête*; **I can't ~ (the sight of) her** je ne peux pas la supporter *or* la sentir* *or* la voir*, je la trouve insupportable; **she can't ~ being laughed at** elle ne supporte pas *or* ne tolère pas qu'on se moque (*subj*) d'elle; **I can't ~ gin/Debussy/wet weather** je déteste le gin/Debussy/la pluie.

c (*withstand*) *pressure, heat* supporter, résister à. **to ~ the strain** *[rope/beam etc]* supporter la tension/le poids *etc*; *[person]* supporter la tension, tenir le coup*; **she stood the journey quite well** elle a bien supporté le voyage; **these cheap shoes won't ~ much wear** ces chaussures bon marché ne vont pas faire beaucoup d'usage; **it won't ~ close examination** cela ne résiste pas à un examen serré; **it won't ~ much more rubbing like that** cela ne résistera pas longtemps si on continue à le frotter comme ça; **the town stood constant bombardment for 2 days** la ville a résisté 2 jours à un bombardement continuel; *see* **test**.

d (*pay for*) payer, offrir. **to ~ sb a meal** payer à déjeuner (*or* dîner) à qn; **to ~ sb a drink** payer à boire à qn; **I'll ~ you an ice cream** je te paie *or* je t'offre une glace; **he stood the next round of drinks** il a payé *or* offert la tournée suivante; **to ~ the cost of sth** payer le coût de qch; *see* **treat**.

e (*phrases*) **to ~ a chance** avoir une bonne chance (*of doing* de faire); **to ~ no chance** ne pas avoir la moindre chance (*of doing* de faire); **to ~ one's ground** (*lit*) tenir bon, ne pas reculer; (*fig*) tenir bon *or* ferme, ne pas lâcher pied; **to ~ (one's) trial** passer en jugement (*for sth* pour qch, *for doing* pour avoir fait).

4 vi a (*be upright; also ~ up*) *[person, animal]* être *or* se tenir debout; *[pole, table etc]* être debout. **the child has learnt to ~** l'enfant sait se tenir debout maintenant; **he is too weak to ~** il est trop faible pour se tenir debout *or* se tenir sur ses jambes; **we had to ~ as far as Calais** nous avons dû rester *or* voyager debout jusqu'à Calais; **you must ~ (up)** *or* **stay ~ing (up) till the music stops** vous devez rester debout jusqu'à ce que la musique s'arrête (*subj*); **to ~ erect** (*stay upright*) rester debout; (*straighten up*) se redresser; **~ (up) straight!** tiens-toi droit(e)!; (*fig*) **to ~ on one's own (two) feet** voler de ses propres ailes, se débrouiller tout seul; **he ~s over 6 feet in his socks** il mesure *or* fait plus de 1 mètre 80 sans chaussures; **the tree ~s 30 metres high** l'arbre mesure *or* fait 30 mètres (de haut); **the chair won't ~ (up) properly** cette chaise ne tient pas bien debout, cette chaise est bancale; **the post must ~ upright** le pieu doit être *or* rester droit; **the house is still ~ing** la maison est encore debout *or* existe toujours *or* est toujours là; **not much still ~s of the walls** il ne reste plus grand-chose des murs; **they didn't leave a stone ~ing of the old town** ils n'ont rien laissé debout dans la vieille ville; *see* **attention, easy, hair** *etc*.

b (*rise: also ~ up*) se lever, se mettre debout. **all ~!** tout le monde debout!; (*more frm*) levez-vous s'il vous plaît!; (*fig*) **to ~ (up) and be counted** déclarer ouvertement sa position.

c (*~ still*) rester (debout), être (debout). **we stood talking for an hour** nous sommes restés là à parler pendant une heure; **he stood in the doorway** il se tenait dans l'embrasure de la porte; **don't ~ there, do something!** ne reste pas là à ne rien faire!; **I left him ~ing on the bridge** je l'ai laissé sur le pont; (*fig*) **he left the others ~ing** il dépassait les autres d'une tête (*fig*); **the man ~ing over there** cet homme là-bas; **~ over there till I'm ready** mets-toi *or* reste là-bas jusqu'à ce que je sois prêt; **he stood there ready to shoot** il était là prêt à tirer; **they stood patiently in the rain** ils attendaient patiemment sous la pluie; **they stood in a circle around the grave** ils se tenaient en cercle autour de la tombe; (*esp US*) **to ~ in line** faire la queue; **the car stood abandoned by the roadside** la voiture était abandonnée au bord de la route; **beads of perspiration stood on his brow** des gouttes de sueur perlaient sur son front; **tears stood in her eyes** elle avait les larmes aux yeux; **~ still!** tenez-vous tranquille!, ne bougez pas!, restez là!; (*fig*) **time seemed to ~ still** le temps semblait s'être arrêté; **~ and deliver!** la bourse ou la vie!; (*lit, fig*) **to ~ fast** *or* **firm** tenir bon *or* ferme, ne pas lâcher pied; (*lit*) **to ~ in sb's way** bloquer *or* barrer le passage à qn; (*fig*) **I won't ~ in your way** je ne vous ferai pas obstacle, je ne vous barrerai pas la route; **nothing now ~s in our way** maintenant la voie est libre; **his age ~s in his way** son âge constitue un sérieux handicap; **to ~ in the way of progress** constituer un obstacle au progrès; **to ~ clear** s'écarter; **you're ~ing on my foot** tu me marches sur le pied; **he stood on the beetle** il a marché sur *or* écrasé le scarabée; (*Aut*) **to ~ on the brakes** appuyer à fond sur *or* écraser la pédale de frein, freiner à mort; (*fig*) **to ~ on ceremony** faire des manières; **to ~ on one's dignity** garder ses distances, faire grand cas de sa dignité; **I won't ~ on my right to do so** je n'insisterai pas sur le fait que j'ai le droit de le faire; **it ~s to reason that ...** il va sans dire que ..., il va de soi que ...; **where do you ~ on this question?** quelle est votre position *or* quel est votre point de vue sur cette question?; **I like to know where I ~** j'aime savoir où j'en suis, j'aime connaître ma situation; **where do you ~ with him?** où en êtes-vous avec lui?, quels sont vos rapports avec lui?; **he ~s alone in this matter** personne ne partage son avis sur cette question; **this ~s alone** c'est unique en son genre; (*fig*) **he ~s (head and shoulders) above all the others** il dépasse tous les autres d'une tête (*fig*).

d (*be situated*) *[town, building, tree]* se trouver; *[object, vehicle]* se trouver, être. **the village ~s in the valley** le village se trouve *or* est (situé) dans la vallée; **the house ~s in its own grounds** la maison est entourée d'un parc *or* se dresse au milieu d'un parc; **3 chairs stood against the wall** il y avait 3 chaises contre le mur; **to let sth ~ in the sun** laisser *or* exposer qch au soleil; (*fig*) **nothing ~s between you and success** rien ne s'oppose à votre réussite; **that was all that stood between him and ruin** c'était tout ce qui le séparait de la ruine.

e (*be mounted, based*) *[statue etc]* reposer (*on* sur); (*fig*) *[argument, case]* reposer, être basé (*on* sur). **the lamp ~s on an alabaster base** la lampe a un pied *or* un support d'albâtre.

f (*be at the moment; have reached*) **to ~ at** *[thermometer, clock]* indiquer; *[offer, price, bid]* être à, avoir atteint; *[score]* être de; **you must accept the offer as it ~s** il faut que vous acceptiez (*subj*) l'offre telle quelle; **the record ~s unbeaten** le record n'a pas encore été battu; **the record stood at 4 minutes for several years** pendant plusieurs années le record est resté à 4 minutes; **sales ~ at 5% up on last year** les ventes sont pour le moment en hausse de 5% sur l'année dernière; (*Banking*) **to have £500 ~ing to one's account** avoir 500 livres en banque *or* à son compte (bancaire); **the amount ~ing to your account** la somme que vous avez à votre compte (bancaire), votre solde *m* de crédit; **as things ~ at the moment** étant donné l'état actuel des choses, les choses étant ce qu'elles sont en ce moment; **how do things ~ between them?** où en sont-ils?; **how do things ~?** où en sont les choses?

g (*remain undisturbed, unchanged*) *[liquid, mixture, dough etc]* reposer; *[tea, coffee]* infuser; *[offer, law, agreement, objection]* rester sans changement, demeurer valable. **let the matter ~ as it is** laissez les choses comme elles sont; **they agreed to let the regulation ~** ils ont décidé de ne rien changer au règlement; **the project will ~ or fall by ...** le succès du projet repose sur ...; **I ~ or fall by this** je me porte personnellement garant de cela.

h (*be*) être. **to ~ accused/convicted of murder** être accusé/déclaré coupable de meurtre; **to ~ in fear of sb/sth** craindre *or* redouter qn/qch; **I ~ corrected** je reconnais m'être trompé, je reconnais mon erreur; **to ~ opposed to sth** être opposé à qch, s'opposer à qch; **they were ~ing ready to leave at a moment's notice** ils étaient *or* se tenaient prêts à partir dans la minute; **to ~ well with sb** être bien vu de qn.

i (*act as*) remplir la fonction de, être. **to ~ guard over sth** monter la garde près de qch, veiller sur qch; **to ~ godfather to sb** être parrain de qn; **to ~ security for sb** se porter caution pour qn; (*Brit Parl*) **to ~ (as a candidate)** être *or* se porter candidat; **he stood (as candidate) for Gloomville** il a été candidat *or* s'est présenté à Gloomville; **to ~ against sb in an election** se présenter contre qn dans une élection; **to ~ for election** se présenter aux élections, être candidat; (*Brit*) **to ~ for re-election** se représenter; **he stood for the council but wasn't elected** il était candidat au poste de conseiller mais n'a pas été élu, il était candidat dans l'élection du conseil mais a été battu.

j (*be likely*) **to ~ to lose** risquer de perdre; **to ~ to win** risquer* de *or* avoir des chances de gagner; **he ~s to make a fortune on it** il pourrait bien faire fortune ainsi.

k (*Naut*) **to ~ (out) to sea** (*move*) mettre le cap sur le large; (*stay*) être *or* rester au large.

►**stand about, stand around** vi rester là, traîner (*pej*). **don't stand about doing nothing!** ne reste pas là à ne rien faire!, ne traîne pas sans rien faire!; **they were standing about wondering what to do** ils restaient là à se demander ce qu'ils pourraient bien faire; **they kept us standing about for hours** ils nous ont fait attendre debout *or* fait faire le pied de grue pendant des heures.

►**stand aside** vi s'écarter, se pousser. **he stood aside to let me pass** il s'est écarté *or* poussé *or* effacé pour me laisser passer; **stand aside!** poussez-vous!, écartez-vous!; (*fig*) **to stand aside in favour of sb** laisser la voie libre à qn, ne pas faire obstacle à qn; **he never stands aside if there is work to be done** il est toujours prêt à travailler quand il le faut.

►**stand back** vi (*move back*) reculer, s'écarter. (*fig*) **you must stand back and get the problem into perspective** il faut que vous preniez (*subj*) du recul pour voir le problème dans son ensemble; **the farm stands back from the motorway** la ferme est à l'écart *or* en retrait de l'autoroute.

►**stand by** 1 vi a (*be onlooker*) rester là (à ne rien faire), se tenir là. **I could not stand by and see him beaten** je ne pouvais rester là à le voir se faire battre sans intervenir; **how could you stand by while they attacked him?** comment pouviez-vous rester là sans rien faire alors qu'ils l'attaquaient?; **he stood by and let me get on with it** il s'est contenté d'assister et m'a laissé faire.

b *[troops]* être en état d'alerte; *[person, ship, vehicle]* (*be ready*) être *or* se tenir prêt; (*be at hand*) attendre *or* être sur place. (*gen*) **stand by!** attention!; (*Aviat*) **stand by for takeoff** paré pour le décollage; (*Naut*) **stand by to drop anchor** paré à mouiller l'ancre; **stand by for further news** tenez-vous prêt à recevoir d'autres nouvelles.

2 vt fus *promise* tenir; *sb else's decision* accepter; *one's own decision* réaffirmer, s'en tenir à; *friend* être fidèle à, ne pas abandonner; *colleague etc* soutenir, défendre. **I stand by what I have said** je m'en tiens à ce que j'ai dit.

3 **stand-by** n *see* **stand-by**.

►**stand down** vi (*Mil*) *[troops]* être déconsigné (en fin d'alerte); (*Jur*) *[witness]* quitter la barre; (*fig*) (*withdraw*) *[candidate]* se désister; (*resign*) *[official, chairman etc]* se démettre de ses fonctions, démissionner. **he stood down in favour of his brother** il s'est désisté en faveur de son frère *or* pour laisser la voie libre à son frère.

►**stand for** vt fus a (*represent*) représenter. **what does U.N.O. stand for?** qu'est-ce que les lettres U.N.O. représentent *or* veulent dire *or* signifient?; **our party stands for equality of opportunity** notre parti est synonyme d'égalité des chances; **I dislike all he stands for** je déteste tout ce qu'il représente *or* incarne; *see also* **stand 4i.** b (*tolerate*) supporter, tolérer. **I won't stand for it!** je ne le supporterai *or* tolérerai *or* permettrai pas!

►**stand in** 1 vi: **to stand in for sb** remplacer qn; **I offered to stand in when he was called away** j'ai proposé d'assurer son remplacement *or* de le remplacer quand il a dû s'absenter. 2 **stand-in** n *see* **stand 2.**

►**stand off** 1 vi a (*Naut*) mettre le cap sur le large. b (*move away*) s'écarter; (*fig: keep one's distance*) se tenir à l'écart (*from* de), garder ses distances (*from* par rapport à). c (*reach stalemate*) aboutir à une impasse. 2 vt sep (*Brit*) *workers* mettre temporairement au chômage. 3 **stand-off** n *see* **stand-off.**

►**stand out** vi a (*project*) *[ledge, buttress]* avancer (*from* sur), faire saillie; *[vein etc]* ressortir, saillir (*on* sur). **to stand out in relief** ressortir, être en relief.

b (*be conspicuous, clear*) ressortir, se détacher, trancher, se découper. **to stand out against the sky** ressortir *or* se détacher sur le ciel; **the yellow stands out against the dark background** le jaune ressort *or* se détache *or* tranche sur le fond sombre; **his red hair stands out in the crowd** ses cheveux roux le font remarquer dans la foule; (*fig*) **his ability stands out** son talent ressort *or* est manifeste; (*fig*) **he stands out above all the rest** il surpasse *or* surclasse tout le monde; (*fig*) **that stands out a mile!*** cela saute aux yeux!, cela crève les yeux!

c (*remain firm*) tenir bon, tenir ferme. **how long can you stand out?** combien de temps peux-tu tenir *or* résister?; **to stand out for sth** revendiquer qch, s'obstiner à demander qch; **to stand out against** *attack* résister à; *demand* s'opposer fermement à.

►**stand over** 1 vi *[items for discussion]* rester en suspens, être remis à plus tard. **let the matter stand over until next week** remettons la question à la semaine prochaine. 2 vt fus *person* surveiller, être sur *or* derrière le dos de. **I hate people standing over me while I work** je déteste avoir quelqu'un sur *or* derrière le dos quand je travaille; **I'll stand over you till you do it** je ne te lâcherai pas jusqu'à ce que tu l'aies fait; **stop standing over him and let him do it himself** arrête de le surveiller et laisse-le faire cela tout seul.

►**stand to** (*Mil*) 1 vi se mettre en état d'alerte. 2 **stand-to** n *see* **stand 2.**

►**stand up** 1 vi (*rise*) se lever, se mettre debout; (*be standing*) *[person]* être debout; *[chair, structure]* être (encore) debout. **she had nothing but the clothes she was standing up in** elle ne possédait que les vêtements qu'elle avait sur le dos; **the soup was so thick the spoon could stand up in it** la soupe était si épaisse qu'on pouvait y faire tenir la cuiller debout; (*fig*) **that argument won't stand up in court** cet argument ne sera pas valable en justice, cet argument sera démoli par l'avocat de la partie adverse; (*fig*) **to stand up and be counted** avoir le courage de ses opinions; *see also* **stand 4a, 4b.**

2 vt sep a (*place upright*) **to stand sth up (on its end)** mettre qch debout; **to stand sth up against a wall** appuyer *or* mettre qch contre un mur; **he stood the child up on the table** il a mis l'enfant debout sur la table.

b (* *fig*) poser un lapin à*, faire faux bond à. **she stood me up twice last week** elle m'a fait faux bond deux fois la semaine dernière.

3 **stand-up** adj *see* **stand-up.**

►**stand up for** vt fus *person* défendre, prendre le parti de, prendre fait et cause pour; *principle, belief* défendre. **you must stand up for what you think is right** vous devez défendre ce qui vous semble juste; **stand up for me if he asks you what you think** prenez ma défense *or* soutenez-moi s'il vous demande votre avis; **to stand up for o.s.** se défendre.

►**stand up to** vt fus *opponent* affronter; (* *fig: in argument etc*) tenir tête à; *heat, cold etc* résister à. **it won't stand up to that sort of treatment** cela ne résistera pas à ce genre de traitement; **the report won't stand up to close examination** le rapport ne résistera pas *or* ne supportera pas un examen serré.

standard ['stændəd] 1 n a (*flag*) étendard *m*; (*Naut*) pavillon *m*.

b (*norm*) norme *f*; (*criterion*) critère *m*; (*for weights and measures*) étalon *m*; (*for silver*) titre *m*; (*fig: intellectual etc*) niveau *m* (voulu). **monetary ~** titre de monnaie; **the metre is the ~ of length** le mètre est l'unité *f* de longueur; (*fig*) **to be** *or* **come up to ~** *[person]* être à la hauteur, être du niveau voulu; *[thing]* être de la qualité voulue, être conforme à la norme; **I'll never come up to his ~** je n'arriverai jamais à l'égaler; **judging by that ~** si l'on en juge selon ce critère; **you are applying a double ~** vous appliquez deux mesures; **his ~s are high** il cherche l'excellence, il ne se contente pas de l'à-peu-près; (*morally, artistically*) **he has set us a high ~** il a établi un modèle difficile à surpasser; **the exam sets a high ~** cet examen exige un niveau élevé; **the ~ of the exam was low** le niveau de l'examen était bas; **to be first-year university ~** être du niveau de première année d'université; **high/low ~ of living** niveau de vie élevé/bas; **their ~ of culture** leur niveau de culture; **to have high moral ~s** avoir un sens moral très développé; **I couldn't accept their ~s** je ne pouvais pas accepter leur échelle de valeurs; *see* **gold** *etc.*

c (*support*) support *m*; (*for lamp, street light*) pied *m*; (*actual streetlight*) pylône *m* d'éclairage; (*water/gas pipe*) tuyau vertical d'eau/de gaz; (*tree, shrub*) arbre *m* de haute tige; *see* **lamp.**

2 adj a *size, height, procedure* ordinaire, normal; *metre, kilogram, measure, weight etc* étalon *inv*; (*Comm: regular*) *design, model, size* standard *inv*; *rate of interest* courant; *reference book, work* classique, de base; (*Ling*) *pronunciation, usage* correct. **it is now ~ practice to do so** c'est maintenant courant *or* la norme (de faire ainsi); **the practice became ~ in the 1940s** cette pratique s'est généralisée *or* répandue dans les années 40; **it's ~ equipment on all their cars** c'est monté en série sur toutes leurs voitures; **a ~ car** une voiture de série; (*Rail*) **~ gauge** écartement normal (*see also* **3**); **he's below ~ height for the police** il n'a pas la taille requise pour être agent de police; **~ time** (l')heure légale; **~ English** (l')anglais correct; **~ French** (le) français correct *or* de l'Académie; **it's the ~ work on Greece** c'est l'ouvrage de base sur la Grèce; (*Statistics*) **~ deviation/error** écart *m*/erreur *f* type; (*Jur*) **~ clause** clause-type *f*; **~ operating procedure** procédure *f* à suivre.

b *shrub* de haute tige. **a ~ rose** un rosier

3 comp ►**standard bearer** porte-étendard *m inv* ►**standard-gauge** (*Rail*) d'écartement normal ►**Standard Grade** (*Scot Scol*) ≃ épreuve *f* du brevet des collèges ►**standard lamp** (*Brit*) lampadaire *m*.

standardization [ˌstændədaɪˈzeɪʃən] n (*see* **standardize**) standardisation *f*; normalisation *f*.

standardize ['stændədaɪz] vt (*gen*) standardiser; *product, terminology* normaliser. (*US Scol*) **~d test** *test de connaissances commun à tous les établissements.*

stand-by ['stændbaɪ] 1 n (*person*) remplaçant(e) *m(f)*; (*US Theat: understudy*) doublure *f*; (*car/battery/boots*) voiture *f*/pile *f*/bottes *fpl* de réserve *or* de secours. **if you are called away you must have a ~** si vous vous absentez, vous devez avoir un(e) remplaçant(e) *or* quelqu'un qui puisse vous remplacer en cas de besoin; **aspirin is a useful ~** l'aspirine est toujours bonne à avoir *or* peut toujours être utile; **lemon is a useful ~ if you have no vinegar** le citron peut être utilisé à la place du vinaigre le cas échéant; **to be on ~** *[troops]* être sur pied d'intervention; *[plane]* se tenir prêt à décoller; *[doctor]* être de garde; (*Mil*) **to be on 24-hour ~** être prêt à intervenir dans les 24 heures; (*Mil*) **to put on ~** mettre sur pied d'intervention.

2 adj *car, battery etc* de réserve; *generator, plan* de secours. (*Aviat*) **a**

~ **ticket** billet *m* sans garantie; ~ **passenger** voyageur *m*, -euse *f* sans garantie; (*Jur, Fin*) ~ **credit** crédit *m* d'appoint; ~ **loan** prêt conditionnel.

standee* [stæn'diː] **n** (*US*) (*at match etc*) spectateur *m*, -trice *f* debout; (*on bus etc*) voyageur *m*, -euse *f* debout.

standing ['stændɪŋ] 1 **adj** a (*upright*) *passenger* debout *inv*; *statue* en pied; *corn, crop* sur pied. (*in bus, theatre*) ~ **room** places *fpl* debout; **"~ room only"** (*seats all taken*) "il n y a plus de places assises"; (*no seats provided*) "places debout seulement"; ~ **stone** pierre levée *or* dressée; **he got a ~ ovation** ils lui ont fait une ovation, ils se sont levés pour l'ovationner *or* l'applaudir; (*Sport*) ~ **jump** saut *m* à pieds joints; ~ **start** (*Sport*) départ *m* debout; (*Aut*) départ arrêté.
b (*permanent*) *army, committee, invitation* permanent; *rule* fixe; *custom* établi, courant; *grievance, reproach* constant, de longue date. ~ **expenses** frais généraux; **it's a ~ joke that he wears a wig** on plaisante constamment à son sujet en prétendant qu'il porte une perruque; **it's a ~ joke** c'est un sujet de plaisanterie continuel; ~ **order** (*Brit Banking*) prélèvement *m* bancaire; (*for goods*) commande *f* permanente; (*Mil, Parl*) ~ **orders** règlement *m*; **to place a ~ order for a newspaper** passer une commande permanente pour un journal.
2 **n** a (*position, importance etc*) [*person*] importance *f*, rang *m*, standing *m*; [*restaurant, business*] réputation *f*, standing; [*newspaper*] importance, réputation, influence *f*. **social ~** rang *or* position *f* social(e), standing; **professional ~** rang *or* standing professionnel; **what's his financial ~?** quelle est sa situation financière?; **his ~ in (public opinion) polls** sa cote de popularité; **what's his ~?** quelle est sa réputation?, que pense-t-on de lui?; **firms of that ~** des compagnies aussi réputées; **a man of (high *or* some *or* good) ~** un homme considéré *or* estimé; **he has no ~ in this matter** il n'a aucune autorité *or* son opinion ne compte pas *or* il n'a pas voix au chapitre dans cette affaire.
b (*duration*) durée *f*. **of 10 years' ~** *friendship* qui dure depuis 10 ans; *agreement, contract* qui existe depuis 10 ans; *doctor, teacher* qui a 10 ans de métier; **of long ~** de longue *or* vieille date; **he has 30 years' ~ in the firm** il a 30 ans d'ancienneté dans la compagnie, il travaille dans la compagnie depuis 30 ans; *see* **long[1]**.
c (*US Sport*) **the ~** le classement.
d (*US Aut*) **"no ~"** "stationnement interdit".

stand-off ['stændɒf] 1 **n** a (*pause: in negotiations etc*) temps *m* d'arrêt. b (*stalemate*) impasse *f*. c (*counterbalancing situation*) contrepartie *f*. 2 **comp ▸ stand-off half** (*Rugby*) demi *m* d'ouverture.

stand-offish [ˌstænd'ɒfɪʃ] **adj** (*pej*) distant, réservé, froid. **don't be so ~!** ne prends pas ton air supérieur!

stand-offishly [ˌstænd'ɒfɪʃlɪ] **adv** (*pej*) d'une manière réservée *or* distante, avec froideur.

stand-offishness [ˌstænd'ɒfɪʃnɪs] **n** (*pej*) froideur *f*, réserve *f*.

standstill ['stændstɪl] **n** arrêt *m*. **to come to a ~** [*person, car*] s'immobiliser; [*production, discussions*] s'arrêter; **to bring to a ~** *car* arrêter; *production, discussion* paralyser; **to be at a ~** [*person, car*] être immobile; [*production, discussion*] être paralysé, être au point mort; **trade is at a ~** les affaires sont dans le marasme complet.

stand-up ['stændʌp] **adj** *collar* droit; *meal etc* (pris) debout. ~ **comedian** *or* **comic** comique *m* (qui se produit en solo); **a ~ fight** (*fisticuffs*) une bagarre en règle *or* violente; (*argument*) une discussion en règle *or* violente.

stank [stæŋk] **pret of stink.**

Stanley ['stænlɪː] **n** ®: ~ **knife** cutter *m*.

stannic ['stænɪk] **adj** stannique.

stanza ['stænzə] **n** (*Poetry*) strophe *f*; (*in song*) couplet *m*.

stapes ['steɪpiːz] **n, pl ~s** *or* **stapedes** [stæ'piːdiːz] étrier *m*.

staphylococcus [ˌstæfɪlə'kɒkəs] **n, pl staphylococci** [ˌstæfɪlə'kɒkaɪ] staphylocoque *m*.

staple[1] ['steɪpl] 1 **adj** (*basic*) *food, crop, industry* principal; *products, foods* de base. ~ **commodity** article *m* de première nécessité; ~ **diet** nourriture *f* de base. 2 **n** a (*Econ*) (*chief commodity*) produit *m or* article *m* de base; (*raw material*) matière première. b (*chief item*) (*Comm: held in stock*) produit *m or* article *m* de base; (*gen: of conversation etc*) élément *or* sujet principal; (*in diet etc*) aliment *m or* denrée *f* de base. c (*Tex: fibre*) fibre *f*.

staple[2] ['steɪpl] 1 **n** (*for papers*) agrafe *f*; (*Tech*) crampon *m*, cavalier *m*. ~ **gun** agrafeuse *f* d'artisan *or* d'atelier. 2 **vt** (*also ~ together*) *papers* agrafer; *wood, stones* cramponner. **to ~ sth on to sth** agrafer qch à qch.

stapler ['steɪplə^r] **n** agrafeuse *f*.

star [stɑː^r] 1 **n** a (*Astron*) étoile *f*, astre *m*; (*Typ etc: asterisk*) astérisque *m*; (*Scol: for merit*) bon point. **morning/evening ~** étoile du matin/du soir; (*US*) **the S~s and Stripes** la Bannière étoilée; (*US Hist*) **the S~s and Bars** le drapeau des États Confédérés; **S~ of David** étoile de David; **the ~ of Bethlehem** l'étoile de Bethléem (*see also* 2); **he was born under a lucky/an unlucky ~** il est né sous une bonne/une mauvaise étoile; **you can thank your (lucky) ~s* that ...** tu peux remercier le ciel *or* bénir ton étoile de ce que ...; (*fig*) **to see ~s*** voir trente-six chandelles; (*horoscope*) **the ~s** l'horoscope *m*; **it was written in his ~s that he would do it** il était écrit qu'il le ferait; **3-~ hotel** hôtel *m* 3 étoiles; (*Brit*) **2-~ petrol** ≃ ordinaire *m*, normal*m*; (*Brit*) **3-** *or* **4-~ petrol** super* *m*; (*gen*) **four-~** de première qualité; (*US*) **four-~ general** général *m* à quatre étoiles; *see* **guiding, pole[2], shooting** *etc*.
b (*Cine, Sport etc: person*) vedette *f*; (*actress*) vedette *f*, star *f*. **the film made him into a ~** le film en a fait une vedette *or* l'a rendu célèbre; *see* **all, film** *etc*.
2 **comp ▸ star anise** anis *m* étoilé **▸ star-chamber adj** (*fig*) secret et arbitraire **▸ star-crossed** maudit par le sort **▸ stardust n** (*fig*) la vie en rose **▸ starfish** étoile *f* de mer **▸ star fruit** carambole *f* **▸ stargazer** (*astronomer*) astronome *mf*; (*astrologer*) astrologue *mf*; (*fish*) uranoscope *m* **▸ stargazing** contemplation *f* des étoiles; (*predictions*) prédictions *fpl* astrologiques; (*fig: dreaming*) rêverie *f*, rêvasserie *f* (*pej*); **to be stargazing** regarder les étoiles; (*fig: daydream*) rêvasser, être dans la lune **▸ stargrass** (*Bot*) herbe étoilée **▸ starlight: by starlight** à la lumière des étoiles **▸ starlit** *night, sky* étoilé; *countryside, scene* illuminé par les étoiles **▸ star-of-Bethlehem** (*Bot*) ornithogale *m*, dame-d'onze-heures **▸ star part** (*Cine, Theat*) premier rôle **▸ a star(ring) role** (*Cine, Theat*) l'un des principaux rôles **▸ star route** (*US Post*) liaison postale **▸ star shell** (*Mil*) fusée éclairante **▸ star sign** signe *m* zodiacal *or* du zodiaque **▸ star-spangled** parsemé d'étoiles; (*US flag, anthem*) **the Star-Spangled Banner** la Bannière étoilée **▸ star-studded** *sky* parsemé d'étoiles; *cast* prestigieux; *play* à la distribution prestigieuse **▸ the star turn** (*Theat, fig*) la vedette **▸ Star Wars** (*gen, Cine, US Mil* *) la guerre des étoiles; (*US Mil* *) **the "Star Wars" plan** *or* **program** le projet de la guerre des étoiles.
3 **vt** a (*decorate with ~s*) étoiler. **lawn ~red with daisies** pelouse parsemée *or* émaillée (*liter*) de pâquerettes.
b (*put asterisk against*) marquer d'un astérisque.
c (*Cine, Theat*) avoir pour vedette. **the film ~s John Wayne** John Wayne est la vedette du film; **~ring Greta Garbo as ...** avec Greta Garbo dans le rôle de ... .
4 **vi** (*Cine, Theat*) être la vedette (*in a film* d'un film); (*fig*) briller. **he ~red as Hamlet** c'est lui qui a joué le rôle de Hamlet.

starboard ['stɑːbəd] (*Naut*) 1 **n** tribord *m*. **to ~** à tribord; **land to ~!** terre par tribord! 2 **adj** *guns, lights* de tribord. **on the ~ beam** par le travers tribord; **on the ~ side** à tribord; *see* **watch[2]**. 3 **vt: to ~ the helm** mettre la barre à tribord.

starch [stɑːtʃ] 1 **n** (*NonC*) (*in food*) amidon *m*, fécule *f*; (*for stiffening*) amidon; (*fig: formal manner*) raideur *f*, manières apprêtées *or* empesées. **he was told to cut out all ~(es)** on lui a dit de supprimer tous les féculents; (*US fig*) **it took the ~ out of him*** cela l'a mis à plat, cela lui a ôté toute son énergie. 2 **comp ▸ starch-reduced** *bread* de régime; *diet* pauvre en féculents. 3 **vt** *collar* amidonner, empeser.

starchy ['stɑːtʃɪ] **adj** *food* féculent; (*fig pej*) *person, attitude* guindé, apprêté, raide.

stardom ['stɑːdəm] **n** (*NonC: Cine, Sport, Theat etc*) célébrité *f*, gloire *f*, vedettariat *m*. **to rise to ~, achieve ~** devenir célèbre *or* une vedette, atteindre la célébrité.

stare [stɛə^r] 1 **n** regard *m* (fixe). **cold/curious/vacant ~** (long) regard froid/curieux/vague.
2 **vi: to ~ at sb** dévisager qn, fixer qn du regard, regarder qn fixement; **to ~ at sth** regarder qch fixement, fixer qch du regard; **to ~ at sb/sth in surprise** regarder qn/qch avec surprise *or* d'un air surpris, écarquiller les yeux devant qn/qch; **they all ~d in astonishment** ils ont tous regardé d'un air ébahi *or* en écarquillant les yeux; **he ~d at me stonily** il m'a regardé d'un air dur; **what are you staring at?** qu'est-ce que tu regardes comme ça?; **it's rude to ~** il est mal élevé de regarder les gens fixement; **to ~ into space** regarder dans le vide *or* dans l'espace, avoir le regard perdu dans le vague.
3 **vt: to ~ sb in the face** dévisager qn, fixer qn du regard, regarder qn dans le blanc des yeux; **where are my gloves? — here, they're staring you in the face!** où sont mes gants? — ils sont là devant ton nez *or* tu as le nez dessus!; **they're certainly in love, that ~s you in the face** ils sont vraiment amoureux, cela crève les yeux; **ruin ~d him in the face** il était au bord de la ruine; **the truth ~d him in the face** la vérité lui crevait les yeux *or* lui sautait aux yeux.

▸ stare out vt sep faire baisser les yeux à.

staring ['stɛərɪŋ] **adj** *crowd* curieux; (*fig*) *colour* criard, voyant, gueulard‡. **his ~ eyes** son regard fixe; (*in surprise*) son regard étonné *or* ébahi; (*in fear*) son regard effrayé; *see* **stark.**

stark [stɑːk] 1 **adj** a (*stiff*) raide, rigide; (*bleak*) *countryside* désolé, morne; *cliff etc* à pic *inv*, escarpé; *décor* austère. (*fig*) **the ~ truth** la vérité telle qu'elle est. b (*utter*) pur, absolu, complet (*f* -ète). **it is ~ folly** c'est de la folie pure; **to be in ~ contrast with** contraster violemment avec. 2 **adv: ~ raving mad*, ~ staring mad*** complètement fou (*f* folle) *or* dingue* *or* cinglé‡; ~ **naked** complètement nu, à poil‡.

starkers‡ ['stɑːkəz] **adj** (*Brit*) nu comme un ver*, à poil‡.

starkly ['stɑːklɪ] **adv** *stand out* d'une façon frappante; *contrast* violemment. ~ **clear** *or* **evident** d'une évidence frappante.

starkness ['stɑːknɪs] **n** (*see* **stark 1a**) raideur *f*, rigidité *f*; désolation *f*.

starless ['stɑːlɪs] **adj** sans étoiles.

starlet ['stɑːlɪt] **n** (*Cine*) starlette *f*.

starling ['stɑːlɪŋ] **n** étourneau *m*, sansonnet *m*.

starry ['stɑːrɪ] 1 **adj** *sky* étoilé, parsemé d'étoiles; *night* étoilé. 2

comp ▸ starry-eyed *person* (*idealistic*) idéaliste; (*innocent*) innocent, ingénu; (*from wonder*) éberlué; (*from love*) éperdument amoureux, ébloui; **in starry-eyed wonder** le regard plein d'émerveillement, complètement ébloui.

start [stɑːt] 1 n a (*beginning*) *[speech, book, film, career etc]* commencement *m*, début *m*; *[negotiations]* ouverture *f*, amorce *f*; (*Sport*) *[race etc]* départ *m*; (*starting line*) (point *m* de) départ. **the ~ of the academic year** la rentrée universitaire et scolaire; **that was the ~ of all the trouble** c'est là que tous les ennuis ont commencé; **at the ~** au commencement, au début; **from the ~** dès le début, dès le commencement; **for a ~** d'abord, pour commencer; **from ~ to finish** du début jusqu'à la fin, de bout en bout, d'un bout à l'autre; **to get off to a good** *or* **brisk** *or* **fast ~** bien commencer, bien démarrer; **to get a good ~ in life** bien débuter dans la vie; **they gave their son a good ~ in life** ils ont fait ce qu'il fallait pour que leur fils débute (*subj*) bien dans la vie; **that was a good ~ to his career** cela a été un bon début *or* un début prometteur pour sa carrière; **to get off to a bad** *or* **slow ~** (*lit, fig*) mal démarrer, mal commencer; **it's off to a good/bad ~** c'est bien/mal parti; **to make a ~** commencer; **to make an early ~** commencer de bonne heure; (*in journey*) partir de bonne heure; **to make a fresh ~** recommencer (à zéro*); (*Sport*) **to be lined up for the ~** être sur la ligne de départ; (*Sport*) **the whistle blew for the ~ of the race** le coup de sifflet a annoncé le départ de la course; (*Sport*) **wait for the ~** attendez le signal du départ; *see* **false** *etc*.

b (*advantage*) (*Sport*) avance *f*; (*fig*) avantage *m*. **will you give me a ~?** est-ce que vous voulez bien me donner une avance?; **to give sb 10 metres' ~** *or* **a 10-metre ~** donner 10 mètres d'avance à qn; (*fig*) **that gave him a ~ over the others in the class** cela lui a donné un avantage sur les autres élèves de sa classe, cela l'a avantagé par rapport aux autres élèves de sa classe.

c (*sudden movement*) sursaut *m*, tressaillement *m*. **to wake with a ~** se réveiller en sursaut; **to give a ~** sursauter, tressaillir; **to give sb a ~** faire sursauter *or* tressaillir qn; **you gave me such a ~!** ce que vous m'avez fait peur!; *see* **fit²**.

2 comp ▸ **start-up** *[machine]* démarrage *m*, mise *f* en route; *[business]* lancement *m*, mise en route; **start-up costs** (*Comm etc*) frais *mpl* de lancement *or* de démarrage; **start-up money** capital *m* initial *or* de lancement.

3 vt a (*begin*) commencer (*to do, doing* à faire, de faire); se mettre (*to do, doing* à faire); *work* commencer, se mettre à; *task* entreprendre; *song* commencer (à chanter), entonner; *attack* déclencher; *bottle* entamer, déboucher; *book, letter [writer]* commencer (à écrire); *[reader]* commencer (à lire). **to ~ a cheque book/a page** commencer *or* prendre un nouveau carnet de chèques/une nouvelle page; **to ~ a journey** partir en voyage; **to get ~ed** *see* **3d**; **he ~ed the day with a glass of milk** il a bu un verre de lait pour bien commencer la journée; **to ~ the day right** bien commencer la journée, se lever du pied droit; **to ~ life as** débuter dans la vie comme; **that doesn't (even) ~ to compare with ...** cela est loin d'être comparable à ..., cela n'a rien de comparable avec ...; **it soon ~ed to rain** il n'a pas tardé à pleuvoir; **I'd ~ed to think you were not coming** je commençais à croire que tu ne viendrais pas; **to ~ again** *or* **afresh** recommencer (*to do* à faire), recommencer à zéro*; **don't ~ that again!** tu ne vas pas recommencer!; **"it's late" he ~ed** "il est tard" commença-t-il.

b (*originate, initiate: often ~ off, ~ up*) *discussion* commencer, ouvrir; *conversation* amorcer, engager; *quarrel, argument, dispute* déclencher, faire naître; *reform, movement, series of events* déclencher; *fashion* lancer; *phenomenon, institution* donner naissance à; *custom, policy* inaugurer; *war* causer; *rumour* donner naissance à, faire naître. **to ~ (up) a fire** (*in grate etc*) allumer un feu, faire du feu; (*accidentally*) mettre le feu, provoquer un incendie; **you'll ~ a fire if you go on doing that!** tu vas mettre le feu à la maison *or* tu vas provoquer un incendie si tu fais ça!; **she has ~ed a baby*** elle est enceinte; *see* **family, slate 1**.

c (*cause to ~; also ~ up*) *engine, vehicle* mettre en marche, démarrer; *clock* mettre en marche; (*also ~ off*) *race* donner le signal du départ. (*fig*) **he ~ed the ball rolling by saying ...** pour commencer, il a dit ...; **he blew the whistle to ~ the runners (off)** il a sifflé pour donner le signal du départ; **he ~ed the new clerk (off) in the sales department** il a d'abord mis *or* affecté le nouvel employé au service des ventes; **they ~ed her (off) as a typist** d'abord *or* pour commencer ils l'ont employée comme dactylo; **to ~ sb (off** *or* **out) on a career** lancer *or* établir qn dans une carrière; **if you ~ him (off) on that subject ...** si tu le lances sur ce sujet ...; **that ~ed him (off) sneezing/remembering** *etc* alors il s'est mis à éternuer/à se souvenir *etc*; **to get ~ed** *see* **3d**; (*lit, fig*) **to ~ a hare** lever un lièvre.

d **to get ~ed** (*vi*) commencer, démarrer; (*vt*) (*gen*) faire commencer, faire démarrer; *engine, vehicle* mettre en marche, faire démarrer; *clock* mettre en marche; *project* faire démarrer; **to get ~ed on (doing) sth** commencer (à faire) qch; **let's get ~ed!** allons-y!, on s'y met!*; **to get sb ~ed on (doing) sth** faire commencer qch à qn; **once I get ~ed I work very quickly** une fois lancé je travaille très vite; **just to get ~ed, they ...** rien que pour mettre l'affaire en route *or* rien que pour démarrer, ils ... .

4 vi a (*also ~ off, ~ out*) *[person]* commencer, s'y mettre; *[speech, programme, meeting, ceremony]* commencer (*with* par). **let's ~!** commençons!, allons-y!, on s'y met!*; **we must ~ at once** il faut commencer *or* nous y mettre immédiatement; **well, to ~ at the beginning** eh bien, pour commencer par le commencement; **it's ~ing (off) rather well/badly** cela s'annonce plutôt bien/mal; **to ~ (off) well in life** bien débuter dans la vie; **to ~ (out** *or* **up) in business** se lancer dans les affaires; **just where the hair ~s** à la naissance des cheveux; **before October ~s** avant le début d'octobre; **to ~ again** *or* **afresh** recommencer (à zéro*); **classes ~ on Monday** les cours commencent *or* reprennent lundi; **the classes ~ (up) again soon** les cours reprennent bientôt, c'est bientôt la rentrée; **~ing from Monday** à partir de lundi; **to ~ (off) by doing** commencer par faire; **~ by putting everything away** commence par tout ranger; **to ~ with sth** commencer *or* débuter par qch; **~ with me!** commencez par moi!; **to ~ with there were only 3 of them, but later ...** (tout) d'abord ils n'étaient que 3, mais plus tard ...; **this is false to ~ with** pour commencer *or* d'abord c'est faux; **we only had 100 francs to ~ with** nous n'avions que 100 F pour commencer *or* au début; **~ on a new page** prenez une nouvelle page; **he ~ed (off) in the sales department/as a clerk** il a débuté dans le service des ventes/comme employé; **he ~ed (off** *or* **out) as a Marxist** il a commencé par être marxiste, au début *or* au départ il a été marxiste; **he ~ed (off) with the intention of writing a thesis** au début son intention était d'écrire *or* il avait l'intention d'écrire une thèse; **he ~ed (out) to say that ...** son intention était de dire que ... .

b (*broach*) **to ~ on a book** *[writer]* commencer (à écrire) un livre; *[reader]* commencer (à lire) un livre; **to ~ on a course of study** commencer *or* entreprendre un programme d'études; **they had ~ed on a new bottle** ils avaient débouché *or* entamé une nouvelle bouteille; **I ~ed on the job last week** (*employment*) j'ai commencé à travailler la semaine dernière; (*task*) je m'y suis mis la semaine dernière; *see also* **start on**.

c (*also ~ up*) *[music, noise, guns]* commencer, retentir; *[fire]* commencer, prendre; *[river]* prendre sa source; *[road]* partir (*at* de); *[political party, movement, custom]* commencer, naître. **that's when the trouble ~s** c'est alors *or* là que les ennuis commencent; **it all ~ed when he refused to pay** toute cette histoire a commencé *or* tout a commencé quand il a refusé de payer.

d (*leave: also ~ off, ~ out*) *[person]* partir, se mettre en route; *[ship]* partir; *[train]* partir, démarrer, se mettre en marche. **to ~ (off** *or* **out) from London/for Paris/on a journey** partir de Londres/pour Paris/en voyage; (*Sport*) **10 horses ~ed and only 3 finished** 10 chevaux ont pris le départ mais 3 seulement ont fini la course; **he ~ed (off** *or* **out) along the corridor** il s'est engagé dans le couloir; **he ~ed (off** *or* **out) down the street** il a commencé à descendre la rue.

e (*also ~ up*) *[car, engine, machine]* démarrer, se mettre en route; *[clock]* se mettre à marcher. **my car won't ~** ma voiture ne veut pas démarrer*.

f (*jump nervously*) *[person]* sursauter, tressaillir; *[animal]* tressaillir, avoir un soubresaut. **to ~ to one's feet** sauter sur ses pieds, se lever brusquement; **he ~ed forward** il a fait un mouvement brusque en avant; (*fig*) **his eyes were ~ing out of his head** les yeux lui sortaient de la tête; **tears ~ed to her eyes** les larmes lui sont montées aux yeux.

g *[timbers]* jouer.

▸ **start back** vi a (*return*) prendre le chemin du retour, repartir. b (*recoil*) *[person, horse etc]* reculer soudainement, faire un bond en arrière.

▸ **start in** vi s'y mettre, s'y coller*. **start in!** allez-y!

▸ **start off** 1 vi *see* **start 4a, 4d**. 2 vt sep *see* **start 3b, 3c**.

▸ **start on** vt fus (*: *pick on, nag*) s'en prendre à; *see also* **start 4b**.

▸ **start out** vi *see* **start 4a, 4d**.

▸ **start up** 1 vi *see* **start 4a, 4c, 4e**. 2 vt sep *see* **start 3b, 3c**. 3 **start-up** n *see* **start 2**.

starter ['stɑːtəʳ] 1 n a (*Sport*) (*official*) starter *m*; (*horse, runner*) partant *m*. (*Sport*) **to be under ~'s orders** *[runner]* être à ses marques; *[horse]* être sous les ordres du starter; (*fig*) **to be a slow ~** être lent au départ *or* à démarrer; (*Scol etc*) **the child was a late ~** cet enfant a mis du temps à se développer; (*fig*) **it's a non-~*** ça ne vaut rien, ça n'a pas l'ombre d'une chance. b (*also ~ button*) (*Aut*) démarreur *m*; (*on machine etc*) bouton *m* de démarrage; (*also ~ motor*) démarreur. c (*Brit: in meal*) hors-d'œuvre *m inv*. **for ~s*** (*food*) comme hors-d'œuvre; (*fig: for a start*) pour commencer, d'abord. 2 comp ▸ **starter flat** appartement *m* idéal pour un premier achat.

starting ['stɑːtɪŋ] comp ▸ **starting block** (*Athletics*) starting block *m*, bloc *m* de départ ▸ **starting gate** (*Racing*) starting-gate *m* ▸ **starting grid** (*Motor Racing*) grille *f* de départ ▸ **starting handle** (*Brit Aut*) manivelle *f* ▸ **starting line** (*Sport*) ligne *f* de départ ▸ **starting pistol** pistolet *m* de starter ▸ **starting point** point *m* de départ ▸ **starting post** (*Sport*) ligne *f* de départ ▸ **starting price** (*St Ex*) prix *m* initial; (*Racing*) cote *f* de départ ▸ **starting salary** salaire *m* d'embauche ▸ **starting stalls** (*Horse-racing*) stalles *fpl* de départ.

startle ['stɑːtl] vt *[sound, sb's arrival]* faire sursauter *or* tressaillir *or* tressauter; *[news, telegram]* alarmer. **it ~d him out of his sleep** cela l'a réveillé en sursaut; **to ~ sb out of his wits** donner un (drôle* de) choc à qn; **you ~d me!** vous m'avez fait peur!

startled ['stɑːtld] **adj** *animal* effarouché; *person* très surpris, saisi, ahuri; *expression, voice* très surpris.

startling ['stɑːtlɪŋ] **adj** (*surprising*) surprenant, saisissant, ahurissant; (*alarming*) alarmant.

startlingly ['stɑːtlɪŋlɪ] **adv**: ~ **blue eyes** yeux *mpl* d'un bleu saisissant; ~ **modern building** bâtiment *m* d'une modernité saisissante; ~ **high price** prix *m* exorbitant *or* ahurissant; ~ **close** à une proximité alarmante.

starvation [stɑː'veɪʃən] 1 **n** (*NonC*) inanition *f*. **they are threatened with** ~ ils risquent de mourir d'inanition *or* de faim, la famine les menace. 2 **comp** *rations, wages* de famine ▸**starvation diet: to be on a starvation diet** (*lit*) être sérieusement *or* dangereusement sous-alimenté; (*fig* *) suivre un régime draconien ▸**starvation level: to be living at starvation level** = **to be on a starvation diet** (*lit*).

starve [stɑːv] 1 **vt** a faire souffrir de la faim; (*deliberately*) affamer. **to ~ sb to death** laisser qn mourir de faim; **to ~ o.s. to death** se laisser mourir de faim; **she ~d herself to feed her children** elle s'est privée de nourriture pour donner à manger à ses enfants; **you don't have to ~ yourself in order to slim** tu peux maigrir sans te laisser mourir de faim; **to ~ sb into submission** soumettre qn par la faim; (*Mil*) **to ~ a town into surrender** amener une ville à se rendre par la famine.

b (*deprive*) priver (*sb of sth* qn de qch). **~d of affection** privé d'affection; **engine ~d of petrol** moteur *m* à sec.

2 **vi** manquer de nourriture, être affamé. **to ~ (to death)** mourir de faim; (*deliberately*) se laisser mourir de faim; *see also* **starving**.

▸**starve out vt sep** *person, animal* obliger à sortir en l'affamant.

starveling ['stɑːvlɪŋ] **n** (*person*) affamé(e) *m(f)*.

starving ['stɑːvɪŋ] **adj** affamé, famélique. (*fig*) **I'm ~*** je meurs de faim, j'ai une faim de loup.

stash* [stæʃ] 1 **vt** (*also* ~ **away**) (*hide*) cacher, planquer‡; (*save up, store away*) mettre à gauche*, mettre de côté. **he had £500 ~ed away** il avait 500 livres (*stored away*) en réserve *or* (*in safe place*) en lieu sûr. 2 **n** (*place*) planque‡ *f*, cachette *f*. **a ~ of jewellery/drugs** des bijoux cachés/des drogues cachées; **a ~ of money** un magot, un bas de laine.

stasis ['steɪsɪs] **n** (*Med, Literat*) stase *f*.

state [steɪt] 1 **n** a (*condition*) état *m*. **~ of alert/emergency/siege/war** état d'alerte/d'urgence/de siège/de guerre; **the ~ of the art** l'état actuel de la technique *or* des connaissances (*see also* 2); **in your ~ of health/mind** dans votre état de santé/d'esprit; **he was in an odd ~ of mind** il était d'une humeur étrange; **you're in no ~ to reply** vous n'êtes pas en état de répondre; (*in bank*) **I'd like to know the ~ of my account** j'aimerais connaître la position de mon compte; (*fig*) **what's the ~ of play?** où en est-on?; **in a good/bad ~ of repair** bien/mal entretenu; **to be in a good/bad ~** *[chair, car, house]* être en bon/mauvais état; *[person, relationship, marriage]* aller bien/mal; **you should have seen the ~ the car was in** vous auriez dû voir l'état de la voiture; **it wasn't in a (fit) ~ to be used** c'était hors d'état de servir, c'était inutilisable; **he's not in a (fit) ~ to drive** il est hors d'état *or* il n'est pas en état de conduire; **what a ~ you're in!** vous êtes dans un bel état!; **he got into a terrible ~ about it*** ça l'a mis dans tous ses états; **don't get into such a ~!*** ne vous affolez pas!; *see* **affair, declare** *etc*.

b (*Pol*) État *m*. **the S~** l'État; (*US*) **the S~s** les États-Unis; (*US*) **the S~ of Virginia** l'État de Virginie; **the affairs of ~** les affaires de l'État; **a ~ within a ~** un État dans l'État; *see* **evidence, minister, police, secretary** *etc*.

c (*US: S~ Department*) **S~** le Département d'État.

d (*rank*) rang *m*. **every ~ of life** tous les rangs sociaux.

e (*NonC: pomp*) pompe *f*, apparat *m*. **the robes of ~** les costumes *mpl* d'apparat; **in ~** en grande pompe, en grand apparat; **to live in ~** mener grand train; *see* **lie¹** *etc*.

2 **comp** *business, documents, secret* d'État; *security, intervention* de l'État; *medicine* étatisé; (*US: often* **S~**) *law, policy, prison, university* de l'État ▸**state apartments** appartements officiels ▸**state banquet** banquet *m* de gala ▸**State Capitol** (*US*) Capitole *m* ▸**state-certified midwife** (*Brit Med*) sage-femme *f* diplômée d'État ▸**state coach** (*Brit*) carrosse *m* d'apparat (*de cérémonie officielle*) ▸**state control** contrôle *m* de l'État; **under state control** = **state-controlled** ▸**state-controlled** étatisé ▸**statecraft** (*NonC*) habileté *f* politique ▸**State Department** (*US*) Département *m* d'État, ≃ ministère *m* des Affaires étrangères ▸**state education** (*Brit*) enseignement public ▸**state-enrolled nurse** (*Brit*) infirmier *m*, -ière *f* auxiliaire, aide-soignante *mf* ▸**state funeral** funérailles *fpl* nationales ▸**statehouse** (*US*) siège *m* de la législature d'un État ▸**State legislature** (*US Jur*) législature *f* de l'État ▸**State line** (*US*) frontière *f* entre les États ▸**state-maintained** (*Brit Scol*) public ▸**state militia** (*US*) milice *f* (*formée de volontaires d'un État*) ▸**state-of-the-art** (*fig: up-to-date*) **adj** *computer, video* dernier cri; (*fig*) **it's state-of-the-art*** c'est ce qui se fait de mieux, c'est le dernier cri ▸**State of the Union Address** (*US Pol*) Discours *m* sur l'état de l'Union ▸**state-owned** étatisé ▸**State police** (*US*) police *f* de l'État; **Michigan State police** la police de l'État du Michigan ▸**state-registered nurse** (*Brit*) infirmier *m*, -ière *f* diplômé(e) d'État ▸**State Representative** (*US Pol*) membre *m* de la Chambre des Représentants d'un État ▸**State rights** (*US*) = **State's rights** ▸**stateroom** *[palace]* grande salle de réception; *[ship, train]* cabine *f* de luxe ▸**state-run** d'état ▸**State's attorney** (*US*) procureur *m* ▸**state school** (*Brit*) école publique ▸**state sector** (*Econ etc*) secteur *m* public ▸**State Senator** (*US Pol*) membre *m* du Sénat d'un État ▸**stateside*** (*US*) aux États-Unis, ≃ chez nous ▸**statesman** *see* **statesman** ▸**state socialism** (*Pol Econ*) socialisme *m* d'État ▸**State's rights** (*US*) droits particuliers de l'État ▸**state-subsidised** subventionné par l'État ▸**state-trading countries** (*Econ*) pays *mpl* à commerce d'État ▸**state trooper** (*US*) ≃ gendarme *m* ▸**State university** (*US*) Université *f* de l'État ▸**state visit: to go on** *or* **make a state visit to a country** se rendre en visite officielle *or* faire un voyage officiel dans un pays ▸**state-wide adj, adv** (*US*) d'un bout à l'autre de l'État.

3 **vt** déclarer, affirmer (*that* que); *one's views, the facts* exposer, donner, formuler; *time, place* fixer, spécifier; *conditions* poser, formuler; *theory, restrictions* formuler; *problem* énoncer, poser. **I also wish to ~ that ...** je voudrais ajouter que ...; **it is ~d in the records that ...** il est écrit *or* mentionné dans les archives que ...; **I have seen it ~d that ...** j'ai lu quelque part que ...; **as ~d above** ainsi qu'il est dit plus haut; **~ your name and address** déclinez vos nom, prénoms et adresse; (*written*) inscrivez vos nom, prénoms et adresse; **cheques must ~ the sum clearly** les chèques doivent indiquer la somme clairement; **he was asked to ~ his case** on lui a demandé de présenter ses arguments; (*Jur*) **to ~ the case for the prosecution** présenter le dossier de l'accusation.

stated ['steɪtɪd] **adj** *date, sum* fixé; *interval* fixe; *limit* prescrit. **on ~ days** à jours fixes; **at the ~ time, at the time ~** à l'heure dite.

statehood ['steɪthʊd] **n** (*NonC*) **to achieve ~** devenir un État.

stateless ['steɪtlɪs] **adj** apatride. **~ person** apatride *mf*.

stateliness ['steɪtlɪnɪs] **n** majesté *f*, caractère imposant.

stately ['steɪtlɪ] **adj** majestueux, imposant. (*Brit*) **~ home** château *m* (*de l'aristocratie*).

statement ['steɪtmənt] **n** a (*NonC*) *[one's views, the facts]* exposition *f*, formulation *f*; *[time, place]* spécification *f*; *[theory, restrictions, conditions]* formulation; *[problem]* énonciation *f*. b (*written, verbal*) déclaration *f*; (*Jur*) déposition *f*. **official ~** communiqué officiel; **to make a ~** (*gen, Press*) faire une déclaration; (*Jur*) faire une déposition, déposer; (*Jur*) **~ of grounds** exposé *m* des motifs. c (*Fin: of accounts etc: bill*) relevé *m*; (*Comm: bill*) facture *f*; (*also* **bank ~**) relevé de compte. d (*Ling*) assertion *f*.

statesman ['steɪtsmən] **n, pl statesmen** homme *m* d'État. (*fig*) **he is a real ~** il est extrêmement diplomate; *see* **elder¹**.

statesmanlike ['steɪtsmənlaɪk] **adj** diplomatique.

statesmanship ['steɪtsmənʃɪp] **n** (*NonC*) habileté *f* politique, diplomatie *f*.

statesmen ['steɪtsmən] **npl of statesman**.

static ['stætɪk] 1 **adj** (*gen*) statique. 2 **n** (*NonC*) a **~s** statique *f*. b (*Elec, Rad, TV etc*) parasites *mpl*; (*fig: criticism etc*) savon‡ *m*, engueulade* *f*. (*US*) **he gave me a lot of ~ about** il m'a drôlement engueulé‡ à propos de.

station ['steɪʃən] 1 **n** a (*place*) poste *m*, station *f*; (*fire ~*) caserne *f* de pompiers; (*lifeboat ~*) centre *m* *or* poste (de secours en mer); (*Mil*) poste (militaire); (*Police*) poste *or* commissariat *m* (de police), gendarmerie *f*; (*Elec: power ~*) centrale *f* (électrique); (*Rad*) station de radio, poste émetteur; (*Austral: sheep/cattle ranch*) élevage *m* (de moutons/de bétail), ranch *m*. **naval ~** station navale; (*Rad*) **foreign ~s** stations étrangères; (*Telec*) **calling all ~s** appel à tous les émetteurs; (*Rel*) **the S~s of the Cross** les Stations de la Croix, le Chemin de (la) Croix; *see* **frontier, petrol, pump¹, service** *etc*.

b (*Rail*) gare *f*; *[underground]* station *f*. **bus** *or* **coach ~** gare routière; **the train came into the ~** le train est entré en gare; (*in underground*) la rame est entrée dans la station; *see* **change** *etc*.

c (*position*) poste *m* (*also Mil*), place *f*, position *f*. **to take up one's ~** prendre position, se placer; **from my ~ by the window** de la fenêtre où je m'étais posté *or* où je me trouvais.

d (*rank*) condition *f*, rang *m*. **one's ~ in life** son rang *or* sa situation social(e), sa place dans la société; **to get ideas above one's ~** avoir des idées de grandeur; **to marry beneath one's ~**† faire une mésalliance.

e (*US Telec*) poste *m*. **give me ~ 101** je voudrais le poste 101.

2 **comp** (*Rail*) *staff, bookstall etc* de (la) gare ▸**station break:** (*US Rad*) **to take a station break** tourner quelques pages de publicité ▸**station master** (*Rail*) chef *m* de gare ▸**station officer** (*Brit Police*) responsable *mf* d'un poste de police ▸**station wag(g)on** (*US Aut*) break *m*, station-wagon *f*.

3 **vt** *people* placer, mettre, poster; *look-out, troops, ship* poster; *tanks, guns* placer, installer, mettre. **to ~ o.s.** se placer, se poster; **to be ~ed at** *[troops, regiment]* être en *or* tenir garnison à; *[ships, sailors]* être en station à.

stationary ['steɪʃənərɪ] **adj** (*motionless*) *person, ship, vehicle etc* stationnaire, immobile; (*fixed*) *crane etc* fixe.

stationer ['steɪʃənəʳ] **n** papetier *m*, -ière *f*. **~'s (shop)** papeterie *f*.

stationery ['steɪʃənərɪ] 1 **n** (*NonC*) papeterie *f*, papier *m* et petits articles de bureau; (*writing paper*) papier à lettres. 2 **comp**

►**Stationery Office:** (*Brit*) **His** (*or* **Her**) **Majesty's Stationery Office** ≃ l'Imprimerie nationale (*fournit aussi de la papeterie à l'administration et publie une gamme étendue d'ouvrages et de brochures didactiques*).

statistic [stə'tɪstɪk] 1 n ~s statistiques *fpl*, chiffres *mpl*; (*hum: woman's*) mensurations *fpl*; **a set of ~s** une statistique; **these ~s are not reliable** on ne peut pas se fier à ces chiffres *or* à ces statistiques; **~s suggest that ...** la statistique *or* les statistiques suggère(nt) que ...; *see* **vital, statistics.** 2 adj = **statistical.**

statistical [stə'tɪstɪkəl] adj *error* de statistique(s); *probability, table* statistique; *expert* en statistique(s).

statistically [stə'tɪstɪkəlɪ] adv statistiquement.

statistician [ˌstætɪs'tɪʃən] n statisticien(ne) *m(f)*.

statistics [stə'tɪstɪks] n (*NonC*) statistique *f*.

stative ['staɪtɪv] adj (*Ling*) ~ **verb** verbe *m* d'état.

stator ['steɪtəʳ] n stator *m*.

statuary ['stætjʊərɪ] 1 adj statuaire. 2 n (*art*) statuaire *f*; (*statues collectively*) statues *fpl*.

statue ['stætjuː] n statue *f*. **the S~ of Liberty** la Statue de la Liberté.

statuesque [ˌstætjʊ'esk] adj sculptural.

statuette [ˌstætjʊ'et] n statuette *f*.

stature ['stætʃəʳ] n stature *f*, taille *f*; (*fig*) calibre *m*, importance *f*, envergure *f*. **of short ~** court de stature *or* de taille; **he is a writer of some ~** c'est un écrivain d'une certaine envergure *or* d'un certain calibre; **his ~ as a painter increased when ...** il a pris de l'envergure *or* de l'importance en tant que peintre quand ...; **moral/intellectual ~** envergure sur le plan moral/intellectuel.

status ['steɪtəs] 1 n, pl ~es a (*economic etc position*) situation *f*, position *f*; (*Admin, Jur*) statut *m*. **social ~** standing *m*; **civil ~** état civil; **what is his (official) ~?** quel est son titre officiel?, quelle est sa position officielle?; **the economic ~ of the country** la situation *or* position économique du pays; **the financial ~ of the company** l'état financier de la compagnie; **the ~ of the black population** la condition sociale *or* (*Admin*) le statut de la population noire; **his ~ as an assistant director** son standing de directeur-adjoint.

b (*prestige*) *[person]* prestige *m*, standing *m*; *[job, post]* prestige. **it is the ~ more than the salary that appeals to him** c'est le prestige plus que le salaire qui a de l'attrait pour lui; **he hasn't got enough ~ for the job** il ne fait pas le poids* pour le poste.

2 comp ►**status report:** (*Mil etc*) **to make a status report on** faire le point sur ►**status symbol** marque *f* de standing, signe extérieur de richesse.

status quo ['steɪtəs'kwəʊ] n statu quo *m*.

statute ['stætjuːt] 1 n (*Jur etc*) loi *f*. **by ~** selon la loi; (*US Jur*) **the ~ of limitations is seven years** au bout de sept ans il y a prescription. 2 comp ►**statute book** ≃ code *m*; **to be on the statute book** figurer dans les textes de loi, ≃ être dans le code ►**statute law** droit écrit.

statutorily ['stætjʊtərəlɪ] adv statutairement.

statutory ['stætjʊtərɪ] adj *duty, right, control* statutaire; *holiday* légal; *offence* prévu *or* défini par un article de loi. **~ body** organisme *m* de droit public; (*US Jur*) **~ change** modification *f* législative; **~ corporation** société *f* d'État; **to have ~ effect** faire force de loi; (*US Jur*) **~ rape** détournement *m* de mineurs; (*fig: token: in company, on committee etc*) **the ~* woman/Black** *etc* la femme/le Noir *etc* de rigueur.

staunch[1] [stɔːntʃ] vt *flow* contenir, arrêter; *blood* étancher; *wound* étancher le sang de.

staunch[2] [stɔːntʃ] adj *support, assistance* sûr, loyal, dévoué; *friend, ally* à toute épreuve.

staunchly ['stɔːntʃlɪ] adv avec dévouement, loyalement.

staunchness ['stɔːntʃnɪs] n dévouement *m*, loyauté *f*.

stave [steɪv] (vb: pret, ptp **stove** *or* **staved**) n *[barrel etc]* douve *f*; (*Mus*) portée *f*; (*Poetry*) stance *f*, strophe *f*.

►**stave in** vt sep défoncer, enfoncer.

►**stave off** vt sep *danger* écarter, conjurer; *threat* dissiper, conjurer; *ruin, disaster, defeat* éviter, conjurer; *hunger* tromper; *attack* parer. **in an attempt to stave off the time when ...** en essayant de retarder le moment où ... .

staves [steɪvz] npl of **staff**[2], **staff**[3].

stay[1] [steɪ] 1 n a séjour *m*. **he is in Rome for a short ~** il est à Rome pour une courte visite *or* un bref séjour; **a ~ in hospital** un séjour à l'hôpital; **will it be a long ~?** est-ce qu'il restera (*or* vous resterez *etc*) longtemps?

b (*Jur*) suspension *f*. **~ of execution** sursis *m* à l'exécution (d'un jugement); **to put a ~ on proceedings** surseoir aux poursuites.

2 comp ►**stay-at-home** casanier *m*, -ière *f*, pantouflard(e)* *m(f)* ►**staying power** résistance *f*, endurance *f*; **he hasn't a lot of staying power** il se décourage facilement.

3 vt a (*check*) arrêter; *disease, epidemic* enrayer; *hunger* tromper; (*delay*) retarder; (*Jur*) *judgment* surseoir à, différer; *proceedings* suspendre; *decision* ajourner, remettre. **to ~ one's hand** se retenir.

b (*last out*) *race* terminer, aller jusqu'au bout de; *distance* tenir. **to ~ the course** (*Sport*) aller jusqu'au bout; (*fig*) tenir bon, tenir le coup*.

4 vi a (*remain*) rester; demeurer. **~ there!** restez là!; **here I am and here I ~** j'y suis j'y reste; **to ~ still, to ~ put*** ne pas bouger; **to ~ for** *or* **to dinner** rester (à) dîner; **to ~ faithful** rester *or* demeurer fidèle; (*Rad*) **~ tuned!** restez à l'écoute, ne quittez pas l'écoute; **to ~ ahead of the others** garder son avance sur les autres; **it is here to ~** c'est bien établi; **he is here to ~** il est là pour de bon; **things can't be allowed to ~ that way** on ne peut pas laisser les choses comme ça; **if the weather ~s fine** si le temps se maintient (au beau); **he ~ed (for) the whole week** il est resté toute la semaine; **he ~ed a year in Paris** il est resté un an à Paris, il a séjourné un an à Paris; *[customers, employees]* **to ~ with a company** rester fidèle à une compagnie.

b (*on visit*) **has she come to ~?** est-ce qu'elle est venue avec l'intention de rester?; **she came to ~ (for) a few weeks** elle est venue passer quelques semaines; **I'm ~ing with my aunt** je loge chez ma tante; **to ~ in a hotel** descendre à l'hôtel; **where do you ~ when you go to London?** où logez-vous quand vous allez à Londres?; **he was ~ing in Paris when he fell ill** il séjournait à Paris quand il est tombé malade.

c (*Scot: live permanently*) habiter.

d (*persevere*) tenir. **to ~ to the finish** tenir jusqu'à la ligne d'arrivée; **to ~ with a scheme*** ne pas abandonner un projet; **~ with it!*** tenez bon!

e (*liter: pause*) s'arrêter.

►**stay away** vi: **he stayed away for 3 years** il n'est pas rentré avant 3 ans; **he stayed away from the meeting** il n'est pas allé (*or* venu) *or* il s'est abstenu d'aller à la réunion; **to stay away from school** ne pas aller à l'école, manquer l'école.

►**stay behind** vi rester en arrière *or* à la fin. **you'll stay behind after school!** tu resteras après la classe!

►**stay down** vi a rester en bas; (*bending*) rester baissé; (*lying down*) rester couché; (*under water*) rester sous l'eau; (*fig Scol*) redoubler. b *[food etc]* **nothing he eats will stay down** il n'assimile rien *or* il ne garde rien de ce qu'il mange.

►**stay in** vi a *[person]* (*at home*) rester à la maison, ne pas sortir; (*Scol*) être en retenue. b *[nail, screw, tooth filling]* tenir.

►**stay out** vi a *[person]* (*away from home*) ne pas rentrer; (*outside*) rester dehors. **get out and stay out!** sortez et ne revenez pas!; **he always stays out late on Fridays** il rentre toujours tard le vendredi; **he stayed out all night** il n'est pas rentré de la nuit; **don't stay out after 9 o'clock** rentrez avant 9 heures. b (*Ind: on strike*) rester en grève. c (*fig*) **to stay out of** *argument* ne pas se mêler de; *prison* éviter; **to stay out of trouble** se tenir tranquille; **you stay out of this!** mêlez-vous de vos (propres) affaires!

►**stay over** vi s'arrêter (un *or* plusieurs jour(s)), faire une halte. **can you stay over till Thursday?** est-ce que vous pouvez rester jusqu'à jeudi?

►**stay up** vi a *[person]* rester debout, ne pas se coucher. **don't stay up for me** ne m'attendez pas pour aller vous coucher; **you can stay up to watch the programme** vous pouvez voir l'émission avant de vous coucher; **we always stay up late on Saturdays** nous veillons *or* nous nous couchons toujours tard le samedi. b (*not fall*) *[trousers, fence etc]* tenir.

stay[2] [steɪ] 1 n a (*for pole, flagstaff etc: also Naut*) étai *m*, hauban *m*; (*for wall*) étai, étançon *m*; (*fig*) soutien *m*, support *m*. b (†: *corsets*) ~s corset *m*. 2 vt (*also* ~ **up**) (*also Naut*) haubaner, étayer.

stayer ['steɪəʳ] n (*horse*) stayer *m*, cheval *m* qui a du fond; (*runner*) coureur *m* qui a du fond *or* de la résistance physique. **he's a ~** (*Sport*) il a du fond, il est capable d'un effort prolongé; (*fig*) il n'abandonne pas facilement, il va jusqu'au bout de ce qu'il entreprend.

STD [ˌestiː'diː] a (*Brit Telec*) (abbr of **subscriber trunk dialling**) automatique *m*. **to phone ~** téléphoner par l'automatique; **~ code** indicatif *m* de zone. b (abbr of **sexually transmitted disease**) M.S.T. *f*. **~ clinic** ≃ service *m* de (dermato-)vénérologie.

stead [sted] n: **in my/his** *etc* ~ à ma/sa *etc* place; **to stand sb in good ~** rendre grand service à qn, être très utile à qn.

steadfast ['stedfəst] adj *person* (*unshakeable*) ferme, résolu, inébranlable; (*constant*) constant, loyal; *intention, desire* ferme; *gaze* ferme, résolu. **~ in adversity/danger** inébranlable au milieu des infortunes/du danger; **~ in love** constant en amour.

steadfastly ['stedfəstlɪ] adv fermement, résolument.

steadfastness ['stedfəstnɪs] n fermeté *f*, résolution *f* (*liter*). **~ of purpose** ténacité *f*.

steadily ['stedɪlɪ] adv a (*firmly*) *walk* d'un pas ferme; *hold, grasp* d'une main ferme; *gaze, look* longuement, sans détourner les yeux; *stay, reply, insist* fermement, avec fermeté. **to stand ~** *[person]* se tenir bien droit sur ses jambes; *[chair]* être stable. b (*constantly, regularly*) *improve, decrease, rise* progressivement, régulièrement; *rain, work, sob, continue* sans arrêt, sans interruption. **the engine ran ~** le moteur marchait sans à-coups.

steadiness ['stedɪnɪs] n a (*firmness: see* **steady 1a**) stabilité *f*; solidité *f*; fermeté *f*, sûreté *f*; caractère sérieux. b (*regularity etc: see* **steady 1b**) constance *f*; uniformité *f*; régularité *f*; stabilité *f*.

steady ['stedɪ] 1 adj a (*firm*) *chair, table, pole* stable, solide; *boat* stable; *hand* ferme, sûr; *gaze* franc (*f* franche); *nerves* solide; *person* sérieux. **to hold** *or* **keep ~** *wobbling object* assujettir; *table etc* (*with hand*) maintenir, (*with wedge*) caler (*see also* **1b**); **he isn't very ~ (on his feet)** il n'est pas très solide sur ses jambes; **the car is not very ~ on**

corners la voiture ne tient pas très bien la route dans les tournants; **he plays a very ~ game** il a un jeu très régulier, il n'y a pas de surprise avec lui; ~ **(on)!*** doucement!, du calme!; (*Naut*) ~ **as she goes!, keep her ~!** comme ça droit!; *see* **ready**.

b (*regular, uninterrupted*) *temperature, purpose, wind* constant; *improvement, decrease* uniforme, constant; *pace, speed, progress* régulier, constant; *job, prices, sales, market* stable; *demand* régulier, constant. **he's got a ~ income** il a un revenu (mensuel) régulier; **to hold** *or* **keep sth ~** *temperature, prices, demand* stabiliser qch; **we were doing a ~ 60 km/h** nous roulions à une vitesse régulière *or* constante de 60 km/h; **there was a ~ downpour for 3 hours** il n'a pas cessé de pleuvoir pendant 3 heures; **a ~ boyfriend** un copain*; **a ~ girlfriend** une copine*.

2 **adv** (*) **to go ~ with sb** sortir avec qn, fréquenter qn; **they've been going ~ for 6 months** ils sortent ensemble depuis 6 mois.

3 **comp** ►**steady-state theory** (*Phys*) théorie *f* de la création continue.

4 **n** (‡) (*male*) copain*; (*female*) copine*.

5 **vt** *wobbling object* assujettir; *chair, table* (*with hand*) maintenir, (*wedge*) caler; *nervous person, horse* calmer. **to ~ o.s.** reprendre son aplomb (*also fig*), se retenir de tomber; **to ~ one's nerves** se calmer (les nerfs); **to have a ~ing effect on sb** (*make less nervous*) calmer qn; (*make less wild*) assagir qn, mettre du plomb dans la cervelle de qn*.

6 **vi** (*also* ~ **up**) (*regain balance*) reprendre son aplomb; (*grow less nervous*) se calmer; (*grow less wild*) se ranger, s'assagir; *[prices, market]* se stabiliser.

steak [steɪk] 1 **n** (*beef*) bifteck *m*, steak *m*; (*of other meat*) tranche *f*; (*of fish*) tranche, darne *f*; *see* **fillet, frying, rump, stew 3** *etc*. 2 **comp** ►**steak and kidney pie/pudding** tourte *f*/pudding *m* à la viande de bœuf et aux rognons ►**steakhouse** ≈ grill-room *m* ►**steak knife** couteau *m* à viande *or* à steak.

steal [stiːl] **pret stole, ptp stolen** 1 **vt** *object, property* voler, dérober (*liter*) (*from sb* à qn); (*fig*) *kiss* voler (*from sb* à qn). **he stole a book from the library** il a volé un livre à la bibliothèque; **he stole money from the till/drawer** *etc* il a volé de l'argent dans la caisse/dans le tiroir *etc*; **to ~ the credit for sth** s'attribuer tout le mérite de qch; **to ~ a glance at** jeter un coup d'œil furtif à, lancer un regard furtif à; **to ~ a march on sb*** gagner *or* prendre qn de vitesse; (*Theat, also fig*) **to ~ the show from sb** ravir la vedette à qn; (*fig*) **he stole the show** il n'y en a eu que pour lui, on n'a eu d'yeux que pour lui; **to ~ sb's thunder** éclipser qn en lui coupant l'herbe sous le pied.

2 **vi** a voler. (*Bible*) **thou shalt not ~** tu ne voleras point.

b (*move silently*) **to ~ up/down/out** *etc* monter/descendre/sortir *etc* à pas furtifs *or* feutrés *or* de loup; **he stole into the room** il s'est glissé *or* faufilé dans la pièce; (*fig*) **a smile stole across her lips** un sourire erra sur ses lèvres; **a tear stole down her cheek** une larme furtive glissa sur sa joue; **the light was ~ing through the shutters** la lumière filtrait à travers les volets.

3 **n** (*US: theft*) vol *m*. (*fig: bargain*) **it's a ~*** c'est une bonne affaire.

►**steal away** 1 **vi** s'esquiver. 2 **vt sep** *child etc* prendre, enlever (*from sb* à qn); *sb's husband* voler, prendre (*from sb* à qn); *sb's affections* détourner.

stealing ['stiːlɪŋ] **n** (*NonC*) vol *m*. ~ **is wrong** c'est mal de voler.

stealth [stelθ] **n**: **by ~** furtivement, à la dérobée.

stealthily ['stelθɪlɪ] **adv** *remove, exchange* furtivement, à la dérobée; *walk, enter, leave* furtivement, à pas furtifs *or* feutrés *or* de loup.

stealthiness ['stelθɪnɪs] **n** caractère furtif, manière furtive.

stealthy ['stelθɪ] **adj** *action* fait en secret *or* à la dérobée, furtif; *entrance, look, movement* furtif. ~ **footsteps** pas furtifs *or* feutrés *or* de loup.

steam [stiːm] 1 **n** (*NonC*) vapeur *f*; (*condensation: on window etc*) buée *f*. **it works by ~** ça marche *or* fonctionne à la vapeur; (*Naut*) **full ~ ahead!** en avant toute!; (*fig*) **the building project is going full ~ ahead** le projet de construction va de l'avant à plein régime; **to get up** *or* **pick up ~** *[train, ship]* prendre de la vitesse; *[driver etc]* faire monter la pression; (*fig*) *[worker, programme, project]* démarrer vraiment* (*fig*); (*fig*) **when she gets up** *or* **picks up ~ she can ...** quand elle s'y met *or* quand elle est lancée elle peut ...; (*fig*) **to run out of ~** *[speaker, worker]* s'essouffler (*fig*); *[programme, project]* tourner court, s'essouffler; **the strike is running out of ~** le mouvement de grève commence à s'essouffler; (*fig*) **under one's own ~** par ses propres moyens; (*fig*) **to let off** *or* **blow off ~*** (*energy*) se défouler*; (*anger*) épancher sa bile.

2 **comp** *boiler, iron, turbine* à vapeur; *bath* de vapeur ►**steamboat** (bateau *m* à) vapeur *m* ►**steam-driven** à vapeur ►**steamed up***: (*fig*) **to get steamed up** se mettre dans tous ses états (*about sth* à propos de qch); **don't get so steamed up about it!** ne te mets pas dans tous tes états pour ça! ►**steam engine** (*Rail*) locomotive *f* à vapeur ►**steam heat** chaleur fournie par la vapeur ►**steam organ** orgue *f* à vapeur ►**steamroller** **n** rouleau compresseur ◊ **vt** (*fig*) *opposition etc* écraser, briser; *obstacles* aplanir; **to steamroller a bill through Parliament** faire approuver un projet de loi au Parlement sans tenir compte de l'opposition; (*fig*) **steamroller tactics** tactiques dictatoriales ►**steamship** paquebot *m*; **steamship company** ligne *f* de paquebots ►**steam shovel** (*US*) excavateur *m*.

3 **vt** passer à la vapeur; (*Culin*) cuire à la vapeur. **~ed pudding** pudding cuit à la vapeur; **to ~ open an envelope** décacheter une enveloppe à la vapeur; **to ~ off a stamp** décoller un timbre à la vapeur.

4 **vi** a *[kettle, liquid, horse, wet clothes]* fumer. **~ing hot** fumant.

b **to ~ along/away** *etc [steamship, train]* avancer/partir *etc*; (* *fig*) *[person, car]* avancer/partir *etc* à toute vapeur*; **they were ~ing along at 12 knots** ils filaient 12 nœuds; **the ship ~ed up the river** le vapeur remontait la rivière; **the train ~ed out of the station** le train est sorti de la gare dans un nuage de fumée; **to ~ ahead** *[steamship]* avancer; (*) *[person]* avancer à toute vapeur*; (* *fig: make great progress*) faire des progrès à pas de géant.

►**steam up** 1 **vi** *[window, mirror]* se couvrir de buée; *[bathroom]* se remplir de buée. 2 **vt sep** embuer. 3 **steamed-up*** **adj** *see* **steam 2**.

steamer ['stiːməʳ] 1 **n** a (*Naut*) (bateau *m* à) vapeur *m*; (*liner*) paquebot *m*. b (*saucepan*) ≈ couscoussier *m*. 2 **comp** ►**steamer rug** (*US*) plaid *m* (pour les genoux).

steamy ['stiːmɪ] **adj** a *atmosphere, heat* humide; *room, window* embué. b (*fig *: erotic*) érotique.

steed [stiːd] **n** (*liter*) coursier *m* (*liter*).

steel [stiːl] 1 **n** a (*NonC*) acier *m*. (*fig*) **to be made of ~** avoir une volonté de fer; **nerves of ~** nerfs *mpl* d'acier; *see* **stainless** *etc*.

b (*sharpener*) aiguisoir *m*, fusil *m*; (*for striking sparks*) briquet† *m*, fusil†; (*liter: sword/dagger*) fer *m*; *see* **cold** *etc*.

2 **comp** (*made of steel*) *knife, tool* d'acier; (*Ind*) *manufacture* de l'acier; (*Ind: gen, also of ~ production*) sidérurgique; (*Ind*) *dispute, strike* des sidérurgistes, des (ouvriers) métallurgistes; (*St Ex*) *shares, prices* de l'acier ►**steel band** steel band *m* ►**steel-clad** bardé de fer ►**steel engraving** gravure *f* sur acier ►**steel grey** gris acier *inv*, gris métallisé *inv* ►**steel guitar** guitare *f* aux cordes d'acier ►**steel helmet** casque *m* ►**steel industry** sidérurgie *f*, industrie *f* sidérurgique ►**steel maker, steel manufacturer** fabricant *m* d'acier, aciériste *m* ►**steel mill** = **steelworks** ►**steel-plated** revêtu d'acier ►**steel tape** (*Carpentry etc*) mètre *m* à ruban métallique ►**steel wool** (*NonC*) (*for floors*) paille *f* de fer; (*for saucepans*) tampon *m* métallique ►**steelworker** sidérurgiste *m*, (ouvrier *m*) métallurgiste *m* ►**steelworks** aciérie *f* ►**steelyard** balance *f* romaine.

3 **vt** (*fig*) **to ~ o.s.** *or* **one's heart to do** s'armer de courage pour faire; **to ~ o.s. against** se cuirasser contre.

steely ['stiːlɪ] 1 **adj** *material, substance* dur comme l'acier; *appearance* de l'acier; *colour* acier *inv*; (*fig*) *person* dur, insensible; *eyes* dur; *gaze, expression* d'acier, dur; *refusal, attitude* inflexible, inébranlable.

2 **comp** ►**steely blue** bleu acier *inv* ►**steely-eyed** au regard d'acier ►**steely grey** gris acier *inv*, gris métallisé *inv* ►**steely-hearted** au cœur d'acier *or* de bronze.

steep¹ [stiːp] **adj** a *slope* raide, abrupt, escarpé; *cliff* à pic, abrupt; *hill* escarpé; *road* raide, escarpé; *stairs* raide. **it's a ~ climb to the top** la montée est raide pour atteindre le sommet; **a ~ path** un raidillon. b (* *fig*) *price* élevé, excessif; *bill* salé*; *story* raide*. **it's rather ~ if he can't even go and see her** c'est un peu raide* *or* fort* qu'il ne puisse même pas aller la voir.

steep² [stiːp] 1 **vt** (*in water, dye etc*) tremper (*in* dans); *washing* faire tremper, mettre à tremper; (*Culin*) macérer, mariner (*in* dans). (*fig*) **~ed in ignorance/vice** croupissant dans l'ignorance/le vice; **~ed in prejudice** imbu de préjugés; **a town ~ed in history** une ville imprégnée d'histoire; **a scholar ~ed in the classics** un érudit imprégné des auteurs classiques. 2 **vi** *[clothes etc]* tremper; (*Culin*) macérer, mariner.

steeple ['stiːpl] 1 **n** clocher *m*, flèche *f*. 2 **comp** ►**steeplechase** steeple(-chase) *m* (*course*) ►**steeplechasing** steeple(-chase) *m* (*sport*) ►**steeplejack** réparateur *m* de hautes cheminées et de clochers.

steeply ['stiːplɪ] **adv**: **to rise** *or* **climb ~** *[road etc]* monter en pente raide; *[prices etc]* monter en flèche.

steepness ['stiːpnɪs] **n** *[road etc]* pente *f* (raide); *[slope]* abrupt *m*.

steer¹ [stɪəʳ] **n** (*ox*) bœuf *m*; (*esp US: castrated*) bouvillon *m*.

steer² [stɪəʳ] 1 **vt** a (*handle controls of*) *ship* gouverner; *boat* barrer.

b (*move, direct*) *ship, car* diriger (*towards* vers); (*fig*) *person* guider; *conversation* diriger. (*Naut*) **to ~ a** *or* **one's course to** faire route vers *or* sur; **to ~ one's way through a crowd** se frayer un passage à travers une foule; **he ~ed her over to the bar** il l'a guidée vers le bar; (*fig*) **he ~d me into a good job** c'est lui qui m'a permis de trouver un bon boulot*.

2 **vi** (*Naut*) tenir le gouvernail *or* la barre, gouverner. **to ~ by the stars** se guider sur les étoiles; **he ~ed for the lighthouse** il a fait route vers *or* il a mis le cap sur le phare; **~ due north!** cap au nord!; **this car/boat doesn't ~ well** cette voiture n'a pas une bonne direction/ce bateau gouverne mal; (*fig*) **to ~ clear of** se tenir à l'écart de, éviter.

3 **n** (*US *: tip*) tuyau* *m*, conseil *m*. **a bum ~** un tuyau qui ne vaut rien.

steerage ['stɪərɪdʒ] (*Naut*) 1 **n** entrepont *m*. 2 **adv** dans l'entrepont, en troisième classe. 3 **comp** ►**steerageway** vitesse minimale de manœuvre.

steering ['stɪərɪŋ] 1 n (*NonC*) (*Aut*) (*action*) conduite *f*; (*mechanism*) direction *f*; (*Naut*) conduite, pilotage *m*. 2 comp ▸**steering arm** (*Aut*) bras *m* de direction ▸**steering column** (*Aut*) colonne *f* de direction ▸**steering committee** (*Admin etc*) comité *m* d'organisation ▸**steering gear** (*Aut*) boîte *f* de direction; (*Naut*) servomoteur *m* de barre *or* de gouvernail; (*Aviat*) direction *f* ▸**steering lock** (*Aut*) (*when driving*) rayon *m* de braquage; (*anti-theft device*) antivol *m* de direction ▸**steering system** (*Aut*) direction *f* ▸**steering wheel** (*Aut*) volant *m*; (*Naut*) roue *f* de barre *or* de timonerie.

steersman ['stɪəzmən] n, pl **steersmen** ['stɪəzmən] (*Naut*) timonier *m*, homme *m* de barre.

stellar ['steləʳ] adj (*lit*) stellaire; (*fig, esp US: superb*) superbe, excellent.

stem[1] [stem] 1 vt a (*stop*) *flow* contenir, arrêter, endiguer; *flood, river* contenir, endiguer; *course of disease* enrayer, juguler; *attack* juguler, stopper, briser. (*fig*) **to ~ the course of events** endiguer la marche des événements; (*fig*) **to ~ the tide** *or* **flow of** endiguer (le flot de). b *ski* ramener *or* écarter en chasse-neige. 2 comp ▸**stem parallel** (*Ski*) stem(m) *m* parallèle ▸**stem turn** (*Ski*) (virage *m* en) stem(m) *m*.

stem[2] [stem] 1 n a *[flower, plant]* tige *f*; *[tree]* tronc *m*; *[fruit, leaf]* queue *f*; *[glass]* pied *m*; *[tobacco pipe]* tuyau *m*; *[feather]* tige, tuyau; (*Handwriting, Printing: of letter*) hampe *f*; (*Mus: of note*) queue; (*Ling: of word*) radical *m*. b (*Naut*) (*timber*) étrave *f*; (*part of ship*) avant *m*, proue *f*. **from ~ to stern** de bout en bout. 2 comp ▸**stem ginger** rhizome *m* de gingembre confit ▸**stem-winder** montre *f* à remontoir. 3 vi: **to ~ from** provenir de, découler de, dériver de.

-stemmed [stemd] adj ending in comps: **short-/thick-stemmed** *pipe* à tuyau court/épais; **thin-/green-stemmed** *plant* à tige fine/verte; **slim-/thick-stemmed** *glass* au pied fin/épais.

stench [stentʃ] n puanteur *f*, odeur nauséabonde *or* fétide.

stencil ['stensl] 1 n (*of metal, cardboard*) pochoir *m*; (*of paper*) poncif *m*; (*in typing etc*) stencil *m*; (*decoration*) peinture *f or* décoration *f* au pochoir. (*Typing*) **to cut a ~** préparer un stencil. 2 vt *lettering, name* peindre *or* marquer au pochoir; (*in typing etc*) *document* polycopier, tirer au stencil.

stenographer [ste'nɒgrəfəʳ] n (*US*) sténographe *mf*.

stenography [ste'nɒgrəfɪ] n (*US*) sténographie *f*.

stentorian [sten'tɔːrɪən] adj de stentor.

step [step] 1 n a (*movement, sound, track*) pas *m*. **to take a ~ back/forward** faire un pas en arrière/en avant; **with slow ~s** à pas lents; (*lit, fig*) **at every ~** à chaque pas; **~ by ~** (*lit*) pas à pas, (*fig*) petit à petit (*see also* **2**); **he didn't move a ~** il n'a pas bougé d'un pas; **we heard ~s in the lounge** nous avons entendu des pas *or* un bruit de pas dans le salon; **we followed his ~s in the snow** nous avons suivi (la trace de) ses pas dans la neige; (*fig*) **to follow in sb's ~s** marcher sur les pas *or* suivre les brisées de qn; (*fig: distance*) **it's a good ~*** *or* **quite a ~* to the village** il y a un bon bout de chemin *or* ça fait une bonne trotte* d'ici au village; (*fig*) **every ~ of the way** *complain etc* continuellement, constamment; *argue, object* point par point; **I'll fight this decision every ~ of the way** je combattrai cette décision jusqu'au bout; *see* **retrace, watch**[2] *etc*.

b (*fig*) pas *m* (*towards* vers); (*measure*) disposition *f*, mesure *f*. **it is a great ~ for the nation to take** c'est pour la nation un grand pas à faire *or* à franchir; **that's a ~ in the right direction** c'est un pas dans la bonne voie; **the first ~s in one's career** les premiers pas *or* les débuts *mpl* de sa carrière; **it's a ~ up in his career** c'est une promotion pour lui; **to take ~s (to do)** prendre des dispositions *or* des mesures (pour faire); **to take legal ~s** avoir recours à la justice, engager des poursuites (*to do* pour faire); **what's the next ~?** qu'est-ce qu'il faut faire maintenant? *or* ensuite?; **the first ~ is to decide ...** la première chose à faire est de décider ...; *see* **false** *etc*.

c (*NonC: in marching, dancing*) pas *m*. **a waltz ~** un pas de valse; **to keep (in) ~** (*in marching*) marcher au pas; (*in dance*) danser en mesure; (*lit, fig*) **to keep ~ with sb** ne pas se laisser distancer par qn; **to fall into ~** se mettre au pas; **to get out of ~** rompre le pas; (*fig*) **to be in ~ with** *[person]* agir conformément à, être au diapason de; *[regulations]* être conforme à; **to be/march** *etc* **out of ~** ne pas être/marcher *etc* au pas; (*Mil*) **to break ~** rompre le pas; (*fig*) **to be out of ~ with** *[person]* être déphasé par rapport à; *[regulations]* ne pas être conforme à; **the unions and their leaders are out of ~** il y a déphasage entre les syndicats et leurs dirigeants.

d (*stair*) marche *f* (*also Climbing*); (*doorstep*) pas *m* de la porte, seuil *m*; (*on bus etc*) marchepied *m*. **(flight of) ~s** (*indoors*) escalier *m*; (*outdoors*) perron *m*, escalier; (*Brit*) **(pair of) ~s** escabeau *m*; **mind the ~** attention à la marche.

2 comp ▸**stepbrother** demi-frère *m* ▸**step-by-step instructions** mode *m* d'emploi point par point ▸**stepchild** beau-fils *m*, belle-fille *f* ▸**stepdaughter** belle-fille *f* ▸**stepfather** beau-père *m* ▸**stepladder** escabeau *m* ▸**stepmother** belle-mère *f* ▸**stepparent** beau-père *m*/belle-mère *f* ▸**stepparents** beaux-parents *mpl* ▸**stepped-up** *campaign, efforts* intensifié; *production, sales* augmenté, accru ▸**stepping stone** (*lit*) pierre *f* de gué; (*fig*) tremplin *m* (*to* pour obtenir, pour arriver à) ▸**stepsister** demi-sœur *f* ▸**stepson** beau-fils *m*.

3 vt a (*place at intervals*) échelonner.

b (*Naut*) *mast* arborer, mettre dans son emplanture.

4 vi faire un *or* des pas, aller, marcher. **~ this way** venez par ici; **to ~ off sth** descendre de qch, quitter qch; **he ~ped into the car/on to the pavement** il est monté dans la voiture/sur le trottoir; **he ~ped into his slippers/trousers** il a mis ses pantoufles/son pantalon; **to ~ on sth** marcher sur qch; **to ~ on the brakes** donner un coup de frein; (*US Aut*) **to ~ on the gas*** appuyer sur le champignon*; (*fig*) **~ on it!*** dépêche-toi!, grouille-toi!*; **to ~ out of line** (*lit*) sortir des rangs; (*fig*) s'écarter du droit chemin (*iro*); **to ~ over sth** enjamber qch; *see* **shoe** *etc*.

▸**step aside** vi s'écarter, se ranger.

▸**step back** vi (*lit*) faire un pas en arrière, reculer. (*fig*) **we stepped back into Shakespeare's time** nous nous sommes reportés quatre siècles en arrière à l'époque shakespearienne.

▸**step down** vi (*lit*) descendre (*from* de); (*fig*) se retirer, se désister (*in favour of sb* en faveur de qn).

▸**step forward** vi faire un pas en avant; (*show o.s., make o.s. known*) s'avancer, se faire connaître; (*volunteer*) se présenter.

▸**step in** vi entrer; (*fig*) intervenir, s'interposer.

▸**step inside** vi entrer.

▸**step out** 1 vi (*go outside*) sortir; (*hurry*) allonger le pas; (*US * fig*) faire la bombe*. 2 vt sep (*measure*) *distance* mesurer en comptant les pas.

▸**step up** 1 vi: **to step up to sb/sth** s'approcher de qn/qch. 2 vt sep *production, sales* augmenter, accroître; *campaign* intensifier; *attempts, efforts* intensifier, multiplier; (*Elec*) *current* augmenter. 3 **stepped-up** adj *see* **step 2**.

Stephen ['stiːvn] n Étienne *m*, Stéphane *m*.

steppe [step] n steppe *f*.

stereo ['stɪərɪəʊ] 1 n a (abbr of **stereophonic**) (*system*) stéréo *f*, stéréophonie *f*; (*record player/radio etc*) chaîne *f*/radio *f etc* stéréophonique *or* stéréo *inv*; (*record/tape etc*) disque *m*/bande *f* magnétique *etc* stéréophonique *or* stéréo. **recorded in ~** enregistré en stéréo(phonie). b abbr of **stereoscope, stereotype** *etc*. 2 comp *record player, cassette recorder, record, tape etc* stéréophonique, stéréo *inv*; *broadcast, recording* en stéréophonie ▸**stereo effects** effet *m* stéréo(phonique) ▸**stereo sound** audition *f* stéréophonique ▸**stereovision** vision *f* stéréoscopique.

stereo... ['stɪərɪəʊ] pref stéréo... .

stereochemistry [ˌstɪərɪə'kemɪstrɪ] n stéréochimie *f*.

stereogram ['stɪərɪəgræm] n, **stereograph** ['stɪərɪəgræf] n stéréogramme *m*.

stereophonic [ˌstɪərɪə'fɒnɪk] adj stéréophonique. **~ sound** audition *f* stéréophonique.

stereoscope ['stɪərɪəskəʊp] n stéréoscope *m*.

stereoscopic [ˌstɪərɪəs'kɒpɪk] adj stéréoscopique.

stereoscopy [ˌstɪərɪ'ɒskəpɪ] n stéréoscopie *f*.

stereotype ['stɪərɪətaɪp] 1 n (*Typ*) cliché *m*; (*process*) clichage *m*; (*fig: Psych, Soc etc*) stéréotype *m*. 2 vt (*Printing*) clicher; (*fig*) stéréotyper.

sterile ['steraɪl] adj (*all senses*) stérile.

sterility [ste'rɪlɪtɪ] n stérilité *f*.

sterilization [ˌsterɪlaɪ'zeɪʃən] n stérilisation *f*.

sterilize ['sterɪlaɪz] vt stériliser.

sterling ['stɜːlɪŋ] 1 n (*NonC*) a (*Econ*) livres *fpl* sterling *inv*. b (*also* **~ silver**) argent fin *or* de bon aloi. 2 adj a *gold, silver* fin, de bon aloi; (*fig*) *qualities, principles, worth, sense* solide, sûr, à toute épreuve; *person* de confiance. **pound ~** livre *f* sterling *inv*; **the ~ area** la zone sterling. b (*also* **~ silver**) d'argent fin *or* de bon aloi.

stern[1] [stɜːn] n (*Naut*) arrière *m*, poupe *f*; (*) *[horse etc]* croupe *f*; (*) *[person]* derrière *m*, postérieur* *m*. (*Naut*) **~ foremost** par l'arrière, en marche arrière; *see* **stem**[2].

stern[2] [stɜːn] adj *person, character* sévère, dur; *glance, expression, face, speech* sévère, sombre; *discipline* sévère, strict; *punishment* sévère, rigoureux; *warning* grave. **he was made of ~er stuff** il était d'une autre trempe, il n'était pas aussi faible qu'on le pensait.

sterna ['stɜːnə] npl of **sternum**.

sternly ['stɜːnlɪ] adv sévèrement, durement, sombrement, strictement, rigoureusement.

sternness ['stɜːnnɪs] n (*see* **stern**[2]) sévérité *f*; dureté *f*; rigueur *f*.

sternum ['stɜːnəm] n, pl **~s** *or* **sterna** sternum *m*.

steroid ['stɪərɔɪd] n stéroïde *m*.

stertorous ['stɜːtərəs] adj stertoreux, ronflant.

stet [stet] 1 impers vb (*Typ*) bon, à maintenir. 2 vt maintenir.

stethoscope ['steθəskəʊp] n stéthoscope *m*.

Stetson ['stetsən] n ® chapeau *m* d'homme à larges bords.

stevedore ['stiːvɪdɔːʳ] n arrimeur *m*, débardeur *m*, docker *m*.

Steven ['stiːvn] n Étienne *m*.

stew [stjuː] 1 n *[meat]* ragoût *m*; *[rabbit, hare]* civet *m*. (*fig*) **to be/get in a ~*** (*trouble*) être/se mettre dans le pétrin*; (*worry*) être/se mettre dans tous ses états; *see* **Irish**. 2 comp ▸**stewpan, stewpot** cocotte *f*. 3 vt *meat* (faire) cuire en ragoût, faire en daube; *rabbit, hare* cuire en civet; *fruit* faire cuire. **~ed fruit** (*gen*) fruits cuits; (*mushy*) **~ed**

apples/rhubarb *etc* compote *f* de pommes/de rhubarbe *etc;* **~ing steak** bœuf *m* à braiser; (*pej*) **~ed tea** thé trop infusé; (*fig: drunk*) **to be ~ed**⁑ être soûl*. 4 **vi** *[meat]* cuire en ragoût *or* à l'étouffée; *[fruit]* cuire; *[tea]* devenir trop infusé. (*fig*) **to let sb ~ in his own juice** laisser qn cuire *or* mijoter dans son jus.

steward ['stjuːəd] **n** (*on estate etc*) intendant *m*, régisseur *m*; (*on ship, plane*) steward *m*; (*in club, college*) intendant, économe *m*; (*at meeting*) membre *m* du service d'ordre; (*at dance*) organisateur *m*. (*at meeting etc*) **the ~s** le service d'ordre; *see* **shop**.

stewardess ['stjʊədes] **n** hôtesse *f*.

stewardship ['stjʊədʃɪp] **n** (*duties*) intendance *f*, économat *m*, fonctions *fpl* de régisseur. **under his ~** quand il était intendant *or* régisseur *or* économe.

stg (*Fin*) **abbr of sterling.**

stick [stɪk] (**vb: pret, ptp stuck**) 1 **n** a (*length of wood*) bâton *m*; (*twig*) petite branche, brindille *f*; (*walking ~*) canne *f*; (*support for peas, flowers etc*) bâton, tuteur *m*, (*taller*) rame *f*; (*for lollipop etc*) bâton; (*Mil, Mus*) baguette *f*; (*Aviat: joy~*) manche *m* à balai; (*Hockey, Lacrosse*) crosse *f*; (*Ice Hockey*) stick *m*. **~s** (*for fire*) du petit bois; (*Sport: hurdles*) haies *fpl*; **a few ~s of furniture** quelques pauvres meubles *mpl*; **every ~ of furniture** chaque meuble; (*pej: backwoods*) **(out) in the ~s*** dans l'arrière-pays, en pleine cambrousse*; (*fig*) **to use** *or* **wield the big ~** manier la trique (*fig*); (*Pol*) faire de l'autoritarisme; **the policy of the big ~** la politique du bâton; (*fig*) **to get (hold of) the wrong end of the ~** mal comprendre; (*US fig*) **to get on the ~**⁑ s'y coller*, s'y mettre; *see* **cleft, drum, shooting** *etc*.

b *[chalk, charcoal, sealing wax, candy]* bâton *m*, morceau *m*; *[dynamite]* bâton; *[chewing gum]* tablette *f*, palette *f* (*Can*); *[celery]* branche *f*; *[rhubarb]* tige *f*. **a ~ of bombs** un chapelet de bombes; **a ~ of parachutists** un groupe de saut; *see* **grease**.

c (*fig *: criticism*) critiques *fpl* désobligeantes. **to give sb a lot of ~** éreinter qn (*for, over* à propos de); **to take** *or* **get a lot of ~** se faire éreinter (*for, over* à propos de).

d (*Brit *: person*) **he is a dull** *or* **dry old ~** il est rasoir*; **he's a funny old ~** c'est un numéro*.

e (*Drugs sl*) stick *m*, joint *m* (*sl*).

2 **comp ►stickball** (*US*) *sorte de base-ball* **►stick insect** phasme *m* **►stick-in-the-mud*** **adj, n** sclérosé(e) *m(f)*, encroûté(e) *m(f)* **►stick-on adj** adhésif **►stickpin** (*US*) épingle *f* de cravate **►stick shift** (*US Aut*) levier *m* de vitesses **►stick-to-itiveness*** (*US*) ténacité *f*, persévérance *f* **►stick-up*** braquage* *m*, hold-up *m* **►stickweed** (*US*) jacobée *f* **►stickwork: his stickwork is very good** *[hockey player etc]* il manie bien la crosse *or* le stick; *[drummer]* il manie bien les baguettes; *[conductor]* il manie bien la baguette.

3 **vt** a (*thrust, stab*) *pin, needle, fork* piquer, enfoncer, planter (*into* dans); *knife, dagger, bayonet* plonger, enfoncer, planter (*into* dans); *spade, rod* planter, enfoncer (*into* dans). **to ~ a pin through sth** transpercer qch avec une épingle; **we found this place by ~ing a pin into the map** nous avons trouvé ce coin en plantant une épingle au hasard sur la carte; **a board stuck with drawing pins/nails** un panneau couvert de punaises/hérissé de clous; **to ~ a pig** égorger un cochon; **to squeal like a stuck pig** brailler comme un cochon qu'on égorge; **I've stuck the needle into my finger** je me suis piqué le doigt avec l'aiguille.

b (*put*) mettre; poser; placer; fourrer. **he stuck it on the shelf/under the table** il l'a mis *or* posé sur l'étagère/sous la table; **to ~ sth into a drawer** mettre *or* fourrer qch dans un tiroir; **to ~ one's hands in one's pockets** mettre *or* fourrer ses mains dans ses poches; **he stuck his head through the window/round the door** il a passé la tête par la fenêtre/dans l'embrasure de la porte; **he stuck his finger into the hole** il a mis *or* fourré son doigt dans le trou; **he stuck the lid on the box** il a mis *or* placé le couvercle sur la boîte; **to ~ one's hat on one's head** mettre son chapeau sur sa tête; **I'll have to ~ a button on that shirt*** il faudra que je mette *or* couse un bouton à cette chemise; **he had stuck £3 on the price*** il avait majoré le prix de 3 livres; **to ~ an advertisement in the paper*** mettre *or* passer une annonce dans le journal; **they stuck him on the committee*** ils l'ont mis (*or* collé*) au comité; (*fig*) **you know where you can ~ that!**⁑, **~ it up your ass!**⁑* tu sais où tu peux te le mettre!⁑; *see* **nose** *etc*.

c (*with glue etc*) coller. **to ~ a poster on the wall/a door** coller une affiche au mur/sur une porte; **to ~ a stamp on a letter** coller un timbre sur une lettre, timbrer une lettre; **you'll have to ~ it with glue/sellotape** il vous faudra le faire tenir avec de la colle/du scotch ®; **"~ no bills"** "défense d'afficher"; **it was stuck fast** c'était bien collé *or* indécollable (*see also* **3e**); (*fig*) **he tried to ~ the murder on his brother**⁑ il a essayé de mettre le meurtre sur le dos de son frère; (*fig*) **you can't ~ that on me!**⁑ vous ne pouvez pas me mettre ça sur le dos!

d (*esp Brit: tolerate*) *sb's presence, mannerisms etc* supporter; *person* souffrir, sentir*, pifer⁑. **I can't ~ it any longer** je ne peux plus le supporter, j'en ai plein le dos*, j'en ai ras le bol⁑; **I wonder how he ~s it at all** je me demande comment il peut tenir le coup*.

e **to be stuck** *[key, lock, door, drawer, gears, valve, lid]* être coincé, être bloqué; *[vehicle, wheels]* être coincé, être bloqué; (*in mud*) être embourbé; (*in sand*) être enlisé; *[machine, lift]* être bloqué, être en panne; **to be stuck fast** être bien coincé *or* bloqué; **to get stuck in the mud** s'embourber, s'enliser dans la boue; **to get stuck in the sand** s'enliser dans le sable; **to be stuck in the lift** être coincé *or* bloqué dans l'ascenseur; **a bone got stuck in my throat** une arête s'est mise en travers de ma gorge; **the train was stuck at the station** le train était bloqué *or* immobilisé en gare; **the car was stuck between two trucks** la voiture était bloquée *or* coincée entre deux camions; (*fig*) **I was stuck in a corner and had to listen to him** j'étais coincé dans un coin et j'ai dû l'écouter; **he was stuck in town all summer** il a été obligé de rester en ville tout l'été; **I'm stuck at home all day** je suis cloué à la maison toute la journée; **we're stuck here for the night** nous allons être obligés de passer la nuit ici; (*fig*) **he's really stuck* on her** il est vraiment entiché d'elle; **the second question stuck* me** j'ai séché* sur la deuxième question; **to be stuck for an answer** ne pas savoir que répondre; (*in crossword puzzle, guessing game, essay etc*) **I'm stuck*** je sèche*; **I'll help you if you're stuck*** je t'aiderai si tu as un problème *or* si tu ne sais pas le faire; **I'm stuck for £10*** il me manque 10 livres; **he's not stuck for money*** ce n'est pas l'argent qui lui manque; **I was stuck* with the job of organizing it all** je me suis retrouvé avec le boulot de tout organiser sur les bras*; **he stuck* me with the bill** il m'a collé* la note; **I was stuck* with the bill** j'ai récolté la note, j'ai dû me farcir la note⁑; **he stuck⁑ me (for) £10 for that old book** il m'a fait payer *or* il m'a pris 10 livres pour ce vieux bouquin; **I was stuck* with him all evening** je l'ai eu sur le dos *or* sur les bras toute la soirée.

4 **vi** a (*embed itself etc*) *[needle, spear]* se planter, s'enfoncer (*into* dans). **he had a knife ~ing in(to) his back** il avait un couteau planté dans le dos.

b (*adhere*) *[glue, paste]* tenir; *[stamp, label]* être collé, tenir (*to* à); (*fig*) *[habit, name etc]* rester. **the paper stuck to the table** le papier a collé *or* s'est collé *or* est resté collé à la table; **the eggs have stuck to the pan** les œufs ont attaché à la casserole; *[food]* **it ~s to your ribs*** ça tient au corps *or* à l'estomac; (*fig*) **the nickname stuck to him** le surnom lui est resté; (*fig*) **to make a charge ~** prouver la culpabilité de quelqu'un.

c (*remain, stay*) rester; (*remain loyal*) rester fidèle (*to* à). **to ~ close to sb** rester aux côtés de qn, ne pas quitter *or* laisser qn; **they stuck to the fox's trail** ils sont restés sur les traces du renard; **I'll ~ in the job for a bit longer** pour le moment je garde ce boulot* *or* je vais rester où je suis; (*fig*) **to ~ to** *or* **by sb through thick and thin** rester fidèle à qn envers et contre tout; **will you ~ by me?** vous ne m'abandonnerez pas?, est-ce que vous me soutiendrez?; (*fig*) **to ~ to sb like a limpet** *or* **a leech** se cramponner à qn, coller à qn comme une sangsue; **she stuck to him all through the tour** elle ne l'a pas lâché d'une semelle pendant toute la tournée; **to ~ to one's word** *or* **promise** tenir parole; **to ~ to one's principles** rester fidèle à ses principes; **to ~ to** *or* **at a job** rester dans un emploi; **~ at it!** persévère!, tiens bon!, ne te laisse pas décourager!; **to ~ to one's post** rester à son poste; (*fig*) **to ~ to one's last** s'en tenir à ce que l'on sait faire; **to ~ to one's guns*** ne pas en démordre; (*fig*) **he stuck to his story** il a maintenu ce qu'il avait dit; **decide what you're going to say then ~ to it** décidez ce que vous allez dire et tenez-vous-y *or* n'en démordez pas; (*fig*) **to ~ to the facts** s'en tenir aux faits; **~ to the point!** ne vous éloignez pas *or* ne sortez pas du sujet!; **to ~ with** *person* (*stay beside*) rester avec, ne pas quitter; *person, brand* (*stay loyal*) rester fidèle; *activity, sport* s'en tenir à; **~ with him!*** ne le perdez pas de vue!

d (*get jammed etc*) *[wheels, vehicle]* se coincer, se bloquer; (*in mud*) s'embourber; (*in sand*) s'enliser; *[key, lock, door, drawer, gears, valve, lid]* se coincer, se bloquer; *[machine, lift]* se bloquer, tomber en panne. **to ~ fast** être bien coincé *or* bloqué; **the car stuck in the mud** la voiture s'est enlisée dans la boue *or* s'est embourbée; **a bone stuck in my throat** une arête s'est mise en travers de ma gorge; (*fig*) **that ~s in my throat** *or* **gizzard*** je n'arrive pas à digérer ça; (*fig*) **the bidding stuck at £100** les enchères se sont arrêtées à 100 livres; **I got halfway through and stuck there** je suis resté coincé à mi-chemin; (*fig*) **he stuck halfway through the second verse** il est resté court *or* en carafe* au milieu de la deuxième strophe; *[house for sale]* **it may ~ for a few weeks, but it'll get sold in the end** ça risque de traîner pendant quelques semaines, mais ça finira par se vendre.

e (*balk*) reculer, regimber (*at, on* devant). **he will ~ at nothing to get what he wants** il ne recule devant rien pour obtenir ce qu'il veut; **he wouldn't ~ at murder** il irait jusqu'au meurtre; **they may ~ on** *or* **at that clause** il se peut qu'ils regimbent (*subj*) devant cette clause.

f (*extend, protrude*) **the nail was ~ing through the plank** le clou dépassait *or* sortait de la planche; **the rod was ~ing into the next garden** la barre dépassait dans le jardin d'à côté.

g (*Cards*) **(I) ~!, I'm ~ing** (je suis) servi.

►stick around* **vi** rester dans les parages; (*be kept waiting*) attendre, poireauter*. **stick around for a few minutes** restez dans les parages un moment; **I was tired of sticking around doing nothing** j'en avais assez de poireauter* sans rien faire.

►stick away vt sep cacher, planquer⁑. **he stuck it away behind the bookcase** il l'a caché *or* planqué⁑ derrière la bibliothèque.

►stick back vt sep a (*replace*) remettre (*into* dans, *on to* sur). b (*with glue etc*) recoller.

►stick down 1 **vi** *[envelope etc]* se coller. 2 **vt sep** a *envelope etc* coller. b (*put down*) poser, mettre. **he stuck it down on the table** il l'a posé *or* mis sur la table. c (*) *notes, details* noter en vitesse. **he stuck down a few dates before he forgot** avant d'oublier il a rapidement noté quelques dates.

►**stick in** 1 **vi** (*) s'y mettre sérieusement; persévérer. **you'll have to stick in if you want to succeed** vous devrez vous y mettre sérieusement si vous voulez réussir; **he stuck in at his maths** il a persévéré en maths. 2 **vt sep** a (*put in*) *needle, pin, fork* piquer, enfoncer, planter; *dagger, knife, bayonet, spade* planter, enfoncer; *photo in album etc* coller. (*fig*) **he stuck in a few quotations*** il a collé* quelques citations par-ci par-là; **try to stick in a word about our book** essaie de glisser un mot sur notre livre; *see* **oar** *etc.* b (*fig*) **to get stuck in*** s'y mettre sérieusement.

►**stick on** 1 **vi** *[label, stamp etc]* rester collé. 2 **vt sep** a *label* coller; *stamp* mettre, coller. b (*put on*) *hat, coat, lid* mettre. **stick on another record** mets un autre disque; (*fig: put the price up*) **to stick it on⁑** augmenter les prix. 3 **stick-on adj** *see* **stick 2**.

►**stick out** 1 **vi** a (*protrude*) *[teeth]* avancer; *[shirttails]* dépasser, sortir; *[rod etc]* dépasser; *[balcony etc]* faire saillie. **his ears stick out** il a les oreilles décollées; **I could see his legs sticking out from under the car** je pouvais voir ses jambes qui sortaient de dessous la voiture; **to stick out beyond sth** dépasser qch; (*fig*) **it sticks out a mile*** ça crève les yeux (*that* que).
b (*persevere etc*) tenir (bon). **can you stick out a little longer?** est-ce que vous pouvez tenir un peu plus longtemps?; **to stick out for more money** tenir bon dans ses revendications pour une augmentation de salaire.
2 **vt sep** a *rod etc* faire dépasser; *one's arm, head* sortir (*of* de). **to stick one's chest out** bomber la poitrine; **to stick one's tongue out** tirer la langue; *see* **neck**.
b (*: *tolerate*) supporter. **to stick it out** tenir le coup.

►**stick through** 1 **vi** (*protrude*) dépasser. 2 **vt sep** *pen, rod, one's finger etc* passer à travers.

►**stick together** 1 **vi** a *[labels, pages, objects]* être collés ensemble. **the pieces won't stick together** les morceaux ne veulent pas rester collés *or* se coller ensemble. b (*stay together*) rester ensemble; (*fig*) se serrer les coudes. **stick together till you get through the park** restez ensemble jusqu'à *or* ne vous séparez pas avant la sortie du parc; (*fig*) **we must all stick together!** nous devons nous serrer les coudes! 2 **vt sep** coller (ensemble).

►**stick up** 1 **vi** a **there was a mast sticking up out of the water** il y avait un mât qui sortait *or* dépassait de l'eau; **his head was sticking up above the crowd** sa tête était visible au-dessus de la foule; **your hair is sticking up** vos cheveux rebiquent*.
b **to stick up for sb*** prendre la défense *or* le parti de qn; **to stick up for o.s.*** défendre ses intérêts, ne pas se laisser faire; **to stick up for one's rights*** défendre ses droits, ne pas se laisser faire; **to stick up to sb⁑** tenir tête à qn.
2 **vt sep** a *notice etc* afficher.
b **to stick up one's hand** lever la main; **stick 'em up!*** haut les mains!; **to stick sb up⁑** dévaliser qn (sous la menace d'un revolver); **they stuck up the bank⁑** ils ont attaqué la banque (à main armée).
3 **stick-up*** **n** *see* **stick 2**.
4 **stuck-up*** **adj** *see* **stuck 2**.

►**stick with vt fus** *see* **stick 1c**.

sticker ['stɪkəʳ] 1 **n** a (*label*) autocollant *m*. **a ban the bomb ~** un autocollant anti-nucléaire; *see* **bill¹**. b (*fig*) **he's a ~*** il n'abandonne pas facilement, il va jusqu'au bout de ce qu'il entreprend. 2 **comp** ►**sticker price** (*US: in car sales*) prix *m* clés en mains.

stickiness ['stɪkɪnɪs] **n** (*see* **sticky a**) caractère poisseux *or* gluant *or* collant; viscosité *f*; moiteur *f*; chaleur *f* et humidité *f*.

sticking ['stɪkɪŋ] **adj in comps: sticking plaster** (*Brit*) sparadrap *m*; **sticking point** (*fig*) point *m* de friction.

stickleback ['stɪklbæk] **n** épinoche *f*.

stickler ['stɪkləʳ] **n: to be a ~ for** *discipline, obedience, correct clothing, good manners* insister sur, tenir rigoureusement à; *etiquette* être à cheval sur, être pointilleux sur; *grammar, spelling* être rigoriste en matière de; *figures, facts* être pointilleux sur le chapitre de, insister sur; **to be a ~ for detail** être tatillon.

sticky ['stɪkɪ] 1 **adj** a *paste, substance* poisseux, gluant; *label* gommé, adhésif; *paint, toffee, syrup* poisseux; *oil* visqueux; *road, surface, pitch* gluant; (*sweaty*) *palm* moite; (*fig*) *climate* chaud et humide. **~ hands** (*with jam etc*) mains *fpl* poisseuses; (*sweaty*) mains moites; (*fig*) **to have ~ fingers*** avoir les doigts crochus*; **~ tape** scotch *m* ®, papier collant, ruban adhésif; **it was a ~ day** il faisait une chaleur moite (ce jour-là).
b (* *fig*) *problem* épineux, délicat; *situation* délicat; *person* peu accommodant, difficile. (*Brit fig*) **to be on a ~ wicket** être dans une situation délicate; **to come to** *or* **meet a ~ end** mal finir; **to have a ~ time** passer un mauvais quart d'heure; (*longer*) connaître des moments difficiles; **he's very ~ about lending his car** il répugne à prêter sa voiture.
2 **comp** ►**sticky-fingered***, **sticky-handed*** (*fig: dishonest*) porté sur la fauche⁑.

stiff [stɪf] 1 **adj** a (*gen*) raide, rigide; *arm, leg* raide, ankylosé; *joint, shoulder, knee* ankylosé; *corpse* rigide, raide; *collar, shirt front* dur, raide; (*starched*) empesé; *door, lock, brush* dur; *dough, paste* dur, ferme, consistant. (*Culin*) **~ eggwhite** blanc d'œuf battu en neige très ferme; **as ~ as a board** *or* **a poker** *or* **a ramrod** raide comme un piquet *or* un échalas *or* la justice; **my leg is ~ today** j'ai une jambe raide aujourd'hui, je remue mal ma jambe aujourd'hui; **you'll be** *or* **feel ~ tomorrow** vous aurez des courbatures *or* vous serez courbatu demain; **he's getting ~ as he grows older** il se raidit avec l'âge, il perd de sa souplesse en vieillissant; **to have a ~ back** avoir mal au dos; **to have a ~ neck** avoir le torticolis (*see also* **2**); **to be ~ with cold** être frigorifié, être engourdi par le froid; **he was ~ with boredom** il s'ennuyait à mort; (*fig*) **to keep a ~ upper lip** rester impassible, garder son flegme; *see* **bore²**, **frozen**, **scare**, **worried** *etc*.
b (*fig*) *bow, smile* froid; *reception* froid, distant; *person* guindé, froid, distant; *resistance* opiniâtre, tenace; *exam, test* difficile; *climb* raide, pénible; *programme, course, task* ardu; *wind, breeze* fort; *price* élevé, excessif; *bill* salé*. **I could do with a ~ drink** je boirais bien quelque chose de fort; **he had a ~ whisky** il a pris un grand verre de whisky *or* un whisky bien tassé; **this book is ~ reading** ce livre n'est pas d'une lecture facile.
2 **comp** ►**stiff-necked** (*fig*) opiniâtre, entêté.
3 **n** a (⁑: *corpse*) macchabée⁑ *m*.
b (⁑: *fool*) **big ~** gros balourd *or* bêta.
c (*US* *) (*tramp*) vagabond *m*, chemineau *m*; (*laborer: also* **working ~**) ouvrier *m* manuel.

stiffen ['stɪfn] (*also* **~ up**) 1 **vt** *card, fabric* raidir, renforcer; (*starch*) empeser; *dough, paste* donner de la consistance à; *limb* raidir; *joint* ankyloser; (*fig*) *morale, resistance etc* affermir. 2 **vi** *[card, fabric]* devenir raide *or* rigide; *[dough, paste]* prendre de la consistance, devenir ferme; *[limb]* se raidir; *[joint]* s'ankyloser; *[door, lock]* devenir dur; *[breeze]* augmenter d'intensité, fraîchir; *[resistance]* devenir opiniâtre; *[morale]* s'affermir. **he ~ed when he heard the noise** il s'est raidi quand il a entendu le bruit.

stiffener ['stɪfənəʳ] **n** a (*starch etc*) amidon *m*. b (*plastic strip: in collar etc*) baleine *f*.

stiffening ['stɪfənɪŋ] **n** (*cloth*) toile *f* (*pour raidir les revers etc*).

stiffly ['stɪflɪ] **adv** *move, turn, bend* raidement, avec raideur; (*fig*) *smile, bow, greet* froidement; *say* sèchement, froidement. **they stood ~ to attention** ils se tenaient au garde-à-vous sans bouger un muscle.

stiffness ['stɪfnɪs] **n** (*see* **stiff**) raideur *f*; rigidité *f*; ankylose *f*; dureté *f*; fermeté *f*, consistance *f*; difficulté *f*, caractère ardu; froideur *f*; caractère guindé *or* distant.

stifle ['staɪfl] 1 **vt** *person* étouffer, suffoquer; *fire* étouffer; *sobs* étouffer, retenir, réprimer; *anger, smile, desire* réprimer. **to ~ a yawn/sneeze** réprimer une envie de bâiller/d'éternuer. 2 **vi** étouffer, suffoquer. 3 **n** (*Anat*) *[horse etc]* grasset *m*.

stifling ['staɪflɪŋ] **adj** *smoke, fumes* suffocant; *heat* étouffant, suffocant. **it's a ~ day*** on étouffe aujourd'hui; **it's ~ in here** on étouffe ici.

stigma ['stɪgmə] **n, pl ~s** *or* **stigmata** [stɪg'mɑːtə] stigmate *m*. (*Rel*) **the stigmata** les stigmates.

stigmatic [stɪg'mætɪk] **adj, n** (*Rel*) stigmatisé(e) *m(f)*.

stigmatize ['stɪgmətaɪz] **vt** (*all senses*) stigmatiser.

stile [staɪl] **n** a (*steps over fence, wall*) échalier *m*; (*turn~*) tourniquet *m* (*porte*). b (*Constr etc: upright*) montant *m*.

stiletto [stɪ'letəʊ] **n, pl ~s** *or* **~es** (*weapon*) stylet *m*; (*Brit: also* **~ heel**) talon *m* aiguille.

still¹ [stɪl] 1 **adv** a (*up to this time*) encore, toujours. **he is ~ in bed** il est encore *or* toujours au lit; **I can ~ remember it** je m'en souviens encore; **he ~ hasn't arrived** il n'est pas encore arrivé, il n'est toujours pas arrivé; **you ~ don't believe me** vous ne me croyez toujours pas; **I ~ have 10 francs left** il me reste encore 10 F; **he's ~ as stubborn as ever** il est toujours aussi entêté.
b (+ **comp adj**) (*even*) encore. **~ better, better ~** encore mieux; **he is tall but his brother is taller ~** *or* **~ taller** lui est grand, mais son frère l'est encore plus.
c (*nonetheless*) quand même, tout de même. **even if it's cold, you'll ~ come** même s'il fait froid vous viendrez, s'il fait froid vous viendrez quand même *or* tout de même; **he's ~ your brother** il n'en est pas moins votre frère; (*US*) **~ and all*** tout compte fait.
2 **conj** néanmoins, quand même. **it's fine — ~, you should take your umbrella** il fait beau — néanmoins, vous devriez prendre votre parapluie *or* vous devriez prendre votre parapluie quand même.

still² [stɪl] 1 **adj** (*motionless*) immobile; (*peaceful*) calme, tranquille; (*quiet*) silencieux; (*not fizzy*) *[drinks]* plat, non gazeux. **keep ~!** reste tranquille!, ne bouge pas!; **all was ~** tout était calme *or* tranquille *or* silencieux; **the ~ waters of the lake** les eaux calmes *or* tranquilles du lac; (*Prov*) **~ waters run deep** il n'est pire eau que l'eau qui dort; **be ~!**† taisez-vous!; (*fig*) **a** *or* **the ~ small voice** la voix de la conscience.
2 **adv** *sit, stand, hold* sans bouger.
3 **comp** ►**stillbirth** (*birth*) mort *f* à la naissance; (*child*) enfant *m(f)* mort-né(e) ►**stillborn** mort-né (*f* mort-née) ►**still life** (**pl ~ ~s**) (*Art*) nature morte.
4 **n** a (*liter*) silence *m*, calme *m*. **in the ~ of the night** dans le

silence de la nuit.

b (*Cine*) photo *f* affichage.

5 vt *anger, fear* calmer; *person* apaiser, tranquilliser; (*silence*) faire taire.

still[3] [stɪl] 1 n (*apparatus*) alambic *m*; (*place*) distillerie *f*. 2 vt distiller.

stillness [ˈstɪlnɪs] n (*see* **still**[2]) immobilité *f*; calme *m*, tranquillité *f*; silence *m*.

stilt [stɪlt] n échasse *f*; (*Archit*) pilotis *m*.

stilted [ˈstɪltɪd] adj *person, wording, style* guindé, emprunté; *manners* guindé, contraint, emprunté; *conversation* guindé; *book etc* qui manque de naturel *or* d'aisance.

stimulant [ˈstɪmjʊlənt] 1 adj stimulant. 2 n (*also fig*) stimulant *m*. (*fig*) **to be a ~ to** stimuler.

stimulate [ˈstɪmjʊleɪt] vt (*also Physiol*) stimuler. **to ~ sb to sth/to do** inciter *or* pousser qn à qch/à faire.

stimulating [ˈstɪmjʊleɪtɪŋ] adj *air* stimulant, vivifiant; *medicine, drink* stimulant, fortifiant; *person, book, film, experience* stimulant, enrichissant, qui fait penser *or* réfléchir; *music* stimulant, exaltant.

stimulation [ˌstɪmjʊˈleɪʃən] n (*stimulus*) stimulant *m*; (*state*) stimulation *f*.

stimulus [ˈstɪmjʊləs] n, pl **stimuli** [ˈstɪmjʊlaɪ] (*Physiol*) stimulus *m*; (*fig*) stimulant *m*. (*fig*) **to be a ~ to** *or* **for** *exports, efforts* stimuler; *imagination* stimuler, enflammer; **it gave trade a new ~** cela a donné une nouvelle impulsion *or* un coup de fouet au commerce; **under the ~ of** stimulé par.

stimy [ˈstaɪmɪ] = **stymie**.

sting [stɪŋ] (vb: pret, ptp **stung**) 1 n a [*insect*] dard *m*, aiguillon *m*. (*fig*) **but there's a ~ in the tail** mais il y a une mauvaise surprise à la fin; (*fig: of plan, draft, legislation etc*) **it's had its ~ removed** on l'a rendu inopérant; (*fig*) **to take the ~ out of** *words* adoucir; *situation* désamorcer.

b (*pain, wound, mark*) [*insect, nettle etc*] piqûre *f*; [*iodine etc*] brûlure *f*; [*whip*] douleur cuisante; (*fig*) [*attack*] mordant *m*, vigueur *f*; [*criticism, remark*] causticité *f*, mordant. **I felt the ~ of the rain on my face** la pluie me cinglait le visage; **the ~ of salt water in the cut** la brûlure de l'eau salée dans la plaie.

c (*esp US* ⁑*: confidence trick*) arnaque* *m*, coup *m* monté.

2 comp ►**stingray** pastenague *f*, terre *f*.

3 vt a [*insect, nettle*] piquer; [*iodine, ointment*] brûler; [*rain, hail, whip*] cingler, fouetter; (*fig*) [*remark, criticism*] piquer au vif, blesser. (*fig*) **stung by remorse** bourrelé de remords; **my remark stung him into action** ma remarque (l'a piqué au vif et) l'a poussé à agir; **he was stung into replying brusquely** piqué *or* blessé, il répondit brusquement; *see* **quick**.

b (⁑) avoir*, estamper*. **he stung me for £10 for that meal** il m'a eu* *or* estampé* en me faisant payer ce repas 10 livres, il a eu le toupet* de me faire payer ce repas 10 livres; **I've been stung!** je me suis fait avoir!* *or* estamper!*, c'était le coup de fusil!*

4 vi a [*insect, nettle*] piquer; [*iodine, ointment*] brûler; [*blow, slap, whip*] provoquer une sensation cuisante; [*remark, criticism*] être cuisant. **that ~s!** ça pique!, ça brûle!

b [*eyes*] cuire, piquer; [*cut, skin*] cuire, brûler. **the fumes made his eyes ~** les fumées picotaient ses yeux.

stingily [ˈstɪndʒɪlɪ] adv *praise* chichement; *spend* avec avarice; *serve* en lésinant.

stinginess [ˈstɪndʒɪnɪs] n [*person*] ladrerie *f*, avarice *f*; [*portion*] insuffisance *f*.

stinging [ˈstɪŋɪŋ] 1 adj *cut, blow, pain* cuisant; (*fig*) *remark, criticism* cuisant, mordant. **~ nettle** ortie *f* brûlante *or* romaine. 2 n (*sensation*) sensation cuisante.

stingy [ˈstɪndʒɪ] adj *person* avare, pingre, ladre; *portion, amount* misérable, insuffisant. **to be ~ with** *food, wine* lésiner sur; *praise* être chiche de; **to be ~ with money** être avare *or* ladre; **he/she is ~** il/elle est pingre, c'est un/une pingre.

stink [stɪŋk] (vb: pret **stank**, ptp **stunk**) 1 n a puanteur *f*, odeur infecte. **what a ~!** ce que ça pue!; (*fig*) **there's a ~ of corruption** cela pue la corruption, cela sent la corruption à plein nez.

b (* *fig: row, trouble*) esclandre *m*, grabuge* *m*. **there was a dreadful ~ about the broken windows** il y a eu du grabuge* à propos des carreaux cassés; **to kick up** *or* **cause** *or* **make a ~** faire toute une scène, râler*; **to kick up a ~ about sth** causer un esclandre à propos de qch, faire du grabuge* à cause de qch.

2 comp ►**stink-bomb** boule puante ►**stink-horn** phallus *m* impudique, satyre puant ►**stinkpot**⁑ salaud⁑ *m*, salope⁑ *f* ►**stinkweed** diplotaxis *m*.

3 vi a puer, empester, chlinguer⁑. **it ~s of fish** cela pue *or* empeste le poisson; **it ~s in here!** cela pue *or* empeste ici!; (*lit, fig*) **it ~s to high heaven*** cela sent à plein nez; (*fig*) **it ~s of corruption** cela pue la corruption, cela sent la corruption à plein nez; (*fig*) **the whole business ~s** toute l'affaire pue *or* est infecte *or* est ignoble; **they're ~ing with money**⁑ ils sont bourrés de fric⁑.

b (⁑*: be very bad*) [*person, thing*] être dégueulasse⁑.

4 vt *room etc* empester.

►**stink out** vt sep *fox etc* enfumer; *room* empester.

stinker⁑ [ˈstɪŋkəʳ] n (*pej*) (*person*) salaud⁑ *m*, salope⁑ *f*; (*angry letter*) lettre *f* d'engueulade⁑. (*gen*) **to be a ~*** [*person*] être affreux, être un salaud (*or* une salope); [*problem, question*] être affreux, être un casse-tête.

stinking [ˈstɪŋkɪŋ] 1 adj *substance* puant; (⁑ *fig*) infect, ignoble, vache⁑. **what a ~**⁑ **thing to do** quelle vacherie!⁑; **to have a ~* cold** avoir un rhume épouvantable *or* un sale* rhume. 2 adv: **to be ~ rich**⁑ être bourré de fric⁑, être plein aux as⁑.

stint [stɪnt] 1 n a ration *f* de travail, besogne assignée. **to do one's ~** (*daily work*) faire son travail quotidien; (*do one's share*) faire sa part de travail; **he does a ~ in the gym/at the typewriter every day** il passe un certain temps chaque jour au gymnase/à la machine; **I've done my ~ at the wheel** j'ai pris mon tour au volant; **I've finished my ~ for today** j'ai fini ce que j'avais à faire aujourd'hui.

b **without ~** *spend* sans compter; *give, lend* généreusement, avec largesse.

2 vt *food* lésiner sur; *compliments* être chiche de. **to ~ sb of sth** mesurer qch à qn; **he ~ed himself in order to feed the children** il s'est privé afin de nourrir les enfants; **he didn't ~ himself** il ne s'est privé de rien.

3 vi: **to ~ on** *food* lésiner sur; *compliments* être chiche de; **to ~ on money** être avare *or* ladre.

stipend [ˈstaɪpend] n (*esp Rel*) traitement *m*.

stipendiary [staɪˈpendɪərɪ] 1 adj *services, official* rémunéré. 2 n personne *f* qui reçoit une rémunération *or* un traitement fixe. (*Brit Jur: also* **~ magistrate**) juge *m* de tribunal de police correctionnelle.

stipple [ˈstɪpl] vt pointiller.

stipulate [ˈstɪpjʊleɪt] 1 vt stipuler (*that* que); *price etc* stipuler, convenir expressément de; *quantity* stipuler, prescrire. 2 vi: **to ~ for sth** stipuler qch, spécifier qch, convenir expressément de qch.

stipulation [ˌstɪpjʊˈleɪʃən] n stipulation *f*. **on the ~ that** ... à la condition expresse que ... (+ *fut or subj*).

stir[1] [stɜːʳ] 1 n a **to give sth a ~** remuer *or* tourner qch.

b (*fig: excitement etc*) agitation *f*, sensation *f*. **there was a great ~ in Parliament about** ... il y a eu beaucoup d'agitation au Parlement à propos de ...; **it caused** *or* **made quite a ~** cela a fait une certaine sensation, cela a eu un grand retentissement, cela a fait du bruit.

2 comp ►**stir-fry** vt faire sauter (en remuant) ◊ adj *vegetables* sauté.

3 vt a *tea, soup* remuer, tourner; *mixture* tourner; *fire* tisonner. **he ~red sugar into his tea** il a remué *or* tourné son thé après y avoir mis du sucre; **she ~red milk into the mixture** elle a ajouté du lait au mélange.

b (*move*) agiter, (faire) bouger, remuer. **the wind ~red the leaves** le vent a agité *or* remué *or* fait trembler les feuilles; **he didn't ~ a finger (to help)** il n'a pas levé *or* remué le petit doigt (pour aider); **nothing could ~ him from his chair** rien ne pouvait le tirer de son fauteuil; **to ~ o.s.*** se secouer, se bouger⁑; (*fig*) **to ~ one's stumps*** se grouiller⁑, agiter ses abattis⁑.

c (*fig*) *curiosity, passions* exciter; *emotions* éveiller; *imagination* stimuler, exciter; *person* émouvoir, exalter. **to ~ sb to do sth** inciter qn à faire qch; **to ~ a people to revolt** inciter un peuple à la révolte; **to ~ sb to pity** émouvoir la compassion de qn; **it ~red his heart** cela lui a remué le cœur; **to ~ sb's blood** réveiller l'enthousiasme de qn; **it was a song to ~ the blood** c'était une chanson enthousiasmante.

4 vi a [*person*] remuer, bouger; [*leaves, curtains etc*] remuer, trembler; [*feelings*] être excité. **I will not ~ from here** je ne bougerai pas d'ici; **he hasn't ~red from the spot** il n'a pas quitté l'endroit; **he wouldn't ~ an inch** il ne voulait pas bouger d'un centimètre; (*fig*) il ne voulait pas faire la moindre concession; **to ~ in one's sleep** bouger en dormant *or* dans son sommeil; **nobody is ~ring yet** personne n'est encore levé, tout le monde dort encore; **nothing was ~ring in the forest** rien ne bougeait dans la forêt; **the curtains ~red in the breeze** la brise a agité les rideaux; **anger ~red within her** la colère est montée en elle.

b (* *fig: try to cause trouble*) essayer de mettre la pagaïe* *or* de causer des problèmes.

►**stir in** vt sep *milk etc* ajouter en tournant.

►**stir round** vt sep (*Culin etc*) tourner.

►**stir up** vt sep *soup etc* tourner, remuer; *fire* tisonner; (*fig*) *curiosity, attention, anger* exciter; *imagination* exciter, stimuler; *memories, the past* réveiller; *revolt* susciter; *hatred* attiser; *mob* ameuter; *opposition, discord* fomenter; *trouble* provoquer; *person* secouer (*fig*). **to stir sb up to sth/to do** pousser *or* inciter qn à qch/à faire.

stir[2]⁑ [stɜːʳ] (*esp US*) 1 n (*prison*) taule⁑ *f or* tôle⁑ *f*. **in ~** en taule⁑, au bloc*. 2 comp ►**stir-crazy**⁑ rendu dingue⁑ par la réclusion.

stirrer* [ˈstɜːrəʳ] n (*troublemater*) fauteur *m* de troubles, fout-la-merde⁑ *m*.

stirring [ˈstɜːrɪŋ] 1 adj *speech, tale, music* émouvant; *years, period* exaltant. 2 n (*first sign*) [*discontent, revolt*] frémissement *m*; [*love*] frisson *m*. **a ~ of interest** un début d'intérêt.

stirrup [ˈstɪrəp] 1 n a [*rider*] étrier *m*. **to put one's feet in the ~s** chausser les étriers. b (*US Climbing*) escarpolette *f*, étrier *m*. c (*Med: for childbirth*) **~s** étriers *mpl*. 2 comp ►**stirrup cup** coup *m* de l'étrier ►**stirrup leather** étrivière *f* ►**stirrup pump** pompe *f* à main portative ►**stirrup strap** = **stirrup leather.**

stitch [stɪtʃ] 1 n (*Sewing*) point *m*; (*Knitting*) maille *f*; (*Surgery*) point de suture; (*sharp pain*) point de côté. (*Prov*) **a ~ in time saves nine** un point à temps en vaut cent; **she put a few ~es in the tear** elle a fait un point à la déchirure; **to put ~es in a wound** suturer *or* recoudre une plaie; (*Med*) **he had 10 ~es** on lui a fait 10 points de suture; (*Med*) **to get one's ~es out** se faire retirer ses fils (de suture); (*fig*) **he hadn't a ~ (of clothing) on*** il était tout nu; **he hadn't a dry ~ on him** il n'avait pas un fil de sec sur le dos; (*fig*) **to be in ~es*** se tenir les côtes, rire à s'en tenir les côtes; **her stories had us in ~es*** ses anecdotes nous ont fait rire aux larmes, ses anecdotes étaient tordantes; *see* **cable, drop** *etc.*

2 vt *seam, hem, garment* (*gen*) coudre; (*on machine*) piquer; *book* brocher; (*Med*) suturer; *see* **hand, machine.**

3 vi coudre.

►**stitch down** vt sep rabattre.

►**stitch on** vt sep *pocket, button* coudre; (*mend*) recoudre.

►**stitch up** vt sep a (*Sewing*) coudre; (*mend*) recoudre; (*Med*) suturer. b (‡ *fig: frame*) monter un coup contre. **I was stitched up** j'ai été victime d'un coup monté.

stitching ['stɪtʃɪŋ] n points *mpl*.

stoat [stəʊt] n hermine *f*.

stock [stɒk] 1 n a (*supply*) *[cotton, sugar, books, goods]* réserve *f*, provision *f*, stock *m* (*Comm*); *[money]* réserve. (*Comm*) **in ~** en stock, en magasin; **out of ~** épuisé; **the shop has a large ~** le magasin est bien approvisionné *or* achalandé*; **coal ~s are low** les réserves *or* les stocks de charbon sont réduit(e)s; (*Theat*) **~ of plays** répertoire *m*; **I've got a ~ of cigarettes** j'ai une provision *or* un stock* de cigarettes; **to get in** *or* **lay in a ~ of** s'approvisionner en *or* de, faire provision de; **it adds to our ~ of facts** cela est un complément à toutes nos données; **a great ~ of learning** un grand fonds d'érudition; (*Ling*) **the linguistic** *or* **word ~** le fonds lexical; **to take ~** (*Comm*) faire l'inventaire; (*fig*) faire le point; (*fig*) **to take ~ of** *situation, prospects etc* faire le point de; *person* jauger, évaluer les mérites de; *see* **dead, surplus** *etc.*

b (*Agr: animals and equipment*) cheptel *m* (vif et mort); (*Agr: also* **live~**) cheptel vif, bétail *m*; (*Rail*) matériel roulant; (*Ind: raw material*) matière première; (*for paper-making*) pâte *f* à papier; *see* **fat, live**[2], **rolling** *etc.*

c (*Fin*) valeurs *fpl*, titres *mpl*; (*company shares*) actions *fpl*. **~s and shares** valeurs (mobilières), titres; **railway ~(s)** actions de chemin de fer; (*fig*) **to put ~ in sth** faire cas de qch; (*fig*) **his ~ has risen** sa cote a remonté; *see* **preference, registered** *etc.*

d (*tree trunk*) tronc *m*; (*tree stump*) souche *f*; (*Horticulture: for grafting*) porte-greffe *m*, ente *f*; *see* **laughing.**

e (*base, stem*) *[anvil]* billot *m*; *[plough]* fût *m*; *[rifle]* fût et crosse *f*; *[plane]* fût, bois *m*; *[whip]* manche *m*; *[fishing rod]* gaule *f*; *[anchor]* jas *m*; *see* **lock**[1] *etc.*

f (*descent, lineage*) souche *f*, lignée *f*, famille *f*. **of good Scottish ~** de bonne souche écossaise; **he comes of farming ~** il vient d'une famille d'agriculteurs, il est d'origine *or* de souche paysanne.

g (*Cards*) talon *m*.

h (*Culin*) bouillon *m*. **chicken ~** bouillon de poulet.

i (*flower*) giroflée *f*, mathiole *f*.

j (*Hist*) **the ~s** le pilori.

k **to be on the ~s** *[ship]* être sur cale; (*fig*) *[book, piece of work, scheme]* être en chantier.

l (*tie*) cravate *f* foulard.

2 adj a (*Comm*) *goods, model* courant, de série; (*Theat*) du répertoire; (*fig: stereotyped*) *argument, joke, excuse, comment* classique, banal. (*Comm*) **~ line** article suivi; **~ size** taille courante *or* normalisée; **she is not ~ size** elle n'est pas une taille courante; **~ phrase** cliché *m*, expression toute faite.

b (*for breeding*) destiné à la reproduction. **~ mare** jument poulinière.

3 comp ►**stock book** livre *m* de magasin ►**stockbreeder** éleveur *m*, -euse *f* ►**stockbreeding** élevage *m* ►**stockbroker** *etc see* **stockbroker** *etc* ►**stock car** (*Rail*) wagon *m* à bestiaux; (*Aut Sport*) stock-car *m*; (*Aut Sport*) **stock-car racing** course *f* de stock-cars ►**stock certificate** (*Fin*) titre *m* ►**stock company** (*Fin*) société *f* par actions, société anonyme (*see also* **joint**); (*US Theat*) compagnie *f or* troupe *f* (de théâtre) de répertoire ►**stock control** (*Comm*) = **stock management** ►**stock cube** (*Culin*) bouillon-cube *m* ►**stock dividend** dividende *m* sous forme d'actions ►**stock exchange** Bourse *f* (des valeurs); **on the stock exchange** à la Bourse ►**stockfish** stockfisch *m* ►**stockholder** actionnaire *mf* ►**stock-in-trade** (*goods*) marchandises *fpl* en magasin *or* en stock; (*tools, materials; also fig: of comedian, writer etc*) outils *mpl* du métier ►**stockjobber** (*Brit*) *intermédiaire qui traite directement avec l'agent de change;* (*US: often pej*) agent *m* de change, agioteur *m* (*often pej*) ►**stock level** (*Comm*) niveau *m* des stocks ►**stock list** (*Fin*) cours *m* de la Bourse; (*Comm*) liste *f* des marchandises en stock, inventaire commercial ►**stockman** gardien *m* de bestiaux ►**stock management** gestion *f* des stocks ►**stock market** Bourse *f*, marché financier; **stock market closing report** compte rendu des cours de clôture ►**stock option** (*US Fin*) droit *m* (préférentiel) de souscription ►**stockpile** vt *food etc* stocker, faire *or* constituer des stocks de; *weapons* amasser, accumuler ◊ vi faire des stocks ◊ n stock *m*, réserve *f* ►**stockpiling** stockage *m*, constitution *f* de stocks ►**stockpot** (*Culin*) marmite *f* de bouillon ►**stockroom** magasin *m*, réserve *f*, resserre *f* ►**stock-still: to stand** *or* **be stock-still** rester planté comme un piquet; (*in fear, amazement*) rester cloué sur place ►**stocktaking** (*Brit Comm*) (*action*) inventaire *m*; **to do stocktaking, be stocktaking** (*Comm*) faire l'inventaire; (*fig*) faire le point ►**stockyard** parc *m* à bestiaux.

4 vt a (*supply*) *shop, larder, cupboard* approvisionner (*with* en); *library/farm* monter en livres/en bétail; *river, lake* peupler (*with* de), empoissonner. **well-~ed** *shop etc* bien approvisionné; *library, farm* bien fourni *or* pourvu *or* monté; *garden* bien fourni; **his memory is ~ed with facts** sa mémoire a emmagasiné des tas de connaissances.

b (*Comm: hold in ~*) *milk, hats, tools etc* avoir, vendre.

►**stock up** 1 vi s'approvisionner (*with, on* en *or* de, *for* pour), faire ses provisions (*with, on* de, *for* pour). 2 vt sep *shop, larder, cupboard, freezer* garnir; *library* accroître le stock de livres de; *farm* accroître le cheptel de; *river, lake* aleviner, empoissonner.

stockade [stɒ'keɪd] 1 n a (*fencing; enclosure*) palissade *f*. b (*US: for military prisoners*) salle *f* de police (*d'une caserne*), bloc‡ *m*. 2 vt palanquer.

stockbroker ['stɒkbrəʊkə^r] 1 n agent *m* de change. 2 comp ►**the stockbroker belt** (*Brit*) la banlieue résidentielle (*des nouveaux riches*) ►**stockbroker Tudor** (*Brit*) *style Tudor des banlieues résidentielles.*

stockbroking ['stɒkbrəʊkɪŋ] n commerce *m* des valeurs en Bourse.

Stockholm ['stɒkhəʊm] n Stockholm.

stockily ['stɒkɪlɪ] adv: **~ built** trapu, râblé.

stockiness ['stɒkɪnɪs] n aspect trapu *or* râblé.

stockinet(te) [ˌstɒkɪ'net] n (*fabric*) jersey *m*; (*knitting stitch*) (point *m* de) jersey.

stocking ['stɒkɪŋ] 1 n bas *m*; *see* **Christmas, nylon** *etc.* 2 comp ►**stocking feet: in one's stocking feet** sans chaussures ►**stocking-filler** tout petit cadeau de Noël ►**stocking mask** bas *m* (*d'un bandit masqué*) ►**stocking stitch** (*Knitting*) (point *m* de) jersey *m*.

stockist ['stɒkɪst] n (*Brit*) revendeur *m*; *see* **sole**[3].

stocky ['stɒkɪ] adj trapu, râblé.

stodge* [stɒdʒ] n (*Brit: NonC*) (*food*) aliment bourratif, étouffe-chrétien* *m inv*; (*in book etc*) littérature *f* indigeste.

stodgy ['stɒdʒɪ] adj (*filling*) *food, diet* bourratif; (*heavy*) *cake* pâteux, lourd; (* *fig*) *book* indigeste; (*) *person* rassis, sans imagination.

stogie, stogy ['stəʊgɪ] n (*US*) cigare *m*.

stoic ['stəʊɪk] 1 n stoïque *mf*. (*Philos*) **S~** stoïcien *m*. 2 adj stoïque. (*Philos*) **S~** stoïcien.

stoical ['stəʊɪkəl] adj stoïque.

stoically ['stəʊɪkəlɪ] adv stoïquement, avec stoïcisme.

stoicism ['stəʊɪsɪzəm] n stoïcisme *m*.

stoke [stəʊk] 1 vt (*also* **~ up**) *fire* garnir, entretenir; *furnace* alimenter; *engine, boiler* chauffer. 2 comp ►**stokehole** (*Naut*) chaufferie *f*; *[boiler, furnace]* porte *f* de chauffe.

►**stoke up** 1 vi (*furnace*) alimenter la chaudière; (*open fire*) entretenir le feu; (* *fig: eat*) se garnir *or* se remplir la panse*. 2 vt sep = **stoke 1.**

stoker ['stəʊkə^r] n (*Naut, Rail etc*) chauffeur *m*.

STOL [stɒl] (*Aviat*) (abbr of **short take-off and landing**) ADAC *m* (*avion à décollage et atterrissage courts*).

stole[1] [stəʊl] n (*Dress*) étole *f*, écharpe *f*; (*Rel*) étole.

stole[2] [stəʊl] pret of **steal.**

stolen ['stəʊlən] ptp of **steal.**

stolid ['stɒlɪd] adj *person* flegmatique, impassible; *manner, voice* imperturbable, impassible.

stolidity [stɒ'lɪdɪtɪ] n, **stolidness** ['stɒlɪdnɪs] n (*see* **stolid**) flegme *m*, impassibilité *f*.

stolidly ['stɒlɪdlɪ] adv flegmatiquement, d'une manière impassible, imperturbablement.

stomach ['stʌmək] 1 n (*Anat*) estomac *m*; (*belly*) ventre *m*. **he was lying on his ~** il était couché *or* allongé sur le ventre, il était à plat ventre; **to have a pain in one's ~** avoir mal à l'estomac *or* au ventre; (*fig*) **I have no ~ for this journey** je n'ai aucune envie de faire ce voyage; **an army marches on its ~** une armée ne se bat pas le ventre creux; *see* **empty, full, lie**[1], **turn, turn over** *etc.*

2 comp *disease* de l'estomac; *ulcer* à l'estomac ►**stomach ache** mal *m* de ventre; **I have (a) stomach ache** j'ai mal au ventre ►**stomach pump** pompe stomacale ►**stomach trouble: he has stomach trouble** il a des ennuis *mpl* gastriques.

3 vt *food* digérer; (*fig*) *behaviour, sb's jokes* encaisser*, digérer*, supporter. (*fig*) **he couldn't ~ this** il n'a pas pu l'encaisser*.

stomatologist [ˌstəʊmə'tɒlədʒɪst] n stomatologiste *mf*, stomatologue *mf*.

stomatology [ˌstəʊmə'tɒlədʒɪ] n stomatologie *f*.

stomp [stɒmp] 1 vi: **to ~ in/out** *etc* entrer/sortir *etc* d'un pas lourd et bruyant; **we could hear him ~ing about** on entendait le bruit lourd de ses pas. 2 vt (*esp US*) **to ~ one's feet** (*in rage*) trépigner; (*in dance*) frapper du pied. 3 n a *[feet]* martèlement *m*. b (*dance*) swing *m*.

stone [stəʊn] 1 n a (*substance; single piece; also gem*) pierre *f*; (*pebble*) caillou *m*; (*on beach etc*) galet *m*; (*commemorative*) stèle *f* (commémorative); (*gravestone*) pierre tombale, stèle *f*. **(made) of ~** de pierre; (*fig*) **within a ~'s throw (of)** à deux pas (de); (*fig*) **to leave no ~ unturned** remuer ciel et terre (*to do* pour faire); **to turn to ~, to change into ~** (vt) pétrifier, changer en pierre; (vi) se pétrifier; *see* **paving, precious, rolling, stand, tomb** *etc*.

b (*in fruit*) noyau *m*.

c (*Med*) calcul *m*. **to have a ~ in the kidney** avoir un calcul dans le rein; **to have a ~ removed from one's kidney** se faire enlever un calcul rénal; *see* **gall**[1] *etc*.

d (pl gen inv) (*Brit: weight*) = *14 livres = 6,348 kg*.

2 comp *building, wall* en pierre ▸**Stone Age** l'âge *m* de (la) pierre ▸**stone-blind** complètement aveugle ▸**stonebreaker** (*person*) casseur *m* de pierres; (*machine*) casse-pierre(s) *m*, concasseur *m* ▸**stone-broke*** (*US*) = **stony-broke*** (*see* **stony 2**) ▸**stonechat** (*Orn*) traquet *m* (pâtre) ▸**stone-cold** complètement froid; **stone-cold sober*** pas du tout ivre ▸**stonecrop** (*Bot*) orpin *m* ▸**stonecutter** (*person*) tailleur *m* de pierre(s) précieuse(s), lapidaire *m*; (*machine*) sciotte *f*, scie *f* (de carrier) ▸**stone-dead** raide mort ▸**stone-deaf** sourd comme un pot ▸**stone fruit** fruit *m* à noyau ▸**stone-ground** *flour, wheat* meulé à la pierre ▸**stonemason** tailleur *m* de pierre(s) ▸**stonewall** vi (*Cricket*) jouer très prudemment; (*fig*) donner des réponses évasives ▸**stoneware** pots *mpl* de grès ▸**stonewashed** *jeans* délavé à la pierre ▸**stonework** maçonnerie *f*.

3 vt a *person, object* lancer *or* jeter des pierres sur, bombarder de pierres. **to ~ sb to death** lapider qn, tuer qn à coups de pierre; (*Brit: excl*) **~ the crows!*** vingt dieux!*

b *date, olive* dénoyauter.

stoned‡ ['stəʊnd] adj (*drunk*) soûl*, complètement rond‡; (*Drugs*) défoncé‡.

stonily ['stəʊnɪlɪ] adv avec froideur, froidement; *stare, look* d'un œil froid.

stony ['stəʊnɪ] 1 adj *path, road, soil* pierreux, caillouteux, rocailleux; *beach* de galets; *substance, texture* pierreux; (*fig*) *person, attitude* dur, insensible; *heart* de pierre, dur; *look, welcome* froid. (*fig*) **to fall on ~ ground** ne rien donner. 2 comp ▸**stony-broke*** (*Brit*) fauché comme les blés* ▸**stony-faced** au visage impassible.

stood [stʊd] pret, ptp of **stand**.

stooge [stuːdʒ] n (*Theat*) comparse *mf*, faire-valoir *m*; (*gen: pej*) laquais *m*.

▸**stooge about‡, stooge around‡** vi rôder, errer.

stook [stuːk] 1 n moyette *f*. 2 vi moyetter.

stool [stuːl] 1 n a tabouret *m*; (*folding*) pliant *m*; (*foot~*) tabouret, marchepied† m. (*fig*) **to fall between two ~s** se retrouver le bec dans l'eau*; *see* **music, piano** *etc*. b (*fig*) *[window]* rebord *m*; (*Med*) selle *f*; (*Bot*) pied *m* (*de plante*), plante *f* mère. 2 comp ▸**stool pigeon*** indicateur *m*, -trice *f*, mouchard(e) *m(f)*; (*in prison*) mouton *m*.

stoolie‡, stooly‡ ['stuːlɪ] n (*US*) = **stool pigeon**.

stoop[1] [stuːp] 1 n a **to have a ~** avoir le dos voûté *or* rond. b *[bird of prey]* attaque *f* plongeante. 2 vi a (*have a ~*) avoir le dos voûté *or* rond, être voûté. b (*also* **~ down**) se baisser, se pencher, se courber; (*fig*) s'abaisser (*to sth* jusqu'à qch, *to do, to doing* jusqu'à faire). (*fig*) **he would ~ to anything** il est prêt à toutes les bassesses. c *[bird of prey]* plonger. 3 vt baisser, courber, incliner.

stoop[2] [stuːp] n (*US*) véranda *f*.

stooping ['stuːpɪŋ] adj *person* penché, courbé; *back* voûté.

stop [stɒp] 1 n a (*halt*) arrêt *m* (*also Ski*); (*short stay*) halte *f*. **we had a ~ of a few days in Arles** nous avons fait une halte de quelques jours à Arles; **we had a ~ for coffee** nous avons fait une pause-café; **they worked for 6 hours without a ~** ils ont travaillé 6 heures d'affilée *or* sans discontinuer; **a 5-minute ~, 5 minutes' ~** 5 minutes d'arrêt; **to be at a ~** *[traffic, vehicle]* être à l'arrêt; *[work, progress, production]* s'être arrêté, avoir cessé; **to come to a ~** *[traffic, vehicle]* s'arrêter; *[work, progress, production]* cesser; **to bring to a ~** *traffic, vehicle* arrêter; *work, progress, production* faire cesser; **to make a ~** *[bus, train]* s'arrêter; *[plane, ship]* faire escale; **to put a ~ to sth** mettre fin à qch, mettre un terme à qch; **I'll put a ~ to all that!** je vais mettre un terme *or* le holà à tout ça!

b (*stopping place*) *[bus, train]* arrêt *m*; *[plane, ship]* escale *f*; *see* **bus, request** *etc*.

c *[organ]* jeu *m*. (*fig*) **to pull out all the ~s** faire un suprême effort, remuer ciel et terre (*to do* pour faire).

d (*Punctuation*) point *m*; (*in telegrams*) stop *m*; *see also* **full**.

e (*device*) (*on drawer, window*) taquet *m*; (*door ~*) butoir *m* de porte; (*on typewriter: also* **margin ~**) margeur *m*; (*Tech*) mentonnet *m*.

f (*Phon*) (consonne *f*) occlusive *f*.

g (*Phot*) diaphragme *m*.

2 comp *button, lever, signal* d'arrêt; (*Phot*) *bath, solution* d'arrêt ▸**stop-and-go** (*US*) *see* **stop-go** ▸**stopcock** robinet *m* d'arrêt ▸**stop consonant** (*Phon*) (consonne *f*) occlusive *f* ▸**stopgap** n bouche-trou *m* ◊ adj *measure, solution* intérimaire ▸**stop-go** *see* **stop-go** ▸**stop-light** (*traffic light*) feu *m* rouge; (*brake light*) feu *m* de stop ▸**stop-off** arrêt *m*, courte halte ▸**stop order** (*St Ex*) ordre *m* stop ▸**stopover** halte *f*; (*Aviat, Rail etc*) **stopover ticket** billet *m* avec faculté d'arrêt ▸**stop-press** (*Brit Press*) (*news*) nouvelles *fpl* de dernière heure; (*as heading*) "dernière heure" ▸**stop sign** (*Aut*) (panneau *m*) stop *m* ▸**stop street** (*US Aut*) rue *f* non prioritaire ▸**stopwatch** chronomètre *m*.

3 vt a (*block*) *hole, pipe* boucher, obturer; (*accidentally*) boucher, bloquer; *leak* boucher, colmater; *jar, bottle* boucher; *tooth* plomber. **to ~ one's ears** se boucher les oreilles; (*fig*) **to ~ one's ears to sth** rester sourd à qch; **to ~ a gap** (*lit*) boucher un trou *or* un interstice; (*fig*) combler une lacune (*see also* **stop 2**); **to ~ the way** barrer le chemin.

b (*halt*) *person, vehicle, ball, machine, process* arrêter; *traffic* arrêter, interrompre; *progress* interrompre; *light* empêcher de passer; *pain, worry, enjoyment* mettre fin à; (*fig: Sport etc: beat*) battre. **to ~ sb short** (*lit*) arrêter qn net *or* brusquement; (*fig: silence*) couper la parole à qn; **to ~ sb (dead) in his tracks** (*lit*) arrêter qn net *or* brusquement; (*fig*) couper qn dans son élan; **he ~ped a bullet*** il a reçu une balle; **the walls ~ some of the noise** les murs arrêtent *or* étouffent *or* absorbent une partie du bruit.

c (*cease*) arrêter, cesser (*doing* de faire). **~ it!** assez!, ça suffit!; **~ that noise!** assez de bruit!; **to ~ work** arrêter *or* cesser de travailler, cesser le travail.

d (*interrupt*) *activity, building, production* interrompre, arrêter; (*suspend*) suspendre; (*Boxing*) *fight* suspendre; *allowance, leave, privileges* supprimer; *wages* retenir; *gas, electricity, water supply* couper. **rain ~ped play** la pluie a interrompu *or* arrêté la partie; **they ~ped £2 out of his wages** ils ont retenu 2 livres sur son salaire; **to ~ one's subscription** résilier son abonnement; **to ~ (payment on) a cheque** faire opposition au paiement d'un chèque; *[bank]* **to ~ payment** suspendre ses paiements; **he ~ped the milk for a week** il a fait interrompre *or* il a annulé la livraison du lait pendant une semaine.

e (*prevent*) empêcher (*sb's doing, sb from doing* qn de faire, *sth happening, sth from happening* que qch n'arrive (*subj*)). **there's nothing to ~ you** rien ne vous en empêche; **he ~ped the house (from) being sold** il a empêché que la maison (ne) soit vendue *or* la vente de la maison.

f (*Mus*) *string* presser; *[trumpet etc]* *hole* boucher, mettre le doigt sur.

4 vi a *[person, vehicle, machine, clock, sb's heart]* s'arrêter. **~ thief!** au voleur!; (*in work etc*) **you can ~ now** vous pouvez (vous) arrêter maintenant; (*in lesson etc*) **we'll ~ here for today** nous nous arrêterons *or* nous nous en tiendrons là pour aujourd'hui; **he ~ped (dead) in his tracks** il s'est arrêté net *or* pile*; **he ~ped in mid sentence** il s'est arrêté au beau milieu d'une phrase; (*fig*) **~ and think** réfléchissez bien; **~ and consider if** *or* **whether ...** réfléchissez si ...; (*fig*) **he never knows where to ~** il ne sait pas s'arrêter; (*fig*) **he will ~ at nothing** il est prêt à tout, il ne recule devant rien (*to do* pour faire); *see* **dead, short** *etc*.

b *[supplies, production, process, music]* s'arrêter, cesser; *[attack, pain, worry, enjoyment, custom]* cesser; *[allowance, privileges]* être supprimé; *[play, programme, concert]* finir, se terminer; *[conversation, discussion, struggle]* cesser, se terminer.

c (*) (*remain*) rester; (*live temporarily*) loger. **~ where you are!** restez là où vous êtes!; **I'm ~ping with my aunt** je loge chez ma tante.

▸**stop away*** vi: **he stopped away for 3 years** il est resté 3 ans sans revenir *or* 3 ans absent; **he stopped away from the meeting** il n'est pas allé (*or* venu) à la réunion, il s'est tenu à l'écart de la réunion.

▸**stop behind*** vi rester en arrière *or* à la fin.

▸**stop by*** vi s'arrêter en passant.

▸**stop down*** vi (*bending*) rester baissé; (*lying down*) rester couché; (*under water*) rester sous l'eau.

▸**stop in*** vi a (*at home*) rester à la maison *or* chez soi, ne pas sortir. b = **stop by***.

▸**stop off** 1 vi s'arrêter; (*on journey*) s'arrêter, faire une courte halte, interrompre son voyage. 2 **stop-off** n *see* **stop 2**.

▸**stop out*** vi rester dehors, ne pas rentrer. **he always stops out late on Fridays** il rentre toujours tard le vendredi.

▸**stop over** 1 vi s'arrêter (un *or* plusieurs jour(s)), faire une halte. 2 **stopover** n, adj *see* **stop 2**.

▸**stop up** 1 vi (*Brit* *) ne pas se coucher, rester debout. **don't stop up for me** ne m'attendez pas pour aller vous coucher. 2 vt sep *hole, pipe* boucher; (*accidentally*) boucher, bloquer, obstruer; *jar, bottle* boucher. **my nose is stopped up** j'ai le nez bouché.

stop-go [stɒp'gəʊ] 1 n (*gen, Econ*) **a period of ~** une période d'activité intense suivie de relâchement. 2 comp ▸**stop-go policy** (*Pol etc*) valse-hésitation *f* en politique.

stoppage ['stɒpɪdʒ] n a (*in traffic, work*) arrêt *m*, interruption *f*, suspension *f*; (*Ftbl etc*) arrêt *m* de jeu; (*strike*) grève *f*; *[leave, wages, payment]* suspension; (*amount deducted*) retenue *f*. (*Ftbl*) **~ time** arrêts *mpl* de jeu; **to play ~ time** jouer les arrêts de jeu. b (*blockage*) obstruction *f*, engorgement *m*; (*Med*) occlusion *f*.

stopper ['stɒpəʳ] 1 n *[bottle, jar]* bouchon *m*; *[bath, basin]* bouchon, bonde *f*. **to take the ~ out of a bottle** déboucher une bouteille; **to put the ~ into a bottle** boucher une bouteille; (*fig*) **to put a ~ on sth*** mettre un terme *or* le holà à qch; *see* **conversation.** 2 **vt** boucher.

stopping ['stɒpɪŋ] 1 **n** a (*NonC: halting etc: see* **stop 3b, 3c, 3d**) arrêt *m*, interruption *f*; suspension *f*; cessation *f*; *[cheque]* arrêt de paiement; (*Mus*) *see* **double.** b (*NonC: blocking: see* **stop 3a**) obturation *f*, bouchage *m*. c *[tooth]* plombage *m*. 2 **comp** ▸**stopping place** (*lay-by etc*) parking *m*; **we were looking for a stopping place** nous cherchions un coin où nous arrêter ▸**stopping train** (train *m*) omnibus *m*.

storage ['stɔːrɪdʒ] 1 **n** a (*NonC*) *[goods, fuel]* entreposage *m*, emmagasinage *m*; *[furniture]* entreposage *m*; *[food, wine]* rangement *m*, conservation *f*; *[radioactive waste]* stockage *m*; *[heat, electricity]* accumulation *f*; *[documents]* conservation *f*. **to put in(to)** ~ entreposer, emmagasiner; *furniture* mettre au garde-meuble; *see* **cold.**

b (*Comput*) (*state*) mémoire *f*; (*action*) mise *f* en mémoire. ~ **capacity** capacité *f* de mémoire.

2 **comp** *problems* d'entreposage, d'emmagasinage; *charges* de magasinage ▸**storage battery** accumulateur *m*, accu* *m* ▸**storage capacity** (*gen*) capacité *f* d'entreposage *or* d'emmagasinage; (*Comput*) *see* **storage 1b** ▸**storage heater** (*also* **electric storage heater**) radiateur *m* électrique par accumulation ▸**storage space** (*in house*) espace *m* de rangement; (*in firm etc*) espace d'emmagasinage ▸**storage tank** *[oil etc]* réservoir *m* d'emmagasinage; *[rainwater]* citerne *f* ▸**storage unit** (*furniture*) meuble *m* de rangement.

store [stɔːʳ] 1 **n** a (*supply, stock, accumulation*) provision *f*, réserve *f*, stock *m*; *[learning, information]* fonds *m*. **to get in** *or* **lay in a** ~ **of sth** faire provision de qch; **to keep a** ~ **of sth** avoir une provision de qch, stocker qch; (*fig*) **to set great** ~**/little** ~ **by sth** faire grand cas/peu de cas de qch, attacher du prix/peu de prix à qch.

b (*supplies*) ~**s** provisions *fpl*; **to take on** *or* **lay in** ~**s** s'approvisionner, faire des provisions.

c (*Brit: depot, warehouse*) entrepôt *m*; (*furniture* ~) garde-meuble *m*; (*in office, factory etc: also* ~**s**) réserve *f*, (*larger*) service *m* des approvisionnements. **ammunition** ~ dépôt *m* de munitions; **to put in(to)** ~ *goods etc* entreposer; *furniture* mettre au garde-meuble; **I am keeping this in** ~ **for winter** je garde cela en réserve pour l'hiver; (*fig*) **I've got a surprise in** ~ **for you** j'ai une surprise en réserve pour vous, je vous réserve une surprise; (*fig*) **what does the future hold** *or* **have in** ~ **for him?, what is in** ~ **for him?** que lui réserve l'avenir?

d (*esp US: shop*) magasin *m*, commerce *m*; (*large*) grand magasin; (*small*) boutique *f*. **book** ~ magasin de livres, librairie *f*; *see* **chain, department, general** *etc*.

2 **comp** (*gen: esp US*) *item, line* de série; (*US: also* **store-bought**) *clothes* de confection *or* de série; *cake* du commerce ▸**storefront** (*US*) devanture *f* ▸**storehouse** entrepôt *m*, magasin *m*; (*fig: of information etc*) mine *f* ▸**storekeeper** magasinier *m*; (*esp US: shopkeeper*) commerçant(e) *m(f)* ▸**storeroom** réserve *f*, magasin *m*.

3 **vt** a (*keep in reserve, collect: also* ~ **up**) *food, fuel, goods* mettre en réserve; *documents* conserver; *electricity, heat* accumuler, emmagasiner; (*fig: in one's mind*) *facts, information* noter *or* enregistrer dans sa mémoire. **this cellar can** ~ **enough coal for the winter** cette cave peut contenir assez de charbon pour passer l'hiver.

b (*place in* ~*: also* ~ **away**) *food, fuel, goods* emmagasiner, entreposer; *one's furniture* mettre au garde-meuble; *crops* mettre en grange, engranger; (*Comput*) mettre en réserve. **he** ~**d the information (away)** (*in filing system etc*) il rangea *or* classa le renseignement; (*in his mind*) il nota le renseignement; **I've got the camping things** ~**d (away) till we need them** j'ai rangé *or* mis de côté les affaires de camping en attendant que nous en ayons besoin; **where do you** ~ **your wine?** où est-ce que vous rangez *or* conservez votre vin?

c (*equip, supply*) *larder etc* approvisionner, pourvoir, munir (*with* de); *mind, memory* meubler (*with* de).

d (*Comput*) mémoriser.

4 **vi: these apples** ~ **well/badly** ces pommes se conservent bien/mal.

▸**store away** **vt sep** *see* **store 3b.**

▸**store up** **vt sep** *see* **store 3a.**

storey, (*US*) **story** ['stɔːrɪ] **n** étage *m*. **on the 3rd** *or* (*US*) **4th** ~ au 3ᵉ (étage); **a 4-storey(ed)** *or* (*US*) **4-storied building** un bâtiment à *or* de 4 étages.

-storeyed, (*US*) **-storied** ['stɔːrɪd] **adj ending in comps** *see* **storey.**

stork [stɔːk] **n** cigogne *f*.

storm [stɔːm] 1 **n** a tempête *f*; (*thunderstorm*) orage *m*; (*on Beaufort scale*) violente tempête. ~ **of rain/snow** tempête de pluie/de neige; **magnetic** ~ orage magnétique; (*Brit fig*) **it was a** ~ **in a teacup** c'était une tempête dans un verre d'eau; *see* **dust, hail¹, sand** *etc*.

b (*fig*) *[arrows, missiles]* pluie *f*, grêle *f*; *[insults, abuse]* torrent *m*; *[cheers, protests, applause, indignation]* tempête *f*. **there was a political** ~ les passions politiques se sont déchaînées; **his speech caused** *or* **raised quite a** ~ son discours a provoqué une véritable tempête *or* un ouragan; **to bring a** ~ **about one's ears** soulever un tollé (général); **a period of** ~ **and stress** une période très orageuse *or* très tourmentée.

c (*Mil*) **to take by** ~ prendre *or* emporter d'assaut; (*fig*) **the play took London by** ~ la pièce a obtenu un succès foudroyant *or* fulgurant à Londres; **he took her by** ~ il a eu un succès foudroyant *or* fulgurant auprès d'elle, elle a eu le coup de foudre pour lui.

2 **comp** *signal, warning* de tempête ▸**storm belt** zone *f* des tempêtes ▸**stormbound** bloqué par la tempête ▸**storm cellar** (*US*) abri *m* tempête, abri cyclonique ▸**storm centre** centre *m* de dépression; (*fig*) centre de l'agitation ▸**storm cloud** nuage orageux; (*fig*) nuage noir *or* menaçant ▸**storm cone** cône *m* de tempête ▸**storm damage** dégâts *mpl* occasionnés par la tempête ▸**storm door** double porte *f* (*à l'extérieur*) ▸**storm drain** égout *m* pluvial ▸**storm lantern** lampe-tempête *f*, lanterne-tempête *f* ▸**storm-lashed** battu par l'orage *or* la tempête ▸**storm petrel** (*Orn, fig*) = **stormy petrel** (*see* **stormy**) ▸**stormproof** à l'épreuve de la tempête ▸**storm sewer** égout *m* pluvial ▸**storm-tossed** ballotté *or* battu par la tempête ▸**storm trooper** (*Mil*) (*gen*) membre *m* d'une troupe d'assaut; (*Nazi*) membre *m* des sections d'assaut nazies ▸**storm troops** troupes *fpl* d'assaut ▸**storm water** eau *f* pluviale ▸**storm window** double fenêtre *f* (*à l'extérieur*).

3 **vt** (*Mil*) prendre *or* emporter d'assaut. (*fig*) **angry ratepayers** ~**ed the town hall** les contribuables en colère ont pris d'assaut *or* ont envahi la mairie.

4 **vi** *[wind]* souffler en tempête, faire rage; *[rain]* tomber à torrents, faire rage; (*fig*) *[person]* fulminer (*with rage etc* de colère *etc*). **to** ~ **at sb** tempêter *or* fulminer contre qn; **to** ~ **(one's way) in/out** *etc* entrer/sortir *etc* comme un ouragan.

storming ['stɔːmɪŋ] **n** (*attack, invasion*) assaut *m*. **the** ~ **of the Bastille** la prise de la Bastille.

stormy ['stɔːmɪ] **adj** *weather, sky* orageux; *sea* houleux, (*stronger*) démonté; (*fig*) *discussion, meeting* houleux, orageux; *glance* noir, fulminant; *temperament, person* violent, emporté. ~ **petrel** (*Orn*) pétrel *m*; (*fig*) enfant *mf* terrible.

story¹ ['stɔːrɪ] 1 **n** a (*account*) histoire *f*. **it's a long** ~ c'est toute une histoire, c'est une longue histoire; **that's not the whole** *or* **full** ~**, that's only part of the** ~ mais ce n'est pas tout; **according to your** ~ d'après ce que vous dites, selon vous; **I've heard his** ~ j'ai entendu sa version des faits; (*fig*) **it's quite another** ~ *or* **a very different** ~ c'est une tout autre histoire; (*fig*) **it's the same old** ~ c'est toujours la même histoire *or* la même chanson*; (*fig*) **these scars tell their own** ~ ces cicatrices parlent d'elles-mêmes *or* en disent long; (*fig hum*) **that's the** ~ **of my life!** ça m'arrive tout le temps!

b (*tale*) histoire *f*, conte *m*; (*legend*) histoire, légende *f*; (*Literat*) histoire, récit *m*; (*short*) nouvelle *f*; (*anecdote, joke*) histoire, anecdote *f*. **there's an interesting** ~ **attached to that** on raconte une histoire intéressante à ce sujet; **or so the** ~ **goes** ou du moins c'est ce que l'on raconte, d'après les on-dit; **he writes stories** il écrit des histoires *or* des nouvelles; **she told the children a** ~ elle a raconté une histoire aux enfants; **do you know the** ~ **about ...?** connaissez-vous l'histoire de ...?; **what a** ~ **this house could tell!** que de choses cette maison pourrait nous (*or* vous *etc*) raconter!; *see* **bedtime, fairy, short** *etc*.

c (*Cine, Literat, Theat etc: plot*) action *f*, intrigue *f*, scénario *m*. **the** ~ **of the play is taken from his book** l'action *or* l'intrigue *or* le scénario de la pièce est emprunté(e) à son livre; **he did the** ~ **for the film** il a écrit le scénario du film.

d (*Press, Rad, TV*) (*event etc*) affaire *f*; (*article*) article *m*. **they devoted 2 pages to the** ~ **of ...** ils ont consacré 2 pages à l'affaire de ...; **did you read the** ~ **on ...?** avez-vous lu l'article sur ...?; **I don't know if there's a** ~ **in it** je ne sais pas s'il y a matière à un article; **he was sent to cover the** ~ **of the refugees** on l'a envoyé faire un reportage sur les réfugiés.

e (** fig*) histoire *f*. **to tell stories** raconter des histoires.

2 **comp** ▸**storyboard** (*Cine, TV*) scénarimage *m*, storyboard *m* ▸**storybook** **n** livre *m* de contes *or* d'histoires ◊ **adj** (*fig*) *situation, love affair* de roman *or* de livre d'histoires; **a meeting with a storybook ending** une rencontre qui se termine comme dans les romans ▸**story line** *[film, book, play]* action *f*, intrigue *f*, scénario *m* ▸**storyteller** conteur *m*, -euse *f*; (**: fibber*) menteur *m*, -euse *f* ▸**story-writer** nouvelliste *mf*.

story² ['stɔːrɪ] **n** (*US*) = **storey.**

stoup [stuːp] **n** (*Rel*) bénitier *m*; (*††: tankard*) pichet *m*.

stout [staʊt] 1 **adj** a (*fat*) gros (*f* grosse), corpulent. **to get** *or* **grow** ~ prendre de l'embonpoint. b (*strong*) *stick* solide; *coat* épais (*f* -aisse), solide; *shoes* robuste, solide; *horse* vigoureux, puissant; *resistance, defence* intrépide, énergique; *soldier* vaillant, intrépide; *supporter* fidèle. **with** ~ **hearts** vaillamment; **he is a** ~ **fellow*** c'est un brave type*, on peut compter sur lui. 2 **comp** ▸**stout-hearted** vaillant, intrépide. 3 **n** (*Brit: beer*) stout *m*, bière brune (*épaisse et forte*).

stoutly ['staʊtlɪ] **adv** *fight, defend, resist* vaillamment, intrépidement; *deny* catégoriquement; *believe, maintain* dur comme fer. ~ **built** *hut etc* solidement bâti; *person* (*strong*) costaud, bien bâti *or* charpenté, de forte carrure; (*fat*) corpulent, gros (*f* grosse).

stoutness ['staʊtnɪs] **n** (*see* **stout**) corpulence *f*, embonpoint *m*; solidité *f*, robustesse *f*; vigueur *f*; puissance *f*; intrépidité *f*; vaillance *f*.

stove¹ [stəʊv] 1 **n** a (*heater*) poêle *m*; *see* **wood.** b (*cooker*) (*solid fuel*) fourneau *m*; (*gas, electricity*) cuisinière *f*; (*small*) réchaud *m*. c (*Ind, Tech*) four *m*, étuve *f*. 2 **comp** ▸**stovepipe** (*lit, also fig: hat*) tuyau *m* de poêle.

stove² [stəʊv] **pret, ptp of stave.**

stow [stəʊ] 1 vt ranger, mettre; (*out of sight: also* ~ **away**) faire disparaître, cacher; (*Naut*) *cargo* arrimer; (*also* ~ **away**) *ropes, tarpaulins etc* ranger. **where can I ~ this?** où puis-je déposer ceci?; ~ **it!**‡ la ferme!‡, ferme-la!‡ 2 comp ▸**stowaway** passager clandestin, passagère clandestine.

▸**stow away** 1 vi s'embarquer clandestinement. **he stowed away to Australia** il s'est embarqué clandestinement pour l'Australie. 2 vt sep (*put away*) ranger, déposer, mettre; (*put in its place*) ranger, placer; (*put out of sight*) faire disparaître, cacher; (‡ *fig*) *meal, food* enfourner*; *see also* **stow 1.** 3 **stowaway** n *see* **stow 2.**

stowage ['stəʊɪdʒ] n (*Naut*) (*action*) arrimage *m*; (*space*) espace *m* utile; (*costs*) frais *mpl* d'arrimage.

strabismus [strə'bɪzməs] n strabisme *m*.

strabotomy [strə'bɒtəmɪ] n strabotomie *f*.

straddle ['strædl] 1 vt *horse, cycle* enfourcher; *chair* se mettre à califourchon *or* à cheval sur; *fence, ditch* enjamber. **to be straddling sth** être à califourchon *or* à cheval sur qch; **the village ~s the border** le village est à cheval sur la frontière; **the enemy positions ~d the river** l'ennemi avait pris position des deux côtés de la rivière; (*Mil: gunnery*) **to ~ a target** encadrer un objectif; (*US fig*) **to ~ an issue** nager entre deux eaux, ménager la chèvre et le chou. 2 vi être à califourchon; (*US * fig*) nager entre deux eaux, ménager la chèvre et le chou. **straddling legs** jambes écartées.

strafe [strɑːf] vt (*Mil etc*) (*with machine guns*) mitrailler au sol; (*with shellfire, bombs*) bombarder, marmiter; (*fig* *) (*punish*) punir; (*reprimand*) semoncer vertement.

strafing ['strɑːfɪŋ] n (*Mil, Aviat*) mitraillage *m* au sol.

straggle ['strægl] vi a *[vines, plants]* pousser tout en longueur, pousser au hasard; *[hair]* être *or* retomber en désordre; *[houses, trees etc]* être épars *or* disséminés; *[village etc]* s'étendre en longueur. **the branches ~d along the wall** les branches tortueuses grimpaient le long du mur; **the village ~s for miles along the road** les maisons du village s'égrènent *or* le village s'étend sur des kilomètres le long de la route; **her hair was straggling over her face** ses cheveux rebelles *or* des mèches folles retombaient en désordre sur son visage.

b *[people, cars, planes]* **to ~ in/out** *etc* entrer/sortir *etc* les uns après les autres *or* par petits groupes (détachés) *or* petit à petit.

▸**straggle away, straggle off** vi se débander *or* se disperser petit à petit.

straggler ['stræglə^r] n (*person*) traînard(e) *m(f)* (*also Mil*); (*plane etc*) avion *etc* isolé (qui traîne derrière les autres); (*Bot*) branche gourmande, gourmand *m*.

straggling ['stræglɪŋ] adj, **straggly** ['stræglɪ] adj qui traîne en longueur; *plant* (qui pousse) tout en longueur; *village* tout en longueur. ~ **hair** cheveux fins rebelles *or* en désordre *or* décoiffés; **a ~ row of houses** un rang de maisons disséminées; **a long ~ line** une longue ligne irrégulière.

straight [streɪt] 1 adj a (*not curved, twisted etc*) *line, stick, limb, edge* droit; *road* droit, rectiligne; *course, route* direct, en ligne droite; *tree, tower* droit, vertical; *chair* à dossier droit; *hair* raide; *stance, posture, back* bien droit; (*Geom*) *angle* plat; *picture* d'aplomb, droit; *rug, tablecloth* droit; *hat* droit, d'aplomb, bien mis. **to put** *or* **set ~** *picture* redresser, remettre d'aplomb; *hat, tie* ajuster; **the picture/your tie isn't ~** le tableau/votre cravate est de travers; **your hem isn't ~** votre ourlet n'est pas rond; (*fig*) **to keep a ~ face** garder son sérieux (*see also* **4**); (*US*) ~ **razor** rasoir *m* à main *or* de coiffeur.

b (*in order*) *room, house, books, one's affairs, accounts* en ordre. **to put** *or* **set** *or* **get ~** *house, room, books* mettre en ordre, mettre de l'ordre dans; *one's affairs, accounts* mettre de l'ordre dans; **to set matters ~** rétablir la vérité, mettre les choses au clair; (*fig*) **let's get this ~** entendons-nous bien sur ce point; **to put** *or* **set sb ~ about sth** éclairer qn sur qch; **to keep sb ~ about sth** empêcher qn de se tromper sur qch; **to put** *or* **set o.s. ~ with sb** faire en sorte de ne pas être en reste avec qn; (*don't owe anything*) **now we're ~** maintenant on est quitte; *see* **record.**

c (*direct, frank*) *person* honnête, franc (*f* franche), loyal; *dealing* loyal, régulier; *answer, question* franc; *look* franc, droit; *denial, refusal* net (*f* nette), catégorique. **to give sb a ~ look** regarder qn droit dans les yeux; ~ **speaking,** ~ **talking** franc-parler *m*; **to play a ~ game** agir loyalement, jouer franc jeu; (*Racing, St Ex etc*) ~ **tip** tuyau* *m* de bonne source.

d (*plain, uncomplicated, undiluted*) *whisky etc* sec, sans eau; (*Theat*) *part, actor* sérieux; (*fig *: pure and simple*) *dishonesty etc* pur et simple, à l'état pur. **a ~ play** une pièce de théâtre proprement dite; (*Pol*) **a ~ fight** une campagne électorale à deux candidats; (*US Pol*) **to vote a ~ ticket** voter pour une liste sans panachage; (*Cards*) ~ **flush** quinte *f* flush; (*fig*) **it was ~* racism** c'était du racisme pur et simple *or* du racisme à l'état pur.

e (‡) (*gen*) normal; (*not homosexual*) hétéro *inv*; (*not a drug addict*) qui ne se drogue pas; (*not a criminal*) honnête, régulier.

2 n a *[racecourse, railway line, river etc]* **the ~** la ligne droite; (*fig*) **now we're in the ~** nous sommes maintenant dans la dernière ligne droite.

b **to cut sth on the ~** couper qch (de) droit fil; **out of the ~** de travers, en biais.

c (*fig*) **to follow** *or* **keep to the ~ and narrow** rester dans le droit chemin; (*fig*) **to keep sb on the ~ and narrow** faire suivre le droit chemin à qn.

3 adv a (*in a ~ line*) *walk, fly* droit, en ligne droite; *grow, stand* (bien) droit; *sit* correctement. **he came ~ at me** il est venu (tout) droit vers moi; **to shoot ~** tirer juste; **I can't see ~*** j'y vois trouble; **the cork shot ~ up in the air** le bouchon est parti droit en l'air; **hold yourself ~** redressez-vous, tenez-vous droit; ~ **above us** juste au-dessus de nous; ~ **across from the house** juste en face de la maison; **to go ~ ahead** *or* ~ **on** aller tout droit; **he looked ~ ahead** il a regardé droit devant lui; **to look sb ~ in the face/the eye** regarder qn bien en face/droit dans les yeux; **the bullet went ~ through his chest** la balle lui a traversé la poitrine de part en part.

b (*directly*) tout droit, tout de suite, sur-le-champ, aussitôt. **he went ~ to London** il est allé directement *or* tout droit à Londres; **go ~ to bed** va droit au lit, va tout de suite te coucher; ~ **after this** tout de suite après; ~ **away,** ~ **off** tout de suite, sur-le-champ; ~ **out,** ~ **off** (*without hesitation*) sans hésiter; (*without beating about the bush*) sans ambages, sans mâcher ses mots; **he read "Hamlet" ~ off** il a lu "Hamlet" d'une seule traite; **to come ~ to the point** en venir droit au fait; (*fig*) ~ **from the horse's mouth** de source sûre; (*fig*) **I let him have it ~ from the shoulder** je le lui ai dit carrément *or* sans mâcher mes mots *or* sans ambages, je le lui ai dit tout cru; **I'm telling you ~, I'm giving it to you ~*** je vous le dis tout net; **give it to me ~*** n'y va pas par quatre chemins*.

c (*phrases*) **to drink one's whisky ~** boire son whisky sec *or* sans eau; (*Theat*) **he played the role ~** il a joué le rôle de façon classique *or* sans modification; *[criminal]* **he's been going ~ for a year now** voilà un an qu'il est resté dans le droit chemin *or* qu'il vit honnêtement.

4 comp ▸**straight-cut tobacco** tabac coupé dans la longueur de la feuille ▸**straightedge** règle large et plate, limande *f* (*Carpentry*) ▸**straight-faced** adv en gardant son (*or* mon *etc*) sérieux ◊ adj qui garde son (*or* mon *etc*) sérieux, impassible ▸**straightforward** *see* **straightforward** ▸**straightjacket** = **straitjacket** ▸**straight-laced** = **strait-laced** ▸**straight-line** *depreciation* constant ▸**straight man** (*Theat*) comparse *m*, faire-valoir *m* ▸**straight-out*** *answer, denial, refusal* net (*f* nette), catégorique; *supporter, enthusiast, communist* sans réserve; *liar, thief* fieffé (*before noun*) ▸**straightway**†† tout de suite, sur-le-champ.

straighten ['streɪtn] 1 vt *wire, nail* redresser, défausser; *hair* décrêper; *road* refaire en éliminant les tournants; *tie, hat* ajuster; *picture* redresser, remettre d'aplomb; *room* mettre de l'ordre dans, mettre en ordre; *papers* ranger. **to ~ one's back** *or* **shoulders** se redresser, se tenir droit; **to ~ the hem of a skirt** arrondir une jupe. 2 vi (*also* ~ **out**) *[road etc]* devenir droit; (*also* ~ **out,** ~ **up**) *[growing plant etc]* pousser droit; (*also* ~ **up**) *[person]* se redresser.

▸**straighten out** 1 vi *see* **straighten 2.** 2 vt sep *wire, nail* redresser, défausser; *road* refaire en éliminant les tournants; (*fig*) *situation* débrouiller; *problem* résoudre; *one's ideas* mettre de l'ordre dans, débrouiller. **he managed to straighten things out*** il a réussi à arranger les choses; **I'm trying to straighten out how much I owe him*** j'essaie de démêler combien je lui dois; **to straighten sb out‡** remettre qn dans la bonne voie; **I'll soon straighten him out!‡** je vais aller le remettre à sa place!, je vais lui apprendre!

▸**straighten up** 1 vi a *see* **straighten 2.** b (*tidy up*) mettre de l'ordre, ranger. 2 vt sep *room, books, papers* ranger, mettre de l'ordre dans.

straightforward [ˌstreɪt'fɔːwəd] adj (*frank*) honnête, franc (*f* franche); (*plain-spoken*) franc, direct; (*simple*) simple. **it's very ~** c'est tout ce qu'il y a de plus simple; **it was ~ racism** c'était du racisme pur et simple *or* du racisme à l'état pur.

straightforwardly [ˌstreɪt'fɔːwədlɪ] adv *answer* franchement, sans détour; *behave* avec droiture, honnêtement. **everything went quite ~** tout s'est bien passé, tout s'est passé sans anicroche*.

straightforwardness [ˌstreɪt'fɔːwədnɪs] n (*see* **straightforward**) honnêteté *f*, franchise *f*; simplicité *f*.

straightness ['streɪtnɪs] n (*frankness*) franchise *f*; (*honesty*) rectitude *f*.

strain[1] [streɪn] 1 n a (*Tech etc*) tension *f*, effort *m*, pression *f*, traction *f*. **the ~ on the rope** la tension de la corde, l'effort *m or* la force exercé(e) sur la corde; **it broke under the ~** cela s'est rompu sous la tension *or* sous l'effort de traction; **that puts a great ~ on the beam** cela exerce une forte pression *or* traction sur la poutre; **to take the ~ off sth** soulager qch, diminuer la tension de qch *or* la pression sur qch; **can you take some of the ~?** pouvez-vous nous (*or* les *etc*) aider à soutenir ceci?; (*fig*) **it put a great ~ on their friendship** cela a mis leur amitié à rude épreuve; **it was a ~ on the economy/their resources** cela grevait l'économie/leurs ressources; **it was a ~ on his purse** cela faisait mal à son portefeuille, cela grevait son budget; *see* **breaking, stand.**

b (*physical*) effort *m* (physique); (*mental*) tension nerveuse; (*overwork*) surmenage *m*; (*tiredness*) fatigue *f*. **the ~(s) of city life** la tension de la vie urbaine; **the ~ of 6 hours at the wheel** la fatigue nerveuse engendrée par 6 heures passées au volant; **listening for 3 hours is a ~** écouter pendant 3 heures demande un grand effort; **all the ~ and struggle of bringing up the family** toutes les tensions et les soucis qui sont le lot d'un parent qui élève ses enfants; **the ~ of climbing the stairs** l'effort requis pour monter l'escalier; **he has been under a great deal of ~** ses nerfs ont été mis à rude épreuve; **the situation put a great ~ on him** *or* **put him under a great ~** la situation l'a épuisé *or* l'a beaucoup fatigué nerveusement; *see* **stress**.

c (*Med: sprain*) entorse *f*, foulure *f*; *see* **eye** *etc*.

d **~s** (*Mus*) accords *mpl*, accents *mpl*; (*Poetry*) accents, chant *m*; **to the ~s of the "London March"** aux accents de la "Marche Londonienne".

2 vt a *rope, beam* tendre fortement *or* excessivement; (*Med*) *muscle* froisser; *arm, ankle* fouler; (*fig*) *friendship, relationship, marriage* mettre à rude épreuve; *resources, savings, budget, the economy* grever; *meaning* forcer; *word* forcer le sens de; *sb's patience* mettre à l'épreuve; *one's authority* outrepasser, excéder. (*Med*) **to ~ one's back** se donner un tour de reins; **to ~ one's heart** se fatiguer le cœur; **to ~ one's shoulder** se froisser un muscle dans l'épaule; **to ~ one's voice** forcer sa voix; **to ~ one's eyes** s'abîmer *or* se fatiguer les yeux; **he ~ed his eyes to make out what it was** il plissa les yeux pour mieux distinguer ce que c'était; **to ~ one's ears to hear sth** tendre l'oreille pour entendre qch; **to ~ every nerve to do** fournir un effort intense pour faire; **to ~ o.s.** (*damage muscle etc*) se froisser un muscle; (*overtire o.s.*) se surmener; (*iro*) **don't ~ yourself!** surtout ne te fatigue pas!

b (†† *or liter*) **to ~ sb to o.s.** *or* **one's heart** serrer qn contre son cœur, étreindre qn.

c (*filter*) *liquid* passer, filtrer; *soup, gravy* passer; *vegetables* (faire) égoutter.

3 vi: **to ~ to do** (*physically*) peiner pour faire, fournir un gros effort pour faire; (*mentally*) s'efforcer de faire; **to ~ at sth** (*pushing/pulling*) pousser/tirer qch de toutes ses forces; (*fig: jib at*) renâcler à qch; [*dog*] **to ~ at the leash** tirer fort sur sa laisse; (*Prov*) **to ~ at a gnat (and swallow a camel)** faire une histoire pour une vétille et passer sur une énormité; (*fig*) **to ~ after sth** faire un grand effort pour obtenir qch; **to ~ under a weight** ployer sous un poids.

►**strain off** vt sep *liquid* vider.

strain² [streɪn] n (*breed, lineage*) race *f*, lignée *f*; [*animal etc*] race *f*; [*virus*] souche *f*; (*tendency, streak*) tendance *f*. **there is a ~ of madness in the family** il y a dans la famille des tendances à *or* une prédisposition à la folie; (*fig*) **there was a lot more in the same ~** il y en avait encore beaucoup du même genre; **he continued in this ~** il a continué sur ce ton *or* dans ce sens.

strained [streɪnd] adj a *arm, ankle* foulé; *muscle* froissé; *eyes* fatigué; *voice* forcé; *smile, laugh, cough* forcé, contraint; *look* contraint; *relations, atmosphere, nerves, person* tendu; *style* affecté. **he has a ~ shoulder/back** il s'est froissé un muscle dans l'épaule/le dos. b *soup, gravy* passé; *vegetables* égoutté; *baby food* en purée.

strainer ['streɪnəʳ] n (*Culin*) passoire *f*; (*Tech*) épurateur *m*.

strait [streɪt] 1 n a (*Geog: also* **~s**) détroit *m*. **the S~ of Gibraltar** le détroit de Gibraltar; **the S~s of Dover** le Pas de Calais; **the S~ of Hormuz** le détroit d'Hormuz *or* d'Ormuz. b (*fig*) **~s** situation *f* difficile; **to be in financial ~s** avoir des ennuis d'argent; *see* **dire**. 2 adj (††) étroit. 3 comp ►**straitjacket** *see* **straitjacket** ►**strait-laced** collet monté *inv*.

straitened ['streɪtnd] adj: **in ~ circumstances** dans la gêne.

straitjacket ['streɪtdʒækɪt] n camisole *f* de force.

strand¹ [strænd] 1 n (*liter: shore*) grève *f*, rivage *m*, rive *f*. 2 vt *ship* échouer; (*also* **to leave ~ed**) *person* laisser en rade* *or* en plan*. **they were (left) ~ed without passports or money** ils se sont retrouvés en rade* *or* coincés sans passeport ni argent; **he took the car and left me ~ed** il a pris la voiture et m'a laissé en plan* *or* en rade*.

strand² [strænd] n [*thread, wire*] brin *m*; [*rope*] toron *m*; [*fibrous substance*] fibre *f*; [*pearls*] rang *m*; (*fig: in narrative etc*) fil *m*, enchaînement *m*. **a ~ of hair** une mèche; (*fig*) **the ~s of one's life** le fil de sa vie.

strange [streɪndʒ] adj a (*alien, unknown*) *language, country* inconnu. **there were several ~ people there** il y avait plusieurs personnes que je ne connaissais pas (*or* qu'il ne connaissait pas *etc*); **don't talk to any ~ men** n'adresse pas la parole à des inconnus; **I never sleep well in a ~ bed** je ne dors jamais bien dans un lit autre que le mien.

b (*odd, unusual*) étrange, bizarre, insolite, surprenant. **it is ~ that** il est étrange *or* bizarre *or* surprenant que + *subj*; **~ to say I have never met her** chose curieuse *or* chose étrange je ne l'ai jamais rencontrée; **~ as it may seem** aussi étrange que cela puisse paraître; **I heard a ~ noise** j'ai entendu un bruit insolite.

c (*unaccustomed*) *work, activity* inaccoutumé. **you'll feel rather ~ at first** vous vous sentirez un peu dépaysé pour commencer.

strangely ['streɪndʒlɪ] adv étrangement, curieusement, bizarrement. **~ enough I have never met her** chose curieuse *or* chose étrange je ne l'ai jamais rencontrée.

strangeness ['streɪndʒnɪs] n étrangeté *f*, bizarrerie *f*, nouveauté *f*.

stranger ['streɪndʒəʳ] 1 n (*unknown*) inconnu(e) *m(f)*; (*from another place*) étranger *m*, -ère *f*. **he is a perfect ~ (to me)** il m'est totalement inconnu; **I'm a ~ here** je ne suis pas d'ici; **I am a ~ to Paris** je ne connais pas Paris; **a ~ to politics** un novice en matière de politique; (*liter*) **he was no ~ to misfortune** il connaissait bien le malheur, il avait l'habitude du malheur; **you're quite a ~!** vous vous faites *or* vous devenez rare!, on ne vous voit plus! 2 comp ►**Strangers' Gallery** (*Brit Parl*) tribune réservée au public.

strangle ['stræŋgl] 1 vt étrangler; (*fig*) *free speech* étrangler, museler; *protests* étouffer. **~d** *person, voice, cry, laugh* étranglé; *sneeze, sob* étouffé, réprimé. 2 comp ►**stranglehold: to have a stranglehold on** (*lit*) tenir à la gorge; (*fig*) tenir à la gorge *or* à sa merci; (*fig: Econ, Comm etc*) **a stranglehold on the market** une domination *or* un quasi-monopole du marché.

strangler ['stræŋgləʳ] n étrangleur *m*, -euse *f*.

strangling ['stræŋglɪŋ] n (*lit*) strangulation *f*, étranglement *m*; (*fig*) étranglement. **there have been several ~s in Boston** plusieurs personnes ont été étranglées à Boston.

strangulate ['stræŋgjʊleɪt] vt (*Med*) étrangler.

strangulation [ˌstræŋgjʊ'leɪʃən] n (*NonC*) strangulation *f*.

strap [stræp] 1 n (*of leather*) lanière *f*, courroie *f*, sangle *f*; (*of cloth*) sangle, bande *f*, courroie; (*on shoe, also Climbing*) lanière; (*on harness etc*) sangle, courroie; (*on suitcase, around book*) sangle, courroie, lanière; (*on garment*) bretelle *f*; (*on shoulder bag, camera etc*) bandoulière *f*; (*watch ~*) bracelet *m*; (*for razor*) cuir *m*; (*in bus, tube*) poignée *f* de cuir; (*Scol*) lanière de cuir; (*Tech*) lien *m*. (*Scol*) **to give sb the ~** administrer une correction à qn (avec une lanière de cuir).

2 comp ►**straphang** voyager debout (dans le métro *etc*) ►**straphanger** (*standing*) voyageur *m*, -euse *f* debout *inv*; (*US: public transport user*) usager *m* des transports en commun.

3 vt a (*tie*) attacher (*sth to sth* qch à qch).

b (*also* **~ up**) *sb's ribs etc* bander *or* maintenir avec une sangle; *suitcase, books* attacher avec une sangle *or* une courroie.

c *child etc* administrer une correction à.

►**strap down** vt sep attacher avec une sangle *or* une courroie.

►**strap in** vt sep *object* attacher avec une sangle *or* une courroie; *child in car, pram etc* attacher avec une ceinture de sécurité *or* un harnais. **he isn't properly strapped in** il est mal attaché, sa ceinture de sécurité *or* son harnais est mal mis(e).

►**strap on** vt sep *object* attacher; *watch* mettre, attacher.

►**strap up** vt sep = **strap 3b**.

strapless ['stræplɪs] adj *dress, bra* sans bretelles.

strapped* [stræpt] adj **to be financially ~, to be ~ for funds** *or* **for cash** être à court (d'argent), être dans l'embarras.

strapper* ['stræpəʳ] n gaillard(e) *m(f)*.

strapping ['stræpɪŋ] 1 adj costaud*, bien découplé *or* charpenté. **a ~ fellow** un grand gaillard. 2 n (*NonC*) a (*for cargo*) courroies *fpl*, sangles *fpl*. b (*Med*) bardages *mpl*.

Strasbourg ['stræzbɜːg] n Strasbourg.

strata ['strɑːtə] npl of **stratum**.

stratagem ['strætɪdʒəm] n stratagème *m*.

strategic(al) [strə'tiːdʒɪk(əl)] adj stratégique. (*US Aviat*) **S~ Air Command** l'aviation militaire stratégique (américaine); **~ business unit** domaine *m* d'activité stratégique; (*US Mil, Space*) **S~ Defense Initiative** Initiative *f* de défense stratégique.

strategically [strə'tiːdʒɪkəlɪ] adv stratégiquement.

strategist ['strætɪdʒɪst] n stratège *m*.

strategy ['strætɪdʒɪ] n stratégie *f*.

stratification [ˌstrætɪfɪ'keɪʃən] n stratification *f*.

stratificational [ˌstrætɪfɪ'keɪʃənl] adj (*Ling*) stratificationnel.

stratify ['strætɪfaɪ] vti stratifier.

stratocruiser ['strætəʊˌkruːzəʳ] n avion *m* stratosphérique.

stratosphere ['strætəʊsfɪəʳ] n stratosphère *f*.

stratospheric [ˌstrætəʊs'ferɪk] adj stratosphérique.

stratum ['strɑːtəm] n, pl **~s** *or* **strata** (*Geol*) strate *f*, couche *f*; (*fig*) couche.

straw [strɔː] 1 n paille *f*. **to drink sth through a ~** boire qch avec une paille; **to draw ~s** tirer à la courte paille; **to draw the short ~** (*lit*) tirer la paille la plus courte; (*fig*) tirer le mauvais numéro; (*fig*) **man of ~** homme *m* de paille; (*fig*) **to clutch** *or* **catch** *or* **grasp at a ~** *or* **~s** se raccrocher désespérément à un semblant d'espoir; (*fig*) **it's a ~ in the wind** c'est une indication des choses à venir; (*fig*) **when he refused, it was the last ~** quand il a refusé, ç'a été la goutte d'eau qui fait déborder le vase; (*excl*) **that's the last ~** *or* **the ~ that breaks the camel's back!** ça c'est le comble!; **I don't care a ~*** je m'en fiche*.

2 comp (*made of ~: gen*) de *or* en paille; *roof* en paille, en chaume ►**strawberry** *see* **strawberry** ►**straw boss** (*US*) sous-chef *m* ►**straw-coloured** paille *inv* ►**straw hat** chapeau *m* de paille ►**straw man** (*fig*) homme *m* de paille ►**straw mat** paillasson *m* ►**straw mattress** paillasse *f* ►**straw poll** = **straw vote** ►**straw-poll elections** (*US Pol*) élection-pilote *or* témoin ►**straw vote** (*fig, esp US*) sondage *m* d'opinion, vote *m* blanc.

strawberry ['strɔːbərɪ] 1 n (*fruit*) fraise *f*; (*plant*) fraisier *m*. **wild ~** fraise des bois, fraise sauvage. 2 comp *jam* de fraises; *ice cream* à la fraise; *tart* aux fraises ►**strawberry bed** fraiseraie *f*, fraisière *f*

►**strawberry blonde** adj blond vénitien *inv* ◊ n blonde *f* qui tire sur le roux ►**strawberry mark** (*Anat*) tache *f* de vin, envie *f* ►**strawberry roan** rouan *m* vineux.

stray [streɪ] 1 n a (*dog, cat, etc*) animal errant *or* perdu; (*sheep, cow etc*) animal égaré; (*child*) enfant *mf* perdu(e) *or* abandonné(e). **this dog is a ~** c'est un chien perdu *or* errant; *see* **waif**.
b (*Rad*) **~s** parasites *mpl*, friture *f*.
2 adj *dog, cat* perdu, errant; *sheep, cow* égaré; *child* perdu, abandonné; (*fig*) *plane, taxi, shot etc* isolé; *thought* inopiné. **a ~ bullet** une balle perdue; **a few ~ houses** quelques maisons isolées *or* éparses; **a few ~ cars** quelques rares voitures; **he was picked up by a ~ motorist** il a été pris par un des rares automobilistes.
3 vi (*also* **~ away**) *[person, animal]* s'égarer; *[thoughts]* vagabonder, errer. (*lit, fig*) **to ~ (away) from** *village, plan, subject* s'écarter de; *course, route* dévier de; **they ~ed into enemy territory** ils se sont égarés *or* ont fait fausse route et se sont retrouvés en territoire ennemi; **his thoughts ~ed to the coming holidays** il se prit à penser aux vacances prochaines.

streak [stri:k] 1 n a (*line, band*) raie *f*, bande *f*; *[ore, mineral]* veine *f*; *[light]* rai(s) *m*, filet *m*; *[blood, paint]* filet. **his hair had ~s of grey in it** ses cheveux commençaient à grisonner; **she had (blond) ~s put in her hair** elle s'est fait faire des mèches (blondes); **a ~ of cloud across the sky** une traînée nuageuse dans le ciel; **a ~ of lightning** un éclair; **he went past like a ~ (of lightning)** il est passé comme un éclair.
b (*fig: tendency*) tendance(s) *f(pl)*, propension *f*. **he has a jealous ~ or a ~ of jealousy** il a des tendances *or* une propension à la jalousie; **she has a ~ of Irish blood** elle a du sang irlandais dans les veines; **a lucky ~, a ~ of luck** une période de chance; **an unlucky ~, a ~ of bad luck** une période de malchance; **a winning ~** (*Sport*) une suite *or* une série de victoires; (*Casino*) une bonne passe; **to be on a winning ~** (*Sport*) accumuler les victoires; (*Casino*) être dans une bonne passe.
2 vt zébrer, strier (*with* de). **mirror ~ed with dirt** miroir zébré de longues traînées sales; **sky ~ed with red** ciel strié *or* zébré de bandes rouges; **cheeks ~ed with tear-marks** joues sillonnées de larmes; **clothes ~ed with mud/paint** vêtements maculés de longues traînées de boue/de peinture; **his hair was ~ed with grey** ses cheveux commençaient à grisonner; **she's got ~ed hair, she's had her hair ~ed** elle s'est fait faire des mèches; **rock ~ed with quartz** roche veinée de quartz; **meat ~ed with fat** viande persillée.
3 vi a (*rush*) **to ~ in/out/past** *etc* entrer/sortir/passer *etc* comme un éclair.
b (**: dash naked*) courir tout nu en public.

streaker* ['stri:kəʳ] n streaker *m*, -euse *f*.

streaky ['stri:kɪ] adj *colour* marbré; *window, mirror, sky* zébré; *rock etc* veiné. (*Brit Culin*) **~ bacon** bacon *m* pas trop maigre, ≃ poitrine *f* salée *or* fumée.

stream [stri:m] 1 n a (*brook*) ruisseau *m*.
b (*current*) courant *m*. **to go with the ~** (*lit*) suivre le fil de l'eau; (*fig*) suivre le courant *or* le mouvement, faire comme tout le monde; (*lit, fig*) **to go against the ~** aller contre le courant *or* à contre-courant; *see* **down¹**, **up**.
c (*flow*) *[water etc]* flot *m*, jet *m*; *[lava]* flot, torrent *m*; *[blood, light]* flot; *[tears]* torrent, ruisseau *m*; *[cold air etc]* courant *m*; *[oaths, curses, excuses]* flot, torrent, déluge *m*; *[cars, trucks]* flot, succession *f*, défilé ininterrompu. **a thin ~ of water** un mince filet d'eau; **the water flowed out in a steady ~** l'eau s'écoulait régulièrement; *[oil]* **to be on ~** être en service; **to come on ~** être mis en service; **to bring the oil on ~** mettre le pipeline en service; **~s of people were coming out** des flots de gens sortaient, les gens sortaient à flots; (*Literat, Psych*) **the ~ of consciousness** la vie mouvante et insaisissable de la conscience, le "stream of consciousness".
d (*Brit Scol*) classe *f* de niveaux. (*Brit Scol*) **divided into 5 ~s** réparti en 5 classes de niveau; **the top/middle/bottom ~** la section forte/moyenne/faible (*de l'ensemble des élèves qui suivent le même programme*).
2 comp ►**streamline** *see* **streamline**.
3 vi a *[water, tears, oil, milk]* ruisseler; *[blood]* ruisseler, dégouliner. **to ~ with blood/tears** *etc* ruisseler de sang/de larmes *etc;* **the fumes made his eyes ~** les émanations l'ont fait pleurer à chaudes larmes; **cold air/sunlight ~ed through the window** l'air froid/le soleil entra à flots par la fenêtre.
b (*in wind etc: also* **~ out**) flotter au vent.
c *[people, cars etc]* **to ~ in/out/past** *etc* entrer/sortir/passer *etc* à flots.
4 vt a **to ~ blood/water** *etc* ruisseler de sang/d'eau *etc*.
b (*Scol*) *pupils* répartir par niveau. **to ~ French** *or* **the French classes** répartir les élèves par niveaux en français.

streamer ['stri:məʳ] n (*of paper*) serpentin *m*; (*banner*) banderole *f*; (*Astron*) flèche lumineuse; (*Press*) manchette *f*.

streaming ['stri:mɪŋ] 1 n (*Scol*) répartition *f* des élèves par niveaux.
2 adj: **I've got a ~ cold** je n'arrête pas de me moucher avec ce rhume.

streamline ['stri:mlaɪn] vt (*Aut, Aviat*) donner un profil aérodynamique à; (*fig*) *organization etc* rationaliser, procéder au dégraissage de.

streamlined ['stri:mlaɪnd] adj (*Aut*) aérodynamique; (*fig*) *organization* rationalisé, dégraissé.

streamlining ['stri:mlaɪnɪŋ] n (*fig: of organization etc*) rationalisation *f*, dégraissage *m*.

street [stri:t] 1 n rue *f*. **I saw him in the ~** je l'ai vu dans la rue; *[demonstrators, protesters]* **to take to the ~s** descendre dans la rue en signe de protestation; **to turn** *or* **put sb (out) into the ~** mettre qn à la rue; (*homeless*) **to be out on the ~(s)** être à la rue, être sans abri; (*fig*) **the man in the ~** l'homme de la rue, Monsieur-tout-le-monde; **a woman of the ~s** une prostituée; **she is on the ~s*, she works the ~s*** elle fait le trottoir*; (*Brit fig*) **that is right up my ~*** cela est tout à fait dans mes cordes; (*Brit fig*) **he is not in the same ~ as you*** il ne vous vient pas à la cheville; (*Brit fig*) **to be ~s ahead of sb*** dépasser qn de loin; (*fig*) **they're ~s apart*** un monde *or* tout les sépare; (*fig*) **~s better*** beaucoup mieux; *see* **back, high, queer, walk** *etc*.
2 comp *noises etc* de la rue; *singer etc* des rues ►**street academy** (*US Scol*) *école privée pour enfants appartenant à une minorité ethnique* ►**street accident** accident *m* de la circulation ►**street arab** gamin(e) *m(f)* des rues ►**streetcar** (*US*) tramway *m* ►**street cleaner** (*person*) balayeur *m*; (*machine*) balayeuse *f* ►**street cred*** *or* **credibility: to have street cred** *or* **credibility** être branché*; **this will do wonders for your street cred** ça fera des merveilles pour ton image de marque ►**street directory** = **street guide** ►**street door** porte *f* sur la rue *or* d'entrée ►**street fighting** (*NonC: Mil*) combats *mpl* de rue ►**street furniture** mobilier *m* urbain ►**street guide** guide *m or* répertoire *m or* index *m* des rues ►**street hawker** colporteur *m* ►**streetlamp** réverbère *m* ►**street level: at street level** au rez-de-chaussée ►**streetlight** = **streetlamp** ►**street lighting** (*NonC*) éclairage *m* des rues *or* de la voie publique ►**street map** plan *m* des rues ►**street market** marché *m* à ciel ouvert ►**street musician** musicien *m* des rues ►**street photographer** photostoppeur *m*, -euse *f* ►**street price** (*US, St Ex*) cours *m* après Bourse *or* hors Bourse ►**street seller** marchand ambulant ►**street sweeper** (*person*) balayeur *m*; (*machine*) balayeuse *f* ►**street trading** vente *f* ambulante *or* dans la rue ►**street urchin** gamin(e) *m(f)* des rues ►**street value** *[drugs]* valeur *f* au niveau du revendeur ►**street vendor** marchand ambulant ►**streetwalker** prostituée *f*, putain‡ *f* ►**streetwise** (*lit*) *child* conscient des dangers de la rue; (*fig*) *worker, policeman* futé, réaliste ►**street worker** (*US Soc*) assistant(e) *m(f)* social(e) pour les jeunes.

strength [streŋθ] n (*NonC*) a *[person, animal, hand, voice, magnet, lens]* force *f*, puissance *f*; (*health*) forces, robustesse *f*; *[enemy, team, nation, one's position]* force; *[building, wall, wood]* solidité *f*; *[shoes, material]* solidité, robustesse; *[wind]* force; *[current]* intensité *f*; *[character, accent, emotion, influence, attraction]* force; *[belief, opinion]* force, fermeté *f*; *[arguments, reasons]* force, solidité; *[protests]* force, vigueur *f*; *[claim, case]* solidité; *[tea, coffee, cigarette]* force; *[sauce]* goût relevé; *[drink]* teneur *f* en alcool; *[solution]* titre *m*. **he hadn't the ~ to lift it** il n'avait pas la force de le soulever; **his ~ failed him** ses forces l'ont abandonné; **give me ~!*** Dieu qu'il faut être patient!; **to get one's ~ back** reprendre des forces, recouvrer ses forces; **to go from ~ to ~** devenir de plus en plus fort; **~ of character** force de caractère; **~ of purpose** résolution *f*, détermination *f*; **~ of will** volonté *f*, fermeté; (*Fin*) **the ~ of the pound** la solidité de la livre; **the pound has gained in ~** la livre s'est consolidée; **to be bargaining** *etc* **from ~** être en position de force pour négocier *etc;* (*fig*) **on the ~ of** en vertu de; *see* **show, tensile** *etc*.
b (*Mil, Naut*) effectif(s) *m(pl)*. **fighting ~** effectif(s) mobilisable(s); **they are below** *or* **under ~** leur effectif n'est pas au complet; **to bring up to ~** compléter l'effectif de; **in** *or* **at full ~** au grand complet; (*fig*) **his friends were there in ~** ses amis étaient là en grand nombre; **to be on the ~** (*Mil*) figurer sur les contrôles; (*gen*) faire partie du personnel.

strengthen ['streŋθən] 1 vt *muscle, limb* fortifier, rendre fort; *eyesight* améliorer; *person* fortifier, remonter, tonifier; (*morally*) fortifier, tonifier, enhardir; *enemy, nation, team, one's position, protest, case* renforcer; (*Fin*) *the pound, stock market* consolider; *building, table* consolider, renforcer; *wall* étayer; *fabric, material* renforcer; *affection, emotion, effect* augmenter, renforcer; *opinion, belief* confirmer, renforcer. 2 vi *[muscle, limb]* devenir fort *or* vigoureux, se fortifier; *[wind]* augmenter, redoubler; *[desire, influence, characteristic]* augmenter; *[prices]* se raffermir.

strengthening ['streŋθənɪŋ] (*see* **strengthen**) 1 n renforcement *m*; consolidation *f*; augmentation *f*. 2 adj fortifiant, remontant, tonifiant. **to have a ~ effect on sth** avoir l'effet de consolider (*or* renforcer *etc*) qch.

strenuous ['strenjʊəs] adj *exercise, work, training* ardu; *game, march* fatigant, qui nécessite *or* exige de l'effort; *life, holiday* très actif; *effort, attempt* acharné, vigoureux; *protest* vigoureux, énergique; *attack, conflict, opposition, resistance* acharné. **I have had a ~ day** je me suis beaucoup dépensé aujourd'hui; **it was all too ~ for me** cela nécessitait trop d'effort pour moi; **I'd like to do something a little less ~** j'aimerais faire quelque chose qui exige (*subj*) un peu moins d'effort; (*Med*) **he mustn't do anything ~** il ne faut pas qu'il se fatigue; **to make ~ efforts to do** faire des efforts acharnés pour faire, s'efforcer avec acharnement de faire.

strenuously ['strenjʊəslɪ] adv *work, protest* énergiquement; *exercise, pull* vigoureusement; *resist, try* avec acharnement.

strenuousness ['strenjʊəsnɪs] n (degré *m* d')effort *m* requis (*of* par).

streptococcal [ˌstreptəʊ'kɒkl] adj, **streptococcic** [ˌstreptəʊ'kɒksɪk] adj streptococcique.

streptococcus [ˌstreptəʊ'kɒkəs] n, pl **streptococci** [ˌstreptəʊ'kɒkaɪ] streptocoque *m*.

streptomycin [ˌstreptəʊ'maɪsɪn] n streptomycine *f*.

stress [stres] 1 n a (*pressure etc*) pression *f*, contrainte *f*, agression *f*, stress *m*; (*Med*) stress; (*also* **mental ~, nervous ~**) tension *f* (nerveuse). **in times of ~** à des moments *or* à une période de grande tension; **under the ~ of circumstances** poussé par les circonstances, sous la pression des circonstances; **the ~es and strains of modern life** toutes les pressions et les tensions de la vie moderne, les agressions de la vie moderne; **to be under ~** *[person]* être stressé; *[relationship]* être tendu; **this put him under great ~** ceci l'a considérablement stressé; **he reacts well under ~** il réagit bien dans des conditions difficiles.
b (*emphasis*) insistance *f*. **to lay ~ on** *good manners, academic subjects etc* insister sur, mettre l'accent sur; *fact, detail* insister sur, faire ressortir.
c (*Ling, Poetry*) (*NonC: gen*) accentuation *f*; (*accent; on syllable*) accent *m*; (*accented syllable*) syllabe accentuée; (*Mus*) accent. (*Ling*) **the ~ is on the first syllable** l'accent tombe sur la première syllabe; *see* **primary, secondary**.
d (*Tech*) effort *m*; charge *f*; travail *m*. **tensile ~** tension *f*; **the ~ acting on a metal** l'effort qui agit sur un métal; **the ~ produced in the metal** le travail du métal; *[beam, metal]* **to be in ~** travailler; **the ~ to which a beam is subjected** la charge qu'on fait subir à une poutre; **a ~ of 500 kilos per square millimetre** une charge de 500 kilos par millimètre carré.
2 comp ►**stress mark** (*Ling*) accent *m* ►**stress quotient: this job has a high stress quotient** ce travail provoque une grande tension nerveuse ►**stress-related** *illness* causé par le stress.
3 vt a (*emphasize*) *good manners, one's innocence* insister sur; *fact, detail* faire ressortir, souligner, attirer l'attention sur.
b (*Ling, Mus, Poetry*) accentuer.
c (*Tech: natural process*) fatiguer, faire travailler; (*Tech: industrial process*) *metal* mettre sous tension.

stressed [strest] adj a (*under stress*) *person* stressé, tendu; *relationship etc* tendu. b (*Ling, Poetry*) accentué.

stressful ['stresfʊl] adj *way of life, circumstances* difficile, qui engendre beaucoup de tension nerveuse, stressant.

stretch [stretʃ] 1 n a (*act, gesture*) étirement *m*; (*distance, span: of wing etc*) envergure *f*. **with a ~ of his arm** en étendant le bras; **to give a rope a ~** étirer une corde; **to give shoes a ~** élargir des chaussures; **there's not much ~ left in this elastic** cet élastique a beaucoup perdu de son élasticité; **there's a lot of ~ in this material** ce tissu donne *or* prête bien; **to be at full ~** *[arms, rope etc]* être complètement tendu; (*fig*) *[engine etc]* tourner à plein; *[factory]* tourner à plein (rendement); *[person]* donner son plein; **by a ~ of the imagination** en faisant un effort d'imagination; **by no ~ of the imagination can one say** ... même en faisant un gros effort d'imagination on ne peut pas dire ...; **not by a long ~**! loin de là!
b (*period of time*) période *f*. **for a long ~ of time** (pendant) longtemps; **for hours at a ~** (pendant) des heures d'affilée *or* sans discontinuer *or* sans interruption; **he read it all in one ~** il l'a tout lu d'une seule traite, il l'a lu (tout) d'une traite; (*Prison sl*) **to do a ~** faire de la prison *or* de la taule‡; **he's done a 10-year ~** il a fait 10 ans de prison *or* taule‡.
c (*area*) étendue *f*; (*part*) partie *f*, bout *m*. **vast ~es of sand/snow** de vastes étendues de sable/de neige; **there's a straight ~ (of road) after you pass the lake** la route est toute droite *or* il y a un bout tout droit une fois que vous avez dépassé le lac; **a magnificent ~ of country** une campagne magnifique; **in that ~ of the river** dans cette partie de la rivière; **for a long ~ the road runs between steep hills** sur des kilomètres la route serpente entre des collines escarpées; (*Racing, Running, also fig*) **to go into the final ~** entrer dans la dernière ligne droite; *see* **home**.
d (*Naut*) bordée *f* (courue sous les mêmes amures).
2 adj *fabric, socks, trousers* extensible; (*elasticated*) élastique. (*on skin*) **~ mark** vergeture *f*.
3 vt a (*make longer, wider etc*) *rope, spring* tendre; *elastic* étirer; *shoe, glove, hat* élargir; (*Med*) *muscle, tendon* distendre; (*fig*) *law, rules* tourner; *meaning* forcer; *one's principles* adapter; *one's authority* outrepasser, excéder. (*fig*) **(if you were) to ~ a point you could say that** ... on pourrait peut-être aller jusqu'à dire que ...; **you could ~ a point and allow him to** ... vous pourriez faire une petite concession et lui permettre de ...; **to ~ the truth** forcer la vérité, exagérer.
b (*extend: often* **~ out**) *wing* déployer; *rope, net, canopy* tendre (*between* entre, *above* au-dessus de); *rug* étendre, étaler; *linen* étendre. (*after sleep etc*) **to ~ o.s.** s'étirer (*see also* **3d**); **he had to ~ his neck to see** il a dû tendre le cou pour voir; **he ~ed (out) his arm to grasp the handle** il tendit *or* allongea le bras pour saisir la poignée; **he ~ed his arms and yawned** il s'étira et bâilla; **he ~ed his leg to ease the cramp** il a étendu *or* allongé la jambe pour atténuer la crampe; (*fig: go for a walk*) **I'm just going to ~ my legs** je vais me dégourdir les jambes; **the blow ~ed him (out) cold** le coup l'a mis K.-O.*; *[rope etc]* **to be fully ~ed** être complètement tendu; *see also* **3c, 3d**.
c (*fig*) *resources, supplies, funds, income* (*make them last*) faire durer, tirer le maximum de; (*put demands on them*) mettre à rude épreuve. **to be fully ~ed** *[engine]* tourner à plein; *[factory]* tourner à plein (rendement); **our supplies/resources** *etc* **are fully ~ed** nos provisions/ressources *etc* sont utilisées au maximum, nos provisions/ressources *etc* ne sont pas élastiques; **we're very ~ed at the moment** on tourne à plein en ce moment; *see also* **3b, 3d**.
d (*fig*) *athlete, student etc* pousser, exiger le maximum de. **the work he is doing does not ~ him enough** le travail qu'il fait n'exige pas assez de lui *or* n'est pas assez astreignant; **to be fully ~ed** travailler à la limite de ses possibilités; **to ~ o.s. too far** vouloir en faire trop; *see also* **3b, 3c**.
4 vi a *[person, animal]* s'étirer. **he ~ed lazily** il s'est étiré paresseusement; **he ~ed across me to get the book** il a tendu le bras devant moi pour prendre le livre.
b (*lengthen*) s'allonger; (*widen*) s'élargir; *[elastic]* s'étirer, se tendre; *[fabric, jersey, gloves, shoes]* prêter, donner.
c (*extend, reach, spread out: often* **~ out**) *[rope etc]* s'étendre, aller; *[forest, plain, procession, sb's authority, influence]* s'étendre. **the rope won't ~ to that post** la corde ne va pas jusqu'à ce poteau; **how far will it ~?** jusqu'où ça va?; (*fig*) **my money won't ~* to a new car** mon budget ne me permet pas d'acheter une nouvelle voiture; **the festivities ~ed (out) into January** les festivités se sont prolongées sur une partie de janvier; **a life of misery ~ed (out) before her** une vie de misère s'étendait *or* s'étalait devant elle.

►**stretch across** vi: **he stretched across and touched her cheek** il a tendu la main et touché sa joue.

►**stretch down** vi: **she stretched down and picked up the book** elle a tendu la main et ramassé le livre, elle a allongé le bras pour ramasser le livre.

►**stretch out** 1 vi *[person, arm etc]* s'étendre, s'allonger; *[countryside etc]* s'étendre. **he stretched (himself) out on the bed** il s'est étendu *or* allongé sur le lit; *see also* **stretch 4c**. 2 vt sep a (*reach*) *arm, hand, foot* tendre, allonger; (*extend*) *leg etc* allonger, étendre; *wing* déployer; *net, canopy, rope* tendre; *rug* étendre, étaler; *linen* étendre; (*lengthen*) *meeting, discussion* prolonger; *story, explanation* allonger; *see also* **stretch 3b**. b = **stretch 3c**.

►**stretch over** vi = **stretch across**.

►**stretch up** vi: **he stretched up to reach the shelf** il s'est étiré pour atteindre l'étagère.

stretcher ['stretʃəʳ] 1 n a (*Med*) brancard *m*, civière *f*.
b (*device*) (*for gloves*) ouvre-gants *m inv*; (*for shoes*) forme *f*; (*for fabric*) cadre *m*; (*for artist's canvas*) cadre, châssis *m*; (*on umbrella*) baleine *f*.
c (*Constr: brick*) panneresse *f*, carreau *m*; (*crosspiece in framework*) traverse *f*; (*crossbar in chair, bed etc*) barreau *m*, bâton *m*; (*cross-plank in canoe etc*) barre *f* de pieds.
2 comp ►**stretcher-bearer** (*Med*) brancardier *m* ►**stretcher case** malade *mf or* blessé(e) *m(f)* qui ne peut pas marcher ►**stretcher party** détachement *m* de brancardiers.
3 vt porter sur un brancard *or* une civière. **the goalkeeper was ~ed off** le gardien de but a été emmené sur un brancard *or* une civière.

stretchy ['stretʃɪ] adj extensible, qui donne, qui prête.

strew [struː] pret **strewed**, ptp **strewed** *or* **strewn** [struːn] vt *straw, sand, sawdust* répandre, éparpiller (*on, over* sur); *flowers, objects* éparpiller, semer (*on, over* sur); *wreckage etc* éparpiller, disséminer (*over* sur); *ground, floor* joncher, parsemer (*with* de); *room, table* joncher (*also fig*).

strewth‡ [struːθ] excl ça alors!*, bon sang!*

striate [straɪ'eɪt] vt strier.

stricken ['strɪkən] 1 (*rare*) ptp of **strike**. 2 adj *person, animal* (*wounded*) gravement blessé; (*ill*) atteint *or* touché par un mal; (*afflicted*) *look, expression* affligé; (*in dire straits*) *person, country, army* très éprouvé; (*damaged*) *city* dévasté, ravagé; *ship* très endommagé; *see also* **strike**.

-stricken ['strɪkən] adj ending in comps frappé de, atteint de, accablé de. **plague-stricken** pestiféré, atteint de la peste, frappé par la peste; *see* **grief** *etc*.

strict [strɪkt] adj a (*severe, stern*) *person, principle, views* strict, sévère; *discipline* strict, sévère, rigoureux; *ban, rule* strict, rigoureux; *order* formel; *etiquette* rigide. **to be ~ with sb** être strict *or* sévère avec *or* à l'égard de qn.
b (*precise*) *meaning* strict (*after noun*); *translation* précis, exact; (*absolute*) *accuracy, secrecy* strict (*before noun*), absolu; *privacy* strict (*before noun*). **in the ~ sense of the word** au sens strict du mot; **there is a ~ time limit on** ... il y a un délai impératif *or* de rigueur en ce qui concerne ...; **the ~ truth** la stricte vérité, l'exacte vérité; (*US Jur*) **~ construction/constructionist** interprétation *f* stricte/interprète *mf* strict(e) (*de la constitution américaine*); (*Jur*) **~ liability**

responsabilité *f* sans faute; *see* **confidence.**

strictly ['strɪktlɪ] **adv** a (*sternly, severely*) *treat, bring up* strictement, d'une manière stricte, sévèrement, avec sévérité, avec rigueur. b (*precisely*) strictement, exactement, rigoureusement; (*absolutely*) strictement, absolument. ~ **confidential/personal** strictement confidentiel/privé; ~ **private and confidential** personnel et confidentiel; ~ **between ourselves** strictement entre nous; ~ **speaking** à strictement *or* à proprement parler; ~ **prohibited** (*gen*) formellement interdit; (*Admin*) interdit à titre absolu; **"smoking ~ prohibited"** "défense formelle de fumer"; *see* **bird.**

strictness ['strɪktnɪs] **n** *[person, principles, views]* sévérité *f*; *[discipline]* sévérité, rigueur *f*; *[translation]* exactitude *f*, précision *f*.

stricture ['strɪktʃəʳ] **n** (*criticism*) critique *f* (hostile) (*on* de); (*restriction*) restriction *f* (*on* de); (*Med*) sténose *f*, rétrécissement *m*.

stridden ['strɪdn] **ptp of stride.**

stride [straɪd] (**vb: pret strode, ptp stridden**) 1 **n** grand pas, enjambée *f*; *[runner]* foulée *f*. **with giant ~s** à pas de géant; **in** *or* **with a few ~s he had caught up with the others** il avait rattrapé les autres en quelques enjambées *or* foulées; (*fig*) **to make great ~s** faire de grands progrès (*in French* en français, *in one's studies* dans ses études, *in doing* pour ce qui est de faire); **to get into one's ~**, (*US*) **to hit one's ~** trouver son rythme, prendre la cadence; **to take in one's ~** *changes etc* accepter sans sourciller *or* sans se laisser abattre; *exam/interrogation etc* passer/subir *etc* comme si de rien n'était; (*gen*) **he took it in his ~** il ne s'est pas laissé abattre, il a fait comme si de rien n'était; (*US fig*) **to be caught off ~** être pris au dépourvu.

2 **vi** marcher à grands pas *or* à grandes enjambées. **to ~ along/in/away** *etc* avancer/entrer/s'éloigner *etc* à grands pas *or* à grandes enjambées; **he was striding up and down the room** il arpentait la pièce.

3 **vt** a *deck, yard, streets* arpenter.

b (†) = **bestride.**

stridency ['straɪdənsɪ] **n** stridence *f*.

strident ['straɪdənt] **adj** strident (*also Phon*).

stridently ['straɪdəntlɪ] **adv** *announce, declare* d'une voix stridente; *hoot, sound, whistle* d'une façon stridente.

strife [straɪf] 1 **n** (*NonC*) conflit *m*, dissensions *fpl*, luttes *fpl*, (*less serious*) querelles *fpl*. (*Pol*) **party crippled by internal ~** parti paralysé par des dissensions *or* des querelles intestines; **industrial ~** conflits sociaux; **domestic ~** querelles de ménage, dissensions domestiques; (*liter*) **to cease from ~** déposer les armes. 2 **comp ►strife-ridden** déchiré par les luttes *or* les conflits.

strike [straɪk] (**vb: pret struck, ptp struck,** (*rare*) **stricken**) 1 **n** a (*act*) coup *m* (frappé); (*Aviat, Mil*) raid *m* (aérien). (*Mil*) **first ~ weapon** arme *f* de première frappe.

b (*Ind*) grève *f* (*of, by* de). **the coal ~** la grève des mineurs; **the electricity/gas ~** la grève (des employés) de l'électricité/du gaz; **the transport/hospital ~** la grève des transports/des hôpitaux; **the Ford ~** la grève chez Ford; **to be (out) on ~** être en grève, faire grève (*for* pour obtenir, *against* pour protester contre); **to go on ~, to come out on ~** se mettre en grève, faire grève; *see* **general, hunger, rail, steel, sympathy** *etc*.

c (*Min, Miner etc: discovery*) découverte *f*. **the rich ~ of oil** la découverte d'un riche gisement de pétrole; **to make a ~** découvrir un gisement; (*fig*) **a lucky ~** un coup de chance.

d (*Fishing: by angler*) ferrage *m*; (*Fishing: by fish*) touche *f*, mordage *m*; (*Baseball, Bowling*) strike *m*. (*US fig*) **you have two ~s against you** tu es mal parti*, ça se présente mal pour toi.

e *[clock]* sonnerie *f* des heures.

2 **comp** (*Ind*) *committee, fund* de grève **►strikebound** bloqué par une (*or* la) grève **►strikebreaker** (*Ind*) briseur *m* de grève **►strikebreaking: he was accused of strikebreaking** on l'a accusé d'être un briseur de grève **►strike clause** (*Ind*) clause *f* en cas de grève **►strike force** (*gen: of police etc*) brigade *f* spéciale, détachement *m*; (*Mil*) force *f* de frappe **►strike fund** (*Ind*) caisse *f* syndicale de grève **►strike leader** (*Ind*) leader *m or* dirigeant *m* des grévistes **►strike pay** (*Ind*) salaire *m* de gréviste.

3 **vt** a (*hit*) *person* frapper, donner un *or* des coup(s) à; *ball* toucher, frapper; *nail, table* frapper sur, taper sur, donner un coup sur, cogner sur; (*Mus*) *string* toucher, pincer; *[snake]* mordre, piquer. **to ~ sth with one's fist, to ~ one's fist on sth** frapper du poing *or* donner un coup de poing sur qch; **to ~ sth with a hammer** frapper *or* taper *or* cogner sur qch avec un marteau, donner un coup de marteau sur qch; (*fig*) **to ~ a man when he is down** frapper un homme à terre; **he struck me (a blow) on the chin** il m'a frappé au menton, il m'a donné un coup de poing au menton; **to ~ the first blow** donner le premier coup, frapper le premier (*or* la première); (*fig*) **to ~ a blow for freedom** rompre une lance pour la liberté; (*fig*) **he struck his rival a shrewd blow by buying the land** il a porté à son rival un coup subtil en achetant la terre; **he struck the knife from his assailant's hand** d'un coup de poing il a fait tomber le couteau de la main de son assaillant; **the pain struck him as he bent down** la douleur l'a saisi quand il s'est baissé; **disease struck the city** la maladie a frappé la ville *or* s'est abattue sur la ville; **to be stricken by** *or* **with remorse** être pris de remords; (*fig*) **the news struck him all of a heap**‡ la nouvelle lui a coupé bras et jambes *or* l'a éberlué*; (*fig*) **he was struck all of a heap**‡ il en est resté baba*; **the city was struck** *or* **stricken by fear** la ville a été prise de peur, la peur s'est emparée de la ville; **to ~ fear into sb('s heart)** remplir (le cœur de) qn d'effroi; **it struck terror and dismay into the whole population** cela a terrorisé la population tout entière.

b (*knock against*) *[person, one's shoulder etc, spade]* cogner contre, heurter; *[car etc]* heurter, rentrer dans*; (*Naut*) *rocks, the bottom* toucher, heurter; (*fig*) *[lightning, light]* frapper. **he struck his head on** *or* **against the table as he fell** sa tête a heurté la table quand il est tombé, il s'est cogné la tête à *or* contre la table en tombant; **the stone struck him on the head** la pierre l'a frappé *or* l'a heurté à la tête; **he was struck by 2 bullets** il a reçu 2 balles; **to be struck by lightning** être frappé par la foudre, être foudroyé; **a piercing cry struck his ear** un cri perçant lui a frappé l'oreille *or* les oreilles; **the horrible sight that struck his eyes** le spectacle horrible qui lui a frappé les yeux *or* le regard *or* la vue.

c (*find, discover*) *gold* découvrir, trouver; (*fig*) *hotel, road* tomber sur, trouver; (*fig*) *difficulty, obstacle* rencontrer. **to ~ oil** (*Miner*) trouver du pétrole; (*fig*) trouver le filon*; (*fig*) **to ~ it rich** faire fortune; *see* **patch.**

d (*make, produce etc*) *coin, medal* frapper; *sparks, fire* faire jaillir (*from* de); *match* frotter, gratter; (*fig*) *agreement, truce* arriver à, conclure. **to ~ a light** allumer une allumette (*or* un briquet *etc*); (*Bot*) **to ~ roots** prendre racine; (*Horticulture*) **to ~ cuttings** faire prendre racine à des boutures; **to ~ an average** établir une moyenne; **to ~ a balance** trouver un équilibre, trouver le juste milieu; **to ~ a bargain** conclure un marché; **to ~ an attitude** poser; **to ~ an attitude of surprise** faire l'étonné(e); *see* **pose.**

e *chord, note* sonner, faire entendre; *[clock]* sonner. (*fig*) **that ~s a chord** cela me dit *or* me rappelle quelque chose; (*fig*) **to ~ a false note** sonner faux; **to ~ a note of warning** donner *or* sonner l'alarme; **the clock struck 3** la pendule a sonné 3 heures; **it has just struck 6** 6 heures viennent juste de sonner; (*Naut*) **to ~ 4 bells** piquer 4.

f (*take down*) *tent* démonter, plier; *sail* amener; *camp* lever; *flag* baisser, amener. (*Theat*) **to ~ the set** démonter le décor.

g (*delete*) *name* rayer (*from* de); *person* (*from list*) rayer; (*from professional register*) radier (*from* de). **the judge ordered the remark to be struck** *or* **stricken from the record** le juge a ordonné que la remarque soit rayée du procès-verbal.

h (*cause to be or become*) rendre (subitement). (*lit, fig*) **to ~ sb dumb** rendre qn muet; **to ~ sb dead** porter un coup mortel à qn; (*fig*) **~ me pink!**‡ j'en suis soufflé!*

i (*make impression on*) frapper; sembler, paraître (*sb* à qn). **I was struck by his intelligence** j'ai été frappé par son intelligence; **I wasn't very struck* with him** il ne m'a pas fait très bonne impression; **to be struck on sb**‡ (*impressed by*) être très impressionné par qn; (*in love with*) être toqué* de qn; **the funny side of it struck me later** le côté drôle de la chose m'est apparu *or* m'a frappé plus tard; **that ~s me as a good idea** cela me semble *or* paraît une bonne idée; **an idea suddenly struck him** soudain il a eu une idée, une idée lui est venue soudain à l'esprit; **it ~s me that** *or* **~s me* he is lying** j'ai l'impression qu'il ment, à mon avis il ment; **how did he ~ you?** quelle impression *or* quel effet vous a-t-il fait?; **how did the film ~ you?** qu'avez-vous pensé du film?

j (*Fishing*) *[angler]* ferrer. **the fish struck the bait** le poisson a mordu à l'appât.

4 **vi** a (*hit*) frapper; (*attack*) (*Mil*) attaquer; *[snake]* mordre, piquer; *[tiger]* sauter sur sa proie; (*fig*) *[disease etc]* frapper; *[panic]* s'emparer des esprits. (*lit, fig*) **to ~ home** frapper *or* toucher juste, faire mouche; (*fig*) **to ~ lucky** avoir de la chance; **he struck at his attacker** il porta un coup à son assaillant; **we must ~ at the root of this evil** nous devons attaquer *or* couper ce mal dans sa racine; (*fig*) **it ~s at the root of our parliamentary system** cela porte atteinte aux fondements mêmes de notre système parlementaire; **his speech ~s at the heart of the problem** son discours porte sur le fond même du problème; **he struck at the heart of the problem** il a mis le doigt sur le fond du problème; **his foot struck against** *or* **on a rock** son pied a buté contre *or* heurté un rocher; **when the ship struck** quand le bateau a touché; **the sun was striking through the mist** le soleil perçait la brume; **the chill struck through to his very bones** le froid a pénétré jusqu'à la moelle de ses os; *see* **iron.**

b *[match]* s'allumer.

c *[clock]* sonner. **has 6 o'clock struck?** est-ce que 6 heures ont sonné?; (*fig*) **his hour has struck** son heure est venue *or* a sonné.

d (*Ind: go on ~*) faire grève (*for* pour obtenir, *against* pour protester contre).

e (*turn, move, go*) aller, prendre. **~ left on leaving the forest** prenez à gauche en sortant de la forêt; **to ~ uphill** se mettre à grimper la côte.

f (*Horticulture: take root*) prendre racine; (*Fishing: seize bait*) mordre.

►strike back vt (*Mil, gen*) rendre les coups (*at sb* à qn), se venger (*at sb* de qn), user de représailles (*at sb* à l'égard de qn).

►strike down vt sep abattre; (*fig*) *[esp disease]* terrasser.

►strike in vi (*fig: interrupt*) interrompre.

►**strike off** 1 vi (*change direction*) prendre, aller. **he struck off across the fields** il a pris *or* il s'en est allé à travers champs. 2 vt sep a *sb's head* trancher, couper; *branch* couper. b (*score out, delete*) (*from list*) rayer. *[doctor etc]* **to be struck off** être radié. c (*Typ*) tirer.

►**strike on** vt fus *idea* avoir; *solution* tomber sur, trouver.

►**strike out** 1 vi a (*hit out*) se débattre. **he struck out wildly** il s'est débattu furieusement; **he struck out at his attackers** il lança une volée de coups dans la direction de ses attaquants. b (*set off*) **to strike out for the shore** *[swimmer]* se mettre à nager *or* *[rower]* se mettre à ramer vers le rivage; (*fig*) **he left the firm and struck out on his own** il a quitté l'entreprise et s'est mis à son compte. 2 vt sep (*delete*) *word, question* rayer.

►**strike through** vt sep = **strike out 2**.

►**strike up** 1 vi *[band etc]* commencer à jouer; *[music]* commencer. 2 vt sep (*Mus*) *[band]* se mettre à jouer; *[singers]* se mettre à chanter. **strike up the band!** faites jouer l'orchestre!; **to strike up an acquaintance** faire *or* lier connaissance (*with sb* avec qn); **to strike up a friendship** lier amitié (*with sb* avec qn).

►**strike upon** vt fus = **strike on**.

striker ['straɪkəʳ] n a (*Ind*) gréviste *mf*. b (*clapper*) frappeur *m*; (*on clock*) marteau *m*; (*on gun*) percuteur *m*. c (*Ftbl*) buteur *m*.

striking ['straɪkɪŋ] 1 adj a (*impressive, outstanding*) frappant, saisissant. b *clock* qui sonne les heures. **the ~ mechanism** la sonnerie des heures. c (*Mil*) *force, power* de frappe. (*Mil, fig*) **within ~ distance** *or* **range of sth** à portée de qch. d (*Ind*) *workers* en grève, gréviste. 2 n a *[coins]* frappe *f*. b *[clock]* sonnerie *f* des heures.

strikingly ['straɪkɪŋlɪ] adv d'une manière frappante *or* saisissante, remarquablement. ~ **beautiful** d'une beauté frappante *or* saisissante, remarquablement beau (*f* belle).

string [strɪŋ] (vb: pret, ptp **strung**) 1 n a (*cord*) ficelle *f*; *[violin, piano, bow, racket etc]* corde *f*; *[puppet]* ficelle, fil *m*; *[apron, bonnet, anorak]* cordon *m*; (*Bot: on bean etc*) fil(s). **a piece of ~** un bout de ficelle; (*fig*) **he had to pull ~s to get the job** il a dû user de son influence *or* se faire pistonner *or* faire jouer le piston pour obtenir le poste; **to pull ~s for sb** exercer son influence pour aider qn, pistonner qn; (*fig*) **with no ~s attached** sans condition(s); (*fig*) **there are no ~s attached** cela ne vous (*or* nous *etc*) engage à rien; **he has got her on a ~** il la tient, il la mène par le bout du nez; **to have more than one ~ to one's bow** avoir plus d'une corde à son arc; **his first ~** sa première ressource; **his second ~** sa deuxième ressource, la solution de rechange; (*Mus*) **the ~s** les cordes, les instruments *mpl* à cordes; *see* **apron, heart** *etc*.

b *[beads, pearls]* rang *m*; *[onions]* chapelet *m*; *[garlic]* chaîne *f*; (*fig*) *[people, vehicles]* file *f*; *[racehorses]* écurie *f*; *[curses, lies, insults, excuses]* kyrielle *f*, chapelet.

c (*Ling*) séquence *f*.

d (*Comput*) chaîne *f*. **a numeric/character ~** une chaîne numérique/de caractères.

e (*Sport*) équipe *f* (provisoire).

2 comp (*Mus*) *orchestra, quartet* à cordes; *serenade, piece* pour cordes ►**string bag** filet *m* à provisions ►**string bean** (*vegetable*) haricot vert; (*US fig: tall thin person*) asperge* *f*, grande perche *f* ►**string correspondent** (*US Press*) correspondant(e) *m(f)* local(e) à temps partiel ►**string(ed) instrument** (*Mus*) instrument *m* à cordes ►**string player** (*Mus*) musicien(ne) *m(f)* qui joue d'un instrument à cordes ►**string-puller**: **he's a string-puller** il n'hésite pas à se faire pistonner *or* à faire jouer le piston ►**string-pulling** le piston ►**string tie** cravate-lacet *f* ►**string vest** tricot *m* (de corps) de coton à grosses mailles.

3 vt a *violin etc* monter; *bow* garnir d'une corde; *racket* corder; *see* **highly**.

b *beads, pearls* enfiler; *rope* tendre (*across* en travers de, *between* entre). **they strung lights in the trees** ils ont suspendu *or* attaché des (guirlandes de) lampions dans les arbres.

c *beans* enlever les fils de.

►**string along*** 1 vi suivre. **to string along with sb** (*accompany*) accompagner qn, aller *or* venir avec qn; (*fig: agree with*) se ranger du côté de *or* à l'avis de qn. 2 vt sep (*pej*) faire marcher, bercer de fausses espérances.

►**string out** 1 vi *[people, things]* s'échelonner (*along a road* le long d'une route). **string out a bit more!** espacez-vous un peu plus! 2 vt sep a *lanterns, washing etc* suspendre; *guards, posts* échelonner. *[people, things]* **to be strung out along the road** être échelonnés *or* s'échelonner le long de la route. b (*fig*) **to be strung out**‡ (*gen*) (*debilitated*) être à plat; (*disturbed*) être perturbé; (*Drugs sl: addicted*) être accroché‡; (*Drugs sl: under influence*) être drogué; (*Drugs sl: with withdrawal symptoms*) être en manque; **strung out‡ on drugs** *etc* abruti par la drogue *etc*.

►**string up** vt sep a *lantern, onions, nets* suspendre (au moyen d'une corde). b (*fig*) **he had strung himself up to do it** il avait aiguisé toutes ses facultés en vue de le faire; **to be strung up (about sth)** être très tendu *or* nerveux (à la pensée de qch). c (*: *hang; lynch*) pendre.

stringed [strɪŋd] adj *see* **string 2**.

-stringed [strɪŋd] adj ending in comps: **4-stringed** à 4 cordes.

stringency ['strɪndʒənsɪ] n (*see* **stringent**) rigueur *f*; irrésistibilité *f*. **in times of economic ~** en période d'austérité.

stringent ['strɪndʒənt] adj (*strict*) *rule, order, law* strict, rigoureux; *measures* énergique, rigoureux; (*compelling*) *reasons, arguments* irrésistible; *necessity* impérieux. (*Fin*) **~ money market** marché financier tendu *or* serré.

stringently ['strɪndʒəntlɪ] adv rigoureusement, strictement.

stringer ['strɪŋəʳ] n (*journalist*) correspondant(e) *m(f)* local(e) à temps partiel.

stringy ['strɪŋɪ] adj *beans, celery, meat* filandreux; *molasses, cooked cheese* filant, qui file; *plant, seaweed* tout en longueur; (*fig*) *person* filiforme.

strip [strɪp] 1 n a *[metal, wood, paper, grass]* bande *f*; *[fabric]* bande, bandelette *f*; *[ground]* bande, langue *f*; *[water, sea]* bras *m*. **a ~ of garden** un petit jardin tout en longueur; **to tear sb off a ~**‡, **to tear a ~ off sb**‡ bien sonner les cloches à qn*.

b (*Aviat: also* **landing ~**) piste *f* d'atterrissage.

c (*also* **comic ~**) = **~ cartoon**; *see* **2**.

d (*Brit Ftbl etc: clothes*) tenue *f*. **the England ~** la tenue de l'équipe (de football) d'Angleterre.

e (*) = **~tease**; *see* **striptease**.

2 comp ►**strip cartoon** (*Brit*) bande dessinée ►**strip club** boîte *f* de striptease ►**strip cropping** (*Agr*) *cultures alternées selon les courbes de niveaux* ►**strip joint** (*US*) = **strip club** ►**strip lighting** (*Brit*) éclairage *m* au néon *or* fluorescent ►**strip mining** (*US*) extraction *f* à ciel ouvert ►**strip poker** strip-poker *m* ►**strip-search** n fouille *f* au corps ◊ vt **he was strip-searched at the airport** on l'a obligé à se dévêtir avant de le fouiller à l'aéroport ►**strip show** strip-tease *m* ►**striptease** *see* **striptease** ►**strip-wash** n (grande) toilette *f* (*surtout d'un malade*) ◊ vt faire la (grande) toilette de.

3 vt a (*remove everything from*) *person* déshabiller, dévêtir; (*often* **~ down**) *room, house* démeubler, vider; *[thieves]* dévaliser, vider; *car, engine, gun* démonter complètement; (*Tech*) *nut, screw, gears* arracher le filet de; *[wind, people, birds]* *branches, bushes* dépouiller, dégarnir; (*take paint etc off*) *furniture, door* décaper. **to ~ sb naked** *or* **to the skin** déshabiller *or* dévêtir qn complètement; **to ~ a bed (down)** défaire un lit complètement; **to ~ (down) the walls** enlever *or* arracher le papier peint; **~ped pine** pin *m* décapé; **~ped pine furniture** vieux meubles en pin décapé.

b (*remove*) *old covers, wallpaper, decorations, ornaments* enlever; *old paint* décaper, enlever. **to ~ the bark from the tree** dépouiller un arbre de son écorce.

c (*deprive etc*) *person, object* dépouiller (*of* de). **to ~ a tree of its bark** dépouiller un arbre de son écorce; **to ~ a room of all its pictures** enlever tous les tableaux dans une pièce; **to ~ sb of his titles/honours** dépouiller qn de ses titres/honneurs; (*Fin*) **to ~ a company of its assets** cannibaliser* une compagnie; *see also* **asset**.

4 vi se déshabiller, se dévêtir; *[striptease artist]* faire du strip-tease. **to ~ naked** *or* **to the skin** se mettre nu; **to ~ to the waist** se déshabiller *or* se dévêtir jusqu'à la ceinture, se mettre torse nu; **to be ~ped to the waist** être nu jusqu'à la ceinture, être torse nu.

►**strip down** 1 vi = **strip off 1**. 2 vt sep (*Tech etc*) *machine, engine, gun* démonter complètement; *see also* **strip 3a**.

►**strip off** 1 vi se déshabiller *or* se dévêtir complètement, se mettre nu. 2 vt sep *buttons, ornaments* enlever, ôter (*from* de); *paper* enlever, arracher (*from* de); *leaves* faire tomber (*from* de); *berries* prendre (*from* de).

stripe [straɪp] n a (*of one colour: also Zool*) raie *f*, rayure *f*. (*pattern*) **~s** (*gen*) rayures; (*Zool*) rayures, zébrures *fpl*; **yellow with a white ~** jaune rayé de blanc; *see* **pin, star** *etc*. b (*Mil*) galon *m*. **to get one's ~s** gagner ses galons; **to lose one's ~s** être dégradé. c (†) (*lash*) coup *m* de fouet; (*weal*) marque *f* (d'un coup de fouet).

striped [straɪpt] adj *fabric, garment* rayé, à raies, à rayures; (*Zool*) rayé, tigré. **~ with red** à raies *or* rayures rouges, rayé de rouge.

stripling ['strɪplɪŋ] n adolescent *m*, tout jeune homme, gringalet *m* (*pej*).

stripper ['strɪpəʳ] n a (*also* **paint-~**) décapant *m*. b (*: *striptease artist*) strip-teaseuse *f*. **male ~** strip-teaseur *m*.

striptease ['strɪptiːz] n strip-tease *m*, effeuillage *m*. **~ artist** strip-teaseuse *f*, effeuilleuse *f*.

stripteaser ['strɪptiːzəʳ] n strip-teaseuse *f*, effeuilleuse *f*.

stripy ['straɪpɪ] adj rayé, à raies, à rayures.

strive [straɪv] pret **strove**, ptp **striven** ['strɪvn] vi a (*try hard*) s'efforcer (*to do* de faire), faire son possible (*to do* pour faire), s'évertuer (*to do* à faire). **to ~ after** *or* **for sth** s'efforcer de *or* faire son possible pour *or* s'évertuer à obtenir qch. b (*liter: struggle, fight*) lutter, se battre (*against, with* contre).

striving ['straɪvɪŋ] n efforts *mpl* (*for* pour obtenir).

strobe [strəʊb] 1 adj *lights* stroboscopique; *see also* **2**. 2 n a (*also* **~ light**, **~ lighting**) lumière *f* stroboscopique. b = **stroboscope**.

stroboscope ['strəʊbəskəʊp] n stroboscope *m*.

strode [strəʊd] pret of **stride**.

stroke [strəʊk] 1 n a (*movement; blow: gen, Billiards, Cricket, Golf, Tennis etc*) coup *m*; (*Swimming: movement*) mouvement *m* des bras (*pour nager*); (*Rowing, Swimming: style*) nage *f*; (*Rowing: movement*) coup de rame *or* d'aviron. **he gave the cat a ~** il a fait une caresse au chat; **with a ~ of his axe** d'un coup de hache; **with a ~ of the pen** d'un trait de plume; **~ of lightning** coup de foudre; (*Golf, Tennis etc*) **good ~!** bien joué!; **to row at 38 ~s to the minute** ramer *or* nager à une cadence de 38 coups d'aviron minute; (*Rowing, fig*) **to set the ~** donner la cadence; **to put sb off his ~** (*Sport*) faire perdre sa cadence *or* son rythme à qn; (*fig*) faire perdre tous ses moyens à qn; **he swam the pool with powerful ~s** il a traversé le bassin d'une manière puissante; *see* **back, breast** *etc.*

b (*fig*) **at a (single) ~, at one ~** d'un (seul) coup; **it was a tremendous ~ to get the committee's agreement** cela a été un coup de maître que d'obtenir l'accord du comité; **he hasn't done a ~ (of work)** il n'a rien fait du tout, il n'en a pas fichu une rame*; **~ of diplomacy** chef-d'œuvre *m* de diplomatie; **~ of genius** trait *m* de génie; **~ of luck** coup de chance *or* de veine; *see* **master** *etc.*

c (*mark*) *[pen, pencil]* trait *m*; *[brush]* touche *f*; (*Typ: oblique*) barre *f*. **thick ~s of the brush** des touches épaisses; (*Typ*) **5 ~ 6** 5 barre 6; *see* **brush** *etc.*

d *[bell, clock]* coup *m*. **on the ~ of 10** sur le coup de 10 heures, à 10 heures sonnantes; **he arrived on the ~** il est arrivé à l'heure exacte; **in the ~ of time** juste à temps.

e (*Med*) attaque *f* (d'apoplexie). **to have a ~** avoir une attaque (d'apoplexie); *see* **heat, sun.**

f (*Tech: of piston*) course *f*. **a two-/four-~ engine** un moteur à deux/quatre temps; *see also* **two.**

g (*Rowing: person*) chef *m* de nage. **to row ~** être chef de nage, donner la nage.

2 **vt** a *cat, sb's hand, one's chin* caresser; *sb's hair* caresser, passer la main dans. (*fig*) **to ~ sb (up) the wrong way** prendre qn à rebrousse-poil *or* à contre-poil.

b (*Rowing*) **to ~ a boat** être chef de nage, donner la nage.

c (*draw line through: also* **~ out**) barrer, biffer, rayer.

d (*Sport*) *ball* frapper.

3 **vi** (*Rowing*) être chef de nage, donner la nage.

►**stroke down** **vt sep** *cat's fur* caresser; *hair* lisser. (*fig*) **to stroke sb down** apaiser *or* amadouer qn.

►**stroke out** **vt sep** = **stroke 2c.**

►**stroke up** **vt sep** *see* **stroke 2a.**

stroll [strəʊl] 1 **n** petite promenade. **to have** *or* **take a ~, to go for a ~** aller faire un tour. 2 **vi** se promener nonchalamment, flâner. **to ~ in/out/away** *etc* entrer/sortir/s'éloigner *etc* sans se presser *or* nonchalamment; **to ~ up and down the street** descendre et remonter la rue en flânant *or* sans se presser *or* nonchalamment.

stroller ['strəʊləʳ] **n** a (*person*) promeneur *m*, -euse *f*, flâneur *m*, -euse *f*. b (*esp US: push chair*) poussette *f*; (*folding*) poussette-canne *f*.

strolling ['strəʊlɪŋ] **adj** *player, minstrel* ambulant.

stroma ['strəʊmə] **n, pl stromata** ['strəʊmətə] stroma *m*.

strong [strɒŋ] 1 **adj** a (*powerful*) fort (*also Mil, Pol, Sport etc*), vigoureux, puissant; (*healthy*) fort, robuste, vigoureux; *heart* robuste, solide; *nerves* solide; *eyesight* très bon (*f* bonne); *leg* vigoureux; *arm, limb* fort, vigoureux; *voice* fort, puissant; *magnet* puissant; *wind* fort; (*Elec*) *current* intense; *lens, spectacles* fort, puissant; (*solid, robust*) *building, wall* solide; *table, shoes, bolt, nail* solide, robuste; *glue* fort; *fabric, material* solide, résistant. **to be (as) ~ as a horse** (*powerful*) être fort comme un bœuf *or* comme un Turc; (*healthy*) avoir une santé de fer; **do you feel ~?** est-ce que vous avez des forces?, est-ce que vous vous sentez en forme?; (*in health*) **when you are ~ again** quand vous aurez repris des forces, quand vous aurez retrouvé vos forces; **she has never been very ~** elle a toujours eu une petite santé; (*fig*) **you need a ~ stomach for that job** il faut avoir l'estomac solide *or* bien accroché* pour faire ce travail; *see* **constitution** *etc.*

b (*fig: morally*) fort, courageux; *character, personality* fort, puissant; *characteristic* marqué, frappant; *accent* fort, marqué; *emotion, desire, interest* vif (*f* vive); *reasons, argument, evidence* solide, sérieux; (*St Ex*) *market* ferme; (*Econ*) *the pound, dollar* solide; *candidate, contender* sérieux, qui a des chances de gagner; *letter* bien senti; *protest* énergique, vigoureux, vif; *measures, steps* énergique; *influence, attraction* fort, profond; (*Mus*) *beat* fort. (*in courage etc*) **you must be ~** soyez courageux, vous devez faire preuve de courage; (*mentally etc*) **he's a very ~ person** c'est un homme bien trempé *or* un homme qui a du ressort; **we are in a ~ position to make them obey** nous sommes bien placés pour les faire obéir; **his ~ suit** (*Cards*) sa couleur forte; (*fig: also* **his ~ point**) son fort; **to be ~ in maths** être fort en maths; **to be ~ on*** (*good at*) être bon en; (*emphasizing*) mettre l'accent sur; **in ~ terms** en termes non équivoques; **~ language** grossièretés *fpl*, propos grossiers; **there are ~ indications that ...** tout semble indiquer que ...; **a ~ effect** beaucoup d'effet; **I had a ~ sense of ...** je ressentais vivement ...; **I've a ~ feeling that ...** j'ai bien l'impression que ...; **he's got ~ feelings on this matter** cette affaire lui tient à cœur; **it is my ~ opinion** *or* **belief that** je suis fermement convaincu *or* persuadé que; **a ~ socialist** un socialiste fervent; **~ supporters of** d'ardents partisans de, des fervents de; **I am a ~ believer in** je crois fermement à *or* profondément à; *see* **case[1]** *etc.*

c (*affecting senses powerfully*) *coffee, cheese, wine, cigarette* fort; (*pej*) *butter* rance; *sauce, taste* fort, relevé; *solution* concentré; *light* fort, vif (*f* vive). **~ drink** alcool *m*, boisson *f* alcoolisée; **his breath is very ~** il a l'haleine forte; **it has a ~ smell** ça sent fort.

d (*in numbers*) **an army 500 ~** une armée (forte) de 500 hommes; **they were 100 ~** ils étaient au nombre de 100.

e (*Ling*) *verb, form* fort.

2 **comp** ►**strong-arm** *see* **strong-arm** ►**strong-armed** aux bras forts ►**strongbox** coffre-fort *m* ►**strong breeze** (*on Beaufort scale*) vent frais ►**strong gale** (*on Beaufort scale*) fort coup de vent ►**stronghold** (*Mil*) forteresse *f*, fort *m*; (*fig*) bastion *m* ►**strong-limbed** aux membres forts *or* vigoureux ►**strongman** (*in circus etc*) hercule *m*; (*fig, Comm, Pol etc*) homme *m* fort ►**strong-minded** *see* **strong-minded** ►**strongroom** (*gen*) chambre *f* forte; (*in bank*) chambre forte, salle *f* des coffres ►**strong-willed** résolu; **to be strong-willed** avoir de la volonté.

3 **adv**: **to be going ~** *[person]* être toujours solide; *[car etc]* marcher toujours bien; *[relationship etc]* aller bien; *[firm, business]* aller bien, être florissant; **that's pitching it** *or* **coming it** *or* **going it a bit ~*** il pousse (*or* vous poussez *etc*) un peu*, il y va (*or* vous y allez *etc*) un peu fort; **to come on ~*** (*gen: be overbearing*) insister lourdement; (*sexually*) aller un peu loin; (*US: make progress*) progresser fortement.

strong-arm* ['strɒŋɑːm] 1 **adj** *method, treatment* brutal. **~ man** gros bras *m* (*fig*); **~ tactics** la manière forte. 2 **vt** faire violence à. **to ~ sb into doing sth** forcer la main à qn pour qu'il fasse qch.

strongly ['strɒŋlɪ] **adv** *fight, attack* avec force, énergiquement; *play* efficacement; *attract, interest, influence, desire* fortement, vivement; *accentuate, remind, indicate* fortement; *protest, defend* énergiquement, vigoureusement; *believe* fermement, profondément; *feel, sense* profondément; *answer* en termes sentis; *constructed, made* solidement. **~ built** *wall, table* solide, robuste; *person* bien bâti, de forte constitution; **a ~-worded letter** une lettre bien sentie; **it smells very ~** cela sent très fort; **it smells ~ of onions** cela a une forte odeur d'oignons.

strong-minded ['strɒŋ'maɪndɪd] **adj** résolu, qui a beaucoup de volonté, qui sait ce qu'il veut.

strong-mindedly ['strɒŋ'maɪndɪdlɪ] **adv** avec une persévérance tenace, avec ténacité.

strong-mindedness ['strɒŋ'maɪndɪdnɪs] **n** volonté *f*, force *f* de caractère.

strontium ['strɒntɪəm] **n** strontium *m*. **~ 90** strontium 90, strontium radio-actif.

strop [strɒp] 1 **n** cuir *m* (à rasoir). 2 **vt** *razor* repasser sur le cuir.

strophe ['strəʊfɪ] **n** strophe *f*.

stroppy* ['strɒpɪ] **adj** (*Brit*) contrariant, difficile. **to get ~** monter sur ses grands chevaux.

strove [strəʊv] **pret of strive.**

struck [strʌk] **pret, ptp of strike.**

structural ['strʌktʃərəl] **adj** a (*gen, also Anat, Bot, Chem etc*) structural; (*Econ, Ling*) structural, structurel; (*relating to structuralism*) structural. **~ psychology/linguistics** psychologie/linguistique structurale; **~ complexity** complexité structurale *or* structurelle *or* de structure; **~ change** changement structural *or* structurel; (*Ling*) **~ analysis/description** *etc* analyse/description *etc* structurale *or* structurelle; **~ unemployment** chômage *m* structurel.

b (*Constr*) *fault etc* de construction. **~ alterations** modifications *fpl* des parties portantes; **~ damage** dégâts *mpl* de structure; **~ steel** acier *m* (de construction); **~ engineer** ingénieur *m* du génie civil; **~ engineering** génie *m* civil.

structuralism ['strʌktʃərəlɪzəm] **n** structuralisme *m*.

structuralist ['strʌktʃərəlɪst] **adj, n** structuraliste (*mf*).

structurally ['strʌktʃərəlɪ] **adv** (*Anat, Bot, Chem etc*) du point de vue de la structure; (*Constr*) du point de vue de la construction, du point de vue des fondations et des murs. **there is nothing ~ wrong with the building** il n'y a rien à redire quant aux fondations et aux murs; **~ sound** (*gen*) bien structuré; (*Constr*) d'une construction solide.

structure ['strʌktʃəʳ] 1 **n** a (*Anat, Bot, Chem, Geol, Ling, Math, Philos, Phys, Psych etc*) structure *f*; (*Literat, Poetry*) structure, composition *f*. **social/administrative ~** structure sociale/administrative.

b (*Constr*) *[building etc]* ossature *f*, carcasse *f*, armature *f*; (*the building, bridge etc itself*) construction *f*, édifice *m*. 2 **vt** structurer.

structured ['strʌktʃəd] **adj** structuré. **~ activity** activité structurée.

struggle ['strʌgl] 1 **n** (*lit, fig*) lutte *f* (*for* pour, *against* contre, *with* avec, *to do* pour faire); (*fight*) bagarre *f*. **to put up a ~** résister (*also fig*), se débattre; **he lost his glasses in the ~** il a perdu ses lunettes dans la bagarre; (*Mil*) **they surrendered without a ~** ils n'ont opposé aucune résistance; **you won't succeed without a ~** vous ne réussirez pas sans vous battre, il faudra vous battre si vous voulez réussir; **her ~ to feed her children** sa lutte quotidienne pour nourrir ses enfants; **the ~ to find somewhere to live** les difficultés qu'on a à trouver *or* le mal qu'il faut se donner pour trouver un logement; **I had a ~ to persuade him** j'ai eu beaucoup de mal à le persuader, je ne l'ai persuadé qu'au prix de grands efforts; **it was a ~ but we made it** cela nous a demandé beaucoup d'efforts mais nous y sommes arrivés.

2 **vi** a (*gen*) lutter (*against* contre, *for* pour); (*fight*) lutter, se battre, résister; (*thrash around*) se débattre, se démener; (*fig: try hard*) se démener, se décarcasser* (*to do* pour faire), s'efforcer (*to do* de faire). **he was struggling with the thief** il était aux prises *or* se battait avec le voleur; **he ~d fiercely as they put on the handcuffs** il a résisté avec acharnement quand on lui a passé les menottes; **he ~d to get free from the ropes** il s'est débattu *or* démené pour se dégager des cordes; **they were struggling for power** ils se disputaient le pouvoir; (*fig*) **he was struggling to make ends meet** il avait beaucoup de mal à joindre les deux bouts, il tirait le diable par la queue; **he is struggling to finish it before tomorrow** il se démène *or* il se décarcasse* pour le terminer avant demain.

b (*move with difficulty*) **to ~ in/out** *etc* entrer/sortir *etc* avec peine *or* à grand-peine; **he ~d up the cliff** il s'est hissé péniblement *or* à grand-peine jusqu'au sommet de la falaise; **he ~d through the tiny window** il s'est contorsionné pour passer par la minuscule fenêtre; **to ~ through the crowd** se frayer péniblement un chemin à travers la foule; **he ~d to his feet** (*from armchair etc*) il s'est levé non sans peine; (*during fight etc*) il s'est relevé péniblement; **he ~d into a jersey** il a enfilé non sans peine un pull-over.

►**struggle along** **vi** (*lit*) avancer avec peine *or* à grand-peine; (*fig: financially*) subsister *or* se débrouiller tant bien que mal.

►**struggle back** **vi** (*return*) revenir (*or* retourner) avec peine *or* à grand-peine. (*fig*) **to struggle back to solvency** s'efforcer de redevenir solvable.

►**struggle on** **vi** a = **struggle along**. b (*continue the struggle*) continuer de lutter, poursuivre la lutte (*against* contre).

►**struggle through** **vi** (*fig*) venir à bout de ses peines, s'en sortir.

struggling ['strʌglɪŋ] **adj** *artist etc* qui tire le diable par la queue.

strum [strʌm] 1 **vt** a *piano* tapoter de; *guitar, banjo etc* gratter de, racler (de). b (*also* **~ out**) *tune* (*on piano*) tapoter; (*on guitar etc*) racler. 2 **vi**: **to ~ on** = **1a**. 3 **n** (*also* **~ming**) *[guitar etc]* raclement *m*.

strumpet†† ['strʌmpɪt] **n** catin *f*.

strung [strʌŋ] **pret, ptp of string**; *see also* **highly, string up** *etc*.

strut¹ [strʌt] **vi** (*also* **~ about, ~ around**) se pavaner. **to ~ in/out/along** *etc* entrer/sortir/avancer *etc* en se pavanant *or* en se rengorgeant *or* d'un air important.

strut² [strʌt] **n** (*support*) étai *m*, support *m*; (*for wall, trench, mine*) étrésillon *m*; (*more solid*) étançon *m*; (*Carpentry*) contrefiche *f*, (*between uprights*) lierne *f*, traverse *f*, entretoise *f*; (*Constr: in roof*) jambe *f* de force.

strychnine ['strɪkniːn] **n** strychnine *f*.

stub [stʌb] 1 **n** *[tree, plant]* souche *f*, chicot *m*; *[pencil, broken stick]* bout *m*, morceau *m*; *[cigarette, cigar]* bout, mégot* *m*; *[tail]* moignon *m*; *[cheque, ticket]* talon *m*. 2 **vt**: **to ~ one's toe/one's foot** se cogner le doigt de pied/le pied (*against* contre). 3 **comp** ►**stub end**: **stub end of a pencil** *etc* bout *m* de crayon *etc*.

►**stub out** **vt sep** *cigar, cigarette* écraser.

stubble ['stʌbl] **n** (*NonC*) (*Agr*) chaume *m*, éteule *f*; (*on chin*) barbe *f* de plusieurs jours. **field of ~** chaume, éteule.

stubbly ['stʌblɪ] **adj** *field* couvert de chaume; *chin, face* mal rasé; *beard* de plusieurs jours; *hair* court et raide, en brosse.

stubborn ['stʌbən] **adj** *person* entêté, têtu, obstiné, opiniâtre; *animal* rétif; *campaign, resistance* opiniâtre, obstiné, acharné; *denial, refusal, insistence* obstiné, opiniâtre; *fever, disease* rebelle, persistant, opiniâtre; *see* **mule¹**.

stubbornly ['stʌbənlɪ] **adv** obstinément, opiniâtrement. **he ~ refused** il a obstinément *or* opiniâtrement refusé, il s'est obstiné à refuser.

stubbornness ['stʌbənnɪs] **n** (*see* **stubborn**) entêtement *m*; obstination *f*; opiniâtreté *f*; acharnement *m*; persistance *f*.

stubby ['stʌbɪ] **adj** *person* trapu, courtaud, boulot (*f* -otte); *finger* épais (*f* -aisse), boudiné; *pencil, crayon* gros et court. **a ~ tail** un bout de queue.

stucco ['stʌkəʊ] 1 **n, pl ~es** *or* **~s** stuc *m*. 2 **comp** de *or* en stuc, stuqué ►**stuccowork** stucage *m*. 3 **vt** stuquer.

stuck [stʌk] 1 **pret, ptp of stick**. 2 **comp** ►**stuck-up*** bêcheur*, prétentieux; **to be stuck-up*** être bêcheur*, faire du chiqué*.

stud¹ [stʌd] 1 **n** (*knob, nail*) clou *m* à grosse tête; (*on door, shield etc*) clou décoratif; (*on boots*) clou à souliers, caboche *f*; (*on football boots*) crampon *m*; (*on tyre, roadway*) clou; (*Aut: cat's-eye*) clou à catadioptre; (*also* **collar ~**) bouton *m* de col; (*in chain*) étai *m*; (*Constr*) montant *m*; (*Tech: double-headed screw*) goujon *m*; (*pivot screw*) tourillon *m*. 2 **vt** *boots, shield, door*, clouter. (*Aut*) **~ded tyre** pneu *m* clouté *or* à clous; (*fig*) **~ded with** parsemé de, émaillé de; **sky ~ded with stars** ciel constellé, ciel parsemé *or* semé *or* piqueté *or* criblé d'étoiles.

stud² [stʌd] 1 **n** a (*racing ~*) écurie *f* (de courses); (*~ farm*) haras *m*. **to be at ~** étalonner. b (*‡: young man*) jeune mec‡ *m*; (*promiscuous*) tombeur* *m*. 2 **comp** ►**studbook** stud-book *m* ►**stud farm** haras *m* ►**stud fee** prix *m* de la saillie ►**studhorse** étalon *m* ►**stud mare** (jument *f*) poulinière *f* ►**stud poker** (*Cards*) *variété de poker*.

student ['stjuːdənt] 1 **n** (*Univ*) étudiant(e) *m(f)*; (*Scol*) élève *mf*, lycéen(ne) *m(f)*. (*Univ*) **medical ~** étudiant(e) en médecine; **~'s book** livre *m* de l'élève; **he is a ~ of bird life** il étudie la vie des oiseaux; **he is a keen ~** il est très studieux.

2 **comp** (*Univ*) *life* étudiant, estudiantin; (*Univ*) *residence, restaurant* universitaire; (*Univ*) *power, unrest* étudiant; *attitudes, opinions* (*Univ*) des étudiants; (*Scol*) des élèves, des lycéens ►**the student community** les étudiants *mpl* ►**student council** (*Brit Scol*) comité *m* des délégués de classe ►**student councillor** (*Scol, Univ*) délégué(e) *m(f)* de classe ►**student driver** (*US*) conducteur *m*, -trice *f* débutant(e) ►**student file** (*US Scol*) dossier *m* scolaire ►**student grant** bourse *f* ►**student ID card** (*US Scol*) carte *f* d'identité scolaire ►**student lamp** (*US*) lampe *f* de bureau (*orientable*) ►**student nurse** (*Med*) élève *mf* infirmier(-ière) ►**student participation** participation *f* étudiante (*Univ*) *or* lycéenne (*Scol*) ►**student teacher** professeur *m* stagiaire, (*in primary school*) instituteur *m*, -trice *f* stagiaire ►**student teaching** stage *m* pédagogique ►**student union** (*in university*) (*club*) club *m* des étudiants; (*trade union*) syndicat *m or* union *f* des étudiants.

studentship ['stjuːdəntʃɪp] **n** bourse *f* (d'études).

studied ['stʌdɪd] **adj** *calm, politeness* étudié, calculé; *insult, avoidance* délibéré, voulu; (*pej*) *pose, style* affecté.

studio ['stjuːdɪəʊ] 1 **n** *[artist, photographer, musician etc]* studio *m*, atelier *m*; (*Cine, Rad, Recording, TV etc*) studio; *see* **mobile, recording** *etc*. 2 **comp** ►**studio apartment** (*US*) studio *m* (*logement*) ►**studio audience** (*Rad, TV*) public *m* (*invité à une émission*) ►**studio couch** divan *m* ►**studio flat** (*Brit*) studio *m* ►**studio portrait** (*Phot*) portrait *m* photographique.

studious ['stjuːdɪəs] **adj** *person* studieux, appliqué; *piece of work, inspection* sérieux, soigné; *effort* assidu, soutenu; *calm, politeness* étudié, calculé; *insult, avoidance* délibéré, voulu.

studiously ['stjuːdɪəslɪ] **adv** (*with care etc*) studieusement; (*deliberately*) d'une manière étudiée *or* calculée *or* délibérée, soigneusement. **he ~ avoided her** il prenait soin de l'éviter; **~ calm** d'un calme étudié.

studiousness ['stjuːdɪəsnɪs] **n** application *f* (*à l'étude*), amour *m* de l'étude.

study ['stʌdɪ] 1 **n** a (*gen, Art, Mus, Phot, Soc etc*) étude *f*. **to make a ~ of sth** faire une étude de qch, étudier qch; **it is a ~ of women in industry** c'est une étude sur les femmes dans l'industrie; **his studies showed that ...** ses recherches *fpl* ont montré que ...; (*fig: model, ideal*) **it is a ~ in social justice** c'est un modèle de justice sociale; (*fig hum*) **his face was a ~** il fallait voir son visage, son visage était un poème*; *see* **brown** *etc*.

b (*NonC*) étude *f*; (*Scol*) études *fpl*. **he spends all his time in ~** il consacre tout son temps à l'étude *or* à ses études, il passe tout son temps à étudier.

c (*room*) bureau *m*, cabinet *m* de travail.

2 **comp** *visit, hour* d'étude; *group* de travail ►**study hall** (*US Scol*) (*gen*) permanence *f*; (*in boarding school*) (salle *f* d')étude *f*; (*US Scol*) **study hall teacher** surveillant(e) *m(f)* d'étude ►**study period** (*Brit*) (heure *f* d')étude *f* surveillée ►**study room** (*Scol*) permanence *f*; (*in boarding school*) (salle *f* d')étude *f* ►**study tour** voyage *m* d'études.

3 **vt** *nature, an author, text* étudier; (*Scol, Univ*) *maths etc* faire des études de, étudier; *project, proposal, map, ground* étudier, examiner soigneusement; *person, sb's face, reactions* étudier, observer attentivement; *stars* observer; *see also* **studied**.

4 **vi** (*gen*) étudier; (*Scol, Univ etc*) étudier, faire ses études. **to ~ hard** travailler dur; **to ~ under sb** *[undergraduate]* suivre les cours de qn; *[postgraduate]* travailler *or* faire des recherches sous la direction de qn; *[painter, composer]* être l'élève de qn; **to ~ for an exam** préparer un examen; **he is ~ing to be a doctor/a pharmacist** il fait des études de médecine/de pharmacie; **he is ~ing to be a teacher** il fait des études pour entrer dans l'enseignement *or* pour devenir professeur.

stuff [stʌf] 1 **n** (*NonC*) a (*gen*) chose *f*, truc* *m*. **look at that ~** regarde ça, regarde ce truc*; **it's dangerous ~** c'est dangereux; **radioactive waste is dangerous ~** les déchets radioactifs sont une substance dangereuse *or* constituent un réel danger; **what's this ~ in this jar?** qu'est-ce que c'est que ça *or* que ce truc* dans ce pot?; **his new book is good ~** son nouveau livre est bien; **there's some good ~ in what he writes** il y a de bonnes choses dans ce qu'il écrit; **his painting is poor ~** sa peinture ne vaut pas grand-chose; **I can't listen to his ~ at all** je ne peux pas souffrir sa musique (*or* sa poésie *etc*); (*pej*) **all that ~ about how he wants to help us** toutes ces promesses en l'air comme quoi il veut nous aider; **that's the ~ (to give them** *or* **to give the troops)!*** bravo, c'est ça!; **~ and nonsense!*** balivernes!; **he is the ~ that heroes are made from**, (*liter*) **he is the ~ of heroes** il a l'étoffe d'un héros; **it is the (very) ~ of life/politics** *etc* c'est l'essence même de la vie/la politique; **he knows his ~*** il connaît son sujet (*or* son métier), il s'y connaît; **do your ~!*** vas-y!, c'est à toi!; **he did his ~ very well*** il s'en est bien sorti; **she's a nice bit of ~‡** c'est une jolie môme* *or* nana‡; *see* **green, hot, stern²** *etc*.

b (*miscellaneous objects*) choses *fpl*; (*jumbled up*) fatras *m*; (*possessions*) affaires *fpl*, fourbi* *m*; (*tools etc*) *[workman]* attirail *m*, affaires, fourbi*. **he brought back a lot of ~ from China** il a rapporté des tas de choses de Chine; **put your ~ away** range tes affaires *or* tes trucs*.

c (*fabric, cloth*) étoffe *f* (*surtout de laine*).

d (*Drugs sl*) (*gen*) came‡ *f*, drogue *f*; (*marijuana*) marijuana *f*, marie-jeanne *f*; (*heroin*) poudre‡ *f*, neige‡ *f*, héroïne *f*.

2 **comp** (†) *dress etc* en laine, en lainage.

3 **vt** a (*fill, pack*) *cushion, quilt, chair, toy, mattress* rembourrer (*with* avec); (*Taxidermy*) *animal* empailler; *sack, box, pockets* bourrer, remplir (*with* de); (*Culin*) *chicken, tomato* farcir (*with* avec); (*stop up*) *hole* boucher (*with* avec); (*cram, thrust*) *objects, clothes, books* fourrer (*in, into* dans). **to ~ one's ears** se boucher les oreilles; **to ~ one's fingers into one's ears** fourrer ses doigts dans ses oreilles; **he ~ed the papers down the drain** il a fait disparaître les papiers dans le tuyau de descente; **he ~ed some money into my hand** il m'a fourré de l'argent dans la main; (*fig*) **he is a ~ed shirt*** il est pompeux; **~ed toy** jouet *m* de peluche; **to ~ o.s. with food, to ~ food into one's mouth** se gaver *or* se bourrer de nourriture; **he was ~ing himself*** il s'empiffrait*; **they ~ed him with morphine** ils l'ont bourré de morphine; **to ~ one's head with useless facts** se farcir *or* se bourrer la tête *or* la mémoire de connaissances inutiles; **he's ~ing you** *or* **your head with silly ideas** il te bourre le crâne *or* il te farcit la cervelle d'idées niaises; **the museum is ~ed with interesting things** le musée est bourré de choses intéressantes; (*US Pol*) **to ~ a ballot box** mettre des bulletins de vote truqués dans une urne; **get ~ed!‡** va te faire cuire un œuf!‡, va te faire foutre!**

b (**: put*) mettre, poser, laisser. **~ your books on the table** mets *or* pose *or* laisse tes livres sur la table; (*fig*) **(you know where) you can ~ that!‡** tu sais où tu peux te le mettre!‡

c (*‡: have sex with*) s'envoyer‡, baiser**.

4 **vi** (**: guzzle*) se gaver, se gorger.

►**stuff away*** **vt sep** *food* enfourner*, engloutir.

►**stuff up** **vt sep** *hole* boucher. **my nose is stuffed up, I'm stuffed up*** j'ai le nez bouché.

stuffily [ˈstʌfɪlɪ] **adv** *say etc* d'un ton désapprobateur.

stuffiness [ˈstʌfɪnɪs] **n** (*in room*) manque *m* d'air; *[person]* pruderie *f*, esprit *m* étriqué *or* vieux jeu *inv*.

stuffing [ˈstʌfɪŋ] **n** *[quilt, cushion, toy, mattress, chair]* bourre *f*, rembourrage *m*, rembourrure *f*; (*Taxidermy*) paille *f*; (*Culin*) farce *f*. (*fig*) **he's got no ~** c'est une chiffe molle; **to knock the ~ out of sb** *[boxer, blow]* dégonfler qn; *[illness, defeat, news]* mettre qn à plat*; (*take down a peg*) remettre qn à sa place.

stuffy [ˈstʌfɪ] **adj** a *room* mal ventilé, mal aéré. **it's ~ in here** on manque d'air *or* on étouffe ici; **it smells ~** ça sent le renfermé. b *person* collet monté *inv*, vieux jeu *inv*; *book, programme etc* ennuyeux et moralisant.

stultify [ˈstʌltɪfaɪ] **vt** *person* abrutir, déshumaniser; *sb's efforts, action* rendre vain; *argument, reasoning, claim* enlever toute valeur à.

stultifying [ˈstʌltɪfaɪɪŋ] **adj** *work* abrutissant, déshumanisant; *atmosphere* débilitant.

stumble [ˈstʌmbl] 1 **n** a (*in walking*) faux pas *m*, trébuchement *m*; *[horse]* faux pas. b **he recited it without a ~** il l'a récité sans trébucher *or* se reprendre une seule fois. 2 **comp** ►**stumbling block** pierre *f* d'achoppement. 3 **vi** a trébucher (*over* sur, contre), faire un faux pas; *[horse]* broncher. **he ~d against the table** il a trébuché *or* fait un faux pas et a heurté la table; **to ~ in/out/along** *etc* entrer/sortir/avancer *etc* en trébuchant. b (*in speech*) trébucher (*at, over* sur). **he ~d through the speech** il a prononcé (*or* lu) le discours d'une voix hésitante *or* trébuchante.

►**stumble across, stumble (up)on** **vt fus** (*fig*) tomber sur.

stumblebum‡ [ˈstʌmbl͵bʌm] **n** (*US*) empoté(e)* *m(f)*, abruti(e)* *m(f)*.

stump [stʌmp] 1 **n** a *[tree]* souche *f*, chicot *m*; *[limb, tail]* moignon *m*; *[tooth]* chicot *m*; *[cigar]* bout *m*, mégot* *m*; *[pencil, chalk, sealing wax, crayon etc]* bout (*qui reste de qch*). (*US*) **to find o.s. up a ~*** ne savoir que répondre, être perplexe.

b (*Cricket*) piquet *m*.

c (*US Pol*) estrade *f* (d'un orateur politique). **to be** *or* **go on the ~** faire campagne, faire une tournée de discours.

d (*fig: legs*) **~s‡** guiboles‡ *fpl*; *see* **stir¹**.

2 **vt** a (**: puzzle*) coller*, faire sécher*. **to be ~ed by sth** être incapable de *or* ne savoir que répondre à qch, sécher* sur qch; (*during quiz, crossword etc*) **I'm ~ed** je sèche*.

b (*Cricket*) mettre hors jeu.

c (*US Pol*) **to ~ a state** faire une tournée électorale dans un état.

3 **vi** a **to ~ in/out/along** *etc* entrer/sortir/avancer *etc* à pas lourds (*heavily*) *or* clopin-clopant* (*limping*).

b (*US * Pol*) faire une tournée électorale.

►**stump up*** (*Brit*) 1 **vi** casquer‡. 2 **vt sep** cracher*, y aller de.

stumpy [ˈstʌmpɪ] **adj** *person* courtaud, boulot (*f* -otte); *object* épais (*f* -aisse) et court.

stun [stʌn] **vt** étourdir, assommer; (*fig: amaze*) abasourdir, stupéfier. **~ grenade** grenade *f* incapacitante *or* paralysante; **~ gun** pistolet *m* hypodermique.

stung [stʌŋ] **pret, ptp of sting.**

stunk [stʌŋk] **ptp of stink.**

stunned [stʌnd] **adj** (*lit*) assommé, étourdi; (*fig*) stupéfait (*by* de).

stunner‡ [ˈstʌnəʳ] **n** (*girl/dress/car etc*) fille *f*/robe *f*/voiture *f* *etc* fantastique* *or* sensationnelle*.

stunning [ˈstʌnɪŋ] **adj** *blow* étourdissant; (*overwhelming*) *news, announcement, event* stupéfiant, renversant; (**: lovely*) *girl, dress, car* sensationnel*, fantastique*.

stunningly [ˈstʌnɪŋlɪ] **adv** *dressed etc* d'une manière éblouissante *or* sensationnelle*.

stunt¹ [stʌnt] 1 **n** (*feat*) tour *m* de force, exploit *m* (*destiné à attirer l'attention du public*); *[stuntman]* cascade *f*; (*Aviat*) acrobatie *f*; *[students]* canular* *m*; (*trick*) truc* *m*, coup monté, combine‡ *f*; (*publicity ~*) truc* publicitaire. **don't ever pull a ~ like that again** ne recommence plus jamais un truc* pareil; **it's a ~ to get your money** c'est un truc* *or* c'est un coup monté pour avoir votre argent; **that was a good ~** c'était un truc* ingénieux *or* une combine‡ ingénieuse.

2 **comp** ►**stunt flier** (*Aviat*) aviateur *m* qui fait de l'acrobatie, aviateur *m* de haute voltige ►**stunt flying** acrobatie aérienne, haute voltige ►**stuntman, stunt woman** (*Cine, TV*) cascadeur *m*, -euse *f*.

3 **vi** *[pilot etc]* faire des acrobaties; (*Cine*) faire le cascadeur.

stunt² [stʌnt] **vt** *growth* retarder, arrêter; *person, plant* retarder la croissance *or* le développement de.

stunted [ˈstʌntɪd] **adj** *person, plant* rabougri, rachitique, chétif.

stupefaction [͵stjuːpɪˈfækʃən] **n** stupéfaction *f*, stupeur *f*.

stupefy [ˈstjuːpɪfaɪ] **vt** *[blow]* étourdir; *[drink, drugs, lack of sleep]* abrutir; (*fig: astound*) stupéfier, abasourdir.

stupefying [ˈstjuːpɪfaɪɪŋ] **adj** (*fig*) stupéfiant, ahurissant.

stupendous [stjuːˈpendəs] **adj** *ceremony, beauty* prodigieux; *victory, achievement* remarquable, extraordinaire; (** fig*) *film, holiday* fantastique*, sensationnel*, formidable*. **a ~ actor** *etc* un acteur *etc* prodigieux, un immense acteur *etc*.

stupendously [stjuːˈpendəslɪ] **adv** formidablement*, d'une manière sensationnelle* *or* fantastique*.

stupid [ˈstjuːpɪd] **adj** stupide, bête, idiot; (*from sleep, drink etc*) abruti, hébété. **don't be ~** ne sois pas bête *or* stupide *or* idiot, ne fais pas l'idiot; **I've done a ~ thing** j'ai fait une bêtise *or* une sottise; **come on, ~*** allez viens, gros bêta* (*f* grosse bêtasse*); **you ~ idiot!*** espèce d'idiot(e)!; **the blow knocked him ~** le coup l'a étourdi; **he drank himself ~** il s'est abruti d'alcool.

stupidity [stjuːˈpɪdɪtɪ] **n** stupidité *f*, sottise *f*, bêtise *f*.

stupidly [ˈstjuːpɪdlɪ] **adv** stupidement, sottement. **I ~ told him your name** j'ai eu la sottise de *or* j'ai été assez bête pour lui dire votre nom.

stupidness [ˈstjuːpɪdnɪs] **n** = **stupidity**.

stupor [ˈstjuːpəʳ] **n** stupeur *f*.

sturdily [ˈstɜːdɪlɪ] **adv** (*see* **sturdy**) robustement; vigoureusement; solidement; énergiquement. **~ built** *person, child* robuste; *chair, cycle* robuste, solide; *house* de construction solide.

sturdiness [ˈstɜːdɪnɪs] **n** (*see* **sturdy**) robustesse *f*; vigueur *f*; solidité *f*.

sturdy [ˈstɜːdɪ] **adj** *person, tree* robuste, vigoureux; *cycle, chair* robuste, solide; (*fig*) *resistance, defence, refusal* énergique, vigoureux. **~ common-sense** gros *or* robuste bon sens.

sturgeon [ˈstɜːdʒən] **n, pl inv** esturgeon *m*.

stutter [ˈstʌtəʳ] 1 **n** bégaiement *m*. **to have a ~** bégayer. 2 **vi** bégayer. 3 **vt** (*also* **~ out**) bégayer, dire en bégayant.

stutterer [ˈstʌtərəʳ] **n** bègue *mf*.

stuttering [ˈstʌtərɪŋ] 1 **n** (*NonC*) bégaiement *m*. 2 **adj** bègue, qui bégaie.

Stuttgart [ˈstʊtgɑːt] **n** Stuttgart.

STV [estiːˈviː] **n** (**abbr of single transferable vote**) *see* **single 3**.

sty¹ [staɪ] **n** *[pigs]* porcherie *f*.

sty², stye [staɪ] **n** (*Med*) orgelet *m*, compère-loriot *m*.

Stygian [ˈstɪdʒɪən] **adj** (*fig*) sombre *or* noir comme le Styx, ténébreux. **~ darkness** ténèbres *fpl* impénétrables, nuit noire.

style [staɪl] 1 **n** a (*gen, Art, Literat, Mus, Sport, Typ etc*) style *m*. **in the ~ of Mozart** dans le style *or* à la manière de Mozart; **building in the Renaissance ~** édifice *m* (de) style Renaissance; **March 6th, old/new ~** 6 mars vieux/nouveau style; **~ of life** *or* **living** style de vie; **he won in fine ~** il l'a emporté haut la main; **I like his ~ of writing** j'aime sa manière d'écrire *or* son style; (*fig*) **I don't like his ~** je n'aime pas son genre; **that house is not my ~*** ce n'est pas mon genre de maison; **that's the ~!*** bravo!; *see* **cramp¹** *etc*.

b (*Dress etc*) mode *f*, genre *m*, modèle *m*; (*Hairdressing*) coiffure *f*. **in the latest ~** (**adv**) à la dernière mode; (**adj**) du dernier cri; **these coats are made in 2 ~s** ces manteaux sont confectionnés en 2 genres *or* en 2 modèles; **the 4 ~s are all the same price** les 4 modèles sont tous au même prix; **I want something in that ~** je voudrais quelque chose dans ce genre-là *or* dans ce goût-là.

c (*NonC: distinction, elegance*) *[person]* allure *f*, chic *m*; *[building, car, film, book]* style *m*, cachet *m*. **that writer lacks ~** cet écrivain manque de style *or* d'élégance, le style de cet écrivain manque de tenue; **to live in ~** mener grand train, vivre sur un grand pied; **he does things in ~** il fait bien les choses; **they got married in ~** ils se sont mariés en grande pompe; **he certainly travels in ~** quand il voyage il fait bien les choses, il voyage dans les règles de l'art.

d (*sort, type*) genre *m*. **just the ~ of book/car I like** justement le genre de livre/de voiture que j'aime.

e (*form of address*) titre *m*.

2 **comp** ►**style book** (*Typ*) manuel *m* des règles typographiques

▸**style sheet** (*Comput*) feuille *f* de style.

3 **vt** a (*call, designate*) appeler. **he ~s himself "Doctor"** il se fait appeler "Docteur"; **the headmaster is ~d "rector"** le directeur a le titre de "recteur"; *see* **self-styled**.

b (*design etc*) *dress, car, boat* créer, dessiner. **to ~ sb's hair** créer une nouvelle coiffure pour qn; **it is ~d for comfort not elegance** c'est un modèle conçu en fonction du confort et non de l'élégance.

c (*Typ*) *manuscript* préparer (*selon le style de l'éditeur*).

styli ['staɪlaɪ] **npl of stylus**.

styling ['staɪlɪŋ] 1 **n** (*NonC*) *[dress]* forme *f*, ligne *f*, façon *f*; *[car]* ligne; (*Hairdressing*) coupe *f*. 2 **comp** *mousse, gel, lotion* coiffant, structurant ▸**styling brush** brosse *f* ronde.

stylish ['staɪlɪʃ] **adj** *person* élégant, qui a du chic; *garment, hotel, district* chic *inv*; *film, book, car* qui a une certaine élégance.

stylishly ['staɪlɪʃlɪ] **adv** *live, dress* élégamment; *travel* dans les règles de l'art.

stylishness ['staɪlɪʃnɪs] **n** élégance *f*, chic *m*.

stylist ['staɪlɪst] **n** (*Literat*) styliste *mf*; (*Dress etc*) modéliste *mf*; (*Hairdressing*) coiffeur *m*, -euse *f*, artiste *mf* (capillaire).

stylistic [staɪ'lɪstɪk] 1 **adj** (*Ling, Literat etc*) stylistique, du style. **~ device** procédé *m* stylistique *or* de style. 2 **n: ~s** stylistique *f*.

stylistically [staɪ'lɪstɪkəlɪ] **adv** stylistiquement.

stylize ['staɪlaɪz] **vt** styliser.

stylus ['staɪləs] **n, pl ~es** *or* **styli** (*tool*) style *m*; *[record player]* pointe *f* de lecture.

stymie ['staɪmɪ] 1 **n** (*Golf*) trou barré. 2 **vt** (*Golf*) barrer le trou à; (* *fig*) coincer*. **I'm ~d*** je suis coincé*, je suis dans une impasse.

styptic ['stɪptɪk] 1 **adj** styptique. **~ pencil** crayon *m* hémostatique. 2 **n** styptique *m*.

Styrofoam ['staɪrə,fəʊm] ® 1 **n** (*US*) polystyrène *m* expansé. 2 **comp** *cup* en polystyrène.

Styx [stɪks] **n** Styx *m*.

suasion ['sweɪʒən] **n** (*also* **moral ~**) pression morale.

suave [swɑːv] **adj** *person* doucereux; *manner, voice* doucereux, onctueux (*pej*). **I didn't like his rather ~ suggestion that ...** je n'ai pas aimé la façon insinuante *or* un peu trop persuasive dont il a suggéré que ... .

suavely ['swɑːvlɪ] **adv** doucereusement, onctueusement (*pej*).

suavity ['swɑːvɪtɪ] **n** (*NonC*) manières doucereuses *or* onctueuses (*pej*).

sub* [sʌb] 1 **abbr of subaltern, subedit, subeditor, sub-lieutenant, submarine (n), subscription, substitute.** 2 **vi: to ~ for sb** remplacer qn, faire une rempla pour qn*.

sub... [sʌb] **pref** sub..., sous-; *see* **subculture** *etc*.

subagent [sʌb'eɪdʒənt] **n** sous-agent *m*.

subalpine ['sʌb'ælpaɪn] **adj** subalpin.

subaltern ['sʌbltən] 1 **n** (*Brit Mil*) *officier d'un rang inférieur à celui de capitaine*. 2 **adj** subalterne.

subaqua [,sʌb'ækwə] **adj: ~ club** club *m* de plongée.

subaqueous ['sʌb'eɪkwɪəs] **adj** subaquatique, aquatique.

subarctic ['sʌb'ɑːktɪk] **adj** subarctique; (*fig*) presque arctique.

subassembly [,sʌbə'semblɪ] **n** sous-assemblée *f*.

subatomic ['sʌbə'tɒmɪk] **adj** subatomique.

sub-basement ['sʌb'beɪsmənt] **n** second sous-sol.

sub-branch ['sʌb'brɑːntʃ] **n** sous-embranchement *m*.

subclass ['sʌb'klɑːs] **n** sous-classe *f*.

subcommittee ['sʌbkə,mɪtɪ] **n** sous-comité *m*; (*larger*) sous-commission *f*. **the Housing S~** la sous-commission du logement.

subconscious ['sʌb'kɒnʃəs] **adj, n** subconscient (*m*).

subconsciously ['sʌb'kɒnʃəslɪ] **adv** de manière subconsciente, inconsciemment.

subcontinent ['sʌb'kɒntɪnənt] **n** sous-continent *m*. **the (Indian) S~** le sous-continent indien.

subcontract ['sʌb'kɒntrækt] 1 **n** sous-traité *m*. 2 [,sʌbkən'trækt] **vt** sous-traiter.

subcontracting ['sʌbkɒn'træktɪŋ] 1 **n** sous-traitance *f*. 2 **adj** *firm* sous-traitant.

subcontractor ['sʌbkən'træktəʳ] **n** sous-entrepreneur *m*, sous-traitant *m*.

subculture ['sʌb'kʌltʃəʳ] **n** (*Soc*) subculture *f*; (*Bacteriology*) culture repiquée.

subcutaneous ['sʌbkjʊ'teɪnɪəs] **adj** sous-cutané.

subcutaneously ['sʌbkjʊ'teɪnɪəslɪ] **adv** en sous-cutané.

subdeacon [,sʌb'diːkən] **n** sous-diacre *m*.

subdeb* ['sʌbdeb], **subdebutante** ['sʌb,debjuːtɑːnt] **n** (*US*) jeune fille *f* qui n'a pas encore fait son entrée dans le monde.

subdistrict ['sʌb,dɪstrɪkt] **n** subdivision *f* d'un quartier.

subdivide [,sʌbdɪ'vaɪd] 1 **vt** subdiviser (*into* en). 2 **vi** se subdiviser.

subdivision ['sʌbdɪ,vɪʒən] **n** subdivision *f*.

subdominant [,sʌb'dɒmɪnənt] **n** (*Ecol*) (espèce *f*) sous-dominante *f*; (*Mus*) sous-dominante *f*.

subdue [səb'djuː] **vt** *people, country* subjuguer, assujettir, soumettre; *feelings, passions, desire* contenir, refréner, maîtriser; *light, colour* adoucir, atténuer; *voice* baisser; *pain* atténuer, amortir.

subdued [səb'djuːd] **adj** *emotion* contenu; *reaction, response* faible, pas très marqué; *voice, tone* bas (*f* basse); *conversation, discussion* à voix basse; *colour* doux (*f* douce); *light, lighting* tamisé, voilé. **she was very ~** elle avait perdu sa vivacité *or* son entrain *or* son exubérance.

subedit ['sʌb'edɪt] **vt** (*Brit: Press, Typ*) corriger, mettre au point, préparer pour l'impression.

subeditor ['sʌb'edɪtəʳ] **n** (*Brit: Press, Typ*) secrétaire *mf* de (la) rédaction.

sub-entry ['sʌb,entrɪ] **n** (*Book-keeping*) sous-entrée *f*.

subfamily ['sʌb,fæmɪlɪ] **n** sous-famille *f*.

subfield ['sʌbfiːld] **n** (*Math*) subdivision *f*.

sub-frame ['sʌbfreɪm] **n** (*Aut*) faux-châssis *m*.

subfusc ['sʌb'fʌsk] **n** toge *f* et mortier noirs.

subgroup ['sʌb,gruːp] **n** sous-groupe *m*.

subhead(ing) ['sʌb,hed(ɪŋ)] **n** sous-titre *m*.

subhuman ['sʌb'hjuːmən] **adj** pas tout à fait humain, moins qu'humain.

subject ['sʌbdʒɪkt] 1 **n** a (*citizen etc*) sujet(te) *m(f)*. **the king and his ~s** le roi et ses sujets; **British ~** sujet britannique; **he is a French ~** (*in France*) c'est un sujet français, il est de nationalité française; (*elsewhere*) c'est un ressortissant français.

b (*Med, Phot, Psych etc: person*) sujet *m*. **he's a good ~ for treatment by hypnosis** c'est un sujet qui répond bien au traitement par l'hypnose; **he's a good ~ for research into hypnosis** c'est un bon sujet d'expérience pour une étude de l'hypnose.

c (*matter, topic: gen, Art, Literat, Mus etc*) sujet *m* (*of, for* de); (*Scol, Univ*) matière *f*, discipline *f*. **to get off the ~** sortir du sujet; **that's off the ~** c'est hors du sujet *or* à côté du sujet; **let's get back to the ~** revenons à nos moutons; **on the ~ of** au sujet de, sur le sujet de; **while we're on the ~ of ...** pendant que nous parlons de ..., à propos de ...; (*Scol, Univ*) **his best ~** sa matière *or* sa discipline forte; *see* **change, drop** *etc*.

d (*reason, occasion*) sujet *m*, motif *m* (*of, for* de). **it is not a ~ for rejoicing** il n'y a pas lieu de se réjouir.

e (*Gram, Logic, Philos*) sujet *m*.

2 **comp** ▸**subject heading** rubrique *f* ▸**subject index** (*in book*) index *m* des matières; (*in library*) fichier *m* par matières ▸**subject matter** (*theme*) sujet *m*; (*content*) contenu *m* ▸**subject pronoun** (*Gram*) pronom *m* sujet.

3 **adj** *people, tribes, state* soumis. **~ to** (*liable to*) (*disease etc*) sujet à; (*flooding, subsidence etc*) exposé à; (*the law, taxation*) soumis à; (*conditional upon*) sous réserve de, à condition de; (*except for*) sous réserve de, sauf; **~ to French rule** sous (la) domination française; **nations ~ to communism** nations *fpl* d'obédience communiste; **our prices are ~ to alteration** nos prix peuvent être modifiés *or* sont donnés sous réserve de modifications; **~ to the approval of the committee** sous réserve de l'approbation du comité; **you may leave the country ~ to producing the necessary documents** vous pouvez quitter le pays à condition de fournir les documents nécessaires; **~ to prior sale** sous réserve de *or* sauf vente antérieure.

4 [səb'dʒekt] **vt** (*subdue*) *country* soumettre, assujettir (*liter*). **to ~ sb to sth** soumettre qn à qch, faire subir qch à qn; **to ~ sth to heat/cold** exposer qch à la chaleur/au froid; **he was ~ed to much criticism** il a été en butte à de nombreuses critiques, il a fait l'objet de nombreuses critiques, il a été très critiqué; **to ~ o.s. to criticism** s'exposer à la critique.

subjection [səb'dʒekʃən] **n** sujétion *f*, soumission *f*. **to hold** *or* **keep in ~** maintenir dans la sujétion *or* sous son joug; **to bring into ~** soumettre, assujettir (*liter*); **they were living in a state of complete ~** ils vivaient dans la sujétion *or* dans la soumission *or* dans les chaînes.

subjective [səb'dʒektɪv] 1 **adj** subjectif; (*Gram*) *case, pronoun* sujet; *genitive* subjectif. 2 **n** (*Gram*) nominatif *m*.

subjectively [səb'dʒektɪvlɪ] **adv** subjectivement.

subjectivism [səb'dʒektɪvɪzəm] **n** subjectivisme *m*.

subjectivity [,səbdʒek'tɪvɪtɪ] **n** subjectivité *f*.

subjoin ['sʌb'dʒɔɪn] **vt** adjoindre, ajouter.

sub judice ['sʌb'dʒuːdɪsɪ] **adj** (*Jur*) **it is ~** l'affaire passe à présent devant les tribunaux.

subjugate ['sʌbdʒʊgeɪt] **vt** *people, country* subjuguer, soumettre, assujettir; *animal, feelings* dompter.

subjugation [,sʌbdʒʊ'geɪʃən] **n** subjugation *f*, assujettissement *m*.

subjunctive [səb'dʒʌŋktɪv] **adj, n** subjonctif (*m*). **in the ~ (mood)** au (mode) subjonctif.

subkingdom ['sʌb,kɪŋdəm] **n** (*Bot, Zool etc*) embranchement *m*.

sublease ['sʌb'liːs] 1 **n** sous-location *f*. 2 **vti** sous-louer (*to* à, *from* à).

sublet ['sʌb'let] (**vb: pret, ptp sublet**) 1 **n** sous-location *f*. 2 **vti** sous-louer (*to* à).

sub-librarian ['sʌblaɪ'breərɪən] **n** bibliothécaire *mf* adjoint(e).

sub-lieutenant ['sʌblef'tenənt] **n** (*Brit Naut*) enseigne *m* de vaisseau (de première classe).

sublimate ['sʌblɪmeɪt] 1 **vt** (*all senses*) sublimer. 2 ['sʌblɪmɪt] **adj, n** (*Chem*) sublimé (*m*).

sublimation [,sʌblɪ'meɪʃən] **n** sublimation *f*.

sublime [sə'blaɪm] 1 **adj** a *being, beauty, work, scenery* sublime; (*: *excellent*) *dinner, hat, person* divin, fantastique*, sensationnel*. b *con-*

tempt, indifference, impertinence suprême (*before noun*), souverain (*before noun*), sans pareil. 2 n sublime *m*. **from the ~ to the ridiculous** du sublime au grotesque.

sublimely [sə'blaɪmlɪ] adv a ~ **beautiful** d'une beauté sublime. b *contemptuous, indifferent* au plus haut point, suprêmement, souverainement. ~ **unaware of** dans une ignorance absolue de.

subliminal [ˌsʌb'lɪmɪnl] adj subliminal. ~ **advertising** publicité insidieuse.

subliminally [ˌsʌb'lɪmɪnəlɪ] adv au-dessous du niveau de la conscience.

sublimity [sə'blɪmɪtɪ] n sublimité *f*.

sublingual [sʌb'lɪŋgwəl] adj sublingual.

submachine gun ['sʌbmə'ʃiːngʌn] n mitraillette *f*.

submarine [ˌsʌbmə'riːn] 1 n a sous-marin *m*. b (*US *: sandwich*) grand sandwich *m* mixte. 2 comp ▸**submarine chaser** chasseur *m* de sous-marins ▸**submarine pen** abri *m* pour sous-marins. 3 adj sous-marin.

submariner [ˌsʌb'mærɪnəʳ] n sous-marinier *m*.

submaxillary [ˌsʌb'mæksɪlərɪ] adj sous-maxillaire.

submediant [ˌsʌb'miːdɪənt] n (*Mus*) sus-dominante *f*.

sub-menu ['sʌbmenjuː] n (*Comput*) sous-menu *m*.

submerge [səb'mɜːdʒ] 1 vt *[flood, tide, sea]* submerger; *field* inonder, submerger. **~d** *rock, wreck etc* submergé; (*fig*) *poor people* déshérité, indigent; *[submarine]* **speed ~d** vitesse *f* en plongée; **to ~ sth in sth** immerger qch dans qch; (*fig*) **to ~ o.s. in sth** se plonger totalement dans qch; (*fig*) **~d in work** submergé *or* débordé de travail. 2 vi *[submarine, diver etc]* s'immerger.

submergence [səb'mɜːdʒəns] n submersion *f*.

submersible [səb'mɜːsəbl] adj, n submersible *(m)*.

submersion [səb'mɜːʃən] n (*see* **submerge**) submersion *f*; immersion *f*.

submission [səb'mɪʃən] n a (*Mil, fig*) soumission (*to* à). **starved/beaten into ~** réduit par la faim/les coups; **to make one's ~ to sb** faire sa soumission à qn. b (*NonC: submissiveness*) soumission *f*, docilité *f*. c (*NonC: see* **submit 1b**) soumission *f*. d *[plan, application etc]* proposition *f*. e (*Jur*) **~s** conclusions *fpl* (*d'une partie*); (*Jur*) **to file ~s with a court** déposer des conclusions auprès d'un tribunal. f (*gen*) **his ~ was that ...** il a allégué *or* avancé que ...; **in my ~** selon ma thèse. g (*Wrestling*) soumission *f*.

submissive [səb'mɪsɪv] adj *person, answer, smile* soumis, docile.

submissively [səb'mɪsɪvlɪ] adv avec soumission, docilement.

submissiveness [səb'mɪsɪvnɪs] n soumission *f*, docilité *f*.

submit [səb'mɪt] 1 vt a **to ~ o.s. to sb/sth** se soumettre à qn/qch. b (*put forward*) *documents, sample, proposal, report, evidence* soumettre (*to* à). **to ~ that** suggérer que; **I ~ that** ma thèse est que. 2 vi (*Mil*) se soumettre (*to* à); (*fig*) se soumettre, se plier (*to* à).

subnormal ['sʌb'nɔːməl] 1 adj *temperature* au-dessous de la normale; *person* subnormal, arriéré. 2 npl: **the mentally/educationally ~** les attardés *or* retardés (sur le plan intellectuel/éducatif).

suborbital ['sʌb'ɔːbɪtəl] adj (*Space*) sous-orbital.

sub-order ['sʌb'ɔːdəʳ] n sous-ordre *m*.

subordinate [sə'bɔːdnɪt] 1 adj *member of staff, rank, position* subalterne; (*Gram*) subordonné. 2 n subordonné(e) *m(f)*, subalterne *mf*. 3 [sə'bɔːdɪneɪt] vt subordonner (*to* à). (*Gram*) **subordinating conjunction** subordonnant *m*, conjonction *f* de subordination.

subordination [səˌbɔːdɪ'neɪʃən] n subordination *f*.

suborn [sə'bɔːn] vt suborner.

subparagraph ['sʌbˌpærəgrɑːf] n sous-paragraphe *m*.

subplot ['sʌbˌplɒt] n (*Literat*) intrigue *f* secondaire.

subpoena [səb'piːnə] (*Jur*) 1 n citation *f*, assignation *f* (*pour le témoin*). 2 vt citer *or* assigner (à comparaître).

subpopulation ['sʌbˌpɒpjʊ'leɪʃən] n subpopulation *f*.

sub post office [sʌb'pəʊstˌɒfɪs] n petit bureau de poste secondaire, petit bureau de poste de quartier *or* de village.

subregion ['sʌbˌriːdʒən] n sous-région *f*.

subrogate ['sʌbrəgɪt] adj subrogé. (*Ling*) ~ **language** langage subrogé.

sub rosa [ˌsʌb'rəʊzə] adv en confidence, sous le sceau du secret.

subroutine [ˌsʌbruː'tiːn] n (*Comput*) sous-programme *m*.

subscribe [səb'skraɪb] 1 vt a *money* donner, verser (*to* à). b *one's signature, name* apposer (*to* au bas de); *document* signer. **he ~s himself John Smith** il signe John Smith. 2 vi verser une somme d'argent, apporter une contribution, cotiser*. **to ~ to** *book, new publication, fund* souscrire à; *newspaper* s'abonner à, être abonné à; *opinion, project, proposal* souscrire à; **I don't ~ to the idea that money should be given to ...** je ne suis pas partisan de donner de l'argent à ... .

subscriber [səb'skraɪbəʳ] 1 n (*to fund, new publication etc*) souscripteur *m*, -trice *f* (*to* de); (*to newspaper, also Telec*) abonné(e) *m(f)* (*to* de); (*to opinion, idea*) adepte *mf*, partisan *m* (*to* de). 2 comp ▸**subscriber trunk dialling** (*abbr* **STD**) (*Brit Telec*) automatique *m*.

subscript ['sʌbskrɪpt] (*Typ*) 1 adj inférieur (*f* -eure). 2 n indice *m*.

subscription [səb'skrɪpʃən] 1 n (*to fund, charity*) souscription *f*; (*to club*) cotisation *f*; (*to newspaper*) abonnement *m*. **to pay one's ~** (*to club*) payer *or* verser sa cotisation; (*to newspaper*) payer *or* régler son abonnement; (*Press*) **to take out a ~ to** s'abonner à. 2 comp ▸**subscription rate** (*Press*) tarif *m* d'abonnement.

subsection ['sʌbˌsekʃən] n (*Jur etc*) subdivision *f*, article *m*.

subsequent ['sʌbsɪkwənt] adj a (*following*) ultérieur (*f* -eure), postérieur (*f* -eure), suivant, subséquent (*frm, Jur*). **on a ~ visit** lors d'une visite postérieure *or* ultérieure; **his ~ visit** sa visite suivante; **~ to his speech** à la suite de son discours; **~ to this** par la suite. b (*resultant*) consécutif, résultant.

subsequently ['sʌbsɪkwəntlɪ] adv par la suite.

subserve [səb'sɜːv] vt (*frm*) favoriser.

subservience [səb'sɜːvɪəns] n (*see* **subservient a**) caractère *m* subalterne; obséquiosité *f*, servilité *f*; asservissement *m* (*to* à).

subservient [səb'sɜːvɪənt] adj a *role* subalterne; (*pej*) *person, manner* obséquieux (*pej*), servile (*pej*); (*to taste, fashion*) asservi (*to* à). b (*frm: useful*) utile (*to* à).

subset ['sʌbˌset] n sous-ensemble *m*.

subside [səb'saɪd] vi *[land, pavement, foundations, building]* s'affaisser, se tasser; *[flood, river]* baisser, décroître; *[wind, anger, excitement]* tomber, se calmer; *[threat]* s'éloigner; *[person]* (*into armchair etc*) s'affaisser, s'écrouler (*into* dans, *on to* sur); (**: keep quiet*) se taire.

subsidence ['sʌbsɪdns, səb'saɪdəns] n *[land, pavement, foundations, building]* affaissement *m*. **"road liable to ~"** ≃ "chaussée instable"; **the crack in the wall is caused by ~** la faille dans le mur est due à l'affaissement du terrain.

subsidiarity [ˌsəbsɪdɪ'ærɪtɪ] n subsidiarité *f*.

subsidiary [səb'sɪdɪərɪ] 1 adj *motive, reason* subsidiaire; *advantage, income* accessoire. (*Fin*) ~ **company** filiale *f*; (*Climbing*) ~ **summit** antécime *f*. 2 n (*Fin*) filiale *f*.

subsidize ['sʌbsɪdaɪz] vt subventionner. **heavily ~d** *agriculture, housing* fortement subventionné.

subsidy ['sʌbsɪdɪ] n subvention *f*. **government** *or* **state ~** subvention de l'État; **there is a ~ on butter** l'État subventionne les producteurs *or* la production de beurre.

subsist [səb'sɪst] vi subsister. **to ~ on bread/£60 a week** vivre de pain/avec 60 livres par semaine.

subsistence [səb'sɪstəns] 1 n a existence *f*, subsistance *f*. **means of ~** moyens *mpl* d'existence *or* de subsistance. b (*also* **~ allowance, ~ benefit**) frais *mpl or* indemnité *f* de subsistance. 2 comp ▸**subsistence crops** cultures *fpl* vivrières de base ▸**subsistence economy** économie *f* de subsistance ▸**subsistence farmer** agriculteur *m* qui produit le minimum vital ▸**subsistence farming** agriculture *f* de subsistance ▸**subsistence level: to live at subsistence level** avoir tout juste de quoi vivre ▸**subsistence wage** salaire tout juste suffisant pour vivre.

subsoil ['sʌbsɔɪl] n (*Agr, Geol*) sous-sol *m*.

subsonic ['sʌb'sɒnɪk] adj subsonique.

subspecies ['sʌb'spiːʃiːz] n, pl inv sous-espèce *f*.

substance ['sʌbstəns] n (*matter, material*) substance *f* (*also Chem, Philos, Phys, Rel etc*); (*essential meaning, gist*) substance, fond *m*, essentiel *m*; (*solid quality*) solidité *f*; (*consistency*) consistance *f*; (*wealth etc*) biens *mpl*, fortune *f*. **that is the ~ of his speech** voilà la substance *or* l'essentiel de son discours; **I agree with the ~ of his proposals** je suis d'accord sur l'essentiel de ses propositions; **the meal had not much ~ (to it)** le repas n'était pas très substantiel; **to lack ~** *[film, book, essay]* manquer d'étoffe; *[argument]* être plutôt mince; *[accusation, claim, allegation]* être sans grand fondement; **in ~** en substance; **a man of ~** (*rich*) un homme riche *or* cossu; (*Jur*) **the ~ of the case** le fond de l'affaire; *see* **sum**.

substandard [ˌsʌb'stændəd] adj *goods* de qualité inférieure; *performance* médiocre; *housing* inférieur aux normes exigées; (*Ling*) non conforme à la langue correcte.

substantial [səb'stænʃəl] adj a (*great, large*) *amount, proportion, part, progress* important, considérable, substantiel (*fig*); *sum, loan* important, considérable, élevé; *proof* solide, concluant; *difference* appréciable; *argument* de poids; *meal* substantiel, copieux; *firm* solide, bien assis; *landowner, farmer, businessman* riche, cossu; *house etc* grand, important. **to be in ~ agreement** être d'accord sur l'essentiel *or* dans l'ensemble; (*Jur*) ~ **damages** dommages-intérêts *mpl* élevés. b (*real*) substantiel, réel.

substantially [səb'stænʃəlɪ] adv a (*considerably*) *improve, contribute, progress* considérablement. ~ **bigger** beaucoup plus grand; ~ **different** très différent; **not ~ different** pas réellement différent. b (*to a large extent*) en grande partie. **this is ~ true** c'est en grande partie vrai; **it is ~ the same book** c'est en grande partie le même livre, ce n'est guère différent de l'autre livre. c *built, constructed* solidement.

substantiate [səb'stænʃɪeɪt] vt fournir des preuves à l'appui de, justifier. **he could not ~ it** il n'a pas pu fournir de preuves.

substantiation [səbˌstænʃɪ'eɪʃən] n preuve *f*, justification *f*.

substantival [ˌsʌbstən'taɪvəl] adj (*Gram*) substantif, à valeur de substantif.

substantive ['sʌbstəntɪv] 1 n (*Gram*) substantif *m*. 2 adj a (*gen*) substantiel; (*existing independently*) indépendant, autonome. b (*Gram*) substantif.

substation ['sʌbˌsteɪʃən] n sous-station *f*.

substitute ['sʌbstɪtjuːt] 1 n (*person: gen, Sport*) remplaçant(e) *m(f)*, suppléant(e) *m(f)* (*for* de); (*thing*) produit *m* de remplacement, succédané *m* (*gen pej*), ersatz *m inv* (*gen pej*) (*for* de); (*Gram*) terme suppléant. **you must find a ~ (for yourself)** vous devez vous trouver un remplaçant, il faut vous faire remplacer; **~s for rubber, rubber ~s** succédanés *or* ersatz de caoutchouc; (*Comm*) **"beware of ~s"** "se méfier des contrefaçons"; **there is no ~ for wool** rien ne peut remplacer la laine; **a correspondence course is no/a poor ~ for personal tuition** les cours par correspondance ne remplacent pas/remplacent mal les cours particuliers; *see* **turpentine** *etc.*

2 **adj** (*Sport*) (à titre de) remplaçant. **~ coffee** ersatz *m inv or* succédané *m* de café; (*Educ*) **~ teacher** suppléant(e) *m(f)*.

3 **vt** substituer (*A for B* A à B), remplacer (*A for B* B par A).

4 **vi**: **to ~ for sb** remplacer *or* suppléer qn.

substitution [ˌsʌbstɪ'tju:ʃən] **n** substitution *f* (*also Chem, Ling, Math etc*), remplacement *m*. **~ of x for y** substitution de x à y, remplacement de y par x.

substratum ['sʌb'strɑ:təm] **n, pl substrata** ['sʌb'strɑ:tə] (*gen, Geol, Ling, Soc etc*) substrat *m*; (*Agr*) sous-sol *m*; (*fig*) fond *m*.

substructure ['sʌbˌstrʌktʃəʳ] **n** infrastructure *f*.

subsume [səb'sju:m] **vt** subsumer.

subsystem [ˌsʌb'sɪstəm] **n** sous-système *m*.

subteen [ˌsʌb'ti:n] **n** (*esp US*) préadolescent(e) *m(f)*.

subtemperate [ˌsʌb'tempərɪt] **adj** subtempéré.

subtenancy ['sʌb'tenənsɪ] **n** sous-location *f*.

subtenant ['sʌb'tenənt] **n** sous-locataire *mf*.

subtend [səb'tend] **vt** sous-tendre.

subterfuge ['sʌbtəfju:dʒ] **n** subterfuge *m*.

subterranean [ˌsʌbtə'reɪnɪən] **adj** souterrain.

subtext ['sʌbtekst] **n** sujet *m* sous-jacent.

subtilize ['sʌtɪlaɪz] **vti** subtiliser.

subtitle ['sʌbˌtaɪtl] (*Cine*) 1 **n** sous-titre *m*. 2 **vt** sous-titrer.

subtitling ['sʌbˌtaɪtlɪŋ] **n** sous-titrage *m*.

subtle ['sʌtl] **adj** *person* subtil (*f* subtile), perspicace, qui a beaucoup de finesse; *mind, intelligence* subtil, fin, pénétrant; *argument, suggestion, analysis, reply* subtil, ingénieux, astucieux; *irony, joke* subtil, fin; *distinction* subtil, ténu; *allusion* subtil, discret (*f* -ète); *charm* subtil, indéfinissable; *perfume* subtil, délicat. (*Cine, Literat, Theat etc*) **it wasn't very ~** c'était un peu gros, c'était cousu de fil blanc.

subtleness ['sʌtlnɪs] **n = subtlety a.**

subtlety ['sʌtltɪ] **n** a (*NonC*: *see* **subtle**) subtilité *f*; perspicacité *f*; finesse *f*; ingéniosité *f*; délicatesse *f*. b **a ~** une subtilité.

subtly ['sʌtlɪ] **adv** subtilement.

subtonic [ˌsʌb'tɒnɪk] **n** sous-tonique *f*.

subtopic ['sʌb'tɒpɪk] **n** sous-thème *m*, subdivision *f* d'un thème.

subtotal [ˌsʌb'təʊtl] **n** total *m* partiel.

subtract [səb'trækt] **vt** soustraire, retrancher, déduire (*from* de).

subtraction [səb'trækʃən] **n** soustraction *f*.

subtropical ['sʌb'trɒpɪkəl] **adj** subtropical.

subtropics [sʌb'trɒpɪks] **npl** régions *fpl* subtropicales.

suburb ['sʌbɜ:b] **n** faubourg *m*. **the ~s** la banlieue; **in the ~s** en banlieue; **the outer ~s** la grande banlieue; **it is now a ~ of London** c'est maintenant un faubourg de Londres, ça fait partie de la banlieue de Londres.

suburban [sə'bɜ:bən] **adj** *house, square, shops, train, residents* de banlieue; *community, development* suburbain, de(s) banlieue(s); (*pej*) *person, attitude, accent* banlieusard (*pej*). **~ spread** *or* **growth** développement *m* suburbain *or* des banlieues.

suburbanite [sə'bɜ:bənaɪt] **n** habitant(e) *m(f)* de la banlieue, banlieusard(e) *m(f)* (*pej*).

suburbanize [sə'bɜ:bənaɪz] **vt** donner le caractère *or* les caractéristiques de la banlieue à, transformer en banlieue.

suburbia [sə'bɜ:bɪə] **n** (*NonC*) la banlieue.

subvention [səb'venʃən] **n** subvention *f*.

subversion [səb'vɜ:ʃən] **n** (*Pol*) subversion *f*.

subversive [səb'vɜ:sɪv] 1 **adj** subversif. 2 **n** (*people*) **~s** éléments *mpl* subversifs.

subvert [səb'vɜ:t] **vt** *the law, tradition* bouleverser, renverser; (*corrupt*) *person* corrompre.

subway ['sʌbweɪ] **n** (*underpass: esp Brit*) passage souterrain; (*railway: esp US*) métro *m*.

sub-zero ['sʌb'zɪərəʊ] **adj** *temperature* au-dessous de zéro.

succeed [sək'si:d] 1 **vi** a (*be successful*) réussir (*in sth* dans qch); (*prosper*) réussir, avoir du succès; *[plan, attempt]* réussir. **to ~ in doing** réussir *or* parvenir *or* arriver à faire; **he ~s in all he does** tout lui réussit, il réussit tout ce qu'il entreprend; (*Prov*) **nothing ~s like success** un succès en entraîne un autre; **to ~ in business/as a politician** réussir *or* avoir du succès en affaires/en tant qu'homme politique; **to ~ in life/one's career** réussir dans la vie/sa carrière.

b (*follow*) succéder (*to* à). **he ~ed (to the throne) in 1911** il a succédé (à la couronne) en 1911; **there ~ed a period of peace** il y eut ensuite une période de paix.

2 **vt** *[person]* succéder à, prendre la suite de; *[event, storm, season etc]* succéder à, suivre. **he ~ed his father as leader of the party** il a succédé à *or* pris la suite de son père à la direction du parti; **he was ~ed by his son** son fils lui a succédé; **as year ~ed year** comme les années passaient, comme les années se succédaient.

succeeding [sək'si:dɪŋ] **adj** (*in past*) suivant, qui suit; (*in future*) à venir, futur. **each ~ year brought** ... chaque année qui passait apportait ...; **each ~ year will bring** ... chacune des années à venir apportera ...; **on 3 ~ Saturdays** 3 samedis consécutifs *or* de suite; **in the ~ chaos** dans la confusion qui a suivi.

success [sək'ses] 1 **n** *[plan, venture, attempt, person]* succès *m*, réussite *f* (*in an exam* à un examen, *in one's aim* dans son but). **his ~ in doing sth** le fait qu'il ait réussi à faire qch; **his ~ in his attempts** la réussite qui a couronné ses efforts; **without ~** sans succès, en vain; **to meet with ~** avoir *or* obtenir *or* remporter du succès; **to have great ~** faire fureur, avoir un succès fou; **to make a ~ of** *project, enterprise* faire réussir, mener à bien; *job, meal, dish* réussir; **we wish you every ~** nous vous souhaitons très bonne chance; **congratulations on your ~** je vous félicite de votre succès, (toutes mes) félicitations pour votre succès; **congratulations on your ~ in obtaining** ... je vous félicite d'avoir réussi à obtenir ...; **he was a ~ at last** il avait enfin réussi, il était enfin arrivé, il avait enfin du succès; **he was a great ~ at the dinner/as Hamlet/as a writer/in business** il a eu beaucoup de succès au dîner/dans le rôle de Hamlet/en tant qu'écrivain/en affaires; **it was a ~** *[holiday, meal, evening, attack]* c'était une réussite, c'était réussi; *[play, book, record]* ça a été couronné de succès; **the hotel was a great ~** on a été très content de l'hôtel; *see* **rate[1] 1a, succeed.**

2 **comp ▸ success story** (histoire *f* d'une) réussite *f*.

successful [sək'sesfʊl] **adj** *plan, venture* couronné de succès, qui a réussi; *businessman* prospère, qui a du succès *or* qui est heureux en affaires; *writer, painter, book* à succès; *candidate* (*in exam*) reçu, admis; (*in election*) élu; *application* couronné de succès; *visit, deal, effort* fructueux, couronné de succès; *marriage, outcome* heureux; *career, business, firm* prospère. **to be ~** réussir (*in an exam/competition etc* à un examen/concours *etc, in one's attempts/life/one's career etc* dans ses efforts/la vie/sa carrière *etc*); *[performer, play etc]* avoir du succès; **to be ~ in doing** réussir *or* parvenir *or* arriver à faire; *see* **bidder.**

successfully [sək'sesfəlɪ] **adv** avec succès. **to do sth ~** faire qch avec succès, réussir à faire qch.

succession [sək'seʃən] **n** a *[victories, disasters, delays, kings]* succession *f*, série *f*, suite *f*. **in ~** (*one after the other*) successivement, l'un(e) après l'autre; (*by turns*) successivement, tour à tour, alternativement; (*on each occasion*) successivement, progressivement; **4 times in ~** 4 fois de suite; **for 10 years in ~** pendant 10 années consécutives *or* 10 ans de suite; **in close** *or* **rapid ~** *walk* à la file; *happen* coup sur coup; **the ~ of days and nights** la succession *or* l'alternance *f* des jours et des nuits.

b (*NonC*) (*act of succeeding: to title, throne, office, post*) succession *f* (*to* à); (*Jur: heirs collectively*) héritiers *mpl*. **he is second in ~ (to the throne)** il occupe la deuxième place dans l'ordre de succession (à la couronne); **in ~ to his father** à la suite de son père.

successive [sək'sesɪv] **adj** *generations, discoveries* successif; *days, months* consécutif. **on 4 ~ days** pendant 4 jours de suite *or* 4 jours consécutifs; **with each ~ failure** à chaque nouvel échec.

successively [sək'sesɪvlɪ] **adv** (*by turns*) successivement, tour à tour, alternativement; (*on each occasion*) successivement, progressivement; (*one after the other*) successivement, l'un(e) après l'autre.

successor [sək'sesəʳ] **n** (*person, thing*) successeur *m* (*to, of* de). **the ~ to the throne** l'héritier *m*, -ière *f* de la couronne; (*Jur*) **~ in title** ayant droit *m*, ayant cause *m*.

succinct [sək'sɪŋkt] **adj** succinct, concis, bref.

succinctly [sək'sɪŋktlɪ] **adv** succinctement, brièvement, en peu de mots.

succinctness [sək'sɪŋktnɪs] **n** concision *f*.

succor ['sʌkəʳ] (*US*) = **succour.**

succotash ['sʌkətæʃ] **n** (*US Culin*) *plat de maïs en grain et de fèves de Lima.*

succour, (*US*) **succor** ['sʌkəʳ] (*liter*) 1 **n** (*NonC*) secours *m*, aide *f*. 2 **vt** secourir, soulager, venir à l'aide de.

succulence ['sʌkjʊləns] **n** succulence *f*.

succulent ['sʌkjʊlənt] 1 **adj** (*also Bot*) succulent. 2 **n** (*Bot*) plante grasse. **~s** plantes grasses, cactées *fpl*.

succumb [sə'kʌm] **vi** (*to temptation etc*) succomber (*to* à); (*die*) mourir (*to* de), succomber.

such [sʌtʃ] 1 **adj** a (*of that sort*) tel, pareil. **~ a book** un tel livre, un livre pareil, un pareil livre, un livre de cette sorte; **~ books** de tels livres, des livres pareils, de pareils livres, des livres de cette sorte; **~ people** de telles gens, des gens pareils, de pareilles gens; **we had ~ a case last year** nous avons eu un cas semblable l'année dernière; **in ~ cases** en pareil cas; **did you ever hear of ~ a thing?** avez-vous jamais entendu une chose pareille?; **there's no ~ thing!** ça n'existe pas! (*see also* **1b**); **there is no ~ thing in France** il n'y a rien de tel en France; **I said no ~ thing!** je n'ai jamais dit cela!, je n'ai rien dit de la sorte!; **no ~ thing!** pas du tout!; **or some ~ (thing)** ou une chose de ce genre; **no ~ book exists** un tel livre n'existe pas; **Robert was ~ a one** Robert était comme ça; **~ was my reply** telle a été ma réponse, c'est ce que j'ai répondu; **~ is not the case** ce n'est pas le cas ici; **~ is life!** c'est la vie!; **it was SUCH weather!** quel temps il a fait!, il a fait un de ces temps!

b (*gen*) ~ **as** tel que, comme; **a friend ~ as Paul, ~ a friend as Paul** un ami tel que *or* comme Paul; **only ~ a fool as Martin would do that** il fallait un idiot comme Martin *or* quelqu'un d'aussi bête que Martin pour faire cela; **~ writers as Molière, Corneille** *etc* des écrivains tels (que) Molière, Corneille *etc;* **until ~ time** jusqu'à ce moment-là; **until ~ time as** ... jusqu'à ce que ... + *subj*; **~ a book as this, a book ~ as this** un livre tel que *or* comme celui-ci; **he's not ~ a fool as you think** il n'est pas aussi *or* si bête que vous croyez; **I'm not ~ a fool as to believe that!** je ne suis pas assez bête pour croire ça!; **there are no ~ things as unicorns** les licornes n'existent pas; **have you ~ a thing as a penknife?** auriez-vous un canif par hasard?; (*question*) **~ as?** comme quoi, par exemple?; **I must buy some more things — ~ as?** je dois acheter plusieurs choses encore – quel genre de choses? *or* quoi encore?; **it is not ~ as to cause concern** cela ne doit pas être une raison d'inquiétude; **his health was ~ as to alarm his wife** son état de santé était de nature à alarmer sa femme; **it caused ~ scenes of grief as are rarely seen** cela a provoqué des scènes de douleur telles qu'on *or* comme on en voit peu; **~ books as I have** le peu de livres *or* les quelques livres que je possède; **you can take my car, ~ as it is** vous pouvez prendre ma voiture pour ce qu'elle vaut; *see* **time** *etc.*

c (*so much*) tellement, tant. **embarrassed by ~ praise** embarrassé par tant *or* tellement de compliments; **he was in ~ pain** il souffrait tellement; **don't be in ~ a rush** ne soyez pas si pressé; **we had SUCH a surprise!** quelle surprise nous avons eue!, nous avons eu une de ces surprises!, nous avons été drôlement surpris!*; **there was ~ a noise that** ... il y avait tellement *or* tant de bruit que ...; **his rage was ~ that ..., ~ was his rage that** ... il était tellement *or* si furieux que ... .

2 **adv** a (*so very*) si, tellement. **he gave us ~ good coffee** il nous a offert un si bon café; **~ big boxes** de si grandes boîtes; **~ a lovely present** un si joli cadeau; **it was SUCH a long time ago!** il y a si *or* tellement longtemps de ça!; **he bought ~ an expensive car that** ... il a acheté une voiture si *or* tellement chère que ... .

b (*in comparisons*) aussi. **I haven't had ~ good coffee for years** ça fait des années que je n'ai pas bu un aussi bon café; **~ lovely children as his** des enfants aussi gentils que les siens.

3 **pron** ceux *mpl*, celles *fpl*. **~ as wish to go** ceux qui veulent partir; **all ~** tous ceux; **I'll give you ~ as I have** je vous donnerai ceux que j'ai *or* le peu que j'ai; **I know of no ~** je n'en connais point; **as ~** (*in that capacity*) à ce titre, comme tel(le), en tant que tel(le); (*in itself*) en soi; **the soldier, as ~, deserves respect** tout soldat, comme tel, mérite le respect; **the work as ~ is boring, but the pay is good** le travail en soi est ennuyeux, mais le salaire est bon; **and as ~ he was promoted** et en tant que tel il a obtenu de l'avancement; **he was a genius but not recognized as ~** c'était un génie mais il n'était pas reconnu pour tel *or* considéré comme tel; **there are no houses as ~** il n'y a pas de maisons à proprement parler; **teachers and doctors and ~(like)*** les professeurs et les docteurs et autres (gens de la sorte); **rabbits and hares and ~(like)*** les lapins, les lièvres et autres animaux de ce genre *or* de la sorte; **shoes and gloves and ~(like)*** les souliers, les gants et autres choses de ce genre *or* de la sorte.

4 **comp** ► **such-and-such adj** tel (et *or* ou tel); **Mr Such-and-such*** Monsieur Untel; **in such-and-such a street** dans telle (et *or* ou telle) rue ► **suchlike*** **adj** de la sorte, de ce genre (*see also* **3**).

suck [sʌk] 1 **n** a **to have a ~ at sth** sucer qch.

b (*at breast*) tétée *f*. **to give ~ to** allaiter, donner le sein à.

2 **comp** ► **sucking-pig** cochon *m* de lait.

3 **vt** *fruit, pencil* sucer; *juice, poison* sucer (*from* de); (*through straw*) *drink* aspirer (*through* avec); *sweet* sucer, suçoter; *[baby] breast, bottle* téter; *[leech]* sucer; *[pump, machine]* aspirer (*from* de). **to ~ one's thumb** sucer son pouce; **child ~ing its mother's breast** enfant qui tète sa mère; **to ~ dry** *orange etc* sucer tout le jus de; (*fig*) *person* (*of money*) sucer jusqu'au dernier sou; (*of energy*) sucer jusqu'à la moelle; (*fig*) **to be ~ed into a situation** être entraîné dans une situation; *see* **teach**.

4 **vi** a *[baby]* téter.

b **to ~ at** *fruit, pencil, pipe* sucer; *sweet* sucer, suçoter.

c (*US* ⁑*: be very bad*) **it ~s!** c'est un tas de conneries!⁑

►**suck down vt sep** *[sea, mud, sands]* engloutir.

►**suck in** 1 **vi** (⁑ *fig*) **to suck in with sb** faire de la lèche à qn⁑, lécher les bottes de qn. 2 **vt sep** *[sea, mud, sands]* engloutir; *[porous surface]* absorber; *[pump, machine]* aspirer; (*fig*) *knowledge, facts* absorber, assimiler.

►**suck off***⁑ **vt sep** tailler une pipe à*⁑.

►**suck out vt sep** *[person]* sucer, faire sortir en suçant (*of, from* de); *[machine]* refouler à l'extérieur (*of, from* de).

►**suck up** 1 **vi** (⁑ *fig*) **to suck up to sb** faire de la lèche à qn⁑, lécher les bottes* de qn. 2 **vt sep** *[person]* aspirer, sucer; *[pump, machine]* aspirer; *[porous surface]* absorber.

sucker ['sʌkəʳ] 1 **n** a (*on machine*) ventouse *f*, suceuse *f*, suçoir *m*; (*plunger*) piston *m*; (*Bot*) surgeon *m*, drageon *m*; *[leech, octopus]* ventouse; *[insect]* suçoir. b (⁑*: person*) poire* *f*, gogo* *m*. **to be a ~ for sth** ne pouvoir résister à qch. 2 **vt** (*US* ⁑*: swindle*) embobiner*. **to get ~ed out of 500 dollars** se faire refaire de 500 dollars.

suckle ['sʌkl] 1 **vt** *child* allaiter, donner le sein à; *young animal* allaiter. 2 **vi** téter.

suckling ['sʌklɪŋ] **n** (*act*) allaitement *m*; (*child*) nourrisson *m*, enfant *mf* à la mamelle.

sucrase ['sju:kreɪz] **n** sucrase *f*, invertase *f*.

sucrose ['su:krəʊz] **n** saccharose *f*.

suction ['sʌkʃən] 1 **n** succion *f*. **it works by ~** cela marche par succion; **to adhere by ~ (on)** faire ventouse (sur). 2 **comp** *apparatus, device* de succion ► **suction disc** ventouse *f* ► **suction pump** pompe aspirante ► **suction shaft** (*Min*) puits *m* d'appel d'air ► **suction valve** clapet *m* d'aspiration.

Sudan [sʊ'dɑ:n] **n: (the) ~** le Soudan.

Sudanese [ˌsu:də'ni:z] 1 **n** a (*person*) Soudanais(e) *m(f)*. b (*Ling*) soudanais *m*. 2 **adj** soudanais.

sudden ['sʌdn] **adj** *movement, pain, emotion, change, decision* soudain, subit, brusque; *death, inspiration* subit; *bend in road, marriage, appointment* imprévu, inattendu. **all of a ~** soudain, tout à coup, tout d'un coup, brusquement; **it's all so ~!** on s'y attendait tellement peu!, c'est arrivé tellement vite!; (*Med*) **~ infant death syndrome** mort *f* subite du nourrisson; (*Sport*) **~ death (play-off)** *coup supplémentaire déterminant le gagnant en cas d'égalité.*

suddenly ['sʌdnlɪ] **adv** brusquement, soudainement, subitement, tout à coup, tout d'un coup, soudain. **to die ~** mourir subitement.

suddenness ['sʌdnnɪs] **n** (*see* **sudden**) soudaineté *f*, brusquerie *f*; caractère subit *or* imprévu *or* inattendu.

suds [sʌdz] **npl** a (*also* **soap~**) (*lather*) mousse *f* de savon; (*soapy water*) eau savonneuse. b (*US* ⁑*: beer*) bière *f*.

sue [su:] 1 **vt** (*Jur*) poursuivre en justice, entamer une action contre, intenter un procès à (*for sth* pour obtenir qch, *over, about* au sujet de). **to ~ sb for damages** poursuivre qn en dommages-intérêts; **to ~ sb for libel** intenter un procès en diffamation à qn; **to be ~d for damages/libel** être poursuivi en dommages-intérêts/en diffamation; **to ~ sb for divorce** entamer une procédure de divorce contre qn. 2 **vi** a (*Jur*) intenter un procès, engager des poursuites. **to ~ for divorce** entamer une procédure de divorce. b (*liter*) **to ~ for peace/pardon** solliciter la paix/le pardon.

suede [sweɪd] 1 **n** daim *m*, cuir suédé. **imitation ~** suédine *f*. 2 **comp** *shoes, handbag, coat, skirt* de daim; *gloves* de suède; *leather* suédé.

suet [sʊɪt] **n** (*Culin*) graisse *f* de rognon. **~ pudding** *gâteau sucré ou salé à base de farine et de graisse de bœuf.*

Suetonius [swi:'təʊnɪəs] **n** Suétone *m*.

Suez ['su:ɪz] **n: ~ Canal** canal *m* de Suez; **Gulf of ~** golfe *m* de Suez; (*Brit Hist*) **before/after ~** avant/après l'affaire de Suez.

suffer ['sʌfəʳ] 1 **vt** a (*undergo*) (*gen*) subir; *hardship, bereavement, martyrdom, torture* souffrir, subir; *punishment, change in circumstances, loss* subir; *damage, setback* essuyer, subir; *pain, headaches, hunger* souffrir de. **he ~ed a lot of pain** il a beaucoup souffert; (*liter*) **to ~ death** mourir; **her popularity ~ed a decline** sa popularité a souffert *or* a décliné.

b (*bear*) *pain* endurer, tolérer, supporter; (*allow*) *opposition, sb's rudeness, refusal etc* tolérer, permettre. **I can't ~ it a moment longer** je ne peux plus le souffrir *or* le tolérer, c'est intolérable, c'est insupportable; **he doesn't ~ fools gladly** il n'a aucune patience pour les imbéciles; (*liter*) **to ~ sb to do** souffrir que qn fasse.

2 **vi** a *[person]* souffrir. **to ~ in silence** souffrir en silence; **to ~ for one's sins** expier ses péchés; **he ~ed for it later** il en a souffert les conséquences *or* il en a pâti plus tard; **you'll ~ for this** il vous en cuira, vous me le paierez; **I'll make him ~ for it!** il me le paiera!

b (*be afflicted by*) **to ~ from** *rheumatism, heart trouble, the cold, hunger* souffrir de; *deafness* être atteint de; *a cold, influenza, frostbite, pimples, bad memory* avoir; **he ~s from a limp/stammer** *etc* il boite/bégaie *etc;* **he was ~ing from shock** il était commotionné; **to ~ from the effects of** *fall, illness* se ressentir de, souffrir des suites de; *alcohol, drug* subir le contrecoup de; **to be ~ing from having done** souffrir *or* se ressentir d'avoir fait; **the child was ~ing from its environment** l'enfant subissait les conséquences fâcheuses de son milieu *or* était la victime de son milieu; **she ~s from lack of friends** son problème c'est qu'elle n'a pas d'amis; **the house is ~ing from neglect** la maison se ressent d'avoir été négligée *or* du manque d'entretien; **his style ~s from over-elaboration** son style souffre *or* a le défaut d'être trop élaboré; *see* **delusion** *etc.*

c (*be injured, impaired*) *[limb]* souffrir, être blessé; *[eyesight, hearing, speech]* souffrir, se détériorer; *[health, reputation, plans, sales, wages]* souffrir, pâtir; *[car, town, house]* souffrir, être endommagé; *[business]* souffrir, péricliter. **your health will ~** votre santé en souffrira *or* en pâtira; **the regiment ~ed badly** le régiment a essuyé de grosses pertes.

sufferance ['sʌfərəns] **n** tolérance *f*, souffrance *f* (*Jur*). **on ~** par tolérance.

sufferer ['sʌfərəʳ] **n** (*from illness*) malade *mf*; (*from misfortune*) victime *f*; (*from accident*) accidenté(e) *m(f)*, victime. **~ from diabetes/AIDS/asthma** *etc*, **diabetes/AIDS/asthma** *etc* **~** diabétique *mf*/sidéen(ne) *m(f)*/asthmatique *mf etc;* (*hum*) **my fellow ~s at the concert** mes compagnons *mpl* d'infortune au concert.

suffering ['sʌfərɪŋ] 1 **n** souffrance(s) *f(pl)*. **"after much ~ patiently**

borne" "après de longues souffrances patiemment endurées"; **her ~ was great** elle a beaucoup souffert. 2 adj souffrant, qui souffre.

suffice [sə'faɪs] (*frm*) 1 vi suffire, être suffisant. **~ it to say** qu'il (me) suffise de dire, je me contenterai de dire. 2 vt suffire à, satisfaire.

sufficiency [sə'fɪʃənsɪ] n (*frm*) quantité suffisante. **a ~ of coal** une quantité suffisante de charbon, suffisamment de charbon, du charbon en quantité suffisante *or* en suffisance; *see* **self**.

sufficient [sə'fɪʃənt] adj (*enough*) *books, money, food, people* assez de, suffisamment de; (*big enough*) *number, quantity* suffisant. **to be ~** être suffisant *or* assez (*for* pour), suffire (*for* à); **I've got ~** j'en ai assez *or* suffisamment; **~ to eat** assez à manger; **he earns ~ to live on** il gagne de quoi vivre; **one meal a day is ~** un repas par jour est suffisant; **one song was ~ to show he couldn't sing** une chanson a suffi à *or* pour démontrer qu'il ne savait pas chanter; **that's quite ~ thank you** cela me suffit, je vous remercie; *see* **self**.

sufficiently [sə'fɪʃəntlɪ] adv suffisamment, assez. **he is ~ clever to do so** il est suffisamment *or* assez intelligent pour le faire; **a ~ large number/quantity** un nombre/une quantité suffisant(e).

suffix ['sʌfɪks] 1 n suffixe *m*. 2 [sʌ'fɪks] vt suffixer (*to* à).

suffocate ['sʌfəkeɪt] 1 vi suffoquer, étouffer; (*fig: with anger, indignation, surprise*) suffoquer (*with* de). 2 vt suffoquer, étouffer; (*fig*) [*anger, indignation, surprise*] suffoquer. **he felt ~d in that small town atmosphere** il étouffait dans cette atmosphère de petite ville.

suffocating ['sʌfəkeɪtɪŋ] adj *heat, atmosphere* étouffant, suffocant; *fumes* suffocant, asphyxiant; (*fig*) étouffant. **it's ~ in here** on étouffe ici.

suffocation [,sʌfə'keɪʃən] n suffocation *f*, étouffement *m*; (*Med*) asphyxie *f*. **to die from ~** mourir asphyxié.

suffragan ['sʌfrəgən] 1 adj suffragant. 2 n: **~ (bishop)** (évêque *m*) suffragant *m*.

suffrage ['sʌfrɪdʒ] n a (*franchise*) droit *m* de suffrage *or* de vote. **universal ~** suffrage universel; **elected by universal ~** élu au suffrage universel. b (*frm: vote*) suffrage *m*, vote *m*.

suffragette [,sʌfrə'dʒet] n suffragette *f*. (*Hist*) **the S~ Movement** le Mouvement des Suffragettes.

suffragist ['sʌfrədʒɪst] n partisan(e) *m(f)* du droit de vote pour les femmes.

suffuse [sə'fju:z] vt [*light*] baigner, se répandre sur; [*emotion*] envahir. **the room was ~d with light** la pièce baignait dans une lumière douce; **~d with red** rougi, empourpré; **eyes ~d with tears** yeux baignés de larmes.

sugar ['ʃʊgə^r] 1 n (*NonC*) sucre *m*. **come here ~!*** viens ici chéri(e)! *or* mon petit lapin en sucre!; **~!*** mince!*; *see* **icing** *etc*.
2 vt *food, drink* sucrer; *see* **pill**.
3 comp ►**sugar almond** = **sugared almond** ►**sugar basin** (*Brit*) sucrier *m* ►**sugar beet** betterave sucrière *or* à sucre ►**sugar bowl** = **sugar basin** ►**sugar cane** canne *f* à sucre ►**sugar-coated** (*lit*) dragéifié; (*fig: falsely pleasant*) doucereux, mielleux ►**sugar cube** morceau *m* de sucre ►**sugar daddy*** (*fig*) vieux protecteur ►**sugared almond** dragée *f* ►**sugar-free** sans sucre ►**sugar loaf** pain *m* de sucre ►**sugar lump** = **sugar cube** ►**sugar maple** (*Can, US*) érable *m* à sucre ►**sugar pea** mange-tout *m inv* ►**sugar plantation** plantation *f* de canne à sucre ►**sugarplum** bonbon *m*, dragée *f* ►**sugar refinery** raffinerie *f* de sucre ►**sugar sifter** saupoudreuse *f*, sucrier *m* verseur ►**sugar tongs** pince *f* à sucre.

sugarless ['ʃʊgəlɪs] adj sans sucre.

sugary ['ʃʊgərɪ] adj *food, drink* (très) sucré; *taste* de sucre, sucré; (*fig pej*) *person, smile* doucereux; *voice* mielleux. (*pej*) **she is rather ~** elle a un petit air sucré, elle est toute sucre tout miel.

suggest [sə'dʒest] vt a (*propose*) suggérer, proposer (*sth to sb* qch à qn); (*pej: hint*) insinuer (*sth to sb* qch à qn). **I ~ that we go to the museum** je suggère *or* je propose qu'on aille au musée; **he ~ed that they (should) go to London** il leur a suggéré *or* proposé d'aller à Londres; **an idea ~ed itself (to me)** une idée m'est venue à l'esprit; **what are you trying to ~?** que voulez-vous dire par là?, qu'insinuez-vous? (*pej*); (*esp Jur*) **I ~ to you that ...** mon opinion est que ... .
b (*imply*) [*facts, data, sb's actions*] suggérer, laisser supposer, sembler indiquer (*that* que); (*evoke*) suggérer, évoquer, faire penser à. **what does that smell ~ to you?** à quoi cette odeur vous fait-elle penser?, qu'est-ce que cette odeur vous suggère? *or* évoque pour vous?; **the coins ~ a Roman settlement** les monnaies suggèrent l'existence d'un camp romain, les monnaies donnent à penser *or* laissent supposer qu'il y a eu un camp romain; **it doesn't exactly ~ a careful man** on ne peut pas dire que cela dénote un homme soigneux.

suggestibility [sə,dʒestɪ'bɪlɪtɪ] n suggestibilité *f*.

suggestible [sə'dʒestɪbl] adj suggestible, influençable.

suggestion [sə'dʒestʃən] n a (*gen*) suggestion *f*; (*proposal*) suggestion, proposition *f*; (*insinuation*) allusion *f*, insinuation *f*. **to make *or* offer a ~** faire une suggestion *or* une proposition; **if I may make a ~** si je peux me permettre de faire une suggestion; **have you any ~s?** avez-vous quelque chose à suggérer?; **my ~ is that ...** je suggère *or* je propose que ...; **there is no ~ of corruption** il ne saurait être question de corruption, rien n'autorise à penser qu'il y ait eu corruption. b (*NonC: Psych etc*) suggestion *f*. **the power of ~** la force de suggestion.
c (*trace*) soupçon *m*, pointe *f*.

suggestive [sə'dʒestɪv] adj suggestif (*also pej*). **to be ~ of** = **suggest b**.

suggestively [sə'dʒestɪvlɪ] adv (*pej*) de façon suggestive.

suggestiveness [sə'dʒestɪvnɪs] n (*pej*) caractère suggestif, suggestivité *f*.

suicidal [,sʊɪ'saɪdl] adj *person, tendency, carelessness* suicidaire. (*fig*) **I feel ~ this morning** j'ai envie de me jeter par la fenêtre (*or* sous un train *or* à l'eau *etc*) ce matin; (*fig*) **that would be absolutely ~!** ce serait un véritable suicide!; **he drives in this ~ way** il conduit comme un fou, s'il voulait se suicider il ne conduirait pas autrement.

suicide ['sʊɪsaɪd] 1 n (*act: lit, fig*) suicide *m*; (*person*) suicidé(e) *m(f)*. **there were 2 attempted ~s** il y a eu 2 tentatives *fpl* de suicide, 2 personnes ont tenté de se suicider; **such an act was political ~** un tel acte représentait un véritable suicide politique, il se suicidait politiquement en faisant cela; (*fig*) **it would be ~ to do so** le faire équivaudrait à un suicide, ce serait se suicider que de le faire; *see* **attempt, commit** *etc*. 2 comp *attack, bomber etc* suicide *inv* ►**suicide attempt, suicide bid** tentative *f* de suicide ►**suicide pact** serment *m* de se suicider ensemble.

suit [su:t] 1 n a (*tailored garment*) (*for man*) costume *m*, complet *m*; (*for woman*) tailleur *m*; (*non-tailored, also for children*) ensemble *m*; [*racing driver, astronaut*] combinaison *f*. **~ of clothes** tenue *f*; **~ of armour** armure complète; (*Naut*) **a ~ of sails** un jeu de voiles; *see* **lounge, trouser** *etc*.
b (*frm: request*) requête *f*, pétition *f*; (*liter: for marriage*) demande *f* en mariage; *see* **press**.
c (*Jur*) poursuite *f*, procès *m*, action *f*. **to bring a ~** intenter un procès (*against sb* à qn), engager des poursuites (*against sb* contre qn); **criminal ~** action criminelle; *see* **file**[2], **law, party** *etc*.
d (*Cards*) couleur *f*. **long *or* strong ~** couleur longue; (*fig*) fort *m*; **short ~** couleur courte; *see* **follow**.
2 vt a (*be convenient, satisfactory for*) [*arrangements, date, price, suggestion*] convenir à, arranger, aller à; [*climate, food, occupation*] convenir à. **it doesn't ~ me to leave now** cela ne m'arrange pas de partir maintenant; **I'll do it when it ~s me** je le ferai quand ça m'arrangera; **such a step ~ed him perfectly *or* just ~ed his book*** une telle mesure lui convenait parfaitement *or* l'arrangeait parfaitement *or* faisait tout à fait son affaire; **~ yourself!*** c'est comme vous voudrez!, faites comme vous voudrez! *or* voulez!; **~s me!*** ça me va!, ça me botte!‡; **it ~s me here** je suis bien ici; *see* **ground**.
b (*be appropriate to*) convenir à, aller à. **the job doesn't ~ him** l'emploi ne lui convient pas, ce n'est pas un travail fait pour lui; **such behaviour hardly ~s you** une telle conduite ne vous va guère *or* n'est guère digne de vous; (*Theat*) **the part ~ed him perfectly** le rôle lui allait comme un gant *or* était fait pour lui; **he is not ~ed to teaching** il n'est pas fait pour l'enseignement; **the hall was not ~ed to such a meeting** la salle n'était pas faite pour *or* ne se prêtait guère à une telle réunion; **it ~s their needs** cela leur convient; **they are well ~ed (to one another)** ils sont faits l'un pour l'autre, ils sont très bien assortis.
c [*garment, colour, hairstyle*] aller à. **it ~s her beautifully** cela lui va à merveille.
d (*adapt*) adapter, approprier (*sth to sth* qch à qch). **to ~ the action to the word** joindre le geste à la parole.
3 vi convenir, aller, faire l'affaire. **will tomorrow ~?** est-ce que demain vous convient? *or* vous va? *or* est à votre convenance?

suitability [,su:tə'bɪlɪtɪ] n (*see* **suitable**) fait *m* de convenir *or* d'aller *or* d'être propice *etc*; [*action, remark, reply, example, choice*] à-propos *m*, pertinence *f*. **I doubt the ~ of these arrangements** je doute que ces dispositions conviennent (*subj*); **his ~ for the position is doubtful** il n'est pas sûr qu'il soit l'homme le plus indiqué pour ce poste.

suitable ['su:təbl] adj *climate, food* qui convient (*for* à); *colour, size* qui va (*for* à); *place, time* propice, adéquat (*for* à); *action, reply, example, remark, choice* approprié (*for* à), pertinent; *clothes* approprié (*for* à), adéquat; (*socially*) convenable. (*gen*) **it's not ~** ça ne convient pas; **the most ~ man for the position** l'homme le plus apte à occuper ce poste, l'homme le plus indiqué pour ce poste; **I can't find anything ~** je ne trouve rien qui me convienne; (*clothes*) je ne trouve rien qui m'aille; **the 25th is the most ~ for me** c'est le 25 qui m'arrange *or* me convient le mieux; **he is not a ~ teacher for such a class** quelqu'un comme lui ne devrait pas enseigner dans une telle classe; **he is not at all a ~ person** ce n'est pas du tout l'homme qu'il faut; **the hall is quite ~ for the meeting** c'est une salle qui se prête bien à ce genre de réunion; **the film isn't ~ for children** ce n'est pas un film pour les enfants; **this gift isn't ~ for my aunt** ce cadeau ne plaira pas à ma tante *or* ne sera pas au goût de ma tante.

suitably ['su:təblɪ] adv *reply* à propos; *explain* de manière adéquate; *thank, apologize* comme il convient (*or* convenait *etc*), comme il se doit (*or* devait *etc*); *behave* convenablement, comme il faut. **he was ~ impressed** il a été favorablement impressionné.

suitcase ['su:tkeɪs] n valise *f*. (*fig*) **to live out of a ~** vivre sans jamais vraiment défaire ses bagages.

suite [swi:t] n a (*furniture*) mobilier *m*; (*rooms: in hotel etc*) appartement *m*, suite *f*. **a dining-room ~** un mobilier *or* un ensemble de salle à manger, une salle à manger; *see* **bedroom, bridal** *etc.* **b** (*Mus*) suite *f.* **c** (*retainers*) suite *f*, escorte *f.*

suiting ['suːtɪŋ] **n** (*NonC: Tex*) tissu *m* pour complet.

suitor ['suːtəʳ] **n** soupirant *m*, prétendant *m*; (*Jur*) plaideur *m*, -euse *f.*

sulcus ['sʌlkəs] **n, pl sulci** ['sʌlsaɪ] scissure *f.*

Suleiman [ˌsuːlɪ'mɑːn] **n: ~ the Magnificent** Soliman *or* Suleyman le Magnifique.

sulfa ['sʌlfə] **n** (*US*) = **sulpha.**

sulfate ['sʌlfeɪt] **n** (*US*) = **sulphate.**

sulfide ['sʌlfaɪd] **n** (*US*) = **sulphide.**

sulfonamide [sʌl'fɒnəmaɪd] **n** (*US*) = **sulphonamide.**

sulfur ['sʌlfəʳ] **n** (*US*) = **sulphur.**

sulfureous [sʌl'fjʊərɪəs] **adj** (*US*) = **sulphureous.**

sulfuric [sʌl'fjʊərɪk] **adj** (*US*) = **sulphuric.**

sulfurous ['sʌlfərəs] **adj** (*US*) = **sulphurous.**

sulk [sʌlk] **1 n** bouderie *f*, maussaderie *f.* **to be in the ~s, to have (a fit of) the ~s** bouder, faire la tête. **2 vi** bouder.

sulkily ['sʌlkɪlɪ] **adv** en boudant, d'un air *or* d'un ton maussade.

sulkiness ['sʌlkɪnɪs] **n** (*state*) bouderie *f*; (*temperament*) caractère boudeur *or* maussade.

sulky ['sʌlkɪ] **adj** boudeur, maussade. **to be** *or* **look ~** faire la tête.

sullen ['sʌlən] **adj** *person, look, smile* maussade, renfrogné; *comment, silence* renfrogné; *horse* rétif; *clouds* menaçant; *sky, countryside, lake* maussade, morne.

sullenly ['sʌlənlɪ] **adv** *say, reply, refuse, deny* d'un ton maussade; *promise, agree* de mauvaise grâce. **he remained ~ silent** il ne s'est pas départi de son air renfrogné *or* maussade et n'a pas ouvert la bouche.

sullenness ['sʌlənnɪs] **n** (*see* **sullen**) maussaderie *f*, humeur *f* maussade, air renfrogné; aspect menaçant *or* maussade *or* morne.

sully ['sʌlɪ] **vt** (*liter*) souiller.

sulpha ['sʌlfə] **n: ~ drug** sulfamide *m.*

sulphate ['sʌlfeɪt] **n** sulfate *m.* **copper ~** sulfate de cuivre.

sulphide ['sʌlfaɪd] **n** sulfure *m.*

sulphonamide [sʌl'fɒnəmaɪd] **n** sulfamide *m.*

sulphur ['sʌlfəʳ] **1 n** soufre *m.* **2 adj** (*colour*) **~ (yellow)** (jaune) soufre. **3 comp ▸sulphur dioxide** anhydride sulfureux **▸sulphur spring** source sulfureuse.

sulphureous [sʌl'fjʊərɪəs] **adj** sulfureux; (*in colour*) couleur de soufre, soufré.

sulphuric [sʌl'fjʊərɪk] **adj** sulfurique.

sulphurous ['sʌlfərəs] **adj** sulfureux.

sultan ['sʌltən] **n** sultan *m.*

sultana [sʌl'tɑːnə] **1 n a** (*fruit*) raisin *m* de Smyrne. **b** (*woman*) sultane *f.* **2 comp ▸sultana cake** (*Culin*) cake *m* (aux raisins de Smyrne).

sultanate ['sʌltənɪt] **n** sultanat *m.*

sultriness ['sʌltrɪnɪs] **n** (*heat*) chaleur étouffante; *[weather]* lourdeur *f.*

sultry ['sʌltrɪ] **adj** *heat* étouffant, suffocant; *weather, air* lourd; *atmosphere* étouffant, pesant; (*fig*) *voice* chaud, sensuel; *person, character* passionné; *look, smile* plein de passion, sensuel, provocant.

sum [sʌm] **1 n** (*total after addition*) somme *f*, total *m* (*of* de); (*amount of money*) somme (d'argent); (*Math: problem*) calcul *m*, opération *f*, (*specifically adding*) addition *f.* (*Scol: arithmetic*) **~s** le calcul; **to do a ~ in one's head** faire un calcul mental *or* de tête; **he is good at ~s** il est bon en calcul; **the ~ of its parts** la somme de ses composants *or* parties; **the ~ of our experience** la somme de notre expérience; **the ~ and substance of what he said** les grandes lignes de ce qu'il a dit; **in ~** en somme, somme toute; *see* **lump[1], round** *etc.*

2 comp ▸summing-up récapitulation *f*, résumé *m* (*also Jur*) **▸sum total** (*amount*) somme totale; (*money*) montant *m* (global); (*fig*) **the sum total of all this was that he ...** le résultat de tout cela a été qu'il ... .

▸sum up 1 vi récapituler, faire un *or* le résumé; (*Jur*) résumer. **to sum up, let me say that ...** en résumé *or* pour récapituler je voudrais dire que ... . **2 vt sep a** (*summarize*) *speech, facts, arguments* résumer, récapituler; *book etc* résumer. **that sums up all I felt** cela résume tout ce que je ressentais. **b** (*assess*) *person* jauger, se faire une idée de; *situation* apprécier d'un coup d'œil. **3 summing-up n** *see* **sum 2.**

sumac(h) ['suːmæk] **n** sumac *m.*

Sumatra [sʊ'mɑːtrə] **n** Sumatra.

Sumatran [sʊ'mɑːtrən] **1 adj** de Sumatra. **2 n** habitant(e) *m(f)* (*or* natif *m*, -ive *f*) de Sumatra.

summarily ['sʌmərɪlɪ] **adv** sommairement.

summarize ['sʌməraɪz] **1 vt** *book, text* résumer; *speech, facts, arguments* résumer, récapituler. **2 vi** faire un résumé.

summary ['sʌmərɪ] **1 n a** (*NonC: see* **summarize**) résumé *m*; récapitulation *f.* **in ~** en résumé. **b** (*printed matter, list etc*) sommaire *m*, résumé *m*; (*Fin: of accounts*) relevé *m.* (*Rad, TV*) **here is a ~ of the news** voici les nouvelles *fpl* en bref. **2 adj** (*all senses*) sommaire.

summat‡ ['sʌmət] **n** (*dial*) = **something.**

summation [sʌ'meɪʃən] **n** (*addition*) addition *f*; (*summing-up*) récapitulation *f*, résumé *m* (*also Jur*).

summer ['sʌməʳ] **1 n** été *m.* **in ~** en été; **in the ~ of 1987** pendant l'été de 1987, en été 1987; (*liter*) **a girl of 17 ~s** une jeune fille de 17 printemps; *see* **high, Indian** *etc.*

2 comp *weather, heat, day, season, activities* d'été, estival; *residence* d'été **▸summer camp** (*US Scol*) colonie *f* de vacances **▸summer clothes** vêtements *mpl* d'été, tenue estivale *or* d'été **▸summer holidays** grandes vacances **▸summerhouse** pavillon *m* (dans un jardin) **▸summer lightning** éclair *m* de chaleur **▸summer resort** station estivale **▸summer school** université *f* d'été **▸summer squash** (*US*) courgette *f* **▸summertime** (*Brit*) (*season*) été *m* **▸summer time** (*by clock*) heure *f* d'été **▸summer visitor** estivant(e) *m(f).*

3 vi (*rare*) passer l'été.

summery ['sʌmərɪ] **adj** d'été.

summit ['sʌmɪt] **1 n** *[mountain]* sommet *m*, cime *f*, faîte *m*; (*fig*) *[power, honours, glory]* sommet, apogée *m*, faîte; *[ambition]* summum *m*; (*Pol*) sommet. (*Pol*) **at ~ level** au plus haut niveau. **2 comp** (*Pol*) *talks* au sommet **▸summit conference** (conférence *f* au) sommet *m* **▸summit meeting** rencontre *f* au sommet.

summitry* ['sʌmɪtrɪ] **n** (*Pol, esp US*) tactique *f* de la rencontre au sommet.

summon ['sʌmən] **vt** *servant, police* appeler, faire venir; (*to meeting*) convoquer (*to* à); *[monarch, president, prime minister]* mander (*to* à); (*Jur*) citer, assigner, appeler en justice (*as* comme); *help, reinforcements* requérir. **the Queen ~ed Parliament** la reine a convoqué le Parlement; **to ~ sb to do** sommer qn de faire; (*Jur*) **to ~ sb to appear** citer *or* assigner qn; (*Mil*) **they ~ed the town to surrender** ils ont sommé la ville de *or* ils ont mis la ville en demeure de se rendre; **I was ~ed to his presence** j'ai été requis de paraître devant lui, il m'a mandé auprès de lui; **to ~ sb in (***or* **down** *etc***)** (*Admin etc*) sommer qn d'entrer (*or* de descendre *etc*); (*gen: informally*) appeler qn.

▸summon up vt sep *one's energy, strength* rassembler, faire appel à; *interest, enthusiasm* faire appel à. **to summon up (one's) courage** faire appel à *or* rassembler tout son courage, s'armer de courage, prendre son courage à deux mains (*to do* pour faire); **he summoned up the courage to fight back** il a trouvé le courage de riposter.

summons ['sʌmənz] **1 n, pl ~es** sommation *f* (*also Mil*), injonction *f*; (*Jur*) assignation *f*, citation *f.* (*Jur*) **to take out a ~ against sb** faire assigner qn; **he got a ~ for drunken driving** il a reçu une citation *or* une assignation pour conduite en état d'ivresse; (*Mil*) **they sent him a ~ to surrender** ils lui ont fait parvenir une sommation de se rendre; *see* **issue, serve. 2 vt** (*Jur*) citer, assigner (*à comparaître*), appeler en justice (*for sth* pour qch).

sumo ['suːməʊ] **n** sumo *m.*

sump [sʌmp] **n** (*Tech*) puisard *m* (*pour eaux-vannes etc*); (*Brit Aut*) carter *m.* **~ oil** huile *f* de carter.

sumptuary ['sʌmptjʊərɪ] **adj** (*frm*) somptuaire. (*Hist*) **~ law** loi *f* somptuaire.

sumptuous ['sʌmptjʊəs] **adj** somptueux, fastueux, luxueux.

sumptuously ['sʌmptjʊəslɪ] **adv** somptueusement.

sumptuousness ['sʌmptjʊəsnɪs] **n** somptuosité *f.*

sun [sʌn] **1 n** soleil *m.* **the ~ is shining** il fait (du) soleil, le soleil brille; **in the ~** au soleil; **right in the ~** en plein soleil; **a place in the ~** (*lit*) un endroit ensoleillé *or* au soleil; (*fig*) une place au soleil; **this room certainly catches the ~** cette pièce reçoit beaucoup de soleil; **to catch the ~** (*get a tan*) prendre des bonnes couleurs; (*get sunburn*) prendre un coup de soleil; **in the July ~** au soleil de juillet; **come out of the ~** ne restez pas au soleil; **the ~ is in my eyes** j'ai le soleil dans les yeux; **he rose with the ~** il se levait avec le soleil; **everything under the ~** tout ce qu'il est possible d'imaginer; **nothing under the ~** rien au monde; **there's no prettier place under the ~** il n'est pas de plus joli coin au monde *or* sur la terre; **no reason under the ~** pas la moindre raison; **there is nothing new under the ~** il n'y a rien de nouveau sous le soleil; *see* **midnight** *etc.*

2 vt: to ~ o.s. *[lizard, cat]* se chauffer au soleil; *[person]* prendre un bain de soleil, lézarder au soleil.

3 comp ▸sunbaked brûlé par le soleil **▸sunbath** bain *m* de soleil **▸sunbathe** prendre un bain *or* des bains de soleil, se (faire) bronzer **▸sunbather** personne *f* qui prend un bain de soleil **▸sunbathing** bains *mpl* de soleil **▸sunbeam** rayon *m* de soleil **▸sunbed** (*in garden etc*) lit *m* pliant; (*with sunray lamp*) lit à ultra-violets **▸the Sunbelt** (*US*) les États *mpl* du Sud et de l'Ouest (*où l'ensoleillement est grand*) **▸sunblind** store *m* **▸sunblock** écran *m* solaire total **▸sun bonnet** capeline *f* **▸sunburn** *etc see* **sunburn** *etc* **▸sunburst** échappée *f* de soleil; **sunburst clock** pendule *f* soleil **▸sun dance** *danse rituelle du solstice chez les Indiens d'Amérique* **▸Sunday** *see* **Sunday ▸sun deck** *[house, hotel etc]* véranda *f*; (*Naut*) pont supérieur *or* des embarcations **▸sundial** cadran *m* solaire **▸sundown** = **sunset ▸sundowner*** (*Austral: tramp*) chemineau *m*, clochard *m*; (*Brit: drink*) *boisson alcoolique prise au coucher du soleil* **▸sun-drenched** inondé de soleil **▸sun dress** robe *f* bain de soleil **▸sundried** séché au soleil **▸sun-filled** ensoleillé, rempli de soleil **▸sunfish** (*Zool*) poisson lune *m* **▸sunflower** (*Bot*) tournesol *m*, soleil *m*; (*Culin*) **sunflower oil/seeds** huile *f*/graines *fpl* de tournesol; (*US*) **the Sunflower State** le Kansas **▸sunglasses** lunettes *fpl* de soleil **▸sun-god** dieu *m* soleil **▸sunhat**

chapeau *m* de soleil *or* de plage ▸**sun helmet** casque colonial ▸**the Sun King** (*Hist*) le Roi-Soleil ▸**sun lamp** lampe *f* à rayons ultraviolets ▸**sunlight** (lumière *f* du) soleil *m*; **in the sunlight** au soleil, à la lumière du soleil ▸**sunlit** ensoleillé ▸**sun lotion** = **suntan lotion** ▸**sun lounge** véranda *f*; (*in health institution etc*) solarium *m* ▸**sun-lounger** fauteuil *m* bain de soleil ▸**sun oil** = **suntan oil** ▸**sun porch** petite véranda (à l'entrée) ▸**sunray lamp** (*Med*) = **sun lamp** ▸**sun-ray treatment** héliothérapie *f* ▸**sunrise** lever *m* du soleil; **sunrise industry** industrie *f* en expansion *or* montante ▸**sunroof** (*Aut*) toit *m* ouvrant ▸**sunset** coucher *m* du soleil; (*US Jur*) **sunset clause** clause *f* de révision; **sunset industry** industrie *f* en déclin; (*US*) **sunset law** *loi qui impose la revue périodique d'un organisme officiel* ▸**sunshade** (*lady's parasol*) ombrelle *f*; (*for eyes*) visière *f*; (*for table, on pram*) parasol *m*; (*in car*) pare-soleil *m inv* ▸**sun-shield** (*Aut*) pare-soleil *m inv* ▸**sunshine** *see* **sunshine** ▸**sunspecs*** = **sunglasses** ▸**sunspot** tache *f* solaire ▸**sunstroke** (*Med*) insolation *f* ▸**sunsuit** costume *m* bain de soleil ▸**suntan** bronzage *m*; **to get a suntan** (se faire) bronzer; **suntan lotion** lotion *f or* lait *m* solaire; **suntan oil** huile *f* solaire ▸**suntanned** bronzé ▸**suntrap** coin très ensoleillé ▸**sun umbrella** parasol *m* ▸**sunup*** = **sunrise** ▸**sun visor** (*for eyes, on cap*) visière *f*; (*Aut*) pare-soleil *m inv* ▸**sun-worship** (*Rel*) culte *m* du Soleil ▸**sun-worshipper** (*Rel*) adorateur *m*, -trice *f* du Soleil; (*fig*) adepte *mf or* fanatique *mf* du soleil.

Sun. abbr of **Sunday**.

sunburn ['sʌnbɜːn] n coup *m* de soleil.

sunburned ['sʌnbɜːnd], **sunburnt** ['sʌnbɜːnt] adj (*tanned*) bronzé, hâlé; (*painfully*) brûlé par le soleil. **to get ~** (*tan*) (se faire) bronzer; (*painfully*) prendre un coup de soleil.

sundae ['sʌndeɪ] n sundae *m*, coupe *f* glacée Chantilly.

Sunday ['sʌndɪ] 1 n a dimanche *m*; *for phrases see* **Saturday**; *see also* **Easter, month, palm²**.
b (*fig: ~ papers*) **the ~s*** les journaux *mpl* du dimanche.
2 comp *clothes, paper* du dimanche; *walk, rest, peace* dominical ▸**Sunday best**: **in one's Sunday best** tout endimanché, en habits du dimanche ▸**Sunday driver, Sunday motorist** (* *pej*) chauffeur *m* du dimanche ▸**Sunday observance** observance *f* du repos dominical ▸**Sunday opening** (*Comm*) l'ouverture des magasins le dimanche, le commerce dominical ▸**Sunday school** école *f* du dimanche, ≃ catéchisme *m*; **Sunday school teacher** catéchiste *mf* (*qui s'occupe de l'école du dimanche*) ▸**Sunday trading** (*Comm*) = **Sunday opening**; **Sunday trading laws** réglementation *f* du commerce dominical.

sunder ['sʌndəʳ] (*liter*) 1 vt séparer, fractionner, scinder. 2 n: **in ~** (*apart*) écartés; (*in pieces*) en morceaux.

sundry ['sʌndrɪ] 1 adj divers, différent. **all and ~** tout le monde, n'importe qui; **to all and ~** à tout venant, à tout le monde, à n'importe qui. 2 npl: **sundries** articles *mpl* divers.

sung [sʌŋ] ptp of **sing**.

sunk [sʌŋk] 1 ptp of **sink¹**. 2 comp ▸**sunk costs** (*Ind*) frais *mpl* fixes, coûts *mpl* constants.

sunken ['sʌŋkən] adj *ship, rock* submergé; *eyes* creux, cave; *cheeks* creux; *garden* en contrebas; *bath* encastré (*au ras du sol*).

sunless ['sʌnlɪs] adj sans soleil.

Sunni ['sʌnɪ] n sunnisme *m*.

sunny ['sʌnɪ] adj *room, situation, month, morning* ensoleillé; *side* (*of street, building etc*) exposé au soleil, ensoleillé; (*fig*) *smile* radieux, épanoui; *person* heureux, épanoui. **to have a ~ disposition** *or* **nature** *or* **personality** être d'un naturel enjoué; **it is ~** *or* **a ~ day** il fait (du) soleil; (*Brit Met*) **~ intervals** *or* **periods** éclaircies *fpl*; (*Met*) **the outlook is ~** on prévoit (le retour) du soleil, on peut s'attendre à un temps ensoleillé; (*fig*) **to be in a ~ mood** être d'une humeur charmante; (*fig*) **he always sees the ~ side of things** il voit tout en rose, il voit tout du bon côté; **he's on the ~ side of fifty*** il est du bon côté de la cinquantaine; (*US Culin*) **eggs ~ side up** œufs *mpl* sur le plat (*frits sans avoir été retournés*).

sunshine ['sʌnʃaɪn] 1 n (*NonC*) (lumière *f* du) soleil *m*. **in the ~** au soleil; (*Met*) **5 hours of ~** 5 heures d'ensoleillement; (*iro*) **he's a real ray of ~ today** il est gracieux comme une porte de prison aujourd'hui; **hallo ~!*** bonjour mon rayon de soleil! 2 comp ▸**sunshine law** (*US*) *loi imposant la publicité des débats pour les décisions administratives* ▸**sunshine roof** (*Aut*) toit *m* ouvrant ▸**the Sunshine State** (*US*) la Floride.

sup [sʌp] 1 vi souper (*on, off* de). 2 vt (*also* **~ up**) boire *or* avaler à petites gorgées. 3 n petite gorgée.

super ['suːpəʳ] 1 adj (*) formidable*, sensationnel*. 2 comp ▸**Super Bowl** (*US Ftbl*) Super Bowl *m* (*championnat de football américain*) ▸**super-duper**‡ formid* *inv*, sensass* *inv*, terrible*. 3 n a (*) abbr of **superintendent** (*of police*) and (*Cine*) **supernumerary**. b (*US: gasoline*) super(carburant) *m*.

super... ['suːpəʳ] pref super..., *e.g.* **~-salesman** super-vendeur *m*; *see also* **superannuate** *etc*.

superable ['suːpərəbl] adj surmontable.

superabundance [ˌsuːpərəˈbʌndəns] n surabondance *f*.

superabundant [ˌsuːpərəˈbʌndənt] adj surabondant.

superannuate [ˌsuːpəˈrænjʊeɪt] vt mettre à la retraite. **~d** retraité, à la *or* en retraite; (*fig*) suranné, démodé.

superannuation [ˌsuːpəˌrænjʊˈeɪʃən] n (*act*) (mise *f* à la) retraite *f*; (*pension*) pension *f* de retraite; (*also* **~ contribution**) versements *mpl or* cotisations *fpl* pour la pension; **~ fund** caisse *f* de retraite.

superb [suːˈpɜːb] adj superbe, magnifique.

superbly [suːˈpɜːblɪ] adv superbement, magnifiquement. **he is ~ fit** il est en pleine forme *or* dans une forme éblouissante.

supercargo ['suːpəˌkɑːgəʊ] n (*Naut*) subrécargue *m*.

supercharged ['suːpətʃɑːdʒd] adj surcomprimé.

supercharger ['suːpətʃɑːdʒəʳ] n compresseur *m*.

supercilious [ˌsuːpəˈsɪlɪəs] adj hautain, dédaigneux.

superciliously [ˌsuːpəˈsɪlɪəslɪ] adv avec dédain, dédaigneusement, d'un air *or* d'un ton hautain.

superciliousness [ˌsuːpəˈsɪlɪəsnɪs] n hauteur *f*, arrogance *f*.

super-class ['suːpəˌklɑːs] n super-classe *f*.

superconductive [ˌsuːpəkənˈdʌktɪv] adj supraconducteur.

superconductivity ['suːpəˌkɒndʌk'tɪvɪtɪ] n supraconductivité *f*.

superconductor [ˌsuːpəkənˈdʌktəʳ] n supraconducteur *m*.

supercool [ˌsuːpəˈkuːl] vt (*Chem*) sous-refroidir.

supercover ['suːpəˌkʌvəʳ] n (*Insurance*) garantie *f* totale, couverture *f* complète.

superego [ˌsuːpərˈiːgəʊ] n sur-moi *m*.

supererogation ['suːpərˌerəˈgeɪʃən] n surérogation *f*.

superette ['suːpəret] n (*US*) petit supermarché *m*, supérette *f*.

superficial [ˌsuːpəˈfɪʃəl] adj superficiel.

superficiality ['suːpəˌfɪʃɪˈælɪtɪ] n caractère superficiel, manque *m* de profondeur.

superficially [ˌsuːpəˈfɪʃəlɪ] adv superficiellement.

superficies [ˌsuːpəˈfɪʃiːz] n, pl inv superficie *f*.

superfine ['suːpəfaɪn] adj *goods, quality* extra-fin, superfin, surfin; (*pej*) *distinction* trop ténu, bien mince.

superfluity [ˌsuːpəˈflʊɪtɪ] n a surabondance *f* (*of* de). b = **superfluousness**.

superfluous [sʊˈpɜːflʊəs] adj *goods, explanation* superflu. **~ hair** poils superflus; **it is ~ to say that ...** je n'ai pas besoin de dire que ..., inutile de dire que ...; **he felt rather ~*** il se sentait de trop.

superfluously [sʊˈpɜːflʊəslɪ] adv d'une manière superflue.

superfluousness [sʊˈpɜːflʊəsnɪs] n caractère superflu.

supergiant [ˌsuːpəˈdʒaɪənt] n (*Astron*) supergéante *f*.

superglue ['suːpəgluː] n ® supercolle *f*.

supergrass ['suːpəgrɑːs] n super-indicateur *m* de police.

superheat [ˌsuːpəˈhiːt] vt surchauffer.

superhighway ['suːpəˌhaɪweɪ] n (*US*) voie *f* express (à plusieurs files).

superhuman [ˌsuːpəˈhjuːmən] adj surhumain.

superimpose [ˌsuːpərɪmˈpəʊz] vt superposer (*on* à). (*Cine, Phot, Typ*) **~d** en surimpression.

superintend [ˌsuːpərɪnˈtend] vt *work, shop, department* diriger; *exam* surveiller; *production* contrôler; *vote-counting* présider à.

superintendence [ˌsuːpərɪnˈtendəns] n (*see* **superintend**) direction *f*; surveillance *f*; contrôle *m*.

superintendent [ˌsuːpərɪnˈtendənt] n a [*institution, orphanage*] directeur *m*, -trice *f*; [*department*] chef *m*. b (*also* **police ~**, **~ of police**) ≃ commissaire *m* (de police).

Superior [sʊˈpɪərɪəʳ] adj: **Lake ~** le lac Supérieur.

superior [sʊˈpɪərɪəʳ] 1 adj a supérieur (*f* -eure) (*to* à); *product, goods* de qualité supérieure; (*pej: smug*) *person* condescendant, suffisant; *air, smile* supérieur, de supériorité, suffisant. **~ in number to** supérieur en nombre à, numériquement supérieur à; **in ~ numbers** en plus grand nombre, plus nombreux; (*Typ*) **~ letter/number** lettre *f*/nombre *m* supérieur(e); **he felt rather ~** il a éprouvé un certain sentiment de supériorité; **in a ~ voice** d'un ton supérieur *or* suffisant; *see* **mother**. b (*Bio, Bot etc*) supérieur (*f* -eure). 2 n (*also Rel*) supérieur(e) *m(f)*.

superiority [sʊˌpɪərɪˈɒrɪtɪ] n supériorité *f* (*to, over* par rapport à). **~ complex** complexe *m* de supériorité.

superjacent [ˌsuːpəˈdʒeɪsənt] adj sus-jacent.

superlative [sʊˈpɜːlətɪv] 1 adj *condition, quality, achievement* sans pareil; *happiness, indifference* suprême; (*Gram*) superlatif. 2 n (*Gram*) superlatif *m*. **in the ~** au superlatif; (*fig*) **he tends to talk in ~s** il a tendance à exagérer.

superlatively [sʊˈpɜːlətɪvlɪ] adv extrêmement, au suprême degré, au plus haut point. **he was ~ fit** il était on ne peut plus en forme; (*iro*) **he is ~ stupid** c'est le roi des imbéciles.

superman ['suːpəmæn] n, pl **supermen** surhomme *m*. (*on TV etc*) **S~** Superman *m*.

supermarket ['suːpəˌmɑːkɪt] n supermarché *m*.

supermen ['suːpəmen] npl of **superman**.

supernal [suːˈpɜːnəl] adj (*liter*) céleste, divin.

supernatural [ˌsuːpəˈnætʃərəl] 1 adj surnaturel. (*fig*) **there's something ~ about it** cela semble presque anormal. 2 n surnaturel *m*.

supernormal [ˌsuːpəˈnɔːməl] adj au-dessus de la normale.

sultry ['sʌltrɪ] adj *heat* étouffant, suffocant; *weather, air* lourd; *atmosphere* étouffant, pesant; (*fig*) *voice* chaud, sensuel; *person, character*

passionné; *look, smile* plein de passion, sensuel, provocant.
supernova [ˌsuːpəˈnəʊvə] n (*Astron*) supernova *f*.
supernumerary [ˌsuːpəˈnjuːmərərɪ] 1 adj (*Admin, Bio etc*) surnuméraire; (*superfluous*) superflu. 2 n (*Admin etc*) surnuméraire *mf*; (*Cine*) figurant(e) *m(f)*.
superorder [ˈsuːpərɔːdəʳ] n super-ordre *m*.
superordinate [ˌsuːpərˈɔːdənɪt] 1 adj dominant, supérieur. 2 n (*Ling*) terme *m* générique.
superphosphate [ˌsuːpəˈfɒsfeɪt] n superphosphate *m*.
superpose [ˌsuːpəˈpəʊz] vt (*also Geom*) superposer (*on* à).
superposition [ˌsuːpəpəˈzɪʃən] n superposition *f*.
superpower [ˈsuːpəpaʊəʳ] n (*Pol*) superpuissance *f*, super-grand *m*.
superscript [ˈsuːpəˌskrɪpt] (*Typ*) 1 adj supérieur. 2 n (*number*) chiffre *m* supérieur; (*letter*) lettre *f* supérieure.
superscription [ˌsuːpəˈskrɪpʃən] n suscription *f*.
supersede [ˌsuːpəˈsiːd] vt *belief, object, order* remplacer; *person* supplanter, prendre la place de. **this edition ~s previous ones** cette édition remplace et annule les précédentes; **~d idea/method** idée/méthode périmée.
supersensitive [ˌsuːpəˈsensɪtɪv] adj hypersensible.
supersonic [ˌsuːpəˈsɒnɪk] adj supersonique. ~ **bang** *or* **boom** bang *m* (supersonique).
supersonically [ˌsuːpəˈsɒnɪkəlɪ] adv en supersonique.
superstar [ˈsuːpəstɑːʳ] n (*Cine, Theat*) superstar *f*; (*Sport*) super-champion(ne) *m(f)*.
superstition [ˌsuːpəˈstɪʃən] n superstition *f*.
superstitious [ˌsuːpəˈstɪʃəs] adj superstitieux.
superstitiously [ˌsuːpəˈstɪʃəslɪ] adv superstitieusement.
superstore [ˈsuːpəstɔːʳ] n (*esp Brit*) hypermarché *m*.
superstratum [ˌsuːpəˈstrɑːtəm] n, pl **~s** *or* **superstrata** [ˌsupəˈstrɑːtə] (*Ling*) superstrat *m*.
superstructure [ˈsuːpəˌstrʌktʃəʳ] n superstructure *f*.
supertanker [ˈsuːpəˌtæŋkəʳ] n pétrolier géant, supertanker *m*.
supertax [ˈsuːpətæks] n tranche *f* supérieure de l'impôt sur le revenu.
supervene [ˌsuːpəˈviːn] vi survenir.
supervention [ˌsuːpəˈvenʃən] n apparition *f*, manifestation *f*.
supervise [ˈsuːpəvaɪz] 1 vt *person, worker* surveiller, avoir l'œil sur; *organization, department* diriger; *work* surveiller, diriger, superviser; *exam* surveiller; (*Univ*) *research* diriger. 2 vi exercer la surveillance, surveiller.
supervision [ˌsuːpəˈvɪʒən] n surveillance *f*, contrôle *m*, direction *f* (*esp Comm*). **under the ~ of** sous la surveillance *or* direction de; **to keep sth under strict ~** exercer une surveillance *or* un contrôle sévère sur qch.
supervisor [ˈsuːpəvaɪzəʳ] n (*gen*) surveillant(e) *m(f)*; (*Comm*) chef *m* de rayon; (*at exam*) surveillant(e); (*Univ*) directeur *m*, -trice *f* *or* patron *m* de thèse.
supervisory [ˈsuːpəvaɪzərɪ] adj *post, duty* de surveillance. **in a ~ capacity** à titre de surveillant.
supine [ˈsuːpaɪn] adj (*lit: also* **lying ~, in a ~ position**) couché *or* étendu sur le dos; (*fig pej*) mou (*f* molle), indolent, mollasse.
supper [ˈsʌpəʳ] 1 n (*main evening meal*) dîner *m*; (*after theatre etc*) souper *m*; (*snack*) collation *f*. **to have ~** dîner (*or* souper *etc*); (*Rel*) **the Last S~** la Cène; (*fig*) **we made him sing for his ~** nous l'avons aidé *etc*, mais c'était donnant donnant; *see* **lord.** 2 comp ►**suppertime** l'heure *f* du dîner (*or* du souper *etc*); **at suppertime** au dîner (*or* souper *etc*).
supplant [səˈplɑːnt] vt *person* supplanter, évincer; *object* supplanter, remplacer.
supple [ˈsʌpl] adj (*lit, fig*) souple. **to become ~(r)** s'assouplir.
supplement [ˈsʌplɪmənt] 1 n (*also Press*) supplément *m* (*to* à); *see* **colour.** 2 [ˈsʌplɪˌment] vt *income* augmenter, arrondir (*by doing* en faisant); *book, information, one's knowledge* ajouter à, compléter.
supplementary [ˌsʌplɪˈmentərɪ] adj supplémentaire, additionnel; (*Geom, Mus*) supplémentaire. ~ **to** en plus de; (*Brit Admin*) ~ **benefit**† allocation *f* supplémentaire (*d'aide sociale*); (*Parl*) ~ **question** question orale; (*Jur*) ~ **scheme** régime *m* complémentaire.
suppleness [ˈsʌplnɪs] n souplesse *f*.
suppletion [səˈpliːʃən] n (*Ling*) suppléance *f*.
suppletive [səˈpliːtɪv] adj (*Ling*) supplétif.
suppliant [ˈsʌplɪənt] adj, n, **supplicant** [ˈsʌplɪkənt] adj, n suppliant(e) *m(f)*.
supplicate [ˈsʌplɪkeɪt] 1 vt supplier, implorer (*sb to do* qn de faire); *mercy etc* implorer (*from sb* de qn). 2 vi: **to ~ for sth** implorer qch.
supplication [ˌsʌplɪˈkeɪʃən] n supplication *f*; (*written*) supplique *f*.
supplier [səˈplaɪəʳ] n (*Comm*) fournisseur *m*.
supply[1] [səˈplaɪ] 1 n a (*amount, stock*) provision *f*, réserve *f*, stock *m* (*also Comm*). **a good ~ of coal** une bonne provision *or* réserve de charbon, un bon stock de charbon; **to get** *or* **lay in a ~ of** faire des provisions de, s'approvisionner de; **to get in a fresh ~ of sth** renouveler sa provision *or* sa réserve *or* son stock de qch, se réapprovisionner de qch; **supplies** (*gen*) provisions, réserves; (*food*) vivres *mpl*; (*Mil*) subsistances *fpl*, approvisionnements *mpl*; **electrical supplies** matériel *m* électrique; **office supplies** fournitures *fpl* *or* matériel de bureau.

b (*NonC: act of ~ing*) *[fuel etc]* alimentation *f*; *[equipment, books etc]* fourniture *f*. **the ~ of fuel to the engine** l'alimentation du moteur en combustible; **the electricity/gas ~** l'alimentation en électricité/gaz; (*Econ*) ~ **and demand** l'offre *f* et la demande; (*Brit*) **Ministry of S~** ≃ services *mpl* de l'Intendance; *see* **short, water** *etc*.

c (*person: temporary substitute*) remplaçant(e) *m(f)*, suppléant(e) *m(f)*. **to teach** *or* **be on ~** faire des suppléances *or* des remplacements.

d (*Parl*) **supplies** crédits *mpl*.

2 comp *train, wagon, truck, convoy* préposé au ravitaillement, ravitailleur; *pharmacist etc* intérimaire ►**supply line** voie *f* de ravitaillement ►**supply management** (*Econ*) régulation *f* de l'offre ►**supply ship** navire ravitailleur ►**supply-side economics** (*Econ*) théorie *f* de l'offre ►**supply teacher** suppléant(e) *m(f)*.

3 vt a (*provide, furnish*) *tools, books, goods* fournir, procurer (*to sb* à qn); (*Comm*) fournir, approvisionner; (*equip*) *person, city* fournir, approvisionner (*with sth* en *or* de qch); (*Mil: with provisions*) ravitailler, approvisionner. (*Comm*) **we ~ most of the local schools** nous fournissons *or* nous approvisionnons la plupart des écoles locales; (*Comm*) **to ~ from stock** livrer sur stock; **sheep ~ wool** les moutons donnent de la laine; **we ~ the tools for the job** nous fournissons *or* nous procurons les outils nécessaires pour faire le travail; **to ~ electricity/gas/water to the town** alimenter la ville en électricité/gaz/eau; **to ~ sb with food** nourrir *or* alimenter qn; **they kept us supplied with milk** grâce à eux nous n'avons jamais manqué de lait; **the car was supplied with a radio** la voiture était munie *or* pourvue d'une radio; **a battery is not supplied with the torch** une pile n'est pas livrée avec la torche; **to ~ sb with information/details** fournir des renseignements/des détails à qn.

b (*make good*) *need, deficiency* suppléer à, remédier à; *sb's needs* subvenir à; *loss* réparer, compenser.

supply[2] [ˈsʌplɪ] adv *move, bend* avec souplesse, souplement.
support [səˈpɔːt] 1 n a (*NonC: lit, fig*) appui *m*, soutien *m*. **he couldn't stand without ~** il ne pouvait pas se soutenir (sur ses jambes); **he leaned on me for ~** il s'est appuyé sur moi; **to give ~ to sb/sth** soutenir qn/qch; **this bra gives good ~** ce soutien-gorge maintient bien la poitrine; (*fig*) **he looked to his friends for ~** il a cherché un soutien *or* un appui auprès de ses amis; **he needs all the ~ he can get** il a bien besoin de tout l'appui qu'on pourra lui donner; **he got a lot of ~ from his friends** ses amis l'ont vraiment soutenu *or* appuyé; **the proposal got no ~** personne n'a parlé en faveur de la proposition; **he spoke in ~ of the motion** il a parlé en faveur de la motion; **in ~ of his theory/claim** à l'appui de sa théorie/revendication; **have I your ~ in this?** est-ce que je peux compter sur votre appui *or* soutien en la matière?; **to give** *or* **lend one's ~ to** prêter son appui à; **that lends ~ to his theory** ceci corrobore *or* vient corroborer sa théorie; **they demonstrated in ~ of the prisoners** ils ont manifesté en faveur des prisonniers, ils ont fait une manifestation de soutien aux prisonniers; **a collection in ~ of the accident victims** une quête au profit des victimes de l'accident; **they stopped work in ~** ils ont cessé le travail par solidarité; **he depends on his father for (financial) ~** il dépend financièrement de son père; (*financial*) **he has no visible means of ~** il n'a pas de moyens d'existence connus; **what means of ~ has he got?** quelles sont ses ressources?; *see* **moral.**

b (*object*) (*gen*) appui *m*; (*Constr, Tech*) support *m*, soutien *m*; (*fig: moral, financial etc*) soutien; (*US Econ: subsidy*) subvention *f*. **use the stool as a ~ for your foot** prenez le tabouret comme appui pour votre pied; **he is the sole (financial) ~ of his family** il est le seul soutien (financier) de sa famille; **he has been a great ~ to me** il a été pour moi un soutien précieux.

2 comp (*Mil etc*) *troops, convoy, vessel* de soutien ►**support hose** = **support stockings** ►**support price** (*Econ*) prix *m* de soutien ►**support stockings** bas *mpl* anti-fatigue.

3 vt a (*hold up*) *[pillar, beam]* supporter, soutenir; *[bridge]* porter; *[person, neck]* soutenir. **the elements necessary to ~ life** les éléments nécessaires à l'entretien de la vie, les éléments vitaux.

b (*uphold*) *motion, theory, cause, party* être pour, être en faveur de, être partisan de; *candidate* soutenir, appuyer, être partisan de; *sb's application, action, protest* soutenir, appuyer; *team* être supporter de, supporter*. **with only his courage to ~ him** avec son seul courage comme soutien, n'ayant de soutien que son courage; **his friends ~ed him in his refusal to obey** ses amis l'ont soutenu *or* l'ont appuyé *or* ont pris son parti lorsqu'il a refusé d'obéir; **the socialists will ~ it** les socialistes seront *or* voteront pour; **I cannot ~ what you are doing** je ne peux pas approuver ce que vous faites; (*Cine, Theat*) **~ed by a cast of thousands** avec le concours de milliers d'acteurs et figurants; **the proofs that ~ my case** les preuves à l'appui de ma cause; (*Econ*) **a subsidy to ~ the price of beef** une subvention pour maintenir le prix du bœuf; (*Ftbl*) **he ~s Celtic** c'est un supporter du Celtic, il supporte* le Celtic.

c (*financially*) subvenir aux besoins de. **he has a wife and 3 children to ~** il doit subvenir aux besoins de sa femme et de ses 3 enfants; **to ~ o.s.** (*gen*) subvenir à ses propres besoins; (*earn one's living*) gagner sa vie; **the school is ~ed by money from ...** l'école reçoit une aide financière de ... .

tenant *m*. **b** (*person*) *[party]* partisan *m*, tenant *m*; *[theory, cause, opinion]* adepte *mf*, partisan, tenant; (*Sport*) supporter *m*. **football ~s** supporters de football.

supporting [sə'pɔːtɪŋ] **adj** *wall* d'appui, de soutènement; (*Cine, Theat*) *role, part* secondaire, de second plan; *actor* qui a un rôle secondaire *or* de second plan. **~ cast** partenaires *mpl*; **~ film** film *m* qui passe en premier; *see* **self.**

supportive [sə'pɔːtɪv] **adj** *colleague, friend, family* qui est d'un grand soutien *or* d'un grand secours; *attitude* positif.

supportively [sə'pɔːtɪvlɪ] **adv** *act, behave* de façon très positive.

supportiveness [sə'pɔːtɪvnɪs] **n** attitude *f* positive, soutien *m*.

suppose [sə'pəʊz] **1 vt a** (*imagine*) supposer (*that* que + *subj*); (*assume, postulate*) supposer (*that* que + *indic*). **~ he doesn't come? — he will — yes but just ~!** et s'il ne vient pas? — il viendra — oui, mais à supposer qu'il ne vienne pas? *or* oui, mais au cas où il ne viendrait pas?; **if we ~ that the two are identical** si nous supposons que les deux sont identiques; (*Math*) **~ A equals B** soit A égale B; **~ ABC a triangle** soit un triangle ABC.

b (*believe, think*) croire, penser, imaginer (*that* que). **what do you ~ he wants?** à votre avis que peut-il bien vouloir?; **I went in, and who do you ~ was there?** je suis entré et devine qui se trouvait là?; **he is (generally) ~d to be rich, it is (generally) ~d that he is rich** il passe pour être riche, on dit qu'il est riche; **I never ~d him (to be) a hero** je n'ai jamais pensé *or* imaginé qu'il fût un héros; **I don't ~ he'll agree, I ~ he won't agree** cela m'étonnerait qu'il soit d'accord, je ne pense pas qu'il soit d'accord, je suppose qu'il ne sera pas d'accord; **I ~ so** probablement, je suppose que oui; **I don't ~ so, I ~ not** je ne (le) pense *or* crois pas, probablement pas; **wouldn't you ~ he'd be sorry?** n'auriez-vous pas pensé qu'il le regretterait?

c (*modal use in pass: "ought"*) **to be ~d to do sth** être censé faire qch; **she was ~d to telephone this morning** elle était censée *or* elle devait téléphoner ce matin; **he isn't ~d to know** il n'est pas censé le savoir; **you're not ~d to do that** il ne vous est pas permis de faire cela; **what's that ~d to mean?** qu'est-ce que tu veux dire par là?

d (*in imperative: "I suggest"*) **~ we go for a walk?** et si nous allions nous promener?; **~ I tell him myself?** et si c'était moi qui le lui disais?

e (*in prp as conj: "if"*) **supposing** si + *indic*, à supposer que + *subj*, supposé que + *subj*; **supposing he can't do it?** et s'il ne peut pas le faire?, et à supposer *or* et supposé qu'il ne puisse le faire?; **even supposing that** à supposer même que + *subj*; **always supposing that** en supposant que + *subj*, en admettant que + *subj*.

f (*presuppose*) supposer. **that ~s unlimited resources** cela suppose des ressources illimitées.

2 vi: you'll come, I ~? vous viendrez, j'imagine? *or* je suppose?; **don't spend your time supposing, do something!** ne passe pas ton temps à faire des suppositions, fais quelque chose!

supposed [sə'pəʊzd] **adj** (*presumed*) présumé, supposé; (*so-called*) prétendu, soi-disant *inv*; *see also* **suppose.**

supposedly [sə'pəʊzɪdlɪ] **adv** soi-disant, à ce que l'on suppose (*or* supposait *etc*). **they were ~ aware of what had happened** ils étaient soi-disant conscients *or* ils étaient censés être conscients de ce qui était arrivé; **he had ~ gone to France** il était censé être allé en France; **did he go? — ~!** est-ce qu'il y est allé? — à ce que l'on suppose! *or* soi-disant!; **~ not** apparemment pas.

supposing [sə'pəʊzɪŋ] **conj** *see* **suppose 1e.**

supposition [ˌsʌpə'zɪʃən] **n** supposition *f*, hypothèse *f*. **that is pure ~** c'est une pure supposition; **on the ~ that ...** à supposer que ... + *subj*, dans la supposition que ... + *subj*; **on this ~** dans cette hypothèse.

suppositional [ˌsʌpə'zɪʃənəl] **adj**, **suppositious** [ˌsʌpə'zɪʃəs] **adj** hypothétique.

supposititious [səˌpɒzɪ'tɪʃəs] **adj** supposé, faux (*f* fausse), apocryphe.

suppository [sə'pɒzɪtərɪ] **n** suppositoire *m*.

suppress [sə'pres] **vt** *abuse, crime* supprimer, mettre fin à; *revolt* réprimer, étouffer; *one's feelings* réprimer, refouler, maîtriser; *yawn, scandal* étouffer; *facts, truth* étouffer, dissimuler, cacher; *newspaper, publication* interdire, supprimer; *evidence* faire disparaître, supprimer; (*Psych*) refouler; (*Elec, Rad etc*) antiparasiter; (**: silence*) *heckler etc* faire taire. **to ~ a cough/sneeze** *etc* se retenir de *or* réprimer une envie de tousser/d'éternuer *etc*.

suppression [sə'preʃən] **n** (*see* **suppress**) suppression *f*; répression *f*; étouffement *m*; dissimulation *f*; interdiction *f*; (*Psych*) refoulement *m*; (*Elec, Rad etc*) antiparasitage *m*.

suppressive [sə'presɪv] **adj** répressif.

suppressor [sə'presəʳ] **n** (*Elec etc*) dispositif *m* antiparasite.

suppurate ['sʌpjʊəreɪt] **vi** suppurer.

suppuration [ˌsʌpjʊə'reɪʃən] **n** suppuration *f*.

supra... ['suːprə] **pref** supra..., sur... .

supranational [ˌsuːprə'næʃənl] **adj** supranational.

suprarenal [ˌsuːprə'riːnl] **adj** surrénal.

suprasegmental [ˌsuːprəseg'mentl] **adj** (*Ling*) suprasegmental.

supremacist [sʊ'preməsɪst] **n** personne *f* qui croit en la suprématie d'un groupe (*or* d'une race *etc*).

supremacy [sʊ'preməsɪ] **n** suprématie *f* (*over* sur); *see* **white.**

supreme [sʊ'priːm] **adj** (*all senses*) suprême. (*Rel*) **the S~ Being** l'Etre suprême; (*Mil*) **S~ Commander** commandant *m* en chef *or* suprême, généralissime *m*; (*Can Jur, US Jur*) **S~ Court** Cour *f* suprême; **to make the ~ sacrifice** faire le sacrifice de sa vie; *see* **reign, soviet** *etc*.

supremely [sʊ'priːmlɪ] **adv** suprêmement.

supremo [sʊ'priːməʊ] **n** (*Brit*) grand chef *m*.

Supt. (*Brit Police*) **abbr of Superintendent.**

sura ['sʊərə] **n** surate *f*.

surcharge ['sɜːtʃɑːdʒ] **1 n** (*extra payment, extra load, also Elec; also Post: overprinting*) surcharge *f*; (*extra tax*) surtaxe *f*. **import ~** surtaxe à l'importation. **2** [sɜː'tʃɑːdʒ] **vt** surcharger; surtaxer.

surd [sɜːd] **1 adj** (*Math*) irrationnel; (*Ling*) sourd. **2 n** (*Math*) quantité *f or* nombre *m* irrationnel(le); (*Ling*) sourde *f*.

sure [ʃʊəʳ] **1 adj a** (*infallible; reliable; safe etc*) *aim, shot, marksman, judgment, method, friend, footing* sûr; *solution, remedy* sûr, infaillible; *facts* sûr, indubitable; *success* assuré, certain.

b (*definite, indisputable*) sûr, certain. **it is ~ that he will come, he is ~ to come** il est sûr *or* certain qu'il viendra; **it is not ~ that he will come, he is not ~ to come** il n'est pas sûr *or* certain qu'il vienne; **it's not ~ yet** ça n'a encore rien de sûr; **it's ~ to rain** il va pleuvoir à coup sûr *or* c'est sûr et certain*; **be ~ to tell me, be ~ and tell me** ne manquez pas de me le dire; **you're ~ of a good meal** un bon repas vous est assuré; **he's ~ of success** il est sûr *or* certain de réussir; **you can't be ~ of him** vous ne pouvez pas être sûr de lui; **I want to be ~ of seeing him** je veux être sûr *or* certain de le voir; **to make ~ of a seat** s'assurer (d')une place; **to make ~ of one's facts** vérifier *or* s'assurer de ce qu'on avance; **better get a ticket beforehand and make ~** il vaut mieux prendre un billet à l'avance pour plus de sûreté *or* pour être sûr*; **did you lock it? — I think so but I'd better make ~** l'avez-vous fermé à clef? — je crois, mais je vais vérifier *or* m'en assurer; **I've made ~ of having enough coffee for everyone** j'ai veillé à ce qu'il y ait assez de café pour tout le monde; **nothing is ~ in this life** dans cette vie on n'est sûr de rien; **~ thing!*** oui bien sûr!, d'accord!; **he is, to be ~, rather tactless** il manque de tact, c'est certain; (*excl*) **well, to be ~!*** bien, ça alors!; **he'll leave for ~** il partira sans aucun doute; **and that's for ~*** ça ne fait aucun doute; **I'll find out for ~** je me renseignerai pour savoir exactement ce qu'il en est; **do you know for ~?** êtes-vous absolument sûr? *or* certain?; **I'll do it next week for ~** je le ferai la semaine prochaine sans faute.

c (*positive, convinced, assured*) sûr (*of* de), certain. **I'm *or* I feel ~ I've seen him** je suis sûr *or* certain de l'avoir vu; **I'm ~ he'll help us** je suis sûr qu'il nous aidera; **I'm not ~** je ne suis pas sûr *or* certain (*that* que + *subj*); **I'm not ~ how/why/when** *etc* je ne sais pas très bien comment/pourquoi/quand *etc*; **I'm not ~ (if) he can** je ne suis pas sûr *or* certain qu'il puisse; **I'm ~ I didn't mean to** je ne l'ai vraiment pas fait exprès; **he says he did it but I'm not so ~ (about that)** il dit que c'est lui qui l'a fait mais je n'en suis pas si sûr (que ça); **I'm going alone! — I'm not so ~ about that!** *or* **don't be so ~ about that!** j'irai seul! — ne le dis pas si vite!; **to be/feel ~ of o.s.** être/se sentir sûr de soi.

2 adv a (**: esp US: certainly*) pour sûr*. **he can ~ play the piano** pour sûr* *or* en tout cas, il sait jouer du piano; **he was ~ drunk, he ~ was drunk** il était drôlement soûl; **will you do it? — ~!** le ferez-vous? — bien sûr! *or* pour sûr!*

b ~ enough (*confirming*) effectivement, en effet, de fait; (*promising*) assurément, sans aucun doute; **~ enough, he did come** comme je l'avais (*or* on l'avait *etc*) bien prévu, il est venu; **and ~ enough he did arrive** et effectivement *or* en effet *or* de fait il est arrivé; **~ enough*, I'll be there** j'y serai sans faute; **it's petrol, ~ enough** c'est effectivement *or* bien de l'essence, c'est de l'essence en effet; **~ enough!** assurément!; (*US **) **he ~ enough made a hash of that** pour sûr qu'il a tout gâché*.

c as ~ as aussi sûr que; **as ~ as my name's Smith** aussi sûr que je m'appelle Smith; **as ~ as fate, as ~ as anything, as ~ as guns*, as ~ as eggs is eggs*** aussi sûr que deux et deux font quatre.

3 comp ► sure enough* (*US*) réel **► sure-fire*** certain, infaillible **► sure-footed** au pied sûr **► sure-footedly** d'un pied sûr.

surely ['ʃʊəlɪ] **adv a** (*expressing confidence: assuredly*) sûrement, certainement; (*expressing incredulity*) tout de même. **~ we've met before?** je suis sûr que nous nous sommes déjà rencontrés!; **~ he didn't say that!** il n'a pas pu dire ça, tout de même!; **there is ~ some mistake** il doit sûrement *or* certainement y avoir quelque erreur; **~ you can do something to help?** il doit bien y avoir quelque chose que vous puissiez faire pour aider; **~ you didn't believe him?** vous ne l'avez pas cru, j'espère; **~ to God‡ *or* to goodness* you knew that!** mais bon sang tu devrais bien le savoir!*; **it must rain soon, ~** il va bien pleuvoir, tout de même; **that's ~ not true** ça ne peut pas être vrai, ça m'étonnerait que ce soit vrai; **~ not!** pas possible!; (*US: with pleasure*) **~!** bien volontiers!

b (*inevitably*) sûrement, à coup sûr. **justice will ~ prevail** la justice prévaudra sûrement.

c *advance, move* (*safely*) sûrement; (*confidently*) avec assurance; *see* **slowly.**

sureness ['ʃʊənɪs] **n** (*certainty*) certitude *f*; (*sure-footedness*) sûreté *f*; (*self-assurance*) assurance *f*, sûreté de soi; *[judgment, method, footing, grip]* sûreté; *[aim, shot]* justesse *f*, précision *f*. **the ~ of his touch** sa sûreté de main.

surety [ˈʃʊərətɪ] **n** a (*Jur*) (*sum*) caution *f*; (*person*) caution, garant(e) *m(f)*. **to go** *or* **stand ~ for sb** se porter caution *or* garant pour qn; **in his own ~ of £1,000** après avoir donné une sûreté personnelle de 1 000 livres. b (††) certitude *f*. **of a ~** certainement.

surf [sɜːf] 1 **n** (*NonC*) (*waves*) vagues *fpl* déferlantes, ressac *m*; (*foam*) écume *f*; (*spray*) embrun *m*. 2 **vi** (*also* **go ~ing**) surfer, pratiquer le surf, faire du surf. 3 **comp ▸ surfboard n** planche *f* de surf ◊ **vi** surfer ▸ **surfboarder** = **surfer** ▸ **surfboarding** = **surfing** ▸ **surf boat** surf-boat *m* ▸ **surfcasting** (*US Sport*) pêche *f* au lancer en mer (*depuis le rivage*) ▸ **surfride** surfer ▸ **surfrider** = **surfer** ▸ **surfriding** = **surfing**.

surface [ˈsɜːfɪs] 1 **n** a *[earth, sea, liquid, object etc]* surface *f*; (*fig*) surface, extérieur *m*, dehors *m*. *[sea, lake etc]* **under the ~** sous l'eau; **to come** *or* **rise to the ~** remonter à la surface; (*fig*) faire surface, se faire jour; **on the ~** (*Naut*) en surface; (*Min: also* **at the ~**) au jour, à la surface; (*fig*) à première vue, au premier abord, en apparence; **on the ~ of the table** sur la surface de la table; **his faults are all on the ~** il a des défauts mais il a bon fond; (*fig*) **I can't get below the ~ with him** je n'arrive pas à le connaître vraiment *or* à aller au-delà des apparences avec lui; (*fig*) **prejudices just below** *or* **beneath the ~** préjugés prêts à faire surface *or* à se faire jour; **the road ~ is icy** la chaussée est verglacée.

b (*Math*) (*area*) surface *f*, superficie *f*, aire *f*; (*side: of solid*) côté *m*, face *f*.

2 **comp ▸ surface-to-air** (*Mil*) sol-air *inv* ▸ **surface-to-surface** (*Mil*) sol-sol *inv*.

3 **adj** a *tension* superficiel (*also fig*); (*Naut*) *vessel etc* de surface; (*Min*) *work* au jour, à la surface. (*Math etc*) **~ area** surface *f*, superficie *f*, aire *f*; (*Post*) **~ mail** courrier *m* par voie de terre; (*by sea*) courrier maritime; **by ~ mail** par voie de terre; (*by sea*) par voie maritime; (*on record player*) **~ noise** grésillements *mpl*; (*Min*) **~ workers** personnel *m* qui travaille au jour *or* à la surface; (*fig*) **it's only a ~ reaction** ce n'est qu'une réaction superficielle.

b (*Phon, Gram*) de surface. **~ structure/grammar** structure *f*/grammaire *f* de surface.

4 **vt** a *road* revêtir (*with* de); *paper* calandrer, glacer.

b (*Naut*) *submarine, object, wreck* amener à la surface.

5 **vi** *[swimmer, diver, whale]* revenir *or* remonter à la surface; *[submarine]* faire surface; (*fig: emerge*) *[news, feeling etc]* faire surface, se faire jour; (** fig*) (*after absence*) réapparaître; (*after hard work*) faire surface.

surfeit [ˈsɜːfɪt] 1 **n** excès *m* (*of* de); (*NonC: satiety*) satiété *f*. **to have a ~ of** avoir une indigestion de (*fig*); **there is a ~ of** il y a par trop de. 2 **vt: to be ~ed with pleasure** être repu de plaisir.

surfer [ˈsɜːfəʳ] **n** surfeur *m*, -euse *f*.

surfing [ˈsɜːfɪŋ] **n** surf *m*; *see* **surf 2**.

surge [sɜːdʒ] 1 **n** (*gen*) mouvement puissant; *[rage, fear, enthusiasm]* vague *f*, montée *f*; (*Elec*) saute *f* de courant; (*fig: in sales etc*) afflux *m*. **the ~ of the sea** la houle; **he felt a ~ of anger** il a senti la colère monter en lui; **there was a ~ of sympathy for him** il y a eu un vif mouvement *or* une vague de sympathie pour lui; **the ~ of people around the car** la foule qui se pressait autour de la voiture; **he was carried along by the ~ of the crowd** il était porté par le mouvement de la foule.

2 **vi** a *[waves]* s'enfler; *[flood, river]* déferler. **the sea ~d against the rocks** la houle battait *or* heurtait les rochers; **the surging sea** la mer houleuse; **the ship ~d at anchor** le bateau amarré était soulevé par la houle; (*Elec*) **the power ~d suddenly** il y a eu une brusque surtension de courant; **the blood ~d to his cheeks** le sang lui est monté *or* lui a reflué au visage; **anger ~d (up) within him** la colère monta en lui.

b *[crowd, vehicles etc]* déferler. **to ~ in/out** *etc* entrer/sortir *etc* à flots; **they ~d round the car** ils se pressaient autour de la voiture; **they ~d forward** ils se sont lancés en avant; (*fig*) **a surging mass of demonstrators** une foule déferlante de manifestants.

surgeon [ˈsɜːdʒən] 1 **n** chirurgien *m*. **she is a ~** elle est chirurgien; **a woman ~** une femme chirurgien; *see* **dental, house, veterinary** *etc.* 2 **comp ▸ surgeon general** (**pl ~s ~**) (*Mil*) médecin-général *m*; (*US Admin*) ministre *m* de la Santé.

surgery [ˈsɜːdʒərɪ] 1 **n** a (*NonC: skill; study; operation*) chirurgie *f*. **it is a fine piece of ~** le chirurgien a fait du beau travail; **to have ~** se faire opérer; *see* **plastic** *etc.* b (*Brit: consulting room*) cabinet *m* (de consultation); (*interview*) consultation *f*. **come to the ~ tomorrow** venez à mon cabinet demain, venez à la consultation demain; **when is his ~?** à quelle heure sont ses consultations?, à quelle heure consulte-t-il?; **during his ~** pendant ses heures de consultation; **there is an afternoon ~** il consulte l'après-midi. 2 **comp ▸ surgery hours** heures *fpl* de consultation.

surgical [ˈsɜːdʒɪkəl] **adj** *operation, intervention, treatment* chirurgical; *instruments* chirurgical, de chirurgie. **~ appliance** appareil *m* orthopédique; **~ cotton** coton *m* hydrophile; **~ dressing** pansement *m*; **~ shock** choc *m* opératoire; (*Brit*) **~ spirit** alcool *m* à 90 (degrés).

surgically [ˈsɜːdʒɪkəlɪ] **adv** chirurgicalement.

Surinam [ˌsʊərɪˈnæm] **n** Surinam *m*.

Surinamese [ˌsʊərɪnæˈmiːz] 1 **n** surinamais(e) *m(f)*. 2 **adj** surinamais.

surliness [ˈsɜːlɪnɪs] **n** caractère *or* air revêche *or* maussade *or* renfrogné.

surly [ˈsɜːlɪ] **adj** revêche, maussade, renfrogné, bourru.

surmise [ˈsɜːmaɪz] 1 **n** conjecture *f*, hypothèse *f*. **it was nothing but ~** c'était entièrement conjectural. 2 [sɜːˈmaɪz] **vt** conjecturer, présumer (*from sth* d'après qch). **to ~ that ...** (*infer*) conjecturer que ..., présumer que ...; (*suggest*) émettre l'hypothèse que ...; **I ~d as much** je m'en doutais.

surmount [sɜːˈmaʊnt] **vt** a (*Archit etc*) surmonter. **~ed by a statue** surmonté d'une statue. b (*overcome*) *obstacle, difficulties, problems* surmonter, venir à bout de.

surmountable [sɜːˈmaʊntəbl] **adj** surmontable.

surname [ˈsɜːneɪm] 1 **n** nom *m* de famille. **name and ~** nom et prénoms. 2 **vt: ~d Jones** nommé *or* dénommé Jones, dont le nom de famille est (*or* était) Jones.

surpass [sɜːˈpɑːs] **vt** *person* surpasser (*in* en); *hopes, expectations* dépasser. (*also iro*) **to ~ o.s.** se surpasser (*also iro*).

surpassing [sɜːˈpɑːsɪŋ] **adj** incomparable, sans pareil.

surplice [ˈsɜːpləs] **n** surplis *m*.

surpliced [ˈsɜːplɪst] **adj** en surplis.

surplus [ˈsɜːpləs] 1 **n, pl ~es** (*Comm, Econ, gen*) surplus *m*, excédent *m*; (*Fin*) boni *m*, excédent. **a tea ~** un surplus *or* un excédent de thé.

2 **adj** (*gen*) *food, boxes etc* en surplus, en trop, de reste; (*Comm, Econ*) en surplus, excédentaire; (*Fin*) de boni, excédentaire. **it is ~ to (our) requirements** cela excède nos besoins; *[book, document etc]* **~ copies** exemplaires *mpl* de passe; **~ stock** surplus *mpl*, stocks *mpl* excédentaires; **American ~ wheat** excédent *m* *or* surplus *m* de blé américain; **his ~ energy** son surcroît d'énergie. 3 **comp ▸ surplus store** magasin *m* de surplus.

surprise [səˈpraɪz] 1 **n** (*emotion: NonC*) surprise *f*, étonnement *m*; (*event etc*) surprise. **much to my ~, to my great ~** à ma grande surprise, à mon grand étonnement; **he stopped in ~** il s'est arrêté sous l'effet de la surprise, étonné il s'est arrêté; **to take by ~** *person* surprendre, prendre au dépourvu; (*Mil*) *fort, town* prendre par surprise; **a look of ~** un regard surpris *or* traduisant la surprise; **imagine my ~ when ...** imaginez quel a été mon étonnement *or* quelle a été ma surprise quand ...; **what a ~!** quelle surprise!; **to give sb a ~** faire une surprise à qn, surprendre qn; **it was a lovely/nasty ~ for him** cela a été pour lui une agréable/mauvaise surprise; **it came as a ~ (to me) to learn that ...** j'ai eu la surprise d'apprendre que ... .

2 **adj** *defeat, gift, visit, decision* inattendu, inopiné. **~ attack** attaque *f* par surprise, attaque brusquée.

3 **vt** a (*astonish*) surprendre, étonner. **he was ~d to hear that ...** il a été surpris *or* étonné d'apprendre que ..., cela l'a surpris *or* étonné d'apprendre que ...; **I shouldn't be ~d if it snowed** cela ne m'étonnerait pas qu'il neige (*subj*); **don't be ~d if he refuses** ne soyez pas étonné *or* surpris s'il refuse, ne vous étonnez pas s'il refuse; **it's nothing to be ~d at** cela n'a rien d'étonnant, ce n'est pas *or* guère étonnant; **I'm ~d at** *or* **by his ignorance** son ignorance me surprend; **I'm ~d at you!** je ne m'attendais pas à cela de vous!, cela me surprend de votre part!; **it ~d me that he agreed** j'ai été étonné *or* surpris qu'il accepte (*subj*), je ne m'attendais pas à ce qu'il accepte (*subj*); (*iro*) **go on, ~ me!** allez, étonne-moi!; **he ~d me into agreeing to do it** j'ai été tellement surpris que j'ai accepté de le faire; *see also* **surprised**.

b (*catch unawares*) *army, sentry* surprendre, attaquer par surprise; *thief* surprendre, prendre sur le fait; (*gen*) surprendre.

surprised [səˈpraɪzd] **adj** surpris, étonné. **you'd be ~ how many people ...** si tu savais combien de gens ...; **he'll surely be on time — you'd be ~!** il sera sûrement à l'heure — n'y compte pas!; *see also* **surprise**.

surprising [səˈpraɪzɪŋ] **adj** surprenant, étonnant. **it is ~ that** il est surprenant *or* étonnant que + *subj*.

surprisingly [səˈpraɪzɪŋlɪ] **adv** *big, sad etc* étonnamment, étrangement. **you look ~ cheerful for someone who ...** vous m'avez l'air de bien bonne humeur pour quelqu'un qui ...; **~ enough, ...** chose étonnante, ...; **not ~ he didn't come** comme on pouvait s'y attendre il n'est pas venu, il n'est pas venu, ce qui n'a rien d'étonnant.

surreal [səˈrɪəl] **adj** surréaliste (*fig*).

surrealism [səˈrɪəlɪzəm] **n** surréalisme *m*.

surrealist [səˈrɪəlɪst] **adj, n** surréaliste (*mf*).

surrealistic [səˌrɪəˈlɪstɪk] **adj** surréaliste.

surrender [səˈrendəʳ] 1 **vi** (*Mil*) se rendre (*to* à), capituler (*to* devant). **to ~ to the police** se livrer à la police, se constituer prisonnier; (*fig*) **to ~ to despair** s'abandonner *or* se livrer au désespoir.

2 **vt** a (*Mil*) *town, hill* livrer (*to* à).

b *firearms* rendre (*to* à); *stolen property, documents, photos* remettre (*to* à); *insurance policy* racheter; *lease* céder; *one's rights, claims, powers, liberty* renoncer à, abdiquer; *hopes* abandonner. (*fig*) **to ~ o.s. to despair/to the delights of sth** s'abandonner *or* se livrer au désespoir/aux plaisirs de qch.

3 **n** a (*Mil etc*) reddition *f* (*to* à), capitulation *f* (*to* devant). **no ~!** on ne se rend pas!; *see* **unconditional**.

b (*giving up*) *[firearms, stolen property, documents]* remise *f* (*to* à);

[insurance policy] rachat *m*; *[one's rights, claims, powers, liberty]* renonciation *f* (*of* à), abdication *f* (*of* de, *to* en faveur de); *[hopes]* abandon *m*; *[lease]* cession *f*; (*return*) restitution *f* (*of* de, *to* à).
4 comp ▸ **surrender value** (*Insurance*) valeur *f* de rachat.

surreptitious [ˌsʌrəp'tɪʃəs] adj *entry, removal* subreptice, clandestin; *movement, gesture* furtif.

surreptitiously [ˌsʌrəp'tɪʃəslɪ] adv *enter, remove* subrepticement, clandestinement; *move* furtivement, sournoisement (*pej*).

surrogacy ['sʌrəgəsɪ] n (*in childbearing*) maternité *f* de substitution.

surrogate ['sʌrəgɪt] 1 n a (*gen: frm*) substitut *m*, représentant *m*. b (*Psych*) substitut *m*. c (*Brit: also* ~ **bishop**) *évêque auxiliaire à qui l'on délègue le pouvoir d'autoriser les mariages sans publication de bans*. d (*US: judge*) *juge chargé de l'homologation de testaments etc*.
2 adj *pleasure etc* de remplacement. ~ **mother** (*Genetics*) mère-porteuse *f*, mère *f* de substitution; (*Psych*) substitut *m* maternel; ~ **motherhood** maternité *f* de substitution. 3 ['sʌrəgeɪt] vi (*be a* ~ *mother*) être mère-porteuse *f or* mère de substitution.

surround [sə'raʊnd] 1 vt entourer; (*totally*) cerner, encercler. ~**ed by** entouré de; (*Mil, Police etc*) **you are** ~**ed** vous êtes cerné *or* encerclé; (*fig*) **to** ~ **o.s. with friends/allies** s'entourer d'amis/d'alliés. 2 n bordure *f*, encadrement *m*; (*Brit: on floor: also* ~**s**) bordure (entre le tapis et le mur).

surrounding [sə'raʊndɪŋ] 1 adj environnant. **the** ~ **countryside** les environs *mpl*, les alentours *mpl*. 2 npl: ~**s** (*surrounding country*) alentours *mpl*, environs *mpl*; (*setting*) cadre *m*, décor *m*; **the** ~**s of Glasgow are picturesque** les alentours *or* les environs de Glasgow sont pittoresques, Glasgow est situé dans un cadre *or* un décor pittoresque; **he found himself in** ~**s strange to him** il s'est retrouvé dans un cadre *or* décor qu'il ne connaissait pas; **animals in their natural** ~**s** des animaux dans leur cadre naturel.

surtax ['sɜːtæks] n (*gen*) surtaxe *f*; (*income tax*) tranche *f* supérieure de l'impôt sur le revenu. **to pay** ~ être dans les tranches supérieures d'imposition.

surtitle ['sɜːˌtaɪtl] npl: ~**s** surtitres *mpl*.

surveillance [sɜː'veɪləns] n surveillance *f*. **to keep sb under** ~ surveiller qn; **under constant** ~ sous surveillance continue.

survey ['sɜːveɪ] 1 n a (*comprehensive view*) *[countryside, prospects, development etc]* vue générale *or* d'ensemble (*of* de). **he gave a general** ~ **of the situation** il a fait un tour d'horizon de la situation, il a passé la situation en revue.
b (*investigation, study*) *[reasons, prices, situation, sales, trends]* enquête *f* (*of* sur), étude *f* (*of* de). **to carry out** *or* **make a** ~ **of** enquêter sur, faire une étude de; ~ **of public opinion** sondage *m* d'opinion.
c (*Surv: of land, coast etc*) (*act*) relèvement *m*, levé *m*; (*report*) levé; *see* **aerial, ordnance**.
d (*Brit: in housebuying*) (*act*) visite *f* d'expert, inspection *f*, examen *m*; (*report*) (rapport *m* d')expertise *f*.
2 comp ▸ **survey course** (*US Univ*) cours *m* d'initiation ▸ **survey ship** bateau *m* hydrographique.
3 [sɜː'veɪ] vt a (*look around at*) *countryside, view, crowd* embrasser du regard; *prospects, trends* passer en revue. **he** ~**ed the scene with amusement** il regardait la scène d'un œil amusé.
b (*examine, study*) *ground before battle etc* inspecter; *developments, needs, prospects* enquêter sur, faire une étude de. **the Prime Minister** ~**ed the situation** le Premier ministre a fait un tour d'horizon de *or* a passé en revue la situation; **the book** ~**s the history of the motorcar** le livre passe en revue *or* étudie dans les grandes lignes l'histoire de l'automobile.
c (*Surv*) *site, land* arpenter, faire le levé de, relever; (*Brit*) *house, building* inspecter, examiner; *country, coast* faire le levé topographique de; *seas* faire le levé hydrographique de.

surveying [sɜː'veɪɪŋ] 1 n (*see* **survey 3c**) a (*act*) arpentage *m*, levé *m*; inspection *f*, examen *m*. b (*science, occupation*) arpentage *m*; topographie *f*; hydrographie *f*. 2 comp *instrument* d'arpentage; *studies* d'arpentage *or* de topographie *or* d'hydrographie.

surveyor [sə'veɪəʳ] n (*Brit: of property, buildings etc*) expert *m*; *[land, site]* (arpenteur *m*) géomètre *m*; *[country, coastline]* topographe *mf*; *[seas]* hydrographe *mf*; *see* **quantity** *etc*.

survival [sə'vaɪvəl] 1 n (*act*) survie *f* (*also Jur, Rel*); (*relic: of custom, beliefs etc*) survivance *f*, vestige *m*. **the** ~ **of the fittest** (*lit: in evolution*) la lutte pour la vie; (*fig*) la loi du plus fort. 2 comp ▸ **survival bag** ≃ couverture *f* de survie ▸ **survival course** cours *m* de survie ▸ **survival kit** kit *m* de survie.

survivalist [sə'vaɪvəlɪst] n (*US*) *personne se protégeant contre une éventuelle attaque nucléaire*.

survive [sə'vaɪv] 1 vi *[person]* survivre (*on* avec); *[house, jewellery, book, custom]* survivre, subsister. **he** ~**d to tell the tale** il a survécu et a pu raconter ce qui s'était passé; **only 3 volumes** ~ il ne reste *or* il ne subsiste plus que 3 tomes; (*iro*) **you'll** ~! vous n'en mourrez pas!; **they don't eat/earn enough to** ~ **on** il ne mangent/gagnent pas assez pour survivre. 2 vt *person* survivre à; *injury, disease* réchapper de; *fire, accident, experience, invasion* survivre à, réchapper de. **he is** ~**d by a wife and 2 sons** sa femme et 2 fils lui survivent.

surviving [sə'vaɪvɪŋ] adj *spouse, children etc* survivant. (*Fin: after merger*) ~ **company** société *f* absorbante.

survivor [sə'vaɪvəʳ] n survivant(e) *m(f)*; (*of accident*) survivant(e), rescapé(e) *m(f)*; (*fig: of regime etc*) rescapé(e). **he's a real** ~! il surmonte toutes les crises.

sus* [sʌs] (*Brit*) 1 n abbr of **suspicion**. (*Brit*) ~ **law** loi *f* autorisant à interpeller des suspects à discrétion. 2 vt = **suss***.

Susan ['suːzn] n Suzanne *f*.

susceptibility [səˌseptə'bɪlɪtɪ] n (*sensitiveness*) vive sensibilité, émotivité *f*, impressionnabilité *f*; (*touchiness*) susceptibilité *f*; (*Med*) prédisposition *f* (*to* à). **his** ~ **to hypnosis** la facilité avec laquelle on l'hypnotise; **his susceptibilities** ses cordes *fpl* sensibles.

susceptible [sə'septəbl] adj (*sensitive, impressionable*) sensible, émotif, impressionnable; (*touchy*) susceptible, ombrageux. **to be** ~ **to** *pain* être (très) sensible à, craindre; *kindness* être sensible à; *suggestion, sb's influence* être ouvert à, être accessible à; (*Med*) *disease* être prédisposé à; *treatment* répondre à; ~ **of** susceptible de.

sushi ['suːʃɪ] n (*NonC*) sushi *m*. ~ **restaurant/bar** restaurant *m*/petit restaurant *m* de sushi.

suspect ['sʌspekt] 1 n suspect(e) *m(f)*.
2 adj *evidence, act* suspect.
3 [səs'pekt] vt a soupçonner (*that* que); *person* soupçonner, suspecter (*pej*) (*of a crime* d'un crime, *of doing* de faire *or* d'avoir fait); *ambush, swindle* flairer, soupçonner. **I** ~ **him of being the author** *[book etc]* je le soupçonne d'en être l'auteur; *[anonymous letter]* je le soupçonne *or* je le suspecte d'en être l'auteur; **he** ~**s nothing** il ne se doute de rien.
b (*think likely*) soupçonner, avoir dans l'idée, avoir le sentiment (*that* que). **I** ~ **he knows who did it** je soupçonne *or* j'ai dans l'idée *or* j'ai le sentiment qu'il sait qui est le coupable; **I** ~**ed as much** je m'en doutais; **he'll come, I** ~ il viendra, j'imagine.
c (*have doubts about*) suspecter, douter de. **I** ~ **the truth of what he says** je doute de *or* je suspecte la vérité de ce qu'il dit.

suspend [səs'pend] vt a (*hang*) suspendre (*from* à). *[particles etc]* **to be** ~**ed in sth** être en suspension dans qch; **a column of smoke hung** ~**ed in the still air** une colonne de fumée flottait dans l'air immobile.
b (*stop temporarily; defer etc*) *publication* suspendre, surseoir; *decision, payment, regulation, meetings, discussions* suspendre; *licence, permission* retirer provisoirement; *bus service* interrompre provisoirement. **to** ~ **judgment** suspendre son jugement; (*Jur*) ~**ed sentence** condamnation *f* avec sursis; (*Jur*) **he received a** ~**ed sentence of 6 months in jail** il a été condamné à 6 mois de prison avec sursis; (*fig hum*) **to be in a state of** ~**ed animation** ne donner aucun signe de vie.
c *employee, office holder, officer etc* suspendre (*from* de); (*Scol, Univ*) exclure temporairement.

suspender [səs'pendəʳ] 1 n a (*Brit*) (*for stockings*) jarretelle *f*; (*for socks*) fixe-chaussette *m*. b (*US: braces*) ~**s** bretelles *fpl*. 2 comp ▸ **suspender belt** (*Brit*) porte-jarretelles *m inv*.

suspense [səs'pens] 1 n (*NonC*) a incertitude *f*, attente *f*; (*in book, film, play*) suspense *m*. **we waited in great** ~ nous avons attendu haletants; **to keep sb in** ~ tenir qn en suspens, laisser qn dans l'incertitude; *[film]* tenir qn en suspens *or* en haleine; **to put sb out of (his)** ~ mettre fin à l'incertitude *or* à l'attente de qn; **the** ~ **is killing me!*** ce suspense me tue! (*also iro*). b (*Admin, Jur*) **to be** *or* **remain in** ~ être (laissé) *or* rester en suspens. 2 comp ▸ **suspense account** (*Book-keeping*) compte *m* d'attente.

suspension [səs'penʃən] 1 n a (*see* **suspend b**) suspension *f*; retrait *m* provisoire; interruption *f* provisoire. b (*see* **suspend c**) suspension *f*; renvoi *m or* exclusion *f* temporaire. c (*Aut, Chem, Tech etc*) suspension *f*. (*Chem*) **in** ~ en suspension. 2 comp ▸ **suspension bridge** pont suspendu ▸ **suspension file** dossier *m* suspendu ▸ **suspension points** (*Gram*) points *mpl* de suspension.

suspensory [səs'pensərɪ] adj *ligament* suspenseur (*m only*); *bandage* de soutien.

suspicion [səs'pɪʃən] n a soupçon *m*; (*NonC*) soupçon(s). **an atmosphere laden with** ~ une atmosphère chargée de soupçons; **above** *or* **beyond** ~ au-dessus *or* à l'abri de tout soupçon; **under** ~ considéré comme suspect; **he was regarded with** ~ on s'est montré soupçonneux à son égard; (*Jur*) **to arrest sb on** ~ arrêter qn sur des présomptions; **on** ~ **of murder** sur présomption de meurtre; **I had a** ~ **that he wouldn't come back** je soupçonnais *or* quelque chose me disait *or* j'avais le sentiment qu'il ne reviendrait pas; **I had no** ~ **that** ... je ne me doutais pas du tout que ...; **I had (my)** ~**s about that letter** j'avais mes doutes quant à cette lettre; **I have my** ~**s about it** j'ai des doutes là-dessus, cela me semble suspect; **he was right in his** ~ **that** ... il avait raison de soupçonner que ..., c'est à juste titre qu'il soupçonnait que ... .
b (*fig: trace, touch*) soupçon *m*.

suspicious [səs'pɪʃəs] adj a (*feeling suspicion*) soupçonneux, méfiant. **to be** ~ **about sb/sth** avoir des soupçons à l'égard de qn/quant à qch, tenir qn/qch pour suspect; **to be** ~ **of** se méfier de. b (*causing suspicion: also* ~**-looking**) *person, vehicle, action* suspect, louche.

suspiciously [səs'pɪʃəslɪ] adv a (*with suspicion*) *examine, glance, ask etc* avec méfiance, soupçonneusement. b (*causing suspicion*) *behave,* *run away etc* d'une manière suspecte *or* louche. **it looks ~ like measles** ça m'a tout l'air d'être la rougeole; **it sounds ~ as though he won't give it back** ça m'a tout l'air de signifier qu'il ne le rendra pas; **he arrived ~ early** il me paraît suspect qu'il soit arrivé si tôt; **he was ~ eager** il était d'un empressement suspect.

suspiciousness [səs'pɪʃəsnɪs] **n** (*NonC*) (*feeling suspicion*) caractère soupçonneux *or* méfiant; (*causing suspicion*) caractère suspect.

suss* [sʌs] **vt** (*Brit*) **to ~ (out)** *situation, plan* piger‡; **I can't ~ him out** je n'arrive pas à le cerner; **he'll ~ you (out) straight away** il va tout de suite comprendre ton jeu; **I've ~ed it out, I've got it ~ed** j'ai pigé‡.

sustain [səs'teɪn] **vt** a *weight, beam etc* supporter; *body* nourrir, sustenter†; *life* maintenir; (*Mus*) *note* tenir, soutenir; *effort, role* soutenir; *pretence* poursuivre, prolonger; *assertion, theory* soutenir, maintenir; *charge* donner des preuves à l'appui de. **that food won't ~ you for long** ce n'est pas cette nourriture qui va vous donner beaucoup de forces; (*Jur*) **objection ~ed** ≃ (objection) accordée; (*Jur*) **the court ~ed his claim** *or* **~ed him in his claim** le tribunal a fait droit à sa revendication; **~ed** *effort, attack* soutenu, prolongé; *applause* prolongé; (*Econ*) **~ed growth** expansion *f* soutenue.
b (*suffer*) *attack* subir; *loss* éprouver, essuyer; *damage* subir, souffrir; *injury* recevoir. **he ~ed concussion** il a été commotionné.

sustainable [səs'teɪnəbəl] **adj** *rate, growth* qui peut être maintenu; *argument* tenable; *energy, source, forest* durable.

sustaining [səs'teɪnɪŋ] **adj** *food* nourrissant, nutritif. (*Mus*) **~ pedal** pédale forte; (*US: Rad, TV*) **~ program** émission non patronnée.

sustenance ['sʌstɪnəns] **n** (*NonC*) a (*nourishing quality*) valeur nutritive; (*food and drink*) alimentation *f*, nourriture *f*. **there's not much ~ in melon** le melon n'est pas très nourrissant *or* nutritif, le melon n'a pas beaucoup de valeur nutritive; **they depend for ~ on, they get their ~ from** ils se nourrissent de; **roots and berries were** *or* **provided their only ~** les racines et les baies étaient leur seule nourriture, pour toute nourriture ils avaient des racines et des baies. b (*means of livelihood*) moyens *mpl* de subsistance.

suttee [sʌ'tiː] **n** (*widow*) (veuve *f*) satî *f inv*; (*rite*) satî *m*.

suture ['suːtʃəʳ] **n** suture *f*.

suzerain ['suːzə,reɪn] **n** suzerain(e) *m(f)*.

suzerainty ['suːzərəntɪ] **n** suzeraineté *f*.

svelte [svelt] **adj** svelte.

SW (*Rad*) (**abbr of short wave**) O.C. *fpl*.

swab [swɒb] 1 **n** (*mop, cloth*) serpillière *f*; (*Naut*) faubert *m*; (*for gun-cleaning*) écouvillon *m*; (*Med: cotton wool etc*) tampon *m*; (*Med: specimen*) prélèvement *m*. (*Med*) **to take a ~ of sb's throat** faire un prélèvement dans la gorge de qn. 2 **vt** a (*also* **~ down**) *floor etc* nettoyer, essuyer; (*Naut*) *deck* passer le faubert sur. b (*also* **~ out**) *gun* écouvillonner; (*Med*) *wound* tamponner, essuyer *or* nettoyer avec un tampon.

swaddle ['swɒdl] 1 **vt** (*in bandages*) emmailloter (*in* de); (*in blankets etc*) emmitoufler* (*in* dans); *baby* emmailloter, langer. 2 **comp** ►**swaddling bands, swaddling clothes** (*liter*) maillot *m*, lange *m*.

swag [swæg] 1 **n** a (‡: *loot*) butin *m*. b (*Austral*) bal(l)uchon* *m*. 2 **comp** ►**swagman*** (*Austral*) chemineau *m*, ouvrier *m* agricole itinérant.

swagger ['swægəʳ] 1 **n** air fanfaron; (*gait*) démarche assurée. **to walk with a ~** marcher en plastronnant *or* d'un air important. 2 **comp** ►**swagger cane** (*Mil*) badine *f*, jonc *m* ►**swagger coat** manteau *m* trois quarts ►**swagger stick** (*US*) = **swagger cane.** 3 **adj** (*Brit* *) chic *inv*. 4 **vi** a (*also* **~ about, ~ along**) plastronner, parader. **to ~ in/out** *etc* entrer/sortir *etc* d'un air fanfaron *or* en plastronnant. b (*boast*) se vanter (*about* de).

swaggering ['swægərɪŋ] 1 **adj** *gait* assuré; *person* fanfaron, qui plastronne; *look, gesture* fanfaron. 2 **n** (*strutting*) airs plastronnants; (*boasting*) fanfaronnades *fpl*.

Swahili [swɑː'hiːlɪ] 1 **adj** swahili, souahéli. 2 **npl** a (*people*) Swahilis *mpl*, Souahélis *mpl*. b (*Ling*) swahili *m*, souahéli *m*.

swain [sweɪn] **n** (†† *or liter*) amant† *m*, soupirant† *m*.

swallow¹ ['swɒləʊ] 1 **n** (*Orn*) hirondelle *f*. (*Prov*) **one ~ doesn't make a summer** une hirondelle ne fait pas le printemps (*Prov*). 2 **comp** ►**swallow dive** (*Brit*) saut *m* de l'ange ►**swallowtail (butterfly)** machaon *m* ►**swallow-tailed coat** (habit *m* à) queue *f* de pie.

swallow² ['swɒləʊ] 1 **n** (*act*) avalement *m*; (*amount*) gorgée *f*. **at** *or* **with one ~** (*drink*) d'un trait, d'un seul coup; (*food*) d'un seul coup. 2 **vi** avaler. (*emotionally*) **he ~ed hard** sa gorge se serra. 3 **vt** a *food, drink, pill* avaler; *oyster* gober. (*fig*) **to ~ the bait** se laisser prendre (à l'appât). b (*fig*) *story* avaler, gober; *insult* avaler, encaisser*; *one's anger, pride* ravaler. **that's a bit hard to ~** c'est plutôt dur à avaler; **they ~ed it whole** ils ont tout avalé *or* gobé.

►**swallow down** **vt sep** avaler.

►**swallow up** **vt sep** (*fig*) engloutir. **the ground seemed to swallow them up** le sol semblait les engloutir; **he was swallowed up in the crowd** il s'est perdu *or* il a disparu dans la foule; **the mist swallowed them up** la brume les a enveloppés; **taxes swallow up half your income** les impôts engloutissent *or* engouffrent la moitié de vos revenus.

swam [swæm] **pret of swim.**

swami ['swɑːmɪ] **n, pl ~es** *or* **~s** pandit *m*.

swamp [swɒmp] 1 **n** marais *m*, marécage *m*. 2 **comp** ►**swamp buggy** (*US*) voiture *f* amphibie ►**swamp fever** paludisme *m*, malaria *f* ►**swampland** (*NonC*) marécages *mpl*. 3 **vt** (*flood*) inonder; *boat* emplir d'eau; (*sink*) submerger; (*fig*) submerger (*with* de). (*fig*) **he was ~ed with requests/letters** il était submergé de requêtes/lettres; **I'm absolutely ~ed* (with work)** je suis débordé (de travail); (*Ftbl etc*) **towards the end of the game they ~ed us** vers la fin de la partie ils ont fait le jeu.

swampy ['swɒmpɪ] **adj** marécageux.

swan [swɒn] 1 **n** cygne *m*. **the S~ of Avon** le cygne de l'Avon (*Shakespeare*). 2 **comp** ►**swan dive** (*US*) saut *m* de l'ange ►**Swan Lake** (*Ballet*) le Lac des Cygnes ►**swan-necked** *woman* au cou de cygne; *tool* en col de cygne ►**swansdown** (*NonC*) (*feathers*) (duvet *m* de) cygne *m*; (*Tex*) molleton *m* ►**swan song** (*fig*) chant *m* du cygne ►**swan-upping** (*Brit*) *recensement annuel des cygnes de la Tamise.* 3 **vi** (*Brit* *) **he ~ned off to London before the end of term** il est parti à Londres sans s'en faire* *or* il est tranquillement parti à Londres avant la fin du trimestre; **he's ~ning around in Paris somewhere** il se balade* quelque part dans Paris sans s'en faire*.

swank* [swæŋk] 1 **n** a (*NonC*) esbroufe* *f*. **out of ~** pour épater*, pour faire de l'esbroufe*. b (*person*) esbroufeur* *m*, -euse* *f*. 2 **vi** faire de l'esbroufe*, chercher à épater* *or* à en mettre plein la vue*. **to ~ about sth** se vanter de qch.

swanky* ['swæŋkɪ] **adj** qui en met plein la vue*.

swannery ['swɒnərɪ] **n** colonie *f* de cygnes.

swap* [swɒp] 1 **n** troc *m*, échange *m*. **it's a fair ~** ça se vaut; (*stamps etc*) **~s** doubles *mpl*. 2 **vt** échanger, troquer (*A for B* A contre B); *stamps, stories* échanger (*with sb* avec qn). **Paul and Martin have ~ped hats** Paul et Martin ont échangé leurs chapeaux; **let's ~ places** changeons de place (l'un avec l'autre); **I'll ~ you!** tu veux échanger avec moi?; *see* **wife.** 3 **vi** échanger.

►**swap over, swap round** **vt sep, vi** changer de place.

SWAPO ['swɑːpəʊ] **n** (**abbr of South-West Africa People's Organization**) S.W.A.P.O. *f*.

sward†† [swɔːd] **n** gazon *m*, pelouse *f*.

swarm¹ [swɔːm] 1 **n** *[bees, flying insects]* essaim *m*; *[ants, crawling insects]* fourmillement *m*, grouillement *m*; *[people]* essaim, nuée *f*, troupe *f*. (*fig*) **in a ~, in ~s** en masse. 2 **vi** a *[bees]* essaimer. b *[crawling insects]* fourmiller, pulluler, grouiller. *[people]* **to ~ in/out** *etc* entrer/sortir *etc* en masse; **they ~ed round** *or* **over** *or* **through the palace** ils ont envahi le palais en masse; **the children ~ed round his car** les enfants s'agglutinaient autour de sa voiture. c (*lit, fig*) *[ground, town, streets]* fourmiller, grouiller (*with* de).

swarm² [swɔːm] **vt** (*also* **~ up**) *tree, pole* grimper à toute vitesse à (*en s'aidant des pieds et des mains*).

swarthiness ['swɔːðɪnɪs] **n** teint basané *or* bistré.

swarthy ['swɔːðɪ] **adj** basané, bistré.

swashbuckler ['swɒʃ,bʌkləʳ] **n** fier-à-bras *m*.

swashbuckling ['swɒʃ,bʌklɪŋ] **adj** *person* fanfaron, qui plastronne; *film* de cape et d'épée.

swastika ['swɒstɪkə] **n** svastika *m* *or* swastika *m*; (*Nazi*) croix gammée.

swat [swɒt] 1 **vt** *fly, mosquito* écraser; (*: *slap*) *table etc* donner un coup sur, taper sur. 2 **n** a **to give a fly a ~, to take a ~ at a fly** donner un coup de tapette à une mouche. b (*also* **fly ~**) tapette *f*.

swath [swɔːθ] **n, pl ~s** [swɔːðz] (*Agr*) andain *m*. **to cut corn in ~s** couper le blé en andains; **to cut a ~ through sth** ouvrir une voie dans qch.

swathe [sweɪð] 1 **vt** (*bind*) emmailloter (*in* de); (*wrap*) envelopper (*in* dans). **~d in bandages** emmailloté de bandages; **~d in blankets** enveloppé *or* emmitouflé* dans des couvertures. 2 **n** = **swath.**

swatter ['swɒtəʳ] **n** (*also* **fly ~**) tapette *f*.

sway [sweɪ] 1 **n** (*NonC*) a (*motion*) *[rope, hanging object, trees]* balancement *m*, oscillation *f*; *[boat]* balancement, oscillations; *[tower block, bridge]* mouvement *m* oscillatoire, oscillation.
b (*liter*) emprise *f*, empire *m* (*over* sur), domination *f* (*over* de). **to hold ~ over** avoir de l'emprise *or* de l'empire sur, tenir sous son emprise *or* son empire *or* sa domination.
2 **comp** ►**sway-backed** ensellé.
3 **vi** *[tree, rope, hanging object, boat]* se balancer, osciller; *[tower block, bridge]* osciller; *[train]* tanguer; *[person]* tanguer, osciller; (*fig: vacillate*) osciller, balancer (*liter*) (*between* entre). **he stood ~ing (about** *or* **from side to side** *or* **backwards and forwards)** il oscillait (sur ses jambes *or* de droite à gauche *or* d'arrière en avant), il tanguait; **to ~ in/out** *etc* (*from drink, injury*) entrer/sortir *etc* en tanguant; (*regally*) entrer/sortir *etc* majestueusement; **he ~ed towards leniency** il a penché pour la clémence.
4 **vt** a *hanging object* balancer, faire osciller; *hips* rouler, balancer; *[wind]* balancer, agiter; *[waves]* balancer, ballotter.
b (*influence*) influencer, avoir une action déterminante sur. **these factors finally ~ed the committee** ces facteurs ont finalement influencé le choix *or* la décision du comité; **I allowed myself to be ~ed** je me suis laissé influencer; **his speech ~ed the crowd** son discours a eu une

action déterminante sur la foule.

Swazi ['swɑːzɪ] 1 n Swazi(e) *m(f)*. 2 adj swazi.

Swaziland ['swɑːzɪˌlænd] n Swaziland *m.*

swear [swɛəʳ] pret **swore**, ptp **sworn** 1 vt a jurer (*on sth* sur qch, *that* que, *to do* de faire); *fidelity, allegiance* jurer. **I ~ it!** je le jure!; **to ~ an oath** (*solemnly*) prêter serment; (*curse*) lâcher *or* pousser un juron; **to ~ (an oath) to do sth** faire (le) serment *or* jurer de faire qch; (*Jur*) **to ~ a charge against sb** accuser qn sous serment; **I could have sworn he touched it** j'aurais juré qu'il l'avait touché; **I ~ he said so!** il l'a dit je vous le jure, je vous jure qu'il l'a dit; **I ~ I've never enjoyed myself more** ma parole, je ne me suis jamais autant amusé; *see also* **black, oath, sworn** *etc.*

b *witness, jury* faire prêter serment à. **to ~ sb to secrecy** faire jurer le secret à qn.

2 vi a (*take solemn oath etc*) jurer. (*Jur*) **do you so ~? — I ~** ≃ dites "je le jure" — je le jure; **he swore on the Bible/by all that he held dear** il a juré sur la Bible/sur tout ce qu'il avait de plus cher; **to ~ to the truth of sth** jurer que qch est vrai; **would you ~ to having seen him?** est-ce que vous jureriez que vous l'avez vu?; **I think he did but I couldn't** *or* **wouldn't ~ to it** il me semble qu'il l'a fait mais je n'en jurerais pas.

b (*curse*) jurer, pester (*at* contre, après); (*blaspheme*) jurer, blasphémer. **don't ~!** ne jure pas!, ne sois pas grossier!; **to ~ like a trooper** jurer comme un charretier; **it's enough to make you ~*** il y a de quoi vous faire râler*.

3 comp ▸**swearword** gros mot, juron *m.*

▸**swear by** vt fus (*fig*) **he swears by vitamin C tablets** il ne jure que par les vitamines C; **I swear by whisky as a cure for flu** pour moi il n'y a rien de tel que le whisky pour guérir la grippe.

▸**swear in** vt sep *jury, witness, president etc* assermenter, faire prêter serment à.

▸**swear off** vt fus *alcohol, tobacco* jurer de renoncer à. **he has sworn off stealing** il a juré de ne plus voler.

▸**swear out** vt sep (*US Jur*) **to swear out a warrant for sb's arrest** obtenir un mandat d'arrêt contre qn en l'accusant sous serment.

sweat [swet] 1 n a sueur *f*, transpiration *f*; (*fig: on walls etc*) humidité *f*, suintement *m*; (*state*) sueur(s). **by the ~ of his brow** à la sueur de son front; **to be dripping** *or* **covered with ~** ruisseler de sueur, être en nage; **to be in a ~** (*lit*) être en sueur, être couvert de sueur; (* *fig*) avoir des sueurs froides; **he was in a great ~ about it** ça lui donnait des sueurs froides; *see* **cold**.

b (*: *piece of work etc*) corvée *f*. **it was an awful ~** on a eu un mal de chien, on en a bavé⁑; **no ~!⁑** pas de problème!

c (⁑) **an old ~** un vétéran, un vieux routier.

2 comp ▸**sweatband** (*in hat*) cuir intérieur; (*Sport*) bandeau *m* ▸**sweat gland** glande *f* sudoripare ▸**sweats*** npl (tenue *f* de) jogging *m* ▸**sweat shirt** sweat-shirt *m* ▸**sweatshop** atelier *m or* usine *f* où les ouvriers sont exploités ▸**sweat-stained** taché *or* maculé de sueur ▸**sweat suit** survêtement *m*, survêt* *m.*

3 vi [*person, animal*] suer (*with, from* de), être en sueur; [*walls*] suer, suinter; [*cheese etc*] suer. **he was ~ing profusely** il suait à grosses gouttes; **to ~ like a bull** suer comme un bœuf; (*fig*) **he was ~ing over his essay*** il suait sur sa dissertation.

4 vt a *person, animal* faire suer *or* transpirer; (*fig*) *workers* exploiter. **~ed goods** marchandises produites par une main-d'œuvre exploitée; **~ed labour** main-d'œuvre exploitée.

b **to ~ blood*** (*work hard*) suer sang et eau (*over sth* sur qch); (*be anxious*) avoir des sueurs froides; **he was ~ing blood over** *or* **about the exam*** l'examen lui donnait des sueurs froides; (*US fig*) **don't ~ it!⁑** calme-toi!, relaxe!*

▸**sweat off** vt sep: **I've sweated off half a kilo** j'ai perdu un demi-kilo à force de transpirer.

▸**sweat out** vt sep *cold etc* guérir en transpirant. (*fig*) **you'll just have to sweat it out*** il faudra t'armer de patience; **they left him to sweat it out*** ils n'ont rien fait pour l'aider.

sweater ['swetəʳ] 1 n tricot *m*, pull-over *m*, pull* *m.* 2 comp ▸**sweater girl** fille bien roulée*.

sweating ['swetɪŋ] n [*person, animal*] transpiration *f*; (*Med*) sudation *f*; [*wall*] suintement *m.*

sweaty ['swetɪ] adj *body* en sueur; *feet* qui suent; *hand* moite (de sueur); *smell* de sueur; *shirt, sock* mouillé *or* maculé de sueur.

Swede [swiːd] n Suédois(e) *m(f)*.

swede [swiːd] n (*esp Brit*) rutabaga *m.*

Sweden ['swiːdən] n Suède *f.*

Swedenborgian [ˌswiːdən'bɔːdʒɪən] adj swedenborgien.

Swedish ['swiːdɪʃ] 1 adj suédois. **~ gymnastics** *or* **movements** gymnastique *f* suédoise; **~ mile** mile *m* suédois (= 10 km). 2 n a **the S~** les Suédois *mpl.* b (*Ling*) suédois *m.*

sweep [swiːp] (vb: pret, ptp **swept**) 1 n a (*with broom etc*) coup *m* de balai. **to give a room a ~ (out)** donner un coup de balai à *or* balayer une pièce; *see* **clean**.

b (*also* **chimney ~**) ramoneur *m*; *see* **black**.

c (*movement*) [*arm*] grand geste; [*sword*] grand coup; [*scythe*] mouvement *m* circulaire; [*net*] coup; [*lighthouse beam, radar beam*] trajectoire *f*; [*tide*] progression *f* irrésistible; (*fig*) [*progress, events*] marche *f*. **in** *or* **with one ~** d'un seul coup; **with a ~ of his arm** d'un geste large; **to make a ~ of the horizon** (*with binoculars*) parcourir l'horizon; [*lighthouse beam*] balayer l'horizon; **to make a ~ for mines** draguer des mines; **the police made a ~ of the district** la police a ratissé le quartier.

d (*range*) [*telescope, gun, lighthouse, radar*] champ *m.* **with a ~ of 180°** avec un champ de 180°.

e (*curve, line*) [*coastline, hills, road, river*] grande courbe; (*Archit*) courbure *f*, voussure *f*; [*curtains, long skirt*] drapé *m.* **a wide ~ of meadowland** une vaste étendue de prairie; (*Aut, Aviat, Naut etc*) **the graceful ~ of her lines** sa ligne aérodynamique *or* son galbe plein(e) de grâce.

f (*) (abbr of **sweepstake**) *see* **2.**

2 comp ▸**sweepback** [*aircraft wing etc*] dessin *m* en flèche arrière, angle *m* flèche ▸**sweep hand** [*clock etc*] trotteuse *f* ▸**sweepstake** sweepstake *m.*

3 vt a *room, floor, street etc* balayer; *chimney* ramoner; (*Naut*) *river, channel* draguer; (*fig*) [*waves, hurricane, bullets, searchlights, skirts*] balayer. **to ~ a room clean** donner un bon coup de balai dans une pièce; (*Naut*) **to ~ sth clean of mines** déminer qch; (*fig*) **he swept the horizon with his binoculars** il a parcouru l'horizon avec ses jumelles; **his eyes/his glance swept the room** il a parcouru la pièce des yeux/du regard; **their fleet swept the seas in search of ...** leur flotte a sillonné *or* parcouru les mers à la recherche de ...; **a wave of indignation swept the city** une vague d'indignation a déferlé sur la ville; *see* **broom** *etc.*

b *dust, snow etc* balayer; (*Naut*) *mines* draguer, enlever. **he swept the rubbish off the pavement** il a enlevé les ordures du trottoir d'un coup de balai; **she swept the snow into a heap** elle a balayé la neige et en a fait un tas; (*fig*) **to ~ sth under the carpet** *or* **rug** tirer le rideau sur qch; **to ~ sth off the table on to the floor** faire tomber qch de la table par terre d'un geste large; **to ~ sth into a bag** faire glisser qch d'un geste large dans un sac; (*fig*) **to ~ everything before one** remporter un succès total, réussir sur toute la ligne; (*fig*) **to ~ the board** remporter un succès complet, tout rafler*; **the socialists swept the board at the election** les socialistes ont remporté l'élection haut la main; (*fig*) **he swept the obstacles from his path** il a balayé *or* écarté les obstacles qui se trouvaient sur son chemin; **the army swept the enemy before them** l'armée a balayé l'ennemi devant elle; **the crowd swept him into the square** la foule l'a emporté *or* entraîné sur la place, il a été pris dans le mouvement de la foule et il s'est retrouvé sur la place; **the wave swept him overboard** la vague l'a jeté par-dessus bord; **the gale swept the caravan over the cliff** la rafale a emporté la caravane et l'a précipitée du haut de la falaise; **the current swept the boat downstream** le courant a emporté le bateau; **to be swept off one's feet** (*by wind, flood etc*) être emporté (*by* par); (*fig*) être enthousiasmé *or* emballé* (*by* par); **the water swept him off his feet** le courant lui a fait perdre pied; (*fig*) **he swept her off her feet** elle a eu le coup de foudre pour lui; (*fig*) **this election swept the socialists into office** *or* **power** cette élection a porté les socialistes au pouvoir avec une forte majorité.

4 vi a (*pass swiftly*) [*person, vehicle, convoy*] **to ~ in/out/along** *etc* entrer/sortir/avancer *etc* rapidement; **the car swept round the corner** la voiture a pris le virage comme un bolide; **the planes went ~ing across the sky** les avions sillonnaient le ciel; **the rain swept across the plain** la pluie a balayé la plaine; **panic swept through the city** la panique s'est emparée de la ville; **plague swept through the country** la peste a ravagé le pays.

b (*move impressively*) [*person, procession*] **to ~ in/out/along** *etc* entrer/sortir/avancer *etc* majestueusement; **she came ~ing into the room** elle a fait une entrée majestueuse dans la pièce; (*fig: Pol*) **to ~ into office** être porté au pouvoir; **the royal car swept down the avenue** la voiture royale a descendu l'avenue d'une manière imposante; (*fig*) **the motorway ~s across the hills** l'autoroute s'élance à travers les collines; **the forests ~ down to the sea** les forêts descendent en pente douce jusqu'au bord de la mer; **the bay ~s away to the south** la baie décrit une courbe majestueuse vers le sud; **the Alps ~ down to the coast** les Alpes descendent majestueusement vers la côte.

▸**sweep along** 1 vi *see* **sweep 4a, 4b.** 2 vt sep [*crowd, flood, current, gale*] emporter, entraîner; [*leaves*] balayer.

▸**sweep aside** vt sep *object, person* repousser, écarter; *suggestion, objection* repousser, rejeter; *difficulty, obstacle* écarter.

▸**sweep away** 1 vi (*leave*) (*rapidly*) s'éloigner rapidement; (*impressively*) s'éloigner majestueusement *or* d'une manière imposante; *see also* **sweep 4b.** 2 vt sep *dust, snow, rubbish* balayer; [*crowd, flood, current, gale*] entraîner. **they swept him away to lunch** ils l'ont entraîné pour aller déjeuner.

▸**sweep down** 1 vi *see* **sweep 4b.** 2 vt sep *walls etc* nettoyer avec un balai; [*flood, gale etc*] emporter. **the river swept the logs down to the sea** les bûches ont flotté sur la rivière jusqu'à la mer.

▸**sweep off** = **sweep away.**

▸**sweep out** 1 vi *see* **sweep 4a, 4b.** 2 vt sep *room, dust, rubbish* balayer.

▸**sweep up** 1 vi a (*with broom etc*) **to sweep up after sb** balayer les débris *or* les saletés de qn; **to sweep up after a party** balayer quand les invités sont partis. b **he swept up to me** il s'est approché de moi (*angrily*) avec furie *or* (*impressively*) majestueusement; **the car swept up to the house** la voiture a remonté l'allée jusqu'à la maison (*fast*) rapidement *or* (*impressively*) d'une manière imposante. 2 **vt sep** *snow, leaves, dust etc* balayer. **she swept up the letters and took them away** elle a ramassé les lettres d'un geste brusque et les a emportées.

sweeper ['swiːpəʳ] **n** a (*worker*) balayeur *m.* b (*machine*) balayeuse *f*; (*carpet* ~) balai *m* mécanique; (*vacuum cleaner*) aspirateur *m.* c (*Ftbl*) arrière *m* volant.

sweeping ['swiːpɪŋ] 1 **adj** a *movement, gesture* large; *bow, curtsy* profond; *glance* circulaire; *coastline* qui décrit une courbe majestueuse; *skirts* qui balaient le sol. b *change, reorganization* radical, fondamental; *reduction* considérable; *price cut* imbattable. (*Pol: at election*) ~ **gains/losses** progression *f*/recul *m* considérable *or* très net(te); ~ **statement,** ~ **generalization** généralisation hâtive; **that's pretty** ~! c'est beaucoup dire! 2 **npl:** ~**s** balayures *fpl*, ordures *fpl*; (*fig: of society etc*) rebut *m.*

sweet [swiːt] 1 **adj** a *taste, tea, biscuit* sucré; *cider, wine, apple, orange etc* doux (*f* douce). **a litre of** ~ **cider** *etc* un litre de cidre *etc* doux; **this cider** *etc* **is too sweet** ce cidre *etc* est trop sucré *or* doux; **to have a** ~ **tooth** être friand de sucreries; **I love** ~ **things** j'aime les sucreries *fpl*; (*Culin*) ~ **and sour** aigre-doux (*f* aigre-douce); **sickly** ~ (*gen*) douceâtre; *smell* fétide.

b (*fig*) *milk, air, breath* frais (*f* fraîche); *water* pur; *soil* sain; *scent* agréable, suave; *sound, voice* harmonieux, mélodieux; *running of engine, machine* sans à-coups; *revenge, success, character, face, smile* doux (*f* douce). (*fig*) **the** ~ **smell of success** la douceur exquise du succès; **it was** ~ **to his ear** c'était doux à son oreille; (*pej*) ~ **words** flagorneries *fpl*; **she is a very** ~ **person** elle est vraiment très gentille, elle est tout à fait charmante; **that was very** ~ **of her** c'était très gentil de sa part; **he carried on in his own** ~ **way** il a continué comme il l'entendait; **he'll do it in his own** ~ **time** il le fera quand ça lui dira*; **he'll please his own** ~ **self** il n'en fera qu'à sa tête; **at his own** ~ **will** à son gré; **to keep sb** ~* cultiver les bonnes grâces de qn; **do keep him** ~!* tu as intérêt à cultiver ses bonnes grâces; **to be** ~ **on sb*** avoir le béguin pour qn*, être amoureux de qn; *see* **Fanny, nothing, sixteen** *etc.*

c (**: attractive*) *child, dog* mignon, adorable, gentil; *house, hat, dress* mignon, gentillet. **a** ~ **old lady** une adorable vieille dame; **what a** ~ **little baby!** le mignon petit bébé!

2 **adv: to smell** ~ sentir bon; **to taste** ~ avoir un goût sucré.

3 **n** (*esp Brit: candy*) bonbon *m*; (*Brit: dessert*) dessert *m.* (*fig*) **the** ~**s of success/solitude** *etc* les délices *fpl* de la réussite/de la solitude *etc;* **come here, (my)** ~* viens ici, mon ange.

4 **comp** ►**sweetbread** ris *m* de veau *or* d'agneau ►**sweetbriar, sweetbrier** églantier odorant ►**sweet chestnut** châtaigne *f*, marron *m* ►**sweetcorn** maïs *m* ►**sweetheart** petit(e) ami(e) *m(f)*, bien-aimé(e)† *m(f)*; **yes sweetheart** oui chéri(e) *or* mon ange *or* mon cœur ►**sweet herbs** fines herbes ►**sweetmeat** sucrerie *f*, confiserie *f* ►**sweet-natured** d'un naturel doux ►**sweet pea** pois *m* de senteur ►**sweet pepper** piment *m* doux, piment (vert *or* rouge) ►**sweet potato** patate *f* (douce) ►**sweet-scented** parfumé, odoriférant, odorant ►**sweetshop** (*Brit*) confiserie *f* (*souvent avec papeterie, journaux et tabac*) ►**sweet-smelling** = **sweet-scented** ►**sweet talk** flagorneries *fpl* ►**sweet-talk** flagorner ►**sweet-tempered** = **sweet-natured** ►**sweet william** œillet *m* de poète.

sweeten ['swiːtn] 1 **vt** a *coffee, sauce etc* sucrer; *air* purifier; *room* assainir. b (*fig*) *person, sb's temper, task* adoucir. c (**: also* ~ **up**) (*give incentive to*) amadouer; (*bribe*) graisser la patte à*; *see* **pill.** 2 **vi** *[person, sb's temper]* s'adoucir.

sweetener ['swiːtnəʳ] **n** a (*for coffee, food*) édulcorant *m.* b (** fig*) (*incentive*) carotte* *f*; (*bribe*) pot-de-vin *m*; (*compensation*) quelque chose *m* pour faire passer la pilule*, lot *m* de consolation.

sweetening ['swiːtnɪŋ] **n** (*NonC*) a (*substance*) édulcorant *m.* b (*see* **sweeten**) sucrage *m*; adoucissement *m.*

sweetie* ['swiːtɪ] **n** a (*person: also* ~**-pie**⁑) **he's/she's a** ~ il/elle est chou*, c'est un ange; **yes** ~ oui mon chou* *or* mon ange. b (*esp Scot: candy*) bonbon *m.*

sweetish ['swiːtɪʃ] **n** au goût sucré, douceâtre (*pej*).

sweetly ['swiːtlɪ] **adv** *sing, play* mélodieusement; *smile, answer* gentiment. **the engine is running** ~ le moteur marche sans à-coups.

sweetness ['swiːtnɪs] **n** (*to taste*) goût sucré; (*in smell*) odeur *f* suave; (*to hearing*) son mélodieux *or* harmonieux; *[person, nature, character, expression]* douceur *f.* (*fig*) **to be all** ~ **and light** être tout douceur.

swell [swel] (**vb: pret swelled, ptp swollen** *or* **swelled**) 1 **n** a *[sea]* houle *f.* **heavy** ~ forte houle; *see* **ground.**

b (*Mus*) crescendo *m inv* (et diminuendo *m inv*); (*on organ*) boîte expressive.

c (**†: stylish person*) personne huppée*, gandin *m* (*pej*). **the** ~**s** les gens huppés*, le gratin*.

2 **adj** a (**: stylish*) *clothes* chic *inv*; *house, car, restaurant* chic, rupin⁑; *relatives, friends* huppé*.

b (**: esp US: excellent*) sensationnel*, formidable*. **a** ~ **guy** un type sensationnel* *or* vachement bien*; **that's** ~ c'est formidable* *or* sensass* *inv.*

3 **comp** ►**swell box** (*Mus*) boîte expressive ►**swellhead*** (*esp US*) bêcheur* *m*, -euse* *f* ►**swellheaded*** bêcheur* ►**swellheadedness*** vanité *f*, suffisance *f.*

4 **vi** a (*also* ~ **up**) *[balloon, tyre, airbed]* (se) gonfler; *[sails]* se gonfler; *[ankle, arm, eye, face]* enfler; *[wood]* gonfler. (*fig*) **to** ~ **(up) with pride** se gonfler d'orgueil; **to** ~ **(up) with rage/indignation** s'emplir de rage/d'indignation.

b (*increase*) *[river]* grossir; *[sound, music, voice]* s'enfler; *[numbers, population, membership]* grossir, augmenter. **the numbers soon** ~**ed to 500** les nombres ont vite augmenté *or* grossi pour atteindre 500, les nombres se sont vite élevés à 500; **the little group soon** ~**ed into a crowd** le petit groupe est vite devenu une foule; **the murmuring** ~**ed to a roar** le murmure s'enfla pour devenir un rugissement.

5 **vt** *sail* gonfler; *sound* enfler; *river, lake* grossir; *number* grossir, augmenter. **this** ~**ed the membership/population to 1,500** ceci a porté à 1 500 le nombre des membres/le total de la population; **population swollen by refugees** population grossie par les réfugiés; **river swollen by rain** rivière grossie par les pluies, rivière en crue; **a second edition swollen by a mass of new material** une deuxième édition augmentée par une quantité de documents nouveaux; **to be swollen with pride** être gonflé *or* bouffi d'orgueil; **to be swollen with rage** bouillir de rage; *see also* **swollen** *etc.*

►**swell out** 1 **vi** *[sails etc]* se gonfler. 2 **vt sep** gonfler.

►**swell up vi** = **swell 4a.**

swelling ['swelɪŋ] 1 **n** a (*Med*) enflure *f*; (*lump*) grosseur *f*; (*bruising*) enflure, tuméfaction *f*; (*on tyre etc*) hernie *f.* b (*NonC: see* **swell 4**) enflement *m*; gonflement *m.* 2 **adj** *jaw etc* qui enfle; *sail* gonflé; *sound, chorus, voices* qui enfle; *line, curve* galbé.

swelter ['sweltəʳ] **vi** étouffer de chaleur.

sweltering ['sweltərɪŋ] **adj** *weather, heat, afternoon* étouffant, oppressant. **it's** ~ **in here** on étouffe de chaleur ici.

swept [swept] 1 **pret, ptp of sweep.** 2 **comp** ►**sweptback** (*Aviat*) en flèche; *hair* rejeté en arrière ►**sweptwing aircraft** avion *m* à ailes en flèche.

swerve [swɜːv] 1 **vi** *[boxer, fighter]* faire un écart; *[ball]* dévier; *[vehicle, ship]* faire une embardée; *[driver]* donner un coup de volant; (*fig*) dévier (*from* de). **the car** ~**d away from the lorry on to the verge** la voiture a fait une embardée pour éviter le camion et est montée sur l'accotement; **he** ~**d round the bollard** il a viré sur les chapeaux de roues autour de la borne lumineuse. 2 **vt** *ball* faire dévier; *car etc* faire faire une embardée à. 3 **n** *[vehicle, ship]* embardée *f*; *[boxer, fighter]* écart *m.*

swift [swɪft] 1 **adj** *reaction, response, revenge, victory* prompt, rapide; *vehicle, journey* rapide; *movement* vif, leste. **they were** ~ **to act** ils ont été prompts à agir, ils ont agi sans tarder; (*liter*) ~ **to anger** prompt à la colère *or* à se mettre en colère. 2 **comp** ►**swift-flowing** au cours rapide ►**swift-footed** (*liter*) au pied léger. 3 **n** (*Orn*) martinet *m.*

swiftly ['swɪftlɪ] **adv** rapidement, vite.

swiftness ['swɪftnɪs] **n** (*see* **swift 1**) rapidité *f*, vitesse *f*; promptitude *f.*

swig* [swɪg] 1 **n** lampée* *f*, (*larger*) coup *m.* **to take a** ~ **at a bottle** boire un coup à même la bouteille. 2 **vt** lamper*.

►**swig down* vt sep** avaler d'un trait.

swill [swɪl] 1 **n** a (*NonC*) (*for pigs etc*) pâtée *f*; (*garbage, slops*) eaux grasses. b **to give sth a** ~ **(out** *or* **down)** = **to swill sth (out** *or* **down)**; *see* **2a.** 2 **vt** a (*also* ~ **out,** ~ **down**) *floor* laver à grande eau; *glass* rincer. b (**: drink*) boire avidement, boire à grands traits.

swim [swɪm] (**vb: pret swam, ptp swum**) 1 **n: to go for a** ~, **to have** *or* **take a** ~ (*in sea etc*) aller nager *or* se baigner; (*in* ~*ming baths*) aller à la piscine; **it's time for our** ~ c'est l'heure de la baignade; **after a 2 km** ~ après avoir fait 2 km à la nage; **Channel** ~ traversée *f* de la Manche à la nage; **it's a long** ~ voilà une bonne *or* longue distance à parcourir à la nage; **I had a lovely** ~ ça m'a fait du bien de nager comme ça; (*fig*) **to be in the** ~ être dans le mouvement.

2 **comp** ►**swimsuit** maillot *m* (de bain).

3 **vi** a *[person]* nager, (*as sport*) faire de la natation; *[fish, animal]* nager. **to go** ~**ming** (*in sea etc*) aller nager, aller se baigner; (*in* ~*ming baths*) aller à la piscine; **to** ~ **away/back** *etc [person]* s'éloigner/revenir *etc* à la nage; *[fish]* s'éloigner/revenir *etc;* **to** ~ **across a river** traverser une rivière à la nage; **he swam under the boat** il est passé sous le bateau (à la nage); **to** ~ **under water** nager sous l'eau; **he had to** ~ **for it** son seul recours a été de se sauver à la nage *or* de se jeter à l'eau et de nager; (*fig*) **to** ~ **with the tide** suivre le courant.

b (*fig*) **the meat was** ~**ming in gravy** la viande nageait *or* baignait dans la sauce; **her eyes were** ~**ming (with tears)** ses yeux étaient noyés *or* baignés de larmes; **the bathroom was** ~**ming** la salle de bains était inondée; **the room was** ~**ming round** *or* ~**ming before his eyes** la pièce semblait tourner autour de lui; **his head was** ~**ming** la tête lui tournait.

4 **vt** *lake, river* traverser à la nage. **it was first swum in 1900** la première traversée à la nage a eu lieu en 1900; **he can** ~ **10 km** il peut faire 10 km à la nage; **he can** ~ **2 lengths** il peut nager *or* faire 2 longueurs; **before he had swum 10 strokes** avant qu'il ait pu faire *or* nager 10 brasses; **I can't** ~ **a stroke** je suis incapable de faire une

brasse; **can you ~ the crawl?** savez-vous nager *or* faire le crawl?

swimmer ['swɪmə^r] **n** nageur *m*, -euse *f*.

swimming ['swɪmɪŋ] **1 n** (*gen*) nage *f*; (*Sport, Scol*) natation *f*. **2 comp ►swimming bath(s)** (*Brit*) piscine *f* **►swimming cap** bonnet *m* de bain **►swimming costume** (*Brit*) maillot *m* (de bain) une pièce **►swimming crab** étrille *f* **►swimming gala** fête *f* de natation **►swimming pool** piscine *f* **►swimming ring** bouée *f* **►swimming suit** maillot *m* (de bain) **►swimming trunks** maillot *m or* caleçon *m or* slip *m* de bain.

swimmingly ['swɪmɪŋlɪ] **adv: to go ~** se dérouler sans accrocs *or* à merveille; **it's all going ~** tout marche comme sur des roulettes.

swindle ['swɪndl] **1 n** escroquerie *f*. **it's a ~** c'est du vol, nous nous sommes fait estamper* *or* rouler*. **2 vt** escroquer, estamper*, rouler*. **to ~ sb out of his money, to ~ sb's money out of him** escroquer de l'argent à qn.

swindler ['swɪndlə^r] **n** escroc *m*.

swine [swaɪn] **1 n, pl inv** (*Zool*) pourceau *m*, porc *m*; (*‡ fig: person*) salaud‡ *m*. **you ~!‡** espèce de salaud!‡ **2 comp ►swineherd††** porcher *m*, -ère *f*.

swing [swɪŋ] (**vb: pret, ptp swung**) **1 n a** (*movement*) balancement *m*; *[pendulum]* (*movement*) mouvement *m* de va-et-vient, oscillations *fpl*; (*arc, distance*) arc *m*; *[instrument pointer, needle]* oscillations; (*Boxing, Golf*) swing *m*. **the ~ of the boom sent him overboard** le retour de la bôme l'a jeté par-dessus bord; **he gave the starting handle a ~** il a donné un tour de manivelle; **the golfer took a ~ at the ball** le joueur de golf a essayé de frapper *or* a frappé la balle avec un swing; **to take a ~ at sb** décocher *or* lancer un coup de poing à qn; (*fig*) **the ~ of the pendulum brought him back to power** le mouvement du pendule l'a ramené au pouvoir; (*Pol*) **the socialists need a ~ of 5% to win the election** il faudrait aux socialistes un revirement d'opinion en leur faveur de l'ordre de 5% pour qu'ils remportent (*subj*) l'élection; (*Pol*) **a ~ to the left** un revirement en faveur de la gauche; (*St Ex*) **the ~s of the market** les fluctuations *fpl or* les hauts et les bas *mpl* du marché.

b (*rhythm*) *[dance etc]* rythme *m*; *[jazz music]* swing *m*. **to walk with a ~ (in one's step)** marcher d'un pas rythmé; **music/poetry with a ~ to it** *or* **that goes with a ~** musique/poésie rythmée *or* entraînante; (*fig*) **to go with a ~** *[evening, party]* marcher du tonnerre*; *[business, shop]* très bien marcher; **to be in full ~** *[party, election, campaign]* battre son plein; *[business]* être en plein rendement, gazer*; **to get into the ~ of things** se mettre dans le bain.

c (*scope, freedom*) **they gave him full ~ in the matter** ils lui ont donné carte blanche en la matière; **he was given full ~ to make decisions** on l'a laissé entièrement libre de prendre des décisions; **he gave his imagination full ~** il a donné libre cours à son imagination.

d (*seat for ~ing*) balançoire *f*. **to have a ~** se balancer, faire de la balançoire; **to give a child a ~** pousser un enfant qui se balance; (*fig*) **what you gain on the ~s you lose on the roundabouts, (it's) ~s and roundabouts*** ce qu'on gagne d'un côté on le perd de l'autre.

e (*also* **~ music**) swing *m*.

2 comp ►swing band (*Mus*) orchestre *m* de swing **►swing bridge** pont tournant **►swing door** (*Brit*) porte battante **►swing music** *see* **swing 1e ►swing-wing** (*Aviat*) à géométrie variable.

3 vi a (*hang, oscillate*) *[arms, legs]* se balancer, être ballant; *[object on rope etc]* se balancer, pendiller, osciller; *[hammock]* se balancer; *[pendulum]* osciller; (*on a swing*) se balancer; (*pivot: also* **~ round**) tourner, pivoter; *[person]* se retourner, virevolter. **he was left ~ing by his hands** il s'est retrouvé seul suspendu par les mains; **to ~ to and fro** se balancer; **the load swung (round) through the air as the crane turned** comme la grue pivotait la charge a décrit une courbe dans l'air; **the ship was ~ing at anchor** le bateau se balançait sur son ancre; **he swung across on the rope** agrippé à la corde il s'est élancé et a *or* est passé de l'autre côté; **the monkey swung from branch to branch** le singe se balançait de branche en branche; **he swung up the rope ladder** il a grimpé prestement à l'échelle de corde; **he swung (up) into the saddle** il a sauté en selle; **the door swung open/shut** la porte s'est ouverte/s'est refermée; **he swung (round) on his heel** il a virevolté.

b (*move rhythmically*) **to ~ along/away** *etc* avancer/s'éloigner *etc* d'un pas rythmé *or* allègre; **the regiment went ~ing past the king** le régiment a défilé au pas cadencé devant le roi; **to ~ into action** *[army etc]* se mettre en branle; (*fig*) passer à l'action; (*fig*) **music that really ~s** musique *f* au rythme entraînant.

c (*change direction: often* **~ round**) *[plane, vehicle]* virer (*to the south etc* au sud *etc*). **the convoy swung (round) into the square** le convoi a viré pour aller sur la place; **the river ~s north here** ici la rivière décrit une courbe *or* oblique vers le nord; (*fig Pol*) **the country has swung to the right** le pays a viré *or* effectué un virage à droite.

d to ~ at a ball frapper *or* essayer de frapper une balle avec un swing; **to ~ at sb** décocher *or* lancer un coup de poing à qn; **he swung at me with the axe** il a brandi la hache pour me frapper.

e (*‡: be hanged*) être pendu. **he'll ~ for it** on lui mettra la corde au cou pour cela; **I'd ~ for him** je le tuerais si je le tenais.

f (*) (*be fashionable*) être branché*, être dans le vent; (*go to parties etc*) partouzer‡.

4 vt a (*move to and fro*) *one's arms, legs, umbrella, hammock* balancer; *object on rope* balancer, faire osciller; *pendulum* faire osciller; *child on swing* pousser; (*brandish*) brandir. **he swung his sword above his head** il a fait un moulinet avec l'épée au-dessus de sa tête; **he swung his axe at the tree** il a brandi sa hache pour frapper l'arbre; **he swung his racket at the ball** il a ramené sa raquette pour frapper la balle; **he swung the box (up) on to the roof of the car** il a envoyé la boîte sur le toit de la voiture; **he swung the case (up) on to his shoulders** il a balancé la valise sur ses épaules; **he swung himself across the stream/over the wall** *etc* il s'est élancé et a franchi le ruisseau/et a sauté par-dessus le mur *etc*; **to ~ o.s. (up) into the saddle** sauter en selle; **to ~ one's hips** rouler *or* balancer les hanches, se déhancher; (*Brit fig*) **to ~ the lead*** tirer au flanc*; *see* **room**.

b (*turn: often* **~ round**) *propeller* lancer; *starting handle* tourner. **to ~ a door open/shut** ouvrir/fermer une porte; **he swung the ship (round) through 180°** il a viré de 180°, il a fait virer (le bateau) de 180°; **he swung the car round the corner** il a viré au coin.

c (*fig: influence*) *election, decision* influencer; *voters* faire changer d'opinion. **his speech swung the decision against us** son discours a provoqué un revirement et la décision est allée contre nous; **he managed to ~ the deal*** il a réussi à emporter l'affaire; **to ~ it on sb‡** tirer une carotte à qn*, pigeonner qn*.

d (*Mus*) *a tune, the classics etc* jouer de manière rythmée.

►swing round 1 vi *[person]* se retourner, virevolter; *[crane etc]* tourner, pivoter; *[ship, plane, convoy, procession]* virer; *[car, truck]* virer, (*after collision etc*) faire un tête-à-queue; (*fig*) *[voters]* virer de bord; *[opinions etc]* connaître un revirement; *see also* **swing 3a, 3c. 2 vt sep** *object on rope etc* faire tourner; *sword, axe* brandir, faire des moulinets avec; *crane etc* faire pivoter; *car, ship, plane, convoy, procession* faire tourner *or* virer; *see also* **swing 4b**.

►swing to vi *[door]* se refermer.

swingeing ['swɪndʒɪŋ] **adj** *blow, attack* violent; *defeat, majority* écrasant; *damages, taxation, price increases* considérable, énorme.

swinger* ['swɪŋə^r] **n: he's a ~** (*with it*) il est branché* *or* dans le vent; (*going to parties*) c'est un partouzard‡ *or* un noceur*; (*sexually*) il couche à droite et à gauche.

swinging ['swɪŋɪŋ] **adj** *step* rythmé; *music* rythmé, entraînant; *rhythm* entraînant, endiablé; (*fig*) (*lively*) dynamique; (*modern, fashionable etc*) dans le vent, à la page. (*US*) **~ door** porte battante; **the party was really ~** la surprise-partie était du tonnerre* *or* à tout casser*; **~ London** le "swinging London"; **London was really ~ then** on rigolait* bien à Londres dans ce temps-là.

swingometer [swɪŋ'ɒmɪtə^r] **n** (*at election*) indicateur *m* de tendances.

swinish‡ ['swaɪnɪʃ] **adj** dégueulasse‡.

swipe [swaɪp] **1 n** (*) (*at ball etc*) grand coup; (*slap*) gifle *f*, calotte* *f*, baffe‡ *f*. **to take a ~ at = to swipe at**; *see* **3**. **2 vt a** (*: *hit*) *ball* frapper à toute volée; *person* calotter* *or* gifler à toute volée. **b** (*‡: steal: often hum*) calotter‡, piquer* (*sth from sb* qch à qn). **3 vi** (*) **to ~ at** *ball etc* frapper *or* essayer de frapper à toute volée; *person* flanquer* une gifle *or* une calotte* à.

swirl [swɜːl] **1 n** (*in river, sea*) tourbillon *m*, remous *m*; *[dust, sand]* tourbillon; *[smoke]* tourbillon, volute *f*; (*fig*) *[cream, ice cream etc]* volute; *[lace, ribbons etc]* tourbillon. **the ~ of the dancers' skirts** le tourbillon *or* le tournoiement des jupes des danseuses. **2 vi** *[water, river, sea]* tourbillonner, faire des remous *or* des tourbillons; *[dust, sand, smoke, skirts]* tourbillonner, tournoyer. **3 vt** *[river etc]* **to ~ sth along/away** entraîner/emporter qch en tourbillonnant; **he ~ed his partner round the room** il a fait tournoyer *or* tourbillonner sa partenaire autour de la salle.

swish [swɪʃ] **1 n** *[whip]* sifflement *m*; *[water, person in long grass]* bruissement *m*; *[grass in wind]* frémissement *m*, bruissement; *[tyres in rain]* glissement *m*; *[skirts]* bruissement, froufrou *m* soyeux. **2 vt a** *whip, cane* faire siffler. **b** (*‡: beat, cane*) administrer *or* donner des coups de trique à. **3 vi** *[cane, whip]* siffler, cingler l'air; *[water]* bruire; *[long grass]* frémir, bruire; *[skirts]* bruire, froufrouter. **4 adj** (*) = **swishy**.

swishy‡ ['swɪʃɪ] **adj** (*Brit: smart*) rupin‡; (*US: effeminate*) efféminé, du genre tapette‡.

Swiss [swɪs] **1 adj** suisse. **~ French/German** suisse romand/allemand; **the ~ Guards** la garde (pontificale) suisse; (*Brit Culin*) **~ roll** gâteau *m* roulé; (*US Culin*) **~ steak** *steak fariné et braisé aux tomates et aux oignons*. **2 n, pl inv** Suisse(sse) *m(f)*. **the ~** les Suisses.

switch [swɪtʃ] **1 n a** (*Elec*) (*gen*) bouton *m* électrique, commande *f* (*esp Tech*); (*for lights*) interrupteur *m*, commutateur *m*; (*Aut: also* **ignition ~**) contact *m*. (*Elec*) **the ~ was on/off** le bouton était sur la position ouvert/fermé, c'était allumé/éteint.

b (*Rail: points*) aiguille *f*, aiguillage *m*.

c (*transfer*) *[opinion]* changement *m*, revirement *m*, retournement *m*; *[allegiance etc]* changement; *[funds]* transfert *m* (*from* de, *to* en faveur de). **his ~ to Labour** son revirement en faveur des travaillistes; (*Bridge: in bidding*) **the ~ to hearts/clubs** (le changement de couleur et) le passage à cœur/trèfle; **the ~ of the 8.30 from platform 4** le changement de voie du train de 8.30 attendu au quai 4; **the ~ of the aircraft from Heathrow to Gatwick because of fog** le détournement sur Gatwick à cause du brouillard de l'avion attendu à Heathrow.

d (*stick*) baguette *f*; (*cane*) canne *f*; (*riding crop*) cravache *f*; (*whip*) fouet *m*.

e *[hair]* postiche *m*.

2 comp ▶**switchback** n (*Brit: at fair; also road*) montagnes *fpl* russes ◊ adj (*up and down*) tout en montées et descentes; (*zigzag*) en épingles à cheveux ▶**switchblade** (**knife**) (*US*) couteau *m* à cran d'arrêt ▶**switchboard** (*Elec*) tableau *m* de distribution; (*Telec*) standard *m*; (*Telec*) **switchboard operator** standardiste *mf* ▶**switch-car** (*for gangster: in escape etc*) voiture-relais *f* ▶**switch hit** vi (*Baseball*) frapper la balle indifféremment de la main droite ou de la main gauche ▶**switch-hitter** (*Baseball*) batteur *m* indifféremment gaucher *or* droitier; (*US* ‡: *bisexual*) bisexuel(le) *m(f)* ▶**switchman** (*Rail*) aiguilleur *m* ▶**switchover**: **the switchover from A to B** le passage de A à B; **the switchover to the metric system** l'adoption *f* du système métrique ▶**switchyard** (*US Rail*) gare *f* de triage.

3 vt a (*transfer*) *one's support, allegiance, attention* reporter (*from* de, *to* sur). (*Ind*) **to ~ production to another factory** transférer la production dans une autre usine; (*Ind*) **to ~ production to another model** (cesser de produire l'ancien modèle et) se mettre à produire un nouveau modèle; **to ~ the conversation to another subject** détourner la conversation, changer de sujet de conversation.

b (*exchange*) échanger (*A for B* A contre B, *sth with sb* qch avec qn); (*also ~* **over**, **~ round**) *two objects, letters in word, figures in column* intervertir, permuter; (*rearrange: also ~* **round**) *books, objects* changer de place. **we had to ~ taxis when the first broke down** nous avons dû changer de taxi quand le premier est tombé en panne; **to ~ plans** changer de projet; **we have ~ed all the furniture round** nous avons changé tous les meubles de place.

c (*Rail*) aiguiller (*to another track* sur une autre voie).

d (*Elec etc*) **to ~ the heater to "low"** mettre le radiateur sur "doux"; **to ~ the radio/TV to another programme** changer de station/de chaîne; *see also* **switch back, switch on** *etc*.

e **to ~ the grass with one's cane** cingler l'herbe avec sa canne; **the cow ~ed her tail** la vache fouettait l'air de sa queue; **he ~ed it out of my hand** il me l'a arraché de la main.

4 vi a (*transfer: also ~* **over**) **Paul ~ed (over) to Conservative** Paul a voté conservateur cette fois; **we ~ed (over) to oil central heating** (nous avons changé et) nous avons maintenant fait installer le chauffage central au mazout; **many have ~ed (over) to teaching** beaucoup se sont recyclés dans l'enseignement.

b *[tail etc]* battre l'air.

▶**switch back** 1 vi (*to original plan, product, allegiance etc*) revenir, retourner (*to* à). (*Rad, TV*) **to switch back to the other programme** remettre l'autre émission. 2 vt sep: **to switch the heater back to "low"** remettre le radiateur sur "doux"; **to switch the light back on** rallumer; **to switch the heater/oven back on** rallumer le radiateur/le four. 3 **switchback** n, adj *see* **switch 2**.

▶**switch off** 1 vi a (*Elec*) éteindre; (*Rad, TV*) éteindre *or* fermer le poste. (*fig*) **when the conversation is boring, he just switches off*** quand la conversation l'ennuie, il décroche*.

b *[heater, oven etc]* **to switch off automatically** s'éteindre tout seul *or* automatiquement.

2 vt sep *light* éteindre; *electricity, gas* éteindre, fermer; *radio, television, heater* éteindre, fermer, arrêter; *alarm clock, burglar alarm* arrêter. (*Rad, TV*) **he switched the programme off** il a fermé *or* éteint le poste; (*Aut*) **to switch off the engine** couper l'allumage, arrêter le moteur; **the oven switches itself off** le four s'éteint automatiquement; (*fig*) **he seems to be switched off* most of the time** il semble être détaché des autres la plupart du temps.

▶**switch on** 1 vi a (*Elec*) allumer; (*Rad, TV*) allumer le poste. b *[heater, oven etc]* **to switch on automatically** s'allumer tout seul *or* automatiquement. 2 vt sep *gas, electricity* allumer; *water supply* ouvrir; *radio, television, heater* allumer, brancher; *engine, machine* mettre en marche. **to switch on the light** allumer; (*fig*) **his music switches me on**‡ sa musique m'excite *or* me rend euphorique; (*fig*) **to be switched on**‡ (*up-to-date*) être branché*, être dans le vent *or* à la page; (*by drugs*) planer*, être sous l'influence de la drogue; (*sexually*) être tout excité *or* émoustillé (*by* par).

▶**switch over** 1 vi a = **switch 4a**. b (*TV/Rad*) changer de chaîne/de station. (*TV/Rad*) **to switch over to the other programme** mettre l'autre chaîne/station. 2 vt sep a *see* **switch 3b**. b (*TV/Rad*) **to switch the programme over** changer de chaîne/de station. 3 **switchover** n *see* **switch 2**.

▶**switch round** 1 vi *[two people]* changer de place (l'un avec l'autre). 2 vt sep *see* **switch 3b**.

Swithin ['swɪðɪn] n Swithin *m or* Swithun *m*. **St. ~'s Day** (jour *m* de) la Saint-Swithin (*15 juillet: pluie de St-Swithin, pluie pour longtemps*).

Switzerland ['swɪtsələnd] n Suisse *f*. **French-/German-/Italian-speaking ~** la Suisse romande/allemande/italienne.

swivel ['swɪvl] 1 n pivot *m*, tourillon *m*. 2 comp *seat, mounting etc* pivotant, tournant ▶**swivel chair** fauteuil pivotant. 3 vt (*also ~* **round**) faire pivoter, faire tourner. 4 vi *[object]* pivoter, tourner.

▶**swivel round** 1 vi pivoter. 2 vt sep = **swivel 3**.

swizz‡ [swɪz] n (*Brit: swindle*) escroquerie *f*. (*disappointment*) **what a ~!** on est eu!*, on s'est fait avoir!*

swizzle ['swɪzl] 1 n (*Brit* ‡) = **swizz**‡. 2 comp ▶**swizzle stick** fouet *m*.

swollen ['swəʊlən] 1 ptp of **swell**. 2 adj *arm, eye, jaw, face* enflé; *stomach* gonflé, ballonné; *river, lake* en crue; *population* accru. **eyes ~ with tears** yeux gonflés de larmes; **to have ~ glands** avoir (une inflammation) des ganglions; *see also* **swell**. 3 comp ▶**swollen-headed*** *etc* = **swellheaded*** *etc; see* **swell 3**.

swoon [swuːn] 1 vi († *or hum: faint*) se pâmer († *or hum*); (*fig*) se pâmer d'admiration (*over sb/sth* devant qn/qch). 2 n († *or hum*) pâmoison *f*. **in a ~** en pâmoison.

swoop [swuːp] 1 n *[bird, plane]* descente *f* en piqué; (*attack*) attaque *f* en piqué (*on* sur); *[police etc]* descente, rafle *f* (*on* dans). **at one (fell) ~** d'un seul coup. 2 vi (*also ~* **down**) *[bird]* fondre, piquer; *[aircraft]* descendre en piqué, piquer; *[police etc]* faire une descente. **the plane ~ed (down) low over the village** l'avion est descendu en piqué au-dessus du village; **the eagle ~ed (down) on the rabbit** l'aigle a fondu *or* s'est abattu sur le lapin; **the soldiers ~ed (down) on the terrorists** les soldats ont fondu sur les terroristes.

swoosh* [swuːʃ] 1 n *[water]* bruissement *m*; *[stick etc through air]* sifflement *m*; *[tyres in rain]* glissement *m*. 2 vi *[water]* bruire. **he went ~ing through the mud** il est passé avec un bruit de boue qui gicle *or* en faisant gicler bruyamment la boue.

swop [swɒp] = **swap**.

sword [sɔːd] 1 n épée *f*. **to wear a ~** porter l'épée; **to put sb to the ~** passer qn au fil de l'épée; **to put up one's ~** rengainer son épée, remettre son épée au fourreau; **those that live by the ~ die by the ~** quiconque se servira de l'épée périra par l'épée; (*fig*) **to turn** *or* **beat one's ~s into ploughshares** forger des socs de ses épées; *see* **cross, point** *etc*.

2 comp *scar, wound* d'épée ▶**sword arm** bras droit ▶**sword dance** danse *f* du sabre ▶**swordfish** poisson-épée *m*, espadon *m* ▶**swordplay**: **there was a lot of swordplay in the film** il y avait beaucoup de duels *or* ça ferraillait dur* dans le film ▶**sword-point**: **at sword-point** à la pointe de l'épée ▶**swordsman**: **to be a good swordsman** être une fine lame ▶**swordsmanship** habileté *f* dans le maniement de l'épée ▶**swordstick** canne *f* à épée ▶**sword-swallower** avaleur *m* de sabres.

swore [swɔːʳ] pret of **swear**.

sworn [swɔːn] 1 ptp of **swear**. 2 adj *evidence, statement* donné sous serment; *enemy* juré; *ally, friend* à la vie et à la mort.

swot* [swɒt] (*Brit*) 1 n (*pej*) bûcheur *m*, -euse *f*, bosseur‡ *m*. 2 vt bûcher*, potasser*. 3 vi bûcher*, potasser*, bosser‡. **to ~ for an exam** bachoter; **to ~ at maths** potasser* *or* bûcher* ses maths.

▶**swot up*** vi, vt sep: **to swot up (on) sth** potasser* qch.

swotting* ['swɒtɪŋ] n bachotage *m*. **to do some ~** bosser‡, bachoter.

swum [swʌm] ptp of **swim**.

swung [swʌŋ] 1 pret, ptp of **swing**. 2 adj (*Typ*) **~ dash** tilde *m*.

sybarite ['sɪbəraɪt] n sybarite *mf*.

sybaritic [ˌsɪbə'rɪtɪk] adj sybarite.

sycamore ['sɪkəmɔːʳ] n sycomore *m*, faux platane.

sycophancy ['sɪkəfənsɪ] n flagornerie *f*.

sycophant ['sɪkəfənt] n flagorneur *m*, -euse *f*.

sycophantic [ˌsɪkə'fæntɪk] adj flagorneur.

Sydney ['sɪdnɪ] n Sydney.

syllabary ['sɪləbərɪ] n syllabaire *m*.

syllabi ['sɪləˌbaɪ] npl of **syllabus**.

syllabic [sɪ'læbɪk] adj syllabique.

syllabification [sɪˌlæbɪfɪ'keɪʃən] n syllabation *f*.

syllabify [sɪ'læbɪfaɪ] vt décomposer en syllabes.

syllable ['sɪləbl] n syllabe *f*. **to explain sth in words of one ~** expliquer qch en petit nègre.

syllabub ['sɪləbʌb] n ≃ sabayon *m*.

syllabus ['sɪləbəs] n, pl **~es** *or* **syllabi** (*Scol, Univ*) programme *m*. **on the ~** au programme.

syllogism ['sɪlədʒɪzəm] n syllogisme *m*.

syllogistic [ˌsɪlə'dʒɪstɪk] adj syllogistique.

syllogize ['sɪlədʒaɪz] vi raisonner par syllogismes.

sylph [sɪlf] 1 n sylphe *m*; (*fig: woman*) sylphide *f*. 2 comp ▶**sylph-like** *woman* gracile, qui a une taille de sylphide; *figure* de sylphide.

sylvan ['sɪlvən] adj (*liter*) sylvestre, des bois.

Sylvester [sɪl'vestəʳ] n Sylvestre *m*.

Sylvia ['sɪlvɪə] n Sylvie *f*.

sylviculture ['sɪlvɪkʌltʃəʳ] n sylviculture *f*.

symbiosis [ˌsɪmbɪ'əʊsɪs] n (*also fig*) symbiose *f*.

symbiotic [sɪmbɪ'ɒtɪk] adj symbiotique.

symbol ['sɪmbəl] n symbole *m*.

symbolic(al) [sɪm'bɒlɪk(əl)] adj symbolique.

symbolically [sɪm'bɒlɪkəlɪ] adv symboliquement.

symbolism ['sɪmbəlɪzəm] n symbolisme *m*.

symbolist ['sɪmbəlɪst] adj, n symboliste *(mf)*.

symbolization [ˌsɪmbəlaɪ'zeɪʃən] n symbolisation *f*.

symbolize ['sɪmbəlaɪz] vt symboliser.

symmetric(al) [sɪ'metrɪk(əl)] adj symétrique.

symmetrically [sɪˈmetrɪkəlɪ] adv symétriquement, avec symétrie.
symmetry [ˈsɪmɪtrɪ] n symétrie *f*.
sympathetic [ˌsɪmpəˈθetɪk] adj (*showing pity*) *person* compatissant (*to, towards* envers); *words, smile, gesture* de sympathie, compatissant; (*kind*) bien disposé, bienveillant (*to* envers, à l'égard de), compréhensif; (*Anat etc*) sympathique. **they were ~ but could not help** ils ont compati mais n'ont rien pu faire pour aider; **you will find him very ~** vous le trouverez bien disposé à votre égard *or* tout prêt à vous écouter; **they are ~ to actors** ils sont bien disposés à l'égard des acteurs.
sympathetically [ˌsɪmpəˈθetɪkəlɪ] adv (*showing pity*) avec compassion; (*kindly*) avec bienveillance; (*Anat etc*) par sympathie.
sympathize [ˈsɪmpəθaɪz] vi: **I do ~ with you!** je vous plains!; **her cousin called to ~** sa cousine est venue témoigner sa sympathie; **I ~ with you in your grief** je m'associe *or* je compatis à votre douleur; **I ~ with you** *or* **what you feel** *or* **what you say** je comprends votre point de vue.
sympathizer [ˈsɪmpəθaɪzəʳ] n a (*in adversity*) personne *f* qui compatit. **he was surrounded by ~s** il était entouré de personnes qui lui témoignaient leur sympathie. b (*fig: esp Pol*) sympathisant(e) *m(f)* (*with* de).
sympathy [ˈsɪmpəθɪ] 1 n a (*pity*) compassion *f*. **please accept my (deepest) ~** *or* **sympathies** veuillez agréer mes condoléances; **to feel ~ for** éprouver *or* avoir de la compassion pour; **to show one's ~ for sb** témoigner sa sympathie à *or* pour qn.
b (*fellow feeling*) solidarité *f* (*for* avec). **the sympathies of the crowd were with him** il avait le soutien de la foule, la foule était pour lui; **I have no ~ with lazy people** je n'ai aucune indulgence pour les gens qui sont paresseux; **he is in ~ with the workers** il est du côté des ouvriers; **I am in ~ with your proposals but ...** je suis en accord avec *or* je ne désapprouve pas vos propositions mais ...; **to come out** *or* **strike in ~ with sb** faire grève en solidarité avec qn.
2 comp ►**sympathy strike** (*Ind*) grève *f* de solidarité.
symphonic [sɪmˈfɒnɪk] adj symphonique. **~ poem** poème *m* symphonique.
symphony [ˈsɪmfənɪ] 1 n symphonie *f*. 2 comp *concert, orchestra* symphonique ►**symphony writer** symphoniste *mf*.
symposium [sɪmˈpəʊzɪəm] n, pl **~s** *or* **symposia** [sɪmˈpəʊzɪə] (*all senses*) symposium *m*.
symptom [ˈsɪmptəm] n (*Med, fig*) symptôme *m*, indice *m*.
symptomatic [ˌsɪmptəˈmætɪk] adj symptomatique (*of* de).
synagogue [ˈsɪnəɡɒɡ] n synagogue *f*.
sync* [sɪŋk] n (abbr of **synchronization**) **in ~** bien synchronisé, en harmonie; (*fig: of people*) **they are in ~** ils sont en harmonie, le courant passe; **out of ~** mal synchronisé, déphasé.
synchromesh [ˌsɪŋkrəʊˈmeʃ] n (*Aut*) synchronisation *f*. **~ on all gears** boîte *f* de vitesse avec tous les rapports synchronisés.
synchronic [sɪŋˈkrɒnɪk] adj (*gen*) synchrone; (*Ling*) synchronique.
synchronicity [sɪŋkrəˈnɪsɪtɪ] n synchronisme *m*.
synchronism [ˈsɪŋkrənɪzəm] n synchronisme *m*.
synchronization [ˌsɪŋkrənaɪˈzeɪʃən] n synchronisation *f*.
synchronize [ˈsɪŋkrənaɪz] 1 vt synchroniser. (*Sport*) **~d swimming** natation *f* synchronisée. 2 vi [*events*] se passer *or* avoir lieu simultanément; [*footsteps etc*] être synchronisés. **to ~ with sth** être synchrone avec qch, se produire en même temps que qch.
synchronous [ˈsɪŋkrənəs] adj synchrone.
syncline [ˈsɪŋklaɪn] n synclinal *m*.
syncopate [ˈsɪŋkəpeɪt] vt syncoper.
syncopation [ˌsɪŋkəˈpeɪʃən] n (*Mus*) syncope *f*.
syncope [ˈsɪŋkəpɪ] n (*Ling, Med*) syncope *f*.
syncretism [ˈsɪŋkrɪtɪzəm] n syncrétisme *m*.
syndic [ˈsɪndɪk] n (*government official*) administrateur *m*, syndic *m*; (*Brit Univ*) membre *m* d'un comité administratif.
syndicalism [ˈsɪndɪkəlɪzəm] n syndicalisme *m*.
syndicalist [ˈsɪndɪkəlɪst] adj, n syndicaliste *(mf)*.
syndicate [ˈsɪndɪkɪt] 1 n a (*Comm etc*) syndicat *m*, coopérative *f*. b [*criminals*] gang *m*, association *f* de malfaiteurs. c (*US Press*) *agence spécialisée dans la vente par abonnements d'articles, de reportages etc.* 2 [ˈsɪndɪkeɪt] vt a (*Press: esp US*) *article etc* vendre *or* publier par l'intermédiaire d'un syndicat de distribution; (*Rad, TV*) *programme* distribuer sous licence. (*Press*) **~d columnist** journaliste *mf* d'agence. b (*Fin*) **to ~ a loan** former un consortium de prêt; **~d loan** prêt *m* consortial. c *workers* syndiquer.
syndrome [ˈsɪndrəʊm] n (*also fig*) syndrome *m*.
synecdoche [sɪˈnekdəkɪ] n synecdoque *f*.
synergism [ˈsɪnəˌdʒɪsəm] n synergie *f*.
synergy [ˈsɪnədʒɪ] n synergie *f*.
synod [ˈsɪnəd] n synode *m*.
synonym [ˈsɪnənɪm] n synonyme *m*.
synonymous [sɪˈnɒnɪməs] adj synonyme (*with* de).
synonymy [sɪˈnɒnəmɪ] n synonymie *f*.
synopsis [sɪˈnɒpsɪs] n, pl **synopses** [sɪˈnɒpsiːz] résumé *m*, précis *m*; (*Cine, Theat*) synopsis *m or f*.
synoptic [sɪˈnɒptɪk] adj synoptique.
synovial [saɪˈnəʊvɪəl] adj (*Anat*) synovial.
syntactic(al) [sɪnˈtæktɪk(əl)] adj syntaxique *or* syntactique.
syntagm [ˈsɪntæm] n, pl **~s, syntagma** [sɪnˈtæɡmə] n, pl **syntagmata** [sɪnˈtæɡmətə] syntagme *m*.
syntagmatic [ˌsɪntæɡˈmætɪk] adj syntagmatique.
syntax [ˈsɪntæks] n syntaxe *f*. (*Comput*) **~ error** erreur *f* de syntaxe.
synthesis [ˈsɪnθəsɪs] n, pl **syntheses** [ˈsɪnθəsiːz] synthèse *f*.
synthesize [ˈsɪnθəsaɪz] vt (*combine*) synthétiser; (*produce*) produire synthétiquement *or* par une synthèse, faire la synthèse de.
synthesizer [ˈsɪnθəsaɪzəʳ] n synthétiseur *m*; *see* **speech**.
synthetic [sɪnˈθetɪk] 1 adj (*all senses*) synthétique. 2 n (*gen*) produit *m* synthétique. (*Tex*) **~s** fibres *fpl* synthétiques, textiles artificiels.
syphilis [ˈsɪfɪlɪs] n syphilis *f*.
syphilitic [ˌsɪfɪˈlɪtɪk] adj, n syphilitique *(mf)*.
syphon [ˈsaɪfən] = **siphon**.
Syria [ˈsɪrɪə] n Syrie *f*.
Syrian [ˈsɪrɪən] 1 adj syrien. **~ Arab Republic** République *f* arabe syrienne. 2 n Syrien(ne) *m(f)*.
syringe [sɪˈrɪndʒ] 1 n seringue *f*. 2 vt seringuer.
syrup [ˈsɪrəp] n sirop *m*; (*Culin: also* **golden ~**) mélasse raffinée.
syrupy [ˈsɪrəpɪ] adj (*lit, fig*) sirupeux.
system [ˈsɪstəm] 1 n a (*structured whole: gen, Anat, Comput, Ling, Med, Pol, Sci, Tech*) système *m*. **a political/economic/social ~** un système politique/économique/social; **solar ~** système solaire; **respiratory/nervous ~** système respiratoire/nerveux; **digestive ~** appareil *m* digestif; **the railway ~** le réseau de chemin de fer; **the Social Security ~** le régime de la Sécurité sociale; (*Comm*) **the Bell ~** la compagnie *or* le réseau Bell; [*rivers*] **the St. Lawrence ~** le Saint-Laurent et ses affluents; (*Geog*) **the urban ~** la trame urbaine; *see* **feudal** *etc*.
b (*gen: method, type, process*) système *m*. **new teaching ~s** nouveaux systèmes d'enseignement.
c (*the body*) organisme *m*. **her ~ will reject it** son organisme le rejettera; **it was a shock to his ~** cela a été une secousse pour son organisme, cela a ébranlé son organisme; (*fig*) **to get sth out of one's ~*** (*gen*) trouver un exutoire à qch; **let him get it out of his ~*** *anger* laisse-le décharger sa bile; *hobby, passion* laisse-le faire — ça lui passera; **he can't get her out of his ~*** il n'arrive pas à l'oublier.
d (*established order*) **the ~** le système; **to get round** *or* **beat** *or* **buck the ~** trouver le joint (*fig*); **down with the ~!** à bas le système!
e (*Comput*) système *m*. **~ disk** disque *m* système; **~ operator** opérateur *m* du système, serveur *m*; *see* **operating c**.
f (*NonC: order*) méthode *f* (*NonC*). **to lack ~** manquer de méthode.
2 comp ►**systems analysis** analyse *f* fonctionnelle ►**systems analyst** analyste *mf* fonctionnel(le) ►**systems desk** pupitre *m* ►**systems engineer** ingénieur *m* système ►**systems programmer** programmeur *m* d'étude ►**systems software** logiciel *m* de base.
systematic [ˌsɪstəˈmætɪk] adj *reasoning, work* systématique, méthodique; *failures* systématique.
systematically [ˌsɪstəˈmætɪkəlɪ] adv (*see* **systematic**) systématiquement; méthodiquement.
systematization [ˌsɪstəmətaɪˈzeɪʃən] n systématisation *f*.
systematize [ˈsɪstəmətaɪz] vt systématiser.
systemic [sɪˈstemɪk] adj a (*gen*) du système; (*Anat*) du système, de l'organisme; *insecticide* systémique. **~ circulation** circulation générale; **~ infection** infection généralisée. b (*Ling*) systémique.

T

T, t [tiː] 1 **n** (*letter*) T, t *m*. **T for Tommy** ≈ T comme Thérèse; (*fig*) **that's it to a T*** c'est exactement cela; **it fits him to a T*** cela lui va comme un gant; *see* **dot.** 2 **comp** ►**T-bar** (**lift**) (*Ski*) téléski *m* à archets ►**T-bone** (**steak**) (*Culin*) steak *m* avec un os en T ►**T-junction** intersection *f* en T ►**T-shaped** en forme de T, en équerre ►**T-shirt** T-shirt *m or* tee-shirt *m* ►**T-square** équerre *f* en T ►**T-stop** (*Phot*) diaphragme *m*.

TA [tiːˈeɪ] **n** a (*Brit Mil*) (**abbr of Territorial Army**) *see* **territorial.** b (*US Univ*) (**abbr of teaching assistant**) *see* **teaching.**

ta⁑ [tɑː] **excl** (*Brit*) merci!

tab¹ [tæb] **n** (*part of garment*) patte *f*; (*loop on garment etc*) attache *f*; (*label*) étiquette *f*; (*on shoelace*) ferret *m*; (*marker: on file etc*) onglet *m*; (*US* *: *café check*) addition *f*, note *f*. **to keep ~s** *or* **a ~ on*** *person* avoir *or* tenir à l'œil*; *thing* avoir l'œil sur*; (*US: lit, fig*) **to pick up the ~*** payer la note *or* l'addition.

tab² [tæb] **n** a (*Comput*) (**abbr of tabulator**) **~ key** touche *f* de tabulation. b **abbr of tablet c.**

tabard [ˈtæbəd] **n** tabard *m*.

Tabasco [təˈbæskəʊ] **n** ® *sauce forte à base de poivrons.*

tabby [ˈtæbɪ] **n** (*also* **~ cat**) chat(te) *m(f)* tigré(e) *or* moucheté(e).

tabernacle [ˈtæbənækl] **n** tabernacle *m*. (*Rel*) **the T~** le tabernacle.

table [ˈteɪbl] 1 **n** a (*furniture, food on it*) table *f*; (*people at ~*) tablée *f*, table. **ironing/bridge/garden ~** table à repasser/de bridge/de jardin; **at ~** à table; **to sit down to ~** se mettre à table; **to lay** *or* **set the ~** mettre la table *or* le couvert; **the whole ~ laughed** toute la tablée *or* la table a ri; (*Parl*) **to lay sth on the ~** remettre *or* ajourner qch; (*Parl*) **the bill lies on the ~** la discussion du projet de loi a été ajournée; (*fig*) **to put sth on the ~** (*Brit: propose*) proposer qch, faire une proposition; (*US: postpone*) ajourner *or* remettre qch; (*fig*) **he slipped me £5 under the ~*** il m'a passé 5 livres de la main à la main; (*fig*) **he was nearly under the ~** un peu plus et il roulait sous la table*; *see* **clear, turn** *etc*.

b *[facts, statistics]* table *f* (*also Math*); *[prices, fares, names]* liste *f*; (*Sport: also* **league ~**) classement *m*. **~ of contents** table des matières; (*Math*) **the two-times ~** la table de (multiplication par) deux; (*Sport*) **we are in fifth place in the ~** nous sommes classés cinquièmes, nous sommes cinquièmes au classement; *see* **log²** *etc*.

c (*Geog*) = **tableland;** *see* **3.**

d (*Rel*) **the T~s of the Law** les Tables de la Loi.

2 **vt** a (*Brit Admin, Parl: present*) *motion etc* présenter, soumettre.

b (*US Admin, Parl: postpone*) *motion etc* ajourner. **to ~ a bill** reporter la discussion d'un projet de loi.

c (*tabulate*) dresser une liste *or* une table de; *results* classifier.

3 **comp** *wine, grapes, knife, lamp* de table ►**Table Bay** (*Geog*) baie *f* de la Table ►**tablecloth** nappe *f* ►**table-cover** tapis *m* de table ►**table cream** (*US*) crème fraîche liquide ►**table d'hôte** **adj** à prix fixe ◊ **n** (**pl ~s d'hôte**) table *f* d'hôte, repas *m* à prix fixe ►**table football** baby-foot *m* ►**tableland** (*Geog*) (haut) plateau *m* ►**table leg** pied *m* de table ►**table linen** linge *m* de table ►**table manners: he has good table manners** il sait se tenir à table ►**tablemat** (*of linen etc*) napperon *m*; (*heat-resistant*) dessous-de-plat *m inv* ►**Table Mountain** (*Geog*) la montagne de la Table ►**table napkin** serviette *f* (de table) ►**table runner** chemin *m* de table ►**table salt** sel fin ►**tablespoon** cuiller *f* de service; (*measurement: also* **tablespoonful**) cuillerée *f* à soupe (*US Culin = 29,5 ml*) ►**table talk** (*NonC*) menus propos *mpl* ►**table tennis** **n** ping-pong *m*, tennis *m* de table ◊ **comp** de ping-pong ►**table-tennis player** joueur *m*, -euse *f* de ping-pong, pongiste *mf* ►**tabletop** dessus *m* de table ►**table turning** (*NonC*) (spiritisme *m* par les) tables *fpl* tournantes ►**tableware** (*NonC*) vaisselle *f*.

tableau [ˈtæbləʊ] **n, pl ~x** *or* **~s** [ˈtæbləʊz] (*Theat*) tableau vivant; (*fig*) tableau.

tablet [ˈtæblɪt] **n** a (*stone: inscribed*) plaque *f* (commémorative); (*Hist: of wax, slate etc*) tablette *f*. b *[chocolate]* tablette *f*. **~ of soap** savonnette *f*. c (*Pharm*) comprimé *m*, cachet *m*; (*for sucking*) pastille *f*. d (*Comput*) tablette *f*.

tabloid [ˈtæblɔɪd] 1 **n** (*Press: also* **~ newspaper**) tabloïd(e) *m*, quotidien *m* populaire (de demi-format). 2 **adj** (*also* **in ~ form**) en raccourci, condensé.

taboo [təˈbuː] 1 **adj, n** (*Rel, fig*) tabou *(m)*. 2 **vt** proscrire, interdire.

tabor [ˈteɪbəʳ] **n** tambourin *m*.

tabu [təˈbuː] = **taboo.**

tabular [ˈtæbjʊləʳ] **adj** tabulaire.

tabulate [ˈtæbjʊleɪt] **vt** *facts, figures* mettre sous forme de table; *results etc* classifier; (*Typ*) mettre en colonnes.

tabulation [ˌtæbjʊˈleɪʃən] **n** (*see* **tabulate**) diposition *f* en listes *or* tables; classification *f*; tabulation *f*.

tabulator [ˈtæbjʊleɪtəʳ] **n** *[typewriter]* tabulateur *m*.

tacheometer [ˌtækɪˈɒmɪtəʳ] **n** tachéomètre *m*.

tachograph [ˈtækəgrɑːf] **n** tachygraphe *m*.

tachometer [tæˈkɒmɪtəʳ] **n** tachymètre *m*.

tachycardia [ˌtækɪˈkɑːdɪə] **n** tachycardie *f*.

tachycardiac [ˌtækɪˈkɑːdɪæk] **adj** tachycardiaque.

tachymeter [tæˈkɪmɪtəʳ] **n** tachéomètre *m*.

tacit [ˈtæsɪt] **adj** (*gen*) tacite; (*Ling*) *knowledge of language* implicite.

tacitly [ˈtæsɪtlɪ] **adv** tacitement.

taciturn [ˈtæsɪtɜːn] **adj** taciturne.

taciturnity [ˌtæsɪˈtɜːnɪtɪ] **n** taciturnité *f*.

Tacitus [ˈtæsɪtəs] **n** Tacite *m*.

tack [tæk] 1 **n** a (*for wood, lino, carpets etc*) broquette *f*; (*for upholstery*) semence *f*; (*US: also* **thumb~**) punaise *f*; *see* **brass.**

b (*Brit Sewing*) point *m* de bâti.

c (*Naut*) bord *m*, bordée *f*. **to make a ~** faire *or* courir *or* tirer un bord *or* une bordée; **to be on a port/starboard ~** être bâbord/tribord amures; (*fig*) **to be on the right/wrong ~** être sur la bonne/mauvaise voie; (*fig*) **to try another ~** essayer une autre tactique.

d (*NonC: for horse*) sellerie *f* (*articles*).

2 **comp** ►**tackroom** sellerie *f* (*endroit*).

3 **vt** a (*also* **~ down**) *wood, lino, carpet* clouer (*avec des broquettes*).

b (*Brit Sewing*) faufiler, bâtir.

4 **vi** (*Naut: make a ~*) faire *or* courir *or* tirer un bord *or* une bordée. **they ~ed back to the harbour** ils sont rentrés au port en louvoyant *or* en tirant des bordées.

►**tack down** **vt sep** (*Brit Sewing*) maintenir en place au point de bâti; *see also* **tack 3a.**

►**tack on** **vt sep** a (*Brit Sewing*) bâtir, appliquer au point de bâti. b (*fig*) ajouter (après coup) (*to* à).

tackiness [ˈtækɪnɪs] **n** (*NonC*) (*see* **tacky**) a viscosité *f*. b (*) ringardise* *f*, mocheté* *f*. c (*) vulgarité *f*.

tacking [ˈtækɪŋ] (*Brit Sewing*) 1 **n** bâtissage *m*, faufilure *f*. **to take out the ~ from sth** défaufiler qch. 2 **comp** ►**tacking stitch** point *m* de bâti.

tackle [ˈtækl] 1 **n** a (*NonC*) (*esp Naut: ropes, pulleys*) appareil *m* de levage; (*gen: gear, equipment*) équipement *m*. **fishing ~** articles *mpl or* matériel *m* de pêche.

b (*Ftbl, Hockey, Rugby etc: action*) tac(k)le *m*; (*US Ftbl: player*) plaqueur *m*.

2 **vt** a (*physically*) (*Ftbl, Hockey, Rugby etc*) tac(k)ler; *thief, intruder* saisir à bras-le-corps.

b (*verbally*) **I'll ~ him about it at once** je vais lui en parler *or* lui en dire deux mots tout de suite; **I ~d him about what he had done** je l'ai questionné sur ce qu'il avait fait.

c *task* s'attaquer à; *problem, question, subject* aborder, s'attaquer à; (*) *meal, food* attaquer*. **he ~d Hebrew on his own** il s'est mis à l'hébreu tout seul.

tacky [ˈtækɪ] **adj** a (*sticky*) *glue* qui commence à prendre; *paint* pas tout à fait sec (*f* sèche); *surface* poisseux, collant. b (*: *ugly, bad quality*) *jewellery, design, hotel, clothes* tocard⁑, ringard*, moche*.

c (*US* *) *person* commun, vulgaire.

taco ['tɑːkəʊ] n, pl ~s (*US*) *crêpe de maïs farcie servie chaude*.

tact [tækt] n (*NonC*) tact *m*, doigté *m*, délicatesse *f*.

tactful ['tæktfʊl] adj *person* délicat, plein de tact; *hint* subtil (*f* subtile), fin; *inquiry, reference* discret (*f* -ète); *answer* plein de tact, diplomatique* (*fig*); *suggestion* plein de tact, délicat. **be ~!** du tact!, un peu de diplomatie!*; **to be ~ with sb** agir envers qn avec tact *or* doigté, ménager qn; **you could have been a bit more ~** tu aurais pu avoir un peu plus de tact *or* de doigté.

tactfully ['tæktfəlɪ] adv avec tact, avec doigté, avec délicatesse.

tactfulness ['tæktfʊlnɪs] n = **tact**.

tactic ['tæktɪk] n (*Mil, fig*) tactique *f*. (*NonC: Mil*) ~s la tactique.

tactical ['tæktɪkəl] adj (*Mil, fig*) *exercise, weapon, value* tactique; *error etc* de tactique; (*skilful*) adroit. ~ **voting** vote *m* tactique.

tactically ['tæktɪkəlɪ] adv (*Mil, fig*) d'un *or* du point de vue tactique. **to vote ~** voter utile.

tactician [tæk'tɪʃən] n (*Mil, fig*) tacticien *m*.

tactile ['tæktaɪl] adj tactile.

tactless ['tæktlɪs] adj *person* peu délicat, qui manque de tact; *hint* grossier; *inquiry, reference* indiscret (*f* -ète); *answer* qui manque de tact, peu diplomatique* (*fig*); *suggestion* peu délicat.

tactlessly ['tæktlɪslɪ] adv sans tact, sans doigté, sans délicatesse.

tactlessness ['tæktlɪsnɪs] n (*see* **tactless**) manque *m* de tact, indélicatesse *f*, grossièreté *f*, manque *m* de diplomatie*.

tadpole ['tædpəʊl] n têtard *m*.

Tadzhik ['tɑːdʒɪk] adj: ~ **SSR**† RSS† *f* du Tadjikistan.

Tadzhikistan [tɑːˌdʒɪkɪ'stɑːn] n Tadjikistan *m*.

tae kwon do ['taɪ'kwɒn'dəʊ] n taekwondo *m*, Tae Kwon Do *m*.

taffeta ['tæfɪtə] n (*NonC*) taffetas *m*.

taffrail ['tæfreɪl] n (*Naut*) couronnement *m*; (*rail*) lisse *f* de couronnement.

Taffy* ['tæfɪ] n (*also* ~ **Jones**) *sobriquet donné à un Gallois*.

taffy ['tæfɪ] n (*US*) bonbon *m* au caramel; (*Can*) tire *f* d'érable.

tag [tæg] 1 n a *[shoelace, cord etc]* ferret *m*; (*on garment etc*) patte *f*, marque *f*; (*label*) étiquette *f*; (*marker: on file etc*) onglet *m*. **all uniforms must have name ~s** chaque uniforme doit être marqué au nom de son propriétaire; *see* **price** *etc*.

b (*quotation*) citation *f*; (*cliché*) cliché *m*, lieu commun; (*catchword*) slogan *m*. (*Ling*) ~ **(question)** question-tag *f*.

c (*NonC: game*) (jeu *m* du) chat *m*.

2 comp ▸**tagboard** (*US*) carton *m* (pour étiquettes) ▸**tag day** (*US*) journée *f* de vente d'insignes (*pour une œuvre*) ▸**tag end** *[speech, performance, programme etc]* fin *f*; *[goods for sale]* restes *mpl* ▸**tag line** *[play]* dernière réplique; *[poem]* dernier vers.

3 vt a *garment* marquer; *bag, box, file* étiqueter; (*US* * *fig*) *car* mettre un papillon* sur; *driver* mettre une contravention à.

b (*: *follow*) suivre; *[detective]* filer.

▸**tag along** vi suivre le mouvement*. **she left and the children tagged along behind her** elle est partie et les enfants l'ont suivie; **the others came tagging along behind** les autres traînaient derrière *or* étaient à la traîne derrière; **she usually tags along (with us)** la plupart du temps elle vient avec nous.

▸**tag on*** 1 vi: **to tag on to sb** coller aux talons de qn*; **he came tagging on behind** il traînait derrière. 2 vt sep (*fig*) ajouter (après coup) (*to* à).

▸**tag out** vt sep (*Baseball*) mettre hors jeu.

tagliatelle [ˌtæljə'telɪ, ˌtæglɪə'telɪ] n (*NonC*) tagliatelles *fpl*.

tagmeme ['tægmiːm] n tagmème *m*.

tagmemics [tæg'miːmɪks] n (*NonC*) tagmémique *f*.

Tagus ['teɪgəs] n Tage *m*.

Tahiti [tə'hiːtɪ] n Tahiti *m*. **in ~** à Tahiti.

Tahitian [tə'hiːʃɪən] 1 adj tahitien. 2 n a Tahitien(ne) *m(f)*. b (*Ling*) tahitien *m*.

t'ai chi (ch'uan) ['taɪdʒiː('tʃwɑːn)] n tai-chi(-chuan) *m*.

tail [teɪl] 1 n a *[animal, aircraft, comet, kite, procession, hair]* queue *f*; *[shirt]* pan *m*; *[coat]* basque *f*; *[ski]* talon *m*. (*lit, fig*) **with his ~ between his legs** la queue entre les jambes; (*fig*) **to keep one's ~ up** ne pas se laisser abattre; (*fig*) **he was right on my ~** il me suivait de très près; (*fig*) **it is a case of the ~ wagging the dog** c'est une petite minorité qui se fait obéir; *see* **nose, sting, turn** *etc*.

b *[coin]* pile *f*. **~s I win!** pile je gagne!

c (*Dress*) **~s*** queue *f* de pie.

d (* *hum: buttocks*) postérieur* *m* (*hum*). (*US*) **a piece of ~**** une fille baisable**.

e (‡) **to put a ~ on sb** faire filer qn.

2 comp ▸**tail assembly** (*Aviat*) dérive *f* ▸**tailback** (*Brit Aut*) bouchon *m*, retenue *f* ▸**tailboard** (*Aut etc*) hayon *m* ▸**tail coat** habit *m* ▸**tail end** *[piece of meat, roll of cloth etc]* bout *m*; *[procession etc]* queue *f*; *[storm, debate, lecture]* toutes dernières minutes, fin *f* ▸**tailgate** (*Brit Aut*) hayon *m* (arrière), 3e (*or* 5e) porte *f*; (*US Aut*) **to tailgate sb*** coller au pare-chocs de qn ▸**tailhopping** (*Ski*) ruade *f* ▸**taillamp, taillight** (*Aut, Rail etc*) feu *m* arrière *inv* ▸**tail-off** diminution *f or* baisse *f* graduelle ▸**tailpiece** (*to speech etc*) appendice *m*; (*to letter*) post-scriptum *m*; (*Typ*) cul-de-lampe *m*; *[violin]* cordier *m* ▸**tailpipe** (*Aut*) tuyau *m* d'échappement ▸**tailplane** (*Aviat*) stabilisateur *m* ▸**tail skid** (*Aviat*) béquille *f* de queue ▸**tailspin** n (*Aviat*) vrille *f*; *[prices]* chute *f* verticale ◊ vi tomber en chute libre; (*Aviat*) **to be in a tailspin** vriller ▸**tail unit** (*Aviat*) empennage *m* ▸**tailwind** vent *m* arrière *inv*.

3 vt a (*) *suspect etc* suivre, filer.

b (*cut tail of*) *animal* couper la queue à; *see* **top¹**.

4 vi: **to ~ after sb** suivre qn tant bien que mal.

▸**tail away** vi *[sounds]* se taire (peu à peu); *[attendance, interest, numbers]* diminuer, baisser (petit à petit); *[novel]* se terminer en queue de poisson.

▸**tail back** 1 vi: **the traffic tailed back to the bridge** le bouchon *or* la retenue remontait jusqu'au pont. 2 **tailback** n *see* **tail 2**.

▸**tail off** 1 vi = **tail away**. 2 **tail-off** n *see* **tail 2**.

-tailed [teɪld] adj ending in comps: **long-tailed** à la queue longue.

tailor ['teɪlər] 1 n tailleur *m*. **~'s chalk** craie *f* de tailleur; **~'s dummy** mannequin *m*; (*fig pej*) fantoche *m*. 2 comp ▸**tailor-made** *garment* fait sur mesure; (*fig*) **the building was tailor-made for this purpose** le bâtiment était fonctionnalisé, le bâtiment était construit spécialement pour cet usage; **a lesson tailor-made for that class** une leçon conçue *or* préparée spécialement pour cette classe; **the job was tailor-made for him** le poste était fait pour lui. 3 vt *garment* façonner; (*fig*) *speech, book, product, service* adapter (*to, to suit* à, *for* pour). **a ~ed skirt** une jupe ajustée.

tailoring ['teɪlərɪŋ] n (*fig*) *[product, service]* personnalisation *f*, adaptation *f* (*to* à).

taint [teɪnt] 1 vt *meat, food* gâter; *water* infecter, polluer; *air, atmosphere* vicier, infecter, polluer; (*fig liter*) *sb's reputation etc* souiller (*liter*). 2 n (*NonC*) (*infection*) infection *f*, souillure *f*; (*decay*) corruption *f*, décomposition *f*; (*fig: of insanity, sin, heresy etc*) tare *f* (*fig*), souillure (*fig liter*).

tainted ['teɪntɪd] adj *food* gâté; *meat* avarié; *water* infecté, pollué; *air, atmosphere* vicié, infecté, pollué; *action, motive* impur; *reputation* entaché, sali, souillé (*liter*); *money* mal acquis; *blood* impur; *family, lineage* sali, souillé (*liter*). **to become ~** *[food]* se gâter; *[meat]* s'avarier; *[water, air etc]* s'infecter, se polluer.

Taiwan ['taɪ'wɑːn] n Taiwan (*no article in French*). **in ~** à Taiwan.

take [teɪk] (vb: pret **took**, ptp **taken**) 1 n a (*Cine, Phot*) prise *f* de vue(s); (*Sound Recording*) enregistrement *m*; (*Fishing, Hunting etc*) prise *f*; (*US Comm: takings*) recette *f*. (*US fig*) **to be on the ~‡** toucher des pots de vin, palper*.

b (*esp US *: share*) part *f*, montant *m* perçu. **the taxman's ~ is nearly 50%** la ponction fiscale s'élève à 50 %.

2 comp ▸**takeaway** (*Brit*) (*food shop*) café *m* qui fait des plats à emporter; (*Brit*) **takeaway food** plats préparés (à emporter); (*Brit*) **takeaway meal** repas *m* à emporter ▸**takedown*** *toy, weapon etc* démontable ▸**take-home pay** salaire net ▸**takeoff** (*Aviat*) décollage *m*; (*Gym, Ski*) envol *m*; (*fig: Econ etc*) démarrage *m*; (*imitation*) imitation *f*, pastiche *m* ▸**takeout** (*US*) = **takeaway**; (*Bridge*) **takeout (bid)** réponse *f* de faiblesse ▸**takeover** (*Pol*) prise *f* du pouvoir; (*Fin*) rachat *m*; **takeover bid** offre publique d'achat, O.P.A. *f* ▸**take-up** souscription *f*.

3 vt a (*gen*) prendre; (*seize*) prendre, saisir. **to ~ sb's hand** prendre la main de qn; **he took me by the arm, he took my arm** il m'a pris le bras; **he took her in his arms** il l'a prise dans ses bras; **to ~ sb by the throat** prendre *or* saisir qn à la gorge; **I ~ a (size) 12 in dresses/a (size) 5 in shoes** *etc* je prends une taille 12 en robes/une pointure 5 en chaussures; *see also* **size 1b**.

b (*extract*) prendre (*from sth* dans qch), tirer (*from sth* de qch); (*remove*) prendre, enlever, ôter (*from sb* à qn); (*without permission*) prendre; (*steal*) prendre, voler. **to ~ sth from one's pocket** prendre qch dans *or* tirer qch de sa poche; **to ~ sth from a drawer** prendre qch dans un tiroir; **the devil ~ it!***† au diable!; **he ~s his examples from real life** il tire ses exemples de la réalité; **I took these statistics from a government report** j'ai tiré ces statistiques d'un rapport gouvernemental; *see* **hand** *etc*.

c (*Math etc: subtract*) soustraire, retrancher, retirer (*from* de). **he took 10 francs off the price** il a rabattu 10 F sur le prix.

d (*capture etc*) (*Mil*) *city, district, hill* prendre, s'emparer de; (*gen*) *suspect, wanted man* prendre, capturer; *fish etc* prendre, attraper; (*sexually*) *woman* prendre; (*Chess*) prendre; *prize* avoir, obtenir, remporter; *degree* avoir, obtenir. **he must be ~n alive** il faut le prendre *or* capturer vivant; (*Cards*) **to ~ a trick** faire une levée; **my ace took his king** j'ai pris son roi avec mon as; **the grocer ~s about £500 per day** l'épicier (se) fait à peu près 500 livres de recette par jour; *see* **fancy, prisoner, surprise** *etc*.

e (*make, have, undertake etc*) *notes, letter, photo, temperature, measurements, lessons, bath, decision, holiday etc* prendre. **the policeman took his name and address** l'agent a pris *or* relevé ses nom et adresse; **he ~s "The Times"** il prend "The Times"; (*Phot*) **he took the cathedral from the square** il a pris la cathédrale vue de la place; **to ~ a ticket for a concert** prendre un billet *or* une place pour un concert; **I'll ~ that one** je prends *or* prendrai celui-là; **to ~ a wife**† prendre femme†; **~ your partners for a waltz** invitez vos partenaires et en avant pour la valse; **you'll have to ~ your chance** il va falloir que tu prennes le risque; **to ~**

sth (up)on o.s. prendre qch sur soi; **to ~ it (up)on o.s. to do** prendre sur soi *or* sous son bonnet de faire; (*Med*) **to ~ cold** prendre froid; **to ~ ill, to be ~n ill** tomber malade; **to ~ fright** prendre peur; *see* **advantage, opportunity, possession, walk 1a** *etc.*

f (*ingest, consume*) *food, drink* prendre. **he ~s sugar in his tea** il prend du sucre dans son thé; **to ~ tea† with sb** prendre le thé avec qn; **to ~ drugs** *[patient]* prendre des médicaments; (*gen*) se droguer; **to ~ morphine** se droguer à la morphine, prendre de la morphine; (*Med*) **"not to be ~n (internally)"** "pour usage externe"; **he took no food for 4 days** il n'a rien mangé *or* pris pendant 4 jours; **how much alcohol has he ~n?** combien d'alcool a-t-il bu? *or* absorbé?; **I can't ~ alcohol** je ne supporte pas l'alcool.

g (*occupy*) *chair, seat* prendre, s'asseoir sur; (*rent*) *house, flat etc* prendre, louer. **to ~ one's seat** s'asseoir; **is this seat ~n?** cette place est-elle prise? *or* occupée?

h (*go by*) *bus, train, plane, taxi* prendre; *road* prendre, suivre. **~ the first on the left** prenez la première à gauche.

i (*negotiate*) *bend* prendre; *hill* grimper; *fence* sauter. **he took that corner too fast** il a pris ce virage trop vite.

j (*Scol, Univ*) (*sit*) *exam, test* passer, se présenter à; (*study*) *subject* prendre, faire. **what are you taking next year?** qu'est-ce que tu prends *or* fais l'an prochain (comme matière)?

k (*tolerate*) accepter. **he won't ~ no for an answer** il n'acceptera pas un refus; **he won't ~ that reply from you** il n'acceptera jamais une telle réponse venant de vous; **I'll ~ no nonsense!** on ne me raconte pas d'histoires!; **I'm not taking any!**⁑ je ne marche pas!*; **I can't ~ it any more** je n'en peux plus; **we can ~ it!** on ne se laissera pas abattre!, on (l')encaissera!*; (*fig*) **he/the car took a lot of punishment** il/la voiture en a beaucoup vu*; *see* **beating, lie down** *etc.*

l (*have as capacity*) contenir, avoir une capacité de. **the bus ~s 60 passengers** l'autobus a une capacité de 60 places; **the hall will ~ 200 people** la salle contient jusqu'à 200 personnes; **the bridge will ~ 10 tons** le pont supporte un poids maximal de 10 tonnes.

m (*receive, accept*) *gift, payment* prendre, accepter; *a bet* accepter; *news* prendre, supporter. **he won't ~ less than £50 for it** il en demande au moins 50 livres; **~ it from me!** croyez-moi!, croyez-moi sur parole!; **(you can) ~ it or leave it** c'est à prendre ou à laisser; **whisky? I can ~ it or leave it*** le whisky? j'aime ça mais sans plus; **she took his death quite well** elle s'est montrée très calme en apprenant sa mort; **she took his death very badly** elle a été très affectée par sa mort; **I wonder how she'll ~ it** je me demande comment elle prendra cela; **you must ~ us as you find us** vous devez nous prendre comme nous sommes; **to ~ things as they come** prendre les choses comme elles viennent*; **you must ~ things as they are** il faut prendre les choses comme elles sont*; **to ~ things** *or* **it** *or* **life easy*** ne pas s'en faire, se le couler douce*; **~ it easy!*** du calme!, t'en fais pas!*; (*handing over task etc*) **will you ~ it from here?** pouvez-vous prendre la suite? *or* la relève?; (*esp US: have a break*) **~ five!*, ~ ten!*** repos!; *see* **amiss, lamb, word** *etc.*

n (*assume*) supposer, imaginer. **I ~ it that ...** je suppose *or* j'imagine que ...; **how old do you ~ him to be?** quel âge lui donnez-vous?; **what do you ~ me for?** pour qui me prenez-vous?; **do you ~ me for a fool?** vous me prenez pour un imbécile?; **I took him for** *or* **to be a doctor** je l'ai pris pour un médecin; **I took him to be foreign** je le croyais étranger; **to ~ A for B** prendre A pour B, confondre A et B; *see* **grant, read[1]** *etc.*

o (*consider*) prendre. **now ~ Ireland** prenons par exemple l'Irlande; **~ the case of ...** prenons *or* prenez le cas de ...; **taking one thing with another ...** tout bien considéré ... .

p (*require*) prendre, demander; (*Gram*) être suivi de. **it ~s time** cela prend *or* demande du temps; **the journey ~s 5 days** le voyage prend *or* demande 5 jours; **it took me 2 hours to do it, I took 2 hours to do it** j'ai mis 2 heures à le faire; **~ your time!** prenez votre temps!; **it won't ~ long** cela ne prendra pas longtemps; **that ~s a lot of courage** cela demande beaucoup de courage; **it ~s a brave man to do that** il faut être courageux pour faire cela; **it ~s some doing*** cela n'est pas facile (à faire); **it ~s some believing*** c'est à peine croyable; **it took 3 policemen to hold him down** il a fallu 3 gendarmes pour le tenir; (*Prov*) **it ~s two to make a quarrel** il faut être au moins deux pour se battre; **he has got what it ~s to do the job** il a toutes les qualités requises pour ce travail; **he's got what it ~s!*** (*courage/talent/perseverance*) ce n'est pas le courage/le talent/la persévérance qui lui manque.

q (*carry*) *child, object* porter, apporter, emporter; *one's gloves, umbrella* prendre, emporter (avec soi); (*lead*) emmener, conduire; (*accompany*) accompagner. **he took her some flowers** il lui a apporté des fleurs; **~ his suitcase upstairs** montez sa valise; **he ~s home £60 a week** il gagne *or* se fait* 60 livres net (*inv*) par semaine; **he took her to the cinema** il l'a emmenée au cinéma; **I'll ~ you to dinner** je vous emmènerai dîner; **they took him over the factory** ils lui ont fait visiter l'usine; **to ~ sb to hospital** transporter qn à l'hôpital; **he took me home in his car** il m'a ramené *or* raccompagné dans sa voiture; **this road will ~ you to Paris** cette route vous mènera à Paris; **this bus will ~ you to the town hall** cet autobus vous conduira à la mairie; (*fig*) **what took you to Lille?** qu'est-ce qui vous a fait aller à Lille?; *see* **post[3], walk** *etc.*

r (*refer*) **to ~ a matter to sb** soumettre une affaire à qn, en référer à qn; **I took it to him for advice** je lui ai soumis le problème pour qu'il me conseille; (*Jur*) **to ~ a case to the High Court** en appeler à la Cour suprême.

4 vi *[fire, vaccination, plant cutting etc]* prendre. (*Phot*) **he ~s well, he ~s a good photo*** il est très photogénique; *see* **kindly** *etc.*

►**take aback** vt sep *see* **aback**.

►**take after** vt fus ressembler à, tenir de.

►**take against** vt fus prendre en grippe.

►**take along** vt sep *person* emmener; *camera etc* emporter, prendre.

►**take apart** 1 vi *[toy, machine etc]* se démonter. 2 vt sep *machine, engine, toy* démonter; (* *fig: criticize harshly*) *plan, suggestion* démanteler, démolir*. **I'll take him apart* if I get hold of him!** si je l'attrape je l'étripe!* *or* je lui fais sa fête!⁑

►**take aside** vt sep *person* prendre à part, emmener à l'écart.

►**take away** 1 vi: **it takes away from its value** cela diminue *or* déprécie sa valeur; **that doesn't take away from his merit** cela n'enlève rien à son mérite. 2 vt sep a (*carry or lead away*) *object* emporter; *person* emmener. (*on book etc*) **"not to be taken away"** "à consulter sur place". b (*remove*) *object* prendre, retirer, enlever (*from sb* à qn, *from sth* de qch); *sb's child, wife, sweetheart* enlever (*from sb* à qn). **she took her children away from the school** elle a retiré ses enfants de l'école. c (*Math*) soustraire, retrancher, ôter (*from* de). (*in counting*) **if you take 3 away from 6 ...** 6 moins 3 ... . 3 **takeaway** adj, n *see* **take 2**.

►**take back** vt sep a *gift, one's wife etc* reprendre. **to take back a** *or* **one's promise** reprendre sa parole; **she took back all she had said about him** elle a retiré tout ce qu'elle avait dit à son sujet; **I take it all back!** je n'ai rien dit! b (*return*) *book, goods* rapporter (*to* à); (*accompany*) *person* raccompagner, reconduire (*to* à). (*fig*) **it takes me back to my childhood** cela me rappelle mon enfance; **that takes me back a few years!** ça me rappelle de vieux souvenirs!

►**take down** 1 vt sep a *vase from shelf etc* descendre (*from, off* de); *trousers* baisser; *picture* décrocher, descendre; *poster* décoller; *see* **peg**. b (*dismantle*) *scaffolding, machine* démonter; *building* démolir. c (*write etc*) *notes, letter* prendre; *address, details* prendre, noter, inscrire. 2 **takedown*** adj *see* **take 2**.

►**take from** vt fus = **take away from**; *see* **take away**.

►**take in** vt sep a *chairs, harvest* rentrer; *person* faire entrer; *lodgers* prendre; *friend* recevoir; *orphan, stray dog* recueillir; *newspaper etc* prendre, recevoir. **she takes in sewing** elle fait *or* prend de la couture à domicile.

b *skirt, dress, waistband* reprendre; (*Knitting*) *stitches* diminuer. (*Climbing*) **to take in the slack on a rope** avaler le mou d'une corde.

c (*include, cover*) couvrir, inclure, englober, embrasser. **we cannot take in all the cases** nous ne pouvons pas couvrir *or* inclure tous les cas; **this takes in all possibilities** ceci englobe *or* embrasse toutes les possibilités; (*fig*) **we took in Venice on the way home** nous avons visité Venise sur le chemin du retour; (*US fig*) **to take in a movie** aller au cinéma.

d (*grasp, understand*) saisir, comprendre. **that child takes everything in** rien n'échappe à cet enfant; **the children were taking it all in** les enfants étaient tout oreilles; **she couldn't take in his death at first** dans les premiers temps elle ne pouvait pas se faire à l'idée de sa mort; **he hadn't fully taken in that she was dead** il n'avait pas (vraiment) réalisé qu'elle était morte; **he took in the situation at a glance** il a apprécié la situation en un clin d'œil.

e (*: *cheat, deceive*) avoir*, rouler*. **I've been taken in** je me suis laissé avoir*, j'ai été roulé*; **he's easily taken in** il se fait facilement avoir*; **to be taken in by appearances** se laisser prendre aux *or* tromper par les apparences; **I was taken in by his disguise** je me suis laissé prendre à son déguisement.

►**take off** 1 vi *[person]* partir (*for* pour); *[aircraft, high jumper etc]* décoller. **the plane took off for Berlin** l'avion s'est envolé pour Berlin.

2 vt sep a (*remove*) *garment* enlever, ôter, retirer; *buttons, price tag, lid* enlever; *telephone receiver* décrocher; *item on menu, train, bus* supprimer. (*Med*) **they had to take his leg off** on a dû l'amputer d'une jambe; (*Comm*) **he took £5 off** il a baissé le prix de *or* il a fait un rabais de 5 livres, il a rabattu 5 livres sur le prix; **her new hairstyle takes 5 years off her*** sa nouvelle coiffure la rajeunit de 5 ans.

b (*lead etc away*) *person, car* emmener. **he took her off to lunch** il l'a emmenée déjeuner; **to take sb off to jail** emmener qn en prison; **he was taken off to hospital** on l'a transporté à l'hôpital; **after the wreck a boat took the crew off** une embarcation est venue sauver l'équipage du navire naufragé; **to take o.s. off** s'en aller.

c (*imitate*) imiter, pasticher.

3 **takeoff** n *see* **take 2**.

►**take on** 1 vi a *[song, fashion etc]* prendre, marcher*.

b (*Brit *: be upset*) s'en faire*.

2 vt sep a (*accept etc*) *work, responsibility* prendre, accepter, se charger de; *bet* accepter; *challenger* (*for game/fight*) accepter de jouer/de se battre contre. **I'll take you on** (*Betting*) je parie avec vous; (*Sport*) je joue contre vous; **he has taken on more than he bargained for** il n'avait pas compté prendre une si lourde responsabilité; **to agree to**

take a job on (*employment*) accepter un poste; (*task*) accepter de se charger d'un travail.

b *employee* prendre, embaucher; *cargo, passenger* embarquer, prendre; *form, qualities* prendre, revêtir.

c (*contend with*) *enemy* s'attaquer à. (*challenge etc*) **he took on the whole committee** il s'est attaqué *or* s'en est pris au comité tout entier.

►**take out** 1 vt sep a (*lead or carry outside*) *prisoner* faire sortir; *chair etc* sortir. **they took us out to see the sights** ils nous ont emmenés visiter la ville; **he took her out to lunch/the theatre** il l'a emmenée déjeuner/au théâtre; **he has often taken her out** il l'a souvent sortie; **I'm going to take the children/dog out** je vais sortir les enfants/le chien.

b (*from pocket, drawer*) prendre (*from, of* dans); (*remove*) sortir, retirer, enlever, ôter (*from, of* de); *tooth* arracher; *appendix, tonsils* enlever; *stain* ôter, enlever (*from* de). **take your hands out of your pockets** sors *or* enlève *or* retire tes mains de tes poches; (*fig*) **that will take you out of yourself a little** cela vous changera un peu les idées; (*fig*) **that sort of work certainly takes it out of you*** il n'y a pas de doute que ces choses-là fatiguent* beaucoup; **when he got the sack he took it out on the dog*** quand il a été mis à la porte il s'est défoulé* sur le chien; **don't take it out on me!*** ce n'est pas la peine de t'en prendre à moi!; **don't take your bad temper out on me*** ne passez pas votre mauvaise humeur sur moi.

c *insurance policy* souscrire à, prendre; *patent* prendre; *licence* se procurer.

d (*Mil **) *target* descendre*, bousiller*.

2 **takeout** adj, n *see* **take 2**.

►**take over** 1 vi [*dictator, army, political party etc*] prendre le pouvoir. **to take over from sb** prendre la relève *or* le relai de qn; **let him take over** cédez-lui la place.

2 vt sep a (*escort or carry across*) **he took me over to the island in his boat** il m'a transporté jusqu'à l'île dans son bateau; **will you take me over to the other side?** voulez-vous me faire traverser?

b (*assume responsibility for*) *business, shop, materials, goods, furniture etc* reprendre; *new car* prendre livraison de; *sb's debts* prendre à sa charge. **he took over the shop from his father** il a pris la suite de son père dans le magasin; **he took over the job from X** c'est lui qui a pris la succession de X; **I took over his duties** je l'ai remplacé dans ses fonctions; **he took over the leadership of the party when Smith resigned** il a remplacé Smith à la tête du parti après la démission de celui-ci.

c (*Fin*) *another company* absorber, racheter. (*fig*) **the tourists have taken over Venice** les touristes ont envahi Venise.

3 **takeover** n, adj *see* **take 2**.

►**take to** vt fus a (*conceive liking for*) *person* se prendre d'amitié pour, se prendre de sympathie pour, sympathiser avec; *game, action, study* prendre goût à, mordre à‡. **I didn't take to the idea** l'idée ne m'a rien dit; **they took to each other at once** ils se sont plu immédiatement; **I didn't take to him** il ne m'a pas beaucoup plu.

b (*start, adopt*) *habit* prendre; *hobby* se mettre à. **to take to drink/drugs** se mettre à boire/à se droguer; **she took to telling everyone ...** elle s'est mise à dire à tout le monde ... .

c **to take to one's bed** s'aliter; **to take to the woods** [*walker*] passer par les bois; [*hunted man*] s'enfuir à travers bois; (*Naut*) **to take to the boats** abandonner *or* évacuer le navire; *see* **heel[1]** *etc*.

►**take up** 1 vi: **to take up with sb** se lier avec qn, se prendre d'amitié pour qn.

2 vt sep a (*lead or carry upstairs, uphill etc*) *person* faire monter; *object* monter.

b (*lift*) *object from ground etc* ramasser, prendre; *carpet* enlever; *roadway, pavement* dépaver; *dress, hem, skirt* raccourcir; *passenger* prendre; (*fig: after interruption*) *one's work, book etc* reprendre, se remettre à, continuer; *conversation, discussion, story* reprendre (le fil de); *see* **cudgel** *etc*.

c (*occupy*) *space* occuper, tenir, prendre; *time* prendre, demander; *attention* occuper, absorber. **he is very taken up** il est très pris; **he is quite taken up with her** il ne pense plus qu'à elle; **he is completely taken up with his plan** il est tout entier à son projet; **it takes up too much room** cela prend *or* occupe trop de place; **it takes up all my free time** cela (me) prend tout mon temps libre.

d (*absorb*) *liquids* absorber. **to take up the slack in a rope** tendre une corde.

e (*raise question of*) *subject* aborder. **I'll take that up with him** je lui en parlerai; **I would like to take you up on something you said earlier** je voudrais revenir sur quelque chose que vous avez dit précédemment.

f (*start, accept*) *hobby, subject, sport, languages etc* se mettre à; *career* embrasser; *method* adopter, retenir; *challenge* relever; *shares* souscrire à; *person* (*as friend*) adopter; (*as protégé*) prendre en main. (*fig*) **I'll take you up on your promise** je mettrai votre parole à l'épreuve; **I'd like to take you up on your offer of free tickets** je voudrais accepter votre offre de places gratuites; **I'll take you up on that some day** je m'en souviendrai à l'occasion, un jour je vous prendrai au mot.

g (*understand*) comprendre. **you've taken me up wrongly** vous m'avez mal compris.

3 **take-up** n *see* **take 2**.

taken [ˈteɪkən] 1 ptp of **take**. 2 adj a *seat, place* pris, occupé. b **to be very ~ with sb/sth** être très impressionné par qn/qch; **I'm not very ~ with him** il ne m'a pas fait une grosse impression; **I'm quite ~ with** *or* **by that idea** cette idée me plaît énormément.

taker [ˈteɪkər] n: **~s of snuff** les gens qui prisent; **drug-~s** les drogués *mpl*; **at £5 he found no ~s** il n'a pas trouvé d'acheteurs *or* de preneurs pour 5 livres; **this suggestion found no ~s** cette suggestion n'a été relevée par personne.

taking [ˈteɪkɪŋ] 1 adj *person, manners* engageant, attirant, séduisant. 2 n a **it is yours for the ~** tu n'as qu'à (te donner la peine de) le prendre. b (*Comm*) **~s** recette *f*. c (*Mil: capture*) prise *f*. d (*Brit Jur*) **~ and driving away a vehicle** vol *m* de véhicule.

talc [tælk] n, **talcum (powder)** [ˈtælkəm (ˌpaʊdər)] n talc *m*.

tale [teɪl] 1 n (*story*) conte *m*, histoire *f*; (*legend*) histoire, légende *f*; (*account*) récit *m*, histoire (*pej*). **"T~s of King Arthur"** "La Légende du Roi Arthur"; **he told us the ~ of his adventures** il nous a fait le récit de ses aventures; **I've heard that ~ before** j'ai déjà entendu cette histoire-là quelque part; **I've been hearing ~s about you** on m'a dit *or* raconté des choses sur vous; **to tell ~s** (*inform on sb*) rapporter, cafarder*; (*to lie*) mentir, raconter des histoires*; (*fig*) **to tell ~s out of school** raconter ce qu'on devait (*or* doit *etc*) taire; **he lived to tell the ~** il y a survécu; *see* **fairy, old, tell 1b, woe** *etc*.

2 comp ►**talebearer** rapporteur *m*, -euse *f*, cafard* *m* ►**talebearing, taletelling** rapportage *m*, cafardage* *m*.

talent [ˈtælənt] 1 n a don *m*, talent *m*; (*NonC*) talent. **to have a ~ for drawing** être doué pour le dessin, avoir un don *or* du talent pour le dessin; **a writer of great ~** un écrivain de grand talent *or* très talentueux; **he encourages young ~** il encourage les jeunes talents; **he is looking for ~ amongst the schoolboy players** il cherche de futurs grands joueurs parmi les lycéens; (*attractive people*) **there's not much ~ here tonight‡** (*amongst the girls*) il n'y a pas grand-chose comme minettes‡ *or* nénettes‡ ici ce soir; (*amongst the boys*) il n'y a pas grand-chose comme types bien* ici ce soir.

b (*coin*) talent *m*.

2 comp ►**talent scout, talent spotter** (*Cine, Theat*) dénicheur *m*, -euse *f* de vedettes; (*Sport*) dénicheur, -euse de futurs grands joueurs.

talented [ˈtæləntɪd] adj *person* talentueux, doué.

tali [ˈteɪlaɪ] npl of **talus**.

talisman [ˈtælɪzmən] n, pl **~s** talisman *m*.

talk [tɔːk] 1 n a conversation *f*, discussion *f*; (*more formal*) entretien *m*; (*chat*) causerie *f*. **during his ~ with the Prime Minister** pendant son entretien avec le Premier ministre; (*esp Pol*) **~s** discussions *fpl*; **peace ~s** conférence *f or* discussions sur la paix; **the Geneva ~s on disarmament** la conférence de Genève sur le désarmement; **I enjoyed our (little) ~** notre causerie *or* notre petite conversation m'a été très agréable; **we've had several ~s about this** nous en avons parlé *or* discuté plusieurs fois; **I must have a ~ with him** (*gen*) il faut que je lui parle (*subj*); (*warning, threatening etc*) j'ai à lui parler; **we must have a ~ some time** il faudra que nous nous rencontrions (*subj*) un jour pour discuter *or* causer.

b (*informal lecture*) exposé *m* (*on* sur); (*less academic or technical*) causerie *f* (*on* sur). **to give a ~** faire un exposé, donner une causerie (*on* sur); **Mr Jones has come to give us a ~ on ...** M. Jones est venu nous parler de ...; **to give a ~ on the radio** parler à la radio.

c (*NonC*) propos *mpl*; (*gossip*) bavardage(s) *m(pl)*; (*pej*) racontars *mpl*. **the ~ was all about the wedding** les propos tournaient autour du mariage; **you should hear the ~!** si tu savais ce qu'on raconte!; **there is (some) ~ of his returning** (*it is being discussed*) il est question qu'il revienne; (*it is being rumoured*) on dit qu'il va peut-être revenir, le bruit court qu'il va revenir; **there was no ~ of his resigning** il n'a pas été question qu'il démissionne (*subj*); **it's common ~ that ...** on dit partout que ..., tout le monde dit que ...; **it's just ~** ce ne sont que des on-dit *or* des racontars *or* des bavardages; **there has been a lot of ~ about her** il a beaucoup été question d'elle; (*pej*) on a raconté beaucoup d'histoires sur elle; **I've heard a lot of ~ about the new factory** j'ai beaucoup entendu parler de la nouvelle usine; **all that ~ about what he was going to do!** toutes ces vaines paroles sur ce qu'il allait faire!; (*pej*) **he's all ~** c'est un grand vantard *or* hâbleur; **it was all (big) ~** tout ça c'était du vent*; **she's/it's the ~ of the town** on ne parle que d'elle/de cela; *see* **baby, idle, small** *etc*.

2 comp ►**talk show** (*Rad*) causerie *f or* tête à tête *m or* entretien *m* (radiodiffusé(e)); (*TV*) causerie *etc* (télévisée).

3 vi a (*speak*) parler (*about, of* de); (*chatter*) bavarder, causer. **he can't ~ yet** il ne parle pas encore; **after days of torture he finally ~ed** après plusieurs jours de torture, il a enfin parlé; **I'll make you ~!** (avec moi) tu vas parler!; **now you're ~ing!*** voilà qui devient intéressant!; **it's easy** *or* **all right for him to ~!** il peut parler!; (*iro*) **look who's ~ing!*, YOU can ~!*** tu peux toujours parler, toi!, qu'est-ce qu'il ne faut pas entendre!; (*fig*) **to ~ through one's hat*** dire n'importe quoi; **he was just ~ing for the sake of ~ing** il parlait pour ne rien dire; **he ~s too much** (*too loquacious*) il parle trop; (*indiscreet*) il ne sait pas se taire; **don't ~ to me like that!** ne me parle pas sur ce ton!; **do what he tells you because he knows what he's ~ing about** fais ce qu'il te

demande parce qu'il sait ce qu'il dit; **he knows what he's ~ing about when he's on the subject of cars** il s'y connaît quand il parle (de) voitures; **he doesn't know what he's ~ing about** il ne sait pas ce qu'il dit; **I'm not ~ing about you** ce n'est pas de toi que je parle, il ne s'agit pas de toi; **he was ~ing of** *or* **about going to Greece** il parlait d'aller en Grèce; (*fig*) **it's not as if we're ~ing about ...** ce n'est pas comme s'il s'agissait de ...; (*fig*) **you're ~ing about a million dollars** ce qui est en jeu, c'est un million de dollars, dites-vous bien qu'il faut escompter un million de dollars; **they ~ed of** *or* **about nothing except ...** ils ne parlaient que de ...; **the marriage was much ~ed of in the town** toute la ville parlait du mariage; **his much ~ed-of holiday never happened** ses fameuses vacances ne sont jamais arrivées; **I'm not ~ing to him any more** je ne lui adresse plus la parole, je ne lui cause plus*; **~ing of films, have you seen ...?** en parlant de *or* à propos de films, avez-vous vu ...?; **~ about a stroke of luck!*** tu parles d'une aubaine!*; *see* **big, tough**.

b (*converse*) parler (*to* à, *with* avec), discuter (*to, with* avec); (*more formally*) s'entretenir (*to, with* avec); (*chat*) causer (*to, with* avec); (*gossip*) parler, causer (*about* de), jaser (*pej*) (*about* sur). **who were you ~ing to?** à qui parlais-tu?; **I saw them ~ing (to each other)** je les ai vus en conversation l'un avec l'autre; **to ~ to o.s.** se parler tout seul; **I'll ~ to you about that tomorrow** je t'en parlerai demain; (*threateningly*) j'aurai deux mots à te dire là-dessus demain; **it's no use ~ing to you** je perds mon temps avec toi; **we were just ~ing of** *or* **about you** justement nous parlions de toi; **the Foreign Ministers ~ed about the crisis in China** les ministres des Affaires étrangères se sont entretenus de la crise chinoise; **I have ~ed with him several times** j'ai eu plusieurs conversations avec lui; **try to keep him ~ing** essaie de le faire parler aussi longtemps que possible; **to get o.s. ~ed about** faire parler de soi; *see* **nineteen** *etc*.

4 **vt** a *a language, slang* parler. **to ~ business/politics** parler affaires/politique; **to ~ nonsense** *or* **rubbish*** *or* **tripe**‡ raconter des idioties, dire n'importe quoi *or* des conneries‡; **he's ~ing sense** c'est la voix de la raison qui parle, ce qu'il dit est le bon sens même; **~ sense!** ne dis pas n'importe quoi!; *see* **hind²**, **shop**, **turkey** *etc*.

b **to ~ sb into doing sth** amener qn à *or* persuader qn de faire qch (*à force de paroles*); **I managed to ~ him out of doing it** je suis arrivé à le dissuader de le faire (en lui parlant); **she ~ed him into a better mood** elle l'a remis de meilleure humeur en lui parlant; **he ~ed himself into the job** il a si bien parlé qu'on lui a offert le poste.

►**talk away** **vi** parler *or* discuter sans s'arrêter, ne pas arrêter de parler. **we talked away for hours** nous avons passé des heures à parler *or* discuter; **she was talking away about her plans when suddenly ...** elle était partie à parler de ses projets quand soudain ... .

►**talk back** **vi** répondre (insolemment) (*to sb* à qn).

►**talk down** 1 **vi**: **to talk down to sb** parler à qn comme à un enfant. 2 **vt sep** a (*silence*) **they talked him down** leurs flots de paroles l'ont réduit au silence. b (*Aviat*) *pilot, aircraft* aider à atterrir par radio-contrôle. c *suicidal person* persuader de ne pas sauter.

►**talk on** **vi** parler *or* discuter sans s'arrêter, ne pas arrêter de parler. **she talked on and on about it** elle en a parlé pendant des heures et des heures.

►**talk out** **vt sep** a (*discuss thoroughly*) **to talk it/things out** mettre les choses au clair. b (*Parl*) **to talk out a bill** prolonger la discussion d'un projet de loi jusqu'à ce qu'il soit trop tard pour le voter. c **to talk o.s. out** parler jusqu'à l'épuisement.

►**talk over** **vt sep** a *question, problem* discuter (de), débattre. **let's talk it over** discutons-en entre nous; **I must talk it over with my wife first** je dois d'abord en parler à ma femme. b = **talk round 1**.

►**talk round** 1 **vt sep**: **to talk sb round** amener qn à changer d'avis, gagner qn à son avis, convaincre *or* persuader qn. 2 **vt fus** *problem, subject* tourner autour de. **they talked round it all evening** ils ont tourné autour du pot toute la soirée.

►**talk up** (*US*) 1 **vi** (*speak frankly*) ne pas mâcher ses mots. 2 **vt fus** *project, book* pousser, vanter.

talkathon ['tɔːkəθɒn] **n** (*US*) débat-marathon *m*.

talkative ['tɔːkətɪv] **adj** bavard, loquace, volubile.

talkativeness ['tɔːkətɪvnɪs] **n** volubilité *f*, loquacité *f* (*liter*).

talker ['tɔːkəʳ] **n** parleur *m*, -euse *f*, causeur *m*, -euse *f*, bavard(e) *m(f)* (*sometimes pej*). **he's a great ~** c'est un grand bavard *or* un causeur intarissable, il a la langue bien pendue*; **he's a terrible ~** c'est un vrai moulin à paroles.

talkie* ['tɔːkɪ] **n** (*Cine*) film parlant. **the ~s** le cinéma parlant; *see* **walkie-talkie**.

talking ['tɔːkɪŋ] 1 **n** bavardage *m*. **he did all the ~** il a fait tous les frais de la conversation; **that's enough ~!** assez de bavardages!, assez bavardé!; **no ~!** défense de parler!, silence (s'il vous plaît). 2 **adj** *doll, parrot, film* parlant. 3 **comp** ►**talking book** livre enregistré ►**talking head** (*TV*) présentateur *m*, -trice *f* en gros plan ►**talking point** sujet *m* de discussion *or* de conversation ►**talking shop*** parlot(t)e *f* ►**talking-to*** attrapade* *f*; **to give sb a (good) talking-to** passer un bon savon à qn*.

tall [tɔːl] 1 **adj** *person* grand, de haute taille; *building etc* haut, élevé. **how ~ is that mast?** quelle est la hauteur de ce mât?; **how ~ are you?** combien mesurez-vous?; **he is 6 feet ~** ≃ il mesure 1 mètre 80; **~ and slim** élancé; **he is ~er than his brother** il est plus grand que son frère; **she is ~er than me by a head** elle me dépasse de la tête; **she wears high heels to make herself look ~er** elle porte des talons hauts pour se grandir; (*fig*) **he told me a ~ story about ...** il m'a raconté une histoire à dormir debout *or* une histoire marseillaise sur ...; **that's a ~ story!** elle est forte, celle-là!*; **that's a ~ order!** c'est demander un peu trop!, c'est pousser (un peu)!*

2 **adv**: **he stands 6 feet ~** il fait 2 mètres; (*fig*) **to stand** *or* **walk ~** garder *or* marcher la tête haute.

3 **comp** ►**tallboy** (*Brit*) commode *f*.

tallness ['tɔːlnɪs] **n** *[person]* grande taille; *[building etc]* hauteur *f*.

tallow ['tæləʊ] **n** suif *m*. **~ candle** chandelle *f*.

tally ['tælɪ] 1 **n** (*Hist: stick*) taille *f* (*latte de bois*); (*count*) compte *m*. **to keep a ~ of** (*count*) tenir le compte de; (*mark off on list*) pointer. 2 **vi** s'accorder (*with* avec), correspondre (*with* à).

tallyho ['tælɪ'həʊ] **excl, n** taïaut (*m*).

talon ['tælən] **n** a *[eagle etc]* serre *f*; *[tiger etc, person]* griffe *f*. b (*Archit, Cards*) talon *m*.

talus ['teɪləs] **n, pl tali** astragale *m*.

tamable ['teɪməbl] **adj** = **tameable**.

tamarin ['tæmərɪn] **n** tamarin *m* (*Zool*).

tamarind ['tæmərɪnd] **n** (*fruit*) tamarin *m*; (*tree*) tamarinier *m*.

tamarisk ['tæmərɪsk] **n** tamaris *m*.

tambour ['tæm,bʊəʳ] **n** (*Archit, Mus*) tambour *m*; (*Embroidery*) métier *m or* tambour à broder.

tambourine [,tæmbə'riːn] **n** tambour *m* de basque, tambourin *m*.

Tamburlaine ['tæmbəleɪn] **n** Tamerlan *m*.

tame [teɪm] 1 **adj** *bird, animal* apprivoisé; (*fig*) *story, match* insipide, fade. **to become** *or* **grow ~(r)** s'apprivoiser; **the sparrows are quite ~** les moineaux sont presque apprivoisés *or* ne sont pas farouches; (*hum*) **let's ask our ~ American** demandons-le à notre Américain de service (*hum*); (*hum*) **I really need a ~ osteopath** ce qu'il me faudrait vraiment c'est un ostéopathe à demeure. 2 **vt** *bird, wild animal* apprivoiser; *esp lion, tiger* dompter; (*fig*) *passion* maîtriser; *person* mater, soumettre.

tameable ['teɪməbl] **adj** (*see* **tame 2**) apprivoisable; domptable.

tamely ['teɪmlɪ] **adv** *agree* docilement. **the story ends ~** l'histoire finit en eau de boudin.

tamer ['teɪməʳ] **n** dresseur *m*, -euse *f*. **lion-~** dompteur *m*, -euse *f* (de lions), belluaire *m*.

Tamerlane ['tæməleɪn] **n** Tamerlan *m*.

Tamil ['tæmɪl] 1 **n** a Tamoul(e) *m(f) or* Tamil(e) *m(f)*. b (*Ling*) tamoul *m or* tamil *m*. 2 **adj** tamoul *or* tamil.

taming ['teɪmɪŋ] **n** (*NonC*) (*gen*) apprivoisement *m*; *[circus animals]* dressage *m*, domptage *m*. **"The T~ of the Shrew"** "La Mégère Apprivoisée".

Tammany ['tæmənɪ] **n** (*US Hist*) *organisation démocrate de New York, souvent impliquée dans des affaires de corruption*.

tammy* ['tæmɪ] **n**, **tam o'shanter** [,tæmə'ʃæntəʳ] **n** béret écossais.

tamp [tæmp] **vt** *earth* damer, tasser; *tobacco* tasser. (*in blasting*) **to ~ a drill hole** bourrer un trou de mine à l'argile *or* au sable.

Tampax ['tæmpæks] **n** ® Tampax *m* ®.

tamper ['tæmpəʳ] 1 **vi**: **to ~ with** *machinery, car, brakes, safe etc* toucher à (*sans permission*); *lock* essayer de crocheter; *document, text* altérer, fausser, falsifier; *accounts* falsifier, fausser, trafiquer; (*Jur*) *evidence* falsifier; (*US*) *jury* soudoyer; *sb's papers, possessions* toucher à, mettre le nez dans*. 2 **comp** ►**tamper-proof** impossible à falsifier.

tampon ['tæmpɒn] **n** (*Med*) tampon *m*.

tan [tæn] 1 **n** (*also* **sun~**) bronzage *m*, hâle *m*. **she's got a lovely ~** elle a un beau bronzage, elle est bien bronzée. 2 **adj** ocre, brun roux *inv*. 3 **vt** a *skins* tanner. (*fig*) **to ~ sb*, to ~ sb's hide (for him)*** rosser qn*, tanner le cuir à qn‡. b *[sun] sunbather, holiday-maker* brunir, bronzer, hâler; *sailor, farmer etc* hâler, basaner, tanner. **to get ~ned** = **to tan**; *see* **4**. 4 **vi** bronzer, brunir.

tandem ['tændəm] 1 **n** tandem *m*. 2 **adv** *ride* en tandem. (*fig*) **to do sth in ~** faire qch en tandem (*with* avec); (*fig*) **to happen in ~** arriver simultanément.

tang [tæŋ] **n** a (*taste*) saveur forte (et piquante); (*smell*) senteur *or* odeur forte (et piquante). **the salt ~ of the sea air** l'odeur caractéristique de la marée. b *[file, knife]* soie *f*.

Tanganyika [,tæŋgə'njiːkə] **n** Tanganyika *m*. **Lake ~** le lac Tanganyika.

tangent ['tændʒənt] **n** (*Math*) tangente *f*. (*fig*) **to go off** *or* **fly off at a ~** partir dans une digression.

tangential [tæn'dʒenʃəl] **adj** tangentiel.

tangentially [tæn'dʒenʃəlɪ] **adv** (*lit*) tangentiellement; (*fig: indirectly*) indirectement.

tangerine [,tændʒə'riːn] 1 **n** (*also* **~ orange**) mandarine *f*. 2 **adj** (*colour*) mandarine *inv*.

tangibility [,tændʒɪ'bɪlɪtɪ] **n** tangibilité *f*.

tangible ['tændʒəbl] **adj** tangible, palpable; *proof, result* tangible; *assets* réel. (*Fin*) **~ net worth** valeur *f* nette réelle.

tangibly ['tændʒəblɪ] **adv** tangiblement, manifestement.

Tangier [tæn'dʒɪəʳ] n Tanger.

tangle ['tæŋgl] 1 n *[wool, string, rope]* enchevêtrement *m*; (*Climbing: in rope*) nœud *m*; *[creepers, bushes, weeds]* fouillis *m*, enchevêtrement; (*fig: muddle*) confusion *f*. **to get into a ~** *[string, rope, wool]* s'entortiller, s'embrouiller, s'enchevêtrer; *[hair]* s'emmêler, s'enchevêtrer; (*fig*) *[accounts etc]* s'embrouiller; *[traffic]* se bloquer; *[person]* s'embrouiller, être empêtré; **he got into a ~ when he tried to explain** il s'est embrouillé dans ses explications; **I'm in a ~ with the accounts** je suis empêtré dans les comptes; **the whole affair was a hopeless ~** toute cette histoire était affreusement confuse *or* était affreusement embrouillée *or* était un véritable embrouillamini*.

2 vt (*also* **~ up**: *lit, fig*) enchevêtrer, embrouiller, emmêler. **~d** *string, rope, wool* embrouillé, enchevêtré, entortillé; *hair* emmêlé, enchevêtré; (*fig: complicated*) *situation, negotiations* embrouillé; (*fig*) **a ~d web of lies** un inextricable tissu de mensonges; **his tie got ~d up in the machine** sa cravate s'est entortillée dans la machine; (*gen*) **to get ~d (up)** = **to get into a tangle** (*see* **1**).

3 vi a (*become tangled*) = **to get into a tangle** (*lit senses*); *see* **1**.

b (* *fig*) **to ~ with sb** se frotter à qn, se colleter avec qn*; **they ~d over whose fault it was** ils se sont colletés* sur la question de savoir à qui était la faute.

tango ['tæŋgəʊ] 1 n, pl **~s** tango *m*. 2 vi danser le tango.

tangy ['tæŋɪ] adj piquant.

tank [tæŋk] 1 n a (*container*) (*for storage*) réservoir *m*, cuve *f*; (*esp for rainwater*) citerne *f*; (*for gas*) réservoir; (*Aut: petrol ~*) réservoir (à essence); (*for transporting*) réservoir, cuve, (*esp oil*) tank *m*; (*for fermenting, processing etc*) cuve (*also Phot*); (*for fish*) aquarium *m*. **fuel ~** réservoir à carburant; *see* **septic** *etc*. b (*Mil*) char *m* (d'assaut *or* de combat), tank *m*. 2 comp (*Mil*) *commander* de char d'assaut *or* de combat; *brigade* de chars d'assaut *or* de combat ►**tank car** (*US Rail*) wagon-citerne *m* ►**tank top** débardeur *m* (*vêtement*) ►**tank town*** (*US fig*) petite ville (perdue) ►**tank trap** (*Mil*) fossé *m* antichar ►**tank truck** (*US*) camion-citerne *m*.

►**tank along*** vi (*esp on road*) foncer*, aller à toute allure*.

►**tank up** 1 vi (*Aut* *) faire le plein; (*Brit fig* ‡: *drink a lot*) se soûler la gueule‡. 2 vt sep (*) *car etc* remplir d'essence. (*Brit fig*) **to be tanked up**‡ être soûl* *or* bituré‡; (*Brit fig*) **to get tanked up**‡ se soûler la gueule‡.

tankard ['tæŋkəd] n chope *f*, pot *m* à bière.

tanker ['tæŋkəʳ] n (*truck*) camion-citerne *m*; (*ship*) pétrolier *m*, tanker *m*; (*aircraft*) avion-ravitailleur *m*; (*Rail*) wagon-citerne *m*.

tankful ['tæŋkfʊl] n: **a ~ of petrol** un réservoir (plein) d'essence; **a ~ of water** une citerne (pleine) d'eau.

tanned [tænd] adj (*also* **sun~**) *sunbather, holiday-maker* bronzé, bruni, hâlé; *sailor, farmer* hâlé, basané, tanné.

tanner¹ ['tænəʳ] n tanneur *m*.

tanner²* ['tænəʳ] n (*Brit*) (ancienne) pièce *f* de six pence.

tannery ['tænərɪ] n tannerie *f* (*établissement*).

tannic ['tænɪk] adj tannique.

tannin ['tænɪn] n tan(n)in *m*.

tanning ['tænɪŋ] n a (*sun~*) bronzage *m*. b *[hides]* tannage *m*. c (‡ *fig: beating*) tannée‡ *f*, raclée* *f*, correction *f*.

Tannoy ['tænɔɪ] n ® (*Brit*) système *m* de haut-parleurs. **on** *or* **over the ~** par le(s) haut-parleur(s).

tansy ['tænzɪ] n tanaisie *f*.

tantalize ['tæntəlaɪz] vt mettre au supplice (*fig*), tourmenter (*par de faux espoirs*).

tantalizing ['tæntəlaɪzɪŋ] adj *offer, suggestion* terriblement tentant; *smell* terriblement appétissant; *slowness etc* désespérant. **it's ~!** c'est terriblement tentant!, (*stronger*) c'est le supplice de Tantale!

tantalizingly ['tæntəlaɪzɪŋlɪ] adv d'une façon cruellement tentante. **~ slowly** avec une lenteur désespérante.

tantalum ['tæntələm] n tantale *m*.

Tantalus ['tæntələs] n Tantale *m*.

tantamount ['tæntəmaʊnt] adj: **~ to** équivalent à; **it's ~ to failure** autant dire un échec, cela équivaut à un échec.

tantrum ['tæntrəm] n (*also* **temper ~**) crise *f* de colère *or* de rage. **to have** *or* **throw a ~** piquer une colère *or* une crise (de rage).

Tanzania [ˌtænzə'nɪə] n Tanzanie *f*. **United Republic of ~** République unie de Tanzanie.

Tanzanian [ˌtænzə'nɪən] 1 adj tanzanien. 2 n Tanzanien(ne) *m(f)*.

Tao ['taʊ] n Tao *m*.

Taoism ['taʊɪzəm] n taoïsme *m*.

Taoist ['taʊɪst] adj, n taoïste (*mf*).

tap¹ [tæp] 1 n a (*Brit: for water, gas etc*) robinet *m*; (*Brit: ~ on barrel etc*) cannelle *f*, robinet, chantepleure *f*; (*plug for barrel*) bonde *f*. **beer on ~** bière *f* en fût; (*fig*) **there are funds/resources on ~** il y a des fonds/des ressources disponibles; (*fig*) **he seems to have unlimited money on ~** il a l'air d'avoir de l'argent en veux-tu en voilà*; (*fig*) **there are plenty of helpers on ~** il y a autant d'assistants que l'on veut.

b (*Telec*) écoute *f* téléphonique.

c (*NonC: also* **~-dancing**) claquettes *fpl*.

2 comp ►**taproom** (*Brit*) salle *f* (de bistro) ►**taproot** (*Bot*) pivot *m*, racine pivotante ►**tap water** (*Brit*) eau *f* du robinet.

3 vt a *cask, barrel* percer, mettre en perce; *pine* gemmer; *other tree* inciser; (*Elec*) *current* capter; *wire* brancher. **to ~ a tree for its rubber, to ~ (off) rubber from a tree** inciser un arbre pour en tirer le latex.

b *telephone* mettre sur écoute; *telephone line* brancher (pour mettre un téléphone sur écoute). **to ~ sb's phone** mettre qn sur table d'écoute; **my phone is being ~ped** mon téléphone est sur écoute.

c (*fig*) *resources, supplies* exploiter, utiliser. **to ~ sb for money*** emprunter *or* taper* de l'argent à qn; **they ~ped her for a loan*** ils lui ont demandé un prêt; **to ~ sb for information** soutirer des informations à qn.

tap² [tæp] 1 n a petit coup, petite tape. **there was a ~ at the door** on a frappé doucement *or* légèrement à la porte.

b (*Mil*) **~s** (*end of the day*) (sonnerie *f* de) l'extinction *f* des feux; (*at funeral*) sonnerie *f* aux morts.

2 comp ►**tap-dance** n claquettes *fpl* ◊ vi faire des claquettes ►**tap-dancer** danseur *m*, -euse *f* de claquettes ►**tap-dancing** *see* **tap¹ 1c**.

3 vi frapper doucement, taper (doucement), tapoter. **to ~ on** *or* **at the door** frapper doucement à la porte.

4 vt frapper doucement, taper (doucement), tapoter. **she ~ped the child on the cheek** elle a tapoté la joue de l'enfant; **he ~ped me on the shoulder** il m'a tapé sur l'épaule; **to ~ in/out a nail** enfoncer/enlever un clou à petits coups.

►**tap out** vt sep a *one's pipe* débourrer; *see also* **tap² 4**. b *signal, code* pianoter. **to tap out a message in Morse** transmettre un message en morse.

tape [teɪp] 1 n a (*gen: of cloth, paper, metal*) ruban *m*, bande *f*; (*for parcels, documents*) bolduc *m*; (*sticky ~*) papier *m* collant, ruban *m* adhésif, scotch *m* ®; (*Med*) sparadrap *m*. **ticker-~** ruban (de papier) perforé; **the message was coming through on the ~** le message nous parvenait sur la bande (perforée); *see* **paper, punch, red**.

b (*Sewing*) (*decorative*) ruban *m*, ganse *f*; (*for binding*) extra-fort *m*.

c (*Sound Recording, Video, Comput: actual tape*) bande *f* magnétique; (*audio cassette*) audiocassette *f*; (*video cassette*) vidéo(cassette) *f*, cassette *f* vidéo. **the ~ is stuck** la bande est coincée; **I'm going to buy a ~** je vais acheter une cassette; (*video ~*) je vais acheter une (vidéo)cassette *or* une cassette vidéo; **bring your ~s** apporte tes cassettes.

d (*Sport*) fil *m* d'arrivée; (*at opening ceremonies*) ruban *m*.

e (*tape measure*) mètre *m* à ruban; (*esp Sewing*) centimètre *m*.

2 comp ►**tape deck** platine *f* de magnétophone ►**tape drive** (*Comput*) dérouleur *m* de bande magnétique ►**tape machine** (*Brit*) téléscripteur *m*, téléimprimeur *m* ►**tape measure** mètre *m* à ruban; (*esp Sewing*) centimètre *m* ►**tape-record** enregistrer (au magnétophone *or* sur bande) ►**tape recorder** magnétophone *m* ►**tape recording** enregistrement *m* (magnétique *or* au magnétophone) ►**tapeworm** ténia *m*, ver *m* solitaire.

3 vt a (*also* **~ up**) *parcel etc* attacher avec du ruban *or* du bolduc; (*with sticky tape*) scotcher*, coller avec du scotch ® *or* du ruban adhésif; (*also* **~ up, ~ together**) *broken vase etc* recoller avec du scotch *etc* . (*Brit fig*) **I've got him ~d*** je sais ce qu'il vaut; **I've got it all ~d*** je sais parfaitement de quoi il retourne*; **they had the game/situation ~d*** ils avaient le jeu/la situation bien en main; **he's got the job ~d*** il sait parfaitement ce qu'il y a à faire, il peut le faire les doigts dans le nez‡.

b (*record*) *song, message* enregistrer (sur bande *or* au magnétophone); *video material* enregistrer. (*Scol etc*) **~d lesson** leçon enregistrée sur bande.

taper ['teɪpəʳ] 1 n (*for lighting*) bougie fine (*pour allumer les cierges, bougies etc*); (*Rel: narrow candle*) cierge *m*. 2 vt *column, table leg, trouser leg, aircraft wing* fuseler; *stick, end of belt* tailler en pointe, effiler; *hair* effiler; *structure, shape* terminer en pointe. 3 vi *[column, table leg, trouser leg]* finir en fuseau; *[stick, end of belt]* s'effiler; *[hair]* être effilé; *[structure, outline]* se terminer en pointe, s'effiler.

►**taper off** 1 vi *[sound]* se taire peu à peu; *[storm]* s'estomper, aller en diminuant; *[speech, conversation]* s'effilocher. **the end tapers off to a point** le bout se termine en pointe. 2 vt sep finir en pointe.

tapered ['teɪpəd] adj *column, table leg, trouser leg* fuselé, en fuseau; *stick* pointu; *hair* effilé; *structure, outline* en pointe. **~ fingers** doigts fuselés.

tapering ['teɪpərɪŋ] adj a **~ fingers** doigts *mpl* fuselés; *see also* **tapered**. b *tariff, rate, charge* dégressif.

tapestry ['tæpɪstrɪ] n tapisserie *f* (*ouvrage en tissu*). **the Bayeux T~** la tapisserie de Bayeux.

tapioca [ˌtæpɪ'əʊkə] n tapioca *m*.

tapir ['teɪpəʳ] n tapir *m*.

tappet ['tæpɪt] n (*Tech*) poussoir *m* (de soupape).

tapping¹ ['tæpɪŋ] n (*NonC*) a *[pine]* gemmage *m*; *[other trees]* incision *f*; *[electric current]* captage *m*. b (*Telec*) **phone ~** écoutes *fpl* téléphoniques.

tapping² ['tæpɪŋ] n (*NonC*) (*noise, act*) tapotement *m*. **~ sound** tapotement.

tar¹ [tɑːʳ] 1 n (*NonC*) goudron *m*; (*on roads*) goudron, bitume *m*. 2

vt *fence etc* goudronner; *road* goudronner, bitumer. **to ~ and feather sb** passer qn au goudron et à la plume; (*fig*) **they're all ~red with the same brush** ils sont tous à mettre dans le même sac*; (*roofing*) **~red felt** couverture *f* bitumée *or* goudronnée.

tar²*† [tɑːʳ] n (*sailor*) mathurin† *m*; *see* **jack**.

taramasalata [ˌtærəməsəˈlɑːtə] n tarama *m*.

tarantella [ˌtærənˈtelə] n tarentelle *f*.

tarantula [təˈræntjʊlə] n, pl ~s *or* **tarantulae** [təˈræntjʊˌliː] tarentule *f*.

tarboosh, tarbush [tɑːˈbuːʃ] n tarbouch(e) *m*.

tardily [ˈtɑːdɪlɪ] adv (*belatedly*) tardivement; (*slowly*) lentement; (*late*) en retard.

tardiness [ˈtɑːdɪnɪs] n (*NonC*) (*slowness*) lenteur *f*, manque *m* d'empressement (*in doing* à faire); (*unpunctuality*) manque de ponctualité.

tardy [ˈtɑːdɪ] adj (*belated*) tardif; (*unhurried*) lent, nonchalant; (*late*) en retard. **to be ~ in doing** faire avec du retard; (*US Scol*) **~ slip** billet *m* de retard.

tare¹ [tɛəʳ] n (*weeds*) ~s†† ivraie *f* (*NonC*: *liter*).

tare² [tɛəʳ] n (*Comm*: *weight*) tare *f* (*poids*).

target [ˈtɑːgɪt] 1 n (*Mil, Sport*: *for shooting practice*; *fig*: *of criticism etc*) cible *f*; (*Mil*: *in attack or mock attack*; *fig*: *objective*) but *m*, objectif *m*. **dead on ~!** pile!; **to be on ~** [*rocket, missile, bombs etc*] suivre la trajectoire prévue; (*fig*) [*remark, criticism*] mettre (en plein) dans le mille; (*in timing etc*) ne pas avoir de retard; (*Comm*) [*sales*] correspondre aux objectifs; [*forecast*] tomber juste; **we're on ~ for sales of £10 million this year** nos ventes devraient atteindre les 10 millions de livres cette année; **they set themselves a ~ of £1,000** ils se sont fixé comme but *or* objectif de réunir (*or* de gagner *etc*) 1.000 livres; **the ~s for production** les objectifs de production; (*Comm*) **our ~ is young people under 20** notre cible *or* le public ciblé, ce sont les jeunes de moins de 20 ans; (*fig*) **an obvious ~** une cible facile.

2 comp *date, amount etc* fixé, prévu ►**target area** (*Mil*) environs *mpl* de la cible ►**target group** groupe *m* cible *inv* ►**target language** langue *f* cible *inv*, langue d'arrivée ►**target practice** (*Mil, Sport*) exercices *mpl* de tir (à la cible) ►**target price** prix indicatif *or* objectif ►**target vehicle** (*Space*) vaisseau-cible *m*.

3 vt a (*Mil etc*) *enemy troops* prendre pour cible, viser; *missile* pointer, diriger.

b (*Comm, TV, Cine*: *aim at*) *market, audience etc* cibler, s'adresser à, prendre pour cible.

c (*Comm, Fin*: *aim for*) *sales, production figures* avoir pour objectif.

d (*direct, send*) *aid, benefits etc* concentrer.

targetable [ˈtɑːgɪtəbl] adj *warhead* dirigeable.

targeting [ˈtɑːgɪtɪŋ] n a (*Mil*) **the ~ of civilian areas** la prise des quartiers civils pour cible. b (*Comm*) ciblage *m*. **the ~ of young people as potential buyers of ...** la prise pour cible des jeunes comme acheteurs potentiels de ... .

Tarheel [ˈtɑːhiːl] n (*US*) habitant(e) *m(f)* de la Caroline du Nord. **the ~ State** la Caroline du Nord.

tariff [ˈtærɪf] 1 n (*Econ*: *taxes*) tarif douanier; (*Comm*: *price list*) tarif, tableau *m* des prix. 2 comp *concession, quota* tarifaire ►**tariff barrier** barrière *f* douanière ►**tariff heading** (*Jur, Fin*) position *f* tarifaire ►**tariff reform** (*Econ*) réforme *f* des tarifs douaniers.

tarmac [ˈtɑːmæk] 1 n a (*esp Brit*: *NonC*: *substance*) **T~** ® macadam *m* goudronné. b (*airport runway*) piste *f*; (*airport apron*) aire *f* d'envol. 2 vt macadamiser, goudronner.

Tarmacadam [ˌtɑːməˈkædəm] n ® = **tarmac a**.

tarn [tɑːn] n petit lac (de montagne).

tarnation‡ [tɑːˈneɪʃən] (*US dial*) 1 n damnation! 2 adj fichu* (*before noun*). 3 adv fichtrement*.

tarnish [ˈtɑːnɪʃ] 1 vt *metal* ternir; *gilded frame etc* dédorer; *mirror* désargenter; (*fig*) *reputation, image, memory* ternir. 2 vi se ternir; se dédorer; se désargenter. 3 n (*NonC*) ternissure *f*; dédorage *m*; désargentage *m*.

tarot [ˈtærəʊ] n (*NonC*) **the ~** le(s) tarot(s) *m(pl)*; **~ card** tarot.

tarp* [tɑːp] n (*US, Austral*) (abbr of **tarpaulin**) bâche *f* (goudronnée).

tarpaulin [tɑːˈpɔːlɪn] n a (*NonC*) toile goudronnée. b (*sheet*) bâche *f* (goudronnée); (*on truck, over boat cargo*) prélart *m*.

tarpon [ˈtɑːpɒn] n tarpon *m*.

tarragon [ˈtærəgən] n estragon *m*. **~ vinegar** vinaigre *m* à l'estragon.

tarring [ˈtɑːrɪŋ] n goudronnage *m*.

tarry¹ [ˈtɑːrɪ] adj *substance* goudronneux, bitumeux; (*tar-stained*) taché *or* plein de goudron.

tarry² [ˈtærɪ] vi (*liter*) (*stay*) rester, demeurer; (*delay*) s'attarder, tarder.

tarsal [ˈtɑːsəl] adj (*Anat*) tarsien.

Tarsus [ˈtɑːsəs] n Tarsus; (*Antiq*) Tarse *f*.

tarsus [ˈtɑːsəs] n, pl **tarsi** [ˈtɑːsaɪ] tarse *m*.

tart¹ [tɑːt] adj *flavour, fruit* âpre, aigrelet, acidulé; (*fig*) *comment* acerbe.

tart² [tɑːt] n a (*esp Brit Culin*) tarte *f*; (*small*) tartelette *f*. **apple ~** tarte(lette) aux pommes. b (‡: *prostitute*) poule‡ *f*, putain‡ *f*.

►**tart up**‡ vt sep (*Brit pej*) *house, car, design, scheme* rénover, retaper, rajeunir. **to tart o.s. up** se faire beau (*or* belle); (*dress*) s'attifer (*pej*); (*make up*) se maquiller outrageusement.

tartan [ˈtɑːtən] 1 n tartan *m*. 2 adj *garment, fabric* écossais. **~ (travelling) rug** plaid *m*.

Tartar [ˈtɑːtəʳ] 1 n a Tartare *mf or* Tatar(e) *m(f)*. b **t~** personne *f* difficile *or* intraitable; (*woman*) mégère *f*, virago *f*; (*fig*) **to catch a t~** trouver à qui parler. 2 adj a (*Geog*) tartare *or* tatar. b (*Culin*) **t~(e) sauce** sauce *f* tartare; **steak t~(e)** (steak *m*) tartare *m*.

tartar [ˈtɑːtəʳ] n (*NonC*: *Chem etc*) tartre *m*; *see* **cream**.

tartaric [tɑːˈtærɪk] adj tartrique.

tartly [ˈtɑːtlɪ] adv aigrement, d'une manière acerbe.

tartness [ˈtɑːtnɪs] n (*lit, fig*) aigreur *f*.

Tarzan [ˈtɑːzən] n Tarzan *m*.

task [tɑːsk] 1 n tâche *f*, besogne *f*, travail *m*; (*Scol*) devoir *m*. **a hard ~** une lourde tâche; **to take sb to ~** prendre qn à partie, réprimander qn (*for, about* pour). 2 vt *sb's brain, patience, imagination* mettre à l'épreuve; *sb's strength* éprouver. **it didn't ~ him too much** cela ne lui a pas demandé trop d'effort. 3 comp ►**task force** (*Mil*) corps *m* expéditionnaire; (*Police*) détachement *m* spécial (*affecté à un travail particulier*) ►**taskmaster**: (*Prov*) **poverty is a hard taskmaster** la misère est un tyran implacable; **he is a hard taskmaster** c'est un véritable tyran, il ne plaisante pas avec le travail.

Tasman [ˈtæzmən] n: **~ Sea** mer *f* de Tasman.

Tasmania [tæzˈmeɪnɪə] n Tasmanie *f*.

Tasmanian [tæzˈmeɪnɪən] 1 adj tasmanien. 2 n Tasmanien(ne) *m(f)*.

tassel [ˈtæsəl] n gland *m*; (*pompon*) pompon *m*.

Tasso [ˈtæsəʊ] n le Tasse.

taste [teɪst] 1 n a (*flavour*) goût *m*, saveur *f*. **it has an odd ~** cela a un drôle de goût; **it has no ~** cela n'a aucun goût *or* aucune saveur; **it left a bad ~ in the mouth** (*lit*) cela m'a (*or* lui a *etc*) laissé un goût déplaisant dans la bouche; (*fig*) j'en ai (*or* il en a *etc*) gardé une amertume.

b (*NonC*: *sense*) goût *m* (*also fig*). **sweet to the ~** (au goût) sucré; (*fig*) **to have (good) ~** avoir du goût, avoir bon goût; **he has no ~** il n'a aucun goût, il a très mauvais goût; **in good/bad ~** de bon/mauvais goût; **in poor** *or* **doubtful ~** d'un goût douteux; **people of ~** les gens de goût.

c **to have a ~ of sth** (*lit*) goûter (à) qch; (*fig*) goûter de qch; **would you like a ~ (of it)?** voulez-vous (y) goûter?; **he had a ~ of the cake** il a goûté au gâteau; **I gave him a ~ of the wine** je lui ai fait goûter le vin; (*fig*) **it gave him a ~ of military life/of the work** cela lui a donné un aperçu *or* un échantillon de la vie militaire/du travail; (*fig*) **he's had a ~ of prison** il a tâté de la prison; (*fig*) **to give sb a ~ of his own medicine** rendre à qn la monnaie de sa pièce; (*fig*) **to give sb a ~ of the whip** montrer à qn ce qui l'attend s'il ne marche pas droit; (*fig*) **a ~ of happiness** une idée du bonheur; (*fig*) **we got a ~ of his anger** il nous a donné un échantillon de sa colère; (*fig*) **it was a ~ of things to come** c'était un avant-goût de l'avenir.

d (*small amount, trace*) **a ~ of** (*gen*) un (tout) petit peu de; [*salt etc*] une pincée de; [*vinegar, cream, brandy*] une goutte de.

e (*liking*) goût *m*, penchant *m* (*for* pour). **it is to my ~** ça me plaît, ça correspond à mon *or* mes goût(s); **to have a ~ for** avoir du goût *or* un penchant pour; **to get** *or* **acquire** *or* **develop a ~ for** prendre goût à; (*Culin*) **sweeten to ~** sucrer à volonté; **it's a matter of ~** c'est affaire de goût; **there's no accounting for ~** des goûts et des couleurs on ne discute pas; **each to his own ~, ~s differ** chacun son goût; **one's ~(s) in music** ses goûts musicaux; **she has expensive ~s** elle a un goût *or* un penchant pour tout ce qui est cher; **he has expensive ~s in cars** il a le goût des voitures de luxe.

2 comp ►**taste bud** papille gustative.

3 vt a (*perceive flavour of*) sentir (le goût de). **I can't ~ the garlic** je ne sens pas (le goût de) l'ail; **I can't ~ anything when I have a cold** je trouve tout insipide quand j'ai un rhume; **you won't ~ it** tu n'en sentiras pas le goût.

b (*sample*) *food, drink* goûter à; (*esp for first time*) goûter de; (*to test quality*) *food* goûter; *wine* (*at table*) goûter; (*at wine-tasting*) déguster; (*fig*) *power, freedom, success* goûter à, connaître. **just ~ this!** goûtez à ça!; **I haven't ~d salmon for years** ça fait des années que je n'ai pas mangé *or* goûté de saumon; **I have never ~d snails** je n'ai jamais mangé d'escargots; **he had not ~d food for a week** il n'avait rien mangé depuis une semaine; **~ the sauce before adding salt** goûtez la sauce avant d'ajouter du sel; **you must ~ my marmalade** je vais vous faire goûter de ma confiture d'oranges; *see* **wine**.

4 vi: **it doesn't ~ at all** cela n'a aucun goût; **to ~ bitter** avoir un goût amer; **to ~ good/bad** avoir bon/mauvais goût; **to ~ of** *or* **like sth** avoir un goût de qch; **it doesn't ~ of anything in particular** cela n'a pas de goût spécial; **it ~s all right to me** d'après moi cela a un goût normal.

tasteful [ˈteɪstfʊl] adj de bon goût, d'un goût sûr, élégant.

tastefully [ˈteɪstfəlɪ] adv avec goût.

tastefulness [ˈteɪstfʊlnɪs] n bon goût, goût sûr.

tasteless [ˈteɪstlɪs] adj *food* fade, insipide, sans saveur; *medicine* qui n'a aucun goût; (*fig*) *remark, decoration etc* de mauvais goût.

tastelessly [ˈteɪstlɪslɪ] adv (*fig*) sans goût, avec mauvais goût.

tastelessness [ˈteɪstlɪsnɪs] n manque *m* de saveur, fadeur *f* (*pej*); (*fig*) mauvais goût.

taster [ˈteɪstəʳ] n a (*person*) dégustateur *m*, -trice *f*. b (*: *foretaste*) avant-goût *m* (*fig*). **that is just a ~** ce n'est qu'un avant-goût *or* qu'un début.

tastiness ['teɪstɪnɪs] n saveur *f* agréable, goût *m* (délicieux).

tasting ['teɪstɪŋ] n dégustation *f*.

tasty ['teɪstɪ] adj *food* savoureux, délicieux; *titbit* succulent; (*well-seasoned*) relevé, bien assaisonné.

tat¹ [tæt] 1 vi faire de la frivolité (*dentelle*). 2 vt faire en frivolité.

tat²* [tæt] n (*NonC: Brit pej: shabby clothes*) friperies *fpl*; (*goods*) camelote* *f*.

ta-ta* ['tæ'tɑː] excl (*Brit*) au revoir!, salut!*

tattered ['tætəd] adj *clothes, flag* en lambeaux, en loques, dépenaillé*; *book, handkerchief* en morceaux, tout déchiré; *sheet of paper, bed linen* en lambeaux, en morceaux; *person* déguenillé, dépenaillé*, loqueteux; *reputation* en miettes.

tatters ['tætəz] npl lambeaux *mpl*, loques *fpl*. **in ~** = **tattered**.

tatting ['tætɪŋ] n (*NonC*) frivolité *f* (*dentelle*).

tattle ['tætl] 1 vi (*gossip*) jaser, cancaner; (*tell secrets*) cafarder*. 2 n (*NonC*) bavardage *m*, commérages *mpl*.

tattler ['tætləʳ] n (*man or woman*) commère *f* (*pej*), concierge* *mf* (*fig pej*).

tattletale ['tætl,teɪl] (*US*) 1 n commère *f* (*pej*), concierge* *mf* (*fig pej*). 2 adj (*fig*) *mark etc* révélateur.

tattoo¹ [tə'tuː] 1 vt tatouer. 2 n tatouage *m*.

tattoo² [tə'tuː] n (*Mil: on drum, bugle*) retraite *f*; (*Brit Mil: spectacle*) parade *f* militaire; (*gen: drumming*) battements *mpl*. **to beat a ~ on the drums** battre le tambour; (*fig*) **his fingers were beating a ~ on the table** il pianotait *or* tambourinait sur la table.

tattooist [tə'tuːɪst] n tatoueur *m*, -euse *f*.

tatty* ['tætɪ] adj (*esp Brit*) *clothes, shoes, leather goods, furniture* fatigué; *paint* écaillé; *house* en mauvais état; *plant, flowers* défraîchi; *poster, book* écorné. **she looked rather ~** elle était plutôt défraîchie.

taught [tɔːt] pret, ptp of **teach**.

taunt [tɔːnt] 1 n raillerie *f*, sarcasme *m*. 2 vt railler, persifler (*liter*). **to ~ sb with cowardice** taxer qn de lâcheté sur un ton railleur *or* persifleur.

taunting ['tɔːntɪŋ] 1 n railleries *fpl*, persiflage *m*, sarcasmes *mpl*. 2 adj railleur, persifleur, sarcastique.

tauntingly ['tɔːntɪŋlɪ] adv d'un ton railleur *or* persifleur *or* sarcastique.

Taurean [,tɔː'riːən] n: **to be a ~** être (du) Taureau.

tauromachy ['tɔːrəmækɪ] n (*liter*) tauromachie *f*.

Taurus ['tɔːrəs] n (*Astron*) le Taureau. **I'm (a) ~** je suis (du) Taureau.

taut [tɔːt] adj (*lit, fig*) tendu.

tauten ['tɔːtn] 1 vt tendre. 2 vi se tendre.

tautly ['tɔːtlɪ] adv (*lit*) *stretch* à fond; (*fig*) *say* d'une voix tendue *or* crispée.

tautness ['tɔːtnɪs] n tension *f* (*d'un cordage etc*).

tautological [,tɔːtə'lɒdʒɪkəl] adj tautologique.

tautology [tɔː'tɒlədʒɪ] n tautologie *f*.

tavern† ['tævən] n taverne† *f*, auberge *f*.

tawdriness ['tɔːdrɪnɪs] n *[goods]* qualité *f* médiocre; *[clothes]* mauvais goût tapageur; *[jewellery]* clinquant *m*; (*fig*) *[motive etc]* indignité *f*.

tawdry ['tɔːdrɪ] adj *goods* de camelote*; *clothes* tapageur, voyant; *jewellery* clinquant; (*fig*) *motive, affair etc* indigne.

tawny ['tɔːnɪ] adj fauve (*couleur*). **tawny owl** chat-huant *m*, chouette *f* (hulotte).

tax [tæks] 1 n (*on goods, services*) taxe *f*, impôt *m*; (*income ~*) impôts, contributions *fpl*. **before/after ~** avant/après l'impôt; **half of it goes in ~** on en perd la moitié en impôts *or* en contributions; **how much ~ do you pay?** combien d'impôts payez-vous?, à quoi se montent vos contributions?; **I paid £3,000 in ~ last year** j'ai payé 3.000 livres d'impôts *or* de contributions l'an dernier; **free of ~** exempt d'impôt, exonéré; **to put *or* place *or* levy a ~ on sth** mettre une taxe *or* un impôt sur qch, taxer *or* imposer qch; **petrol ~, ~ on petrol** taxe *or* droit *m* sur l'essence; (*fig*) **it was a ~ on his strength** cela a mis ses forces à l'épreuve.

2 comp *system, incentive etc* fiscal ►**tax accountant** conseiller fiscal ►**tax adjustment** redressement *m* ►**tax allowance** abattement *or* dégrèvement fiscal ►**tax authority** Administration *f* fiscale, Trésor *m* (public) ►**tax avoidance** évasion *f* fiscale (légale) ►**tax band** = **tax bracket** ►**tax base** assiette *f* de l'impôt ►**tax bite** ponction *f* fiscale, prélèvement *m* fiscal ►**tax bracket** tranche *f* du barème fiscal ►**tax break** (*US*) réduction *f* d'impôt, avantage *m* fiscal ►**tax burden** charge fiscale ►**tax code** (*Brit*) code *m* des impôts ►**tax coding** indice *m* d'abattement fiscal ►**tax-collecting** perception *f* (des impôts) ►**tax collector** percepteur *m* ►**tax credit** crédit *m* d'impôt ►**tax-deductible** sujet à dégrèvements (d'impôts) ►**tax disc** (*Brit Aut*) vignette *f* (automobile) ►**tax evader** fraudeur *m*, -euse *f* fiscal(e) ►**tax evasion** fraude fiscale, évasion fiscale ►**tax-exempt** (*US*) = **tax-free** ►**tax exemption** exonération *f* d'impôt ►**tax exile** personne *f* fuyant le fisc; **to become a tax exile** s'expatrier pour raisons fiscales ►**tax form** feuille *f* d'impôts ►**tax-free** (*Brit*) exempt d'impôts, exonéré ►**tax haven** paradis fiscal ►**tax immunity** immunité fiscale ►**tax levy** prélèvement fiscal ►**tax liability** assujettissement *m* à l'impôt ►**taxman*** percepteur *m* ►**taxmanship*** connaissance *f* de la fiscalité, art *m* de se défendre contre le fisc ►**tax net**: **to bring sb/sth within the tax net** ramener qn/qch dans une fourchette imposable *or* dans la première tranche imposable ►**taxpayer** contribuable *mf*; **the British taxpayer has to pay for it** ce sont les contribuables britanniques qui doivent payer; (*Fin, Admin*) **taxpayer list** rôle *m* (des impôts) ►**tax purposes**: **for tax purposes** pour des raisons fiscales ►**tax rebate** dégrèvement fiscal ►**tax refugee** = **tax exile** ►**tax relief** dégrèvement *or* allègement fiscal ►**tax return** (feuille *f* de) déclaration *f* de revenus *or* d'impôts ►**tax revenue** recettes *fpl* fiscales ►**tax shelter** échappatoire fiscale ►**tax year** exercice *m* fiscal, année *f* fiscale.

3 vt a *goods etc* taxer, imposer; *income, profits, person* imposer; (*fig*) *patience* mettre à l'épreuve; *strength* éprouver. **he is very heavily ~ed** il paie beaucoup d'impôts, il est lourdement imposé; **they are being ~ed out of existence** ils paient tant d'impôts qu'ils ont de la peine à survivre; *see also* **taxing**.

b **to ~ sb with sth** taxer *or* accuser qn de qch; **to ~ sb with doing** accuser qn de faire (*or* d'avoir fait).

taxable ['tæksəbl] adj *income etc* imposable. **~ amount** base *f* d'imposition.

taxation [tæk'seɪʃən] 1 n (*NonC*) (*act*) taxation *f*; (*taxes*) impôts *mpl*, contributions *fpl*; *see* **double, immunity**. 2 comp *authority, system* fiscal.

taxeme ['tæksiːm] n taxème *m*.

taxi ['tæksɪ] 1 n, pl ~s *or* ~es taxi *m*. **by ~** en taxi. 2 comp *charges etc* de taxi ►**taxicab** taxi *m* ►**taxi dancer*** (*US*) taxi-girl *f* ►**taxi driver** chauffeur *m* de taxi ►**taxi fare** (*gen*) tarif *m* de taxi; **I haven't got the taxi fare** je n'ai pas de quoi payer le taxi ►**taxi man*** = **taxi driver** ►**taximeter** taximètre *m*, compteur *m* (de taxi) ►**taxi rank**, (*esp Scot*) **taxi stance**, (*US*) **taxi stand** station *f* de taxis ►**taxiway** (*Aviat*) taxiway *m*. 3 vi a *[aircraft]* se déplacer *or* rouler (lentement) au sol. **the plane ~ed along the runway** l'avion a roulé *or* s'est déplacé lentement le long de la piste. b (*go by taxi*) aller en taxi.

taxidermist ['tæksɪdɜːmɪst] n empailleur *m*, -euse *f*, naturaliste *mf*.

taxidermy ['tæksɪdɜːmɪ] n empaillage *m*, naturalisation *f*, taxidermie *f*.

taxing ['tæksɪŋ] adj (*mentally*) ardu; (*physically*) pénible, malaisé.

taxonomist [tæk'sɒnəmɪst] n taxonomiste *mf*.

taxonomy [tæk'sɒnəmɪ] n taxonomie *f*.

TB [tiː'biː] n abbr of **tuberculosis**.

tbsp. n, pl ~ *or* ~s abbr of **tablespoonful**.

TCE [tiːsiː'iː] n (abbr of **ton coal equivalent**) TEC *f* (*abrév de tonne équivalent charbon*).

Tchaikovsky [tʃaɪ'kɒfskɪ] n Tchaïkovski *m*.

TD [tiː'diː] n a (*Brit*) abbr of **Territorial Decoration**. b (*US Ftbl*) abbr of **touchdown**. c (*US*) (abbr of **Treasury Department**) *see* **treasury**.

te [tiː] n (*Mus*) si *m*.

tea [tiː] 1 n a (*plant, substance*) thé *m*. **she made a pot of ~** elle a fait du thé; (*fig*) **I wouldn't do it for all the ~ in China** je ne le ferais pour rien au monde; (*fig*) **~ and sympathy** réconfort *m*; *see* **cup** *etc*.

b (*esp Brit: meal*) thé *m*; (*for children*) ≈ goûter *m*. **to have ~** prendre le thé; *[children]* goûter; *see* **high** *etc*.

c (*herbal*) infusion *f*, tisane *f*; *see* **beef** *etc*.

2 comp ►**tea bag** sachet *m* de thé ►**tea ball** (*US*) boule *f* *or* infuseur *m* à thé ►**tea boy** (*Brit*) jeune garçon *m* préposé au thé ►**tea break** (*Brit*) pause-thé *f*; **to have a tea break** faire la pause-thé ►**tea caddy** boîte *f* à thé ►**teacake** (*Brit*) petit pain brioché ►**teacart** (*US*) = **tea trolley** ►**tea chest** caisse *f* (à thé) ►**teacloth** (*Brit: for dishes*) torchon *m* (à vaisselle); (*for table*) nappe *f* (à thé); (*for trolley, tray*) napperon *m* ►**tea cosy** (*Brit*) couvre-théière *m inv*, cache-théière *m inv* ►**teacup** tasse *f* à thé (*see also* **read¹, storm**) ►**teacupful** tasse *f* (à thé *or* à café) (*mesure*) ►**tea dance** thé dansant ►**teahouse** maison *f* de thé (*en Chine ou au Japon*) ►**tea infuser** (*Brit*) boule *f* *or* infuseur *m* à thé ►**teakettle** (*US*) bouilloire *f* ►**tea lady** (*Brit*) préposée *f* au thé ►**tea leaf** feuille *f* de thé (*see also* **read¹**) ►**tea party** thé *m* (*réception*) ►**tea-plant** arbre *m* à thé ►**tea plate** petite assiette ►**teapot** théière *f* ►**tearoom** salon *m* de thé ►**tea rose** rose-thé *f* ►**tea service, tea set** service *m* à thé ►**teashop** (*Brit*) pâtisserie-salon de thé *f* ►**teaspoon** petite cuiller, cuiller à thé *or* à café ►**teaspoonful** cuillerée *f* à café ►**tea strainer** passoire *f* (à thé), passe-thé *m inv* ►**tea table**: **they sat at the tea table** ils étaient assis autour de la table mise pour le thé; **the subject was raised at the tea table** on en a discuté pendant le thé; **to set the tea table** mettre la table pour le thé ►**tea-things**: **where are the tea-things?** où est le service à thé?; **to wash up the tea-things** faire la vaisselle après le thé ►**teatime** l'heure *f* du thé ►**tea towel** (*Brit*) torchon *m* (à vaisselle) ►**tea tray** plateau *m* (à thé) ►**tea trolley** (*Brit*) table roulante ►**tea urn** fontaine *f* à thé ►**tea wagon** (*US*) = **tea trolley**.

teach [tiːtʃ] pret, ptp **taught** 1 vt (*gen*) apprendre (*sb sth, sth to sb* qch à qn); (*Scol, Univ etc*) enseigner (*sb sth, sth to sb* qch à qn). **to ~ sb (how) to do** apprendre à qn à faire; **I'll ~ you what to do** je t'apprendrai ce qu'il faut faire; **he ~es French** il enseigne le français; **he taught her French** il lui a appris *or* enseigné le français; (*US*) **to ~ school** (*in primary school*) être instituteur (*or* institutrice); (*in secondary school*) être professeur; **to ~ o.s. (to do) sth** apprendre (à faire) qch tout seul; (*fig*) **I'll ~ you a lesson!** je vais t'apprendre!; **that will ~ him a lesson!**,

that will ~ him (a thing or two)! cela lui donnera une bonne leçon, cela lui servira de leçon; **that will ~ you to mind your own business!** ça t'apprendra à te mêler de tes affaires!; **I'll ~ you (not) to speak to me like that!** je vais t'apprendre à me parler sur ce ton!; **you can't ~ him anything about cars** il n'a rien à apprendre de personne en matière de voitures; (*Brit: loc*) **don't ~ your grandmother to suck eggs!**‡ on n'apprend pas à un vieux singe à faire des grimaces!*; (*Prov*) **you can't ~ an old dog new tricks** ce n'est pas à son (*or* mon *etc*) âge qu'on apprend de nouveaux trucs.

2 **vi** enseigner. **he always wanted to ~** il a toujours eu le désir d'enseigner; **he had been ~ing all morning** il avait fait cours *or* fait la classe toute la matinée.

3 **comp ▸teach-in** séance *f* d'études, séminaire *m* (*sur un thème*).

teachability [ˌtiːtʃə'bɪlɪtɪ] **n** (*esp US*) *[child]* aptitude *f* à apprendre.

teachable ['tiːtʃəbl] **adj** (*esp US*) *child* scolarisable; *subject* enseignable. **he's not ~** on ne peut rien lui apprendre.

teacher ['tiːtʃəʳ] 1 **n** (*in secondary school; also private tutor*) professeur *m*; (*in primary school*) instituteur *m*, -trice *f*, maître *m* d'école, maîtresse *f* d'école; (*in special school, prison*) éducateur *m*, -trice *f*; (*gen: member of teaching profession*) enseignant(e) *m(f)*. **she is a maths ~** elle est professeur de maths; **~'s (hand)book** livre *m* du maître; (*collectively*) **the ~s accepted the government's offer** les enseignants ont *or* le corps enseignant a accepté l'offre du gouvernement; **the ~s' strike** la grève des enseignants; **the ~s' dispute** le conflit des enseignants; *see also* **2**.

2 **comp ▸teacher certification** (*US*) habilitation *f* (à enseigner) **▸teacher education** (*US*) formation *f* pédagogique (des maîtres) **▸teacher evaluation** (*US Scol, Univ*) appréciations *fpl* sur les professeurs (*par les étudiants ou par l'administration*) **▸teacher-pupil ratio** taux *m* d'encadrement; **a high/low teacher-pupil ratio** un fort/faible taux d'encadrement **▸teacher's aide** (*US*) assistant(e) *m(f)* du professeur (*or* de l'instituteur) **▸teacher(s') training** (*Brit*) formation *f* pédagogique (des maîtres); **teacher(s') training college** (*for primary teachers*) ≃ école *f* normale (primaire); (*for secondary*) ≃ centre *m* pédagogique régional de formation des maîtres; **to be at teacher(s') training college** suivre une formation pédagogique (*non universitaire*); **to do one's teacher(s') training** suivre une formation pédagogique; **teacher training certificate** diplôme *m* habilitant à enseigner; **to get one's teachers' training certificate** *or* **qualification** (*primary schools*) ≃ sortir de l'école normale (primaire); (*secondary schools*) ≃ avoir son C.A.P.E.S. *etc.*

teaching ['tiːtʃɪŋ] 1 **n** a (*NonC: act, profession*) enseignement *m*. **he's got 16 hours ~ a week** il a 16 heures de cours par semaine; **to go into ~** entrer dans l'enseignement; (*for backward pupil*) **extra ~** soutien *m* (*in* en); (*Educ*) **T~ of English as a Foreign Language** anglais *m* langue étrangère; (*Educ*) **T~ of English as a Second Language** anglais *m* deuxième langue; *see* **team**.

b (*also* ~s) *[philosopher, sage etc]* enseignements *mpl* (*liter*) (*on, about* sur).

2 **comp ▸teaching aid** outil *m* pédagogique **▸teaching aids** matériel *m* pédagogique **▸teaching assistant** (*US*) étudiant(e) *m(f)* chargé(e) de travaux dirigés **▸teaching equipment** = **teaching aids** **▸teaching hospital** centre *m* hospitalo-universitaire (*abbr* C.H.U. *m*) **▸teaching job** poste *m* d'enseignant **▸teaching machine** machine *f* à enseigner **▸teaching position, teaching post** poste *m* d'enseignant **▸teaching practice** stage *m* de formation des maîtres **▸the teaching profession** (*activity*) l'enseignement *m*; (*in secondary schools only*) le professorat; (*teachers collectively*) le corps enseignant, les enseignants *mpl* **▸teaching staff** personnel *m* enseignant, enseignants *mpl*, équipe *f* pédagogique.

teak [tiːk] **n** teck *m or* tek *m*.

teal [tiːl] **n, pl ~** *or* **~s** sarcelle *f*.

team [tiːm] 1 **n** (*Sport, gen*) équipe *f*; *[horses, oxen]* attelage *m*. **football ~** équipe de football; **our research ~** notre équipe de chercheurs.

2 **comp ▸team games** jeux *mpl* d'équipe **▸team-mate** coéquipier *m*, -ière *f* **▸team member** (*Sport*) équipier *m*, -ière *f* **▸team spirit** (*NonC*) esprit *m* d'équipe **▸team teaching** (*NonC*) enseignement *m* en équipe **▸teamwork** (*NonC*) collaboration *f* (d'équipe). 3 **vt** (*also* **~ up**) *actor, worker* mettre en collaboration (*with* avec); *clothes, accessories* associer (*with* avec).

▸team up 1 **vi** *[people]* faire équipe (*with* avec, *to do* pour faire); *[colours]* s'harmoniser (*with* avec); *[clothes, accessories, furnishings etc]* s'associer (*with* avec). **he teamed up with them to get ...** il s'est allié à eux pour obtenir ... . 2 **vt sep** = **team 3**.

teamster ['tiːmstəʳ] **n** (*US*) routier *m or* camionneur *m* syndiqué.

tear¹ [tɛəʳ] (**vb: pret tore, ptp torn**) 1 **n** déchirure *f*, accroc *m*. **to make a ~ in sth** déchirer qch; **it has a ~ in it** c'est déchiré, il y a un accroc dedans.

2 **comp ▸tearaway** (*Brit*) casse-cou *m inv* **▸tear-off** amovible; **tear-off calendar** éphéméride *f* **▸tear sheet** feuillet *m* détachable.

3 **vt** a (*rip*) *cloth, garment* déchirer, faire un trou *or* un accroc à; *flesh, paper* déchirer. **to ~ a hole in** faire une déchirure *or* un accroc à, faire un trou dans; **he tore it along the dotted line** il l'a déchiré en suivant le pointillé; **to ~ to pieces** *or* **to shreds** *or* **to bits*** *paper* déchirer en menus morceaux; *garment* mettre en pièces *or* lambeaux; *prey* mettre en pièces; (*fig*) *play, performance* éreinter; *argument, suggestion* démolir; **to ~ sth loose** arracher qch; **to ~ (o.s.) loose** se libérer; **to ~ open** *envelope* déchirer; *letter* déchirer l'enveloppe de; *parcel* ouvrir en déchirant l'emballage de; **clothes torn to rags** vêtements mis en lambeaux; (*Med*) **to ~ a muscle** se déchirer un muscle; **I tore my hand on a nail** je me suis ouvert la main sur un clou; (*fig*) **that's torn it!***, (*US*) **that ~s it!*** voilà qui flanque tout par terre!*; *see* **shred**.

b (*fig*) **to be torn by war/remorse** *etc* être déchiré par la guerre/le remords *etc;* **to be torn between two things/people** être tiraillé par *or* balancer entre deux choses/personnes; **I'm very much torn** j'hésite beaucoup (entre les deux).

c (*snatch*) arracher (*from sb* à qn, *out of or off or from sth* de qch). **he tore it out of her hand** il le lui a arraché des mains; **he was torn from his seat** il a été arraché de son siège.

4 **vi** a *[cloth etc]* se déchirer.

b **he tore at the wrapping paper** il a déchiré l'emballage (impatiemment); **he tore at the earth with his bare hands** il a griffé la terre de ses mains nues.

c (*rush*) **to ~ out/down** *etc* sortir/descendre *etc* à toute allure *or* à toute vitesse; **he tore up the stairs** il a monté l'escalier quatre à quatre; *[person, car]* **to ~ along the road** filer à toute allure le long de la route; **they tore after him** ils se sont lancés *or* précipités à sa poursuite; (*fig*) **to ~ into sb*** (*attack verbally*) s'en prendre violemment à qn; (*scold*) passer un savon à qn*.

▸tear apart **vt sep** déchirer; (*fig: divide*) *team, couple etc* déchirer. **his love for Julie is tearing him apart** son amour pour Julie le déchire.

▸tear away 1 **vi** *[person]* partir comme un bolide; *[car]* démarrer en trombe. 2 **vt sep** (*lit, fig*) arracher (*from sb* à qn, *from sth* de qch). (*fig*) **I couldn't tear myself away from it/him** je n'arrivais pas à m'en arracher/à m'arracher à lui. 3 **tearaway** **n** *see* **tear¹ 2**.

▸tear down **vt sep** *poster, flag* arracher (*from* de); *building* démolir.

▸tear off 1 **vi** = **tear away 1**. 2 **vt sep** a *label, wrapping* arracher (*from* de); *perforated page, calendar leaf* détacher (*from* de); *see* **strip**. b (*: *write hurriedly*) *letter etc* bâcler*, torcher*. 3 **tear-off** **adj** *see* **tear 2**.

▸tear out 1 **vi** *see* **tear¹ 4c**. 2 **vt sep** arracher (*from* de); *cheque, ticket* détacher (*from* de). **to tear sb's eyes out** arracher les yeux à qn; **to tear one's hair out** s'arracher les cheveux.

▸tear up **vt sep** a *paper etc* déchirer, mettre en morceaux *or* en pièces; (*fig*) *contract* déchirer (*fig*); *offer* reprendre. b *stake, weed, shrub* arracher; *tree* déraciner.

tear² [tɪəʳ] 1 **n** larme *f*. **in ~s** en larmes; **there were ~s in her eyes** elle avait les larmes aux yeux; **she had ~s of joy in her eyes** elle pleurait de joie; **near** *or* **close to ~s** au bord des larmes; **to burst** *or* **dissolve into ~s** fondre en larmes; **the memory/thought/sight brought ~s to his eyes** à ce souvenir/cette pensée/ce spectacle il eut les larmes aux yeux; **the film/book/experience brought ~s to his eyes** le film/le livre/cette expérience lui a fait venir les larmes aux yeux; *see* **shed** *etc.*

2 **comp ▸tear bomb** grenade *f* lacrymogène **▸teardrop** larme *f* **▸tear duct** conduit *m* lacrymal **▸tear gas** gaz *m* lacrymogène **▸tear-jerker***: **the film/book** *etc* **was a real tear-jerker** c'était un film/roman *etc* tout à fait du genre à faire pleurer dans les chaumières **▸tear-stained** barbouillé de larmes.

tearful ['tɪəfʊl] **adj** *look* larmoyant, (*stronger*) éploré; *face* en larmes; (*whining*) *voice, story, plea* larmoyant (*pej*), pleurnichard* (*pej*). **she was very ~** elle a beaucoup pleuré; **in a ~ voice** avec des larmes dans la voix; (*whining*) d'une voix pleurnicharde* (*pej*).

tearfully ['tɪəfəlɪ] **adv** les larmes aux yeux, en pleurant; (*whining*) en pleurnichant* (*pej*).

tearing ['tɛərɪŋ] 1 **n** déchirement *m*. 2 **adj**: **a ~ sound** un craquement; (*fig*) **to be in a ~ hurry*** être terriblement pressé.

tearless ['tɪəlɪs] **adj** sans larmes.

tearlessly ['tɪəlɪslɪ] **adv** sans larmes, sans pleurer.

tease [tiːz] 1 **n** (*person*) (*gen*) taquin(e) *m(f)*; (*sexual*) allumeur *m*, -euse *f*. 2 **vt** a (*playfully*) taquiner; (*cruelly*) tourmenter; (*sexually*) allumer. b (*Tech*) *cloth* peigner; *wool* carder.

▸tease out **vt sep** *tangle of wool, knots, matted hair* débrouiller *or* démêler (patiemment). (*fig*) **to tease sth out of sb** tirer les vers du nez à qn.

teasel ['tiːzl] **n** (*Bot*) cardère *f*; (*Tech*) carde *f*.

teaser ['tiːzəʳ] **n** a (*person*) (*gen*) taquin(e) *m(f)*; (*sexual*) allumeur *m*, -euse *f*. b (*problem*) problème *m* (difficile); (*tricky question*) colle* *f*.

teasing ['tiːzɪŋ] 1 **n** (*NonC*) taquineries *fpl*. 2 **adj** taquin.

teasingly ['tiːzɪŋlɪ] **adv** en plaisantant, par plaisanterie.

Teasmade, Teasmaid ['tiːzmeɪd] **n** ® *machine à faire le thé*.

teat [tiːt] **n** *[animal]* tétine *f*, tette *f*; *[esp cow]* trayon *m*; *[woman]* mamelon *m*, bout *m* de sein; (*Brit: of baby's bottle*) tétine; (*dummy*) tétine; (*Tech*) téton *m*.

teazel, teazle ['tiːzl] **n** = **teasel**.

tech* [tek] **n** a (*Brit*) (**abbr of technical college**) ≃ CET *m*. b (**abbr of technology**) *see* **high**.

technecium [tek'ni:sıəm] n technécium *m*.
technical ['teknıkəl] adj (*gen*) technique. (*Brit*) ~ **college** collège *m* (d'enseignement) technique; ~ **drawing** dessin *m* technique; ~ **hitch** incident *m or* ennui *m* technique; (*US*) ~ **institute** *or* **school** ≈ I.U.T. *m*, institut *m* universitaire de technologie; (*Sport*) ~ **knock-out** knock-out *m* technique; (*Jur*) ~ **offence** contravention *f*; (*Jur*) **judgment quashed on a ~ point** arrêt cassé pour vice de forme; (*gen*) **it's just a ~ point** c'est juste un point de détail; (*US Air Force*) ~ **sergeant** sergent-chef *m*.
technicality [,teknı'kælıtı] n a (*NonC*) technicité *f*. b (*detail/word/difficulty/fault*) détail *m*/terme *m*/difficulté *f*/ennui *m* technique. **I don't understand all the technicalities** certains détails techniques m'échappent. c (*Jur*) **he got off on a ~** il a été acquitté sur un argument de droit.
technically ['teknıkəlı] adv a (*from technical point of view*) *perfect etc* techniquement, sur le plan technique. **he spoke very ~** il s'est exprimé en termes très techniques. b (*strictly speaking*) en théorie, en principe. ~ **you're right, but ...** en théorie *or* en principe vous avez raison, mais ... .
technician [tek'nıʃən] n technicien(ne) *m(f)*.
Technicolor ['teknı,kʌləʳ] ® 1 n Technicolor *m* ®. **in ~** en Technicolor. 2 adj *film* en Technicolor.
technique [tek'ni:k] n technique *f*. (*Sport etc*) **he's got good ~** sa technique est bonne.
techno... ['teknəʊ] pref techno... .
technocracy [tek'nɒkrəsı] n technocratie *f*.
technocrat ['teknəʊkræt] n technocrate *mf*.
technocratic [,teknə'krætık] adj technocratique.
technological [,teknə'lɒdʒıkəl] adj technologique.
technologically [teknə'lɒdʒıklı] adv technologiquement, sur le plan technologique. ~ **speaking** technologiquement parlant, du point de vue technologique.
technologist [tek'nɒlədʒıst] n technologue *mf*.
technology [tek'nɒlədʒı] n technologie *f*. (*Brit*) **Minister/Ministry of T~** ministre *m*/ministère *m* des Affaires technologiques; **the new ~** la novotique, les nouvelles technologies; *see* **high**.
technostructure ['teknəʊ,strʌktʃəʳ] n technostructure *f*.
techy ['tetʃı] adj = **tetchy**.
tectonic ['tektɒnık] adj tectonique.
tectonics ['tektɒnıks] n (*NonC*) tectonique *f*.
Ted [ted] n a (dim of **Edward** *or* **Theodore**) Ted *m*. b (*) = **teddy-boy**; *see* **teddy**.
ted [ted] vt faner.
tedder ['tedəʳ] n (*machine*) faneuse *f*; (*person*) faneur *m*, -euse *f*.
teddy ['tedı] 1 n a **T~** (dim of **Edward** *or* **Theodore**) Teddy *m*. b (*underwear*) teddy *m*. 2 comp ▸**teddy (bear)** nounours *m* (*baby talk*), ours *m* en peluche ▸**teddy-boy**† (*Brit*) ≈ blouson noir.
tedious ['ti:dıəs] adj ennuyeux, assommant*.
tediously ['ti:dıəslı] adv d'une façon ennuyeuse *or* assommante*. ~ **long** d'une longueur assommante*.
tediousness ['ti:dıəsnıs] n, **tedium** ['ti:dıəm] n (*NonC*) ennui *m*, caractère *m* assommant*.
tee [ti:] (*Golf*) 1 n tee *m*. 2 vt *ball* placer sur le tee.
▸**tee off** 1 vi partir du tee. 2 vt sep (‡) (*US: annoy*) embêter*, casser les pieds à*; (*US fig: begin*) démarrer*.
▸**tee up** vi placer la balle sur le tee.
tee-hee ['ti:'hi:] (vb: pret, ptp **tee-heed**) 1 excl hi-hi! 2 n (petit) ricanement *m*. 3 vi ricaner.
teem [ti:m] vi a *[crowds, fish, snakes etc]* grouiller, fourmiller, pulluler. *[river, street etc]* **to ~ with** grouiller de, fourmiller de; **his brain ~s with ideas** il déborde d'idées. b **it was ~ing (with rain), the rain was ~ing down** il pleuvait à verse *or* à seaux.
teeming ['ti:mıŋ] adj a *crowd* grouillant, fourmillant, pullulant; *street* grouillant de monde, fourmillant; *river* grouillant de poissons. b ~ **rain** pluie battante *or* diluvienne.
teen [ti:n] (abbr of **teenage**) adj a * *magazine, fashion* ado* *inv*. b **in his ~ years** au cours de son adolescence; *see* **teens**.
teenage ['ti:neıdʒ] adj *boy, girl* jeune, adolescent (*de 13 à 19 ans*); *behaviour, view* adolescent, d'adolescent, de jeune; *fashions* pour jeunes, pour adolescents.
teenager ['ti:n,eıdʒəʳ] n jeune *mf*, adolescent(e) *m(f)*.
teens [ti:nz] npl jeunesse *f*, adolescence *f* (*de 13 à 19 ans*). **he is still in his ~** il est encore adolescent; **he is just out of his ~** il a à peine vingt ans; **he is in his early/late ~** il a un peu plus de treize ans/un peu moins de vingt ans.
teensy(weensy)‡ ['ti:nzı('wi:nzı)] adj = **teeny 1**.
teeny* ['ti:nı] 1 adj (*also* ~**weeny**‡) minuscule, tout petit, tout petit petit*. 2 n (*also* ~**-bopper***) ado* *mf*, jeune *mf* (*d'une douzaine d'années*).
teepee ['ti:pi:] n = **tepee**.
tee-shirt ['ti:ʃɜ:t] n tee-shirt *m or* T-shirt *m*.
teeter ['ti:təʳ] 1 vi *[person]* chanceler; *[pile]* vaciller. (*fig*) **to ~ on the edge** *or* **brink of** être prêt à tomber dans. 2 comp ▸**teeter totter** (*US*) *jeu de bascule*.
teeth [ti:θ] npl of **tooth**.
teethe [ti:ð] vi faire *or* percer ses dents.
teething ['ti:ðıŋ] 1 n poussée *f* des dents, dentition *f*. 2 comp ▸**teething ring** anneau *m* (*de bébé qui perce ses dents*) ▸**teething troubles** (*fig*) difficultés *fpl* initiales.
teetotal ['ti:'təʊtl] adj *person* qui ne boit jamais d'alcool; *league* anti-alcoolique.
teetotaler ['ti:'təʊtləʳ] n (*US*) = **teetotaller**.
teetotalism ['ti:'təʊtəlızəm] n abstention *f* de toute boisson alcoolique.
teetotaller, (*US*) **teetotaler** ['ti:'təʊtləʳ] n personne *f* qui ne boit jamais d'alcool.
TEFL ['tefl] n (*Educ*) (abbr of **Teaching of English as a Foreign Language**) *see* **teaching**.
Teflon ['teflɒn] n ® Téflon *m* ®.
tegument ['tegjʊmənt] n tégument *m*.
te-hee ['ti:'hi:] = **tee-hee**.
Teheran [tɛə'rɑ:n] n Téhéran.
tel. (abbr of **telephone (number)**) tél.
Tel Aviv ['telə'vi:v] n Tel-Aviv.
tele... ['telı] pref télé... .
telebanking ['telı,bæŋkıŋ] n opérations *fpl* bancaires à distance (*à partir de son domicile ou d'un bureau*).
telecamera ['telı,kæmərə] n caméra *f* de télévision, télécaméra *f*.
telecast ['telıkɑ:st] 1 n émission *f* de télévision. 2 vt diffuser.
telecommunication ['telıkə,mju:nı'keıʃən] n (gen pl) télécommunications *fpl*. ~**s satellite** satellite *m* de télécommunication; *see* **post³**.
telecommute* ['telıkə,mju:t] vi télétravailler.
telecommuter* ['telıkə,mju:təʳ] n télétravailleur *m*.
telecommuting* ['telıkə,mju:tıŋ] n télétravail *m*.
Telecopier ['telı,kɒpıəʳ] n ® télécopieur *m*.
telecopy ['telı,kɒpı] n télécopie *f*.
telefacsimile [,telıfæk'sımılı] n télécopie *f*.
telefax ['telıfæks] n télécopie *f*.
telefilm ['telıfılm] n téléfilm *m*, film *m* pour la télévision.
telegenic [,telı'dʒenık] adj télégénique.
telegram ['telıgræm] n télégramme *m*; (*Diplomacy, Press*) dépêche *f*, câble *m*.
telegraph ['telıgrɑ:f] 1 n télégraphe *m*. 2 comp *message, wires* télégraphique ▸**telegraph pole, telegraph post** poteau *m* télégraphique. 3 vti télégraphier.
telegrapher [tı'legrəfəʳ] n télégraphiste *mf*.
telegraphese [,telıgrɑ:'fi:z] n (*NonC*) style *m* télégraphique.
telegraphic [,telı'græfık] adj télégraphique.
telegraphically [,telı'græfıkəlı] adv télégraphiquement.
telegraphist [tı'legrəfıst] n télégraphiste *mf*.
telegraphy [tı'legrəfı] n télégraphie *f*.
telekinesis [,telıkı'ni:sıs] n (*NonC*) télékinésie *f*.
telekinetic [,telıkı'netık] adj télékinétique.
Telemachus [tə'leməkəs] n Télémaque *m*.
telemeeting ['telı,mi:tıŋ] n téléréunion *f*.
Telemessage ['telı,mesıdʒ] n ® (*Brit*) télémessage *m*.
telemeter [tı'lemıtəʳ] n télémètre *m*.
telemetric [,telı'metrık] adj télémétrique.
telemetry [tı'lemıtrı] n télémétrie *f*.
teleological [,telıə'lɒdʒıkl] adj téléologique.
teleology [,telı'ɒlədʒı] n téléologie *f*.
telepath ['teləpæθ] n télépathe *mf*.
telepathic [,telı'pæθık] adj télépathique. (*iro*) **I'm not ~!*** je ne suis pas devin!
telepathically [,telı'pæθıkəlı] adv par télépathie, télépathiquement.
telepathist [tı'lepəθıst] n télépathe *mf*.
telepathy [tı'lepəθı] n télépathie *f*.
telephone ['telıfəʊn] 1 n téléphone *m*. **on the ~** au téléphone; **to be on the ~** (*speaking*) être au téléphone; (*be a subscriber*) avoir le téléphone (chez soi).
2 vt *person* téléphoner à, appeler (au téléphone); *message, telegram* téléphoner (*to* à).
3 vi téléphoner.
4 comp ▸**telephone answering machine** répondeur *m* téléphonique ▸**telephone book** = **telephone directory** ▸**telephone booth** (*US*), **telephone box** (*Brit*) cabine *f* téléphonique ▸**telephone call** coup *m* de téléphone*, appel *m* téléphonique ▸**telephone directory** annuaire *m* (du téléphone) ▸**telephone exchange** central *m* téléphonique ▸**telephone kiosk** = **telephone booth** ▸**telephone line** ligne *f* téléphonique ▸**telephone message** message *m* téléphonique ▸**telephone number** numéro *m* de téléphone ▸**telephone operator** standardiste *mf*, téléphoniste *mf* ▸**telephone sales** = **telesales** ▸**telephone service** service *m* des téléphones; **our country has an excellent telephone service** le téléphone marche très bien dans notre pays ▸**telephone subscriber** abonné(e) *m(f)* au téléphone ▸**telephone-tapping** mise *f* sur écoute (téléphonique).
telephonic [,telı'fɒnık] adj téléphonique.
telephonist [tı'lefənıst] n (*esp Brit*) téléphoniste *mf*.

telephony [tɪ'lefənɪ] n téléphonie *f*.
telephoto ['telɪˌfəʊtəʊ] adj: ~ **lens** téléobjectif *m*.
telephotograph [ˌtelɪ'fəʊtəgræf] n téléphotographie *f*.
telephotography [ˌtelɪfə'tɒgrəfɪ] n (*NonC*) téléphotographie *f*.
teleport ['telɪpɔːt] vt téléporter.
teleportation [ˌtelɪpɔː'teɪʃən] n télékinésie *f*.
teleprint ['telɪˌprɪnt] vt (*Brit*) transmettre par téléscripteur.
teleprinter ['telɪˌprɪntə^r] n (*Brit*) téléscripteur *m*, Télétype *m* ®.
teleprompter ['telɪˌprɒmptə^r] n téléprompteur *m*.
telesales ['telɪseɪlz] npl vente *f* par téléphone, télévente *f*. ~ **staff** vendeurs *mpl*, -euses *fpl* par téléphone, télévendeurs *mpl*, -euses *fpl*; ~ **department** service *m* des ventes par téléphone.
telescope ['telɪskəʊp] 1 n (*reflecting*) télescope *m*; (*refracting*) lunette *f* d'approche, longue-vue *f*; (*Astron*) lunette astronomique, télescope. 2 vi *[railway carriages etc]* se télescoper; *[umbrella]* se plier. **parts made to** ~ pièces *fpl* en télescope. 3 vt télescoper.
telescopic [ˌtelɪ'skɒpɪk] adj télescopique. ~ **lens** téléobjectif *m*; ~ **sight** viseur *m*; ~ **umbrella** parapluie pliant *or* télescopique.
teletex ['telətekѕ] n Télétex *m* ®.
Teletext ['telətekst] n ® télétexte *m*, vidéotex *m* diffusé.
telethon ['teləθɒn] n (*TV*) téléthon *m*.
Teletype ['telɪtaɪp] ® 1 vt transmettre par Télétype®. 2 n Télétype *m* ®.
teletypewriter [ˌtelɪ'taɪpraɪtə^r] n ® (*US*) téléscripteur *m*, Télétype *m* ®.
televangelist [ˌtelɪ'vændʒəlɪst] n (*esp US*) télévangéliste *mf*.
teleview ['teləvjuː] vi (*US*) regarder la télévision.
televiewer ['telɪˌvjuːə^r] n téléspectateur *m*, -trice *f*.
televiewing ['telɪˌvjuːɪŋ] n (*NonC: watching TV*) la télévision. **this evening's** ~ **contains** ... le programme de (la) télévision pour ce soir comprend ... .
televise ['telɪvaɪz] vt téléviser.
television ['telɪˌvɪʒən] 1 n télévision *f*; (~ *set*) télévision, téléviseur *m*, poste *m* (de télévision). **on** ~ à la télévision, à la télé*; **colour** ~ télévision (en) couleur.
2 comp *actor, camera, studio* de télévision; *report, news, serial* télévisé; *film, script* pour la télévision ►**television broadcast** émission *f* de télévision ►**television cabinet** meuble-télévision *m* ►**television lounge** *[hotel etc]* salle *f* de télévision ►**television programme** émission *f* de télévision ►**television rights** droits *mpl* d'antenne ►**television room** = **television lounge** ►**television screen** écran *m* de télévision *or* de téléviseur; **on the television screen** sur le petit écran ►**television set** télévision *f*, téléviseur *m*, poste *m* (de télévision).
televisual [ˌtelɪ'vɪʒjʊəl] adj télévisuel.
telex ['teleks] 1 n télex *m*. 2 vt télexer, envoyer par télex. 3 comp ►**telex operator** télexiste *mf*.
tell [tel] pret, ptp **told** 1 vt a (*gen*) dire (*that* que). ~ **me your name** dites-moi votre nom; **I told him how pleased I was** je lui ai dit combien *or* à quel point j'étais content; **I told him what/where/how/why** je lui ai dit *or* expliqué ce que/où/comment/pourquoi; **I told him the way to London, I told him how to get to London** je lui ai expliqué comment aller à Londres; **he told himself it was only a game** il s'est dit que ce n'était qu'un jeu; **I am glad to** ~ **you that** ... je suis heureux de pouvoir vous dire *or* annoncer que ...; **to** ~ **sb sth again** répéter *or* redire qch à qn; **something** ~**s me he won't be pleased** quelque chose me dit qu'il ne sera pas content; **let me** ~ **you that you are quite mistaken** permettez-moi de vous dire que vous vous trompez lourdement; **I won't go, I** ~ **you!** je n'irai pas, te dis-je!, puisque je te dis que je n'irai pas!; **there was terrible trouble, I can** ~ **you!** il y avait des tas de difficultés, c'est moi qui te le dis!*; **I can't** ~ **you how grateful I am** je ne saurais vous dire à quel point je suis reconnaissant; **don't** ~ **me you've lost it!** tu ne vas pas me dire que *or* ne me dis pas que tu l'as perdu!; **I told you so!** je te l'avais bien dit!; ... **or so I've been told** ... ou du moins c'est ce qu'on m'a dit; **I could** ~ **you a thing or two about him** je pourrais vous en dire long sur lui; **I('ll)** ~ **you what*, let's go for a swim!** tiens, si on allait se baigner!; **you're** ~**ing me!*** à qui le dis-tu!; **you** ~ **me!** je n'en sais rien!; ~ **me another!*** à d'autres!*
b (*relate*) dire, raconter; *story, adventure* raconter (*to* à); *a lie, the truth* dire; (*divulge*) *secret* dire, révéler; *sb's age* révéler; *the future* prédire. **to** ~ **sb's fortune** dire la bonne aventure à qn; **to** ~ **fortunes** dire la bonne aventure; **to** ~ **(you) the truth, truth to** ~ à vrai dire; **to** ~ **it like it is*** ne pas avoir peur de dire la vérité, ne pas mâcher ses mots; **can you** ~ **the time?**, (*US*) **can you** ~ **time?** sais-tu lire l'heure?; **can you** ~ **me the time?** peux-tu me dire l'heure (qu'il est)?; **clocks** ~ **the time** les horloges indiquent l'heure; **that** ~**s me all I need to know** maintenant je sais tout ce qu'il me faut savoir; **it** ~**s its own tale** *or* **story** ça dit bien ce que ça veut dire; **the lack of evidence** ~**s a tale** *or* **story** le manque de preuve est très révélateur; **his actions** ~ **us a lot about his motives** ses actes nous en disent long sur ses motifs; **she was** ~**ing him about it** elle lui en parlait, elle était en train de le lui raconter; ~ **me about it*** (*lit*) raconte-moi ça; (*iro*) ne m'en parle pas; **I told him about what had happened** je lui ai dit *or* raconté ce qui était arrivé; (*indicating authorship*) **"by J. Smith, as told to W. Jones"** ≃ "par J. Smith avec la collaboration de W. Jones"; *see* **picture, tale**.
c (*distinguish*) distinguer, voir; (*know*) savoir. **to** ~ **right from wrong** démêler *or* distinguer le bien du mal; **I can't** ~ **them apart** je ne peux pas les distinguer (l'un de l'autre); **how can I** ~ **what he will do?** comment puis-je savoir ce qu'il va faire?; **there's no** ~**ing what he might do** impossible de dire *or* savoir ce qu'il pourrait faire; **I couldn't** ~ **how it was done** je ne pourrais pas dire comment ça a été fait; **no one can** ~ **what he'll say** personne ne peut savoir ce qu'il va dire; **you can** ~ **he's clever by the way he talks** on voit bien qu'il est intelligent à la façon dont il parle; **I can't** ~ **the difference** je ne vois pas la différence (*between* entre); **you can't** ~ **much from his letter** sa lettre n'en dit pas très long.
d (*command*) dire, ordonner (*sb to do* à qn de faire). **do as you are told** fais ce qu'on te dit; **I told him not to do it** je lui ai dit de ne pas le faire, je lui ai défendu de le faire.
e **there were 30 books all told** il y avait 30 livres en tout.
f (*††: count*) compter, dénombrer. **to** ~ **one's beads** dire *or* égrener *or* réciter son chapelet.
2 vi a parler (*of, about* de). (*fig*) **the ruins told of a long-lost civilization** les ruines témoignaient d'une civilisation depuis longtemps disparue; **his face told of his sorrow** sa douleur se lisait sur son visage; **more than words can** ~ plus qu'on ne peut (*or* que je ne peux *etc*) dire.
b (*know*) savoir. **how can I** ~? comment le saurais-je?; **I can't** ~ je n'en sais rien; **who can** ~? qui sait?; **you never can** ~ on ne sait jamais; **you can't** ~ **from his letter** on ne peut pas savoir d'après sa lettre.
c (*be talebearer*) **I won't** ~! je ne le répéterai à personne!; **to** ~ **on sb*** rapporter *or* cafarder* contre qn; **don't** ~ **on us!*** ne nous dénonce pas!
d (*have an effect*) se faire sentir (*on sb/sth* sur qn/qch). **breeding** ~**s** quand on a de la classe cela se sent toujours; **his influence must** ~ son influence ne peut que se faire sentir; **his age is beginning to** ~ il commence à accuser son âge; **his age told against him** il était handicapé par son âge.
3 comp ►**telltale** n rapporteur *m*, -euse *f*, cafard* *m* ◊ adj *mark etc* révélateur (*f* -trice), éloquent.
►**tell off** 1 vt sep a (*: *reprimand*) gronder, attraper* (*sb for sth* qn pour qch, *for doing* pour avoir fait). **to be told off** se faire attraper*.
b (†) (*select etc*) *person* affecter (*for sth* à qch), désigner (*to do* pour faire); (*check off*) dénombrer. 2 **telling-off*** n *see* **telling**.
teller ['telə^r] n (*Banking*) caissier *m*, -ière *f*; *[votes]* scrutateur *m*, -trice *f*. (*US Pol*) ~ **vote** vote *m* à bulletin secret (*dans une assemblée*); *see* **story** *etc*.
telling ['telɪŋ] 1 adj *figures, point, detail* révélateur (*f* -trice), éloquent; *argument, style* efficace; *blow* bon, bien assené. 2 n (*NonC*) *[story etc]* récit *m*, narration *f*. **it lost nothing in the** ~ c'était tout aussi bien quand on l'entendait raconter. 3 comp ►**telling-off*** attrapade* *f*; **to get/give a good telling-off** recevoir/passer un bon savon* (*from* de, *to* à).
tellurium [te'lʊərɪəm] n tellure *m*.
telly* ['telɪ] n (*Brit*) (abbr of **television**) télé* *f*. **on the** ~ à la télé.
temerity [tɪ'merɪtɪ] n (*NonC*) audace *f*, témérité *f*.
temp* [temp] (*Brit*) (abbr of **temporary**) 1 n intérimaire *mf*, secrétaire *mf etc* qui fait de l'intérim. 2 vi faire de l'intérim, travailler comme intérimaire.
temper ['tempə^r] 1 n a (*NonC: nature, disposition*) tempérament *m*, caractère *m*, humeur *f*; (*NonC: mood*) humeur; (*fit of bad* ~) (accès *m or* crise *f* de) colère *f*. **he has a very even** ~ il est d'un caractère *or* d'un tempérament *or* d'une humeur très égal(e); **to have a hot** *or* **quick** ~ être soupe au lait; **to have a nasty** *or* **foul** *or* **vile** ~ avoir un sale caractère, avoir un caractère de chien* *or* de cochon*; **he was in a foul** ~ il était d'une humeur massacrante; **to be in a good/bad** ~ être de bonne/mauvaise humeur; **to keep one's** ~ garder son calme, se maîtriser; **to lose one's** ~ se mettre en colère; **to be in/get into a** ~ être/se mettre en colère (*with sb* contre qn, *over or about sth* à propos de qch); **to put sb into a** ~ mettre qn en colère; ~, ~! ne nous mettons pas en colère!; **in a fit of** ~ **he** ... dans un accès de colère il ...; **he flew into a** ~ il a explosé *or* éclaté; *see* **tantrum**.
b *[metal]* trempe *f*.
2 vt *metal* tremper; (*fig*) *effects, rigours, passions* tempérer (*with* par).
tempera ['tempərə] n (*NonC: Art*) détrempe *f*.
temperament ['tempərəmənt] n (*NonC*) (*nature*) tempérament *m*, nature *f*; (*moodiness, difficult* ~) humeur *f*, tendance *f* au caprice. **the artistic** ~ le tempérament artiste; **an outburst of** ~ une saute d'humeur.
temperamental [ˌtempərə'mentl] adj a *person, horse* fantasque, capricieux, d'humeur instable; (*fig*) *machine, device* capricieux. b (*innate*) *ability, tendency* naturel, inné.
temperamentally [ˌtempərə'mentəlɪ] adv a (*unpredictably*) *behave* capricieusement. b (*by nature*) ~ **suited/unsuited to a job** de nature à/pas de nature à faire un travail; ~, **he is more like** ... au niveau tempérament, il ressemble plus à ... .
temperance ['tempərəns] 1 n (*NonC*) modération *f*; (*in drinking*) tempérance *f*. 2 comp *movement, league* antialcoolique; *hotel* où l'on

ne sert pas de boissons alcoolisées.

temperate ['tempərɪt] adj a (*Geog, Met*) *climate, country etc* tempéré. **~ zone** zone tempérée. b (*mild etc*) *character, nature* modéré, mesuré; *reaction, attitude* modéré, plein de modération. c (*not overindulging*) *person* (*gen*) qui fait preuve de modération, frugal; (*with alcohol*) qui fait preuve de tempérance, sobre; *desire, appetite* modéré.

temperature ['temprɪtʃər] 1 n température *f*. **at a ~ of** ... à une température de ...; **to have** *or* **run a ~** avoir de la température *or* de la fièvre; **to take sb's ~** prendre la température de qn; *see* **high 1b**. 2 comp *change etc* de température ▸**temperature chart** (*Med*) feuille *f* de température.

-tempered ['tempəd] adj ending in comps: **even-tempered** d'humeur égale; *see* **bad, good** *etc*.

tempest ['tempɪst] n (*liter*) tempête *f*, orage *m*.

tempestuous [tem'pestjʊəs] adj *weather* de tempête; *wind* de tempête, violent; (*fig*) *meeting, scene* orageux, agité; *character, person* passionné.

tempestuously [tem'pestjʊəslɪ] adv (*fig*) orageusement, de façon tempétueuse. **the sea crashed ~ against the cliffs** la mer tempétueuse s'abattait contre les falaises.

tempi ['tempiː] (*Mus*) npl of **tempo**.

temping ['tempɪŋ] n (*Brit*) intérim *m*.

Templar ['templər] n = **Knight Templar**; *see* **knight**.

template ['templɪt] n a (*pattern: woodwork, patchwork etc*) gabarit *m*. b (*Constr: beam*) traverse *f*. c (*Comput*) patron *m*.

temple¹ ['templ] n (*Rel*) temple *m*. (*Brit Jur*) **the T~** ≃ le Palais (de Justice).

temple² ['templ] n (*Anat*) tempe *f*.

templet ['templɪt] n = **template**.

tempo ['tempəʊ] n, pl **~s** *or* (*Mus*) **tempi** (*Mus, fig*) tempo *m*.

temporal ['tempərəl] adj (*Gram, Rel*) temporel; (*Anat*) temporal.

temporarily ['tempərərɪlɪ] adv *agree, appoint, decide* provisoirement, temporairement; *lame, blind, disappointed* pendant un certain temps, pendant un moment.

temporary ['tempərərɪ] adj *job, worker* temporaire; *secretary* intérimaire; *teacher* suppléant; *ticket, licence* valide à titre temporaire; *decision, solution, method, powers* provisoire, temporaire; *building* provisoire; *relief, improvement* passager. **~ road surface** revêtement *m* provisoire; **~ injunction** interdiction *f* provisoire *or* temporaire.

temporize ['tempəraɪz] vi a (*procrastinate*) chercher à gagner du temps, atermoyer; (*parley, deal*) transiger, composer par expédient (*with sb* avec qn, *about sth* sur qch); (*effect compromise*) pactiser, transiger, composer (*with sb* avec qn). **to ~ between two people** faire accepter un compromis à deux personnes. b (*pej: bend with circumstances*) faire de l'opportunisme.

tempt [tempt] vt a tenter, séduire. **to ~ sb to do** donner à qn l'envie *or* la tentation de faire; **try and ~ her to eat a little** tâchez de la persuader de manger un peu; **may I ~ you to a little more wine?** puis-je vous offrir un petit peu plus de vin?; **I am very ~ed to accept** je suis très tenté d'accepter; **I'm very ~ed** c'est très tentant; **he was ~ed into doing it** il n'a pas pu résister à la tentation de le faire; (*hum*) **don't ~ me!** n'essaie pas de me tenter!; *see* **sorely**. b († *or Bible: test*) tenter, induire en tentation. (*common usage*) **to ~ Providence** *or* **fate** tenter la Providence.

temptation [temp'teɪʃən] n tentation *f*. **to put ~ in sb's way** exposer qn à la tentation; **lead us not into ~** ne nous laissez pas succomber à la tentation; **there is a great ~ to assume** ... il est très tentant de supposer ...; **there is no ~ to do so** on n'est nullement tenté de le faire.

tempter ['temptər] n tentateur *m*.

tempting ['temptɪŋ] adj (*gen*) tentant; *food* appétissant.

temptingly ['temptɪŋlɪ] adv d'une manière tentante. **the sea was ~ near** la mer était tout près et c'était bien tentant.

temptress ['temptrɪs] n tentatrice *f*.

tempura [tem'pʊərə] n (*NonC*) tempura *f*.

ten [ten] 1 adj dix *inv*. **about ~ books** une dizaine de livres; **the T~ Commandments** les dix commandements *mpl*.

2 pron dix *mfpl*. **there were ~** il y en avait dix; **there were about ~** il y en avait une dizaine.

3 n dix *m inv*. **~s of thousands of** ... des milliers (et des milliers) de ...; **hundreds, ~s and units** les centaines, les dizaines et les unités; **to count in ~s** compter par dizaines; (*fig*) **~ to one he won't come** je parie qu'il ne viendra pas; (*fig*) **they're ~ a penny** il y en a tant qu'on en veut, il y en a à la pelle*; (*Aut*) **to drive with one's hands at ~ to two** conduire avec les mains à dix heures dix; *for other phrases see* **number** *and* **six**.

4 comp ▸**ten-cent store** (*US*) bazar *m* ▸**tenfold** adj décuple ◊ adv au décuple; **to increase tenfold** décupler ▸**ten-gallon hat** (*US*) ≃ chapeau *m* de cowboy ▸**ten-metre line** (*Rugby*) ligne *f* de dix mètres ▸**tenpin** quille *f*; (*Brit*) **tenpin bowling**, (*US*) **tenpins** bowling *m* (à dix quilles).

tenable ['tenəbl] adj *position etc* défendable. **it's just not ~** ça ne peut vraiment pas se défendre.

tenacious [tɪ'neɪʃəs] adj tenace, obstiné, entêté.

tenaciously [tɪ'neɪʃəslɪ] adv avec ténacité, obstinément.

tenacity [tɪ'næsɪtɪ] n (*NonC*) ténacité *f*.

tenancy ['tenənsɪ] n location *f*. **during my ~ of the house** pendant que j'étais locataire de la maison; **~ agreement** contrat *m* de location; **to take on the ~ of a house** prendre une maison en location; **to give up the ~ of a house** résilier un contrat de location; **the new law relating to tenancies** la nouvelle loi relative aux locations.

tenant ['tenənt] 1 n locataire *mf*. 2 comp ▸**tenant farmer** métayer *m*, tenancier *m* ▸**tenant in common** (*Jur*) indivisaire *mf*. 3 vt *property* habiter comme locataire.

tenantry ['tenəntrɪ] n (*NonC: collective*) (ensemble *m* des) tenanciers *mpl* (d'un domaine).

tench [tentʃ] n, pl inv tanche *f*.

tend¹ [tend] vt *sheep, shop* garder; *invalid* soigner; *machine* surveiller; *garden* entretenir; *piece of land* (*to grow food*) travailler, cultiver.

▸**tend to** vt fus (*take care of*) s'occuper de; *see also* **tend²**.

tend² [tend] vi *[person]* avoir tendance, tendre, incliner (*to do* à faire); *[thing]* avoir tendance (*to do* à faire). **to ~ towards** avoir des tendances à, incliner à *or* vers; **he ~s to be lazy** il a tendance *or* il tend à être paresseux, il est enclin à la paresse; **he ~s to(wards) fascism** il a des tendances fascistes, il incline au *or* vers le fascisme; **I ~ to think that** ... j'incline *or* j'ai tendance à penser que ...; **that ~s to be the case with such people** c'est en général le cas avec des gens de cette sorte; **it is a grey ~ing to blue** c'est un gris tirant sur le bleu.

tendency ['tendənsɪ] n tendance *f*. **to have a ~ to do** avoir tendance à faire; **there is a ~ for business to improve** les affaires ont tendance *or* tendent à s'améliorer; (*St Ex*) **a strong upward ~** une forte tendance à la hausse; **the present ~ to(wards) socialism** les tendances socialistes actuelles.

tendentious [ten'denʃəs] adj tendancieux.

tendentiously [ten'denʃəslɪ] adv tendancieusement.

tendentiousness [ten'denʃəsnɪs] n caractère tendancieux.

tender¹ ['tendər] n (*Rail*) tender *m*; (*boat*) (*for passengers*) embarcation *f*; (*for supplies*) ravitailleur *m*.

tender² ['tendər] 1 vt (*proffer*) *object* tendre, offrir; *money, thanks, apologies* offrir. **to ~ one's resignation** donner sa démission (*to sb* à qn); **"please ~ exact change"** "prière de faire l'appoint". 2 vi (*Comm*) faire une soumission (*for sth* pour qch). 3 n a (*Comm*) soumission *f*. **to make** *or* **put in a ~ for sth** faire une soumission pour qch, soumissionner qch; **to invite ~s for sth, put sth out to ~** mettre qch en adjudication. b (*Fin*) **legal ~** cours légal; **that coin is no longer legal ~** cette pièce n'a plus cours. 4 comp ▸**tender offer** (*US St Ex*) offre *f* publique d'achat, O.P.A. *f*.

tender³ ['tendər] 1 adj a (*gen*) tendre; *skin, flower* délicat, fragile; *meat, vegetable, shoots* tendre; *spot, bruise, heart* sensible; *conscience, subject* délicat. (*sore*) **~ to the touch** sensible au toucher; (*liter*) **of ~ years** *or* **age** d'âge tendre.

b (*affectionate*) *person, memories, thoughts, words* tendre, doux (*f* douce); *look, voice* tendre, caressant; *greeting, farewell, embrace* tendre.

2 comp ▸**tenderfoot** (pl **~s**) novice *mf*, nouveau *m*, nouvelle *f* ▸**tender-hearted** sensible, compatissant; **to be tender-hearted** être un cœur tendre ▸**tender-heartedness** (*NonC*) compassion *f*, sensibilité *f* ▸**tenderloin** (*meat*) filet *m*; (*US fig*) quartier *m* louche (*où la police est corrompue*).

tenderer ['tendərər] n soumissionnaire *mf*.

tenderize ['tendəraɪz] vt (*Culin*) attendrir.

tenderizer ['tendəraɪzər] n (*Culin*) (*mallet*) attendrisseur *m*; (*spices*) épices *fpl* pour attendrir la viande.

tenderly ['tendəlɪ] adv tendrement, avec tendresse.

tenderness ['tendənɪs] n (*NonC*) a (*gen*) tendresse *f*; *[skin]* délicatesse *f*; *[flower etc]* fragilité *f*; *[meat etc]* tendreté *f*; *[bruise etc]* sensibilité *f*. b (*emotion*) tendresse *f* (*towards* envers).

tendon ['tendən] n tendon *m*.

tendril ['tendrɪl] n (*Bot*) vrille *f*.

tenebrous ['tenɪbrəs] adj (*liter*) ténébreux.

tenement ['tenɪmənt] n (*apartment*) appartement *m*, logement *m*; (*block: also* **~ house**) immeuble *m* (*généralement ancien*).

Tenerife [ˌtenə'riːf] n Tenerife.

tenet ['tenət] n principe *m*, doctrine *f*.

Tenn. (*US*) abbr of **Tennessee**.

tenner* ['tenər] n (*Brit*) (billet *m* de) dix livres; (*US*) (billet de) dix dollars.

Tennessee [ˌtenɪ'siː] n Tennessee *m*. **in ~** dans le Tennessee.

tennis ['tenɪs] 1 n (*NonC*) tennis *m*. **a game of ~** une partie de tennis. 2 comp *player, racket, club* de tennis ▸**tennis ball** balle *f* de tennis ▸**tennis camp**: (*US*) **to go to tennis camp** faire un stage de tennis ▸**tennis court** (court *m or* terrain *m* de) tennis *m inv* ▸**tennis elbow** (*Med*) synovite *f* du coude ▸**tennis shoe** (chaussure *f* de) tennis *m*.

tenon ['tenən] n tenon *m*.

tenor ['tenər] 1 n a (*general sense*) *[speech, discussion]* sens *m*, substance *f*; (*course*) *[one's life, events, developments]* cours *m*. b (*exact wording*) teneur *f*. c (*Mus*) ténor *m*. 2 adj (*Mus*) *voice, part* de ténor; *aria* pour ténor; *recorder, saxophone etc* ténor *inv*. **the ~ clef**

la clef d'ut quatrième ligne.

tense[1] [tens] n (*Gram*) temps *m*. **in the present ~** au temps présent.

tense[2] [tens] 1 adj *rope, muscles, person, voice* tendu; *period* de tension; *smile* crispé; (*Ling*) *vowel* tendu. **in a voice ~ with emotion** d'une voix étranglée par l'émotion; **they were ~ with fear/anticipation** *etc* ils étaient crispés de peur/par l'attente *etc;* **things were getting rather ~** l'atmosphère devenait plutôt électrique; **the evening was rather ~** tout le monde était très tendu toute la soirée. 2 vt *muscles* tendre. **to ~ o.s.** se tendre. 3 vi *[muscles, person, animal]* se tendre.

►**tense up** 1 vi se crisper. 2 vt: **you're all tensed up** tu es sur les nerfs.

tensely ['tenslı] adv *say* d'une voix tendue. **they waited/watched ~** ils attendaient/regardaient, tendus.

tenseness ['tensnıs] n (*NonC: lit, fig*) tension *f*.

tensile ['tensaıl] adj *material* extensible, élastique. **~ strength** force *f* de tension; **high-~ steel** acier *m* de haute tension; *see* **stress.**

tension ['tenʃən] 1 n (*NonC*) tension *f*. 2 comp ►**tension headache** (*Med*) mal *m* de tête (dû à la tension nerveuse).

tent [tent] 1 n tente *f*. 2 comp ►**tented arch** (*Archit*) ogive *f* ►**tent peg** (*Brit*) piquet *m* de tente ►**tent pole, tent stake** (*US*) montant *m* de tente ►**tent trailer** caravane *f* pliante. 3 vi camper.

tentacle ['tentəkl] n (*also fig*) tentacule *m*.

tentative ['tentətıv] adj *suggestion, gesture, smile* timide, hésitant; *voice* hésitant; *scheme* expérimental; *conclusion, solution, plan* provisoire. **everything is very ~ at the moment** rien n'est encore décidé pour le moment; **a ~ offer** (*of help etc*) une offre hésitante; (*to buy etc*) une offre provisoire; **it's only a ~ suggestion but you ...** si je peux me permettre une suggestion, vous ...; **she is a very ~ person** elle n'a aucune confiance en elle-même.

tentatively ['tentətıvlı] adv (*gen*) non sans hésitation; *try, act* expérimentalement, à titre d'essai; *decide* provisoirement; *say, suggest, smile, walk* timidement, non sans hésitation.

tenterhooks ['tentəhʊks] npl: **to be/keep sb on ~** être/tenir qn sur des charbons ardents *or* au supplice.

tenth [tenθ] 1 adj dixième. 2 n dixième *mf*; (*fraction*) dixième *m*. **nine-~s of the book** les neuf dixièmes du livre; **nine-~s of the time** la majeure partie du temps; *for other phrases see* **sixth.**

tenuity [te'njʊıtı] n (*NonC*) ténuité *f*.

tenuous ['tenjʊəs] adj *link, distinction* ténu; *evidence, plot* mince; *existence* précaire.

tenuously ['tenjʊəslı] adv de manière ténue *or* précaire.

tenure ['tenjʊəʳ] n (*Univ etc*) fait *m* d'être titulaire; (*feudal*) tenure *f*; *[land, property]* bail *m*. *[employee]* **to have ~** être titulaire; **to get ~** être titularisé; **to hope for ~** espérer être titularisé; **the system of ~** le système des emplois *or* postes permanents; (*US Univ*) **~ track position** poste *m* avec possibilité de titularisation; *[appointment etc]* **the ~ is for 2 years** la période de jouissance est de 2 ans; **during his ~ of office** pendant qu'il était en fonction; *see* **security.**

tenured ['tenjʊəd] adj *professor etc* titulaire. **he has a ~ position** il est titulaire de son poste.

tepee ['ti:pi:] n tipi *m*.

tepid ['tepıd] adj (*lit, fig*) tiède.

tepidity [te'pıdıtı] n (*NonC*) tiédeur *f*.

tepidly ['tepıdlı] adv (*fig*) *agree etc* sans grand enthousiasme.

tepidness ['tepıdnıs] n (*NonC*) = **tepidity.**

Ter (*Brit*) = **Terr.**

terbium ['tɜ:bıəm] n terbium *m*.

tercentenary [,tɜ:sen'ti:nərı] adj, n tricentenaire (*m*).

tercet ['tɜ:sıt] n (*Poetry*) tercet *m*; (*Mus*) triolet *m*.

Teresa [tə'ri:zə] n Thérèse *f*.

term [tɜ:m] 1 n a (*gen, Admin, Fin, Jur, Med*) (*limit*) terme *m*; (*period*) période *f*, terme (*Jur*). **to put** *or* **set a ~ to sth** mettre *or* fixer un terme à qch; (*Fin, Med*) **at ~** à terme; **in the long ~** à long terme (*see also* **long-term**); **in the medium ~** à moyen terme (*see also* **medium 3**); **in the short ~** dans l'immédiat (*see also* **short 2**); **during his ~ of office** pendant la période où il exerçait ses fonctions; **elected for a 3-year ~** élu pour une durée *or* période de 3 ans; **~ of imprisonment** peine *f* de prison.

b (*Scol, Univ*) trimestre *m*; (*Jur*) session *f*. (*Scol, Univ*) **the autumn/spring/summer ~** le premier/second *or* deuxième/troisième trimestre; **in ~(time), during ~(time)** pendant le trimestre; **out of ~(time)** pendant les vacances (scolaires *or* universitaires).

c (*Math, Philos*) terme *m*. **A expressed in ~s of B** A exprimé en fonction de B; (*fig*) **in ~s of production we are doing well** sur le plan de la production nous avons de quoi être satisfaits; **he sees art in ~s of human relationships** pour lui l'art est fonction des relations humaines; **to look at sth in ~s of the effect it will have/of how it ...** considérer qch sous l'angle de l'effet que cela aura/de la façon dont cela ...; **we must think in ~s of ...** il faut penser à ...; (*consider the possibility of*) il faut envisager (la possibilité de) ...; **price in ~s of dollars** prix *m* exprimé en dollars.

d (*conditions*) **~s** (*gen*) conditions *fpl*; *[contracts etc]* termes *mpl*; (*Comm etc*) prix *m(pl)*, tarif *m*; **you can name your own ~s** vous êtes libre de stipuler vos conditions; **on what ~s?** à quelles conditions?; **not on any ~s** à aucun prix, à aucune condition; **they accepted him on his own ~s** ils l'ont accepté sans concessions de sa part; **to compete on equal** *or* **the same ~s** rivaliser dans les mêmes conditions *or* sur un pied d'égalité; **to compete on unequal** *or* **unfair ~s** ne pas rivaliser dans les mêmes conditions, ne pas bénéficier des mêmes avantages; **to lay down** *or* **dictate ~s to sb** imposer des conditions à qn; **to come to ~s with** *person* arriver à un accord avec; *problem, situation* accepter; **under the ~s of the contract** d'après les termes du contrat; (*Jur*) **~s and conditions** modalités *fpl*; **~s of surrender** conditions *or* termes de la reddition; **it is not within our ~s of reference** cela n'entre pas dans les termes de notre mandat; **~s of sale** conditions de vente; **~s of payment** conditions *or* modalités de paiement; **credit ~s** conditions de crédit; (*Comm*) **we offer it on easy ~s** nous offrons des facilités *fpl* de paiement; **our ~s for full board** notre tarif pension complète; **"inclusive ~s: £20"** "20 livres tout compris".

e (*relationship*) **to be on good/bad ~s with sb** être en bons/mauvais termes *or* rapports avec qn; **they are on the best of ~s** ils sont au mieux, ils sont en excellents termes; **they're on fairly friendly ~s** ils ont des rapports assez amicaux *or* des relations assez amicales; *see* **equal, nod 2, speaking.**

f (*expression, word*) terme *m*, expression *f*, mot *m*. **technical/colloquial ~** terme technique/familier; **in plain** *or* **simple ~s** en termes simples *or* clairs; **he spoke of her in glowing ~s** il a parlé d'elle en termes très chaleureux; *see* **uncertain.**

2 comp *exams etc* trimestriel ►**term insurance** assurance-vie *f* temporaire ►**term paper** (*US Univ etc*) dissertation *f* trimestrielle ►**termtime** (période *f or* durée *f* du) trimestre (*see also* **1b**) ►**term-time employment** (*US Univ*) emploi *m* pour étudiant (rémunéré par l'université).

3 vt appeler, nommer. **what we ~ happiness** ce que nous nommons *or* appelons le bonheur; **it was ~ed a compromise** ce fut qualifié de compromis.

termagant ['tɜ:məgənt] n harpie *f*, mégère *f*.

terminal ['tɜ:mınl] 1 adj a (*last*) *part, stage* terminal; *illness, cancer* incurable; *patient* en phase terminale, incurable; *ward, hospital* pour malades incurables; *situation* sans issue. (*Rail*) **~ point, ~ station** terminus *m*; **~ velocity** (*Phys*) vitesse finale; (*Aviat*) vitesse maximale. b (*Ling*) *string, element, symbol* terminal. c (*termly*) trimestriel. 2 n a (*air ~*) aérogare *f*; (*Rail, coach*) (gare *f*) terminus *m inv*; (*Underground: terminus*) (gare) terminus; (*Underground: at beginning of line*) tête *f* de ligne. **container ~** terminus de containers; **oil ~** terminal *m* pétrolier. b (*Elec*) borne *f*. c (*Comput*) terminal *m*. **dumb/intelligent ~** terminal passif/intelligent.

terminally ['tɜ:mınlı] adv: **the ~ ill** les malades au stade terminal *or* en phase terminale, ceux qui sont condamnés.

terminate ['tɜ:mıneıt] 1 vt terminer, mettre fin à, mettre un terme à; *contract* résilier, dénoncer. 2 vi se terminer, finir (*in* en, par).

termination [,tɜ:mı'neıʃən] n fin *f*, conclusion *f*; *[contract]* résiliation *f*, dénonciation *f*; (*Gram*) terminaison *f*. **~ of employment** licenciement *m*, résiliation *f* du contrat de travail; **~ (of pregnancy)** interruption *f* de grossesse.

termini ['tɜ:mıni:] npl of **terminus.**

terminological [,tɜ:mınə'lɒdʒıkəl] adj terminologique.

terminologist [,tɜ:mı'nɒlədʒıst] n terminologue *mf*.

terminology [,tɜ:mı'nɒlədʒı] n terminologie *f*.

terminus ['tɜ:mınəs] n, pl **~s** *or* **termini** terminus *m inv*.

termite ['tɜ:maıt] n termite *m*, fourmi blanche.

tern [tɜ:n] n hirondelle *f* de mer, sterne *f*.

ternary ['tɜ:nərı] adj ternaire.

Terr (*Brit*) (abbr of **Terrace**) *forme utilisée dans les adresses sur les enveloppes.*

terrace ['terəs] 1 n (*Agr, Geol etc*) terrasse *f*; (*raised bank*) terre-plein *m*; (*patio, veranda, balcony, roof*) terrasse; (*Brit: row of houses*) rangée *f* de maisons (*attenantes les unes aux autres*). (*Brit Sport*) **the ~s** les gradins *mpl*. 2 comp ►**terrace cultivation** culture *f* en terrasses ►**terrace house** (*Brit*) maison *f* en mitoyenneté. 3 vt *hillside* arranger en terrasses. **~d** *garden, hillside* en terrasses; (*Brit*) *house* en mitoyenneté.

terracotta ['terə'kɒtə] 1 n terre cuite. 2 comp (*made of ~*) en terre cuite; (*colour*) ocre brun *inv*.

terra firma ['terə'fɜ:mə] n terre *f* ferme.

terrain [te'reın] n terrain *m* (*sol*).

terrapin ['terəpın] n tortue *f* d'eau douce.

terrazzo [te'rætsəʊ] n sol *m* de mosaïque.

terrestrial [tı'restrıəl] adj terrestre.

terrible ['terəbl] adj a *accident, disaster* terrible, effroyable, atroce; *heat, pain* atroce, affreux, terrible; *poverty, conditions* effroyable; *holiday, disappointment, report* affreux, abominable, épouvantable. b (*emphatic*) **to be a ~ fool/bore** être terriblement bête/ennuyeux; **it is a ~ shame** c'est vraiment dommage.

terribly ['terəblı] adv a (*very*) drôlement*, rudement*, terriblement; (*pej*) atrocement*, affreusement, horriblement. b (*very badly*) *play, sing* affreusement *or* épouvantablement mal.

terrier ['terıəʳ] n a terrier *m*. b (*Brit Mil sl*) **the ~s** la territoriale*, les territoriaux *mpl*.

terrific [tə'rɪfɪk] **adj** a (*terrifying*) terrifiant, épouvantable. b (*: *extreme etc*) *amount, size, height* énorme, fantastique; *speed* fou (*f* folle), incroyable; *noise* énorme, épouvantable, incroyable; *hill, climb* terriblement *or* incroyablement raide; *heat, cold* terrible, épouvantable; *anxiety* terrible; *pleasure* énorme, formidable*, terrible*. c (*: *excellent*) *result, news, game* formidable*, sensationnel*.

terrifically* [tə'rɪfɪkəlɪ] **adv** a (*extremely*) *good etc* terriblement, incroyablement; *bad etc* horriblement, épouvantablement. b (*very well*) *sing, play* formidablement bien*.

terrify ['terɪfaɪ] **vt** terrifier. **to ~ sb out of his wits** rendre qn fou (*f* folle) de terreur; **to be terrified of** avoir une peur folle de.

terrifying ['terɪfaɪɪŋ] **adj** terrifiant, épouvantable, terrible.

terrifyingly ['terɪfaɪɪŋlɪ] **adv** *loud, near* épouvantablement; *bellow etc* de façon terrifiante.

territorial [ˌterɪ'tɔːrɪəl] 1 **adj** territorial. **~ waters** eaux territoriales; (*Brit*) **T~ Army** armée territoriale. 2 **n** (*Brit Mil*) **T~** territorial *m*; **the T~s** l'armée territoriale, la territoriale*, les territoriaux.

territory ['terɪtərɪ] **n** territoire *m*.

terror ['terə^r] 1 **n** a (*NonC*) terreur *f*, épouvante *f*. **they were living in ~** ils vivaient dans la terreur; **they fled in ~** épouvantés, ils se sont enfuis; **he went *or* was in ~ of his life** il craignait fort pour sa vie, il avait la terreur d'être assassiné; **to go *or* live in ~ of sb/sth** vivre dans la terreur de qn/qch, avoir extrêmement peur de qn/qch; **I have a ~ of flying** monter en avion me terrifie; *see* **hold 3d, reign.**

b (*person*) terreur* *f*. **he was the ~ of the younger boys** il était la terreur des plus petits*; **he's a ~ on the roads*** c'est un danger public sur les routes; **that child is a (real *or* little *or* holy) ~*** cet enfant est une vraie (petite) terreur*.

2 **comp** ►**terror-stricken, terror-struck** épouvanté.

terrorism ['terərɪzəm] **n** (*NonC*) terrorisme *m*. **an act of ~** un acte de terrorisme.

terrorist ['terərɪst] 1 **n** terroriste *mf*. 2 **adj** *attack, group, activities* terroriste; *act* de terrorisme. **~ bombing** attentat *m* à la bombe.

terrorize ['terəraɪz] **vt** terroriser.

terry ['terɪ] **n** (*also* **~ cloth, ~ towelling**) tissu *m* éponge.

terse [tɜːs] **adj** laconique, brusque (*pej*).

tersely ['tɜːslɪ] **adv** laconiquement, avec brusquerie (*pej*).

terseness ['tɜːsnɪs] **n** laconisme *m*, brusquerie *f* (*pej*).

tertiary ['tɜːʃərɪ] 1 **adj** (*gen, also Geol*) tertiaire; (*Educ*) post-scolaire. **~ college** établissement *m* d'enseignement post-scolaire; **~ education** enseignement *m* post-scolaire; **~ industries** entreprises *fpl* du tertiaire; **~ sector** (secteur *m*) tertiaire *m*. 2 **n** (*Geol*) tertiaire *m*; (*Rel*) tertiaire *mf*.

Terylene ['terəliːn] (*Brit*) ® 1 **n** tergal *m* ®. 2 **comp** en tergal.

TESL [tesl] **n** (**abbr of Teaching of English as a Second Language**) *see* **teaching.**

Tessa ['tesə] **n** (**abbr of Tax Exempt Special Savings Account**) *compte de dépôt aux intérêts libres d'impôts si le capital reste bloqué.*

tessellated ['tesɪleɪtɪd] **adj** *pavement* en mosaïque.

tessellation [ˌtesɪ'leɪʃən] **n** (*NonC*) mosaïque *f*.

tessitura [ˌtesɪ'tʊərə] **n** tessiture *f*.

test [test] 1 **n** a (*gen, Ind, Tech etc: on product, vehicle, weapon etc*) essai *m*. **the aircraft has been grounded for ~s** l'avion a été retiré de la circulation pour (être soumis à) des essais *or* des vérifications; **to run a ~ on a machine** tester *or* contrôler une machine; **nuclear ~s** essais nucléaires.

b (*Med: on blood, urine*) analyse *f*; (*Med: on organ*) examen *m*; (*Pharm, Chem*) analyse, test *m*. **urine ~** analyse d'urine; **to do a ~ for sugar** faire une analyse pour déterminer la présence *or* le taux de glucose; **hearing ~** examen de l'ouïe; **they did a ~ for diphtheria** ils ont fait une analyse pour voir s'il s'agissait de la diphtérie; (*Med*) **he sent a specimen to the laboratory for ~s** il a envoyé un échantillon au laboratoire pour analyses; **they did ~s on the water to see whether ...** ils ont analysé l'eau pour voir si ...; (*Med*) **the Wasserman ~** la réaction Wasserman.

c (*of physical or mental quality, also Psych*) **they are trying to devise a ~ to find suitable security staff** ils essaient de concevoir un test permettant de sélectionner le personnel de gardiennage; **it's a ~ of his strength** cela teste ses forces; (*fig*) **a ~ of strength** une épreuve de force; **a ~ of his powers to survive in ...** une épreuve permettant d'établir s'il pourrait survivre dans ...; **it wasn't a fair ~ of her linguistic abilities** cela n'a pas permis d'évaluer correctement ses aptitudes linguistiques; **if we apply the ~ of visual appeal** si nous utilisons le critère de l'attrait visuel; *see* **acid, endurance, intelligence** *etc*.

d (*Scol, Univ*) (*written*) devoir *m or* exercice *m* de contrôle, interrogation *f* écrite; (*oral*) interrogation orale. **practical ~** épreuve *f* pratique.

e (*driving ~*) (examen *m* du) permis *m* de conduire. **my ~ is on Wednesday** je passe mon permis mercredi; **to pass/fail the ~** être reçu/échouer au permis (de conduire).

f (*NonC*) **to put to the ~** mettre à l'essai *or* à l'épreuve; **to stand the ~** *[person]* se montrer à la hauteur*; *[machine, vehicle]* résister aux épreuves; **it has stood the ~ of time** cela a (bien) résisté au passage du temps.

g (*Brit Sport*) = **~ match;** *see* **2.**

2 **comp** *shot etc* d'essai; *district, experiment, year* test *inv* ►**test ban treaty** (*Nucl Phys, Pol*) traité *m* d'interdiction d'essais nucléaires ►**test bore** *[oil]* sondage *m* de prospection ►**test card** (*Brit TV*) mire *f* ►**test case** (*Jur*) conflit-test *m or* affaire-test *f* (destiné(e) à faire jurisprudence); **the strike is a test case** c'est une grève-test ►**test data** (*Comput*) données *fpl* d'essai ►**test-drill** *[oil company]* **vi** se livrer à des forages d'essai ►**test drive n** (*Aut*) essai *m* de route ►**test-drive vt** (*by prospective buyer*) essayer; (*by manufacturer*) mettre au banc d'essai, faire faire un essai de route à ►**test film** (*Cine*) bout *m* d'essai ►**test flight** (*Aviat*) vol *m* d'essai ►**test gauge** bande *f* étalon ►**test-market vt** commercialiser à titre expérimental ►**test match** (*Brit: Cricket, Rugby*) ≃ match international ►**test paper** (*Scol*) interrogation écrite; (*Chem*) (papier) réactif *m* ►**test pattern** (*US TV*) = **test card** ►**test piece** (*Mus*) morceau imposé ►**test pilot** (*Aviat*) pilote *m* d'essai ►**test run** (*lit*) essai *m*; (*fig*) période *f* d'essai ►**test strip** bande *f* d'essai ►**test tube** éprouvette *f*; **test-tube baby** bébé-éprouvette *m*.

3 **vt** *machine, weapon, tool* essayer; *vehicle* essayer, mettre à l'essai; *aircraft* essayer, faire faire un vol d'essai à; (*Comm*) *goods* vérifier; (*Chem*) *metal, liquid* analyser; (*Med*) *blood, urine* faire une (*or* des) analyse(s) de; *new drug etc* expérimenter; (*Psych*) *person, animal* tester; (*gen*) *person* mettre à l'épreuve; *sight, hearing* examiner; *intelligence* mettre à l'épreuve, mesurer; *sb's reactions* mesurer; *patience, nerves* éprouver, mettre à l'épreuve. **they ~ed the material for resistance to heat** ils ont soumis le matériau à des essais destinés à vérifier sa résistance à la chaleur; **these conditions ~ a car's tyres/strength** ces conditions mettent à l'épreuve les pneus/la résistance d'une voiture; **to ~ metal for impurities** analyser un métal pour déterminer la proportion d'impuretés qu'il contient; **to ~ the water** *[chemist etc]* analyser l'eau; *[bather etc]* prendre la température de l'eau, voir si l'eau est bonne; (*fig: Pol etc*) prendre la température d'une assemblée (*or* d'un groupe *etc*), se faire une idée de la situation; (*Med*) **they ~ed him for diabetes** ils l'ont soumis à des analyses pour établir s'il avait le diabète; **they ~ed the child for hearing difficulties** ils ont fait passer à l'enfant un examen de l'ouïe; **to ~ sb for drugs/alcohol** faire subir un contrôle de dopage/un Alcootest ® à qn; **they ~ed the children in geography** ils ont fait subir aux enfants une interrogation *or* un exercice de contrôle en géographie; **they ~ed him for the job** ils lui ont fait passer des tests d'aptitude pour le poste; (*fig*) **it is a ~ing time for us all** c'est une période éprouvante pour nous tous.

4 **vi: to ~ for sugar** faire une recherche de sucre; **he ~ed positive for drugs** son contrôle de dopage était positif; **they were ~ing for a gas leak** ils faisaient des essais pour découvrir une fuite de gaz; (*Telec etc*) **"~ing, ~ing"** ≃ "un, deux, trois".

►**test out vt sep** *machine, weapon, tool* essayer; *vehicle* essayer, mettre à l'essai; *aircraft* essayer, faire faire un vol d'essai à.

testament ['testəmənt] **n** (*all senses*) testament *m*. **the Old/New T~** l'Ancien/le Nouveau Testament.

testamentary [ˌtestə'mentərɪ] **adj** testamentaire.

testator [tes'teɪtə^r] **n** testateur *m*.

testatrix [tes'teɪtrɪks] **n** testatrice *f*.

tester[1] ['testə^r] **n** (*person*) contrôleur *m*, -euse *f*; (*machine etc*) appareil *m* de contrôle.

tester[2] ['testə^r] **n** (*over bed*) baldaquin *m*, ciel *m* de lit.

testes ['testiːz] **npl of testis.**

testicle ['testɪkl] **n** testicule *m*.

testification [ˌtestɪfɪ'keɪʃən] **n** déclaration *or* affirmation solennelle.

testify ['testɪfaɪ] 1 **vt** (*Jur etc*) témoigner, déclarer *or* affirmer sous serment (*that* que). (*gen*) **as he will ~** comme il en fera foi. 2 **vi** (*Jur etc*) porter témoignage, faire une déclaration sous serment. **to ~ against/in favour of sb** déposer contre/en faveur de qn; **to ~ to sth** (*Jur*) attester qch; (*gen*) témoigner de qch.

testily ['testɪlɪ] **adv** d'un ton *or* d'un air irrité.

testimonial [ˌtestɪ'məʊnɪəl] **n** (*character etc reference*) recommandation *f*, certificat *m*; (*gift*) témoignage *m* d'estime (*offert à qn par ses collègues etc*). **as a ~ to our gratitude** en témoignage de notre reconnaissance.

testimony ['testɪmənɪ] **n** (*Jur*) témoignage *m*, déposition *f*; (*statement*) déclaration *f*, attestation *f*. **in ~ whereof** en foi de quoi.

testing ['testɪŋ] 1 **n** *[vehicle, machine etc]* mise *f* à l'essai; (*Chem, Pharm*) analyse *f*; *[new drug]* expérimentation *f*; *[person]* (*gen*) mise *f* à l'épreuve; (*Psych*) test(s) *m(pl)*; *[sight, hearing]* examen *m*; *[intelligence, patience etc]* mise à l'épreuve; *[sb's reactions]* mesure *f*, évaluation *f*. **nuclear ~** essais *mpl* nucléaires. 2 **comp** ►**testing bench** banc *m* d'essai ►**testing ground** (*lit, fig*) banc *m* d'essai.

testis ['testɪs] **n, pl testes** testicule *m*.

testosterone [te'stɒstərəʊn] **n** testostérone *f*.

testy ['testɪ] **adj** irritable, grincheux.

tetanus ['tetənəs] 1 **n** tétanos *m*. 2 **comp** *symptom* tétanique; *epidemic* de tétanos; *vaccine, injection* antitétanique.

tetchily ['tetʃɪlɪ] **adv** irritablement.

tetchiness ['tetʃɪnɪs] **n** (*Brit*) (*NonC*) irritabilité *f*.

tetchy ['tetʃɪ] adj (*Brit*) irritable, grincheux.
tête-à-tête ['teɪtɑː'teɪt] 1 adv en tête à tête, seul à seul. 2 n, pl ~ *or* **tête-à-têtes** tête-à-tête *m inv.*
tether ['teðəʳ] 1 n longe *f*. (*fig*) **to be at the end of one's ~** être à bout (de patience *or* de nerfs), être au bout de son rouleau*. 2 vt (*also* **~ up**) *animal* attacher (*to* à).
tetragon ['tetrəgən] n quadrilatère *m*.
tetrahedron [ˌtetrə'hiːdrən] n, pl ~s *or* **tetrahedra** [ˌtetrə'hiːdrə] tétraèdre *m*.
tetrameter [te'træmɪtəʳ] n tétramètre *m*.
Teutonic [tjʊ'tɒnɪk] adj teutonique.
Tex. (*US*) abbr of **Texas.**
Texan ['teksən] 1 adj texan. 2 n Texan(e) *m(f)*.
Texas ['teksəs] n Texas *m*. **in ~** au Texas.
text [tekst] 1 n (*gen, also Comput*) texte *m*. 2 comp ▸**textbook** manuel *m* scolaire, livre *m* scolaire; (*fig*) **a textbook case** *or* **example of** ... un exemple classique *or* typique de ...; (*fig*) **a textbook landing/dive** *etc* un atterrissage/plongeon *etc* modèle ▸**text editor** (*Comput*) éditeur *m* de texte(s).
textile ['tekstaɪl] adj, n textile (*m*). **~s** *or* **the ~ industry** (l'industrie *f*) textile *m*.
textual ['tekstjʊəl] adj a *error* de texte; *copy, translation* textuel. b (*Ling*) *analysis, meaning* textuel.
textually ['tekstjʊəlɪ] adv textuellement, mot à mot.
texture ['tekstʃəʳ] n *[cloth]* texture *f*; *[minerals, soil]* texture *f*, structure *f*, contexture *f*; *[skin, wood, paper, silk etc]* grain *m*; (*fig*) structure, contexture.
textured ['tekstʃəd] adj (*see* **texture**) *paint* granité. **beautifully ~** de belle texture, d'un beau grain; **rough-/smooth-~** d'une texture grossière/fine, d'un grain grossier/fin; **~ vegetable protein** fibre *f* végétale protéique.
TGIF [ˌtiːdʒiːaɪ'ef] (*loc, hum*) (abbr of **Thank God it's Friday**) Dieu merci c'est vendredi.
TGWU [ˌtiːdʒiːdʌbljuː'juː] n (*Brit*) (abbr of **Transport and General Workers' Union**) *syndicat.*
Thai [taɪ] 1 adj thaïlandais; (*Ling*) thaï *inv*. 2 n a Thaïlandais(e) *m(f)*. b (*Ling*) thaï *m*.
Thailand ['taɪlænd] n Thaïlande *f*.
thalamus ['θæləməs] n, pl **thalami** ['θæləÖmaɪ] thalamus *m*.
thalassemia [tælə'siːmɪə] n thalassémie *f*.
thalidomide [θə'lɪdəʊmaɪd] ® 1 n thalidomide *f* ®. 2 comp ▸**thalidomide baby** (petite) victime *f* de la thalidomide.
thallium ['θælɪəm] n thallium *m*.
Thames [temz] n Tamise *f*. (*fig*) **he'll never set the ~ on fire** il n'a pas inventé la poudre *or* le fil à couper le beurre.
than [ðæn], *weak form* [ðən] conj a que. **I have more ~ you** j'en ai plus que toi; **he is taller ~ his sister** il est plus grand que sa sœur; **he has more brains ~ sense** il a plus d'intelligence que de bon sens; **more unhappy ~ angry** plus malheureux que fâché; **you'd be better going by car ~ by bus** tu ferais mieux d'y aller en voiture plutôt qu'en autobus; **I'd do anything rather ~ admit it** je ferais tout plutôt que d'avouer cela; **no sooner did he arrive ~ he started to complain** il n'était pas plus tôt arrivé *or* il était à peine arrivé qu'il a commencé à se plaindre; **it was a better play ~ we expected** la pièce était meilleure que nous ne l'avions prévu.
b (*with numerals*) de. **more/less ~ 20** plus/moins de 20; **less ~ half** moins de la moitié; **more ~ once** plus d'une fois.
thank [θæŋk] 1 vt remercier, dire merci à (*sb for sth* qn de *or* pour qch, *for doing* de faire, d'avoir fait). **I cannot ~ you enough** je ne saurais assez vous remercier; **do ~ him for me** remerciez-le bien de ma part; **~ you** merci; **~ you very much** merci bien (*also iro*), merci beaucoup, merci mille fois; **~ you for the book/for helping us** merci pour le livre/de nous avoir aidés; **with ~s** avec tous mes (*or* nos) remerciements; **no ~ you** (non) merci; **without so much as a ~ you** sans même dire merci; **~ you for nothing!*** je te remercie! (*iro*); **~ goodness*, ~ heaven(s)*, ~ God*** Dieu merci; **~ goodness you've done it!*** Dieu merci tu l'as fait!; (*fig*) **you've got him to ~ for that** c'est à lui que tu dois cela; **he's only got himself to ~** il ne peut s'en prendre qu'à lui-même; **he won't ~ you for that!** ne t'attends pas à ce qu'il te remercie! *or* te félicite!; **I'll ~ you to mind your own business!** je vous prierai de vous mêler de ce qui vous regarde!
2 npl a **~s** remerciements *mpl*; (*excl*) **~s!*** merci!; **~s very much!*, ~s a lot!*** merci bien (*also iro*), merci beaucoup, merci mille fois; **~s a million*** merci mille fois; **many ~s for all you've done** merci mille fois pour ce que vous avez fait; **many ~s for helping us** merci mille fois de nous avoir aidés; **with ~s** avec tous mes (*or* nos) remerciements; **with my warmest** *or* **best ~s** avec mes remerciements les plus sincères; **give him my ~s** transmettez-lui mes remerciements, remerciez-le de ma part; **to give ~s to God** rendre grâces à Dieu; **~s be to God!** Dieu soit loué!; **that's all the ~s I get!** c'est comme ça qu'on me remercie!
b **~s to** prep grâce à; **~s to you/your brother/his help** *etc* grâce à toi/ton frère/son aide *etc;* **no ~s to you!** ce n'est pas grâce à toi!
3 comp ▸**thank offering** = **thanks offering** ▸**thanksgiving** action *f* de grâce(s); (*Can, US*) **Thanksgiving (Day)** *fête nationale* ▸**thanks offering** action *f* de grâce(s) (*don*) ▸**thank-you: and now a special thank-you to John** et maintenant je voudrais remercier tout particulièrement John; **a thank-you card** une carte de remerciement.
thankful ['θæŋkfʊl] adj reconnaissant (*for* de). **he was ~ to sit down** il s'est assis avec soulagement; **we were ~ for your umbrella!** nous avons vraiment béni votre parapluie!; **let us be ~ that he didn't know** estimons-nous heureux qu'il ne l'ait pas su; **I was ~ that he hadn't seen me** j'ai été bien content *or* je me suis félicité qu'il ne m'ait pas vu; *see* **mercy.**
thankfully ['θæŋkfəlɪ] adv (*gratefully*) avec reconnaissance; (*with relief*) avec soulagement; (*fortunately*) heureusement.
thankfulness ['θæŋkfʊlnɪs] n (*NonC*) gratitude *f*, reconnaissance *f*.
thankless ['θæŋklɪs] adj ingrat.
that [ðæt], *weak form* [ðət] 1 dem adj, pl **those** a (*unstressed*) ce, (*before vowel and mute "h"*) cet, *f* cette, *mfpl* ces. **~ noise** ce bruit; **~ man** cet homme; **~ car** cette voiture; **those books** ces livres; **those houses** ces maisons; **how's ~ work of yours getting on?** et ce travail, comment ça va?*; **I love ~ house of yours!** votre maison, je l'adore!; **~ awful dog of theirs** ce sale chien qu'ils ont*; **where's ~ son of his?** où est-il, ce fameux fils?, où est-il, son fichu* fils? (*pej*); **what about ~ £5 I lent you?** et ces 5 livres que je t'ai prêtées?
b (*stressed; or as opposed to* **this, these**) ce ... là, cette ... là, ces ... là. **I mean THAT book** c'est de ce livre-là que je parle; **I like ~ photo better than this one** je préfère cette photo-là à celle-ci; **~ hill over there** la *or* cette colline là-bas; **(on) ~ Saturday** ce samedi-là; **everyone agreed on ~ point** tout le monde était d'accord là-dessus; **the leaf was blowing this way and ~** la feuille tournoyait de-ci de-là; **she ran this way and ~** elle courait dans tous les sens; **there's little to choose between this author and ~ (one)** il n'y a pas grande différence entre cet auteur-ci et l'autre.
2 dem pron, pl **those** a cela, ça; ce. **what's ~?** qu'est-ce que c'est que ça?; **who's ~?** (*gen*) qui est-ce?; (*on phone*) qui est à l'appareil?; **is ~ you Paul?** c'est toi Paul?; **~'s what they've been told** c'est *or* voilà ce qu'on leur a dit; **~'s the boy I told you about** c'est *or* voilà le garçon dont je t'ai parlé; **those are my children** ce sont mes enfants; (*pointing out*) voilà mes enfants; **do you like ~?** vous aimez ça? *or* cela?; **~'s fine!** c'est parfait!; **~'s enough!** ça suffit!; **what do you mean by ~?** qu'est-ce que vous voulez dire par là?; **she's not as stupid as (all) ~** elle n'est pas si bête que ça; **I prefer ~ to this** je préfère cela à ceci; **as for ~!** pour ce qui est de ça!, quant à cela!; **~'s it** (*the job's finished*) ça y est; (*that's what I want*) voilà, c'est cela; (*that's all*) c'est tout; (*I've had enough*) ça suffit; **you're not going and ~'s ~!** tu n'y vas pas un point c'est tout!; **well, ~'s ~!** eh bien voilà!; **so ~ was ~** les choses se sont arrêtées là; **if it comes to ~, why did you go?** mais en fait, est-ce que tu avais besoin d'y aller?; **so it has come to ~!** on en est donc là!, voilà donc où on en est (arrivé)!; **before/after ~** avant/après cela; **with** *or* **at ~ she burst into tears** là-dessus *or* sur ce, elle a éclaté en sanglots; **and there were 6 of them at ~!** et en plus ils étaient 6!; **~ is (to say)** ... c'est-à-dire ...; **we were talking of this and ~** nous bavardions de choses et d'autres; **do it like ~** fais-le comme ça; **let's leave it at ~ for today** ça suffit pour aujourd'hui; **he went on about loyalty and all ~*** il parlait de loyauté et patati et patata*; **did he go? — ~ he did!†** y est-il allé? — pour sûr!†
b (*~ one*) celui-là *m*, celle-là *f*, ceux-là *mpl*, celles-là *fpl*. **I prefer this to ~** je préfère celui-ci à celui-là (*or* celle-ci à celle-là); **those over there** ceux-là (*or* celles-là) là-bas; **not THOSE!** pas ceux-là (*or* celles-là)!
c (*before rel pron*) **those who** ... ceux *mpl* (*or* celles *fpl*) qui ...; **those who came** ceux qui sont venus; **those which are here** ceux (*or* celles) qui sont ici; **there are those who say** certains disent, il y a des gens qui disent.
3 adv a (*so*) si, aussi. **it's ~ high** c'est haut comme ça; **it's not ~ cold!** il ne fait pas si froid que ça!; **I couldn't go ~ far** je ne pourrais pas aller aussi loin que ça; **I can't carry ~ much** je ne peux pas porter autant que ça; **he was at least ~ much taller than me** il me dépassait de ça au moins.
b (**: so very*) **it was ~ cold!** il faisait un de ces froids!; **it was ~ cold we had to stay indoors** il faisait tellement froid que nous avons dû rester à la maison; **I was ~ tired I fell asleep** je me suis endormi tellement j'étais fatigué; **he was ~ ill!** il était vraiment malade, il n'était pas bien du tout.
4 rel pron a (*nominative*) qui; (*accusative*) que. **the man ~ came to see you** l'homme qui est venu vous voir; **the letter ~ I sent yesterday** la lettre que j'ai envoyée hier; **and Martin, idiot ~ he is, didn't tell me** et Martin, cet imbécile, ne me l'a pas dit; **fool ~ I am!** imbécile que je suis!
b (*with prep*) lequel *m*, laquelle *f*, lesquels *mpl*, lesquelles *fpl*. **the men ~ I was speaking to** les hommes auxquels je parlais; **the box ~ you put it in** la boîte dans laquelle vous l'avez mis; **the girl/the book ~ I told you about** la jeune fille/le livre dont je vous ai parlé; **not ~ I know of** pas que je sache.
c (*in expressions of time*) où. **the evening ~ we went to the opera** le soir où nous sommes allés à l'opéra; **during the years ~ he'd been abroad** pendant les années où il était à l'étranger; **the summer ~ it was**

so hot l'été où il a fait si chaud.

5 conj a que. **he said ~ he had seen her** il a dit qu'il l'avait vue, il a dit l'avoir vue; **he was speaking so softly ~ I could hardly hear him** il parlait si bas que je l'entendais à peine; **not ~ I want to do it** non (pas) que je veuille le faire; **what's the matter? – it's ~ I don't know the way** qu'est-ce qu'il y a? – c'est que je ne sais pas comment y aller; **supposing ~** à supposer que + *subj*; **it is natural ~ he should refuse** il est normal qu'il refuse (*subj*); **in ~ he might refuse** en ce sens qu'il pourrait refuser; **~ he should behave like this is incredible** il est incroyable qu'il se conduise de cette façon; **~ he should behave like this!** dire qu'il peut se conduire ainsi!; **oh ~ we could!** si seulement nous pouvions!; *see* **would** *etc.*

b (*so that: liter, frm*) afin que + *subj.* **so ~, in order ~** pour que + *subj*, afin que + *subj*.

thatch [θætʃ] 1 n (*NonC*) chaume *m*. (*fig*) **his ~ of hair*** sa crinière. 2 vt *roof* couvrir de chaume; *cottage* couvrir en chaume. **~ed roof** toit *m* de chaume; **~ed cottage** chaumière *f*.

thatcher ['θætʃəʳ] n couvreur *m* (de toits de chaume).

Thatcherism ['θætʃə,rɪzəm] n Thatchérisme *m*.

thatching ['θætʃɪŋ] n (*NonC*) a (*craft*) couverture *f* de toits de chaume. b (*material*) chaume *m*.

thaw [θɔː] 1 n (*Met*) dégel *m*; (*fig: Pol etc*) détente *f*. (*fig: Econ*) **economic** *etc* **~** assouplissement *m* des restrictions concernant la vie économique *etc*. 2 vt (*also* **~ out**) *ice* faire dégeler, faire fondre; *snow* faire fondre; *frozen food* décongeler, dégeler. 3 vi (*also* **~ out**) *[ice]* fondre, dégeler; *[snow]* fondre; *[frozen food]* décongeler, dégeler. (*fig*) **he began to ~*** (*get warmer*) il a commencé à se dégeler* *or* à se réchauffer; (*grow friendlier*) il a commencé à se dégeler* *or* à se dérider; (*Met*) **it's ~ing** il dégèle.

the [ðiː], *weak form* [ðə] 1 def art a le, la, (*before vowel or mute "h"*) l', les. **of ~, from ~** du, de la, de l', des; **to ~, at ~** au, à la, à l', aux; **~ prettiest** le plus joli, la plus jolie, les plus joli(e)s; **~ poor** les pauvres *mpl*.

b (*neuter*) **~ good and ~ beautiful** le bien et le beau; **translated from ~ German** traduit de l'allemand; **it is ~ unusual that is frightening** c'est ce qui est inhabituel qui fait peur.

c (*with musical instruments*) **to play ~ piano** jouer du piano.

d (*with sg noun denoting whole class*) **~ aeroplane is an invention of our century** l'avion est une invention de notre siècle.

e (*distributive use*) **50p ~ pound** 50 pence la livre; **2 dollars to ~ pound** 2 dollars la livre; **paid by ~ hour** payé à l'heure; **30 miles to ~ gallon** ≃ 9,3 litres au 100 (km).

f (*with names etc*) **Charles ~ First/Second/Third** Charles premier/deux/trois; **~ Browns** les Brown; **~ Bourbons** les Bourbons.

g (*stressed*) **THE Professor Smith** le célèbre professeur Smith; **he's THE surgeon here** c'est lui le grand chirurgien ici; **it's THE restaurant in this part of town** c'est le meilleur restaurant du quartier; **he's THE man for the job** c'est le candidat idéal pour ce poste; **it was THE colour last year** c'était la couleur à la mode l'an dernier; **it's THE book just now** c'est le livre à lire en ce moment.

h (*other special uses*) **~ cheek of it!** ce toupet!*; **he hasn't ~ sense to refuse** il n'a pas assez de bon sens pour refuser; **I'll see him in ~ summer** je le verrai cet été; **~ dictionary for the nineties** le dictionnaire des années quatre-vingt-dix; **he's got ~ measles*** il a la rougeole; **well, how's ~ leg?*** eh bien, et cette jambe?*

2 adv: **~ more he works ~ more he earns** plus il travaille plus il gagne d'argent; **~ sooner ~ better** le plus tôt sera le mieux; **all ~ better!** tant mieux!; **it will be all ~ more difficult** cela sera d'autant plus difficile; **it makes me all ~ more proud** je n'en suis que plus fier; **he was none ~ worse for it** il ne s'en est pas trouvé plus mal pour ça.

theater (*US*) = **theatre**.

theatre ['θɪətəʳ] (*Brit*) 1 n a (*place*) théâtre *m*, salle *f* de spectacle; (*drama*) théâtre. **I like the ~** j'aime le théâtre; **to go to the ~** aller au théâtre *or* au spectacle; **it makes good ~** c'est du bon théâtre.

b (*large room*) salle *f* de conférences. (*Univ etc*) **lecture ~** amphithéâtre *m*, amphi* *m*.

c (*Med: also* **operating ~**) salle *f* d'opération. *[patient]* **he is in (the) ~** il est sur la table d'opération.

d (*Mil etc*) théâtre *m*. **~ of operations/war** théâtre des opérations/des hostilités.

2 comp (*Theat*) *programme, ticket* de théâtre; *visit* au théâtre; *management* du théâtre; (*Med*) *staff, nurse* de la salle d'opération; *job, work* dans la salle d'opération ▸**theatre company** (*Theat*) troupe *f* de théâtre ▸**theatregoer** habitué(e) *m(f)* du théâtre ▸**theatre-in-the-round** (pl **~s-~-~-~**) le théâtre en rond ▸**theatreland: London's theatreland** le Londres des théâtres ▸**theatre lover** amateur *m* de théâtre ▸**theatre workshop** atelier *m* de théâtre.

theatrical [θɪ'ætrɪkəl] 1 adj théâtral (*also fig pej*). **~ company** troupe *f* de théâtre. 2 npl: **~s** théâtre *m* (d'amateurs); **he does a lot of (amateur) ~s** il fait beaucoup de théâtre d'amateurs; (*fig pej*) **what were all those ~s about?** pourquoi toute cette comédie?

theatricality [θɪ,ætrɪ'kælɪtɪ] n (*also fig pej*) théâtralité *f*.

theatrically [θɪ'ætrɪkəlɪ] adv théâtralement (*also fig pej*).

Thebes [θiːbz] n Thèbes.

thee [ðiː] pron (††, *liter, dial*) te; (*before vowel*) t'; (*stressed; after prep*) toi.

theft [θeft] n vol *m*.

their [ðɛəʳ] poss adj a leur (*f inv*). **they've broken ~ legs** ils se sont cassé la jambe; **THEIR house** leur maison à eux (*or* à elles). b (*singular usage*) son, sa, ses. **somebody rang – did you ask them ~ name?** quelqu'un a téléphoné – est-ce que tu lui as demandé son nom?

theirs [ðɛəz] poss pron a le leur, la leur, les leurs. **this car is ~** cette voiture est à eux (*or* à elles) *or* leur appartient *or* est la leur; **this music is ~** cette musique est d'eux; **a friend of ~** un de leurs amis, un ami à eux (*or* à elles)*; **I think it's one of ~** je crois que c'est un(e) des leurs; **your house is better than ~** votre maison est mieux que la leur; **it's no fault of ~** ce n'est pas de leur faute; (*pej*) **that car of ~** leur fichue* voiture; **that stupid son of ~** leur idiot de fils; **the house became ~** la maison est devenue la leur; **no advice of ~ could prevent him ...** aucun conseil de leur part ne pouvait l'empêcher de ...; (*frm*) **it is not ~ to decide** il ne leur appartient pas de décider; **~ is a specialized department** leur section est une section spécialisée.

b (*singular usage*) le sien, la sienne, les sien(ne)s. **if anyone takes one that isn't ~** si jamais quelqu'un en prend un qui n'est pas à lui.

theism ['θiːɪzəm] n théisme *m*.

theist ['θiːɪst] adj, n théiste (*mf*).

theistic(al) [θiː'ɪstɪk(əl)] adj théiste.

them [ðem], *weak form* [ðəm] 1 pers pron pl a (*direct*) (*unstressed*) les; (*stressed*) eux *mpl*, elles *fpl*. **I have seen ~** je les ai vu(e)s; **I know HER but I don't know THEM** je la connais, elle, mais eux (*or* elles) je ne les connais pas; **if I were ~** si j'étais à leur place, si j'étais eux (*or* elles); **it's ~!** ce sont eux (*or* elles)!, les voilà!

b (*indirect*) leur. **I gave ~ the book** je leur ai donné le livre; **I'm speaking to ~** je leur parle.

c (*after prep etc*) eux, elles. **I'm thinking of ~** je pense à eux (*or* elles); **as for ~** quant à eux (*or* elles); **younger than ~** plus jeune qu'eux (*or* elles); **they took it with ~** ils l'ont emporté (avec eux).

d (*phrases*) **both of ~** tous (*or* toutes) les deux; **several of ~** plusieurs d'entre eux (*or* elles); **give me a few of ~** donnez-m'en quelques-un(e)s; **every one of ~ was lost** ils furent tous perdus, elles furent toutes perdues; **I don't like either of ~** je ne les aime ni l'un(e) ni l'autre; **none of ~ would do it** aucun d'entre eux (*or* aucune d'entre elles) n'a voulu le faire; **it was very good of ~** c'était très gentil de leur part; (*fig pej*) **he's one of ~*** je (*or* tu) vois le genre!*

2 pers pron sg (*see* **1**) le, la l'; lui. **somebody rang – did you ask ~ their name?** quelqu'un a téléphoné – est-ce que tu lui as demandé son nom?; **if anyone asks why I took it, I'll tell ~ ...** si jamais quelqu'un demande pourquoi je l'ai pris, je lui dirai ...; **if anyone arrives early ask ~ to wait** si quelqu'un arrive tôt, fais-le attendre.

thematic [θɪ'mætɪk] adj thématique.

theme [θiːm] 1 n a thème *m*, sujet *m*. b (*Mus*) thème *m*, motif *m*. c (*Ling*) thème *m*. d (*US Scol: essay*) rédaction *f*. 2 comp ▸**theme park** parc *m* à thème ▸**theme song** chanson *f* de la bande originale (*d'un film etc*); (*US: signature tune*) indicatif *m* (musical); (*fig*) refrain *m* (habituel), leitmotiv *m* ▸**theme tune** air *m* de la bande originale (*d'un film etc*).

themself* [ðəm'self] pers pron sg (*reflexive: direct and indirect*) se; (*emphatic*) lui-même *m*, elle-même *f*; (*after prep*) lui *m*, elle *f*. **somebody who could not defend ~** quelqu'un qui ne pouvait pas se défendre; **somebody who doesn't care about ~** quelqu'un qui ne prend pas soin de sa propre personne.

themselves [ðəm'selvz] pers pron pl (*reflexive: direct and indirect*) se; (*emphatic*) eux-mêmes *mpl*, elles-mêmes *fpl*; (*after prep*) eux, elles. **they've hurt ~** ils se sont blessés, elles se sont blessées; **they said to ~** ils (*or* elles) se sont dit; **they saw it ~** ils l'ont vu eux-mêmes; **they were talking amongst ~** ils discutaient entre eux; **these computers can reprogram ~** ces ordinateurs peuvent se reprogrammer automatiquement; **anyone staying here will have to cook for ~** les gens qui logent ici doivent faire leur propre cuisine; **(all) by ~** tout seuls, toutes seules.

then [ðen] 1 adv a (*at that time*) alors, à ce moment(-là), en ce temps(-là). **we had 2 dogs ~** nous avions alors 2 chiens, nous avions 2 chiens à cette époque-là *or* à ce moment-là *or* en ce temps-là; **I'm going to London and I'll see him ~** je vais à Londres et je le verrai à ce moment-là; **(every) now and ~** de temps en temps, de temps à autre; **~ and there, there and ~** sur-le-champ, séance tenante.

b (*after prep*) **from ~ on(wards)** dès lors, dès cette époque(-là) *or* ce moment(-là) *or* ce temps(-là), à partir de cette époque(-là) *or* ce moment(-là); **before ~** avant cela *or* ce moment-là *or* ce temps-là; **by ~ I knew ...** à ce moment-là, je savais déjà ...; **I'll have it finished by ~** je l'aurai fini d'ici là; **since ~** depuis ce moment-là *or* cette époque-là *or* ce temps-là *or* lors; **between now and ~** d'ici là; **(up) until ~** jusque-là, jusqu'alors.

c (*next, afterwards*) ensuite, puis, alors. **he went first to London ~ to Paris** il est allé d'abord à Londres, puis *or* et ensuite à Paris; **and ~ what?** et puis après?; **now this ~ that** tantôt ceci, tantôt cela.

d (*in that case*) en ce cas, donc, alors. **~ it must be in the sitting**

room alors ça doit être au salon; **if you don't want that ~ what do you want?** si vous ne voulez pas de ça, alors que voulez-vous donc?; **but ~ that means that** ... mais c'est donc que ...; **someone had already warned you ~?** on vous avait donc déjà prévenu?; **now ~ what's the matter?** alors qu'est-ce qu'il y a?

e (*furthermore; and also*) et puis, d'ailleurs, aussi. **(and) ~ there's my aunt** et puis il y a ma tante; **... and ~ it's none of my business** ... et d'ailleurs *or* et puis cela ne me regarde pas; **... and ~ again** *or* **... but ~ he might not want to go** ... remarquez, il est possible qu'il ne veuille pas y aller; **... and ~ again** *or* **... but ~ he has always tried to help us** ... et pourtant, il faut dire qu'il a toujours essayé de nous aider.

2 **adj** (*before noun*) d'alors, de l'époque, du moment. **the ~ Prime Minister** le Premier ministre d'alors *or* de l'époque.

thence [ðens] (†, *frm, liter*) 1 **adv** (*from there*) de là, de ce lieu-là; (*therefore*) par conséquent, pour cette raison. 2 **comp ►thenceforth, thenceforward** dès lors.

theocracy [θɪˈɒkrəsɪ] **n** théocratie *f*.

theocratic [θɪəˈkrætɪk] **adj** théocratique.

theodolite [θɪˈɒdəlaɪt] **n** théodolite *m*.

theologian [θɪəˈləʊdʒɪən] **n** théologien(ne) *m(f)*.

theological [θɪəˈlɒdʒɪkəl] **adj** théologique. **~ college** séminaire *m*.

theology [θɪˈɒlədʒɪ] **n** théologie *f*; *see* **liberation**.

theorem [ˈθɪərəm] **n** théorème *m*.

theoretic(al) [θɪəˈretɪk(əl)] **adj** théorique.

theoretically [θɪəˈretɪkəlɪ] **adv** théoriquement.

theoretician [ˌθɪərəˈtɪʃən] **n**, **theorist** [ˈθɪərɪst] **n** théoricien(ne) *m(f)*.

theorize [ˈθɪəraɪz] 1 **vi** *[scientist, psychologist etc]* élaborer une (*or* des) théorie(s) (*about* sur). **it's no good just theorizing about it** ce n'est pas la peine de faire des grandes théories là-dessus*. 2 **vt**: **to ~ that** émettre l'hypothèse que.

theory [ˈθɪərɪ] **n** théorie *f*. **in ~** en théorie.

theosophical [θɪəˈsɒfɪkəl] **adj** théosophique.

theosophist [θɪˈɒsəfɪst] **n** théosophe *mf*.

theosophy [θɪˈɒsəfɪ] **n** théosophie *f*.

therapeutic [ˌθerəˈpjuːtɪk] **adj** *method, result* thérapeutique. **~ community** communauté *f* thérapeutique.

therapeutical [ˌθerəˈpjuːtɪkəl] **adj** thérapeutique.

therapeutics [ˌθerəˈpjuːtɪks] **n** (*NonC*) thérapeutique *f*.

therapist [ˈθerəpɪst] **n** (*gen*) thérapeute *mf*; *see* **occupational** *etc*.

therapy [ˈθerəpɪ] **n** (*gen, also Psych*) thérapie *f*. (*fig*) **it's good ~** c'est très thérapeutique.

there [ðɛəʳ] 1 **adv** a (*place*) y (*before vb*), là. **we shall soon be ~** nous y serons bientôt, nous serons bientôt là, nous serons bientôt arrivés; **put it ~** posez-le là; **when we left ~** quand nous en sommes partis, quand nous sommes partis de là; **on ~** là-dessus; **in ~** là-dedans; **back** *or* **down** *or* **over ~** là-bas; **he lives round ~** il habite par là; (*further away*) il habite par là-bas; **somewhere round ~** quelque part par là; **here and ~** çà et là, par-ci par-là; **from ~** de là; **they went ~ and back in 2 hours** ils ont fait l'aller et retour en 2 heures; *see* **here**.

b **~ is** il y a, il est (*liter*); **~ are** il y a; **once upon a time ~ was a princess** il y avait *or* il était une fois une princesse; **~ will be dancing later** plus tard on dansera; **~ is a page missing** il y a une page qui manque; **~ are 3 apples left** il reste 3 pommes, il y a encore 3 pommes; **~ comes a time when** ... il vient un moment où ...; **~'s no denying it** c'est indéniable.

c (*in existence*) **this road isn't meant to be ~!** cette route ne devrait pas exister! *or* être là!; **if the technology is ~, someone will use it** si la technologie existe, quelqu'un l'utilisera.

d (*other uses*) **~'s my brother!** voilà mon frère!; **~ are the others!** voilà les autres!; **~ he is!** le voilà!; **~ you are** (*I've found you*) (ah) vous voilà!; (*offering sth*) voilà; **that man ~ saw it all** cet homme-là a tout vu; **hey you ~!** hé *or* ho toi, là-bas!*; **hurry up ~!** dépêchez-vous, là-bas!; **~'s my mother calling me** il y a *or* voilà ma mère qui m'appelle; **~'s the problem** là est *or* c'est *or* voilà le problème; **I disagree with you ~** là je ne suis pas d'accord avec vous; **you've got me ~!** alors là, ça me dépasse!*; **but ~ again, he should have known better** mais là encore, il aurait dû se méfier; **you press this switch and ~ you are!** tu appuies sur ce bouton et ça y est!; **~ you are, I told you that would happen** voilà *or* tiens, je t'avais dit que ça allait arriver; **~ they go!** les voilà!; (*fig*) **I had hoped to finish early, but ~ you go** j'espérais finir tôt mais tant pis; (*fig*) **~ you go again*, complaining about** ... ça y est, tu recommences à te plaindre de ...; (*fig*) **~ he goes again!*** ça y est, il recommence!; (*fig*) **he's all ~*** c'est un malin, il n'est pas idiot; **he's not all ~*** (*gen*) il est un peu demeuré; *[old person]* il n'a plus toute sa tête.

2 **excl**: **~, what did I tell you?** alors, qu'est-ce que je t'avais dit?; **~, ~, don't cry!** allons, allons, ne pleure pas!; **~, drink this** allez *or* tenez, buvez ceci; **~ now, that didn't hurt, did it?** voyons, voyons *or* eh bien, ça n'a pas été si douloureux que ça, si?

3 **comp ►thereabouts** (*place*) par là, près de là, dans le voisinage; (*degree etc*) à peu près, environ; **£5 or thereabouts** environ 5 livres **►thereafter** (*frm*) par la suite **►thereat** (*frm*) (*place*) là; (*time*) là-dessus **►thereby** de cette façon, de ce fait, par ce moyen; **thereby hangs a tale!** c'est toute une histoire! **►therefore** *see* **therefore** **►therefrom** (*frm*) de là **►therein** (*frm*) (*in that regard*) à cet égard, en cela; (*inside*) (là-)dedans **►thereof** (*frm*) de cela, en; **he ate thereof** il en mangea **►thereon** (*frm*) (là-)dessus **►thereto** (*frm*) y **►theretofore** (*frm*) jusque-là **►thereunder** (*frm*) (là) en-dessous **►thereupon** (*then*) sur ce; (*on that subject*) là-dessus, à ce sujet **►therewith** (*frm*) (*with that*) avec cela, en outre; (*at once*) sur ce.

therefore [ˈðɛəfɔːʳ] **conj** donc, par conséquent, pour cette raison.

there's [ðɛəz] = **there is, there has**; *see* **be, have**.

therm [θɜːm] **n** = 1,055 X 10⁸ joules; (*formerly*) thermie *f*.

thermal [ˈθɜːməl] 1 **adj** a (*Elec, Phys*) thermique; *paper* thermosensible, à sensibilité thermique. **~ imaging** thermographie *f*; **~ barrier** barrière *f* thermique; **~ breeder, ~ reactor** réacteur *m* thermique; **British ~ unit** (**abbr of BTU**) = 252 calories. b *treatment etc* thermal. **~ baths** thermes *mpl*; **~ spring** source thermale. c *underwear etc* en thermolactyl ® *or* rhovilon ®. 2 **n** (*Met*) courant ascendant (d'origine thermique), ascendance *f* thermique.

thermic [ˈθɜːmɪk] **adj** = **thermal 1a**.

thermionic [ˌθɜːmɪˈɒnɪk] 1 **adj** *effect, emission* thermoionique. **~ valve,** (*US*) **~ tube** tube *m* électronique. 2 **n** (*NonC*) **~s** thermoionique *f*.

thermo... [ˈθɜːməʊ] **pref** therm(o)... .

thermocouple [ˈθɜːməʊkʌpl] **n** thermocouple *m*.

thermodynamic [ˈθɜːməʊdaɪˈnæmɪk] 1 **adj** thermodynamique. 2 **n** (*NonC*) **~s** thermodynamique *f*.

thermoelectric [ˈθɜːməʊɪˈlektrɪk] **adj** thermoélectrique.

thermograph [ˈθɜːməʊgrɑːf] **n** thermographe *m*.

thermography [θɜːˈmɒgrəfɪ] **n** thermographie *f*.

thermometer [θəˈmɒmɪtəʳ] **n** thermomètre *m*.

thermonuclear [ˈθɜːməʊˈnjuːklɪəʳ] **adj** thermonucléaire.

thermopile [ˈθɜːməʊpaɪl] **n** pile *f* thermoélectrique.

thermoplastic [ˈθɜːməʊˈplæstɪk] **n** thermoplastique *m*.

thermoplasticity [ˌθɜːməʊplæˈstɪsɪtɪ] **n** (*NonC*) thermoplasticité *f*.

Thermopylae [θəˈmɒpəliː] **n** les Thermopyles.

Thermos [ˈθɜːməs] **n** ® thermos *m or f inv* ®. **~ flask** bouteille *f* thermos.

thermosiphon [ˌθɜːməʊˈsaɪfən] **n** thermosiphon *m*.

thermostat [ˈθɜːməstæt] **n** thermostat *m*.

thermostatic [ˌθɜːməˈstætɪk] **adj** thermostatique.

thermotherapy [ˌθɜːməʊˈθerəpɪ] **n** thermothérapie *f*.

thesaurus [θɪˈsɔːrəs] **n, pl ~es** *or* **thesauri** [θɪˈsɔːraɪ] (*gen*) trésor *m* (*fig*); (*lexicon etc*) dictionnaire *m* synonymique; (*Comput*) thesaurus *m*.

these [ðiːz] **pl of this**.

theses [ˈθiːsiːz] **npl of thesis**.

Theseus [ˈθiːsɪəs] **n** Thésée *m*.

thesis [ˈθiːsɪs] **n, pl theses** [ˈθiːsiːz] thèse *f*.

Thespian [ˈθespɪən] 1 **adj** (*liter or hum*) dramatique, de Thespis. **his ~ talents** son talent de comédien. 2 **n** (*liter or hum: actor*) comédien(ne) *m(f)*.

Thessalonians [ˌθesəˈləʊnɪənz] **npl** Thessaloniciens *mpl*.

they [ðeɪ] **pers pron pl** a ils *mpl*, elles *fpl*; (*stressed*) eux *mpl*, elles *fpl*. **~ have gone** ils sont partis, elles sont parties; **there ~ are!** les voilà!; **~ are teachers** ce sont des professeurs; **THEY know nothing about it** eux, ils n'en savent rien. b (*people in general*) on. **~ say that** ... on dit que ... . c (*singular usage*) il *m*, elle *f*; (*stressed*) lui *m*, elle *f*. **sb called but ~ didn't give their name** quelqu'un a appelé, mais il *or* elle n'a pas donné son nom.

they'd [ðeɪd] = **they had, they would**; *see* **have, would**.

they'll [ðeɪl] = **they will**; *see* **will**.

they're [ðɛəʳ] = **they are**; *see* **be**.

they've [ðeɪv] = **they have**; *see* **have**.

thiamine [ˈθaɪəmiːn] **n** thiamine *f*.

thick [θɪk] 1 **adj** a (*in shape*) *finger, wall, line, slice, layer, glass, waist, jersey, cup* épais (*f* -aisse); *thread, book, lips, nose, wool, string* épais, gros (*f* grosse); *print* épais, gras (*f* grasse). **to grow** *or* **become ~(er)** *[waist]* (s')épaissir; *[branch]* grossir; **a wall 50 cm ~** un mur de 50 cm d'épaisseur, un mur épais de 50 cm; **the ice was 10 cm ~** la glace avait 10 cm d'épaisseur; (*with pen, brush etc*) **a ~ stroke** un trait épais, un gros trait; (*Brit*) **to give sb a ~ ear*** frotter les oreilles à qn*; (*Brit fig*) **that's a bit ~!*** ça c'est un peu fort!* *or* violent!* *or* raide!*; *see* **skin**.

b (*in consistency etc*) *soup, cream, gravy* épais (*f* -aisse), consistant; *honey* dur; *oil, mud, eyelashes, eyebrows* épais; *fog, smoke* dense, épais; *forest, vegetation, foliage* épais, touffu, dense; *hedge* (bien) fourni, touffu; *beard, hair* épais, touffu; *crowd* dense. **to grow** *or* **become** *or* **get ~(er)** *[soup, cream etc]* épaissir; *[honey]* durcir; *[fog, smoke]* devenir plus dense, s'épaissir; *[vegetation etc]* s'épaissir, devenir plus dense *or* touffu; **to make ~(er)** *soup, sauce* épaissir; **the air is very ~ in here** on manque d'air ici; **the air was ~ with smoke** (*at a party etc*) la pièce était enfumée; (*during fire etc*) l'air était plein d'une fumée épaisse; **the air was ~ with insults** les insultes volaient; **the furniture was ~ with dust** les meubles étaient couverts d'une épaisse couche de poussière; **the road was ~ with cars** la rue était encombrée de voitures; **the town was ~ with tourists** la ville était envahie de touristes; **the leaves were ~ on the ground** les feuilles couvraient le sol d'une couche épaisse; (*fig*) **antique shops are ~ on the ground around here*** il y a pléthore de magasins d'antiquités par ici; **in a ~ voice** (*from headcold, fear*) d'une voix voilée; (*from drink*) d'une voix pâteuse; (*fig*) **they are as ~ as thieves** ils s'entendent comme larrons en foire; **he's very ~* with Paul, Paul and he are very ~*** lui et Paul sont comme les deux doigts de la main.

c (*Brit *: stupid*) bête, obtus, borné. **he's as ~ as a brick‡** *or* **as ~ as two short planks‡** il est bête comme ses pieds*.

2 **adv** *spread, lie etc* en couche épaisse; *cut* en tranches épaisses. **the snow fell ~** la neige tombait dru; **blows/arrows fell ~ and fast** les coups/flèches pleuvaient (de partout); (*fig*) **he lays it on a bit ~*** il exagère *or* pousse* un peu.

3 **n** *[finger, leg etc]* partie charnue. **in the ~ of the crowd** au plus fort *or* épais de la foule; **in the ~ of the fight** en plein cœur de la mêlée; **they were in the ~ of it** ils étaient en plein dedans; **through ~ and thin** à travers toutes les épreuves, contre vents et marées.

4 **comp ►thickheaded*** (*Brit*) bête, obtus, borné **►thick-knit adj** gros (*f* grosse), en grosse laine ◊ **n** gros chandail, chandail en grosse laine **►thick-lipped** aux lèvres charnues, lippu **►thickset** (*and small*) trapu, râblé; (*and tall*) bien bâti, costaud* **►thick-skinned** *orange* à la peau épaisse; (*fig*) *person* peu sensible; **he's very thick-skinned** c'est un dur, rien ne le touche **►thick-skulled*, thick-witted*** = **thickheaded***.

thicken ['θɪkən] 1 **vt** *sauce* épaissir, lier. 2 **vi** *[branch, waist etc]* s'épaissir; *[crowd]* grossir; *[sauce etc]* épaissir; (*fig*) *[mystery]* s'épaissir; *see* **plot**.

thickener ['θɪkənəʳ] **n** épaississant *m*.

thicket ['θɪkɪt] **n** fourré *m*, hallier *m*.

thickie‡ ['θɪkɪ] = **thicky**.

thickly ['θɪklɪ] **adv** *spread* en une couche épaisse; *cut* en tranches épaisses, en morceaux épais; *speak, say* (*from headcold, fear*) d'une voix voilée; (*from drink*) d'une voix pâteuse. **~ spread with butter** couvert d'une épaisse couche de beurre; **~ covered with** *or* **in dust** couvert d'une épaisse couche de poussière; **the snow fell ~** la neige tombait dru; **~ populated region** région *f* à forte concentration de population; **~ wooded** très boisé.

thickness ['θɪknɪs] **n** a (*NonC*) *[wall etc]* épaisseur *f*; *[lips etc]* épaisseur, grosseur *f*; *[fog, forest]* épaisseur, densité *f*; *[hair]* épaisseur, abondance *f*. b (*layer*) épaisseur *f*. **3 ~es of material** 3 épaisseurs de tissu.

thicko‡ ['θɪkəʊ], **thicky‡** ['θɪkɪ] **n** idiot(e) *m(f)*, crétin(e)* *m(f)*.

thief [θi:f] **n, pl thieves** voleur *m*, -euse *f*. (*Prov*) **once a ~ always a ~** qui a volé volera (*Prov*); (*Prov*) **set a ~ to catch a ~** à voleur voleur et demi (*Prov*); **stop ~!** au voleur!; **thieves' cant** argot *m* du milieu; **thieves' kitchen** repaire *m* de brigands; *see* **honour, thick** *etc*.

thieve [θi:v] **vti** voler.

thievery ['θi:vərɪ] **n** (*NonC*) vol *m*.

thieves [θi:vz] **npl of thief.**

thieving ['θi:vɪŋ] 1 **adj** voleur. (*Mus*) **the T~ Magpie** la Pie voleuse. 2 **n** (*NonC*) vol *m*.

thievish† ['θi:vɪʃ] **adj** voleur, de voleur.

thigh [θaɪ] 1 **n** cuisse *f*. 2 **comp ►thighbone** fémur *m* **►thigh boots** cuissardes *fpl*.

thimble ['θɪmbl] **n** dé *m* (à coudre).

thimbleful ['θɪmblfʊl] **n** (*fig*) doigt *m*, goutte *f*.

thin [θɪn] 1 **adj** a *finger, wall, slice, layer, line, wool, ice* mince; *cup, glass* fin; *paper, waist, lips, nose* mince, fin; *fabric, garment, blanket* mince, léger; *arm, leg, person* mince, maigre (*slightly pej*). **~ string** petite ficelle; *[person]* **to get ~(ner)** maigrir, s'amaigrir; **as ~ as a rake** *or* **a lath** maigre comme un clou; (*with pen*) **a ~ stroke** un trait mince *or* fin, un délié; (*fig*) **it's the ~ end of the wedge** c'est s'engager sur la pente savonneuse; *see* **ice, skin** *etc*.

b *soup, gravy* clair, clairet, peu épais (*f* -aisse); *cream, honey* liquide; *mud* peu épais, liquide; *oil* peu épais; *beard, hair, eyelashes, eyebrows, hedge* clairsemé; *fog, smoke* fin, léger; *crowd* épars; *voice* grêle, fluet; *blood* appauvri, anémié. **to grow** *or* **become** *or* **get ~ner** *[fog, crowd]* se disperser, s'éclaircir; **to make ~ner** *soup, sauce* éclaircir, délayer; *plants, trees* éclaircir; **he's rather ~ on top*** il perd ses cheveux, il se dégarnit; **at 20,000 metres the air is ~** à 20.000 mètres l'air est raréfié; (*fig*) **to disappear** *or* **vanish into ~ air** se volatiliser, disparaître (d'un seul coup) sans laisser de traces, disparaître comme par magie; (*fig*) **to appear out of ~ air** apparaître comme par magie *or* tout seul; (*fig*) **to produce** *or* **conjure sth out of ~ air** faire apparaître qch comme par magie; **doctors are ~ on the ground here*** les médecins sont rares par ici.

c (*fig*) *profits* maigre; *excuse, story, argument* peu convaincant; *plot* squelettique. **his disguise was rather ~** son déguisement a été facilement percé à jour; **to have a ~ time of it*** passer par une période plutôt pénible *or* difficile.

2 **adv** *spread* en une couche mince; *cut* en tranches *or* morceaux minces.

3 **comp ►thin-lipped** aux lèvres minces *or* fines; (*with rage etc*) les lèvres pincées **►thin-skinned** *orange etc* à la peau mince *or* fine; (*fig*) *person* susceptible.

4 **vt** *paint* étendre, délayer; *sauce* allonger, délayer, éclaircir; *trees, hair* éclaircir.

5 **vi** *[fog, crowd]* se disperser, s'éclaircir; *[numbers]* se réduire, s'amenuiser. **his hair is ~ning** il perd ses cheveux, il se dégarnit.

►thin down 1 **vi** *[person]* maigrir. 2 **vt sep** *paint* étendre, délayer; *sauce* allonger.

►thin out 1 **vi** *[crowd, fog]* se disperser, s'éclaircir. 2 **vt sep** *seedlings, trees* éclaircir; *numbers, population* réduire; *crowd* disperser; *workforce* réduire, dégraisser.

thine [ðaɪn] (*†† or liter*) 1 **poss pron** le tien, la tienne, les tiens, les tiennes. 2 **poss adj** ton, ta, tes.

thing [θɪŋ] **n** a (*gen sense*) chose *f*; (*object*) chose, objet *m*. **surrounded by beautiful ~s** entouré de belles choses *or* de beaux objets; **~ of beauty** bel objet, belle chose; **such ~s as money, fame ...** des choses comme l'argent, la gloire ...; **he's interested in ideas rather than ~s** ce qui l'intéresse ce sont les idées et non pas les objets; **~s of the mind appeal to him** il est attiré par les choses de l'esprit; **the ~ he loves most is his car** ce qu'il aime le plus au monde c'est sa voiture; **what's that ~?** qu'est-ce que c'est que cette chose-là? *or* ce machin-là?* *or* ce truc-là?*; **the good ~s in life** les plaisirs *mpl* de la vie; **he thinks the right ~s** il pense comme il faut; **she likes sweet ~s** elle aime les sucreries *fpl*; **she has been seeing ~s** elle a eu des visions; **you've been hearing ~s!** tu as dû entendre des voix!

b (*belongings etc*) **~s** affaires *fpl*; **have you put away your ~s?** as-tu rangé tes affaires?; **to take off one's ~s** se débarrasser de son manteau *etc*; **do take your ~s off!** débarrassez-vous (donc)!; **have you got your swimming ~s?** as-tu tes affaires de bain?; **have you got any swimming ~s?** as-tu ce qu'il faut pour aller te baigner?; **where are the first-aid ~s?** où est la trousse de secours?

c (*affair, item, circumstance*) chose *f*. **I've 2 ~s still to do** j'ai encore 2 choses à faire; **the ~s she said!** les choses qu'elle a pu dire!; **the next ~ to do is ...** ce qu'il y a à faire maintenant c'est ...; **the best ~ would be to refuse** le mieux serait de refuser; (*iro*) **that's a fine** *or* **nice ~ to do!** c'est vraiment la chose à faire! (*iro*); **what sort of (a) ~ is that to say to anyone?** ça n'est pas une chose à dire (aux gens); **the last ~ on the agenda** le dernier point à l'ordre du jour; **you take the ~ too seriously** tu prends la chose trop au sérieux; **you worry about ~s too much** tu te fais trop de soucis; **I must think ~s over** il faut que j'y réfléchisse; **how are ~s with you?** et vous, comment ça va?; **how's ~s?*** comment va?*; **as ~s are** dans l'état actuel des choses; **~s are going from bad to worse** les choses vont de mal en pis; **since that's how ~s are** puisque c'est comme ça, puisqu'il en est ainsi; **I believe in honesty in all ~s** je crois à l'honnêteté en toutes circonstances; **to expect great ~s of sb/sth** attendre beaucoup de qn/qch; **they were talking of one ~ and another** ils parlaient de choses et d'autres; **taking one ~ with another** à tout prendre, somme toute; **the ~ is to know when he's likely to arrive** ce qu'il faut c'est savoir *or* la question est de savoir à quel moment il devrait en principe arriver; **the ~ is this:** ... voilà de quoi il s'agit: ...; **the ~ is, she'd already seen him** (ce qu'il y a) c'est qu'elle l'avait déjà vu, mais elle l'avait déjà vu; **it's a strange ~, but** ... c'est drôle, mais ...; **it is one ~ to use a computer, quite another to know how it works** utiliser un ordinateur est une chose, en connaître le fonctionnement en est une autre; **for one ~, it doesn't make sense** d'abord *or* en premier lieu, ça n'a pas de sens; **and (for) another ~, I'd already spoken to him** et en plus, je lui avais déjà parlé; **it's a good ~ I came** heureusement que je suis venu; **he's on to a good ~*** il a trouvé le filon*; **it's the usual ~, he hadn't checked the petrol** c'est le truc* *or* le coup* classique, il avait oublié de vérifier l'essence; **that was a near** *or* **close ~** (*accident*) vous l'avez (*or* il l'a *etc*) échappé belle; (*result of race, competition etc*) il s'en est fallu de peu; **it's just one of those ~s** ce sont des choses qui arrivent; **it's just one damn ~ after another*** les embêtements se succèdent; **I didn't understand a ~ of what he was saying** je n'ai pas compris un mot de ce qu'il disait; **I hadn't done a ~ about it** je n'avais strictement rien fait; **he knows a ~ or two** il s'y connaît; **he's in London doing his own ~*** il est à Londres et fait ce qui lui plaît *or* chante*; **she's gone off to do her own ~*** elle est partie chercher sa voie *or* faire ce qui lui plaît; **she has got a ~ about spiders*** elle a horreur des araignées, elle a la phobie des araignées; **he has got a ~ about blondes*** il est obsédé par les blondes; **he made a great ~ of my refusal*** quand j'ai refusé il en a fait toute une histoire *or* tout un plat*; **don't make a ~ of it!*** n'en fais pas tout un plat!*, ne monte pas ça en épingle!; **he had a ~* with her two years ago** il a eu une liaison avec elle il y a deux ans; **he's got a ~* for her** il en pince pour elle*; **Mr T~* rang up** Monsieur Chose* *or* Monsieur Machin* a téléphoné; *see* **equal, first, such** *etc*.

d (*person, animal*) créature *f*. **(you) poor little ~!** pauvre petit(e)!; **poor ~, he's very ill** le pauvre, il est très malade; **she's a spiteful ~** c'est une rosse*; **you horrid ~!*** chameau!*; **I say, old ~*** dis donc (mon) vieux.

e (*best, most suitable etc* ~) **that's just the ~ for me** c'est tout à fait *or* justement ce qu'il me faut; **just the ~!, the very ~!** (*of object*) voilà tout à fait *or* justement ce qu'il me (*or* nous *etc*) faut!; (*of idea, plan*) c'est l'idéal!; **yoga is the ~ nowadays** le yoga c'est la grande mode aujourd'hui; **it's the in ~*** c'est le truc* à la mode; **that's not the ~ to** do cela ne se fait pas; it's quite the ~ nowadays ça se fait beaucoup aujourd'hui; I don't feel quite the ~* today je ne suis pas dans mon assiette aujourd'hui; he looks quite the ~* in those trousers il est très bien *or* chic avec ce pantalon; this is the latest ~ in ties c'est une cravate dernier cri.

thingamabob*, **thingumabob*** [ˈθɪŋəmɪbɒb] n, **thingumajig*** [ˈθɪŋəmɪdʒɪg] n, **thingummy*** [ˈθɪŋəmɪ] n, **thingummyjig*** [ˈθɪŋəmɪdʒɪg] n = thingy.

thingy* [ˈθɪŋɪ] n (*object*) machin* *m*, truc* *m*, bidule* *m*; (*person*) Machin(e)* *m(f)*, trucmuche‡ *mf*.

think [θɪŋk] (vb: pret, ptp thought) 1 n (*) I'll have a ~ about it j'y penserai; to have a good ~ about sth bien réfléchir à qch; you'd better have another ~ about it tu ferais bien d'y repenser; he's got another ~ coming! il se fait des illusions!, il faudra qu'il y repense! (*subj*).

2 comp ►think tank* groupe *m or* cellule *f* de réflexion.

3 vi a (*gen*) penser, réfléchir. ~ carefully réfléchissez bien; ~ twice before agreeing réfléchissez-y à deux fois avant de donner votre accord; ~ again! (*reflect on it*) repensez-y!; (*have another guess*) ce n'est pas ça, recommence!; let me ~ que je réfléchisse*, laissez-moi réfléchir; to ~ aloud penser tout haut; to ~ big* avoir de grandes idées; (*iro*) I don't ~!* ça m'étonnerait!

b (*devote thought to*) penser, songer, réfléchir (*of, about* à). I was ~ing about *or* of you yesterday je pensais *or* songeais à vous hier; I ~ of you always je pense toujours à toi; you can't ~ of everything on ne peut pas penser à tout; I've too many things to ~ of *or* about just now j'ai trop de choses en tête en ce moment; he's always ~ing of *or* about money, he ~s of *or* about nothing but money il ne pense qu'à l'argent; come to ~ of it, when you ~ about it en y réfléchissant (bien); what else is there to ~ about? c'est ce qu'il y a de plus important *or* intéressant; (you) ~ about it!, († *or liter*) ~ on it! pensez-y!, songez-y!; I'll ~ about it j'y penserai, j'y songerai, je vais y réfléchir; I'll have to ~ about it il faudra que j'y réfléchisse *or* pense (*subj*); that's worth ~ing about cela mérite réflexion; it's not worth ~ing about ça ne vaut pas la peine d'y penser; there's so much to ~ about il y a tant de choses à prendre en considération; you've given us so much to ~ about vous nous avez tellement donné matière à réfléchir; what are you ~ing about? à quoi pensez-vous?; what were you ~ing of! *or* about! où avais-tu la tête?; it doesn't bear ~ing of! c'est trop affreux d'y penser; I'm ~ing of *or* about resigning je pense à donner ma démission; he was ~ing of *or* about suicide il pensait au suicide; I wouldn't ~ of such a thing! ça ne me viendrait jamais à l'idée!; would YOU ~ of letting him go alone? vous le laisseriez partir seul, vous?; sorry, I wasn't ~ing pardon, je n'ai pas réfléchi; I didn't ~ to ask *or* of asking if you ... je n'ai pas eu l'idée de demander si tu ...; and to ~ of her going there alone! quand on pense qu'elle y est allée toute seule!, (et) dire qu'elle y est allée toute seule!

c (*remember, take into account*) penser (*of* à). he ~s of nobody but himself il ne pense qu'à lui; he's got his children to ~ of *or* about il faut qu'il pense (*subj*) à ses enfants; ~ of the cost of it rends-toi compte de la dépense!; to ~ of *or* about sb's feelings considérer les sentiments de qn; that makes me ~ of the day when ... cela me fait penser au *or* me rappelle le jour où ...; I can't ~ of her name je n'arrive pas à me rappeler son nom; I couldn't ~ of the right word le mot juste ne me venait pas.

d (*imagine*) to ~ of imaginer; ~ of me in a bikini! imagine-moi en bikini!; ~ of what might have happened imagine ce qui aurait pu arriver; just ~! imagine un peu!; (just) ~, we could go to Spain rends-toi compte, nous pourrions aller en Espagne.

e (*devise etc*) to ~ of avoir l'idée de; I was the one who thought of inviting him c'est moi qui ai eu l'idée de l'inviter; what will he ~ of next? qu'est-ce qu'il va encore inventer?; he has just thought of a clever solution il vient de trouver une solution astucieuse; ~ of a number pense à un chiffre.

f (*have as opinion*) penser (*of* de). to ~ well *or* highly *or* a lot of sb/sth penser le plus grand bien de qn/qch, avoir une haute opinion de qn/qch; he is very well thought of in France il est très respecté en France; to my way of ~ing à mon avis; that may be his way of ~ing, but ... c'est peut-être comme ça qu'il voit les choses, mais ...; I don't ~ much of him je n'ai pas une haute opinion de lui; I don't ~ much of that idea cette idée ne me dit pas grand-chose; to ~ better of doing sth décider à la réflexion de ne pas faire qch; he thought (the) better of it il a changé d'avis; to ~ the best/the worst of sb avoir une très haute/très mauvaise opinion de qn; to ~ nothing of doing sth (*do as a matter of course*) trouver tout naturel de faire qch; (*do unscrupulously*) n'avoir aucun scrupule à faire qch; ~ nothing of it! mais je vous en prie!, mais pas du tout!; *see* fit¹.

4 vt a (*be of opinion, believe*) penser, croire, trouver. I ~ so/not je pense *or* crois que oui/non; I rather ~ so j'ai plutôt l'impression que oui; I thought as much!, I thought so! je m'y attendais!, je m'en doutais!; I hardly ~ it likely that ... cela m'étonnerait beaucoup que ... + *subj*; she's pretty, don't you ~? elle est jolie, tu ne trouves pas?; I don't know what to ~ je ne sais (pas) qu'en penser; I ~ it will rain je pense *or* crois qu'il va pleuvoir; I don't ~ he came je ne pense *or* crois pas qu'il soit venu; I don't ~ he will come je ne pense pas qu'il vienne *or* qu'il viendra; what do you ~? qu'est-ce que tu (en) penses?; (*iro*) what do YOU ~? qu'est-ce que tu crois, toi?; what do you ~ of him? comment le trouves-tu?; I can guess what you are ~ing je devine ta pensée; what do you ~ I should do? que penses-tu *or* crois-tu que je doive faire?; who do you ~ you are? pour qui te prends-tu?; I never thought he'd look like that je n'aurais jamais cru qu'il ressemblerait à ça; you must ~ me very rude vous devez me trouver très impoli; he ~s he is intelligent, he ~s himself intelligent il se croit *or* se trouve intelligent; they are thought to be rich ils passent pour être riches; I didn't ~ to see you here je ne m'attendais pas à vous voir ici (*see also* 4d); he ~s money the whole time* il ne pense qu'argent*; *see* world.

b (*conceive, imagine*) (s')imaginer. ~ what we could do with that house! imagine ce que nous pourrions faire de cette maison!; I can't ~ what he means! je ne vois vraiment pas ce qu'il veut dire!; you would ~ he'd have known that already on aurait pu penser qu'il le savait déjà; anyone would ~ he owns the place! il se prend pour le maître des lieux celui-là!; who would have thought it! qui l'aurait dit!; to ~ that she's only 10 et dire qu'elle n'a que 10 ans, quand on pense qu'elle n'a que 10 ans; to ~ evil thoughts avoir de mauvaises pensées.

c (*reflect*) penser à. just ~ what you're doing! pense un peu à ce que tu fais!; we must ~ how we may do it il faut nous demander comment nous allons pouvoir le faire; I was ~ing (to myself) how ill he looked je me disais qu'il avait l'air bien malade.

d (*remember*) did you ~ to bring it? tu n'as pas oublié de l'apporter?; I didn't ~ to let him know il ne m'est pas venu à l'idée *or* je n'ai pas eu l'idée de le mettre au courant.

►**think back** vi repenser (*to* à), essayer de se souvenir (*to* de) *or* se rappeler. he thought back, and replied ... il a fait un effort de mémoire, et a répliqué ... .

►**think out** vt sep *problem, proposition* réfléchir sérieusement à, étudier; *plan* élaborer, préparer; *answer, move* réfléchir sérieusement à, préparer. that needs thinking out il faut y réfléchir à fond; well-thought-out bien conçu.

►**think over** vt sep *offer, suggestion* (bien) réfléchir à, peser. think things over carefully first pèse bien le pour et le contre auparavant; I'll have to think it over il va falloir que j'y réfléchisse.

►**think through** vt sep *plan, proposal* examiner en détail *or* par le menu, considérer dans tous ses détails.

►**think up** vt sep *plan, scheme, improvement* avoir l'idée de; *answer, solution* trouver; *excuse* inventer. who thought up that idea? qui a eu cette idée?; what will he think up next? qu'est-ce qu'il va encore bien pouvoir inventer?

thinkable [ˈθɪŋkəbl] adj pensable, concevable, imaginable. it's not ~ that il n'est pas pensable *or* concevable *or* imaginable que + *subj*.

thinker [ˈθɪŋkəʳ] n penseur *m*, -euse *f*.

thinking [ˈθɪŋkɪŋ] 1 adj *being, creature* rationnel. to any ~ person, this ... pour toute personne qui réfléchit, ceci ...; to put on one's ~ cap réfléchir, cogiter* (*hum*). 2 n (*act*) pensée *f*, réflexion *f*; (*thoughts collectively*) opinions *fpl* (*on, about* sur). I'll have to do some (hard) ~ about it il va falloir que j'y réfléchisse sérieusement; current ~ on this les opinions actuelles là-dessus; *see* wishful.

thinly [ˈθɪnlɪ] adv *cut* en tranches minces *or* fines; *spread* en une couche mince. he sowed the seeds ~ il a fait un semis clair; a ~ populated district une région à la population éparse *or* clairsemée; ~ clad insuffisamment vêtu; ~ wooded area zone peu boisée; a criticism ~ disguised as a compliment une critique à peine déguisée en compliment; a ~ veiled *or* disguised accusation une accusation à peine voilée; a ~ veiled attempt une tentative mal dissimulée.

thinner [ˈθɪnəʳ] 1 n (*for paint etc*) diluant *m*. 2 adj compar of thin.

thinness [ˈθɪnnɪs] n (*NonC: see* thin 1a, b) minceur *f*; finesse *f*; légèreté *f*; maigreur *f*.

third [θɜːd] 1 adj troisième. in the presence of a ~ person en présence d'une tierce personne *or* d'un tiers; (*Gram*) in the ~ person à la troisième personne; ~ time lucky! la troisième fois sera (*or* a été *etc*) la bonne; the ~ finger le majeur, le médius; (*US*) to be a ~ wheel tenir la chandelle; *see also* 4; *for other phrases see* sixth.

2 n a troisième *mf*; (*fraction*) tiers *m*; (*Mus*) tierce *f*; *for phrases see* sixth.

b (*Univ: degree*) ≃ licence *f* sans mention.

c (*Aut: ~ gear*) troisième vitesse *f*. in ~en troisième.

d (*Comm*) ~s articles *mpl* de troisième choix *or* de qualité inférieure.

3 adv a (*in race, exam, competition*) en troisième place *or* position. he came *or* was placed ~ il s'est classé troisième.

b (*†: Rail*) to travel ~ voyager en troisième.

c = thirdly.

4 comp ►Third Age troisième âge *m* ►third-class *see* third-class ►third-degree: (*Med*) third-degree burns brûlures *fpl* au troisième degré; to give sb the third degree* (*torture*) passer qn à tabac‡; (*question closely*) cuisiner‡ qn ►the Third Estate le Tiers État ►third party (*Jur*) tierce personne, tiers *m*; third-party (indemnity) insurance (assurance *f*) responsabilité civile ►third-rate de qualité très inférieure ►Third World n Tiers-Monde *m*, tiers monde *m*; ◊ adj *poverty etc* du Tiers-Monde.

third-class ['θɜːd'klɑːs] 1 *adj* (*lit*) de troisième classe; *hotel* de troisième catégorie, de troisième ordre; (†: *Rail*) *ticket, compartment* de troisième (classe); (*fig pej*) *meal, goods* de qualité très inférieure. (†: *Rail*) **~ seat** troisième *f*; (*Univ*) **~ degree** *see* **2.** 2 *n* (*Univ: also* **~ degree**) ≃ licence *f* sans mention. 3 *adv* a (†: *Rail*) **to travel ~** voyager en troisième. b (*US Post*) tarif *m* "imprimés".

thirdly ['θɜːdlɪ] *adv* troisièmement, en troisième lieu.

thirst [θɜːst] 1 *n* (*lit, fig*) soif *f* (*for* de). **I've got a real ~ on (me)*** j'ai la pépie*. 2 *vi* (*lit, fig: liter*) avoir soif (*for* de). **~ing for revenge** assoiffé de vengeance; **~ing for blood** altéré *or* assoiffé de sang.

thirstily ['θɜːstɪlɪ] *adv drink* avidement.

thirsty ['θɜːstɪ] *adj person, animal* qui a soif, (*stronger*) assoiffé; (*fig*) *land* desséché. (*lit, fig*) **to be ~** avoir soif (*for* de); **it makes you ~, it's ~ work** ça donne soif.

thirteen [θɜː'tiːn] 1 *adj* treize *inv*. 2 *n* treize *m inv*; *for phrases see* **six.** 3 *pron* treize *mfpl*. **there are ~** il y en a treize.

thirteenth ['θɜː'tiːnθ] 1 *adj* treizième. 2 *n* treizième *mf*; (*fraction*) treizième *m*; *for phrases see* **sixth.**

thirtieth ['θɜːtɪɪθ] 1 *adj* trentième. 2 *n* trentième *mf*; (*fraction*) trentième *m*; *for phrases see* **sixth.**

thirty ['θɜːtɪ] 1 *adj* trente *inv*. **about ~ books** une trentaine de livres. 2 *n* trente *m inv*. **about ~** une trentaine; *for other phrases see* **sixty.** 3 *pron* trente *mfpl*. **there are ~** il y en a trente. 4 *comp* ▸**thirty-second note** (*US Mus*) triple croche *f* ▸**Thirty-Share Index** (*Brit*) *indice des principales valeurs industrielles* ▸**the Thirty Years War** (*Hist*) la guerre de Trente Ans.

this [ðɪs] 1 *dem adj, pl* **these** a ce, (*before vowel and mute "h"*) cet, *f* cette, *pl* ces. **who is ~ man?** qui est cet homme?; **whose are these books?** à qui sont ces livres?; **these photos you asked for** les photos que vous avez réclamées; **~ week** cette semaine; **~ time last week** la semaine dernière à pareille heure; **~ time next year** l'année prochaine à la même époque; **~ coming week** la semaine prochaine *or* qui vient; **it all happened ~ past half-hour** tout est arrivé dans la demi-heure qui vient de s'écouler; **I've been waiting ~ past half-hour** voilà une demi-heure que j'attends, j'attends depuis une demi-heure; **how's ~ hand of yours?** et votre main, comment va-t-elle?; **~ journalist (bloke) you were going out with*** ce journaliste, là, avec qui tu sortais*; **~ journalist came up to me in the street*** il y a un journaliste qui est venu vers moi dans la rue.

b (*stressed; or as opposed to that, those*) ce *or* cet *or* cette *or* ces ... -ci. **I mean THIS book** c'est de ce livre-ci que je parle; **I like ~ photo better than that one** je préfère cette photo-ci à celle-là; **~ chair (over) here** cette chaise-ci; **the leaf was blowing that way and ~** la feuille tournoyait de-ci de-là; **she ran that way and ~** elle courait dans tous les sens.

2 *dem pron, pl* **these** a ceci, ce. **what is ~?** qu'est-ce que c'est (que ceci)?; **whose is ~?** à qui appartient ceci?; **who's ~?** (*gen*) qui est-ce?; (*US: on phone*) qui est à l'appareil?; **~ is it** (*gen*) c'est cela; (*agreeing*) exactement, tout à fait; (*before action*) (cette fois,) ça y est; **~ is my son** (*in introduction*) je vous présente mon fils; (*in photo etc*) c'est mon fils; **~ is the boy I told you about** c'est *or* voici le garçon dont je t'ai parlé; (*on phone*) **~ is Joe Brown** ici Joe Brown, Joe Brown à l'appareil; **~ is Tuesday** nous sommes mardi; **but ~ is May** mais nous sommes en mai; **~ is what he showed me** voici ce qu'il m'a montré; **~ is where we live** c'est ici que nous habitons; **I didn't want you to leave like ~!** je ne voulais pas que tu partes comme ça!; **it was like ~** ... voici comment les choses se sont passées ...; **do it like ~** faites-le comme ceci; **after ~ things got better** après ceci les choses se sont arrangées; **before ~ I'd never noticed him** je ne l'avais jamais remarqué auparavant; **it ought to have been done before ~** cela devrait être déjà fait; **we were talking of ~ and that** nous parlions de choses et d'autres; **so it has come to ~!** nous en sommes donc là!; **at ~ she burst into tears** sur ce, elle éclata en sanglots; **with ~ he left us** sur ces mots il nous a quittés; **what's all ~ I hear about your new job?** qu'est-ce que j'apprends, vous avez un nouvel emploi?

b (**~ one**) celui-ci *m*, celle-ci *f*, ceux-ci *mpl*, celles-ci *fpl*. **I prefer that to ~** je préfère celui-là à celui-ci (*or* celle-là à celle-ci); **how much is ~?** combien coûte celui-ci (*or* celle-ci)?; **these over here** ceux-ci (*or* celles-ci); **not THESE!** pas ceux-ci (*or* celles-ci)!

3 *adv*: **it was ~ long** c'était aussi long que ça; **he had come ~ far** il était venu jusqu'ici; (*in discussions etc*) il avait fait tant de progrès; **~ much is certain** ... un point est acquis ...; **~ much we do know:** ... tout au moins nous savons ceci: ...; **he has left, ~ much we do know** il est parti, ça nous le savons (déjà); **I can't carry ~ much** je ne peux pas porter (tout) ceci; **he was at least ~ much taller than me** il était plus grand que moi d'au moins ça.

thistle ['θɪsl] 1 *n* chardon *m*. 2 *comp* ▸**thistledown** duvet *m* de chardon.

thistly ['θɪslɪ] *adj ground* couvert de chardons.

thither ['ðɪðəʳ] (†, *liter, frm*) 1 *adv* là, y; *see* **hither.** 2 *comp* ▸**thitherto** jusqu'alors.

tho(') [ðəʊ] *abbr of* **though.**

thole¹ [θəʊl] *n* (*Naut*) tolet *m*.

thole² [θəʊl] *vt* (††, *dial*) supporter.

Thomas ['tɒməs] *n* Thomas *m*; *see* **doubt 3.**

thong [θɒŋ] *n* [*whip*] lanière *f*, longe *f*; (*on garment*) lanière, courroie *f*.

Thor [θɔːʳ] *n* (*Myth*) T(h)or *m*.

thoraces ['θɔːrəˌsiːz] *npl of* **thorax.**

thoracic [θɔː'ræsɪk] *adj* thoracique.

thorax ['θɔːræks] *n, pl* **~es** *or* **thoraces** thorax *m*.

thorium ['θɔːrɪəm] *n* thorium *m*.

thorn [θɔːn] 1 *n* (*spike*) épine *f*; (*NonC: hawthorn*) aubépine *f*. (*fig*) **to be a ~ in sb's side** *or* **flesh** être une source d'irritation constante pour qn; **that was the ~ in his flesh** c'était sa bête noire; *see* **rose².** 2 *comp* ▸**thorn apple** stramoine *f*, pomme épineuse ▸**thornback (ray)** (*fish*) raie bouclée ▸**thorn bush** buisson *m* d'épine.

thornless ['θɔːnlɪs] *adj* sans épines, inerme (*Bot*).

thorny ['θɔːnɪ] *adj* (*lit, fig*) épineux.

thorough ['θʌrə] 1 *adj work, worker* consciencieux; *search, research* minutieux; *knowledge, examination* profond, approfondi, ample. **to give sth a ~ cleaning/wash** *etc* nettoyer/laver *etc* qch à fond; **he's a ~ rascal** c'est un coquin fieffé; **he's making a ~ nuisance of himself** il se rend totalement insupportable; **I felt a ~ idiot** je me sentais complètement idiot.

2 *comp* ▸**thoroughbred** *adj horse* pur-sang *inv*; *other animal* de race ◊ *n* (*horse*) (cheval *m*) pur-sang *m inv*; (*other animal*) bête *f* de race; (*fig: person*) **he's a real thoroughbred** il a vraiment de la classe *or* de la branche ▸**thoroughfare** (*street*) rue *f*; (*public highway*) voie publique; **"no thoroughfare"** "passage interdit" ▸**thoroughgoing** *examination, revision* complet (*f* -ète); *believer* convaincu; *hooligan* vrai (*before noun*); *rogue, scoundrel* fieffé.

thoroughly ['θʌrəlɪ] *adv wash, clean* à fond; *examine, investigate, study* à fond, minutieusement, dans le détail; *understand* parfaitement; (*very*) tout à fait, tout, tout ce qu'il y a de*. **to search ~** *house* fouiller de fond en comble; *drawer* fouiller à fond; **I ~ agree** je suis tout à fait d'accord; **~ clean** tout propre, tout à fait propre; **he's ~ nasty** il est tout ce qu'il y a de* déplaisant.

thoroughness ['θʌrənɪs] *n* (*NonC*) [*worker*] minutie *f*; [*knowledge*] ampleur *f*. **the ~ of his work/research** la minutie qu'il apporte à son travail/sa recherche.

those [ðəʊz] *pl of* **that.**

thou¹ [ðaʊ] *pers pron* (†, *liter*) tu; (*stressed*) toi.

thou²* [θaʊ] *n, pl* **~** *or* **~s** *abbr of* **thousand, thousandth.**

though [ðəʊ] 1 *conj* a (*despite the fact that*) bien que + *subj*, quoique + *subj*, malgré le fait que + *subj*, encore que + *subj*. **~ it's raining** bien qu'il pleuve, malgré la pluie; **~ poor they were honest** ils étaient honnêtes bien que *or* quoique *or* encore que pauvres.

b (*even if*) **I will do it ~ I (should) die in the attempt** je le ferai, dussé-je y laisser la vie; **strange ~ it may seem** si *or* pour étrange que cela puisse paraître; **(even) ~ I shan't be there I'll think of you** je ne serai pas là mais je n'en penserai pas moins à toi; (*liter*) **what ~ they are poor** malgré *or* nonobstant (*liter*) leur misère.

c **as ~** comme si; **it looks as ~** il semble que + *subj*; *see also* **as.**

2 *adv* pourtant, cependant. **it's not easy ~** ce n'est pourtant pas facile, pourtant ce n'est pas facile; **did he ~!*** ah bon!, tiens tiens!

thought [θɔːt] 1 *pret, ptp of* **think.**

2 *n* a (*NonC*) (*gen*) pensée *f*; (*reflection*) pensée, réflexion *f*, méditation *f*; (*daydreaming*) rêverie *f*; (*thoughtfulness*) considération *f*. **to be lost** *or* **deep in ~** être absorbé par ses pensées (*or* par la rêverie), être plongé dans une méditation (*or* dans une rêverie); **after much ~** après mûre réflexion, après y avoir beaucoup réfléchi; **he acted without ~** il a agi sans réfléchir; **without ~ for** *or* **of himself he** ... sans considérer son propre intérêt il ...; **he was full of ~ for her welfare** il se préoccupait beaucoup de son bien-être; **you must take ~ for the future** il faut penser à l'avenir; **he took** *or* **had no ~ for his own safety** il n'avait aucun égard pour sa propre sécurité; **to give ~ to sth** bien réfléchir à qch, mûrement réfléchir sur qch; **I didn't give it a moment's ~** je n'y ai pas pensé une seule seconde; **I gave it no more ~, I didn't give it another ~** je n'y ai pas repensé; **don't give it another ~** n'y pensez plus; **further ~ needs to be given to these problems** ceci nécessite une réflexion plus approfondie sur les problèmes.

b (*idea*) pensée *f*, idée *f*; (*opinion*) opinion *f*, avis *m*; (*intention*) intention *f*, idée. **it's a happy ~** voilà une idée qui fait plaisir; **what a ~!*** imagine un peu!; **what a horrifying ~!*** quel cauchemar!; **what a frightening ~!*** c'est à faire peur!*; **what a lovely ~!*** comme ça serait bien!; **what a brilliant ~!*** quelle idée de génie!; **that's a ~!*** tiens, mais c'est une idée!; **it's only a ~** ce n'est qu'une idée; **the mere ~ of it frightens me** rien que d'y penser *or* rien qu'à y penser j'ai peur; **he hasn't a ~ in his head** il n'a rien dans la tête; **my ~s were elsewhere** j'avais l'esprit ailleurs; **he keeps his ~s to himself** il garde ses pensées pour lui, il ne laisse rien deviner *or* paraître de ses pensées; **the T~s of Chairman Mao** les pensées du Président Mao; **contemporary/scientific ~ on the subject** les opinions des contemporains/des scientifiques sur la question; **the ~ of Nietzsche** la pensée de Nietzsche; **I had ~s** *or* **some ~ of going to Paris** j'avais vaguement l'idée *or* l'intention d'aller à Paris; **he gave up all ~(s) of marrying her** il a renoncé à toute idée de l'épouser; **his one ~ is to win the prize** sa seule pensée *or* idée est de remporter le prix; **it's the ~ that counts** c'est l'intention qui compte; **to**

read sb's ~s lire (dans) la pensée de qn; *see* **collect²**, **penny**, **second¹** *etc.*

c (*adv phrase*) **a ~** un peu, un tout petit peu; **it is a ~ too large** c'est un (tout petit) peu trop grand.

3 comp ▸**thought-provoking** qui pousse à la réflexion, stimulant ▸**thought-read** vi lire (dans) la pensée de qn ▸**thought-reader** liseur *m*, -euse *f* de pensées; (*fig*) **he's a thought-reader** il lit dans la pensée des gens; (*fig*) **I'm not a thought-reader** je ne suis pas devin ▸**thought reading** divination *f* par télépathie ▸**thought transference** transmission *f* de pensée.

thoughtful [ˈθɔːtfʊl] adj a *person* (*pensive*) pensif, méditatif; (*in character*) sérieux, réfléchi; *book, remark, research* profond, sérieux, (bien) réfléchi. **he was looking ~ about it** il avait l'air de méditer là-dessus; **at this, he looked ~** à ces mots il a pris un air pensif; **he's a ~ boy** c'est un garçon réfléchi *or* sérieux. b (*considerate*) *person* prévenant, attentionné; *act, remark* plein de délicatesse; *invitation* gentil. **how ~ of you!** comme c'est (*or* c'était) gentil à vous!; **to be ~ of others** être plein d'égards pour autrui, être attentif à autrui.

thoughtfully [ˈθɔːtfəlɪ] adv a (*pensively*) *ask, say* pensivement. b (*considerately*) avec prévenance. **he ~ booked tickets for us as well** il a eu la prévenance de louer des places pour nous aussi.

thoughtfulness [ˈθɔːtfʊlnɪs] n (*NonC: see* **thoughtful**) a (*look*) air pensif *or* méditatif; (*character*) caractère réfléchi *or* sérieux. b (*consideration*) prévenance *f*, considération *f*.

thoughtless [ˈθɔːtlɪs] adj *behaviour, words, answer* étourdi, irréfléchi, inconsidéré; *person* étourdi, irréfléchi, malavisé. **a ~ action** une étourderie; **he's very ~** il se soucie fort peu des autres.

thoughtlessly [ˈθɔːtlɪslɪ] adv (*carelessly*) à l'étourdie, étourdiment, à la légère; (*inconsiderately*) négligemment, insouciamment.

thoughtlessness [ˈθɔːtlɪsnɪs] n (*NonC*) (*carelessness*) étourderie *f*, légèreté *f*; (*lack of consideration*) manque *m* de prévenance *or* d'égards.

thousand [ˈθaʊzənd] 1 adj mille *inv*. **a ~ men** mille hommes; **about a ~ men** un millier d'hommes; **a ~ years** mille ans, un millénaire; **a ~ thanks!** mille fois merci!; **two ~ pounds** deux mille livres; (*fig*) **I've got a ~ and one things to do** j'ai mille et une choses à faire. 2 n mille *m inv*. **a ~, one ~** mille; **a** *or* **one ~ and one** mille (et) un; **a ~ and two** mille deux; **five ~** cinq mille; **about a ~, a ~ odd** un millier; (*Comm*) **sold by the ~** vendu par mille; **~s of people** des milliers de gens; **they came in their ~s** ils sont venus par milliers. 3 comp ▸**thousandfold** adj multiplié par mille ◊ adv mille fois autant ▸**Thousand Island dressing** mayonnaise relevée de ketchup *etc.*

thousandth [ˈθaʊzən*t*θ] 1 adj millième. 2 n millième *mf*; (*fraction*) millième *m*.

Thrace [θreɪs] n Thrace.

thraldom [ˈθrɔːldəm] n (*NonC: liter*) servitude *f*, esclavage *m*.

thrall [θrɔːl] n (*liter: lit, fig*) (*person*) esclave *mf*; (*state*) servitude *f*, esclavage *m*. (*fig*) **to be in ~ to** être esclave de.

thrash [θræʃ] 1 vt a (*beat*) rouer de coups, rosser; (*as punishment*) donner une bonne correction à; (**: Sport etc*) battre à plate(s) couture(s), donner une bonne correction à. **they nearly ~ed the life out of him, they ~ed him to within an inch of his life** ils ont failli le tuer à force de coups. b (*move wildly*) **the bird ~ed its wings (about)** l'oiseau battait *or* fouettait l'air de ses ailes; **he ~ed his arms/legs (about)** il battait des bras/des jambes. c (*Agr*) = **thresh**. 2 vi battre violemment (*against* contre). 3 n a (*Brit ‡: party*) sauterie* *f*. b (*Mus*) (*also* **~ metal**) thrash *m*.

▸**thrash about, thrash around** 1 vi (*struggle*) se débattre. **he thrashed about with his stick** il battait l'air de sa canne. 2 vt sep *one's legs, arms* battre de; *stick* agiter; *see also* **thrash 1b**.

▸**thrash out*** vt sep *problem, difficulty* (*discuss*) débattre de; (*solve*) démêler. **they managed to thrash it out** ils ont réussi à démêler le problème (*or* aplanir la difficulté *etc*).

thrashing [ˈθræʃɪŋ] n correction *f*, rossée* *f*; (**: Sport etc*) correction (*fig*), dérouillée‡ *f*. **to give sb a good ~** rouer qn de coups; (*as punishment; also Sport*) donner une bonne correction à qn.

thread [θred] 1 n a (*gen, also Sewing etc*) fil *m*. **nylon ~** fil de nylon; (*fig*) **to hang by a ~** ne tenir qu'à un fil; (*fig*) **to lose the ~ (of what one is saying)** perdre le fil de son discours; (*fig*) **to pick up** *or* **take up the ~ again** retrouver le fil; (*fig*) **a ~ of light** un (mince) rayon de lumière.

b *[screw]* pas *m*, filetage *m*. **screw with left-hand ~** vis filetée à gauche.

c (*US: clothes*) **~s‡** fringues‡ *fpl*, frusques‡ *fpl*.

2 vt *needle, beads* enfiler. **to ~ sth through a needle/over a hook/into a hole** faire passer qch à travers le chas d'une aiguille/par un crochet/par un trou; **to ~ a film on to a projector** monter un film sur un projecteur; **he ~ed his way through the crowd** il s'est faufilé à travers la foule; **the car ~ed its way through the narrow streets** la voiture s'est faufilée dans les petites rues étroites.

3 vi a = **to ~ one's way**; *see* **2**.

b *[needle, beads]* s'enfiler; *[tape, film]* passer.

4 comp ▸**threadbare** *rug, clothes* usé, râpé, élimé; *room* défraîchi; (*fig*) *joke, argument, excuse* usé, rebattu ▸**threadlike** filiforme ▸**threadworm** (*Med*) oxyure *m*.

threat [θret] n (*lit, fig*) menace *f*. **to make a ~ against sb** proférer une menace à l'égard de qn; **under (the) ~ of** menacé de; **it is a grave ~ to civilization** cela constitue une sérieuse menace pour la civilisation, cela menace sérieusement la civilisation.

threaten [ˈθretn] 1 vt menacer (*sb with sth* qn de qch, *to do* de faire). **to ~ violence** proférer des menaces de violence; **species ~ed with extinction, ~ed species** espèce menacée, espèce en voie de disparition *or* d'extinction; (*fig*) **it is ~ing to rain** la pluie menace. 2 vi *[storm, war, danger]* menacer.

threatening [ˈθretnɪŋ] adj *gesture, tone, words* de menace, menaçant; *letter* de menaces; (*fig*) *weather, clouds* menaçant; *news* de mauvais augure. (*Psych*) **to find sb ~** se sentir menacé par qn.

threateningly [ˈθretnɪŋlɪ] adv *say* d'un ton menaçant, avec des menaces dans la voix; *gesticulate* d'une manière menaçante. **~ close** dangereusement près.

three [θriː] 1 adj trois *inv*.

2 n trois *m inv*. (*Pol*) **the Big T~** les Trois Grands; (*Sport*) **let's play best of ~** (*after first game*) jouons la revanche et la belle; (*after second game*) jouons la belle; **they were playing best of ~** ils jouaient deux jeux et la belle; *see* **two**; *for other phrases see* **six**.

3 pron trois *mfpl*. **there are ~** il y en a trois.

4 comp ▸**three-act play** pièce *f* en trois actes ▸**three-card monte** (*US*) bonneteau *m* ▸**three-cornered** triangulaire ▸**three-cornered hat** tricorne *m* ▸**three-D, 3-D** (abbr of **three dimensions, three-dimensional**): *picture, film* **(in) three-D** en trois dimensions, en 3-D ▸**three-day event** (*Horse-riding*) concours *m* complet ▸**three-day eventer** (*Horse-riding*) cavalier *m*, -ière *f* de concours complet ▸**three-day eventing** (*Horse-riding*) concours *m* complet ▸**three-dimensional** *object* à trois dimensions, tridimensionnel; *picture, film* en trois dimensions ▸**threefold** adj triple, triplé ◊ adv trois fois autant ▸**three-legged** *table* à trois pieds; *animal* à trois pattes ▸**three-legged race** (*Sport*) course *f* de pieds liés ▸**three-line** *see* **whip** ▸**three-martini lunch*** (*US fig: expense-account lunch*) déjeuner *m* d'affaires (*qui passe dans les notes de frais*) ▸**threepence** *see* **threepence** ▸**threepenny** *see* **threepenny** ▸**three-phase** (*Elec*) triphasé ▸**three-piece suite** salon *m* comprenant canapé et deux fauteuils ▸**three-pin plug** *see* **pin 1b** ▸**three-ply** *wool* à trois fils ▸**three-point landing** (*Aviat*) atterrissage *m* trois points ▸**three-point turn** (*Aut*) demi-tour *m* en trois manœuvres ▸**three-quarter** adj *portrait* de trois-quarts; *sleeve* trois-quarts *inv* ◊ n (*Rugby*) trois-quarts *m inv* ▸**three-quarters** n trois quarts *mpl* ◊ adv **the money is three-quarters gone** les trois quarts de l'argent ont été dépensés; **three-quarters full/empty** aux trois-quarts plein/vide ▸**three-ring circus** (*lit*) cirque *m* à trois pistes; (*US fig **) véritable cirque (*fig*) ▸**threescore** adj, n († *or liter*) soixante (*m*) ▸**threescore and ten** adj, n († *or liter*) soixante-dix (*m*) ▸**three-sided** *object* à trois côtés, à trois faces; *discussion* à trois ▸**threesome** (*people*) groupe *m* de trois, trio *m*; (*game*) partie *f* à trois; **we went in a threesome** nous y sommes allés à trois ▸**three-way** *split, division* en trois; *discussion* à trois ▸**three-wheeler** (*car*) voiture *f* à trois roues; (*tricycle*) tricycle *m*.

threepence [ˈθrepəns] n (*Brit*) trois anciens pence.

threepenny [ˈθrepənɪ] (*Brit*) 1 adj à trois pence. (*Mus*) **the T~ Opera** L'Opéra de quat'sous. 2 n (*also* **~ bit** *or* **piece**) ancienne pièce de trois pence.

threnody [ˈθrenədɪ] n (*lit*) mélopée *f*; (*fig*) lamentations *fpl*.

thresh [θreʃ] vt (*Agr*) battre.

thresher [ˈθreʃəʳ] n (*person*) batteur *m*, -euse *f* (en grange); (*machine*) batteuse.

threshing [ˈθreʃɪŋ] (*Agr*) 1 n battage *m*. 2 comp ▸**threshing machine** batteuse *f*.

threshold [ˈθreʃhəʊld] 1 n seuil *m*, pas *m* de la porte. **to cross the ~** franchir le seuil; (*fig*) **on the ~ of** au bord *or* au seuil de; (*Psych*) **above the ~ of consciousness** supraliminaire; **below the ~ of consciousness** subliminaire; **to have a high/low pain ~** avoir un seuil de tolérance à la douleur élevé/peu élevé. 2 comp ▸**threshold agreement** accord *m* d'indexation des salaires sur les prix ▸**threshold policy** = **threshold wage policy** ▸**threshold price** prix *m* de seuil ▸**threshold wage policy** politique *f* d'indexation des salaires sur les prix.

threw [θruː] pret of **throw**.

thrice [θraɪs] adv trois fois.

thrift [θrɪft] 1 n (*NonC*) économie *f*. 2 comp ▸**thrift shop** *petite boutique d'objets d'occasion gérée au profit d'œuvres charitables.*

thriftiness [ˈθrɪftɪnɪs] n = **thrift**.

thriftless [ˈθrɪftlɪs] adj imprévoyant, dépensier.

thriftlessness [ˈθrɪftlɪsnɪs] n (*NonC*) imprévoyance *f*.

thrifty [ˈθrɪftɪ] adj économe.

thrill [θrɪl] 1 n frisson *m*, sensation *f*, émotion *f*. **a ~ of joy** un frisson de joie; **with a ~ of joy he ...** en frissonnant de joie, il ...; **what a ~!** quelle émotion!; **she felt a ~ as his hand touched hers** un frisson l'a traversée *or* elle s'est sentie électrisée quand il lui a touché la main; **it gave me a big ~** ça m'a vraiment fait quelque chose!*; **to get a ~ out of doing sth** se procurer des sensations fortes en faisant qch; **the film was packed with** *or* **full of ~s** c'était un film à sensations.

2 vt *person, audience, crowd* électriser, transporter. **his glance ~ed her** son regard l'a enivrée; **I was ~ed (to bits*)!** j'étais aux anges!*; **I was ~ed to meet him** ça m'a vraiment fait plaisir *or* fait quelque chose* de le rencontrer.
3 vi tressaillir *or* frissonner (de joie).

thriller ['θrɪləʳ] n (*novel/play/film*) roman *m*/ pièce *f*/film *m* à suspense.

thrilling ['θrɪlɪŋ] adj *play, film, journey* palpitant; *news* saisissant.

thrive [θraɪv] pret **throve** *or* **thrived**, ptp **thrived** *or* **thriven** ['θrɪvn] vi *[person, animal]* se développer bien, être florissant de santé; *[plant]* pousser *or* venir bien; *[business, industry]* prospérer; *[businessman]* prospérer, réussir. **children ~ on milk** le lait est excellent pour les enfants; **he ~s on hard work** le travail lui réussit.

thriving ['θraɪvɪŋ] adj *person, animal* robuste, florissant de santé; *plant* robuste; *industry, businessman* prospère, florissant.

throat [θrəʊt] n (*external*) gorge *f*; (*internal*) gorge, gosier *m*. **to take sb by the ~** prendre qn à la gorge; **I have a sore ~** j'ai mal à la gorge, j'ai une angine; **he had a fishbone stuck in his ~** il avait une arête de poisson dans le gosier; (*fig*) **that sticks in my ~** je n'arrive pas à accepter *or* avaler* ça; (*fig*) **to thrust** *or* **ram** *or* **force** *or* **shove* sth down sb's ~** rebattre les oreilles de qn avec qch; **they are always at each other's ~(s)** ils sont toujours à se battre; *see* **clear, cut, frog[1], jump.**

throaty ['θrəʊtɪ] adj guttural, de gorge.

throb [θrɒb] 1 n *[heart]* pulsation *f*, battement *m*; *[engine]* vibration *f*; *[drums, music]* rythme *m* (fort); *[pain]* élancement *m*. **a ~ of emotion** un frisson d'émotion. 2 vi *[heart]* palpiter; *[voice, engine]* vibrer; *[drums]* battre (en rythme); *[pain]* lanciner. **a town ~bing with life** une ville vibrante d'animation; **the wound ~bed** la blessure me (*or* lui *etc*) causait des élancements; **my head/arm is ~bing** j'ai des élancements dans la tête/dans le bras; **we could hear the music ~bing in the distance** nous entendions au loin le rythme marqué *or* les flonflons *mpl* de la musique.

throes [θrəʊz] npl: **in the ~ of death** dans les affres de la mort, à l'agonie; **in the ~ of war/disease/a crisis** *etc* en proie à la guerre/la maladie/une crise *etc*; **in the ~ of an argument/quarrel/debate** au cœur d'une discussion/d'une dispute/d'un débat; **while he was in the ~ of (writing) his book** pendant qu'il était aux prises avec la rédaction de son livre; **while we were in the ~ of deciding what to do** pendant que nous débattions de ce qu'il fallait faire.

thrombocyte ['θrɒmbəsaɪt] n thrombocyte *m*.

thrombosis [θrɒm'bəʊsɪs] n, pl **thromboses** [θrɒm'bəʊsi:z] thrombose *f*.

throne [θrəʊn] n (*all senses*) trône *m*. **to come to the ~** monter sur le trône; **on the ~** sur le trône; *see* **power.**

throng [θrɒŋ] 1 n foule *f*, multitude *f*, cohue *f* (*pej*). 2 vi affluer, se presser (*towards* vers, *round* autour de, *to see* pour voir). 3 vt: **people ~ed the streets** la foule se pressait dans les rues; **to be ~ed (with people)** *[streets, town, shops]* être grouillant de monde; *[room, bus, train]* être plein de monde, être bondé *or* comble.

thronging ['θrɒŋɪŋ] adj *crowd, masses* grouillant, pullulant.

throttle ['θrɒtl] 1 n (*Aut, Tech: also* **~ valve**) papillon *m* des gaz; (*Aut: accelerator*) accélérateur *m*. **to give an engine full ~** accélérer à fond; **at full ~** à pleins gaz; **to open the ~** accélérer, mettre les gaz; **to close the ~** réduire l'arrivée des gaz. 2 vt *person* étrangler, serrer la gorge de.

►**throttle back, throttle down** 1 vi mettre le moteur au ralenti. 2 vt sep *engine* mettre au ralenti.

through, (*US*) **thru** [θru:] phr vb elem 1 adv a (*place, time, process*) **the nail went (right) ~** le clou est passé à travers; **just go ~** passez donc; **to let sb ~** laisser passer qn; **you can get a train right ~ to London** on peut attraper un train direct pour Londres; (*in exam*) **did you get ~?, are you ~?** as-tu été reçu?, as-tu réussi?; **did you stay all ~?** es-tu resté jusqu'à la fin?; **we're staying ~ till Tuesday** nous restons jusqu'à mardi; **he slept all night ~** il ne s'est pas réveillé de la nuit; **I knew all ~ that this would happen** je savais depuis le début que cela se produirait; **to be wet ~** *[person]* être trempé (jusqu'aux os); *[clothes]* être trempé, être (bon) à essorer; **soaked ~ and ~** complètement trempé; **I know it ~ and ~** je le connais par cœur; **he's a liar ~ and ~** il ment comme il respire; **he's a Scot ~ and ~** il est écossais jusqu'au bout des ongles; **read it (right) ~ to the end, read it right ~** lis-le en entier *or* jusqu'au bout *or* de bout en bout; **I read the letter ~ quickly** j'ai lu la lettre rapidement; *see* **go through, see through** *etc*.
b (*Brit Telec*) **to put sb ~ to sb** passer qn à qn; **I'll put you ~ to her** je vous la passe; **you're ~ now** vous avez votre correspondant; **you're ~ to him** il est en ligne.
c (**: finished*) **I'm ~** ça y est (j'ai fini)*; **are you ~?** ça y est (tu as fini)?*; **I'm not ~ with you yet** je n'en ai pas encore fini *or* terminé avec vous; **are you ~ with that book?** ce livre, c'est fini?, tu n'as plus besoin de ce livre?; **he told me we were ~** il m'a dit qu'on allait casser* *or* que c'était fini entre nous; **he's ~ with her** il l'a plaquée*, lui et elle, c'est fini; **I'm ~ with football!** le football, (c'est) fini!*
2 prep a (*place*) à travers. **a stream flows ~ the garden** un ruisseau traverse le jardin *or* coule à travers le jardin; **the stream flows ~ it** le ruisseau le traverse *or* coule à travers; **water poured ~ the roof** le toit laissait passer des torrents d'eau; **to go ~ a forest** traverser une forêt; **to get ~ a hedge** passer au travers d'une haie; **they went ~ the train, looking for ...** ils ont fait tout le train, pour trouver ...; **he went right ~ the red light** il a carrément grillé le feu rouge; **to hammer a nail ~ a plank** enfoncer un clou à travers une planche; **he was shot ~ the head** on lui a tiré une balle dans la tête; **to look ~ a window/telescope** regarder par une fenêtre/dans un télescope; **go and look ~ it** (*of hole, window etc*) va voir ce qu'il y a de l'autre côté; **I can hear them ~ the wall** je les entends de l'autre côté du mur; **to go ~ sb's pockets** fouiller les poches de qn, faire les poches de qn*; **he has really been ~ it*** il en a vu de dures*; **he is ~ the first part of the exam** il a réussi à la première partie de l'examen; **I'm half-way ~ the book** j'en suis à la moitié du livre; **to speak ~ one's nose** parler du nez; *see* **get through, go through, see through** *etc*.
b (*time*) pendant, durant. **all** *or* **right ~ his life, all his life ~** pendant *or* durant toute sa vie, sa vie durant; **he won't live ~ the night** il ne passera pas la nuit; (*US*) **(from) Monday ~ Friday** de lundi (jusqu')à vendredi; **he stayed ~ July** il est resté pendant tout le mois de juillet *or* jusqu'à la fin de juillet; **he lives there ~ the week** il habite là pendant la semaine.
c (*indicating means, agency*) par, par l'entremise *or* l'intermédiaire de, grâce à, à cause de. **to send ~ the post** envoyer par la poste; **it was all ~ him that I got the job** c'est grâce à lui *or* par son entremise *or* par son intermédiaire que j'ai eu le poste; **it was all ~ him that I lost the job** c'est à cause de lui que j'ai perdu le poste; **I heard it ~ my sister** je l'ai appris par ma sœur; **~ his own efforts** par ses propres efforts; **it happened ~ no fault of mine** ce n'est absolument pas de ma faute si c'est arrivé; **absent ~ illness** absent pour cause de maladie; **to act ~ fear** agir par peur *or* sous le coup de la peur; **he was exhausted ~ having walked all the way** il était épuisé d'avoir fait tout le chemin à pied; **~ not knowing the way he ...** parce qu'il ne connaissait pas le chemin il ... .
3 adj *carriage, train, ticket* direct. *[train]* **~ portion** rame directe; **"no ~ way"** "impasse"; **all the ~ traffic has been diverted** toute la circulation de passage a été détournée.
4 comp ►**throughout** *see* **throughout** ►**throughput** (*Comput*) débit *m*; (*Ind*) consommation *f* de *or* en matières premières (*en un temps donné*) ►**through street** (*US*) rue *f* prioritaire ►**throughway** (*US*) voie *f* rapide *or* express.

throughout [θrʊ'aʊt] 1 prep a (*place*) partout dans. **~ the world** partout dans le monde, dans le monde entier; **at schools ~ France** dans les écoles de toute la France. b (*time*) pendant, durant. **~ his life** durant toute sa vie, sa vie durant; **~ his career/his story** tout au long de sa carrière/son récit. 2 adv (*everywhere*) partout; (*the whole time*) tout le temps.

throve [θrəʊv] pret of **thrive.**

throw [θrəʊ] (vb: pret **threw**, ptp **thrown**) 1 n *[javelin, discus]* jet *m*; (*Wrestling*) mise *f* à terre; (*Ftbl: also* **~-in**) remise *f* en jeu. **give him a ~** laisse-lui la balle/le ballon *etc*; (*Sport*) **it was a good ~** c'était un bon jet; **with one ~ of the ball he ...** avec un seul coup il ...; (*in table games*) **you lose a ~** vous perdez un tour; (*at fair etc*) **50p a ~** 50 pence la partie; (*fig*) **at 10 dollars a ~*** (à) 10 dollars pièce *or* chacun(e); *see* **stone.**
2 comp ►**throwaway** adj *bottle, packaging* à jeter; *remark, line* qui n'a l'air de rien ◊ n (*esp US: leaflet etc*) prospectus *m*, imprimé *m*; **the throwaway society** la société des produits à jeter ►**throwback:** *[characteristic, custom etc]* **it's a throwback to** ça nous (*or* les *etc*) ramène à ►**throw-in** (*Ftbl*) remise *f* en jeu ►**throw-off** (*Handball*) engagement *m* ►**throw-out** (*Handball*) renvoi *m* de but.
3 vt a (*cast*) *object, stone* lancer, jeter (*to, at* à); *ball, javelin, discus, hammer* lancer; *dice* jeter. **he threw a towel at her** il lui a jeté *or* envoyé une serviette à la tête; **they were ~ing stones at the cat** ils jetaient *or* lançaient des pierres au chat; **he threw the ball 50 metres** il a lancé la balle à 50 mètres; **he threw it across the room** il l'a jeté *or* lancé à l'autre bout de la pièce; (*at dice*) **to ~ a six** avoir un six; (*fig*) **to ~ the book at sb*** (*in accusing, reprimanding*) ne rien laisser passer à qn; (*in punishing, sentencing*) donner *or* coller* le maximum à qn; *see* **water** *etc*.
b (*hurl violently*) *[explosion, car crash etc]* projeter; (*in fight, wrestling*) envoyer au sol (*or* au tapis); *[horse] rider* démonter, désarçonner. **the force of the explosion threw him into the air/across the room** la force de l'explosion l'a projeté en l'air/à l'autre bout de la pièce; **he was ~n clear of the car** il a été projeté hors de la voiture; **to ~ o.s. to the ground/at sb's feet/into sb's arms** se jeter à terre/aux pieds de qn/dans les bras de qn; **to ~ o.s. on sb's mercy** s'en remettre à la merci de qn; (*fig*) **she really threw herself at him*** *or* **at his head*** elle s'est vraiment jetée à sa tête; (*fig*) **he threw himself into the job** il s'est mis *or* attelé à la tâche avec enthousiasme; **he threw himself into the task of clearing up** il y est allé de tout son courage pour mettre de l'ordre.
c (*direct*) *light, shadow, glance* jeter; *slides, pictures* projeter; *kiss* envoyer (*to* à); *punch* lancer (*at* à). **to ~ one's voice** *projeter sa voix de façon à ce qu'elle semble provenir d'une autre direction; see* **light[1]** *etc*.
d (*put suddenly, hurriedly*) jeter (*into* dans, *over* sur). **to ~ sb into jail** jeter qn en prison; **to ~ a bridge over a river** jeter un pont sur une rivière; **to ~ a question at sb** poser une question à qn à brûle-

pourpoint; **to ~ into confusion** *person* jeter la confusion dans l'esprit de; *meeting, group* semer la confusion dans; **it ~s the emphasis on ...** cela met l'accent sur ...; **it threw the police off the trail** cela a dépisté la police; **to ~ open** *door, window* ouvrir tout grand; (*fig*) *house, gardens* ouvrir au public; *race, competition etc* ouvrir à tout le monde; **to ~ a party*** organiser *or* donner *or* offrir une petite fête (*for sb* en l'honneur de qn); (*lose deliberately*) **to ~ a race*** *etc* perdre délibérément une course *etc; see* **blame, doubt, fit2, relief** *etc.*

e *switch* actionner.

f *pottery* tourner; *silk* tordre.

g (*: *disconcert*) déconcerter, décontenancer, désorienter, dérouter. **I was quite ~n when he ...** je n'en suis pas revenu *or* je suis resté baba* quand il ... .

►**throw about, throw around** vt sep *litter, confetti* éparpiller. **don't throw it about or it might break** ne t'amuse pas à le lancer, ça peut se casser; **they were throwing a ball about** ils jouaient à la balle; (*in boat, old bus etc*) **to be thrown about** être ballotté; **to throw one's money about** dépenser (son argent) sans compter; (*fig*) **to throw one's weight about** faire l'important; **to throw o.s. about** se débattre.

►**throw aside** vt sep (*lit*) jeter de côté; (*fig*) rejeter, repousser.

►**throw away** 1 vt sep a *rubbish, cigarette end* jeter; (*fig*) *one's life, happiness, health* gâcher; *talents* gaspiller, gâcher; *sb's affection* perdre; *money, time* gaspiller, perdre; *chance* gâcher, perdre, laisser passer. **to throw o.s. away** gaspiller ses dons (*on sb* avec qn). b (*esp Theat*) *line, remark* (*say casually*) laisser tomber; (*lose effect of*) perdre tout l'effet de. 2 **throwaway** adj, n *see* **throw 2**.

►**throw back** 1 vt sep a (*return*) *ball etc* renvoyer (*to* à); *fish* rejeter; (*fig*) *image* renvoyer, réfléchir. b *head, hair* rejeter en arrière; *shoulders* redresser. **to throw o.s. back** se (re)jeter en arrière. c *enemy etc* repousser. (*fig*) **to be thrown back upon sth** être obligé de se rabattre sur qch. 2 **throwback** n *see* **throw 2**.

►**throw down** vt sep *object* jeter; *weapons* déposer. **to throw o.s. down** se jeter à terre; **to throw down a challenge** lancer *or* jeter un défi; *[rain]* **it's really throwing it down*** il pleut à seaux, il tombe des cordes.

►**throw in** 1 vi (*US*) **to throw in with sb** rallier qn.

2 vt sep a *object into box etc* jeter; (*Ftbl*) *ball* remettre en jeu; *one's cards* jeter (sur la table). (*fig*) **to throw in one's hand** *or* **the sponge** *or* **the towel** abandonner (la partie); *see* **lot**.

b (*fig*) *remark, question* interposer. **he threw in a reference to it** il l'a mentionné en passant.

c (*fig*) (*as extra*) en plus; (*included*) compris. **with £5 thrown in** avec 5 livres en plus *or* par-dessus le marché; (*included*) **with meals thrown in** (les) repas compris; **if you buy a washing machine they throw in a packet of soap powder** si vous achetez une machine à laver ils vous donnent un paquet de lessive en prime; **we had a cruise of the Greek Islands with a day in Athens thrown in** nous avons fait une croisière autour des îles grecques avec en prime un arrêt d'un jour à Athènes.

2 **throw-in** n *see* **throw 2**.

►**throw off** vt sep a (*get rid of*) *burden, yoke* rejeter, se libérer de, se débarrasser de; *clothes* enlever *or* quitter *or* ôter (en hâte), se débarrasser brusquement de; *disguise* jeter; *pursuers, dogs* perdre, semer*; *habit, tendency, cold, infection* se débarrasser de. b (*) *poem, composition* faire *or* écrire au pied levé.

►**throw on** vt sep *coal, sticks* ajouter; *clothes* enfiler *or* passer à la hâte. **she threw on some lipstick*** elle s'est vite mis *or* passé un peu de rouge à lèvres.

►**throw out** vt sep a jeter dehors; *rubbish, old clothes etc* jeter, mettre au rebut; *person* (*lit*) expulser, mettre à la porte, vider*; (*fig: from army, school etc*) expulser, renvoyer; *suggestion* rejeter, repousser; (*Parl*) *bill* repousser. (*fig*) **to throw out one's chest** bomber la poitrine. b (*say*) *suggestion, hint, idea, remark* laisser tomber; *challenge* jeter, lancer. c (*make wrong*) *calculation, prediction, accounts, budget* fausser. d (*disconcert*) *person* désorienter, déconcerter.

►**throw over** vt sep *plan, intention* abandonner, laisser tomber*; *friend, boyfriend etc* laisser tomber*, lâcher*, plaquer** (*for sb else* pour qn d'autre).

►**throw together** vt sep a (*pej: make hastily*) *furniture, machine* faire à la six-quatre-deux*; (*) *essay* torcher. **he threw a few things together and left at once** il a rassemblé quelques affaires *or* jeté quelques affaires dans un sac et il est parti sur-le-champ. b (*fig: by chance*) *people* réunir (par hasard). **they were thrown together, fate had thrown them together** le hasard les avait réunis.

►**throw up** 1 vi (*vomit*) vomir. 2 vt sep a (*into air*) *ball etc* jeter *or* lancer en l'air. **he threw the book up to me** il m'a jeté *or* lancé le livre; **he threw up his hands in despair** il a levé les bras de désespoir. b (*produce, bring to light etc*) produire. **the meeting threw up several good ideas** la réunion a produit quelques bonnes idées, quelques bonnes idées sont sorties de la réunion. c (*reproach*) **to throw sth up to sb** jeter qch à la figure *or* au visage de qn, reprocher qch à qn. d (*vomit*) vomir. e (*: *abandon, reject*) *job, task, studies* lâcher, abandonner; *opportunity* laisser passer.

thrower ['θrəʊəʳ] n lanceur *m*, -euse *f*; *see* **discus** *etc.*

throwing ['θrəʊɪŋ] n (*Sport*) **hammer/javelin ~** le lancer du marteau/du javelot.

thrown [θrəʊn] ptp of **throw**.

thru [θruː] (*US*) = **through**.

thrum [θrʌm] vti = **strum**.

thrush1 [θrʌʃ] n (*Orn*) grive *f*.

thrush2 [θrʌʃ] n (*Med*) muguet *m*; (*Vet*) échauffement *m* de la fourchette.

thrust [θrʌst] (vb: pret, ptp **thrust**) 1 n a (*push*) poussée *f* (*also Mil*); (*stab: with knife, dagger, stick etc*) coup *m*; (*with sword*) botte *f*; (*fig: remark*) pointe *f*. (*fig*) **that was a ~ at you** ça c'était une pointe dirigée contre vous, c'est vous qui étiez visé; *see* **cut**.

b (*NonC*) *[propeller, jet engine, rocket]* poussée *f*; (*Archit, Tech*) poussée; (* *fig: drive, energy*) dynamisme *m*, initiative *f*. (*fig*) **the main ~ of his speech** l'idée maîtresse de son discours.

2 vt a pousser brusquement *or* violemment; *finger, stick* enfoncer; *dagger* plonger, enfoncer (*into* dans, *between* entre); *rag etc* fourrer (*into* dans). **he ~ the box under the table** (*moved*) il a poussé *or* fourré* la boîte sous la table; (*hid*) il a vite caché la boîte sous la table; **he ~ his finger into my eye** il m'a mis le doigt dans l'œil; **he ~ the letter at me** il m'a brusquement mis la lettre sous le nez; **to ~ one's hands into one's pockets** enfoncer les mains dans ses poches; **he had a knife ~ into his belt** il avait un couteau glissé dans sa ceinture; **he ~ his head through the window** il a mis *or* passé la tête par la fenêtre; **he ~ the book into my hand** il m'a fourré le livre dans la main; **to ~ one's way** *see* **3a**.

b (*fig*) *job, responsibility* imposer (*upon sb* à qn); *honour* conférer (*on* à). **some have greatness ~ upon them** certains ont de la grandeur sans la rechercher; **I had the job ~ (up)on me** on m'a imposé ce travail; **to ~ o.s. (up)on sb** imposer sa présence à qn.

3 vi a (*also* **~ one's way**) **to ~ in/out** *etc* entrer/sortir *etc* en se frayant un passage; **he ~ past me** il a réussi à passer (*or* il m'a dépassé) en me bousculant; **to ~ through a crowd** se frayer un passage dans la foule.

b (*Fencing*) allonger une botte.

►**thrust aside** vt sep *object, person* écarter brusquement, pousser brusquement à l'écart; (*fig*) *objection, suggestion* écarter *or* rejeter violemment.

►**thrust forward** vt sep *object, person* pousser en avant (brusquement). **to thrust o.s. forward** s'avancer brusquement, se frayer *or* s'ouvrir un chemin; (*fig*) se mettre en avant, se faire valoir.

►**thrust in** 1 vi (*lit: also* **thrust one's way in**) s'introduire de force; (*fig: interfere*) intervenir. 2 vt sep *stick, pin, finger* enfoncer; *rag* fourrer dedans*; *person* pousser (violemment) à l'intérieur *or* dedans.

►**thrust out** vt sep a (*extend*) *hand* tendre brusquement; *legs* allonger brusquement; *jaw, chin* projeter en avant. b (*push outside*) *object, person* pousser dehors. **he opened the window and thrust his head out** il a ouvert la fenêtre et passé la tête dehors.

►**thrust up** vi *[plants etc]* pousser vigoureusement.

thruster ['θrʌstəʳ] n a (*pej*) **to be a ~** se mettre trop en avant, être arriviste. b (*rocket*) (micro)propulseur *m*.

thrustful* ['θrʌstfʊl] adj = **thrusting**.

thrustfulness* ['θrʌstfʊlnɪs] n (*NonC*) dynamisme *m*, initiative *f*, arrivisme *m* (*pej*).

thrusting ['θrʌstɪŋ] adj dynamique, entreprenant; (*pej*) qui se fait valoir, qui se met trop en avant.

thruway ['θruːweɪ] n (*US*) voie *f* rapide *or* express.

Thucydides [θuː'sɪdɪdiːz] n Thucydide *m*.

thud [θʌd] 1 n bruit sourd, son mat. **I heard the ~ of gunfire** j'entendais gronder sourdement les canons. 2 vi faire un bruit sourd, rendre un son mat (*on, against* en heurtant); *[guns]* gronder sourdement; (*fall*) tomber avec un bruit sourd. *[person]* **to ~** *or* **to go ~ding in/out** *etc* entrer/sortir *etc* à pas pesants.

thug [θʌg] n voyou *m*, gangster *m*; (*at demonstrations*) casseur *m*; (*term of abuse*) brute *f*.

thuggery ['θʌgərɪ] n (*NonC*) brutalité *f*, violence *f*.

Thule ['θjuːlɪ] n (*also* **ultima ~**) Thulé.

thulium ['θjuːlɪəm] n thulium *m*.

thumb [θʌm] 1 n pouce *m*. (*fig*) **to be under sb's ~** être sous la coupe de qn; **she's got him under her ~** elle le mène par le bout du nez; (*fig*) **to be all (fingers and) ~s** être très maladroit; **he gave me the ~s up (sign)*** (*all going well*) il m'a fait signe que tout allait bien; (*to wish me luck*) il m'a fait signe pour me souhaiter bonne chance; **he gave me the ~s down (sign)*** il m'a fait signe que ça n'allait pas (*or* que ça n'avait pas bien marché); *see* **finger, rule, twiddle** *etc.*

2 comp *nail, print* du pouce ►**thumb index** répertoire *m* à onglets ►**thumbnail sketch** (*fig*) croquis *m* sur le vif ►**thumbscrew** (*Tech*) vis *f* à papillon *or* à ailettes; (*Hist: torture*) **thumbscrews** poucettes *fpl* ►**thumbstall** poucier *m* ►**thumbtack** (*US*) punaise *f*.

3 vt a *book, magazine* feuilleter. **well ~ed** tout écorné (par l'usage); **to ~ one's nose** faire un pied de nez (*at sb* à qn).

b (*) **to ~ a lift** *or* **a ride** (*gen*) faire du stop* *or* de l'auto-stop; **he ~ed a lift to Paris** il est allé à Paris en stop* *or* en auto-stop; **I managed at last to ~ a lift** je suis enfin arrivé à arrêter *or* à avoir une voiture.

►**thumb through** vt fus *book* feuilleter; *card index* consulter rapidement.

thump [θʌmp] 1 n (*blow: with fist/stick etc*) (grand) coup *m* de poing/de canne *etc;* (*sound*) bruit lourd et sourd. **to fall with a ~** tomber lourdement; **to give sb a ~** assener un coup à qn. 2 vt (*gen*) taper sur; *door* cogner à, taper à. **I could have ~ed him!*** je l'aurais giflé! *or* bouffé!⁑ 3 vi a cogner, frapper (*on* sur, *at* à); *[heart]* battre fort, (*with fear*) battre la chamade. **he was ~ing on the piano** il tapait (comme un sourd) sur le piano, il jouait comme un forcené. b *[person]* **to ~ in/out** *etc* entrer/sortir *etc* en martelant le pavé (*or* le plancher); (*at a run*) entrer/sortir *etc* en courant bruyamment.
▸**thump out** vt sep: **to thump out a tune on the piano** marteler un air au piano.

thumping⁑ ['θʌmpɪŋ] adj (*also* **~ great**) énorme, monumental*, phénoménal.

thunder ['θʌndəʳ] 1 n (*NonC*) tonnerre *m*; *[applause]* tonnerre, tempête *f*; *[hooves]* retentissement *m*, fracas *m*; *[passing vehicles, trains]* fracas, bruit *m* de tonnerre. **there's ~ about** le temps est à l'orage; **there's ~ in the air** il y a de l'orage dans l'air; **I could hear the ~ of the guns** j'entendais tonner les canons; **with a face like ~** le regard noir (de colère); *see* **black 1e, peal, steal.**
2 comp ▸**thunderbolt** coup *m* de foudre; (*fig*) coup de tonnerre ▸**thunderclap** coup *m* de tonnerre (*lit*) ▸**thundercloud** nuage orageux; (*fig*) nuage noir ▸**thunderstorm** orage *m* ▸**thunderstruck** (*fig*) abasourdi, ahuri, stupéfié.
3 vi (*Met*) tonner; *[guns]* tonner; *[hooves]* retentir. **the train ~ed past** le train est passé dans un grondement de tonnerre; (*liter, fig: be vehement*) **to ~ against sth/sb** tonner *or* fulminer contre qch/qn.
4 vt (*also* **~ out**) *threat, order* proférer d'une voix tonitruante. **"no!" he ~ed** "non!" tonna-t-il *or* dit-il d'une voix tonitruante; **the crowd ~ed their approval** la foule a exprimé son approbation dans un tonnerre d'applaudissements et de cris.

thunderer ['θʌndərəʳ] n: **the T~** le dieu de la Foudre et du Tonnerre, Jupiter tonnant.

thundering ['θʌndərɪŋ] adj a **in a ~ rage** *or* **fury** dans une colère noire, fulminant; **in a ~ temper** d'une humeur massacrante. b (*: *also* **~ great**) énorme, monumental*, phénoménal. **it was a ~ success** ça a eu un succès fou *or* un succès monstre.

thunderous ['θʌndərəs] adj *welcome, shouts* étourdissant. **~ acclaim** ovation *f*; **~ applause** tonnerre *m* d'applaudissements.

thundery ['θʌndərɪ] adj orageux.

Thur abbr of **Thursday**.

thurible ['θjʊərɪbl] n encensoir *m*.

thurifer ['θjʊərɪfəʳ] n thuriféraire *m*.

Thurs. abbr of **Thursday**.

Thursday ['θɜːzdɪ] n jeudi *m*; *see* **Maundy;** *for phrases see* **Saturday**.

thus [ðʌs] adv (*in this way*) ainsi, comme ceci, de cette façon, de cette manière; (*consequently*) ainsi, donc, par conséquent. **~ far** (*up to here/now*) jusqu'ici; (*up to there/then*) jusque-là.

thwack [θwæk] 1 n (*blow*) grand coup; (*with hand*) claque *f*, gifle *f*; (*sound*) claquement *m*, coup sec. 2 vt frapper vigoureusement, donner un coup sec à; (*slap*) donner une claque à.

thwart¹ [θwɔːt] vt *plan* contrecarrer, contrarier; *person* contrecarrer *or* contrarier les projets de. **to be ~ed at every turn** voir tous ses plans contrariés l'un après l'autre.

thwart² [θwɔːt] n (*Naut*) banc *m* de nage.

thy [ðaɪ] poss adj (††, *liter, dial*) ton, ta, tes.

thyme [taɪm] n thym *m*. **wild ~** serpolet *m*.

thymus ['θaɪməs] n, pl **~es** *or* **thymi** ['θaɪmaɪ] thymus *m*.

thyroid ['θaɪrɔɪd] 1 n (*also* **~ gland**) thyroïde *f*. 2 adj thyroïde.

thyroxin(e) [θaɪ'rɒksɪn] n thyroxine *f*.

thyself [ðaɪ'self] pers pron (††, *liter, dial*) (*reflexive*) te; (*emphatic*) toi-même.

ti [tiː] n (*Mus*) si *m*.

tiara [tɪ'ɑːrə] n *[lady]* diadème *m*; *[Pope]* tiare *f*.

Tiber ['taɪbəʳ] n Tibre *m*.

Tiberias [taɪ'bɪərɪæs] n: **Lake ~** le lac de Tibériade.

Tiberius [taɪ'bɪərɪəs] n Tibère *m*.

Tibet [tɪ'bet] n Tibet *m*.

Tibetan [tɪ'betən] 1 adj tibétain, du Tibet. 2 n a Tibétain(e) *m(f)*. b (*Ling*) tibétain *m*.

tibia ['tɪbɪə] n, pl **~s** *or* **tibiae** ['tɪbɪ,iː] tibia *m*.

tic [tɪk] 1 n tic *m* (nerveux). 2 comp ▸**tic-tac-toe** (*US*) ≈ (jeu *m* de) morpion *m*.

tich⁑ [tɪtʃ] n bout *m* de chou*, microbe* *m* (*also pej*).

tichy⁑ ['tɪtʃɪ] adj (*also* **~ little**) minuscule.

tick¹ [tɪk] 1 n a *[clock]* tic-tac *m*.
b (*Brit *: instant*) instant *m*. **just a ~!, half a ~!** une minute!, un instant!; **in a ~, in a couple of ~s** en un rien de temps, en moins de deux, en un clin d'œil; **it won't take a ~** *or* **two ~s** c'est l'affaire d'un instant, il y en a pour une seconde; **I shan't be a ~** j'en ai pour une seconde.
c (*mark*) coche *f*. **to put** *or* **mark a ~ against sth** cocher qch.
2 comp ▸**ticktack** (*Racing*) signaux *mpl* (des bookmakers) ▸**ticktack man** (*Brit*) aide *m* de bookmaker ▸**tick-tack-toe** (*US*) ≈ (jeu *m* de) morpion *m* ▸**tick-tock** *[clock]* tic-tac *m*.
3 vt (*Brit*) *name, item, answer* cocher; (*Scol: mark right*) marquer juste. (*on form etc*) **please ~ where appropriate** cochez la (*or* les) case(s) correspondante(s).
4 vi *[clock, bomb etc]* faire tic-tac, tictaquer. (*fig*) **I don't understand what makes him ~*** il est un mystère pour moi; **I wonder what makes him ~*** je me demande comment il fonctionne.
▸**tick away** 1 vi *[clock etc]* continuer son tic-tac; *[taximeter]* tourner; *[time]* s'écouler. 2 vt sep: **the clock ticked the hours away** la pendule marquait les heures.
▸**tick by** vi *[time]* s'écouler.
▸**tick off** 1 vt sep a (*Brit*) (*lit*) *name, item* cocher; (*fig: enumerate*) *reasons, factors etc* énumérer. b (*Brit *: reprimand*) attraper, passer un savon à*. c (*US *: annoy*) embêter*, casser les pieds à*. 2 **ticking-off*** n *see* **ticking² 2.**
▸**tick over** vi (*Brit*) *[engine]* tourner au ralenti; *[taximeter]* tourner; *[business etc]* aller *or* marcher doucettement.

tick² [tɪk] n (*Zool*) tique *f*.

tick³* [tɪk] n (*Brit: credit*) crédit *m*. **on ~** à crédit; **to give sb ~** faire crédit à qn.

tick⁴ [tɪk] n (*NonC: cloth*) toile *f* (à matelas); (*cover*) housse *f* (pour matelas).

ticker ['tɪkəʳ] 1 n a (*esp US*) téléscripteur *m*, téléimprimeur *m*. b (⁑) (*watch*) tocante* *f*; (*heart*) cœur *m*, palpitant⁑ *m*. 2 comp ▸**ticker-tape** (*NonC*) bande *f* de téléscripteur *or* téléimprimeur; (*US: at parades etc*) ≈ serpentin *m*; (*US*) **to get a ticker-tape welcome** être accueilli par une pluie de serpentins.

ticket ['tɪkɪt] 1 n a (*Aviat, Cine, Rail, Theat etc: also for football match etc*) billet *m*; (*for bus, tube*) ticket *m*; (*Comm: label*) étiquette *f*; (*counterfoil*) talon *m*; (*from cash register*) ticket, reçu *m*; (*for cloakroom*) ticket, numéro *m*; (*for left-luggage*) bulletin *m*; (*for library*) carte *f*; (*from pawnshop*) reconnaissance *f* (du mont-de-piété). **to buy a ~** prendre un billet; **coach ~** billet de car; **admission by ~ only** entrée réservée aux personnes munies d'un billet; (*fig*) **that's (just) the ~!*** c'est ça!, voilà ce qu'il nous faut!; *see* **return, season** *etc.*
b (*: *for fine*) P.-V. *m*, papillon *m*. **I found a ~ on the windscreen** j'ai trouvé un papillon sur le pare-brise; **to get a ~ for parking** attraper un P.-V. pour stationnement illégal; **to give sb a ~ for parking** mettre un P.-V. à qn pour stationnement illégal.
c (*certificate*) *[pilot]* brevet *m*. *[ship's captain]* **to get one's ~** passer capitaine.
d (*US Pol: list*) liste *f* (électorale). **he is running on the Democratic ~** il se présente sur la liste des démocrates; *see* **straight.**
2 comp ▸**ticket agency** (*Theat*) agence *f* de spectacles; (*Rail etc*) agence de voyages ▸**ticket barrier** (*Brit Rail*) portillon *m* (d'accès) ▸**ticket collector** contrôleur *m* ▸**ticket holder** personne munie d'un billet ▸**ticket inspector** = **ticket collector** ▸**ticket office** bureau *m* de vente des billets, guichet *m* ▸**ticket-of-leave**† (*Brit Jur*) libération conditionnelle; (*Brit Jur*) **ticket-of-leave man**† libéré conditionnel ▸**tick-et tout** *see* **tout 1.**
3 vt a *goods* étiqueter.
b (*US*) *traveller etc* donner un billet à. **passengers ~ed on these flights** voyageurs en possession de billets pour ces vols.
c (*US: fine*) mettre un P.-V. à.

ticking¹ ['tɪkɪŋ] n (*NonC: Tex*) toile *f* (à matelas).

ticking² ['tɪkɪŋ] 1 n *[clock]* tic-tac *m*. 2 comp ▸**ticking-off** (*Brit* *) attrapade* *f*; **to give sb a ticking-off** passer un savon à qn*, attraper qn; **to get a ticking-off** recevoir un bon savon*, se faire attraper.

tickle ['tɪkl] 1 vt (*lit*) *person, dog* chatouiller, faire des chatouilles* à; (*please*) *sb's vanity, palate etc* chatouiller; (*: *delight*) *person* plaire à, faire plaisir à; (*: *amuse*) amuser, faire rire. **to ~ sb's ribs, to ~ sb in the ribs** chatouiller les côtes à qn; **to be ~d to death⁑, to be ~d pink⁑** être heureux comme tout, être aux anges; *see* **fancy** *etc.* 2 vi chatouiller. 3 n chatouillement *m*, chatouilles* *fpl*. **he gave the child a ~** il a chatouillé l'enfant, il a fait des chatouilles* à l'enfant; **to have a ~ in one's throat** avoir un chatouillement dans la gorge; *see* **slap.**

tickler* ['tɪkləʳ] n (*Brit*) (*question, problem*) colle* *f*; (*situation*) situation délicate *or* épineuse.

tickling ['tɪklɪŋ] 1 n chatouillement *m*, chatouille(s)* *f(pl)*. 2 adj *sensation* de chatouillement; *blanket* qui chatouille; *cough* d'irritation.

ticklish ['tɪklɪʃ] adj, **tickly*** ['tɪklɪ] adj a *sensation* de chatouillement; *blanket* qui chatouille; *cough* d'irritation. *[person]* **to be ~** être chatouilleux, craindre les chatouilles*. b (*touchy*) *person, sb's pride* chatouilleux; (*difficult*) *situation, problem, task* épineux, délicat.

ticky-tacky ['tɪkɪ,tækɪ] (*US*) 1 adj de pacotille. 2 n pacotille *f*.

tidal ['taɪdl] adj *force* de la marée; *river, inland sea, estuary* qui a des marées. **~ wave** raz-de-marée *m inv*; (*fig: of enthusiasm, protest etc*) immense vague *f*, flot *m*; **~ basin** bassin *m* de marée.

tidbit ['tɪdbɪt] n (*esp US*) = **titbit.**

tiddler* ['tɪdləʳ] n (*Brit*) (*stickleback*) épinoche *f*; (*tiny fish*) petit poisson; (*small child*) petit(e) mioche* *m(f)*.

tiddly ['tɪdlɪ] 1 adj (*: *esp Brit*) pompette*, éméché*. 2 comp ▸**tiddlywinks** jeu *m* de puce.

tide [taɪd] 1 n marée *f*. **at high/low ~** à marée haute/basse; **the ~ is on the turn** la mer est étale; **the ~ turns at 3 o'clock** la marée commence à monter (*or* à descendre) à 3 heures; (*fig*) **the ~ has turned, there has been a turn of the ~** la chance a tourné, la chance est passée de notre (*or* leur *etc*) côté; (*fig*) **to go with the ~** suivre le courant; (*fig*) **to go against the ~** aller à contre-courant; **the ~ of events** le cours *or* la marche des événements; **the rising ~ of public impatience** l'exaspération grandissante et généralisée du public; *see* **time**.

2 **comp** ▸**tideland** laisse *f* ▸**tideline, tidemark** laisse *f* de haute mer, ligne *f* de (la) marée haute; (*esp Brit hum: on neck, in bath*) ligne de crasse ▸**tide table** échelle *f* des marées ▸**tidewater** (*Brit*) (eaux *fpl* de) marée *f*; (*US*) côte *f* ▸**tideway** (*channel*) chenal *m* de marée; (*tidal part of river*) section (d'un cours d'eau) soumise à l'influence des marées; (*current*) flux *m*.

3 **vt: to ~ sb over a difficulty** dépanner qn lors d'une difficulté, tirer qn d'embarras provisoirement; **it ~d him over till payday** ça lui a permis de tenir *or* ça l'a dépanné en attendant d'être payé.

▸**tide over vt sep: to tide sb over** permettre à qn de tenir, dépanner qn.

...tide ['taɪd] **n ending in comps** saison *f*. **Eastertide** (la saison de) Pâques *m*; *see* **Whit** *etc*.

tidily ['taɪdɪlɪ] **adv** *arrange, fold* soigneusement, avec soin; *write* proprement. **she is always ~ dressed** elle est toujours correctement vêtue *or* toujours mise avec soin; **try to dress more ~** tâche de t'habiller plus correctement *or* d'apporter plus de soin à ta tenue.

tidiness ['taɪdɪnɪs] **n** (*NonC*) *[room, drawer, desk, books]* ordre *m*; *[handwriting, schoolwork]* propreté *f*. **what I like about him is his ~** ce que j'aime chez lui, c'est son sens de l'ordre; **the ~ of his appearance** sa tenue soignée.

tidings ['taɪdɪŋz] **npl** (*liter*) nouvelle(s) *f(pl)*.

tidy ['taɪdɪ] 1 **adj** a *room, drawer, cupboard* bien rangé, ordonné, en ordre; *desk, objects, books* bien rangé, en ordre; *dress, appearance, hair* net, soigné; *handwriting, schoolwork* net, propre; *habits* d'ordre; *person* (*in appearance*) soigné; (*in character*) ordonné, méthodique. **to make *or* get a room ~** ranger une pièce, mettre de l'ordre dans une pièce; **try to make your writing tidier** tâche d'écrire plus proprement; **to make o.s. ~** s'arranger, remettre de l'ordre dans sa toilette; **to have a ~ mind** avoir l'esprit méthodique.

b (*) *sum, amount, income* rondelet, coquet, joli; *speed* bon. **it cost a ~ bit *or* a ~ penny** ça lui (*or* nous *etc*) a coûté une jolie somme; **it took a ~ bit of his salary** ça lui a pris un bon morceau de son salaire.

2 **n** vide-poches *m inv*; *see* **sink**[2] *etc*.

3 **comp** ▸**tidy-out*, tidy-up*: to have a tidy-out *or* tidy-up** faire du rangement *or* une séance de rangement; **to give sth a (good) tidy-out *or* tidy-up** ranger qch à fond.

4 **vt** (*also* **~ up**) *drawer, cupboard, books, clothes* ranger, mettre de l'ordre dans; *desk* ranger, mettre de l'ordre sur. **to ~ o.s. (up)** s'arranger, remettre de l'ordre dans sa toilette; **to ~ (up) one's hair** arranger sa coiffure, remettre de l'ordre dans sa coiffure.

▸**tidy away vt sep** ranger.

▸**tidy out** 1 **vt sep** *cupboard, drawer* vider pour y mettre de l'ordre. 2 **tidy-out* n** *see* **tidy 3**.

▸**tidy up** 1 **vi** (*tidy room etc*) (tout) ranger; (*tidy o.s.*) s'arranger. 2 **vt sep = tidy 4**. 3 **tidy-up* n** *see* **tidy 3**.

tie [taɪ] 1 **n** a (*cord etc*) *[garment, curtain]* attache *f*; *[shoe]* lacet *m*, cordon *m*; (*Brit: neck~*) cravate *f*; (*fig: bond, link*) lien *m*; (*fig: restriction*) entrave *f*. (*on invitation*) **black ~** ≃ smoking *m*; (*Dress*) **white ~** habit *m*; (*fig*) **the ~s of blood** les liens du sang; **family ~s** (*links*) liens de famille *or* de parenté; (*responsibilities*) attaches familiales; **she finds the children a great ~** avec les enfants elle n'est pas libre, les enfants l'accaparent beaucoup; *see* **old**.

b (*esp Sport*) (*draw*) égalité *f* (de points); (*drawn match*) match nul; (*drawn race/competition*) course *f*/concours *m* dont les vainqueurs sont ex æquo. **the match ended in a ~, the result (of the match) was a ~** les deux équipes ont fait match nul *or* ont terminé le match à égalité; **to play off a ~** (*second match*) rejouer un match nul; (*third match*) jouer la belle; (*Scol, Sport etc*) **there was a ~ for second place** il y avait deux ex æquo en seconde position; **the election ended in a ~** les candidats ont obtenu le même nombre de voix.

c (*Sport: match*) match *m* de championnat; *see* **cup**.

d (*Mus*) liaison *f*.

e (*Archit*) tirant *m*, entrait *m*.

f (*US Rail*) traverse *f*.

2 **comp** ▸**tieback** (*curtain*) rideau *m* bonne femme; (*cord, rope for curtain*) embrasse *f* ▸**tie-break(er)** (*Tennis*) tie-break *m*; (*in quiz/game*) question *f*/épreuve *f* subsidiaire ▸**tie-clasp, tie-clip** fixe-cravate *m* ▸**tie-dye** nouer-lier-teindre (*méthode consistant à cacher certaines parties du tissu en le nouant ou en le liant*) ▸**tie-in** (*link*) lien *m*, rapport *m* (*with* avec); (*US Comm: sale*) vente jumelée *or* par lots; (*US Comm: article*) lot *m* ▸**tie-on** *label* à œillet ▸**tiepin** épingle *f* de cravate ▸**tie-rod** (*Archit, Aut*) tirant *m* ▸**tie-tack** (*US*) = **tie-clasp** ▸**tie-up** (*connection*) lien *m* (*with* avec, *between* entre); (*Fin: merger*) fusion *f* (*with* avec, *between* entre); (*Comm: joint venture between two companies*) accord *m*, entente *f*, association *f*, lien *m* (*with* avec, *between* entre); (*US: stoppage*) interruption *f*, arrêt *m*; (*traffic*) embouteillage *m*.

3 **vt** a (*fasten*) attacher (*to* à); *shoelace, necktie, rope* attacher, nouer; *parcel* attacher, ficeler; *ribbon* nouer, faire un nœud à; *shoes* lacer. **to ~ sb's hands** (*lit*) attacher *or* lier les mains de qn; (*fig*) lier les mains de *or* à qn; (*lit, fig*) **his hands are ~d** il a les mains liées; (*lit, fig*) **to be ~d hand and foot** avoir pieds et poings liés; **to ~ sth in a bow, to ~ a bow in sth** faire un nœud avec qch; **to ~ a knot in sth** faire un nœud à qch; *[rope etc]* **to get ~d in knots** se nouer, faire des nœuds; (*fig*) **to get ~d in knots* to ~ o.s. in knots*** s'embrouiller; *see* **apron**.

b (*link*) lier (*to* à); (*restrict*) restreindre, limiter; (*Mus*) lier. **the house is ~d to her husband's job** la maison est liée au travail de son mari; **I'm ~d to the house/my desk all day** je suis retenu *or* cloué à la maison/mon bureau toute la journée; **are we ~d to this plan?** sommes-nous obligés de nous en tenir à ce projet?

4 **vi** a *[shoelace, necktie, rope]* se nouer.

b (*draw*) (*Sport etc*) faire match nul; (*in competition*) être ex æquo; (*in election*) obtenir le même nombre de voix. (*Sport*) **we ~d with them 4-all** nous avons fait match nul 4 partout; (*in race, exam, competition*) **they ~d for first place** ils ont été premiers ex æquo.

▸**tie back** 1 **vt sep** *curtains* retenir par une embrasse, attacher sur les côtés; *hair* nouer (en arrière). 2 **tieback n** *see* **tie 2**.

▸**tie down vt sep** *object, person, animal* attacher. (*fig*) **he didn't want to be tied down** il ne voulait pas perdre sa liberté; **to tie sb down to a promise** obliger qn à tenir sa promesse; **can you tie him down to these conditions?** pouvez-vous l'astreindre à ces conditions?; **we can't tie him down to a date/a price** nous n'arrivons pas à lui faire fixer une date/un prix; **I shan't tie you down to 6 o'clock** il n'est pas nécessaire que ce soit à 6 heures; **I don't want to tie myself down to going** je ne veux pas m'engager à y aller *or* me trouver contraint d'y aller.

▸**tie in** 1 **vi** a (*be linked*) être lié (*with* à). **it all ties in with what they plan to do** tout est lié à ce qu'ils projettent de faire; **this fact must tie in somewhere** ce fait doit bien avoir un rapport quelque part.

b (*be consistent*) correspondre (*with* à), concorder, cadrer (*with* avec). **it doesn't tie in with what I was told** ça ne correspond pas à *or* ça ne cadre pas avec *or* ça ne concorde pas avec ce que l'on m'a dit.

2 **vt sep: I'm trying to tie that in with what he said** j'essaie de voir la liaison *or* le rapport entre ça et ce qu'il a dit; **can you tie the visit in with your trip to London?** pouvez-vous combiner la visite et *or* avec votre voyage à Londres?

3 **tie-in n** *see* **tie 2**.

▸**tie on** 1 **vt sep** *label etc* attacher (avec une ficelle). (*fig: get drunk*) **to tie one on*** se cuiter*, se soûler*. 2 **tie-on adj** *see* **tie 2**.

▸**tie together vt sep** *objects, people* attacher ensemble.

▸**tie up** 1 **vi** (*Naut*) accoster.

2 **vt sep** a (*bind*) *parcel* ficeler; *prisoner* attacher, ligoter; (*tether*) *boat, horse* attacher (*to* à). (*fig*) **there are a lot of loose ends to tie up** il y a beaucoup de points de détail à régler avant d'en avoir fini; (*fig: muddled*) **to get (o.s.) all tied up*** s'embrouiller.

b *capital, money* immobiliser.

c (*fig: conclude*) *business deal etc* conclure. **it's all tied up now** tout est réglé maintenant, c'est une chose réglée maintenant, nous avons (*or* il a *etc*) tout réglé.

d (**: pass only: occupied*) **he is tied up all tomorrow** il est pris *or* occupé toute la journée de demain; **he is tied up with the manager** il est occupé avec le directeur; **we are tied up for months to come** nous avons un emploi du temps très chargé pour les mois qui viennent; **he's rather tied up with a girl in Dover** une jeune fille de Douvres l'accapare en ce moment.

e (*pass only: linked*) **this company is tied up with an American firm** cette compagnie a des liens avec *or* est liée à une firme américaine; **his illness is tied up* with the fact that his wife has left him** sa maladie est liée au fait que sa femme l'a quitté.

f (*US: obstruct, hinder*) *traffic* obstruer, entraver; *production, sales* arrêter momentanément; *project, programme* entraver. **to get tied up** *[traffic]* se bloquer; *[production, sales]* s'arrêter; *[project, programme]* être suspendu.

3 **tie-up n** *see* **tie 2**.

tied [taɪd] **adj** a (*Sport: equal*) **to be ~** être à égalité. b (*Mus*) *note* lié. c (*Brit*) **~ cottage** logement *m* de fonction (*d'ouvrier agricole etc*); *[pub]* **it's a ~ house** ils ne vendent qu'une marque de bière. d (*Fin*) *loan* conditionnel. e (*busy*) pris. **we are very ~ in the evenings** nous sommes rarement libres le soir; **she is very ~ by the children** elle est très prise par les enfants; **he isn't ~ at all** il n'a aucune attache, rien ne le retient; *see also* **tie up** *etc*.

tier [tɪəʳ] 1 **n** (*in stadium, amphitheatre*) gradin *m*; (*level*) niveau *m*; (*part of cake*) étage *m*. (*Theat*) **grand ~** balcon *m*; (*Theat*) **upper ~** seconde galerie; **to arrange in ~s** (*gen*) étager, disposer par étages; *seating* disposer en gradins; **to rise in ~s** s'étager; **a three-~ system** un système à trois niveaux. 2 **vt** *seats etc* disposer en gradins. **~ed seating** places assises en gradins *or* en amphithéâtre; **three-~ed cake** ≃ pièce montée à trois étages.

Tierra del Fuego [tɪ,erədel'fweɪgəʊ] **n** Terre de Feu *f*.

tiff [tɪf] **n** prise *f* de bec*.

tiffin† ['tɪfɪn] **n** (*Brit: mot anglo-indien*) repas *m* de midi.

tig [tɪg] n = tag 1c.

tiger ['taɪgəʳ] 1 n tigre *m* (*also fig*). **she fought like a ~** elle s'est battue comme une tigresse; (*fig*) **he has a ~ by the tail** il a déclenché quelque chose dont il n'est plus maître. 2 comp ▸**tiger lily** lis tigré ▸**tiger moth** écaille *f* (*papillon*) ▸**tiger's eye (stone)** œil *m* de tigre.

tight [taɪt] 1 adj a (*not loose*) *rope* raide, tendu; *skirt, trousers* serré, étroit; (*too ~*) étriqué, (trop) juste, trop étroit; *belt, shoes* qui serre, trop juste; *tap, screw, lid, drawer* dur; *bend in road* raide; *knot, weave, knitting* serré; *restrictions, control* sévère, strict, rigoureux; *programme, schedule* serré, minuté, très chargé; *competition* serré. **as ~ as a drum** tendu comme un tambour; **my shoes are (too) ~** mes chaussures me serrent; **it should be fairly ~ over the hips** cela devrait être relativement ajusté sur les hanches; **it's a ~ fit** c'est juste; **to keep (a) ~ hold** *or* **a ~ grasp on sth** (*lit*) bien tenir qch, serrer qch; (*fig*) avoir *or* tenir qch en main; **it will be ~ but I think we'll make it in time** ce sera juste mais je crois que nous y arriverons; (*fig*) **to be in a ~ corner** *or* **situation** se trouver dans une situation difficile; *see* **skin, spot, squeeze** *etc*.

b (*not leaky*) *boat, container, joint* étanche. **air~** hermétique, étanche (à l'air); *see* **water** *etc*.

c *credit* serré, resserré; *business* difficile; *budget* juste, serré; *transaction, deal* qui laisse peu de marge. **money is very ~** (*Econ*) l'argent est rare; (*at home*) les finances sont très justes *or* serrées; *[person]* **to be ~ (with one's money)** être avare *or* radin*, ne pas les lâcher facilement*.

d (*: *drunk*) soûl*, gris*, rond*. **to get ~** prendre une cuite*, se cuiter‡.

e (*: *Mus*) *band* bien synchro* *or* synchronisé.

2 adv *grasp* bien, solidement; *close* bien, hermétiquement; *squeeze* très fort; *knit* serré. **screw the nut up ~** serrez l'écrou à bloc; **don't fasten** *or* **tie it too ~** ne le serrez pas trop (fort); **to pack sth ~** bien emballer *or* empaqueter qch; *see* **hold, sit, sleep** *etc*.

3 comp ▸**tight end** (*US Ftbl*) ailier *m* ▸**tight-fisted** avare, radin*, près de son argent* ▸**tight-fitting** *garment* ajusté, collant; *lid, stopper* qui ferme bien ▸**tight-knit** (*fig*) *family* uni; *programme, schedule* serré ▸**tight-lipped: to maintain a tight-lipped silence, to be very tight-lipped** ne pas desserrer les lèvres *or* les dents (*about sth* au sujet de qch); (*from anger etc*) **he stood there tight-lipped** il se tenait là avec un air pincé; **in tight-lipped disapproval** d'un air de réprobation ▸**tightrope** corde *f* raide, fil *m*; (*fig*) **to be on** *or* **walking a tightrope** marcher sur une corde raide; **tightrope walker** funambule *mf* ▸**tightwad**‡ (*US*) radin(e)* *m(f)*.

4 npl: **~s** collant(s) *m(pl)*.

tighten ['taɪtn] 1 vt (*often ~ up*) *rope* tendre; *coat, skirt, trousers* ajuster, rétrécir; *screw, wheel, grasp, embrace* resserrer; *legislation, restrictions, regulations, control* renforcer; (*Econ*) *credit* resserrer. (*lit, fig*) **to ~ one's belt** se serrer la ceinture; (*fig: increase pressure*) **to ~ the screws on** augmenter la pression sur. 2 vi (*also ~ up*) *[rope]* se tendre, se raidir; *[screw, wheel]* se resserrer; *[restrictions, regulations]* être renforcé.

▸**tighten up** 1 vi a = **tighten 2**. b (*fig*) **to tighten up on security/immigration** devenir plus strict *or* sévère en matière de sécurité/d'immigration; **the police are tightening up on shoplifters** la police renforce la lutte contre les voleurs à l'étalage. 2 vt sep *see* **tighten 1**.

tightening ['taɪtnɪŋ] n (*see* **tighten**) ajustage *m*; resserrement *m*; renforcement *m*. (*Econ*) **~ of credit** resserrement *m* de crédit.

tightly ['taɪtlɪ] adv = **tight 2**.

tightness ['taɪtnɪs] n *[dress, trousers]* étroitesse *f*; *[screw, lid, drawer]* dureté *f*; *[restrictions, control]* rigueur *f*, sévérité *f*. **he felt a ~ in his chest** il s'est senti la poitrine oppressée.

tigress ['taɪgrɪs] n tigresse *f*.

Tigris ['taɪgrɪs] n Tigre *m*.

tikka ['tiːkə] n: **chicken/lamb ~** poulet *m*/mouton *m* tikka.

tilde ['tɪldə] n tilde *m*.

tile [taɪl] 1 n (*on roof*) tuile *f*; (*on floor, wall, fireplace*) carreau *m*. (*Brit fig*) **to be out on the ~s*, to spend** *or* **have a night on the ~s*** faire la noce* *or* la bombe*; (*fig*) **he's got a ~ loose**‡ il lui manque une case*. 2 vt *roof* couvrir de tuiles; *floor, wall, fireplace* carreler. **~d** *roof* en tuiles; *floor, room etc* carrelé.

tiling ['taɪlɪŋ] n a (*activity, skill*) *[roof]* pose *f* des tuiles; *[floor, wall etc]* carrelage *m*. b (*tiles collectively*) *[roof]* tuiles *fpl*; *[floor, wall]* carrelage *m*, carreaux *mpl*.

till[1] [tɪl] = **until**.

till[2] [tɪl] n caisse *f* (enregistreuse); (*old-fashioned type*) tiroir-caisse *m*; (*takings*) caisse. **pay at the ~** payez à la caisse; (*fig*) **caught with one's hand in the ~** pris sur le fait, pris en flagrant délit.

till[3] [tɪl] vt (*Agr*) labourer.

tillage ['tɪlɪdʒ] n (*act*) labour *m*, labourage *m*; (*land*) labour, guéret *m*.

tiller[1] ['tɪləʳ] n (*Agr*) laboureur *m*.

tiller[2] ['tɪləʳ] n (*Naut*) barre *f* (*du gouvernail*).

tilt [tɪlt] 1 n a (*tip, slope*) inclinaison *f*. **it has a ~ to it, it's on a** *or* **the ~** c'est incliné, ça penche. b (*Hist*) (*contest*) joute *f*; (*thrust*) coup *m* de lance. (*fig*) **to have a ~ at** décocher des pointes à; **(at) full ~** à toute vitesse, à fond de train. 2 comp ▸**tilt-top table** table *f* rabattable (*toutes inclinaisons*). 3 vt (*often ~ over*) *object, one's head* pencher, incliner; *backrest* incliner. **to ~ one's hat over one's eyes** rabattre son chapeau sur les yeux; **to ~ one's chair (back)** se balancer sur sa chaise. 4 vi a (*gen*) s'incliner; (*also ~ over*) pencher, être incliné. b (*Hist*) jouter (*at* contre); *see* **windmill**.

tilted ['tɪltɪd] adj penché, incliné.

tilth [tɪlθ] n (*soil*) couche *f* arable; (*tilling*) labourage *m*.

timber ['tɪmbəʳ] 1 n a (*NonC*) (*wood*) bois *m* d'œuvre, bois de construction; (*trees collectively*) arbres *mpl*, bois. (*excl*) **~!** attention (à l'arbre qui tombe)!, gare!; **land under ~** futaie *f*, terre boisée (*pour l'abattage*). b (*beam*) madrier *m*, poutre *f*; (*Naut*) membrure *f*. 2 comp *fence etc* en bois ▸**timberland** (*NonC*) région boisée (*pour l'abattage*) ▸**timber line** ligne supérieure de la forêt ▸**timber merchant** (*Brit*) marchand *m* de bois, négociant *m* en bois ▸**timber wolf** loup *m* (gris) ▸**timberyard** (*Brit*) chantier *m* de bois. 3 vt *tunnel etc* boiser. **~ed** *house* en bois; *land, hillside* boisé; *see* **half**.

timbering ['tɪmbərɪŋ] n (*NonC*) boisage *m*.

timbre ['tæ̃mbrə, 'tɪmbəʳ] n (*gen, also Phon*) timbre *m*.

timbrel ['tɪmbrəl] n tambourin *m*.

Timbuktu [ˌtɪmbʌk'tuː] n Tombouctou *m* (*also fig*).

time [taɪm] 1 n a (*NonC: gen*) temps *m*. **~ and space** le temps et l'espace; **~ flies** le temps passe vite; **only ~ will tell** ≃ qui vivra verra; **~ will show if ...** le temps dira si ..., on saura avec le temps si ...; **for all ~** pour toujours; **in ~, with ~, in process of ~, in the course of ~, as ~ goes (***or* **went) by** avec le temps, à la longue; **it takes ~ for it to change** (*a few minutes*) ça ne change pas tout de suite; (*longer*) ça ne change pas du jour au lendemain; **it takes ~ to change people's ideas** changer les idées des gens demande *or* prend du temps; **at this point in ~** à l'heure qu'il est, en ce moment; **from ~ out of mind** de temps immémorial, de toute éternité; (*Prov*) **~ and tide wait for no man** les événements n'attendent personne; (*Prov*) **~ is money** le temps c'est de l'argent; (*liter*) **to take T~ by the forelock** saisir l'occasion aux cheveux; *see* **immemorial, test, unity** *etc*.

b (*NonC: more specifically*) temps *m*. **I've no ~ for that sort of thing** (*lit*) je n'ai pas le temps de faire ce genre de chose; (*fig*) ce genre de chose m'agace; **I've no ~ for people like him** les gens comme lui m'énervent, je ne supporte pas les gens comme lui; **I've got a lot of ~* for him** je le trouve très bien; **it didn't leave him much ~ for sleep** ça ne lui a guère laissé le temps de dormir; **I've enough ~** *or* **I have the ~ to go there** j'ai le temps d'y aller; **we've got plenty of ~, we've all the ~ in the world** nous avons tout notre temps; **you've got plenty of ~ to wait for me** vous avez bien le temps de m'attendre; **I can't find ~ to do** *or* **for (doing) the garden** je n'arrive pas à trouver le temps de m'occuper du jardin; **there's no ~ to lose** *or* **to be lost** il n'y a pas de temps à perdre; **to make up for lost ~** rattraper le temps perdu; **what a waste of ~!** quelle perte de temps!, que de temps perdu!; **in no ~ at all, in less than no ~** en un rien de temps, en moins de deux*; **he had ~ on his hands** *or* **~ to spare** il avait du temps de reste *or* du temps devant lui; **~ hung heavy (on his hands)** le temps lui durait *or* pesait, il trouvait le temps long; **I spent a lot of ~ preparing this, it took me a lot of ~ to prepare this** il m'a fallu pas mal de temps pour le préparer, le préparer m'a pris pas mal de temps; **he spent all/half his ~ reading** il a passé tout son temps/la moitié de son temps à lire; **I had to stand for part** *or* **some of the ~** j'ai dû rester debout (pendant) une partie du temps; **part** *or* **some of the ~ he looks cheerful but most of the ~ he doesn't** parfois *or* quelquefois *or* par moments il a l'air gai, mais la plupart du temps il a l'air triste; **he spends the best part of his ~ in London** il passe la meilleure partie *or* la plus grande partie de son temps à Londres, il passe le plus clair de son temps à Londres; **half the ~* she's drunk** la moitié du temps elle est ivre; **the letter was in my pocket all the ~** la lettre était dans ma poche (pendant) tout ce temps-là; **all the ~ he knew who had done it** il savait dès le début qui l'avait fait; **I can't be impartial all (of) the ~** je ne peux pas être tout le temps impartial; **take your ~** prenez votre temps; **take your ~ over it!** mettez-y le temps qu'il faudra!; (*fig*) **it took me all my ~ to finish it** j'ai eu du mal à le finir; **to take ~ out to do sth** (*gen*) trouver le temps de faire qch; (*during career*) se mettre en congé *or* en disponibilité pour faire qch; (*during studies*) interrompre ses études pour faire qch; **your ~ is up** (*in exam, prison visit etc*) c'est l'heure; (*Telec*) votre temps de communication est écoulé; **my ~ is my own** mon temps m'appartient, je suis maître de mon temps; **free ~, ~ off** temps libre; **he'll tell you in his own good ~** il vous le dira quand bon lui semblera; **all in good ~!** chaque chose en son temps!; **let me know in good ~** prévenez-moi à temps; **he arrived in good ~ for the start of the match** il est arrivé en avance pour le début du match; **a race against ~** une course contre la montre; **he was working against ~ to finish it** il travaillait d'arrache-pied pour le terminer à temps; **for the ~ being** pour le moment; *see* **bide, make 1f, play, spare, waste** *etc*.

c (*NonC: period, length of ~*) **for a ~** pendant un (certain) temps; **a long ~** longtemps; **a long ~ ago** il y a longtemps; **a short ~** peu de temps; **a short ~ later** peu (de temps) après; **for a short ~ we thought that ...** nous avons (pendant) un moment pensé que ...; **he hasn't been seen for a long ~** on ne l'a pas vu depuis longtemps, ça fait longtemps qu'on ne l'a pas vu; **it will be a long ~ before I see her again** je ne la reverrai pas de longtemps; **long ~ no see!*** tiens! un revenant!*; **it will be a long ~ before I do that again** je ne recommencerai pas de si tôt; **it's a long ~ since he left** il y a bien longtemps qu'il est parti; **you took a long ~ to get here** *or* **getting here** tu as mis longtemps pour *or* à venir; **what a (long) ~ you've been!** vous y avez mis le temps!, il vous en a fallu du temps!; **it takes a long ~ for that drug to act** ce médicament met du temps à agir; **it took a very long ~ for that to happen** ceci n'est arrivé que très longtemps après, il a fallu attendre longtemps pour que cela arrive (*subj*); **in a short ~ they were all gone** quelques moments plus tard ils avaient tous disparu; **I have been learning French for a long ~** j'apprends le français depuis longtemps; **he had to stay in bed for a long ~** il a dû rester longtemps au lit; **for a long ~ (to come) he will wonder ...** il se demandera (pendant) longtemps ...; **for a long ~ (past) he has been unable to work** il a longtemps été hors d'état de travailler (*see also* **long**); **I waited for some ~** j'ai attendu assez longtemps *or* pas mal de temps*; **I waited for some considerable ~** j'ai attendu un temps considérable; **after some little ~** après un certain temps; **some ~ ago** il y a quelque temps *or* un certain temps; **it won't be ready for some ~ (yet)** ce ne sera pas prêt avant un certain temps *or* avant pas mal de temps*; **some ~ before the war** quelque temps avant la guerre; **some ~ next year/in 1996** dans le courant de l'année prochaine/de l'année 1996; **in no ~ at all, in next to no ~, in less than no ~** en un rien de temps, en moins de deux*; **he did it in half the ~ it took you** il l'a fait deux fois plus vite *or* en deux fois moins de temps que vous; **it is only a matter** *or* **question of ~ (before the bridge collapses)** ce n'est qu'une question de temps (avant que le pont ne s'écroule); **he is coming in 2 weeks' ~** il vient dans 2 semaines; (*frm*) **within the agreed ~** dans les délais convenus; (*US*) **to buy sth on ~** acheter qch à tempérament; **what ~ did he do it in?** il a mis combien de temps?; **the winner's ~ was 12 seconds** le temps du gagnant était 12 secondes; **cooking ~ 25 minutes** temps de cuisson 25 minutes; *[prisoner]* **to do ~*** faire de la taule‡; (*US: hurry*) **to make ~** se dépêcher; (*US*) **he's making ~ with her‡** il essaie de la tomber‡; *see* **extra, record, serve** *etc.*

d (*NonC: period worked*) **to be on** *or* **to work full ~** travailler à plein temps *or* à temps plein (*see also* **full 4**); **to be on ~ and a half** faire des heures supplémentaires payées une fois et demie le tarif normal *or* à 150 %; **Sunday working is paid at double ~** les heures du dimanche sont payées *or* comptées double; **in the firm's ~, in company ~** pendant les heures de service; **in** *or* (*US*) **on one's own ~** après les heures de service; *see* **half, part-time, short** *etc.*

e (*epoch, era: often pl*) époque *f.* **in medieval ~s** à l'époque médiévale; **in Gladstone's ~** du temps de Gladstone; **in olden ~s, in ~s past, in former ~s** dans le temps, jadis; **~ was when one could ...** il fut un temps où l'on pouvait ...; **in my ~ it was all different** de mon temps c'était complètement différent; **I've seen some strange things in my ~** j'ai vu des choses étranges dans ma vie; **that was before my ~** (*before I was born*) je n'étais pas encore né, c'était avant ma naissance; (*before I came here*) je n'étais pas encore là; **in ~(s) of peace** en temps de paix; **peace in our ~** la paix de notre vivant; **it will last our ~** cela durera aussi longtemps que nous; (*fig*) **he is ahead of** *or* **in advance of** *or* **before his ~, he was born before his ~** il est en avance sur son époque; **to keep up with** *or* **move with the ~s** être de son époque, vivre avec son époque, être à la page; **to be behind the ~s** être vieux jeu* *inv*; **the ~s we live in** l'époque où nous vivons; **at the best of ~s** (déjà) quand tout va bien; **~s are hard** les temps sont durs; **those were tough ~s** la vie n'était pas facile de ce temps-là; **they lived through some terrible ~s in the war** ils ont connu des moments terribles *or* ils en ont vu de dures* pendant la guerre; **to have a poor** *or* **rough** *or* **bad** *or* **thin** *or* **tough* ~ (of it)** en voir de dures*; **I gave him a bad ~ of it** je lui ai fait passer un mauvais quart d'heure; (*longer*) je lui ai fait *or* mené la vie dure; **what great ~s we've had!** c'était la belle vie! *or* le bon temps!; **to have a good ~ (of it)** bien s'amuser; **it was a tense ~ for all of us** cela a été une période très tendue pour nous tous; *see* **big, injury, old 1e, sign.**

f (*by clock*) heure *f.* **what is the ~?, what ~ is it?** quelle heure est-il?; **what ~ do you make it?, what do you make the ~?** quelle heure avez-vous?; **have you got the right ~?** est-ce que vous avez l'heure exacte *or* juste?; **the ~ is 4.30** il est 4 heures et demie; **what ~ is he arriving at?** à quelle heure est-ce qu'il arrive?; **he looked at the ~** il a regardé l'heure; **that watch keeps good ~** cette montre est toujours à l'heure; **there's a ~ and a place for everything** il y a un temps pour tout; (*fig*) **to pass the ~ of day** bavarder un peu, échanger quelques mots (*with sb* avec qn); **I wouldn't give him the ~ of day** je ne m'arrêterais même pas pour lui dire bonjour; **at this ~ of (the) night** à cette heure de la nuit; **at any ~ of the day or night** à n'importe quelle heure du jour ou de la nuit; **at any ~ during school hours** n'importe quand pendant les heures d'ouverture de l'école; **open at all ~s** ouvert à toute heure; (*Brit: in pub*) **~ gentlemen please!** on ferme!; (*US*) **it's midnight by Eastern ~** il est minuit, heure de la côte est; **it was 6 o'clock Paris ~** il était 6 heures, heure de Paris; **ahead of ~** en avance; **behind ~** en retard; **just in ~** juste à temps (*for sth* pour qch, *to do* pour faire); **on ~** à l'heure; **the trains are on ~** *or* **up to ~, the trains are running to ~** les trains sont à l'heure; **it's near my train ~** c'est presque l'heure de mon train; **it's ~ for tea, it's tea~** c'est l'heure du thé; **it's ~ to go** c'est l'heure de partir, il est temps de partir; **it's ~ I was going, it's ~ for me to go** il est temps que je m'en aille; **it's about ~ he was here** il serait temps *or* il commence à être temps qu'il arrive (*subj*); **it's ~ somebody taught him a lesson** il est grand temps que quelqu'un lui donne (*subj*) une bonne leçon; **not before ~!, (and) about ~ too!** et ce n'est pas trop tôt!; *see* **Greenwich, high, tell** *etc.*

g (*moment, point of ~*) moment *m.* **at the** *or* **that ~** à ce moment-là; **at this ~** en ce moment; **at the present ~** en ce moment, actuellement; **at this particular ~** à ce moment précis; **at (any) one ~** à un moment donné; **sometimes ... at other ~s** quelquefois ... d'autres fois; **at all ~s** à tous moments; **I have at no ~ said that** je n'ai jamais dit cela, à aucun moment je n'ai dit cela; **at ~s** par moments; **I could hit him at ~s, there are ~s when I could hit him** il y a des moments où je pourrais le gifler; **at his ~ of life** à son âge; **he came at a very inconvenient ~** il est arrivé à un moment tout à fait inopportun, il a mal choisi son moment pour arriver; **he may come (at) any ~** il peut arriver d'un moment à l'autre; **come (at) any ~** venez n'importe quand, venez quand vous voudrez; **it may happen any ~ now** cela peut arriver d'un moment à l'autre; (*US*) **any~ soon*** d'un jour *or* d'un moment à l'autre; **at this ~ of year** à cette époque de l'année, à cette saison; **to do two things at the same ~** faire deux choses à la fois; **they arrived at the same ~ as we did** ils sont arrivés en même temps que nous; **but at the same ~, you must admit that ...** mais pourtant *or* cependant, il faut avouer que ...; **by the ~ I had finished** le temps que je termine (*subj*), quand j'eus *or* j'ai eu (enfin) terminé; **by this** *or* **that ~ they had drunk all the wine** à ce moment-là ils avaient déjà bu tout le vin; **you must be cold by this ~** vous devez avoir froid maintenant; **by this ~ next year** dans un an; **this ~ tomorrow** demain à cette heure-ci; **this ~ last year** l'année dernière à cette époque-ci; **this ~ last week** il y a exactement huit jours; **(in) between ~s** entre-temps; **from ~ to ~** de temps en temps; **from that ~** *or* **this ~ on he was ...** à partir de ce moment il fut ...; **from this ~ on I shall do what you tell me** désormais *or* dorénavant je ferai ce que tu me diras; **until such ~ as** jusqu'à ce que + *subj*, en attendant que + *subj*; **this is no ~ for quarrelling** ce n'est pas le moment de se disputer; **to choose one's ~** choisir son moment; **now's your ~ to tell him** c'est maintenant que vous devriez (le) lui dire; **now's the ~ to do it** c'est maintenant le moment de le faire; **at Christmas ~** à (la) Noël; **to die before one's ~** mourir avant l'âge; **his ~ is drawing near** *or* **approaching** son heure *or* sa fin est proche; **his ~ has come** son heure est venue *or* est arrivée *or* a sonné; **when the ~ comes** quand le moment viendra; **when the ~ is right** quand ce sera le bon moment; **the ~ has come to do ...** il est temps de faire ...; **the ~ has come for us to leave** il est temps que nous partions (*subj*); **it's ~ to get up** c'est l'heure de nous (*or* vous *etc*) lever; *see* **given, proper** *etc.*

h (*occasion*) fois *f.* **this ~** cette fois; **(the) next ~ you come** la prochaine fois que vous viendrez; **every** *or* **each ~** chaque fois; **give me beer every ~!*** rien ne vaut une bonne bière!, donnez-moi de la bière à tous les coups!*; **several ~s** plusieurs fois; **at other ~s** d'autres fois; **at various ~s in the past** plusieurs fois déjà; **at odd ~s I've wondered ...** il m'est arrivé parfois de me demander ...; **many a ~, many ~s** maintes fois, bien des fois, très souvent; **~ after ~, ~s without number, ~ and (~) again** maintes et maintes fois, à plusieurs reprises; **hundreds of ~s*** vingt *or* trente-six *or* cent fois; **(the) last ~** la dernière fois; **there's always a first ~** il y a un début à tout; **the previous ~, the ~ before** la fois d'avant, la dernière fois; **come back some other ~** revenez une autre fois; **some ~ or other I'll do it** un jour ou l'autre je le ferai; **I remember the ~ when he told me about it** je me rappelle le jour où il me l'a dit; **the ~s I've told him that!*** je le lui ai dit je ne sais combien de fois!; **the ~s I've sat here!*** toutes les fois que je me suis assis ici!; **one at a ~** un(e) par un(e), un(e) à un(e), un(e) seul(e) à la fois; **for weeks at a ~** pendant des semaines entières; **one can use the machine for 10 francs a ~** ça coûte 10 F chaque fois que l'on se sert de la machine.

i (*multiplying*) fois *f.* **2 ~s 3 is 6** 2 fois 3 (font) 6; **10 ~s as big as, 10 ~s the size of** 10 fois plus grand que; **it's worth 10 ~s as much** ça vaut 10 fois plus; *see* **times.**

j (*Mus etc*) mesure *f.* **in ~** en mesure (*to, with* avec); **to be out of ~** ne pas être en mesure (*with* avec); **three-four ~** mesure à trois temps; **to keep ~** rester en mesure; *see* **beat, mark[1].**

2 vt a (*choose ~ of*) *invasion, visit* fixer (*for* à), prévoir (*for* pour); *remark, interruption* choisir *or* calculer le moment de. **it was ~d to begin at ...** le commencement était fixé *or* prévu pour ...; **you ~d that perfectly!** c'est tombé à point nommé!, vous ne pouviez pas mieux calculer *or* choisir votre moment!; **well-~d** *remark, entrance* tout à fait opportun, tombé à point nommé; *blow* bien calculé.

b (*count ~ of*) *race, runner, worker etc* chronométrer; *programme, ceremony, piece of work* minuter. **to ~ sb over 1,000 metres** chronométrer (le temps de) qn sur 1.000 mètres; **~ how long it takes you** notez le temps qu'il vous faut pour le faire; **to ~ an egg** minuter la cuisson d'un œuf.

3 comp ▸time and motion study (*Ind*) étude *f* des cadences **▸time bomb** bombe *f* à retardement **▸time capsule** capsule *f* témoin (*devant servir de document historique*) **▸time card** (*Ind*) feuille *f or* fiche *f* de présence *or* de pointage ▸**time clock** (*Ind etc*) (*machine itself*) enregistreur *m* de temps; **they were standing near the time clock** ils se tenaient près du pointage ▸**time-consuming** qui prend du temps ▸**time deposit** (*US Fin*) dépôt *m* à terme ▸**time discount** (*US Comm*) remise *f* pour paiement anticipé ▸**time draft** (*US Fin*) traite *f* à délai de date ▸**time exposure** (*Phot*) pose *f* ▸**time-filler** manière *f* de passer le temps *or* de s'occuper ▸**time frame** délais *mpl* ▸**time fuse** détonateur *m or* fusée *f* à retard *or* à retardement ▸**time-honoured** consacré (par l'usage) ▸**timekeeper** (*watch*) montre *f*; (*stopwatch*) chronomètre *m*; (*Sport: official*) chronométreur *m* (officiel); *[person]* **to be a good timekeeper** être toujours à l'heure ▸**timekeeping** (*Sport*) chronométrage *m*; (*at work*) **I'm trying to improve my timekeeping** j'essaie d'être plus ponctuel ▸**time-lag** (*between events etc*) décalage *m*, retard *m*; (*between countries*) décalage horaire ▸**time-lapse photography** accéléré *m* ▸**time limit** (*period*) délai *m* fixé; (*Jur*) délai de forclusion; (*deadline*) date *f* limite; **to put** *or* **set a time limit on sth** fixer un délai *or* une limite de temps pour qch; **within a certain time limit** dans un certain délai; **without a time limit** sans limitation de temps ▸**time loan** (*US Fin*) emprunt *m* à terme ▸**time lock** fermeture *f* à mouvement d'horlogerie ▸**time machine** (*Science Fiction*) machine *f* à remonter le temps ▸**timeout** (*esp US*) temps *m* mort; (*Chess*) temps de repos ▸**timepiece** (*gen*) mécanisme *m* d'horlogerie; (*watch*) montre *f*; (*clock*) horloge *f* ▸**time-saver: it is a great time-saver** ça fait gagner beaucoup de temps ▸**time-saving adj** qui fait gagner du temps ◊ **n** économie *f or* gain *m* de temps ▸**timescale** durée *f*, période *f*; **our timescale for this project is 10 to 15 years** nous nous situons dans une perspective de 10 à 15 ans ▸**timeserver** (*pej*) opportuniste *mf* ▸**time-serving** (*pej*) **adj** opportuniste ◊ **n** opportunisme *m* ▸**time share vt** (*Comput*) utiliser *or* exploiter en temps partagé; *holiday home* avoir en multipropriété ◊ **n** maison *f* (*or* appartement *m*) en multipropriété ▸**time-sharing** (*Comput*) (exploitation *f or* travail *m* en) temps partagé; (*holiday home*) multipropriété *f* ▸**time sheet** (*Ind etc*) feuille *f* de présence ▸**time signal** (*Rad*) signal *m* horaire ▸**time signature** (*Mus*) indication *f* de la mesure ▸**time slice** (*Comput*) tranche *f* de temps ▸**time span** période *f* de temps ▸**time study** = **time and motion study** ▸**time switch** *[electrical apparatus]* minuteur *m*; (*for lighting*) minuterie *f* ▸**timetable n** (*Rail etc*) (indicateur *m*) horaire *m*; (*Scol*) emploi *m* du temps; (*Ftbl: also* **fixtures timetable**) calendrier *m* des rencontres ◊ **vt** *visit, course* établir un emploi du temps pour ▸**time travel** (*Science Fiction*) voyage *m* dans le temps ▸**time trial** (*Motor Racing*) course *f* contre la montre ▸**time-warp** distorsion *f* du temps; **it's like going into** *or* **living in a time-warp** on a l'impression d'avoir fait un bond en arrière (*or* en avant) dans le temps *or* d'avoir fait un bond dans le passé (*or* le futur) ▸**time-wasting adj** qui fait perdre du temps ◊ **n** perte *f* de temps ▸**timeworn** *stones etc* usé par le temps; *idea* rebattu ▸**time zone** fuseau *m* horaire.

timeless [ˈtaɪmlɪs] **adj** éternel.

timeliness [ˈtaɪmlɪnɪs] **n** (*NonC*) à-propos *m*, opportunité *f*.

timely [ˈtaɪmlɪ] **adj** à propos, opportun.

timer [ˈtaɪməʳ] **n** (*Culin etc*) compte-minutes *m inv*; (*with sand in it*) sablier *m*; (*on machine, electrical device etc*) minuteur *m*; (*Aut*) distributeur *m* d'allumage; *see* **old**.

times‡ [taɪmz] **vt** (*multiply*) multiplier.

timid [ˈtɪmɪd] **adj** (*shy*) timide; (*unadventurous*) timoré, craintif; (*cowardly*) peureux.

timidity [tɪˈmɪdɪtɪ] **n** (*NonC: see* **timid**) timidité *f*; caractère timoré *or* craintif; caractère peureux.

timidly [ˈtɪmɪdlɪ] **adv** (*see* **timid**) timidement; craintivement; peureusement.

timidness [ˈtɪmɪdnɪs] **n** = **timidity**.

timing [ˈtaɪmɪŋ] 1 **n** a *[musician etc]* sens *m* du rythme. **a good comedian depends on his (sense of)** ~ un bon comédien doit minuter très précisément son débit; **the actors' ~ was excellent throughout the play** le minutage des acteurs était excellent tout au long de la pièce; ~ **is very important in formation flying** la synchronisation est capitale dans les vols en formation; **the ~ of the demonstration** (*date/hour*) la date/l'heure de cette manifestation; (*programme of various stages*) le minutage de cette manifestation; **he arrived just when the meal was ready: I had to admire his** ~ il est arrivé au moment précis où le repas était prêt, il ne pouvait pas mieux *or* je dois dire qu'il a su choisir son moment.

b (*Aut*) réglage *m* de l'allumage. (*Aut*) **to set the** ~ régler l'allumage.

c (*Ind, Sport*) chronométrage *m*.

2 **comp** ▸**timing device, timing mechanism** *[bomb etc]* mouvement *m* d'horlogerie; *[electrical apparatus]* minuteur *m*.

Timor [ˈtiːmɔːʳ, ˈtaɪmɔːʳ] **n** Timor. **in** ~ à Timor.

timorous [ˈtɪmərəs] **adj** timoré, craintif.

timorously [ˈtɪmərəslɪ] **adv** craintivement.

Timothy [ˈtɪməθɪ] **n** Timothée *m*.

timothy [ˈtɪməθɪ] **n** (*Bot*) fléole *f* des prés.

timpani [ˈtɪmpənɪ] **npl** timbales *fpl*.

timpanist [ˈtɪmpənɪst] **n** timbalier *m*.

tin [tɪn] 1 **n** a (*NonC*) étain *m*; (*~plate*) fer-blanc *m*.

b (*esp Brit: can*) boîte *f* (*en fer-blanc*). ~ **of salmon** boîte de saumon.

c (*for storage*) boîte *f* (de fer). **cake** ~ boîte à gâteaux.

d (*Brit Culin*) (*mould: for cakes etc*) moule *m*; (*dish: for meat etc*) plat *m*. **cake** ~ moule à gâteau; **meat** *or* **roasting** ~ plat à rôtir.

2 **vt** a (*put in ~s*) *food etc* mettre en boîte(s) *or* en conserve; *see also* **tinned**.

b (*coat with ~*) étamer.

3 **comp** (*made of ~*) en étain, d'étain; (*made of ~plate*) en *or* de fer-blanc ▸**tin can** boîte *f* (en fer-blanc) ▸**tin ear***: (*US*) (*Mus*) **he has a tin ear** il n'a pas d'oreille; (*fig*) **to develop a tin ear** faire la sourde oreille (*for* à) ▸**tinfoil** (*NonC*) papier *m* d'étain, papier (d')aluminium ▸**tin god**: (*fig*) **(little) tin god** idole *f* de pacotille ▸**tin hat** casque *m* ▸**tin lizzie*** (*car*) (*model T Ford*) Ford *f* Lizzie; (*old banger*) vieille bagnole* *f* ▸**tin mine** mine *f* d'étain ▸**tin opener** (*Brit*) ouvre-boîte(s) *m* ▸**Tin Pan Alley** (*Mus, fig*) l'industrie *f* de la musique populaire ▸**tinplate** (*NonC*) fer-blanc *m* ▸**tinpot*** *car, bike* qui ne vaut pas grand-chose, en fer-blanc; *dictator, government* de pacotille; **a tinpot little town** un petit bled* ▸**tinsmith** ferblantier *m* ▸**tin soldier** soldat *m* de plomb ▸**tintack** (*Brit*) clou *m* de tapissier, semence *f* ▸**tin whistle** flûteau *m*.

tincture [ˈtɪŋktʃəʳ] 1 **n** (*Pharm*) teinture *f*; (*fig*) nuance *f*, teinte *f*. ~ **of iodine** teinture d'iode. 2 **vt** (*lit, fig*) teinter (*with* de).

tinder [ˈtɪndəʳ] 1 **n** (*NonC*) (*in tinderbox*) amadou *m*; (*small sticks*) petit bois (*NonC*). **as dry as** ~ sec (*f* sèche) comme de l'amadou. 2 **comp** ▸**tinderbox** briquet *m* (à amadou); (*fig: esp Pol*) poudrière *f*.

tine [taɪn] **n** *[fork]* dent *f*, fourchon *m*; *[antler]* andouiller *m*.

ting [tɪŋ] 1 **n** tintement *m*. 2 **vi** tinter. 3 **vt** faire tinter. 4 **comp** ▸**ting-a-ling** *[telephone, doorbell]* dring dring *m*; *[handbell, tiny bells]* drelin drelin *m*.

tinge [tɪndʒ] (*lit, fig*) 1 **n** teinte *f*, nuance *f*. 2 **vt** teinter (*with* de).

tingle [ˈtɪŋgl] 1 **vi** (*prickle*) picoter, fourmiller; (*fig: thrill*) vibrer, frissonner. **her face was tingling** le visage lui picotait *or* lui cuisait; **her cheeks were tingling with cold** le froid lui piquait *or* lui brûlait des joues; **my fingers are tingling** j'ai des picotements *or* des fourmis dans les doigts; **the toothpaste makes my tongue** ~ le dentifrice me pique la langue; **he was tingling with impatience** il brûlait d'impatience. 2 **n** (*sensation*) picotement *m*, fourmillement *m*, sensation cuisante; (*thrill*) frisson *m*. (*sound*) **to have a ~ in one's ears** avoir les oreilles qui tintent.

tingling [ˈtɪŋglɪŋ] 1 **n** (*NonC*) = **tingle 2**. 2 **adj** = **tingly**.

tingly [ˈtɪŋglɪ] **adj** *sensation* cuisant, de picotement, de fourmillement. **my arm is** *or* **feels** ~ j'ai des fourmis *or* des fourmillements dans le bras.

tinker [ˈtɪŋkəʳ] 1 **n** a (*esp Brit: gen*) romanichel(le) *m(f)* (*often pej*); (*specifically mending things*) rétameur *m* (ambulant); (**: child*) polisson(ne) *m(f)*. (*fig*) **it's not worth a ~'s cuss** *or* **~'s damn** ça ne vaut pas tripette* *or* un clou*; **I don't care** *or* **give a ~'s cuss** *or* **~'s damn** je m'en fiche*, je m'en soucie comme de l'an quarante; **~, tailor, soldier, sailor ...** ≈ il m'aime un peu, beaucoup, passionnément ... .

b **to have a ~ (with)*** bricoler*.

2 **vi** a (*also* **~ about**) bricoler, s'occuper à des bricoles. **he was ~ing (about) with the car** il bricolait la voiture; **stop ~ing with that watch!** arrête de tripoter* cette montre!

b (*fig*) **to ~ with** *contract, wording, report etc* (*change*) faire des retouches à, remanier; (*dishonestly*) tripatouiller*.

tinkle [ˈtɪŋkl] 1 **vi** tinter. 2 **vt** faire tinter. 3 **n** a tintement *m*. (*Brit Telec*) **to give sb a ~*** donner *or* passer un coup de fil à qn*. b (**: baby talk: passing water*) pipi* *m*.

tinkling [ˈtɪŋklɪŋ] 1 **n** (*NonC*) tintement *m*. 2 **adj** *bell* qui tinte; *stream* qui clapote, qui gazouille.

tinned [tɪnd] **adj** (*Brit*) *fruit, salmon* en boîte, en conserve. ~ **goods** *or* **food** conserves *fpl*; **it's only** ~ ce n'est qu'une boîte de conserve.

tinnitus [tɪˈnaɪtəs] **n** acouphène *m*.

tinny [ˈtɪnɪ] **adj** *sound* métallique, grêle; *taste* métallique; (** pej*) *car, typewriter etc* de camelote*. ~ **piano** casserole* *f*.

tinsel [ˈtɪnsəl] **n** (*NonC*) guirlandes *fpl* de Noël (argentées), clinquant *m* (*also fig pej*).

tint [tɪnt] 1 **n** teinte *f*, nuance *f*; (*for hair*) shampooing colorant; *see* **flesh**. 2 **vt** teinter (*with* de). **to ~ one's hair** se faire un shampooing colorant.

tintinnabulation [ˈtɪntɪˌnæbjʊˈleɪʃən] **n** tintinnabulement *m*.

Tintoretto [ˌtɪntəˈretəʊ] **n** le Tintoret.

tiny [ˈtaɪnɪ] **adj** tout petit, minuscule. **a ~ little man** un tout petit bonhomme.

tip[1] [tɪp] 1 **n** (*end*) *[stick, pencil, ruler, wing, finger, nose]* bout *m*; *[sword, knife, asparagus]* pointe *f*; *[iceberg, mountain]* pointe, cime *f*; *[ski]* pointe, spatule *f*; *[tongue]* pointe (*also Phon*), bout; (*metal etc end piece*) *[shoe]* bout, pointe; *[cigarette]* bout; (*filter ~*) bout (filtre); *[umbrella, cane]* embout *m*; *[billiard cue]* procédé *m*. **from ~ to toe** de la tête aux pieds; **he stood on the ~s of his toes** il s'est dressé sur la pointe des pieds; **he touched it with the ~ of his toe** il l'a touché du bout de l'orteil; (*fig*) **I've got it on** *or* **it's on the ~ of my tongue** je l'ai sur le bout de la langue; (*fig*) **it's just the ~ of the iceberg** c'est seulement la partie émergée de l'iceberg, ça n'est rien comparé au reste; *see* **fingertip, wing** *etc* .

2 vt (*put ~ on*) mettre un embout à; (*cover ~ of*) recouvrir le bout de. (*Brit*) **~ped cigarettes** cigarettes *fpl* (à bout) filtre *inv*; **~ped with steel, steel-~ped** ferré, qui a un embout de fer.

3 comp ▸**tiptoe:** n **on tiptoe** sur la pointe des pieds ◊ vi **to tiptoe in/out** *etc* entrer/sortir *etc* sur la pointe des pieds ▸**tiptop*** de premier ordre, excellent, de toute première*.

tip² [tɪp] 1 n a (*tap*) tape *f*, petit coup.

b (*gratuity*) pourboire *m*. (*in restaurant*) **the ~ is included** le service est compris.

c (*hint, information*) suggestion *f*, tuyau* *m*; (*advice*) conseil *m*; (*Horse Racing*) tuyau*. **"~s for the handyman"** "les trucs du bricoleur"; **that horse is a hot ~ for the 3.30** ce cheval a une première chance dans la course de 15 h 30; **take my ~** suivez mon conseil.

2 comp ▸**tip-off: to give sb a tip-off** (*gen*) prévenir qn, donner *or* filer un tuyau* à qn; (*Police*) avertir *or* prévenir qn (*par une dénonciation*).

3 vt a (*tap, touch*) toucher (légèrement), effleurer. **to ~ one's hat to sb** mettre *or* porter la main à son chapeau pour saluer qn.

b (*reward*) donner un pourboire à. **he ~ped the waiter 5 francs** il a donné 5 F de pourboire au garçon.

c (*Horse Racing, gen*) pronostiquer. **to ~ the winner** pronostiquer le cheval gagnant; **he ~ped Blue Streak for the 3.30** il a pronostiqué la victoire de Blue Streak dans la course de 15 h 30; **to ~ sb the wink* about sth** filer un tuyau* à qn sur qch; (*fig*) **they are ~ped to win the next election** on pronostique qu'ils vont remporter les prochaines élections; **Paul was ~ped for the job** on avait pronostiqué que Paul serait nommé.

tip³ [tɪp] 1 n (*Brit*) (*for coal*) terril *m*; (*for rubbish*) décharge *f*, dépotoir *m*; (* *fig: untidy place*) (véritable) dépotoir.

2 comp ▸**tip-cart** tombereau *m* ▸**tipcat** (jeu *m* du) bâtonnet *m* ▸**tipstaff** *see* **tipstaff** ▸**tip-up seat** (*in theatre etc*) siège *m* rabattable; (*in taxi, underground etc*) strapontin *m* ▸**tip-up truck** camion *m* à benne (basculante).

3 vt (*incline, tilt*) pencher, incliner; (*overturn*) faire basculer, renverser; (*pour, empty*) *liquid* verser (*into* dans, *out of* de); *load, sand, rubbish* déverser, déposer; *clothes, books etc* déverser (*into* dans, *out of* de). **he ~ped the water out of the bucket** il a vidé le seau; **to ~ sb off his chair** renverser *or* faire basculer qn de sa chaise; **they ~ped him into the water** ils l'ont fait basculer *or* tomber dans l'eau; **the car overturned and they were ~ped into the roadway** la voiture s'est retournée et ils se sont retrouvés sur la chaussée; **to ~ the scales at 90 kg** peser 90 kg; (*fig*) **to ~ the scales** faire pencher la balance (*in sb's favour* en faveur de qn, *against sb* au détriment de qn); (*US*) **to ~ one's hand*** *or* **one's mitt‡** dévoiler son jeu (involontairement).

4 vi a (*incline*) pencher, être incliné; (*overturn*) se renverser, basculer. **"no ~ping", "~ping prohibited"** "défense de déposer des ordures".

b **it's ~ping with rain*** il pleut des cordes, ça dégringole*.

▸**tip back, tip backward(s)** 1 vi *[chair]* se rabattre en arrière; *[person]* se pencher en arrière, basculer (en arrière). 2 vt sep *chair* rabattre *or* faire basculer (en arrière).

▸**tip down*** vti sep (*of rain*) **it's tipping (it) down** il pleut des cordes, ça dégringole*.

▸**tip forward(s)** 1 vi *[chair]* se rabattre en avant; *[person]* se pencher en avant. 2 vt sep *chair* rabattre *or* faire basculer (en avant); *car seat* rabattre (en avant).

▸**tip off** 1 vt sep (*gen*) donner *or* filer un tuyau* à (*about sth* sur qch); *police* prévenir *or* avertir (*par une dénonciation*). 2 **tip-off** n *see* **tip² 2.**

▸**tip out** vt sep *liquid, contents* vider; *load* décharger, déverser. **they tipped him out of his chair/out of bed** ils l'ont fait basculer de sa chaise/du lit.

▸**tip over** 1 vi (*tilt*) pencher; (*overturn*) basculer. 2 vt sep faire basculer.

▸**tip up** 1 vi *[table etc]* (*tilt*) pencher, être incliné; (*overturn*) basculer; *[box, jug]* se renverser; *[seat]* se rabattre; *[truck]* basculer. 2 vt sep (*tilt*) *table etc* incliner; *jug, box* pencher, incliner; *person* faire basculer. 3 **tip-up** adj *see* **tip³ 2.**

tipper ['tɪpəʳ] n a (*vehicle*) camion *m* à benne (basculante); (*back of vehicle*) benne *f* (basculante). b **he is a good** *or* **big ~*** il a le pourboire facile.

tippet ['tɪpɪt] n (*also* **fur ~**) étole *f* (de fourrure).

Tipp-Ex ['tɪpeks] ® 1 n Tipp-Ex *m* ®. 2 vt: **to tippex sth (out)** tippexer qch, effacer qch au Tipp-Ex.

tipple ['tɪpl] 1 vi picoler*. 2 n (*hum*) **gin is his ~** ce qu'il préfère boire c'est du gin.

tippler ['tɪpləʳ] n picoleur* *m*, -euse* *f*.

tipsily ['tɪpsɪlɪ] adv *walk* en titubant légèrement. **... he said tipsily ...** dit-il un peu ivre.

tipstaff ['tɪpstɑːf] n (*Brit Jur*) huissier *m*.

tipster ['tɪpstəʳ] n (*Horse Racing*) pronostiqueur *m*.

tipsy ['tɪpsɪ] adj gai, éméché, parti*. **to get ~** devenir gai; (*Brit*) **~ cake** (sorte *f* de) baba *m* au rhum.

tirade [taɪ'reɪd] n diatribe *f*.

tire¹ ['taɪəʳ] n (*US*) = **tyre.**

tire² ['taɪəʳ] 1 vt fatiguer; (*weary*) fatiguer, lasser. 2 vi se fatiguer; se lasser. **he ~s easily** il se fatigue vite, il est vite fatigué; **he never ~s of telling us how ...** il ne se lasse jamais de nous dire comment ... .

▸**tire out** vt sep épuiser, éreinter, claquer*, crever*. **to be tired out** être épuisé *or* éreinté *or* claqué* *or* crevé*, ne plus tenir debout.

tired ['taɪəd] adj *person* fatigué; (*weary*) las (*f* lasse); *movement, voice* las. **I'm ~ of waiting** j'en ai assez d'attendre, je suis las *or* fatigué d'attendre; **to be ~ of sth/sb** en avoir assez de qch/qn; **to get ~ of** commencer à en avoir assez de, se lasser de; **I'm ~ of telling you** je me tue à vous le répéter; **to be ~ to death* of sth** en avoir par-dessus la tête *or* en avoir vraiment marre de qch; **you make me ~!*** tu me fatigues!, tu me casses les pieds!*; **the same ~ clichés** les mêmes clichés rebattus; (*fig*) **a ~ lettuce leaf** une feuille de laitue défraîchie; (*hum: drunk*) **~ and emotional*** ivre, gris.

tiredly ['taɪədlɪ] adv *reply* d'une voix fatiguée; *walk* d'un pas lourd, avec une démarche fatiguée.

tiredness ['taɪədnɪs] n (*see* **tired**) fatigue *f*; lassitude *f*.

tireless ['taɪəlɪs] adj infatigable, inlassable.

tirelessly ['taɪəlɪslɪ] adv infatigablement, inlassablement.

tiresome ['taɪəsəm] adj (*annoying*) agaçant, ennuyeux; (*boring*) ennuyeux, assommant.

tiresomeness ['taɪəsəmnɪs] n (*see* **tiresome**) caractère agaçant *or* ennuyeux.

tiring ['taɪərɪŋ] adj fatigant.

tiro ['taɪərəʊ] n = **tyro.**

Tirol [tɪ'rəʊl] n = **Tyrol.**

tisane [tɪ'zæn] n tisane *f*.

tissue ['tɪʃuː] 1 n (*cloth*) tissu *m*, étoffe *f*; (*Anat, Bio*) tissu; (*paper handkerchief*) mouchoir *m* en papier, kleenex *m* ®; (*toilet paper*) papier *m* hygiénique; (*fig: web, mesh*) tissu, enchevêtrement *m*. **a ~ of lies** un tissu de mensonges. 2 comp ▸**tissue culture** culture *f* de tissus ▸**tissue paper** (*NonC*) papier *m* de soie.

tit¹ [tɪt] n (*Orn*) mésange *f*; *see* **blue** *etc.*

tit² [tɪt] n: **~ for tat!** un prêté pour un rendu!; **I'll give him ~ for tat** je lui rendrai la pareille, je lui revaudrai ça; **~-for-tat killings/reprisals** meurtres *mpl* en riposte *or* en représailles/représailles *fpl* en riposte.

tit³*‡ [tɪt] n a (*breast*) nichon‡ *m*, néné* *m*. **to get on sb's ~s** taper sur le système à qn. b (*idiot*) abruti(e)‡ *m(f)*, con(ne)‡ *m(f)*.

Titan ['taɪtən] n (*also fig:* **t~**) Titan *m*.

titanic [taɪ'tænɪk] adj a titanesque. b (*Chem*) au titane.

titanium [tɪ'teɪnɪəm] n titane *m*.

titbit ['tɪtbɪt] n (*esp Brit*) *[food]* friandise *f*, bon morceau; *[gossip]* potin *m*; (*in newspaper*) entrefilet croustillant. (*snack with drinks*) **~s** amuse-gueule *mpl*; (*in telling news etc*) **I've saved the ~ for the end** j'ai gardé le détail le plus croustillant pour la fin.

titchy‡ ['tɪtʃɪ] adj = **tichy.**

titfer‡ ['tɪtfəʳ] n (*Brit: hat*) galurin *m*.

tithe [taɪð] n dîme *f*.

Titian ['tɪʃən] 1 n Titien *m*. 2 adj: **t~** blond vénitien *inv*.

titillate ['tɪtɪleɪt] vt titiller.

titillation [ˌtɪtɪ'leɪʃən] n titillation *f*.

titivate ['tɪtɪveɪt] 1 vi se pomponner, se bichonner. 2 vt bichonner, pomponner.

title ['taɪtl] 1 n a *[person]* titre *m*. **what ~ should I give him?** comment dois-je l'appeler?; **I don't know his exact ~** je ne connais pas son titre exact; **George III gave him a ~** Georges III lui a conféré un titre *or* l'a titré *or* l'a anobli; **this earned him the ~ of "King of the Ring"** cela lui a valu le titre de "Roi du Ring".

b (*Sport*) titre *m*. **to win/hold the ~** remporter/détenir le titre; *see* **world.**

c *[book etc]* titre *m*. **under the ~ of** sous le titre de.

d (*Cine, TV*) **the ~s** (*credit ~s*) le générique; (*subtitles*) les sous-titres *mpl*.

e (*Jur*) droit *m*, titre *m* (*to sth* à qch).

2 comp ▸**title deed** titre *m* (constitutif) de propriété ▸**title fight** (*Boxing*) match *m* de championnat ▸**title holder** (*Sport*) détenteur *m*, -trice *f or* tenant(e) *m(f)* du titre ▸**title page** page *f* de titre ▸**title role** (*Cine, Theat*) rôle *m* du personnage qui donne son nom à la pièce, ≃ rôle principal.

3 vt *book etc* intituler.

titled ['taɪtld] adj *person* titré.

titmouse ['tɪtmaʊs] n mésange *f*.

titrate ['taɪtreɪt] vt titrer (*Chem*).

titter ['tɪtəʳ] 1 vi rire sottement (*at* de), glousser. 2 n gloussement *m*, petit rire sot.

tittle ['tɪtl] 1 n brin *m*, grain *m*; *see* **jot.** 2 comp ▸**tittle-tattle** n (*NonC*) cancans *mpl*, potins *mpl* ◊ vi cancaner, jaser.

titty*‡ ['tɪtɪ] n roploplo‡ *m*, néné‡ *m*. **tough ~!** *or* **titties!** pas de pot!*

titular ['tɪtjʊləʳ] adj *possessions, estate* titulaire; *ruler, leader* nominal.

Titus ['taɪtəs] n Tite *m*.

tizzy* ['tɪzɪ] n affolement* *m*, panique* *f*. to be in/get into a ~ être/se mettre dans tous ses états.

TM [ti:'em] n a (abbr of transcendental meditation) *see* transcendental. b (abbr of trademark) MD.

TN (*US Post*) abbr of Tennessee.

TNT [ti:en'ti:] n (abbr of trinitrotoluene) T.N.T. *m*.

to [tu:, *weak form* tə] (phr vb elem) 1 prep a (*direction, movement*) à; vers; en; chez. he went ~ the door il est allé à la porte; ~ it y; I've been ~ it j'y suis allé; he was walking slowly ~ the door il marchait lentement vers la porte; to go ~ school/town aller à l'école/en ville; he came over ~ where I was standing il est venu (jusqu')à l'endroit où je me trouvais; to go ~ the doctor('s) aller chez le docteur; let's go ~ John's allons chez Jean; ~ the left à gauche; ~ the west à l'ouest; to fall ~ the ground tomber par *or* à terre; to turn a picture ~ the wall retourner un tableau contre le mur; he was sitting with his back ~ me il était assis le dos tourné vers moi.

b (*in geog names*) (*countries: gen; also fem French provinces, islands and fem US states*) en; (*countries: all plurals, and masc sing with initial consonant*) au *or* aux; (*towns: gen; also masc islands*) *à;* (*most departments; also masc French regions, Brit counties, masc US states and islands with "île" in name*) dans le (*or* la *or* l' *or* les). ~ England/France *etc* en Angleterre/France *etc;* ~ Iran/Israel *etc* en Iran/Israël *etc;* ~ Brittany/Provence *etc* en Bretagne/Provence *etc;* ~ Sicily/Crete *etc* en Sicile/Crète *etc;* ~ Louisiana/Virginia *etc* en Louisiane/Virginie *etc;* ~ Japan/the United States *etc* au Japon/aux États-Unis *etc;* ~ London/Paris *etc* à Londres/Paris *etc;* ~ le Havre au Havre; ~ Cuba/Malta *etc* à Cuba/Malte *etc;* ~ the Drôme/the Var *etc* dans la Drôme/le Var *etc;* ~ Seine-et-Marne *etc* en Seine-et-Marne *etc;* ~ Poitou/Berry *etc* dans le Poitou/le Berry *etc;* ~ Sussex/Yorkshire *etc* dans le Sussex/le Yorkshire *etc;* ~ the Isle of Man/the Ile de Ré *etc* dans l'île de Man/l'île de Ré *etc;* the road ~ London la route de Londres; on the way ~ Paris sur la route de Paris, en allant à Paris; boats ~ and from Calais les bateaux à destination ou en provenance de Calais.

c (*as far as*) (jusqu')à. to count (up) ~ 20 compter jusqu'à 20; it comes ~ £20 ça fait 20 livres en tout, ça s'élève à 20 livres; it is 90 km ~ Paris (*from here*) nous sommes à 90 km de Paris; (*from there*) c'est à 90 km de Paris; it's correct ~ a millimetre c'est exact à un millimètre près; they perished ~ a man pas un seul n'a survécu; 8 years ago ~ the day il y a 8 ans jour pour jour; ~ this day jusqu'à ce jour, jusqu'à aujourd'hui; I didn't stay ~ the end je ne suis pas resté jusqu'à la fin; from morning ~ night du matin (jusqu')au soir; from Monday ~ Friday du lundi au vendredi; from day ~ day de jour en jour; from town ~ town de ville en ville; from time ~ time de temps en temps; from bad ~ worse de mal en pis; there were 50 ~ 60 people il y avait (de) 50 à 60 personnes, il y avait entre 50 et 60 personnes.

d (*marking dative*) à. to give sth ~ sb donner qch à qn; I gave them ~ him je les lui ai donnés; give it ~ me donnez-le-moi; the man I sold it ~ l'homme à qui *or* auquel je l'ai vendu; she said ~ herself elle s'est dit; that belongs ~ him cela lui appartient; what's it ~ you?, what does it matter ~ you? qu'est-ce que cela peut vous faire?; be nice ~ her sois gentil avec elle; it's a great help ~ me cela m'est très utile; known ~ the Ancients connu des anciens.

e (*in dedications etc*) "~ my wife Anne" "à ma femme, Anne"; dedicated ~ the memory of dédié à la mémoire de; here's ~ you! à la vôtre!; ~ absent friends! (buvons) à la santé des absents!; to erect a statue ~ sb ériger une statue en l'honneur de qn.

f (*against, next to*) à; contre. back ~ back dos à dos; bumper ~ bumper pare-chocs contre pare-chocs; to clasp sb ~ one's heart serrer qn sur son cœur.

g (*in time phrases*) 20 (minutes) ~ 2 2 heures moins 20; at (a) quarter ~ 4 à 4 heures moins le quart; it's (a) quarter ~ il est moins le quart; it was 10 ~ il était moins 10.

h (*in proportions, equivalences etc*) A is ~ B as C is ~ D A est à B ce que C est à D; to bet 10 ~ 1 parier 10 contre 1; by a majority of 10 ~ 7 avec une majorité de 10 contre 7; they won by 4 goals ~ 2 ils ont gagné 4 (buts) à 2; one person ~ a room une personne par chambre; 200 people ~ the square km 200 personnes au km carré; how many miles ~ the gallon? ≈ combien de litres au cent?; 6 francs ~ the dollar 6 francs le dollar.

i (*in comparison with*) inferior/superior ~ inférieur (*f* -eure)/supérieur (*f* -eure) à; that's nothing ~ what is to come ce n'est rien à côté de ce qui va venir; he's famous (compared) ~ what he used to be 10 years ago il est célèbre en comparaison de *or* à côté de ce qu'il était il y a 10 ans; I prefer bridge ~ chess je préfère le bridge aux échecs.

j (*concerning*) what would you say ~ a beer? que diriez-vous d'une bière?; there's nothing ~ it il n'y a rien de plus facile; that's all there is ~ it (*it's easy*) ça n'est pas plus difficile que ça; (*no ulterior motive etc*) c'est aussi simple que ça; (*Comm*) "~ repairing cooker: 1,000 francs" "remise en état d'une cuisinière: 1.000 F"; (*Comm*) ~ services rendered pour services rendus.

k (*according to*) ~ the best of my recollection (pour) autant que je m'en souvienne; ~ all intents and purposes à toutes fins utiles; ~ all appearances selon toute apparence; ~ my mind, ~ my way of thinking à mon avis; it's not ~ my taste ce n'est pas à mon goût; in time ~ the music en mesure avec la musique; cheque ~ the value of £100 chèque de 100 livres; (*Math*) 3 ~ the 4th, 3 ~ the power 4 3 (à la) puissance 4; ~ some degree dans une certaine mesure.

l (*of*) de. assistant ~ the manager adjoint(e) *m(f)* du directeur; secretary ~ the board secrétaire *mf* (auprès) du comité de gestion; ambassador ~ France ambassadeur *m* en France; ambassador ~ King Paul ambassadeur auprès du roi Paul; wife ~ Mr Milton femme *f* de M. Milton; he has been a good friend ~ us il a été pour nous un ami fidèle.

m (*of purpose, result*) ~ my delight/surprise à ma grande joie/surprise; ~ this end à cet effet, dans ce but; it is ~ his credit c'est tout à son honneur; the water had changed ~ ice l'eau s'était changée en glace *or* avait gelé; his love turned ~ hatred son amour a tourné à la haine; frozen ~ death mort de froid; it comes ~ the same thing ça revient au même *or* à la même chose.

2 particle (*forming infin*) a (*shown in French by vb ending*) ~ be être; ~ eat manger; ~ hear him talk, you'd think ... à l'entendre, on croirait ...; he woke up ~ find ... en se réveillant il a trouvé ... .

b (*with ellipsis of vb*) he asked me to come but I didn't want ~ il m'a demandé de venir mais je n'ai pas voulu; I'll try ~ j'essaierai; I'd love ~ ce sera(it) avec plaisir; I didn't mean ~ je ne l'ai pas fait exprès; I forgot ~ j'ai oublié.

3 adv: to push the door ~ fermer la porte (en la poussant); when the door is ~ quand la porte est fermée; to go ~ and fro *[person]* aller et venir; *[machine part etc]* avoir un mouvement de va-et-vient; *[train, bus etc]* faire la navette (*between* entre); he was walking ~ and fro il faisait les cent pas, il se promenait de long en large; *see* come to *etc*.

4 comp ►-to-be comp ending futur (*see* mother *etc*); husband-to-be futur mari ►to-do*: to make a to-do faire des embarras *or* des histoires*; she made a great to-do about it elle en a fait tout un plat*; what a to-do! quelle histoire!, quelle affaire! ►to-ing and fro-ing allées et venues *fpl*.

toad [təʊd] 1 n crapaud *m* (*also fig*). 2 comp ►toad-in-the-hole (*Brit Culin*) *saucisses cuites au four dans de la pâte à crêpes* ►toadstool (*poisonous*) champignon vénéneux ► (*edible*) champignon *m*.

toady ['təʊdɪ] 1 n flagorneur *m*, -euse *f*, lèche-bottes* *mf inv*. 2 vi être flagorneur. to ~ to sb flagorner qn, flatter qn bassement, lécher les bottes de qn*.

toadying ['təʊdɪɪŋ] n, **toadyism** ['təʊdɪɪzəm] n (*NonC*) flagornerie *f*.

toast [təʊst] 1 n a (*NonC: Culin*) pain grillé, toast *m*. you've burnt the ~ tu as laissé brûler le pain *or* les toasts; a piece *or* slice of ~ une tartine grillée, un (morceau de) toast, une rôtie; sardines on ~ sardines *fpl* sur toast *or* sur canapé; (*fig*) you've got him on ~* vous le tenez; *see* warm.

b (*drink, speech*) toast *m*. to drink a ~ to sb porter un toast à qn *or* en l'honneur de qn, boire à la santé *or* au succès de qn; they drank his ~ in champagne ils lui ont porté un toast au champagne; here's a ~ to all who ... levons nos verres en l'honneur de tous ceux qui ...; to propose *or* give a ~ to sb porter un toast à qn *or* en l'honneur de qn; she was the ~ of the town elle était la coqueluche *or* la vedette de la ville.

2 comp ►toasting fork fourchette *f* à griller le pain ►toastmaster animateur *m* pour réceptions et banquets ►toast rack porte-toasts *m inv*.

3 vt a *bread etc* (faire) griller. ~ed cheese toast *m* au fromage; (*fig*) he was ~ing his toes by the fire il se chauffait *or* se rôtissait les pieds auprès du feu.

b (*propose ~ to*) porter un toast à; (*drink ~ to*) *person* boire à la santé de *or* au succès de, porter un toast à; *event, victory* arroser (*in champagne etc* au champagne *etc*).

toaster ['təʊstər] n grille-pain *m inv* (*électrique*).

toastie, toasty ['təʊstɪ] n ≈ croque-monsieur *m*.

tobacco [tə'bækəʊ] 1 n, pl ~s *or* ~es tabac *m*. 2 comp *leaf, smoke, plantation, company* de tabac; *pouch* à tabac; *industry* du tabac ►tobacco jar pot *m* à tabac ►tobacco plant (pied *m* de) tabac *m* ►tobacco planter propriétaire *m* d'une plantation de tabac.

tobacconist [tə'bækənɪst] n (*esp Brit*) marchand(e) *m(f)* de tabac, buraliste *mf*. ~'s (shop) (bureau *m or* débit *m* de) tabac *m*.

Tobago [tə'beɪgəʊ] n Tobago; *see* Trinidad.

toboggan [tə'bɒgən] 1 n toboggan *m*; (*on runners*) luge *f*; (*Sport*) luge. 2 comp *race* de luge; de toboggan ►toboggan run piste *f* de luge (*or* de toboggan). 3 vi a (*also* go ~ing) faire du toboggan *or* de la luge; (*Sport*) luger. he ~ed down the hill il a descendu la colline en toboggan *or* en luge. b (*fig*) *[prices, sales, numbers etc]* dégringoler.

toby jug ['təʊbɪˌdʒʌg] n chope *f* à effigie humaine.

toccata [tə'kɑ:tə] n toccata *f*.

tocsin ['tɒksɪn] n tocsin *m*.

tod‡ [tɒd] n (*Brit*) on one's ~ tout seul (*f* toute seule).

today [tə'deɪ] 1 adv aujourd'hui (*also fig*). it rained all (day) ~ il a plu toute la journée aujourd'hui; a week ago ~ il y a huit jours aujourd'hui; ~ week, a week (from) ~ aujourd'hui en huit; early ~ aujourd'hui de bonne heure; what day is it ~? quel jour est-on *or* est-ce aujourd'hui?; what date is it ~? quelle est la date aujourd'hui?; (*fig*) ~ you can't dismiss anyone without a good reason aujourd'hui on ne peut renvoyer personne sans motif; (*fig*) here ~ and gone tomorrow ça va ça vient.

2 n aujourd'hui *m* (*also fig*). **what day is ~?** quel jour est-on *or* est-ce aujourd'hui?; ~ **is Friday** aujourd'hui c'est vendredi; **what is ~'s date?** quelle est la date aujourd'hui?; ~ **is the 4th** aujourd'hui c'est le 4; ~ **is very wet** il pleut beaucoup aujourd'hui; ~ **was a bad day for me** aujourd'hui ça s'est mal passé pour moi; **~'s paper** le journal d'aujourd'hui; (*fig*) **the writers of ~** les écrivains d'aujourd'hui.

toddle ['tɒdl] 1 vi a *[child]* **to ~ in/out** *etc* entrer/sortir *etc* à pas hésitants; **he has begun to ~, he is just toddling** il fait ses premiers pas. b (* *hum*) (*go*) aller; (*stroll*) se balader*; (*leave: also* **~ off**) se sauver*, se trotter‡. 2 n (*hum*) **to go for a ~‡** aller faire un petit tour *or* une petite balade*.

toddler ['tɒdləʳ] n tout(e) petit(e) *m(f)* (qui commence à marcher), bambin* *m*. **he's only a ~** il est encore tout petit; **she has one baby and one ~** elle a un bébé et un petit qui commence juste à marcher.

toddy ['tɒdɪ] n ≈ grog *m*.

TOE [tiːəʊ'iː] n (abbr of **ton oil equivalent**) TEP *f* (*abrév de tonne équivalent pétrole*).

toe [təʊ] 1 n (*Anat*) orteil *m*, doigt *m* de pied; *[sock, shoe]* bout *m*. **big/little ~** gros/petit orteil; **to tread** *or* **step on sb's ~s** (*lit, fig*) marcher sur les pieds de qn; (*fig*) **to keep sb on his ~s** forcer qn à rester vigilant *or* alerte; (*fig*) **that will keep you on your ~s!** ça t'empêchera de t'endormir!, ça te fera travailler!; *see* **tip[1], top[1]**.

2 comp ►**toecap: reinforced toecap** bout dur *or* renforcé (*de soulier*) ►**toe-clip** (*Cycling*) cale-pied *m inv* ►**toehold** (*lit*) prise *f* (pour le pied); (*fig*) **to have a toehold in** avoir un pied dans ►**toenail** ongle *m* de l'orteil *or* du pied ►**toe-piece** (*Ski*) butée *f* ►**toerag‡** petit(e) con(ne)‡ *m(f)*, trou *m* du cul**‡**.

3 vt (*touch/push*) toucher/pousser du bout de l'orteil. **to ~ the line** *or* (*US*) **mark** (*in race*) se ranger sur la ligne de départ; (*fig*) se mettre au pas, se plier; (*Pol*) **to ~ the party line** ne pas s'écarter de *or* suivre la ligne du parti.

-toed [təʊd] adj ending in comps: **three-toed** à trois orteils.

toff‡† [tɒf] n (*Brit*) aristo‡ *m*, dandy* *m*.

toffee ['tɒfɪ] (*Brit*) 1 n caramel *m* (au beurre). (*fig*) **he can't do it for ~*** il n'est pas fichu* de le faire. 2 comp ►**toffee apple** pomme caramélisée ►**toffee-nosed‡** (*pej*) bêcheur*, qui fait du chiqué*.

tofu ['təʊˌfuː, 'tɒˌfuː] n tofu *m*, fromage *m* de soja.

tog* [tɒg] 1 vt: **to ~ up** *or* **out** nipper*, fringuer‡; **to be all ~ged up** *or* **out (in one's best clothes)** être bien fringué‡ *or* sapé‡, être sur son trente et un. 2 n: **~s** fringues‡ *fpl*.

toga ['təʊgə] n toge *f*.

together [tə'geðəʳ] (*phr vb elem*) 1 adv a ensemble. **I've seen them ~** je les ai vus ensemble; (*fig*) **we're in this ~** nous sommes logés à la même enseigne; (*fig pej*) **they were both in it ~** ils avaient partie liée tous les deux; **you must keep ~** vous devez rester ensemble, vous ne devez pas vous séparer; **tie the ropes ~** nouez les cordes; **~ with what you bought yesterday that makes ...** avec ce que vous avez acheté hier ça fait ...; **(taken) ~ with the previous figures, these show that ...** ces chiffres, considérés conjointement avec les précédents, indiquent que ...; **he, ~ with his colleagues, accepted ...** lui, ainsi que ses collègues, a accepté ...; **if you look at the reports ~** si vous considérez les rapports conjointement; **they belong ~** *[objects]* ils vont ensemble; *[people]* ils sont faits l'un pour l'autre; *see* **bang together, gather together, live together** *etc*.

b (*simultaneously*) en même temps, à la fois, simultanément; *sing, play, recite* à l'unisson. **the shots were fired ~** les coups de feu ont été tirés simultanément *or* en même temps; **they both stood up ~** ils se sont tous les deux levés en même temps; **don't all speak ~** ne parlez pas tous à la fois; **all ~ now!** (*shouting, singing*) tous en chœur maintenant!; (*pulling*) (oh!) hisse!; (*Mus*) **you're not ~** vous n'êtes pas à l'unisson.

c (*continuously*) **for days/weeks ~** (pendant) des jours entiers/des semaines entières; **for 5 weeks ~** (pendant) 5 semaines de suite *or* d'affilée.

d (* *fig*) **to get it ~, to get one's act ~** s'organiser; **let's get it ~** il faut qu'on s'organise, il faut qu'on essaie d'y voir plus clair; **she's got it ~** c'est quelqu'un d'équilibré.

2 adj (*‡: *well adjusted*) *person* équilibré. **a ~ person** quelqu'un d'équilibré.

togetherness [tə'geðənɪs] n (*NonC*) (*unity*) unité *f*; (*friendliness*) camaraderie *f*.

toggle ['tɒgl] 1 n (*Naut*) cabillot *m*; (*on garment*) bouton *m* de duffel-coat. 2 comp ►**toggle joint** (*Tech*) genouillère *f* ►**toggle key** (*Comput*) touche *f* à bascule ►**toggle switch** (*Elec*) bouton *m* à bascule.

Togo ['təʊgəʊ] n Togo *m*.

toil[1] [tɔɪl] 1 n (*NonC*) (dur) travail *m*, labeur *m* (*liter*). 2 vi a (*work hard: also* **~ away**) travailler dur (*at, over* à, *to do* pour faire), peiner (*at, over* sur, *to do* pour faire). b (*move with difficulty*) *[person, horse, vehicle]* **to ~ along/up** *etc* avancer/monter *etc* péniblement *or* avec peine.

toil[2] [tɔɪl] n (*fig liter: snare, net*) **~s** rets *mpl*; (*fig*) **in the ~s of** dans les rets de.

toilet ['tɔɪlɪt] 1 n a (*dressing etc, dress*) toilette *f*. b (*lavatory*) toilettes *fpl*, cabinets *mpl*, waters* *mpl*. **"T~s"** "Toilettes"; **to go to the ~** aller aux toilettes *or* aux cabinets *or* aux waters*; **to put sth down the ~** jeter qch dans la cuvette des cabinets.

2 comp ►**toilet bag** sac *m* de toilette ►**toilet case** trousse *f* de toilette ►**toilet paper** (*NonC*) papier *m* hygiénique ►**toilet requisites** (*Comm*) articles *mpl* de toilette ►**toilet roll** rouleau *m* de papier hygiénique ►**toilet seat** siège *m* des cabinets ►**toilet soap** savonnette *f*, savon *m* de toilette ►**toilet table** table *f* de toilette ►**toilet tissue** (*NonC*) = **toilet paper** ►**toilet-train: to toilet-train a child** apprendre à un enfant à être propre ►**toilet training** apprentissage *m* de la propreté ►**toilet water** eau *f* de toilette.

toiletries ['tɔɪlɪtrɪz] npl articles *mpl* de toilette.

toilette [twɑː'let] n = **toilet 1a**.

toilsome ['tɔɪlsəm] adj (*liter*) pénible, épuisant.

toke [təʊk] n (*US Drugs sl*) bouffée *f*.

token ['təʊkən] 1 n a (*sign, symbol*) marque *f*, témoignage *m*, gage *m*; (*keepsake*) souvenir *m*; (*metal disc: for travel, telephone etc*) jeton *m*; (*voucher, coupon*) bon *m*, coupon *m*; (*gift ~*) bon-cadeau *m*. **milk ~** bon de lait; **as a ~ of, in ~ of** en témoignage de, en gage de; (*fig*) **by the same ~** de même; *see* **book, record** *etc*. b (*Ling*) occurrence *f*. 2 adj *support, payment, strike* symbolique, de pure forme. **they put up a ~ resistance** ils ont opposé un semblant de résistance pour la forme; (*Parl*) **~ vote** vote *m* de crédits (dont le montant n'est pas définitivement fixé); (*pej*) **the ~ woman on the committee** la femme-alibi du comité.

tokenism ['təʊkənɪzəm] n politique *f* de pure forme.

Tokyo ['təʊkjəʊ] n Tokyo.

told [təʊld] pret, ptp of **tell**.

Toledo [tɒ'leɪdəʊ] n Tolède.

tolerable ['tɒlərəbl] adj a (*bearable*) tolérable, supportable. b (*fairly good*) passable, assez bon. **the food is ~** on y mange passablement, on n'y mange pas trop mal.

tolerably ['tɒlərəblɪ] adv *work etc* passablement; *certain, competent* à peu près. **he plays ~ (well)** il joue passablement, il ne joue pas trop mal.

tolerance ['tɒlərəns] n tolérance *f*, indulgence *f*; (*Med, Tech*) tolérance.

tolerant ['tɒlərənt] adj tolérant, indulgent (*of sth* de qch; *of sb* à l'égard de qn; (*Med*) *of* à). **to be ~ of sth** tolérer qch.

tolerantly ['tɒlərəntlɪ] adv d'une manière tolérante, avec indulgence.

tolerate ['tɒləreɪt] vt *heat, pain* supporter; *insolence, injustice* tolérer, supporter; (*Med, Tech*) tolérer.

toleration [ˌtɒlə'reɪʃən] n (*NonC*) tolérance *f*.

toll[1] [təʊl] 1 n (*tax, charge*) péage *m*. (*fig*) **the war took a heavy ~ of** *or* **among the young men** la guerre a fait beaucoup de victimes parmi les jeunes, les jeunes ont payé un fort tribut à la guerre; **it took (a) great ~ of his strength** cela a sérieusement ébranlé *or* sapé ses forces; **it took a ~ of his savings** cela a fait un gros trou dans ses économies; **we must reduce the accident ~ on the roads** il nous faut réduire le nombre des victimes de la route; **the ~ of dead and injured has risen** le nombre des morts et des blessés a augmenté.

2 comp ►**tollbar** barrière *f* de péage ►**tollbooth** poste *m* de péage ►**tollbridge** pont *m* à péage ►**toll call** (*US Telec*) appel *m* longue distance ►**toll-free** (*US Telec*) adv sans payer la communication ◊ adj gratuit; **toll-free number** (*US Telec*) ≃ numéro *m* vert ►**tollgate** = **tollbar** ►**tollhouse** maison *f* de péager ►**tollkeeper** péager *m*, -ère *f* ►**toll road, tollway** route *f* à péage.

toll[2] [təʊl] 1 vi *[bell]* sonner. **for whom the bell ~s** pour qui sonne le glas. 2 vt *bell, the hour* sonner; *sb's death* sonner le glas pour.

tolley ['tɒlɪ] n (*marble*) calot *m*.

Tolstoy ['tɒlstɔɪ] n Tolstoï *m*.

Tom [tɒm] 1 n a (dim of **Thomas**) Thomas *m*. (*fig*) **(any) ~, Dick or Harry** n'importe qui, le premier venu; *see* **peep[1]**. b (*US* ‡: *pej: also* **Uncle ~**) Oncle Tom *m*, bon nègre. 2 comp ►**Tom Thumb** Tom-pouce *m*; (*in French tale*) le Petit Poucet.

tom [tɒm] n (*cat*) matou *m*. **~ cat** (*cat*) matou *m*; (*US* ‡: *man*) coureur *m* de jupons, cavaleur* *m*.

tomahawk ['tɒməhɔːk] n tomahawk *m*, hache *f* de guerre.

tomato [tə'mɑːtəʊ] (*US*) [tə'meɪtəʊ] 1 n, pl **~es** (*fruit, plant*) tomate *f*. 2 comp ►**tomato juice** jus *m* de tomates ►**tomato ketchup** ketchup *m* ►**tomato paste** = **tomato purée** ►**tomato plant** tomate *f* ►**tomato purée** purée *f* de tomates ►**tomato sauce** sauce *f* tomate.

tomb [tuːm] 1 n tombeau *m*, tombe *f*. 2 comp ►**tombstone** pierre tombale, tombe *f*.

tombac, tombak ['tɒmbæk] n (*NonC*) tombac *m*, laiton *m*.

tombola [tɒm'bəʊlə] n (*Brit*) tombola *f*.

tomboy ['tɒmbɔɪ] n garçon manqué.

tomboyish ['tɒmbɔɪɪʃ] adj de garçon manqué.

tomboyishness ['tɒmbɔɪɪʃnɪs] n (*NonC*) manières *fpl* de garçon manqué.

tome [təʊm] n tome *m*, gros volume.

tomfool ['tɒm'fuːl] adj absurde, idiot.

tomfoolery [tɒm'fuːlərɪ] n (*NonC*) niaiserie(s) *f(pl)*, âneries *fpl*.

Tommy ['tɒmɪ] 1 n (dim of Thomas) Thomas *m*; (*Brit Mil **: also **t~**) tommy* *m*, soldat *m* britannique. 2 comp ►**tommy gun** mitraillette *f* ►**tommyrot*** (*NonC*) bêtises *fpl*, âneries *fpl*.

tomography [tə'mɒgrəfɪ] n tomographie *f*.

tomorrow [tə'mɒrəʊ] 1 adv demain (*also fig*). **all (day)** ~ toute la journée (de) demain; **a week ago** ~ il y aura huit jours demain; **a week (from)** ~ demain en huit; **he'll have been here a week** ~ cela fera huit jours demain qu'il est là; **see you ~!** à demain!; **early** ~ demain de bonne heure; **what day will it be ~?** quel jour serons-nous demain?; **what date will it be ~?** quelle sera la date demain?; (*fig*) ~ **we will see cities where forests stand today** demain nous verrons des villes là où se dressent des forêts aujourd'hui; *see* **today**.

2 n demain *m* (*also fig*). **the day after** ~ après-demain; **what day will** ~ **be?** quel jour serons-nous demain?; ~ **will be Saturday** demain ce sera samedi; **what date will** ~ **be?** quelle est la date de demain?; ~ **will be the 5th** demain ce sera le 5; **I hope** ~ **will be dry** j'espère qu'il ne pleuvra pas demain; ~ **will be a better day for you** les choses iront mieux pour vous demain; (*loc*) ~ **never comes** demain n'arrive jamais; (*loc*) ~ **is another day!** ça ira peut-être mieux demain!; **~'s paper** le journal de demain; (*fig*) **the writers of** ~ les écrivains *mpl* de demain *or* de l'avenir; (*fig*) **like** *or* **as if there was no ~*** *spend, drive* sans se soucier du lendemain; *eat, drink* comme si c'était la dernière fois; (*fig*) **brighter ~s** des lendemains qui chantent.

3 comp ►**tomorrow morning/afternoon/evening** demain matin/après-midi/soir ►**tomorrow week** demain en huit.

tomtit ['tɒmtɪt] n mésange *f*.

tomtom ['tɒmtɒm] n tam-tam *m*.

ton [tʌn] 1 n a (*weight*) tonne *f* (*Brit* = *1016,06 kg*; *Can, US etc* = *907,20 kg*). **metric** ~ tonne (= *1.000 kg*); **a 7-~ truck** un camion de 7 tonnes; (*fig*) **it weighs a ~, it's a ~ weight** c'est du plomb; (*fig*) **~s of*** beaucoup de, des tas de*. b (*Naut*) (*also* **register** ~) tonneau *m* (= *2,83 m³*); (*also* **displacement** ~) tonne *f*; **a 60,000-~ steamer** un paquebot de 60.000 tonnes. c (*‡*: *hundred*) **a** ~ cent; (*Aut* ‡ *etc*) **to do a** ~ **(up)** faire du cent soixante à l'heure. 2 comp ►**ton-up boys‡** (*Brit: motorcyclists*) motards* *mpl*, fous *mpl* de la moto.

tonal ['təʊnl] adj tonal.

tonality [təʊ'nælɪtɪ] n tonalité *f*.

tondo ['tɒndəʊ] n, pl **tondi** ['tɒndi:] tondo *m*.

tone [təʊn] 1 n a (*in sound: also Ling, Mus*) ton *m*; (*Telec: also of radio, record player etc*) tonalité *f*; [*musical instrument*] sonorité *f*. **to speak in low ~s** *or* **in a low** ~ parler à voix basse *or* doucement; **to speak in angry ~s, to speak in an angry** ~ **(of voice)** parler sur le ton de la colère; **don't speak to me in that** ~ **(of voice)!** ne me parlez pas sur ce ton!; **in friendly ~s, in a friendly** ~ sur un ton amical; (*Ling*) **rising/falling** ~ ton montant/descendant; *see* **dialling, engaged** *etc*.

b (*in colour*) ton *m*. **a two-~ car** une voiture de deux tons.

c (*general character*) ton *m*. **what was the** ~ **of his letter?** quel était le ton de sa lettre?; **we were impressed by the whole** ~ **of the school** nous avons été impressionnés par la tenue générale de l'école; (*Fin*) **the** ~ **of the market** la tenue du marché; **to raise/lower the** ~ **of sth** rehausser/rabaisser le ton de qch.

d (*NonC: class, elegance*) classe *f*. **it gives the restaurant ~, it adds** ~ **to the restaurant** cela donne de la classe au restaurant.

e (*Med, Physiol: of muscles etc*) tonus *m*, tonicité *f*.

2 comp ►**tone arm** [*record player*] bras *m* de lecture ►**tone colour** (*Mus*) timbre *m* ►**tone control** (**knob**) [*record player etc*] bouton *m* de tonalité ►**tone-deaf: to be tone-deaf** ne pas avoir d'oreille ►**tone-deafness** manque *m* d'oreille ►**tone language** (*Ling*) langue *f* à tons ►**tone poem** poème *m* symphonique ►**tone row, tone series** (*Mus*) série *f* (de notes).

3 vi [*colour*] s'harmoniser (*with* avec).

►**tone down** vt sep *colour* adoucir; *sound* baisser; *radio etc* baisser (le son de); (*fig*) *criticism, effect* atténuer, adoucir; *attitude, language* atténuer, modérer; *policy* modérer, mettre en sourdine.

►**tone in** vi s'harmoniser (*with* avec).

►**tone up** vt sep *muscles, the system* tonifier.

toneless ['təʊnlɪs] adj *voice* blanc (*f* blanche), sans timbre.

tonelessly ['təʊnlɪslɪ] adv *speak* d'une voix blanche.

toner ['təʊnəʳ] n (*for photocopier, printer*) encre *f*, toner *m*; (*cosmetic*) (lotion *f*) tonique *m*.

Tonga ['tɒŋə] n Tonga *fpl*.

tongs [tɒŋz] npl (*also* **pair of** ~) pinces *fpl*; (*for coal*) pincettes *fpl*; (*for sugar*) pince *f* (à sucre); (*curling* ~) fer *m* (à friser); *see* **hammer**.

tongue [tʌŋ] 1 n a (*Anat, Culin*) langue *f*; [*shoe*] languette *f*; [*bell*] battant *m*; (*fig: of flame, land; also on tool, machine etc*) langue. **to put out** *or* **stick out one's** ~ tirer la langue (*at sb* à qn); [*dog, person*] **his** ~ **was hanging out** il tirait la langue; [*hounds*] **to give** ~ donner de la voix; (*fig*) **to lose/find one's** ~ perdre/retrouver sa langue; **with his** ~ **in his cheek**, ~ **in cheek** ironiquement, en plaisantant; **I'm going to let him feel** *or* **give him the rough side of my** ~† je vais lui faire comprendre comment je m'appelle; **keep a civil** ~ **in your head!** tâchez d'être plus poli!; (*fig*) **I can't get my** ~ **round it** je n'arrive pas à le prononcer correctement; *see* **cat, hold, tip¹, wag¹** *etc*.

b (*language*) langue *f*. (*Rel*) **to speak in ~s** avoir le don (surnaturel) de s'exprimer dans des langues inconnues; *see* **mother** *etc*.

2 comp ►**tongue-and-groove** (*Carpentry*) *see* **tongue-and-groove** ►**tongue depressor** (*Med*) spatule *f* (*pour déprimer la langue*) ►**tongue-in-cheek** *remark etc* ironique (*see also* **1**) ►**tongue-lashing*** engueulade‡ *f*; **to give sb/get a tongue-lashing** engueuler qn‡/se faire engueuler‡ ►**tongue-tied** (*fig*) muet (*fig*); (*fig*) **tongue-tied from shyness/fright/astonishment** *etc* muet de timidité/peur/stupeur *etc*, trop timide/effrayé/abasourdi *etc* pour parler ►**tongue twister** phrase *f* (*or* nom *etc*) très difficile à prononcer.

3 vt (*Mus*) *note* attaquer en coup de langue.

tongue-and-groove ['tʌŋgən'gru:v] 1 n (*also* ~ **boarding** *or* **strips**) planches *fpl* à rainure et languette. ~ **joint** assemblage *m* à rainure et languette. 2 vt *wall* revêtir de planches à rainure et languette.

-tongued [tʌŋd] adj ending in comps qui a la langue ..., *e.g.* **sharp-tongued** qui a la langue acérée.

tonguing ['tʌŋɪŋ] n (*Mus*) (technique *f* du) coup de langue.

tonic ['tɒnɪk] 1 adj (*Ling, Med, Mus, Physiol*) tonique. ~ **water** *see* **2b**; ~ **wine** vin *m* tonique; (*Mus*) ~ **sol-fa** solfège *m*. 2 n a (*Med*) tonique *m*, fortifiant *m*. (*lit, fig*) **you need a** ~ il vous faut un bon tonique; (*fig*) **it was a real** ~ **to see him** cela m'a vraiment remonté le moral de le voir. b (*also* ~ **water, Indian** ~) ≃ Schweppes *m* ®; **gin and** ~ gin-tonic *m*. c (*Mus*) tonique *f*.

tonicity [tɒ'nɪsɪtɪ] n tonicité *f*.

tonight [tə'naɪt] adv, n (*before bed*) ce soir; (*during sleep*) cette nuit.

tonnage ['tʌnɪdʒ] n (*Naut: all senses*) tonnage *m*.

tonne [tʌn] n tonne *f*.

tonneau ['tʌnəʊ] n, pl **~s** *or* **~x** ['tʌnəʊ] (*Aut: also* ~ **cover**) bâche *f* (*de voiture de sport*).

-tonner ['tʌnəʳ] n ending in comps: **a 10-tonner** (*truck*) un (camion de) 10 tonnes.

tonometer [təʊ'nɒmɪtəʳ] n (*Mus*) diapason *m* de Scheibler; (*Med*) tonomètre *m*.

tonsil ['tɒnsl] n amygdale *f*. **to have one's ~s out** *or* **removed** être opéré des amygdales.

tonsillectomy [ˌtɒnsɪ'lektəmɪ] n amygdalectomie *f*.

tonsillitis [ˌtɒnsɪ'laɪtɪs] n (*NonC*) angine *f*, amygdalite *f*. **he's got** ~ il a une angine, il a une amygdalite (*frm*).

tonsorial [tɒn'sɔ:rɪəl] adj (*hum*) de barbier.

tonsure ['tɒnʃəʳ] 1 n tonsure *f*. 2 vt tonsurer.

tontine [tɒn'ti:n] n tontine *f*.

Tony ['təʊnɪ] n a (dim of **Anthony**) Antoine *m*. b (*Theat*, pl **~s** *or* **Tonies**: *also* ~ **award**) Tony *m* (*Oscar du théâtre décerné à Broadway*).

too [tu:] adv a (*excessively*) trop, par trop (*liter*). **it's** ~ **hard for me** c'est trop difficile pour moi; **it's** ~ **hard for me to explain** c'est trop difficile pour que je puisse vous l'expliquer; **that case is** ~ **heavy to carry** cette valise est trop lourde à porter; **it's** ~ **heavy for me to carry** c'est trop lourd à porter pour moi; **he's** ~ **mean to pay for it** il est trop pingre pour le payer; **that's** ~ **kind of you!** vous êtes vraiment trop aimable!; **I'm not** ~ **sure about that** je n'en suis pas très certain; ~ **true!***, ~ **right!*** que oui!*, et comment!*; **it's just ~-~!‡** en voilà un chichi!*; *see* **good, many, much, none** *etc*.

b (*also*) aussi; (*moreover*) en plus, par-dessus le marché, de plus, en outre. **I went** ~ moi aussi j'y suis allé; **you** ~ **can own a car like this** vous aussi vous pouvez être le propriétaire d'une voiture comme celle-ci; **HE can swim** ~ lui aussi sait nager; **he can SWIM** ~ il sait nager aussi, il sait aussi *or* également nager; **they asked for a discount** ~! et en plus *or* et par-dessus le marché ils ont demandé un rabais!; **and then, ~, there's the question of ...** et puis il y a également la question de ... .

took [tʊk] pret of **take**.

tool [tu:l] 1 n (*gen, Tech*) outil *m* (de travail); (*fig: book etc*) outil, instrument *m*. **set of ~s** panoplie *f* d'outils; **garden ~s** outils *or* ustensiles *mpl* de jardinage; (*lit, fig*) **these are the ~s of my trade** voilà les outils de mon métier; **he was merely a** ~ **of the revolutionary party** il n'était que l'outil *or* l'instrument du parti révolutionnaire; (*fig*) **a** ~ **in the hands of** un instrument dans les mains de; *see* **down¹, machine, workman** *etc*.

2 comp ►**toolbag** trousse *f* à outils ►**toolbox** boîte *f or* mallette *f or* caisse *f or* coffre *m* à outils ►**toolcase** = **toolbag, toolbox** ►**tool-chest** = **toolbox** ►**toolhouse** = **toolshed** ►**toolkit** trousse *f* à outils; (*Comput*) valise *f* ►**toolmaker** (*Ind*) outilleur *m* ►**toolmaking** (*Ind*) montage *m* et réglage *m* des machines-outils ►**toolroom** (*Ind*) atelier *m* d'outillage ►**toolshed** cabane *f* à outils.

3 vt (*gen*) travailler, ouvrager; *silver* ciseler; *leather* repousser.

4 vi (*Aut*) **to** ~ **along/past*** rouler/passer tranquillement *or* pépère‡.

►**tool up** 1 vt sep (*Ind*) équiper, outiller. 2 vi [*factory etc*] s'équiper, s'outiller; (*fig*) se préparer.

tooled [tu:ld] adj (*gen*) ouvragé; *silver* ciselé; *leather* repoussé; *book cover* en cuir repoussé.

tooling ['tu:lɪŋ] n (*on book-cover etc*) repoussé *m*; (*on silver*) ciselure *f*.

toot [tu:t] 1 n [*car horn*] coup *m* de klaxon; [*whistle*] coup de sifflet; [*trumpet, flute*] note *f* (brève). 2 vi klaxonner, corner; donner un coup de sifflet; jouer une note. 3 vt (*Aut*) **to** ~ **the horn** klaxonner, corner.

tooth [tu:θ] 1 n, pl **teeth** *[person, animal, comb, saw etc]* dent *f*. **front ~** dent de devant; **back ~** molaire *f*; **to have a ~ out** se faire arracher une dent; **to mutter sth between one's teeth** *or* **between clenched teeth** grommeler qch entre ses dents; **to set** *or* **grit one's teeth** serrer les dents; (*lit, fig*) **to bare** *or* **show one's teeth** montrer les dents; **in the teeth of the wind** contre le vent; **in the teeth of the opposition** en dépit de *or* malgré l'opposition; **~ and nail** avec acharnement, farouchement; (*fig*) **to get one's teeth into sth** se mettre à fond à qch, se mettre à faire qch pour de bon; **there's nothing you can get your teeth into** (*of food etc*) ce n'est pas très substantiel; (*fig*) il n'y a là rien de substantiel *or* solide; (*fig*) **the legislation has no teeth** la législation est impuissante; (*fig*) **to give a law teeth** renforcer le pouvoir d'une loi; (*fig*) **to cast** *or* **throw sth in sb's teeth** jeter qch à la tête de qn, reprocher qch à qn; **to be fed up** *or* **sick to the (back) teeth of sth**‡ en avoir marre* *or* ras le bol‡ de qch; *see* **chatter, edge, long**[1] *etc.*

2 comp ▸**toothache** mal *m or* rage *f* de dents; **to have toothache** avoir mal aux dents ▸**toothbrush** brosse *f* à dents ▸**toothbrush moustache** moustache *f* en brosse ▸**toothcomb** (*also* **fine toothcomb**) *see* **fine**[2] **3** ▸**toothpaste** (pâte *f*) dentifrice *m* ▸**toothpick** cure-dent *m* ▸**tooth powder** poudre *f* dentifrice.

toothed [tu:θt] adj *wheel, leaf* denté.

-toothed [tu:θt] adj ending in comps: **big-toothed** aux grandes dents.

toothless ['tu:θlɪs] adj édenté; (*fig: powerless*) *organization* impuissant, sans pouvoir; *treaty, agreement* inefficace.

toothsome ['tu:θsəm] adj savoureux, succulent.

toothy ['tʊθɪ] adj *[person]* **to be ~** arborer une belle rangée de dents, avoir des dents de cheval (*pej*); **he gave me a ~ smile** il m'a souri découvrant largement ses dents.

tootle ['tu:tl] 1 n *[trumpet, flute, car-horn]* notes *fpl* (brèves); (*tune*) petit air. 2 vi a (*toot: Aut*) klaxonner, corner; (*Mus*) jouer un petit air. b (*Aut* *) **to ~ along/past** *etc* rouler/passer *etc* gaiement *or* sans s'en faire*. 3 vt *trumpet, flute etc* jouer un peu de.

toots‡ ['tʊts] n ma belle*.

tootsie‡, **tootsy**‡ ['tʊtsɪ] n a (*toe*) doigt *m* de pied; (*foot*) peton* *m*, pied *m*. b (*girl*) jolie nana‡. **hi ~!** salut ma belle!*

top[1] [tɒp] 1 n a (*highest point*) *[mountain, tree]* sommet *m*, faîte *m*, cime *f*; *[hill, head]* sommet, haut *m*; *[ladder, stairs, page, wall, cupboard]* haut; *[wave]* crête *f*; *[box, container]* dessus *m*; *[list, table, classification, queue]* tête *f*; (*surface*) surface *f*. **at the ~ of** *hill, mountain* au sommet de; *stairs, ladder, building, page* en haut de; *list, queue, division, league* en tête de; *street etc* en haut de, au bout de; *garden* au fond de; *profession, career* au faîte de; **it's near the ~ of the pile** c'est vers le haut de la pile; **it's at the ~ of the pile** c'est en haut *or* au sommet de la pile; (*fig*) **at the ~ of the pile*** *or* **heap*** en haut de l'échelle; **6 lines from the ~ of page 7** 6e ligne à partir du haut de la page 7; **the ~ of the milk** la crème du lait; (*Scol*) **to be at the ~ of the class** être premier de la classe; **it's ~ of the pops this week** c'est en tête du hit-parade *or* numéro un au hit-parade cette semaine; **the men at the ~** les dirigeants *mpl*, les responsables *mpl*, ceux qui sont au pouvoir *or* à la tête; **the men at the ~ don't care about it** en haut lieu ils ne s'en soucient guère; **he was sitting at the ~ of the table** il était assis à la place d'honneur; **at the ~ of one's voice** à tue-tête; **to come** *or* **rise** *or* **float to the ~** remonter à la surface, surnager; **it was floating on ~ of the water** cela flottait sur l'eau; (*Mil*) **to go over the ~** monter à l'assaut; (*fig: too many*) **we've got 5 over the ~*** nous en avons 5 de trop; (*fig*) **to be over the ~*** *[film, book]* dépasser la mesure; *[person]* en faire trop*, exagérer; *[act, opinion]* être excessif; (*fig*) **to get to** *or* **reach the ~, to make it to the ~** (*gen*) réussir, aller loin; (*in hierarchy etc*) arriver en haut de l'échelle; **from ~ to toe, from the ~ of his head to the tip of his toes** de la tête (jusqu')aux pieds; **from ~ to bottom** *paint* complètement, de haut en bas; *cover* entièrement; *search a person* des pieds à la tête; *search a house* de fond en comble; **he's saying that off the ~ of his head*** il dit ça comme ça (mais il n'en est pas certain), il parle sans savoir ce qu'il dit (*pej*); **the system is rotten from ~ to bottom** le système tout entier est pourri; (*Ir*) **the ~ of the morning to you!** je vous souhaite bien le bonjour!; (*Brit Aut*) **in ~ = in top gear** (*see* **2**); **he's (the) ~s**‡ il est champion*; *see* **blow**[1], **tree, up** *etc.*

b **on (the) ~ of** sur; **on ~ of it, on (the) ~** (en) dessus; **it's the one on (the) ~** c'est celui qui est en dessus; **take the plate on the ~** prends l'assiette du dessus; (*fig*) **he came out on ~** il a eu le dessus, il l'a emporté; **let's go up on ~** (*in bus*) on va en haut; (*in ship*) on va sur le pont; (*fig*) **to live on ~ of each other** vivre les uns sur les autres; (*fig*) **in such a small flat the children are always on ~ of us** dans un appartement si petit, les enfants sont toujours dans nos jambes; (*fig*) **to be on ~ of the world** être aux anges; **to be on the ~ of one's form** être au meilleur de sa forme; (*fig*) **he's on ~ of things now*** il s'en sort très bien *or* il domine bien la situation maintenant; (*after breakdown, bereavement*) il a repris le dessus maintenant; **things are getting on ~ of her*** elle est dépassée, elle ne sait plus où donner de la tête; (*fig*) **the lorry was right on ~ of the car in front** le camion touchait presque la voiture de devant; **by the time I saw the car, it was practically on ~ of me** quand j'ai vu la voiture elle était pratiquement sur moi; **he bought another car on ~ of the one he's got already** il a acheté une autre auto en plus de celle qu'il a déjà; **then on ~ of all that he refused to help us** et puis par-dessus le marché il a refusé de nous aider.

c (*upper part, section*) *[car etc]* toit *m*; *[bus]* étage supérieur; (*open ~*) impériale *f*; *[garment, pyjamas, bikini]* haut *m*; *[plant, vegetable]* fane *f*. (*on box etc*) "~" "dessus", "haut"; (*Aut*) **a sliding** *or* **sunshine ~** un toit ouvrant; (*on bus*) **seats on ~** places *fpl* à l'étage supérieur; **we saw London from the ~ of a bus** nous avons vu Londres du haut d'un bus; **I want a ~ to go with this skirt** je voudrais un haut qui aille avec cette jupe; **the table ~ is made of oak** le plateau de la table est en chêne; **the table ~ is scratched** le dessus de la table est rayé; **she hasn't got much up ~** (*: *she is stupid*) ce n'est pas une lumière*; (‡: *she has small breasts*) elle est plate comme une limande* *or* une planche à repasser*; *see* **big** *etc.*

d (*cap, lid*) *[box]* couvercle *m*; *[bottle]* (*screw-on*) bouchon *m*; (*snap-on*) capsule *f*; *[pen]* capuchon *m*.

2 adj (*highest*) *shelf, drawer* du haut; *floor, storey* dernier; (*highest in rank etc*) premier; (*best*) (le) meilleur. **the ~ step** la dernière marche (d'en haut); *[paint]* **the ~ coat** la dernière couche (*see also* **3**); **the ~ right-hand corner** le coin en haut à droite; (*Mus*) **the ~ note** la note la plus haute; **at the ~ end of the scale** en haut de l'échelle; **a car at the ~ end of the range** une voiture haut de gamme; **~ prices** prix *mpl* maximums *or* maxima; **we pay ~ price(s) for old clocks** nous offrons les meilleurs prix pour les vieilles horloges; (*US*) **to pay ~ dollar for sth** payer qch au prix fort; **at ~ speed** à toute vitesse; (*Brit Aut*) **in ~ gear** (*four-speed box*) en quatrième; (*five-speed box*) en cinquième; **in** *or* **on ~ form** en pleine forme; (*Scol*) **he was** *or* **came ~ in maths** il a été premier en maths; **the ~ mark** la meilleure note; (*fig*) **~ marks for efficiency** vingt sur vingt pour efficacité; (*Scol*) **in the ~ class** (*secondary school*) ≃ en terminale; (*primary*) ≃ au cours moyen deux; (*~ stream*) dans le premier groupe; (*Mus*) **the ~ 10** les dix premiers du Top; **the ~ 30** (*singles*) ≃ le Top 50; (*albums*) le Top 30; **the ~ men in the party** les dirigeants *mpl* du parti; **one of the ~ pianists** un des plus grands pianistes; **a ~ job, one of the ~ jobs** un des postes les plus prestigieux; **~ management** cadres *mpl* supérieurs; **the newspaper for ~ people** le journal de l'élite; **it's ~ security** c'est top secret; *see also* **3, whack 1c**.

3 comp ▸**top banana**‡ (*US*) (*gen*) gros bonnet; (*Theat*) comique *m* principal ▸**top boots** bottes *fpl* à revers ▸**top brass*** (*fig*) huiles* *fpl* ▸**topcoat** (*Dress*) pardessus *m*, manteau *m* ▸**top copy** original *m* ▸**top-dog*** adj (*US*) le meilleur; **he's top dog around here** c'est lui qui commande ici *or* qui fait la pluie et le beau temps ici ▸**top-down information** information *f* descendante ▸**top-drawer*** (*socially*) aristocratique; (*in quality, achievement*) de tout premier rang; **he's out of the top drawer** il est de bonne famille, il fait partie du gratin* ▸**top-dress** (*Agr*) fumer en surface ▸**top dressing** fumure *f* en surface ▸**topflight*** de premier ordre, excellent ▸**top hand*** (*US*) collaborateur *m* de premier plan ▸**top hat** (chapeau *m*) haut-de-forme *m* ▸**top-hatted** en (chapeau) haut-de-forme ▸**top-heavy** *structure etc* trop lourd du haut; (*fig*) *organization* mal équilibré ▸**top-hole***† (*Brit*) de première*, au poil* ▸**topknot** (*hair*) toupet *m*, houppe *f*; (*ribbons etc*) coque *f*; (*bird's feathers*) aigrette *f* ▸**top-level** *meeting, talks, discussion* au plus haut niveau; *decision* pris au plus haut niveau *or* au sommet ▸**top-liner*** (*Brit Theat*) (artiste *mf* en) tête *f* d'affiche ▸**top-loader** machine *f* à laver à chargement par le dessus ▸**top-loading** *washing machine* à chargement par le dessus ▸**topmast** (*Naut*) mât *m* de hune ▸**topmost** le plus haut ▸**topnotch***† = **topflight*** ▸**top-ranking** (très) haut placé ▸**topsail** (*Naut*) hunier *m* ▸**top-secret** ultra-secret (*f* ultra-secrète), top secret (*f* top secrète) ▸**top-security wing** *[prison]* quartier *m* de haute surveillance ▸**topside** n (*Brit Culin*) gîte *m* (à la noix); (*Naut*) haut *m*, accastillage *m* ◊ adj (*US* *) *official etc* haut placé, de haut niveau ▸**topsider*** (*US*) personnage haut placé ▸**topsoil** terre *f*; (*Agr*) couche *f* arable ▸**top spin** (*Tennis*) lift *m* ▸**top-up**: **can I offer you a top-up?** je vous en remets?; (*Aut*) **the battery/oil needs a top-up** il faut remettre de l'eau dans la batterie/remettre de l'huile; **top-up loan** prêt *m* complémentaire; **top-up policy** rallonge *f* de police.

4 vt a (*remove ~ from*) *tree* étêter, écimer; *plant* écimer; *radish, carrot etc* couper *or* enlever les fanes de; (‡: *behead*) *person* couper le cou à*; (‡: *kill*) *person* buter‡. **to ~ and tail fruit** préparer des fruits (*en les équeutant etc*).

b (*form ~ of*) surmonter. **~ped by a dome** surmonté d'un dôme.

c (*exceed*) dépasser. **we have ~ped last year's sales figures** nous avons dépassé les chiffres de vente de l'année dernière; **the fish ~ped 10 kg** le poisson pesait *or* faisait plus de 10 kg; **to ~ sb in height** dépasser qn en hauteur; (*fig*) **and to ~ it all** ... et pour couronner le tout ..., et pour comble ...; **that ~s the lot!*** c'est le bouquet!*

d (*pass ~ of*) *hill* franchir le sommet de; *ridge* franchir.

e (*be at ~ of*) *pile* être au sommet de; *list, queue* être en tête de *or* à la tête de. (*Theat*) **to ~ the bill** être en tête d'affiche, tenir la vedette.

▸**top off** 1 vi (*reach peak*) *[sales, production etc]* atteindre son (*or* leur) maximum (et se stabiliser). 2 vt sep terminer, compléter. **we topped off the meal with a glass of cognac** nous avons couronné *or* complété le repas par un verre de cognac.

▸**top out** vi (*Constr*) terminer le gros œuvre; (*Comm*) *[rate, price, cost]* plafonner, atteindre son point le plus élevé.

►**top up** (*Brit*) 1 vi (*Aut*) **to top up with oil** remettre *or* rajouter de l'huile. 2 vt sep *cup, glass* remplir (à nouveau); (*Aut*) *battery* remettre de l'eau dans. **I've topped up the petrol in your tank** j'ai rajouté *or* remis de l'essence dans votre réservoir; **I've topped up your coffee** je vous ai remis du café; (*fig*) **her parents top up her grant** ses parents lui donnent de l'argent en complément de sa bourse; **can I top you up?*** je vous en remets? 3 **top-up** n *see* **top 3**.

top[2] [tɒp] n (*toy*) toupie *f*; *see* **sleep, spinning**.

topaz [ˈtəʊpæz] n topaze *f*.

tope† [təʊp] vi picoler.

topee [ˈtəʊpiː] n casque colonial.

toper† [ˈtəʊpəʳ] n grand buveur.

topiary [ˈtəʊpɪərɪ] n (*NonC*) art *m* topiaire.

topic [ˈtɒpɪk] n [*essay, speech*] sujet *m*; (*for discussion*) sujet de discussion, thème *m*; (*Scol, esp Brit: project*) dossier *m*; (*Ling*) thème *m*.

topical [ˈtɒpɪkəl] adj d'actualité.

topicality [ˌtɒpɪˈkælɪtɪ] n (*NonC*) actualité *f*.

topless [ˈtɒplɪs] adj *costume* sans haut; *girl* aux seins nus; *beach* seins nus; *bar* où les serveuses ont les seins nus. ~ **swimsuit** monokini* *m*.

topographer [təˈpɒgrəfəʳ] n topographe *mf*.

topographic(al) [ˌtɒpəˈgræfɪk(l)] adj topographique.

topography [təˈpɒgrəfɪ] n topographie *f*.

topper* [ˈtɒpəʳ] n a (*hat*) (chapeau *m*) haut-de-forme *m*. b (*US*) **the ~* was that ...** le comble *or* le plus fort, c'est que ... .

topping [ˈtɒpɪŋ] 1 adj (*Brit* *†) épatant*. 2 n (*for pizza*) garniture *f*. (*NonC*) **chocolate/orange** ~ crème *f* au chocolat/à l'orange (*dont on nappe un dessert*); **dessert with a ~ of whipped cream** dessert *m* nappé de crème fouettée.

topple [ˈtɒpl] 1 vi (*lose balance*) [*person*] basculer, culbuter, perdre l'équilibre; [*pile*] basculer; (*fall: also* ~ **over**, ~ **down**) [*person*] tomber; [*pile etc*] s'effondrer, se renverser; [*empire, dictator, government*] tomber. **to ~ over a cliff** tomber du haut d'une falaise. 2 vt sep *object* faire tomber, faire basculer, renverser; *government, ruler* renverser, faire tomber.

topsy-turvy [ˈtɒpsɪˈtɜːvɪ] adj, adv sens dessus dessous, à l'envers. **to turn everything ~** tout mettre sens dessus dessous, tout bouleverser *or* chambouler*; **everything is ~** tout est sens dessus dessous; (*fig*) c'est le monde à l'envers *or* renversé.

toque [təʊk] n toque *f*.

tor [tɔːʳ] n butte *f* (rocheuse).

torch [tɔːtʃ] 1 n (*flaming*) torche *f*, flambeau *m* (*also fig*); (*Brit: electric*) lampe *f* de poche, lampe *or* torche électrique. **the house went up like a ~** la maison s'est mise à flamber comme du bois sec; (*fig*) **he still carries a ~ for her*** il en pince toujours pour elle*; *see* **Olympic**. 2 comp ►**torchbearer** porteur *m* de flambeau *or* de torche ►**torchlight**: **by torchlight** à la lumière des flambeaux (*or* d'une lampe de poche); **torchlight procession** retraite *f* aux flambeaux ►**torch singer** (*US*) chanteuse *f* tragique ►**torch song** chanson *f* d'amour tragique.

tore [tɔːʳ] pret of **tear[1]**.

toreador [ˈtɒrɪədɔːʳ] n toréador *m*.

torero [təˈrɛərəʊ] n torero *m*.

torment [ˈtɔːment] 1 n tourment *m* (*liter*), supplice *m*. **to be in ~** être au supplice; **the ~s of jealousy** les affres *fpl* de la jalousie; **to suffer ~s** souffrir le martyre. 2 [tɔːˈment] vt (*cause pain to*) tourmenter, torturer, martyriser; (*harass*) *person, animal* harceler, tourmenter. (*fig*) **to ~ o.s.** se tourmenter, se torturer; **~ed by jealousy** torturé *or* rongé par la jalousie.

tormentor [tɔːˈmentəʳ] n persécuteur *m*, -trice *f*, (*stronger*) bourreau *m*.

torn [tɔːn] ptp of **tear[1]**.

tornado [tɔːˈneɪdəʊ] n, pl ~s *or* ~es tornade *f*.

Toronto [təˈrɒntəʊ] n Toronto.

torpedo [tɔːˈpiːdəʊ] 1 n, pl ~es (*weapon, fish*) torpille *f*. 2 comp ►**torpedo attack**: **to make a torpedo attack** attaquer à la torpille ►**torpedo boat** torpilleur *m*, vedette *f* lance-torpilles ►**torpedo tube** (tube *m*) lance-torpilles *m inv*. 3 vt torpiller (*also fig*).

torpid [ˈtɔːpɪd] adj engourdi, torpide.

torpidity [tɔːˈpɪdɪtɪ] n, **torpor** [ˈtɔːpəʳ] n torpeur *f*, engourdissement *m*.

torque [tɔːk] 1 n (*Phys*) moment *m* de torsion; (*Aut*) couple *m* moteur; (*Hist: collar*) torque *m*. 2 comp ►**torque converter** (*Aut*) convertisseur *m* de couple ►**torque spanner, torque wrench** clef *f* dynamométrique.

torrent [ˈtɒrənt] n torrent *m* (*also fig*). **the rain was coming down in ~s** il pleuvait à torrents.

torrential [tɒˈrenʃəl] adj torrentiel.

torrid [ˈtɒrɪd] adj *climate, heat* torride; (*fig*) *passion, love affair* ardent. (*Geog*) **the T~ Zone** la zone intertropicale.

torsi [ˈtɔːsɪ] npl of **torso**.

torsion [ˈtɔːʃən] 1 n torsion *f*. 2 comp ►**torsion balance** balance *f* de torsion ►**torsion bar** barre *f* de torsion.

torso [ˈtɔːsəʊ] n, pl ~s *or* (*rare*) **torsi** (*Anat*) torse *m*; (*Sculp*) buste *m*.

tort [tɔːt] n (*Jur*) acte délictuel *or* quasi-délictuel. (*US Jur*) **~s lawyer** *avocat spécialisé en droit civil*.

tortilla [tɔːˈtiːə] n tortilla *f*.

tortoise [ˈtɔːtəs] 1 n tortue *f*. 2 comp ►**tortoiseshell** n écaille *f* (de tortue) ◊ comp *ornament, comb* en *or* d'écaille; *spectacles* à monture d'écaille ►**tortoiseshell (butterfly)** (papillon *m*) grande tortue ►**tortoiseshell (cat)** chat *m* écaille-de-tortue.

tortuous [ˈtɔːtjʊəs] adj *path* tortueux, sinueux; *methods, argument* tortueux, détourné; *mind* tortueux, retors (*pej*).

torture [ˈtɔːtʃəʳ] 1 n torture *f*, supplice *m*. **to put sb to (the) ~** torturer qn, faire subir des tortures à qn; (*fig*) **it was sheer ~!** c'était un vrai supplice! 2 comp ►**torture chamber** chambre *f* de torture. 3 vt (*lit*) torturer; (*fig*) torturer, mettre à la torture *or* au supplice; *senses etc* mettre au supplice; *language* écorcher; *meaning* dénaturer; *tune* massacrer. (*fig*) **to ~ o.s.** se torturer; **~d by doubt** torturé *or* tenaillé par le doute.

torturer [ˈtɔːtʃərəʳ] n tortionnaire *m*, bourreau *m*.

Tory [ˈtɔːrɪ] (*Pol*) 1 n tory *m*, conservateur *m*, -trice *f*. 2 adj *party, person, policy* tory *inv*, conservateur (*f* -trice).

Toryism [ˈtɔːrɪɪzəm] n (*Pol*) torysme *m*.

tosh‡ [tɒʃ] n (*NonC*) bêtises *fpl*, blagues *fpl*. (*excl*) ~! allons (donc)!

toss [tɒs] 1 n a (*throw*) lancement *m*; (*by bull*) coup *m* de cornes. (*from horse*) **to take a ~** faire une chute, être désarçonné; **with a ~ of his head** d'un mouvement brusque de la tête; **I don't give a ~‡** je m'en contrefous‡, j'en ai rien à branler** (*about* de).

b [*coin*] coup *m* de pile ou face; (*Sport: at start of match*) tirage *m* au sort. **they decided it by the ~ of a coin** ils l'ont décidé à pile ou face; **to win/lose the ~** (*gen*) gagner/perdre à pile ou face; (*Sport*) gagner/perdre au tirage au sort; *see* **argue**.

2 comp ►**toss-up** [*coin*] coup *m* de pile ou face; (*fig*) **it was a toss-up between the theatre and the cinema** le théâtre ou le cinéma, ça nous (*or* leur *etc*) était égal *or* c'était kif-kif*; **it's a toss-up whether I go or stay** que je parte ou que je reste (*subj*), c'est un peu à pile ou face.

3 vt *ball etc* lancer, jeter (*to* à); (*Brit*) *pancake* faire sauter; *salad* retourner, remuer; *head, mane* rejeter en arrière; [*bull*] projeter en l'air; [*horse*] désarçonner, démonter. **to ~ sb in a blanket** faire sauter qn dans une couverture; (*Culin*) ~ **in butter** ajoutez un morceau de beurre et remuez; **they ~ed a coin to decide who should stay** ils ont joué à pile ou face pour décider qui resterait; **I'll ~ you for it** on le joue à pile ou face; **the sea ~ed the boat against the rocks** la mer a projeté *or* envoyé le bateau sur les rochers; **the boat was ~ed by the waves** le bateau était agité *or* ballotté par les vagues; *see* **caber**.

4 vi a (*often* ~ **about**, ~ **around**) [*person*] s'agiter; [*plumes, trees*] se balancer; [*boat*] tanguer. **he was ~ing (about *or* around) in his sleep** il s'agitait dans son sommeil, son sommeil était agité; **he was ~ing and turning all night** il n'a pas arrêté de se tourner et se retourner toute la nuit.

b (*often* ~ **up**) jouer à pile ou face. **let's ~ (up) for it** on le joue à pile ou face; **they ~ed (up) to see who would stay** ils ont joué à pile ou face pour savoir qui resterait.

►**toss about, toss around** 1 vi *see* **toss 4a**. 2 vt sep *boat etc* ballotter, faire tanguer; *plumes, branches* agiter. (*fig*) **to toss one's money about** jeter l'argent par les fenêtres.

►**toss aside** vt sep *object* jeter de côté; (*fig*) *person, helper* repousser; *suggestion, offer* rejeter, repousser; *scheme* rejeter.

►**toss away** vt sep jeter.

►**toss back** vt sep *ball etc* renvoyer; *hair, mane* rejeter en arrière. (*fig*) **they were tossing ideas back and forth** ils échangeaient toutes sortes d'idées.

►**toss off** 1 vi (**: *masturbate*) se branler** 2 vt sep a *drink* lamper, avaler d'un coup; *essay, letter, poem* écrire au pied levé, torcher (*pej*). b (**: *masturbate*) branler**, faire une branlette à**. **to toss o.s. off** = **toss off 1**.

►**toss out** vt sep *rubbish* jeter; *person* mettre à la porte, jeter dehors.

►**toss over** vt sep lancer. **toss it over!** envoie!, lance!

►**toss up** 1 vi *see* **toss 4b**. 2 vt sep *object* lancer, jeter (*into the air* en l'air). 3 **toss-up** n *see* **toss 2**.

tosser** [tɒsəʳ] n (*Brit*) branleur** *m*.

tot[1] [tɒt] n a (*child: also* **tiny** ~) petit(e) enfant *m(f)*, tout(e) petit(e) *m(f)*, bambin *m*. b (*esp Brit: drink*) **a ~ of whisky** un petit verre de whisky; **just a ~** juste une goutte *or* une larme.

tot[2]* [tɒt] (*esp Brit*) 1 vt (*also* ~ **up**) additionner, faire le total de. 2 vi: **it ~s up to £5** ça fait 5 livres en tout, ça se monte *or* ça s'élève à 5 livres; **I'm just ~ting up** je fais le total.

total [ˈtəʊtl] 1 adj *sum, amount, quantity* total, global; *eclipse, war* total; *failure, silence* total, complet (*f* -ète), absolu. **the ~ losses/sales/debts** le total des pertes/ventes/dettes; **it was a ~ loss** on a tout perdu; **to be in ~ ignorance of sth** être dans l'ignorance la plus complète de qch, ignorer complètement qch; **they were in ~ disagreement** ils étaient en complet désaccord; (*memory*) ~ **recall** remémoration totale; *see* **abstainer, abstinence**.

2 n a (montant *m*) total *m*, somme *f* (totale). **it comes to a ~ of £5, the ~ comes to £5** le total s'élève à 5 livres, cela fait 5 livres en tout; *see* **grand, sum**.

b **in ~** au total.

3 vt a (*add: also* ~ **up**) *figures, expenses* totaliser, faire le total de, additionner.
b (*amount to*) s'élever à. **that ~s £5** cela fait 5 livres (en tout), cela s'élève à 5 livres; **the class ~led 40** il y avait 40 élèves en tout dans la classe.
c (*US* ⁑: *wreck*) *car* bousiller*, démolir.

totalitarian [ˌtəʊtælɪˈtɛərɪən] adj, n totalitaire (*mf*).

totalitarianism [ˌtəʊtælɪˈtɛərɪənɪzəm] n totalitarisme *m*.

totality [təʊˈtælɪtɪ] n totalité *f*.

totalizator [ˈtəʊtəlaɪzeɪtəʳ] n a (*adding etc machine*) (appareil *m*) totalisateur *m*, machine totalisatrice. b (*Betting: esp Brit*) pari mutuel.

totalize [ˈtəʊtəlaɪz] vt totaliser, additionner.

totalizer [ˈtəʊtəlaɪzəʳ] n = **totalizator**.

totally [ˈtəʊtəlɪ] adv totalement, entièrement, complètement.

tote[1]* [təʊt] 1 n abbr of **totalizator b**. 2 comp ▸**tote board** tableau *m* totalisateur. 3 vt (*US*) **to ~ up** additionner.

tote[2] [təʊt] 1 vt (*: *carry*) *gun, object* porter. **I ~d it around all day** je l'ai coltiné* *or* trimballé* toute la journée. 2 comp ▸**tote bag** (*esp US*) (sac *m*) fourre-tout* *m*.

totem [ˈtəʊtəm] n totem *m*. ~ **pole** mât *m* totémique.

totemic [təʊˈtemɪk] adj totémique.

totter [ˈtɒtəʳ] vi *[person]* chanceler, vaciller, tituber; *[object, column, chimney stack]* chanceler, vaciller; (*fig*) *[company, government]* chanceler. **to ~ in/out** *etc* entrer/sortir *etc* en titubant *or* d'un pas chancelant.

tottering [ˈtɒtərɪŋ] adj, **tottery** [ˈtɒtərɪ] adj chancelant.

toucan [ˈtuːkən] n toucan *m*.

touch [tʌtʃ] 1 n a (*sense of* ~) toucher *m*. **Braille is read by ~** le braille se lit au toucher; **soft to the ~** doux (*f* douce) au toucher; **the cold ~ of marble** le toucher froid du marbre.
b (*act of ~ing*) contact *m*, toucher *m*; (*light brushing*) frôlement *m*, effleurement *m*; *[instrumentalist, typist]* toucher; *[artist]* touche *f*. **the slightest ~ might break it** le moindre contact pourrait le casser; **to give sb a ~ on the arm** toucher le bras de qn; **I felt a ~ on my arm** j'ai senti qu'on me touchait le bras; **at the ~ of her hand, he ...** au contact de sa main, il ...; **with the ~ of a finger** à la simple pression d'un doigt; **at the ~ of a switch** au simple contact d'un bouton; **she felt the ~ of the wind on her cheek** elle sentait le contact *or* la caresse du vent sur sa joue; **he altered it with a ~ of the brush/pen** il l'a modifié d'un coup de pinceau/d'un trait de plume; **to have a light ~** *[pianist, typist]* avoir le toucher léger; *[typewriter]* avoir une frappe légère; **you can see the master's ~ in this portrait** vous pouvez voir la touche du maître dans ce portrait; (*lit, fig*) **to put the final *or* finishing ~(es) to sth, to give sth the final *or* finishing ~(es)** mettre la dernière main à qch; **it has the ~ of genius** cela porte le sceau du génie; **he lacks the human *or* personal ~** il est trop impersonnel *or* froid, il manque de chaleur humaine; **it's the human *or* personal ~ that makes his speeches so successful** c'est la note personnelle qui fait que ses discours ont tant de succès; **that's the Nelson ~** c'est du Nelson (tout pur); **you've got the right ~ with him** vous savez vous y prendre avec lui.
c (*small amount*) ~ **of** un tout petit peu de; **a ~ of colour/gaiety** une touche de couleur/de gaieté; **a ~ of sadness/humour** une pointe *or* une note de tristesse/d'humour; **it is a ~ (too) expensive** c'est un tout petit peu (trop) cher; **there's a ~ of spring in the air** ça sent le printemps; **there's a ~ of frost/cold in the air** il pourrait bien geler/faire froid; **he got a ~ of the sun** il a pris un petit coup de soleil; **to have a ~ of flu** être un peu grippé; **to have a ~ of rheumatism** faire un peu de rhumatisme; **it needs a ~ of paint** il faudrait y passer une petite couche de peinture.
d (*contact, communication*) **to be/keep in ~ with sb** être/rester en contact *or* en rapport *or* en relation avec qn; **I'll be in ~!** je t'écrirai! (*or* je te téléphonerai!); **keep in ~!** tiens-nous au courant!, écris de temps en temps!; **to be out of ~ with sb, to have lost ~ with sb** avoir perdu le contact avec qn, ne plus être en contact *or* en rapport *or* en relation avec qn; **to be out of ~ *or* to have lost ~ with the political situation** ne plus être au courant de la situation politique, être déphasé en matière de politique*; **to lose ~ with reality *or* the facts** ne plus avoir le sens des réalités; (*fig*) **he's completely out of ~, he has lost ~ with what is going on** il est complètement déphasé*, il n'est plus dans le coup*; **we're very much out of ~ here** nous sommes coupés de tout ici; **to get in(to) ~ with sb** se mettre en rapport *or* en relation avec qn, prendre contact avec qn, joindre *or* contacter* qn; **you can get in(to) ~ with me at this number** vous pouvez me joindre *or* m'atteindre *or* me contacter* à ce numéro; **you ought to get in ~ with the police** vous devriez prendre contact avec *or* contacter* la police; **to lose ~ with sb** perdre le contact avec qn; **they lost ~ (with each other) long ago** il y a bien longtemps qu'ils ne sont plus en relation *or* en rapport; **I'll put you in ~ with him** je vous mettrai en rapport *or* en relation avec lui.
e (*Ftbl, Rugby*) touche *f*. **the ball went into ~** le ballon est sorti en touche; **it is in ~** il y a touche; **to kick for ~, to kick the ball into ~** envoyer le ballon en touche.
f (⁑: *borrowing etc*) **he has made a ~** il a tapé* quelqu'un; **he's good for a ~, he's a soft *or* an easy ~** il est toujours prêt à se laisser taper*.
2 comp ▸**touch-and-go: it's touch-and-go with the sick man** le malade est entre la vie et la mort; **it was touch-and-go whether she did it** elle a été à deux doigts de ne pas le faire; **it was touch-and-go until the last minute** l'issue est restée incertaine jusqu'au bout ▸**touchdown** (*Aviat, Space*) (*on land*) atterrissage *m*; (*on sea*) amerrissage *m*; (*on moon*) alunissage *m*; (*US Ftbl*) essai *m* ▸**touch football** (*US*) *variante du jeu de football* ▸**touch judge** (*Rugby*) juge *m* de touche ▸**touchline** (*Ftbl etc*) (ligne *f* de) touche *f* ▸**touchpaper** papier nitraté ▸**touch-sensitive** *screen* tactile; *key* à effleurement ▸**touchstone** (*lit, fig*) pierre *f* de touche ▸**touch-type** taper au toucher ▸**touch-typing** dactylographie *f* au toucher ▸**touch-typist** dactylo* *f* qui tape au toucher ▸**touchwood** amadou *m*.
3 vt a (*come into contact with*) toucher; (*brush lightly*) frôler, effleurer. **"do not ~ the goods"** "ne touchez pas les *or* aux marchandises"; **he ~ed it with his finger** il l'a touché du doigt; **he ~ed her arm** il lui a touché le bras, il l'a touchée au bras; **his hand ~ed mine** sa main a touché *or* frôlé *or* effleuré la mienne; **to ~ one's hat to sb** saluer qn en portant la main à son chapeau; **I can ~ the bottom** je peux toucher le fond, j'ai pied; **the ship ~ed the bottom** le bateau a touché; **his feet are not ~ing the ground** ses pieds ne touchent pas terre; (*Aviat*) **to ~ ground** atterrir, toucher le sol; *see* **wood**.
b (*tamper with*) toucher à. **don't ~ that switch!** ne touchez pas à ce bouton!; **don't ~ that!** n'y touchez pas!; **the burglars didn't ~ the safe** les cambrioleurs n'ont pas touché au coffre-fort; **I didn't ~ it!** je n'y ai pas touché!; **I didn't ~ him!** je n'ai pas touché (à) un cheveu de sa tête, je ne lui ai rien fait; ~ **nothing till the police arrive** ne touchez à rien avant l'arrivée de la police.
c (*fig*) toucher à. **their land ~es ours** leur terre touche à *or* est contiguë à la nôtre; **Switzerland ~es Italy** la Suisse et l'Italie sont limitrophes *or* ont une frontière commune; **the ship ~ed Bordeaux** le bateau a fait escale à *or* a touché Bordeaux; **to ~ base** se mettre à jour *or* au courant; **he merely ~ed the problem of racism** il n'a fait qu'effleurer le problème du racisme; **the frost ~ed the plants** la gelée a abîmé les plantes; **the fire didn't ~ the paintings** l'incendie a épargné les tableaux; **they can't ~ you if you don't break the law** ils ne peuvent rien contre vous *or* rien vous faire si vous respectez la loi; (*in exam*) **I didn't ~ the 3rd question** je n'ai pas touché à la 3e question; **he won't ~ anything illegal** si c'est illégal il n'y touchera pas; **water won't ~ these stains** l'eau n'agira pas sur ces taches; **the steak is so tough the knife just won't ~ it** le bifteck est si dur que le couteau n'arrive pas à l'entamer *or* à y pénétrer; **clouds ~ed with pink** nuages à reflets roses; *see* **barge**.
d (*gen neg*) *food, drink* toucher à. **he didn't ~ his meal** il n'a pas touché à son repas; **I never ~ onions** je ne mange jamais d'oignons; **I won't ~ gin** je ne boirai pas *or* je ne prendrai pas de gin.
e (*equal, rival*) valoir, égaler. **her cooking doesn't *or* can't ~ yours** sa cuisine est loin de valoir la tienne; **there's no pianist to ~ him, there's nobody to ~ him as a pianist, nobody can ~ him as a pianist** personne ne peut l'égaler *or* il est sans égal comme pianiste; **there's nothing to ~ hot whisky for a cold** rien ne vaut un grog au whisky pour guérir un rhume.
f (*concern*) toucher, concerner, regarder. **it ~es us all closely** cela nous touche *or* nous concerne tous de très près; **if it ~es the national interest** s'il y va de l'intérêt national.
g (*move emotionally*) toucher. **we were very ~ed by your letter** nous avons été très touchés de votre lettre.
h (*) **to ~ sb for a loan** taper* qn; **I ~ed him for £10** je l'ai tapé* de 10 livres.
4 vi a *[hands, ends etc]* se toucher; *[lands, gardens, areas]* se toucher, être contigus (*f* -guës). (*fig*) **to ~ (up)on a subject** effleurer un sujet.
b (*meddle*) **don't ~!** n'y touchez pas!, ne touchez pas!; **"do not ~"** "défense de toucher".

▸**touch at** vt fus (*Naut*) toucher (à), faire escale à.

▸**touch down** 1 vi a (*Aviat, Space*) (*on land*) atterrir, toucher le sol; (*on sea*) amerrir; (*on moon*) alunir. b (*Rugby, US Ftbl*) marquer un essai; (*behind one's own goal-line*) toucher la balle dans l'en-but. 2 vt sep (*Rugby etc*) **to touch the ball down** marquer un essai; (*behind one's own goal-line*) toucher la balle dans l'en-but. 3 **touchdown** n *see* **touch 2**.

▸**touch off** vt sep *fuse, firework* faire partir; *mine etc* faire exploser *or* détoner *or* partir; *explosion* déclencher; (*fig*) *crisis, riot* faire éclater, déclencher; *reaction, scene, argument* provoquer, déclencher.

▸**touch up** vt sep a *painting, photo* retoucher. b (⁑: *sexually*) peloter⁑.

touché [tuːˈʃeɪ] excl (*Fencing*) touché!; (*fig*) très juste!

touched [tʌtʃt] adj (*moved*) touché (*by* de); (*: *mad*) toqué*, timbré*.

touchiness [ˈtʌtʃɪnɪs] n (*NonC*) susceptibilité *f*.

touching [ˈtʌtʃɪŋ] 1 adj touchant, attendrissant. 2 prep concernant, touchant (†, *liter*).

touchingly [ˈtʌtʃɪŋlɪ] adv d'une manière touchante.

touchy [ˈtʌtʃɪ] adj *person* susceptible (*about* sur la question *or* le chapitre de), chatouilleux, ombrageux; *matter, issue, problem* délicat, épineux; *business, situation* délicat. **he's very ~** il se vexe *or* s'offense pour un rien.

tough [tʌf] 1 adj a (*strong*) *cloth, steel, leather, garment etc* solide, résistant; (*pej*) *meat* dur, coriace. (*hum: of meat etc*) **it's as ~ as old boots** c'est de la semelle.

b (*of person: strong*) (*physically*) robuste, résistant; (*mentally*) solide, endurant. **you have to be ~ to do that kind of work** il faut de la résistance *or* il ne faut pas être une mauviette pour faire ce genre de travail; (*hum*) **as ~ as old boots*** coriace.

c (*of person: hard in character*) dur, tenace; *criminal, gangster* endurci. **as ~ as nails** dur à cuire; **he is a ~ man to deal with** il ne fait pas souvent de concessions; **~ guy** dur *m*; (*pej*) **they're a ~ lot, they're ~ customers** ce sont des durs à cuire*; **to get ~ with sb*** (commencer à) se montrer dur pour *or* envers qn.

d (*hard*) *resistance, struggle, opposition* acharné, âpre; *journey* rude, fatigant, pénible; *task* dur, rude, pénible; *obstacle* rude, sérieux; *problem* épineux; *regulations* sévère; *conditions* dur, sévère. **it's ~ work** c'est un travail dur *or* pénible, ce n'est pas du gâteau* *or* de la tarte*; **rugby is a ~ game** le rugby n'est pas un sport de *or* pour fillettes; **to take a ~ line (with sb)** employer la manière forte (avec qn).

e (*: *unfortunate*) **that's ~** c'est vache*; **to have a ~ time of it*** en voir de dures*; **it was ~ on the others** c'était vache* pour les autres; **~ luck** déveine* *f*, manque *m* de pot*; **~ luck!** (*pity*) pas de veine!, manque de pot!*; (*you'll have to put up with it*) tant pis pour vous!; **that's ~ luck on him** il n'a pas de veine *or* de pot*; **~ shit!**‡ démerdez-vous!‡, tant pis pour vous!

2 n (*) dur *m*.

3 adv: **to talk** *or* **act ~** jouer au dur.

4 vt (*fig*) **to ~ it out*** (*hold out*) tenir bon, faire front; (*rough it*) vivre à la dure.

5 comp ▸**tough-minded** dur (à cuire) ▸**tough-mindedness** dureté *f*.

toughen ['tʌfn] (*also* ~ **up**) 1 vt *metal, glass, cloth, leather* rendre plus solide, renforcer; *person* endurcir, aguerrir; *conditions* rendre plus sévère. **~ed glass** verre trempé. 2 vi [*metal, glass, cloth, leather*] devenir plus solide; [*person*] s'endurcir, s'aguerrir; [*conditions, regulations*] devenir plus sévère.

toughly ['tʌflɪ] adv *fight, oppose* avec acharnement, âprement; *speak, answer* durement, sans ménagement. **it is ~ made** c'est du solide.

toughness ['tʌfnɪs] n (*NonC: see* **tough**) solidité *f*, résistance *f*; dureté *f*, endurance *f*; acharnement *m*, âpreté *f*; caractère *m* pénible *or* rude; caractère épineux; sévérité *f*; ténacité *f*.

toupee ['tu:peɪ] n postiche *m*.

tour ['tʊəʳ] 1 n (*journey*) voyage *m*, périple *m*; (*by team, actors, musicians etc*) tournée *f*; (*by premier, visiting statesman etc*) visite officielle, tournée de visites; (*of town, factory, museum etc*) visite, tour *m*; (*package ~*) voyage organisé; (*day ~*) excursion *f*. (*Hist*) **the Grand T~** le tour de l'Europe; **they went on a ~ of the Lake District** ils ont fait un voyage *or* un périple dans la région des Lacs; **we went on** *or* **made a ~ of the Loire castles** nous avons visité *or* fait* les châteaux de la Loire; **they went on a ~ to Spain** ils sont allés en voyage organisé *or* ils ont fait un voyage organisé en Espagne; **the ~ includes 3 days in Venice** le voyage comprend 3 jours à Venise; **to go on a ~ round the world** faire le tour du monde; **to go on a walking/cycling ~** faire une randonnée à pied/en bicyclette; (*sign on coach*) **"on ~"** "excursion"; (*Sport, Theat etc*) **to go on ~** faire une tournée; **to be on ~** être en tournée; (*Theat etc*) **to take a company on ~** emmener une troupe en tournée; **to take a play on ~** donner une pièce en tournée; **~ of inspection** tournée d'inspection; (*Mil etc*) **~ of duty** période *f* de service; *see* **conduct** *etc*.

2 comp ▸**tour guide** (*person*) guide *mf* ▸**tour operator** (*Brit*) (*bus company*) compagnie *f* de cars (faisant des voyages organisés); (*travel agency*) tour-opérateur *m*, voyagiste *m*.

3 vt *district, town, exhibition, museum, factory* visiter. **they are ~ing France** ils visitent la France, ils font du tourisme en France; (*Sport, Theat*) ils sont en tournée en France; **the play is ~ing the provinces** la pièce tourne en province *or* est en tournée en province.

4 vi: **to go ~ing** voyager, faire du tourisme; **they went ~ing in Italy** ils sont allés visiter l'Italie, ils ont fait du tourisme en Italie.

tourer ['tʊərəʳ] n (*car*) voiture *f* de tourisme; (*caravan*) caravane *f*.

touring ['tʊərɪŋ] 1 n (*NonC*) tourisme *m*, voyages *mpl* touristiques. 2 adj *team* en tournée. **~ car** voiture *f* de tourisme; (*Theat*) **~ company** (*permanently*) troupe ambulante; (*temporarily*) troupe en tournée. 3 comp ▸**touring bindings** (*Ski*) fixations *fpl* de randonnée.

tourism ['tʊərɪzəm] n tourisme *m*.

tourist ['tʊərɪst] 1 n touriste *mf*. **"T~s' Guide to London"** "Guide touristique de Londres"; (*Sport: touring team*) **the ~s** les visiteurs *mpl*, l'équipe *f* en tournée. 2 comp *class, ticket* touriste *inv*; *season* des touristes ▸**tourist agency** agence *f* de tourisme ▸**tourist bureau** = **tourist office** ▸**tourist court** (*US*) motel *m* ▸**tourist home** (*US*) *maison dans laquelle des chambres sont louées aux touristes* ▸**tourist information (centre), tourist (information) office** office *m* de tourisme, syndicat *m* d'initiative ▸**tourist trade** tourisme *m* ▸**tourist traffic** flot *m* *or* afflux *m* des touristes (en voiture) ▸**tourist trap** attrape-touristes *m*. 3 adv *travel* en classe touriste.

touristas [tʊ'rɪstəs] npl (*US*) **the ~**‡ la diarrhée, la courante‡.

touristy* ['tʊərɪstɪ] adj (*pej*) trop touristique.

tournament ['tʊənəmənt] n (*Hist, gen*) tournoi *m*. **chess/tennis ~** tournoi d'échecs/de tennis.

tourney ['tʊənɪ] n (*Hist*) tournoi *m*.

tourniquet ['tʊənɪkeɪ] n (*Med*) tourniquet *m*, garrot *m*.

tousle ['taʊzl] vt *hair* ébouriffer; *clothes* chiffonner, friper, froisser; *bed, bedclothes* mettre en désordre.

tousled ['taʊzld] adj *person* échevelé; *hair* ébouriffé, échevelé; *clothes* chiffonné, fripé, froissé; *bed, bedclothes* en désordre.

tout [taʊt] 1 n (*gen*) vendeur ambulant; (*for custom*) racoleur *m*; (*for hotels*) rabatteur *m*; (*Racing*) pronostiqueur *m*; (*also* **ticket ~**) revendeur *m* de billets (*au marché noir*). 2 vt *wares* vendre (avec insistance); *tickets* revendre (*au marché noir*). 3 vi raccrocher les passants; (*Horse Racing*) vendre des pronostics. **to ~ for custom** raccrocher *or* racoler *or* accoster les clients, courir après la clientèle; **the taxi drivers were ~ing for the hotels** les chauffeurs de taxi racolaient des clients pour les hôtels.

▸**tout about, tout (a)round** vt sep *wares* vendre (avec insistance). **he has been touting those books about for weeks*** ça fait des semaines qu'il essaie de placer *or* de caser* ces livres.

tow[1] [təʊ] 1 n a (*act*) remorquage *m*; (*line*) câble *m* de remorquage; (*vehicle etc towed*) véhicule *m* en remorque. (*lit*) **to give sb a ~, to have sb in ~** remorquer qn; (*fig*) **he had a couple of girls in ~*** il avait deux filles dans son sillage (*fig*); **to be on ~** (*Brit*) *or* **in ~** (*US*) être en remorque; (*sign*) **"on ~"** "véhicule en remorque"; **to take a car in ~** prendre une voiture en remorque.

b (*ski ~*) téléski *m*, tire-fesses* *m*.

2 comp ▸**towaway zone** (*US Aut*) zone *f* de stationnement interdit (avec mise en fourrière) ▸**tow bar** barre *f* de remorquage ▸**towboat** remorqueur *m* ▸**tow car** (*esp US*) voiture remorqueuse ▸**towing-line, towing-rope** câble *m* de remorquage ▸**towing-truck** dépanneuse *f* ▸**towline** = **towing-line** ▸**towpath** chemin *m* de halage ▸**towrope** = **towing-rope** ▸**tow-start:** (*Aut*) **to give sb a tow-start** faire démarrer qn en remorque ▸**tow truck** (*US*) dépanneuse *f*.

3 vt *boat, vehicle* remorquer (*to, into* jusqu'à); *caravan, trailer* tirer, tracter; *barge* haler.

▸**tow away** vt sep *vehicle* remorquer; [*police*] emmener en fourrière.

tow[2] [təʊ] 1 n (*Tex*) filasse *f*, étoupe *f* (blanche). 2 comp ▸**tow-haired, tow-headed** aux cheveux (blond) filasse.

towage ['təʊɪdʒ] n remorquage *m*.

toward(s) [tə'wɔ:d(z)] prep a (*of direction*) vers, du côté de, dans la direction de. **if he comes ~ you** s'il vient vers vous *or* dans votre direction *or* de votre côté; **his back was ~ the door** il tournait le dos à la porte; (*fig*) **we are moving ~ a solution/war** *etc* nous nous acheminons vers une solution/la guerre *etc*; **they have begun negotiations ~ an agreement on ...** ils ont entamé des négociations en vue d'un accord sur ...; **he is saving ~ a new car** il fait des économies pour (acheter) une nouvelle voiture; **I'll put the prize money ~ a new car** le prix servira à m'acheter une nouvelle voiture; **all donations will go ~ a new roof** tous les dons serviront à l'achat d'un nouveau toit.

b (*of time*) vers. **~ 10 o'clock** vers *or* sur le coup de 10 heures, sur les 10 heures; **~ the end of the century** vers la fin du siècle.

c (*of attitude*) envers, à l'égard de. **his attitude ~ them** son attitude envers eux *or* à leur égard; **my feelings ~ him** mes sentiments à son égard *or* envers lui *or* pour lui.

towel ['taʊəl] 1 n serviette *f* (de toilette); (*dish ~, tea ~*) torchon *m*; (*for hands*) essuie-mains *m inv*; (*for glasses*) essuie-verres *m inv*; (*sanitary ~*) serviette hygiénique; *see* **bath** *etc*. 2 comp ▸**towel rail** porte-serviettes *m inv* ▸**towel ring** anneau *m* porte-serviette. 3 vt frotter avec une serviette. **to ~ o.s. dry** *or* **down** se sécher *or* s'essuyer avec une serviette.

towelling ['taʊəlɪŋ] 1 n a (*NonC*) tissu *m* éponge. b (*rubbing with towel*) **to give sb a ~ (down)** frictionner qn avec une serviette. 2 comp *robe etc* en *or* de tissu éponge.

tower ['taʊəʳ] 1 n tour *f*. **the T~ of Babel** la tour de Babel; **the T~ of London** la Tour de Londres; **church ~** clocher *m*; **water ~** château *m* d'eau; (*fig*) **he is a ~ of strength** il est ferme comme un roc, c'est un roc; **he proved a ~ of strength to me** il s'est montré un soutien précieux pour moi.

2 comp ▸**tower block** (*Brit*) immeuble-tour *m*, tour *f* (d'habitation).

3 vi [*building, mountain, cliff, tree*] se dresser de manière imposante. **I saw him ~ing in the doorway** j'ai vu sa silhouette imposante dans l'embrasure de la porte; **the new block of flats ~s above** *or* **over the church** le nouvel immeuble écrase l'église; **he ~ed over her** elle était toute petite à côté de lui; (*fig*) **he ~s above** *or* **over his colleagues** il domine de très haut ses collègues.

▸**tower up** vi [*building, cliff etc*] se dresser de manière imposante, s'élever très haut.

towering ['taʊərɪŋ] adj *building, mountain, cliff* très haut, imposant; *tree* énorme, imposant; *ambition etc* démesuré. **he saw a ~ figure** il vit une silhouette imposante; (*fig*) **in a ~ rage** dans une colère noire.

town [taʊn] 1 n ville *f*. **he lives in (a) ~** il habite en ville *or* à la ville; **she lives in a little ~** elle habite (dans) une petite ville; **there is more work in the ~ than in the country** il y a plus de travail en ville *or* à la ville qu'à la campagne; **guess who's in ~!** devine qui vient d'arriver en ville!; **he's out of ~** il n'est pas là, il est en déplacement; (*US*) **he's from out of ~** il n'est pas d'ici, il est étranger à la ville; **to go (in)to ~, to go down~** aller en ville; **to go up to ~** monter en ville; **the whole ~ is talking about it** toute la ville en parle; (*Univ*) **~ and gown** les citadins *mpl* et les étudiants *mpl*; **a country ~** une ville de province; **let's go out on the ~*** on va faire une descente en ville* (*hum*); (*fig*) **to have a night on the ~*** faire la noce* *or* la bombe*; (*fig*) **he really went to ~ on that essay*** il a mis le paquet* quand il a écrit cette dissertation; **they went to ~ on their daughter's wedding*** ils n'ont pas fait les choses à moitié *or* ils n'ont pas lésiné pour le mariage de leur fille; *see* **man, new, talk** *etc*.

2 comp ▸**town-and-country planning** aménagement *m* du territoire ▸**town centre** centre-ville *m* ▸**town clerk** ≃ secrétaire *m* de mairie ▸**town council** (*Brit*) conseil municipal ▸**town councillor** (*Brit*) conseiller *m*, -ère *f* municipal(e) ▸**town crier** (*Hist*) crieur public ▸**town-dweller** citadin(e) *m(f)* ▸**town hall** (*Brit*) ≃ mairie *f*, hôtel *m* de ville ▸**town house** (*gen*) maison *f* de ville; (*terraced house*) maison en mitoyenneté; (*more imposing*) hôtel particulier ▸**town life** vie urbaine ▸**town meeting** (*US*) assemblée générale des habitants d'une localité ▸**town planner** (*Brit*) urbaniste *mf* ▸**town planning** (*Brit*) urbanisme *m* ▸**townsfolk** = **townspeople** ▸**township** *see* **township** ▸**townsman** citadin *m*, habitant *m* de la ville *or* des villes; **my fellow townsmen** mes concitoyens *mpl* ▸**townspeople** citadins *mpl*, habitants *mpl* de la ville *or* des villes ▸**townswoman** citadine *f*, habitante *f* de la ville *or* des villes.

townee* [taʊ'niː] n, (*US*) **townie*** ['taʊnɪ] n (*pej*) pur citadin; (*Univ sl*) citadin.

townscape ['taʊnskeɪp] n paysage *or* panorama urbain.

township ['taʊnʃɪp] n commune *f*, municipalité *f*.

toxaemia, (*US*) **toxemia** [tɒk'siːmɪə] n toxémie *f*.

toxic ['tɒksɪk] adj toxique. **~ waste** déchets *mpl* toxiques; **~ shock syndrome** toxic shock syndrome *m*.

toxicological [ˌtɒksɪkə'lɒdʒɪkəl] adj toxicologique.

toxicologist [ˌtɒksɪ'kɒlədʒɪst] n toxicologue *mf*.

toxicology [ˌtɒksɪ'kɒlədʒɪ] n toxicologie *f*.

toxin ['tɒksɪn] n toxine *f*.

toxoplasmosis [ˌtɒksəʊplæz'məʊsɪs] n toxoplasmose *f*.

toy [tɔɪ] 1 n jouet *m*. 2 comp *house, truck, stove, railway* miniature; *trumpet* d'enfant ▸**toybox** boîte *f or* coffre *m* à jouets ▸**toy boy*** (*fig*) petit minet* *m* ▸**toy car** petite auto ▸**toychest** = **toybox** ▸**toy dog** (*fig*) chien *m* d'appartement ▸**toy maker** fabricant *m* de jouets ▸**toyshop** magasin *m* de jouets ▸**toy soldier** petit soldat ▸**toy train** petit train; (*electric*) train électrique. 3 vi: **to ~ with** *object, pen, sb's affections etc* jouer avec; *idea, scheme* caresser; **to ~ with one's food** manger du bout des dents, chipoter, picorer.

tpi [tiːpiː'aɪ] n (*Comput*) (abbr of **tracks per inch**) pistes *fpl* par pouce.

trace¹ [treɪs] 1 n a (*gen*) trace *f*. **there were ~s of the cave having been lived in** il y avait des traces d'habitation dans la grotte; **the police could find no ~ of the thief** la police n'a trouvé aucune trace du voleur; **~s of an ancient civilization** la trace *or* les vestiges *mpl* d'une ancienne civilisation; **to vanish/sink without ~** disparaître/sombrer sans laisser de traces; **there is no ~ of it now** il n'en reste plus trace maintenant; **we have lost all ~ of them** nous avons complètement perdu leur trace; **~s of arsenic in the stomach** traces d'arsenic dans l'estomac; **without a ~ of ill-feeling** sans la moindre rancune.

b (*US: trail*) piste *f*.

2 comp ▸**trace element** oligo-élément *m*.

3 vt a (*draw*) *curve, line etc* tracer, esquisser, dessiner; (*with tracing paper etc*) décalquer.

b (*follow trail of*) suivre la trace de; (*and locate*) *person* retrouver, dépister; *object* retrouver. **ask the police to help you ~ him** demandez à la police de vous aider à le retrouver; **they ~d him as far as Paris but then lost him** ils ont pu suivre sa trace jusqu'à Paris mais l'ont perdu par la suite; **I can't ~ your file at all** je ne trouve pas (de) trace de votre dossier; **I can't ~ his having been in touch with us** je n'ai aucune indication *or* mention du fait qu'il nous ait contactés.

▸**trace back** 1 vi (*esp US*) **this traces back to the loss of ...** ceci est imputable à la perte de ... .

2 vt sep: **to trace back one's ancestry** *or* **descent** *or* **family to** faire remonter sa famille à, établir que sa famille remonte à; **they traced the murder weapon back to a shop in Leeds** ils ont réussi à établir que l'arme du crime provenait d'un magasin de Leeds; **we traced him back to Paris, then the trail ended** (en remontant la filière) nous avons retrouvé sa trace à Paris mais, là, la piste s'est perdue; **this may be traced back to the loss of ...** ceci peut être attribué à *or* est attribuable *or* imputable à la perte de ... .

▸**trace out** vt sep tracer.

trace² [treɪs] n *[harness]* trait *m*; *see* **kick**.

traceable ['treɪsəbl] adj: **it is ~** on peut le retrouver.

tracer ['treɪsəʳ] n (*person*) traceur *m*, -euse *f*; (*instrument*) roulette *f*, traçoir *m*; (*Biochemistry*) traceur; (*also* **~ bullet**) balle traçante; (*also* **~ shell**) obus traçant.

tracery ['treɪsərɪ] n (*NonC*) (*Archit*) réseau *m* (*de fenêtre ajourée*); *[veins on leaves]* nervures *fpl*; *[frost on window etc]* dentelles *fpl*.

trachea [trə'kɪə] n, pl **~s** *or* **tracheae** [træ'kiːiː] trachée *f*.

tracheotomy [ˌtrækɪ'ɒtəmɪ] n trachéotomie *f*.

trachoma [træ'kəʊmə] n trachome *m*.

tracing ['treɪsɪŋ] 1 n (*process: NonC*) calquage *m*; (*result*) calque *m*. 2 comp ▸**tracing paper** papier-calque *m inv*, papier *m* à décalquer.

track [træk] 1 n a (*mark, trail, also Climbing*) trace *f*; *[animal]* trace, piste *f*, foulée *f*; *[person]* trace, piste; *[tyres, wheels]* trace; *[boat]* sillage *m*; (*route: on radar screen; also of bullet, comet, rocket, hurricane etc*) trajectoire *f*. **the hurricane destroyed everything in its ~** l'ouragan a tout détruit sur son passage; **a ~ of muddy footprints across the floor** des traces de pas boueuses sur le plancher; **to follow in sb's ~s** (*lit*) suivre la trace de qn; (*fig*) suivre la voie tracée par qn, suivre *or* marcher sur les traces de qn; **to be on sb's ~(s)** être sur la piste de qn; **he had the police on his ~(s)** la police était sur sa piste; **they got on to his ~ very quickly** ils ont très vite trouvé sa piste; **to put** *or* **throw sb off the ~** désorienter qn; **to cover (up)** *or* **hide one's ~s** (*lit*) couvrir sa marche; (*fig*) couvrir sa marche, brouiller les pistes; (*fig*) **to be on the right ~** être sur la bonne voie; **to put sb on the right ~** mettre qn dans la bonne voie; (*fig*) **to be on the wrong ~, to be off the ~** faire fausse route; (*fig*) **you're away off the ~!** vous êtes tout à fait à côté!, vous n'y êtes pas du tout!; **to keep ~ of** *spacecraft etc* suivre; (*fig*) *events* suivre (la marche *or* le fil de); *developments, situation* suivre, rester au courant de; **they kept ~ of him till they reached the wood** ils ont suivi sa trace jusqu'au bois; (*fig*) **I kept ~ of her until she got married** je suis resté en contact avec elle *or* au courant de ce qu'elle faisait jusqu'à son mariage; **I've lost ~ of what he's doing** je ne suis plus au courant de ce qu'il fait; **to lose ~ of** *spacecraft etc* perdre; (*fig*) *developments, situation* ne plus suivre, ne plus être au courant de; *events* perdre le fil de; **they lost ~ of him in the woods** ils ont perdu sa trace une fois arrivés au bois; **I lost ~ of her after the war** j'ai perdu tout contact avec elle *or* je l'ai perdue de vue après la guerre; **don't lose ~ of him** (*lit*) ne perdez pas sa trace; (*fig*) ne le perdez pas de vue; **I've lost ~ of those books** je ne sais plus *or* j'ai oublié où sont ces livres; **to lose all ~ of time** perdre la notion du temps; **keep ~ of the time** n'oubliez pas l'heure; **I've lost ~ of what he is saying** j'ai perdu le fil de ce qu'il dit, je ne suis plus ce qu'il dit; (*fig*) **we must be making ~s*** il faut qu'on se sauve* (*subj*); **he made ~s for the hotel*** il a filé à l'hôtel; *see* **change, inside, stop**.

b (*path*) chemin *m*, sentier *m*, piste *f*. **sheep ~** piste à moutons; **mule ~** chemin *or* sentier muletier; **from there on, the road became nothing but a ~** à partir de là, la route n'était plus carrossable; *see* **beaten, cart, dirt** *etc*.

c (*Rail*) voie *f* (ferrée), rails *mpl*. **to leave the ~(s)** quitter les rails, dérailler; **to cross the ~** traverser la voie; **single-~ line** ligne *f* à voie unique; (*US fig*) **to live on the wrong side of the ~s** vivre dans les quartiers pauvres; *see* **one**.

d (*Sport*) piste *f*. **motor-racing ~** autodrome *m*; **dog-racing ~** cynodrome *m*; *see* **race¹** *etc*.

e *[electronic tape, CD, computer disk]* piste *f*; *[long-playing record]* plage *f*; (*fig: piece of music*) morceau *m*. **4-~ tape** bande *f* à 4 pistes; *see* **sound¹**.

f (*Aut etc*) (*tyre tread*) chape *f*; (*space between wheels*) écartement *m*; (*also* **caterpillar ~**) chenille *f*.

g (*US Scol*) classe *f* de niveaux. **divided into 5 ~s** répartis en 5 classes de niveaux; **the top/middle/bottom ~** la section forte/moyenne/faible (*de l'ensemble des élèves qui suivent le même programme*).

h (*Drugs sl*) **~s** marques *fpl* de piqûres.

2 comp ▸**track athletics** (*Sport*) athlétisme *m* sur piste ▸**track event** (*Sport*) épreuve *f* sur piste ▸**tracklayer** (*US Rail*) = **trackman** ▸**track lighting** rampe *f* de spots ▸**track maintenance** (*Rail*) entretien *m* de la voie ▸**trackman** (*US Rail*) responsable *m* de l'entretien de la voie ▸**track meet** (*US Sport*) réunion sportive sur piste ▸**track race** (*Sport*) course *f* sur piste ▸**track racing** (*Sport*) courses *fpl* sur piste ▸**track record:** (*Sport, also fig*) **to have a good track record** avoir eu de bons résultats ▸**track rod** (*Brit*) biellette *f* de connexion ▸**track shoe** chaussure *f* de course ▸**track shot** (*Cine*) travel(l)ing *m* ▸**tracksuit** survêtement *m* ▸**track system** (*US Scol*) système *m* de répartition des élèves par niveaux ▸**trackwalker** (*US Rail*) = **trackman**.

3 vt *animal* suivre à la piste *or* à la trace, suivre la trace de; *person, vehicle* suivre la trace de; *hurricane, rocket, spacecraft, comet* suivre la trajectoire de. **to ~ dirt over the floor** laisser des traces sales sur le plancher.

4 vi *[camera]* faire un travel(l)ing.

▸**track down** vt sep *animal, wanted man* traquer et capturer; *lost object, lost person, reference, quotation* (finir par) retrouver *or* localiser.

tracked [trækt] adj: **~ vehicle** véhicule *m* à chenilles.

tracker ['trækəʳ] 1 n (*Hunting*) traqueur *m*; (*gen*) poursuivant(e) *m(f)*. 2 comp ▸**tracker dog** chien policier.

tracking ['trækɪŋ] adj (*Elec*) **~ device** dispositif *m* de pistage; (*Cine*) **~**

shot travel(l)ing *m*; (*Space*) ~ **station** station *f* d'observation (de satellites).

trackless ['træklɪs] adj *forest, desert* sans chemins; *vehicle* sans chenilles.

tract[1] [trækt] 1 n a *[land, water]* étendue *f*; *[coal etc]* gisement *m*; (*US: housing estate*) lotissement *m*. **vast ~s of wilderness** de vastes zones *fpl or* étendues désertiques. b (*Anat*) **digestive/respiratory ~** appareil *or* système digestif/respiratoire. 2 comp ►**tract house** (*US*) pavillon *m* (*dans un lotissement*).

tract[2] [trækt] n (*pamphlet*) tract *m*; (*Rel*) traité *m*.

tractable ['træktəbl] adj *person* accommodant, souple; *animal* docile; *material* malléable; *problem* soluble, résoluble.

Tractarian [træk'tɛərɪən] adj, n (*Rel*) tractarien(-ienne) *m(f)*.

Tractarianism [træk'tɛərɪənɪzəm] n (*Rel*) tractarianisme *m*.

traction ['trækʃən] 1 n (*NonC: all senses*) traction *f*. (*Tech*) **electric/steam ~** traction électrique/à vapeur. 2 comp ►**traction engine** locomobile *f*.

tractive ['træktɪv] adj de traction.

tractor ['træktəʳ] 1 n tracteur *m*. 2 comp ►**tractor drive** (*Comput*) dispositif *m* d'entraînement à picots ►**tractor driver** conducteur *m*, -trice *f* de tracteur ►**tractor-trailer** (*US*) semi-remorque *m*.

trad* [træd] adj (*esp Mus*) abbr of **traditional**.

tradable ['treɪdəbl] adj (*esp US: Econ, Fin*) commercialisable.

trade [treɪd] 1 n a (*NonC: commerce*) commerce *m*, affaires *fpl*; (*illegal*) trafic *m*. (*Econ*) **overseas ~** commerce extérieur; **it's good for ~** ça fait marcher le commerce; **the fur ~** l'industrie *f* de la fourrure; **the wool ~, the ~ in wool** le commerce de la laine; **he's in the wool ~** il est négociant en laine; **the drug ~, the ~ in drugs** le trafic de la drogue; **they do a lot of ~ with** ils font beaucoup de commerce *or* d'affaires avec, ils commercent beaucoup avec; **~ has been good** *or* **brisk** les affaires ont été bonnes, le commerce a bien marché; **to do a good** *or* **brisk** *or* **roaring ~** vendre beaucoup (*in* de); (*Brit*) **Board of T~**, (*US*) **Department of T~** ministère *m* du Commerce; **Secretary (of State) for T~, Minister of T~** ministre *m* du Commerce; (*Brit*) **Department of T~ and Industry** ≃ ministère *m* (du Commerce et) de l'Industrie; *see* **rag**[1], **tourist** *etc*.

b (*job, skill*) métier *m*. **he is a butcher by ~** il est boucher de son métier *or* de son état; (*hum*) **he's a doctor by ~** il est médecin de son état; **to put sb to a ~**† mettre qn en apprentissage; **she wants him to learn a ~** elle veut qu'il apprenne un métier; (*lit, fig*) **he's in the ~** il est du métier; (*lit, fig*) **as we say in the ~** comme on dit dans le jargon du métier, pour employer un terme technique; **known in the ~ as ...** que les gens du métier appellent ...; **special terms for the ~** tarif spécial pour les membres de la profession; *see* **stock, tool, trick** *etc*.

c = **trade wind**; *see* 2.

d (*swap*) échange *m*. **to do a ~ with sb for sth** faire l'échange de qch avec qn.

2 comp (*gen*) *exchanges, visits* commercial; (*Publishing*) *press, publications* professionnel, spécialisé ►**trade agreement** accord *m* commercial ►**trade association** association commerciale ►**trade barriers** barrières douanières ►**trade bill** effet *m* de commerce ►**trade cycle** (*Econ*) cycle *m* économique ►**trade deficit** balance *f* (commerciale) déficitaire, déficit extérieur ►**the Trade Descriptions Act** (*Brit*) *la loi protégeant les consommateurs contre la publicité et les appellations mensongères* ►**trade discount** remise *f* au détaillant ►**trade fair** foire(-exposition) commerciale ►**trade figures** (*Econ*) résultats *mpl* (financiers) ►**trade gap** déficit *m* commercial *or* de la balance commerciale ►**trade-in** (*Comm*) reprise *f*; **he took my old machine as a trade-in** il m'a repris ma vieille machine; **trade-in allowance** reprise *f*; **trade-in price/value** prix *m*/valeur *f* à la reprise ►**trade journal** revue professionnelle ►**trademark** n marque *f* (de fabrique) ◊ vt *product, goods* apposer une marque sur; *symbol, word* déposer; **registered trademark** marque déposée ►**trade mission** mission *f* commerciale ►**trade name** nom *m* de marque ►**trade-off** (*exchange*) échange *m* (*between* entre); (*balancing*) compromis *m*, concessions mutuelles ►**trade paper** = **trade journal** ►**trade plate** (*Aut*) ≃ plaque *f* W, plaque d'immatriculation provisoire ►**trade price** prix *m* de gros ►**trade returns** (*Econ*) = **trade figures** ►**trade route** route commerciale ►**trade school** collège *m* technique ►**trade secret** (*Comm, Ind, also fig*) secret *m* de fabrication ►**tradesman** commerçant *m*; (*skilled worker*) ouvrier *m* qualifié ►**tradesman's** *or* **tradesmen's entrance** entrée *f* de service *or* des fournisseurs ►**tradespeople** commerçants *mpl* ►**trade(s) union** syndicat *m*; **trade(s) union membership** adhésion *f* à un syndicat; (*number of members*) nombre *m* de syndiqués; (*Brit*) **the Trades Union Congress** la confédération des syndicats britanniques ►**trade(s) unionism** syndicalisme *m* ►**trade(s) unionist** syndicaliste *mf* ►**tradeswoman** commerçante *f*; (*skilled worker*) ouvrière *f* qualifiée ►**trade talks** (*Pol etc*) négociations commerciales ►**trade wind** (*Geog*) (vent) alizé *m*.

3 vi a *[firm, country, businessman]* faire le commerce (*in* de), commercer, avoir *or* entretenir des relations commerciales (*with* avec). **he ~s as a wool merchant** il est négociant en laine; (*fig*) **to ~ (up)on sb's kindness** abuser de la gentillesse de qn.

b (*US: of private individual*) faire ses achats (*with* chez, à), être client(e) (*with* chez).

c (*St Ex*) *[currency, commodity]* **to be trading at** se négocier à; *see* **cease**.

d (*exchange*) échanger, troquer (*with sb* avec qn).

4 vt (*exchange*) **to ~ A for B** échanger *or* troquer A contre B; **I ~d my knife with him for his marbles** je lui ai donné mon canif en échange de ses billes.

►**trade in** vt sep *car, television etc* faire reprendre. **I've traded it in for a new one** je l'ai fait reprendre quand j'en ai acheté un nouveau.

►**trade off** 1 vt sep a (*balance*) **to trade off A against B** accepter que A compense B. b (*exchange*) **to trade off one thing against** *or* **for another** échanger *or* troquer une chose contre une autre. 2 **trade-off** n *see* **trade 2**.

trader ['treɪdəʳ] n a commerçant(e) *m(f)*, marchand(e) *m(f)*; (*bigger*) négociant(e) *m(f)*; (*street ~*) vendeur *m*, -euse *f* de rue; (*US St Ex*) contrepartiste *m*. **wool ~** négociant en laine; *see* **slave** *etc*. b (*ship*) navire marchand *or* de la marine marchande.

tradescantia [,trædəs'kæntɪə] n tradescantia *m*.

trading ['treɪdɪŋ] 1 n (*NonC*) (*in shops: business*) commerce *m*, affaires *fpl*; (*on larger scale*) commerce, négoce *m*; (*between countries*) commerce, échanges *mpl* (commerciaux); (*St Ex*) transactions *fpl*, opérations *fpl*. (*St Ex*) **~ was brisk yesterday** l'activité a été soutenue hier.

2 comp *port, centre* de commerce ►**trading capital** capital *m* engagé, capital de roulement ►**trading estate** (*Brit*) zone artisanale et commerciale ►**trading nation** nation commerçante ►**trading partner** partenaire commercial ►**trading post** (*esp Can, US*) comptoir *m* (commercial) ►**trading profits:** (*Fin, Ind*) **trading profits for last year** bénéfices obtenus pour l'exercice de l'année écoulée ►**trading stamp** timbre-prime *m* ►**trading standards** normes *fpl* de conformité; **trading standards office** ≃ Direction *f* de la Consommation et de la Répression des Fraudes.

tradition [trə'dɪʃən] n tradition *f*. **according to ~** selon la tradition *or* la coutume; **it's in the (best) ~ of** c'est dans la (plus pure) tradition de; **~ has it that ...** la tradition veut que ...; **it is a ~ that ...** il est de tradition que ... + *subj*; **the ~ that ...** la tradition selon laquelle ... *or* qui veut que ... .

traditional [trə'dɪʃənl] adj traditionnel. **it is ~ for them to do that** chez eux il est de tradition de faire ça; **they wore the ~ red cloaks** ils portaient les capes rouges traditionnelles *or* les traditionnelles capes rouges.

traditionalism [trə'dɪʃnəlɪzəm] n traditionalisme *m*.

traditionalist [trə'dɪʃnəlɪst] adj, n traditionaliste *(mf)*.

traditionally [trə'dɪʃnəlɪ] adv traditionnellement.

traduce [trə'dju:s] vt (*frm*) calomnier, diffamer.

Trafalgar [trə'fælgəʳ] n: **Battle of ~** bataille *f* de Trafalgar.

traffic ['træfɪk] (vb: pret, ptp **trafficked**) 1 n (*NonC*) a (*Aut*) circulation *f*; (*Aviat, Naut, Rail, Telec*) trafic *m*. **road ~** circulation routière; **rail ~** trafic ferroviaire; (*Aut*) **holiday ~** circulation des grands départs *or* des grandes rentrées, rush *m* des vacances; (*Aut*) **the ~ is very light** il y a très peu de circulation; **there's a lot of ~** *or* **the ~ is heavy this morning** (*Aut*) il y a beaucoup de circulation ce matin; (*Aviat, Naut, Rail*) le trafic est intense ce matin; **the bridge is closed to heavy ~** *or* **is open to light ~ only** l'accès au pont est interdit aux poids lourds; **~ is building up/falling off** (*Aut*) la circulation s'intensifie/se dégage; (*Aviat, Naut, Rail*) le trafic s'intensifie/se raréfie; (*Aut*) **the build-up** *or* **backlog of ~ extends to the bridge** le bouchon s'étire jusqu'au pont; (*Aut*) **~ out of/into Paris** la circulation dans le sens Paris-province/province-Paris; **~ coming into London should avoid Putney Bridge** il est recommandé aux automobilistes se rendant à Londres d'éviter Putney Bridge; **~ in and out of Heathrow Airport** le trafic à destination et en provenance de l'aéroport de Heathrow; (*Naut*) **~ in** *or* **using the Channel** trafic *or* navigation *f* en Manche; *see* **tourist** *etc*.

b (*trade*) commerce *m* (*in* de); (*pej*) trafic *m* (*in* de). **the drug ~** le trafic de la drogue *or* des stupéfiants.

2 comp ►**traffic circle** (*US*) rond-point *m*, sens *m* giratoire ►**traffic control** (*Aut*) prévention routière; (*Aviat, Naut, Rail*) contrôle *m* du trafic ►**traffic controller** (*Aviat*) contrôleur *m*, -euse *f* de la navigation aérienne, aiguilleur *m* du ciel ►**traffic control tower** (*Aviat*) tour *f* de contrôle ►**traffic cop*** (*esp US*) = **traffic policeman** ►**traffic diversion** déviation *f* ►**traffic duty:** (*Police*) **to be on traffic duty** faire la circulation ►**traffic holdup** bouchon *m* (*de circulation*) ►**traffic island** (*Brit*) refuge *m* ►**traffic jam** embouteillage *m*, bouchon *m* ►**traffic lights** feux *mpl* de signalisation; **to go through the traffic lights at red** passer au rouge, griller le feu rouge; **the traffic lights were (at) green** le feu était (au) vert ►**traffic offence** (*Jur*) infraction *f* au code de la route ►**traffic pattern** (*Aviat*) couloir *m or* position *f* d'approche ►**traffic police** (*speeding etc*) police *f* de la route; (*points duty etc*) police de la circulation ►**traffic policeman** (*gen*) ≃ agent *m* de police; (*on points duty*) agent de la circulation ►**traffic regulations** réglementation *f* de la circulation ►**traffic sign** panneau *m* de signalisation, poteau indicateur; **international traffic signs** signalisation routière internationale ►**traffic signals** = **traffic lights** ►**traffic warden** (*Brit*) contractuel(le) *m(f)*.

3 vi: **to ~ in sth** faire le commerce *or* le trafic (*pej*) de.

trafficator† ['træfɪkeɪtəʳ] n (*Brit*) flèche *f* (de direction)†.

trafficker ['træfɪkəʳ] n trafiquant(e) *m(f)* (*in* en).

tragedian [trə'dʒiːdɪən] n (*writer*) auteur *m* tragique; (*actor*) tragédien *m*.

tragedienne [trə,dʒiːdɪ'en] n tragédienne *f*.

tragedy ['trædʒɪdɪ] n (*gen, Theat*) tragédie *f*. **the ~ of it is that ...** ce qui est tragique, c'est que ...; **it is a ~ that ...** il est tragique que ... + *subj*.

tragic ['trædʒɪk] adj (*gen, Theat*) tragique.

tragically ['trædʒɪkəlɪ] adv tragiquement.

tragicomedy ['trædʒɪ'kɒmɪdɪ] n tragi-comédie *f*.

tragicomic ['trædʒɪ'kɒmɪk] adj tragi-comique.

trail [treɪl] 1 n a (*of blood, smoke: also from plane, comet etc*) traînée *f*. **a long ~ of refugees** une longue file *or* colonne de réfugiés; **to leave a ~ of destruction** tout détruire sur son passage; **his illness brought a series of debts in its ~** sa maladie a amené dans son sillage une série de dettes; *see* **vapour** *etc*.

b (*tracks: gen*) trace *f*; (*Hunting*) piste *f*, trace(s), foulée *f*. (*lit, fig*) **to be on the ~ of sb** être sur la piste de qn; **I'm on the ~ of that book you want** j'ai trouvé trace *or* j'ai retrouvé la trace du livre que vous voulez; *see* **hot** *etc*.

c (*path, road*) sentier *m*, chemin *m*; *see* **blaze²**, **nature**.

d (*Ski, Climbing*) trace *f*; (*cross country skiing*) piste *f* de fond. **to break a ~** faire la trace, tracer.

2 comp ►**trail bike*** moto *f* de moto-cross ►**trailblazer** (*fig*) pionnier *m*, -ière *f* ►**trailblazing** (*fig*) innovateur *m* (*f* -trice) ►**trailbreaker** (*esp US*) = **trailblazer** ►**trail mix** mélange *m* de fruits secs (*raisins secs, noisettes, banane séchée, noix de coco etc*).

3 vt a (*follow*) suivre la piste de; (*fig: lag behind*) être dépassé par.

b (*drag, tow*) *object on rope, toy cart etc* tirer, traîner; (*Aut*) *caravan, trailer, boat* tirer, tracter. **he was ~ing his schoolbag behind him** il traînait son cartable derrière lui; **the children ~ed dirt all over the carpet** les enfants ont couvert le tapis de traces sales; **to ~ one's fingers through** *or* **in the water** laisser traîner ses doigts dans l'eau; **don't ~ your feet!** ne traîne pas les pieds!

c (*Mil*) *rifle etc* porter à la main.

d (*announce as forthcoming*) donner un avant-goût de.

e (*Hort*) **to ~ a plant over a fence** *etc* faire grimper une plante par-dessus une clôture *etc*.

4 vi a *[object]* traîner; *[plant]* ramper. **your coat is ~ing in the mud** ton manteau traîne dans la boue; **smoke ~ed from the funnel** une traînée de fumée s'échappait de la cheminée; (*fig Sport*) **they were ~ing by 13 points** ils étaient en retard de 13 points; (*Ftbl*) **they are ~ing at the bottom of the league** ils traînent en bas de division.

b **to ~ along/in/out** *etc* (*move in straggling line*) passer/entrer/sortir *etc* à la queue leu leu *or* en file; (*move wearily*) passer/entrer/sortir *etc* en traînant les pieds.

►**trail away, trail off** vi *[voice, music]* s'estomper.

trailer ['treɪləʳ] 1 n a (*Aut: behind car, van, truck*) remorque *f*; (*esp US: caravan*) caravane *f*. b (*Cine, TV*) bande-annonce *f*. c (*Phot: end of film roll*) amorce *f* (en fin d'un rouleau). 2 comp ►**trailer camp, trailer court, trailer park** (*US*) camp *m* de caravaning ►**trailer tent** tente *f* remorque.

trailing ['treɪlɪŋ] adj *hair, blanket etc* traînant; *plant* rampant. (*Aviat*) **~ edge** bord *m* de fuite.

train [treɪn] 1 n a (*Rail*) train *m*; (*in underground*) rame *f*, métro *m*. **to go by ~** prendre le train; **to go to London by ~** prendre le train pour aller à Londres, aller à Londres en train *or* par le train; **to travel by ~** voyager par le train *or* en train; **on** *or* **in the ~** dans le train; **to transport by ~** transporter par voie ferroviaire; *see* **express, freight, slow** *etc*.

b (*procession*) file *f*; (*entourage*) suite *f*, équipage *m*; *[camels]* caravane *f*, file; *[mules]* train *m*, file; *[vehicles etc]* cortège *m*, file. **he arrived with 50 men in his ~** il arriva avec un équipage de 50 hommes; (*fig*) **the war brought famine in its ~** la guerre amena la famine dans son sillage *or* entraîna la famine; *see* **baggage** *etc*.

c (*line, series*) suite *f*, série *f*, succession *f*; *[gunpowder]* traînée *f*. **in an unbroken ~** en succession ininterrompue; **a ~ of events** une suite d'événements; **it broke** *or* **interrupted his ~ of thought** cela est venu interrompre le fil de sa *or* ses pensée(s); **I've lost my ~ of thought** je ne retrouve plus le fil de ma *or* mes pensée(s); (*fig*) **it is in ~** c'est en préparation, c'est en marche; **to set sth in ~** mettre qch en marche *or* en mouvement.

d *[dress, robe]* traîne *f*.

e (*Tech*) train *m*. **~ of gears** train de roues d'engrenage.

2 comp (*Ind*) *dispute, strike etc* des cheminots, des chemins de fer ►**trainband** (*Hist*) milice *f* ►**trainbearer** dame *f or* demoiselle *f* d'honneur; (*little boy*) page *m* ►**train crash** accident *m* de chemin de fer, (*more serious*) catastrophe *f* ferroviaire ►**train ferry** ferry-boat *m* ►**trainman** (*US Rail*) cheminot *m* ►**train oil** huile *f* de baleine ►**train service**: **there is a very good train service to London** les trains pour Londres sont très fréquents; **there is an hourly train service to London** il y a un train pour Londres toutes les heures; **do you know what the train service is to London?** connaissez-vous l'horaire des trains pour Londres? ►**train set** train *m* électrique (*jouet*) ►**train-spotter** passionné(e) *m(f)* de trains ►**train-spotting**: **to go train-spotting** observer les trains (*pour identifier les divers types de locomotives*) ►**train-workers** employés *mpl* des chemins de fer, cheminots *mpl*.

3 vt a (*instruct*) *person, engineer, doctor, nurse, teacher, craftsman, apprentice* former; *employee, soldier* former, instruire; (*Sport*) *player* entraîner, préparer; *animal* dresser; *voice* travailler; *ear, mind, memory* exercer. **he is ~ing someone to take over from him** il forme son successeur; (*housetrain*) **to ~ a puppy/child** apprendre à un chiot/à un enfant à être propre; **to ~ an animal to do** apprendre à *or* dresser un animal à faire; **to ~ sb to do** apprendre à qn à faire; (*professionally*) former qn à faire, préparer qn à faire; **to ~ o.s. to do** s'entraîner *or* s'exercer à faire; **to ~ sb in a craft** apprendre un métier à qn, préparer qn à un métier; **he was ~ed in weaving** *or* **as a weaver** il a reçu une formation de tisserand; **to ~ sb in the use of sth** *or* **to use sth** apprendre à qn à utiliser qch, instruire qn dans le maniement de qch; **where were you ~ed?** où avez-vous reçu votre formation?; *see also* **trained**.

b (*direct etc*) *gun, camera, telescope etc* braquer (*on* sur). **to ~ a plant along a wall** faire grimper une plante le long d'un mur.

4 vi a recevoir une (*or* sa) formation; (*Sport*) s'entraîner (*for* pour), se préparer (*for* à). **to ~ as** *or* **~ to be a teacher/secretary** *etc* recevoir une formation de professeur/de secrétaire *etc*; **where did you ~?** où avez-vous reçu votre formation?

b (*Rail: go by ~*) aller en train.

►**train up** vt sep former, préparer.

trained [treɪnd] adj *person* compétent, qualifié (*for* pour, en matière de); *engineer* diplômé, breveté; *nurse* diplômé, qualifié; *teacher* habilité à enseigner; *animal* dressé. **to the ~ eye/ear** pour un œil/une oreille exercé(e); **she has a ~ voice** elle a pris des leçons de chant; **he isn't ~ for this job** il n'a pas la formation voulue pour ce poste, il n'est pas qualifié pour ce poste; **we need a ~ person for the job** nous avons besoin de quelqu'un qui soit qualifié pour ce poste *or* qui ait la compétence voulue pour ce poste; **they employ only ~ personnel** ils n'emploient que du personnel qualifié; **he is not ~ at all** il n'a reçu aucune formation professionnelle; **well-~** *employee, worker* qui a reçu une bonne formation; *butler, valet, maid* stylé; *child* bien élevé; *animal* bien dressé; (*iro*) **she's got a well-~ husband** son mari est bien dressé.

trainee [treɪ'niː] 1 n (*gen*) stagiaire *mf*; (*US Police, Mil etc*) jeune recrue *f*. **sales/management ~** stagiaire de vente/de direction. 2 adj (*gen*) stagiaire, en stage; (*in trades*) en apprentissage. **~ typist** dactylo* *f* stagiaire; **~ hairdresser** apprenti(e) coiffeur *m*, -euse *f*.

traineeship [treɪ'niːʃɪp] n stage *m*, stage d'emploi-formation (*Admin*).

trainer ['treɪnəʳ] n a *[athlete, football team, racehorse]* entraîneur *m*; (*Cycling etc*) soigneur *m*; (*in circus*) dresseur *m*, -euse *f*, (*esp of lions*) dompteur *m*, -euse *f*. b (*Aviat*) (*flight simulator*) simulateur *m* de vol; (*also* **~ aircraft**) avion-école *m*. c (*Brit: shoe*) chaussure *f* de sport.

training ['treɪnɪŋ] 1 n *[person, engineer, doctor, nurse, teacher, craftsman]* formation *f*; *[employee, soldier]* formation, instruction *f*; (*Sport*) entraînement *m*, préparation *f*; *[animal]* dressage *m*. (*Sport*) **to be out of ~** avoir perdu la forme; (*Sport*) **to be in ~** (*preparing o.s.*) être en cours d'entraînement *or* de préparation; (*on form*) être en forme; (*Sport*) **to be in ~ for sth** s'entraîner pour *or* se préparer à qch; **staff ~** formation du personnel; **she has had some secretarial ~** elle a suivi quelques cours de secrétariat; **it is good ~** c'est un bon apprentissage *or* entraînement; *see* **teacher, toilet, voice** *etc*.

2 comp ►**training camp** camp *m* d'entraînement ►**training centre** (*gen*) centre *m* de formation; (*Sport*) centre (d'entraînement) sportif ►**training college** (*gen*) école spécialisée *or* professionnelle; **(teacher) training college** *see* **teacher 2** ►**training course** cours *m(pl)* professionnel(s) ►**training manual** manuel *m or* cours *m* d'instruction ►**training plane** avion-école *m* ►**training scheme** programme *m* de formation *or* d'entraînement ►**training ship** navire-école *m* ►**training shoe** = **trainer**.

traipse* [treɪps] vi: **to ~ in/out** *etc* entrer/sortir *etc* d'un pas traînant *or* en traînassant*; **they ~d in wearily** ils sont entrés en traînant les pieds; **to ~ around** *or* **about** se balader*, déambuler; **we've been traipsing about the shops all day** nous avons traîné *or* traînassé* dans les magasins toute la journée.

trait [treɪt] n trait *m* (*de caractère*).

traitor ['treɪtəʳ] n traître *m*. **to be a ~ to one's country/to a cause** trahir sa patrie/une cause; **to turn ~** passer à l'ennemi.

traitorous ['treɪtərəs] adj traître (*f* traîtresse), déloyal, perfide.

traitorously ['treɪtərəslɪ] adv traîtreusement, perfidement, en traître (*or* en traîtresse).

traitress ['treɪtrɪs] n traîtresse *f*.

trajectory [trə'dʒektərɪ] n trajectoire *f*.

tram [træm] 1 n a (*Brit: also* **~car**) tram(way) *m*. **to go by ~** prendre le tram. b (*Min*) berline *f*, benne roulante. 2 comp ►**tramline** (*Brit*) = **tramway**; (*Brit Tennis*) **tramlines** lignes *fpl* de côté ►**tramway** (*Brit*) (*rails*) voie *f* de tramway; (*route*) ligne *f* de tramway.

trammel ['træməl] (*liter*) 1 vt entraver. 2 npl: **~s** entraves *fpl*.

tramp [træmp] 1 n a (*sound*) **the ~ of feet** le bruit de pas.

b (*hike*) randonnée *f* (à pied), excursion *f*, promenade *f*. **to go for a ~** (aller) faire une randonnée *or* une excursion; **after a 10-hour ~** après 10 heures de marche (à pied); **it's a long ~** c'est long à faire à pied.
c (*vagabond*) chemineau *m*, clochard(e) *m(f)*, vagabond(e) *m(f)*.
d (*pej: woman*) **she's a ~*** elle est coureuse*.
e (*also* **~ steamer**) tramp *m*.
2 **vi**: **to ~ along** (*hike*) poursuivre son chemin à pied; (*walk heavily*) marcher d'un pas lourd; *[soldiers etc]* marteler le pavé *or* la route; **to ~ up and down** faire les cent pas; **he was ~ing up and down the platform** il arpentait le quai d'un pas lourd.
3 **vt**: **to ~ the streets** battre le pavé; **I ~ed the town looking for the church** j'ai parcouru la ville à pied pour trouver l'église.
►**tramp down, tramp in** vt sep tasser du pied.

trample ['træmpl] 1 **vt**: **to ~ (underfoot)** *sth on ground etc* piétiner, fouler aux pieds; (*fig*) *person, conquered nation* fouler aux pieds, bafouer; *sb's feelings* bafouer; *objections etc* passer outre à; **he ~d the stone into the ground** il a enfoncé du pied la pierre dans le sol; **he was ~d by the horses** il a été piétiné par les chevaux. 2 **vi**: **to ~ in/out** *etc* entrer/sortir *etc* d'un pas lourd; (*lit, fig*) **to ~ on** = **to trample (underfoot)**; *see* **1**. 3 **n** (*act: also* **trampling**) piétinement *m*; (*sound*) bruit *m* de pas.

trampoline ['træmpəlɪn] 1 **n** trampoline *m*. 2 **vi** (*also* **to go trampolining**) faire du trampoline.

trance [trɑːns] **n** (*Hypnosis, Rel, Spiritualism etc*) transe *f*; (*Med*) catalepsie *f*; (*fig: ecstasy*) transe, extase *f*. **to go** *or* **fall into a ~** (*Hypnosis, Rel, Spiritualism etc*) entrer en transe; (*Med*) tomber en catalepsie; (*fig*) entrer en transe, tomber en extase; *[hypnotist]* **to put sb into a ~** faire entrer qn en transe.

tranche [trɑːnʃ] **n** (*Econ etc*) tranche *f*.

trannie*, **tranny*** ['trænɪ] **n abbr of transistor (radio)**.

tranquil ['træŋkwɪl] **adj** tranquille, paisible, serein.

tranquillity, (*US also*) **tranquility** [træŋ'kwɪlɪtɪ] **n** tranquillité *f*, calme *m*.

tranquillize, (*US also*) **tranquilize** ['træŋkwɪlaɪz] **vt** (*Med*) mettre sous tranquillisants.

tranquillizer, (*US also*) **tranquilizer** ['træŋkwɪlaɪzəʳ] **n** tranquillisant *m*, calmant *m*.

trans. **abbr of transitive, transport(ation), translation, translator, transfer(red)**.

trans... [trænz] **pref** trans... . **the T~-Canada Highway** la route transcanadienne.

transact [træn'zækt] **vt** *business* traiter, régler, faire.

transaction [træn'zækʃən] **n** (*gen: also in bank, shop etc*) opération *f*, affaire *f*; (*Econ, Fin, St Ex*) transaction *f*; (*gen*) opération, affaire; (*NonC*) conduite *f*, gestion *f*. **we have had some ~s with that firm** nous avons fait quelques opérations *or* quelques affaires avec cette société; **cash ~** opération au comptant; **the ~s of the Royal Society** (*proceedings*) les travaux *mpl* de la Royal Society; (*minutes*) les actes *mpl* de la Royal Society.

transactional [træn'zækʃənl] **adj** transactionnel. (*Psych*) **~ analysis** analyse transactionnelle.

transalpine ['trænz'ælpaɪn] **adj** transalpin.

transatlantic ['trænzət'læntɪk] **adj** transatlantique.

transceiver [træn'siːvəʳ] **n** (*Rad*) émetteur-récepteur *m*.

transcend [træn'send] **vt** *belief, knowledge, description* transcender, dépasser; (*excel over*) surpasser; (*Philos, Rel*) transcender.

transcendence [træn'sendəns] **n**, **transcendency** [træn'sendənsɪ] **n** transcendance *f*.

transcendent [træn'sendənt] **adj** transcendant.

transcendental [ˌtrænsen'dentl] **adj** transcendantal. **~ meditation** méditation transcendantale.

transcendentalism [ˌtrænsen'dentəlɪzəm] **n** transcendantalisme *m*.

transcontinental ['trænzˌkɒntɪ'nentl] **adj** transcontinental.

transcribe [træn'skraɪb] **vt** (*gen, also Phon*) transcrire.

transcript ['trænskrɪpt] **n** (*gen*) transcription *f*; (*US Univ*) (copie *f* de) dossier *m* complet de la scolarité.

transcription [træn'skrɪpʃən] **n** (*gen, also Phon*) transcription *f*. (*Phon*) **narrow/broad ~** transcription étroite/large.

transduce [trænz'djuːs] **vt** transformer, convertir.

transducer [trænz'djuːsəʳ] **n** (*also Comput*) transducteur *m*.

transduction [trænz'dʌkʃən] **n** transduction *f*.

transect [træn'sekt] **vt** sectionner (transversalement).

transept ['trænsept] **n** transept *m*.

transfer [træns'fɜːʳ] 1 **vt** *employee, civil servant, diplomat* transférer, muter (*to* à); *soldier, player, prisoner* transférer (*to* à); *passenger* transférer (*to* à), transborder; *object, goods* transférer (*to sb* à qn, *to a place* à un lieu), transporter (*to a place* dans un lieu), transmettre (*to sb* à qn); *power* faire passer (*from* de, *to* à); *ownership* transférer (*from* de, *to* à); *money* virer (*from* de, *to, into* à, sur); *vote* reporter (*to* sur); *design, drawing* reporter, décalquer (*to* sur). (*Brit Telec*) **to ~ the charges** téléphoner en P.C.V.; (*Brit Telec*) **~red charge call** communication *f* en P.C.V.; *[telephone operator]* **I'm ~ring you now** je vous mets en communication maintenant; (*notice*) **business ~red to ...** (*office*) bureaux transférés à ...; (*shop*) magasin transféré à ...; **to ~ one's affection to sb** reporter son *or* ses affection(s) sur qn.
2 **vi** *[employee, civil servant, diplomat]* être transféré *or* muté (*to* à); *[soldier, player, prisoner, offices]* être transféré (*to* à); (*US Univ: change universities*) faire un transfert (pour une autre université). (*Univ etc*) **he's ~red from Science to Geography** il ne fait plus de science, il s'est réorienté en géographie; **to ~ from one train/plane etc to another** être transféré *or* transbordé d'un train/avion *etc* à un autre; **we had to ~ to a bus** nous avons dû changer et prendre un car.
3 ['trænsfɜːʳ] **n** a (*gen*) transfert *m*; *[employee, diplomat]* transfert, mutation *f*; *[soldier, player, prisoner]* transfert; *[passenger]* transfert, transbordement *m*; *[object, goods]* transfert, transport *m*, transmission *f*; *[money]* virement *m*; (*Pol: of power*) passation *f*; (*Jur: document*) transfert, translation *f* (*Jur*). **to pay sth by bank ~** payer qch par virement bancaire; (*Jur*) **~ of ownership** transfert *or* translation de propriété (*from* de, *to* à); (*Jur*) **application for ~ of proceedings** demande *f* de renvoi devant une autre juridiction; (*Ftbl etc*) **to ask for a ~** demander un transfert.
b (*picture, design etc*) (*rub-on type*) décalcomanie *f*; (*stick-on*) autocollant *m*; (*sewn-on*) décalque *m*.
c (*Coach, Rail: also* **~ ticket**) billet *m* de correspondance.
4 ['trænsfɜːʳ] **comp** ►**transfer desk** guichet *m* de transit ►**transfer fee** (*Ftbl etc*) (prix *m* du) transfert *m* ►**transfer lounge** salle *f* de transit ►**transfer passenger** passager *m* en transit ►**transfer season** (*Ftbl*) période *f* des transferts ►**transfer student** (*US Univ*) étudiant(e) *m(f)* venant d'une autre université ►**transfer tax** (*Fin*) droit *m* de mutation.

transferable [træns'fɜːrəbl] **adj** transmissible. **not ~** strictement personnel; **~ vote** voix *f* reportée (*sur un second candidat*).

transferee [ˌtrænsfɜː'riː] **n** (*Jur*) cessionnaire *mf*, bénéficiaire *mf*.

transference ['trænsfərəns] **n** (*NonC*) a = **transfer 3**; *see also* **thought**. b (*Psych*) transfert *m*.

transferor, transferrer [træns'fɜːrəʳ] **n** (*Jur*) cédant(e) *m(f)*.

transfiguration [ˌtrænsfɪgə'reɪʃən] **n** (*gen, also Rel*) transfiguration *f*.

transfigure [træns'fɪgəʳ] **vt** transfigurer.

transfix [træns'fɪks] **vt** (*lit*) transpercer. (*fig*) **to be** *or* **stand ~ed** être cloué sur place; **to be ~ed with horror** être cloué au sol d'horreur, être paralysé par l'horreur.

transform [træns'fɔːm] 1 **vt** (*gen*) transformer, métamorphoser (*into* en); (*Chem, Elec, Math, Phys*) convertir, transformer (*into* en); (*Gram*) transformer (*into* en). **to ~ o.s. into, to be ~ed into** se transformer en. 2 ['trænsfɔːm] **n** (*US Ling*) transformation *f*.

transformation [ˌtrænsfə'meɪʃən] **n** (*see* **transform 1**) transformation *f*, métamorphose *f*; conversion *f*; (*Ling*) transformation.

transformational [ˌtrænsfə'meɪʃənl] **adj** (*Ling*) transformationnel.

transformer [træns'fɔːməʳ] 1 **n** (*Elec*) transformateur *m*. 2 **comp** ►**transformer station** poste *m* de transformateurs.

transfuse [træns'fjuːz] **vt** (*Med, fig*) transfuser.

transfusion [træns'fjuːʒən] **n** (*Med, fig*) transfusion *f*. **blood ~** transfusion sanguine *or* de sang; **to give sb a ~** faire une transfusion à qn.

transgress [træns'gres] 1 **vt** transgresser, enfreindre, violer. 2 **vi** pécher.

transgression [træns'greʃən] **n** (*sin*) péché *m*, faute *f*; (*NonC*) transgression *f*.

transgressor [træns'gresəʳ] **n** (*gen: of law etc*) transgresseur *m* (*liter*); (*Rel: sinner*) pécheur *m*, -eresse *f*.

tranship [træn'ʃɪp] **vt** = **transship**.

transhipment [træn'ʃɪpmənt] **n** = **transshipment**.

transience ['trænzɪəns] **n** caractère *m* éphémère *or* transitoire.

transient ['trænzɪənt] 1 **adj** transitoire, éphémère, passager. 2 **n** (*US: in hotel etc*) client(e) *m(f)* de passage.

transistor [træn'zɪstəʳ] **n** (*Elec*) transistor *m*; (*also* **~ radio, ~ set**) transistor.

transistorize [træn'zɪstəraɪz] **vt** transistoriser. **~d** transistorisé, à transistors.

transit ['trænzɪt] 1 **n** (*NonC*) (*gen*) transit *m*; (*Astron*) passage *m*. **in ~** en transit. 2 **comp** *goods, passengers* en transit; *documents, port, visa* de transit ►**transit camp** (*Mil etc*) camp volant ►**transit lounge** (*Aviat*) salle *f* de transit.

transition [træn'zɪʃən] 1 **n** transition *f* (*from* de, *to* à). 2 **comp** *period* de transition.

transitional [træn'zɪʃənəl] **adj** *period, government* de transition; *measures* transitoire.

transitive ['trænzɪtɪv] **adj** transitif.

transitively ['trænzɪtɪvlɪ] **adv** transitivement.

transitivity [ˌtrænsɪ'tɪvɪtɪ] **n** (*Gram*) transitivité *f*.

transitory ['trænzɪtərɪ] **adj** transitoire, éphémère, passager.

Transkei [træn'skaɪ] **n** Transkei *m*.

translatable [trænz'leɪtəbl] **adj** traduisible.

translate [trænz'leɪt] 1 **vt** a (*gen, Ling, also Comput*) traduire (*from* de, *into* en). **how do you ~ "weather"?** quelle est la traduction de "weather"?, comment traduit-on "weather"?; **the word is ~d as ...** le mot se traduit par ...; **which when ~d means ...** ce que l'on peut traduire par ...; (*fig*) **to ~ ideas into actions** passer des idées aux actes; **the figures, ~d in terms of hours lost, mean** ... exprimés *or* traduits en termes d'heures perdues, ces chiffres signifient ... . **b** (*Rel*) *bishop, relics* transférer; (*convey to heaven*) ravir. **2** **vi** *[person]* traduire; *[word, book]* se traduire. **it won't ~** c'est intraduisible.

translation [trænzˈleɪʃən] **n** **a** traduction *f* (*from* de, *into* en); (*Scol etc*) version *f*. **the poem loses in ~** le poème perd à la traduction; **it is a ~ from the Russian** c'est traduit du russe. **b** (*Rel*) *[bishop]* translation *f*; *[relics]* transfert *m*; (*conveying to heaven*) ravissement *m*.

translator [trænzˈleɪtəʳ] **n** (*person*) traducteur *m*, -trice *f*; (*machine*) traducteur *m*. (*Comput*) **~ (program)** programme *m* de traduction.

transliterate [trænzˈlɪtəreɪt] **vt** translit(t)érer.

transliteration [ˌtrænzlɪtəˈreɪʃən] **n** translit(t)ération *f*.

translucence [trænzˈluːsns] **n** translucidité *f*.

translucent [trænzˈluːsnt] **adj, translucid** [trænzˈluːsɪd] **adj** translucide.

transmigrate [ˈtrænzmaɪˈgreɪt] **vi** *[soul]* transmigrer; *[people]* émigrer.

transmigration [ˌtrænzmaɪˈgreɪʃən] **n** *[soul]* transmigration *f*; *[people]* émigration *f*.

transmissible [trænzˈmɪsəbl] **adj** transmissible.

transmission [trænzˈmɪʃən] **1** **n** (*gen*) transmission *f*; (*US: gearbox*) boîte *f* de vitesses. **2** **comp ▸ transmission cable** (*Aut*) câble *m* de transmission **▸ transmission shaft** arbre *m* de transmission.

transmit [trænzˈmɪt] **1** **vt** (*gen, Aut, Med, Phys etc*) transmettre; (*Rad, Telec, TV*) émettre, diffuser; *see* **sexually**. **2** **vi** (*Rad, Telec, TV*) émettre, diffuser.

transmitter [trænzˈmɪtəʳ] **n** **a** (*Rad*) émetteur *m*. **b** (*in telephone*) capsule *f* microphonique. **c** (*transmitting device*) transmetteur *m*.

transmitting [trænzˈmɪtɪŋ] **1** **adj** (*Telec*) *set, station* émetteur (*f* -trice). **2** **n** (*gen, Med, Phys*) = **transmission 1**.

transmogrify [trænzˈmɒgrɪfaɪ] **vt** (*hum*) métamorphoser, transformer (*into* en).

transmutable [trænzˈmjuːtəbl] **adj** transmuable *or* transmutable.

transmutation [ˌtrænzmjuːˈteɪʃən] **n** transmutation *f*.

transmute [trænzˈmjuːt] **vt** transmuer *or* transmuter (*into* en).

transom [ˈtrænsəm] **n** **a** (*crosspiece*) traverse *f*, imposte *f*. **b** (*US: in window*) vasistas *m*.

transonic [trænˈsɒnɪk] **adj** = **transsonic**.

transparency [trænsˈpærənsɪ] **n** **a** (*NonC*) transparence *f*. **b** [trænsˈpɛərənsɪ] (*Brit Phot*) diapositive *f*; (*for overhead projector*) transparent *m*. **colour ~** diapositive en couleur.

transparent [trænsˈpærənt] **adj** (*all senses*) transparent.

transparently [trænsˈpærəntlɪ] **adv** (*fig*) manifestement. **it is ~ clear** *or* **obvious** il est manifestement *or* tout à fait clair.

transpierce [trænsˈpɪəs] **vt** transpercer.

transpiration [ˌtrænspɪˈreɪʃən] **n** transpiration *f*.

transpire [trænsˈpaɪəʳ] **1** **vi** **a** **(impers vb)** (*become known*) s'ébruiter; (*happen*) se passer, arriver. **it ~d that** ... on a appris par la suite que ... . **b** (*Bot, Physiol*) transpirer. **2** **vt** transpirer.

transplant [trænsˈplɑːnt] **1** **vt** *plant, population* transplanter; (*Med*) transplanter, greffer; *seedlings etc* repiquer. **2** [ˈtrænsplɑːnt] **n** (*Med*) transplantation *f*, greffe *f*. **he's had a heart ~** on lui a fait une greffe du cœur *or* une transplantation cardiaque.

transplantation [ˌtrænsplɑːnˈteɪʃən] **n** (*see* **transplant 1**) transplantation *f*; repiquage *m*.

transponder [trænˈspɒndəʳ] **n** transpondeur *m*.

transport [ˈtrænspɔːt] **1** **n** **a** *[goods, parcels etc]* transport *m*. **road/rail ~** transport par route/par chemin de fer; **by road ~** par route; **by rail ~** par chemin de fer; (*Brit*) **Minister/Department of T~** ministre *m*/ministère *m* des Transports; **have you got any ~ for this evening?*** tu as une voiture pour ce soir? **b** (*esp Mil: ship/plane/train*) navire *m*/avion *m*/train *m* de transport. **c** (*fig*) *[delight etc]* transport *m*; *[fury etc]* accès *m*. **2** **comp** *costs, ship, plane etc* de transport; *system, dispute, strike* des transports **▸ transport café** (*Brit*) routier *m*, restaurant *m* de routiers **▸ Transport Police** (*Brit*) ≃ la police des chemins de fer. **3** [trænsˈpɔːt] **vt** (*lit, fig*) transporter.

transportable [trænsˈpɔːtəbl] **adj** transportable.

transportation [ˌtrænspɔːˈteɪʃən] **n** (*act of transporting*) transport *m*; (*means of transport*) moyen *m* de transport; *[criminals]* transportation *f*. (*US*) **Secretary/Department of T~** ministre *m*/ministère *m* des Transports.

transporter [trænsˈpɔːtəʳ] **n** (*Mil: vehicle, ship*) transport *m*; (*plane*) avion *m* de transport; (*car* ~) (*Aut*) camion *m* *or* (*Rail*) wagon *m* pour transport d'automobiles.

transpose [trænsˈpəʊz] **vti** transposer. **transposing instrument** instrument *m* transpositeur.

transposition [ˌtrænspəˈzɪʃən] **n** transposition *f*.

transsexual [trænzˈseksjʊəl] **n** transsexuel(le) *m(f)*.

transsexualism [trænzˈseksjʊəlɪzəm] **n** transsexualisme *m*.

transship [trænsˈʃɪp] **vt** transborder.

transshipment [trænsˈʃɪpmənt] **n** transbordement *m*.

trans-Siberian [trænzsaɪˈbɪərɪən] **adj** transsibérien.

transsonic [trænzˈsɒnɪk] **adj** transsonique.

transubstantiate [ˌtrænsəbˈstænʃɪeɪt] **vt** transsubstantier.

transubstantiation [ˈtrænsəbˌstænʃɪˈeɪʃən] **n** transsubstantiation *f*.

Transvaal [ˈtrænzvɑːl] **n** Transvaal *m*.

transversal [trænzˈvɜːsəl] (*Geom*) **1** **adj** transversal. **2** **n** (ligne *f*) transversale *f*.

transversally [trænzˈvɜːsəlɪ] **adv** transversalement.

transverse [ˈtrænzvɜːs] **1** **adj** (*gen, Geom*) transversal; (*Anat*) transverse. (*Aut*) **~ engine** moteur *m* transversal; (*Mus*) **~ flute** flûte *f* traversière. **2** **n** (*gen*) partie transversale; (*Geom*) axe transversal.

transversely [trænzˈvɜːslɪ] **adv** transversalement.

transvestism [trænzˈvestɪzəm] **n** travestisme *m*.

transvestite [trænzˈvestaɪt] **n** travesti(e) *m(f)* (*Psych*).

Transylvania [ˌtrænsɪlˈveɪnɪə] **n** Transylvanie *f*.

trap [træp] **1** **n** **a** (*gen*) piège *m*; (*gin* ~) collet *m*; (*covered hole*) trappe *f*; (*fig*) piège, traquenard. **lion** *etc* **~** piège à lions *etc*; (*lit, fig*) **to set** *or* **lay a ~** tendre un piège (*for sb* à qn); (*lit, fig*) **to catch in a ~** prendre au piège; **we were caught like rats in a ~** nous étions faits comme des rats; (*fig*) **he fell into the ~** il est tombé dans le piège; **it's a ~** c'est un piège; *see* **man, mouse, radar, speed** *etc*.

b (~ *door*) trappe *f* (*also Theat*); (*Greyhound Racing*) box *m* de départ; (*Shooting*) ball-trap *m*; (*in drainpipe*) siphon *m*; (*‡: mouth*) gueule‡ *f*. **shut your ~!‡** ta gueule!‡, la ferme!‡; **keep your ~ shut (about it)‡** ferme ta gueule‡ (là-dessus).

c (*carriage*) charrette anglaise, cabriolet *m*.

d (*luggage*) **~s** bagages *mpl*.

2 **comp ▸ trap door** trappe *f* **▸ trapshooting** ball-trap *m*.

3 **vt** **a** (*lit, fig: snare*) *animal, person* prendre au piège. **they ~ped him into admitting that** ... il est tombé dans leur piège et a admis que ... .

b (*immobilize, catch, cut off*) *person, vehicle, ship* bloquer, immobiliser; *gas, liquid* retenir; *object* coincer (*in sth* dans qch). **20 miners were ~ped** 20 mineurs étaient bloqués *or* murés (au fond); **~ped by the flames** cerné par les flammes; **the climbers were ~ped on a ledge** les alpinistes étaient bloqués sur une saillie; **to ~ one's finger in the door** se coincer *or* se pincer le doigt dans la porte; (*Sport*) **to ~ the ball** bloquer le ballon.

trapeze [trəˈpiːz] **1** **n** trapèze *m* (*de cirque*). **2** **comp ▸ trapeze artist** trapéziste *mf*, voltigeur *m*, -euse *f*.

trapezium [trəˈpiːzɪəm] **n, pl ~s** *or* **trapezia** [trəˈpiːzɪə] trapèze *m* (*Math*).

trapezius [trəˈpiːzɪəs] **n, pl ~es** (muscle *m*) trapèze *m*.

trapezoid [ˈtræpɪzɔɪd] **1** **n** trapèze *m* (*Math*). **2** **adj** trapézoïdal.

trapper [ˈtræpəʳ] **n** trappeur *m*.

trappings [ˈtræpɪŋz] **npl** (*for horse*) harnachement *m*; (*dress ornaments*) ornements *mpl*, apparat *m*, atours† *mpl*. (*fig*) **shorn of all its ~** débarrassé de toutes ses fioritures; (*fig*) **if you look beneath the ~** si on regarde derrière la façade; **with all the ~ of kingship** avec tout le cérémonial afférent à la royauté; **all the ~ of success** tous les signes extérieurs du succès.

Trappist [ˈtræpɪst] **1** **n** trappiste *m*. **2** **adj** de la Trappe.

trapse* [treɪps] **vi** = **traipse**.

trash [træʃ] **1** **n** (*refuse: esp US*) ordures *fpl*; (*pej: worthless thing*) camelote* *f*; (*nonsense*) inepties *fpl*; (*‡ pej: people*) racaille *f* (*NonC*). (*fig*) **this is ~** ça ne vaut rien (du tout); (*esp goods*) c'est de la camelote*; (*message, letter, remark etc*) c'est de la blague*; **he talks a lot of ~** il ne raconte que des inepties, ce qu'il dit c'est de la blague*; *[people]* **they're just ~‡** c'est de la racaille; **he's ~‡** c'est un moins que rien; *see* **white**.

2 **comp ▸ trash can** (*US*) poubelle *f*, boîte *f* à ordures **▸ trash heap** (*lit*) tas *m* d'ordures, dépotoir *m*; (*fig*) **the trash heap of history** les oubliettes *or* la poubelle de l'histoire.

3 **vt** (*US* *) **a** (*vandalize*) saccager.

b (*criticize*) débiner*, dénigrer.

4 **vi** (*US* *) commettre des actes de vandalisme.

trasher* [ˈtræʃəʳ] **n** (*US*) vandale *m*.

trashy [ˈtræʃɪ] **adj** *goods* de camelote*, de pacotille; *novel, play* de quatre sous; *film, speech, opinion, ideas* qui ne vaut rien (du tout).

Trasimene [ˈtræzɪmiːn] **n: Lake ~** lac *m* Trasimène.

trauma [ˈtrɔːmə] **1** **n, pl ~s** *or* **traumata** [ˈtrɔːmətə] (*Med, Psych*) trauma *m*; (*fig*) traumatisme *m*. **2** **comp ▸ trauma centre** (*US Med*) service *m* de traumatologie.

traumatic [trɔːˈmætɪk] **adj** (*Med*) traumatique; (*Psych, fig*) traumatisant.

traumatism [ˈtrɔːmətɪzəm] **n** traumatisme *m*.

traumatize [ˈtrɔːmətaɪz] **vt** traumatiser.

traumatized [ˈtrɔːmətaɪzd] **adj** traumatisé.

travail†† [ˈtræveɪl] **1** **n** labeur *m*; (*in childbirth*) douleurs *fpl* de l'enfantement. **2** **vi** peiner; (*in childbirth*) être en couches.

travel [ˈtrævl] **1** **vi** **a** (*journey*) voyager, faire un *or* des voyage(s), aller. **they have ~led a lot** ils ont beaucoup voyagé, ils ont fait beaucoup de voyages; **they have ~led a long way** ils sont venus de loin; (*fig*) ils ont fait beaucoup de chemin; **he is ~ling in Spain just now** il est en voyage en Espagne en ce moment; **as he was ~ling across France** pendant qu'il voyageait à travers la France; **to ~ through a region** traverser une région; (*visit*) visiter *or* parcourir une région; **to ~ round the world** faire le tour du monde; **to ~ light** voyager avec peu de bagages; **I like ~ling by car** j'aime voyager en voiture; **he ~s to work by car** il va au travail en voiture; *[food, wine]* **it ~s well** ça supporte bien le voyage.

b (*Comm*) voyager, être représentant. **he ~s for a Paris firm** il voyage pour *or* il représente une société parisienne; **he ~s in soap** il est représentant en savon.

c (*move, go*) *[person, animal, vehicle]* aller; *[object]* aller, passer; *[machine part, bobbin, piston etc]* se déplacer. **to ~ at 80 km/h** faire du 80 km/h; **you were ~ling too fast** vous alliez trop vite; **he was really ~ling!*** il roulait drôlement vite!*; **this car can certainly ~*** c'est une voiture qui a du nerf*; **light ~s at (a speed of)** ... la vitesse de la lumière est de ...; **news ~s fast** les nouvelles se propagent *or* circulent vite; **the news ~led to Rome** la nouvelle s'est propagée jusqu'à Rome; **the boxes ~ along a moving belt** les boîtes passent sur une *or* se déplacent le long d'une chaîne; **this part ~s 3 cm** cette pièce se déplace de 3 cm *or* a une course de 3 cm; (*fig*) **his eyes ~led over the scene** son regard se promenait *or* il promenait son regard sur le spectacle; **her mind ~led over recent events** elle a revu en esprit les événements récents.

2 vt: **to ~ a country/district** parcourir un pays/une région; **they ~ the road to London every month** ils font la route de Londres tous les mois; **a much-~led road** une route très fréquentée; **they ~led 300 km** ils ont fait *or* parcouru 300 km.

3 n a (*NonC*) le(s) voyage(s) *m(pl)*. **to be fond of ~** aimer voyager, aimer le(s) voyage(s); **~ was difficult in those days** les voyages étaient difficiles *or* il était difficile de voyager à l'époque; **~ broadens the mind** les voyages ouvrent l'esprit.

b **~s** voyages *mpl*; **his ~s in Spain** ses voyages en Espagne; **he's off on his ~s again** il repart en voyage; **if you meet him on your ~s** (*lit*) si vous le rencontrez au cours de vos voyages; (*fig hum*) si vous le rencontrez au cours de vos allées et venues.

c *[machine part, piston etc]* course *f*.

4 comp *allowance, expenses* de déplacement; *scholarship etc* de voyages ▸**travel agency** agence *f* de voyages *or* de tourisme ▸**travel agent** agent *m* de voyages ▸**travel book** récit *m* de voyages ▸**travel brochure** dépliant *m* touristique ▸**travel bureau** = **travel agency** ▸**travel film** film *m* de voyage; (*documentary*) documentaire *m* touristique ▸**travel insurance** assurance *f* voyage ▸**travel organization** organisme *m* de tourisme ▸**travel-sick, travel sickness: to be travel-sick, to suffer from travel sickness** (*in car/plane/boat*) avoir le mal de la route/de l'air/de mer; **travel-sickness pill** comprimé *m* contre le mal de la route (*or* de l'air *etc*) ▸**travel-stained** sali par le(s) voyage(s) ▸**travel voucher** bon *m* de voyage ▸**travel-weary, travel-worn** fatigué par le(s) voyage(s).

travelator ['trævəleɪtəʳ] n tapis *m or* trottoir *m* roulant.

travelled, (*US*) **traveled** ['trævld] adj (*also* **well-~**) *person* qui a beaucoup voyagé; *see also* **travel 2**.

traveller, (*US*) **traveler** ['trævləʳ] 1 n a voyageur *m*, -euse *f*; (*commercial ~*) voyageur *m or* représentant *m* de commerce, V.R.P. *m*. (*Comm*) **he is a ~ in soap** il est représentant en savon. b (*Brit: gypsies*) **~s** gens *mpl* du voyage. 2 comp ▸**traveller's cheque,** (*US*) **traveler's check** chèque *m* de voyage, traveller's check *or* chèque ▸**travel(l)er's joy** (*Bot*) clématite *f* des haies.

travelling, (*US*) **traveling** ['trævlɪŋ] 1 n (*NonC*) voyage(s) *m(pl)*. 2 adj *circus, troupe* ambulant; *crane* mobile. (*Brit*) **~ people** les gens *mpl* du voyage; (*Comm*) **~ salesman** voyageur *m or* représentant *m* de commerce, V.R.P. *m*. 3 comp *bag, rug, scholarship* de voyage; *expenses, allowance* de déplacement ▸**travelling clock** réveil *m or* pendulette *f* de voyage.

travelogue, (*US*) *also* **travelog** ['trævəlɒg] n (*talk*) compte rendu *m* de voyage; (*film*) documentaire *m* touristique; (*book*) récit *m* de voyage.

traverse ['trævəs] 1 vt (*gen, Climbing, Ski*) traverser; *[searchlights]* balayer. 2 vi (*Climbing, Ski*) faire une traversée, traverser. 3 n (*line*) transversale *f*; (*crossbar, crossbeam; also across rampart, trench etc*) traverse *f*; (*Archit*) galerie transversale; (*Climbing, Ski*) traversée *f*.

travesty ['trævɪstɪ] 1 n (*Art, Literat etc*) parodie *f*, pastiche *m*; (*pej*) parodie *f*, simulacre *m*, travestissement *m*. (*pej*) **it was a ~ of freedom/peace** c'était un simulacre de liberté/de paix; **it was a ~ of justice** c'était un simulacre de justice *or* un travestissement de la justice *or* une parodie de la justice. 2 vt travestir, déformer, falsifier.

trawl [trɔːl] 1 n (*also* **~ net**) chalut *m*; (*fig: search*) recherche *f*. 2 vi pêcher au chalut. **to ~ for herring** pêcher le hareng au chalut; (*fig*) **to ~ for sth** être en quête de qch. 3 vt *net* traîner, tirer. (*fig*) **to ~ a place/the papers for sth** ratisser un endroit/éplucher les journaux à la recherche de qch.

trawler ['trɔːləʳ] 1 n (*ship, man*) chalutier *m*. 2 comp ▸**trawler fisherman** pêcheur *m* au chalut ▸**trawler owner** propriétaire *mf* de chalutier.

trawling ['trɔːlɪŋ] n (*NonC*) chalutage *m*, pêche *f* au chalut.

tray [treɪ] 1 n (*for carrying things*) plateau *m*; (*for storing things*) (*box-type*) boîte *f* (de rangement); (*basket-type*) corbeille *f* (de rangement); (*drawer-type*) tiroir *m*; (*of eggs, in chocolate box*) plateau; (*in bird or animal cage*) plaque *f*, plateau; *see* **ash²**, **ice** *etc*. 2 comp ▸**traycloth** napperon *m*.

treacherous ['tretʃərəs] adj *person, action, answer* traître (*f* traîtresse), déloyal, perfide; (*fig*) *ground, surface, weather* traître; *memory* infidèle. **road conditions** *or* **the roads are ~** il faut se méfier de l'état des routes.

treacherously ['tretʃərəslɪ] adv traîtreusement, perfidement. **the roads are ~ slippery** les routes sont dangereusement glissantes.

treachery ['tretʃərɪ] n traîtrise *f*, déloyauté *f*.

treacle ['triːkl] (*Brit*) 1 n (*also* **black ~**) mélasse *f*. 2 comp ▸**treacle pudding** pudding *m* à la mélasse raffinée ▸**treacle tart** tarte *f* à la mélasse raffinée.

treacly ['triːklɪ] adj (*fig*) sirupeux.

tread [tred] (vb: pret **trod**, ptp **trodden**) 1 n a (*NonC*) (*footsteps*) pas *mpl*; (*sound*) bruit *m* de pas.

b *[tyre]* bande *f* de roulement; *[stair]* giron *m*; *[shoe]* semelle *f*; (*belt over tractor etc wheels*) chenille *f*.

2 comp ▸**treadmill** (*mill*) trépigneuse *f*; (*Hist: punishment*) manège *m* de discipline; (*for exercise*) tapis *m* de jogging; (*fig*) **he hated the treadmill of life in the factory** il détestait la morne *or* mortelle routine du travail d'usine ▸**tread pattern** (*Aut*) sculpture *f*.

3 vi marcher. **to ~ on sth** mettre le pied sur qch, marcher sur qch; (*deliberately*) **he trod on the cigarette end** il a écrasé le mégot du pied; (*fig*) **to ~ on sb's heels** suivre *or* serrer qn de près, talonner qn; (*lit, fig*) **to ~ carefully** *or* **softly** *or* **warily** avancer avec précaution, y aller doucement; *see* **toe** *etc*.

4 vt *path, road* suivre, parcourir (*à pied*). **he trod the streets looking for somewhere to live** il a erré dans les rues *or* il a battu le pavé à la recherche d'un logis; **to ~ sth underfoot** fouler qch aux pieds, piétiner qch; **to ~ grapes** fouler du raisin; **~ the earth (in** *or* **down) round the roots** tassez la terre du pied autour des racines; **he trod his cigarette end into the mud** il a enfoncé du pied son mégot dans la boue; **you're ~ing mud into the carpet** tu mets *or* tu étales de la boue sur le tapis; **to ~ water** (*pret, ptp gen* **treaded**) faire du sur-place (*dans l'eau*); **well-trodden path** (*lit*) sentier *m* bien tracé; (*fig*) sentier battu; (*Theat:* †† *or liter*) **to ~ the boards** faire du théâtre; (†† *or liter: dance*) **to ~ a measure** danser.

▸**tread down** vt sep tasser *or* presser du pied. **the grass was trodden down** l'herbe avait été piétinée *or* foulée.

▸**tread in** vt sep *root, seedling* consolider en tassant tout autour la terre du pied.

treadle ['tredl] 1 n pédale *f* (*de tour, de machine à coudre etc*). 2 comp *machine* à pédale. 3 vi actionner la pédale, pédaler.

Treas. abbr of **Treasurer**.

treason ['triːzn] n trahison *f*. **high ~** haute trahison.

treasonable ['triːzənəbl] adj *thought, action* qui constitue une trahison.

treasure ['treʒəʳ] 1 n trésor *m* (*also fig*). **yes my ~** oui mon trésor; **~s of medieval art** les trésors *or* les joyaux *mpl* de l'art médiéval; **she's a ~** (*gen*) elle est adorable; (*of servant etc*) c'est une perle.

2 comp ▸**treasure-house** (*lit*) trésor *m* (*lieu*); (*fig: of library, museum etc*) mine *f*, trésor; **she's a real treasure-house of information** c'est un puits de science, c'est une mine d'érudition ▸**treasure hunt** chasse *f* au trésor ▸**treasure-trove** (*NonC*) trésor *m* (*dont le propriétaire est inconnu*).

3 vt a (*value greatly*) *object, sb's friendship, opportunity etc* tenir beaucoup à, attacher une grande valeur à. **this is my most ~d possession** c'est ce que je possède de plus précieux.

b (*keep carefully: also* **~ up**) *object, money, valuables* garder précieusement, prendre grand soin de; *memory, thought* conserver précieusement, chérir.

treasurer ['treʒərəʳ] n trésorier *m*, -ière *f* (*d'une association etc*).

treasury ['treʒərɪ] 1 n a **the T~** la Trésorerie, ≃ le ministère des Finances; (*US*) **Secretary/Department of the T~** ministre *m*/ministère *m* des Finances. b (*place*) trésorerie *f*; (*fig: book*) trésor *m*. 2 comp ▸(*Brit Parl*) **Treasury bench** banc *m* des ministres ▸**treasury bill** (*US*) ≃ bon *m* du Trésor ▸**Treasury Department** (*US*) ministère *m* de l'Économie et des Finances ▸**treasury note** ≃ bon *m* du Trésor ▸**Treasury Secretary** (*US*) ministre *m* de l'Économie et des Finances.

treat [triːt] 1 vt a *person* traiter, agir envers, se conduire envers; *animal* traiter; *object, theme, suggestion* traiter, examiner. **to ~ sb well** bien traiter qn, bien agir *or* se conduire envers qn; **to ~ sb badly** mal agir *or* se conduire envers qn, traiter qn fort mal; **to ~ sb like a child/a dog** traiter qn en enfant/comme un chien; **he ~ed me as though I was to blame** il s'est conduit envers moi comme si c'était ma faute; **you should ~ your mother with more respect** vous devriez montrer plus de respect envers votre mère; **you should ~ your books with more care** tu devrais faire plus attention à *or* prendre plus de soin de tes livres; **the article ~s the problems of race relations with fresh insight** cet article traite *or* analyse *or* examine les problèmes des rapports interraciaux de façon nouvelle *or* originale et pénétrante; **he ~s the subject very objectively** il traite le sujet avec beaucoup d'objectivité; **he ~ed the whole thing as a joke** il a pris tout cela à la plaisanterie.

b *wood, soil, substance* traiter (*with sth* à qch); (*Med*) traiter, soigner (*sb for sth* qn pour qch). **they ~ed him/the infection with**

penicillin ils l'ont soigné/ont soigné l'infection à la pénicilline.

c (*pay for etc*) **to ~ sb to sth** offrir *or* payer* qch à qn; **to ~ o.s. to sth** s'offrir *or* se payer* qch; **I'll ~ you to a drink** je t'offre *or* te paie* un verre, je régale*.

2 vi a (*negotiate*) **to ~ with sb** traiter avec qn (*for sth* pour qch); **to ~ for peace** engager des pourparlers en vue de la paix.

b (*discuss*) *[book, article etc]* **to ~ of** traiter (de), examiner.

3 n a (*pleasure*) plaisir *m*; (*outing*) sortie *f*; (*present*) cadeau *m*. **I've got a ~ for you** j'ai une bonne surprise pour toi; **what a ~!** quelle aubaine!, chouette* alors!; **it's a ~ in store** c'est un plaisir à venir; **it was a great ~ (for us) to see them again** ça nous a vraiment fait plaisir de les revoir, ça a été une joie de les revoir; **what would you like as a ~ for your birthday?** qu'est-ce qui te ferait plaisir pour ton anniversaire?; **it is a ~ for her to go out to a meal** elle se fait une joie de *or* c'est tout un événement* pour elle de dîner en ville; **let's give the children a ~** faisons (un) plaisir *or* une gâterie aux enfants, gâtons un peu les enfants; **I want to give her a ~** je veux lui faire plaisir; **to give o.s. a ~** s'offrir un petit extra, s'offrir quelque chose; **the school ~ was a visit to the seaside** la fête de l'école a consisté en une excursion au bord de la mer; **to stand ~** inviter; **to stand sb a ~** (*gen*) offrir *or* payer* quelque chose à qn; (*food, drink only*) régaler* qn; **this is to be my ~** c'est moi qui offre *or* qui paie*; (*food, drink only*) c'est moi qui régale*.

b (*Brit* ‡: *adv phrase*) **a ~** à merveille; **the garden is coming on a ~** le jardin avance à merveille; **the plan worked a ~** le projet a marché comme sur des roulettes.

treatise ['tri:tɪz] n (*Literat*) traité *m* (*on* de).

treatment ['tri:tmənt] 1 n (*gen, Chem, etc*) traitement *m*; (*Med*) traitement, soins *mpl*. **his ~ of his parents/the dog** la façon dont il traite (*or* traitait) ses parents/le chien; **his ~ of this subject in his book** la façon dont il traite ce sujet dans son livre; **he got very good ~ there** (*gen*) on l'a très bien traité là-bas; (*Med*) il a été très bien traité *or* soigné là-bas; **to give sb preferential ~** accorder à qn un traitement préférentiel *or* un régime de faveur; **he needs medical ~** il a besoin de soins médicaux *or* d'un traitement; **they refused him ~** ils ont refusé de le soigner; **he is having (a course of) ~ for kidney trouble** il suit un traitement *or* il est sous traitement pour ennuis rénaux; (*fig*) **to give sb the ~**‡ en faire voir de dures* *or* de toutes les couleurs* à qn; *see* **respond**.

2 comp ▸**treatment room** (*Med*) salle *f* de soins.

treaty ['tri:tɪ] 1 n a traité *m* (*with* avec, *between* entre). (*Pol*) **to make a ~ with sb** conclure *or* signer un traité avec qn. b (*NonC*) **to sell a house by private ~** vendre une maison par accord privé. 2 comp ▸**treaty obligations** obligations conventionnelles.

treble ['trebl] 1 adj a (*triple: all senses*) triple. (*in numerals*) **~ seven five four** (77754) triple sept *or* trois fois sept cinq quatre, sept cent soixante-dix-sept cinquante-quatre; **the amount is in ~ figures** le montant dépasse la centaine; (*in football pools*) **the ~ chance** *méthode de pari en football*. b (*Mus*) *voice* de soprano (*voix d'enfant*); *part* pour *or* de soprano. **the ~ clef** la clef de sol. 2 n a (*Mus: part, singer*) soprano *m*. b (*Sound Recording*) aigus *mpl*. c (*drink*) triple *m*. d (*Darts*) triple *m*. 3 adv (*thrice*) trois fois plus que. 4 vti tripler.

trebly ['treblɪ] adv triplement, trois fois plus.

tree [tri:] (vb: pret, ptp **treed**) 1 n a arbre *m*. **cherry ~** cerisier *m*; (*Bible*) **the ~ of life** l'arbre de vie; (*Bible*) **the ~ of knowledge of good and evil** l'arbre de la science du bien et du mal; (*Rel* ††: *the Cross*) **the ~** l'arbre de la Croix; (*fig*) **to be at** *or* **to have reached the top of the ~** être arrivé en haut de l'échelle (*fig*); (*fig*) **to be up a ~**‡ être dans le pétrin; *see* **apple, bark¹, bark², family, plum** *etc*.

b (*shoe ~*) embauchoir *m*; (*cobbler's last*) forme *f*.

c (*Ling*) arbre *m*.

d *[saddle]* arçon *m* (de la selle).

2 comp ▸**tree-covered** boisé ▸**tree-creeper** grimpereau *m* ▸**tree diagram** (*Ling*) représentation *f* en arbre ▸**tree fern** fougère *f* arborescente ▸**tree frog** rainette *f*, grenouille *f* arboricole ▸**tree of heaven** (*Bot*) ailante *m* ▸**tree house** cabane construite dans un arbre ▸**tree lawn** (*US*) plate-bande plantée d'arbres (*entre la rue et le trottoir*) ▸**tree line** limite *f* des arbres ▸**tree-lined** bordé d'arbres ▸**tree-runner** (*bird*) sittelle *f* ▸**tree surgeon** arboriculteur *m*, -trice *f* (qui s'occupe du traitement des arbres malades) ▸**tree surgery** arboriculture *f* (spécialisée dans le traitement des arbres malades) ▸**treetop** sommet *m or* cime *f* d'un arbre; **in the treetops** au sommet *or* à la cime des arbres ▸**tree trunk** tronc *m* d'arbre.

3 vt forcer à se réfugier dans un arbre.

treeless ['tri:lɪs] adj sans arbres, dépourvu d'arbres, déboisé.

trefoil ['trefɔɪl] n (*Archit, Bot*) trèfle *m*. **~ leaf** feuille *f* de trèfle.

trek [trek] 1 vi a (*go slowly*) cheminer, avancer avec peine; (*as holiday: also* **to go ~king**) faire du trekking *or* de la randonnée; (*go on long, difficult journey*) faire un périple; (*Hist: go by oxcart*) voyager en char à bœufs; *see* **pony**. b (*: *walk*) se traîner. **I had to ~ over to the library** il a fallu que je me traîne (*subj*) jusqu'à la bibliothèque. 2 n (*hike*) trek *m*, trekking *m*, randonnée *f*; (*long, difficult journey*) périple *m*; (*leg of journey*) étape *f*; (*by oxcart*) voyage *m* en char à bœufs; (*: *walk*) balade* *f*. **it was quite a ~* to the hotel** il y avait un bon bout de chemin* à faire jusqu'à l'hôtel.

trekking ['trekɪŋ] n trekking *m*, randonnée *f*. **to go ~** faire du trekking *or* de la randonnée; **to go on a ~ holiday** partir en vacances faire de la randonnée.

trellis ['trelɪs] 1 n treillis *m*, (*tougher*) treillage *m*; (*NonC: also* **~work**) treillage. 2 vt treillisser, treillager.

tremble ['trembl] 1 vi (*from fear*) trembler, frémir, frissonner; (*from excitement, passion*) frémir, trembler; (*from cold*) trembler, frissonner, grelotter; *[hand]* trembler; *[voice]* (*with fear, age*) trembler, chevroter; (*with passion*) vibrer; *[ground, building]* trembler, être secoué; *[engine, ship]* vibrer, trépider. **I ~ to think what might have happened** je frémis rien qu'à la pensée de ce qui aurait pu arriver; **what will he do next? — I ~ to think!** qu'est-ce qu'il va encore faire? — j'en frémis d'avance; **he ~d at the thought** il a frémi rien que d'y penser.

2 n (*see* **1**) tremblement *m*; frémissement *m*; frissonnement *m*; vibration(s) *f(pl)*; trépidation(s) *f(pl)*. **to be all of a ~*** trembler comme une feuille, trembler de la tête aux pieds.

trembling ['tremblɪŋ] (*see* **tremble 1**) 1 adj tremblant; frémissant; frissonnant; grelottant; chevrotant; vibrant; trépidant. 2 n (*NonC*) tremblement *m*; frémissement *m*; frissonnement *m*; *see* **fear**.

tremendous [trə'mendəs] adj (*huge*) *difference, number, size, pleasure* énorme; (*dreadful*) *storm, explosion, blow* terrible, épouvantable; *victory* foudroyant; *speed* fou (*f* folle); (*: *excellent*) formidable*, sensationnel*. **a ~ crowd** un monde fou; **a ~ success** un succès fou *or* à tout casser*; **we had a ~ time*** on s'est drôlement bien amusé*.

tremendously [trə'mendəslɪ] adv énormément, terriblement, extrêmement.

tremolo ['treməlәʊ] n (*Mus*) trémolo *m*.

tremor ['tremə^r] n tremblement *m*; *see* **earth**.

tremulous ['tremjʊləs] adj (*timid*) *person* timide, craintif, effarouché; *smile* timide, incertain; (*trembling*) (*from fear*) *person* tremblant, frissonnant, frémissant; *voice* tremblant, chevrotant; (*from excitement, passion*) *person* frémissant, frissonnant; *voice* vibrant; *hand* tremblant; *handwriting* tremblé.

tremulously ['tremjʊləslɪ] adv *say, answer, suggest* en tremblant, en frémissant, timidement; *smile* d'une façon incertaine, timidement.

trench [trenʃ] 1 n tranchée *f* (*also Mil*); (*wider*) fossé *m*. **he fought in the ~es** il était dans les tranchées *or* a fait la guerre des tranchées.

2 comp ▸**trench coat** trench-coat *m* ▸**trench fever** (*Med*) typhus *m* exanthématique, rickettsiose *f* ▸**trench knife** couteau *m* (à double tranchant) ▸**trench warfare** (*Mil*) guerre *f* de tranchées. 3 vt (*dig trenches in*) creuser une *or* des tranchée(s) dans; (*Mil: surround with trenches*) *one's position etc* retrancher. 4 vi creuser une *or* des tranchée(s).

trenchant ['trenʃənt] adj incisif, mordant.

trenchantly ['trenʃəntlɪ] adv d'un ton incisif *or* mordant.

trencher ['trenʃə^r] 1 n tranchoir *m*. 2 comp ▸**trencherman**: **he is a good** *or* **great** *or* **hearty trencherman** il a un sacré coup de fourchette*.

trend [trend] 1 n (*tendency*) tendance *f* (*towards* à); (*Geog*) *[coast, river, road]* direction *f*, orientation *f*; (*fashion*) mode *f*, vogue *f*. (*Fin etc*) **upward/downward ~** tendance à la hausse/à la baisse; **there is a ~ towards doing/away from doing** on a tendance à faire/à ne plus faire; **the latest ~s in swimwear** la mode la plus récente en maillots de bain; **the ~ of events** le cours *or* la tournure des événements; **to set a ~** donner le ton; (*fashion*) lancer une mode; **to buck the ~** aller *or* agir à contre-courant; **~s in popular music** les tendances de la musique populaire; *see* **market, reverse** *etc*.

2 comp ▸**trendsetter** (*person*) personne *f* qui donne le ton (*or* qui lance une mode); (*garment etc*) article *m* dernier cri *inv* ▸**trend-setting** n innovation *f* ◊ adj innovateur (*f* -trice), qui donne le ton (*or* lance une mode).

3 vi *[river, road]* **to ~ northwards/southwards** *etc* aller vers le nord/le sud *etc*; *[events, opinions]* **to ~ towards sth** tendre vers qch.

trendiness* ['trendɪnɪs] n fait *m* d'être branché* *or* dans le vent.

trendy* ['trendɪ] 1 adj *clothes* branché*, dernier cri *inv*; *opinions* dans le vent*, d'avant-garde, avancé; *behaviour, religion* à la mode, dans le vent*; *person* branché*, dans le vent*; *restaurant etc* branché*. **he's got quite a ~ image** il fait très branché*. 2 n branché(e)* *m(f)*, personne *f* dans le vent.

trepan [trɪ'pæn] 1 vt *metal plate etc* forer; (*Med*) trépaner. 2 n (*for quarrying etc*) foreuse *f*, trépan *m*; (*Med*) trépan.

trephine [tre'fi:n] (*Med*) 1 vt trépaner. 2 n trépan *m*.

trepidation [ˌtrepɪ'deɪʃən] n (*fear*) vive inquiétude; (*excitement*) agitation *f*.

trespass ['trespəs] 1 n a (*NonC: Jur: illegal entry*) entrée non autorisée. b (††, *Rel: sin*) offense *f*, péché *m*. **forgive us our ~es** pardonnez-nous nos offenses. 2 vi a s'introduire sans permission. **"no ~ing"** "entrée interdite", "propriété privée"; **you're ~ing** vous êtes dans une propriété privée; **to ~ on** *sb's land* s'introduire *or* se trouver sans permission dans *or* sur; (*fig*) *sb's hospitality, time* abuser de; *sb's privacy* s'ingérer dans; *sb's rights* empiéter sur. b (††, *Rel*) **to ~ against** *person* offenser; *law* enfreindre; **as we forgive them that ~**

against us comme nous pardonnons à ceux qui nous ont offensés.

trespasser ['trespəsər] n a intrus(e) *m(f)* (dans une propriété privée). **"~s will be prosecuted"** "défense d'entrer sous peine de poursuites". b (††, *Rel: sinner*) pécheur *m*, -eresse *f*.

tress [tres] n (*liter*) boucle *f* de cheveux. **~es** chevelure *f*.

trestle ['tresl] 1 n tréteau *m*, chevalet *m*. 2 comp ▸**trestle bridge** pont *m* sur chevalets ▸**trestle table** table *f* à tréteaux.

trews [tru:z] npl pantalon écossais (étroit).

tri... [traɪ] pref tri... .

Triad ['traɪæd] n Triade *f*.

triad ['traɪəd] n (*gen*) triade *f*; (*Mus*) accord parfait.

trial ['traɪəl] 1 n a (*Jur*) (*proceedings*) procès *m*; (*NonC*) jugement *m*. **the ~ lasted a month** le procès a duré un mois; **famous ~s** procès *or* causes *fpl* célèbres; **a new ~ was ordered** la révision du procès a été demandée; **at the ~ it emerged that ...** au cours du procès *or* à l'audience il est apparu que ...; **during his ~ he claimed that ...** pendant son procès il a affirmé que ...; **~ by jury** jugement par jury; **to be** *or* **go on ~** passer en jugement *or* en justice (*see also* **1b**); **to put sb on ~** faire passer qn en jugement; **to be sent for ~** être traduit en justice (*to* devant), être inculpé; **to be on ~ for theft** être jugé pour vol; **he was on ~ for his life** il encourait la peine de mort; **to bring sb to ~** faire passer qn en jugement *or* en justice; **to come up for ~** *[case]* passer au tribunal; *[person]* passer en jugement; *see* **commit, stand.**

b (*test*) *[machine, vehicle, drug etc]* essai *m*. **~s** (*Ftbl etc*) match *m* de sélection; (*Athletics etc*) épreuve *f* de sélection; **sheepdog ~s** concours *m* de chiens de berger; **horse ~s** concours hippique; **~ of strength** épreuve de force; **to have a ~ of strength with sb** lutter de force avec qn, se mesurer à qn; **by (a system of) ~ and error** par tâtonnements, en tâtonnant; **it was all ~ and error** on a procédé uniquement par tâtonnements; **to take sb/sth on ~** prendre qn/qch à l'essai; *[machine, method, employee]* **to be on ~** être à l'essai; **to give sb a ~** mettre qn à l'essai.

c (*hardship*) épreuve *f*; (*nuisance*) souci *m*. **the ~s of old age** les afflictions *fpl or* les vicissitudes *fpl* de la vieillesse; **the interview was a great ~** l'entrevue a été une véritable épreuve *or* a été très éprouvante; **he is a ~ to his mother** il est un souci perpétuel pour sa mère, il donne beaucoup de soucis à sa mère; **what a ~ you are!** ce que tu es agaçant! *or* exaspérant!; *see* **tribulation.**

2 comp *flight, period etc* d'essai; *offer, marriage* à l'essai ▸**trial attorney** (*US Jur*) avocat *m* qui plaide à l'audience ▸**trial balance** (*Fin*) balance *f* d'inventaire ▸**trial balloon** (*US*) (*lit, fig*) ballon *m* d'essai ▸**trial basis**: **on a trial basis** à titre d'essai ▸**trial court** (*US, Can*) cour *f* jugeant en première instance ▸**trial division** (*US, Can: Jur*) division *f or* tribunal *m* de première instance ▸**trial jury** (*US Jur*) jury *m* (dans un procès) ▸**trial run** *[machine etc]* essai *m*; (*fig*) période *f* d'essai, répétition *f*.

triangle ['traɪæŋgl] n (*Math, Mus, fig*) triangle *m*; (*drawing instrument*) équerre *f*; *see* **eternal.**

triangular [traɪ'æŋgjʊlər] adj triangulaire.

triangulate [traɪ'æŋgjʊleɪt] vt trianguler.

triangulation [traɪ,æŋgjʊ'leɪʃən] n triangulation *f*.

Triassic [traɪ'æsɪk] adj (*Geol*) *period* triasique.

triathlon [traɪ'æθlən] n triathlon *m*.

tribal ['traɪbəl] adj *customs, dance, life, system* tribal; *warfare* entre tribus.

tribalism ['traɪbəlɪzəm] n tribalisme *m*.

tribe [traɪb] 1 n (*gen, Bot, Zool*) tribu *f*; (* *fig*) tribu, smala* *f*. **the twelve T~s of Israel** les douze tribus d'Israël. 2 comp ▸**tribesman** membre *m* d'une (*or* de la) tribu.

tribo... ['traɪbəʊ] pref tribo... . **~electricity** tribo-électricité *f*.

tribulation [,trɪbjʊ'leɪʃən] n affliction *f*, souffrance *f*. **(trials and) ~s** tribulations *fpl*; **in times of ~** en période d'adversité, en temps de malheurs.

tribunal [traɪ'bju:nl] n (*gen, Jur, fig*) tribunal *m*. **~ of inquiry** commission *f* d'enquête.

tribune ['trɪbju:n] n (*platform*) tribune *f* (*also fig*); (*Hist, gen: person*) tribun *m*.

tributary ['trɪbjʊtərɪ] 1 adj tributaire. 2 n (*river*) affluent *m*; (*state, ruler*) tributaire *m*.

tribute ['trɪbju:t] n tribut *m*, hommage *m*; (*esp Hist: payment*) tribut. **to pay ~ to** payer tribut à, rendre hommage à; (*Hist etc*) payer (le) tribut à; **it is a ~ to his generosity that nobody went hungry** qu'aucun n'ait souffert de la faim témoigne de sa générosité; *see* **floral.**

trice [traɪs] 1 n: **in a ~** en un clin d'œil, en moins de deux* *or* de rien. 2 vt (*Naut: also* **~ up**) hisser.

Tricel ['traɪsel] ® 1 n Tricel *m* ®. 2 comp *shirt etc* de *or* en Tricel.

tricentenary [,traɪsen'ti:nərɪ], **tricentennial** [,traɪsen'tenɪəl] adj, n tricentenaire (*m*). **~ celebrations** fêtes *fpl* du tricentenaire.

triceps ['traɪseps] n, pl **~** *or* **~es** triceps *m*.

trick [trɪk] 1 n a (*dodge, ruse*) ruse *f*, astuce *f*, truc* *m*; (*prank, joke, hoax*) tour *m*, farce *f*, blague* *f*; *[conjurer, juggler, dog etc]* tour; (*special skill*) truc. **it's a ~ to make you believe ...** c'est une ruse *or* une astuce *or* un truc* pour vous faire croire ...; **he got it all by a ~** il a tout obtenu par une ruse *or* un stratagème *or* une combine⁑; **a dirty** *or* **low** *or* **shabby** *or* **nasty ~** un sale tour, un tour de cochon*; **a ~ of the trade** une ficelle du métier; **it's a ~ of the light** c'est une illusion d'optique; **he's up to his (old) ~s again** il fait de nouveau des siennes*; **how's ~s?*** alors, quoi de neuf?, alors, ça gaze?*; (*fig*) **he knows a ~ or two*** c'est un petit malin; **I know a ~ worth two of that*** je connais un tour *or* un truc* bien meilleur encore que celui-là; **that will do the ~*** ça fera l'affaire, c'est juste ce qu'il faut; **I'll soon get the ~ of it*** je vais bientôt prendre le pli *or* le truc*; (*US*) **~ or treat!** donnez-moi quelque chose ou je vous joue un tour! (*expression employée par les enfants qui font la quête la veille de la Toussaint*); *see* **bag, card[1], conjuring, play** *etc.*

b (*peculiarity*) particularité *f*; (*habit*) habitude *f*, manie *f*; (*mannerism*) tic *m*. **he has a ~ of scratching his ear when puzzled** il a le tic de se gratter l'oreille quand il est perplexe; **he has a ~ of arriving just when I'm making coffee** il a le don *or* le chic* d'arriver au moment où je fais du café; **this horse has a ~ of stopping suddenly** ce cheval a la manie de s'arrêter brusquement; **these things have a ~ of happening just when you don't want them to** ces choses-là se produisent comme par magie *or* ont le don de se produire juste quand on ne le veut pas; **history has a ~ of repeating itself** l'histoire a le don de se répéter.

c (*Cards*) levée *f*, pli *m*. **to take a ~** faire une levée *or* un pli; (*fig*) **he never misses a ~** rien ne lui échappe.

2 comp ▸**trick cushion** (*or* **spoon** *etc*) attrape *f* ▸**trick-cyclist** cycliste-acrobate *mf*; (*Brit* ⁑: *psychiatrist*) psy⁑ *m*, psychiatre *mf* ▸**trick photograph** photographie truquée ▸**trick photography** truquage *m* photographique ▸**trick question** question-piège *f* ▸**trick rider** (*on horse*) voltigeur *m*, -euse *f* (à cheval) ▸**trick riding** voltige *f* (à cheval).

3 vt (*hoax, deceive*) attraper, avoir*, rouler*; (*swindle*) escroquer. **I've been ~ed!** on m'a eu!* *or* roulé!*; **to ~ sb into doing** amener qn à faire par la ruse; **to ~ sb out of sth** obtenir qch de qn *or* soutirer qch à qn par la ruse.

▸**trick out, trick up** vt sep parer (*with* de). **the ladies tricked out in all their finery** les dames sur leur trente et un *or* tout endimanchées.

trickery ['trɪkərɪ] n (*NonC*) ruse *f*, supercherie *f*, fourberie *f*. **by ~** par ruse.

trickiness ['trɪkɪnɪs] n (*NonC*) (*see* **tricky**) caractère délicat *or* épineux, difficulté *f*; caractère rusé *or* retors.

trickle ['trɪkl] 1 n *[water, blood etc]* filet *m*. **the stream has shrunk to a mere ~** le ruisseau n'est plus qu'un filet d'eau; **a ~ of people** quelques (rares) personnes *fpl*; **there was a ~ of news from the front line** il y avait de temps en temps des nouvelles du front; **there was a steady ~ of cash/offers/letters** l'argent/les offres/les lettres arrivai(en)t en petit nombre mais régulièrement.

2 comp ▸**trickle charger** (*Elec*) chargeur *m* à régime lent ▸**trickle-down theory** (*US Econ*) *théorie économique selon laquelle la richesse finit par toucher les plus pauvres.*

3 vi *[water etc]* (*drop slowly*) couler *or* tomber goutte à goutte; (*flow slowly*) dégoutter, dégouliner, couler en un filet. **tears ~d down her cheeks** les larmes coulaient *or* dégoulinaient le long de ses joues; **the rain ~d down his neck** la pluie lui dégoulinait dans le cou; **the stream ~d along over the rocks** le ruisseau coulait faiblement sur les rochers; (*fig*) *[people]* **to ~ in/out/away** *etc* entrer/sortir/s'éloigner *etc* par petits groupes *or* les uns après les autres; (*Ftbl*) **the ball ~d into the net** le ballon a roulé doucement dans le filet; **money ~d into the fund** les contributions au fonds arrivaient lentement; **money ~d out of his account** son compte se dégarnissait lentement (mais régulièrement), une succession de petites sorties (d'argent) dégarnissait lentement son compte; **letters of complaint are still trickling into the office** quelques lettres de réclamation continuent à arriver de temps en temps au bureau.

4 vt *liquid* faire couler goutte à goutte, faire dégouliner *or* dégoutter (*into* dans, *out of* de).

▸**trickle away** vi *[water etc]* s'écouler doucement *or* lentement *or* goutte à goutte; *[money etc]* disparaître *or* être utilisé peu à peu; *see also* **trickle 3.**

trickster ['trɪkstər] n a (*dishonest*) filou *m*; *see* **confidence.** b (*magician etc*) illusionniste *mf*.

tricksy* ['trɪksɪ] adj *person* (*mischievous*) filou*; (*scheming*) retors.

tricky ['trɪkɪ] adj *problem, situation* délicat, épineux, difficile; *job, task* difficile, délicat, plein de pièges *or* de complications; (*pej*) *person* rusé, retors. **he's a ~ man to deal with** (*scheming*) avec lui il faut se méfier; (*difficult, touchy*) il n'est pas commode.

tricolo(u)r ['trɪkələr] n (drapeau *m*) tricolore *m*.

tricorn ['traɪkɔ:n] 1 adj à trois cornes. 2 n tricorne *m*.

trictrac ['trɪktræk] n trictrac *m*.

tricuspid [traɪ'kʌspɪd] adj tricuspide.

tricycle ['traɪsɪkl] n tricycle *m*.

trident ['traɪdənt] n trident *m*.

tridentine [traɪ'dentaɪn] adj tridentin.

tridimensional [,traɪdɪ'menʃənl] adj tridimensionnel, à trois dimensions.

triennial [traɪ'enɪəl] 1 adj triennal; (*Bot*) trisannuel. 2 n (*Bot*) plante trisannuelle.

triennially [traɪ'enɪəlɪ] adv tous les trois ans.

Trier [trɪəʳ] n Trèves.
trier ['traɪəʳ] n: **to be a ~** être persévérant, ne pas se laisser rebuter.
Trieste [tri:'est] n Trieste.
trifle ['traɪfl] 1 n a bagatelle *f*. **it's only a ~** (*object, sum of money etc*) c'est une bagatelle, ce n'est rien, c'est bien peu de chose; (*remark, event etc*) c'est une vétille, il n'y a pas de quoi fouetter un chat; **he worries over ~s** il se fait du mauvais sang pour un rien; **£5 is a mere ~** 5 livres est une bagatelle *or* une misère *or* trois fois rien; **he bought it for a ~** il l'a acheté pour une bagatelle *or* une bouchée de pain *or* trois fois rien.
b (*adv phrase*) **a ~** un peu, un rien, un tantinet; **it's a ~ difficult** c'est un peu *or* un rien *or* un tantinet difficile.
c (*Culin*) ≃ diplomate *m*.
2 vi: **to ~ with** *person, sb's affections, trust etc* traiter à la légère, se jouer de; **he's not to be ~d with** il ne faut pas le traiter à la légère; **to ~ with one's food** manger du bout des dents, chipoter.
►**trifle away** vt sep *time* perdre; *money* gaspiller.
trifler ['traɪfləʳ] n (*pej*) fantaisiste *mf*, fumiste *mf*.
trifling ['traɪflɪŋ] adj insignifiant.
trifocal [traɪ'fəʊkəl] 1 adj à triple foyer, trifocal. 2 n (*lens*) verre *m* à triple foyer. **~s** lunettes à triple foyer *or* trifocales.
trifoliate [traɪ'fəʊlɪɪt] adj à trois feuilles, trifolié.
triforium [traɪ'fɔ:rɪəm] n, pl **triforia** [traɪ'fɔ:rɪə] triforium *m*.
triform ['traɪfɔ:m] adj à *or* en trois parties.
trigger ['trɪgəʳ] 1 n *[gun]* détente *f*, gâchette *f*; *[tool]* déclic *m*. **to press** *or* **pull** *or* **squeeze the ~** appuyer sur la détente *or* la gâchette; **he's quick** *or* **fast on the ~*** (*lit*) il n'attend pas pour tirer; (*fig*) il réagit vite. 2 comp ►**trigger finger** index *m* (*avec lequel on appuie sur la gâchette*) ►**trigger-happy*** *person* à la gâchette facile, prêt à tirer pour un rien; (*fig*) *nation etc* prêt à presser le bouton *or* à déclencher la guerre pour un rien ►**trigger price** prix *m* minimum à l'importation. 3 vt (*also* **~ off**) *explosion* déclencher; *revolt* déclencher, provoquer; *protest* soulever; *reaction* provoquer.
trigonometric(al) [,trɪgənə'metrɪk(əl)] adj trigonométrique.
trigonometry [,trɪgə'nɒmɪtrɪ] n trigonométrie *f*.
trigram ['traɪgræm] n trigramme *m*.
trigraph ['traɪgræf] n trigramme *m*.
trike* [traɪk] n abbr of **tricycle**.
trilateral [,traɪ'lætərəl] adj trilatéral.
trilby ['trɪlbɪ] n (*Brit: also* **~ hat**) chapeau *m* mou.
trilingual [,traɪ'lɪŋgwəl] adj trilingue.
trilith ['traɪlɪθ] n trilithe *m*.
trilithic [traɪ'lɪθɪk] adj en forme de trilithe.
trilithon [traɪ'lɪθɒn, 'traɪlɪ,θɒn] n = **trilith**.
trill [trɪl] 1 n (*Mus: also of bird*) trille *m*; (*Ling*) consonne roulée. 2 vi (*Mus: also of bird*) triller. 3 vt a (*gen*) triller. **"come in" she ~ed** "entrez" roucoula-t-elle. b (*Phon*) **to ~ one's r's** rouler les r; **~ed r** r roulé *or* apical.
trillion ['trɪljən] n (*Brit*) trillion *m*; (*US*) billion *m*. (*fig **) **there are ~s of places I want to go** il y a des milliers d'endroits où j'aimerais aller.
trilogy ['trɪlədʒɪ] n trilogie *f*.
trim [trɪm] 1 adj *appearance, person, clothes* net, soigné; *ship, garden, house* bien tenu, en bon ordre, coquet. **she has a ~ figure** elle a la taille svelte *or* bien prise; **the car has ~ lines** cette voiture a une ligne très pure; **it's a ~ little boat** c'est un petit bateau coquet *or* pimpant.
2 n a (*NonC*) (*condition*) état *m*, ordre *m*. **in (good) ~** *garden, house etc* en (bon) état *or* ordre; *person, athlete* en (bonne) forme; *[athlete etc]* **to get into ~** se remettre en forme; **to get things into ~** mettre de l'ordre dans les choses; (*Naut*) **the ~ of the sails** l'orientation *f* des voiles.
b (*cut*) (*at hairdressers*) coupe *f* (d')entretien. **to have a ~** se faire rafraîchir les cheveux, se faire faire une coupe d'entretien; **to give sth a ~** = **to trim sth**; *see* **4a**.
c (*around window, door*) moulures *fpl*; (*Aut: inside*) aménagement intérieur; (*Aut: outside*) finitions extérieures; (*on dress etc*) garniture *f*. **car with blue (interior) ~** voiture à habillage intérieur bleu.
3 comp ►**trimline phone, trimphone** ® appareil *m* (téléphonique) compact.
4 vt a (*cut*) *beard* tailler, couper légèrement; *hair* rafraîchir; *wick, lamp* tailler, moucher; *branch, hedge, roses* tailler (légèrement); *piece of wood, paper* couper les bords de, rogner. **to ~ one's nails** se rogner *or* se couper les ongles; **to ~ costs** réduire les dépenses; **to ~ the workforce** dégraisser le personnel, faire des dégraissages; **to ~ the edges of sth** couper *or* rogner les bords de qch; **to ~ the ragged edge off sth** ébarber qch.
b (*decorate*) *hat, dress* garnir, orner (*with* de); *Christmas tree* décorer (*with* de). **to ~ the edges of sth with sth** border qch de qch; (*US*) **to ~ a store window** composer un étalage, décorer une vitrine de magasin.
c *boat, aircraft* équilibrer; *sail* gréer, orienter. (*fig*) **to ~ one's sails** réviser ses positions, corriger le tir.
►**trim away** vt sep enlever aux ciseaux (*or* au couteau *or* à la cisaille).
►**trim down** vt sep *wick* tailler, moucher.
►**trim off** vt sep = **trim away**.
trimaran ['traɪməræn] n trimaran *m*.
trimester [trɪ'mestəʳ] n trimestre *m*.
trimmer ['trɪməʳ] n a (*beam*) linçoir *m or* linsoir *m*. b (*for trimming timber*) trancheuse *f* (*pour le bois*). c (*Elec*) trimmer *m*, condensateur *m* ajustable (d'équilibrage). d (*person adapting views: pej*) opportuniste *mf*.
trimming ['trɪmɪŋ] n a (*on garment, sheet etc*) parement *m*; (*braid etc*) passementerie *f* (*NonC*). (*fig: accessories*) **it's £100 without the ~s** cela coûte 100 livres sans les extra. b (*Culin*) garniture *f*, accompagnement *m*. **roast beef and all the ~s** du rosbif avec la garniture habituelle. c (pl: *pieces cut off*) **~s** chutes *fpl*, rognures *fpl*. d (*esp US: defeat*) raclée* *f*, défaite *f*. e (*cutting back*) réduction *f*, élagage *m*; *[staff]* compression *f*, dégraissage *m*.
trimness ['trɪmnɪs] n *[garden, boat, house]* aspect net *or* soigné. **the ~ of his appearance** son aspect soigné *or* coquet *or* pimpant; **the ~ of her figure** la sveltesse de sa silhouette.
trinary ['traɪnərɪ] adj trinaire.
Trinidad ['trɪnɪdæd] n (l'île *f* de) la Trinité. **~ and Tobago** Trinité et Tobago *f*.
Trinidadian [,trɪnɪ'dædɪən] 1 adj de la Trinité. 2 n habitant(e) *m(f)* de la Trinité.
trinitrotoluene [traɪ,naɪtrəʊ'tɒljʊi:n] n trinitrotoluène *m*.
trinity ['trɪnɪtɪ] 1 n trinité *f*. (*Rel*) **the Holy T~** la Sainte Trinité. 2 comp ►**Trinity (Sunday)** la fête de la Trinité ►**Trinity term** (*Univ*) troisième trimestre *m* (de l'année universitaire).
trinket ['trɪŋkɪt] n (*knick-knack*) bibelot *m*, babiole *f* (*also pej*); (*jewel*) colifichet *m* (*also pej*); (*on chain*) breloque *f*.
trinomial [traɪ'nəʊmɪəl] n (*Math*) trinôme *m*.
trio ['trɪəʊ] n trio *m*.
triode ['traɪəʊd] n (*Elec*) triode *f*.
triolet ['tri:əʊlet] n triolet *m*.
trip [trɪp] 1 n a (*journey*) voyage *m*; (*excursion*) excursion *f*. **he's away on a ~** il est (parti) en voyage; **we did the ~ in 10 hours** nous avons fait le voyage *or* le trajet en 10 heures; **there are cheap ~s to Spain** on organise des voyages à prix réduit en Espagne; **we went on** *or* **took a ~ to Malta** nous sommes allés (en voyage) à Malte; **we took** *or* **made a ~ into town** nous sommes allés en ville; **he does 3 ~s to Scotland a week** il va en Écosse 3 fois par semaine; **I don't want another ~ to the shops today** je ne veux pas retourner dans les magasins aujourd'hui; **after 4 ~s to the kitchen he ...** après 4 voyages à la cuisine il ...; *see* **business, coach, day, round** *etc*.
b (*Drugs sl*) trip *m* (*sl*). **to be on a ~** faire un trip; **to have a bad ~** faire un trip qui tourne mal.
c (*stumble*) faux pas; (*in wrestling etc*) croche-pied *m*, croc-en-jambe *m*; (*fig; mistake*) faux pas, erreur *f*, gaffe* *f*.
2 comp ►**trip hammer** marteau *m* à bascule *or* à soulèvement ►**tripwire** fil *m* de détente.
3 vi a (*stumble: also* **~ up**) trébucher (*on, over* contre, sur), buter (*on, over* contre), faire un faux pas. **he ~ped and fell** il a trébuché *or* il a fait un faux pas et il est tombé.
b (*go lightly and quickly*) **to ~ along/in/out** *etc* marcher/entrer/sortir *etc* d'un pas léger *or* sautillant; **the words came ~ping off her tongue** elle l'a dit sans la moindre hésitation.
c (*Drugs sl*) faire un trip (*sl*), flipper‡.
4 vt a (*make fall: also* **~ up**) faire trébucher; (*deliberately*) faire un croche-pied *or* un croc-en-jambe à. **I was ~ped (up)** on m'a fait un croche-pied *or* un croc-en-jambe.
b (*Tech*) *mechanism* déclencher, mettre en marche.
c (†: *dance*) **to ~ the light fantastic*** danser.
►**trip over** vi trébucher, faire un faux pas.
►**trip up** 1 vi a = **trip 3a**. b (*fig*) faire une erreur, gaffer*. 2 vt sep faire trébucher; (*deliberately*) faire un croche-pied *or* un croc-en-jambe à; (*fig: in questioning etc*) prendre en défaut, désarçonner (*fig*).
tripartite [,traɪ'pɑ:taɪt] adj triparti, tripartite.
tripe [traɪp] n (*NonC*) (*Culin*) tripes *fpl*; (*: *esp Brit: nonsense*) bêtises *fpl*, inepties *fpl*, idioties *fpl*. **what absolute ~!*** quelles bêtises! quelles foutaises!‡; **it's a lot of ~*** tout ça c'est de la foutaise*; **this book is ~*** ce livre est complètement inepte.
triphase ['traɪfeɪz] adj (*Elec*) triphasé.
triphthong ['trɪfθɒŋ] n triphtongue *f*.
triplane ['traɪ,pleɪn] n triplan *m*.
triple ['trɪpl] 1 adj triple (*gen before noun*). **the T~ Alliance** la Triple-Alliance; **the T~ Entente** la Triple-Entente; (*Mus*) **in ~ time** à trois temps; **they require ~ copies of every document** ils demandent trois exemplaires de chaque document. 2 comp ►**triple-digit** (*US*) adj (*gen*) à trois chiffres; (*inflation*) égal *or* supérieur à 100 % ►**triple glazing** triple vitrage *m* ►**triple jump** (*Sport*) triple saut *m* ►**triple jumper** (*Sport*) (*definition*) spécialiste *mf* du triple saut; (*taking part in an athletics meeting*) concurrent(e) *m(f)* du triple saut. 3 n triple *m*. 4 adv trois fois plus que. 5 vti tripler.
triplet ['trɪplɪt] n (*Mus*) triolet *m*; (*Poetry*) tercet *m*. (*persons*) **~s** triplé(e)s *m(f)pl*.
triplex ['trɪpleks] 1 adj triple. 2 n ® (*Brit*) **T~ (glass)** Triplex *m* ®, verre Sécurit *m* ®.

triplicate ['trɪplɪkɪt] 1 adj en trois exemplaires. 2 n a in ~ en trois exemplaires. b (*third copy*) triplicata *m*.
triploid ['trɪplɔɪd] adj triploïde.
triply ['trɪplɪ] adv triplement.
tripod ['traɪpɒd] n trépied *m*.
Tripoli ['trɪpəlɪ] n Tripoli.
tripos ['traɪpɒs] n (*Cambridge Univ*) examen *m* pour le diplôme de B.A. avec mention.
tripper ['trɪpəʳ] n (*Brit*) touriste *mf*, vacancier *m*, -ière *f*; (*on day trip*) excursionniste *mf*.
triptych ['trɪptɪk] n triptyque *m*.
trireme ['traɪri:m] n trirème *f*.
trisect [traɪ'sekt] vt diviser en trois parties (égales).
Tristan ['trɪstən] n Tristan *m*.
trisyllabic ['traɪsɪ'læbɪk] adj trisyllabe, trisyllabique.
trisyllable [,traɪ'sɪləbl] n trisyllabe *m*.
trite [traɪt] adj *subject, design* banal. ~ **remark** banalité *f*, lieu commun.
tritely ['traɪtlɪ] adv banalement.
triteness ['traɪtnɪs] n (*NonC*) banalité *f*.
tritium ['trɪtɪəm] n tritium *m*.
triton ['traɪtn] n (*all senses*) triton *m*. **T~** Triton *m*.
tritone ['traɪtəʊn] n (*Mus*) triton *m*.
triturate ['trɪtʃəreɪt] vt triturer, piler.
trituration [,trɪtʃə'reɪʃən] n trituration *f*, pilage *m*.
triumph ['traɪʌmf] 1 n (*emotion*) sentiment *m* de triomphe; (*victory*) triomphe *m*, victoire *f*; (*success*) triomphe, réussite *f*, succès triomphal; (*Roman Hist*) triomphe. **in ~** en triomphe; **it was a ~ for ...** cela a été un triomphe *or* un succès triomphal pour ...; **it is a ~ of man over nature** c'est le triomphe de l'homme sur la nature; **his ~ at having succeeded** sa satisfaction triomphante d'avoir réussi. 2 vi (*lit, fig*) triompher (*over* de).
triumphal [traɪ'ʌmfəl] adj triomphal.
triumphant [traɪ'ʌmfənt] adj *homecoming* triomphal; *team, army* triomphant, victorieux; *look, smile* triomphant, de triomphe.
triumphantly [traɪ'ʌmfəntlɪ] adv *return, march* en triomphe, triomphalement; *answer, announce* d'un ton triomphant, triomphalement.
triumvirate [traɪ'ʌmvɪrɪt] n triumvirat *m*.
triune ['traɪju:n] adj (*Rel*) trin.
trivet ['trɪvɪt] n (*over fire*) trépied *m*, chevrette *f*; (*on table*) dessous-de-plat *m inv*.
trivia ['trɪvɪə] npl bagatelles *fpl*, futilités *fpl*, fadaises *fpl*.
trivial ['trɪvɪəl] adj *sum, amount, loss* insignifiant, dérisoire; *reason, excuse* insignifiant, sans valeur; *remark, comment* sans importance *or* valeur; *film, book* banal, sans originalité *or* intérêt. **a ~ mistake** une faute légère *or* sans gravité, une peccadille.
triviality [,trɪvɪ'ælɪtɪ] n a (*NonC: see* **trivial**) caractère insignifiant *or* dérisoire; manque *m* d'importance *or* de valeur *or* d'intérêt; banalité *f*. b **trivialities** bagatelles *fpl*, futilités *fpl*, fadaises *fpl*.
trivialization [,trɪvɪəlaɪ'zeɪʃən] n banalisation *f*.
trivialize ['trɪvɪəlaɪz] vt banaliser.
trivially ['trɪvɪəlɪ] adv de façon banalisée.
triweekly ['traɪ'wi:klɪ] 1 adv (*thrice weekly*) trois fois par semaine; (*every three weeks*) toutes les trois semaines. 2 adj *event, visit* qui se produit trois fois par semaine (*or* toutes les trois semaines).
trochaic [trɒ'keɪɪk] adj trochaïque.
trochee ['trəʊki:] n trochée *m*.
trod [trɒd] pret of **tread**.
trodden ['trɒdn] ptp of **tread**.
troglodyte ['trɒglədaɪt] n troglodyte *m*.
troika ['trɔɪkə] n (*also Pol*) troïka *f*.
Troilus ['trɔɪləs] n: ~ **and Cressida** Troïlus *m* et Cressida *f*.
Trojan ['trəʊdʒən] 1 adj troyen. (*Hist*) **the ~ Horse** le cheval de Troie; **the ~ War** la guerre de Troie. 2 n Troyen(ne) *m(f)*; *see* **work**.
troll [trəʊl] n troll *m*.
trolley ['trɒlɪ] 1 n (*esp Brit*) (*for luggage*) chariot *m* (à bagages), (*two-wheeled*) diable *m*; (*for shopping*) poussette *f*, (*in supermarket*) chariot, caddie *m*; (*tea ~*) table roulante, chariot à desserte, (*in office*) chariot à boissons; (*for stretcher etc*) chariot; (*in mine, quarry etc*) benne roulante; (*Rail*) wagonnet *m*; (*on tramcar*) trolley *m*; (*US: tramcar*) tramway *m*, tram *m*. (*Brit* ‡: *mad*) **to be/go off one's ~** être/devenir barjo(t)‡, onduler/commencer à onduler de la toiture‡. 2 comp ▸**trolley bus** trolleybus *m* ▸**trolley car** (*US*) tramway *m*, tram *m* ▸**trolley line** (*US*) (*rails*) voie *f* de tramway; (*route*) ligne *f* de tramway ▸**trolley pole** perche *f* de trolley.
trollop ['trɒləp] n traînée‡ *f*.
trombone [trɒm'bəʊn] n trombone *m* (*Mus*).
trombonist [trɒm'bəʊnɪst] n tromboniste *mf*.
troop [tru:p] 1 n [*people*] bande *f*, groupe *m*; [*animals*] bande, troupe *f*; [*scouts*] troupe; (*Mil: of cavalry*) escadron *m*. (*Mil*) **~s** troupes. 2 comp *movements etc* de troupes ▸**troop carrier** (*Aut*) transport *m* de troupes; (*Naut*) transport *m* (*navire*); (*Aviat*) avion *m* de transport militaire ▸**troopship** transport *m* (*navire*) ▸**troop train** train *m* militaire. 3 vi: **to ~ in/past** *etc* entrer/passer *etc* en bande *or* en groupe; **they all ~ed over to the window** ils sont tous allés s'attrouper près de la fenêtre. 4 vt (*Brit Mil*) **to ~ the colour** faire la parade du drapeau; (*ceremony*) **~ing the colour** le salut au drapeau (*le jour de l'anniversaire officiel de la Reine*).
trooper ['tru:pəʳ] n (*Mil*) soldat *m* de cavalerie; (*US: state ~*) ≃ C.R.S. *m*; *see* **swear**.
trope [trəʊp] n trope *m*.
trophy ['trəʊfɪ] n (*Hunting, Mil, Sport, also fig*) trophée *m*.
tropic ['trɒpɪk] 1 n tropique *m*. **T~ of Cancer/Capricorn** tropique du cancer/du capricorne; **in the ~s** sous les tropiques. 2 adj (*liter*) = **tropical**.
tropical ['trɒpɪkəl] adj *plant, region* tropical, des tropiques; *heat, rain* tropical.
tropism ['trəʊpɪzəm] n tropisme *m*.
troposphere ['trɒpəsfɪəʳ] n troposphère *f*.
Trot* [trɒt] n (*pej*) (abbr of **Trotskyist**) trotskyste *mf*.
trot [trɒt] 1 n (*pace*) trot *m*. **to go at a ~** [*horse*] aller au trot, trotter; [*person*] trotter; **to go for a ~** (aller) faire du cheval; (*fig*) **5 days/whiskies** *etc* **on the ~*** 5 jours/whiskies *etc* de suite *or* d'affilée; **he is always on the ~*** il court tout le temps, il n'a pas une minute de tranquillité; **to keep sb on the ~** ne pas accorder une minute de tranquillité à qn; **to have the ~s**‡ (*diarrhoea*) avoir la courante‡. 2 vi [*horse*] trotter; [*person*] trotter, courir. [*person*] **to ~ in/past** *etc* entrer/passer *etc* au trot *or* en courant *or* d'un pas pressé. 3 vt *horse* faire trotter.
▸**trot along** vi a = **trot over**. b = **trot away**.
▸**trot away, trot off** vi partir *or* s'éloigner (au trot *or* en courant), filer*.
▸**trot out** vt sep *excuses, reasons* débiter; *names, facts etc* réciter d'affilée.
▸**trot over, trot round** vi aller, courir. **she trotted over** *or* **round to the grocer's** elle a fait un saut *or* a couru chez l'épicier.
troth†† [trəʊθ] n promesse *f*, serment *m*; **by my ~** pardieu††; *see* **plight²**.
Trotsky ['trɒtskɪ] n Trotski *m*.
Trotskyism ['trɒtskɪɪzəm] n trotskisme *m*, trotskysme *m*.
Trotskyist ['trɒtskɪɪst], **Trotskyite** ['trɒtskɪaɪt] adj, n trotskiste *(mf)*, trotskyste *(mf)*.
trotter ['trɒtəʳ] n a (*horse*) trotteur *m*, -euse *f*. b (*Culin*) **pig's/sheep's ~s** pieds *mpl* de porc/de mouton.
trotting ['trɒtɪŋ] n (*Sport*) trot *m*. ~ **race** course *f* de trot.
troubadour ['tru:bədɔ:ʳ] n troubadour *m*.
trouble ['trʌbl] 1 n a (*NonC: difficulties, unpleasantness*) ennuis *mpl*, difficulté *f*. **to be in ~** avoir des ennuis, être en difficulté; **you're in ~ now** ce coup-ci tu as des ennuis *or* tu as des problèmes; **he's in ~ with the boss** il a des ennuis avec le patron; **to get into ~ (with sb)** s'attirer des ennuis (avec qn); **he got into ~ for doing that** il a eu *or* il s'est attiré des ennuis pour (avoir fait) cela, il s'est fait attraper pour (avoir fait) ça; **to get sb into ~** causer des ennuis à qn, mettre qn dans le pétrin; (*euph*) **to get a girl into ~*** mettre une (jeune) fille dans une position intéressante (*euph*); **to get sb/get (o.s.) out of ~** tirer qn/se tirer d'affaire; **to make ~** causer des ennuis (*for sb* à qn); **you're making ~ for yourself** tu t'attires des ennuis; **I don't want any ~** je ne veux pas d'ennuis; **it's asking for ~** c'est se chercher des ennuis; **he goes around looking for ~** il cherche les ennuis; **he'll give you ~** il vous donnera du fil à retordre; **here comes ~!*** aïe! des ennuis en perspective!; **there's ~ brewing** il y a de l'orage dans l'air; *see* **mean, meet¹** *etc*.
b (*NonC: bother, effort*) mal *m*, peine *f*. **it's no ~** cela ne me dérange pas; **it's no ~ to do it properly** ce n'est pas difficile de le faire comme il faut; **it's not worth the ~** cela ne *or* n'en vaut pas la peine; **he/it is more ~ than he/it is worth** ça ne vaut pas la peine de s'embêter avec lui/ça; **nothing is too much ~ for her** elle se dévoue *or* se dépense sans compter; **I had all that ~ for nothing** je me suis donné tout ce mal pour rien; **you could have saved yourself the ~** tu aurais pu t'éviter cette peine; **he went to enormous ~ to help us** il s'est donné un mal fou *or* il s'est mis en quatre pour nous aider; **to go to the ~ of doing, to take the ~ to do** se donner la peine *or* le mal de faire; **he went to** *or* **took a lot of ~ over his essay** il s'est vraiment donné beaucoup de mal pour sa dissertation, il s'est vraiment beaucoup appliqué à sa dissertation; **I don't want to put you to the ~ of writing** je ne veux pas qu'à cause de moi vous vous donniez (*subj*) le mal d'écrire; **I'm putting you to** *or* **giving you a lot of ~** je vous donne beaucoup de mal, je vous dérange beaucoup; **it's no ~ at all!** je vous en prie!, ça ne me dérange pas du tout!
c (*difficulty, problem*) ennui *m*, difficulté *f*, problème *m*; (*misfortune*) ennui *m*, souci *m*, peine *f*; (*nuisance*) souci, embarras *m*, ennui. **what's the ~?** qu'est-ce qu'il y a?, qu'est-ce qui ne va pas?, qu'est-ce que tu as?; **that's (just) the ~!** c'est ça l'ennui!; **the ~ is that** ... l'ennui *or* le problème (c')est que ...; **the ~ with you is that you can never face the facts** l'ennui avec toi *or* ton défaut c'est que tu ne regardes jamais les choses en face; **the carburettor is giving us ~** nous avons des problèmes *or* des ennuis de carburateur; **the technician is trying to locate the ~** le technicien essaie de localiser la panne *or* le problème; **there has been ~ between them ever since** depuis, ils

s'entendent mal; **he caused ~ between them** il a semé la discorde entre eux; **I'm having ~ with my eldest son** mon fils aîné me donne des soucis *or* me cause des ennuis; **the child is a ~ to his parents** l'enfant est un souci pour ses parents; **that's the least of my ~s** c'est le cadet de mes soucis; **he had ~ in tying his shoelace** il a eu du mal à attacher son lacet; **did you have any ~ in getting here?** est-ce que vous avez eu des difficultés *or* des problèmes en venant?; **now your ~s are over** vous voilà au bout de vos peines; **his ~s are not yet over** il n'est pas encore au bout de ses peines, il n'est pas encore sorti de l'auberge; **family ~s** ennuis domestiques *or* de famille; **money ~s** soucis *or* ennuis d'argent *or* financiers; (*Med*) **I have back ~, my back is giving me ~** j'ai mal au dos, mon dos me fait souffrir; **kidney/chest ~** ennuis rénaux/pulmonaires; (*Aut*) **we've got engine ~** nous avons des ennuis de moteur, il y a quelque chose qui ne vas pas dans le moteur; *see* **heart**.

d (*political, social unrest*) conflits *mpl*, troubles *mpl*. **they're having a lot of ~ in Southern Africa** il y a des troubles étendus *or* il y a beaucoup d'agitation *or* la situation est très tendue en Afrique australe; (*Ir Hist*) **the T~s** les troubles; **labour ~s** conflits du travail, troubles sociaux; **he caused a lot of ~ between unions and management** il a causé de nombreux désaccords *or* beaucoup de friction entre les syndicats et le patronat; **there's ~ at the factory** ça chauffe* à l'usine.

2 **comp** ▸**trouble-free** *period, visit* sans ennuis *or* problèmes *or* soucis; *car* qui ne tombe jamais en panne; *university* non contestataire ▸**troublemaker** fauteur *m*, -trice *f* de troubles, perturbateur *m*, -trice *f* ▸**troublemaking** n comportement *m* perturbateur ◊ **adj** perturbateur *m* (*f* -trice) ▸**troubleshoot** *etc see* **troubleshoot** *etc* ▸**troublesome** *see* **troublesome** ▸**trouble spot** point *m* de conflit, point chaud *or* névralgique.

3 **vt** a (*worry*) inquiéter; (*inconvenience*) gêner; (*upset*) troubler. **his eyes ~ him** ses yeux lui posent des problèmes; **the heat ~d us** la chaleur nous a gênés; **do these headaches ~ you often?** est-ce que vous souffrez souvent de ces maux de tête?; **there's one detail that ~s me** il y a un détail qui me gêne; **nothing ~s him** il ne se fait jamais de souci; *see also* **troubled**.

b (*bother*) déranger. **I am sorry to ~ you** je suis désolé de vous déranger; **does it ~ you if ...** est-ce que cela vous dérange si ... + *indic or* que ... + *subj*; **don't ~ yourself!** ne vous dérangez pas!, ne vous tracassez pas!; **he didn't ~ himself to reply** il ne s'est pas donné la peine de répondre; **may I ~ you for a light?** puis-je vous demander du feu?; **I'll ~ you to show me the letter!** vous allez me faire le plaisir de me montrer la lettre!; **I shan't ~ you with the details** je vous ferai grâce des détails, je vous passerai les détails.

4 **vi** se déranger. **please don't ~!** ne vous dérangez pas!, ne vous donnez pas cette peine-là!; **don't ~ about me** ne vous faites pas de souci pour moi; **to ~ to do** se donner la peine *or* le mal de faire.

troubled ['trʌbld] **adj** *person* inquiet (*f* -ète), préoccupé; *look, voice* inquiet; *life, sleep* agité, orageux; *water* trouble. **to be ~ about sth** s'inquiéter de qch, être préoccupé par qch; **we live in ~ times** nous vivons à une époque agitée *or* mouvementée *or* de troubles; **he's ~ with rheumatism** il souffre de rhumatisme; *see* **fish, oil**.

troubleshoot ['trʌbl,ʃu:t] **vi** (*gen, also Ind, Pol*) (intervenir pour) régler un problème *or* (*stronger*) une crise; (*Tech, Aut etc*) localiser une panne.

troubleshooter ['trʌbl,ʃu:tə^r] **n** (*gen*) expert *m* (appelé en cas de crise); *[conflict]* médiateur *m*; (*Tech, Aut*) spécialiste *mf* (pour localiser la panne).

troubleshooting ['trʌbl,ʃu:tɪŋ] **n** (*see* **troubleshoot**) intervention *f* pour régler un problème *or* une crise; localisation *f* d'une panne.

troublesome ['trʌblsəm] **adj** *person* pénible, difficile (à supporter); *request* gênant, embarrassant; *task* ennuyeux, pénible; *cough* gênant, incommodant. **his back is ~** son dos le fait souffrir; **how ~!** quel ennui!

troublous ['trʌbləs] **adj** (*liter*) trouble, agité.

trough [trɒf] **n** a (*depression*) dépression *f*, creux *m*; (*between waves*) creux (d'une vague); (*channel*) chenal *m*; (*fig*) point bas. (*Met*) **~ of low pressure** dépression, zone *f* dépressionnaire. b (*drinking ~*) abreuvoir *m*; (*feeding ~*) auge *f*; (*kneading ~*) pétrin *m*.

trounce [traʊns] **vt** (*thrash*) rosser, rouer de coups; (*Sport: defeat*) écraser, battre à plate(s) couture(s).

troupe [tru:p] **n** (*Theat*) troupe *f*.

trouper ['tru:pə^r] **n** (*Theat*) acteur *m*, -trice *f*, artiste *mf* (*qui fait partie d'une troupe de théâtre*). (*fig*) **an old ~** un vieux de la vieille.

trouser ['traʊzə^r] (*esp Brit*) 1 **npl**: **~s** pantalon *m*; **a pair of ~s** un pantalon; **long ~s** pantalon long; **short ~s** culottes courtes; *see* **wear**.

2 **comp** ▸**trouser clip** pince *f* à pantalon ▸**trouser leg** jambe *f* de pantalon ▸**trouser press** presse *f* à pantalons ▸**trouser suit** (*Brit*) tailleur-pantalon *m*.

trousseau ['tru:səʊ] **n, pl ~s** *or* **~x** ['tru:səʊ] trousseau *m* (*de jeune mariée*).

trout [traʊt] 1 **n, pl ~** *or* **~s** truite *f*. 2 **comp** ▸**trout fisherman** pêcheur *m* de truites ▸**trout fishing** pêche *f* à la truite ▸**trout rod** canne *f* à truite, canne spéciale truite ▸**trout stream** ruisseau *m* à truites.

trove [trəʊv] **n** *see* **treasure 2**.

trow†† [traʊ] **vti** croire.

trowel ['traʊəl] **n** (*Constr*) truelle *f*; (*gardening*) déplantoir *m*; *see* **lay on**.

Troy [trɔɪ] **n** Troie.

troy [trɔɪ] **n** (*also* **~ weight**) troy *m*, troy-weight *m*, poids *m* de Troy.

truancy ['truənsɪ] **n** (*Scol*) absentéisme *m* (scolaire). **he was punished for ~** il a été puni pour avoir manqué les cours *or* pour s'être absenté.

truant ['truənt] 1 **n** (*Scol*) élève *mf* absentéiste *or* absent(e) sans autorisation. **to play ~** manquer les cours, faire l'école buissonnière; **he's playing ~ from the office today** (il n'est pas au bureau aujourd'hui,) il fait l'école buissonnière. 2 **adj** (*liter*) *thought* vagabond. 3 **comp** ▸ (*US*) **truant officer** *fonctionnaire chargé de faire respecter les règlements de la scolarisation*.

truce [tru:s] **n** trêve *f*. *[enemies etc]* **to call a ~** conclure *or* établir une trêve; (*fig*) **to call a ~ to sth** faire trêve à qch.

Trucial ['tru:ʃəl] **adj**: **~ States** États *mpl* de la Trêve.

truck[1] [trʌk] 1 **n** a (*NonC*) (*barter*) troc *m*, échange *m*; (*payment*) paiement *m* en nature. (*fig*) **to have no ~ with** refuser d'avoir affaire à. b (*US: vegetables*) produits *mpl etc* maraîchers. 2 **comp** ▸**truck farm** (*US*) jardin maraîcher ▸**truck farmer** maraîcher *m*, -ère *f* ▸**truck farming** culture *f* maraîchère ▸**truck garden** = **truck farm**.

truck[2] [trʌk] 1 **n** (*esp US: lorry*) camion *m*; (*Rail*) wagon *m* à plate-forme, truck *m*; (*luggage handcart*) chariot *m* à bagages, (*two-wheeled*) diable *m*. 2 **vti** (*esp US*) camionner. 3 **comp** ▸**truckdriver** (*esp US*) camionneur *m*, routier *m* ▸**truckload** plein camion ▸**truckman** (*US*) = **truckdriver** ▸**truck stop** (*US*) routier *m*, restaurant *m* de routiers.

truckage ['trʌkɪdʒ] **n** (*US*) camionnage *m*.

trucker ['trʌkə^r] **n** a (*esp US: truck driver*) camionneur *m*, routier *m*. b (*US: market gardener*) maraîcher *m*.

trucking ['trʌkɪŋ] **n** (*US*) camionnage *m*.

truckle ['trʌkl] 1 **vi** s'humilier, s'abaisser (*to* devant). 2 **comp** ▸**truckle bed** lit *m* gigogne *inv*.

truculence ['trʌkjʊləns] **n** brutalité *f*, agressivité *f*.

truculent ['trʌkjʊlənt] **adj** brutal, agressif.

truculently ['trʌkjʊləntlɪ] **adv** brutalement, agressivement.

trudge [trʌdʒ] 1 **vi**: **to ~ in/out/along** *etc* entrer/sortir/marcher *etc* péniblement *or* en traînant les pieds; **we ~d round the shops** nous nous sommes traînés de magasin en magasin; **he ~d through the mud** il pataugeait (péniblement) dans la boue. 2 **vt**: **to ~ the streets/the town** *etc* se traîner de rue en rue/dans toute la ville *etc*. 3 **n** marche *f* pénible.

true [tru:] 1 **adj** a (*exact, accurate*) *story, news, rumour, statement* vrai, véridique; *description, account, report* fidèle, exact, véridique; *copy* conforme; *statistics, measure* exact. **it all turned out to be ~** il s'est finalement trouvé que tout était vrai; **that's ~!** c'est vrai!; **too ~!*** ah oui alors!, je ne te le fais pas dire!; **we mustn't generalize, it's ~, but ...** il ne faut pas généraliser, d'accord *or* c'est vrai, mais ...; **that's wrong! — ~, but ...** c'est faux! — d'accord, *or* c'est juste, *or* c'est vrai, mais ...; **can it be ~ that** est-il possible que + *subj*; **it is ~ that** il est vrai que + *indic*; **is it ~ that** est-il vrai que + *indic or subj*; **it's not ~ that** il n'est pas vrai que + *indic or subj*; **if it is ~ that** s'il est vrai que + *indic or subj*; **to come ~** se réaliser; **the same holds ~ for** il en va *or* est de même pour, c'est aussi vrai pour; **I certify that this is a ~ likeness of X** je certifie que cette photographie présente une parfaite ressemblance avec X; *see* **good** *etc*.

b (*real, genuine*) *repentance, sympathy, friendship* réel, vrai (*before noun*), véritable, authentique. **what is the ~ situation?** quelle est la situation réelle?, quelle est en réalité la situation?; **the one ~ God** le seul vrai Dieu, le seul Dieu véritable; **the T~ Cross** la vraie Croix; **the frog is not a ~ reptile** la grenouille n'est pas vraiment un reptile; **he is a ~ scholar** c'est un vrai *or* véritable savant; **he has been a ~ friend to me** il a été un vrai *or* véritable ami pour moi; **spoken like a ~ Englishman!** voilà qui est parler en vrai *or* véritable Anglais!; **~ love** (*emotion*) le grand amour; (*lover*) bien-aimé(e) *m(f)*; **~ north** le nord vrai *or* géographique.

c (*faithful*) **to be ~ to sb/sth** être fidèle à qn/qch; **there were 60 of them, all good men and ~** ils étaient 60, tous loyaux et braves; **~ to life** conforme à la réalité, réaliste; **to be** *or* **run ~ to type** être conforme au type *or* typique; **~ to type, he refused to help** comme on aurait pu s'y attendre, il a refusé de prêter son aide; **that was ~ to form** ça, c'était typique *or* à prévoir; **the horse ran ~ to form** le cheval a fait une course digne de lui.

d *surface, join* plan, uniforme; *wall, upright* vertical, d'aplomb; *beam* droit; *wheel* dans l'axe.

e (*Mus*) *voice, instrument, note* juste.

2 **n**: **out of ~** *upright, wall* pas d'aplomb; *beam* tordu, gauchi; *surface* gondolé; *join* mal aligné; *wheel* voilé, faussé.

3 **adv** *aim, sing* juste. **to breed ~** se reproduire selon le type parental; **tell me ~** dis-moi la vérité; *see* **ring**[2].

4 **comp** ▸**true-blue*** loyal ▸**true-born** véritable, vrai, authentique ▸**true-bred** de race pure, racé ▸**true-false test** questionnaire *m or* test *m* du type "vrai ou faux" ▸**true-hearted** loyal, sincère ▸**true-life*** vrai, vécu.

truffle ['trʌfl] **n** truffe *f*.

trug [trʌg] n (*Brit*) corbeille *f* de jardinier.
truism ['tru:ɪzəm] n truisme *m*.
truly ['tru:lɪ] adv (*genuinely*) *love, believe, admire* vraiment, réellement; (*faithfully*) *reflect, show* fidèlement; (*truthfully*) *answer, tell* franchement; (*without doubt*) *wonderful, awful* vraiment, véritablement. **tell me ~** dis-moi la vérité; **he did say so, ~ (he did)!** il l'a dit, je te jure!*; **really and ~?** vraiment?, vraiment vrai?*; **he's a ~ great writer** c'est véritablement un grand écrivain; **a ~ terrible film** un vrai *or* véritable navet, un film vraiment mauvais; **well and ~** bel et bien; (*letter ending*) **yours ~** je vous prie d'agréer l'expression de mes sentiments respectueux *or* (*man to woman*) de mes très respectueux hommages; **nobody knows it better than yours ~*** personne ne le sait mieux que votre humble serviteur (*hum*).
trump[1] [trʌmp] 1 n (*Cards*) atout *m*. **spades are ~(s)** atout pique; **what's ~(s)?** quel est l'atout?; **the three of ~(s)** le trois d'atout; (*fig*) **he had a ~ up his sleeve** il avait un atout en réserve; (*fig*) **he was holding all the ~s** il avait tous les atouts dans son jeu; (*Brit fig*) **to turn up ~s*** faire des merveilles; *see* **no.** 2 comp ▸**trump card** (*fig*) carte *f* maîtresse, atout *m*. 3 vt (*Cards*) couper, prendre avec l'atout. (*fig*) **to ~ sb's ace** faire encore mieux que qn.
▸**trump up** vt sep *charge, excuse* forger *or* inventer (de toutes pièces).
trump[2] [trʌmp] n (*liter*) trompette *f*. **the Last T~** la trompette du Jugement (dernier).
trumpery ['trʌmpərɪ] 1 n (*NonC*) (*showy trash*) camelote* *f* (*NonC*); (*nonsense*) bêtises *fpl*. 2 adj (*showy*) criard; (*paltry*) insignifiant, sans valeur.
trumpet ['trʌmpɪt] 1 n a (*instrument*) trompette *f*. b (*player*) (*in orchestra*) trompettiste *mf*, (*Mil etc: trumpeter*) trompette *m*. c (*~-shaped object*) cornet *m*; *see* **ear**[1]. d *[elephant]* barrissement *m*. 2 comp ▸**trumpet blast** coup *m or* sonnerie *f* de trompette ▸**trumpet call** (*lit*) = **trumpet blast**; (*fig*) vibrant appel (*for* pour). 3 vi *[elephant]* barrir. 4 vt trompeter.
trumpeter ['trʌmpɪtə[r]] n trompette *m*.
trumpeting ['trʌmpɪtɪŋ] n *[elephant]* barrissement(s) *m(pl)*.
truncate [trʌŋ'keɪt] vt (*gen, also Comput*) tronquer.
truncating [trʌŋ'keɪtɪŋ] n (*Comput*) troncation *f*.
truncheon ['trʌntʃən] n (*weapon*) matraque *f*; (*Brit: for directing traffic*) bâton *m* (*d'agent de police*).
trundle ['trʌndl] 1 vt (*push/pull/roll*) pousser/traîner/faire rouler bruyamment. 2 vi: **to ~ in/along/down** entrer/passer/descendre lourdement *or* bruyamment.
trunk [trʌŋk] 1 n (*Anat, Bot*) tronc *m*; *[elephant]* trompe *f*; (*luggage*) malle *f*; (*US Aut*) coffre *m*, malle. **~s** (*swimming*) slip *m or* maillot *m* de bain; (*underwear*) slip (d'homme); (*Telec* †) l'inter *m*; *see* **subscriber.** 2 comp ▸**trunk call** (*Brit Telec*) communication interurbaine ▸**trunk curl** (*Gymnastics*) = **sit-up;** *see* **sit 3** ▸**trunk line** (*Telec*) inter *m*, téléphone interurbain; (*Rail*) grande ligne ▸**trunk road** (*Brit*) (route *f*) nationale *f*.
trunnion ['trʌnɪən] n tourillon *m*.
truss [trʌs] 1 n *[hay etc]* botte *f*; *[flowers, fruit on branch]* grappe *f*; (*Constr*) ferme *f*; (*Med*) bandage *m* herniaire. 2 vt *hay* botteler; *chicken* trousser; (*Constr*) armer, renforcer.
▸**truss up** vt sep *prisoner* ligoter.
trust [trʌst] 1 n a (*NonC: faith, reliance*) confiance *f* (*in* en). **position of ~** poste *m* de confiance; **breach of ~** abus *m* de confiance; **to have ~ in sb/sth** avoir confiance en qn/qch; **to put** *or* **place one's ~ in sb/sth** faire confiance *or* se fier à qn/qch; **to take sth on ~** accepter qch de confiance *or* les yeux fermés; **you'll have to take what I say on ~** il vous faudra me croire sur parole; (*without payment*) **he gave it to me on ~** il me l'a donné sans me faire payer tout de suite.
b (*Jur*) fidéicommis *m*. **to set up a ~ for sb** instituer un fidéicommis à l'intention de qn; **to hold sth/leave money in ~ for one's children** tenir qch/faire administrer un legs par fidéicommis à l'intention de ses enfants.
c (*charge, responsibility*) charge *f*, devoir *m*, obligation *f*. **to give sth into sb's ~** confier qch à la charge de qn.
d (*Comm, Fin*) trust *m*, cartel *m*; *see* **brain, investment, unit** *etc*.
2 comp ▸**trust account** (*Banking*) compte *m* en fidéicommis ▸**trustbuster** (*US*) fonctionnaire *m* chargé de la lutte antitrust ▸**trust company** société *f* fiduciaire ▸**trust fund** fonds *m* en fidéicommis ▸**trust territory** (*Pol*) territoire *f* sous tutelle ▸**trustworthy** *see* **trustworthy.**
3 vt a (*believe in, rely on*) *person, object* avoir confiance en, se fier à; *method, promise* se fier à. **don't you ~ me?** tu n'as pas confiance (en moi)?; **he is not to be ~ed** on ne peut pas lui faire confiance; **you can ~ me** vous pouvez avoir confiance en moi; **you can ~ me with your car** tu peux me confier ta voiture, tu peux me prêter ta voiture en toute confiance; **he's not to be ~ed with a knife** il ne serait pas prudent de le laisser manipuler un couteau; **can we ~ him to do it?** peut-on compter sur lui pour le faire?; **the child is too young to be ~ed on the roads** l'enfant est trop petit pour qu'on le laisse (*subj*) aller dans la rue tout seul; **I can't ~ him out of my sight** j'ai si peu confiance en lui que je ne le quitte pas des yeux; (*iro*) **~ you!*** ça ne m'étonne pas de toi!, (pour) ça on peut te faire confiance! (*iro*); (*iro*) **~ him to break it!*** pour casser quelque chose on peut lui faire confiance!; **he can be ~ed to do his best** on peut être sûr qu'il fera de son mieux; **you can't ~ a word he says** impossible de croire deux mots de ce qu'il raconte; **I wouldn't ~ him as far as I can throw him*** je n'ai absolument aucune confiance en lui.
b (*entrust*) confier (*sth to sb* qch à qn).
c (*hope*) espérer (*that* que). **I ~ not** j'espère que non.
4 vi: **to ~ in sb** se fier à qn, s'en remettre à qn; **let's ~ to luck** *or* **to chance** essayons tout de même, tentons notre chance, tentons le coup*; **I'll have to ~ to luck to find the house** il faudra que je m'en remette à la chance pour trouver la maison.
trusted ['trʌstɪd] adj *friend, servant* en qui l'on a toute confiance; *method* éprouvé.
trustee [trʌs'ti:] 1 n a (*Jur*) fidéicommissaire *m*, curateur *m*, -trice *f*. (*Jur, Fin*) **~ in bankruptcy** ≃ syndic *m* de faillite. b *[institution, school]* administrateur *m*, -trice *f*. **the ~s** le conseil d'administration. c (*US Univ*) membre *m* du conseil d'université. 2 comp ▸**Trustee Savings Bank** (*Brit*) ≃ Caisse *f* d'Épargne.
trusteeship [trʌs'ti:ʃɪp] n a (*Jur*) fidéicommis *m*, curatelle *f*. b *[institution etc]* poste *m* d'administrateur. **during his ~** pendant qu'il était administrateur.
trustful ['trʌstfʊl] adj confiant.
trustfully ['trʌstfəlɪ] adv avec confiance.
trusting ['trʌstɪŋ] adj = **trustful.**
trustworthiness ['trʌst,wɜ:ðɪnɪs] n (*NonC*) *[person]* loyauté *f*, fidélité *f*; *[statement]* véracité *f*.
trustworthy ['trʌst,wɜ:ðɪ] adj *person* digne de confiance; *report, account* fidèle, exact.
trusty ['trʌstɪ] 1 adj († *or hum*) sûr, loyal, fidèle. **my ~ sword** ma fidèle épée. 2 n (*in prison*) détenu *m* bénéficiant d'un régime de faveur.
truth [tru:θ] 1 n, pl **~s** [tru:ðz] a (*NonC*) vérité *f*. **you must always tell the ~** il faut toujours dire la vérité; **to tell you the ~** *or* **to tell, he ...** à vrai dire, *or* à dire vrai, il ...; **the ~ of it is that** la vérité c'est que; **there's no ~ in what he says** il n'y a pas un mot de vrai dans ce qu'il dit; **there's some ~ in that** il y a du vrai dans ce qu'il dit (*or* dans ce que vous dites *etc*); (*Prov*) **~ will out** la vérité finira (toujours) par se savoir; (*Jur*) **the ~, the whole ~ and nothing but the ~** la vérité, toute la vérité et rien que la vérité; **the honest ~** la pure vérité, la vérité vraie*; **the plain unvarnished ~** la vérité toute nue, la vérité sans fard; **in (all) ~** en vérité, à vrai dire.
b vérité *f*; *see* **home.**
2 comp ▸**truth drug** sérum *m* de vérité.
truthful ['tru:θfʊl] adj *person* qui dit la vérité; *statement, account* véridique, vrai; *portrait* fidèle.
truthfully ['tru:θfəlɪ] adv *answer* véridiquement, sans mentir. **I don't mind, ~** sincèrement, ça m'est égal.
truthfulness ['tru:θfʊlnɪs] n (*NonC*) véracité *f*.
try [traɪ] 1 n a (*attempt*) essai *m*, tentative *f*. **to have a ~** essayer (*at doing* de faire); **to give sth a ~** essayer qch; **he had a ~ for the job** il s'est présenté pour le poste; **it was a good ~** il a (*or* tu as *etc*) vraiment essayé; **it's worth a ~** cela vaut le coup d'essayer; **to do sth at the first ~** faire qch du premier coup; **after 3 tries he gave up** après avoir essayé 3 fois, il a abandonné.
b (*Rugby*) essai *m*. **to score a ~** marquer un essai.
2 comp ▸**try-on*: it's a try-on** c'est du bluff ▸**tryout** essai *m*.
3 vt a (*attempt*) essayer, tâcher (*to do* de faire); (*seek*) chercher (*to do* à faire). **~ to eat** *or* **~ and eat some of it** essaie *or* tâche d'en manger un peu; **he was ~ing to understand** il essayait de *or* tâchait de *or* cherchait à comprendre; **it's ~ing to rain*** il a l'air de vouloir pleuvoir*; **I'll ~ anything once** je suis toujours prêt à faire un essai; (*warning*) **just you ~ it!** essaie donc un peu!, essaie un peu pour voir!*; **you've only tried 3 questions** vous avez seulement essayé de répondre à 3 questions; **have you ever tried the high jump?** as-tu déjà essayé le saut en hauteur?; **to ~ one's best** *or* **one's hardest** faire de son mieux, faire tout son possible (*to do* pour faire); **to ~ one's hand at sth/at doing** s'essayer à qch/à faire.
b (*sample, experiment with*) *method, recipe, new material, new car etc* essayer. **have you tried these olives?** avez-vous goûté à *or* essayé ces olives?; **won't you ~ me for the job?** vous ne voulez pas me faire faire un essai?; **have you tried aspirin?** avez-vous essayé (de prendre de) l'aspirine?; **~ pushing that button** essayez de presser ce bouton; **I tried 3 hotels but they were all full** j'ai essayé 3 hôtels mais ils étaient tous complets; **to ~ the door** essayer d'ouvrir la porte; **~ this for size** essaie cela pour voir si c'est ta taille (*garment*) *or* si c'est ta pointure (*shoe*) *or* si ça marche (*spanner, screw etc*); (* *fig: offering any object*) essaie ça pour voir; (*when suggesting sth*) écoute ça un peu.
c (*test, put strain on*) *person, sb's patience, strength, endurance* mettre à l'épreuve, éprouver; *vehicle, plane* tester; *machine, gadget* tester, mettre à l'essai; *eyes, eyesight* fatiguer. **to ~ one's strength against sb** se mesurer à qn; **to ~ one's luck** tenter sa chance, tenter le coup; **this material has been tried and tested** ce tissu a subi tous les tests; **he was tried and found wanting** il ne s'est pas montré à la hauteur, il n'a pas répondu à ce qu'on attendait de lui; **they have been sorely tried** ils ont

été durement éprouvés; *see* **well.**

d (*Jur*) *person, case* juger. **to ~ sb for theft** juger qn pour vol; (*Mil*) **he was tried by court-martial** il est passé en conseil de guerre.

4 **vi** essayer. **~ again!** recommence!, refais un essai!; **just you ~!** essaie donc un peu!, essaie un peu pour voir!*; **I didn't even ~ (to)** je n'ai même pas essayé; **I couldn't have done that (even) if I'd tried** je n'aurais pas pu faire cela même si je l'avais voulu; **to ~ for a job/a scholarship** essayer d'obtenir un poste/une bourse.

►**try on** 1 **vt sep** a *garment, shoe* essayer. **try this on for size** essayez cela pour voir si c'est votre taille (*garment*) *or* pointure (*shoe*). b (*) **to try it on with sb** essayer de voir jusqu'où l'on peut pousser qn; (*sexually*) faire des avances à qn; **he's trying it on** il essaie de voir jusqu'où il peut aller (*fig*); **he's trying it on to see how you'll react** il essaie de voir comment tu vas réagir; **don't try anything on!** ne fais pas le malin! 2 **try-on*** **n** *see* **try 2.**

►**try out** 1 **vt sep** *machine, new material* essayer, faire l'essai de; *new drug, new recipe, method, solution* essayer; *new teacher, employee etc* mettre à l'essai. **try it out on the cat first** essaie d'abord de voir quelle est la réaction du chat. 2 **tryout** **n** *see* **try 2.**

►**try over** **vt sep** (*Mus*) essayer.

trying ['traɪɪŋ] **adj** *person* fatigant, pénible; *work* ennuyeux, fastidieux, pénible; *experience* pénible, douloureux. **to have a ~ time** passer un (*or* des) moment(s) difficile(s) *or* pénible(s); (*longer*) avoir une mauvaise période.

tryst†† [trɪst] **n** a (*meeting*) rendez-vous *m* (d'amour). b (*also* **~ing place**) lieu *m* de rendez-vous (d'amour).

tsar [zɑːʳ] **n** tsar *m*.

tsarina [zɑː'riːnə] **n** tsarine *f*.

tsarist ['zɑːrɪst] **n, adj** tsariste (*mf*).

tsetse fly ['tsetsɪflaɪ] **n** mouche *f* tsé-tsé *inv*.

tsp. **pl tsp.** *or* **tsps.** (**abbr of teaspoon(ful)**) cuil. *f* à café.

T T [tiː'tiː] **adj** a **abbr of teetotal, teetotaler.** b (**abbr of tuberculin tested**) *see* **tuberculin.** c (*US Post*) (**abbr of Trust Territory**) *see* **trust.**

TU [ti'juː] **n** (**abbr of Trade(s) Union**) *see* **trade.**

tub [tʌb] 1 **n** (*gen, also in washing machine*) cuve *f*; (*for washing clothes*) baquet *m*; (*for flowers*) bac *m*; (*also* **bath~**) tub *m*, (*in bathroom*) baignoire *f*; (*: *boat*) sabot* *m*, rafiau* *m or* rafiot* *m*; (*for cream etc*) (petit) pot *m*. (*Brit*) **to have a ~*** prendre un bain (*or* un tub). 2 **comp** ►**tub-thumper** (*Brit fig*) orateur *m* démagogue ►**tub-thumping** (*Brit fig*) **n** (*NonC*) démagogie *f* ◊ **adj** démagogique.

tuba ['tjuːbə] **n, pl ~s** *or* (*frm*) **tubae** ['tjuːbiː] tuba *m*.

tubby* ['tʌbɪ] **adj** rondelet, dodu, replet (*f* -ète) (*esp of woman*).

tube [tjuːb] 1 **n** (*gen, Anat, Telec, TV*) tube *m*; *[tyre]* chambre *f* à air. (*Brit: the underground*) **the ~** le métro; (*Brit*) **to go by ~** prendre le métro; (*television*) **the ~*** la télé*; *see* **inner** *etc.* 2 **comp** ►**tube station** (*Brit*) station *f* de métro.

tubeless ['tjuːblɪs] **adj** *tyre* sans chambre à air.

tuber ['tjuːbəʳ] **n** (*Bot, Anat*) tubercule *m*.

tubercle ['tjuːbɜːkl] **n** (*Anat, Bot, Med*) tubercule *m*.

tubercular [tjʊ'bɜːkjʊləʳ] **adj** (*Anat, Bot, Med*) tuberculeux.

tuberculin [tjʊ'bɜːkjʊlɪn] **n** tuberculine *f*. **~-tested cows** vaches tuberculinisées; **~-tested milk** ≃ lait certifié.

tuberculosis [tjʊˌbɜːkjʊ'ləʊsɪs] **n** tuberculose *f*. **he's got ~** il a la tuberculose, il est tuberculeux; **~ sufferer** tuberculeux *m*, -euse *f*.

tuberculous [tjʊ'bɜːkjʊləs] **adj** = **tubercular.**

tubing ['tjuːbɪŋ] **n** (*NonC*) (*tubes collectively*) tubes *mpl*, tuyaux *mpl*; (*substance*) tube, tuyau. **rubber ~** tube *or* tuyau en caoutchouc.

tubular ['tjuːbjʊləʳ] **adj** tubulaire. (*Mus*) **~ bells** carillon *m* (d'orchestre).

tubule ['tjuːbjʊl] **n** (*Anat*) tube *m*.

TUC [tiːjuː'siː] **n** (*Brit*) (**abbr of Trades Union Congress**) TUC *m* (*fédération des syndicats britanniques*).

tuck [tʌk] 1 **n** a (*Sewing etc*) rempli *m*. **to put** *or* **take a ~ in sth** faire un rempli dans qch.

b (*Brit Scol: NonC: food*) boustifaille‡ *f*.

2 **comp** ►**tuckbox** (*Brit Scol*) boîte *f* à provisions ►**tuck-in*** bon repas, festin *m* (*hum*); **they had a (good) tuck-in** ils ont vraiment bien mangé ►**tuck-shop** (*Brit Scol*) comptoir *m or* boutique *f* à provisions.

3 **vt** a (*gen*) mettre. **to ~ a blanket round sb** envelopper qn dans une couverture; **he ~ed the book under his arm** il a mis *or* rangé le livre sous son bras; **he ~ed his shirt into his trousers** il a rentré sa chemise dans son pantalon; **he was sitting with his feet ~ed under him** il avait les pieds repliés sous lui.

b (*Sewing*) faire un rempli dans.

4 **vi: to ~ into a meal*** attaquer un repas.

►**tuck away** **vt sep** a (*put away*) mettre, ranger. **tuck it away out of sight** cache-le; **the hut is tucked away among the trees** la cabane se cache *or* est cachée *or* est perdue parmi les arbres. b (*: *eat*) bouffer‡.

►**tuck in** 1 **vi** (*: *eat*) (bien) boulotter*. **tuck in!** allez-y, mangez! 2 **vt sep** *shirt, flap, stomach* rentrer; *bedclothes* border. **to tuck sb in** border qn. 3 **tuck-in*** **n** *see* **tuck 2.**

►**tuck under** **vt sep** *flap* rentrer.

►**tuck up** **vt sep** *skirt, sleeves* remonter; *hair* relever; *legs* replier. **to tuck sb up (in bed)** border qn (dans son lit).

tucker[1]†† ['tʌkəʳ] **n** (*Dress*) fichu *m*; *see* **bib.**

tucker[2]* ['tʌkəʳ] **vt** (*US*) fatiguer, crever*. **~ed (out)*** épuisé, éreinté, vanné.

Tudor ['tjuːdəʳ] **adj** (*Archit*) Tudor *inv*; *period* des Tudors; *see* **stockbroker.**

Tue(s). **abbr of Tuesday.**

Tuesday ['tjuːzdɪ] **n** mardi *m*; *see* **shrove;** *for phrases see* **Saturday.**

tufa ['tjuːfə] **n** tuf *m* calcaire.

tuffet ['tʌfɪt] **n** *[grass]* touffe *f* d'herbe; (*stool*) (petit) tabouret *m*.

tuft [tʌft] **n** touffe *f*. (*Orn*) **~ of feathers** huppe *f*, aigrette *f*; **~ of hair** (*on top of head*) épi *m*; (*anywhere on head*) touffe de cheveux.

tufted ['tʌftɪd] **adj** *grass* en touffe; *bird* huppé. **~ duck** (fuligule *m*) morillon *m*.

tug [tʌg] 1 **n** a (*pull*) (petite) saccade *f*, (petit) coup *m*. **to give sth a ~** tirer sur qch; **I felt a ~ at my sleeve/on the rope** j'ai senti qu'on me tirait par la manche/qu'on tirait sur la corde; (*fig*) **parting with them was quite a ~** les quitter a été un vrai déchirement. b (*also* **~boat**) remorqueur *m*. 2 **comp** ►**tug-of-love*** *lutte acharnée entre les parents pour avoir la garde d'un enfant* ►**tug-of-war** (*Sport*) lutte *f* à la corde; (*fig*) lutte (acharnée *or* féroce). 3 **vt** (*pull*) *rope, sleeve etc* tirer sur; (*drag*) tirer, traîner; (*Naut*) remorquer. **to ~ sth up/down** faire monter/faire descendre qch en le tirant *or* traînant. 4 **vi** tirer fort *or* sec (*at, on* sur).

tuition [tjʊ'ɪʃən] **n** (*NonC*) cours *mpl*. **private ~** cours *mpl* particuliers (*in* de); (*Scol etc*) **~ fees** frais *mpl* de scolarité.

tulip ['tjuːlɪp] **n** tulipe *f*. **~ tree** tulipier *m*.

tulle [tjuːl] **n** tulle *m*.

tumble ['tʌmbl] 1 **n** a (*fall*) chute *f*, culbute *f*; *[acrobat etc]* culbute, cabriole *f*. **to have** *or* **take a ~** faire une chute *or* une culbute; (*fig*) **they had a ~ in the hay** ils ont folâtré dans le foin.

b (*confused heap*) amas *m*. **in a ~** en désordre.

2 **comp** ►**tumbledown** en ruine(s), délabré ►**tumble-dry** faire sécher dans le sèche-linge ►**tumble(r) dryer** séchoir rotatif ►**tumbleweed** (espèce *f* d')amarante *f*.

3 **vi** a (*fall*) faire une chute, tomber, dégringoler; (*trip*) trébucher (*over* sur); *[river, stream]* descendre en cascade; *[prices]* chuter, dégringoler; (*fig*) *[person, ruler etc]* faire la culbute; *[acrobat etc]* faire des culbutes *or* des cabrioles. **he ~d out of bed** il est tombé du lit (*see also* **3b**); **to ~ head over heels** faire la culbute, culbuter; **to ~ downstairs** culbuter *or* dégringoler dans l'escalier; **he ~d over a chair** il a trébuché sur une chaise; **he ~d over the cliff/into the river** il est tombé du haut de la falaise/dans la rivière; **the clothes ~d out of the cupboard** la pile de vêtements a dégringolé quand on a ouvert le placard; **the tumbling waters of the Colorado River** les eaux tumultueuses du Colorado; (*fig*) **to ~ into war/depression** basculer dans la guerre/la dépression.

b (*rush*) se jeter. **he ~d into bed** il s'est jeté au lit; **he ~d out of bed** il a bondi hors du lit; **they ~d out of the car** ils ont déboulé de la voiture.

c (*Brit * fig: realize*) **to ~ to sth** réaliser* qch; **then I ~d (to it)** c'est alors que j'ai pigé*.

4 **vt** a *pile, heap* renverser, faire tomber, faire culbuter; *hair* ébouriffer; *books, objects* jeter en tas *or* en vrac. **~d** *room* en désordre; *bed* tout défait; *clothes* chiffonnés.

b *[washing machine]* faire tourner (dans un tambour).

►**tumble about, tumble around** 1 **vi** *[puppies, children]* gambader, s'ébattre, folâtrer; *[acrobat]* cabrioler. 2 **vt sep** *books, objects* mélanger.

►**tumble down** 1 **vi** *[person]* faire une chute *or* une culbute, culbuter. *[building etc]* **to be tumbling down** tomber en ruine(s), menacer ruine. 2 **tumbledown** **adj** *see* **tumble 2.**

►**tumble out** 1 **vi** *[objects, contents]* tomber en vrac, s'éparpiller. 2 **vt sep** *objects, contents* faire tomber en vrac.

►**tumble over** 1 **vi** culbuter. 2 **vt sep** renverser, faire tomber, faire culbuter.

tumbler ['tʌmbləʳ] **n** (*glass*) verre *m* (droit); (*of plastic, metal*) gobelet *m*; (*in lock*) gorge *f* (de serrure); (*tumble dryer*) tambour *m or* séchoir *m* (à linge) à air chaud; (*Tech etc: revolving drum*) tambour rotatif; (*acrobat*) acrobate *mf*; (*pigeon*) pigeon culbutant. (*Elec*) **~ switch** interrupteur *m* à bascule.

tumbrel ['tʌmbrəl] **n, tumbril** ['tʌmbrɪl] **n** tombereau *m*.

tumefaction [ˌtjuːmɪ'fækʃən] **n** tuméfaction *f*.

tumescent [tjuː'mesnt] **adj** tumescent.

tumid ['tjuːmɪd] **adj** (*Med*) tuméfié; (*fig*) ampoulé.

tummy* ['tʌmɪ] **n** ventre *m*. **~ache** mal *m* de ventre; **~ tuck** plastie *f* abdominale; **to have a ~ tuck** se faire retendre le ventre.

tumour, (*US*) **tumor** ['tjuːməʳ] **n** tumeur *f*.

tumuli ['tjuːmjʊlaɪ] **npl of tumulus.**

tumult ['tjuːmʌlt] **n** (*uproar*) tumulte *m*; (*emotional*) émoi *m*. **in a ~** dans le tumulte; (*emotionally*) en émoi.

tumultuous [tjuː'mʌltjʊəs] **adj** (*gen*) tumultueux; *welcome* débordant; *applause, cheers* frénétique.

tumultuously [tjuː'mʌltjʊəslɪ] **adv** tumultueusement.

tumulus ['tjuːmjʊləs] **n, pl tumuli** tumulus *m*.

tun [tʌn] n fût *m*, tonneau *m*.
tuna ['tju:nə] n, pl ~ or ~s (*also* ~ **fish**) thon *m*; *see* **blue, long.**
tundra ['tʌndrə] n toundra *f*.
tune [tju:n] 1 n a (*melody*) air *m*. **he gave us a ~ on the piano** il nous a joué un air au piano; **there's not much ~ to it** ce n'est pas très mélodieux; **to the ~ of** *sing* sur l'air de; *march, process* aux accents de; (*fig*) **repairs** *etc* **to the ~ of £300** réparations *etc* s'élevant à la coquette somme de 300 livres; (*fig*) **to change one's ~, to sing another** *or* **a different ~** changer de ton; (*fig*) **to call the ~** (*give orders*) commander; (*take decisions*) décider; *see* **dance 3**.
b (*NonC*) **to be in ~** *[instrument]* être accordé; *[singer]* chanter juste; **to be out of ~** *[instrument]* être désaccordé; *[singer]* chanter faux; **to sing/play in ~** chanter/jouer juste; **to sing/play out of ~** chanter/jouer faux; (*fig*) **to be in/out of ~ with** être en accord/ désaccord avec.
2 comp ▸**tune-up** (*Aut*) réglage *m*, mise *f* au point.
3 vt (*Mus*) accorder; (*Rad, TV: also* ~ **in**) régler (*to* sur); (*Aut*) régler, mettre au point. (*Rad*) **you are ~d (in) to ...** vous êtes à l'écoute de ...; *see* **stay¹**.
▸**tune in** (*Rad, TV*) 1 vi se mettre à l'écoute (*to* de). **tune in again tomorrow** soyez de nouveau à l'écoute demain; **thousands tuned in** des milliers de gens se sont mis à l'écoute (*to see/hear* pour voir/écouter).
2 vt sep (*Rad, TV*) régler (*to* sur). **predatory fish are tuned in to all movement in the sea around them** les poissons prédateurs captent les ondes émises par tout mouvement dans la mer; (*fig: aware of*) **to be tuned in to** *new developments, sb's feelings* être conscient de; *other people* être à l'écoute de; (*fig*) **he is/isn't tuned in**‡ il est/n'est pas dans la course*; *see also* **tune 3**.
▸**tune out*** (*US fig*) 1 vi faire la sourde oreille. 2 vt sep a ne pas faire attention à, faire la sourde oreille à. b **he's tuned out** il n'est pas branché*.
▸**tune up** 1 vi (*Mus*) accorder son (*or* ses) instrument(s). 2 vt sep (*Mus*) accorder; (*Aut*) mettre au point. 3 **tune-up** n *see* **tune 2**.
tuneful ['tju:nfʊl] adj *voice, music, instrument, opera* mélodieux; *singer* à la voix mélodieuse.
tunefully ['tju:nfəlɪ] adv mélodieusement.
tunefulness ['tju:nfʊlnɪs] n (*see* **tuneful**) caractère mélodieux; voix mélodieuse.
tuneless ['tju:nlɪs] adj peu mélodieux, discordant.
tunelessly ['tju:nlɪslɪ] adv *sing, play* faux.
tuner ['tju:nəʳ] 1 n (*person*) accordeur *m*; (*Rad: also* **stereo** ~) syntoniseur *m*, syntonisateur *m* (*Can*); (*knob*) bouton *m* de réglage; *see* **piano.** 2 comp ▸**tuner amplifier** radio-ampli *m*.
tungsten ['tʌŋstən] n (*NonC*) tungstène *m*. ~ **lamp/steel** lampe *f*/acier *m* au tungstène.
tunic ['tju:nɪk] n tunique *f*.
tuning ['tju:nɪŋ] 1 n (*Mus*) accord *m*; (*Rad, TV*) réglage *m*; (*Aut*) réglage(s), mise *f* au point. 2 comp ▸**tuning fork** (*Mus*) diapason *m* ▸**tuning key** (*Mus*) accordoir *m* ▸**tuning knob** (*Rad etc*) bouton *m* de réglage.
Tunis ['tju:nɪs] n Tunis.
Tunisia [tju:'nɪzɪə] n Tunisie *f*.
Tunisian [tju:'nɪzɪən] 1 adj tunisien. 2 n Tunisien(ne) *m(f)*.
tunnel ['tʌnl] 1 n (*gen, Rail*) tunnel *m*; (*Min*) galerie *f*. **to make a ~** = **to tunnel** (*see* **3**); *see also* **channel.**
2 comp ▸**tunnel effect** (*Phys*) effet *m* tunnel ▸**tunnel vision** (*Opt*) rétrécissement *m* du champ visuel; (*fig*) **to have tunnel vision** avoir une vision étroite des choses, avoir des vues étroites.
3 vi *[people, rabbits etc]* percer *or* creuser un *or* des tunnel(s) *or* des galeries (*into* dans, *under* sous). **to ~ in/out** *etc* entrer/sortir *etc* en creusant un tunnel.
4 vt percer *or* creuser un *or* des tunnel(s) dans. **a mound ~led by rabbits** un monticule dans lequel les lapins ont percé *or* creusé des galeries; **shelters ~led out of the hillside** des abris creusés à flanc de colline; **to ~ one's way in** *etc* = **to tunnel in** *etc* (*see* **3**).
tunny ['tʌnɪ] n , pl ~ *or* **tunnies** = **tuna.**
tuppence ['tʌpəns] n (**abbr of twopence**) deux pence *mpl*. (*fig*) **it's not worth ~*** ça ne vaut pas un radis*; **I don't care ~*** je m'en fiche (comme de l'an quarante)*.
tuppenny ['tʌpənɪ] adj (**abbr of twopenny**) à *or* de deux pence. (*fig*) **~-ha'penny** de rien du tout*, de deux sous.
turban ['tɜ:bən] 1 n turban *m*. 2 vt: **~ed** *person, head* enturbanné.
turbid ['tɜ:bɪd] adj turbide.
turbidity [tɜ:'bɪdɪtɪ] n turbidité *f*.
turbine ['tɜ:baɪn] n turbine *f*. **steam/gas ~** turbine à vapeur/à gaz.
turbo ['tɜ:bəʊ] n = **turbofan.** (*Aut*) ~ **engine** moteur *m* turbo.
turbo... ['tɜ:bəʊ] pref turbo... .
turbocharged ['tɜ:bəʊ,tʃɑ:dʒd] adj: ~ **engine** moteur *m* turbo.
turbofan [,tɜ:bəʊ'fæn] n (*fan*) turbofan *m*; (*also* ~ **engine**) turbofan *m*, turboventilateur *m*.
turbogenerator [,tɜ:bəʊ'dʒenə,reɪtəʳ] n turbogénérateur *m*.
turbojet ['tɜ:bəʊ'dʒet] n (*also* ~ **engine**) turboréacteur *m*; (*also* ~ **aircraft**) avion *m* à turboréacteur.
turboprop ['tɜ:bəʊ'prɒp] n (*also* ~ **engine**) turbopropulseur *m*; (*also* ~ **aircraft**) avion *m* à turbopropulseur.
turbosupercharger [,tɜ:bəʊ'su:pə,tʃɑ:dʒəʳ] n turbocompresseur *m* de suralimentation.
turbot ['tɜ:bət] n, pl ~ *or* ~s turbot *m*.
turbulence ['tɜ:bjʊləns] n (*NonC*) turbulence *f* (*also Aviat*); *[waves, sea]* agitation *f*.
turbulent ['tɜ:bjʊlənt] adj *crowd, class, passions, person, personality, mood* turbulent; *waves, sea* agité.
turd** [tɜ:d] n merde** *f*; (*person*) con‡ *m*, couillon‡ *m*.
tureen [tə'ri:n] n soupière *f*.
turf [tɜ:f] 1 n, pl ~s *or* **turves** a (*NonC: grass*) gazon *m*; (*one piece*) motte *f* de gazon; (*NonC: peat*) tourbe *f*; (*Sport*) turf *m*. (*Sport*) **the ~** le turf. b (*US* ‡) *[gang etc]* territoire *m or* secteur *m* réservé. *[prostitute]* **on the ~**‡ sur le trottoir*. 2 comp ▸**turf accountant** (*Brit*) bookmaker *m*. 3 vt a (*also* ~ **over**) *land* gazonner. b (*Brit* *) (*throw*) balancer*, jeter; (*push*) pousser; (*put*) mettre, flanquer*.
▸**turf in*** vt sep (*Brit*) *objects* balancer* dedans. (*fig: give up*) **he turfed it all in**‡ il a tout laissé tomber*.
▸**turf out*** vt sep (*Brit*) *objects* sortir; (*throw away*) bazarder*; *person* flanquer à la porte*, virer*; (‡) *suggestion* démolir*.
Turgenev [tur'geɪnɪv] n Tourgueniev *m*.
turgid ['tɜ:dʒɪd] adj turgide; (*fig*) *style, language* boursouflé, ampoulé.
Turin [tjʊə'rɪn] n Turin. **the ~ Shroud** le suaire de Turin.
Turk [tɜ:k] n Turc *m*, Turque *f*. (*fig: esp Pol*) **young ~** jeune Turc.
Turkey ['tɜ:kɪ] n Turquie *f*.
turkey ['tɜ:kɪ] 1 n, pl ~ *or* ~s a dindon *m*, dinde *f*; (*Culin*) dinde. (*US fig*) **to talk ~*** parler net *or* franc; *see* **cold.** b (*esp US: Cine, Theat* *: *flop*) four* *m*. c (‡: *awkward person*) balourd *m*. 2 comp ▸**turkey buzzard** vautour *m* aura ▸**turkey cock** dindon *m*.
Turkish ['tɜ:kɪʃ] 1 adj turc (*f* turque). 2 comp ▸**Turkish bath** bain *m* turc ▸**Turkish coffee** café *m* turc ▸**Turkish delight** (*Culin: NonC*) lo(u)koum *m* ▸**Turkish towel** serviette *f* éponge *inv* ▸**Turkish towelling** (*NonC*) tissu *m* éponge (*NonC*). 3 n (*Ling*) turc *m*.
Turkmen ['tɜ:kmen] n: ~ **SSR**† RSS† *f* du Turkménistan.
turmeric ['tɜ:mərɪk] n (*NonC*) curcuma *m*, safran *m* des Indes.
turmoil ['tɜ:mɔɪl] n agitation *f*, trouble *m*; (*emotional*) trouble, émoi *m*. **everything was in a ~** c'était le bouleversement *or* le chambardement* le plus complet.
turn [tɜ:n] 1 n a (*movement: of wheel, handle etc*) tour *m*. **to give sth a ~** tourner qch (une fois); **to give a screw a ~** donner un tour de vis; **with a ~ of his head he could see ...** en tournant la tête il voyait ...; (*Culin*) **done to a ~** à point; *see* **hand.**
b (*change: of direction, condition*) tournure *f*; (*bend: in road etc*) tournant *m*, virage *m*; (*Ski*) virage. **to make a ~** *[person, vehicle]* tourner; *[road, ship]* virer; **"no left ~"** "défense de tourner à gauche"; **take the next left ~** prenez la prochaine (route) à gauche; (*walk*) **to go for** *or* **take a ~ in the park** aller faire un tour dans le parc; **the milk is on the ~** le lait commence à tourner; **at the ~ of the century** en début (*or* en fin) de siècle; (*specifically*) fin dix-neuvième et début vingtième *etc*; **at the ~ of the year** vers la fin de l'année, en fin d'année; (*fig*) **at every ~** à tout instant; **things took a new ~** les choses ont pris une nouvelle tournure; **events took a tragic ~** les événements ont pris un tour *or* une tournure tragique; *[events]* **to take a ~ for the worse** s'aggraver; **to take a ~ for the better** s'améliorer; **the patient took a ~ for the worse/better** l'état du malade s'est aggravé/amélioré; *see* **tide.**
c (*Med: crisis*) crise *f*, attaque *f*; (*fright*) coup *m*. **he had one of his ~s last night** il a eu une nouvelle crise *or* attaque la nuit dernière; **she has giddy** *or* **dizzy ~s** elle a des vertiges; **it gave me quite a ~*, it gave me a nasty ~*** ça m'a fait un coup*.
d (*action etc*) **to do sb a good ~** rendre un service à qn; **to do sb a bad ~** jouer un mauvais tour à qn; **that's my good ~ for the day** j'ai fait ma bonne action *or* B.A.* pour la journée; (*Prov*) **one good ~ deserves another** un prêté pour un rendu (*Prov*); **it has served its ~** ça a fait son temps.
e (*esp Brit: Theat etc*) numéro *m*. **to do a ~** faire un numéro; *see* **star.**
f (*Mus*) doublé *m*.
g (*in game, queue, series*) tour *m*. **it's your ~** c'est votre tour, c'est à vous; **it's your ~ to play** (c'est) à vous de jouer; **whose ~ is it?** (*gen*) c'est à qui le tour?; (*in game*) c'est à qui de jouer?, c'est à qui le tour?; **wait your ~** attendez votre tour; **they answered in ~** ils ont répondu chacun à leur tour, ils ont répondu à tour de rôle; **they played in ~** *or* **by ~s** ils ont joué à tour de rôle; **I feel hot and cold by ~s** *or* **in ~** j'ai tour à tour trop chaud et trop froid; **and he, in ~, said ...** et lui, à son tour, a dit ...; (*answering*) et lui, il a répliqué ...; **~ (and ~) about** à tour de rôle; **to take it ~ (and ~) about to do sth, to take ~s at doing sth, to take it in ~(s) to do sth** faire qch à tour de rôle; **take it in ~s!** chacun son tour!; **to take ~s at the wheel** se relayer au volant; **to take a ~ at the wheel** faire un bout de conduite*; (*Mil etc*) **~ of duty** tour *m* de garde *or* de service; (*fig*) **to speak** *or* **talk out of ~** commettre une indiscrétion.
h (*tendency etc*) tendance *f*, tournure *f* d'esprit, mentalité *f*. **to be of** *or* **have a scientific ~ of mind** avoir l'esprit *or* une tournure d'esprit scientifique; **to be of** *or* **have a cheerful ~ of mind** être d'une disposition

or d'une nature joyeuse; **to have a strange ~ of mind** avoir une mentalité bizarre; **~ of phrase, ~ of style** tournure, tour *m* de phrase; **there's an old-fashioned ~ to her speech** sa façon de parler a un tour démodé; **to have a good ~ of speed** être rapide.

2 comp ▸**turnabout** *see* **turnabout** ▸**turnaround** *see* **turnaround** ▸**turncoat** renégat(e) *m(f)* ▸**turndown** *see* **turndown** ▸**turnkey** geôlier *m*, -ière *f* ▸**turnkey factory** usine *f* clés en main ▸**turn-off** *see* **turn-off** ▸**turn-on** *see* **turn-on** ▸**turnout** *see* **turnout** ▸**turnover** *see* **turnover** ▸**turnpike** (*barrier*) barrière *f* de péage; (*US: road*) autoroute *f* à péage ▸**turnround** = **turnaround** ▸**turn signal** (*US Aut*) clignotant *m* ▸**turnstile** tourniquet *m* (*barrière*); **turntable** *[record player]* platine *f*; (*for trains, cars etc*) plaque tournante ▸**turntable ladder** échelle pivotante ▸**turn-up** *see* **turn-up**.

3 vt a *handle, knob, screw, key, wheel* tourner; (*mechanically etc*) faire tourner. **~ it to the left** tournez-le vers la gauche; **~ the wheel right round** faites faire un tour complet à la roue; **what ~s the wheel?** qu'est-ce qui fait tourner la roue?; (*Aut*) **he ~ed the wheel sharply** il a donné un brusque coup de volant; **you can ~ it through 90°** on peut le faire pivoter de 90°; **~ the key in the lock** ferme (la porte) à clef; *see* **somersault**.

b *page* tourner; *mattress, pillow, collar, the soil, steak, record* retourner. **to ~ one's ankle** se tordre la cheville; **it ~s my stomach** cela me soulève le cœur, cela m'écœure; *see* **inside, upside down**.

c (*change position of, direct*) *car, object* tourner (*towards* vers); *gun, hose, searchlight* braquer (*on sb* sur qn); *thoughts, attention* tourner, diriger (*towards* vers). **to ~ a picture to the wall** tourner un tableau face au mur; **~ the switch to "on"** ouvrez le commutateur; **~ the knob to "high"** tournez le bouton jusqu'à "fort"; **~ it to "wash"** mettez-le en position "lavage"; **to ~ the lights low** baisser les lumières; **~ your face this way** tourne le visage de ce côté-ci; **he ~ed his back on us** (*lit*) il nous a tourné le dos; (*fig*) il s'est mis à nous battre froid; **he ~ed his back on the past** il a tourné la page (*fig*); **as soon as he ~s his back, as soon as his back is ~ed** dès qu'il a le dos tourné; (*fig*) **without ~ing a hair** sans sourciller, sans broncher; (*fig*) **to ~ the other cheek** tendre l'autre joue; **he ~ed his hand to writing** il s'est mis à écrire; **he can ~ his hand to anything** il sait tout faire; (*fig*) **I'm trying to ~ an honest penny** j'essaie de me faire de l'argent honnêtement; (*fig*) **to ~ the tables** renverser les rôles, retourner la situation (*on sb* aux dépens de qn); **he ~ed his steps to the sea** il a dirigé ses pas vers la mer; **they ~ed his argument against him** ils ont retourné son raisonnement contre lui; **they ~ed him against his father** ils l'ont fait se retourner contre *or* ils l'ont monté contre son père; *see* **account, advantage, heat** *etc*.

d (*deflect*) *blow* parer, détourner. **he ~ed the beggar from the door** il a chassé le mendiant; **nothing will ~ him from his purpose** rien ne l'écartera *or* ne le détournera de son but; **to ~ sb from doing** dissuader qn de faire.

e (*shape*) *wood, metal* tourner. **a well-~ed leg** une jambe faite au tour; (*fig*) **well-~ed phrase** expression bien tournée.

f (*go round*) **to ~ the corner** (*lit*) tourner au *or* le coin de la rue; (*fig*) passer le moment critique; *[patient]* passer le cap; **he has** *or* **is ~ed 40** il a 40 ans passés; **it's ~ed 3 o'clock** il est 3 heures passées.

g (*transform*) changer, transformer (*into* en); (*translate*) traduire (*into* en); *milk* faire tourner. **she ~ed him into a frog** elle l'a changé en grenouille; **they ~ed the land into a park** ils ont transformé le terrain en parc; **the experience ~ed him into an old man** cette expérience a fait de lui un vieillard; **an actor ~ed writer** un acteur devenu écrivain; (*fig*) **~ your talents into hard cash** faites travailler vos talents pour vous; **to ~ a book into a play/film** adapter un livre pour la scène/l'écran; **to ~ verse into prose** mettre de la poésie en prose; **to ~ sth black** noircir qch; **it ~ed him green with envy** cela l'a fait verdir de jalousie, il en était vert de jalousie; **we were ~ed sick by the sight** le spectacle nous a rendus malades; **to ~ a boat adrift** faire partir un bateau à la dérive; *see* **loose** *etc*.

4 vi a (*move round; rotate, revolve*) *[handle, knob, wheel, screw, key]* tourner; *[person]* se tourner (*to, towards* vers), (*right round*) se retourner. **~ to face me** tourne-toi vers moi; **he ~ed and saw me** il s'est retourné et m'a vu; **he ~ed to me and smiled** il s'est tourné vers moi et a souri; **he ~ed to look at me** il s'est retourné pour me regarder; **he ~ed to lie on his other side** il s'est tourné pour changer de côté; **the earth ~s on its axis** la terre tourne autour de son axe; (*fig*) **my head is ~ing** j'ai la tête qui tourne; **his stomach ~ed at the sight** le spectacle lui a retourné l'estomac *or* soulevé le cœur; (*depend*) **to ~ on sth** dépendre de qch, reposer sur qch; **it all ~s on whether he has the money** tout dépend s'il a l'argent ou non; **to ~ tail (and run)** prendre ses jambes à son cou; **he would ~ in his grave if he knew ...** il se retournerait dans sa tombe s'il savait ...; *see* **toss, turtle**.

b (*move in different direction*) *[person, vehicle, aircraft]* (*change course*) tourner; (*reverse direction*) faire demi-tour; *[ship]* virer; *[road, river]* faire un coude; *[wind]* tourner, changer; *[tide]* changer de direction. **~ to page 214** allez (à la) page 214; (*Mil*) **right ~!** à droite, droite!; **to ~ (to the) left** tourner à gauche; **~ first right** prenez la première à droite; **they ~ed and came back** ils ont fait demi-tour *or* fait volte-face et ils sont revenus (sur leurs pas); **the car ~ed at the end of the street** (*turned round*) la voiture a fait demi-tour au bout de la rue; (*turned off*) la voiture a tourné au bout de la rue; (*Aut*) **there's nowhere to ~** il n'y a pas d'endroit où faire demi-tour; **the car ~ed into a side street** la voiture a tourné dans une rue transversale; **our luck has ~ed** la chance a tourné pour nous; **the conversation ~ed on the election** la conversation en est venue à l'élection; **the dog ~ed on him** le chien l'a attaqué; **they ~ed on him and accused him of treachery** ils s'en sont pris à lui et l'ont accusé de trahison; (*fig*) **to ~ against sb** se retourner contre qn; (*fig*) **he didn't know which way to ~** il ne savait plus où donner de la tête; **he ~ed to me for advice** il s'est tourné vers *or* adressé à moi pour me demander conseil; **where can I ~ for money?** où pourrais-je trouver de l'argent?; **he ~ed to politics** il s'est tourné vers la politique; **he ~ed to drink** il s'est mis à boire; **farmers are ~ing from industrial to organic methods** les fermiers délaissent l'agriculture industrielle pour (se tourner vers) l'agriculture biologique; **our thoughts ~ to those who ...** nos pensées vont à *or* se tournent vers ceux qui ...; *see* **tide**.

c (*become*) **to ~ into** devenir; **he ~ed into a frog** il se changea *or* se métamorphosa en grenouille; **he ~ed into an old man overnight** il est devenu vieux en l'espace d'une nuit; **to ~ to stone** se changer en pierre, se pétrifier; **his admiration ~ed to scorn** son admiration se changea en *or* tourna au *or* fit place au mépris; (*fig*) **his knees ~ed to water** *or* **jelly** ses genoux se sont dérobés sous lui; **the weather has ~ed cold** le temps s'est rafraîchi; **to ~ black** noircir; **to ~ angry** se mettre en colère; **to ~ traitor** (*Mil, Pol*) se vendre à l'ennemi; (*gen*) se mettre à trahir; **to ~ communist** devenir communiste; **to ~ Catholic** se convertir au catholicisme; **to ~ professional** passer *or* devenir professionnel.

d *[leaves]* jaunir; *[milk]* tourner; *[weather]* changer.

▸**turn about, turn around** (*see also* **turn round**) 1 vi *[person]* se retourner, faire volte-face; *[vehicle]* faire demi-tour; *[object]* tourner. (*Mil*) **about turn!** demi-tour! 2 vt sep a (*lit*) tourner (dans l'autre sens). b (*fig*) (*change mind, tactics etc*) **to turn sb around** faire changer d'avis à qn; **to turn things around** renverser la situation. 3 **turnabout** n, **turnaround** n *see* **turnabout, turnaround**.

▸**turn aside** 1 vi (*lit, fig*) se détourner (*from* de). 2 vt sep détourner.

▸**turn away** 1 vi se détourner (*from* de). 2 vt sep a *head, face, eyes, gun* détourner. **turn the photograph away from the light** tourne la photographie de telle façon qu'elle ne soit pas exposée à la lumière. b (*reject*) *person* (*gen*) renvoyer, (*stronger*) chasser; *salesman at door* envoyer promener; *offer* refuser, rejeter. **they're turning business** *or* **customers away** ils refusent des clients.

▸**turn back** 1 vi a *[traveller]* revenir, rebrousser chemin, faire demi-tour; *[vehicle]* faire demi-tour; (*fig: reverse a decision*) tourner bride. (*fig*) **there is no turning back** on ne peut pas retourner en arrière. b **to turn back to page 100** revenir à la page 100. 2 vt sep a (*fold, bend*) *bedclothes, collar* rabattre; *corner of page* relever, replier. b (*send back*) *person, vehicle* faire faire demi-tour à. c *clock, hands of clock* reculer (*to* jusqu'à). (*fig*) **if only we could turn the clock back** si seulement on pouvait remonter le (cours du) temps; **it has turned the clock back 50 years** cela nous (*or* vous *etc*) a fait revenir en arrière de 50 ans.

▸**turn down** 1 vt sep a (*fold, bend*) *bedclothes* rabattre, retourner; *collar* rabattre. **to turn down the corner of the page** corner la page. b (*reduce*) *gas, heat, lighting, radio, music* baisser. c (*refuse*) *offer, suggestion, loan, suitor* rejeter, repousser; *candidate, volunteer* refuser. d (*place upside down*) *playing card* retourner (face contre table). 2 vi *[sales]* fléchir, chuter, baisser. 3 **turndown** n, adj *see* **turndown**.

▸**turn in** 1 vi a *[car, person]* **to turn in to a driveway** entrer *or* tourner dans une allée. b **his toes turn in** il a les pieds tournés en dedans. c (**: go to bed*) aller se coucher. 2 vt sep a **to turn in the ends of sth** rentrer les bouts de qch; **to turn one's toes in** tourner les pieds en dedans. b (**: surrender, return*) *borrowed goods, equipment* rendre (*to* à); *wanted man* livrer (à la police); *stolen goods* apporter à la police.

▸**turn off** 1 vi a *[person, vehicle]* tourner.

b *[heater, oven etc]* **to turn off automatically** s'éteindre automatiquement.

c (*‡ fig: lose interest*) décrocher*.

2 vt sep *water* fermer; *tap* fermer; *light* éteindre; *electricity, gas* éteindre, fermer; (*at main*) *all services* couper; *radio, television, heater* éteindre, fermer, arrêter. (*Rad, TV*) **he turned the programme off** il a fermé *or* éteint le poste; (*Aut*) **to turn off the engine** couper l'allumage, arrêter le moteur; **the oven turns itself off** le four s'éteint tout seul *or* automatiquement; (*fig*) **the way he smiled turned me off‡** sa façon de sourire m'a totalement rebuté *or* (*stronger*) m'a dégoûté*.

3 **turn-off** n *see* **turn-off**.

▸**turn on** 1 vi a *[heater, oven etc]* **to turn on automatically** s'allumer automatiquement. b (*Rad, TV*) allumer le poste. 2 vt sep a *tap* ouvrir; *water* faire couler; *gas, electricity* allumer; *radio, television, heater* allumer; (*at main*) *all services* brancher; *engine, machine* mettre en marche. **to turn on the light** allumer; (*fig*) **to turn on the charm*** (se mettre à) faire du charme*. b (**: excite: gen*) exciter. **she ~s him on** elle l'excite; **this music turns me on‡** cette musique me fait quelque chose*; (*fig*) **to be turned on‡** (*up-to-date*) être branché* *or* dans le vent; (*by drugs*) planer*; (*sexually*) être (tout) excité *or* émoustillé* (*by* par). 3 **turn-on**⁑ n *see* **turn-on**.

▶**turn out** 1 vi a (*from bed*) se lever; (*from house*) sortir; *[guard]* (aller) prendre la faction; *[troops etc]* aller au rassemblement. **not many people turned out to see her** peu de gens sont venus la voir.
b *[car, pedestrian]* **to turn out of a driveway** sortir d'une allée.
c **his toes turn out** il tourne les pieds en dehors, il a les pieds en canard.
d (*transpire; end*) se révéler, s'avérer. **it turned out that she had not seen her** il s'est avéré qu'elle ne l'avait pas vue; **it turned out to be true** cela s'est avéré juste; **it turned out to be wrong** cela s'est révélé faux; **it turned out to be harder than we thought** cela s'est révélé *or* avéré plus difficile que l'on ne pensait; **he turned out to be a good student** il s'est révélé bon étudiant; **as it turned out, nobody came** en l'occurrence *or* en fin de compte personne n'est venu; **it all depends how things turn out** tout dépend de la façon dont les choses vont se passer; **everything will turn out all right** tout finira bien.
2 vt sep a *light* éteindre; *gas* éteindre, fermer.
b **to turn one's toes out** marcher en canard, tourner les pieds en dehors.
c (*empty out*) *pockets, suitcase* retourner, vider; *contents* vider (*of* de); *room, cupboard* nettoyer à fond; *cake, jelly* démouler (*on to* sur, *of* de); (*expel*) *person* mettre à la porte; *tenant* expulser. **they turned him out of the house** ils l'ont mis à la porte; **to turn sb out of his job** renvoyer qn.
d *troops, police* envoyer. **to turn out the guard** faire sortir la garde.
e (*produce*) *goods* fabriquer, produire. **the college turns out good teachers** le collège forme de bons professeurs.
f **to be well turned out** être élégant.
3 **turnout** n *see* **turnout**.

▶**turn over** 1 vi a *[person]* se retourner; *[car etc]* se retourner, faire un tonneau; *[boat]* se retourner, chavirer. **turn over and go to sleep!** (re)tourne-toi et dors!; **the barrel turned over and over** le tonneau faisait des tours sur lui-même; **my stomach turned over** (*at gruesome sight*) j'ai eu l'estomac retourné; (*from fright etc*) mon sang n'a fait qu'un tour; (*Aut*) **the engine was turning over** le moteur était *or* tournait au ralenti.
b (*in reading*) tourner la page. (*in letter etc*) **please turn over** (*abbr* **PTO**) tournez s'il vous plaît (*abbr T.S.V.P.*).
2 vt sep a *page* tourner; *mattress, patient, earth, playing card, plate* retourner. (*fig*) **to turn over an idea in one's mind** retourner *or* ressasser une idée dans sa tête; *see* **leaf**.
b (*hand over*) *object* rendre; *person* livrer (*to* à).
3 vt fus: **the firm turns over £10,000 a week** l'entreprise réalise un chiffre d'affaires de 10.000 livres par semaine.
4 **turnover** n *see* **turnover**.

▶**turn round** 1 vi a *[person]* se retourner; (*change direction*) *[person, vehicle]* faire demi-tour; (*rotate*) *[object]* tourner. **to turn round and round** tourner *or* tournoyer sur soi-même; **turn round and look at me** retournez-vous et regardez-moi; **he turned round and came back** il a fait demi-tour et est revenu; (*fig*) **he turned round and said he was leaving** il a subitement annoncé qu'il partait.
b (*load/unload and leave*) *[ship, plane]* décharger (*or* recharger) et repartir.
2 vt sep a *one's head* tourner; *person, object* tourner, retourner; *vehicle, ship, aircraft* faire faire demi-tour à. **he turned the car round** il a fait demi-tour; (*fig: unload and send on its way*) **to turn a ship/plane round** charger (*or* décharger) un navire/avion; (*Comm*) **to turn an order round** exécuter *or* traiter une commande.
b (*fig*) (*change mind, tactics etc*) **to turn sb round** faire changer qn d'avis; **to turn things/the economy round** renverser la situation/la tendance de l'économie; *[text]* **if you turned this round a bit it would be very funny** si vous formuliez cela un peu différemment, ce pourrait être très drôle.

▶**turn up** 1 vi a (*arrive*) arriver, s'amener; (*be found*) être trouvé *or* retrouvé; *[playing card]* sortir. **something will turn up** on va bien trouver quelque chose; **I've lost my job — something will turn up (for you)** j'ai perdu mon poste — tu finiras par trouver quelque chose; *[person, lost object]* **to turn up again** refaire surface; *see* **trump**[1].
b (*point upwards*) remonter, être relevé. **his nose turns up** il a le nez retroussé *or* en trompette.
c *[prices]* remonter. **profits have turned up in the last quarter** les bénéfices sont en hausse au dernier trimestre.
2 vt sep a *collar, sleeve* remonter. **to have a turned-up nose** avoir le nez retroussé *or* en trompette; (*fig: disgust*) **it really turns me up**⁑ ça me débecte⁑; (*Brit fig: stop*) **turn it up!**⁑ y en a marre!⁑, la ferme!⁑; *see also* **nose**.
b *buried object* déterrer; (*fig: find*) *lost object, reference* déterrer, dénicher. **a survey turned up more than 3,000 people suffering from ...** une enquête a révélé que plus de 3.000 personnes souffraient de ... .
c *heat, gas* monter, mettre plus fort; *radio, television* mettre plus fort. (*Rad, TV etc*) **to turn up the sound** augmenter *or* monter le volume.
3 **turn-up** n *see* **turn-up**.

turnabout ['tɜːnəbaʊt] n (*lit, fig*) volte-face *f inv*.

turnaround ['tɜːnəraʊnd] n (*lit, fig*) volte-face *f inv*; (*place for turning vehicle*) endroit *m* pour manœuvrer; (*unloading time etc*) *[plane, truck]* rotation *f*; *[ship]* estarie *f*, starie *f*. ~ **time** (*Comm: of order*) temps *m* d'exécution; (*Comput*) temps de retournement; **the ~ time for our trucks is 3 hours** nos camions opèrent des rotations de 3 heures.

turndown ['tɜːndaʊn] 1 n a *[sales, rate, tendency]* fléchissement *m*, (tendance *f* à la) baisse *f*. b (*rejection*) refus *m*. 2 adj *flap* à rabattre. ~ **collar** col *m* rabattu.

turner ['tɜːnəʳ] n tourneur *m*.

turnery ['tɜːnərɪ] n atelier *m* de tournage.

turning ['tɜːnɪŋ] 1 n a (*side road*) route (*or* rue) latérale; (*fork*) embranchement *m*; (*bend in road, river*) coude *m*. **take the second ~ on the left** prenez la deuxième à gauche. b (*NonC: Tech*) tournage *m*. 2 comp ▶**turning circle** (*Aut*) rayon *m* de braquage ▶**turning lathe** (*Tech*) tour *m* ▶**turning point**: (*fig*) **he was at a turning point in his career** il était à un tournant de sa carrière; **that was the turning point in her life** ce fut le moment décisif de sa vie.

turnip ['tɜːnɪp] n navet *m*.

turn-off ['tɜːnɒf] n a (*Aut*) embranchement *m* (*où il faut tourner*). b (⁑) **it's a (real) ~!** c'est vraiment à vous rebuter! *or* (*stronger*) dégoûter!*; (*sexually also*) c'est vraiment pas sexy!*

turn-on⁑ ['tɜːnɒn] n: **it's a (real) ~!** c'est excitant!; (*for men also*) ça me fait bander!⁂

turnout ['tɜːnaʊt] n a (*attendance*) assistance *f*. **what sort of a ~ was there?** combien y avait-il de gens (dans l'assistance)?; **there was a good ~** beaucoup de gens sont venus; (*Brit*) **~ at the polls**, (*US*) **voter ~** (taux *m* de) participation électorale; **high/low ~ at the polls** fort/faible taux de participation électorale. b (*clean-out*) nettoyage *m*. **to have a good ~ of a room/cupboard** nettoyer une pièce/un placard à fond. c (*Ind: output*) production *f*. d (*Dress*) tenue *f*.

turnover ['tɜːn,əʊvəʳ] n a (*Comm etc*) *[stock, goods]* rotation *f*; *[shares]* mouvement *m*; (*total business done*) chiffre *m* d'affaires. **a profit of £4,000 on a ~ of £40,000** un bénéfice de 4.000 livres pour un chiffre d'affaires de 40.000 livres; **he sold them cheaply hoping for a quick ~** il les a vendus bon marché pour les écouler rapidement. b *[staff, workers]* renouvellement *m*, rotation *f*. **there is a high** *or* **rapid (rate of) ~ in that firm** cette maison connaît de fréquents changements *or* renouvellements de personnel. c (*Culin*) chausson *m*. **apple ~** chausson aux pommes.

turnround = **turnaround**.

turn-up ['tɜːnʌp] n a (*Brit*) *[trousers]* revers *m*. b (*) **that was a ~ (for the books)!** ça a été une belle surprise!

turpentine ['tɜːpəntaɪn] n (essence *f* de) térébenthine *f*. ~ **substitute** white-spirit *m*.

turpitude ['tɜːpɪtjuːd] n turpitude *f*.

turps* [tɜːps] n abbr of **turpentine**.

turquoise ['tɜːkwɔɪz] 1 n (*stone*) turquoise *f*; (*colour*) turquoise *m*. 2 adj *necklace, ring* de turquoise(s); (*colour*) turquoise *inv*.

turret ['tʌrɪt] 1 n (*Archit, Mil, Phot, Tech*) tourelle *f*. 2 comp ▶**turret gun** canon *m* de tourelle.

turreted ['tʌrɪtɪd] adj à tourelles.

turtle ['tɜːtl] 1 n tortue marine. (*fig*) **to turn ~** chavirer, se renverser; *see* **mock**. 2 comp ▶**turtledove** tourterelle *f* ▶**turtleneck (sweater)** (*Brit*) (pull-over *m* à) encolure montante *or* col *m* cheminée; (*US*) (pull-over *m* à) col roulé ▶**turtle soup** consommé *m* à la tortue.

Tuscan ['tʌskən] 1 adj toscan. 2 n a Toscan(e) *m(f)*. b (*Ling*) toscan *m*.

Tuscany ['tʌskənɪ] n Toscane *f*.

tush [tʌʃ] excl bah!

tusk [tʌsk] n défense *f* (*d'éléphant etc*).

tusker ['tʌskəʳ] n éléphant *m* (*or* sanglier *m etc*) adulte (*qui a ses défenses*).

tussle ['tʌsl] 1 n (*struggle*) lutte *f* (*for* pour); (*scuffle*) mêlée *f*. **to have a ~ with sb** en venir aux mains avec qn; (*verbally*) avoir une prise de bec* avec qn. 2 vi se battre (*with sb* avec qn, *for sth* pour qch). **to ~ over sth** se disputer qch.

tussock ['tʌsək] n touffe *f* d'herbe.

tut [tʌt] (*also* **tut-tut**) 1 excl allons allons!, allons donc! 2 vi: **he (tut-)~ted at the idea** à cette idée il a eu une exclamation désapprobatrice.

Tutankhamen [,tuːtən'kɑːmen] n, **Tutankhamun** [,tuːtənkɑː'muːn] n Toutankhamon *m*.

tutelage ['tjuːtɪlɪdʒ] n tutelle *f*.

tutelary ['tjuːtɪlərɪ] adj tutélaire.

tutor ['tjuːtəʳ] 1 n (*private teacher*) professeur *m* (particulier) (*in* en), (*full-time*) précepteur *m*, -trice *f*; (*Brit Univ*) directeur *m*, -trice *f* d'études; (*Brit Scol: also* **form ~**) professeur *m* principal; (*in prison*) éducateur *m*, -trice *f*. 2 comp ▶**tutor group** (*Brit Scol*) classe *f* ▶**tutor period** (*Brit Scol*) cours *m* avec le professeur principal (*en début de journée*) ▶**tutor room** (*Brit Scol*) salle *f* de classe (*affectée à une classe particulière*). 3 vt donner des leçons particulières *or* des cours particuliers à. **to ~ sb in Latin** donner des cours particuliers de latin à qn.

tutorial [tjuː'tɔːrɪəl] 1 adj *system, class* de travaux pratiques *or*

dirigés; *duties* de directeur d'études. 2 n (*Univ*) travaux pratiques *or* dirigés (*in* de).
tutoring ['tju:tərɪŋ] n cours *mpl* particuliers (*in* de); (*remedial*) cours *mpl* de soutien (*in* de).
tutti-frutti ['tʊtɪ'frʊtɪ] n plombières *f*.
tutu ['tu:tu:] n tutu *m*.
tuwhit-tuwhoo [tʊ'wɪttʊ'wu:] n hou-hou *m*.
tuxedo [tʌk'si:dəʊ] n (*US*) smoking *m*.
TV* [ˌti:'vi:] 1 n (abbr of **television**) télé* *f*; *see* **television**. 2 comp ▸**TV dinner** repas congelé (sur un plateau); *see also* **television**.
TVEI [ˌti:vi:i:'aɪ] n (*Brit*) (abbr of **technical and vocational educational initiative**) *plan de formation pour les jeunes*.
TVP [ˌti:vi:'pi:] n (abbr of **textured vegetable protein**) *see* **textured**.
twaddle ['twɒdl] n (*NonC*) âneries *fpl*, balivernes *fpl*, fadaises *fpl*.
twain [tweɪn] npl: **the ~††** les deux; (*loc*) **and never the ~ shall meet** et les deux sont inconciliables.
twang [twæŋ] 1 n [*wire, string*] son *m* (de corde pincée); (*tone of voice*) ton nasillard, nasillement *m*. **to speak with a ~** nasiller, parler du nez; **he has an American ~** il a le nasillement américain dans la voix. 2 vt *guitar etc* pincer les cordes de, gratter de. 3 vi [*wire, bow*] vibrer.
twangy ['twæŋɪ] adj *noise* de corde pincée; *voice, tone* nasillard.
'twas†† [twɒz] = **it was**; *see* **be**.
twat ** [twæt] n a (*genitals*) con* *m*; (*woman*) gonzesse* *f*. b (*pej: person*) pauvre con(ne)* *m(f)*.
tweak [twi:k] 1 vt *sb's ear, nose* tordre; *rope etc, sb's hair* tirer (d'un coup sec). 2 n coup sec. **to give sth a ~** = **to tweak sth**; *see* **1**.
twee* [twi:] adj (*Brit pej*) *person* chichiteux, mignard; *remark* mièvre; *room etc* à la décoration maniérée; *decoration* maniéré, un peu cucul*.
tweed [twi:d] 1 n tweed *m*. (*suit*) **~s** costume *m* de tweed. 2 comp *jacket etc* de *or* en tweed.
tweedy ['twi:dɪ] adj *material* qui ressemble au tweed. (*pej*) **she's one of these ~ ladies*** elle a le genre dame bien et tweeds cossus.
'tween [twi:n] prep (*liter*) = **between**.
tweeny* ['twi:nɪ] n (*Brit*) bonne *f*.
tweet [twi:t] 1 n (*also* **~-~**) gazouillis *m*, gazouillement *m*, pépiement *m*. 2 vi gazouiller, pépier.
tweeter ['twi:tər] n haut-parleur *m* aigu, tweeter *m*.
tweeze* [twi:z] vt *eyebrows etc* épiler.
tweezers ['twi:zəz] npl (*also* **pair of ~**) pince *f* fine, pince à épiler.
twelfth [twelfθ] 1 adj douzième. **T~ Night** la fête des Rois. 2 n douzième *mf*; (*fraction*) douzième *m*; *for phrases see* **sixth**.
twelve [twelv] 1 adj douze *inv*. 2 n douze *m inv*; *see* **o'clock**; *for other phrases see* **six**. 3 pron douze *mfpl*. **there are ~** il y en a douze. 4 comp ▸**twelvemonth††** année *f*, an *m* ▸**twelve-tone** (*Mus*) dodécaphonique.
twentieth ['twentɪɪθ] 1 adj vingtième. 2 n vingtième *mf*; (*fraction*) vingtième *m*; *for phrases see* **sixth**.
twenty ['twentɪ] 1 adj vingt *inv*. **about ~ books** une vingtaine de livres.
2 n vingt *m*. **about ~** une vingtaine; *for other phrases see* **sixty**.
3 pron vingt *mfpl*. **there are ~** il y en a vingt.
4 comp ▸**twenty-first** (*birthday*) vingt et unième anniversaire *m*; (*birthday party*) **I'm having my twenty-first on Saturday** je fête mes 21 ans *or* mon 21e anniversaire samedi ▸**twenty-four hours** (*whole day*) vingt-quatre heures *fpl*; *open etc* **twenty-four hours a day** vingt-quatre heures sur vingt-quatre; (*Comm*) **twenty-four hour service** service jour et nuit, "service 24 heures sur 24" ▸**twenty-one** (*Cards*) vingt-et-un *m* (*jeu*) ▸**twenty-twenty vision**: **to have twenty-twenty vision** avoir dix dixièmes à chaque œil ▸**twenty-two metre line** (*Rugby*) ligne *f* des vingt-deux mètres.
twerp* [twɜ:p] n andouille* *f*, idiot(e) *m(f)*.
twice [twaɪs] adv deux fois. **~ as much, ~ as many** deux fois plus; **~ as much bread** deux fois plus de pain; **~ as long as ...** deux fois plus long que ...; **she is ~ your age** elle a deux fois votre âge, elle a le double de votre âge; **~ 2 is 4** deux fois 2 font 4; **~ weekly, ~ a week** deux fois la *or* par semaine; (*fig*) **he didn't have to be asked ~** il ne s'est pas fait prier; **he's ~ the man you are** il te vaut bien, il vaut beaucoup mieux que toi; **since the operation she is ~ the woman she was** depuis son opération, elle est deux fois mieux qu'avant; *see* **once, think**.
twiddle ['twɪdl] 1 vt *knob* tripoter, manier. (*fig*) **to ~ one's thumbs** se tourner les pouces. 2 vi: **to ~ with sth** jouer avec *or* tripoter qch. 3 n: **to give sth a ~** donner plusieurs petits tours à qch.
twig[1] [twɪg] n brindille *f*, petite branche.
twig[2]* [twɪg] vti (*Brit: understand*) piger*, comprendre.
twilight ['twaɪlaɪt] 1 n (*evening*) crépuscule *m* (*also fig*); (*morning*) aube *f* naissante. **at ~** (*evening*) au crépuscule, à la tombée du jour; (*morning*) à l'aube naissante; **in the ~** dans le demi-jour *or* la semi-obscurité *or* la pénombre; (*fig*) **in the ~ of history** dans les brumes *fpl* de l'histoire. 2 comp ▸**twilight world** monde *m* nébuleux ▸**twilight zone** (*fig*) zone *f* floue.
twilit ['twaɪlɪt] adj (*lit*) *sky, place* crépusculaire; (*fig*) nébuleux.
twill [twɪl] n (*Tex*) sergé *m*.
'twill [twɪl] = **it will**; *see* **will**.
twin [twɪn] 1 n jumeau *m*, -elle *f*; *see* **identical, Siamese**. 2 adj *son, brother* jumeau; *daughter, sister* jumelle; (*Brit*) *town* jumelé. **~ boys** jumeaux *mpl*; **~ girls** jumelles *fpl*; (*fig*) **they're ~ souls** ce sont deux âmes sœurs. 3 comp ▸**twin-bedded room** (*Brit: in hotel*) chambre *f* à deux lits ▸**twin beds** lits *mpl* jumeaux ▸**twin-cylinder** adj à deux cylindres ◊ n moteur *m* à deux cylindres ▸**twin-engined** bimoteur ▸**twin-screw** à deux hélices ▸**twinset** (*Brit*) twin-set *m*; (*Brit pej*) **she's rather twin-set-and-pearls*** elle est du genre petite bourgeoise rangée ▸**twin-tub** machine *f* à laver à deux cuves. 4 vt *town etc* jumeler (*with* avec).
twine [twaɪn] 1 n (*NonC*) ficelle *f*. 2 vt (*weave*) tresser; (*roll*) entortiller, enrouler (*round* autour de). **she ~d her arms round his neck** elle lui a enlacé le cou de ses bras. 3 vi [*plant, coil*] s'enrouler (*round* autour de); [*river, road*] serpenter, zigzaguer.
twinge [twɪndʒ] n: **a ~ (of pain)** un élancement, un tiraillement; **a ~ of conscience** *or* **remorse** *or* **guilt** un (petit) remords; **to feel a ~ of remorse/shame** éprouver un certain remords/une certaine honte; **to feel a ~ of regret** *or* **sadness** avoir un pincement au cœur.
twining ['twaɪnɪŋ] adj *plant* volubile (*Bot*).
twinkle ['twɪŋkl] 1 vi [*star, lights*] scintiller, briller; [*eyes*] briller, pétiller. 2 n [*star, lights*] scintillement *m*; [*eyes*] éclat *m*, pétillement *m*. **... he said with a ~ (in his eye)** ... dit-il avec un pétillement (malicieux) dans les yeux; **he had a ~ in his eye** il avait les yeux pétillants (de malice); **in a ~, in the ~ of an eye** en un clin d'œil.
twinkling ['twɪŋklɪŋ] 1 adj (*see* **twinkle 1**) scintillant, brillant; pétillant. 2 n: **in the ~ of an eye** en un clin d'œil.
twinning ['twɪnɪŋ] n [*towns*] jumelage *m*.
twirl [twɜ:l] 1 n [*body*] tournoiement *m*; [*dancer*] pirouette *f*; (*in writing*) fioriture *f*. **to give sth a ~** = **to twirl sth**; *see* **3**. 2 vi (*also* **~ round**) [*cane, lasso, dancer*] tournoyer; [*handle, knob*] pivoter. 3 vt (*also* **~ round**) *cane, lasso* faire tournoyer; *knob, handle* faire pivoter; *moustache* tortiller.
twirler* ['twɜ:lər] n (*US*) majorette *f*.
twirp* [twɜ:p] n = **twerp***.
twist [twɪst] 1 n a (*action*) torsion *f*; (*Med*) entorse *f*, foulure *f*. **to give a ~ to** *knob, handle* faire pivoter, faire tourner; *wire* tordre; *one's ankle* se tordre, se fouler; **he put a ~ on the ball** il a imprimé une rotation à la balle; **with a quick ~ (of the wrist)** d'un rapide tour de poignet.
b (*coil*) rouleau *m*; (*in road*) tournant *m*, virage *m*; (*in river*) coude *m*; (*in wire, flex, cord*) tortillon *m*; (*fig*) (*of events*) tournure *f*; (*of meaning*) distorsion *f*. **a ~ of yarn** une torsade *or* un cordonnet de fil; **sweets in a ~ of paper** des bonbons dans un tortillon de papier *or* une papillote; **a ~ of lemon** un zeste de citron; **the road is full of ~s and turns** la route est pleine de tournants *or* de virages, la route fait des zigzags; **to take a ~ round a post with a rope** faire passer une corde autour d'un poteau; **the story has an unexpected ~ to it** l'histoire comporte un coup de théâtre; **he gave a new ~ to this old plot** il a donné un tour nouveau à cette vieille intrigue; (*fig*) **to get (o.s.) into a ~*, to get one's knickers in a ~*** s'énerver; (*fig*) **to go round the ~*** devenir dingue*, perdre la boule*; **to drive sb round the ~*** faire tourner qn en bourrique*.
c (**: cheat*) **what a ~!** on s'est fait avoir!*; **it's a ~!** c'est de la triche!*
d (*dance*) twist *m*. **to do the ~** twister.
2 comp ▸**twist grip** [*motorcycle*] poignée *f* d'accélération *or* (*gear change*) de changement de vitesses.
3 vt a (*interweave*) *threads, strands, ropes, wires* entortiller, tresser; (*turn round on itself*) *thread, rope, wire, one's handkerchief* tordre; (*coil*) enrouler (*round* autour de); (*turn*) *knob, handle* tourner; *top, cap* tourner, visser; (*deform*) *metal etc* tordre, déformer; (*fig*) *meaning* déformer, fausser, altérer; *words* déformer. [*rope etc*] **to get ~ed** s'entortiller; **he ~ed the strands into a cord** il a entortillé *or* tressé les fils pour en faire une corde; **he ~ed the paper into a ball** il a tirebouchonné le papier pour en faire une boule; **you've ~ed it out of shape** tu l'as déformé en le tordant, tu l'as tordu; **~ the cap clockwise** vissez la capsule dans le sens des aiguilles d'une montre; **to ~ the top off a jar** dévisser le couvercle d'un bocal (pour l'enlever); **to ~ one's ankle** se tordre *or* se fouler la cheville; **to ~ one's neck** se tordre le cou, attraper le torticolis; **to ~ sb's arm** (*lit*) tordre le bras à qn; (*fig*) forcer la main à qn; **he ~ed his mouth scornfully** il eut un rictus méprisant; **limbs ~ed by arthritis** des membres tordus par l'arthrite; **his face was ~ed with pain/rage** ses traits étaient tordus par la douleur/la fureur; **you're ~ing everything I say** tu déformes tout ce que je dis; *see* **finger, twisted** *etc*.
b (**: cheat*) rouler*, avoir*.
4 vi a [*flex, rope etc*] s'entortiller, s'enrouler; [*socks, trousers*] tirebouchonner; [*one's ankle etc*] se tordre. **to ~ round sth** s'enrouler autour de qch; **the road ~s (and turns) through the valley** la route zigzague *or* serpente à travers la vallée; **the motorbike ~ed through the traffic** la moto louvoyait *or* zigzaguait parmi la circulation.
b (*dance the ~*) twister.
▸**twist about, twist around** vi [*rope etc*] tortiller; [*road etc*] tortiller, zigzaguer, serpenter.

►**twist off** 1 vi: **the top twists off** le couvercle se dévisse. 2 vt sep *branch* enlever en tordant; *bottle-top* enlever en dévissant.
►**twist out** 1 vi: **he twisted out of their grasp** il s'est dégagé de leur étreinte. 2 vt sep *object* enlever en tournant.
►**twist round** 1 vi *[road etc]* tortiller, zigzaguer, serpenter; *[person]* se retourner. 2 vt sep *rope, wire* enrouler; *knob, handle,* tourner; *top, cap* tourner, visser; *one's head, chair* tourner.
►**twist up** 1 vi *[ropes etc]* s'entortiller, s'emmêler; *[smoke]* monter en volutes. 2 vt sep *ropes, threads* entortiller, emmêler.
twisted ['twɪstɪd] adj *key, rod, metal, beam* tordu; *wire, rope, flex, cord* tordu, emmêlé, entortillé; *wrist, ankle* tordu, foulé; (*fig*) *logic* faux (*f* fausse); *mind* tordu, mal tourné; (*dishonest*) malhonnête; *lawyer, politician* véreux.
twister* ['twɪstəʳ] n a (*Brit: crook*) escroc *m* (*lit, fig*). b (*US: tornado*) tornade *f*.
twisting ['twɪstɪŋ] 1 n (*gen*) torsion *f*; *[meaning]* déformation *f*. 2 adj *path* sinueux, en zigzag.
twit[1] [twɪt] vt (*tease*) taquiner (*about, with* sur, à propos de).
twit[2]* [twɪt] n (*Brit: fool*) idiot(e) *m(f)*, crétin(e) *m(f)*.
twitch [twɪtʃ] 1 n (*nervous movement*) tic *m*; (*pull*) coup *m* sec, saccade *f*. **I've got a ~ in my eyelid** j'ai l'œil qui saute; **he has a (nervous) ~ in his cheek** il a un tic à la joue; **with one ~ (of his hand) he freed the rope** il a dégagé la corde d'une saccade; **he gave the rope a ~** il a tiré d'un coup sec sur la corde; **a ~ of the whip** un (petit) coup de fouet.

2 vi a *[person, animal, hands]* avoir un mouvement convulsif; (*permanent condition*) avoir un tic; *[face, mouth, cheek, eyebrow, muscle]* se convulser, se contracter (convulsivement); *[dog's nose etc]* remuer, bouger.

b (*fig: be nervous*) s'agiter.

3 vt *rope etc* tirer d'un coup sec, donner un coup sec à. **he ~ed it out of her hands** il le lui a arraché des mains; **the dog ~ed its nose/its ears** le nez/les oreilles du chien a/ont remué *or* bougé.

►**twitch away** vt sep arracher d'un petit geste (*from sb* à qn).
twitchy* ['twɪtʃɪ] adj (*lit*) agité; (*fig: nervous*) nerveux.
twitter ['twɪtəʳ] 1 vi *[bird]* gazouiller, pépier; *[person]* (*chatter*) parler avec agitation (*about* de), jacasser (*pej*) (*about* sur); (*be nervous*) s'agiter (nerveusement). 2 n *[birds]* gazouillis *m*, gazouillement *m*, pépiement *m*. (*fig*) **to be in a ~ (about sth)*** être tout sens dessus dessous* (à cause de qch).
'twixt [twɪkst] prep (†† *or liter*) = **betwixt.**
two [tu:] 1 adj deux *inv*; *see* **mind** *etc.*

2 n deux *m inv*. **to cut sth in ~** couper qch en deux; **~ by ~** deux par deux, deux à deux; **in ~s** par deux; **in ~s and threes** deux ou trois à la fois, par petits groupes; **they're ~ of a kind** ils se ressemblent (tous les deux); (*fig*) **to put ~ and ~ together** faire le rapport (entre deux *or* plusieurs choses); **~'s company** on est mieux à deux; **~'s company, three's a crowd** quand il y a trois personnes, il y en a une de trop; *see* **one**; *for other phrases see* **six.**

3 pron deux *mfpl*. **there are ~** il y en a deux.

4 comp ►**two-bit*** adj (*esp US pej*) de pacotille ►**two-bits** (*US*) 25 cents *mpl* ►**two-by-four*** (*US fig*) (*small*) exigu (*f* -uë); (*unimportant*) minable ►**two-chamber system** (*Parl*) bicamérisme *m* ►**two-colour process** (*Phot*) bichromie *f* ►**two-cycle** (*US*) = **two-stroke** ►**two-cylinder** (*Aut*) à deux cylindres ►**two-door** (*Aut*) à deux portes ►**two-edged** (*lit, fig*) à double tranchant ►**two-faced** (*fig*) hypocrite ►**twofer*** (*US*) deux articles *mpl* pour le prix d'un ►**two-fisted*** (*US*) vigoureux, costaud* ►**twofold** adj double ◊ adv au double ►**two-handed** *sword* à deux mains; *saw* à deux poignées; *card game* à deux joueurs ►**two-legged** bipède ►**two-party** (*Pol*) biparti *or* bipartite ►**twopence** (*Brit*) deux pence (*see also* **tuppence**) ►**two-phase** (*Elec*) diphasé ►**two-piece: two-piece (suit)** (*man's*) costume *m* (deux-pièces); (*woman's*) tailleur *m* (deux-pièces); **two-piece (swimsuit)** deux-pièces *m inv*, bikini *m* ►**two-pin plug** *see* **pin 1b** ►**two-ply** *cord, rope* à deux brins; *wool* à deux fils; *wood* à deux épaisseurs ►**two-seater** adj à deux places ◊ n (*car*) voiture *f or* (*plane*) avion *m* à deux places ►**two-sided:** (*fig*) **this is a two-sided problem** ce problème peut être appréhendé de deux façons ►**twosome** (*people*) couple *m*; (*game*) jeu *m or* partie *f* à deux; **we went in a twosome** nous y sommes allés à deux ►**two-star (petrol)** (*Brit*) (essence *f*) ordinaire *f* ►**two-storey** à deux étages ►**two-stroke:** (*Aut*) **two-stroke (engine)** moteur *m* à deux temps, deux-temps *m inv*; **two-stroke (mixture/fuel)** mélange *m*/carburant *m* pour moteur à deux-temps ►**two-tier financing** (*Fin*) financement *m* à deux étages ►**two-time:** vt **she found out he was two-timing her*** elle a découvert qu'il sortait *or* qu'il la trompait avec une autre ◊ adj (*US*) **two-time loser**⁑ (*crook etc*) repris *m* de justice; (*divorcee*) homme *m* (*or* femme *f*) deux fois divorcé(e) ►**two-timer**⁑ (*US*) (*gen*) traître *m*; (*in marriage*) mari *m* (*or* femme *f*) infidèle ►**two-tone** (*in colour*) de deux tons; (*in sound*) à deux tons ►**two-way** (*Elec*) *switch* à deux départs; (*Aut*) *street* à double sens; *traffic* dans les deux sens; *exchange, negotiations* bilatéral; **a two-way mirror** miroir *m* sans tain; **a two-way radio** un émetteur-récepteur ►**two-wheeler** deux-roues *m inv*.

twopenny ['tʌpənɪ] 1 adj (*Brit*) à *or* de deux pence. **~ piece** pièce *f* de deux pence. 2 comp ►**twopenny-halfpenny*** (*fig*) de rien du tout*, de deux sous.
'twould†† [twʊd] = **it would;** *see* **would.**
TX (*US Post*) abbr of **Texas.**
tycoon [taɪ'ku:n] n: **(business *or* industrial) ~** gros *or* important homme d'affaires; **oil** *etc* **~** magnat *m or* roi *m* du pétrole *etc.*
tyke* [taɪk] n (*dog*) cabot *m* (*pej*); (*child*) môme *mf*.
tympana ['tɪmpənə] npl of **tympanum.**
tympani ['tɪmpənɪ] n = **timpani.**
tympanic [tɪm'pænɪk] adj: **~ membrane** tympan *m*.
tympanist ['tɪmpənɪst] n = **timpanist.**
tympanum ['tɪmpənəm] n, pl **~s** *or* **tympana** (*Anat, Archit, Zool*) tympan *m*; (*Mus*) tymbale *f*.
type [taɪp] 1 n a (*gen, Bio, Soc etc*) type *m*; (*sort*) genre *m*, espèce *f*, sorte *f*; (*make of machine, coffee etc*) marque *f*; *[aircraft, car]* modèle *m*. **books of all ~s** des livres de toutes sortes *or* de tous genres *or* de toutes espèces; **a new ~ of plane, a new ~ plane*** un nouveau modèle d'avion; **a gruyère-~ cheese** un fromage genre gruyère*; **what ~ do you want?** vous en (*or* le *or* la *etc*) voulez de quelle sorte?; **what ~ of car is it?** quel modèle de voiture est-ce?; **what ~ of man is he?** quel genre *or* type d'homme est-ce?; **what ~ of dog is he?** qu'est-ce que c'est comme (race de) chien?; **you know the ~ of thing I mean** vous voyez (à peu près) ce que je veux dire; **he's not that ~ of person** ce n'est pas son genre; **I know his ~!** je connais les gens de son genre *or* espèce; (*person*) **a queer ~*** un drôle de numéro*; **he's not my ~*** il n'est pas mon genre*; **it's my ~ of film** c'est le genre de film que j'aime *or* qui me plaît; *see* **true.**

b (*typical example*) type *m* (même), exemple *m* même. **to deviate from the ~** s'éloigner du type ancestral; **she was the very ~ of English beauty** c'était le type même *or* l'exemple même de la beauté anglaise; *see* **revert.**

c (*Ling*) (*gen*) type *m*; (*also* **word-~**) vocable *m*.

d (*Typ*) (*one letter*) caractère *m*; (*letters collectively*) caractères, type *m*. **to set ~** composer; **to set sth (up) in ~** composer qch; **in ~** composé; **to keep the ~ set up** conserver la forme; **in large/small ~** en gros/petits caractères; **in italic ~** en italiques; *see* **bold** *etc.*

2 comp ►**type-cast:** (*Theat etc*) **to be type-cast as** être enfermé dans le rôle de ►**typecasting: to avoid typecasting** éviter les stéréotypes ►**typeface** (*Typ*) œil *m* de caractère ►**typescript** (*NonC*) manuscrit *or* texte dactylographié, tapuscrit *m* ►**typeset** composer ►**typesetter** (*person*) compositeur *m*, -trice *f*; (*machine*) linotype *f* ►**typesetting** (*NonC*) composition *f* ►**typewrite** taper (à la machine) ►**typewriter** machine *f* à écrire (*see also* **memory**) ►**typewriting** dactylographie *f* ►**typewritten** tapé (à la machine), dactylographié.

3 vt a *blood sample etc* classifier. (*Theat etc*) **he is now ~d as the kindly old man** on ne lui donne plus que les rôles de doux vieillard; (*Theat*) **I don't want to be ~d** je ne veux pas me cantonner dans un (seul) rôle.

b *letter etc* taper (à la machine).

4 vi *[typist etc]* taper à la machine. **"clerk: must be able to ~"** "employé(e) de bureau sachant la dactylo".

►**type out** vt sep a *notes, letter* taper (à la machine). b *error* effacer (à la machine).
►**type over** vt sep = **type out b.**
►**type up** vt sep *notes* taper (à la machine).
typhoid ['taɪfɔɪd] 1 n (*also* **~ fever**) (fièvre *f*) typhoïde *f*. 2 comp *symptom, victim* de la typhoïde; *inoculation* anti-typhoïdique ►**Typhoid Mary*** (*US fig*) source *f* d'infection.
typhoon [taɪ'fu:n] n typhon *m*.
typhus ['taɪfəs] n typhus *m*.
typical ['tɪpɪkəl] adj *behaviour, speech* typique, caractéristique (*of* de); *case, example* typique, type *inv*. **~ of** typique de; **it was a ~ day in spring** c'était un jour de printemps comme il y en a tant; **the ~ Frenchman** le Français type *or* typique; **he's a ~ teacher** c'est le type même du professeur; **with ~ modesty he said** ... avec sa modestie habituelle il a dit ...; **this is ~ rudeness on his part** c'est une grossièreté qui est bien de lui; **that's ~ of him!** c'est bien *or* tout à fait (de) lui!; (*iro*) **~!** étonnant! (*iro*), ça ne m'étonne pas!, le coup classique!
typically ['tɪpɪkəlɪ] adv typiquement. **he is ~ English** il est typiquement anglais, c'est l'Anglais type *or* typique; **it's ~ French to do that** c'est très *or* bien français de faire ça; **it was ~ wet that day** il pleuvait beaucoup ce jour-là, comme d'habitude; **he was ~ rude to us** il s'est conduit envers nous avec sa grossièreté habituelle.
typify ['tɪpɪfaɪ] vt *[behaviour, incident, object]* être caractéristique de; *[person]* avoir le type même de.
typing ['taɪpɪŋ] 1 n (*NonC*) a (*skill*) dactylo *f*, dactylographie *f*. **to learn ~** apprendre à taper (à la machine), apprendre la dactylo *or* la dactylographie. b **there were several pages of ~ to read** il y avait plusieurs pages dactylographiées à lire. 2 comp *lesson, teacher* de dactylo, de dactylographie ►**typing error** faute *f* de frappe ►**typing paper** papier *m* machine ►**typing pool** bureau *m or* pool *m* des dactylos, dactylo* *f*; **she works in the typing pool** elle est à la dactylo*; **to send sth to the typing pool** envoyer qch à la dactylo* ►**typing**

speed: her typing speed is 60 elle tape 60 mots à la minute.
typist ['taɪpɪst] **n** dactylo *mf*, dactylographe *mf*; *see* **shorthand**.
typo ['taɪpəʊ] **n** (*US: error*) coquille *f* (typographique).
typographer [taɪ'pɒgrəfəʳ] **n** typographe *mf*.
typographic(al) [ˌtaɪpə'græfɪk(əl)] **adj** typographique.
typography [taɪ'pɒgrəfɪ] **n** typographie *f*.
typological [ˌtaɪpə'lɒdʒɪkəl] **adj** typologique.
typology [taɪ'pɒlədʒɪ] **n** typologie *f*.
tyrannic(al) [tɪ'rænɪk(əl)] **adj** tyrannique.
tyrannically [tɪ'rænɪkəlɪ] **adv** tyranniquement.
tyrannicide [tɪ'rænɪsaɪd] **n** (*act*) tyrannicide *m*; (*person*) tyrannicide *mf*.
tyrannize ['tɪrənaɪz] 1 **vi: to ~ over sb** tyranniser qn. 2 **vt** tyranniser.
tyrannous ['tɪrənəs] **adj** tyrannique.
tyrannously ['tɪrənəslɪ] **adv** tyranniquement.
tyranny ['tɪrənɪ] **n** tyrannie *f*.
tyrant ['taɪrənt] **n** tyran *m*.
Tyre [taɪəʳ] **n** (*Geog*) Tyr.
tyre ['taɪəʳ] 1 **n** pneu *m*; *see* **spare** *etc.* 2 **comp** ►**tyre gauge** manomètre *m* (pour pneus) ►**tyre lever** démonte-pneu *m* ►**tyremaker** fabricant *m* de pneus, pneumaticien *m* ►**tyre pressure** pression *f* des pneus ►**tyre valve** valve *f* (de gonflage).
tyro ['taɪrəʊ] **n** novice *mf*, débutant(e) *m(f)*.
Tyrol [tɪ'rəʊl] **n** Tyrol *m*.
Tyrolean [ˌtɪrə'li(:)ən] 1 **adj** tyrolien. (*Climbing*) ~ **traverse** tyrolienne *f*. 2 **n** Tyrolien(ne) *m(f)*.
Tyrolese [ˌtɪrə'li:z] = **Tyrolean.**
Tyrrhenian [tɪ'ri:nɪən] **adj: ~Sea** mer *f* Tyrrhénienne.
tzar [zɑ:ʳ] **n** = **tsar.**
tzarina [zɑ:'ri:nə] **n** = **tsarina.**
tzarist ['zɑ:rɪst] **n, adj** = **tsarist.**
tzetze fly ['tsetsɪflaɪ] **n** = **tsetse fly.**

U

U, u [ju:] 1 n a (*letter*) U, u *m*. **U for Uncle** ≃ U comme Ursule. b (*Brit Cine*) (**abbr of Universal**) ≃ tous publics. **it's a U film** c'est un film pour tous publics. 2 **comp** ▸**U-bend** (*in pipe*) coude *m*; (*Brit: in road*) coude, virage *m* en épingle à cheveux ▸**U-boat** sous-marin allemand ▸**U-shaped** en (forme de) U ▸**U-turn** (*Aut*) demi-tour *m*; (*fig*) revirement *m*, volte-face *f* (*on* au sujet de); (*Aut*) **"no U-turns"** "défense de faire demi-tour"; (*fig*) **to make a U-turn on sth** faire volte-face au sujet de qch. 3 **adj** (*Brit* *†: *upper-class*) *word, accent, behaviour* distingué. **non-U*** commun; **it's not very U* to do that** cela manque de distinction que de faire ça.

UAE [ju:eɪ'i:] n (**abbr of United Arab Emirates**) *see* **united 2**.

UB40 [ˌju:bi:'fɔ:tɪ] n (*Brit*) (**abbr of Unemployment Benefit 40**) *carte de demandeur d'emploi*. (*: *unemployed people*) ~**s** chômeurs *mpl*, demandeurs *mpl* d'emploi.

ubiquitous [ju:'bɪkwɪtəs] **adj** doué d'ubiquité, omniprésent.

ubiquity [ju:'bɪkwɪtɪ] **n** ubiquité *f*, omniprésence *f*.

UCCA ['ʌkə] n (*Brit*) (**abbr of Universities Central Council for Admissions**) *service central des inscriptions universitaires*. ~ **form** ≃ dossier *m* d'inscription universitaire.

U.D.A. [ju:di:'eɪ] n (*Brit*) (**abbr of Ulster Defence Association**) *see* **Ulster**.

U.D.C. [ju:di:'si:] n (*Brit Local Govt*) (**abbr of Urban District Council**) *see* **urban**.

udder ['ʌdəʳ] **n** pis *m*, mamelle *f*.

UDI [ju:di:'aɪ] n (*Brit Pol*) (**abbr of unilateral declaration of independence**) *see* **unilateral**.

U.D.R. [ju:di:'ɑ:ʳ] n (*Brit*) (**abbr of Ulster Defence Regiment**) *see* **Ulster**.

UEFA [jʊ'eɪfə] n (*Ftbl*) (**abbr of Union of European Football Associations**) U.E.F.A. *f*.

UFO [ˌju:e'fəʊ, 'ju:fəʊ] n (**abbr of unidentified flying object**) OVNI *m*.

Uganda [ju:'gændə] **n** Ouganda *m*.

Ugandan [ju:'gændən] 1 **adj** ougandais. 2 **n** Ougandais(e) *m(f)*.

UGC [ju:dʒi:'si:] n (*Brit Educ*) (**abbr of University Grants Committee**) *see* **university**.

ugh [ɜ:h] **excl** pouah!

ugli ['ʌglɪ] **n, pl** ~**s** *or* ~**es** tangelo *m*.

uglify ['ʌglɪfaɪ] **vt** enlaidir, rendre laid.

ugliness ['ʌglɪnɪs] n (*NonC*) laideur *f*.

ugly ['ʌglɪ] **adj** *person, appearance* laid, vilain; *custom, vice etc* particulièrement déplaisant, répugnant; *war* qui n'est pas beau à voir, (*stronger*) horrible; *expression* menaçant; *situation* très inquiétant; *wound* vilain (*before n*). **as ~ as sin** laid comme un pou *or* un singe; **an ~ rumour** de vilains bruits; **it is an ~ sight** ce n'est pas beau à voir; **there was an ~ incident** *or* **scene** il y a eu un sale incident; **"blackmail" is an ~ word** "chantage" est un bien vilain mot; ~ **customer*** sale individu *m*, sale type* *m*; (*fig*) ~ **duckling** vilain petit canard; **he gave me an ~ look** il m'a regardé d'un sale œil; (*fig*) *[person]* **to grow** *or* **turn ~, to cut up ~*** se faire menaçant, montrer les dents; **the whole business is taking an ~ turn** l'affaire prend une sale tournure; *see* **mood**.

UHF [ju:eɪ'tʃef] n (**abbr of ultra high frequency**) UHF *f*.

uh-huh ['ʌˌhʌ] **excl** oui oui.

UHT [ju:eɪ'tʃti:] **adj** (**abbr of ultra heat treated**) *milk etc* U.H.T. *inv*, longue-conservation *inv*.

uh-uh ['ʌˌʌ] **excl** (*warning*) hé!

U.K. [ju:'keɪ] n (**abbr of United Kingdom**) Royaume-Uni *m*.

uke* [ju:k] **n abbr of ukulele**.

Ukraine [ju:'kreɪn] **n: the ~** l'Ukraine *f*.

Ukrainian [ju:'kreɪnɪən] 1 **adj** ukrainien. ~ **S.S.R.** R.S.S. *f* d'Ukraine. 2 n (*person*) Ukrainien(ne) *m(f)*; (*Ling*) ukrainien *m*.

ukulele [ˌju:kə'leɪlɪ] **n** guitare hawaïenne.

ULC [ju:el'si:] n (*US*) (**abbr of ultra-large carrier**) superpétrolier *m*.

ulcer ['ʌlsəʳ] n (*Med*) ulcère *m*; (*fig*) plaie *f*.

ulcerate ['ʌlsəreɪt] 1 **vt** ulcérer. ~**d** ulcéreux. 2 **vi** s'ulcérer.

ulceration [ˌʌlsə'reɪʃən] **n** ulcération *f*.

ulcerative ['ʌlsəˌreɪtɪv] **adj** ulcératif.

ulcerous ['ʌlsərəs] **adj** (*having ulcers*) ulcéreux; (*causing ulcers*) ulcératif.

ullage ['ʌlɪdz] n (*Customs*) manquant *m*.

ulna ['ʌlnə] **n, pl** ~**s** *or* **ulnae** ['ʌlni:] cubitus *m*.

Ulster ['ʌlstəʳ] 1 n a (province *f* de l')Ulster *m*. b (*coat*) **u~** ulster *m*. 2 **comp** de l'Ulster ▸**Ulster Defence Association** *organisation paramilitaire protestante* ▸**Ulster Defence Regiment** *section de l'armée britannique en Irlande du Nord* ▸**Ulsterman** habitant *m or* natif *m* de l'Ulster ▸**Ulster Volunteer Force** *armée volontaire en Irlande du Nord* ▸**Ulsterwoman** habitante *f or* native *f* de l'Ulster.

ulterior [ʌl'tɪərɪəʳ] **adj** ultérieur (*f* -eure). ~ **motive** motif secret, arrière-pensée *f*.

ultimata [ˌʌltɪ'meɪtə] **npl of ultimatum**.

ultimate ['ʌltɪmɪt] 1 **adj** a (*final*) *aim, destiny, solution* final; *decision, result, outcome* final, définitif; *victory, defeat* final, ultime; *control, authority* suprême. (*Mil, fig*) **the ~ deterrent** l'ultime moyen *m* de dissuasion; (*Mil, fig*) **the ~ weapon** l'arme *f* suprême; **the ~ beneficiary/loser is ...** en fin de compte, le bénéficiaire/le perdant est ...; **he came to the ~ conclusion that ...** il a finalement conclu que ...; **what is your ~ ambition in life?** quelle est votre suprême ambition dans la vie?; **they had no ~ hope of escape** en fin de compte ils n'avaient aucun espoir de s'évader; **death is the ~ sacrifice** la mort est le sacrifice suprême *or* l'ultime sacrifice.

b (*best, most effective*) suprême. **we have produced the ~ sports car** nous avons fabriqué ce qu'il y a de mieux comme voiture de sport; **the ~ insult** l'insulte *f* suprême; **the ~ (in) luxury/generosity** le summum du luxe/de la générosité; **the ~ (in) selfishness/bad manners** le comble de l'égoïsme/de l'impolitesse.

c (*basic*) *principle, cause, truth* fondamental, premier. (*Gram*) ~ **constituent** constituant *m* ultime.

d (*furthest*) (*gen*) le plus éloigné, le plus distant; *boundary of universe* le plus reculé; *ancestor* le plus éloigné. **the ~ origins of man** les origines premières de l'homme; **the ~ frontiers of knowledge** les confins *mpl* du savoir.

2 **n: it's the ~ in comfort** c'est le fin du fin dans le domaine du confort, c'est le nec-plus-ultra du confort (*see also* **1b**).

ultimately ['ʌltɪmɪtlɪ] **adv** (*in the end, at last*) finalement, à la fin; (*eventually*) par la suite; (*fundamentally*) en fin de compte, en définitive, en dernière analyse. **he did ~ arrive** il a fini par arriver, il est finalement arrivé; **we will ~ build a block of flats here** nous envisageons de construire un immeuble ici par la suite; **it may ~ be possible** ce n'est pas impossible à une date ultérieure; **it ~ depends on you** en définitive *or* en dernière analyse *or* en fin de compte cela dépend de vous; ~, **we are all descended from Adam and Eve** en dernière analyse, nous descendons tous d'Adam et d'Ève.

ultimatum [ˌʌltɪ'meɪtəm] **n, pl** ~**s** *or* **ultimata** ultimatum *m*. **to give/deliver** *or* **issue an ~** donner/adresser un ultimatum (*to* à).

ultimo ['ʌltɪməʊ] **adv** (*Comm*) du mois dernier. **the 25th ~** le 25 du mois dernier.

ultra... ['ʌltrə] **pref** ultra..., hyper..., *e.g.* ~**fashionable** du tout dernier cri, très à la mode; ~**sensitive** ultra-sensible, hypersensible; ~**rich** richissime.

ultrahigh ['ʌltrə'haɪ] **adj:** ~ **frequency** très haute fréquence.

ultralarge ['ʌltrə'lɑ:dʒ] **adj** extra-grand. (*US: Aut: tanker*) ~ **carrier** superpétrolier *m*.

ultralight ['ʌltrə'laɪt] 1 **adj** ultra-léger. 2 n (*Aviat*) U.L.M. *m*, ultra-léger-motorisé *m*.

ultramarine [ˌʌltrəmə'ri:n] **adj, n** (bleu) outremer (*m*) *inv*.

ultramodern ['ʌltrə'mɒdən] **adj** ultramoderne.

ultramontane [ˌʌltrə'mɒnteɪn] **adj, n** ultramontain(e) *m(f)*.

ultramontanism [ˌʌltrə'mɒntɪnɪzəm] **n** ultramontanisme *m*.

ultrashort ['ʌltrə'ʃɔ:t] **adj** ultra-court.

ultrasonic [ˌʌltrə'sɒnɪk] 1 **adj** ultrasonique. 2 n (*NonC*) ~**s** science *f* des ultrasons.

ultrasound ['ʌltrəsaʊnd] **n** ultrasons *mpl*; (*also* ~ **scan** *or* **picture**) échographie *f*. ~ **scanner** générateur *m* d'ondes ultrasonores.

ultraviolet [ˌʌltrə'vaɪəlɪt] **adj** ultra-violet. (*Med*) **to have ~ treatment** se faire traiter aux rayons ultra-violets; ~ **radiation** rayons *mpl* ultra-violets.

ultra vires [ˌʌltrə'vaɪəri:z] **adv, adj** (*Jur*) au-delà des pouvoirs.

ululate ['ju:ljʊleɪt] **vi** *[owl]* (h)ululer; *[dog]* hurler.

ululation [ˌju:ljʊ'leɪʃən] **n** (*see* **ululate**) (h)ululement *m*; hurlement *m*.

Ulysses [ju:'lɪsi:z] **n** Ulysse *m*.

um [ʌm] **1 interj** euh. **2 vi: to ~ and err*** se tâter*, hésiter; **after a lot of ~ming and erring* he decided to buy it** après beaucoup d'hésitations il se décida à l'acheter.

umber ['ʌmbəʳ] **adj, n** (terre *f* d')ombre *(f)*, terre *(f)* de Sienne; *see* **burnt**.

umbilical [ˌʌmbɪ'laɪkəl] **adj** ombilical. ~ **cord** cordon ombilical.

umbilicus [ˌʌmbɪ'laɪkəs] **n, pl umbilici** [ˌʌmbə'laɪsaɪ] ombilic *m*, nombril *m*.

umbrage ['ʌmbrɪdʒ] **n** (*NonC*) ombrage *m* (*fig*), ressentiment *m*. **to take ~** prendre ombrage, se froisser (*at* de).

umbrella [ʌm'brelə] **1 n a** (*gen*) parapluie *m*; (*against sun*) parasol *m*. **to put up/put down an ~** ouvrir/fermer un parapluie; **beach ~** parasol; (*Mil*) **air ~** écran *m* de protection aérienne; (*fig*) **under the ~ of** sous les auspices *or* l'égide de. **b** *[jellyfish]* ombrelle *f*. **2 comp ▸umbrella pine** pin *m* parasol **▸umbrella stand** porte-parapluies *m inv*. **3 adj: ~ body** *or* **organization** organisme *m* qui en chapeaute plusieurs autres; **an ~ project** un projet-cadre; **an ~ term** un terme général.

Umbria ['ʌmbrɪə] **n** Ombrie *f*.

Umbrian ['ʌmbrɪən] **1 adj** ombrien. **2 n** Ombrien(ne) *m(f)*.

umlaut ['ʊmlaʊt] **n** (*vowel change: NonC*) inflexion *f* vocalique; (*diaeresis*) tréma *m*.

umpire ['ʌmpaɪəʳ] **1 n** arbitre *m*. **2 vt** arbitrer. **3 vi** servir d'arbitre, être l'arbitre.

umpteen* ['ʌmpti:n] **adj** beaucoup de, je ne sais combien de. **I've told you ~ times** je te l'ai dit maintes et maintes fois *or* je ne sais combien de fois *or* trente-six fois *or* cent fois; **he had ~ books** il avait je ne sais combien de livres *or* des quantités de livres.

umpteenth* ['ʌmpti:nθ] **adj** (é)nième.

UN [ju:'en] **n** (**abbr of United Nations**) O.N.U. *f*.

'un [ən] **pron** (**abbr of one**) **he's a good ~** c'est un brave type*; **little ~** petiot(e) *m(f)*.

un... [ʌn] **pref** dé..., dés..., dis..., in..., mal... .

unabashed ['ʌnə'bæʃt] **adj** nullement décontenancé *or* intimidé. **"yes" he said ~** "oui" dit-il sans se décontenancer *or* sans perdre contenance *or* sans se laisser intimider.

unabated ['ʌnə'beɪtɪd] **adj: to remain** *or* **continue ~** (*gen*) rester inchangé; **the fighting continued ~ well into the next day** les combats ont continué le lendemain sans perdre de leur intensité; **with ~ interest** avec toujours autant d'intérêt; **his ~ enthusiasm for the scheme** l'enthousiasme qu'il continuait à exprimer pour le projet.

unabbreviated ['ʌnə'bri:vɪeɪtɪd] **adj** non abrégé, sans abréviation.

unable ['ʌn'eɪbl] **adj: to be ~ to do** (*gen*) ne (pas) pouvoir faire; (*not know how to*) ne pas savoir faire; (*be incapable of*) être incapable de faire; (*be prevented from*) être dans l'impossibilité de faire, ne pas être en mesure de faire.

unabridged ['ʌnə'brɪdʒd] **adj** intégral, non abrégé. **~ edition/version** édition/version intégrale.

unaccented ['ʌnæk'sentɪd] **adj, unaccentuated** ['ʌnæk'sentjʊeɪtɪd] **adj** *voice, speech* sans accent; *syllable* inaccentué, non accentué, atone.

unacceptable ['ʌnək'septəbl] **adj** *offer, suggestion* inacceptable; *amount, degree, extent, level* inadmissible. **it's quite ~ that we should have to do this** il est inadmissible que nous ayons à le faire; **the ~ face of capitalism** la face honteuse du capitalisme.

unacceptably ['ʌnək'septəblɪ] **adv** *dangerous, risky etc* à un point inacceptable *or* inadmissible. **he suggested, quite ~, doing it later** il a suggéré de le faire plus tard, ce qui était bien entendu inacceptable *or* inadmissible.

unaccommodating ['ʌnə'kɒmədeɪtɪŋ] **adj** (*disobliging*) désobligeant; (*not easy to deal with*) peu accommodant.

unaccompanied ['ʌnə'kʌmpənɪd] **adj** *person, child, luggage* non accompagné; (*Mus*) *singing* sans accompagnement, a cappella; *instrument* seul.

unaccomplished [ˌʌnə'kʌmplɪʃt] **adj a** (*unfinished*) *work, task, journey* inaccompli, inachevé; *project, desire* inaccompli, non réalisé. **b** (*untalented*) *person* sans talents; *performance* médiocre.

unaccountable ['ʌnə'kaʊntəbl] **adj** inexplicable.

unaccountably ['ʌnə'kaʊntəblɪ] **adv** inexplicablement.

unaccounted ['ʌnə'kaʊntɪd] **adj: 2 passengers are still ~ for** 2 passagers n'ont toujours pas été retrouvés; **£5 is still ~ for** il manque encore 5 livres; **this is ~ for in the report** ceci n'est pas expliqué dans le rapport.

unaccustomed ['ʌnə'kʌstəmd] **adj** *slowness, charm* inaccoutumé, inhabituel. **to be ~ to (doing) sth** ne pas avoir l'habitude de (faire) qch; (*hum*) **~ as I am to public speaking** ... n'ayant pas l'habitude de prendre la parole en public ... .

unacknowledged ['ʌnək'nɒlɪdʒd] **adj** *letter* resté sans réponse, dont on n'a pas accusé réception; *mistake, help, services* non reconnu (publiquement); *child* non reconnu.

unacquainted ['ʌnə'kweɪntɪd] **adj: to be ~ with the facts** ignorer les faits, ne pas être au courant des faits; **she is ~ with poverty** elle ne sait pas ce que c'est que la pauvreté, elle ne connaît pas la pauvreté; **to be ~ with sb** ne pas avoir fait la connaissance de qn; **they are ~** ils ne se connaissent pas.

unadaptable ['ʌnə'dæptəbl] **adj** inadaptable, peu adaptable.

unadapted ['ʌnə'dæptɪd] **adj** mal adapté, inadapté (*to* à).

unaddressed ['ʌnə'drest] **adj** sans adresse, qui ne porte pas d'adresse.

unadjusted [ˌʌnə'dʒʌstɪd] **adj** non corrigé. **seasonally ~ employment figures** statistiques *fpl* du chômage non corrigées des variations saisonnières.

unadopted ['ʌnə'dɒptɪd] **adj a** *child* qui n'est pas adopté. **many children remain ~** beaucoup d'enfants ne trouvent pas de parents adoptifs. **b** (*Brit*) **~ road** route non prise en charge par la commune.

unadorned ['ʌnə'dɔ:nd] **adj** sans ornement, tout simple; (*fig*) *truth* pur, tout nu. **beauty ~** la beauté toute simple *or* sans artifice *or* sans fard.

unadulterated ['ʌnə'dʌltəreɪtɪd] **adj** pur, naturel; *wine* non frelaté; (*fig*) *bliss, nonsense* pur (et simple).

unadventurous ['ʌnəd'ventʃərəs] **adj** *person, career, design, theatre production* conventionnel, qui manque d'audace. **where food is concerned, he is very ~** pour ce qui est de la nourriture, il n'aime pas essayer quelque chose de nouveau.

unadventurously ['ʌnəd'ventʃərəslɪ] **adv** *dressed, decorated* de façon conventionnelle; *choose, decide* par manque d'audace *or* d'imagination.

unadvertised ['ʌn'ædvətaɪzd] **adj** *meeting, visit* sans publicité, discret (*f* -ète).

unadvised ['ʌnəd'vaɪzd] **adj** *person* qui n'a pas reçu de conseils; (*ill-advised*) *person* malavisé, imprudent; *measures* inconsidéré, imprudent.

unaesthetic [ˌʌni:s'θetɪk] **adj** inesthétique, peu esthétique.

unaffected ['ʌnə'fektɪd] **adj a** (*sincere*) *person* naturel, simple; *behaviour* non affecté; *style* sans recherche, simple. **b** non affecté. **~ by damp/cold** non affecté par l'humidité/le froid, qui résiste à l'humidité/au froid; **~ by heat** inaltérable à la chaleur; **our plans were ~ by the strike** nos plans sont restés inchangés malgré la grève; **they are ~ by the new legislation** ils ne sont pas affectés *or* touchés par la nouvelle législation. **c he was quite ~ by her sufferings** ses souffrances ne l'ont pas touché *or* l'ont laissé froid; **he remained ~ by all the noise** il était indifférent à tout ce bruit.

unaffectedly ['ʌnə'fektɪdlɪ] **adv** *behave* sans affectation; *dress* simplement. **she was ~ pleased** elle était sincèrement contente.

unaffiliated ['ʌnə'fɪlɪeɪtɪd] **adj** non affilié (*to* à).

unafraid ['ʌnə'freɪd] **adj** sans peur, qui n'a pas peur. **to be ~ of (doing) sth** ne pas avoir peur de (faire) qch.

unaided ['ʌn'eɪdɪd] **adj: his ~ work** le travail qu'il a fait (*or* avait fait *etc*) tout seul *or* sans être aidé; **he did it ~** il l'a fait tout seul *or* sans être aidé; **by his own ~ efforts** par ses propres efforts *or* moyens.

unaired [ˌʌn'ɛəd] **adj** non aéré.

unalike ['ʌnə'laɪk] **adj** peu ressemblant. **the two children are so ~** les deux enfants se ressemblent si peu.

unalloyed ['ʌnə'lɔɪd] **adj** *happiness* sans mélange, parfait; *metal* non allié.

unalterable [ʌn'ɒltərəbl] **adj** *rule* invariable, immuable; *fact* certain; *emotion, friendship* inaltérable.

unalterably [ʌn'ɒltərəblɪ] **adv** invariablement, immuablement.

unaltered ['ʌn'ɒltəd] **adj** inchangé, non modifié, tel quel. **his appearance was ~** physiquement il n'avait pas changé *or* il était toujours le même.

unambiguous ['ʌnæm'bɪgjʊəs] **adj** *wording* non ambigu (*f* -guë), non équivoque, clair; *order, thought* clair.

unambiguously ['ʌnæm'bɪgjʊəslɪ] **adv** sans ambiguïté, sans équivoque.

unambitious ['ʌnæm'bɪʃəs] **adj** *person* sans ambition, peu ambitieux; *plan* modeste.

un-American ['ʌnə'merɪkən] **adj** (*anti-American*) antiaméricain; (*not typical*) peu *or* pas américain.

unamiable ['ʌn'eɪmɪəbl] **adj** désagréable, peu aimable.

unamused ['ʌnə'mju:zd] **adj** qui n'est pas amusé. **the story left her ~** l'histoire ne l'a pas amusée du tout, elle n'a pas trouvé l'histoire amusante du tout.

unanimity [ˌju:nə'nɪmɪtɪ] **n** (*NonC*) unanimité *f*.

unanimous [ju:'nænɪməs] **adj** *group, decision* unanime. **the committee was ~ in its condemnation of this** *or* **in condemning this** les membres du comité ont été unanimes pour *or* à condamner cela, les membres du comité ont condamné cela à l'unanimité; **it was accepted by a ~ vote** cela a été voté à l'unanimité.

unanimously [ju:'nænɪməslɪ] **adv** *agree, condemn* à l'unanimité, unanimement; *vote* à l'unanimité.

unannounced ['ʌnə'naʊnst] **1 adj** *guest, call etc* imprévu. **2 adv**

arrive, enter etc sans se faire annoncer; (*in less formal situations*) sans prévenir.
unanswerable [ʌn'ɑːnsərəbl] **adj** *question* à laquelle il est impossible de répondre; *argument* irréfutable, incontestable.
unanswered ['ʌn'ɑːnsəd] **adj** *letter, request, question* (qui reste) sans réponse; *problem, puzzle* non résolu; *criticism, argument* non réfuté; *prayer* inexaucé; (*Jur*) *charge* irréfuté. **her letter remained ~** sa lettre est restée sans réponse; **there was a pile of ~ letters on his desk** sur son bureau, il y avait une pile de lettres en attente *or* une pile de lettres auxquelles il n'avait pas (encore) répondu.
unappealing ['ʌnə'piːlɪŋ] **adj** peu attirant, peu attrayant.
unappetizing ['ʌn'æpɪtaɪzɪŋ] **adj** (*lit, fig*) peu appétissant.
unappreciated ['ʌnə'priːʃɪeɪtɪd] **adj** *person* méconnu, incompris; *offer, help* non apprécié.
unappreciative ['ʌnə'priːʃɪətɪv] **adj** *audience* froid, indifférent. **to be ~ of sth** ne pas apprécier qch, rester indifférent à qch.
unapproachable ['ʌnə'prəʊtʃəbl] **adj** d'un abord difficile, inabordable.
unapt ['ʌn'æpt] **adj** (*inappropriate*) inapproprié.
unarguable ['ʌn'ɑːgjʊəbl] **adj** incontestable.
unarguably ['ʌn'ɑːgjʊəblɪ] **adv** incontestablement.
unarmed ['ʌn'ɑːmd] **1 adj** *person* non armé; *combat* sans armes. **he is ~** il n'est pas armé. **2 adv** sans armes.
unashamed ['ʌnə'ʃeɪmd] **adj** *pleasure, greed* effronté, impudent. **he was quite ~ about it** il n'en avait absolument pas honte; **he was an ~ believer in magic** il croyait à la magie et ne s'en cachait pas.
unashamedly ['ʌnə'ʃeɪmɪdlɪ] **adv** *say, suggest* sans honte, sans vergogne. **he was ~ delighted about it** il ne cherchait nullement à déguiser la joie que cela lui procurait; **he was ~ selfish** il était d'un égoïsme éhonté, il était égoïste sans vergogne; **he was ~ a liar** c'était un menteur éhonté *or* effronté, il mentait sans vergogne *or* effrontément.
unasked ['ʌn'ɑːskt] **1 adj**: **this was ~ for** on ne l'avait pas demandé; **~ question** question *f* implicite *or* non formulée. **2 adv**: **she did it ~** elle l'a fait sans qu'on le lui ait demandé *or* de son propre chef; **he came in ~** il est entré sans y avoir été invité.
unaspirated ['ʌn'æspəreɪtɪd] **adj** (*Phon*) non aspiré.
unassailable [ˌʌnə'seɪləbl] **adj** *fortress* imprenable; *position, reputation* inattaquable; *argument, reason* irréfutable, inattaquable. **he is quite ~ on that point** ses arguments sont irréfutables sur ce point, on ne peut pas l'attaquer sur ce point.
unassisted ['ʌnə'sɪstɪd] **1 adv** tout seul, sans être aidé. **2 adj** tout seul.
unassuming ['ʌnə'sjuːmɪŋ] **adj** sans prétentions, modeste.
unassumingly ['ʌnə'sjuːmɪŋlɪ] **adv** modestement, sans prétentions.
unattached ['ʌnə'tætʃt] **adj** *part etc* non attaché (*to* a), libre (*to* de); (*fig*) *person, group* indépendant (*to* de); (*not married etc*) libre, sans attaches; (*Jur*) non saisi.
unattainable ['ʌnə'teɪnəbl] **adj** *place, objective, person* inaccessible.
unattended ['ʌnə'tendɪd] **adj a** (*not looked after*) *shop, machine* (laissé) sans surveillance; *luggage* laissé sans surveillance, abandonné; *child* sans surveillance, (tout) seul. **do not leave your luggage ~** surveillez toujours vos bagages; **~ to** négligé. **b** (*unaccompanied*) *king etc* seul, sans escorte.
unattractive ['ʌnə'træktɪv] **adj** *appearance, house, idea* peu attrayant, peu séduisant; *person, character* déplaisant, peu sympathique.
unattractiveness ['ʌnə'træktɪvnɪs] **n** (*NonC*) manque *m* d'attrait *or* de beauté.
unauthenticated ['ʌnɔː'θentɪkeɪtɪd] **adj** *evidence* non établi; *signature* non authentifié.
unauthorized ['ʌn'ɔːθəraɪzd] **adj** (*gen*) *action* non autorisé, (fait) sans autorisation. **this was ~** cela a été fait sans autorisation; **~ absence** absence *f* irrégulière; (*Jur*) **~ signature** signature *f* usurpatoire.
unavailable ['ʌnə'veɪləbl] **adj** *funds* indisponible; (*Comm*) *article* épuisé, qu'on ne peut se procurer; *person* indisponible, qui n'est pas disponible *or* libre.
unavailing ['ʌnə'veɪlɪŋ] **adj** *effort* vain, inutile; *remedy, method* inefficace.
unavailingly ['ʌnə'veɪlɪŋlɪ] **adv** en vain, sans succès.
unavoidable [ˌʌnə'vɔɪdəbl] **adj** inévitable. **it is ~ that** il est inévitable que + *subj*.
unavoidably [ˌʌnə'vɔɪdəblɪ] **adv** inévitablement. **he was ~ delayed** il a été retardé pour des raisons indépendantes de sa volonté, il a été malencontreusement retardé.
unaware ['ʌnə'wɛəʳ] **adj**: **to be ~ of sth** ignorer qch, ne pas être conscient de qch, ne pas avoir conscience de qch; **to be ~ that** ignorer que, ne pas savoir que; **"stop" he said, ~ of the danger** "arrête" dit-il, ignorant *or* inconscient du danger; **I was not ~ that** je n'étais pas sans savoir que; **he is politically quite ~** il n'a aucune conscience politique, il n'est pas politisé; **he is socially quite ~** il n'est pas sensibilisé aux problèmes sociaux.
unawareness [ˌʌnə'wɛənɪs] **n** ignorance *f*.
unawares ['ʌnə'wɛəz] **adv a** (*by surprise*) à l'improviste, au dépourvu. **to catch *or* take sb ~** prendre qn à l'improviste *or* au dépourvu. **b** (*not realizing*) inconsciemment, par mégarde.
unbacked ['ʌn'bækt] **adj** (*Fin*) à découvert.
unbalance ['ʌn'bæləns] **1 vt** déséquilibrer. **2 n** déséquilibre *m*.
unbalanced ['ʌn'bælənst] **adj a** mal équilibré; (*mentally*) déséquilibré. **his mind was ~** il était déséquilibré. **b** (*Fin*) *account* non soldé.
unbandage ['ʌn'bændɪdʒ] **vt** *limb, wound* débander; *person* ôter ses bandages *or* ses pansements à.
unbaptized ['ʌnbæp'taɪzd] **adj** non baptisé.
unbar ['ʌn'bɑːʳ] **vt** *door* débarrer, enlever la barre de.
unbearable [ʌn'bɛərəbl] **adj** insupportable.
unbearably [ʌn'bɛərəblɪ] **adv** insupportablement. **~ selfish** d'un égoïsme insupportable, insupportablement égoïste; **it's ~ hot/cold today** aujourd'hui il fait une chaleur/un froid insupportable.
unbeatable ['ʌn'biːtəbl] **adj** imbattable.
unbeaten ['ʌn'biːtn] **adj** *army, player, team* invaincu; *record, price* non battu.
unbecoming ['ʌnbɪ'kʌmɪŋ] **adj** *garment* peu seyant, qui ne va *or* ne sied pas; (*fig*) *behaviour* malséant, inconvenant.
unbeknown(st) ['ʌnbɪ'nəʊn(st)] **adj, adv**: **~ to** à l'insu de.
unbelief ['ʌnbɪ'liːf] **n** (*also Rel*) incrédulité *f*. **in ~, with an air of ~** d'un air incrédule.
unbelievable [ˌʌnbɪ'liːvəbl] **adj** incroyable. **it is ~ that** il est incroyable que + *subj*.
unbelievably [ˌʌnbɪ'liːvəblɪ] **adv** incroyablement. **~ selfish** d'un égoïsme incroyable; **~, he refused** aussi incroyable que cela puisse paraître, il a refusé.
unbeliever ['ʌnbɪ'liːvəʳ] **n** (*also Rel*) incrédule *mf*.
unbelieving ['ʌnbɪ'liːvɪŋ] **adj** (*also Rel*) incrédule.
unbelievingly ['ʌnbɪ'liːvɪŋlɪ] **adv** d'un air incrédule.
unbend ['ʌn'bend] **pret, ptp unbent 1 vt** *pipe, wire* redresser, détordre. **2 vi** *[person]* se détendre. **he unbent enough to ask me how I was** il a daigné me demander comment j'allais.
unbending [ʌn'bendɪŋ] **adj** non flexible, rigide; (*fig*) *person, attitude* inflexible, intransigeant.
unbias(s)ed [ʌn'baɪəst] **adj** impartial.
unbidden [ʌn'bɪdn] **adv**: **she did it ~** elle l'a fait sans qu'on le lui ait demandé *or* de son propre chef; **he came in ~** il est entré sans y avoir été invité.
unbind ['ʌn'baɪnd] **pret, ptp unbound vt** (*free*) délier; (*untie*) dénouer, défaire; (*unbandage*) débander; *see also* **unbound**.
unbleached ['ʌn'bliːtʃt] **adj** *linen* écru; *hair* non décoloré.
unblemished [ʌn'blemɪʃt] **adj** (*lit, fig*) sans tache.
unblinking [ʌn'blɪŋkɪŋ] **adj** *person* imperturbable, impassible. **he gave me an ~ stare, he looked at me with ~ eyes** il m'a regardé sans ciller (des yeux).
unblock ['ʌn'blɒk] **vt** *sink, pipe* déboucher; *road, harbour, traffic* dégager.
unblushing [ʌn'blʌʃɪŋ] **adj** effronté, éhonté.
unblushingly [ʌn'blʌʃɪŋlɪ] **adv** sans rougir (*fig*), effrontément.
unbolt ['ʌn'bəʊlt] **vt** *door* déverrouiller, tirer le verrou de; *beam* déboulonner.
unborn ['ʌn'bɔːn] **adj** *child* qui n'est pas encore né; *generation* à venir, futur.
unbosom [ʌn'bʊzəm] **vt**: **to ~ o.s. to sb** ouvrir son cœur à qn, se confier à qn.
unbound ['ʌn'baʊnd] **1 pret, ptp of unbind. 2 adj** *prisoner, hands, feet* non lié; *seam* non bordé; *book* broché, non relié; *periodical* non relié.
unbounded [ʌn'baʊndɪd] **adj** *joy, gratitude* sans borne, illimité; *conceit, pride* démesuré.
unbowed ['ʌn'baʊd] **adj** (*fig*) insoumis, invaincu. **with head ~** la tête haute.
unbreakable ['ʌn'breɪkəbl] **adj** incassable; (*fig*) *promise, treaty* sacré.
unbreathable ['ʌn'briːðəbl] **adj** irrespirable.
unbribable ['ʌn'braɪbəbl] **adj** incorruptible, qui ne se laisse pas acheter.
unbridled [ʌn'braɪdld] **adj** (*fig*) débridé, déchaîné, effréné.
unbroken ['ʌn'brəʊkən] **adj** *crockery, limb* non cassé; *seal* intact, non brisé; *skin* intact, non déchiré; *ice* non rompu, continu, intact; (*fig*) *promise* tenu; *series, silence, sleep* ininterrompu; *record* non battu; *horse* indompté; *voice* qui n'a pas mué. **his spirit remained ~** il ne se découragea pas; (*Aut*) **~ line** ligne continue; **descended in an ~ line from Edward VII** descendu en ligne directe d'Édouard VII.
unbuckle ['ʌn'bʌkl] **vt** déboucler.
unbundle [ʌn'bʌndl] **vt** (*gen*) séparer, dégrouper; (*after a buyout*) vendre par appartements; *price* (*into separate items*) détailler, tarifer séparément.
unburden [ʌn'bɜːdn] **vt** *conscience* soulager; *heart* épancher. **to ~ o.s.** s'épancher (*to sb* avec qn, dans le sein de qn), se livrer (*to sb* à qn); **to ~ o.s. of sth** se décharger de qch.
unburied ['ʌn'berɪd] **adj** non enterré, non enseveli.
unbusinesslike [ʌn'bɪznɪslaɪk] **adj** *trader, dealer* qui n'a pas le sens des affaires, peu commerçant; *transaction* irrégulier; (*fig*) *person* qui manque de méthode *or* d'organisation; *report* peu méthodique.
unbutton ['ʌn'bʌtn] **1 vt** *coat* déboutonner. (** fig*) **to ~ o.s.** se déboutonner; (** fig: unrestrained*) **~ed** sans retenue. **2 vi** (** fig*) *[person]* se déboutonner.

uncalled-for [ʌn'kɔːldfɔːʳ] adj *criticism* injustifié; *remark* déplacé. **that was quite ~** vous n'aviez nullement besoin de faire (*or* dire) ça.
uncannily [ʌn'kænɪlɪ] adv *silent, cold* mystérieusement, sinistrement; *alike* étrangement.
uncanny [ʌn'kænɪ] adj *sound* mystérieux, étrange, inquiétant; *atmosphere* étrange, qui donne le frisson; *mystery, event, question, resemblance, accuracy, knack* troublant. **it's ~ how he does it** je ne m'explique vraiment pas comment il peut le faire.
uncap ['ʌn'kæp] vt *bottle* décapsuler.
uncared-for ['ʌn'kɛədfɔːʳ] adj *garden, building* négligé, (laissé) à l'abandon; *appearance* négligé, peu soigné; *child* laissé à l'abandon, délaissé.
uncaring [ˌʌn'kɛərɪŋ] adj insensible, indifférent.
uncarpeted ['ʌn'kɑːpɪtɪd] adj sans tapis.
uncashed [ʌn'kæʃəd] adj *cheque* non encaissé.
uncatalogued ['ʌn'kætəlɒgd] adj qui n'a pas été catalogué.
uncaught ['ʌn'kɔːt] adj *criminal* qui n'a pas été appréhendé *or* pris.
unceasing [ʌn'siːsɪŋ] adj incessant, continu, continuel.
unceasingly [ʌn'siːsɪŋlɪ] adv sans cesse, continuellement.
uncensored ['ʌn'sensəd] adj *letter* non censuré; *film, book* non censuré, non expurgé.
unceremonious ['ʌnˌserɪ'məʊnɪəs] adj brusque.
unceremoniously ['ʌnˌserɪ'məʊnɪəslɪ] adv sans cérémonie, brusquement, avec brusquerie.
uncertain [ʌn'sɜːtn] adj *person* incertain, qui n'est pas sûr *or* certain; *voice, smile, steps* incertain, mal assuré, hésitant; *age, date, weather* incertain; *result, effect* incertain, aléatoire; *temper* inégal. **it is ~ whether** il n'est pas certain *or* sûr que + *subj*; **he is ~ whether** il ne sait pas au juste si + *indic*, il n'est pas sûr que + *subj*; **to be ~ about sth** être incertain de qch, ne pas être certain *or* sûr de qch, avoir des doutes sur qch; **he was ~ about what he was going to do** il était incertain de ce qu'il allait faire, il ne savait pas au juste ce qu'il allait faire; **in no ~ terms** en des termes on ne peut plus clairs.
uncertainly [ʌn'sɜːtnlɪ] adv d'une manière hésitante.
uncertainty [ʌn'sɜːtntɪ] n incertitude *f*, doute(s) *m(pl)*. **in order to remove any ~** pour dissiper des doutes éventuels; **in view of this ~** *or* **these uncertainties** en raison de l'incertitude dans laquelle nous nous trouvons *or* de ces incertitudes.
uncertificated ['ʌnsə'tɪfɪkeɪtɪd] adj (*gen*) non diplômé; *secondary teacher* non certifié.
uncertified ['ʌn'sɜːtɪfaɪd] adj *document etc* non certifié. (*US*) **~ teacher** ≃ maître *m* auxiliaire.
unchain ['ʌn'tʃeɪn] vt (*fig*) *passions, reaction* déchaîner; (*lit*) *dog* lâcher.
unchallengeable ['ʌn'tʃælɪndʒəbl] adj indiscutable, incontestable.
unchallenged ['ʌn'tʃælɪndʒd] 1 adj *leader, rights, superiority* incontesté, indiscuté; *statement, figures* non contesté, non controversé; (*Jur*) *witness* non récusé. 2 adv: **I cannot let that go ~** je ne peux pas laisser passer ça sans protester; **he slipped ~ through the enemy lines** il a passé au travers des lignes ennemies sans être interpellé.
unchangeable [ʌn'tʃeɪndʒəbl] adj invariable, immuable.
unchanged ['ʌn'tʃeɪndʒd] adj inchangé.
unchanging [ʌn'tʃeɪndʒɪŋ] adj invariable, immuable.
uncharacteristic [ˌʌnkærɪktə'rɪstɪk] adj peu caractéristique, peu typique. **that is ~ of him** ça ne lui ressemble pas.
uncharacteristically [ˌʌnkærɪktə'rɪstɪklɪ] adv: **~ rude/generous** d'une grossièreté/générosité peu caractéristique *or* peu typique; **to behave ~** se comporter de façon peu caractéristique *or* peu typique.
uncharged ['ʌn'tʃɑːdʒd] adj (*Elec*) non chargé; (*Jur*) non accusé; *gun* non chargé.
uncharitable [ʌn'tʃærɪtəbl] adj peu charitable.
uncharitably [ʌn'tʃærɪtəblɪ] adv peu charitablement.
uncharted ['ʌn'tʃɑːtɪd] adj *region, island* inexploré; *spot, city* qui n'est pas sur la carte; *sea, waters* dont on n'a pas dressé la carte. (*fig*) **we're sailing in ~ waters** nous ne savons pas bien où nous allons.
unchaste ['ʌn'tʃeɪst] adj non chaste, lascif.
unchecked ['ʌn'tʃekt] adj a (*unrestrained*) *anger* non maîtrisé, non réprimé. (*Mil*) **they advanced ~ for several kilometres** ils ont fait plusieurs kilomètres sans rencontrer d'opposition; **this practice continued ~ for several years** cette pratique s'est poursuivie sans la moindre opposition *or* s'est poursuivie impunément pendant des années. b (*not verified*) *figures, statement* non vérifié; *typescript* non relu.
unchivalrous ['ʌn'ʃɪvəlrəs] adj peu galant, discourtois.
unchristian ['ʌn'krɪstjən] adj peu chrétien, contraire à l'esprit chrétien. (*fig: uncivilized*) **at an ~ hour** à une heure indue *or* impossible*.
uncial ['ʌnsɪəl] 1 adj oncial. 2 n onciale *f*.
uncircumcised ['ʌn'sɜːkəmsaɪzd] adj incirconcis.
uncivil ['ʌn'sɪvɪl] adj incivil (*f* incivile), impoli (*to sb* envers qn).
uncivilized ['ʌn'sɪvɪlaɪzd] adj (*lit*) *country, people etc* barbare, inculte; (*fig*) *behaviour* barbare, grossier; *amount, length of time etc* impossible*. **~ hour** heure indue; **what an ~ thing to do!** quelle grossièreté!; **how ~ of him!** comme c'est grossier de sa part!
uncivilly [ʌn'sɪvɪlɪ] adv impoliment.
unclad ['ʌn'klæd] adj sans vêtements, nu.
unclaimed ['ʌn'kleɪmd] adj *property, prize* non réclamé; *right* non revendiqué.
unclasp ['ʌn'klɑːsp] vt *necklace* défaire, dégrafer; *hands* ouvrir.
unclassed ['ʌn'klɑːst] adj non classé.
unclassified ['ʌn'klæsɪfaɪd] adj *items, papers* non classé, non classifié; *road* non classé; (*fig: not secret*) *information* non (classé) secret (*f* -ète). (*Brit Univ*) **~ degree** *licence sans mention accordée lorsque toutes les épreuves n'ont pas été passées*.
uncle ['ʌŋkl] n a oncle *m*. **yes ~** oui tonton, oui mon oncle; (*US fig*) **to say** *or* **cry ~*** s'avouer vaincu, demander grâce; (*US*) **U~ Sam** l'oncle Sam (*personnification des U.S.A.*); (*US pej*) **U~ Tom** bon nègre; see **Dutch**.
b (*Brit* ‡: *pawnbroker*) ma tante‡ (*mont-de-piété.*)
unclean ['ʌn'kliːn] adj (*lit*) sale, malpropre; (*fig, Rel*) impur.
unclear [ˌʌn'klɪəʳ] adj qui n'est pas clair *or* évident; *result, outcome* incertain. **it is ~ whether he is coming or not** on ne sait pas encore très bien s'il va venir ou pas.
unclench ['ʌn'klentʃ] vt desserrer.
unclimbed ['ʌn'klaɪmd] adj *mountain, peak* vierge.
uncloak ['ʌn'kləʊk] vt (*fig*) *person* démasquer; *mystery, plot* dévoiler.
unclog ['ʌn'klɒg] vt *pipe* déboucher; *wheel* débloquer.
unclothe ['ʌn'kləʊð] vt déshabiller, dévêtir.
unclothed ['ʌn'kləʊðd] adj sans vêtements, nu.
unclouded ['ʌn'klaʊdɪd] adj *sky* sans nuages, dégagé; *liquid* clair, limpide; (*fig*) *happiness* sans nuages, parfait; *future* sans nuages.
unco ['ʌŋkəʊ] adv (*Scot*) très, extrêmement.
uncoil ['ʌn'kɔɪl] 1 vt dérouler. 2 vi se dérouler.
uncollectable ['ʌnkə'lektəbl] adj *tax* (très) difficile à percevoir.
uncollected ['ʌnkə'lektɪd] adj *tax* non perçu; *bus fare* non encaissé; *luggage, lost property* non réclamé; *refuse* non ramassé, non enlevé.
uncoloured, (*US*) **uncolored** ['ʌn'kʌləd] adj (*colourless*) non coloré; (*black and white*) en noir et blanc; *hair* non teint; (*fig*) *judgment, description* objectif, impartial. (*fig*) **~ by** non déformé *or* faussé par.
uncombed ['ʌn'kəʊmd] adj *hair, wool* non peigné.
un-come-at-able* ['ʌnkʌm'ætəbl] adj inaccessible.
uncomely ['ʌn'kʌmlɪ] adj *person* laid, peu joli; *clothes* peu seyant.
uncomfortable [ʌn'kʌmfətəbl] adj *shoes, lodgings* inconfortable, peu confortable; *position* inconfortable, incommode; *person* (*physically*) qui n'est pas bien *or* à l'aise; (*uneasy*) mal à l'aise; *silence* gênant, pesant; *afternoon etc* désagréable, pénible. **this chair is very ~** on est très mal dans ce fauteuil, ce fauteuil n'est pas du tout confortable; **you look ~ in that chair** vous n'avez pas l'air bien (assis) dans ce fauteuil; (*fig*) **to feel ~ about sth** se sentir gêné *or* mal à l'aise au sujet de qch; **I had an ~ feeling that he was watching me** j'avais l'impression déconcertante qu'il me regardait; **I had an ~ feeling that he would change his mind** je ne pouvais pas m'empêcher de penser qu'il allait changer d'avis; **to make things** *or* **life ~ for sb** faire *or* créer des ennuis à qn; **to have an ~ time** passer un mauvais quart d'heure; (*longer*) connaître des moments difficiles.
uncomfortably [ʌn'kʌmfətəblɪ] adv *hot* désagréablement; *seated* inconfortablement, peu confortablement, mal; *dressed* mal, inconfortablement; (*uneasily*) *think* avec une certaine inquiétude; *say* avec gêne. **the bullet went past ~ close** la balle est passée un peu trop près à mon (*or* son *etc*) goût.
uncommitted ['ʌnkə'mɪtɪd] adj *person, party* non engagé, libre; *literature* non engagé; *attitude* neutraliste.
uncommon [ʌn'kɒmən] 1 adj (*unusual*) rare, peu commun, peu fréquent; (*outstanding*) rare, singulier, extraordinaire. **it is not ~ for this to happen** il n'est pas rare que cela arrive (*subj*), cela arrive assez souvent. 2 adv (*) singulièrement, extraordinairement.
uncommonly [ʌn'kɒmənlɪ] adv *kind, hot* singulièrement, extraordinairement. **not ~** assez souvent.
uncommunicative ['ʌnkə'mjuːnɪkətɪv] adj peu communicatif, peu expansif, renfermé. **on this issue he proved very ~** sur cette question il s'est montré très réservé.
uncomplaining ['ʌnkəm'pleɪnɪŋ] adj qui ne se plaint pas, patient, résigné.
uncomplainingly ['ʌnkəm'pleɪnɪŋlɪ] adv sans se plaindre, patiemment.
uncompleted ['ʌnkəm'pliːtɪd] adj inachevé.
uncomplicated [ʌn'kɒmplɪkeɪtɪd] adj peu compliqué, simple.
uncomplimentary ['ʌnˌkɒmplɪ'mentərɪ] adj peu flatteur.
uncomprehending ['ʌnˌkɒmprɪ'hendɪŋ] adj: **he stood there, quite ~** il restait là, n'y comprenant rien; **she gave a polite, but ~ smile** elle a souri poliment, mais manifestement sans comprendre.
uncomprehendingly ['ʌnˌkɒmprɪ'hendɪŋlɪ] adv sans comprendre.
uncompromising [ʌn'kɒmprəmaɪzɪŋ] adj *person, attitude* intransigeant, inflexible; *sincerity, honesty* absolu.
uncompromisingly [ʌn'kɒmprəmaɪzɪŋlɪ] adv *say* en se refusant à toute concession. **~ loyal** d'une loyauté intransigeante.
unconcealed ['ʌnkən'siːld] adj *object* non caché, non dissimulé; *joy* évident, non dissimulé.

unconcern ['ʌnkən'sɜːn] **n** (*calm*) calme *m*; (*in face of danger*) sang-froid *m*; (*lack of interest*) indifférence *f*, insouciance *f*.
unconcerned ['ʌnkən'sɜːnd] **adj** (*unworried*) imperturbable (*by* devant), qui ne s'inquiète pas (*by, about* de); (*unaffected*) indifférent (*by* à), insouciant (*by* de). **he went on speaking,** ~ il a continué de parler sans se laisser troubler.
unconcernedly ['ʌnkən'sɜːnɪdlɪ] **adv** sans s'inquiéter, sans se laisser troubler, avec indifférence, avec insouciance.
unconditional ['ʌnkən'dɪʃənl] **adj** inconditionnel, sans condition, sans réserve. (*Jur*) ~ **discharge** libération inconditionnelle; (*Mil*) ~ **surrender** reddition *f* sans condition.
unconditionally ['ʌnkən'dɪʃnəlɪ] **adv** (*gen*) inconditionnellement; *surrender, accept* inconditionnellement, sans conditions.
unconfined ['ʌnkən'faɪnd] **adj** *space* illimité, sans bornes; *animal* en liberté.
unconfirmed ['ʌnkən'fɜːmd] **adj** *report, rumour* non confirmé.
uncongenial ['ʌnkən'dʒiːnɪəl] **adj** *person* peu sympathique, antipathique; *work, surroundings* peu agréable.
unconnected ['ʌnkə'nektɪd] **adj** *events, facts* sans rapport (*with* avec); *languages* sans connexion, d'origine différente; *ideas* décousu, sans suite; (*Elec*) débranché.
unconquerable [ʌn'kɒŋkərəbl] **adj** *army, nation, mountain* invincible; *difficulty* insurmontable; *tendency* irrépressible, incorrigible.
unconquered [ʌn'kɒŋkəd] **adj** *land* qui n'a pas été conquis; *mountain* invaincu.
unconscionable [ʌn'kɒnʃnəbl] **adj** déraisonnable.
unconscious [ʌn'kɒnʃəs] **1 adj a** (*Med*) sans connaissance, (*having fainted*) évanoui. **he was** ~ **for 3 hours** il est resté sans connaissance *or* évanoui pendant 3 heures; **to become** ~ perdre connaissance; **knocked** ~ assommé. **b** (*unaware*) *person* inconscient (*of* de); *humour etc* inconscient, involontaire; *desire, dislike* inconscient. **to be** ~ **of sth** être inconscient de qch, ne pas avoir conscience de qch; (*Psych*) **the** ~ **mind** l'inconscient *m*. **2 n** (*Psych*) inconscient *m*.
unconsciously [ʌn'kɒnʃəslɪ] **adv** inconsciemment, sans s'en rendre compte. **he made an** ~ **funny remark** il a fait une remarque dont l'humour lui a échappé.
unconsciousness [ʌn'kɒnʃəsnɪs] **n** (*NonC*) **a** (*Med*) perte *f* de connaissance, (*specifically fainting*) évanouissement *m*. **b** (*unawareness*) inconscience *f*.
unconsidered ['ʌnkən'sɪdəd] **adj** *remark, action* inconsidéré, irréfléchi. ~ **trifles** des vétilles sans importance.
unconstitutional ['ʌn,kɒnstɪ'tjuːʃənl] **adj** inconstitutionnel, anticonstitutionnel.
unconstitutionally [ʌn,kɒnstɪ'tjuːʃnəlɪ] **adv** inconstitutionnellement, anticonstitutionnellement.
unconstrained ['ʌnkən'streɪnd] **adj** *person* non contraint, libre; *behaviour* aisé; *act* spontané.
unconsummated [ʌn'kɒnsʌmeɪtəd] **adj** *marriage, relationship etc* non consommé.
uncontested ['ʌnkən'testɪd] **adj** incontesté; (*Parl*) *seat* non disputé, remporté sans opposition.
uncontrollable ['ʌnkən'trəʊləbl] **adj** *child, animal* indiscipliné, impossible; *desire, emotion* irrésistible, irrépressible, qui ne peut être contenu *or* maîtrisé; *epidemic, price rise, inflation* qui ne peut être enrayé, qui ne peut être freiné. **he was seized with** ~ **laughter** le fou rire l'a pris; ~ **fits of rage** emportements *mpl*; **to have an** ~ **temper** ne pas être toujours maître de soi, ne pas savoir se contrôler.
uncontrollably ['ʌnkən'trəʊləblɪ] **adv** (*gen*) irrésistiblement. **to laugh** ~ avoir le fou rire; **she was crying** ~ elle pleurait sans pouvoir s'arrêter *or* se dominer; **the fire raged** ~ on n'arrivait pas à maîtriser l'incendie; **the car skidded** ~ le conducteur a dérapé et a perdu le contrôle de sa voiture; **inflation is rising** ~ l'inflation augmente irrésistiblement.
uncontrolled ['ʌnkən'trəʊld] **adj** *emotion, desire* non contenu, non maîtrisé, effréné; *price rises* effréné; *inflation* galopant, incontrôlé.
uncontroversial ['ʌn,kɒntrə'vɜːʃəl] **adj** qui ne prête pas à controverse, non controversable.
unconventional ['ʌnkən'venʃənl] **adj** peu conventionnel, original.
unconventionality ['ʌnkən,venʃə'nælɪtɪ] **n** originalité *f*, caractère *m* peu conventionnel.
unconventionally ['ʌnkən'venʃnəlɪ] **adv** de manière peu conventionnelle.
unconverted ['ʌnkən'vɜːtɪd] **adj** (*Fin, Rel, gen*) non converti.
unconvinced ['ʌnkən'vɪnst] **adj** non convaincu, sceptique. **to be** *or* **remain** ~ ne pas être convaincu *or* persuadé (*of sth* de qch), avoir des doutes (*of sth* sur qch).
unconvincing ['ʌnkən'vɪnsɪŋ] **adj** peu convaincant.
unconvincingly ['ʌnkən'vɪnsɪŋlɪ] **adv** *speak, argue* d'un ton *or* d'une manière peu convaincant(e).
uncooked ['ʌn'kʊkt] **adj** non cuit, cru.
uncool* ['ʌn'kuːl] **adj** *person* pas branché*, pas cool*; *action, thing* pas cool*.
uncooperative ['ʌnkəʊ'ɒpərətɪv] **adj** peu coopératif.
uncooperatively ['ʌnkəʊ'ɒpərətɪvlɪ] **adv** de façon peu coopérative.
uncoordinated ['ʌnkəʊ'ɔːdɪneɪtɪd] **adj** non coordonné.
uncork ['ʌn'kɔːk] **vt** déboucher, enlever le bouchon de.
uncorrected ['ʌnkə'rektɪd] **adj** non corrigé.
uncorroborated ['ʌnkə'rɒbəreɪtɪd] **adj** non corroboré, sans confirmation.
uncorrupted ['ʌnkə'rʌptɪd] **adj** non corrompu.
uncountable ['ʌn'kaʊntəbl] **adj a** (*innumerable*) innombrable, incalculable. **b** (*Ling*) ~ **noun** nom *m* non dénombrable.
uncounted ['ʌn'kaʊntɪd] **adj** qui n'a pas été compté; (*fig: innumerable*) innombrable.
uncouple ['ʌn'kʌpl] **vt** *carriage* dételer; *train, engine* découpler; *trailer* détacher.
uncouth [ʌn'kuːθ] **adj** *person, behaviour* grossier, fruste.
uncover [ʌn'kʌvər] **vt** découvrir.
uncovered [ʌn'kʌvəd] **adj** découvert; (*Fin*) à découvert.
uncritical ['ʌn'krɪtɪkəl] **adj** *person* dépourvu d'esprit critique; *attitude, approach, report* non critique. **to be** ~ **of** manquer d'esprit critique à l'égard de.
uncritically ['ʌn'krɪtɪkəlɪ] **adv** sans (faire preuve d')esprit critique.
uncross ['ʌn'krɒs] **vt** décroiser.
uncrossed ['ʌn'krɒst] **adj** décroisé; *cheque* non barré.
uncrowded ['ʌn'kraʊdɪd] **adj** où il n'y a pas trop de monde.
uncrowned ['ʌn'kraʊnd] **adj** non couronné, sans couronne. (*fig*) **the** ~ **king of** le roi sans couronne de.
uncrushable ['ʌn'krʌʃəbl] **adj** *fabric, dress* infroissable. **he's quite** ~ il ne se laisse jamais abattre.
UNCTAD, Unctad ['ʌŋktæd] **n** (**abbr of United Nations Conference on Trade and Development**) Congrès *m* des Nations Unies sur le commerce et le développement.
unction ['ʌŋkʃən] **n** (*all senses*) onction *f*.
unctuous ['ʌŋktjʊəs] **adj** (*pej*) onctueux, mielleux.
unctuously ['ʌŋktjʊəslɪ] **adv** (*pej*) onctueusement, avec onction.
unctuousness ['ʌŋktjʊəsnɪs] **n** (*NonC: pej*) manières onctueuses.
uncultivated ['ʌn'kʌltɪveɪtɪd] **adj** *land, person, mind* inculte; *voice, accent* qui manque de raffinement.
uncultured ['ʌn'kʌltʃəd] **adj** *person, mind* inculte; *voice, accent* qui manque de raffinement.
uncurl ['ʌn'kɜːl] **1 vt** *wire, snake* dérouler. **to** ~ **one's legs** déplier ses jambes. **2 vi** [*snake etc*] se dérouler.
uncut ['ʌn'kʌt] **adj** (*gen*) non coupé; *hedge* non taillé; *crops* sur pied; *diamond* brut; *gem, stone* non taillé; *edition, film, play* sans coupures, intégral.
undamaged [ʌn'dæmɪdʒd] **adj** *goods* non endommagé, en bon état; *reputation* intact; (*Psych*) non affecté.
undamped ['ʌn'dæmpt] **adj** (*fig*) *enthusiasm, courage* non refroidi, intact.
undated ['ʌn'deɪtɪd] **adj** non daté, sans date.
undaunted ['ʌn'dɔːntɪd] **adj** non intimidé, non effrayé (*by* par), inébranlable. **he was** ~ **by their threats** leurs menaces ne l'effrayaient pas; **he carried on** ~ il a continué sans se laisser intimider *or* démonter.
undeceive ['ʌndɪ'siːv] **vt** détromper, désabuser (*liter*).
undecided ['ʌndɪ'saɪdɪd] **adj** *person* indécis, irrésolu; *question* indécis; *weather* incertain. **that is still** ~ cela n'a pas encore été décidé; **I am** ~ **whether to go or not** je n'ai pas décidé si j'irai ou non.
undeclared ['ʌndɪ'klεəd] **adj** (*Customs*) non déclaré.
undefeated ['ʌndɪ'fiːtɪd] **adj** invaincu.
undefended ['ʌndɪ'fendɪd] **adj** (*Mil etc*) sans défense, non défendu; (*Jur*) *suit* où on ne présente pas de défense, où le défendeur s'abstient de plaider.
undefiled ['ʌndɪ'faɪld] **adj** (*liter: lit, fig*) pur, sans tache. ~ **by any contact with ...** qui n'a pas été contaminé *or* souillé par le contact de ... .
undefined [,ʌndɪ'faɪnd] **adj** *word, condition* non défini; *sensation etc* indéterminé, vague.
undelivered ['ʌndɪ'lɪvəd] **adj** non remis, non distribué. **if** ~ **return to sender** ≃ en cas d'absence, prière de retourner à l'expéditeur.
undemanding ['ʌndɪ'mɑːndɪŋ] **adj** *person* peu exigeant, facile; *work, course* peu astreignant; *book, film* facile.
undemocratic [,ʌndemə'krætɪk] **adj** antidémocratique.
undemonstrative ['ʌndɪ'mɒnstrətɪv] **adj** réservé, peu démonstratif, peu expansif.
undeniable [,ʌndɪ'naɪəbl] **adj** indéniable, incontestable.
undeniably [,ʌndɪ'naɪəblɪ] **adv** incontestablement, indiscutablement. **it is** ~ **true that** il est incontestable *or* indiscutable que.
undenominational ['ʌndɪ,nɒmɪ'neɪʃənl] **adj** non confessionnel.
undependable ['ʌndɪ'pendəbl] **adj** *person* sur qui on ne peut compter, à qui on ne peut se fier; *information* peu sûr; *machine* peu fiable.
under ['ʌndər] **1 adv a** (*beneath*) au-dessous, en dessous. **he stayed** ~ **for 3 minutes** (*under water*) il est resté sous l'eau pendant 3 minutes; (*under anaesthetic*) il est resté sous l'effet de l'anesthésie *or* il est resté anesthésié pendant 3 minutes; (*Comm etc*) **as** ~ comme ci-dessous; **he lifted the rope and crawled** ~ il a soulevé la corde et il est passé par-dessous en se traînant; *see* **down[1], go under** *etc*.
b (*less*) au-dessous. **children of 15 and** ~ les enfants de 15 ans et

au-dessous; **10 degrees** ~ 10 degrés au-dessous de zéro.

2 **prep** a (*beneath*) sous. ~ **it** dessous; ~ **the table/sky/umbrella** sous la table/le ciel/le parapluie; **he came out from** ~ **the bed** il est sorti de dessous le lit; **the book slipped from** ~ **his arm** le livre a glissé de sous son bras; **it's** ~ **there** c'est là-dessous; **he went and sat** ~ **it** il est allé s'asseoir dessous; **to stay** ~ **water** rester sous l'eau; ~ **the microscope** au microscope; *for other phrases see* **breath, cover, wing** *etc.*

b (*less than*) moins de; (*in series, rank, scale etc*) au-dessous de. **to be** ~ **age** avoir moins de dix-huit ans, être mineur (*see also* **underage**); **children** ~ **15** enfants de moins de *or* enfants au-dessous de 15 ans (*see also* **3**); **the** ~**-15s** *etc* les moins de 15 *etc* ans; **it sells at** ~ **£10** cela se vend à moins de 10 livres; **there were** ~ **50 of them** il y en avait moins de 50; **any number** ~ **10** un chiffre au-dessous de 10; **in** ~ **2 hours** en moins de 2 heures; **those** ~ **the rank of captain** ceux au-dessous du grade de capitaine.

c (*fig*) sous. ~ **the Tudors** sous les Tudors; ~ **the circumstances** dans les circonstances; ~ **an assumed name** sous un faux nom; **you'll find him** ~ **"plumbers" in the book** vous le trouverez sous "plombiers" dans l'annuaire; **sent** ~ **plain cover** envoyé sous pli discret; (*Agr*) ~ **wheat** en blé; ~ **sentence of death** condamné à mort; (*Mil etc*) **to serve** ~ **sb** servir sous les ordres de qn; **he had 50 men** ~ **him** il avait 50 hommes sous ses ordres; ~ **the command of** sous les ordres de; **to study** ~ **sb** *[undergraduate]* suivre les cours de qn; *[postgraduate]* faire des recherches *or* travailler sous la direction de qn; *[painter, composer]* être l'élève de qn; **this department comes** ~ **his authority** cette section relève de sa compétence; (*Comput*) **to run** ~ **CP/M** fonctionner sous CP/M; *for other phrases see* **control, impression, obligation** *etc.*

d (*according to*) en vertu de, conformément à, selon. ~ **article 25** en vertu de *or* conformément à l'article 25; ~ **French law** selon la législation française; ~ **the terms of the contract** aux termes du contrat, selon *or* suivant les termes du contrat; ~ **his will** selon son testament.

3 **comp** ► **under-the-counter** *see* **under-the-counter.**

4 **pref** a (*below*) sous-; *see* **underfloor, undersea** *etc.*

b (*insufficiently*) sous-, *eg* ~**nourished** sous-alimenté; ~**used/appreciated** *etc* qui n'est pas assez utilisé/apprécié *etc; see* **undercharge, undercooked** *etc.*

c (*junior*) sous-, *eg* ~**gardener** sous-jardinier *m*; *see* **under-secretary** *etc.*

underachieve [ˌʌndərəˈtʃiːv] **vi** (*Scol*) être sous-performant, ne pas obtenir les résultats correspondant à son niveau d'intelligence.

underachiever [ˌʌndərəˈtʃiːvəʳ] **n** (*Scol*) (*Brit*) élève *mf* sous-performant(e); (*US*) élève très médiocre.

underage [ˌʌndərˈeɪdʒ] **adj** *person* mineur. ~ **drinking** consommation *f* d'alcool par les mineurs.

underarm [ˌʌndərˈɑːm] 1 **adv** (*Sport etc*) *throw, bowl* par en-dessous. 2 **adj** a *throw etc* par en-dessous. b *deodorant* pour les aisselles; *hair* des aisselles, sous les bras. ~ **odour** odeur *f* de transpiration sous les aisselles.

underbade [ˌʌndəˈbeɪd] **pret of underbid.**

underbelly [ˈʌndəbelɪ] **n** (*Anat*) bas-ventre *m*. (*fig*) **the (soft)** ~ le point vulnérable.

underbid [ˌʌndəˈbɪd] **pret underbade** *or* **-bid, ptp underbidden** *or* **-bid vti** (*Bridge: also* ~ **one's hand**) annoncer au-dessous de sa force.

underbody [ˈʌndəbɒdɪ] **n** (*Aut*) dessous *m* de caisse.

underbrush [ˈʌndəbrʌʃ] **n** (*US: NonC*) sous-bois *msg*, broussailles *fpl*.

undercapitalized [ˈʌndəˈkæpɪtəlaɪzd] **adj: to be** ~ *[businessman]* ne pas disposer de fonds suffisants; *[project etc]* ne pas être doté de fonds suffisants.

undercarriage [ˈʌndəkærɪdʒ] **n** (*Aviat*) train *m* d'atterrissage.

undercharge [ˈʌndəˈtʃɑːdʒ] **vt** ne pas faire payer assez à. **he** ~**d me by £2** il aurait dû me faire payer 2 livres de plus.

underclass [ˈʌndəklɑːs] **n** (*in society*) classe *f* (sociale) très défavorisée, ≃ quart-monde *m*.

underclassman [ˈʌndəˈklɑːsmən] **n** (*US Univ*) étudiant *m* de première *or* deuxième année.

underclothes [ˈʌndəkləʊðz] **npl, underclothing** [ˈʌndəkləʊðɪŋ] **n** (*NonC*) = **underwear.**

undercoat [ˈʌndəkəʊt] **n** *[paint]* couche *f* de fond; (*US Aut*) couche *f* antirouille (du châssis).

undercoating [ˈʌndəkəʊtɪŋ] **n** (*NonC: US Aut*) couche *f* antirouille (du châssis).

undercooked [ˈʌndəˈkʊkt] **adj** pas assez cuit.

undercover [ˌʌndəˈkʌvəʳ] **adj** secret (*f* -ète), clandestin. ~ **agent** *or* **man** *or* **policeman** agent secret.

undercurrent [ˈʌndəˌkʌrənt] **n** (*in sea*) courant *m* (sous-marin); (*fig*) *[feeling etc]* courant sous-jacent.

undercut [ˌʌndəˈkʌt] **pret, ptp undercut** 1 **vt** a (*Comm: sell cheaper than*) *competitor* vendre moins cher que. b (*fig, esp Econ: undermine, reduce*) *the dollar, incomes* réduire la valeur de. **inflation** ~**s spending power** l'inflation réduit le pouvoir d'achat. c (*Sport*) *ball* lifter. 2 **n** (*Culin*) (morceau *m* de) filet *m*.

underdeveloped [ˈʌndədɪˈveləpt] **adj** (*Econ*) sous-développé; (*Anat, Physiol*) qui n'est pas complètement développé *or* formé; (*Phot*) insuffisamment développé.

underdog [ˈʌndədɒg] **n: the** ~ (*in game, fight*) celui (*or* celle) qui perd, le perdant (*or* la perdante); (*predicted loser*) celui (*or* celle) que l'on donne perdant(e); (*economically, socially*) l'opprimé *m*.

underdone [ˈʌndəˈdʌn] **adj** *food* pas assez cuit; (*Brit*) *steak etc* saignant.

underdrawers [ˈʌndədrɔːz] **npl** (*US*) caleçon *m*, slip *m* (*pour homme*).

underdressed [ˌʌndəˈdrest] **adj: to be** ~ ne pas être vêtu avec l'élégance requise.

underemphasize [ˌʌndərˈemfəsaɪz] **vt** ne pas donner l'importance nécessaire à.

underemployed [ˌʌndərɪmˈplɔɪd] **adj** *person, equipment, building* sous-employé; *resources* sous-exploité. **I'm** ~ **half the time** bien souvent je suis sous-employé *or* je ne suis pas assez occupé.

underemployment [ˌʌndərɪmˈplɔɪmənt] **n** *[person etc]* sous-emploi *m*; *[resources]* sous-exploitation *f*.

underestimate [ˌʌndərˈestɪmɪt] 1 **n** sous-estimation *f*. 2 **vt** [ˌʌndərˈestɪmeɪt] *size, numbers, strength* sous-estimer; *person* sous-estimer, mésestimer.

underestimation [ˌʌndərestɪˈmeɪʃən] **n** sous-estimation *f*.

underexpose [ˌʌndərɪksˈpəʊz] **vt** (*Phot*) sous-exposer.

underexposed [ˌʌndərɪksˈpəʊzd] **adj** (*Phot*) sous-exposé.

underexposure [ˌʌndərɪksˈpəʊʒəʳ] **n** (*Phot*) sous-exposition *f*.

underfed [ˌʌndəˈfed] (**pret, ptp of underfeed**) **adj** sous-alimenté.

underfeed [ˌʌndəˈfiːd] **pret, ptp underfed vt** sous-alimenter.

underfeeding [ˌʌndəˈfiːdɪŋ] **n** sous-alimentation *f*.

underfelt [ˈʌndəfelt] **n** *[carpet]* thibaude *f*.

underfinanced [ˌʌndəfaɪˈnænst] **adj: to be** ~ *[businessman]* ne pas disposer de fonds suffisants; *[project etc]* ne pas être doté de fonds suffisants.

underfloor [ˈʌndəflɔːʳ] **adj** (*gen*) *pipes etc* qui se trouve sous le plancher *or* le sol. ~ **heating** chauffage *m* par le plancher *or* par le sol.

underflow [ˈʌndəfləʊ] **n** (*in sea*) courant *m* (sous-marin); (*fig*) *[feeling etc]* courant sous-jacent.

underfoot [ˈʌndəˈfʊt] **adv** (*gen*) sous les pieds. **to trample sth** ~ fouler qch aux pieds; **it is wet** ~ le sol est humide.

underfunded [ˌʌndəˈfʌndɪd] **adj: to be** ~ *[businessman]* ne pas disposer de fonds suffisants; *[project etc]* ne pas être doté de fonds suffisants.

underfunding [ˌʌndəˈfʌndɪŋ] **n** manque *m* de financement.

undergarment [ˈʌndəgɑːmənt] **n** sous-vêtement *m*.

undergo [ˌʌndəˈgəʊ] **pret underwent, ptp undergone vt** *test, change, modification,* (*Med*) *operation, examination* subir; *suffering* éprouver; (*Med*) *treatment* suivre. **it is** ~**ing repairs** c'est en réparation.

undergraduate [ˌʌndəˈgrædjʊɪt] 1 **n** étudiant(e) *m(f)* (*qui prépare la licence*). 2 **comp** *life* étudiant, estudiantin; *circles* étudiant; *rooms* pour étudiants, d'étudiants; *opinion* des étudiants; *grants, income* d'étudiants; *attitude* d'étudiant; *course* pour étudiants de licence.

underground [ˈʌndəgraʊnd] 1 **adj** *work* sous terre, souterrain; *explosion, cable* souterrain; (*fig*) *organization* clandestin, secret (*f* -ète); *press* clandestin; (*Art, Cine*) underground *inv*, d'avant-garde. ~ **car park** parking *m* souterrain; ~ **railway** métro *m*; (*fig: US Hist: for slaves*) **the** ~ **railroad** *filière clandestine pour aider les esclaves noirs à fuir le Sud;* (*fig*) ~ **movement** mouvement clandestin; (*in occupied country*) résistance *f*.

2 **adv** sous (la) terre; (*fig*) clandestinement, secrètement. **it is 3 metres** ~ c'est à 3 mètres sous (la) terre; *[wanted man]* **to go** ~ entrer dans la clandestinité; *[guerilla]* prendre le maquis.

3 **n** (*Brit: railway*) métro *m*. **by** ~ en métro; **the** ~ (*Mil, Pol etc*) la résistance; (*Art etc*) mouvement *m* underground *or* d'avant-garde.

undergrowth [ˈʌndəgrəʊθ] **n** (*NonC*) broussailles *fpl*, sous-bois *msg*.

underhand [ˌʌndəˈhænd] **adj, underhanded** [ˌʌndəˈhændɪd] **adj** (*US*) (*pej*) en sous-main, en dessous, sournois. ~ **trick** fourberie *f*.

underhandedly [ˌʌndəˈhændɪdlɪ] **adv** (*pej*) sournoisement, en dessous, en sous-main.

underinsure [ˌʌndərɪnˈʃʊəʳ] **vt** sous-assurer. **to be** ~**d** ne pas être suffisamment couvert par son *or* l'assurance; **if only you hadn't been** ~**d** si seulement vous n'aviez pas été sous-assuré; **the premises are** ~**d** les locaux ne sont pas suffisamment couverts par l'assurance.

underinvest [ˌʌndərɪnˈvest] **vi** (*Econ, Fin*) sous-investir.

underinvestment [ˌʌndərɪnˈvestmənt] **n** (*Econ, Fin*) sous-investissement *m*.

underlay [ˌʌndəˈleɪ] 1 **pret of underlie.** 2 [ˈʌndəleɪ] **n** *[carpet]* thibaude *f*.

underlie [ˌʌndəˈlaɪ] **pret underlay, ptp underlain vt** être à la base de, sous-tendre.

underline [ˌʌndəˈlaɪn] **vt** (*lit, fig*) souligner.

underling [ˈʌndəlɪŋ] **n** (*pej*) subalterne *m*, sous-fifre* *m inv* (*pej*).

underlining [ˌʌndəˈlaɪnɪŋ] **n** (*NonC*) soulignage *m*, soulignement *m*.

underlip [ˈʌndəlɪp] **n** lèvre *f* inférieure.

underlying [ˌʌndəˈlaɪɪŋ] **adj** (*gen, also Gram, Jur*) sous-jacent.

undermanned [ˌʌndəˈmænd] **adj** (*gen, also Mil*) *office, post etc* à court de personnel; (*Mil*) *ship, plane* à court d'équipage.

undermentioned [ˌʌndəˈmenʃənd] adj (cité) ci-dessous.
undermine [ˌʌndəˈmaɪn] vt (*lit*) *cliffs* miner, saper; (*fig*) *influence, power, authority* saper, ébranler; *health* miner, user; *effect* amoindrir.
undermost [ˈʌndəməʊst] adj le plus bas.
underneath [ˈʌndəˈniːθ] 1 prep sous, au-dessous de. **stand ~ it** mettez-vous dessous; **from ~ the table** de dessous la table. 2 adv (en) dessous. **the one ~** celui d'en dessous. 3 adj d'en dessous. 4 n dessous *m*.
undernourish [ˌʌndəˈnʌrɪʃ] vt sous-alimenter.
undernourished [ˌʌndəˈnʌrɪʃt] adj sous-alimenté.
undernourishment [ˌʌndəˈnʌrɪʃmənt] n sous-alimentation *f*.
underoccupied [ˌʌndərˈɒkjʊpaɪd] adj *accommodation* insuffisamment occupé; *person* qui n'a pas assez à faire.
underpaid [ˌʌndəˈpeɪd] (pret, ptp of **underpay**) adj sous-payé; *worker* sous-rémunéré, sous-payé.
underpants [ˈʌndəpænts] npl caleçon *m*, slip *m* (*pour hommes*).
underpart [ˈʌndəpɑːt] n partie *f* inférieure.
underpass [ˈʌndəpɑːs] n (*for cars*) passage *m* inférieur (*de l'autoroute*); (*for pedestrians*) passage souterrain.
underpay [ˌʌndəˈpeɪ] pret, ptp **underpaid** vt sous-payer; *worker* sous-rémunérer, sous-payer.
underperform [ˌʌndəpəˈfɔːm] vi (*St Ex*) mal se comporter, faire une contre-performance. **the stock has ~ed on the Brussels stock market** le titre ne s'est pas comporté comme il aurait dû à la Bourse de Bruxelles.
underpin [ˌʌndəˈpɪn] vt *wall* étayer; *building* reprendre en sous-œuvre; (*fig*) *project etc* étayer.
underplay [ˌʌndəˈpleɪ] vt (*gen*) minimiser, réduire l'importance de. **he rather ~ed it** il n'a pas insisté là-dessus, il a minimisé la chose; (*Theat*) **to ~ a role** jouer un rôle avec beaucoup de retenue.
underpopulated [ˌʌndəˈpɒpjʊleɪtɪd] adj sous-peuplé.
underprice [ˌʌndəˈpraɪs] vt mettre un prix trop bas à.
underpriced [ˌʌndəˈpraɪst] adj *goods* en vente à un prix inférieur à sa vraie valeur. **at £3 this book is ~** le prix de 3 livres est trop bas pour ce livre.
underpricing [ˌʌndəˈpraɪsɪŋ] n tarification *f* trop basse.
underprivileged [ˌʌndəˈprɪvɪlɪdʒd] 1 adj (*economically, socially*) *families* économiquement faible, déshérité; *countries* déshérité. 2 npl: **the ~** les économiquement faibles *mpl*.
underproduce [ˌʌndəprəˈdjuːs] vti (*Econ, Ind*) sous-produire.
underproduction [ˌʌndəprəˈdʌkʃən] n (*Econ, Ind*) sous-production *f*.
underqualified [ˈʌndəˈkwɒlɪˌfaɪd] adj: **to be ~** ne pas avoir les compétences *fpl* nécessaires (*for* pour).
underrate [ˌʌndəˈreɪt] vt *size, numbers, strength* sous-estimer; *person* sous-estimer, méconnaître.
underrated [ˌʌndəˈreɪtɪd] adj *play, book, actor* méconnu, sous-estimé. **he's very ~** il est vraiment méconnu, on le sous-estime vraiment.
underreact [ˌʌndəriːˈækt] vi réagir mollement.
underreaction [ˌʌndəriːˈækʃən] n réaction *f* molle.
underripe [ˌʌndəˈraɪp] adj *fruit* vert, qui n'est pas mûr; *cheese* qui n'est pas fait.
underscore [ˌʌndəˈskɔːʳ] vt (*lit*) souligner; (*fig*) souligner, mettre en évidence.
underscoring [ˌʌndəˈskɔːrɪŋ] n (*NonC*) (*see* **underscore**) soulignement *m*, soulignage *m*; mise *f* en évidence.
undersea [ˈʌndəsiː] adj sous-marin.
underseal [ˈʌndəsiːl] (*Brit Aut*) 1 vt *car* traiter contre la rouille (le châssis de). 2 n couche *f* antirouille (du châssis).
undersealing [ˈʌndəsiːlɪŋ] n (*Brit Aut*) couche *f* antirouille (du châssis).
under-secretary [ˌʌndəˈsekrətrɪ] n sous-secrétaire *mf*.
undersell [ˌʌndəˈsel] pret, ptp **undersold** vt *competitor* vendre moins cher que. (*fig*) **to ~ oneself** ne pas se montrer à sa juste valeur.
undersexed [ˌʌndəˈsekst] adj a (*having a low sex drive*) de faible libido. **to be ~** avoir une faible libido. b (*unsatisfied*) frustré.
undershirt [ˈʌndəʃɜːt] n (*US*) maillot *m* de corps.
undershoot [ˌʌndəˈʃuːt] pret, ptp **undershot** vt (*Aviat*) **to ~ the runway** atterrir avant d'atteindre la piste.
undershorts [ˈʌndəʃɔːts] npl (*US*) caleçon *m*, slip *m* (*pour hommes*).
undershot [ˈʌndəʃɒt] (pret, ptp of **undershoot**) adj *water wheel* à aubes.
underside [ˈʌndəsaɪd] n dessous *m*.
undersigned [ˈʌndəsaɪnd] adj, n (*Jur, frm*) soussigné(e) *m(f)*. **I, the ~, declare ...** je soussigné(e) déclare ... .
undersized [ˌʌndəˈsaɪzd] adj de (trop) petite taille, trop petit.
underskirt [ˈʌndəskɜːt] n (*Brit*) jupon *m*.
underslung [ˌʌndəˈslʌŋ] adj *car* surbaissé.
undersoil [ˈʌndəsɔɪl] n sous-sol *m* (*Agr*).
undersold [ˌʌndəˈsəʊld] pret, ptp of **undersell**.
underspending [ˌʌndəˈspendɪŋ] n (*Admin*) fait *m* de ne pas dépenser entièrement les crédits disponibles.
understaffed [ˌʌndəˈstɑːft] adj à court de personnel.
understand [ˌʌndəˈstænd] pret, ptp **understood** 1 vt a *person, words, meaning, painting, difficulty* comprendre; *action, event* comprendre, s'expliquer. **this can be understood in several ways** cela peut se comprendre de plusieurs façons; **that is easily understood** c'est facile à comprendre, cela se comprend facilement; **to make o.s. understood** se faire comprendre; **do I make myself understood?** est-ce que je me fais bien comprendre?; **that's quite understood!** c'est entendu!; **it must be understood that** il faut (bien) comprendre que; (*frm*) **it being understood that your client is responsible** à condition que votre client accepte (*subj*) la responsabilité; **do you ~ why/how/what?** est-ce que vous comprenez pourquoi/comment/ce que?; **that's what I can't ~** voilà ce que je ne comprends pas *or* ce qui me dépasse; **I can't ~ it!** je ne comprends pas!; **I can't ~ a word of it** je n'y comprends rien; **I can't ~ his agreeing to do it** je n'arrive pas à comprendre *or* je ne m'explique pas qu'il ait accepté de le faire; **I quite ~ that you don't want to come** je comprends très bien que vous n'ayez pas envie de venir; **you don't ~ the intricacies of the situation** vous ne comprenez pas *or* vous ne vous rendez pas compte de la complexité de la situation; **my wife doesn't ~ me** ma femme ne me comprend pas.
b (*believe etc*) (croire) comprendre. **I understood we were to be paid** j'ai cru comprendre que nous devions être payés; **I ~ you are leaving today** il paraît que vous partez aujourd'hui, si je comprends bien vous partez aujourd'hui; (*frm: in business letter etc*) **we confirm our reservation and we ~ (that) the rental will be ...** nous confirmons notre réservation, étant entendu que la location s'élèvera à ...; **am I to ~ that ...?** dois-je comprendre que ...?; **she is understood to have left the country, it is understood that she has left the country** il paraît *or* on pense généralement *or* on croit qu'elle a quitté le pays; **he let it be understood that** il a donné à entendre *or* il a laissé entendre que; **we were given to ~ that ...** on nous a donné à entendre que ..., on nous a fait comprendre que ... .
c (*imply, assume*) *word etc* sous-entendre. **to be understood** *[arrangement, price, date]* ne pas être spécifié; (*Gram*) être sous-entendu; **it was understood that he would pay for it** (*it was assumed*) on présumait qu'il le paierait; (*it was agreed*) il était entendu qu'il le paierait; *see also* **understood**.
2 vi comprendre. **now I ~!** je comprends *or* j'y suis maintenant!; **there's to be no noise, (do you) ~! *or* is that understood?** pas de bruit, c'est bien compris! *or* tu entends!; **he was a widower, I ~** il était veuf, si j'ai bien compris *or* si je ne me trompe (pas).
understandable [ˌʌndəˈstændəbl] adj *person, speech* compréhensible, intelligible; *behaviour* compréhensible, naturel, normal; *pride, sorrow etc* compréhensible, naturel. **it is ~ that** on comprend *or* il est normal que + *subj*; **that's ~** ça se comprend.
understandably [ˌʌndəˈstændəblɪ] adv a *speak, explain* d'une façon compréhensible. b (*naturally, of course*) naturellement; (*rightly*) à juste titre. **~, he refused** il a refusé, naturellement *or* comme on pouvait s'y attendre *or* et ça se comprend; **he's ~ angry** il est furieux, et à juste titre *or* et ça se comprend.
understanding [ˌʌndəˈstændɪŋ] 1 adj *person* compréhensif (*about* à propos de); *smile, look* compatissant, bienveillant.
2 n a (*NonC*) compréhension *f*, entendement *m*, intelligence *f*. **he has good ~** il comprend vite; **he had a good ~ of the problems** il comprenait bien les problèmes; **his ~ of the problems/of children** sa compréhension des problèmes/des enfants, sa faculté de comprendre les problèmes/les enfants; **the age of ~** l'âge *m* de discernement; **it's beyond ~** cela dépasse l'entendement.
b (*agreement*) accord *m*; (*arrangement*) arrangement *m*. **to come to an ~ with sb** s'entendre *or* s'arranger avec qn; **I have an ~ with the local shop** je me suis entendu avec le magasin du coin; **there is an ~ between us that ...** il est entendu entre nous que ...; **on the ~ that** à condition que + *subj*.
c (*NonC: concord*) entente *f*, bonne intelligence. **this will encourage ~ between our nations** ceci favorisera l'entente entre nos nations.
understandingly [ˌʌndəˈstændɪŋlɪ] adv avec bienveillance, en faisant preuve de compréhension.
understate [ˌʌndəˈsteɪt] vt minimiser, réduire l'importance de.
understated [ˌʌndəˈsteɪtɪd] adj (*gen*) discret (*f* -ète); *fashion detail, collar etc* discret, d'une élégance discrète. **~ black dress** petite robe *f* noire toute simple.
understatement [ˈʌndəˌsteɪtmənt] n affirmation *f* en dessous de la vérité; (*Ling*) litote *f*. **to say he is clever is rather an ~** dire qu'il est intelligent n'est pas assez dire *or* ne suffit pas; **that's an ~** c'est peu dire, vous pouvez le dire, le terme est faible; **that's the ~ of the year!*** c'est bien le moins qu'on puisse dire!
understeer [ˈʌndəˌstɪəʳ] vi braquer insuffisamment.
understood [ˌʌndəˈstʊd] 1 ptp of **understand**. 2 adj (*agreed*) entendu, convenu; (*Gram*) sous-entendu. **it is an ~ thing that he can't always be there** il est bien entendu qu'il ne peut pas toujours être là; *see also* **understand**.
understudy [ˈʌndəstʌdɪ] (*Theat*) 1 n doublure *f*. 2 vt *actor* doubler; *part* doubler un acteur dans.
undersubscribed [ˌʌndəsəbˈskraɪbd] (*St Ex*) adj non couvert, non entièrement souscrit.
undertake [ˌʌndəˈteɪk] pret **undertook**, ptp **undertaken** vt *task* entreprendre; *duty* se charger de; *responsibility* assumer; *obligation* contracter. **to ~ to do** promettre *or* se charger de faire, s'engager à faire.

undertaker [ˈʌndəteɪkəʳ] n entrepreneur *m or* ordonnateur *m* des pompes funèbres. **the ~'s** les pompes *fpl* funèbres, le service des pompes funèbres.

undertaking [ˌʌndəˈteɪkɪŋ] n a (*task, operation*) entreprise *f*. **it is quite an ~** ce n'est pas une petite affaire, c'est toute une entreprise. b (*promise*) promesse *f*, engagement *m*. **to give an ~** promettre (*that* que; *to do* de faire); **I can give no such ~** je ne peux rien promettre de la sorte.

undertax [ˌʌndəˈtæks] vt *person* imparer insuffisamment; *goods* taxer insuffisamment. **he was ~ed by £5000** on lui a fait payer 5 000 livres d'impôts de moins qu'on ne l'aurait dû.

under-the-counter [ˌʌndəðəˈkaʊntəʳ] 1 adj en douce. 2 adv clandestinement, en douce.

undertone [ˈʌndətəʊn] n a **to say sth in an ~** dire qch à mi-voix. b **an ~ of criticism** des critiques cachées *or* sous-jacentes; **it has ~s of dishonesty** cela implique quelque chose de malhonnête.

undertow [ˈʌndətəʊ] n (*lit*) courant *m* sous-marin (*provoqué par le retrait de la vague*); (*fig*) tension *f*.

underuse [ˌʌndəˈjuːz] 1 vt utiliser insuffisamment; *see also* **underutilize**. 2 [ˌʌndəˈjuːs] n utilisation *f* insuffisante, sous-utilisation *f*, sous-emploi *m*.

underused [ˌʌndəˈjuːzd] adj *resources, facilities* insuffisamment utilisé; *see also* **underutilized. seriously** *or* **grossly ~** loin d'être suffisamment utilisé.

underutilization [ˌʌndəjuːtɪlaɪˈzeɪʃən] n (*see* **underutilized**) sous-exploitation *f*, utilisation *f* insuffisante, sous-utilisation *f*, sous-emploi *m*.

underutilize [ˌʌndəˈjuːtɪlaɪz] vt (*see* **underutilized**) sous-exploiter, utiliser insuffisamment, sous-utiliser, sous-employer.

underutilized [ˌʌndəˈjuːtɪlaɪzd] adj *potential, talent, resources* sous-exploité, utilisé insuffisamment; *space, facilities, equipment* sous-employé, sous-utilisé, utilisé insuffisamment.

undervalue [ˌʌndəˈvæljuː] vt *help, contribution* sous-estimer; *person* sous-estimer, mésestimer.

undervalued [ˌʌndəˈvæljuːd] adj *help, contribution* sous-estimé; *person, helper* sous-estimé, mésestimé. **this house is ~** cette maison vaut plus que son prix; **it's ~ by about £1000** cela vaut environ 1 000 livres de plus.

undervest [ˈʌndəvest] n maillot *m* de corps.

underwater [ˈʌndəˈwɔːtəʳ] 1 adj sous-marin. 2 adv sous l'eau.

underway [ˌʌndəˈweɪ] adj *see* **way 1k**.

underwear [ˈʌndəwɛəʳ] n (*NonC: gen, also men's*) sous-vêtements *mpl*; (*women's only*) dessous *mpl*, lingerie *f* (*NonC*).

underweight [ˌʌndəˈweɪt] adj a *goods* d'un poids insuffisant. **it's 50 grams ~** il manque 50 grammes. b *[person]* **to be ~** ne pas peser assez, être trop maigre; **she's 20 lbs ~** elle pèse ≃ 9 kilos de moins que son poids normal.

underwired [ˌʌndəˈwaɪəd] adj *bra* avec armature.

underworld [ˈʌndəwɜːld] 1 n a (*Myth: hell*) **the ~** les enfers *mpl*. b (*criminal*) **the ~** le milieu, la pègre. 2 comp *organization, personality* du milieu; *connections* avec le milieu; *attack* organisé par le milieu.

underwrite [ˌʌndəˈraɪt] pret **underwrote,** ptp **underwritten** vt a (*Insurance*) *policy* réassurer; *risk* assurer contre, garantir; *amount* garantir. b (*St Ex*) *share issue* garantir (une *or* l'émission de). c (*Comm, Fin*) *project, enterprise* soutenir *or* appuyer (financièrement). d (*support*) *decision, statement etc* soutenir, souscrire à.

underwriter [ˈʌndəˌraɪtəʳ] n a (*Insurance*) assureur *m*. b (*St Ex*) syndicataire *m*.

underwritten [ˈʌndəˈrɪtn] ptp of **underwrite**.

underwrote [ˈʌndəˈrəʊt] pret of **underwrite**.

undeserved [ˈʌndɪˈzɜːvd] adj immérité.

undeservedly [ˈʌndɪˈzɜːvɪdlɪ] adv *reward, punish* à tort, indûment; *be rewarded, punished* sans l'avoir mérité, indûment.

undeserving [ˈʌndɪˈzɜːvɪŋ] adj *person* peu méritant; *cause* peu méritoire. **~ of** indigne de, qui ne mérite pas.

undesirable [ˈʌndɪˈzaɪərəbl] 1 adj peu souhaitable, (*stronger*) indésirable. **it is ~ that** il est peu souhaitable que + *subj*; (*Admin, Jur*) **~ alien** étranger *m*, -ère *f* indésirable. 2 n indésirable *mf*.

undetected [ˈʌndɪˈtektɪd] adj non décelé, non détecté, non découvert. **to go ~** passer inaperçu.

undetermined [ˈʌndɪˈtɜːmɪnd] adj (*unknown*) indéterminé, non connu; (*uncertain*) irrésolu, indécis.

undeterred [ˈʌndɪˈtɜːd] adj non découragé. **to carry on ~** continuer sans se laisser décourager *or* comme si de rien n'était.

undeveloped [ˈʌndɪˈveləpt] adj *fruit, intelligence, part of body* qui ne s'est pas développé; *film* non développé; *land, resources* non exploité.

undeviating [ʌnˈdiːvɪeɪtɪŋ] adj *path* droit; *policy, course* constant.

undiagnosed [ʌnˈdaɪəgnəʊzd] adj (*lit, fig*) non diagnostiqué.

undies* [ˈʌndɪz] npl dessous *mpl*, lingerie *f* (*NonC*).

undigested [ˈʌndaɪˈdʒestɪd] adj non digéré.

undignified [ʌnˈdɪgnɪfaɪd] adj qui manque de dignité. **how ~!** quel manque de dignité!

undiluted [ˈʌndaɪˈluːtɪd] adj *concentrate* non dilué; *pleasure* sans mélange; *nonsense* pur.

undiminished [ˈʌndɪˈmɪnɪʃt] adj non diminué.

undimmed [ˈʌnˈdɪmd] adj *lamp* qui n'a pas été mis en veilleuse; *headlight* qui n'est pas en code; *colour, metal, beauty* non terni; *sight* aussi bon qu'auparavant. **my memory of it is ~** je m'en souviens avec précision.

undiplomatic [ˈʌnˌdɪpləˈmætɪk] adj *person* peu diplomate; *action, answer* peu diplomatique.

undipped [ˈʌnˈdɪpt] adj (*Aut*) **his headlights were ~** il était en phares, il n'était pas en code; **to drive on ~ headlights** conduire avec ses phares allumés.

undiscerning [ˈʌndɪˈsɜːnɪŋ] adj qui manque de discernement.

undischarged [ˈʌndɪsˈtʃɑːdʒd] adj *bankrupt* non réhabilité; *debt* non acquitté, impayé.

undisciplined [ʌnˈdɪsɪplɪnd] adj indiscipliné.

undisclosed [ˈʌndɪsˈkləʊzd] adj non révélé, non divulgué.

undiscovered [ˈʌndɪsˈkʌvəd] adj (*not found*) non découvert; (*unknown*) inconnu. **the treasure remained ~ for 700 years** le trésor n'a été découvert que 700 ans après.

undiscriminating [ˈʌndɪsˈkrɪmɪneɪtɪŋ] adj qui manque de discernement.

undisguised [ˈʌndɪsˈgaɪzd] adj (*lit, fig*) non déguisé.

undismayed [ˈʌndɪsˈmeɪd] adj non découragé, non consterné. **he was quite ~ by the news** la nouvelle ne l'a nullement consterné; **... he said ~** ... dit-il sans se laisser décourager *or* intimider.

undisputed [ˈʌndɪsˈpjuːtɪd] adj incontesté.

undistinguished [ˈʌndɪsˈtɪŋgwɪʃt] adj (*in character*) médiocre, quelconque; (*in appearance*) peu distingué.

undisturbed [ˈʌndɪsˈtɜːbd] adj a (*untouched*) *papers, clues* non dérangé, non déplacé; (*uninterrupted*) *sleep* non troublé, paisible. **to work ~** travailler sans être dérangé. b (*unworried*) non inquiet (*f* -ète), calme. **he was ~ by the news** la nouvelle ne l'a pas inquiété.

undivided [ˈʌndɪˈvaɪdɪd] adj indivisé, entier; (*unanimous*) unanime. **your ~ attention** toute votre attention.

undo [ˈʌnˈduː] pret **undid,** ptp **undone** vt *button, garment, knot, parcel, box, knitting* défaire; *good effect* détruire, annuler; *mischief, wrong* réparer; *see also* **undone**.

undocumented [ʌnˈdɒkjʊmentɪd] adj *event etc* sur lequel on ne possède pas de témoignages; (*US*) *person* sans papiers.

undoing [ˈʌnˈduːɪŋ] n (*NonC*) ruine *f*, perte *f*. **that was his ~** c'est ce qui l'a perdu, c'est ce qui a causé sa perte.

undomesticated [ˈʌndəˈmestɪkeɪtɪd] adj *animal* non domestiqué; *person* qui ne sait pas faire le ménage.

undone [ˈʌnˈdʌn] 1 ptp of **undo**. 2 adj *button, garment, knot, parcel* défait; *task* non accompli. **to come ~** se défaire; **to leave sth ~** ne pas faire qch; (*†† or hum*) **I am ~!** je suis perdu!

undoubted [ʌnˈdaʊtɪd] adj indubitable, certain.

undoubtedly [ʌnˈdaʊtɪdlɪ] adv indubitablement, sans aucun doute.

undramatic [ˈʌndrəˈmætɪk] adj peu dramatique.

undreamed-of [ʌnˈdriːmdɒv] adj, **undreamt-of** [ʌnˈdremtɒv] adj (*unhoped for*) inespéré; (*unsuspected*) insoupçonné, qui dépasse l'imagination.

undress [ʌnˈdres] 1 vt déshabiller. **to get ~ed** se déshabiller; *see also* **undressed**. 2 vi se déshabiller. 3 n (*also Mil*) **in a state of ~** en petite tenue.

undressed [ʌnˈdrest] 1 pret, ptp of **undress 1, 2**. 2 adj a *salad* non assaisonné. b *wound* non pansé; *see also* **dress 3**.

undrinkable [ˈʌnˈdrɪŋkəbl] adj (*unpalatable*) imbuvable; (*poisonous*) non potable.

undue [ˈʌnˈdjuː] adj (*gen*) excessif; *anger, haste etc* indu, excessif. **I hope this will not cause you ~ inconvenience** j'espère que cela ne vous causera pas trop d'inconvénients.

undulate [ˈʌndjʊleɪt] vi onduler, ondoyer.

undulating [ˈʌndjʊleɪtɪŋ] adj *movement* ondoyant, onduleux; *aspect* onduleux; *line* sinueux, onduleux; *countryside* vallonné.

undulation [ˌʌndjʊˈleɪʃən] n ondulation *f*, ondoiement *m*.

undulatory [ˈʌndjʊlətrɪ] adj ondulatoire.

unduly [ˈʌnˈdjuːlɪ] adv trop, excessivement. **he was not ~ worried** il n'était pas inquiet outre mesure.

undying [ʌnˈdaɪɪŋ] adj (*fig*) éternel.

unearned [ˈʌnˈɜːnd] adj *money* non gagné; (*fig*) *praise, reward* immérité. **~ income** rentes *fpl*; **~ increment** plus-value *f*.

unearth [ˈʌnˈɜːθ] vt déterrer; (*fig*) déterrer, dénicher, découvrir.

unearthly [ʌnˈɜːθlɪ] adj (*gen*) surnaturel, mystérieux; (*threatening*) sinistre; (** fig*) impossible*. **~ hour** heure *f* impossible *or* indue.

unease [ʌnˈiːz] n inquiétude *f*, malaise *m* (*at, about* devant).

uneasily [ʌnˈiːzɪlɪ] adv (*ill-at-ease*) avec gêne; (*worriedly*) avec inquiétude; *sleep* mal, d'un sommeil agité.

uneasiness [ʌnˈiːzɪnɪs] n (*NonC*) inquiétude *f*, malaise *m* (*at, about* devant).

uneasy [ʌnˈiːzɪ] adj *calm, peace, truce* troublé, difficile; *silence* gêné; *sleep, night* agité; *conscience* non tranquille; *person* (*ill-at-ease*) mal à l'aise, gêné; (*worried*) inquiet (*f* -ète) (*at, about* devant, de), anxieux. **to grow** *or* **become ~ about sth** commencer à s'inquiéter au sujet de qch; **I have an ~ feeling that he's watching me** j'ai l'impression déconcertante qu'il me regarde; **I had an ~ feeling that he would**

change his mind je ne pouvais m'empêcher de penser qu'il allait changer d'avis.
uneatable ['ʌn'iːtəbl] adj immangeable.
uneaten ['ʌn'iːtn] adj non mangé, non touché.
uneconomic(al) ['ʌn,iːkə'nɒmɪk(əl)] adj *machine, car* peu économique; *work, method* peu économique, peu rentable. **it is ~ to do that** il n'est pas économique *or* rentable de faire cela.
unedifying ['ʌn'edɪfaɪɪŋ] adj peu édifiant.
unedited [ʌn'edɪtɪd] adj *film* non monté; *essays, works* non édité; *tape* non mis au point.
uneducated ['ʌn'edjʊkeɪtɪd] adj *person* sans instruction; *letter, report* informe, plein de fautes, (*badly written*) mal écrit; *handwriting* d'illettré; *speech, accent* populaire.
unemotional ['ʌnɪ'məʊʃənl] adj (*having little emotion*) peu émotif, peu émotionnable; (*showing little emotion*) *person, voice, attitude* qui ne montre *or* ne trahit aucune émotion, impassible; *reaction* peu émotionnel; *description, writing* neutre, dépourvu de passion.
unemotionally ['ʌnɪ'məʊʃnəlɪ] adv avec impassibilité.
unemployable ['ʌnɪm'plɔɪəbl] adj incapable de travail.
unemployed ['ʌnɪm'plɔɪd] 1 adj *person* en *or* au chômage, sans travail *or* emploi; *machine, object* inutilisé, dont on ne se sert pas; (*Fin*) *capital* qui ne travaille pas. **~ person** chômeur *m*, -euse *f*, (*esp Admin*) demandeur *m* d'emploi; (*Econ*) **the numbers ~** les inactifs *mpl*. 2 npl: **the ~** les chômeurs *mpl*, les sans-emploi *mpl* (*esp Admin*) les demandeurs *mpl* d'emploi; **the young ~** les jeunes *mpl* sans emploi *or* au chômage.
unemployment ['ʌnɪm'plɔɪmənt] 1 n (*NonC*) chômage *m*. **to reduce** *or* **cut ~** réduire le chômage *or* le nombre des chômeurs, résorber le chômage; **~ has risen** le chômage *or* le nombre des chômeurs a augmenté. 2 comp ▸**unemployment benefit** (*Brit*), **unemployment compensation** (*US*) allocation *f* de chômage ▸**unemployment figures** statistiques *fpl* du chômage, nombre *m* des chômeurs ▸**unemployment rate: an unemployment rate of 10%** *or* **of 1 in 10** un taux de chômage de 10%.
unencumbered ['ʌnɪn'kʌmbəd] adj non encombré (*with* de).
unending [ʌn'endɪŋ] adj interminable, sans fin.
unendurable ['ʌnɪn'djʊərəbl] adj insupportable, intolérable.
unenforceable ['ʌnɪn'fɔsəbl] adj *law etc* inapplicable.
unengaged ['ʌnɪn'geɪdʒd] adj libre.
un-English ['ʌn'ɪŋglɪʃ] adj peu anglais, pas anglais.
unenlightened ['ʌnɪn'laɪtnd] adj peu éclairé, rétrograde.
unenterprising ['ʌn'entəpraɪzɪŋ] adj *person* peu entreprenant, qui manque d'initiative; *policy, act* qui manque d'audacité *or* de hardiesse.
unenthusiastic ['ʌnɪn,θuːzɪ'æstɪk] adj peu enthousiaste. **you seem rather ~ about it** ça n'a pas l'air de vous enthousiasmer *or* de vous emballer*.
unenthusiastically ['ʌnɪn,θuːzɪ'æstɪkəlɪ] adv sans enthousiasme.
unenviable ['ʌn'envɪəbl] adj peu enviable.
unequal ['ʌn'iːkwəl] adj *size, opportunity, work* inégal. **to be ~ to a task** ne pas être à la hauteur d'une tâche.
unequalled ['ʌn'iːkwəld] adj *skill, enthusiasm, footballer, pianist* inégalé, sans égal, qui n'a pas son égal; *record* inégalé.
unequally ['ʌn'iːkwəlɪ] adv inégalement.
unequivocal ['ʌnɪ'kwɪvəkəl] adj sans équivoque. **he gave him an ~ "no"** il lui a opposé un "non" catégorique *or* sans équivoque.
unequivocally ['ʌnɪ'kwɪvəkəlɪ] adv sans équivoque.
unerring ['ʌn'ɜːrɪŋ] adj *judgment, accuracy* infaillible; *aim, skill, blow* sûr.
unerringly ['ʌn'ɜːrɪŋlɪ] adv (*see* **unerring**) infailliblement; d'une manière sûre.
UNESCO [juː'neskəʊ] n (abbr of **United Nations Educational, Scientific and Cultural Organization**) U.N.E.S.C.O. *f*.
unescorted [,ʌnes'kɔːtɪd] adj, adv a (*Mil, Naut*) sans escorte. b (*unaccompanied by a male partner*) sans cavalier.
unessential ['ʌnɪ'senʃəl] 1 adj non essentiel, non indispensable. 2 npl: **the ~s** tout ce qui n'est pas essentiel *or* indispensable, le superflu.
unesthetic [,ʌniːs'θetɪk] adj = **unaesthetic**.
unethical ['ʌn'eθɪkəl] adj peu éthique, immoral.
uneven ['ʌn'iːvən] adj (*gen*) inégal; *path* inégal, raboteux; *ground* inégal, accidenté; *quality, pulse, work* inégal, irrégulier; *number* impair. (*Aut*) **the engine sounds ~** il y a des à-coups dans le moteur, le moteur ne tourne pas rond.
unevenly ['ʌn'iːvənlɪ] adv (*see* **uneven**) inégalement; irrégulièrement.
unevenness ['ʌn'iːvənnɪs] n (*NonC: see* **uneven**) inégalité *f*; irrégularité *f*.
uneventful ['ʌnɪ'ventfʊl] adj *day, meeting, journey* sans incidents, sans histoires, peu mouvementé; *life* calme, tranquille, peu mouvementé; *career* peu mouvementé.
uneventfully ['ʌnɪ'ventfʊlɪ] adv *take place, happen* sans incidents, sans histoires.
unexceptionable [,ʌnɪk'sepʃnəbl] adj irréprochable.
unexceptional [,ʌnɪk'sepʃənl] adj qui n'a rien d'exceptionnel.
unexciting ['ʌnɪk'saɪtɪŋ] adj *time, life, visit* peu passionnant, peu intéressant; *food* ordinaire.
unexpected ['ʌnɪks'pektɪd] adj *arrival* inattendu, inopiné; *result, change* inattendu, imprévu; *success, happiness* inattendu, imprévu, inespéré. **it was all very ~** on ne s'y attendait pas du tout.
unexpectedly ['ʌnɪks'pektɪdlɪ] adv alors qu'on ne s'y attend (*or* attendait *etc*) pas, subitement. **to arrive ~** arriver à l'improviste *or* inopinément.
unexpired ['ʌnɪks'paɪəd] adj non expiré, encore valide.
unexplained ['ʌnɪks'pleɪnd] adj inexpliqué.
unexploded ['ʌnɪks'pləʊdɪd] adj non explosé, non éclaté.
unexploited ['ʌnɪks'plɔɪtɪd] adj inexploité.
unexplored ['ʌnɪks'plɔːd] adj inexploré.
unexposed ['ʌnɪks'pəʊzd] adj (*Phot*) *film* vierge.
unexpressed ['ʌnɪks'prest] adj inexprimé.
unexpurgated ['ʌn'ekspɜːgeɪtɪd] adj non expurgé, intégral.
unfading [ʌn'feɪdɪŋ] adj (*fig*) *hope* éternel; *memory* impérissable, ineffaçable.
unfailing [ʌn'feɪlɪŋ] adj *supply* inépuisable, intarissable; *zeal* inépuisable; *optimism* inébranlable; *remedy* infaillible.
unfailingly [ʌn'feɪlɪŋlɪ] adv infailliblement, immanquablement.
unfair ['ʌn'fɛəʳ] adj *person* injuste (*to sb* envers qn, à l'égard de qn); *decision, arrangement, deal* injuste, inéquitable; *competition, play, tactics* déloyal. **~ dismissal** licenciement *m* abusif; **it's ~ that** ce n'est pas juste *or* il est injuste que + *subj*; **it is ~ of her to do so** il est injuste qu'elle agisse ainsi, ce n'est pas juste de sa part d'agir ainsi.
unfairly ['ʌn'fɛəlɪ] adv *decide* injustement; *play* déloyalement; *dismissed* abusivement.
unfairness ['ʌn'fɛənɪs] n (*see* **unfair**) injustice *f*; déloyauté *f*.
unfaithful ['ʌn'feɪθfʊl] adj infidèle (*to* à).
unfaithfully ['ʌn'feɪθfəlɪ] adv infidèlement, avec infidélité.
unfaithfulness ['ʌn'feɪθfʊlnɪs] n infidélité *f*.
unfaltering [ʌn'fɔːltərɪŋ] adj *step, voice* ferme, assuré.
unfalteringly [ʌn'fɔːltərɪŋlɪ] adv *speak* d'une voix ferme *or* assurée; *walk* d'un pas ferme *or* assuré.
unfamiliar ['ʌnfə'mɪljəʳ] adj *place, sight* peu familier, étrange, inconnu; *person, subject* peu familier, inconnu, mal connu. **to be ~ with sth** mal connaître qch.
unfamiliarity ['ʌnfə,mɪlɪ'ærɪtɪ] n (*NonC*) aspect étrange *or* inconnu.
unfashionable ['ʌn'fæʃnəbl] adj *dress, subject* démodé, qui n'est plus à la mode, passé de mode; *district, shop, hotel* peu chic *inv*. **it is ~ to speak of ...** ça ne se fait plus de parler de ... .
unfasten ['ʌn'fɑːsn] vt *garment, buttons, rope* défaire; *door* ouvrir, déverrouiller; *bonds* défaire, détacher; (*loosen*) desserrer.
unfathomable [ʌn'fæðəməbl] adj (*lit, fig*) insondable.
unfathomed ['ʌn'fæðəmd] adj (*lit, fig*) insondé.
unfavourable, (*US*) **unfavorable** ['ʌn'feɪvərəbl] adj *conditions, report, impression, outlook, weather* défavorable; *moment* peu propice, inopportun; *terms* désavantageux; *wind* contraire.
unfavourably, (*US*) **unfavorably** ['ʌn'feɪvərəblɪ] adv défavorablement. **I was ~ impressed** j'ai eu une impression défavorable; **to regard sth ~** être défavorable *or* hostile à qch.
unfazed* ['ʌn'feɪzd] adj (*US*) imperturbable. **it left him quite ~** ça ne lui a rien fait, il n'a pas bronché.
unfeeling [ʌn'fiːlɪŋ] adj insensible, impitoyable, dur.
unfeelingly [ʌn'fiːlɪŋlɪ] adv sans pitié, impitoyablement.
unfeigned [ʌn'feɪnd] adj non simulé, sincère.
unfeignedly [ʌn'feɪnɪdlɪ] adv sincèrement, vraiment.
unfeminine [ʌn'femɪnɪn] adj peu féminin.
unfettered ['ʌn'fetəd] adj (*liter: lit, fig*) sans entrave. **~ by** libre de.
unfilial ['ʌn'fɪljəl] adj peu filial.
unfinished ['ʌn'fɪnɪʃt] adj *task, essay* inachevé, incomplet (*f* -ète). **I have 3 ~ letters** j'ai 3 lettres à finir; **we have some ~ business** nous avons une affaire (*or* des affaires) à régler; **the U~ Symphony** la Symphonie inachevée; *[piece of handcraft etc]* **it looks rather ~** c'est mal fini, la finition laisse à désirer.
unfit ['ʌn'fɪt] 1 adj a (*incompetent*) inapte, impropre (*for* à; *to do* à faire); (*unworthy*) indigne (*to do* de faire). **he is ~ to be a teacher** il ne devrait pas enseigner; **he was ~ to drive** il n'était pas en état de conduire; **he is ~ for work** il n'est pas en état de reprendre le travail; **~ for military service** inapte au service militaire; **the doctor declared him ~ for the match** le docteur a déclaré qu'il n'était pas en état de jouer; **~ for habitation** inhabitable; **~ for consumption** impropre à la consommation; **~ to eat** (*unpalatable*) immangeable; (*poisonous*) non comestible; **~ for publication** impropre à la publication, impubliable; **road ~ for lorries** route impraticable aux camions.
b (*not physically fit*) qui n'est pas en forme.
2 vt rendre inapte (*for* à; *to do* à faire).
unfitness ['ʌn'fɪtnɪs] n inaptitude *f* (*for* à; *to do* à faire); (*ill health*) incapacité *f*.
unfitted [ʌn'fɪtɪd] adj inapte (*for* à; *to do* à faire).
unfitting [ʌn'fɪtɪŋ] adj *language, behaviour* peu *or* guère convenable, inconvenant; *ending, result* mal approprié.
unfix ['ʌn'fɪks] vt détacher, enlever; (*Mil*) *bayonets* remettre.
unflagging [ʌn'flægɪŋ] adj *person, devotion, patience* infatigable, inlassable; *enthusiasm* inépuisable; *interest* soutenu jusqu'au bout.

unflaggingly [ʌn'flægɪŋlɪ] adv infatigablement, inlassablement.
unflappability* [ˌʌnflæpə'bɪlɪtɪ] n (NonC) calme m, flegme m.
unflappable* ['ʌn'flæpəbl] adj imperturbable, qui ne perd pas son calme, flegmatique.
unflattering ['ʌn'flætərɪŋ] adj *person, remark, photo, portrait* peu flatteur. **he was very ~ about it** ce qu'il en a dit n'avait rien de flatteur *or* n'était pas flatteur; **she wears ~ clothes** elle porte des vêtements qui ne la mettent guère en valeur *or* qui ne l'avantagent guère.
unflatteringly ['ʌn'flætərɪŋlɪ] adv d'une manière peu flatteuse.
unfledged ['ʌn'fledʒd] adj (*fig*) *person, organization, movement* qui manque d'expérience. **an ~ youth** un garçon sans expérience, un blanc-bec (*pej*).
unflinching ['ʌn'flɪntʃɪŋ] adj *expression, determination* stoïque. **she was ~ in her desire to succeed** elle était absolument déterminée à réussir.
unflinchingly ['ʌn'flɪntʃɪŋlɪ] adv stoïquement, sans broncher.
unflyable ['ʌn'flaɪəbl] adj *plane* qu'on ne peut pas faire voler.
unfocu(s)sed [ˌʌn'fəʊkəst] adj *camera* pas mis au point; *gaze, eyes* dans le vague; (*fig*) *aims, desires etc* flou, vague.
unfold [ʌn'fəʊld] **1** vt *napkin, map, blanket* déplier; *wings* déployer; (*fig*) *plans, ideas* exposer; *secret* dévoiler, révéler. **to ~ a map on a table** étaler une carte sur une table; **to ~ one's arms** décroiser les bras. **2** vi *[flower]* s'ouvrir, s'épanouir; *[view, countryside]* se dérouler, s'étendre; *[story, film, plot]* se dérouler.
unforced [ʌn'fɔːst] adj *smile, laugh* naturel. (*Sport*) **~ error** faute *f* directe.
unforeseeable ['ʌnfɔː'siːəbl] adj imprévisible.
unforeseen ['ʌnfɔː'siːn] adj imprévu.
unforgettable ['ʌnfə'getəbl] adj (*gen*) inoubliable; (*for unpleasant things*) impossible à oublier.
unforgettably [ˌʌnfə'getəblɪ] adv: **~ beautiful/clear** d'une beauté/clarté inoubliable; **~ ugly/dirty** d'une laideur/saleté frappante.
unforgivable ['ʌnfə'gɪvəbl] adj impardonnable.
unforgivably ['ʌnfə'gɪvəblɪ] adv impardonnablement.
unforgiven ['ʌnfə'gɪvən] adj non pardonné.
unforgiving ['ʌnfə'gɪvɪŋ] adj implacable, impitoyable.
unforgotten ['ʌnfə'gɒtn] adj inoublié.
unformed ['ʌn'fɔːmd] adj informe.
unforthcoming ['ʌnfɔːθ'kʌmɪŋ] adj *reply, person* réticent (*about* sur). **he was very ~ about it** il s'est montré très réticent, il s'est montré peu disposé à en parler.
unfortified ['ʌn'fɔːtɪfaɪd] adj (*Mil*) sans fortifications, non fortifié.
unfortunate [ʌn'fɔːtʃnɪt] **1** adj *person* malheureux, malchanceux; *coincidence* malheureux, fâcheux, regrettable; *circumstances* triste; *event* fâcheux, malencontreux; *incident, episode* fâcheux, regrettable; *remark* malheureux, malencontreux. **it is most ~ that** il est très malheureux *or* regrettable que + *subj*; **how ~!** quel dommage!; **he has been ~** il n'a pas eu de chance. **2** n malheureux *m*, -euse *f*.
unfortunately [ʌn'fɔːtʃnɪtlɪ] adv malheureusement, par malheur. **an ~ worded document** un document rédigé de façon malencontreuse.
unfounded ['ʌn'faʊndɪd] adj *rumour, allegation, belief* dénué de tout fondement, sans fondement; *criticism* injustifié.
unframed ['ʌn'freɪmd] adj *picture* sans cadre.
unfreeze ['ʌn'friːz] pret **unfroze**, ptp **unfrozen** **1** vt (*lit*) dégeler; (*Econ, Fin*) débloquer. **2** vi dégeler.
unfreezing ['ʌn'friːzɪŋ] n (*Econ*) *[prices, wages]* déblocage *m*.
unfrequented ['ʌnfrɪ'kwentɪd] adj peu fréquenté.
unfriendliness ['ʌn'frendlɪnɪs] n (*NonC*) froideur *f* (*towards* envers).
unfriendly ['ʌn'frendlɪ] adj *person, reception* froid; *attitude, behaviour, act, remark* inamical, (*stronger*) hostile. **to be ~ to(wards) sb** manifester de la froideur *or* de l'hostilité à qn, ne pas être très gentil avec qn.
unfrock ['ʌn'frɒk] vt défroquer.
unfroze ['ʌn'frəʊz] pret of **unfreeze**.
unfrozen ['ʌn'frəʊzn] ptp of **unfreeze**.
unfruitful ['ʌn'fruːtfʊl] adj stérile, infertile; (*fig*) infructueux.
unfruitfully ['ʌn'fruːtfʊlɪ] adv (*fig*) en vain, sans succès.
unfulfilled ['ʌnfʊl'fɪld] adj *promise* non tenu; *ambition* inaccompli, non réalisé; *desire* insatisfait; *condition* non rempli; *prophecy* non réalisé. *[person]* **to feel ~** se sentir frustré, éprouver un sentiment d'insatisfaction.
unfulfilling ['ʌnfʊl'fɪlɪŋ] adj peu satisfaisant. **he finds it ~** ça ne le satisfait pas pleinement.
unfunny* ['ʌn'fʌnɪ] adj qui n'est pas drôle, qui n'a rien de drôle.
unfurl [ʌn'fɜːl] **1** vt déployer. **2** vi se déployer.
unfurnished ['ʌn'fɜːnɪʃt] adj non meublé.
ungainliness [ʌn'geɪnlɪnɪs] n (*NonC*) gaucherie *f*.
ungainly [ʌn'geɪnlɪ] adj gauche, disgracieux, dégingandé.
ungallant ['ʌn'gælənt] adj peu *or* guère galant, discourtois.
ungenerous ['ʌn'dʒenərəs] adj **a** (*miserly*) peu généreux, parcimonieux. **b** (*uncharitable*) mesquin, méchant.
ungentlemanly [ʌn'dʒentlmənlɪ] adj peu *or* guère galant, discourtois.
un-get-at-able* ['ʌnget'ætəbl] adj inaccessible.
ungird ['ʌn'gɜːd] pret, ptp **ungirt** vt détacher.
unglazed ['ʌn'gleɪzd] adj *door, window* non vitré; *picture* qui n'est pas sous verre; *pottery* non vernissé, non émaillé; *photograph* mat; *cake* non glacé.
unglued ['ʌn'gluːd] adj (*gen*) sans colle. (*US fig*) **to come ~*** *[house etc]* s'écrouler; *[person]* flancher*, craquer*.
ungodliness [ʌn'gɒdlɪnɪs] n (*NonC*) impiété *f*.
ungodly [ʌn'gɒdlɪ] adj *person, action, life* impie, irréligieux; (* *fig*) impossible*. **~ hour** heure indue.
ungovernable [ʌn'gʌvənəbl] adj *people, country* ingouvernable; *desire, passion* irrépressible. **he has an ~ temper** il n'est pas toujours maître de lui-même.
ungracious ['ʌn'greɪʃəs] adj *person* peu gracieux, incivil (*f* incivile); *smile, remark, gesture* peu gracieux, peu aimable. **it would be ~ to refuse** on aurait mauvaise grâce à refuser.
ungraciously ['ʌn'greɪʃəslɪ] adv avec mauvaise grâce.
ungrammatical ['ʌngrə'mætɪkəl] adj incorrect, non grammatical, agrammatical.
ungrammatically ['ʌngrə'mætɪkəlɪ] adv incorrectement, agrammaticalement.
ungrateful [ʌn'greɪtfʊl] adj *person* ingrat, peu reconnaissant (*towards* envers); *task* ingrat.
ungratefully [ʌn'greɪtfəlɪ] adv avec ingratitude.
ungrudging ['ʌn'grʌdʒɪŋ] adj *person, contribution* généreux; *help* donné sans compter; *praise, gratitude* très sincère.
ungrudgingly [ʌn'grʌdʒɪŋlɪ] adv *give* généreusement; *help* de bon cœur, sans compter.
unguarded ['ʌn'gɑːdɪd] adj (*Mil etc*) sans surveillance; (*fig*) *remark* irréfléchi, imprudent. **in an ~ moment** dans un moment d'inattention.
unguent ['ʌŋgwənt] n onguent *m*.
ungulate ['ʌŋgjʊleɪt] **1** adj ongulé. **2** n animal ongulé. **~s** les ongulés *mpl*.
unhallowed [ʌn'hæləʊd] adj non consacré, profane.
unhampered ['ʌn'hæmpəd] adj non entravé (*by* par), libre.
unhand [ʌn'hænd] vt (†† *or hum*) lâcher.
unhandy* [ʌn'hændɪ] adj gauche, maladroit.
unhappily [ʌn'hæpɪlɪ] adv (*miserably*) d'un air malheureux, sur un ton malheureux; (*unfortunately*) malheureusement.
unhappiness [ʌn'hæpɪnɪs] n (*NonC*) tristesse *f*, chagrin *m*.
unhappy [ʌn'hæpɪ] adj *person* (*sad*) triste, malheureux; (*ill-pleased*) mécontent; (*worried*) inquiet (*f* -ète); (*unfortunate*) malheureux, malchanceux; *childhood* malheureux; *remark, choice* malheureux, malencontreux; *coincidence* malheureux, regrettable, fâcheux; *circumstances* triste. **to make sb ~** rendre qn malheureux, faire de la peine à qn; **this ~ state of affairs** cette situation regrettable *or* déplorable *or* fâcheuse; **we are ~ about the decision** la décision nous inquiète; **I feel ~ about leaving him alone** je n'aime pas le laisser seul, cela m'inquiète de le laisser seul.
unharmed ['ʌn'hɑːmd] adj *person* sain et sauf, indemne; *thing* intact, non endommagé. **he escaped ~** il en est sorti indemne *or* sain et sauf.
unharness ['ʌn'hɑːnɪs] vt dételer (*from* de).
unhealthy [ʌn'helθɪ] adj *person, appearance, complexion* maladif; *air, place, habit* malsain; (*fig*) *curiosity* malsain, morbide. (*fig: dangerous*) **it's getting rather ~ around here*** les choses commencent à se gâter par ici; **the car sounds a bit ~*** le moteur fait un bruit qui ne me plaît pas.
unheard ['ʌn'hɜːd] **1** adj non entendu. **he was condemned ~** il a été condamné sans avoir été entendu. **2** comp ▶ **unheard-of** inouï, sans précédent; **it's quite unheard-of for such a thing to happen** ce genre de chose n'arrive pratiquement jamais *or* est sans précédent.
unhedged ['ʌn'hedʒd] adj (*esp US*) *venture, bet* hasardeux, à découvert.
unheeded ['ʌn'hiːdɪd] adj (*ignored*) négligé, ignoré; (*unnoticed*) inaperçu. **this warning went ~** on n'a pas prêté attention à *or* on n'a pas tenu compte de *or* on a ignoré cet avertissement; **it must not go ~** il faut en tenir compte, il faut y prêter attention.
unheeding ['ʌn'hiːdɪŋ] adj insouciant (*of* de), indifférent (*of* à). **they passed by ~** ils sont passés à côté sans faire attention.
unhelpful ['ʌn'helpfʊl] adj *person* peu serviable, peu obligeant; *advice, book, tool* qui n'aide guère, qui n'apporte rien d'utile. **I found that very ~** ça ne m'a pas aidé du tout, je ne suis pas plus avancé.
unhelpfully ['ʌn'helpfʊlɪ] adv *say, suggest* sans apporter quoi que ce soit d'utile.
unhelpfulness [ʌn'helpfʊlnɪs] n (*see* **unhelpful**) manque *m* de serviabilité; inutilité *f*.
unheralded ['ʌn'herəldɪd] adj sans tambour ni trompette.
unhesitating [ʌn'hezɪteɪtɪŋ] adj *reply, reaction* immédiat, prompt; *person* résolu, ferme, qui n'hésite pas. **his ~ generosity** sa générosité spontanée.
unhesitatingly [ʌn'hezɪteɪtɪŋlɪ] adv sans hésitation, sans hésiter.
unhindered ['ʌn'hɪndəd] adj *progress* sans obstacles, sans encombre, sans entrave; *movement* libre, sans encombre. **to go ~** passer librement *or* sans rencontrer d'obstacles *or* sans encombre; **he worked ~** il a travaillé sans être dérangé (*by* par).
unhinge [ʌn'hɪndʒ] vt enlever de ses gonds, démonter; (*fig*) *mind* déranger; *person* déséquilibrer.
unhinged ['ʌn'hɪndʒd] adj (*mad*) déséquilibré, dingue*. **he's ~** il est

déséquilibré *or* dingue*, il a le cerveau détraqué.
unhitch ['ʌn'hɪtʃ] vt *rope* décrocher, détacher; *horse* dételer.
unholy [ʌn'həʊlɪ] adj impie, profane; (* *fig*) impossible*. ~ **hour*** heure indue.
unhook ['ʌn'hʊk] vt *picture from wall* décrocher (*from* de); (*undo*) *garment* dégrafer.
unhoped-for [ʌn'həʊptfɔːʳ] adj inespéré.
unhopeful [ʌn'həʊpfʊl] adj *prospect, start* peu prometteur; *person* pessimiste, qui n'a guère d'espoir.
unhorse ['ʌn'hɔːs] vt désarçonner, démonter.
unhurried ['ʌn'hʌrɪd] adj *person* posé, pondéré, qui prend son temps; *steps, movement* lent; *reflection* mûr (*before n*), long (*f* longue); *journey* fait sans se presser. **after ~ consideration** après avoir longuement *or* posément considéré; **they had an ~ meal** ils ont mangé sans se presser.
unhurriedly ['ʌn'hʌrɪdlɪ] adv posément, en prenant son temps, sans se presser.
unhurt ['ʌn'hɜːt] adj indemne, sain et sauf. **to escape ~** sortir indemne *or* sain et sauf.
unhygienic ['ʌnhaɪ'dʒiːnɪk] adj contraire à l'hygiène, non hygiénique.
uni* ['juːnɪ] n (abbr of **university**) ≃ fac* *f*.
uni... ['juːnɪ] pref uni..., mono... .
unicameral ['juːnɪ'kæmərəl] adj (*Parl*) unicaméral.
UNICEF ['juːnɪsef] n (abbr of **United Nations Children's Fund**) U.N.I.C.E.F. *f*.
unicellular ['juːnɪ'seljʊləʳ] adj unicellulaire.
unicorn ['juːnɪkɔːn] n licorne *f*.
unicycle ['juːnɪˌsaɪkl] n monocycle *m*.
unidentified ['ʌnaɪ'dentɪfaɪd] adj *butterfly, person* non identifié. ~ **flying object** (*abbr* **UFO**) objet volant non identifié (*abbr* **OVNI** *m*).
unidirectional [ˌjuːnɪdɪ'rekʃənl] adj unidirectionnel.
unification [ˌjuːnɪfɪ'keɪʃən] n unification *f*.
uniform ['juːnɪfɔːm] 1 n uniforme *m*. **in ~** en uniforme; (*Mil etc*) **in full ~** en grand uniforme; **out of ~** *policeman, soldier* en civil; *schoolboy* en habits de tous les jours. 2 adj *length* uniforme; *colour, shade* pareil, même; *temperature* constant. **to make ~** uniformiser. 3 comp *trousers etc* d'uniforme.
uniformed ['juːnɪfɔːmd] adj a (*Police*) *officer* en tenue. ~ **branch** (catégorie *f* du) personnel *m* en tenue; ~ **staff** personnel en tenue. b *organization* qui porte un uniforme.
uniformity [ˌjuːnɪ'fɔːmɪtɪ] n (*NonC*) uniformité *f*.
uniformly ['juːnɪfɔːmlɪ] adv uniformément, sans varier.
unify ['juːnɪfaɪ] vt unifier. ~ **ing** *factor, force, theme etc* unificateur (*f* -trice).
unilateral ['juːnɪ'lætərəl] adj unilatéral. ~ **declaration of independence** proclamation unilatérale d'indépendance; ~ **disarmament** désarmement unilatéral.
unilateralism ['juːnɪ'lætərəlɪzəm] n adhésion *f* au désarmement unilatéral.
unilateralist ['juːnɪ'lætərəlɪst] n partisant *m* du désarmement unilatéral.
unilaterally ['juːnɪ'lætərəlɪ] adv unilatéralement.
unimaginable [ˌʌnɪ'mædʒnəbl] adj inimaginable, inconcevable.
unimaginably ['ʌnɪ'mædʒnəblɪ] adv *awful* inconcevablement; *beautiful* extraordinairement.
unimaginative ['ʌnɪ'mædʒnətɪv] adj peu imaginatif, qui manque d'imagination.
unimaginatively ['ʌnɪ'mædʒnətɪvlɪ] adv d'une manière peu imaginative, sans imagination.
unimaginativeness ['ʌnɪ'mædʒnətɪvnɪs] n manque *m* d'imagination.
unimpaired ['ʌnɪm'peəd] adj *quality* non diminué; *health, mental powers, hearing* aussi bon qu'auparavant; *prestige* intact, entier. **his sight is ~** sa vue ne s'est pas détériorée *or* n'a pas été affectée, sa vue est aussi bonne qu'auparavant, il a conservé toute sa vue.
unimpeachable [ˌʌnɪm'piːtʃəbl] adj *reputation, conduct, honesty* irréprochable, inattaquable; *references* irréprochable, impeccable; *evidence* irrécusable; *source* sûr.
unimpeded ['ʌnɪm'piːdɪd] adj libre, sans contrainte(s).
unimportant ['ʌnɪm'pɔːtənt] adj peu important, sans importance, insignifiant. **it's quite ~** ça n'a pas d'importance, c'est sans importance.
unimposing ['ʌnɪm'pəʊzɪŋ] adj peu imposant, peu impressionnant.
unimpressed ['ʌnɪm'prest] adj (*by sight, size, pleas etc*) peu impressionné (*by* par); (*by explanation, argument*) peu convaincu (*by* par). **I was ~** ça ne m'a pas impressionné *or* convaincu.
unimpressive ['ʌnɪm'presɪv] adj *person, amount* peu *or* guère impressionnant, insignifiant; *sight, achievement, result* peu *or* guère impressionnant, peu frappant; *argument, performance* peu convaincant.
unimproved ['ʌnɪm'pruːvd] adj *situation, position, work, health, appearance, condition* qui ne s'est pas amélioré, inchangé; *land* en friche; *method* non amélioré; *team* qui ne joue pas mieux qu'avant. *[invalid]* **he is ~** son état de santé ne s'est pas amélioré *or* demeure inchangé.
unincorporated [ˌʌnɪn'kɔːpəreɪtɪd] adj non incorporé (*in* dans); (*Comm, Jur*) non enregistré.
uninfluential ['ʌnɪnflʊ'enʃəl] adj sans influence, qui n'a pas d'influence.
uninformative ['ʌnɪn'fɔːmətɪv] adj *report, document, account* qui n'apprend rien. **he was very ~** il a été très réservé, il ne nous (*or* leur *etc*) a rien appris d'important.
uninformed ['ʌnɪn'fɔːmd] adj *person* mal informé, mal renseigné (*about* sur), qui n'est pas au courant (*about* de); *opinion* mal informé.
uninhabitable ['ʌnɪn'hæbɪtəbl] adj inhabitable.
uninhabited ['ʌnɪn'hæbɪtɪd] adj *house* inhabité; *island* désert, inhabité.
uninhibited ['ʌnɪn'hɪbɪtɪd] adj *person* sans inhibitions, qui n'a pas d'inhibitions, sans complexes*; *impulse, desire* non refréné; *dance* sans retenue.
uninitiated ['ʌnɪ'nɪʃɪeɪtɪd] 1 adj non initié (*into* à), qui n'est pas au courant (*into* de). 2 npl: **the ~** (*Rel*) les profanes *mpl*; (*gen*) les non-initiés *mpl*, les profanes; (*fig*) **it is complicated for the ~** c'est bien compliqué pour ceux qui ne s'y connaissent pas *or* qui ne sont pas au courant.
uninjured ['ʌn'ɪndʒəd] adj qui n'est pas blessé, indemne, sain et sauf. **he was ~ in the accident** il est sorti indemne *or* sain et sauf de l'accident.
uninspired ['ʌnɪn'spaɪəd] adj qui n'est pas inspiré, qui manque d'inspiration.
uninspiring ['ʌnɪn'spaɪərɪŋ] adj qui n'est pas *or* guère inspirant.
uninsured ['ʌnɪn'ʃʊəd] adj non assuré (*against* contre).
unintelligent ['ʌnɪn'telɪdʒənt] adj inintelligent.
unintelligible ['ʌnɪn'telɪdʒəbl] adj inintelligible.
unintelligibly ['ʌnɪn'telɪdʒəblɪ] adv inintelligiblement.
unintended ['ʌnɪn'tendɪd] adj, **unintentional** ['ʌnɪn'tenʃənl] adj involontaire, non intentionnel, inconscient. **it was quite ~** ce n'était pas fait exprès.
unintentionally ['ʌnɪn'tenʃnəlɪ] adv involontairement, sans le vouloir, sans le faire exprès.
uninterested [ʌn'ɪntrɪstɪd] adj indifférent (*in* à).
uninteresting ['ʌn'ɪntrɪstɪŋ] adj *book, account, activity* inintéressant, dépourvu d'intérêt; *person* ennuyeux; *offer* non intéressant.
uninterrupted ['ʌnˌɪntə'rʌptɪd] adj ininterrompu, continu.
uninterruptedly ['ʌnˌɪntə'rʌptɪdlɪ] adv sans interruption.
uninvited ['ʌnɪn'vaɪtɪd] adj *person* qui n'a pas été invité; *criticism* gratuit. **to arrive ~** arriver sans avoir été invité *or* sans invitation; **to do sth ~** faire qch sans y avoir été invité.
uninviting ['ʌnɪn'vaɪtɪŋ] adj peu attirant, peu attrayant; *food* peu appétissant.
union ['juːnjən] 1 n a (*gen, also Pol*) union *f*; (*marriage*) union, mariage *m*. **postal/customs ~** union postale/douanière; (*US*) **the U~** les États-Unis *mpl*; **U~ of Soviet Socialist Republics**† Union des Républiques socialistes soviétiques†; **U~ of South Africa**† Union d'Afrique du Sud†; (*Univ*) **the (Students') U~** l'Association *f* des Étudiants; (*fig*) **in perfect ~** en parfaite harmonie; **in ~ there is strength** l'union fait la force; *see* **state**.
b (*Ind: also* **trade ~**, (*US*) **labor ~**) syndicat *m*. **~s and management** ≃ les partenaires *mpl* sociaux; **to join a ~** adhérer à un syndicat, se syndiquer; **to join the U~ of Miners** adhérer au Syndicat des mineurs; **to belong to a ~** faire partie d'un syndicat, être membre d'un syndicat; **the government has challenged the power of the ~s** le gouvernement s'est attaqué à la toute-puissance des syndicats.
c (*Tech: for pipes etc*) raccord *m*.
2 comp (*Ind*) *card, leader, movement* syndical; *headquarters* du syndicat; *factory etc* syndiqué ►**union catalog** (*US*) catalogue *m* combiné (*de plusieurs bibliothèques*) ►**Union Jack** (*Brit*) Union Jack *m* (*drapeau du Royaume-Uni*) ►**union member** (*Ind*) membre *m* du syndicat, syndiqué(e) *m(f)* ►**union membership** (*members collectively*) membres *mpl* du *or* des syndicat(s); (*number of members*) effectifs *mpl* du *or* des syndicat(s) (*see also* **membership**) ►**union rate** (*Ind*) tarif *m* syndical ►**union school** (*US*) *lycée dont dépendent plusieurs écoles appartenant à un autre secteur* ►**union shop** (*US*) atelier *m* d'ouvriers syndiqués ►**union suit** (*US*) combinaison *f*.
unionism ['juːnjənɪzəm] n (*Ind*) syndicalisme *m*; (*Pol*) unionisme *m*.
unionist ['juːnjənɪst] n a (*Ind: trade ~*) membre *m* d'un syndicat, syndiqué(e) *m(f)*. **the militant ~s** les syndicalistes *mpl*, les militants syndicaux. b (*Pol: Ir, US etc*) unioniste *mf*.
unionization [ˌjuːnjənaɪ'zeɪʃən] n syndicalisation *f*.
unionize ['juːnjənaɪz] (*Ind*) 1 vt syndiquer. 2 vi se syndiquer.
uniparous [juː'nɪpərəs] adj (*Zool*) unipare; (*Bot*) à axe principal unique.
unique [juː'niːk] adj (*sole*) unique; (*outstanding*) unique, exceptionnel. ~ **selling point** avantage *m* unique; ~ **selling proposition** offre *f* exclusive *or* spéciale.
uniquely [juː'niːklɪ] adv exceptionnellement.
uniqueness [juː'niːknɪs] n caractère unique *or* exceptionnel.
unisex ['juːnɪseks] adj unisexe.
unison ['juːnɪsn, 'juːnɪzn] n (*gen, also Mus*) unisson *m*. **in ~** (*sing*) à l'unisson; **"yes" they said in ~** "oui" dirent-ils en chœur *or* tous ensemble; **to act in ~** agir de concert.
unit ['juːnɪt] 1 n a (*gen, Admin, Elec, Math, Mil, etc*) unité *f*; (*Univ etc*) unité de valeur, U.V. *f*. **administrative/linguistic/monetary ~** unité

administrative/linguistique/monétaire; ~ **of length** unité de longueur; *see* **thermal** *etc.*

b (*complete section, part*) bloc *m*, groupe *m*, élément *m*. **compressor ~** groupe *m* compresseur; **generative ~** groupe *m* électrogène; **the lens ~ of a camera** l'objectif *m* d'un appareil photographique; **you can buy the furniture in ~s** vous pouvez acheter le mobilier par éléments; *see* **kitchen, sink**[2] *etc.*

c (*building(s)*) locaux *mpl*; (*offices*) bureaux *mpl*; (*for engineering etc*) bloc *m*; (*for sport, activity*) centre *m*; (*looking after the public*) service *m*. **assembly/operating ~** bloc de montage/opératoire; **X-ray ~** service de radiologie; **sports ~** centre sportif; **the library/laboratory ~** la bibliothèque/les laboratoires *mpl*; **the staff accommodation ~** les logements *mpl* du personnel; *see also* **1d**.

d (*group of people*) unité *f*; (*in firm*) service *m*. **research ~** unité *or* service de recherches; (*Soc*) **family ~** groupe familial.

2 comp ►**unit furniture** mobilier *m* par éléments ►**unit-linked policy** (*Brit Ins*) *assurance-vie avec participation aux bénéfices d'un fonds commun de placement* ►**unit of account** *[European Community]* unité *f* de compte ►**unit price** prix *m* unitaire ►**unit rule** (*US Pol*) *règlement selon lequel la délégation d'un État à une convention vote en bloc suivant la majorité de ses membres* ►**unit trust** (*Brit Fin*) ≃ fond *m* commun de placement; (*company*) société *f* d'investissement à capital variable, SICAV *f*.

Unitarian [ˌjuːnɪˈtɛərɪən] adj, n (*Rel*) unitaire (*mf*), unitarien(ne) *m(f)*.

Unitarianism [ˌjuːnɪˈtɛərɪənɪzəm] n (*Rel*) unitarisme *m*.

unitary [ˈjuːnɪtərɪ] adj unitaire.

unite [juːˈnaɪt] 1 vt a (*join*) *countries, groups* unir; (*marry*) unir, marier. **to ~ A and B/A with B** unir A et B/A à B. b (*unify*) *party, country* unifier. 2 vi s'unir (*with sth* à qch; *with sb* à *or* avec qn; *against* contre; *in doing, to do* pour faire). **women of the world ~!** femmes du monde entier, unissez-vous!

united [juːˈnaɪtɪd] 1 adj (*Pol, gen*) uni; (*unified*) unifié; *front* uni; *efforts* conjugué. **by a ~ effort they ...** en unissant *or* en conjuguant leurs efforts ils ..., par leurs efforts conjugués ils ...; (*Prov*) **~ we stand, divided we fall** l'union fait la force. 2 comp ►**United Arab Emirates** Émirats *mpl* arabes unis ►**United Arab Republic** République Arabe Unie ►**United Kingdom (of Great Britain and Northern Ireland)** Royaume-Uni *m* (de Grande-Bretagne et d'Irlande du Nord) ►**United Nations (Organization)** (Organisation *f* des) Nations unies ►**United States (of America)** États-Unis *mpl* (d'Amérique).

unity [ˈjuːnɪtɪ] n unité *f*; (*fig*) harmonie *f*, accord *m*. (*Theat*) **~ of time/place/action** unité de temps/de lieu/d'action; (*Prov*) **~ is strength** l'union fait la force; **to live in ~** vivre en harmonie (*with* avec).

univalent [ˈjuːnɪˈveɪlənt] adj univalent.

univalve [ˈjuːnɪvælv] 1 adj univalve. 2 n mollusque *m* univalve.

universal [ˌjuːnɪˈvɜːsəl] 1 adj *language, remedy, suffrage, protest* universel. **such beliefs are ~** de telles croyances sont universelles *or* sont répandues dans le monde entier; **he's a ~ favourite** tout le monde l'aime *or* le trouve sympa*; **its use has become ~** son emploi s'est répandu *or* s'est généralisé dans le monde entier, son emploi s'est universalisé *or* est devenu universel; **to make sth ~** universaliser qch, rendre qch universel, généraliser qch; **~ joint** (joint *m* de) cardan *m*; (*US Comm*) **U~ Product Code** code *m* à barres; **~ time** temps universel. 2 n (*Philos*) universel *m*. (*Philos, Ling*) **~s** universaux *mpl*.

universality [ˌjuːnɪvɜːˈsælɪtɪ] n (*NonC*) universalité *f*.

universalize [ˌjuːnɪˈvɜːsəlaɪz] vt universaliser, rendre universel.

universally [ˌjuːnɪˈvɜːsəlɪ] adv (*throughout the world*) universellement, dans le monde entier. (*by everybody*) **~ praised** loué par chacun *or* de tout le monde.

universe [ˈjuːnɪvɜːs] n univers *m*.

university [ˌjuːnɪˈvɜːsɪtɪ] 1 n université *f*. **to be at/go to ~** être/aller à l'université *or* à la Fac*; **to study at ~** faire des études universitaires; *see* **open, residence**.

2 comp *degree, town, library* universitaire; *professor, student* d'université, de Fac* ►**Universities Central Council on Admissions** (*Brit*) *service central des inscriptions universitaires* ►**university education**: **he has a university education** il a fait des études universitaires ►**university entrance** entrée *f* à l'université; **university entrance examination** (*gen*) examen *m* d'entrée à l'université; (*for a limited number of places*) concours *m* d'entrée à l'université ►**University Grants Committee** (*Brit*) *commission gouvernementale responsable de la dotation des universités* ►**university place** place *f* dans une université.

unjust [ˈʌnˈdʒʌst] adj injuste (*to* envers).

unjustifiable [ʌnˈdʒʌstɪfaɪəbl] adj injustifiable.

unjustifiably [ʌnˈdʒʌstɪfaɪəblɪ] adv sans justification.

unjustified [ˈʌnˈdʒʌstɪfaɪd] adj (*gen*) injustifié; (*Typ*) non justifié.

unjustly [ˈʌnˈdʒʌstlɪ] adv injustement.

unkempt [ˈʌnˈkempt] adj *appearance* négligé, débraillé; *hair* mal peigné, ébouriffé; *clothes, person* débraillé.

unkind [ʌnˈkaɪnd] adj *person, behaviour* peu aimable, pas gentil, (*stronger*) cruel, méchant; *remark* méchant, peu gentil; *climate* rigoureux, rude; *fate* cruel. **to be ~** être peu aimable *or* pas gentil *or* cruel (*to sb* avec *or* envers qn); (*verbally*) être méchant (*to sb* avec *or* envers qn); **he was ~ enough to say ...** il a eu la méchanceté de dire ...

unkindly [ʌnˈkaɪndlɪ] 1 adv *speak, say* méchamment, (*stronger*) avec malveillance; *behave* méchamment, (*stronger*) cruellement. **don't take it ~ if ...** ne soyez pas offensé si ..., ne le prenez pas en mauvaise part si ...; **to take ~ to sth** accepter qch difficilement. 2 adj *person* peu aimable, peu gentil; *remark* méchant, peu gentil; *climate* rude. **in an ~ way** méchamment, avec malveillance.

unkindness [ʌnˈkaɪndnɪs] n a (*NonC*) *[person, behaviour]* manque *m* de gentillesse, (*stronger*) méchanceté *f*; *[words, remark]* méchanceté; *[fate]* cruauté *f*; *[weather]* rigueur *f*. b (*act of ~*) méchanceté *f*, action *or* parole méchante.

unknot [ˈʌnˈnɒt] vt dénouer, défaire (le nœud de).

unknowable [ˈʌnˈnəʊəbl] adj inconnaissable.

unknowing [ˈʌnˈnəʊɪŋ] adj inconscient. **... he said, all ~ ...** dit-il, sans savoir ce qui se passait.

unknowingly [ˈʌnˈnəʊɪŋlɪ] adv inconsciemment.

unknown [ˈʌnˈnəʊn] 1 adj inconnu. **it was ~ to him** cela lui était inconnu, il l'ignorait, il n'en savait rien; **~ to him the plane had crashed** l'avion s'était écrasé, ce qu'il ignorait; **~ to me, he bought ...** à mon insu, il a acheté ...; **a substance ~ to science** une substance inconnue de *or* ignorée de la science; (*Math, fig*) **~ quantity** inconnue *f*; **he's an ~ quantity** il représente une inconnue; (*Mil*) **the U~ Soldier** *or* **Warrior** le Soldat inconnu; (*Jur*) **murder by person or persons ~** meurtre *m* dont l'auteur est (*or* les auteurs sont) inconnu(s).

2 n a **the ~** (*Philos, gen*) l'inconnu *m*; (*Math, fig*) l'inconnue *f*; **voyage into the ~** voyage dans l'inconnu; **in space exploration there are many ~s** dans l'exploration de l'espace il y a de nombreuses inconnues.

b (*person, actor etc*) inconnu(e) *m(f)*. **they chose an ~ for the part of Macbeth** ils ont choisi un inconnu pour jouer le rôle de Macbeth.

unlace [ˈʌnˈleɪs] vt délacer, défaire (le lacet de).

unladen [ˈʌnˈleɪdn] adj *ship* à vide. **~ weight** poids *m* à vide.

unladylike [ˈʌnˈleɪdɪlaɪk] adj *girl, woman* mal élevée, qui manque de distinction; *manners, behaviour* peu distingué. **it's ~ to yawn** une jeune fille bien élevée ne bâille pas.

unlamented [ˈʌnləˈmentɪd] adj non regretté. **he died ~** on ne pleura pas sa mort.

unlatch [ˈʌnˈlætʃ] vt ouvrir, soulever le loquet de.

unlawful [ˈʌnˈlɔːfʊl] adj *act, means* illégal, illicite; *marriage* illégitime. (*Jur*) **~ assembly** (*outdoors*) attroupement séditieux; (*indoors*) réunion illégale.

unlawfully [ˈʌnˈlɔːfəlɪ] adv illégalement, illicitement.

unleaded [ˈʌnˈledɪd] 1 adj *petrol* sans plomb. 2 n (*also* **~ petrol**) essence *f* sans plomb.

unlearn [ˈʌnˈlɜːn] pret, ptp **unlearned** *or* **unlearnt** vt désapprendre.

unlearned [ˈʌnˈlɜːnɪd] adj ignorant, illettré.

unleash [ˈʌnˈliːʃ] vt *dog* détacher, lâcher; *hounds* découpler; (*fig*) *anger etc* déchaîner, déclencher.

unleavened [ˈʌnˈlevnd] adj *bread* sans levain, azyme (*Rel*). (*fig*) **~ by any humour** qui n'est pas égayé par le moindre trait d'humour.

unless [ənˈles] conj à moins que ... (ne) + *subj*, à moins de + *infin*. **I'll take it, ~ you want it** je vais le prendre, à moins que vous (ne) le vouliez; **take it, ~ you can find another** prenez-le, à moins d'en trouver un autre; **I won't do it ~ you phone me** je ne le ferai que si tu me téléphones; **I won't go ~ you do** je n'irai que si tu y vas, toi aussi; **~ I am mistaken** à moins que je (ne) me trompe, si je ne me trompe (pas); **~ I hear to the contrary** sauf avis contraire, sauf contrordre; (*Admin, Comm, Pharm etc*) **~ otherwise stated** sauf indication contraire.

unlettered [ˈʌnˈletəd] adj illettré.

unliberated [ˈʌnˈlɪbəreɪtɪd] adj *woman etc* qui n'est pas libéré *or* émancipé.

unlicensed [ˈʌnˈlaɪsənst] adj *activity* illicite, non autorisé; *vehicle* sans vignette. (*Brit*) **~ premises** établissement qui n'a pas de licence de débit de boissons.

unlikable [ˈʌnˈlaɪkəbl] adj = **unlikeable**.

unlike [ˈʌnˈlaɪk] 1 adj dissemblable (*also Math, Phys*), différent. **they are quite ~** ils ne se ressemblent pas du tout.

2 prep à la différence de, contrairement à. **~ his brother, he ...** à la différence de *or* contrairement à son frère, il ...; **it's quite ~ him to do that** ça ne lui ressemble pas *or* ça n'est pas dans ses habitudes *or* ça n'est pas (du tout) son genre de faire cela; **how ~ George!** on ne s'attendait pas à ça de la part de Georges!; **your house is quite ~ mine** votre maison n'est pas du tout comme la mienne *or* est très différente de la mienne; **the portrait is quite ~ him** le portrait ne lui ressemble pas, le portrait est très peu ressemblant.

unlikeable [ˈʌnˈlaɪkəbl] adj *person* peu sympathique; *town, thing* peu agréable.

unlikelihood [ʌnˈlaɪklɪhʊd] n, **unlikeliness** [ʌnˈlaɪklɪnɪs] n (*NonC*) improbabilité *f*.

unlikely [ʌnˈlaɪklɪ] adj *happening, outcome* improbable, peu probable; *explanation* peu plausible, invraisemblable; (*hum*) *hat etc* invraisemblable. **it is ~ that she will come, she is ~ to come** il est improbable *or* peu probable qu'elle vienne, il y a peu de chances pour qu'elle vienne; **she is ~ to succeed** elle a peu de chances de réussir; **that is ~ to happen**

cela ne risque guère d'arriver; **it is most ~** c'est fort *or* très improbable; **it is not ~ that** il est assez probable que + *subj*, il se pourrait bien que + *subj*, il n'est pas impossible que + *subj*; **in the ~ event of his accepting** au cas *or* dans le cas fort improbable où il accepterait; **it looks an ~ place for mushrooms** ça ne me paraît pas être un endroit à champignons; **the most ~ men have become prime minister** des hommes que rien ne semblait destiner à de telles fonctions sont devenus premier ministre; **she married a most ~ man** on ne s'attendait vraiment pas à ce qu'elle épouse (*subj*) un homme comme lui; **she wears the most ~ clothes** elle s'habille d'une façon on ne peut plus invraisemblable.

unlimited [ʌn'lɪmɪtɪd] **adj** *time, resources, opportunities* illimité; *patience, power* illimité, sans bornes.

unlined ['ʌn'laɪnd] **adj** *garment, curtain* sans doublure; *face* sans rides; *paper* uni, non réglé.

unlisted ['ʌn'lɪstɪd] **adj** qui ne figure pas sur une liste; (*St Ex*) non inscrit à la cote; (*US Telec*) qui ne figure pas dans l'annuaire, qui est sur la liste rouge. (*US Telec*) **to go ~** se faire mettre sur la liste rouge; (*Brit*) **~ building** édifice non classé.

unlit ['ʌn'lɪt] **adj** *lamp* non allumé; *road* non éclairé; *vehicle* sans feux.

unload ['ʌn'ləʊd] **1 vt** *ship, cargo, truck, rifle, washing machine* décharger; (*fig: get rid of*) se débarrasser de, se défaire de; (*St Ex*) se défaire de. **to ~ sth on (to) sb** se décharger de qch sur qn. **2 vi** *[ship, truck]* être déchargé, déposer son chargement.

unloaded ['ʌn'ləʊdɪd] **adj** *gun* qui n'est pas chargé; *truck, ship* qui est déchargé.

unloading ['ʌn'ləʊdɪŋ] **n** déchargement *m*.

unlock ['ʌn'lɒk] **1 vt** *door, box* ouvrir; (*fig*) *heart* ouvrir; *mystery* résoudre; *secret* révéler. **the door is ~ed** la porte n'est pas fermée à clef. **2 vi** *[lock, box, door]* s'ouvrir.

unlooked-for [ʌn'lʊktfɔːʳ] **adj** inattendu, inespéré.

unloose ['ʌn'luːs] **vt**, **unloosen** [ʌn'luːsn] **vt** *rope* relâcher, détendre; *knot* desserrer; *prisoner* libérer, relâcher; *grasp* relâcher, desserrer.

unlovable ['ʌn'lʌvəbl] **adj** peu *or* guère attachant.

unloved ['ʌn'lʌvd] **adj** mal aimé.

unlovely ['ʌn'lʌvlɪ] **adj** déplaisant.

unloving ['ʌn'lʌvɪŋ] **adj** peu affectueux, froid.

unluckily [ʌn'lʌkɪlɪ] **adv** malheureusement, par malheur. **~ for him** malheureusement pour lui; **the day started ~** la journée a mal commencé.

unluckiness [ʌn'lʌkɪnɪs] **n** manque *m* de chance *or* de veine*.

unlucky [ʌn'lʌkɪ] **adj** *person* malchanceux, qui n'a pas de chance *or* de veine*; *coincidence, event* malencontreux; *choice, decision* malheureux; *moment* mal choisi, mauvais; *day* de malchance, de déveine*; *omen* néfaste, funeste; *object, colour, number, action* qui porte malheur. **he is always ~** il n'a jamais de chance; **he tried to get a seat but he was ~** il a essayé d'avoir une place mais il n'y est pas arrivé; **he was just ~** il n'a pas eu de chance *or* de veine*; **he was ~ enough to meet her** il a eu la malchance *or* la déveine* de la rencontrer; **how ~ for you!** vous n'avez pas de chance! *or* de veine!*, ce n'est pas de chance pour vous!; **it was ~ (for her) that her husband should walk in just then** malheureusement pour elle son mari est entré à cet instant précis, elle n'a pas eu de chance *or* de veine* que son mari soit entré à cet instant précis; **it is ~ to walk under a ladder** ça porte malheur de passer sous une échelle.

unmade ['ʌn'meɪd] **1 pret, ptp of unmake.** **2 adj** *bed* non encore fait, défait; *road* non goudronné.

un-made-up ['ʌnmeɪd'ʌp] **adj** *face, person* non maquillé, sans maquillage.

unmake ['ʌn'meɪk] **pret, ptp unmade vt** défaire; (*destroy*) détruire, démolir.

unman ['ʌn'mæn] **vt** faire perdre courage à, émasculer (*fig*).

unmanageable [ʌn'mænɪdʒəbl] **adj** *vehicle, boat* difficile à manœuvrer, peu maniable; *animal* indocile; *person, child* impossible, difficile; *parcel, size, amount* peu maniable; *hair* difficile à coiffer, rebelle.

unmanly ['ʌn'mænlɪ] **adj** (*cowardly*) lâche; (*effeminate*) efféminé.

unmanned ['ʌn'mænd] **adj** *tank, ship* sans équipage; *spacecraft* inhabité. (*Space*) **~ flight** vol *m* sans équipage; **the machine was left ~ for 10 minutes** il n'y a eu personne au contrôle de la machine pendant 10 minutes; **the telephone was left ~** il n'y avait personne pour prendre les communications; **he left the desk ~** il a laissé le guichet sans surveillance; **3 of the positions were ~** 3 des positions n'étaient pas occupées; *see also* **unman**.

unmannerliness [ʌn'mænəlɪnɪs] **n** (*NonC*) manque *m* de savoir-vivre, impolitesse *f*.

unmannerly [ʌn'mænəlɪ] **adj** mal élevé, impoli, discourtois.

unmapped ['ʌn'mæpt] **adj** dont on n'a pas établi *or* dressé la carte.

unmarked ['ʌn'mɑːkt] **adj** (*unscratched etc*) sans tache, sans marque; *body, face* sans marque; (*unnamed*) *linen, suitcase* non marqué, sans nom; (*uncorrected*) *essay* non corrigé; (*Ling*) non marqué; (*Sport*) *player* démarqué. **~ police car** voiture (de police) banalisée.

unmarketable ['ʌn'mɑːkɪtəbl] **adj** invendable.

unmarriageable ['ʌn'mærɪdʒəbl] **adj** immariable.

unmarried ['ʌn'mærɪd] **adj** célibataire, qui n'est pas marié. **~ mother** mère *f* célibataire, fille-mère *f* (*pej*); **the ~ state** le célibat.

unmask ['ʌn'mɑːsk] **1 vt** (*lit, fig*) démasquer. **2 vi** ôter son masque.

unmatched ['ʌn'mætʃt] **adj** sans pareil, sans égal, incomparable.

unmeant ['ʌn'ment] **adj** qui n'est pas voulu, involontaire.

unmemorable ['ʌn'memərəbl] **adj** *book, film etc* qui ne laisse pas un souvenir impérissable. **an ~ face** un visage quelconque *or* le genre de visage que l'on oublie facilement.

unmentionable [ʌn'menʃnəbl] **1 adj** *object* dont il ne faut pas faire mention; *word* qu'il ne faut pas prononcer. **it is ~** il ne faut pas en parler. **2 n** (*hum*) **~s*** sous-vêtements *mpl*, dessous *mpl*.

unmerciful [ʌn'mɜːsɪfʊl] **adj** impitoyable, sans pitié (*towards* pour).

unmercifully [ʌn'mɜːsɪfəlɪ] **adv** impitoyablement, sans pitié.

unmerited ['ʌn'merɪtɪd] **adj** immérité.

unmethodical ['ʌnmɪ'θɒdɪkəl] **adj** peu méthodique.

unmindful [ʌn'maɪndfʊl] **adj**: **~ of** oublieux de, indifférent à, inattentif à.

unmistakable ['ʌnmɪs'teɪkəbl] **adj** *evidence, sympathy* indubitable; *voice, accent, walk* qu'on ne peut pas ne pas reconnaître. **the house is quite ~** vous ne pouvez pas ne pas reconnaître la maison, vous ne pouvez pas vous tromper de maison.

unmistakably ['ʌnmɪs'teɪkəblɪ] **adv** manifestement, sans aucun doute, indubitablement.

unmitigated [ʌn'mɪtɪgeɪtɪd] **adj** *terror, admiration* non mitigé, absolu; *folly* pur; *disaster* total. **it is ~ nonsense** c'est complètement idiot *or* absurde; **he is an ~ scoundrel/liar** c'est un fieffé coquin/menteur.

unmixed ['ʌn'mɪkst] **adj** pur, sans mélange.

unmolested ['ʌnmə'lestɪd] **adj** (*unharmed*) indemne, sain et sauf; (*undisturbed*) (laissé) en paix, tranquille.

unmortgaged ['ʌn'mɔːgɪdʒd] **adj** libre d'hypothèques, non hypothéqué.

unmotivated ['ʌn'məʊtɪveɪtɪd] **adj** immotivé, sans motif.

unmounted ['ʌn'maʊntɪd] **adj** (*without horse*) sans cheval, à pied; *gem* non serti, non monté; *picture, photo* non monté *or* collé sur carton; *stamp* non collé dans un album.

unmourned ['ʌn'mɔːnd] **adj** non regretté. **he died ~** on ne pleura pas sa mort.

unmoved ['ʌn'muːvd] **adj** insensible, indifférent (*by* à), qui n'est pas ému (*by* par). **he was ~ by her tears** ses larmes ne l'ont pas ému *or* touché; **it leaves me ~** cela me laisse indifférent *or* froid.

unmusical ['ʌn'mjuːzɪkəl] **adj** *sound* peu mélodieux, peu harmonieux; *person* peu musicien, qui n'a pas d'oreille.

unmuzzle ['ʌn'mʌzl] **vt** (*lit, fig*) démuseler.

unnam(e)able ['ʌn'neɪməbl] **adj** innommable.

unnamed ['ʌn'neɪmd] **adj** *fear, object* innommé; *author, donor* anonyme.

unnatural [ʌn'nætʃrəl] **adj** anormal, non naturel; *habit, vice, love* contre nature, pervers; *relationship* contre nature; (*affected*) *style, manner* affecté, forcé, qui manque de naturel. **it is ~ for her to be so unpleasant** il n'est pas normal *or* naturel qu'elle soit si désagréable.

unnaturally [ʌn'nætʃrəlɪ] **adv** anormalement; (*affectedly*) d'une manière affectée *or* forcée. **it was ~ silent** un silence anormal régnait; **not ~ we were worried** nous étions naturellement inquiets, bien entendu, nous étions inquiets.

unnavigable ['ʌn'nævɪgəbl] **adj** non navigable.

unnecessarily [ʌn'nesɪsərɪlɪ] **adv** *do, say* inutilement, pour rien. **he is ~ strict** il est sévère sans nécessité *or* plus que raison.

unnecessary [ʌn'nesɪsərɪ] **adj** (*useless*) inutile; (*superfluous*) superflu. **all this fuss is quite ~** c'est faire beaucoup d'histoires pour rien; **it is ~ to add that ...** (il est) inutile d'ajouter que ...; **it is ~ for you to come** il n'est pas nécessaire *or* il est inutile que vous veniez (*subj*).

unneighbourly, (*US*) **unneighborly** ['ʌn'neɪbəlɪ] **adj** peu sociable, qui n'agit pas en bon voisin. **this ~ action** cette action mesquine de la part de mon (*or* son *etc*) voisin.

unnerve ['ʌn'nɜːv] **vt** troubler, (*less strong*) déconcerter, dérouter.

unnerved ['ʌn'nɜːvd] **adj** troublé, (*less strong*) déconcerté, démonté.

unnerving ['ʌn'nɜːvɪŋ] **adj** troublant, (*less strong*) déconcertant.

unnervingly ['ʌn'nɜːvɪŋlɪ] **adv**: **~ quiet/calm** d'un calme/sang-froid déconcertant.

unnoticed ['ʌn'nəʊtɪst] **adj** inaperçu, inobservé. **to go ~** passer inaperçu.

unnumbered ['ʌn'nʌmbəd] **adj** *page* sans numéro, qui n'a pas été numéroté; *house* sans numéro; (*liter: innumerable*) innombrable.

UNO ['juːnəʊ] **n** (**abbr of United Nations Organization**) O.N.U. *f*.

unobjectionable ['ʌnəb'dʒekʃnəbl] **adj** *thing* acceptable; *person* à qui on ne peut rien reprocher.

unobservant ['ʌnəb'zɜːvənt] **adj** peu observateur (*f* -trice), peu perspicace.

unobserved ['ʌnəb'zɜːvd] **adj** inaperçu, inobservé. **he escaped ~** il s'est échappé sans être vu; **to go ~** passer inaperçu.

unobstructed ['ʌnəb'strʌktɪd] **adj** *pipe* non bouché, non obstrué; *path, road* dégagé, libre. **the driver has an ~ view to the rear** le conducteur a une excellente visibilité à l'arrière.

unobtainable ['ʌnəb'teɪnəbl] **adj** (*Comm etc*) impossible à obtenir *or* à se procurer. (*Telec*) **the number is ~** il est impossible d'obtenir le numéro.

unobtrusive [ˈʌnəbˈtruːsɪv] adj *person* discret (*f* -ète), effacé; *object* discret, pas trop visible; *smell, remark* discret.

unobtrusively [ˈʌnəbˈtruːsɪvlɪ] adv discrètement.

unoccupied [ˈʌnˈɒkjʊpaɪd] adj *person* inoccupé, désœuvré, qui n'a rien à faire; *house* inoccupé, inhabité; *seat* libre, qui n'est pas pris; *post* vacant; (*Mil*) *zone* libre.

unofficial [ˈʌnəˈfɪʃəl] adj *report, information, news* officieux, non officiel; *visit* privé. **in an ~ capacity** à titre privé *or* personnel *or* non officiel; (*Ind*) **~ strike** grève *f* sauvage.

unofficially [ˈʌnəˈfɪʃəlɪ] adv (*see* **unofficial**) officieusement, non officiellement.

unopened [ˈʌnˈəʊpənd] adj non ouvert, qui n'a pas été ouvert. **the book lay ~ all day** le livre est resté fermé toute la journée; **the bottle was ~** la bouteille n'avait pas été ouverte.

unopposed [ˈʌnəˈpəʊzd] adj (*Parl, gen*) sans opposition; (*Mil*) sans rencontrer de résistance. (*Parl*) **the bill was given an ~ second reading** le projet de loi a été accepté sans opposition à la deuxième lecture.

unorganized [ˈʌnˈɔːgənaɪzd] adj (*gen, Bio, Ind*) inorganisé; (*badly organized*) *event etc* mal organisé; *essay* qui manque d'organisation; *person* qui ne sait pas s'organiser, qui manque d'organisation.

unoriginal [ˈʌnəˈrɪdʒɪnəl] adj *person, work* qui manque d'originalité, peu original; *style, remark* banal; *idea* peu original, banal.

unorthodox [ˈʌnˈɔːθədɒks] adj (*gen*) peu orthodoxe; (*Rel*) hétérodoxe.

unostentatious [ˈʌn,ɒstənˈteɪʃəs] adj discret (*f* -ète), sans ostentation, simple.

unostentatiously [ˈʌn,ɒstənˈteɪʃəslɪ] adv discrètement, sans ostentation.

unpack [ˈʌnˈpæk] 1 vt *suitcase* défaire; *belongings* déballer. **to get ~ed** déballer ses affaires. 2 vi défaire sa valise, déballer ses affaires.

unpacking [ˈʌnˈpækɪŋ] n (*NonC*) déballage *m*. **to do one's ~** déballer ses affaires.

unpaid [ˈʌnˈpeɪd] adj *bill* impayé; *debt* non acquitté; *work, helper* non rétribué; *leave* non payé. **to work ~** travailler à titre bénévole, travailler gracieusement *or* gratuitement.

unpalatable [ʌnˈpælɪtəbl] adj *food* qui n'a pas bon goût, peu agréable à manger; (*fig*) *fact, report* désagréable, dur à digérer* *or* à avaler*; *truth* désagréable à entendre.

unparalleled [ʌnˈpærəleld] adj *beauty, wit* incomparable, sans égal; *success* hors pair; *event* sans précédent. **~ in the history of ...** sans précédent dans l'histoire de ... .

unpardonable [ʌnˈpɑːdnəbl] adj impardonnable, inexcusable. **it's ~ of him to have taken it** il est impardonnable de l'avoir pris.

unpardonably [ʌnˈpɑːdnəblɪ] adv inexcusablement. **~ rude** d'une impolitesse impardonnable *or* inexcusable.

unparliamentary [ˈʌn,pɑːləˈmentərɪ] adj antiparlementaire, indigne d'un parlementaire; (*fig*) injurieux, grossier.

unpatented [ˈʌnˈpeɪtntɪd] adj *invention* non breveté.

unpatriotic [ˈʌn,pætrɪˈɒtɪk] adj *person* peu patriote; *act, speech* antipatriotique.

unpatriotically [ˈʌn,pætrɪˈɒtɪkəlɪ] adv antipatriotiquement.

unpaved [ˈʌnˈpeɪvd] adj non pavé.

unperceived [ˈʌnpəˈsiːvd] adj inaperçu.

unperforated [ˈʌnˈpɜːfəreɪtɪd] adj non perforé.

unperturbed [ˈʌnpəˈtɜːbd] adj (*gen*) imperturbable. **~ by** non déconcerté *or* découragé par; **he was ~ by this failure** cet échec ne l'a pas découragé; **~ by this failure, he ...** sans se laisser décourager par cet échec, il ... .

unpick [ˈʌnˈpɪk] vt *seam* découdre, défaire; *stitch* défaire.

unpin [ˈʌnˈpɪn] vt détacher (*from* de); *sewing, one's hair* enlever les épingles de.

unplaced [ˈʌnˈpleɪst] adj (*Sport*) *horse* non placé; *athlete* non classé.

unplanned [ˈʌnˈplænd] adj *occurrence* imprévu; *baby* non prévu.

unplayable [ˈʌnˈpleɪəbl] adj injouable.

unpleasant [ʌnˈpleznt] adj *person* déplaisant, désagréable; *house, town* peu attrayant, déplaisant; *smell, taste* désagréable; *surprise, weather* désagréable, mauvais; *remark* désagréable, déplaisant, désobligeant; *experience, situation* désagréable, fâcheux. **he was very ~ to her** il a été très désagréable *or* déplaisant avec elle, il a été très désobligeant envers elle; **he had an ~ time** il a passé un mauvais quart d'heure; (*longer*) il a passé de mauvais moments.

unpleasantly [ʌnˈplezntlɪ] adv *reply* désagréablement; *behave, smile* de façon déplaisante. **the bomb fell ~ close** la bombe est tombée un peu trop près à mon (*or* son *etc*) goût.

unpleasantness [ʌnˈplezntnɪs] n *[experience, person]* caractère *m* désagréable; *[place, house]* aspect *or* caractère déplaisant; (*quarrelling*) discorde *f*, friction *f*, dissension *f*. **there has been a lot of ~ recently** il y a eu beaucoup de frictions *or* dissensions ces temps derniers; **after that ~ at the beginning of the meeting** après cette fausse note au début de la réunion.

unpleasing [ʌnˈpliːzɪŋ] adj déplaisant.

unplug [ˈʌnˈplʌg] vt (*Elec*) débrancher.

unplumbed [ˈʌnˈplʌmd] adj *depth, mystery* non sondé.

unpoetic(al) [ˈʌnpəʊˈetɪk(əl)] adj peu poétique.

unpolished [ˈʌnˈpɒlɪʃt] adj *furniture* non ciré, non astiqué; *floor, shoes* non ciré; *glass* dépoli; *silver* non fourbi; *diamond* non poli; (*fig*) *person* qui manque d'éducation *or* de savoir-vivre; *manners* peu raffiné; *style* qui manque de poli.

unpolluted [ˈʌnpəˈluːtɪd] adj *air, river* non pollué; (*fig*) *mind* non contaminé, non corrompu.

unpopular [ˈʌnˈpɒpjʊləʳ] adj *person, decision, style, model* impopulaire. **this measure was ~ with the workers** cette mesure était impopulaire chez les ouvriers, les ouvriers n'ont pas bien accueilli cette mesure; **to make o.s. ~** se rendre impopulaire; **he is ~ with his colleagues** ses collègues ne l'aiment pas beaucoup, il n'est pas très populaire *or* il est impopulaire auprès de ses collègues; **I'm rather ~ with him just now*** je ne suis pas très bien vu de lui *or* je n'ai pas la cote* auprès de lui en ce moment.

unpopularity [ˈʌn,pɒpjʊˈlærɪtɪ] n (*NonC*) impopularité *f*.

unpopulated [ˈʌnˈpɒpjʊleɪtɪd] adj inhabité.

unpractical [ˈʌnˈpræktɪkəl] adj *method, project, suggestion* qui n'est pas pratique; *tool* peu pratique. **he's very ~** il manque tout à fait de sens pratique, il n'a pas du tout l'esprit pratique.

unpractised, (*US*) **unpracticed** [ʌnˈpræktɪst] adj *person* inexpérimenté, inexpert; *movement etc* inexpert, inhabile; *eye, ear* inexercé.

unprecedented [ʌnˈpresɪdəntɪd] adj sans précédent.

unpredictability [ˈʌnprɪdɪktəˈbɪlɪtɪ] n imprévisibilité *f*.

unpredictable [ˈʌnprɪˈdɪktəbl] adj *event, consequence, reaction* imprévisible, impossible à prévoir; *person* aux réactions imprévisibles; *weather* incertain. **he is quite ~** il a des réactions imprévisibles, on ne sait jamais ce qu'il va faire *or* comment il va réagir.

unpredictably [ˈʌnprɪˈdɪktəblɪ] adv de façon imprévisible.

unprejudiced [ʌnˈpredʒʊdɪst] adj *person* impartial, sans parti pris, sans préjugés; *decision, judgment* impartial, sans parti pris.

unpremeditated [ˈʌnprɪˈmedɪteɪtɪd] adj non prémédité.

unprepared [ˈʌnprɪˈpɛəd] adj *meal etc* qui n'est pas préparé *or* prêt; *speech* improvisé. **I was ~ for the exam** je n'avais pas suffisamment préparé l'examen; **he began it quite ~** il l'a commencé sans préparation *or* sans y être préparé; **to catch sb ~** prendre qn au dépourvu; **he was ~ for the news** il ne s'attendait pas à la nouvelle, la nouvelle l'a pris au dépourvu *or* l'a surpris.

unpreparedness [ˈʌnprɪˈpɛərɪdnɪs] n (*NonC*) manque *m* de préparation, impréparation *f*.

unprepossessing [ˈʌn,priːpəˈzesɪŋ] adj *appearance* peu avenant. **he is ~** il présente* mal, il fait mauvaise impression; **it is ~** ça ne paie pas de mine.

unpresentable [ˈʌnprɪˈzentəbl] adj *person, thing* qui n'est pas présentable.

unpretentious [ˈʌnprɪˈtenʃəs] adj sans prétention(s).

unpriced [ˈʌnˈpraɪst] adj *goods* dont le prix n'est pas marqué.

unprincipled [ʌnˈprɪnsɪpld] adj peu scrupuleux, sans scrupules.

unprintable [ˈʌnˈprɪntəbl] adj (*lit*) impubliable; (*fig*) licencieux, obscène, scabreux. (*hum*) **his comments were quite ~** je ne peux vraiment pas répéter ce qu'il a dit.

unprivileged [ˈʌnˈprɪvɪlɪdʒd] adj (*gen*) défavorisé; (*Econ*) économiquement faible.

unproductive [ˈʌnprəˈdʌktɪv] adj *capital, soil* improductif; *discussion, meeting, work* stérile, improductif.

unprofessional [ˈʌnprəˈfeʃənl] adj *attitude, familiarity* contraire au code professionnel. **~ conduct** manquement *m* aux devoirs de la profession.

unprofitable [ˈʌnˈprɒfɪtəbl] adj (*gen*) peu rentable, peu profitable; *job* peu lucratif.

unprofitably [ˈʌnˈprɒfɪtəblɪ] adv sans profit.

unpromising [ˈʌnˈprɒmɪsɪŋ] adj peu prometteur.

unpromisingly [ˈʌnˈprɒmɪsɪŋlɪ] adv de façon peu prometteuse.

unprompted [ˈʌnˈprɒmptəd] 1 adj *remark, offer etc* non sollicité. 2 adv: **he did it ~** il l'a fait sans que rien ne lui soit demandé.

unpronounceable [ˈʌnprəˈnaʊnsəbl] adj imprononçable.

unprotected [ˈʌnprəˈtektɪd] adj *person, town* sans défense; *sex* sans protection; (*without roof etc*) *house* découvert; (*bare*) *wood* sans protection; (*open to weather*) *plant* exposé aux conditions extérieures.

unprovided-for [ʌnprəˈvaɪdɪd,fɔːʳ] adj *person* sans ressources.

unprovoked [ˈʌnprəˈvəʊkt] 1 adj *attack* sans provocation. **he was ~** on ne l'avait pas provoqué. 2 adv: **he said that ~** il a dit ça sans avoir été provoqué.

unpublishable [ˈʌnˈpʌblɪʃəbl] adj impubliable.

unpublished [ˈʌnˈpʌblɪʃt] adj inédit.

unpunctual [ˈʌnˈpʌŋktjʊəl] adj peu ponctuel, qui n'est jamais à l'heure.

unpunctuality [ˈʌn,pʌŋktjʊˈælɪtɪ] n (*NonC*) manque *m* de ponctualité.

unpunished [ˈʌnˈpʌnɪʃt] adj impuni. **to go ~** rester impuni.

unputdownable* [ˈʌn,pʊtˈdaʊnəbl] adj *book* inlâchable*.

unqualified [ˈʌnˈkwɒlɪfaɪd] adj a *craftsman, player* non qualifié; *teacher, engineer, nurse* non diplômé. **no ~ person will be considered** les candidats n'ayant pas les diplômes requis ne seront pas considérés; **he is ~ for the job** (*no paper qualifications*) il n'a pas les titres *or* le(s) di-

plôme(s) requis *or* il ne remplit pas les conditions requises pour ce poste; (*unsuitable*) il n'a pas les qualités requises pour tenir le poste; **he is ~ to judge** il n'est pas qualifié *or* compétent pour juger.
b (*absolute*) *acceptance, support, approval* inconditionnel, sans réserve; *praise* non mitigé, sans réserve; *success* formidable, fou (*f* folle); (**: utter*) *idiot* fini, achevé; *rogue, liar* fieffé (*before n*). **an ~ "yes"/"no"** un "oui"/"non" inconditionnel.
c (*Gram*) *noun* non qualifié.

unquenchable [ʌn'kwentʃəbl] **adj** (*lit, fig*) insatiable.

unquenched [ʌn'kwentʃt] **adj** *fire* non éteint; *desire* inassouvi. **~ thirst** soif non étanchée; (*fig*) soif inassouvie.

unquestionable [ʌn'kwestʃənəbl] **adj** *fact, authority* incontestable, indiscutable; *honesty, sincerity* hors de doute, certain.

unquestionably [ʌn'kwestʃənəblɪ] **adv** indiscutablement.

unquestioned [ʌn'kwestʃənd] **adj** qui n'est pas mis en question *or* en doute, incontesté, indiscuté.

unquestioning [ʌn'kwestʃənɪŋ] **adj** *acceptance* inconditionnel; *belief, faith, obedience* aveugle, total; *devotion* total. **an ~ supporter of ...** un(e) inconditionnel(le) de ... .

unquiet ['ʌn'kwaɪət] 1 **adj** *person, mind* inquiet (*f* -ète), tourmenté; *times* agité, troublé. 2 **n** inquiétude *f*; agitation *f*.

unquote ['ʌn'kwəʊt] **adv** (*in dictation*) fermez les guillemets; (*in report, lecture*) fin de citation.

unquoted ['ʌn'kwəʊtɪd] **adj** (*St Ex*) non coté.

unravel [ʌn'rævəl] 1 **vt** *material* effiler, effilocher; *knitting* défaire; *threads* démêler; (*fig*) *mystery* débrouiller, éclaircir; *plot* dénouer. 2 **vi** s'effiler, s'effilocher.

unread ['ʌn'red] **adj** *book, newspaper* qui n'a pas été lu. **he left the letter ~** il a laissé la lettre sans la lire; **the book lay ~ on the table** le livre est resté sur la table sans avoir été lu.

unreadable ['ʌn'ri:dəbl] **adj** *handwriting* illisible; *book* illisible, pénible à lire.

unreadiness ['ʌn'redɪnɪs] **n** (*NonC*) impréparation *f*.

unready ['ʌn'redɪ] **adj** mal préparé, qui n'est pas prêt. **he was ~ for what happened next** il ne s'attendait pas à ce qui est arrivé ensuite, ce qui est arrivé ensuite l'a pris au dépourvu.

unreal ['ʌn'rɪəl] **adj** a irréel. **it all seemed rather ~ to me** tout cela me paraissait quelque peu irréel, j'avais l'impression de rêver. b (*) (*extraordinary*) incroyable; (*difficult*) incroyablement difficile.

unrealistic ['ʌnrɪə'lɪstɪk] **adj** *person, project* peu réaliste, irréaliste. **it's a bit ~ to expect him to do it at once** ce serait trop demander que d'espérer qu'il le fasse aussitôt, il serait déraisonnable d'espérer qu'il le fasse aussitôt.

unrealistically ['ʌnrɪə'lɪstɪkəlɪ] **adv** *hard, expensive etc* excessivement, déraisonnablement.

unreality ['ʌnrɪ'ælɪtɪ] **n** (*NonC*) irréalité *f*.

unrealizable ['ʌnrɪə'laɪzəbl] **adj** irréalisable.

unrealized ['ʌn'ri:əlaɪzd] **adj** *plan, ambition* qui n'a pas été réalisé; *objective* qui n'a pas été atteint.

unreason ['ʌn'ri:zn] **n** (*NonC*) déraison *f*, manque *m* de bon sens.

unreasonable [ʌn'ri:znəbl] **adj** *person, suggestion* qui n'est pas raisonnable, déraisonnable; *demand, length of time* excessif, démesuré; *price* qui n'est pas raisonnable, exorbitant, exagéré. **at this ~ hour** à cette heure indue; **it is ~ to expect him to accept** on ne peut pas raisonnablement compter qu'il acceptera.

unreasonableness [ʌn'ri:znəblnɪs] **n** (*NonC*) *[person]* attitude *f* déraisonnable; *[demand, price]* caractère *m* exorbitant *or* excessif.

unreasonably [ʌn'ri:znəblɪ] **adv** déraisonnablement, excessivement, exagérément.

unreasoning [ʌn'ri:znɪŋ] **adj** *emotion, action* irraisonné; *person* qui ne raisonne pas.

unreclaimed ['ʌnrɪ'kleɪmd] **adj** *land* (*from forest*) non défriché; (*from sea*) non asséché.

unrecognizable ['ʌn'rekəgnaɪzəbl] **adj** méconnaissable, qui n'est pas reconnaissable.

unrecognized ['ʌn'rekəgnaɪzd] **adj** *value, worth, talent* méconnu; (*Pol*) *government, régime* non reconnu. **he walked ~ down the street** il a descendu la rue (à pied) sans être reconnu *or* sans que personne ne le reconnaisse.

unrecorded ['ʌnrɪ'kɔ:dɪd] **adj** a *event, deed, decision* non mentionné, qui n'est pas dans les archives, non enregistré. b (*on tape etc*) *song, programme* non enregistré.

unredeemed ['ʌnrɪ'di:md] **adj** *object from pawn* non dégagé; *debt* non remboursé, non amorti; *bill* non honoré; *mortgage* non purgé; *promise* non tenu; *obligation* non rempli; *sinner* non racheté; *fault* non réparé; *failing* non racheté, non compensé (*by* par).

unreel [ʌn'rɪəl] 1 **vt** *film* dérouler; *thread* dérouler, dévider; *fishing line* dérouler, lancer. 2 **vi** se dérouler; se dévider.

unrefined ['ʌnrɪ'faɪnd] **adj** *petroleum, metal* brut, non raffiné; *sugar* non raffiné; *person, manners, speech* qui manque de raffinement, fruste.

unreflecting ['ʌnrɪ'flektɪŋ] **adj** a *person* irréfléchi, impulsif; *act, emotion* irraisonné. b *surface* non réfléchissant.

unreformed ['ʌnrɪ'fɔ:md] **adj** *person* non amendé; *institution* non réformé.

unregarded ['ʌnrɪ'gɑ:dɪd] **adj** dont on ne tient pas compte, dont on ne fait pas cas. **his generosity went quite ~** sa générosité est passée inaperçue.

unregistered ['ʌn'redʒɪstəd] **adj** *birth* non déclaré; *car* non immatriculé; (*Post*) non recommandé.

unregretted ['ʌnrɪ'gretɪd] **adj** *person, act, words* que l'on ne regrette pas. **he died ~** on n'a pas pleuré sa mort.

unrehearsed ['ʌnrɪ'hɜ:st] **adj** *performance* sans répétition; *speech, reply* improvisé, spontané; *incident, effect* imprévu, inattendu.

unrelated ['ʌnrɪ'leɪtɪd] **adj**: **to be ~ to** *[facts, events]* n'avoir aucun rapport avec, être sans rapport avec; *[person]* n'avoir aucun lien de parenté avec; **the two events are quite ~** il n'y a aucun rapport entre les deux événements; **the two Smiths are ~** il n'y a aucun lien de parenté entre les deux Smith, les deux Smith ne sont pas parents entre eux.

unrelenting ['ʌnrɪ'lentɪŋ] **adj** implacable.

unreliability ['ʌnrɪˌlaɪə'bɪlɪtɪ] **n** (*NonC*) *[person]* manque *m* de sérieux; *[machine]* manque *m* de fiabilité.

unreliable ['ʌnrɪ'laɪəbl] **adj** *person* sur qui on ne peut compter, qui manque de sérieux; *company, firm* qui n'est pas sérieux, qui n'inspire pas confiance; *car, machine, map* peu fiable; *news* sujet à caution, de source douteuse; *source of information* douteux. **he's very ~** on ne peut vraiment pas compter sur lui *or* se fier à lui *or* avoir confiance en lui; **my watch is ~** je ne peux pas me fier à ma montre.

unrelieved ['ʌnrɪ'li:vd] **adj** *pain* constant, que rien ne soulage; *gloom, anguish* constant, que rien ne vient dissiper. **~ grey/black** gris/noir uniforme; **~ boredom** ennui mortel; **bare landscape ~ by any trees** paysage nu dont l'uniformité n'est même pas rompue par la présence d'arbres.

unremarkable ['ʌnrɪ'mɑ:kəbl] **adj** médiocre, non remarquable, quelconque.

unremarked ['ʌnrɪ'mɑ:kt] **adj** inaperçu.

unremitting ['ʌnrɪ'mɪtɪŋ] **adj** *kindness, help, effort* inlassable, infatigable; *hatred* opiniâtre, constant. **he was ~ in his attempts to help us** il s'est inlassablement efforcé de nous aider.

unremittingly ['ʌnrɪ'mɪtɪŋlɪ] **adv** sans cesse, sans relâche, inlassablement.

unremunerative ['ʌnrɪ'mju:nərətɪv] **adj** peu rémunérateur (*f* -trice), mal payé; (*fig*) peu fructueux, peu rentable.

unrepaid ['ʌnrɪ'peɪd] **adj** *loan* non remboursé.

unrepealed ['ʌnrɪ'pi:ld] **adj** non abrogé.

unrepeatable ['ʌnrɪ'pi:təbl] **adj** *offer, bargain* unique, exceptionnel; *comment* trop grossier pour être répété. **what she said is ~** je n'ose répéter ce qu'elle a dit.

unrepentant ['ʌnrɪ'pentənt] **adj** impénitent. **he is quite ~ about it** il ne manifeste pas le moindre repentir, il n'en a nullement honte.

unreported ['ʌnrɪ'pɔ:tɪd] **adj** *crime, attack, accident etc* non signalé. *[crime etc]* **to go ~** ne pas être signalé.

unrepresentative ['ʌnˌreprɪ'zentətɪv] **adj** peu représentatif (*of* de).

unrepresented ['ʌnˌreprɪ'zentɪd] **adj** non représenté, sans représentant.

unrequited ['ʌnrɪ'kwaɪtɪd] **adj** non partagé, qui n'est pas payé de retour.

unreserved ['ʌnrɪ'zɜ:vd] **adj** *seat* non réservé; *admiration* entier, sans réserve.

unreservedly ['ʌnrɪ'zɜ:vɪdlɪ] **adv** *speak* franchement, sans réserve; *approve, agree, accept* sans réserve, entièrement.

unresisting ['ʌnrɪ'zɪstɪŋ] **adj** *person* qui ne résiste pas, soumis; *attitude, obedience* soumis.

unresolved ['ʌnrɪ'zɒlvd] **adj** non résolu.

unresponsive ['ʌnrɪs'pɒnsɪv] **adj** qui ne réagit pas. **~ to** insensible à; **he was fairly ~ when I spoke to him about it** il n'a pas beaucoup réagi quand je lui en ai parlé; **the engine was ~** le moteur n'était pas nerveux.

unrest [ʌn'rest] **n** (*NonC*) agitation *f*, (*stronger*) troubles *mpl*.

unrestrained ['ʌnrɪ'streɪnd] **adj** *feelings* non contenu, non refréné; *language, behaviour* outrancier. **he was very ~** (*gen*) il a donné libre cours à sa colère (*or* son indignation *etc*), (*specifically speaking*) il n'a pas mâché ses mots.

unrestrainedly [ˌʌnrɪ'streɪnədlɪ] **adv** sans retenue.

unrestricted ['ʌnrɪ'strɪktɪd] **adj** *time, power* sans restriction, illimité; *access* libre.

unrevealed ['ʌnrɪ'vi:ld] **adj** non révélé.

unrewarded ['ʌnrɪ'wɔ:dɪd] **adj** *person, effort* non récompensé, sans récompense. **to go ~** rester sans récompense.

unrewarding ['ʌnrɪ'wɔ:dɪŋ] **adj** *work, activity* (*unproductive*) infructueux, qui ne donne rien; (*unfulfilling*) ingrat, qui n'en vaut pas la peine; (*financially*) peu rémunérateur (*f* -trice).

unrighteous [ʌn'raɪtʃəs] 1 **adj** impie, pervers. 2 **npl**: **the ~** les impies *mpl*.

unrighteousness [ʌn'raɪtʃəsnɪs] **n** (*NonC*) perversité *f*.

unripe ['ʌn'raɪp] **adj** vert, qui n'est pas mûr.

unrivalled, (*US*) *also* **unrivaled** [ʌn'raɪvəld] **adj** sans égal, sans concurrence, incomparable.

unroadworthy ['ʌn'rəʊd,wɜːðɪ] adj *car* qui n'est pas en état de marche.
unrobe ['ʌn'rəʊb] 1 vi se dévêtir, se dépouiller de ses vêtements (*de cérémonie*); (*undress*) se déshabiller. 2 vt dépouiller de ses vêtements (*de cérémonie*), dévêtir; (*undress*) déshabiller.
unroll ['ʌn'rəʊl] 1 vt dérouler. 2 vi se dérouler.
unromantic ['ʌnrəʊ'mæntɪk] adj *place, landscape, words* peu romantique; *person* terre à terre, prosaïque, peu romantique.
unrope ['ʌn'rəʊp] vi (*Climbing*) se décorder.
UNRRA [,juːenɑːrɑːr'eɪ] n (abbr of **United Nations Relief and Rehabilitation Administration**) Administration *f* des Nations unies pour le secours et la reconstruction.
unruffled ['ʌn'rʌfld] adj *hair* lisse; *water* lisse, non ridé; *person* calme, imperturbable, qui ne se départ pas de son calme. **to carry on ~** continuer sans se laisser déconcerter *or* sans sourciller.
unruled ['ʌn'ruːld] adj *paper* uni, non réglé.
unruly [ʌn'ruːlɪ] adj *child* indiscipliné, turbulent; *hair* indiscipliné. **~ behaviour** indiscipline *f*.
unsaddle ['ʌn'sædl] vt *horse* desseller; *rider* désarçonner.
unsafe ['ʌn'seɪf] adj a (*dangerous*) *machine, car* dangereux, peu sûr; *ladder* dangereux, instable; *structure, bridge* dangereux, non solide; *journey* périlleux, risqué; *toy* dangereux; *method* peu sûr. (*gen*) **~ to eat** *or* **drink** impropre à la consommation; *water* **~ to drink** non potable. b (*in danger*) en danger. **to feel ~** ne pas se sentir en sécurité.
unsaid ['ʌn'sed] (pret, ptp of **unsay**) adj inexprimé, passé sous silence. **much was left ~** on a passé beaucoup de choses sous silence, il restait beaucoup de choses à dire; **that would have been better left ~** il aurait mieux valu passer cela sous silence *or* ne pas dire cela, ce n'était pas une chose à dire.
unsalaried ['ʌn'sælərɪd] adj non rémunéré.
unsaleable ['ʌn'seɪləbl] adj invendable.
unsalted ['ʌn'sɔːltɪd] adj (*gen*) sans sel, non salé; *butter* sans sel, doux.
unsanitary [ʌn'sænɪtərɪ] adj = **insanitary**.
unsatisfactory ['ʌn,sætɪs'fæktərɪ] adj peu satisfaisant, qui laisse à désirer.
unsatisfied ['ʌn'sætɪsfaɪd] adj *person* insatisfait, mécontent (*with* de); (*unconvinced*) non convaincu, non persuadé; *desire* insatisfait, inassouvi; *curiosity, need, demand, appetite* non satisfait.
unsatisfying ['ʌn'sætɪsfaɪɪŋ] adj *result* peu satisfaisant; *work* ingrat, qui donne peu de satisfaction; *food* peu nourrissant.
unsaturated ['ʌn'sætʃəreɪtɪd] adj (*Chem*) non saturé.
unsavoury, (*US*) **unsavory** ['ʌn'seɪvərɪ] adj *food* mauvais au goût; *smell* nauséabond; (*fig*) *person, district* peu recommandable; *reputation* équivoque, louche; *subject* plutôt répugnant, très déplaisant. **an ~ business** une sale affaire.
unsay ['ʌn'seɪ] pret, ptp **unsaid** vt se dédire de. **you can't ~ it now** tu ne peux plus te rétracter *or* te dédire; *see also* **unsaid**.
unscathed ['ʌn'skeɪðd] adj (*physically*) indemne; (*psychologically*) non affecté (*by* par). **to escape ~** s'en sortir sans une égratignure *or* sain et sauf *or* indemne.
unscented [ʌn'sentɪd] adj non parfumé.
unscholarly ['ʌn'skɒləlɪ] adj *person* peu érudit, peu savant; *work* qui manque d'érudition.
unschooled ['ʌn'skuːld] adj *person* qui n'a pas d'instruction; *horse* qui n'a pas été dressé. **~ in** qui n'a rien appris de, ignorant en matière de *or* pour ce qui est de.
unscientific ['ʌn,saɪən'tɪfɪk] adj *method, approach* peu scientifique; *person* qui manque d'esprit scientifique; (*fig*) peu méthodique.
unscramble ['ʌn'skræmbl] vt (*Telec*) déchiffrer.
unscratched ['ʌn'skrætʃt] adj *surface* non rayé, intact; *person* indemne, sain et sauf. **to escape ~** s'en sortir sans une égratignure.
unscrew ['ʌn'skruː] 1 vt dévisser. 2 vi se dévisser.
unscripted ['ʌn'skrɪptɪd] adj (*Rad, TV*) improvisé, non préparé d'avance.
unscrupulous [ʌn'skruːpjʊləs] adj *person* dénué de scrupules, sans scrupules, malhonnête, indélicat; *act* malhonnête, indélicat.
unscrupulously [ʌn'skruːpjʊləslɪ] adv sans scrupule(s), peu scrupuleusement.
unscrupulousness [ʌn'skruːpjʊləsnɪs] n (*NonC*) *[person]* manque *m* de scrupules *or* de délicatesse; *[act]* malhonnêteté *f*, manque de délicatesse.
unseal ['ʌn'siːl] vt (*open*) ouvrir, décacheter; (*take seal off*) desceller.
unseasonable [ʌn'siːznəbl] adj *fruit etc* hors de saison. **the weather is ~** ce n'est pas un temps de saison.
unseasonably [ʌn'siːznəblɪ] adv: **it was ~ warm/cold** ce temps tiède/froid n'était pas de saison.
unseasoned ['ʌn'siːznd] adj *timber* vert, non conditionné; *food* non assaisonné.
unseat ['ʌn'siːt] vt *rider* désarçonner; (*Parl*) *Member of Parliament* faire perdre son siège à, sortir.
unseaworthy ['ʌn'siː,wɜːðɪ] adj qui n'est pas en état de naviguer *or* en mesure de tenir la mer.
unsecured ['ʌnsɪ'kjʊəd] adj (*Fin*) à découvert, sans garantie.
unseeded [ʌn'siːdɪd] adv (*Tennis etc*) *player* non classé.
unseeing ['ʌn'siːɪŋ] adj (*lit, fig*) aveugle.
unseemliness [ʌn'siːmlɪnɪs] n (*see* **unseemly**) inconvenance *f*, manque *m* de bienséance; indécence *f*; grossièreté *f*.
unseemly [ʌn'siːmlɪ] adj *behaviour* inconvenant, malséant; *dress* inconvenant, indécent; *language* inconvenant, grossier.
unseen ['ʌn'siːn] 1 adj (*invisible*) invisible; (*unnoticed*) inaperçu. (*esp Brit: Scol, Univ*) **~ translation** version *f* (*sans préparation*). 2 adv (*invisibly*) invisiblement; (*unnoticed*) inaperçu; *escape* sans être vu. 3 n a (*esp Brit: Scol, Univ*) version *f* (*sans préparation*). b **the ~** le monde occulte.
unselfconscious ['ʌn,self'kɒnʃəs] adj naturel. **he was very ~ about it** cela ne semblait nullement le gêner *or* l'intimider.
unselfconsciously ['ʌn,self'kɒnʃəslɪ] adv avec naturel, sans la moindre gêne.
unselfish ['ʌn'selfɪʃ] adj *person* généreux; *act* désintéressé, généreux.
unselfishly ['ʌn'selfɪʃlɪ] adv sans penser à soi, généreusement.
unselfishness ['ʌn'selfɪʃnɪs] n (*NonC*) *[person]* générosité *f*; *[act]* désintéressement *m*, générosité.
unsentimental ['ʌn'sentɪmentl] adj *person* qui ne se laisse pas influencer par ses sentiments, non sentimental; *account, story* dénué de (tout) sentiment, non sentimental.
unserviceable ['ʌn'sɜːvɪsəbl] adj inutilisable, hors d'état de fonctionner.
unsettle ['ʌn'setl] vt *person, weather* perturber; *stomach* déranger.
unsettled ['ʌn'setld] adj a *person* perturbé; *weather, future* incertain; *market* instable; *question* pendant, qui n'a pas été décidé; *account* impayé, non acquitté; (*Med*) *stomach* dérangé. **he feels ~ in his job** il n'est pas vraiment satisfait de son emploi. b (*without settlers*) *territory* inhabité, sans habitants.
unsettling ['ʌn'setlɪŋ] adj *news* inquiétant; *influence, effect* perturbateur (*f* -trice).
unsex ['ʌn'seks] vt faire perdre sa masculinité (*or* féminité) à; (*make impotent*) rendre impuissant.
unsexed ['ʌn'sekst] adj: **~ chicks** poussins *mpl* au sexage desquels on n'a pas procédé.
unshackle ['ʌn'ʃækl] vt ôter les fers à, désenchaîner; (*fig*) émanciper, libérer.
unshaded ['ʌn'ʃeɪdɪd] adj (*in sunlight*) non ombragé, en plein soleil; *lamp* sans abat-jour; *part of drawing or map etc* non hachuré.
unshak(e)able ['ʌn'ʃeɪkəbl] adj inébranlable.
unshak(e)ably ['ʌn'ʃeɪkəblɪ] adv *certain, convinced* au plus haut point.
unshaken ['ʌn'ʃeɪkən] adj *resolve* inébranlable; *person* non déconcerté.
unshaven ['ʌn'ʃeɪvn] adj non rasé; (*bearded*) barbu.
unsheathe ['ʌn'ʃiːð] vt dégainer.
unship ['ʌn'ʃɪp] vt *cargo* décharger; débarquer.
unshockable ['ʌn'ʃɒkəbl] adj: **he is (completely) ~** il n'est choqué par rien.
unshod ['ʌn'ʃɒd] adj *horse* qui n'est (*or* n'était *etc*) pas ferré; *person* déchaussé, pieds nus.
unshrinkable ['ʌn'ʃrɪŋkəbl] adj irrétrécissable (au lavage).
unsighted ['ʌn'saɪtɪd] adj (*unseen*) qui n'est pas en vue, que l'on n'a pas vu. (*unable to see sth*) **the goalkeeper was ~ by a defender** le gardien de but était privé de vision par un défenseur.
unsightliness [ʌn'saɪtlɪnɪs] n (*NonC*) aspect disgracieux, laideur *f*.
unsightly [ʌn'saɪtlɪ] adj disgracieux, laid. **he has an ~ scar on his face** une cicatrice lui dépare le visage.
unsigned ['ʌn'saɪnd] adj non signé, sans signature.
unsinkable ['ʌn'sɪŋkəbl] adj insubmersible; (*fig: esp Pol*) inattaquable.
unskilful, (*US*) **unskillful** ['ʌn'skɪlfʊl] adj (*clumsy*) maladroit; (*inexpert*) malhabile, inexpert.
unskilfully, (*US*) **unskillfully** ['ʌn'skɪlfəlɪ] adv (*clumsily*) avec maladresse; (*inexpertly*) malhabilement.
unskilled ['ʌn'skɪld] adj (*gen*) inexpérimenté, inexpert; (*Ind*) *work* de manœuvre, ne nécessitant pas de connaissances professionnelles spéciales. **~ worker** manœuvre *m*, ouvrier *m*, -ière *f* non spécialisé(e).
unskimmed ['ʌn'skɪmd] adj *milk* non écrémé, entier.
unsmiling [ʌn'smaɪlɪŋ] adj *person* qui ne sourit pas, peu souriant.
unsmilingly [ʌn'smaɪlɪŋlɪ] adv sans (le) sourire.
unsociability ['ʌn,səʊʃə'bɪlɪtɪ] n (*NonC*) insociabilité *f*.
unsociable [ʌn'səʊʃəbl] adj insociable, sauvage. **he's very ~** il est vraiment insociable *or* sauvage; **I'm feeling rather ~ this evening** je n'ai guère envie de voir des gens ce soir.
unsocial [ʌn'səʊʃəl] adj: **to work ~ hours** travailler en dehors des heures normales.
unsold ['ʌn'səʊld] adj invendu.
unsoldierly ['ʌn'səʊldʒəlɪ] adj *behaviour, emotion* indigne d'un soldat; *appearance* peu militaire, peu martial; *person* qui n'a pas l'esprit *or* la fibre militaire.
unsolicited ['ʌnsə'lɪsɪtɪd] adj non sollicité.
unsolvable ['ʌn'sɒlvəbl] adj insoluble, qu'on ne peut résoudre.
unsolved ['ʌn'sɒlvd] adj non résolu, inexpliqué; *crossword* non terminé. **one of the great ~ mysteries** une des grandes énigmes.
unsophisticated ['ʌnsə'fɪstɪkeɪtɪd] adj *person* (*in taste, lifestyle*) sim-

ple; (*in attitude*) simple, naturel; (*in appearance*) qui n'est pas sophistiqué; *style, room* simple; *film, book, song, machine* simple, qui n'est pas compliqué. **an ~ wine** un petit vin sans prétention.

unsought [ˈʌnˈsɔːt] **adj** (*also* **~-for**) non recherché, non sollicité.

unsound [ˈʌnˈsaʊnd] **adj** *health* précaire, chancelant; *heart* non solide; *constitution, teeth, lungs, fruit, tree* qui n'est pas sain; *timber* pourri, gâté; *structure, floor, bridge* en mauvais état, peu solide; *bank, business, organization* peu solide; *alliance, investment* peu sûr, hasardeux; *reasoning, judgment, argument* mal fondé, spécieux, boiteux, peu valable; *policy, decision, step, advice, opinion* peu sensé, peu judicieux; *case, training* peu solide; *claim, title* peu valable, peu acceptable; *statesman, player* incompétent. (*Jur*) **of ~ mind** qui ne jouit pas de toutes ses facultés mentales; **the book is ~ on some points** certains aspects de ce livre sont discutables, certains arguments de ce livre sont spécieux *or* boiteux.

unsparing [ʌnˈspɛərɪŋ] **adj** **a** (*lavish*) prodigue (*of* de), généreux. **to be ~ in one's efforts to do** ne pas ménager ses efforts pour faire. **b** (*cruel*) impitoyable, implacable.

unsparingly [ʌnˈspɛərɪŋlɪ] **adv** *give* généreusement, avec prodigalité, avec largesse; *work* inlassablement.

unspeakable [ʌnˈspiːkəbl] **adj** (*work*) indicible, ineffable, indescriptible; (*bad*) indescriptible, innommable. **it's ~!** les mots me manquent!, c'est dégoûtant!

unspeakably [ʌnˈspiːkəblɪ] **adv** *dirty* indescriptiblement; *suffer* affreusement. **~ bad** affreusement mauvais, exécrable.

unspecifically [ˈʌnspəˈsɪfɪkəlɪ] **adv** *talk etc* en restant dans le vague, sans entrer dans les détails.

unspecified [ˈʌnˈspesɪfaɪd] **adj** non spécifié.

unspectacular [ˈʌnspekˈtækjʊləʳ] **adj** *performance, math, results, work* peu remarquable.

unspent [ˈʌnˈspent] **adj** *money, funds* non dépensé, qui reste.

unspoiled [ˈʌnˈspɔɪld] **adj**, **unspoilt** [ˈʌnˈspɔɪlt] **adj** *paint, dress etc* intact, qui n'est pas abîmé; *countryside, beauty, view* qui n'est pas déparé *or* défiguré; *style* naturel; *child* qui reste naturel. **~ by** non gâché par; **he remained ~ by his great success** malgré son grand succès il restait aussi simple qu'avant.

unspoken [ˈʌnˈspəʊkən] **adj** *word* non prononcé; *thought* inexprimé; *consent* tacite.

unsporting [ˈʌnˈspɔːtɪŋ] **adj**, **unsportsmanlike** [ˈʌnˈspɔːtsmənlaɪk] **adj** (*Sport, gen*) déloyal. **to be ~** (*not play fair*) être déloyal, ne pas jouer franc jeu, ne pas être sport *inv*; (*be bad loser*) être mauvais joueur; **that's very ~ of you** ce n'est pas très chic de votre part.

unspotted [ˈʌnˈspɒtɪd] **adj** (*lit, fig*) sans tache, immaculé.

unstable [ˈʌnˈsteɪbl] **adj** (*all senses*) instable.

unstained [ˈʌnˈsteɪnd] **adj** (*not coloured*) *furniture, floor* non teinté; (*clean*) *garment, surface* immaculé, sans tache; *reputation* non terni, sans tache.

unstamped [ˈʌnˈstæmpt] **adj** *letter* non affranchi, non timbré; *document, passport* non tamponné.

unstated [ʌnˈsteɪtɪd] **adj** *agreement, assumption, understanding* inexprimé, sous-entendu; *reason* inexprimé.

unstatesmanlike [ˈʌnˈsteɪtsmənlaɪk] **adj** peu diplomatique.

unsteadily [ˈʌnˈstedɪlɪ] **adv** *walk* d'un pas chancelant *or* incertain; *say* d'une voix mal assurée.

unsteadiness [ˈʌnˈstedɪnɪs] **n** (*see* **unsteady**) manque *m* de stabilité; manque d'assurance; irrégularité *f*.

unsteady [ˈʌnˈstedɪ] **adj** *ladder, structure* instable, branlant; *hand* mal assuré, tremblant; *step, gait, voice* mal assuré, chancelant; *flame* vacillant; *rhythm* irrégulier; (*fig: unreliable*) peu sûr, inconstant, changeant; *mind* irrésolu, instable. **to be ~ on one's feet** ne pas très bien tenir sur ses jambes, marcher d'un pas chancelant *or* incertain; (*from drink*) tituber, chanceler.

unstick [ˈʌnˈstɪk] **pret, ptp unstuck** **1** **vt** décoller. **to come unstuck** *[stamp, notice]* se décoller; (*) *[plan]* tomber à l'eau*; **he certainly came unstuck* over that scheme** il est vraiment tombé sur un bec* pour ce qui est de ce projet. **2** **vi** se décoller.

unstinted [ʌnˈstɪntɪd] **adj** *praise* sans réserve; *generosity* sans bornes; *efforts* illimité, incessant.

unstinting [ʌnˈstɪntɪŋ] **adj** *person* prodigue (*of* de), généreux; *praise* sans réserve; *kindness, generosity* sans bornes. **to be ~ in one's efforts to do** ne pas ménager ses efforts pour faire; **to be ~ in one's praise of** chanter les louanges de.

unstitch [ˈʌnˈstɪtʃ] **vt**: **to come ~ed** se découdre.

unstop [ˈʌnˈstɒp] **vt** *sink* déboucher, désobstruer; *bottle* déboucher, décapsuler.

unstoppable* [ˈʌnˈstɒpəbl] **adj** qu'on ne peut pas arrêter.

unstrap [ˈʌnˈstræp] **vt**: **to ~ A from B** détacher A de B, défaire les sangles qui attachent A à B.

unstressed [ˈʌnˈstrest] **adj** *syllable* inaccentué, atone.

unstring [ˈʌnˈstrɪŋ] **pret, ptp unstrung** **vt** *violin, racket* enlever *or* détendre les cordes de; *beads* désenfiler; (*fig*) *person* démoraliser.

unstructured [ˈʌnˈstrʌktʃəd] **adj** peu structuré.

unstrung [ˈʌnˈstrʌŋ] **adj** *violin, racket* dont on a enlevé les cordes, dont les cordes sont détendues; (*fig*) démoralisé.

unstuck [ˈʌnˈstʌk] **pret, ptp of unstick**.

unstudied [ˈʌnˈstʌdɪd] **adj** naturel, spontané.

unsubdued [ˈʌnsəbˈdjuːd] **adj** (*lit, fig*) indompté.

unsubsidized [ˈʌnˈsʌbsɪdaɪzd] **adj** non subventionné, qui ne reçoit pas de subvention.

unsubstantial [ˈʌnsəbˈstænʃəl] **adj** *structure* peu solide, léger; *meal* peu substantiel, peu nourrissant; *argument* peu solide, sans substance; *evidence* insuffisant.

unsubstantiated [ˈʌnsəbˈstænʃɪeɪtɪd] **adj** *accusation* non prouvé; *testimony, rumour* non confirmé, non corroboré.

unsubtle [ʌnˈsʌtl] **adj** lourd.

unsuccessful [ˈʌnsəkˈsesfʊl] **adj** *negotiation, venture, visit, meeting* infructueux, qui est un échec; *attempt* vain, infructueux; *candidate* refusé, malheureux; *application* refusé, non retenu; *writer, painter, book* qui n'a pas de succès; *firm* qui ne prospère pas; *marriage, outcome* malheureux. **to be ~** échouer, ne pas réussir; **to be ~ in doing sth** ne pas réussir *or* ne pas arriver à faire qch; **he is ~ in everything he does** rien ne lui réussit; **he was ~ in his exam** il a échoué à *or* il n'a pas été reçu à son examen; **I tried to speak to him but I was ~** j'ai essayé de lui parler mais sans succès *or* mais en vain *or* mais je n'ai pas pu; **after 3 ~ attempts, he ...** après avoir essayé 3 fois sans succès il ..., après avoir échoué 3 fois il ... .

unsuccessfully [ˈʌnsəkˈsesfəlɪ] **adv** en vain, sans succès.

unsuitability [ˈʌnˌsuːtəˈbɪlɪtɪ] **n**: **he was rejected on the grounds of ~ (for the job)** il n'a pas été retenu parce qu'il n'avait pas le profil requis (pour l'emploi).

unsuitable [ˈʌnˈsuːtəbl] **adj** *climate, food, place, time, arrangement* qui ne convient pas; *moment* inopportun; *colour, size* qui ne va pas; *clothes* peu approprié, inadéquat, (*socially*) non convenable; *action, reply, example, device* peu approprié, inopportun; *language, attitude* inconvenant. **to be ~ for** *[clothes, language, date]* ne pas convenir à; *[film, book]* ne pas être (conseillé) pour; **he is ~ for the post** ce n'est pas l'homme qu'il faut pour le poste; **he married a very ~ girl** il a épousé une fille qui n'était pas du tout faite pour lui *or* qui ne lui convenait pas du tout.

unsuitably [ˈʌnˈsuːtəblɪ] **adv** *behave, dress* pas comme il faut.

unsuited [ˈʌnˈsuːtɪd] **adj**: **~ to** *or* **for** *person* inapte à; *thing* impropre à; **~ to do** inapte *or* impropre à faire; **they are ~ (to each other)** ils ne sont pas compatibles, ils ne vont pas bien ensemble.

unsullied [ˈʌnˈsʌlɪd] **adj** sans souillure, sans tache.

unsung [ˈʌnˈsʌŋ] **adj** (*liter*) *hero, exploits* méconnu.

unsupported [ˈʌnsəˈpɔːtɪd] **adj** *structure* non soutenu, non étayé; *statement* non confirmé, non corroboré; *hypothesis* non vérifié, non soutenu; *candidate* sans appui, sans soutien; *troops* non soutenu; *mother, family* sans soutien financier.

unsure [ˈʌnˈʃʊəʳ] **adj** *person* incertain (*of, about* de); *memory* peu fidèle. **to be ~ of o.s.** ne pas être sûr de soi, manquer d'assurance.

unsurmountable [ˈʌnsəˈmaʊntəbl] **adj** insurmontable.

unsurpassable [ˈʌnsəˈpɑːsəbl] **adj** insurpassable.

unsurpassed [ˈʌnsəˈpɑːst] **adj** non surpassé (*in* en).

unsurprising [ˈʌnsəˈpraɪzɪŋ] **adj** sans surprise.

unsurprisingly [ˈʌnsəˈpraɪzɪŋlɪ] **adv**: **~, he left immediately** comme on pouvait s'y attendre, il est parti tout de suite; **not ~, he did it rather well** chose étonnante, il l'a plutôt bien fait.

unsuspected [ˈʌnsəsˈpektɪd] **adj** insoupçonné.

unsuspecting [ˈʌnsəsˈpektɪŋ] **adj** qui ne se méfie pas, qui ne se doute de rien. **and he, quite ~, said ...** et lui, ne se doutant de rien *or* sans la moindre méfiance, dit ... .

unsuspicious [ˈʌnsəsˈpɪʃəs] **adj** (*feeling no suspicion*) peu soupçonneux, peu méfiant; (*arousing no suspicion*) qui n'a rien de suspect, qui n'éveille aucun soupçon. **~-looking** tout à fait ordinaire.

unsweetened [ˈʌnˈswiːtnd] **adj** non sucré, sans sucre.

unswerving [ʌnˈswɜːvɪŋ] **adj** *resolve* inébranlable; *loyalty* inébranlable, à toute épreuve.

unswervingly [ʌnˈswɜːvɪŋlɪ] **adv**: **~ loyal** totalement dévoué (*to* à); **to hold ~ to one's course** poursuivre inébranlablement son but, ne pas se laisser détourner de son but.

unsympathetic [ˈʌnˌsɪmpəˈθetɪk] **adj** indifférent (*to* à), peu compatissant, incompréhensif; (*unlikeable*) antipathique. **he was quite ~ when we ...** il n'a pas du tout compati quand nous ...; (*stronger*) il n'a pas manifesté la moindre compassion quand nous ... .

unsympathetically [ˈʌnˌsɪmpəˈθetɪkəlɪ] **adv** froidement; (*stronger*) sans (manifester) la moindre compassion.

unsystematic [ˈʌnˌsɪstɪˈmætɪk] **adj** *work, reasoning* peu systématique, peu méthodique.

unsystematically [ˈʌnˌsɪstɪˈmætɪkəlɪ] **adv** sans système, sans méthode.

untainted [ˈʌnˈteɪntɪd] **adj** (*lit*) *meat, butter* frais (*f* fraîche); (*fig*) *reputation* intact, non terni, sans tache; *person, mind* non corrompu (*by* par), pur.

untam(e)able [ˈʌnˈteɪməbl] **adj** *bird, wild animal* inapprivoisable; *large or fierce animal* non dressable; *esp lion, tiger* indomptable.

untamed [ˈʌnˈteɪmd] **adj** *animal etc* sauvage, inapprivoisé, farouche; *esp lion, tiger* indompté; *passion* violent, fougueux.

untangle ['ʌn'tæŋgl] vt *rope, wool, hair* démêler; *mystery* débrouiller, éclaircir; *plot* dénouer.

untanned ['ʌn'tænd] adj *hide* non tanné; *person* non bronzé.

untapped ['ʌn'tæpt] adj *resources* inexploité.

untarnished ['ʌn'tɑːnɪʃt] adj (*lit, fig*) non terni, sans tache.

untasted ['ʌn'teɪstɪd] adj *food, delights* auquel on n'a pas goûté. **the food lay ~ on the plate** le repas restait dans l'assiette; **he left the meal ~** il n'a pas goûté au repas.

untaught ['ʌn'tɔːt] adj (*uneducated*) sans instruction, ignorant; (*natural, innate*) spontané, inné, naturel.

untaxable ['ʌn'tæksəbl] adj *income* non imposable; *goods* exempt de taxes.

untaxed ['ʌn'tækst] adj *goods* exempt de taxes, non imposé; *income* non imposable, exempté d'impôts; *car* sans vignette.

unteachable ['ʌn'tiːtʃəbl] adj *person* à qui on ne peut rien apprendre; *pupil* réfractaire à tout enseignement; *subject* impossible à enseigner, qui ne se prête pas à l'enseignement.

untempered ['ʌn'tempəd] adj *steel* non revenu.

untenable ['ʌn'tenəbl] adj *position* intenable; *opinion* insoutenable.

untenanted ['ʌn'tenəntɪd] adj inoccupé, sans locataire(s).

untended ['ʌn'tendɪd] adj (*unwatched*) sans surveillance; (*unmaintained*) *garden etc* mal entretenu.

untested ['ʌn'testɪd] adj *person, theory, method* qui n'a pas été mis à l'épreuve; *product, weapon, invention* qui n'a pas été essayé; *new drug* non encore expérimenté; (*Psych*) non testé.

unthinkable [ʌn'θɪŋkəbl] 1 adj impensable, inconcevable. **it is ~ that** il est impensable *or* inconcevable que + *subj*. 2 n: **the ~** l'impensable *m*, l'inconcevable *m*.

unthinking ['ʌn'θɪŋkɪŋ] adj irréfléchi, étourdi.

unthinkingly ['ʌn'θɪŋkɪŋlɪ] adv sans réfléchir, étourdiment.

unthought-of [ʌn'θɔːtɒv] adj auquel on n'a pas pensé *or* songé.

unthread ['ʌn'θred] vt *needle, pearls* désenfiler.

untidily [ʌn'taɪdɪlɪ] adv *work, live* sans méthode, sans ordre; *write* sans soin, de manière brouillonne. **to dress ~** s'habiller sans soin; **she was ~ dressed** elle était habillée à la diable; **she dresses ~** elle fait débraillé, elle s'habille sans soin; **his books lay ~ about the room** ses livres jonchaient la pièce.

untidiness [ʌn'taɪdɪnɪs] n (*NonC*) *[room]* désordre *m*; *[dress]* désordre, (*habitual*) débraillé *m*; *[person]* (*in dress, appearance*) débraillé; (*in habits*) manque *m* d'ordre.

untidy [ʌn'taɪdɪ] adj a *person* (*in appearance*) dont les vêtements sont (*or* étaient *etc*) en désordre, (*habitually*) débraillé; (*in character*) désordonné, brouillon. **she looked ~** ses vêtements étaient en désordre; (*slovenly*) elle faisait débraillé. b *appearance* négligé, désordonné; *clothes* en désordre, (*habitually*) débraillé, mal tenu; *hair* ébouriffé, mal peigné; *writing* brouillon; *work, page* sale, brouillon; *room* en désordre, en pagaïe*; *desk* en désordre, mal rangé.

untie ['ʌn'taɪ] vt *knot* défaire; *string* dénouer, défaire; *parcel* défaire, ouvrir; *prisoner, hands* délier, détacher; *bonds* défaire, détacher.

until [ən'tɪl] 1 prep jusqu'à. **~ such time as** (*in future*) jusqu'à ce que + *subj*, en attendant que + *subj*; (*in past*) avant que + *subj*; **~ the next day** jusqu'au lendemain; **from morning ~ night** du matin (jusqu')au soir; **~ now** jusqu'ici, jusqu'à maintenant; **~ then** jusque-là; **not ~** (*in future*) pas avant; (*in past*) ne ... que; **it won't be ready ~ tomorrow** ce ne sera pas prêt avant demain; **he didn't leave ~ the following day** il n'est parti que le lendemain; **the work was not begun ~ 1986** ce n'est qu'en 1986 que les travaux ont commencé; **I had heard nothing of it ~ 5 minutes ago** j'en ai seulement entendu parler *or* j'en ai entendu parler pour la première fois il y a 5 minutes.

2 conj (*in future*) jusqu'à ce que + *subj*, en attendant que + *subj*; (*in past*) avant que + *subj*. **wait ~ I come** attendez que je vienne; **~ they built the new road** avant qu'ils (ne) fassent la nouvelle route; **~ they build the new road** en attendant qu'ils fassent la nouvelle route; **he laughed ~ he cried** il a ri aux larmes; **not ~** (*in future*) pas avant que + (ne) + *subj*, tant que ... ne ... pas + *indic*; (*in past*) tant que ... ne ... pas + *indic*; **he won't come ~ you invite him** il ne viendra pas avant que vous (ne) l'invitiez *or* avant d'être invité, il ne viendra pas tant que vous ne l'inviterez pas; **they did nothing ~ we came** ils n'ont rien fait tant que nous n'avons pas été là; **do nothing ~ I tell you** ne faites rien avant que je (ne) vous le dise *or* tant que je ne vous l'aurai pas dit; **do nothing ~ you get my letter** ne faites rien avant d'avoir reçu ma lettre; **wait ~ you get my letter** attendez d'avoir reçu ma lettre; **don't start ~ I come** ne commencez pas avant que j'arrive (*subj*), attendez-moi pour commencer.

untilled ['ʌn'tɪld] adj non labouré, non cultivé, inculte.

untimely [ʌn'taɪmlɪ] adj *spring, weather* prématuré, précoce; *moment* inopportun, mal choisi; *arrival* inopportun, intempestif; *death* prématuré; *remark* inopportun, déplacé, intempestif. **to come to an ~ end** *[person]* mourir prématurément *or* avant son temps; *[project]* être enterré prématurément.

untiring [ʌn'taɪərɪŋ] adj *person, efforts* infatigable, inlassable. **to be ~ in one's efforts to do** s'efforcer infatigablement *or* inlassablement de faire.

untiringly [ʌn'taɪərɪŋlɪ] adv infatigablement, inlassablement.

unto ['ʌntʊ] prep (*liter*) = **to, towards**.

untogether* [,ʌntə'geðə^r] adj *[person]* **to be ~** (*disorganized*) ne pas être au point*; (*unstable*) être paumé*.

untold ['ʌn'təʊld] adj a *story* jamais raconté; *secret* jamais dévoilé *or* divulgué. **that story remains ~** cette histoire n'a encore jamais été racontée; **to leave sth ~** passer qch sous silence. b (*incalculable*) *amount, loss, wealth* incalculable; *agony, joy* indicible, indescriptible.

untouchable [ʌn'tʌtʃəbl] 1 adj intouchable. 2 n (*in India*) intouchable *mf*, paria *m*; (*fig*) paria.

untouched ['ʌn'tʌtʃt] adj a auquel on n'a pas touché. (*Comm*) **~ by hand** sans manipulation directe; **he left his meal ~, his meal lay ~** il n'a pas touché à son repas. b (*safe*) *person* indemne; *thing* intact; (*unaffected*) insensible, indifférent (*by* à).

untoward [,ʌntə'wɔːd] adj fâcheux, malencontreux.

untrained ['ʌn'treɪnd] adj *worker, teacher* qui n'a pas reçu de formation professionnelle, sans formation; *mind* non formé; *voice* non travaillé; *animal* non dressé. **to the ~ ear** à l'oreille inexercée; *[pianist etc]* **he's quite ~** il n'a jamais reçu de leçons *or* de formation, c'est un amateur.

untrammelled, (*US*) **untrammeled** [ʌn'træməld] adj non entravé (*by* par), libre (*by* de).

untranslatable ['ʌntrænz'leɪtəbl] adj intraduisible.

untravelled ['ʌn'trævld] adj *road* peu fréquenté; *person* qui n'a pas voyagé.

untreated [ʌn'triːtɪd] adj (*Med*) *illness, injury* qui n'est pas soigné, non soigné; *wood, soil, sewage, chemicals* non traité.

untried ['ʌn'traɪd] adj *product, weapon, invention* qui n'a pas été essayé; *person, method* qui n'a pas été mis à l'épreuve; (*Jur*) *case, person* non jugé. **he was condemned ~** il a été condamné sans jugement.

untrodden ['ʌn'trɒdn] adj (*liter*) *path* peu fréquenté; *region, territory* inexploré, vierge; *snow* non foulé, vierge.

untroubled ['ʌn'trʌbld] adj tranquille, calme, paisible. **~ by the thought of ...** nullement troublé à la pensée de ...; **to be ~ by the news** rester impassible en apprenant la nouvelle.

untrue ['ʌn'truː] adj *statement* faux (*f* fausse), erroné, inexact; *rumour* faux; *instrument* qui n'est pas juste, inexact; *reading* erroné, inexact; *lover etc* infidèle (*to* à), déloyal (*to* envers). **it is ~ that** il est faux *or* il n'est pas vrai que + *subj*.

untrustworthy ['ʌn'trʌst,wɜːðɪ] adj *person* indigne de confiance; *witness* récusable; *book* auquel on ne peut se fier; *source of information* douteux.

untruth ['ʌn'truːθ] n, pl **~s** ['ʌn'truːðz] contre-vérité *f*, (*stronger*) mensonge *m*; (*NonC*) fausseté *f*.

untruthful ['ʌn'truːθfʊl] adj *statement* mensonger; *person* menteur, qui ne dit pas la vérité.

untruthfully ['ʌn'truːθfəlɪ] adv en mentant, (*more formally*) mensongèrement.

untruthfulness ['ʌn'truːθfʊlnɪs] n (*NonC*) fausseté *f*, caractère mensonger.

untuneful ['ʌn'tjuːnfʊl] adj peu harmonieux.

untutored ['ʌn'tjuːtəd] adj *person* peu instruit, dont les connaissances sont rudimentaires; *work* qui dénote des connaissances rudimentaires; *taste* non formé.

untwine ['ʌn'twaɪn] vt défaire, détortiller.

untwist ['ʌn'twɪst] vt (*untangle*) *rope, threads, wool* démêler, détortiller; (*straighten out*) *flex, rope* détordre; (*unravel*) *rope, wool* défaire; (*unscrew*) *bottle-top* dévisser.

untypical ['ʌn'tɪpɪkəl] adj peu typique, peu caractéristique (*of* de). **it's ~ of him** ce n'est pas de lui, ce n'est pas son genre.

unusable ['ʌn'juːzəbl] adj inutilisable.

unused ['ʌn'juːzd] adj a (*new*) *clothes* neuf (*f* neuve), qui n'a pas été porté; *machine* neuf, qui n'a pas servi; (*not in use*) *resources, talent* inutilisé; (*Ling*) inusité. b ['ʌn'juːst] **to be ~ to (doing) sth** être peu habitué à (faire) qch, ne pas avoir l'habitude de (faire) qch; **I am quite ~ to it now** j'en ai perdu l'habitude, je n'en ai plus l'habitude.

unusual [ʌn'juːʒʊəl] adj (*rare*) peu commun, inhabituel; (*exceptional*) exceptionnel; (*strange*) insolite, étrange, bizarre. **it is ~ for him to be early** il est exceptionnel *or* rare qu'il arrive (*subj*) de bonne heure, il n'arrive pas de bonne heure d'habitude, il n'est pas dans ses habitudes d'arriver de bonne heure; **it's not ~ for him to be late** *or* **that he should be late** il n'est pas rare qu'il soit en retard, il lui arrive souvent d'être en retard; **that's ~ for him!** ce n'est pas dans ses habitudes!, on ne s'attend pas à ça de lui!

unusually [ʌn'juːʒʊəlɪ] adv a (*more than one normally finds*) *tall, dark, handsome etc* exceptionnellement, extraordinairement. b (*more than normally for this person*) *cheerful, silent, early etc* exceptionnellement, anormalement. **~ early** exceptionnellement tôt, plus tôt que de coutume *or* d'ordinaire.

unutterable [ʌn'ʌtərəbl] adj *joy, boredom* indicible, indescriptible; (*) *idiot, fool* fini, achevé.

unvaried [ʌn'vɛərɪd] adj uniforme, qui manque de variété, monotone (*pej*). **the menu was ~ from one week to the next** le menu ne changeait pas d'une semaine à l'autre.

unvarnished ['ʌn'vɑːnɪʃt] adj *wood* non verni; *pottery* non vernissé;

(*fig*) *account, description* simple, sans fard, sans embellissements. **the ~ truth** la vérité pure et simple, la vérité toute nue.
unvarying [ʌnˈvɛərɪɪŋ] **adj** invariable, constant.
unvaryingly [ʌnˈvɛərɪɪŋlɪ] **adv** invariablement.
unveil [ʌnˈveɪl] **vt** dévoiler.
unveiling [ʌnˈveɪlɪŋ] **n** dévoilement *m*; (*ceremony*) inauguration *f*.
unventilated [ˈʌnˈventɪleɪtɪd] **adj** sans ventilation.
unverifiable [ˈʌnˈverɪfaɪəbl] **adj** invérifiable.
unverified [ˈʌnˈverɪfaɪd] **adj** non vérifié.
unversed [ˈʌnˈvɜːst] **adj**: **~ in** peu versé dans.
unvoiced [ˈʌnˈvɔɪst] **adj** **a** *opinion, sentiment* inexprimé. **b** (*Phon*) *consonant* non voisé, sourd.
unwaged [ˈʌnˈweɪdʒd] **npl** (*Admin*) **the ~** les sans-emploi, étudiants et retraités *mpl*.
unwanted [ˈʌnˈwɒntɪd] **adj** *clothing, article* superflu, dont on ne se sert pas, dont on n'a pas besoin; *child* non désiré, non souhaité; *effect* non recherché. **he felt ~** (*in conversation etc*) il avait l'impression de gêner *or* d'être de trop; (*unloved*) il avait l'impression que personne ne l'aimait; *see* **hair**.
unwarlike [ˈʌnˈwɔːlaɪk] **adj** peu guerrier, peu belliqueux, pacifique.
unwarrantable [ʌnˈwɒrəntəbl] **adj** *intrusion etc* injustifiable. **it is quite ~ that ...** il est tout à fait injustifiable que ... + *subj*.
unwarrantably [ʌnˈwɒrəntəblɪ] **adv** de façon injustifiable.
unwarranted [ʌnˈwɒrəntɪd] **adj** injustifié.
unwary [ʌnˈwɛərɪ] **adj** *person* qui n'est pas sur ses gardes, sans méfiance, imprudent; *action, decision* imprudent.
unwashed [ˈʌnˈwɒʃt] **1** **adj** *hands, object* non lavé; *person* qui ne s'est pas lavé. **2** **n** (*hum*) **the great ~*** la racaille, la populace.
unwavering [ʌnˈweɪvərɪŋ] **adj** *faith, resolve, devotion* inébranlable; *gaze* fixe; *concentration* qui ne faiblit pas. **to follow an ~ course** poursuivre inébranlablement son but, aller droit au but, ne pas se laisser détourner de son but.
unwaveringly [ʌnˈweɪvərɪŋlɪ] **adv** *follow, continue* inébranlablement; *say* fermement; *gaze* fixement.
unweaned [ˈʌnˈwiːnd] **adj** non sevré.
unwearable [ˈʌnˈwɛərəbl] **adj** *clothes, colour* pas mettable.
unwearied [ʌnˈwɪərɪd] **adj**, **unwearying** [ʌnˈwɪərɪɪŋ] **adj** infatigable, inlassable. **to be ~ in one's efforts to do** s'efforcer infatigablement *or* inlassablement de faire.
unwed† [ˈʌnˈwed] **adj** = **unmarried**.
unweighting [ˈʌnˈweɪtɪŋ] **n** (*Ski*) allègement *m*.
unwelcome [ʌnˈwelkəm] **adj** *visitor, gift* importun; *news, delay, change* fâcheux. **the money was not ~** l'argent était le bienvenu; **they made us feel most ~** ils nous ont très mal accueillis, ils nous ont bien fait sentir que nous les importunions.
unwelcoming [ˈʌnˈwelkəmɪŋ] **adj** *person, place* peu accueillant.
unwell [ˈʌnˈwel] **adj** souffrant, indisposé. **to feel ~** ne pas se sentir très bien.
unwholesome [ˈʌnˈhəʊlsəm] **adj** *atmosphere, climate* malsain, insalubre; *thoughts, interest* malsain, morbide; *influence* malsain, pernicieux, nocif; *food* malsain.
unwieldy [ʌnˈwiːldɪ] **adj** *tool, sword, parcel* peu maniable, difficile à manier; *person* lourd, qui se déplace avec peine; *method* maladroit.
unwilling [ˈʌnˈwɪlɪŋ] **adj**: **to be ~ to do** (*reluctant*) être peu disposé à faire; (*refuse*) ne pas vouloir faire, refuser de faire; **I am ~ for him to go** je ne veux pas qu'il y aille; **her ~ helper/accomplice** son aide/complice malgré lui.
unwillingly [ˈʌnˈwɪlɪŋlɪ] **adv** à contrecœur, de mauvaise grâce, contre son gré.
unwillingness [ˈʌnˈwɪlɪŋnɪs] **n** (*NonC*) **his ~ to help is surprising** il est étonnant qu'il ne soit pas disposé à aider.
unwind [ˈʌnˈwaɪnd] **pret, ptp unwound** **1** **vt** dérouler. **2** **vi** se dérouler; (** fig: relax*) se détendre, se relaxer.
unwisdom [ˈʌnˈwɪzdəm] **n** (*NonC*) manque *m* de bon sens, imprudence *f*.
unwise [ˈʌnˈwaɪz] **adj** *person* imprudent, malavisé; *move, decision* imprudent, peu judicieux. **it would be ~ to do** on serait malavisé de faire, il serait imprudent de faire.
unwisely [ˈʌnˈwaɪzlɪ] **adv** imprudemment.
unwitting [ʌnˈwɪtɪŋ] **adj** involontaire; *action* non intentionnel, involontaire. **he was the ~ victim of** il a été la victime involontaire de, il a été sans le savoir la victime de.
unwittingly [ʌnˈwɪtɪŋlɪ] **adv** involontairement, sans le savoir, par mégarde.
unwomanly [ʌnˈwʊmənlɪ] **adj** peu féminin.
unwonted [ʌnˈwəʊntɪd] **adj** (*rare*) peu commun; (*unusual for this person*) inaccoutumé.
unworkable [ˈʌnˈwɜːkəbl] **adj** *suggestion, method* impraticable; *mine* inexploitable; *substance, fabric* rebelle. *[idea, scheme etc]* **it's ~** ça ne marchera jamais; **it was ~** ça ne pouvait pas marcher.
unworldly [ˈʌnˈwɜːldlɪ] **adj** *person* détaché de ce monde, qui n'a pas les pieds sur terre, peu réaliste, naïf (*f* naïve); *beauty* céleste, qui n'est pas de ce monde; *idealism, preoccupations* détaché de ce monde.
unworthiness [ʌnˈwɜːðɪnɪs] **n** manque *m* de mérite.
unworthy [ʌnˈwɜːðɪ] **adj** indigne (*of* de, *to do* de faire). **it is ~ of you** c'est indigne de vous.
unwounded [ˈʌnˈwuːndɪd] **adj** non blessé, indemne, valide.
unwrap [ˈʌnˈræp] **vt** défaire, ouvrir.
unwritten [ˈʌnˈrɪtn] **adj** *song, folk tale* non écrit; *agreement* verbal. **it is an ~ law** *or* **rule that ...** il est tacitement admis que ... .
unyielding [ʌnˈjiːldɪŋ] **adj** *person* inflexible, qui ne cède pas; *substance* très dur; *structure* rigide.
unyoke [ˈʌnˈjəʊk] **vt** dételer.
unzip [ˈʌnˈzɪp] **vt** ouvrir (la fermeture éclair ® de). **can you ~ me?** peux-tu défaire ma fermeture éclair?
up [ʌp] (*phr vb elem*) **1** **adv** **a** (*gen*) en haut, en l'air. **he threw the ball ~** il a jeté la balle en l'air; **hold it ~ higher** tiens-le plus haut; **~ there** là-haut; **~ in the air** en l'air; **~ in the sky** (là-haut) dans le ciel; **~ in the mountains** dans les montagnes; **from ~ on the hill** (du haut) de la colline; **~ on deck** sur le pont; **~ on the hill** en haut de la colline, sur la colline; **~ on top of the cupboard** sur le placard; **~ at the top of the tree** en haut *or* au sommet de l'arbre; **it's ~ on top** c'est là-haut; **~ above** au-dessus; **~ above sth** au-dessus de qch; **he lives 5 floors ~** il habite au 5e étage; **the people 3 floors ~ from me** les gens qui habitent 3 étages au-dessus de chez moi; **all the way ~** jusqu'en haut, jusqu'au sommet; **I met him on my way ~** je l'ai rencontré en montant; **I was on my way ~ to see you** je montais vous voir; **a little farther ~** (*on wall etc*) un peu plus haut; (*along bench etc*) un peu plus loin; **sit close ~ to me** assieds-toi tout près de moi; **he came ~ to me** il s'est approché de moi, il est venu vers moi; **I saw the car and walked ~ to it** j'ai vu la voiture et m'en suis approché; **his hand has been ~ for a long time** il a la main levée depuis longtemps; **with his head ~ (high)** la tête haute; **the blinds were ~** les stores étaient levés; **he sat in the car with the windows ~** il était assis dans la voiture avec les vitres levées *or* fermées; **this zip won't stay ~** cette fermeture éclair ne veut pas rester fermée; **the ladder was ~ against the wall** l'échelle était appuyée contre le mur (*see also* **1h**); **set the box ~ on end** mets la boîte debout; **it was ~ on end** c'était debout; (*on parcel*) **"this side ~"** "haut"; **sit still for a while, you've been ~ and down all evening** assieds-toi un moment, tu n'as pas arrêté (de) toute la soirée; **to jump ~ and down** sauter; **to walk ~ and down** faire les cent pas; *see also* **climb, face up to, hand up, halfway** *etc*.

b (*out of bed*) **to be ~** être levé, être debout *inv*; **(get) ~!** debout!, levez-vous!; **we were ~ at 7** nous étions levés *or* debout à 7 heures; **I was still ~ at midnight** j'étais encore debout *or* je ne m'étais toujours pas couché à minuit; **he's always ~ early** il est toujours levé *or* il se lève toujours de bonne heure; **I was ~ late this morning** je me suis levé tard ce matin; **I was ~ late last night** je me suis couché tard hier soir; **he was ~ all night** il ne s'est pas couché de la nuit; **she was ~ all night looking after her child** elle ne s'est pas couchée de la nuit *or* elle a veillé toute la nuit pour s'occuper de son enfant; **he was ~ and down all night** il n'a pas arrêté de se lever toute la nuit; **she was ~ and about** *or* **and doing* at 7 o'clock** elle était debout *or* sur pied et à l'ouvrage à 7 heures; *[sick person]* **to be ~ and about again** être de nouveau sur pied; *see also* **get up**.

c (*fig*) **when the sun was ~** quand le soleil était levé, après le lever du soleil; **the tide is ~** la marée est haute; **the river is ~** la rivière a monté; **the road is ~** la route est en travaux; (*Parl*) **the House is ~** la Chambre ne siège pas; **the temperature was ~ in the forties** la température dépassait quarante degrés; **~ with Joe Bloggs!** vive Joe Bloggs!; **~ with Celtic!** allez Celtic!, tous pour Celtic!; **to be ~ (on horseback)** être à cheval; **a horse with Smith ~** un cheval monté par Smith; (*in meeting etc*) **let's go and sit ~ front** allons nous asseoir devant (*see also* **up-front**); **he's ~ at the top of the class** il est en tête de (sa) classe; **he was ~ with** *or* **among the leaders** il était dans les premiers; **he's well ~ in Latin** (*place in class*) il a une bonne place *or* il est bien placé en latin; (*knows a lot*) il est fort *or* calé* en latin; **I'm ~ with him in maths** nous nous valons en maths, nous sommes au même niveau *or* de la même force en maths; **I'm not very well ~ in what's been going on** je ne suis pas vraiment au fait de ce qui s'est passé; (*Univ*) **when I was ~*** quand j'étais étudiant *or* à la Fac*; **~ in London** à Londres; **~ in Scotland** en Écosse; **he's ~ from Birmingham** il vient *or* il arrive de Birmingham; **he's ~ in Leeds for the weekend** il passe le weekend à Leeds; **I come ~ to town every week** je viens en ville toutes les semaines; **we're ~ for the day** nous sommes venus passer la journée; **I was on my way ~ to London** j'allais à Londres, j'étais en route pour Londres; **~ north** dans le nord; **I'll play you 100 ~** je vous fais une partie en 100, le premier qui a 100 points gagne; **Chelsea were 3 goals ~** Chelsea menait par 3 buts; **we were 20 points ~ on them** nous avions 20 points d'avance sur eux; **to be one ~ on sb*** faire mieux que qn; **to be** *or* **come ~ before Judge X** *[accused person]* comparaître devant le juge X; *[case]* être jugé par le juge X; **his blood is ~** il a le sang qui bout; **his temper is ~** il est en colère; *[invalid]* **he's been rather ~ and down recently** il a eu des hauts et des bas récemment; **what's ~?*** (*what's happening*) qu'est-ce qu'il y a?; (*what's wrong*) qu'est-ce qui ne va pas?; **what's ~ with him?*** qu'est-ce qu'il a?, qu'est-ce qui lui prend?; **what's ~ with the car/your leg?*** qu'est-ce qu'elle a, votre voiture?/votre jambe?; **I know there's some-**

thing ~* (*happening*) je sais qu'il se passe quelque chose; (*wrong*) je sais qu'il y a quelque chose qui ne va pas; **there's something ~ with Paul*** il y a quelque chose qui ne va pas *or* qui ne tourne pas rond* chez Paul; **there's something ~ with the engine*** il y a quelque chose qui ne tourne pas rond* dans le moteur; **there's something ~ with my leg*** j'ai quelque chose à la jambe, ma jambe me tracasse; (*US*) **a bourbon (straight) ~*** un bourbon sans glace *or* sans glaçons; (*US*) **two fried eggs, ~*** deux œufs sur le plat, non retournés; **I have 10 bucks ~* on that horse** j'ai parié 10 dollars sur ce cheval; *for other phrases see* **arm²**, **hard** *etc*.

d (*more, higher etc*) **to be ~** *[prices, salaries, shares, numbers]* avoir augmenté, avoir monté (*by* de); *[temperature, water level]* avoir monté (*by* de); **potatoes are ~ again** les pommes de terre ont encore augmenté; **the standard is ~** le niveau est plus élevé; **it is ~ on last year** cela a augmenté par rapport à l'an dernier.

e (*upwards*) **from £2 ~** à partir de 2 livres; **from (the age of) 13 ~** à partir de (l'âge de) 13 ans; **from his youth ~** dès sa jeunesse.

f (*installed, built etc*) **we've got the curtains/pictures ~ at last** nous avons enfin posé les rideaux/accroché les tableaux; **the shutters are ~** les volets sont posés *or* (*closed*) mis *or* fermés; **the new building isn't ~ yet** le nouveau bâtiment n'est pas encore construit; **the tent isn't ~ yet** la tente n'est pas encore plantée; **look, the flag is ~!** regarde, le drapeau est hissé!; **the notice about the outing is ~** l'excursion est affichée.

g (*finished*) **his leave/visit is ~** sa permission/sa visite est terminée; **it is ~ on the 20th** ça se termine *or* ça finit le 20; **when 3 days were ~** au bout de 3 jours; **time's ~!** c'est l'heure!; **it's all ~ with him*** il est fichu*; *see* **game¹** *etc*.

h **to be ~ against difficulties** se heurter à *or* être aux prises avec des difficultés; **you don't know what you're ~ against!** tu n'as pas idée des difficultés qui t'attendent!; **he's ~ against stiff competition** il a affaire à forte partie *or* à des concurrents sérieux; **he's ~ against a very powerful politician** il a contre lui un homme politique très puissant; **we're really ~ against it** nous allons avoir du mal à nous en sortir.

i (*as far as*) **~ to** jusqu'à; **~ to** *or* **till** *or* **until now** jusqu'à maintenant, jusqu'ici; **~ to here** jusqu'ici; **~ to there** jusque-là; **what page are you ~ to?** à quelle page en êtes-vous?; **~ to and including chapter 5** jusqu'au chapitre 5 inclus; **to be ~ to one's knees/waist** *etc* **in water** avoir de l'eau jusqu'aux genoux/jusqu'à la taille *etc;* **to count ~ to 100** compter jusqu'à 100; **he'll pay ~ to £10** il paiera jusqu'à 10 livres.

j (*depending on*) **it's ~ to you to decide** c'est à vous de décider; **it's ~ to you whether you go or not** c'est à vous de décider si vous y allez ou non; **shall I do it? — it's ~ to you** je le fais? — faites comme vous voulez *or* faites commes vous l'entendez *or* (c'est) à vous de décider *or* ça ne tient qu'à vous; **if it were ~ to me ...** s'il n'en tenait qu'à moi ..., si c'était moi qui décidais ...; **it's ~ to us to help him** c'est à nous de l'aider, il nous appartient de l'aider.

k (*busy doing etc*) **what is he ~ to?** qu'est-ce qu'il fait? *or* fabrique?*, qu'est-ce qu'il peut bien faire?; **he's ~ to something** il manigance *or* mijote quelque chose, il a quelque chose en tête; **what have you been ~ to recently?** qu'est-ce que vous devenez ces temps-ci?; **what have you been ~ to?** qu'est-ce que tu as manigancé? *or* fabriqué?*; **what are you ~ to with that knife?** qu'est-ce que tu fais *or* fabriques* avec ce couteau?; **he's ~ to no good** *[child]* il prépare quelque sottise; *[adult]* il mijote quelque mauvais coup; *see* **mischief** *etc*.

l (*equal to*) **to be ~ to a task** être à la hauteur d'une tâche; **is he ~ to advanced work?** est-il capable de faire des études supérieures?; **it isn't ~ to his usual standard** d'habitude il fait mieux que ça, il nous a habitués à mieux; **are you feeling ~ to going for a walk?** est-ce que tu te sens d'attaque à faire une promenade?; **I just don't feel ~ to it** je ne m'en sens pas le courage; **he really isn't ~ to going back to work yet** il n'est vraiment pas encore en état de reprendre le travail; **it's not ~ to much** ça ne vaut pas grand-chose.

2 **prep: to be ~ a tree/~ a ladder** être dans un arbre/sur une échelle; **to go ~ the stairs** monter les marches d'un escalier, monter l'escalier; **to go ~ the street** monter la rue; **to climb ~ a cliff** escalader une falaise; **to climb ~ a tree** grimper dans *or* sur un arbre; **to run ~ a hill** monter une colline en courant; **to sail ~ a river** remonter une rivière en bateau; **he pointed ~ the hill/the stairs** il indiqua du doigt le haut de la colline/de l'escalier; **the car drove ~ the road** la voiture a remonté la rue; **the house is ~ that road** la maison est dans cette rue; **they live just ~ the road** ils habitent un peu plus haut *or* plus loin dans la (même) rue; **put it ~ your sleeve** mets-le dans ta manche; **~ hill and down dale** par monts et par vaux; **he travelled ~ and down the country** il parcourait le pays; **people ~ and down the country are saying ...** un peu partout dans le pays *or* aux quatre coins du pays il y a des gens qui disent ...; **he walked ~ and down the street** il a fait les cent pas dans la rue, il a arpenté la rue; **I've been ~ and down the stairs all evening** je n'ai pas arrêté de monter et descendre les escaliers de toute la soirée; **further ~ the page** plus haut sur la même page; **~ yours!**‡** va te faire foutre!**‡**; *see* **halfway**.

3 **n** a **~s and downs** (*in road etc*) accidents *mpl*; (*fig: in life, health etc*) hauts *mpl* et bas *mpl*; **after many ~s and downs** après bien des hauts et des bas, après maintes vicissitudes; **his career had its ~s and downs** il a connu des hauts et des bas *or* des succès et des revers dans sa carrière, sa carrière a connu des hauts et des bas.

b **he's on the ~ and ~*** (*Brit*) tout va de mieux en mieux pour lui; (*US*) il est tout à fait honnête, on peut compter sur lui; **it's on the ~ and ~*** (*Brit*) ça s'améliore; (*US*) c'est tout à fait honnête, c'est dans les règles; (*US*) **he's on the ~*** il fait des progrès, il est en progrès.

4 **adj** a (*Brit Rail*) **the ~ train** le train qui va à Londres; **the ~ platform** le quai du train pour Londres.

b (*elated*) **to be ~*** être en forme.

c (*Comput: functioning*) opérationnel. **to be ~ and running** (*Comput*) être opérationnel; (*gen*) *[project, system etc]* être en route; **to get sth ~ and running** (*Comput, gen*) mettre en route.

5 **vi** (‡ *hum*) **he ~ped and hit him** il a bondi et l'a frappé; **I ~ped and told him what I thought of him** sans plus attendre je lui ai dit ses quatre vérités; **he ~ped and went** *or* **offed** sans faire ni une ni deux il a fichu le camp*.

6 **vt** a (*: *raise*) (*gen*) augmenter; *prices, wages etc* augmenter; (*on scale, in hierarchy etc*) relever.

b (*Naut*) **to ~ anchor** lever l'ancre.

7 **comp ▸up-and-coming** *politician, businessman, actor* plein d'avenir, plein de promesses, qui monte; *rival* qui monte **▸up-and-down** *movement* ascendant et descendant, de va-et-vient; (*fig*) *career, business* qui a des hauts et des bas; *progress* en dents de scie **▸up-and-under** (*Rugby*) chandelle *f*, up and under *m* **▸up-and-up** = **up and up** (*see* **3b**) **▸up-beat** **n** (*Mus*) levé *m* **▸up beat*** **adj** (*fig*) optimiste **▸up-bow** (*Mus*) poussé *m* **▸up-current** (*Aviat*) courant (d'air) ascendant **▸up-draft** (*US*) = **up-current** **▸up-front** *see* **up-front** **▸up-market** *goods, car* haut de gamme *inv*; *newspaper* sérieux; *programme* (plutôt) intellectuel *or* raffiné; *area* select **▸up-to-date** *see* **up-to-date** **▸up-to-the-minute** de dernière heure.

upbraid [ʌp'breɪd] **vt** réprimander, morigéner, faire des reproches à. **to ~ sb for doing** reprocher à qn de faire (*or* d'avoir fait).

upbringing ['ʌpbrɪŋɪŋ] **n** éducation *f*. **he owed his success to his ~** il devait son succès à l'éducation qu'il avait reçue *or* à la manière dont il avait été élevé.

upchuck‡ ['ʌptʃʌk] **vi** (*US*) dégueuler‡, vomir.

upcoming ['ʌpkʌmɪŋ] **adj** (*US*) imminent, prochain.

upcountry [ʌp'kʌntrɪ] 1 **adv** *go* vers l'intérieur (d'un pays); *be* à l'intérieur. 2 **adj** de l'intérieur (*d'un pays*).

update [ʌp'deɪt] 1 **vt** (*gen, also Comput*) mettre à jour. **to ~ sb on sth** mettre qn au courant de qch. 2 ['ʌpdeɪt] **n** mise *f* à jour; (*Comput*) *[software package]* actualisation *f*, update *m*.

upend [ʌp'end] **vt** *box etc* mettre debout; (*fig*) *system etc* renverser, bouleverser, chambouler*.

up-front* [ʌp'frʌnt] 1 **adj** a (*esp US: open, frank*) franc (*f* franche), ouvert. b (*esp US: important*) important. c (*paid in advance*) payé d'avance. 2 **adv** a (*in advance*) *pay etc* d'avance. b (*esp US: openly*) ouvertement.

upgrade ['ʌpgreɪd] 1 **n** rampe *f*, montée *f*. (*fig*) **to be on the ~** *[business]* être en progrès; *[price]* augmenter, être en hausse; *[sick person]* être en voie de guérison. 2 ['ʌp'greɪd] **adv** (*US*) = **uphill 1**. 3 [ʌp'greɪd] **vt** a (*improve*) améliorer; (*modernize*) moderniser; (*Comput*) augmenter la puissance de. b (*raise, promote*) *employee* promouvoir; *job, post* revaloriser. **I have been ~d** je suis monté en grade, j'ai été promu. 4 **comp ▸upgradeable** (*Comput*) extensible.

upheaval [ʌp'hiːvəl] **n** a (*NonC*) (*gen*) bouleversement *m*; (*esp Pol*) perturbations *fpl*; (*moving things around: in home, office etc*) branle-bas *m*, remue-ménage *m*. **it caused a lot of ~** cela a tout perturbé. b (*disturbing event*) crise *f*, (*stronger*) cataclysme *m*. c (*Geol*) soulèvement *m*.

uphill ['ʌp'hɪl] 1 **adv** a **to go ~** *[road]* aller en montant, monter; *[car]* monter (la côte). b (*Ski*) en amont. 2 **adj** a *road* qui monte; (*fig*) *task* pénible, difficile, ardu. **it's ~ all the way** ça monte tout le long; (*fig*) c'est une lutte continuelle *or* incessante; (*fig*) **it's an ~ battle/struggle (trying to find a job/flat)** c'est une bataille/lutte difficile (que d'essayer de trouver un emploi/appartement); (*fig*) **we're fighting an ~ battle against corruption** nous menons une bataille incessante contre la corruption. b (*Ski*) en amont.

uphold [ʌp'həʊld] **pret, ptp upheld vt** *institution, person* soutenir, donner son soutien à; *law* faire respecter, maintenir; (*Jur*) *verdict* confirmer, maintenir.

upholder [ʌp'həʊldəʳ] **n** défenseur *m*.

upholster [ʌp'həʊlstəʳ] **vt** recouvrir. (*fig hum*) **she is fairly well ~ed*** elle est assez bien rembourrée*.

upholsterer [ʌp'həʊlstərəʳ] **n** tapissier *m*.

upholstery [ʌp'həʊlstərɪ] **n** a (*NonC*) (*trade*) tapisserie *f* (*art, métier*). b (*covering*) (*cloth*) tissu *m* d'ameublement; (*leather*) cuir *m*; (*in car*) garniture *f*.

upkeep ['ʌpkiːp] **n** *[family, house, car, garden]* entretien *m*. **~ (costs)** frais *mpl* d'entretien.

upland ['ʌplənd] 1 **n** (*also* **~s**) hautes terres *fpl*, hauteurs *fpl*, plateau(x) *m(pl)*. 2 **adj** des hautes terres, du *or* des plateau(x), des hauteurs.

uplift ['ʌplɪft] 1 n (*fig*) sentiment *m* d'élévation morale *or* spirituelle. 2 comp ▶**uplift bra** soutien-gorge *m* qui maintient bien la poitrine. 3 [ʌp'lɪft] vt a (*lit*) *arm, face* ~**ed** levé. b (*fig: spiritually, emotionally*) *soul* élever; *person* élever (l'âme *or* l'esprit *or* les sentiments de), grandir. **to feel ~ed** se sentir grandi. c (*fig: improve living conditions*) améliorer le cadre de vie de.

uplifting ['ʌp'lɪftɪŋ] adj (*fig*) (*edifying*) édifiant; (*cheering*) *film etc* réjouissant.

uplighter ['ʌpˌlaɪtəʳ] n applique *f* murale (*qui dirige la lumière en hauteur*).

upmost ['ʌpməʊst] = **uppermost**.

upon [ə'pɒn] prep = **on 2**.

upper ['ʌpəʳ] 1 adj *part, section, floor* supérieur (*f* -eure), du dessus, au-dessus; *lip, jaw, stratum, deck* supérieur; (*in geographical names*) haut; (*fig: in rank etc*) supérieur. **the temperature is in the ~ thirties** la température dépasse trente-cinq degrés; **the ~ (reaches of the) Thames** la haute Tamise; **the ~ classes** les couches supérieures de la société (*see also* **3**); **in the ~ (income) brackets** aux revenus élevés; *see* **hand 1b**.

2 n a [*shoe*] empeigne *f*. (*fig*) **to be (down) on one's ~s*** manger de la vache enragée, être dans la purée*.

b (*US Rail **) couchette *f* supérieure.

c (*‡: drug, pill*) stimulant *m*, excitant *m*.

3 comp ▶**upper atmosphere** couche *f* supérieure de l'atmosphère ▶**upper case** (*Typ*) haut *m* de casse; **upper-case letter** majuscule *f* ▶**Upper Chamber** = **Upper House** ▶**upper circle** (*Brit Theat*) deuxième balcon *m* ▶**upper-class** adj aristocratique ▶**upperclassman** (*US Univ*) étudiant *m* de troisième *or* quatrième année ▶**upper-crust*** adj aristocratique; (*fig*) **the upper crust*** le gratin* ▶**uppercut** (*Boxing*) uppercut *m* ▶**the Upper House** (*Parl*) (*gen*) la Chambre haute; (*in Britain*) la Chambre des Lords; (*in France, in the US etc*) le Sénat ▶**upper-income bracket** tranche *f* des revenus élevés ▶**upper middle class** haute bourgeoisie ▶**upper school** (*Scol*) (*gen*) grandes classes *fpl*; (*Scol Admin: top section*) (classe *f*) terminale *f* ▶**upper sixth (form)** (*Brit Scol*) (classe *f*) terminale *f* ▶**Upper Volta** Haute-Volta *f*.

uppermost ['ʌpəməʊst] 1 adj (*highest*) le plus haut, le plus élevé; (*on top*) en dessus. **the thought of it was ~ in my mind** j'y pensais avant tout autre chose, c'était au premier plan de mes pensées. 2 adv en dessus.

uppish* ['ʌpɪʃ], **uppity‡** ['ʌpɪtɪ] adj prétentieux, bêcheur*, arrogant, crâneur*. **to get ~** monter sur ses ergots; **to get ~ with sb** traiter qn de haut.

upraise [ʌp'reɪz] vt élever, lever. **~d** *hand, arm etc* levé.

uprate [ʌp'reɪt] adj: **~ tax brackets** tranches *fpl* les plus imposées.

upright ['ʌpraɪt] 1 adj (*erect*) *person, structure* droit, vertical; *piano* droit; (*fig: honest*) droit, honnête, probe. **~ freezer** congélateur-armoire *m*. 2 adv *stand* droit; *place* droit, verticalement. 3 n a [*door, window*] montant *m*, pied-droit *m* (*Archit*); [*goal-post*] montant de but. b (*piano*) piano droit.

uprightly ['ʌpˌraɪtlɪ] adv honnêtement, avec droiture.

uprightness ['ʌpˌraɪtnɪs] n (*NonC*) honnêteté *f*, droiture *f*.

uprising ['ʌpraɪzɪŋ] n soulèvement *m*, insurrection *f*, révolte *f* (*against* contre).

upriver ['ʌp'rɪvəʳ] 1 adv *be* en amont (*from* de); *sail* vers l'amont; *swim* contre le courant. 2 adj d'amont.

uproar ['ʌprɔːʳ] n (*NonC*) tumulte *m*. **this caused an ~, at this there was (an) ~** (*shouting*) cela a déclenché un véritable tumulte; (*protesting*) cela a déclenché une tempête de protestations; **the hall was in (an) ~** (*shouting*) le tumulte régnait dans la salle; (*protesting*) toute la salle protestait bruyamment; (*disturbance*) la plus vive agitation régnait dans la salle; **the meeting ended in (an) ~** la réunion s'est terminée dans le tumulte.

uproarious [ʌp'rɔːrɪəs] adj *meeting, evening, discussion* désopilant, tordant*; *joke, mistake* hilarant; *laughter* éclatant. **~ success** grand succès *m* comique.

uproariously [ʌp'rɔːrɪəslɪ] adv *laugh* aux éclats; *greet* avec de grands éclats de rire. **~ funny** désopilant.

uproot [ʌp'ruːt] vt (*lit, fig*) déraciner.

upsa-daisy* ['ʌpsəˌdeɪzɪ] excl (*baby talk*) allez, hop!

upscale* ['ʌp'skeɪl] adj classe*.

upset [ʌp'set] pret, ptp **upset** 1 vt a (*overturn*) *cup etc* renverser; *boat* faire chavirer; (*spill*) *milk, contents* renverser, répandre. (*fig*) **that ~ the applecart*** ça a tout fichu par terre*, ça a chamboulé* tous mes (*or* ses *etc*) projets.

b (*fig*) *plan, timetable* déranger, bouleverser; *system* déranger; *calculation* fausser; *stomach, digestion* déranger; *person* (*offend*) vexer; (*grieve*) faire de la peine à; (*annoy*) contrarier, fâcher, indisposer; (*make ill*) rendre malade. **don't ~ yourself** ne vous tracassez pas, ne vous en faites pas*, ne vous faites pas de bile*; **now you've ~ him** maintenant il est vexé; **onions always ~ me** *or* **my digestion** *or* **my stomach** les oignons me rendent malade, je ne supporte pas les oignons.

2 adj a *person* (*offended*) vexé; (*grieved*) peiné, attristé, triste; (*annoyed*) fâché, contrarié, ennuyé; (*ill*) indisposé, souffrant. **to get ~** se vexer; devenir triste; se fâcher; **he looked terribly ~** il avait l'air bouleversé *or* tout chaviré*; **what are you so ~ about?** qu'est-ce qui ne va pas?

b *stomach, digestion* dérangé.

3 ['ʌpset] comp ▶**upset price** (*at auction: esp US*) mise *f* à prix.

4 ['ʌpset] n (*upheaval*) désordre *m*, remue-ménage *m*; (*in plans etc*) bouleversement *m*, changement *m* soudain (*in* de); (*emotional*) chagrin *m*; (**: quarrel*) brouille *f*. **to have a stomach ~** avoir l'estomac dérangé, avoir une indigestion.

upsetting [ʌp'setɪŋ] adj (*offending*) vexant; (*saddening*) triste, (*stronger*) affligeant; (*annoying*) contrariant, fâcheux, ennuyeux.

upshot ['ʌpʃɒt] n résultat *m*, aboutissement *m*, conséquence *f*. **the ~ of it all was ...** le résultat de tout cela a été ...; **in the ~** à la fin, en fin de compte.

upside down ['ʌpsaɪd'daʊn] 1 adv à l'envers. **to hold a book ~** tenir un livre à l'envers; **to turn ~** *box, book* retourner; (*fig*) *room, drawer, cupboard* mettre sens dessus dessous; *life* bouleverser; (*) *plans* flanquer à l'eau*. 2 adj *book* à l'envers; *cup* retourné; (*in disorder*) *room etc* sens dessus dessous. (*Culin*) **pineapple ~ cake** gâteau renversé à l'ananas.

upstage ['ʌp'steɪdʒ] 1 adv (*Theat*) *be, stand* au fond de la scène; *go* vers le fond de la scène; *enter* par le fond de la scène. 2 adj (** fig*) hautain, prétentieux, crâneur*. 3 vt éclipser, souffler la vedette à.

upstairs ['ʌp'stɛəz] 1 adv en haut (*d'un escalier*). **he's ~** il est en haut; **to go ~** monter (l'escalier); **he ran ~** il a monté l'escalier quatre à quatre; **to take ~** *person* faire monter; *luggage etc* monter; **the people ~** les gens du dessus; **the room ~** la pièce d'en haut *or* à l'étage; (*fig*) **he's not got much ~*** il n'est pas très intelligent, ça ne tourne pas très fort là-haut*; *see* **kick**. 2 n: **the house has no ~** la maison est de plain-pied *or* n'a pas d'étage; **the ~ belongs to another family** l'étage *m* appartient à une autre famille. 3 ['ʌpstɛəz] adj *flat, neighbour* du dessus; *room* d'en haut, à l'étage. **I prefer an ~ room** je préfère une chambre à l'étage *or* en étage.

upstanding [ʌp'stændɪŋ] adj a (*erect*) qui se tient droit. (*frm*) **be ~** levez-vous. b (*well-built*) bien bâti, bien campé; (*honest*) droit, honnête, probe. **a fine ~ young man** un jeune homme très bien.

upstart ['ʌpstɑːt] n parvenu(e) *m(f)*, arriviste *mf*.

upstate ['ʌp'steɪt] (*US*) 1 adv *go* vers l'intérieur (*d'un État des États-Unis*); *be* à l'intérieur. 2 adj de l'intérieur. **~ New York** la partie nord de l'État de New York (*située loin de l'agglomération new-yorkaise*).

upstream ['ʌp'striːm] 1 adv *be* en amont (*from* de); *sail* vers l'amont; *swim* contre le courant. 2 adj d'amont. **~ industries** industries *fpl* en amont.

upstretched [ʌp'stretʃt] adj: **with arms ~** les bras tendus en l'air.

upstroke ['ʌpstrəʊk] n (*with pen*) délié *m*; [*piston etc*] course *f* ascendante.

upsurge ['ʌpsɜːdʒ] n [*feeling*] vague *f*, accès *m*; [*interest*] renaissance *f*, recrudescence *f*, regain *m*.

upswept [ˌʌp'swept] adj a (*Aut, Aviat*) profilé. b *hair* relevé sur la tête.

upswing ['ʌpswɪŋ] n (*lit*) mouvement *m* ascendant, montée *f*; (*fig*) amélioration *f* notable; (*Econ*) redressement *m*, reprise *f* (*in* de).

upsy-daisy* ['ʌpsəˌdeɪzɪ] excl = **upsa-daisy**.

uptake ['ʌpteɪk] n a (*understanding*) **to be quick on the ~*** avoir l'esprit vif *or* rapide, comprendre *or* saisir vite; **to be slow on the ~*** être lent à comprendre *or* à saisir. b (*Tech: intake*) consommation *f*. c (*Marketing*) **the ~ on the new product** l'intérêt suscité par le nouveau produit.

upthrust ['ʌpθrʌst] n (*gen, Tech*) poussée *f* ascendante; (*Geol*) soulèvement *m*.

uptight* [ʌp'taɪt] adj a (*tense*) très tendu, crispé; (*touchy*) susceptible; (*conventional*) collet monté *inv*. **to get ~** (*tense*) se crisper (*about* à propos de); (*upset*) se froisser (*about* à propos de). b (*US: having no money*) à court d'argent.

uptime ['ʌpˌtaɪm] n [*machine, computer*] temps *m* *or* durée *f* de fonctionnement.

up-to-date [ˌʌptə'deɪt] adj a (*updated*) *report, file* à jour. b (*most recent*) *report, assessment, information* très (*or* le plus) récent. c (*modern*) *building, course* moderne; *attitude, person* moderne, dans le vent, à la page; *see also* **date¹ 1c**.

uptorn [ʌp'tɔːn] adj *tree* déraciné, arraché.

uptown ['ʌp'taʊn] (*US*) 1 adv dans les quartiers chics. 2 adj des quartiers chics.

upturn [ʌp'tɜːn] 1 vt retourner, mettre à l'envers; (*overturn*) renverser. **~ed nose** nez retroussé. 2 ['ʌptɜːn] n amélioration *f* (*in* de).

UPW [ˌjuːpiː'dʌbljuː] n (*Brit*) (abbr of **Union of Post Office Workers**) *syndicat*.

upward ['ʌpwəd] 1 adj *movement* ascendant, ascensionnel; *pull, thrust* vers le haut, ascensionnel; *trend* à la hausse; *slope* qui monte; *glance* levé. (*Soc*) **~ mobility** mobilité *f* sociale ascendante, possibilités *fpl* d'ascension sociale. 2 adv = **upwards**.

upwardly [ˈʌpwədlɪ] adv (*Soc*) ~ **mobile** (npl) mobiles *mpl* sociaux ascendants; (adj) à mobilité sociale ascendante.

upwards [ˈʌpwədz] (*phr vb elem*) adv *move, walk* en montant, vers le haut. **to look** ~ regarder en haut *or* vers le haut; **looking** ~ les yeux levés, la tête levée; **place the book face** ~ posez le livre face en dessus, posez le livre à l'endroit; **he was lying face** ~ il était couché sur le dos; **to slope gently** ~ monter en pente douce; (*fig*) **prices from 10 francs** ~ prix à partir de 10 F; **from childhood** ~ dès sa jeunesse; **and** ~ et plus, et au-dessus; ~ **of 3,000** 3000 et plus.

upwind [ˈʌpˈwɪnd] adv contre le vent, du côté du vent. **to be** ~ **of** être dans le vent par rapport à.

uraemia [jʊˈriːmɪə] n urémie *f*.

uraemic [jʊˈriːmɪk] adj urémique.

Ural [ˈjʊərəl] n: **the** ~ **Mountains, the** ~**s** les monts *mpl* Oural, l'Oural *m*.

uranalysis [ˌjʊərəˈnælɪsɪs] n, pl **uranalyses** [ˌjʊərəˈnælɪsiːz] (*Med*) analyse *f* d'urine.

uranium [jʊəˈreɪnɪəm] 1 n uranium *m*. 2 comp ►**uranium-bearing** *rock* uranifère.

Uranus [jʊəˈreɪnəs] n (*Myth*) Uranus *m*; (*Astron*) Uranus *f*.

urban [ˈɜːbən] adj urbain. **in** ~ **areas** dans les zones urbaines; ~ **blight** dégradation *f* *or* pollution *f* urbaine; (*Admin*) ~ **conservation area** secteur sauvegardé; (*Admin*) ~ **development zone** ≈ zone *f* à urbaniser en priorité, Z.U.P. *f*; (*Brit*) ~ **district council** conseil *m* de district urbain; ~ **guerilla** guérillero *m* urbain; ~ **renewal** rénovations urbaines; ~ **sprawl** étalement urbain; ~ **studies** étude *f* de l'environnement urbain.

urbane [ɜːˈbeɪn] adj urbain, courtois.

urbanite [ˈɜːbənaɪt] n (*US*) citadin(e) *m(f)*.

urbanity [ɜːˈbænɪtɪ] n (*NonC*) urbanité *f*, courtoisie *f*.

urbanization [ˌɜːbənaɪˈzeɪʃən] n urbanisation *f*.

urbanize [ˈɜːbənaɪz] vt urbaniser.

urchin [ˈɜːtʃɪn] n polisson(ne) *m(f)*, garnement *m*; *see* **sea, street.**

Urdu [ˈʊəduː] n ourdou *m*.

urea [ˈjʊərɪə] n urée *f*.

uremia [jʊˈriːmɪə] *etc* = **uraemia** *etc*.

ureter [jʊˈriːtəʳ] n uretère *m*.

urethra [jʊˈriːθrə] n, pl ~**s** *or* **urethrae** [jʊˈriːθriː] urètre *m*.

urge [ɜːdʒ] 1 n désir ardent, forte envie, démangeaison* *f* (*to do* de faire). **to feel** *or* **have the** ~ **to do** éprouver une forte envie de faire, avoir vivement envie de faire, être démangé* par une envie de faire; *see* **sex.**

2 vt *person* pousser, exhorter (*to do* à faire), presser, conseiller vivement (*to do* de faire); *caution, remedy, measure* préconiser, conseiller vivement, recommander avec insistance; *excuse* faire valoir; *point* insister sur. **I** ~ **you to write at once, write at once I** ~ **you** je ne saurais trop vous conseiller d'écrire immédiatement; **I** ~**d him not to go** je lui ai vivement déconseillé d'y aller; **he needed no urging** il ne s'est pas fait prier; **to** ~ **that sth (should) be done** recommander vivement que *or* insister pour que qch soit fait; **"do it now!" he** ~**d** "faites-le tout de suite!" insista-t-il; **he** ~**d acceptance of the report** il a vivement recommandé *or* préconisé l'acceptation du rapport; **to** ~ **patience on sb** exhorter qn à la patience; **they** ~**d this policy on the Government** ils ont fait pression sur le gouvernement pour qu'il adopte (*subj*) cette politique; **to** ~ **sb back/in/out** *etc* presser qn de revenir/ d'entrer/de sortir *etc*.

►**urge on** vt sep *horse* presser, pousser, talonner; *person* faire avancer; *troops* pousser en avant, faire avancer; (*fig*) *worker* aiguillonner, presser; *work* activer, hâter; (*Sport*) *team* animer, encourager. **to urge sb on to (do) sth** inciter qn à (faire) qch.

urgency [ˈɜːdʒənsɪ] n (*NonC*) *[case etc]* urgence *f*; *[tone, entreaty]* insistance *f*. **a matter of** ~ une affaire urgente; **there's no** ~ ce n'est pas urgent, cela ne presse pas; **with a note of** ~ **in his voice** avec insistance.

urgent [ˈɜːdʒənt] adj *need* urgent, pressant; *case, attention, letter, message* urgent; *tone* insistant; *plea, entreaty, request* pressant. ~ **steps** *or* **measures** mesures urgentes *or* d'urgence; **it's** ~! c'est urgent!, ça urge!*; **how** ~ **is it?** est-ce que c'est très urgent?, est-ce que ça presse?; **is it** ~? est-ce (vraiment) urgent?, y a-t-il urgence?; **it's not** ~ ce n'est pas urgent, cela ne presse pas, cela peut attendre; **it is** ~ **that he should go** il doit y aller d'urgence, il est urgent qu'il y aille; **to be in** ~ **need of** avoir un besoin urgent de; **the most** ~ **thing is to get help to them** le plus urgent est de leur faire parvenir des secours; **he demands an** ~ **answer** il exige qu'on lui réponde d'urgence *or* de toute urgence *or* sans délai; **he was very** ~ **about the need for action** il les (*or* nous *etc*) a pressés instamment d'agir, il a préconisé la nécessité d'agir.

urgently [ˈɜːdʒəntlɪ] adv *need* sans délai; *request* d'urgence, de toute urgence; *plead* instamment. **we must talk** ~ il faut qu'on parle de toute urgence *or* sans plus attendre; **he is** ~ **in need of medical attention** son état demande des soins urgents; **please reply** ~ nous vous serions reconnaissants de bien vouloir répondre dans les plus brefs délais.

uric [ˈjʊərɪk] adj urique.

urinal [ˈjʊərɪnl] n (*place*) urinoir *m*; (*in street*) vespasienne *f*; (*receptacle*) urinal *m*.

urinalysis [ˌjʊərɪˈnælɪsɪs] n, pl **urinalyses** [ˌjʊərɪˈnælɪsiːz] = **uranalysis.**

urinary [ˈjʊərɪnərɪ] adj urinaire.

urinate [ˈjʊərɪneɪt] vi uriner.

urine [ˈjʊərɪn] n urine *f*.

urn [ɜːn] n a (*vase etc*) urne *f*; (*funeral* ~) urne (funéraire). b **tea** ~ fontaine *f* à thé.

urogenital [ˌjʊərəʊˈdʒenɪtl] adj urogénital.

urological [ˌjʊərəʊˈlɒdʒɪkl] adj urologique.

urologist [jʊəˈrɒlədʒɪst] n urologue *mf*.

urology [jʊəˈrɒlədʒɪ] n urologie *f*.

Ursa [ˈɜːsə] n (*Astron*) ~ **Major/Minor** la Grande/Petite Ourse.

urticaria [ˌɜːtɪˈkeərɪə] n urticaire *f*.

Uruguay [ˈjʊərəgwaɪ] n Uruguay *m*.

Uruguayan [ˌjʊərəˈgwaɪən] 1 adj uruguayen, de l'Uruguay. 2 n Uruguayen(ne) *m(f)*.

US [juːˈes] (abbr of **United States**) U.S.A. *mpl*, É.U.(A.) *mpl*.

us [ʌs] pers pron a nous. **he hit** ~ il nous a frappés; **give it to** ~ donnez-le-nous; **in front of** ~ devant nous; **let** ~ *or* **let's go!** allons-y!; **younger than** ~ plus jeune que nous; **both of** ~ nous deux, tous (*or* toutes) les deux; **several of** ~ plusieurs d'entre nous; **he is one of** ~ il est des nôtres; **as for** ~ **English, we** ... nous autres Anglais, nous ...; **we took the books with** ~ nous avons emporté les livres. b (‡) me, moi. **give** ~ **a bit!** donne-m'en un morceau!, donne-moi-z-en!‡; **give** ~ **a look!** fais voir!

USA [juːesˈeɪ] n a (abbr of **United States of America**) U.S.A. *mpl*, É.U.A. *mpl*. b (abbr of **United States Army**) *armée de terre des États-Unis*.

usable [ˈjuːzəbl] adj utilisable. **no longer** ~ hors d'usage.

U.S.A.F. [juːeseɪˈef] n (abbr of **United States Air Force**) *armée de l'air des États-Unis*.

usage [ˈjuːzɪdʒ] n (*NonC*) a (*custom*) usage *m*, coutume *f*; (*Ling*) usage. b (*treatment*) *[tool, machine, chair etc]* manipulation *f*; *[person]* traitement *m*. **it's had some rough** ~ ça a été bousculé, on s'en est mal servi; **kind** ~ gentillesse *f*.

usance [ˈjuːzəns] n (*Fin*) usance *f*.

USDA [ˌjuːesdiːˈeɪ] n (abbr of **United States Department of Agriculture**) *see* **agriculture.**

USDAW [ˌjuːesdiːeɪˈdʌbljuː] n (*Brit*) (abbr of **Union of Shop Distributive and Allied Workers**) *syndicat*.

USDI [ˌjuːesdiːˈaɪ] n (abbr of **United States Department of the Interior**) *see* **interior.**

use [juːs] 1 n a (*NonC: using*) usage *m*, emploi *m*, utilisation *f*. **the** ~ **of steel in industry** l'emploi de l'acier dans l'industrie; **to learn the** ~ **of** apprendre à se servir de; **care is necessary in the** ~ **of firearms** il faut prendre des précautions quand on utilise des *or* on se sert d'armes à feu; **directions for** ~ mode *m* d'emploi; **for your (own) personal** ~ à votre usage personnel; **"for the** ~ **of teachers only"** *book, equipment* "à l'usage des professeurs seulement"; *car park, room* "réservé aux professeurs"; **to keep sth for one's own** ~ réserver qch à son usage personnel; **for** ~ **in case of emergency** à utiliser en cas d'urgence; **fit for** ~ en état de servir; **ready for** ~ prêt à servir *or* à l'emploi; **for general/household** ~ à usage général/domestique; **for** ~ **in schools/the home** destiné à être utilisé dans les écoles/à la maison; (*Med*) **for external** ~ à usage externe; **to improve with** ~ s'améliorer à l'usage; **in** ~ *machine* en usage, utilisé; *word* en usage, usité; **no longer in** ~, **now out of** ~ *machine* hors d'usage, qui n'est plus utilisé; *word* qui ne s'emploie plus, inusité; (*on machine, lift etc*) **"out of** ~**"** "en dérangement"; **it's gone out of** ~ on ne l'emploie plus; **in general** ~ d'usage *or* d'emploi courant; **it is in daily** ~ on s'en sert tous les jours; **to come into** ~ entrer en usage; **to go out of** ~ tomber en désuétude; **to put sth into** ~ commencer à se servir de qch; **to make** ~ **of** se servir de, faire usage de, utiliser; **to make good** ~ **of, to put to good** ~ *machine, time, money* faire un bon emploi de, tirer parti de; *opportunity, facilities* mettre à profit, tirer parti de.

b (*way of using*) emploi *m*, utilisation *f*; (*need*) besoin *m*. **a new** ~ **for** un nouvel emploi de, une nouvelle utilisation de; **it has many** ~**s** cela a beaucoup d'emplois; **I'll find a** ~ **for it** je trouverai un moyen de m'en servir, j'en trouverai l'emploi; **I've no further** ~ **for it** je ne m'en sers plus, je n'en ai plus besoin; (*fig*) **I've no** ~ **for that sort of behaviour!*** je n'ai que faire de ce genre de conduite!; **I've no** ~ **for him at all!*** il m'embête!*

c (*NonC: usefulness*) **to be of** ~ servir, être utile (*for sth, to sth* à qch, *to sb* à qn); **to be (of) no** ~ ne servir à rien; **this is no** ~ **any more** ce n'est plus bon à rien; **what's the** ~ **of all this?** à quoi sert tout ceci?; **is this (of) any** ~ **to you?** est-ce que cela peut vous être utile? *or* vous servir?; **can I be (of) any** ~? puis-je être *or* me rendre utile?; **he's no** ~ il est incapable, il est nul; **he's no** ~ **as a goalkeeper** il ne vaut rien comme gardien de but; **you're no** ~ **to me if you can't spell** vous ne m'êtes d'aucune utilité si vous faites des fautes d'orthographe; **this tool has its** ~**s** cet outil a son utilité; **he has his** ~**s** il est utile par certains côtés; **a lot of** ~ **that will be to you!*** ça te fera une belle jambe!*; **there's** *or* **it's no** ~ **you(r) protesting** il ne vous sert à rien de protester; **it's no** ~ **trying to reason with him** il ne sert à rien d'essayer de le raisonner, on perd son temps à essayer de le raisonner; **it's no** ~,

he won't listen ça ne sert à rien *or* c'est inutile, il ne veut rien entendre; **it's no ~, we must start work** tout ça c'est bien joli mais il faut nous mettre au travail; **you won't get it, it is no ~** tu ne l'auras pas, rien à faire; **what's the ~ of telling him not to, he never takes any notice** à quoi bon lui dire d'arrêter, il ne prête jamais attention; **I've told him fifty times already, what's the ~?** je le lui ai dit trente-six fois déjà, pour ce que ça a servi.

d (*NonC*) usage *m.* **to have the ~ of a garage** avoir l'usage d'un garage, pouvoir se servir d'un garage; **with ~ of kitchen** avec usage *or* jouissance de la cuisine; **he gave me the ~ of his car** il m'a permis de me servir de sa voiture; **to have lost the ~ of one's arm** avoir perdu l'usage de son bras; **to have the full ~ of one's faculties** jouir de toutes ses facultés.

e (*frm: custom*) coutume *f*, habitude *f*; (*Rel, Soc*) usage *m.* **this has long been his ~** telle est son habitude depuis longtemps.

2 [ju:z] **vt** a *object, tool* se servir de, utiliser, employer; *force, discretion* user de; *opportunity* profiter de; *method, means* employer; *sb's name* faire usage de. **he ~d a knife to open it** il s'est servi d'un couteau *or* il a utilisé un couteau *or* il a pris un couteau pour l'ouvrir; **it is ~d for opening bottles** on s'en sert pour ouvrir les bouteilles; **are you using this?** vous servez-vous de ceci?, avez-vous besoin de ceci?; **have you ~d a gun before?** vous êtes-vous déjà servi d'un fusil?; **the money is to be ~d to build a new hospital** l'argent servira à construire un nouvel hôpital *or* à la construction d'un nouvel hôpital; **he ~d his shoe as a hammer** il s'est servi de son soulier comme marteau. **I ~ that as a table** ça me sert de table; **ointment to be ~ed sparingly** crème à utiliser en couche légère; **I don't ~ my French much** je ne me sers pas beaucoup de mon français; **I don't want to ~ the car** je ne veux pas prendre la voiture; **he said I could ~ his car** il a dit que je pouvais me servir de *or* prendre sa voiture; **no longer ~ed** *tools, machine, room* qui ne sert plus; *word* qui ne s'emploie plus, inusité; **he wants to ~ the bathroom** il veut aller aux toilettes; **someone is using the bathroom** il y a quelqu'un aux toilettes; **~ your head!** *or* **brains!** réfléchis un peu!, tu as une tête, c'est pour t'en servir!; **~ your eyes!** ouvre l'œil!; **I feel I've just been ~ed** j'ai l'impression qu'on s'est tout bonnement servi de moi; **I could ~ a drink!*** je prendrais bien un verre!; **this house could ~ a bit of paint!*** une couche de peinture ne ferait pas de mal à cette maison!; *see also* **used**.

b (*also* **~ up**) user, consommer; prendre. **this car ~s (up) too much petrol** cette voiture use *or* consomme trop d'essence; **have you ~d (up) all the paint?** avez-vous utilisé toute la peinture?, avez-vous fini la peinture?; **you can ~ (up) the left-overs in a casserole** vous pouvez utiliser les restes pour faire un ragoût.

c (*treat*) *person* traiter, agir envers. **to ~ sb well** bien traiter qn, bien agir envers qn; **he was badly ~d** on a mal agi envers lui, on a abusé de sa bonne volonté.

3 **aux vb**: **I ~d to see her every week** je la voyais toutes les semaines; **I ~d to swim every day** je me baignais *or* j'avais l'habitude de me baigner tous les jours; **I ~d not** *or* **I use(d)n't*** *or* **I didn't ~* to smoke** (autrefois) je ne fumais pas; **what ~d he to** *or* **what did he ~* to do on Sundays?** qu'est-ce qu'il faisait (d'habitude) le dimanche?; **things aren't what they ~d to be** les choses ne sont plus ce qu'elles étaient.

4 **vi** (*Drugs sl*) se droguer, se camer⁑.

►**use up** **vt sep** *food* consommer entièrement, finir; *objects, ammunition, one's strength, resources, surplus* épuiser; *money* dépenser. **to use up the scraps** utiliser les restes; **it is all used up** c'est épuisé, il n'en reste plus; *see also* **use 2b**.

used [ju:zd] **adj** a *stamp* oblitéré; *car* d'occasion. b [ju:st] (*accustomed*) **to be ~ to (doing) sth** être habitué à (faire) qch, avoir l'habitude de (faire) qch; **I'm not ~ to it** je n'en ai pas l'habitude, je n'y suis pas habitué; **to get ~ to** s'habituer à; **you'll get ~ to it** vous vous y ferez.

use(d)n't ['ju:snt] = **used not**; *see* **use 3**.

useful ['ju:sfʊl] **adj** *tool, chair, book* utile; *discussion, time* utile, profitable; *attempt* honorable. **it is ~ for him to be able to ...** il est très utile qu'il puisse ...; **to make o.s. ~** se rendre utile, donner un coup de main*; **to come in ~** être utile; **that knife will come in ~** ce couteau pourra nous rendre service; **to be ~ to sb** *[person]* rendre service à qn; *[advice, knowledge, tool]* être utile à qn, rendre service à qn; (*iro*) **that's ~!** nous voilà bien avancés!; **this machine has a ~ life of 10 years** cette machine peut donner 10 ans de satisfaction *or* de service; **it has reached the end of its ~ life** ce n'est plus bon *or* utile à grand-chose; **he's a ~ man to know** c'est un homme utile à connaître *or* qu'il est bon de connaître; **it's a ~ thing to know** c'est bon à savoir; **he's a ~ player** c'est un joueur compétent; **he's quite ~ with his fists** il sait bien se servir de ses poings; **he's ~ with a gun** il sait manier un fusil.

usefully ['ju:sfəlɪ] **adv** utilement.

usefulness ['ju:sfʊlnɪs] **n** (*NonC*) utilité *f*; *see* **outlive**.

useless ['ju:slɪs] **adj** *tool* inutile; (*unusable*) inutilisable; *advice, suggestion* inutile, qui ne vaut rien; *person* incompétent; *remedy* inefficace; *volunteer* incapable; *effort* inutile, vain. **this is a ~ machine** c'est une machine inutile *or* qui ne sert à rien; **this machine is ~ without a handle** cette machine est inutilisable sans une manivelle, on ne peut pas se servir de cette machine sans une manivelle; **shouting is ~** (il est) inutile de crier, il ne sert à rien de crier, ce n'est pas la peine de crier; **he's ~ as a goalkeeper** il ne vaut rien comme gardien de but; **he's absolutely ~*** c'est un cas désespéré, il est complètement nul.

uselessly ['ju:slɪslɪ] **adv** inutilement.

uselessness ['ju:slɪsnɪs] **n** (*NonC*) *[tool, advice etc]* inutilité *f*; *[remedy]* inefficacité *f*; *[person]* incompétence *f*.

user ['ju:zəʳ] 1 **n** a *[public service, telephone, road, train, dictionary]* usager *m*; *[machine, tool]* utilisateur *m*, -trice *f*; *[electricity, gas]* usager, utilisateur; (*Comput*) utilisateur *m.* **car ~** automobiliste *mf*; **computer ~s** ceux qui utilisent un ordinateur, utilisateurs d'ordinateurs.

b (*Drugs*) usager *m*, consommateur *m.* **heroin ~** héroïnomane *mf*.

2 **comp** ►**user-definable, user-defined** (*Comput*) touche *f* définissable par l'utilisateur ►**user-friendliness** (*Comput*) convivialité *f*; *[machine, dictionary etc]* facilité *f* d'utilisation ►**user-friendly** (*Comput*) convivial; (*gen*) facile à utiliser; **we want to make the store more user-friendly for shoppers** nous voulons rendre le magasin plus accueillant pour les clients ►**user name** (*Comput*) nom *m* de l'utilisateur.

USES [ˌju:esi:'es] **n** (**abbr of United States Employment Service**) *see* **employment**.

USGS [ˌju:esdʒi:'es] **n** (**abbr of United States Geological Survey**) *see* **geological**.

usher ['ʌʃəʳ] 1 **n** (*in law courts etc*) huissier *m*; (*doorkeeper*) portier *m*; (*at public meeting*) membre *m* du service d'ordre; (*in theatre, church*) placeur *m.* 2 **vt**: **to ~ sb out/along** *etc* faire sortir/avancer *etc* qn; **to ~ sb into a room** introduire *or* faire entrer qn dans une salle; **to ~ sb to the door** reconduire qn à la porte.

►**usher in** **vt sep** *person* introduire, faire entrer; (*fig*) *period, season* inaugurer, commencer. **it ushers in a new era** cela annonce *or* inaugure une nouvelle époque, cela marque le début d'une ère nouvelle; **it ushered in a new reign** cela inaugura un nouveau règne, ce fut l'aurore d'un nouveau règne; **the spring was ushered in by storms** le début du printemps fut marqué par des orages.

usherette [ˌʌʃə'ret] **n** (*Cine, Theat*) ouvreuse *f*.

USM [ju:es'em] **n** (**abbr of United States Mint**) *Hôtel de la Monnaie américain*.

USN [ju:es'en] **n** (**abbr of United States Navy**) *marine de guerre des États-Unis*.

USP [ju:es'pi:] **n** (**abbr of unique selling point**) *see* **unique**.

USPHS [ˌju:espi:eɪtʃ'es] **n** (**abbr of United States Public Health Service**) *see* **public**.

USS [ju:es'es] **n abbr of United States Ship** (*or* **Steamer**).

U.S.S.R.† [ˌju:eses'ɑ:ʳ] (**abbr of Union of Soviet Socialist Republics**†) U.R.S.S. *f*.

usu. **abbr of usual(ly)**.

usual ['ju:ʒʊəl] 1 **adj** (*gen*) habituel; *price* habituel, courant; *word* usuel, courant. **my ~ grocer** mon épicier habituel; **his ~ drink is beer** d'habitude il boit de la bière; **this is not my ~ brand** ce n'est pas la marque que je prends d'habitude *or* habituellement; **it wasn't his ~ car** ce n'était pas la voiture qu'il prenait d'habitude *or* à l'ordinaire; **come at the ~ time** venez à l'heure habituelle, venez à la même heure que d'habitude; **7 o'clock is my ~ time to get up** en général *or* d'habitude, je me lève à 7 heures; **it is the ~ practice** c'est ce qui se fait d'habitude; **his ~ practice was to rise at 6** il avait l'habitude de se lever à 6 heures; **as is ~ with such machines it broke down** comme toutes les machines de ce genre elle est tombée en panne; **as is ~ on these occasions** comme le veut la coutume en ces occasions; **he was on his ~ good behaviour** il se tenait bien, comme d'habitude; **with his ~ tact** avec son tact habituel, avec le tact qui le caractérise *or* qui est le sien; **he'll soon be his ~ self again** il retrouvera bientôt sa santé (*or* sa gaieté *etc*); **as ~, as per ~*** comme d'habitude, comme à l'ordinaire; **he's late — as ~!** il est en retard — comme toujours! *or* comme d'habitude!; (*Comm*) **"business as ~"** "la vente *or* les affaires continue(nt)"; **more than ~** plus que d'habitude *or* d'ordinaire *or* de coutume; **it's quite ~ for this to happen** ça arrive souvent, ça n'a rien d'inhabituel; **it's ~ to ask first** il est préférable *or* de règle de demander d'abord; **it's not ~ for him to be late** il est rare qu'il soit en retard, il n'est pas en retard d'habitude; **it's the ~ thing** c'est comme toujours! ça ne change jamais; **he said the ~ things about ...** il a dit ce qu'il est d'usage *or* de règle de dire à propos de ...; **it was the ~ kind of party** c'était une soirée typique *or* une soirée comme tant d'autres; *see* **channel**.

2 **n** (**: drink*) **you know my ~** vous savez ce que je prends d'habitude; **the ~ please!** comme d'habitude s'il vous plaît!

usually ['ju:ʒʊəlɪ] **adv** habituellement, d'habitude, généralement, ordinairement, d'ordinaire, à l'ordinaire. **I ~ go on Wednesdays** j'y vais généralement *or* ordinairement le mercredi, habituellement *or* d'habitude *or* d'ordinaire j'y vais le mercredi; **what do you ~ do?** qu'est-ce que vous faites d'habitude? *or* d'ordinaire? *or* à l'ordinaire?; **more than ~ careful** encore plus prudent que d'habitude *or* d'ordinaire *or* de coutume.

usufruct ['ju:zjʊfrʌkt] **n** (*Jur*) usufruit *m*.

usufructuary [ˌju:zjʊ'frʌktjʊərɪ] (*Jur*) 1 **n** usufruitier *m*, -ière *f*. 2 **adj** usufruitier.

usurer ['juːʒərər] n usurier *m*, -ière *f*.
usurious [juː'zjʊərɪəs] adj usuraire.
usurp [juː'zɜːp] vt usurper.
usurpation [ˌjuːzɜː'peɪʃən] n (*NonC*) usurpation *f*.
usurper [juː'zɜːpər] n usurpateur *m*, -trice *f*.
usurping [juː'zɜːpɪŋ] adj usurpateur (*f* -trice).
usury ['juːʒʊrɪ] n (*NonC: Fin*) usure *f*.
UT (*US*) abbr of **Utah**.
Utah ['juːtɔː] n Utah *m*. **in ~** dans l'Utah.
utensil [juː'tensl] n ustensile *m*; *see* **kitchen**.
uteri ['juːtəˌraɪ] npl of **uterus**.
uterine ['juːtəraɪn] adj utérin.
uterus ['juːtərəs] n, pl **uteri** utérus *m*.
utilitarian [ˌjuːtɪlɪ'tɛərɪən] 1 adj utilitaire. 2 n utilitariste *mf*.
utilitarianism [ˌjuːtɪlɪ'tɛərɪənɪzəm] n (*NonC*) utilitarisme *m*.
utility [juː'tɪlɪtɪ] 1 n a (*NonC*) utilité *f*. b (*public ~*) service *m* public. 2 adj *goods* utilitaire, fonctionnel; *vehicle* utilitaire. 3 comp ► **utility room** ≈ buanderie *f* ► **utility software** (*Comput*) logiciel *m* utilitaire.
utilizable ['juːtɪˌlaɪzəbl] adj utilisable.
utilization [ˌjuːtɪlaɪ'zeɪʃən] n (*see* **utilize**) utilisation *f*; exploitation *f*.
utilize ['juːtɪlaɪz] vt *object, facilities, equipment* utiliser, se servir de; *situation, resources, talent, person* utiliser, tirer parti de, exploiter; *space* utiliser, tirer parti de.
utmost ['ʌtməʊst] 1 adj a (*greatest*) le plus grand; *skill* suprême; *danger* extrême. **with the ~ speed** à toute vitesse; **with the ~ candour** en toute franchise, avec la plus grande franchise; **with the ~ possible care** avec le plus grand soin possible, aussi soigneusement que possible; **it is of the ~ importance that** ... il est extrêmement important que ... + *subj*; **it's a matter of the ~ importance** c'est une affaire de la plus haute importance *or* d'une importance capitale.
b (*furthest*) le plus éloigné, extrême. **to the ~ ends of the earth** aux quatre coins de la terre.
2 n: **to do one's ~ to do** faire tout son possible *or* tout ce qu'on peut pour faire; **to the ~ of one's ability** à la limite de ses capacités, au mieux de ses possibilités; **that is the ~ I can do** c'est absolument tout ce que je peux faire, je ne peux absolument pas faire plus *or* mieux; **to the ~** au plus haut degré, au plus haut point; **at the ~** au maximum, tout au plus.
Utopia [juː'təʊpɪə] n utopie *f*.
Utopian [juː'təʊpɪən] 1 adj utopique. 2 n utopiste *mf*.
Utopianism [juː'təʊpɪənɪzəm] n utopisme *m*.
utricle ['juːtrɪkl] n utricule *m*.
Uttar Pradesh ['ʊtə'prɑːdeʃ] n Uttar Pradesh *m*.
utter[1] ['ʌtər] adj *candour, sincerity, disaster* complet (*f* -ète), total, absolu; *madness* pur; *idiot, brute, fool* fini, parfait (*before n*), achevé. **an ~ rogue/liar** un fieffé coquin/menteur; **it was ~ nonsense!** c'était complètement absurde, ça n'avait aucun sens; **he's an ~ stranger** il m'est complètement inconnu.
utter[2] ['ʌtər] vt *word* prononcer, proférer; *cry* pousser; *threat, insult* proférer; *libel* publier; *counterfeit money* émettre, mettre en circulation. **he didn't ~ a word** il n'a pas dit un seul mot, il n'a pas soufflé mot.
utterance ['ʌtərəns] n a (*remark etc*) paroles *fpl*, déclaration *f*. b (*NonC*) *[facts, theory]* énonciation *f*; *[feelings]* expression *f*. **to give ~ to** exprimer. c (*style of speaking*) élocution *f*, articulation *f*. **to have a clear/defective ~** bien/mal articuler. d (*Ling*) énoncé *m*.
utterly ['ʌtəlɪ] adv complètement, totalement, tout à fait.
uttermost ['ʌtəməʊst] = **utmost**.
UV [juː'viː] adj (abbr of **ultraviolet**) UV.
UVA, UV-A [juːviː'eɪ] adj (abbr of **ultraviolet radiation** *with a range of 320-380 nanometres*) UVA (*inv*). **~ rays** (rayons *mpl*) UVA *mpl*.
UVB, UV-B [juːviː'biː] adj (abbr of **ultraviolet radiation** *with a range of 280-320 nanometres*) UVB (*inv*). **~ rays** (rayons *mpl*) UVB *mpl*.
UVF [juːviː'ef] n abbr of **Ulster Volunteer Force**.
uvula ['juːvjʊlə] n, pl **~s** *or* **uvulae** ['juːvjʊˌliː] luette *f*, uvule *f*.
uvular ['juːvjʊlər] adj (*Anat, Phon*) uvulaire. ~ **"r"** "r" grasseyé.
uxorious [ʌk'sɔːrɪəs] adj excessivement dévoué *or* soumis à sa femme.
uxoriousness [ʌk'sɔːrɪəsnɪs] n (*NonC*) dévotion excessive à sa femme.
Uzbek ['ʊzbek] adj: **~ S.S.R.**† R.S.S.† *f* d'Ouzbékistan.
Uzbekistan [ˌʌzbekɪ'stɑːn] n Ouzbékistan *m*.

V

V, v [viː] **1** n **a** (*letter*) V, v *m*. **V for Victor, V for Victory** ≃ V comme Victor. **b** (**abbr of vide** = **see**) V, voir. **c** (**abbr of versus**) contre. **d** (*esp Bible*) **abbr of verse. e abbr of very. f** (**abbr of volt**) V. **2 comp ▸V1** (*Mil Hist*) V1 *m* (*bombe volante utilisée par les Allemands en 1944-45*) **▸V8 (engine)** (*Aut*) moteur *m* à huit cylindres en V **▸V and A** (*Brit*) (**abbr of Victoria and Albert Museum**) *musée à Londres* **▸V-neck** décolleté *m* en V *or* en pointe **▸V-necked** à encolure en V *or* en pointe **▸V-shaped** en (forme de) V **▸V-sign: to give the V-sign** (*for victory*) faire le V de la victoire; (*rudely*) faire un geste obscène de la main.

VA [viːˈeɪ] n (*US*) **a** (**abbr of Veterans Administration**) *see* **veteran. b** (*Post*) **abbr of Virginia.**

Va. (*US*) **abbr of Virginia.**

vac* [væk] n (*Brit Univ*) (**abbr of vacation**) vacances *fpl* (universitaires).

vacancy [ˈveɪkənsɪ] n **a** (*in boarding house*) chambre *f* à louer. **"no vacancies"** "complet"; **have you any vacancies for August?** est-ce qu'il vous reste des chambres (libres) pour le mois d'août? **b** (*job*) poste *m* vacant *or* libre, vacance *f*. **"no vacancies"** "pas d'embauche"; **"~ for a typist"** "on cherche dactylo"; **they have vacancies for typists** ils ont des postes de dactylo à pourvoir, ils cherchent (à embaucher) des dactylos; **we have a ~ for a keen young man** nous cherchons un jeune homme dynamique; **to fill a ~** *[employer]* pourvoir un poste vacant; *[employee]* être nommé à un poste vacant; **we are looking for sb to fill a ~ in our sales department** nous cherchons à pourvoir le poste vacant dans notre département de ventes. **c** (*NonC: emptiness*) vide *m*. **d** (*NonC: lack of intelligence*) esprit *m* vide, stupidité *f*.

vacant [ˈveɪkənt] adj **a** (*unoccupied*) *job, post* vacant, libre, à pourvoir *or* remplir; *room, house* inoccupé, libre; *seat* libre, disponible. **to become** *or* **fall ~** devenir vacant (*or* libre *etc*); (*Press*) **"situations ~"** "offres d'emploi"; **a ~ space** un espace libre; *[land]* **a ~ lot** (*gen*) un terrain inoccupé; (*for sale*) un terrain à vendre; (*Univ etc: on course*) **a ~ place** place *f* libre *or* disponible; (*Jur*) **with ~ possession** avec libre possession, avec jouissance immédiate. **b** (*empty*) *hours* creux, de loisir; *mind* inoccupé, vide; *stare* vague; *person* (*stupid*) stupide, niais; (*dreamy*) sans expression, rêveur, distrait.

vacantly [ˈveɪkəntlɪ] adv **a** (*dreamily*) d'un air rêveur *or* distrait *or* absent. **to gaze ~ into space** fixer le vide, avoir le regard perdu dans le vide. **b** (*stupidly*) (*gen*) d'une manière stupide *or* niaise; *say etc* d'un ton stupide *or* niais.

vacate [vəˈkeɪt] vt *room, seat, job* quitter. **to ~ a house** quitter une maison, déménager (d'une maison); **to ~ one's post** démissionner; **this post will soon be ~d** ce poste sera bientôt vacant *or* à pourvoir; **to ~ the premises** vider les lieux.

vacation [vəˈkeɪʃən] **1** n **a** (*esp Brit*) (*Univ*) vacances *fpl*; (*Jur*) vacations *fpl or* vacances judiciaires; *see* **long**[1] *etc*. **b** (*US*) vacances *fpl*. **on ~** en vacances; **on his ~** pendant ses vacances; **to take a ~** prendre des vacances; **where are you going for your ~?** où allez-vous passer vos vacances? **2 comp ▸vacation course** cours *mpl* de vacances **▸vacation trip** voyage *m* de vacances. **3** vi (*US*) passer des (*or* ses *etc*) vacances.

vacationer [vəˈkeɪʃənəʳ] n, **vacationist** [vəˈkeɪʃənɪst] n (*US*) vacancier *m*, -ière *f*.

vaccinate [ˈvæksɪneɪt] vt vacciner (*against* contre). **to get ~d** se faire vacciner; **have you been ~d against ...?** est-ce que vous êtes vacciné contre ...?

vaccination [ˌvæksɪˈneɪʃən] n vaccination *f* (*against* contre). **smallpox ~** vaccination contre la variole; **to have a ~ against ...** se faire vacciner contre ... .

vaccine [ˈvæksiːn] n vaccin *m*; (*Comput*) logiciel *m* anti-virus. **polio ~** vaccin contre la polio; **~-damaged** victime d'encéphalo-myélite vaccinale.

vacillate [ˈvæsɪleɪt] vi hésiter (*between* entre). **she ~d so long over accepting that ...** elle s'est demandé si longtemps si elle allait accepter ou non que ... .

vacillating [ˈvæsɪleɪtɪŋ] **1** adj irrésolu, indécis, qui hésite. **2** n vacillation *f*, irrésolution *f*, indécision *f*.

vacillation [ˌvæsɪˈleɪʃən] n indécision *f*.

vacua [ˈvækjʊə] npl of **vacuum.**

vacuity [væˈkjuːɪtɪ] n vacuité *f*. (*silly remarks*) **vacuities** niaiseries *fpl*, remarques *fpl* stupides.

vacuous [ˈvækjʊəs] adj *face, eyes, stare* vide, sans expression; *remark* bête, vide de sens; *life* vide de sens.

vacuum [ˈvækjʊm] **1** n **a** (pl **~s** *or* (*frm*) **vacua**: *Phys*) vacuum *m*. (*fig*) **in a ~** dans le vide; *see* **nature. b** (*gen*) vide *m*. **their departure left a ~** leur départ a laissé un (grand) vide; **a cultural ~** un vide culturel. **c** (*: **~ cleaner**) aspirateur *m*. **to give sth a ~** = **to ~ sth**; *see* **3. 2 comp** *brake, pump, tube* à vide **▸vacuum bottle** (*US*) = **vacuum flask ▸vacuum cleaner** aspirateur *m* **▸vacuum extraction** (*Med*) (*abortion*) I.V.G. *f* par aspiration; (*birth*) naissance *f* par ventouse **▸vacuum flask** (*Brit*) bouteille *f* thermos ®, thermos *m or f inv* **▸vacuum-packed** emballé sous vide. **3** vt (*also* **~-clean**) *carpet* passer à l'aspirateur; *room* passer l'aspirateur dans.

vade mecum [ˈvɑːdɪˈmeɪkʊm] n vade-mecum *m inv*.

vagabond [ˈvægəbɒnd] **1** n vagabond(e) *m(f)*; (*tramp*) chemineau *m*, clochard(e) *m(f)*. **2** adj *life* errant, de vagabondage; *thoughts* vagabond; *habits* irrégulier.

vagary [ˈveɪgərɪ] n caprice *m*.

vagi [ˈveɪdʒaɪ] npl of **vagus.**

vagina [vəˈdʒaɪnə] n, pl **~s** *or* **vaginae** [vəˈdʒaɪniː] vagin *m*.

vaginal [vəˈdʒaɪnəl] adj (*gen*) *infection etc* vaginal. **~ discharge** pertes blanches; **~ smear** frottis *m* vaginal.

vagrancy [ˈveɪgrənsɪ] n (*also Jur*) vagabondage *m*.

vagrant [ˈveɪgrənt] **1** n vagabond(e) *m(f)*; (*tramp*) clochard(e) *m(f)*, mendiant(e) *m(f)*, chemineau *m*; (*Jur*) vagabond(e). **2** adj vagabond, errant.

vague [veɪg] adj **a** (*not clear: gen*) vague; *outline, photograph* flou, imprécis; *direction, question, account* vague, imprécis; *sensation, feeling* vague, confus, imprécis; *memory, impression* flou, confus. **there's a ~ resemblance** il y a une vague ressemblance; **her reply was ~** sa réponse manquait de clarté *or* de précision; **I haven't the vaguest idea (about it)** je n'en ai pas la moindre idée; **I had a ~ idea** *or* **feeling she would come** je pensais vaguement *or* j'avais comme une idée* qu'elle viendrait; **he was ~ about the time he would be arriving at** (*didn't say exactly*) il n'a pas (bien) précisé l'heure de son arrivée; (*didn't know exactly*) il n'était pas sûr de l'heure à laquelle il arriverait; **I'm still very ~ about all this** je n'ai pas encore compris tout ça; **I'm still very ~ about how it happened** je ne sais pas encore exactement comment ça s'est passé; **I'm very ~ about Greek politics** je ne m'y connais pas très bien en politique grecque.

b (*absent-minded*) *person* distrait. **he's always rather ~** il est toujours distrait *or* dans la lune; **she's getting rather ~ these days** elle ne s'y retrouve plus très bien *or* elle perd un peu la tête maintenant; **to look ~** avoir l'air vague *or* distrait; **to have a ~ look in one's eyes** avoir l'air vague.

vaguely [ˈveɪglɪ] adv **a** (*not clearly*) *speak, remember, look, resemble* vaguement; *understand* confusément, vaguement. **they're ~ similar** ils se ressemblent vaguement; **it's only ~ like yours** ça ne ressemble pas beaucoup au tien; **it's ~ blue** c'est bleuâtre, c'est plutôt bleu; **there's something ~ sinister about him** il y a quelque chose de vaguement *or* légèrement sinistre en lui. **b** (*not alertly*) *smile etc* d'un air vague *or* distrait.

vagueness [ˈveɪgnɪs] n **a** *[photograph etc]* imprécision *f*, manque *m* de précision *or* de netteté; *[question, account, memory]* manque *m* de précision; *[feeling, sensation]* caractère *m* imprécis, vague *m*. **b** (*absent-mindedness*) distraction *f*. **his ~ is very annoying** c'est agaçant qu'il soit si étourdi *or* distrait *or* tête en l'air*.

vagus [ˈveɪgəs] n, pl **vagi** nerf *m* vague *or* pneumogastrique.

vain [veɪn] adj **a** (*useless, empty*) *attempt* vain (*before n*), inutile;

hope vain, futile; *promise* vide, illusoire; *words* creux; *display, ceremony* futile. **in ~** en vain, vainement, inutilement; **it was all in ~** cela n'a servi à rien, c'était inutile *or* en vain; **she tried in ~ to open the door** elle a essayé en vain d'ouvrir la porte; **I looked for him in ~, he had already left** j'ai eu beau le chercher, il était déjà parti; **all his (*or* my *etc*) efforts were in ~** c'était peine perdue; **to take God's name in ~** blasphémer le nom de Dieu; (*hum*) **we've been taking your name in ~!** nous venons de parler de vous! b (*conceited*) vaniteux.

vainglorious [veɪn'glɔːrɪəs] adj orgueilleux, vaniteux, prétentieux.

vainglory [veɪn'glɔːrɪ] n (*NonC*) orgueil *m*, vanité *f*, prétention *f*.

vainly ['veɪnlɪ] adv a (*to no effect*) en vain, vainement, inutilement. b (*conceitedly*) vaniteusement, avec vanité.

valance ['væləns] n (*round bed frame*) tour *m or* frange *f* de lit; (*round bed canopy*) lambrequin *m*.

vale [veɪl] n (*liter*) val *m* (*liter*), vallée *f*. (*fig*) **this ~ of tears** cette vallée de larmes.

valediction [ˌvælɪ'dɪkʃən] n a (*farewell*) adieu(x) *m(pl)*. b (*US Scol*) discours *m* d'adieu.

valedictorian [ˌvælɪdɪk'tɔːrɪən] n (*US Scol*) major *m* de la promotion (*qui prononce le discours d'adieu*).

valedictory [ˌvælɪ'dɪktərɪ] 1 adj d'adieu. 2 n (*US Scol*) discours *m* d'adieu.

valence ['veɪləns] n a (*esp US*) = **valency**. b (*Bio*) atomicité *f*.

Valencia [ba'lenθjə] n Valence (*en Espagne*).

valency ['veɪlənsɪ] n (*Chem*) valence *f*.

valentine ['væləntaɪn] n a **V~** Valentin(e) *m(f)*; **St V~'s Day** la Saint-Valentin. b (*also* **~ card**) carte *f* de la Saint-Valentin (*envoyée comme gage d'amour*). **will you be my ~?** ≃ c'est toi que j'aime (*écrit sur une carte*).

valerian [və'lɪərɪən] n valériane *f*.

valet ['væleɪ] 1 n a (*person: in hotel or household*) valet *m* de chambre. **~ parking** service *m* de garage des voitures. b (*rack for clothes*) valet *m*. 2 ['vælɪt] vt *man* servir comme valet de chambre; *clothes* entretenir. **dry cleaner with ~ing service** pressing *m*.

valetudinarian ['vælɪˌtjuːdɪ'nɛərɪən] adj, n valétudinaire (*mf*).

Valhalla [væl'hælə] n Walhalla *m*.

valiant ['væljənt] adj *action* courageux, brave. **our ~ soldiers** nos vaillants *or* valeureux soldats (*liter*); **he made a ~ effort to save the child** il a tenté avec courage de sauver l'enfant; **he made a ~ effort to smile** il a fait un gros effort pour sourire.

valiantly ['væljəntlɪ] adv vaillamment, courageusement.

valid ['vælɪd] adj a (*Jur etc*) *claim, contract, document* valide, valable. **passport ~ for all countries** passeport valable pour tous pays; **~ passport** passeport valable *or* valide *or* en règle; **ticket ~ for one week** billet bon *or* valable *or* valide pour une semaine; **no longer ~** *ticket, document* périmé. b *excuse* valable; *argument, reasoning* solide, valable, bien fondé.

validate ['vælɪdeɪt] vt *claim, document* valider; *theory, argument* prouver la justesse de; (*Comput*) valider. **this will ~ all he says** cela va prouver la justesse de tout ce qu'il affirme.

validation [ˌvælɪ'deɪʃən] n *[claim etc]* validation *f*.

validity [və'lɪdɪtɪ] n *[document, claim]* validité *f*; *[argument]* justesse *f*.

valise [və'liːz] n sac *m* de voyage; (*Mil*) sac (de soldat).

Valium ['vælɪəm] n ® Valium *m* ®. **to be on ~** être sous Valium.

Valkyrie ['vælkɪrɪ] n Walkyrie *f or* Valkyrie *f*.

valley ['vælɪ] n vallée *f*, val *m* (*liter*); (*small, narrow*) vallon *m*. **the Seine/Rhône** *etc* **~** la vallée de la Seine/du Rhône *etc*; **the Loire ~** la vallée de la Loire; (*between Orléans and Tours*) le Val de Loire; *see* **lily**.

valor ['vælər] n (*US*) = **valour**.

valorous ['vælərəs] adj (*liter*) valeureux (*liter*), vaillant (*liter*).

valour, (*US*) **valor** ['vælər] n (*liter*) courage *m*, bravoure *f*, valeur *f*.

valuable ['væljʊəbl] 1 adj *jewel, painting* de (grande) valeur, de grand prix; *help, advice, team member, time* précieux. 2 n: **~s** objets *mpl* de valeur; **all her ~s were stolen** on lui a volé tous les objets de valeur *or* tout ce qui avait de la valeur.

valuation [ˌvæljʊ'eɪʃən] n a *[house, property, painting etc]* expertise *f*, évaluation *f*, estimation *f*; (*value decided upon*) appréciation *f*, évaluation, estimation. **to have a ~ done** faire expertiser *or* évaluer quelque chose; **what is the ~?** à combien l'appréciation s'élève-t-elle?, à combien est-ce estimé *or* évalué? b *[person, sb's character, work etc]* appréciation *f*. **to take sb at his own ~** prendre qn pour celui qu'il croit être.

valuator ['væljʊeɪtər] n expert *m* (en estimations de biens mobiliers).

value ['væljuː] 1 n a (*gen*) valeur *f*; (*usefulness, worth*) valeur, utilité *f*. **her education has been of no ~ to her** son éducation ne lui a rien valu *or* ne lui a servi à rien; **to set great ~ on sth** attacher *or* accorder une grande valeur à qch.

b (*worth in money*) valeur *f*. **to gain (in) ~** prendre de la valeur; **to lose (in) ~** se déprécier; **increase in ~** hausse *f or* augmentation *f* de valeur, appréciation *f*; **loss of ~** perte *f or* diminution *f* de valeur, dépréciation *f*; **he paid the ~ of the cup he broke** il a remboursé (le prix de) la tasse qu'il a cassée; **of little ~** de peu de valeur; **of no ~** sans valeur; **to be of great ~** valoir cher; **it's good ~ (for money)** on en a pour son argent, le rapport qualité-prix est bon (*esp Comm*); **to get good ~ for money** en avoir pour son argent; **the large packet is the best ~** le grand paquet est le plus avantageux; **to put a ~ of £20 on sth** évaluer *or* estimer qch à 20 livres; **to put a ~ on sth** évaluer qch; **to set a low ~ on sth** attacher peu de valeur à qch; **to put too high/too low a ~ on sth** surestimer/sous-estimer qch; **goods to the ~ of £100** marchandises d'une valeur de 100 livres; **cheque to the ~ of £100** chèque au montant de 100 livres; *see* **street**.

c (*moral worth*) *[person]* valeur *f*, mérite *m*. **to appreciate sb at his proper ~** estimer *or* apprécier qn à sa juste valeur.

d (*moral standards*) **~s** valeurs *fpl*; *see* **Victorian**.

e (*Math, Mus, Painting, Phon*) valeur *f*.

2 comp ▸**value added tax** (*abbr* **V.A.T.**) (*Brit*) taxe *f* sur la valeur ajoutée (*abbr* **T.V.A.**) ▸**value judgment** (*fig*) jugement *m* de valeur.

3 vt a (*estimate worth of*) *house, jewels, painting* évaluer, estimer (*at* à), expertiser. **the house was ~d at £80,000** la maison a été estimée *or* évaluée à 80 000 livres; **he had it ~d** il l'a fait expertiser.

b (*appreciate etc*) *friendship* apprécier; *comforts* apprécier, faire grand cas de; *liberty, independence* tenir à. **if you ~ your life** si vous tenez à la vie; **I greatly ~ all you have done** je vous suis très reconnaissant de *or* pour tout ce que vous avez fait; **we ~ your opinion** votre avis nous importe beaucoup; **he is someone we all ~** nous l'apprécions tous beaucoup.

valued ['væljuːd] adj *friend, customer* précieux; *colleague* estimé.

valueless ['væljʊlɪs] adj sans valeur.

valuer ['væljʊər] n expert *m* (en estimations de biens mobiliers).

valve [vælv] n (*Anat*) valvule *f*; (*Bot, Zool*) valve *f*; (*Tech*) *[machine]* soupape *f*, valve; *[air chamber, tyre]* valve; (*Electronics, Rad*) lampe *f*; *[musical instrument]* piston *m*. **inlet/outlet ~** soupape d'admission/d'échappement; **exhaust ~** clapet *m* d'échappement; (*Mus*) **~ horn/trombone** cor/trombone à pistons; *see* **safety, suction** *etc*.

valvular ['vælvjʊlər] adj valvulaire.

vamoose‡ [və'muːs] vi filer*, décamper*. ~! fiche le camp!*

vamp¹ [væmp] 1 n (*woman*) vamp *f*. 2 vt vamper*. 3 vi jouer la femme fatale.

vamp² [væmp] 1 vt (*repair*) rafistoler; (*Mus*) improviser. 2 vi (*Mus*) improviser des accompagnements. 3 n *[shoe]* devant *m*.

vampire ['væmpaɪər] n (*lit, fig*) vampire *m*. **~ bat** vampire (*chauve-souris*).

van¹ [væn] 1 n a (*Aut*) (*Brit: smallish*) camionnette *f*, fourgonnette *f*; (*Brit, US: large*) camion *m*, fourgon *m*; *see* **removal** *etc*. b (*Brit Rail*) fourgon *m*; *see* **guard, luggage** *etc*. c (*) (**abbr of caravan**) caravane *f*; (*gipsy's*) roulotte *f*. 2 comp ▸**van-boy** livreur *m* ▸**van-driver** chauffeur *m* de camion ▸**van-man** = **van-boy** ▸**van pool** (*US*) pool *m* de transport (*grâce auquel plusieurs personnes se servent d'une même camionnette pour se rendre à leur travail*).

van² [væn] n **abbr of vanguard**.

van³ [væn] n (*Tennis*) (**abbr of advantage 1b**) **~ in/out** avantage *m* dedans/dehors.

vanadium [və'neɪdɪəm] n vanadium *m*.

Vancouver [væn'kuːvər] n Vancouver. **~ Island** (île *f* de) Vancouver.

vandal ['vændəl] n vandale *mf*. (*Hist*) **V~** Vandale *mf*.

vandalism ['vændəlɪzəm] n vandalisme *m*.

vandalistic [ˌvændə'lɪstɪk] adj destructeur (*f* -trice), de vandale.

vandalize ['vændəlaɪz] vt *painting, building, phone box* saccager.

vane [veɪn] n *[windmill]* aile *f*; *[propeller]* pale *f*; *[turbine]* aube *f*; *[quadrant etc]* pinnule *f*, lumière *f*; *[feather]* barbe *f*; (*also* **weather ~**) girouette *f*.

vanguard ['vængɑːd] n a (*Mil, Naut*) avant-garde *f*. **in the ~ (of)** en tête (de). b (*fig*) avant-garde *f*. **in the ~ of progress** à l'avant-garde *or* à la pointe du progrès.

vanilla [və'nɪlə] 1 n vanille *f*. 2 comp *cream, ice* à la vanille ▸**vanilla pod** gousse *f* de vanille ▸**vanilla sugar** sucre vanillé.

vanillin [væ'nɪlɪn] n vanilline *f*.

vanish ['vænɪʃ] 1 vi (*gen*) disparaître (*from* de); *[obstacles, fears]* disparaître, se dissiper. **to ~ into thin air** se volatiliser, disparaître sans laisser de traces; **he/it had ~ed from sight** il/cela avait disparu, il/cela était introuvable; **he/it has ~ed from the face of the earth** il/cela a disparu sans laisser de traces; **he ~ed into the distance** il s'est évanoui dans le lointain; **he said goodbye and ~ed into the house** il a dit au revoir et il est rentré précipitamment dans la maison; **I've got to ~!*** il faut que je file!* *or* que je m'éclipse!*

2 comp ▸**vanishing act***: (*fig*) **to do a vanishing act** s'éclipser* ▸**vanishing cream**† crème *f* de jour ▸**vanishing point** point *m* de fuite ▸**vanishing trick** tour *m* de passe-passe.

vanished ['vænɪʃt] adj *empire, custom etc* disparu.

vanity ['vænɪtɪ] 1 n (*NonC*) a (*conceit*) vanité *f*. **I may say without ~** je peux dire sans (vouloir) me vanter. b (*worthlessness*) vanité *f*, futilité *f*. **all is ~** tout est vanité. 2 comp ▸**vanity bag** sac *m* (de soirée) ▸**vanity box, vanity case** mallette *f* pour affaires de toilette, vanity-case *m* ▸**vanity mirror** (*in car etc*) miroir *m* de courtoisie ▸**vanity press** (*Publishing*) maison *f* d'édition à compte d'auteur ▸**vanity unit** (*in bathroom*) élément *m* de salle de bains à lavabo encastré.

vanquish ['væŋkwɪʃ] vt vaincre.
vanquisher ['væŋkwɪʃəʳ] n vainqueur *m*.
vantage ['vɑːntɪdʒ] 1 n a avantage *m*, supériorité *f*. b (*Tennis*) avantage *m*. ~ **Miss Wade** avantage Mademoiselle Wade; *see also* **van**[3].
2 comp ▸**vantage ground** (*Mil*) position stratégique *or* avantageuse ▸**vantage point** (*fig*) position avantageuse, bonne place.
Vanuatu ['vænuːˌætuː] n: **Republic of** ~ (République *f* de) Vanuatu.
vapid ['væpɪd] adj *remark, conversation* fade, sans intérêt, insipide; *style* plat.
vapidity [væ'pɪdɪtɪ] n *[conversation]* insipidité *f*; *[style]* platitude *f*.
vapor ['veɪpəʳ] n (*US*) = **vapour**.
vaporization [ˌveɪpəraɪ'zeɪʃən] n vaporisation *f*.
vaporize ['veɪpəraɪz] 1 vt vaporiser. 2 vi se vaporiser.
vaporizer ['veɪpəraɪzəʳ] n (*gen, Chem*) vaporisateur *m*, vaporiseur *m*; (*Med: for inhalation*) inhalateur *m*; (*for perfume*) atomiseur *m*.
vaporous ['veɪpərəs] adj vaporeux.
vapour, (*US*) **vapor** ['veɪpəʳ] 1 n a (*Phys: also mist etc*) vapeur *f*; (*on glass*) buée *f*. b **to have the** ~**s**† avoir des vapeurs†. 2 comp ▸**vapour bath** bain *m* de vapeur ▸**vapour trail** (*Aviat*) traînée *f* de condensation. 3 vi (*US* ⁑: *boast*) fanfaronner.
variability [ˌvɛərɪə'bɪlɪtɪ] n variabilité *f*.
variable ['vɛərɪəbl] 1 adj (*gen*) variable; *weather* variable, incertain, changeant; *mood* changeant; *work* de qualité inégale. 2 n (*gen*) variable *f*. 3 comp ▸**variable pitch propeller** hélice *f* à pas variable ▸**variable type** (*Comput*) type *m* de variable.
variance ['vɛərɪəns] n a désaccord *m*, différend *m*. *[people]* **to be at** ~ être en désaccord; **to be at** ~ **with sb about sth** avoir un différend avec qn sur qch; **this is at** ~ **with what he said earlier** ceci ne s'accorde pas avec *or* ceci contredit ce qu'il a dit auparavant. b (*Math*) variance *f*. c (*Jur*) différence *f*, divergence *f*. **there is a** ~ **between the two statements** les deux dépositions ne s'accordent pas *or* ne concordent pas.
variant ['vɛərɪənt] 1 n (*gen, Ling etc*) variante *f*. 2 adj a (*alternative*) différent. ~ **reading** variante *f*. b (*Ling*) variant. c (*diverse*) différent, divers, varié.
variation [ˌvɛərɪ'eɪʃən] n (*gen, Bio, Chem, Met, Mus, Phys*) variation *f*; (*in opinions, views*) fluctuation(s) *f(pl)*, changements *mpl*.
varicoloured, (*US*) **varicolored** ['vɛərɪˌkʌləd] adj multicolore, bigarré; (*fig*) divers.
varicose ['værɪkəʊs] adj *ulcer* variqueux. ~ **veins** varices *fpl*.
varied ['vɛərɪd] adj varié, divers.
variegated ['vɛərɪgeɪtɪd] adj bigarré, diapré (*liter*); (*Bot*) panaché.
variegation [ˌvɛərɪ'geɪʃən] n bigarrure *f*, diaprure *f* (*liter*).
variety [və'raɪətɪ] 1 n a (*diversity*) variété *f* (*in* dans), diversité *f*. **children like** ~ les enfants aiment la variété *or* ce qui est varié; **it lacks** ~ ça n'est pas assez varié; **they have increased in number and** ~ ils sont devenus plus nombreux et plus variés; (*Prov*) ~ **is the spice of life** il faut de tout pour faire un monde.
b **a wide** *or* **great** *or* **large** ~ **of** ... un grand nombre de ...; **dolphins produce a** ~ **of noises** les dauphins émettent différents bruits *or* un certain nombre de bruits; **for a** ~ **of reasons** pour diverses raisons; **it offers a** ~ **of careers** cela offre un grand choix de carrières.
c (*Bio: subdivision*) variété *f*. **new plant** ~ obtention *f or* nouveauté *f* végétale.
d (*type, kind*) type *m*, espèce *f*. **many varieties of socialist(s)** de nombreux types (différents) de socialistes, de nombreuses espèces (différentes) de socialistes; **books of the paperback** ~ des livres du genre livre de poche.
e (*NonC: Theat*) variétés *fpl*.
2 comp (*Theat*) *actor, artiste etc* de variétés, de music-hall ▸**variety meats** (*US Culin*) abats *mpl* (*de boucherie*) ▸**variety show** (*Theat*) spectacle *m* de variétés *or* de music-hall; (*Rad, TV*) émission *f* de variétés ▸**variety store** (*US*) ≃ prisunic *m* ▸**variety theatre** (théâtre *m* de) variétés *fpl* ▸**variety turn** (*Brit*) numéro *m* (de variétés *or* de music-hall).
variola [və'raɪələ] n variole *f*, petite vérole.
various ['vɛərɪəs] adj (*different*) divers, différent; (*several*) divers (*before n*), plusieurs. **the** ~ **meanings of a word** les divers sens d'un mot; **at** ~ **times** (*different*) en diverses occasions; (*several*) à plusieurs reprises; ~ **people have told me** ... plusieurs *or* diverses personnes m'ont dit ... .
variously ['vɛərɪəslɪ] adv (*in various ways*) diversement, de différentes *or* diverses façons; (*at different times*) à différents moments. **I've heard it** ~ **suggested that** ... j'ai entendu dire de sources diverses que ... .
varmint*† ['vɑːmɪnt] n polisson(ne) *m(f)*, vaurien(ne) *m(f)*.
varnish ['vɑːnɪʃ] 1 n (*lit, fig*) vernis *m*; (*on pottery*) vernis, émail *m*; *see* **nail, spirit**. 2 vt *furniture, painting* vernir; *pottery* vernisser. **to** ~ **one's nails** se vernir les ongles; (*fig*) **to** ~ **the truth** maquiller la vérité.
varnishing ['vɑːnɪʃɪŋ] n vernissage *m*. (*Art*) ~ **day** (le jour du) vernissage.
varsity ['vɑːsɪtɪ] 1 n a (*Brit Univ* *) fac* *f*. b (*US Univ: Sport*) équipe *f* de première catégorie (*représentant un établissement d'enseignement*). 2 comp ▸**varsity match** match *m* (entre les universités d'Oxford et de Cambridge) ▸**varsity sports** (*US*) sports *mpl* pratiqués entre équipes de différents établissements.
vary ['vɛərɪ] 1 vi varier, changer, se modifier. **to** ~ **with the weather** changer selon le temps; **to** ~ **from sth** différer de qch; **opinions** ~ **on this point** les opinions varient sur ce point. 2 vt *programme, menu* varier; *temperature* faire varier, (*directly*) varier.
varying ['vɛərɪɪŋ] adj qui varie, variable. **with** ~ **degrees of success** avec plus ou moins de succès.
vascular ['væskjʊləʳ] adj vasculaire.
vas deferens ['væs 'defəˌrenz] n, pl **vasa deferentia** ['veɪsə ˌdefə'renʃɪə] (*Anat*) canal *m* déférent.
vase [vɑːz] n vase *m*. **flower** ~ vase à fleurs.
vasectomy [væ'sektəmɪ] n vasectomie *f*. **to have a** ~ avoir une vasectomie.
Vaseline ['væsɪliːn] ® 1 n vaseline *f*. 2 vt enduire de vaseline.
vasoconstrictor [ˌveɪzəʊkən'strɪktəʳ] n vaso-constricteur *m*.
vasodilator [ˌveɪzəʊdaɪ'leɪtəʳ] n vaso-dilatateur *m*.
vasomotor [ˌveɪzəʊ'məʊtəʳ] adj vaso-moteur (*f* -trice).
vassal ['væsəl] adj, n (*Hist, fig*) vassal (*m*).
vassalage ['væsəlɪdʒ] n vassalité *f*, vasselage *m*.
vast [vɑːst] adj (*gen*) vaste (*usu before n*); *area, size* vaste, immense; *quantity, reserve* vaste, énorme. **a** ~ **amount of** énormément de; ~ **knowledge** de vastes connaissances; **to a** ~ **extent** dans une très large *or* grande mesure; **a** ~ **success** un succès énorme; ~ **sums (of money)** des sommes folles; **at** ~ **expense** à grands frais.
vastly ['vɑːstlɪ] adv *grateful, amused* infiniment; *rich* extrêmement, immensément. **he was** ~ **mistaken** il se trompait du tout au tout; ~ **improved** infiniment meilleur.
vastness ['vɑːstnɪs] n immensité *f*.
VAT [viːeɪ'tiː, væt] n (*Brit*) (**abbr of value added tax**) T.V.A. *f*. ~-**registered** enregistré à la T.V.A.; ~ **return** formulaire *m* de déclaration de la T.V.A.
vat [væt] n cuve *f*, bac *m*.
Vatican ['vætɪkən] 1 n Vatican *m*. 2 comp *policy etc* du Vatican ▸**Vatican City** la cité du Vatican ▸**the Vatican Council** le concile (de) Vatican II.
vaudeville ['vəʊdəvɪl] (*esp US*) 1 n spectacle *m* de variétés *or* de music-hall. 2 comp *show, singer* de variétés, de music-hall.
vaudevillian [ˌvəʊdə'vɪlɪən] (*US*) 1 n (*writer*) auteur *m* de variétés; (*performer*) acteur *m*, -trice *f* de variétés. 2 adj de variétés.
vaudevillist ['vəʊdəvɪlɪst] n (*US*) = **vaudevillian**.
vault[1] [vɔːlt] n a (*Archit*) voûte *f*. (*liter*) **the** ~ **of heaven** la voûte céleste. b (*Anat*) voûte *f*. **cranial** ~ voûte cranienne. c (*cellar*) cave *f*. d (*in bank*) (*strongroom*) chambre forte; (*safe deposit box room*) salle *f* des coffres. **it's lying in the** ~**s of the bank** c'est dans les coffres de la banque. e (*burial chamber*) caveau *m*. **buried in the family** ~ inhumé dans le caveau de famille.
vault[2] [vɔːlt] 1 vi (*gen*) sauter; (*Sport*) sauter (à la perche). **to** ~ **over sth** sauter qch (d'un bond); *see* **pole**[1]. 2 vt (*gen*) sauter d'un bond; (*Sport*) franchir. 3 n saut *m*.
vaulted ['vɔːltɪd] adj (*Archit*) voûté, en voûte.
vaulting[1] ['vɔːltɪŋ] n (*Archit*) voûte(s) *f(pl)*.
vaulting[2] ['vɔːltɪŋ] n (*Sport*) exercice *m or* pratique *f* du saut. ~ **horse** cheval *m* d'arçons.
vaunt [vɔːnt] vt (*liter*) (*boast about*) vanter; (*praise*) vanter, faire l'éloge de. **much** ~**ed** tant vanté, dont on (*or* il *etc*) fait tant l'éloge.
V.C. [viː'siː] n a (*Brit*) (**abbr of Victoria Cross**) *see* **Victoria**. b (*Univ*) (**abbr of vice-chancellor**) *see* **vice-**. c (*US: in Vietnam*) **abbr of Vietcong**.
V.C.R. [viːsiː'ɑːʳ] n (**abbr of video cassette recorder**) *see* **video**.
VD [viː'diː] n (*Med*) (**abbr of venereal disease**) *see* **venereal**.
VDU [viːdiː'juː] n (*Comput*) (**abbr of visual display unit**) console *f* (de visualisation).
veal [viːl] n veau *m* (*Culin*). ~ **cutlet** escalope *f* de veau; *see* **fillet**.
vector ['vektəʳ] 1 n a (*Bio, Math*) vecteur *m*. b (*Aviat*) direction *f*. 2 comp (*Math*) vectoriel. 3 vt (*Aviat*) radioguider.
vectorial [vek'tɔːrɪəl] adj vectoriel.
veep⁑ [viːp] n (*US: from* **VP**) = **vice-president**; *see* **vice-**.
veer [vɪəʳ] 1 vi a *[wind]* (*change direction*) tourner (*to the north* vers le nord, au nord), changer de direction; *[ship]* virer (de bord); *[car, road]* virer. **the car** ~**ed off the road** la voiture a quitté la route. b (*change etc*) changer. **he** ~**ed round to my point of view** changeant d'opinion il s'est rallié à mon point de vue; **he** ~**ed off** *or* **away from his subject** il s'est éloigné de son sujet; **her feelings for him** ~**ed between tenderness and love** les sentiments qu'elle lui portait oscillaient entre la tendresse et l'amour. 2 vt a (*Naut*) *cable* filer. b *ship, car* faire virer.
veg* [vedʒ] n (**abbr of vegetables**) légumes *mpl*.
▸**veg out**⁑ vi (*esp US*) glander⁑.
vegan ['viːgən] n, adj végétalien(ne) *m(f)*.
veganism ['viːgənɪzəm] n végétalisme *m*.
vegeburger ['vedʒɪˌbɜːgəʳ] n burger *m* végétarien.
vegetable ['vedʒtəbl] 1 n a légume *m*. **early** ~**s** primeurs *fpl*. b (*generic term: plant*) végétal *m*, plante *f*. c (*fig pej: brain-damaged etc person*) épave *f*. **he's just a** ~* ce n'est plus qu'une épave, il n'a plus l'usage de ses facultés. 2 comp *oil, matter* végétal ▸**vegetable dish**

plat *m* à légumes, légumier *m* ▸ **vegetable garden** (jardin *m*) potager *m* ▸ **vegetable kingdom** règne végétal ▸ **vegetable knife** couteau *m* à éplucher ▸ **vegetable marrow** (*esp Brit*) courge *f* ▸ **vegetable patch** carré *m* de légumes ▸ **vegetable salad** salade *f or* macédoine *f* de légumes ▸ **vegetable slicer** coupe-légumes *m inv* ▸ **vegetable soup** soupe *f* aux *or* de légumes.
vegetarian [ˌvedʒɪˈtɛərɪən] **adj, n** végétarien(ne) *m(f)*.
vegetarianism [ˌvedʒɪˈtɛərɪənɪzəm] **n** végétarisme *m*.
vegetate [ˈvedʒɪteɪt] **vi** végéter, moisir*.
vegetated [ˈvedʒɪteɪtɪd] **adj** avec de la végétation. **sparsely/densely** ~ à (la) végétation rare/dense.
vegetation [ˌvedʒɪˈteɪʃən] **n** (*NonC*) végétation *f*.
vegetative [ˈvedʒɪtətɪv] **adj** (*Bio, fig*) végétatif.
veggie* [ˈvedʒɪ] **n, adj** a (**abbr of vegetarian**) végétarien(ne) *m(f)*. b (*esp US*) (**abbr of vegetable**) légume *m*.
veggieburger [ˈvedʒɪˌbɜːdəʳ] **n = vegeburger.**
vehemence [ˈviːɪməns] **n** *[feelings]* ardeur *f*, intensité *f*, véhémence *f*; *[actions]* violence *f*, fougue *f*, véhémence.
vehement [ˈviːɪmənt] **adj** *feelings, speech* ardent, passionné, véhément; *attack* violent, impétueux.
vehemently [ˈviːɪməntlɪ] **adv** *speak* avec passion, avec véhémence; *attack* avec violence.
vehicle [ˈviːɪkl] **n** a (*Aut, Rail etc*) véhicule *m*; (*very large*) engin *m*. **"closed to ~s"** "interdit à la circulation"; *see* **commercial**. b (*Chem, Art, Pharm etc; also fig*) véhicule *m*. **a ~ of** *or* **for communication** un véhicule de la communication.
vehicular [vɪˈhɪkjʊləʳ] **adj** de véhicules, de voitures. **~ traffic** circulation *f*.
veil [veɪl] 1 **n** (*gen*) voile *m*; (*on hat*) voilette *f*; (*fig*) voile. (*Rel*) **to take the ~** prendre le voile; (*fig liter*) **beyond the ~** dans l'au-delà; **to wear a ~** être voilé; (*fig*) **to draw/throw a ~ over** mettre/jeter un voile sur; **under the ~ of** sous le voile de; **~ of mist** voile de brume. 2 **vt** voiler, couvrir d'un voile; (*fig*) *truth, facts* voiler; *feelings* voiler, dissimuler. **the clouds ~ed the moon** les nuages voilaient la lune.
veiled [veɪld] **adj** *person, hint, reference* voilé; *meaning, warning, threat* voilé, caché.
veiling [ˈveɪlɪŋ] **n** (*on hat etc*) voilage *m*; (*fig*) *[truth, facts]* dissimulation *f*.
vein [veɪn] **n** a (*in body, insect wing*) veine *f*; (*in leaf*) nervure *f*. (*suicide*) **to open a ~** s'ouvrir les veines; **he has French blood in his ~s** il a du sang français dans les veines; *see* **varicose**.
b (*in stone etc: gen*) veine *f*; (*of ore etc*) filon *m*, veine. (*fig*) **there's a ~ of truth in what he says** il y a un fond de vérité dans ce qu'il dit; (*fig*) **there's a ~ of commonsense/dishonesty** *etc* **in the family** il y a un fond de bon sens/de malhonnêteté *etc* que l'on retrouve chez tous les membres de la famille.
c (*style etc*) style *m*; (*mood*) esprit *m*, humeur *f*, disposition *f*. **in a humorous/revolutionary** *etc* **~** dans un esprit humoristique/révolutionnaire *etc;* **in the same ~, in a similar ~** dans le même esprit; **in a realistic ~** dans un style réaliste.
veined [veɪnd] **adj** *hand, marble* veiné; *stone* marbré; *leaf* nervuré.
veining [ˈveɪnɪŋ] **n** *[marble]* veinures *fpl*; *[stone]* marbrures *fpl*; *[leaf]* nervures *fpl*; *[marble-effect paper]* dessin *mpl* marbrés.
veinule [ˈveɪnjuːl] **n** veinule *f*.
vela [ˈviːlə] **npl of velum.**
velar [ˈviːləʳ] **adj** vélaire.
Velcro [ˈvelkrəʊ] **n** ® Velcro *m* ®.
veld(t) [velt] **n** veld(t) *m*.
vellum [ˈveləm] 1 **n** vélin *m*. 2 **comp** *binding* de vélin ▸ **vellum paper** papier *m* vélin.
velocipede† [vəˈlɒsɪpiːd] **n** vélocipède† *m*.
velocity [vɪˈlɒsɪtɪ] **n** vélocité *f*, vitesse *f*.
velodrome [ˈviːləˌdrəʊm] **n** vélodrome *m*.
velour(s) [vəˈlʊəʳ] **n** (*for clothes*) velours *m* rasé; (*for upholstery*) velours épais.
velum [ˈviːləm] **n, pl vela** (*Anat*) voile *m* du palais.
velvet [ˈvelvɪt] 1 **n** a (*gen*) velours *m*. (*fig*) **to be on ~*** jouer sur le *or* du velours*; *see* **black, iron.** b (*US: unearned income*) bénéfice *m* non salarial. 2 **comp** *dress* de velours ▸ **velvet tread:** (*fig*) **with a velvet tread** à pas de velours, à pas feutrés.
velveteen [ˈvelvɪtiːn] **n** velvet *m*.
velvety [ˈvelvɪtɪ] **adj** *surface, texture, material* velouteux, velouté; *sauce, voice* velouté.
vena cava [ˈviːnəˈkeɪvə] **n, pl venae cavae** [ˈviːniːˈkeɪviː] veine *f* cave.
venal [ˈviːnl] **adj** vénal.
venality [viːˈnælɪtɪ] **n** vénalité *f*.
vend [vend] **vt** (*Jur*) vendre.
vendee [venˈdiː] **n** (*Jur*) acquéreur *m*.
vendetta [venˈdetə] **n** vendetta *f*.
vending [ˈvendɪŋ] **n** vente *f*. **~ machine** distributeur *m* automatique.
vendor [ˈvendəʳ] **n** a (*gen*) marchand(e) *m(f)*. **ice-cream** *etc* **~** marchand(e) de glaces *etc; see* **news, street.** b (*machine*) distributeur *m* automatique. c [ˈvendɔːʳ] (*Jur*) vendeur *m*.
veneer [vəˈnɪəʳ] 1 **n** placage *m*; (*fig*) apparence *f*, vernis *m*. **with** *or* **under a ~ of** sous un vernis de. 2 **vt** plaquer.
venerable [ˈvenərəbl] **adj** vénérable.
venerate [ˈvenəreɪt] **vt** vénérer.
veneration [ˌvenəˈreɪʃən] **n** vénération *f*.
venereal [vɪˈnɪərɪəl] **adj** vénérien. **~ disease** (*abbr* **V.D.**) maladie vénérienne.
venereology [vɪˌnɪərɪˈɒlədʒɪ] **n** vénér(é)ologie *f*.
venery [ˈvenərɪ] **n** a (*liter: hunting*) vénerie *f*. b (††: *debauchery*) débauche *f*.
Venetia [vɪˈniːʃə] **n** Vénétie *f* (*Hist*).
Venetian [vɪˈniːʃən] 1 **adj** vénitien, de Venise. **~ glass** cristal *m* de Venise; **~ blind** store vénitien. 2 **n** Vénitien(ne) *m(f)*.
Veneto [ˈvɛːneto] **n** Vénétie *f* (*moderne*).
Venezuela [ˌveneˈzweɪlə] **n** Venezuela *m*.
Venezuelan [ˌveneˈzweɪlən] 1 **adj** vénézuélien. 2 **n** Vénézuélien(ne) *m(f)*.
vengeance [ˈvendʒəns] **n** vengeance *f*. **to take ~ (up)on** se venger de *or* sur; **to take ~ for** tirer vengeance de; (*fig*) **with a ~** pour de bon*.
vengeful [ˈvendʒfʊl] **adj** vengeur (*f* -eresse).
venial [ˈviːnɪəl] **adj** (*also Rel*) véniel.
veniality [ˌviːnɪˈælɪtɪ] **n** caractère véniel.
Venice [ˈvenɪs] **n** Venise.
venire [vɪˈnaɪrɪ] (*US Jur*) 1 **n** liste *f* des jurés assignés. 2 **comp** ▸ **venireman** juré *m* nommé par assignation.
venison [ˈvenɪsən] **n** venaison *f*.
venom [ˈvenəm] **n** (*lit, fig*) venin *m*.
venomous [ˈvenəməs] **adj** (*lit, fig*) venimeux. (*fig*) **~ tongue** langue *f* de vipère.
venomously [ˈvenəməslɪ] **adv** d'une manière venimeuse, haineusement.
venous [ˈviːnəs] **adj** (*Anat, Bot*) veineux.
vent [vent] 1 **n** (*for gas, liquid*) (*hole*) orifice *m*; (*pipe*) conduit *m*; (*in chimney*) tuyau *m*; *[volcano]* cheminée *f*; (*in barrel*) trou *m*; (*in coat*) fente *f*. (*fig*) **to give ~ to** donner *or* laisser libre cours à. 2 **vt** *barrel etc* pratiquer un trou dans; (*fig*) *one's anger etc* décharger (*on* sur). 3 **comp** ▸ **vent glass** (*Aut*) déflecteur *m*.
ventilate [ˈventɪleɪt] **vt** *room* aérer, ventiler; *tunnel* ventiler; *blood* oxygéner; (*fig*) *question* livrer à la discussion; *grievance* étaler au grand jour.
ventilation [ˌventɪˈleɪʃən] **n** ventilation *f*. **~ shaft** conduit *m* d'aération *or* de ventilation.
ventilator [ˈventɪleɪtəʳ] **n** ventilateur *m*; (*Aut: also* **~ window**) déflecteur *m*.
ventricle [ˈventrɪkl] **n** ventricule *m*.
ventriloquism [venˈtrɪləkwɪzəm] **n** ventriloquie *f*.
ventriloquist [venˈtrɪləkwɪst] **n** ventriloque *mf*. **~'s dummy** poupée *f* de ventriloque.
ventriloquy [venˈtrɪləkwɪ] **n** ventriloquie *f*.
venture [ˈventʃəʳ] 1 **n** a (*project*) entreprise *f*, projet *m*; (*business operation*) entreprise. **it was a risky ~** c'était une entreprise assez risquée *or* assez hasardeuse; **the success of his first artistic/film** *etc* **~** le succès de sa première entreprise artistique/cinématographique *etc;* **all his business ~s failed** toutes ses entreprises en matière de commerce *or* toutes ses tentatives commerciales ont échoué; **this is a new ~ in publishing** ceci constitue quelque chose de nouveau *or* un coup d'essai en matière d'édition.
b (*journey etc*) voyage *m* aventureux (*to* vers), aventures *fpl*.
c **at a ~** au hasard.
2 **comp** ▸ **venture capital** (*Econ*) capital-risques *m* ▸ **venture capitalist** (*Econ*) spécialiste *mf* du capital-risques.
3 **vt** *life* risquer, exposer, hasarder (*liter*); *fortune, opinion, reputation* risquer, hasarder; *explanation, estimate* hasarder, avancer. **when I asked him that, he ~d a guess** quand je lui ai posé la question, il a hasardé *or* avancé une réponse; **to ~ to do** oser faire, se permettre de faire; **he ~d the opinion that** il a hasardé une opinion selon laquelle, il s'est permis d'observer que, il a osé observer que; **I ~d to write to you** je me suis permis de vous écrire (à tout hasard); **... but he did not ~ to speak** ... mais il n'a pas osé parler; (*Prov*) **nothing ~d nothing gained** qui ne risque rien n'a rien (*Prov*).
4 **vi** s'aventurer, se risquer. **to ~ in/out/through** *etc* se risquer à entrer/sortir/traverser *etc;* **to ~ out of doors** se risquer à sortir; **to ~ into town/into the forest** s'aventurer *or* se hasarder dans la ville/dans la forêt; **they ~d on a programme of reform** ils ont essayé de mettre sur pied *or* d'entreprendre un ensemble de réformes; **when we ~d on this** quand nous avons entrepris cela, quand nous nous sommes lancés là-dedans.
▸**venture forth vi** (*liter*) se risquer à sortir.
venturesome [ˈventʃəsəm] **adj** *person* aventureux, entreprenant; *action* risqué, hasardeux.
venue [ˈvenjuː] **n** (*gen*) lieu *m* (de rendez-vous); (*Jur*) lieu du procès, juridiction *f*. **the ~ of the meeting is ...** la réunion aura lieu à ... .
Venus [ˈviːnəs] **n** (*Astron, Myth*) Vénus *f*. (*Bot*) **~ fly-trap** dionée *f*.
Venusian [vɪˈnjuːzɪən] **adj** vénusien.
veracious [vəˈreɪʃəs] **adj** véridique.

veracity [vəˈræsɪtɪ] n véracité *f.*

veranda(h) [vəˈrændə] n véranda *f.*

verb [vɜːb] (*Gram*) 1 n verbe *m*; *see* **auxiliary** *etc.* 2 comp ▶ **verb phrase** syntagme *m* verbal.

verbal [ˈvɜːbəl] 1 adj a *statement, agreement, promise, error* verbal, oral; *confession* oral; *translation* mot à mot, littéral. ~ **memory** mémoire auditive. b (*Gram*) verbal. 2 n (*US Jur* *) aveux *mpl* faits oralement (*et servant de témoignage dans un procès*).

verbalize [ˈvɜːbəlaɪz] vt *feelings etc* traduire en paroles, exprimer.

verbally [ˈvɜːbəlɪ] adv verbalement, oralement.

verbatim [vɜːˈbeɪtɪm] 1 adj textuel, mot pour mot. 2 adv textuellement, mot pour mot.

verbena [vɜːˈbiːnə] n (*genus*) verbénacées *fpl*; (*plant*) verveine *f.*

verbiage [ˈvɜːbɪɪdʒ] n verbiage *m.*

verbless [ˈvɜːblɪs] adj sans verbe.

verbose [vɜːˈbəʊs] adj verbeux, prolixe.

verbosely [vɜːˈbəʊslɪ] adv avec verbosité, verbeusement.

verbosity [vɜːˈbɒsɪtɪ] n verbosité *f.*

verdant [ˈvɜːdənt] adj (*liter*) verdoyant.

verdict [ˈvɜːdɪkt] n a (*Jur*) verdict *m.* ~ **of guilty/not guilty** verdict de culpabilité/de non-culpabilité; *see* **bring in.** b *[doctor, electors, press etc]* verdict *m*, jugement *m*, décision *f.* **to give one's ~ about** *or* **on** se prononcer sur.

verdigris [ˈvɜːdɪgrɪs] adj, n vert-de-gris (*m*) *inv.*

verdure [ˈvɜːdjʊəʳ] n (*liter*) verdure *f.*

verge [vɜːdʒ] n a **on the ~ of doing** sur le point de faire; **on the ~ of ruin/despair/a nervous breakdown** au bord de la ruine/du désespoir/de la dépression nerveuse; **on the ~ of sleep** *or* **of falling asleep** sur le point de s'endormir; **on the ~ of tears** au bord des larmes, sur le point de pleurer; **on the ~ of a discovery** à la veille d'une découverte; **on the ~ of retirement/old age** au seuil de la retraite/vieillesse; **people living on the ~ of starvation** les gens que menace la famine, les gens qui risquent de mourir de faim.

b (*Brit: of road*) bas-côté *m*, accotement *m*, bord *m.* **the car mounted the ~** la voiture est montée sur le bas-côté *or* l'accotement; **pull over on to the ~** arrêtez-vous sur le bas-côté; (*Aut*) **"soft ~s"** "accotement non stabilisé".

c (*edge: gen*) bord *m*; (*round flowerbed*) bordure *f* en gazon; *[forest]* orée *f.*

▶ **verge on** vt fus *[ideas, actions]* approcher de, côtoyer. **this verges on the ridiculous** c'est au bord du ridicule, cela frise le ridicule, ce n'est pas loin d'être ridicule; **shyness verging on hostility** une timidité qui approche de l'hostilité *or* qui côtoie l'hostilité *or* qui est presque de l'hostilité; **he's verging on bankruptcy** il est au bord de la faillite; **she is verging on fifty** elle frise la cinquantaine; **she was verging on madness** elle frôlait la folie.

verger [ˈvɜːdʒəʳ] n (*Rel*) bedeau *m*; (*ceremonial*) huissier *m* à verge.

Vergil [ˈvɜːdʒɪl] n Virgile *m.*

Vergilian [vəˈdʒɪlɪən] adj virgilien.

verifiability [ˌverɪfaɪəˈbɪlɪtɪ] n vérifiabilité *f.*

verifiable [ˈverɪfaɪəbl] adj vérifiable.

verification [ˌverɪfɪˈkeɪʃən] n (*check*) vérification *f*, contrôle *m*; (*proof*) vérification.

verifier [ˈverɪfaɪəʳ] n (*Comput*) vérificatrice *f.*

verify [ˈverɪfaɪ] vt *statements, information, spelling* vérifier; *documents* contrôler; *suspicions, fears* vérifier, confirmer.

verily† [ˈverɪlɪ] adv en vérité.

verisimilitude [ˌverɪsɪˈmɪlɪtjuːd] n vraisemblance *f.*

veritable [ˈverɪtəbl] adj véritable, vrai (*before n*).

verity [ˈverɪtɪ] n (*liter*) vérité *f.*

vermicelli [ˌvɜːmɪˈselɪ] n vermicelle(s) *m(pl).*

vermicide [ˈvɜːmɪsaɪd] n vermicide *m.*

vermifugal [ˈvɜːmɪfjuːgəl] adj vermifuge.

vermifuge [ˈvɜːmɪfjuːdʒ] n vermifuge *m.*

vermilion [vəˈmɪljən] adj, n vermillon (*m*) *inv.*

vermin [ˈvɜːmɪn] collective n (*animals*) animaux *mpl* nuisibles; (*insects*) vermine *f* (*NonC*), parasites *mpl*; (*pej: people*) vermine (*NonC*), racaille *f* (*NonC*), parasites.

verminous [ˈvɜːmɪnəs] adj *person, clothes* pouilleux, couvert de vermine; *disease* vermineux.

Vermont [vɜːˈmɒnt] n Vermont *m.* **in ~** dans le Vermont.

vermouth [ˈvɜːməθ] n vermout(h) *m.*

vernacular [vəˈnækjʊləʳ] 1 n a (*Ling*) (*native speech*) langue *f* vernaculaire, dialecte *m*; (*jargon*) jargon *m.* b (*Archit*) architecture *f* populaire (*typique d'une région ou d'un pays*). **in the local ~** dans le style local. 2 adj *crafts* indigène, du pays; *language* vernaculaire, du pays. ~ **architecture** = **vernacular 1b.**

vernal [ˈvɜːnl] adj *equinox* vernal; (*liter*) *flowers* printanier.

Verona [vəˈrəʊnə] n Vérone.

veronica [vəˈrɒnɪkə] n a (*plant*) véronique *f.* b (*name*) **V~** Véronique *f.*

verruca [veˈruːkə] n, pl **verrucae** [veˈruːsiː] *or* **~s** verrue *f* (*gen plantaire*).

Versailles [veəˈsaɪ] n Versailles.

versatile [ˈvɜːsətaɪl] adj *person* aux talents variés, doué en tous genres; *mind* souple; *genius* universel, encyclopédique; (*Bot, Zool*) versatile.

versatility [ˌvɜːsəˈtɪlɪtɪ] n *[person]* variété *f* de talents, faculté *f* d'adaptation; *[mind]* souplesse *f*; (*Bot, Zool*) versatilité *f.*

verse [vɜːs] 1 n a (*stanza*) *[poem]* strophe *f*; *[song]* couplet *m.* b (*NonC: poetry*) poésie *f*, vers *mpl.* **in ~** en vers; *see* **blank, free** *etc.* c *[Bible, Koran]* verset *m*; *see* **chapter.** 2 comp *drama etc* en vers.

versed [vɜːst] adj (*also* **well-~**) versé (*in* dans). **not (well-)~** peu versé.

versification [ˌvɜːsɪfɪˈkeɪʃən] n versification *f*, métrique *f.*

versifier [ˈvɜːsɪfaɪəʳ] n (*pej*) versificateur *m*, -trice *f* (*pej*).

versify [ˈvɜːsɪfaɪ] 1 vt versifier, mettre en vers. 2 vi faire des vers.

version [ˈvɜːʃən] n a (*account*) version *f*; (*interpretation*) interprétation *f.* b (*variant*) *[text]* version *f*, variante *f*; *[car]* modèle *m.* c (*translation*) version *f*, traduction *f*; *see* **authorize.**

verso [ˈvɜːsəʊ] n verso *m.*

versus [ˈvɜːsəs] prep a (*in comparison*) par opposition à. **statements about public ~ private ownership** les déclarations concernant la propriété publique par opposition à la propriété privée *or* opposant la propriété publique à la propriété privée; **the question of electricity ~ gas for cooking** la question de l'électricité par rapport au gaz *or* de l'électricité comparée au gaz pour la cuisine.

b (*in sporting event*) contre. **the England ~ Spain match** le match Angleterre-Espagne *or* de l'Angleterre contre l'Espagne *or* opposant l'Angleterre à l'Espagne.

c (*in dispute, competition*) **it's management ~ workers** c'est la direction contre les ouvriers, la direction s'oppose aux ouvriers; **the 1960 Nixon ~ Kennedy election** l'élection qui en 1960 a opposé Nixon à Kennedy.

d (*Jur*) **Jones ~ Smith** Jones contre Smith.

vertebra [ˈvɜːtɪbrə] n, pl **vertebrae** [ˈvɜːtɪbriː] *or* **~s** vertèbre *f.*

vertebral [ˈvɜːtɪbrəl] adj vertébral.

vertebrate [ˈvɜːtɪbrət] adj, n vertébré (*m*).

vertex [ˈvɜːteks] n, pl **~es** *or* **vertices** [ˈvɜːtɪsiːz] (*gen, Geom*) sommet *m*; (*Anat*) vertex *m.*

vertical [ˈvɜːtɪkəl] 1 adj *line, plane* (*also Comm, Econ*) vertical. (*Comm, Econ*) ~ **analysis/integration/mobility/planning** analyse *f*/intégration *f*/mobilité *f*/planification *f* verticale; ~ **cliff** falaise *f* à pic; ~ **take-off aircraft** avion *m* à décollage vertical. 2 n verticale *f.* **out of** *or* **off the ~** décalé par rapport à *or* écarté de la verticale.

vertically [ˈvɜːtɪkəlɪ] adv verticalement.

vertiginous [vɜːˈtɪdʒɪnəs] adj vertigineux.

vertigo [ˈvɜːtɪgəʊ] n, pl **~es** *or* **vertigines** [vɜːˈtɪdʒɪˌniːz] vertige *m.* **to suffer from ~** avoir des vertiges.

verve [vɜːv] n verve *f*, brio *m.*

Very [ˈvɪərɪ] adj (*Mil*) ~ **light** fusée éclairante; ~ **pistol** pistolet *m* lance-fusées.

very [ˈverɪ] 1 adv a (*extremely*) très, fort, bien. ~ **amusing** très *or* fort *or* bien amusant; **to be ~ careful** faire très *or* bien attention; **I am ~ cold/hot** j'ai très froid/chaud; **are you tired? — ~/not ~** êtes-vous fatigué? — très/pas très; ~ **well written/made** très bien écrit/fait; ~ **well, if you insist** (très) bien, si vous insistez; ~ **little** très peu; ~ **little milk** très peu de lait; **it is not ~ likely** ce n'est pas très probable, c'est peu probable; (*Rel*) **the V~ Reverend ...** le Très Révérend ...; (*Rad*) ~ **high frequency** (ondes *fpl*) ultra-courtes *fpl*; (*Electronics*) ~ **high/low frequency** très haute/basse fréquence.

b (*absolutely*) tout, de loin. ~ **best quality** toute première qualité; ~ **last/first** tout dernier/premier; **she is the ~ cleverest in the class** elle est de loin la plus intelligente de la classe; **give it me tomorrow at the ~ latest** donnez-le-moi demain au plus tard *or* demain dernier délai; **at midday at the ~ latest** à midi au plus tard; **at the ~ most/least** tout au plus/moins; **to be in the ~ best of health** être en excellente santé; **they are the ~ best of friends** ils sont les meilleurs amis du monde.

c ~ **much** beaucoup, bien; **thank you ~ much** merci beaucoup; **I liked it ~ much** je l'ai beaucoup aimé; **he is ~ much better** il va beaucoup mieux; ~ **much bigger** beaucoup *or* bien plus grand; ~ **much respected** très *or* fort respecté; **he is ~ much the more intelligent of the two** il est de beaucoup *or* de loin le plus intelligent des deux; **he doesn't work ~ much** il ne travaille pas beaucoup, il travaille peu; (*emphatic "yes"*) ~ **much so!** absolument!

d (*for emphasis*) **the ~ same day** le jour même, ce jour-là; **the ~ same hat** exactement le même chapeau; **the ~ next day** le lendemain même, dès le lendemain; **I took the ~ next train** j'ai pris le premier train; **the ~ next shop we come to** le prochain magasin; **the ~ next person to do this was ...** la personne qui a fait cela tout de suite après était ... (*see also* **next**); *see* **own.**

2 adj a (*precise, exact*) même, exactement, justement. **that ~ day/moment** ce jour/cet instant même; **on the ~ spot** à l'endroit même *or* précis; **his ~ words** ses propos mêmes; **the ~ thing/man I need** tout à fait *or* justement la chose/l'homme qu'il me faut; **the ~ thing!** (*what I need*) c'est justement ce qu'il me faut!; (*of suggestion, solution*) c'est idéal!; **to catch in the ~ act** prendre en flagrant délit (*of stealing etc* de vol *etc*).

b (*extreme*) tout. **at the ~ end** *[play, year]* tout à la fin; *[garden, road]* tout au bout; **at the ~ back** tout au fond; **to the ~ end** jusqu'au bout; **in the ~ depths of the sea/forest** au plus profond de la mer/la forêt.

c (*mere*) seul. **the ~ word** le mot seul, rien que le mot; **the ~ thought of** la seule pensée de, rien que de penser à; **the ~ idea!** quelle idée alors!

d (*liter*) **he is a ~ rascal** *or* **the veriest rascal** c'est un fieffé coquin.

vesicle ['vesɪkl] **n** vésicule *f*.

vesper ['vespəʳ] **n**: **~s** vêpres *fpl*; **to ring the ~ bell** sonner les vêpres.

vessel ['vesl] **n** a (*Naut*) vaisseau *m*, navire *m*, bâtiment *m*. b (*Anat, Bot*) vaisseau *m*; *see* **blood.** c (*liter: receptacle*) vaisseau *m* (*liter*), récipient *m*, vase *m*. **drinking ~** vaisseau.

vest[1] [vest] 1 **n** a (*Brit*) *[child, man]* tricot *m* de corps; *[woman]* chemise *f* américaine. b (*US*) gilet *m*. 2 **comp** ►**vest pocket n** (*US*) poche *f* de gilet ►**vest-pocket adj** (*US*) *calculator etc* de poche; (*fig: tiny*) minuscule.

vest[2] [vest] **vt** (*frm*) **to ~ sb with sth, to ~ sth in sb** investir qn de qch, assigner qch à qn; **the authority ~ed in me** l'autorité dont je suis investi; (*Comm, Fin*) **~ed interests** droits *mpl* acquis; (*fig*) **he has a ~ed interest in the play since his daughter is acting in it** il est directement intéressé dans la pièce, étant donné que sa fille y joue.

vestal ['vestl] **adj**: **~ virgin** vestale *f*.

vestibular [ve'stɪbjʊləʳ] **adj** (*Anat*) vestibulaire.

vestibule ['vestɪbjuːl] **n** *[house, hotel]* vestibule *m*, hall *m* d'entrée; *[church]* vestibule; (*Anat*) vestibule.

vestige ['vestɪdʒ] **n** a (*trace, remnant*) vestige *m*. **~s of past civilisations** vestiges de civilisations disparues; (*fig*) **not a ~ of truth/commonsense** pas un grain de vérité/de bon sens; **a ~ of hope** un reste d'espoir. b (*Anat, Bio: organ*) organe *m* rudimentaire *or* atrophié. **the ~ of a tail** une queue rudimentaire *or* atrophiée.

vestigial [ves'tɪdʒɪəl] **adj** rudimentaire, atrophié.

vesting ['vestɪŋ] **n** (*Insurance*) acquisition *f* de droits.

vestment ['vestmənt] **n** *[priest]* vêtement sacerdotal; (*ceremonial robe*) habit *m* de cérémonie.

vestry ['vestrɪ] **n** (*part of church*) sacristie *f*; (*meeting*) assemblée paroissiale, conseil paroissial.

vesture ['vestʃəʳ] **n** (*NonC: liter*) vêtements *mpl*.

Vesuvius [vɪ'suːvɪəs] **n** Vésuve *m*.

vet [vet] 1 **n** a (**abbr of veterinary surgeon, veterinarian**) vétérinaire *mf*. b (*US* *) (**abbr of veteran**) ancien combattant *m*.

2 **vt** *text* corriger, revoir; *application* examiner de près *or* minutieusement; *person* examiner soigneusement *or* de près; *figures, calculations* vérifier; *report* (*check*) vérifier le contenu de; (*approve*) approuver. **wage claims are ~ted by the union** les revendications salariales doivent d'abord recevoir l'approbation du syndicat; **his wife ~s his contracts** sa femme vérifie *or* contrôle ses contrats; **you'll have to ~ it very carefully** vous devrez le vérifier très soigneusement; **the purchases are ~ted by a committee** les achats doivent d'abord être approuvés par un comité; **the director ~ted him for the job** le directeur l'a examiné sous tous les angles avant de lui offrir le poste; **we have ~ted him thoroughly** nous nous sommes renseignés de façon approfondie à son sujet.

vetch [vetʃ] **n** vesce *f*.

veteran ['vetərən] 1 **n** a (*gen*) vétéran *m*. b (*Mil: also* **war ~**) ancien combattant *m*. (*US*) **V~s Administration** *ministère des anciens combattants;* (*US*) **V~s Day** le onze novembre (*anniversaire de l'armistice*). 2 **adj** (*experienced*) chevronné, expérimenté. **she is a ~ campaigner for women's rights** elle fait campagne depuis toujours pour les droits de la femme; **a ~ car** une voiture d'époque (*avant 1919*); **a ~ teacher/golfer** *etc* un vétéran de l'enseignement/du golf *etc*.

veterinarian [ˌvetərɪ'nɛərɪən] **n** (*esp US*) vétérinaire *mf*.

veterinary ['vetərɪnərɪ] **adj** *medicine, science* vétérinaire. (*esp Brit*) **~ surgeon** vétérinaire *mf*.

veto ['viːtəʊ] 1 **n, pl ~es** (*act, decision*) veto *m*; (*power*) droit *m* de veto. **to use one's ~** exercer son droit de veto; **to put a ~ on** mettre son veto à. 2 **vt** (*Pol etc, also fig*) mettre *or* opposer son veto à.

vetting ['vetɪŋ] **n** *[text]* correction *f*, révision *f*; *[application, candidate]* examen *m* minutieux; *[figures]* vérification *f*; *see* **positive, security.**

vex [veks] **vt** contrarier, ennuyer, fâcher.

vexation [vek'seɪʃən] **n** (*NonC*) ennui *m*, tracas *m*.

vexatious [vek'seɪʃəs] **adj** *thing* contrariant, ennuyeux; *person* tracassier, contrariant.

vexed [vekst] **adj** a (*annoyed*) fâché (*with sb* contre qn, avec qn, *at sth* de qch). **to get ~** se fâcher. b **a ~ question** une question controversée; **we live in ~ times** nous traversons une époque difficile.

vexing ['veksɪŋ] **adj** a (*annoying*) = **vexatious.** b (*puzzling*) *question, issue* frustrant.

VG (*Scol etc*) (**abbr of very good**) T.B., très bien.

VGA [ˌviːdʒiː'eɪ] **n** (**abbr of video gate array**) **~ card** carte *f* VGA.

VHF [viːeɪtʃ'ef] **n** (**abbr of very high frequency**) V.H.F. *f*.

VHS [viː'eɪtʃ'es] **n** (**abbr of video home system**) VHS.

VI (*US Post*) **abbr of Virgin Islands.**

via ['vaɪə] **prep** a (*lit: by way of*) via, par. **a ticket to Vienna ~ Frankfurt** un billet pour Vienne via Francfort; **the journey takes 9 hours ~ Ostend** le voyage prend neuf heures via Ostende *or* (si l'on passe) par Ostende; **you should go ~ Paris** vouz devriez passer par Paris; **we went home ~ the pub** nous sommes passés par le pub *or* nous nous sommes arrêtés au pub avant de rentrer. b (*fig: by way of*) par. **to send a message ~ the computer** envoyer un message par l'ordinateur. c (*by means of*) au moyen de, grâce à. **the launch was detected ~ a satellite** le lancement a été détecté au moyen de *or* grâce à un satellite.

viability [ˌvaɪə'bɪlɪtɪ] **n** (*see* **viable**) viabilité *f*; chances *fpl* de succès.

viable ['vaɪəbl] **adj** *company, policy, service, product* viable; *project, programme, method* qui a des chances de réussir. **it's not a ~ proposition** ce n'est pas viable.

viaduct ['vaɪədʌkt] **n** viaduc *m*.

vial ['vaɪəl] **n** (*liter*) fiole *f*; (*Pharm*) ampoule *f*.

viands ['vaɪəndz] **npl** (*liter*) aliments *mpl*.

viaticum [vaɪ'ætɪkəm] **n, pl viatica** [vaɪ'ætɪkə] *or* **~s** viatique *m*.

vibes* [vaɪbz] **npl** a (**abbr of vibrations**) (*from band, singer*) atmosphère *f*, ambiance *f*. (*between individuals*) **I got good ~ from her** entre nous, le courant est passé; **the ~ are wrong** ça ne gaze pas*. b **abbr of vibraphone.**

vibrancy ['vaɪbrənsɪ] **n** *[voice]* résonance *f*; *[speech]* vigueur *f*; *[light, colours]* éclat *m*; *[person, language]* vivacité *f*.

vibrant ['vaɪbrənt] **adj** *voice, speech* vibrant; *light, colours* vif (*f* vive); *person, language* vivant, vif. (*fig*) **to be ~ with** vibrer de.

vibraphone ['vaɪbrəfəʊn] **n** vibraphone *m*.

vibrate [vaɪ'breɪt] 1 **vi** (*quiver*) vibrer (*with* de); (*resound*) retentir (*with* de); (*fig*) frémir, vibrer (*with* de). 2 **vt** faire vibrer.

vibration [vaɪ'breɪʃən] **n** vibration *f*.

vibrato [vɪ'brɑːtəʊ] (*Mus*) 1 **n** vibrato *m*. 2 **adv** avec vibrato.

vibrator [vaɪ'breɪtəʳ] **n** a (*Elec*) vibrateur *m*. b (*massager, also sexual*) vibromasseur *m*.

vibratory ['vaɪbrətərɪ] **adj** vibratoire.

viburnum [vaɪ'bɜːnəm] **n** viorne *f*.

vicar ['vɪkəʳ] **n** a (*C of E*) pasteur *m* (*de l'Église anglicane*). **good evening ~** bonsoir pasteur. b **~ apostolic** vicaire *m* apostolique; **~ general** (*pl* **~s ~**) grand vicaire, vicaire général; **the V~ of Christ** le vicaire de Jésus-Christ.

vicarage ['vɪkərɪdʒ] **n** presbytère *m* (*de l'Église anglicane*).

vicarious [vɪ'kɛərɪəs] **adj** a (*delegated*) délégué. **to give ~ authority to** déléguer son autorité à. b (*for others*) *work* fait à la place d'un autre. **the ~ suffering of Christ** les souffrances que le Christ subit pour autrui; **I got ~ pleasure out of it** j'en ai retiré indirectement du plaisir.

vicariously [vɪ'kɛərɪəslɪ] **adv** *experience* indirectement; *authorize* par délégation, par procuration.

vice[1] [vaɪs] 1 **n** (*NonC: depravity*) vice *m*; (*evil characteristic*) vice; (*less strong*) défaut *m*. *[dog, horse etc]* **he has no ~s** il n'est pas vicieux. 2 **comp** ►**Vice Squad** (*Police*) brigade mondaine *or* des mœurs.

vice[2], (*US*) vise [vaɪs] **n** (*Tech*) étau *m*; *see* **grip** *etc*.

vice[3] ['vaɪsɪ] **prep** (*frm*) à la place de.

vice- [vaɪs] **pref** vice-. **~admiral** vice-amiral *m* d'escadre; (*Sport*) **~captain** capitaine *m* adjoint; **~chairman** vice-président(e) *m(f)*; **~chairmanship** vice-présidence *f*; **~chancellor** (*Univ*) ≃ président(e) *m(f)* d'université; (*Jur*) vice-chancelier *m*; **~consul** vice-consul *m*; **vice-premier** Premier ministre *m* adjoint; **~presidency** vice-présidence *f*; **~president** vice-président(e) *m(f)*; (*US Pol*) **V~President Smith** le vice-président Smith; (*US Pol*) **~presidential** vice-présidentiel; (*US Pol*) **~presidential candidate** candidat(e) *m(f)* à la vice-présidence; (*Scol*) **~principal** (*gen*) directeur *m*, -trice *f* adjoint(e); *[lycée]* censeur *m*; *[college]* principal(e) *m(f)* adjoint(e); **~regal** de *or* du vice-roi.

viceroy ['vaɪsrɔɪ] **n** vice-roi *m*.

vice versa ['vaɪsɪ'vɜːsə] **adv** vice versa, inversement.

vicinity [vɪ'sɪnɪtɪ] **n** (*nearby area*) voisinage *m*, environs *mpl*, alentours *mpl*; (*closeness*) proximité *f*. **in the ~** dans les environs, à proximité; **in the ~ of the town** aux alentours de la ville, à proximité de la ville; **it's something in the ~ of £100** c'est aux alentours de 100 livres; **in the immediate ~** dans les environs immédiats; **the immediate ~ of the town** les abords *mpl* de la ville.

vicious ['vɪʃəs] **adj** *remark, look, criticism* méchant, malveillant, haineux; *kick, attack* brutal, violent; *habit* vicieux, pervers; *animal* vicieux, rétif. **to have a ~ tongue** être mauvaise langue, avoir une langue de vipère; **~ circle** cercle vicieux.

viciously ['vɪʃəslɪ] **adv** (*see* **vicious**) méchamment, avec malveillance, haineusement; brutalement, violemment.

viciousness ['vɪʃəsnɪs] **n** (*see* **vicious**) méchanceté *f*, malveillance *f*; brutalité *f*, violence *f*.

vicissitude [vɪ'sɪsɪtjuːd] **n** vicissitude *f*.

victim ['vɪktɪm] **n** (*lit, fig*) victime *f*. **the accident/bomb ~s** les victimes de l'accident/de l'explosion; **many of the Nazi ~s, many of the ~s of the Nazis** de nombreuses victimes des Nazis; **to be the** *or* **a ~ of** être victime de; **to fall (a) ~ to** devenir la victime de; (*fig: to sb's charms etc*) succomber à.

victimization [ˌvɪktɪmaɪ'zeɪʃən] **n** représailles *fpl* (*subies par un ou plusieurs des responsables*). **the dismissed worker alleged ~** l'ouvrier qu'on avait licencié a prétendu être victime de représailles; **the result was further ~** ceci a mené à d'autres représailles; **there must be no ~**

of strikers on ne doit pas exercer de représailles contre les grévistes.
victimize ['vɪktɪmaɪz] **vt** faire une victime de, prendre pour *or* en victime; (*Ind: after strike*) exercer des représailles sur. **to be ~d** être victime de représailles.
victimless ['vɪktɪmlɪs] **adj: ~ crime** *crime dans lequel toutes les parties sont consentantes.*
victor ['vɪktəʳ] **n** vainqueur *m*. **to emerge the ~ over sb** remporter la victoire sur qn.
Victoria [vɪk'tɔːrɪə] **1 n a** (*name*) Victoria *f*; (*Australian state*) Victoria *m*. **Lake ~** le lac Victoria. **b** (*carriage*) **v~** victoria *f*. **2 comp ▸Victoria Falls** chutes *fpl* de Victoria **▸Victoria Cross** (*abbr* **V.C.**) (*Brit Mil*) Croix *f* de Victoria (*la plus haute décoration militaire*).
Victorian [vɪk'tɔːrɪən] **1 n** Victorien(ne) *m(f)*. **2 adj** victorien. (*Brit*) **~ values** les valeurs *fpl* (rigoristes) de l'époque victorienne.
Victoriana [vɪk,tɔːrɪ'ɑːnə] **n** (*NonC*) objets victoriens, antiquités victoriennes.
victorious [vɪk'tɔːrɪəs] **adj** *army* victorieux, vainqueur (*m only*); *shout* de victoire. **to be ~ (in)** sortir victorieux (de).
victoriously [vɪk'tɔːrɪəslɪ] **adv** victorieusement.
victory ['vɪktərɪ] **n** victoire *f*. **to gain** *or* **win a ~ over** remporter une victoire sur; *see* **winged**.
victual ['vɪtl] **1 vt** approvisionner, ravitailler. **2 vi** s'approvisionner, se ravitailler. **3 npl: ~s** victuailles *fpl*, vivres *mpl*.
victualler ['vɪtləʳ] **n** fournisseur *m* (de provisions); *see* **license**[1].
vid* [vɪd] **n** (**abbr of video**) vidéo *f* (*film*).
vide ['vɪdeɪ] **impers vb** (*frm*) voir, Cf.
videlicet [vɪ'diːlɪset] **adv** (*frm*) c'est-à-dire, à savoir.
video ['vɪdɪəʊ] **1 n a** (*NonC*) vidéo *f*; (*machine*) magnétoscope *m*; (*cassette*) vidéocassette *f*, cassette *f* vidéo; (*film*) vidéo. **I've got it on ~, I've got a ~ of it** je l'ai en vidéo; **get a ~ for tonight** loue une vidéo(cassette) *or* un film en vidéo pour ce soir; **to make a ~ of sth, to record sth on ~** enregistrer qch sur magnétoscope, faire une vidéo de qch.
b (*US: television*) télévision *f*, télé* *f*.
2 comp (*on video*) *film, entertainment* en vidéo; *facilities* vidéo *inv*; (*US: on television*) *film etc* télévisé **▸video art** art *m* vidéo *inv* **▸video camera** caméra *f* vidéo *inv* **▸video cassette** vidéocassette *f*, cassette *f* vidéo **▸video (cassette** *or* **tape) recorder** magnétoscope *m* **▸video (cassette** *or* **tape) recording** enregistrement *m* en vidéo *or* magnétoscopique **▸video clip** clip *m* vidéo *inv* **▸video club** vidéoclub *m* **▸video conference** visioconférence *f*, vidéoconférence *f* **▸video conferencing** (système *m* de) visioconférence *f or* vidéoconférence *f* **▸video disk** vidéodisque *m* **▸video disk player** lecteur *m* de vidéodisque **▸video film** film *m* vidéo *inv* **▸video frequency** vidéo fréquence *f* **▸video game** jeu *m* vidéo *inv* **▸video library** vidéothèque *f* **▸video nasty*** vidéocassette *f* à caractère violent (*or* pornographique) **▸videophone** vidéophone *m*, visiophone *m* **▸video player** magnétoscope *m* **▸video shop** vidéoclub *m* **▸video tape** bande *f* vidéo *inv*; (*cassette*) vidéocassette *f* **▸videotape vt** enregistrer sur magnétoscope **▸videotext** Vidéotex *m* ®.
3 vt (*from TV*) enregistrer (sur magnétoscope); (*with camcorder*) faire une vidéo de, filmer.
Videotex ['vɪdɪəteks] **n** ® Vidéotex *m* ®.
vie [vaɪ] **vi** rivaliser, lutter. **to ~ with sb for sth** lutter avec qn pour (avoir) qch, disputer qch à qn; **to ~ with sb in doing** rivaliser avec qn pour faire; **they ~d with each other in their work** ils travaillaient à qui mieux mieux.
Vienna [vɪ'enə] **1 n** Vienne (*en Autriche*). **2 comp** (*gen*) viennois, de Vienne **▸vienna roll** (*Culin*) pain *m* viennois.
Viennese [,vɪə'niːz] **1 adj** viennois. **2 n, pl inv** Viennois(e) *m(f)*.
Vietcong, Viet Cong [,vjet'kɒŋ] **1 n** (*group*) Viêt-cong *m*; (*individual:* **pl inv**) Viêt-cong. **2 adj** Viêt-cong *inv*.
Viet Nam, Vietnam ['vjet'næm] **n** Viêt-Nam *m*. **North/South ~** Viêt-Nam du Nord/du Sud; **the ~ war** la guerre du Viêt-Nam.
Vietnamese [,vjetnə'miːz] **1 adj** vietnamien. **North/South ~** nord-/sud-vietnamien. **2 n a (pl inv)** Vietnamien(ne) *m(f)*. **North/South ~** Nord-/Sud-Vietnamien(ne) *m(f)*. **b** (*Ling*) vietnamien *m*.
view [vjuː] **1 n a** (*ability to see*) vue *f*. **it blocks the ~** ça bouche la vue, on ne peut pas voir; **he has a good ~ of it from his window** de sa fenêtre, il le voit bien; **the ship came into ~** le navire est apparu; **I came in ~ of the lake** je suis arrivé devant *or* en vue du lac; **the cameraman had a job keeping the plane in ~** le caméraman avait du mal à ne pas perdre l'avion de vue; **if your hands are often in ~** si vos mains sont souvent en évidence, si on voit souvent vos mains; **in full ~ of thousands of people** devant des milliers de gens, sous les yeux de milliers de gens; **in full ~ of the house** devant la maison; **the house is within ~ of the sea** de la maison, on voit la mer; **all the people within ~** tous ceux qu'on pouvait voir (*or* qui pouvaient voir); **when it is exposed to ~** quand c'est visible *or* en évidence; **the pictures are on ~** les tableaux sont exposés; **the house will be on ~ tomorrow** on pourra visiter la maison demain; **hidden from ~** caché aux regards; **it is lost to ~** on ne le voit plus; **to keep sth out of ~** cacher qch (aux regards).
b (*sight, prospect*) vue *f*, panorama *m*. **there is a splendid ~ from here** d'ici la vue *or* le panorama est splendide; **the ~ from the top** la vue *or* le panorama d'en haut; **a trip to see the ~s** une excursion pour admirer les belles vues; **room with a sea ~** *or* **a ~ of the sea** chambre avec vue sur la mer; **a good ~ of the sea** une belle vue de la mer; **a ~ over the town** une vue générale de la ville; **a** *or* **the back/front ~ of the house** la maison vue de derrière/devant; **this is a side ~** c'est une vue latérale; **I got a side ~ of the church** j'ai vu l'église de côté; **it will give you a better ~** vous verrez mieux comme ça.
c (*photo etc*) vue *f*, photo *f*. **50 ~s of Paris** 50 vues *or* photos de Paris; **I want to take a ~ of the palace** je veux photographier le palais.
d (*opinion*) opinion *f*, avis *m*, vues *fpl*. **her ~s on politics/education** ses opinions politiques/sur l'éducation; **an exchange of ~s** un échange de vues *or* d'opinions; **in my ~** à mon avis; **that is my ~** voilà mon opinion *or* mon avis *or* mes vues là-dessus, voilà ce que j'en pense; **my personal ~ is that he ...** à mon avis, il ..., personnellement, je pense qu'il ...; **it's just a personal ~** ce n'est qu'une opinion personnelle; **the Government ~ is that one must ...** selon le gouvernement *or* dans l'optique gouvernementale, on doit ...; **the generally accepted ~ is that he ...** selon l'opinion généralement répandue, il ...; **each person has a different ~ of democracy** chacun comprend la démocratie à sa façon; **one's ~ of old age changes** les idées que l'on se fait de la vieillesse évoluent; **I cannot accept this ~** je trouve cette opinion *or* cette façon de voir les choses inacceptable; **I've changed my ~ on this** j'ai changé d'avis là-dessus; (*in exam question*) **give reasons for your ~s** justifiez votre réponse; **I have no strong ~s on that** je n'ai pas d'opinion bien arrêtée *or* précise là-dessus; **to take** *or* **hold ~s on sth** avoir un avis *or* une opinion *or* des idées sur qch; **to hold** *or* **take the ~ that ...** penser que ..., estimer que ..., considérer que ...; **we don't take that ~** nous avons une opinion différente là-dessus; **I take a similar ~** je partage cet avis; **he takes a gloomy/optimistic ~ of society** il est très pessimiste/optimiste en ce qui concerne la société; **to take a dim** *or* **poor ~ of sth** apprécier qch médiocrement; *see* **point**.
e (*way of looking at sth*) vue *f*. **an idealistic ~ of the world** une vue *or* une vision idéaliste du monde; **a general** *or* **an overall ~ of the problem** une vue d'ensemble *or* générale du problème; **a clear ~ of the facts** une idée claire des faits.
f in ~ of his refusal étant donné son refus, vu son refus; **in ~ of this** ceci étant; **in ~ of the fact that ...** étant donné que ..., vu que ... .
g (*intention*) **with this (aim** *or* **object** *etc*) **in ~** dans ce but, à cette fin; **with the ~ of doing, with a ~ to doing** en vue de faire, dans l'intention de faire, afin de faire; **negotiations with a ~ to a permanent solution** des négociations en vue d'une solution permanente; **what end has he in ~?** quel est son but?, que désire-t-il?; **he has in ~ the purchase of the house** il envisage d'acheter la maison; **I don't teach only with the exams in ~** je ne pense pas uniquement aux examens quand je fais mes cours; **he has the holiday in ~ when he says ...** il pense aux vacances quand il dit ... .
2 comp ▸Viewdata ® (*Phot*) ≃ Minitel ® **▸viewfinder** viseur *m* **▸viewphone** vidéophone *m*, visiophone *m* **▸viewpoint** (*lit, fig*) point *m* de vue.
3 vt a (*look at, see*) voir. **London ~ed from the air** Londres vu d'avion, Londres à vol d'oiseau.
b (*inspect, examine*) examiner, inspecter; *slides, microfiches* visionner; *object for sale* inspecter; *house, castle* visiter.
c (*TV*) regarder. **I recorded it to ~ it later on** je l'ai enregistré pour le regarder plus tard.
d (*think of, understand*) considérer, envisager. **to ~ sb/sth as ...** considérer qn/qch comme ...; **it can be ~ed in many different ways** on peut l'envisager *or* l'examiner sous plusieurs angles; **how do you ~ that?** qu'est-ce que vous en pensez?, quelle est votre opinion là-dessus?; **he ~s it very objectively** il se montre très objectif; **the management ~ed the scheme favourably** la direction a été favorable au projet; **they ~ the future with alarm** ils envisagent l'avenir avec inquiétude.
4 vi (*TV*) regarder la télévision.
viewer ['vjuːəʳ] **n a** (*TV*) téléspectateur *m*, -trice *f*. **b** (*for slides*) visionneuse *f*; (*viewfinder*) viseur *m*.
viewership ['vjuːəʃɪp] **n** (*US TV*) **to score a good** *or* **a wide ~** obtenir un bon indice d'écoute.
viewing ['vjuːɪŋ] **1 n a** (*TV*) **there's no good ~ tonight** il n'y a rien de bon à la télévision ce soir; **your ~ for the weekend** vos programmes du week-end; **golf makes excellent ~** le golf produit un excellent spectacle de télévision. **b** (*in house-buying*) **"early ~ essential"** "à visiter aussi tôt que possible". **c** (*watching*) observation *f*. **2 comp** (*Astron etc*) *conditions* d'observation; (*TV*) *patterns* d'écoute; *habits* des téléspectateurs **▸viewing audience** (*TV*) téléspectateurs *mpl* **▸viewing figures** (*TV*) nombre *m* de téléspectateurs, taux *m* d'écoute **▸viewing gallery** (*in building*) galerie *f* **▸viewing public** (*TV*) téléspectateurs *mpl* **▸viewing time** (*TV*) heure *f* d'écoute.
viggerish* ['vɪgərɪʃ] **n** (*US*) pourcentage *m*, bénéfice *m* (*sur un pari, un prêt*).
vigil ['vɪdʒɪl] **n** (*gen*) veille *f*; (*by sickbed, corpse etc*) veillée *f*; (*Rel*) vigile *f*; (*Pol*) manifestation *f* silencieuse. **to keep ~ over sb** veiller qn; **a long ~** une longue veille, de longues heures sans sommeil; (*Pol*) **to hold a ~** manifester en silence.

vigilance ['vɪdʒɪləns] n vigilance *f*.
vigilant ['vɪdʒɪlənt] adj vigilant, attentif.
vigilante [ˌvɪdʒɪ'læntɪ] n membre *m* d'un groupe d'autodéfense *or* de légitime défense. ~ **group** groupe *m* d'autodéfense *or* de légitime défense.
vigilantly ['vɪdʒɪləntlɪ] adv avec vigilance, attentivement.
vignette [vɪ'njet] n (*in books*) vignette *f*; (*Painting, Phot*) portrait *m* en buste dégradé; (*character sketch*) esquisse *f* de caractère.
vigor ['vɪgəʳ] n (*US*) = **vigour**.
vigorous ['vɪgərəs] adj (*gen*) vigoureux; *government, supporter, measure* vigoureux, énergique; *defence, attempt* énergique.
vigorously ['vɪgərəslɪ] adv *nod, shake hands, nudge* vigoureusement, énergiquement; *fight, protest, defend* énergiquement.
vigour, (*US*) **vigor** ['vɪgəʳ] n (*physical or mental strength*) vigueur *f*, énergie *f*; (*health*) vigueur, vitalité *f*; (*sexual*) vigueur.
Viking ['vaɪkɪŋ] 1 adj *art, customs etc* viking. ~ **ship** drakkar *m*. 2 n Viking *mf*.
vile [vaɪl] adj a (*base, evil*) *motive, action, traitor etc* vil (*f* vile), infâme, ignoble. b (*extremely bad*) *food, drink, taste, play* abominable, exécrable; *smell* abominable, infect; *weather* infect, abominable. **to be in a ~ temper** être d'une humeur massacrante.
vilely ['vaɪllɪ] adv vilement, bassement.
vileness ['vaɪlnɪs] n vilenie *f*, bassesse *f*.
vilification [ˌvɪlɪfɪ'keɪʃən] n diffamation *f*, calomnie *f*.
vilify ['vɪlɪfaɪ] vt calomnier, diffamer.
villa ['vɪlə] n (*in town*) pavillon *m* (*de banlieue*); (*in country*) maison *f* de campagne; (*by sea*) villa *f*.
village ['vɪlɪdʒ] 1 n village *m*, bourgade *f*, patelin* *m*. 2 comp *well* du village ►**village green** pré communal ►**village idiot** idiot *m* du village ►**village school** école *f* de *or* du village.
villager ['vɪlɪdʒəʳ] n villageois(e) *m(f)*.
villain ['vɪlən] n (*scoundrel*) scélérat *m*, vaurien *m*; (*in drama, novel*) traître(sse) *m(f)*; (**: rascal*) coquin(e) *m(f)*; (*Police etc sl: criminal*) bandit *m*. (*fig*) **he's the ~ (of the piece)** c'est lui le coupable.
villainous ['vɪlənəs] adj *act, conduct* ignoble, infâme; (**: bad*) *coffee, weather* abominable, infect. ~ **deed** infamie *f*.
villainously ['vɪlənəslɪ] adv d'une manière ignoble.
villainy ['vɪlənɪ] n infamie *f*, bassesse *f*.
-ville‡ [vɪl] noun and adj ending in comps, *e.g.* **squaresville** les ringards‡; **it's dullsville** on s'ennuie vachement‡.
villein ['vɪlɪn] n (*Hist*) vilain(e) *m(f)*, serf *m*, serve *f*.
villus ['vɪləs] n, pl **villi** ['vɪlaɪ] villosité *f*.
vim* [vɪm] n (*NonC*) énergie *f*, entrain *m*. **full of ~** plein d'entrain.
vinaigrette [ˌvɪneɪ'gret] n (*Culin*) vinaigrette *f*.
Vincent ['vɪnsənt] n Vincent *m*.
vindaloo [ˌvɪndə'luː] n *type de curry très épicé*.
vindicate ['vɪndɪkeɪt] vt a *person* (*prove innocent*) justifier. **this ~d him** (*proved him right*) cela a prouvé qu'il avait eu raison. b *opinion, action* justifier; *rights* faire valoir.
vindication [ˌvɪndɪ'keɪʃən] n justification *f*, défense *f*. **in ~ of** en justification de, pour justifier.
vindictive [vɪn'dɪktɪv] adj vindicatif.
vindictively [vɪn'dɪktɪvlɪ] adv vindicativement.
vindictiveness [vɪn'dɪktɪvnɪs] n caractère vindicatif.
vine [vaɪn] 1 n (*grapevine*) vigne *f*; (*similar plant*) plante *f* grimpante *or* rampante. 2 comp *leaf, cutting* de vigne ►**vine grower** viticulteur *m*, vigneron *m* ►**vinegrowing** viticulture *f*; **vine-growing district** région *f* viticole ►**vine harvest** vendange(s) *f(pl)* ►**vineyard** *see* **vineyard**.
vinegar ['vɪnɪgəʳ] n vinaigre *m*; *see* **cider, oil** *etc*.
vinegary ['vɪnɪgərɪ] adj acide, qui a le goût du vinaigre, qui sent le vinaigre; (*fig*) *remark* acide, acidulé.
vinery ['vaɪnərɪ] n (*hothouse*) serre *f* où l'on cultive la vigne; (*vineyard*) vignoble *m*.
vineyard ['vɪnjəd] n vignoble *m*.
viniculture ['vɪnɪkʌltʃəʳ] n viticulture *f*.
vino* ['viːnəʊ] n pinard‡ *m*, vin *m*.
vinous ['vaɪnəs] adj vineux.
vintage ['vɪntɪdʒ] 1 n (*harvesting*) vendange(s) *f(pl)*, récolte *f*; (*season*) vendanges *fpl*; (*year*) année *f*, millésime *m*. **what ~ is this wine?** ce vin est de quelle année?; **1966 was a good ~** 1966 était une bonne année (*pour le vin*); (*wine*) **the 1972 ~** le vin de 1972.
2 comp ►**vintage car** voiture *f* d'époque (*construite entre 1919 et 1930*) ►**vintage wine** grand vin, vin de grand cru ►**vintage year**: **a vintage year for burgundy** une bonne année pour le bourgogne.
3 adj a (*very old*) très ancien, antique. (*fig hum*) **this typewriter is a ~ model** cette machine à écrire est une antiquité *or* une pièce de musée.
b (*best, most typical*) typique. **it was ~ Churchill** c'était du Churchill des meilleures années.
vintner ['vɪntnəʳ] n négociant *m* en vins.
vinyl ['vaɪnɪl] 1 n vinyle *m*. 2 comp *tiles* de *or* en vinyle; *paint* vinylique.
viol ['vaɪəl] n viole *f*. ~ **player** violiste *mf*.
viola[1] [vɪ'əʊlə] 1 n (*Mus*) alto *m*. 2 comp ►**viola d'amore** viole *f* d'amour ►**viola da gamba** viole *f* de gambe ►**viola player** altiste *mf*.
viola[2] ['vaɪəʊlə] n (*flower*) (*sorte de*) pensée *f*; (*genus*) violacée *f*.
violate ['vaɪəleɪt] vt a (*disobey etc*) *law, rule* contrevenir à, violer, enfreindre; *agreement* violer, enfreindre; *the Commandments* violer, transgresser. b (*show disrespect for*) *principles, honour* bafouer; *human rights, civil rights* violer; *public order, property, frontier* ne pas respecter. c (*disturb*) *peace* troubler, perturber. **to ~ sb's privacy** (*in room etc*) déranger le repos de qn; *[detective, reporter etc]* (*in private life*) déranger qn dans sa vie privée. d (*desecrate*) *place* violer, profaner; *tomb* violer. e (*rape*) violer, violenter.
violation [ˌvaɪə'leɪʃən] n a (*act of violating: see* **violate** a) contravention *f*, violation *f*; infraction *f*. **in ~ of** en contravention de. b (*Jur: esp US: minor offence*) contravention *f*, infraction *f*; (*US: on parking meter*) dépassement *m*. c (*rape*) viol *m*.
violator ['vaɪəleɪtəʳ] n a (*gen*) violateur *m*. b (*Jur: esp US: offender*) contrevenant *m*. **~s will be prosecuted** toute violation fera l'objet de poursuites.
violence ['vaɪələns] n (*gen*) violence *f*. **by ~** par la violence; **a climate of ~** un climat de violence; **we are witnessing an escalation of ~** nous assistons à une escalade de la violence; **~ began** *or* **erupted when ...**, **there was an outbreak of ~ when ...** de violents incidents *mpl or* des bagarres *fpl* ont éclaté quand ...; **racial ~** violence raciste; **all the ~ on the screen today** toute la violence *or* toutes les scènes de violence à l'écran aujourd'hui; **terrorist ~** actes *mpl* de violence terroristes; **police ~** violence de la police; **act of ~** acte de violence; (*Jur*) **crime of ~** voie *f* de fait; (*Jur*) **robbery with ~** vol *m* avec coups et blessures; (*fig*) **to do ~ to sb/sth** faire violence à qn/qch.
violent ['vaɪələnt] adj (*gen*) violent; *attack, blow* violent, brutal; *halt, change* brutal; *temper* violent, coléreux; *colour* criard. **~ clashes with the police** violents affrontements avec la police; **~ scenes** scènes *fpl* de violence; **~ criminal** criminel *m* coupable d'actes de violence; **to be ~ with sb** se montrer violent avec qn, user de violence avec qn; **to die a ~ death** mourir de mort violente; **to have a ~ temper** avoir un tempérament violent; **to be in a ~ temper** être dans une colère noire *or* dans une rage folle; **by ~ means** par la violence; **a ~ dislike (for)** une vive aversion (pour *or* envers).
violently ['vaɪələntlɪ] adv (*gen*) violemment; *struggle, criticize, react* violemment, avec violence; (*severely*) *angry* violemment, terriblement; *ill* terriblement. **she was shivering/trembling ~** elle était secouée de frissons/tremblements violents; **to behave ~** se montrer violent; **to fall ~ in love with** tomber follement amoureux de; **to die ~** mourir de mort violente.
violet ['vaɪəlɪt] 1 n (*Bot*) violette *f*; (*colour*) violet *m*. 2 adj violet.
violin [ˌvaɪə'lɪn] 1 n violon *m*; *see* **first**. 2 comp *sonata, concerto* pour violon ►**violin case** étui *m* à violon ►**violin player** violoniste *mf*.
violinist [ˌvaɪə'lɪnɪst] n violoniste *mf*.
violist [vɪ'əʊlɪst] n (*US*) altiste *mf*.
violoncellist [ˌvaɪələn'tʃelɪst] n violoncelliste *mf*.
violoncello [ˌvaɪələn'tʃeləʊ] n violoncelle *m*.
VIP [viːaɪ'piː] (**abbr of very important person**) 1 n V.I.P. *m inv*, personnage *m* de marque, personnalité *f*. 2 adj *visitors etc* de marque, très important. (*in airport*) **~ lounge** salon *m* d'accueil (réservé aux personnages de marque); **to give sb/get the ~ treatment** traiter qn/être traité comme un personnage de marque.
viper ['vaɪpəʳ] n (*Zool, fig*) vipère *f*.
viperish ['vaɪpərɪʃ] adj de vipère (*fig*).
virago [vɪ'rɑːgəʊ] n, pl **~es** *or* **~s** mégère *f*, virago *f*.
viral ['vaɪərəl] adj viral.
Virgil ['vɜːdʒɪl] n Virgile *m*.
virgin ['vɜːdʒɪn] 1 n (fille *f*) vierge *f*; garçon *m* vierge. **she/he is a ~** elle/il est vierge; (*Astrol, Astron*) **the V~** la Vierge; (*Rel*) **the (Blessed) V~** la (Sainte) Vierge; **the V~ Mary** la Vierge Marie. 2 adj *person* vierge; (*fig*) *forest, land, olive oil, page, wool* vierge; *freshness, sweetness* virginal. **~ snow** neige fraîche; (*Geog*) **the V~ Islands** les îles *fpl* Vierges.
virginal ['vɜːdʒɪnl] 1 adj virginal. 2 n (*Mus*) **~(s)** virginal *m*.
Virginia [və'dʒɪnjə] 1 n Virginie *f*. **in ~** en Virginie. 2 comp ►**virginia creeper** (*Brit*) vigne *f* vierge ►**Virginia tobacco** Virginie *m*, tabac *m* blond.
Virginian [və'dʒɪnjən] 1 n Virginien(ne) *m(f)*. 2 adj de Virginie.
virginity [vɜː'dʒɪnɪtɪ] n virginité *f*. **to lose one's ~** perdre sa virginité.
Virgo ['vɜːgəʊ] n (*Astron*) la Vierge. **I'm (a) ~** je suis (de la) Vierge.
Virgoan [vɜː'gəʊən] n: **to be a ~** être (de la) Vierge;
virgule ['vɜːgjuːl] n (*US Typ*) barre *f* oblique.
virile ['vɪraɪl] adj (*lit, fig*) viril (*f* virile).
virility [vɪ'rɪlɪtɪ] n virilité *f*.
virologist [ˌvaɪə'rɒlədʒɪst] n virologue *mf*.
virology [ˌvaɪə'rɒlədʒɪ] n virologie *f*.
virtual ['vɜːtjʊəl] adj a (*in reality*) **he is the ~ leader** en fait *or* en pratique c'est lui le chef, c'est lui le vrai chef; (*almost*) **a ~ monopoly/impossibility** un quasi-monopole/une quasi-impossibilité; **it's a ~ revolution** il s'agit presque *or* pratiquement d'une révolution; **it came to a ~ standstill** cela s'est presque complètement arrêté; **it was a ~**

failure ça a été pratiquement *or* virtuellement un échec; **this memo is a ~ insult** cette note équivaut pratiquement *or* quasiment à une insulte.
b (*Comput, Phys*) *memory, image* virtuel. **~ reality** réalité *f* virtuelle.

virtually ['vɜːtjʊəlɪ] adv (*in reality*) en fait, en pratique; (*almost*) pratiquement, quasiment. **he is ~ the leader** en fait *or* en pratique c'est lui le chef, c'est lui le vrai chef; **it's ~ the same thing** c'est pratiquement *or* quasiment la même chose, cela revient au même; **to be ~ certain** être pratiquement sûr; **he ~ confessed** il a pratiquement avoué; **it is ~ impossible to do that** il est pratiquement *or* quasiment *or* virtuellement impossible de faire cela; **~ nothing happened** il ne s'est pratiquement rien passé; **he started with ~ nothing** il est parti de presque rien.

virtue ['vɜːtjuː] n a (*good quality*) vertu *f*. **to make a ~ of necessity** faire de nécessité vertu.
b (*NonC: chastity*) vertu *f*, chasteté *f*. **a woman of easy ~** une femme de petite vertu.
c (*advantage*) mérite *m*, avantage *m*. **this set has the ~ of being portable** ce poste a l'avantage d'être portatif; **it has the ~ of clarity** ça a l'avantage d'être clair *or* de la clarté; **he has the ~ of being easy to understand** il a le mérite d'être facile à comprendre; **there is no ~ in doing that if it is unnecessary** il n'y a aucun mérite à faire cela si ce n'est pas nécessaire; **this method has no ~s over the others** cette méthode n'a pas d'avantages particuliers par rapport aux autres.
d (*NonC: power*) pouvoir *m*, efficacité *f*. **healing ~** pouvoir thérapeutique.
e **in** *or* **by ~ of** en vertu de, en raison de; **by ~ of the fact that ...** en vertu *or* en raison du fait que ...; **by ~ of being British, he ...** en vertu *or* en raison du fait qu'il était britannique, il ... .

virtuosity [,vɜːtjʊ'ɒsɪtɪ] n virtuosité *f*.

virtuoso [,vɜːtjʊ'əʊzəʊ] 1 n, pl **~s** *or* **virtuosi** [,vɜːtjʊ'əʊzɪ] (*esp Mus*) virtuose *mf*. **a violin ~** un(e) virtuose du violon. 2 adj *performance* de virtuose. **a ~ violinist** un(e) virtuose du violon.

virtuous ['vɜːtjʊəs] adj vertueux.

virtuously ['vɜːtjʊəslɪ] adv vertueusement.

virulence ['vɪrʊləns] n virulence *f*.

virulent ['vɪrʊlənt] adj virulent.

virulently ['vɪrʊləntlɪ] adv avec virulence.

virus ['vaɪərəs] n, pl **~es** virus *m* (*also fig, Comput*). **rabies ~** virus de la rage *or* rabique; **~ disease** maladie virale *or* à virus.

visa ['viːzə] 1 n, pl **~s** a (*in passport*) visa *m* (*de passeport*). **entrance/exit ~** visa d'entrée/de sortie; **to get an Egyptian ~** obtenir un visa pour l'Égypte. b (*credit card*) **V~ (card)** ® carte *f* Visa ®, ≃ Carte Bleue ®. 2 vt viser.

visage ['vɪzɪdʒ] n (*liter*) visage *m*, figure *f*.

vis-à-vis ['viːzəviː] 1 prep (+ *person*) vis à vis de; (+ *thing*) par rapport à, devant. **~ the West** vis à vis de l'Occident. 2 n (*person placed opposite*) vis-à-vis *m*; (*person of similar status*) homologue *mf*.

viscera ['vɪsərə] npl viscères *mpl*.

visceral ['vɪsərəl] adj viscéral.

viscid ['vɪsɪd] adj visqueux (*lit*).

viscose ['vɪskəʊs] 1 n viscose *f*. 2 adj visqueux (*lit*).

viscosity [vɪs'kɒsɪtɪ] n viscosité *f*.

viscount ['vaɪkaʊnt] n vicomte *m*.

viscountcy ['vaɪkaʊntsɪ] n vicomté *f*.

viscountess ['vaɪkaʊntɪs] n vicomtesse *f*.

viscounty ['vaɪkaʊntɪ] n = **viscountcy**.

viscous ['vɪskəs] adj visqueux, gluant.

vise [vaɪs] (*US*) = **vice**².

visé ['viːzeɪ] (*US*) = **visa a**.

visibility [,vɪzɪ'bɪlɪtɪ] n visibilité *f*. (*Met*) **good/poor** *or* **low ~** bonne/mauvaise visibilité; **~ is down to** *or* **is only 20 metres** la visibilité ne dépasse pas 20 mètres.

visible ['vɪzəbl] adj a (*able to be seen*) visible. **~ to the naked eye** visible à l'œil nu; **it was not ~ to a passer-by** un passant ne pouvait pas l'apercevoir; **to become ~** apparaître; (*Econ*) **~ exports** exportations *fpl* visibles. b (*obvious*) visible, manifeste. **there was a ~ mark on the carpet** il y avait une marque bien visible sur le tapis; **with ~ impatience** avec une impatience visible *or* manifeste; **there is no ~ reason/difference** *etc* on ne voit pas très bien la raison/la différence *etc*; **it serves no ~ purpose** on n'en voit pas vraiment l'utilité; (*Jur*) **with no ~ means of support** sans ressources apparentes.

visibly ['vɪzəblɪ] adv (*lit*) visiblement; (*fig*) manifestement, visiblement.

Visigoth ['vɪzɪgɒθ] n Wisigoth *mf*.

vision ['vɪʒən] 1 n a (*NonC*) vision *f*, vue *f*; (*fig: foresight*) vision, prévoyance *f*. **his ~ is very bad** sa vue est très mauvaise; **within/outside range of ~** à portée de/hors de vue; (*fig*) **a man of great ~** un homme qui voit loin; **his ~ of the future** la façon dont il voit (*or* voyait) l'avenir; *see* **field**.
b (*in dream, trance*) vision *f*, apparition *f*. **it came to me in a ~** j'en ai eu une vision; **to have** *or* **see ~s** avoir des visions; **to have ~s of wealth** avoir des visions de richesses; **she had ~s of being drowned** elle s'est vue noyée.
2 comp ►**vision mixer** (*Cine, TV*) (*machine*) mixeur *m* (d'images); (*person*) **"vision-mixer: Alexander Anderson"** "mixage d'images par Alexander Anderson" ►**vision-mixing** (*Cine, TV*) mixage *m* d'images.
3 vt (*US*) envisager.

visionary ['vɪʒənərɪ] adj, n visionnaire (*mf*).

visit ['vɪzɪt] 1 n (*call, tour*) visite *f*; (*stay*) séjour *m*. **to pay a ~ to** *person* rendre visite à; *place* aller à; (*fig*) **to pay a ~*** aller au petit coin*; **to be on a ~ to** *person* être en visite chez; *place* faire un séjour à; **he went on a two-day ~ to Paris** il est allé passer deux jours à Paris; **I'm going on a ~ to Glasgow next week** j'irai à Glasgow la semaine prochaine; **on a private/an official ~** en visite privée/officielle; **his ~ to Paris lasted 3 days** son séjour à Paris a duré 3 jours.
2 vt a (*go and see*) *person* aller voir, (*more formally*) rendre visite à; *sick person* aller voir, (*more formally*) visiter; *town* aller à, faire un petit tour à; *museum, zoo* aller à, visiter; *theatre* aller à.
b (*go and stay with*) *person* faire un séjour chez; (*go and stay in*) *town, country* faire un séjour à (*or* en).
c (*formally inspect*) *place* inspecter, faire une visite d'inspection à; *troops* passer en revue. (*Jur*) **to ~ the scene of the crime** se rendre sur les lieux du crime.
d (†: *afflict; inflict*) *person* punir (*with* de). **to ~ the sins of the fathers upon the children** punir les enfants pour les péchés de leurs pères.
3 vi a **I'm just ~ing** je ne suis que de passage.
b (*US: chat*) bavarder.

►**visit with** vt fus (*US*) *person* passer voir.

visitation [,vɪzɪ'teɪʃən] n a (*by official*) visite *f* d'inspection; [*bishop*] visite pastorale; (*pej hum: prolonged visit*) visite trop prolongée. (*Rel*) **the V~ of the Blessed Virgin Mary** la Visitation de la Vierge. b (*calamity*) punition *f* du ciel.

visiting ['vɪzɪtɪŋ] 1 n: **I find ~ a nuisance** cela m'ennuie de faire des visites. 2 comp *friends* de passage; *lecturer etc* invité, de l'extérieur ►**visiting card** (*Brit*) carte *f* de visite ►**visiting fireman*** (*US fig: iro*) visiteur *m* de marque ►**visiting hours** heures *fpl* de visite ►**visiting nurse** (*US*) infirmière *f* à domicile ►**visiting professor** (*Univ*) professeur associé ►**visiting teacher** (*US*) ≃ visiteuse *f* scolaire ►**visiting team** (*Sport*) visiteurs *mpl* ►**visiting terms: I know him but I'm not on visiting terms with him** je le connais, mais nous ne nous rendons pas visite ►**visiting time** = **visiting hours**.

visitor ['vɪzɪtəʳ] n a (*guest*) invité(e) *m(f)*. **to have a ~** recevoir *or* avoir une visite; **to have ~s** avoir des visites *or* de la visite; **we've had a lot of ~s** nous avons eu beaucoup de visites; **have your ~s left?** est-ce que tes invités sont partis?; (*fig iro*) **we seem to have had a ~ during the night** quelqu'un a voulu nous rendre visite cette nuit; **~s' book** livre *m* d'or; (*in hotel*) registre *m*.
b (*client*) (*in hotel*) client(e) *m(f)*; (*at exhibition*) visiteur *m*; (*tourist*) voyageur *m*, -euse *f*, visiteur. **~s to London** visiteurs de passage à Londres; **~s to the castle** les personnes visitant le château; **~ centre** hall *m* *or* centre *m* d'accueil (*sur un site historique avec exposition, diaporama, cafétéria etc*); (*Parl etc*) **~s' gallery** tribune *f* du public; **~'s tax** taxe *f* de séjour; *see* **health, passport, prison**.

visor ['vaɪzəʳ] n visière *f*; *see* **sun**.

vista ['vɪstə] n (*view*) vue *f*; (*survey*) (*of past*) vue, image *f*; (*of future*) perspective *f*, horizon *m*. (*fig*) **to open up new ~s** ouvrir de nouveaux horizons *or* de nouvelles perspectives.

visual ['vɪzjʊəl] 1 adj *field, memory* visuel; *landing etc* à vue; *nerve* optique. **~ aid** support visuel; **to teach with ~ aids** enseigner par des méthodes visuelles *or* avec des supports visuels; **~ artist** créateur *m*, -trice *f* d'œuvre plastique; **~ arts** arts *mpl* plastiques; (*Comput*) **~ display unit** console *f* de visualisation, visuel *m*; **within ~ range** à portée de vue. 2 npl: **~s** (*display material*) support(s) *m(pl)* visuel(s); [*video game, film etc*] images *fpl*.

visualization [,vɪzjʊəlaɪ'zeɪʃən] n visualisation *f*.

visualize ['vɪzjʊəlaɪz] vt a (*recall*) *person, sb's face* se représenter, évoquer. b (*imagine*) *sth unknown* s'imaginer; *sth familiar* se représenter. **try to ~ a million pounds** essayez de vous imaginer un million de livres; **I ~d him working at his desk** je me le suis représenté travaillant à son bureau. c (*foresee*) envisager, prévoir. **we do not ~ many changes** nous n'envisageons pas beaucoup de changements.

visually ['vɪzjʊəlɪ] adv visuellement. (*Admin*) **~ handicapped** mal voyant; **the ~ handicapped** les mal-voyants *mpl*.

vital ['vaɪtl] 1 adj a (*of life*) vital. **~ force** force vitale; **~ parts** organes vitaux; **~ spark** étincelle *f* de vie; **~ statistics** [*population*] statistiques *fpl* démographiques; (*: *woman's*) mensurations *fpl*. b (*essential*) *supplies, resources* vital, essentiel, indispensable; (*very important*) *problem, matter, question* vital, fondamental. **of ~ importance** d'une importance capitale; **your support is ~ to us** votre soutien nous est indispensable; **it is ~ that ...** il est indispensable *or* vital que ... + *subj*. c (*fatal*) *wound* mortel; *error* fatal. d (*lively*) énergique, plein d'entrain. 2 n: **the ~s** (*Anat*) les organes vitaux; (*fig*) les parties essentielles.

vitality [vaɪ'tælɪtɪ] n (*lit, fig*) vitalité *f*.

vitalize ['vaɪtəlaɪz] vt (*lit*) vivifier; (*fig*) mettre de la vie dans, animer.

vitally ['vaɪtəlɪ] adv *necessary* absolument; *urgent* extrêmement. **it is ~**

needed c'est vital, on en a un besoin vital; **this problem is ~ important** ce problème est d'une importance capitale; **it is ~ important that we arrive on time** il est absolument indispensable *or* il faut absolument que nous arrivions (*subj*) à l'heure.

vitamin [ˈvɪtəmɪn] 1 n vitamine *f*. ~ **A/B** *etc* vitamine A/B *etc*; **with added ~s** vitaminé. 2 comp *content* en vitamines; *tablets* de vitamines ▸**vitamin deficiency** carence *f* en vitamines; **vitamin deficiency disease** avitaminose *f* ▸**vitamin-enriched** vitaminé ▸**vitamin pill** comprimé *m* de vitamines ▸**vitamin-rich** riche en vitamines ▸**vitamin tablet** = **vitamin pill**.

vitaminize [ˈvɪtəmɪnaɪz] vt incorporer des vitamines dans. **~d food** nourriture vitaminée.

vitiate [ˈvɪʃɪeɪt] vt (*all senses*) vicier.

viticulture [ˈvɪtɪkʌltʃəʳ] n viticulture *f*.

vitreous [ˈvɪtrɪəs] adj a *china, rock, electricity* vitreux; *enamel* vitrifié. b (*Anat*) vitré. ~ **humour** humeur vitrée.

vitrifaction [ˌvɪtrɪˈfækʃən] n, **vitrification** [ˌvɪtrɪfɪˈkeɪʃən] n vitrification *f*.

vitrify [ˈvɪtrɪfaɪ] 1 vt vitrifier. 2 vi se vitrifier.

vitriol [ˈvɪtrɪəl] n (*Chem, fig*) vitriol *m*.

vitriolic [ˌvɪtrɪˈɒlɪk] adj (*Chem*) de vitriol; (*fig*) venimeux, mordant.

vitriolize [ˈvɪtrɪəlaɪz] vt vitrioler.

vitro [ˈvɪtrəʊ] *see* **in vitro**.

vituperate [vɪˈtjuːpəreɪt] 1 vt injurier, vitupérer contre. 2 vi vitupérer.

vituperation [vɪˌtjuːpəˈreɪʃən] n vitupérations *fpl*.

vituperative [vɪˈtjuːpərətɪv] adj injurieux.

Vitus [ˈvaɪtəs] n *see* **saint**.

viva[1] [ˈviːvə] 1 excl vive! 2 n vivat *m*.

viva[2] [ˈvaɪvə] n (*Brit Univ*) épreuve *f* orale, oral *m*.

vivacious [vɪˈveɪʃəs] adj vif, enjoué, qui a de la vivacité, animé; (*Bot*) vivace.

vivaciously [vɪˈveɪʃəslɪ] adv avec vivacité, avec verve.

vivacity [vɪˈvæsɪtɪ] n vivacité *f*; (*in words*) verve *f*.

vivarium [vɪˈvɛərɪəm] n, pl ~s *or* **vivaria** [vɪˈvɛərɪə] vivarium *m*; (*for fish, shellfish*) vivier *m*.

viva voce [ˈvaɪvəˈvəʊsɪ] 1 adj oral, verbal. 2 adv de vive voix, oralement. 3 n (*Brit Univ*) épreuve orale, oral *m*.

vivid [ˈvɪvɪd] adj a (*bright*) *colour, light* vif (*f* vive), éclatant; *tie etc* voyant. **a ~ blue dress** une robe d'un bleu éclatant. b (*lively*) *memory* net, vif (*f* vive), précis; *imagination* vif; *dream* impressionnant; *description* vivant, frappant; *example, comparison* frappant; *language* vivant, coloré; *lesson* vivant.

vividly [ˈvɪvɪdlɪ] adv a *coloured* de façon éclatante; *shine* avec éclat. b *describe, recount* de façon frappante *or* vivante; *express* de façon vivante *or* colorée. **he remembered/pictured it ~** il le revoyait/l'imaginait comme s'il y était.

vividness [ˈvɪvɪdnɪs] n *[colour]* vivacité *f*, éclat *m*; *[light]* éclat, clarté *f*; *[style]* clarté, vigueur *f*.

vivify [ˈvɪvɪfaɪ] vt vivifier, ranimer.

viviparous [vɪˈvɪpərəs] adj vivipare.

vivisect [ˌvɪvɪˈsekt] vt pratiquer la vivisection sur.

vivisection [ˌvɪvɪˈsekʃən] n vivisection *f*.

vivisectionist [ˌvɪvɪˈsekʃənɪst] n, **vivisector** [ˈvɪvɪsektəʳ] n (*scientist*) vivisecteur *m*; (*supporter*) partisan(e) *m(f)* de la vivisection.

vixen [ˈvɪksn] n (*Zool*) renarde *f*; (*woman*) mégère *f*.

viz [vɪz] adv (**abbr of vide licet** = **namely**) c.-à-d., c'est-à-dire.

vizier [vɪˈzɪəʳ] n vizir *m*.

VLF [viːelˈef] n (**abbr of very low frequency**) *see* **very**.

vocab* [ˈvəʊkæb] (**abbr of vocabulary**) voca* *m*.

vocable [ˈvəʊkəbl] n vocable *m*.

vocabulary [vəʊˈkæbjʊlərɪ] n (*gen*) vocabulaire *m*; (*in textbook*) (*bilingual*) lexique *m*, vocabulaire; (*technical*) lexique, glossaire *m*.

vocal [ˈvəʊkəl] 1 adj a (*Anat*) vocal. ~ **c(h)ords** cordes vocales. b *communication* oral, verbal. ~ **music** musique vocale; (*Mus*) ~ **score** partition chorale. c (*voicing one's opinions*) *group, person* qui se fait entendre; (*noisy*) bruyant. **Women's Lib are getting very ~** le M.L.F. commence à faire du bruit *or* à se faire entendre. 2 n (*Mus*) **~(s)** chant *m*. **lead ~s** chanteur (-euse) *m(f)*; **backing ~s** chœurs *mpl*.

vocalic [vəʊˈkælɪk] adj vocalique.

vocalisation [ˌvəʊkəlaɪˈzeɪʃən] n vocalisation *f*.

vocalist [ˈvəʊkəlɪst] n chanteur *m*, -euse *f* (*dans un groupe*).

vocalize [ˈvəʊkəlaɪz] 1 vt *one's opinions* exprimer; *consonant* vocaliser; *language* écrire en marquant des points-voyelles. 2 vi (*Ling*) se vocaliser; (*Mus*) vocaliser, faire des vocalises.

vocally [ˈvəʊkəlɪ] adv vocalement, oralement.

vocation [vəʊˈkeɪʃən] n (*Rel etc*) vocation *f*. **to have a ~ for teaching** avoir la vocation de l'enseignement.

vocational [vəʊˈkeɪʃənl] adj professionnel. (*Scol etc*) ~ **course** (*period*) stage *m* de formation professionnelle; (*subject*) matière *f* ayant une utilité dans la vie professionnelle; ~ **guidance** orientation professionnelle; ~ **training** formation professionnelle.

vocative [ˈvɒkətɪv] 1 n vocatif *m*. **in the ~** au vocatif. 2 adj (*gen*) vocatif. ~ **ending** flexion *f* du vocatif; ~ **case** vocatif *m*.

vociferate [vəʊˈsɪfəreɪt] vi vociférer, brailler*.

vociferation [vəʊˌsɪfəˈreɪʃən] n vocifération *f*.

vociferous [vəʊˈsɪfərəs] adj bruyant.

vociferously [vəʊˈsɪfərəslɪ] adv bruyamment, en vociférant.

vodka [ˈvɒdkə] n vodka *f*.

vogue [vəʊg] 1 n a (*fashion*) mode *f*, vogue *f*. **wigs were the ~** *or* **in ~ then** les perruques étaient alors à la mode *or* en vogue; **to be all the ~** faire fureur; **to come into ~** devenir à la mode; **to go out of ~** passer de mode; **the current ~ for mini-skirts** la vogue que connaissent actuellement les mini-jupes. b (*popularity*) vogue *f*, popularité *f*. **to have a great ~** être très en vogue. 2 adj attrib à la mode, en vogue.

voice [vɔɪs] 1 n a (*gen*) voix *f*; (*pitch, quality*) voix, ton *m*. **in a deep ~** d'une voix grave; **at the top of one's ~** à tue-tête; **to raise/lower one's ~** élever/baisser la voix; **keep your ~ down** ne parle pas trop fort; (*fig*) **he likes the sound of his own ~** il aime s'écouter parler; **his ~ has broken** il a mué, sa voix a mué; **a ~ could be heard at the back of the room** on entendait une voix au fond de la salle; **three ~s were raised in protest about the heating** trois personnes se sont plaintes du chauffage; **to have a ~ in the matter** avoir voix au chapitre; **they acclaimed him with one ~** ils ont été unanimes à l'acclamer; **to give ~ to** exprimer; (*liter*) **to listen to the ~ of a friend** écouter les conseils *or* la voix d'un ami; **the ~ of reason** la voix de la raison; **the ~ of God** la voix de Dieu; *see* **find, lose, loud** *etc*.

b (*Mus*) voix *f*. **tenor/bass ~** voix de ténor/de basse; **a piece for ~ and piano** un morceau pour voix et piano; **to be in good ~** être en voix; **he has a lovely ~** il a une belle voix.

c (*Gram*) voix *f*. **active/passive ~** voix active/passive; **in the active/passive ~** à l'actif/au passif.

d (*Phon*) voix *f*.

2 comp ▸**voice-activated** à commande vocale ▸**voice box** (*Anat*) larynx *m* ▸**voice-over** (*TV*) commentaire *m* (voix hors champ) ▸**voice parts** (*Mus*) parties vocales ▸**voiceprint** empreinte *f* vocale ▸**voice production** diction *f*, élocution *f* ▸**voice range** étendue *f* de la voix ▸**voice recognition** reconnaissance *f* vocale ▸**voice synthesis** synthèse *f* vocale ▸**voice training** *[actor etc]* cours *mpl* de diction *or* d'élocution; *[singer]* cours de chant ▸**voice vote** (*US Pol etc*) vote *m* par acclamation.

3 vt a (*express*) *feelings, opinion* exprimer, formuler.

b (*Ling*) *consonant* voiser, sonoriser. **~d consonant** consonne sonore *or* voisée.

c (*Mus*) accorder.

-voiced [vɔɪst] adj ending in comps: **low-/warm-voiced** à voix basse/chaude.

voiceless [ˈvɔɪslɪs] adj a (*lit: Med etc*) aphone; (*fig*) *minority etc* qui ne peut s'exprimer, sans voix. b (*Phon*) *consonant* sourd, non-voisé.

voicing [ˈvɔɪsɪŋ] n (*Phon*) sonorisation *f*, voisement *m*.

void [vɔɪd] 1 n (*lit, fig*) vide *m*. (*fig*) **an aching ~** un grand vide; **to fill the ~** combler le vide. 2 adj a (*frm: vacant*) *space* vide; *job* vacant. ~ **of** dépourvu de. b (*Jur*) nul. **to make ~** rendre nul; *see* **null**. c (*Cards*) **to be ~ in** avoir chicane à. 3 vt a (*remove*) évacuer (*from* de). b (*excrete*) évacuer; (*vomit*) vomir. c (*Jur*) annuler, rendre nul.

voile [vɔɪl] n voile *m* (*Tex*).

Voivodina, Vojvodina [ˌvɔɪvəˈdiːnə] n Vojvodine *f*, Vojvodina *f*.

vol. abbr of **volume**.

volatile [ˈvɒlətaɪl] adj (*Chem*) volatil (*f* volatile); (*fig*) *political situation* explosif; (*changeable*) *person* versatile; (*lively*) pétillant de vie; (*transient*) fugace.

volatility [ˌvɒləˈtɪlɪtɪ] n (*Chem*) volatilité *f*; (*fickleness*) inconstance *f*, versatilité *f*; (*liveliness*) entrain *m*.

volatilize [vɒˈlætəlaɪz] 1 vt volatiliser. 2 vi se volatiliser, s'évaporer.

vol-au-vent [ˈvɒləʊˌvɑ̃ː,ˈvɒləˌvɒn] n vol-au-vent *m*. **chicken/mushroom ~** vol-au-vent au poulet/aux champignons.

volcanic [vɒlˈkænɪk] adj (*lit, fig*) volcanique.

volcano [vɒlˈkeɪnəʊ] n, pl ~**es** *or* ~**s** volcan *m*.

vole[1] [vəʊl] n (*Zool*) campagnol *m*; *see* **water**.

vole[2] [vəʊl] (*Cards*) 1 n vole *f*. 2 vi faire la vole.

Volga [ˈvɒlgə] n Volga *f*.

volition [vɒˈlɪʃən] n volition *f*, volonté *f*. **of one's own ~** de son propre gré.

volley [ˈvɒlɪ] 1 n a (*Mil*) volée *f*, salve *f*; *[stones]* grêle *f*; (*fig*) *[insults]* bordée *f*, torrent *m*; *[questions]* feu *m* roulant; *[applause]* salve. **to fire a ~** tirer une salve. b (*Sport*) volée *f*. **half ~** demi-volée *f*. 2 comp ▸**volleyball** volley(-ball) *m*; **volleyball player** volleyeur *m*, -euse *f*. 3 vt a (*Mil*) tirer une volée de; (*fig*) *insults* lâcher un torrent *or* une bordée de. b (*Sport*) *ball* reprendre de volée, attraper à la volée. 4 vi a (*Mil*) tirer par salves. b (*Sport*) renvoyer une volée.

volleyer [ˈvɒlɪəʳ] n (*Tennis*) volleyeur *m*, -euse *f*.

volt [vəʊlt] 1 n volt *m*. 2 comp ▸**volt meter** voltmètre *m*.

voltage [ˈvəʊltɪdʒ] n voltage *m*, tension *f*. **high/low ~** haute/basse tension.

voltaic [vɒlˈteɪɪk] adj voltaïque.

volte-face [ˈvɒltˈfɑːs] n, pl inv volte-face *f inv*. (*lit, fig*) **to make a ~** faire volte-face.

volubility [ˌvɒljʊˈbɪlɪtɪ] n volubilité *f*, loquacité *f*.

voluble ['vɒljʊbl] adj volubile, loquace.

volubly ['vɒljʊblɪ] adv avec volubilité, avec faconde.

volume ['vɒlju:m] 1 n a (*book*) volume *m*; (*one in a set*) volume, tome *m*. ~ **one/two** tome premier/second; ~ **three/four** *etc* tome trois/quatre *etc*; **in 6 ~s** en 6 volumes; **a 2-~ dictionary** un dictionnaire en 2 volumes; (*fig*) **to write ~s** écrire des volumes; (*fig*) **to speak** *or* **say ~s** en dire long (*about* sur).
b (*size: gen, also Phys*) volume *m*. **the gas expanded to twice its original ~** le gaz s'est dilaté et a doublé de volume; **production ~** volume de la production; **the ~ of imports/exports** le volume des importations/exportations; **the ~ of protest has increased since ...** les protestations ont pris de l'ampleur depuis ... .
c (*space inside: of tank, container*) capacité *f*. (*fig: large amount*) **~s of** (*gen*) beaucoup de; **~s of smoke** nuages *mpl* de fumée; **~s of tears** flots *mpl* de larmes.
d (*sound*) volume *m*, puissance *f*. (*Rad, TV*) **to turn the ~ up/down** augmenter/diminuer le volume.
2 comp ▸**volume control** (*Rad, TV*) bouton *m* de réglage du volume.

volumetric [ˌvɒljʊ'metrɪk] adj volumétrique.

voluminous [və'lu:mɪnəs] adj volumineux.

voluntarily ['vɒləntərɪlɪ] adv (*willingly*) volontairement, de mon (*or* son *etc*) plein gré; (*without payment*) bénévolement.

voluntary ['vɒləntərɪ] 1 adj a (*not obligatory*) *confession, statement* volontaire, spontané; *contribution, movement* volontaire; *pension scheme etc* facultatif. ~ **euthanasia** euthanasie *f* volontaire.
b (*unpaid*) *service* bénévole. (*Soc*) ~ **agency**, (*Admin*) ~ **body** organisation *f* bénévole; ~ **help** (*person*) bénévole *mf*; (*assistance*) aide *f* bénévole, bénévolat *m*; (*US Med*) ~ **hospital** hôpital *m* de l'assistance publique; (*Comm, Fin*) ~ **liquidation** dépôt *m* de bilan; **to go into ~ liquidation** déposer son bilan; (*US Jur*) ~ **manslaughter** homicide *m* volontaire; (*Soc*) ~ **organization** organisation bénévole; (*Brit*) ~ **school** école *f* libre; (*Brit*) **V~ Service Overseas** ≈ coopération *f* technique à l'étranger; ~ **work** travai *m* bénévole, bénévolat *m*; **she does ~ work in a hospital** elle travaille bénévolement *or* comme bénévole dans un hôpital; ~ **worker** bénévole *mf*.
2 n (*Mus, Rel*) morceau *m* d'orgue.

volunteer [ˌvɒlən'tɪər] 1 n (*gen, Mil*) volontaire *mf*; (*voluntary helper*) bénévole *mf*.
2 adj a (*having offered to do sth*) *group* de volontaires; *driver, ticket-seller* qui se porte (*or* s'est porté *etc*) volontaire.
b (*unpaid*) *helper etc* bénévole. (*US*) **the V~ State** le Tennessee.
3 vt donner *or* offrir de son plein gré. **they ~ed 5 pounds a week to the fund** ils ont offert de contribuer 5 livres par semaine au fonds; **they ~ed to carry it all back** ils ont offert de tout remporter; **to ~ information** fournir (spontanément) un renseignement; **"there were 7 of them" he ~ed** "ils étaient 7" dit-il spontanément.
4 vi (*Mil*) s'engager comme volontaire (*for* dans). (*gen*) **to ~ for sth** s'offrir *or* se proposer pour (faire) qch.

voluptuous [və'lʌptjʊəs] adj voluptueux, sensuel.

voluptuously [və'lʌptjʊəslɪ] adv voluptueusement.

voluptuousness [və'lʌptjʊəsnɪs] n volupté *f*, sensualité *f*.

volute [və'lu:t] n (*Archit*) volute *f*.

voluted [və'lu:tɪd] adj (*Archit*) en volute.

vomit ['vɒmɪt] 1 n vomissement *m*, vomi *m*. 2 vt (*lit, fig*) vomir. **to ~ out** *or* **up** *or* (*liter*) **forth** vomir. 3 vi vomir.

vomiting ['vɒmɪtɪŋ] n vomissements *mpl*.

voodoo ['vu:du:] 1 adj vaudou *inv*. 2 n vaudou *m*. 3 vt envoûter.

voracious [və'reɪʃəs] adj *appetite, person* vorace; *reader* avide.

voraciously [və'reɪʃəslɪ] adv *eat* voracement, avec voracité; *read* avidement, avec voracité.

voracity [vɒ'ræsɪtɪ] n (*lit, fig*) voracité *f*.

vortex ['vɔ:teks] n, pl **vortices** ['vɔ:tɪsi:z] *or* **~es** (*lit*) vortex *m*, tourbillon *m*; (*fig*) tourbillon.

votary ['vəʊtərɪ] n (*liter*) fervent(e) *m(f)* (*of* de).

vote [vəʊt] 1 n a (*gen, also Pol*) vote *m*; (*expression of opinion*) vote, suffrage *m*; (*franchise*) droit *m* de vote *or* de suffrage. **to give the ~ to the under twenty-ones** accorder le droit de vote aux moins de vingt et un ans; **one man, one ~** ≈ suffrage *m* universel, une seule voix par électeur; **~s for women!** droit de vote pour les femmes!; **to put to the ~** mettre au vote *or* aux voix; **the matter was settled by ~** on a réglé la question en la mettant au vote *or* aux voix; **to take a ~** (*gen*) voter (*on* sur); (*Admin, Pol*) procéder au vote (*on* sur); **after the ~** après le scrutin; ~ **of censure** *or* **no confidence** motion *f* de censure; **to pass a ~ of censure** voter la censure; ~ **of confidence** vote de confiance; **to ask for a ~ of confidence** poser la question de confiance; **to pass a ~ of confidence (in)** passer un vote de confiance (à l'égard de); **(to pass a) ~ of thanks** (faire un) discours *m* de remerciement.
b (*vote cast*) voix *f*, vote *m*. **to give one's ~ to** donner sa voix à, voter pour; **to win ~s** gagner des voix; **to count the ~s** compter les voix *or* les votes; (*Pol*) dépouiller le scrutin; **he has my ~** je voterai pour lui; ~ **for/against sth** voix pour/contre qch; **elected by a majority ~** élu au vote majoritaire; **they won by a two-thirds ~** ils ont remporté les deux tiers des voix; **he'll win/lose the Massachusetts ~** il va remporter/perdre le Massachusetts; (*Pol*) **the Labour ~** les voix travaillistes; *see* **casting, floating** *etc*.
c (*money allotted*) crédits votés.
2 comp ▸**vote-catching** adj (*pej*) électoraliste ▸**vote winner*** argument *m* électoral décisif.
3 vt a (*approve*) *bill, treaty* voter. **the committee ~d to request a subsidy** le comité a voté une demande d'une subvention.
b (*cast ~ for*) voter. **to ~ Socialist** voter socialiste; ~ **Smith at the next election!** votez Smith aux prochaines élections!
c (*elect*) élire. **he was ~d chairman** il a été élu président; (*fig*) **the group ~d her the best cook** le groupe l'a proclamée la meilleure cuisinière; **I ~ we go to the pictures** je propose que l'on aille au cinéma.
4 vi voter (*for* pour, *against* contre), donner sa voix (*for sb* à qn, *for sth* pour qch); (*in general election etc*) aller aux urnes, voter. **the country ~s in 3 weeks** les élections ont lieu dans 3 semaines; **to ~ for the Socialists** voter pour les socialistes; ~ **for Smith!** votez Smith!; **to ~ on sth** mettre qch au vote; (*fig*) **to ~ with one's feet** partir en signe de mécontentement, montrer son désaccord en partant.
▸**vote down** vt sep rejeter (*par le vote*).
▸**vote in** vt sep *law* adopter, voter; *person* élire.
▸**vote out** vt sep *amendment* ne pas voter, ne pas adopter, rejeter, repousser; *M.P., chairman etc* ne pas réélire, sortir*. **he was voted out (of office)** il n'a pas été réélu; **he was voted out by a large majority** il a été battu à une forte majorité; **the electors voted the Conservative government out** les électeurs ont rejeté le gouvernement conservateur.
▸**vote through** vt sep *bill, motion* voter, ratifier.

voter ['vəʊtər] 1 n électeur *m*, -trice *f*. 2 comp ▸**voter registration** (*US Pol*) inscription *f* sur les listes électorales; **voter registration card** carte *f* d'électeur; *see* **turnout**.

voting ['vəʊtɪŋ] 1 n vote *m*; scrutin *m*. **the ~ went against him** le vote lui a été défavorable; **the ~ took place yesterday** le scrutin a eu lieu hier. 2 comp ▸**voting booth** isoloir *m* ▸**voting machine** (*US*) machine *f* pour enregistrer les votes ▸**voting paper** bulletin *m* de vote ▸**voting rights** droit *m* de vote ▸**voting share** (*Fin*) action *f* avec droit de vote.

votive ['vəʊtɪv] adj votif.

vouch [vaʊtʃ] vi: **to ~ for sb/sth** se porter garant de qn/qch, répondre de qn/qch; **to ~ for the truth of** garantir la vérité de.

voucher ['vaʊtʃər] n a (*for cash, meals, petrol*) bon *m*; *see* **luncheon**. b (*receipt*) reçu *m*, récépissé *m*; (*for debt*) quittance *f*. c (*proof*) pièce justificative.

vouchsafe [vaʊtʃ'seɪf] vt *reply* accorder; *help, privilege* accorder, octroyer. (*frm*) **to ~ to do** accepter gracieusement de faire; (*pej*) condescendre à faire; **it is not ~d to everyone to understand such things** il n'est pas donné à tout le monde de comprendre ce genre de choses; **he hasn't ~d an answer** il n'a pas jugé bon de nous donner une réponse.

vow [vaʊ] 1 n vœu *m*, serment *m*. **to take a ~** faire vœu (*to do* de faire, *of sth* de qch); **the ~s which he took when ...** les vœux qu'il a faits quand ...; (*Rel*) **to take one's ~s** prononcer ses vœux; **to make a ~ = to ~** (*see* **2**); ~ **of celibacy** vœu de célibat; **she swore a ~ of secrecy** elle a juré *or* elle a fait le serment de ne le divulguer à personne; *see* **break** *etc*. 2 vt a (*publicly*) jurer (*to do* de faire, *that* que); *obedience, loyalty* faire vœu de. **to ~ vengeance on sb** jurer de se venger de qn. b (*to oneself*) se jurer (*to do* de faire, *that* que). **he ~ed (to himself) that he would remain there** il s'est juré d'y rester.

vowel ['vaʊəl] 1 n voyelle *f*. 2 comp *system, sound* vocalique ▸**vowel shift** mutation *f* vocalique.

voyage ['vɔɪɪdʒ] 1 n (*Naut*) voyage *m* par mer, traversée *f*; (*fig*) voyage. **to go on a ~** partir en voyage (par mer); **the ~ across the Atlantic** la traversée de l'Atlantique; **the ~ out** le voyage d'aller; **the ~ back** *or* **home** le voyage de retour; **on the ~ out/home** à l'aller/au retour; ~ **of discovery** voyage d'exploration. 2 vt (*Naut*) traverser, parcourir. 3 vi a (*Naut*) voyager par mer. **to ~ across** traverser. b (*US Aviat*) voyager par avion.

voyager ['vɔɪədʒər] n (*traveller*) passager *m*, -ère *f*, voyageur *m*, -euse *f*; (*Hist: explorer*) navigateur *m*.

voyageur [ˌvɔɪə'dʒɜ:] n (*Can Hist*) trappeur *m* (*or* batelier *m etc*) assurant la liaison entre différents comptoirs.

voyeur [vwɑ:'jɜ:r] n voyeur *m*.

voyeurism ['vwɑ:jɜ:ˌrɪzəm] n voyeurisme *m*.

voyeuristic [ˌvwɑ:jɜ:'rɪstɪk] adj *personality* de voyeur, qui tend vers le voyeurisme; *film* qui tend vers le voyeurisme; *person* voyeur (*f* -euse).

V.P. [vi:'pi:] n (*US*) (abbr of **Vice-President**) *see* **vice**.

VR [vi:'ɑ:r] n (abbr of **virtual reality**) *see* **virtual**.

vs (abbr of **versus**) VS, contre.

V.S.O. [vi:es'əʊ] n (*Brit*) (abbr of **Voluntary Service Overseas**) ≈ coopération *f* technique à l'étranger.

VT (*US Post*) abbr of **Vermont**.

Vt. (*US*) abbr of **Vermont**.

VTOL [ˌvi:ti:əʊ'el] (abbr of **vertical takeoff and landing**) n a ~ **(aircraft)** ADAV *m*, VTOL *m*. b (*technique*) décollage *m* et atterrissage *m* verticaux.

Vulcan ['vʌlkən] n (*Myth*) Vulcain *m*.

vulcanite ['vʌlkənaɪt] n ébonite *f*.
vulcanization [ˌvʌlkənaɪ'zeɪʃən] n vulcanisation *f*.
vulcanize ['vʌlkənaɪz] vt vulcaniser.
vulcanologist [ˌvʌlkə'nɒlədʒɪst] n vulcanologue *m*.
vulcanology [ˌvʌlkə'nɒlədʒɪ] n vulcanologie *f*.
vulgar ['vʌlgəʳ] adj a (*pej: unrefined*) *person, action, language, clothes* vulgaire, grossier. ~ **ostentation** ostentation grossière; ~ **word** gros mot, grossièreté *f*. b (††: *of the common people*) vulgaire, commun. ~ **Latin** latin *m* vulgaire; **the ~ tongue** la langue commune. c (*Math*) ~ **fraction** fraction *f* ordinaire.
vulgarian [vʌl'gɛərɪən] n (*pej*) personne *f* vulgaire, parvenu *m*.
vulgarism ['vʌlgərɪzəm] n (*uneducated expression*) vulgarisme *m*; (*swearword*) gros mot, grossièreté *f*.
vulgarity [vʌl'gærɪtɪ] n vulgarité *f*, grossièreté *f*.
vulgarization [ˌvʌlgəraɪ'zeɪʃən] n vulgarisation *f*.
vulgarize ['vʌlgəraɪz] vt a (*make known*) vulgariser, populariser. b (*make coarse*) rendre vulgaire.
vulgarly ['vʌlgəlɪ] adv a (*generally*) vulgairement, communément. b (*coarsely*) vulgairement, grossièrement.
Vulgate ['vʌlgɪt] n Vulgate *f*.
vulnerability [ˌvʌlnərə'bɪlɪtɪ] n vulnérabilité *f*.
vulnerable ['vʌlnərəbl] adj (*also Bridge*) vulnérable. **to find sb's ~ spot** trouver le point faible de qn.
vulture ['vʌltʃəʳ] n (*also fig*) vautour *m*. (*Orn*) **black ~** moine *m*.
vulva ['vʌlvə] n, pl **vulvae** ['vʌlviː] *or* **~s** vulve *f*.
vying ['vaɪɪŋ] n rivalité*f*, concurrence *f*.

W

W, w ['dʌbljʊ] n a (*letter*) W, w *m*. **W for Willie** ≃ W comme William. b (abbr of **watt**) W. c (abbr of **west**) O., ouest.
W. abbr of **Wales** *or* **Welsh**.
WA (*US*) abbr of **Washington**.
wacky‡ ['wækɪ] adj (*US*) farfelu*, fou-fou* (*f* fofolle*).
wad [wɒd] 1 n a (*plug, ball*) [*cloth, paper*] tampon *m*; [*putty, chewing gum*] boulette *f*; (*for gun*) bourre *f*; [*straw*] bouchon *m*. **a ~ of cotton wool** un tampon d'ouate; **a ~ of tobacco** (*uncut*) une carotte de tabac; (*for chewing*) une chique de tabac. b (*bundle*) [*papers, documents*] paquet *m*, tas *m*, pile *f*, (*tied together*) liasse *f*; [*banknotes*] liasse. 2 vt a (*also* ~ **up**) *paper etc* faire un tampon de; *putty etc* faire une boulette de. b *garment* doubler d'ouate, ouater; *quilt* rembourrer. c (*also* ~ **up**) *hole, crack* boucher avec un tampon *or* avec une boulette.
wadding ['wɒdɪŋ] n (*NonC*) (*raw cotton or felt; also for gun*) bourre *f*; (*gen: for lining or padding*) rembourrage *m*, capiton *m*; (*for garments*) ouate *f*.
waddle ['wɒdl] 1 vi [*duck*] se dandiner; [*person*] se dandiner, marcher come un canard. **to ~ in/out/across** *etc* entrer/sortir/traverser *etc* en se dandinant. 2 n dandinement *m*.
wade [weɪd] 1 vi a **to ~ through water/mud** avancer *or* marcher *or* patauger dans l'eau/la boue; **to ~ through long grass** avancer *or* marcher dans l'herbe haute; **he ~d ashore** il a regagné la rive à pied; (*fig*) **to ~ into sb*** (*attack physically*) se jeter *or* tomber *or* se ruer sur qn; (*attack verbally*) tomber sur qn, prendre qn à partie; (*scold*) engueuler‡ qn; **to ~ into a meal*** attaquer un repas*; **I managed to ~ through his book*** j'ai réussi à lire son livre, mais ça a été laborieux; **it took me an hour to ~ through your essay*** il m'a fallu une heure pour venir à bout de votre dissertation; **he was wading through his homework*** il faisait ses devoirs lentement et méthodiquement.
b (*paddle: for fun*) barboter.
2 vt *stream* passer *or* traverser à gué.
►**wade in**‡ vi (*in fight/argument etc*) se mettre de la partie (*dans une bagarre/dispute etc*).
wader ['weɪdəʳ] n (*boot*) cuissarde *f*, botte *f* de pêcheur; (*bird*) échassier *m*.
wadge [wɒdʒ] n = **wodge**.
wadi ['wɒdɪ] n, pl **~es** oued *m*.
wading ['weɪdɪŋ] 1 n (*NonC*) barbotage *m*, pataugeage *m*. 2 comp ►**wading bird** échassier *m* ►**wading pool** (*US*) petit bassin.
wafer ['weɪfəʳ] 1 n a (*Culin*) gaufrette *f*; (*Rel*) (pain *m* d')hostie *f*; (*seal*) cachet *m* (*de papier rouge*). b (*Comput, Electronics*) tranche *f*. **silicon ~** tranche de silicium. 2 comp ►**wafer-thin** mince comme du papier à cigarette *or* comme une pelure d'oignon.
wafery ['weɪfərɪ] adj = **wafer-thin**; *see* **wafer 2**.
waffle¹ ['wɒfl] n (*Culin*) gaufre *f*. **~ iron** gaufrier *m*.
waffle²* ['wɒfl] (*Brit*) 1 n (*NonC*) (*wordiness*) verbiage *m*; (*padding*) remplissage *m*, délayage *m*, rabâchage *m*. **there's too much ~ in this essay** il y a trop de remplissage dans cette dissertation, vous avez (*or* il a *etc*) trop allongé la sauce* dans cette dissertation. 2 vi (*in conversation*) parler pour ne rien dire, parler dans le vague; (*in speech, book, essay*) faire du remplissage, allonger la sauce*. **he was waffling on about the trouble he'd had** il parlait interminablement de ses problèmes.
waffler* ['wɒfləʳ] n (*Brit*) personne *f* qui fait du verbiage.
waft [wɑːft] 1 vt *smell, sound* porter, apporter; (*also* ~ **along**) *boat* faire avancer, pousser; *clouds* faire glisser *or* avancer. 2 vi [*sounds, smell*] flotter; [*corn etc*] ondoyer. 3 n [*air, scent*] (petite) bouffée *f*.
wag¹ [wæg] 1 vt agiter, remuer. **the dog ~ged its tail (at me)** le chien a agité *or* remué la queue (en me voyant); **he ~ged his finger/his pencil at me** il a agité le doigt/son crayon dans ma direction; **to ~ one's head** hocher la tête. 2 vi [*tail*] remuer, frétiller. (*fig*) **his tongue never stops ~ging** il a la langue bien pendue, il ne s'arrête jamais de bavarder; **the news set tongues ~ging** la nouvelle a fait marcher les langues *or* a fait jaser (les gens). 3 n [*tail*] remuement *m*, frétillement *m*. **with a ~ of its tail** en remuant *or* agitant la queue. 4 comp ►**wagtail** (*Orn*) hoche-queue *m*, lavandière *f*.
wag²† [wæg] n (*joker*) plaisantin *m*, farceur *m*, -euse *f*.
wage [weɪdʒ] 1 n salaire *m*, paye *f or* paie *f*; [*domestic servant*] gages *mpl*. **hourly/weekly ~** salaire horaire/hebdomadaire; **I've lost 2 days' ~s** j'ai perdu 2 jours de salaire *or* de paye; **his week's ~s** son salaire *or* sa paye de la semaine; **his ~ is** *or* **his ~s are £150 per week** il touche un salaire de 150 livres par semaine, il gagne *or* est payé 150 livres par semaine; **he gets a good ~** il est bien payé, il a un bon salaire; (*Bible*) **the ~s of sin is death** la mort est le salaire du péché; *see* **living**.
2 comp ►**wage(s) bill** masse *f* salariale ►**wage(s) claim** (*Brit*), **wage demand** revendication *f* salariale ►**wage(s) clerk** employé(e) *m(f)* aux salaires, ≃ aide-comptable *mf* ►**wage differential** écart *m* salarial *or* de salaires ►**wage drift** dérapage *m* de salaire ►**wage earner** salarié(e) *m(f)*; **she is the family wage earner** c'est elle qui fait vivre sa famille *or* qui est le soutien de sa famille; **we are both wage earners** nous gagnons tous les deux notre vie ►**wage(s) freeze** blocage *m* des salaires ►**wage increase** augmentation *f or* hausse *f* de salaire ►**wage packet** (*lit*) enveloppe *f* de paye; (*fig*) paye *f or* paie *f* ►**wage-price spiral** spirale *f* prix-salaires ►**wage-push inflation** inflation *f* par les salaires ►**wage rates** taux *m* des salaires ►**wage restraint** limitation *f* des salaires ►**wage rise** = **wage increase** ►**wage scale** échelle *f* des salaires ►**wage(s) settlement** accord *m* salarial ►**wage(s) slip** bulletin *m* de salaire, fiche *f* de paye ►**wage spread** (*US*) éventail *m* des salaires ►**wage-stop** (*Brit Soc Admin*) *principe selon lequel les sans-travail ne peuvent toucher une allocation de chômage plus élevée qu'un salaire éventuel* ►**wage worker** (*US*) = **wage earner**.
3 vt: **to ~ war** faire la guerre (*against* à, contre); **to ~ a campaign** faire campagne (*against* contre), mener une campagne (*for* pour).
wager ['weɪdʒəʳ] 1 vt parier (*on* sur, *that* que). 2 n pari *m*. **to lay a ~** faire un pari.
waggish ['wægɪʃ] adj badin, facétieux.
waggishly ['wægɪʃlɪ] adv d'une manière facétieuse, d'un ton facétieux *or* badin.
waggle ['wægl] 1 vt *pencil, branch* agiter; *loose screw, button* faire jouer. **it was waggling its tail** il agitait *or* remuait la queue, il frétillait de la queue; **to ~ one's hips** tortiller des hanches; **my finger hurts if you ~ it like that** j'ai mal quand vous me tortillez le doigt comme ça. 2 vi [*tail*] remuer, frétiller; [*tooth*] branler. 3 n: **to give sth a ~** agiter *or* remuer qch.
waggon ['wægən] 1 n (*horse- or ox-drawn*) chariot *m*; (*truck*) camion *m*; (*Brit Rail*) wagon *m* (de marchandises); (**: car*) auto *f*, bagnole *f*; (*US: also* **station ~**) break *m*; (*tea trolley*) table roulante, (*larger: for tea urn*) chariot. (*US: police van*) **the ~*** le panier à salade*; (*fig*) **to go/be on the ~*** ne plus/ne pas boire (d'alcool), se mettre/être au régime sec; **he's off the ~ (again)*** il s'est remis à boire; *see* **station** *etc*.
2 comp ►**waggonload** (*Agr*) charretée *f*; (*Rail*) wagon *m* ►**waggon train** (*US Hist*) convoi *m* de chariots.
waggoner ['wægənəʳ] n roulier *m*, charretier *m*.
waggonette [ˌwægə'net] n break *m* (*hippomobile*).
Wagnerian [vɑːg'nɪərɪən] adj wagnérien.
wagon ['wægən] n (*esp US*) = **waggon**.
waif [weɪf] n enfant *mf* misérable; (*homeless*) enfant abandonné(e). **~s and strays** enfants abandonnés.
wail [weɪl] 1 n [*person*] gémissement *m*, plainte *f*; [*baby*] vagissement *m*; [*wind*] gémissement, plainte; [*siren*] hurlement *m*. **to give a ~** pousser un gémissement *or* un vagissement, gémir, vagir. 2 vi [*person*] gémir, pousser un *or* des gémissement(s); (*cry*) pleurer; (*whine*) pleurnicher; [*baby*] vagir; [*wind*] gémir; [*siren*] hurler; [*bagpipes etc*] gémir.
wailing ['weɪlɪŋ] 1 n (*NonC*) [*person*] (*gen*) gémissements *mpl*, plaintes *fpl*, pleurs *mpl*; (*whining*) pleurnicheries *fpl*; [*baby*] vagissements *mpl*; [*wind*] gémissements, plainte; [*siren*] hurlement *m*.

2 adj *voice, person* gémissant; *sound* plaintif. **the W~ Wall** le mur des Lamentations.

wain [weɪn] n (*liter*) chariot *m*. (*Astron*) **Charles's W~** le Chariot de David, la Grande Ourse.

wainscot ['weɪnskət] n lambris *m* (*en bois*).

wainscot(t)ing ['weɪnskətɪŋ] n lambrissage *m* (*en bois*).

waist [weɪst] 1 n a (*Anat, Dress*) taille *f*. **he put his arm round her ~** il l'a prise par la taille; **she measures 70 cm round the ~** elle fait 70 cm de tour de taille; **they were stripped to the ~** ils étaient nus jusqu'à la ceinture, ils étaient torse nu; **he was up to the** *or* **his ~ in water** l'eau lui arrivait à la ceinture *or* à mi-corps.

b (*fig*) étranglement *m*, resserrement *m*; *[violin]* partie resserrée de la table.

c (*US*) (*blouse*) corsage *m*, blouse *f*; (*bodice*) corsage, haut *m*.

2 vt *jacket etc* cintrer.

3 comp ▸**waistband** ceinture *f* (*de jupe etc*) ▸**waistcoat** (*Brit*) gilet *m* ▸**waistline** taille *f*; (*hum*) **I've got to think of my waistline** je dois faire attention à ma ligne ▸**waist measurement, waist size** tour *m* de taille ▸**waist slip** jupon *m*.

-waisted ['weɪstɪd] adj ending in comps: **to be slim-waisted** avoir la taille fine; **high-/low-waisted dress** robe *f* à taille haute/basse; *see* **shirt**.

wait [weɪt] 1 n a attente *f*. **you'll have a 3-hour ~** vous aurez 3 heures d'attente, vous devrez attendre (pendant) 3 heures; **it was a long ~** il a fallu attendre longtemps, l'attente a été longue; **there was a 20-minute ~ between trains** il y avait 20 minutes de battement *or* d'attente entre les trains; (*on coach journey etc*) **there is a half-hour ~ at Leeds** il y a un arrêt d'une demi-heure *or* une demi-heure d'arrêt à Leeds; **during the ~ between the performances** pendant le battement *or* la pause entre les représentations; **to be** *or* **lie in ~** guetter, être à l'affût; **to be** *or* **lie in ~ for sb** *[huntsman, lion]* guetter qn; *[bandits, guerrillas]* dresser un guet-apens *or* une embuscade à qn; **the journalists lay in ~ for him as he left the theatre** les journalistes l'attendaient (au passage) à sa sortie du théâtre *or* le guettaient à sa sortie du théâtre.

b (*Brit*) **the ~s** les chanteurs *mpl* de Noël (*qui vont de porte en porte*).

2 comp ▸**wait-and-see policy** *or* **tactics** (*Pol etc*) attentisme *m* ▸**wait-listed:** (*Travel*) **to be wait-listed on a flight** être sur la liste d'attente d'un vol.

3 vi a attendre. **to ~ for sb/sth** attendre qn/qch; **~ for it!*** (*order to wait*) attendez!; (*guess what*) devinez quoi!*; **to ~ for sb to leave, to ~ until sb leaves** attendre le départ de qn, attendre que qn parte; **could you ~ a moment?** vous pouvez patienter un moment?; **~ till you're old enough** attends d'être assez grand; **can you ~ till 10 o'clock?** pouvez-vous attendre jusqu'à 10 heures?; **we ~ed and ~ed** nous avons attendu à n'en plus finir; **just you ~!** tu vas voir ce que tu vas voir!; (*threateningly*) tu ne perds rien pour attendre!; **just ~ till your father finds out!** attends un peu que ton père apprenne ça!; **~ and see!** attends (voir)! (*see also* **2**); **we'll just have to ~ and see** il va falloir attendre, il va falloir voir venir; **~ and see what happens next** attendez voir ce qui va se passer; **to keep sb ~ing** faire attendre qn; **don't keep us ~ing** ne te fais pas attendre, ne nous fais pas attendre; **I was kept ~ing in the corridor** on m'a fait attendre dans le couloir, j'ai fait le pied de grue dans le couloir; (*Comm*) **"repairs while you ~"** "réparations à la minute"; (*Comm*) **they do it while you ~** ils le font à la minute; (*loc*) **everything comes to him who ~s** tout vient à point à qui sait attendre (*Prov*); **he didn't ~ to be told twice** il ne se l'est pas fait dire deux fois; **that was worth ~ing for** cela valait la peine d'attendre; **I just can't ~ for next Saturday!** je meurs d'impatience *or* d'envie d'en être à samedi prochain!; **I can't ~ to see him again!** (*longingly*) je meurs d'envie de le revoir!; **I can't ~ for the day when this happens** je rêve du jour où cela arrivera; **the Conservatives can't ~ to reverse this policy** les conservateurs brûlent de révoquer cette politique; **parcel ~ing to be collected** colis *m* en souffrance; **all that can ~ till tomorrow** tout cela peut attendre jusqu'à demain.

b servir. **to ~ (at table)** servir à table, faire le service.

4 vt a *signal, orders, one's turn, chance* attendre. **I ~ed 2 hours** j'ai attendu (pendant) 2 heures; **~ a moment!** (attendez) un instant! *or* une minute!; (*interrupting, querying*) minute!*; **to ~ one's moment** *or* **time** attendre son heure (*to do* pour faire); **we'll ~ lunch for you** nous vous attendrons pour nous mettre à table.

b (*US*) **to ~ table** servir à table, faire le service.

▸**wait about, wait around** vi attendre; (*loiter*) traîner. **to wait about for sb** attendre qn, faire le pied de grue pour qn; **the job involves a lot of waiting about** on perd beaucoup de temps à attendre dans ce métier; **you can't expect him to wait about all day while you ...** tu ne peux pas exiger qu'il traîne (*subj*) toute la journée à t'attendre pendant que tu ... .

▸**wait behind** vi rester. **to wait behind for sb** rester pour attendre qn.

▸**wait in** vi rester à la maison (*for sb* pour attendre qn).

▸**wait on** vt fus a *[servant]* servir, être de service auprès de; (*at table*) servir. **I'm not here to wait on him!** je ne suis pas sa bonne! (*or* son valet de chambre!); **she waits on him hand and foot** elle est aux petits soins pour lui. b (*frm*) = **wait upon a**.

▸**wait out** vt sep: **to wait it out** patienter.

▸**wait up** vi (*not go to bed*) ne pas se coucher, veiller. **we waited up till 2 o'clock** nous avons veillé *or* attendu jusqu'à 2 heures, nous ne nous sommes pas couchés avant 2 heures; **she always waits up for him** elle attend toujours qu'il rentre (*subj*) pour se coucher, elle ne se couche jamais avant qu'il ne soit rentré; **don't wait up (for me)** couchez-vous sans m'attendre; **you can wait up to see the programme** tu peux voir le programme avant de te coucher, tu peux rester debout pour voir le programme.

▸**wait upon** vt fus a (*frm*) *[ambassador, envoy etc]* présenter ses respects à. b = **wait on a**.

waiter ['weɪtəʳ] n garçon *m* (de café), serveur *m*. **~!** garçon!; *see* **dumb, head, wine**.

waiting ['weɪtɪŋ] 1 n (*NonC*) attente *f*. (*Aut*) **"no ~"** "stationnement strictement interdit"; **all this ~!** ce qu'on attend!, dire qu'il faut attendre si longtemps!; (*frm*) **to be in ~ on sb** être attaché au service de qn; *see* **lady**. 2 adj qui attend. 3 comp ▸**waiting game:** (*fig*) **to play a waiting game** (*gen*) attendre son heure; (*in diplomacy, negotiations etc*) mener une politique d'attente, se conduire en attentiste ▸**waiting list** liste *f* d'attente ▸**waiting room** (*Rail, Bus etc*) salle *f* d'attente; *[office, surgery etc]* salon *m* d'attente.

waitress ['weɪtrɪs] n serveuse *f*. **~!** Mademoiselle (s'il vous plaît)!

waive [weɪv] vt (*Jur*) *claim, right, privilege* renoncer à, abandonner; *condition, age limit* ne pas insister sur, abandonner; *principle* déroger à, renoncer à.

waiver ['weɪvəʳ] n (*Jur: see* **waive**) renonciation *f* (*of* à); abandon *m* (*of* de).

wake¹ [weɪk] n *[ship]* sillage *m*, eaux *fpl*. (*fig*) **in the ~ of the storm** à la suite de l'orage, après l'orage; **in the ~ of the army** dans le sillage *or* sur les traces de l'armée; **the war brought famine in its ~** la guerre a amené la famine dans son sillage; **to follow in sb's ~** marcher sur les traces de qn *or* dans le sillage de qn.

wake² [weɪk] (vb: pret **woke, waked**, ptp **waked, woken, woke**) 1 n a (*over corpse*) veillée *f* mortuaire.

b (*N Engl*) **W~s (Week)** *semaine f de congé annuel dans le nord de l'Angleterre*.

2 vi (*also* **~ up**) se réveiller, s'éveiller (*from* de). **~ up!** réveille-toi!; (* *fig: think what you're doing*) mais enfin réveille-toi! *or* ouvre les yeux!; **to ~ from sleep** se réveiller, s'éveiller, sortir du sommeil; **to ~ (up) from a nightmare** (*lit*) se réveiller d'un cauchemar; (*fig*) sortir d'un cauchemar; **she woke (up) to find them gone** en se réveillant *or* à son réveil elle s'est aperçue qu'ils étaient partis; **he woke up (to find himself) in prison** il s'est réveillé en prison; **he woke up to find himself rich** à son réveil il était riche; (*fig*) **to ~ (up) to sth** prendre conscience de *or* se rendre compte de *or* s'apercevoir de qch; **to ~ (up) from one's illusions** revenir de ses illusions; (*fig: stirred himself*) **he suddenly woke up and started to work hard** il s'est tout à coup réveillé *or* remué *or* secoué et s'est mis à travailler dur; (*fig: understood*) **he suddenly woke up and realized that ...** tout à coup ses yeux se sont ouverts *or* dessillés et il s'est rendu compte que ... .

3 vt (*also* **~ up**) *person* réveiller (*from* de), tirer du sommeil; (*fig*) *memories* (r)éveiller, ranimer; *desires* éveiller, provoquer, exciter. **a noise that would ~ the dead** un bruit à réveiller les morts; (*fig*) **he needs something to ~ him up** il aurait besoin d'être secoué.

wakeful ['weɪkfʊl] adj *person* (*awake*) éveillé, qui ne dort pas; (*alert*) vigilant; *hours etc* sans sommeil. **to have** *or* **spend a ~ night** passer une nuit blanche.

wakefulness ['weɪkfʊlnɪs] n (*sleeplessness*) insomnie *f*; (*watchfulness*) vigilance *f*.

waken ['weɪkən] vti = **wake²**.

waker ['weɪkəʳ] n: **to be an early ~** se réveiller tôt, être matinal.

wakey-wakey‡ ['weɪkɪ'weɪkɪ] excl réveillez-vous!, debout!

waking ['weɪkɪŋ] 1 adj: **in one's ~ hours** pendant les heures de veille; **he devoted all his ~ hours to ...** il consacrait chaque heure de sa journée à ...; **~ or sleeping, he ...** (qu'il soit) éveillé ou endormi, il ... .

2 n (état *m* de) veille *f*. **between ~ and sleeping** entre la veille et le sommeil, dans un (état de) demi-sommeil.

Waldorf ['wɔːldɔːf] n (*Culin*) **~ salad** salade *f* Waldorf (*composée de pommes, noix et céleri liés avec une mayonnaise*).

wale [weɪl] n (*US*) = **weal¹**.

Wales [weɪlz] n pays *m* de galles; **in ~** au pays de Galles; **North/South ~** le Nord/le Sud du pays de Galles; (*Brit*) **Secretary of State for ~** ministre *m* chargé du pays de Galles; *see* **prince**.

walk [wɔːk] 1 n a promenade *f*; (*ramble*) randonnée *f*; (*~ing race*) épreuve *f* de marche. **to go for a ~, to take** *or* **have a ~** se promener, faire une promenade, (*shorter*) faire un tour; **(go) take a ~!*** fous le camp!‡, dégage!*; **let's have a little ~** promenons-nous un peu, allons faire un petit tour; **he had a long ~** il s'est promené longtemps, il a fait une grande promenade, il a fait une vraie randonnée; **we went on a long ~ to see the castle** nous avons fait une excursion (à pied) pour visiter le château; **to take sb for a ~** emmener qn se promener *or* en promenade; **to take the dog for a ~** promener le chien; **he did a 10-km ~ each day** il faisait chaque jour une promenade de 10 km; **the house is 10 minutes' ~ from here** la maison est à 10 minutes de marche d'ici *or* à 10 minutes à pied d'ici; **it's only a short ~ to the shops** il n'y a pas loin à marcher jusqu'aux magasins, il n'y a pas loin pour aller aux magasins; **there's a nice ~ by the river** il y a une jolie promenade à faire le long de la rivière; (*US fig: easily*) **in a ~*** *win* dans un fauteuil; *do sth* les doigts dans le nez; *see* **sponsor**.

b (*gait*) démarche *f*, façon *f* de marcher. **I knew him by his ~** je l'ai reconnu à sa démarche *or* à sa façon de marcher.

c **he slowed down to a ~** il a ralenti pour aller au pas; **you've plenty of time to get there at a ~** vous avez tout le temps qu'il faut pour y arriver sans courir; **he went at a quick ~** il marchait d'un pas rapide.

d (*avenue*) avenue *f*, promenade *f*; (*path in garden*) allée *f*; (*path in country*) chemin *m*, sentier *m*; (*US: sidewalk*) trottoir *m*. (*fig*) **from all ~s of life** de toutes conditions sociales.

2 **comp** ▸**walkabout*** (*Australia*) voyage *m* (d'aborigène) dans le désert; *[president, celebrity]* bain *m* de foule; **to go** *or* **be on a walkabout*** (*Australia*) (**: go for a walk*) partir se balader* dans la campagne; *[president, celebrity]* prendre un bain de foule ▸**walkaway*** (**victory** *or* **win**) (*US*) victoire *f* dans un fauteuil* ▸**walk-in** *wardrobe, cupboard, larder* de plain-pied; *[flat, house]* **in walk-in condition** habitable de suite ▸**walk(ing)-on part** (*Theat etc*) rôle *m* de figurant(e) ▸**walkout** (*strike*) grève *f* surprise; (*from meeting, lecture etc*) départ *m* (en signe de protestation); **to stage a walkout** *[workers]* faire une grève surprise; *[students, delegates etc]* partir (en signe de protestation) ▸**walkover** (*Racing*) walk-over *m*; (*fig*) **it was a walkover!*** (*game etc*) c'était une victoire facile! *or* dans un fauteuil!*; (*exam etc*) c'était un jeu d'enfant!, c'était simple comme bonjour!; (*Sport*) **it was a walkover for Smith*** Smith a gagné dans un fauteuil* *or* haut la main ▸**walk-up** (*US*) (*house*) immeuble *m* sans ascenseur; (*apartment*) appartement *m* dans un immeuble sans ascenseur ▸**walkway** passage *m* pour piétons.

3 **vi** **a** (*gen*) marcher; (*not run*) aller au pas, ne pas courir. **I haven't ~ed since the accident** je n'ai pas (re)marché depuis l'accident; **I can't ~ as I used to** je n'ai plus mes jambes d'autrefois; (*loc*) **you must ~ before you can run** on apprend petit à petit; **she ~s in her sleep** elle est somnambule; **she was ~ing in her sleep** elle marchait en dormant; **don't ~ on the new rug** ne marche pas sur le nouveau tapis; **I'll ~ with you** je vais vous accompagner; **to ~ across/down** *etc* traverser/descendre *etc* (à pied *or* sans courir); **he ~ed up/down the stairs** (*gen*) il a monté/descendu l'escalier; (*didn't run*) il a monté/descendu l'escalier sans courir; **he was ~ing up and down** il marchait de long en large, il faisait les cent pas; **you should always WALK across the road** on ne doit jamais traverser la rue en courant; **~, don't run** ne cours pas; (*fig*) **my pen seems to have ~ed*** mon stylo a fichu le camp*.

b (*not ride or drive*) aller à pied; (*go for a ~*) se promener, faire une promenade; *[ghost]* apparaître. **they ~ed all the way to London** ils ont fait tout le chemin à pied jusqu'à Londres; **I always ~ home** je rentre toujours à pied; **shall we ~ a little?** si nous faisions quelques pas?, si nous marchions un peu?, si nous nous promenions un peu?; **they were out ~ing** ils étaient partis se promener (à pied).

4 **vt** **a** *distance* faire à pied. **he ~s 5 km every day** il fait 5 km (de marche) à pied par jour; **you can ~ it in a couple of minutes** vous y serez en deux minutes à pied, à pied cela vous prendra deux minutes, à pied vous en avez pour deux minutes; **he ~ed it in 10 minutes** il l'a fait à pied en 10 minutes, il lui a fallu 10 minutes à pied; (*fig: it was easy*) **he ~ed it*** cela a été un jeu d'enfant pour lui.

b *town etc* parcourir. **to ~ the streets** se promener dans les rues; (*to fill in time*) flâner dans les rues; (*from poverty*) errer dans les rues, battre le pavé; *[prostitute]* faire le trottoir; **he ~ed the town looking for a dentist** il a parcouru la ville en tous sens à la recherche d'un dentiste; **they ~ed the countryside in search of ...** ils ont battu la campagne à la recherche de ...; **to ~ the plank** subir le supplice de la planche (*sur un bateau de pirates*); **the policeman was ~ing his beat** l'agent de police faisait sa ronde; **I've ~ed this road many times** j'ai pris cette route (à pied) bien des fois.

c (*cause to ~*) *person* faire marcher, faire se promener, promener; *dog* promener; *horse* conduire à pied. **I ~ed him round the garden till he was calmer** je me suis promené avec lui dans le jardin jusqu'à ce qu'il se calme (*subj*); **the nurse ~ed him down the ward to exercise his legs** l'infirmière l'a fait marcher *or* se promener dans la salle pour qu'il s'exerce (*subj*) les jambes; **I ~ed him round Paris** je l'ai promené dans Paris; **he seized my arm and ~ed me across the room** il m'a pris par le bras et m'a fait traverser la pièce; **to ~ sb in/out** *etc* faire entrer/sortir *etc* qn; **I'll ~ you to the station** je vais vous accompagner (à pied) à la gare; **to ~ sb home** raccompagner qn (chez lui *or* elle); **he ~ed her to her car** il l'a raccompagnée jusqu'à sa voiture; **I had to ~ my cycle home** j'ai dû pousser ma bicyclette jusqu'à la maison; **to ~ a cooker/chest of drawers across a room** pousser une cuisinière/une commode petit à petit d'un bout à l'autre d'une pièce (*en la faisant pivoter d'un pied sur l'autre*); **they ~ed him off his feet** ils l'ont tellement fait marcher qu'il ne tenait plus debout.

▸**walk about** **1** **vi** aller et venir, se promener, circuler. **2** **walkabout*** **n** *see* **walk 2**.

▸**walk across** **vi** (*over bridge etc*) traverser. **to walk across to sb** s'approcher de qn, se diriger vers qn.

▸**walk around** **vi** = **walk about 1**.

▸**walk away** **1** **vi** partir, filer*. **to walk away from sb** s'éloigner de qn, quitter qn; **he walked away with the wrong coat** il s'est trompé de manteau en partant; **to walk away from an accident** sortir indemne d'un accident; (*fig: win easily*) **to walk away with sth** gagner *or* remporter qch haut la main; **I did the work but he walked away with all the credit** c'est moi qui ai fait tout le travail et c'est lui qui a reçu tous les éloges. **2** **walkaway*** **n, adj** *see* **walk 2**.

▸**walk back** **vi** revenir, rentrer, retourner; (*specifically on foot*) revenir *or* rentrer *or* retourner à pied.

▸**walk in** **1** **vi** entrer. **"please walk in"** "prière d'entrer", "entrez sans frapper"; **who should walk in but Paul!** et voilà que Paul est entré (à ce moment-là)!, et qui entre sur ces entrefaites? Paul!; **he just walked in and took all my jewels** il n'a eu qu'à (se donner la peine d')entrer pour prendre tous mes bijoux; **he just walked in and gave me the sack** il est entré sans crier gare et m'a annoncé qu'il me mettait à la porte; **to walk in on sb** entrer sans prévenir. **2** **walk-in** **adj** *see* **walk 2**.

▸**walk into** **vt fus** **a** *trap, ambush* tomber dans. **you really walked into that one!*** tu es vraiment tombé *or* tu as vraiment donné dans le panneau!; **he wondered what he had walked into** il se demandait dans quelle galère il s'était laissé entraîner. **b** (*bump into*) *person, lamppost, table* se cogner à, rentrer dans*; (**: meet*) tomber sur. **c** (*find easily*) *job* trouver sans problème *or* facilement.

▸**walk off** **1** **vi** **a** = **walk away 1**. **b** (*steal*) **to walk off with sth** barboter⁑ *or* faucher⁑ qch. **2** **vt sep** *excess weight* perdre en marchant. **to walk off a headache** prendre l'air *or* faire une promenade pour se débarrasser d'un mal de tête.

▸**walk off with*** **vt fus** = **walk away with***.

▸**walk on** **1** **vi** (*Theat*) être figurant(e), jouer les utilités. **2** **walk(ing)-on** **adj** *see* **walk 2**. **3** **walker-on** **n** *see* **walker 2**.

▸**walk out** **1** **vi** (*go out*) sortir; (*go away*) partir; (*as protest*) partir (en signe de protestation); (*go on strike*) se mettre en grève, faire grève. (*fig*) **you can't walk out now!** tu ne peux pas partir comme ça!, tu ne peux pas tout laisser tomber* comme ça!; **her husband has walked out** son mari l'a quittée *or* plaquée⁑; **they walked out of the discussion** ils ont quitté la séance de discussion (en signe de protestation). **2** **walkout** **n** *see* **walk 2**.

▸**walk out on*** **vt fus** *boyfriend, business partner* laisser tomber*, plaquer⁑.

▸**walk out with†** **vt fus** (*Brit: court*) fréquenter†.

▸**walk over** **1** **vi** passer (à pied), faire un saut (à pied). **I'll walk over tomorrow morning** j'y passerai *or* j'y ferai un saut (à pied) demain matin; **he walked over to me and said ...** il s'est approché de moi et a dit ... . **2** **vt fus** (*****) **a** (*defeat easily*) battre haut la main. **b** (*treat badly: also* **walk all over**) marcher sur les pieds de. **she lets him walk all over her** elle se laisse marcher sur les pieds (sans jamais lui faire de reproche). **3** **walkover** **n** *see* **walk 2**.

▸**walk through** **1** **vt fus** (*Theat*) répéter les mouvements de. **2** **walk-through** **n** répétition *f* technique.

▸**walk up** **1** **vi** (*go upstairs etc*) monter; (*approach*) s'approcher (*to sb* de qn). (*at fair etc*) **walk up, walk up!** approchez, approchez! **2** **walk-up** **n** *see* **walk 2**.

walkathon* ['wɔːkəθɒn] **n** (*US*) marathon *m* (de marche).

walker ['wɔːkə^{r}] **1** **n** **a** (*esp Sport*) marcheur *m*, -euse *f*; (*for pleasure*) promeneur *m*, -euse *f*. **he's a good/bad ~** il est bon/mauvais marcheur; **he's a fast ~** il marche vite; *see* **sleep, street** *etc*. **b** (*support frame*) (*for convalescents etc*) déambulateur *m*; (*for babies*) trotte-bébé *m*. **2** **comp** ▸**walker-on** (*Theat*) figurant(e) *m(f)*, comparse *mf*.

walkie-talkie ['wɔːkɪ'tɔːkɪ] **n** talkie-walkie *m*.

walking ['wɔːkɪŋ] **1** **n** **a** (*NonC*) marche *f* à pied, promenade(s) *f(pl)* (à pied); (*as a constitutional*) footing *m* (*NonC*); *see* **sleep** *etc*.

b (*Sport*) marche *f* (athlétique); (*Basketball*) marcher *m*.

2 **adj** ambulant. (*Mil*) **the ~ wounded** les blessés capables de marcher; **he is a ~ encyclopedia** c'est une encyclopédie vivante; **he is a ~ miracle** c'est un miracle ambulant, il revient de loin.

3 **comp** ▸**walking distance**: **it is within walking distance (of the house)** on peut facilement y aller à pied (de la maison); **5 minutes' walking distance away** à 5 minutes de marche ▸**walking holiday**: **we had a walking holiday in the Tyrol** pour nos vacances nous avons fait de la marche dans le Tyrol ▸**walking-on** (*Theat*) **adj** *see* **walk 2** ▸**walking pace**: **at a walking pace** au pas ▸**walking papers***: (*US*) **to give sb his walking papers*** renvoyer qn, mettre *or* flanquer* qn à la porte ▸**walking race** épreuve *f* de marche ▸**walking shoes** chaussures *fpl* de marche ▸**walking stick** canne *f* ▸**walking tour** *or* **trip**: **to be on a walking tour** *or* **trip** faire une longue randonnée à pied.

Walkman ['wɔːkmən] **n, pl Walkman personal stereos** ® Walkman *m* ®, baladeur *m*, somnambule *m* (*Can*).

Walkyrie [vælˈkɪərɪ] **n** Valkyrie *f*.

wall [wɔːl] **1** **n** (*gen*) mur *m* (*also fig*); (*interior; also of trench, tunnel*) paroi *f*; (*round garden, field*) mur (de clôture); (*round city, castle etc*) murs, remparts *mpl*, murailles *fpl*; (*Anat*) paroi; *[tyre]* flanc *m*; (*fig: of smoke, mountains etc*) mur *m*, muraille *f*. **within the (city) ~s** dans les murs, dans la ville; **the Great W~ of China** la grande muraille de Chine; **the Berlin W~** le mur de Berlin; **the north ~ of the Eiger** la face nord *or* la paroi nord de l'Eiger; **they left only the bare ~s standing** ils n'ont laissé que les murs; (*Econ*) **a high tariff ~** une barrière douanière élevée; (*loc*) **~s have ears** les murs ont des oreilles; *[prisoner]* **to go over the ~** s'évader, faire la belle‡; (*fig*) **to go to the ~** *[person]* perdre la partie; (*go bankrupt*) faire faillite; *[plan, activity]* être sacrifié; **it's always the weakest to the ~** ce sont toujours les plus faibles qui écopent*; **it is a case of the weakest to the ~** les plus faibles doivent céder le pas; (*fig*) **he had his back to the ~, he was up against the ~** il avait le dos au mur, il était acculé; **to get sb up against the ~, to drive** *or* **push sb to the ~** acculer qn, mettre qn au pied du mur; (*fig*) **to bang** *or* **knock** *or* **beat one's head against a (brick) ~** se cogner *or* se taper la tête contre les murs; (*fig*) **to come up against a (blank) ~, to come up against a stone** *or* **brick ~** se heurter à un mur; **to drive** *or* **send sb up the ~*** rendre qn dingue‡, en faire voir de toutes les couleurs* à qn; (*US fig*) **off the ~*** dingue*, bizarre; *see* **party**.

2 **comp** *decoration, clock, map* mural ►**wall bars** espalier *m* (*pour exercices de gymnastique*) ►**wallboard** (*US*) plaque *f* de plâtre ►**wall chart** planche murale (*gravure*) ►**wallcovering** tapisserie(s) *f(pl)* *or* tenture(s) *f(pl)* murale(s) ►**wall cupboard** placard mural *or* suspendu ►**wall-eyed** qui louche, qui a un œil qui dit zut à l'autre* ►**wallflower** (*Bot*) giroflée *f*; (*fig*) **to be a wallflower** faire tapisserie ►**wall lamp, wall light** applique *f* (*lampe*) ►**wall lighting** éclairage *m* par appliques ►**wall-mounted** *clock, phone* mural ►**wallpaper n** papier peint ◊ **vt** tapisser (de papier peint); (*pej*) **wallpaper music*** musique *f* d'ambiance (enregistrée) ►**wall socket** (*Elec*) prise *f* (murale) ►**Wall Street** (*US*) Wall Street *m* (la Bourse de New York) ►**wall to wall: to carpet sth wall to wall** recouvrir qch de moquette; **wall-to-wall carpet(ing)** moquette *f*.

3 **vt** *garden* entourer d'un mur, construire un mur autour de; *city* fortifier, entourer de murs *or* de remparts. **~ed garden** jardin clos; **~ed town** ville fortifiée.

►**wall in vt sep** *garden etc* entourer d'un mur.

►**wall off vt sep** *plot of land* séparer par un mur.

►**wall up vt sep** *doorway, window* murer, condamner; *person, relics* murer, emmurer.

wallaby ['wɒləbɪ] **n, pl wallabies** *or* ~ wallaby *m*.

wallah ['wɒlə] **n** (*Hist: Anglo-Indian*) **the laundry** *etc* ~ le préposé au blanchissage *etc*.

wallet ['wɒlɪt] **n** portefeuille *m*; (††: *of pilgrims etc*) besace *f*.

Walloon [wɒ'lu:n] 1 **adj** wallon. 2 **n** a Wallon(ne) *m(f)*. b (*Ling*) wallon *m*.

wallop ['wɒləp] 1 **n** a (*: *in fight, as punishment*) coup *m*, beigne‡ *f*, torgnole‡ *f*; (*in accident*) coup, gnon‡ *m*; (*sound*) fracas *m*, boucan* *m*. **to give sb a ~** flanquer une beigne‡ *or* une torgnole‡ à qn; **~!** vlan!; **it hit the floor with a ~** vlan! c'est tombé par terre, c'est tombé par terre avec un grand fracas. b (*Brit* ‡: *beer*) bière *f*. 2 **vt** (*) *person* flanquer une raclée* *or* une rossée* à qn; *ball, object* taper sur, donner un *or* des grand(s) coup(s) dans. 3 **adv: he went ~ into the wall*** il est rentré* en plein dans le mur.

walloping‡ ['wɒləpɪŋ] 1 **adj** sacré* (*before n*), formidable, phénoménal. **~ big** vachement grand‡. 2 **n** raclée* *f*, rossée* *f*. **to give sb a ~** (*punish*) flanquer une raclée* *or* une rossée* à qn; (*Sport etc: beat*) enfoncer* qn, battre qn à plate(s) couture(s).

wallow ['wɒləʊ] 1 **vi** *[person, animal]* se vautrer (*in* dans); *[ship]* être ballotté; (*fig*) (*in vice, sin*) se vautrer (*in* dans); (*in self-pity etc*) se complaire (*in* à). 2 **n** (*pool, bog etc*) mare *f* bourbeuse; (*in bath*) séjour *m* prolongé.

wally‡ ['wɒlɪ] **n** idiot* *m*. **to be a ~** être bête* *or* idiot*; **you look a right ~!** tu as vraiment l'air bête* *or* l'air d'un con‡!

walnut ['wɔ:lnʌt] 1 **n** noix *f*; (*also* **~ tree**) noyer *m*; (*NonC: wood*) noyer. 2 **comp** *table etc* de *or* en noyer; *cake* aux noix; *oil* de noix.

Walpurgis [væl'pʊəgɪs] **n: ~ Night** la nuit de Walpurgis.

walrus ['wɔ:lrəs] **n, pl ~es** *or* ~ morse *m* (*Zool*). (*hum*) **~ moustache** moustache *f* à la gauloise.

waltz [wɔ:ls] 1 **n** valse *f*. (*US fig*) **it was a ~!*** c'était du gâteau* *or* de la tarte*. 2 **vi** valser, danser la valse. (*fig*) (*gaily*) **to ~ in/out** *etc* entrer/sortir *etc* d'un pas joyeux *or* dansant; (*brazenly*) entrer/sortir *etc* avec désinvolture; **she ~ed in without even knocking*** elle a fait irruption sans même frapper; **he ~ed off with the prize*** il a gagné le prix haut la main; (*fig*) **he ~ed* into the job** il a obtenu le poste les mains dans les poches. 3 **vt: he ~ed her round the room** il l'a entraînée dans une valse tout autour de la pièce; (*fig: in delight etc*) il s'est mis à danser de joie avec elle.

waltzer ['wɔ:lsəʳ] **n** a (*dancer*) valseur *m*, -euse *f*. b (*at fairground*) Mont-Blanc *m*.

wampum ['wɒmpəm] **n** a (*beads*) wampum *m*. b (*US* ‡: *money*) pognon‡ *m*, fric‡ *m*.

WAN [wæn] **n** (**abbr of wide area network**) grand réseau *m*.

wan [wɒn] **adj** *complexion, sky, light* pâle, blême, blafard; *person, look* triste; *smile* pâle, faible. *[sky etc]* **to grow ~** pâlir, blêmir.

wand [wɒnd] **n** *[conjurer, fairy]* baguette *f* (magique); *[usher, steward, sheriff]* verge *f*, bâton *m*.

wander ['wɒndəʳ] 1 **n** tour *m*, balade* *f*. **to go for a ~ around the town/the shops** aller faire un tour en ville/dans les magasins.

2 **comp** ►**wanderlust** envie *f* de voir le monde, bougeotte* *f*.

3 **vi** a *[person]* errer, aller sans but; (*for pleasure*) flâner; *[thoughts]* errer, vagabonder, vaguer; *[river, road]* serpenter, faire des méandres. **he ~ed through the streets** il errait *or* allait sans but *or* flânait de par les rues, il se promenait au hasard des rues; **his glance ~ed round the room** son regard errait dans la pièce.

b (*stray*) s'égarer. **to ~ from the subject** s'écarter du sujet; **his eyes ~ed from the page** son regard distrait s'est écarté de la page; **his thoughts ~ed back to his youth** ses pensées se sont distraitement reportées à sa jeunesse; **his attention ~ed** il était distrait, il n'arrivait pas à fixer son attention *or* à se concentrer; **sorry, my mind was ~ing** excusez-moi, j'étais distrait; **his mind ~ed to the day when ...** il repensa par hasard au jour où ...; (*pej*) **his mind is ~ing, his wits are ~ing, he's ~ing*** (*from fever*) il délire, il divague; (*from old age*) il divague, il déraille*; **don't take any notice of what he says, he's just ~ing*** ne faites pas attention à ce qu'il dit, il radote.

c (*go casually*) **to ~ in/out/away** *etc* entrer/sortir/partir *etc* sans se presser *or* d'un pas nonchalant; **they ~ed round the shop** ils ont flâné dans le magasin; **let's ~ down to the café** descendons tranquillement *or* tout doucement au café.

4 **vt** parcourir au hasard, errer dans. **to ~ the streets** aller au hasard des rues, errer dans les rues; **to ~ the hills/the countryside** se promener au hasard *or* errer dans les collines/dans la campagne; **to ~ the world** courir le monde, rouler sa bosse*.

►**wander about, wander around vi** (*aimlessly*) aller sans but, se promener au hasard, errer; (*casually*) aller sans se presser *or* d'un pas nonchalant, flâner.

►**wander off vi** partir; (*get lost*) s'égarer. **he wandered off the path** il s'est écarté du chemin.

wanderer ['wɒndərəʳ] **n** vagabond(e) *m(f)* (*also pej*). (*hum*) **the ~'s returned!** tiens! — un revenant!

wandering ['wɒndərɪŋ] 1 **adj** *way of life, person* errant, vagabond; *river, road* qui serpente, en lacets; *tribe* nomade; *glance* errant, distrait; *imagination, thoughts* vagabond; (*pej*) *speech* diffus. **the W~ Jew** le Juif errant; **~ minstrel** ménestrel ambulant. 2 **npl: ~s** (*journeyings*) voyages *mpl* à l'aventure, vagabondages *mpl*; (*fig: in speech etc*) divagations *fpl*.

wane [weɪn] 1 **vi** *[moon]* décroître, décliner, être à son déclin; *[enthusiasm, interest, emotion]* diminuer; *[strength, reputation, popularity, empire]* décliner, être en déclin. 2 **n: to be on the ~ = to wane**; *see* **1**.

wangle* ['wæŋgl] 1 **n** combine* *f*. **it's a ~** c'est une combine*; **he got it by a ~** il se l'est procuré par le système D*, il l'a eu par une combine*.

2 **vt** a (*get*) se débrouiller pour avoir; (*without paying*) carotter*, resquiller*. **to ~ sth for sb** se débrouiller pour obtenir qch pour qn, carotter* qch pour qn; **can you ~ me a free ticket?** est-ce que tu peux m'avoir une place gratuite? *or* me resquiller* une place?; **I'll ~ it somehow** je me débrouillerai pour arranger ça, je goupillerai* ça; **he ~d £10 out of his father** il a soutiré *or* carotté* 10 livres à son père; **he ~d his way into the hall** il s'est faufilé dans la salle.

b (*fake*) *results, report, accounts* truquer*, cuisiner*.

3 **vi: to ~ in** *etc* = **to ~ one's way in** *etc; see* **2a**.

wangler* ['wæŋgləʳ] **n** (*see* **wangle 2a**) débrouillard(e)* *m(f)*; carotteur* *m*, -euse* *f*, resquilleur* *m*, -euse* *f*.

wangling* ['wæŋglɪŋ] **n** (*NonC*) système D* *m*, carottage* *m*, resquille* *f*.

waning ['weɪnɪŋ] (*see* **wane**) 1 **n** (*NonC*) décroissement *m*; déclin *m*; diminution *f*. 2 **adj** *moon* à son déclin; *enthusiasm, interest* qui diminue; *strength, reputation, popularity, empire* déclinant, sur son déclin.

wank‡‡ [wæŋk] (*Brit*) 1 **vi** se branler‡‡, se faire une branlette‡‡ 2 **n: to have a ~ = to wank**.

wanker‡‡ ['wæŋkəʳ] **n** (*Brit fig*) branleur‡‡ *m*.

wanly ['wɒnlɪ] **adv** *shine* avec une clarté pâle *or* blême; *smile, look, say* tristement, faiblement.

wanness ['wɒnnɪs] **n** *[person]* tristesse *f*; *[complexion]* pâleur *f*.

want [wɒnt] 1 **n** a (*NonC: lack*) manque *m*. **for ~ of** faute de, par manque de; **for ~ of anything better** faute de mieux; **for ~ of anything better to do** faute d'avoir quelque chose de mieux à faire; **for ~ of something to do he ...** comme il n'avait rien à faire il ..., par désœuvrement il ...; **it wasn't for ~ of trying that he ...** ce n'était pas faute d'avoir essayé qu'il ...; **there was no ~ of enthusiasm** ce n'était pas l'enthousiasme qui manquait, l'enthousiasme ne faisait pas défaut.

b (*NonC: poverty, need*) pauvreté *f*, besoin *m*, misère *f*. **to be** *or* **live in ~** être dans le besoin, être nécessiteux; **to be in ~ of sth** avoir besoin de qch.

c (*gen pl: requirement, need*) **~s** besoins *mpl*; **his ~s are few** il a peu de besoins, il n'a pas besoin de grand-chose; **it fills** *or* **meets a long-felt ~** cela comble enfin cette lacune.

2 **comp** ►**want ad** (*US Press*) demande *f* (*for* de).

3 **vt** a (*wish, desire*) vouloir, désirer (*to do* faire). **what do you**

~? que voulez-vous?, que désirez-vous?; **what do you ~ with** *or* **of him?** qu'est-ce que vous lui voulez?; **what do you ~ to do tomorrow?** qu'est-ce que vous avez envie de faire demain?, qu'est-ce que vous voulez *or* désirez faire demain?; **I don't ~ to!** je n'en ai pas envie!; (*more definite*) je ne veux pas!; **all I ~ is a good sleep** tout ce que je veux, c'est dormir longtemps; **he ~s success/popularity** il veut *or* désire *or* ambitionne le succès/la popularité; **I ~ your opinion on this** je voudrais votre avis là-dessus; **what does he ~ for that picture?** combien veut-il *or* demande-t-il pour ce tableau?; **I ~ you to tell me ...** je veux que tu me dises ...; **I ~ the car cleaned** je veux qu'on nettoie (*subj*) la voiture; **I always ~ed a car like this** j'ai toujours souhaité avoir une *or* j'ai toujours eu envie d'une voiture comme ça; **I was ~ing to leave** j'avais envie de partir; **to ~ in/out*** *etc* vouloir entrer/sortir *etc*; (*fig*) **he ~s out*** il ne veut plus continuer, il veut laisser tomber*; **you're not ~ed here** on n'a pas besoin de vous ici, on ne veut pas de vous ici; **I know when I'm not ~ed!*** je me rends compte que je suis de trop; **where do you ~ this table?** où voulez-vous (qu'on mette) cette table?; (*fig*) **you've got him where you ~ him** vous l'avez coincé*, vous le tenez à votre merci; (*iro*) **you don't ~ much!** il n'en faut pas beaucoup pour vous faire plaisir! *or* vous satisfaire! (*iro*); (*sexually*) **to ~ sb** désirer qn.

b (*seek, ask for*) demander. **the manager ~s you in his office** le directeur veut vous voir *or* vous demande dans son bureau; **you're ~ed on the phone** on vous demande au téléphone; **to be ~ed by the police** être recherché par la police; **"~ed for murder"** "recherché pour meurtre"; **"good cook ~ed"** "on demande une bonne cuisinière"; *see also* **wanted**.

c (*gen Brit*) (*need*) *[person]* avoir besoin de; *[task]* exiger, réclamer; (**: ought*) devoir (*to do* faire). **we have all we ~** nous avons tout ce qu'il nous faut; **just what I ~(ed)!** exactement ce qu'il me faut!; **you ~ a bigger hammer if you're going to do it properly** tu as besoin de *or* il te faut un marteau plus grand pour faire cela correctement; **what do you ~ with a house that size?** pourquoi as-tu besoin d'une *or* veux-tu une maison aussi grande?; **such work ~s good eyesight** un tel travail exige *or* réclame *or* nécessite une bonne vue; **the car ~s cleaning** la voiture a besoin* d'être lavée, il faudrait laver la voiture; **your hair ~s combing** tu as besoin de te peigner, il faudrait que tu te peignes (*subj*), tu devrais te peigner; **that child ~s a smacking** cet enfant a besoin d'une *or* mérite une fessée, une fessée ne ferait pas de mal à cet enfant; **you ~ to be careful with that!*** fais attention à ça!, fais gaffe‡ à ça!; **you ~ to see his new boat!*** il faudrait que tu voies son nouveau bateau!, tu devrais voir son nouveau bateau!

d (*lack*) **he ~s talent** il manque de talent, le talent lui fait défaut; **this shirt ~s a button** il manque un bouton à cette chemise; **the carpet ~s 5 cm to make it fit** il manque 5 cm pour que le tapis soit de la bonne dimension; **it ~ed only his agreement** il ne manquait que son accord; **it ~s 12 minutes to midnight** dans 12 minutes il sera minuit.

4 vi (*be in need*) être dans le besoin *or* la misère, être nécessiteux. (*lack*) **to ~ for sth** manquer de qch, avoir besoin de qch; **they ~ for nothing** il ne leur manque rien, ils ne manquent de rien, ils n'ont besoin de rien; *see* **waste**.

wanted ['wɒntɪd] adj a *criminal* recherché par la police. **"~ for murder"** "recherché pour meurtre"; **the ~ man** le suspect, l'homme que la police recherche (*or* recherchait); (*Police*) **~ notice** avis *m* de recherche; *see also* **want 3b**. b (*Press*) **"~"** "demandes" *fpl*; **to put in a ~ advertisement** mettre une petite annonce sous la rubrique "demandes".

wanting ['wɒntɪŋ] 1 adj a (*missing*) **the end of the poem is ~** il manque la fin du poème, la fin du poème manque; **a sense of compassion is ~ in the novel** le roman manque *or* est dépourvu d'un sens de la charité; **the necessary funds were ~** les fonds nécessaires faisaient défaut *or* manquaient.

b (*lacking in, short of*) **~ in** qui manque de, déficient en; **he was ~ in courage** il manquait de courage, le courage lui manquait *or* lui faisait défaut; (*loc*) **he was tried and found ~** il a été mis à l'épreuve et jugé insuffisant; **it was tried and found ~** on s'est aperçu que ce n'était pas suffisamment bien; (*pej*) **he is a bit ~*** il est simplet, il lui manque une case‡.

2 prep (*without*) sans; (*minus*) moins.

wanton ['wɒntən] 1 adj a (*pej*) *woman* dévergondé; *thoughts* impudique, libertin. b (*liter: capricious*) *person, breeze* capricieux. **a ~ growth of weeds** des mauvaises herbes luxuriantes *or* exubérantes. c (*gratuitous*) *cruelty, destruction* gratuit, injustifié, absurde. 2 n (††) dévergondée *f*, femme légère.

wantonly ['wɒntənlɪ] adv (*see* **wanton**) de façon dévergondée; impudiquement; capricieusement; *destroy, spoil etc* gratuitement, de façon injustifiée.

wantonness ['wɒntənnɪs] n (*NonC: see* **wanton**) dévergondage *m*; caprices *mpl*; *[cruelty, destruction]* gratuité *f*, absurdité *f*.

war [wɔːʳ] 1 n guerre *f*. **to be at ~** être en (état de) guerre (*with* avec); *[country]* **to go to ~** se mettre en guerre, entrer en guerre (*against* contre, *over* à propos de); *[soldier]* **to go (off) to ~** partir pour la guerre, aller à la guerre; (*Mil, also fig*) **to make ~ on** faire la guerre à; **~ of attrition** guerre d'usure; **the W~s of the Roses** la guerre des Deux-Roses; **the Great W~** la Grande Guerre, la guerre de 14 *or* de 14-18; **the (American) W~ of Independence** la guerre de Sécession; **the period between the ~s** (*1918-39*) l'entre-deux-guerres *m inv*; (*Brit*) **the W~ Office**, (*US*) **the W~ Department** le ministère de la Guerre; (*Mil, fig*) **to carry** *or* **take the ~ into the enemy's camp** passer à l'attaque, prendre l'offensive, porter la guerre chez l'ennemi; (*fig*) **it was ~ to the knife** *or* **the death between them** c'était une lutte à couteaux tirés entre eux; (*fig*) **~ of words** guerre de paroles; (*fig*) **you've been in the ~s again*** tu t'es encore fait amocher‡ *or* estropier; *see* **cold, nerve, state** *etc*.

2 comp *conditions, debt, crime, criminal, orphan, widow, wound, zone* de guerre ► **war bond** (*US Hist*) titre *m* d'emprunt de guerre (*pendant la Deuxième Guerre mondiale*) ► **war bride** mariée *f* de la guerre ► **war chest** (*US Pol etc*) caisse spéciale (d'un parti politique pour les élections) ► **war clouds** (*fig*) nuages avant-coureurs de la guerre ► **war correspondent** (*Press, Rad, TV*) correspondant *m* de guerre ► **war cry** cri *m* de guerre ► **war dance** danse guerrière ► **war-disabled** mutilé(e)s *m(f)pl or* invalides *mfpl* de guerre ► **warfare** (*NonC*) (*Mil*) guerre *f* (*NonC*); (*fig*) lutte *f* (*against* contre); **class warfare** lutte *f* des classes ► **war fever** psychose *f* de guerre ► **war footing: on a war footing** sur le pied de guerre ► **war games** (*Mil: for training*) kriegspiel *m*; (*Mil: practice manoeuvres*) manœuvres *fpl* militaires; (*board games*) jeux *mpl* de stratégie militaire ► **warhead** ogive *f*; **nuclear warhead** ogive *f or* tête *f* nucléaire ► **warhorse** cheval *m* de bataille; (*fig*) **an old warhorse** un vétéran, un(e) dur(e) à cuire* ► **warlike** guerrier, belliqueux ► **war lord** chef *m* militaire, seigneur *m* de la guerre ► **war memorial** monument *m* aux morts ► **warmonger(ing)** *see* **warmonger(ing)** ► **war paint** peinture *f* de guerre (*des Indiens*); (*fig hum: make-up*) maquillage *m*, peinturlurage *m* (*pej*) ► **warpath:** (*fig*) **to be on the warpath** être sur le sentier de la guerre, chercher la bagarre* ► **war record: what is his war record?** qu'est-ce qu'il a fait pendant la guerre?; **he has a good war record** son état de service pendant la guerre est tout à fait honorable ► **warship** navire *m or* vaisseau *m* de guerre ► **wartime** (*NonC: n*) temps *m* de guerre; (*comp*) de guerre; **in wartime** en temps de guerre ► **war-torn** déchiré par la guerre ► **war-weary** las (*f* lasse) de la guerre ► **war whoop** (*US*) cri *m* de guerre ► **the war-wounded** les blessés *mpl* de guerre.

3 vi faire la guerre (*against* à).

warble[1] ['wɔːbl] n a (*abcess*) *[cattle]* var(r)on *m*. b (*on horse's back*) callosité *f*.

warble[2] ['wɔːbl] 1 n gazouillis *m*, gazouillements *mpl*. 2 vi *[bird]* gazouiller; *[person]* roucouler. 3 vt (*also* **~ out**) chanter en gazouillant.

warbler ['wɔːbləʳ] n fauvette *f*, pouillot *m*.

warbling ['wɔːblɪŋ] n gazouillis *m*, gazouillement(s) *m(pl)*.

ward [wɔːd] 1 n a (*Jur: person*) pupille *mf*. **~ of court** pupille sous tutelle judiciaire; **in ~** sous tutelle judiciaire; *see* **watch**[2]. b (*Brit: Local Government*) section électorale. c *[hospital]* salle *f*, (*separate building*) pavillon *m*; *[prison]* quartier *m*. 2 comp ► **ward heeler** (*US Pol pej*) agent *or* courtier électoral ► **wardroom** (*Naut*) carré *m* ► **ward round** (*Med*) visite *f* (*de médecin hospitalier*).

►**ward off** vt sep *blow, danger* parer, éviter; *illness* éviter.

warden ['wɔːdn] n *[institution]* directeur *m*, -trice *f*; *[city, castle]* gouverneur *m*; *[park, game reserve]* gardien *m*, -ienne *f*; *[youth hostel]* père *m or* mère *f* aubergiste; (*US: prison governor*) directeur, -trice; *[student residence etc]* directeur *m*, -trice *f* de foyer universitaire; (*Brit: on hospital board etc*) membre *m* du conseil d'administration; (*Brit: air-raid ~*) préposé(e) *m(f)* à la défense passive; (*traffic ~*) contractuel(le) *m(f)*. (*Brit*) **W~ of the Cinque Ports** gouverneur des Cinque Ports; *see* **church, fire** *etc*.

warder ['wɔːdəʳ] n a (*esp Brit:* †) gardien *m or* surveillant *m* (de prison). b (*esp US*) (*in building*) concierge *m*; (*in museum*) gardien *m* (de musée).

wardress ['wɔːdrɪs] n (*esp Brit*) gardienne *f or* surveillante *f* (de prison).

wardrobe ['wɔːdrəʊb] 1 n (*cupboard*) armoire *f*, penderie *f*, garde-robe *f*; (*clothes*) garde-robe; (*Theat*) costumes *mpl*. (*Cine, Theat*) **Miss X's ~ by ...** costumes de Mlle X par ..., Mlle X est habillée par ... . 2 comp ► **wardrobe mistress** (*Theat*) costumière *f* ► **wardrobe trunk** malle *f* penderie.

...ward(s) [wəd(z)] suf vers, dans la *or* en direction de. **townward(s)** vers la ville, dans la *or* en direction de la ville; *see* **backward(s), downward(s)** *etc*.

wardship ['wɔːdʃɪp] n (*NonC*) tutelle *f*.

...ware [wɛəʳ] n ending in comps: (*NonC*) **kitchenware** articles *mpl* de cuisine; (*NonC*) **silverware** argenterie *f*; *see* **hard** *etc*.

warehouse ['wɛəhaʊs] 1 n, pl **warehouses** ['wɛəˌhaʊzɪz] entrepôt *m*, magasin *m*. 2 ['wɛəhaʊz] vt entreposer, mettre en magasin, emmagasiner. 3 comp ► **warehouseman** magasinier *m*.

warehousing ['wɛəhaʊzɪŋ] n (*Comm*) entreposage *m*, magasinage *m*.

wares [wɛəz] npl marchandises *fpl*.

warily ['wɛərɪlɪ] adv (*see* **wary**) avec prudence, avec circonspection; avec précaution. ... **she said ~** ... dit-elle *or* avança-t-elle avec précaution.

wariness ['wɛərɪnɪs] n (*NonC: see* **wary**) prudence *f*, circonspection *f*; précaution *f*.

warlock ['wɔːlɒk] n sorcier *m*.

warm [wɔːm] 1 adj a (assez) chaud. **I am ~** j'ai (assez) chaud; **this room is quite ~** il fait (assez) chaud *or* il fait bon dans cette pièce; **a ~ iron/oven** un fer/four moyen; **the iron/oven is ~** le fer/four est (assez) chaud; **a ~ fire** un bon feu; **I am as ~ as toast** je suis chaud comme une caille*; **it's ~, the weather is ~** il fait chaud; **it's too ~ in here** il fait trop chaud ici, on étouffe ici; **it's nice and ~ in here** il fait bon ici, il fait agréablement chaud ici; **in ~ weather** par temps chaud; (*Met*) **~ front** front chaud; **the water is just ~** l'eau est juste chaude *or* n'est pas très chaude; **this coffee's only ~** ce café n'est pas assez chaud *or* est tiède; **to get sth ~** (ré)chauffer qch; **to get** *or* **grow ~** *[person]* se (ré)chauffer; *[water, object]* chauffer; (*in guessing etc games*) **you're getting ~(er)!** tu chauffes!; **to keep sth ~** *or* **in a ~ place** tenir qch au chaud; **keep me ~** tiens-moi chaud; (*of sick person*) **keep him ~** ne le laissez pas prendre froid; **this scarf keeps me ~** cette écharpe me tient chaud; **you've got to keep yourself ~** surtout ne prenez pas froid; **it's ~ work** c'est du travail qui donne chaud; **the trail is still ~** les traces sont récentes; (*fig*) **to make things ~ for sb** mener la vie dure à qn, en faire voir de dures* à qn; **things got too ~ for him** ça chauffait* trop *or* ça bardait‡ trop à son goût.

b (*fig*) *colour, shade* chaud; *voice, tone* chaud, chaleureux, entraînant; *dispute, discussion* chaud, vif, animé; *temperament* chaud, vif; *feelings* chaud, chaleureux; *apologies, thanks* vif; *greeting, welcome, congratulations, encouragement* cordial, chaleureux; *applause* chaleureux, enthousiaste; *supporter, admirer* ardent, chaud, enthousiaste. **they have a very ~ relationship** ils ont beaucoup d'affection l'un pour l'autre; **she is a very ~ person, she has a very ~ nature** *or* **heart** elle est très chaleureuse *or* affectueuse (de nature), elle est pleine de chaleur; (*in letter*) **"with ~est wishes"** "avec tous mes vœux les plus amicaux".

2 comp ►**warm-blooded** (*Zool*) à sang chaud; (*fig*) ardent, sensuel, qui a le sang chaud ►**warm-hearted** chaleureux, affectueux ►**warm-up*** (*Sport*) échauffement *m*; (*Rad, Theat, TV etc*) mise en train; **warm-up exercises** exercices *mpl* d'échauffement.

3 n (*) **to give sth a ~** (ré)chauffer qch; **come and have a ~ by the fire** viens te (ré)chauffer près du feu; **come inside and sit in the ~** entrez vous asseoir au chaud.

4 vt (*also* **~ up**) *person, room* réchauffer; *water, food* (ré)chauffer, faire (ré)chauffer; *coat, slippers* (ré)chauffer. **to ~ o.s.** se (ré)chauffer; **to ~ one's feet/hands** se (ré)chauffer les pieds/les mains; (*fig*) **the news ~ed my heart** la nouvelle m'a (ré)chauffé le cœur; *see* **cockle**.

5 vi a (*also* **~ up**) *[person]* se (ré)chauffer; *[water, food, clothing]* chauffer; *[room, bed]* se réchauffer, devenir plus chaud.

b (*fig*) **to ~ to an idea** s'enthousiasmer peu à peu pour une idée; **I ~ed to him, my heart ~ed to him** je me suis pris de sympathie pour lui; **to ~ to one's subject** se laisser entraîner par son sujet, traiter son sujet avec un enthousiasme grandissant.

►**warm over, warm through** vt sep *food* faire (ré)chauffer.

►**warm up** 1 vi a = **warm 5a**. b *[engine, car]* se réchauffer; *[athlete, dancer]* s'échauffer; *[discussion]* s'échauffer, s'animer; *[audience]* devenir animé. **the party was warming up** la soirée commençait à être pleine d'entrain, la soirée chauffait*; **the game is warming up** la partie commence à devenir excitante; **things are warming up** ça commence à s'animer *or* à chauffer*. 2 vt sep *person, room* réchauffer; *water, food* (ré)chauffer, faire (ré)chauffer; *coat, slippers* (ré)chauffer; *engine, car* faire chauffer; *discussion* animer; (*Theat etc*) *audience* mettre en train. 3 **warm-up*** n *see* **warm 2**. 4 **warming-up** adj *see* **warming 2**.

warming ['wɔːmɪŋ] 1 adj *drink* qui réchauffe; (*fig: heart~*) qui réchauffe le cœur, réconfortant. 2 comp ►**warming oven** four *m* à réchauffer ►**warming pan** bassinoire *f* ►**warming-up exercises** exercices *mpl* d'échauffement.

warmly ['wɔːmlɪ] adv *clothe, wrap up* chaudement; (*fig*) *congratulate, welcome* chaudement, chaleureusement, cordialement; *applaud* chaleureusement, avec enthousiasme; *thank, recommend* vivement, chaudement. **the sun shone ~** le soleil était chaud; **tucked up ~ in bed** bordé bien au chaud dans son lit.

warmonger ['wɔːˌmʌŋgəʳ] n belliciste *mf*.

warmongering ['wɔːˌmʌŋgərɪŋ] 1 adj belliciste. 2 n (*NonC*) propagande *f* belliciste.

warmth [wɔːmθ] n (*NonC: see* **warm 1a, 1b**) chaleur *f*; vivacité *f*; cordialité *f*.

warn [wɔːn] vt prévenir, avertir (*of* de, *that* que). **to ~ the police** alerter la police; **you have been ~ed!** vous êtes averti! *or* prévenu!; **to ~ sb against doing** *or* **not to do** conseiller *or* recommander à qn de ne pas faire, déconseiller à qn de faire; **to ~ sb off** *or* **against sth** mettre qn en garde contre qch, déconseiller qch à qn.

warning ['wɔːnɪŋ] 1 n a (*act*) avertissement *m*; (*in writing*) avis *m*, préavis *m*; (*signal: also Mil*) alerte *f*, alarme *f*; (*Met*) avis. **it fell without ~** c'est tombé inopinément; **they arrived without ~** ils sont arrivés à l'improviste *or* sans prévenir; **he left me without ~** il m'a quitté sans me prévenir; **let this be a ~ to you** que cela vous serve d'avertissement; **thank you for the ~** merci de m'avoir prévenu *or* averti; **there was a note of ~ in his voice** il y avait une mise en garde dans le ton qu'il a pris; **to take ~ from** tirer la leçon de; **his employer gave him a ~ about lateness** son patron lui a donné un avertissement à propos de son manque de ponctualité; **to give a week's ~** prévenir huit jours à l'avance; (*more formal*) donner un délai de huit jours; (*in writing*) donner un préavis de huit jours; **I gave you due ~ (that)** je vous avais bien prévenu (que); (*Met*) **gale/storm ~** avis de grand vent/de tempête; (*Mil*) **4 minute ~** alerte de 4 minutes.

2 adj *glance, cry* d'avertissement. **~ device** dispositif *m* d'alarme, avertisseur *m*; **~ light** voyant *m* (avertisseur), avertisseur lumineux; **~ notice** avis *m*, avertissement *m*; **~ shot** (*gen, Mil*) coup tiré en guise d'avertissement; (*Naut*) coup *m* de semonce; (*fig*) avertissement; **~ sign** panneau avertisseur; (*Aut*) **~ triangle** triangle *m* de présignalisation; **... he said in a ~ tone** *or* **voice ...** dit-il pour mettre en garde.

warp [wɔːp] 1 n a (*Tex*) chaîne *f*; (*fig: essence, base*) fibre *f*. b (*distortion*) (*in wood*) gauchissement *m*, voilure *f*; (*in metal*) voilure; (*Sound-Recording*) voile *m* (d'un disque); *see* **time**. 2 vt *wood* gauchir, voiler; *metal, aircraft wing, tennis racket* voiler; (*fig*) *judgment* fausser, pervertir; *mind, character, person* pervertir. **he has a ~ed mind, his mind is ~ed** il a l'esprit tordu; **he has a ~ed sense of humour** il a un sens de l'humour morbide; **he gave us a ~ed account of ...** il nous a fait un récit tendancieux de ... . 3 vi gauchir, se voiler; se fausser, se pervertir; devenir débauché *or* corrompu.

warrant ['wɒrənt] 1 n a (*NonC: justification*) justification *f*, droit *m*. **he has no ~ for saying so** il ne s'appuie sur rien pour justifier cela.

b (*Comm, Fin etc: certificate*) (*for payment or services*) bon *m*; (*guarantee*) garantie *f*; (*Customs*) warrant *m*; (*Mil*) brevet *m*; (*Jur, Police*) mandat *m*. (*Jur*) **there is a ~ out against him, there is a ~ out for his arrest** on a émis un mandat d'arrêt contre lui; (*Police*) **let me see your ~** je veux voir votre mandat (d'arrêt *or* de perquisition *etc*); *see* **death, search**.

2 comp ►**warrant officer** (*Mil*) adjudant *m* (*auxiliaire de l'officier*) ►**warrant sale** (*Scot Jur*) vente *f* forcée *or* judiciaire.

3 vt a (*justify*) *action, assumption, reaction, behaviour* justifier, légitimer. **the facts do not ~ it** les faits ne le justifient pas *or* ne le permettent pas.

b (*guarantee*) garantir. **I'll ~ (you) he won't do it again!** je vous assure *or* promets *or* certifie qu'il ne recommencera pas!

warrantable ['wɒrəntəbl] adj justifiable, légitime.

warranted ['wɒrəntɪd] adj a (*justified*) justifié. b (*guaranteed*) garanti.

warrantee [ˌwɒrən'tiː] n (*Jur*) créancier *m*, -ière *f*.

warranter, warrantor ['wɒrəntəʳ] n (*Jur*) garant(e) *m(f)*, débiteur *m*, -trice *f*.

warranty ['wɒrəntɪ] n autorisation *f*, droit *m*; (*Comm, Jur*) garantie *f*.

warren ['wɒrən] n *[rabbits]* terriers *mpl*, garenne *f*; (*fig*) (*overcrowded house, tenement*) taupinière *f* (*fig*); (*part of town*) dédale *m*, labyrinthe *m*. **a ~ of little streets** un dédale *or* un labyrinthe de petites rues.

warring ['wɔːrɪŋ] adj *nations* en guerre; (*fig*) *interests* contradictoires, contraires; *ideologies* en conflit, en opposition.

warrior ['wɒrɪəʳ] n guerrier *m*, -ière *f*; *see* **unknown**.

Warsaw ['wɔːsɔː] n Varsovie. **the ~ Pact countries** les pays du pacte de Varsovie.

wart [wɔːt] 1 n (*Med*) verrue *f*; (*Bot*) excroissance *f*; (*on wood*) loupe *f*. (*fig*) **~s and all** sans aucune flatterie, sans aucun embellissement. 2 comp ►**wart hog** phacochère *m*.

warty ['wɔːtɪ] adj couvert de verrues, verruqueux.

wary ['wɛərɪ] adj *person* prudent, sur ses gardes, circonspect; *voice, look* prudent; *manner* précautionneux. **to be ~ about sb/sth** se méfier de qn/qch; **to be ~ of doing sth** hésiter beaucoup à faire qch; **it's best to be ~ here** il vaut mieux être prudent *or* être sur ses gardes *or* prendre ses précautions ici; **to keep a ~ eye on sb/sth** avoir l'œil sur qn/qch, surveiller qn/qch de près.

was [wɒz] pret of **be**.

wash [wɒʃ] 1 n a **to give sth a ~** laver qch; **to have a ~** se laver, faire sa toilette; **to have a quick ~** se débarbouiller, faire un brin de toilette; (*notice*) **"~ and brush-up: 16p"** ≃ "serviette et savon: 16 pence"; **it needs a ~** cela a besoin d'être lavé, il faut laver cela; **your face needs a ~** il faut que tu te laves (*subj*) la figure *or* que tu te débarbouilles (*subj*); **to send sheets to the ~** envoyer des draps au blanchissage *or* à la laverie; **in the ~** (*in basket etc*) au sale; (*in tub, washing machine*) à la lessive; **the colours ran in the ~** cela a déteint à la lessive *or* au lavage; (*fig*) **it will all come out in the ~*** (*be known*) on finira bien par savoir ce qu'il en est; (*be all right*) ça finira par se tasser* *or* s'arranger; *see* **car**.

b = **washing 1b**.

c *[ship]* sillage *m*, remous *m*; (*sound: of waves etc*) clapotis *m*.

d (*layer of paint: for walls etc*) badigeon *m*. **to give the walls a blue ~** badigeonner les murs en *or* de bleu; *see* **whitewash** *etc*.

e (*Art*) lavis *m*. **to put a ~ on a drawing** laver un dessin.

f (*Pharm*) solution *f*; *see* **eye, mouth**.

g (*Brit Geog*) **the W~** le golfe du Wash.

2 **comp** ▸ **wash-and-wear** *shirt* sans entretien ▸ **washbasin** (*Brit*) (cuvette *f* de) lavabo *m* ▸ **washboard** planche *f* à laver (*also Mus*) ▸ **washbowl** = **washbasin** ▸ **washcloth** (*esp US*) gant *m* de toilette ▸ **washday** jour *m* de lessive ▸ **washdown: to give sth a washdown** laver qch à grande eau ▸ **wash drawing** (*Art*) (dessin *m* au) lavis *m* ▸ **wash-hand basin** = **washbasin** ▸ **wash house** lavoir *m* ▸ **wash leather** (*Brit*) peau *f* de chamois ▸ **wash-out*** (*event, play*) fiasco *m*, désastre *m*; (*person*) zéro *m*, nullité *f* ▸ **washrag** (*US*) gant *m* de toilette ▸ **washroom** toilettes *fpl* ▸ **washstand** lavabo *m*; (*unplumbed*) console *f* de toilette ▸ **washtub** (*bath*) tub *m*; (*for clothes*) baquet *m*, bassine *f*.

3 **vt** a (*gen*) laver. **to ~ o.s.** *[person]* se laver, faire sa toilette; *[cat]* faire sa toilette; **to ~ one's hair** se laver la tête, se faire un shampooing; **to ~ one's hands** se laver les mains; (*fig*) **to ~ one's hands of sth** se laver les mains de qch; (*fig*) **to ~ one's hands of sb** se désintéresser de qn; **to ~ a child's face** laver le visage d'un enfant, débarbouiller un enfant; **he ~ed the dirt off his hands** il s'est lavé les mains (pour en enlever la saleté); **to ~ the dishes** faire la vaisselle; **to ~ the clothes** faire la lessive; **to ~ sth with detergent/in hot water** nettoyer qch avec du détergent/à l'eau chaude; (*fig*) **to ~ one's dirty linen in public** laver son linge sale en public; **he ~ed the floor clean** il a bien nettoyé *or* lavé le sol; **the rain ~ed it clean** la pluie l'a lavé; **the rain ~ed the car clean of mud** la pluie a fait partir toute la boue de la voiture; (*fig*) **to be ~ed clean** *or* **free of sin** être lavé de tout péché.

b *[river, sea, waves, current]* (*carry away*) emporter, entraîner; (*carry ashore*) rejeter; (*flow over*) baigner; (*scoop out*) creuser. **several barrels were ~ed ashore** plusieurs tonneaux ont échoué *or* ont été rejetés sur la côte; **to be ~ed out to sea** être emporté par la mer, être entraîné vers le large; **to be ~ed overboard** être emporté par une vague; **the raft was ~ed downstream** le radeau a été emporté *or* entraîné en aval; **the Atlantic ~es its western shores** la côte ouest est baignée par l'Atlantique; **the water ~ed a channel through the sand** l'eau a creusé un chenal dans le sable; *see* **overboard**.

c (*Min*) *earth, gravel, gold, ore* laver; (*Chem*) *gas* épurer. **to ~ walls with distemper** badigeonner des murs, passer des murs au badigeon, peindre des murs à la détrempe; **to ~ brass with gold** couvrir du cuivre d'une pellicule d'or.

4 **vi** a (*have a ~*) *[person]* se laver, faire sa toilette; *[cat]* faire sa toilette*; (*do the washing*) laver, faire la lessive. **he ~ed in cold water** il s'est lavé à l'eau froide; **this fabric will/won't ~** ce tissu est/n'est pas lavable; (*Brit fig*) **that just won't ~!*** ça ne prend pas!; **that excuse won't ~ with him*** cette excuse ne prendra pas *or* ne marchera pas avec lui, on ne lui fera pas avaler cette excuse.

b *[waves, sea, flood, river]* **to ~ against** *cliffs, rocks* baigner; *lighthouse, boat* clapoter contre; **to ~ over sth** balayer qch; **let the music ~ over you** laisse-toi bercer par la musique.

▸**wash away** 1 **vi** (*with soap*) s'en aller *or* partir au lavage; (*with water*) s'en aller *or* partir à l'eau. 2 **vt sep** a *[person] stain* enlever *or* faire partir au lavage; *mud* enlever à l'eau; (*fig*) *sins* laver. **the rain washed the mud away** la pluie a fait partir la boue. b *[river, current, sea]* (*carry away*) emporter; (*destroy*) éroder, dégrader; *footprints etc* balayer, effacer. **the boat was washed away** le bateau a été emporté; **the river washed away part of the bank** la rivière a érodé *or* dégradé une partie de la rive.

▸**wash down** 1 **vt sep** a *deck, car* laver (à grande eau); *wall* lessiver. b *medicine, pill* faire descendre (*with* avec); *food* arroser (*with* de). c *[rain, flood, river]* emporter, entraîner. 2 **washdown n** *see* **wash 2**.

▸**wash in vt sep** *[sea, tide]* rejeter (sur le rivage).

▸**wash off** 1 **vi** (*from clothes*) s'en aller *or* partir au lavage (*with soap*) *or* à l'eau (*with water*); (*from walls*) partir au lessivage. **it won't wash off** ça ne s'en va pas, ça ne part pas, c'est indélébile; (*from hands*) **it will wash off** ça partira quand tu te laveras (*or* je me laverai *etc*) les mains. 2 **vt sep** (*from clothes*) faire partir au lavage (*with soap*) *or* à l'eau (*with water*); (*from wall*) faire partir en lessivant.

▸**wash out** 1 **vi** a *[stain]* s'en aller *or* partir au lavage (*with soap*) *or* à l'eau (*with water*); *[dye, colours]* passer au lavage. **this stain won't wash out** cette tache ne s'en va pas *or* ne part pas, cette tache est indélébile.

b (*US* ‡) **he washed out of university** il s'est fait recaler aux examens de la fac*.

2 **vt sep** a (*remove*) *stain* enlever *or* faire partir au lavage (*with soap*) *or* à l'eau (*with water*).

b (*clean*) *bottle, pan* laver.

c (*fig: spoil*) perturber; (*: *cancel*) rendre impossible. (*fig: by rain*) **the match was washed out** (*prevented*) le match a été annulé *or* n'a pas eu lieu à cause de la pluie; (*halted*) la pluie a perturbé *or* interrompu le match; **his illness has washed out* any chance of a holiday this year** sa maladie a anéanti toute possibilité de vacances cette année; **our plans were washed out* by the change in the exchange rate** nos projets sont partis à vau-l'eau avec le nouveau taux de change; (*tired etc*) **to be/look/feel washed out*** être/avoir l'air/se sentir complètement lessivé*.

d (*fig: pale*) **washed-out** *colour* délavé.

3 **wash-out* n** *see* **wash 2**.

▸**wash through vt sep** *clothes* laver rapidement, passer à l'eau.

▸**wash up** 1 **vi** a (*Brit: wash dishes*) faire *or* laver la vaisselle. b (*US: have a wash*) se débarbouiller, faire un brin de toilette. 2 **vt sep** a (*Brit*) *plates, cups* laver. **to wash up the dishes** faire *or* laver la vaisselle. b *[sea, tide]* rejeter (sur le rivage). c (*: *finish: gen pass*) **to be (all) washed up** *[plan, scheme]* être fichu*, être tombé à l'eau*; *[marriage, relationship]* être en ruines; **Paul and Anne are all washed up** tout est fini entre Paul et Anne; (*tired etc*) **to be/feel/look washed up** être/se sentir/avoir l'air lessivé*. 3 **washing-up n, adj** *see* **washing 2**.

washable ['wɒʃəbl] **adj** lavable, lessivable.

washer ['wɒʃəʳ] 1 **n** a (*Tech*) rondelle *f*, joint *m*; (*in tap*) rondelle. b (*washing machine*) machine *f* à laver; (*Aut: for windscreen*) lave-glace *m inv*; *see* **dish, wind**[1] *etc*. 2 **comp** ▸ **washer-dryer** machine *f* lavante-séchante ▸ **washerwoman** laveuse *f* (de linge).

washing ['wɒʃɪŋ] 1 **n** a (*act*) *[car]* lavage *m*; *[clothes]* lessive *f*, blanchissage *m*; *[walls]* lessivage *m*. **I do a big ~ on Mondays** je fais une grande lessive le lundi, le lundi est mon jour de grande lessive; *see* **brain**.

b (*NonC: clothes*) linge *m*, lessive *f*. **to do the ~** faire la lessive, laver le linge; **put your jeans in the ~** mets tes jeans au sale; **your shirt is in the ~** ta chemise est à la lessive.

2 **comp** ▸ **washing day** jour *m* de lessive ▸ **washing line** corde *f* à linge ▸ **washing machine** machine *f* à laver, lave-linge *m* ▸ **washing powder** (*Brit*) lessive *f* (en poudre), détergent *m* ▸ **washing soda** cristaux *mpl* de soude ▸ **washing-up** (*Brit*) vaisselle *f* (*à laver etc*); **to do the washing-up** faire *or* laver la vaisselle; **look at all that washing-up!** regarde tout ce qu'il y a comme vaisselle à faire! *or* à laver!; **washing-up bowl** bassine *f*, cuvette *f*; **washing-up liquid** produit *m* pour la vaisselle, (produit) lave-vaisselle *m inv*; **washing-up water** eau *f* de vaisselle.

Washington ['wɒʃɪŋtən] **n** (*city, state*) Washington *m*. **in ~ (State)** dans le Washington.

washy ['wɒʃɪ] **adj** = **wishy-washy**.

wasn't ['wɒznt] = **was not**; *see* **be**.

wasp [wɒsp] 1 **n** a guêpe *f*. **~'s nest** guêpier *m*. b (*US* *) (**abbr of White Anglo-Saxon Protestant**) **W~** *or* **WASP** blanc protestant, blanche protestante. 2 **comp** ▸ **wasp-waisted** à taille de guêpe.

waspish ['wɒspɪʃ] **adj** grincheux, hargneux.

waspishly ['wɒspɪʃlɪ] **adv** avec hargne.

wassail†† ['wɒseɪl] 1 **n** (*festivity*) beuverie *f*; (*drink*) bière épicée. 2 **vi** faire ribote†.

wast†† [wɒst] **2nd pers sg pret of be**.

wastage ['weɪstɪdʒ] 1 **n** (*NonC*) *[resources, energy, food, money]* gaspillage *m*; *[time]* perte *f*, gâchage *m*; (*amount lost from container*) fuites *fpl*, pertes *fpl*; (*rejects*) déchets *mpl*; (*as part of industrial process etc*) déperdition *f*; (*Comm: through pilfering etc*) coulage *m*. **such a ~ of good men** un tel gaspillage de talent; **there is a huge ~ of energy/money** on gaspille énormément d'énergie/d'argent; **the amount of ~ that goes on in large establishments** le gaspillage *or* le gâchis qui se produit dans les grands établissements; *see* **waste**.

2 **comp** ▸ **wastage rate: the wastage rate among students/entrants to the profession** le pourcentage d'étudiants qui abandonnent en cours d'études/de ceux qui abandonnent en début de carrière.

waste [weɪst] 1 **n** a (*NonC*) *[resources, energy, food, money]* gaspillage *m*, gâchis *m*; *[time]* perte *f*. **to go** *or* **run to ~** être gaspillé, se perdre inutilement; *[land]* tomber en friche, être à l'abandon; **there's too much ~ in this firm** il y a trop de gaspillage dans cette compagnie; **we must reduce the ~ in the kitchens** nous devons diminuer le gaspillage *or* le gâchis dans les cuisines; **it's a ~ of manpower** c'est un gaspillage de ressources humaines; **it's a ~ of money to do that** on gaspille de l'argent en faisant cela, on perd de l'argent à faire cela; **that machine was a ~ of money** cela ne valait vraiment pas la peine d'acheter cette machine, on a vraiment fichu de l'argent en l'air* en achetant cette machine; **it's a ~ of effort** c'est un effort inutile *or* perdu; **it's a ~ of time!** c'est une perte de temps!, c'est du temps perdu!; **it's a ~ of time doing that** on perd son temps à faire *or* en faisant cela; **it's a ~ of time and energy** c'est peine perdue; **it's a ~ of breath** c'est perdre sa salive, c'est dépenser sa salive pour rien; **what a ~!** quel gaspillage!

b (*NonC:* **~ material**: *also* (*US*) **~s**) déchets *mpl*; (*household ~*) ordures *fpl* (ménagères); (*water*) eaux sales *or* usées. **industrial/kitchen ~** déchets industriels/domestiques; **nuclear/metal ~** déchets nucléaires/de métal; *see* **cotton**.

c (*expanse: often pl*) terres désolées, désert *m*; (*in town*) terrain *m* vague. **~s** *or* **a ~ of snow and ice** un désert immense de neige et de glace.

2 **adj** *energy, heat* perdu; *food* superflu, inutilisé; *water* usé, sale; *land, ground* inculte, en friche; *region, district* à l'abandon, désolé. (*gen, also Physiol*) **~ material, ~ matter** déchets *mpl*; **~ products** (*Ind*) déchets *mpl* de fabrication; (*Physiol*) déchets (de l'organisme); **a piece of ~ land** un terrain vague (*see also* **3**); **"The W~ Land"** "la Terre désolée"; **to lay ~** ravager, dévaster.

3 **comp** ▸ **wastebasket** corbeille *f* (à papier) ▸ **wastebin** (*Brit*)

(*wastebasket*) corbeille *f* (à papier); (*in kitchen*) boîte *f* à ordures, poubelle *f* ►**waste disposal unit** broyeur *m* d'ordures ►**wasteland** (*gen*) terres *fpl* à l'abandon *or* en friche; (*in town*) terrain *m* vague; (*after holocaust*) désert *m* ►**waste management** gestion *f* des déchets ►**wastepaper** vieux papiers *mpl*, papier(s) de rebut; **wastepaper basket** = **wastebasket** ►**waste pipe** (tuyau *m* de) vidange *f*.

4 **vt** a *resources, food, electricity, energy etc* gaspiller; *time* perdre; *opportunity* perdre, laisser passer. **to ~ one's money** gaspiller de l'argent, ficher de l'argent en l'air* (*on sth* pour qch, *on doing* pour faire); **nothing is ~d in this firm** il n'y a aucun gaspillage *or* il n'y a aucun gâchis *or* rien ne se perd dans cette entreprise; **we ~d 9 litres of petrol** nous avons gaspillé *or* perdu 9 litres d'essence, nous avons dépensé 9 litres d'essence pour rien; **I ~d a whole day on that journey** j'ai perdu toute une journée avec ce voyage; **you're wasting your breath!** tu dépenses ta salive pour rien!, tu perds ton temps!; **I won't ~ my breath discussing that** je ne vais pas perdre mon temps *or* me fatiguer à discuter cela; **you're wasting your time trying** tu essaies en pure perte, tu perds ton temps à essayer; **to ~ no time in doing** ne pas perdre de temps à faire; **the sarcasm was ~d on him** il n'a pas compris *or* saisi le sarcasme; **caviar is ~d on him** il ne sait pas apprécier le caviar, ça ne vaut pas la peine de lui donner du caviar; **~d effort** des efforts inutiles *or* vains; **a ~d life** une vie gâchée; **his attempts to placate her were ~d** il a essayé en vain de l'amadouer, ses efforts pour l'amadouer n'ont rien donné *or* ont été en pure perte.

b **~d by disease** (*emaciated*) décharné par la maladie; (*withered*) atrophié par la maladie; (*‡: exhausted*) **~d** lessivé*, crevé‡.

c (*‡: kill*) zigouiller‡, supprimer*.

5 **vi** *[food, goods, resources]* se perdre, être gaspillé. **you mustn't let it ~** il ne faut pas le laisser perdre; (*Prov*) **~ not want not** l'économie protège du besoin.

►**waste away** **vi** dépérir. (*iro*) **you're not exactly wasting away!** tu ne fais pas précisément pitié à voir! (*iro*).

wasted ['weɪstɪd] **adj** *limb* (*emaciated*) décharné; (*withered*) atrophié.

wasteful ['weɪstfʊl] **adj** *person* gaspilleur; *process* peu économique, peu rentable. **~ expenditure** gaspillage *m*, dépenses excessives *or* inutiles; **~ habits** gaspillage; **to be ~ of sth** *[person]* gaspiller qch; *[method, process]* mal utiliser qch.

wastefully ['weɪstfəlɪ] **adv**: **to spend/buy/throw away ~** faire du gaspillage en dépensant/achetant/jetant, dépenser/acheter/jeter bêtement; **to use sth ~** ne pas utiliser qch au mieux, gaspiller qch.

wastefulness ['weɪstfʊlnɪs] **n** (*NonC*) *[person]* manque *m* d'économie; *[process]* manque de rentabilité.

waster* ['weɪstər] **n** = **wastrel**.

wasting ['weɪstɪŋ] **adj** *disease* qui ronge, qui mine.

wastrel ['weɪstrəl] **n** (*spendthrift*) dépensier *m*, -ière *f*, panier percé *m*; (*good-for-nothing*) propre *mf* à rien.

watch¹ [wɒtʃ] 1 **n** montre *f*. **by my ~** à ma montre; *see* **stop, wrist**.

2 **comp** *chain, glass* de montre ►**watchband** bracelet *m* de montre ►**watchmaker** horloger *m*, -ère *f* ►**watchmaking** horlogerie *f* ►**watch pocket** gousset *m* ►**watch strap** = **watchband**.

watch² [wɒtʃ] 1 **n** a (*NonC*) (*vigilance*) vigilance *f*; (*act of watching*) surveillance *f*. **to keep ~** faire le guet; **to keep (a) close ~ on** *or* **over** surveiller de près *or* avec vigilance; **to set a ~ on sth/sb** faire surveiller qch/qn; (*frm*) **to keep ~ and ward over sth** surveiller qch avec vigilance; **to be under ~** être sous surveillance; **to be on the ~** (*Mil etc*) monter la garde; (*gen*) guetter, faire le guet; **to be on the ~ for sb/sth** guetter qn/qch; **to be on the ~ for danger** être sur ses gardes à cause d'un danger éventuel; **to be on the ~ for bargains** être à l'affût des bonnes affaires.

b (*Naut: period of duty*) quart *m*. **to be on ~** être de quart; (*fig: † or liter*) **the long ~es of the night** les longues nuits sans sommeil; *see* **dog**.

c (*Mil*) (*group of men*) garde *f* (*Mil*), quart *m* (*Naut*); (*one man*) sentinelle *f* (*Mil*), homme *m* de quart (*Naut*). (*Naut*) **the port ~** les bâbordais *mpl*; **the starboard ~** les tribordais *mpl*; (*Hist*) **the ~** le guet, la ronde; *see* **officer**.

2 **comp** ►**Watch Committee** (*Brit Hist*) *comité m qui veille au maintien de l'ordre dans une commune* ►**watchdog** *see* **watchdog** ►**watchman** (*gen*) gardien *m*; (*night watchman*) veilleur *m or* gardien de nuit ►**watch night service** (*Rel*) ≃ messe *f* de minuit de la Saint-Sylvestre ►**watchtower** tour *f* de guet ►**watchword** (*password*) mot *m* de passe; (*fig: motto*) mot d'ordre.

3 **vt** a *event, match, programme, TV, ceremony* regarder; *person* regarder, observer, (*spy on*) surveiller, observer, épier; *suspect, suspicious object, house, car* surveiller; *expression, birds, insects etc* observer; *notice board, small ads etc* consulter régulièrement; *political situation, developments* surveiller, suivre de près. **~ me, ~ what I do** regarde-moi (faire), regarde ce que je fais, observe-moi; **~ how he does it** regarde *or* observe comment il s'y prend; **~ the soup to see it doesn't boil over** surveille la soupe pour qu'elle ne se sauve (*subj*) pas; **to ~ sb do** *or* **doing sth** regarder qn faire qch; **to ~ sb like a hawk** surveiller qn de (très) près; **have you ever ~ed an operation?** avez-vous déjà vu une opération? *or* assisté à une opération?; **we are being ~ed** (*gen*) on nous observe *or* surveille *or* épie; (*by police, detective etc*) on nous surveille; **to ~ sb's movements** surveiller *or* épier les allées et venues de qn; **he needs ~ing** il faut le surveiller, il faut l'avoir à l'œil; **~ tomorrow's paper** ne manquez pas de lire le journal de demain; (*Prov*) **a ~ed pot never boils** marmite surveillée ne bout jamais; **"~ this space"** "?" (*annonce d'une publicité ou d'informations à venir*); *see* **bird**.

b (*guard: Mil etc*) monter la garde devant, garder; (*take care of*) *child, dog* surveiller, s'occuper de; *luggage, shop* surveiller, garder.

c (*be careful of, mind*) faire attention à. **~ that knife!** (fais) attention avec ce couteau!; **~ that sharp edge!** (fais) attention au bord coupant!; **~ your head!** attention *or* gare à votre tête!; **to ~ one's step** (*lit*) faire attention *or* regarder où on met le pied; (*fig*) se surveiller (*dans ses paroles ou ses actes*); (*fig*) **~ your step!, ~ how you go!*, ~ yourself!** (fais) attention!, fais gaffe!‡; **we'll have to ~ the money carefully** il faudra que nous fassions attention à *or* surveillions nos dépenses; **to ~ sb's interests** veiller sur les intérêts de qn, prendre soin des intérêts de qn; **I must ~ the** *or* **my time as I've a train to catch** il faut que je surveille (*subj*) l'heure car j'ai un train à prendre; **he works well but does tend to ~ the clock** il travaille bien mais il a tendance à surveiller la pendule; **to ~ what one says** parler avec précaution, faire attention à ce que l'on dit; **~ what you're doing!** fais attention (à ce que tu fais)!; **~ it!*** (*warning*) attention!, fais gaffe!‡; (*threat*) attention!, gare à toi!; **~ your language!** surveille ton langage!; **~ you don't burn yourself** faites attention de *or* prenez garde de ne pas vous brûler, attention, ne vous brûlez pas!; **~ (that) he does all his homework** veillez à ce qu'il fasse *or* assurez-vous qu'il fait tous ses devoirs.

d (*look for*) *opportunity* guetter. **he ~ed his chance and slipped out** il a guetté *or* attendu le moment propice et s'est esquivé.

4 **vi** regarder; (*be on guard*) faire le guet, monter la garde; (*Rel etc: keep vigil*) veiller; (*pay attention*) faire attention. **he has only come to ~** il est venu simplement pour regarder *or* simplement en spectateur; **to ~ by sb's bedside** veiller au chevet de qn; **to ~ over** *person* surveiller; *thing* surveiller, garder; *sb's rights, safety* protéger, surveiller; **somebody was ~ing at the window** quelqu'un les (*or* me *etc*) regardait de la fenêtre; **to ~ for sth/sb** (*wait for*) guetter qch/qn; (*be careful of*) faire attention à; **he's ~ing to see what you're going to do** il attend pour voir ce que vous allez faire; **~ and you'll see how it's done** regarde et tu vas voir comme cela se fait; **he'll be here soon, just (you) ~** attends, il sera bientôt là; *see* **brief**.

►**watch out** **vi** (*keep a look-out*) faire le guet; (*fig: take care*) faire attention, prendre garde. **watch out for the signal** guettez *or* attendez le signal; **watch out!** attention!, fais gaffe!‡; (*as menace*) attention!, gare à toi!; **watch out for cars when crossing the road** faites attention *or* prenez garde aux voitures en traversant la rue; **to watch out for thieves** être sur ses gardes contre les voleurs; **watch out for trouble if ...** préparez-vous *or* attendez-vous à des ennuis si ... .

watchable ['wɒtʃəbl] **adj** (*TV*) qui se laisse regarder.

watchdog ['wɒtʃdɒg] 1 **n** (*lit*) chien *m* de garde; (*fig*) gardien(ne) *m(f)*. 2 **comp** *group etc* qui veille ►**watchdog committee** comité *m* de vigilance. 3 **vt** (*US* *) *events, developments* suivre de près.

watcher ['wɒtʃər] **n** (*observer*) observateur *m*, -trice *f*; (*hidden or hostile*) guetteur *m*; (*spectator*) spectateur *m*, -trice *f*; (*onlooker*) curieux *m*, -euse *f*. (*Pol*) **China ~** spécialiste *mf* des questions chinoises; **Kremlin ~** kremlinologiste *mf*, kremlinologue *mf*; *see* **bird**.

watchful ['wɒtʃfʊl] **adj** vigilant, attentif. **to keep a ~ eye on sth/sb** garder qch/qn à l'œil, avoir l'œil sur qch/qn; **under the ~ eye of ...** sous l'œil vigilant de ... .

water ['wɔːtər] 1 **n** a (*NonC: gen*) eau *f*. **I want a drink of ~** je voudrais de l'eau *or* un verre d'eau; **to turn on the ~** (*at main*) ouvrir l'eau; (*from tap*) ouvrir le robinet; **hot and cold ~ in all rooms** eau courante chaude et froide dans toutes les chambres; **the road is under ~** la route est inondée, la route est recouverte par les eaux; **to swim under ~** nager sous l'eau; **to go by ~** voyager par bateau; **the island across the ~** l'île de l'autre côté de l'eau; **we spent an afternoon on the ~** nous avons passé un après-midi sur l'eau; **there's 3 metres of ~ here, the ~ is 3 metres deep here** ici l'eau est profonde de 3 mètres, il y a ici 3 mètres (de profondeur) d'eau *or* 3 mètres de fond; (*tide*) **at high/low ~** à marée haute/basse, à mer pleine/basse; *[ship]* **to make ~** faire eau (*see also* **1c**); **it won't hold ~** *[container, bucket]* cela n'est pas étanche, l'eau va fuir; (*fig*) *[plan, suggestion, excuse]* cela ne tient pas debout, cela ne vaut rien; (*fig*) **a lot of ~ has passed under the bridge since then** il est passé beaucoup d'eau sous les ponts depuis ce temps-là; (*fig*) **that's ~ under the bridge, all ~ under the bridge** tout ça c'est du passé; **he spends money like ~** il jette l'argent par les fenêtres, l'argent lui fond entre les mains; (*fig*) **to pour** *or* **throw cold ~ on sth** se montrer peu enthousiaste pour qch; (*fig*) **it's like ~ off a duck's back*** c'est comme si on chantait, c'est comme de l'eau sur le dos d'un canard; **lavender/rose ~** eau de lavande/de rose; *see* **deep, fire, fish** *etc*.

b *[spa, lake, river, sea]* **~s** eaux *fpl*; **to take** *or* **drink the ~s** prendre les eaux, faire une cure thermale; **in French ~s** dans les eaux (territoriales) françaises; **the ~s of the Rhine** l'eau *or* les eaux du Rhin; *see* **territorial** *etc*.

c (*Med, Physiol*) **to make** *or* **pass ~** uriner; (*in labour*) **her** *or* **the ~s**

broke la poche des eaux s'est rompue; ~ **on the knee** épanchement *m* de synovie; ~ **on the brain** hydrocéphalie *f*.

2 **comp** *pressure, pipe, vapour* d'eau; *pump, mill* à eau; *plant etc* aquatique; (*Ind*) *dispute, strike* des employés de l'eau ▸**water bailiff** garde-pêche *m inv* ▸**water bed** matelas *m* d'eau ▸**water beetle** gyrin *m*, tourniquet *m* ▸**water bird** oiseau *m* aquatique ▸**water biscuit** craquelin *m* ▸**water blister** (*Med*) ampoule *f*, phlyctène *f* ▸**water boatman** (*Zool*) notonecte *m or f* ▸**waterborne** flottant; *boats* à flot; *goods* transporté par voie d'eau; *disease* d'origine hydrique ▸**water bottle** (*gen: plastic*) bouteille *f* (en plastique); *[soldier etc]* bidon *m*; *[cyclist, peasant]* bidon *m*, (*smaller*) gourde *f* (*see* **hot 3**) ▸**water buffalo** (*Indian*) arni *m*; (*Indonesian*) kérabau *m* ▸**water butt** citerne *f* (à eau de pluie) ▸**water cannon** canon *m* à eau ▸**water carrier** (*person*) porteur *m*, -euse *f* d'eau; (*container*) bidon *m* à eau; **the Water Carrier** (*Astrol, Astron*) le Verseau ▸**water cart** (*for streets*) arroseuse *f* (*municipale*); (*for selling*) voiture *f* de marchand d'eau ▸**water chestnut** macle *f*, châtaigne *f* d'eau ▸**water clock** horloge *f* à eau ▸**water closet** (*abbr* **W.C.**) cabinet(s) *m(pl)*, waters *mpl*, W.-C. *mpl* ▸**watercolour n** (*painting*) aquarelle *f* ◊ **adj** à l'aquarelle; **watercolours** (*paints*) couleurs *fpl* à l'eau *or* pour aquarelle; **painted in watercolours** peint à l'aquarelle ▸**watercolourist** aquarelliste *mf* ▸**water-cooled** à refroidissement par eau ▸**water-cooler** distributeur *m* d'eau réfrigérée ▸**water-cooling** refroidissement *m* par eau ▸**watercourse** cours *m* d'eau ▸**watercress** cresson *m* (de fontaine) ▸**water diviner** sourcier *m*, -ière *f*, radiesthésiste *mf* ▸**water divining** art *m* du sourcier, radiesthésie *f* ▸**waterfall** chute *f* d'eau, cascade *f* ▸**water fountain** jet *m* d'eau ▸**waterfowl** (*sg*) oiseau *m* d'eau; (*collective pl*) gibier *m* d'eau ▸**waterfree** sans eau, anhydre ▸**waterfront** (*at docks etc*) quais *mpl*; (*sea front*) front *m* de mer ▸**water gas** gaz *m* à l'eau ▸**water glass** (*tumbler*) verre *m* à eau ▸**waterglass** (*NonC: Chem*) silicate *m* de potasse ▸**water heater** chauffe-eau *m inv* ▸**water hen** poule *f* d'eau ▸**water hole** point *m* d'eau, mare *f* ▸**water ice** (*Brit Culin*) sorbet *m* ▸**water jacket** (*Aut etc*) chemise *f* d'eau ▸**water jump** (*Racing*) rivière *f*, brook *m* ▸**water level** (*gen*) niveau *m* de l'eau; (*Aut: of radiator*) niveau *m* d'eau ▸**water lily** nénuphar *m* ▸**waterline** (*Naut*) ligne *f* de flottaison; (*left by tide, river*) = **watermark** ▸**waterlogged** *wood* imprégné d'eau; *shoes* imbibé d'eau; *land, pitch* détrempé ▸**water main** conduite principale d'eau ▸**waterman** batelier *m* ▸**watermark** (*in paper*) filigrane *m*; (*left by tide*) laisse *f* de haute mer; (*left by river*) ligne *f* des hautes eaux; **above/below the watermark** au-dessus/au-dessous de la laisse de haute mer *or* de la ligne des hautes eaux ▸**water-meadow** prairie souvent inondée, noue *f* ▸**watermelon** pastèque *f*, melon *m* d'eau ▸**water meter** compteur *m* d'eau ▸**water nymph** naïade *f* ▸**water pistol** pistolet *m* à eau ▸**water polo** water-polo *m* ▸**water power** énergie *f* hydraulique, houille blanche ▸**waterproof adj** *material* imperméable; *watch* étanche ◊ **n** imperméable *m* ◊ **vt** imperméabiliser; **waterproof sheet** (*for bed*) alaise *f*; (*tarpaulin*) bâche *f* ▸**waterproofing** (*NonC*) (*process*) imperméabilisation *f*; (*quality*) imperméabilité *f* ▸**water purifier** (*device*) épurateur *m* d'eau; (*tablet*) cachet *m* pour purifier l'eau ▸**water-rail** (*bird*) râle *m* (d'eau) ▸**water rat** rat *m* d'eau ▸**water rate** (*Brit*) taxe *f* sur l'eau ▸**water-repellent adj** hydrofuge, imperméable ◊ **n** hydrofuge *m* ▸**water-resistant** *ink etc* qui résiste à l'eau, indélébile; *material* imperméable ▸**watershed** (*Geog*) ligne *f* de partage des eaux; (*fig*) moment critique *or* décisif, grand tournant ▸**waterside n** bord *m* de l'eau ◊ **adj** *flower, insect* du bord de l'eau; *landowner* riverain; **at** *or* **on** *or* **by the waterside** au bord de l'eau, sur la berge; **along the waterside** le long de la rive ▸**water-ski n** ski *m* nautique (*objet*) ◊ **vi** faire du ski nautique ▸**water-skier** skieur *m*, -euse *f* nautique ▸**water-skiing** (*NonC*) ski *m* nautique (*sport*) ▸**water snake** serpent *m* d'eau ▸**water softener** adoucisseur *m* d'eau ▸**water-soluble** soluble dans l'eau ▸**water sports** sports *mpl* nautiques ▸**waterspout** (*on roof etc*) (tuyau *m* de) descente *f*; (*Met*) trombe *f* ▸**water supply** (*for town*) approvisionnement *m* en eau, distribution *f* des eaux; (*for house etc*) alimentation *f* en eau; (*for traveller*) provision *f* d'eau; **the water supply was cut off** on avait coupé l'eau ▸**water system** (*Geog*) réseau *m* hydrographique; (*for house, town*) = **water supply** ▸**water table** (*Geog*) niveau *m* hydrostatique ▸**water tank** réservoir *m* d'eau, citerne *f* ▸**watertight** *container* étanche; (*fig*) *excuse, plan* inattaquable, indiscutable; (*lit*) **watertight compartment** compartiment *m* étanche; (*fig*) **in watertight compartments** séparé par des cloisons étanches ▸**water tower** château *m* d'eau ▸**water vole** rat *m* d'eau ▸**water waggon** (*US*) voiture-citerne *f* (à eau) ▸**waterway** voie *f* navigable ▸**waterweed** élodée *f* ▸**waterwheel** roue *f* hydraulique ▸**water wings** bouée *f*, flotteurs *mpl* de natation ▸**water workers** (*Ind*) employés *mpl* de l'eau ▸**waterworks** (*system*) système *m* hydraulique; (*place*) station *f* hydraulique; (*fig: cry*) **to turn on the waterworks*** se mettre à pleurer à chaudes larmes *or* comme une Madeleine*; (*Brit Med euph*) **to have something wrong with one's waterworks*** avoir des ennuis de vessie.

3 **vi** *[eyes]* larmoyer, pleurer. **his mouth ~ed** il a eu l'eau à la bouche; **it made his mouth ~** cela lui a fait venir l'eau à la bouche.

4 **vt** *plant, garden* arroser; *animal* donner à boire à, faire boire; *wine, milk* couper (d'eau), baptiser*. (*Tex*) **~ed silk** soie moirée; **the river ~s the whole province** le fleuve arrose *or* irrigue toute la province.

▸**water down vt sep** *milk, wine* couper (d'eau), baptiser*; (*fig*) *story* édulcorer; *effect* atténuer, affaiblir.

watered [ˈwɔːtɪd] 1 **adj** a *milk etc* coupé d'eau. b *silk etc* moiré. c (*US*) ~ **stock** (*cattle*) bétail *m* gorgé d'eau (avant la pesée); (*St Ex*) actions *fpl* gonflées (sans raison). 2 **comp** ▸**watered-down** (*lit*) *milk, wine etc* coupé d'eau; (*fig*) *version, account* édulcoré.

Watergate [ˈwɔːtəgeɪt] **n** (*fig*) Watergate *m* (*scandale politique*).

watering [ˈwɔːtərɪŋ] 1 **n** *[streets, plants]* arrosage *m*; *[fields, region]* irrigation *f*. **frequent ~ is needed** il est conseillé d'arroser fréquemment, des arrosages fréquents sont recommandés. 2 **comp** ▸**watering can** arrosoir *m* ▸**watering hole** (*for animals*) point *m* d'eau; (* *fig*) bar *m* ▸**watering place** (*for animals*) point *m* d'eau; (*spa*) station thermale, ville *f* d'eaux; (*seaside resort*) station *f* balnéaire; (*fig hum*) bar *m*.

Waterloo [ˌwɔːtəˈluː] **n** Waterloo. **Battle of ~** bataille *f* de Waterloo; (*fig*) **to meet one's ~** essuyer un revers irrémédiable.

watery [ˈwɔːtərɪ] **adj** *substance* aqueux, qui contient de l'eau; *eyes* larmoyant, humide; *district, ground* détrempé, saturé d'eau; *sky, moon* qui annonce la pluie; (*pej*) *tea, coffee* trop faible; *soup* trop liquide; *taste* fade, insipide; *colour* délavé, pâle. (*liter*) **in his ~ grave** dans l'onde qui est son tombeau.

watt [wɒt] **n** (*Elec*) watt *m*.

wattage [ˈwɒtɪdʒ] **n** (*Elec*) puissance *f or* consommation *f* en watts.

wattle [ˈwɒtl] **n** a (*NonC: woven sticks*) clayonnage *m*. ~ **and daub** clayonnage enduit de torchis. b *[turkey, lizard]* caroncule *f*; *[fish]* barbillon *m*.

wave [weɪv] 1 **n** a (*at sea*) vague *f*, lame *f*; (*on lake*) vague; (*on beach*) rouleau *m*; (*on river, pond*) vaguelette *f*; (*in hair*) ondulation *f*, cran *m*; (*on surface*) ondulation; (*fig: of dislike, enthusiasm, strikes, protests etc*) vague. (*liter*) **the ~s** les flots *mpl*, l'onde *f*; (*fig*) **to make ~s** créer des remous; **her hair has a natural ~ (in it)** ses cheveux ondulent naturellement *or* ont un cran naturel; (*Mil*) **the first ~ of the attack** la première vague d'assaut; **to come in ~s** *[people]* arriver par vagues; *[explosions etc]* se produire par vagues; (*fig: Cine etc*) **the new ~** la nouvelle vague; *see* **crime, heat, permanent** *etc*.

b (*Phys, Rad, Telec etc*) onde *f*. **long ~** grandes ondes; **medium/short ~** ondes moyennes/courtes; *see* **light[1], shock[1], sound[1]** *etc*.

c (*gesture*) geste *m or* signe *m* de la main. **he gave me a cheerful ~** il m'a fait un signe joyeux de la main; **with a ~ of his hand** d'un geste *or* signe de la main, en agitant la main.

2 **comp** ▸**waveband** (*Rad etc*) bande *f* de fréquences ▸**wave energy** énergie *f* des vagues ▸**wave guide** (*Electronics*) guide *m* d'ondes ▸**wavelength** (*Phys*) longueur *f* d'ondes; (*fig*) **we're not on the same wavelength** nous ne sommes pas sur la même longueur d'ondes* ▸**wave mechanics** (*NonC: Phys*) mécanique *f* ondulatoire ▸**wave power** énergie *f* des vagues.

3 **vi** a *[person]* faire signe de la main; *[flag]* flotter (au vent); *[branch, tree]* être agité; *[grass, corn]* onduler, ondoyer. **to ~ to sb** (*in greeting*) saluer qn de la main, faire bonjour (*or* au revoir) de la main à qn; (*as signal*) faire signe à qn (*to do* de faire).

b *[hair]* onduler, avoir un *or* des cran(s).

4 **vt** a *flag* agiter, faire claquer, brandir; *handkerchief etc* agiter; (*threateningly*) *stick, sword* brandir. **to ~ one's hand to sb** faire signe de la main à qn; **he ~d the ticket at me furiously** il a agité vivement le ticket sous mon nez; **to ~ goodbye to sb** dire au revoir de la main à qn, agiter la main en signe *or* guise d'adieu; **he ~d his thanks** il a remercié d'un signe de la main, il a agité la main en signe *or* guise de remerciement; **to ~ sb back/through/on** *etc* faire signe à qn de reculer/de passer/d'avancer *etc;* **he ~d the car through the gates** il a fait signe à la voiture de franchir les grilles.

b *hair* onduler.

▸**wave about, wave around vt sep** *object* agiter dans tous les sens. **to wave one's arms about** gesticuler, agiter les bras dans tous les sens.

▸**wave aside, wave away vt sep** *person, object* écarter *or* éloigner d'un geste; *objections* écarter (d'un geste); *offer, sb's help etc* rejeter *or* refuser (d'un geste).

▸**wave down vt sep: to wave down a car** faire signe à une voiture de s'arrêter.

▸**wave off vt sep** faire au revoir à.

wavelet [ˈweɪvlɪt] **n** vaguelette *f*.

waver [ˈweɪvəʳ] **vi** *[flame, shadow]* vaciller, osciller; *[voice]* trembler, trembloter; *[courage, determination]* vaciller, chanceler; *[person]* (*weaken*) lâcher pied, flancher*; (*hesitate*) vaciller, hésiter, balancer (*between* entre). **he ~ed in his resolution** sa résolution chancelait; **he is beginning to ~** il commence à ne plus être aussi décidé *or* à flancher*.

waverer [ˈweɪvərəʳ] **n** indécis(e) *m(f)*, irrésolu(e) *m(f)*.

wavering [ˈweɪvərɪŋ] 1 **adj** *flame, shadow* vacillant, oscillant; *voice* tremblant, tremblotant; *courage, determination* vacillant, chancelant. 2 **n** (*NonC: see* **waver**) vacillation *f*, oscillations *fpl*; tremblement *m*; hésitation(s) *f(pl)*.

wavy [ˈweɪvɪ] 1 **adj** *hair, surface* ondulé; *line* onduleux. 2 **comp**

►**wavy-haired** aux cheveux ondulés.

wax[1] [wæks] 1 n (*NonC*) cire *f*; (*for skis*) fart *m*; (*in ear*) cérumen *m*, (bouchon *m* de) cire. **he was ~ in their hands** c'était une vraie pâte molle entre leurs mains; *see* **bee, sealing** *etc.* 2 comp *candle, doll, seal, record* de *or* en cire ►**wax(ed) paper** papier paraffiné *or* sulfurisé ►**waxwing** (*bird*) jaseur *m* ►**waxworks** (*pl: figures*) personnages *mpl* en cire; (*sg: wax museum*) musée *m* de cire. 3 vt *floor, furniture* cirer, encaustiquer; *skis* farter; *shoes, moustache* cirer; *thread* poisser; *car* lustrer. **to ~ one's legs** s'épiler les jambes à la cire; **~ed cotton** coton *m* huilé; **~ed jacket** veste *f* de *or* en coton huilé.

wax[2] [wæks] vi *[moon]* croître. *[feelings, issues etc]* **to ~ and wane** croître et décroître; († *or hum*) **to ~ merry/poetic** *etc* devenir d'humeur joyeuse/poétique *etc;* **to ~ eloquent** déployer toute son éloquence (*about, over* à propos de); *see* **enthusiastic.**

waxen ['wæksən] adj (*of wax:* †) de *or* en cire; (*like wax*) cireux.

waxing ['wæksɪŋ] n (*gen*) cirage *m*; *[skis]* fartage *m*.

waxy ['wæksɪ] adj *substance, texture* cireux; *complexion, colour* cireux, jaunâtre; *potato* ferme, pas farineux.

way [weɪ] 1 n a (*road etc*) chemin *m*, voie *f*. **follow the ~ across the fields** suivez le chemin qui traverse les champs *or* à travers champs; **they drove a ~ through the hills** ils ont fait un chemin *or* fait une route *or* ouvert un passage à travers les collines; **the Appian W~** la voie Appienne; (*Rel*) **the W~ of the Cross** le chemin de la Croix; **private/public ~** voie privée/publique; **they live over** *or* **across the ~** ils habitent en face (*from* de); **the ~ is obstructed by roadworks** le chemin *or* la voie *or* le passage est bloqué(e) par les travaux; (*fig*) **the middle ~** (*compromise*) la solution intermédiaire; (*happy medium*) le juste milieu; *see* **parting, pave, permanent** *etc.*

b (*route*) chemin *m* (*to* de, vers). **which is the ~ to the town hall?** pouvez-vous m'indiquer le chemin *or* la direction de la mairie?; **he talked all the ~ to the theatre** il a parlé pendant tout le chemin jusqu'au théâtre; **there are houses all the ~** il y a des maisons tout le long du chemin; **it rained all the ~** il a plu pendant tout le chemin; (*fig*) **I'm with you all the ~*** je suis entièrement d'accord avec vous (*see also* **1e**); **we have gone** *or* **taken the wrong ~** nous nous sommes trompés de chemin, nous avons pris le mauvais chemin; (*fig*) **the ~ to success** le chemin du succès; **the shortest** *or* **quickest ~ to Leeds** le chemin le plus court pour aller à Leeds; **I went the long ~ round** j'ai pris le chemin le plus long; **on the ~ to London we met ...** en allant à Londres *or* en route pour Londres nous avons rencontré ...; **it's on the ~ to the station** c'est sur le chemin de la gare; **we met several people on** *or* **along the ~** nous avons rencontré plusieurs personnes en route *or* chemin faisant; **on the ~ here I saw ...** en venant (ici) j'ai vu ...; **you pass it on your ~ home** vous passez devant en rentrant chez vous; **I must be on my ~** il faut que je parte *or* que je me mette en route; **to start on one's ~** se mettre en route; **he went on his ~, content** il s'est remis en route *or* il est reparti satisfait; **he is on the ~ to fame** il est sur le chemin de la gloire, il est en passe de devenir célèbre; **he went by ~ of Glasgow** il est passé par Glasgow, il y est allé via Glasgow; **they met a tramp by the ~** en chemin *or* sur leur route *or* chemin faisant ils ont rencontré un vagabond; (*fig*) **by the ~, what did he say?** à propos, qu'est-ce qu'il a dit?; **oh and by the ~ ...** oh à propos ..., oh pendant que j'y pense ...; **he mentioned it by the ~** il l'a mentionné en passant; (*fig*) **that is by the ~** tout ceci est secondaire *or* entre parenthèses, je signale ceci au passage *or* en passant; **the village is quite out of the ~** le village est vraiment à l'écart *or* isolé; (*fig*) **it's nothing out of the ~** cela n'a rien de spécial *or* d'extraordinaire, c'est très quelconque; **it's an out-of-the-~ subject** c'est un sujet peu commun, c'est un sujet qui sort des sentiers battus; **I'll take you home if it's not out of my ~** je vous ramènerai si c'est sur mon chemin *or* si cela ne me fait pas faire un détour; (*fig*) **to go out of one's ~ to do sth** se donner du mal pour faire qch, faire un effort particulier pour faire qch; **he went out of his ~ to help us** il s'est donné du mal *or* il s'est coupé en quatre* pour nous aider; **don't go out of your ~ to do it** ne vous dérangez pas pour le faire; **to lose the** *or* **one's ~** perdre son chemin (*to* en allant à); **to ask the** *or* **one's ~** demander son chemin (*to* pour aller à); **I know the** *or* **my ~ to the station** je connais le chemin de la gare, je sais comment aller à la gare; (*fig*) **she knows her ~ about** elle sait se retourner *or* se débrouiller; **they went their own ~s** *or* **their separate ~s** (*lit*) ils sont partis chacun de leur côté; (*fig*) chacun a suivi son chemin; (*fig*) **he went his own ~** il a fait à son idée *or* à sa guise, il n'en a fait qu'à sa tête; (*fig*) **he has gone the ~ of his brothers** il a fait comme ses frères; **to make one's ~ towards ...** se diriger vers ...; **he made his ~ through the forest** il a traversé la forêt; (*fig*) **he had to make his own ~ in Hollywood** il a dû faire son chemin tout seul à Hollywood; *see* **find, point, see**[1]**, work** *etc.*

c (*route: + adv or prep*) chemin *m*, route *f*. **the ~ back** le chemin *or* la route du retour; **the ~ back to the station** le chemin pour retourner à la gare; **on the ~ back he met ...** au retour *or* sur le chemin du retour *or* en revenant il a rencontré ...; **he made his ~ back to the car** il est retourné (*or* revenu) vers la voiture; **the ~ down** le chemin pour descendre, la descente; **I don't know the ~ down** je ne sais pas par où on descend; **the ~ forward is dangerous** le chemin devient dangereux plus loin; **the ~ in** l'entrée *f*; **"~ in"** "entrée"; **I'm looking for a ~ in/out** je cherche un moyen d'entrer/de sortir; **do you know the ~ into/out of this building?** savez-vous par où on entre dans/sort de ce bâtiment?; *[fashion etc]* **it's on the ~ in** c'est la nouvelle mode; **it's on the ~ out** c'est passé de mode; **the ~ out** la sortie; **"~ out"** "sortie"; **you'll see it on the** *or* **your ~ out** vous le verrez en sortant; (*fig*) **there is no ~ out of** *or* **no ~ round this difficulty** il n'y a pas moyen de se sortir de la difficulté *or* de contourner la difficulté; (*fig*) **there's no other ~ out** il n'y a pas d'autre façon de s'en sortir *or* d'autre solution; **the ~ through the forest is clearly marked** le chemin à travers la forêt est clairement indiqué; **"no ~ through"** "sans issue"; **the ~ up** le chemin pour monter, la montée (*also Climbing*); **I don't know the ~ up** je ne sais pas par où on monte.

d (*path*) **to be in sb's ~** barrer le passage à qn; **to be in the ~** (*lit*) bloquer *or* barrer le passage; (*fig*) gêner; **am I in the** *or* **your ~?** (*lit*) est-ce que je vous empêche de passer?; (*fig*) est-ce que je vous gêne?; **it's not in the ~** *or* **it's out of the ~ over there** ça ne gêne pas là-bas; **to get out of the ~** se ranger, s'écarter (du chemin); **(get) out of the** *or* **my ~!** pousse-toi!, écarte-toi!, laisse-moi passer!; **to get out of sb's ~** laisser passer qn, céder le pas à qn; **I couldn't get out of the ~ of the car in time** je n'ai pas pu m'écarter de la voiture à temps; **get it out of the ~!** poussez-le!, écartez-le!; **as soon as I've got the exam out of the ~** dès que je serai débarrassé de l'examen; **keep matches out of children's ~** *or* **out of the ~ of children** ne laissez pas les allumettes à la portée des enfants; **to keep out of sb's ~** éviter qn; **keep (well) out of his ~ today!** ne te frotte pas à lui aujourd'hui!; **he kept well out of the ~** il a pris soin de rester à l'écart; **to put sth out of the ~** ranger qch, écarter qch; **put it out of the ~ in the cupboard** range-le dans le placard; **he wants his wife out of the ~*** il veut se débarrasser de sa femme; **to put difficulties in sb's ~** créer des difficultés à qn; **he put me in the ~ of one or two good bargains** il m'a permis de profiter de *or* il m'a indiqué quelques bonnes affaires; **to make ~ for sb** faire place à qn, s'écarter pour laisser passer qn; (*fig*) laisser la voie libre à qn; **make ~!** écartez-vous!; **make ~ for the king!** place au roi!; **he made ~ for the ambulance** il s'est écarté pour laisser passer l'ambulance; (*fig*) **this made ~ for a return to democracy** ceci a ouvert la voie à *or* préparé le terrain pour la restauration de la démocratie; **to push** *or* **force** *or* **thrust** *or* **elbow one's ~ through a crowd** se frayer un chemin à travers une foule; **to hack** *or* **cut one's ~ through the jungle** s'ouvrir un chemin à la hache dans la jungle; **to crawl/limp** *etc* **one's ~ to the door** ramper/boiter *etc* jusqu'à la porte; **he talked his ~ out of the difficulty** il s'est sorti de cette difficulté avec de belles paroles; *see* **give, open, right** *etc.*

e (*distance*) distance *f*. **to be a long ~ off** *or* **away** être loin; **a long ~ off I could hear ...** j'entendais au loin ...; **a little ~ away** *or* **off** pas très loin, à une courte distance; **it's a long** *or* **good ~ to London** Londres est loin, ça fait loin pour aller à Londres*; **it's a long** *or* **quite a ~ from here to London** cela fait loin d'ici à Londres; **the roots go a long ~ down** les racines descendent loin; **it's a long ~ from here** c'est loin d'ici; **he's a long ~ from home** il est loin de chez lui; (*fig*) **you're a long ~ out** vous êtes loin du compte; (*fig*) **they've come a long ~** ils ont fait du chemin; **we've a long ~ to go** (*lit*) nous avons encore une grande distance à parcourir *or* un grand bout de chemin à faire; (*fig*) (*not got enough*) nous sommes encore très loin du compte; (*still more efforts to make*) nous ne sommes pas au bout de nos peines; **your work has still a long ~ to go** vous avez encore de grands efforts à faire dans votre travail; (*fig*) **it should go a long ~/some ~ towards paying the bill** cela devrait couvrir une grande partie/une partie de la facture; **it should go a long ~/some way towards improving relations between the two countries** cela devrait améliorer considérablement/contribuer à améliorer les rapports entre les deux pays; **he makes a little go a long ~** il tire le meilleur parti de ce qu'il a; **a little kindness goes a long ~** un peu de gentillesse facilite bien des choses; **he is a long ~ from understanding why I did it** il est loin d'avoir compris pourquoi je l'ai fait; **it's a long ~ from what we want** ce n'est pas du tout ce qu'on veut; **it's a long ~ from being finished** c'est loin d'être terminé; **is it finished? — not by a long ~!** est-ce terminé? — loin de là *or* tant s'en faut!; **is this what you want? — not by a long ~** c'est cela que vous voulez? — mais pas du tout *or* absolument pas!; **it's better by a long ~** c'est nettement mieux; (*fig: have sex*) **to go all the ~* with sb** coucher* avec qn, aller jusqu'au bout avec qn.

f (*direction*) direction *f*, sens *m*. **this ~** par ici; **"this ~ for** *or* **to the cathedral"** "vers la cathédrale"; **the leaf was blowing this ~ and that** la feuille tournoyait de-ci de-là *or* par-ci par-là; **he ran this ~ and that** il courait dans tous les sens; **turn round this ~ for a moment** tourne-toi par ici un instant; **which ~ did he go?** par où est-il passé?, dans quelle direction est-il parti?; **which ~ do we go from here?** (*lit*) par où passons-nous maintenant?, quel chemin prenons-nous maintenant?; (*fig*) quelle voie devons-nous choisir maintenant?, que faire maintenant?; **are you going my ~?** est-ce que vous allez dans la même direction que moi?; (*fig*) **everything's going his ~ just now*** tout lui sourit *or* lui réussit en ce moment; **he went that ~** il est allé *or* parti par là; **she didn't know which ~ to look** elle ne savait pas où regarder; **he looked the other ~** il a détourné les yeux; **he never looks my ~** il ne regarde jamais dans ma direction; **I'll be down** *or* **round your ~**

tomorrow je serai près de chez vous *or* dans vos parages demain; **if he comes your ~ again** s'il revient dans vos parages; **if the chance comes your ~** si jamais vous en avez l'occasion; **it's out** *or* **over Oxford ~** c'est du côté d'Oxford; (*fig*) **he's in a fair ~ to succeed** il est en passe de réussir; **you're wearing your hat the wrong ~ round** vous avez mis votre chapeau à l'envers *or* dans le mauvais sens; **the right ~ up** dans le bon sens; **the wrong ~ up** sens dessus dessous; **his jersey is the right/wrong ~ out** son chandail est à l'endroit/à l'envers; **turn the box the other ~ round** tourne la boîte dans l'autre sens; **he didn't hit her, it was the other ~ round** ce n'est pas lui qui l'a frappée, c'est juste le contraire; **a one-~ street** une rue à sens unique; **a three-~ discussion** une discussion à trois participants; **a four-~ radio link-up** une liaison radio à quatre voies; *see* **rub up** *etc*.

g (*manner, method, course of action*) façon *f*, méthode *f*, manière *f*, moyen *m*. **there are ~s and means** il y a différents moyens (*of doing* de faire); **we haven't the ~s and means to do it** nous n'avons pas les ressources suffisantes pour le faire; **W~s and Means Committee** (*Brit Admin*) la Commission des Finances; (*US Pol*) *commission des finances de la Chambre des Représentants (examinant les recettes)*; **we'll find a ~ to do** *or* **of doing it** nous trouverons un moyen *or* une façon de le faire; **love will find a ~** l'amour finit toujours par triompher; **(in) this/that ~** comme ceci/cela, de cette façon, de cette manière; (*on label*) **"this ~ up"** "dessus", "haut"; **that's the ~ to do it** voilà comment il faut s'y prendre, c'est ainsi qu'il faut (le) faire; (*encouraging*) **that's the ~!**, (*also US*) **that's the ~ to go!*** voilà c'est bien!; (*of sb's death*) **that's the ~ to go!** c'est une belle mort!; (*of sb's death*) **what a ~ to go!** quelle façon de mourir!; **do it your own ~** fais-le comme tu veux *or* à ta façon; **he has his own ~ of doing things** il a sa façon à lui de faire les choses; **the French ~ of life** la manière de vivre des Français, la vie française; (*fig*) **such shortages are a ~ of life** de telles pénuries sont entrées dans les mœurs *or* font partie de la vie de tous les jours; **to get one's own ~** arriver à ses fins; **to want one's own ~** vouloir imposer sa volonté, ne vouloir en faire qu'à sa tête; **Arsenal had it all their own ~ in the second half** Arsenal a complètement dominé le match pendant la deuxième mi-temps; **I won't let him have things all his own ~** je ne vais pas faire ses quatre volontés* *or* lui passer tous ses caprices; (*hum: to seduce*) **to have** *or* **get one's evil** *or* **wicked ~ with sb** arriver à ses fins avec qn; **my ~ is to get the personnel together first** ma méthode consiste à rassembler d'abord le personnel; **to my ~ of thinking** à mon avis; **her ~ of looking at it** son point de vue sur la question; **that's the ~ the money goes** c'est à ça que l'argent passe; **what an odd ~ to behave!** quelle drôle de façon de se conduire!; **whatever ~ you like to look at it** de quelque façon que vous envisagiez (*subj*) la chose; **it's just the ~ things are** c'est la vie; **that's the ~ of the world!** ainsi va le monde!; **it's just the ~ I'm made** c'est comme ça que je suis; **leave it all the ~ it is** laisse les choses comme elles sont *or* telles quelles; **the ~ things are going we shall have nothing left** du train où vont les choses il ne nous restera rien; **that's always the ~** c'est toujours comme ça; **that's always the ~ with him** c'est toujours comme ça *or* toujours pareil avec lui; **it was this ~ ...** voici comment cela s'est passé ...; **to do sth the right/wrong ~** faire qch bien/mal; **there's a right and a wrong ~ of doing everything** il y a toujours une bonne et une mauvaise façon de faire quelque chose; **he said it in such a ~ that ...** il l'a dit d'un tel ton *or* d'une telle façon *or* d'une telle manière que ...; **in a general ~ it's true** c'est vrai en général; **once in a ~ we ...** (une fois) de temps en temps nous ...; **it was by ~ of being a joke** c'était en guise de plaisanterie, c'était entendu comme une plaisanterie; **I did it by ~ of discovering what ...** je l'ai fait pour découvrir *or* afin de découvrir ce que ...; **I met him by the ~ of work** je l'ai rencontré dans *or* par mon travail; *see* **either**.

h **no ~!*** pas question!*; (*refusal*) **there's no ~* I'm doing that** il n'est pas question que je fasse ça; (*disbelief*) **there's no ~* that is a man!** il n'est pas possible que ce soit un homme!; (*disagreement*) **there's no ~* I said that!** je n'ai sûrement pas *or* je n'ai jamais dit ça!

i (*state; condition; degree*) état *m*. **things are in a bad ~** tout va mal; **he is in a bad ~** il va mal; **the car is in a very bad ~** la voiture est en piteux état; **she was in a terrible ~** (*physically*) elle était dans un état terrible; (*agitated*) elle était dans tous ses états; **there are no two ~s about it** c'est absolument clair; **one ~ or (an)other you must ...** d'une façon ou d'une autre vous devez ...; **it doesn't matter one ~ or the other** cela n'a pas d'importance, de toutes façons; **2 days** *etc* **one ~ or the other won't make much difference** 2 jours *etc* de plus ou de moins ne changeront pas grand-chose; (*Racing*) **each ~** gagnant ou placé; **you can't have it both** *or* **all ~s** il faut choisir; **they live in quite a small ~** ils vivent modestement, ils ont un petit train de vie *or* un train de vie modeste; (*fig*) **in a small ~ he contributed to ...** il a apporté sa petite contribution à ...; **in a small ~ it did make a difference** cela a quand même fait une petite différence; **he deals in quite a big ~** il fait de grosses affaires; **he does things in a big ~** il fait les choses en grand; **he is a bookseller in a big ~** c'est un gros libraire; **we lost in a really big ~** nous avons vraiment beaucoup perdu; **in the ordinary ~ of things** à l'ordinaire, normalement; **he's not a plumber in the ordinary ~** ce n'est pas un plombier ordinaire *or* comme les autres *or* au sens traditionnel du mot; **she's good/bad/clever** *etc* **that ~** elle est bonne/mauvaise/douée *etc* pour ce genre de choses; *see* **family** *etc*.

j (*custom, habit, manner of behaving*) coutume *f*, habitude *f*, manière *f*, façon *f*. **the ~s of the Spaniards** les coutumes espagnoles; **the good old ~s** les coutumes du bon vieux temps; **the ~s of God and men** les voies *fpl* de Dieu et de l'homme; **they mistrusted his foreign ~s** ils se méfiaient de ses habitudes d'étranger; **he has an odd ~ of scratching his chin when he laughs** il a une drôle de façon *or* manière de se gratter le menton quand il rit; **he is very slow in his ~s** il est très lent dans ce qu'il fait, il fait tout très lentement; **he is amusing in his (own) ~** il est amusant à sa façon; **in his own small ~ he helped a lot of people** dans la mesure de ses modestes moyens il a aidé beaucoup de gens; **that's not my ~** ce n'est pas mon genre, ce n'est pas ma façon de faire; **it's not my ~ to show my feelings** ce n'est pas mon genre *or* dans mes habitudes d'exprimer ce que je ressens; **it's only his (little) ~** c'est comme ça qu'il est, voilà comment il est; **she has a (certain) ~ with her** elle sait persuader; **he has a ~ with people** il sait (comment) s'y prendre avec les gens, les gens le trouvent sympathique; **to have a ~ with words** (*be eloquent*) bien savoir manier les mots *or* le langage; (*iro*) avoir une façon toute personnelle de s'exprimer (*iro*); **he has got a ~ with cars** il sait (comment) s'y prendre avec les voitures; **to mend** *or* **improve one's ~s** s'amender, acheter une conduite*; **to get into/out of the ~ of doing** prendre/perdre l'habitude de faire.

k (*respect, detail, particular*) égard *m*, point *m*. **in some ~s** à certains égards; **in many ~s** à bien des égards; **in more ~s than one** à plus d'un titre; **can I help you in any ~?** puis-je vous aider en quoi que ce soit?, puis-je faire quelque chose pour vous aider?; **in every ~ possible, in every possible ~** *help* dans la mesure du possible; *try* de toutes les façons possibles; **does that in any ~ explain it?** est-ce là une explication satisfaisante?; **he's in no ~** *or* **not in any ~ to blame** ce n'est vraiment pas sa faute, ce n'est aucunement sa faute; **not in any ~!** en aucune façon!, pas le moins du monde!; **without in any ~ wishing to do so** sans vouloir le moins du monde le faire; **he's right in a** *or* **one ~** il a raison dans un certain sens; **what is there in the ~ of books?** qu'est-ce qu'il y a comme livres?, qu'est-ce qu'il y a à lire?

l (*Naut*) **to gather/lose ~** prendre/perdre de la vitesse; **to have ~ on** avoir de l'erre; **to be under ~** (*Naut*) faire route, être en route; (*fig*) *[train, coach]* être en route; *[journey, meeting, discussion]* être en cours; *[plans]* être en voie de réalisation *or* d'exécution; **to get under ~** (*Naut*) appareiller, lever l'ancre; (*fig*) *[person]* se mettre en route, partir; (*Aut etc*) se mettre en route, démarrer; *[meeting, discussion]* démarrer; *[plan, project]* démarrer, commencer à se réaliser *or* à être exécuté; **they got the ship under ~** ils ont appareillé; **things are getting under ~ at last** cela commence enfin à prendre tournure; **to get sth under ~** *meeting etc* faire démarrer qch; *project etc* mettre qch en train; **to be (well) on one's ~ (to success, victory** *etc***)** être sur la voie (du succès, de la victoire *etc*).

m (*Shipbuilding*) **~s** cale *f*.

2 **adv** (*) très loin. **~ over there** très loin là-bas; **~ down below** très loin en bas, bien plus bas; **~ up in the sky** très haut dans le ciel; **~ back/over = away back/over** (*see* **away 1a**); **~ out to sea** loin au large; **you're ~ out in your calculations** tu es très loin de compte dans tes calculs (*see also* **3**).

3 **comp** ▸**waybill** (*Comm*) récépissé *m* ▸**wayfarer** *etc see* **wayfarer** *etc* ▸**waylay** *see* **waylay** ▸**way-out*** *clothes, ideas, behaviour* (*odd*) excentrique; (*great*) super* *inv*, formidable; *guess* très loin de compte ▸**way port** port *m* intermédiaire ▸**wayside** *see* **wayside** ▸**way station** (*US*) (*Rail*) petite gare; (*fig: stage*) étape *f* ▸**way train** (*US*) omnibus *m*.

wayfarer [ˈweɪˌfɛərəʳ] **n** voyageur *m*, -euse *f*.

wayfaring [ˈweɪˌfɛərɪŋ] **n** voyages *mpl*.

waylay [weɪˈleɪ] **pret, ptp waylaid vt** (*attack*) attaquer, assaillir; (*speak to*) arrêter au passage.

wayside [ˈweɪsaɪd] 1 **n** bord *m or* côté *m* de la route. **along the ~** le long de la route; **by the ~** au bord de la route; **to fall by the ~** (*liter: err, sin*) quitter le droit chemin; (*not complete course: of contestant etc*) abandonner en route; (*be cancelled or postponed: of project etc: also* **go by the ~**) tomber à l'eau; (*gen*) **it went by the ~** on a dû laisser tomber. 2 **comp** *plant, café* au bord de la route.

wayward [ˈweɪwəd] **adj** *person* qui n'en fait qu'à sa tête; *horse* rétif.

waywardness [ˈweɪwədnɪs] **n** (*NonC*) fait *m* de n'en faire qu'à sa tête; caractère *m* rebelle *or* rétif.

WBA n (**abbr of World Boxing Association**) WBA *f*.

W.C. [ˈdʌblju(ː)ˈsiː] **n** (*Brit*) (**abbr of water closet**) W.-C. *mpl*, waters *mpl*.

we [wiː] **pers pron pl** (*unstressed, stressed*) nous. **WE don't do that** nous, nous ne faisons pas ce genre de choses; **~ went to the pictures** nous sommes allés *or* on est allé* au cinéma; **~ French** nous autres Français; **as ~ say in England** comme on dit (chez nous) en Angleterre; **~ all make mistakes** tout le monde peut se tromper; **~ the teachers understand that ...** nous autres professeurs, nous comprenons que ...; **~ three have already discussed it** nous en avons déjà discuté à nous trois, nous trois en avons déjà discuté; **"~ are convinced" said the king** "nous sommes convaincu" dit le roi.

WEA [ˈdʌbljuːiːˈeɪ] **n** (*Brit*) (**abbr of Workers' Educational Association**)

Association d'éducation populaire.

weak [wi:k] 1 adj a (*physically*) *person, animal* faible, qui manque de forces; *join, beam, structure, material* faible, fragile, qui manque de solidité; (*morally etc*) *person* faible, mou (*f* molle); *army, country, team* faible, sans défense; *government* faible, impuissant; *excuse, argument, evidence* faible, réfutable, peu convaincant; *intellect* faible. **to grow ~(er)** *[person]* s'affaiblir, faiblir; *[structure, material]* faiblir, perdre de sa solidité; *[voice]* faiblir, devenir plus faible; *[influence, power]* baisser, diminuer; **his health is ~** il a une santé fragile *or* délicate; **~ from** *or* **with hunger** affaibli par la faim; **~ from** *or* **with fright** les jambes molles de peur; **to have a ~ heart** être cardiaque, avoir le cœur faible *or* malade; **to have ~ lungs** *or* **a ~ chest** avoir les poumons fragiles, être faible des bronches; **to have a ~ stomach** *or* **digestion** avoir l'estomac fragile; **to have ~ eyes** *or* **eyesight** avoir la vue faible, avoir une mauvaise vue; **to have a ~ chin/mouth** avoir le menton fuyant/la bouche tombante; **in a ~ voice** d'une voix fluette *or* faible; **to be ~ in the head*** être faible d'esprit, être débile*; **his knees felt ~, he went ~ at the knees** ses genoux se dérobaient sous lui, il avait les jambes molles *or* comme du coton*; **he is ~ in maths** il est faible en maths; **~ point** *or* **spot** point *m* faible; (*fig*) **the ~ link in the chain** le point faible; (*US*) **the ~ sister*** le faiblard*, la faiblarde* (dans un groupe); **you're too ~ with her** tu te montres trop faible envers elle; *see* **constitution, sex, wall** *etc.*

b *coffee, tea* léger, faible; *solution, mixture, drug, lens, spectacles, magnet* faible; (*Elec*) *current* faible; (*Econ*) *the pound, dollar* faible. (*Gram*) **~ verb** verbe *m* faible.

2 n: **the ~** les faibles *mpl.*

3 comp ▸**weak-kneed** (*fig*) mou (*f* molle), lâche, faible ▸**weak-minded** faible *or* simple d'esprit ▸**weak-willed** faible, velléitaire.

weaken ['wi:kən] 1 vi *[person]* (*in health*) s'affaiblir, faiblir; (*in resolution*) faiblir, flancher*; (*relent*) se laisser fléchir; *[structure, material]* faiblir, perdre de sa solidité, commencer à fléchir; *[voice]* faiblir, baisser; *[influence, power]* baisser, diminuer; *[country, team]* faiblir; *[prices]* fléchir. **the price of tin has ~ed further** le cours de l'étain a de nouveau faibli *or* a accentué son repli.

2 vt *person* (*physically*) affaiblir, miner; (*morally, politically*) affaiblir; *join, structure, material* enlever de la solidité à; *heart* fatiguer; *country, team, government* affaiblir, rendre vulnérable; *defence, argument, evidence* affaiblir, enlever du poids *or* de la force à; *coffee, solution, mixture* couper, diluer; (*Econ*) *the pound, dollar* affaiblir, faire baisser.

weakening ['wi:kənɪŋ] 1 n *[health, resolution]* affaiblissement *m*; *[structure, material]* fléchissement *m*, fatigue *f*. 2 adj *effect* affaiblissant, débilitant; *disease, illness* débilitant, qui mine.

weakling ['wi:klɪŋ] n (*physically*) gringalet *m*, mauviette *f*; (*morally etc*) faible *mf*, poule *f* mouillée.

weakly ['wi:klɪ] 1 adj faible, maladif, chétif. 2 adv *move* faiblement, sans forces; *speak* faiblement, mollement.

weakness ['wi:knɪs] n (*see* **weak**) faiblesse *f*; fragilité *f*; mollesse *f*; impuissance *f*. **it's one of his ~es** c'est là un de ses points faibles; **to have a ~ for** avoir un faible pour.

weal¹ [wi:l] n (*on skin*) marque *f* d'un coup de fouet (*or* de bâton *etc*), zébrure *f*.

weal²†† [wi:l] n bien *m*, bonheur *m*. **the common ~** le bien public; **~ and woe** le bonheur et le malheur.

weald [wi:ld] n (*wooded country*) pays boisé; (*open country*) pays découvert.

wealth [welθ] 1 n (*NonC*) (*fact of being rich*) richesse *f*; (*money, possessions, resources*) richesses, fortune *f*; (*natural resources etc*) richesse(s). **a man of great ~** un homme puissamment riche; **"The W~ of Nations"** "la Richesse des Nations"; **the ~ of the oceans** les richesses *or* les riches ressources *fpl* des océans; **the mineral ~ of a country** les richesses minières d'un pays; (*fig*) **a ~ of ideas** une profusion *or* une abondance d'idées, des idées en abondance *or* à profusion. 2 comp ▸**wealth tax** (*Brit*) impôt *m* sur la fortune.

wealthy ['welθɪ] 1 adj *person, family* riche, fortuné, nanti; *country* riche. 2 npl: **the ~** les riches *mpl.*

wean [wi:n] vt *baby* sevrer; (*fig: from bad habits etc*) détacher, détourner (*from, off* de). **I've managed to ~ him off gin** je l'ai habitué à se passer de gin; **I ~ed her off the idea of going to Greece** je l'ai dissuadée de partir pour la Grèce.

weaning ['wi:nɪŋ] n sevrage *m*.

weapon ['wepən] n (*lit, fig*) arme *f*. **~ of offence/defence** arme offensive/défensive.

weaponry ['wepənrɪ] n (*NonC: collective*) (*gen: arms*) armes *fpl*; (*Mil*) matériel *m* de guerre, armements *mpl*.

wear [wɛəʳ] (vb: pret **wore**, ptp **worn**) 1 n (*NonC*) a (*act of wearing*) port *m*, fait *m* de porter; (*use*) usage *m*; (*deterioration through use*) usure *f*. **clothes for everyday ~** vêtements pour tous les jours; **clothes for evening ~** tenue *f* de soirée; (*shop notice*) tenues de soirée; **for evening ~ we suggest ...** comme tenue de soirée nous suggérons ...; **it isn't for town ~** ce n'est pas une tenue de ville, cela ne se porte pas en ville; **it is compulsory ~ for officers** le port en est obligatoire pour les officiers; **what is the correct ~ for these occasions?** quelle est la tenue convenable pour de telles occasions?, qu'est-ce qui est de mise en de telles occasions?; **this carpet has seen** *or* **had some hard ~** ce tapis a beaucoup servi; **to be in constant ~** *[garment]* être porté continuellement; *[tyres etc]* être en usage continuel, être continuellement utilisé; **this material will stand up to a lot of ~** ce tissu fera beaucoup d'usage *or* résistera bien à l'usure; **there is still some ~ left in it** (*garment*) c'est encore mettable; (*carpet, tyre*) cela fera encore de l'usage; **he got 4 years' ~ out of it** cela lui a fait *or* duré 4 ans; (*US*) **wear resistant** inusable; **it has had a lot of ~ and tear** c'est très usagé, cela a été beaucoup porté *or* utilisé; **fair** *or* **normal ~ and tear** usure normale; **the ~ and tear on the engine** l'usure du moteur; **to show signs of ~, to look the worse for ~** *[clothes, shoes, carpet]* commencer à être défraîchi *or* fatigué; *[tyres, machine]* commencer à être fatigué *or* usagé; (*fig*) **he was (looking) somewhat the worse for ~*** il n'était pas très frais.

b (*esp Comm: clothes collectively*) vêtements *mpl*. **children's ~** vêtements pour enfants; **summer ~** vêtements d'été; **ski ~** vêtements de ski; *see* **foot, sport** *etc.*

2 vt a *garment, flower, sword, watch, spectacles* porter; *beard, moustache* porter, avoir; (*fig*) *smile* avoir, arborer; *look* avoir, afficher. **he was ~ing a hat** il avait *or* il portait un chapeau, il avait mis un chapeau; **I never ~ a hat** je ne mets *or* porte jamais de chapeau; **hats are now rarely worn** les chapeaux ne se portent plus guère aujourd'hui; **what shall I ~?** qu'est-ce que je vais mettre?; **I've nothing to ~, I haven't got a thing to ~** je n'ai rien à me mettre; **I haven't worn that for ages** cela fait des siècles que je ne l'ai pas mis *or* porté; **Eskimos don't ~ bikinis** les Esquimaudes ne portent jamais de bikini; **she was ~ing blue** elle était en bleu; **what the well-dressed woman is ~ing this year** ce que la femme élégante porte cette année; **he ~s good clothes** il est bien habillé, il s'habille bien; **she ~s her hair long** elle a les cheveux longs; **she ~s her hair in a bun** elle porte un chignon; **I never ~ scent** je ne me parfume jamais, je ne me mets jamais de parfum; **she was ~ing make-up** elle (s')était maquillée; **she was ~ing lipstick** elle s'était *or* elle avait mis du rouge à lèvres; **to ~ the crown** être sur le trône; (*fig*) **she's the one who ~s the trousers** *or* **the pants*** c'est elle qui porte la culotte* *or* qui commande; **she wore a frown** elle fronçait les sourcils; **he wore a look** *or* **an air of satisfaction, he wore a satisfied look on his face** son visage exprimait la satisfaction, il affichait *or* avait un air de satisfaction; **she ~s her age** *or* **her years well** elle porte bien son âge, elle est encore bien pour son âge; *see* **heart** *etc.*

b (*rub etc*) *clothes, fabric, stone, wood* user; *groove, path* creuser peu à peu. **to ~ a hole in sth** trouer *or* percer peu à peu qch, faire peu à peu un trou dans *or* à qch; **to ~ sth into holes** faire des trous à qch; **the knife blade was worn thin** la lame du couteau s'était amincie à l'usage; **the rug was worn thin** *or* **threadbare** le tapis était usé jusqu'à la corde *or* complètement râpé; **he had worn himself to a shadow** il s'était fatigué au point de n'être plus que l'ombre de lui-même; **worn with care** usé *or* rongé par les soucis; *see also* **frazzle, work, worn** *etc.*

c (*Brit *: tolerate, accept*) tolérer. **he won't ~ that** il n'acceptera jamais, il ne marchera pas*; **the committee won't ~ another £100 on your expenses** vous ne ferez jamais avaler au comité 100 livres de plus pour vos frais*.

3 vi a (*last*) *[clothes, carpet, tyres etc]* faire de l'usage, résister à l'usure. **a good tweed will ~ forever** un bon tweed ne s'use jamais *or* est inusable; **these shoes will ~ for years** ces chaussures dureront *or* feront des années; **that dress/carpet has worn well** cette robe/ce tapis a bien résisté à l'usure *or* a fait beaucoup d'usage; (*fig*) **theory/friendship that has worn well** théorie/amitié intacte en dépit du temps; **that car has worn well*** cette voiture est quand même encore en bon état; **she has worn well*** elle est bien conservée.

b (*rub etc thin*) *[garment, fabric, stone, wood]* s'user. **the trousers have worn at the knees** le pantalon est usé aux genoux; **to ~ into holes** se trouer; **the rock has worn smooth** la roche a été polie par le temps; **the material has worn thin** le tissu est râpé; (*fig*) **that excuse has worn thin!** cette excuse ne prend plus!; **my patience is ~ing thin** je suis presque à bout de patience; **discipline was ~ing thin** il n'y avait pratiquement plus de discipline, la discipline commençait à pâtir sérieusement.

c *[day, year, sb's life]* **to ~ towards its end** *or* **towards a close** tirer à sa fin.

▸**wear away** 1 vi *[wood, metal]* s'user; *[cliffs etc]* être rongé *or* dégradé; *[inscription, design]* s'effacer. 2 vt sep user; ronger, dégrader; effacer.

▸**wear down** 1 vi *[heels, pencil etc]* s'user; *[resistance, courage]* s'épuiser. 2 vt sep *materials* user; *patience, strength* user, épuiser; *courage, resistance* miner. (*fig*) **the hard work was wearing him down** le travail l'usait *or* le minait; **they wore him down with constant pestering until he finally agreed** ils n'ont cessé de l'importuner jusqu'à ce qu'il finisse par accepter *or* jusqu'à ce qu'il accepte (*subj*) de guerre lasse.

▸**wear off** 1 vi *[colour, design, inscription]* s'effacer, disparaître; *[pain]* disparaître, passer; *[anger, excitement]* s'apaiser, passer; *[effects]* se dissiper, disparaître; *[anaesthetic]* se dissiper. **the novelty has worn off** cela n'a plus l'attrait de la nouveauté. 2 vt sep effacer par l'usure, faire disparaître.

►**wear on** vi *[day, year, winter etc]* avancer; *[battle, war, discussions etc]* se poursuivre. **as the years wore on** à mesure que les années passaient, avec le temps.

►**wear out** 1 vi *[clothes, material, machinery]* s'user; *[patience, enthusiasm]* s'épuiser. 2 vt sep a *shoes, clothes* user; *one's strength, reserves, materials, patience* épuiser. b (*exhaust*) *person, horse* épuiser. **to wear one's eyes out** s'user les yeux *or* la vue; **to wear o.s. out** s'épuiser, s'exténuer (*doing* à faire); **to be worn out** être exténué *or* éreinté. 3 **worn-out** adj *see* **worn**.

►**wear through** 1 vt sep trouer, percer. 2 vi se trouer (*par usure*).

wearable ['wɛərəbl] adj *garment* mettable.

wearer ['wɛərəʳ] n: **will the ~ of the green coat please come forward?** la personne vêtue du *or* portant le manteau vert aurait-elle l'obligeance de s'avancer?; **these shoes will delight the ~** ces chaussures feront la joie de la personne *or* de celui (*or* de celle) qui les portera; **as all uniform ~s know ...** comme tous ceux qui portent l'uniforme le savent ...; **direct from maker to ~** directement du fabricant au client.

wearied ['wɪərɪd] adj (*tired*) *person, animal, smile, look* las (*f* lasse); *sigh* de lassitude.

wearily ['wɪərɪlɪ] adv *say* d'un ton las *or* fatigué, avec lassitude; *sigh, smile, look* d'un air las *or* fatigué, avec lassitude; *move* péniblement.

weariness ['wɪərɪnɪs] n (*see* **weary**) lassitude *f*, fatigue *f*, épuisement *m*; abattement *m*; ennui *m*; *see* **world**.

wearing ['wɛərɪŋ] adj épuisant, lassant.

wearisome ['wɪərɪsəm] adj (*tiring*) fatigant, épuisant; (*boring*) ennuyeux, lassant, fastidieux.

weary ['wɪərɪ] 1 adj (*tired*) *person, animal* las (*f* lasse), fatigué, épuisé; *smile, look* las; (*dispirited*) *person* las, abattu; *sigh* de lassitude; (*tiring*) *journey, wait* fatigant, épuisant; (*irksome*) ennuyeux, lassant. **to be/grow ~ of (doing) sth** être las/se lasser de (faire) qch; **~ of life** dégoûté *or* las de vivre; **~ of waiting** las *or* fatigué d'attendre; **~ with walking** fatigué *or* las à force d'avoir marché; **4 ~ hours** 4 heures mortelles; **10 ~ miles** 10 milles épuisants; *see* **world**. 2 vi se lasser (*of sth* de qch, *of doing* de faire). 3 vt (*tire*) fatiguer, lasser; (*try patience of*) lasser, agacer, ennuyer (*with* à force de); *see also* **wearied**.

weasel ['wi:zl] 1 n, pl ~ *or* ~s belette *f*; (*fig pej: person*) fouine *f* (*fig pej*). 2 comp ►**weasel words*** (*US fig*) paroles *fpl* ambiguës *or* équivoques. 3 vi (*US *: also* **~-word**) (*speaking*) s'exprimer de façon ambiguë *or* équivoque. **to ~ out of sth** (*extricate o.s.*) se sortir *or* se tirer de qch en misant sur l'ambiguïté; (*avoid it*) éviter qch en misant sur l'ambiguïté.

weather ['weðəʳ] 1 n temps *m*. **~ permitting** si le temps le permet; **what's the ~ like?, what's the ~ doing?*** quel temps fait-il?; **it's fine/bad ~** il fait beau/mauvais, le temps est beau/mauvais; **I don't like the ~ much** je n'aime pas ce genre de temps; **summer ~** temps d'été *or* estival; **in this ~** par ce temps, par un temps comme ça; **in hot ~** par temps chaud, en période de chaleur; **in all ~s** par tous les temps; (*fig*) **to be under the ~*** être mal fichu*, ne pas être dans son assiette; *see* **heavy, wet**.

2 vt a (*survive*) *tempest, hurricane* essuyer, réchapper à; (*fig*) *crisis* survivre à, réchapper à, surmonter. **to ~ a storm** (*lit*) essuyer une tempête, réchapper à une tempête; (*fig*) tenir le coup, ne pas succomber.

b (*expose to ~*) *wood etc* faire mûrir. **~ed rocks** rochers exposés aux intempéries; **rocks ~ed by rain and wind** rochers patinés *or* érodés par la pluie et par le vent.

3 vi *[wood]* mûrir; *[rocks]* s'effriter.

4 comp *knowledge, map, prospects* météorologique; *conditions, variations* atmosphérique; (*Naut*) *side, sheet* du vent ►**weather-beaten** *person, face* hâlé, tanné; *building* dégradé par les intempéries; *stone* effrité par les intempéries ►**weatherboard(ing)** (*Brit: NonC*) planches *fpl* de recouvrement ►**weather-bound** immobilisé *or* retenu par le mauvais temps ►**Weather Bureau** (*US*), **Weather Centre** (*Brit*) Office national de la météorologie ►**weather chart** carte *f* du temps, carte météorologique ►**weather check** (bref) bulletin *m* météo *inv* ►**weather cock** girouette *f* ►**weather eye:** (*fig*) **to keep a weather eye on sth** surveiller qch; (*fig*) **to keep one's weather eye open** veiller au grain (*fig*) ►**weather forecast** prévisions *fpl* météorologiques, météo* *f* (*NonC*) ►**weather forecaster, weatherman*** météorologue *m*, météorologiste *m* ►**weatherproof** adj *clothing* imperméable; *house* étanche ◊ vt *clothing* imperméabiliser; *house* rendre étanche ►**weather report** bulletin *m* météo(rologique), météo* *f* (*NonC*) ►**weather ship** navire *m* météo *inv* ►**the weather situation** le temps (qu'il fait *or* fera *etc*) ►**weather station** station *f or* observatoire *m* météorologique ►**weather strip** bourrelet *m* (*pour porte etc*) ►**weather vane** = **weather cock** ►**weather-worn** = **weather-beaten**.

weave [wi:v] (vb: **pret wove, ptp woven**) 1 n tissage *m*. **loose/tight ~** tissage lâche/serré; **a cloth of English ~** du drap tissé en Angleterre.

2 vt *threads, cloth, web* tisser; *strands* entrelacer; *basket, garland, daisies* tresser; (*fig*) *plot* tramer, tisser; *story* inventer, bâtir. **to ~ flowers into one's hair** entrelacer des fleurs dans ses cheveux; **to ~ details into a story** introduire *or* incorporer des détails dans une histoire; **to ~ one's way** *see* **3c**.

3 vi a (*Tex etc*) tisser.

b *[road, river, line]* serpenter.

c (pret, ptp gen **weaved**) **to ~ (one's way) through the crowd** se faufiler à travers la foule; **the drunk man ~d (his way) across the room** l'ivrogne a titubé *or* zigzagué à travers la pièce; **the car was weaving (its way) in and out through the traffic** la voiture se faufilait *or* se glissait à travers la circulation; **the boxer was weaving in and out skilfully** le boxeur s'engageait et se dégageait adroitement; (*fig*) **let's get weaving!*** allons, remuons-nous!

weaver ['wi:vəʳ] n (*person*) tisserand(e) *m(f)*; (*also* **~bird**) tisserin *m*.

weaving ['wi:vɪŋ] 1 n (*NonC: see* **weave**) tissage *m*; tressage *m*; entrelacement *m*. 2 comp ►**weaving mill** (atelier *m* de) tissage *m*.

web [web] 1 n (*fabric*) tissu *m*; *[spider]* toile *f*; (*between toes etc*) *[animals etc]* palmure *f*; *[humans]* palmature *f*; (*fig: of lies etc*) tissu. 2 comp ►**web(bed) feet** *or* **toes: to have web(bed) feet** *or* **toes, to be web-footed** *or* **web-toed** *[animal]* être palmipède, avoir les pieds palmés; *[human]* avoir une palmature.

webbing ['webɪŋ] n (*NonC*) (*fabric*) toile forte en bande; (*on chair*) sangles *fpl*; (*on bird's, animal's foot*) palmure *f*; (*on human foot*) palmature *f*.

we'd [wi:d] = **we had, we should, we would;** *see* **have, should, would**.

Wed. abbr of **Wednesday**.

wed [wed] pret **wedded**, ptp **wedded**, (*rare*) **wed** 1 vt (*marry*) épouser, se marier avec; *[priest]* marier; (*fig*) *things, qualities* allier. (*fig*) **she is ~ded to her work** elle ne vit que pour son travail, elle se consacre entièrement à son travail; **his cunning, ~ded to ambition, led to ...** sa ruse, alliée à l'ambition, a conduit à ... . 2 vi se marier. 3 npl: **the newly-~s** les jeunes *or* nouveaux mariés.

wedded ['wedɪd] adj *person* marié; *bliss, life* conjugal. **his (lawful) ~ wife** sa légitime épouse; **the ~ couple** les mariés *mpl*.

wedding ['wedɪŋ] 1 n (*ceremony*) mariage *m*, noces *fpl*. **silver/golden ~** noces d'argent/d'or; **they had a quiet ~** ils se sont mariés dans l'intimité, le mariage a été célébré dans l'intimité; **they had a church ~** ils se sont mariés à l'église; *see* **civil**.

2 comp *cake, night* de noces; *present* de mariage, de noces; *invitation* de mariage; *ceremony, march* nuptial ►**wedding anniversary** anniversaire *m* de mariage ►**wedding band** = **wedding ring** ►**wedding breakfast** lunch *m* de mariage; (*less elegant*) repas *m* de noces ►**wedding day: their wedding day** le jour de leur mariage ►**wedding dress** robe *f* de mariée ►**wedding guest** invité(e) *m(f)* (*à un mariage*) ►**wedding ring** alliance *f*, anneau *m* de mariage.

wedel ['veɪdl] vi (*Ski*) godiller.

wedeln ['veɪdln] n (*Ski*) godille *f*.

wedge [wedʒ] 1 n a (*for holding sth steady; under wheel etc, also Golf*) cale *f*; (*for splitting wood, rock*) coin *m*. (*fig*) **to drive a ~ between two people** brouiller deux personnes; *see* **thin**.

b (*piece: of cake, pie etc*) part *f*, morceau *m*.

c (*Ski*) chasse-neige *m*; (*Climbing*) coin *m*de bois.

d ~s (*~-heeled shoe*) chaussures *fpl* à semelles compensées.

2 comp ►**wedge-heeled** à semelles compensées ►**wedge-shaped** en forme de coin ►**wedge-soled** = **wedge-heeled**.

3 vt (*fix*) *table, wheels* caler; (*stick, push*) enfoncer (*into* dans, *between* entre). **to ~ a door open/shut** maintenir une porte ouverte/fermée à l'aide d'une cale; **the door was ~d** on avait mis une cale à la porte; **he ~d the table leg to hold it steady** il a calé le pied de table; **I can't move this, it's ~d** je n'arrive pas à l'enlever, c'est coincé; **to ~ a stick into a crack** enfoncer un bâton dans une fente; **the car was ~d between two trucks** la voiture était coincée entre deux camions; **he managed to ~ another book into the bookcase** il a réussi à faire rentrer *or* à enfoncer *or* à fourrer* un autre livre dans la bibliothèque.

►**wedge in** 1 vi *[person]* se glisser. 2 vt sep (*into case, box etc*) *object* faire rentrer, enfoncer, fourrer*; (*into car, onto seat etc*) *person* faire rentrer; *several people* entasser. **to be wedged in** être coincé.

wedlock ['wedlɒk] n (*NonC*) mariage *m*. **to be born out of ~** être (un) enfant naturel.

Wednesday ['wenzdeɪ] n mercredi *m*; *see* **ash²**; *for other phrases see* **Saturday**.

wee¹ [wi:] adj (*Scot*) tout petit. **a ~ bit** un tout petit peu.

wee²* [wi:] n, vi: **to (have a) ~** faire pipi*.

weed [wi:d] 1 n a mauvaise herbe; (** pej: person*) mauviette *f*; (**: marijuana*) herbe *f* (*sl*). (*hum*) **the ~*** le tabac. b **(widow's) ~s** vêtements *mpl* de deuil; **in widow's ~s** en deuil. 2 comp ►**weedhead** (*Drugs sl*) consommateur *m* de la marijuana ►**weed-killer** désherbant *m*, herbicide *m*. 3 vt désherber; (*hoe*) sarcler.

►**weed out** vt sep *plant* enlever, arracher; (*fig*) *weak candidates* éliminer (*from* de); *troublemakers* expulser (*from* de); *old clothes, books* trier et jeter.

weeding ['wi:dɪŋ] n (*NonC*) désherbage *m*; (*with hoe*) sarclage *m*. **I've done some ~** j'ai un peu désherbé.

weedy ['wi:dɪ] adj *ground* couvert de mauvaises herbes, envahi par les mauvaises herbes; (*fig pej*) *person* qui a l'air d'une mauviette.

week [wi:k] 1 n semaine *f*. **in a ~** dans une semaine *or* une huitaine, dans huit jours; **what day of the ~ is it?** quel jour de la semaine sommes-nous?; **~ in ~ out** chaque semaine, semaine après semaine, pendant des semaines; **~ after ~** semaine après semaine; **this ~** cette semaine; **next/last** ~ la semaine prochaine/dernière; **the** ~ **before last** l'avant-dernière semaine; **the** ~ **after next** pas la semaine prochaine, celle d'après; **by the end of the** ~ **he had** ... à la fin de la semaine il avait ...; **in the middle of the** ~ vers le milieu *or* dans le courant de la semaine; **twice a** ~ deux fois par semaine; **this time next** ~ dans huit jours à la même heure; **this time last** ~ il y a huit jours à la même heure; **today** ~, **a** ~ **today, this day** ~ (d')aujourd'hui en huit; **tomorrow** ~, **a** ~ **tomorrow** (de) demain en huit; **yesterday** ~, **a** ~ **(past) yesterday** il y a eu une semaine hier; **Sunday** ~, **a** ~ **on Sunday** (de) dimanche en huit; **every** ~ chaque semaine; **two** ~**s ago** il y a deux semaines, il y a quinze jours; **in 3** ~**s' time** dans *or* d'ici 3 semaines; **it lasted (for)** ~**s** cela a duré des semaines (et des semaines); **the first time** *etc* **in** ~**s** la première fois *etc* depuis des semaines; **the** ~ **ending May 6th** la semaine qui se termine le 6 mai; **he owes her 3** ~**s' rent** il lui doit 3 semaines de loyer; **paid by the** ~ payé à la semaine; **the working** ~ la semaine de travail; **a 36-hour** ~ une semaine de 36 heures; **a three-day** ~ une semaine (de travail) de trois jours; **a** ~**'s wages** le salaire hebdomadaire *or* de la *or* d'une semaine; *see* **Easter.**

2 **comp** ►**weekday** **n** jour *m* de semaine, (*esp Comm*) jour ouvrable ◊ **comp** *activities, timetable* de la semaine; **(on) weekdays** en semaine, (*esp Comm*) les jours ouvrables.

weekend ['wiːk'end] 1 **n** week-end *m*, fin *f* de semaine. **(at)** ~**s** en fin de semaine, pendant le(s) week-end(s); **what are you doing at the** ~? qu'est-ce que tu vas faire pendant le week-end?; **we're going away for the** ~ nous partons en week-end; **to take a long** ~ prendre un week-end prolongé; **they had Tuesday off so they made a long** ~ **of it** comme ils ne devaient pas travailler mardi ils ont fait le pont. 2 **comp** *visit, programme* de *or* du week-end ►**weekend bag, weekend case** sac *m* de voyage, mallette *f* ►**weekend cottage** maison *f* de campagne. 3 **vi** passer le week-end.

weekender ['wiːk'endəʳ] **n** personne *f* partant (*or* partie) en week-end. **the village is full of** ~**s** le village est plein de gens qui sont venus pour le week-end.

weekly ['wiːklɪ] 1 **adj** *wages, visit* de la semaine, hebdomadaire; *journal* hebdomadaire. 2 **adv** (*once a week*) chaque semaine, une fois par semaine; (*same day each week*) tous les huit jours. **twice** ~ deux fois par semaine. 3 **n** (*magazine*) hebdomadaire *m*.

weenie* ['wiːnɪ] **n** (*US Culin*) = **wienie.**

weeny* ['wiːnɪ] 1 **adj** tout petit, petit petit*. 2 **comp** ►**weeny-bopper*** enfant *mf* (de 8 à 12 ans).

weep [wiːp] **pret, ptp wept** 1 **vi** *[person]* pleurer, verser des larmes; *[walls, sore, wound etc]* suinter. **to** ~ **for joy** pleurer de joie; **to** ~ **for sb/sth** pleurer qn/qch; **to** ~ **over sth** pleurer *or* se lamenter sur qch; **she wept to see him leave** elle a pleuré de le voir partir; **I could have wept!** j'en aurais pleuré! 2 **vt** *tears* pleurer, verser, répandre. **to** ~ **one's eyes out** pleurer à chaudes larmes; *see* **bucket.** 3 **n: to have a good** ~ pleurer à chaudes larmes *or* un bon coup; **to have a little** ~ pleurer un peu, verser quelques larmes.

weeping ['wiːpɪŋ] 1 **n** (*NonC*) larmes *fpl*. **we heard the sound of** ~ on entendait quelqu'un qui pleurait. 2 **adj** *person* qui pleure; *walls, wound* suintant. ~ **willow** saule *m* pleureur.

weepy ['wiːpɪ] 1 **adj** *voice* larmoyant; *film etc* mélo*, sentimental. *[person]* **to be** *or* **feel** ~ avoir envie de pleurer, être au bord des larmes. 2 **n** (*Brit: film, book*) mélo* *m*, film *m* (*or* livre *m*) sentimental.

weever ['wiːvəʳ] **n** (*fish*) vive *f*.

weevil ['wiːvəl] **n** charançon *m*.

weewee* ['wiːwiː] (*baby talk*) 1 **n** pipi* *m*. 2 **vi** faire pipi*.

weft [weft] **n** (*Tex*) trame *f*.

weigh [weɪ] 1 **vt** a (*lit, fig*) peser. **to** ~ **o.s.** se peser; **to** ~ **sth in one's hand** soupeser qch; **it** ~**s 9 kilos** ça pèse 9 kilos; **how much** *or* **what do you** ~? combien est-ce que vous pesez?; (*fig*) **that argument doesn't** ~ **anything with me** cet argument n'a aucun poids à mes yeux; **to** ~ **one's words** peser ses mots; **to** ~ **(up) A against B** mettre en balance A et B; **to** ~ **(up) the pros and cons** peser le pour et le contre.

b (*Naut*) **to** ~ **anchor** lever l'ancre.

2 **vi** *[object, responsibilities]* peser (*on* sur). **this box** ~**s fairly heavy** cette boîte pèse assez lourd; **the fear of cancer** ~**s on her** *or* **on her mind all the time** la peur du cancer la tourmente constamment; **there's something** ~**ing on her mind** quelque chose la préoccupe *or* la tracasse; **these factors do not** ~ **with him** ces facteurs ne comptent pas *or* n'ont aucun poids à ses yeux; **the economic climate** ~**s heavily against having children** le climat économique dissuade d'avoir des enfants.

3 **comp** ►**weighbridge** pont-bascule *m* ►**weigh-in** (*Sport*) pesage *m*.

►**weigh down** 1 **vi** peser *or* appuyer de tout son poids (*on sth* sur qch). (*fig*) **this sorrow weighed down on her** ce chagrin la rongeait *or* la minait. 2 **vt sep** faire plier *or* ployer, courber; (*fig*) accabler, tourmenter. **the fruit weighed the branch down** la branche ployait *or* pliait sous le poids des fruits; **he was weighed down with parcels** il pliait sous le poids des paquets; **to be weighed down by** *or* **with responsibilities** être accablé *or* surchargé de responsabilités; **to be weighed down with fears** être en proie à toutes sortes de peurs.

►**weigh in** 1 **vi** *[boxer, jockey etc]* se faire peser. **to weigh in at 70 kilos** peser 70 kilos avant le match *or* la course; (*fig*) **he weighed in with the fact that** ... il est intervenu dans le débat avec un argument de poids: le fait que ... . 2 **vt sep** *boxer, jockey* peser (*avant le match ou la course*). 3 **weigh-in n** *see* **weigh 3.**

►**weigh out vt sep** *sugar etc* peser.

►**weigh up vt sep** (*consider*) examiner, calculer; (*compare*) mettre en balance (*A with B, A against B* A et B); (*assess*) *person, the opposition* juger, sonder. **I'm weighing up whether to go or not** je me tâte pour savoir si j'y vais ou non; *see also* **weigh 1a.**

weighing ['weɪɪŋ] **in comps:** ~ **machine** (*gen*) balance *f*; (*for heavy loads*) bascule *f*.

weight [weɪt] 1 **n** a (*NonC*) poids *m*; (*Phys: relative* ~) pesanteur *f*. (*Phys*) **atomic** ~ poids atomique; **to be sold by** ~ se vendre au poids; **what is your** ~? combien pesez-vous?, quel poids faites-vous?; **my** ~ **is 60 kilos** je pèse 60 kilos; **it is 3 kilos in** ~ ça pèse 3 kilos; **what a** ~ **it is!** que c'est lourd!; **they are the same** ~ ils font le même poids; ~ **when empty** poids à vide; (*fig*) **it is worth its** ~ **in gold** cela vaut son pesant d'or; **to be under**~**/over**~ être trop maigre/trop gros (*f* grosse); **to put on** *or* **gain** ~ grossir, prendre du poids; **to lose** ~ maigrir, perdre du poids; **he put** *or* **leaned his full** ~ **on the handle** il a pesé *or* appuyé de tout son poids sur la poignée; **he put his full** ~ **behind the blow** il a frappé de toutes ses forces; (*fig*) **to throw one's** ~ *or* **to put all one's** ~ **behind sth/sb** apporter personnellement tout son soutien à qch/à qn; **feel the** ~ **of this box!** soupesez-moi cette boîte!; *see* **pull, throw about** *etc*.

b (*fig*) *[argument, words, public opinion, evidence]* poids *m*, force *f*; *[worry, responsibility, years, age]* poids. **to lend** *or* **give** ~ **to sth** donner du poids à qch; **to carry** ~ *[argument, factor]* avoir du poids (*with* pour); *[person]* avoir de l'influence; **we must give due** ~ **to his arguments** nous devons donner tout leur poids à ses arguments; *see* **mind.**

c (*for scales, on clock etc*) poids *m*. ~**s and measures** poids et mesures; *see* **paper, put** *etc*.

2 **comp** ►**weight lifter** (*Sport*) haltérophile *m* ►**weight lifting** haltérophilie *f* ►**weight training** musculation *f* (*avec des poids*) ►**weightwatcher: he's a weightwatcher** (*actively slimming*) il suit un régime amaigrissant; (*figure-conscious*) il surveille son poids.

3 **vt** (*sink*) lester avec un poids (*or* une pierre *etc*); (*hold down*) retenir *or* maintenir avec un poids (*or* une pierre *etc*). (*fig*) **the situation was heavily** ~**ed in his favour/against him** la situation lui était nettement favorable/défavorable.

►**weight down vt sep** (*sink*) lester avec un poids (*or* une pierre *etc*); (*hold down*) retenir *or* maintenir avec un poids (*or* une pierre *etc*).

weighted ['weɪtɪd] **adj** pondéré. ~ **average** moyenne *f* pondérée.

weightiness ['weɪtɪnɪs] **n** (*NonC: see* **weighty**) lourdeur *f*; caractère probant; importance *f*, gravité *f*.

weighting ['weɪtɪŋ] **n** a (*on salary*) indemnité *f*, allocation *f*. **London** ~ indemnité de résidence pour Londres. b (*Scol*) coefficient *m*. c (*Econ*) coefficient *m*, pondération *f*.

weightless ['weɪtlɪs] **adj** (*Space*) en état d'apesanteur.

weightlessness ['weɪtlɪsnɪs] **n** apesanteur *f*.

weighty ['weɪtɪ] **adj** *load* pesant, lourd; (*fig*) *burden, responsibility* lourd; *argument, matter* de poids; *reason* probant; *consideration, deliberation* mûr; *problem* grave, important.

Weimar ['vaɪmɑːr] **n** Weimar. **the** ~ **Republic** la république de Weimar.

weir [wɪəʳ] **n** barrage *m*.

weird [wɪəd] **adj** (*eerie*) surnaturel, mystérieux; (*odd*) bizarre, étrange, curieux, singulier.

weirdly ['wɪədlɪ] **adv** (*see* **weird**) mystérieusement; bizarrement, étrangement, curieusement, singulièrement.

weirdness ['wɪədnɪs] **n** étrangeté *f*.

weirdo‡ ['wɪədəʊ] **n, weirdy** ['wɪədɪ] **n** drôle d'oiseau* *m*, (*man only*) drôle de mec‡ *m*.

welch* [welʃ] **vi** = **welsh*.**

welcome ['welkəm] 1 **adj** a *reminder, interruption* opportun. *[guest, helper, food, change, decision]* **to be** ~ être le (*or* la) bienvenu(e); ~! soyez le bienvenu (*or* la bienvenue *etc*)!; ~ **to our house** nous sommes enchantés de vous avoir chez nous, (*more frm*) bienvenue chez nous; (*on notice*) "~ **to England!**" "bienvenue en Angleterre!"; **to make sb** ~ faire bon accueil à qn; (*fig*) **to put out the** ~ **mat for sb** faire un accueil chaleureux à qn; **I didn't feel very** ~ j'ai eu l'impression que je n'étais pas le bienvenu, je me suis senti de trop; **a cup of coffee is always** ~ une tasse de café est toujours la bienvenue; **it was** ~ **news/a** ~ **sight** nous avons été (*or* il a été *etc*) heureux de l'apprendre/de le voir; **it was a** ~ **gift** ce cadeau était le bienvenu, ce cadeau m'a (*or* lui a *etc*) fait bien plaisir; **it was a** ~ **relief** j'ai été (*or* il a été *etc*) vraiment soulagé.

b (*answer to thanks*) **you're** ~! il n'y a pas de quoi!, c'est moi qui vous remercie!, de rien!; **you're** ~ **to try** je vous en prie, essayez; (*iro*) libre à vous d'essayer; **you're** ~ **to use my car** n'hésitez pas à prendre ma voiture; **you're** ~ **to anything you need from here** tout ce qui est ici est à votre entière disposition; **you're** ~ **to any help I can give you** si je peux vous être utile, ce sera avec plaisir.

2 **n** accueil *m*. **to bid sb** ~ souhaiter la bienvenue à qn; **to give sb a warm** ~ faire un accueil chaleureux à qn; **they gave him a great** ~ ils

lui ont fait fête; **I got a fairly cold ~** j'ai été accueilli *or* reçu plutôt froidement; **words of ~** paroles *fpl* d'accueil, mots *mpl* de bienvenue; **what sort of a ~ will this product get from the housewife?** comment la ménagère accueillera-t-elle ce produit?; *see* **outstay.**

3 **vt** *person, delegation, group of people* (*greet, receive*) accueillir; (*greet warmly*) faire bon accueil à, accueillir chaleureusement; (*bid welcome*) souhaiter la bienvenue à; *sb's return, news, suggestion, change* se réjouir de. **he ~d me in** il m'a chaleureusement invité à entrer; (*TV etc*) **please ~ Linda Anderson!** on applaudit Linda Anderson!; **we would ~ your views on ...** nous serions heureux de connaître vos vues sur ...; **I'd ~ a cup of coffee** je prendrais volontiers une tasse de café, je ne dirais pas non à une tasse de café; *see* **open.**

►**welcome back vt sep: they welcomed him back after his journey** ils l'ont accueilli chaleureusement *or* ils lui ont fait fête à son retour de voyage.

welcoming ['welkəmɪŋ] **adj** *smile, handshake* accueillant; *ceremony, speeches* d'accueil. **the ~ party was waiting at the airport** la délégation venue les accueillir attendait à l'aéroport.

weld [weld] 1 **n** soudure *f*. 2 **vt** *metal, rubber, seam, join* souder; (*also* **~ together**) *pieces, parts* souder, assembler; (*fig*) *groups, parties* cimenter l'union de; *ideas* amalgamer, réunir. **to ~ sth on to sth** souder qch à qch; **the hull is ~ed throughout** la coque est complètement soudée; (*fig*) **he ~ed them (together) into a united party** il en a fait un parti cohérent. 3 **vi** souder.

welder ['weldəʳ] **n** (*person*) soudeur *m*; (*machine*) soudeuse *f*.

welding ['weldɪŋ] 1 **n** (*NonC*) (*Tech*) soudage *m*; (*fig*) *[parties]* union *f*; *[ideas]* amalgame *m*. 2 **comp** *process* de soudure, de soudage ►**welding torch** chalumeau *m*.

welfare ['welfɛəʳ] 1 **n a** (*gen*) bien *m*; (*comfort*) bien-être *m*; (*US*) aide *f* sociale. **the nation's ~, the ~ of all** le bien public; **the physical/spiritual ~ of the young** la santé physique/morale des jeunes; **I'm anxious about his ~** je suis inquiet pour son bien *or* bien-être; **to look after sb's ~** avoir la responsabilité de qn; *see* **child** *etc.*

b public/social ~ assistance publique/sociale; **to be on (the) ~*** toucher les prestations sociales, recevoir l'aide sociale; **to live on (the) ~*** vivre aux dépens de l'État.

2 **comp** *milk, meals* gratuit ►**welfare benefits** avantages *mpl* sociaux ►**welfare centre** centre *m* d'assistance sociale ►**welfare check** (*US*) chèque *m* d'allocations ►**welfare hotel** (*US*) *foyer où sont hébergés temporairement ceux qui bénéficient de l'aide sociale* ►**welfare mother** (*US*) mère seule qui bénéficie de l'aide sociale ►**welfare payments** prestations sociales ►**Welfare State: the establishment of the Welfare State in Great Britain** l'établissement de l'État-providence *m* en Grande-Bretagne; **thanks to the Welfare State, they ...** grâce à la Sécurité sociale et autres avantages sociaux, ils ...; **Britain is a welfare state** l'État-providence a été institué en Grande-Bretagne ►**welfare work** travail social ►**welfare worker** ≈ travailleur *m*, -euse *f* social(e).

welfarism ['welfɛərɪzəm] **n** (*US Pol*) théorie *f* de l'État-providence.

welfarist ['welfɛərɪst] **adj, n** (*US Pol*) partisan *m* de l'État-providence.

welfarite* ['welfɛəraɪt] **n** (*US pej*) personne *f* qui bénéficie de l'aide sociale.

well[1] [wel] 1 **n** (*for water, oil*) puits *m*; *[staircase, lift]* cage *f*; (*shaft between buildings*) puits, cheminée *f*; (*Brit Jur*) barreau *m*. (*fig*) **this book is a ~ of information** ce livre est une mine de renseignements; *see* **ink, oil** *etc.* 2 **comp** ►**welldigger** puisatier *m* ►**wellhead, wellspring** (*lit, fig*) source *f* ►**well water** eau *f* de puits. 3 **vi** (*also* **~ up**) *[tears, emotion]* monter. **tears ~ed (up) in her eyes** les larmes lui montèrent aux yeux; **anger ~ed (up) within him** la colère sourdit (*liter*) *or* monta en lui.

►**well out vi** *[spring]* sourdre; *[tears, blood]* couler (*from de*).

well[2] [wel] 1 **adv, compar better, superl best a** (*satisfactorily, skilfully etc*) *behave, sleep, eat, treat, remember* bien. **he sings as ~ as he plays** il chante aussi bien qu'il joue; **he sings as ~ as she does** il chante aussi bien qu'elle; **~ done!** bravo!; **~ played!** bien joué!; **everything is going ~** tout va bien; **the evening went off very ~** la soirée s'est très bien passée; **to do ~ in one's work** bien réussir dans son travail; **to do ~ at school** bien marcher à l'école; **he did very ~ for an 8-year-old** il s'est bien débrouillé pour un enfant de 8 ans; **he did quite ~, he came out of it quite ~** il ne s'en est pas mal sorti, il ne s'est pas mal débrouillé; **the patient is doing ~** le malade est en bonne voie; **he did ~ after the operation but ...** il s'est bien rétabli après l'opération mais ...; **you did ~ to come at once** vous avez bien fait de venir tout de suite; **you would do ~ to think about it** vous feriez bien d'y penser; **to do as ~ as one can** faire de son mieux; **he did himself ~** il ne s'est privé de rien, il s'est traité comme un prince; **to do ~ by sb** bien agir *or* être généreux envers qn; **you're ~ out of it!** c'est une chance que tu n'aies plus rien à voir avec cela (*or* lui *etc*); **how ~ I understand!** comme je vous (*or* le *etc*) comprends!; **I know the place ~** je connais bien l'endroit; **~ I know it!** je le sais bien!, je ne le sais que trop!; *see also* **5.**

b (*intensifying: very much; thoroughly*) bien. **it was ~ worth the trouble** cela valait bien le dérangement *or* la peine de se déranger; **he is ~ past** *or* **over fifty** il a largement dépassé la cinquantaine; **~ over 1,000 people** bien plus de 1.000 personnes; **it's ~ past 10 o'clock** il est bien plus de 10 heures; **it continued ~ into 1984** cela a continué pendant une bonne partie de 1984; **~ above ...** bien au-dessus de ...; **~ and truly** bel et bien; **he could ~ afford to pay for it** il avait largement les moyens de le payer; **lean ~ forward** penchez-vous bien en avant.

c (*with good reason; with equal reason*) **you may ~ be surprised to learn that** vous serez sans aucun doute surpris d'apprendre que; **one might ~ ask why** on pourrait à juste titre demander pourquoi; **you might ~ ask!** belle question!, c'est vous qui me le demandez!; **you could ~ refuse to help them** vous pourriez à juste titre refuser de les aider; **he couldn't very ~ refuse** il ne pouvait guère refuser; **we may as ~ begin now** autant (vaut) commencer maintenant, nous ferions aussi bien de commencer maintenant; **you might (just) as ~ say that ...** autant dire que ...; **you may as ~ tell me the truth** autant me dire la vérité, tu ferais aussi bien de me dire la vérité; **shall I go? — you may** *or* **might as ~** j'y vais? — tant qu'à faire, allez-y!*; **we might (just) as ~ have stayed at home** autant valait rester à la maison, nous aurions aussi bien fait de ne pas venir; **she apologized, as ~ she might** elle a présenté ses excuses, comme il se devait; **she apologized — ~ she might!** elle a présenté ses excuses — c'était la moindre des choses!; *see* **pretty.**

d (*in addition*) **as ~** (*also*) aussi; (*on top of all that*) par-dessus le marché; **I'll take those as ~** je prendrai ceux-là aussi; **and it rained as ~!** et par-dessus le marché il a plu!; **by night as ~ as by day** de jour comme de nuit, aussi bien de jour que de nuit; **as ~ as his dog he has 2 rabbits** en plus de son chien il a 2 lapins; **on bikes as ~ as in cars** à vélo aussi bien qu'en voiture, à vélo comme en voiture; **I had Paul with me as ~ as Lucy** j'avais Paul aussi en même temps que Lucy; **all sorts of people, rich as ~ as poor** toutes sortes de gens, tant riches que pauvres.

2 **excl** (*surprise*) tiens!, eh bien!; (*relief*) ah bon!, eh bien!; (*resignation*) enfin!; (*dismissively*) bof!* (*resuming after interruption*) **~, as I was saying ...** donc, comme je disais ..., je disais donc que ...; (*hesitation*) **~ ...** c'est que ...; **he has won the election! — ~, ~(, ~)!** il a été élu! — tiens, tiens(, tiens)!; **~?** eh bien?, et alors?; **~, who would have thought it?** tiens! *or* eh bien! qui l'aurait jamais cru?; **~ I never!*, ~, what do you know!*** pas possible!, ça par exemple!, bien ça alors!; **I intended to do it — ~, have you?** j'avais l'intention de le faire — et alors?; **~, what do you think of it?** eh bien! qu'en dites-vous?; **~, here we are at last!** eh bien! nous voilà enfin!; **~, there's nothing we can do about it** enfin, on n'y peut rien; **~, you may be right** qui sait, vous avez peut-être raison; **very ~ then** (bon) d'accord; **you know Paul? ~, he's getting married** vous connaissez Paul? eh bien il se marie; **are you coming? — ~ ... I've got a lot to do here** vous venez? — c'est que ... j'ai beaucoup à faire ici.

3 **adj, compar better, superl best a** bien; bon. (*Prov*) **all's ~ that ends well** tout est bien qui finit bien (*Prov*); (*Mil*) **all's ~!** tout va bien!; **all is not ~ with her** il y a quelque chose qui ne va pas, elle traverse une mauvaise passe; **it's all very ~ to say that** c'est bien beau *or* joli de dire cela; **that's all very ~ but ..., that's all ~ and good but ...** tout ça c'est bien joli *or* beau mais ...; **if you want to do it, ~ and good** si vous voulez le faire je ne vois pas d'inconvénient; **it would be ~ to start early** on ferait bien de partir tôt; **it is as ~ to remember** il y a tout lieu de se rappeler; **it's as ~ not to offend her** il vaudrait mieux ne pas la froisser; **it would be just as ~ for you to stay** vous feriez tout aussi bien de rester; **it's ~ for you that nobody saw you** heureusement pour vous qu'on ne vous a pas vu, vous avez de la chance *or* c'est heureux pour vous qu'on ne vous ait pas vu.

b (*healthy*) **how are you? — very ~, thank you** comment allez-vous? — très bien, merci; **I hope you're ~** j'espère que vous allez bien; **to feel ~** se sentir bien; **to get ~** se remettre; **get ~ soon!** remets-toi vite!; **people who are ~ do not realize ...** les gens qui se portent bien *or* qui sont en bonne santé ne se rendent pas compte ... .

4 **n: to think/speak ~ of** penser/dire du bien de; **I wish you ~!** je vous souhaite de réussir!, bonne chance!; **somebody who wishes you ~** quelqu'un qui vous veut du bien; **to leave ~ alone** laisser les choses telles qu'elles sont; (*Prov*) **let** *or* **leave ~ alone** le mieux est l'ennemi du bien (*Prov*).

5 **pref: well-** bien; **~-chosen/dressed** *etc* bien choisi/habillé *etc; see also* **6.**

6 **comp** ►**well-adjusted** *person* posé, équilibré ►**well-advised** *action, decision* sage, prudent; **you would be well advised to go** vous auriez (tout) intérêt à partir ►**well-aimed** *shot* bien visé; *remark* qui porte ►**well-appointed** *house, room* bien équipé ►**well-argued** *case, report* bien argumenté ►**well-attended** *meeting, lecture* qui attire beaucoup de monde, qui a du succès; *show, play* couru ►**well-balanced** (*lit*) bien équilibré; (*fig*) *person, diet* bien équilibré; *paragraph, sentence* bien agencé ►**well-behaved** *child* sage, qui se conduit bien; *animal* obéissant, discipliné ►**well-being** bien-être *m* ►**wellborn** bien né, de bonne famille ►**well-bred** (*of good family*) de bonne famille; (*courteous*) bien élevé; *animal* de bonne race ►**well-built** *building* bien construit, solide; *person* bien bâti, solide, costaud* ►**well-chosen** bien choisi; **in a few well-chosen words** en quelques mots bien choisis ►**well-cooked** *meat* bien cuit ►**well-defined** *colours, distinctions* bien défini; *photo, outline* net; *problem* bien défini,

précis ▸**well-deserved** bien mérité ▸**well-developed** (*Anat*) bien développé; *person* bien fait; *plan* bien développé; *argument, idea* bien exposé ▸**well-disposed** bien disposé (*towards* envers) ▸**well-documented** *case, work* bien documenté; **his life is well-documented** on a beaucoup de renseignements *or* documents sur sa vie ▸**well-dressed** bien habillé, bien vêtu ▸**well-earned** bien mérité ▸**well-educated** cultivé, instruit ▸**well-equipped** bien équipé; (*esp with tools*) *person* bien outillé; *factory* bien équipé, doté d'un équipement important; **to be well equipped to do** *[person]* avoir ce qu'il faut pour faire; *[factory]* être parfaitement équipé pour faire ▸**well-favoured**†† beau (*f* belle) ▸**well-fed** bien nourri ▸**well-fixed:** (*US*) **to be well-fixed*** (*well-to-do*) être nanti, vivre dans l'aisance; **we're well-fixed* for food** nous avons largement assez à manger ▸**well-formed** (*Ling*) bien formé, grammatical ▸**well-formedness** grammaticalité *f* ▸**well-founded** *suspicion* bien fondé, légitime ▸**well-groomed** *person* soigné; *hair* bien coiffé; *horse* bien pansé ▸**well-grounded** *suspicion* bien fondé, légitime; **he is well grounded in history** il a des bases solides en histoire ▸**well-heeled*** nanti, fort à l'aise ▸**well-informed** bien informé, bien renseigné (*about* sur); (*knowledgeable*) *person* instruit; (*Pol, Press*) **well-informed circles** milieux bien informés ▸**well-intentioned** bien intentionné ▸**well-judged** *remark, criticism* bien vu, judicieux; *shot, throw* bien visé, bien vu; *estimate* juste ▸**well-kept** *house, garden* bien entretenu, bien tenu; *hands, nails* soigné; *hair* bien entretenu; *secret* bien gardé ▸**well-knit** (*fig*) *person, body* bien bâti; *arguments, speech* bien enchaîné; *scheme* bien conçu ▸**well-known** (*famous*) bien connu, célèbre; **it's a well-known fact that** ... tout le monde sait que ... ▸**well-liked** apprécié ▸**well-loved** bien aimé ▸**well-made** bien fait ▸**well-managed** bien mené ▸**well-mannered** qui a de bonnes manières, bien élevé ▸**well-marked** (*fig*) marqué, prononcé, distinct ▸**well-meaning** *person* bien intentionné; *remark, action* fait avec les meilleures intentions ▸**well-meant** fait avec les meilleures intentions ▸**well-nigh** presque ▸**well-nourished** bien nourri ▸**well-off:** (*rich*) **to be well-off** vivre dans l'aisance, être riche *or* aisé *or* bien nanti; **the less well-off** ceux qui ont de petits moyens; (*fortunate*) **you don't know when you're well-off** tu ne connais pas ton bonheur; **she's well-off without him** c'est un bon débarras pour elle ▸**well-oiled** (*lit*) bien graissé; (*: *drunk*) pompette* ▸**well-padded*** rembourré ▸**well-paid** bien payé, bien rémunéré ▸**well-preserved** *building, person* bien conservé ▸**well-proportioned** bien proportionné ▸**well-read** cultivé ▸**well-respected** très respecté *or* considéré ▸**well-rounded** *style* harmonieux; *sentence* bien tourné ▸**well-spent** *time* bien employé, bien utilisé; *money* utilement dépensé (*see also* **money**) ▸**well-spoken** *person* qui parle bien, qui a une élocution soignée; *words* bien choisi, bien trouvé; **well-spoken-of** dont on dit du bien ▸**well-stocked** *shop, larder* bien approvisionné; *river, lake* bien empoissonné ▸**well-tempered:** (*Mus*) **the Well-tempered Klavier** le Clavecin bien tempéré ▸**well-thought-of** *person* (bien) considéré, dont on a bonne opinion; *thing* bien considéré, bien apprécié ▸**well-thought-out** bien conçu ▸**well-thumbed** qui a fait de l'usage ▸**well-timed** *remark, entrance* tout à fait opportun, tombé à point nommé; *blow* bien calculé ▸**well-to-do** aisé, riche; **to be well-to-do** vivre dans l'aisance, être riche *or* aisé *or* nanti ▸**well-tried** *method* éprouvé, qui a fait ses preuves ▸**well-trodden** *path* battu ▸**well-turned** *phrase* bien tourné ▸**well-wishers** npl amis *mpl*; (*unknown*) amis *or* admirateurs *mpl* inconnus; (*Pol: supporters*) sympathisants *mpl*; **he got many letters from well-wishers** il a reçu de nombreuses lettres d'encouragement ▸**well-woman clinic** ≃ centre *m* gynécologique et de dépistage ▸**well-worn** *path* battu; *carpet, clothes* usagé; (*fig*) *phrase, expression* banal, usagé, rebattu; ▸**well-written** bien écrit.

we'll [wiːl] = **we shall, we will**; *see* **shall, will**.

Wellington ['welɪŋtən] n (*in N.Z.*) Wellington.

wellington ['welɪŋtən] n (*Brit: also* ~ **boot**) botte *f* de caoutchouc.

Wellsian ['welzɪən] adj de (H.G.) Wells.

welly* ['welɪ] n, pl **wellies** (*Brit*) ~ **boots, wellies** bottes *f* de caoutchouc, caoutchoucs *mpl*.

Welsh [welʃ] 1 adj gallois. (*Brit*) ~ **dresser** vaisselier *m*; (*Pol*) ~ **Nationalism/Nationalist** nationalisme *m*/nationaliste *mf* gallois(e); (*Brit Pol*) the ~ **Office** le ministère des Affaires galloises. 2 n a (*pl*) **the** ~ les Gallois *mpl*. b (*Ling*) gallois *m*. 3 comp ▸**Welshman** Gallois *m* ▸**Welsh rabbit, Welsh rarebit** (*Culin*) toast *m* au fromage ▸**Welshwoman** Galloise *f*.

welsh* [welʃ] vi: **to** ~ **on sb** (*gen*) lever le pied* en emportant l'argent de qn; (*in gambling*) lever le pied* en emportant l'enjeu de qn.

welt [welt] n *[shoe]* trépointe *f*; (*weal*) marque *f* de coup, zébrure *f*.

welter ['weltəʳ] 1 n *[objects, words, ideas]* fatras *m*. (*fig*) **a** ~ **of conflicting interests** un tourbillon d'intérêts contradictoires; **in a** ~ **of blood** dans un bain de sang; **in a** ~ **of mud** dans un véritable bourbier. 2 vi (*in blood*) baigner (*in* dans); (*in mud*) se vautrer, se rouler (*in* dans).

welterweight ['weltəweɪt] (*Boxing*) 1 n poids *m* welter. 2 comp *champion, fight* poids welter *inv*.

wen [wen] n loupe *f*, kyste sébacé. (*fig*) **the Great W~** Londres.

wench [wentʃ] († *or hum*) 1 n jeune fille *f*, jeune femme *f*. 2 vi: **to go** ~**ing** courir le jupon.

wend [wend] vt: **to** ~ **one's way** aller son chemin, s'acheminer (*to, towards* vers); **to** ~ **one's way back from** s'en revenir de.

Wendy house ['wendɪ,haʊs] n (*Brit*) modèle *m* réduit de maison (*jouet d'enfant*).

went [went] pret of **go**.

wept [wept] pret, ptp of **weep**.

were [wɜːʳ] pret of **be**.

we're [wɪəʳ] = **we are**; *see* **be**.

weren't [wɜːnt] = **were not**; *see* **be**.

werewolf ['wɪəwʊlf] n, pl **werewolves** ['wɪəwʊlvz] loup-garou *m*.

wert†† [wɜːt] 2nd pers sg pret of **be**.

Wesleyan ['wezlɪən] 1 n disciple *m* de Wesley. 2 adj de Wesley, wesleyen. ~ **Methodists** méthodistes *mpl* wesleyens.

west [west] 1 n ouest *m*. **to the** ~ **of** à l'ouest de; **in the** ~ **of Scotland** dans l'ouest de l'Écosse; **house facing the** ~ maison exposée à l'ouest *or* au couchant; *[wind]* **to veer to the** ~, **to go into the** ~ tourner à l'ouest; **the wind is in the** ~ le vent est à l'ouest; **the wind is (coming** *or* **blowing) from the** ~ le vent vient *or* souffle de l'ouest; **to live in the** ~ habiter dans l'ouest; **the W~** (*Pol*) l'Occident *m*, l'Ouest *m*; (*US Geog*) l'Ouest; *see* **wild** *etc*.

2 adj ouest *inv*, de *or* à l'ouest. ~ **wind** vent *m* d'ouest; ~ **coast** côte ouest *or* occidentale; **on the** ~ **side** du côté ouest; **room with a** ~ **aspect** pièce exposée à l'ouest *or* au couchant; (*Archit*) ~ **transept/door** transept *m*/portail *m* ouest; **in** ~ **Devon** dans l'ouest du Devon; **in** ~ **Leeds** dans les quartiers ouest de Leeds; **in the** ~ **Atlantic** dans l'Atlantique ouest; *see also* **4**.

3 adv *go* à l'ouest, vers l'ouest, en direction de l'ouest; *be, lie* à *or* dans l'ouest. **the town lies** ~ **of the border** la ville est située à l'ouest de la frontière; **we drove** ~ **for 100 km** nous avons roulé pendant 100 km en direction de l'ouest; **go** ~ **till you get to Crewe** allez en direction de l'ouest jusqu'à Crewe; (*fig*) **to go** ~* *[thing]* être fichu* *or* perdu; *[person]* passer l'arme à gauche*; **further** ~ plus à l'ouest; **to sail due** ~ aller droit vers l'ouest; (*Naut*) avoir le cap à l'ouest; ~ **by south** ouest quart sud-ouest.

4 comp ▸**West Africa** Afrique occidentale ▸**West African** adj de l'Afrique occidentale, ouest-africain ◊ n habitant(e) *m(f)* de l'Afrique occidentale ▸**West Bank: the West Bank (of the Jordan)** la Cisjordanie ▸**West Berlin** Berlin-Ouest ▸**West Berliner** n habitant(e) *m(f)* de Berlin-Ouest ▸**westbound** *traffic, vehicles* (se déplaçant) en direction de l'ouest; *carriageway* ouest *inv* ▸**the West Country** (*Brit*) le sud-ouest de l'Angleterre ▸**the West End** (*gen*) les beaux quartiers *mpl* (*situés à l'ouest*); (*in London*) le West End, (*centre touristique et commercial de Londres*) ▸**Westender** (*gen*) habitant(e) *m(f)* des beaux quartiers (*situés à l'ouest*); (*in London*) habitant(e) *m(f)* du West End ▸**west-facing** exposé (*or* orienté) à l'ouest *or* au couchant ▸**West German** adj allemand de l'ouest ▸**West Germany** Allemagne *f* de l'Ouest ▸**West Indian** adj antillais ◊ n Antillais(e) *m(f)* ▸**West Indies** Antilles *fpl* ▸**west-north-west** n ouest-nord-ouest *m* ◊ adj (de l' *or* à l')ouest-nord-ouest *inv* ◊ adv vers l'ouest-nord-ouest ▸**West Point** (*US*) école *f* militaire, ≃ Saint-Cyr ▸**west-south-west** n ouest-sud-ouest ◊ adj (de l' *or* à l')ouest-sud-ouest *inv* ◊ adv vers l'ouest-sud-ouest ▸**West Virginia** Virginie-Occidentale *f*; **in West Virginia** en Virginie-Occidentale.

westerly ['westəlɪ] 1 adj *wind* de l'ouest; *situation* à l'ouest, au couchant. **in a** ~ **direction** en direction de l'ouest, vers l'ouest; ~ **longitude** longitude *f* ouest *inv*; ~ **aspect** exposition *f* à l'ouest *or* au couchant. 2 adv vers l'ouest.

western ['westən] 1 adj (de l')ouest *inv*. **in** ~ **France** dans la France de l'ouest; **the** ~ **coast** la côte ouest *or* occidentale; **house with a** ~ **outlook** maison exposée à l'ouest *or* au couchant; ~ **wall** mur exposé à l'ouest *or* au couchant; **W~ Europe** Europe occidentale; **the W~ Church** l'Église *f* d'Occident, l'Église latine; *see* **country**.

2 n (*film*) western *m*; (*novel*) roman-western *m*.

3 comp ▸**Western Australia** Australie-Occidentale *f* ▸**Western Isles** (*Brit*) Hébrides *fpl* ▸**westernmost** le plus à l'ouest, le plus occidental ▸**Western omelet** (*US Culin*) omelette *f* au jambon avec oignons et poivrons ▸**western roll** (*Sport*) saut *m* en rouleau ▸**western writer** écrivain *m* de (roman-)westerns.

westerner ['westənəʳ] n homme *m* *or* femme *f* de l'ouest, habitant(e) *m(f)* de l'ouest; (*Pol*) Occidental(e) *m(f)*.

westernization [,westənaɪ'zeɪʃən] n occidentalisation *f*.

westernize ['westənaɪz] vt occidentaliser. **to become** ~**d** s'occidentaliser.

Westminster ['west,mɪnstəʳ] n (*Brit Parl*) Westminster *m* (*le Parlement britannique*).

westward ['westwəd] 1 adj à l'ouest. 2 adv (*also* ~**s**) vers l'ouest.

wet [wet] 1 adj a *object, roof* (tout) mouillé; *grass* mouillé, (*damp*) humide; *clothes, nappy, baby* mouillé, (*stronger*) trempé. **the roads are very** ~ les routes sont très humides *or* mouillées; **the road is slippery when** ~ la chaussée est glissante par temps de pluie; **the ink is still** ~ l'encre n'est pas encore sèche; **the paint is** ~ la peinture est fraîche; (*notice*) "~ **paint**" "attention à *or* prendre garde à la peinture"; *[person]* **to be** ~ **to the skin** *or* ~ **through** être trempé jusqu'aux os; **my shirt is wringing** ~ ma chemise est complètement trempée *or* est à tordre; **to get** ~ se mouiller; **to get one's feet** ~ se mouiller les pieds;

don't get your shoes ~ ne mouille pas tes souliers; **cheeks ~ with tears** joues baignées de larmes; (*fig*) **he's still ~ behind the ears*** il manque d'expérience, il est encore bleu*; **it grows in ~ places** ça pousse dans les endroits humides; *see* **soaking**.

b (*of weather*) **it is ~** il pleut, le temps est pluvieux; **it's going to be ~** le temps est à la pluie, il va pleuvoir; **a ~ day** un jour de pluie, un jour pluvieux; **on ~ days** les jours de pluie; **it's a very ~ climate** c'est un climat très humide *or* pluvieux; **in ~ weather** quand le temps est pluvieux, par temps humide *or* pluvieux; **the ~ season** la saison des pluies, la saison pluviale *or* humide.

c (*Brit* ‡: *silly, spineless*) **he's really ~** c'est une vraie lavette*, il est vraiment nouille*.

d (*US: against prohibition*) *town, state* où la vente des boissons alcoolisées est autorisée.

e (*US fig: quite wrong*) **you're all ~!*** tu te fiches complètement dedans*, tu as tort.

2 comp ▸**wetback*** (*US*) ouvrier agricole mexicain (*entré illégalement aux États-Unis*) ▸**wet blanket** (*fig*) rabat-joie *m inv*, trouble-fête *mf inv* ▸**wet dock** (*Naut*) bassin *m* à flot ▸**wet dream** pollution *f or* éjaculation *f* nocturne ▸**wet fish** poisson *m* frais ▸**wetlands** (*esp US*) marécages *mpl* ▸**the wet look** (*Fashion*) le look brillant ▸**wet-nurse** n nourrice *f* ◊ vt servir de nourrice à, élever au sein ▸**wetsuit** combinaison *f or* ensemble *m* de plongée.

3 n a **the ~** (*rain*) la pluie; (*damp*) l'humidité *f*; **it got left out in the ~** c'est resté dehors sous la pluie (*or* à l'humidité); **come in out of the ~** ne restez pas sous la pluie, entrez.

b (‡ *pej: spineless person*) lavette* *f*, nouille* *f*.

c (*Brit Pol* *) modéré *m* (du parti Conservateur).

4 vt mouiller. **to ~ one's lips** se mouiller les lèvres; (*fig*) **to ~ one's whistle*†** boire un coup*, en siffler un*; **to ~ o.s.** *or* **one's pants** mouiller sa culotte; **to ~ the bed** mouiller le lit.

5 vi (*: *urinate*) faire pipi*.

wether [ˈweðəʳ] n bélier châtré, mouton *m*.

wetness [ˈwetnɪs] n humidité *f*. **the ~ of the weather** le temps pluvieux.

wetting [ˈwetɪŋ] n: **to get a ~** se faire arroser; **to give sth/sb a ~** arroser qch/qn.

WEU (abbr of **Western European Union**) UEO *f*.

we've [wiːv] = **we have**; *see* **have**.

whack [wæk] 1 n a (*blow*) grand coup; (*sound*) coup sec, claquement *m*. **to give sth/sb a ~** donner un grand coup à qch/qn; (*excl*) **~!** vlan!; (*US*) **out of ~‡** détraqué, déglingué*. b (*: *attempt*) **to have a ~ at doing** essayer de faire; **I'll have a ~ at it** je vais tenter le coup*. c (*Brit* *: *share*) part *f*. **you'll get your ~*** tu auras ta part; **to pay one's ~*** payer sa part; **to pay top** *or* **the full ~* for sth** payer qch plein pot*; **you'll get £15,000 a year, top ~*** tu auras 15 000 livres par an, grand maximum*. 2 vt *thing, person* donner un (*or* des) grand(s) coup(s) à; (*spank*) fesser; (‡: *defeat*) donner une raclée à, flanquer une déculottée* *or* une dérouillée‡ à.

whacked* [ˈwækt] adj (*Brit fig: exhausted*) crevé*, claqué*.

whacker‡ [ˈwækəʳ] n (*Brit*) (*fish etc*) poisson *m etc* énorme; (*lie*) mensonge *m* énorme.

whacking [ˈwækɪŋ] 1 n (*spanking*) fessée *f*; (*beating: lit, fig*) raclée* *f*. **to give sb/sth a ~** = **to whack sb/sth**; *see* **whack**. 2 adj (*: *esp Brit: also* **~ big***, **~ great***) énorme.

whacky‡ [ˈwækɪ] adj = **wacky**.

whale [weɪl] 1 n, pl **~s** *or* **~** baleine *f*. b (*fig*) **we had a ~ of a time*** on s'est drôlement* bien amusé; **a ~ of a difference*** une sacrée* différence; **a ~ of a lot of*** ... vachement* de ..., une sacrée* quantité de ... . 2 comp ▸**whaleboat** (*Naut*) baleinière *f* ▸**whalebone** fanon *m* de baleine; (*NonC: Dress*) baleine *f* ▸**whale calf** baleineau *m* ▸**whale oil** huile *f* de baleine ▸**whalewatching**: **to go whalewatching** aller regarder les baleines. 3 vi: **to go whaling** aller à la pêche à la baleine, aller pêcher la baleine.

whaler [ˈweɪləʳ] n (*man*) pêcheur *m* de baleine; (*ship*) baleinier *m*.

whaling [ˈweɪlɪŋ] 1 n (*NonC*) pêche *f* à la baleine. 2 comp *industry* baleinier ▸**whaling ship** baleinier *m* ▸**whaling station** port baleinier.

wham [wæm] excl vlan!

whammy [ˈwæmɪ] n (*US*) mauvais sort *m*, poisse* *f*.

whang [wæŋ] 1 n bruit retentissant. 2 vt donner un coup dur et sonore à. 3 vi faire un bruit retentissant.

wharf [wɔːf] n, pl **~s** *or* **wharves** quai *m* (*pour marchandises*).

wharfage [ˈwɔːfɪdʒ] n (*NonC*) droits *mpl* de quai.

wharves [wɔːvz] npl of **wharf**.

what [wɒt] 1 adj a (*interrog, also indirect speech: which*) quel. **~ play did you see?** quelle pièce avez-vous vue?; **~ news did he bring?** quelles nouvelles vous a-t-il données?; **~ books do you want?** quels livres voulez-vous?; **~ time is it?** quelle heure est-il?; **he told me ~ time it was** il m'a dit l'heure (qu'il était); **~ one* are you looking for?** lequel (*or* laquelle) cherchez-vous?; **she showed me ~ book it was** elle m'a montré quel livre c'était.

b (*exclamatory*) quel; que. **~ a man!** quel homme!; **~ a pity!** quel dommage!; **~ a nuisance!** que c'est ennuyeux!; **~ fools we are!** que nous sommes bêtes!; **~ a huge house!** quelle maison immense!; **~ a nice house you have!** que vous avez une jolie maison!, quelle jolie maison vous avez!; **~ a lot of people!** que de monde!; (*iro*) **~ an excuse!** quelle excuse!; *see also* **3**.

c (*as much or as many as*) tout ... que. **give me ~ books you have about it** donnez-moi tous les livres en votre possession qui s'y rapportent; **I gave him ~ money I had** je lui ai donné tout l'argent que j'avais; **~ little I said** le peu que j'ai dit; **~ little help I could give** l'aide que j'ai apportée si petite soit-elle.

2 pron a (*interrog*) (*subject*) qu'est-ce qui; (*object*) (qu'est-ce) que; (*after prep*) quoi. **~ did you do?** qu'est-ce que vous avez fait?, qu'avez-vous fait?; **~'s happened?, ~'s up?*** qu'est-ce qu'il y a?, qu'est-ce qui arrive? *or* se passe?; **~ does it matter?** qu'est-ce que ça fait?; **~'s that?** (*gen*) qu'est-ce que c'est que ça?; (*on not hearing*) comment?, qu'est-ce que tu as (*or* il a *etc*) dit?; **~'s that book?** quel est ce livre?, qu'est-ce que c'est que ce livre?; **~ is his address?** quelle est son adresse?; **~ is this called?** comment ça s'appelle?; **~'s the French for "pen"?** comment dit-on "pen" en français?; **~ can we do?** que pouvons-nous faire?; **~ the heck*** *or* **hell‡** *etc* **did he say?** qu'est-ce qu'il a bien pu raconter?; **oh ~ the hell!‡** oh après tout qu'est-ce que ça peut bien foutre!‡, oh je m'en fous!‡; **~ do 2 and 2 make?** que font 2 et 2?; **~'s the use of that?** à quoi ça sert?; **~ does he owe his success to?** à quoi doit-il son succès?; **~ is wealth without happiness?** qu'est-ce que la richesse sans le bonheur?; **~ were you talking about?** de quoi parliez-vous?; **~ will it cost?** combien est-ce que ça coûtera?, ça coûtera combien?; **you told him WHAT?** quoi! qu'est-ce que vous lui avez dit?; **it's WHAT?** c'est quoi?; (*esp Brit*) **it's getting late, ~?*†** il se fait tard, pas vrai?

b (*fixed interrog phrases*) **~ about a drink?** si on buvait quelque chose?; (*in bar etc*) si on prenait un verre?; **~ about Robert?** et Robert?; **~ about writing that letter?** et si vous écriviez cette lettre?; **~ about the money you owe me?** et l'argent que vous me devez?; **~ about it?, ~ of it?, so ~?*** et alors?; **you ~?** (*: *expressing surprise*) c'est pas vrai!*, ah bon!*; (‡: **~** *did you say?*) hein?*; **~ about** *or* **of the danger involved?** et les risques que l'on court?; **~ for?** pourquoi? (*see also* **4**); **~ did you do that for?** pourquoi avez-vous fait ça?; **are you coming/do you want it** *or* **~?** tu viens/tu le veux ou quoi?; **~ if we were to go and see him?** et si on allait le voir?; **... but ~ if we were to do it all the same?** ... que se passerait-il si on le faisait quand même?; **~ if it rains?** et s'il pleut?; (*liter*) **~ though there may be** *or* **there are dangers** et qu'importent les dangers!

c (*indirect use*) (*subject*) ce qui; (*object*) ce que. **I wonder ~ will happen** je me demande ce qui va arriver; **tell us ~ you're thinking about** dites-nous ce à quoi vous pensez; **he asked me ~ she'd told me** il m'a demandé ce qu'elle m'avait dit; **I don't know ~ that book is** je ne sais pas ce que c'est que ce livre *or* quel est ce livre; **he knows ~'s ~** il s'y connaît, il connaît son affaire; **he just doesn't know ~'s ~** il n'a aucune idée, il est complètement dépassé*; **I'll show them ~'s ~** je vais leur montrer de quoi il retourne *or* de quel bois je me chauffe*.

d (*rel use etc: that which*) (*subject*) ce qui; (*object*) ce que. **~ is done is done** ce qui est fait est fait; **~ I need is ...** ce dont j'ai besoin c'est ...; **~ can be changed is ...** ce que l'on peut changer c'est ...; **~ I like is coffee** ce que j'aime c'est le café; **I don't know who is doing ~** je ne sais pas qui fait quoi; **they raped, pillaged and God knows** *or* **I don't know ~** ils ont violé, pillé et Dieu sait *or* je ne sais plus quoi; **I know ~ ..., (I'll) tell you ~ ...** tu sais quoi ..., j'ai une idée ...; **he's not ~ he was 5 years ago** il n'est plus ce qu'il était il y a 5 ans; **Paris isn't ~ it was** Paris n'est plus ce qu'il était; **I've no clothes except ~ I'm wearing** je n'ai d'autres vêtements que ceux que je porte; **do ~ you will** faites ce que vous voudrez; **say ~ you like** vous pouvez dire ce que vous voudrez *or* voulez.

e (*fixed phrases*) **and ~ is more** et qui plus est; **and ~ is worse** et ce qui est pire; **and, ~ is less common, there was ...** et, ce qui est plus inhabituel *or* et, chose plus inhabituelle, il y avait ...; **... and ~ have you*, ... and ~ not*** ... et je ne sais quoi encore; **~ with the suitcase and the box he could hardly ...** avec la valise et la boîte en plus, il ne pouvait guère ...; **~ with the heatwave and the financial crisis** entre la vague de chaleur et la crise financière, étant donné la vague de chaleur et la crise financière; **~ with one thing and another** avec ceci et cela; (*after listing things*) avec tout ça; **never a day passes but ~ it rains*** il ne se passe pas de jour qu'il ne pleuve; **not but ~ that wouldn't be a good thing** non que cela soit une mauvaise chose.

3 excl: **~! no butter!** quoi! *or* comment! pas de beurre!; **he's getting married — ~!** il se marie — quoi!; **~-ho!*†** ohé bonjour!

4 comp ▸**what-d'ye-call-her***, **what's-her-name*** la fille Machin*; (*married woman*) Madame Machin* ▸**what-d'ye-call-him***, **what's-his-name*** Machin* *m*, Machin Chouette* *m* ▸**what-d'ye-call-it***, **what's-it***, **what's-its-name*** machin* *m*, truc* *m*, bidule‡ *m* ▸**what's-it: Mr What's-it*** Monsieur Machin (Chose)* ▸**whate'er** (*liter*), **whatsoe'er** (*liter*), **whatsoever** (*emphatic*) = **whatever** ▸**whatever** *see* **whatever** ▸**what-for***: **to give sb what-for** passer un savon à qn* ▸**whatnot** *see* **whatnot**.

whatever [wɒtˈevəʳ] 1 adj a (*gen*) **~ book you choose** quel que soit le livre que vous choisissiez (*subj*); **any box of ~ size** n'importe quelle boîte quelle qu'en soit la taille; **give me ~ money you've got** donne-moi (tout) ce que tu as comme argent; **he agreed to make ~ repairs might prove necessary** il a accepté de faire toutes réparations reconnues nécessaires (quelles qu'elles soient); **you'll have to change ~ plans you've made** il vous faudra changer les projets que vous avez faits (quels qu'ils soient).

b (*: *emphatic interrog*) ~ **books have you been reading?** qu'est-ce que vous êtes allé lire?, vous avez lu de drôles de livres!*; ~ **time is it?** quelle heure peut-il bien être?

2 **adv**: ~ **the weather** quel que soit le temps qu'il fasse; ~ **the news from the front, they** ... quelles que soient les nouvelles du front, ils ...; **I'll take anything ~ that you can spare** je prendrai tout ce dont vous n'avez pas besoin (quoi que ce soit); **I've no money ~** je n'ai pas un sou, je n'ai pas le moindre argent; **there's no doubt ~ about it** cela ne fait pas le moindre doute *or* aucun doute *or* pas l'ombre d'un doute; **nothing ~** rien du tout, absolument rien; **did you see any? — none ~!** tu en as vu? — non, absolument aucun!; **in no case ~ shall we agree to see** ... en aucun cas nous n'accepterons de voir ...; **has he any chance ~?** a-t-il la moindre chance?

3 **pron** a (*no matter what*) quoi que + *subj*. ~ **happens** quoi qu'il arrive; ~ **you (may) find** quoi que vous trouviez; ~ **it may be** quoi que ce soit; ~ **he may mean** quel que soit ce qu'il veut dire; ~ **it** *or* **that means** *or* **may mean** *or* **meant** quel que soit le sens du mot (*or* de la phrase *etc*); (*hum, iro*) maintenant, allez savoir ce que ça veut dire; **I'll pay ~ it costs** je paierai ce que ça coûtera; ~ **it costs, get it** achète-le quel qu'en soit le prix; ~ **he said before, he won't now do it** quoi qu'il ait dit auparavant, il ne le fera pas maintenant.

b (*anything that*) tout ce que. **do ~ you please** faites ce que vous voulez *or* voudrez; **we shall do ~ seems necessary** nous ferons le nécessaire; **Monday or Tuesday, ~ suits you best** lundi ou mardi, ce qui *or* le jour qui vous convient le mieux; ~ **you say, sir** comme monsieur voudra; (*iro*) **I tell you I'm ill! — ~ you say** je te dis que je suis malade! — bien sûr, puisque tu le dis (*iro*).

c (*: *emphatic interrog*) ~ **did you do?** qu'est-ce que vous êtes allé faire?; ~ **did you say that for?** pourquoi êtes-vous allé dire ça?

d (*other similar things*) **the books and the clothes and ~** les livres et les vêtements et ainsi de suite *or* et tout ce qui s'ensuit *or* et que sais-je encore.

whatnot* ['wɒtnɒt] **n** a (*furniture*) étagère *f*. b = **what-d'ye-call-it;** *see* **what 4.** c (*and other things*) **and ~** et ainsi de suite, et tout ce qui s'ensuit.

wheat [wi:t] 1 **n** (*NonC*) blé *m*, froment *m*. (*fig*) **to separate** *or* **divide the ~ from the chaff** séparer le bon grain de l'ivraie. 2 **comp** *flour* de blé, de froment; *field* de blé, à blé ►**wheat country: it's wheat country** c'est une terre à blé ►**wheatear** (*Orn*) traquet *m* (motteux) ►**wheatgerm** (*NonC*) germes *mpl* de blé ►**wheatmeal** farine brute (à 80%); **wheatmeal bread** ≃ pain *m* de campagne ►**wheat sheaf** gerbe *f* de blé.

wheaten ['wi:tn] **adj** de blé, de froment.

wheedle ['wi:dl] **vt** cajoler, câliner. **to ~ sth out of sb** obtenir *or* tirer qch de qn par des cajoleries *or* des câlineries; **to ~ sb into doing** cajoler *or* câliner qn pour qu'il fasse, amener qn à force de cajoleries *or* câlineries à faire.

wheedling ['wi:dlɪŋ] 1 **adj** câlin, enjôleur. 2 **n** cajolerie(s) *f(pl)*, câlinerie(s) *f(pl)*.

wheel [wi:l] 1 **n** a (*gen*) roue *f*; *[trolley, toy]* roulette *f*; (*Naut*) (roue de) gouvernail *m*; (*Aut: steering ~*) volant *m*; (*spinning ~*) rouet *m*; (*potter's ~*) tour *m* (de potier); (*in roulette etc*) roue; (*Hist: torture instrument*) roue. ~ **of fortune** roue de la fortune; **big ~** (*in fairground etc*) grande roue; (*: *important person*) huile* *f*; **at the ~** (*Naut*) au gouvernail; (*Aut: also* **behind the ~**) au volant; (*US*) **are you on ~s?*** vous êtes motorisé?*; (*fig*) **it was hell on ~s‡** c'était absolument infernal, c'était un vrai cauchemar; **to take the ~** (*Naut*) prendre le gouvernail; (*Aut: also* **to get behind the ~**) se mettre au volant; (*Hist*) **to break sb on the ~** rouer qn; (*fig*) **the ~s of government** les rouages *mpl* du gouvernement; (*fig*) **to oil** *or* **grease the ~s** huiler les rouages; (*fig*) **there are ~s within ~s** c'est plus compliqué que ça ne paraît, il y a toutes sortes de forces en jeu; (*fig*) **the ~ has come full circle** la boucle est bouclée; *see* **shoulder, spoke¹** *etc*.

b (‡: *car*) **(set of) ~s** bagnole* *f*.

c (*Mil etc*) **to make a right/left ~** effectuer une conversion à droite/à gauche.

2 **comp** ►**wheelbarrow** brouette *f* ►**wheelbase** (*Aut*) empattement *m* ►**wheel brace** (*Aut*) clef *f* en croix ►**wheelchair** fauteuil roulant; **wheelchair olympics†** jeux *mpl* olympiques pour handicapés; (*hum*) **when I'm in a wheelchair** ... quand je serai dans une petite voiture* ... ►**wheel clamp** sabot *m* (de Denver) ►**wheel horse*** (*US fig*) cheval *m* de labour (*fig*) ►**wheelhouse** (*Naut*) timonerie *f* ►**wheelspin** (*Aut*) patinage *m* ►**wheelwright** charron *m*.

3 **vt** *barrow, pushchair, bed* pousser, rouler; *cycle* pousser; *child* pousser (dans un landau *etc*). **to ~ a trolley into/out of a room** rouler *or* pousser un chariot dans/hors d'une pièce; **they ~ed the sick man over to the window** ils ont poussé le malade (dans son fauteuil roulant *or* sur son lit roulant) jusqu'à la fenêtre; (*fig: bring*) **he ~ed‡ out an enormous box** il a sorti une boîte énorme; ~ **him in!‡** amenez-le!

4 **vi** (*also ~* **round**) *[birds]* tournoyer; *[windmill sails etc]* tourner (en rond); *[person]* se retourner (brusquement), virevolter; (*Mil*) effectuer une conversion; *[procession]* tourner. (*Mil*) **right ~!** à droite!; (*fig*) **he is always ~ing and dealing*** il est toujours en train de manigancer quelque chose *or* de chercher des combines*.

wheeled [wi:ld] **adj** *object* à roues, muni de roues. **three-~** à trois roues.

wheeler ['wi:ləʳ] **n** (*pej*) **~-(and-)dealer*** affairiste *m*; (*pej*) **~-dealing*** = **wheeling and dealing.**

-wheeler ['wi:ləʳ] **n ending in comps: four-wheeler** voiture *f* à quatre roues; *see* **two** *etc*.

wheeling ['wi:lɪŋ] **n** (*pej*) **~ and dealing*** brassage *m* d'affaires louches, combines* *fpl*; **there has been a lot of ~ and dealing* over the choice of candidate** le choix du candidat a donné lieu à toutes sortes de combines* *or* manigances *fpl or* micmacs* *mpl*.

wheeze [wi:z] 1 **n** a respiration bruyante *or* sifflante. b (‡†: *Brit: scheme*) truc* *m*, combine* *f*. c (*US* *: *saying*) dicton *m*, adage *m*. 2 **vi** *[person]* respirer bruyamment *or* comme un asthmatique, avoir du mal à respirer; *[animal]* souffler, ahaner. 3 **vt** (*also ~* **out**) **"yes," he ~d** "oui," dit-il d'une voix rauque; **the old organ ~d out the tune** le vieil orgue a joué le morceau dans un bruit de soufflerie.

wheezy ['wi:zɪ] **adj** *person* poussif, asthmatique; *voice* d'asthmatique; *animal* poussif; *organ etc* asthmatique (*fig*).

whelk [welk] **n** bulot *m*, buccin *m*.

whelp [welp] 1 **n** (*animal*) petit(e) *m(f)*; (*pej: youth*) petit morveux. 2 **vi** (*of animals*) mettre bas.

when [wen] 1 **adv** quand. ~ **did it happen?** quand *or* à quelle époque *or* à quel moment cela s'est-il passé?, cela s'est passé quand?*; ~ **does the train leave?** quand *or* à quelle heure part le train?; ~ **is your birthday?** quand est votre anniversaire?, quelle est la date de votre anniversaire?; ~ **was the wheel invented?** de quand date l'invention de la roue?, quand la roue a-t-elle été inventée?; ~ **did Columbus cross the Atlantic?** quand *or* en quelle année Christophe Colomb a-t-il traversé l'Atlantique?; **I don't know ~ we'll see him again** je ne sais pas quand nous le reverrons; **~'s the wedding?** à quand le mariage?; ~ **does snow first fall?** vers quelle date la neige commence-t-elle à tomber?; ~ **can you use the definite article with this word?** quand peut-on employer l'article défini avec ce mot?; **do you know ~ he first met her?** savez-vous quand il a fait sa connaissance?; **do you know ~ is the best time to call on her?** savez-vous quel est le meilleur moment pour lui rendre visite?; **he didn't tell me ~ she would telephone** il ne m'a pas dit quand *or* quel jour (*or* à quelle heure) elle téléphonerait; **he told me ~ to meet him** *or* **~ I should meet him** il m'a dit quand (je devais) le rencontrer; **did he say ~ he'd be back?** a-t-il dit quand il serait de retour?; **let me know ~ you want your holidays** faites-moi savoir quand *or* à quelle date vous voulez vos congés; **till ~?** jusqu'à quand?; **he's got to go by ~?** il faut qu'il soit parti quand?; **since ~ has he got a car?** depuis quand a-t-il une voiture?; (*iro*) **since ~?*** depuis quand?*

2 **conj** a (*at the time that*) quand, lorsque. ~ **I heard his voice I smiled** quand *or* lorsque j'ai entendu sa voix j'ai souri; **he waved ~ he saw me** il a fait signe de la main quand *or* lorsqu'il m'a vu; ~ **I was a child there was no TV** quand *or* lorsque j'étais enfant il n'y avait pas de télé*; ~ **(he was) just a child he** ... alors qu'il n'était qu'un enfant il ..., tout enfant il ...; **he did it ~ (he was) a student at Oxford** il l'a fait quand *or* lorsqu'il était étudiant à Oxford; ~ **(it is) finished the bridge will measure** ... une fois terminé, le pont mesurera ...; **let me know ~ she comes** faites-moi savoir quand elle arrivera; ~ **speaking German I often make mistakes** quand je parle allemand je fais souvent des fautes; ~ **writing to her, remember to say** ... quand vous lui écrirez n'oubliez pas de dire ...; **go ~ you like** partez quand vous voulez *or* voudrez; **I'll still love you ~ you're old and grey** je t'aimerai encore quand tu seras vieille et que tu auras les cheveux gris; **he's only happy ~ drunk** il n'est heureux que lorsqu'il est ivre.

b (*on or at which*) **on the day ~ I met him** le jour où je l'ai rencontré; **at the time ~ I should have been at the station** au moment *or* à l'heure où j'aurais dû être à la gare; **it was in spring, ~ the trees are green** c'était au printemps, au moment *or* à l'époque où les arbres sont verts; (*every Saturday*) **on Saturday(s), ~** ... le samedi, quand ...; (*each Saturday that* ...) **on Saturday(s) ~** ... les samedis où ...; (*last Saturday*) **on Saturday, ~** ... samedi, quand ...; **he arrived at 8 o'clock, ~ traffic is at its peak** il est arrivé à 8 heures, heure à laquelle la circulation est la plus intense; **at the very moment ~ I was about to leave** juste au moment où j'allais partir; **one day ~ the sun was shining** un jour que *or* où le soleil brillait; **it was one of those days ~ everything is quiet** c'était un de ces jours où tout est calme; **this is a time ~ we must speak up for our principles** c'est dans un moment comme celui-ci qu'il faut défendre nos principes; **there are times ~ I wish I'd never met him** il y a des moments où je regrette de l'avoir jamais connu; **he left in June, since ~ we have not heard from him** il est parti en juin et nous sommes sans nouvelles depuis *or* et depuis lors nous sommes sans nouvelles; **it will be ready on Saturday, until ~ we must** ... ce sera prêt samedi et en attendant nous devons ...; (*pouring drinks etc*) **say ~!*** vous me direz ... .

c (*the time that*) **he told me about ~ you got lost in Paris** il m'a raconté le jour *or* la fois* où vous vous êtes perdu dans Paris; **she spoke of ~ they had visited London** elle a parlé de la semaine (*or* du jour) où ils avaient visité Londres; **now is ~ I need you most** c'est maintenant que j'ai le plus besoin de vous; **that's ~ the train leaves** c'est l'heure à laquelle le train part; **that's ~ Napoleon was born** c'est l'année (*or* le jour) où Napoléon est né; **that's ~ you ought to try to be patient** c'est le moment d'essayer de faire preuve de patience; **that was ~ the trouble started** c'est alors que les ennuis ont commencé.

d (*after*) quand, une fois que. **~ you read the book you'll know why** quand vous lirez le livre vous saurez pourquoi; **~ you've read the book you'll know why** quand vous aurez lu le livre vous saurez pourquoi; **~ they had left he telephoned me** après leur départ *or* après qu'ils furent partis il m'a téléphoné; **~ they had finished the coffee she offered them some brandy** après qu'ils eurent fini *or* quand ils eurent fini le café elle leur a offert du cognac; **~ you've been to Greece you ...** quand *or* une fois que vous êtes allé en Grèce vous ..., après être allé en Grèce vous ...; **~ he had seen her he slipped away** après l'avoir vue il s'est esquivé; **~ he had sat down he began to talk** une fois assis il commença de parler; **you may ask questions ~ he's finished** vous pouvez poser vos questions quand il aura fini *or* après qu'il aura fini.

e (*each time that, whenever*) quand, lorsque, chaque fois que. **~ it rains I wish I were in Italy** quand il pleut je regrette de ne pas être en Italie; **~ the moon is full** à la pleine lune; **I take aspirin ~ I have a headache** je prends un cachet d'aspirine quand j'ai mal à la tête; **my heart sinks ~ he says "it reminds me ..."** j'ai le cœur qui défaille chaque fois qu'il dit "ça me rappelle ...".

f (*whereas; although*) alors que. **he walked ~ he could have taken the bus** il est allé à pied alors qu'il aurait pu prendre le bus; **he walked ~ I would have taken the bus** il est allé à pied tandis que *or* alors que moi j'aurais pris le bus.

g (*considering that*) quand, alors que, étant donné que. **what are you doing indoors ~ you could be out in the sun?** que fais-tu dans la maison quand *or* alors que tu pourrais profiter du soleil dehors?; **how can you understand ~ you won't listen?** comment pouvez-vous comprendre quand *or* si vous n'écoutez pas?; **what's the good of trying ~ I know I can't do it?** à quoi sert d'essayer quand *or* étant donné que je sais que je ne peux pas le faire?; **fancy going to Blackpool ~ you could have gone to Mexico!** quelle idée d'aller à Blackpool quand vous auriez pu aller au Mexique!

h (*and then*) quand. **he had just sat down ~ the phone rang** il venait juste de s'asseoir quand le téléphone a sonné; **hardly had I got back ~ I had to leave again** je venais à peine de rentrer quand j'ai dû repartir; **I was about to leave ~ I remembered ...** j'étais sur le point de partir quand je me suis rappelé ... .

3 **n**: **I want to know the ~ and the how of all this** je veux savoir quand et comment tout ça est arrivé.

4 **comp ▸whene'er** (*liter*) = **whenever ▸whenever** *see* **whenever ▸whensoe'er** (*liter*), **whensoever** (*emphatic*) = **whenever**.

whence [wens] **adv, conj** (*liter*) d'où.

whenever [wen'evə^r] 1 **conj** a (*at whatever time*) quand. **come ~ you wish** venez quand vous voulez *or* voudrez; **you may leave ~ you're ready** vous pouvez partir quand vous serez prêt.

b (*every time that*) quand, chaque fois que, toutes les fois que. **come and see us ~ you can** venez nous voir quand vous le pouvez; **~ I see a black horse I think of Jenny** chaque fois que *or* toutes les fois que je vois un cheval noir je pense à Jenny; **~ it rains the roof leaks** chaque fois qu'il pleut le toit laisse entrer l'eau; **~ people ask him he says ...** quand on lui demande il dit ...; **~ you touch it it falls over** on n'a qu'à le toucher et il tombe.

2 **adv** (*) mais quand donc. **~ did you do that?** mais quand donc est-ce que vous avez fait ça?*; **last Monday, or ~** lundi dernier, ou je ne sais quand; **I can leave on Monday, or Tuesday, or ~** je peux partir lundi, ou mardi, ou un autre jour *or* ou n'importe quand.

where [wεə^r] 1 **adv** (*in or to what place*) où. **~ do you live?** où habitez-vous?; **~ are you going (to)?** où allez-vous?; **I wonder ~ he is** je me demande où il est; **~'s the theatre?** où est le théâtre?; **~ are you from?, ~ do you come from?** d'où venez-vous?, vous venez d'où?; **~ have you come from?** d'où est-ce que vous arrivez?, vous arrivez d'où?; **I don't know ~ I put it** je ne sais pas où je l'ai mis; **you saw him near ~?** vous l'avez vu près d'où?; **he was going towards ~?** il allait vers où?; **~ have you got to in the book?** où est-ce que vous en êtes de votre livre?; (*fig*) **~ do I come into it?** qu'est-ce que je viens faire dans tout ça?, quel est mon rôle dans tout ça?; **~'s the difference?** où voyez-vous une différence?; **~ should we be if ...?** où serions-nous si ...?

2 **conj** a (*gen*) (là) où. **stay ~ you are** restez (là) où vous êtes; **there is a garage ~ the 2 roads intersect** il y a un garage au croisement des 2 routes; **there is a school ~ our house once stood** il y a une école là où *or* à l'endroit où se dressait autrefois notre maison, à l'emplacement de notre maison il y a une école; **go ~ you like** allez où vous voulez *or* voudrez; **it is coldest ~ there are no trees for shelter** c'est là où il n'y a pas d'arbre pour abriter (du vent) qu'il fait le plus froid; **I'm at the stage ~ I could ...** j'en suis à un point tel que je pourrais ...; **the book is not ~ I left it** le livre n'est pas (là) où je l'avais laissé; **it's not ~ I expected to see it** je ne m'attendais pas à le voir là; **Lyons stands ~ the Saône meets the Rhône** Lyon se trouve au confluent de la Saône et du Rhône.

b (*in etc which*) où. **the house ~ he was born** la maison où il est né, sa maison natale; **in the place ~ there used to be a church** à l'endroit où il y avait une église; **he put it down there, ~ the box is now** il l'a mis là, à l'endroit où se trouve maintenant la boîte; **England is ~ you'll find this sort of thing most often** c'est en Angleterre que vous trouverez le plus fréquemment cela.

c (*the place that*) là que. **this is ~ the car was found** c'est là qu'on a retrouvé la voiture; **this is ~ we got to in the book** c'est là que nous en sommes du livre; **that's ~ you're wrong!** c'est là que vous vous trompez!, voilà votre erreur!; **so that's ~ my gloves have got to!** voilà où sont passés mes gants!; (*fig*) **that's ~** *or* **there's* ~ things started to go wrong** c'est là que les choses se sont gâtées; **this is ~** *or* **here's* ~ you've got to make your own decision** là il faut que tu décides (*subj*) tout seul; **that's ~ I meant** c'est là que je voulais dire; **he went up to ~ she was sitting** il s'est approché de l'endroit où elle était assise; **I walked past ~ he was standing** j'ai dépassé l'endroit où il se tenait; **from ~ I'm standing I can see ...** d'où *or* de là où je suis je peux voir ... .

d (*wherever etc*) là où. **you'll always find water ~ there are trees** vous trouverez toujours de l'eau là où il y a des arbres; **~ there is kindness, there you will find ...** là où il y a de la gentillesse, vous trouverez ... .

e (*whereas*) alors que. **he walked ~ he could have taken the bus** il est allé à pied alors qu'il aurait pu prendre le bus; **he walked ~ I would have taken the bus** il est allé à pied alors que *or* tandis que moi j'aurais pris le bus.

3 **n**: **I want to know the ~ and the why of it** je veux savoir où et pourquoi c'est arrivé.

4 **comp ▸whereabouts** *see* **whereabouts ▸whereas** (*while*) alors que, tandis que; (*in view of the fact that*) attendu que, considérant que; (*although*) bien que + *subj*, quoique + *subj* **▸whereat** (*liter*) sur quoi, après quoi, et sur ce, et là-dessus **▸whereby conj** (*frm*) par quoi, par lequel (*or* laquelle *etc*), au moyen duquel (*or* de laquelle *etc*) **▸wherefore†† conj** (*for that reason*) et donc, et pour cette raison (*see also* **why 4**) ◊ **adv** (*why*) pourquoi **▸wherein interrog adv** (††) en quoi, dans quoi ◊ **conj** (*frm*) où, en quoi, dans quoi, dans lequel (*or* laquelle *etc*) **▸whereof** (*frm, liter*) de quoi, dont, duquel (*or* de laquelle *etc*) **▸whereon conj** (*frm, liter*) sur quoi, sur lequel (*or* laquelle *etc*) **▸wheresoe'er** (*liter*), **wheresoever** (*emphatic*) = **wherever ▸whereto** (*frm*) et dans ce but, et en vue de ceci **▸whereupon** sur quoi, après quoi, et sur ce, et là-dessus **▸wherever** *see* **wherever ▸wherewith** (*frm, liter*) avec quoi, avec lequel (*or* laquelle *etc*) **▸wherewithal** moyens *mpl*, ressources *fpl* nécessaires; **he hasn't the wherewithal to buy it** il n'a pas les moyens de l'acheter, il n'a pas ce qu'il lui faut pour l'acheter.

whereabouts ['wεərəbaʊts] 1 **adv** où (donc). **~ did you put it?** où (donc) l'as-tu mis? 2 **n**: **to know sb's/sth's ~** savoir où est qn/qch; **his ~ are unknown** personne ne sait où il se trouve.

wherever [wεər'evə^r] 1 **conj** a (*no matter where*) où que + *subj*. **~ I am I'll always remember** où que je sois, je n'oublierai jamais; **~ you go I'll go too** où que tu ailles *or* partout où tu iras, j'irai; **I'll buy it ~ it comes from** je l'achèterai d'où que cela provienne *or* quelle qu'en soit la provenance; **~ it came from, it's here now!** peu importe d'où cela vient, c'est là maintenant!

b (*anywhere, in or to whatever place*) (là) où. **sit ~ you like** asseyez-vous (là) où vous voulez; **go ~ you please** allez où bon vous semblera; **we'll go ~ you wish** nous irons (là) où vous voudrez; **he comes from Barcombe, ~ that is** il vient d'un endroit qui s'appellerait Barcombe.

c (*everywhere*) partout où. **~ you see this sign, you can be sure that ...** partout où vous voyez ce signe, vous pouvez être sûr que ...; **~ there is water available** partout où il y a de l'eau.

2 **adv** (*) mais où donc. **~ did you get that hat?** mais où donc avez-vous déniché ce chapeau?*; **I bought it in London or Liverpool or ~** je l'ai acheté à Londres, Liverpool ou Dieu sait où.

whet [wet] 1 **vt** *tool* aiguiser, affûter; *desire, appetite, curiosity* aiguiser, stimuler. 2 **comp ▸whetstone** pierre *f* à aiguiser.

whether ['weðə^r] **conj** a si. **I don't know ~ it's true or not, I don't know ~ or not it's true** je ne sais pas si c'est vrai ou non; **you must tell him ~ you want him (or not)** il faut que tu lui dises si oui ou non tu as besoin de lui; **I don't know ~ to go or not** je ne sais pas si je dois y aller ou non; **it is doubtful ~** il est peu probable que + *subj*; **I doubt ~** je doute que + *subj*; **I'm not sure ~** je ne suis pas sûr si + *indic or* que + *subj*.

b que + *subj*. **~ it rains or (~ it) snows I'm going out** qu'il pleuve ou qu'il neige je sors; **~ you go or not, ~ or not you go** que tu y ailles ou non.

c soit. **~ today or tomorrow** soit aujourd'hui soit demain; **~ before or after** soit avant soit après; **~ with or without an umbrella** avec ou sans parapluie; **I shall help you ~ or no** de toute façon *or* quoi qu'il arrive (*subj*) je vous aiderai.

whew [hwju:] excl (*relief, exhaustion*) ouf!; (*surprise, admiration*) fichtre!*

whey [weɪ] n petit-lait *m*.

which [wɪtʃ] 1 adj a (*in questions etc*) quel. **~ card did he take?** quelle carte a-t-il prise?, laquelle des cartes a-t-il prise?; **I don't know ~ book he wants** je ne sais pas quel livre il veut; **~ one?** lequel (*or* laquelle)?; **~ one of you?** lequel (*or* laquelle) d'entre vous?; **~ Smith do you mean?** quel Smith voulez-vous dire?

b **in ~ case** auquel cas; ... **Paris, ~ city I know well** ... Paris, ville que je connais bien; **he spent a week here, during ~ time** ... il a passé une semaine ici au cours de laquelle ...; **he used "peradventure", ~ word** ... il a employé "peradventure", mot qui ... .

2 pron a (*in questions etc*) lequel *m*, laquelle *f*. **~ is the best of these maps?**, **~ of these maps is the best?** quelle est la meilleure de ces cartes?, laquelle de ces cartes est la meilleure?; **~ have you taken?** lequel (*or* laquelle) avez-vous pris(e)?; **~ of you two is taller?** lequel de vous deux est le plus grand?, qui est le plus grand de vous deux?; **~ are the ripest apples?** quelles sont les pommes les plus mûres?, quelles pommes sont les plus mûres?; **~ would you like?** lequel aimeriez-vous?; **~ of you are married?** lesquels d'entre vous sont mariés?; **~ of you owns the red car?** lequel d'entre vous est le propriétaire de la voiture rouge?

b (*the one or ones that*) (*subject*) celui (*or* celle *or* ceux *or* celles) qui; (*object*) celui *etc* que. **I don't mind ~ you give me** vous pouvez me donner celui que vous voudrez (ça m'est égal); **I don't mind ~** ça m'est égal; **show me ~ is the cheapest** montrez-moi celui qui est le moins cher; **I can't tell** *or* **I don't know ~ is ~** je ne peux pas les distinguer; **tell me ~ are the Frenchmen** dites-moi lesquels sont les Français; **I know ~ I'd rather have** je sais celui que je préférerais; **ask him ~ of the books he'd like** demandez-lui parmi tous les livres lequel il voudrait.

c (*that*) (*subject*) qui; (*object*) que; (*after prep*) lequel (*or* laquelle *or* lesquels *or* lesquelles). **the book ~ is on the table** le livre qui est sur la table; **the apple ~ you ate** la pomme que vous avez mangée; **the house towards ~ she was going** la maison vers laquelle elle se dirigeait; **the film of ~ he was speaking** le film dont il parlait; **opposite ~** en face duquel (*or* de laquelle *etc*); **the book ~ I told you about** le livre dont je vous ai parlé; **the box ~ you put it in** la boîte dans laquelle vous l'avez mis.

d (*and that*) (*subject*) ce qui; (*object*) ce que; (*after prep*) quoi. **he said he knew her, ~ is true** il a dit qu'il la connaissait, ce qui est vrai; **she said she was 40, ~ I don't believe** elle a dit qu'elle avait 40 ans, ce que *or* chose que je ne crois pas *or* mais je n'en crois rien; **you're late, ~ reminds me** ... vous êtes en retard, ce qui me fait penser ...; ... **upon ~ she left the room** ... sur quoi *or* et sur ce elle a quitté la pièce; ... **of ~ more later** ... ce dont je reparlerai plus tard, ... mais je reviendrai là-dessus plus tard; **from ~ we deduce that** d'où *or* et de là nous déduisons que; **after ~ we went to bed** après quoi nous sommes allés nous coucher.

whichever [wɪtʃ'evəʳ] 1 adj a (*that one which*) **~ method is most successful should be chosen** on devrait choisir la méthode garantissant les meilleurs résultats, peu importe laquelle; **take ~ book you like best** prenez le livre que vous préférez(, peu importe lequel); **I'll have ~ apple you don't want** je prendrai la pomme que *or* dont vous ne voulez pas; **keep ~ one you prefer** gardez celui que vous préférez; **go by ~ route is the most direct** prenez la route la plus directe, peu importe laquelle; **do it in ~ way you can** faites-le comme vous pourrez.

b (*no matter which*) (*subject*) quel que soit ... qui + *subj*; (*object*) quel que soit ... que + *subj*. **~ dress you wear** quelle que soit la robe que tu portes; **~ book is left** quel que soit le livre qui reste; **~ book is chosen** quel que soit le livre choisi; (*fig*) **~ way you look at it** de quelque manière que vous le considériez (*subj*).

2 pron a (*the one which*) (*subject*) celui *m* qui, celle *f* qui; (*object*) celui que, celle que. **~ is best for him** celui (*or* celle) qui lui convient le mieux; **~ you choose will be sent to you at once** celui (*or* celle) que vous choisirez vous sera expédié(e) immédiatement; **~ of the books is selected** le livre qui sera sélectionné quel qu'il soit; **choose ~ is easiest** choisissez (celui qui est) le plus facile; **on Thursday or Friday, ~ is more convenient** jeudi ou vendredi, le jour qui vous conviendra le mieux; **A or B, ~ is the greater** A ou B, à savoir le plus grand des deux; **at sunset or 7pm, ~ is the earlier** au coucher du soleil ou à 19 heures au plus tard, selon la saison.

b (*no matter which one*) (*subject*) quel *m* que soit celui qui + *subj*, quelle *f* que soit celle qui + *subj*; (*object*) quel que soit celui que + *subj*, quelle que soit celle que + *subj*. **~ of the two books he chooses, it won't make a lot of difference** quel que soit le livre qu'il choisisse, cela ne fera pas beaucoup de différence; **~ of the methods is chosen, it can't affect you much** quelle que soit la méthode choisie, ça ne vous affectera pas beaucoup.

whiff [wɪf] 1 n a (*puff*) *[smoke, hot air etc]* bouffée *f*; (*smell*) odeur *f*. **a ~ of chloroform** une bouffée *or* petite dose de chloroforme; **a ~ of garlic/seaweed** *etc* une bouffée d'ail/de varech *etc*; **after a few ~s he put out the cigarette** après quelques bouffées il a éteint la cigarette; **one ~ of this is enough to kill you** il suffit de respirer ça une fois pour mourir; **I caught a ~ of gas** j'ai senti l'odeur du gaz; **take a ~ of this!*** renifle ça! b (**: bad smell*) **what a ~!*** ce que ça sent mauvais! 2 vi (*) sentir mauvais.

whiffet ['wɪfɪt] n (*US pej*) morveux⁑ *m*, -euse⁑ *f*.

whiffy* ['wɪfɪ] adj qui sent mauvais.

Whig [wɪg] adj, n (*Pol Hist*) whig (*m*).

while [waɪl] 1 conj a (*during the time that*) pendant que. **it happened ~ I was out of the room** c'est arrivé pendant que *or* alors que j'étais hors de la pièce; **can you wait ~ I telephone?** pouvez-vous attendre pendant que je téléphone?; **she fell asleep ~ reading** elle s'est endormie en lisant; **~ you're away I'll write some letters** pendant ton absence *or* pendant que tu seras absent j'écrirai quelques lettres; **don't drink ~ on duty** ne buvez pas pendant le service; **"heels repaired ~ you wait"** "talon minute"; **~ you're up you could close the door** pendant que *or* puisque tu es debout tu pourrais fermer la porte; **and ~ you're about it** et pendant que vous y êtes.

b (*as long as*) tant que. **~ there's life there's hope** tant qu'il y a de la vie il y a de l'espoir; **it won't happen ~ I'm here** cela n'arrivera pas tant que je serai là; **~ I live I shall make sure that** ... tant que *or* aussi longtemps que je vivrai je ferai en sorte que ... .

c (*although*) quoique + *subj*, bien que + *subj*. **~ I admit he is sometimes right** ... tout en admettant *or* quoique j'admette qu'il ait quelquefois raison ...; **~ there are a few people who like that sort of thing** ... bien qu'il y ait un petit nombre de gens qui aiment ce genre de chose ... .

d (*whereas*) alors que, tandis que. **she sings quite well, ~ her sister can't sing a note** elle ne chante pas mal alors que *or* tandis que sa sœur ne sait pas chanter du tout.

2 comp ▸**while-you-wait heel repairs** ≃ talon minute.

3 n a **a ~** quelque temps; **a short ~, a little ~** un moment, un instant; **a long ~, a good ~** (assez) longtemps; **after a ~** quelque temps après, au bout de quelque temps; **let's stop for a ~** arrêtons un moment *or* (*longer*) quelque temps; **for a ~ I thought** ... j'ai pensé un moment ..., (*longer*) pendant quelque temps j'ai pensé ...; **it takes quite a ~ to ripen** cela met assez longtemps à mûrir; **once in a ~** (une fois) de temps en temps; **(in) between ~s** entre-temps; *see* **worth**.

b **he looked at me (all) the ~** *or* **the whole ~** il m'a regardé pendant tout ce temps-là.

▸**while away** vt sep (faire) passer.

whiles [waɪlz] adv (*dial, esp Scot*) quelquefois, de temps en temps.

whilst [waɪlst] conj = **while 1**.

whim [wɪm] n caprice *m*, fantaisie *f*, lubie *f*. **to be full of ~s** être capricieux *or* fantasque; **it's just a (passing) ~** c'est une lubie qui lui (*or* te *etc*) passera; **he gives in to her every ~** il lui passe tous ses caprices, il fait ses quatre volontés*; **as the ~ takes him** comme l'idée lui prend.

whimper ['wɪmpəʳ] 1 n (faible) gémissement *m*, (faible) geignement *m*, plainte inarticulée. ... **he said with a ~** ... dit-il d'un ton larmoyant, ... gémit-il, ... pleurnicha-t-il (*pej*); (*fig*) **without a ~** sans se plaindre. 2 vi *[person, baby]* gémir *or* geindre faiblement, pleurnicher (*pej*); *[dog]* gémir, pousser de petits cris plaintifs. 3 vt: **"no," he ~ed** "non," gémit-il *or* pleurnicha-t-il (*pej*), "non," dit-il d'un ton larmoyant.

whimpering ['wɪmpərɪŋ] 1 n geignements *mpl*, gémissements *mpl*. 2 adj *tone, voice* larmoyant, pleurnicheur (*pej*); *person, animal* qui gémit faiblement.

whimsical ['wɪmzɪkəl] adj *person* fantasque; *smile, look* étrange, curieux; *idea* saugrenu; *story, book* étrange, fantaisiste.

whimsicality [,wɪmzɪ'kælɪtɪ] n a (*NonC*) caractère fantasque *or* fantaisiste *or* curieux. b **whimsicalities** idées (*or* actions *etc*) bizarres *or* saugrenues.

whimsically ['wɪmzɪkəlɪ] adv *say, suggest* de façon saugrenue; *smile, look* étrangement, curieusement; *muse, ponder* malicieusement.

whimsy ['wɪmzɪ] n (*whim*) caprice *m*, fantaisie *f*, lubie *f*; (*NonC: whimsicality*) caractère *m* fantaisiste.

whimwhams* ['wɪm,wæmz] npl (*US*) trouille⁑ *f*, frousse* *f*.

whin [wɪn] n (*Bot*) ajonc *m*.

whine [waɪn] 1 n *[person, child, dog]* gémissement prolongé; (*fig: complaint*) plainte *f*; *[bullet, shell, siren, machine]* plainte stridente *or* monocorde. ... **he said in a ~** ... se lamenta-t-il, ... dit-il d'une voix geignarde; (*fig*) **it's another of his ~s about taxes** le voilà qui se répand encore en lamentations sur ses impôts; (*fig*) **I'm tired of all his ~s** j'en ai assez de ses jérémiades *fpl*.

2 vi *[person, dog]* geindre, gémir; (*fig: complain*) se lamenter; *[siren]* gémir. (*fig*) **to ~ about sth** se lamenter sur qch; **don't come whining to me about it** ne venez pas vous plaindre à moi, ne venez pas me faire vos doléances.

3 vt: **"it's happened again," he ~d** "ça a recommencé," se lamenta-t-il *or* dit-il d'une voix geignarde.

whinge* ['wɪndʒ] (*Brit*) 1 vi se lamenter (*about* sur), geindre*. **stop ~ing** arrête de geindre *or* de te plaindre. 2 n: **he was having a real ~** il n'arrêtait pas de grogner.

whingeing* ['wɪndʒɪŋ] (*Brit*) 1 adj geignard, plaintif (*f* -ive). 2 n gémissements *mpl*, plaintes *fpl*.

whining ['waɪnɪŋ] 1 n *[person, child]* gémissements continus, pleurnicheries *fpl*, jérémiades *fpl*; *[dog]* gémissements; (*fig: complaining*) plaintes continuelles, jérémiades, lamentations *fpl*. 2 adj *voice* geignard, pleurard; *child* geignard, pleurnicheur; *dog* qui gémit.

whinny ['wɪnɪ] 1 n hennissement *m*. 2 vi hennir.

whip [wɪp] 1 n a fouet *m*; (*riding* ~) cravache *f*.
b (*Parl*) (*person*) whip *m*, chef *m* de file (*député chargé par son parti d'assurer la discipline à l'intérieur du groupe parlementaire*); (*Brit: summons*) convocation *f*. **three-line** ~ convocation impérative (*pour voter*).
c (*Culin: dessert*) crème *f or* mousse *f* instantanée.
2 comp ▸**whipcord** (*Tex*) whipcord *m* ▸**whip hand**: (*fig*) **to have the whip hand** être le maître, avoir le dessus; **to have the whip hand over sb** avoir la haute main sur qn ▸**whiplash** (*blow from whip*) coup *m* de fouet; (*fig: in car accident*) coup *m* du lapin*, syndrome cervical traumatique; **whiplash injury to the neck** lésion *f* traumatique des vertèbres cervicales; (*fig*) **he felt the whiplash of fear** il fut saisi d'une peur cinglante ▸**whip-round*** (*Brit*) collecte *f*; **to have a whip-round* for sb/sth** faire une collecte pour qn/qch.
3 vt a *person, animal, child* fouetter; (*Culin*) *cream* fouetter, battre au fouet; *egg white* battre en neige; (*fig*) (*defeat*) battre à plate(s) couture(s); (*criticize severely*) critiquer vivement, cingler, éreinter. **the rain ~ped her face** la pluie lui cinglait *or* fouettait la figure; **to ~ sb into a frenzy** mettre qn hors de ses gonds.
b (*fig *: defeat*) battre à plates coutures.
c (*seize etc*) **to ~ sth out of sb's hands** enlever brusquement *or* vivement qch des mains de qn; **he ~ped a gun out of his pocket** il a brusquement sorti un revolver de sa poche; **he ~ped the letter off the table** il a prestement fait disparaître la lettre qui était (restée) sur la table.
d (*Brit *: steal*) faucher*, piquer‡. **somebody's ~ped my watch!** quelqu'un m'a fauché* *or* piqué‡ ma montre!
e *cable, rope* surlier; (*Sewing*) surfiler.
4 vi: **to ~ along/away** *etc* filer/partir *etc* à toute allure *or* comme un éclair; **the car ~ped round the corner** la voiture a pris le tournant à toute allure; **the wind ~ped through the trees** le vent s'élançait à travers les arbres; **the rope broke and ~ped across his face** la corde a cassé et lui a cinglé le visage.

▸**whip away** 1 vi *see* **whip 4**. 2 vt sep (*remove quickly*) *[person]* enlever brusquement *or* vivement, faire disparaître; *[wind etc]* emporter brusquement.

▸**whip back** vi *[broken rope, cable etc]* revenir brusquement en arrière.

▸**whip in** 1 vi a *[person]* entrer précipitamment *or* comme un éclair. b (*Hunting*) être piqueur. 2 vt sep a (*Hunting*) *hounds* ramener, rassembler; (*Parl*) *members voting* battre le rappel de; (*fig*) *voters, supporters* rallier. b (*Culin*) **whip in the cream** incorporez la crème avec un fouet.

▸**whip off** vt sep *garment etc* ôter *or* enlever en quatrième vitesse*; *lid, cover* ôter brusquement.

▸**whip on** vt sep a *garment etc* enfiler en quatrième vitesse. b (*urge on*) *horse* cravacher.

▸**whip out** 1 vi *[person]* sortir précipitamment. 2 vt sep *knife, gun, purse* sortir brusquement *or* vivement (*from* de).

▸**whip over*** vi = **whip round 1b**.

▸**whip round** 1 vi a (*turn quickly*) *[person]* se retourner vivement; *[object]* pivoter brusquement. b (*) **he's just whipped round to the grocer's** il est juste allé faire un saut à l'épicerie; **whip round to your aunt's and tell her** ... va faire un saut *or* cours chez ta tante lui dire ... .
2 **whip-round*** n *see* **whip 2**.

▸**whip through** vt fus *book* parcourir rapidement; *homework, task* expédier, faire en quatrième vitesse.

▸**whip up** vt sep a *emotions, enthusiasm, indignation* donner un coup de fouet à, fouetter, attiser; *support, interest* donner un coup de fouet à, stimuler. b *cream, egg whites* fouetter, battre au fouet. (*fig*) **to whip up a meal*** préparer un repas en vitesse; **can you whip us up something to eat?*** est-ce que vous pourriez nous faire à manger* *or* nous préparer un morceau en vitesse? c (*snatch up*) saisir brusquement.

whipper ['wɪpəʳ] comp ▸**whipper-in** (pl ~s-~) piqueur *m* ▸**whippersnapper** (†, *hum*) freluquet *m*.

whippet ['wɪpɪt] n whippet *m*.

whipping ['wɪpɪŋ] 1 n (*as punishment*) correction *f*. **to give sb a ~** fouetter qn, donner le fouet à qn, donner des coups de fouet à qn. 2 comp ▸**whipping boy** (*fig*) bouc *m* émissaire ▸**whipping cream** (*Culin*) crème fraîche (*à fouetter*) ▸**whipping post** poteau *m* (*où étaient attachées les personnes qu'on fouettait*) ▸**whipping top** toupie *f*.

whippoorwill ['wɪp,pʊə,wɪl] n engoulevent *m* d'Amérique du Nord.

whir [wɜːʳ] = **whirr**.

whirl [wɜːl] 1 n *[leaves, papers, smoke]* tourbillon *m*, tournoiement *m*; *[sand, dust, water]* tourbillon. (*fig*) **a ~ of parties and dances** un tourbillon de surprises-parties et de bals; **the whole week was a ~ of activity** nous n'avons (*or* ils n'ont *etc*) pas arrêté de toute la semaine; **the social ~** la vie mondaine; **her thoughts/emotions were in a ~** tout tourbillonnait dans sa tête/son cœur; **my head is in a ~** la tête me tourne; (*fig*) **to give sth a ~*** essayer qch.
2 comp ▸**whirlpool** tourbillon *m*; (*US*) **whirlpool bath** bain *m* à remous ▸**whirlwind** n tornade *f*, trombe *f* (*see also* **sow²**) ◊ adj (*fig*) éclair* *inv*.
3 vi a (*spin: also ~* **round**) *[leaves, papers, smoke, dancers]* tourbillonner, tournoyer; *[sand, dust, water]* tourbillonner; *[wheel, merry-go-round, spinning top]* tourner. **they ~ed past us in the dance** ils sont passés près de nous en tourbillonnant pendant la danse; **the leaves ~ed down** les feuilles tombaient en tourbillonnant; **my head is ~ing (round)** la tête me tourne; **her thoughts/emotions were ~ing** tout tourbillonnait dans sa tête/son cœur, ses pensées/ses émotions étaient en désarroi.
b (*move rapidly*) **to ~ along** aller à toute vitesse *or* à toute allure; **to ~ away** *or* **off** partir à toute vitesse *or* à toute allure.
4 vt *[wind] leaves, smoke* faire tourbillonner, faire tournoyer; *dust, sand* faire tourbillonner. **he ~ed his sword round his head** il a fait tournoyer son épée au-dessus de sa tête; **they ~ed us round the Louvre** ils nous ont fait visiter le Louvre à toute vitesse; **the train ~ed us up to London** le train nous a emportés à Londres (à toute allure).

▸**whirl round** 1 vi (*turn suddenly*) *[person]* se retourner brusquement, virevolter; *[revolving chair etc]* pivoter; *see also* **whirl 3a**. 2 vt sep a *[wind] leaves, smoke* faire tourbillonner, faire tournoyer; *dust, sand* faire tourbillonner. b *sword, object on rope etc* faire tournoyer; *revolving chair etc* faire pivoter.

whirligig ['wɜːlɪgɪg] n (*toy*) moulin *m* à vent; (*merry-go-round*) manège *m*; (*beetle*) tourniquet *m*, gyrin *m*; (*fig: of events etc*) tourbillon *m*. **the smoke moved in a ~ towards** ... la fumée allait en tourbillonnant *or* en tournoyant dans la direction de ... .

whirlybird* ['wɜːlɪbɜːd] n (*US*) hélico* *m*, hélicoptère *m*, banane* *f*.

whirr [wɜːʳ] 1 vi *[bird's wings, insect's wings]* bruire; *[cameras, machinery]* ronronner, (*louder*) vrombir; *[propellers]* vrombir. **the helicopter went ~ing off** l'hélicoptère est parti en vrombissant. 2 n *[bird's wings, insect's wings]* bruissement *m* (d'ailes); *[machinery]* ronronnement *m*, (*louder*) vrombissement *m*; *[propellers]* vrombissement.

whisk [wɪsk] 1 n a (*egg ~*) fouet *m* (à œufs), (*rotary*) batteur *m* à œufs. **give the mixture a good ~** bien battre le mélange.
b (*for sweeping*) époussette *f*; (*fly~*) émouchoir *m*, chasse-mouches *m inv*.
c **with a ~ of his tail, the horse** ... d'un coup de queue, le cheval ... .
2 vt a (*Brit Culin*) (*gen*) battre au fouet; *egg whites* battre en neige. **~ the eggs into the mixture** incorporez les œufs dans le mélange avec un fouet *or* en remuant vigoureusement.
b **the horse ~ed its tail** le cheval fouettait l'air de sa queue.
c **to ~ sth out of sb's hands** enlever brusquement *or* vivement qch des mains de qn; **she ~ed the letter off the table** elle a prestement fait disparaître la lettre de la table; **he ~ed it out of his pocket** il l'a brusquement sorti de sa poche; **he ~ed the vacuum cleaner round the flat** il a passé l'aspirateur dans l'appartement en deux temps trois mouvements*; **the lift ~ed us up to the top floor** l'ascenseur nous a emportés jusqu'au dernier étage à toute allure; **he was ~ed into a meeting** on l'a brusquement entraîné dans une réunion; **he ~ed her off to meet his mother** il l'a emmenée illico* faire la connaissance de sa mère.
3 vi: **to ~ along/in/out** *etc* filer/entrer/sortir *etc* à toute allure; **she ~ed out of the room** elle a quitté brusquement la pièce.

▸**whisk away** vt sep *flies* chasser d'un coup d'émouchoir; *dust, crumbs* enlever d'un coup d'époussette; (*fig*) *cloth, dishes* faire disparaître.

▸**whisk off** vt sep *flies* chasser d'un coup d'émouchoir; *dust* enlever d'un coup d'époussette; *lid, cover* ôter brusquement; *garment* enlever *or* ôter en quatrième vitesse; *see also* **whisk 2c**.

▸**whisk together** vt sep (*Culin*) mélanger en fouettant *or* avec un fouet.

▸**whisk up** vt sep (*Culin*) fouetter; *see also* **whisk 2c**.

whisker ['wɪskəʳ] n *[animal, man]* poil *m*. **~s** (*side ~s*) favoris *mpl*; (*beard*) barbe *f*; (*moustache*) moustache(s) *f(pl)*; *[animal]* moustaches; **he won the race by a ~** il s'en est fallu d'un cheveu *or* d'un poil* qu'il ne perde la course; (*fig*) **they came within a ~* of being** ... il s'en est fallu d'un cheveu qu'ils ne soient ... .

whiskered ['wɪskəd] adj (*see* **whisker**) *man* qui a des favoris (*or* une barbe *or* des moustaches).

whiskey (*Ir, US*), **whisky** (*Brit, Can*) ['wɪskɪ] 1 n (*gen*) whisky *m*; (*Brit esp*) scotch *m*; (*US esp*) bourbon *m*. **a ~ and soda** un whisky soda; *see* **sour**. 2 comp *flavour* de whisky.

whisper ['wɪspəʳ] 1 vi *[person]* chuchoter, parler à voix basse; *[leaves, water]* chuchoter, murmurer. **to ~ to sb** parler *or* chuchoter à l'oreille de qn, parler à voix basse à qn; **it's rude to ~** c'est mal élevé de chuchoter à l'oreille de quelqu'un; **you'll have to ~** il faudra que vous parliez (*subj*) bas.
2 vt chuchoter, dire à voix basse (*sth to sb* qch à qn, *that* que). **he ~ed a word in my ear** il m'a dit *or* soufflé quelque chose à l'oreille; **to ~ sweet nothings to sb** susurrer des mots doux à (l'oreille de) qn; (*fig*) **I've heard it ~ed that he's gone away** j'ai entendu dire qu'il est parti; (*fig*) **it is being ~ed that** ... le bruit court que ..., on dit que ... .
3 n (*low tone*) chuchotement *m*; *[wind, leaves, water]* murmure *m*, bruissement *m*; (*fig: rumour*) bruit *m*, rumeur *f*. **I heard a ~** j'ai entendu un chuchotement, j'ai entendu quelqu'un qui parlait à voix

basse; **a ~ of voices** des chuchotements; **to say/answer in a ~** dire/répondre à voix basse; **to speak in a ~** parler bas *or* à voix basse; **her voice scarcely rose above a ~** sa voix n'était guère qu'un murmure; (*fig*) **not a ~ to anyone!** n'en soufflez mot à personne!; (*fig*) **I've heard a ~ that he won't come back** j'ai entendu dire qu'il ne reviendrait pas; **there is a ~ that ..., the ~ is going round that ...** le bruit court que ..., on dit que ... .

whispering ['wɪspərɪŋ] 1 adj *person* qui chuchote, qui parle à voix basse; *leaves, wind, stream* qui chuchote, qui murmure. **~ voices** des chuchotements *mpl*. 2 n *[voice]* chuchotement *m*; *[leaves etc]* chuchotement, bruissement *m*, murmure *m*, chuchotis *m*; (*fig*) (*gossip*) médisances *fpl*; (*rumours*) rumeurs *fpl* insidieuses. (*fig*) **there has been a lot of ~ about them** toutes sortes de rumeurs insidieuses ont couru sur leur compte. 3 comp ▸**whispering campaign** (*fig*) campagne (diffamatoire) insidieuse ▸**whispering gallery** galerie *f* à écho.

whist [wɪst] n (*Brit*) whist *m*. **~ drive** tournoi *m* de whist.

whistle ['wɪsl] 1 n a (*sound*) (*made with mouth*) sifflement *m*, (*jeering*) sifflet *m*; (*made with a ~*) coup *m* de sifflet; *[train, kettle, blackbird]* sifflement. **the ~s of the audience** (*cheering*) les sifflements d'admiration du public; (*booing*) les sifflets du public; **to give a ~** (*gen*) siffler; (*blow a ~*) donner un coup de sifflet.

b (*object: also of kettle etc*) sifflet *m*; (*Mus: also* **penny ~**) flûteau *m*. **a blast on a ~** un coup de sifflet strident; **the referee blew his ~** l'arbitre a donné un coup de sifflet *or* a sifflé; **the referee blew his ~ for half-time** l'arbitre a sifflé la mi-temps; **it broke off as clean as a ~** ça a cassé net; (*fig*) **to blow the ~ on sth**‡ tirer la sonnette d'alarme (au sujet de qch); (*fig*) **to blow the ~ on sb*** dénoncer qn; (*fig*) **he blew the ~ on it**‡ (*informed on it*) il a dévoilé le pot aux roses; (*stopped it*) il y a mis le holà.

2 comp ▸**whistle blower*** (*fig*) personne *f* qui tire la sonnette d'alarme ▸**whistle-stop** (*fig: Pol etc*) *see* **whistle-stop**.

3 vi *[person]* siffler, (*tunefully, light-heartedly*) siffloter; (*blow a ~*) donner un coup de sifflet, siffler; *[bird, bullet, wind, kettle, train]* siffler. **he ~d to his dog** il a sifflé son chien; **he ~d at** *or* **for me to stop** il a sifflé pour que je m'arrête (*subj*); **he ~d for a taxi** il a sifflé un taxi; **the boy was whistling at all the pretty girls** le garçon sifflait toutes les jolies filles; **the referee ~d for a foul** l'arbitre a sifflé une faute; **the crowd ~d at the referee** la foule a sifflé l'arbitre; **the audience booed and ~d** les spectateurs ont hué et sifflé; **the audience cheered and ~d** les spectateurs ont manifesté leur enthousiasme par des acclamations et des sifflements; **he strolled along whistling (away) gaily** il flânait en sifflotant gaiement; (*fig*) **he's whistling in the dark** il fait (*or* dit) ça pour se rassurer, il essaie de se donner du courage; (*fig*) **he can ~ for it!*** il peut se fouiller!* *or* se brosser!*, il peut toujours courir!*; **an arrow ~d past his ear** une flèche a sifflé à son oreille; **the cars ~d by us** les voitures passaient devant nous à toute allure.

4 vt *tune* siffler, (*casually, light-heartedly*) siffloter. **to ~ a dog back/in** *etc* siffler un chien pour qu'il revienne/entre (*subj*) *etc*.

▸**whistle up** vt sep *dog, taxi* siffler. (*fig*) **he whistled up 4 or 5 people to give us a hand*** il s'est débrouillé pour dégoter* 4 ou 5 personnes prêtes à nous donner un coup de main; **can you whistle up another blanket or two?*** vous pouvez dégoter* encore une ou deux couvertures?

whistle-stop ['wɪsl,stɒp] 1 n visite *f* éclair *inv* (*dans une petite ville au cours d'une campagne électorale*). 2 adj: **he made a ~ tour of Virginia** il a fait à toute allure le tour de la Virginie; (*US*) **a ~ town** une petite ville *or* un petit trou* (*où le train s'arrête*). 3 vi (*US*) faire une tournée électorale.

Whit [wɪt] 1 n la Pentecôte. 2 comp *holiday etc* de Pentecôte ▸**Whit Monday/Sunday** le lundi/dimanche de Pentecôte ▸**Whitsun(tide)** les fêtes *fpl* de (la) Pentecôte, la Pentecôte ▸**Whit Week** la semaine de Pentecôte.

whit [wɪt] n: **there was not a ~ of truth in it** il n'y avait pas un brin de vérité là-dedans; **he hadn't a ~ of sense** il n'avait pas un grain de bon sens; **it wasn't a ~ better after he'd finished** quand il a eu terminé ce n'était pas mieux du tout; **I don't care a ~** ça m'est profondément égal, je m'en moque complètement.

white [waɪt] 1 adj a (*gen*) *bread, hair, wine, meat, metal, rabbit* blanc (*f* blanche). (*Culin*) **~ sauce** béchamel *f*, sauce blanche; **as ~ as a sheet** pâle comme un linge; **~ as a ghost** pâle comme la mort; **as ~ as snow** blanc comme (la) neige; **to be ~ with fear/anger** être blanc *or* blême *or* pâle de peur/colère; **to go** *or* **turn ~** (*with fear, anger*) blêmir, pâlir, blanchir; *[hair]* blanchir; *[object]* devenir blanc, blanchir; **he went ~ with fear** il a blêmi de peur; **this detergent gets the clothes ~r than ~** ce détergent lave encore plus blanc; **~ blood cell, ~ corpuscle** globule blanc; **a ~ Christmas** un Noël sous la neige; (*fig*) **to show the ~ feather** caner*, se dégonfler*; (*Mil etc*) **the ~ flag** le drapeau blanc; **~ frost** gelée blanche; (*fig*) **a ~ lie** un pieux mensonge; *[blind person]* **~ stick** canne *f* blanche; **~ wedding** mariage *m* en blanc; *see also* **3** *etc*.

b (*racially*) *person, face, skin, race* blanc (*f* blanche). **a ~ man** un Blanc; **a ~ woman** une Blanche; **the ~ South Africans** les Blancs d'Afrique du Sud; **~ supremacy** la suprématie de la race blanche; (*pej*) **~ trash** les petits Blancs pauvres; *see also* **3** *etc*.

2 n a (*colour*) blanc *m*; (*whiteness*) blancheur *f*; *[egg, eye]* blanc; (**: white wine*) blanc *m*. **to be dressed in ~** être vêtu de blanc; (*linen etc*) **the ~s** le (linge) blanc; (*clothes*) **tennis ~s** tenue *f* de tennis; **his face was a deathly ~** son visage était d'une pâleur mortelle; **the sheets were a dazzling ~** les draps étaient d'une blancheur éclatante; (*Mil etc*) **don't fire till you see the ~s of their eyes** ne tirez qu'au dernier moment; *see* **black** *etc*.

b (*person of ~ race*) Blanc *m*, Blanche *f*. (*US pej*) **poor ~** (petit) Blanc *m or* (petite) Blanche *f* pauvre (du Sud).

3 comp ▸**whitebait** blanchaille *f*; (*Culin*) petite friture *f* ▸**whitecaps** (*at sea*) moutons *mpl* ▸**white coffee** café *m* au lait ▸**white-collar: a white-collar job** un emploi dans un bureau; **white-collar union** *syndicat d'employé(e)s de bureau ou de cols blancs;* **white-collar worker** employé(e) *m(f)* de bureau, col *m* blanc ▸**whited sepulchre** (*fig*) sépulcre blanchi, hypocrite *mf* ▸**white dwarf** (*Astron*) naine blanche ▸**white elephant** (*fig*) (*ornament etc*) objet *m* superflu; (*building etc*) réalisation coûteuse et sans (grande) utilité; (*fig*) **it's a white elephant** c'est tout à fait superflu, on n'en a pas besoin; **white elephant stall** étalage *m* d'objets superflus ▸**white-faced** blême, pâle ▸**white fox** (*animal*) renard *m* polaire; (*skin, fur*) renard blanc ▸**white gold** or blanc ▸**white goods** (*Comm*) (*linens*) linge blanc; (*domestic appliances*) appareils ménagers ▸**white-haired** *person* aux cheveux blancs; *animal* à poil blanc, aux poils blancs ▸**Whitehall** *see* **Whitehall** ▸**white-headed** *person* aux cheveux blancs; *bird* à tête blanche; (*fig*) **the white-headed boy** l'enfant chéri ▸**white heat** (*Phys*) chaude blanche, chaleur *f* d'incandescence; **to raise metal to a white heat** chauffer un métal à blanc; (*fig*) **the indignation of the crowd had reached white heat** l'indignation de la foule avait atteint son paroxysme ▸**white hope:** (*fig*) **to be the white hope of** être le grand espoir de, être l'espoir numéro un de ▸**white horses** (*at sea*) = **whitecaps** ▸**white-hot** chauffé à blanc ▸**the White House** (*US*) la Maison Blanche ▸**white knight** (*St Ex*) chevalier *m* blanc ▸**white lead** blanc *m* de céruse ▸**white light** (*Phys*) lumière blanche ▸**white-livered** (*fig liter*) poltron, couard ▸**white magic** magie blanche ▸**white meter** (*Elec*) compteur *m* bleu; **meter heating** chauffage *m* par accumulateur ▸**the White Nile** le Nil Blanc ▸**white noise** (*Acoustics*) son *m* blanc ▸**whiteout:** (*Met*) **there is a whiteout** il y a le jour blanc ▸**white owl** (*Orn*) harfang *m*, chouette blanche ▸**white paper** (*Parl*) livre *m* blanc (*on* sur) ▸**white pepper** (*Culin*) poivre *m* blanc ▸**white plague** (*US: tuberculosis*) tuberculose *f* pulmonaire ▸**white raisin** (*US*) raisin sec de Smyrne ▸**White Russia** Russie Blanche ▸**White Russian** adj russe blanc (*f* russe blanche) ◊ n Russe blanc, Russe blanche ▸**white sale** (*Comm*) vente *f* de blanc ▸**white sapphire** saphir blanc ▸**white sauce** (*Culin*) béchamel *f*, sauce *f* blanche ▸**White Sea** mer *f* Blanche ▸**white shark** requin *m* blanc ▸**white slavery, the white slave trade** la traite des blanches ▸**white spirit** (*Brit*) white-spirit *m* ▸**white-tailed eagle** orfraie *f*, pygargue *m* ▸**whitethorn** (*Bot*) aubépine *f* ▸**whitethroat** (*Orn*) (*Old World warbler*) grisette *f*; (*American sparrow*) moineau *m* d'Amérique ▸**white tie** (*Dress*) habit *m*; **it was a white-tie affair** l'habit était de rigueur ▸**whitewall (tire)** (*US Aut*) pneu *m* à flanc blanc ▸**whitewash** *see* **whitewash** ▸**white water** (*esp Sport*) eau *f* vive ▸**white whale** baleine *f* blanche ▸**whitewood** bois *m* blanc.

Whitehall ['waɪt,hɔːl] n Whitehall *m* (*siège m des ministères et des administrations publiques*).

whiten ['waɪtn] vti blanchir.

whitener ['waɪtnəʳ] n (*for coffee etc*) succédané *m* de lait en poudre; (*for clothes*) agent *m* blanchissant.

whiteness ['waɪtnɪs] n (*see* **white 1**) blancheur *f*, blanc *m*, couleur blanche; pâleur *f*; aspect *m* blême.

whitening ['waɪtnɪŋ] n (*NonC*) a (*act*) *[wall etc]* blanchiment *m*; *[linen]* blanchiment, décoloration *f*; *[hair]* blanchissement *m*. b (*substance: for shoes, doorsteps etc*) blanc *m*.

whitewash ['waɪtwɒʃ] 1 n a (*NonC: for walls etc*) lait *m or* blanc *m* de chaux.

b (*fig*) **the whole episode was a ~ of the government's inefficiency** tout l'épisode était une mise en scène pour camoufler la carence du gouvernement; (*fig*) **the article in the paper was nothing but a ~ of his doubtful character** l'article du journal ne visait qu'à blanchir sa réputation douteuse.

c (*US Sport* ‡) raclée* *f*.

2 vt a *wall etc* blanchir à la chaux, chauler.

b (*fig*) *sb's reputation, career, motives* blanchir; *sb's faults, happening* justifier (par des arguments fallacieux); *person* blanchir, disculper, réhabiliter. (*fig*) **they tried to ~ the whole episode** ils se sont livrés à une entreprise de justification de toute l'affaire, ils ont essayé de peindre l'affaire sous les traits les plus anodins.

c (*US Sport* ‡) écraser complètement*.

whitey‡ ['waɪtɪ] n (*esp US: pej*) (*individual*) Blanc *m*, Blanche *f*; (*Whites collectively*) les Blancs *mpl*.

whither ['wɪðəʳ] adv (*liter*) où. (*in headlines, titles etc*) **"~ the Government now?"** "où va le gouvernement?"

whiting[1] ['waɪtɪŋ] n, pl ~ (*fish*) merlan *m*.

whiting[2] ['waɪtɪŋ] n (*NonC: for shoes, doorsteps etc*) blanc *m*.

whitish ['waɪtɪʃ] adj blanchâtre.

whitlow ['wɪtləʊ] n panaris *m*.

Whitsun ['wɪtsn] n *see* **Whit.**

whittle ['wɪtl] vt *piece of wood* tailler au couteau. **to ~ sth out of a piece of wood, to ~ a piece of wood into sth** tailler qch au couteau dans un morceau de bois.

►**whittle away** 1 vi: **to whittle away at sth** tailler qch au couteau. 2 vt sep = **whittle down.**

►**whittle down** vt sep *wood* tailler; (*fig*) *costs, amount* amenuiser, réduire.

whiz, whizz [wɪz] 1 n a (*sound*) sifflement *m*.
b (*US* ‡) champion* *m*, as *m*. **he's a ~ at tennis** au tennis il est champion* *or* c'est un as.
2 comp ►**whizz-bang**‡ n (*Mil sl: shell*) obus *m*; (*firework*) pétard *m* ◊ adj (*US: excellent*) du tonnerre* ►**whizz kid*** phénomène *m*.
3 vi aller à toute vitesse en sifflant, filer à toute allure *or* comme une flèche. **to ~ *or* go ~ing through the air** fendre l'air (en sifflant); (*Aut*) **to ~ along/past** *etc* filer/passer *etc* à toute vitesse *or* à toute allure; **I'll just ~ over to see him*** je file* le voir; **he ~ed up to town for the day*** il a fait un saut en ville pour la journée.
4 vt a (‡) (*throw*) lancer, filer‡; (*transfer quickly*) apporter. **~ the book over to me** lance-moi le livre, file-moi‡ le livre; **he ~ed it round to us as soon as it was ready** il nous l'a vite apporté *or* passé dès que c'était prêt.
b (*also* **~ up**: *in blender*) mixer.

WHO [ˌdʌbljuːeɪtʃ'əʊ] n (abbr of **World Health Organization**) O.M.S. *f*.

who [huː] 1 pron a (*interrog: remplace aussi "whom" dans le langage parlé*) (qui est-ce) qui; (*after prep*) qui. **~'s there?** qui est là?; **~ are you?** qui êtes-vous?; **~ has the book?** (qui est-ce) qui a le livre?; **~ does he think he is?** il se prend pour qui?, pour qui se prend-il?; (*indignantly*) **~ is he to tell me ...?** de quel droit est-ce qu'il me dit ...?; **you can't sing — WHO can't?** tu es incapable de chanter – ah bon!, tu crois ça!; **~ came with you?** (qui est-ce) qui est venu avec vous?; **~ should it be but Robert!** qui vois-je? Robert!; **I don't know ~'s ~ in the office** je ne connais pas très bien les gens au bureau; **"W~'s W~"** ≃ "Bottin Mondain"; **~(m) did you see?** vous avez vu qui?, qui avez-vous vu?; **~(m) did you speak to?** à qui avez-vous parlé?, vous avez parlé à qui?; **~'s the book by?** le livre est de qui?; **~(m) were you with?** vous étiez avec qui?; **you-know-~ said ...** qui-vous-savez a dit ... .
b (*rel*) qui. **my aunt ~ lives in London** ma tante qui habite à Londres; **he ~ wishes to object must do so now** quiconque désire élever une objection doit le faire maintenant; **those ~ can swim** ceux qui savent nager; (*liter*) **~ is not with me is against me** celui qui *or* quiconque n'est pas pour moi est contre moi.
2 comp ►**whodun(n)it*** roman *m* (*or* film *m* *or* feuilleton *m* *etc*) policier (à énigme) ►**whoever** *see* **whoever** ►**whoe'er** (*liter*), **whosoe'er** (*liter*), **whosoever** (*emphatic*) = **whoever.**

whoa [wəʊ] excl (*also* **~ there**) ho!, holà!

who'd [huːd] = **who had, who would;** *see* **who.**

whoever [huː'evəʳ] pron (*remplace aussi "whomever" dans le langage parlé*) a (*anyone that*) quiconque. **~ wishes may come with me** quiconque le désire peut venir avec moi; **you can give it to ~ wants it** vous pouvez le donner à qui le veut *or* voudra; **~ finds it can keep it** quiconque *or* celui qui le trouvera pourra le garder; **~ said that was an idiot** celui qui a dit ça était un imbécile; **ask ~ you like** demandez à qui vous voulez *or* voudrez.
b (*no matter who*) (*subject*) qui que ce soit qui + *subj*; (*object*) qui que ce soit que + *subj*. **~ you are, come in!** qui que vous soyez, entrez!; **~ he marries, it won't make much difference** qui que ce soit qu'il épouse (*subj*) *or* quelle que soit celle qu'il épouse (*subj*), ça ne fera pas beaucoup de différence.
c (*: *interrog: emphatic*) qui donc. **~ told you that?** qui donc vous a dit ça?, qui a bien pu vous dire ça?; **~ did you give it to?** vous l'avez donné à qui?

whole [həʊl] 1 adj a (*entire*) (+ *sing n*) tout, entier; (+ *plur n*) entier. **along its ~ length** sur toute sa longueur; **~ villages were destroyed** des villages entiers ont été détruits; **the ~ road was like that** toute la route était comme ça; **the ~ world** le monde entier; **he used a ~ notebook** il a utilisé un carnet entier; **he swallowed it ~** il l'a avalé tout entier; **the pig was roasted ~** le cochon était rôti tout entier; **we waited a ~ hour** nous avons attendu une heure entière *or* toute une heure; **it rained 3 ~ days** il a plu 3 jours entiers; **but the ~ man eludes us** mais l'homme tout entier reste un mystère pour nous; **is that the ~ truth?** est-ce que c'est bien toute la vérité?; **but the ~ point of it was to avoid that** mais tout l'intérêt de la chose était d'éviter cela; **with my ~ heart** de tout mon cœur; **he took the ~ lot** il a pris le tout; **the ~ lot of you** vous tous, tous tant que vous êtes; **it's a ~ lot better*** c'est vraiment beaucoup mieux; **there are a ~ lot of things I'd like to tell her** il y a tout un tas de choses que j'aimerais lui dire; **to go the ~ hog*** aller jusqu'au bout, ne pas faire les choses à moitié (*see also* **3**); (*US*) **to go (the) ~ hog* for sb/sth** essayer par tous les moyens de conquérir qn/d'obtenir qch.
b (*intact, unbroken*) intact, complet (*f* -ète). **not a glass was left ~ after the party** il ne restait pas un seul verre intact après la surprise-partie; **keep the egg yolks ~** gardez les jaunes intacts, veillez à ne pas crever les jaunes; **he has a ~ set of Dickens** il a une série complète des œuvres de Dickens; **to our surprise he came back ~** à notre grande surprise il est revenu sain et sauf; **the seal on the letter was still ~** le sceau sur la lettre était encore intact; (*US fig*) **made out of ~ cloth** inventé de toutes pièces; **~ milk** lait entier; (*Mus*) **~ note** ronde *f*; (*Math*) **~ number** nombre entier; (*US Mus*) **~ step** = **~ tone; ~ tone** ton entier; (††: *healed*) **his hand was made ~** sa main a été guérie.
2 n a (*the entire amount of*) **the ~ of the morning** tout le matin; **the ~ of the time** tout le temps; **the ~ of the apple was bad** la pomme toute entière était gâtée; **the ~ of Paris was snowbound** Paris était complètement bloqué par la neige; **the ~ of Paris was talking about it** dans tout Paris on parlait de ça; **nearly the ~ of our output this year** presque toute notre production *or* presque la totalité de notre production cette année; **he received the ~ of the amount** il a reçu la totalité de la somme; **on the ~** dans l'ensemble.
b (*complete unit*) tout *m*. **four quarters make a ~** quatre quarts font un tout *or* un entier; **the ~ may be greater than the sum of its parts** le tout peut être plus grand que la somme de ses parties; **the estate is to be sold as a ~** la propriété doit être vendue en bloc; **considered as a ~ the play was successful, although some scenes ...** dans l'ensemble *or* prise dans son ensemble la pièce était un succès, bien que certaines scènes ... .
3 comp ►**wholefood(s)** aliments *mpl* complets ►**wholefood restaurant** restaurant *m* qui n'utilise que des aliments complets ►**wholegrain** adj *bread, flour, rice* complet ►**wholehearted** *approval, admiration* sans réserve(s); **they made a wholehearted attempt ...** ils ont essayé de tout cœur ... ►**wholeheartedly** de tout cœur, à fond ►**whole-hog*** (*esp US*) adj *support* sans réserve(s), total; *supporter* acharné, ardent (*before n*) ◊ adv à fond, jusqu'au bout ►**whole-hogger***: (*esp US*) **to be a whole-hogger** (*gen*) se donner entièrement à ce qu'on fait; (*Pol*) être jusqu'au-boutiste *mf* ►**wholemeal** (*Brit*) *flour* brut; *bread* ≃ complet ►**wholesale** *etc see* **wholesale** *etc* ►**wholesome** *food, life, thoughts, book, person* sain; *air, climate* sain, salubre; *exercise, advice* salutaire ►**wholesomeness** (*see* **wholesome**) caractère *m* *or* nature *f* sain(e); salubrité *f*; caractère salutaire ►**whole-wheat** *flour* brut; *bread* ≃ complet.

wholesale ['həʊlseɪl] 1 n (*NonC: Comm*) (vente *f* en) gros *m*. **at *or* by ~** en gros.
2 adj a (*Comm*) *price, firm, trade* de gros. **~ dealer, ~ merchant, ~ trader** grossiste *mf*, marchand(e) *m(f)* en gros; **~ market** marché *m* de gros; (*US Fin*) **~ price index** indice *m* des prix de gros.
b (*fig*) *slaughter, destruction* systématique, en masse; *rejection, criticism, acceptance* en bloc. **there has been ~ sacking of unskilled workers** il y a eu des licenciements en masse parmi les manœuvres; **there is a ~ campaign in the press against ...** il y a une campagne systématique *or* généralisée dans la presse contre ...; **there was a ~ attempt to persuade the public that ...** on a essayé par tous les moyens de persuader le public que ... .
3 adv a (*Comm*) *buy, sell* en gros. **I can get it for you ~** je peux vous le faire avoir au prix de gros.
b (*fig*) en masse, en série, en bloc. **such houses are being destroyed ~** de telles maisons sont détruites en série; **these proposals were rejected ~** toutes ces propositions ont été rejetées en bloc; **workers are being dismissed ~** on procède en ce moment à des licenciements en masse.

wholesaler ['həʊlseɪləʳ] n (*Comm*) grossiste *mf*, marchand(e) *m(f)* en gros.

wholism ['həʊlɪzəm] n = **holism.**

wholistic [həʊ'lɪstɪk] adj = **holistic.**

who'll [huːl] = **who will, who shall;** *see* **who.**

wholly ['həʊlɪ] adv complètement, entièrement, tout à fait. (*Jur, Econ*) **~-owned subsidiary** filiale *f* à cent pour cent.

whom [huːm] 1 pron a (*interrog: souvent remplacé par "who" dans le langage parlé*) qui. **~ did you see?** qui avez-vous vu?; **by ~ is the book?** de qui est le livre?; **with ~?** avec qui?; **to ~?** à qui?; *see also* **who 1a.** b (*rel*) **my aunt, ~ I love dearly** ma tante, que j'aime tendrement; **those ~ he had seen recently** ceux qu'il avait vus récemment; **the man to ~** l'homme à qui, l'homme auquel; **the man of ~** l'homme dont; (*liter*) **~ the gods love die young** ceux qui sont aimés des dieux meurent jeunes. 2 comp ►**whomever,** (*emphatic*) **whomsoever** *accusative case of* **whoever, whosoever.**

whomping* ['wɒmpɪŋ] adj (*US*) (*also* **~ big*, ~ great***) énorme.

whoop [huːp] 1 n cri *m* (*de joie, de triomphe*); (*Med*) toux aspirante (de la coqueluche). **with a ~ of glee/triumph** avec un cri de joie/de triomphe. 2 vi pousser des cris; (*Med*) avoir des quintes de toux coquelucheuse. 3 vt: **to ~ it up**‡ faire la noce* *or* la bringue‡, bien se marrer‡. 4 comp ►**whooping cough** coqueluche *f*.

whoopee [wʊ'piː] 1 excl hourra!, youpi! 2 n: **to make ~**‡ faire la noce* *or* la bringue‡, bien se marrer‡. 3 comp ►**whoopee cushion*** (*US*) coussin(-péteur) *m* de farces et attrapes.

whoops [wuːps] excl (*also* **~-a-daisy**) (*avoiding fall etc*) oups!, houp-là!; (*lifting child*) houp-là!, hop-là!

whoosh [wuːʃ] 1 excl zoum! 2 n: **the ~ of sledge runners in the snow** le bruit des patins de luges glissant sur la neige, le glissement des patins de luges sur la neige. 3 vi: **the car ~ed past** la voiture est passée à toute allure dans un glissement de pneus.

whop‡ [wɒp] vt (*beat*) rosser*; (*defeat*) battre à plate(s) couture(s).

whopper* ['wɒpəʳ] n (*car/parcel/nose etc*) voiture *f*/colis *m*/nez *m etc* énorme; (*lie*) mensonge *m* énorme.

whopping ['wɒpɪŋ] 1 adj (*: *also* ~ **big**, ~ **great**) énorme. 2 n (‡) raclée* *f*.

whore [hɔːʳ] 1 n (‡ *pej*) putain‡ *f*. 2 comp ▸**whorehouse‡** bordel‡ *m* ▸**whoremonger†** fornicateur *m*; (*pimp*) proxénète *m*, souteneur *m*. 3 vi (*lit: also* **go whoring**) courir la gueuse, se débaucher. (*fig liter*) **to ~ after sth** se prostituer pour obtenir qch.

who're ['huːəʳ] = **who are**; *see* **who**.

whorish‡ ['hɔːrɪʃ] adj de putain‡, putassier**‡*.

whorl [wɜːl] n *[fingerprint]* volute *f*; *[spiral shell]* spire *f*; (*Bot*) verticille *m*. **~s of meringue/cream** des tortillons *mpl* de meringue/crème.

whortleberry ['wɜːtlbərɪ] n myrtille *f*.

who's [huːz] = **who is, who has**; *see* **who**.

whose [huːz] 1 poss pron à qui. **~ is this?** à qui est ceci?; **I know ~ it is** je sais à qui c'est; **~ is this hat?** à qui est ce chapeau?; **here's a lollipop each — let's see ~ lasts longest!** voici une sucette chacun — voyons celle de qui durera le plus longtemps!

2 poss adj a (*interrog*) à qui, de qui. **~ hat is this?** à qui est ce chapeau?; **~ son are you?** de qui êtes-vous le fils?; **~ book is missing?** c'est le livre de qui qui manque?, qui n'a pas (*or* n'a pas remis *etc*) son livre?; **~ fault is it?** à qui la faute?

b (*rel use*) dont, de qui. **the man ~ hat I took** l'homme dont j'ai pris le chapeau; **the boy ~ sister I was talking to** le garçon à la sœur duquel *or* à la sœur de qui je parlais; **those ~ passports I've got here** ceux dont j'ai les passeports ici.

whosever [huː'zevəʳ] poss pron = **of whomever** (*see* **whoever**). **~ book you use, you must take care of it** peu importe à qui est le livre dont tu te sers, il faut que tu en prennes soin.

who've [huːv] = **who have**; *see* **who**.

why [waɪ] 1 adv (*for what reason, with what purpose etc*) pourquoi. **~ did you do it?** pourquoi l'avez-vous fait?; **I wonder ~ he left her** je me demande pourquoi il l'a quittée; **I wonder ~** je me demande pourquoi; **he told me ~ he did it** il m'a dit pourquoi il l'a fait *or* la raison pour laquelle il l'a fait; **~ not?** pourquoi pas?; **~ not phone her?** pourquoi ne pas lui téléphoner?; **~ ask her when you don't have to?** pourquoi le lui demander quand vous n'êtes pas obligé de le faire?

2 excl eh bien!, tiens! **~, what's the matter?** eh bien, qu'est-ce qui ne va pas?; **~, it's you!** tiens, c'est vous!; **~, it's quite easy!** voyons donc, ce n'est pas difficile!

3 conj: **the reasons ~ he did it** les raisons pour lesquelles il l'a fait; **there's no reason ~ you shouldn't try again** il n'y a pas de raison (pour) que tu n'essayes (*subj*) pas de nouveau; **that's (the reason) ~** voilà pourquoi; **that is ~ I never spoke to him again** c'est pourquoi je ne lui ai jamais reparlé.

4 n: **the ~(s) and (the) wherefore(s)** les causes *fpl* et les raisons *fpl*; **the ~ and (the) how** le pourquoi et le comment.

5 comp ▸**whyever*** (*interrog: emphatic*) pourquoi donc; **whyever did you do it?*** pourquoi donc est-ce que vous avez fait ça?, pourquoi est-ce que vous êtes allé faire ça?*

WI [ˌdʌbljuː'aɪ] n a (*Brit*) (abbr of **Women's Institute**) *see* **woman**. b (*US*) abbr of **Wisconsin**. c (abbr of **West Indies**) *see* **west**.

wibbly-wobbly* [ˌwɪblɪ'wɒblɪ] adj = **wobbly**.

wick [wɪk] n mèche *f*. (*fig*) **he gets on my ~‡** il me tape sur le système*, il me court sur le haricot‡.

wicked ['wɪkɪd] adj a (*iniquitous*) *person* mauvais, méchant, malfaisant; *act, behaviour* mauvais, vilain (*before n*), inique; *system, policy* inique, pernicieux. **he is a very ~ man** il est foncièrement méchant *or* mauvais; **that was a ~ thing to do!** c'était vraiment méchant; **it was a ~ attempt to get rid of him** cette tentative d'élimination était dictée par la méchanceté.

b (*bad, unpleasant*) *blow, wound* vilain (*before n*); *pain* cruel, violent; *satire, criticism, comment* méchant. **a ~ waste** un scandaleux gâchis; **he has a ~ temper** il a un caractère épouvantable; **it's ~ weather*** il fait un temps affreux *or* un très vilain temps; **this is a ~ car to start*** faire démarrer cette voiture est une véritable plaie*.

c (*mischievous etc*) *smile, look, remark, suggestion* malicieux. **he's a ~ little boy** c'est un petit malicieux *or* coquin; **he's got a ~ sense of humour** il a un humour très malicieux *or* espiègle.

d (*: *skilful*) **that was a ~ shot!** quel beau coup!; **he plays a ~ game** il a un jeu du tonnerre*; **the way he got out of that affair was really ~**la façon dont il s'est sorti de cette histoire, chapeau!*

e (‡: *excellent*) super* *inv*, extra* *inv*.

wickedly ['wɪkɪdlɪ] adv a (*evilly*) *behave* vilainement, très mal. **he ~ destroyed ...** il a poussé la méchanceté jusqu'à détruire ... . b (*mischievously*) *look, smile, suggest* malicieusement. c (*: *skilfully*) *play, manage etc* comme un chef*, formidablement* bien.

wickedness ['wɪkɪdnɪs] n *[behaviour, order, decision, person]* méchanceté *f*, cruauté *f*, vilenie *f*; *[murder]* horreur *f*, atrocité *f*; *[look, smile, suggestion]* malice *f*; *[waste]* scandale *m*.

wicker ['wɪkəʳ] 1 n (*NonC*) (*substance*) osier *m*; (*objects: also* **~work**) vannerie *f*. 2 comp (*also* **~work**) *basket, chair* d'osier, en osier.

wicket ['wɪkɪt] 1 n a (*door, gate*) (petite) porte *f*, portillon *m*; (*for bank teller etc*) guichet *m*. b (*Cricket*) (*stumps etc*) guichet *m*; (*pitch between them*) terrain *m* (*entre les guichets*); *see* **losing, sticky**. 2 comp ▸**wicket-keeper** (*Cricket*) gardien *m* de guichet.

wickiup ['wɪkɪˌʌp] n (*US*) hutte *f* de branchages.

widdershins ['wɪdəʃɪnz] adv (*esp Scot*) = **withershins**.

wide [waɪd] 1 adj *road, river, strip* large; *margin* grand; *garment* large, ample, flottant; *ocean, desert* immense, vaste; *circle, gap, space* large, grand; (*fig*) *knowledge* vaste, grand, très étendu; *choice, selection* grand, considérable; *survey, study* de grande envergure. **how ~ is the room?** quelle est la largeur de la pièce?, quelle largeur a la pièce?; **it is 5 metres ~** cela a *or* fait 5 mètres de large; **the ~ Atlantic** l'immense *or* le vaste Atlantique; **no one/nowhere in the whole ~ world** personne/nulle part au monde; (*Cine*) **~ screen** écran *m* panoramique; **she stared, her eyes ~ with fear** elle regardait, les yeux agrandis de peur *or* par la peur; **... mouth ~ with astonishment ...** bouche bée de stupeur; **a man with ~ views** *or* **opinions** un homme aux vues larges; **he has ~ interests** il a des goûts très éclectiques; **to a ~ extent** dans une large mesure; **in the widest sense of the word** au sens le plus général *or* le plus large du mot; **it has a ~ variety of uses** cela se prête à une grande variété d'usages; **the shot/ball/arrow was ~** le coup/la balle/la flèche est passé(e) à côté; **it was ~ of the target** c'était loin de la cible; *see* **mark²** *etc*.

2 adv *aim, shoot, fall* loin du but. **the bullet went ~** la balle est passée à côté; **he flung the door ~** il a ouvert la porte en grand; **they are set ~ apart** *[trees, houses, posts]* ils sont largement espacés; *[eyes]* ils sont très écartés; **he stood with his legs ~ apart** il se tenait debout les jambes très écartées; **to open one's eyes ~** ouvrir grand les yeux *or* ses yeux en grand; (*at dentist's*) **"open ~!"** "ouvrez grand!"; *see* **far, open**.

3 comp ▸**wide-angle lens** (*Phot*) objectif *m* grand-angulaire, objectif grand angle *inv* ▸**wide area network** (*Comput*) grand réseau *m* ▸**wide-awake** (*lit*) bien *or* tout éveillé; (*fig*) éveillé, alerte, vif ▸**wide-bodied** *or* **wide-body aircraft** avion *m* à fuselage élargi, gros-porteur *m* ▸**wide boy‡** (*Brit pej*) escroc *m*, filou *m*, requin* *m* ▸**wide-eyed** adj (*in naïveté*) aux yeux grands ouverts *or* écarquillés; (*in fear, surprise*) aux yeux agrandis *or* écarquillés ◊ adv les yeux écarquillés; **in wide-eyed amazement** les yeux agrandis par la stupeur ▸**wide-mouthed** *person* qui a une grande bouche; *river* à l'embouchure large; *cave* avec une vaste entrée; *bottle* au large goulot; *bag* large du haut ▸**wide-ranging** *mind, report, survey* de grande envergure; *interests* divers, variés ▸**widespread** *arms* en croix; *availability* courant; *wings* déployé; *belief, opinion* très répandu; *confusion* général.

-wide [waɪd] adj, adv ending in comps *see* **country, nation** *etc*.

widely ['waɪdlɪ] adv a *scatter, spread* partout, sur une grande étendue; *travel* beaucoup; *differ* largement, radicalement. **~ different cultures** des cultures radicalement différentes; **the trees were ~ spaced** les arbres étaient largement espacés.

b (*fig: extensively*) généralement. **it is ~ believed that ...** on pense communément *or* généralement que ...; **~-held opinions** des opinions très répandues; **he is ~ known for his generosity** sa réputation de générosité est bien connue, il est bien connu pour sa générosité; **he is ~ known to be the author of ...** comme presque tout le monde le sait, c'est lui l'auteur de ...; **to be ~ read** *[author, book]* être très lu; *[reader]* avoir beaucoup lu (*in sth* qch), être très cultivé.

widen ['waɪdn] 1 vt *circle, gap, space* élargir, agrandir; *road, river, strip, garment* élargir; *margin* augmenter; *knowledge* accroître, élargir; *survey, study* accroître la portée de. (*in election etc*) **to ~ one's lead over sb** accroître son avance sur qn. 2 vi (*also* ~ **out**) s'élargir; s'agrandir.

wideness ['waɪdnɪs] n largeur *f*.

widgeon ['wɪdʒən] n canard siffleur.

widget* ['wɪdʒɪt] n (*US*) (*device*) gadget *m*; (*thingummy*) truc* *m*, machin* *m*.

widow ['wɪdəʊ] 1 n veuve *f*. **W~ Smith†** la veuve Smith; (*fig*) **she's a golf ~** elle ne voit jamais son mari qui est toujours à jouer au golf, son mari la délaisse pour aller jouer au golf; **~'s peak** pousse *f* de cheveux en V sur le front; (*Admin*) **~'s pension** *or* **benefit** ≈ allocation *f* veuvage; (*US*) **~'s walk** belvédère *m* (*construit sur le faîte d'une maison côtière*); *see* **grass, mite, weed** *etc*. 2 vt: **to be ~ed** *[man]* devenir veuf; *[woman]* devenir veuve; **she was ~ed in 1975** elle est devenue veuve en 1975, elle a perdu son mari en 1975; **she has been ~ed for 10 years** elle est veuve depuis 10 ans; **he lives with his ~ed mother** il vit avec sa mère qui est veuve.

widower ['wɪdəʊəʳ] n veuf *m*.

widowhood ['wɪdəʊhʊd] n veuvage *m*.

width [wɪdθ] 1 n a (*NonC*) *[road, river, strip, bed, ocean, desert, gap, space, margin]* largeur *f*; *[garment]* ampleur *f*; *[circle]* largeur, diamètre *m*. **what is the ~ of the room?** quelle est la largeur de la pièce?, quelle largeur a la pièce?; **it is 5 metres in ~, its ~ is 5 metres, it has a ~ of 5 metres** cela a *or* fait 5 mètres de large; **measure it across its ~**

prends la mesure en largeur. **b** (*of cloth*) largeur *f*, lé *m*. **you'll get it out of one** ~ une largeur *or* un lé te suffira. **2** comp ▸ **widthways, widthwise** en largeur.

wield [wi:ld] vt *sword, axe, pen, tool* manier; (*brandish*) brandir; *power, authority, control* exercer.

wiener* ['wi:nəʳ] (*US*) **1** n saucisse *f* de Francfort. **2** comp ▸ **wiener schnitzel** ['vi:nə'ʃnɪtsəl] escalope *f* viennoise.

wienie* ['wi:nɪ] n (*US*) saucisse *f* de Francfort.

wife [waɪf] pl **wives** **1** n **a** (*spouse*) femme *f*, (*esp Admin*) épouse *f*; (*married woman*) femme mariée. **his second** ~ sa deuxième *or* seconde femme, la femme qu'il a (*or* avait *etc*) épousée en secondes noces; **the farmer's/butcher's** *etc* ~ la fermière/bouchère *etc*; **the** ~⁑ la patronne*; **he decided to take a** ~ il a décidé de se marier *or* de prendre femme†; **to take sb to** ~† prendre qn pour femme; **wives whose husbands have reached the age of 65** les femmes mariées dont les maris ont atteint 65 ans; (*US Jur*) ~**'s equity** part *f* de la communauté revenant à la femme en cas de divorce; **"The Merry Wives of Windsor"** "Les Joyeuses Commères de Windsor"; *see* **working** *etc*.

b († *or** *dial: woman*) bonne femme*. **she's a poor old** ~ c'est une pauvre vieille; *see* **old** *etc*.

2 comp ▸ **wife-swapping** échange *m* de partenaires (*par deux couples*).

wifely ['waɪflɪ] adj *duties, virtues* conjugal; *feelings, wisdom* d'une bonne épouse.

wig [wɪg] **1** n (*gen*) perruque *f*; (*hairpiece*) postiche *m*; (⁑: *hair*) tignasse* *f*. **2** comp ▸ **wigmaker** perruquier *m*, -ière *f*.

wigeon ['wɪdʒən] n = **widgeon**.

wigging⁑ ['wɪgɪŋ] n (*Brit: scolding*) attrapade⁑ *f*, réprimande *f*. **to give sb a** ~ passer un savon* à qn; **to get a** ~ se faire enguirlander*.

wiggle ['wɪgl] **1** vt *pencil, stick* agiter; *toes* agiter, remuer; *loose screw, button, tooth* faire jouer. **to** ~ **one's hips** tortiller des hanches; **my finger hurts if you** ~ **it like that** j'ai mal quand vous me tortillez le doigt comme ça; **he** ~**d his finger at me warningly** il a agité l'index en ma direction en guise d'avertissement. **2** vi *[loose screw etc]* branler; *[tail]* remuer, frétiller; *[rope, snake, worm]* se tortiller. **she** ~**d across the room** elle a traversé la pièce en se déhanchant *or* en tortillant des hanches. **3** n: **to walk with a** ~ marcher en se déhanchant, marcher en tortillant des hanches; **to give sth a** ~ = **to wiggle sth**; *see* **1**.

wiggly ['wɪglɪ] adj *snake, worm* qui se tortille. **a** ~ **line** un trait ondulé.

wight†† [waɪt] n être *m*.

wigwam ['wɪgwæm] n wigwam *m*.

wilco [ˌwɪl'kəʊ] adv (*Telec*) message reçu.

wild [waɪld] **1** adj **a** (*not domesticated etc*) *animal* sauvage; (*wary*) farouche; *plant, tribe, man, land, countryside* sauvage. ~ **beast** (*gen*) bête *f* sauvage; (*dangerous*) bête féroce; ~ **duck** canard *m* sauvage; ~ **flowers** fleurs *fpl* des champs, fleurs sauvages; ~ **goat** *etc* chèvre *f etc* sauvage; ~ **rabbit** lapin *m* de garenne; ~ **boar** sanglier *m*; **he's still too** ~ **to let you get near him** il est encore trop farouche pour te laisser t'approcher de lui; **the plant in its** ~ **state** la plante à l'état sauvage; **it was growing** ~ ça poussait à l'état sauvage; **a** ~ **stretch of coastline** une côte sauvage; (*fig*) ~ **horses wouldn't make me tell you** je ne te le dirais pour rien au monde; (*fig*) **to sow one's** ~ **oats** jeter sa gourme, (*stronger*) faire les quatre cent coups; (*US*) ~ **and woolly*** fruste, primitif; *see also* **2** *and* **rose²**, **run**, **strawberry** *etc*.

b (*rough*) *wind* violent, furieux, de tempête; *sea* déchaîné, gros (*f* grosse), en furie. **in** ~ **weather** par gros temps; **the weather was** ~ il faisait très gros temps; **it was a** ~ **night** le vent faisait rage cette nuit-là.

c (*unrestrained*) *appearance* farouche; *laughter, anger* fou (*f* folle); *idea, plan* fou, extravagant, abracadabrant; *imagination, enthusiasm* débordant, délirant; *life* de bâtons de chaise; *evening, party* fou. **his hair was** ~ **and uncombed** il avait les cheveux en bataille; **there was** ~ **confusion at the airport** la confusion la plus totale régnait à l'aéroport; **he took a** ~ **swing at his opponent** il a lancé le poing en direction de son adversaire; **he had a** ~ **look in his eyes** il avait une lueur sauvage *or* farouche dans les yeux; **he was** ~ **in his youth, he had a** ~ **youth** il a fait les quatre cent coups dans sa jeunesse, il a eu quelques années folles quand il était jeune; **a whole gang of** ~ **kids** toute une bande de casse-cou; **we had some** ~ **times together** nous avons fait bien des folies ensemble; **those were** ~ **times** l'époque était rude; **there were moments of** ~ **indignation** par moments ils étaient fous d'indignation; **he had some** ~ **scheme for damming the river** il avait un projet complètement fou *or* abracadabrant *or* extravagant pour barrer le fleuve; **there was a lot of** ~ **talk about ...** on a agité des tas d'idées folles au sujet de ...; **they made some** ~ **promises** ils ont fait quelques promesses insensées *or* folles *or* extravagantes; **that is a** ~ **exaggeration** c'est une énorme exagération; **to make a** ~ **guess** risquer *or* émettre à tout hasard une hypothèse (*at sth* sur qch).

d (*excited*) comme fou (*f* folle); (*enthusiastic*) fou, dingue* (*about* de); (*angry*) (fou) furieux, dingue*. **the dog went** ~ **when he saw his master** le chien est devenu comme fou quand il a vu son maître; **the audience went** ~ **with delight** le public a hurlé de joie; **his fans went** ~ **when he appeared** la folie a gagné les fans* quand il est apparu; **he was** ~ **with joy** il ne se tenait plus de joie; **he was** ~ **with anger/indignation** il était fou de rage/d'indignation; **to be** ~ **about sb/sth*** être dingue* de qn/qch; **I'm not** ~ **about it*** ça ne m'emballe* pas beaucoup; **it's enough to drive you** ~**!*** c'est à vous rendre dingue!*; **he was absolutely** ~* **when he heard about it** il était absolument hors de lui quand il l'a su.

2 comp ▸ **wildcard** (*Comput*) caractère *m* de remplacement ▸ **wildcat** *see* **wildcat** ▸ **wild-eyed** (*mad*) au regard fou; (*grief-stricken*) aux yeux hagards, au regard égaré; **in wild-eyed terror** une terreur folle dans les yeux ▸ **wildfire: to spread like wildfire** se répandre comme une traînée de poudre ▸ **wildfowl** (*one bird*) oiseau *m* sauvage; (*collectively*) oiseaux sauvages; (*Hunting*) gibier *m* à plume ▸ **wildfowling: to go wildfowling** chasser (le gibier à plumes) au tir ▸ **wild-goose chase:** (*fig*) **it proved to be a wild-goose chase** l'aventure a fini en eau de boudin*; **he sent me off on a wild-goose chase** il m'a fait courir partout pour rien ▸ **wildlife: he's interested in wildlife** il s'intéresse à la faune et à la flore; **the wildlife of Central Australia** la faune et la flore d'Australie centrale; **wildlife sanctuary** réserve *f* naturelle ▸ **the Wild West** (*US*) le Far West ▸ **Wild West show** (*US*) spectacle *m* sur le thème du Far West.

3 n: **the call of the** ~ l'appel *m* de la nature; (*natural habitat*) **in the** ~ dans la nature; **he went off into the** ~**s** il est parti vers des régions sauvages *or* reculées; **he lives in the** ~**s of Alaska** il vit au fin fond de l'Alaska; (*fig*) **we live out in the** ~**s** nous habitons en pleine brousse.

wildcat ['waɪldˌkæt] **1** n, pl ~**s** *or* ~ **a** (*animal*) chat *m* sauvage; (*fig: person*) personne *f* féroce. **b** (*US*) (*oil well*) forage *m* dans un terrain vierge. **2** adj **a** (*US*) (*unsound*) *scheme, project* insensé; (*financially*) financièrement douteux. **b** (*Ind*) ~ **strike** grève *f* sauvage. **3** vi (*US: for oil*) entreprendre un forage dans un terrain vierge.

wildcatter* ['waɪldˌkætəʳ] n (*striker*) gréviste *mf*; (*Fin*) spéculateur *m*.

wildebeest ['wɪldɪbi:st] n, pl ~**s** *or* ~ gnou *m*.

wilderness ['wɪldənɪs] n (*gen*) étendue déserte, région reculée *or* sauvage; (*Bible: also fig*) désert *m*; (*overgrown garden*) jungle *f*. **a** ~ **of snow and ice** de vastes étendues de neige et de glace; **a** ~ **of empty seas** des kilomètres et des kilomètres de mer; (*fig*) **a** ~ **of streets/ruins** un désert de rues/de ruines; (*Bible*) **to preach in the** ~ prêcher dans le désert; (*fig*) **to be in the** ~ faire sa traversée du désert; **this garden is a** ~ ce jardin est une vraie jungle.

wildly ['waɪldlɪ] adv *[wind, sea etc] blow, gust, rage* violemment, furieusement; *[person] behave* de façon extravagante; *wave, gesticulate, talk* fiévreusement; *applaud, cheer* follement, frénétiquement; *protest* violemment. **her heart was beating** ~ son cœur battait violemment *or* à se rompre; **he looked at them** ~ il leur a jeté un regard fou; **he hit out** ~ il lançait des coups dans tous les sens *or* au hasard; **to shoot** ~ tirer au hasard; **you're guessing** ~ tu dis ça tout à fait au hasard; ~ **happy** follement heureux; ~ **delighted** aux anges; **I'm not** ~ **pleased about it*** ce n'est pas que ça me fasse très plaisir; **they were rushing about** ~ ils se précipitaient dans tous les sens.

wildness ['waɪldnɪs] n *[land, countryside, scenery]* aspect *m* sauvage; *[tribe, people]* sauvagerie *f*; *[wind, sea]* fureur *f*, violence *f*; *[appearance]* désordre *m*; *[imagination]* extravagance *f*; *[enthusiasm]* ferveur *f*. **the** ~ **of the weather** le sale temps qu'il fait (*or* faisait *etc*).

wiles [waɪlz] npl artifices *mpl*, manège *m*; (*stronger*) ruses *fpl*.

wilful, (*US*) **willful** ['wɪlfʊl] adj *person, character* entêté, têtu, obstiné; *action* voulu, volontaire, délibéré; *murder* prémédité; *damage, destruction* commis avec préméditation.

wilfully, (*US*) **willfully** ['wɪlfəlɪ] adv (*obstinately*) obstinément, avec entêtement, avec obstination; (*deliberately*) à dessein, délibérément, de propos délibéré.

wilfulness, (*US*) **willfulness** ['wɪlfʊlnɪs] n *[person]* obstination *f*, entêtement *m*; *[action]* caractère délibéré *or* intentionnel.

wiliness ['waɪlɪnɪs] n ruse *f* (*NonC*), astuce *f* (*NonC*).

will [wɪl] **1** modal aux vb (2nd pers sg **wilt††**; neg **will not** often abbr to **won't**) (*see also* **would**) **a** (*used to form fut tense*) **he will speak** il parlera, (*near future*) il va parler; **don't worry, he will come** ne vous inquiétez pas, il ne manquera pas de venir *or* il viendra sans faute; **you'll regret it some day** tu le regretteras un jour; **we will come too** nous viendrons (nous) aussi; **you won't lose it again, will you?** tu ne le perdras plus, n'est-ce pas?; **you will come to see us, won't you?** vous viendrez nous voir, n'est-ce pas?; **will he come too? — yes he will** est-ce qu'il viendra (lui) aussi? — oui; **I'll go with you — no you won't!** je vais vous accompagner — non, certainement pas! *or* en aucun cas!; **they'll arrive tomorrow — will they?** ils arriveront demain — ah bon? *or* c'est sûr?; **I don't think he'll do it tomorrow** je ne pense pas qu'il le fasse demain; (*in commands*) **you will speak to no one** ne parlez à personne, vous ne parlerez à personne; **will you be quiet!** veux-tu (bien) te taire!

b (*indicating conjecture*) **that will be the postman** ça doit être le facteur, c'est *or* voilà sans doute le facteur; **that will have been last year, I suppose** c'était l'année dernière, sans doute; **she'll be about forty** elle doit avoir quarante ans environ *or* la quarantaine; **she'll have forgotten all about it by now** elle aura tout oublié à l'heure qu'il est.

c (*indicating willingness*) **I will help you** je vous aiderai, je veux bien vous aider; **will you help me? — yes I will/no I won't** tu veux m'aider? — oui je veux bien/non je ne veux pas; **if you'll help me I think we can do it** si vous voulez bien m'aider, je crois que nous y arriverons; **won't you come with us?** tu ne veux pas venir (avec nous)?; **will you have a cup of coffee?** voulez-vous *or* prendrez-vous un petit café?; **won't you have a drink?** vous prendrez bien un verre?; (*in requests*) **will you please sit down!** voulez-vous vous asseoir, s'il vous plaît!; **just a moment, will you?** un instant, s'il vous plaît; (*in marriage service*) **I will** oui; **I WILL see him!** on ne m'empêchera pas de le voir!; **I won't have it!** je ne tolère pas ça!, je n'admets pas ça!; **the window won't open** la fenêtre ne s'ouvre pas *or* ne veut pas s'ouvrir; **do what you will** faites ce que vous voulez *or* comme vous voulez; **come when you will** venez quand vous voulez; **look where you will** regardez où bon vous semble.

d (*indicating habit, characteristic: gen present tense in French*) **he will sit for hours doing nothing** il reste assis pendant des heures à ne rien faire; **this bottle will hold one litre** cette bouteille contient un litre *or* fait le litre; **the car will do 150 km/h** cette voiture fait 150 km/h; **he WILL talk all the time!** il ne peut pas s'empêcher *or* s'arrêter de parler!; **if you WILL tell her all I say to you** si tu insistes pour *or* si tu t'entêtes à lui raconter tout ce que je te dis; **I WILL call him Richard, though his name's actually Robert** il faut toujours que je l'appelle (*subj*) Richard bien qu'en fait il s'appelle Robert; (*loc*) **boys will be boys** il faut (bien) que jeunesse se passe (*loc*); **accidents will happen** il y aura toujours des accidents, on ne peut pas empêcher les accidents.

2 **pret, ptp willed vt** a (*wish, intend*) vouloir (*that* que + *subj*). **God has ~ed it so** Dieu a voulu qu'il en soit ainsi; **it is as God ~s** c'est la volonté de Dieu; **you must ~ it really hard if you wish to succeed** pour réussir il faut le vouloir très fort; **to ~ sb's happiness** vouloir le bonheur de qn.

b (*urge etc by willpower*) **he was ~ing her to accept** il l'adjurait intérieurement d'accepter; **he ~ed himself to stand up** il fit un suprême effort pour se mettre debout.

c (*Jur: leave in one's will*) léguer (*sth to sb* qch à qn).

3 **n** a (*faculty*) volonté *f*; (*wish*) volonté, désir *m*. **he has a strong ~, he has a ~ of his own** il est très volontaire; **a ~ of iron, an iron ~** une volonté de fer; **to have a weak ~** manquer de volonté; **the ~ to live** la volonté de survivre; (*Prov*) **where there's a ~ there's a way** vouloir c'est pouvoir (*Prov*); **the ~ of God** la volonté de Dieu, la volonté divine; **it is the ~ of the people that ...** la volonté du peuple est que ... + *subj*; (*frm*) **what is your ~?** quelle est votre volonté?; (*frm*) **it is my ~ that he should leave** je veux qu'il parte; **you must take the ~ for the deed** il faut juger la chose sur l'intention; **Thy ~ be done** que Ta volonté soit faite; **at ~** (*as much as you like*) à volonté; (*whenever you like*) quand vous le voulez; **to choose/borrow** *etc* **at ~** choisir/emprunter *etc* à volonté; **you are free to leave at ~** vous êtes libre de partir quand vous voulez; **to do sth against one's ~** faire qch à son corps défendant *or* à contre-cœur; **with the best ~ in the world** avec la meilleure volonté du monde; **to work with a ~** travailler avec détermination *or* ardeur; *see* **free, goodwill, ill, sweet** *etc*.

b (*Jur*) testament *m*. **the last ~ and testament of ...** les dernières volontés de ...; **he left it to me in his ~** il me l'a légué par testament, il me l'a laissé dans son testament.

4 **comp ▸ willpower** volonté *f*, vouloir *m*.

willful ['wɪlfʊl] *etc* (*US*) = **wilful** *etc*.

William ['wɪljəm] **n** Guillaume *m*. **~ the Conqueror** Guillaume le Conquérant; **~ of Orange** Guillaume d'Orange; **~ Tell** Guillaume Tell.

willie‡ ['wɪlɪ] **n** a (*Brit*) zizi* *m*. b (*npl*): **to have the ~s** avoir les chocottes‡ *fpl*; **it gives me the ~s** ça me donne les chocottes‡.

willing ['wɪlɪŋ] 1 **adj** a **to be ~ to do** être prêt *or* disposé à faire, vouloir bien faire, faire volontiers; **I'm quite ~ to tell him** je veux bien le lui dire, je ne demande pas mieux que de le lui dire; **he wasn't very ~ to help** il n'était pas tellement prêt à aider; **those who are ~ and able to go** ceux qui veulent et qui peuvent y aller; **God ~** si Dieu le veut.

b *helper, worker* bien disposé, de bonne volonté. **a few ~ men** quelques hommes de bonne volonté; **~ hands helped him to his feet** des mains secourables se tendirent et l'aidèrent à se lever; **there were plenty of ~ hands** il y avait beaucoup d'offres d'assistance; **he's very ~** il est plein de bonne volonté; (*fig*) **the ~ horse** la bonne âme (qui se sacrifie toujours).

c (*voluntary*) *obedience, help, sacrifice* spontané.

2 **n: to show ~** faire preuve de bonne volonté.

willingly ['wɪlɪŋlɪ] **adv** (*with goodwill*) volontiers, de bon cœur *or* gré; (*voluntarily*) volontairement, spontanément. **will you help? — ~!** peux-tu nous aider? — volontiers!; **did he do it ~ or did you have to make him?** l'a-t-il fait de lui-même *or* volontairement *or* spontanément ou bien vous a-t-il fallu le forcer?

willingness ['wɪlɪŋnɪs] **n** bonne volonté; (*enthusiasm*) empressement *m* (*to do* à faire). **I don't doubt his ~, just his competence** ce n'est pas sa bonne volonté que je mets en doute mais sa compétence; **I was grateful for his ~ to help** je lui étais reconnaissant de bien vouloir m'aider *or* de son empressement à m'aider; **in spite of the ~ with which she agreed** malgré la bonne volonté qu'elle a mise à accepter, malgré son empressement à accepter.

will-o'-the-wisp ['wɪləðə'wɪsp] **n** (*lit, fig*) feu follet *m*.

willow ['wɪləʊ] 1 **n** (*tree*) saule *m*; (*wood*) (bois *m* de) saule (*NonC*); (*for baskets etc*) osier *m*. (*fig: cricket/baseball bat*) **the ~*** la batte (de cricket/de baseball); *see* **pussy, weeping.** 2 **comp** *bat etc* de *or* en saule; *basket* d'osier, en osier **▸ willowherb** (*Bot*) épilobe *m* **▸ willow pattern** motif *m* chinois (dans les tons bleus); **willow pattern china** porcelaine *f* à motif chinois **▸ willow warbler** (*Orn*) pouillot *m* fitis.

willowy ['wɪləʊɪ] **adj** *person* svelte, élancé; *object* fin, mince.

willy* ['wɪlɪ] **n** = **willie a**.

willy-nilly ['wɪlɪ'nɪlɪ] **adv** bon gré mal gré.

wilt[1]†† [wɪlt] **2nd pers sg of will 1**.

wilt[2] [wɪlt] 1 **vi** *[flower]* se faner, se flétrir; *[plant]* se dessécher, mourir; *[person]* (*grow exhausted*) s'affaiblir, s'alanguir; (*lose courage*) fléchir, être pris de découragement; *[effort, enthusiasm etc]* diminuer. **the guests began to ~ in the heat of the room** la chaleur de la pièce commençait à incommoder les invités; **he ~ed visibly when I caught his eye** son visage s'est décomposé quand il a vu mon regard.

2 **vt** *flower* faner, flétrir; *plant* dessécher.

Wilts [wɪlts] **abbr of Wiltshire.**

wily ['waɪlɪ] **adj** rusé, astucieux, malin (*f* -igne). **he's a ~ old devil*** *or* **bird*** *or* **fox*, he's as ~ as a fox** c'est un malin *or* un vieux roublard‡ *or* un vieux renard.

wimp* [wɪmp] **n** (*pej*) mauviette *f*, femmelette *f*, poule *f* mouillée.

▸wimp out‡ vi se dégonfler.

wimpish* ['wɪmpɪʃ] **adj** *behaviour, reaction* de mauviette. **his ~ friend** sa mauviette d'ami.

wimpishly* ['wɪmpɪʃlɪ] **adv** *say* misérablement; *behave* comme une mauviette.

wimple ['wɪmpl] **n** guimpe *f*.

wimpy* ['wɪmpɪ] **adj** = **wimpish**.

win [wɪn] (**vb: pret, ptp won**) 1 **n** (*Sport etc*) victoire *f*. **another ~ for Scotland** une nouvelle victoire pour l'Écosse; **it was a convincing ~ for France** la victoire revenait indiscutablement à la France; **to have a ~** gagner; **to back a horse for a ~** jouer un cheval gagnant.

2 **vi** a (*in war, sport, competition etc*) gagner, l'emporter. **to ~ by a length** gagner *or* l'emporter d'une longueur; **go in and ~!** vas-y et ne reviens pas sans la victoire!; **he was playing to ~** il jouait pour gagner; **who's ~ning?** qui est-ce qui gagne?; **to ~ hands down*** gagner les doigts dans le nez‡, gagner haut la main, (*esp in race*) arriver dans un fauteuil; (*US Sport*) **~, place and show** gagnant, placé et troisième; (*in reluctant agreement*) **you ~!** soit! tu as gagné!; **I** (*or* **you** *etc*) **(just) can't ~** j'ai (*or* on a *etc*) toujours tort.

b **to ~ free** *or* **loose** se dégager (*from sth* de qch).

3 **vt** a (*gain victory in*) *war, match, competition, bet* gagner; *race* gagner, enlever. **to ~ the day** (*Mil*) remporter la victoire; (*gen*) l'emporter.

b (*compete for and get*) *prize* gagner, remporter; *victory* remporter; *scholarship* obtenir; *sum of money* gagner. **he won it for growing radishes** il l'a gagné *or* remporté *or* eu pour sa culture de radis; **he won £5 from her at cards** il lui a gagné 5 livres aux cartes; **his essay won him a trip to France** sa dissertation lui a valu un voyage en France.

c (*obtain etc*) *fame, fortune* trouver; *sb's attention* capter, captiver; *sb's friendship* gagner; *sb's esteem* gagner, conquérir; *sympathy, support, admirers, supporters* s'attirer; *coal, ore etc* extraire (*from* de). **to ~ friends** se faire des amis; **to ~ a name** *or* **a reputation (for o.s.)** se faire un nom *or* une réputation (*as* en tant que); **this won him the friendship of ...** ceci lui a gagné *or* valu l'amitié de ...; **this won him the attention of the crowd** ça lui a valu l'attention de la foule; **this manoeuvre won him the time he needed** cette manœuvre lui a valu d'obtenir le délai dont il avait besoin; **to ~ sb's love/respect** se faire aimer/respecter de qn; **to ~ sb to one's cause** gagner *or* rallier qn à sa cause; (†) **to ~ a lady** *or* **a lady's hand (in marriage)** obtenir la main d'une demoiselle.

d (*reach*) *summit, shore, goal* parvenir à, arriver à. **he won his way to the top of his profession** il a durement gagné sa place au sommet de sa profession.

▸win back vt sep *cup, trophy* reprendre (*from* à); *gaming loss etc* recouvrer; *land* reconquérir (*from* sur), reprendre (*from* à); *sb's favour, support, esteem, one's girlfriend etc* reconquérir. **I won the money back from him** j'ai repris l'argent qu'il m'avait gagné.

▸win out vi a l'emporter, gagner. b = **win through**.

▸win over, win round vt sep *person* convaincre, persuader; *voter* gagner à sa cause. **I won him over to my point of view** je l'ai gagné à ma façon de voir; **the figures won him over to our way of thinking** les statistiques l'ont fait se rallier à notre façon de voir; **I won him over eventually** j'ai fini par le convaincre *or* le persuader; **to win sb over to doing sth** convaincre *or* persuader qn de faire qch.

▸win through vi y arriver, y parvenir, réussir (à la fin). **you'll win through all right!** tu y arriveras!, tu en viendras à bout!; (*in competition etc*) **he won through to the second round** il a gagné le premier tour.

wince [wɪns] 1 **vi** (*flinch*) tressaillir; (*grimace*) grimacer (de douleur *or* dégoût *etc*). **he ~d at the thought/at the sight** cette pensée/ce spectacle l'a fait tressaillir *or* grimacer; **he ~d as I touched his injured arm** il a sursauté *or* il a fait une grimace de douleur lorsque j'ai touché son bras blessé; **without wincing** sans broncher *or* sourciller. 2 **n** tressaillement *m*, crispation *f*; (*grimace*) grimace *f* (de douleur *or* dégoût *etc*). **to give a ~ = to wince;** *see* **1.**

winch [wɪntʃ] 1 **n** treuil *m*. 2 **vt: to ~ sth up/down** *etc* monter/descendre *etc* qch au treuil; **they ~ed him out of the water** ils l'ont hissé hors de l'eau au treuil.

Winchester ['wɪntʃɪstəʳ] **n** ® (*Comput*) ~ **(disk)** disque *m* Winchester; ~ **(rifle)** (carabine *f*) Winchester *f*.

wind¹ [wɪnd] 1 **n** a vent *m*. **high ~** grand vent, vent violent *or* fort; **following ~** vent arrière; **the ~ is rising/dropping** le vent se lève/tombe; **the ~ was in the east** le vent venait de l'est *or* était à l'est; **where is the ~?, which way is the ~?** d'où vient le vent?; **to go/run like the ~** aller/filer comme le vent; **between ~ and water** (*Naut*) près de la ligne de flottaison; (*fig*) sur la corde raide; (*Naut*) **to sail into the ~** avancer contre le vent; **to sail close to the ~** (*Naut*) naviguer au plus près; (*fig: nearly break law*) friser l'illégalité; (*fig: in jokes etc*) friser la vulgarité; (*Naut*) **to run before the ~** avoir vent arrière; (*fig*) **to take the ~ out of sb's sails** couper l'herbe sous le pied de qn; **to see how the ~ blows** *or* **lies** (*Naut*) prendre l'aire du vent; (*fig*) voir la tournure que prennent (*or* vont prendre *etc*) les choses, prendre le vent; (*fig*) **the ~ of change is blowing** un grand courant d'air frais souffle; (*fig*) **there's something in the ~** il y a quelque chose dans l'air, il se prépare quelque chose; (*fig*) **to get ~ of sth** avoir vent de qch; **he threw caution to the ~s** il a fait fi de toute prudence; *see* **ill, north, sail** *etc*.

b (*breath*) souffle *m*. **he has still plenty of ~** il a encore du souffle; **he had lost his ~** il avait perdu le souffle *or* perdu haleine; **to knock the ~ out of sb** *[blow]* couper la respiration *or* le souffle à qn; *[fighter]* mettre qn hors d'haleine; *[fall, exertion]* essouffler qn, mettre qn hors d'haleine; **to get one's ~ back** reprendre (son) souffle, reprendre haleine; (*fig pej*) **it's all ~** ce n'est que du vent, c'est du vent; (*Brit fig*) **to put the ~ up sb*** flanquer la frousse à qn*; (*Brit*) **to get/have the ~ up*** attraper/avoir la frousse* (*about* à propos de); *see* **second, sound²** *etc*.

c (*Med*) vents *mpl*, gaz *mpl*. **the baby has got ~** le bébé a des vents; **to break ~** lâcher un vent, avoir des gaz; **to bring up ~** avoir un renvoi.

d (*Mus*) **the ~** les instruments *mpl* à vent.

2 **comp** *erosion etc* éolien ▸**windbag*** (*fig pej*) moulin *m* à paroles ▸**wind-bells** = **wind-chimes** ▸**windblown** *person, hair* ébouriffé par le vent; *tree* fouetté par le vent ▸**wind-borne** *seeds, pollen* transporté *or* porté par le vent ▸**windbreak** (*tree, fence etc*) abat-vent *m inv*; (*for camping etc*) pare-vent *m inv* ▸**Windbreaker** ® = **windcheater** ▸**windburn** (*Med*) brûlure *f* épidermique (due au vent) ▸**windburned** bruni ▸**windcheater** (*Brit*) anorak léger, coupe-vent *m inv* ▸**windchill factor** (*Met*) facteur *m* d'abaissement de la température dû au vent ▸**wind-chimes** carillon éolien ▸**wind cone** manche *f* à air ▸**wind deflector** (*Aut*) déflecteur *m* ▸**windfall** (*lit*) fruit(s) abattu(s) par le vent; (*fig*) aubaine *f*, manne *f* (tombée du ciel); (*Econ*) **windfall profit** profit *m* d'aubaine ▸**wind farm** éoliennes *fpl*, installation *f* d'éoliennes ▸**windflower** anémone *f* ▸**wind gauge** anémomètre *m* ▸**wind instrument** (*Mus*) instrument *m* à vent ▸**windjammer** (*Naut*) grand voilier (de la marine marchande) ▸**wind machine** (*Theat, Cin*) *machine qui produit du vent ou le bruit du vent* ▸**windmill** moulin *m* à vent; (*fig*) **to tilt at** *or* **fight windmills** se battre contre les moulins à vent; (*Volleyball*) **windmill service** service *m* balancier ▸**windpipe** (*Anat*) trachée *f* ▸**wind power** énergie *f* éolienne ▸**windproof adj** protégeant du vent, qui ne laisse pas passer le vent ◊ **vt** protéger du *or* contre le vent ▸**windscreen** (*esp Brit Aut*) pare-brise *m inv*; **windscreen washer** lave-glace *m inv*; **windscreen wiper** essuie-glace *m inv* ▸**windshield** (*US*) = **windscreen** ▸**windsleeve, windsock** = **wind cone** ▸**windstorm** vent *m* de tempête ▸**windsurf** *etc see* **windsurf** *etc* ▸**windswept** venteux, battu des vents, balayé par le(s) vent(s) ▸**wind tunnel** (*Phys*) tunnel *m* aérodynamique; **there was a wind tunnel between the two tower blocks** il y avait un courant d'air à renverser les gens entre les deux tours ▸**windward** *see* **windward**.

3 **vt** a **to ~ sb** *[blow etc]* couper la respiration *or* le souffle à qn; *[fighter]* mettre qn hors d'haleine; *[fall, exertion]* essouffler qn, mettre qn hors d'haleine; **he was ~ed by the blow, the blow ~ed him** le coup lui a coupé le souffle *or* la respiration; **he was quite ~ed by the climb** l'ascension l'avait essoufflé *or* mis hors d'haleine; **I'm only ~ed** j'ai la respiration coupée, c'est tout.

b *horse* laisser souffler.

c (*Hunting: scent*) avoir vent de.

d **to ~ a baby** faire faire son rot* *or* son renvoi à un bébé.

wind² [wɪnd] **pret, ptp winded** *or* **wound vt: to ~ the horn** sonner du cor; (*Hunting*) sonner de la trompe.

wind³ [waɪnd] **(vb: pret, ptp wound)** 1 **n** a (*bend: in river etc*) tournant *m*, coude *m*.

b **to give one's watch a ~** remonter sa montre; **give the handle another ~ or two** donne un ou deux tours de manivelle de plus.

2 **vt** a (*roll*) *thread, rope etc* enrouler (*on* sur, *round* autour de); (*wrap*) envelopper (*in* dans). **to ~ wool (into a ball)** enrouler de la laine (pour en faire une pelote); **~ this round your head** enroule-toi ça autour de la tête; **with the rope wound tightly round his waist** la corde bien enroulée autour de la taille, la corde lui ceignant étroitement la taille; **she wound a shawl round the baby, she wound the baby in a shawl** elle a enveloppé le bébé dans un châle; **to ~ one's arms round sb** enlacer qn; **the snake/rope wound itself round a branch** le serpent/la corde s'est enroulé(e) autour d'une branche; **he slowly wound his way home** il s'en revint lentement chez lui, il prit lentement le chemin du retour; *see also* **3** *and* **finger** *etc*.

b *clock, watch, toy* remonter; *handle* donner un (*or* des) tour(s) de.

3 **vi** (*also* **~ its way**) *[river, path]* **to ~ along** serpenter, faire des zigzags; **the road ~s through the valley** la route serpente à travers la vallée, la route traverse la vallée en serpentant; **the procession wound through the town** la procession a serpenté à travers la ville; **the line of cars wound slowly up the hill** les voitures ont lentement gravi la colline en une file ondulante *or* sinueuse; **to ~ up/down** *[path etc]* monter/descendre en serpentant *or* en zigzags; *[stairs, steps]* monter/descendre en tournant; *[snake, ivy etc]* **to ~ round sth** s'enrouler autour de qch.

▸**wind down** 1 **vi** a *see* **wind³ 3.** b (*: *relax*) se détendre, se relaxer*. c (*fig*) **to be winding down** *[event]* tirer à sa fin; *[energy, enthusiasm, interest]* diminuer, être en perte de vitesse. 2 **vt sep** a (*on rope/winch etc*) faire descendre (au bout d'une corde/avec un treuil *etc*). b *car window* baisser. c (*fig*) *department, service etc* réduire progressivement (en vue d'un démantèlement éventuel).

▸**wind forward vt sep** = **wind on.**

▸**wind off vt sep** dérouler, dévider.

▸**wind on vt sep** enrouler.

▸**wind up** 1 **vi** a *see* **wind³ 3.**

b *[meeting, discussion]* se terminer, finir (*with* par). **they wound up in Cannes** ils ont fini *or* ils se sont retrouvés à Cannes; **he wound up as a doctor** il a fini (comme) médecin; (*fig: finish in possession of*) **to wind up with sth** se retrouver avec qch.

c (*in debate*) **he wound up for the Government** c'est lui qui a résumé la position du gouvernement dans le discours de clôture.

2 **vt sep** a *object on rope/winch etc* faire monter (au bout d'une corde/avec un treuil *etc*); (*fig: end*) *meeting, speech* clôturer, clore, terminer (*with* par); (*Comm*) *business* liquider. **to wind up one's affairs** liquider ses affaires; (*Banking*) **to wind up an account** clôturer *or* clore un compte.

b *car window* monter, fermer.

c *watch etc* remonter. (*fig: tense*) **to be wound up*** être tendu *or* crispé (*about* à propos de); **it gets me all wound up (inside)***ça me retourne*.

d (*tease*) *person* faire marcher*.

3 **winding-up n** *see* **winding 3.**

4 **wind-up n** (*practical joke*) blague* *f*, bobard* *m*.

winder ['waɪndəʳ] **n** *[watch etc]* remontoir *m*; (*for car windows*) lève-glace *m*, lève-vitre *m*; (*for thread etc*) dévidoir *m*; (*person*) dévideur *m*, -euse *f*.

winding ['waɪndɪŋ] 1 **adj** *road* sinueux, tortueux; *river* sinueux, qui serpente. **a ~ staircase** un escalier tournant. 2 **n** a (*NonC: see* **wind³ 2**) enroulement *m*; enveloppement *m*; remontage *m*; (*onto bobbin*) bobinage *m*. b **~(s)** *[road]* zigzags *mpl*; *[river]* méandres *mpl*. 3 **comp** ▸**winding sheet** linceul *m* ▸**winding-up** *[meeting, account]* clôture *f*; *[business, one's affairs]* liquidation *f*; (*Jur, Fin*) **winding-up arrangements** concordat *m*.

windlass ['wɪndləs] **n** guindeau *m*, treuil *m*.

windless ['wɪndlɪs] **adj** sans vent. **it was a ~ day** il n'y avait ce jour-là pas un brin *or* un souffle de vent.

window ['wɪndəʊ] 1 **n** a (*gen, also Comput*) fenêtre *f*; (*in car, train*) vitre *f*, glace *f*; (~ *pane*) vitre, carreau *m*; (*stained-glass* ~) vitrail *m*, (*larger*) verrière *f*; *[shop]* vitrine *f*, devanture *f*, (*more modest*) étalage *m*; *[café etc]* vitrine; (*in post office, ticket office etc*) guichet *m*; (*in envelope*) fenêtre. **I saw her at the ~** je l'ai vue à la fenêtre (*or* à la vitre); **don't lean out of the ~** ne te penche pas par la fenêtre; (*in train, car etc*) ne te penche pas en dehors; **to look/throw** *etc* **out of the ~** regarder/jeter *etc* par la fenêtre; (*in car etc*) regarder/jeter dehors; (*fig*) **to go** *or* **fly** *or* **disappear out of the ~** s'évanouir, se volatiliser; **well, there's another plan out the ~!*** eh bien, voilà encore un plan de fichu* *or* qui tombe à l'eau; **the ~s look out on to fields** les fenêtres donnent sur *or* ont vue sur des champs; **to break a ~** casser une vitre *or* un carreau; **to clean the ~s** nettoyer *or* laver les carreaux; (*Comm*) **to put sth in the ~** mettre qch en vitrine *or* à la devanture; (*Comm*) **I saw it in the ~** je l'ai vu à l'étalage *or* à la devanture *or* en vitrine; (*Comm*) **the ~s are lovely at Christmas time** les vitrines sont très belles au moment de Noël; (*Comm*) **in the front of the ~** sur le devant de la vitrine; (*fig*) **there is perhaps a ~ of opportunity to change ...** nous avons peut-être maintenant la possibilité de changer ... .

b (*Space: also* **launch ~**) fenêtre *f or* créneau *m* de lancement.

2 **comp** ▸**window box** jardinière *f* (*à plantes*) ▸**window cleaner** (*person*) laveur *m*, -euse *f* de vitres *or* carreaux; (*substance*) produit *m* à nettoyer les vitres *or* carreaux ▸**window-cleaning: to do the window-cleaning** faire les vitres *or* carreaux ▸**window dresser** (*Comm*) étalagiste *mf* ▸**window dressing** (*Comm*) composition *f* d'étalage; **she is learning window dressing** elle fait des études d'étalagiste; (*fig pej*) **it's just window dressing** ce n'est qu'une façade

► **window envelope** enveloppe *f* à fenêtre ► **window frame** châssis *m* (de fenêtre) ► **window ledge** = **windowsill** ► **window pane** vitre *f*, carreau *m* ► **window seat** (*in room*) banquette *f* (située sous la fenêtre); (*in vehicle*) place *f* côté fenêtre *inv* ► **window shade** (*US*) store *m* ► **window-shopper**: **she's a great window-shopper** elle adore faire du lèche-vitrines ► **window-shopping** lèche-vitrines *m*; **to go window-shopping** faire du lèche-vitrines ► **windowsill** (*inside*) appui *m* de fenêtre; (*outside*) rebord *m* de fenêtre ► **window winder** (*Aut*) lève-glace *m*, lève-vitre *m*.

windsurf ['wɪndsɜːf] **vi** (*also:* **go ~ing**) faire de la planche à voile.

Windsurfer ['wɪndsɜːfəʳ] **n** ® (*board*) planche *f* à voile; (*person*) (véli)planchiste *mf*.

windsurfing ['wɪndsɜːfɪŋ] **n** planche *f* à voile (*sport*).

windward ['wɪndwəd] **1 adj** qui est au vent *or* contre le vent, qui est du côté du vent. (*Geog*) **the W~ Islands** les îles *fpl* du Vent. **2 adv** du côté du vent, au vent, contre le vent. **3 n** côté *m* du vent. **to look to ~** regarder dans la direction du vent; **to get to ~ of sth** se mettre contre le vent par rapport à qch.

windy ['wɪndɪ] **adj a** *place* battu *or* balayé par les vents, venteux, exposé au vent, éventé; *day, weather* de (grand) vent. **it's ~ today** il fait *or* il y a du vent aujourd'hui, le vent souffle aujourd'hui. **b** (*Brit* * *fig: scared*) **to be/get ~ about sth** paniquer* à cause de qch. **c** (*US* *: *wordy*) *person, speech* verbeux.

wine [waɪn] **1 n** vin *m*. **elderberry ~** vin de sureau.
2 vt: **to ~ and dine sb** emmener qn faire un dîner bien arrosé.
3 vi: **to ~ and dine** faire un dîner bien arrosé.
4 comp *bottle, cellar* à vin; (*colour*) lie de vin *inv or* lie-de-vin *inv* ► **wine bar** ≃ pub *m* ► **winebibber** grand(e) buveur *m*, -euse *f* (de vin) ► **wine-bottling** mise *f* en bouteilles (du vin) ► **wine box** cubitainer *m* ® ► **wine cask** fût *m*, tonneau *m* (à vin) ► **wine-coloured** lie de vin *inv or* lie-de-vin *inv* ► **wine cooler** rafraîchisseur *m* à vin ► **wineglass** verre *m* à vin ► **wine grower** viticulteur *m*, -trice *f*, vigneron(ne) *m(f)* ► **winegrowing n** viticulture *f*, culture *f* de la vigne ◊ **adj** *district, industry* vinicole, viticole ► **wine list** carte *f* des vins ► **wine merchant** (*Brit*) marchand(e) *m(f)* de vin; (*on larger scale*) négociant(e) *m(f)* en vins ► **wine press** pressoir *m* (à vin) ► **wine-shop** boutique *f* du marchand de vin ► **wineskin** outre *f* à vin ► **wine taster** (*person*) dégustateur *m*, -trice *f* (de vins); (*cup etc*) tâte-vin *m inv* ► **wine tasting** dégustation *f* (de vins) ► **wine vinegar** vinaigre *m* de vin ► **wine waiter** sommelier *m*.

wined up* ['waɪnd'ʌp] **adj** (*US*) bourré‡, noir*.

winery ['waɪnərɪ] **n** (*US*) établissement *m* vinicole.

wing [wɪŋ] **1 n a** (*gen, Zool; also of plane*) aile *f*. **to be on the ~** être en vol, voler; **to shoot a bird on the ~** tirer un oiseau au vol *or* à la volée; *[bird]* **to take ~** prendre son vol *or* son essor, s'envoler; (*fig*) **he** *or* **his heart took ~** son cœur s'emplit de joie; (*fig: vanish*) **to take ~s** disparaître, s'envoler, fondre comme neige au soleil; (*fig*) **to take sb under one's ~** prendre qn sous son aile; (*fig*) **on the ~s of fantasy** sur les ailes de l'imagination; (*fig*) **fear lent** *or* **gave him ~s** la peur lui donnait des ailes; (*Aviat: insignia*) **~s** insigne *m* (de pilote); (*fig*) **to earn** *or* **win** *or* **get one's ~s** faire ses preuves, gagner ses éperons, prendre du grade *or* du galon; *see* **clip²**, **spread** *etc*.
b (*Pol*) aile *f*. **on the left/right ~ of the party** sur l'aile gauche/droite du parti.
c (*Sport*) (*person*) ailier *m*, aile *m*. **~ (three-quarter)** trois-quarts aile *m*; **left/right ~** ailier gauche/droit; **he plays (on the) left ~** il est ailier gauche.
d (*Brit: of car*) aile *f*; *[armchair]* oreille *f*, oreillard *m*.
e *[building, mansion]* aile *f*.
f (*of organization etc*) aile *f*. **it is the political ~ of this terrorist group** c'est l'aile politique de ce groupe terroriste.
2 npl (*Theat*) **the ~s** les coulisses *fpl*, la coulisse; **to stand** *or* **stay in the ~s** (*Theat*) se tenir dans les coulisses; (*fig*) rester dans la (*or* les) coulisse(s); (*fig*) **to wait in the ~s for sb to do sth** attendre dans la *or* les coulisse(s) que qn fasse qch.
3 comp ► **wing case** (*Zool*) élytre *m* ► **wing chair** bergère *f* à oreilles ► **wing collar** col cassé ► **wing commander** (*Aviat*) lieutenant-colonel *m* (de l'armée de l'air) ► **wing flap** (*Aviat*) aileron *m* ► **wing-footed** (*liter*) aux pieds ailés ► **wing-forward** (*Rugby*) ailier *m* ► **wing mirror** (*Brit Aut*) rétroviseur *m* de côté ► **wing nut** papillon *m*, écrou *m* à ailettes ► **wingspan, wingspread** envergure *f* ► **wing three-quarter** (*Rugby*) trois-quarts aile *m* ► **wing tip** bout *m* de l'aile.
4 vt a (*wound*) *bird* blesser *or* toucher (à l'aile); *person* blesser au bras (*or* à la jambe *etc*).
b (*liter*) **to ~ an arrow at sth** darder une flèche en direction de qch; (*liter*) **fear ~ed his steps** la peur lui donnait des ailes; **to ~ one's way** = **to wing**; *see* **4**.
c (*US*) *[actor, speaker etc]* **to ~ it*** improviser.
5 vi (*also* **~ one's way**) voler. **they ~ed over the sea** ils ont survolé la mer.

wingding‡ ['wɪŋ,dɪŋ] **n** (*US*) fête *f*, boum* *f*.

winge* ['wɪndʒ] **vi** = **whinge**.

winged [wɪŋd] **adj** *creature, god, statue* ailé. **the W~ Victory of Samothrace** la Victoire de Samothrace.

-winged [wɪŋd] **adj ending in comps**: **white-winged** aux ailes blanches.

winger ['wɪŋəʳ] **n** (*Sport*) ailier *m*. (*Pol*) **the left-/right-~s** ceux qui sont de gauche/droite.

wingless ['wɪŋlɪs] **adj** sans ailes; *insect* aptère.

wink [wɪŋk] **1 n** clin *m* d'œil; (*blink*) clignement *m*. **to give sb a ~** faire un clin d'œil à qn; **with a ~** en clignant de l'œil; **in a ~, as quick as a ~** en un clin d'œil; **I didn't get a ~ of sleep** je n'ai pas fermé l'œil (de la nuit); *see* **forty, sleep, tip²** *etc*. **2 vi** *[person]* faire un clin d'œil (*to, at* à); (*blink*) cligner des yeux; *[star, light]* clignoter. (*fig*) **to ~ at sth** fermer les yeux sur qch, prendre qch à la légère. **3 vt**: **to ~ one's eye** faire un clin d'œil (*at sb* à qn); **to ~ one's eyes** cligner des yeux; **to ~ a tear back** *or* **away** cligner de l'œil pour chasser une larme.

winker ['wɪŋkəʳ] **n** (*Brit Aut*) clignotant *m*.

winking ['wɪŋkɪŋ] **1 adj** *light, signal* clignotant. **2 n** clins *mpl* d'œil; (*blinking*) clignements *mpl* d'yeux. **it was as easy as ~** c'était simple comme bonjour.

winkle ['wɪŋkl] **1 n** (*Brit*) bigorneau *m*. **2 vt**: **to ~ sth out of sth/sb** extirper qch de qch/qn. **3 comp** ► **winkle pickers*** (*Brit: shoes*) chaussures *fpl* pointues.

winnable ['wɪnəbl] **adj** gagnable.

winner ['wɪnəʳ] **n** (*in fight, argument*) vainqueur *m*; (*Sport*) gagnant(e) *m(f)*, vainqueur; (*in competitions etc*) gagnant(e); (*horse/car/essay etc*) (cheval *m*/voiture *f*/composition *f etc*) gagnant(e). **to be the ~** gagner; (*Tennis*) **that ball was a ~** cette balle était imparable; (*fig*) **his latest disc/show is a ~*** son dernier album/spectacle va faire un malheur*; (*fig*) **he's a ~!*** il est sensass!‡; **he picked** *or* **spotted the ~** (*Racing*) il a choisi le cheval gagnant; (*fig*) il a tiré le bon numéro; **I think he's on to a ~** (*will win*) je crois qu'il va gagner; (*has chosen ~*) je crois qu'il a tiré le bon numéro.

winning ['wɪnɪŋ] **1 adj a** *person, dog, car etc* gagnant; *blow, stroke, shot etc* décisif, de la victoire. **the ~ goal came in the last 5 minutes** le but qui a décidé de la victoire a été marqué dans les 5 dernières minutes. **b** (*captivating*) *person* charmant, adorable; *smile, manner* charmeur, engageant. **the child has ~ ways, the child has a ~ way with him** cet enfant a une grâce irrésistible. **2 npl** (*Betting etc*) **~s** gains *mpl*. **3 comp** ► **winning post** poteau *m* d'arrivée.

winningly ['wɪnɪŋlɪ] **adv** d'une manière charmeuse, d'un air engageant.

Winnipeg ['wɪnɪpeg] **n** Winnipeg.

winnow ['wɪnəʊ] **vt** *grain* vanner. (*fig liter*) **to ~ truth from falsehood** démêler le vrai d'avec le faux.

winnower ['wɪnəʊəʳ] **n** (*person*) vanneur *m*, -euse *f*; (*machine*) tarare *m*.

wino‡ ['waɪnəʊ] **n** poivrot* *m*, ivrogne *mf*.

winsome ['wɪnsəm] **adj** séduisant, engageant, charmeur.

winsomely ['wɪnsəmlɪ] **adv** d'une manière séduisante, d'un air engageant.

winsomeness ['wɪnsəmnɪs] **n** (*NonC*) charme *m*, séduction *f*.

winter ['wɪntəʳ] **1 n** hiver *m*. **in ~** en hiver; **in the ~ of 1977** pendant l'hiver de 1977; **"A W~'s Tale"** "Le Conte d'hiver".
2 comp *weather, day, season, temperatures, activities, residence* d'hiver, hivernal ► **winter ascent** (*Climbing*) hivernale *f* ► **winter clothes** vêtements *mpl* d'hiver ► **winter depression** blues *m* de l'hiver ► **wintergreen** (*Bot*) gaulthérie *f*; **oil of wintergreen** essence *f* de wintergreen ► **winter holidays** vacances *fpl* d'hiver ► **winterkill** (*US*) **vt** *plant* tuer par le gel ◊ **vi** être tué par le gel ► **Winter Olympics** (*Sport*) Jeux *mpl* olympiques d'hiver ► **winter sleep** sommeil hibernal, hibernation *f* ► **winter sports** sports *mpl* d'hiver ► **wintertime** hiver *m*.
3 vi hiverner, passer l'hiver.
4 vt *animals* hiverner.

winterize ['wɪntəraɪz] **vt** (*US*) préparer pour l'hiver.

wintry ['wɪntrɪ] **adj** *sky, weather* d'hiver, hivernal; (*fig*) *smile, gesture* glacial. **in ~ conditions** par un temps hivernal; **~ conditions on the roads** conditions hasardeuses sur les routes (dues au temps hivernal).

wipe [waɪp] **1 n** coup *m* de torchon (*or* d'éponge *etc*). **to give sth a ~** donner un coup de torchon (*or* d'éponge *etc*) à qch.
2 comp ► **wipe-out** (*destruction*) destruction *f*, annihilation *f*; (*US Windsurfing*) chute *f*, gamelle* *f*.
3 vt a *table, dishes, floor* essuyer (*with* avec). **to ~ one's hands/face/eyes** s'essuyer les mains/le visage/les yeux (*on* sur, *with* avec); **to ~ one's feet** (*with towel*) s'essuyer les pieds; (*on mat*) s'essuyer les pieds, essuyer ses pieds; **to ~ one's nose** se moucher; **to ~ one's bottom** s'essuyer; **he ~d the glass dry** il a soigneusement essuyé le verre; **to ~ the blackboard** effacer *or* essuyer *or* nettoyer le tableau; (*fig*) **to ~ the slate clean** passer l'éponge, tout effacer (*fig*); (*fig*) **to ~ the floor with sb*** réduire qn en miettes*.
b (*Comput, TV, Sound Recording etc*) *tape, disk, video* effacer. **to ~ sth from a tape** *etc* effacer qch sur une bande *etc*.

►**wipe away vt sep** *tears* essuyer; *marks* effacer.

►**wipe down vt sep** *surface, wall etc* essuyer.

►**wipe off vt sep** effacer. **that will ~ the smile off her face!*** après ça on va voir si elle a toujours le sourire!

►**wipe out** 1 vt sep a *container* bien essuyer; *writing, error etc* effacer; (*fig*) *insult* effacer, laver; *debt* amortir; *the past, memory* oublier, effacer. **to wipe out an old score** régler une vieille dette (*fig*). b (*annihilate*) *town, people, army* anéantir. c *opposing team* écraser. **to wipe sb out*** *[person]* régler son compte à qn; *[event, news]* anéantir qn. 2 **wipe-out** n *see* **wipe 2**.

►**wipe up** 1 vi essuyer la vaisselle. 2 vt sep essuyer.

wiper ['waɪpəʳ] n (*cloth*) torchon *m*; (*Brit Aut*) essuie-glace *m inv*. (*Brit Aut*) ~ **arm** bras *m* d'essuie-glace.

wire ['waɪəʳ] 1 n a (*NonC: substance*) fil *m* (métallique *or* de fer); (*Elec*) fil (électrique); (*piece of* ~) fil; (*snare*) collet *m*, lacet *m*; (~ *fence*) grillage *m*, treillis *m* métallique. **copper** ~ fil de cuivre; **telephone** ~**s** fils téléphoniques; **cheese** ~ fil à couper; (*fig*) **he had to pull** ~**s to get the job** il a dû user de son influence *or* se faire pistonner *or* faire jouer le piston pour obtenir le poste; (*fig*) **to pull** ~**s for sb** exercer son influence pour aider qn, pistonner qn; (*fig*) **they got their** ~**s crossed*** il y a eu malentendu, ils se sont mal compris; (*more generally*) ils n'étaient pas sur la même longueur d'onde; (*US*) **to work** *etc* **down to the** ~* travailler *etc* jusqu'au bout *or* jusqu'au dernier moment; (*US fig*) **to go down to the** ~* (*of competition*) entrer dans sa phase finale; (*US fig*) **to come in** *or* **get in (just) under the** ~* arriver de justesse; *see* **barbed, live**[2] *etc*.

b (*telegram*) télégramme *m*.

c (*US **: spectacles*) ~**s** lunettes *fpl* à monture d'acier.

2 comp *object, device* de *or* en fil de fer ►**wire brush** brosse *f* métallique ►**wire cutters** cisaille *f*, pince coupante ►**wire-drawer, wire-drawing machine** étireuse *f* ►**wire gauge** calibre *m* (pour fils métalliques) ►**wire gauze** toile *f* métallique ►**wire glass** (*US*) verre armé ►**wire-haired terrier** terrier *m* à poils durs ►**wireman** (*US*) cableur *m* ►**wiremesh, wire netting** (*NonC*) treillis *m* métallique, grillage *m* ►**wire-puller: he's a wire-puller** il n'hésite pas à se faire pistonner *or* à faire jouer le piston ►**wire-pulling** le piston ►**wire rope** câble *m* métallique ►**wire service** (*US: Press etc*) agence *f* de presse utilisant des téléscripteurs ►**wiretap** vi mettre un (*or* des) téléphone(s) sur écoute ◊ vt mettre sur écoute ►**wiretapping** mise *f* sur écoute d'une ligne téléphonique ►**wire wool** paille *f* de fer ►**wireworks** tréfilerie *f*.

3 vt a (*also* ~ **up**) *opening, fence* grillager; *flowers, beads* monter sur fil de fer; (*Elec*) *house* faire l'installation électrique de; *circuit* installer. **to** ~ **sth to sth** relier *or* rattacher qch à qch (*avec du fil de fer*); (*Elec*) brancher qch sur qch, relier qch à qch; **to** ~ **a room (up) for sound** sonoriser une pièce; **it's all** ~**d (up) for television** l'antenne (réceptrice *or* émettrice) de télévision est déjà installée; **to be** ~**d** (*for cable TV*) être raccordé; (*bugged*) être équipé de micros cachés; (*US fig: tense*) ~**d-up**⁑ surexcité, tendu.

b (*telegraph*) télégraphier (*to* à).

4 vi télégraphier.

►**wire together** vt sep *objects* attacher (avec du fil de fer).

►**wire up** vt sep = **wire 3a**.

wireless ['waɪəlɪs] (*esp Brit*) 1 n a (*NonC:* ~ *telegraphy*) télégraphie *f* sans fil, T.S.F. *f*. **to send a message by** ~ envoyer un sans-fil; **they were communicating by** ~ ils communiquaient par sans-fil.

b (†*:* ~ *set*) (poste *m* de) T.S.F.† *f*. **on the** ~ à la T.S.F.

2 comp (†) *station, programme* radiophonique ►**wireless broadcast**† émission *f* de T.S.F.† ►**wireless message** radiogramme *m*, radio *m*, sans-fil *m* ►**wireless operator** radiotélégraphiste *mf*, radio *mf* ►**wireless room** cabine *f* radio *inv* ►**wireless set**† poste *m* de T.S.F.† ►**wireless telegraph, wireless telegraphy** télégraphie *f* sans fil, T.S.F. *f*, radiotélégraphie *f* ►**wireless telephone** téléphone *m* sans fil ►**wireless telephony** téléphonie *f* sans fil, radiotéléphonie *f*.

wiring ['waɪərɪŋ] n (*NonC: Elec*) installation *f* (électrique). **to have the** ~ **redone** faire refaire l'installation électrique (*in* de).

wiry ['waɪərɪ] adj *hair* dru; *animal* nerveux (*fig*); *person* noueux, maigre et nerveux.

Wisconsin [wɪs'kɒnsɪn] n Wisconsin *m*. **in** ~ dans le Wisconsin.

wisdom ['wɪzdəm] 1 n (*NonC*) *[person]* sagesse *f*; *[action, remark]* prudence *f*. 2 comp ►**wisdom tooth** dent *f* de sagesse.

wise[1] [waɪz] 1 adj (*sagacious*) *person* sage; *look, nod* averti; *thoughts, sayings* sage, avisé; (*learned*) savant; (*prudent*) prudent; (*judicious*) *action, remark* judicieux, sensé. **a** ~ **man** (*sagacious*) un sage; (*learned*) un savant, un érudit; (*Bible*) **the (Three) W**~ **Men** les (trois) rois mages; **he grew** ~**r with age** il s'est assagi avec l'âge *or* en vieillissant; **it wasn't very** ~ **to tell him that** ce n'était pas très judicieux *or* prudent de lui dire ça; **he was** ~ **enough to refuse** il s'est montré assez sage *or* prudent pour refuser, il a eu la sagesse *or* la prudence de refuser; **you would be** ~ **to do ...** il serait sage *or* prudent que tu fasses ...; **how** ~ **of you!** vous avez eu bien raison; **the wisest thing to do is ...** ce qu'il y a de plus sage à faire est ...; **to be** ~ **after the event** avoir raison après coup; **I'm none the wiser** ça ne m'avance pas beaucoup, je n'en sais pas plus pour autant; **nobody will be any the wiser if you ...** personne n'en saura rien *or* ne s'apercevra de rien si tu ...; ~ **guy*** gros malin*, type* *m* qui fait le malin; **to put sb** ~ **to sth*** mettre qn au courant *or* au parfum* de qch; **to be** ~ **to sth*** être au courant de qch; **to get** ~ **to sb*** piger* ce que veut (*or* fait) qn, piger* le petit jeu de qn.

2 comp ►**wiseacre** puits *m* de science (*iro*) ►**wisecrack*** n vanne⁑ *f* ◊ vi faire *or* sortir une (*or* des) vanne(s)⁑; **"need any help?" he wisecracked** "z'avez besoin de mes services?"* plaisanta-t-il.

►**wise up**⁑ 1 vi (*US*) **to wise up to sth** se mettre au parfum⁑ de qch, piger* qch. 2 vt sep: **to wise sb up** mettre qn au parfum* (*about* de); **to get wised up about sth** se faire mettre au parfum* de qch.

wise[2] [waɪz] n: **in no** ~ aucunement, en aucune façon *or* manière; **in this** ~ ainsi, de cette façon *or* manière.

...wise [waɪz] adv ending in comps a en ce qui concerne, du point de vue de, pour ce qui est de, côté*. **healthwise he's fine but moneywise things aren't too good** du point de vue santé *or* côté* santé ça va, mais pour ce qui est de l'argent *or* côté* argent ça ne va pas trop bien. b à la manière de, dans le sens de *etc; see* **clockwise, lengthways** *etc*.

wisely ['waɪzlɪ] adv (*sagaciously*) sagement; (*prudently*) prudemment, judicieusement. **he loved her not** ~ **but too well** il l'aimait follement dans tous les sens du terme; **he didn't behave very** ~ sa conduite n'a guère été prudente *or* judicieuse.

wish [wɪʃ] 1 vt a (*desire*) souhaiter, désirer. **I** ~ **that you** + *cond* je voudrais que vous + *subj*; **I** ~ **to be told when he comes** je souhaite *or* désire être informé de sa venue; **I** ~ **to be alone** je souhaite *or* désire *or* voudrais être seul; **he did not** ~ **it** il ne le souhaitait *or* désirait pas; **what do you** ~ **him to do?** que voudrais-tu *or* souhaites-tu *or* désires-tu qu'il fasse?; **I** ~ **I'd gone with you** j'aurais bien voulu vous accompagner, je regrette de ne pas vous avoir accompagné; **I** ~ **you had left with him** j'aurais bien voulu que tu sois parti avec lui, je regrette que tu ne sois pas parti avec lui; **I** ~ **I hadn't said that** je regrette d'avoir dit cela; **I** ~ **you'd stop talking!** tu ne peux donc pas te taire!; **I only** ~ **I'd known about that before!** si seulement j'avais su ça avant!, comme je regrette de n'avoir pas su ça avant!; **I** ~ **I could!** si seulement je pouvais!; **I** ~ **to heaven* he hadn't done it** mais bon sang* pourquoi est-il allé faire ça?; **I** ~ **it weren't so** si seulement il pouvait ne pas en être ainsi.

b (*desire for sb else*) souhaiter, vouloir; (*bid*) souhaiter. **he doesn't** ~ **her any ill** *or* **harm** il ne lui veut aucun mal; **I** ~ **you well** *or* **I** ~ **you (good) luck in what you're trying to do** je vous souhaite de réussir dans ce que vous voulez faire; (*iro*) **I** ~ **you well of it!, I** ~ **you luck of it!** je te souhaite bien du plaisir!; **he** ~**ed us (good) luck as we left** il nous a souhaité bonne chance au moment de partir; ~ **me luck!** souhaite-moi bonne chance!; **to** ~ **sb good morning** dire bonjour à qn, souhaiter *or* donner le bonjour à qn († *or hum*); **to** ~ **sb good-bye** dire au revoir à qn; **to** ~ **sb a happy birthday** souhaiter bon anniversaire à qn; **I** ~ **you every happiness!** je vous souhaite d'être très heureux!; **he** ~**ed us every happiness** il nous a fait tous ses souhaits de bonheur.

c (* *fig*) **the bike was** ~**ed on (to) me** je n'ai pas pu faire autrement que d'accepter le vélo; **the job was** ~**ed on (to) me** c'est un boulot qu'on m'a collé*; **I wouldn't** ~ **that on (to) anybody** c'est quelque chose que je ne souhaiterais pas à mon pire ennemi; **I wouldn't** ~ **him on anybody** je ne souhaiterais sa présence à personne; **I got her kids** ~**ed on (to) me for the holiday** elle m'a laissé ses gosses sur les bras pendant les vacances*.

2 vi faire un vœu. **you must** ~ **as you eat it** fais un vœu en le mangeant; **to** ~ **for sth** souhaiter qch; **I** ~**ed for that to happen** j'ai souhaité que cela se produise; **she's got everything she could** ~ **for** elle a tout ce qu'elle peut désirer; **what more could you** ~ **for?** que pourrais-tu souhaiter de plus?; **it's not everything you could** ~ **for** ce n'est pas l'idéal.

3 n a (*desire, will*) désir *m*. **what is your** ~**?** que désirez-vous?; (*liter or hum*) **your** ~ **is my command** vos désirs sont pour moi des ordres; **it has always been my** ~ **to do that** j'ai toujours désiré faire *or* eu envie de faire cela; **he had no great** ~ **to go** il n'avait pas grande envie d'y aller; **to go against sb's** ~**es** contrecarrer les désirs de qn; **he did it against my** ~**es** il l'a fait contre mon gré.

b (*specific desire*) vœu *m*, souhait *m*. **to make a** ~ faire un vœu; **the fairy granted him 3** ~**es** la fée lui accorda 3 souhaits; **his** ~ **came true, his** ~ **was granted, he got his** ~ son vœu *or* souhait s'est réalisé; **you shall have your** ~ ton souhait sera réalisé *or* te sera accordé, ton vœu sera exaucé.

c **give him my good** *or* **best** ~**es** (*in conversation*) faites-lui mes amitiés; (*in letter*) transmettez-lui mes meilleures pensées; **he sends his best** ~**es** (*in conversation*) il vous fait ses amitiés; (*in letter*) il vous envoie ses meilleures pensées; **best** ~**es** *or* **all good** ~**es for a happy birthday** tous mes (*or* nos) meilleurs vœux pour votre anniversaire; **(with) best** ~**es for a speedy recovery/your future happiness** tous mes (*or* nos) vœux de prompt rétablissement/de bonheur; **(with) best** ~**es for Christmas and the New Year** (nos) meilleurs vœux pour Noël et la nouvelle année; **(with) best** ~**es to both of you on your engagement** meilleurs vœux (de bonheur) à tous deux à l'occasion de vos fiançailles; **(with) best** ~**es for a happy holiday** je vous souhaite (*or* nous vous souhaitons) d'excellentes vacances; (*in letter*) **with best** ~**es from, with all good** ~**es from** bien amicalement; **the Queen sent a message of good** ~**es on Independence Day** la reine a envoyé des vœux pour le jour de l'Indépendance; **they came to offer him their best** ~**es on the occasion of ...** ils sont venus lui offrir leurs meilleurs vœux pour ... .

4 comp ▸**wishbone** fourchette *f*; (*Sport*) wishbone *m* ▸**wish fulfilment** (*Psych*) accomplissement *m* de désir ▸**wish list** liste *f* de souhaits; **what is your wish list?** quels sont vos souhaits?; **top of my wish list** mon souhait le plus cher.

wishful [ˈwɪʃfʊl] adj: **to be ~ to do** *or* **of doing** avoir envie de faire; **it's ~ thinking if you believe that** si tu crois cela c'est que tu prends tes désirs pour la réalité *or* c'est que tu t'aveugles sur la réalité des choses.

wishy-washy* [ˈwɪʃɪˌwɒʃɪ] adj *colour* délavé; *speech, style, taste* fade, insipide, fadasse*; *person* sans aucune personnalité, falot, fadasse*.

wisp [wɪsp] n *[straw]* brin *m*; *[hair]* fine mèche; *[thread]* petit bout; *[smoke]* mince volute *f*. **a little ~ of a girl** une fillette menue.

wispy [ˈwɪspɪ] adj *straw, hair* fin; *smoke* mince, fin. **a ~ little old lady** une vieille dame menue.

wistaria [wɪsˈtɛərɪə] n, **wisteria** [wɪsˈtɪərɪə] n glycine *f*.

wistful [ˈwɪstfʊl] adj nostalgique, mélancolique, rêveur.

wistfully [ˈwɪstfəlɪ] adv avec nostalgie *or* mélancolie, avec une tristesse rêveuse.

wistfulness [ˈwɪstfʊlnɪs] n *[person]* caractère *m* mélancolique; *[look, smile, voice]* nostalgie *f*, mélancolie *f*, regret *m*.

wit[1] [wɪt] vi (*Jur etc*) **to ~** ... à savoir ..., c'est à dire ... .

wit[2] [wɪt] n a (*gen pl: intelligence*) **~(s)** esprit *m*, intelligence *f*, astuce *f*; **mother ~, native ~** bon sens, sens commun; **he hadn't the ~** *or* **he hadn't enough ~ to hide the letter** il n'a pas eu l'intelligence *or* la présence d'esprit de cacher la lettre; **you'll need all your ~s about you** *or* **you'll need to use all your ~s if you're to avoid being seen** il va te falloir toute ta présence d'esprit pour éviter d'être vu; **keep your ~s about you!** restez attentif!; **use your ~s!** sers-toi de ton intelligence!; **it was a battle of ~s (between them)** ils jouaient au plus fin; **he lives by** *or* **on his ~s** c'est un chevalier d'industrie, il vit d'expédients; **to collect** *or* **gather one's ~s** rassembler ses esprits; **the struggle for survival sharpened his ~s** la lutte pour la vie lui avivait l'esprit; **he was at his ~s' end** il ne savait plus que faire, il ne savait plus à quel saint se vouer; **I'm at my ~s' end to know what to do** je ne sais plus du tout ce que je dois faire; **to be/go out of one's ~s** être/devenir fou (*f* folle); **she was nearly out of her ~s with worry about him** elle était si inquiète pour lui qu'elle en devenait folle.

b (*NonC: wittiness*) esprit *m*. **the book is full of ~** le livre est très spirituel *or* est plein d'esprit; **he has a ready** *or* **pretty ~** il a beaucoup d'esprit, il est très spirituel; **in a flash of ~ he said** ... obéissant à une inspiration spirituelle il a dit ...; **this flash of ~ made them all laugh** ce trait d'esprit les a tous fait rire.

c (*person*) homme *m* d'esprit, femme *f* d'esprit; (*Hist, Literat*) bel esprit.

witch [wɪtʃ] 1 n sorcière *f*; (*fig: charmer*) ensorceleuse *f*, magicienne *f*. (*fig*) **she's an old ~** c'est une vieille sorcière; **~es' sabbath** sabbat *m* (de sorcières). 2 comp ▸**witchcraft** sorcellerie *f* ▸**witch doctor** sorcier *m* (*de tribu*) ▸**witch-elm** = **wych-elm** ▸**witch hazel** hamamélis *m* ▸**witch hunt** (*fig: esp Pol*) chasse *f* aux sorcières ▸**witching hour**: **the witching hour of midnight** minuit, l'heure fatale, minuit, l'heure du crime (*hum*).

witchery [ˈwɪtʃərɪ] n sorcellerie *f*; (*fig: fascination*) magie *f*, ensorcellement *m*, envoûtement *m*.

with [wɪð, wɪθ] (*phr vb elem*) 1 prep a (*indicating accompaniment, relationship*) avec, à. **I was ~ her** j'étais avec elle; **go ~ your brother** va avec ton frère, accompagne ton frère; **he lives ~ his aunt** (*in his house*) il habite avec sa tante; (*in her house*) il habite chez *or* avec sa tante; **she was staying ~ friends** elle passait quelque temps chez des amis; **he's ~ IBM** il travaille chez IBM; **a scientist ~ ICI** un chercheur de ICI; **I'll be ~ you in a minute** je suis à vous dans un instant; **I have no money ~ me** je n'ai pas d'argent sur moi; **she had her umbrella ~ her** elle avait pris son parapluie; **he took it away ~ him** il l'a emporté avec lui; **he went off ~ it** il est parti avec; **she left the child ~ her aunt** elle a laissé l'enfant avec sa tante *or* à la garde de sa tante; **mix the red ~ the blue** mélange le rouge et le bleu *or* le rouge avec le bleu; **just mix the red ~ it** tu n'as qu'à mélanger le rouge avec; **hold my gloves, I can't drive ~ them on** tiens mes gants, je ne peux pas conduire avec; **do you take sugar ~ coffee?** prenez-vous du sucre dans *or* avec votre café?; **that problem is always ~ us** ce problème ne nous lâche pas; **~ "Hamlet" it's the best play he wrote** c'est, avec "Hamlet", la meilleure pièce qu'il ait écrite; **fill it up ~ petrol** faites le plein d'essence; **they loaded the truck ~ coal** ils ont chargé le camion de charbon.

b (*agreement, harmony*) avec. **to agree ~ sb** être d'accord avec qn; **can you carry the committee ~ you?** le comité vous suivra-t-il?; **the hat doesn't go ~ the dress** le chapeau ne va pas avec la robe; **are you ~ us then?** alors vous êtes des nôtres?; **I'm ~ you in what you say** je suis d'accord avec ce que vous dites; **I'm ~ you all the way** je suis avec vous cent pour cent; **I'm ~ you** (*I agree*) je suis d'accord; (*: *I understand*) je vois*, je vous suis; **he just wasn't ~ us*** (*didn't understand*) il ne voyait* pas du tout; (*wasn't paying attention*) il était tout à fait ailleurs; (*up-to-date*) **to be ~ it**‡ *[person]* être dans le vent* *or* dans la course‡; *[clothes etc]* être dans le vent* *or* du dernier cri (*see also* **2**); **to get ~ it**‡ se mettre dans la course‡.

c (*descriptive: having etc*) à, qui a, avec. **the man ~ the beard** le barbu, l'homme à la barbe; **the boy ~ brown eyes** le garçon aux yeux marron; **passengers ~ tickets** ... voyageurs *mpl* en possession de *or* munis de billets ...; **the house ~ the green shutters** la maison aux volets verts; **I want a coat ~ a fur collar** je veux un manteau avec un *or* à col de fourrure; **a room ~ a view of the sea** une chambre avec vue sur la mer *or* qui a vue sur la mer; **machine ~ the latest features** machine *f* munie des derniers perfectionnements.

d (*manner*) avec, de. **~ my whole heart** de tout mon cœur; **I'll do it ~ pleasure** je le ferai avec plaisir; **~ a shout of joy he sprang up** (en) poussant un cri de joie il a sauté sur ses pieds; **he welcomed us ~ open arms** il nous a accueillis à bras ouverts; **~ all speed** à grande allure, à toute vitesse; **I did it ~ a lot of trouble** je l'ai fait avec beaucoup de difficultés; **~ no trouble at all he** ... sans la moindre difficulté il ...; **he made it ~ great care** il l'a fait avec un soin infini; **... he said ~ a smile** ... dit-il en souriant *or* avec un sourire; **she turned away ~ tears in her eyes** elle s'est détournée, les larmes aux yeux.

e (*means, instrument*) avec, de. **cut it ~ a knife** coupe-le avec un couteau; **he was writing ~ a pencil** il écrivait avec un crayon; **I saw it ~ my own eyes** je l'ai vu de mes propres yeux; **take it ~ both hands** prenez-le à deux mains; **he walks ~ a stick** il marche avec une *or* à l'aide d'une canne; **cover it ~ a cloth** couvre-le d'une *or* avec une serviette.

f (*cause*) avec, de. **trembling ~ fear** tremblant de peur; **he jumped ~ joy** il a sauté de joie; **the hills are white ~ snow** les monts sont blancs de neige; **he's in bed ~ flu** il est retenu au lit par la grippe; **he went down ~ measles** il a attrapé la rougeole; **she was sick ~ fear** elle était malade de peur; **~ the elections no one talks anything but politics** avec les élections on ne parle plus que politique; **~ the price of food these days you can't expect that** ... au prix où est la nourriture de nos jours comment voulez-vous que ... (+ *subj*); **I couldn't see him ~ so many people there** il y avait tellement de monde que je n'ai pas pu le voir; **~ so much happening it was difficult to** ... il se passait tellement de choses qu'il était difficile de ...; **it varies ~ the weather** ça change avec le temps; **this period ended ~ the outbreak of war** cette période s'est terminée avec le début de la guerre; **it all started ~ his attempt to cut prices** tout a commencé quand il a essayé de réduire les prix.

g (*opposition*) avec, contre. **they were at war ~ Spain** ils étaient en guerre avec *or* contre l'Espagne; **the war ~ Japan** la guerre avec *or* contre le Japon; **he had an argument ~ his brother** il a eu une dispute avec son frère; **in competition ~** en concurrence avec; **he was struggling ~ the intruder** il était en train de se colleter avec l'intrus.

h (*separation*) **to part ~ sb** se séparer de qn; **he won't part ~ it** il ne veut pas s'en séparer; **I can't dispense ~ that** je ne peux pas me passer de ça.

i (*in regard to*) avec, de. **the trouble ~ Paul is that** ce qu'il y a avec Paul c'est que; **it's a habit ~ him** c'est une habitude chez lui; **be patient ~ her** sois patient avec elle; **she's good ~ children** elle sait bien s'occuper des enfants; **what do you want ~ that book?** qu'est-ce que tu veux faire de ce livre?; **be honest ~ me** dites-moi les choses franchement; **what's the matter ~ you?** qu'est-ce que tu as?, qu'est-ce qui te prend?; **what's up ~ Paul?*, what's ~ Paul?*** qu'est-ce qu'il a, Paul?*, qu'est-ce qui lui prend, Paul?*; **he was pleased ~ what he saw** il était satisfait *or* content de ce qu'il voyait.

j (*indicating time*) avec. **he rose ~ the sun** il se levait avec le jour; **~ the approach of winter** à l'approche de l'hiver, l'hiver approchant; **it lessened ~ time** cela a diminué avec le temps; **~ these words he left us** à ces mots *or* sur ces mots *or* là-dessus *or* sur ce il nous a quittés; **~ that he closed the door** sur ce *or* là-dessus il a fermé la porte.

k (*despite*) malgré. **~ all his faults I still like him** malgré tous ses défauts *or* il a beau avoir des défauts je l'aime bien quand même; **~ all that he is still the best we've got** malgré tout ça il est encore le meilleur que nous ayons; **~ all your intelligence, you** ... intelligent comme vous l'êtes, vous ... .

l (*in exclamatory phrases*) **away ~ you!** allez-vous-en!; **away ~ him!** qu'on l'emmène (*subj*)!; **down ~ traitors!** à bas les traîtres!; **off ~ his head!** qu'on lui coupe (*subj*) la tête!

2 comp ▸**with-it**‡ *person* dans le vent*, dans la course‡; *ideas, dress, school, firm etc* dans le vent*.

withal†† [wɪˈðɔːl] adv en outre, de plus.

withdraw [wɪθˈdrɔː] pret **withdrew**, ptp **withdrawn** 1 vt *person, hand, money, application, troops* retirer (*from* de); *permission, help* retirer (*from* à); *ambassador, representative* rappeler; *accusation, opinion, suggestion, statement* retirer, rétracter; *claim* retirer, renoncer à; *order* annuler; (*Med*) *drugs* arrêter; (*Comm*) *goods* retirer de la vente; (*Fin*) *banknotes* retirer de la circulation. (*Jur*) **to ~ a charge** retirer une accusation.

2 vi *[troops etc]* reculer, se retirer, se replier (*from* de); *[person]* (*move away*) se retirer; (*retract offer, promise etc*) se rétracter, se dédire; *[candidate, competitor]* se retirer, se désister (*from* de, *in favour of sb* en faveur de qn). (*Mil*) **to ~ to a new position** se replier; **he withdrew a few paces** il a reculé de quelques pas; **you can't ~ now!** tu ne peux plus te dédire *or* plus reculer maintenant!; **I ~ from the game** je me retire de la partie, j'abandonne; (*fig*) **to ~ into o.s.** se replier sur soi-même.

withdrawal [wɪθ'drɔːəl] 1 n a (*NonC: act of withdrawing: see* **withdraw**) retrait *m*; rappel *m*; rétraction *f*; annulation *f*. **they demand the ~ of the troops** ils exigent le retrait des troupes; **the army's ~ to new positions** le repli de l'armée sur de nouvelles positions; **the candidate's ~** le désistement du candidat. b (*Med, Psych*) repli *m* sur soi-même; (*with symptoms*) (état *m* de) manque *m*. 2 comp ►**withdrawal symptoms** (*Med, Psych*) symptômes *mpl* de l'état de manque *or* du manque, malaise *m* de la privation; **to have** *or* **be suffering from withdrawal symptoms** être en (état de) manque.

withdrawn [wɪθ'drɔːn] 1 ptp of **withdraw**. 2 adj (*reserved*) *person* renfermé.

withe [wɪθ] n = **withy**.

wither ['wɪðəʳ] 1 vi *[plant]* se flétrir, se faner, s'étioler, dépérir; *[person, limb]* (*from illness*) s'atrophier; (*from age*) se ratatiner; (*fig*) *[beauty]* se faner; *[hope, love, enthusiasm]* s'évanouir. 2 vt *plant* flétrir, faner; *limb* atrophier, ratatiner; *beauty* altérer, faner; *hope etc* détruire petit à petit. **he ~ed her with a look** il l'a regardée avec un profond mépris, son regard méprisant lui a donné envie de rentrer sous terre.

►**wither away** vi *[plant]* se dessécher, mourir; *[beauty]* se faner complètement, s'évanouir; *[hope etc]* s'évanouir.

withered ['wɪðəd] adj *flower, leaf, plant* flétri, fané, desséché; *arm, leg* atrophié; *face* fané, flétri. **a ~ old woman** une vieille femme toute desséchée.

withering ['wɪðərɪŋ] 1 n *[plant]* dépérissement *m*; *[limb]* atrophie *f*; *[beauty]* déclin *m*; *[hope, love, enthusiasm]* évanouissement *m*. 2 adj *heat* desséchant; *tone, look* profondément méprisant; *remark, criticism* cinglant, blessant.

witheringly ['wɪðərɪŋlɪ] adv *say, look* avec un profond mépris.

withers ['wɪðəz] npl garrot *m* (*du cheval*).

withershins ['wɪðəʃɪnz] adv dans le sens opposé au mouvement apparent du soleil.

withhold [wɪθ'həʊld] pret, ptp **withheld** vt *money from pay etc* retenir (*from sth* de qch); *payment, decision* remettre, différer; *one's consent, permission, one's help, support* refuser (*from sb* à qn); *facts, truth, news* cacher, taire (*from sb* à qn). (*US*) **~ing tax** retenue *f* à la source; **he withheld his tax in protest against ...** il a refusé de payer ses impôts pour protester contre ... .

within [wɪð'ɪn] (*phr vb elem*) 1 adv dedans, à l'intérieur. **from ~** de l'intérieur.

2 prep a (*inside*) à l'intérieur de. **~ the box** à l'intérieur de la boîte; **~ it** à l'intérieur; **~ (the boundary of) the park** à l'intérieur du parc, dans les limites du parc; **here ~ the town** à l'intérieur même de la ville; **~ the city walls** à l'intérieur des murs (de la ville), dans l'enceinte de la ville; **a voice ~ him said ...** une voix en lui a dit ... .

b (*~ limits of*) **to be ~ the law** être dans (les limites de) la légalité; **to live ~ one's income** vivre selon ses moyens; **~ the range of the guns** à portée de(s) canon(s); **the coast was ~ sight** la côte était à portée de la vue *or* en vue; **they were ~ sight of the town** ils étaient en vue de la ville; (*fig*) **he was ~ reach** *or* **sight of his goal** il touchait au but; *see* **call, province, reach.**

c (*in measurement, distances*) **~ a kilometre of the house** à moins d'un kilomètre de la maison; **we were ~ a mile of the town** nous étions à moins d'un mille de la ville; **correct to ~ a centimetre** correct à un centimètre près; *see* **inch.**

d (*in time*) **~ a week of her visit** (*after*) moins d'une semaine après *or* (*before*) avant sa visite; **I'll be back ~ an hour** *or* **the hour** je serai de retour d'ici une heure *or* dans l'heure qui suit; **they arrived ~ minutes (of our call)** ils sont arrivés très peu de temps après (notre appel); **he returned ~ the week** il est revenu avant la fin de la semaine; **~ 2 years from now** d'ici 2 ans; **"use ~ 3 days of opening"** ≃ "se conserve encore 3 jours au réfrigérateur après ouverture"; (*Comm*) **~ a period of 4 months** dans un délai de 4 mois; **~ the stipulated period** dans les délais stipulés; *see* **living.**

3 adj (*Jur*) **the ~ instrument** le document ci-inclus.

without [wɪð'aʊt] (*phr vb elem*) 1 adv (*liter*) à l'extérieur, au dehors. **from ~** de l'extérieur, de dehors.

2 prep a sans. **~ a coat** sans manteau; **~ a coat or hat** sans manteau ni chapeau; **he went off ~ it** il est parti sans; **~ any money** sans argent, sans un *or* le sou*; **he is ~ friends** il n'a pas d'amis; **with or ~ sugar?** avec ou sans sucre?; **~ so much as a phone call** sans même un malheureux coup de fil; **~ a doubt** sans aucun doute; **~ doubt** sans doute; **not ~ some difficulty** non sans difficulté; **do it ~ fail** ne manquez pas de le faire, faites-le sans faute; **he was quite ~ shame** il n'avait aucune honte; **~ speaking, he ...** sans parler, il ...; **~ anybody knowing** sans que personne le sache; **to go ~ sth, to do ~ sth** se passer de qch.

b (††: *outside*) au *or* en dehors de, à l'extérieur de.

3 conj (*dial or* ‡: *unless*) à moins que + *subj*, à moins de + *infin*.

withstand [wɪθ'stænd] pret, ptp **withstood** vt résister à.

withy ['wɪðɪ] n brin *m* d'osier.

witless ['wɪtlɪs] adj sot (*f* sotte), stupide. **to scare sb ~** faire une peur bleue à qn; **to be scared ~** être pris d'une peur panique.

witness ['wɪtnɪs] 1 n a (*Jur etc: person*) témoin *m*. (*Jur*) **~ for the defence/prosecution** témoin à décharge/à charge; **there were 3 ~es to this event** cet événement a eu 3 témoins, 3 personnes ont été témoins de cet événement; **he was a ~ to** *or* **of this incident** il a été témoin de cet incident; **the ~es to his signature** les témoins (certifiant sa signature); **in front of 2 ~es** en présence de 2 témoins; (*Jur*) **to call sb as ~** citer qn comme témoin; (*Jur*) **"your ~"** "le témoin est à vous"; *see* **eye.**

b (*esp Jur: evidence*) témoignage *m*. **in ~ of** en témoignage de; **in ~ whereof** en témoignage de quoi, en foi de quoi; **to give ~ on behalf of/against** témoigner en faveur de/contre, rendre témoignage pour/contre; **to bear** *or* **be ~ to sth** témoigner de qch, attester qch; **he took this as ~ of her good faith** cela a été pour lui le témoignage *or* l'attestation *f* de sa bonne foi; **I took it as ~ of the fact that ...** j'ai pensé que cela attestait le fait que ...; (*fig*) **her clothes were ~ to her poverty** ses vêtements révélaient *or* attestaient sa pauvreté; **he has his good points, (as) ~ his work for the blind** il a ses bons côtés, témoin *or* comme le prouve *or* à preuve* ce qu'il fait pour les aveugles; **~ the case of X** voyez *or* regardez *or* témoin le cas de X.

2 comp ►**witness box** (*Brit*), **witness stand** (*US*) barre *f* des témoins; **in the witness box** *or* **stand** à la barre.

3 vt a (*see*) être témoin de (*esp Jur*), assister à. **did anyone ~ the theft?** quelqu'un a-t-il été témoin du vol?; **the accident was ~ed by several people** plusieurs personnes ont été témoins de l'accident.

b (*fig*) (*see*) voir; (*notice*) *change, improvement* remarquer. (*fig*) **a building/a century which has ~ed ...** un bâtiment/un siècle qui a vu ... .

c (*esp Jur*) *document* attester *or* certifier l'authenticité de. **to ~ sb's signature** être témoin, signer comme témoin.

4 vi (*Jur*) **to ~ to sth** témoigner de qch, attester qch; **he ~ed to having seen the accident** il a témoigné *or* attesté avoir vu l'accident *or* qu'il a vu l'accident; **to ~ against sb** témoigner contre qn.

-witted ['wɪtɪd] adj ending in comps à l'esprit ... . **quick-witted** à l'esprit vif; *see* **slow** *etc*.

witter* ['wɪtəʳ] vi (*Brit*) **to ~ on about sth*** parler interminablement de qch; **stop ~ing (on)*** arrête de parler pour ne rien dire.

witticism ['wɪtɪsɪzəm] n mot *m* d'esprit, bon mot.

wittily ['wɪtɪlɪ] adv spirituellement, avec beaucoup d'esprit. **... he said ~** ... dit-il avec beaucoup d'esprit.

wittiness ['wɪtɪnɪs] n (*NonC*) esprit *m*, humour *m*.

wittingly ['wɪtɪŋlɪ] adv sciemment, en toute connaissance de cause.

witty ['wɪtɪ] adj spirituel, plein d'esprit. **~ remark** mot *m* d'esprit.

wives [waɪvz] npl of **wife**.

wiz [wɪz] n (*US*) as *m*, crack* *m*.

wizard ['wɪzəd] n magicien *m*, enchanteur *m*, sorcier *m*. (*fig*) **he is a financial ~** il a le génie de la finance, c'est un génie *or* il est génial en matière financière; **he is a ~ with a paintbrush/slide rule** c'est un champion* *or* un as du pinceau/de la règle à calcul; **he's a ~ at chess** c'est un as *or* un crack* aux échecs; (*Brit: excl*) ~!† au poil!*

wizardry ['wɪzədrɪ] n (*NonC*) magie *f*, sorcellerie *f*; (*fig*) génie *m*. **it is a piece of ~** c'est génial; **this evidence of his financial ~** cette preuve de son génie en matière financière.

wizened ['wɪznd] adj ratatiné, desséché.

wk abbr of **week**.

W.O. [ˌdʌblju:'əʊ] n (*Mil*) (abbr of **warrant officer**) *see* **warrant**.

woa [wəʊ] excl = **whoa**.

woad [wəʊd] n guède *f*.

wobble ['wɒbl] 1 vi a *[jelly, one's hand, pen, voice]* trembler; *[object about to fall, pile of rocks]* osciller, remuer dangereusement; *[cyclist etc]* osciller; *[tightrope walker, dancer]* chanceler; *[table, chair]* branler, être branlant *or* instable; *[compass needle]* osciller; *[wheel]* avoir du jeu. **the table was wobbling** la table branlait; **this table ~s** cette table est branlante *or* bancale, cette table n'est pas stable; **the cart ~d through the streets** la charrette est passée dans les rues en bringuebalant *or* en cahotant.

b (* *fig: hesitate*) vaciller, osciller, hésiter (*between* entre).

2 vt faire trembler; faire osciller; faire remuer dangereusement; faire branler.

3 n: **to walk with a ~** avoir une démarche chancelante, marcher d'un pas chancelant; **this chair has a ~** cette chaise est branlante *or* bancale; (*Aut*) **wheel ~** shimmy *m*.

wobbly ['wɒblɪ] 1 adj *hand, voice* tremblant; *jelly* qui tremble; *table, chair* bancal, branlant; *object about to fall* qui oscille *or* remue dangereusement, branlant; *wheel* qui a du jeu. **to be ~ = to wobble** (*see* **wobble 1**); **he's rather ~ still after his illness** il est encore faible après sa maladie; **his legs are a bit ~, he's a bit ~ on his legs** il flageole un peu sur ses jambes; **I'm rather ~ on this bike** je n'arrive pas à trouver mon équilibre *or* je suis en équilibre instable sur cette bicyclette. 2 n: **to throw a ~*** piquer une crise*; (*US Hist*) **the Wobblies*** l'I.W.W. (*Industrial Workers of the World: mouvement syndicaliste du début du XXᵉ siècle*).

wodge [wɒdʒ] n (*Brit*) gros morceau.

woe [wəʊ] 1 n malheur *m*. († *or hum*) **~ is me!** pauvre de moi!; **~ betide the man who ...** malheur à celui qui ...; **he told me his ~s** *or* **his tale of ~** il m'a fait le récit de ses malheurs *or* tribulations *fpl*; **it was such a tale of ~ that** c'était une litanie si pathétique que. 2 comp

▸**woebegone** désolé, abattu.

woeful [ˈwəʊfʊl] adj *person, smile, look, gesture* malheureux, très triste; *news, story, sight* affligeant, très triste; *incident, state of affairs* malheureux, cruel.

woefully [ˈwəʊfəlɪ] adv a *say, look* (très) tristement. b (*unfortunately*) malheureusement. **the house is ~ lacking in modern conveniences** le confort moderne fait cruellement défaut à cette maison.

wog** [wɒg] n (*Brit pej*) sale étranger *m*, -ère *f*, métèque* *m* (*pej*).

wok [wɒk] n wok *m*.

woke [wəʊk] pret of wake².

woken [ˈwəʊkn] ptp of wake².

wold [wəʊld] n haute plaine, plateau *m*.

wolf [wʊlf] 1 n, pl **wolves** loup *m*. **she-~** louve *f*; (*fig*) **a ~ in sheep's clothing** un loup déguisé en brebis; (*fig*) **that will keep the ~ from the door** cela nous (*or* les *etc*) mettra au moins à l'abri du besoin; (*fig*) **he's a ~*** c'est un tombeur de femmes*; *see* **cry, lone** *etc*. 2 comp ▸**wolf call** (*US*) = **wolf whistle** ▸**wolf cub** (*also Scouting* †) louveteau *m* ▸**wolfhound** chien-loup *m* ▸**wolf pack** bande *f* de loups ▸**wolfsbane** (*Bot*) aconit *m* ▸**wolf whistle** n (*fig*) sifflement admiratif (*à l'adresse d'une fille*); **he gave a wolf whistle, he wolf-whistled** il a sifflé la fille. 3 vt (*also* **~ down**) engloutir.

wolfish [ˈwʊlfɪʃ] adj vorace.

wolfishly [ˈwʊlfɪʃlɪ] adv voracement.

wolfram [ˈwʊlfrəm] n wolfram *m*, tungstène *m*.

wolverine [ˈwʊlvəriːn] 1 n a (*Zool*) glouton *m*, carcajou *m*. b (*US*) **W~** habitant(e) *m(f)* du Michigan. 2 comp ▸**the Wolverine State** (*US*) le Michigan.

wolves [wʊlvz] npl of wolf.

woman [ˈwʊmən], pl **women** 1 n femme *f*. **young ~** jeune femme; **come along, young ~!** allez mademoiselle, venez!; **my good ~**† ma bonne†; (*hum: wife*) **the little ~**** ma (*or* sa *etc*) légitime**; **the ~ must be mad*** celle-là*, elle doit être folle; **~ of the world** femme du monde; **Paul and all his women** Paul et toutes ses maîtresses; **he runs after women** c'est un coureur de jupons, il court (après) les femmes; **~ is a mysterious creature** la femme est une créature mystérieuse; (*loc*) **a ~'s place is in the home** la place d'une femme est au foyer (*loc*); (*loc*) **a ~'s work is never done** on n'a jamais fini de faire le ménage, on trouve toujours à faire dans une maison; **she's her own ~** elle est son propre maître; **she's a career ~** c'est une femme qui consacre beaucoup d'énergie à sa carrière, elle est (assez) ambitieuse dans sa vie professionnelle; **~ to ~** (adj, adv) entre femmes; **a ~ of the world** une femme d'expérience; **she's the ~ for the job** c'est la femme qu'il (nous *or* leur *etc*) faut pour ce travail; **a ~ of letters** une femme de lettres; **I've got a ~ who comes in 3 times a week** j'ai une femme de ménage qui vient 3 fois par semaine; **women's liberation** la libération de la femme; **Women's (Liberation) Movement, Women's Lib** mouvement *m* de libération de la femme, M.L.F. *m*; **Women's Libber** féministe *mf*; **Women's Centre** ≃ centre *m* d'accueil de femmes; **she belongs to a women's group** elle est membre d'un groupe féministe; (*Brit*) **the Greenham women** les femmes de Greenham (Common); (*Press*) **women's page** la page des lectrices; **women's rights** les droits *mpl* de la femme; **women's suffrage** le droit de vote pour les femmes; **women's team** équipe féminine; (*Brit*) **Women's Institute** *association f de femmes de tendance plutôt traditionaliste*; *see* **old** *etc*.

2 adj: **he's got a ~ music teacher** il a un professeur de musique femme, son professeur de musique est une femme; **~ worker** ouvrière *f*; **women doctors think that ...** les femmes médecins pensent que ...; **women often prefer women doctors** les femmes préfèrent souvent les médecins femmes; **he's got a ~ driver** son chauffeur est une femme; **women drivers are generally maligned** on calomnie généralement les femmes au volant; **~ friend** amie *f*.

3 comp ▸**woman-hater** misogyne *mf* ▸**womanhood** *see* **womanhood** ▸**womankind** *see* **womankind** ▸**womanlike** adj féminin, de femme ◊ adv d'une manière très féminine ▸**woman police constable** (*Brit*) femme *f* agent de police ▸**womenfolk** les femmes *fpl*.

womanhood [ˈwʊmənhʊd] n (*NonC: feminine nature*) féminité *f*. **to reach ~** devenir une femme.

womanish [ˈwʊmənɪʃ] adj (*gen pej*) *man* efféminé; *quality, behaviour* de femme.

womanize [ˈwʊmənaɪz] vi courir les femmes.

womanizer [ˈwʊmənaɪzəʳ] n coureur *m* de jupons.

womankind [ˈwʊmənkaɪnd] n les femmes *fpl* (*en général*).

womanliness [ˈwʊmənlɪnɪs] n (*NonC*) féminité *f*, caractère féminin.

womanly [ˈwʊmənlɪ] adj *figure, bearing* féminin, de femme; *behaviour* digne d'une femme. **~ kindness/gentleness** gentillesse/douceur toute féminine.

womb [wuːm] 1 n utérus *m*, matrice *f*; (*fig*) (*of nature*) sein *m*; (*of earth*) sein, entrailles *fpl*. 2 comp ▸**womb-leasing** location *f* d'utérus.

wombat [ˈwɒmbæt] n wombat *m*, phascolome *m*.

women [ˈwɪmɪn] npl of woman.

won [wʌn] pret, ptp of win.

wonder [ˈwʌndəʳ] 1 n a (*NonC*) émerveillement *m*, étonnement *m*. **to be lost in ~** être muet d'étonnement *or* d'admiration, être émerveillé *or* ébloui; **he watched, lost in silent ~** il regardait en silence, émerveillé *or* ébloui; **the sense of ~ that children have** la faculté d'être émerveillé qu'ont les enfants; **... he said in ~ ...** dit-il d'une voix remplie d'étonnement.

b (*sth wonderful*) merveille *f*, prodige *m*, miracle *m*. **the ~ of electricity** le miracle de l'électricité; **the ~s of science/medicine** les prodiges *or* les miracles de la science/de la médecine; **the Seven W~s of the World** les sept merveilles du monde; **he promised us ~s** il nous a promis monts et merveilles; (*iro*) **~s will never cease** c'est un miracle!, cela tient du miracle! (*iro*); **the ~ of it all is that ...** le plus étonnant dans tout cela c'est que ...; **it's a ~ that he didn't fall** c'est extraordinaire qu'il ne soit pas tombé, on se demande comment il a fait pour ne pas tomber; **it's a ~ to me that ...** je n'en reviens pas que ... + *subj*; **he paid cash for a ~!*** et miracle, il a payé comptant!; **if for a ~ he ...** si par extraordinaire il ...; **no ~ he came late, it's no ~ (that) he came late** ce n'est pas étonnant qu'il soit arrivé en retard *or* s'il est arrivé en retard; **no ~!** cela n'a rien d'étonnant!, pas étonnant!*; **he failed, and little** *or* **small ~!** il a échoué, ce qui n'est guère étonnant!; **it's little** *or* **small ~ that ...** il n'est guère étonnant que ... + *subj*; *see* **nine, work** *etc*.

2 comp ▸**wonderland** pays *m* merveilleux; **"Alice in Wonderland"** "Alice au pays des merveilles" ▸**wonderstruck** frappé d'étonnement, émerveillé, ébloui ▸**wonder-worker**: **he is a wonder-worker** il accomplit de vrais miracles; **this drug/cure is a wonder-worker** c'est un remède/une cure miracle.

3 vi a (*marvel*) s'étonner, s'émerveiller. **the shepherds ~ed at the angels** les bergers émerveillés regardaient les anges; **I ~ at your rashness** votre audace m'étonne *or* me surprend; **I ~ (that) you're still able to work** je ne sais pas comment vous faites pour travailler encore; **I ~ (that) he didn't kill you** cela m'étonne qu'il ne vous ait pas tué; **do you ~** *or* **can you ~ at it?** est-ce que cela vous étonne?; **he'll be back, I shouldn't ~** cela ne m'étonnerait pas qu'il revienne.

b (*reflect*) penser, songer. **his words set me ~ing** ce qu'il a dit m'a laissé songeur; **it makes you ~** cela donne à penser; **I was ~ing about what he said** je pensais *or* songeais à ce qu'il a dit; **I'm ~ing about going to the pictures** j'ai à moitié envie d'aller au cinéma; **he'll be back – I ~!** il reviendra – je me le demande!

4 vt se demander. **I ~ who he is** je me demande qui il est, je serais curieux de savoir qui il est; **I ~ what to do** je ne sais pas quoi faire; **I ~ where to put it** je me demande où (je pourrais) le mettre; **he was ~ing whether to come with us** il se demandait s'il allait nous accompagner; **I ~ why!** je me demande pourquoi!

wonderful [ˈwʌndəfʊl] adj (*astonishing*) merveilleux, étonnant, extraordinaire; (*miraculous*) miraculeux; (*excellent*) merveilleux, magnifique, formidable*, sensationnel*. **we had a ~ time** ça a été merveilleux; **isn't it ~!** c'est formidable!* *or* sensationnel!*; (*iro*) ce n'est pas extraordinaire ça! (*iro*); **~ to relate, he ...** (et) chose étonnante, il ... .

wonderfully [ˈwʌndəfəlɪ] adv (+ *adj*) merveilleusement; (+ *vb*) à merveille, admirablement. **it was ~ hot all day** il a fait merveilleusement chaud toute la journée; **she manages ~ considering how handicapped she is** elle se débrouille admirablement *or* à merveille si l'on considère combien elle est handicapée; **he looks ~ well** il a très bonne mine.

wondering [ˈwʌndərɪŋ] adj (*astonished*) étonné; (*thoughtful*) songeur, pensif.

wonderingly [ˈwʌndərɪŋlɪ] adv (*with astonishment*) avec étonnement, d'un air étonné; (*thoughtfully*) songeusement, pensivement.

wonderment [ˈwʌndəmənt] n = **wonder 1a**.

wondrous [ˈwʌndrəs] 1 adj (*liter*) merveilleux. 2 adv († *or liter*) merveilleusement. **~ well** à merveille.

wondrously [ˈwʌndrəslɪ] adv (*liter*) = **wondrous 2**.

wonky* [ˈwɒŋkɪ] adj (*Brit*) *chair, table* bancal; *machine* qui ne tourne pas rond*, déréglé, détraqué. (*fig*) **it's a bit ~** *[sentence, pattern, ideas etc]* il y a quelque chose qui cloche*; **their marriage is rather ~ at the moment** leur mariage traverse une mauvaise passe en ce moment; **he's feeling rather ~ still** il se sent encore un peu patraque* *or* vaseux*; **the grammar is a bit ~** la syntaxe est un peu boiteuse, ce n'est pas très grammatical; **your hat's a bit ~** votre chapeau est mis de travers *or* de traviole*; **to go ~** *[car, machine]* se détraquer; *[TV picture etc]* se dérégler; *[piece of handicraft, drawing]* aller de travers.

wont [wəʊnt] 1 adj: **to be ~ to do** avoir coutume *or* avoir l'habitude de faire. 2 n coutume *f*, habitude *f* (*to do* de faire). **as was my ~** ainsi que j'en avais l'habitude, comme de coutume.

won't [wəʊnt] = **will not**; *see* **will**.

wonted [ˈwəʊntɪd] adj (*liter*) habituel, coutumier.

woo [wuː] vt *woman* faire la cour à, courtiser; (*fig*) *influential person* rechercher les faveurs de; *voters, audience* chercher à plaire à; *fame, success* rechercher, poursuivre. (*fig*) **he ~ed them with promises of ...** il cherchait à s'assurer leurs faveurs *or* à leur plaire en leur promettant ... .

wood [wʊd] 1 n a (*NonC: material*) bois *m*. (*fig*) **to touch ~**, (*US*) **to knock on ~** toucher du bois; **touch ~!**, (*US*) **knock on ~!** touchons *or* je touche du bois!; *see* **dead, hard, soft** *etc*.

b (*forest*) bois *m*. ~s bois *mpl*; **a pine (*or* beech *etc*) ~** un bois de pins (*or* de hêtres *etc*), une pinède (*or* une hêtraie *etc*); (*fig*) **he can't see the ~ for the trees** les arbres lui cachent la forêt; (*fig*) **we're out of the ~(s) now** on est au bout du tunnel maintenant; (*fig*) **we're not out of the ~(s) yet** on n'est pas encore tiré d'affaire *or* sorti de l'auberge; *see* **neck**.

c (*cask*) **drawn from the ~** tiré au tonneau; **aged in the ~** vieilli au tonneau; **wine in the ~** vin *m* au tonneau.

d (*Mus*) **the ~s** les bois *mpl*.

e (*Golf*) bois *m*; (*Bowls*) boule *f*. (*Golf*) **a number 2 ~** un bois 2.

2 **comp** *floor, object, structure* de bois, en bois; *fire* de bois; *stove* à bois ►**wood alcohol** esprit-de-bois *m*, alcool *m* méthylique ►**wood anemone** anémone *f* des bois ►**woodbine** *see* **woodbine** ►**wood block** bois *m* de graveur ►**wood-burning stove** poêle *m* à bois ►**wood carving** (*act: NonC*) sculpture *f* sur bois; (*object*) sculpture en bois ►**woodchuck** marmotte *f* d'Amérique ►**woodcock** (*Orn*) bécasse *f* ►**woodcraft** (*NonC*) connaissance *f* des bois ►**woodcut** gravure *f* sur bois ►**woodcutter** bûcheron *m*, -onne *f* ►**woodcutting** (*Art: act, object*) gravure *f* sur bois; (*in forest*) abattage *m* des arbres ►**wood engraving** gravure *f* sur bois ►**woodland n** (*NonC*) région boisée, bois *mpl* ◊ **comp** *flower, path etc* des bois ►**woodlark** (*Orn*) alouette *f* des bois ►**woodlouse** (**pl woodlice**) cloporte *m* ►**woodman** (**pl woodmen**) forestier *m* ►**wood nymph** (*Myth*) dryade *f*, nymphe *f* des bois ►**woodpecker** (*Orn*) pic *m* ►**woodpigeon** (*Orn*) (pigeon *m*) ramier *m* ►**woodpile** tas *m* de bois ►**wood pulp** pulpe *f*, pâte *f* à papier ►**wood shavings** copeaux *mpl* (de bois) ►**woodshed** bûcher *m* ►**woodsman** (**pl woodsmen**) (*US*) = **woodman** ►**wood trim** (*US*) boiseries *fpl* ►**woodwind** (*Mus*) (*one instrument*) bois *m*; (*collective pl*) bois *mpl* ►**wood wool** (*NonC*) copeaux *mpl* de bois ►**woodwork** (*NonC*) *see* **woodwork** ►**woodworm** ver *m* du bois; **the table has got woodworm** la table est piquée des vers *or* mangée aux vers *or* vermoulue.

woodbine ['wʊdbaɪn] **n** chèvrefeuille *m*.

wooded ['wʊdɪd] **adj** boisé. **thickly/sparsely ~** très/peu boisé.

wooden ['wʊdn] 1 **adj** (*lit*) de bois, en bois; (*fig*) *movement, gesture* raide; *acting, performance* raide, qui manque de naturel; *look* sans expression, inexpressif, impassible. **~ face** visage *m* de bois; **the W~ Horse of Troy** le cheval de Troie; (*US pej*) **~ Indian**⁑ (*constrained*) personne *f* raide comme la justice; (*dull*) personne terne *or* ennuyeuse; **~ leg** jambe *f* de bois; (*US fig*) **~ nickel*** objet *m* sans valeur; **to try to sell sb ~ nickels*** essayer de rouler qn; **~ spoon** cuiller *f* de *or* en bois (*also Rugby, fig*). 2 **comp** ►**wooden-headed** idiot, imbécile.

woodenly ['wʊdnlɪ] **adv** *say* impassiblement.

woodsy ['wʊdzɪ] **adj** (*US*) *countryside* boisé; *flowers etc* des bois.

woodwork ['wʊdwɜːk] **n** a (*craft, subject*) (*carpentry*) menuiserie *f*; (*cabinet-making*) ébénisterie *f*. b (*in house*) (*beams etc*) charpente *f*; (*doors, skirting boards, window frames etc*) boiseries *fpl*. (*fig pej*) **to come out of the ~*** sortir d'un peu partout, apparaître comme par miracle. c (* *Ftbl*) bois *mpl*, poteaux *mpl* (de but).

woody ['wʊdɪ] **adj** *countryside* boisé; *plant, stem, texture* ligneux; *odour* de *or* du bois.

wooer† ['wuːəʳ] **n** prétendant *m*.

woof[1] [wʊf] **n** (*Tex*) trame *f*.

woof[2] [wʊf] 1 **n** *[dog]* aboiement *m*. 2 **vi** aboyer. ~, ~! oua, oua!

woofer ['wʊfəʳ] **n** haut-parleur *m* grave, woofer *m*.

wool [wʊl] 1 **n** a laine *f*. **he was wearing ~** il portait de la laine *or* des lainages; **a ball of ~** une pelote de laine; **knitting/darning ~** laine à tricoter/repriser; (*fig*) **to pull the ~ over sb's eyes** en faire *or* laisser accroire à qn; **the sweater is all ~ *or* pure ~** le pull-over est pure laine; (*US fig*) **all ~ and a yard wide*** authentique, de première classe; *see* **dye, steel** *etc*.

b (⁑: *hair*) tifs *mpl*.

2 **comp** *cloth* de laine; *dress* en *or* de laine ►**wool fat** suint *m* ►**wool-gathering** (*fig*) manque *m* d'attention; (*fig*) **to be *or* go wool-gathering** être dans les nuages, rêvasser ►**wool-grower** éleveur *m*, -euse *f* de moutons à laine ►**wool-lined** doublé laine ►**wool merchant** négociant(e) *m(f)* en laines, lainier *m*, -ière *f* ►**the Woolsack** (*Brit Parl*) le Sac de Laine (*siège du Lord Chancellor à la chambre des Lords*) ►**woolshed** lainerie *f* ►**wool shop** magasin *m* de laines ►**wool trade** commerce *m* de la laine.

woollen, (*US*) *also* **woolen** ['wʊlən] 1 **adj** *cloth* de laine; *garment* en *or* de laine, de *or* en lainage. **~ cloth, ~ material** lainage *m*, étoffe *f* de laine; **~ goods** lainages; **the ~ industry** l'industrie lainière; **~ manufacturer** fabricant(e) *m(f)* de lainages. 2 **npl**: **~s** lainages *mpl*.

woolliness, (*US*) *also* **wooliness** ['wʊlɪnɪs] **n** (*fig: see* **woolly**) caractère confus *or* nébuleux; verbosité *f*.

woolly, (*US*) *also* **wooly** ['wʊlɪ] 1 **adj** *material, garment, appearance, sheep* laineux; (*fig*) *clouds* cotonneux; (*also* **~-headed, ~-minded**) *ideas* confus, nébuleux; *essay, book, speech* verbeux; *see* **wild**. 2 **n** (*Brit *: jersey etc*) tricot *m*, pull *m*. **woollies***, (*US*) *also* **woolies*** lainages *mpl*; **winter woollies*** lainages d'hiver.

woops* [wʊps] **excl** = **whoops***.

woozy⁑ ['wuːzɪ] **adj** dans les vapes⁑, tout chose*; (*tipsy*) éméché; *ideas* confus, nébuleux; *outline* estompé, flou. **this cold makes me feel ~** je suis complètement abruti par ce rhume.

wop⁑ [wɒp] **n** (*pej*) Rital⁑ *m*, Italien *m*.

Worcester ['wʊstəʳ] **n**: **~ sauce** *sauce épicée au soja et au vinaigre*.

word [wɜːd] 1 **n** a (*gen*) mot *m*; (*spoken*) mot, parole *f*. *[song etc]* **~s** paroles; **the written/spoken ~** ce qui est écrit/dit; **by ~ of mouth** de vive voix (*see also* **2**); **angry ~s** mots prononcés sous le coup de la colère; **fine ~s** de belles paroles; (*iro*) **fine *or* big ~s!** belles paroles!, toujours les grands mots!; **a man of few ~s** un homme peu loquace; **in ~ and deed** en parole et en fait; **~ for ~** *repeat, copy out* mot pour mot, textuellement; *translate* mot à mot, littéralement; *review, go over* mot par mot (*see also* **2**); **in other ~s** autrement dit; **in a ~** en un mot; **tell me in your own ~s** dis-le moi à ta façon; **what's the ~ for "banana" in German?, what's the German ~ for "banana"?** comment dit-on "banane" en allemand?; **the French have a ~ for it** les Français ont un mot pour dire cela; **in the ~s of Racine** comme dit Racine, selon les mots de Racine; **I can't put my thoughts/feelings into ~s** je ne trouve pas les mots pour exprimer ce que je pense/ressens; **I can't find ~s *or* I have no ~s to tell you how ...** je ne saurais vous dire comment ...; **~s fail me!** j'en perds la parole!, je ne sais plus que dire!; **without a ~, he left the room** il a quitté la pièce sans dire un mot; **with these ~s, he sat down** sur ces mots il s'est assis; **it's too stupid for ~s** c'est vraiment trop stupide; **boring is not the ~ for it!** ennuyeux est trop peu dire!; **"negligent" is a better ~ for it** "négligent" serait plus juste *or* serait plus près de la vérité; **she disappeared, there's no other ~ for it *or* that's the only ~ for it** elle a disparu, c'est bien le mot *or* on ne peut pas dire autrement; **or ~s to that effect** ou du moins ça revenait au même; **those were his very ~s** ce sont ses propres paroles, c'est ce qu'il a dit mot pour mot *or* textuellement; **it all came out in a flood of ~s** il (*or* elle *etc*) nous a tout raconté dans un flot *or* déluge de paroles; **I told him in so many ~s that ...** je lui ai carrément dit que ..., sans y aller par quatre chemins je lui ai dit que ...; **he didn't say so in so many ~s** il n'a pas dit ça explicitement, ce n'est pas exactement ce qu'il a dit (mais cela revenait au même); **I'll give you a ~ of warning** je voudrais juste vous mettre en garde; **after these ~s of warning** après cette mise en garde; **a ~ of advice** un petit conseil; **a ~ of thanks** un mot de remerciement; **a ~ to new fathers** quelques conseils aux nouveaux pères; **he won't hear a ~ against her** il n'admet absolument pas qu'on la critique (*subj*); **nobody had a good ~ to say about him (*or* it)** personne n'a trouvé la moindre chose à dire en sa faveur; **to put in a (good) ~ for sb** dire *or* glisser un mot en faveur de qn; **Mr Martin will now say a few ~s** M. Martin va maintenant prendre la parole; **I want a ~ with you** j'ai à vous parler; **can I have a ~?** puis-je vous dire un mot (en privé)?, auriez-vous un moment?; **I'll have a ~ with him about it** je lui en toucherai un mot, je vais lui en parler; **I had a ~ with him about it** je lui en ai parlé brièvement; **I remember every ~ he said** je me souviens de ce qu'il a dit mot pour mot; **I didn't breathe a ~** je n'ai pas soufflé mot; **I never said a ~** je n'ai rien dit du tout, je n'ai pas ouvert la bouche; **he didn't say a ~ about it** il n'en a absolument pas parlé; **I can't get a ~ out of him** je ne peux rien en tirer (,il reste muet); **you took the ~s right out of my mouth** c'est exactement ce que j'allais dire, vous avez dit ce que j'avais sur la langue; **you put ~s into my mouth!** vous me faites dire ce que je n'ai pas dit!; **by *or* through ~ of mouth** de vive voix; (*quarrel*) **to have ~s with sb** avoir des mots avec qn*, se disputer avec qn; **from the ~ go** dès le début *or* le commencement; **there's no such ~ as "impossible"** "impossible" n'est pas français; *see* **believe, breathe, eat, edge** *etc*.

b (*message*) mot *m*; (*NonC: news*) nouvelles *fpl*. **~ came from headquarters that ...** le quartier général nous (*or* leur *etc*) a fait dire *or* nous (*or* les *etc*) a prévenus que ...; **~ came that ...** on a appris que ...; **to send ~ that** faire savoir *or* faire dire que; **there's no ~ from John yet** on est toujours sans nouvelles de Jean; **I'm hoping for ~ about it tomorrow** j'espère que j'aurai des nouvelles demain *or* que demain je saurai ce qui se passe; **I hope he'll bring us ~ of Liline** j'espère qu'il nous apportera des nouvelles de Liline; (*rumour*) **the ~ was that he had left** le bruit courait qu'il était parti; *see* **leave**.

c (*watchword, slogan*) mot *m* d'ordre. **their new ~ is democracy**la démocratie est à l'ordre du jour.

d (*promise etc: NonC*) parole *f*, promesse *f*. **~ of honour** parole d'honneur; **a man of his ~** un homme de parole; **his ~ is his bond** il n'a qu'une parole; **he is as good as his ~** on peut le croire sur parole; **he was as good as his ~** il a tenu (sa) parole; **to give one's ~** donner sa parole (d'honneur) (*to sb* à qn, *that* que); **I give you my ~ for it** je vous en donne ma parole; **to break one's ~** manquer à sa parole; **to go back on one's ~** retirer *or* rendre *or* reprendre sa parole; **to keep one's ~** tenir (sa) parole; **to hold sb to his ~** contraindre qn à tenir sa promesse; **to take sb at his ~** prendre qn au mot; **it was his ~ against mine** c'était sa parole contre la mienne; **I've only got her ~ for it** c'est elle qui le dit, je n'ai aucune preuve; **you'll have to take his ~ for it** il vous faudra le croire sur parole; **take my ~ for it, he's a good man** croyez-m'en, c'est un brave homme; (*excl*) **(upon) my ~!*** ma parole!

e (*command*) (mot *m* d')ordre *m*; (*pass~*) mot de passe. **the ~ of command** l'ordre; **his ~ is law** c'est lui qui fait la loi; **he gave the ~ to advance** il a donné l'ordre *or* le signal d'avancer; *see* **say**.

f (*Rel*) **the W~** (*logos*) le Verbe; (*the Bible, the Gospel; also* **the**

W~ of God) le Verbe (de Dieu), la parole de Dieu.

g (*Comput*) mot *m*.

2 **comp** ►**word-blind** dyslexique ►**word-blindness** dyslexie *f* ►**wordbook** lexique *m*, vocabulaire *m* ►**word class** (*Gram*) catégorie *f* grammaticale ►**wordcount** (*Comput*) nombre *m* de mots ►**word formation** (*Ling*) formation *f* des mots ►**word-for-word** *analysis* mot par mot; **a word-for-word translation** une traduction mot-à-mot, un mot-à-mot ►**word game** jeu *m* avec des mots ►**word list** (*in exercise etc*) liste *f* de mots; (*in dictionary*) nomenclature *f* ►**word-of-mouth adj** verbal, oral ►**word order** (*Gram*) ordre *m* des mots ►**word-perfect: to be word-perfect in sth** savoir qch sur le bout du doigt ►**word picture: to give a word picture of sth** faire le tableau de qch, dépeindre qch ►**wordplay** jeu *m* sur les mots, jeu de mots ►**word processing** traitement *m* de texte; **word-processing package** système *m* de traitement de texte ►**word processor** machine *f* de traitement de texte ►**wordsmith** *see* **wordsmith** ►**word-type** (*Ling*) vocable *m* ►**wordwrap** (*Comput*) retour *m* (automatique) à la ligne.

3 **vt** *document, protest* formuler, rédiger, libeller (*Admin*). **he had ~ed the letter very carefully** il avait choisi les termes de la lettre avec le plus grand soin; **well ~ed** bien tourné; **I don't know how to ~ it** je ne sais pas comment le formuler.

wordiness ['wɜːdɪnɪs] **n** verbosité *f*.

wording ['wɜːdɪŋ] **n** *[letter, speech, statement]* termes *mpl*, formulation *f*; (*Jur, Admin*) rédaction *f*; *[official document]* libellé *m*. **the ~ of the last sentence is clumsy** la dernière phrase est maladroitement exprimée *or* formulée; **the ~ is exceedingly important** le choix des termes est extrêmement important; **change the ~ slightly** changez quelques mots (ici et là); **a different ~ would make it less ambiguous** ce serait moins ambigu si on l'exprimait autrement.

wordless ['wɜːdlɪs] **adj** *admiration, resentment* muet.

wordlessly ['wɜːdlɪslɪ] **adv** sans prononcer un mot.

wordsmith ['wɜːdsmɪθ] **n** manieur *m* de mots. **he's a skilled ~** il sait tourner ses phrases, (*stronger*) il a le génie des mots.

wordy ['wɜːdɪ] **adj** verbeux.

wore [wɔː^{r}] **pret of wear.**

work [wɜːk] 1 **n** a (*NonC: gen*) travail *m*, œuvre *f*. **to be at ~** travailler, être à l'œuvre *or* au travail; **he was at ~ on another picture** il travaillait sur un autre tableau; **there are subversive forces at ~ here** des forces subversives sont en jeu *or* à l'œuvre; **to start ~, to set to ~** se mettre au travail *or* à l'œuvre; **to set to ~ mending** *or* **to mend the fuse** entreprendre de *or* se mettre à réparer le fusible; **they set him to ~ mending the fence** ils lui ont donné pour tâche de réparer la barrière; **he does his ~ well** il travaille bien, il fait du bon travail; **good ~**! bien travaillé!, bravo!; **it's good ~** c'est du bon ouvrage *or* travail; **that's a good piece of ~** c'est du bon travail; **he's a nasty piece of ~*** c'est un sale type*; **he's doing useful ~ there** il fait œuvre utile *or* du bon travail là-bas; **she put a lot of ~ into it** elle a passé beaucoup de temps dessus; **there's still a lot of ~ to be done on it** il reste encore beaucoup à faire; **I've got some more ~ for you** j'ai encore du travail pour vous; **I'm trying to get some ~ done** j'essaie de travailler un peu; **~ has begun on the new bridge** les travaux du nouveau pont ont commencé, on a commencé la construction du nouveau pont; (*Comm, Fin*) **~ in progress** travaux *mpl* en cours; **it's women's ~** c'est un travail de femme; (*iro*) **it's nice ~ if you can get it!*** c'est une bonne planque pour ceux qui ont de la veine!*; **it's quite easy ~** ce n'est pas difficile à faire; **it's hot ~** ça donne chaud; **to make short** *or* **quick ~ of sth** faire qch très rapidement; **there's been some dirty ~* here!** il y a quelque chose de pas catholique là-dessous!; **it's obviously the ~ of a professional** c'est manifestement l'œuvre d'un professionnel *or* un travail de professionnel; **you'll have your ~ cut out** ça ne va pas être facile, tu auras du pain sur la planche *or* de quoi t'occuper (*to do* pour faire); *see* **short 1a, thirsty** *etc.*

b (*as employment*) travail *m*. **to go to ~** aller travailler, aller à l'usine (*or* au bureau *etc*); **on his way to ~** en allant à son travail (*or* au bureau *etc*); (*more formally, Admin*) en se rendant à son lieu de travail; **he's looking for ~** il cherche du travail *or* de l'emploi; **he's at ~ at the moment** il est au bureau (*or* à l'usine *etc*) en ce moment; **he is in regular ~** il a un emploi régulier; **to be out of ~** être en *or* au chômage *or* sans emploi; (*Econ, Admin*) **numbers out of ~** inactifs *mpl*; **to put** *or* **throw sb out of ~** réduire qn au chômage; **this decision threw a lot of men out of ~** cette décision a fait beaucoup de chômeurs; **600 men were thrown out of ~** 600 hommes ont été licenciés *or* ont perdu leur emploi; **he's off ~ today** il n'est pas allé (*or* venu) travailler aujourd'hui; **he has been off ~ for 3 days** il est absent depuis 3 jours; **a day off ~** un jour de congé; **I've got time off ~** j'ai du temps libre; **where is his (place of) ~?** où est son travail?*, où travaille-t-il?; **domestic ~** travaux domestiques; **office ~** travail de bureau; **I've done a full day's ~** (*lit*) j'ai fait ma journée; (*fig*) j'ai eu une journée bien remplie, je n'ai pas perdu mon temps aujourd'hui; (*fig*) **it's all in a day's ~** ça n'a rien d'extraordinaire; (*US*) **"work wanted"** "demandes d'emploi"; *see* **day, social** *etc.*

c (*product*) ouvrage *m*, œuvre *f*; *[seamstress etc]* ouvrage. **the ~s of God** les œuvres de Dieu; **good ~s** bonnes œuvres; **his life's ~** l'œuvre de sa vie; **his ~ will not be forgotten** son œuvre restera dans la mémoire des hommes; **each man will be judged by his ~s** chaque homme sera jugé selon ses œuvres; **it was a ~ of skill and patience** c'était un ouvrage qui faisait preuve d'habileté et de patience.

d (*Art, Literat, Mus*) œuvre *f*; (*on specific subject*) ouvrage *m*. **a ~ of art** une œuvre d'art; **the complete ~s of Corneille** les œuvres complètes de Corneille; **Camus' last ~** la dernière œuvre de Camus; **a ~ on Dickens** un ouvrage sur Dickens; **it's one of the few ~s he has written on ...** c'est l'un des quelques ouvrages qu'il ait écrits sur ...; **this ~ was commissioned by ...** cette œuvre a été commandée par ...; **~s of fiction/reference** ouvrages de fiction/référence; **he sells a lot of his ~** il vend beaucoup de tableaux (*or* de livres *etc*).

e **(pl) ~s** (*gen, Admin, Mil*) travaux *mpl*; *[clock, machine etc]* mécanisme *m*. **building ~s** travaux de construction; **road ~s** travaux d'entretien *or* de réfection de la route; (*fig*) **they gave him the ~s⁑** ils lui en ont fait voir de dures*, il a eu droit à un interrogatoire (*or* une engueulade⁑ *etc*) en règle; (*murdered him*) ils l'ont descendu⁑, ils lui ont fait la peau⁑; (*fig*) **the whole ~s*** tout le tremblement*, tout le tralala*; (*US fig*) **to put in the ~s*** jouer le grand jeu; *see* **public, spanner** *etc.*

f *see* **works.**

2 **comp** ►**workaday** *see* **workaday** ►**workaholic** *see* **workaholic** ►**workbag** sac *m* à ouvrage ►**workbasket** corbeille *f* à ouvrage ►**workbench** établi *m* ►**workbook** (*exercise book*) cahier *m* d'exercices; (*manual*) manuel *m*; (*work record book*) cahier de préparations, cahier-journal *m* ►**workbox** boîte *f* à ouvrage ►**work-camp** (*prison*) camp *m* de travail forcé; (*voluntary*) chantier *m* de travail (bénévole) ►**workday adj** = **workaday; n a workday of 8 hours** une journée de travail de 8 heures; **Saturday is a workday** (*gen*) on travaille le samedi; (*Comm*) le samedi est un jour ouvrable ►**work-desk** bureau *m* de travail ►**work ethic** attitude *f* moraliste envers le travail ►**work experience** stage *m* ►**work file** (*Comput*) fichier *m* de travail ►**work force** (*Econ, Ind*) main-d'œuvre *f*, personnel *m* ►**workhorse** cheval *m* de labour; (*fig*) battant *m* ►**workhouse** (*Brit Hist*) hospice *m*; (*US Jur*) maison *f* de correction ►**work-in** (*Ind*) ≃ occupation *f* du lieu de travail (par la main-d'œuvre) ►**work load: his work load is too heavy** il a trop de travail; **they were discussing work loads** ils discutaient de la répartition du travail ►**workman** (**pl workmen**) *see* **workman** ►**workmate** camarade *mf* de travail ►**workout** (*Sport*) séance *f* d'entraînement ►**workpeople** travailleurs *mpl*, ouvriers *mpl* ►**work permit** permis *m* de travail ►**work prospects** *[course, training]* débouchés *mpl*; *[student]* perspectives *fpl* ►**workroom** salle *f* de travail ►**work-rule** (*US Ind*) = **work-to-rule** ►**work sheet** (*Comput*) feuille *f* de programmation ►**workshop** atelier *m* ►**work-shy: to be workshy** être rebuté par le travail, être fainéant ►**work station** poste *m* de travail ►**work-study student** (*US Univ*) étudiant(e) *m(f)* ayant un emploi rémunéré par l'université ►**work surface** = **worktop** ►**worktable** table *f* de travail ►**worktop** plan *m* de travail ►**work-to-rule** (*Brit Ind*) grève *f* du zèle ►**work week:** (*US*) **a work week of 38 hours** une semaine de 38 heures ►**work-worn** *hands* usé par le travail; *see also* **works 2.**

3 **vi** a (*gen*) travailler. **to ~ hard** travailler dur; **to ~ like a Trojan** travailler comme un forçat *or* un bœuf; (*Ind*) **to ~ to rule** faire la grève du zèle; **he ~s in engineering** il est ingénieur; **he prefers to ~ in wood/clay** il préfère travailler avec le bois/la terre glaise; **he prefers to ~ in oils** il aime mieux faire de la peinture à l'huile; **he is ~ing at his maths** il travaille ses maths; **he ~ed on the car all morning** il a travaillé sur la voiture toute la matinée; (*fig*) **I've been ~ing on him but haven't yet managed to persuade him** j'ai bien essayé de le convaincre mais je n'y suis pas encore arrivé; **he's ~ing at** *or* **on his memoirs** il travaille à ses mémoires; **the police are ~ing on the case** la police enquête sur l'affaire; **have you solved the problem? — we're ~ing on it** avez-vous résolu le problème? — on y travaille *or* on cherche; **they are ~ing on the principle that ...** ils partent du principe que ...; **there are not many facts/clues** *etc* **to ~ on** on manque de faits/d'indices *etc* sur lesquels on puisse se baser *or* qui puissent servir de point de départ; **he has always ~ed for/against such a reform** il a toujours lutté pour/contre une telle réforme; **we are ~ing towards a solution/an agreement** *etc* nous nous dirigeons petit à petit vers une solution/un accord *etc; see* **overtime** *etc.*

b *[mechanism, watch, machine, car, switch]* marcher; *[drug, medicine]* agir, faire (son) effet, opérer; *[yeast]* fermenter; *[scheme, arrangement]* marcher. **the lift isn't ~ing** l'ascenseur ne marche pas *or* est en panne; **it ~s off the mains/on electricity/off a battery** ça marche sur le secteur/à l'électricité/sur pile; **my brain doesn't seem to be ~ing today** mon cerveau n'a pas l'air de fonctionner aujourd'hui; **the spell ~ed** le charme a fait son effet; **the plan ~ed like a charm** tout s'est déroulé exactement comme prévu; **it just won't ~** ça ne marchera pas *or* jamais; (*fig*) **that ~s both ways** c'est à double tranchant.

c (*move*) *[face, mouth]* se contracter, se crisper. **his tie had ~ed round to the back of his neck** sa cravate avait tourné et lui pendait dans le dos; **dust has ~ed into the mechanism** de la poussière s'est introduite *or* s'est glissée dans le mécanisme; **water has ~ed through the roof** de l'eau s'est infiltrée par le toit; **the wind has ~ed round to the south** le vent a petit à petit tourné au sud; *see* **loose.**

d (*also* ~ **one's way**) avancer (*towards* vers). **he ~ed carefully along to the edge of the cliff** il s'est approché du bord de la falaise en prenant bien garde de ne pas tomber; *see also* **4d**.

4 **vt** a (*cause to* ~) *person, staff* faire travailler; *mechanism, machine* faire marcher, actionner. **he ~s his staff too hard** il exige trop de travail de son personnel, il surmène son personnel; **he ~s himself too hard** il se surmène (*see also* **4b**); **he's ~ing himself to death** il se tue à la tâche; **can you ~ the sewing machine?** sais-tu te servir de la machine à coudre?; **the machine is ~ed by electricity** la machine marche à l'électricité; *see* **finger**.

b (*achieve by* ~) *miracle* faire, accomplir; *change* apporter. **to ~ wonders** *or* **marvels** *[person]* faire des merveilles; *[drug, medicine, action, suggestion etc]* faire merveille; **he ~ed his passage to Australia** il a payé son passage en travaillant à bord du bateau sur lequel il a gagné l'Australie; **to ~ one's way through college** travailler pour payer ses études (*see also* **4d**); (*fig*) **he has managed to ~ his promotion*** il s'est débrouillé pour obtenir son avancement; **can you ~ it* so that she can come too?** pouvez-vous faire en sorte qu'elle puisse venir aussi?; **I'll ~ it* if I can** si je peux m'arranger pour le faire je le ferai; **he ~ed his audience (up) into a frenzy of enthusiasm** il est arrivé par degrés à soulever l'enthousiasme de son auditoire; **he ~ed himself (up) into a rage** il s'est mis dans une colère noire; *see* **oracle**.

c (*operate, exploit*) *mine, land* exploiter, faire valoir. (*Comm*) **this representative ~s the south-east region** ce représentant couvre la région du sud-est.

d (*manoeuvre etc*) **to ~ a ship into position** exécuter une manœuvre pour placer un bateau en position (opérationnelle); **he ~ed the rope gradually through the hole** il est petit à petit arrivé à faire passer la corde dans le trou; **he ~ed his hands free** il est arrivé à délier ses mains; **to ~ sth loose** arriver à desserrer qch; **he ~ed the lever up and down** il a levé et baissé le levier plusieurs fois; **she ~ed the hook carefully out of the cloth** en s'y prenant minutieusement elle a réussi à enlever le crochet du tissu; **he ~ed the incident into his speech** il s'est arrangé pour introduire *or* parler de l'incident dans son discours; **he ~ed his way along to the edge of the roof** il s'est approché graduellement du rebord du toit; **I saw him ~ing his way round towards me** je l'ai vu qui s'approchait de moi petit à petit.

e (*make, shape*) *metal, wood, leather etc* travailler, façonner; *dough, clay* travailler, pétrir; *object* façonner (*out of* dans); (*sew*) coudre; (*embroider*) *design etc* broder. (*Culin*) ~ **the butter and sugar together** travaillez bien le beurre et le sucre; ~ **the flour in gradually** incorporez la farine petit à petit.

►**work away** vi: **they worked away all day** ils ont passé toute la journée à travailler; **she was working away at her embroidery** elle continuait à faire sa broderie.

►**work down** vi *[stockings etc]* glisser.

►**work in** 1 vi a *[dust, sand etc]* s'introduire, s'insinuer. b (*cooperate etc*) **she works in with us as much as possible** elle collabore avec nous autant que possible; **this doesn't work in with our plans for ...** ceci ne cadre pas *or* ne concorde pas avec nos projets pour ...; **that'll work in quite well** ça cadrera très bien. 2 **vt sep** *bolt, nut, stick etc* introduire petit à petit; *reference, quotation, subject etc* glisser, introduire. **we'll work in a mention of it somewhere** on s'arrangera pour le mentionner quelque part; *see also* **work 4e**. 3 **work-in** n *see* **work 2**.

►**work off** 1 vi *[nut, handle etc]* se détacher. 2 **vt sep** a *debt, obligation* acquitter en travaillant. b *one's surplus fat* se débarrasser de; *weight* éliminer; *frustration, rage* passer, assouvir. **to work off one's energy** dépenser son surplus d'énergie; **don't work off your annoyance on me!** ne passe pas ta mauvaise humeur sur moi!; **he worked it all off doing the gardening** il s'est défoulé en faisant du jardinage.

►**work out** 1 vi a *[plan, arrangement]* aboutir, réussir, marcher; *[puzzle, problem, sum]* se résoudre exactement, marcher*. **what does the total work out at?** cela s'élève à *or* fait combien en tout?; **it works out at 5 apples per child** ça fait 5 pommes par enfant; **it's all working out as planned** tout se déroule comme prévu; **things didn't work out (well) for her** les choses ont plutôt mal tourné pour elle; **their marriage didn't work out** leur mariage n'a pas marché*; **it will work out right in the end** tout finira (bien) par s'arranger; **how did it work out?** comment ça a marché?*; **it hasn't worked out that way** les choses se sont passées autrement, il en est allé autrement.

b *[athlete, boxer etc]* s'entraîner.

2 **vt sep** a *calculation, equation* résoudre; *answer, total* trouver; *code* déchiffrer; *problem* résoudre; *puzzle* faire, résoudre; *plan, scheme, idea* élaborer, mettre au point; *settlement* (*details*) mettre au point; (*differences of opinion*) régler. **I'll have to work it out** (*gen*) il faut que je réfléchisse; (*counting*) il faut que je calcule; **who worked all this out?** qui a eu l'idée de tout ça?; **can you work out where we are on the map?** peux-tu découvrir où nous sommes sur la carte?; **he worked out why she'd gone** il a fini par découvrir pourquoi elle était partie; **I can't work it out** ça me dépasse.

b (*exhaust resources of*) *mine, land* épuiser.

c *one's anger etc* (*express*) donner libre cours à; (*get rid of*) passer, assouvir. **to work out one's energy** dépenser son surplus d'énergie; (*anger, frustration etc*) **he worked it all out doing the gardening** il s'est défoulé en faisant du jardinage; **don't work out your annoyance on me!** ne passe pas ta mauvaise humeur sur moi!

3 **workout** n *see* **work 2**.

►**work over*** **vt sep** (*beat up*) passer à tabac, tabasser*.

►**work round** vi (*in conversation, negotiations etc*) **you'll have to work round to that subject tactfully** il faudra que vous abordiez (*subj*) ce sujet avec tact; **what are you working round to?** où voulez-vous en venir?; *see also* **work 3c**.

►**work up** 1 vi a **events were working up to a climax** on était au bord de la crise, une crise se préparait; **the book works up to a dramatic ending** l'auteur a su amener un dénouement dramatique; (*in conversation etc*) **to work up to sth** en venir à qch, préparer le terrain pour qch; **what is he working up to?** où veut-il bien en venir?; **I thought he was working up to a proposal** je croyais qu'il préparait le terrain pour faire sa demande.

b *[garment etc]* remonter.

2 **vt sep** *trade, business* développer. **he worked the firm up from almost nothing into a major company** en partant pratiquement de rien il a réussi à faire de cette firme une compagnie de grande envergure; **he worked his way up to the top of his firm** il a gravi un à un tous les échelons de la hiérarchie dans son entreprise; **he worked his way up from office boy to managing director** il est devenu P.D.G. après avoir commencé au bas de l'échelle en tant que garçon de bureau; **he worked his way up from nothing** il est parti de rien et s'est élevé à la force du poignet; (*Comm*) **he's trying to work up a connection in Wales** il essaie d'établir une liaison au pays de Galles; **he worked the crowd up into a fury** il a déchaîné la fureur de la foule; **to work up an appetite** s'ouvrir l'appétit; **I can't work up much enthusiasm for the plan** je n'arrive pas à m'enthousiasmer beaucoup pour ce projet; **can't you work up a little more interest in it?** tu ne pourrais pas t'y intéresser un petit peu plus?; **to work o.s. up, to get worked up** se mettre dans tous ses états, s'énerver.

-work [wɜːk] **n ending in comps: cement-work** le ciment; **lattice-work** le treillis.

workable [ˈwɜːkəbl] **adj** a *scheme, arrangement, solution, suggestion* possible, réalisable. **it's just not ~** ça ne marchera jamais. b *mine, land* exploitable.

workaday [ˈwɜːkədeɪ] **adj** *clothes* de travail, de tous les jours; *event* banal, courant.

workaholic* [ˌwɜːkəˈhɒlɪk] **n** bourreau *m or* drogué(e) *m(f)* de travail.

worker [ˈwɜːkəʳ] 1 **n** (*gen, Ind, Agr etc*) ouvrier *m*, -ière *f*; (*esp Pol*) travailleur *m*, -euse *f*. **woman ~** ouvrière; **he's a good ~** il travaille bien; **he's a fast ~** (*lit*) il travaille vite; (* *fig*) il ne perd pas de temps; **all the ~s in this industry** tous ceux qui travaillent dans cette industrie; (*Ind*) **management and ~s** patronat *m* et travailleurs *or* ouvriers; **we rely on volunteer ~s** nous dépendons de travailleurs bénévoles; **office ~** employé(e) *m(f)* de bureau; **research ~** chercheur *m*, -euse *f*; (*Brit*) **Workers' Educational Association** ≃ Association *f* d'éducation populaire.

2 **comp** ►**worker ant** ouvrière *f*, fourmi *f* neutre ►**worker bee** (abeille *f*) ouvrière *f* ►**worker director** (*Ind*) ouvrier *m* faisant partie du conseil d'administration ►**worker participation** (*Ind*) participation *f* des travailleurs *or* ouvriers ►**worker priest** prêtre-ouvrier *m*.

working [ˈwɜːkɪŋ] 1 **adj** *clothes, lunch, dinner, group* de travail; *model* qui marche; *partner, population* actif. **~ capital** fonds *mpl* de roulement; **the ~ class** la classe ouvrière (*see also* **2**); (*Pol: collectively*) **the ~ classes** le prolétariat; (*Brit*) **a ~ day of 8 hours** une journée de travail de 8 heures; **during** *or* **in ~ hours** pendant les heures de travail, pendant le service; (*Brit*) **Saturday is a ~ day** (*gen*) on travaille le samedi; (*Comm*) le samedi est un jour ouvrable; (*Comput*) **~ disk** disque *m* de travail; (*gen*) **~ life** vie *f* active; **she spent most of her ~ life abroad** elle a passé la plus grande partie de sa vie active à l'étranger; **a long and strenuous ~ life** une longue vie de labeur; **~ drawing** épure *f*; **good ~ environment** bonnes conditions de travail; **~ expenses** *[mine, factory]* frais *mpl* d'exploitation; *[salesman]* frais; **~ hypothesis** hypothèse *f* de travail; (*Pol etc*) **to have a ~ majority** avoir une majorité suffisante; (*Ind, Soc etc*) **the ~ man will not accept ...** les ouvriers *mpl or* les travailleurs *mpl* n'accepteront pas ...; **he's an ordinary ~ man** c'est un simple ouvrier; **he's a ~ man now** il travaille maintenant, il gagne sa vie maintenant; (*Brit*) **~ party** (*gen*) groupe *m* de travail, (*grander*) commission *f* d'enquête; (*squad: of soldiers*) escouade *f*; **a ~ wife** une femme mariée qui travaille; **she is an ordinary ~ woman** c'est une simple ouvrière; **she is a ~ woman** elle travaille, elle gagne sa vie; (*Comm, Press, Soc etc*) **the ~ woman** la femme active; *see* **order**.

2 **comp** ►**working-class** *origins, background, accent, suburb* ouvrier, prolétarien; **he is working-class** il appartient à la classe ouvrière.

3 **n** a **~s** (*mechanism*) mécanisme *m*; *[government, organization]* rouages *mpl*; (*Min*) chantier *m* d'exploitation; **I don't understand the ~s of her mind** je ne comprends pas ce qui se passe dans sa tête.

b (*NonC*) (*work*) travail *m*; *[machine etc]* fonctionnement *m*; *[yeast]* fermentation *f*; *[mine, land]* exploitation *f*, faire-valoir *m*; *[metal, wood, leather, clay, dough]* travail; (*Sewing*) couture *f*; (*embroidery*) broderie *f*.

workman ['wɜːkmən], pl **workmen** 1 n a (*gen, Comm, Ind etc*) ouvrier *m*. **a ~ came to fix the roof** un ouvrier est venu réparer le toit; (*Prov*) **a bad ~ blames his tools** les mauvais ouvriers se plaignent toujours de leurs outils (*Prov*); **workmen's compensation** pension *f* d'invalidité (*pour ouvriers*).
b **to be a good ~** bien travailler, avoir du métier.
2 comp ► **workmanlike** *person, attitude* professionnel; *object, product, tool* bien fait, soigné; (*fig*) *attempt* sérieux; **it was a workmanlike essay** c'était une dissertation honnête *or* bien travaillée; **he made a workmanlike job of it** il a fait du bon travail; **he set about it in a very workmanlike way** il s'y est pris comme un vrai professionnel.

workmanship ['wɜːkmənʃɪp] n *[craftsman]* métier *m*, maîtrise *f*; *[artefact]* exécution *f or* fabrication *f* soignée. **this example of his ~** cet exemple de sa maîtrise *or* de son habileté professionnelle *or* de ce qu'il est capable de faire; **a chair of fine ~** une chaise faite avec art; **a superb piece of ~** un *or* du travail superbe.

workmen ['wɜːkmən] npl of **workman**.

works [wɜːks] 1 n sing or pl (*Brit Ind etc: factory*) usine *f*; (*processing plant etc*) installations *fpl*. **gas~** usine à gaz; **steel~** aciérie *f*; **irrigation ~** installations d'irrigation, barrage *m*; **water~** station *f* hydraulique; **price ex ~** prix *m* sortie d'usine. 2 comp *entrance, car park, canteen* de l'usine; *car* de l'entreprise; (*as opposed to staff*) des ouvriers ► **works committee, works council** comité *m* d'entreprise ► **works manager** chef *m* d'exploitation.

world [wɜːld] 1 n a (*gen, Geog etc*) monde *m*. **all over the ~, all the ~ over** dans le monde entier; **to go round the ~, to go on a trip round the ~** *or* **a round-the-~ tour** faire le tour du monde, voyager autour du monde; **a round-the-~ cruise** une croisière autour du monde; **to see the ~** voir du pays, courir le monde; **the most powerful nation in the ~** la nation la plus puissante du monde; **it is known throughout the ~** c'est connu dans le monde entier, c'est universellement connu; **our company leads the ~ in shoe manufacturing** notre compagnie est à la pointe de l'industrie de la chaussure dans le monde; **~s out in space** mondes extra-terrestres; **to be alone in the ~** être seul au monde; **it's a small ~!** (que) le monde est petit!; **the New W~** le Nouveau Monde; **the ancient ~** le monde antique, l'antiquité *f*; **the English-speaking ~** le monde anglophone; **the ~ we live in** le monde où nous vivons; **in the ~ of tomorrow** dans le monde de demain; **since the ~ began, since the beginning of the ~** depuis que le monde est monde; **it's not the end of the ~** ça pourrait être bien pire; (*Rel*) **~ without end** dans les siècles des siècles; **he is a citizen of the ~** c'est un citoyen du monde; **his childhood was a ~ of hot summers and lazy days** son enfance était un univers d'étés brûlants et de journées oisives; (*fig*) **he lives in a ~ of his own, he lives in another ~** il vit dans un monde à lui, il plane; (*fig*) **to be dead to the ~** (*asleep*) dormir profondément; (*drunk*) être ivre mort; *see* **dead 1b, fire 1a, old, old-world**.
b (*emphatic phrases*) **to think the ~ of sb** ne jurer que par qn; **she's** *or* **she means all the ~ to him** elle est tout pour lui; (*fig*) **on top of the ~*** aux anges; **it did him a** *or* **the ~ of good** ça lui a fait énormément de bien *or* un bien fou*; **there's a ~ of difference between Paul and Richard** il y a un monde entre Paul et Richard; **their views are ~s apart** leurs opinions sont diamétralement opposées; (*fig*) **they were ~s apart** (*gen*) ils n'avaient rien en commun, tout les séparait; (*in opinion etc*) ils étaient diamétralement opposés; **it was for all the ~ as if ...** c'était exactement *or* tout à fait comme si ...; **I'm the ~'s worst cook** il n'y a pas au monde pire cuisinière que moi; **I'd give the ~ to know ...** je donnerais tout au monde pour savoir ...; **it's what he wants most in (all) the ~** c'est ce qu'il veut plus que tout au monde; **in the whole (wide) ~ you won't find a better man than he is** nulle part au monde vous ne trouverez un meilleur homme que lui; **nowhere in the ~, nowhere in the whole (wide) ~** nulle part au monde; **I wouldn't do it for (anything in) the ~, nothing in the ~ would make me do it** je ne le ferais pour rien au monde, je ne le ferais pas pour tout l'or du monde; **what/where/why/how in the ~ ...?** que/où/pourquoi/comment diable* ...?; **where in the ~ has he got to?** où a-t-il bien pu passer?, où diable* est-ce qu'il est passé?
c (*this life etc*) monde *m*; (*Rel: as opposed to spiritual life*) siècle *m*, monde; (*domain, realm*) monde, univers *m*. **in this ~** ici-bas, en ce (bas) monde; (*fig*) **it's out of this ~*** c'est extraordinaire, c'est sensationnel*; **the next ~, the ~ to come** l'au-delà, l'autre monde; **he's gone to a better ~** il est parti pour un monde meilleur; **he's not long for this ~** il n'en a plus pour longtemps (à vivre); (*Rel*) **in the ~** dans le siècle; (*Rel*) **the ~, the flesh and the devil** les tentations *fpl* du monde, de la chair et du diable; **to bring a child into the ~** mettre un enfant au monde; **to come into the ~** venir au monde, naître; **the ~ of nature** le monde de la nature; **the business/sporting ~** le monde des affaires/du sport; **in the university ~** dans les milieux universitaires; **in the ~ of music** dans le monde de la musique; **the ~ of dreams** l'univers *or* le monde des rêves; **in the best of all possible ~s** dans le meilleur des mondes (possibles); *see* **best, other**.
d (*society etc*) monde *m*. **to go up in the ~** faire du chemin (*fig*); **to come down in the ~** déchoir; **he has come down in the ~** il a connu de meilleurs jours; **to make one's way in the ~** faire son chemin dans le monde; **he had the ~ at his feet** il avait le monde à ses pieds; **you have to take the ~ as you find it** il faut prendre le monde comme il est *or* les choses comme elles sont; **the ~ and his wife** absolument tout le monde, tout le monde sans exception; **you know what the ~ will say if ...** tu sais ce que les gens diront si ...; **the Rockefellers/Mr Smiths** *etc* **of this ~** des gens comme les Rockefeller/M. Smith *etc; see* **man**.
2 comp *power, war, proportions* mondial; *record, tour* du monde; *language* universel ► **the World Bank** (*Fin*) la Banque mondiale, la Banque internationale pour la reconstruction et le développement ► **world-beater*:** (*fig*) **it's a world-beater** cela a eu un succès fou* ► **World Boxing Association** World Boxing Association *f* (*association américaine de boxe*) ► **world boxing champion** champion *m* du monde de boxe ► **world champion** (*Sport*) champion *m* du monde ► **world championship** championnat *m* du monde ► **world class** n sportif (-ive) *m(f)* de niveau international ► **world-class** adj *player, team etc* de niveau international; *statesman, politician* de carrure internationale ► **World Council of Churches** Conseil *m* œcuménique des Églises ► **the World Court** (*Jur*) la Cour internationale de justice ► **the World Cup** (*Ftbl*) la Coupe du monde ► **World Fair** (*Comm*) Exposition Internationale ► **world-famous** de renommée mondiale, célèbre dans le monde entier ► **World Health Organization** Organisation mondiale de la santé ► **world music** world music *f* ► **world scale: on a world scale** à l'échelle mondiale ► **World Series** (*US Baseball*) championnat *m* national de baseball ► **world-shaking** stupéfiant ► **World title** (*Sport*) titre *m* de champion du monde; (*Boxing*) **the world title fight** le championnat du monde ► **World War One/Two** la Première/Deuxième *or* Seconde Guerre mondiale ► **world-weariness** dégoût *m* du monde ► **world-weary** las (*f* lasse) du monde ► **world-wide** adj mondial, universel ◊ adv *be known* mondialement, universellement; *travel* à travers le monde, partout dans le monde.

worldliness ['wɜːldlɪnɪs] n *[person]* attachement *m* aux biens de ce monde; (*Rel*) mondanité *f*.

worldly ['wɜːldlɪ] 1 adj *matters, pleasures* de ce monde, terrestre; *attitude* matérialiste; *person* (*acquisitive etc*) attaché aux biens de ce monde; (*experienced*) qui a l'expérience du monde; (*Rel*) mondain, temporel. **his ~ goods** sa fortune, ses biens temporels. 2 comp ► **worldly-minded** attaché aux biens de ce monde ► **worldly-wisdom** expérience *f* du monde, savoir-faire *m* ► **worldly-wise** qui a l'expérience du monde.

worm [wɜːm] 1 n a (*gen: earth~ etc*) ver *m* (de terre); (*in fruit etc*) ver; (*maggot*) asticot *m*; (*fig: person*) minable* *mf*, miteux* *m*, -euse* *f*. (*fig*) **the ~ has turned** il en a eu (*or* j'en ai eu *etc*) assez de se (*or* me *etc*) faire marcher dessus; (*US fig*) **a can of ~s*** un véritable guêpier (*fig*); (*fig*) **the ~ in the apple** *or* **bud** le ver dans le fruit (*fig*); **you ~!*** misérable!; *see* **book, glow, silk** *etc*.
b (*Med*) **~s** vers *mpl*; **to have ~s** avoir des vers.
2 comp ► **worm-cast** déjections *fpl* de ver ► **worm drive** (*Tech*) transmission *f* par vis sans fin; (*Comput*) unité *f* à disques inscriptibles une seule fois ► **worm-eaten** *fruit* véreux; *furniture* mangé aux vers, vermoulu; (*fig*) désuet (*f* -ète), suranné ► **worm gear** (*Tech*) engrenage *m* à vis sans fin ► **wormhole** piqûre *f or* trou *m* de ver ► **worm(ing) powder** (*Vet*) poudre *f* vermifuge ► **wormlike** vermiculaire, vermiforme ► **worm's eye view*** (*Phot, Cine*) contre-plongée *f*; (*fig*) point *m* de vue des humbles; (*fig*) **a worm's-eye view of what is going on** un humble aperçu de ce qui se passe ► **wormwood** *see* **wormwood**.
3 vt a (*wriggle*) **to ~ o.s.** *or* **one's way along/down/across** *etc* avancer/descendre/traverser *etc* à plat ventre *or* en rampant; **he ~ed his way through the narrow window** il a réussi en se tortillant à passer par la lucarne; (*fig*) **he ~ed his way into our group** il s'est insinué *or* immiscé dans notre groupe; **to ~ one's way into sb's heart** trouver le chemin du cœur de qn.
b (*extract*) **to ~ sth out of sb** soutirer qch à qn; **I'll ~ it out of him somehow** je m'arrangerai pour lui tirer les vers du nez.
c (*rid of ~s*) *dog etc* débarrasser de ses vers.

wormwood ['wɜːmwʊd] n armoise *f*. (*fig*) **it was ~ to him** cela le mortifiait.

wormy ['wɜːmɪ] adj *fruit* véreux; *furniture* vermoulu, mangé aux vers; *soil* plein de vers; *shape* vermiculaire.

worn [wɔːn] 1 ptp of **wear**. 2 adj *garment, carpet, tyre, hands, machine part* usé; *person* las (*f* lasse); *see also* **wear**. 3 comp ► **worn-out** *garment, carpet, tyre* usé jusqu'à la corde; *tool, machine part* complètement usé; *person* épuisé, fourbu, éreinté; *see also* **wear**.

worried ['wʌrɪd] adj inquiet (*f* -ète). **to be ~ about sth** être inquiet au sujet de *or* pour qch; **~ sick** *or* **stiff** *or* **to death*** fou (*f* folle) d'inquiétude; **where shall I put it? — I'm not ~, just leave it there** où est-ce que je pose ça? — oh!, ça n'a pas beaucoup d'importance, laisse-le là; **you had me ~ (for a minute)** tu m'as fait peur; *see also* **worry**.

worrier ['wʌrɪəʳ] n anxieux *m*, -euse *f*, inquiet *m*, -ète *f*. **he's a dreadful ~** c'est un éternel inquiet.

worrisome ['wʌrɪsəm] adj inquiétant.

worry ['wʌrɪ] 1 n souci *m*. **the ~ of having to find the money** le souci d'avoir à trouver l'argent; **he hasn't any worries** il est sans souci; **to**

make o.s. sick with ~ se faire un sang d'encre, se ronger les sangs (*about, over* au sujet de, pour); **that's the least of my worries** c'est le cadet *or* le dernier de mes soucis; **what's your ~?*** qu'est-ce qui ne va pas?; **he is a constant ~ to his parents** il est un perpétuel souci pour ses parents; **it is a great ~ to us all, it's causing us a lot of ~** cela nous fait faire *or* nous cause *or* nous donne beaucoup de souci(s); **what a ~ it all is!** tout ça c'est bien du souci!

2 comp ► **worry beads** ≃ komboloï *m* ► **worry line*** ride *f* (*causée par l'inquiétude*) ► **worryguts*, worrywart*** anxieux *m*, -euse *f*, éternel inquiet, éternelle inquiète.

3 vi a se faire du souci, s'inquiéter, s'en faire* (*about, over* au sujet de, pour), (*stronger*) se tourmenter, se faire de la bile *or* du mauvais sang (*about, over* pour, au sujet de). **don't ~ about me** ne vous faites pas de souci *or* ne vous inquiétez pas *or* ne vous en faites pas* pour moi *or* à mon sujet; **she worries about her health** sa santé la tracasse; **I've got enough to ~ about without that (as well)** j'ai déjà assez de soucis (comme ça); **there's nothing to ~ about** il n'y a aucune raison de vous inquiéter; (*iro*) **I should ~!*** je ne vois pas pourquoi je m'en ferais!*; **I'll punish him if I catch him, don't you ~!*** je le punirai si je l'y prends, (ne) t'en fais pas!*; **not to ~!** tant pis — ce n'est pas grave!

b **to ~ at sth** = **to ~ sth**; *see* **4b**.

4 vt a (*make anxious*) inquiéter, tracasser. **it worries me that he should believe ...** cela m'inquiète qu'il puisse croire ...; **the whole business worries me to death*** j'en suis fou d'inquiétude; **don't ~ yourself about it** ne te fais pas de mauvais sang *or* de bile pour ça; **don't ~ your head!** ne vous mettez pas martel en tête; **she worried herself sick over it all** elle s'est rendue malade à force de se faire du souci pour tout ça, elle s'est rongé les sangs à propos de tout ça; **what's ~ing you?** qu'est-ce qui ne va pas?; *see also* **worried**.

b [*dog etc*] *bone, rat, ball* prendre entre les dents et secouer, jouer avec; *sheep* harceler. **he kept ~ing the loose tooth with his tongue** il n'arrêtait pas d'agacer avec sa langue la dent qui branlait.

►**worry along** vi continuer à se faire du souci.

►**worry at** vt fus *problem* ressasser.

worrying ['wʌrɪɪŋ] 1 adj inquiétant. **the ~ thing is that he ...** ce qui m'inquiète *or* ce qui est inquiétant c'est qu'il ...; **to have a ~ time** passer un mauvais quart d'heure, (*longer*) en voir de dures*. 2 n: **~ does no good** il ne sert à rien de se faire du souci; **all this ~ has aged him** tout le souci qu'il s'est fait l'a vieilli; *see* **sheep**.

worse [wɜːs] 1 adj, compar of **bad** *and* **ill** pire, plus mauvais (*than* que). **your essay is ~ than his** votre dissertation est plus mauvaise que la sienne; **his is bad but yours is ~** la sienne est mauvaise mais la vôtre est pire; **you're ~ than he is!** tu es pire que lui!; **and, (what's) ~ ...** et, qui pis est ...; **it's ~ than ever** c'est pire *or* pis (*liter*) que jamais; **it could have been ~** ç'aurait pu être pire; **things couldn't be ~** ça ne pourrait pas aller plus mal; **~ things have happened** on a vu pire; (*fig hum*) **~ things happen at sea*** ce n'est pas le bout du monde, il y a pire; **and, to make matters** *or* **things ~, he ...** et, pour comble de malheur, il ...; **you've only made matters** *or* **things** *or* **it ~** tu n'as fait qu'aggraver la situation (*or* ton cas) *or* qu'envenimer les choses; **he made matters ~ for himself by refusing** il a aggravé son cas en refusant; **things will get ~ before they get better** les choses iront plus mal avant d'aller mieux; **it gets ~ and ~** ça ne fait qu'empirer, ça va de mal en pis *or* de pis en pis; **he is getting ~** (*in behaviour, memory, faculties*) il ne s'améliore *or* s'arrange pas; (*in health*) il va de plus en plus mal, son état ne fait que s'aggraver *or* qu'empirer; **to get ~** [*rheumatism etc*] empirer; [*climate, weather, food*] se détériorer, se gâter; [*economic situation, conditions*] se détériorer, empirer; **the smell is getting ~** ça sent de plus en plus mauvais; **I feel slightly ~** je me sens légèrement moins bien *or* plutôt plus mal; **business is ~ than ever** les affaires vont plus mal que jamais; **it will be the ~ for you if ...** c'est vous qui serez perdant si ...; **so much the ~ for him!** tant pis pour lui!; **he's none the ~ for his fall** il ne s'est pas ressenti de sa chute; **he's none the ~ for it** il ne s'en porte pas plus mal; **the house would be none the ~ for a coat of paint** une couche de peinture ne ferait pas de mal à cette maison; **to be the ~ for drink** être éméché *or* (*stronger*) ivre; **~ luck!*** hélas!; *see* **wear 1a**.

2 adv, compar of **badly** *and* **ill** *sing, play etc* plus mal. **he did it ~ than you did** il l'a fait plus mal que toi; **it hurts ~ than ever** ça fait plus mal que jamais; **that child behaves ~ and ~** cet enfant se conduit de mal en pis; **you might do ~ than to accept** accepter n'est pas ce que vous pourriez faire de pire; **you might** *or* **could do ~** vous pourriez faire pire *or* pis (*liter*); **he is ~ off than before** (*gen*) il se retrouve dans une situation pire qu'avant, il se retrouve encore plus mal en point qu'avant; (*financially*) il y a perdu; **I like him none the ~ for that** je ne l'en aime pas moins pour ça; **I shan't think any the ~ of you for it** je n'en aurai pas une moins bonne opinion de toi pour ça; **it's raining ~ than ever** il pleut pire *or* pis que jamais; **she hates me ~ than before** elle me déteste encore plus qu'avant; **he was taken ~ during the night** son état a empiré *or* s'est aggravé pendant la nuit.

3 n pire *m*. **I have ~ to tell you** je ne vous ai pas tout dit, il y a pire encore; **there's ~ to come** on n'a pas vu le pire; **~ followed** ensuite cela a été pire; **there has been a change for the ~** (*gen*) il y a eu une détérioration très nette de la situation; (*Med*) il y a eu une aggravation très nette de son état; *see* **bad**.

worsen ['wɜːsn] 1 vi [*situation, conditions, weather*] empirer, se détériorer, se dégrader; [*sb's state, health*] empirer, s'aggraver; [*illness*] s'aggraver; [*chances of success*] diminuer, se gâter; [*relationship*] se détériorer, se gâter, se dégrader. 2 vt empirer, rendre pire.

worsening ['wɜːsnɪŋ] n (*see* **worsen**) détérioration *f*, dégradation *f*; aggravation *f*; diminution *f*.

worship ['wɜːʃɪp] 1 n a (*Rel*) adoration *f*, culte *m*, vénération *f*; (*organized ~*) culte, office *m*; (*gen: of person*) adoration, culte; (*of money, success etc*) culte. **form of ~** liturgie *f*; (*Rel*) **place of ~** édifice consacré au culte, église *f*, temple *m*; (*Rel*) **hours of ~** heures *fpl* des offices; *see* **hero** *etc*.

b (*esp Brit: in titles*) **His W~ (the Mayor)** Monsieur le maire; **Your W~** (*to Mayor*) Monsieur le Maire; (*to magistrate*) Monsieur le Juge.

2 vt (*Rel*) *God, idol etc* adorer, vénérer, rendre un culte à; (*gen*) adorer, vénérer, avoir un culte pour, vouer un culte à; *money, success etc* avoir le culte de. **he ~ped the ground she trod on** il vénérait jusqu'au sol qu'elle foulait.

3 vi (*Rel*) faire ses dévotions (*at* à); (*fig*) **to ~ at the altar of power/fame** avoir le culte du pouvoir/de la renommée, vouer un culte au pouvoir/à la renommée.

worshipful ['wɜːʃɪpfʊl] adj (*esp Brit: in titles*) **the W~ Mayor of ...** Monsieur le maire de ...; **the W~ Company of Goldsmiths** l'honorable compagnie des orfèvres.

worshipper ['wɜːʃɪpəʳ] n (*Rel, fig*) adorateur *m*, -trice *f*. (*in church*) **~s** fidèles *mpl*.

worst [wɜːst] 1 adj, superl of **bad** *and* **ill** le (*or* la) pire, le (*or* la) plus mauvais(e). **that was the ~ hotel we found** c'est le plus mauvais hôtel que nous ayons trouvé; **the ~ film I've ever seen** le plus mauvais film que j'aie jamais vu; **the ~ student in the class** le plus mauvais élève de la classe; **that was his ~ mistake** cela a été son erreur la plus grave; **it was the ~ thing he ever did** c'est la pire chose qu'il ait jamais faite; **it was the ~ winter for 20 years** c'était l'hiver le plus rude depuis 20 ans; **he felt ~ when ...** il s'est senti le plus mal quand ...; **she arrived at the ~ possible time** elle n'aurait pas pu arriver à un plus mauvais moment *or* à un moment plus inopportun, elle n'aurait pas pu plus mal tomber; **he chose the ~ possible job for a man with a heart condition** pour quelqu'un qui souffre du cœur il n'aurait pas pu choisir un emploi plus contre-indiqué; (*US fig*) **in the ~ way*** désespérément, terriblement.

2 adv, superl of **badly** *and* **ill** le plus mal. **they all sing badly but he sings ~ of all** ils chantent tous mal mais c'est lui qui chante le plus mal de tous; **the ~-dressed man in England** l'homme le plus mal habillé d'Angleterre; **he came off ~** c'est lui qui s'en est le plus mal sorti; **such people are the ~ off** ce sont ces gens-là qui souffrent le plus *or* sont le plus affectés; **it's my leg that hurts ~ of all** c'est ma jambe qui me fait le plus mal; **that boy behaved ~ of all** ce garçon a été le pire de tous.

3 comp ► **worst-case** (*Econ, Mil, Pol etc: in planning*) *hypothesis, projection, guess* le (*or* la) plus pessimiste; **the worst-case scenario** le pire qui puisse arriver;

4 n pire *m*, pis *m* (*liter*). **the ~ that can happen** le pire *or* la pire chose *or* le pis (*liter*) qui puisse arriver; **at (the) ~** au pis aller; **to be at its (***or* **their) ~** [*crisis, storm, winter, epidemic*] être à *or* avoir atteint son (*or* leur) paroxysme *or* son (*or* leur) point culminant; [*situation, conditions, relationships*] n'avoir jamais été aussi mauvais; **at the ~ of the storm/epidemic** au plus fort de l'orage/de l'épidémie; **things** *or* **matters were at their ~** les choses ne pouvaient pas aller plus mal; **the ~ is yet to come** il faut s'attendre à pire, on n'a pas encore vu le pire; **the ~ was yet to come** le pire devait arriver ensuite, on n'avait pas encore vu le pire; **he feared the ~** il craignait le pire; **the ~ of it is that ...** le pire c'est que ...; **... and that's not the ~ of it!** ... et il y a pire encore!; **that's the ~ of ...** ça c'est l'inconvénient de ...; (*Brit*) **if the ~ comes to the ~**, (*US*) **if ~ comes to ~** en mettant les choses au pis, même en envisageant le pire; **the ~ hasn't come to the ~ yet** ce pourrait encore être pire, la situation n'est pas désespérée; **to get the ~ of it** *or* **of the bargain*** être le perdant, avoir la mauvaise part; **do your ~!** vous pouvez toujours essayer!; **it brings out the ~ in me** ça réveille en moi les pires instincts; *see* **think 3f**.

5 vt battre, avoir la supériorité sur. **to be ~ed** avoir le dessous.

worsted ['wʊstɪd] 1 n worsted *m*. 2 comp *suit etc* en worsted.

worth [wɜːθ] 1 n a (*value*) valeur *f*. **what is its ~ in today's money?** ça vaut combien *or* quelle est sa valeur en argent d'aujourd'hui?; **its ~ in gold** sa valeur (en) or; **a book/man** *etc* **of great ~** un livre/homme *etc* de grande valeur; **I know his ~** je sais ce qu'il vaut; **he showed his true ~** il a montré sa vraie valeur *or* ce dont il était capable.

b (*quantity*) **he bought 20 pence ~ of sweets** il a acheté pour 20 pence de bonbons; **50 pence ~, please** (pour) 50 pence s'il vous plaît; *see* **money, penny** *etc*.

2 adj a (*equal in value to*) **to be ~** valoir; **the book is ~ £10** le livre vaut 10 livres; **it can't be ~ that!** ça ne peut pas valoir autant!; **what** *or* **how much is it ~?** ça vaut combien?; **I don't know what it's ~ in terms of cash** je ne sais pas combien ça vaut en argent *or* quel prix ça pourrait aller chercher; **how much is the old man ~?** à combien

s'élève la fortune du vieux?; **he's ~ millions** sa fortune s'élève à plusieurs millions; **it's ~ a great deal** ça a beaucoup de valeur, ça vaut cher; **it's ~ a great deal to me** ça a beaucoup de valeur pour moi; **what is his friendship ~ to you?** quel prix attachez-vous à son amitié?; **it's more than my life is ~ to do that** ma vie ne vaudrait pas la peine d'être vécue si je faisais ça, je ne peux pas risquer de faire ça; **it's as much as my job is ~ to show him that** lui montrer ça est un coup à perdre mon emploi*; **to be ~ one's weight in gold** valoir son pesant d'or; **it's not ~ the paper it's written on** ça ne vaut pas le papier sur lequel c'est écrit; **this pen is ~ 10 of any other make** ce stylo en vaut 10 d'une autre marque; **one Scotsman's ~ 3 Englishmen** un Écossais vaut 3 Anglais; **tell me about it — what's it ~ to you?!*** dites-le-moi — vous donneriez combien pour le savoir? *or* (vous êtes prêt à payer) combien?*; **I'll give you my opinion for what it's ~** je vais vous dire ce que j'en pense, prenez-le pour ce que ça vaut; **he was running/shouting for all he was ~** il courait/criait comme un perdu *or* de toutes ses forces; **to try for all one is ~ to do sth** faire absolument tout son possible pour faire qch.

b (*deserving, meriting*) **it's ~ the effort** ça mérite qu'on fasse l'effort; **it was well ~ the trouble** ça valait bien le dérangement *or* la peine qu'on se dérange (*subj*); **it's not ~ the time and effort involved** c'est une perte de temps et d'effort; **it's ~ reading/having** *etc* ça vaut la peine d'être lu/d'en avoir un *etc;* **it's not ~ having** ça ne vaut rien*; **that's ~ knowing** c'est bon à savoir; **it's ~ thinking about** ça mérite réflexion; **it's ~ going to see the film just for the photography** rien que pour la photographie le film mérite *or* vaut la peine d'être vu; (*Prov*) **what is ~ doing is ~ doing well** ce qui vaut la peine d'être fait vaut la peine d'être bien fait (*Prov*); **it's ~ it** ça vaut la peine *or* le coup*; **will you go? — is it ~ it?** tu iras? — est-ce que ça en vaut la peine?; **life isn't ~ living** la vie ne vaut pas la peine d'être vécue; **she/it** *etc* **makes (my) life ~ living** elle/cela *etc* est ma raison de vivre; **the museum is ~ a visit** le musée vaut la visite; **it is ~ while to study the text** on gagne à étudier le texte, c'est un texte qui mérite d'être étudié; **it would be ~ (your) while to go and see him** vous gagneriez à aller le voir; **it's not ~ (my) while waiting for him** je perds (*or* perdrais) mon temps à l'attendre; **it's not ~ while** ça ne vaut pas le coup*; **it wasn't ~ his while to take the job** il ne gagnait rien à accepter l'emploi, ça ne valait pas le coup* qu'il accepte (*subj*) l'emploi; **I'll make it ~ your while*** je vous récompenserai de votre peine, vous ne regretterez pas de l'avoir fait.

3 comp ▶**worthwhile** *visit* qui en vaut la peine; *book* qui mérite d'être lu; *film* qui mérite d'être vu; *work, job, occupation, life, career* utile, qui a un sens, qui donne des satisfactions; *contribution* notable, très valable; *cause* louable, digne d'intérêt; **he is a worthwhile person to go and see** c'est une personne qu'on gagne à aller voir; **I want the money to go to someone worthwhile** je veux que l'argent aille à quelqu'un qui le mérite *or* à une personne méritante.

worthily ['wɜːðɪlɪ] adv dignement.

worthiness ['wɜːðɪnɪs] n (*see* **worthy 1b**) caractère *m* digne *or* brave; caractère louable *or* noble.

worthless ['wɜːθlɪs] adj *object, advice, contribution* qui ne vaut rien; *effort* vain. **he's a ~ individual** il ne vaut pas cher, il n'est bon à rien; **he's not completely ~** il n'est pas complètement dénué de qualités.

worthlessness ['wɜːθlɪsnɪs] n *[object, advice]* absence totale de valeur; *[effort]* inutilité *f*; *[person]* absence totale de qualités.

worthy ['wɜːðɪ] 1 adj a (*deserving*) digne (*of* de). **to be ~ of sth/sb** être digne de qch/qn, mériter qch/qn; **to be ~ to do** être digne de faire, mériter de faire; **he found a ~ opponent** *or* **an opponent ~ of him** il a trouvé un adversaire digne de lui; **it is ~ of note that ...** il est bon de remarquer que ...; **nothing ~ of mention** rien de notable; **~ of respect** digne de respect; **~ of praise** louable, digne d'éloge.

b (*meritorious*) *person* digne (*before n*), brave; *motive, cause, aim, effort* louable, noble. **the ~ people of Barcombe** les dignes *or* braves habitants *mpl* de Barcombe; **the ~ poor** les pauvres méritants.

2 n (*respectable citizen*) notable *m*; (*hum iro*) brave homme *m*, brave femme *f*. **a Victorian ~** un notable sous le règne de Victoria; (*hum iro*) **the village worthies** les dignes *or* braves habitants *mpl* du village.

wot [wɒt] 1 vti (††) sais, sait. **God ~** Dieu sait. 2 (⁑) = **what**.

Wotan ['vəʊtɑːn] n Wotan *m*.

wotcha⁑ ['wɒtʃə], **wotcher⁑** ['wɒtʃəʳ] excl (*Brit*) salut!

would [wʊd] 1 modal aux vb (cond of **will**; neg **would not** often abbr to **wouldn't**) a (*used to form cond tenses*) **he would do it if you asked him** il le ferait si vous le lui demandiez; **he would have done it if you had asked him** il l'aurait fait si vous le lui aviez demandé; **I wondered if you'd come** je me demandais si vous viendriez *or* si vous alliez venir; **I thought you'd want to know** j'ai pensé que vous aimeriez le savoir; **who would have thought it?** qui l'aurait pensé?; **you'd never guess** *or* **know she had false teeth** jamais on ne croirait qu'elle a de fausses dents; **so it would seem** c'est bien ce qu'il semble; **you would think she had enough to do without ...** on pourrait penser qu'elle a assez à faire sans ... .

b (*indicating conjecture*) **it would have been about 8 o'clock when he came** il devait être 8 heures à peu près quand il est venu, il a dû venir vers 8 heures; **he'd have been about fifty if he'd lived** il aurait eu la cinquantaine s'il avait vécu; **he'd be about 50, but he doesn't look it** il doit avoir dans les 50 ans, mais il ne les fait pas*; **I saw him come out of the shop — when would this be?** je l'ai vu sortir du magasin — quand est-ce que c'était?

c (*indicating willingness*) **I said I would do it** je lui ai dit que je le ferais *or* que je voulais bien le faire; **he wouldn't help me** il ne voulait pas m'aider, il n'a pas voulu m'aider; **the car wouldn't start** la voiture n'a pas démarré *or* n'a pas voulu démarrer; **if you would come with me, I'd go to see him** si vous vouliez bien m'accompagner, j'irais le voir; **what would you have me do?** que voulez-vous que je fasse?; **would you like some tea?** voulez-vous *or* voudriez-vous du thé?; **would you like to go for a walk?** voulez-vous faire une promenade?, est-ce que vous aimeriez faire une promenade?; (*in requests*) **would you please leave!** voulez-vous partir, s'il vous plaît!; (*frm*) **would you be so kind as to tell him** auriez-vous l'amabilité *or* la gentillesse de le lui dire; **would you mind closing the window please** voulez-vous fermer la fenêtre, s'il vous plaît.

d (*indicating habit, characteristic*) **he would always read the papers before dinner** il lisait toujours *or* il avait l'habitude de lire les journaux avant le dîner; **50 years ago the streets would be empty on Sundays** il y a 50 ans, les rues étaient vides le dimanche; **you WOULD go and tell her!** c'est bien de toi d'aller le lui dire!*, il a fallu que tu ailles le lui dire!; **you would!*** c'est bien de toi!*, ça ne m'étonne pas de toi!; **it WOULD have to rain!** il pleut, naturellement!, évidemment il fallait qu'il pleuve!

e (*expressing preferences*) **I wouldn't have a vase like that in my house** je n'aurais pas ce vase chez moi!; **I would never marry in church**je ne me marierais jamais à l'église.

f (*giving advice*) **I wouldn't worry, if I were you** à ta place, je ne m'inquiéterais pas; **I would wait and see what happens first**à ta place j'attendrais de voir ce qui se passe.

g (*subj uses: liter*) **would to God she were here!** plût à Dieu qu'elle fût ici!; **would that it were not so!** si seulement cela n'était pas le cas!; **would I were younger!** si seulement j'étais plus jeune!

2 comp ▶**would-be poet/teacher** personne *f* qui veut être poète/professeur; (*pej*) prétendu *or* soi-disant poète/professeur *m*.

wouldn't ['wʊdnt] = **would not**; *see* **would**.

would've ['wʊdəv] = **would have**; *see* **would**.

wound¹ [wuːnd] 1 n (*lit, fig*) blessure *f*; (*esp Med*) plaie *f*. **bullet/knife ~** blessure causée par une balle/un couteau; **he had 3 bullet ~s in his leg** il avait été blessé par 3 balles à la jambe; **chest/head ~** blessure *or* plaie à la poitrine/tête; **the ~ is healing up** la plaie se cicatrise; *see* **lick, salt** *etc.* 2 vt (*lit, fig*) blesser. **he was ~ed in the leg/in his self esteem** il était blessé à la jambe/dans son amour-propre; **the bullet ~ed him in the shoulder** la balle l'a atteint *or* l'a blessé à l'épaule; **her feelings were** *or* **she was ~ed by this remark** elle a été profondément blessée par cette remarque; *see also* **wounded**.

wound² [waʊnd] pret, ptp of **wind²**, **wind³**.

wounded ['wuːndɪd] 1 adj *soldier* blessé; (*fig*) *vanity etc* blessé. **a ~ man** un blessé. 2 npl: **the ~** les blessés *mpl*; *see* **walking, war** *etc.*

wounding ['wuːndɪŋ] adj blessant.

wove [wəʊv] pret of **weave**.

woven ['wəʊvən] ptp of **weave**.

wow* [waʊ] 1 excl sensass!⁑, terrible!* 2 n a **it's a ~!** c'est sensationnel!* *or* terrible!* b (*Acoustics*) pleurage *m*, baisse *f* de hauteur du son. 3 vt (*: *make enthusiastic*) emballer*.

WP [ˌdʌbljuːˈpiː] a (abbr of **weather permitting**) si le temps le permet. b abbr of **word processing**. c abbr of **word processor**.

wpb* n (abbr of **wastepaper basket**) *see* **waste**.

WPC [ˌdʌbljuːpiːˈsiː] n (abbr of **Woman Police Constable**) *see* **woman**.

wpm (abbr of **words per minute**) mots/minute.

WRAC [ræk] n (*Brit*) (abbr of **Women's Royal Army Corps**) *section féminine de l'armée britannique*.

wrack¹ [ræk] vt = **rack¹ 3**.

wrack² [ræk] n = **rack²**.

wrack³ [ræk] n (*seaweed*) varech *m*.

WRAF [ræf] n (*Brit*) (abbr of **Women's Royal Air Force**) *section féminine de l'armée de l'air britannique*.

wraith [reɪθ] n apparition *f*, spectre *m*. **~-like** spectral.

wrangle ['ræŋgl] 1 n altercation *f*, dispute *f*. **the ~s within the party** les disputes à l'intérieur du parti. 2 vi se disputer, se chamailler* (*about, over* à propos de). **they were wrangling over** *or* **about who should pay** ils n'arrivaient pas à s'entendre pour décider qui payerait.

wrangler ['ræŋgləʳ] n (*Cambridge Univ*) ≃ major *m*; (*US: cowboy*) cowboy *m*.

wrangling ['ræŋglɪŋ] n (*quarrelling*) disputes *fpl*.

wrap [ræp] 1 n (*shawl*) châle *m*; (*stole, scarf*) écharpe *f*; (*cape*) pèlerine *f*; (*coat*) manteau *m*; (*housecoat etc*) peignoir *m*; (*rug, blanket*) couverture *f*. **~s** (*outdoor clothes*) vêtements chauds; (*outer covering: on parcel etc*) emballage *m*; (*fig*) **to keep a scheme under ~s** ne pas dévoiler un projet; (*fig*) **when the ~s come off** quand le voile est levé; (*fig: Cine*) **it's a ~*** c'est dans la boîte*.

2 comp ▶**wraparound** *or* **wrapover skirt/dress** jupe *f*/robe *f* portefeuille *inv* ▶**wrapround rear window** (*Aut*) lunette *f* arrière panoramique ▶**wrap-up*** (*US*) (*summary*) résumé *m*, reprise *f* en

bref; (*concluding event*) conclusion *f*, aboutissement *f*.
3 vt (*cover*) envelopper (*in* dans); (*pack*) *parcel, gift* emballer, empaqueter (*in* dans); (*wind*) *tape, bandage* enrouler (*round* autour de). (*Culin*) **~ the chops in foil** enveloppez les côtelettes dans du papier d'aluminium; **chops ~ped in foil** côtelettes *fpl* en papillotes; (*in shops*) **shall I ~ it for you?** est-ce que je vous l'enveloppe?, est-ce que je vous fais un paquet?; **she ~ped the child in a blanket** elle a enveloppé l'enfant dans une couverture; **~ the rug round your legs** enroulez la couverture autour de vos jambes, enveloppez vos jambes dans la couverture; **he ~ped his arms round her** il l'a enlacée; **~ped bread/cakes** *etc* pain *m*/gâteaux *mpl* pré-emballé(s) *or* pré-empaqueté(s); (*fig*) **the town was ~ped in mist** la brume enveloppait la ville; **the whole affair was ~ped in mystery** toute l'affaire était enveloppée *or* entourée de mystère; (*fig*) **he ~ped‡ the car round a lamppost** il a encadré* un lampadaire; *see* **gift**.

►**wrap up** 1 vi a (*dress warmly*) s'habiller chaudement, s'emmitoufler. **wrap up well!** couvrez-vous bien!
b (*Brit* ‡: *be quiet*) se taire, la fermer‡, la boucler‡. **wrap up!** la ferme!‡, boucle-la!‡
2 vt sep a *object* envelopper (*in* dans); *parcel* emballer, empaqueter (*in* dans); *child, person* (*in rug etc*) envelopper; (*in clothes*) emmitoufler; (*fig: conceal*) *one's intentions* dissimuler. **wrap yourself up well!** couvrez-vous bien!; (*fig*) **he wrapped up his meaning in unintelligible jargon** il a entortillé ce qu'il voulait dire dans un jargon tout à fait obscur; **he wrapped it up a bit*, but what he meant was ...** il ne l'a pas dit franchement *or* il l'a enrobé un peu *or* il a quelque peu tourné autour du pot*, mais ce qu'il voulait dire c'est ...; **tell me straight out, don't try to wrap it up*** dis-le moi carrément, n'essaie pas de me dorer la pilule.
b (*fig: engrossed*) **to be wrapped up in one's work** être absorbé par *or* ne vivre que pour son travail; **to be wrapped up in sb** penser constamment à qn; **he is quite wrapped up in himself** il ne pense qu'à lui-même; **they are wrapped up in each other** ils vivent entièrement l'un pour l'autre, ils n'ont d'yeux que l'un pour l'autre.
c (*: *conclude*) *deal* conclure. **he hopes to wrap up his business there by Friday evening** il espère conclure *or* régler ce qu'il a à y faire d'ici vendredi soir; **let's get all this wrapped up** finissons-en avec tout ça; **he thought he had everything wrapped up** il pensait avoir tout arrangé *or* réglé; (*esp US: fig*) **to wrap up the evening's news** résumer les informations de la soirée.
3 **wrap-up** n *see* **wrap 2**.

wrapper ['ræpəʳ] n a [*sweet, chocolate, chocolate bar*] papier *m*; [*parcel*] papier d'emballage; [*newspaper for post*] bande *f*; [*book*] jaquette *f*, couverture *f*. b (*US: garment*) peignoir *m*.

wrapping ['ræpɪŋ] 1 n [*parcel*] papier *m* (d'emballage); [*sweet, chocolate*] papier. 2 comp ►**wrapping paper** (*brown paper*) papier *m* d'emballage, papier kraft; (*decorated paper*) papier (pour) cadeau.

wrath [rɒθ] n (*liter*) colère *f*, courroux *m* (*liter*).

wrathful ['rɒθfʊl] adj (*liter*) courroucé (*liter*).

wrathfully ['rɒθfəlɪ] adv (*liter*) avec courroux (*liter*).

wreak [riːk] vt *one's anger etc* assouvir (*upon sb* sur qn); *destruction* entraîner violemment. **to ~ vengeance** *or* **revenge** assouvir une vengeance (*on sb* sur qn); (*lit*) **to ~ havoc** faire des ravages, dévaster; (*fig*) **this ~ed havoc with their plans** cela a bouleversé *or* a chamboulé* tous leurs projets.

wreath [riːθ] n, pl **~s** [riːðz] [*flowers*] guirlande *f*, couronne *f*; (*funeral ~*) couronne; [*smoke*] volute *f*, ruban *m*; [*mist*] nappe *f* (*mince*). **laurel ~** couronne de laurier; (*ceremony*) **the laying of ~s** le dépôt de gerbes *fpl* au monument aux morts.

wreathe [riːð] 1 vt a (*garland*) *person* couronner (*with* de); *window etc* orner (*with* de). (*fig*) **valley ~d in mist** vallée enveloppée de brume; **hills ~d in cloud** collines *fpl* dont le sommet disparaît dans les nuages; **his face was ~d in smiles** son visage était rayonnant. b (*entwine*) *flowers, ribbons* enrouler (*round* autour de), tresser, entrelacer.
2 vi [*smoke*] **to ~ upwards** s'élever en tournoyant.

wreck [rek] 1 n a (*~ed ship*) épave *f*, navire naufragé; (*act, event*) naufrage *m*; (*fig: of hopes, plans, ambitions*) naufrage, effondrement *m*, anéantissement *m*. **to be saved from the ~** réchapper du naufrage; **the ~ of the Hesperus** le naufrage de l'Hespérus; **sunken ~s in the Channel** des épaves englouties au fond de la Manche; **the ship was a total ~** le navire a été entièrement perdu.
b (*accident: Aut, Aviat, Rail*) accident *m*; (*~ed train/plane/car etc*) train *m*/avion *m*/voiture *f etc* accidenté(e), épave *f*; (*building*) ruines *fpl*, décombres *mpl*. (*Rail*) **there has been a ~ near Stratford** il y a eu un accident de chemin de fer près de Stratford; **the car was a complete ~** la voiture était bonne à mettre à la ferraille *or* à envoyer à la casse.
c (*person*) **he was a ~** il était l'ombre de lui-même; **he looks a ~** on dirait une loque, il a une mine de déterré; **a ~ of humanity, a human ~** une épave, une loque humaine.
2 vt a *ship* provoquer le naufrage de; *train, plane, car* [*bomb, terrorist, accident*] détruire; [*driver, pilot*] démolir; *building* démolir; *mechanism* détraquer, abîmer, bousiller*, esquinter*; *furniture etc* casser, démolir. [*ship, sailor*] **to be ~ed** faire naufrage; **the plane was completely ~ed** il n'est resté que des débris de l'avion; **in his fury he ~ed the whole house** dans sa rage il a tout démoli *or* cassé dans la maison.
b (*fig*) *marriage, friendship* briser, être la ruine de; *career* briser; *plans, hopes, ambitions* ruiner, anéantir, annihiler; *negotiations, discussions* faire échouer, saboter; *health* ruiner. **this ~ed his chances of success** cela a anéanti ses chances de succès; **it ~ed my life** cela a brisé ma vie, ma vie en a été brisée.

wreckage ['rekɪdʒ] n (*NonC*) a (*wrecked ship*) épave *f*, navire naufragé; (*pieces from this*) débris *mpl*; (*Aut, Aviat, Rail etc*) débris; [*building*] décombres *mpl*. (*Aviat, Rail*) **~ was strewn over several kilometres** les débris étaient disséminés sur plusieurs kilomètres; **there are still several bodies in the charred ~** les corps de plusieurs victimes se trouvent encore parmi les débris (*or* décombres) calcinés. b (*act*) [*ship*] naufrage *m*; [*train*] déraillement *m*; (*fig: of hopes, ambitions, plans*) anéantissement *m*.

wrecked [rekt] adj *ship* naufragé; *train, car* complètement démoli, accidenté; (*Admin*) *plan* anéanti.

wrecker ['rekəʳ] n a (*gen*) destructeur *m*, démolisseur *m*; (*Hist: of ships*) naufrageur *m*. b (*in salvage*) (*person*) sauveteur *m* (d'épave); (*boat*) canot *or* bateau sauveteur; (*truck*) dépanneuse *f*. c (*US*) (*in demolition*) [*buildings*] démolisseur *m*; [*cars*] marchand(e) *m(f)* de ferraille.

wrecking ['rekɪŋ] 1 n (*act*) [*ship*] naufrage *m*; [*train*] déraillement *m*; (*fig*) [*hopes, ambitions, plans*] anéantissement *m*. 2 comp ►**wrecking ball** boulet *m* de démolition ►**wrecking bar** (pince *f* à) levier *m* ►**wrecking crane** (*Rail*) grue *f* de levage.

wren [ren] n a (*bird*) roitelet *m*, troglodyte *m*. b (*Brit Navy*) **W~** Wren *f* (*auxiliaire féminine de la marine royale britannique*).

wrench [rentʃ] 1 n a (*tug*) mouvement violent de torsion; (*Med*) entorse *f*; (*fig: emotional*) déchirement *m*. **he gave the handle a ~** il a tiré de toutes ses forces sur la poignée; **the ~ of parting** le déchirement de la séparation; **it was a ~ when she saw him leave** cela a été un déchirement quand elle l'a vu partir.
b (*tool*) clef *f or* clé *f* (à écrous), tourne-à-gauche *m*; (*Aut: for wheels*) clef en croix. (*US fig*) **to throw a ~ into the works** mettre des bâtons dans les roues; **to throw a ~ into the economy** porter un coup très dur à l'économie; *see* **monkey**.
2 vt *handle etc* tirer violemment sur. **to ~ sth (away) from sb** *or* **from sb's grasp** arracher qch des mains de qn; (*Med*) **to ~ one's ankle** se tordre la cheville; **to ~ sth off** *or* **out** *or* **away** arracher qch (*of, from* de); **he ~ed (himself) free** il s'est dégagé avec un mouvement violent; **to ~ a box open** ouvrir de force une boîte.

wrest [rest] vt *object* arracher violemment (*from sb* des mains de qn); *secret, confession* arracher (*from sb* à qn); *power, leadership, title* ravir (*from sb* à qn). **he managed to ~ a living from the poor soil** à force de travail et de persévérance il a réussi à tirer un revenu du maigre sol.

wrestle ['resl] 1 vi lutter (corps à corps) (*with sb* contre qn); (*Sport*) lutter à main plate *or* corps à corps, pratiquer la lutte; (*as staged fight*) catcher (*with sb* contre qn). (*fig*) **to ~ with** *problem, one's conscience, sums, device* se débattre avec; *difficulties* se débattre contre, se colleter avec; *temptation, illness, disease* lutter contre; **the pilot ~d with the controls** le pilote se débattait avec les commandes; (*fig*) **she was wrestling with her suitcases** elle peinait avec ses valises, elle avait bien du mal à porter ses valises.
2 vt *opponent* lutter contre; (*Sport*) rencontrer à la lutte *or* au catch.
3 n lutte *f*. **to have a ~ with sb** lutter avec qn.

wrestler ['resləʳ] n (*Sport*) lutteur *m*, -euse *f*; (*in staged fight*) catcheur *m*, -euse *f*.

wrestling ['reslɪŋ] 1 n (*Sport: NonC*) lutte *f* (à main plate); (*staged fighting*) catch *m*. (*Sport*) **Graeco-Roman ~** lutte gréco-romaine. 2 comp ►**wrestling hold** prise *f* de catch *or* de lutte à main plate ►**wrestling match** match *m or* rencontre *f* de catch *or* de lutte à main plate.

wretch [retʃ] n (*unfortunate*) pauvre hère *m*, pauvre diable *m*, (pauvre) malheureux *m*, -euse *f*; (*pej*) scélérat(e) *m(f)*, misérable *mf*; (*hum*) affreux *m*, -euse *f*, misérable. **he's a filthy ~*** c'est un salaud‡; **you ~!** misérable!; **cheeky little ~!** petit polisson!, petit misérable!

wretched ['retʃɪd] adj a *person* (*very poor*) misérable; (*unhappy*) malheureux, misérable; (*depressed*) déprimé, démoralisé; (*ill*) malade, mal fichu. **the ~ beggars** les pauvres gueux *mpl*, les miséreux *mpl*; (*conscience-stricken etc*) **I feel ~ about it** je me sens vraiment coupable.
b (*poverty-stricken, miserable*) *life, conditions, houses* misérable; (*shamefully small*) *wage* de misère, dérisoire, minable; *sum, amount* misérable (*before n*), insignifiant, minable, dérisoire. **in ~ poverty** dans une misère noire; **~ clothes** vêtements misérables *or* miteux, guenilles *fpl*; **~ slums** taudis *mpl* misérables *or* lamentables; **the ~ of the earth** les déshérités de la terre.
c (*contemptible*) *behaviour, remark* mesquin; (*very bad*) *weather, holiday, meal, results* minable*, lamentable, affreux, pitoyable; (*: *annoying*) maudit (*before n*), fichu* (*before n*). **that was a ~ thing to do** c'était vraiment mesquin de faire ça, il devrait (*or* vous devriez *etc*) avoir honte d'avoir fait ça; **what ~ luck!** quelle déveine!*; **there were**

some ~ questions in the exam il y avait quelques questions impossibles *or* épouvantables à l'examen; **I'm a ~ player** je suis un piètre joueur, je joue très mal; **they played a ~ game** ils ont très mal joué; **where's that ~ pencil?*** où est ce fichu* *or* maudit crayon?; **that ~ dog of his*** son maudit chien; **then the ~ woman had to apologize to us!** ensuite la malheureuse femme a dû nous présenter ses excuses!

wretchedly ['retʃɪdlɪ] **adv** (*very poorly*) *live* misérablement, pauvrement; (*unhappily*) *weep, apologize, look* misérablement, pitoyablement; *say, explain* d'un ton pitoyable; (*contemptibly*) *treat, behave* mesquinement, abominablement; *pay* lamentablement, très mal, chichement; (*very badly*) *perform, play, sing* lamentablement, très mal. **~ clad** misérablement vêtu; **his wage is ~ small** son salaire est vraiment dérisoire.

wretchedness ['retʃɪdnɪs] **n** (*extreme poverty*) misère *f*, extrême pauvreté *f*; (*unhappiness*) extrême tristesse *f*; (*shamefulness*) *[amount, wage, sum]* caractère *m* dérisoire *or* pitoyable, extrême modicité *f*; *[act, behaviour]* mesquinerie *f*; (*poor quality*) *[meal, hotel, weather]* extrême médiocrité *f*, caractère minable *or* pitoyable. **his ~ at having to do this** le sentiment de culpabilité et d'impuissance qu'il éprouvait devant la nécessité de faire cela.

wrick [rɪk] 1 **vt** (*Brit*) **to ~ one's ankle** se tordre la cheville; **to ~ one's neck** attraper un torticolis. 2 **n** entorse *f*; (*in neck*) torticolis *m*.

wriggle ['rɪgl] 1 **n**: **with a ~ he freed himself** il s'est dégagé d'un mouvement du corps; **to give a ~ = to wriggle**; *see* 2.

2 **vi** *[worm, snake, eel]* se tortiller; *[fish]* frétiller; *[person]* (*restlessly*) remuer, gigoter*, se trémousser; (*in embarrassment*) se tortiller; (*squeamishly*) frissonner, tressaillir; (*excitedly*) frétiller. **to ~ along/down** *etc [worm etc]* avancer/descendre *etc* en se tortillant; *[person]* avancer/descendre *etc* à plat ventre *or* en rampant; **the fish ~d off the hook** le poisson a réussi à se détacher de l'hameçon, le poisson frétillait tellement qu'il s'est détaché de l'hameçon; **she managed to ~ free** elle a réussi à se dégager en se tortillant *or* en se contorsionnant; **he ~d through the hole in the hedge** il s'est faufilé *or* s'est glissé dans le trou de la haie (en se tortillant); **do stop wriggling (about)!** arrête de te trémousser *or* de gigoter* comme ça!, tiens-toi tranquille!

3 **vt**: **to ~ one's toes/fingers** remuer *or* tortiller les orteils/les doigts; **to ~ one's way along** *etc* = **to ~ along** *etc*; *see* 2.

►**wriggle about, wriggle around** **vi** *[worm, snake, eel]* se tortiller; *[fish, tadpole]* frétiller; *[person]* se trémousser, gigoter*; *see also* **wriggle 2**.

►**wriggle out** **vi** *[worm etc]* sortir; *[person]* se dégager. **the snake wriggled out of the cage** le serpent s'est coulé hors de la cage; **the fish wriggled out of my hand** le poisson m'a glissé des mains *or* m'a glissé entre les doigts; (*fig*) **to wriggle out of a difficulty** esquiver une difficulté; **to wriggle out of a task/a responsibility/the blame** *etc* se dérober à *or* esquiver une tâche/une responsabilité/la réprobation *etc*; **he'll manage to wriggle out of it somehow** il trouvera bien un moyen de s'esquiver *or* de se défiler*, il se ménagera bien une porte de sortie.

wriggler ['rɪglə^r] **n** a *[child etc]* **he's a dreadful ~** il n'arrête pas de gigoter*, il ne se tient jamais tranquille. b (*mosquito larva*) larve *f* de moustique.

wriggly ['rɪglɪ] **adj** *worm, eel, snake* qui se tortille; *fish* frétillant; *child* remuant, qui gigote* *or* se trémousse.

wring [rɪŋ] (**vb: pret, ptp wrung**) 1 **n**: **to give clothes a ~** essorer des vêtements.

2 **vt** a (*squeeze, twist*) serrer, tordre. **to ~ a chicken's neck** tordre le cou à un poulet; **I'll ~ your neck if I catch you!*** je te tordrai le cou si je t'y prends!*; **to ~ one's hands** se tordre les mains (de désespoir); **he wrung my hand, he wrung me by the hand** il m'a serré longuement la main; (*fig*) **a story to ~ one's heart** une histoire à vous fendre le cœur.

b (*also* **~ out**) *wet clothes, rag, towel* essorer; *water* exprimer (*from sth* de qch). (*on label*) **"do not ~"** "ne pas essorer"; **~ a cloth out in cold water and apply to forehead** faites une compresse avec un linge mouillé dans de l'eau froide et appliquez-la sur le front.

c (*fig: extort: also* **~ out**) arracher, extorquer. **they wrung a confession/the truth from** *or* **out of him** ils lui ont arraché une confession/la vérité; **he wrung £10 out of me** il m'a extorqué *or* soutiré* 10 livres; **I'll ~ it out of him!** je vais lui tirer les vers du nez!, je vais le faire parler!; **they managed to ~ out of him what had happened** ils sont arrivés non sans peine à lui faire dire *or* avouer ce qui s'était passé.

►**wring out** **vt sep** a = **wring 2b, 2c**. b (**: exhausted*) **to be wrung out** être lessivé* *or* vidé* *or* moulu.

wringer ['rɪŋə^r] **n** essoreuse *f* (à rouleaux). **to put sth through the ~** essorer qch (*à la machine*).

wringing ['rɪŋɪŋ] **adj** (*also* **~ wet**) *garment* trempé, à tordre*; *person* trempé jusqu'aux os.

wrinkle ['rɪŋkl] 1 **n** a (*on skin, fruit*) ride *f*; (*in socks, cloth, rug etc*) pli *m*. b (‡) (*tip*) tuyau*; (*good idea*) combine‡ *f*. 2 **vt** (*also* **~ up**) *skin* rider; *forehead* plisser; *nose* froncer; *fruit* rider, ratatiner; *rug, sheet* plisser, faire des plis dans. 3 **vi** *[sb's brow]* se plisser, se contracter; *[nose]* se plisser, se froncer; *[rug]* faire des plis; *[socks]* être en accordéon.

►**wrinkle down** **vi** *[stockings etc]* tomber en accordéon.

►**wrinkle up** 1 **vi** *[skirt, sweater]* remonter en faisant des plis; *[rug]* faire des plis; *[sb's brow, nose]* se plisser. 2 **vt sep** = **wrinkle 2**.

wrinkled ['rɪŋkld] **adj** *skin, face* ridé; *brow, nose* plissé, froncé; *apple* ridé, ratatiné; *sheet, rug, sweater, skirt* qui fait des plis; *stocking, sock* qui fait l'accordéon. **a ~ old woman** une vieille femme toute ratatinée *or* desséchée.

wrinkly ['rɪŋklɪ] 1 **adj** = **wrinkled**. 2 **npl** (*pej: old people*) **wrinklies** les vioques‡ *mpl*.

wrist [rɪst] 1 **n** poignet *m*. 2 **comp** ►**wristband** *[shirt etc]* poignet *m*; *[watch etc]* bracelet *m* ►**wrist joint** articulation *f* du poignet ►**wrist loop** (*Climbing*) dragonne *f* ►**wrist watch** montre-bracelet *f*.

wristlet ['rɪstlɪt] 1 **n** bracelet *m* (de force). 2 **comp** ►**wristlet watch** montre-bracelet *f*.

writ[1] [rɪt] **n** (*Jur*) acte *m* judiciaire; (*for election*) *lettre officielle émanant du président de la Chambre des communes, demandant qu'on procède à des élections.* **to issue a ~ against sb** assigner qn (en justice); **to issue a ~ for libel against sb** assigner qn en justice pour diffamation; **to serve a ~ on sb, to serve sb with a ~** assigner qn; **~ of attachment** commandement *m* de saisie; **~ of execution** titre *m* exécutoire; **~ of habeas corpus** ordre *m* (écrit) d'habeas corpus; **~ of subpoena** assignation *f or* citation *f* (en justice).

writ[2] [rɪt] (††) a **pret, ptp of write**. b (*liter*)**~ large** (*very obvious*) en toutes lettres (*fig*); (*exaggerated*) poussé à l'extrême.

write [raɪt] **pret wrote, ptp written** 1 **vt** a (*gen*) écrire; *cheque, list* faire, écrire; *prescription, certificate* rédiger; *bill* faire. **did I ~ that?** j'ai écrit ça, moi?; **how is it written?** comment (est-ce que) ça s'écrit?; **you must print, not ~ your name** il ne faut pas écrire votre nom en cursive mais en caractères d'imprimerie; (*liter*) **it is written "thou shalt not kill"** il est écrit "tu ne tueras point"; (*fig*) **his guilt was written all over his face** la culpabilité se lisait sur son visage; (*fig*) **he had "policeman" written all over him*** cela sautait aux yeux qu'il était policier.

b *book, essay, poem* écrire; *music, opera* écrire, composer. **you could ~ a book about all that is going on here** on pourrait écrire *or* il y aurait de quoi écrire un livre sur tout ce qui se passe ici.

c (*Comput*) *program, software etc* écrire, rédiger; *see* **read**.

2 **vi** a (*gen*) écrire. **he can read and ~** il sait lire et écrire; **~ on both sides of the paper** écrivez des deux côtés de la feuille; **as I ~, I can see ...** en ce moment même, je peux voir ...; **this pen ~s well** ce stylo écrit bien.

b (*as author*) **he had always wanted to ~** il avait toujours voulu écrire *or* être écrivain; **he ~s for a living** il est écrivain de métier *or* de profession; **he ~s about social policy** il écrit sur les *or* il traite des questions de politique sociale; **he ~s for "The Times"** il écrit dans le "Times"; **he ~s on foreign policy for "The Guardian"** il écrit des articles de politique étrangère dans le "Guardian"; **what shall I ~ about?** sur quoi est-ce que je vais écrire?

c (*correspond*) écrire (*to* à). **he wrote to tell us that ...** il (nous) a écrit pour nous dire que ...; (*Comm*) **~ for our brochure** demandez notre brochure; **I've written for a form** j'ai écrit pour leur demander un formulaire; *see* **home**.

3 **comp** ►**write-in** (*US Pol*) (*insertion of name*) inscription *f*; (*name itself*) nom inscrit ►**write-off** *see* **write-off** ►**write-protected** (*Comput*) protégé contre l'écriture ►**write-protect notch** (*Comput: on disk*) encoche *f* de barrage d'écriture ►**write-up** *see* **write-up**.

►**write away** **vi** (*Comm etc*) écrire (*to* à). **to write away for** *information, application form, details* écrire pour demander; *goods* commander par lettre.

►**write back** **vi** répondre (*par lettre*).

►**write down** **vt sep** a écrire; (*note*) noter; (*put in writing*) mettre par écrit. **write it down at once or you'll forget** écrivez-le *or* notez-le tout de suite sinon vous oublierez; **write all your ideas down and send them to me** mettez toutes vos idées par écrit et envoyez-les moi; **it was all written down for posterity** c'était tout consigné pour la postérité; (*fig*) **I had written him down as useless*** je m'étais mis dans la tête qu'il n'était bon à rien. b (*Comm etc: reduce price of*) réduire le prix de.

►**write in** 1 **vi**: **listeners are invited to write in with their suggestions** nos auditeurs sont invités à nous envoyer leurs suggestions; **a lot of people have written in to complain** beaucoup de gens nous ont écrit pour se plaindre; **to write in for sth** écrire pour demander qch. 2 **vt sep** *word, item on list etc* insérer, ajouter; (*US Pol*) *candidate's name* inscrire. **to write sth into an agreement** *or* **contract** (*at the outset*) stipuler qch dans un contrat; (*add*) ajouter qch à un contrat. 3 **write-in n** *see* **write 3**.

►**write off** 1 **vi** = **write away**.

2 **vt sep** a (*write quickly*) *letter etc* écrire en vitesse *or* d'une traite.

b *debt* passer aux profits et pertes; (*fig*) considérer comme perdu *or* gâché, mettre une croix* sur, faire son deuil* de. **they wrote off £20,000** ils ont passé 20.000 livres aux profits et pertes; (*Comm*) **the operation was written off as a total loss** ils ont décidé de mettre un terme à l'opération qui se révélait une perte sèche; (*fig*) **I've written off the whole thing as a dead loss** j'en ai fait mon deuil*, j'ai fait une croix dessus*; (*fig*) **we've written off the first half of the term** nous considérons la première moitié du trimestre comme perdue *or* gâchée;

(*fig*) **he had been written off as a failure** on avait décidé qu'il ne ferait jamais rien de bon; **they had written off all the passengers (as dead)** ils tenaient tous les passagers pour morts; **the insurance company decided to write off his car** la compagnie d'assurances a décidé que la voiture était irréparable; **he wrote his car off* in the accident** il a complètement bousillé* sa voiture dans l'accident; **the boat was completely written off*** le bateau a été complètement détruit *or* a été une perte totale.
3 **write-off** n *see* **write-off**.

►**write out** vt sep a *one's name and address, details etc* écrire; *cheque, list* faire, écrire; *prescription, bill* rédiger; *bill* faire. b (*copy*) *notes, essay etc* recopier, mettre au net *or* au propre; *recipe* copier, relever. **write out the words 3 times each** copiez chaque mot 3 fois. c (*TV, Rad*) *character* retirer (de la distribution *or* du générique). **she was written out of the series after a year** on a retiré son nom de la distribution de l'émission au bout d'un an, elle ne figure plus au générique après un an de cette émission.

►**write up** 1 vi = **write away**. 2 vt sep a *notes, diary* mettre à jour; (*write report on*) *happenings, developments* faire un compte rendu de; (*record*) (*Chem etc*) *experiment* rédiger; (*Archeol etc*) *one's findings* consigner. **he wrote up the day's events in the ship's log** il a inscrit *or* consigné dans le journal de bord les événements de la journée; **she wrote it up for the local paper** elle en a fait le compte rendu pour le journal local. b (*praise*) écrire un article élogieux (*or* une lettre élogieuse) sur. 3 **write-up** n *see* **write-up**.

write-off ['raɪtɒf] n (*Comm*) perte sèche; (*Fin: tax*) déduction fiscale. **to be a ~** *[car]* être irréparable, être bon pour la casse *or* la ferraille; *[project, operation]* n'avoir abouti à rien, se révéler une perte de temps; **the whole afternoon was a ~** l'après-midi a été une perte de temps totale (du commencement à la fin).

writer ['raɪtəʳ] n a (*of letter, book etc*) auteur *m*; (*as profession*) écrivain *m*, auteur. **the (present) ~ believes ...** l'auteur croit ...; **a thriller ~** un auteur de romans policiers; **he is a ~** il est écrivain, c'est un écrivain; **to be a good ~** (*of books*) être un bon écrivain, écrire bien; (*in handwriting*) écrire bien, avoir une belle écriture; **to be a bad ~** (*of books*) écrire mal, être un écrivailleur *or* un écrivassier; (*in handwriting*) écrire mal *or* comme un chat; **~'s block** hantise *f* de la page blanche (*qui paralyse l'écrivain*); **~'s cramp** crampe *f* des écrivains; (*Scot Jur*) **W~ to the Signet** ≈ notaire *m*; *see* **hack²**, **letter** *etc*.
b (*Comput: of program etc*) auteur *m*.

write-up ['raɪtʌp] n (*gen, also Comput*) description *f*; (*review: of play etc*) compte rendu *m*, critique *f*; (*report: of event etc*) compte rendu, exposé *m*. **there's a ~ about it in today's paper** il y a un compte rendu dans le journal d'aujourd'hui; **the play got a good ~** la pièce a eu de bonnes critiques.

writhe [raɪð] vi se tordre; (*fig*) frémir. **it made him ~** (*in pain*) il s'est tordu de douleur; (*from disgust*) il a frémi de dégoût; (*from embarrassment*) il ne savait plus où se mettre; **he ~d under the insult** il a frémi sous l'injure.

►**writhe about, writhe around** vi (*in pain*) se tordre dans des convulsions; (*to free o.s.*) se contorsionner en tous sens.

writing ['raɪtɪŋ] 1 n a (*NonC: hand~, sth written*) écriture *f*. **there was some ~ on the page** il y avait quelque chose d'écrit sur la page; **I could see the ~ but couldn't read it** je voyais bien qu'il y avait quelque chose d'écrit mais je n'ai pas pu le déchiffrer; **I can't read your ~** je n'arrive pas à déchiffrer votre écriture; **in his own ~** écrit de sa main; (*fig*) **he saw the ~ on the wall** il a vu le signe sur le mur.
b (*NonC: written form*) écrit *m*. **I'd like to have that in ~** j'aimerais avoir cela par écrit; **get his permission in ~** obtenez sa permission par écrit; **evidence in ~ that ...** preuve par écrit *or* littérale que ...; **to put sth in ~** mettre qch par écrit.
c (*NonC: occupation of writer*) **he devoted his life to ~** il a consacré sa vie à son œuvre d'écrivain; **~ is his hobby** écrire est son passe-temps favori; **he earns quite a lot from ~** ses écrits lui rapportent pas mal d'argent.
d (*output of writer*) écrits *mpl*, œuvres *fpl*. **there is in his ~ evidence of a desire to ...** on trouve dans ses écrits la manifestation d'un désir de ...; **the ~s of H. G. Wells** les œuvres de H. G. Wells.
e (*NonC: act*) **he learns reading and ~** il apprend à lire et à écrire; **~ is a skill which must be learned** écrire est un art qui requiert un apprentissage; **the ~ of this book took 10 years** écrire ce livre a pris 10 ans.
2 comp ►**writing case** (*Brit*) correspondancier *m*, nécessaire *m* de correspondance ►**writing desk** secrétaire *m* (*bureau*) ►**writing lesson** leçon *f* d'écriture ►**writing pad** bloc *m* de papier à lettres, bloc-notes *m* ►**writing paper** papier *m* à lettres ►**writing room** (*in hotel etc*) salon *m* d'écriture ►**writing table** bureau *m*.

written ['rɪtn] 1 ptp of **write**. 2 adj *reply, inquiry, request* écrit, par écrit; *French, English etc* écrit. **~ exam** épreuve écrite, écrit *m*; **~ proof** *or* **evidence** pièce *f* justificative; (*Parl*) **~ question** question écrite; *see* **hand** *etc*.

WRNS [renz] n (*Brit*) (abbr of **Women's Royal Naval Service**) *service des auxiliaires féminines de la marine royale britannique*.

wrong [rɒŋ] 1 adj a (*wicked*) mal *inv*; (*unfair*) injuste. **it is ~ to lie, lying is ~** c'est mal de mentir; **it is ~ for her to have to beg, it is ~ that she should have to beg** il est injuste qu'elle soit obligée de mendier; **you were ~ to hit him, it was ~ of you to hit him** tu n'aurais pas dû le frapper, tu as eu tort de le frapper; **what's ~ with going to the pictures?** quel mal y a-t-il à aller au cinéma?; **there's nothing ~ with** *or* **in (doing) that** il n'y a rien à redire à ça, je n'y vois aucun mal (*see also* **1c**).
b (*mistaken, incorrect*) *belief, guess* erroné; *answer, solution, calculation, sum* faux (*f* fausse), inexact, incorrect; (*Mus*) *note* faux; (*unsuitable, inconvenient*) qui n'est pas ce qu'il faut (*or* fallait *etc*). **my clock/watch is ~** mon réveil/ma montre n'est pas à l'heure; **you're quite ~** vous vous trompez, vous avez tort, vous faites erreur; (*iro*) **how ~ can you get!*** comme on peut se tromper!; **he was ~ in deducing that ...** il a eu tort de déduire que ...; **I was ~ about him** je me suis mépris *or* trompé sur son compte; **he got all his sums ~** toutes ses opérations étaient fausses; **the Chancellor got his sums ~*** le chancelier de l'Échiquier a fait une erreur *or* s'est trompé dans ses calculs; **you've got your facts ~** ce que vous avancez est faux; **he got the figures ~** il s'est trompé dans les chiffres; **they got it ~ again** ils se sont encore trompés; **he told me the ~ time** (*gen*) il ne m'a pas donné l'heure exacte; (*for appointment etc*) il ne m'a pas donné la bonne heure; **it happened at the ~ time** c'est arrivé à un moment inopportun; **the letter has the ~ date on it** ils se sont trompés de date sur la lettre; **the ~ use of drugs** l'usage abusif des médicaments; (*Telec*) **to get a ~ number** se tromper de numéro; (*Telec*) **that's the ~ number** ce n'est pas le bon numéro; **he got on the ~ train** il s'est trompé de train, il n'a pas pris le bon train; **it's the ~ road for Paris** ce n'est pas la bonne route pour Paris; (*fig*) **you're on the ~ road** *or* **track** vous faites fausse route; **I'm in the ~ job** ce n'est pas le travail qu'il me faut; (*also hum*) j'aurais vraiment dû faire autre chose, je me suis trompé de voie; **she married the ~ man** elle n'a pas épousé l'homme qu'il lui fallait; **you've got** *or* **picked the ~ man if you want someone to mend a fuse** vous tombez mal si vous voulez quelqu'un qui puisse réparer un fusible; **he's got the ~ kind of friends** il a de mauvaises fréquentations; **that's the ~ kind of plug** ce n'est pas la prise qu'il faut, ce n'est pas la bonne sorte de prise; **to say the ~ thing** dire ce qu'il ne fallait pas dire, faire un impair; **you've opened the packet at the ~ end** vous avez ouvert le paquet par le mauvais bout *or* du mauvais côté; **that's quite the ~ way to go about it** ce n'est pas comme ça qu'il faut s'y prendre *or* qu'il faut le faire, vous vous y prenez (*or* il s'y prend *etc*) mal; **a piece of bread went down the ~ way** j'ai (*or* il a *etc*) avalé une miette de pain de travers; **he was on the ~ side of the road** il était du mauvais côté de la route; **he got out of the train on the ~ side** il est descendu du train à contre-voie; (*fig*) **he got out of bed on the ~ side, he got out of the ~ side of the bed** il s'est levé du pied gauche; **the ~ side of the cloth** le mauvais côté *or* l'envers *m* du tissu; **he's on the ~ side of forty** il a dépassé la quarantaine; (*fig*) **to get on the ~ side of sb** se faire mal voir de qn; (*rub sb up the wrong way*) prendre qn à rebrousse-poil; **you've put it back in the ~ place** vous l'avez mal remis, vous ne l'avez pas remis là où il fallait; *see also* **end, side, stick, way** *etc*.
c (*amiss*) qui ne va pas. **something's ~** *or* **there's something ~ (with it** *or* **him** *etc*) il y a quelque chose qui ne va pas; **something's ~ with my leg** j'ai quelque chose à la jambe, ma jambe me tracasse; **something's ~ with my watch** ma montre ne marche pas comme il faut; **what's ~?** qu'est-ce qui ne va pas?; **there's nothing ~** ça va, tout va bien; **nothing ~, I hope?** tout va bien *or* pas d'ennuis, j'espère; **there's nothing ~ with it** (*theory, translation*) c'est tout à fait correct; (*method, plan*) c'est tout à fait valable; (*machine, car*) ça marche très bien; **there's nothing ~ with hoping that ...** il n'y a pas de mal à espérer que ...; **there's nothing ~ with him** il va très bien, il est en parfaite santé; **there's something ~ somewhere** il y a quelque chose qui cloche* là-dedans; **what's ~ with you?** qu'est-ce que vous avez?; **what's ~ with your arm?** qu'est-ce que vous avez au bras?; **what's ~ with the car?** qu'est-ce qu'elle a, la voiture?, qu'est-ce qui cloche* dans la voiture?; **he's ~ in the head*** il a le cerveau dérangé *or* fêlé*.
2 adv *answer, guess* mal, incorrectement. **you've spelt it ~** vous l'avez mal écrit; **you're doing it all ~** vous vous y prenez mal; **you did ~ to refuse** vous avez eu tort de refuser; **you've got the sum ~** vous vous êtes trompé dans votre calcul, vous avez fait une erreur de calcul; (*misunderstood*) **you've got it all ~*** vous n'avez rien compris; **don't get me ~*** comprends-moi bien; **she took me up ~** elle n'a pas compris ce que je voulais dire; **to go ~** (*on road*) se tromper de route, faire fausse route; (*in calculations, negotiations etc*) se tromper, faire une faute *or* une erreur; (*morally*) mal tourner; *[plan]* mal tourner; *[business deal etc]* tomber à l'eau; *[machine, car]* tomber en panne; *[clock, watch etc]* battre la breloque, se détraquer; **you can't go ~** (*on road*) c'est très simple, il est impossible de se perdre; (*in method etc*) c'est simple comme bonjour; (*in choice of job, car etc*) (de toute façon) c'est un bon choix; **you can't go ~ with a Super Deluxe** (de toute façon) une Super Deluxe, c'est un bon choix; **you won't go far ~ if you ...** vous ne pouvez guère vous tromper si vous ...; **something went ~ with the gears** quelque chose s'est détraqué *or* a foiré* dans l'embrayage; **something must have gone ~** il a dû arriver quelque chose; **nothing can go**

~ **now** tout doit marcher comme sur des roulettes maintenant; **everything went ~ that day** tout est allé mal *or* de travers ce jour-là.

3 **n** a (*evil*) mal *m*. **to do ~** mal agir; (*fig*) **he can do no ~ in her eyes** tout ce qu'il fait est bien à ses yeux *or* trouve grâce à ses yeux; *see also* **right.**

b (*injustice*) injustice *f*, tort *m*. **he suffered great ~** il a été la victime de graves injustices; **to right a ~** réparer une injustice; (*Prov*) **two ~s don't make a right** on ne répare pas une injustice par une autre (injustice); **you do me ~ in thinking ...** vous êtes injuste envers moi *or* vous me faites tort en pensant ...; **he did her ~**† il a abusé d'elle.

c **to be in the ~** être dans son tort, avoir tort; **to put sb in the ~** mettre qn dans son tort.

4 **vt** traiter injustement, faire tort à. **you ~ me if you believe ...** vous êtes injuste envers moi si vous croyez ... .

5 **comp** ►**wrongdoer** malfaiteur *m*, -trice *f* ►**wrongdoing** (*NonC*) méfaits *mpl* ►**wrong-foot** (*Ftbl, Tennis*) prendre à contre-pied ►**wrong-headed** buté.

wrongful ['rɒŋfʊl] **adj** injustifié. (*Jur*) ~ **arrest** arrestation *f* arbitraire; (*Ind*) ~ **dismissal** renvoi injustifié.

wrongfully ['rɒŋfəlɪ] **adv** à tort.

wrongly ['rɒŋlɪ] **adv** a (*incorrectly*) *state, allege, multiply* incorrectement, inexactement; *treat* injustement; *accuse* faussement, à tort; *answer, guess, translate* mal, incorrectement, pas comme il faut; *position, insert* mal, pas comme il faut. **the handle has been put on ~** le manche n'a pas été mis comme il faut *or* a été mal mis; **you have been ~ informed** on vous a mal renseigné; ~ **dismissed** renvoyé injustement *or* à tort; **he behaved quite ~ when he said that** il a eu tort de dire ça; *see* **rightly.** b (*by mistake*) par erreur. **it was ~ put in this drawer** on l'a mis dans ce tiroir par erreur.

wrongness ['rɒŋnɪs] **n** (*incorrectness*) *[answer]* inexactitude *f*; (*injustice*) injustice *f*; (*evil*) immoralité *f*.

wrote [rəʊt] **pret of write.**

wrought [rɔːt] 1 **pret, ptp** †† **of work** (*liter*) **he ~ valiantly** il a œuvré vaillamment; **the destruction ~ by the floods** les ravages provoqués par l'inondation. 2 **adj** *iron* forgé; *silver* ouvré. 3 **comp** ►**wrought iron** fer forgé ►**wrought-iron adj** *gate, decoration* en fer forgé ►**wrought-ironwork** ferronnerie *f* ►**wrought-up: to be wrought-up** être très tendu.

wrung [rʌŋ] **pret, ptp of wring.**

WRVS [ˌdʌbljuːɑːviː'es] **n** (*Brit*) (**abbr of Women's Royal Voluntary Service**) *service d'auxiliaires bénévoles au service de la collectivité.*

wry [raɪ] **adj** *comment, humour, joke* désabusé, empreint d'une ironie désabusée. **a ~ smile** un sourire forcé *or* désabusé; **with a ~ shrug of his shoulders he ...** d'un haussement d'épaules désabusé il ...; **to make a ~ face** faire la grimace.

wryly ['raɪlɪ] **adv** avec une ironie désabusée.

WS [ˌdʌbljuː'es] **n** (*Scot Jur*) (**abbr of Writer to the Signet**) *see* **writer.**

wt abbr of weight.

WV (*US*) **abbr of West Virginia.**

WWF n (**abbr of Worldwide Fund for Nature**) WWF *m*.

WY (*US*) **abbr of Wyoming.**

wych-elm ['wɪtʃ'elm] **n** orme blanc *or* de montagne.

wynd [waɪnd] **n** (*Scot*) venelle *f*.

Wyoming [waɪ'əʊmɪŋ] **n** Wyoming *m*. **in ~** dans le Wyoming.

WYSIWYG ['wɪzɪwɪg] **n** (*Comput*) (**abbr of what you see is what you get**) WYSIWYG *m*, ce que vous voyez est ce que vous aurez.

X, x [eks] (vb: pret, ptp **x-ed, x'ed**) 1 n a (*letter*) X, x *m*; (*Math, fig*) x; (*at the end of a letter: kiss*) bises *fpl*, (*several kisses*) grosses bises. **X for X-ray** ≃ X comme Xavier; **he signed his name with an X** il a signé d'une croix *or* en faisant une croix; **for x years** pendant x années; **Mr X** Monsieur X; **x-axis** axe *m* des x; **X-chromosome** chromosome *m* X; **X marks the spot** l'endroit est marqué d'une croix; *see* **X-ray**. b (*Brit Cine* †) **X-certificate,** (*US*) **X-rated** classé X, ≃ interdit aux moins de 18 ans. (*fig*) **X-rated** *book, language etc* obscène, porno*. 2 vt marquer d'une croix.

►**x out** vt sep *mistake* raturer (par une série de croix).

xenon ['zenɒn] n xénon *m*.

xenophobe ['zenəfəʊb] adj, n xénophobe *(mf)*.

xenophobia [ˌzenə'fəʊbɪə] n xénophobie *f*.

xenophobic [ˌzenə'fəʊbɪk] adj xénophobe.

Xenophon ['zenəfən] n Xénophon *m*.

xerography [zɪə'rɒgrəfɪ] n xérographie *f*.

Xerox ['zɪərɒks] ® 1 n (*machine*) photocopieuse *f*; (*reproduction*) photocopie *f*. 2 vt (faire) photocopier, prendre *or* faire une photocopie de, copier*. 3 vi se faire *or* se laisser photocopier.

Xerxes ['zɜːksiːz] n Xerxès *m*.

XL [ˌek'sel] (abbr of **extra large**) XL.

Xmas ['eksməs, 'krɪsməs] n abbr of **Christmas**.

X-ray ['eksˌreɪ] 1 n (*ray*) rayon *m* X; (*photograph*) radiographie *f*, radio* *f*. **to have an ~** se faire radiographier, se faire faire une radio*. 2 vt *heart, envelope* radiographier, faire une radio de*; *person* radiographier, faire une radio à*. 3 comp radioscopique, radiographique ►**X-ray diagnosis** radiodiagnostic *m* ►**X-ray examination** examen *m* radioscopique, radio* *f* ►**X-ray photo, X-ray picture** (*on film*) radiographie *f*, radio* *f*; (*on screen*) radioscopie*f*, radio* ►**X-ray treatment** radiothérapie *f*.

xylograph ['zaɪləgrɑːf] n xylographie *f*.

xylographic [ˌzaɪlə'græfɪk] adj xylographique.

xylography [zaɪ'lɒgrəfɪ] n xylographie *f*.

xylophone ['zaɪləfəʊn] n xylophone *m*.

xylophonist [zaɪ'lɒfənɪst] n joueur *m* de xylophone.

Y

Y, y [waɪ] n (letter) Y, y m. **Y for Yellow** ≈ Y comme Yvonne; **y-axis** axe m des y; **Y-chromosome** chromosome m Y; **Y-fronts** npl ® slip m (d'homme); **Y-shaped** en (forme d')Y.

yacht [jɒt] 1 n (sails or motor) yacht m; (sails) voilier m. 2 vi: **to go ~ing** faire de la navigation de plaisance or de la voile or du yachting m. 3 comp ►**yacht club** yacht-club m, cercle m nautique or de voile ►**yacht race** course f de yachts or de voiliers ►**yachtsman** (in race, professional) navigateur m; (amateur) plaisancier m ►**yachtswoman** navigatrice f; plaisancière f.

yachting ['jɒtɪŋ] 1 n navigation f de plaisance, yachting m, voile f. 2 comp cruise en yacht; cap de marin; magazine etc de la voile ►**yachting circles**: **in yachting circles** dans les milieux de la voile or de la navigation de plaisance ►**yachting coast**: **it's not a yachting coast** ce n'est pas une côte propice au yachting or à la navigation de plaisance.

yack*, **yackety-yak*** [jæk], ['jækɪtɪ'jæk] (pej) 1 vi caqueter, jacasser. 2 n caquetage m.

yah [jɑː] excl beuh!

yahoo [jɑː'huː] n butor m, rustre m.

yak[1] [jæk] n (Zool) yak m or yack m.

yak[2]* [jæk] = **yackety-yak**.

Yale [jeɪl] n ®: **~ lock** serrure f à barillet or à cylindre.

yam [jæm] n (plant, tuber) igname f; (US: sweet potato) patate douce.

yammer* ['jæmə'ʳ] vi geindre.

yang [jæŋ] n (Philos) yang m.

Yangtze ['jæŋksɪ] n Yang Tsé Kiang m.

Yank* [jæŋk] (abbr of **Yankee**) 1 adj amerloque‡, ricain‡ (pej). 2 n Amerloque‡ mf, Ricain(e)‡ m(f) (pej).

yank [jæŋk] 1 n coup sec, saccade f. 2 vt tirer d'un coup sec.

►**yank off*** vt sep a (detach) arracher or extirper (d'un coup sec). b **to yank sb off to jail** embarquer* qn en prison.

►**yank out*** vt sep arracher or extirper (d'un coup sec).

Yankee* ['jæŋkɪ] 1 n Yankee mf. 2 adj yankee (f inv). **"~ Doodle"** air populaire de la Révolution américaine.

yap [jæp] 1 vi [dog] japper; (*) [person] jacasser. 2 n jappement m.

yapping ['jæpɪŋ] 1 adj dog jappeur; person jacasseur. 2 n jappements mpl; jacasserie f.

Yarborough ['jɑːbrə] n (Bridge etc) main ne contenant aucune carte supérieure au neuf.

yard[1] [jɑːd] 1 n a yard m (91,44 cm), ≈ mètre m. **one ~ long** long d'un yard or d'un mètre; **20 ~s away from us** à 20 mètres de nous; **he can't see a ~ in front of him** il ne voit pas à un mètre devant lui; (Sport) **to run a hundred ~s, to run in the hundred ~s or hundred ~s' race** ≈ courir le cent mètres; **to buy cloth by the ~** acheter de l'étoffe au mètre; **how many ~s would you like?** quel métrage désirez-vous?

b (fig) **he pulled out ~s of handkerchief** il a sorti un mouchoir d'une longueur interminable; **a word a ~ long** un mot qui n'en finit plus; **an essay ~s long** une dissertation-fleuve; **with a face a ~ long** faisant un visage long d'une aune, faisant une tête longue comme ça; **sums by the ~** des calculs à n'en plus finir.

c (Naut) vergue f.

2 comp ►**yardarm** (Naut) bout m de vergue ►**yardstick** (fig) mesure f.

yard[2] [jɑːd] 1 n a [farm, hospital, prison, school etc] cour f; (surrounded by the building: in monastery, hospital etc) préau m. **back~** arrière-cour f; see **farm** etc.

b (work-site) chantier m; (for storage) dépôt m. **builder's/shipbuilding ~** chantier de construction/de construction(s) navale(s); **timber~** dépôt de bois; **coal/contractor's ~** dépôt de charbon/de matériaux de construction; see **dock[1]**, **goods** etc.

c (Brit) **the Y~, Scotland Y~** Scotland Yard m, ≈ le Quai des Orfèvres; **to call in the Y~** demander l'aide de Scotland Yard.

d (US) (garden) jardin m; (field) champ m.

e (enclosure for animals) parc m; see **stock**.

2 comp ►**yardbird‡** (US) (soldier) bidasse m empôté (qui est souvent de corvée); (convict) taulard‡ m ►**yardmaster** (US Rail) chef m de triage ►**yard sale** (US) vente f d'objets usagés (chez un particulier).

yardage ['jɑːdɪdʒ] n longueur f en yards, ≈ métrage m.

yarn [jɑːn] 1 n a fil m; (Tech: for weaving) filé m. **cotton/nylon** etc **~** fil de coton/de nylon etc. b (tale) longue histoire; see **spin**. 2 vi raconter or débiter des histoires.

yarrow ['jærəʊ] n mille-feuille f, achillée f.

yashmak ['jæʃmæk] n litham m.

yaw [jɔː] vi (Naut) (suddenly) faire une embardée, embarder; (gradually) dévier de la route; (Aviat, Space) faire un mouvement de lacet.

yawl [jɔːl] n (Naut) (sailing boat) yawl m; (ship's boat) yole f.

yawn [jɔːn] 1 vi a [person] bâiller. **to ~ with boredom** bâiller d'ennui. b [chasm etc] s'ouvrir. 2 vt: **to ~ one's head off** bâiller à se décrocher la mâchoire; **"no" he ~ed** "non" dit-il en bâillant or dans un bâillement. 3 n bâillement m. **to give a ~** bâiller; **the film is one long ~*** le film est ennuyeux de bout en bout or fait bâiller; see **stifle**.

yawning ['jɔːnɪŋ] 1 adj chasm béant; person qui bâille. 2 n bâillements mpl.

yaws [jɔːz] n (Med) pian m.

yd abbr of **yard**.

ye[1] [jiː] pers pron (††, liter, dial) vous. **~ gods!*** grands dieux!*, ciel! (hum).

ye[2] [jiː] def art (††: the) ancienne forme écrite de **the**.

yea [jeɪ] (††: yes) 1 particle oui. **whether ~ or nay** que ce soit oui ou (que ce soit) non. 2 adv (liter: indeed) voire, et même. 3 n oui m. **the ~s and the nays** les voix fpl pour et les voix contre, les oui mpl et les non.

yeah* [jɛə] particle ouais*, oui. (iro) **oh ~?** et puis quoi encore?

year [jɪəʳ] 1 n a an m, année f. **last ~** l'an dernier, l'année dernière; **this ~** cette année; **next ~** l'an prochain, l'année prochaine, l'année qui vient; (loc) **this ~, next ~, sometime, never!** ≈ un peu, beaucoup, passionnément, à la folie, pas du tout!; **every ~, each ~** tous les ans, chaque année; **every other ~, every second ~** tous les deux ans; **3 times a ~** 3 fois l'an or par an; **in the ~ of grace** en l'an de grâce; **in the ~ of Our Lord** en l'an or en l'année de Notre Seigneur; **in the ~ 1869** en 1869; **in the ~ two thousand** en l'an deux mille; **~ by ~, from ~ to ~** d'année en année; **from one ~ to the other** d'une année à l'autre; **~ in, ~ out** année après année; **all the ~ round, from ~('s) end to ~('s) end** d'un bout de l'année à l'autre; **over the ~s, as (the) ~s go** (or **went**) **by** au cours or au fil des années; **taking one ~ with another, taking the good ~s with the bad** bon an mal an; **~s (and ~s) ago** il y a (bien) des années; **for ~s together** plusieurs années de suite; **to pay by the ~** payer à l'année; **document valid one ~** document valide un an; **a ~ last January** il y a eu un an au mois de janvier (dernier); **a ~ in January, a ~ next January** il y aura un an en janvier (prochain); **they have not met for ~s** ils ne se sont pas vus depuis des années; (fig) **I've been waiting for you for ~s*** ça fait une éternité que je t'attends; **sentenced to 15 ~s' imprisonment** condamné à 15 ans de prison; (Prison) **he got 10 ~s** il a attrapé 10 ans; **he is 6 ~s old** il a 6 ans; **in his fortieth ~** dans sa quarantième année; **it costs £50 a ~** cela coûte 50 livres par an; **he earns £15,000 a ~** il gagne 15.000 livres par an; **a friend of 30 ~s' standing** un ami de 30 ans or que l'on connaît (or connaissait etc) depuis 30 ans; **it has taken ~s off my life!, it has put ~s on me!** cela m'a vieilli de cent ans!; **that new hat takes ~s off her** ce nouveau chapeau la rajeunit; see **after**, **donkey**, **New Year**, **old** etc.

b (age) **from his earliest ~s** dès son âge le plus tendre; **he looks old for his ~s** il fait or paraît plus vieux que son âge; **young for his ~s** jeune pour son âge; **she is very active for a woman of her ~s** elle est très active pour (une femme de) son âge; **well on in ~s** d'un âge avancé; **to get on in ~s** prendre de l'âge; (liter) **to grow in ~s** avancer en âge; **to reach ~s of discretion** arriver à l'âge adulte (fig).

c (Scol, Univ) année f. **he is first in his ~** il est le premier de son

année; **she was in my ~ at school** elle était de mon année au lycée; **he's in the second ~** (*Univ*) il est en deuxième année; (*secondary school*) ≈ il est en cinquième.
d *[coin, stamp, wine]* année *f*.
2 comp ►**yearbook** annuaire *m* (*d'une université, d'un organisme etc*) ►**year end** (*Comm, Fin*) clôture *f or* fin *f* de l'exercice; **year-end report/accounts** rapport *m*/comptes *mpl* de fin d'exercice ►**year head** (*Brit Scol*) conseiller *m*, -ère *f* (principal(e)) d'éducation ►**year(-)long** qui dure (*or* durait *etc*) un an ►**year-round** qui dure toute l'année ►**year tutor** (*Brit Scol*) = **year head**.

yearling [ˈjɪəlɪŋ] **1 n** animal *m* d'un an; (*racehorse*) yearling *m*. **2 adj** (âgé) d'un an.

yearly [ˈjɪəlɪ] **1 adj** annuel. **2 adv** annuellement. **twice ~** deux fois par an.

yearn [jɜːn] **vi a** (*feel longing*) languir (*for, after* après), aspirer (*for, after* à). **to ~ for home** avoir la nostalgie de chez soi *or* du pays; **to ~ to do** avoir très envie *or* mourir d'envie de faire, aspirer à faire. **b** (*feel tenderness*) s'attendrir, s'émouvoir (*over* sur).

yearning [ˈjɜːnɪŋ] **1 n** désir ardent *or* vif (*for, after* de, *to do* de faire), envie *f* (*for, after* de, *to do* de faire), aspiration *f* (*for, after* vers, *to do* à faire). **2 adj** *desire* vif (*f* vive), ardent; *look* plein de désir *or* de tendresse.

yearningly [ˈjɜːnɪŋlɪ] **adv** (*longingly*) avec envie, avec désir; (*tenderly*) avec tendresse, tendrement.

yeast [jiːst] **n** (*NonC*) levure *f*. **dried ~** levure déshydratée.

yeasty [ˈjiːstɪ] **adj a** (*frothy*) écumeux, mousseux; (*frivolous*) superficiel, sans consistance, frivole. **b ~ taste** goût *m* de levure.

yec(c)h⁑ [jek] **excl** (*US*) berk! *or* beurk!

yec(c)hy⁑ [ˈjekɪ] **adj** (*US*) dégueulasse⁑, dégoûtant.

yegg⁑ [jeg] **n** (*US: also* **yeggman**⁑) cambrioleur *m*, casseur⁑ *m*.

yell [jel] **1 n** hurlement *m*, cri *m*. **to give a ~** pousser un hurlement *or* un cri; **a ~ of fright** un hurlement *or* un cri d'effroi; **a ~ of laughter** un grand éclat de rire; (*US Univ*) **college ~** ban *m* d'étudiants; (*fig*) **it was a ~!**⁑ c'était à se tordre!*; (*fig*) **he's a ~**⁑ il est tordant*. **2 vi a** (*also* **~ out**) hurler (*with* de). **to ~ at sb** crier après qn; **to ~ with laughter** rire bruyamment *or* aux éclats. **b** (*: *weep*) beugler⁑, hurler. **3 vt a** (*also* **~ out**) hurler, crier. **"stop it!" he ~ed** "arrêtez!" hurla-t-il. **b** (*: *weep*) **she was ~ing her head off** elle beuglait⁑ comme un veau, elle hurlait.

yelling [ˈjelɪŋ] **1 n** hurlements *mpl*, cris *mpl*. **2 adj** hurlant.

yellow [ˈjeləʊ] **1 adj a** (*colour*) *object etc* jaune; *hair, curls* blond. **to go** *or* **turn** *or* **become** *or* **grow ~** devenir jaune, jaunir; **the ~ races** les races *fpl* jaunes; (*Ind, Ecol*) **~ rain** pluie *f* jaune; *see also* **2** *and* **canary, line** *etc*.
b (*fig pej: cowardly*) lâche, froussard*, trouillard⁑. **there was a ~ streak in him** il y avait un côté lâche *or* froussard* *or* trouillard⁑ en lui.
2 comp ►**yellowback**† (*pej*) roman *m* à sensation ►**yellow-belly**⁑ (*pej*) froussard(e)* *m(f)*, trouillard(e)⁑ *m(f)* ►**yellow card** (*Ftbl*) carton *m* jaune ►**yellow-dog contract** (*US Ind Hist*) contrat *m* interdisant de se syndiquer (*aujourd'hui illégal*) ►**yellow fever** (*Med*) fièvre *f* jaune ►**yellow flag** (*Naut*) pavillon *m* de quarantaine ►**yellowhammer** (*Orn*) bruant *m* jaune ►**yellow jack*** (*Naut*) = **yellow flag** ►**yellow metal** (*gold*) métal *m* jaune; (*brass*) cuivre *m* jaune, métal Muntz ►**yellow ochre** jaune *m* d'ocre ►**yellow pages** (*Telec*) pages *fpl* jaunes (de l'annuaire) ►**yellow peril** (*fig*) péril *m* jaune ►**Yellow River** le fleuve Jaune ►**Yellow Sea** la mer Jaune ►**yellow soap** savon *m* de Marseille ►**yellow spot** (*Anat*) tache *f* jaune ►**yellow wagtail** (*Orn*) bergeronnette *f* flavéole; *see* **line 1a**.
3 n (*colour; also of egg*) jaune *m*.
4 vi jaunir.
5 vt jaunir. **paper ~ed with age** papier jauni par le temps.

yellowish [ˈjeləʊɪʃ] **adj** tirant sur le jaune, jaunâtre (*pej*).

yellowness [ˈjeləʊnɪs] **n** (*NonC*) **a** (*colour*) *[object]* couleur *f* jaune, jaune *m*; *[skin]* teint *m* jaune. **b** (* *pej: cowardice*) lâcheté *f*, trouillardise⁑ *f*.

yellowy [ˈjeləʊɪ] **adj** = **yellowish**.

yelp [jelp] **1 n** *[dog]* jappement *m*; *[fox, person]* glapissement *m*. **2 vi** japper; glapir.

yelping [ˈjelpɪŋ] **1 n** *[dog]* jappement *m*; *[fox, person]* glapissement *m*. **2 adj** *dog* jappeur; *fox, person* glapissant.

Yemen [ˈjemən] **n** Yémen *m*.

Yemeni [ˈjemənɪ], **Yemenite** [ˈjemənaɪt] **1 adj** yéménite. **2 n** Yéménite *mf*.

yen[1] [jen] **n, pl inv** (*money*) yen *m*.

yen[2]* [jen] **n** désir *m* intense, grande envie (*for* de). **to have a ~ to do** avoir (grande) envie de faire.

yenta* [ˈjentə] **n** (*US pej*) commère *f*.

yeoman [ˈjəʊmən] **pl yeomen 1 n a** (*Hist: freeholder*) franc-tenancier *m*. **b** (*Brit Mil*) cavalier *m*; *see* **yeomanry**. **2 comp** ►**yeoman farmer** (*Hist*) franc-tenancier *m*; (*modern*) propriétaire exploitant ►**Yeoman of the Guard** (*Brit*) hallebardier *m* de la garde royale ►**yeoman service**: (*fig*) **to do** *or* **give yeoman service** rendre des services inestimables.

yeomanry [ˈjəʊmənrɪ] **n** (*NonC*) **a** (*Hist*) (classe *f* des) francs-tenanciers *mpl*. **b** (*Brit Mil*) *régiment m de cavalerie (volontaire)*.

yeomen [ˈjəʊmən] **npl of yeoman**.

yep* [jep] **particle** ouais*, oui.

yes [jes] **1 particle** (*answering affirmative question*) oui; (*answering neg question*) si. **do you want some? — ~!** en voulez-vous? – oui!; **don't you want any? — ~ (I do)!** vous n'en voulez pas? – (mais) si!; **to say ~** dire oui; **he says ~ to everything** il dit oui à tout; **~ certainly** mais oui, certes oui; **~ and no** oui et non; (*Brit* †) **~, rather*** bien sûr (que oui); (*contradicting*) **oh ~, you DID say that** si si *or* mais si, vous avez bien dit cela; **~?** (*awaiting further reply*) (ah) oui?, et alors?; (*answering knock at door*) oui?, entrez!; **waiter! — ~ sir?** garçon! – (oui) Monsieur?
2 n oui *m inv*. **he gave a reluctant ~** il a accepté de mauvaise grâce; **he answered with ~es and noes** il n'a répondu que par des oui et des non.
3 comp ►**yes man** (* *pej*) béni-oui-oui* *m inv* (*pej*); **he's a yes man** il dit amen à tout ►**yes-no question** (*Ling*) interrogation *f* par oui ou non.

yeshiva [jəˈʃiːvə] **n, pl yeshivahs** *or* **yeshivoth** [jəˈʃiːvɒθ] (*US*) école *f or* université *f* juive.

yesterday [ˈjestədeɪ] **1 adv a** hier. **it rained ~** il a plu hier; **all (day) ~** toute la journée d'hier; **he arrived only ~** il n'est arrivé qu'hier; **a week (from) ~** d'hier en huit; **a week (past) ~** il y a eu hier huit jours; **I had to have it by ~** *or* **no later than ~** il fallait que je l'aie hier au plus tard; **late ~** hier dans la soirée; *see* **born**.
b (*fig: in the past*) hier, naguère. **towns which ~ were villages** des villes qui étaient hier *or* naguère des villages.
2 n a hier *m*. **~ was the second** c'était hier le deux; **~ was Friday** c'était hier vendredi; **~ was very wet** il a beaucoup plu hier; **~ was a bad day for him** la journée d'hier s'est mal passée pour lui; **the day before ~** avant-hier *m*; **where's ~'s news-paper?** où est le journal d'hier?
b (*fig*) hier *m*, passé *m*. **the great men of ~** tous les grands hommes du passé *or* d'hier; **all our ~s** tout notre passé.
3 comp ►**yesterday afternoon** hier après-midi ►**yesterday evening** hier (au) soir ►**yesterday morning** hier matin ►**yesterday week** il y a eu hier huit jours.

yesternight [ˈjestəˈnaɪt] **n, adv** (††, *liter*) la nuit dernière, hier soir.

yesteryear [ˈjestəˈjɪəʳ] **n** (††, *liter*) les années passées. **the snows of ~** les neiges d'antan.

yet [jet] **1 adv a** (*also* **as ~**) (*by this time, still, thus far, till now*) encore, toujours, jusqu'ici, jusqu'à présent; (*by that time, still, till then*) encore, toujours, jusqu'alors, jusque-là. **they haven't (as) ~ returned** *or* **returned (as) ~** ils ne sont pas encore *or* ne sont toujours pas revenus; **they hadn't (as) ~ managed to do it** ils n'étaient pas encore *or* toujours pas arrivés à le faire; **the greatest book (as) ~ written** le plus beau livre écrit jusqu'ici *or* jusqu'à présent; **no one has come (as) ~** personne n'est encore venu, jusqu'à présent *or* jusqu'ici personne n'est venu; **no one had come (as) ~** jusqu'alors *or* jusque-là personne n'était (encore) venu; **I have ~ to see** (*or* **receive** *etc*) **one** je n'en ai encore jamais vu (*or* reçu *etc*).
b (*so far; already; now*) maintenant; alors; déjà; encore. **has he arrived ~?** est-il déjà arrivé?; **no, not ~** non, pas encore; **I wonder if he's come ~** je me demande s'il est déjà arrivé *or* s'il est arrivé maintenant; **not (just) ~** pas tout de suite, pas encore, pas pour l'instant; **don't come in (just) ~** n'entrez pas tout de suite *or* pas encore *or* pas pour l'instant; **must you go just ~?** faut-il que vous partiez (*subj*) déjà?; **I needn't go (just) ~** je n'ai pas besoin de partir tout de suite; **that won't happen (just) ~, that won't happen ~ awhile(s)** ça n'est pas pour tout de suite.
c (*still, remaining*) encore (maintenant). **they have a few days ~** ils ont encore *or* il leur reste encore quelques jours; **there's another bottle ~** il reste encore une bouteille; **half is ~ to be built** il en reste encore la moitié à construire; **places ~ to be seen** des endroits qui restent (encore) à voir; **he has ~ to learn** il a encore à apprendre, il lui reste à apprendre; (*liter*) **she is ~ alive** elle est encore vivante, elle vit encore.
d (*with compar: still, even*) encore. **this is ~ more difficult** ceci est encore plus difficile; **he wants ~ more money** il veut encore plus *or* encore davantage d'argent.
e (*in addition*) encore, de plus. **~ once more** encore une fois, une fois de plus; **another arrived and ~ another** il en est arrivé un autre et encore un autre.
f (*before all is over*) encore, toujours. **he may come ~** *or* **~ come** il peut encore *or* toujours venir; **he could come ~** il pourrait bien encore *or* toujours venir; **I'll speak to her ~** je finirai bien par lui parler; **I'll do it ~** j'y arriverai bien quand même.
g (*frm*) **nor ~** ni, et ... non plus, ni même, et ... pas davantage; **I do not like him nor ~ his sister** je ne les aime ni lui ni sa sœur, je ne l'aime pas et sa sœur non plus *or* et sa sœur pas davantage; **not he nor ~ I** ni lui ni moi; **they did not come nor ~ (even) write** ils ne sont pas venus et ils n'ont même pas écrit.
2 conj (*however*) cependant, pourtant; (*nevertheless*) toutefois, néanmoins, malgré tout, tout de même. **(and) ~ everyone liked her** (et) pourtant *or* néanmoins tout le monde l'aimait, mais tout le monde

l'aimait quand même; **(and) ~ I like the house** (et) malgré tout *or* (et) pourtant *or* (et) néanmoins j'aime bien la maison; **it's strange ~ true** c'est étrange mais pourtant vrai *or* mais vrai tout de même.

yeti ['jetɪ] n yéti *m*.

yew [ju:] n (*also* ~ **tree**) if *m*; (*wood*) (bois *m* d')if.

Y.H.A. [ˌwaɪeɪtʃ'eɪ] n (*Brit*) (abbr of **Youth Hostels Association**) ≃ F.U.A.J. *f* (*Fédération unie des auberges de jeunesse*).

Yid** [jɪd] n (*pej*) youpin(e)** *m(f)* (*pej*), Juif *m*, Juive *f*.

Yiddish ['jɪdɪʃ] 1 adj yiddish *inv*. 2 n (*Ling*) yiddish *m*.

yield [ji:ld] 1 n *[earth]* production *f*; *[land, farm, field, orchard, tree]* rendement *m*, rapport *m*, récolte(s) *f(pl)*; *[mine, oil well]* débit *m*; *[labour]* produit *m*, rendement; *[an industry]* production, rendement; *[tax]* recettes *fpl*, rapport, revenu *m*; *[business, shares]* rapport, rendement, revenu. ~ **per acre** rendement à l'hectare.

2 vt a (*produce, bear; bring in*) *[earth]* produire; *[farm, field, land, orchard, tree]* rendre, produire, donner, rapporter; *[mine, oil well]* débiter; *[labour, an industry]* produire; *[business, investments, tax, shares]* rapporter. **to ~ a profit** rapporter un profit *or* un bénéfice; **that land ~s no return** cette terre ne rend pas, cette terre ne produit *or* rapporte rien; (*Fin*) **shares ~ing high interest** actions *fpl* à gros rendement; **shares ~ing 10%** actions qui rapportent 10%; **it will ~ the opportunity of** cela fournira l'occasion de; **to ~ results** donner *or* produire des résultats; **this ~ed many benefits** bien des bénéfices en ont résulté.

b (*surrender*) *fortress, territory* céder, livrer, abandonner (*to* à); *ownership, rights* céder (*to* à), renoncer à (*to* en faveur de). (*Mil, fig*) **to ~ ground to sb** céder du terrain à qn; (*fig*) **to ~ the floor to sb** laisser la parole à qn; **to ~ a point to sb** concéder un point à qn, céder à qn sur un point; **if he ~s this point** s'il admet *or* concède ce point, s'il cède sur ce point; (*Aut*) **to ~ the right of way to sb** laisser *or* céder la priorité à qn; (*frm*) **to ~ obedience/thanks to sb** rendre obéissance/grâces à qn (*frm*).

3 vi a (*give produce; bring in revenue: see* **2a** *for typical subjects*) rendre; rapporter; donner; produire; débiter. **field that ~s well** champ qui rapporte *or* qui donne un bon rendement, champ qui rend bien; **land that ~s poorly** terre qui rend peu *or* mal.

b (*surrender, give way*) céder (*to* devant, à), se rendre (*to* à). **we shall never ~** nous ne céderons jamais, nous ne nous rendrons jamais; **they begged him but he would not ~** ils l'ont supplié mais il n'a pas cédé *or* il ne s'est pas laissé fléchir; (*Mil etc*) **they ~ed to us** ils se rendirent à nous; **to ~ to force** céder devant la force; **to ~ to superior forces** céder devant *or* à des forces supérieures; **to ~ to superior numbers** céder au nombre; **to ~ to reason** se rendre à la raison; **to ~ to sb's entreaties** céder aux prières *or* instances de qn; **to ~ to sb's threats** céder devant les menaces de qn; **to ~ to sb's argument** se rendre aux raisons de qn; **the disease ~ed to treatment** le mal a cédé aux remèdes; **to ~ to temptation** succomber à la tentation; (*liter*) **he ~ed to nobody in courage** il ne le cédait à personne en courage; **I ~ to nobody in my admiration for ...** personne plus que moi n'admire ... .

c (*give way*) *[branch, door, ice, rope]* céder; *[beam]* céder, fléchir; *[floor, ground]* s'affaisser; *[bridge]* céder, s'affaisser. **to ~ under pressure** céder à la pression.

►**yield up** vt sep (*liter*) abandonner, céder, livrer. **to yield o.s. up to temptation** succomber *or* s'abandonner *or* se livrer à la tentation; **to yield up the ghost** rendre l'âme.

yielding ['ji:ldɪŋ] 1 adj a (*fig*) *person* complaisant, accommodant. b (*lit: see* **yield 3c**) qui cède, qui fléchit; *ground, surface* mou (*f* molle), élastique. 2 n *[person]* soumission *f*; *[town, fort]* reddition *f*, capitulation *f*; *[right, goods]* cession *f*.

yin [jɪn] n (*Philos*) yin.

yippee* [jɪ'pi:] excl hourra!

Y.M.C.A. [ˌwaɪemsi:'eɪ] n (abbr of **Young Men's Christian Association**) Y.M.C.A. *m*.

yob(bo)* ['jɒb(əʊ)] n (*Brit pej*) loubard *m*.

yock* [jɒk] (*US*) 1 n gros rire *m*, rire gras. 2 vt: **to ~ it up** rigoler*, s'esclaffer.

yod [jɒd] n (*Ling*) yod *m*.

yodel ['jəʊdl] 1 vi jodler *or* iodler, faire des tyroliennes. 2 n (*song, call*) tyrolienne *f*.

yoga ['jəʊgə] n yoga *m*.

yoghourt, yog(h)urt ['jəʊgət] n yaourt *m or* yog(h)ourt *m*. **~-maker** yaourtière *f*.

yogi ['jəʊgɪ] n, pl ~s *or* **yogin** ['jəʊgɪn] yogi *m*.

yo-heave-ho ['jəʊ'hi:v'həʊ] excl (*Naut*) ho hisse!

yoke [jəʊk] 1 n, pl ~s *or* ~ a (*for oxen*) joug *m*; (*for carrying pails*) palanche *f*, joug; (*on harness*) support *m* de timon. b (*fig: dominion*) joug *m*. **to come under the ~ of** tomber sous le joug de; **to throw off** *or* **cast off the ~** briser *or* secouer *or* rompre le joug. c (pl inv) (*pair*) attelage *m*, paire *f*, couple† *m*. **a ~ of oxen** une paire de bœufs. d *[dress, blouse]* empiècement *m*. e (*Constr*) *[beam]* moise *f*, lien *m*; (*Tech*) bâti *m*, carcasse *f*. 2 comp ►**yoke oxen** bœufs *mpl* d'attelage. 3 vt (*also* ~ **up**) *oxen* accoupler; *ox etc* mettre au joug; *pieces of machinery* accoupler; (*fig: also* ~ **together**) unir. **to ~ oxen (up) to the plough** atteler des bœufs à la charrue.

yokel ['jəʊkəl] n (*pej*) rustre *m*, péquenaud *m*.

yolk [jəʊk] n (*Bio*) vitellus *m*; (*Culin*) jaune *m* (d'œuf). (*Bio*) ~ **sac** membrane *f* vitelline.

Yom Kippur [ˌjɒmkɪ'pʊəʳ] n Yom Kippur *m*.

yon [jɒn] adj (††, *liter, dial*) = **yonder 2**.

yonder ['jɒndəʳ] 1 adv là(-bas). **up ~** là-haut; **over ~** là-bas; **down ~** là-bas en bas. 2 adj (*liter*) ce ... -là, ce ... là-bas. **from ~ house** de cette maison-là, de cette maison là-bas.

yonks* [jɒŋks] npl: **for ~** très longtemps; **I haven't seen him for ~** ça fait une éternité *or* une paye* que je ne l'ai pas vu.

yoof* [ju:f] n = **youth**.

yoo-hoo* ['ju:'hu:] excl ohé! (vous *or* toi là-bas!), hou hou!

YOP† [waɪəʊ'pi:, jɒp] (*Brit*) n a (abbr of **Youth Opportunities Programme**) ≃ Plan *m* Avenirs Jeunes. b [jɒp] jeune stagiaire *mf* (*dans le cadre du Plan Avenirs Jeunes*).

yore [jɔ:ʳ] n (*liter*) **of ~** d'antan (*liter*), (d')autrefois; **in days of ~** au temps jadis.

Yorks [jɔ:ks] abbr of **Yorkshire**.

Yorkshire ['jɔ:kʃəʳ] n Yorkshire *m*. (*Brit Culin*) ~ **pudding** *pâte à crêpe cuite qui accompagne un rôti de bœuf;* ~ **terrier** yorkshire-terrier *m*.

you [ju:] 1 pers pron a (*subject*) tu, vous, (*pl*) vous; (*object or indirect object*) te, vous, (*pl*) vous; (*stressed and after prep*) toi, vous, (*pl*) vous. **~ are very kind** tu es très gentil, vous êtes très gentil(s); **I shall see ~ soon** je te *or* je vous verrai bientôt, on se voit bientôt; **this book is for ~** ce livre est pour toi *or* vous; **take them with ~** emportez-les avec vous; **she is younger than ~** elle est plus jeune que toi *or* vous; **~ and yours** toi et les tiens, vous et les vôtres; **all of ~** vous tous; **all ~ who came here** vous tous qui êtes venus ici; **~ who know him** toi qui le connais, vous qui le connaissez; **~ French** vous autres Français; **~ and I will go together** toi *or* vous et moi, nous irons ensemble; **there ~ are!** (*you've arrived*) te *or* vous voilà!, (*take this*) voici!, tiens!, tenez!; **if I were ~** (si j'étais) à ta *or* votre place, si j'étais toi *or* vous; **between ~ and me** (*lit*) entre toi *or* vous et moi; (*in secret*) entre nous, de toi *or* vous à moi; **~ fool (~)!** imbécile (que tu es)!, espèce d'imbécile!; **~ darling!** tu es un amour!; **it's ~** c'est toi *or* vous; **~ there!** toi *or* vous là-bas!; **never ~ mind*** (*don't worry*) ne t'en fais pas*, ne vous en faites pas*; (*it's not your business*) ça ne te *or* vous regarde pas, mêle-toi de tes *or* mêlez-vous de vos affaires; **don't ~ go away** ne pars pas, toi!, ne partez pas, vous!; **there's a fine house for ~!** en voilà une belle maison!; **now YOU say something** maintenant à toi *or* à vous de parler; (††, *dial*) **sit ~ down** assieds-toi, asseyez-vous.

b (*one, anyone*) (*nominative*) on; (*accusative, dative*) vous, te. **~ never know, ~ never can tell** on ne sait jamais; **~ go towards the church** vous allez *or* on va vers l'église; **~ never know your (own) luck** on ne connaît jamais son bonheur *or* sa chance; **fresh air does ~ good** l'air frais (vous *or* te) fait du bien.

2 comp ►**you-all*** (*US*) vous (*pl*) ►**you-know-who*** qui-vous-savez, qui-tu-sais.

you'd [ju:d] = **you had, you would**; *see* **have, would**.

you'll [ju:l] = **you will**; *see* **will**.

young [jʌŋ] 1 adj *man, tree, country* jeune; *vegetable, grass* nouveau (*before vowel* nouvel; *f* nouvelle); *appearance, smile* jeune, juvénile. **~ people** jeunes *mpl*, jeunes gens, jeunesse *f*; **~ lady** (*unmarried*) jeune fille *f*, demoiselle *f*; (*married*) jeune femme *f*; **they have a ~ family** ils ont de jeunes enfants; **listen to me, ~ man** écoutez-moi, jeune homme; **her ~ man**† son amoureux, son petit ami; **~ in heart** jeune de cœur; **he is ~ for his age** il est jeune pour son âge, il paraît *or* fait plus jeune que son âge; **he is very ~ for this job** il est bien jeune pour ce poste; **to marry ~** se marier jeune; **he is 3 years younger than you** il est plus jeune que vous de 3 ans, il a 3 ans de moins que vous, il est votre cadet de 3 ans; **my younger brother** mon frère cadet; **my younger sister** ma sœur cadette; **the younger son of the family** le cadet de la famille; **I'm not so ~ as I was** je n'ai plus (mes) vingt ans (*fig*); **in my ~ days** dans ma jeunesse, dans mon jeune temps, quand j'étais jeune; **in my younger days** quand j'étais plus jeune; **to grow** *or* **get younger** rajeunir; **if I were younger** si j'étais plus jeune; **if I were 10 years younger** si j'avais 10 ans de moins; **you're only ~ once** jeunesse n'a qu'un temps; **you ~ scoundrel!** petit *or* jeune voyou!; **~ Mr Brown, Mr Brown the younger** le jeune M. Brown; (*as opposed to his father*) M. Brown fils; **Pitt the Younger** le second Pitt; **Pliny the Younger** Pline le Jeune; **the ~ moon** la nouvelle lune; **the night is ~** (*liter*) la nuit n'est pas très avancée; (* *hum*) on a toute la nuit devant nous*; **the younger generation** la jeune génération, la génération montante; (*Brit Jur*) **~ offender** jeune délinquant(e) *m(f)*; (*Brit Jur*) **~ offenders institution** centre *m* de détention pour mineurs; **the ~ idea** (*lit*) ce que pensent les jeunes; (*fig*) la jeune génération; **Y~ France** la jeune génération en France; **he has a very ~ outlook** il a des idées très jeunes; **that dress is too ~ for her** cette robe est *or* fait trop jeune pour elle; **~ wine** vin vert; (*fig*) **~ blood** sang nouveau *or* jeune; *see* **hopeful** *etc*.

2 collective npl a (*people*) **the ~** les jeunes *mpl*, les jeunes gens, la jeunesse; **~ and old** les (plus) jeunes comme les (plus) vieux, tout le monde; **a mother defending her ~** une mère qui défend ses petits *or* sa nichée (*fig*); **books for the ~** livres pour les jeunes *or* la jeunesse.

b *[animal]* petits *mpl.* **cat with ~** chatte pleine.
3 **comp ▸young-looking** qui a (*or* avait *etc*) l'air jeune; **she's very young-looking** elle a l'air *or* elle fait très jeune.

youngish ['jʌŋɪʃ] **adj** assez jeune.

youngster ['jʌŋstəʳ] **n** (*boy*) jeune garçon *m*, jeune *m*; (*child*) enfant *mf*.

your [jʊəʳ] **poss adj** a ton, ta, tes; votre, vos. **~ book** ton *or* votre livre; **YOUR book** ton livre à toi, votre livre à vous; **~ table** ta *or* votre table; **~ friend** ton ami(e), votre ami(e); **~ clothes** tes *or* vos vêtements; **this is the best of ~ paintings** c'est ton *or* votre meilleur tableau; **give me ~ hand** donne-moi *or* donnez-moi la main; **you've broken ~ leg!** tu t'es cassé la jambe!; *see* **majesty, worship** *etc.*
b (*one's*) son, sa, ses; ton *etc,* votre *etc.* **you give him ~ form and he gives you ~ pass** on lui donne son formulaire et il vous remet votre laissez-passer; **exercise is good for ~ health** l'exercice est bon pour la santé.
c (*typical*) ton *etc,* votre *etc.* **so these are ~ country pubs?** alors c'est ça, vos bistros* de campagne?; **~ ordinary Englishman will always prefer ...** l'Anglais moyen préférera toujours ... .

you're [jʊəʳ] = **you are;** *see* **be.**

yours [jʊəz] **poss pron** le tien, la tienne, les tiens, les tiennes; le vôtre, la vôtre, les vôtres. **this is my book and that is ~** voici mon livre et voilà le tien *or* le vôtre; **this book is ~** ce livre est à toi *or* à vous, ce livre est le tien *or* le vôtre; **is this poem ~?** ce poème est-il de toi? *or* de vous?; **when will the house become ~?** quand est-ce que la maison deviendra (la) vôtre?; **she is a cousin of ~** c'est une de tes *or* de vos cousines; **that is no business of ~** cela ne te *or* vous regarde pas, ce n'est pas ton *or* votre affaire; **it's no fault of ~** ce n'est pas de votre faute (à vous); (*Comm*) **~ of the 10th inst** votre honorée du 10 courant (*Comm*); **no advice of ~ could prevent him** aucun conseil de votre part ne pouvait l'empêcher; **it is not ~ to decide** ce n'est pas à vous de décider, il ne vous appartient pas de décider; **~ is a specialized department** votre section est une section spécialisée; (*pej*) **that dog of ~** ton *or* votre sacré‡ *or* fichu* chien; **that stupid son of ~** ton *or* votre idiot de fils; **that temper of ~** ton *or* votre sale caractère; (*in pub etc*) **what's ~?** qu'est-ce que tu prends? *or* vous prenez?; *see* **affectionately, ever, you** *etc.*

yourself [jə'self] **pers pron, pl yourselves** [jə'selvz] (*reflexive: direct and indirect*) te, vous, (*pl*) vous; (*after prep*) toi, vous, (*pl*) vous; (*emphatic*) toi-même, vous-même, (*pl*) vous-mêmes. **have you hurt ~?** tu t'es fait mal?, vous vous êtes fait mal?; **are you enjoying ~?** tu t'amuses bien?, vous vous amusez bien?; **were you talking to ~?** tu te parlais à toi-même?, tu te parlais tout seul?, vous vous parliez à vous-même?, vous vous parliez tout seul?; **you never speak about ~** tu ne parles jamais de toi, vous ne parlez jamais de vous; **you ~ told me, you told me ~** tu me l'as dit toi-même, vous me l'avez dit vous-même; **(all) by ~** tout seul; **did you do it by ~?** tu l'as *or* vous l'avez fait tout seul?; **you will see for ~** tu verras toi-même, vous verrez vous-même; **someone like ~*** quelqu'un comme vous; **people like yourselves*** des gens comme vous; **how's ~?‡** et toi, comment (ça) va?*; **how are you? — fine and ~?*** comment vas-tu? — très bien et toi?; **you are not (quite) ~ today** tu n'es pas dans ton assiette *or* vous n'êtes pas dans votre assiette aujourd'hui; *see* **among(st).**

youth [ju:θ] 1 **n** a (*NonC*) jeunesse *f*. **in (the days of) my ~** dans ma jeunesse, lorsque j'étais jeune, au temps de ma jeunesse; **in early ~** dans la première *or* prime jeunesse; **he has kept his ~** il est resté jeune; (*Prov*) **~ will have its way** *or* **its fling** il faut que jeunesse se passe; *see* **first.**
b (*pl* **youths** [ju:ðz]: *young man*) jeune homme *m*. **~s** jeunes gens *mpl*.
c (*collective: young people*) jeunesse *f*, jeunes *mpl*, jeunes gens *mpl*. **she likes working with (the) ~** elle aime travailler avec les jeunes; **the ~ of a country** la jeunesse d'un pays; **the ~ of today are very mature** les jeunes d'aujourd'hui sont très mûrs, la jeunesse aujourd'hui est très mûre.
2 **comp** de jeunes, de jeunesse **▸youth club** foyer *m or* centre *m* de jeunes **▸Youth Employment Service** (*Brit*) service *m* d'orientation professionnelle pour les jeunes **▸youth leader** animateur *m*, -trice *f* de groupes de jeunes **▸the Hitler Youth Movement** les Jeunesses hitlériennes **▸youth orchestra** orchestre *m* de jeunes **▸Youth Training Scheme**† (*Brit*) ≈ pacte *m* national pour l'emploi des jeunes; *see* **hostel.**

youthful ['ju:θfʊl] **adj** *person, looks, fashion* jeune; *air, mistake* de jeunesse; *quality, freshness* juvénile. **she looks ~** elle a l'air jeune, elle a un air de jeunesse.

youthfulness ['ju:θfʊlnɪs] **n** jeunesse *f*. **~ of appearance** air *m* jeune *or* de jeunesse.

you've [ju:v] = **you have;** *see* **have.**

yow [jaʊ] **excl** aïe!

yowl [jaʊl] 1 **n** *[person, dog]* hurlement *m*; *[cat]* miaulement *m*. 2 **vi** *[person, dog]* hurler (*with, from* de); *[cat]* miauler.

yowling ['jaʊlɪŋ] **n** *[person, dog]* hurlements *mpl*; *[cat]* miaulements *mpl*.

yo-yo ['jəʊjəʊ] **n** ® a yo-yo *m* ®. b (*US* ‡: *fool*) ballot* *m*, poire* *f*.

yr **abbr of year.**

Y.T.S.† ['waɪti:'es] **n** (*Brit*) (**abbr of Youth Training Scheme**) *see* **youth.**

ytterbium [ɪ'tɜ:bɪəm] **n** ytterbium *m*.

yttrium ['ɪtrɪəm] **n** yttrium *m*.

yuan [ju:æn] **n, pl inv** yuan *m*.

yucca ['jʌkə] **n** yucca *m*.

yuck‡ [jʌk] **excl** berk! *or* beurk!, pouah!

yucky‡ ['jʌkɪ] **adj** dégueulasse‡, dégoûtant.

Yugoslav ['ju:gəʊ'slɑ:v] 1 **adj** yougoslave. 2 **n** Yougoslave *mf*.

Yugoslavia ['ju:gəʊ'slɑ:vɪə] **n** Yougoslavie *f*.

Yugoslavian ['ju:gəʊ'slɑ:vɪən] **adj** yougoslave.

yuk* [jʌk] = **yuck.**

yukky* ['jʌkɪ] = **yucky.**

Yukon ['ju:kɒn] **n** Yukon *m*. **~ Territory** (territoire *m* du) Yukon.

Yule [ju:l] 1 **n** (†) Noël *m*. 2 **comp ▸Yule log** bûche *f* de Noël **▸Yuletide**† (époque *f* de) Noël *f*.

yummy‡ ['jʌmɪ] 1 **adj** *food* délicieux. 2 **excl** miam-miam!*

yum-yum‡ ['jʌm'jʌm] **excl** = **yummy 2.**

yup* [jʌp] **particle** (*US*) ouais*, oui.

yuppie* ['jʌpɪ] 1 **n** (**abbr of young urban** *or* **upwardly mobile professional**) yuppie *mf* (*jeune cadre dynamique et ambitieux*). 2 **adj** *car, clothes* de yuppie; *bar, restaurant, area, flat* de yuppies. **~ flu*** *troubles d'ordre viral associés au stress.*

yuppified* ['jʌpɪ,faɪd] **adj** *bar, restaurant, area, flat* transformé en bar (*or* restaurant *etc*) de yuppies. **he is becoming more and more ~** il se transforme de plus en plus en yuppie.

yuppy* ['jʌpɪ] **n** = **yuppie.**

Y.W.C.A. [,waɪdʌblju:si:'eɪ] **n** (**abbr of Young Women's Christian Association**) Y.W.C.A. *m*.

Z

Z, z [zed], (*US*) [ziː] 1 **n** (*letter*) Z, z *m*. **Z for Zebra** ≃ Z comme Zoé. 2 **comp** ▸**z-axis** axe *m* des z ▸**Z-car** ≃ voiture *f* pie *inv* (*de la police*).
Zacharias [ˌzækəˈraɪəs] **n** Zacharie *m*.
zaftig* [ˈzɑːftɪk] **adj** (*US*) jolie et bien en chair.
Zaire [zɑːˈiːəʳ] **n** Zaïre *m*.
Zairian [zɑːˈiːərɪən] 1 **n** Zaïrois(e) *m(f)*. 2 **adj** zaïrois.
Zambesi, Zambezi [zæmˈbiːzɪ] **n** Zambèze *m*.
Zambia [ˈzæmbɪə] **n** Zambie *f*.
Zambian [ˈzæmbɪən] 1 **n** Zambien(ne) *m(f)*. 2 **adj** zambien.
zany [ˈzeɪnɪ] 1 **adj** dingue*, toqué*, cinglé*. 2 **n** (*Theat*) bouffon *m*, zan(n)i *m* (*Theat Hist*).
Zanzibar [ˈzænzɪbɑːʳ] **n** Zanzibar *m*.
zap* [zæp] 1 **excl** vlan!, bing! 2 **vt** a (*destroy*) *town* ravager, bombarder; *person* supprimer*, descendre*. b (*delete*) *word, data* supprimer. c (*astonish*) épater*. d (*send quickly*) **I'll ~ it out to you straight away** je vais vous l'expédier tout de suite. 3 **vi** a (*move quickly*) *[car]* foncer. **we had to ~ down to London** nous avons dû filer à Londres à toute vitesse; **to ~ along** *[car]* foncer, gazer*; *[project]* gazer*, rouler*. b (*TV*) **to ~ from channel to channel** zapper* d'une chaîne à l'autre.
zapped* [zæpt] **adj** (*exhausted*) claqué*, crevé*, vanné*.
zapper* [ˈzæpəʳ] **n** (*TV: remote control*) télécommande *f*.
zappy* [ˈzæpɪ] **adj** *person* plein d'entrain *or* d'allant; *style of writing* qui a du punch; *car* rapide, qui fonce *or* gaze*.
Zarathustra [ˌzærəˈθuːstrə] **n** Zarathoustra *m or* Zoroastre *m*.
zeal [ziːl] **n** (*NonC*) a (*religious fervour*) zèle *m*, ferveur *f*. b (*enthusiasm*) zèle *m*, ardeur *f* (*for* pour), empressement *m* (*for* à).
zealot [ˈzelət] **n** a fanatique *mf*, zélateur *m*, -trice *f* (*liter*) (*for* de). b (*Jewish Hist*) **Z~** zélote *mf*.
zealotry [ˈzelətrɪ] **n** fanatisme *m*.
zealous [ˈzeləs] **adj** (*fervent*) zélé; (*devoted*) dévoué, empressé. **~ for the cause** plein de zèle *or* d'ardeur *or* d'enthousiasme pour la cause.
zealously [ˈzeləslɪ] **adv** (*fervently*) avec zèle, avec ferveur, avec ardeur; (*stronger*) avec fanatisme; (*devotedly*) avec zèle, avec empressement.
zebra [ˈzebrə, ˈziːbrə] **pl ~** *or* **~** 1 **n** zèbre *m*. 2 **comp** ▸**zebra crossing** (*Brit*) passage *m* pour piétons ▸**zebra stripes** zébrures *fpl*; **with zebra stripes** zébré.
zebu [ˈziːbuː] **n** zébu *m*.
Zechariah [ˌzekəˈraɪə] **n** = **Zacharias**.
zed [zed] **n**, (*US*) **zee** [ziː] **n** (la lettre) z *m*.
Zen [zen] **n** Zen *m*. **~ Buddhism** bouddhisme *m* zen; **~ Buddhist** bouddhiste *(mf)* zen.
zenana [zeˈnɑːnə] **n** zénana *m*.
zenith [ˈzenɪθ] **n** (*Astron*) zénith *m*; (*fig*) zénith, apogée *m*, faîte *m*. **at the ~ of his power** au zénith *or* à l'apogée *or* au faîte de son pouvoir.
Zephaniah [ˌzefəˈnaɪə] **n** Sophonie *m*.
zephyr [ˈzefəʳ] **n** zéphyr *m*.
zeppelin [ˈzeplɪn] **n** zeppelin *m*.
zero [ˈzɪərəʊ] **pl ~s** *or* **~es** 1 **n** a (*point on scale*) zéro *m*. **15 degrees below ~** 15 degrés au-dessous de zéro; **absolute ~** zéro absolu; (*fig*) **his chances of success sank to ~** ses chances de réussite se réduisirent à zéro.
b (*esp US: cipher, numeral etc*) zéro *m*. **row of ~s** série *f* de zéros.
2 **comp** *tension, voltage* nul (*f* nulle) ▸**zero altitude** (*Aviat*) altitude *f* zéro; **to fly at zero altitude** voler en rase-mottes, faire du rase-mottes ▸**zero-base** (*US*) **vt** (*fig*) *question, issue* reprendre à zéro, réexaminer point par point ▸**zero-G*, zero-gravity** impesanteur *f* ▸**zero growth** (*Econ*) taux *m* de croissance zéro, croissance *f* économique zéro ▸**zero hour** (*Mil*) l'heure *f* H; (*fig*) le moment critique *or* décisif ▸**the zero option** (*Pol*) l'option *f* zéro ▸**zero point** point *m* zéro ▸**zero population growth** accroissement *m* démographique nul ▸**zero-rated (for VAT)** exempt de TVA, ne pas être assujetti à la TVA ▸**zero-rating** exemption *f* de TVA, non-assujettissement *m* à la TVA ▸**zero-sum** (*US*) **adj** à *or* de somme nulle.
▸**zero in** **vi**: **to zero in on sth** (*move in on*) se diriger droit vers *or* sur qch, piquer droit sur qch; (*fig: identify*) mettre le doigt sur qch, identifier qch; (*fig: concentrate on*) se concentrer sur qch, faire porter tous ses efforts sur qch; (*fig: in attacking speech etc*) **he zeroed in on those who ...** il s'en est pris tout particulièrement à ceux qui ... .
zest [zest] **n** (*NonC*) a (*gusto*) entrain *m*, élan *m*, enthousiasme *m*. **to fight with ~** combattre avec entrain; **he ate it with great ~** il l'a mangé avec grand appétit; **~ for living** goût *m* pour la vie, appétit *m* de vivre. b (*fig*) saveur *f*; piquant *m*. **story full of ~** histoire savoureuse; **it adds ~ to the episode** cela donne une certaine saveur *or* du piquant à l'histoire. c (*Culin*) *[orange, lemon]* zeste *m*.
zestful [ˈzestfʊl] **adj** plein d'entrain, enthousiaste.
zestfully [ˈzestfəlɪ] **adv** avec entrain *or* enthousiasme *or* élan.
Zetland [ˈzetlənd] **n** Zetland *fpl*.
Zeus [zjuːs] **n** Zeus *m*.
zidovudine [zaɪˈdɒvjʊˌdiːn] **n** zidovudine *f*.
zigzag [ˈzɪgzæg] 1 **n** zigzag *m*. 2 **adj** *path, course, line* en zigzag; *road* en lacets; *pattern, design* à zigzags. 3 **adv** en zigzag. 4 **vi** zigzaguer, faire des zigzags. **to ~ along** avancer en zigzaguant, marcher *etc* en zigzag; **to ~ out/through** *etc* sortir/traverser *etc* en zigzaguant.
zilch* [zɪltʃ] **n** (*esp US*) rien, zéro, que dalle*. **he's a real ~** c'est un zéro*.
zillion* [ˈzɪljən] **adj, n, pl ~s** *or* **~** (*US*) **a ~ dollars** des millions *mpl* et des millions de dollars; **~s of problems, a ~ problems** des tas *mpl* de problèmes.
Zimbabwe [zɪmˈbɑːbwɪ] **n** Zimbabwe *m*.
Zimbabwean [zɪmˈbɑːbwɪən] 1 **adj** zimbabwéen. 2 **n** Zimbabwéen(ne) *m(f)*.
zimmer [ˈzɪməʳ] **n** ® déambulateur *m*.
zinc [zɪŋk] 1 **n** (*NonC*) zinc *m*. 2 **comp** *plate, alloy* de zinc; *roof* zingué ▸**zinc blende** blende *f* ▸**zinc chloride** chlorure *m* de zinc ▸**zinc dust** limaille *f* de zinc ▸**zinc ointment** pommade *f* à l'oxyde de zinc ▸**zinc oxide** oxyde *m* de zinc ▸**zinc sulphate** sulfate *m* de zinc ▸**zinc white** = **zinc oxide**.
zing [zɪŋ] 1 **n** a (*noise of bullet*) sifflement *m*. b (**NonC*) entrain *m*. 2 **vi** *[bullet, arrow]* siffler. **the bullet ~ed past his ear** la balle lui a sifflé à l'oreille; **the cars ~ed past** les voitures sont passées dans un bruit strident.
zinnia [ˈzɪnɪə] **n** zinnia *m*.
Zion [ˈzaɪən] **n** Sion *m*.
Zionism [ˈzaɪənɪzəm] **n** sionisme *m*.
Zionist [ˈzaɪənɪst] 1 **adj** sioniste. 2 **n** Sioniste *mf*.
zip [zɪp] 1 **n** a (*Brit: also* **~ fastener**) fermeture *f* éclair ®, fermeture à glissière. **pocket with a ~** poche *f* à fermeture éclair ®, poche zippée*.
b (*sound of bullet*) sifflement *m*.
c (**NonC: energy etc*) entrain *m*, élan *m*. **put a bit of ~ into it** activez-vous!
2 **comp** ▸**zip code** (*US Post*) code *m* postal ▸**zip fastener** = **zip 1a** ▸**zip gun** (*US*) pistolet *m* bricolé *or* artisanal ▸**zip-on** à fermeture éclair ®.
3 **vt** a (*close: also* **~ up**) *dress, bag* fermer avec une fermeture éclair ® *or* à glissière.
b **she ~ped open her dress/bag** *etc* elle a ouvert la fermeture éclair ® *or* à glissière de sa robe/de son sac *etc*.
4 **vi** (*) *[car, person]* **to ~ in/out/past/up** *etc* entrer/sortir/passer/monter *etc* comme une flèche.
▸**zip on** 1 **vi** s'attacher avec une fermeture éclair ® *or* fermeture à glissière. 2 **vt sep** attacher avec une fermeture éclair ® *or* fermeture à glissière. 3 **zip-on** **adj** *see* **zip 2**.
▸**zip up** 1 **vi** *[dress etc]* se fermer avec une fermeture éclair ® *or* fermeture à glissière. 2 **vt sep** **can you zip me up?** tu peux m'aider avec la fermeture éclair ®?; *see also* **zip 3a**.

zipper [ˈzɪpəʳ] n (*esp US*) = **zip 1a**.
zippy‡ [ˈzɪpɪ] adj *person* plein d'entrain *or* d'allant.
zircon [ˈzɜːkən] n zircon *m*.
zirconium [zɜːˈkəʊnɪəm] n zirconium *m*.
zit* [zɪt] n (*esp US*) bouton *m* (*sur la peau*).
zither [ˈzɪðəʳ] n cithare *f*.
zodiac [ˈzəʊdɪæk] n zodiaque *m*; *see* **sign**.
zodiacal [zəʊˈdaɪəkəl] adj du zodiac. ~ **light** lumière *f* zodiacale.
zoftig‡ [ˈzɒftɪk] = **zaftig**‡.
zombie [ˈzɒmbɪ] n (* *fig pej*) automate *mf*, mort(e) *m(f)* vivant(e); (*lit*) zombi *m*.
zonal [ˈzəʊnl] adj zonal.
zone [ˈzəʊn] 1 n a (*Astron, Geog, Math etc*) zone *f*; (*esp Mil*) (*area*) zone; (*subdivision of town*) secteur *m*. **it lies within the ~ reserved for** ... cela se trouve dans le secteur *or* la zone réservé(e) à ...; *see* **battle, danger, enterprise, time** *etc*. b (*US: also* **postal delivery** ~) zone *f* (postale). 2 comp ▸**zone defence** (*Basketball*) défense *f* de zone. 3 vt a (*divide into ~s*) *area* diviser en zones; *town* diviser en secteurs. b **this district has been ~d for industry** c'est une zone réservée à l'implantation industrielle.
zoning [ˈzəʊnɪŋ] n répartition *f* en zones.
zonked‡ [zɒŋkt] adj (*also:* ~ **out**) (*exhausted*) crevé*, claqué*; (*on drugs*) défoncé‡; (*US: drunk*) bourré‡, saoul.
zoo [zuː] n zoo *m*. ~ **keeper** gardien(ne) *m(f)* de zoo.
zoological [ˌzəʊəˈlɒdʒɪkəl] adj zoologique. ~ **gardens** jardin *m or* parc *m* zoologique.
zoologist [ˌzəʊˈɒlədʒɪst] n zoologiste *mf*.
zoology [zəʊˈɒlədʒɪ] n zoologie *f*.
zoom [zuːm] 1 n a (*sound*) vrombissement *m*, bourdonnement *m*. b (*Aviat: upward flight*) montée *f* en chandelle. c (*Phot: also* ~ **lens**) zoom *m*. 2 vi a *[engine]* vrombir, bourdonner. b **to ~ away/through** *etc* démarrer/traverser *etc* en trombe*; **the car ~ed past us** la voiture est passée en trombe devant nous. c (*Aviat*) *[plane]* monter en chandelle.
▸**zoom in** vi (*Cine*) faire un zoom (*on* sur).
zoomorphic [ˌzəʊəʊˈmɔːfɪk] adj zoomorphe.
zoophyte [ˈzəʊəˌfaɪt] n zoophyte *m*.
zoot* [zuːt] in comps: **zoot-suit*** costume *m* zazou; **zoot-suiter*** zazou *m*.
Zoroaster [ˌzɒrəʊˈæstəʳ] n Zoroastre *m or* Zarathoustra *m*.
Zoroastrianism [ˌzɒrəʊˈæstrɪənɪzəm] n Zoroastrisme *m*.
zucchini [zuːˈkiːnɪ] n, pl ~ *or* ~**s** (*US*) courgette *f*.
Zuider Zee [ˈzaɪdəˈziː] n Zuiderzee *m*.
Zulu [ˈzuːluː] 1 adj zoulou (*f inv*). 2 n a Zoulou *mf*. b (*Ling*) zoulou *m*. 3 comp ▸**Zululand** Zoulouland *m*.
Zurich [ˈzjʊərɪk] n Zurich. **Lake** ~ le lac de Zurich.
zwieback [ˈzwiːbæk] n (*US*) biscotte *f*.
zygote [ˈzaɪgəʊt] n zygote *m*.

APPENDICES

ANNEXES

CONTENTS

SOMMAIRE

THE FRENCH VERB

LE VERBE FRANÇAIS

FORMATION OF COMPOUND TENSES

Most verbs form their compound tenses using the verb *avoir,* except in the reflexive form. Simple tenses of the auxiliary are followed by the past participle to form the compound tenses shown below (the verb *avoir* is given as an example):

AVOIR			+ PAST PARTICIPLE	COMPOUND TENSES OF VERBS
PRESENT	j' tu il nous vous ils	**ai** **as** **a** **avons** **avez** **ont**		= PERFECT (*chanter* = il **a chanté**) (*boire* = il **a bu**) (*avoir* = il **a eu**) (*être* = il **a été**)
IMPERFECT	j' tu il nous vous ils	**avais** **avais** **avait** **avions** **aviez** **avaient**		= PLUPERFECT (il **avait chanté,** il **avait bu,** il **avait eu,** il **avait été**)
FUTURE	j' tu il nous vous ils	**aurai** **auras** **aura** **aurons** **aurez** **auront**		= FUTURE PERFECT (il **aura chanté,** il **aura bu,** il **aura eu,** il **aura été**)
CONDITIONAL (PRESENT)	j' tu il nous vous ils	**aurais** **aurais** **aurait** **aurions** **auriez** **auraient**	**+ PAST PARTICIPLE** (chanté) (bu) (eu) (été)	= PAST CONDITIONAL (this tense is rarely studied but the forms are not rare) (il **aurait chanté,** il **aurait bu,** il **aurait eu,** il **aurait été**)
PAST HISTORIC	j' tu il nous vous ils	**eus** **eus** **eut** **eûmes** **eûtes** **eurent**		= PAST ANTERIOR (rare as a spoken form) (il **eut chanté,** il **eut bu,** il **eut eu,** il **eut été**)
IMPERATIVE		**aie** **ayons** **ayez**		= PAST IMPERATIVE (rare) (**aie chanté, aie bu, aie eu, aie été**)
PRESENT PARTICIPLE		**ayant**		= SECOND FORM OF PAST PARTICIPLE (**ayant chanté, ayant bu, ayant eu, ayant été**)
SUBJUNCTIVE (PRESENT)	que j' que tu qu'il que nous que vous qu'ils	**aie** **aies** **ait** **ayons** **ayez** **aient**		= PAST SUBJUNCTIVE (rare as spoken form) (qu'il **ait chanté,** qu'il **ait bu,** qu'il **ait eu,** qu'il **ait été**)
SUBJUNCTIVE (IMPERFECT) (rare)	que j' que tu qu'il que nous que vous qu'ils	**eusse** **eusses** **eût** **eussions** **eussiez** **eussent**		= PLUPERFECT SUBJUNCTIVE (very rare, even in the written form) (qu'il **eût chanté,** qu'il **eût bu,** qu'il **eût eu,** qu'il **eût été**)

COMPOUND TENSES OF AVOIR: formed with *avoir,* and the past participle *(eu, eue).*

INDICATIVE

PRESENT	PERFECT
j'arrive	je suis arrivé
tu arrives	tu es arrivé
il arrive	il est arrivé
nous arrivons	nous sommes arrivés
vous arrivez	vous êtes arrivés
ils arrivent	ils sont arrivés

IMPERFECT	PLUPERFECT
j'arrivais	j'étais arrivé
tu arrivais	tu étais arrivé
il arrivait	il était arrivé
nous arrivions	nous étions arrivés
vous arriviez	vous étiez arrivés
ils arrivaient	ils étaient arrivés

PAST HISTORIC	PAST ANTERIOR
j'arrivai	je fus arrivé
tu arrivas	tu fus arrivé
il arriva	il fut arrivé
nous arrivâmes	nous fûmes arrivés
vous arrivâtes	vous fûtes arrivés
ils arrivèrent	ils furent arrivés

FUTURE	FUTURE PERFECT
j'arriverai [aRiv(ə)Rɛ]	je serai arrivé
tu arriveras	tu seras arrivé
il arrivera	il sera arrivé
nous arriverons [aRiv(ə)Rɔ̃]	nous serons arrivés
vous arriverez	vous serez arrivés
ils arriveront	ils seront arrivés

SUBJUNCTIVE

PRESENT

que j'arrive
que tu arrives
qu'il arrive
que nous arrivions
que vous arriviez
qu'ils arrivent

IMPERFECT

que j'arrivasse
que tu arrivasses
qu'il arrivât
que nous arrivassions
que vous arrivassiez
qu'ils arrivassent

PAST

que je sois arrivé
que tu sois arrivé
qu'il soit arrivé
que nous soyons arrivés
que vous soyez arrivés
qu'ils soient arrivés

PLUPERFECT

que je fusse arrivé
que tu fusses arrivé
qu'il fût arrivé
que nous fussions arrivés
que vous fussiez arrivés
qu'ils fussent arrivés

CONDITIONAL

PRESENT

j'arriverais [aRivRɛ]
tu arriverais
il arriverait
nous arriverions [aRivəRjɔ̃]
vous arriveriez
ils arriveraient

PAST I

je serais arrivé
tu serais arrivé
il serait arrivé
nous serions arrivés
vous seriez arrivés
ils seraient arrivés

PAST II

je fusse arrivé
tu fusses arrivé
il fût arrivé
nous fussions arrivés
vous fussiez arrivés
ils fussent arrivés

	PRESENT	PAST
IMPERATIVE	arrive arrivons arrivez	sois arrivé soyons arrivés soyez arrivés
PARTICIPLE	arrivant	arrivé, ée étant arrivé
INFINITIVE	arriver	être arrivé

NB The verbs *jouer, tuer* etc. are regular: e.g. *je joue, je jouerai; je tue, je tuerai.*

INDICATIVE

PRESENT	PERFECT
je me repose	je me suis reposé
tu te reposes	tu t'es reposé
il se repose	il s'est reposé
nous nous reposons	nous nous sommes reposés
vous vous reposez	vous vous êtes reposés
ils se reposent	ils se sont reposés

IMPERFECT	PLUPERFECT
je me reposais	je m'étais reposé
tu te reposais	tu t'étais reposé
il se reposait	il s'était reposé
nous nous reposions	nous nous étions reposés
vous vous reposiez	vous vous étiez reposés
ils se reposaient	ils s'étaient reposés

PAST HISTORIC	PAST ANTERIOR
je me reposai	je me fus reposé
tu te reposas	tu te fus reposé
il se reposa	il se fut reposé
nous nous reposâmes	nous nous fûmes reposés
vous vous reposâtes	vous vous fûtes reposés
ils se reposèrent	ils se furent reposés

FUTURE	FUTURE PERFECT
je me reposerai	je me serai reposé
tu te reposeras	tu te seras reposé
il se reposera	il se sera reposé
nous nous reposerons	nous nous serons reposés
vous vous reposerez	vous vous serez reposés
ils se reposeront	ils se seront reposés

SUBJUNCTIVE

PRESENT	IMPERFECT
que je me repose	que je me reposasse
que tu te reposes	que tu te reposasses
qu'il se repose	qu'il se reposât
que nous nous reposions	que nous nous reposassions
que vous vous reposiez	que vous vous reposassiez
qu'ils se reposent	qu'ils se reposassent

PAST	PLUPERFECT
que je me sois reposé	que je me fusse reposé
que tu te sois reposé	que tu te fusses reposé
qu'il se soit reposé	qu'il se fût reposé
que nous nous soyons reposés	que nous nous fussions reposés
que vous vous soyez reposés	que vous vous fussiez reposés
qu'ils se soient reposés	qu'ils se fussent reposés

CONDITIONAL

PRESENT	PAST I	PAST II
je me reposerais	je me serais reposé	je me fusse reposé
tu te reposerais	tu te serais reposé	tu te fusses reposé
il se reposerait	il se serait reposé	il se fût reposé
nous nous reposerions	nous nous serions reposés	nous nous fussions reposés
vous vous reposeriez	vous vous seriez reposés	vous vous fussiez reposés
ils se reposeraient	ils se seraient reposés	ils se fussent reposés

	PRESENT	PAST
IMPERATIVE	repose-toi reposons-nous reposez-vous	unused
PARTICIPLE	se reposant	s'étant reposé
INFINITIVE	se reposer	s'être reposé

conjugation 2 — **FINIR:** regular verbs ending in **-ir**

INDICATIVE

PRESENT	PERFECT
je finis	j'ai fini
tu finis	tu as fini
il finit	il a fini
nous finissons	nous avons fini
vous finissez	vous avez fini
ils finissent	ils ont fini

IMPERFECT	PLUPERFECT
je finissais	j'avais fini
tu finissais	tu avais fini
il finissait	il avait fini
nous finissions	nous avions fini
vous finissiez	vous aviez fini
ils finissaient	ils avaient fini

PAST HISTORIC	PAST ANTERIOR
je finis	j'eus fini
tu finis	tu eus fini
il finit	il eut fini
nous finîmes	nous eûmes fini
vous finîtes	vous eûtes fini
ils finirent	ils eurent fini

FUTURE	FUTURE PERFECT
je finirai	j'aurai fini
tu finiras	tu auras fini
il finira	il aura fini
nous finirons	nous aurons fini
vous finirez	vous aurez fini
ils finiront	ils auront fini

SUBJUNCTIVE

PRESENT	IMPERFECT	PAST	PLUPERFECT
que je finisse	que je finisse	que j'aie fini	que j'eusse fini
que tu finisses	que tu finisses	que tu aies fini	que tu eusses fini
qu'il finisse	qu'il finît	qu'il ait fini	qu'il eût fini
que nous finissions	que nous finissions	que nous ayons fini	que nous eussions fini
que vous finissiez	que vous finissiez	que vous ayez fini	que vous eussiez fini
qu'ils finissent	qu'ils finissent	qu'ils aient fini	qu'ils eussent fini

CONDITIONAL

PRESENT	PAST I	PAST II
je finirais	j'aurais fini	j'eusse fini
tu finirais	tu aurais fini	tu eusses fini
il finirait	il aurait fini	il eût fini
nous finirions	nous aurions fini	nous eussions fini
vous finiriez	vous auriez fini	vous eussiez fini
ils finiraient	ils auraient fini	ils eussent fini

IMPERATIVE

PRESENT	PAST
finis	aie fini
finissons	ayons fini
finissez	ayez fini

PARTICIPLE

PRESENT	PAST
finissant	fini, ie
	ayant fini

INFINITIVE

PRESENT	PAST
finir	avoir fini

		INDICATIVE			
		present 1st person	present 3d person	imperfect	past historic
3	**placer**	je place [plas] nous plaçons [plasɔ̃]	il place ils placent	je plaçais	je plaçai
		NB Verbs in ***-ecer*** (e.g. *dépecer*) are conjugated like ***placer*** and ***geler.*** Verbs in ***-écer*** (e.g. *rapiécer*) are conjugated like ***céder*** and ***placer.***			
	bouger	je bouge [buʒ] nous bougeons [buʒɔ̃]	il bouge ils bougent	je bougeais nous bougions	je bougeai
		NB Verbs in ***-éger*** (e.g. *protéger*) are conjugated like ***bouger*** and ***céder.***			
4	**appeler**	j'appelle [apɛl] nous appelons [ap(ə)lɔ̃]	il appelle ils appellent	j'appelais	j'appelai
	jeter	je jette [ʒɛt] nous jetons [ʒ(ə)tɔ̃]	il jette ils jettent	je jetais	je jetai
5	**geler**	je gèle [ʒɛl] nous gelons [ʒ(ə)lɔ̃]	il gèle ils gèlent	je gelais nous gelions [ʒəljɔ̃]	je gelai
	acheter	j'achète [aʃɛt] nous achetons [aʃ(ɛ)tɔ̃]	il achète ils achètent	j'achetais [aʃtɛ] nous achetions	j'achetai
	Also verbs in ***-emer*** (e.g. *semer*), ***-ener*** (e.g. *mener*), ***-eser*** (e.g. *peser*), ***-ever*** (e.g. *lever*) etc. NB Verbs in ***-ecer*** (e.g. *dépecer*) are conjugated like ***geler*** and ***placer.***				
6	**céder**	je cède [sɛd] nous cédons [sedɔ̃]	il cède ils cèdent	je cédais nous cédions	je cédai
	Also verbs in ***-é*** + consonant(s) + ***-er*** (e.g. *célébrer, lécher, déléguer, préférer* etc). NB Verbs in ***-éger*** (e.g. *protéger*) are conjugated like ***céder*** and ***bouger.*** Verbs in ***-écer*** (e.g. *rapiécer*) are conjugated like ***céder*** and ***placer.***				
7	**épier**	j'épie [epi] nous épions [epjɔ̃]	il épie ils épient	j'épiais nous épiions [epijɔ̃]	j'épiai
	prier	je prie [pʀi] nous prions [pʀijɔ̃]	il prie ils prient	je priais nous priions [pʀijjɔ̃]	je priai
8	**noyer**	je noie [nwa] nous noyons [nwajɔ̃]	il noie ils noient	je noyais nous noyions [nwajjɔ̃]	je noyai
	Also verbs in ***-uyer*** (e.g. *appuyer*). N.B. ***Envoyer*** has in the future tense : *j'enverrai,* and in the conditional : *j'enverrais.*				
	payer	je paie [pɛ] or je paye [pɛj] nous payons [pɛjɔ̃]	il paie or il paye ils paient or ils payent	je payais nous payions [pɛjjɔ̃]	je payai
	Also all verbs in ***-ayer.***				

future	CONDITIONAL present	SUBJUNCTIVE present	IMPERATIVE present	PARTICIPLES present past
je placerai [plasʀɛ]	je placerais	que je place que nous placions	place plaçons	plaçant placé, ée
je bougerai [buʒʀɛ]	je bougerais	que je bouge que nous bougions	bouge bougeons	bougeant bougé, ée
j'appellerai [apɛlʀɛ]	j'appellerais	que j'appelle que nous appelions	appelle appelons	appelant appelé, ée
je jetterai [ʒɛtʀɛ]	je jetterais	que je jette que nous jetions	jette jetons	jetant jeté, ée
je gèlerai [ʒɛlʀɛ]	je gèlerais	que je gèle que nous gelions	gèle gelons	gelant gelé, ée
j'achèterai [aʃɛtʀɛ]	j'achèterais	que j'achète que nous achetions	achète achetons	achetant acheté, ée
je céderai [sɛdʀɛ ; sedʀɛ] [1]	je céderais [1]	que je cède que nous cédions	cède cédons	cédant cédé, ée
j'épierai [epiʀɛ]	j'épierais	que j'épie	épie épions	épiant épié, iée
je prierai [pʀiʀɛ]	je prierais	que je prie	prie prions	priant prié, priée
je noierai [nwaʀɛ]	je noierais	que je noie	noie noyons	noyant noyé, noyée
je paierai [pɛʀɛ] or je payerai [pɛjʀɛ] nous paierons or nous payerons	je paierais or je payerais	que je paie or que je paye	paie or paye payons	payant payé, payée

1. Actually pronounced as though there were a grave accent on the future and the conditional *(je cèderai, je cèderais)*, rather than an acute.

INDICATIVE

PRESENT	PERFECT
je vais [vɛ]	je suis allé
tu vas	tu es allé
il va	il est allé
nous allons [alɔ̃]	nous sommes allés
vous allez	vous êtes allés
ils vont [vɔ̃]	ils sont allés
IMPERFECT	**PLUPERFECT**
j'allais [alɛ]	j'étais allé
tu allais	tu étais allé
il allait	il était allé
nous allions [aljɔ̃]	nous étions allés
vous alliez	vous étiez allés
ils allaient	ils étaient allés
PAST HISTORIC	**PAST ANTERIOR**
j'allai	je fus allé
tu allas	tu fus allé
il alla	il fut allé
nous allâmes	nous fûmes allés
vous allâtes	vous fûtes allés
ils allèrent	ils furent allés
FUTURE	**FUTURE PERFECT**
j'irai [iʀɛ]	je serai allé
tu iras	tu seras allé
il ira	il sera allé
nous irons	nous serons allés
vous irez	vous serez allés
ils iront	ils seront allés

SUBJUNCTIVE

PRESENT

que j'aille [aj]
que tu ailles
qu'il aille
que nous allions
que vous alliez
qu'ils aillent

IMPERFECT

que j'allasse [alas]
que tu allasses
qu'il allât
que nous allassions
que vous allassiez
qu'ils allassent

PAST

que je sois allé
que tu sois allé
qu'il soit allé
que nous soyons allés
que vous soyez allés
qu'ils soient allés

PLUPERFECT

que je fusse allé
que tu fusses allé
qu'il fût allé
que nous fussions allés
que vous fussiez allés
qu'ils fussent allés

ALLER

CONDITIONAL

PRESENT

j'irais
tu irais
il irait
nous irions
vous iriez
ils iraient

PAST I

je serais allé
tu serais allé
il serait allé
nous serions allés
vous seriez allés
ils seraient allés

PAST II

je fusse allé
tu fusses allé
il fût allé
nous fussions allés
vous fussiez allés
ils fussent allés

	PRESENT	PAST
IMPERATIVE	va allons allez	sois allé soyons allés soyez allés

	PRESENT	PAST
PARTICIPLE	allant	allé, ée étant allé

	PRESENT	PAST
INFINITIVE	aller	être allé

		INDICATIVE			
		present 1st person	present 3d person	imperfect	past historic
10	haïr	je hais ['ɛ] nous haïssons [aisɔ̃]	il hait [ɛ] ils haïssent [ais]	je haïssais nous haïssions	je haïs ['ai] nous haïmes
11	courir	je cours [kuʀ] nous courons [kuʀɔ̃]	il court ils courent	je courais [kuʀɛ] nous courions	je courus
12	cueillir	je cueille [kœj] nous cueillons [kœjɔ̃]	il cueille ils cueillent	je cueillais nous cueillions [kœjjɔ̃]	je cueillis
13	assaillir	j'assaille nous assaillons [asajɔ̃]	il assaille ils assaillent	j'assaillais nous assaillions [asajjɔ̃]	j'assaillis
14	servir	je sers [sɛʀ] nous servons [sɛʀvɔ̃]	il sert ils servent [sɛʀv]	je servais nous servions	je servis
15	bouillir	je bous [bu] nous bouillons [bujɔ̃]	il bout ils bouillent [buj]	je bouillais nous bouillions [bujjɔ̃]	je bouillis
16	partir	je pars [paʀ] nous partons [paʀtɔ̃]	il part ils partent [paʀt]	je partais nous partions	je partis
	sentir	je sens [sɑ̃] nous sentons [sɑ̃tɔ̃]	il sent ils sentent [sɑ̃t]	je sentais nous sentions	je sentis
17	fuir	je fuis [fɥi] nous fuyons [fɥijɔ̃]	il fuit ils fuient	je fuyais nous fuyions [fɥijjɔ̃]	je fuis nous fuîmes
18	couvrir	je couvre nous couvrons	il couvre ils couvrent	je couvrais nous couvrions	je couvris
19	mourir	je meurs [mœʀ] nous mourons [muʀɔ̃]	il meurt ils meurent	je mourais [muʀɛ] nous mourions	je mourus
20	vêtir	je vêts [vɛ] nous vêtons [vɛtɔ̃]	il vêt ils vêtent [vɛt]	je vêtais nous vêtions	je vêtis [veti] nous vêtîmes
21	acquérir	j'acquiers [akjɛʀ] nous acquérons [akeʀɔ̃]	il acquiert ils acquièrent	j'acquérais [akeʀɛ] nous acquérions	j'acquis
22	venir	je viens [vjɛ̃] nous venons [v(ə)nɔ̃]	il vient ils viennent [vjɛn]	je venais nous venions	je vins [vɛ̃] nous vînmes [vɛ̃m]

future	CONDITIONAL present	SUBJUNCTIVE present	IMPERATIVE present	PARTICIPLES present past
je haïrai [ˈaiʀɛ]	je haïrais	que je haïsse	hais haïssons	haïssant haï, haïe [ˈai]
je courrai [kuʀʀɛ]	je courrais	que je coure	cours courons	courant couru, ue
je cueillerai	je cueillerais	que je cueille	cueille cueillons	cueillant cueilli, ie
j'assaillirai	j'assaillirais	que j'assaille	assaille assaillons	assaillant assailli, ie
je servirai	je servirais	que je serve	sers servons	servant servi, ie
je bouillirai	je bouillirais	que je bouille	bous bouillons	bouillant bouilli, ie
je partirai	je partirais	que je parte	pars partons	partant parti, ie
je sentirai	je sentirais	que je sente	sens sentons	sentant senti, ie
je fuirai	je fuirais	que je fuie	fuis fuyons	fuyant fui, fuie
je couvrirai	je couvrirais	que je couvre	couvre couvrons	couvrant couvert, erte [kuvɛʀ, ɛʀt]
je mourrai [muʀʀɛ]	je mourrais	que je meure	meurs mourons	mourant mort, morte [mɔʀ, mɔʀt]
je vêtirai	je vêtirais	que je vête	vêts vêtons	vêtant vêtu, ue [vety]
j'acquerrai [akɛʀʀɛ]	j'acquerrais	que j'acquière	acquiers acquérons	acquérant acquis, ise [aki, iz]
je viendrai [vjɛ̃dʀɛ]	je viendrais	que je vienne	viens venons	venant venu, ue

		INDICATIVE			
		present 1st person	present 3d person	imperfect	past historic
23	**pleuvoir**	(impersonal)	il pleut [plø]	il pleuvait	il plut
24	**prévoir**	je prévois [pʀevwa] nous prévoyons [pʀevwajɔ̃]	il prévoit ils prévoient	je prévoyais nous prévoyions [pʀevwajjɔ̃]	je prévis
25	**pourvoir**	je pourvois nous pourvoyons	il pourvoit ils pourvoient	je pourvoyais nous pourvoyions	je pourvus
26	**asseoir**	j'assieds [asjɛ] nous asseyons [asɛjɔ̃] or j'assois nous assoyons	il assied ils asseyent [asɛj] or il assoit ils assoient	j'asseyais nous asseyions or j'assoyais nous assoyions	j'assis
27	**mouvoir**	je meus [mø] nous mouvons [muvɔ̃]	il meut ils meuvent [mœv]	je mouvais nous mouvions	je mus [my] nous mûmes
28	**recevoir**	je reçois [ʀ(ə)swa] nous recevons [ʀ(ə)səvɔ̃]	il reçoit ils reçoivent [ʀəswav]	je recevais nous recevions	je reçus [ʀ(ə)sy]
	devoir				
29	**valoir**	je vaux [vo] nous valons [valɔ̃]	il vaut ils valent [val]	je valais nous valions	je valus
	équivaloir				
	prévaloir				
	falloir	(impersonal)	il faut [fo]	il fallait [falɛ]	il fallut
30	**voir**	je vois [vwa] nous voyons [vwajɔ̃]	il voit ils voient	je voyais nous voyions [vwajjɔ̃]	je vis
31	**vouloir**	je veux [vø] nous voulons [vulɔ̃]	il veut ils veulent [vœl]	je voulais nous voulions	je voulus
32	**savoir**	je sais [sɛ] nous savons [savɔ̃]	il sait ils savent [sav]	je savais nous savions	je sus
33	**pouvoir**	je peux [pø] or je puis nous pouvons [puvɔ̃]	il peut ils peuvent [pœv]	je pouvais nous pouvions	je pus

NB ***Émouvoir*** and ***promouvoir*** have the past participles *ému, e* and *promu, e* respectively.

future	CONDITIONAL present	SUBJONCTIVE present	IMPERATIVE present	PARTICIPLE present / past
il pleuvra	il pleuvrait	qu'il pleuve [plœv]	does not exist	pleuvant plu (no feminine)
je prévoirai	je prévoirais	que je prévoie [pʀevwa]	prévois prévoyons	prévoyant prévu, ue
je pourvoirai	je pourvoirais	que je pourvoie	pourvois pourvoyons	pourvoyant pourvu, ue
j'assiérai [asjeʀɛ] or j'asseyerai [asɛjʀɛ] or j'assoirai NB *j'asseyerai* is old-fashioned.	j'assiérais or j'assoirais	que j'asseye [asɛj] or que j'assoie [aswa]	assieds asseyons or assois assoyons	asseyant assis, ise or assoyant assis, ise
je mouvrai [muvʀɛ]	je mouvrais	que je meuve que nous mouvions	meus mouvons	mouvant mû, mue [my]
je recevrai	je recevrais	que je reçoive que nous recevions	reçois recevons	recevant reçu, ue
				dû, due
je vaudrai [vodʀɛ]	je vaudrais	que je vaille [vaj] que nous valions [valjɔ̃]	vaux valons	valant valu, ue
				équivalu (no feminine)
		que je prévale	does not exist	prévalu (no feminine)
il faudra [fodʀa]	il faudrait	qu'il faille [faj]		does not exist fallu (no feminine)
je verrai [veʀɛ]	je verrais	que je voie [vwa] que nous voyions [vwajjɔ̃]	vois voyons	voyant vu, vue
je voudrai [vudʀɛ]	je voudrais	que je veuille [vœj] que nous voulions [vuljɔ̃]	veux or veuille voulons	voulant voulu, ue
je saurai [soʀɛ]	je saurais	que je sache [saʃ] que nous sachions	sache sachons	sachant su, sue
je pourrai [puʀɛ]	je pourrais	que je puisse [pɥis] que nous puissions	not used	pouvant pu

INDICATIVE		SUBJUNCTIVE
PRESENT	**PERFECT**	**PRESENT**
j'ai [e; ɛ]	j'ai eu	que j'aie [ɛ]
tu as [a]	tu as eu	que tu aies
il a [a]	il a eu	qu'il ait
nous avons [avɔ̃]	nous avons eu	que nous ayons [ɛjɔ̃]
vous avez [ave]	vous avez eu	que vous ayez
ils ont [ɔ̃]	ils ont eu	qu'ils aient
IMPERFECT	**PLUPERFECT**	**IMPERFECT**
j'avais	j'avais eu	que j'eusse [ys]
tu avais	tu avais eu	que tu eusses
il avait	il avait eu	qu'il eût [y]
nous avions	nous avions eu	que nous eussions [ysjɔ̃]
vous aviez	vous aviez eu	que vous eussiez
ils avaient	ils avaient eu	qu'ils eussent
PAST HISTORIC	**PAST ANTERIOR**	**PAST**
j'eu [y]	j'eus eu	que j'aie eu
tu eus	tu eus eu	que tu aies eu
il eut	il eut eu	qu'il ait eu
nous eûmes [ym]	nous eûmes eu	que nous ayons eu
vous eûtes [yt]	vous eûtes eu	que vous ayez eu
ils eurent [yʀ]	ils eurent eu	qu'ils aient eu
FUTURE	**FUTURE PERFECT**	**PLUPERFECT**
j'aurai [ɔʀɛ]	j'aurai eu	que j'eusse eu
tu auras	tu auras eu	que tu eusses eu
il aura	il aura eu	qu'il eût eu
nous aurons	nous aurons eu	que nous eussions eu
vous aurez	vous aurez eu	que vous eussiez eu
ils auront	ils auront eu	qu'ils eussent eu

conjugations 35 to 37

		INDICATIVE			
		present — 1st person	present — 3d and 2nd persons	imperfect	past historic
35	**conclure**	je conclus [kɔ̃kly] nous concluons [kɔ̃klyɔ̃]	il conclut ils concluent	je concluais nous concluions	je conclus
36	**rire**	je ris [ʀi] nous rions [ʀijɔ̃]	il rit ils rient	je riais nous riions [ʀjjɔ̃]	je ris
37	**dire**	je dis [di] nous disons [dizɔ̃]	il dit vous dites [dit] ils disent [diz]	je disais nous disions	je dis
	suffire	je suffis [syfi] nous suffisons [syfizɔ̃]	il suffit ils suffisent [syfiz]	je suffisais nous suffisions	je suffis

NB ***Exclure*** is conjugated like ***conclure***: past participle *exclu, ue*; ***inclure*** is conjugated like ***conclure*** except for the past participle *inclus, use*.

NB ***Médire, contredire, dédire, interdire, prédire*** are conjugated like ***dire*** except for the 2nd person plural of the present tense: *médisez, contredisez, dédisez, interdisez, prédisez*.

NB ***Confire*** is conjugated like ***suffire*** except for the past participle *confit, ite*.

CONDITIONAL

PRESENT	PAST I	PAST II
j'aurais	j'aurais eu	j'eusse eu
tu aurais	tu aurais eu	tu eusses eu
il aurait	il aurait eu	il eût eu
nous aurions	nous aurions eu	nous eussions eu
vous auriez	vous auriez eu	vous eussiez eu
ils auraient	ils auraient eu	ils eussent eu

	PRESENT	PAST
IMPERATIVE	aie [ɛ] ayons [ɛjɔ̃] ayez [eje]	aie eu ayons eu ayez eu
PARTICIPLE	ayant	eu, eue [y] ayant eu
INFINITIVE	avoir	avoir eu

irregular verbs ending in **-re**

future	**CONDITIONAL** present	**SUBJUNCTIVE** present	**IMPERATIVE** present	**PARTICIPLES** present / past
je conclurai	je conclurais	que je conclue	conclus concluons	concluant conclu, ue
je rirai	je rirais	que je rie	ris rions	riant ri (no feminine)
je dirai	je dirais	que je dise	dis disons dites	disant dit, dite
je suffirai	je suffirais	que je suffise	suffis suffisons	suffisant suffi (no feminine)

		INDICATIVE			
		present 1st person	present 3d person	imperfect	past historic
38	**nuire**	je nuis [nɥi] nous nuisons [nɥizɔ̃]	il nuit ils nuisent [nɥiz]	je nuisais nous nuisions	je nuisis

Also the verbs ***luire, reluire.***

		present 1st person	present 3d person	imperfect	past historic
	conduire	je conduis nous conduisons	il conduit ils conduisent	je conduisais nous conduisions	je conduisis

Also the verbs ***construire, cuire, déduire, détruire, enduire, induire, instruire, introduire, produire, réduire, séduire, traduire.***

		present 1st person	present 3d person	imperfect	past historic
39	**écrire**	j'écris [ekʀi] nous écrivons [ekʀivɔ̃]	il écrit ils écrivent [ekʀiv]	j'écrivais nous écrivions	j'écrivis
40	**suivre**	je suis [sɥi] nous suivons [sɥivɔ̃]	il suit ils suivent [sɥiv]	je suivais nous suivions	je suivis
41	**rendre**	je rends [ʀɑ̃] nous rendons [ʀɑ̃dɔ̃]	il rend ils rendent [ʀɑ̃d]	je rendais nous rendions	je rendis

Also the verbs ending in ***-andre*** (e.g. *répandre*), ***-erdre*** (e.g. *perdre*), ***-ondre*** (e.g. *répondre*), ***-ordre*** (e.g. *mordre*).

		present 1st person	present 3d person	imperfect	past historic
	rompre	je romps [ʀɔ̃] nous rompons [ʀɔ̃pɔ̃]	il rompt ils rompent [ʀɔ̃p]	je rompais nous rompions	je rompis

Also the verbs ***corrompre*** and ***interrompre.***

		present 1st person	present 3d person	imperfect	past historic
	battre	je bats [ba] nous battons [batɔ̃]	il bat ils battent [bat]	je battais nous battions	je battis
42	**vaincre**	je vaincs [vɛ̃] nous vainquons [vɛ̃kɔ̃]	il vainc ils vainquent [vɛ̃k]	je vainquais nous vainquions	je vainquis
43	**lire**	je lis [li] nous lisons [lizɔ̃]	il lit ils lisent [liz]	je lisais nous lisions	je lus
44	**croire**	je crois [kʀwa] nous croyons [kʀwajɔ̃]	il croit ils croient	je croyais nous croyions [kʀwajjɔ̃]	je crus nous crûmes
45	**clore**	je clos [klo]	il clôt ils closent [kloz] (rare)	je closais (rare)	not applicable
46	**vivre**	je vis [vi] nous vivons [vivɔ̃]	il vit ils vivent [viv]	je vivais nous vivions	je vécus [veky]
47	**moudre**	je mouds [mu] nous moulons [mulɔ̃]	il moud ils moulent [mul]	je moulais nous moulions	je moulus

NB Most forms of this verb are rare except *moudre, moudrai(s), moulu, e.*

		present 1st person	present 3d person	imperfect	past historic
48	**coudre**	je couds [ku] nous cousons [kuzɔ̃]	il coud ils cousent [kuz]	je cousais nous cousions	je cousis [kuzi]

future	CONDITIONAL present	SUBJUNCTIVE present	IMPERATIVE present	PARTICIPLES present past
je nuirai	je nuirais	que je nuise	nuis nuisons	nuisant nui (no feminine)
je conduirai	je conduirais	que je conduise	conduis conduisons	conduisant conduit, ite
j'écrirai	j'écrirais	que j'écrive	écris écrivons	écrivant écrit, ite
je suivrai	je suivrais	que je suive	suis suivons	suivant suivi, ie
je rendrai	je rendrais	que je rende	rends rendons	rendant rendu, ue
je romprai	je romprais	que je rompe	romps rompons	rompant rompu, ue
je battrai	je battrais	que je batte	bats battons	battant battu, ue
je vaincrai	je vaincrais	que je vainque	vaincs vainquons	vainquant vaincu, ue
je lirai	je lirais	que je lise	lis lisons	lisant lu, ue
je croirai	je croirais	que je croie	crois croyons	croyant cru, crue
je clorai (rare)	je clorais	que je close	clos	closant (rare) clos, close
je vivrai	je vivrais	que je vive	vis vivons	vivant vécu, ue
je moudrai	je moudrais	que je moule	mouds moulons	moulant moulu, ue
je coudrai	je coudrais	que je couse	couds cousons	cousant cousu, ue

		INDICATIVE			
		present 1st person	present 3d person	imperfect	past historic
49	**joindre**	je joins [ʒwɛ̃] nous joignons [ʒwaɲɔ̃]	il joint ils joignent [ʒwaɲ]	je joignais nous joignions [ʒwaɲjɔ̃]	je joignis
50	**traire**	je trais [tʀɛ] nous trayons [tʀɛjɔ̃]	il trait ils traient	je trayais nous trayions [tʀɛjjɔ̃]	not applicable
51	**absoudre**	j'absous [ɑpsu] nous absolvons [ɑpsɔlvɔ̃]	il absout ils absolvent [ɑpsɔlv]	j'absolvais nous absolvions	j'absolus [apsɔly] (rare)

NB 1. ***Dissoudre*** is conjugated like ***absoudre***; ***résoudre*** is conjugated like ***absoudre***, but the past historic *je résolus* is current. ***Résoudre*** has two past participles: *résolu, ue (problème résolu)*, and *résous, oute* (*brouillard résous en pluie* [rare]).

52	**craindre**	je crains [kʀɛ̃] nous craignons [kʀɛɲɔ̃]	il craint ils craignent [kʀɛɲ]	je craignais nous craignions [kʀɛɲjɔ̃]	je craignis
	peindre	je peins [pɛ̃] nous peignons [pɛɲɔ̃]	il peint ils peignent [pɛɲ]	je peignais nous peignions [pɛɲjɔ̃]	je peignis
53	**boire**	je bois [bwa] nous buvons [byvɔ̃]	il boit ils boivent [bwav]	je buvais nous buvions	je bus
54	**plaire**	je plais [plɛ] nous plaisons [plɛzɔ̃]	il plaît ils plaisent [plɛz]	je plaisais nous plaisions	je plus

NB The past participle of ***plaire, complaire, déplaire*** is generally invariable.

	taire	je tais nous taisons	il tait ils taisent	je taisais nous taisions	je tus
55	**croître**	je croîs [kʀwa] nous croissons [kʀwasɔ̃]	il croît ils croissent [kʀwas]	je croissais nous croissions	je crûs nous crûmes

NB Like ***accroître***, the past participle of ***décroître*** is *décru, e*.

	accroître	j'accrois nous accroissons	il accroît ils accroissent	j'accroissais	j'accrus nous accrûmes
56	**mettre**	je mets [mɛ] nous mettons [metɔ̃]	il met ils mettent [mɛt]	je mettais nous mettions	je mis
57	**connaître**	je connais [kɔnɛ] nous connaissons [kɔnɛsɔ̃]	il connaît ils connaissent [kɔnɛs]	je connaissais nous connaissions	je connus
58	**prendre**	je prends [pʀɑ̃] nous prenons [pʀənɔ̃]	il prend ils prennent [pʀɛn]	je prenais nous prenions	je pris
59	**naître**	je nais [nɛ] nous naissons [nɛsɔ̃]	il naît ils naissent [nɛs]	je naissais nous naissions	je naquis [naki]

NB ***Renaître*** has no past participle.

future	**CONDITIONAL** present	**SUBJUNCTIVE** present	**IMPERATIVE** present	**PARTICIPLES** present past
je joindrai	je joindrais	que je joigne	joins joignons	joignant joint, jointe
je trairai	je trairais	que je traie	trais trayons	trayant trait, traite
j'absoudrai	j'absoudrais	que j'absolve	absous absolvons	absolvant absous[1], oute [apsu, ut]
je craindrai	je craindrais	que je craigne	crains craignons	craignant craint, crainte
je peindrai	je peindrais	que je peigne	peins peignons	peignant peint, peinte
je boirai	je boirais	que je boive que nous buvions	bois buvons	buvant bu, bue
je plairai	je plairais	que je plaise	plais plaisons	plaisant plu (no feminine)
je tairai	je tairais	que je taise	tais taisons	taisant tu, tue
je croîtrai	je croîtrais	que je croisse	croîs croîssons	croissant crû, crue
j'accroîtrai	j'accroîtrais	que j'accroisse	accrois accroissons	accroissant accru, ue
je mettrai	je mettrais	que je mette	mets mettons	mettant mis, mise
je connaîtrai	je connaîtrais	que je connaisse	connais connaissons	connaissant connu, ue
je prendrai	je prendrais	que je prenne que nous prenions	prends prenons	prenant pris, prise
je naîtrai	je naîtrais	que je naisse	nais naissons	naissant né, née

1. The past participle forms *absout, dissout,* with a final *t,* are often preferred.

INDICATIVE

PRESENT	PERFECT
je fais [fɛ]	j'ai fait
tu fais	tu as fait
il fait	il a fait
nous faisons [f(ə)zɔ̃]	nous avons fait
vous faites [fɛt]	vous avez fait
ils font [fɔ̃]	ils ont fait

IMPERFECT	PLUPERFECT
je faisais [f(ə)zɛ]	j'avais fait
tu faisais	tu avais fait
il faisait	il avait fait
nous faisions [fəzjɔ̃]	nous avions fait
vous faisiez [fəzje]	vous aviez fait
ils faisaient	ils avaient fait

PAST HISTORIC	PAST ANTERIOR
je fis	j'eus fait
tu fis	tu eus fait
il fit	il eut fait
nous fîmes	nous eûmes fait
vous fîtes	vous eûtes fait
ils firent	ils eurent fait

FUTURE	FUTURE PERFECT
je ferai [f(ə)ʀɛ]	j'aurai fait
tu feras	tu auras fait
il fera	il aura fait
nous ferons [fʀɔ̃]	nous aurons fait
vous ferez	vous aurez fait
ils feront	ils auront fait

SUBJUNCTIVE

PRESENT

que je fasse [fas]
que tu fasses
qu'il fasse
que nous fassions
que vous fassiez
qu'ils fassent

IMPERFECT

que je fisse [fis]
que tu fisses
qu'il fît
que nous fissions
que vous fissiez
qu'ils fissent

PAST

que j'aie fait
que tu aies fait
qu'il ait fait
que nous ayons fait
que vous ayez fait
qu'ils aient fait

PLUPERFECT

que j'eusse fait
que tu eusses fait
qu'il eût fait
que nous eussions fait
que vous eussiez fait
qu'ils eussent fait

CONDITIONAL

PRESENT

je ferais [f(ə)ʀɛ]
tu ferais
il ferait
nous ferions [fəʀjɔ̃]
vous feriez
ils feraient

PAST I

j'aurais fait
tu aurais fait
il aurait fait
nous aurions fait
vous auriez fait
ils auraient fait

PAST II

j'eusse fait
tu eusses fait
il eût fait
nous eussions fait
vous eussiez fait
ils eussent fait

IMPERATIVE

PRESENT	PAST
fais	aie fait
faisons	ayons fait
faites	ayez fait

PARTICIPLE

PRESENT	PAST
faisant [f(ə)zɑ̃]	fait
	ayant fait

INFINITIVE

PRESENT	PAST
faire	avoir fait

conjugation 61 — **ÊTRE**

INDICATIVE

PRESENT	PERFECT
je suis [sɥi]	j'ai été
tu es [ɛ]	tu as été
il est [ɛ]	il a été
nous sommes [sɔm]	nous avons été
vous êtes [ɛt]	vous avez été
ils sont [sɔ̃]	ils ont été

IMPERFECT	PLUPERFECT
j'étais [etɛ]	j'avais été
tu étais	tu avais été
il était	il avait été
nous étions [etjɔ̃]	nous avions été
vous étiez	vous aviez été
ils étaient	ils avaient été

PAST HISTORIC	PAST ANTERIOR
je fus [fy]	j'eus été
tu fus	tu eus été
il fut	il eut été
nous fûmes	nous eûmes été
vous fûtes	vous eûtes été
ils furent	ils eurent été

FUTURE	FUTURE PERFECT
je serai [s(ə)ʀɛ]	j'aurai été
tu seras	tu auras été
il sera	il aura été
nous serons [s(ə)ʀɔ̃]	nous aurons été
vous serez	vous aurez été
ils seront	ils auront été

SUBJUNCTIVE

PRESENT

que je sois [swa]
que tu sois
qu'il soit
que nous soyons [swajɔ̃]
que vous soyez
qu'ils soient

IMPERFECT

que je fusse
que tu fusses
qu'il fût
que nous fussions
que vous fussiez
qu'ils fussent

PAST

que j'aie été
que tu aies été
qu'il ait été
que nous ayons été
que vous ayez été
qu'ils aient été

PLUPERFECT

que j'eusse été
que tu eusses été
qu'il eût été
que nous eussions été
que vous eussiez été
qu'ils eussent été

CONDITIONAL

PRESENT

je serais [s(ə)ʀɛ]
tu serais
il serait
nous serions [səʀjɔ̃]
vous seriez
ils seraient

PAST I

j'aurais été
tu aurais été
il aurait été
nous aurions été
vous auriez été
ils auraient été

PAST II

j'eusse été
tu eusses été
il eût été
nous eussions été
vous eussiez été
ils eussent été

IMPERATIVE

PRESENT	PAST
sois [swa]	aie été
soyons [swajɔ̃]	ayons été
soyez [swaje]	ayez été

PARTICIPLE

PRESENT	PAST
étant	été [ete]
	ayant été

INFINITIVE

PRESENT	PAST
être	avoir été

RULES OF AGREEMENT FOR PAST PARTICIPLE

The past participle is a form of the verb which does not vary according to tense or person, but which is more like an adjective, in that it may agree in gender and number with the word to which it refers.

PAST PARTICIPLE AGREEMENT DEPENDING ON USAGE

without auxiliary (adjectival use)	• **agreement** with the word it refers to *une affaire bien partie* (agrees with *affaire,* feminine singular)

with *être*	• **agreement** with the subject of **être** *les hirondelles sont revenues* (agrees with *hirondelles,* feminine plural)
with *avoir*	• **agreement** with the direct object, provided the direct object preceeds the past participle *je les ai crus* (agrees with *les,* masculine plural) *la lettre qu'il a écrite* (agrees with *que,* referring back to *lettre,* feminine singular) • **no agreement,** then, in the following cases: *nous avons couru* (no direct object) *elles ont pris la clé* (direct object follows past participle)

with *s'être*	**as with *être***	• if the verb is reflexive, the past participle agrees with the subject *ils se sont enrhumés* (agrees with *ils,* masculine plural)
	as with *avoir*	• if the reflexive pronoun is the indirect object, any agreement is with the preceding direct object *la bosse qu'il s'est faite* (agrees with *que,* referring back to *bosse,* feminine singular) **no agreement,** then, if the direct object follows the past participle *ils se sont lavés les mains* (the object being *les mains*)

LE VERBE ANGLAIS

THE ENGLISH VERB

L'anglais comprend de nombreux verbes forts ou irréguliers (dont nous donnons la liste ci-dessous, § 7) ainsi que de nombreuses variantes orthographiques (voir au § 8), mais à chacun des temps la conjugaison reste la même pour toutes les personnes sauf pour la troisième personne du singulier au présent de l'indicatif.

Les notes qui suivent se proposent de résumer la structure et les formes du verbe anglais.

1 LE MODE INDICATIF

PRÉSENT	FORMATION	Le présent de l'indicatif a la même forme que l'infinitif présent à toutes les personnes sauf à la troisième personne du singulier, à laquelle vient s'ajouter un *s*, ex. : *he sells.*
	verbes se terminant par une sifflante ou une chuintante	Dans les cas où l'infinitif se termine par une sifflante ou une chuintante on intercale un *e*, ex. : *kisses, buzzes, rushes, touches.*
	verbes se terminant par consonne + y	Les verbes qui se terminent en consonne + *y* changent cet *y* en *ies* à la troisième personne du singulier, ex. : *tries, pities, satisfies.* REMARQUE. Là où le *y* est précédé d'une voyelle, on applique la règle générale, ex. : *pray — he prays, annoy — she annoys.*
	Formes irrégulières	• Le verbe *to be* a des formes irrégulières pour toutes les personnes : I am, you are, he is, we are, you are, they are. • Trois autres verbes ont une forme irrégulière à la troisième personne du singulier : do he does have he has go he goes
IMPARFAIT PASSÉ SIMPLE PARTICIPE PASSÉ	FORMATION	L'imparfait, le passé simple et le participe passé ont, en anglais, la même forme. On les construit en ajoutant *ed* au radical de l'infinitif, ex. : *paint — I painted — painted.*
	verbes se terminant par un *e* muet	On ajoute *d* à l'infinitif des verbes qui se terminent par un *e* muet, ex. : *bare — I bared — bared, move — I moved — moved, revise — I revised — revised.*
	verbes irréguliers	Pour les verbes irréguliers, voir la liste ci-dessous, § 7.
TEMPS COMPOSÉS ou PASSÉS	FORMATION	Les temps composés du passé se forment à l'aide de l'auxiliaire *to have* suivi du participe passé.
	PASSÉ COMPOSÉ	Présent de *to have* + participe passé. ex. : *I have painted.*
	PLUS-QUE-PARFAIT	Passé de *to have* + participe passé, ex. : *I had painted.*
FUTUR	FUTUR SIMPLE	Le futur se forme à l'aide de *will* suivi de l'infinitif, ex. : *I will do it.* Dans la langue soignée, on utilise *shall* à la première personne du singulier et du pluriel, ex. : *we shall see to it.*
	FUTUR ANTÉRIEUR	L'auxiliaire *to have* accompagné de *will* (ou de *shall* dans la langue soignée) et du participe passé du verbe conjugué s'emploie pour le futur antérieur, ex. : *I will have finished.*
FORME PROGRESSIVE	Il existe également en anglais, au mode indicatif, une forme progressive qui se forme avec l'auxiliaire *to be*, conjugué au temps approprié et suivi du participe présent, ex. : *I am waiting, we were hoping, they will be leaving, they would still have been waiting, I had been painting all day.* Ce système diffère dans une certaine mesure du système français, qui a parfois comme équivalent la formule « être en train de » suivie de l'infinitif.	

2 LE CONDITIONNEL

PRÉSENT	Le conditionnel se forme à l'aide de *would* suivi de l'infinitif, ex. : *I would go.* Dans la langue soignée, on utilise *should* à la première personne du singulier et du pluriel, ex. : *we should see it.*
PASSÉ	L'auxiliaire *to have* accompagné de *would* (ou de *should* dans la langue soignée) et du participe passé du verbe conjugué s'emploie pour le conditionnel passé, ex. : *I would have paid.*

3 LE MODE SUBJONCTIF

PRÉSENT	Au présent et à toutes les personnes, le subjonctif a la même forme que l'infinitif, ex. : *(that) I go, (that) she go* etc.
IMPARFAIT	A l'imparfait, *to be* est l'unique verbe qui ait une forme irrégulière. Cette forme est *were* pour toutes les personnes : ex. : *(that) I were, (that) we were* etc.
Emploi	Le subjonctif est peu utilisé en anglais. Il faut cependant noter que le subjonctif s'emploie obligatoirement en anglais dans : *if I were you, were I to attempt it* (l'emploi de *was* étant considéré comme incorrect dans ces expressions, ainsi que dans d'autres expressions analogues). Le subjonctif se rencontre aussi dans l'expression figée *so be it* et dans le langage juridique ou officiel, ex. : *it is agreed that nothing be done, it was resolved that the pier be painted* (quoique *should be done* et *should be painted* soient également corrects).

4 LE MODE IMPÉRATIF

FORMATION	Il n'y a qu'une forme de l'impératif, qui est en fait celle de l'infinitif, ex. : *tell me, come here, don't do that.*

5 LE GÉRONDIF ET LE PARTICIPE PRÉSENT

FORMATION	Le gérondif et le participe présent ont la même forme en anglais. Ils s'obtiennent en ajoutant la désinence *-ing* au radical de l'infinitif, ex. : *washing, sending, passing.* Pour les variantes orthographiques voir paragraphe 8.

6 LA VOIX PASSIVE

FORMATION	La voix passive se forme exactement comme en français avec le temps approprié du verbe *to be* et le participe passé : ex. : *we are forced to, he was killed, they had been injured, the company will be taken over, it ought to have been rebuilt, were it to be agreed.*

7 VERBES FORTS OU IRRÉGULIERS

INFINITIF	PRÉTÉRIT	PARTICIPE PASSÉ
abide	abode or abided	abode or abided
arise	arose	arisen
awake	awoke or awaked	awoken, or awaked
be	was, were	been
bear	bore	borne
beat	beat	beaten
become	became	become
beget	begot, begat††	begotten
begin	began	begun
bend	bent	bent
beseech	besought	besought
bet	bet or betted	bet or betted
bid	bade or bid	bid or bidden
bind	bound	bound
bite	bit	bitten
bleed	bled	bled
blow	blew	blown
break	broke	broken
breed	bred	bred
bring	brought	brought
build	built	built
burn	burned or burnt	burned or burnt
burst	burst	burst
buy	bought	bought
can	could	—
cast	cast	cast
catch	caught	caught
chide	chid	chidden or chid
choose	chose	chosen
cleave[1] *(fendre)*	clove or cleft	cloven or cleft
cleave[2] *(s'attacher)*	cleaved	cleaved
cling	clung	clung
come	came	come
cost	cost or costed	cost or costed
creep	crept	crept
cut	cut	cut
deal	dealt	dealt
dig	dug	dug
dive	dived, (US) dove	dived
do	did	done
draw	drew	drawn
dream	dreamed or dreamt	dreamed or dreamt
drink	drank	drunk
drive	drove	driven
dwell	dwelled or dwelt	dwelled or dwelt
eat	ate	eaten

INFINITIF	PRÉTÉRIT	PARTICIPE PASSÉ
fall	fell	fallen
feed	fed	fed
feel	felt	felt
fight	fought	fought
find	found	found
flee	fled	fled
fling	flung	flung
fly	flew	flown
forbid	forbad(e)	forbidden
forget	forgot	forgotten
forsake	forsook	forsaken
freeze	froze	frozen
get	got	got, (US) gotten
gild	gilded	gilded or gilt
gird	girded or girt	girded or girt
give	gave	given
go	went	gone
grind	ground	ground
grow	grew	grown
hang	hung, Jur hanged	hung, Jur hanged
have	had	had
hear	heard	heard
heave	heaved, (Naut) hove	heaved, (Naut) hove
hew	hewed	hewed or hewn
hide	hid	hidden
hit	hit	hit
hold	held	held
hurt	hurt	hurt
keep	kept	kept
kneel	knelt	knelt
know	knew	known
lade	laded	laden
lay	laid	laid
lead	led	led
lean	leaned or leant	leaned or leant
leap	leaped or leapt	leaped or leapt
learn	learned or learnt	learned or learnt
leave	left	left
lend	lent	lent
let	let	let
lie	lay	lain
light	lit or lighted	lit or lighted
lose	lost	lost
make	made	made
may	might	—
mean	meant	meant

INFINITIF	PRÉTÉRIT	PARTICIPE PASSÉ
meet	met	met
mow	mowed	mown or mowed
pay	paid	paid
put	put	put
quit	quit or quitted	quit or quitted
read [ri:d]	read [red]	read [red]
rend	rent	rent
rid	rid	rid
ride	rode	ridden
ring[2]	rang	rung
rise	rose	risen
run	ran	run
saw	sawed	sawed or sawn
say	said	said
see	saw	seen
seek	sought	sought
sell	sold	sold
send	sent	sent
set	set	set
sew	sewed	sewed or sewn
shake	shook	shaken
shave	shaved	shaved or shaven
shear	sheared	sheared or shorn
shed	shed	shed
shine	shone	shone
shoe	shod	shod
shoot	shot	shot
show	showed	shown or showed
shrink	shrank	shrunk
shut	shut	shut
sing	sang	sung
sink	sank	sunk
sit	sat	sat
slay	slew	slain
sleep	slept	slept
slide	slid	slid
sling	slung	slung
slink	slunk	slunk
slit	slit	slit
smell	smelled or smelt	smelled or smelt
smite	smote	smitten
sow	sowed	sowed or sown
speak	spoke	spoken

INFINITIF	PRÉTÉRIT	PARTICIPE PASSÉ
speed	speeded or sped	speeded or sped
spell	spelled or spelt	spelled or spelt
spend	spent	spent
spill	spilled or spilt	spilled or spilt
spin	spun or span††	spun
spit	spat	spat
split	split	split
spoil	spoiled or spoilt	spoiled or spoilt
spread	spread	spread
spring	sprang	sprung
stand	stood	stood
stave	stove or staved	stove or staved
steal	stole	stolen
stick	stuck	stuck
sting	stung	stung
stink	stank	stunk
strew	strewed	strewed or strewn
stride	strode	stridden
strike	struck	struck
string	strung	strung
strive	strove	striven
swear	swore	sworn
sweep	swept	swept
swell	swelled	swollen
swim	swam	swum
swing	swung	swung
take	took	taken
teach	taught	taught
tear	tore	torn
tell	told	told
think	thought	thought
thrive	throve or thrived	thriven or thrived
throw	threw	thrown
thrust	thrust	thrust
tread	trod	trodden
wake	woke or waked	woken or waked
wear	wore	worn
weave	wove or weaved	woven or weaved
weep	wept	wept
win	won	won
wind	wound	wound
wring	wrung	wrung
write	wrote	written

REMARQUE. Ne sont pas compris dans cette liste les verbes formés avec un préfixe. Pour leur conjugaison, se référer au verbe de base, ex. : pour *forbear* voir ***bear***, pour *understand* voir ***stand.***

8 VERBES FAIBLES PRÉSENTANT DES VARIANTES ORTHOGRAPHIQUES

TERMINAISON DES VERBES À L'INFINITIF	VARIANTE ORTHOGRAPHIQUE AU PARTICIPE PASSÉ ET AU GÉRONDIF	EXEMPLE		
		INFINITIF	PARTICIPE PASSÉ	GÉRONDIF
Les verbes se terminant par une seule consonne précédée d'une seule voyelle accentuée	redoublent la consonne devant la désinence *ed* ou *ing*.	sob wed lag control dim tan tap prefer pat	sobbed wedded lagged controlled dimmed tanned tapped preferred patted	sobbing wedding lagging controlling dimming tanning tapping preferring patting
		(En revanche *to cook* devient *cooked — cooked* parce qu'il comporte une voyelle longue, et *fear* qui comporte une diphtongue donne *feared — fearing.*)		
Les verbes qui se terminent en *c*	changent le *c* en *ck* devant les désinences *ed* et *ing*.	frolic traffic	frolicked trafficked	frolicking trafficking
Les verbes terminés par la consonne *l* ou *p* précédée d'une voyelle non accentuée	redoublent la consonne au participe passé et au gérondif en anglais britannique, mais restent inchangés en anglais américain.	grovel travel worship	(Brit) grovelled (US) groveled (Brit) travelled (US) traveled (Brit) worshipped (US) worshiped	(Brit) grovelling (US) groveling (Brit) travelling (US) traveling (Brit) worshipping (US) worshiping
		N.B. La même différence existe entre les formes substantivées de ces verbes : (Brit) traveller, worshipper; (US) traveler, worshiper		
Lorsque le verbe se termine par un *e* muet,	le *e* muet disparaît en faveur de la désinence *ed* ou *ing*.	invite rake smile move	invited raked smiled moved	inviting raking smiling moving
		(Le *e* muet se conserve toutefois dans les verbes *dye, singe,* etc. et dans une série peu nombreuse de verbes se terminant en *oe : dyeing, singeing, hoeing.*)		
Si le verbe se termine en *y*,	le *y* devient *ied* pour former le prétérit et le participe passé.	worry pity falsify try	worried — worried pitied — pitied falsified — falsified tried — tried	Le gérondif de ces verbes est parfaitement régulier, ex. : *worrying, trying,* etc.
Gérondif des verbes monosyllabiques *die, lie, vie*				dying, lying, vying.

9 VERBES ANGLAIS À PARTICULE

vi verbe intransitif. ex. : ► **blow off** dans *his hat blew off.*

vt sep verbe transitif séparable. ex. : ► **blow off** dans *the wind blew off his hat* ou *the wind blew his hat off.* Le complément d'objet du verbe peut se mettre soit après la particule, soit entre les deux éléments du verbe en les séparant. Cette dernière structure est d'ailleurs obligatoire lorsque le complément d'objet est un pronom : *the wind blew it off.*

vt fus verbe transitif fusionné. ex. : ► **admit to** dans *he admitted to the theft.* Le complément d'objet ne peut jamais s'intercaler entre les deux éléments du verbe, même lorsqu'il s'agit d'un pronom : *he admitted to it.*

REMARQUE. Pour beaucoup de verbes qui indiquent un mouvement ou une direction, les verbes à particule correspondants n'ont pas été dissociés de l'article principal, car ils peuvent être déduits des illustrations fournies. Ainsi, à partir de

> **crawl** 2 vi a ... **to ~ in/out** *etc* entrer/sortir *etc* en rampant *or* à quatre pattes...

vous pouvez construire : *to crawl across* (traverser en rampant), *to crawl down* (descendre en rampant), etc.

NUMBERS AND DATES

NOMBRES ET DATES

NOMBRES ET DATES
NUMBERS AND DATES

1 CARDINAL AND ORDINAL NUMBERS NOMBRES CARDINAUX ET ORDINAUX

Cardinal numbers		Les nombres cardinaux	Ordinal numbers	Les nombres ordinaux
nought	0	zéro		
one	1	(m) un, (f) une	first	(m) premier, (f) -ière
two	2	deux	second	deuxième
three	3	trois	third	troisième
four	4	quatre	fourth	quatrième
five	5	cinq	fifth	cinquième
six	6	six	sixth	sixième
seven	7	sept	seventh	septième
eight	8	huit	eighth	huitième
nine	9	neuf	ninth	neuvième
ten	10	dix	tenth	dixième
eleven	11	onze	eleventh	onzième
twelve	12	douze	twelfth	douzième
thirteen	13	treize	thirteenth	treizième
fourteen	14	quatorze	fourteenth	quatorzième
fifteen	15	quinze	fifteenth	quinzième
sixteen	16	seize	sixteenth	seizième
seventeen	17	dix-sept	seventeenth	dix-septième
eighteen	18	dix-huit	eighteenth	dix-huitième
nineteen	19	dix-neuf	nineteenth	dix-neuvième
twenty	20	vingt	twentieth	vingtième
twenty-one	21	vingt et un	twenty-first	vingt et unième
twenty-two	22	vingt-deux	twenty-second	vingt-deuxième
twenty-three	23	vingt-trois		
thirty	30	trente	thirtieth	trentième
thirty-one	31	trente et un	thirty-first	trente et unième
thirty-two	32	trente-deux		
forty	40	quarante	fortieth	quarantième
fifty	50	cinquante	fiftieth	cinquantième
sixty	60	soixante	sixtieth	soixantième
seventy	70	soixante-dix	seventieth	soixante-dixième
eighty	80	quatre-vingt(s)	eightieth	quatre-vingtième
ninety	90	quatre-vingt-dix	ninetieth	quatre-vingt-dixième
ninety-nine	99	quatre-vingt-dix-neuf		
a (or one) hundred	100	cent	hundredth	centième
a hundred and one	101	cent un	hundred and first	cent unième
a hundred and two	102	cent deux		
a hundred and ten	110	cent dix	hundred and tenth	cent dixième
a hundred and eighty-two	182	cent quatre-vingt-deux		

Cardinal numbers		Les nombres cardinaux	Ordinal numbers	Les nombres ordinaux
two hundred	200	deux cents	two hundredth	deux centième
two hundred and one	201	deux cent un		
two hundred and two	202	deux cent deux		
three hundred	300	trois cents	three hundredth	trois centième
four hundred	400	quatre cents	four hundredth	quatre centième
five hundred	500	cinq cents	five hundredth	cinq centième
six hundred	600	six cents	six hundredth	six centième
seven hundred	700	sept cents	seven hundredth	sept centième
eight hundred	800	huit cents	eight hundredth	huit centième
nine hundred	900	neuf cents	nine hundredth	neuf centième
a (or one) thousand	1,000 French 1 000	mille	thousandth	millième
a thousand and one	1,001 French 1 001	mille un		
a thousand and two	1,002 French 1 002	mille deux		
two thousand	2,000 French 2 000	deux mille	two thousandth	deux millième
ten thousand	10,000 French 10 000	dix mille		
a (or one) hundred thousand	100,000 French 100 000	cent mille		
a (or one) million (see note **b**)	1,000,000 French 1 000 000	un million (voir note **b**)	millionth	millionième
two million	2,000,000 French 2 000 000	deux millions	two millionth	deux millionième

NOTES ON USAGE OF THE CARDINAL NUMBERS

[a] To divide the larger numbers clearly, a space or a point is used in French where English places a comma:

English 1,000 French 1 000 or 1.000
English 2,304,770 French 2 304 770 or 2.304.770

(This does not apply to dates: see below.)

[b] **1 000 000:** In French, the word *million* is a noun, so the numeral takes *de* when there is a following noun:

un million de fiches
trois millions de maisons détruites

[c] **One,** and the other numbers ending in *one,* agree in French with the noun (stated or implied):

une maison, un employé, il y a cent une personnes.

REMARQUES SUR LES NOMBRES CARDINAUX

[a] Alors qu'un espace ou un point est utilisé en français pour séparer les centaines des milliers, l'anglais utilise la virgule à cet effet ;

français 1 000 (ou 1.000) anglais 1,000
français 2 304 770 (ou 2.304.770) anglais 2,304,770

(Cette règle ne s'applique pas aux dates. Voir ci-dessous.)

[b] En anglais, le mot *million* (ainsi que *mille* et *cent*) n'est pas suivi de *of* lorsqu'il accompagne un nom:

a million people,
a hundred houses,
a thousand people.

NOTES ON USAGE OF THE ORDINAL NUMBERS
REMARQUES SUR LES NOMBRES ORDINAUX

[a] **Abbreviations:** English 1st, 2nd, 3rd, 4th, 5th, etc. French (m) 1er, (f) 1re, 2e, 3e, 4e, 5e and so on.

[b] **First,** and the other numbers ending in *first,* agree in French with the noun (stated or implied):
La première maison, le premier employé, la cent et unième personne.

[c] See also the notes on dates, below.
Voir aussi ci-dessous le paragraphe concernant les dates.

2 FRACTIONS — LES FRACTIONS

one half, a half	$\frac{1}{2}$	(m) un demi, (f) une demie
one and a half helpings	$1\frac{1}{2}$	une portion et demie
two and a half kilos	$2\frac{1}{2}$	deux kilos et demi
one third, a third	$\frac{1}{3}$	un tiers
two thirds	$\frac{2}{3}$	deux tiers
one quarter, a quarter	$\frac{1}{4}$	un quart
three quarters	$\frac{3}{4}$	trois quarts
one sixth, a sixth	$\frac{1}{6}$	un sixième
five and five sixths	$5\frac{5}{6}$	cinq et cinq sixièmes
one twelfth, a twelfth	$\frac{1}{12}$	un douzième
seven twelfths	$\frac{7}{12}$	sept douzièmes
one hundredth, a hundredth	$\frac{1}{100}$	un centième
one thousandth, a thousandth	$\frac{1}{1000}$	un millième

3 DECIMALS — LES DÉCIMALES

In French, a comma is written where English uses a point:

Alors que le français utilise la virgule pour séparer les entiers des décimales, le point est utilisé en anglais à cet effet :

English/Anglais		French/Français
3.56 (three point five six)	=	3,56 (trois virgule cinquante-six)
.07 (point nought seven)	=	0,07 (zéro virgule zéro sept)

4 NOMENCLATURE — NUMÉRATION

3,684 is a four-digit number
It contains 4 units, 8 tens, 6 hundreds and 3 thousands
The decimal .234 contains 2 tenths, 3 hundredths and 4 thousandths

3.684 est un nombre à quatre chiffres
4 est le chiffre des unités, 8 celui des dizaines, 6 celui des centaines et 3 celui des milliers
la fraction décimale 0,234 contient 2 dixièmes, 3 centièmes et 4 millièmes

5 PERCENTAGES / LES POURCENTAGES

$2\frac{1}{2}$% two and a half per cent	Deux et demi pour cent
18% of the people here are over 65	Ici dix-huit pour cent des gens ont plus de soixante-cinq ans
Production has risen by 8%	La production s'est accrue de huit pour cent
(See also the main text of the dictionary.)	*(Voir aussi dans le corps du dictionnaire.)*

6 SIGNS / LES SIGNES

addition sign	+	signe plus, signe de l'addition
plus sign (e.g. + 7 = plus seven)	+	signe plus (ex. : + 7 = plus 7)
subtraction sign	−	signe moins, signe de la soustraction
minus sign (e.g. − 3 = minus three)	−	signe moins (ex. : − 3 = moins 3)
multiplication sign	×	signe de la multiplication
division sign	÷	signe de la division
square root sign	$\sqrt{}$ (french $\sqrt[2]{}$)	signe de la racine carrée
infinity	∞	symbole de l'infini
sign of identity, is equal to	≡	signe d'identité
sign of equality, equals	=	signe d'égalité
is approximately equal to	≈	signe d'équivalence
sign of inequality, is not equal to	≠	signe de non-égalité
is greater than	>	plus grand que
is less than	<	plus petit que

7 CALCULATION / LE CALCUL

$8+6=14$ eight and (or plus) six are (or make) fourteen	huit et (ou plus) six font (ou égalent) quatorze
$15-3=12$ fifteen take away (or fifteen minus) three equals twelve, three from fifteen leaves twelve	trois ôté de quinze égalent douze, quinze moins trois égalent douze
$3\times3=9$ three threes are nine, three times three is nine	trois fois trois égalent neuf, trois multiplié par trois égalent neuf
$32\div8=4$ thirty-two divided by eight is (or equals) four	trente-deux divisé par huit égalent quatre
$3^2=9$ three squared is nine	trois au carré égale neuf
$2^5=32$ two to the power of five (or to the fifth) is (or equals) thirty-two	deux à la puissance cinq égale trente-deux
$\sqrt{16}=4$ the square root of sixteen is four	la racine carrée de seize ($\sqrt[2]{16}$) est quatre

9 TIMES — L'HEURE

TIMES	L'HEURE
2 hours 33 minutes and 14 seconds	deux heures trente-trois minutes et quatorze secondes
half an hour	une demi-heure
a quarter of an hour	un quart d'heure
three quarters of an hour	trois quarts d'heure
what's the time?	quelle heure est-il?
what time do you make it?	quelle heure avez-vous?
have you the right time?	avez-vous l'heure exacte?
I make it 2.20	d'après ma montre il est 2 h 20
my watch says 3.37	il est 3 h 37 à ma montre
it's 1 o'clock	il est une heure
it's 2 o'clock	il est deux heures
it's 5 past 4	il est quatre heures cinq
it's 10 to 6	il est six heures moins dix
it's half past 8	il est huit heures et demie
it's a quarter past 9	il est neuf heures et quart
it's a quarter to 2	il est deux heures moins le quart
at 10 a.m.	à dix heures du matin
at 4 p.m.	à quatre heures de l'après-midi
at 11 p.m.	à onze heures du soir
at exactly 3 o'clock, at 3 sharp, at 3 on the dot	à trois heures exactement, à trois heures précises
the train leaves at 19.32	le train part à dix-neuf heures trente-deux
(at) what time does it start?	à quelle heure est-ce que cela commence?
it is just after 3	il est trois heures passées
it is nearly 9	il est presque neuf heures
about 8 o'clock	aux environs de huit heures
at (or by) 6 o'clock at the latest	à six heures au plus tard
have it ready for 5 o'clock	tiens-le prêt pour 5 heures
it is full each night from 7 to 9	c'est plein chaque soir de 7 à 9
"closed from 1.30 to 4.30"	« fermé de une heure et demie à quatre heures et demie »
until 8 o'clock	jusqu'à huit heures
it would be about 11	il était environ 11 heures, il devait être environ 11 heures
it would have been about 10	il devait être environ dix heures
at midnight	à minuit
before midday, before noon	avant midi

10 DATES — LES DATES

DATES	LES DATES
NB The days of the week and the months start with a small letter in French: lundi, mardi, février, mars.	N.B. Contrairement au français, les jours de la semaine et les mois prennent une majuscule en anglais : Monday, Tuesday, February, March.
the 1st of July, July 1st	le 1er juillet
the 2nd of May, May 2nd	le 2 mai
on June 21st, on the 21st (of) June	le 21 juin
on Monday	lundi
he comes on Mondays	il vient le lundi
"closed on Fridays"	« fermé le vendredi »
he lends it to me from Monday to Friday	il me le prête du lundi au vendredi
from the 14th to the 18th	du 14 au 18
what's the date?, what date is it today?	quelle est la date d'aujourd'hui ?
today's the 12th	aujourd'hui nous sommes le 12
one Thursday in October	un jeudi en octobre
about the 4th of July	aux environs du 4 juillet
1978 nineteen (hundred and) seventy-eight	mille neuf cent soixante-dix-huit, dix-neuf cent soixante-dix-huit
4 B.C., B.C. 4	4 av. J.-C.
70 A.D., A.D. 70	70 ap. J.-C.
in the 13th century	au XIIIe siècle
in (or during) the 1930s	dans (ou pendant) les années 30
in 1940 something	en 1940 et quelques
HEADING OF LETTERS:	EN-TÊTE DE LETTRES :
19th May 1993	le 19 mai 1993
(See also the main text of the dictionary.)	*(Voir aussi dans le corps du dictionnaire.)*

WEIGHTS, MEASURES AND TEMPERATURES

POIDS, MESURES ET TEMPÉRATURES

1. LINEAR MEASURES - MESURES DE LONGUEUR
   SURVEYORS' MEASURES - MESURES D'ARPENTAGE
2. SQUARE MEASURES - MESURES DE SUPERFICIE
3. CUBIC MEASURES - MESURES DE VOLUME
   MEASURES OF CAPACITY - MESURES DE CAPACITÉ
4. WEIGHTS - POIDS
   METRIC SYSTEM - SYSTÈME MÉTRIQUE
   AVOIRDUPOIS SYSTEM - SYSTÈME AVOIRDUPOIS
5. TEMPERATURES - TEMPÉRATURES

WEIGHTS AND MEASURES — POIDS ET MESURES

NOTES

1. Metric system

Measures formed with the following prefixes are mostly omitted:

REMARQUES

1. Le système métrique

La plupart des mesures formées à partir des préfixes suivants ont été omises :

deca-	10 times	10 fois	*déca-*
hecto-	100 times	100 fois	*hecto-*
kilo-	1000 times	1 000 fois	*kilo-*
déci-	one tenth	un dixième	*déci-*
centi-	one hundredth	un centième	*centi-*
mil(l)i-	one thousandth	un millième	*mil(l)i-*

2. US measures

In the US, the same system as that which applies in Great Britain is used for the most part; the main differences are mentioned below.

2. Mesures nord-américaines

Les mesures britanniques sont valables pour les USA dans la majeure partie des cas. Les principales différences sont énumérées ci-dessous.

3. The numerical notation of measures:

Numerical equivalents are shown in standard English notation when they are translations of French measures and in standard French notation when they are translations of English measures;
e.g. 1 millimetre (millimètre) = 0.03937 inch
should be read in French as 0,03937 pouce.
e.g. 1 inch (pouce) = 2,54 centimetres
should be read in English as 2.54 centimètres.

3. Notation graphique des équivalences de mesures :

Les équivalences sont notées en anglais lorsqu'elles traduisent des mesures françaises et en français lorsqu'elles se rapportent à des mesures anglaises :
ex. 1 millimetre (millimètre) = 0.03937 inch
doit se lire en français 0,03937 pouce.
ex. 1 inch (pouce) = 2,54 centimètres
doit se lire en anglais 2.54 centimetres.

[1] LINEAR MEASURES — MESURES DE LONGUEUR

metric system / système métrique	1 millimetre US millimeter	(millimètre)	**mm**	0.03937 inch
	1 centimetre US centimeter	(centimètre)	**cm**	0.3937 inch
	1 metre US meter	(mètre)	**m**	39.37 inches = 1.094 yards
	1 kilometre US kilometer	(kilomètre)	**km**	0.6214 mile (5/8 mile)
French non-metric measures / mesures françaises non métriques	1 nautical mile	1 mille marin		= 1 852 mètres
	1 knot	1 nœud		= 1 mille/heure

British system / système britannique	1 inch	(pouce)		**in**	2,54 centimètres
	1 foot	(pied)	= 12 inches	**ft**	30,48 centimètres
	1 yard	(yard)	= 3 feet	**yd**	91,44 centimètres
	1 furlong		= 220 yards		201,17 mètres
	1 mile	(mile)	= 1,760 yards	**m** ou **ml**	1,609 kilomètres

surveyors' measures / mesures d'arpentage	1 link	= 7.92 inches	=	20,12 centimètres
	1 rod (or pole, perch)	= 25 links	=	5,029 mètres
	1 chain	= 22 yards = 4 rods	=	20,12 mètres

[2] SQUARE MEASURES — MESURES DE SUPERFICIE

metric system / système métrique	1 square centimetre US square centimeter	(centimètre carré)		**cm²**	0.155 square inch
	1 square metre US square meter	(mètre carré)		**m²**	10.764 square feet = 1.196 square yards
	1 square kilometre US square kilometer	(kilomètre carré)		**km²**	0.3861 square mile = 247.1 acres
	1 are	(are)	= 100 square metres	**a**	119.6 square yards
	1 hectare	(hectare)	= 100 ares	**ha**	2.471 acres
British system / système britannique	1 square inch	(pouce carré)		**in²**	6,45 cm²
	1 square foot	(pied carré)	= 144 square inches	**ft²**	929,03 cm²
	1 square yard	(yard carré)	= 9 square feet	**yd²**	0,836 m²
	1 square rod		= 30.25 square yards		25,29 m²
	1 acre		= 4,840 square yards	**a**	40,47 ares
	1 square mile	(mile carré)	= 640 acres	**m²** ou **ml²**	2,59 km²

3 CUBIC MEASURES — MESURES DE VOLUME

metric system / système métrique	1 cubic centimetre US cubic centimeter	(centimètre cube)		**cm^3**	0.061 cubic inch
	1 cubic metre US cubic meter	(mètre cube)		**m^3**	35.315 cubic feet 1.308 cubic yards
British system / système britannique	1 cubic inch			**in^3**	16,387 cm^3
	1 cubic foot	(pied cube)	= 1,728 cubic inches	**ft^3**	0,028 m^3
	1 cubic yard	(yard cube)	= 27 cubic feet	**yd^3**	0,765 m^3
	1 register ton	(tonne)	= 100 cubic feet		2,832 m^3

4 MEASURES OF CAPACITY — MESURES DE CAPACITÉ

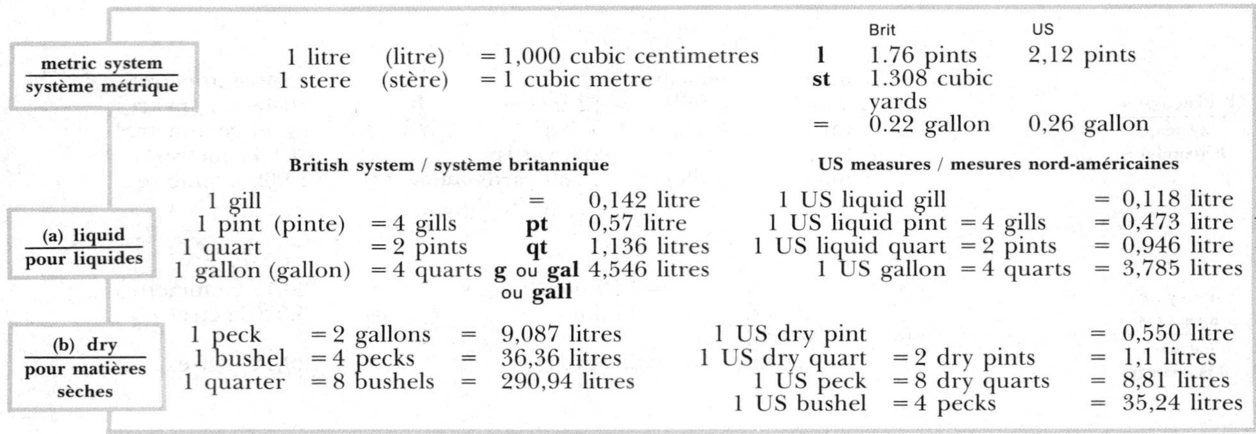

					Brit	US
metric system / système métrique	1 litre	(litre)	= 1,000 cubic centimetres	**l**	1.76 pints	2,12 pints
	1 stere	(stère)	= 1 cubic metre	**st**	1.308 cubic yards	
				=	0.22 gallon	0,26 gallon

British system / système britannique

(a) liquid / pour liquides	1 gill		=		0,142 litre
	1 pint (pinte)	= 4 gills		**pt**	0,57 litre
	1 quart	= 2 pints		**qt**	1,136 litres
	1 gallon (gallon)	= 4 quarts		**g** ou **gal** ou **gall**	4,546 litres
(b) dry / pour matières sèches	1 peck	= 2 gallons	=		9,087 litres
	1 bushel	= 4 pecks	=		36,36 litres
	1 quarter	= 8 bushels	=		290,94 litres

US measures / mesures nord-américaines

(a) liquid / pour liquides	1 US liquid gill		= 0,118 litre
	1 US liquid pint	= 4 gills	= 0,473 litre
	1 US liquid quart	= 2 pints	= 0,946 litre
	1 US gallon	= 4 quarts	= 3,785 litres
(b) dry / pour matières sèches	1 US dry pint		= 0,550 litre
	1 US dry quart	= 2 dry pints	= 1,1 litres
	1 US peck	= 8 dry quarts	= 8,81 litres
	1 US bushel	= 4 pecks	= 35,24 litres

5 WEIGHTS — POIDS

metric system / système métrique

1 gram or gramme	(gramme)		french **g** Brit **g** or **gr**	15.4 grains
1 kilogram or kilogramme	(kilogramme)		**kg**	2.2046 pounds
1 quintal	(quintal)	= 100 kilogrammes	**q**	220.46 pounds
1 metric ton	(tonne)	= 1 000 kilogrammes	**t**	0.9842 ton

Avoirdupois system / système avoirdupoids

British system / système britannique

1 grain	(grain)		**gr**	0,0648 gramme
1 drachm or dram		= 27.34 grains	**dr**	1,772 grammes
1 ounce	(once)	= 16 drachms	**oz**	28,35 grammes
1 pound	(livre)	= 16 ounces	**lb**	453,6 grammes = 0,453 kilogramme
1 stone		= 14 pounds	**st**	6,348 kilogrammes
1 quarter		= 28 pounds		12,7 kilogrammes
1 hundredweight		= 112 pounds	**cwt**	50,8 kilogrammes
1 (long) ton	(tonne)	= 2,240 pounds	**t**	1 016,05 kilogrammes

US measures / mesures nord-américaines

1 (short) hundredweight	= 100 pounds	45,36 kilogrammes
1 (short) ton	= 2000 pounds,	907,18 kilogrammes

6 TEMPERATURES — TEMPÉRATURES

$$59\,°F = (59 - 32) \times \frac{5}{9} = 15\,°C$$

A rough-and-ready way of converting centigrade to Fahrenheit and vice versa: start from the fact that

10 °C = 50 °F

thereafter for every 5 °C add 9 °F.

Thus :

15 °C = (10 + 5) = (50 + 9) = 59 °F
68 °F = (50 + 9 + 9)
= (10 + 5 + 5) = 20 °C

$$20\,°C = (20 \times \frac{9}{5}) + 32 = 68\,°F$$

Une manière rapide de convertir les centigrades en Fahrenheit et vice versa : en prenant pour base

10 °C = 50 °F

5 °C équivalent à 9 °F.

Ainsi :

15 °C = (10 + 5) = (50 + 9) = 59 °F
68 °F = (50 + 9 + 9)
= (10 + 5 + 5) = 20 °C

TABLE DES MATIÈRES

CONTENTS

Photocomposition Morton Word Processing Ltd, Scarborough
Imprimé en France par Maury-Imprimeur S.A. – Malesherbes

Dépôt légal juin 1993

Abréviations utilisées dans le dictionnaire | Abbreviations used in the dictionary

Abréviations utilisées dans le dictionnaire		Abbreviations used in the dictionary
abréviation	*abrév, abbr*	abbreviated, abbreviation
adjectif	*adj*	adjective
administration	*Admin*	administration
adverbe	*adv*	adverb
agriculture	*Agr*	agriculture
anatomie	*Anat*	anatomy
antiquité	*Antiq*	ancient history
approximativement	*approx*	approximately
archéologie	*Archéol, Archeol*	archaeology
architecture	*Archit*	architecture
argot	*arg*	slang
article	*art*	article
astrologie	*Astrol*	astrology
astronomie	*Astron*	astronomy
attribut	*attrib*	predicative
automobile	*Aut*	automobiles
auxiliaire	*aux*	auxiliary
aviation	*Aviat*	aviation
biologie	*Bio*	biology
botanique	*Bot*	botany
britannique, Grande-Bretagne	*Brit*	British, Great Britain
canadien, Canada	*Can*	Canadian, Canada
chimie	*Chim, Chem*	chemistry
cinéma	*Ciné, Cine*	cinema
commerce	*Comm*	commerce
mots composés	*comp*	compound, in compounds
comparatif	*compar*	comparative
informatique	*Comput*	computing
conditionnel	*cond*	conditional
conjonction	*conj*	conjunction
construction	*Constr*	building trade
cuisine	*Culin*	cookery
défini	*déf, def*	definite
démonstratif	*dém, dem*	demonstrative
dialectal, régional	*dial*	dialect
diminutif	*dim*	diminutive
direct	*dir*	direct
écologie	*Ecol*	ecology
économique	*Écon, Econ*	economics
écossais, Écosse	*Écos*	Scottish, Scotland
enseignement	*Éduc, Educ*	education
par exemple	*eg*	for example
électricité, électronique	*Élec, Elec*	electricity, electronics
épithète	*épith*	before noun
surtout	*esp*	especially
et cetera	*etc*	etcetera
euphémisme	*euph*	euphemism
par exemple	*ex*	for example
exclamation	*excl*	exclamation
féminin	*f*	feminine
figuré	*fig*	figuratively
finance	*Fin*	finance
féminin pluriel	*fpl*	feminine plural
formel, langue soignée	*frm*	formal language
football	*Ftbl*	football
fusionné	*fus*	fused
futur	*fut*	future
en général, généralement	*gén, gen*	in general, generally
géographie	*Géog, Geog*	geography
géologie	*Géol, Geol*	geology
géometrie	*Géom, Geom*	geometry
grammaire	*Gram*	grammar
gymnastique	*Gym*	gymnastics
héraldique	*Hér, Her*	heraldry
histoire	*Hist*	history
humoristique	*hum*	humorous
impératif	*impér, imper*	imperative
impersonnel	*impers*	impersonal
industrie	*Ind*	industry
indéfini	*indéf, indef*	indefinite
indicatif	*indic*	indicative
indirect	*indir*	indirect
infinitif	*infin*	infinitive
inséparable	*insep*	inseparable
interrogatif	*interrog*	interrogative
invariable	*inv*	invariable
irlandais, Irlande	*Ir*	Irish, Ireland
ironique	*iro*	ironic
irrégulier	*irrég*	irregular
droit, juridique	*Jur*	law, legal
linguistique	*Ling*	linguistics
littéral, au sens propre	*lit*	literally
littéraire	*liter*	literary
littérature	*Literat*	literature
littéraire	*littér*	literary
littérature	*Littérat*	literature
locutions	*loc*	locution
masculin	*m*	masculine
mathématique	*Math*	mathematics
médecine	*Méd, Med*	medicine